BRITANNICA

BOOK OF

THE YEAR

Encyclopædia
Britannica, Inc.

Chicago
Auckland
London
Madrid
Manila
Paris
Rome
Seoul
Sydney
Tokyo
Toronto

Encyclopædia Britannica and the editors of the *Britannica Book of the Year* are proud to present the annual compilation of the trends, developments, and facts of 1994—our 58th edition. And what a year it was! Watershed elections in South Africa, unimaginable bloodshed in Rwanda, and old politicians rejected in the United States and Italy. The world lost notables like Richard Nixon, Jacqueline Kennedy Onassis, and Kim Il Sung; gained heroes like Hakeem Olajuwon, Taslima Nasrin, and Tom Hanks; regained figures like Jean-Bertrand Aristide and Helmut Kohl; feted Bonnie Blair, Whitney Houston, and Frank Gehry; celebrated the birth of a new country (Palau) and two new chemical elements (numbers 110 and 111); and marked the anniversaries of D-Day, the tulip, and, yes, Barbie.

This year's edition features the work of some 70 new contributors. Sir Peter Ustinov, actor, public figure, and citizen of the world, shares his observations about the year in our keynote COMMENTARY. We have also added eight Spotlight features in WORLD AFFAIRS to draw attention to important regional topics; for example, "The New Middle East," "Africa's Second Liberation," and "Asian Values."

Regular readers will note a number of changes in the 1995 yearbook. SPORTS AND GAMES now features an introductory essay on general issues as well as new coverage of judo, sumo, Australian rules football, equestrian show jumping and dressage, and Little League baseball. We also have special coverage of two top sporting events of the year—the Olympic Winter Games and the World Cup football (soccer) competition—as well as the top nonevent: the U.S. baseball strike. LITERATURE gains a few words on Netherlandic, Turkish, Persian, and Arabic letters as well as coverage of important writing in English outside the U.K., the U.S., and Canada. MUSIC includes expanded coverage of the genres of popular and world music; THEATRE applauds Toronto's featured billing in that field; and MOTION PICTURES is accompanied by a special report on Hollywood's challenge to the film industry worldwide. A new section, AUCTIONS AND COLLECTIONS, brings together coverage of art auctions, rare books, philately, and numismatics and adds a discussion of other collectibles (what is the most ever paid for a corset?) and a celebration of Sotheby's 250th anniversary.

You'll find full coverage of a once-in-a-millennium event, the crash of Comet Shoemaker-Levy 9 into Jupiter (as well as biographies of the comet's discoverers), and features on the effects of digital photography on our perceptions of reality and the controversy over "repressed memories." We have a new section on PALEONTOLOGY. You can learn about Prozac (a drug that bears an uncanny resemblance to "soma," the substance dreamed up by Aldous Huxley, born 100 years ago this year) and Jules Verne's eerily accurate technological vision of the 20th century in a newly discovered manuscript.

RELIGION has a new table on church membership in the U.S. to complement the widely consulted table of religious affiliation by continental areas. The social status of women and children worldwide is examined in two features, and two other articles provide historical background on the conflict between Hutu and Tutsi in Rwanda and the white settlement of South Africa.

We have retitled our business section BUSINESS AND INDUSTRY REVIEW and added coverage of retailing, paper and pulp, apparel, and housewares, as well as light metals, advanced composite materials, and metalworking. In ECONOMIC AFFAIRS look also for a fascinating account of the world's new stock exchanges.

We have also made visual improvements in the book. Tables have been redesigned, and several have been changed to charts so as to better present the essence of the data. Layouts have changed too, most visibly in SPORTING RECORD but also in the placement of photographs throughout the book. Photos include the unforgettable work of Sebastião Salgado and the late Kevin Carter. Six maps were specially compiled for this volume.

Cataloging what's new in our book is not in any way to diminish the importance of the regular features of *Britannica Book of the Year*, of course, especially the authoritative and incomparable BRITANNICA WORLD DATA.

Surely you will find yourself returning time and time again to the *Britannica Book of the Year* during 1995. I also hope that if you have suggestions about how the book could be of even greater value to you, you will write and let us know.

Enjoy!

Charles P. Trumbull, Editor

CONTENTS

77

278

186

112

290

473

Toward the Age of Common Sense

BY SIR PETER USTINOV

I am not one of those who can easily tell the difference between year and year, like a meteorologist with reliable charts to go by. I am not even one who can refer to a kind of event or quirk of fashion as typically '70s or '80s. All I am capable of is sensing the prevalent groundswells of life and registering, on occasion, the undertow, which is often contradictory.

We are in the midst of an enormous revolution in collective behaviour, one which is too often judged by old criteria. It all began, within living memory, with the sudden dissolution of one of the most rigidly controlled autocracies the world has ever known, the Soviet Union. It was as if the nation had responded to some physical law, like the boiling point, and simply vanished. Abruptly, in a world which had obeyed a general tendency to unify and coalesce, a large number of new republics were born, all enjoying a precarious independence as though they had found themselves in the middle of the last century.

The example was followed by others who felt cheated of their moment of self-identity in history. Slovakia decided to secede from its Czech sister, and the horror of Yugoslavia must be invoked as the most lamentable example of blood carelessly and brutally spilled during these enormous upheavals. I would go as far as to say that in Prague, suddenly released from the doctrinaire bonds of communism, the mob reacted, perhaps for the first time in history, with the intelligence of an individual. There were no excesses; no proof was needed of what was happening; joy and relief created their own congenial climate.

Mikhail Gorbachev will certainly go down in history as the great pioneer who made this extraordinary reassessment possible. It matters little that he is suffering from a temporary eclipse in his own country. He launched a new way of thinking of which we all are the beneficiaries, and nothing parochial politics can do is capable of tarnishing his example. There will always be those of limited vision who believe that the Cold War was won by the West and that it constituted a victory over the heresy of communism, to be celebrated as such. To be so shortsighted would be to judge by outmoded standards, as I have mentioned above. Gorbachev's importance was not merely to re-create Russia out of the embers of the Soviet Union but actually to be the first to hazard the opinion that the nuclear deterrent, so favoured by hawks in both camps, was a lunacy and an odious reflection on the humanity of all nations.

Chernobyl was a frightening warning. The idea of millions of deliberate Chernobyls, killing and distorting life on a huge scale, was an idea too horrible to contemplate, and yet its possibility had been entertained by rational people. The automatic result of this renunciation of the advantages of nuclear weaponry by the major powers, and the beginning

The protean Sir Peter Ustinov is known throughout the world as an actor on stage and screen (numbering two Academy Awards and a New York Drama Critics' Circle Award among his honours), a playwright, and a director of theatrical productions, operas, and motion pictures. Forbes FYI *recently titled an interview with him "The Greatest Living Raconteur"; he delights audiences around the world with his witty one-man show. Ustinov has served as goodwill ambassador for UNICEF since 1969 and chancellor of the University of Durham since 1992. He was knighted in 1990 and is a member of the French Academy. In addition to his stage works, Ustinov has written short stories and novels and contributes a regular column to* The European. *A collection of these commentaries was published in 1991 under the same title,* Ustinov at Large.

SEBASTIÃO SALGADO

A boy prays with his fellow Muslim soldiers in the breakaway Russian republic of Chechnya. After a period during which the world saw diverse nationalities gathered together in large, multinational states, many peoples have begun to assert their separate identities.

SEAN RAMSAY—JB PICTURES

of the gradual dismantling of their huge arsenals, was the signal for another phenomenon to begin, a respect for human life in those parts of the world most capable of ending it on a large scale. This unexpected respect for the sanctity of life, coupled with growing political pressure from Green parties and ecological groups like Greenpeace, has resulted in a totally changed attitude toward military intervention and the military in general. A new role is being invented for NATO, without much success now that the Warsaw Pact has disappeared into thin air. There is, in fact, something a little pathetic about vast armies left without opponents worthy of them. In NATO's case there is the paradoxical sight of old enemies applying desperately to join, finally underscoring its utter uselessness, at least in the role for which it was constituted. Another case, that of the U.S. armed forces, is at least as difficult to resolve. The imaginative tiptoe diplomacy of Jimmy Carter, Sam Nunn, and Colin Powell in Haiti in 1994 was followed by an enormous show of military might. This time, however, unlike Panama of a few years back, the might was used only as a demonstration of the power behind the tiptoes. The airborne troops landed and, their mandate not being immediately clear, they had for a time to watch local police brutality without intervening. Eventually it turned into a successful mission, however, with the reestablishment of an elected authority, to be followed by the gradual evacuation of the armada to leave the country to whatever devices lie within its competence.

Other spheres of international intervention in 1994 were not so happy. In Rwanda the French risked setting a danger-ous example but succeeded in demonstrating that it is the duty of responsible governments in the midst of the present moral confusion to act responsibly. The fact that they did something was, in itself, a welcome change from the general paralysis gripping other large nations. In Somalia the muddle of the attempted reconciliation between armed intervention and humanitarian action had not been resolved, with the result that a violent punitive expedition against clandestine but popular leaders was thwarted, the troops withdrawn, and the peacekeepers left more or less at the mercy of the gangster bosses.

The acme of mismanagement in 1994 was reached in Bosnia. Once again a compromise was sought between the military and those dispensing humanitarian aid. The result was a hybrid force confronting those who expected and feared old-fashioned ruthlessness but received only shadow-boxing. It was too easy for the disreputable to deliberately misunderstand the rules of this new game of symbolic strength, with every finger forbidden contact with the trigger and only intangible moral ascendancy as the force to be reckoned with. We know the results. Some spectacular but halfhearted air strikes against meticulously specific targets and entire groups of thinly armed UN peacekeepers taken hostage temporarily in order to prevent this from happening again. NATO, left to its own untried devices, would presumably have known what to do under such provoking circumstances, but driven into endless and fruitless consultation with the UN as a senior partner, it was frustrated and finally worse than useless.

In an African refugee camp a worker with Médecins sans Frontières removes the body of a dead child. Since its founding in France in the late 1960s, the aid group has sent medical personnel to Afghanistan, Liberia, Peru, and Somalia—wherever their humanitarian services have been needed.

STEELE-PERKINS—MAGNUM

As an unarmed apostle of peace, the secretary-general of the UN was somehow less convincing in 1994 than was Mahatma Gandhi half a century ago, a business suit carrying less weight than a loincloth and dispassionate logic less weight than serene conviction. The cumulative effect of these half measures and counterfeit toughness was to leave the frightening impression that perhaps millions of men had died in vain during the most recent of wars "to end all wars," and that, compared with the spineless posture of these modern self-styled peacekeepers, the appeasers of Munich, Neville Chamberlain and Édouard Daladier, appeared in retrospect as merely cautious.

Of course, it is easy to criticize when one has no responsibility, and it may well be that the present anomalies are all a result of the profound changes to which the societies of the more evolved sections of our planet have submitted. There is a general increase in sensitivity toward the value of human life, and the threats to the well-being of the community are suddenly clearly defined. For the first time in history, if one excepts the unique example of the International Red Cross, which succeeded in enforcing accepted standards for the treatment of prisoners of war, there have come into being movements born of the guilty conscience of the human animal, such as Médecins sans Frontières, volunteer medics in explosive parts of the world; Greenpeace, vigilantes raising objections to errors of ecological judgments on the part of governments and businesses; and Amnesty International, an organization recording man's inhumanity to man. The very existence of such international bodies, to say nothing of the Green parties in various parliaments, in which for the first time concern for the health of our environment achieves a response from voters, is symptomatic of an extraordinary reassessment of responsibility in human affairs.

The terrifying advance of AIDS has created an enemy for the human animal far more tangible than the traditional rivalry between nations. It arrived at the very moment in history when humankind was being asked for the first time to contemplate a future without enemies, a far more formidable task than it at first appeared. From time immemorial enmity has been a fact of life. It has polarized our endeavours and created targets for our energy. And it is good for business. What Dwight D. Eisenhower so graphically described as the military-industrial complex was the logical consequence of the concern for defense which was a priority at a time in which the enemies were allowed to flourish. Since then the military-industrial complex has priced itself out of the market with the endless need for weapons of ever greater sophistication. Now that the latest combat aircraft costs 10 times what it did in even recent memory, there is a sudden need for stringent economy in an area traditionally outside normal strictures. Besides that, the chronic absence of rivals has sounded more than a warning note to all those industries reliant on pessimism for their very existence.

In the new pattern of nationalism, there is no country left which is fully independent. Even the mighty United States is required to consult before exercising its rights as an independent nation. Those countries which have recently acquired

9

independence often find themselves in fact less independent than they were before their gesture of liberation. A flag unlike any other, an anthem with unique words, and a worthless currency all one's own are not valid proof of national identity. This can only come through interdependence, a sane evolution of independence with secure modern structures, where national identity is respected and a fair share in increasing mutual prosperity is guaranteed.

The tendency toward internationalization is irreversible because it is an economic necessity, and economics governs the ebb and flow of human intercourse where military might and colonialism did in a previous era. If this were not so, why was the League of Nations created at the end of World War I, a prototype, imperfect and dangerously ahead of its time, destroyed by the swan song of old-style empires and the upstart dictators who sought to revive them? It took another terrible war to build up momentum for a new surge of hope, in the shape of the UN. It, too, is living through moments of danger, but what a triumph of the will that it exists at all! The UN survives because there is an urgent desire for its survival, as an outcome of that universality of purpose desired by all sane inhabitants of the globe, concerned with people and not with monstrous excrescence such as ethnic cleansing and other antediluvian forms of racism.

Already commerce is international, and the close examination of a recently purchased product often reveals that it may have been built anywhere but in its country of origin. Once business is international, it follows that crime is automatically international too. The police are still shaking themselves free of their parochial shackles. Interpol is authorized to work only in a consultative capacity for the time being. And certainly a form of an internationally approved legal system is a crying necessity for dealing with organized crime stretching over national borders. The farce of instituting tribunals to deal with war crimes in former Yugoslavia is an example of the creaking mechanism operative at this time in such urgent matters. In this case it is obviously not facilitated by the fact that many potential war criminals are engaged in a parody of peace talks, and it will be difficult to recognize accepted negotiating delegates as criminals once peace has been established.

But, you may ask, once all is subjected to this new, as yet uncertain, atmosphere of cooperation toward an ultimate raising of living standards everywhere, a technological breakthrough for changing conventional concepts of unemployment, of jobs, of all human activity, even of leisure, what is there left for those who still dream of glory, of service to a country, to a flag? Little wars and isolated outbursts of turbulence will go on as long as there are communities still rooted in their tribal past, playing old games by old rules, matches and return matches with bullets as arguments and death as the scorer. In the more evolved parts of the globe, the elements in human nature which still hanker for victory and the clash of arms, the Olympic Games, the World Cup, and other safety valves, are there in force to ensure an outlet for high spirits. The sight of an athlete on the victor's podium, eyes blurred with tears and mouth stumbling over the words of an anthem unknown to a majority of spectators, should be enough to slake the thirst for restrained heroics, and athletes, embracing, united by

> # We
> do not inherit the world from our parents, but rather we are lent it by our children.
> —*African proverb*

their disciplines rather than divided by their nationalities, more than a hint of a new spirit animating this aging world.

We were not born with prejudice, which develops through family life and education and seems much like the sediment in any bottle of fine wine. However, the fact that children left to their own devices are free from it should be an example and a warning to us all. The old African proverb which says that we do not inherit the world from our parents but rather are lent it by our children is particularly apt. The fact that this piece of subtle and searching wisdom comes to us from the most troubled and the most perplexing of this earth's continents is very revealing.

In an ideal world, every living being would be everyone's responsibility. In a real, yet changing world, we are shyly edging toward such a distant possibility. Love of country is normal. Patriotism which leads to others' being hurt is no longer acceptable. The young are invariably in advance of where we stood at the same age. They are often skeptical of the values we piously handed down to them, and this is all to the good. Experience is something which may well have to be acquired, but so much has changed fundamentally since we acquired ours that it may not be apposite today. Politicians are far too glib about the rise of crime in the young and tend to advocate sterner penalties, more prisons, and a galaxy of lazy solutions to problems which have their roots in boredom, in the chronic lack of horizons, in the penury of oxygen for the imagination. Here is the real clash of generations, opposing the hardened mental arteries of those still addicted to a dull, conventional view of things and those impatient with what they are told and eager to obey their own instincts, which suggest that life must be richer than it is allowed to appear.

As one who is privileged to be chancellor of an outstanding university, may I say that I have the greatest respect for the motives and impulses of the young. They may make mistakes at times, but that capacity is also enjoyed by the old. On the other hand, their sense of adventure, if allowed to burgeon, is a constant source of wonder, as is the clarity of their vision and their optimism even under the pall of authoritative discouragement.

Sometimes, listening to the admonitions of those old before their time, laying down the law in some parliament or congress or chamber of deputies, we might easily get the impression that nothing really evolves, nothing really moves forward. Believe me, it does. The proof? Sixty-seven years ago there was a picture on the wall of my first classroom. It was of Jesus Christ leading a Boy Scout by the hand and showing the boy with his other hand the extent of the British Empire on the map. The expression on the Lord's face could best be described as reverent ecstasy. There was no doubt whose side He was on. Once again, in the early '20s, a French politician made a vibrant oration describing the swelling pride in a mother's heart when she inadvertently discovered that the Unknown Soldier was none other than her missing son. It is difficult to understand today how such tasteless nonsense could have been taken seriously only just over half a century ago. If standards have changed so rapidly, is there any limit for our future hopes? In all probability, the coming generation will take as normal that which we welcome with such trepidation and incredulity today, an age of common sense.

Chronology of 1994

JANUARY

1 Mexican peasants revolt in Chiapas. A group of uniformed Mexican peasants, calling themselves the Zapatista National Liberation Army (EZLN), caught the government completely off guard when they attacked and captured four towns in the southeastern state of Chiapas. In a written statement the rebels called for the resignation of Pres. Carlos Salinas de Gortari, urged free elections, and demanded an end to the government's alleged discrimination against the region's Indians. The EZLN began its insurrection on January 1 because the North American Free Trade Agreement (NAFTA) took effect on that date. The rebels cited NAFTA as another instance of government policy that further enriched the wealthy while ignoring the plight of the poor. Although outgunned and outmanned by superior government forces, the EZLN vowed to broaden the conflict. On January 6 three bombs exploded near Mexico City, the capital. Two days later a bomb was detonated in Acapulco and four others in or near the capital. On January 10 the president ordered a cease-fire and gave Manuel Camacho Solís, the former foreign relations minister, broad authority to negotiate a peace settlement with the Indians.

Saudi Arabia to implement budget cuts. During a nationally broadcast address, King Fahd of Saudi Arabia informed his Cabinet that a world surplus of oil had depressed prices to such an extent that the government would have to trim its annual budget by 20%. The monarch did not specify which areas of spending would be curtailed, but analysts surmised that the country's vast social welfare system and its

military procurement program were likely to be substantially affected.

2 Hundreds killed in Afghan capital. Afghan officials reported that more than 600 people had been killed or wounded during the first 36 hours of intense fighting in the capital city of Kabul. Most of the civilian casualties were victims of misdirected rebel rockets, mortars, and artillery shells that landed in residential areas. Following the 1992 overthrow of Mohammad Najibullah, the Soviet-installed president, rival factions took over various areas of the city and continued to battle for supremacy. Pres. Burhanuddin Rabbani, who headed a fragile Islamic coalition government, accused Gen. 'Abd ar-Rashid Dostam of having launched the latest offensive in order that the government might once again come under communist control.

3 Indians riot in Venezuelan prison. At least 122 inmates were killed during a vicious ethnic feud that erupted in a federal prison in Maracaibo, Venezuela, located about 520 km (325 mi) west of Caracas, the capital. The riot, which appeared to be planned vengeance for the decapitation of a Guajiro Indian inmate the previous week, allegedly began when 400 Indians broke out of their cell blocks and hurled firebombs into areas occupied by non-Indian prisoners. Some of the victims burned to death; others were shot, stabbed, drowned, lynched, mutilated, or decapitated. Few, if any, of those who died were Indians. The National Guard finally restored order after battling the inmates for five hours.

5 France moves to deport illegal aliens. Charles Pasqua, the Cabinet minister responsible for implementing France's immigration policy, declared that "the world will get the message" when the government begins deporting planeloads, boatloads, and trainloads of illegal immigrants. Conceding that in the future France would face immigration problems even greater than those encountered in the past, Pasqua justified the nation's new laws and immigration policies, which took effect on January 1, as the only way to stop a massive influx of immigrants from North Africa and the republics of the former Soviet Union, where thousands saw no hope in a future at home. The government estimated that between 100,000 and 150,000 aliens were entering and staying in France illegally each year.

8 Fierce fires ravage Sydney area. Thousands of people were forced to flee their homes in the suburbs of Sydney, Australia, as firestorms continued to rage out of control on an 800-km (500-mi) front for the third straight day. The director of the New South Wales state brushfire services described the blaze as the worst in Australia in 200 years. The arrival of light rains on January 10 aided the 7,000 firefighters as they gradually brought under control the 130 fires still burning; some had almost certainly been set by arsonists.

9 BCCI officer to be charged in the U.S. U.S. federal prosecutors revealed that an agreement had been reached with Sheikh Zaid ibn Sultan an-Nahayan, president of the United Arab Emirates (U.A.E.) and ruler of Abu Dhabi (one of the seven Persian Gulf states that constitute the U.A.E.), to extradite Swaleh Naqvi to the U.S. to face charges of massive fraud. As chief executive of the Luxembourg-based Bank of Credit and Commerce International (BCCI), Naqvi possessed extensive knowledge about the bank's international dealings and could presumably explain the disappearance of some $20 billion before the bank's global operations were shut down in 1991. U.S. investigators were especially eager to learn the degree to which BCCI influenced First American Bankshares Inc. in Washington, D.C., after it had secretly and illegally purchased the bank. As part of a broad agreement, Sheikh Zaid received assurances that he would face no civil or criminal charges in the U.S. even though he had been BCCI's largest shareholder and had been sued by trustees of First American for $1.5 billion.

The bodies of men presumed to be rebels lie in Ocosingo, in southeastern Mexico. Peasants began attacks on January 1 and took four towns before being driven out by government troops.

11

10 **Guatemala seeks lasting peace.** After five days of discussions, Guatemalan officials and representatives of the three-army leftist guerrilla movement agreed on a new framework for negotiating an end to over 30 years of violent conflict. A broad-based assembly, headed by Roman Catholic Bishop Rodolfo Quezada Toruño, a veteran negotiator, had been empowered to make recommendations for solving the country's social and human rights problems, which were key issues in the civil strife. Jean Arnault, an on-site UN negotiator, expressed hope that a peace settlement could be signed before the end of the year.

11 **New Russian assembly convenes.** Members of both chambers of Russia's newly constituted Federal Assembly gathered in separate buildings in Moscow amid hope that the proceedings would be less raucous than those that had characterized the former Congress of People's Deputies. The 178 members of the Federation Council (upper house) included two members from each of the nation's 89 regions and territories. In his opening address, Pres. Boris Yeltsin asked the delegates for their cooperation, but he also made it clear that he was completely prepared for confrontation. In addressing the less powerful State Duma (lower house), Prime Minister Viktor Chernomyrdin indicated that the government would continue its program of reforms without resorting to "shock therapy" tactics. First Deputy Prime Minister Yegor Gaidar was the leader of Russia's Choice, a reformist party that held about 16% of the seats in the Duma. The anti-Yeltsin forces were dominated by Vladimir Zhirinovsky, a flamboyant ultranationalist who apparently aspired to the presidency. Among the assembly's top priorities was the passage of laws that defined the functions and authority of the various branches of the newly structured government.

13 **Italian prime minister resigns.** Carlo Ciampi tendered his resignation after less than nine tumultuous months as prime minister of Italy. Since February 1992 several thousand Italians had been implicated in corruption, including five former prime ministers, about 200 members of Parliament, and numerous prominent businessmen. The cases of alleged bribery, extortion, fraud, embezzlement, and illegal political contributions were said to involve billions of dollars. On January 16 Pres. Oscar Luigi Scalfaro dissolved Parliament and called for new elections in March. With countless old-guard politicians discredited beyond redemption, no one could predict with confidence what the political landscape would look like after the election.

14 **Ukraine surrenders nuclear arms.** Ukrainian Pres. Leonid Kravchuk, Russian Pres. Boris Yeltsin, and U.S. Pres. Bill Clinton signed an agreement in Moscow that would, it was hoped, lead to the transfer of Ukraine's nuclear weapons to Russia, where they would be destroyed. In exchange, Ukraine would

(From left) U.S. Pres. Bill Clinton, Russian Pres. Boris Yeltsin, and Ukrainian Pres. Leonid Kravchuk shake hands at the signing of an accord on January 14. Ukraine agreed to give up its nuclear weapons in return for aid.
WALKER—GAMMA LIAISON

receive nuclear fuel and guarantees of security. The country, which was the second largest of the former Soviet republics, was in a state of near economic collapse. With its currency reserves virtually exhausted, inflation raging out of control, the production of energy far below normal, and large factories idle or barely functioning, the country desperately needed help to extricate itself from the economic quagmire that was devouring it. Divesting itself of nuclear weapons in exchange for Russian help seemed to be Ukraine's best hope for recovery.

17 **Quake devastates Los Angeles.** Millions of residents of southern California were terrorized by a disastrous predawn earthquake initially measuring 6.6—and later upgraded to 6.8—on the Richter scale. The quake, which was centred some 32 km (20 mi) northwest of Los Angeles, sent freeway overpasses crashing to the ground, totally demolished multistory buildings, and ignited numerous fires. At least 61 persons were reported killed. Hundreds of thousands of people were without water or electricity. In recent years there had been more severe earthquakes in southern California, but none had occurred in such a heavily populated area. Authorities quickly moved to take control of the situation by declaring a state of emergency and imposing a dusk-to-dawn curfew. Construction engineers estimated that it would take months to restore the freeways, which were a vital part of the region's transportation network. On February 12 President Clinton signed an $8.6 billion relief bill for the state of California for what some believed was the costliest natural disaster in U.S. history.

26 **Legislature ousts Belarus leader.** The Parliament of Belarus voted 209–36 to unseat Stanislau Shushkevich, chairman of the Supreme Soviet (head of state). The legislators, who had been elected before the breakup of the Soviet Union, were overwhelmingly opposed to Shushkevich's efforts to introduce reforms that would establish a free-market economy. They also sought closer alignment with Russia's foreign policies. Parliamentarians who supported Shushkevich denounced his ouster as a betrayal of the nation's sovereignty. The leader of the Belarusian Popular Front, disheartened by the turn of events, declared that the new leadership would now bring Belarus "into the Russian empire."

30 **Algerian military loses its power.** Algeria took a significant step toward returning to political normalcy by naming Liamine Zeroual to a three-year term as president. The appointment was the first of a series of steps leading to the election of a new national legislature. Algeria had plunged into political turmoil in December 1991 when Muslim fundamentalists, in the first round of voting for the National Assembly, stunned almost everyone by capturing 44% of the seats outright. In other races that required a runoff because no candidate had won an absolute majority of the vote, the Islamic Salvation Front had done so well that the fundamentalists were virtually certain, in the final round of voting, to take over the government and establish an Islamic state. At that juncture the army, backed by secularists, forced Pres. Chadli Bendjedid to resign. It then set up a High State Council to run the country, declared a state of emergency, and canceled the second round of the election. During the two years of conflict that followed, paramilitary death squads tracked down and killed suspected rebels, and Muslim guerrillas succeeded in assassinating government officials. At least 2,000 lives were estimated to have been lost to such violence.

FEBRUARY

1 **Lasso named to new UN rights post.** UN Secretary-General Boutros Boutros-Ghali nominated José Ayala Lasso to be the first United Nations high commissioner for human rights. However, members of several human rights organizations were highly critical of the appointment because Ayala had served as foreign minister under a repressive military regime in his native Ecuador. During the 1993 UN General Assembly debate that preceded the creation of the new agency, there was wide disagreement on what the functions of the commission should be and what authority it should have. Because these differences were never resolved, the UN mandate establishing the commission did not specify the circumstances under which it could initiate an investigation of suspected violations of human rights or whether it could act only with the approval of UN organizations to which the nations in question belonged.

3 **U.S. ends Vietnam trade embargo.** President Clinton officially ended the 19-year-old U.S. trade embargo against Vietnam, thereby paving the way for the eventual restoration of full diplomatic relations between the two countries. For the present, each nation would conduct business through a liaison office in the other's capital. Indirectly addressing the concerns of the families of more than 2,000 Americans missing in action during the Vietnam War, Clinton remarked that he was absolutely convinced that lifting the embargo was the most efficacious way of learning the fate of the military personnel still unaccounted for. U.S. businessmen had long argued that the embargo was an anachronism that barred them from investing in Vietnam's rapidly expanding economy.

Russian military to help Shevardnadze. Russian Pres. Boris Yeltsin and Georgian Pres. Eduard Shevardnadze signed a series of agreements in the Georgian capital city of Tbilisi. These included a treaty that extended the life of three Russian military bases in Georgia beyond the year 1995. Russia would also train and supply the Georgian army. Small groups of protesters denounced "Russian imperialism" and Shevardnadze's "betrayal of the country's independence." Factions within Russia's legislature also opposed the treaty, reportedly because they feared Russia could become embroiled in Georgia's effort to reestablish control over Abkhazia and South Ossetia, two strongholds of armed secessionists. Georgia had earlier asked for and received Russian military assistance in Abkhazia after promising to strengthen ties with other former Soviet republics by becoming a member of the Commonwealth of Independent States.

Court favours Chad in border dispute. The International Court of Justice, popularly known as the World Court, ruled 16–1 that Libya had no legal basis to support its claim to the 120,000-sq km (45,000-sq mi) Aozou Strip. Libya and Chad had both laid claim to the long stretch of land, which over the years had been the scene of fierce military engagements. In 1983 Libya, supported by its allies in northern Chad, had won effective control over the whole northern half of Chad, but the Chadian army gradually reoccupied the territory. In 1990 both parties in the dispute agreed to let the World Court, the judicial arm of the United Nations, decide the case. The court concluded that the border had been definitively fixed in 1955 when Libya signed a treaty with France, which at the time claimed Chad as an overseas colony.

6 **Costa Ricans elect new president.** After an intense and sometimes virulent campaign, José María Figueres Olsen, the candidate of the National Liberation Party, won slightly less than 50% of the popular vote and was elected to a four-year term as the president of Costa Rica. Figueres, whose father had drawn up the Central American nation's blueprint for democracy and welfare, was scheduled to succeed Pres. Rafael Calderón Fournier on May 8. The Costa Rican constitution did not permit the head of state and government to seek reelection.

Ahtisaari wins the presidency of Finland. Martti Ahtisaari, leader of the Social Democratic Party, won 54% of the vote in a runoff election to become president of Finland.

His opponent, Defense Minister Elisabeth Rehn, had surprised nearly everyone by finishing ahead of nine other candidates in the January 16 election. Ahtisaari indicated that he would involve himself in domestic issues in an effort to revitalize the nation's moribund economy. Prime Minister Esko Aho, however, pointedly remarked that the government's domestic policies would remain intact. By tradition, the Finnish president was responsible for the conduct of foreign policy and the prime minister for domestic affairs.

9 **Accord initialed by Israel and PLO.** Yasir Arafat, chairman of the Palestine Liberation Organization (PLO), and Shimon Peres, foreign minister of Israel, initialed a document in Cairo that resolved all the problems "either completely in detail or in principle" that had impeded implementation of the accord signed in September 1993 in Washington, D.C. That historic agreement granted self-government to Palestinians in occupied Gaza and the West Bank. As a first step, Palestinians would govern all of Gaza and the city of Jericho in the West Bank. Whether the Palestinians would exercise jurisdiction beyond the city's limits was a matter still to be negotiated. The timetable for total Israeli withdrawal from Gaza and Jericho would depend on how quickly practical problems involving the transfer of power could be settled. Final ratification of the accord by both sides did not appear to present any serious problem.

17 **Bosnian Serbs yield to threats.** Ethnic Serbs living in Bosnia and Herzegovina began to withdraw

Citizens move along a street in Sarajevo, the capital of Bosnia and Herzegovina, after Serbs had stopped shelling the city. The attackers began a withdrawal of their artillery from the hills around the city on February 17.

their heavy artillery from the hills surrounding Sarajevo, the besieged capital. On Nov. 9, 1993, NATO had issued an ultimatum that included threats to launch air strikes to silence the weapons if they were not put under UN control or moved 20 km (12 mi) away from the city by February 20. The ferocious fighting in Bosnia involved Serbs, Croats, and Muslims who were battling each other in shifting alliances to establish control over various regions of the country. NATO intervened after the Serbs had rejected repeated demands that they stop shelling the virtually defenseless city. Numerous reports of hate-inspired atrocities had evoked worldwide pleas that something be done to end the slaughter, especially of innocent civilians. The best hope for peace appeared to rest on the willingness of all parties to accept a division of the republic into autonomous ethnic regions.

22 **CIA agent charged with spying.** Aldrich Ames, a former member of the Soviet counterintelligence unit of the U.S. Central Intelligence Agency, was arrested by federal authorities in Washington, D.C., and charged with spying for Moscow, both before and after the breakup of the Soviet Union. Ames allegedly had received as much as $2.7 million for passing on highly secret information and for identifying agents employed abroad by the U.S. Ten of the agents were reportedly arrested and shot. Ames's wife, who had once been a CIA informer, was also arrested. The damage Ames had inflicted on U.S. intelligence operations was said to be catastrophic. The CIA itself was accused of inexcusable laxity for having failed to investigate the opulent lifestyle of Ames and his wife, which could not have been supported by a conventional income.

Peruvian army officers guilty of murder. A military court in Lima, Peru, sentenced two army majors, described as leaders of an assassination squad, to 20 years in prison for their roles in the 1992 murders of nine students and a teacher at the Enrique Guzmán y Valle National Education University. The victims had been shot in the head and their bodies burned. The army general in charge of intelligence planning was also implicated in the killings and was given a five-year sentence. Six others were sent to prison for periods ranging from 4 to 15 years. The case had been kept alive by the weekly magazine *Sí*, which disclosed the site where some of the victims were buried. Peruvian Pres. Alberto Fujimori expressed hope that U.S. criticism of his country's human rights record would now

be muffled and that Washington would release millions of dollars in urgently needed aid.

23 **Yeltsin's archrivals get amnesty.** Members of Russia's State Duma, the lower house of the nation's legislature, in a calculated act of defiance, approved a sweeping amnesty that included the release from prison of Pres. Boris Yeltsin's most intransigent opponents—those who had led an armed revolt against his government in October 1993. The vote was 253–67. On February 26 Ruslan Khasbulatov, the former speaker of parliament, and Aleksandr Rutskoy, the former vice president, were among those who were set free. Both had been captured with their armed supporters after Russian troops shelled and attacked the White House (the parliament building). The assault claimed 140 lives. Shortly before the prisoners walked out of the prison, Russia's chief

prosecutor, a Yeltsin supporter, resigned because there was no legal way he could accede to the president's request and halt the release.

Marcos estate ordered to pay $1.2 billion. A 10-member federal jury in Hawaii, having heard a class-action suit filed against Ferdinand Marcos, ordered his estate to pay some 10,000 plaintiffs exemplary damages (extraordinarily large punitive damages, allowable in certain cases) amounting to $1.2 billion. The jury had concluded that the former president of the Philippines bore responsibility for the numerous murders,

rapes, acts of torture, and other violations of human rights that had occurred after his declaration of martial law in 1972. The Marcos estate would also be liable for compensatory damages, the size of which had not yet been determined. Despite the court's decision, there were serious doubts that the plaintiffs would ever receive any money because the Philippine government had thus far failed to locate the billions of dollars Marcos allegedly looted from the national treasury before his ouster from power in 1986.

25 **Israeli murders Arabs in Hebron.** Baruch Goldstein, a U.S.-born medical doctor and an Israeli right-wing extremist, opened fire with an automatic weapon on a dense crowd of Palestinians worshiping at the Cave of the Patriarchs mosque in Hebron. About 30–40 persons were slain and some 150 wounded. Goldstein had apparently entered

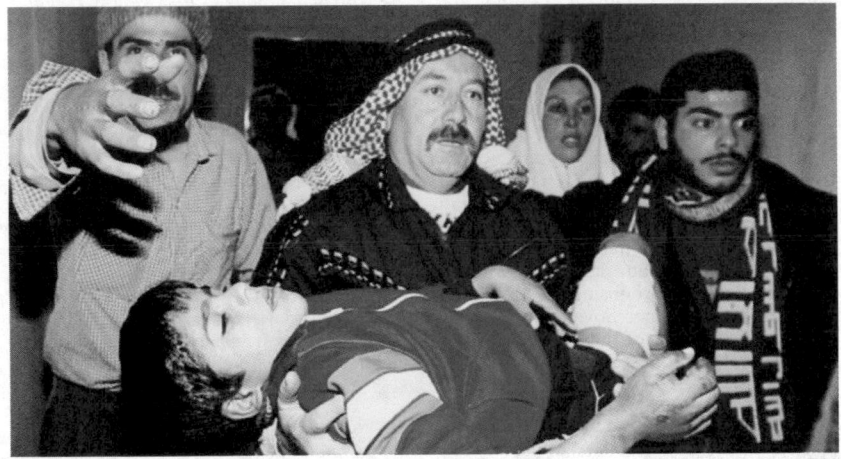

A father carries his wounded son from the Cave of the Patriarchs in Hebron in the West Bank. An Israeli settler opened fire in the mosque on February 25, killing and wounding Palestinians.
JACQUELINE ARZT—AP

the mosque with his weapon in full view without arousing the suspicion of Israeli security guards. The massacre that followed was the worst act of violence in the West Bank since Israel occupied the territory in 1967. After the first wave of shock and terror had passed, infuriated worshipers sprang toward Goldstein and beat him to death. Israeli Prime Minister Yitzhak Rabin called the massacre "a loathsome criminal act of murder." The anti-Israeli rioting that quickly erupted in the occupied territories was expected; less expected were the angry protests of Arabs in parts of Israel proper.

MARCH

1 **EU welcomes three new nations.** The European Union (EU), formerly known as the European Community (EC), reached agreement with Austria, Finland, and Sweden on terms for their admission into the organization at the beginning of the new year. All of the approved applicants, however, still had to have the accord formally ratified by their re-

spective national legislatures. Negotiations with Norway were put on hold because of a dispute over fishing rights in the North Sea. Spain and Portugal had expanded the EC to 12 members by joining the group in 1986. The ultimate goal of the EU was to unite all of Western Europe in a free-trade zone with a common currency and a unified foreign policy.

2 **Mexico agrees to assist Chiapas.** Representatives of the Mexican government and of Indians from the impoverished state of Chiapas announced a tentative agreement that would, it was hoped, end the Indians' two-month-old insurrection and gradually improve the economic and political climate of their region. The package of promised reforms, which had to be submitted to various Indian communities for approval, included new rights for Indians, land reform, a series of new social programs, and changes in the political and judicial structures of Chiapas. Subcomandante Marcos, the nom de guerre of the leader of the rebel Zapatista National Liberation Army, indicated that his followers would not lay down their arms until the government's promises had been spelled out in greater detail and Mexican law changed to ensure greater democracy on a national scale. Proponents of change accused the Institutional Revolutionary Party (PRI) of Pres. Carlos Salinas de Gortari, which had dominated Mexican politics for 65 years, of resorting to fraudulent elections to retain power.

3 **Vatican establishes ties with Jordan.** The Vatican officially reported that it had established diplomatic ties with the Hashemite Kingdom of Jordan to reinforce "the relationship of respect and friendship which already exists between the two sides." The move had long been expected because the Vatican had already established diplomatic missions in Arab nations that had a Catholic presence far less conspicuous than that in Jordan. The Vatican and Jordan also shared a deep concern about the status of Jerusalem, which was sacred to Jews, Muslims, and Christians alike. Even though Israel occupied the entire city after seizing control of east Jerusalem from Jordan during the 1967 Arab-Israeli war, Jordan still claimed a protectorate over the Dome of the Rock and the Al Aqsa Mosque, two sites sacred to Muslims. The future status of Jerusalem, which Israel had designated as its national capital, was one of the most delicate and intractable problems standing in the way of a comprehensive peace settlement in the Middle East.

4 **Ukraine begins shipping warheads.** Implementing a January agreement signed in Moscow by Ukrainian Pres. Leonid Kravchuk and Russian Pres. Boris Yeltsin, Ukraine sent the first shipment of 60 nuclear warheads to Russia for dismantling. Ukraine had pledged to divest itself of all of its 1,600 nuclear weapons at staggered intervals. The U.S. had played a pivotal role in the negotiations by promising to provide $350 million to Russia to help defray the cost of rendering the weapons useless.

World Trade Center bombers convicted. A federal jury in New York City found four Arab immigrants guilty of the February 1993 bombing of the World Trade Center in Manhattan. The huge explosion, detonated in an underground garage, killed six persons, injured more than 1,000, and caused hundreds of millions of dollars in damage. The alleged mastermind of the plot and one of his associates were still at large. A seventh suspect was to be tried separately. The four convicted terrorists included Mohammad A. Salameh, who was found guilty on 10 counts. He was convicted of renting the apartment where the explosives were mixed and of renting the van that carried the bomb into the garage. Mahmud Abouhalima, convicted on nine counts, was part of the small group that constructed the bomb. Nidal A. Ayyad, a chemical

engineer, was identified as the person who procured the explosives. Ahmad M. Ajaj, found guilty on 10 counts, provided the manual of instructions for making the bomb. During the five-month trial, some 200 witnesses had been put on the stand and more than 1,000 exhibits placed in evidence. Sheikh Omar Abdel-Rahman, a radical Muslim cleric, and 14 others were scheduled to go on trial in September. All were believed to be terrorists involved in a similar plot to bomb the United Nations building and other targets in New York City.

11 **Agreement to reduce Polish debt.** Western banks agreed, after four years of negotiations, to reorganize Poland's huge foreign debt in such a way that its obligations would be reduced by more than 40%. Poland's economic situation had become so dire that its leaders had little choice but to default on the nation's debt for several years. Although each of the many banks that had granted loans to Poland would have to study and approve the agreement in the months ahead, Poland was expected to experience a significant upturn in its economy within a year or so.

12 **Anglican Church ordains women.** With the ordination of 32 women as priests of the Church of England, the Anglican Church abandoned a tradition that had been honoured for more than 450 years. The women were ordained by Bishop Barry Rogerson in Bristol Cathedral. Even though the General Synod of the Anglican Church had declared in 1975 that it found no theological basis for excluding women from the priesthood, many Anglicans were deeply perturbed by the announcement. Their number included some 700 clergymen who warned that they would leave the church and convert to Roman Catholicism if such ordinations took place. Pope John Paul II, whose opposition to women priests was clear and unswerving, viewed the ordinations as "a profound obstacle to every hope of reunion between the Catholic Church and the Anglican communion." The archbishops

of Canterbury and York, both of whom attended the ordination ceremony, issued a joint statement urging church members to show "generosity, tolerance, courtesy, and loving patience with each other."

14 **Moravcik becomes prime minister.** Leaders of five political parties in Slovakia approved the appointment of Jozef Moravcik as the nation's new prime minister. Moravcik, the last foreign minister of Czechoslovakia before its breakup in January 1993, replaced Vladimir Meciar, who had been ousted on March 11 when the parliament rejected his leadership by a 78–2 vote of no confidence. There were 56 abstentions. Meciar had been widely criticized for antidemocratic policies that led many members of his own Movement for a Democratic Slovakia to desert him. He had also created political turmoil by publicly feuding with Pres. Michal Kovac. The new prime minister faced the urgent and daunting task of reconciling various political interests so that measures could be taken to shore up democracy and foster economic reforms.

23 **PRI candidate slain in Mexico.** Luis Colosio, the presidential candidate of Mexico's ruling Institutional Revolutionary Party (PRI), was shot and killed as he was leaving a campaign rally in Tijuana. Colosio, whom Pres. Carlos Salinas de Gortari had handpicked as his successor, was virtually guaranteed the presidency because the PRI had monopolized all branches of the government for more than six decades. Accused of the assassination was a young local pacifist, identified as Mario Aburto Martínez, who had no known connection to any group opposed to the government. On March 29 Salinas selected Ernesto Zedillo Ponce de León, who had been manager of Colosio's campaign, to be the PRI's new presidential candidate.

25 **U.S. ends mission in Somalia.** Fifteen months after spearheading Operation Restore Hope in Somalia, the U.S. quietly withdrew its last Marine combat units from the country. At

PETERSON—GAMMA LIAISON

The last of the U.S. troops in Somalia leave on March 25. The U.S. forces, which had entered Somalia on Dec. 9, 1992, to prevent mass starvation, relinquished their operations to a United Nations force.

one time the U.S. presence had numbered some 28,000 personnel. About 19,000 United Nations troops still remained in Somalia, but there was growing evidence that whatever progress had been made to ameliorate the chaotic political situation was proving to be not much more than a passing phenomenon. The main goal of the operation, however, had been successful. Hundreds of thousands of Somalis had been saved from starvation, and the warring factions had been sufficiently contained—despite numerous ugly incidents—to permit the distribution of food and medicines to those in desperate need.

28 **Uganda to get new constitution.** Enthusiastic voters went to the polls in Uganda for the first time in 14 years to elect a constituent assembly. More than 1,500 candidates had campaigned on a nonparty basis for the 214 elected seats. Supporters of Pres. Yoweri Museveni won 114 seats; the president was further allowed to appoint 10 members of his choosing. The assembly would also include two representatives from each of the four main political parties and 56 persons representing the special interests of such groups as women, youth, and

French students protest a measure allowing employers to pay below-minimum wages to workers under 25 years of age. The decree was revoked on March 30.

BASSIGNAC/TURPIN/VAN DER STOCKT—GAMMA LIAISON

labour unions. The assembly was expected to complete its draft of a new constitution in about six months. Only then would the people return to the polls to elect a president and members of the parliament.

30 **France bows to student protests.** French Prime Minister Édouard Balladur yielded to student demands and revoked a government decree that would have allowed employers to hire young people at less than the minimum wage. Faced with an unemployment rate that exceeded 12% overall and 25% for those under 25, the government had viewed the new law as a positive step that would create job opportunities for the young. The students, however, took to the streets of Paris and a dozen other cities to denounce the decree as discriminatory. On March 28 the government tried to mollify the protesters by agreeing to suspend the edict until a more satisfying proposal could be drawn up, but the students insisted that the decree be stricken from the books. The government then took a new tack to help resolve the unemployment problem by offering employers a $175 monthly subsidy for providing first-time jobs to those under 25.

APRIL

5 **Turkey adopts austerity program.** Prime Minister Tansu Ciller announced a series of austerity measures designed to alleviate the nation's severe economic problems. Inflation had reached an annual rate exceeding 70%, and the national budget deficit had soared to more than $8.5 billion by the end of 1993. In addition, the country's trade and balance of payments deficits had reached record heights. To reverse this negative trend, Ciller pledged to shut down unprofitable state industries, give high priority to a program of privatization, freeze wages, and increase the cost of tobacco, gasoline, and other items sold by the government. There would also be a one-time tax on the assets of banks and corporations. The government also devalued the lira for the second time since January, pegging the exchange rate at 32,000 liras to one U.S. dollar. The leader of the Motherland Party, which represented the strongest challenge to Ciller's True Path Party, characterized the austerity measures as a bad copy of a similar program in 1980 that led to a military coup.

6 **Two presidents killed in crash.** Cyprien Ntaryamira and Juvénal Habyarimana, the respective presidents of Burundi and Rwanda, were killed when their plane crashed as it was landing in Kigali, Rwanda's capital. Eight others aboard the plane also died. The circumstances of the incident were unclear, but there were suspicions that the plane might have been brought down by ground fire or a missile. The two African leaders, both Hutu, were returning from Tanzania, where they had conferred with other African leaders on ways to end the incessant bloody feuding between Tutsi and Hutu tribesmen in their respective countries.

8 **Japanese prime minister resigns.** Morihiro Hosokawa, who had become prime minister of Japan in August 1993, abruptly resigned amid allegations that he or close associates had profited illegally from a large loan proffered by executives of a trucking company in the early 1980s. As head of the Japan New Party, Hosokawa had led a broad-based seven-party coalition government that was united by its determination to prevent the scandal-ridden Liberal-Democratic Party from regaining power. During the 38 years it had controlled the government, the LDP had become so corrupted by money politics that many longtime members deserted the party in disgust. On April 25, with Hosokawa gone, the lower house of the Diet (parliament) elected Tsutomu Hata, a member of Shinseito (Japan Renewal Party), prime minister. Like Hosokawa, he was a former member of the LDP and had served in Hosokawa's Cabinet as deputy prime minister and foreign minister. On April 26, even before he was formally appointed to his new post by the emperor, Hata faced a major political crisis: the Social Democrats withdrew from the coalition. That left Hata without a majority in the lower house and with an uncertain future as head of the government.

10 **NATO cripples Serb offensive.** U.S. military aircraft assigned to NATO forces in Europe attacked Bosnian Serb positions near Gorazde on orders from the United Nations commander in Bosnia and Herzegovina. The Serbs, choosing to ignore UN Secretary-General Boutros Boutros-Ghali's warning of possible military reprisals if they did not halt their offensive, continued their two-week assault against the Muslim enclave with artillery and armoured vehicles. Gorazde, which the

UN had designated one of the six "safe zones" in the war-ravaged country, was home to some 65,000 people. That small community included an estimated 40,000 Muslim refugees who had fled to Gorazde when their own towns were seized by the Serbs. The Serb commander condemned the UN for supporting the NATO attack, saying that the UN had violated its own principles and had taken sides in the civil war by supporting the Muslims. The U.S. ambassador to the UN responded that the air strikes were basically undertaken to protect UN peacekeeping forces in Gorazde.

11 **Florida sues the U.S. government.** Lawton Chiles, the governor of Florida, filed a lawsuit against the U.S. government to seek reimbursement for the hundreds of millions of dollars the state had been forced to spend on illegal immigrants. Following an analysis of the state's finances, Florida claimed that it had spent nearly $900 million on some 350,000 undocumented immigrants during 1993. As a consequence, the state's hospitals, schools, and prisons were underfunded, and legal residents had only limited access to certain government services. The financial burden of caring for huge numbers of illegal aliens, the state argued, should be borne by the federal government because it had not taken adequate steps to control its borders.

15 **World trade pact finally signed.** The seventh series of international trade talks under the so-called Uruguay round of the General Agreement on Tariffs and Trade (GATT) that began in Punta del Este in 1986 reached a successful conclusion in Marrakech, Morocco. The complexity of the numerous issues that took years to resolve was evident in the final document, which filled 22,000 pages. When representatives of 125 nations signed the accord, GATT went out of existence and was replaced by the World Trade Organization, which would bear responsibility for overseeing compliance with the new regulations. The pact, designed to liberalize international trade by, among other things, eliminating tariffs, was expected to have an impact of immense proportions and improve the economies of countries all over the world. Even though most of the signatory nations had not yet formally ratified the pact, it was scheduled to take effect on Jan. 1, 1995.

CIS strengthens unity at Moscow summit. The 12 nations constituting the Commonwealth of Independent States became more cohesive during their meeting in Moscow by consolidating Russia's position of preeminence in the organization and by establishing an Interstate Economic Commission, headquartered in Minsk, the capital of Belarus, to facilitate the eventual formation of a custom-free union. Three days earlier Russia and Belarus had signed a treaty that would progressively give Russia control over Belarus' monetary system.

20 **Russia receives $1.5 billion loan.** The International Monetary Fund (IMF) released a $1.5 billion loan to Russia to support the country's economic reform and stabilization program during the current year. A similar sum had been lent to Russia in June 1993 as part of an overall effort to assist Russia and the new democracies of Eastern Europe. The director of the IMF remarked that the loan was justified because Russian monetary policy had undergone a spectacular change for the better during the 10 months following receipt of the initial loan. Russia was also expected to reap economic benefits by having its $84 billion foreign debt rescheduled.

22 **Richard Nixon dies from stroke.** Richard Nixon, the 37th president (1969–74) of the United States, died in a New York City hospital four days after suffering a severe stroke at home. According to his wishes, no aggressive measures were taken to prolong his life after he lapsed into a coma. The funeral was held on April 27 in Yorba Linda, Calif., on the grounds of the Richard Nixon Library and Birthplace; the house where Nixon was born stands on the same site. During the funeral ceremony, presided over by evangelist Billy Graham, a longtime family friend, eulogies were delivered by President Clinton; Henry Kissinger, Nixon's secretary of state and foreign policy adviser; Bob Dole, the minority leader in the Senate; and Pete Wilson, the governor of California. Nixon had specified in his will that he did not want a formal state funeral in Washington, D.C.

24 **Calderón wins in El Salvador.** In a runoff election for the presidency of El Salvador, Armando Calderón Sol of the ruling Nationalist Republican Alliance (Arena) coasted to victory with 68% of the popular vote. His opponent was Rubén Zamora, candidate of the leftist Democratic Convergence coali-

tion. In the March 20 election, Calderón had fallen just short of an absolute majority, which would have made a runoff unnecessary. The March election had been the first since the United Nations brokered a peace accord in January 1992 that ended a 12-year-old civil war. The Farabundo Martí National Liberation Front guerrillas had accepted the peace settlement in exchange for certain guarantees, including the opportunity to seek elective office. When Calderón took office on June 1, Arena would control 39 of the 84 seats in the Legislative Assembly. However, with the promised support of the National Conciliation Party, which won four seats, Calderón would operate with a very slim majority.

26 **A historic vote in South Africa.** For the first time in South Africa's history, people of all races went to the polls to elect their national and regional leaders. The balloting, which ended on April 29, signaled an end of three centuries of white minority rule and the extinction of apartheid—a system of racial separation that had been institutionalized

Black South African voters wait in a long line. The voting, which began on April 26, was the first in which citizens of all races could cast ballots in a national election and represented the beginning of majority rule.
BROOKS KRAFT—SYGMA

by the National Party in 1948. Despite preelection violence, mainly on the part of white extremists, South African blacks (75% of the population), whites (over 13%), Coloureds (mixed race, over 8%), and Indians (near 3%) brought about an

astonishing transformation in the nation's political life. When the final election tallies had been completed, Nelson Mandela's African National Congress was awarded 252 seats in the National Assembly, the National Party of former prime minister F.W. de Klerk 82, and Mangosuthu Buthelezi's Inkatha Freedom Party 43. (Buthelezi, a political rival of Mandela, had waited until April 19 before deciding that his Zulu-based party would not boycott the election.) Four other parties shared the remaining 23 seats. On May 9 Mandela, who had been imprisoned for 27 years until 1990 for opposing the all-white government, was elected president, unopposed, by the National Assembly. The next day he took the presidential oath of office in the presence of dignitaries from more than 130 nations. His Cabinet included de Klerk as second deputy president and Buthelezi as minister of home affairs.

27 **Syria and Russia sign accords.** A series of accords was signed in Damascus that helped revitalize relations between Syria and Russia and enhanced the latter's image as a broker

in the quest for a Middle East peace settlement. Moscow deflected criticism of its arms deal with Syria by saying that it would supply Syria only with defensive weapons and with spare parts for Soviet-made equipment it already possessed. The two nations also agreed to expand trade and cooperate more fully in other areas.

28 **Teamsters settle bitter strike.** The International Brotherhood of Teamsters, which had called a strike on April 6 after four months of failed negotiations with 22 trucking companies, approved a compromise settlement that ended a bitter and complex labour dispute. The 24-day work stoppage was the longest in the U.S. union's history. A critical issue had been management's decision to replace full-time drivers with lower-wage part-time employees in order to cut operating costs on loads delivered to multiple destinations. Many transport companies had gone out of business in recent years because the cost of doing business had become intolerable. Competition also intensified after the industry was deregulated in 1980 and more independent truckers took to the roads. The terms of the settlement excluded the hiring of part-time drivers but included a no-strike clause and allowed more freight to be shipped by rail rather than by trucks. Although some 75,000 truckers, dockworkers, delivery drivers, warehouse workers, and mechanics were expected back at work within a few days, the Teamsters had good reason to worry about how much business they had lost permanently to nonunion truckers in the strike.

29 **Rwanda engulfed in violence.** Boutros Boutros-Ghali, secretary-general of the United Nations, urged the UN Security Council to consider taking "forceful action" to end the wanton massacre of Hutu and Tutsi civilians in Rwanda. A tidal wave of violence had engulfed the capital city of Kigali immediately after Pres. Juvénal Habyarimana, a Hutu, was killed in a suspicious plane crash on April 6. In the week that followed, an estimated 10,000–20,000 civilians were slain, many by marauding bands of Tutsi and Hutu armed with machetes, spears, bows and arrows, clubs, and guns. The Rwandan Patriotic Front (Tutsi guerrillas) added a new dimension to the conflict by laying siege to Kigali. With the situation totally out of control, Belgium, France, and the U.S. dispatched troops to the area to evacuate their nationals. UN peacekeepers on the ground did their best to succour the victims with food and medicines. Meanwhile, vast numbers of Rwandans were fleeing the country, most notably to neighbouring Tanzania, where at least 250,000 had massed by the end of the month. Besides the thousands of civilians buried in mass graves to prevent the spread of disease, the death list included high government officials, nuns and priests, and persons working in hospitals and relief agencies. Because the majority Hutu (90%) and minority Tutsi had never been able to agree on an equitable sharing of power, ethnic animosities continued to smoulder. Outside observers believed that Rwanda's ethnic and political problems would continue to be explosive issues even if the UN-brokered cease-fire and peace accord signed in August 1993 were reestablished.

MAY

3 **Netherlands election is inconclusive.** Dutch voters were so divided in their loyalties that the results of the national election left many wondering what kind of government The Netherlands would have. The ruling coalition, which included the Christian Democratic Appeal (CDA) and the Labour Party, was clearly destroyed, but no party emerged with enough strength to claim a mandate to rule. The Labour Party, under the leadership of Deputy Prime Minister Willem ("Wim") Kok, received the greatest support and a projected 37 seats in the 150-seat Second Chamber (lower house of parliament). The CDA was expected to hold on to 34 seats, leaving the former coalition 5 seats short of a majority and with 32 fewer seats than it had controlled before the election. Prime Minister Ruud Lubbers' government had lost popular support in large part because it had cut social programs and introduced other belt-tightening measures to curb The Netherlands' growing budget deficit. The next ruling coalition—which would not likely take shape without long and laborious negotiations—would likely include the Democrats 66 party, a left-leaning group that was expected to occupy about 24 seats in the lower house.

4 **Israeli and PLO leaders sign accord.** During a meeting in Cairo, Yasir Arafat, chairman of the Palestine Liberation Organization, and Yitzhak Rabin, prime minister of Israel, signed a long-delayed accord that resolved a number of outstanding details on Palestinian self-rule in the Gaza Strip and in Jericho, a city located in the West Bank. During the gradual transfer of power to Palestinian civil authorities, Israel would continue to have overall responsibility for security matters and authority over Jewish settlements in the occupied territories.

5 **Yemen torn apart by civil war.** Yemen, a republic situated at the southern end of the Arabian Peninsula, was plunged into civil war because of a dispute over the sharing of power between the north and the south, which had been two separate republics before agreeing to unite in 1990. Hoping to end the fighting quickly, northern forces loyal to Pres. Ali Abdallah Salih launched an offensive against outnumbered southern troops supporting Vice Pres. Ali Salim al-Baidh. He had been head of the Marxist-oriented People's Democratic Republic of Yemen before unification. By the end of the month, thousands of Yemenis had been killed or wounded in the fighting, and northern troops were poised about 16 km (10 mi) from Aden, the most important city in the south. A spokesman for the north urged the United Nations not to jeopardize the nation's unity by intervening in the conflict.

6 **Tunnel links Britain and France.** Queen Elizabeth II of the U.K. and Pres. François Mitterrand of France formally inaugurated the Channel Tunnel (Eurotunnel), a 50-km (31-mi)-long rail tunnel beneath the English Channel, in a ceremony in Calais, France. The project was hailed as one of the great engineering successes of the century. After construction began in 1987, it gradually became clear that the project would take a year and a half longer than planned. Its final cost would be about $15 billion, more than double the original estimate. Paying customers would begin using the high-speed Eurostar rail system in about six months, pending the installation and testing of safety systems. Full service, which included the transport of passengers in their automobiles, was set for the summer of 1995.

TIM GRAHAM—SYGMA

Queen Elizabeth II of the U.K. (second from right) and French Pres. François Mitterrand (sixth from right) attend the ceremony in Calais, France, on May 6 inaugurating the rail tunnel beneath the English Channel. Construction of the 50-km (31-mi) tunnel began in 1987.

Haiti faces broader new trade embargo.
The United Nations Security Council voted unanimously to expand its trade embargo against Haiti in an effort to force the military regime to relinquish power and allow Jean-Bertrand Aristide to return from exile and assume the presidency. After easily winning the December 1990 democratic election, Aristide had held office for about eight months before being ousted in a military coup. The Security Council also set a May 21 deadline for Haiti to comply with the UN-sponsored agreement Aristide and Lieut. Gen. Raoul Cédras, the de facto ruler of the country, had signed in New York in July 1993. Under terms of that accord, the military would step down and Aristide would return to Haiti as president. Instead, a powerful pro-military group of senators openly defied the Security Council on May 11 by naming Émile Jonassaint, an elderly Supreme Court justice, provisional president.

Colombia legalizes private use of drugs.
Colombia's Constitutional Court voted 5–4 to legalize the personal use of marijuana, cocaine, and other drugs. The decision, which startled U.S. and Colombian officials who had fought for years to curtail the use of such drugs, could be reversed only by amendment of the nation's constitution. Pres. César Gaviria Trujillo called the court's ruling absurd. The country's chief prosecuting attorney, however, had taken the position that efforts to stop drug use had been a failure and that the decriminalization of drugs should be seriously considered. Germany's Federal Constitutional Court had recently ruled that possessing or importing small quantities of marijuana and hashish was not illegal. After marijuana was legalized in The Netherlands in 1976, hundreds of cafés and other establishments openly included a wide variety of drugs among the other items they offered for sale.

8 **Pérez elected Panamanian president.**
Ernesto Pérez Belladares, a millionaire banker running under the banner of the Democratic Revolutionary Party, defeated six other candidates in a race for the presidency of Panama. Although he was supported by only one-third of the electorate, a runoff was not required. His strongest challenge had come from Mireya Moscoso de Gruber, who received 29% of the vote. Singer-actor Rubén Blades made a serious run for the presidency, but he finished third with 17% of the vote. Incumbent Pres. Guillermo Endara Galimany was not directly involved in the election because, by law, he could serve only one five-year term. During the campaign Pérez Belladares promised to better the lives of the country's poorest citizens through social programs and the creation of more jobs.

11 **Berlusconi takes helm in Italy.**
A new political era dawned in Italy when Silvio Berlusconi took the oath of office as prime minister. The ceremony not only apparently closed a chapter on a government besmirched by blatant corruption; it also marked a return to the past because, for the first time since the end of World War II, neo-Fascists were elevated to positions in the Cabinet.

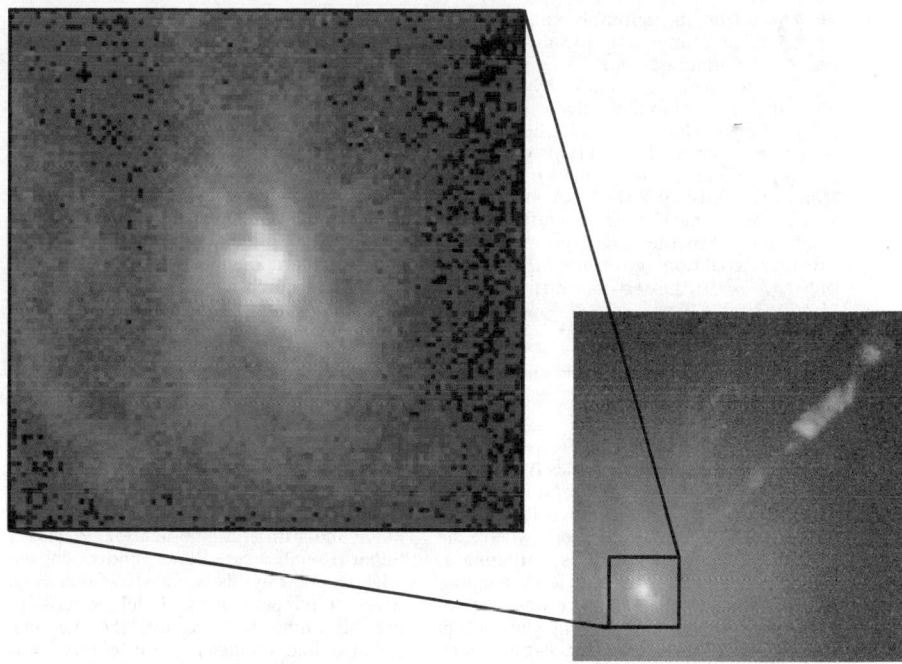

Images of the centre of galaxy M87 made by the Hubble Space Telescope reveal a disk of gas, the rapid rotation of which suggests a massive black hole. The finding was announced May 25.
HOLLAND FORD (STSCI/JHU), NASA, ET AL

Before the March elections Berlusconi's Forza Italia party formed a coalition with the neo-Fascist National Alliance (formerly known as the Italian Social Movement) and the Northern League. Campaigning under the name Alliance for Freedom, the coalition won an absolute majority in the national Chamber of Deputies. After bitter wrangling, all agreed to offer Berlusconi the prime ministership. He responded by awarding high Cabinet posts to members of the Northern League and the National Alliance.

17 **Voters oust president of Malawi.**
In Malawi's first multiparty elections, nonagenarian Pres. Hastings Kamuzu Banda was defeated by Bakili Muluzi, candidate of the United Democratic Front. Muluzi had formerly been secretary-general of the ruling Malawi Congress Party. Banda, self-declared president for life, had exercised dictatorial powers since 1964, when the African republic became independent from Britain. The electorate, however, had paved the way for his removal in June 1993 by passing a referendum establishing a multiparty political system.

25 **Hubble proves Einstein's theory.**
During a news conference in Washington, D.C., Holland Ford, an astronomer at the Space Telescope Institute and Johns Hopkins University, Baltimore, Md., announced that the Hubble Space Telescope had provided "conclusive evidence of a supermassive black hole" in the centre of galaxy M87 in the constellation Virgo. Confirmation of the existence of such a phenomenon, predicted by Albert Einstein in his theory of general relativity, had eluded scientists for decades. Some black holes are thought to form from massive stars that became unstable and gravitationally collapsed inward upon themselves after exhausting their internal

thermonuclear fuel. Other kinds may form at the centres of galaxies when large volumes of interstellar matter collect under the influence of gravity and collapse. In either case, the weight of the matter falling in from all sides compresses the matter at the centre of the collapsing region to zero volume and infinite density. Gravity becomes so intense that nothing, not even light, can escape.

26 **Clinton alters his China policy.**
President Clinton announced that he had decided to sign an executive order extending for one year China's most-favoured-nation trade status even though it had failed to make "overall significant progress" in respecting the human rights of its citizens. Clinton revised his policy even further by declaring that China's observance of human rights, which previously had been a key issue in determining its trade status, would henceforth be treated as a separate matter. The U.S., however, would continue to pressure China to comply with the United Nations Universal Declaration of Human Rights. It would also, among other things, resist the importation of goods produced in Chinese prisons.

Antarctic whale sanctuary established.
During its annual meeting in Mexico, the International Whaling Commission voted 23–1, with six abstentions, to bar permanently all commercial whalers from the waters south of Africa, Australia, and South America, a major feeding ground for many types of whales. All stocks of whales in the area, except the minke, had been reduced to a fraction of their population. Japan, the only nation actively fighting the establishment of a vast whale sanctuary covering nearly one-quarter of the world's oceans, argued that a ban on hunting minke was an emotional decision unjustified by scientific data.

29 **Socialists triumph in Hungary.** The Hungarian Socialist (former Communist) Party staged a spectacular political comeback by winning, after the final runoff elections, a total of 209 of the 386 elective seats in the National Assembly. Eight additional seats were filled by appointment. The Alliance of Free Democrats finished a weak second with 70 seats. The Hungarian Democratic Forum, which had been the senior partner in the previous coalition government, retained only 37 seats. Observers attributed the election results to widespread dissatisfaction with Hungary's efforts to adopt a free-market economy. During a special party congress on June 4, the Socialists officially named Gyula Horn as their choice for prime minister. Late in June the entire assembly was expected to confirm Horn as head of government.

30 **Pope bans ordination of women.** Pope John Paul II emphatically reaffirmed the position that women cannot be ordained priests in the Roman Catholic Church. In a letter addressed to Catholic bishops throughout the world, the pontiff endeavoured to end a debate that had engrossed a large number of bishops, priests, nuns, and laypeople. The central message of the pope's letter read: "Wherefore, in order that all doubt may be removed regarding a matter of great importance, a matter which pertains to the church's divine constitution itself, in virtue of my ministry of confirming the brethren, I declare that the church has no authority whatsoever to confer priestly ordination on women and that this judgment is to be definitively held by all the church's faithful."

JUNE

3 **Crimea acknowledges ties to Ukraine.** A dispute over the status of the Crimean Peninsula was officially resolved and a crisis averted when the Ukraine government and its autonomous region of Crimea signed a joint communiqué affirming that Crimea was part of Ukraine. The issue was especially important to Ukraine because the Black Sea Fleet, which Russia and Ukraine both claimed, was based in Crimea. The communiqué also noted that differences between Crimean and Ukrainian laws would be resolved by a joint committee. On May 20 Crimea's local legislature had taken the region a step closer to total independence by reconfirming (69–2) a constitution that had been adopted in 1992 but was suspended a few days later when Ukraine gave in to several Crimean demands.

4 **Rights in East Timor discussed.** A private conference on Indonesia's observance of human rights in East Timor, a former Portuguese colony seized by Indonesia in 1976, concluded in Manila despite government efforts to ban the meeting. Indonesia claimed East Timor as its 27th province, but the United Nations had repeatedly refused to acknowledge the legitimacy of the claim. Local resistance had been resolute throughout the years, and Indonesian troops had reportedly killed one-sixth of the population. President Suharto, embarrassed and annoyed by the adverse publicity his country was receiving, urged Philippine Pres. Fidel Ramos to use his authority to cancel the meeting. Suharto had implied that if nothing was done, he might choose to aid the Muslim separatists fighting in the southern part of the Philippines. Ramos issued an injunction, but it was invalidated by the Supreme Court. The president, however, was able to deny visas to overseas delegates and to order the deportation of foreign delegates already in the country. The wife of French Pres. François Mitterrand, made aware of the situation, canceled plans to attend the conference.

6 **Allies remember Normandy landing.** Various heads of state and government, representatives of the Allies whose troops had participated in the historic 1944 D-Day invasion of Normandy during World War II, gathered in France to commemorate the 50th anniversary of the event, which led to the liberation of Western Europe and contributed to the defeat of Nazi Germany. Some 30,000 elderly veterans also traveled to Normandy to remember and pay homage to those who had given their lives to set others free. On June 5, 38 veterans of the 82nd Airborne Division, some in their 80s, were warmly cheered as they dropped from the sky in multicoloured parachutes in a reenactment of their hazardous Normandy landing behind enemy lines 50 years earlier. Other veterans in battle gear waded ashore to commemorate the launching of Operation Overlord, the largest amphibious invasion in history. French Pres. François Mitterrand presided over the largest of the anniversary celebrations at Omaha Beach. Among the many other remembrances that took place at various locations was a visit by President Clinton to the Normandy American Cemetery near Omaha Beach, where more than 9,000 U.S. soldiers were buried. The president remarked, "These are the fathers we never knew, the uncles we never met, the friends who never returned, the heroes we can never repay."

10 **Muslim Brotherhood under attack.** The Egyptian government stepped up its campaign against the Muslim Brotherhood, a powerful antigovernment organization that sought to win converts to Islamic fundamentalism by gaining control of charitable institutions and by influencing university faculties, professional groups, local government officials, labour leaders, and others of like status. The ultimate goal of the Brotherhood, officially outlawed in Egypt in 1954, was to turn Egypt into an Islamic republic. Pres. Hosni Mubarak, who had no such wishes for his country, was concerned that the vast sums of money the Brotherhood received from Saudi Arabia and other Persian Gulf states and its adherents, numbering in the hundreds of thousands and growing, posed a greater threat than did the terrorist groups that shared the Brotherhood's vision of the kind of state Egypt should be.

U.S. puts new pressure on General Cédras. President Clinton, determined to dislodge the military regime in Haiti headed by Lieut. Gen. Raoul Cédras, added two new elements to the list of economic sanctions already in place. He ordered an immediate ban on all financial transactions between the two countries, thereby making it impossible for wealthy Haitians, many of whom profited from the military government, to withdraw funds from their U.S. accounts

LES STONE—SYGMA

Haitian children wait in line to receive drinking water. On June 10 the U.S. government further tightened sanctions against the island nation in an effort to bring down its military government.

or transfer funds out of Haiti for deposit in the U.S. The ban would affect hundreds of millions of dollars. Clinton also called a halt to all commercial flights between the U.S. and Haiti. On June 12 it was unofficially reported that some 30 Latin-American countries had privately informed U.S. officials that they were prepared to support a military invasion of Haiti if economic sanctions did not bring down its military rulers. That same day Émile Jonassaint, Haiti's provisional president, declared a state of emergency.

12 New European Parliament elected. The 12 nations of the European Union finished their two-stage balloting for representation in the European Parliament without giving any political bloc a majority of the 567 seats. The left-of-centre groups, which included an assortment of socialists, communists, and environmentalists, won 242 seats. Right-of-centre groups captured 229 seats, and nonaffiliated groups won 96 seats. Both of the major blocs were expected to woo the uncommitted, but neither group was confident it would be able to command an absolute majority of 284 seats when Parliament convened.

15 Israel and Vatican affirm ties. After years of often bitter antagonism between Jews and the Roman Catholic Church, the Vatican and Israel simultaneously announced the establishment of full diplomatic relations. Following the lead of virtually all other states with diplomats accredited to Israel, the Vatican announced that its embassy would be located in an area administered by Tel Aviv rather than in Jerusalem. Even though Jerusalem had been officially designated Israel's capital, most nations tried not to become directly involved in the sensitive issue of the ancient city's status. When the Vatican agreed to establish diplomatic relations with Israel, it was given no guarantees that it would have an active voice in future discussions about the status of Jerusalem.

17 O.J. Simpson accused of murder. Hall of Fame professional football player and television personality O.J. Simpson was formally charged in Los Angeles with murdering his former wife Nicole Brown Simpson and Ronald Goldman, who was at Nicole's house the night of June 12 when the murders were committed. After a preliminary evaluation of the evidence, the police ordered Simpson, by now a prime suspect, to turn himself in. While his lawyers were discussing the situation, Simpson slipped away and became a fugitive from justice. Hours later a longtime friend, driving along a Los Angeles freeway, contacted police by car telephone to say that Simpson was with him in the car holding a gun to his head. Millions sat transfixed in front of their television sets as helicopter crews beamed live pictures of the car leisurely moving through traffic while police vehicles followed at a discreet distance. After returning to his home, Simpson surrendered to authorities. He hired a team of prominent defense attorneys and at his arraignment pleaded not guilty. Legal squabbles over the admissibility of evidence and jury selection dragged on for

Former football star, television personality, and actor O.J. Simpson appears in a mug shot. On June 17 Simpson was charged with the murder of his former wife Nicole and a friend, Ronald Goldman.
LAPD—GAMMA LIAISON

months. No murder case in U.S. history had ever received such sensational pretrial publicity, sparked so much discussion, or generated so many news stories, editorials, magazine articles, television interviews, and even "instant" books.

19 Samper wins Colombian election. Ernesto Samper Pizano, candidate of the ruling Liberal Party, narrowly defeated Andres Pastrana Arango, the Conservative Party candidate, in a runoff election for the presidency of Colombia. Samper, scheduled to begin his four-year term on August 7, would succeed César Gaviria Trujillo, who was excluded by law from seeking reelection. Analysts attributed the low voter turnout (45%) to a general lack of interest in the outcome. Both candidates, whose political parties had dominated national politics since the 1950s, had pledged to continue the gradual process of economic liberalization initiated by Gaviria and to push for a negotiated peace settlement with leftist rebels. Samper supported an increase in social expenditures to create jobs and raise the living standard of the poor. He also advocated caution on such policies as privatization and the lowering of trade barriers. Neither of the two candidates spoke much about Colombia's notorious illegal drug trade even though there was a widely held belief that high government officials were being bought off by drug kingpins.

21 Indonesia clamps down on press. The Indonesian government notified three popular publications that their licenses had been revoked. News of the crackdown came as a shock to the hundreds of thousands who had come to rely on *Tempo*, *Editor*, and *DeTik* as dependable sources of information about their country. Many who were angry about the closures accused President Suharto of depriving the public of legitimate news and reversing his policy of gradually relaxing government censorship of the press. *Editor*, a news magazine, and *DeTik*, a tabloid that had approached a circulation of nearly 500,000 in little more than a year, were

suppressed "for covering political events without appropriate licenses." *Tempo*, which did have such authority, was reportedly shut down for its coverage of a sensitive story: a Cabinet-level squabble involving Minister of Research and Technology B.J. Habibie and Finance Minister Mar'ie Muhammad over the cost of refitting 39 former East German warships that had been purchased on Habibie's authority.

23 French troops cross into Rwanda. The French government ordered some 2,500 marines and Foreign Legionnaires to cross the Zairean border into Rwanda to protect refugees, missionaries, and the wounded from indiscriminate massacre at the hands of warring Hutu and Tutsi tribesmen. More than 200,000 Rwandans had already lost their lives. The French minister of defense explained that Operation Turquoise was launched "to protect threatened civilians, not for war operations or military assistance." Its purpose, he reiterated, was to put a stop to genocide by moving noncombatants to safer areas close to the border in Zaire.

29 Socialist is chosen to lead Japan. In a move that stunned Japan, the lower house of the Diet (parliament) elected (261–214) Tomiichi Murayama, the leader of the Social Democratic Party of Japan (SDPJ), prime minister. He replaced Tsutomu Hata, a reformist who had resigned on June 25, and gave Japan its first socialist prime minister since 1948. To win the prime ministership, Murayama agreed to accept the Liberal-Democratic Party (LDP) as partners in his coalition government in exchange for their support. Until that moment such a coalition would have been the most unlikely of scenarios. During the LDP's long hold on power, its most formidable opposition had come from the SDPJ, which opposed the LDP on virtually every major issue. The SDPJ, moreover, had joined the coalition government of Prime Minister Morihiro Hosokawa when the scandal-riddled LDP fell from power in July 1993. The partners in the new government, however, were united in their opposition to political reforms that were likely to diminish their representation in the Diet. Murayama also backed away from the anti-U.S., anti-nuclear power, pro-North Korea positions that had characterized the SDPJ in the past. Murayama, inaugurated on June 30, awarded 13 of the 20 Cabinet posts to members of the LDP.

30 Hong Kong votes for democracy. Hong Kong's 60-member Legislative Council ignored dire threats from Beijing (Peking) by approving a proposal that would expand democratic participation in the process by which council members were elected. Gov. Chris Patten had disregarded China's vigorous objections, saying that the people of Hong Kong desired greater democracy, which would guarantee Hong Kong's economic future. Because China threatened to dismantle Hong Kong's political structure after it gained sovereignty over the territory on July 1, 1997, some segments of the business community, with an eye to the future, leaned toward compliance with China's wishes.

JULY

1 **Arafat warmly welcomed in Gaza.** Fulfilling a dream he had nurtured for decades, Yasir Arafat, chairman of the Palestine Liberation Organization, crossed the Egyptian border and entered the Gaza Strip, the homeland of his ancestors. It was a momentous event for hundreds of thousands of Palestinians who, as a result of the accord Arafat had signed with Israel, would begin adjusting to self-rule under the Palestine National Authority (PNA). Despite the general jubilation that marked Arafat's arrival, he was protected by extremely tight security because certain Palestinian extremists, opposed to any compromise with Israel, considered him a traitor to their cause. Four days later Arafat made his first trip in 27 years to Jericho in the West Bank, where he was sworn in as head of the PNA. Jericho had been granted the same degree of independence as Gaza.

2 **Cambodia reports attempted coup.** Officials of the Cambodian government reported that a coup led by Prince Norodom Chakrapong, the estranged son of King Norodom Sihanouk, and Gen. Sin Song—both members of the Cabinet—had been foiled when government troops intercepted 200–300 dissident soldiers in armoured vehicles and trucks as they were advancing on Phnom Penh, the capital. The coup had been planned to occur while the king was in China for treatment of prostate cancer. After many hours of telephone conversations that involved the king, the queen, Chakrapong, government officials, and the U.S. ambassador, Chakrapong was allowed to board a plane and go into exile in Malaysia. Gen. Sin Song was placed under arrest.

4 **Rwandan refugees inundate Zaire.** The Rwandan Patriotic Front captured Kigali, the national capital, then directed its offensive against other parts of the country still under government control. Although the Tutsi rebels comprised less than 15% of the population, their professionally trained, highly motivated troops

easily overwhelmed the national army, which was under Hutu command. The three-month-long civil war had already created unspeakable suffering. An estimated 200,000–500,000 people had been killed, and up to two million Rwandans had sought safety across the border in Zaire, where thousands were dying from starvation and disease. A spokesperson for the UN High Commissioner for Refugees described the situation as "absolutely catastrophic." One member of an on-site British relief agency characterized the plight of the refugees as "a disaster on a scale not witnessed in modern times." For untold thousands water, food, and medical supplies arrived too late to save their lives.

8 **Kim Il Sung dies in Pyongyang.** North Korea's official news agency informed the nation on July 9 that "Great Leader" Kim Il Sung had died the previous day of an apparent heart attack. The year after Korea was divided into two separate states (1948), Kim gained absolute power in the Democratic People's Republic of Korea as chairman of the Korean Workers' (Communist) Party. At his death Kim, who had named his son Kim Jong Il heir-designate, left North Korea's economy in shambles, in great part because his country had become more and more isolated from the international community. Shortly before his unexpected death, Kim had agreed, for the first time, to discuss reconciliation with the president of South Korea and to seek to resolve the tense international crisis over North Korea's nuclear program.

10 **Kuchma wins Ukrainian election.** In a runoff election for the presidency of Ukraine, Leonid Kuchma defeated incumbent Pres. Leonid Kravchuk by capturing 52% of the vote. An analysis of the results showed that a vast proportion of the electorate had voted along ethnic lines. In the predominantly Russian-speaking eastern regions of Ukraine and in Crimea, where 70% of the population was ethnic Russian, Kuchma won about

90% of the vote. In some districts in the western part of the country, which were heavily populated by ethnic Ukrainians, he failed to win even 5% of the vote. Kuchma, who had formerly been head of the Soviet Union's largest missile plant, campaigned on a promise to reform and invigorate the country's pitiful economy by forging closer ties with Russia. During the previous year Ukraine's industrial output had declined 40%, and nearly half of the workforce was unemployed.

Lukashenka coasts to victory in Belarus. In a runoff election to choose Belarus' first president, Aleksandr Lukashenka, a former communist, overwhelmed Prime Minister Vyacheslau Kebich by capturing more than 80% of the popular vote. The landslide victory was viewed by many observers as a mass protest against the status quo. Lukashenka had campaigned on a promise to root out corruption, which was rampant among government officials, to imprison Kebich, and to dismiss anyone who had ties to his administration. Although Lukashenka had no significant experience in either domestic or foreign affairs, he made lavish promises to rebuild the country's shattered economy, create jobs, provide for the elderly, and stifle inflation, which had been averaging about 10% a week. Lukashenka also declared that there was no solution to the nation's severe problems other than closer ties with Russia.

12 **Employees buy United Airlines.** After seven years of sporadic negotiations, employees of United Airlines (UAL) bought controlling interest (55%) in the world's largest carrier. The $4.9 billion investment made by the company's 54,000 employees included wage and benefit concessions ranging from 8.25% for nonunion workers to 15.7% for pilots over a period of 5½ years. Under terms of the agreement, the employees would have a significant albeit indirect role in decision making because the three persons they selected to sit on the 12-person board of directors would have veto power over such proposals as the sale of company assets and the expansion of its operations. Even so, some investment advisers with intimate knowledge of the highly competitive airline industry were reluctant to predict that the new owners would, in the years ahead, be happy with the decision they had made. The new chairman of UAL would be Gerald Greenwald, a former executive at Chrysler Corp.

18 **UN retains sanctions on Iraq.** The United States and Great Britain, which had veto power over UN Security Council resolutions, took a firm stand against the removal of UN-imposed economic sanctions on Iraq. The U.S. ambassador to the UN argued that Iraq had made only token gestures to meet UN conditions for removing restrictions on its trade and oil sales and had not, therefore, earned favourable consideration. China, France, Russia, and some Third World nations holding seats on the Security Council pushed in vain for a statement

SEBASTIÃO SALGADO

Bodies of Rwandans who had tried to flee their country lie scattered along a road. On July 4 the minority Tutsi rebels captured the capital, Kigali, creating thousands of additional refugees.

acknowledging that Iraq had made sufficient progress to justify a loosening of the sanctions. The Russian representative issued a separate statement in which he encouraged Iraq to satisfy the UN conditions and urged the Security Council to revoke the sanctions as soon as the UN Special Committee on Iraq declared that the installation of a system to monitor Iraqi weapons had been completed.

21 **Tony Blair to lead Labour Party.** The electoral college of Great Britain's Labour Party selected Tony Blair to be its party leader. He succeeded John Smith, who had died in May. Political analysts expressed a belief that Blair provided the Labour Party with a good chance of regaining control of the government for the first time since 1979. They cited the substantial decline in Prime Minister John Major's popularity, broad dissatisfaction with the Conservative government, and Blair's decision to back away from such traditional Labour policies as increased taxation to finance social programs and support for trade unions in their disputes with industry. The next parliamentary election had to be called no later than mid-1997.

22 **Gambian military seizes power.** Sir Dawda Jawara, president of The Gambia since 1970, was overthrown in a coup organized by junior army officers. The country's four or five new military rulers immediately suspended the constitution, outlawed political parties,

imposed a curfew, and set up a Provisional Council of the Armed Forces. They also promised to set a date for the restoration of democracy. Sir Dawda and his sizable entourage were taken aboard a visiting U.S. warship and set ashore in neighbouring Senegal, where they were granted temporary political asylum.

28 **Congress passes anticrime bill.** After months of contentious congressional debate, conferees from the U.S. Senate and House of Representatives reached agreement on anticrime legislation that President Clinton hailed as "the toughest, largest, smartest federal attack on crime in the history of our country." Some members of Congress continued to ridicule the bill, especially for financing social welfare programs as deterrents to crime. The entire anticrime program would cost $30.2 billion. The money would put 100,000 new police officers on the nation's streets, finance new prisons, pay for crime-prevention and rehabilitation programs, and provide scholarships for students willing to commit themselves to a career in law enforcement. In addition, the bill banned the manufacture, sale, and possession of 19 types of assault weapons and extended the federal death penalty to some 60 crimes. It also required mandatory life imprisonment for persons convicted of three serious felonies.

29 **Taiwan amends its constitution.** The National Assembly of the Republic of China in Taiwan

passed 10 constitutional amendments after three months of tumultuous confrontation between the ruling Kuomintang (KMT; Nationalist Party) and the opposition Democratic Progressive Party and its allies. One amendment provided for the direct election of the president and vice president, a right previously invested in the National Assembly. Another change would permit overseas nationals to cast ballots in that election. The conditions for recalling a president were also modified. Henceforth a president could not be removed from office without a two-thirds vote of the Assembly and the approval of a majority of voters. Only one KMT-sponsored amendment failed. It called for the simultaneous election of the president and the National Assembly to avoid fundamental changes in the government during a president's term in office.

31 **UN approves invasion of Haiti.** Frustrated in its attempt to persuade the military government of Haiti to step down and allow the Rev. Jean-Bertrand Aristide to assume the presidency, which he had won in the December 1990 election, the United Nations Security Council authorized (12–0, with 2 abstentions) a United States-led military invasion of the country if the sanctions already in place failed to force the junta to relinquish power. Gen. Raoul Cédras and his associates, however, were not given a specific deadline after which they would be taken into custody by invading foreign troops.

AUGUST

3 **Breyer joins U.S. Supreme Court.** During a private ceremony conducted by Chief Justice William Rehnquist, Stephen Breyer officially became a member of the U.S. Supreme Court. He had asked to take the oath of office before the formal White House ceremony on August 12 so that he could begin selecting his staff and have access to material on cases awaiting decision by the court. In July the Senate Judiciary Committee had questioned Breyer, the chief judge of the U.S. Court of Appeals for the First Circuit, on a wide variety of issues before unanimously recommending that he be confirmed by the entire Senate. Only nine senators opposed the appointment. Breyer replaced retired justice Harry Blackmun.

10 **Germany seizes nuclear material.** In a sting operation carried out at the Munich airport, German police seized 370–430 g (12–14 oz) of plutonium-239, an isotope used in the manufacture of nuclear weapons. One Colombian and two Spaniards were arrested after they arrived aboard a Lufthansa flight from Moscow. Three other incidents that occurred between May 10 and August 12 involved smaller amounts of smuggled nuclear material. The first case involved a German businessman with apparent ties to Iraq. Police found six grams of ^{239}Pu in his home in Tengen. In June the discovery in Landshut of about nine grams of highly enriched uranium-235 led to the arrest of one Czech, four

Slovaks, and one German. On August 12 a German carrying a tiny quantity of nuclear material was arrested in Bremen. All the nuclear material was believed to have been smuggled out of Russia or one of the other former Soviet republics. Russian authorities promised to track down the source of the smuggled material.

14 **Sudan nabs notorious terrorist.** Ilich Ramírez Sánchez, an international terrorist known as Carlos, or "the Jackal," was apprehended in The Sudan and turned over to French authorities. The next day he was flown to France to face murder charges and other charges. Carlos, a native of Venezuela, had been sought by Western intelligence agencies for some 20 years even though he had apparently given up his terrorist activities. One of his most sensational successes was the 1975 kidnapping of 11 OPEC ministers who were meeting in Vienna. Three persons were killed, but Carlos and his accomplices hijacked a plane and took the oil ministers to Algeria, where they were released after the payment of a $20 million ransom. Carlos was most closely linked to Arab groups, but at various times communist regimes in Eastern Europe protected him, if only because he was creating havoc in Western Europe.

16 **Dominican Republic ends crisis.** Three months after winning what was widely viewed as a fraudulent

election, Joaquín Balaguer was sworn in as president of the Dominican Republic. The frail 87-year-old politician had held the office for 20 of the previous 28 years. On August 10 Balaguer and opposition party leaders had reached a compromise that allowed Balaguer to remain in office until new elections were held in November 1995. Four days later a special constitutional assembly added an amendment to the constitution that postponed the election until May 1996.

17 **Lesotho's king ousts Mokhehle.** Prime Minister Ntsu Mokhehle and his Cabinet were dismissed by King Letsie III of Lesotho on the grounds that the people were dissatisfied with the nation's first democratically elected government. On August 19 a provisional council was appointed to run the country until new elections were held at a still-unspecified date. The king's action was widely seen as an attempt to return power to his father, Moshoeshoe II, who had been deposed by the military in 1990 and temporarily exiled.

19 **Sri Lankans elect Kumaratunga.** Chandrika Bandaranaike Kumaratunga, candidate of the nine-party People's Alliance, was sworn in as prime minister of Sri Lanka. Although the alliance failed to win an absolute majority in the August 16 parliamentary elections, it captured 105 of the 225 seats—11 more than the United National Party, which had controlled the government for 17 years. Kumaratunga's father and mother had both held the post of prime minister. Under Sri Lanka's political system, Pres. Dingiri Wijetunga, whose term did not expire until the end of the year, could have selected anyone to be prime minister. He named Kumaratunga after Prime Minister Ranil Wickremasinghe announced that he would oppose any other choice.

U.S. policy on Cuban refugees is changed. President Clinton, fearful that thousands of Cuban refugees in unseaworthy vessels were heading for the United States with the approval of Cuban Pres. Fidel Castro, announced that Cuban refugees would no longer automatically be granted asylum in the U.S. Instead, those picked up at sea by the U.S. Navy or Coast Guard and those reaching U.S. shores would be sent to holding camps. Some would be routed to the U.S. naval base at Guantánamo Bay in Cuba. On August 20 Clinton increased the pressure on Castro by prohibiting charter flights to Cuba and by outlawing cash transfers, which had been providing Cuba with an estimated $500 million a year in hard currency. Clinton remarked, "The solution to Cuba's many problems is not an uncontrolled exodus. It is freedom and democracy for Cuba."

21 **PRI retains Mexican presidency.** Ernesto Zedillo Ponce de Léon, candidate of Mexico's long-ruling Institutional Revolutionary Party (PRI), won the presidency in balloting that observers reported was virtually free of the blatant fraud that had characterized most past elections. The PRI had not lost the presidency since the party was founded in 1929. Zedillo's closest rival was Diego Fernández de Cevallos of the National Action Party. He won the support of about 27% of the electorate. Zedillo

was expected to take over the reins of government from Pres. Carlos Salinas de Gortari on December 1. Incomplete results of the parliamentary elections indicated that the PRI would still control the Senate and the Chamber of Deputies.

22 **Kok takes over in Netherlands.** Nearly four months after parliamentary elections, Willem ("Wim") Kok, leader of the left-wing Labour Party, took the oath of office as prime minister of The Netherlands. His three-party coalition included the right-wing Liberal Party and the leftist Democrats 66 bloc. For the first time in decades, the Christian Democratic Appeal became the party in opposition. Kok had insisted that all the partners in his coalition endorse his political program, which was designed to increase employment, lower taxes, and cut the national budget. The government would continue to provide free education for undergraduates, but in the future those wishing to pursue graduate degrees would have to pay their own way.

30 **Papua New Guinea holds election.** Following an order of the Supreme Court, Papua New Guinea's unicameral National Parliament held an election for the prime ministership. The vote was 69–32 in favour of Sir Julius Chan. He succeeded Paias Wingti, who had been elected in 1992. In September 1993 Wingti resigned overnight and was reelected the next morning. He employed this strategy in hopes of taking advantage of a provision in the law that protected a new prime minister from a no-confidence vote for the first 18 months of his tenure in office. The Supreme Court, after ruling that such tactics violated the spirit of the constitution, ordered a new election. Wingti then decided to step aside. After assuming office, Chan announced that his top priority would be to end the six-year-

old civil war in Bougainville, the largest of the Solomon Islands, which were part of Papua New Guinea.

31 **IRA proclaims a new cease-fire.** Affirming a new determination to rely on political solutions to end the conflict in Northern Ireland, the outlawed Provisional wing of the Irish Republican Army (IRA) announced a complete cessation of military operations against the British government and its troops in Northern Ireland. Since 1969 some 3,000 people, mostly civilians, had been killed there in sectarian fighting between Roman Catholics and local Protestant paramilitary units backed up by British soldiers. For months there had been unofficial reports of high-level meetings, many in secret, to find a formula for settling the dispute over who should rule Northern Ireland. Despite all efforts to resolve the impasse, the basic problem remained; the majority of people in Northern Ireland were Protestant and presumably wished to remain British, while the IRA and its supporters contended that the Irish republic comprised the entire island.

Russia meets deadline for troop pullout. Adhering to a time schedule agreed to in July, Russia withdrew the last of its troops from Estonia and Latvia. The future status of retired Russian soldiers who wished to remain in prosperous Estonia had been settled earlier; all could apply for permanent residence, but Estonia would have the right, after reviewing each case individually, to deport criminals and others judged to be detrimental to the country. The first total withdrawal of Russian military personnel from the Baltics had occurred in Lithuania in August 1993, and Russian forces left Poland the following month. On August 31 the final contingent of Russian troops departed from Berlin, Russia's last base on German soil.

ALON REININGER—CONTACT PRESS IMAGES

Cubans trying to reach Florida on a homemade raft are picked up by the U.S. Coast Guard. On August 19 Pres. Bill Clinton announced that the U.S. would begin to hold Cuban refugees in camps rather than grant them automatic asylum.

SEPTEMBER

6 **Nigerian ruler proclaims dictatorship.** Gen. Sani Abacha, who had been ruling oil-rich Nigeria since November 1993 as chairman of the Provisional Ruling Council, assumed dictatorial powers. The previous day oil workers had ended a two-month strike that failed to force Abacha to turn over the reins of government to Moshood ("MKO") Abiola, who was in prison facing charges of treason. He had been arrested after apparently winning the presidential election in June 1993. The National Defense and Security Council annulled the election "so as to protect our legal system and the judiciary from being ridiculed." After assuming absolute power, Abacha declared that his government was beyond the jurisdiction of the courts and that persons taken into custody could be detained for three months without being charged. He also muzzled the press by shutting down leading newspapers and magazines.

7 **Barbados chooses a new government.** Owen Arthur took the oath of office as prime minister of Barbados one day after his Barbados Labour Party soundly defeated the ruling Democratic Labour Party (DLP) by winning 19 of the 28 seats in the lower House of the Assembly. The DLP, which had held uninterrupted power for a decade, captured eight seats and the National Democratic Party one. Arthur, who was trained as an economist, promised that his government would give top priority to lowering unemployment, which stood at 22%.

9 **Accord reached on Cuban refugees.** After more than a week of negotiations in New York City, the U.S. and Cuba reached agreement on a new refugee policy that would end the recent tidal wave of Cubans fleeing to the U.S. In the future a minimum of 20,000 Cubans a year would be permitted to enter the U.S. legally as long as Cuba took steps to stem the tide of illegal emigrants heading for the U.S. The number of economic refugees had reached such unmanageable proportions in recent weeks that President Clinton had felt compelled on August 19 to announce that, beginning immediately, the nation's 28-year-old policy of granting asylum to any Cuban reaching U.S. shores was no longer in effect. Henceforth, Cubans picked up at sea, often crowded aboard unseaworthy boats or on makeshift rafts, would be transported directly to holding camps at U.S. bases in Panama or Guantánamo Bay, Cuba.

13 **Disputes mar Cairo conference.** The third UN-sponsored International Conference on Population and Development ended in Cairo after nine days of often bitter debate over such issues as sexual morality, family planning, and the legitimacy and desirability of abortion as a means of birth control. The Roman Catholic Church, some Latin-American countries, and several predominantly Islamic nations generally strongly opposed certain specific policies (or the ambiguity of statements) contained in a proposed Program of Action to stabilize the world's population. The Sudan, a largely Islamic country, was one of 11 countries that did not send delegates to the conference. It boycotted the meeting, it said, because the outcome would result "in the spread of immoral and irreligious values." Those who argued that the lot of impoverished nations would improve significantly if the birthrate was

Delegates confer during the UN population conference, which ended in Cairo on September 13. There were sharp disagreements on the roles of family planning versus economic development.
DONNA DECESARE—IMPACT VISUALS

controlled encountered challenges from others who cited history as proof that birthrates invariably drop when nations emerge from widespread poverty. Much greater emphasis, they contended, should be placed on economic development as a vital element in stabilizing the world's population. Before the conference ended, the Vatican surprised many by endorsing 8 of the 16 chapters that constituted the new UN statement of policy on population.

16 **Exxon fined billions for oil spill.** In Anchorage, Alaska, a federal jury fined Exxon Corp. a record $5 billion in punitive damages for the oil spill in Prince William Sound that resulted when the supertanker *Exxon Valdez* ran aground in 1989. The money would go to some 34,000 fishermen and to others who claimed in a lawsuit that they had suffered substantial losses because of the pollution. Lawyers for Exxon announced that they would appeal the jury's decision.

18 **Haiti's military junta to step down.** President Clinton announced on national television that Haiti's military rulers had defused a tense situation by agreeing to relinquish power by October 15, thus allowing Pres. Jean-Bertrand Aristide to return to Haiti to assume the

JEFFREY MARKOWITZ—SYGMA

(From left) U.S. Sen. Sam Nunn, Gen. Colin Powell, and former president Jimmy Carter report on their mission to Haiti. On Sept. 18 it was announced that Haiti's military leaders would quit.

presidency that he had held before being ousted in a September 1991 military coup. The agreement was reached while U.S. warplanes were flying toward Haiti to carry out the first phase of a military operation to remove by force Lieut. Gen. Raoul Cédras and other members of the junta. The top U.S. negotiators in Port-au-Prince were former president Jimmy Carter, Sen. Sam Nunn, and Colin Powell, the former chairman of the Joint Chiefs of Staff. On September 19 U.S. troops landed in Haiti to work in close cooperation with local military and police forces "to promote freedom and democracy and to forge a sustained and mutually beneficial relationship between the governments, people, and institutions of Haiti and the United States." Once deployed, the U.S. soldiers obeyed orders and did not interfere on occasions when street violence, including brutal, wanton beatings, occurred. Recognizing the absurdity of the situation, the U.S. later changed its policy and ordered its troops to take command.

21 **Scientists find remarkable fossil.** Timothy D. White, a paleontologist at the University of California at Berkeley and the leader of an international group of scientists working in Ethiopia, announced the discovery of ancient fossils belonging to apelike creatures that were the ancestors of modern humans (*Homo sapiens*). The 4.4 million-year-old fossils represented an entirely new species that was a million years older than the partial skeleton of Lucy, a hominid (upright-walking primate) discovered in Ethiopia in 1974. An analysis of the newly discovered fossils appeared to support the theory that humans and apes evolved from a common ancestor that lived some four million to six million years ago.

26 **Quebec to vote on sovereignty.** Jacques Parizeau, whose separatist Parti Québécois (PQ) had won 77 of the 125 seats in the province's National Assembly on September 12, was sworn in as premier of Quebec. Despite the PQ's overwhelming success in gaining control of the Assembly, its percentage of the popular vote was only a fraction of a percentage point greater than that of the Liberal Party, which won only 47 seats. The Liberal Party had run the government for nine years. Parizeau's victory meant, among other things, that Canadians would once again face the possibility that the mainly French-speaking voters of Quebec would opt for sovereignty when given a choice in a provincial referendum to be held in 1995.

Saudi Arabia arrests Islamic militants. The government of Saudi Arabia publicly confirmed press reports that 110 Islamic militants had been recently arrested for plotting to spread sedition and destabilize the country. Although the Saudi government was alert to possible threats coming from leftist secularists, extreme right-wing religious zealots appeared to present a more immediate threat to the status quo. They were blamed for social unrest inside Saudi Arabia and were responsible for serious conflicts in such Arab nations as Egypt, Algeria, and Tunisia.

U.S. health care debate reaches impasse. George Mitchell, speaking as majority leader of the U.S. Senate, announced that national health care legislation was a dead issue during the current session of Congress. President Clinton had made universal health care a major goal of his Democratic administration, but he was unable to overcome the opposition that surfaced in many different quarters. Given the complexity of the problems that had to be solved and the conflicting interests that had to be reconciled, it became clearer each day that passage of comprehensive health care legislation was not close at hand. Most legislators, however, agreed that health care reforms were badly needed and would in time become law, if not on a national scale then locally, in a variety of ways, by individual states.

29 **Americas now free of poliovirus.** The Pan American Health Organization declared that paralytic poliomyelitis (polio) had been eradicated in North and South America and in the Caribbean. Health officials coupled the announcement with a caution that the disease could reappear unless a serious effort was made to totally eradicate the disease through an extensive program of immunization. Some 120,000 cases of polio were still reported each year, mostly in less developed countries.

Claes named as NATO secretary-general. All 16 nations belonging to NATO approved the appointment of Willy Claes as the organization's new secretary-general. Claes, who was Belgium's deputy prime minister and foreign minister, replaced Manfred Wörner, who had died in August. The U.S. was not an enthusiastic supporter of Claes because the Belgian government, of which he was part, had refused to sell ammunition to Great Britain during the Persian Gulf war. In addition, Claes's Flemish Socialist Party had created discord by opposing the deployment of U.S. missiles in Europe in the 1980s.

30 **Arabs relax their boycott of Israel.** Six Arab nations belonging to the Gulf Cooperation Council (GCC) declared that they would no longer blacklist companies doing business with Israel. The Arab nations' 46-year-old ban on direct trade with Israel remained in force, but the GCC planned to call on the Arab League to rescind the ban entirely. Egypt became the first Arab nation to violate the boycott deliberately after it signed a peace treaty with Israel in 1979. The boycott was further weakened in September 1993 when Israel and the Palestine Liberation Organization signed a declaration of peace. Since that time the Arab boycott had become something of an anachronism because there were numerous indications that Israel and its longtime foes were prepared to negotiate a step-by-step permanent peace settlement.

OCTOBER

3 **Cardoso wins the election in Brazil.** A runoff election for the presidency of Brazil was avoided when Fernando Cardoso won a majority of the valid votes cast. (Because voting was mandatory in Brazil, a large number of ballots were left blank or declared invalid.) Cardoso's closest rival in the field of eight was Luis Inácio Lula da Silva ("Lula") of the Workers Party, who had been considered the front-runner until Cardoso resigned as finance minister in March and declared his intention to run for the presidency even though many Brazilians scarcely knew his name. His surge in popularity was attributed to the success of measures he had drafted as finance minister to curb rampant inflation, which by election day was at its lowest level in years. Cardoso was scheduled to assume office on Jan. 1, 1995.

4 **Dispute over missile sales settled.** After negotiations in Washington, D.C., the U.S. and China signed an agreement that ended a festering debate over China's alleged violation of a treaty that prohibited the sale of certain high-technology items to other countries. China had not formally signed the 1987 international agreement, known as the Missile Technology Control Regime (MTCR), but it had agreed in 1992 to adhere to its provisions. The U.S. contended that China had reneged on its promise by selling M-11 missile components to Pakistan—a charge both countries denied. China further contended that the M-11 missiles had a shorter range and a smaller payload than the limits set by the MTCR. The dispute was resolved when China accepted the more-restrictive interpretation of the treaty and the U.S. removed its one-year-old ban on the sale of high-tech equipment that China wished to purchase.

5 **Police find the bodies of 53 cultists.** Swiss police in two small villages found the bodies of 48 members of the Order of the Solar Temple, an international religious cult. An examination of the bodies indicated that the cultists had died by suicide, from bullets fired into their heads, or by suffocation. The corpses of five other members of the cult were discovered in Quebec. The residences occupied by the cultists in Switzerland and Canada had been set ablaze by several devices connected to gasoline and benzine. The badly burned body of Luc Jouret, the Belgian founder of the cult, had to be identified through dental records. He had warned his followers that an apocalypse was near because humans had polluted the environment.

7 **U.S. responds to new Iraqi threat.** President Clinton ordered the immediate dispatch of additional Marine and navy forces to the Persian Gulf to counter a new military threat posed by Iraqi Pres. Saddam Hussein. Just hours earlier Saddam had issued orders for two

The USS *George Washington* moves through the Suez Canal on its way to the Persian Gulf. On October 7 U.S. Pres. Bill Clinton ordered troops to the area to counter a buildup of Iraqi forces.
TOM HARTWELL—SABA

divisions of Republican Guard troops to move toward the Kuwaiti border, where 50,000 Iraqi soldiers were already stationed. The sudden buildup raised the possibility that Saddam was planning, for unknown reasons, another invasion of Kuwait. In 1990 some 350,000 Iraqis had invaded and annexed Kuwait until U.S.-led United Nations forces launched a massive and devastating counteroffensive. The most recent crisis subsided when Saddam ordered his troops to pull back from the Kuwaiti border. The retreat followed reports that 28 U.S. ships, about 650 planes, and an additional 40,000 troops were either heading for Kuwait or already in place.

15 **Aristide gets warm welcome home.** Two days after Haiti's most powerful military figures were flown into exile in Panama, Jean-Bertrand Aristide returned to Haiti aboard a U.S. government plane. As tens of thousands of jubilant supporters cheered, Aristide was reinstalled as president in Port-au-Prince, the capital. Under heavy security he addressed an ecstatic crowd at the National Palace. His message, intended to bring peace and stability to a nation that had been terrorized for three years, was delivered in French, Creole, and English: "No to violence, no to vengeance, yes to reconciliation." On October 26 the president announced that he had selected Smarck Michel to be prime minister. The appointment of the U.S.-educated commodities trader who advocated a free market indicated that revitalization of the country's economy would be one of the government's top priorities.

16 **Vote weakens Kohl government.** Germany's coalition government suffered a serious setback in parliamentary elections, but it managed to maintain control of the Bundestag (lower house) with a slim majority of 10 seats.

Chancellor Helmut Kohl's Christian Democratic Union and its sister party, the Christian Social Union, together won 294 of the 672 seats. Kohl's coalition ally, the Free Democratic Party, captured 47 seats, giving the government a total of 341. The opposition Social Democratic Party emerged with 252 seats, the Greens/ Alliance '90 party with 49, and the Party of Democratic Socialism with 30. The combined total of seats occupied by the opposition came to 331. Kohl, who was reelected on November 15, was expected to surpass Konrad Adenauer's postwar record 14-year tenure during his new four-year term as chancellor.

Macedonia holds first national election. Kiro Gligorov, candidate of the Alliance for Macedonia—a three-party coalition governing the country—was easily reelected to a five-year term as president. The election was the first in Macedonia since it became independent in 1991 with the breakup of Yugoslavia. Gligorov won more than 52% of the vote, while Ljubisa Georgievski of the Internal Macedonian Revolutionary Organization–Democratic Party for Macedonian National Unity won about 14.5%. Only 10 of the nearly 1,800 candidates seeking election to the unicameral 120-seat Assembly won their contests outright. All other races were to be decided in later runoff elections. Officials of an international team of observers conceded that the election process had been flawed, but they would not side with those demanding that the results be voided. Instead, they expressed optimism that most of the problems that had surfaced during the first round of voting would be solved before the final round of balloting took place.

19 **New book creates a firestorm.** Bookstores throughout the U.S. began selling a highly controversial new book entitled *The Bell Curve: Intelli-*

gence and Class Structure in American Life. The uproar it created generated scores of television interviews and discussions, numerous newspaper and magazine articles, and countless letters to the editor. Among those who spoke out, many vigorously condemned the book's basic premises and conclusions, while others defended the book as fundamentally sound. Its coauthors, Harvard University professor Richard Herrnstein and social scientist Charles Murray, argued that a person's intelligence, or cognitive ability, was largely determined by heredity. As a consequence, better educational opportunities could have only limited value in improving these abilities. The most heated debate raged over one chapter that claimed that blacks as a group scored lower on intelligence tests than whites and Asians and would, predictably, as a group, earn less during their working years than other groups. The authors emphasized that their findings applied only to groups, not to individuals. Any one person, they pointed out, could outscore and outperform any other individual regardless of their respective backgrounds.

21 **U.S. and North Korea sign pact.** After three weeks of intense negotiations in Geneva, the United States and North Korea signed an agreement that set forth a timetable for the complete dismantling of North Korea's nuclear program. There had been worldwide concern over Pyongyang's refusal to allow the International Atomic Energy Agency (IAEA) to inspect certain sites where, it was believed, nuclear weapons were being developed. Although North Korea repeatedly denied the charge, suspicions that it had in fact launched such a program had been reinforced when it announced in March 1993 that it was withdrawing from the Nuclear Non-proliferation Treaty. Key provisions of the agreement signed in Geneva included a U.S. commitment to oversee the construction in North Korea of two 1,000-MW light-water nuclear reactors, financed mainly by Japan and South Korea; a cessation of all activity at a graphite-moderated reactor in Yongbyon and of construction work at other reactor sites; a guaranteed supply of oil from the U.S.; and full access to all of North Korea's nuclear facilities by IAEA inspectors after the light-water reactors came on-line.

23 **New rice increases output by 20%.** During a meeting of agricultural experts and World Bank officials in Washington, D.C., Ken Fisher, director of research at the International Rice Research Institute in the Philippines, revealed that a new variety of rice had been developed that would increase harvests by at least 20%. He estimated that the increased yield would eventually feed an additional 500 million people in several years, after the rice plants became commercially available. At the same meeting, Lester R. Brown, the president of the Worldwatch Institute and an expert on world grain supplies, pointed out that the demand for rice would increase significantly with rising populations in Asia. He also noted that the amount of land devoted to rice cultivation was gradually shrinking in many places to make room for factories and other buildings.

Israeli Prime Minister Yitzhak Rabin (left) shakes hands with Jordan's King Hussein as U.S. Pres. Bill Clinton applauds. The two Middle Eastern countries signed a treaty of peace on October 26.

PATRICK ROBERT—SYGMA

marked its relationship with Israel. Egypt had been the first in 1979. President Clinton was among the 4,500 guests who attended the signing ceremony, which took place under heavy security. The peace treaty resolved long-standing disputes over land and water and called for the establishment of full diplomatic relations within a month. The two countries also pledged to work together on joint projects and cooperate in a wide variety of other areas. Both King Hussein of Jordan and Prime Minister Yitzhak Rabin of Israel spoke of the numerous benefits each country would reap with the advent of peace.

25 **Vatican and PLO establish ties.** In an apparent effort to increase its influence and diplomatic presence in the Holy Land, the Vatican established "permanent and official" relations with the Palestine Liberation Organization (PLO). Although the action fell well short of recognition of a Palestinian state, the Vatican somewhat balanced out its formal relations with Israel by agreeing to maintain

contact with the PLO through the Holy See's embassy in Tunisia. At the same time, the Vatican continued to defend the inalienable right of Palestinians to freedom and independence.

26 **Israel and Jordan embrace peace.** Jordan became the second Arab nation formally to end the state of war and hostility that for 46 years had

29 **Pretoria responds to criticism.** Thabo Mbeki, first deputy president of South Africa, announced that Pres. Nelson Mandela's administration would respond to widespread criticism that government officials were living lives of luxury while the country was heavily burdened with debts and a large segment of the population was mired in poverty. As part of a general plan to trim expenses, the salaries of the president and two deputy presidents would be cut by 20%, and the civil service bureaucracy would become substantially leaner. During an interview Mandela had remarked that high salaries and luxurious living had undermined the government's credibility when it asked South Africans "to tighten their belts." He also called for the privatization of many government-owned enterprises in order to encourage private investment in South Africa and acquire capital for financing social programs.

NOVEMBER

1 **Canada revamps immigration rules.** After years of welcoming more immigrants per capita than any other major industrialized nation, Canada announced that it was revising its immigration laws. Tighter limits would be placed on the total number of immigrants admitted into the country (215,000 in 1995), and preference would be given to those with higher education or skills that would benefit the nation's economy. Consequently, by the year 2000, the percentage of family-sponsored immigrants would decline from 51% to 44% of all those granted permanent residence. Spouses and children of immigrants already settled in Canada would continue to be admitted without restrictions, but all other relatives would be placed in a special category and subjected to quotas.

2 **Japanese approve political reforms.** The final version of a package of broad political reforms, which had wide popular support, was approved by Japan's House of Representatives in the hope that a restructuring of the electoral system would rid the country of blatant corruption. The upper chamber, the House of Councillors, added its approval on November 21. The new legislation would introduce single-seat electoral constituencies, which would break the power of large political parties that could no longer depend solely on seats awarded by proportional representation. Corporate

contributions to individual candidates were to be restricted, but government subsidies would help compensate for the shortfall in financing campaigns. In addition, urban areas, long underrepresented, were set to have a greater voice in the Diet, which would have 500 members in the House of Representatives rather than 511 after the new laws took effect on December 25.

8 **Republicans triumph nationwide.** Scoring one of the most decisive political victories in modern U.S. history, the Republican Party won control of both houses of Congress for the first time in 40 years. The landslide was so complete that not one Republican senator, congressman, or governor seeking reelection was defeated. The Republicans gained eight Senate seats, giving them control by a margin of 53–47. They also gained 53 seats in the House, bringing their new total to 230; the Democrats won 204 seats, and an independent, one. All 11 first-term senators would be Republicans, as would 73 of the 88 first-term members of the House. For the first time since 1862, a speaker of the House went down to defeat. Thomas Foley's loss was just as shocking as that of Dan Rostenkowski. The 36-year tenure of the powerful chairman of the Ways and Means Committee was ended by a young, virtually unknown, underfunded political neophyte. Jack Brooks of Texas, a 42-year veteran in the House and chairman of the

New York Gov. Mario Cuomo concedes defeat in his bid for a fourth term. Cuomo was one of several prominent Democrats who lost to Republicans in the November 8 elections.

MARK PETERSON—SABA

Judiciary Committee, also went down to defeat. The success of Republicans at the state level was equally impressive. After ousting 11 Democratic governors, they were in a position to set the agenda for 30 states. The Democrats also lost the governorship in Maine when an independent swept to victory. Rep. Newt Gingrich led the

Republican attack on President Clinton and his fellow Democrats. He pledged that the old ways of doing business would be a thing of the past the moment he became speaker of the House.

9 **Kumaratunga easily wins election.** Sri Lankan Prime Minister Chandrika Kumaratunga became president after winning 62% of the popular vote during national elections. Her rival, Srima Dissanayake, ran as a candidate of the United National Party. Kumaratunga, leader of the People's Alliance coalition, finished first in all but one of the nation's 160 electoral districts. On November 15, three days after being sworn into office, the new president appointed her mother, Sirimavo Bandaranaike, prime minister—a position she had filled twice before.

10 **Iraq recognizes Kuwait border.** The Iraqi Revolutionary Command Council issued a declaration, signed by Pres. Saddam Hussein, officially recognizing the sovereignty of Kuwait, the integrity of its borders, and its political independence. If Iraq hoped that its formal recognition of Kuwait would move the United Nations to drop its economic sanctions, it was doomed to disappointment. On November 14 the U.S. ambassador to the UN presented the Security Council with evidence that Saddam had spent more than $500 million on dozens of luxurious palaces for family members while millions of Iraqis were still living in poverty. The Security Council left the sanctions in place.

13 **Sweden to join European Union.** Given their choice in a national referendum, 52.2% of Swedish voters opted for membership in the European Union (EU). Subsequent ratification by the Riksdag (parliament) followed as a matter of course. Finland and Austria, which earlier in the year had approved similar referenda, would join Sweden as official members of the EU on Jan. 1, 1995. Late in November a majority of Norway's electorate voted to keep the country outside the EU.

15 **Congress Party ousted in Nepal.** Preliminary results of parliamentary elections in Nepal indicated that the United Marxist-Leninist (UML) alliance had won 88 seats in the House of Representatives, a net gain of 20. The Nepali Congress Party (NCP) finished second and lost control of the government. The 83 seats it had won represented a net loss of 35. Its poor showing at the polls was attributed to intraparty bickering and charges of corruption. The National Democratic Party captured 20 seats, and several minor parties won a total of 14. In order to form a workable coalition, the UML—whose policies resembled those of social democrats more than those of hardline communists—was expected to seek allies among disaffected NCP members.

APEC agrees to liberalize its trade laws. At the end of a two-day conference in Bogor, Indon., the leaders of the 18 economic powers formally committed to Asia-Pacific Economic Cooperation (APEC) signed an agreement to liberalize trade by gradually eliminating barriers to free trade and by opening up investment opportunities by the year 2020. The U.S. and Japan, ranking first and second in world trade, gave APEC the economic base it needed to develop its full potential. Other economies represented in APEC included those of Australia, Brunei, Canada, Chile, China, Hong Kong, Indonesia, Malaysia, Mexico, New Zealand, Papua New Guinea, Philippines, Singapore, South Korea, Taiwan, and Thailand. As a group, the members of APEC represented 38% of the world's population, 41% of global trade, and 50% of the world's gross national product.

16 **Ukraine to become nuclear free.** The Supreme Council (parliament) of Ukraine voted overwhelmingly to add the country's name to those of other nations formally committed to observing the Nuclear Non-proliferation Treaty. The decision obliged Ukraine, once the world's third largest nuclear power, with 1,800 nuclear warheads, to proclaim itself a nuclear-free zone and recognize that only five nations could legitimately possess nuclear weapons: China, France, Great Britain, Russia, and the U.S. Russia's implementation of the Strategic Arms Reduction Talks treaty (START I) and ratification of START II by the U.S. and Russia had been held up until Ukraine agreed to sign the Nuclear Nonproliferation Treaty. Among the safeguards Ukraine had demanded were a guarantee that its borders and independence would be respected and that no nations would ever use nuclear weapons against it.

17 **Ireland's prime minister resigns.** Albert Reynolds, leader of the Fianna Fail party, resigned as prime minister of Ireland one day after leading members of the Labour Party, junior partners in the ruling coalition, quit their Cabinet posts. Reynolds had raised the ire of Dick Spring, the deputy prime minister and foreign minister, by announcing on November 11 the nomination of Harry Whelehan, the nation's attorney general, to the post of president of the High Court. Spring had accused Whelehan of ignoring for seven months repeated requests from the police in Northern Ireland to extradite a Roman Catholic priest charged with child molestation. The nomination of Whelehan and his elevation to the High Court on November 15 was so resented by the Labour Party that it resolved to bring down the government by deserting the coalition. The priest had already gone voluntarily to Northern Ireland, where he was sentenced to four years in prison.

20 **Fragile peace accord in Angola.** After yearlong negotiations in Lusaka, the capital of Zambia, the government of Angola and the rebel National Union for the Total Independence of Angola (UNITA) signed their third peace treaty since 1989. Expectations that this treaty would hold were based on the fact that, for the first time, UNITA was guaranteed a share of power in national, regional, and local governments. The United Nations also promised to deploy some 7,000 armed peacekeepers throughout the country once there was evidence that the peace settlement was holding firm. Optimism about the future, however, was muted because Jonas Savimbi, the leader of UNITA, did not attend the meeting, prompting Pres. José Eduardo dos Santos to refrain from personally signing the treaty. During the 19 years of civil war, an estimated 500,000 Angolans had been killed.

27 **Uruguayans reelect former leader.** In an uncommon procedure that permitted political parties to field more than one candidate for an elective office—thereby eliminating primary contests—Uruguay's Colorado Party won a plurality of 32.2% of the popular vote in national elections. By rule, the most popular of the Colorado Party's three candidates, former president Julio María Sanguinetti, became head of state and government. The National (Blanco) Party, led by Alberto Volonte, finished in second place with 31.1% of the vote. Although the Broad Front finished in third place, its popular support fell just 1.5% below that of the victorious Colorado Party. It was expected that when ballots cast for candidates seeking election to the Chamber of Deputies were tallied, the three major parties would have relatively equal representation.

As host, Indonesian President Suharto speaks at the Asia-Pacific Economic Cooperation forum on November 15. The 18 member states agreed to ambitious goals of trade liberalization.
HALSTEAD—GAMMA LIAISON

DECEMBER

1 U.S. Senate ratifies GATT accord. Eight months after U.S. trade officials had given their approval to a new General Agreement on Tariffs and Trade (GATT), the Senate ratified the 125-nation accord by a vote of 76–24. The House of Representatives had led the way two days earlier by approving the legislation 288–146. President Clinton signed the bill on December 8. Most other GATT nations were expected to ratify the new accord before it went into effect on Jan. 1, 1995, under the new name World Trade Organization (WTO). Because the WTO apparatus was authorized to settle disputes, some U.S. legislators feared that the U.S. could have decisions forced upon it that it found unacceptable or that were incompatible with U.S. laws. In response to such concerns, a provision in the treaty allowed any country to withdraw from the WTO six months after giving notice.

WHO to direct a new AIDS program. During a meeting in Paris on World AIDS Day, UN Secretary-General Boutros Boutros-Ghali told delegates from 42 nations that previous efforts to conquer AIDS had been largely unsuccessful because there had been too little consultation and

Élysées, Paris' most famous boulevard, to protest what they considered to be a tepid response by those in positions to do much more to attack the AIDS epidemic.

3 Opposition party wins Taipei post. Scoring its most significant political victory to date, the opposition Democratic Progressive Party (DPP) won the race for mayor of Taipei, the capital of Taiwan. Its candidate, Chen Shui-bian, was a well-known member of the National Assembly. The success of his campaign was cited as evidence that multiparty democracy was taking firm root in Taiwan. The victory also gave the DPP a conspicuous platform from which to challenge for the presidency in 1996. The ruling Kuomintang (KMT; Nationalist Party), however, continued to dominate the political scene. James Soong, its candidate for governor, faced election for the first time and was returned to office in a landslide. (The governor had previously been appointed by the president). Wu Den-yih gave the KMT another important victory with his election as mayor of Kaohsiung, Taiwan's second largest city. Political analysts interpreted the election results as a general desire for controlled change that would not destabilize the

of the ruling Institutional Revolutionary Party (PRI), had been fraudulent, the EZLN refused to recognize the legitimacy of his governorship and, in a separate ceremony, installed Amado Avendaño of the Democratic Revolutionary Party as chief executive officer of the state. On October 15 Subcomandante Marcos, the leader of the EZLN, had threatened to turn not only Chiapas but all of Mexico into a battleground if Robledo was inaugurated.

Turkey imprisons eight of its legislators. Turkish Prime Minister Tansu Ciller's campaign against Kurdish separatists took on a new dimension with the sentencing of eight members of the National Assembly to prison for consorting with members of the outlawed Kurdish Workers' Party (PKK). Five of those convicted received 15-year terms. Earlier in 1994 Ciller had ordered 300,000 troops to wipe out PKK strongholds in Turkey's southeastern provinces. She also suspended parliamentary immunity and ordered the arrest of six members of the Democratic Party, a pro-Kurdish group said to be a front for the PKK. The conflict between Kurds and government forces had claimed an estimated 13,000 lives over a period of 10 years.

A Chechen fights amid the rubble of the streets of Grozny, his republic's capital. On December 11 the Russian army invaded Chechnya, a largely Muslim region that had unilaterally declared its independence in 1991.
PAUL LOWE—MAGNUM

cooperation among various groups working on the same tasks. To remedy this situation, Peter Piot, the associate director of the World Health Organization's (WHO's) AIDS program since 1992, was appointed head of a new UN agency on December 12. Its main responsibility would be to coordinate the work of six international organizations devoted to all aspects of AIDS research. Members of Act Up, a militant group demanding that more be done to combat AIDS, lay down on the Champs-

country. Many voters apparently also had misgivings about the DPP's call for Taiwan independence.

8 Tensions mount in Chiapas area. The formal inauguration of Eduardo Robledo Rincón as governor of the Mexican state of Chiapas threatened to revive the civil conflict initiated by the rebel Zapatista National Liberation Army (EZLN) in January. Claiming that the August election of Robledo, a member

9 Cuban refugees in Panama riot. U.S. officials reported that order had been restored at four U.S.-controlled Cuban refugee bases in Panama after a full day of sporadic rioting. The violence appeared to be the result of frustration among the 8,500 detainees who had grown weary of their confinement and primitive conditions and were anxious about their future. All had hoped to enter the U.S. as legal immigrants. Among the hundreds injured during the melee were 25 military personnel and 19 Cubans who required hospitalization. Most of their wounds had been inflicted by rocks, bricks, or bottles. About 1,000 Cubans took advantage of the confusion to escape from the camps, but virtually all were back in camp within a short time.

10 **Japanese political parties merge.** The alignment of political forces in Japan underwent a dramatic change with the official inauguration of the New Frontier Party (Shinshinto) in Yokohama. The new party represented the merger of nine parties: Shinseito, Komeito, Japan New Party, Democratic Socialist Party, and five smaller groups. The organization committee, which included representatives of all nine parties, was headed by Ichiro Ozawa, who had deserted the scandal-ridden Liberal-Democratic Party (LDP) to articulate his views as a member of the opposition. His mentor in the LDP had been Shin Kanemaru, who had left politics in disgrace. The New Frontier was committed to "unwavering reform" and "responsible politics," but it had not yet taken a position on certain specific issues. Toshiki Kaifu, a former LDP prime minister, was elected leader of the party by a vote of 131–83. Ozawa was chosen to be its secretary-general.

11 **Russian army invades Chechnya.** Russian Pres. Boris Yeltsin, having warned the federated republic of Chechnya that military force would be used to prevent its secession, ordered the Russian army to attack. The predominantly Muslim Chechen population was a fiercely independent group with a long history of animosity toward outsiders. Their president, Dzhokhar Dudayev, had declared independence unilaterally in 1991. The situation was highly explosive because the area was rich in oil and the main oil pipeline from the Caspian oil fields of Azerbaijan passed through the republic. On December 16 Russian Major Gen. Ivan Babichev dramatically halted his tank division about 32 km (20 mi) from Grozny, the Chechen capital. He told the people that he could not bring himself "to use the army against peaceful civilians." Despite numerous international efforts to establish a cease-fire, Russian troops entered Grozny on December 31 after the city had been severely damaged by air strikes and heavy artillery.

Americas to form own free-trade zone. During its three-day meeting in Miami, Fla., the leaders of 34 Western Hemisphere nations endorsed the creation of a Free Trade Area of the Americas (FTAA). The only independent nation in the Americas not invited to participate was Cuba. If negotiations went smoothly, the FTAA would be a reality by the year 2005 and would be the largest trade organization in the world. It had a combined annual purchasing power of $13 trillion. Plans called for much smaller regional trade agreements already functioning in South America to be incorporated into the FTAA. The North American Free Trade Agreement (NAFTA), which regulated trade between Canada, the U.S., and Mexico, was expected to serve as a guide when the FTAA began drafting its regulations.

On the final day of the meeting, the three members of NAFTA invited Chile to join the organization.

17 **North Korea downs U.S. aircraft.** An unarmed U.S. Army OH-58 Kiowa reconnaissance helicopter was shot down by North Korea approximately five kilometres (three miles) north of the demilitarized zone that separated North and South Korea. The incident threatened to negate the improvement in relations between the U.S. and North Korea following the October settlement of a dispute over North Korea's nuclear program. One of the U.S. chief warrant officers was killed in the crash, the other taken into custody. The U.S. claimed that the pilots were on a routine training mission and had probably strayed into North Korea airspace because the normally familiar terrain was covered with snow. Repeated U.S. requests that the matter be resolved quickly went unanswered until December 22, when the remains of David Hilemon were turned over to U.S. authorities. Bobby Hall, the second pilot, appeared to be in good health when he was set free on December 30.

18 **Ex-communists win in Bulgaria.** The Bulgarian Socialist (former communist) Party led by Zhan Videnov won control of the nation's 240-seat unicameral legislature by capturing a substantial plurality of the popular vote. Among the 48 other political parties that contested the election, the Union of Democratic Forces, which was strongly anticommunist, had the most support—about 25% of all the votes cast. Prime Minister Lyuben Berov's resignation on September 2 was accepted by Parliament on September 8. Pres. Zhelyu Zhelev bided his time, then dissolved Parliament on December 17 and ordered new elections. Berov had led a nonparty government of technocrats for nearly two years with little success. Videnov, however, spoke confidently of his ability to solve Bulgaria's problems, "not by returning to the past but by moving forward." Because he was not an ardent advocate of the free market, Bulgaria seemed likely to remain one of the least privatized nations in Eastern Europe.

20 **Cease-fire announced in Bosnia.** Former U.S. president Jimmy Carter announced that government leaders in Bosnia and Herzegovina and representatives of the Bosnian Serbs had agreed to a four-month cease-fire beginning December 23. Earlier in the year Carter, acting as peacemaker in a private capacity, had had similar successes in North Korea and Haiti. The situation in Bosnia and Herzegovina had so frustrated UN officials that there were serious discussions about a total withdrawal of its peacekeeping force. Typical of the problems it faced was the capture of UN personnel, who were taken hostage and dispersed to strategic areas to deter the UN from launching air strikes against Serb positions. The UN sense of hopelessness was further heightened when the "safe zones" it had set up to protect civilians came under Serb attack. All the while, U.S. and UN military leaders were at odds over what policies to pursue.

The bodies of hijackers are removed from an Air France plane. Militants opposed to the Algerian government hijacked the aircraft in Algiers on December 24.
T. ORBAN/B. BISSON—SYGMA

22 **Facing defeat, Berlusconi quits.** Italy was once again plunged into political turmoil when Prime Minister Silvio Berlusconi tendered his resignation after just seven months in office. He urged Pres. Oscar Scalfaro to call new elections in order to foster the democratic process rather than search for someone capable of forming a new coalition government. Berlusconi felt compelled to resign in the face of three upcoming motions of no confidence, one of which was directed by a leader of one of the parties in his own coalition. He remained as prime minister in a caretaker capacity.

24 **French plane seized in Algiers.** Four heavily armed gunmen seized control of an Air France Airbus A-300 as it began to taxi to the runway at the international airport in Algiers, the capital of Algeria. The 227 passengers and 12 crew members aboard were scheduled to fly to Orly Airport outside Paris. The terrorists released dozens of Algerian passengers almost immediately and distributed head scarfs to women who remained aboard—an indication that the terrorists were probably Islamic fundamentalists. On December 26, after three passengers had been killed, the Algerian and French governments allowed the plane, which had been surrounded by police, to fly to Marseille, France. As darkness began to settle over the airport, French paramilitary commandos stormed the plane and killed the four gunmen. Some passengers, crew members, and police were injured, but none was killed. While the hijacking was still in progress, the Armed Islamic Group claimed responsibility, explaining that the action was in reprisal for France's "unconditional political, military, and economic aid" to the Algerian government, which it had vowed to overthrow. French authorities reported on December 27 that the government had received word that the terrorists had planned to blow up the plane over Paris. After the crisis ended, police searched the plane and found 20 sticks of dynamite.

Disasters

The loss of life and property from disasters in 1994 included the following:

Aviation

January 3, Near Irkutsk, Siberia. A TU-154 Russian jetliner with one of its three engines ablaze plowed through farm buildings and power lines before crashing in a field and bursting into flames moments after takeoff; all 120 persons aboard perished, and another fatality was reported on the ground.

January 5, Florida. A twin-engine plane crashed on a rural road in the Orlando area after experiencing engine trouble shortly after takeoff; 10 persons were killed, including a newlywed couple and a number of their relatives.

January 12, Cuzco, Peru. A helicopter with 15 military personnel aboard crashed on the airport runway; all aboard were killed.

February 25, Near Carpish Pass, Peru. The wreckage of a passenger plane carrying 29 persons was discovered in a remote, cloud-shrouded area of the eastern Andes a day after it lost radio contact and disappeared; there were no survivors of the crash.

March 14, Off the coast of Kenya. A U.S. Air Force AC-130 gunship carrying weapons to support the international effort in Mogadishu, Somalia, crashed some 20 m (66 ft) from the shoreline; 11 of the 14 crew members aboard were killed.

March 17, Nagorno-Karabakh, Azerbaijan. An Iranian transport plane carrying the families of diplomats home from Moscow to Tehran to celebrate the Muslim New Year went down in the disputed, heavily Armenian enclave; the craft, which carried 32 persons, mostly women and children, reportedly lost cabin pressure before it crashed, claiming the lives of all aboard.

March 23, Near Novokuznetsk, Siberia. A Russian A-310 Airbus slammed into a snow-covered hillside and exploded after disappearing from radar tracking screens. The pilot, who had apparently turned over the cockpit controls to his teenage son and daughter while he and the copilot visited with the passengers, was unable to reach the controls in time to steer the plummeting aircraft out of a fatal nosedive, which resulted in the deaths of all 75 persons aboard the half-empty plane.

March 23, Pope Air Force Base, North Carolina. Two air force planes, one an F-16 Fighting Falcon and the other a C-130 Hercules transport plane, collided in midair when both attempted to land simultaneously; the two fighter pilots ejected to safety and the C-130 cargo plane was able to land safely with its crew, but the F-16 exploded, crashed, skidded down the tarmac in the form of a giant fireball, and slammed into a C-141 Star-Lifter transport plane with hundreds of paratroopers on board. The death toll on the ground was 23, and 85 were badly injured, most of them with severe burns.

April 1, Near Djanet, Alg. A helicopter crashed with 14 persons aboard; there were no survivors.

April 26, Nagoya, Japan. A China Airlines A-300 Airbus crash-landed and exploded on the tarmac shortly after an inexperienced copilot at the controls struggled to land the jet as its computerized controls tried to abort the landing and gain altitude; only 7 of the 271 persons aboard survived the fiery explosion. In early May it was also revealed that the copilot had a blood level of alcohol that was in excess of Japan's standards for drunken driving.

Late April, West Kalimantan, Indon. A plane crash claimed the lives of 10 persons, but a lone survivor was found crawling through the bush five days later.

May 6/7, Near Kinshasa, Zaire. A twin-engine plane carrying at least nine officials from Zaire, Tunisia, and Uganda crashed in a swamp; besides the various government officials, an unspecified number of passengers were on the flight; apparently all perished.

June 2, Western Scotland. A helicopter carrying high-ranking MI-5 officers and senior members of the special branch of the Royal Ulster Constabulary to a security conference exploded in a fireball before crashing in heavy fog on the tip of the Mull of Kintyre; none of the 29 persons aboard survived.

June 6, Near Xian (Sian), China. A Chinese jetliner en route to Guangzhou (Canton) crashed moments after takeoff; all 160 persons aboard perished.

June 7, Near Abidjan, Côte d'Ivoire. An Air Ivoire Fokker F-27 crashed on its approach to the capital; 17 persons were killed.

June 18, Near Washington, D.C. A plane carrying Mexican fans to a World Cup soccer match between Mexico and Norway crashed in the woods in heavy fog while making its final approach to Dulles Airport outside Washington, D.C.; all 12 persons aboard the aircraft were killed.

July 1, Tidjikya, Mauritania. An Air Mauritania passenger plane crashed while attempting to land during a sandstorm; 94 of the 101 persons aboard lost their lives.

July 2, Charlotte, N.C. A USAir DC-9 jetliner with 57 persons aboard crashed during a thunderstorm while making its approach to the Charlotte-Douglas International Airport; 37 persons were killed despite the pilots' desperate efforts to reverse the aircraft's downward spiral. Experts believed that wind shear was a possible cause of the crash.

July 19, Near Colón, Panama. A plane carrying 21 persons exploded and crashed shortly after takeoff; all aboard perished, and investigators were concerned that a bomb may have been aboard the aircraft.

August 5, Bada, Siberia. A Russian military transport plane crashed upon landing at the Bada airport; 47 persons aboard perished.

August 21, Near Agadir, Morocco. A Royal Air Maroc passenger plane crashed in the Atlas Mountains; all 44 persons aboard the aircraft were killed, including 16 foreign tourists and a Kuwaiti prince and his wife. Government allegations that the pilot was suicidal could not be proved.

September 8, Near Aliquippa, Pa. A USAir Boeing 737 inexplicably nose-dived to the ground and exploded while approaching the Greater Pittsburgh International Airport, a scheduled stop en route to its final destination in Florida; all 132 persons aboard were killed.

September 26, Near Vanavara, Siberia. A Russian Yak-40 plane carrying 26 persons crashed while preparing for an emergency landing during a storm; there were no survivors.

October 12, Central Iran. A commuter plane crashed in the Karkas Mountains; all 66 persons aboard perished.

October 29, Near Irkutsk. A four-engine Russian plane crashed; 21 persons were killed.

October 31, Near Roselawn, Ind. A Chicago-bound commuter plane carrying 68 persons crashed and burned in a cornfield after descending from 3,050 m (10,000 ft) to 2,440 m (8,000 ft) during a torrential downpour; no one survived the crash, which investigators believed was probably caused by ice buildup on the aircraft's wings.

November 1, Off the coast of Cozumel, Mexico. A helicopter carrying 14 persons plunged into the Caribbean Sea shortly after its pilot had reportedly experienced mechanical failure; all aboard were killed.

December 13, Near Morrisville, N.C. A commuter plane crashed in a heavily wooded area while preparing to land at the Raleigh-Durham Airport; of the 20 persons aboard the craft, 15 were killed when the plane plummeted to the ground in fog and rain, apparently after experiencing an engine flameout.

December 29, Near Van, Turkey. An aircraft whose pilot had aborted two landings crashed during a third attempt in a blinding snowstorm; of the 76 persons aboard the aircraft, which was severed into three parts, 54 persons were killed and 22 were injured.

Fires and Explosions

January 16, Tetouan, Morocco. A fire that swept through a steam bath claimed the lives of 24 persons; 15 were treated for smoke inhalation.

Mid-February, Yuanshi (Yuan-shih) county, Hubei (Hupeh) province, China. Several crates of firecrackers exploded at a market; 16 persons were killed and 7 were injured in the blast.

March 20, Dhaka, Bangladesh. A gas cylinder belonging to a balloon vendor exploded near a tap where women and children were waiting in line to collect water; more than 18 persons were killed, and 15 were seriously injured.

March 29, Kashmir, India. An explosion tore through an army explosives depot; at least 15 military personnel were killed in the inferno.

March 30, Idil, Sirnak province, Turkey. A passenger minibus traveling on a country road struck a mine planted on a bridge by separatist Kurdish guerrillas; 15 persons were killed, and one was wounded.

Late April, Near Galashki, Russia. An apparent engine defect caused a bus to erupt in flames; at least 31 persons lost their lives, and 27 were injured.

July 1, Vitória, Brazil. A fireworks stall exploded at an outdoor antique market and touched off other fires in adjacent buildings and in cars passing through the marketplace; at least 30 persons were killed, and some 40 were injured.

July 3–10, Southern and eastern Spain. The worst wildfires in 20 years, resulting from extraordinarily dry weather coupled with torrid temperatures, incinerated more than 150,000 ha (370,500 ac) of pine and eucalyptus forest and claimed the lives of 14 firefighters and 7 others.

REGION BEAL—PITTSBURGH POST GAZETTE/SYGMA

Investigators study the wreckage of an airplane that crashed in Pennsylvania on September 8. All 132 people on the USAir flight were killed when the plane suddenly dived to the ground.

Rescuers search for victims in Durunkah, Egypt, after a fire on November 2. More than 500 people were killed when floodwaters spread burning fuel from an explosion at a fuel-storage complex.

TOM HARTWELL—SABA

July 6, Near Glenwood Springs, Colo. A firestorm on Storm King Mountain claimed the lives of 14 of 52 smoke jumpers who were trapped when the relatively contained wildfire exploded into a major conflagration as it was fueled by 80-km/h (50-mph) winds.

July 18, Buenos Aires, Arg. An explosion in a Jewish community centre claimed the lives of nearly 100 persons; authorities believed that a bomb planted by terrorists had triggered the blast.

Mid-August, Seoul, South Korea. A fire swept through a hostess bar; 14 persons were killed.

September 7, Moscow. At least three explosions ripped through a two-story building that housed a sports club, a municipal maintenance office, and the passport division of a neighbouring police station; the unexplained blast killed as many as 10 persons and injured 27.

Early October, Uttar Pradesh, India. An explosion in a fireworks factory claimed the lives of 26 persons and critically injured 27; many of the victims were children.

October 24, Chungju Lake, South Korea. A fire swept through a pleasure boat, and the vessel was engulfed in flames; at least 20 persons were killed, and 12 were missing.

October 26, Bihar, India. A fire that raced through one coach of a train claimed the lives of at least 28 persons.

November 2, Durunkah, Egypt. A raging fire broke out at a fuel-storage complex when torrential rains caused the main bridge to the complex to collapse on an oil depot. Floodwaters spread blazing fuel from the damaged depot on the village; more than 500 persons were killed, and at least 200 homes were incinerated.

November 27, Liaoning (Liao-ning) province, China. A blazing fire swept through a dance hall in Fuxin (Fu-hsin) filled with students from a local technical school; 233 students perished, and only 16 escaped from the structure, which had one small entrance door and small, out-of-reach windows.

November 30, Shantung (Shan-tung) province, China. A raging hotel fire claimed the lives of 38 persons and injured 11; it took nearly 100 firefighters to bring the conflagration under control.

December 8, Karamay (K'o-la-ma-i), Xinjiang Uygur (Sinkiang Uighur) Autonomous Region, China. A movie theatre filled with more than 800 persons, at least 500 of them schoolchildren and their teachers, was engulfed in flames as patrons watched a cultural performance; at least 300 persons, most of them children, lost their lives.

Marine

January 1, Mid-North Atlantic Ocean. A mammoth cargo ship sank during a fierce storm; res-

cuers found empty life rafts and concluded that all 36 persons aboard the vessel had drowned.

January 15, Near Chimagurhi, India. Two passenger ferries carrying Hindu pilgrims collided in thick fog in the Bay of Bengal; one boat was severed in two, and at least 100 passengers from that vessel were feared drowned.

Late January, South China Sea. An oil tanker with 10 crewmen aboard inexplicably exploded and tore in two; all crew members were feared dead.

February 3, Off the coast of Land's End, England. A bulk carrier sank during a violent storm packing hurricane-force winds after reporting that it was taking on huge amounts of water through a damaged hold; the 27 crewmen aboard the vessel were lost at sea.

Mid-February, Off the coast of Ranong, Thailand. A boat that may have been overloaded capsized; more than 200 Burmese workers were feared drowned.

February 21, Off the coast of The Bahamas. An overcrowded boat carrying illegal Haitian migrants sank in shark-infested waters; some 24 passengers were feared dead.

March 7, Lake Victoria, Kenya. An overloaded ferry carrying passengers, timber, and corn (maize) capsized and sank during a storm; at least 40 persons were missing and believed drowned.

March 13, Bosporus, Turkey. The collision of an oil tanker and a dry cargo ship in the busy waterway resulted in an oil spill and a raging fire aboard the tanker; at least 17 crewmen were killed, and 16 were missing.

March 20, Off the coast of Masirah, Oman. A supertanker filled with millions of gallons of oil exploded and caught fire at sea; as the vessel with 18 dead crewmen aboard tried to dock, various states refused to allow it into port because of fears of pollution.

March 30, Off the coast of Toulon, France. A submerged French nuclear submarine, powered by a pressurized, water-cooled nuclear reactor, limped back to port after a pipe burst and released superheated steam into the vessel's turbine compartment; 10 sailors conducting routine inspections were burned to death or asphyxiated.

April 8, Central Philippines. A wooden boat carrying 15 fishermen sank after being swamped by Typhoon Owen; only one person survived.

April 22, Off the coast of al-Basit, Syria. An overloaded fishing boat carrying elementary schoolchildren and teachers capsized; of the 55 persons aboard the vessel, 36 children and 5 teachers perished.

April 29, Off the coast of Mombasa, Kenya. A ferry packed with commuters capsized and sank when panic-stricken upper-deck passengers ran

to one side of the boat after the helmsman experienced difficulty steering; at least 272 persons were killed in what was the country's worst ferry disaster to date.

May 17, Near Libreville, Gabon. A canoe carrying illegal immigrants capsized off the coast during a storm; some 50 persons perished.

May 24, Off the coast of the Dominican Republic. A small boat carrying more than 100 illegal immigrants to Puerto Rico capsized in the Mona Passage; at least 40 persons drowned.

June 12, Off the coast of Somalia. A dhow filled with refugees from Yemen capsized off the northern coast of Somalia; at least 50 persons were feared drowned.

June 20, Off the coast of South Africa. The Chinese tanker *Apollo Sea* sank off the Cape of Good Hope and produced a massive oil spill near Dassen Island, the breeding grounds of the endangered jackass penguin; 37 crew members were killed, and some 1,600 jackass penguins drowned after being coated with oil.

Early July, Off the coast of Haiti. Hundreds of boats containing some 5,000 Haitian refugees set sail for the U.S.; the massive exodus in overcrowded, rickety boats resulted in the deaths of at least 200 persons in numerous tragedies at sea.

July 9, China. A bus that was being ferried across the Yangtze River (Chang Jiang) slid off the boat and plunged into the water; at least 50 persons drowned.

July 13, Off the coast of Havana. A stolen wooden tugboat with 63 refugees aboard sank; the leaking vessel was submerged after a pursuing vessel struck its stern; 31 persons, mostly women and children, drowned.

August 20, Chandpur, Bangladesh. A ferry carrying some 250 passengers overturned in strong currents and was drawn underwater by a whirlpool while it prepared to dock; more than 200 persons were feared drowned.

Early September, Off the coast of Cape Town. An iron-ore carrier, the *Iron Antonis,* apparently sustained a crack during a storm and sank in the Atlantic Ocean; all 24 crewmen abandoned the vessel and drowned.

September 28, Off the coast of Turku, Fin. The *Estonia,* a massive passenger-and-car ferry, rapidly sank in the Baltic Sea during a roaring storm accompanied by high winds of up to 100 km/h (62 mph) and choppy seas as high as 10 m (33 ft); the roll-on, roll-off vessel apparently began taking on water when the large hydraulic loading door in the bow was ripped off during the pounding storm. While many of the passengers slept below, the ferry heaved to its port side and sank, stern first, in the chilly (10° C [50° F]) water; of the more than 1,040 passengers believed aboard, only about 140 survived.

October 16, Near Madarbari Island, Bangladesh. A ferry carrying nearly 200 persons, 165 of them members of a wedding party, capsized and sank in choppy waters; more than 100 persons were feared drowned.

November 11, Off the coast of Johore, Malaysia. A small boat packed with Indonesian illegal workers was swamped by waves and capsized; 37 of the 87 persons aboard the craft drowned.

December 2, Near Rosario, Phil. A ferry and a freight tanker collided near the mouth of Manila Bay; 34 persons aboard the ferry were known dead, and 113 were missing and presumed drowned.

December 9, North Atlantic Sea. A Ukrainian cargo ship sank after being battered by huge waves and fierce winds; 2 of the 31 seamen aboard the boat were rescued, but rescuers were unable to save others clinging to life rafts because of the turbulent waters.

Mining and Tunneling

January 24, Heilongjiang (Heilungkiang) province, China. A powerful gas explosion at the Xiji (Hsi-chi) coal mine claimed the lives of 47 miners and left 32 missing and presumed dead.

January 25, West Bengal, India. Lethal carbon monoxide emissions from a fire that was caused by a short circuit killed 55 miners at a coal mine near Asansol.

January 27, Newkenda, India. A fire in a coal mine trapped 55 miners for two days; all perished.

March 6, Jilin (Kirin) province, China. A predawn explosion at the Liaowang coal and gas field claimed the lives of 12 miners.

April, China. Several gas explosions during the first three months of the year reportedly killed at least 700 Chinese coal miners despite the closing in February of some 2,000 mines in Heilongjiang province for safety reasons.

Mid-May, Jiangxi (Kiangsi) province, China. A powerful gas explosion killed 38 coal miners in underground tunnels.

Early August, Queensland, Australia. A series of gas explosions trapped 11 miners underground; all succumbed to the toxic fumes.

August 29, Mindanao Island, Philippines. A powerful gas explosion ripped through the country's largest coal mine near Malangas; 90 of 170 miners working underground were killed.

Early September, Slov'yanoserbsk, Ukraine. An explosion in a coal mine claimed the lives of 24 miners and injured 15; methane gas was suspected as a cause of the blast.

Natural

January 7, Bicol, Phil. A violent storm lashed the area, causing landslides and flooding; at least 23 fatalities were attributed to the weather system, which hit the town of Manito hardest, leaving 15 persons known dead and 30 missing.

Mid-January, U.S. A bitter arctic cold wave that stretched from the Midwest to the Eastern Seaboard paralyzed the regions with temperatures that plummeted to record-breaking lows, notably in such cities as Pittsburgh, Pa. ($-30°$ C [$-22°$ F]); Akron, Ohio, and Clarksburg, W.Va. ($-32°$ C [$-25°$ F]); and Indianapolis, Ind. ($-33°$ C [$-27°$ F]); more than 140 deaths were attributed to the deep freeze.

Mid-January, Northern and northwestern Bangladesh. A severe cold snap killed 29 persons, mostly destitute children and elderly people living in slums.

January 17, Los Angeles. A strong predawn earthquake of magnitude 6.8 violently shook the area, claimed the lives of 61 persons, injured more than 9,000, and resulted in $13 billion–$20 billion in damages; the temblor caused sections of the Santa Monica, Golden State, Antelope Valley, and Simi Valley freeways to collapse; multiple fires resulting from gas leaks, including those that destroyed some 70 homes in Sylmar; the derailment of a 64-car train between Northridge and Chatsworth; and the collapse of offices, plants, and apartment buildings, notably a three-story apartment in Northridge (close to the epicentre in the San Fernando Valley), where 16 persons were killed when the building crumpled. Many of the 25,000 left homeless camped in parks and shelters as powerful aftershocks reverberated.

January 21, Halmahera, Indonesia. A strong earthquake of magnitude 6.8 jolted the Moluccan island, reduced some of the buildings to rubble, and claimed the lives of at least seven persons.

Early February, Southwestern Colombia. Heavy rains produced flooding that destroyed some 1,400 homes and claimed the lives of at least 19 persons; hard hit was the town of Florida, which was ravaged by the floodwaters.

February 2–4, Madagascar. Cyclone Geralda, which was billed as the "cyclone of the century," lashed the island with torrential rains and winds of up to 350 km/h (220 mph); the brutal storm killed at least 70 persons; left some 500,000 homeless, including 80,000 in the worst-hit town of Toamasina; sank seven ships; flooded 70% of the farmlands; and devastated 95% of the main commercial port.

February 4, Virginia, South Africa. The wall of a gold-treatment dam collapsed and unleashed a huge wave of toxic mine refuse; at least 12 persons were known dead, and 82 were missing and presumed dead.

Mid-February, Peru. Torrential rains caused severe flooding and mud slides; at least 50 persons were killed, and more than 5,000 families were left homeless.

February 16, Sumatra, Indonesia. A powerful earthquake of magnitude 7.2 violently shook Lam-

pung province and devastated 75% of the mountain town of Liwa, which was beset by thundering landslides; the temblor claimed the lives of at least 215 persons.

March, Kyrgyzstan. A series of landslides killed nearly 100 persons during the month.

March 27, Alabama, Georgia, North Carolina, South Carolina, and Tennessee. A series of violent thunderstorms and ferocious tornadoes wreaked widespread destruction across the five states and claimed the lives of at least 42 persons; hardest hit were the town of Piedmont, Ala., where a tornado killed at least 19 Palm Sunday worshipers at the Goshen Methodist Church, and the Georgia counties of Bartow, Pickens, Lumpkin, White, and Habersham, where at least 13 persons lost their lives.

Late March, Nampula province, Mozambique. A brutal cyclone lashed the northern province with punishing winds that claimed the lives of at least 34 persons, destroyed thousands of homes and farmlands, and left some 1.5 million persons homeless.

Mid-April, Brazil. A thundering landslide killed at least 19 miners at an Amazon tin mine.

April 17, Bangladesh. Tropical storms accompanied by gale-force winds crushed homes, uprooted trees, and claimed the lives of at least 29 persons near the coast of the Bay of Bengal; 200 fishermen in the town of Cox's Bazar were also missing and feared drowned.

May 2, Southeastern Bangladesh. A roaring cyclone whipped up winds of up to 290 km/h (180 mph), rampaged through the islands of Kutubdia, Maheshkhali, Ukhia, and St. Martin, and claimed the lives of 233 persons; a new storm-warning system aided early evacuation and was credited with keeping the death toll to a relatively low number, although the figure was expected to rise after destruction in remote areas had been assessed.

May 27, Sabaragamuva province, India. A huge landslide triggered by incessant rains entombed at least 15 persons.

Late-May, Northern India. A record-breaking heat wave gripped New Delhi and the western state of Rajasthan; at least 161 deaths were attributed to the searing temperature, which reached 49° C (120° F).

June 3, Eastern Java, Indonesia. Two predawn earthquakes caused a series of tidal waves to lash the island; hardest hit was Banyuwangi, where more than 200 sleeping residents were killed.

June 6, Southwestern Colombia. An earthquake followed by a massive avalanche of rocks, ice, and mud buried dozens of villages in the Cauca and Huila regions; though the official death toll was placed at 269, other reports estimated that as many as 1,000 persons, many of them Páez and Guambiano Indians, succumbed.

Mid-June, Southern China. Torrential summer rains produced massive flooding in Guangdong (Kwangtung) and Guangxi (Kwangsi); as many as 400 persons were believed dead, and housing, industry, and agriculture sustained sizable damages.

Late June–mid-July, India. Torrential monsoon rains caused massive flooding; some 500 lives were lost, and precious crops were destroyed.

Early July, Georgia, Alabama, and Florida. Tropical Storm Alberto stalled over the Southern states and dumped as much as 61 cm (24 in) of rain in some areas of Georgia, where at least 32 persons lost their lives. At least one person died in Alabama, and 31 deluged counties across the three states were declared federal disaster areas.

Early July, Philippines. Relentless rains triggered heavy flooding in nine provinces, where 68 persons were killed. The government pledged relief funds of $2.8 million to assuage the calamitous devastation.

Early August, Taiwan. A ferocious typhoon packing winds of up to 137 km/h (85 mph) claimed the lives of 10 persons, injured 41, severed power lines, and blew down hundreds of trees.

Mid-August, Beijing (Peking). A suffocating heat wave claimed the lives of at least 104 persons.

August 18, Northern Algeria. A strong earthquake of magnitude 5.6 killed at least 171 persons, left some 15,500 persons homeless, and reduced mud-brick homes to rubble in the Mascara region.

August 20–21, Zhejiang (Chekiang) province, China. Typhoon Fred assaulted the eastern province with driving rain, which pounded the area for 43 consecutive hours; the brutal storm killed some 1,000 persons and caused damages in excess of $1.1 billion.

August 26, Baluchistan province, Pak. Rampaging floodwaters swept away a minibus carrying 24 persons, including 16 children; all drowned.

August 27–28, Central Moldova. Several days of torrential rains triggered severe flooding; at least 50 persons lost their lives in the central Hincesti region, which was declared a disaster area.

Late August, Niger. Severe flooding led to the deaths of 40 persons and prompted some 30,000 to abandon their homes.

September 23, Algeria. Floods caused by torrential rains claimed the lives of at least 29 persons.

Late September, Pampanga province, Phil. Heavy rains caused the Mt. Pinatubo volcano to unleash an avalanche of mud and rocks that killed 23 persons and buried more than 1,300 homes in the Porac and Bacolor districts; some 10,000 persons fled high-risk areas.

October 4, Kuril Islands. An earthquake of magnitude 8.2 struck the sparsely populated chain of islands and claimed the lives of 16 Russian soldiers stationed there.

October 16–19, Houston, Texas. As much as 76 cm (30 in) of rain soaked Houston's San Jacinto River Basin, causing massive flooding that submerged homes and highways and claimed the lives of at least 10 persons.

October 23, Manila. Typhoon Teresa battered the main island of Luzon, killing 25 persons, including 16 crewmen from an oil tanker that broke in two during the storm, leaving thousands homeless, and downing trees and power lines.

November 4–5, Northern Italy. Torrential rains produced the worst flooding in more than 80 years; in the hardest-hit region of Piedmont, at least 57 persons were killed as the floodwaters obliterated homes and highways and destroyed communications links. Authorities feared the death toll could rise as high as 100 after rescuers reached and searched villages isolated by the storm.

November 13–19, Haiti, Cuba, Florida, and North Carolina. Tropical Storm Gordon unleashed its fury on Haiti, where more than 200 persons were killed, before battering Cuba, heading northeast across southern Florida, and crossing into the North Atlantic to briefly threaten North Carolina's Outer Banks before making a U-turn back to Florida and weakening into a tropical depression. The zigzagging storm claimed the lives of at least 537 persons. At least $200 million in damages occurred in Florida alone.

Mid-November, Northern Somalia. A cyclone killed at least 30 persons and injured hundreds.

November 15, Mindoro, Phil. An earthquake of magnitude 6.7 spawned tidal waves up to 15 m (49 ft) high that subsumed houses in the town of Baco, where the corpses of children were later discovered hanging from trees; at least 60 persons lost their lives, and 130 were injured as more than 700 aftershocks (one of which measured 5.1) reverberated.

Late November, Djibouti. Torrential rains forced thousands to evacuate their homes; 20 persons were killed in the southern region of Hol-Hol.

November 22, Java. A volcanic eruption on Mt. Merapi killed at least 31 persons and buried dozens who were trapped in homes built on the slopes of the country's most active volcano.

Late December, Philippines. Tropical Storm Axel vented its fury on the country and claimed the lives of at least 15 persons and injured some 40.

Railroad

March 8, Near Durban, South Africa. A commuter train that was traveling at an accelerated speed around a sharp turn derailed and fell into a gorge; at least 88 persons were known dead, and more than 350 were injured in Natal province's worst railroad accident.

March 21, Shaba, Zaire. A train derailment between Lubumbashi and Lubudi claimed the lives of 43 persons and injured several.

April 3, Near Sohawa, Pak. A passenger train traveling to Rawalpindi from Lahore derailed and plunged down a steep hill; at least 13 persons lost their lives, and some 100 were injured.

May 15, Near Pinlong township, Myanmar (Burma). A train that was heavily loaded with passengers and rice derailed en route to Kayah state; 25 persons were killed, and 38 were injured.

Early August, Southwestern Russia. A commuter train slammed into five freight cars that broke away from a freight train and derailed; 21 persons were killed in the accident, and at least 80 were injured.

August 13, Near Tbilisi, Georgia. A passenger train rammed a stationary freight train because of a faulty signal; at least 22 persons were killed, and some 16 were injured.

August 21, Tunisia. A collision between two passenger trains between the villages of Kalaa Kebira and Kalaa Seghira resulted in 21 deaths and 89 injuries.

Late September, Southern Angola. A train derailment claimed the lives of at least 140 persons, and 80 were injured.

October 20, Near Beijing. A freight train plowed into a commuter bus at an unguarded railroad crossing; at least 17 persons were killed, and 30 were injured.

December 2, Near Szolnok, Hung. An express train derailed, causing some of its cars to slam into a building; at least 20 persons were entombed under rubble.

December 30, Myanmar. A passenger train derailed while crossing a bridge in the northern part of the country; at least 102 persons were killed and 53 were injured when one of the cars plunged into a ravine and another was left dangling from the bridge.

Traffic

Mid-January, Southwestern Hungary. A cable that was securing some six tons of sheet metal to the trailer of a truck became loose, and several metal sheets were released into the pathway of a bus; 11 persons were killed.

January 10, Bali, Indonesia. A bus carrying mainly French tourists plunged into a ravine near Kintamali; 10 tourists lost their lives, and 17 were injured.

January 14, Bihar, India. A small bus carrying 60 persons careened into a dry riverbed; all 40 passengers inside the vehicle were killed, but the 20 persons riding atop the vehicle survived the crash.

January 14, Tak province, Thailand. An 18-wheel truck that was barreling down a dark highway collided head-on with a tour bus; at least 37 persons were killed, and 3 were injured.

February 5, Kerala, India. A head-on collision between a bus and a truck carrying inflammable coir resulted in at least 40 fatalities when the fuel tank of the bus exploded on impact.

February 10, Sumatra. A bus plunged into a ravine in the village of Gulbong; 36 persons were killed, and 11 were injured when the vehicle left the road during bad weather.

March 9, Near Barstow, Calif. A pickup truck carrying 20 persons, including at least 19 Salvadorans, veered off the road and rammed into a culvert after the driver apparently fell asleep; 12 of the Salvadorans were killed in the crash, but the driver survived.

March 14, Near Nashik, India. A bus transporting mainly women and children fell off a bridge and plunged into the Kadva River; at least 65 persons were killed, and 11 were injured.

March 20, al-'Ayn, Abu Dhabi. A tractor-trailer transporting fertilizer slammed into a passenger pickup in heavy fog; 19 Pakistanis were killed.

April 14, Near Karnal, India. A private bus carrying 120 members of a wedding party toppled into a canal; more than 80 persons lost their lives.

April 16, Near Dhobi, India. A crowded bus fell into the Moma River after smashing into guardrails; at least 20 persons were killed, and 20 were injured.

April 16, Near Bogotá, Colombia. A multi vehicle accident involving a cargo truck, a car, and a small bus claimed the lives of at least 22 persons who were incinerated in the inferno.

Early May, Andhra Pradesh, India. Separate road accidents involving two wedding parties claimed the lives of 48 persons.

May 2, Gdansk, Poland. A bus crash killed 30 passengers riding in the vehicle.

Mid-May, Near Cairo. A truck that was transporting children who were observing the feast of Eid al-Adha by visiting the graves of their relatives went out of control and careened into an irrigation canal; 18 youngsters lost their lives in the crash.

May 23, Western Nepal. A bus traveling on a mountain road veered off the pavement and plunged 300 m (984 ft) down the slope; 22 persons were killed, and 24 were injured.

May 26, Eastern Transvaal, South Africa. A bus fell into a reservoir; 32 persons drowned.

May 29, Central Kenya. An overcrowded bus carrying more than 70 passengers overturned; 18 schoolchildren and a teacher were killed.

Late June, Mirerswarai, Bangladesh. Two buses collided head-on; 22 persons were killed, most of them members of a bridal party, and 80 were injured, 12 of them seriously.

July 3, Weatherford, Texas. An 18-wheel tractor-trailer rear-ended a van, causing the van to burst into flames; 14 persons in the van were killed, and 5 were injured, including the truck driver.

July 3, Near Snyder, Texas. A tractor-trailer plowed into a pickup truck carrying three adults and 12 children, who were seated in the bed of the vehicle; 11 persons were killed in the crash.

Early August, Near Umzimkulu, South Africa. A bus transporting high-school students slammed into a rock formation; 10 persons were killed, and 78 were injured.

August 21, Near Wenatchee, Wash. A car crossing into another lane rammed into a car; 11 persons died in the collision.

August 26, Near Silvan, Turkey. A crowded bus crashed into a military vehicle and exploded; 30 persons, many of them women and children on the bus, lost their lives, and 25 were injured.

September 25, Near Presidente Prudente, Brazil. A bus transporting 45 persons to a political rally in São Paulo plowed through a bridge guardrail after the driver lost control of the vehicle on a steep descent; 31 persons were killed when the bus plunged into the river, and 14 were injured.

December 13, Northeastern Brazil. A bus full of Christmas shoppers collided with a tanker truck; 13 persons lost their lives, and 29 were injured.

December 25, Côte d'Ivoire. A bus carrying schoolchildren home for Christmas skidded off a coastal road and plunged into a ravine after swerving to avoid a parked vehicle; the accident, which occurred in heavy fog, killed 21 persons and injured 49.

December 28, Near Maturín, Venezuela. A speeding passenger bus rammed a bus that had stopped to assist yet another bus disabled along the roadside. The bus that was struck was shoved into an oil pipeline, which exploded on impact; at least 30 persons aboard that vehicle were incinerated, and 15 were injured.

Miscellaneous

January 26, Nice, France. The concrete roof of a supermarket collapsed on shoppers and sales staff; at least 10 persons were killed, and some 90 were injured.

Late January, Near Delhi, India. Some 13 villagers, who stole what they thought was liquor but was actually a poisonous chemical from a disabled tanker, succumbed to the toxic substance after drinking it; 37 were hospitalized.

February 15, Hunan province, China. A throng of passengers changing trains in the crowded railway station at Hengyang (Heng-yang) stampeded in a rush to return to the city of Guangzhou (Canton) following the Chinese New Year holiday; more than 40 persons died in the crush.

May 23, Mina, Saudi Arabia. Pilgrims attending the annual hajj (pilgrimage to Mecca) stampeded during a symbolic ritual that involved throwing stones at three piles of rocks to cast out the devil; some 270 persons were trampled to death in the melee.

A helicopter hovers over a section of a bridge that fell into the Han River in Seoul, South Korea, on October 21. At least 32 people died when their vehicles were thrown into the water.
AFP

July 14, Motta Visconti, Italy. A home for the elderly was leveled after a gas explosion ripped through the concrete structure and claimed the lives of 27 residents; the blast occurred while workers were repairing sewage pipes.

July 14, Bombay. Heavy rains saturated a five-story building, which collapsed; 14 persons were killed, and 13 were injured.

Mid-July, Near Khartoum, The Sudan. At least 22 passengers stranded in the desert after the bus they were riding in became lost in a sandstorm died of thirst and starvation.

August 12, Brazzaville, Congo. A group of Roman Catholics gathered outside a church to witness a claim that a preacher would perform miracles surged, and 142 believers, most of them children, were trampled.

Early October, Guangdong (Kwangtung) province, China. A suspension bridge collapsed at an amusement park; at least 38 tourists were hurled to their death in the lake below.

October 21, Seoul. A 48-m (157-ft)-long section of a steel-girdered bridge sheared neatly from the main structure the morning after the bridge had undergone repair work. The span floated after falling into the Han River, but at least 10 vehicles were spilled into the water; 32 or more persons were feared dead.

Mid-November, Central Nepal. A party of mountain climbers, including nine Germans, a Swiss, and their Nepalese guide, fell to their death while descending from the summit of Mount Pisang; all 11 were roped together and were killed after some members of the group slipped and sent the entire party down the slope and over a sheer drop.

Mid-November, Bihar, India. Locally made liquor killed at least 50 persons who drank the spirits.

November 18, Turkey. An outbreak of mushroom poisoning killed at least 18 persons and caused illness in 175; government officials banned wild mushroom hunting in the wake of the deaths.

November 23, Nagpur, India. A stampede by protesters attempting to force their way through a police cordon guarding a state legislature building killed at least 130 persons who were trampled.

Mid-December, Morelos, Mexico. A lethal concoction of mescal and methanol sold as liquor by bootleggers claimed the lives of at least 28 persons who imbibed the deadly brew.

Mid-December, Luanda, Angola. Home brew laced with methyl alcohol claimed the lives of at least 50 persons who drank the lethal concoction.

People of 1994

NOBEL PRIZES

Prize for Peace

Controversy surrounded the Nobel Committee's decision to award the 1994 Nobel Prize for Peace to ("in alphabetical order") Palestine Liberation Organization (PLO) Chairman Yasir Arafat, Israeli Foreign Minister Shimon Peres, and Israeli Prime Minister Yitzhak Rabin "for their efforts to create peace in the Middle East." Criticism was aimed not only at the choice of Arafat, whose organization's primary aim had once been Israel's destruction, but also at Rabin and Peres, who had led offensives against Israel's neighbours. The prize was intended "to honour a political act which called for great courage on both sides" and to "serve as an encouragement to all the Israelis and Palestinians who are endeavouring to establish lasting peace in the region."

The Israeli Labour Party government's decision to negotiate with the PLO was met with fierce opposition. After Arafat and Rabin signed the Sept. 13, 1993, peace agreement with a historic handshake, militant forces on both sides tried to shatter the delicate accord.

Arafat and Rabin both were born in the Middle East and grew up enemies. Arafat was born Rahman 'abd ar-Ra'uf al-Qudwah in Palestine on Aug. 24, 1929. Upon graduating with a degree in civil engineering from the University of Cairo in 1956, he joined the Egyptian army and fought in the Suez. While working as an engineer in Kuwait, he helped found al-Fatah, which became the military arm of the PLO, and in 1968 he gained the PLO chairmanship. Long considered a chief proponent of terrorism, Arafat was sometimes a target of it himself. His tendencies, at times, to act alone and to compromise won him enemies from within his own camp. Nevertheless, six months after the state of Palestine was declared in 1988, he was elected president of its provisional government.

Rabin, born in Jerusalem on March 1, 1922, made his career in the military (1941–68), joining the Jewish Defense Forces against the Nazi-sponsored French regime in World War II, directing the defense of Jerusalem in Israel's war of independence (1948), and planning the winning strategy for the Six-Day War (1967). He was ambassador to the United States (1968–73) before entering politics as a Labour Party member. After a brief stint as minister of labour under Prime Minister Golda Meir, he himself became prime minister in June 1974. It was he who ordered a daring raid (July 1976) to rescue hostages seized by Palestinian terrorists and held at the airport at Entebbe, Uganda. Rabin was forced to resign his post in April 1977, but he regained the leadership of his party and the job of prime minister in June 1992.

Born Shimon Perski in Wolozin, Poland (now Volozhin, Belarus), on Aug. 15, 1923, Peres immigrated to Palestine with his family in 1934. His mentor in the Zionist movement was David Ben-Gurion, Israel's first prime minister, who in 1948 put Peres in charge of the navy. From 1952 to 1965 he held various defense offices, with responsibility for increasing weapons production and initiating a nuclear program. Peres led the Labour Party from 1977 to 1992 but served only briefly as prime minister (1984–86). When Rabin recaptured the Labour leadership in 1992, Peres was named foreign minister. Although for many years he and Rabin had clashed over their party's direction, they agreed at last to put old rivalries aside to pursue a legacy of peace.

(MARGARET BARLOW)

Prize for Economics

John F. Nash of Princeton University, John C. Harsanyi of the University of California at Berkeley, and Reinhard Selten of the University of Bonn, Germany, shared the 1994 Nobel Memorial Prize in Economic Science for their achievements in establishing the foundations of what is known as game theory. Game theory, the Royal Swedish Academy of Sciences noted, "emanates from studies of games such as chess or poker," in which "players have to think ahead [and] devise a strategy based on expected countermoves from the other player. Such strategic interaction also characterizes many economic situations, and game theory has therefore proved to be very useful in economic analysis."

Game theory has transformed modern business, replacing the classical economics of pure competition. It was invented in the 1940s by John von Neumann and Oskar Morgenstern. Much of its formal mathematical basis was set forth by Nash in "Non-cooperative Games," his doctoral dissertation at Princeton University. Nash's equilibrium theory is still taught to determine when to stop changing bargaining strategies. It was his assumption that all players are rivals, using what they know about one another to operate in their own self-interest.

Nash was born in 1928 in Bluefield, W.Va., and studied mathematics at the Carnegie Institute of Technology (now Carnegie Mellon University; B.S., M.S., 1948) and at Princeton (Ph.D., 1950). In 1951 he joined the staff of the Massachusetts Institute of Technology, but after an illness in the late 1950s, he returned to Princeton as a visiting scholar.

Born in 1920 in Budapest, Harsanyi earned a doctorate (1947) in mathematics from the University of Budapest. He arrived in the United States in 1956 as a Rockefeller fellow at Stanford University (Ph.D., 1959) and was a research associate (1957) at Yale University before joining the faculty of the Haas School of Business at the University of California at Berkeley in 1964. He remained there until 1990, when he became professor emeritus. After the late 1960s, when he enhanced Nash's model by introducing the predictability of rivals' actions based on the chance that they would choose one move or countermove over another, Harsanyi's work embraced ethics as well as game theory. Among his contributions were formal investigations concerning appropriate behaviour and correct social choices among competitors. His numerous publications include *A General Theory of Equilibrium Selection in Games* (1988), co-written with Selten.

Selten, the first German to receive the economics prize, was born in Breslau (now Wrocław, Poland) in 1930 and studied mathematics at the University of Frankfurt/Main (Diplom, 1957). He, too, expanded upon Nash's model in the 1960s, first by establishing theories for discriminating between reasonable and unreasonable game outcomes and later by incorporating the concept that strategies develop over time. In numerous publications he has explored mathematical systems in economics. He was a visiting professor at the University of California at Berkeley in the late 1960s and taught at the Free University of Berlin and the University of Bielefeld before joining the faculty at Bonn in 1984. Interested in applications of his work outside the field of economics, he participated in a 1976 conference at which game theory was used to predict (with limited success) future developments in the Middle East.

(MARGARET BARLOW)

(From left) PLO head Yasir Arafat and Israel's Foreign Minister Shimon Peres and Prime Minister Yitzhak Rabin show the Nobel Peace Prizes they shared for agreements on Palestinian self-rule.

Kenzaburō Ōe appears with his wife at ceremonies honouring him as the winner of the Nobel Prize for Literature. The writer was known primarily for his fiction about postwar Japan.

TOBBE GUSTAVSSON—REPORTAGEBILD/PHOTOREPORTERS

Prize for Literature

Japanese novelist Kenzaburō Ōe, who gave a voice to the darkness that gripped the soul of his nation in the aftermath of war, was awarded the 1994 Nobel Prize for Literature. Referring to the impact on Ōe and his generation of Japan's defeat in World War II and the subsequent occupation, the Swedish Academy of Letters wrote, "The humiliation took a firm grip on him and has coloured much of his work."

Born on Jan. 31, 1935, he was 10 when the emperor of Japan surrendered and the U.S. occupation forces arrived at Ōe's mountain village on the island of Shikoku. Years later, when he was a student (1954–59) of French literature at the University of Tokyo, he wrote to express his anger and betrayal over these events. Short stories such as "Shiiku" (1958; "The Catch," 1959), for which he won the Akutagawa Prize, symbolized the disillusionment that pervaded postwar Japan. Always a voracious reader, he was influenced by many French- and English-language writers, including Mark Twain, whose antiestablishment Huckleberry Finn was an early hero to Ōe.

Two powerful books embodied primary themes that dominated Ōe's work. *Hiroshima nōto* (1965; *Hiroshima Notes,* 1981) was based on 1963 interviews with atomic-bomb survivors and chronicled courage in the face of hopeless destruction. In *Kojinteki na taiken* (1964; *A Personal Matter,* 1968), Ōe probed his desperate struggle to come to terms with his first-born son's severe brain damage. After his plot to take the child's life fails, he decides to let him live and accepts his obligation to love and nourish the boy. The novel, winner of the 1964 Shinchō Prize, was the first of several autobiographical stories in which his son appeared.

While his essays often drew criticism for their preoccupation with left-leaning politics, Ōe's style was praised for its brilliance and energy. It was in short-fiction collections such as *Warera no kyōki o ikinobiru michi o oshieyo* (1969; *Teach Us to Outgrow Our Madness,* 1977) and *Nan to mo shirenai mirai ni* (1983; *The Crazy Iris and Other Stories of the Atomic Aftermath,* 1985) that he displayed the "poetic force" commended by the academy. Ōe's novel *Man'en gannen no futtōbōru* (1967; *The Silent Cry,* 1974), which won a Tanizaki Prize, was singled out by the academy as "one of his major works. At first glance it appears to concern an unsuccessful revolt, but fundamentally the novel deals with people's relationships . . . in a confusing world in which knowledge, passions, dreams, ambitions, and attitudes merge into each other."

Expressing surprise at the academy's announcement, Ōe commemorated two compatriots, saying that they shared the prize in a symbolic way. Kōbō Abe, author of the surrealistic *Suna no onna* (1962; *The Woman in the Dunes,* 1964), and Masuji Ibuse, who wrote about the victims of the atomic bomb in *Kuroi ame* (1966; *Black Rain,* 1969), had both died in 1993. The only other Japanese writer to have won the Nobel literature prize was Yasunari Kawabata, in 1968.

(MARGARET BARLOW)

Prize for Chemistry

An organic chemist, George A. Olah of the University of Southern California (USC) won the 1994 Nobel Prize for Chemistry for discovering how to extend the life span of an elusive family of compounds that appear for only a split second in the intermediate stages of chemical reactions. Use of his technique finally provided proof that those chemical intermediates, termed carbocations, really do exist. "Olah's discovery completely transformed the scientific study of the elusive carbocations," said the Royal Swedish Academy of Sciences in its citation. It allowed chemists to study the structure of carbocations, improve their understanding of the manner in which organic compounds react to produce products, and find ways of manipulating reactions to yield desired products. Olah's work led to many industrial applications, including syntheses of high-strength plastics and lead-free high-octane gasoline.

Olah became interested in carbocations while still in his native country of Hungary. He was born May 22, 1927, in Budapest and received his Ph.D. in 1949 from the Technical University of Budapest. After holding various positions at the university, he served as head of the department of organic chemistry and associate director of the central research institute of the Hungarian Academy of Sciences. Following the 1956 Hungarian revolution and the subsequent defeat by Soviet troops, Olah fled the country and began work at a Dow Chemical Co. laboratory in Ontario, where he developed the techniques for stabilizing and isolating carbocations. He served on the faculty of Case Western Reserve University, Cleveland, Ohio, from 1965 to 1977. Olah then moved to USC and in 1991 became director of the Loker Hydrocarbon Research Institute.

Carbocations are positively charged fragments of hydrocarbon molecules whose properties had puzzled chemists since the 1920s and '30s. At that time chemists had only a poor understanding of the way that reactions actually proceed. In a reaction, chemicals called reactants interact to form products, new compounds having structures and properties that can be much different from those of the reactants. The earliest studies of organic reactions made chemists realize that in some reactions the products could not possibly form in a single step. Rather, intermediate products must form and disappear as the reaction proceeds, as no other mechanism could account for some of the dramatic structural changes that were seen to take place in the transformation from reactants to products. Chemists theorized that the intermediates in hydrocarbon reactions would be positively charged hydrocarbon molecules, or carbocations. Since most chemical reactions proceed quickly, carbocations had to form and disappear in millionths of a second. Chemists thought that it would be impossible to isolate and study carbocations because they would vanish long before any analytical technique could be completed.

Olah's method for extending the life span of carbocations from millionths of a second to months was relatively simple. He prepared stable carbocations by dissolving hydrocarbon compounds in cold solutions of powerful acids such as that made by mixing hydrogen fluoride and antimony pentafluoride. Such "superacids" are much stronger than conventional acids like the sulfuric acid used in automobile storage batteries. The technique produced high concentrations of stable carbocations that could be studied with conventional analytical tools. Some of the early analyses, which were conducted by Olah's group, brought additional surprises. Ever since the 1860s it had been believed that carbon could form no more than four chemical bonds with other atoms—the basis for the carbon atom centred tetrahedral structure well known to chemists. Analysis showed, however, that some carbocations were pentahedral or hexahedral, capable of forming additional bonds.   (MICHAEL WOODS)

Prize for Physics

Two scientists, one American and one Canadian, shared the 1994 Nobel Prize for Physics for developing neutron scattering, a powerful technique that uses nuclear radiation to analyze the innermost structure and properties of matter. The Royal Swedish Academy of Sciences, in awarding the prize, said that the pioneering work of Clifford G. Shull and Bertram N. Brockhouse was of major theoretical and practical importance. Neutron scattering allowed scientists to peer into the atomic structure of bulk matter and begin to understand interactions that determine the properties of solid and liquid materials. Neutron-scattering studies were important in the development of magnetic materials in computer data-storage devices, new superconducting materials that lose electrical resistance without deep cooling, and better catalysts for cleaning up automobile exhausts. They even contributed to elucidating the structure of disease-causing viruses.

Brockhouse and Shull conducted their research independently in the 1940s and '50s at two of the earliest nuclear reactors built in Canada and the U.S. Brockhouse worked at the Chalk River reactor in Ontario, Shull at Oak Ridge National Laboratory in Tennessee. The reactors supplied beams of neutrons—electrically neutral subatomic particles emitted during radioactive decay—that the two scientists exploited in their research. As early as the 1930s physicists had dreamed of using neutrons to study the atomic structure of materials. They knew that neutrons, like other subatomic particles, have the ability to behave as both particles and waves. When neutrons strike a sample of matter, they penetrate, collide with the nuclei of the constituent atoms, and then diffract, or scatter, in a characteristic pattern that depends on their wavelike behaviour. The resulting diffraction pattern provides detailed information about the composition of the material under study, specifically the way that its atoms are arranged in space in relation to each other.

In 1946 Shull joined a group of Oak Ridge physicists, headed by E.O. Wollan, who were trying to use neutron-diffraction patterns to locate the three-dimensional positions of atoms in solid materials. A similar technique, based on X-rays, already was in use. But X-ray diffraction could not determine the location of hydrogen atoms, which are an important component of many inorganic materials and all organic molecules found

Bertram N. Brockhouse (left) receives the Nobel Prize for Physics from King Carl XVI Gustaf of Sweden. The Canadian shared the award with U.S. scientist Clifford G. Shull.

GUNNAR ASK—REPORTAGEBILD/PHOTOREPORTERS

in living things. Unlike neutrons, which deflect off the nucleus of an atom, X-rays deflect off the orbiting electrons. Hydrogen has just one electron around its nucleus and thus is scarcely noticeable on X-ray diffraction patterns.

"Similar efforts were being made elsewhere," the Royal Swedish Academy said, "but it was the Wollan-Shull group and later Shull in collaboration with other researchers that proceeded most purposely and achieved results with surprising rapidity." Nuclear reactors produce neutrons that move at different speeds. Researchers, in contrast, needed beams of neutrons that were monochromatic—all traveling at essentially the same speed. Shull's group solved the problem by passing the mixed beams through crystals of sodium chloride and other materials. The crystals separated neutrons of different speeds into separate, monochromatic beams. Shull and his colleagues studied neutron diffraction in very simple crystals, thus establishing the basis for interpreting diffraction patterns from more complicated materials. They also developed a neutron-scattering technique to probe the structure of magnetic materials, a task that could not be done with X-ray diffraction.

Shortly after Shull began his work, Brockhouse initiated studies that led to development of neutron spectroscopy, the technique that brought his share of the Nobel Prize. "During a hectic period between 1955 and 1960 Brockhouse's pioneering work was without parallel within neutron spectroscopy," the Royal Swedish Academy said. Scientists already knew that atoms in the innermost structure of materials vibrate or oscillate. Vibrations induced in one atom cause neighbouring atoms to resonate, so that the entire crystal vibrates in a unique pattern determined by its atomic structure. Knowledge about a material's vibrational energy is extremely important because it helps to determine how well a material will conduct electricity or heat. Brockhouse's neutron spectroscopy technique provided a way for scientists to measure vibrational energy.

He devised an apparatus, similar to that developed by Shull, for obtaining monochromatic beams of neutrons and passed them through samples of crystalline material. When the neutrons collided with an atom, they lost energy and set up vibrations in the crystal structure of the material. Brockhouse also developed a device, called the triple-axis spectrometer, that measured the amount of energy that neutrons lost as a result of scattering. He realized that the lost energy could be interpreted as energy absorbed by the sample in the creation of phonons. Phonons are units of vibrational energy that proved to be of great use in evaluating the properties of different materials.

Brockhouse was born July 15, 1918, in Lethbridge, Alta. He received a Ph.D. in 1950 from the University of Toronto. That same year he began a long career at the Chalk River Nuclear Laboratories operated by Atomic Energy of Canada Limited. He joined the faculty of McMaster University, Hamilton, Ont., in 1962, where he helped to establish a program in solid-state physics. Shull was born Sept. 23, 1915, in Pittsburgh, Pa. He received his Ph.D. in 1941 from New York University. After working as a research physicist for a private firm, Shull served as chief physicist at the Oak Ridge National Laboratory from 1946 to 1955. He then joined the faculty of the Massachusetts Institute of Technology as professor of physics.   (MICHAEL WOODS)

Prize for Physiology or Medicine

Two American researchers, Alfred G. Gilman and Martin Rodbell, shared the 1994 Nobel Prize for Physiology or Medicine for discovering G proteins, molecules that allow cells to respond to chemical signals such as hormones, neurotransmitters, and growth factors from a variety of the body's tissues. G proteins proved to be the missing link in a biochemical information-processing system in which cells react to incoming signals in ways that give rise to such fundamental life processes as metabolism, vision, smell, and cognition. Diseases can result from disturbances in the way that G proteins pass on, or transduce, incoming signals. Rodbell retired in June 1994 as head of the laboratory of signal transduction at the National Institute of Environmental Health Sciences (NIEHS), a U.S. government agency located in Research Triangle Park, N.C. Gilman was with the University of Texas Southwestern Medical Center in Dallas.

Long before Rodbell and Gilman began their work, conducted independently in the 1960s and '70s, scientists knew that cells use hormones and other chemical messengers to communicate with one another and coordinate their activities. The American scientist Earl W. Sutherland, Jr., won the 1971 Nobel Prize for Physiology or Medicine for showing that most hormones, which he called "first messengers," carry signals to the outer surface of the cell membrane in animals. Rather than entering the cells directly, the hormone molecules attach to special receptor sites on the cell surface, and the cell responds by producing a "second messenger," the compound cyclic adenosine monophosphate (cAMP), which acts inside the cell. Molecules of cAMP relay the final signals that alter function within the cell. Humans respond to fright, for instance, by producing the hormone epinephrine (adrenaline), which signals heart muscle cells to produce cAMP, which causes the heart muscle to beat faster and stronger.

Beginning in the late 1960s, Rodbell, then working at the National Institutes of Health (NIH), Bethesda, Md., showed that this communication process requires cooperation between three separate components. They are the cell surface receptor, a transducer that relays information from the receptor, and an amplifier that produces large quantities of second-messenger molecules like cAMP. Rodbell was among the first to realize that the receptor and amplifier were separate entities. But his major contribution was the discovery of a separate transducer function in cell communication that explained the way in which information passed between receptor and amplifier. Rodbell showed that the transducer worked only in the presence of an energy-rich molecule called guanosine triphosphate (GTP).

Gilman and his associates, working in the 1970s at the University of Virginia, Charlottesville, determined the chemical nature of Rodbell's mysterious transducer. They studied mutated cells that could not respond to outside chemical signals. The cells, nevertheless, had a normal receptor mechanism for accepting signals from a first messenger and a normal ability to generate cAMP as a second messenger. Gilman showed that the cells lacked a functional transducer mechanism that relayed the signal from receptor to amplifier. He further established that the missing component was a protein, found in normal cells, and showed that its transfer to defective cells restored signal transmission. By 1980 Gilman's group had purified the protein, allowing its properties to be studied. Researchers found that the protein exists in the cell membrane in an inactive form until a signal arrives and binds to the membrane. Then the protein rapidly changes into an active form by binding to GTP. This association with GTP led to the protein's name, the G protein. The activated G protein then shuttles from the receptor system to the amplifier system, turning on production of large amounts of the second messenger cAMP. After a few seconds the G protein reverts to an inactive form and awaits another activating signal.

Scientists subsequently identified about 100 kinds of cell receptors that rely on G proteins for transducing signals into cellular action. G proteins in the cells of the eye's retina, for instance, transduce the light signals that the brain interprets as images. Other G proteins work in olfactory cells and taste cells, help regulate the overall metabolic activity of cells, and help control cell division and specialization.

"Many symptoms of disease are explained by an altered function of G-proteins," said the Nobel Assembly at the Karolinska Institute, a biomedical research centre in Stockholm that selects winners of the medicine prize. The toxin produced by cholera bacteria, for instance, prevents one kind of G protein from reverting to an inactive form. Stuck in the "on" position, it causes the severe loss of water and salts that dehydrates and kills many cholera victims. Abnormal activity of G proteins may be involved in cancer, diabetes, skeletal diseases, and other health problems.

Rodbell was born Dec. 1, 1925, in Baltimore, Md. He received his Ph.D. in 1954 from the University of Washington and held positions in the U.S. and Switzerland. From 1970 to 1985 he headed laboratories at NIH and then joined NIEHS as scientific director. Gilman was born July 1, 1941, in New Haven, Conn. He received M.D. and Ph.D. degrees in 1969 from Case Western Reserve University, Cleveland, Ohio. From 1971 to 1981 he served on the faculty of the University of Virginia School of Medicine in Charlottesville. In 1981 Gilman moved to the University of Texas Southwestern Medical Center, where he served as professor and chairman of pharmacology. He also was coeditor and coauthor of a noted, regularly revised textbook on drug action, *The Pharmacological Basis of Therapeutics,* which was originated by his father, Alfred, also a pharmacologist.

(MICHAEL WOODS)

BIOGRAPHIES

Adams, Gerry

In 1994 Gerry Adams joined the long list of international figures who made the change from alleged terrorist to peacemaker. On August 31 the Irish Republican Army (IRA) announced a cease-fire. As president of the IRA's political wing, Sinn Fein, Adams was a central figure in bringing it about.

Gerard Adams was born in Belfast, Northern Ireland, on Oct. 6, 1948, into a prominent Irish nationalist family with ties to the IRA. Although Adams denied being a member of the IRA, it was widely believed that by 1972 he had become a member of the IRA's army council and its commander in Belfast. He was one of the first people to be imprisoned when the British government introduced internment without trial for suspected terrorists. During the course of his three years' imprisonment, he collected his sole criminal conviction: for attempting to escape.

In 1981 Adams persuaded Sinn Fein to widen its strategy and enter candidates in both local and national elections. He was elected an MP in 1983, but he refused to take the oath of allegiance and never took his seat. (He lost his seat in 1992.) As an MP, Adams was frequently invited to condemn violence, but he always refused.

In 1991, however, Adams started shifting Sinn Fein's strategy toward negotiation. He wrote to trade-union and church leaders and to politicians in both London and Dublin, saying that Sinn Fein wanted to join peace talks. He also began a series of secret negotiations with John Hume, the leader of the nationalist Social Democratic and Labour Party, which had always opposed violence and the IRA. In 1993 the British government admitted that it had conducted indirect negotiations with Sinn Fein through intermediaries.

In December 1993 British Prime Minister John Major and Irish Prime Minister Albert Reynolds agreed on a common strategy for considering the future of Northern Ireland, the so-called Downing Street Declaration. Adams stepped up his campaign to win international respect. In January 1994 he obtained a visa to visit the U.S., where he appeared on a number of television and radio interview programs. At the same time, Adams was barred from British radio and TV under the terms of an exclusion order and broadcasting ban. (Intriguingly, his statements could be read on the air by actors.)

Meanwhile, Adams was involved in intensive debates inside Sinn Fein and the IRA over their response to the Downing Street Declaration. Finally came the announcement of a cease-fire. Within three weeks the broadcasting ban had been ended; within seven weeks the exclusion order had been lifted. The scene was set for Adams' new role as principal Sinn Fein negotiator in talks about the long-term future of Northern Ireland.

(PETER KELLNER)

Alberts, Bruce

If the new president of the National Academy of Sciences (NAS), Bruce Alberts, had his way, scientific literacy would soon become one of the nation's leading concerns. A strong advocate of improving science education in primary and secondary schools, Alberts arrived (1993) at the prestigious organization in Washington, D.C., eager to promote this message. Only one year into his six-year term as president, he had already made his presence felt with his unpretentious manner and self-deprecating humour.

Though a life devoted to scientific research could be demanding, Alberts combined a vital career as a research scientist with one as an administrator involved in educational projects. As a professor of biochemistry and biophysics at the University of California at San Francisco, Alberts spent many years investigating the role of certain proteins in chromosomal replication and served as department chairman. He was also coauthor of *Molecular Biology of the Cell* (1983), a widely used textbook. Alberts channeled his boundless energy and enthusiasm for science into the establishment of a variety of educational endeavours, including City Science, a program to improve science instruction in the San Francisco elementary school system. He influenced national efforts to address scientific literacy by serving on the advisory board of the National Science Resources Center, a joint project of the NAS and the Smithsonian Institution, as well as on the board of the National Academy of Sciences' National Committee on Science Education Standards and Assessment. In 1988 he became head of the Commission on Life Sciences of the National Research Council (NRC—the operating arm of the NAS and its affiliated institutions, the National Academy of Engineering and the Institute of Medicine).

Bruce Michael Alberts was born on April 14, 1938, in Chicago, Ill. He earned an A.B. in biochemical sciences from Harvard College in 1960 and received a doctorate in biophysics from Harvard University in 1965. Alberts taught at Princeton University until 1976, when he moved to the University of California at San Francisco.

Elected to membership in the NAS in 1981, Alberts became its 20th president, succeeding geophysicist Frank Press. Alberts' major concern was running the NRC, which prepared hundreds of scientific, medical, and technical reports each year under contract from the government and private sources. In the midst of all that the post required, Alberts nonetheless maintained his passion for reforming science education and undertook the groundwork necessary for the NAS/NRC to move ahead toward the establishment of a national science-education program.

(MARY JANE FRIEDRICH)

Annenberg, Walter H.

In 1994 many people considered the life of Walter Annenberg an American success story: an immigrant's son who gained renown as a publisher, an ambassador, an art collector, and one of the most important philanthropists in the U.S. It was also the story of a quiet boy with a speech impediment who lived in the shadow of his flamboyant father until he took over the family's scandal-plagued legacy and turned it into one of the most profitable communications empires in the country.

Annenberg was born into a life of ease and privilege on March 13, 1908, in Milwaukee, Wis. His father, Moses ("Moe") Annenberg, an immigrant from East Prussia, had been the general-circulation manager of Hearst newspapers, but he made his fortune after he took control of the popular horse-racing publications the *Daily Racing Form* and *Morning Telegraph,* as well as a wire service that sent racetrack results to betting parlours nationwide. Annenberg joined the family business in 1928. He was a company vice president when his father was indicted (1939) for tax evasion and bribery. Annenberg was also indicted, but the charges against him were later dropped, and upon his father's death (1942) shortly after being paroled, he gained full control of what was left of Triangle Publications, Inc. Although the company was deep in debt, Annenberg turned it around quickly by taking it in new directions in publishing and in radio and television. The cornerstone of its fortune was laid in 1953 when Annenberg merged several local TV publications into one national magazine, *TV Guide,* which came to be one of the most popular magazines in the U.S. He also served as the editor and publisher of the *Philadelphia Inquirer* (which his father had purchased in 1936). In 1969, after his friend Richard Nixon was elected president, Annenberg was appointed ambassador to the Court of St. James's, where he served until 1974.

Annenberg sold his interests in Triangle for a reported $3.2 billion in 1988 and turned his energies to philanthropy and art collecting. He purchased numerous high-priced pieces in the soaring art market of the 1980s, notably Pablo Picasso's "At the Lapin Agile" for $40.7 million in 1989. Annenberg made headlines when he announced that after his death his collection—Impressionist and Postimpressionist works worth an estimated $1 billion—would be donated to the Metropolitan Museum of Art in New York City.

It was as a philanthropist that Annenberg gained wide respect late in life. He founded the Annenberg School for Communication at the University of Pennsylvania (his alma mater) in 1958, and he went on to donate to hundreds of organizations, large and small. By 1993 the Annenberg Foundation, worth about $1.6 billion, was one of the nation's wealthiest. That year it was announced that he was donating $500 million toward efforts to reform the public schools.

(CHERYL L. COLLINS)

Aristide, Jean-Bertrand

On Oct. 15, 1994, just over three years after a coup had forced him to flee, Pres. Jean-Bertrand Aristide returned to Haiti, urging, "No to violence, no to vengeance, yes to reconciliation." Whether it would prove to be a triumphant return remained to be seen.

Aristide had been elected in Haiti's first free democratic election on Dec. 16, 1990, with an overwhelming 67% of the vote. His inauguration on Feb. 7, 1991, represented a victory for Lavalas (which means "flood" or "torrent" in Creole), Haiti's mass movement that had drafted Aristide to run. In his seven months as president, Aristide proposed raising the minimum wage, initiated a literacy campaign, dismantled the repressive system of rural section chiefs, and oversaw a drastic reduction in human rights violations. The coup of Sept. 30, 1991, led by the military and financed by members of Haiti's small elite, declared that such reforms would not be tolerated. On his return from exile in the U.S., Aristide, who for 20 years had aligned himself with the poor and disenfranchised and often criticized the church hierarchy and the country's powerful elite—regardless of the risks to himself—faced a peculiar challenge. He was constitutionally prohibited from a second term and, despite promises of millions of dollars in aid, none had arrived by year's end. What could he accomplish in his remaining 15 months that would transform the compromises he had been forced to accept into boons for the movement that had nurtured him?

Aristide was born on July 15, 1953, in Port Salut. He attended a school in Port-au-Prince run by the Roman Catholic Salesian order, where he exhibited a great aptitude for language and a sharp intelligence. In 1966 he moved to the Salesian seminary at Cap-Haïtien and began to prepare for the priesthood. In 1975 Aristide first aligned himself with the poor and Ti Legliz ("Little Church"), which sprang from liberation theology. He returned from his novitiate year in the Dominican Republic to Port-au-Prince to study psychology (B.A., 1979) at the state university. The late 1970s was a time of increasing militancy against the brutal regime of Jean-Claude Duvalier. Aristide, responsible for programming at Radio Cacique (the Roman Catholic radio station), urged change and often found himself at odds with his superiors. Encouraged by them to leave the country, he spent most of the next six years studying biblical theology abroad. He visited Haiti briefly in 1982 for his ordination by the progressive Bishop Willy Romélus. He returned to Haiti in 1985, eventually becoming parish priest at St. Jean Bosco, a centre of resistance in Port-au-Prince. In 1986, the year Duvalier was driven from power, Aristide survived the first of many assassination attempts, was cautioned about his outspoken political views by the Salesians, and founded the orphanage Lafanmi Selavi. During the next several years he continued to anger the church hierarchy and the military. An attempt in 1987 to transfer him to a less central parish in the countryside failed when his supporters occupied Port-au-Prince's cathedral. An attack on a 1988 mass he was celebrating left 13 people dead and more than 70 injured. He was reprimanded, and the Salesians expelled him in late 1988. (He stopped celebrating mass or preaching in public in order not to anger the hierarchy.) In 1990, when a notorious Duvalierist announced his candidacy for president, progressive-centre forces united to urge Aristide to run for the office. After his election the Vatican continued to pressure Aristide to leave the priesthood. In November 1994 Aristide formally requested that he be relieved of his priestly duties. (ELLEN FINKELSTEIN)

Barbie

In March 1959 the first Barbie doll was unveiled at a toy fair in New York City. She was the brainchild of Ruth Handler, who along with her husband, Elliot, cofounded Mattel Creations (later Mattel, Inc.) in 1945. While raising her two children, Barbara and Kenneth, Handler noticed how much her daughter liked to play make-believe with paper dolls, often assigning them adult roles. Inspired by this and by a German comic strip character named Lilli, to which Mattel bought the rights, Handler created the three-dimensional Barbie doll (named after her daughter). In 1961 her son had his name immortalized in plastic when the Ken doll, Barbie's significant other, was introduced. Handler believed that allowing little girls to imagine the future with pretend play was an important part of growing up. What emerged was what came to be the world's most popular doll, including four younger siblings, a pantheon of friends, and a proliferation of accessories—each sold separately, of course. As Barbie turned 35, however, she found that along with her designer clothes, motor homes, and product endorsements came her share of controversy.

Barbie began life as a teenage fashion model. Over the years she became a ballerina, registered nurse, American Airlines stewardess, surgeon, and U.S. Air Force pilot. In 1992 she ran for president, but she lost, possibly because, after 20 years of silence, her first utterances (much to the dismay of feminists) included the words, "Math class is tough." In 1991 Mattel took action against Kenner Products' Miss America doll, citing copyright infringement. Versions of Miss America—which was manufactured in China—were subsequently seized by the U.S. Customs Service and stored in a government warehouse. A year later Mattel settled a similar suit against Hasbro Inc., which agreed to change its popular British Sindy doll to look less like Barbie.

By 1994 it seemed that Barbie herself could not be stopped and would continue her reign as the queen of dolldom. Since 1959 more than 800 million dolls in the Barbie family had been sold. Adult collectors invested thousands of dollars in special-issue Barbies. She had had more than 500 professions and could be found in more than 140 countries in the guise of several nationalities. However, it was unlikely that she would ever be seen in Kuwait after she was banned by a top Muslim official in August 1994. Barbie's curvacious figure had often been chastised for providing girls with an unrealistic body image. On the other hand, a group of Finnish scientists declared that she was anorexic.

After losing $113 million in 1987 on unsuccessful new product lines, Mattel found that it was more profitable to increase promotion of the Barbie franchise, and in 1993 sales of Barbie paraphernalia exceeded $1 billion. In celebration of Barbie's 35th birthday in 1994, Mattel reissued a replica of the original 1959 doll, and in October her life was chronicled in the book *Forever Barbie: The Unauthorized Biography of a Real Doll,* by M.G. Lord. (ANTHONY L. GREEN)

Battle, Kathleen

In February 1994 New York City's Metropolitan Opera issued the terse announcement that it had fired Kathleen Battle, considered by many to be one of the finest sopranos singing today, for what it termed "unprofessional actions." Opera fans around the world were stunned, and a journalistic firestorm fueled by speculation and rumour ensued in which the media dug up accounts concerning the prima donna's alleged maltreatment of all ranks of opera personnel, from wigmasters and stagehands to entire casts.

Kathleen Deanne Battle was born on Aug. 13, 1948, in Portsmouth, Ohio. As a child and young adult she was both a good student and a good singer, but her ambitions were not grand. She was awarded a scholarship to the University of Cincinnati College-Conservatory of Music, but she chose to major in music education rather than risk the possibility of failure and disappointment inherent in a performance career. In 1971, with both bachelor's and master's degrees, Battle set out to teach music to Cincinnati's inner-city youth. While teaching, she continued to study voice privately, which resulted in an audition with Thomas Schippers (then conductor of the Cincinnati Symphony Orchestra). He was so moved by Battle's remarkable voice that he hired the almost totally inexperienced singer to perform at the 1972 Festival of Two Worlds in Spoleto, Italy. Battle's debut at the festival in Brahms's *Ein deutsches Requiem* was very well received. Not long after, Schippers introduced Battle to the conductor James Levine, who was to become influential in her performing career, and by 1978 she was singing supporting roles in major U.S. opera houses. That same year she made her debut at the Met as the Shepherd in Wagner's *Tannhäuser.* Critics immediately recognized that Battle's lyric soprano was exceptionally pure and that it retained its perfection at both ends of her two and one-half octave range, from low A to high E. She dispatched the virtuosic coloratura of Handel and Purcell; excelled in such Mozart roles as Susanna in *The Marriage of Figaro,* Zerlina in *Don Giovanni,* and Despina in *Così fan tutte;* and was celebrated for her interpretation of African-American spirituals. Her extensive discography also included the music of Donizetti, Richard Strauss, George Gershwin, and others.

After the Met's dismissal of Battle, doomsayers predicted that her performing career might be over. However, she remained highly popular with the public—all of Battle's recordings continued to sell extremely well—and it seemed likely that concert halls and other opera houses might be happy to have her, despite the allegations of bad behaviour. After all, she has been described as the "best coloratura in the world."

(ELIZABETH LASKEY)

Berlusconi, Silvio

Since the end of World War II, Italy had had more than 50 governments and more than its share of colourful and controversial politicians. In the elections of March 1994, the victory of the coalition led by the Forza Italia party introduced yet another player to the great game of Italian politics—Italy's new prime minister, Silvio Berlusconi.

A 58-year-old business tycoon and founder and leader of Forza Italia, Berlusconi brought to the political arena the same skills he had used in building a vast financial empire, portraying himself and his party as an efficient and businesslike alternative to the corruption and cronyism endemic in Italian politics. Many observers pointed out, however, that Berlusconi had benefited from the same system that he promised to reform and suggested that his web of business interests would conflict with his duties as prime minister.

Berlusconi was born on Sept. 29, 1936, in Milan. After graduating from the University of Milan, he entered the property-development business, where he took advantage of the booming Milanese real estate market to amass a considerable fortune by the 1970s. Berlusconi soon decided to expand the scope of his business interests. In 1974 he created Telemilano, a cable television firm, and four years later he mounted the first direct challenge to the national television monopoly. By 1980 he had established Canale 5, the first commercial television network in Italy. He also steadily diversified his business holdings, acquiring department stores, movie theatres, publishing companies, and the AC Milan soccer team. He consolidated his empire under the umbrella of the Fininvest holding company, a vast conglomerate that grew to control more than 150 businesses.

In January 1994 Berlusconi turned his talents to politics. Bribery and corruption scandals had devastated the ruling coalition of Christian Democrats and Socialists. Amid popular cries for reform, Berlusconi founded Forza Italia and announced his candidacy for the national legislature. Running on a platform of free enterprise and individual initiative, he inveighed against bureaucracy and governmental interference in private business. To this end he allied himself with the right-wing Northern League and the neo-Fascist National Alliance. In the March 28 elections, this coalition, known as the Freedom Alliance, won a majority of seats in the Chamber of Deputies. As leader of the majority party of the ruling coalition, he was sworn in as prime minister on April 28.

The new prime minister's honeymoon was short-lived, however. Opponents charged Berlusconi with conflicts of interest, and in December magistrates formally questioned him regarding past business practices. Faced with a no-confidence vote, Berlusconi resigned on December 22, although he remained at the head of a caretaker government. (JOHN H. MATHEWS)

Black, Conrad

In 1994 financier Conrad Black, whose inherited wealth and acquisitive nature helped establish him as an international press baron, expanded his already vast empire by purchasing the *Chicago Sun-Times* newspaper. As head of one of Canada's largest conglomerates, he was a symbol of Canadian capitalism. Black began in 1967 as part-owner and operator of two small Quebec weeklies. By 1972 he owned 21 local papers across Canada, and during the next 20 years, he built a media empire of almost 250 newspapers worldwide. By 1994 Black controlled the *London Daily Telegraph,* the Fairfax Group in Australia, the *Jerusalem Post,* Southam Press in Canada, and nearly 100 local dailies in the United States.

Born on Aug. 25, 1944, in Montreal, Conrad Moffat Black was the son of George Black, a major shareholder and director of Canada's Argus Corp. Conrad grew up in Toronto, and his ambition was to become head of Argus. When he assumed control of the corporation in 1978, Argus was an investment holding company with token control of several Canadian corporations, including Hollinger Mines, Dominion Stores (a grocery chain), Standard Broadcasting, and Massey-Ferguson (a farm equipment company). Black's goal was to transform Argus from a holding company to an operating company and to reposition it in the newspaper business. Partly to achieve this end, he divested Argus of Massey-Ferguson in 1980 and dismantled Dominion Stores by selling or closing many outlets. Hollinger became the principal shareholder of Argus, and the name of the corporation was changed in 1986 to Hollinger Inc. Problems erupted in 1986 when Hollinger withdrew more than $50 million in surplus from the Dominion Stores pension fund with the approval of the Pension Commission of Ontario. The union representing the Dominion Stores employees sued the commission. The dispute was settled when Hollinger and the employees agreed to share the surplus equally.

Black received a B.A. in history and political science from Carleton University, Ottawa (1965), and a law degree from Laval University, Quebec City (1970). His thesis for his M.A. in history from McGill University, Montreal (1973), was a biography of former Quebec premier Maurice Duplessis; published in 1977, it came to be considered a definitive work. Black, who enjoyed expressing his thoughts on politics and business, was a columnist for the *Toronto Globe and Mail Report on Business Magazine*. He was also noted for his excellent memory, which served him well in recalling and recounting in great detail the story of his business dealings in his autobiography, *A Life in Progress* (1993).

Black received the Order of Canada in 1990 and became a member of the Privy Council of Canada in 1992. (DIANE LOIS WAY)

Blades, Rubén

In May 1994, 20 years after moving to the U.S., Rubén Blades, the Panamanian-born, Harvard-trained lawyer and internationally known salsa singer, composer, political activist, and Hollywood actor, returned to Panama to run for the presidency. As the populist candidate of Papa Egoró (Mother Earth), the party that he had formed during a brief return to Panama in 1991, Blades campaigned with songs and guitar, attracting support from those disillusioned with corrupt politicians. His campaign, however, was underfinanced, and although Blades proved a popular candidate, some thought that his extended absence from the country had left him out of touch. In the May 8 elections, he placed third, winning only 17% of the vote.

Blades was born in Panama City, Panama, on July 16, 1948. His St.-Lucian-born father was a police detective and bongo player, and his Cuban-born mother was a musician and an actress on radio soap operas. Blades initially played the guitar and sang North American rock and roll, but he later composed and performed songs of political protest. Blades graduated with a law degree from the University of Panama in 1972. Shortly thereafter, he and his family were sent into exile when his father (a former member of the secret police) ran afoul of Manuel Noriega, then head of military intelligence.

After settling in New York City, Blades sang and composed as a member of the Willie Colón combo. He left Colón in 1982 to form a new group, Seis del Solar. The band's salsa music incorporated rock and jazz elements, and vibraphones replaced traditional trumpets and trombones. His album *Buscando América* was named a top-10 album of 1984. At the height of his popularity, Blades took a break from his musical career to earn a master's degree (1985) in international law from Harvard University. His first film, *Crossover Dreams,* was released in 1985. In 1987 Blades won a Grammy award for his album *Escenas,* in which Linda Ronstadt joined him in a Spanish duet. His music echoed such social issues as the Iran-contra affair and the AIDS crisis.

After Blades embarked on a film career, he received praise for his performances in such films as *The Milagro Beanfield War* (1988), *Disorganized Crime* (1989), *The Two Jakes* (1990), *The Lemon Sisters* (1990), *Mo' Better Blues* (1990), *The Super* (1991), and *Color of Night* (1994). Blades also composed the musical score for the film *Q & A* (1990).   (NAOMI BERNARDS POLONSKY)

Blair, Bonnie Kathleen
After her career-topping performances in 1994, U.S. speed skater Bonnie Blair was hailed as the most successful American woman in Olympic Games history. At 19 she first gained acclaim by winning the world overall short-track title in 1986 at Chamonix, France, and a year later she twice clocked the world-record time for the 500 m on the standard circuit.

Blair's era of Olympic glory began in 1988 at Calgary, Alta., when she not only won the 500 m with a time that remained on the record books for the next two Games but also took third place in the 1,000 m. Specializing as a sprinter, she won the world sprint championship with a record points score in 1989 at Heerenveen, Neth., and recaptured the title at Calgary in 1994, again with record aggregate points. On March 26, during the latter tournament, she became the first woman to skate 500 m in less than 39 seconds.

On the Hamar track near Lillehammer, Norway, Blair in 1994 successfully defended her 1,000-m title to win the fifth Olympic gold medal of her career, surpassing the previous U.S. women's Olympic record of four gold medals held jointly by track sprinter Evelyn Ashford, swimmer Janet Evans, and diver Pat McCormick. She achieved this by winning the 500 m at three consecutive Games and the 1,000 m twice. A 1,000-m bronze at Calgary in 1988 brought her total Olympic medals tally to six. Blair's 500-m success in 1994 made her the only speed skater of either sex to have won the same event in three successive Olympics.

Blair was born at Cornwall, N.Y., on March 18, 1964. She was coached mainly by Nick Thometz, who was also an Olympic speed skater. Her height of 1.7 m (5 ft 7 in) and weight of 60 kg (132 lb) gave her a slender appearance that masked a well-developed strength in calves and thighs. Her commendably smooth motion usually seemed almost silent, with what sound the skating strokes emitted muffled by the roar of the crowd. Moving about a minute a mile faster than a track athlete (a speed skater being the fastest human over level ground), Blair learned how to counter the extra wind resistance to best advantage with an accentuated crouching, streamlined, gliding style. Her graceful body roll with pronounced lean even at top speed was what her well-informed fans best appreciated.   (HOWARD BASS)

Bouchard, Lucien
In 1990 the Bloc Québécois was formed in Canada to promote sovereignty for the province of Quebec on the federal level. In the federal election of 1993, the Bloc Québécois surprised many Canadians by winning 54 ridings (districts) in Quebec to become the official opposition in the House of Commons. The party leader, Lucien Bouchard, became leader of the opposition.

Bouchard began his career in politics as a member of the Progressive Conservative Party. Then in 1988 Prime Minister Brian Mulroney invited Bouchard to join his Cabinet. After being appointed secretary of state, Bouchard won a seat in the House of Commons from the Quebec

riding of Lac-Saint-Jean. He was made minister of the environment in 1989. Bouchard's aim in entering politics was to help in salvaging the Meech Lake accord, a constitutional agreement that would have recognized Quebec as a distinct society. When the failure of the accord seemed inevitable in 1990, Bouchard resigned from the Cabinet and the Progressive Conservative caucus to become an independent member. He decided to remain in politics to work for the sovereignty of Quebec, and later in 1990 he was a founding member of the Bloc Québécois.

Born in Saint-Coeur-de-Marie, Que., on Dec. 22, 1938, Bouchard received a degree in social sciences (1960) and a degree in law (1963) from Laval University. After being called to the bar in 1964, he practiced law in Chicoutimi, Que., until 1985. During those years he was called upon several times to work for the provincial government. From 1970 to 1976 he was chairman of the Quebec Educational Arbitration Board, which had been set up to ensure uniform working conditions in the provincial education sector. He served as chief counsel for the Cliche Commission of Inquiry into the Construction Industry (1974–75), which examined the problems of the James Bay hydroelectric project. Bouchard was coauthor of the *Martin-Bouchard Report (1977–78)* on reforming negotiation procedures for public sector employees. From 1978 to 1981 he coordinated Quebec's negotiations with its employees.

In 1985 Bouchard became Canadian ambassador to France. In that role he promoted the interests of Canada and of Quebec. He helped organize the first Francophone summit in Paris (1986) and was chairman of the preparation committee for the second Francophone summit in Quebec City (1987).

Late in 1994 Bouchard was stricken with necrotizing myositis, a virulent bacterial infection. After several operations, including the amputation of a leg, he was reported to be recovering and was expected to continue as leader of the opposition.   (DIANE LOIS WAY)

Braxton, Anthony
The two-hour, three-LP piece *For Four Orchestras,* composed by Anthony Braxton and recorded in 1978 by 160 musicians and 4 conductors, was to have been the first composition in a series. A subsequent work, Braxton anticipated, would involve simultaneous orchestras in separate cities linked by television; after that, he would compose a work for linked orchestras on several planets and, by 1995, a work for linked orchestras in several galaxies, assuming that humankind's progress in space travel could keep up with him. Instead, reality caught up with Braxton. He had to finance the four-orchestra recording himself, and though he was among the leading free-jazz improvisers on saxophones, clarinets, and flutes and leader of a topflight quartet, raising money through concert fees was a losing battle. By the early 1980s the Braxton family was living in poverty in upstate New York, in a telephoneless house heated by burning logs in a fireplace.

If that was a low point of Braxton's career, a high point came in 1994 with the release of one of his finest recordings, *Duo (London) 1993,* with fellow saxophone virtuoso Evan Parker, and with a five-year MacArthur Foundation fellowship. The prize came shortly after the second book about him, *New Musical Figurations: Anthony Braxton's Cultural Critique* by Ronald M. Radano, was published and in the midst of his term as chairman of the music department at Wesleyan University, Middletown, Conn. What brought about this upswing in Braxton's life was dedication.

Braxton was born on June 4, 1945, in Chicago, where he began playing alto saxophone in his teens, and in 1966 he joined the groundbreaking free-jazz cooperative Association for the Advancement of Creative Musicians. He quickly grew into an original player and was the first to record an entire album of unaccompanied saxophone solos. After 1969, when he went to Paris, he became an avant-garde hero while recording with the likes of free improvisers, pianists Muhal Richard Abrams and Dave Brubeck, the Globe Unity Orchestra, and bop musicians.

Meanwhile, inspired by John Cage and Karlheinz Stockhausen, among others, Braxton also composed prolifically for chamber settings, for orchestras, for 100 tubas, and for 4 amplified shovels and a coal pile. His compositions were titled with abstract diagrams and written in coloured graphs; they were also almost never played. That situation would change in 1995, however, when CDs were to be released of his *Composition 174* for 10 percussionists and tape; *Composition 175,* "storytelling music"; and *Trilium M,* the first of his operas to be documented. "I feel the millennium that's coming will reflect on the beautiful universal 'balances' that will make up new evolutionary processes," he said. "My hope is to be part of these dynamic universal processes."

(JOHN LITWEILER)

Breyer, Stephen
In recent years, nominations to the U.S. Supreme Court have often been fraught with controversy, with partisan politics taking the place of well-reasoned consideration of the potential justice's merits. Democrats and Republicans alike have accused each other of attempting to politicize the judiciary, and confirmation hearings have sometimes degenerated into ad hominem attacks instead of explorations of judicial philosophy. Pres. Bill Clinton's nomination of Stephen Breyer in 1994 to fill the seat of retiring Justice Harry Blackmun appeared to be an effort to break this cycle. Breyer was viewed as a moderate, acceptable to both Republicans and Democrats. His formidable intellect and legal acumen were tempered by a generous dose of pragmatism unencumbered by any pronounced ideological position, giving him a reputation as a consensus builder. Breyer's supporters expected him to reach out to the centrist wing of the court, as well as providing a moderate counterweight to the conservative constitutional formalism of the court's current intellectual leader, Justice Antonin Scalia.

Stephen Gerald Breyer was born on Aug. 15, 1938, in San Francisco. He received an undergraduate degree from Stanford University and spent two years as a Marshall scholar at Oxford before attending Harvard Law School. Following his graduation from Harvard in 1964, Breyer clerked for Supreme Court Justice Arthur Goldberg, where he further developed his philosophy of neopragmatism and helped write the landmark right-to-privacy decision in *Griswold* v. *Connecticut.* Breyer then spent three years as a special assistant to the U.S. assistant attorney general before returning to Harvard as a professor.

At Harvard, Breyer wrote extensively on antitrust and administrative law. He also served as an assistant special prosecutor (1973) during the Watergate hearings. In 1979 he was appointed chief counsel to the Senate Judiciary Committee, where he helped draft legislation on fair-housing law and deregulation of the airline and trucking industries, as well as making the acquaintance of Sen. Edward Kennedy, who was to become one of his strongest supporters. In 1980, with bipartisan support, Breyer was confirmed as judge of the U.S. Court of Appeals for the First Circuit. As a federal judge, Breyer gained a reputation as a centrist. His pragmatism took precedence over any broad constitutional vision, and his reliance on empirical data in shaping his opinions led critics to claim that his judicial philosophy was determined more by economic considerations and cost-benefit analysis than by concern for people. However, Breyer himself stated that he was skeptical about the benefits of economic pragmatism outside antitrust and regulatory law, and he demonstrated a passion for First Amendment rights. Breyer also served on the U.S. Sentencing Commission, created to determine how severely federal crimes should be punished.

Breyer was confirmed with little difficulty. His freedom from ideological bias assuaged conservative fears of a doctrinaire liberal on the court, while liberals were eager to support a moderate whose intellectual firepower might match Scalia's. Observers of the court predicted that Breyer would continue his role as a consensus builder, drawing the court toward his own brand of pragmatism and moderation. (JOHN H. MATHEWS)

Cardoso, Fernando Henrique
Not long after the military took control of the government in Brazil in 1964, a young sociologist was blindfolded, arrested, and interrogated. After being blacklisted from teaching in the state university system he went into exile and continued his academic work, in which he examined the relationship between the less developed, "dependent," nations and the dominant West. He gained a reputation as a brilliant sociologist and became one of the leading lights of Brazil's left-wing intellectual opposition. That he would run for president soon after the reestablishment of civilian rule might not be surprising, but that he would do so with the overwhelming support of the nation's business establishment—and that foreign multinational corporations would beat a path to his door soon after his election—might be. Yet Fernando Cardoso had shown that he was willing to defy expectations.

Fernando Henrique Cardoso was born in Rio de Janeiro on June 18, 1931, to a well-to-do military family. He became a professor of sociology at the University of São Paulo in 1958. After he left the country in 1964, he taught at universities in Santiago, Chile, and Paris. Upon his return to Brazil in 1968 Cardoso founded a research institute, the Brazilian Centre for Analysis and Planning, which was bombed by right-wing terrorists in the early 1970s.

Cardoso entered politics in 1986 when he won a seat as senator from São Paulo; he gained a reputation as a centrist who was willing to compromise. In 1988 he cofounded the centre-left Party of Brazilian Social Democracy, which ran on a clean-government platform. In 1992, after Pres. Fernando Collor de Mello was impeached on corruption charges and Itamar Franco took over, Cardoso resigned his Senate seat and joined the Cabinet as foreign minister. In May 1993 Cardoso allowed himself to be drafted as finance minister—the fourth in 13 months. He oversaw the complicated political negotiations that produced the Real Plan, an anti-inflation package that introduced a new currency, the real.

In March 1994 Cardoso announced his bid for the presidency, and he stepped down from his post as finance minister. Inflation was running at 45% in June, and when the Real Plan went into effect on July 1, Cardoso was trailing his closest opponent by 20 points. As inflation plummeted to less than 2% in September, however, his popularity soared. Many observers suspected that the business sector had held a lid on prices to boost Cardoso's campaign and, further, that painful economic restructuring loomed after the election.

During his campaign Cardoso had called for moving Brazil away from a state-dominated economy and toward increased foreign investment, more rapid privatization of state-owned companies, and large-scale funding of education and social services. Many of Cardoso's beliefs had changed over time, but his commitment to improving the living standards of the nation's poor had not, even though he had come to believe that a free-market economy was the best means to that end. (CHERYL L. COLLINS)

Caruso, David
After emerging from virtual obscurity in late 1993 to become the actor labeled "TV's hunkiest tough guy" by early 1994 only to be branded a television pariah by late summer, Golden Globe winner David Caruso experienced firsthand the seesawing fortunes of a U.S. actor—all in one dizzying year. The up-from-the-streets, flame-haired Method actor helped propel the unconventional television drama "NYPD Blue" into the ratings stratosphere in its first season with his portrayal of John Kelly, a tough-on-the-outside, in-control homicide detective with a tormented yet sensitive soul. When the show, produced by Steven Bochco, first debuted in the fall of 1993, it generated strident condemnations from religious leaders and other conservatives, boycotts by affiliates of parent company ABC, and cancellations by major commercial advertisers because of its unabashed use of explicit language, sexual situations, and posterior nudity. These taboos had not been extensively breached before on a prime-time network television show. As the season progressed, however, the show won kudos from Viewers for Quality Television, the People's Choice awards, the Golden Globe awards, and Humanitas. By the end of the season, in May 1994, the show had set new standards of excellence for the medium, and it had garnered a record 26 Emmy-award nominations.

During the summer of 1994 the industry was abuzz with the news that the reportedly temperamental and headstrong Caruso had demanded a hefty pay raise. Though he had proven his star quality with an Emmy nomination for best actor in a drama, Caruso's demand was not met. His character, facing banishment to another precinct, quit the force and was written out of the show after the first four episodes. It was not only the salary dispute that prompted Caruso to leave, however, but also the hope of following in his matinee idols' footsteps. Like two other famous Hollywood redheads, James Cagney and Spencer Tracy, who influenced his acting style, Caruso wanted to make good as a leading man in feature films. Many wondered if the somewhat baby-faced actor could make the transition smoothly, when many other performers had failed. In the meantime, Caruso had filmed two yet-to-be-released motion-picture thrillers for which he reportedly received between $1 million and $2 million each. One feature, *Kiss of Death,* was a remake of the 1947 classic, which had made a star of unknown Richard Widmark.

Caruso was born on Jan. 17, 1956, in New York City to an Italian-American father and an Irish-American mother. He had no formal training as an actor but earned cash by posing as an extra in police lineups—his first "acting jobs." In 1978 he moved to California, where he spent the next 15 years playing bit parts in such films as *First Blood* (1982), *An Officer and a Gentleman* (1982), and *Mad Dog and Glory* (1993) before his meteoric rise in "NYPD Blue." (SUSAN RAPP)

Castro, Fidel
On Aug. 11, 1994, Cuban Pres. Fidel Castro indicated in a speech that his government was lifting restrictions on those wishing to leave the country. In short order, thousands of people took him at his word and set sail for Florida in makeshift rafts and homemade boats. Not since 1980 had there been such a massive exodus from the Caribbean nation. True to form, Castro and his Cuban government were making themselves a thorn in the side of the United States.

Castro was a man under considerable pressure in 1994. The son of a Spanish immigrant farm worker, Fidel Castro Ruz was born near Birán, Oriente province, on Aug. 13, 1926/27. He became a political activist as a student, joining the Cuban People's Party about 1947. He obtained a law degree in 1950 and was a candidate in the 1952 elections for a seat in the House of Representatives. On March 10, 1952, however, Gen. Fulgencio Batista overthrew the government. In 1953 Castro began to organize a revolution against Batista, but he was unsuccessful and was subsequently jailed. Released under a 1955 amnesty, Castro went to Mexico, where he organized the next steps of his revolution. In December 1956 he led a small force into Cuba. Aided by waning internal support for the government and by successive military victories, Castro and his forces—reduced to only about 1,000 men—forced Batista to flee. Castro took control of Havana on Jan. 2, 1959, and became prime minister in February. In 1976 he became the president of Cuba.

Castro and his 26th of July Movement, with the Communist Party of Cuba in the lead, attempted to move Cuba from a corrupt dictatorship to a showplace socialist state. He rooted out capitalism and tried to precipitate socialist revolution elsewhere in the hemisphere, meanwhile relying increasingly on the financial support of the U.S.S.R. and its allies. On the positive side, Cubans under Castro were better educated and healthier than almost any other Latin Americans; all education and health services were provided free of charge, and citizens were guaranteed employment.

Over time, the economy was unable to keep pace with the swelling population and especially with the growing number of young people. Cuba became a drain on the resources of the Soviet Union, and Castro could no longer rely on $6 billion in annual subsidies after the U.S.S.R. was dissolved in 1991. Few expected *el líder* to survive the domino-like toppling of communist regimes.

Dire economic and social conditions in Cuba led to increased dissent among the citizenry and growing pressure on Castro to move on. Still, he managed to cling to power, partly by moving tentatively in the direction of a market economy and partly by fostering tourism in order to cover the catastrophic shortfalls in sugar revenues. Meanwhile, the U.S., influenced by its large, conservative Cuban émigré community, came in for its share of criticism for what Spain's *El País* called a "policy of strangulation"—which was providing the perfect scapegoat on which Castro could blame his economic woes.

In late December 1993 Castro's daughter, Alina Fernández Revuelta, had embarrassed her father by seeking asylum in the U.S., where she was publicly critical of the way her homeland was being run. Tensions in Havana boiled over on Aug. 5, 1994, when Cubans rioted during the first massive antigovernment demonstration in 35 years. Some observers saw Castro's lifting of the ban on emigration a week later as the punitive reaction of a desperate man. Still, speculation flared anew that the wily revolutionary might pull it off once again. (ANTHONY L. GREEN)

Claes, Willy
Following the collapse of communism in the Soviet Union and the subsequent dissolution of the Warsaw Pact, the North Atlantic Treaty Organization (NATO) appeared to be an alliance without a mission. However, as the disintegration of the Soviet empire spawned a variety of separatist movements and the conflict in former Yugoslavia threatened to engulf the Balkans, NATO once again emerged as a significant international institution. In late 1994 a new leader took on the task of leading NATO into the 21st century. On September 29, following the death of Secretary-General Manfred Wörner (*see* OBITUARIES), the North Atlantic Council chose Willy Claes, the Belgian minister of foreign affairs, as the new secretary-general of NATO.

Claes was an unusual selection as leader of the world's most powerful military alliance. A lifelong socialist, he had spoken out against the deployment of U.S. missiles in Europe during the 1980s and had been a senior figure in the Belgian government that had refused to take part in the Persian Gulf war. As a member of the European Union's Council of Ministers, he had also spoken strongly against Europe's ineffectuality in dealing with the conflict in former Yugoslavia.

Claes was born in Hasselt, Belgium, on Nov. 24, 1938. After studying at the Free University of Brussels, he was elected to the Hasselt City Council (1964). A Flemish Socialist, Claes entered national politics in 1968 when he was elected to the parliament. He became spokesman for the Belgian Socialist Party in 1971 and was named minister of education the following year. In 1973 Claes accepted appointment as minister of economic affairs, and he was praised for his handling of the 1973–74 oil crisis.

After his party's return to power, Claes again served as minister of economic affairs (1977–82). In 1979 he was also appointed deputy prime minister, a post he held five times. Claes developed a reputation as a talented diplomat, and he was enlisted by King Baudouin to aid in the formation of a coalition government during a period of political turmoil in the 1980s. In 1992, following a third term as economics minister, Claes became minister of foreign affairs. That same year, he was elected chairman of the Party of European Socialists.

Following his appointment as secretary-general of NATO, Claes reaffirmed his commitment to the alliance as the bedrock of European security. By year's end, the war in Bosnia still raged and a new conflict had broken out in the Chechnya region of Russia. What role NATO would play in these conflicts was still open to question, but they both symbolized the type of confrontation that the new secretary-general would have to face in the future. (JOHN H. MATTHEWS)

Crossan, John Dominic
"Jesus was not born of a virgin, not born of David's lineage, not born in Bethlehem," and "there was no stable, no shepherds, no star, no Magi, no massacre of the infants, and no flight into Egypt." These assertions were made not by a fire-breathing atheist but by John Dominic Crossan, a bookish Roman Catholic teaching biblical studies at DePaul University in Chicago. In 1994 his research came "out of the ivory towers" with publication of the volume *Jesus: A Revolutionary Biography,* with the theories that he and the 73 other members of the Jesus Seminar put forth in a book titled *The Five Gospels: What Did Jesus Really Say?* and with a discussion of his own work by other scholars in a collection titled *Jesus and Faith: A Conversation on the Work of John Dominic Crossan.*

Born on Feb. 17, 1934, in Ireland, Crossan moved to the U.S. in 1951 and began his study of the life and teachings of Jesus. In 1969, while on the faculty of the Chicago Catholic Theological Union, he resigned from the Servite priesthood. As he explained later, he "wanted to be free from the irritation of having been trained to think critically but being in constant trouble for doing it."

Crossan first gained notice outside academe with a 1992 work, *The Historical Jesus: The Life of a Mediterranean Jewish Peasant.* The book sold more than 60,000 copies, a surprise to Crossan, whose previous works had sold about 2,000 copies each. That book, and its 1994 successor, made Crossan one of the key figures in the latest version of an old controversy—trying to separate the Jesus of history from the Jesus of the Gospels.

In Crossan's view, "Jesus' divine origins are just as fictional or mythological as those of Octavius. Neither should be taken literally, both must be taken metaphorically." Crossan said that his views need not be taken to mean that the Bible was worthless or that Jesus was not unique. "I see no problem with the [biblical] stories as metaphors and myths," he said. "I want people to face the truth about the relationship between history and faith, and not to let one masquerade for the other."

Amid the flurry of analyses of his works and those of his colleagues in both the academic and popular media, Crossan began work on another major volume, this one dealing with the early years of Christianity. "We're talking about the period before Paul," Crossan told *Publishers Weekly*. "Right now, we only see early Christianity through his glasses. I think there is plenty to learn about those immediate decades following Christ's death." (DARRELL J. TURNER)

Curien, Hubert
Physicists suffering from evaporated research funding in 1994 focused their attention on one of the few remaining oases of Big Science, the Large Hadron Collider (LHC) planned for the European Laboratory for Particle Physics (CERN) near Geneva, and on the new president of the CERN Council, Hubert Curien. When money in the U.S. for the Superconducting Super Collider (SSC) particle accelerator being built near Waxahachie, Texas, dried up in 1993, it dashed the hopes of particle physicists worldwide for probing beyond the so-called standard model—the successful but incomplete theory of the fundamental constituents of matter and their interactions—toward a more satisfactory and inclusive theory and for answering such basic questions as why quarks, electrons, and other fundamental particles have the masses they do.

Those hopes were revived in June 1994 when council delegates from 17 of the 19 supporting nations of CERN voted to include the construction of the LHC in the laboratory's basic program. Curien, who took office as council president in January, had been instrumental in rallying support for the LHC and in convincing scientists and government leaders that data from the collider would be their best bet for unraveling some of the mysteries of subatomic physics. At the end of the June meeting he expressed his belief that "there are no major obstacles, but some more effort and a little time is needed" before unanimous approval could be sought at a later session of the council. That consensus came in December, allowing plans for the LHC to proceed. Many American scientists who had been slated to work on the defunct SSC were already employed at CERN, so building the LHC meant brighter future opportunities for them as well as for colleagues who would have the chance for collaborative research.

Curien was born on Oct. 30, 1924, in Cornimont, France. He was educated in Paris and earned a doctorate in physics, with an emphasis on mineralogy and crystallography, at the University of Paris in 1951. Shortly thereafter he joined the faculty of science at the university, where he stressed the need for a return to basic research in physics. While crusading for that cause, Curien served as director general of France's National Centre for Scientific Research (1969–73), president of the National Centre for Space Studies (1976–84), and council chairman of the European Space Agency (1981–84). In 1984 Curien parlayed his reputation as a defender of basic research into a seat in the French government as minister of research and technology. He occupied that position for two years and then returned to the post from 1988 to 1993. During his ministerial service Curien succeeded in spurring an increase in government funding of nearly 8% for civilian research and development.

Even before the final CERN vote, scientists and engineers were designing and testing accelerator magnets for the LHC. The activity represented a significant step toward achieving the high energy collisions between protons (and, later, between heavy atomic nuclei) that would be needed to find some of the exotic new particles thought to lie beyond the standard model. Although installation of the LHC was not scheduled to begin until the year 2000, the interim survival of CERN as the world's premier particle-physics institution would depend heavily on the continued efforts of Curien, its champion of basic science.

(SUSAN RAPP)

Dion, Céline
By 1994 Canadian singer Céline Dion had reached her goal of becoming an international pop music star. Her first success outside her native Quebec was at the Tokyo Song Festival in 1982. There she won the Musician's Prize and the gold medal for best song with "Tellement j'ai d'amour pour toi." Dion's fame soon extended to audiences in Europe and the U.S., and in 1983 she was the first Canadian to earn a gold record in France with her song "D'amour ou d'amitié." Two years later Dion had a six-week run at the Olympia in Paris. Her recording of "Ne partez pas sans moi" won the 1987 Eurovision Song Contest. Audiences in the U.S. heard Dion sing the closing song in Steven Spielberg's animated film *An American Tail: Fievel Goes West* (1991), and in 1993 her recording with Peabo Bryson of the title song for the animated Disney film *Beauty and the Beast* won a Grammy award for best pop duo. Earlier that year, Dion performed in the U.S. at Pres. Bill Clinton's inauguration gala.

Born on March 30, 1968, in Charlemagne, Que., Dion grew up in a musical family. As a child she performed in her parents' restaurant. Dion's mother wrote "Ce n'était qu'un rêve" and sent her daughter's recording of the song to impresario René Angélil. He launched Dion's career when she was 13 years old. Her extraordinary voice and simplicity delighted Canadians. In 1983 she won Quebec's Felix Awards for best female performer and discovery of the year. She was featured in an episode of the Canadian Broadcasting Corporation's French-language program *Les Beaux Dimanches.* The clergy chose Dion to represent young people for Pope John Paul II's 1984 visit to Quebec, and she sang "Une colombe" for him at Montreal's Olympic Stadium.

By age 18, Dion had become determined to shed her "good girl" image. She took a one-year career break and reemerged with a new look and new music. Sporting short hair and sequined dresses, she sang songs with upbeat rhythms, and she began to record in English. Her first English-language recording, "Where Does My Heart Beat Now?" (1990), was released in 16 countries. In 1993 Dion performed in her first English-language television special, *The Colour of My Love*. In a much-publicized ceremony, she married longtime manager Angélil in December 1994.

Dion, who was once called *la p'tite Québécoise*, had won 15 Felix Awards by 1991, the year she won the Juno Award for best female performer. At the World Music Awards in 1992, she won the award for best-selling Canadian female recording artist. Although she recorded in English, she considered herself to be a francophone, and in 1990 she refused to accept the Felix Award for anglophone artist of the year. Other French albums included *Dion chante Plamondon* (1991) and *Des mots qui sonnent* (1994). (DIANE LOIS WAY)

Downer, Alexander John Gosse

Political dynasties are rare in Australia, where the widespread egalitarian ethos works against inherited wealth and power. Thus, when Alexander Downer became leader of the Liberal Party of Australia on May 23, 1994, he faced not only a party in disarray but also the burden of a distinguished background. Downer's father, Sir Alexander Downer, had been a Cabinet minister in Sir Robert Menzies' government and Australia's High Commissioner in London. His grandfather, Sir John Downer, was one of the founding fathers of the Australian Commonwealth and a senator in the Australian Parliament. Downer's first tasks as Liberal leader were to distance himself from accusations of being born with a silver spoon in his mouth and to rebut the charge of having no experience of grassroots life.

Public opinion polls soon put Downer and his conservative party ahead of Prime Minister Paul Keating and his Australian Labor Party government. Downer made a series of mistakes in his handling of Aboriginal policy, however, and by the end of the year the trend was reversed. Downer's troubles began when he said that a Liberal government would consider scrapping the Native Title Act, under which Aborigines were encouraged to take up large-scale outback land ownership. He made matters worse by a visit to settlements in the Alice Springs area, where what he saw at Kintore, Desert Bore, Areyonga, Yuendumu, and Utopia so unnerved him that he made a series of contradictory and confusing statements, causing his approval rating of 53% at the beginning of the trip to dive to only 34% by the time he returned home. Downer's many supporters brushed off the nosedive in the polls. Chastened nonetheless, he was even more resolved than ever to bring true former prime minister Bob Hawke's prophecy that Downer would be Australia's next prime minister. To this end the Liberal leader took up an aggressive position, replying to ridicule in kind and drawing attention to Keating's 1994 purchase of a $2 million home in which to house his French clock collection.

Downer was born on Sept. 9, 1951, went to school at Geelong Grammar, and continued his education in England at Radley College and the University of Newcastle upon Tyne. He began his working career as an economist with the Westpac Bank; however, he moved quickly to the Ministry of Foreign Affairs and served as a diplomat in Australian embassies in Belgium and Luxembourg. In December 1984 he was elected to Parliament, where his boyish good humour, confidence, and frank reaction to the difficulties that crossed his path endeared him to his party. As the Adelaide *Advertiser* put it, he showed up most other Canberra politicians by getting out into the real world to study problems head on. (A.R.G. GRIFFITHS)

Doyle, Roddy

Irish schoolteacher-turned-novelist Roddy Doyle was busy on both sides of the Atlantic in 1994. In January he toured the U.S. to support the American release of his novel *Paddy Clarke Ha Ha Ha* (1993), which had won the 1993 Booker Prize. His fourth novel was set in the 1960s in a fictional working-class area of northern Dublin and examined the cruelty inflicted upon children by other children. The protagonist, 10-year-old Paddy Clarke, feared his classmates' ostracism, especially after the breakup of his parents' marriage. In mid-1994 Doyle watched as his BBC drama "Family" generated heated controversy throughout conservative Ireland. The program shed harsh light on a family's struggle with domestic violence and alcoholism and portrayed the bleaker side of life in a housing project, the same venue he had used in his earlier, more comedic Barrytown trilogy.

Doyle's unvarnished depiction of the working-class world was a hallmark of his work, and he often alienated critics, many of whom chastised him for his harsh "docu-journalism." The soft-spoken and reserved Doyle proved, however, that it was possible to convey the undiluted truth and still be popular, especially among the very class of people whose lives he chronicled. Doyle's distinctively Irish settings, style, mood, and phrasing made him a favourite fiction writer in his own country as well as overseas.

The second of four children of a printer and a homemaker, Doyle was born in 1958 in Dublin. After majoring in English and geography at University College, Dublin, he taught the subjects for 14 years at Greendale Community School, a Dublin grade school. During the summer break of his third year of teaching, Doyle began writing seriously. In the early 1980s he wrote a heavily political satire, *Your Granny's a Hunger Striker*, but it was never published.

The first editions of the comedy *The Commitments* (1987) were published through his own company, King Farouk, until a London-based publisher took over. The work was the first installment of his internationally acclaimed Barrytown trilogy, which was completed by *The Snapper* (1990) and *The Van* (1991). The trilogy centred on the ups and downs of the never-say-die Rabbitte family, who tempered the bleakness of life in an Irish slum with familial love and understanding. The first two parts of the trilogy were also made into popular international films in the 1990s. By the end of 1994 a movie script for *The Van* had been completed, and Doyle had secured a reputation as a well-respected, if controversial, literary figure. (SUSAN RAPP)

Dudayev, Dzhokhar

If you asked a Muscovite in 1994 to describe the Chechens—who number some 1.3 million and live north of the Caucasus Mountains—you might hear characterizations as diverse as "proud Caucasian warriors," "gangsters from the south," "staunch defenders of Islam," or "a historically oppressed people." Similar things were being said about Dzhokhar Dudayev, the president of Chechnya (Chechenia), who declared the republic independent from Russia in 1991 and who has been a major thorn in Moscow's side ever since.

Dzhokhar Musaevich Dudayev was born in February 1944, during the enforced deportation of his family (together with the entire Chechen and Ingush nations, on Joseph Stalin's orders) from their native village of Yalkhori in the Chechen-Ingush autonomous oblast. He spent the first 13 years of his life in Kazakhstan. Following the 1957 repatriation of the Chechens and Ingush, he studied at evening school in Chechen-Ingushetia and qualified as an electrician. He entered flying school and graduated from the Tambov Higher Military Aviation School for Pilots in 1966. He joined the Communist Party of the Soviet Union in 1968.

Dudayev served in a heavy bomber unit of the Soviet air force in Siberia and Ukraine. He studied at the Gagarin Air Force Academy (1971–74) and rose steadily in the air force, assuming command of the strategic air base at Tartu, Estonia, in 1987 with the rank of major general.

Dudayev retired from the air force in May 1990 and returned to Grozny, the Chechen capital, to devote himself to local politics. In November 1990 he was elected head of the Executive Committee of the unofficial opposition All-National Congress of the Chechen People, which advocated sovereignty for Chechnya as a separate republic within the U.S.S.R. When the communist leadership of the Chechen-Ingush republic publicly expressed its support for the Moscow putsch in August 1991, it was forced to step down. Dudayev was elected Chechen president in October 1991 and unilaterally declared Chechnya's secession from the Russian Federation. Russia refused to recognize this move, but hesitated to use force against the secessionists.

Dudayev's aggressively nationalistic, anti-Russian policies soon began to undermine Chechnya's economy and, Russian observers claimed, transformed the region into a gangsters' paradise. In 1993 the Chechen parliament attempted to organize a referendum on public confidence in Dudayev on the grounds that he had failed to consolidate Chechnya's independence. He retaliated by dissolving parliament and other organs of power. Beginning in early summer 1994, armed Chechen opposition groups with Russian military and financial backing tried repeatedly, but without success, to depose Dudayev by force. In late November, Russian Pres. Boris Yeltsin issued an ultimatum to Dudayev and the opposition to lay down their arms. Russian tanks and troops entered Chechnya to quell the rebellion in December but found the tough mountain people an even match. Fierce fighting, most of it centred in Grozny, continued through the end of the year. (ELIZABETH FULLER)

Freud, Lucian

In late 1993, the Metropolitan Museum of Art in New York City opened a major exhibition of paintings by artist Lucian Freud. Best known as a figure painter, Freud aroused controversy because he often portrayed his subjects naked. In many of the large, later paintings, he represented the raw physical characteristics as well as the inner tensions of his subjects. Adding to the sombre realism of his figures was the dingy setting of the Paddington (London) studio where he had worked for many years. In addition, a show of Freud's early works at the Robert Miller Gallery, also in New York City, ended in January 1994. Although his earlier drawings and paintings were generally smaller, they displayed a similar intensity to those shown at the Met.

Freud was born in Berlin on Dec. 8, 1922. His father, Ernst, an architect, was the youngest son of Sigmund Freud, the famed father of psychoanalysis. The family moved to London about 10 years later. At school he developed a passion for horses and did some early drawings and sculptures of this subject. Later, as an art student, he was as much known for his unconventional behaviour as for his drawing talent. As a teenager he unexpectedly joined the Merchant Navy and, while attending the East Anglian School of Painting and Drawing, he accidentally set fire to the school with a cigarette. He was something of a boy wonder, and when he was 17 his first published sketch (a self-portrait) appeared in an avant-garde literary magazine.

Freud took a long painting trip to Paris and Greece after World War II. Back in London, he began laying the groundwork for his distinctive style in a series of paintings of his first wife, Kitty. Thereafter the subjects of his figure paintings—often nude—were his friends (many of whom were artists) and relatives, including his children. These works were not conventional portraits, and because they are more about paint than about a specific person, their titles seldom reveal the sitter's identity. The paintings show no attempt by the artist to idealize or prettify the subject. Rather, his style was described as creating flesh with paints. His unusual, coarse, personal style of painting made people curious about the artist, but Freud always guarded his privacy and rarely gave interviews.

Although he had been an important artist in England for many years, Freud's work first became widely known in the U.S. through a 1987 retrospective exhibition at the Hirschhorn Museum in Washington, D.C. In the catalog for this exhibit, art critic Robert Hughes called the artist "the greatest living realist painter." In fact, Freud belonged to no "school" of art, and his highly individualistic style did not fit nicely into any particular category. (MARGARET BARLOW)

Gaarder, Jostein

When it first appeared in the United States in September 1994, *Sophie's World* was already something of a phenomenon—and a surprise to the Norwegian high-school teacher, Jostein Gaarder, who wrote it. Originally published in Norway in 1991, the book established its international fame in Germany, where it climbed to the top of *Der Spiegel*'s best-seller list and stayed there for most of the year. *Sophie* was expected in British bookstores in January 1995, and rights had been sold to publishers in most European countries as well as in Turkey, Israel, Japan, South Korea, China, and Brazil.

Gaarder was born on Aug. 8, 1952, in Oslo Norway. He studied the history of ideas, religion, and Nordic literature at the University of Oslo. After graduation in 1976, he worked as a secondary-school teacher of philosophy, religion, and literature in Oslo and Bergen. He began his literary career gradually, lecturing occasionally, submitting articles and poems to newspapers, and coauthoring textbooks. Gaarder debuted as an author of fiction with two short stories published in 1982 and 1986 and followed those with two children's books, *Barna fra Sukhavati* ("The Children from Sukhavati") in 1987 and *Froskeslottet* ("The Frog Palace") in 1988. In both books a fantasy world was set against the real world, giving the central characters the opportunity to explore and question ideas and values. In 1990 came *Kabalmysteriet* ("The Patience Mystery"), featuring a boy, Hans Thomas, and his father on a journey searching for the boy's mother, who had been lost eight years earlier. Gaarder felt that young Hans Thomas needed a greater understanding of philosophy, and this was how he came to write his history of philosophy in *Sophie's World*.

Scoffed at by many critics (*The Times* called it "a potted philosophy primer masquerading as a novel of ideas"), Gaarder's best-seller undoubtedly owed its popularity to its cross-genre and cross-generational appeal. The central character is Sophie, a 14-year-old schoolgirl, who one day receives an unsigned note containing two questions: "Who are you?" and "Where does the world come from?" This leads her—and the reader—into an examination of the history of Western philosophy, from the pre-Socratics to Hegel, Kierkegaard, and Sartre. As was his style in other books, Gaarder spiced the plot of *Sophie's World* with an element of mystery and dosed out the philosophy sections in a gentle and accessible way.

Gaarder's next novel, *Julemysteriet* (1992; "Christmas Magic"), was a journey through the history of Christianity, while *I et speil, I en gate* (1993; "Through a Glass, Darkly") took its title from a line in the Bible and was written as a dialogue between an angel and a girl dying of cancer. The author received several prizes in Norway and Germany for children's literature.

In a lecture at the Oslo Book Fair, Gaarder argued for the introduction of philosophy in schools from the age of 10, when children still retained their curiosity. He felt that confronting and exploring issues such as "Who am I?" and "Where does the world come from?" were important for young people striving to find themselves in a complicated world. (IRENE GARLAND)

Gehry, Frank

In designing the new American Center in Paris, which opened in June 1994, Frank Gehry created an exciting space for promoting U.S. culture. The complex, which included galleries and studios, two small theatres, apartments, and a language school, incorporated several of Gehry's distinguishing characteristics.

Typical of Gehry's work, the American Center appeared to be a cluster of functional buildings instead of one monolithic structure. Large window areas overlooked the bustling city outside. Structural elements were emphasized. Open passageways invited movement and conversation. References to older architectural forms abounded. For example, the popular French mansard roof form appeared on the lower stories of one facade and again, around the corner, in tall, sloping windows.

For a 1994 office building in a historic district of Prague, Gehry also played with earlier forms from nearby 18th- and 19th-century buildings to create a late 20th-century landmark. Other recent Gehry projects included a fish restaurant in Japan, the Vitra Design Museum in Germany, and a theatre at Euro Disneyland Paris.

Frank Owen Gehry was born in Toronto on Feb. 28, 1929. His family immigrated to Los Angeles in 1947. Gehry studied architecture at the University of Southern California (1949–51; 1954) and city planning at Harvard University (1956–57). Before establishing his own firm, Frank O. Gehry & Associates, in 1962, he worked for several other architects. Southern California remained his home and his headquarters.

Gehry's early designs were influenced by Frank Lloyd Wright. In the mid-1960s he began producing the novel structures that established his reputation as a maverick. Gehry's output was prolific, often controversial. He steered away from modern glass boxes, conceiving each design as a sculptural form. His office was filled with large and small models.

For Gehry, architectural space was meant to stimulate its inhabitants. The lively campus he created for Loyola Marymount Law School (1981–84) in downtown Los Angeles inspired a more dynamic on-campus spirit. Even when the client was a large corporation, structures were human-sized. For the Rouse Co. headquarters (Columbia, Md., 1974), he clustered a number of small buildings, one for each corporate division.

Gehry won numerous honours and was a visiting professor at several universities. His design work was not limited to architecture. He did installations for several large art exhibitions, including "The Treasures of Tutankhamen" (1978). His love of inexpensive, functional materials led to the creation of lines of cardboard furniture, Easy Edges (1969–73) and Experimental Edges (1979–82). (MARGARET BARLOW)

Gong Li

When Gong Li's (Kung Li's) sensuous smile first appeared in close-up in *Red Sorghum*, a legend was born. A major event at the 1988 Berlin Film Festival, *Red Sorghum* was the first directorial effort of Zhang Yimou (Chang Yi-mou), whose work as a cinematographer on Chen Kaige's (Ch'en K'ai ke's) *The Yellow Earth* (1984) had helped launch a new wave of filmmakers from China known as the "Fifth Generation." International audiences had tended to view contemporary Chinese cinema as boring and propagandistic. The "Fifth Generation" brought back sensuality, talent, and emotion to their national cinema, and Gong Li came to symbolize this new sensibility. It was this happy combination of glamour and historical significance that propelled the 22-year-old acting student to centre stage, where she was meant to stay.

Gong Li was born on Dec. 31, 1965, in Shenyang, Liaoning province. She was the youngest of five children in a family of academics. In 1985 Gong Li was admitted to the prestigious Central Drama Academy in Beijing. It was during her second year that Zhang, who was interviewing young actresses for the part of the rebellious young bride in *Red Sorghum*, noticed her. Not only did Gong Li get the job, but she also got the man. The romance with director-Pygmalion Zhang (who was still married at the time) both scandalized and delighted fans throughout East Asia.

Zhang Yimou's and Gong Li's careers grew together—with *Ju Dou* (1990) and *Raise the Red Lantern* (1991). In these films, Gong Li played a spirited young woman who, forced to marry the wrong man, fights for her right to independence and sexual pleasure, but pays dearly. She was soon wooed by Hong Kong producers and landed her first comic role in *Terra-Cotta Warrior* (1990), in which she is pursued throughout the centuries by a faithful lover played by Zhang. She also appeared in parodic gangster movies, light-hearted dramas, and kung fu comedies.

It was, however, with mainland directors that she did her best work. In Zhang's *Qiu Ju Goes to Court* (1992; also known as *The Story of Qiu Ju*) she played a decidedly unglamorous country wife, who, though heavily pregnant during most of the

MIRAMAX

film, stubbornly wages a fight against the local bureaucracy. The film was a triumph at the Venice Film Festival, where it received the Golden Lion and Gong Li was given the best actress award. In *Farewell, My Concubine*, which won the Palme d'Or at Cannes in 1993, Chen Kaige cast her as a shrewd, single-minded, yet sensitive prostitute, who gets her man and forces him out of an ambiguous relationship with a fellow Peking Opera singer but is betrayed by him during the Cultural Revolution. In 1994 Zhang's *To Live*, which covered the life of a couple between the 1940s and the 1970s, allowed her to explore new dimensions of her art: not only does she age significantly, but she also evolves from the long-suffering wife of a patrician gambler to a plain, yet energetic, peasant woman who supports two children and a whimsical husband who has found peace in her old age. In addition to her glamour, talent, and magnetic screen presence, Gong Li's phenomenal popularity was due to her modernity. She was an incarnation of the new Chinese woman standing for herself through the tortuous meanders of melodramatic conventions, bureaucratic procedures, and the changing winds of history. (BÉRÉNICE REYNAUD)

Habibie, B(achruddin) J(usuf)

An aircraft engineer seemed an unlikely central figure in the closure of outspoken publications, a billion-dollar controversy over used warships, and the removal of powerful ex-generals from the top of Indonesia's ruling Golkar political organization. Yet all three of these events were linked to B.J. Habibie, Indonesia's research and technology minister and the former chief of research and development at Messerschmitt-Bölkow-Blohm in Germany.

During Golkar's 1993 central-board elections, Habibie helped the children and allies of President Suharto rise to top positions, easing out long-standing military-backed power brokers. In June 1994 a tabloid and two newsmagazines were closed after reporting Cabinet disagreement over Habibie's plan to refurbish 39 vessels bought from the former East German navy at his initiative. The Finance Ministry balked at the cost and the armed forces felt that its turf had been violated. Habibie still got more than $400 million for refurbishing.

Habibie was born on June 25, 1936, in Parepare, South Sulawesi. He met Suharto in 1949 when the general was posted to the province. Suharto became a family friend and took a personal interest in Habibie's development after the boy's father died. Brilliant in science and mathematics, Habibie studied at the prestigious Bandung Institute of Technology and the Technische Hochschule in Aachen, Germany, graduating in 1960. He then did research at the Hochschule before becoming head of research at Messerschmitt in 1966.

Suharto took power in 1966, and in 1974 he asked Habibie to return to Indonesia to help build advanced industries. Suharto assured him that he could do whatever was needed to accomplish that goal. Initially assigned to the state oil company Pertamina, Habibie became a government adviser and chief of a new aerospace company in 1976.

Two years later he became research minister and head of the Agency for Technology Evaluation and Application. He oversaw 10 "strategic" ventures: in aircraft, shipbuilding, train cars, steel, electronics, telecommunications equipment, heavy machinery, explosives, small arms, and ammunition. His agency also funded genetics research. In November 1993 he unveiled the first Indonesian-developed plane, which he helped design. He also brokered a $34 billion gas deal with the United States.

Habibie wanted Indonesia to climb the technology ladder as rising costs forced labour-intensive industries out. He believed his enterprises would spawn high-tech ventures in the private sector. Indonesian technocrats and the World Bank expressed misgivings about costs and viability, however. Military brass resented having to buy equipment from Habibie's firms. Nevertheless, Suharto's support helped the energetic minister generally get his way.

In 1990 Habibie was appointed head of the Indonesian Muslim Intellectuals Association to boost the influence of Muslims, who constituted about 90% of Indonesians, in a government traditionally dominated by Christian technocrats. Habibie was viewed as one of several possible successors to Suharto, whose sixth five-year term would end in 1998. (RICARDO L. SALUDO)

Hanks, Tom

For his gripping portrayal in the film *Philadelphia*—as a gay, AIDS-stricken lawyer embroiled in a discrimination suit against the law firm that had fired him—U.S. actor Tom Hanks was presented in 1994 with both the Academy Award and the Golden Globe award. The dramatic role, for which he shed 35 pounds and thinned his hair, was a vast departure from his many performances in light comedies. Hanks had built a loyal following by portraying characters that blended qualities of Jimmy Stewart and Clark Gable—the amiable, affable, and approachable boy-next-door with good looks and charm.

Thomas J. Hanks was born on July 9, 1956, in Concord, Calif. He was a shy, responsible child who frequently traveled with his father after his parents divorced in 1961. As an undergraduate at California State University, Hanks was attracted to acting because he thought it would provide an opportunity for him to express himself flamboyantly. During 1976–78 he dropped out of school to become an acting intern at what was then the Great Lakes Shakespeare Festival in Lakewood, Ohio. After winning the Cleveland Critics Circle award for playing Proteus in *The Two Gentlemen of Verona,* Hanks received his first taste of the adulation accorded an actor. Two years after arriving (1978) in New York City, Hanks landed the part of cross-dresser Kip Wilson in the television show "Bosom Buddies." Hanks's flair for light comedy was admired by director Ron Howard, who helped expand Hanks's career into motion pictures with *Splash* (1984), a blockbuster romantic comedy about a mermaid in love with a human. During the following decade, Hanks further sharpened his considerable talents in such mediocre films as *The Man with One Red Shoe* (1985), *The Money Pit* (1986), *Punchline* (1988), and *The Bonfire of the Vanities* (1990).

His nomination for an Academy Award as best actor in the 1988 comedy *Big* and the success of *A League of Their Own* (1992) marked Hanks as a major Hollywood leading-man-in-waiting. It was not until 1993, however, that he cemented his reputation as a serious actor. In that year he starred as a widower who discovered his true love via a radio talk show in the megahit movie *Sleepless in Seattle* and then as the lead in *Philadelphia*. In the summer of 1994, Hanks portrayed the title role in the film *Forrest Gump,* which was released to overwhelming critical and popular acclaim. His character, an ever hopeful, guileless, simple-minded man on whom fate smiled, philosophized that "Life is like a box of chocolates: you never know what you're gonna get." Most movie audiences agreed that Tom Hanks was blessed with the best of the box in 1994. (SUSAN RAPP)

Herzog, Roman

When the time came to choose a candidate for Germany's first postunification presidential election, Chancellor Helmut Kohl (*q.v.*) and his ruling Christian Democratic Union (CDU) sought out an easterner as a gesture to promote harmony within the country. The CDU was trailing in the polls, and a general election loomed on the horizon in October. While the post of president was largely ceremonial, Kohl's ability to replace the outgoing president, Richard von Weizsäcker, with his own candidate was seen as a test of the chancellor's political muscle. His choice—Steffen Heitmann, the justice minister for the state of Saxony—had proved a poor one. Heitmann, an inexperienced politician, came under intense criticism in 1993 when he voiced some extreme and unpopular opinions on subjects that included Naziism and immigrants. He then withdrew from the race. Kohl fared better with his replacement nominee, old crony Roman Herzog, the president of Germany's Federal Constitutional Court.

A few weeks before the May 1994 presidential election, Herzog created his own bit of controversy. A magazine quoted him as saying that foreigners living in Germany who turned down the opportunity for citizenship should return to their own countries. Herzog claimed that his comment had been interpreted incorrectly, but the damage was done. When a special 1,324-member electoral college assembled in the Reichstag in Berlin on May 23 to choose a new president, it took three rounds of voting before Herzog received the required majority for the victory. The narrow margin by which he was elected—Herzog received 696 votes, while his nearest rival had 605—proved to be prophetic; the CDU-led coalition squeaked through the October election with a 10-seat majority in the federal legislature.

Herzog was born April 5, 1934, in Landshut, Bavaria. He began his career in law in 1966 as a professor at the Free University in Berlin. He moved on to the College of Administration in Speyer, where he met Kohl, who was then the premier of the state of Rhineland-Palatinate. In 1973 he became Kohl's permanent representative in Bonn and then served in a series of government posts, ultimately becoming the minister of the interior of Baden-Württemberg. Kohl appointed him to the Federal Constitutional Court in 1983, and in 1987 he became its president.

While Herzog was generally considered to be a conservative, his court had a history of returning some surprisingly liberal decisions. Attacked even before the start of his five-year term by Social Democrats, who said that he had failed to denounce right-wing extremism in his acceptance speech, Herzog pledged to speak for all of Germany. But many others felt that a man who could modestly ask the Polish people "for forgiveness for what Germans did to you"—as Herzog did in a speech at the monument to the World War II Warsaw Uprising in the Polish capital on August 1—might be just the kind of president they needed to represent the newly reunited Germany in the newly uniting Europe. (ANTHONY G. CRAINE)

Heym, Stefan

Never one to be inhibited by public opinion or government disapproval, the German writer Stefan Heym spent most of his life provoking controversy, and 1994 was no different. Running on the parliamentary slate of the Party of Democratic Socialism—the reformed Communist Party—the 81-year-old maverick became the oldest member of Germany's Bundestag (lower house of the parliament).

Heym—the name is a pseudonym—was born Helmut Flieg in Chemnitz, Germany, on April 10, 1913. After being dismissed from his local high school for writing an ironic antiwar poem, he went to Berlin to finish school. When the Nazis seized power in 1933 and he learned that the Gestapo was searching for him, the 20-year-old fled into Czechoslovakia. Once safe in Prague he wrote to his parents to tell them where he was, but in order to shield them from danger he signed himself "Stefan Heym." (The name Heym, which he chose on the spur of the moment, means "home" and reflected his homesickness.)

After managing to survive in Prague for two years by writing articles for the local German press, Heym won a scholarship offered by the University of Chicago. Living in a fraternity house, he earned his bachelor's and master's degrees with a thesis on Heinrich Heine. By 1942 he had become a U.S. citizen and published a novel, *Hostages,* written in English. This became a best-seller and was made into a Hollywood film.

In 1945, toward the end of World War II, Heym returned to Germany as a soldier in the U.S. Army. Being a dedicated leftist, however, he opposed the army's policy on Germany's postwar future. After the war he tried to support himself as a novelist, but he found that he was blacklisted because of his political views. Unable to make a living in the United States, Heym moved to the German Democratic Republic and took citizenship there in 1953. Although he was genuinely supportive of the Communist "East German experiment," he was also committed to open discussions of controversial subjects, such as the crimes of Stalinism.

Heym's notorious frankness prompted the continual surveillance he was given in East Germany. (Heym once offered coffee to the plainclothesmen who were keeping him under 24-hour watch.) Still, he continued to write in English, and his international prominence protected him to some extent from government wrath. Even after the Berlin Wall was erected in 1961, he was able to travel to the West in order to meet with publishers and give public readings. It was only in 1969 that he was forced to pay a steep fine for having one of his books printed in the West after it had been banned by the East German government.

When the Communist regime collapsed, Heym became a prominent spokesman for those who wished to retain some form of "socialism with a human face." On these grounds he opposed the reunification of Germany. Elected from a Berlin district to the Bundestag in 1994, he was asked what he planned to say in his opening speech as parliamentary elder. The answer: "You can expect some surprises." (DIETLIND LERNER)

Heyman, I. Michael

On Sept. 19, 1994, the Smithsonian Institution inducted I. Michael Heyman, law professor and former chancellor of the University of California at Berkeley, as its chief executive officer. As 10th secretary of the cultural and scientific institution, Heyman would oversee the management of its exhibitions and research operations, as well as the maintenance of the vast collections housed in the Smithsonian's many museums. This jovial native New Yorker brought to his new job a long history of administrative and fund-raising expertise as well as experience in dealing with a great variety of scientific and policy issues.

Ira Michael Heyman was born in New York City on May 30, 1930. Despite an early interest in science—he qualified to enter the prestigious Bronx High School of Science but transferred to a private school so that he could play football and basketball—he studied government at Dartmouth College, Hanover, N.H., receiving a B.A. in 1951. After serving as a U.S. Marine Corps officer during the Korean War, he entered Yale University Law School, where he became editor of the *Yale Law Journal.* He graduated in 1956, and from 1958 to 1959 he served as chief law clerk for Chief Justice Earl Warren.

Heyman began his teaching career at the University of California at Berkeley as an acting professor of law in 1959 and became a full professor in 1961 and a professor of law and city and regional planning in 1966. He served as chancellor of the university from 1980 to 1990, during which time he restructured and revitalized the biosciences programs. While at that post, he also became a successful fund-raiser and helped supervise the museums the university maintained.

Throughout his career Heyman involved himself in a wide range of issues by both serving on and chairing numerous committees dealing with civil rights, land use, and environmental concerns. In the year before his appointment to the Smithsonian, he was deputy assistant secretary for policy at the U.S. Department of the Interior, acting as counselor to Secretary of the Interior Bruce Babbitt on such issues as the Endangered Species Act. He also served on the Smithsonian's Board of Regents from 1990 to 1994, an involvement that thoroughly acquainted him with the institution.

The 148-year-old Smithsonian Institution, considered the "nation's attic" by some, is a complex of 16 museums and galleries and the National Zoological Park, most of which are located in Washington, D.C. Affiliated scientific and cultural research facilities are located in eight states and Panama. Heyman's goals for his tenure as secretary included converting the Smithsonian's rich stores of information to digital form so that electronic access to them could be made available.

(MARY JANE FRIEDRICH)

Hopkins, Sir Anthony

Having overcome alcohol and other personal demons to attain in midlife the stature so long predicted for him, British actor Anthony Hopkins secured a place in the firmament with an Oscar for his portrayal of Hannibal Lecter in *The Silence of the Lambs* (1991) and with two more extraordinary performances in 1993-94 films: as writer C.S. Lewis in *Shadowlands* and as Stevens the butler, whom Hopkins described as "pathologically afraid to love," in *The Remains of the Day.*

Repressed emotion has been central to Hopkins' best performances but not always to his stormy life. The son of a baker, he was born on Dec. 31, 1937, in Port Talbot, Wales, the hometown of actor Richard Burton, who was both Hopkins' inspiration and the standard against which his career had often been measured. After a lonely, undistinguished youth, Hopkins attended the Cardiff (Wales) College of Music and Drama and the Royal Academy of Dramatic Art, London. Following a stint in regional theatre, he was asked in 1965 to join the National Theatre (NT), where, understudying Laurence Olivier in *The Dance of Death* (1967), he won rave reviews and was designated by critics as the heir apparent to Burton and Olivier. (He had the temerity to audition for Olivier's company with an Othello monologue at a time when Olivier himself was playing the role.) In 1968 he made his film debut in *The Lion in Winter.*

An early 1970s clash with an NT director sent Hopkins to the U.S., first to New York City, where he triumphed on Broadway in *Equus*, then to Los Angeles, where, increasingly self-destructive, he finally faced his alcoholism, supported by his second wife, Jennifer. A decade of mixed performances in film and on television followed—strong work in *Magic* (1978) and *The Elephant Man* (1980) and an Emmy for his portrayal of Adolf Hitler in "The Bunker" (1981) were compromised by appearances in films unworthy of his talent. In the mid-1980s Hopkins made a triumphant return to the NT, alternating the roles of King Lear and Antony in 200 performances and winning accolades as the unscrupulous media magnate in *Pravda.* That role, like his postfeminist powder keg in the film *The Good Father* (1986), set the stage for his portrayal of the gentlemanly psychopath Lecter, which resulted in international stardom and another plum role in *Howards End* (1992).

Where once Hopkins' obsession with technique had been too obvious, these later performances were seamless, his smallest gestures and looks conveying layers of meaning, volcanic emotion percolating beneath the surface ("the lava doesn't erupt but it moves," Lauren Bacall once said of Hopkins). A Method actor known to read over his part as many as 150 times, Hopkins found a way to express what he called the "black anger" within him with great brilliance. For his achievements he was made a Knight of the British Empire in 1987. In the latter part of 1994 Hopkins appeared in the film *The Road to Wellville* and made his stage directorial debut in *August,* in which he also acted.

(JEFF WALLENFELDT)

Houston, Whitney

By 1994 velvety-voiced vocalist Whitney Houston had seen seven consecutive singles reach the top of *Billboard*'s Hot 100 chart and had accomplished more in a decade than most artists achieved in a lifetime. Her first three albums sold more than 40 million copies, and she scored a string of number one hits, beginning in 1985 with "Saving All My Love for You" and culminating in 1992 with "I Will Always Love You." By 1994 Houston had also garnered several American Music Awards and five Grammy awards, and she was presented with the trophy as the best-selling pop artist of the year at the Monte Carlo Music Awards festival.

Whitney Houston was born on Aug. 9, 1963, in Newark, N.J. Her family included her cousin and professional singer Dionne Warwick and Whitney's mother and singing coach, Emily "Cissy" Houston, whose vocal group, the Sweet Inspirations, sang backup for Aretha Franklin. While still in high school, Houston served as a backup for Chaka Khan and Lou Rawls and modeled for fashion magazines. When she was 19, Houston showcased her soaring soprano voice at a New York City nightclub and was brought to the attention of Clive Davis, the president of Arista Records, Inc. After signing her to a recording contract, Davis groomed the gospel-based singer for crossover pop success. Her debut album, *Whitney Houston* (1985), yielded three number-one singles. She attracted a large following with love ballads, and the song "Greatest Love of All" became her signature.

In 1992 Houston made her motion-picture debut in *The Bodyguard,* portraying a spoiled superstar who required protection when her life was threatened. Although critics gave the film lukewarm reviews, *The Bodyguard* was an enormous box office success and featured Houston's biggest hit to date, "I Will Always Love You." The song was originally written and recorded by Dolly Parton, but Houston's rendition stayed at number one longer than any other single had before—a record 14 weeks—and the sound track of the film sold more than 28 million copies. In September, when life began imitating art, Houston obtained a restraining order against a man accused of stalking her.

In July 1992, just months prior to her film debut, Houston married hip-hop singer Bobby Brown. She gave birth to a daughter the following year. In 1994 Houston was featured in an AT&T ad campaign, and she launched a world tour during the last half of the year. She also considered such projects as producing a gospel album and appearing in remakes of *Cinderella* and *A Star Is Born.*

(ANTHONY L. GREEN)

Kagame, Paul

The dominant figure to emerge from the tragedy in Rwanda in 1994 was Paul Kagame, the architect of the successful military campaign waged by the Tutsi-dominated Rwandan Patriotic Front (FPR) to gain control of the country from the Hutu majority after the genocidal bloodbath that followed the death of Pres. Juvénal Habyarimana in April. As hundreds of thousands of the minority Tutsi and their Hutu allies perished at the hands of Hutu militia, Kagame and his rebel army renewed the civil war they had begun in October 1990. Outnumbered by as many as 20,000 soldiers, Kagame's force of 10,000–14,000 executed the general's "deliberately protracted" strategy to perfection. The FPR minimized its casualties by avoiding direct assaults on the enemy. Instead it hammered government strongholds with artillery for days but left corridors through which the enemy could flee, abandoning their heavy armaments, when their stocks and will were depleted. By early July the FPR's siege of the capital, Kigali, was complete, and in a matter of weeks the country was under FPR control. The new government included a Hutu president and prime minister, but real power appeared to rest with Kagame, who, at age 37, assumed the titles of vice president and minster of defense.

Kagame was born about 1957 in southern Rwanda and grew up in exile in Uganda. His parents had taken him there as a young child when Hutu violence toward the Tutsi flared in 1959 during the buildup to Rwandan independence from Belgium. In Uganda he studied at Makerere University, Kampala, before joining the forces of Yoweri Museveni, who overthrew Ugandan Pres. Milton Obote in 1986. Kagame became Museveni's chief of intelligence and gained a reputation for incorruptibility and severity by enforcing a stringent code of behaviour; he earned the nickname Commander Pilate (after Pontius Pilate). Many Ugandans resented the Rwandan presence in their country, however, and as the 1980s closed, Kagame and three other expatriate Rwandan military leaders plotted an invasion of their homeland. In 1990, while Kagame was studying at the U.S. Army Command and General Staff College in Ft. Leavenworth, Kansas, that invasion—mostly involving Tutsi veterans of the Ugandan army—was undertaken and repulsed. In the process the other three members of the FPR command were killed. Kagame assumed direction of the civil war, which was suspended in August 1993 by a peace agreement that promised—but never delivered—real power sharing.

Assuming power in the aftermath of the Hutu massacres of the Tutsi in 1994, Kagame stood firmly against random Tutsi reprisals. In interviews he said that he was determined to bring an end to the cycles of violence. He also called on the Tutsi and Hutu to live together as one people.

(JEFF WALLENFELDT)

Kernot, Cheryl

As one of the foremost Australian role models for young women, Cheryl Kernot—senator from Queensland and leader of the Australian Democrats (AD)—highlighted the contribution made by women climbing the ladder of success. In 1994 she launched an "Inspiring Women" calendar for 1995, with herself as Miss April under the rubric "Strength and Courage." Kernot said that she hoped the calendar would send the message to women that success and inspiration were not necessarily synonymous with fame and wealth and that happiness was not just about being thin or fashionable. She ended by quoting Emmeline Pankhurst: "Women will only be truly successful when no one is surprised that they are successful."

Kernot was born Dec. 5, 1948, in Maitland, New South Wales. After graduating with a Bachelor of Arts degree and Diploma of Education from the Universities of Sydney and Newcastle, she taught in secondary schools for 10 years and worked in the communications industry as a freelance radio producer.

The most popular chief of any Australian political party, she became AD leader after 81% of the full membership elected her in May 1993. She had joined the Democrats in 1979 (two years after its founding), in part because she was attracted to an organization that right from the start had set up party administrative processes that were very appealing to women. In an early speech to the Australian Federation of University Women in Brisbane, Kernot recalled that because of the party's relative youth, the Democrats had not formed links with unions, business, or farmer organizations and had never had to battle with the sort of vested interests and entrenched male hierarchies that existed in other places. She was the party's representative in a Young Political Leaders' exchange tour of the U.S. in 1986, and in 1990 she was elected to the Senate on her fourth attempt. In late 1993 Kernot was heavily involved in the successful passage of the historic Native Title (Mabo) legislation, acting as a behind-the-scenes negotiator between the government, the Senate independents, and Aboriginal groups.

Later, addressing the Harvard Club of Australia in Brisbane on Oct. 1, 1994, Kernot drew attention to her own main political preoccupation, the widening gap between the "haves" and the "have nots" in Australia. With the major parties doing battle for the political middle ground, she said, both the government and the opposition coalition were essentially locked into policies and programs that were the most welcome to the greatest number of voters. This ensured that neither of the major parties wanted or would dare to enter into public dialogue with the people of Australia about the fairest way of raising sufficient revenues to continue to fund the services of a civilized society. In 1994 Senator Kernot kept faith with the Australian Democrats' traditional motto, "Keep the Bastards Honest."   (A.R.G. GRIFFITHS)

Kim Jong Il

In North Korea he was hailed as "Dear Leader," "Guiding Focus," "Bright Star of the Country," and, following his father's death, "Great Successor." Elsewhere, however, people often did not know what to believe about him. Although his true nature and intentions remained obscure, Kim Jong Il was set to take control of the world's most isolated, secretive, and unpredictable nation and to fulfill the dynastic aspirations of his father, Kim Il Sung, the only leader that North Korea had ever known.

Legends in North Korea surrounding his birth indicated the status accorded Kim Jong Il. It was said that he was born on Feb. 16, 1942, in a log cabin on Mount Paekdu (a sacred site that in popular myth was the birthplace of the first Koreans). At the time, his father was coordinating the guerrilla war against the Japanese. His birth, allegedly, had been foretold by a swallow from heaven. The day he was born a single star hung over the mountain, and the moment was announced by the appearance of a double rainbow. (The lone star over Mount Paekdu became a visual symbol of the younger Kim, and the cabin was designated as a pilgrimage site.)

It was thought, however, that Kim Jong Il actually was born in Khabarovsk, Siberia, U.S.S.R., where his parents had sought refuge from the invading Japanese. Kim was his father's firstborn son. When he was six his father took control of North Korea; the following year his mother died. Kim attended elite schools in the capital city of Pyongyang while his father continued to consolidate power and fostered the personality cult that would persist until his death.

After Kim graduated from Kim Il Sung University, Pyongyang, in 1964, he went to work for the Korean Workers' (communist) Party. In 1975 he became a member of the Politburo. His star rose in 1980 when he was officially designated his father's successor. In 1991 he was named supreme commander of the armed forces. Kim reportedly had been running the nation's day-to-day operations for some time before his father's death in July 1994.

Kim Jong Il took centre stage at a time when the nation's economy was contracting, its funds depleted, and its nuclear program facing international condemnation. Kim had previously avoided contact with foreign dignitaries, had rarely traveled outside of the country, and had not been part of the high-level negotiations that revolved around the Nuclear Non-proliferation Treaty. Rumours, disinformation, and speculation depicted Kim as either a bloodthirsty terrorist whose nefarious deeds included a 1983 bombing in Burma (now Myanmar) that killed 17 South Korean government officials, as a power-hungry autocrat who nonetheless liked to spend time partying, or as an amicable man given to making self-deprecating comments on his diminutive stature.

Kim dropped from sight after his father's funeral, fueling rumours that he was unable to consolidate power or was seriously ill following a car accident—or both. At year's end he had not yet formally taken control.

(CHERYL L. COLLINS)

Kohl, Helmut

The election in November 1994 of Helmut Kohl as chancellor of Germany demonstrated that the 64-year-old politician was a survivor. Despite winning confirmation by the slimmest margin of his long political career, Kohl claimed that his fragile coalition government would hold together. As he began his 13th year as head of government, Kohl reflected that his mentor, former chancellor Konrad Adenauer, had won his first election by a narrow margin and went on to rule Germany for 14 years, a record that Kohl was eager to break.

Kohl and his Christian Democratic Union (CDU) faced a vastly different Germany from the one Adenauer had beheld in 1949; indeed, the political landscape of the country had changed drastically since Kohl himself had taken office. German reunification, long a dream of Kohl's, had occurred in 1990, but the financial and social problems resulting from it had not ended. Efforts to integrate the economically depressed former East Germany with the prosperous West had brought public debt to unprecedented levels, while those who had lived under communism often found it difficult to adjust to a society driven by a market economy.

Kohl was born in Ludwigshafen am Rhein, Germany, on April 3, 1930. He studied at the University of Frankfurt and received a Ph.D. from the University of Heidelberg in 1958. Entering politics the next year, he was elected to the Rhineland-Palatinate state legislature. He became minister-president (prime minister) of that state in 1969 and served until 1976 when he was elected to the Bundestag (parliament), where he became Christian Democratic floor leader. After losing his bid for chancellor in the 1976 election, Kohl did not run again until 1982, when changes in the makeup of the coalition government resulted in his confirmation as chancellor. He was reelected in 1987 and 1990.

As 1994 began, however, Kohl was running behind in the polls. His main opponent, Rudolf Scharping of the Social Democratic Party, was benefiting from disenchantment with the political status quo. Unemployment had hit record levels, and the recession that plagued Germany for much of 1993 was showing no signs of letting up. Unification was continuing to drain funds from the German treasury, while Germany's allies urged that the German government become a more active player in the European and international arena. The spring brought a change in fortune for Kohl and his party, however. The economy began a powerful recovery and, as Scharping made several errors and misjudgments, the experienced Kohl began to be viewed as a steadying influence. In the national elections on October 16 the German voters narrowed the CDU-led coalition's majority in the Bundestag to 10 seats from 134. A month later the Bundestag elected Kohl to his fourth term as prime minister by only one vote more than the required majority.

(JOHN H. MATHEWS)

Koss, Johann Olav

The highlight of the outstanding ice speed skating career of Norway's Johann Olav Koss came on Feb. 20, 1994, when he won the stamina-sapping 10,000-m race in the Winter Olympics at Hamar, Norway. His time of 13 min 30.55 sec lowered the record for the distance by an incredible margin of almost 13 seconds. He had clocked the previous best time three years earlier at Heerenveen, Neth. The feat put beyond doubt the fact that the 25-year-old medical student was the world's best long-distance skater. Clinching a third world record in eight days, he had set new marks earlier of 6 min 34.96 sec for the 5,000 m and 1 min 51.29 sec for the 1,500 m. Not since 1980, when Eric Heiden of the U.S. won five Olympic gold medals at Lake Placid, N.Y., had there been a comparable accomplishment in the sport.

A previous victory in the 1,500 m in the 1992 Olympics at Albertville, France, brought Koss's tally of Olympic gold medals to four. Other major achievements included three overall world championship titles—in 1990, 1991, and 1994. There was little doubt, however, that Koss's amazing Olympic 10,000 m would remain etched more indelibly in his memory than anything else.

"I had hoped to beat the world record, but never dreamed I would do it by so much," he reflected. "It took quite a while afterwards to understand fully what I had achieved." He was determined to produce an exceptionally fast start and admitted afterward that his pace in the opening laps "actually scared me a bit." Even so, he went on to make a grueling event almost look easy. "I did not conscientiously use extra power at the outset. I was just gliding. It was fantastic." The 12,000 onlookers who packed the arena, including Norway's Crown Prince Haakon Magnus, offered the kind of inspiration that only a host nation could provide. "It's only once in a lifetime that you experience such an atmosphere, such good ice and, at the same time, be in such good form," said Koss.

The three Olympic titles at one tournament equaled the performance of his fellow countryman, Hjalmar Andersen, who tripled in Oslo in 1952. Norway's cultural affairs minister announced that a new sculpture of Koss would be erected next to that of Andersen at the Hamar rink. Koss's 10,000-m time was three full minutes faster than that of Andersen, who, at the age of 70, presented Koss's medal.

Koss, who was born on Oct. 29, 1968, wore specially developed lightweight one-piece skates for the Olympic competition. Designed by Finn Halvarsen, a former Norwegian national coach, they weighed some 200 g (7.1 oz) less than those of his rivals. Koss's humanitarian side was demonstrated by an altruistic gesture after the Winter Games, when he donated substantial victory bonuses of about $30,000 to the Olympic Aid fund. Some of the money was destined to help relieve suffering in Bosnia and Herzegovina, the capital of which, Sarajevo, had been the site of the 1984 Winter Games.

(HOWARD BASS)

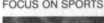

FOCUS ON SPORTS

Kuchma, Leonid Danylovych
In the Ukrainian presidential elections of July 1994, Leonid Kuchma achieved a surprising victory over the incumbent—and first—Ukrainian president, Leonid Kravchuk, by sweeping the industrial cities of eastern Ukraine and the Crimea and dividing the vote in central Ukraine. During the campaign he persistently advocated closer ties with Russia, a policy that endeared him to the former communists and alienated him from the major nationalist centres of western Ukraine. Though Russian was his native tongue, Kuchma was able to demonstrate an adequate command of the Ukrainian language in his campaign speeches. He had served his country earlier as prime minister, from October 1992 to September 1993.

The new Ukrainian president represented a new breed of politician, that of the industrial managers of the Soviet era. Though Kuchma was born in the village of Chaykino, in the north-central province of Chernihiv on Aug. 9, 1938,

AP/WIDE WORLD

his technical career blossomed in the industrial heartland of Dnipropetrovsk. He graduated in 1960 with a degree in mechanical engineering from Dnipropetrovsk State University.

From 1960 to 1975 Kuchma progressed steadily as an engineer, senior engineer, and assistant chief designer at the construction works in the city of Dnipropetrovsk. He served as Communist Party secretary at the works from 1975 to 1982, and in 1982 he was promoted to the position of first deputy general designer. During those years he also worked at a top secret post (even the precise dates were never made known) as a technical manager at Baykonyr, Kazakhstan, the centre of the Soviet space program. Kuchma's most prestigious position in management was from 1986 to 1992, when he served as the general director of the world's largest rocket construction firm, in Dnipropetrovsk.

During his time as prime minister of Ukraine, Kuchma often professed himself frustrated with the difficulties in implementing significant reforms and with what he perceived as a lack of substantial aid from the West. Reflecting his management skills, he was appointed chairman of the Ukrainian Union of Industrialists and Entrepreneurs in December 1993. He was also a recipient of the Lenin Prize and in 1994 held the position of professor at Dnipropetrovsk State University and academician of the Engineering Academy of Ukraine. (DAVID R. MARPLES)

Kumaratunga, Chandrika Bandaranaike
Even in South Asian politics, where women recently had risen to leadership positions, the situation that evolved in Sri Lanka in 1994 was unique. In November a mother and daughter took over the country's two top governmental positions, that of president and prime minister. Elected president was Chandrika Bandaranaike Kumaratunga, the incumbent prime minister and the daughter of two prime ministers: her father, Solomon Bandaranaike, who served in the 1950s, and her mother, Sirimavo Bandaranaike, who served as the world's first elected woman prime minister in the 1960s and '70s and was appointed to the post again after her daughter won the presidency.

The women leaders of South Asian countries were often the widows or daughters of slain political leaders, and Kumaratunga was no exception. Both her father and her husband, a film actor who had risen in politics, were killed by assassins. Even her rival for the presidency was a widow—of Gamini Dissanayake, who was assassinated only weeks before the election by a suicide bomber, alleged to be a Tamil rebel.

Kumaratunga became prime minister in August when the People's Alliance (PA), the political party she led, ousted the long-entrenched United National Party (UNP) in national elections. She had run on a platform of alleviating widespread poverty and ending the bloody civil conflict with the Tamil rebels. Analysts saw the war-weariness of the people as a factor in her election victory. Kumaratunga also vowed to eliminate the nearly dictatorial powers of the presidency—invoked by the UNP when it came to power 17 years earlier—and to make the position ceremonial. It was expected that once she had accomplished this, she would switch positions with her mother and lead the country as prime minister.

Kumaratunga was born on June 29, 1945, in Colombo, Sri Lanka (then Ceylon). She formulated some of her political philosophy during her university days in Paris, and she later recalled that she had once stood at the barricades during a student uprising. She received a degree in political science from the University of Paris and also studied developmental economics, law, and political journalism. During 1988–91 she was a research fellow at the Institute of Commonwealth Studies, University of London. Significant positions that she held before becoming prime minister included chairperson and managing director of *Dinakara Sinhala Daily News Paper* (1977–85), vice president of the Sri Lanka Mahajana Party (SLMP; 1984), and president of SLMP (1986). In 1994 she was the vice president of the PA and deputy leader of the Sri Lanka Freedom Party, part of the PA coalition. (MARVIN MARTIN)

Lara, Brian
In the space of 50 glorious days of dominance, Brian Lara broke the two most coveted batting records in cricket. On April 18, 1994, in Antigua, the West Indian left-hander scored 375, beating the 365 not out of Sir Garfield Sobers in 1958; and on June 6, at the Edgbaston ground in Birmingham, England, Lara made the highest individual score in first-class cricket with an unbeaten innings of 501 for his county, Warwickshire, against Durham. It was Lara's seventh century in eight innings, a record of sustained run-scoring that not even Sir Don Bradman, the greatest of all batsmen, had been able to match.

Lara was still just 25 years old, but if he never made another run, he had already established himself as one of the greats, a worthy inheritor of the tradition of West Indian batting set by Everton Weekes, Viv Richards, and Clive Lloyd. Lara was smaller than all of these, but he relied on timing, a high back lift, and iron-firm wrists rather than brute strength for his power, and his rate of scoring—a run a minute during his 501—was all the more phenomenal because he did not look aggressive either on or off the field. Though not short of self-confidence, he had none of Richards' swagger. But, like all the great batsmen, he played straight and late.

Lara was born on May 2, 1969, in Cantaro, Trinidad, one of a family of 11, and was a natural games player in his youth, a member of the national under-14 association football (soccer) team, and a useful tennis player. But, as with most West Indian children, cricket was his great love. Under the guidance of the former Test left-hander Joey Carew, the boy quickly became the talk of the Caribbean—destined to lead West Indies into the next decade. It did not happen immediately. Lara was selected for West Indies first at age 21, but he did not make his mark until three years later.

There was no doubt about Lara's talent, but his concentration was erratic and his patience limited. The first sign that he was starting to overcome those failings came in Sydney, Australia, in 1993, when his innings of 277—full of delicate late cuts, full-blooded drives, and flicks of his hips, his trademark shot—heralded the arrival of a new force in Test cricket.

Despite the adulation, the fame, and the growing fortune, Lara remained a shy, modest, amusing man, aware of his gifts, but not conceitedly so. The only dangers to an assured rise into the ranks of the very greatest players lay in the expectations that his phenomenal feats had prompted and the staleness that often comes from playing too much cricket. By the middle of the summer, he was nursing a knee injury and complaining of fatigue, but his mere presence lifted Warwickshire to an historic treble in domestic competitions in England. There seemed to be no limit to what Lara could achieve over the next decade or to the pleasure he would bring to those fortunate enough to watch him bat.

(ANDREW LONGMORE)

Leakey, Richard
In January 1994 Richard Leakey resigned from his position as director of the Kenya Wildlife Service (KWS), after being accused of arrogance, corruption, and racism by high-ranking Kenyan officials. The famed paleontologist and conservationist was caught up in this political maelstrom while still learning to walk on artificial limbs, the result of a plane crash the previous September in which he lost both legs.

Following Leakey's resignation, Kenyan Pres. Daniel arap Moi recalled him to his position at the beginning of March, but Leakey, a white Kenyan citizen, resigned once again two weeks later, citing unacceptable government restrictions as the reason for his abrupt departure. His successor, David Western, was also a white Kenyan and a well-known conservationist.

Leakey was first appointed director of the KWS in 1989 by President Moi. He was given broad powers and was widely praised for reducing corruption within KWS, instituting and maintaining a strong policy against ivory poachers, and restoring the security of the national parks. Described as unconventional, tough, and abrasive, Leakey was a strong presence in the Kenyan government, devoted to the preservation of Kenya's wildlife and sanctuaries. As director, however, he made enemies by resisting the efforts of politicians to obtain land from wildlife sanctuaries for commercial purposes.

Leakey's supporters claimed that his departure would hurt Kenya, a country that was regarded as a world leader in wildlife conservation. In fact, Kenya's $450 million-per-year tourism industry was based on its marine and animal parks. Foreign donors expressed concern about the political turmoil surrounding the KWS, and the Kenyan government became apprehensive about losing overseas loans and other monetary support for wildlife conservation, much of which had actually been attracted by Leakey.

Leakey was born on Dec. 19, 1944, in Nairobi, Kenya, to noted anthropologists Mary and Louis S.B. Leakey. He was initially reluctant to follow in his parents' footsteps and in 1961 started his own safari business in Kenya. While exploring the Lake Natron area in 1963, he found an australopithecine jaw and decided that he would indeed become an anthropologist. He then went to London, where he completed a two-year secondary education program in six months. However, he became low on funds, lost interest in academics, and returned to Kenya.

Leakey became best known in the scientific world for his work at the Koobi Fora site on the shores of Lake Turkana in Kenya. This site, which had yielded a remarkable collection of fossils, compelled scholars to revise their views on human development. With his wife, Meave G. Leakey, he coedited volume one of *Koobi Fora Research Projects* (1978). Leakey's other writing includes three books in collaboration with the sci-

LIZ GILBERT—SYGMA

ence writer Roger Lewin: *Origins* (1977), *People of the Lake: Mankind and Its Beginnings* (1978), and *Origins Reconsidered: In Search of What Makes Us Human* (1992).   (AMANDA E. FULLER)

Lepage, Robert
Quebec's Renaissance man—author, director, designer, and actor—Robert Lepage continued in 1994 to surprise and amaze audiences as the theatrical wizard who masterfully translated ideas into images and made his plays seem like intricate puzzles. *Tectonic Plates* (1988) dealt with the collision of French Canadian and Scottish cultures. Two pianos gliding across the stage symbolized the continents of Europe and North America. The bombing of Hiroshima was the metaphor in *The Seven Streams of the River Ota* (1994). This play, set in the home of a Jewish Czech photographer living in Japan, revealed the story line through a series of flashbacks. Lepage's play *Polygraphe* was a metaphysical detective story sparked by the murder of one of his friends.

Born in 1957 in Quebec City, Robert Lepage graduated in 1978 from Conservatoire d'Art Dramatique de Quebec and then studied in Paris with Swiss director Alain Knapp. Lepage became a skilled performer in comic improvisational theatre before joining Théâtre Repère in Quebec (1982). This theatre, founded by Jacques Lessard, relied on the active involvement of actors to discover the key, object, or pattern necessary to develop the production. In 1985 Lepage became artistic director of the company. From 1989 to 1993 he was head of the French theatre section of the National Arts Centre in Ottawa. In 1994 he returned to Quebec City to found a new theatre company, Ex Machina.

Lepage was noted for surprising juxtapositions in his plays. In *Needles and Opium* (1991), French poet and filmmaker Jean Cocteau and U.S. jazz trumpeter Miles Davis exchanged places. Lepage envisioned both these men in 1949 traveling between New York and Paris at the same time, both addicted to drugs. He also believed in producing plays in more than one language, making the actors devise methods to project the meaning to the audience without translation. In 1989 he produced Shakespeare's *Romeo and Juliet* in a combination of English and French. His *Dragon's Trilogy* (1985) was staged partly in Chinese. He won the Dora Mavor Moore Award for his direction of the *Trilogy* (1988). In 1992 Lepage sparked controversy at the British National Theatre by setting Shakespeare's *A Midsummer Night's Dream* in a mud bath.

In 1993 Lepage directed the Canadian Opera Company's production of Béla Bartók's *Bluebeard's Castle* and Arnold Schoenberg's *Erwartung*. He also directed Richard Wagner's *Ring* cycle in

Paris. In a lighter vein, he designed a Montreal show for British rock star Peter Gabriel. As an actor, Lepage starred in his one-man plays *Needles and Opium* and *Vinci* (1985). In 1988 he played the role of Pilate in the film *Jesus of Montreal*.

For his contribution to the performing arts in Canada, Robert Lepage received the National Arts Centre Award in 1994.   (DIANE LOIS WAY)

Lin, Maya
For sculptor/architect Maya Lin, 1994 was a busy year. In August her translucent clock, Eclipsed Time, was installed in the ceiling of Penn Station in New York City. Looking much like a flying saucer, the 4.3-m (14-ft)-wide elliptical frosted glass clock was illuminated from above. A metal disk, moving slowly across the glowing oval, cast an ever-changing shadow on the numerals below (12:00 was a total eclipse). She also saw the completion of her first two houses, one on each coast.

Lin was a college senior in 1981 when her design was chosen for the Vietnam Veterans Memorial in Washington, D.C. In the years that followed, Lin showed great versatility, refusing to become typecast as a creator of memorials.

Lin was born on Oct. 5, 1959, in Athens, Ohio. Her parents, Julia Chang Lin, a poet, and Henry

KEVIN FITZSIMONS

Huan Lin, a ceramicist, emigrated to the U.S. from China in the 1940s. As a child, Lin enjoyed spending time alone, reading, hiking, and making pottery in her father's studio. A high-school course on existentialism and its fascination with death sparked her interest in cemeteries and memorial statuary.

For a class assignment while studying architecture at Yale University, Lin was required to enter the nationwide Vietnam memorial competition. Her design consisted of two low black granite walls that intersected to form a wide "V." Engraved on the mirrorlike stone surface were the names of the more than 58,000 U.S. dead and missing-in-action who served in the Vietnam War. When Lin's winning entry was announced, a number of veterans' groups and others protested. Eventually, a compromise was reached, and a traditional statue depicting three servicemen with a flag was commissioned to stand at the entrance to the memorial site. After its dedication in 1982, however, Lin's wall became one of the city's most visited and most moving tourist attractions.

After graduating from Yale, Lin attended Harvard University. She retreated from the spotlight to work briefly for a Boston architectural firm before returning to Yale for graduate studies (1983–86). Lin then struck out on her own, working out of a New York City loft studio. Her vastly different designs included an earth sculpture for the University of Michigan (1994) and a corporate logo. Concentrating on sculpture much of the time, Lin completed numerous small pieces and two important large commissions—the Civil Rights Memorial in Montgomery, Ala. (1989), and The Women's Table at Yale (1993). She also designed a loft conversion for the Museum for African Art in New York City (1993).

(MARGARET BARLOW)

Lukashenka, Aleksandr Hrygorevich
Throughout the former communist states of Eastern Europe, ex- or pro-communists were returning to power. Still, Aleksandr Lukashenka was a surprising newcomer to the Belarusian political scene in 1994, emphatically winning the runoff presidential election on July 10 against Prime Minister Vyacheslav Kebich, a man who had controlled the politics of the country through strong backing in parliament. Lukashenka was known to the population only because of his role as chairman of the parliamentary commission on corruption. During the campaign, he propagated a simple message: return to a "clean" government; remove corrupt officials from office and bring to trial those who had abused their position; and move the country closer to its Russian neighbour in orientation.

Lukashenka was born in the village of Kopys, Orshanske raion, Vicebsk (Vitebsk) oblast in

1954. He graduated from the Mahilau (Mogilyov) Teaching Institute and the Belarusian Agricultural Academy. In 1975–77 he was an instructor of political affairs of the Western border district (he spent a total of five years in the army). Subsequently, he held a series of minor posts in the Komsomol (Young Communist League) and raion organizations in the Shklau region of Mahilau oblast. From 1982 through 1990 Lukashenka held leading management and Communist Party posts at collective and state farms and at a construction materials combine in the Shklau region. He was elected to the Supreme Soviet (parliament) in 1990 from Tuisvwal district.

In the parliament Lukashenka created a faction called Communists for Democracy. He was the only deputy to oppose the December 1991 agreement that effectively dissolved the Soviet Union. He maintained close association with "conservative" Communist factions, such as the Belaya Rus Slavic Congress and the Union of Officers, and prior to the Belarusian election was known to have links with similar groups in Russia. In May 1994 Vladimir Zhirinovsky's (*q.v.*) Liberal Democratic Party of Russia (LDPR) arranged a press conference for Lukashenka in Moscow after he addressed the State Duma with an appeal for the formation of a new Slavic Union.

Despite such associations, Lukashenka was best described as unpredictable. He was something of a novice in the affairs of state and had made several contradictory statements and radical shifts of direction. He was committed to economic and monetary union with Russia and possibly favoured political union, but he balked at weakening Belarusian independence and found close relations with Russian Pres. Boris Yeltsin difficult to achieve. Despite a proclaimed opposition to privatization and market reformers, he kept some promarket politicians in high office. The pro-Communist Lukashenka might be characterized as a gradualist with a clear preference for a powerful executive.   (DAVID R. MARPLES)

McEntire, Reba

"Everyone's going to OD on Reba," joked country music singer Reba McEntire near the beginning of the year. McEntire, already considered the reigning queen of country, did indeed spend more time in the limelight in 1994 than ever before. She released *Read My Mind*, her 22nd album; published *Reba: My Story*, a best-selling autobiography; starred in *Is There Life Out There?*, a made-for-TV movie, and a TV music special; appeared in the films *North* and *The Little Rascals;* won a Grammy award and a Country Music Association (CMA) award for her collaboration with Linda Davis on "Does He Love You"; and planned an ambitious concert tour.

McEntire was born on March 28, 1954, in McAlester, Okla. The daughter of a world-champion steer roper, she too did some rodeo performing. She joined her first band while in the ninth grade but scored her first big break in music when she was asked to sing the national anthem at the 1974 National Finals Rodeo. Her performance impressed country music star Red Steagall, who helped McEntire record a demo that led to a contract with Mercury Records. Six years after her first single, "I Don't Want to Be a One Night Stand" (1976), she topped the charts with "Can't Even Get the Blues." Other hits followed, but McEntire longed to have more control of her own career and to recapture a more traditional country music sound. She moved to the MCA label in 1984, started coproducing her albums, and topped the charts seven times by the end of 1986. She was the first woman to win six CMA award nominations in one year and was crowned CMA's best female vocalist an unprecedented four years straight (1984–87).

With her musical destiny now resting in her own hands, McEntire expanded into business and acting. Along with second husband and manager Narvel Blackstock, McEntire built an empire that included a talent-management firm, a construction company, a horse farm, and a jet charter service. She made her film debut in the 1990 science-fiction thriller *Tremors.* Then, in March 1991, the euphoria of success was abruptly in-

AP/WIDE WORLD

terrupted when a plane carrying her tour manager and seven band members crashed near San Diego, Calif. McEntire was criticized when, within a month of their deaths, she was back on stage performing with new musicians. She answered the criticism—first by explaining that work helped her deal with the loss, then by releasing the album *For My Broken Heart*. The album paid tribute to the crash victims.

During 1994 her book remained on the *New York Times* best-seller list for 16 weeks. To date McEntire had won at least 30 major awards and sold more than 20 million albums.

(ANTHONY G. CRAINE)

Mbeki, Thabo

On May 10, 1994, Thabo Mbeki was sworn in as first deputy president in the first democratically elected government of South Africa. Regarded as a person of original thought and considerable diplomatic and political skills, Mbeki combined these attributes with urbanity, charm, and calmness as well as toughness.

Mbeki was born in Idutywa, Transkei, on June 18, 1942. His father, a longtime leader in the Eastern Cape African National Congress (ANC), was sentenced to life imprisonment on Robben Island with Nelson Mandela in 1964, released in November 1987, and named deputy president of the Senate in 1994.

Mbeki attended schools in Transkei, including the well-known Lovedale secondary school in Alice. He joined the ANC Youth League in 1956, and in 1959 he participated in a student strike that caused the school to be closed. Already he had impressed observers with his leadership qualities; "he was a very good judge of people" recalled one.

Continuing studies at home, he was also active in the ANC after it was banned in South Africa in 1960. He served (1961) as secretary of the African Students Association, left South Africa illegally in 1962, and enrolled at the University of Sussex, Brighton, England, from which he graduated with an M.A. in economics in 1966. He worked for the ANC in London (1967–70) and then underwent military training in the Soviet Union.

Though criticized in the late 1960s by ANC cadres in Africa for spending time in Europe, Mbeki moved rapidly up in the ANC hierarchy. From 1971 he served in Lusaka, Zambia, as assistant secretary to its Revolutionary Council, becoming the youngest member of the national executive (1975) and political secretary to Pres. Oliver Tambo (1978).

Though he once wrote that "modern capitalism has outlived its usefulness," Mbeki became identified with a more moderate position. When he became chairperson of the ANC in 1993, a South African newspaper complimented him as "the suave jet-setting intellectual."

During the 1970s Mbeki undertook missions for the ANC in Botswana, Swaziland, and Nigeria in order to work with black youth who had left South Africa. In the 1980s he played a key role in the discussions with South African businessmen in Lusaka in September 1985 and with other leading white South Africans in Dakar, Senegal, in July 1987, which paved the way toward South African Pres. F.W. de Klerk's initiation of negotiations with the ANC in 1990.

From 1990 Mbeki participated in those negotiations, which led to the adoption of a new interim constitution. In 1993 he was elected to succeed the ailing Tambo as ANC chairperson.

(MARTIN LEGASSICK)

Miller, Shannon

During the 1992 summer Olympic Games in Barcelona, Spain, a 15-year-old U.S. gymnast, Shannon Miller, drew worldwide notice by earning two silver medals and three bronzes—more than any other U.S. athlete won at Barcelona. By 1994 she had secured more Olympic and world championship medals than any other U.S. gymnast in history.

Miller was born on March 10, 1977, in Rolla, Mo. At an early age she began taking gymnastics classes and competing. She won her first junior division meet when she was 11, scoring three firsts at the 1988 U.S. Classic. When she was 13, she won the all-around title at the Catania Cup competition in Italy by gaining gold medals in the vault, beam, and floor-exercise events and a silver in the uneven bars. She continued to accumulate honours during the following years, frequently winning the all-around title.

Unlike many gymnasts, Miller did not have a specialty—she was noted for her versatility. At the 1991 world championships, she was the first-ever U.S. female gymnast to qualify for all four of the individual events. She succeeded in winning two silver medals there. After the Olympics, Miller really came into her own; from 1992 to 1994, she dominated women's gymnastics. She possessed the petite physical proportions that were ideally suited for the sport, and she was able to execute all the maneuvers with precise technical expertise. Her performances were also enhanced by her dynamic, yet graceful, ballet-inspired style.

In late 1994 she experienced some setbacks, however. At the Goodwill Games in St. Petersburg, Russia, she failed to take the all-around title; it was the first time in two years that anyone had been able to defeat her in that category. Even more devastating was the gold-medal sweep by another U.S. gymnast, Dominique Dawes, at the national gymnastics championships in August. Gymnastics enthusiasts murmured that Miller's age (17) and size (nearly 1.5 m [5 ft]—tall by gymnastics standards) had begun to be a handicap. In November she withdrew from the world team championships, citing exhaustion. With the 1996 Olympics drawing nearer, however, the history-making gymnast seemed determined to win her spot on the U.S. Olympic team.

(ELIZABETH LASKEY)

Mirren, Helen

Despite the fact that Helen Mirren had been an established and highly respected stage, screen, and television actress for more than two decades, it was not until she starred in "Prime Suspect," the highest rated PBS "Mystery" series show ever, that she gained her widest recognition in the United States. As Detective Chief Inspector Jane Tennison in the Emmy award-winning miniseries, she became—as *Newsweek* magazine put it—"the PBS pinup woman of the decade." Though considered sexy, she was not a stereotypical pinup, however. In "Prime Suspect" she was ruthless in her ambition, often looked exhausted, and could face the most gruesome of murder scenes without flinching. Hollywood was said to be interested in filming an American version of the miniseries but, ironically—and typically—Mirren's role would be played by someone thought to have more box-office appeal.

Mirren was born in London in 1946 of a Russian-born father (until she was 10 her last name was Mironoff) and a Scottish mother. When she was 18, she played Cleopatra in a National Youth Theatre production and attracted favourable attention, but she did not immediately pursue an acting career. Instead, at her parents' urging, she attended teacher-training college and qualified as a teacher. She then began to get acting jobs and before long joined the Royal Shakespeare Company. She spent a large part of the next 15 years there, appearing in such roles as Cressida in *Troilus and Cressida* and Cleopatra in *Antony and Cleopatra*. She also spent a year touring Africa and North America with Peter Brook's experimental theatre troupe.

Mirren's motion-picture career began with *A Midsummer Night's Dream* in 1968. She followed that with appearances in over 20 more films, among them *The Long Good Friday* (1980), *Excalibur* (1981), *Cal* (1984), for which she won the best actress award at the Cannes Film Festival, *White Nights* (1985), *The Mosquito Coast* (1986), the controversial *The Cook, The Thief, His Wife, and Her Lover* (1989), and *The Hawk* (1994). In addition to the three "Prime Suspect" miniseries, her television credits include "The Country Wife," "Blue Remembered Hills," and "Cause Célèbre."

In 1994 Mirren returned to the London stage with a brilliant portrayal of the mercurial, love-struck Natalya Petrovna in Ivan Turgenev's *A Month in the Country*. Her film *The Madness of King George* was released late in the year, and a fourth "Prime Suspect" miniseries was being planned.   (BARBARA WHITNEY)

Morceli, Noureddine

"I am gifted by God," Noureddine Morceli was frequently heard to say. By the end of 1994 the Algerian track star's accomplishments had reached proportions befitting his statement. In August, after breaking the outdoor world record for 3,000 m (7 min 25.11 sec), he could claim five middle-distance world records. The others were (outdoor) the 1,500 m (3 min 28.86 sec) and the mile (3 min 44.39 sec) and (indoor) the 1,000 m (2 min 15.26 sec) and the 1,500 m (3 min 34.16 sec).

Morceli was named Athlete of the Year by *Track & Field News* in 1993 and 1994 and by the International Athletic Foundation in 1994. In that two-year period, he lost only once, at 800 m. As he set his sights on more records, most notably the 800-m, the 2,000-m, and 5,000-m events, his driving force was a deeply rooted dedication to bring glory to his country and Islam.

Morceli and his twin sister, Zahia, were born Feb. 20, 1970, in Tenes, Alg. They and their seven siblings were raised in strict adherence to the tenets of Islam, and Morceli's religious devotion remained strong. During the sacred holy days of Ramadan he would fast from sunrise to sunset despite the rigours of training.

Morceli claimed he could not remember when he did not want to run. At the age of seven he was inspired by his brother Abderrahmane, a world-class runner who finished fourth in the 1,500 m in the 1977 World Cup. Later his brother would become Morceli's coach. In the early 1980s Morceli came to idolize Said Aouita, a Moroccan who won the gold medal in the 5,000 m in the 1984 Olympics Games.

By age 17 Morceli had taken second place in the 1,500 m in the world junior championships. A year later he enrolled at Riverside (Calif.) Community College, which had been recommended for its coaching and track facilities. He spent two years there, at the end of which he had run the world's fastest 1,500 m for 1990. From that time there was no stopping him. At age 20 he was ranked first in the world in the 1,500 m. In 1992 he added the outdoor world record for the 1,500 m, in 1993 for the mile, and in 1994 for the 3,000 m.

As Morceli looked forward to the 1995 season, sportswriters unabashedly proclaimed him the greatest runner in the world or even the greatest of all time. Perhaps his spirit was best exemplified

by his winning performance in the 1994 Grand Prix. Racked with flu, weakened and hacking, he not only ran but left the field behind at the finish.
(MARVIN MARTIN)

Murayama, Tomiichi

The election in June 1994 of Tomiichi Murayama as Japan's first Socialist prime minister in 47 years surprised everyone, including himself. With no previous experience in government or international affairs and little economic expertise, the self-effacing Murayama, the third prime minister in a year, was viewed as another titular head of another shaky coalition. An unorthodox alliance was formed between the Social Democratic Party of Japan (SDPJ) and their ideological foes in the Liberal-Democratic Party (LDP). The two groups that over the years had opposed each other on such vital issues as diplomacy, security, and taxation, now joined forces to block the ambitions of LDP renegade Ichiro Ozawa and to keep at bay the increasingly powerful reformists. The dubious arrangement was viewed as an opportunistic sell-out and a shameless grab for power.

Against all predictions, however, the new government did well during its first months in office. Various contested political and economic reforms were cleared and trade agreements approved. Murayama's deft pragmatism on key policy issues guided the Socialists to tough sacrifices and made them come to terms with such realities as Japan's post–World War II military posture in the proliferation of UN peacekeeping missions, and the use of nuclear power. The deep split between his own party and the LDP was papered over by concessions on these issues, but by year's end Murayama once more looked vulnerable with the unraveling of unity within his own party and divisions emerging within the coalition while the opposition gained new coherence. Although the LDP and the SDPJ moved closer at the centres of power, their local organizations remained far apart. This boded ill for the 1995 elections, which were to be contested under a new electoral system that depended on strategic cooperation.

Murayama was born in Oita prefecture on March 3, 1924, one of 11 children born to a poor fisherman. After graduating from Meiji University, Tokyo, in 1946, he returned to Oita to work as an activist in the local fishermen's union. The majority of Murayama's political career was spent in relative obscurity. He worked his way up from councilman in 1955 to prefectural assemblyman in 1963, then was elected to the lower House of the Diet (parliament) in 1972, where he served seven terms. Murayama moved into the limelight when, as a compromise candidate, he was coaxed into the chairmanship of the fractious SDPJ in September 1993. To his critics, the main assets of the prime minister seemed to be a lack of firm policies and the manner of a kind, bushy-browed grandpa. But he also profited from a good understanding of parliamentary tactics. Murayama's habits were homespun and modest, untainted by the sex and money scandals that had undone his predecessors.   (GERD LARSSON)

Nakajima, Hiroshi

In January 1988 the executive board of the World Health Organization (WHO), reviewed the credentials of various candidates before recommending that Hiroshi Nakajima be elected WHO's fourth director general. Four months later the general assembly of WHO approved the recommendation and on July 21 Nakajima became the first Japanese to head a United Nations agency.

Nakajima was born in Chiba City on May 16, 1928. He studied at Tokyo Medical College and the University of Paris, where he specialized in neuro-psychopharmacology. After joining WHO in 1973, he spent several years at the organization's headquarters in Geneva. From 1979 to 1988 he was assigned to the Philippines, where he carried out WHO's health programs as director of its Western Pacific region. As his second term in Manila was drawing to a close, WHO was preparing to celebrate its 40th anniversary and choose a replacement for Halfdan Mahler of Denmark, whose third five-year term as director general was due to expire in May 1988. WHO's

executive board reviewed Nakajima's record of service and concluded that he had the qualifications to succeed Mahler.

Some months after assuming office, Nakajima returned to Japan to ask for greater cooperation and assistance. He also urged the government to be more aggressive in promoting WHO's health programs. Nakajima launched campaigns to fight infectious diseases, especially AIDS, malaria, tuberculosis, and dengue fever. He also put great emphasis on preventive medicine in the form of vaccinations for children. His enthusiasm for such programs derived in part from his visits to remote areas in Africa and elsewhere.

Nakajima's election to a second term seemed to be taken for granted until June 1992, when Muhammad Abdelmoumene, an Algerian neurosurgeon, announced his candidacy for director general. (He had been second in command at WHO until Nakajima fired him). Abdelmoumene's chief support came from the U.S., France, and other European countries. An unexpectedly bitter battle ensued. While Japan lobbied hard in support of Nakajima, his critics charged that he lacked management skills, leadership qualities, and an ability to formulate and enunciate ideas. Nakajima was also accused of bypassing budgetary procedures in allocating WHO funds. Critics claimed that, because of such "problems," WHO was in disarray and morale was low in regional offices and research agencies. At the same time, some Western media accused Japan of threatening to slash imports from less developed countries that did not support Nakajima's reelection. Japan vehemently denied this and all the other charges. In January 1993 WHO's executive board recommended (18–13) that Nakajima be given a second term. When the World Health Assembly convened in May 1993, Japan and its Third World allies prevailed. Nakajima was reelected by a vote of 93–58. In August 1994 he traveled to Japan for the 10th international conference on AIDS. Among the 10,000 public health officials, researchers, patients, and journalists in attendance were representatives of WHO, who had prepared extensive data on the current status of AIDS around the world.

(TAKUJI MIWA)

Nasrin, Taslima

In early August 1994 the Bangladeshi feminist author Taslima Nasrin, disguised in the traditional shrouding dress of Muslim women, made her way through Dhaka and onto a plane. Thus began her flight to sanctuary in Sweden. Left behind was a major fundamentalist Islamic uprising demanding her death for "blasphemous" writings and statements. Militant Muslims had issued a series of *fatwas*, or religious decrees, against Nasrin, and a bounty was offered to her killer.

Nasrin had been enraging strict Muslims for several years. In her columns, poems, and fiction, she wrote withering diatribes against the oppression of women and the Islamic code that made them virtually the chattel of men. Her subject matter became increasingly sexual, and her condemnation of men was unrelenting. She wore her hair short, smoked cigarettes, and eschewed women's traditional Muslim dress. In 1992 fundamentalists attacked bookstores carrying her works.

It was not until the fall of 1993 that she became an international cause célèbre. At that time the first *fatwa* was issued against her in reaction to her novel *Lajja* (1993; *Shame*), which depicts the persecution of a Hindu family by Muslims.

The real fundamentalist explosion came in May 1994, when she was quoted in the Calcutta *Statesman* as saying that the Qur'an "should be revised thoroughly." This brought larger and more vociferous demonstrations, demanding that the government put Nasrin to death. She insisted that her statement referred to the Shari'ah, the Islamic code of law, rather than the Qur'an itself. The outcry against her went unabated, however, and the government called for her arrest, invoking a 19th-century blasphemy law. After about two months in hiding, Nasrin appeared in court. She was released on bail and allowed to keep her passport. A few days later she left the country. In Sweden she remained in hiding while stat-

SHAHIDUL ALAM—DRIK PICTURE LIBRARY

STEPHEN DUNN—ALLSPORT

ing that, when it was safe, she would return to Bangladesh to continue her battle for women's rights. The Bangladeshi government, meanwhile, sought a court order for her return. Unfazed, she went even further and in November declared that the Qur'an had only historical value.

Nasrin was born Aug. 25, 1962, in the town of Mymensingh, then in East Pakistan. Her father was a doctor, and she also became a doctor, working in a family planning clinic in Mymensingh until she was reassigned to a government clinic in Dhaka in 1990. She left the national medical service in 1993. Nasrin was married and divorced twice.

Comparisons with the author Salman Rushdie, also in hiding from Islamic fundamentalists, were inevitable, but Nasrin made a clear distinction between herself and Rushdie. In October 1993 she was quoted as saying, "He has apologized. I have not and will not."   (MARVIN MARTIN)

Novak, Michael

The modern state "is an overpromiser and an underachiever and ultimately a fraud. It is bound to disappoint, to embitter, to divide, to engender corrosive cynicism." These provocative remarks were made by Michael Novak, lay theologian, economist, and political philosopher, at the announcement in March of his having been selected 1994 recipient of the Templeton Prize for Progress in Religion. Established in 1972 by financier John Marks Templeton, the award—the largest annual monetary prize in the world—was worth about $1 million in 1994.

Novak's works crossed boundaries in political ideology and subject matter. He supported the presidential campaigns of both George McGovern and Ronald Reagan, was an active critic of both the Vietnam War and the American Catholic bishops' pastoral letters on nuclear weapons and the U.S. economy, and wrote on subjects ranging from ethnicity to sports.

Novak was born on Sept. 9, 1933, in a blue-collar community in Johnstown, Pa. He graduated from Holy Cross Seminary at the University of Notre Dame, Stonehill College in North Easton, Mass., and Gregorian University in Rome. He transferred to Catholic University in Washington, D.C., in 1958 and left the Congregation of Holy Cross in 1960, within months after ordination as a priest. He was accepted to Harvard on a graduate fellowship later that year and published his first novel, *The Tiber Was Silver,* in 1961.

Novak covered the Second Vatican Council for several periodicals in 1963–64 and wrote a major report on the second session, *The Open Church* (1964). He became a professor of religious studies at Stanford University that year, and in 1967 visited three of his students in Vietnam, where

he also served as a monitor of national elections. From 1968 to 1972 he taught at the State University of New York at Old Westbury.

During the 1970s Novak helped launch the Hastings Institute, a study centre for bioethics, and a humanities program for the Rockefeller Foundation and accepted the post of resident scholar in religion and public policy for the American Enterprise Institute in Washington, a position he still held in 1994. His writings appeared regularly in both the liberal journal *Christianity and Crisis* and the conservative *National Review.*

By the 1980s Novak was widely considered a "neoconservative," a former leftist now critical of that political perspective. In 1981 he was appointed U.S. ambassador for the UN Human Rights Commission. His 1982 book, *The Spirit of Democratic Capitalism,* was considered a seminal work in the theology of economics; other works include *Belief and Unbelief* (1965), *Vietnam: Crisis of Conscience* (1967, with Rabbi Abraham J. Heschel and Protestant theologian Robert McAfee Brown), and *The Catholic Ethic and the Spirit of Capitalism* (1993).   (DARRELL J. TURNER)

Olajuwon, Hakeem

In June 1994 Nigerian-American basketball player Hakeem ("The Dream") Olajuwon made his long-time dream come true by leading the Houston Rockets to victory in the National Basketball Association (NBA) championship series over the New York Knicks. As his first championship title, it capped a milestone year in which he was named Most Valuable Player, Defensive Player of the Year (for the second time), and MVP of the NBA finals. Extremely versatile throughout the regular season, he was a top-ranking player in the major categories of scoring points (27.3 per game), capturing rebounds (11.9), blocking shots (3.71), and making steals (1.6).

The 2.13-m, 116-kg (7-ft, 255-lb) centre, whose surname Olajuwon in his native Yoruban language means "being on top," was no stranger to these heights. During his 10-year career in the NBA, he played in nine all-star games and repeatedly led the league in blocked shots and rebounds.

Olajuwon's ascendancy as one of the finest players in the league coincided with the reemergence of the centre as the dominant position in the NBA. Not since the late 1970s had a centre—generally a team's tallest player—led a club to the NBA finals. For almost two decades team leaders had been smaller guards and forwards, such as superstar guard Michael Jordan of the Chicago Bulls, who retired in 1993. The first season after Jordan's retirement from basketball culminated in a championship matchup between two of the best centres in the league—Olajuwon and the Knicks's Patrick Ewing.

Hakeem Abdul Olajuwon was born on Jan. 21, 1963, in Lagos, Nigeria, where his family owned a cement business. Until age 15 he was unfamiliar with the sport of basketball, instead playing association football (soccer) and team handball at Moslem Teachers College in Lagos. Two years later he was recruited to play basketball in the U.S. with the National Collegiate Athletic Association (NCAA) at the University of Houston, Texas. In his first collegiate season, the Houston Cougars competed in the semifinals of the 1982 NCAA tournament. The next year, Houston returned to the Final Four but lost the championship game; even so, Olajuwon was awarded the Final Four MVP. In 1984 Houston again advanced to the final game, and again the championship title eluded Olajuwon, who battled his rival Ewing, centre for the victorious Georgetown Hoyas.

Olajuwon left college when he was selected first in the 1984 NBA draft, two spots ahead of Jordan, with whom, a decade later, he shared a life-time field-goal percentage of .516. In Olajuwon's first season with the Houston Rockets, the team reached the play-offs, and in his second year they narrowly failed to clinch the championship. His dream was finally fulfilled in 1994 when Houston defeated New York 90–84 in the final game of the seven-game series.   (TOM MICHAEL)

Ozawa, Ichiro

Ichiro Ozawa, architect of Japan's unfolding political realignment, lost his hold on the levers of government with the formation of the new Socialist-led government in June 1994. Most observers expected Ozawa to be back in control following elections in 1995. He was, after all, thought to be the most influential politician Japan had produced in recent years and the only one with a clear-cut vision of where he was headed.

Ozawa was born into the family of a powerful party politician on May 24, 1942. At 27 he inherited a lower house seat for the Iwate prefecture. After studying economics at Keio University, Tokyo, and law at Nihon University, Tokyo, Ozawa was primed for a political career. When his father died in 1968, he hitched his fortunes to Kakuei Tanaka, a Liberal-Democratic Party (LDP) strongman and onetime prime minister. Ozawa stayed close to Tanaka despite his involvement in bribery scandals, then shifted his allegiance to the new king-maker, Shin Kanemaru. Taking his cue from these backroom power brokers, Ozawa became a prodigious fund-raiser.

In the late 1970s, Ozawa served as vice minister of the Science and Technology Agency and of Construction. He was also minister of home affairs (1985–86) in the Cabinet of Prime Minister Yasuhiro Nakasone. From 1989 to 1991 he held the post of secretary-general of the LDP. After walking out on his own party in the summer of 1993 over the question on political reform, Ozawa put together Shinseito (Japan Renewal Party)—a seven-group coalition that toppled the Liberal Democrats, who had held power for 38 years. Through the subsequent administrations of prime ministers Morihiro Hosokawa and Tsutomu Hata, which passed the electoral reforms he had sought, Ozawa was top policymaker. His dictatorial management came under fire, however, after the Social Democratic Party of Japan left the ruling coalition in April 1994, thereby forcing it to resign. Ozawa then set up the Kaikaku (Reform) parliamentary group in order to launch a major new anti-LDP party. Consequently, Ozawa was a prime mover in organizing Shinshinto (New Frontier Party), a merger of nine political parties, which was formally inaugurated on December 10.

Ozawa's grand goals, to create "real parliamentary politics" and a new foreign policy, had been taking shape for two decades. He laid out his prescription for national renewal in his best-selling book, *Blueprint for a New Japan.* It called for Japan to become "a normal nation" and assume responsibilities in the international community, not only as an economic power but also as a political and military one. Ozawa urged Japan to be aggressive in seeking a permanent seat on the UN Security Council and to amend the post-World War II constitution, which prohibited the country from military engagements, so that Japan could participate in UN peacekeeping missions that involved actual or potential conflict. To free Japan from bureaucratic stranglehold, he wanted decentralization and deregulation. He also envisaged new political stability with two big central parties alternating in office and a strengthened presidential-style prime minister heading a British-style Cabinet. Only time would tell how successful Ozawa's plans for Japan would be.

(GERD LARSSON)

Pasqua, Charles

At the end of 1994 things were looking good for Interior Minister Charles Pasqua, France's *premier flic,* or "top cop." The international assassin Carlos "the Jackal" was safely under lock and key, the French government had scored victories against Algerian and Kurdish terrorists, and he had virtually run the government during the vacation month of August. Even with his reputation as a tough law-and-order advocate whose main concern had been the stemming of illegal Arab immigration and Islamic activism, Pasqua nevertheless moved comfortably among the more traditional politicians, including Socialist Pres. François Mitterrand, and was a key factor in the Socialist-conservative "cohabitation" government. Together with Prime Minister Édouard Balladur, Pasqua topped the polls as France's most popular politician.

Pasqua was born on April 18, 1927, in Grasse on the French Riviera, the younger son of Corsican parents. His father, a policeman, was a member of the Resistance, as was an uncle who was deported by the Nazis in 1942. By age 15 Pasqua was a courier for the local Resistance network. He never completed his law studies, instead becoming a jack-of-all-trades (a wine trader, a private detective, and eventually sales director for the pastis company Ricard). His colourful Marseillais accent later became a crucial element of his popularity, although it had earned him many snubs during his early political career.

By the late 1940s he was an active militant in Gen. Charles de Gaulle's Rally of the French People. Pasqua created the Service d'Action Civique (SAC) in 1958 to protect Gaullist personalities from terrorist bombings and attacks by French-Algerian right-wing colonists. By the time SAC leaders had been proved to have been involved in a series of gory murders in 1973, Pasqua had long left their leadership, but these associations came often to haunt him. Neither Pres. Georges Pompidou nor his successor, Valéry Giscard d'Estaing, offered him a ministerial portfolio.

When Prime Minister Jacques Chirac resigned in 1976, Pasqua became his main ally within the neo-Gaullist party Rally for the Republic. A brilliant campaigner and political strategist, he helped Chirac win the crucial job of mayor of Paris in 1977, then masterminded a series of attacks to challenge Giscard that cost the latter the presidency in the 1981 elections. Once Giscard was out of the way, Chirac was established as the natural leader of the right wing, and he duly appointed Pasqua as his interior minister in 1986. When Mitterrand won the presidency, Pasqua forged a good relationship with Balladur. In 1993 Pasqua was instrumental in convincing Chirac to refuse another cohabitation prime ministership, suggesting Balladur in his place.

By year-end 1994 Pasqua had still not announced whether he would support Chirac or Balladur in the May 1995 presidential election, while his own name started appearing in polls as a possible candidate. Now the strongest kingmaker in France, he was expected to support the candidate that would promise him the office of prime minister.   (ANNE-ELLSABETH MOUTET)

Pearl Jam

One of the most popular rock bands in the United States, Pearl Jam not only wrote songs about perceived injustices but also, in June and July 1994, actually testified before a congressional subcommittee about such matters. For their summer concert tour the group planned to set ticket prices at about $20, well below the typical rate of $50, simultaneously hoping to scale the average service fee of $6 down to less than $2. When Ticketmaster Corp., the nation's largest ticket broker, refused to comply with the service-fee reduction, the band canceled its summer tour and in May filed a complaint with the U.S. Department of Justice, asserting that Ticketmaster held a national monopoly on ticket distribution.

It was not the first time that Pearl Jam had challenged convention, nor was it the last. In an unusual move the band's third studio album, *Vitalogy,* was released as a vinyl record in November 1994, a couple of weeks before the compact disc was made available. Despite their superstar stature as a band that typically performed sold-out shows in large sports arenas, they occasionally scheduled last-minute concerts at small venues and experimented with alternative forms of ticket distribution—such as organizing ticket lotteries (thus bypassing Ticket Master), imposing two-ticket limits on sales, and offering local fan-club members opportunities to purchase tickets before the general public.

The real power of Pearl Jam, of course, lay in their angst-ridden music and intense onstage showmanship. The most visible member of the group, vocalist Eddie Vedder (b. Dec. 23, 1965, Evanston, Ill.), wrote despairing lyrics about adolescent abuse that complemented his brooding baritone voice. Other members included guitarists Stone Gossard and Mike McCready and bassist Jeff Ament. Drummers Dave Krusen and Dave Abbruzzese left the band in 1991 and 1994, respectively.

Pearl Jam, named after a preserve Vedder's great-grandmother made, was formed in 1991 in Seattle, Wash., at the epicentre of the burgeoning grunge scene in alternative rock. Gossard and Ament had previously played together in Seattle with the bands Green River (1984–88) and Mother Love Bone (1988–90). After being joined by McCready, the trio circulated a demo tape of Gossard's music that caught the attention of Vedder, then living in San Diego, Calif. The tape formed the basis of the band's first album, *Ten,* which, after its release in September 1991, became one of the most successful debuts of a rock group.

Pearl Jam's stock rose even higher with their subsequent concert tours, music videos, and various musical side projects. Their second album, *Vs.,* met with even greater critical acclaim and popularity than *Ten* had, instantly topping the music charts and selling 350,000 copies on the first day of its release in October 1993. In another unconventional move, the album was issued without accompanying singles or music videos.

(TOM MICHAEL)

Prescott, John

In an era when politicians in many countries were becoming as bland and manufactured as processed cheese, many people took special pleasure in John Prescott's election as deputy leader of the U.K.'s Labour Party in July 1994. Prescott's robust manner, working-class roots, and trade union background provided an ideal foil for the party's new leader, the middle-class, Oxford-educated lawyer Tony Blair.

Prescott was born on May 31, 1938, at Prestatyn, North Wales. His grandfather was a coal miner; his father a railwayman. After leaving school at the age of 15, Prescott worked for two years as a trainee chef and then as a steward (1955–63) on Cunard Line passenger ships. He became active in the Labour Party and the National Union of Seamen. In March 1966 he stood unsuccessfully for the House of Commons. Three months later he helped to organize a seamen's strike, although Labour Prime Minister Harold Wilson condemned the "tightly-knit group of politically motivated men" behind the strike.

Wilson's rebuke, however, did nothing to prevent Prescott's being nominated for the safe Labour constituency of Hull East, which he won

K.N. NG/EDIE BASKIN—ONYX

in 1970. Prescott displayed many of the traits of a left-winger, notably in his opposition to the U.K. membership in the European Communities. He was never a standard, bash-the-party-leadership left-winger, however, and by 1981 he began to distance himself from the far left. In 1983 he backed Neil Kinnock's campaign for the party leadership and was rewarded with a place in Kinnock's shadow cabinet. In 1988 relations between the two men came close to a breaking point when Prescott unsuccessfully challenged Kinnock's incumbent deputy, Roy Hattersley, for his job.

After Labour lost the 1992 general elections, Kinnock and Hattersley stepped down, and Prescott stood again for the deputy leadership. He was defeated by Margaret Beckett but soon established a rapport with Labour's new leader, John Smith. (*See* OBITUARIES.) In the fall of 1993, Smith entrusted Prescott with making a speech to close the debate on reforms to the party constitution. Prescott's syntax and grammar were terrible, but his passion swayed a number of undecided votes, and he was deservedly given the credit for the victory.

When Smith died suddenly in May 1994, Prescott ran for both leader and deputy leader. Blair won the leadership easily, but Prescott defeated Beckett for the deputy leadership by 57–43%. He quickly proved an indispensable ally to Blair, supporting him in his policy initiatives and launching a campaign to overhaul Labour's organization and increase its membership.

(PETER KELLNER)

Price, Nick
In 1982, 26-year-old Nick Price held a three-stroke lead with six holes left to play in one of golf's premier events, the British Open. But then he faltered, and Tom Watson beat him by one stroke. Watson, having also won the 1982 U.S. Open, became only the sixth player ever to win consecutive major tournaments. Twelve years would pass before that exclusive back-to-back club would admit another member: Price, who endured a lengthy period of frustration before being named the best golfer in the world in 1994.

Nicholas Raymond Leige Price was born Jan. 28, 1957, in Durban, South Africa. His family moved to Southern Rhodesia (now Zimbabwe), where he began playing golf at the age of eight. At age 17 he traveled to the U.S. and won the Junior World tournament in San Diego, Calif. Price spent the next year (1975) playing on the South African and European tours as an amateur. He served two years in the Rhodesian Air Force as a pilot and then rejoined the European tour as a professional in 1977. He joined the Professional Golfers' Association of America (PGA) tour full-time in 1983 and showed great promise, winning the World Series of Golf that year by four strokes over Jack Nicklaus. In the years that followed, Price was hailed by his peers as one of the best, and most likable, golfers on the tour. From 1983 to 1990 he earned nearly $1.9 million. After winning the World Series, however, he did not capture another PGA tour event for eight years.

Finally, in 1991 his name topped the leader board twice, and he earned a career-high $714,-000. But it was his first-place finish at the PGA championship in 1992 that marked the beginning of an incredible 24-month run in which he won 16 times and finished in the top 10 in 37 of 59 tournaments. The 15th win came in July 1994 at the British Open in Turnberry, Scotland, where Price avenged his 1982 heartbreak by sinking a spectacular 18-m (60-ft) putt for an eagle on the second-to-last hole, a shot that clinched his victory. Then, in August at the PGA championship in Tulsa, Okla., he shot an 11-under-par 269—the lowest score ever recorded in a U.S. major tournament (Masters, U.S. Open, and PGA)—to win by an amazing margin of six strokes and become the seventh golfer to win back-to-back majors. The win propelled Price to the top position of the Sony world rankings. The next day he underwent minor surgery. Less than a month later he won the Bell Canadian Open at Oakville, Ont. Price finished 1994 as the top money winner of the PGA tour, having earned nearly $1.5 million.

(ANTHONY G. CRAINE)

Proulx, E. Annie
E. Annie Proulx did not follow the customary advice to writers to "write about what you know." She preferred to write about what interested her—what she would *like* to know—and she enjoyed going to new places and writing about what she found there. Thus, for her second novel, *The Shipping News,* she made a number of trips to the Newfoundland coast and just hung around—watching the people, listening to them, and absorbing the atmosphere. She learned about the traditional life there and the ways that life was changing, and she found names for her characters in phone books and on bulletin boards. Her methods proved successful. For her novel about a Brooklyn, N.Y.-born newspaperman who moves to Newfoundland with his two daughters and his aunt, Proulx—after having already won the *Chicago Tribune*'s Heartland Prize, the *Irish Times* International Fiction Prize, and the National Book Award—was the recipient of the 1994 Pulitzer Prize for Fiction.

Edna Annie Proulx was born Aug. 22, 1935, in Norwich, Conn., and grew up in various towns in New England and North Carolina. She earned two degrees in history—a bachelor's degree from the University of Vermont in 1969 and a master's from Sir George Williams University, Montreal, in 1973. She was married and divorced three times, raised three sons, and for 19 years supported herself by writing magazine articles. She had written her first story at the age of 10, while she was sick in bed with chicken pox, and her first published short story appeared when she was in her early 20s. When she later returned to writing stories, they were all published, and in 1988 a collection, *Heart Songs and Other Stories,* came out.

At the suggestion of an editor, she turned to novel writing. *Postcards*—which, in its illustration of the years from World War II to the 1990s in the rural U.S., features a New England farm family losing its home—was published in 1992. For that book, Proulx in 1993 captured the PEN/Faulkner Award for Fiction.

Proulx credited her mother, a painter, with teaching her how to see—to look carefully at the smallest detail of everything—and she learned her lessons well. Her work was highly praised for its vivid depiction of locale and character and, in addition, for its dark, offbeat humour. As of 1994 a third novel was more than half-finished, and several others already formed in her mind were waiting their turn. Proulx obviously would be taking many more trips to interesting new places.

(BARBARA WHITNEY)

Qiao Shi
If the arrangements for political succession that senior leader Deng Xiaoping (Teng Hsiao-p'ing) had in place in 1994 came unstuck, 70-year-old Qiao Shi (Ch'iao Shih) would have a good shot at the top leadership position in China. Qiao Shi was number three in the Chinese political hierarchy, a member of the powerful Political Bureau Standing Committee, and chairman of the National People's Congress (NPC). He had used the latter post to enhance his domestic political standing and acquire needed foreign exposure.

Born in Shanghai in 1924 as Jiang Zhitong (Chiang Chih-t'ung), he changed his name after joining the Communist Party of China (CPC) in 1940. A graduate of East China Associated University, Qiao Shi worked in the Shanghai CPC underground before 1949. He then spent several years in East China and the Northeast, working for a time at the Anshan Iron and Steel Co. His specialty was apparently security and intelligence. In 1963 Qiao Shi was transferred to the CPC headquarters in Beijing (Peking). For the next 20 years he worked in the International Liaison Department (ILD) of the Central Committee, becoming its head in 1982. Responsible for managing relations with other communist and revolutionary parties, the ILD was in the thick of the intrigues and polemics that characterized the era of the cold war between China and the Soviet Union.

In 1982 Qiao Shi's career took off when he was elected to the Central Committee. He successively headed the party's General Office, Orga-

nization Department, Political and Legal Affairs Commission, and possibly the secret police and the People's Armed Police. Qiao Shi was elected to the Political Bureau in September 1985 and to its inner core, the Standing Committee, two years later. His most important post was that of secretary of the Central Discipline Inspection Commission in charge of attacking rampant corruption. In April 1986 Qiao Shi received his first government post as a deputy premier of the State Council. In 1992 he became chairman of the National People's Congress (China's nominal parliament) and, along with General Secretary Jiang Zemin (Chiang Tse-min) and Premier Li Peng (Li P'eng), one of the nation's ruling triumvirate.

During Qiao Shi's tenure, the NPC slowly became a forum for limited debate on policy issues. By emphasizing the need to strengthen China's legal order, Qiao Shi enhanced the role of the NPC and obliquely called into question the political primacy of the CPC. For this reason, student democracy leader Wang Dan (Wang Tan) remarked, "Although Qiao Shi is a master of illusions, it's possible that he could lead China toward more enlightened rule." In 1993, as head of China's parliament, Qiao Shi toured Southeast Asia, and in 1994 he visited Germany, Austria, Switzerland, Australia, New Zealand, Fiji, Argentina, and Brazil. If Jiang Zemin were to falter after Deng Xiaoping's death, Qiao Shi could become primus inter pares in a post-Deng collective leadership.

(STEVEN I. LEVINE)

Quindlen, Anna
In September 1994 *New York Times* syndicated columnist Anna Quindlen—stating that when she got comfortable in a job it was time to move on to the next challenge—announced that at the end of the year she would be leaving the paper to pursue a full-time career as a novelist. She had already had two novels published. Her first—*Object Lessons,* a coming-of-age story—appeared in 1991 and became a best-seller. The experience of temporarily dropping out of college to care for her mother as she was dying of cancer formed the basis of her second novel, *One True Thing* (1994). In addition, two collections of her columns and a children's book were published.

One of the most successful columnists in the U.S., Quindlen was valued for seeming to speak directly to each of her readers about the issues that concerned them, and she brought an insightful, personal view to political, especially gender, issues. Although she had been mentioned as a possible future *Times* executive editor, she felt that continuing her work at the paper would not leave time for the commitment she wanted to make to her fiction writing and to her family.

Quindlen was born July 8, 1953, in Philadelphia. She began her newspaper career as a part-time reporter for the *New York Post* when she was still a student at Barnard College, New York City, and her first story was published in *Seventeen* magazine when she was a junior. She received a B.A. degree in 1974 and went to work at the paper full-time. In 1977 she moved to the *New York Times* to be a general assignment and city hall reporter, and from 1981 to 1983, when she became deputy metropolitan editor, she wrote the biweekly column "About New York." In 1985 Quindlen left the *Times* to stay home with her two young sons and work on a novel, but she returned in late 1986 to write the "Life in the 30's" column. Within two years it was being published in some 60 newspapers. The birth of her daughter in late 1988 led her to quit again, but a year later she was lured back to the *Times,* this time with an offer to write a column on the op-ed page. "Public & Private" began early in 1990, and her popularity continued to grow. In 1992 Quindlen won the Pulitzer Prize for commentary, only the third woman to win the prize in that category.

In her final column, on December 14, Quindlen paid tribute to the "everyday angels" who, through their efforts to give help selflessly where it is needed, make it possible to believe in the essential goodness of people. "I leave you with good tidings of great joy," she wrote. "Those who shun the prevailing winds of cynicism and anomie can truly fly."

(BARBARA WHITNEY)

Reinsdorf, Jerry

It was a turbulent year for the American "national pastime" as players of major league baseball went on strike in August 1994 after failing to negotiate a new labour contract with team owners. During the strike many fans came to realize that professional baseball was no longer just a game but a fast-growing, multibillion-dollar monopoly that enjoyed an antitrust exemption. The one who perhaps best typified the modern sports executive was Jerry Reinsdorf, owner of the Chicago White Sox (from 1981) and of the Chicago Bulls (from 1985), a franchise of the National Basketball Association (NBA). He was one of the most powerful representatives of baseball's 28-team ownership bloc, who precipitated the strike with their proposal for a cap on players' salaries and for revenue-sharing that would aid ball clubs in smaller media markets.

Reinsdorf emerged in 1992 as one of the most persuasive owners in baseball, spearheading the replacement of baseball commissioner Fay Vincent with ally Bud Selig, owner of the Milwaukee Brewers. Reinsdorf was also an influential owner in the NBA. Over the wishes of the league in the early 1990s, he secured a lucrative television contract for the Bulls with the Chicago-based superstation WGN.

With an estimated personal worth between $60 million and $90 million, Reinsdorf was respected for his financial expertise, as well as for his winning teams. He helped transform the White Sox into division champions (1983 and 1993) and the Bulls into three-time NBA champions (1991–93). His dual sports holdings conveniently converged in 1993 when Bulls superstar Michael Jordan retired from basketball to pursue a lifelong dream to play professional baseball and Reinsdorf enrolled him in the White Sox minor-league system.

Despite these successes Reinsdorf was often vilified by fans for his laserlike focus on the economic bottom line. In 1988, threatening to relocate the White Sox to St. Petersburg, Fla., he persuaded Illinois politicians to help finance a new stadium, allowing him to tear down beloved Comiskey Park. The new publicly funded Comiskey Park, which opened in 1991, was subsidized by taxpayers and contained a large number of premium-priced seats. Similarly, in 1994 he unveiled the new United Center, featuring 216 luxury suites, to replace Chicago Stadium for the Bulls.

Reinsdorf was born in Brooklyn, N.Y., on Feb. 25, 1936. After graduating from George Washington University (B.A., 1957) and from Northwestern University Law School (1960), he became a lawyer for the Internal Revenue Service, where he arranged tax shelters for corporations. In 1973 he cofounded Balcor Co., one of the nation's first firms to specialize in real-estate partnerships. After it became a huge success, he sold it to American Express for $53 million in 1982; he eventually left the company in 1987.

(TOM MICHAEL)

Romário

Idolized by the public, the despair of authority—Brazilian association football (soccer) player Romário de Souza Faria was one of the sport's most colourful players. In 1994 he led Brazil to victory and won the Golden Ball as the most gifted performer in the World Cup.

Romário was born on Jan. 29, 1966, and brought up in Villa Pena, a Rio de Janeiro suburb. His first income was derived from cleaning car windshields at traffic lights. It was not until his father took him along to see the Olaria football club that any thoughts of a career in professional sports emerged.

He signed with Olaria and developed rapidly. In a friendly match against Vasco da Gama he scored four times, a feat that persuaded Vasco to sign him. He won two championships with the team and scored 73 goals in 123 matches. Selected for the 1988 Brazilian Olympic team, he was leading goal scorer in the competition, and Brazil took the silver medal. In 1989 Brazil won the América Cup, with Romário scoring the only goal in the final against Uruguay.

Romário then transferred to the Dutch club PSV Eindhoven. PSV captured the League and Cup championships in his first season (1987–88), though Romário was already giving clear indications that he wanted to make a name for himself, not necessarily for the team. His control, mobility, and vision—allied to strength and fine body balance plus a surprisingly long stride—made him a potent striker. But he was disinterested in training, which he considered a waste of energy, and was fined for throwing temper tantrums, failing to report on time, complaining of the cold, and flying to Rio de Janeiro at every conceivable excuse. Though immensely popular with spectators, he was disliked by his fellow players and made no attempt to learn Dutch. His goal-scoring prowess, however, was undeniable. In five seasons he scored 125 goals for PSV.

In March 1990, having already been banned from three internationals for being sent off against Chile for fighting, Romário broke his leg. He was clearly far from being match fit for the 1990 World Cup in Italy.

Romário had a disagreement with the Brazilian coach before the start of the qualifying matches for the 1994 World Cup because he wanted to select his own team. He was brought back for the crucial match with Uruguay and scored twice to guarantee Brazil a place in the finals. In the U.S. he behaved himself on and off the field and was the second-highest scorer, with five goals.

Had the World Cup matured him? Perhaps not. In August he reported back 23 days late for preseason training with the Spanish club Barcelona, to which he had transferred in 1993, and was fined £50,000. Romário said that he was overseeing his Romário Foundation, a project to help Rio street children.

(JACK ROLLIN)

Rose, Sir Michael

In January 1994 Lieut. Gen. Sir Michael Rose assumed one of the toughest and most delicate military commands in the world: leading the UN forces in Bosnia and Herzegovina. Within weeks he had won praise from around the world for his ability to combine diplomatic skills with military judgment.

Rose was born in Quetta, India (now in Pakistan), on Jan. 5, 1940. After studying at the University of Oxford and the Sorbonne, he was commissioned (1964) into the Coldstream Guards. He first saw active service in Aden (now part of Yemen), where the transition from colonial rule to independence (1967) was accompanied by considerable violence. In 1968 Rose joined the fabled Special Air Services (SAS), with whom he conducted a number of undercover operations in Northern Ireland, the Middle East, and East Asia. In 1976 he surfaced as a squadron commander in Northern Ireland. Although some British troops were accused of operating a shoot-to-kill policy, Rose acquired a reputation for insisting that all counterterrorist operations had to operate strictly within the law and under political control.

On April 30, 1980, six Arab terrorists occupied the Iranian embassy in London, seizing 27 hostages. Six days later, after the murder of one hostage and the breakdown of negotiations to secure the release of the rest, Rose led a rescue team of SAS officers. They abseiled into the embassy, freed all the remaining hostages, and killed five terrorists. The assault, shown live on television, greatly enhanced the reputation of the SAS in general and Rose in particular.

Two years later Rose played a prominent role in the recapture of the Falkland Islands/Islas Malvinas from Argentina. He led the operation that regained Mt. Kent, overlooking the capital, and subsequently negotiated the Argentine surrender that ended the war. In 1990 he was appointed director of the Army Staff College, with instructions to modernize its courses and shift its emphasis toward small-scale local wars and counterterrorist operations.

His appointment as UN commander in Bosnia gave him a chance to use his experience. He quickly became convinced that he did not have enough troops to guarantee keeping the peace. Partly as a result, he sought to talk, rather than fight, his way out of problems. This provoked criticism from some quarters that he was too slow to launch air strikes against Serbian positions.

Rose repeatedly called for an increase in his 10,000-strong force, especially the 3,700-strong British contingent. He also entered the argument over whether the UN should lift its arms embargo on Bosnia. He said that if the embargo were lifted, his troops would be placed in an impossible position and would have to withdraw. On October 17, the UN announced that Rose would leave Bosnia in January 1995, at the end of his 12-month term.

(PETER KELLNER)

Sanders, Barry

A favourite activity of fans of the National Football League (NFL) was to debate who was the best running back of all time. The usual candidates included Jim Brown, O.J. Simpson, and Walter Payton. But after the 1994 season, fans would have to give Barry Sanders serious consideration. In his sixth year with the Detroit Lions, Sanders rushed for a career high 1,883 yd on 331 carries, an average of 5.7 yd per carry. Not only did he lead the league in rushing, but his performance was the fourth best in NFL history.

A stocky, thick-legged back, Sanders could use power to defeat would-be tacklers, but his real gift was the darting feints and spins that left defenders grasping air. He could change direction seemingly without losing speed, and on the faster artificial grass he looked like a whirling dervish. Sanders was on the home carpet of the Silverdome when he had the best game of his pro career against the Tampa Bay Buccaneers on November 13, rushing for 237 yd on 26 carries.

Sanders was born July 16, 1968, in Wichita, Kan. A deeply religious person who tithed to his church in Wichita, he learned about the value of humility and hard work from his parents while growing up with eight sisters and two brothers. These lessons proved valuable when Sanders' talents were initially ignored. He had learned his quicksilver moves on the sandlots, but in high school his small stature of 1.73 m (5 ft 8 in) discouraged coaches from playing him at running back until the last five games of his senior year. The startling 1,417 yd that Sanders gained in those games, however, was enough to earn him a football scholarship to Oklahoma State University (OSU). For most of his first two years there Sanders found himself limited to returning kicks, while All-American halfback Thurman Thomas got the handoffs. Sanders was a junior in 1988 when he finally became the starting halfback and had what was probably the greatest single season in college football. He rushed for 2,628 yd—the best single-season rushing performance in the history of the National Collegiate Athletic Association—and broke 33 other records as well. Not surprisingly, Sanders easily won the Heisman Trophy that year as the nation's best college football player. When OSU was put on probation the next year, Sanders declared himself eligible for the professional draft and was selected by the Detroit Lions as the third overall pick.

Sanders' first year in the NFL was an enormous success. He rushed for 1,470 yd (a Detroit Lions single-season record), averaged more than 5 yd per carry, caught 24 passes, and scored 14 touchdowns. At the end of the season he was named rookie of the year and made the All-Pro team. Sanders had rushed for more than 1,000 yd in each of the first six years of his professional career, a feat exceeded only by Eric Dickerson.

(JAMES HENNELLY)

Santer, Jacques

"The right man in the right place at the right time," as he was called by British Prime Minister John Major, or the lowest common denominator, as others said of him, Jacques Santer came to the presidency of the European Commission as a compromise choice. He was selected for a five-year term by the European Council, the heads of government of the 12 member nations of the European Union (EU), at a special meeting on July 15, 1994, and confirmed by a majority of only 22 votes in the 567-seat European Parliament one week later. Santer was drafted after Major had vetoed the selection of Belgian Prime Minister Jean-Luc Dehaene, whose candidacy had been advanced by France and Germany.

Santer, who was reelected in June 1994 to his third term as prime minister of Luxembourg, would assume the reins of the EU administration in January 1995, at a crucial time in the EU's movement toward political and economic integration. The Maastricht Treaty, which established the ground rules for that integration, was scheduled for review in 1996. Several of the "Euroskeptical" signees had begun to waver as the Commission, Parliament, and member nations battled over sharing power. Even if Santer might lack the commanding presence of his predecessor, France's Jacques Delors (for 10 years the voice of EU centralization), his skills as a quiet conciliator would still be much in demand. It was under his guidance, during Luxembourg's six-month stewardships of the rotating presidency of the European Council, that essential agreements were reached—in 1985 and 1991—concerning a single economic market and the Maastricht Treaty, respectively. Santer's vision was of a federalized, "non-Napoleonic" Europe ("The more Europe is decentralized, the stronger it is," he said)—not the predominant view. Holding his own with influential Eurocrats such as the U.K.'s Sir Leon Brittan, within the Commission and outside it, would require statesmanship of the highest order.

Born on May 18, 1937, in Wasserbillig, Luxembourg, Santer graduated from the Athénée de Luxembourg, studied law at the Universities of Strasbourg and Paris (with a degree from the latter), and attended the Institute of Political Science in Paris. Shortly after beginning his law career, he entered politics, serving the Christian Social People's Party as its parliamentary secretary (1966–72; becoming Luxembourg's secretary of state for social and cultural affairs in the last year), secretary-general (1972–74), and ultimately president (1974–82). In 1975 he became a member of the European Parliament and was reelected in 1979 and 1984. He was elected Luxembourg's prime minister in 1984 and at different times during his three terms took on the additional portfolios of Finance and Communications, Treasury, and Cultural Affairs. From 1987 to 1990 he also assumed the leadership of the European People's Party, the coalition that united Christian Democratic and Christian Social parties in the European Parliament. (JEFF WALLENFELDT)

Sa'ud, al-Walid ibn Talal ibn Abdulaziz as-, Prince

In what was called a modern-day fairy tale, but also might turn out to be a shrewd business move, a wealthy prince in 1994 came to the rescue of an American company in trouble. Saudi Prince Walid made a large investment in Euro Disneyland Paris, which was suffering from severe financial difficulties, partly brought on by lower-than-expected attendance. The parent-company stock, Euro Disney S.C.A., had fallen by 20%, and the theme park had lost more than $1 billion since its opening in 1992. Prince Walid, the nephew of Saudi Arabia's King Fahd, invested $400 million in the troubled venture, part of his long-term goal of attaining $5 billion in wealth by 1998.

Prince al-Walid ibn Talal ibn Abdulaziz as-Sa'ud was born in 1954 in Riyadh, Saudi Arabia, and reared there and in Beirut, Lebanon. He attended Menlo College in Menlo Park, Calif., and Syracuse (N.Y.) University, where he studied business and social science. In 1980, allegedly with $15,000 given to him by his father and a 130-room palace against which he could borrow, Prince Walid set out to make his fortune by negotiating big deals at bargain prices. In 1990–91 he bought nearly a 15% interest in the Citicorp banking group for about $800 million, a sum that he parlayed into nearly $2 billion. In addition, he held an 11% interest in the Saks Fifth Avenue retail chain. As the chairman of United Saudi Commercial Bank, a small but highly efficient and profitable concern, Prince Walid led a number of takeovers, including the 1993 acquisition of Panda Supermarket Co., which, after merging with Al-Azizia Supermarket Co., recorded a 10-fold increase in profitability in the first six months of 1994. In July Prince Walid acquired a 50% interest in the Fairmont Group of hotels in the U.S., and in September he completed a deal for a 25% stake in Canada's Four Seasons Hotels. In October he successfully negotiated the takeover of Saudi Livestock Co.

Perhaps the prince's most highly publicized deal, however, was the 24% interest he bought in Euro Disneyland Paris. His plan was to turn the park around financially by investing another $100 million inthe construction of a nearby convention centre, which, it was thought, would help draw conventioneers and their families to the theme park. If all went well, both Prince Walid and Euro Disneyland Paris would benefit. (ANTHONY L. GREEN)

Schuller, Gunther

Of Reminiscences and Reflections by Gunther Schuller is a work filled with unique, changing sound colours, "a hazy exercise in luxuriant orchestration," according to one critic. Dedicated to Schuller's wife, who died in 1992, it was performed only by the Louisville Orchestra, conducted by the composer, before it won the 1994 Pulitzer Prize for musical composition. If only a comparative handful of people heard the work, many may have applauded the award, considering Schuller's extraordinarily diverse half century of composing, playing, producing, teaching, and conducting music.

Gunther Alexander Schuller, who was born in New York City on Nov. 22, 1925, began composing music at age 11, "which is rather late; I mean, Mozart started at three or four," and won the disapproval of his father, a violinist in the New York Philharmonic, because of his fondness for jazz. As "one of the original dropouts," Schuller left high school at 17 to play French horn in the Cincinnati Symphony Orchestra. While playing French horn in the orchestra of the Metropolitan Opera (1945–59), he wrote music for chamber groups and orchestras, including *Seven Studies on Themes of Paul Klee,* possibly his best-known work. As a "conservative radical" composer, he championed "third-stream" music, which joined jazz improvisation to classical composition, as in his *Conversations* and *Abstraction* for, respectively, the Modern Jazz Quartet and alto saxophonist Ornette Coleman with string quartets. He also composed the opera *The Visitation* during the height of the civil rights movement; it recast K., the protagonist of Franz Kafka's *The Trial,* as a contemporary African-American.

Schuller's preoccupation with American music resulted in the book *Early Jazz* (1968), the first volume of a proposed historical trilogy. As president of the New England Conservatory of Music (1967–77), he added jazz artists and a third-stream department to the faculty. He also organized a series of ensembles to preserve distinctively American music in danger of being neglected: bands to play swing music, country fiddle music, and the music of Duke Ellington and of the Paul Whiteman orchestra; the most noted of these groups was his New England Conservatory Ragtime Ensemble, a leading factor in the 1970s revival of ragtime music. After his conservatory years he composed his second, third, and fourth symphonies and several concertos, published the second volume of his history of jazz, *The Swing Era* (1989), and supervised the completion and performance of a major unfinished jazz work, *Epitaph,* by Charles Mingus.

In the 1990s Schuller composed, ran his GM recording company, and transcribed music and conducted for the Smithsonian Institution's Jazz Repertory project. The MacArthur Foundation "genius grant" that he received in 1991 had a five-year limit, but there seemed to be no limits to Schuller's energy and creative ingenuity. (JOHN LITWEILER)

Shalala, Donna Edna

As the debate over health care came to centre court in the U.S. Congress in 1994, one of the Clinton administration's key players was Secretary of Health and Human Services (HHS) Donna Shalala. Whether battling Beltway gridlock or opponents as a teenaged tennis champion, Shalala, a respected academic and the first woman to head a Big Ten university, had always been a fierce, principled competitor. Born on Feb. 14, 1941, in Cleveland, Ohio, where her father, a real-estate salesman, was one of the leaders of the Syrian-Lebanese community, Shalala had a strong female role model in her mother, a physical education teacher who attained a law degree while holding two jobs and raising Shalala and her twin sister.

After graduating from Western College for Women, Oxford, Ohio (B.A., 1962), Shalala served two years in the Peace Corps in Iran, then attended Syracuse (N.Y.) University (master of social sciences, 1968; Ph.D., 1970). She aspired to a career in journalism, but when a job interview with the *New York Times* ended with the advice that she seek a position with a small-town newspaper, Shalala pursued an academic career, teaching at the City University of New York's (CUNY's) Bernard M. Baruch College, then at Columbia University, New York City. She also served as a director and treasurer of the Municipal Assistance Corp., which helped rescue New York City from bankruptcy. From 1977 to 1980 she served in the administration of Pres. Jimmy Carter as an assistant secretary in the Department of Housing and Urban Development.

Returning to academia, Shalala became, at age 39, the president of Hunter College, CUNY. At Hunter she added to her reputation as a committed feminist by overseeing dramatic increases in the percentages of female and minority faculty and administrators. In 1988 she became the chancellor of the University of Wisconsin at Madison, one of the largest universities in the U.S. Confronted by a campus afflicted with racial tension, she instituted the "Madison Plan," which increased recruitment of minority students and faculty and reflected her commitment to a "multiethnic, multiracial, multicultural" academic environment. Also seeking to improve the university's image by reversing the woeful fortunes of its football team, she hired a new athletic director and a new head coach, who led the team to a Rose Bowl victory in January 1994. By that time, however, Shalala had moved on to head HHS, the nation's principal agency for protecting health and providing human services, with responsibility for administering Social Security, Medicare, the National Institutes of Health, and the Food and Drug Administration. Shalala has faced every challenge with the same determination that prompted New York Yankees' owner George Steinbrenner, the coach of the girls' softball team that Shalala once led to the city championship in Cleveland, to call her "one of the toughest competitors that I have ever seen." (JEFF WALLENFELDT)

Shoemaker, Carolyn and Eugene, and Levy, David

For six days between July 16 and 22, 1994, Carolyn Shoemaker, her husband Eugene, and fellow comet hunter David Levy peered anxiously through telescopes to watch the estimated 21 major fragments of the comet they had jointly discovered—Shoemaker-Levy 9—pummel the planet Jupiter. Following months of speculation as to what the impacts would entail, the event itself proved equal to the most optimistic predictions. From the atmosphere of a bruised and battered Jupiter arose tall, bright plumes that left broad, dark stains beneath them, providing a spectacular show for sky watchers around the world. (*See* ASTRONOMY.)

The team discovered the fragmented comet in orbit around Jupiter in March 1993 at the Palomar Observatory in southern California. The find was certainly not the first for the veteran comet spotters: as of late 1994 Carolyn had 32 comet discoveries to her credit, more than anyone alive and only five less than the all-time record held by the 19th-century amateur astronomer Jean-Louis Pons. Eugene (Gene to his acquaintances) was credited with 29, and Levy with 21, of which 13 were in collaboration with the Shoemakers.

Of the three team members only Gene was formally trained as a scientist. Born April 28, 1928, in Los Angeles, Calif., Eugene Merle Shoemaker received a bachelor's degree in geology from the California Institute of Technology and a doctorate from Princeton University. He worked for the U.S. Geological Survey (USGS) from 1948 to 1993, serving thereafter as scientist emeritus.

In the 1960s Gene established the astrogeology branch of the USGS and subsequently its astrogeology centre at Flagstaff, Ariz. He was noted for helping to confirm the impact origin (rather than volcanic origin) of the site now known as Meteor Crater in Arizona and for his work with the National Aeronautics and Space Administration (NASA) on lunar exploration missions.

Carolyn Spellman Shoemaker was born in Gallup, N.M., June 24, 1929. She received bachelor's and master's degrees from Chico (Calif.) State College, having studied history, political science, and English literature. She and Gene were married on Aug. 18, 1951. After teaching high school for a year, Carolyn remained at home to raise their three children. Not until the children left home did she begin helping her husband to search for asteroids and comets, a task at which she became an expert. In 1980 Carolyn accepted a position as a visiting scientist with the astrogeology branch of the USGS and in 1989 also began serving as research professor of astronomy at Northern Arizona University. Both Carolyn and Gene were on the staff of Lowell Observatory, Flagstaff.

Amateur astronomer David Levy met the Shoemakers in 1988 as a result of a comet he had discovered and they were tracking. Born in Montreal on May 22, 1948, Levy developed an interest in astronomy at an early age. In college, however, he studied English literature, receiving a bachelor's degree from Acadia (Nova Scotia) University and a master's degree from Queen's University, Kingston, Ont. A science writer by trade, he was the author of 11 books on astronomy, including his latest, *The Quest for Comets* (1994), and contributed a monthly column to the magazine *Sky and Telescope*. He noted that, although Shoemaker-Levy 9 had made a forceful impact on Jupiter, its reverberations on Earth were even greater, as the widely reported summer event rekindled popular interest in the starry skies above. (MARY JANE FRIEDRICH)

Soros, George

Whenever turbulence struck world money markets, financial dealers traditionally asked two questions: would currency values change and what would happen to interest rates? During the early 1990s a third question acquired equal importance: what was George Soros doing?

Soros' status as an almost mythical financier was established in September 1992, when the British government devalued the pound sterling. Through his Quantum group of companies, Soros had sold some $15 billion worth of sterling during the days preceding devaluation, much of it purchased with borrowed money. Afterward, Soros bought back pounds, paid back the money he had borrowed, and made a profit of about $1 billion. Other people also profited from the pound's fall, but the scale of Soros's operations dwarfed those of everyone else. In 1994, however, his instincts appeared to fail him—at least temporarily—as he speculated that the dollar would rise in value against the Japanese yen. Instead, the dollar fell all year, and the Quantum Fund lost some $600 million in February and possibly another $400 million in the autumn.

Soros was born in Budapest into a prosperous Jewish family on Aug. 12, 1930. His upbringing was disrupted by the Nazis' arrival in 1944. The family split up and used false papers to avoid being sent to concentration camps. In 1947 the family moved to London. Soros studied philosophy under Karl Popper (*see* OBITUARIES) at the London School of Economics, but he abandoned his plans to become a philosopher and joined the London merchant bank Singer & Friedlander. In 1956 he moved to New York City, where he worked initially as an analyst of European securities and rapidly made his mark.

In 1969 he established the Quantum Fund, which subsequently spawned a range of associated companies. His daring investment decisions caused the funds to grow rapidly, but not all his gambles succeeded. He correctly foresaw the worldwide stock market crash of October 1987—but wrongly predicted that Japanese stocks would fall hardest of all.

By 1979 he had decided to use some of his profits to create a network of philanthropic organizations. Much of the work of the Soros Foundations was directed at Eastern Europe—starting with Hungary, where he awarded scholarships, provided technical assistance, and helped modernize schools and businesses. Even though Hungary was still a communist state, Soros obtained guarantees that his foundation could operate without government interference.

As the Cold War ended and the Soviet regime collapsed, Soros established foundations in Poland, Czechoslovakia, Yugoslavia, and Russia. Some critics argued that he was being inconsistent—condemning "short-termism" in Western governments while making money from short-term currency speculation. However, he continued to spend significant sums to help establish democracy in Eastern Europe. Although Soros' critics suggested that his 1994 losses could signal a real change of fortune, admirers predicted that he would be back on top just as quickly. (PETER KELLNER)

Steel, Danielle

In 1994 U.S. publishing phenomenon Danielle Steel saw her 32nd novel, *Accident,* occupy the *Publishers Weekly* list of best-selling hardcover fiction for 15 consecutive weeks. Most critics gave tepid reviews to what they called the formulaic themes in Steel's romance novels, which featured strong yet glamorous women overcoming major obstacles or ordeals to secure a career, love, and a family. Her fans, however, devoured her every novel and helped drive each to the top of the best-seller lists. Her admirers, consisting of almost equal numbers of males and females, enjoyed the exotic locales, historical ambiance, and, most important, the happy endings in her cathartic books.

Danielle Fernande Schuelein-Steel was born on Aug. 14, 1947, in New York City. She was an only child, and after her parents divorced she was reared by relatives and family employees in Paris and New York City. Steel was a lonely child who immersed herself in poetry and books, especially those by her favourite author, French novelist Colette. By the age of 15, Steel had graduated from the Lycée Français, and in 1963 she enrolled in the Parsons School of Design, in New York. Illness prevented her from finishing her studies, but when she recovered, Steel married a wealthy French banker. In 1968 she was hired as a vice president of public relations for the advertising agency Supergirls, Ltd., in New York City.

When the firm floundered in 1971, Steel turned to writing novels and poetry. Her first paperback novel, *Going Home,* was published in 1973 but sold only moderately well. Steel also began writing copy for the Grey Advertising Agency in San Francisco. After divorcing and remarrying and while raising her children, Steel continued to write but did not achieve much success until the publication of her fourth novel, *The Promise* (1978), an instant best-seller that was followed by a slew of best-selling paperbacks. Her first hardcover novel, *The Ring* (1980), a multigenerational, international saga, was also quite successful. Though she published a book of poetry, *Love: Poems* (1981), contributed to the nonfiction book *Having a Baby* (1984), and wrote the Max and Martha series of children's books in 1989, Steel pleased her core of fans most with a string of novels about bittersweet love. Several of her works became popular television movies, including *Kaleidoscope, Jewels,* and *Crossings*.

Steel, however, had no desire to emulate the jet-setting lifestyle of her heroines; she spent most of her time at home with her nine children and third husband. By the end of 1994, she had more than 125 million books in print and no plans to stop crafting her unique blend of juicy dialogue, strongly defined characters, and twisting plots. (SUSAN RAPP)

Uchida, Shungiku

In Japan, as elsewhere, success was part luck, part talent, and part hard work. For singer, dancer, author, and cartoonist Shungiku Uchida, it also included a calculated flouting of social proprieties to shock her devotees. In 1994 she won Japan's version of the French literary prize *Deux Magots* for two best-sellers. The first, a titillating yet disturbing autobiographical novel, sold 300,000 copies after its appearance in late 1993. By July 1994 it had gone into 18 printings. The other, *We Are Reproducing,* consisted of a series of *manga* (comics) on pregnancy, birth, and bringing up an illegitimate baby. Noted religious anthropologist Shinichi Nakagawa, a one-man jury, selected Uchida for "openly and frankly portraying life and sex, . . . at times even making men fear the reality so tenderly described."

Uchida reinforced her individuality and defied convention by insisting on spelling her name "Shungicu." A vivacious entertainer noted for her colourful costumes and rhythmic dances, she frequently appeared in funky concerts and was a featured vocalist with Avecs, her own Latin band.

Uchida was born in Nagasaki on Aug. 7, 1959. Her father deserted the family when she and a younger sister were in primary school. Sometime later, her mother, a dance teacher and bar hostess, began living with a fellow dance instructor. When Shungicu was forced to sleep with her stepfather, her mother did not interfere. One of Shungicu's happiest memories from those unhappy days was receiving a ream of rough paper from her fourth grade teacher for saying, in response to a question, that her dream was to become a *manga-ka* (cartoonist).

Shungicu dropped out of high school in her second year and worked in a restaurant, in a bar, in a printshop, and as a domestic. At times she slept under a bridge. Five years later she left Nagasaki for Tokyo with her beloved *manga* and $7,000 in savings.

Shungicu's first collection of *manga,* entitled *Shungicu,* was an instant hit when it appeared in 1984. Blending sex with what she described as "gag nonsense" that did not offend readers, she won a huge following matched by few others in the crowded field of Japanese *manga-ka*. One of Shungicu's best works was *Minami-kun's Sweetheart,* a *manga* portraying an amiable girl, Chiyomi, who suddenly shrinks to the size of a doll but continues to develop normally. From her place inside Minami-kun's pocket, she accompanies him everywhere he goes. She talks to him from the palm of his hand and sleeps on his pillow beside his head. They fall in love, but she is fatally injured when he is struck by a car and she is thrown to the ground. The romantic fantasy was made into a popular television drama in 1994.

In less than 10 years Shungicu produced more than 60 books, including three collections of essays. Her *manga* books include *A Working Girl's Thoughts, You Gotta Shungicu, The Living Dress, Strange Fruit, Unobserved Foot Beat, Fantasy of an Ordinary Young Girl,* and *Coelacanth Romance.* (KAY K. TATEISHI)

Yanni

For the New Age composer/performer known only as Yanni, 1994 was a very good year. Although from the mid-1980s his nine previous albums had sold some 6 million copies, he became a superstar after March 1994, when Public Broadcasting Service stations repeatedly aired his 90-minute special, "Yanni in Concert: Live at the Acropolis," during national pledge week. The program elicited record-breaking contributions from viewers and became one of the most successful programs ever shown on public television. The television spectacular, which Yanni coproduced, starred the self-taught keyboardist and composer, accompanied by the Royal Philharmonic Concert Orchestra and his own percussive six-piece band in a triumphant performance in his native land, Greece.

Three days after its commercial release in the U.S., the album *Yanni Live at the Acropolis* began to climb *Billboard* magazine's charts; both album and video later went platinum. Public demand for more of Yanni and his romantic, arpeggio-infused instrumental music brought about brisk sales of his earlier releases; his 64 subsequent concerts throughout the U.S. in 1994 were virtually sold out. Plans were made for a world tour.

Yanni Chryssomallis was born to a middle-class family in Kalamata, Greece, on Nov. 14, 1954. As an adolescent, he was a member of the Greek national swimming team, breaking the national freestyle record at age 14. Yanni went to the U.S. at age 18 to attend the University of Minnesota, from which he graduated in 1976 with a B.A. in psychology. A founding member of the rock band Chameleon, he launched his solo recording career in 1980 with the instrumental album *Optimystique*. *Reflections of Passion* (1990) sold 1.8 million copies; both *Dare to Dream* (1992) and *In My Time* (1993) were nominated for Grammy awards. Although unable to read music or to notate it, Yanni composed music for films and television. A naturalized U.S. citizen, he lived in California, where he recorded for his Private Music label.

In performance, Yanni exuded sincerity and almost diffident charm. From time to time, he tossed his mane of shoulder-length black hair and smiled almost shyly, displaying dazzling white teeth beneath an upper lip adorned with a bristling black mustache. Lean and tanned, Yanni had a straightforward, calm glance and a self-contained expression. He usually wore either all white or all black, sometimes favouring a romantic-looking shirt with billowy sleeves. Occasionally while performing, either seated at an acoustic piano or standing at one of several synthesizers, he would close his eyes and shake his head slightly, as if basking in the musical energy and love being exchanged between him and his audience. When Yanni spoke briefly to his audience in fluent, lightly-accented English, he shared his thoughts on creativity and his belief in the oneness of all people.   (NAOMI BERNARDS POLONSKY)

Yegorova, Lyubov
A women's cross-country skier from Russia, Lyubov Yegorova became one of the two most decorated performers in the 1994 Olympic Winter Games at Lillehammer, Norway, by winning three gold medals and a silver. These, with the three golds and two silvers she had acquired in 1992 at Albertville, France, brought her Olympic career total to six gold and three silver medals, an achievement bettered only by the 10 accumulated by her former national team colleague Raisa Smetanina. Only one other Winter Games athlete had captured as many gold medals—the Soviet speed skater Lydia Skoblikova, who amassed six in 1960 and 1964.

Yegorova was born May 5, 1966, in Tomsk, Siberia. In 1982 she moved to Leningrad (now St. Petersburg), where she trained arduously on the local ski course. Joining the World Cup circuit in 1987, she did not make her first real impact until she finished third overall in 1991 and then repeated the feat the following season. She became World Cup winner in 1993 and finished second in 1994. In addition to placing first in 10 cup events during those momentous four years, Yegorova took the 30-km freestyle in the 1991 world championships at Val di Fiemme, Italy, and was a member of the winning relay team. In the 1993 championships at Falun, Sweden, she helped retain the relay title.

Of average build—1.67 m (5 ft 5¾ in) tall and weighing 54 kg (119 lb)—Yegorova developed admirable stamina and versatility, excelling over both the shortest and longest distances, as evidenced in her Olympic performances. In 1992 her first three gold medals were won in the freestyle 10 km, 15 km, and 4 × 5-km relay. In 1994 her three golds came in the 5 km, 10-km pursuit, and relay. She planned to extend her Olympic participation and perhaps shatter all previous records at the 1998 Winter Games in Nagano, Japan.

Resolved to comply with husband Igor Sysoyev's wishes, Yegorova aspired to become a mother before Nagano. "Before then, I would like to take a season off to relax," she said. Asked if she would like her hoped-for child to become a serious skier, she expressed a preference for dancing. "Competitive skiing is too difficult," explained Yegorova, a philosophy clearly not applicable to herself.
(HOWARD BASS)

Zedillo, Ernesto
When Mexican presidential candidate Luis Donaldo Colosio was assassinated on March 23, 1994, while campaigning in Tijuana, campaign manager

SERGIO DORANTES—SYGMA

Ernesto Zedillo Ponce de León stepped in to replace him as the candidate of the Institutional Revolutionary Party (PRI). The PRI, which had governed Mexico for more than 60 years, was expected to continue to operate in a similar fashion. Zedillo's refreshing campaign, however, centred on promises to open and modernize Mexico's economy. Though not with as wide a margin as predicted, Zedillo on August 21 defeated eight other candidates with 50.18% of the vote to become Mexico's newest president. Mexico's economic future and its ability to respond to the demands of open trade in the 21st century rested squarely on Zedillo's shoulders.

Zedillo, the son of an electrician, was born on Dec. 27, 1951, in Mexico City. After spending most of his childhood in Mexicali, just south of the California border, he returned to Mexico City in 1965 to attend the National Polytechnic Institute. A decisive moment in Zedillo's career came when he joined the PRI in 1971. After obtaining his doctorate in economics from Yale University and working for Mexico's central bank, he was appointed undersecretary of planning and budgetary control in 1987 by Carlos Salinas de Gortari, Mexico's president-elect from the PRI. In that position Zedillo earned his reputation as an economic wizard and technocrat by reducing the inflation rate from 160% to only about 8% in five years. He also helped Mexico achieve its first balanced budget. Becoming secretary of education in 1992, Zedillo overhauled the public school system by decentralizing it and giving each of the 31 states more responsibility and control over their own schools.

Against a tense economic backdrop of lingering recession, hesitant foreign investors, high interest rates, and a devalued peso, Zedillo's challenge after taking office on December 1 was to spur Mexico's economy and to combat unemployment. He also promised to spend more money on education, health, and basic services while remaining within the constraints of a balanced budget. Zedillo's hopes of an early start were quickly dashed, however. The stock market plunged, and on December 20 the government was forced to devalue the peso by about 14% against the U.S. dollar and then allow it to float. By year's end, despite an economic restructuring plan and promises of support from other nations, the value of the peso had dropped by more than 40%.   (SUSAN RAPP)

Zhirinovsky, Vladimir
When Vladimir Zhirinovsky's Liberal Democratic Party won 22.8% of the vote in the Russian parliamentary elections in December 1993, the West gasped. It had previously not taken much notice of the man known for his boorish, bullying behaviour or for his promise to create a

dictatorship when elected president, and they had not listened very closely to his threats to expand the borders of Russia to include Alaska and Finland, use large fans to blow radioactive waste into the Baltic states, and reduce crime by instituting summary executions. People did not know if they should take his high-decibel nationalistic comments seriously.

Much of Vladimir Volfovich Zhirinovsky's personal history was vague, unknown, or disputed. It was known that he was born on April 26, 1946, in Alma-Ata (now Almaty), Kazakhstan. He left at age 18 to attend Moscow State University, where he studied Turkish and other languages. After graduating about 1969, he went to work as a translator in Turkey, whence he was expelled in murky circumstances eight months later. He went on to earn a law degree, working first in a state-run law firm (where he was asked to resign) and then at the Mir publishing company. When the local council held elections in 1987, Zhirinovsky sought to run as the firm's candidate and as an independent, but he was disallowed by the Communist Party and Mir, which cited a letter from his previous employer that questioned his ethics. Zhirinovsky was not deterred. In the spring of 1990 he was asked to become the chairman of the Liberal Democratic Party, but by October his views had provoked his expulsion. In the spring of 1991 Zhirinovsky created his own party—and took his previous party's name. In June 1991 he ran for the presidency and won some six million votes, which placed him third.

A figure as colourful as Zhirinovsky was bound to be the object of rumour and speculation. It was widely reported that his career could only have been possible under the auspices of the KGB. Documents surfaced that showed that the surname of his father, who was killed the year he was born, had originally been Eidelshtein, that Zhirinovsky had changed his name at age 18, and that he had been a member of a state-sponsored Jewish group in the late 1980s. Given his rabid Russian nationalism and broad anti-Semitic asides and the support they drew from large segments of the population, the charge that he was Jewish was significant. Zhirinovsky, however, heatedly denied that he was Jewish or that he had been affiliated with the KGB.

The facts did not always seem to matter. Zhirinovsky's campaign proclamations that he was "the last hope of a cheated and humiliated people" and "the very same as you" and his promise to "bring Russia up off its knees" resonated more keenly among many voters than did those of more conventional politicians. "If there were a healthy economy and security for the people, I would lose all the votes I have," he said.
(CHERYL L. COLLINS)

OBITUARIES

Abs, Hermann Josef, German banker (b. Oct. 15, 1901, Bonn, Germany—d. Feb. 5, 1994, Bad Soden, Germany), was a dominant figure in the West German "economic miracle" following World War II, most notably in his role as deputy supervisory board chairman (1948–57) of the Kreditanstalt für Wiederaufbau (Credit Institute for Reconstruction) and then as spokesman for the managing board (1957–67), chairman of the supervisory board (1967–76), and honorary chairman (1976–94) of the powerful Deutsche Bank. Abs studied law for a year before obtaining a post with a merchant bank in 1929. He worked and studied international banking in Germany, France, Britain, and the U.S. until 1938, when he joined the managing board of the Deutsche Bank in Berlin. Abs, a devout Roman Catholic, never became a member of the National Socialist Party, and this, along with his close personal association with Chancellor Konrad Adenauer, quickly gained him a central role in the nation's postwar economic redevelopment. While with the Kreditanstalt, Abs supervised the distribution of Marshall Plan funds to West German industry, and in 1951–53 he led the delegation that renegotiated national war debts. When the Deutsche Bank reopened in Frankfurt in 1957, Abs took control of the new board. He also served successfully on the boards of more than two dozen companies until a 1965 law (unofficially dubbed the Abs law) limited the number of corporate chairmanships an individual could hold simultaneously.

Acton, Sir Harold Mario Mitchell, British writer and connoisseur (b. July 5, 1904, Villa La Pietra, near Florence, Italy—d. Feb. 27, 1994, Villa La Pietra), was "the consummate aesthete of his generation," more admired for his exuberant dilettantism while a student at the University of Oxford in the 1920s and for his lifelong charm than for his many books. The son of an Anglo-Italian father and American mother, Acton went from a privileged childhood at a Tuscan villa to Eton College and Christ Church, Oxford. At Oxford he founded a literary magazine and led a circle of friends that included Graham Greene, Kenneth Clarke, and Evelyn Waugh, who reportedly used Acton as the model for the aesthete Anthony Blanche in *Brideshead Revisited.* From 1932 to 1939 Acton lived in China, lecturing on English literature, translating classical Chinese drama, and collecting art. After serving in the British Royal Air Force in World War II, he returned to the family estate overlooking Florence. He spent the remainder of his life writing, overseeing his extensive art collection, and lavishly entertaining international celebrities, artists, and dignitaries. Acton's books include *The Last Medici* (1932); *Peonies and Ponies* (1941), recounting his years in China; the nonfictional *Tuscan Villas* (1973) and *Florence: A Travellers' Companion* (1986); collections of poetry and fiction; two works on the Bourbons of Naples; and a two-volume autobiography, *Memoirs of an Aesthete* (1948) and *More Memoirs of an Aesthete* (1970). He was knighted in 1974. Acton bequeathed his estate—estimated to be worth between $100 million and $500 million—to New York University.

Afanasyev, Viktor Grigoryevich, Russian journalist (b. Nov. 18, 1922, Aktamysh, Tatar A.S.S.R., Russian Soviet Federated Socialist Republic—d. April 10, 1994, Moscow, Russia), as deputy editor (1968–74) and editor in chief (1976–89) of the daily newspaper *Pravda* and editor in chief (1974–76) of the journal *Kommunist,* was the official voice of the Communist Party of the Soviet Union (CPSU) for more than two decades. Afanasyev joined the army in 1940 and the CPSU in 1943. He graduated from the correspondence division of the Chita Pedagogical Institute in 1950, and three years later he left the army to teach at the Pedagogical Institute in Chelyabinsk. Afanasyev was named head of the department of scientific socialism at the CPSU's Academy of Social Sciences in 1960. In 1968 he was appointed deputy editor of *Pravda,* where he remained except for his brief stint at *Kommunist.* He was elected corresponding member of the Academy of Sciences of the U.S.S.R. in 1972 and made a member of the CPSU Central Committee in 1976. During his years at *Pravda,* Afanasyev, a close associate of Soviet Pres. Leonid Brezhnev and a dedicated communist, built the party newspaper into a powerful and well-respected hard-line publication. In the 1970s readership reportedly reached some 10 million, but it began to decline under Pres. Mikhail Gorbachev's glasnost policies in the late 1980s. In 1989 Afanasyev was removed from his post and given a sinecure at the Academy of Sciences.

Anderson, Lindsay Gordon, British stage and film director (b. April 17, 1923, Bangalore, India—d. Aug. 30, 1994, near Angoulême, France), as one of the original Angry Young Men, made his distaste for conformity and England's class consciousness the constant theme of his often anarchic works. While attending Wadham College, Oxford, Anderson cofounded and coedited the film magazine *Sequence,* and he later wrote for such publications as *Sight and Sound* and *New Statesman.* He began his career in film by directing documentaries, including *Thursday's Children* (1954), which won an Academy Award. Anderson was part of the Free Cinema movement, which featured contemporary urban working-class themes. He worked in television and the theatre before making his feature debut with *This Sporting Life* (1963), a classic social realist drama about a rugby player, adapted by David Storey from his novel. His second feature film, *If . . .* (1968), was about rebellious students who challenge the establishment at a British boarding school. Anderson, who had a long association with London's Royal Court Theatre, became its associate artistic director (1969–75) and directed the premieres of many of Storey's stage productions there—among them, *In Celebration* (1969), *Home* (1970), and *The Changing Room* (1971). Subsequent films were *O Lucky Man!* (1973), *In Celebration* (1974), *Britannia Hospital* (1982), and *The Whales of August* (1987). "Glory! Glory!"— a two-part television series satirizing TV evangelists—was made in 1989. Anderson also occasionally acted, appearing in cameo parts in several films and playing a Cambridge schoolmaster in *Chariots of Fire* (1981).

Ball, George Wildman, U.S. government official and lawyer (b. Dec. 21, 1909, Des Moines, Iowa—d. May 26, 1994, New York, N.Y.), as undersecretary of state (1961–66) in the administrations of John F. Kennedy and Lyndon B. Johnson, vociferously objected to increasing U.S. troop involvement in Vietnam and warned both presidents that the U.S. could not win a guerrilla war. His prophetic counsel was ignored, however, and U.S. involvement escalated from 400 "advisers" to more than 500,000 ground troops. After earning a law degree from Northwestern University in Chicago, Ball practiced law there and became a supporter of Adlai Stevenson, the governor of Illinois. When Stevenson ran for the presidency in 1952, 1956, and 1960, Ball served as national director of Volunteers for Stevenson and was propelled into politics. Ball joined the Kennedy administration as undersecretary of state for economic affairs but was soon elevated to undersecretary of state and advised Kennedy during the 1962 Cuban missile crisis. Ball resigned in 1966 to return to his law practice but served as the U.S. ambassador to the United Nations in 1968. His dovish views on Vietnam became known with the publication in 1971 of the sensitive Pentagon Papers. Ball was the author of five books, including *Diplomacy for a Crowded World* (1976), *Error and Betrayal in Lebanon* (1984), and *The Passionate Attachment* (1992), an examination of U.S.-Israeli relations.

Balsam, Artur, Polish-born U.S. pianist (b. Feb. 8, 1906, Warsaw, Poland, Russian Empire—d. Sept. 1, 1994, New York, N.Y.), was an accomplished soloist, accompanist for violin and cello, and chamber musician whose elegant interpretations of Mozart, Beethoven, and Haydn sonatas distinguished his vast repertoire. Balsam received his musical training in Lodz, Poland, where he made his concert debut at the age of 12. He attended the Lodz Conservatory and the Berlin State Academy of Music and was the winner of the 1930 International Piano Competition and the 1931 Mendelssohn Prize. The following year he toured with violinist Yehudi Menuhin in the U.S., his permanent home after the rise of the Nazis. He recorded about 250 works, notably the complete set of Mozart violin and piano sonatas (with Oscar Shumsky), the Beethoven violin sonatas (with Joseph Fuchs), and cello sonatas (with Zara Nelsova). During the 1960s he performed as a member of a trio with violinist William Kroll and cellist Benar Heifetz. He also taught at Boston University, the Manhattan School of Music, New York City, and the Philadelphia Academy of Music. From 1956 to 1992 he headed a chamber music summer school in Maine.

Barrault, Jean-Louis, French actor and director (b. Sept. 8, 1910, Le Vésinet, France—d. Jan. 22, 1994, Paris, France), mounted acclaimed productions of both classical and modern avant-garde plays that helped revive the theatre in post-World War II Paris. Barrault studied at the Théâtre de l'Atelier with Charles Dullin, who directed his stage debut in 1931. An accomplished mime (and a student of Étienne Decroux), Barrault produced a pantomime version of William Faulkner's *As I Lay Dying* (1935) and captured international attention for his portrayal of a mime in the film *Les Enfants du paradis* (1944; *The Children of Paradise*). In 1940 he joined the Comédie Française and married Madeleine Renaud, who was 10 years his senior and had been a leading actress with the company since 1921. Six years later Barrault left to form their own theatrical company at the Théâtre Marigny. There he produced, directed, and acted in a mixed repertoire of classics by Shakespeare, Molière, Chekhov, and Marivaux, along with modern scripts by Jean Anouilh, Samuel Beckett, Jean Genet, and Eugène Ionesco (*q.v.*) and adaptations of works by Voltaire, Jean-Paul Sartre, Franz Kafka, and others. Barrault was invited to take command at the state-funded Odéon (later renamed the Théâtre de France) in 1958, but he was abruptly dismissed when he expressed support for the 1968 student uprising, in which the theatre was badly damaged. His career was not set back, however, and he and Renaud continued to work at the Théâtre des Nations (1965–67; 1972–74), the Théâtre d'Orsay (1974–81), and the Théâtre du Rond-Point (from 1981). In addition to starring in many of her husband's productions, Renaud made more than 20 motion pictures, including *Jean de la lune* (1931) and *La Lumière du lac* (1988). Barrault appeared in more than three dozen films (most made before 1960) and published several books on the theatre and an autobiography. Both Barrault and Renaud were elected to the Legion of Honour. She died on Sept. 23, 1994, just nine months after her husband's death.

Belluschi, Pietro, Italian-born architect (Aug. 18, 1899, Ancona, Italy—d. Feb. 14, 1994, Portland, Ore.), designed the Equitable Life Assurance Building (1944–47), in Portland, a sleek office tower of aluminum and glass that served as one of the earliest and finest examples of the International Style of architecture, but with a series of magnificent domestic and religious structures that relied on the use of indigenous materials, notably woods, he later became most closely identified as the premier regional designer of the Pacific Northwest. Before traveling to the U.S. as an exchange student in 1923, Belluschi studied engineering at the University of Rome. He attended Cornell University, Ithaca, N.Y., before settling in Portland and working for Albert E. Doyle, a prominent architect there. After Doyle's death Belluschi emerged (1928) as the firm's chief designer. In 1943 he purchased the company and renamed it for himself. In Portland he created such prized structures as the Portland Art Museum (1930–38), Sutor House (1938), St. Thomas More Chapel (1939–41), and Zion Lutheran Church (1950), examples of his principle of "eloquent simplicity." From 1951 to 1965 Belluschi headed the School of Architecture and Planning at the Massachusetts Institute of Technology, and he continued to collaborate with leading architectural firms. He codesigned such New York City landmarks as the Juilliard School of Music, Lincoln Center, and the Pan Am (now Met Life) Building and such San Francisco buildings as the Bank of America World Headquarters and St. Mary's Cathedral. In 1972 Belluschi was the recipient of the Gold Medal of the American Institute of Architects, and in 1991 he was awarded the National Medal of the Arts.

Benson, Ezra Taft, U.S. agronomist and religious leader (b. Aug. 4, 1899, Whitney, Idaho—d. May 30, 1994, Salt Lake City, Utah), as president (1985–94) of the Church of Jesus Christ of Latter-day Saints, stressed the importance of the *Book of Mormon,* one of four volumes of church scripture, and increased church membership from 5.9 million to 8.7 million. During the 1960s and '70s, Benson aroused controversy both inside and outside the church by endorsing the right-wing John Birch Society, by denouncing the civil-rights

operators, who received larger payments for taking farmland out of production. After returning to the church, Benson ascended to the presidency of the Council of the Twelve Apostles in 1973, thus assuring his elevation to the presidency of the church in 1985 upon the death of Spencer Kimball. Benson's leadership came under attack in 1993 when one of his grandsons revealed that Benson had not been able to speak or recognize relatives since being stricken by a severe illness in 1989.

Bill, Max, Swiss graphic artist, industrial designer, architect, sculptor, and painter (b. Dec. 22, 1908, Winterthur, Switz.—d. Dec. 9, 1994, Berlin, Germany), advocated modern design with austere geometric forms and sophisticated, disciplined advertising designs. Among the last surviving students of the Bauhaus art movement, Bill studied architecture, metalwork, stage design, and painting while attending the Bauhaus school from 1927 to 1929. He set up his own art studio in Zürich in 1930 but earned his living mainly by designing advertisements. One of his most famous sculptures was a work in brass entitled "Konstruktion aus drei Kreisscheiben" (1945–46). His designs, however, were usually more eclectic in concept and constructed from more unconventional materials. His hard-edged, sometimes impersonal creations were designed on mathematical concepts and were made of plaster, metal, wood, and stone. Among his works were wall sprockets, a clock, a bridge, furniture, a movie theatre, a house, and most notably the College of Design in Ulm, Germany. These works earned him recognition as a leader of the Concrete and Constructivist

Ezra Taft Benson (centre), who became president of the Church of Jesus Christ of Latter-day Saints in 1985, died in May at age 94. In the 1950s he served as U.S. secretary of agriculture.

TOM SMART—GAMMA LIAISON

movement as "a communist program," and by criticizing the women's movement. His position in the church hierarchy was assured because he was the great-grandson of Mormon church pioneer Ezra T. Benson, who accompanied Brigham Young to the Great Salt Lake in 1847. Benson served as a Mormon missionary for two years before graduating with honours (1927) from Brigham Young University, Provo, Utah, and earning a master's degree in farm economics from Iowa State College. In 1943 he was appointed to the ranks of the Council of the Twelve Apostles, second in rank to the First Presidency, which consisted of the president and his two-man council. Benson gained national prominence while serving (1953–61) as secretary of agriculture in the administration of Pres. Dwight D. Eisenhower, and he became the first Mormon to attain Cabinet status. He was unsuccessful, however, in his effort to strengthen family farms; his policies, in fact, bolstered big

art movements. Bill also taught (1951–56) and planned the curriculum at the College of Design and served (1967–71) as a member of the Swiss parliament. His highly admired sculptures could be seen in cities worldwide. In 1993 Bill was awarded the Imperial Prize for sculpture by the emperor of Japan.

Bloch, Robert Albert, U.S. writer (b. April 5, 1917, Chicago, Ill.—d. Sept. 23, 1994, Los Angeles, Calif.), crafted dozens of screenplays, mysteries, fantasies, and essays but was best remembered for his spine-tingling psychological tales of horror and suspense, most notably the classic *Psycho* (1959), a cult favourite that was adapted for Alfred Hitchcock's 1960 film of the same title. Bloch, who relied on elements of surprise rather than scenes of graphic violence or mythological forces to terrorize and captivate readers, was also one of the first writers to delve into the criminal mind.

His style, which was influenced by the writings of his mentor, H.P. Lovecraft, was also the model for horror specialist Stephen King and science-fiction writer Ray Bradbury. Bloch worked for an advertising agency while writing stories for the magazine *Weird Tales.* He also wrote 39 episodes for the radio program "Stay Tuned for Terror" and established his reputation through multiple broadcasts and republications of the story "Yours Truly, Jack the Ripper." In 1953 he quit his job to become a full-time writer. After publishing his first novel, *The Scarf* (1947), Bloch began a prolific career writing for television, radio, and film. Some of his screenplays include *Torture Garden* (1967), *The House That Dripped Blood* (1970), and *Asylum* (1972).

Bondarchuk, Sergey, Soviet film director and actor (b. Sept. 25, 1920, Belozerka, Ukraine—d. Oct. 20, 1994, Moscow, Russia), as one of the most prominent and successful film directors in the U.S.S.R., gained fame for his large-scale battle-filled epics. Bondarchuk had attended a theatre school before his studies were interrupted by World War II. After being discharged from the army in 1946, he enrolled in the acting department at the All-Union State Institute of Cinematography in Moscow, where he studied under Sergey Gerasimov. During Bondarchuk's final year, Gerasimov had the class rehearse a script for a film he was preparing, and Bondarchuk read well enough to be cast in the film, *The Young Guard* (1948). He went on to gain wide recognition for his performance in the title role in *Taras Shevchenko* (1951). His depiction of the Ukrainian poet was considered one of his finest performances and won him the title People's Artist of the Soviet Union in 1952. Bondarchuk went on to star in a number of films, including a highly praised *Othello* (1956). He played a former prisoner of war returning home in a televised version of a short story, but he was so unhappy with the result that he decided to direct a film version himself. The critically acclaimed *Destiny of a Man* (1959) marked his debut as director and earned him the Lenin Prize in 1960. The theme of war ran through many of the films he directed. Perhaps his best-known work was *War and Peace* (1967), a four-part epic in which he played the role of Pierre Bezukhov; the film, edited for foreign release, won an Academy Award. The ambitious *Waterloo* (1970) followed. Bondarchuk joined the Communist Party of the Soviet Union in 1970 and the following year became the secretary of the Union of Cinematographers. In later years he became a symbol of conservatism, and in 1986 he was voted out of office. Bondarchuk's last film was *Boris Godunov* (1986). In 1994 he called for government support of and protection for the Russian film industry.

Boros, Julius Nicholas, U.S. golfer (b. March 3, 1920, Fairfield, Conn.—d. May 28, 1994, near Fort Lauderdale, Fla.), was a consistent player whose trademark rhythmic and relaxed swing helped him win 18 Professional Golfers' Association of America (PGA) titles, including two U.S. Open championships (1952 and 1963), during a career that spanned a quarter century. Boros, who worked as an accountant before turning professional at the age of 30, was largely self-taught. His masterly touch was also instrumental in making him one of the best wedge shot players of all time. Boros was also a member of the 1959, 1963, 1965, and 1967 Ryder Cup teams. He was inducted into the PGA Hall of Fame in 1974 and the World Golf Hall of Fame in 1982, five years after he retired from the professional tour.

Borotra, Jean-Robert, French tennis player (b. Aug. 13, 1898, Arbonne, near Biarritz, France—d. July 17, 1994, Arbonne), was one of the renowned "Four Musketeers"—Borotra, René Lacoste, Jacques Brugnon, and Henri Cochet—who dominated amateur tennis in the 1920s and early '30s. As a group they won the Davis Cup for France for six consecutive years (1927–32) and reached the finals in 1925, 1926, and 1933. As an individual Borotra won 19 Grand Slam titles. Nicknamed "the Bounding Basque," he was as well known for his exuberance and his omnipresent blue beret as for his unorthodox serve-and-volley style of play. He won the French championship nine times—singles in 1924 and 1931, men's doubles in 1925, 1928, 1929, 1934, and 1936, and mixed doubles in 1927 and 1934; six All-England (Wimbledon) titles—singles in 1924 and 1926, doubles in 1925, 1932, and 1933, and mixed doubles in 1925; the U.S. mixed doubles in 1926; and three Australian titles in 1928—

ALLSPORT/HULTON DEUTSCH

singles, doubles, and mixed doubles. He also won the French indoor championship 12 times, was on the Davis Cup team as late as 1947, and played competitive tennis into his 80s. Borotra trained as a civil engineer and was a company director for more than 40 years (1930–75). He was minister of sport (1940–42) in the Vichy government of Nazi-occupied France, but his wartime collaboration had little effect on his reputation or his popularity. Borotra was awarded the Legion of Honour and was elected to the International Tennis Hall of Fame (1976).

Boulle, Pierre-François-Marie-Louis, French novelist (b. Feb. 20, 1912, Avignon, France—d. Jan. 30, 1994, Paris, France), was best known for two vastly different novels, *Le Pont de la rivière Kwaï* (1952; *The Bridge on the River Kwai;* film adaptation, 1957), a World War II tale of morality and madness among British troops in a Japanese prison camp, and the science-fiction fable *La Planète des singes* (1963; *Planet of the Apes*). The film adaptation of the latter (1968) spawned several sequels and a television series. Boulle trained as an electrical engineer in Paris, but in 1938 he moved to Malaysia to work on a rubber plantation. During World War II he was an intelligence agent in Southeast Asia. In 1942 he was captured while on a mission in French Indochina, but he escaped in 1944. After the war he returned to France to try his hand at writing. His first novel, *William Conrad* (1950), which concerned a German spy in wartime Britain, introduced the issues of morality and honour that he expanded in later books. In *River Kwai* Boulle examined the plight of British soldiers compelled by their own commanding officer's obsessive work ethic and misplaced sense of honour to build a bridge for their Japanese captors. The book, which was translated into more than 20 languages, caused an international sensation, as did the Academy Award-winning film based on it. Boulle's other works include *La Face* (1953; *The Face*), *Aux sources de la rivière Kwaï* (1967; *My Own River Kwai*), *Les Oreilles de jungle* (1972; *Ears of the Jungle*), *Le Bon Leviathan* (1978; *The Good Leviathan*), and *À nous deux, Satan* (1992).

Brazzi, Rossano, Italian actor (b. Sept. 18, 1916, Bologna, Italy—d. Dec. 24, 1994, Rome, Italy), personified the handsome heartbreaker and romantic aristocrat in over 200 films, most of them made in the U.S. In 1939 he gave up a promising law career to debut in *The Trial and Death of Socrates.* Though he was a reigning screen idol by the 1940s, Brazzi secretly worked with Resistance fighters in Rome during World War II. After the war, his popularity declined in Italy, but he became immensely popular in the U.S., notably as Émile de Becque in *South Pacific* (1958). The blue-eyed sex symbol's first Hollywood film appearance was as the professor in *Little Women* (1949), a performance that so enraptured his fans that they later mobbed Brazzi at his Los Angeles motel, seeking autographs and other souvenirs. Brazzi found widespread fame portraying swashbuckling playboys in such films as *The Barefoot Contessa* (1954), *Three Coins in the Fountain* (1954), *Summertime* (1955), *Count Your Blessings* (1959), *The Great Waltz* (1972), and *White Telephone* (1976). By the late 1960s, he returned to Italy to work in television and film, but the success he enjoyed in Hollywood eluded him. In 1984 Brazzi was indicted along with 36 others for international drug and weapons smuggling; the charges against him, however, were later dropped. Brazzi was working on a film when he was hospitalized with a viral infection that disabled his nervous system and eventually claimed his life.

Brooks, Cleanth, U.S. educator, author, and critic (b. Oct. 16, 1906, Murray, Ky.—d. May 10, 1994, New Haven, Conn.), helped to establish New Criticism, a theory of literary analysis that dominated the teaching of literature at U.S. universities for two decades after World War II. Brooks downplayed consideration of biographical and historical influences and championed a "close reading" of literary texts, emphasizing careful structural analysis. He earned a B.A. (1928) from Vanderbilt University, Nashville, Tenn., before coming under the influence of the Fugitives, a literary group that included John Crowe Ransom and Robert Penn Warren. After further study at Tulane University, New Orleans, La. (M.A., 1929), he became a Rhodes scholar at the University of Oxford. Brooks then taught at Louisiana State University (1932–47), where he edited the influential *Southern Review* with Warren, his longtime colleague and with whom he coauthored *Understanding Poetry* (1938). That book and Brooks's *Modern Poetry and the Tradition* (1939) and *The Well Wrought Urn* (1947) were cornerstones of New Criticism. Ransom called Brooks "the most expert living 'reader' or interpreter of difficult verse." He also wrote several insightful studies of the cultural milieu of William Faulkner, chief among them *William Faulkner: The Yoknapatawpha Country* (1963). Brooks taught at Yale University (1947–75), was much in demand as a visiting professor, and served as the cultural attaché at the U.S. embassy in London (1964–66). In 1985 he was named Jefferson lecturer. His last books were *On the Prejudices, Predilections, and Firm Beliefs of William Faulkner* (1987) and *Historical Evidence and the Reading of Seventeenth-Century Poetry* (1991).

Bukowski, Charles, U.S. poet, novelist, and screenwriter (b. Aug. 16, 1920, Andernach, Germany—d. March 9, 1994, San Pedro, Calif.), probed into the life of the inner city and the inner self and described what he found there in uncompromising, often crude, language. A cult figure, first in Europe and, after the success of his screenplay for the motion picture *Barfly* (1987), in the U.S. as well, Bukowski parlayed his life of hard drinking and womanizing into a literary genre. Born in the German Rhineland of a U.S. occupation soldier and his German wife, Bukowski moved to Los Angeles when he was two. His childhood was marred by an abusive father, and after a short stint at a local college and a few years in New York trying to become a writer, Bukowski embarked on what was essentially a 10-year drinking binge, finally arriving at the brink of death in the charity ward of a Los Angeles hospital with an ulcerated liver in

1956. He achieved his first successes in local and underground publications. Los Angeles publisher John Martin recognized the peculiar genius of the self-described "dirty old man" and established Black Sparrow Press to publish Bukowski's works. Bukowski's poetry appeared in dozens of volumes, including *Flower, Fist and Bestial Wail* (1960) and *Poems Written Before Jumping out of an 8 Story Window* (1968); his novels and short-story collections include *Notes of a Dirty Old Man* (1969), *Post Office* (1971), *Erections, Ejaculations, Exhibitions, and General Tales of Ordinary Madness* (1972), *Factotum* (1975), and *Ham on Rye* (1982). He completed a mystery novel, *Pulp,* just before his death. Although he was too much of an underground figure ever to have won wide critical acclaim, Bukowski was reportedly selling one million books a year worldwide.

Burle Marx, Roberto, Brazilian landscape architect (b. Aug. 4, 1909, São Paulo, Brazil—d. June 4, 1994, near Rio de Janeiro, Brazil), transformed his native land by replacing European-style formal gardens with lush tropical native flora. A Renaissance man—sculptor, jewelry designer, ceramicist, amateur opera singer, and painter—Burle Marx fashioned gardens with the eye of an abstract artist. While studying (1928) art in Berlin, he became entranced with the tropical plants populating that city's botanical garden, and he began studies at Dahlem Botanical Gardens. After returning to Brazil, he converted his home into a tropical plant paradise, eventually surrounding it with 800,000 sq m (8.6 million sq ft) of gardens brimming with thousands of rare species. He was particularly fond of Brazilian orchids, palms, water lilies, and bromeliads. Some of his most breathtaking commissions included Rio's Flamengo Park, a 122-ha (300-ac) expanse of land reclaimed from the sea, which included lawns, playing fields, an artificial beach, and an automobile parkway; the hanging gardens of the Ministry of Foreign Affairs in Brasília; and the Brazilian pavilion at the Brussels International Exposition of 1958. He also did landscaping for the UNESCO Building, Paris (1963); the U.S. embassy, Brasília (1967, 1972); the Iranian embassy, Brasília (1971); and the international airport, Rio de Janeiro (1978). He was one of the first to criticize the destruction of rain forests, and he protested against the government's move to enclose parks behind cast-iron fences, which he viewed as sequestering the city in a cage.

Busby, Sir Matthew ("MATT"), Scottish footballer (b. May 26, 1909, Bellshill, Lanarkshire, Scotland—d. Jan. 20, 1994, Manchester, England), was the revered manager (1945–69), general manager (1969–71), director (1971–83), and president (1980–93) of the Manchester United association football (soccer) team; as manager he steered that club to win two Football Association (FA) Cup titles (1948 and 1963), five English Football League championships (1952, 1956, 1957, 1965, and 1967), and the 1968 European Cup. Perhaps his greatest challenge came in February 1958 when the plane in which the club was traveling crashed on takeoff near Munich, Germany. Busby was critically injured, and eight first-string players of the young team that had come to be known as the "Busby Babes" were among the 23 people killed. By the end of that season, however, the surviving players and their hastily recruited reinforcements had reached the FA Cup semifinals, and within 10 years the rebuilt side had captured the European Cup. Busby, the son of a Lanarkshire coal miner who died in World War I, briefly worked in the mines until he won a place with Manchester City in 1929. He was a moderately successful player with City and then with Liverpool (1936–39) and was selected to play for Scotland in 1934. After serving as a physical training instructor in the British army during World War II, he accepted the post of manager at Manchester United, which at that time was languishing in obscurity and near bankruptcy. Busby was particularly known for his skill at recruiting young talent and for introducing a fast-moving, attacking style of play. He was made Commander of the Order of the British Empire in 1958 and was knighted in 1968.

Calloway, Cab (CABELL CALLOWAY III), U.S. entertainer (b. Dec. 25, 1907, Rochester, N.Y.—d. Nov. 18, 1994, Hockessin, Del.), plied his uniquely full and rich singing voice, swinging rhythms, and flamboyant stage manner to become one of the swing era's top bandleaders, then won further fame on the musical stage in notable revivals of *Porgy and Bess* and *Hello, Dolly!* His first hit record, "Minnie the Moocher" (1931), with Calloway and his band exchanging nonsense "hi-de-hi-de-hi-de-ho" lyrics, led to a series of successes with barely disguised drug ditties ("Reefer Man," "Kickin' the Gong Around") and Calloway-composed scat-singing tunes ("Zaz Zu Zaz," "Get That Hi-De-Ho in Your Soul"). Tall, clad in a tuxedo (usually white), his long black hair flying and wide mouth in a teeth-baring grin, he cavorted in front of his band in high-energy shows; he portrayed himself as the heppest of hep cats, talking "jive" language and instructing squares with his "Hepsters Dictionary" and "Swingformation Bureau"

REUTERS/BETTMANN

booklets. In an era of pallid, high-pitched male singers, Calloway stood out for his wide range and robust style, yet he was also a moving ballad singer on occasion. Raised in Baltimore, Md., he followed his sister, singer Blanche Calloway, to Chicago, where he briefly attended Crane College and sang in clubs. By 1929 he was in New York, performing on Broadway in *Connie's Hot Chocolates*. The next year his band began starring at The Cotton Club. He hired excellent musicians (including tenor saxophonists Ben Webster and Chu Berry and bassist Milt Hinton) and molded his band into a powerful, tightly disciplined unit. Abetted by radio, films (beginning with *The Big Broadcast* in 1932), and much touring, they remained one of the most popular jazz bands until the post-World War II decline of ballrooms and big bands. Calloway returned to the musical stage to play the charismatic hedonist Sportin' Life in *Porgy and Bess,* touring the world in the opera's revival in the mid-1950s. He then portrayed Cornelius Vandergelder in the 1967 all-black revival of *Hello, Dolly!* Though semi-retired in the 1970s and '80s, he continued to play concerts and appeared in the film *The Blues Brothers* (1980). Calloway's autobiography, *Of Minnie the Moocher & Me,* appeared in 1976.

Camargo, Iberê Bassanti, Brazilian artist (b. Nov. 18, 1914, Restinga Sêca, Brazil—d. Aug. 9, 1994, Pôrto Alegre, Brazil), was a leading Abstract Expressionist painter who experimented with colour and form, using bold gestures and heavy paint encrusted on huge canvases. Camargo, who confessed that his first toys were a pencil and paper, was a loner who drew inspiration from childhood memories of his native countryside. After study-

ing at a local art school, he continued his education (1939) at the Institute of Fine Arts in Pôrto Alegre before attending the National School of Fine Arts in Rio de Janeiro. He launched a professional career as a printmaker and returned to the National School of Fine Arts as the inaugural teacher of printmaking. Camargo dabbled in figurative and Constructivist art before exploring the limits of Abstract Expressionism. His style, initially typified by a light-hued pallette, was later marked by gloomy dark colours, anthropomorphic forms, and monstrous figures that produced an unsettling effect. Camargo, who saw himself as a cyclist peddling against the wind, also frequently used cyclists as a theme. His lack of artistic conformity—he would not bend to producing fashionable Surrealist-inspired fantastic art or to Brazilian abstract and conceptual art—resulted in the exclusion of his works from a retrospective of Latin-American art mounted in the U.S. and Europe.

Candy, John Franklin, Canadian comedian (b. Oct. 31, 1950, Newmarket, Ont.—d. March 4, 1994, Durango, Mexico), created such kooky characters as slick television personality Johnny La Rue, ghoulish Dr. Tongue, and polka clarinetist Yosh Shmenge for the satirical comedy show "SCTV" before delighting film audiences as a bumbling yet lovable nerd, notably in such smash hits as *Planes, Trains and Automobiles* (1987) and *Uncle Buck* (1989). Though Candy's girth (he weighed more than 136 kg [300 lb] at his death) was a key component in his comedy routines, he attempted numerous diets without lasting success. Beginning in 1972, the genial performer honed his comedic gifts as a member of the Second City improvisational troupes in Chicago and Toronto. Candy joined Second City's "SCTV" series as a regular skit performer and writer in 1977, and he won two Emmy awards for his scripts. After appearing in supporting roles in such films as *The Blues Brothers* (1980), *Stripes* (1981), and *National Lampoon's Vacation* (1983), Candy achieved star status as the sex-obsessed brother of Tom Hanks in *Splash* (1984). Among his other film credits are *Who's Harry Crumb?* (1989), *Delirious* (1991), *Only the Lonely* (1991), *Once Upon a Crime* (1992), and *Cool Runnings* (1993). Candy was also part owner of the Canadian Football League's Toronto Argonauts. At the time of his death—he died in his sleep of a heart attack—Candy was on location filming *Wagons East.*

Canetti, Elias, Bulgarian-born novelist and playwright (b. July 25, 1905, Ruse, Bulg.—d. Aug. 14, 1994, Zürich, Switz.), was awarded the 1981 Nobel Prize for Literature for his explorations of the behaviour and emotions of crowds and

analyses of the individual's position in society. Born into a family of Sephardic Jews, Canetti migrated with his parents when he was six, to Manchester, England, and two years later, after the death of his father, he moved with his brother and mother to Vienna. His mother taught him German, the language of his books. He was educated in Zurich, Frankfurt, and Vienna and received (1929) a doctorate in chemistry from the University of Vienna. In 1927 Canetti witnessed a protest march during which Vienna's Palace of Justice was set on fire and 90 demonstrators were killed. This incident crystallized his interest in crowds and power. He planned an eight-novel series on extremes in human behaviour; only one was written, *Die Blendung* (1935; *Auto da Fé,* also published as *The Tower of Babel*), a nightmarish story of a scholar whose life ends in madness and conflagration. After the Nazi takeover of Austria, Canetti moved to England. There he began the work that resulted—after 10 years of research and 10 years of writing—in *Masse und Macht* (1960; *Crowds and Power*). His interest in the psychopathology of power was also evident in his three plays—*Hochzeit* (1932; *The Wedding*), *Komödie der Eitelkeit* (1950; *Comedy of Vanity*), and *Die Befristeten* (1964; *The Numbered,* also published as *Life-Terms*). Also published were such nonfiction works as *Der Ohrenzeuge—Fünfzig Charaktere* (1974; *Earwitness: Fifty Characters*), a book of character sketches; *Aufzeichnungen 1942–1972* (1973; *The Human Province*), excerpts from his notebooks; three volumes of autobiography: *Die gerettete Zunge* (1977; *The Tongue Set Free*), *Die Fackel im Ohr* (1980; *The Torch in My Ear*), and *Das Augenspiel* (1985; *The Play of The Eyes*); and *Die Fliegenpein* (1992; *The Agony of Flies*), was a collection of aphorisms. A fourth volume of autobiography awaited publication.

Carmet, Jean-Gabriel-Edmond, French actor (b. April 25, 1920, Tours, France—d. April 20, 1994, Sèvres, near Paris, France), appeared in some 200 motion pictures in a career that spanned 50 years. Carmet began as a stagehand and comedian in revues such as the Branquignols troupe (1948). His first screen role was as a member of a crowd in Marcel Carné's *Les Enfants du paradis* (1944; *Children of Paradise*). For the next quarter century, the short, stocky actor appeared in dozens of films, particularly comedies, building a recognizable persona as a French Everyman. Beginning in 1970, however, Carmet tackled more serious roles as directors began using his deceptive on-screen ordinariness to good effect in such films as *Le Grand Blond avec une chaussure noire* (1972; *The Tall Blond Man with One Black Shoe*), *Dupont-Lajoie* (1974), *La Victoire en chantant* (1976; *Black and White in Colour*), *Violette Nozière* (1977; *Violette*), and *Buffet froid* (1979; *Cold Cuts*). He won two César awards from the French cinema academy for best supporting actor for *Les Misérables* (1982) and *Merci la vie* (1992; *Thank You, Life*) as well as the academy's lifetime achievement award in 1993. Carmet's last screen role was in *Germinal* (1993).

Carter, Kevin, South African photojournalist (b. Sept. 13, 1960, Johannesburg, South Africa—d. July 27, 1994, Johannesburg), recorded on film the racial strife and political chaos of his native South Africa, but he captured international attention and the 1994 Pulitzer Prize for a haunting photograph of a vulture patiently watching a starving Sudanese child. Despite his own comfortable suburban childhood, Carter rejected the inequities of apartheid in his native land at an early age. He was drafted into the South African Defense Force and then secured (1983) a job as a sports photographer with the *Sunday Express* newspaper. In 1984 he switched to the Johannesburg *Star* and joined other young white photojournalists who risked imprisonment and death to expose the evils of apartheid. Later he worked for the *Sunday Tribune,* the *Weekly Mail,* and Reuters international news agency. Many of his photographs were picked up all over the world, notably his Pulitzer Prize winner, which was taken during a short foray into The Sudan, and his picture of an anguished South African neo-Nazi

Kevin Carter's photograph of a starving Sudanese girl being watched by a vulture won the Pulitzer Prize for feature photography in 1994. The 33-year-old South African photographer committed suicide in July.

KEVIN CARTER—SYGMA

facing death at the hands of a dimly seen black police officer. Carter, who was increasingly depressed by the violence and suffering he had witnessed and despondent over the shooting death of his friend and colleague Ken Oosterbroek, took his own life.

Cernik, Oldrich, Czechoslovak politician (b. Oct. 27, 1921, Ostrava, Czech.—d. Oct. 19, 1994, Prague, Czech Republic), was one of the architects of the brief period of economic and political reform in 1968 known as the Prague Spring. Cernik, a miner's son, went at age 16 to work in the steel mills around heavily industrialized Ostrava. After joining the Communist Party in 1945, he began (1949) to work in the organization; his ascent was rapid and by 1956 he had become a member of the party's Central Committee. He studied engineering by correspondence and earned a degree in 1964. Cernik gained a reputation as an able technocrat, and in 1960 he was named minister of fuel. He joined forces with others who believed in the decentralization of the state's economy and worked as a behind-the-scenes player in attempts to advance reform. In 1966 he was elected to the party's Presidium. In April 1968 Cernik was appointed prime minister by party president Alexander Dubcek. Cernik was considered a centrist and a master at conciliation. After Warsaw Pact troops occupied Prague in August, he and a handful of other politicians were handcuffed and led away to the Soviet Union. Upon his return, he tried to maintain a balancing act, calling upon his countrymen to cooperate and publicly supporting the country's accord with Moscow while also promising to continue economic reform. In 1969 he was named prime minister of the new federal government of Czechoslovakia, and he actively disassociated himself from the "errors" that he and others had committed. His about-face was insufficient; in January 1970 he was forced out as prime minister and by the end of the year expelled from the party. Cernik's attempts to rekindle his

political career after the fall of the communist regime in 1989 were unsuccessful.

Chacel, Rosa Clotilde Cecilia María del Carmen, Spanish novelist and poet (b. June 3, 1898, Valladolid, Spain—d. July 27, 1994, Madrid, Spain), as a member of the Generation of 1927, balanced her dense narrative style with surrealist imagery and psychological insights. Chacel studied painting and sculpture in Madrid, but ill health forced her to quit school in 1918. In 1922 she and her husband, the painter Timoteo Pérez Rubio, moved to Rome, where Chacel taught at the Spanish Academy and wrote her first novel, *Estación: ida y vuelta* (1930; "Station/Season, Round Trip"). After returning to Spain in 1927, she wrote a volume of sonnets, *A la orilla de un pozo* (1936; "At the Well's Edge"). During the Spanish Civil War, Chacel took her son to France, while Pérez Rubio stayed in Madrid to assist in the rescue of the art collection at the Prado Museum from the wartime violence. The family went into exile in South America in 1940. There Chacel published little of the poetry she wrote but continued to release essays, short stories, and novels, notably *Memorias de Leticia Valle* (1945; *Memoirs of Leticia Valle*) and *La sinrazón* (1960; "Without Reason"). She settled permanently in Spain after her husband's death in 1977. Chacel's later writings include fiction, essays, two autobiographical works, a study of her husband's paintings, and the verse collection *Poesia (1931–1991)* (1992). Chacel spent two years (1959–61) in New York City on a Guggenheim fellowship, won the National Award for Spanish Letters, and received the Gold Medal for Fine Arts from King Juan Carlos I shortly before her death.

Childress, Alice, U.S. playwright, novelist, and actress (b. Oct. 12, 1916, Charleston, S.C.—d. Aug. 14, 1994, New York, N.Y.), addressed racial issues frankly and honestly in works that drew on the African-American experience and featured

sensitive portrayals and finely crafted characterizations. Childress, who was reared in Harlem, New York City, performed with the American Negro Theater in both Broadway and Off-Broadway venues during the 1940s. She wrote, directed, and starred in her first play, *Florence* (produced 1949), and enhanced her reputation with the play *Trouble in Mind* (produced 1955; revised and published 1971). The latter satiric play-within-a-play poked fun at white liberals and condemned racial stereotyping in the performing arts. Whereas *Wedding Band* (1966) focused on interracial love, *String* (1969) and *Wine in the Wilderness* (1969) dealt with other racial themes. Many of her plays featured music, including *Just a Little Simple* (produced 1950; based on Langston Hughes's *Simple Speaks His Mind*), *Gold Through the Trees* (produced 1952), *The African Garden* (produced 1971), *Gullah* (produced 1984; based on her 1977 play *Sea Island Song*), and *Moms* (produced 1986). Other novels were written for adolescents, notably *A Hero Ain't Nothin' but a Sandwich* (1973), a story about a teenage drug addict, and *Rainbow Jordan* (1981), which explored the struggles of poor black urban youth. Two plays, *When the Rattlesnake Sounds* (1975) and *Let's Hear It for the Queen* (1976), were also written for juveniles. Childress' straightforward language was often targeted by censors. Among her other novels were *A Short Walk* (1979) and *Those Other People* (1989).

Chung Il Kwon, Korean army officer and politician (b. Nov. 21, 1917, North Hamgyong province, Korea—d. Jan. 17, 1994, Hawaii), was the commander of South Korean troops during some of the most intense fighting with North Korean and Chinese forces during the Korean War (1950–53), and he was hailed as a national hero for his brilliant tactical skills. He led the army during the September 1950 UN landing at Inchon, which crippled the North Korean offensive. Chung was a 1940 graduate of Tokyo's Military Academy and served in Japan's Imperial army during World War II. He then joined the Chinese Nationalist army before entering the South Korean army. Chung retired from the military in 1957 as a four-star general. During the 1960s he was ambassador to the U.S., France, and several Latin-American countries. He served as prime minister (1964–70) under Pres. Park Chung Hee, who had seized power in 1961. Chung then held a number of government posts before Chun Doo Hwan assumed the presidency in 1980.

Clavell, James, British-born U.S. novelist (b. Oct. 10, 1924, Sydney, Australia—d. Sept. 6, 1994, Vevey, Switz.), used his gifts as a storyteller to create long, richly detailed historical adventure novels set in exotic locales. Though his books were not popular with the critics, they were best-sellers; some 21 million copies were sold during his 40-year career. At the age of nine months, Clavell was taken to England from Australia, where his father—a Royal Navy officer—was stationed. During World War II he joined the Royal Artillery, and in 1942 he was captured by the Japanese in Java. He spent 3½ years in the infamous Changi prison camp near Singapore, which was so brutal that only 10,000 of its 150,000 inmates survived. Clavell left military service in 1946 after a motorcycle accident left him with a limp. He held various odd jobs before discovering an interest in films and working first as a film distributor and then, after moving to the U.S., in television production in New York and as a screenwriter in Hollywood. He wrote screenplays for such films as *The Fly* (1958) and *Watusi* (1959), was one of the writers of *The Great Escape* (1963), and wrote, produced, and directed *Five Gates to Hell* (1959), *Walk like a Dragon* (1960), *To Sir with Love* (1966), and *The Last Valley* (1969). He became a U.S. citizen in 1963. During a 1960 screenwriters' strike, Clavell wrote his first novel, *King Rat* (1962, filmed 1965), based on his prison camp experiences. *Tai-Pan* (1966), *Shogun* (1975), and *Noble House* (1981), all of them set in the Far East, became best-sellers and were filmed as television miniseries; *Shogun* (1980) was second only to *Roots* in TV audience ratings. Clavell's later books include *Whirlwind* (1986) and *Gai-Jin* (1993).

Clemo, Reginald John ("JACK"), British poet (b. March 11, 1916, near St. Austell, Cornwall, England—d. July 25, 1994, Weymouth, Dorset, England), despite deafness (from about 1936) and recurrent attacks of blindness that began in childhood and left him sightless by 1956, wrote deeply personal poetry in which he explored the austere harshness of his Cornish birthplace, the spiritual influence of his physical handicaps, the quest that led to his religious conversion, and, eventually, the peace and happiness he found in his marriage at age 52. Clemo was the son of a clay-kiln worker and had no formal education after age 13. In 1948 he published a novel, *Wilding Graft,* and the first of two autobiographies, *Confession of a Rebel,* appeared in 1949. His first book of poems, *The Clay Verge* (1951), was imbued with a love of Cornwall and its people. He followed with a volume of theological essays, *The Invading Gospel* (1958), and two more volumes of poetry, *The Map of Clay* (1961) and *Cactus on Carmel* (1967). After Clemo's marriage to an art teacher in 1968, his poetry showed greater warmth and a sense of redemption. Later works include the verse collections *The Echoing Tip* (1971), *Broad Autumn* (1975), and *Approach to Murano* (1993) and an autobiography, *The Marriage of a Rebel* (1980).

Cobain, Kurt, U.S. musician (b. Feb. 20, 1967, Aberdeen, Wash.—d. April 5, 1994, Seattle, Wash.), as the anointed angst-ridden poet of the so-called Generation X and lead guitarist and singer of the grunge rock band Nirvana, bespoke a deeply personal despair that struck a chord of fellowship among young adults struggling with their own frustrations. Cobain, a troubled youth, turned to music and then heroin as a source of consolation. He and bass player Chris Novoselic formed Nirvana in 1986, and after employing several different drummers, they recruited Dave Grohl in 1989 to complete the trio. The band, whose style derived from punk rock, combined the fury of that genre (they often smashed their equipment during performances) with a deafening sound of anguished lyrics, a signature that together with their torn jeans and flannel shirts ushered in what became known as grunge rock. In 1989 Nirvana (minus Grohl) released its first album, *Bleach,* and gained a counterculture following among college students. Their second album, *Nevermind* (1991), featured the strident lyrics of "Smells like Teen Spirit," which became

REUTERS/BETTMANN

something of an official anthem for their fans. Cobain's unexpected rise to stardom—the album went triple platinum—elevated him to a prominence he abhorred. In Nirvana's next blockbuster album, *In Utero* (1993), he railed against his fame, "I do not want what I have got." He and his wife, Courtney Love, also a heroin addict, temporarily lost custody of their daughter when Love admitted having taken the drug during her pregnancy. His wife was also lead singer of the neo-punk band Hole. In March 1994, while Nirvana was touring Europe, Cobain was rushed to a hospital after slipping into a drug-and-alcohol-induced coma. On April 8, some three days after Cobain took his life, his body, with a gunshot wound to the head, was discovered.

Colosio Murrieta, Luis Donaldo, Mexican politician (b. Feb. 10, 1950, Magdalena de Kino, Sonora, Mexico—d. March 23, 1994, Tijuana, Mexico), was designated (Nov. 28, 1993) by Pres. Carlos Salinas de Gortari as his handpicked successor, making him the governing Institutional Revolutionary Party (PRI) candidate and the odds-on favourite to win the August 1994 elections. Colosio, a 1972 graduate of the Technological Institute of Higher Studies in Monterrey, joined the PRI that same year. After earning a graduate degree (1977) from the University of Pennsylvania in regional and urban development, he became a protégé of Salinas, and in 1979 he joined the Secretariat of Budget and Planning under his mentor. Colosio was elected to Congress in 1985 and in 1987 became a member of the PRI's national executive committee before

winning election to the Senate in 1988. That same year he became Salinas' presidential campaign manager when the latter was named the PRI's candidate by Pres. Miguel de la Madrid. Colosio's political reputation was tarnished when Salinas emerged victorious by a narrow margin only after a suspicious malfunction of the PRI-controlled Federal Electoral Commission's computer. When he was named head of the party, however, Colosio pledged to spearhead electoral reform and attempted to distance himself from the authoritarian rule of the PRI, in power since 1929. In 1992 Colosio headed the newly created Social Development Secretariat (Sedesol), a program designed to address poverty. His promises of social reform, however, did not prevent the January 1994 uprising in the state of Chiapas, one of the chief beneficiaries of Sedesol. While campaigning as a man of the people and one dedicated to democracy, Colosio appeared without the protection of bodyguards. As a result, he proved an easy target for the assassin who gunned him down at a campaign rally.

Cooper, Dame Whina, New Zealand Maori activist (b. Dec. 9, 1895, Panguru, Northland region, N.Z.—d. March 26, 1994, Panguru), campaigned throughout her life for land rights and social justice for the aboriginal Maori people. As the daughter of the tribal chief Heremia Te Wake, Cooper was a highly visible leader. At age 18 she led her first protest—concerning the draining of a local swamp. She trained as a teacher at St. Joseph's College and later worked as a storekeeper and postmistress. After the death of her second husband, William Cooper, in 1949, she resumed her role as a social activist. In 1951 she was elected the first president of the Maori Women's Welfare League, through which she fought for better health care and for an increased role for women in the debate over native rights. Two years later she became a justice of the peace. In 1975 Cooper established the group Te Roopu o te Matakite and, despite the need for a cane, walked the length of North Island at the head of the month-long Maori Land Reform March. She was created Dame Commander of the Order of the British Empire in 1981 and was made a member of the Order of New Zealand in 1991.

Copleston, Frederick Charles, British Jesuit priest and scholar (b. April 10, 1907, Taunton, Somerset, England—d. Feb. 3, 1994, London, England), wrote the nine-volume work *A History of Philosophy* (1946–74), a concise, clearly written, and objective overview that became a standard introductory philosophy text for thousands of university students, particularly in its U.S. paperback edition (1962–77). Copleston attended Marlborough College, from which he was expelled after he converted from Anglicanism to Roman Catholicism, and St. John's College, Oxford. He joined the Society of Jesus in 1930 and was ordained in 1937. In 1939 he was named professor of the history of philosophy at Heythrop College (later a school of the University of London). He retained that position until he was elevated to principal of Heythrop (1970–74) and dean of the faculty of theology (1972–74). He also taught metaphysics on a regular basis at the Gregorian University in Rome (1952–69) and served as a visiting professor at the University of Santa Clara, Calif. (1975–82). In 1946 Copleston published *A History of Philosophy: Greece and Rome,* the first book of what he originally envisioned as a three-volume survey. His other books include *Nietzsche* (1942), *Philosophies and Cultures* (1980), and *Philosophy in Russia* (1986), which many scholars felt should have been released as volume 10 in the *History* series. Copleston was made Commander of the Order of the British Empire in 1993.

Cotten, Joseph, U.S. actor (b. May 15, 1905, Petersburg, Va.—d. Feb. 6, 1994, Los Angeles, Calif.), was an accomplished Broadway star and a silver screen matinee idol whose elegant mannerisms, handsome looks, and low-key yet compelling dramatic performances earned him both popular and critical acclaim. Cotten, tall and wavy-haired and distinguished by a trace of a Southern drawl, was a major player from 1937 in Orson Welles's Mercury Theater radio ensemble before appearing in the benchmark Broadway production of *The Philadelphia Story* (1939–40) opposite Katharine Hepburn. He secured his reputation, however, starring in three classics by Welles, beginning with his film debut as a drama critic in *Citizen Kane* (1941), followed by *The Magnificent Ambersons* (1942) and *Journey into Fear* (1942). Cotten then starred as the likable yet murderous Uncle Charlie in the Alfred Hitchcock thriller *Shadow of a Doubt* (1943), a serious Scotland Yard detective in *Gaslight* (1944), and a shell-shocked veteran in *I'll Be Seeing You* (1945). He often played the romantic lead, notably opposite such stars as Ingrid Bergman in *Under Capricorn* (1949), Joan Fontaine in *September Affair* (1950), and Jennifer Jones in *Duel in the Sun* (1946) and *Portrait of Jenny* (1948). For his role in the latter, as an artist mesmerized and inspired by the model for one of his paintings, he won the best actor award at the Venice Film Festival. Cotten was superb in *The Third Man* (1949), but his screen career declined sharply in the 1950s, and he appeared mainly in westerns and Italian films. Later films credits include *Hush . . . Hush, Sweet Charlotte* (1961), *The Great Sioux Massacre* (1965), *Airport '77* (1977), and *Heaven's Gate* (1980). A stroke in 1981 left him temporarily speechless and ended his acting career.

Curry, John Anthony, British figure skater (b. Sept. 9, 1949, Birmingham, England—d. April 15, 1994, Binton, Warwickshire, England), came to be known as "the Nureyev of the ice" as he defied conventional wisdom within the sporting establishment and revolutionized men's figure skating with a combination of graceful athleticism and innovative choreography derived from classical ballet. As a boy, Curry studied figure skating because his father considered ballet too effeminate. He won his first skating trophy in 1965 and captured the British national championship five times between 1970 and 1975. In the early 1970s he acquired an American financial sponsor and began training in the U.S. Despite solid compulsory figures and inspired free skating, Curry repeatedly failed to win in international competitions, as tradition-bound judges downgraded his performances and favoured his more athletic competitors. He persevered, however, and in 1976, after toning down his routine somewhat, he finally triumphed, winning the European championship, the Olympic gold medal, and the world championship within a three-month period. In later years, as director of his own professional skating company, Curry worked closely with ballet choreographers, including Kenneth MacMillan, Twyla Tharp, John Butler, and Peter Martins. He also performed occasionally off the ice—as an actor and a dancer—and in 1978 he founded a skating school in New York City. Curry was made an Officer of the Order of the British Empire in 1976. Diagnosed with AIDS, he retired from skating in 1991.

Cushing, Peter Wilton, British actor (b. May 26, 1913, Kenley, Surrey, England—d. Aug. 11, 1994, Canterbury, Kent, England), raised the horror film to an art form with his many portrayals of Baron Frankenstein, Dr. Van Helsing, and similar characters in such classics of the genre as *The Revenge of Frankenstein* (1958), *Dracula* (1958), *The Brides of Dracula* (1960), *Frankenstein Must Be Destroyed* (1969), *The House That Dripped Blood* (1971), and *Frankenstein and the Monster from Hell* (1974). Although the gaunt, elegant Cushing appeared in some 100 motion pictures in his 50-year career, he found his true métier in the horror movies made by Hammer Films, beginning with *The Curse of Frankenstein* (1957). He was also successful as Sherlock Holmes in *The Hound of the Baskervilles* (1959) and in a television series a decade later, as Dr. Who in *Dr. Who and the Daleks* (1965) and *Daleks—Invasion Earth 2150 A.D.* (1966), and as Grand Moff Tarkin in *Star Wars* (1977). Cushing made his professional stage debut with the Worthing Repertory Company in 1935 and his Hollywood film debut four years later in *The Man in the Iron Mask*. His early work was mainly in classical stage and screen roles, no-

CAMERA PRESS/GLOBE PHOTOS

tably as Osric in the 1948 film version of *Hamlet*, but his career took off with his award-winning performance as Winston Smith in a 1954 BBC television adaptation of George Orwell's *Nineteen Eighty-four*. Cushing continued to act through the 1980s and published two volumes of memoirs.

Degrelle, Léon Joseph Marie, Belgian fascist (b. June 15, 1906, Bouillon, Belgium—d. March 31, 1994, Málaga, Spain), was perhaps his country's best-known World War II Nazi collaborator, leader of the fascist Rexist Party of Belgium, and commander of the Walloon (French-speaking Belgian) troops in the German army. Degrelle, the son of a prosperous brewer, attended the University of Louvain. In 1930 he founded the Rexists as an extreme right-wing Roman Catholic populist movement, and in the 1936 national election the party unexpectedly won more than 10% of the vote and 21 of the 202 seats in Parliament. After the Rexists broke with the more moderate Roman Catholics, Degrelle lost influence until the German invasion of Belgium inspired him to collaborate with the occupation forces. In 1941 he founded the Walloon Legion, which was later attached to the Waffen-SS on the Russian front. He won the Iron Cross and was decorated by Adolf Hitler personally. After the war Degrelle was tried in absentia and sentenced to death, but he had fled to Spain, where Gen. Francisco Franco rejected Belgian demands for his extradition. In 1954 Degrelle became a Spanish citizen under the name Léon José de Ramírez Reina.

Delvaux, Paul, Belgian painter (b. Sept. 23, 1897, Antheit, Liège, Belgium—d. July 20, 1994, Veurne, Belgium), in his mature works visually conveyed a dreamlike state, often juxtaposing nude, doe-eyed women with skeletons and other incongruous images in settings of richly detailed classical architecture. Delvaux studied architecture and painting at the Académie des Beaux-Arts in Brussels. As a young artist, he experimented with Expressionism and Impressionism. In the early 1930s, however, he was introduced to the Surrealist works of Salvador Dalí, René Magritte, E.L.T. Mesens, Max Ernst, and Giorgio de Chirico, whose use of imagery was especially influential. Although Delvaux rejected being labeled, he was well established within the Surrealist movement by 1936, when he exhibited his paintings in a joint show with Magritte. The first major retrospective of Delvaux's paintings was held in Brussels in 1944–45; soon after, he was the subject of a documentary art film. From 1950 to 1962 he was a professor of painting at the École Nationale Supérieure d'Art et d'Architecture in

Brussels. In 1982 the Paul Delvaux Museum, devoted exclusively to his work, opened in Sint-Idesbald on the North Sea coast. Delvaux and his wife eventually retired to Veurne, an isolated Flemish village, to escape the glare of publicity. He continued to paint until his eyesight failed in the late 1980s.

Doisneau, Robert, French photographer (b. April 14, 1912, Gentilly, near Paris, France—d. April 1, 1994, Paris), immortalized the spirit of post-World War II Paris through black-and-white photographs that captured the romance, humour, and poignancy embodied in the lives of ordinary people caught in the act of doing ordinary things. Although he was eventually forced to reveal that one of his best-known pictures—a couple kissing in a crowded street—was staged with paid models, Doisneau created candid images that conveyed the spontaneity and absurdity of everyday life to "show the world as I would like it to be at all times." After studying lithography and engraving at the École Estienne in Paris, he laboured as a photographer's assistant and worked in the advertising department of the Renault automobile factory (1934–39). During the German occupation he fought with the French army and put his skills to use forging papers for the Resistance. After the war he earned a living as a fashion photographer for *Vogue* magazine, a portraitist of Parisian artists and intellectuals, and a commercial photographer, but he continued to work as a freelance photojournalist, wandering the streets of Paris on a daily basis taking pictures that appeared in the pages of *Life* and other international publications. Doisneau's images, which were first exhibited at the Museum of Modern Art in New York City in 1951, were later exhibited throughout the U.S. and France and were collected into numerous books.

Ellison, Ralph Waldo, U.S. writer and educator (b. March 1, 1914, Oklahoma City, Okla.—d. April 16, 1994, New York, N.Y.), spent seven years writing his seminal novel, *Invisible Man* (1952), which explored through the eyes of a nameless black narrator the sense of racial alienation experienced by blacks and the social forces that conspire to deny all individuals an identity. His work, which was immediately recognized as a classic, earned him a National Book Award in 1953 and a permanent niche as one of the most important American writers of the 20th century. Ellison, who attended Tuskegee (Ala.) Institute, from 1933 to 1936, began writing short stories while serving in the Merchant Marine during World War II. *Invisible Man* told the story of a young black man who experienced rejection by both blacks and whites as he pursued university studies in the South and traveled north to become a political activist. Ellison, who produced two volumes of essays, *Shadow and Act* (1964) and *Going to the Territory* (1986), spent the remainder of his life working on a second novel, which was unpublished at the time of his death. He taught creative writing at New York University besides serving as a visiting scholar at various universities. Ellison influenced such writers as Joseph Heller and Kurt Vonnegut.

Ellul, Jacques César, French sociopolitical scientist and Protestant theologian (b. Jan. 6, 1912, Bordeaux, France—d. May 19, 1994, Bordeaux), warned against the dangers of a society in which all human activity was determined according to absolute technical efficiency. His antitechnological views, particularly as expressed in his best-known book, *La Technique: ou l'enjeu du siècle* (1954; *The Technological Society,* 1964), were especially popular among rebellious young Americans in the late 1960s. Ellul's theories were largely grounded in his dual interest in Marxism (which he later renounced) and an austere Protestantism found in the Reformed Church, both of which he discovered while a student. After completing his studies at the Universities of Bordeaux and Paris, Ellul lectured at the Universities of Montpellier (1937–38) and Strasbourg (1938–40). During World War II he joined (1940) the French Resistance, and later he tried his hand at politics as deputy mayor of Bordeaux (1944–47). He soon abandoned his attempt at a political solution to social problems, however, and returned to the University of Bordeaux as a professor of law (1946–80) and as professor of history at the affiliated Institute of Political Studies (1947–80). Ellul was also a consultant to the Ecumenical World Council of Churches (1947–53) and a member of the National Council of the Reformed Church in France (1950–70). His other books include *Le Fondement théologique du droit* (1946; *The Theological Foundation of Law,* 1960), *L'Illusion politique* (1965; *The Political Illusion,* 1967), and *L'Ethique de la liberté* (1973; *The Ethics of Freedom,* 1976).

Enwonwu, Benedict Chuka, Nigerian artist (b. July 14, 1921, Onitsha, Nigeria—d. Feb. 5, 1994, Lagos, Nigeria), gained international recognition in the 1950s and '60s for figurative sculptures and paintings in which he combined classical Western training with traditional African elements. Enwonwu first showed artistic promise while at Nigeria's Government College. He won a scholarship to study in England, where he attended Goldsmith's College, London (1944), Ruskin College, Oxford (1944–46), and the Slade College of Art in London (1946–48). In 1946 he participated in a UN-sponsored international exhibition in Paris; two years later he held his first one-man show in London. Enwonwu was soon known as a major artist, and in 1957 Queen Elizabeth II posed for him for a controversial bronze sculpture that graced the entrance to the Nigerian parliament building. In 1959 he returned to Nigeria as official art adviser to the federal government. He quit public service in 1971 to serve as a visiting professor of African studies at Howard University, Washington, D.C., and as professor of fine arts at the University of Ife, Nigeria. He retired in 1975. Enwonwu's other notable works include the carved doors of the chapel for the Apostolic Delegation in Lagos and an elegant bronze figure of a woman donated by the Nigerian government to the UN headquarters in New York City in 1966. He was made a Member of the Order of the British Empire in 1958 and received the Nigerian National Merit Award in 1980.

Erikson, Erik Homburger, German-born psychoanalyst (b. June 15, 1902, Frankfurt am Main, Germany—d. May 12, 1994, Harwich, Mass.), profoundly influenced the study of human development with the 1950 publication of *Childhood and Society,* in which he divided human development, from infancy to old age, into eight stages. Each of these stages in the life cycle, he theorized, presented a crisis resolution that was influenced by culture, society, and history and contributed to the individual's ability to grow and change. Erikson also coined the term *identity crisis,* a personal psychosocial conflict that shaped a distinct aspect of personality. Though he was a disciple of Sigmund Freud, Erikson departed from Freud's theory that the ego was fixed in early childhood. Erikson's psychobiographies of Martin Luther, *Young Man Luther* (1958), and Mohandas K. Gandhi, *Gandhi's Truth on the Origins of Militant Nonviolence* (1969), interpreted their lives in terms of their psychological development. The latter book won Erikson a Pulitzer Prize and a National Book Award in 1970.

When he was 68, Erikson divulged the secret behind his own identity crisis: his birth was the result of his Danish Lutheran mother's extramarital affair with a Danish man. He never knew his father. From the age of three, however, Erikson carried the name of his stepfather, a German Jew, and was known as Erik Homburger. This dual identity disturbed him emotionally. After graduating from high school, he traveled in Europe before settling in Vienna. He was 25 when Anna Freud became his psychoanalyst. He trained at the Vienna Psychoanalytic Institute and became a full member in 1933, the year he fled from Hitler's Europe to the U.S. There, with neither a medical nor a university degree, he practiced child psychoanalysis in Boston and served on the faculties at Harvard Medical School (1935–36), Yale School of Medicine (1936–39), and the

NEWSWEEK

University of California at Berkeley (1939–50). His studies concentrated on those living on the fringes of society, and he was known especially for his observations of the Yurok tribe of northern California. He repeatedly found that similar problems are approached in various ways by different societies. Erikson left Berkeley after refusing to sign a loyalty oath and joined the Austen Riggs Center in Stockbridge, Mass. In 1960 he returned to Harvard, and in 1970 he was made professor emeritus.

Faubus, Orval Eugene, U.S. politician (b. Jan. 7, 1910, Greasy Creek, Ark.—d. Dec. 14, 1994, Conway, Ark.), as governor (1954–67) of Arkansas, defied a 1957 federal court order to desegregate schools and called out the Arkansas National Guard to "prevent violence" by blocking the access of nine black students to Little Rock Central High School; his action was countered by Pres. Dwight D. Eisenhower, who mobilized 1,200 U.S. Army paratroopers to usher the students into the school. Faubus, the son of a poor farmer, was a southern populist who supported New Deal policies. After his election as governor, he appointed six black men to the Democratic State Committee, a move that triggered a charge during his 1956 reelection campaign that he was "soft" on racism. The following year—after the entire Arkansas legislature signed the Southern Manifesto, which attacked the Supreme Court's desegregation law as "naked judicial power"—Faubus determined that his political survival depended on stopping desegregation. His actions attracted national television attention and set the stage for the South's resistance to integration. After leaving office in 1967, Faubus worked as a bank clerk and made three (1970, 1974, and 1986) unsuccessful bids for the governorship. He defended his record in *The Faubus Years* (1991).

Feather, Leonard Geoffrey, British jazz critic and songwriter (b. Sept. 13, 1914, London, England—d. Sept. 22, 1994, Los Angeles, Calif.), compiled the standard reference work *The Encyclopedia of Jazz* (1955), a several-times revised and expanded work offering histories, musical analyses, and thousands of biographies, and he served (from the 1960s until the 1990s) as the influential jazz critic for the *Los Angeles Times.* Feather contributed articles on music to the British publication *Melody Maker* before he embarked on a career as a record producer and migrated to the U.S. in the late 1930s. While serving as a publicist for Duke Ellington during the early 1940s, he bit-

terly feuded with jazz traditionalists who decried the emergence of bebop, a style he highly praised in his well-regarded book *Inside Be-bop* (1949). Besides composing such songs as "Evil Gal Blues" and "Blowtop Blues," which Dinah Washington recorded, and "How Blue Can You Get?," a B.B. King hit, Feather played piano on recordings by major artists. During his tenure at the *Los Angeles Times,* Feather championed younger musicians and harshly criticized avant-garde jazz. He also taught at various universities in California.

Firkusny, Rudolf, Czech-born U.S. pianist (b. Feb. 11, 1912, Napajedla, Moravia, Austria-Hungary [now Czech Republic]—d. July 19, 1994, Staatsburg, N.Y.), had an elegant, patrician style and was a champion of the music of his compatriots; early in his career he also composed. As a child he began studies with Czech composer Leos Janacek; other preparation included the study of composition with Josef Suk and piano with Alfred Cortot and Artur Schnabel. Firkusny began performing as a child prodigy in the musical capitals of Europe in the early 1920s and made his debut in London in 1933 and in New York City in 1938. Escaping the Nazis, he had settled in New York by 1941 and later became a U.S. citizen. Although he was praised for his performances of Mozart, Beethoven, and Brahms, he became best known as an interpreter of the Czech masters Bedrich Smetana, Dvorak, Janacek, and his friend Bohuslav Martinu, who wrote a number of works for Firkusny. He also frequently performed works by other 20th-century composers. He collaborated with orchestras, both in the U.S. and elsewhere, and was known especially for his performances of Dvorak's neglected piano concerto. Among his recordings were the complete piano works of Janacek. He taught at the Juilliard School, New York City, and in Aspen, Colo. After the fall of the communist regime in Czechoslovakia at the end of the 1980s, Firkusny returned to his homeland to perform for the first time in some 44 years. He received a number of honours and was made a member of the Order of Tomas Masaryk, the Czechoslovak patriot and an early sponsor.

Francis, Samuel Lewis ("SAM"), U.S. painter (b. June 25, 1923, San Mateo, Calif.—d. Nov. 4, 1994, Santa Monica, Calif.), applied coloured stains to pure white canvases to create a luminescent effect that was rooted in the subtle influences of French and Japanese painting. After 1970, however, his works became more bold; heavy stripes were complemented with splattered drips and blobs in contrasting colours. Francis, who initially studied medicine, took up painting in a hospital while recovering from spinal tuberculosis, an affliction that resulted from an airplane crash when he was serving with the U.S. Air Force during World War II. He studied at the California School of Fine Art, San Francisco, before moving (1950) to Paris to attend Fernand Léger's private academy. Though Francis was associated with the second generation of New York Abstract Expressionist painters—those artists who relied on an emotional approach to the conception and execution of their works—he cultivated his style in Paris, where he was inspired by the works of Cézanne, Monet, and Matisse, especially the latter's expressions of pure colour. In 1952 Francis established an international reputation with his first one-man show in Paris; he made his New York City debut in 1956 with a solo exhibition at the Martha Jackson Gallery. The following year he visited East Asia, gaining insight into Japanese art and Buddhist meditative techniques. In the late 1950s Francis completed commissions for murals at the Sofu School of flower arrangement in Tokyo and at the Chase Manhattan Bank in New York City. He returned (1960s) to California and took up residence in the Los Angeles area. He was a founding trustee of the Museum of Contemporary Art in Los Angeles.

Gerulaitis, Vitas, U.S. tennis player (b. July 26, 1954, Brooklyn, N.Y.—d. Sept. 18, 1994, Southampton, N.Y.), by means of his court-sweeping speed, precision shots, and dependable forehand, ranked among the top 10 professional tennis players from 1977 to 1982; he won only one Grand Slam event, however, the 1977 Australian Open singles title. The shaggy-haired Gerulaitis was one of the circuit's most visible personalities, and his high-spirited lifestyle ensured that his name remained in the headlines. During his 14-year career he won 27 singles and 9 doubles tournaments. Gerulaitis captured the 1975 Wimbledon doubles championship and the Italian Open twice (1977 and 1979); he reached the finals in the 1979 U.S. Open and 1980 French Open. During the 1980s Gerulaitis admitted that he had been treated for drug abuse, and in 1983 he was implicated but never charged in a cocaine-dealing conspiracy. After his retirement in 1985, Gerulaitis began a career as a sports announcer and later made a comeback as a player on the senior circuit. He was found dead after a faulty propane heater leaked lethal fumes into the heating and air-conditioning system of a friend's home where he was staying.

Goren, Shlomo, Israeli cleric (b. 1917, Zambrow, Poland—d. Oct. 29, 1994, Tel Aviv, Israel), was an important and often controversial figure in Israel's religious and military establishment. Goren, born in Poland, moved with his family to Palestine in 1925. He entered the yeshiva at age 12, and by age 17 he had published his first religious article and was considered a prodigy. About 1936 Goren joined the Haganah, the underground military organization that fought the British in Palestine. As a soldier in the Palestine war of 1948–49, Goren was often asked to help resolve specific questions concerning religious observance under wartime conditions, and in 1948 the chief rabbis in Israel named him chief chaplain of the new state's army. In that position he was often noted for his bravery, accompanying troops to the front and at times going behind enemy lines to bring back the dead for burial; he rose to the rank of brigadier general. He retired from the army in 1972, and in that year Goren was elected Israel's chief Ashkenazic rabbi. His decisions were considered attempts to reconcile religious teaching and technological progress, and he often clashed with the chief rabbi of the Sephardic tradition. Goren served in that post until 1983, yet he continued to offer his opinions into the 1990s. He bitterly opposed accommodation with the Palestine Liberation Organization; he made headlines in late 1993 when he "ruled" that soldiers could disobey orders and refuse to dismantle settlements in the West Bank, and in 1994 he pronounced that religious law commanded Jews to kill Yasir Arafat. Goren wrote many religious articles and essays, including his commentary on the Talmud, *Ha-Yerushalmi ha-Meforash* (1961), a volume that won the Israel prize.

Goria, Giovanni Giuseppe, Italian politician (b. July 30, 1943, Asti, Italy—d. May 21, 1994, Asti), was Italy's finance minister (1982–87, 1992–93) as well as the country's youngest post-World War II prime minister (July 1987–March 1988). He resigned from the Cabinet in February 1993 when he was caught up in a widespread government corruption investigation. Goria joined the Christian Democratic Party at age 17 and entered local politics in Asti soon after studying for a degree in economics at the University of Turin. He was elected to the national Chamber of Deputies in 1976 and was appointed undersecretary for the budget in 1981. Although Goria had no political power base within the Christian Democrats, his youth, good looks, and relative success as a pragmatic finance minister made him an acceptable compromise choice to lead the country after Socialist Prime Minister Bettino Craxi's resignation forced a snap election in June 1987. Goria submitted his own resignation in February 1988 after a rebellious Parliament had rejected his proposed budget bill 17 times in three weeks. His resignation was not accepted initially, and he remained in office for another month. He was elected to the European Parliament in 1989, returned to Rome as agriculture minister in 1991, and rejoined the Finance Ministry the next year. In February 1994 he was brought to trial on corruption charges. Goria, who strongly denied the accusations of bribery and corruption, was acquitted of one charge; another was still pending at the time of his death.

Gottman, Jean-Iona, French geographer (b. Oct. 10, 1915, Kharkov, Ukraine, Russian Empire—d. Feb. 28, 1994, Oxford, England), introduced the concept and term *megalopolis* (from an ancient Greek concept) to describe a densely populated social and economic entity encompassing two or more cities and the increasingly urbanized space between them. After a four-year study of the region stretching from Boston to Washington, D.C., Gottman published *Megalopolis: The Urbanized Northeastern Seaboard of the United States* (1961), in which he concluded that this fusion of cities "was the cradle of a new order in the organization of inhabited space." Gottman was reared by relatives in Paris after his Ukrainian-Jewish parents were killed in 1917. He was at the Sorbonne as a student (1934–37) and researcher (1937–41), but he was forced out during the World War II German occupation of France. In 1941 he moved to the U.S., where he was a government consultant (1942–44), an associate professor at Johns Hopkins University, Baltimore, Md. (1943–48), and a member of the Institute for Advanced Study, Princeton, N.J. (1942–65). He later taught at the University of Paris (1948–56), served as director of the École Pratique des Hautes Études in Paris (1960–84), and eventually settled at the University of Oxford as professor of geography (1968–83), professor emeritus (1983–94), and fellow of Hertford College (1968–94). Gottman's other books include *Virginia at Mid-Century* (1955) and *Megalopolis Revisited* (1987).

Greenberg, Clement, U.S. art critic (b. Jan. 16, 1909, New York, N.Y.—d. May 7, 1994, New York), exerted extraordinary influence over postwar North American art as a champion of both Abstract Expressionism and one of the movement's chief exponents, Jackson Pollock. His patronage was essential to elevating the emerging movement into a major art form, and his critical essays in the *Partisan Review* and his role as art critic for the *Nation* magazine, two powerful cultural publications, made him the chief arbiter of art in the late 1930s, '40s, and '50s. Greenberg's own artistic talents were discouraged by his parents, who destroyed all of his drawings. The experience was instrumental in laying the foundation for Greenberg's theory on the mutual antagonism between art and the average person. After graduating from Syracuse (N.Y.) University (1930), he returned to New York City and translated books. While working for the government as a customs clerk, he began to write essays that espoused a formal approach to looking at art, the so-called Greenberg formalism. In addition to shaping the career of Pollock, Greenberg helped promote Helen Frankenthaler, Mark Rothko, Jules Olitski, and David Smith. He routinely visited galleries and artists' studios, where he offered his advice. Greenberg disavowed such movements as Pop and Conceptual Art and wrote little after the 1960s.

Habyarimana, Juvénal, Rwandan army officer and politician (b. March 8, 1937?, Gasizi, Gisenyi province, Ruanda-Urundi—d. April 6, 1994, near Kigali, Rwanda), ruled Rwanda almost single-handedly for more than 20 years after he seized power in a bloodless coup on July 5, 1973. Habyarimana studied humanities and mathematics at St. Paul's College and medicine at Lovanium University, both in Belgian Congo (now Zaire). He returned home in 1960 to begin training for the National Guard in Kigali. Although he was a member of the Hutu majority ethnic group, he proved to be an effective officer against insurgents from both the Hutu and the Tutsi minority. He rapidly rose through the ranks, becoming chief of staff (1963–65) and then minister of defense and police chief of staff (1965–73). In April 1973 he was promoted to major general; three months later he led a group of disgruntled Hutu officers in the overthrow of Pres. Grégoire Kayibanda. Habyarimana initially banned all political activity. In 1975 he established the National Revolutionary Movement for Development, with himself as sole leader of the single-party state. He gradually allowed more civilian involvement, however, and after the country's first multiparty elections in 1992, he was forced to relinquish some power to the new Tutsi prime minister. Habyarimana and Pres. Cyprien Ntaryamira, the Hutu leader of neighbouring Burundi, were returning from ongoing peace talks between the two ethnic groups when their plane was shot down. The death of the two Hutu presidents under suspicious circumstances ignited the simmering tensions between the Hutu and Tutsi and led to the massacres and the mass exodus from Rwanda.

Hawkins, Frederick ("ERICK"), U.S. modern dancer and choreographer (b. April 23, 1909, Trinidad, Colo.—d. Nov. 23, 1994, New York, N.Y.), was the first male dancer in Martha Graham's dance company; he later formed and danced in his own company. When he was a student at Harvard, reading Greek, Hawkins saw a performance by Harald Kreutzberg, a German modern dancer, and decided to make dance his career. After graduation (1930) he studied with Kreutzberg for two months in Austria. He moved to New York in 1934, studied ballet at George Balanchine and Lincoln Kirstein's newly formed School of American Ballet, and the following year began dancing with the American Ballet. In 1936 he also became a member of Ballet Caravan; Hawkins' first choreography, *Show Piece* (1937), was created for that company. After having performed (1938) as a guest artist with Graham's company, Hawkins began a relationship with her and in 1939 joined her company. They were married in 1948. In addition to creating leading roles in such Graham works as *El Penitente, Appalachian Spring,* and *Night Journey,* he handled the company's administrative work. He also presented some of his own works in her programs. In 1951 he left the company to organize his own group, which eventually became the Erick Hawkins Dance Company. He and Graham were divorced in 1954. Hawkins' works were deeply influenced by American Indian rituals, folklore, Zen Buddhism, Western and Eastern philosophies, and Asian theatre. His dances—among them, *Here and Now with Watchers* (1957), *To Everybody Out There* (1964), *Angels of the Inmost Heaven* (1972), *Parson Weems and the Cherry Tree* (1975), and *Death Is the Hunter* (1975)—employed his Normative Theory of Movement; the body movement was free, simple, and natural—unforced. Hawkins received the National Medal of Arts in October 1994.

Hebblethwaite, Peter, British writer (b. Sept. 30, 1930, Ashton-under-Lyne, Lancashire, England—d. Dec. 18, 1994, Oxford, England), was considered the foremost "Vaticanologist" in the English-speaking world and wrote the definitive biographies of two popes—*John XXIII: Pope of the Council* (1984; U.S. title, *Pope John XXIII: Shepherd of the Modern World,* 1985) and *Paul VI: The First Modern Pope* (1993). Hebblethwaite was educated in England and France, joined the Society of Jesus in 1948, and was ordained a priest in 1963. His attendance at the final sessions of the Second Vatican Council sparked his interest in the papacy and the modernization then taking place in the church. Hebblethwaite was editor of the Jesuit magazine *The Month* from 1965 to 1973. In 1974, unhappy with the church's slow progress on liberalization, he left the priesthood and married. He then was assistant editor of *The Frontier* (1974–76), a lecturer at Wadham College, Oxford (1976–79), and (from 1979) a writer for the *National Catholic Reporter.* Among his other books were *The Year of Three Popes* (1978) and *The Next Pope,* to be published posthumously. Hebblethwaite was a contributor to *Britannica Book of the Year* for some 25 years.

Hiller, Lejaren, U.S. composer (b. Feb. 23, 1924, New York City—d. Jan. 26, 1994, Buffalo, N.Y.), was a pioneer in computer music. From childhood Hiller was interested in both science and music, and he pursued a dual career for much of his life. He graduated from Princeton University with degrees in chemistry (Ph.D., 1947) but also studied composition with Roger Sessions and Milton Babbitt. After a five-year stint as a research chemist in industry, during which time he continued to compose and saw his first works performed publicly, Hiller joined the chemistry department at the University of Illinois at Urbana-Champaign. Working there on the ILLIAC IV, the first large-scale university computer, Hiller recognized certain parallels between computer applications in science and the process of composing. In collaboration with Leonard Isaacson, he wrote the *Illiac Suite for String Quartet* (1956), in which many compositional decisions were given to the computer to make in conformity with a set of rules or weighted probabilities set down by the composer. Other major works included *Computer Cantata* for soprano, tape, and chamber ensemble (1963), *Algorithms I–III* (1968–72), and (with John Cage) *HPSCHD* (1968), a deliberately chaotic work for 1–7 harpsichords (playing pieces of Mozart) and 1–51 channels of taped sound. Hiller also wrote chamber music for traditional instruments as well as a variety of theatre, motion-picture, and television music. He directed the University of Illinois electronic music studio until 1968, when he moved to the State University of New York at Buffalo. There he taught composition and codirected (with Lukas Foss) the Center for the Creative and Performing Arts.

Hoad, Lewis Alan ("LEW"), Australian tennis player (b. Nov. 23, 1934, Sydney, Australia—d. July 3, 1994, Fuengirola, Spain), with his frequent doubles partner and sometime rival Ken Rosewall, dominated amateur tennis in the mid-1950s. The "Sydney twins," as the two were labeled almost from the beginning, led Australia to the Davis Cup championship in 1953, 1955, and 1956. Hoad won 13 Grand Slam events: the Australian singles (1956) and men's doubles (1953, 1956, and 1957); the French singles (1956), doubles (1953), and mixed doubles (1954); the All-England (Wimbledon) singles (1956 and 1957) and doubles (1953, 1955, and 1956); and the U.S. doubles (1956). At his peak in 1956, he captured 15 singles and 17 doubles titles, and he just missed a Grand Slam sweep when he lost the French doubles (with Ashley Cooper) in the final and then lost the U.S. singles final to Rosewall. Hoad turned professional in 1957. He was known for the strength of his wrists and the power of his serve; however, recurring back problems ended his career and plagued his attempted comeback (1968–72). In 1968 Hoad and his wife opened a tennis camp in Spain. He was inducted into the International Tennis Hall of Fame in 1980. In January 1994

Hoad was diagnosed with a rare, virulent form of leukemia.

Hodgkin, Dorothy Mary Crowfoot, British chemist (b. May 12, 1910, Cairo, Egypt—d. July 29, 1994, Shipston-on-Stour, Warwickshire, England), won the 1964 Nobel Prize for Chemistry for her work in determining the atomic structure of vitamin B_{12} and other important biochemical compounds. Hodgkin studied chemistry at Somerville College, Oxford (B.A., 1931; B.Sc., 1932), and the University of Cambridge (Ph.D., 1937), but most of her research was in X-ray crystallography, which was more closely linked to physics than to chemistry. She returned to Somerville College as a tutor in 1935; she became a fellow the following year and remained there until 1977. Hodgkin then became

UPI/BETTMANN

fellow by special election (1977–82) at Oxford's Wolfson College. She remained active as chancellor (1970–88) and honorary fellow (from 1988) at the University of Bristol. In the 1930s and early '40s, Hodgkin began work on an X-ray analysis of the atomic structure of penicillin and of insulin (though it took nearly 35 years to finally accomplish the latter). From 1948 to 1956 she concentrated her crystallographic research on vitamin B_{12}, an enormously complex nonprotein compound crucial to the treatment of pernicious anemia. She also did research into other compounds, including cholesterol and vitamin D. Hodgkin was a founder (1957) of the Pugwash Conference on Science and World Affairs, Wolfson research professor of the Royal Society (1960–77), a member of the Order of Merit (1965), and the winner of numerous international awards.

Honecker, Erich, German political leader (b. Aug. 25, 1912, Neunkirchen, Germany—d. May 29, 1994, Santiago, Chile), was first secretary of the Socialist Unity (Communist) Party (SED) and thus head of state of the German Democratic Republic (GDR; East Germany) from 1971 to 1989. Honecker's career was inextricably linked with the Berlin Wall, the supreme emblem of the Cold War, from 1961 (when he was placed in charge of its construction) through 1989 (when it was physically breached in the bloodless revolution that overthrew his communist regime) to 1993 (when criminal charges that he had issued "shoot-to-kill" orders to East German border guards were dropped because he was dying of cancer). Honecker, who was the son of communist activists, joined the Young Pioneers at age 10 and left school to work four years later. After Adolf Hitler's accession to power (1933), he organized anti-Nazi opposition in northern Germany. He was arrested in 1935 and in 1937

was sentenced to 10 years' imprisonment, a sentence that probably spared him from being shot in later crackdowns on the opposition. He was released in 1945 and was the founding chairman of the Free German Youth Movement (1946–55). As the new GDR was forming, Honecker rose rapidly in the SED. By 1967 he was the designated successor to the East German leader, Walter Ulbricht, who resigned under pressure in 1971. As head of state Honecker took advantage of West Germany's policy of accommodation and signed the Basic Treaty by which Bonn recognized East Germany's existence as an independent nation. For a time he successfully balanced the GDR's ties to the Soviet Union and to West Germany, which he visited in 1987. Internal unrest grew, however, and thousands of East Germans fled to the West, despite Honecker's tightfisted rule, tough emigration restrictions, and reported shootings. Honecker could not withstand the fall of communism throughout Eastern Europe, and in October 1989 he resigned. He took refuge on a Soviet military base near Berlin to avoid criminal prosecution for manslaughter and treason. In 1991 he fled to Moscow, where he sought asylum in the Chilean embassy. Honecker was deported to reunified Germany in 1992, but in January 1993 a Berlin court ruled that he was too ill to stand trial, and he was allowed to emigrate to Chile, where members of his family resided.

Houser, Allan C., U.S. sculptor and painter (b. June 30, 1914, Apache, Okla.—d. Aug. 22, 1994, Santa Fe, N.M.), was a Chiricahua Apache who played a pivotal role in the development of native American Indian art. His works, including murals, watercolours, and sculptures made of stone, wood, and bronze, depicted such familiar Indian themes as mother and child, fire dancers, and warriors on horseback. Houser attended the School of Indian Art in Santa Fe before working for the Federal Works Progress Administration in the 1930s. He taught for some 20 years at such schools as the Intermountain Indian School, Brigham City, Utah, and the Institute of American Indian Arts, Santa Fe, before retiring in 1975 to devote himself completely to sculpture. In 1992 he was awarded the National Medal of Arts, and in April 1994 he presented first lady Hillary Rodham Clinton with "May We Have Peace," a 3.4-m (11-ft) bronze sculpture of an Indian holding aloft a sacred pipe.

Ionesco, Eugène (EUGEN IONESCU), Romanian-born French dramatist (b. Nov. 26, 1912, Slatina, Romania—d. March 28, 1994, Paris, France), was a pioneer in the nonrepresentational Theatre of the Absurd, using social parody and broad slapstick to examine ordinary people trying to cope with the relentless anxiety of modern life, the absurdity of bourgeois social conventions, and the impossibility of meaningful communication. Beginning with his first one-act "antiplay," *La Cantatrice chauve* (1950; *The Bald Soprano*), Ionesco turned audience expectations and conventional stage techniques upside down, reducing conversation to tedious platitudes and turning an existential pessimism about the human condition into uproarious "tragic farce." In the play's most famous scene, two strangers exchange clichéd pleasantries until they stumble upon the discovery that they are apparently husband and wife. Ionesco, the son of a Romanian father and a French mother, was educated at the Universities of Bucharest and Paris and spent his early years shifting between residence in Romania and France. While working as a proofreader in Paris soon after World War II, he decided to learn English. The stilted sentences and banal platitudes he encountered in his English grammar book served as the inspiration for *The Bald Soprano,* which opened in Paris to almost universal ridicule. By the late 1950s, however, Ionesco was recognized as a brilliant innovator, and his fanciful, minimalist style was increasingly imitated. His most popular full-length work, *Le Rhinocéros* (1959; *Rhinoceros*), was successfully staged in Paris by Jean-Louis Barrault (*q.v.*), in London starring Sir Laurence Olivier, and on Broadway with Zero Mostel. In the play Berenger, the "unheroic hero," struggles against the pressure to conform

JERRY BAUER

with society as his friends and neighbours gradually change into mindless, bellowing pachyderms. Ionesco's other plays include *La Leçon* (1951; *The Lesson*), *Les Chaises* (1952; *The Chairs*), *Amédée* (1954), and *Le Roi se meurt* (1962; *Exit the King*). He continued to write in the 1970s, but his later works were less witty and were more concerned with an exploration of the subconscious. Ionesco also published essays, children's books, a personal journal, and a novel. He was elected to the French Academy in 1970.

Jarman, Derek, British filmmaker (b. Jan. 31, 1942, Northwood, Middlesex, England—d. Feb. 19, 1994, London, England), crafted highly personal avant-garde motion pictures through which he sought to "demystify homosexuality" and explore human experience from a uniquely gay perspective. While Jarman often used classical plays or historical personages as the basis for his work, it was said that all of his films were in some way "about" homosexuality. Jarman studied at King's College, London, and the Slade School of Fine Art. He had some success as a painter and as a set designer for the Royal Ballet, the English National Opera, and other arts companies. After designing sets for two films by the controversial director Ken Russell, Jarman tried his hand at moviemaking. The result, *Sebastiane* (1975), was a low-budget portrait of the early Christian martyr and featured male nudity, homoerotic themes, and Latin dialogue in a Super-8 format. Jarman's other films (many of which were shot on a shoestring budget with Super-8 or 16-mm rather than conventional 35-mm stock) include *Jubilee* (1977), *The Tempest* (1979), *Caravaggio* (1986), *War Requiem* (1989), *Edward II* (1991), and *Wittgenstein* (1993). *Blue* (1993), which was made when Jarman was nearly blind, featured an unchanging plain blue screen and a spoken narrative of the director's own thoughts and feelings about his battle with AIDS. *Glitterbug,* a compilation of fragments from old home movies that was commissioned for television, was previewed shortly before his death. Jarman also wrote several books, including two volumes of memoirs, *Modern Nature* (1992) and *At Your Own Risk* (1992).

Jerne, Niels Kaj, British-Danish immunologist (b. Dec. 23, 1911, London, England—d. Oct. 7, 1994, Castillon-du-Gard, France), was a corecipient—with César Milstein and Georges Köhler—of the 1984 Nobel Prize for Physiology or Medicine for his theories of immunology and the effect they had on research. These theories proposed that the body uses a preexisting, immensely diverse repertoire of antibodies to recognize invading organisms and other foreign substances and provided explanations for the way the immune system develops and for the system of interactions in which the immune system is activated when it is needed and then is inactivated. Jerne grew up in Denmark and was educated first in The Netherlands, studying physics at the University of Leiden, and later at the University of Copenhagen, from which he received his medical degree (1951). From 1943 to 1956 he was a researcher at the Danish State Serum Institute, and he then spent six years (1956–62) as the chief medical officer of the World Health Organization. Jerne taught biophysics at the University of Geneva (1960–62), was chairman of the microbiology department at the University of Pittsburgh, Pa. (1962–66), and was professor of experimental therapy at J.W. Goethe University and director of the Paul Ehrlich Institute in Frankfurt am Main, Germany (1966–69). He then served (1969–80) as director of the Basel (Switz.) Institute for Immunology, which he helped establish, and taught (1981–82) at the Pasteur Institute in Paris. Jerne was a member of the American Academy of Arts and Sciences and a foreign associate of the National Academy of Sciences.

Jobim, Antônio Carlos, Brazilian songwriter and composer (b. Jan. 25, 1927, Rio de Janeiro, Brazil–d. Dec. 8, 1994, New York, N.Y.), transformed the extroverted rhythms of the Brazilian samba into an intimate music, the *bossa nova* ("new wrinkle" or "wave"), which became internationally popular in the 1960s. A guitarist and pianist since boyhood, he performed in Rio clubs before becoming music director of Odeon Records. In 1958 João Gilberto's recording of Jobim's song "Chega de Saudade" ("No More Blues") was released. The record was a hit in Brazil, and in 1959 Jobim and Luís Bonfá became noted for their score for *Orfeo negro* (*Black Orpheus*), which won an Academy Award as best foreign film. Jobim's worldwide success soon followed. He maintained a second home in the U.S., where bossa nova's fusion of understated samba pulse (quiet percussion, unamplified guitars playing subtly complex rhythms), gentle singing (Jobim often worked with lyricist Vinícius de Morais), and the melodic and sophisticated harmonies of cool jazz found a long-lasting niche in popular music. He appeared at Carnegie Hall in 1962 with his leading jazz interpreters, tenor saxophonist Stan Getz and guitarist Charlie Byrd; collaborated on the *Frank Sinatra & Antonio Carlos Jobim* and *Getz/Gilberto* albums; recorded albums under his own name; and composed classical works and film scores. Hundreds of performers recorded his more than 400 songs, including "Samba de uma nota só" ("One-Note Samba"), "Desafinado" ("Slightly out of Tune"), "Meditação" ("Meditation"), "Corcovado" ("Quiet Nights of Quiet Stars"), "Garota de Ipanema" ("The Girl from Ipanema"), "Wave," and "Dindi."

Joseph of Portsoken, Keith Sinjohn Joseph, Baron, British politician (b. Jan. 17, 1918, London, England—d. Dec. 10, 1994, London), converted (during the 1980s) the British Conservative Party under Prime Minister Margaret Thatcher from Keynesian demand management to Friedmanite free-market monetarism. Hailed as one of the sharpest intellects in the government and a fervent disciple of the free market, Joseph managed to free industry from governmental controls. Some of his views, particularly concerning social services, were very controversial. Joseph believed in building self-reliance within an economy based mainly on highly competitive free enterprise. On the other hand, Joseph was also labeled the "mad monk" because of his conscientious attempts to end the vicious cycle of poverty, dependence on the welfare state, and deprivation of the inner cities. Although Joseph achieved many of his dreams, he openly regretted some of his decisions. He designed a new form of taxation that provided grants for those with substandard incomes. Joseph was a brilliant student, becoming (1947) a fellow of All Souls, University of Oxford. He served as a Conservative member of Parliament (1956–87), secretary of state for health and social services (1970–74), secretary of state for industry (1979–81), and secretary of state for education (1981–86). Thatcher relied heavily on Joseph, one of the so-called "architects of Thatcherism," and she called him her oldest political ally and mentor. An honest, forceful, and utterly committed man of ideas, Joseph was at the same time shy and diffident and was therefore never seriously expected to take over as prime minister. In 1987 he was made life peer. In 1993 he survived a severe stroke, which left him wheelchair-bound. Joseph died of chest complications from that stroke.

Julia, Raul (Raúl Rafael Carlos Julia y Arcelay), Puerto Rican-born U.S. actor (b. March 9, 1940, San Juan, P.R.—d. Oct. 24, 1994, New York, N.Y.), was a dashing and handsome Latin stage and film star, whose versatility stretched from drama to farcical comedy; his compelling film performance as Valentín, a South American political prisoner incarcerated with a homosexual window dresser (William Hurt) in *Kiss of the Spider Woman* (1985), was one of his most admired screen roles, but he also achieved popular acclaim with his comedic portrayal as the lusty family patriarch, Gomez, in the macabre and wildly successful *The Addams Family* (1991) and its sequel, *Addams Family Values* (1993). After graduating from the University of Puerto Rico, Julia pursued an acting career while appearing in a nightclub act. He arrived (1964) in New York City and gained renown as Macduff in *Macbeth* (1966) and as the title character in *Othello* (1979) in Joseph Papp's New York Shakespeare Festival. On Broadway he earned four Tony award nominations for his roles as Proteus in *Two Gentlemen of Verona* (1971), Charley in a revival of *Where's Charley?* (1974), Mack the Knife in an experimental production of *The Threepenny Opera* (1976), and a Fellini-like film director in *Nine* (1982). His real-life role as an activist—he tirelessly campaigned to end world hunger and poverty—drew him to social-activist film roles. In *Romero* (1989) he portrayed El Salvador's assassinated Archbishop Oscar Romero, and in the made-for-cable-television film *The Burning Season* (1994) he starred as the martyred Brazilian labour leader and environmentalist Chico Mendes. Julia's commanding presence, athleticism, and vitality were showcased in such stage productions as *Betrayal* (1980) and *Arms and the Man* (1985) and in such films as *Eyes of Laura Mars* (1978), *One from the Heart* (1982), *The Morning After* (1986), and *Presumed Innocent* (1990). For a brief time during the early 1970s, he also appeared as the handyman Rafael on TV's "Sesame Street." Julia, who died following a stroke, was reportedly battling cancer.

Kienholz, Edward, U.S. artist (b. Oct. 23, 1927, Fairfield, Wash.—d. June 10, 1994, Hope, Idaho), crafted elaborately detailed three-dimensional environmental- or theatrical-style assemblages that served as harsh indictments of American society. His most famous walk-in tableaux included "Roxy's," a replica of a 1943 Nevada bordello; "Back Seat Dodge '38," featuring a couple in a sexual embrace; and "The Beanery," a reproduction of a decrepit bar complete with 17 sculpted patrons, piped-in smells, jukebox music, and background conversation. Critics labeled some of Kienholz' works repulsive or pornographic. The Vietnam War, death, and mental illness were subjects of his social and political concerns. The tools of his trade included discarded mannequins and stuffed animals, as well as furniture, bones, carpets, and fake blood. Kienholz was initially a painter, but in 1953 he moved to Los Angeles, where he began producing large wooden reliefs for walls. In 1956 he helped found the Ferus Gallery, an avant-garde studio, which exhibited his three-dimensional works. His often controversial sculptures set him apart from his contemporaries. After leaving Los Angeles in 1960, Kienholz divided his time between residences in Berlin and Hope. He credited his fifth wife, Nancy Reddin Kienholz, a photojournalist, as a collaborator after their marriage in 1973. Together they operated the Faith and Charity in Hope Gallery, where exhibitions of established and emerging artists were held. His works found their way into private collections and museums around the world.

Kim Il Sung (KIM SUNG JU), Korean dictator (b. April 15, 1912, near Pyongyang, Korea [now North Korea]—d. July 8, 1994, Pyongyang), ruled the Democratic Republic of Korea (North Korea) with an iron fist from the time it was established in 1948 until his sudden death from a heart attack. As premier (1948–72) and president (1972–94), the "Great Leader" promoted a successful cult of personality that imparted on him "godlike qualities." As a consequence, he was able to cow political adversaries at home and preside unchallenged over one of the communist world's most isolated and repressive societies.

In 1925 Kim's family moved to Manchuria from Korea, which had been occupied by Japan since 1910. As a young man Kim joined the anti-Japanese resistance movement and appropriated the name of Kim Il Sung, a legendary guerrilla hero. While in the Soviet Union, where he had been sent for political and military training, he joined the local Communist Party. During World War II he served in the Soviet army. Following Japan's surrender in 1945, Korea was effectively divided at the 38th parallel; Soviet troops were stationed in the North and U.S. troops in the South. In 1948 the Soviet forces departed, leaving Kim as the head of a communist state, and in 1949 he became chairman of the Korean Workers' (communist) Party. Hoping to reunify Korea by force, Kim ordered his army to invade the South in June 1950, thereby igniting the Korean War. North Korea received massive support from Chinese troops, while South Korea got the backing of UN forces made up largely of U.S. soldiers. The conflict ended three years later in a stalemate. An estimated three million–four million people were killed, yet Korea remained divided.

During the decades that followed, relations with China and the U.S.S.R. cooled. Kim was held responsible for several acts of international terrorism, including the assassination of 17 South Korean officials during a presidential state visit to Burma (now Myanmar) in 1983 and the 1987 bombing of a South Korean commercial plane that killed 115 persons. Shortly before his death, Kim agreed to an unprecedented meeting with South Korean Pres. Kim Young Sam. An international crisis had developed over North Korea's withdrawal from the Nuclear Non-proliferation Treaty and Kim's refusal to allow UN inspection of several facilities that were believed to have the capability of producing nuclear weapons. In 1972 Kim designated his eldest son, Kim Jong Il, as his successor.

FRANCOIS LOCHON—GAMMA LIAISON

Kim Il Sung was the leader of North Korea from its founding in 1948 until his death in July at age 82. Even though he headed a repressive regime, Kim was a cult figure to many North Koreans.

Kim Sang-Man, Korean publisher (b. Jan. 19, 1910, Puan, North Cholla province, Korea—d. Jan. 26, 1994, Seoul, South Korea), as the publisher of *Dong-A Ilbo,* the country's most influential newspaper, was an intrepid defender of the freedom of the press. While conforming to the press censorship imposed by the dictatorial regimes of Presidents Park Chung Hee and Chun Doo Hwan, Kim quietly and shrewdly gained international support for resisting the measure. During a 1974 showdown between the Park government and striking *Dong-A Ilbo* journalists, who objected to censorship and the presence of Korean Central Intelligence Agency (KCIA) agents in newspaper offices, Kim used his international contacts to bring pressure on the government, which had threatened to suspend the paper. Though Park withdrew the KCIA agents, he ordered a complete commercial advertising boycott. Kim's stature was such that ordinary blue-collar workers joined intellectuals in buying newspaper advertising space to show their support for press freedom. The paper was brought to the brink of bankruptcy, and Kim was forced to let some reporters go and reassign others. During Chun's social purification campaign, a number of reporters were fired, but Kim found jobs for many of them in special research departments. Kim, who joined *Dong-A Ilbo* in 1949, served as executive director, president, publisher, chairman, and, from 1981, chairman emeritus. He was a graduate of the London School of Economics. He was named a Commander of the British Empire in 1974 and a honourary Knight of the British Empire in 1981.

Kirby, Jack (JACOB KURTZBERG), U.S. comic-book artist (b. Aug. 28, 1917, New York, N.Y.—d. Feb. 6, 1994, Thousand Oaks, Calif.), as the undisputed king of the comics, helped create some 400 characters, including such unforgettable superheroes as Captain America, Spiderman, the Incredible Hulk, and the Fantastic Four; during the 1950s and '60s, he reinvented those invincible characters by endowing them with a measure of human vulnerability. Kirby left high school at the age of 16 and worked in Max Fleisher's animation studio on Betty Boop and Popeye cartoon material before teaming up with Joe Simon in 1941. Together for 15 years, they collaborated on *Captain America,* featuring the nation's top Nazi combatant; the *Boy Commandos,* about a team of young soldiers; and *My Date,* the first romance comic book. In 1959 Kirby, who had dissolved his partnership with Simon in 1956, joined the Marvel Comics Group and teamed up with writer-editor Stan Lee. Their blockbuster hits included *Silver Surfer, Mighty Thor, Iron Man,* and *X-Men* besides *The Incredible Hulk, The Fantastic Four,* and the revival in 1964 of *Captain America.* Kirby's artistic genius was captured in his brilliantly coloured, larger-than-life superhero depictions, which elevated action drawing to a new level. Other innovations included exploding panels, double-page spreads, and ultimately a book-length format. He also produced (1970) *The Fourth World* series for DC Comics. In 1993, some seven years after he published his last full comic book, Kirby's peers voted him the most influential of all creators.

Knoll, Erwin, Austrian-born U.S. editor (b. July 17, 1931, Vienna, Austria—d. Nov. 2, 1994, Madison, Wis.), as editor of the political magazine *The Progressive,* was known for his commitment to civil liberties and nonviolence and his opposition to capital punishment, nuclear weapons, and U.S. intervention abroad. Knoll gained international attention in 1979 when he refused a government request that an article supposedly revealing hydrogen bomb design secrets be withheld, and the government secured a court order prohibiting publication—an act of prior restraint unprecedented in U.S. history. He contended that all the information was in the public domain, and after six months—following a Madison newspaper's publication of a letter containing some of that information—the Justice Department relented, and the article was printed. Knoll was reared and educated in New York—his family had fled the Nazis and moved to the U.S. when he was nine—and he received a B.A. from New York University in 1953. He also did graduate work in political science at George Washington University, Washington, D.C. He worked for the *Washington Post* (1957–63) and the Newhouse National News Service (1963–68) before becoming the Washington editor of *The Progressive* in 1968 and then moving to Madison in 1973 to be its editor. His opposition to the 1991 Gulf war—almost singular among U.S. editors—led to appearances on the PBS "MacNeil/Lehrer NewsHour." Knoll's several books included *Scandal in the Pentagon* (1969; coauthor with William McGaffin), *War Crimes and the American Conscience* (1970; coeditor), and *No Comment* (1984; editor). He left a book about capital punishment unfinished.

Kohr, Leopold, Austrian-born social philosopher (b. Oct. 5, 1909, Oberndorf, Austria—d. Feb. 26, 1994, Gloucester, England), expounded on "the beauty of the small," particularly in his major work, *The Breakdown of Nations* (1957). Kohr's philosophy, which was based on the premise that human stability and prosperity are best served by small-scale political, social, and economic institutions, was later popularized in E.F. Schumacher's *Small Is Beautiful* (1973). Kohr studied law and economics in Innsbruck, Vienna, and London. In 1938 he moved to North America, where he taught economics at Rutgers University, New Brunswick, N.J. (1946–54), and the University of Puerto Rico (1955–73). He later settled in Britain and lectured on political philosophy at the University of Wales in Aberystwyth (1968–77). Kohr blamed widespread modern problems such as crime and poverty on the rise of "national and urban giantism," which had replaced earlier city-states, and he fiercely opposed the political and economic unification of Europe. His other books include *Development Without Aid* (1973) and *The Inner City* (1988).

Lancaster, Burton Stephen ("BURT"), U.S. motion-picture actor (b. Nov. 2, 1913, New York, N.Y.—d. Oct. 20, 1994, Los Angeles, Calif.), brought a strong, intelligent presence to the screen in a diverse array of emotion-packed roles, ranging from those in Hollywood westerns to European art films, but he was perhaps best remembered for his Academy Award-winning performance as a fiery evangelist and con man in *Elmer Gantry* (1960). Tall, lithe, and distinguished by his winning smile, Lancaster first played to audiences as part of a two-man acrobatic team in a traveling circus. After the act was dissolved, he held various jobs in Chicago before serving in World War II. When the war ended, he won a small part in a Broadway production of *A Sound of Hunting* (1945). Lancaster made his screen debut in *The Killers* (1946) and became an overnight sensation with his charisma and handsome ruggedness. He then starred in a number of thrillers and melodramas, including *Brute Force* (1947), *Sorry, Wrong Number* (1948), and *Criss Cross* (1949), and such adventures as *The Flame and the Arrow* (1950) and *The Crimson Pirate* (1952). More complex roles followed, and Lancaster gave compelling performances in *Come Back, Little Sheba* (1952), *The Rose Tattoo* (1955), and *From Here to Eternity* (1953), which featured a steamy beach

WASSER—GAMMA LIAISON

scene with Deborah Kerr. In 1948 Lancaster and his agent Harold Hecht founded an independent production company, which turned out a string of starring vehicles for him. Among them was *Sweet Smell of Success* (1957), with Lancaster portraying a brutal, Walter Winchell-like gossip columnist. He poignantly portrayed loneliness as an inhabitant of a hotel in *Separate Tables* (1958) and as an inmate in *Birdman of Alcatraz* (1962), which led to his role as a prince in *The Leopard* (1963), directed by Luchino Visconti. Lancaster returned to Hollywood to make *Seven Days in May* (1964), *The Professionals* (1966), and the hugely successful *Airport* (1970) before starring as the haunted professor in another Visconti film, *Conversation Piece* (1974). In 1976 he appeared in both Bernardo Bertolucci's *1900* and Robert Altman's *Buffalo Bill and the Indians*. Lancaster also won acclaim for his performances in *Atlantic City* (1981), *Tough Guys* (1986), and *Field of Dreams* (1989), his last big-screen film. Off-screen Lancaster supported the NAACP and served as president (1968–70) and as a board member (1968–92) of the American Civil Liberties Union Foundation of Southern California.

Lantz, Walter, U.S. animator (b. April 27, 1900, New Rochelle, N.Y.—d. March 22, 1994, Burbank, Calif.), created an unforgettable stable of cartoon characters, notably the rambunctious, red-headed Woody Woodpecker, an irascible bird-brain who delighted viewers with his staccato "Ha-ha-ha-Ha-ha!" merriment; Lantz also made animation history in 1930 with the production of the first Technicolor cartoon, which graced the opening sequence of the film *King of Jazz.* Lantz launched his career in 1915 as an office boy in the art department of the *New York American* before dabbling in animation in 1916 and finding his niche (1922) at Bray Studios in New York City, where he collaborated on *The Katzenjammer*

Kids, Krazy Kat, Happy Hooligan, and *Mutt and Jeff* cartoons. After moving to California in 1927, Lantz served as a gagman for Mack Sennett and Hal Roach before working (1928–38) for Universal Studios. There he took over the *Oswald the Lucky Rabbit* cartoon series and developed such characters as Andy Panda, Winchester the Tortoise, Homer Pigeon, Inspector Willoughby, and Chilly Willy (a pint-sized penguin). Woody Woodpecker, his most enduring character, made his film debut in a bit part in the 1940 cartoon short *Knock, Knock* and became a featured film character and, beginning in 1957, a television star on "The Woody Woodpecker Show." Lantz's inspiration for Woody was a pesky woodpecker that disturbed his honeymoon. His wife, Grace, provided Woody's distinctive voice for most of his adventures. During his more than 60-year career, Lantz produced more than 800 short films, and his cartoons were translated into more than 60 languages and seen in some 70 countries. He closed his studio in 1975, and in 1979 the Academy of Motion Picture Arts and Sciences presented him with a life achievement Oscar in recognition of his superb craftsmanship.

Lasch, Christopher, U.S. social critic and academic (b. June 1, 1932, Omaha, Neb.—d. Feb. 14, 1994, Pittsford, N.Y.), penned stinging indictments of contemporary American culture as the author of several books, most notably the 1979 best-seller *The Culture of Narcissism,* in which he decried a self-absorbed society that failed to develop a self-awareness and instead depended on consumer purchases, demography, opinion polls, and government to define itself. His controversial views on the erosion of society attracted the attention of U.S. Pres. Jimmy Carter, who consulted Lasch for his famous "national malaise" speech. Lasch proposed that Americans embrace such basics as self-reliance, family, nature, community, and the work ethic to counteract the alienation and despair he found prevalent in society. After graduating summa cum laude from Harvard University, Lasch earned an M.A. (1955) in history and a Ph.D. (1961). He taught at the University of Iowa (1961–66), Northwestern University, Evanston, Ill. (1966–70), and the University of Rochester, N.Y. (1970 until his death). His book, *The Minimal Self* (1984) was a successful sequel to *The Culture of Narcissism* and attacked the false prophets of the New Left. Lasch himself had initially been leftist in his leanings but adopted a more centrist view. Some of his other works include *The American Liberals and the Russian Revolution* (1962), *The Agony of the American Left* (1969), *Haven in a Heartless World* (1977), and *The Revolt of the Elites and the Betrayal of Democracy,* which was to be published posthumously.

Lebow, Fred (FISCHL LEBOWITZ), Romanian-born sports figure (b. June 3, 1932, Arad, Rom.—d. Oct. 9, 1994, New York, N.Y.), was a visionary and ambitious organizer who built the New York City Marathon—the first such race of its kind—from a small contest with limited appeal to a premier event, attracting thousands of international participants. Lebow, an Orthodox Jew, immigrated to the U.S. during the 1960s. He left Nazi-occupied Romania before the Soviet occupation at the end of World War II and lived in Czechoslovakia, The Netherlands, and Ireland before finding a permanent home in New York City. He worked in the garment district and became a distance runner to gain stamina for playing tennis. In 1970, with $300 of his own capital, Lebow initiated the first New York City Marathon, which involved about 127 runners in four circumnavigations of Central Park. Six years later, he expanded the race to include all five of New York City's boroughs, and some 2,000 runners covered the course. In 1985 the event was the largest marathon in the world. Lebow, who was stricken with brain cancer in 1990, nonetheless organized and ran the 1992 marathon while battling the disease. He was inducted into the U.S. National Track Hall of Fame shortly before his death.

Lejeune, Jérôme-Jean-Louis-Marie, French geneticist (b. June 13, 1926, Montrouge, France—

d. April 3, 1994, Paris, France), identified (1959) the human chromosomal abnormality linked to Down syndrome, or trisomy 21, one of the most common forms of mental retardation and the first chromosomal disorder to be positively identified. Lejeune's discovery marked a turning point in the new science of cytogenetics (the scientific study of genetic variations at the chromosomal level). Lejeune attended the University of Paris (M.D., 1951; Ph.D., 1960). In the early 1950s he began research into inheritance patterns of Down syndrome in twins at the National Centre for Scientific Research (CNRS) in Paris. In 1959, just three years after the correct number of human chromosomes (46; 23 pairs) had been discovered, he demonstrated that children with Down syndrome had an extra chromosome 21, making three where there would normally be a pair. The term *trisomy* was coined to describe this condition. He later identified several other chromosomal aberrations, notably the cause of the syndrome known as *cri du chat,* which is associated with severe mental retardation. He served as director of research at the CNRS from 1963 and held the post of professor of fundamental genetics at the Faculty of Medicine in Paris from 1964. A devout antiabortion activist, Lejeune was named to the Pontifical Academy of Sciences in 1974, and shortly before his death he was appointed by Pope John Paul II to head the newly formed Pontifical Academy for Life.

Leonov, Leonid Maksimovich, Russian novelist and playwright (b. May 31 [May 19, Old Style], 1899, Moscow, Russia—d. Aug. 8, 1994, Moscow), was admired for the intricate structure of his best narratives and for his ability to convey the complex moral and spiritual dilemmas faced by his characters. His multilayered, psychological approach was strongly influenced by—and often compared to—that of Fyodor Dostoyevsky. Leonov went to school in Moscow and published his first stories in a newspaper in Arkhangelsk, where his father, the poet Maksim L. Leonov, had been exiled. He served as a soldier and journalist in the Red Army during the Russian Civil War (1918–20). In 1924, after publishing several more short stories and novellas, Leonov established his literary reputation with his epic first novel, *Barsuki* (*The Badgers,* 1947), and with *Vor* (1927; *The Thief,* 1931), a pessimistic tale set in the Moscow criminal underworld. Other major works include *Sot* (1930; *Soviet River,* 1932), *Skutarevsky* (1932; Eng. trans., 1936), and *Doroga na okean* (1935; *Road to the Ocean,* 1944). In the 1930s and '40s his fiction conformed somewhat more closely to the prevalent style of Socialist Realism, as did his 12 plays, 11 of which were staged in Moscow. His last major novel, *Russky les* (1953; *The Russian Forest,* 1966), won the Lenin Prize in 1957. Leonov devoted the remainder of his life to revising his earlier works. He was elected to the U.S.S.R. Academy of Sciences in 1972.

Levitt, William Jaird, U.S. builder and developer (b. Feb. 11, 1907, New York, N.Y.—d. Jan. 28, 1994, Manhasset, N.Y.), as the pioneering president of Levitt & Sons, Inc., dramatically altered the U.S. residential suburban landscape with single-family, mass-produced, 74-sq m (800-sq ft) homes. His dwellings both provided an affordable source of housing for returning World War II servicemen and served as the cookie-cutter prototype for Levittown, a model village on Long Island, New York, that Levitt built on the site of a potato farm. While his brother, Alfred, designed the houses and his father, Abraham, focused on landscaping, William Levitt concentrated on organizing, financing, advertising, and sales. After the booming success of the first Levittown (1947–51), which included more than 17,000 homes, Levitt constructed (1951–56) a second Levittown in Bucks county, Pa. He was credited with innovating efficient and cost-effective construction techniques and with uniquely patterning the suburbs with his massive tracts of uniform houses. Levitt was at the same time criticized for the mass-produced appearance of his units, for refusing to sell to blacks, and for not supporting housing for the poor. Levitt erected the New Jersey

Levittown in 1958 and went on to build various other projects before selling his concern in 1968 to International Telephone and Telegraph for $92 million. In a number of business reverses in the 1970s and '80s, Levitt lost much of his wealth.

Liu Haisu, Chinese painter and teacher (b. 1895?, Wujin [Wu-chin], Jiangsu [Chiang-su] province, China—d. Aug. 7, 1994, Shanghai, China), combined traditional Chinese painting methods with European techniques, especially those of van Gogh and Cézanne, and promoted this style as a model for revolutionizing art education in China. As the leader of art schools in Shanghai and Nanjing (Nanking), Liu exerted extraordinary influence. The scion of a distinguished literary family, Liu studied calligraphy under Kang Youwei (K'ang Yu-wei) and traditional landscape and flower painting under Wu Changshi (Wu Ch'angshih) and Chen Hengke (Ch'en Heng-k'e). At age 13, however, Liu set out on his own to pursue a less formal education. He became one of the founders of the Shanghai Academy, the first art college in modern China. During the 1920s and '30s he organized several important national and international exhibitions and toured Japan and Europe, where he studied Western techniques and exhibited his own works. As a teacher, Liu maintained that painters should combine a knowledge of formal art theory with their natural talent and personal judgment, a departure from the Chinese tradition of copying the compositions and techniques of old masters. His works in traditional Chinese style were free-flowing and brilliant in colour. His landscapes focused on rocks and trees, and some of his paintings featured eagles and lions.

Lleras Restrepo, Carlos, Colombian politician (b. April 12, 1908, Bogotá, Colombia—d. Sept. 27, 1994, Bogotá), served as president of Colombia 1966–70 and fostered economic union in Latin America as the driving force behind the Andean Pact, an agreement that forged trade links between Venezuela, Colombia, Peru, Bolivia, and Chile. Lleras Restrepo, a dyed-in-the-wool liberal, practiced law before gaining political prominence as head of the Liberal Party in 1941 and again from 1948 to 1950. His second term as party president began after his predecessor, Jorge Gaitán, was assassinated, an event that touched off a decade of violent unrest between the Liberals and Conservatives in Colombia. After his home was burned to the ground, Lleras Restrepo spent two years in exile in Mexico. His bid for the presidency in 1978 was not supported by the party. Nonetheless, he remained active both in politics and as a journalist, writing for his magazine *Nueva Frontera.*

Lutoslawski, Witold, Polish composer and conductor (b. Jan. 25, 1913, Warsaw, then in the Russian Empire—d. Feb. 7, 1994, Warsaw, Poland), attempted to create a "new musical language" by incorporating elements of folk songs, 12-tone serialism, atonal counterpoint, and controlled improvisations reminiscent of aleatory (chance) compositions while retaining elements of harmony and melodic form. Lutoslawski started composing as a child, but he did not begin formal training until age 15. He studied mathematics at the University of Warsaw and received diplomas in piano (1936) and composition (1937) from the Warsaw Conservatory. During the Nazi occupation of Poland, he performed in clandestine concerts and, with fellow composer Andrzej Panufnik, played piano duets in cafés; these often included proscribed music. Lutoslawski's prewar compositions (most notably the 1938 *Symphonic Variations*) were primarily conventional neoclassical pieces, often infused with traditional folk tunes. When his *Symphony No. 1* (begun in 1941) had its premiere in 1948, however, the new communist government denounced the piece as "formalist" and banned Lutoslawski's increasingly avant-garde works from public performance. He earned a living writing children's songs and scores for motion pictures until these restrictions were eased in the mid 1950s. Although Lutoslawski wrote some vocal and chamber music, he was best known for his orchestral compositions, including *Concerto for Orchestra* (1954), *Funeral Music* (1958), *Venetian Games* (1961), *Concerto for Piano and Orchestra* (1988), and four symphonies, the last of which had its world premiere in 1993.

Lwoff, André Michel, French scientist (b. May 8, 1902, Ainay-le-Château, France—d. Sept. 30, 1994, Paris, France), shared the 1965 Nobel Prize for Physiology or Medicine with François Jacob and Jacques Monod. Their research established how the genetic material of certain bacteria-infecting viruses that have become incorporated into the chromosome of their host cell can be passed along in a noninfective state to succeeding generations of bacteria and then reactivated to produce infective viral particles. Lwoff graduated from the University of Paris in 1921, the same year he joined the Pasteur Institute. He earned medical and science doctorates at Paris in 1927 and 1932, respectively. Lwoff was appointed head of the laboratory at the Pasteur Institute in 1929, and in 1938 he became the head of the microbiology and physiology department. During World War II, he was an active member of the Resistance and was awarded the Grand Cross of the Legion of Honour and the Medal of the Resistance. From 1959 to 1968 he chaired the microbiology department at the Sorbonne. Lwoff's work on viral interactions with host cells greatly influenced cancer research and resulted in his appointment (1968) as director of the Cancer Research Institute at Villejuif, France, a position he held until his retirement in 1972. In later years Lwoff became involved in various movements, ranging from family planning to the control and banning of chemical and biological weapons. His writings include *Biological Order* (1962) and *Jeux et combats* (1981; "Games and Combats").

Lynch, Charles Birchell, Canadian journalist and author (b. Dec. 3, 1919, Cambridge, Mass.—d. July 21, 1994, Ottawa, Ont.), was a gifted storyteller who attracted a wide and loyal readership as the longtime (1958–84) Ottawa syndicated columnist for Southam News Services. Lynch's folksy approach endeared him to English-speaking readers throughout much of the country. In his political commentaries, he boasted of "slipping the readers mickeys of information along with the entertainment." A veteran journalist, Lynch was working as a Reuters correspondent (1943–58) when he reported the D-Day (1944) Normandy landing of Allied troops. The globe-trotting reporter also covered the war crimes trials in Nürnberg before joining Southam. His five-times-a-week column established him as a personality, and the engaging raconteur branched out into radio and television, where his bespectacled, bearded, and rotund figure became a familiar fixture. He was also the author of several books related to Ottawa politics, among them *You Can't Print That!* (1983), *Our Retiring Prime Minister* (1983), and *A Funny Way to Run a Country* (1986). Lynch, who was forced into retirement in 1984, continued to pursue a freelance writing career. He was made an Officer of the Order of Canada in 1977.

McRae, Carmen, U.S. vocalist (b. April 8, 1922, New York, N.Y.—d. Nov. 10, 1994, Beverly Hills, Calif.), mingled subtle technique and a dry contralto voice with swing, edgy wit, and a thoughtful ballad approach to become one of the most admired jazz singers of her generation. Compared with such contemporaries as Sarah Vaughan and Ella Fitzgerald, McRae had a narrow vocal range, yet her stylistic ingenuity, generally unsentimental manner, and care for the meanings of lyrics made her distinctive. She studied piano in her youth and won an amateur talent contest singing at the Apollo Theatre in Harlem in 1939; not long thereafter she met the innovative Billie Holiday, who became the major influence on her style. After touring (1946–47) with the Mercer Ellington band, she spent a crucial formative 3½ years in Chicago before returning to New York and winning a New Star award from *Down Beat* magazine. She began her prolific solo recording career about 1953 and soon was working with top arrangers such as Tadd Dameron and Ralph Burns and collaborating with Sammy Davis, Jr. (1957–58; *Boy Meets Girl* and *Porgy and Bess*) and Dave Brubeck (1960–61). Instrumentalists such as tenor saxophonists Ben Webster and Zoot Sims and the Quincy Jones and Kenny Clarke–Francy Boland big bands sometimes accompanied her (the great drummer Clarke had been her first husband). Typically, though, on record and on her many nightclub and concert tours, she was accompanied by piano trios. Among her last projects, before she retired in 1991, were recorded tributes to Vaughan and composer Thelonious Monk.

Mancini, Enrico ("HENRY"), U.S. composer (b. April 16, 1924, Cleveland, Ohio—d. June 14, 1994, Los Angeles, Calif.), revolutionized film scoring by incorporating elements of jazz into his enduring melodies; he won four Academy Awards—for the songs "Moon River" (1961) and "Days of Wine and Roses" (1962) and for film scores for *Breakfast at Tiffany's* (1961) and *Victor/Victoria* (1982)—besides garnering 20 Grammy awards and collecting eight gold records. His other hits included the title song from the film *Charade,* the *Pink Panther* film theme song, and the "Peter Gunn" television theme song. Mancini's musical education began with flute lessons from his father, but in time the piano became his instrument of choice. He briefly attended the Carnegie Institute of Technology in Pittsburgh, Pa., where Max Adkins, conductor of the Stanley Theater pit band, encouraged him to produce arrangements for that group. Mancini's studies at the Juilliard School of Music in New York City were interrupted by duty in the army air force during World War II. While in the service, however, he met Glenn Miller, and after the war he joined Miller's band as an arranger and pianist. Mancini wrote music for radio before composing scores for such films as *The Glenn Miller Story* (1954), *The Benny Goodman Story* (1956), and *Touch of Evil* (1958). He teamed up with television producer Blake Edwards in 1958, rocketed to fame with his brassy "Peter Gunn" and "Mr. Lucky" theme songs, and wrote the scores for all of Edwards' films, notably *The Great Race, Darling Lili, 10, S.O.B., Sunset,* and the *Pink Panther* series. Besides composing the scores for more than 80 films, he also conducted sellout concerts. At the time of his death, Mancini was working on a stage adaptation of *Victor/Victoria.*

Mann, Gottfried Angelo ("Golo"), German-born historian (b. March 27, 1909, Munich, Germany—d. April 7, 1994, Leverkusen, Germany), was best known for his classic text *Deutsche Geschichte des 19. und 20. Jahrhunderts* (1958; *The History of Germany Since 1789,* 1968) and for his somewhat unorthodox conviction that National Socialism was "an historically unique phenomenon, dependent on an individual and on a moment," rather than an expression of the German national character. Mann, who was the son of the Nobel Prize-winning novelist Thomas Mann, studied philosophy at the Universities of Munich, Berlin, and Heidelberg (Ph.D., 1932). After leaving Germany with his family in 1933, he taught German literature and history at Rennes (France) University (1935–36) and edited (1937–40) a Swiss literary journal, *Mass und Wert.* He was interned by the Nazis in 1940, but he escaped and moved to the U.S., where he taught at Olivet (Mich.) College (1942–43) and Claremont (Calif.) Men's College (1947–57). He returned to Germany in 1958 and was professor of history and political science at Stuttgart Technical University from 1960 until he retired from academia in 1964. Later he worked as a television commentator. Mann's other published works include *Wallenstein: Sein Leben erzählt* (1971; *Wallenstein: His Life Narrated,* 1976) and an autobiography, *Erinnerungen und Gedanken: Eine Jugend in Deutschland* (1986; *Reminiscences and Reflections: A Youth in Germany,* 1990). He won the Goethe Prize in 1985.

Marty, François Cardinal, French Roman Catholic prelate (b. May 18, 1904, Pachins, France—d. Feb. 16, 1994, near Villefranche-de-Rouergue, France), as archbishop of Paris (1968–81), was primate of France during the months of civil and political unrest in 1968 and the difficult years thereafter. Marty received a doctorate in theology from the Catholic Institute in Toulouse. He was ordained in 1930, made bishop of Saint-Flour in 1952, and elevated to archbishop of Rheims in 1960. He was created cardinal in April 1969, a year after taking his post as head of the French church at Notre-Dame. Marty was a vigorous advocate for disaffected labourers and for non-Christian immigrant workers. In 1962 he was asked by Pope John XXIII to prepare a report for the Second Vatican Council on teaching the gospel to the working class. Upon taking his post as archbishop of Paris, he reduced the church hierarchy and introduced a more conciliatory, activist approach to the ministry. Marty retired to a Dominican convent in 1981.

Masina, Giulia Anna ("Giulietta"), Italian actress (b. Feb. 22, 1921, San Giorgio di Piano, near Bologna, Italy—d. March 23, 1994, Rome, Italy), was artistic muse, adviser, and frequent leading lady for her husband of 50 years, the acclaimed filmmaker Federico Fellini, who dedicated his body of work to her. Masina worked as a stage and radio actress while attending the University of Rome and made her professional debut in 1939. In 1942 she performed in a radio play by Fellini, whom she married the following year. Masina's first major screen role was as the ingenuous waif Gelsomina in Fellini's *La Strada* (1954; "The Road"). Three years later she won the best actress award at the Cannes Film Festival for her portrayal of the naive prostitute in *Le notti di Cabiria* (*The Nights of Cabiria*). She also drew accolades for *Il bidone* (1955; *The Swindle*), *Giulietta degli spiriti* (1965; *Juliet of the Spirits*), and *Ginger e Fred* (1985; *Ginger and Fred*). She occasionally worked with other directors, notably Alberto Lattuada in *Senza pietà* (1948; *Without Pity*) and Roberto Rossellini in *Europa '51* (1952; *The Greatest Love*). Masina succumbed to cancer less than five months after her husband's death.

Maung Maung, U, Burmese politician (b. Jan. 11, 1925, Mandalay, Burma [now Myanmar]—d. July 2, 1994, Yangon [Rangoon], Myanmar), was a Western-educated lawyer, judge, and government official before being named the civilian president of Burma on Aug. 19, 1988. His attempts at reform were undermined, however, by his long-time association with the 26-year dictatorial rule of Gen. Ne Win, and he was unable to prevent the September 18 military coup. Maung Maung fought with the Burmese nationalists during and after World War II. After Burma gained independence from Britain (1948), he studied law at the University of Rangoon, was called to the bar at Lincoln's Inn in London, and studied further at the University of Utrecht, Neth., and Yale University, where he later taught political science and Southeast Asian studies. In Burma in the 1950s he practiced law, founded the *Guardian Magazine* (1954) and *Guardian* newspaper (1956), and served in Prime Minister U Nu's civilian administration. After a 1962 coup brought Gen. Ne Win to power, Maung Maung was named supreme court chief justice and appointed to the central committee of the Burma Socialist Program Party. Ne Win unexpectedly resigned on July 23, 1988, but his successor, U Sein Lwin, was forced out by antigovernment riots after about two and a half weeks. As president, Maung Maung lifted martial law, released political prisoners, and declared a free press, but the riots continued until the military stepped in after only one month.

May, Peter Barker Howard, English cricketer (b. Dec. 31, 1929, Reading, Berkshire, England—d. Dec. 27, 1994, Liphook, Hampshire, England), was widely regarded as England's finest post-World War II batsman. In his first-class career (1948–63)—all as an amateur—May scored 85 centuries and 27,592 runs (average 51), including 4,537 runs (average 46.77) and 13 centuries in 66 Test matches. At age 14 while at Charterhouse, he led that public school's batting average in his first year. He was a blue for three years at the University of Cambridge, which he attended after his wartime service in the Royal Navy. May debuted with Surrey in 1950 (he was captain from 1957). He was selected to play for England against South Africa in 1951 and scored 138 runs in his first innings. In 1957 he triumphed against West Indies, when he made a career high 285 not out and 411 in partnership with Colin Cowdrey, a fourth-wicket record in any Test and a record for any England wicket that still stood at the time of his death. From 1955 to 1961, he was England captain a record 41 times, with 20 wins, 10 losses, and 11 draws. In 1963, two years after ill health and the pressures of his work as a broker with Lloyd's of London led to his early retirement from Test cricket, May retired from first-class cricket. Later he served the Marylebone Cricket Club as president (1980–81) and had a somewhat less successful stint as the chairman of selectors (1982–88). May was made Commander of the Order of the British Empire in 1981.

May, Rollo Reece, U.S. psychologist and author (b. April 21, 1909, Ada, Ohio—d. Oct. 22, 1994, Tiburon, Calif.), was known as the father of existential psychotherapy. He was one of the first to abandon Freudian theories of human nature, and in his humanistic approach to therapy, he stressed that anxiety could be harnessed and used as a positive force and that people could use their inner resources in making the choices that guide the direction of their lives. May presented his views in a number of popular books, including *The Meaning of Anxiety* (1950), *Man's Search for Himself* (1953), *Love and Will* (1969), *Power and Innocence* (1972), and *The Courage to Create* (1975). May earned (1930) a bachelor's degree from Oberlin (Ohio) College and became a teacher of English at an American college in Greece. During holidays he attended psychoanalyst Alfred Adler's seminars in Vienna and was inspired to study theology. He returned (1933) to the U.S. and entered Union Theological Seminary, receiving a bachelor of divinity degree in 1938. After serving as a Congregationalist minister for two years, he resigned his ministry to study psychology at Columbia University, New York City. He contracted tuberculosis, however, and was given only a 50–50 chance of surviving. He realized that his personal struggle against death would do more than medical care would to determine whether he lived, and this solidified his existentialist views. He received his Ph.D. in 1949. Over the years May was on the faculty of the William Alanson White Institute of Psychiatry, Psychology, and Psychoanalysis and was a lecturer at the New School for Social Research, both in New York City, and was a visiting professor at such universities as Harvard, Yale, and Princeton.

Mercouri, Melina (Maria Amalia Mercouris), Greek actress and politician (b. Oct. 18, 1925, Athens, Greece—d. March 6, 1994, New York, N.Y), burst onto the international scene in the

ALAIN KELER—SYGMA

role of Ilya, the flamboyant, good-hearted prostitute in the film *Never on Sunday* (1960); in later years as Greece's minister of culture (1981–89; 1993–94), she used her fame as an actress in her crusade to repatriate Greek antiquities. Mercouri studied drama at the National Theatre in Athens (1943–46), made her stage debut in 1944, and established her reputation as Blanche in Tennessee Williams' *A Streetcar Named Desire* (1949). Her first screen appearance in *Stella* (1955) drew little attention. In 1965 she married the French-born U.S. director Jules Dassin, who made her a star in *Never on Sunday* and many of her other memorable films, including *Phaedra* (1962), *Topkapi* (1964), and *A Dream of Passion* (1978). She also re-created her most famous role in a Broadway musical adaptation, *Ilya, Darling* (1967). Mercouri, who was the daughter of a former government minister and the granddaughter of a long-time mayor of Athens, was abroad in 1967 when a military coup toppled the Greek government. She fought tirelessly against the junta, defiantly naming her 1971 autobiography *I Was Born Greek* after she was deprived of her citizenship. She triumphantly returned to Athens after the junta collapsed (1974) and, running as a socialist, was elected to Parliament three years later. As minister of culture, Mercouri devoted much of her energy to a worldwide campaign for the return of the Elgin Marbles, sculptures removed from the Parthenon and placed in the British Museum in the early 19th century.

Morgan, Henry (HENRY LERNER VON OST), U.S. radio announcer and television personality (b. March 31, 1915, New York, N.Y.—d. May 19, 1994, New York), singed the airwaves with his savage wit as the sardonic host of "Here's Morgan," which showcased his gifts as a mordant ad-libber; his irrepressible satiric commentary was so biting and irreverent that it even extended to network sponsors advertising Life Savers, Oh! Henry candy bars, and Schick razors and was the source of his blacklisting during the 1950s communist witch-hunts. At the age of 18 Morgan held court as the youngest radio announcer in the U.S. He worked in Philadelphia, New York City, Duluth, Minn., and Boston before launching his own show in the 1940s. After serving in the army air forces during World War II, he returned to the airwaves and continued to dispense his unique brand of humour. Though he was blacklisted, he did find work on television as the star of "Henry Morgan's Talent Hunt" (1951) and "Here's Morgan" (1953) and as a regular panelist on "I've Got a Secret" and "What's My Line?"

Morgan, William Wilson, U.S. astronomer (b. Jan. 3, 1906, Bethesda, Tenn.—d. June 21, 1994, Williams Bay, Wis.), discovered the spiral shape of the Milky Way Galaxy after years of observing and analyzing the distances and arrangements of stars. Morgan's feat was complicated because our solar system lies within the Milky Way, thus making outside telescopic observation of its configuration impossible. With Philip C. Keenan he had developed the MK (for Morgan Keenan) system for using observations of stars' spectra to determine their luminosity and therefore their distance from Earth, and in 1943 he published *An Atlas of Stellar Spectra*, a classification guide. Using the MK system, he estimated the distances of bright stars within the Milky Way. In 1951 at an American Astronomical Society meeting, Morgan received a standing ovation when he revealed that the structure of the Milky Way Galaxy includes two spiral arms and provided evidence for a third arm. After earning a Ph.D. (1931) from the University of Chicago, Morgan spent his entire career associated with his alma mater and its Yerkes Observatory, of which he was director from 1960 to 1963. An astronomical morphologist, Morgan devoted his career to studying and classifying stars and galaxies, and he also proved the existence of super-giant galaxies. Morgan, who was a member of the National Academy of Sciences and the American Academy of Arts, was the recipient of the Bruce Gold Medal from the Astronomical Society of the Pacific and the Herschel Medal from the Royal Astronomical Society of London.

Moschino, Franco, Italian fashion designer (b. Feb. 27, 1950, Abbiategrasso, Italy—d. Sept. 18, 1994, Annone di Brianza, Italy), as the irreverent enfant terrible of the fashion industry, poked fun at the excesses of the 1980s with his "tongue in chic" designs, most memorably creating suits festooned with cutlery, jackets with faucet handles or dice used as buttons, coats and hats made from teddy bears, expensive linen shirts embroidered with outrageous puns and slogans, dresses that looked like shopping bags, and ball gowns assembled from plastic garbage bags. After studying painting at the Academy of Fine Arts in Milan, Moschino found work in the fashion industry as a freelance illustrator. He designed for Cadette, the Italian clothing company, before launching his own label in 1983. His company, Moonshadow, had annual revenues in excess of £150 million from two main line collections and six complementary lines. His designs, which were inspired by the Surrealist movement of the 1920s, found acceptance among pop stars such as Madonna, Tina Turner, and Yoko Ono; royalty, including Princess Caroline of Monaco and Diana, Princess of Wales; and people on the street, though the latter could rarely afford his pricey ensembles. His mocking disdain for the industry earned Moschino both ridicule and respect among his contemporaries. He died after suffering complications from an abdominal tumour.

Mpetha, Oscar Mafakafaka, South African political activist (b. Aug. 5, 1909, Transkei, South Africa—d. Nov. 15, 1994, Cape Town, South Africa), was a founder of South Africa's trade union movement during the 1940s who became famous for his groundbreaking efforts on behalf of the mainly black Food and Canning Workers' Union. Mpetha qualified as a road master and began working as an assistant foreman; in 1940 he organized and led a movement calling for higher wages for road labourers. He also made a name for himself as a strong voice against apartheid. Mpetha joined the African National Congress (ANC) about 1951 and quickly rose to become chairman of its Cape Province unit. He served in that post until the ANC was banned by the government in 1960. Following the 1960 Sharpeville shootings, Mpetha was detained for four years and then briefly went underground. Resurfacing in the 1970s as a trade union and community leader on the Cape, Mpetha was repeatedly detained and his labour organizations banned. Then in 1980 during a confrontation between residents of the Crossroads squatter camp and police, Mpetha was arrested for provoking the unrest and later charged with terrorism and murder. Mpetha spent three years in prison before the murder charges were dropped. He was sentenced to five years for terrorism, however, which he served at Pollsmoor Prison, where ANC veterans Nelson Mandela and Walter Sisulu were incarcerated. While out on appeal in August 1983, Mpetha was elected one of three copresidents of the United Democratic Front, an alliance of antiapartheid forces. After Mpetha was released in 1989, he fought for the release of Mandela. Despite Mpetha's extremely poor health—his legs were amputated as a result of severe diabetes—he continued to travel and speak throughout the country.

Murchison, Ira, U.S. track star (b. Feb. 6, 1933, Chicago, Ill.—d. March 28, 1994, Harvey, Ill.), burst forth from the starting block with such lightning-quick speed that he was dubbed the "human Sputnik" by Soviet admirers and at 1.62 m (5 ft 4 in) tall was one of the shortest of the great sprinters. In 1951 Murchison reigned as Illinois high-school champion in the 100- and 220-yd dashes, but he reached the pinnacle of his career in 1956 when he ran the leadoff leg of the U.S. 400-m relay at the Olympic Games in Melbourne, Australia, and helped propel his team to a gold medal victory in a world and Olympic record time of 39.5 sec. That year he also jointly held the world 100-m record (10.2 sec) with Bobby Morrow and tied a day-old record (10.1) set by Willie Williams. In 1958 he ran for Western Michigan University and was the NCAA 100-yd champion with a time of 9.5 sec. The following year, however, after

Murchison underwent surgery for colon cancer, his sprinting career ended. He later coached high-school and college track teams in Chicago.

Natwick, Mildred, U.S. actress (b. June 19, 1905, Baltimore, Md.—d. Oct. 25, 1994, New York, N.Y.), specialized in portraying mischievous spinsters and likable eccentric characters on stage and television and in films. She was best remembered as the medium in the stage and television production of *Blithe Spirit* (1941 and 1956, respectively), a mystery writer and amateur sleuth paired with Helen Hayes in the television series "The Snoop Sisters" (1973–74), and Jane Fonda's fun-loving mother in *Barefoot in the Park* (1967), a role that earned her an Academy Award nomination for best supporting actress. With her sharply defined features and twinkling eyes, Natwick became a Broadway regular, appearing in supporting roles in some 40 productions after making her debut in *Carry Nation* (1932). Following her film debut in *The Long Voyage Home* (1940), Natwick showcased her talents in *The Enchanted Cottage* (1945), *The Late George Apley* (1947), *The Trouble With Harry* (1955), *If It's Tuesday This Must Be Belgium* (1969), *Daisy Miller* (1974), and *Dangerous Liaisons* (1988).

Nelson, Harriet (PEGGY LOU SNYDER) U.S. singer and actress (b. July 18, 1909, Des Moines, Iowa—d. Oct. 2, 1994, Laguna Beach, Calif.), became an American icon of motherhood as the radio and television matriarch who starred with her real-life family—husband Ozzie and sons David and Ricky—in the situation comedy "The Adventures of Ozzie and Harriet." The show, which debuted on radio in 1944 before moving to television in 1952, aired until 1966, making it one of the longest-running family comedies. While singing under the name Harriet Hilliard, she met and married (1935) Ozzie, a bandleader. They appeared on the Red Skelton radio program during the 1940s and won an audience following with their unsophisticated and playful humour. When "The Adventures of Ozzie and Harriet" first aired, David and Ricky were portrayed by child actors, but the boys began playing themselves in 1949. The show was billed as "radio's favorite family," and they capitalized on its popularity by making a film, *Here Come the Nelsons* (1952). She later appeared (1973) with her husband in the short-lived series "Ozzie's Girls," but was rarely seen after his death in 1975. Ten years later, Ricky was killed in a plane crash.

Nicol, Davidson Sylvester Hector Willoughby (ABIOSEH NICOL), Sierra Leonean diplomat and writer (b. Sept. 14, 1924, Freetown, Sierra Leone—d. Sept. 20, 1994, Cambridge, England), enjoyed a varied career as a medical researcher, physician, academic, diplomat, and writer. After attending the University of London, where he studied medicine, Nicol earned a B.A. (1947) in natural science and doctorates in medicine and biochemistry from Christ's College, Cambridge. There he conducted research on the chemical structure of insulin in the human body, and he wrote and lectured widely on medical and scientific topics. In 1957 Nicol became a fellow of Christ's College, the first black African to achieve this distinction. Nicol returned to Sierra Leone in 1958 as a senior pathologist, but in 1960 he was appointed principal of the Fourah Bay College in Freetown, a position he held for eight years. He began a distinguished diplomatic career in 1969, when he was appointed Sierra Leone's ambassador to the UN. In 1970 he became president of the UN Security Council, and he served (1972–82) as executive director of the United Nations Institute for Training and Research. From 1983 to 1987 he was president of the World Federation of UN Associations. Nicol, writing under the pen name Abioseh Nicol, won the 1952 Margaret Wrong Prize and Medal for Literature in Africa. His works include *Two African Tales* (1965) and *The Truly Married Woman, and Other Stories* (1965). He edited *Paths to Peace: The UN Security Council and Its Presidency* (1981) and coedited *Creative Women in Changing Societies: A Quest for Alternatives* (1982).

Nixon, Richard Milhous, 37th president (1969–74) of the United States (b. Jan. 9, 1913, Yorba Linda, Calif.—d. April 22, 1994, New York, N.Y.), as leader of the nation, displayed formidable expertise in foreign policy by establishing détente with the Soviet Union, initiating rapprochement with China, and bringing the Vietnam War to an end. When his involvement in the cover-up of the Watergate scandal became known and he faced the threat of impeachment, he also became the first U.S. president to resign from office. He earlier had served (1953–61) as vice president under Pres. Dwight D. Eisenhower.

Nixon, the son of a grocer who operated a modest business, was reared in Whittier, Calif. His mother's strong religious convictions influenced his decision to attend Whittier College, a Quaker institution. He was awarded a scholarship to Duke University Law School, Durham, N.C., and after graduation (1937) returned to Whittier to practice law. There he courted Thelma Ryan, affectionately known as Pat, and the couple married in 1940. During World War II Nixon served as an aviation ground officer in the United States Navy.

After returning to civilian life, Nixon was twice elected (1947 and 1949) to the U.S. House of Representatives. A conservative Republican who gained political prominence with a staunch domestic anticommunist stance, Nixon was Alger Hiss's most hostile interrogator at a 1948 hearing of the House Un-American Activities Committee. Nixon's leading role in the investigation and subsequent indictment of Hiss brought him national attention. In 1950 Nixon defeated former actress Helen Gahagan Douglas for a Senate seat after branding her a "pink lady." In turn, she indelibly labeled Nixon "Tricky Dick." Eisenhower selected Nixon as his running mate in 1952, but after Nixon was accused of financial impropriety, Eisenhower asked him to step aside. Instead, Nixon successfully defended himself on television in the memorable "Checkers" speech, in which he deflected criticism by adamantly refusing to return his children's dog, Checkers, which had been a gift from a well-wisher.

After Eisenhower suffered a heart attack during his first term in office, Nixon gained valuable experience in foreign affairs by traveling extensively and making a number of crucial contacts. In 1958 he made a whirlwind Latin-American tour against a backdrop of violent demonstrations, and the following year in Moscow he engaged Nikita S. Khrushchev in the famed "kitchen debate," which took place in a model kitchen at a U.S. exposition.

In 1960 Nixon became the Republican presidential candidate but lost to Democrat John F. Kennedy by a mere 112,000 votes of the 68 million cast. Two years later Nixon lost his bid to unseat Democrat Edmund G. ("Pat") Brown in a race for the governorship of California. Temporarily retreating from politics, he resumed his law career in New York City. He remained politically active behind the scenes as a loyal party fund-raiser, however, and remained in the public eye as the author of *Six Crises* (1962) and as an engaging and sought-after public speaker.

With the Vietnam War raging, Nixon made capital of his foreign affairs expertise and was proclaimed the 1968 Republican presidential candidate; he narrowly defeated Democratic challenger Hubert H. Humphrey. After assuming office he announced the Nixon Doctrine, a plan to reduce U.S. military forces abroad by offering smaller countries military and economic aid to defend themselves. He gradually withdrew U.S. ground troops from Vietnam while replacing U.S. combat squadrons with South Vietnamese troops, who were fortified with U.S. supplies and air support.

Nixon's accomplishments in foreign policy included the reopening of direct communications with China in 1972 after a 21-year lapse in relations and his May 1972 visit to Moscow, the first by a U.S. president. His trip yielded a U.S.-Soviet strategic arms limitation agreement, a bilateral trade accord, and plans for joint scientific and space cooperation.

At home Nixon was bedeviled by persistent inflation. Though he tried to trim federal expenditures, his administration's annual budget deficits became the largest in history up to that time. He twice (1971 and 1973) devalued the dollar and introduced (Aug. 15, 1971) a New Economic Policy, which included unprecedented peacetime wage and price controls. Nixon's four appoint-

ments to the Supreme Court helped move the court toward "strict constructionism."

Nixon defeated his 1972 Democratic challenger, Sen. George S. McGovern, in one of the largest landslide victories in U.S. presidential history. Aided by Henry A. Kissinger, who as national security adviser conducted intensive negotiations with the North Vietnamese, Nixon effectively ended U.S. participation in the Vietnam War in January 1973, but bombing raids on neighbouring Cambodia continued until August 15. His administration had come under attack when it was revealed in July that the U.S. Air Force had secretly bombed the Viet Cong in Cambodia in 1969 and 1970 and had, together with the Department of Defense, falsified reports to hide the action.

Nixon's second term in office was dominated by the Watergate scandal, which erupted in March 1973 when investigations into the 1972 burglary and wiretapping of the Democratic National Committee headquarters in the Watergate complex in Washington, D.C., revealed that Nixon's administration was criminally involved in the break-in and cover-up. Following the indictment and conviction of several of Nixon's closest aides in July 1974, and after the House of Representatives had voted three articles of impeachment against him, Nixon resigned (August 9). He acknowledged that he had directed the FBI away from inquiries leading to the White House and had actively participated in the cover-up. He had also attempted to prevent the release of secretly recorded White House tapes that revealed his involvement. Nixon was granted a pardon by his successor, Gerald R. Ford, and retired to the seclusion of his estate in San Clemente, Calif. In 1976 he was disbarred in New York state.

Despite his ignominy, Nixon in his later years gained stature as a senior statesman. Besides advising a succession of presidents, he wrote nine more books. The last, *Beyond Peace,* was completed shortly before his death. Nixon, who declined a state funeral, was buried beside his wife at his birthplace. His family announced plans, however, to continue his 20-year battle for control of 3,000 hours of White House tapes and some 150,000 pages of presidential papers that many believed could further tarnish his reputation.

(TOP LEFT AND BOTTOM) UPI/BETTMANN; (TOP RIGHT) JEAN-PIERRE LAFFONT—SYGMA

Richard M. Nixon, 37th president of the United States, died on April 22 at age 81. In 1956 (top left), Vice President Nixon and Pres. Dwight D. Eisenhower celebrated reelection. The president was surrounded by his family (top right) when, faced with impeachment, he announced his resignation effective Aug. 9, 1974. In February 1972 (bottom), during one of his many productive foreign visits, Nixon and his national security adviser, Henry A. Kissinger (right), met with Mao Zedong, chairman of the Chinese Communist Party (centre), and Premier Zhou Enlai (left) in Beijing.

Nizer, Louis, British-born U.S. lawyer (b. Feb. 6, 1902, London, England—d. Nov. 10, 1994, New York, N.Y.), was a legal wizard who was an expert on contract, libel, copyright, divorce, plagiarism, and antitrust law. He used his spellbinding oratorical skills to influence juries while defending such celebrities as Charlie Chaplin, Salvador Dalí, Mae West, and Johnny Carson. After graduating (1924) from Columbia Law School, Nizer set up (1926) a law practice that evolved into the prestigious New York firm of Phillips, Nizer, Benjamin, Krim, and Ballon. In 1962 Nizer won a $3.5 million libel judgment (reduced to $550,000 on appeal) for John Henry Faulk, a CBS radio and television personality. This case was credited with ending blacklisting in the broadcast industry. Nizer was a gifted raconteur, toastmaster, and speaker, who recounted some of his most celebrated cases in the best-selling *My Life in Court* (1961). Two other volumes in the same vein, *The Jury Returns* (1966) and *Reflections Without Mirrors* (1978), received little critical acclaim. Nizer worked until shortly before his death.

Nyandoro, George Bodzo, Zimbabwean nationalist (b. July 8, 1926, Marandellas district, Southern Rhodesia—d. June 24, 1994, Harare, Zimbabwe), was a founding member of the Southern Rhodesian African National Congress (ANC) and one of the earliest leaders in the fight for independence and black majority rule in what was then a British crown colony. Nyandoro was a member of the Shona ethnic group and grandson of the leader of an unsuccessful revolt against the British in 1896–97. After training as a bookkeeper, he became involved in the trade union and independence movements. In the mid-1950s he was secretary-general of the British African National Voice Association, founding vice president of the African National Youth League, and cofounder of the ANC. He also toured rural areas, inciting local opposition to restrictive land laws. In 1959 Nyandoro was among hundreds of black nationalists arrested and detained without trial. Four years later he was released to seek medical treatment in Britain for tuberculosis of the spine. In 1964 he moved to Zambia, where he worked for the banned Zimbabwe African People's Union (ZAPU). Nyandoro later quit ZAPU to form the breakaway Front for the Liberation of Zimbabwe (1971), but he returned home to take a ministerial post in Bishop Abel Muzorewa's transitional government (1979). When Nyandoro was not offered a role in Pres. Robert Mugabe's first postindependence administration, he left government and became a successful businessman.

Odinga, (Ajuma) Oginga, Kenyan politician (b. October 1911?, Sakwa, Central Nyanza, East African Protectorate [now in Kenya]—d. Jan. 20, 1994, Kisumu, Kenya), was a leader in the struggle for Kenyan independence from Britain, but he later organized left-wing opposition to the single-party rule of Pres. Jomo Kenyatta's Kenya African National Union (KANU). Odinga graduated from Makerere University College, Kampala, Uganda, and was a teacher and headmaster until he entered politics in 1947. As a prominent member of the Luo, Kenya's second largest ethnic group, he recruited Luo support for the independence movement and served (1952–57) as president of the Luo Union. From 1960 he was vice president of KANU, and after Kenya gained independence he was the new nation's minister for home affairs (1963–64) and vice president (1964–66). Odinga considered many of Kenyatta's policies too moderate, however, and in 1966 he broke away to form the more radical Kenya People's Union (KPU). In 1969 the KPU was banned and Odinga was placed in detention. He rejoined KANU after his release (1971), but he was effectively blocked by Kenyatta and his followers from running in elections or participating actively in politics. Odinga was expelled from the party and briefly imprisoned in 1982. In 1991 he was a founding member of the opposition Forum for the Restoration of Democracy, and the next year he placed third in Kenya's first multiparty presidential election. Odinga's autobiography, *Not Yet Uhuru,* was published in 1967.

THE MARK SHAW COLLECTION/PHOTO RESEARCHERS

Onassis, Jacqueline Bouvier Kennedy, U.S. first lady (b. July 28, 1929, East Hampton, N.Y.—d. May 19, 1994, New York, N.Y.), redefined the role of first lady with her dignified elegance, magnetic charm, trend-setting style, and especially her cool composure after the assassination (Nov. 22, 1963) of her husband, Pres. John F. Kennedy; though she was a shy and private person, she remained an enigmatic public figure throughout her life first as a widow and devoted mother and then as "Jackie O," wife of Greek shipping magnate Aristotle Onassis. Jacqueline Lee Bouvier was the daughter of Janet Lee and John Vernou Bouvier III. Her parents divorced, but Bouvier received a privileged education and graduated from Miss Porter's School before attending Vassar College, Poughkeepsie, N.Y., and the Sorbonne and earning a B.A. from George Washington University, Washington, D.C., in 1951. She won *Vogue* magazine's Prix de Paris award, but instead of accepting the prize—a yearlong job that required shuttling between Paris and New York—she toured Europe. After returning to the U.S., she became an inquiring photographer for the *Washington Times-Herald.* She met the dashing and politically ambitious Kennedy at a dinner party in 1952, and she accepted his telegraphed proposal in May 1953. They were married on September 12 of that year, and though she was apolitical, her impeccable manners and quiet counsel provided the perfect compliment to the senator from Massachusetts. After a miscarriage and a stillbirth, Kennedy gave birth to daughter Caroline in 1957, and she was pregnant with son John Jr. when her husband was elected president in 1960.

In her role as first lady, she charmed foreign dignitaries with her command of languages and endeared herself to the American public. She restored the White House to its federalist glory and conducted a television tour through the refurbished residence. For this she received an Emmy award for public service. Kennedy was also responsible for setting fashion styles, wearing Oleg Cassini creations and the pillbox hat that became her trademark. In 1963, the year Jacqueline Kennedy was voted the most admired woman in the U.S., she gave birth to a son, Patrick, who lived for only 39 hours. Her image was most vividly branded into the memory of Americans, however, as she appeared in her pink blood-stained suit following the assassination of her husband and as the black-veiled widow who walked in the funeral entourage and later prompted her young son to salute as his father's casket passed by on its way

to burial. She felt that her most important role was as a mother, and she protectively shielded her children from the glare of public scrutiny. During her lifetime she refused to discuss the intimate aspects of her married life with Kennedy, including rumours of his unfaithfulness. She did, however, record tapes on the subject of his assassination, but they were not to be opened until 50 years following the death of their last surviving child.

She married Onassis in 1968 and moved to Greece. Rumours circulated that they were on the brink of divorce when Onassis died in 1975. Onassis' daughter, Christina, paid her stepmother $26 million from his estate. Jacqueline Onassis returned to New York City and joined the publishing house of Doubleday as a book editor. She became a familiar figure with her large sunglasses, bouffant hairstyle, and signature scarfs. From 1975 she was romantically linked with businessman Maurice Tempelsman, who was at her side when she succumbed to non-Hodgkin's lymphoma. She was buried, at her own request, in Arlington National Cemetery beside John F. Kennedy.

O'Neill, Thomas Philip, Jr. ("Tip"), U.S. politician (b. Dec. 19, 1912, Cambridge, Mass.—d. Jan. 5, 1994, Boston, Mass.), was a dyed-in-the-wool liberal Democrat who exerted considerable political clout as a longtime representative (1953–87) from Massachusetts and as the longest-serving (1977–86) speaker of the U.S. House of Representatives. O'Neill, whose career spanned the era from New Deal liberalism to Ronald Reagan conservatism, was an old-style, behind-the-scenes politician who insisted that "all politics is local." A white-haired, cigar-chomping, larger-than-life figure, O'Neill was a shrewd manipulator who marshaled support in the back rooms of the Capitol rather than on the House floor. In 1967 he became the first member of the House leadership to oppose Pres. Lyndon Johnson vocally on the Vietnam War. O'Neill served as House majority whip in 1971 and majority leader in 1972 before being elevated to speaker. He earned the respect of his younger colleagues for approving legislative reform, including institution of a new ethics code and a limit on outside income. Even a Republican-sponsored advertisement featuring a O'Neill look-alike who was meant to symbolize a bloated, free-wheeling Congress not only failed to detract from O'Neill's popularity but rather enhanced it. He appeared on television commercials for a credit card company and played a cameo role on the TV comedy "Cheers." A best-selling

BRUCE HOERTEL

autobiography, *Man of the House,* was published in 1987, and publication of a book of his anecdotes and lore, *All Politics Is Local,* coincided with his death.

Onetti, Juan Carlos, Uruguayan-born novelist (b. July 1, 1909, Montevideo, Uruguay—d. May 30, 1994, Madrid, Spain), chronicled human struggles with alienation and hopelessness amid the decay of modern urban life. In a series of complex existential novels and short stories, many of which were set in the mythical town of Santa María, he fused fantasy and reality in a nihilistic view of city life devoid of spiritual meaning. For many years Onetti moved back and forth between Uruguay and Argentina, working as a journalist for the Reuters news agency in Montevideo (1942–43) and Buenos Aires (1943–46). He was also editor (1939–42) of the respected Montevideo weekly magazine *Marcha* and later (1946–55) of the Argentine magazine *Vea y lea.* After settling in Montevideo, he was named (1957) director of the city's municipal library system. He was imprisoned briefly in 1974 after a literary jury on which he served awarded a prize to a work deemed unacceptable by the Uruguayan military government. In 1975 he went into self-imposed exile in Spain, where he eventually became a citizen. Onetti's first short story appeared in the Argentine newspaper *La prensa* in 1933, while his first short novel, *El pozo* (*The Pit*), was published in Montevideo in 1939. Other novels include *Tierra de nadie* (1941; *No Man's Land*), *La vida breve* (1950; *A Brief Life*), *El astillero* (1961; *The Shipyard*), *Juntacadáveres* (1964; *Body Snatcher*), and *Cuando y no importe* (1993; "What's the Use"). He also wrote several volumes of short stories and essays, notably *Réquiem por Faulkner* (1975; "Requiem for Faulkner"). Onetti received the national literary award of Uruguay in 1963 and the Cervantes Prize, Spain's top literary honour, in 1980.

Osborne, John James, British playwright and film producer (b. Dec. 12, 1929, London, England—d. Dec. 24, 1994, Shropshire, England), revolutionized the British drama by spearheading the "Angry Young Men" movement with his landmark play *Look Back in Anger* (1956). The frustrations portrayed by the play's hero, Jimmy Porter, an underemployed man in his 20s who finds post-World War II England greatly lacking in opportunity, were acutely mirrored in London society and echoed in Osborne's motto, "Damn you, England." Osborne managed to steer generations of British playwrights away from the long-established tradition of portraying the upper classes and their boring, strangled way of life. He opened up the world of British theatre to the gritty "kitchen sink" reality of urban life and the tough lower classes that increasingly inhabited London. In his passionate monologues and throughout his memoirs, Osborne poured out his ire in spiteful outbursts against women, especially his four ex-wives. The fiery and prolific writer crafted several highly successful plays, including *Luther* (1961), for which he won a Tony award, *Inadmissible Evidence* (1964), *A Patriot for Me* (1965), *Time Present* (1968), *The Hotel in Amsterdam* (1968), and *Déjàvu* (1991), a reexamination of the characters originally introduced in *Look Back in Anger.* He produced such films as *The Entertainer* (1960), based on his 1957 play of the same name, and *Tom Jones* (1963), for which he won an Academy Award. Osborne wrote his first play, *The Devil Inside Him* (1950), with mentor Stella Linden. He provided demanding roles for actors and was credited with restoring the tirade (a passionately scathing speech) as a respectable dramatic element. In his 1981 autobiography, *A Better Class of Person,* Osborne attacked the mediocrity of the lower middle classes, discussed his mother's negative influence, and attempted to justify his volatile temperament. Osborne wrote two books in the 1990s, *Almost a Gentleman* (1991) and *Damn You,*

England (1994). Suffering from complications of diabetes, Osborne died of heart failure.

Parish, Sister (DOROTHY MAY KINNICUTT), U.S. interior designer (b. July 15, 1910, Morristown, N.J.—d. Sept. 8, 1994, Dark Harbor, Maine), created ageless atmospheres that appealed to both women and men and dictated style on both sides of the Atlantic with her traditional designs; she was renowned for the quality of her work, and her homey yet sophisticated touch marked the residences of such industrialists and politicians as the Astors, the Rockefellers, the Gettys, and, most prominently, first lady Jacqueline Kennedy (*see* OBITUARIES: *Onassis, Jacqueline*), for whom Parish redecorated the White House. Parish, who became identified by her childhood nickname, Sister, was the daughter of a stockbroker and was raised in baronial splendour. Four years after both her father and her husband, also a stockbroker, were devastated by the stock market crash of 1929, Parish opened a small interior design shop in Far Hills, N.J. She was partial to the understated English country house look, and her combinations of Colefax and Fowler chintzes, overstuffed armchairs, and brocade sofas with such unexpected items as patchwork quilts, four-poster beds, knitted throws, and rag rugs led to her being credited with ushering in what became known as American country style during the 1960s. In 1962 Albert Hadley became her partner, and the firm of Mrs. Henry Parish II Interiors was renamed Parish-Hadley to reflect the change. The patrician designer remained a mainstay of the company into her 80s.

Pass, Joe (JOSEPH ANTHONY JACOBI PASSALAQUA), U.S. guitarist (b. Jan. 13, 1929, New Brunswick, N.J.—d. May 23, 1994, Los Angeles, Calif.), was a technically skilled jazz virtuoso who overcame drug addiction to become an internationally renowned sideman, performing with such jazz greats as Oscar Peterson, Ella Fitzgerald, and Sarah Vaughn. He was also a spellbinding soloist whose fluid fingering and impassioned improvisations defined his incomparable artistry. Pass, a self-taught guitarist, was given his first instrument at the age of nine and was performing with big-name bands by the time he was a teenager. Though his career was stalled by heroin addiction and a five-year jail sentence, he kicked his habit after enrolling in the Synanon drug-rehabilitation program and emerged from obscurity with the 1973 release of a solo album, *Virtuoso.* That same year he became a member of a celebrated trio that included pianist Oscar Peterson and the bassist Niels-Henning Orsted Pedersen. Pass then found recording opportunities with Norman Granz, producer and head of Pablo Records, and worked as a regular member of a studio band. In later years, however, it was his work as a concert soloist that made him a standout.

Pauling, Linus Carl, U.S. chemist (b. Feb. 28, 1901, Portland, Ore.—d. Aug. 19, 1994, Big Sur, Calif.), was a towering figure in the scientific community and the only solo winner of two Nobel Prizes in different categories. He was awarded the 1954 Nobel Prize for Chemistry for discoveries on the nature of chemical bonding, work that was instrumental in describing the structure and shape of molecules, including the complex molecules of living tissues, and he received the 1962 Nobel Prize for Peace as a tireless crusader against the use of warfare, especially nuclear weapons, as a means of resolving international disputes. Pauling, the son of a pharmacist, shared his father's fascination with chemistry. After earning a B.S. (1922) in chemical engineering from Oregon State Agricultural College, Pauling took a Ph.D. (1925) in physical chemistry from the California Institute of Technology, where he taught and conducted research until 1963. An insightful and brilliant researcher who easily recognized interrelationships, Pauling was the first to apply the principles of quantum mechanics to the structure of molecules and effectively used a variety of data to calculate the lengths and angles of the bonds that exist between the atoms in a molecule and ultimately to develop a theoretical framework for understand-

JOE MCNALLY

ing the forces that hold atoms together. He put forth his findings in *The Nature of the Chemical Bond, and the Structure of Molecules and Crystals* (1939), undoubtedly the most influential chemistry textbook of the early to mid-20th century.

Pauling was also a leader in the movement against nuclear weapons testing in the 1950s and '60s. During the McCarthy era of communist witch-hunts, Pauling's passport was revoked for two years. He also submitted an anti-bomb-testing petition to the UN with the signatures of more than 11,000 scientists, a move that was credited with helping to persuade the U.S., U.K., and Soviet Union to initial the 1963 atmospheric test ban treaty. His pacifist views were echoed in his denunciation of the Vietnam War, a stand for which he was widely criticized. He aroused controversy during the 1970s with his zealous advocacy of vitamin C, taken in large doses, as a cure-all for a variety of conditions, ranging from the common cold to cancer. His bold experimentation and courage in pursuing unorthodox ideas led him to discoveries in molecular biology, notably the identification of the genetic defect in the hemoglobin molecule that is the cause of sickle-cell anemia. He was at the forefront in efforts to unravel the structure of DNA, a feat ultimately accomplished by James Watson and Francis Crick. During his remarkable career, Pauling was a member of the Center for the Study of Democratic Institutions, Santa Barbara, Calif., a faculty member of Stanford University, and, at the time of his death, director of research at the Linus Pauling Institute of Science and Medicine, Palo Alto, Calif.

Peppard, George, U.S. actor (b. Oct. 1, 1928, Detroit, Mich.—d. May 8, 1994, Los Angeles, Calif.), rocketed to fame after starring opposite Audrey Hepburn in the 1961 film classic *Breakfast at Tiffany's* and enhanced his reputation in such films as *How the West Was Won* (1962), *The Carpetbaggers* (1964), and *The Blue Max* (1966). When he lost his box-office appeal, he turned to television, appearing in a succession of tough-guy roles, most notably as cigar-chewing soldier of fortune John ("Hannibal") Smith in the action- and violence-packed adventure series "The A-Team" (1983–87). Peppard studied Method acting at Lee Strasberg's Actors Studio, made his film debut in *The Strange One* (1957), and enjoyed a stint on Broadway in *The Pleasure of His Company* (1958) before securing supporting film roles in *Pork Chop Hill* (1959) and *Home from the Hill* (1960). Other television characters Peppard created were an insurance investigator on "Banacek" (1972–74) and a neurosurgeon on "Doctors' Hospital" (1975–76). In 1992 Peppard had a cancerous tumour removed from his lung but still embarked on a tour of *The Lion in Winter*.

Phoumi Vongvichit, Laotian political leader (b. April 6, 1909, French Indochina?—d. Jan. 7, 1994), was a longtime communist and a leader in the Pathet Lao (Land of Lao) revolutionary movement against French colonial rule; he eventually became acting president (1986–91) of the Lao People's Democratic Republic. Phoumi reportedly was born into an affluent family and educated at Vientiane College. He joined Lao Issara (Free Laos) in 1950, and when the movement split in two in the mid-1950s, he was named deputy leader of the more radical Stalinist faction, Pathet Lao. In 1961 he represented the Pathet Lao in negotiations at the international peace conference in Geneva. For more than a decade thereafter, he served a series of coalition governments in such posts as deputy prime minister, foreign minister, and minister of culture and fine arts. When the Pathet Lao seized power in 1975, Phoumi became education minister, with jurisdiction over the "reeducation" of thousands of royalist supporters of the previous government. He was named interim president in 1986 after Prince Souphanouvong resigned that office, and he retired five years later.

Pinay, Antoine, French politician (b. Dec. 30, 1891, Saint-Symphorien-sur-Coise, France—d. Dec. 13, 1994, Saint-Chamond, France), engineered the recovery of the French economy after World War II by adamantly pursuing an anti-inflationary policy, a stance that was unpopular among economists of his day. Pinay's visionary approach to this daunting task brought inflation under control in France for the first time since World War II. In 1960, while serving as finance minister, Pinay introduced a new franc, deflating the standard franc by removing the last two zeroes. For this monumental deed, Pinay earned the moniker "the man who saved the franc." Though he held a series of governmental posts ranging from secretary of state (1949) to minister of foreign affairs (1955–56) to France's first ombudsman (1973–74), Pinay's highest yet briefest office was as prime minister, which he held from March to December 1952. In that post, Pinay introduced successful austerity measures and issued the "emprunt Pinay," a bond that allowed French citizens who had hidden away gold and cash during the war to convert their caches into legal, tax-exempt savings. He later served (1964–73) as president of regional economic development for Rhône-Alpes. Earlier, Pinay had earned the Croix de Guerre for heroism during World War I, had managed a tannery (1919–48), and had aided the Resistance fighters during World War II. He served as mayor of Saint-Chamond from 1929 to 1977. The man whose name became synonymous with strong currency died peacefully just days before his 103rd birthday.

Popper, Sir Karl Raimund, Austrian-born British philosopher (b. July 28, 1902, Vienna, Austria-Hungary—d. Sept. 17, 1994, Croydon, Surrey, England), believed that knowledge—particularly scientific knowledge—evolves from individual experience and cannot be verified through inductive reasoning. Popper postulated that since no one can ever observe and verify all possible evidence to prove a scientific hypothesis correct, it is necessary only to discover one observed exception to the hypothesis to prove it false. He rejected as "pseudoscience" any system of beliefs that could not pass this "falsifiability criterion" and that relied on predetermined "laws" of human behaviour. These included logical positivism, metaphysics, Marxism, fascism, and Freudian psychoanalysis. In the 1980s many conservative politicians seized on his contention that government should avoid evil rather than seek social reform by actively pursuing good. Popper was educated at the University of Vienna (Ph.D., 1928) and worked for a time under the psychiatrist Alfred Adler. He first presented his theories in the highly regarded *Logik der Forschung* (1934; *The Logic of Scientific Discovery,* 1959). Three years later he immigrated to New Zealand, where he taught philosophy at Canterbury University College, Christchurch, until he accepted a post at the London School of Economics (1945). Popper formally retired in 1969, but he continued to write and lecture in England, the U.S., Australia, and New Zealand. His other principal books include *The Open Society and Its Enemies* (1945), *The Poverty of Historicism* (1957), *Unended Quest: An Intellectual Autobiography* (1976), and *A World of Propensities* (1990). Popper was knighted in 1965, elected a fellow of the Royal Society in 1976, and made a Companion of Honour in 1982.

Porritt, Arthur Espie Porritt, Baron, New Zealand-born physician and statesman (b. Aug. 10, 1900, Wanganui, N.Z.—d. Jan. 1, 1994, London, England), after a long career with the British monarchy as surgeon to King George VI (1946–52) and sergeant surgeon to Queen Elizabeth II (1952–67), served as the first native-born governor-general of New Zealand (1967–72). Porritt studied at Otago University, and in 1923 he was awarded a Rhodes scholarship to Magdalen College, Oxford. He completed his medical training in London at St. Mary's Hospital, where he remained on the surgical staff until 1965. After serving at the front in the Royal Army Medical Corps during World War II, he remained an RAMC consultant until 1967. He was also president of the Royal College of Surgeons (1960–63), the British Medical Association (1960–61), and the Royal Society of Medicine (1966–67). Despite his innumerable international honours, in New Zealand Porritt was perhaps better known as a former Olympic athlete. A champion runner both in New Zealand and at Oxford, he led his native country's national Olympic team as captain in 1924 and 1928 and as manager in 1936. In 1924 Porritt took the bronze medal in the 100-m race behind the great Harold Abrahams and American Jackson Scholz. He was a longtime member of the International Olympic Committee (1934–67) and chairman of the Commonwealth Games (1945–66). Porritt was created a baronet in 1963 and awarded a life peerage in 1973.

Potter, Dennis Christopher George, British dramatist (b. May 17, 1935, Berry Hill, near the Forest of Dean, Gloucestershire, England—d. June 7, 1994, Ross-on-Wye, Herefordshire, England), wrote television dramas that challenged the conventions of the medium as well as the expectations of the audience. He often used shocking themes, fantasy sequences, and musical interludes (in which the actors lip-synched to old recordings of period songs) to break the dramatic mood and to provide running commentary on the characters and on the real world beyond the play. After graduating from New College, Oxford (B.A., 1959), Potter made documentaries for BBC television. In 1961 he was stricken with psoriatic arthropathy, a painful and crippling disease of the joints and skin that plagued him for the rest of his life. Unable to work for long periods, he became a television critic and dramatist. His first teleplays, "Vote Vote Vote for Nigel Barton" and "Stand Up, Nigel Barton," were broadcast in December 1965. "Pennies from Heaven" (1978), a six-part serial about a Depression-era sheet-music salesman deluded by his fantasies of love, established Potter's reputation both for quality and for controversy, although his 1981 film adaptation was a failure. "The Singing Detective" (1986), his best-known and most obviously autobiographical teleplay, concerns a novelist suffering with psoriatic arthropathy who lies helpless in a hospital bed dreaming of his childhood in the Forest of Dean, mentally rewriting a pulp-fiction detective novel, and hallucinating fantastic musical numbers. Potter's other teleplays include "Brimstone and Treacle" (written in 1976 but not televised until 1987 because its subject matter was deemed sacrilegious), "Blue Remembered Hills" (1979), "Blade on the Feather" (1984), "Christabel" (1989), "Blackeyes" (1989), and "Lipstick on Your Collar" (1993). He also wrote novels, a stage play, and screenplays, notably *Gorky Park* (1983) and *Dreamchild* (1985). In a television interview in April 1994, Potter announced that he was dying of pancreatic and liver cancer. He spent the last weeks of his life caring for his wife (who died of cancer one week before Potter) and completing two final teleplays: "Karaoke" and "Cold Lazarus."

Primus, Pearl, U.S. dancer, choreographer, and teacher (b. Nov. 29, 1919, Trinidad—d. Oct. 29, 1994, New Rochelle, N.Y.), pioneered the use of authentic African elements in her works and influenced a number of black dancers and choreographers, among them Alvin Ailey and Donald McKayle. Primus moved with her family to the U.S. when she was three. She planned to be a doctor and studied biology at Hunter College, New York City, receiving a bachelor's degree. She sought laboratory work but could not find a job open to blacks, so she applied to the National Youth Administration and was placed in a dance group. She made her solo performing debut in 1943 with the New Dance Group and soon was appearing at Café Society Downtown, one of the first fully integrated nightclubs. She founded (1944) her own company, which performed on Broadway and toured the U.S. Primus had begun using African themes in her choreography, notably her first major work, *African Ceremonial* (1944), and in 1948 she was awarded a Rosenwald fellowship and studied dance in Africa. She made several more trips over the following years and eventually, in 1978, earned a Ph.D. in African and Caribbean studies. In 1954 she married Percival Borde, a dancer she had met on a trip to Trinidad, and they frequently performed and toured together. In addition to African themes, Primus often incorporated experiences of U.S. blacks in her dances. In the mid-1940s she created *Strange Fruit,* which depicted a woman's reactions to a lynching, and *The Negro Speaks of Rivers,* which was inspired by a poem by Langston Hughes and portrayed the difficulty of life along the Mississippi. *Michael, Row Your Boat Ashore* (1979) was about the mother of a Birmingham, Ala., church-bombing victim. Primus danced until 1980 and thereafter directed a black studies program at the State University of New York at Buffalo and taught ethnic studies at five Massachusetts colleges. Among the awards she received was the National Medal of the Arts in 1991.

Rani, Devika, Indian actress (b. March 30, 1908, Waltair, Andhra Pradesh, India—d. March 9, 1994, Bangalore, India), was one of India's most esteemed movie stars in the 1930s and early '40s and, with her husband, the filmmaker Himanshu Rai, was founder of Bombay Talkies studio. Rani was the grandniece of the Nobel Prize-winning poet Rabindranath Tagore and the daughter of an eminent surgeon. While in London studying architecture, textiles, and art design, she met Rai, who hired her as a set and costume consultant. They were married in 1929 and worked in Germany for several months. Rani made her cinema debut opposite her husband in *Karma* (1933), the first Indian film released in English and the first to feature a kissing scene. On their return to Bombay (1934), the couple founded Bombay Talkies, employing German and British technicians and having as its mission the production of socially relevant films. Rani was admired both for her luminous beauty and for her sensitive acting in such films as *Achhut Kanya* (1936; "The Untouchable Girl"), *Jeevan Prabhat* (1937), *Nirmala* (1938), and *Durga* (1939). After Rai's death (1940), Rani remained at the head of Bombay Talkies until she retired to Bangalore with her second husband, the artist Svetoslav Roerich, in 1945. She was honoured by the Indian government with the Padma Shri, one of the highest civilian awards, and she was the first recipient of the Dada Saheb Phalke prize for her lifetime achievement in Indian cinema.

Ray, Dixy Lee (Margaret Ray), U.S. zoologist and government official (b. Sept. 3, 1914, Tacoma, Wash.—d. Jan. 2, 1994, Fox Island, near Seattle, Wash.), was a colourful and outspoken supporter of the nuclear industry, critic of the environmental movement, and proponent of making science more accessible to nonscientists. A childhood fascination with the sea led to academic degrees in zoology from Mills College, Oakland, Calif. (B.A., 1937), and Stanford University (Ph.D., 1945). A specialist in marine crustacea, Ray joined the faculty of the University of Washington, where she taught for 27 years. In 1963 Ray accepted the directorship of the Pacific Science Center in Seattle, which she developed into a major facility for publicizing and popularizing science. Although she had served on numerous federal advisory groups, Ray first moved to the nation's capital in August 1972 after she was selected by Pres. Richard Nixon to be a member of the Atomic Energy Commission (AEC), the first woman to be appointed to a full five-year term; she succeeded James Schlesinger as chairman of that body the following year. Ray's unconventional lifestyle (she lived in a house trailer with her two dogs, which she occasionally took to the office with her) provided piquant contrast to the stereotypical Washington bureaucracy. Following the breakup of the AEC into two agencies in 1974, Ray moved to the Department of State and served as assistant secretary in charge of the Bureau of Oceans, International Environmental and Scientific Affairs. She resigned in 1975 in protest against a lack of support from Secretary of State Henry A. Kissinger. Returning to Washington state, Ray was elected governor in 1977 and served one four-year term. In addition to writing many scientific papers, Ray was coauthor of two books on the excesses of the environmental movement, *Trashing the Planet* (1990) and *Environmental Overkill* (1993).

Raye, Martha (Margaret Teresa Yvonne Reed), U.S. entertainer (b. Aug. 27, 1916, Butte, Mont.—d. Oct. 19, 1994, Los Angeles, Calif.), established her reputation as an irrepressible comic in a career that encompassed radio shows, theatre, film, and entertaining U.S. troops stationed overseas. Raye began performing at the age of three, when she joined the family vaudeville act. She made her feature film debut in *Rhythm on the Range* (1936), scoring a success with her rendition of the song "Mr. Paganini." Raye appeared in such films as *College Holiday* (1936), *Waikiki Wedding* (1937), *Give Me a Sailor* (1938), *Keep 'Em Flying* (1941), and *Hellzapoppin* (1941). She drew praise for her performance opposite Charlie Chaplin in *Monsieur Verdoux* (1947), which was widely regarded as her best film. Raye also performed in the theatre, notably as Ginger Rogers' replacement in *Hello, Dolly!* (1967), and in *No, No, Nanette* (1972). Raye made few films in her later years, but she continued to work in burlesque shows, nightclubs, radio, and television. On TV she was well known for her "Big Mouth" advertisements for a dental adhesive. For working tirelessly with the United Service Organizations (USO) during World War II, the Korean War, and the Vietnam War, she was awarded the Jean Hersholt Humanitarian Award in 1969. She sued the makers of the film *For the Boys* (1991), claiming the story line was based on her USO experiences, but the suit was later dismissed. Raye married for the seventh time in 1991; she wed her manager, who was 33 years her junior. In 1993 she was awarded the Presidential Medal of Freedom.

Redhead, Brian, British journalist and broadcaster (b. Dec. 28, 1929, Newcastle upon Tyne, Northumberland, England—d. Jan. 23, 1994, Macclesfield, Cheshire, England), as chief presenter of BBC radio's popular "Today" program from 1975, was for millions of devoted listeners "the voice of the morning." Redhead studied history at Downing College, Cambridge, before joining the editorial staff of the *Manchester Guardian* in 1954. Within five years he was features editor, and after the newspaper (renamed *The Guardian*) relocated to London, he was made the northern editor. In 1969 he was promoted to editor of *The Guardian*'s sister paper, the *Manchester Evening*

News. Over the years he simultaneously pursued a career in broadcasting, with a series of regional radio and television programs. When his application for editor of *The Guardian* was rejected, he left print journalism to take the job on "Today." Redhead, a lively and relentless interviewer, often irritated his political guests, but his incisive questions and animated personality made his early-morning broadcast required listening in the halls of government. In later years he also produced radio documentaries on religion.

Rey, Fernando (FERNANDO CASADO ARAMBILLET VEIGA), Spanish actor (b. Sept. 20, 1917, La Coruña, Spain—d. March 9, 1994, Madrid, Spain), excelled at portraying suave, complex villains, especially in a series of motion pictures directed by Luis Buñuel in the 1970s, but he was perhaps best known to English-speaking audiences for his role as the French drug baron Alain Charnier in *The French Connection* (1971) and its 1975 sequel. Rey was born into a prosperous family and studied architecture at the University of Madrid until he quit to fight on the Republican side in the Spanish Civil War (1936–39). He began working as a movie extra in 1936, and by 1960 the multilingual Rey had achieved moderate success acting in low-budget pictures and dubbing foreign films into Spanish. His breakthrough came as the lecherous Don Jaime in Buñuel's *Viridiana* (1961). Rey superbly captured Buñuel's vision of privileged decadence and obsession in their later collaborations, *Tristana* (1970), *Le Charme discret de la bourgeoisie* (1972; *The Discreet Charm of the Bourgeoisie*), and *Cet obscur objet du désir* (1977; *That Obscure Object of Desire*). Rey appeared in more than 100 other movies, including Orson Welles's *Chimes at Midnight* (1966), Lina Wertmüller's *Seven Beauties* (1975), and Carlos Saura's *Elisa, vida mia* (1977; *Elisa, My Love*), for which he won the best actor award at the Cannes Film Festival. He also starred as Don Quixote on Spanish television in 1992. Rey's last film, *Al otro lado del túnel* (*The Other Side of the Tunnel*), was released shortly before his death.

Rincón de Gautier, Felisa, Puerto Rican politician (b. 1897?, Ceiba, P.R.—d. Sept. 16, 1994, San Juan, P.R.), served as a popular mayor of San Juan (1946–69) after helping in the 1932 campaign in which women succeeded in gaining the right to vote. Rincón de Gautier was the daughter of a lawyer. She left school at age 15 to care for seven younger siblings. A social activist, Rincón de Gautier entered politics and lobbied for child care programs, centres for the elderly, and legal aid for the poor. Her social programs earned her support among San Juan's poor, who affectionately addressed her as Doña Fela. Appointed mayor in 1946, Rincón de Gautier was returned to office in succeeding elections, winning votes with her Wednesday open-house public forums at the city hall and her attention to public works, including housing, hospitals, schools, and sanitation. She did not seek reelection in 1968 but continued to maintain an interest in politics. At the age of 95, she served as the oldest delegate to the Democratic national convention, held in New York City.

Rodney, Red (ROBERT CHUDNICK), U.S. trumpeter and bandleader (b. Sept. 27, 1927, Philadelphia, Pa.—d. May 27, 1994, Boynton Beach, Fla.), was a brilliant jazz improviser who performed with the swing bands of Jimmy Dorsey, Gene Krupa, Woody Herman, and Benny Goodman before finding his niche as a member (1949–51) of Charlie Parker's bebop quintet. Rodney, distinguished by his flaming red hair, was also the first white bebop trumpeter. His innovative playing style was marked by his brilliant technique and purity of tone. After receiving his first trumpet as a bar mitzvah gift, Rodney adopted the romantic style of trumpeter Harry James before becoming obsessed with the emergence of bebop, a jazz style that relies heavily on complicated melodic and harmonic improvisations. By age 21, Rodney was a sensational player, and he was recruited by Parker to fill the seat vacated by Miles Davis. Rodney's heroin addiction, however, blighted the first half of his career. In the 1960s he played with bands in Las Vegas, Nev., and underwent drug rehabilitation. He also ran afoul of the law when he impersonated a general and stole $10,000 and some secret documents from the safe at an Atomic Energy Commission facility. While spending three years in prison, Rodney earned his law degree but was unable to practice because of his felony conviction. In 1980 Rodney formed a band with multi-instrumentalist Ira Sullivan. He took up the flügelhorn and returned to glory as a skilled ballad player, in demand worldwide.

Roland, Gilbert (LUIS ANTONIO DÁMASO DE ALONSO), U.S. actor (b. Dec. 11, 1905, Ciudad Juárez, Mexico—d. May 15, 1994, Beverly Hills, Calif.), specialized in portraying charismatic and dashing Latin lovers, most notably in the 1927 silent-film classic *Camille* opposite Norma Talmadge, but he was also featured in swashbuckling talkie roles, including that of the Spanish sea captain in *The Sea Hawk* (1940), a matador in *The Bullfighter and the Lady* (1951), and a Mexican rebel leader in *Bandido* (1956). The son and grandson of Spanish bullfighters, Roland also trained as a torero before his family fled the Mexican Revolution and moved to Texas. The mature-looking Roland moved to Los Angeles on his own as a young teen and began appearing as an extra in Hollywood films. The enduring character actor, who was distinguished by a trim mustache, made more than 100 films, including *She Done Him Wrong* (1933), *Captain Kidd* (1945), *We Were Strangers* (1949), *The Bad and the Beautiful* (1952), and *The Big Circus* (1959). During the 1950s and '60s he became a familiar figure on television on such shows as "Alfred Hitchcock Presents," "The Alfred Hitchcock Hour," and "The Fugitive."

Romero, Cesar, U.S. actor (b. Feb. 15, 1907, New York, N.Y.—d. Jan. 1, 1994, Santa Monica, Calif.), was a tall, debonair, and mustachioed film veteran whose diverse career encompassed roles as ingratiating playboys, engaging bandits, and likable scoundrels; he was best remembered for his portrayal of the Joker, an archvillain and master of puns on television's "Batman," and the silver screen's Cisco Kid, a Mexican rogue. Romero's good looks coupled with his Cuban heritage seemed likely to result in his being typecast as a "Latin lover," but his screen persona was more akin to a light parody of a gigolo. A onetime professional dancer, Romero made his film debut in 1934 in *The Thin Man.* After appearing opposite Marlene Dietrich in *The Devil Is a Woman* (1935), his first leading role, Romero seldom starred as a leading man and almost never got the girl. He appeared with Shirley Temple in *Wee Willie Winkie* (1937) and *The Little Princess* (1939) and with Sonja Henie in *Happy Landing* (1938) and *Wintertime* (1943). Romero was also featured in such musicals as *The Great American Broadcast* (1941), *Weekend in Havana* (1941), and *Springtime in the Rockies* (1942). He starred as the Joker in the film version of *Batman* (1966), reprising his role from the campy television series that ran from 1966 to 1968. Some of Romero's other credits include *Diamond Jim* (1935), *The Return of the Cisco Kid* (1939), *The Gay Caballero* (1940), *Tall, Dark and Handsome* (1941), *Around the World in 80 Days* (1956), and *Donovan's Reef* (1963). During the 1980s he portrayed Jane Wyman's husband on the television evening soap opera "Falcon Crest."

Rozhdestvensky, Robert Ivanovich, Russian poet (b. June 20, 1932, Kosikha, Altay *kray,* Russian S.F.S.R., U.S.S.R.—d. Aug. 19/20, 1994, Moscow, Russia), was one of a group of young Russian poets who broke away from the strictures of Socialist Realism in the 1950s and '60s and wrote unconventional verse filled with romanticism and introspection. Rozhdestvensky began writing poetry as a boy and published his first collection, *Flagi vesny* (1955; *Flags of Spring*), several months before he graduated from the Maksim Gorky Institute of World Literature in Moscow. Along with his better-known contemporary, Yevgeny Yevtushenko, he came of age in the era of artistic freedom that followed Joseph Stalin's death (1953). Despite the political idealism and literary experimentation evident in his early work, Rozhdestvensky never openly criticized the Soviet government, and his poetry remained officially acceptable during the more restrictive 1960s and '70s when others, even Yevtushenko, were in disfavour. Among his other collections were *Rovesniku* (1962; *To My Contemporary*), *Posvyashcheniye* (1970; *The Dedication*), and *Za dvadtsat let* (1973; *In the Twenty Years*). The narrative poem *Rekviyem* (1961; *Requiem*) was set to music, as were many of his short love lyrics. Rozhdestvensky was a member of the Communist Party of the Soviet Union from 1977 and was awarded the Lenin Prize in 1979.

Rubin, Jerry, U.S. political activist turned businessman (b. July 14, 1938, Cincinnati, Ohio—d. Nov. 28, 1994, Los Angeles, Calif.), gained his widest renown from the anti-Vietnam War protests during the 1968 Democratic national convention in Chicago and the subsequent "Chicago Seven" trial, in which—after one defendant was removed to be tried separately—he and six others were tried on charges of conspiracy to incite violence and crossing state lines with intent to riot. After a long trial punctuated with taunts and outbursts from the defendants, they were acquitted of conspiracy, but five were convicted of incitement, and all—plus their lawyers—were cited for contempt some 200 times. The convictions were later overturned. Rubin attended Oberlin (Ohio) College, graduated from the University of Cincinnati, and studied at Hebrew University in Jerusalem before briefly attending the University of California at Berkeley. Radicalized by the Free Speech Movement and a trip to Cuba, he helped found the Youth International Party, better known as the Yippies, and was one of the leaders of the 1967 antiwar march on the Pentagon. During the 1968 election campaign, he staged acts of street theatre such as promoting the Yippie candidate—a pig named Pigasus. Rubin moved away from radical politics during the 1970s and turned his attention to the human-potential movement, sampling, for example, yoga, est, meditation, bioenergetics, and Rolfing. In the 1980s he organized networking seminars in New York City for young Wall Street professionals, and he and fellow former Chicago Seven defendant Abbie Hoffman engaged in a series of "Yippie Versus Yuppie" debates. In 1991 he moved to Los Angeles to market a nutritional drink that contained bee pollen and ginseng. Rubin died of a heart attack two weeks after being hit by a car while jaywalking.

Rudolph, Wilma Glodean, U.S. runner (b. June 23, 1940, Clarksville, Tenn.—d. Nov. 12, 1994, Brentwood, Tenn.), was a phenomenal sprinter who overcame crippling childhood illnesses to become the first American woman to capture three track-and-field gold medals at a single Olympics. In the 1960 Olympics in Rome she won the 100-m dash (tying the world record of 11.3 sec in a semifinal race) and the 200-m dash, and she anchored the triumphant U.S. 4 × 100-m relay team (which set a world record of 44.4 sec in a semifinal race). Rudolph, a sickly child who conquered scarlet fever, double pneumonia, and the temporary paralysis of her left leg, wore a leg brace and then an orthopedic shoe until she discarded the shoe to play basketball, her first love. In high school, her basketball coach dubbed the lanky, 1.85-m (6-ft) scoring machine (she had 803 points in 25 games as a junior) "Skeeter" because, he said, "You're little, you're fast and you always get in my way." She attended Tennessee State University from 1957 to 1961. In 1956, weighing less than 46 kg (100 lb), she won a bronze medal in the 4 × 100-m relay at the Olympic Games in Melbourne, Australia. For the 1960 Olympics she bulked up to 59 kg (130 lb). After retiring as a runner, Rudolph established a foundation for underprivileged children; served as a goodwill ambassador to French West Africa; coached briefly at DePauw University, Greencastle, Ind.; and held various corporate business positions. In 1977 her inspirational autobiography, *Wilma,* was published and made into a television movie.

MARK KAUFFMAN—LIFE MAGAZINE

Rudolph, who was Amateur Athletic Union 100-yd dash champion from 1959 to 1962, was inducted into the U.S. National Track and Field Hall of Fame in 1974.

Rühmann, Heinz, German actor (b. March 7, 1902, Essen, Germany—d. Oct. 4, 1994, Berg, near Starnberg, Germany), had a motion-picture career that spanned more than 60 years and 100 films and was one of his country's most beloved stars. Specializing in roles as the little man whose optimism and humour enable him to defeat adversity, he came to be considered a comic institution and was voted most popular actor in Germany at least a dozen times. Rühmann began his career as a stage actor in 1920 and made his film debut in 1926 in *Das deutsche Mutterherz* ("The German Mother Heart"). He became a star after his performance in his first talking picture, *Die Drei von der Tankstelle* (1930; "Three from the Gas Station"). Such films as *Der Mann, der seinen Mörder sucht* (1931; "Looking for His Murderer") and *Der Mann, der Sherlock Holmes war* (1937; "The Man Who Was Sherlock Holmes") made Rühmann so popular that Nazi authorities pressured him to divorce his wife, who was half Jewish. He did so in 1938—after 14 years of marriage—but he helped her escape to Sweden, and after World War II they appeared on television together. Rühmann then directed a few films, but acting remained his principal focus. Among his postwar acting successes were *Charleys Tante* (1955; "Charley's Aunt"), *Der Hauptmann von*

Köpenick (1956; "The Captain from Köpenick"), and *Der Brave Soldat Schwejk* (1960; "The Good Soldier Schweik"). Rühmann became known to English-speaking audiences through his role in the motion picture *Ship of Fools* (1965). In 1993 he appeared in *In weiter Ferne, so nah!* ("Far Away, So Close"), thus becoming one of the very few silent-film performers to remain active in the 1990s.

Rusk, (David) Dean, U.S. diplomat (b. Feb. 9, 1909, Cherokee county, Ga.—d. Dec. 20, 1994, Athens, Ga.), as U.S. secretary of state (1961–69) during the John F. Kennedy and Lyndon B. Johnson administrations, gave unwavering support for U.S. involvement in the Vietnam War amidst massive protests at home as the war escalated and U.S. participation increased. After graduating (1931) from Davidson (N.C.) College, Rusk attended St. John's College, Oxford, as a Rhodes scholar and earned (1934) an M.A. in philosophy, politics, and economics. He taught at Mills College, Oakland, Calif., from 1934 to 1940, when he was called to active duty in the U.S. Army. During World War II, Rusk served Gen. Joseph W. Stilwell as deputy chief of staff for the China-Burma-India theatre and rose to the rank of colonel before leaving the military in 1946. That year he joined the State Department and held a variety of posts before being recruited by Kennedy in 1961 to head the department. In this role he served as advisor to the president during the showdown with Moscow known as the 1962

Cuban Missile Crisis. U.S. aerial photographs revealed that the Soviets were constructing missile-launching installations in Cuba. Kennedy ordered a naval blockade and threatened military reprisals, after which Soviet leader Nikita S. Khrushchev agreed to remove the missiles under UN supervision. In his 1990 memoirs, *As I Saw It,* Rusk recounted his assessment of the situation: "We are eyeball to eyeball, and the other fellow just blinked." He helped negotiate some of the first arms-control accords with Moscow. After stepping down as secretary of state, Rusk taught international law at the University of Georgia until he retired in 1984.

Sablon, Jean, French singer and songwriter (b. March 25, 1906, Nogent-sur-Marne, near Paris, France—d. Feb. 24, 1994, Cannes-la-Bocca, France), was an elegant crooner whose matinee-idol looks (enhanced by his trademark thinly clipped mustache), mellow baritone voice, and intimate use of a microphone charmed audiences in the U.S. and Europe and earned him the nickname "the French Bing Crosby." Sablon made his professional debut in a Parisian operetta in 1923, and by 1931 he was a sought-after cabaret and music-hall singer. In the 1930s he added popular jazz recordings to his repertoire. He also toured and sang regularly on the radio in England, Brazil, and the U.S., where he was performing when World War II broke out in 1939. On his return to Europe (1945), he was initially derided for his Americanized style and dubbed "the singer without a voice" because of his use of the newfangled microphone, but his romantic vocals soon won over French audiences. Sablon gave his last public performance in Rio de Janeiro in 1983, two years after marking his 75th birthday with a concert at New York City's Lincoln Center.

Sallal, 'Abd Allah as-, Yemeni army officer and politician (b. 1917?, San'a', Yemen—d. March 5, 1994, San'a'), was the first president and prime minister of the Yemen Arab Republic (North Yemen) after having led a military coup against the last imam, Saif al-Islam Muhammad al-Badr, on Sept. 27, 1962; Sallal himself was overthrown on Nov. 5, 1967. As a youth Sallal was selected by the monarchy for special military training in Iraq. On his return to Yemen in 1939, he was briefly imprisoned for political reasons. He later spent seven years in jail (1948–55), but he was released by then Crown Prince Badr, who made him governor of Hodeida (1959–61) and promoted him to brigadier. When Badr succeeded to the throne on Sept. 18, 1962, he appointed Sallal chief of staff. Within 10 days a military coup had overthrown the monarchy and installed Sallal as president, with Egyptian military, political, and economic aid. His rule became increasingly tenuous, however, as royalist forces, supported by Saudi Arabia, continued to promote civil unrest. When Egypt withdrew its backing in 1967, moderate republicans staged a bloodless coup while Sallal was on a visit to Iraq. He did not return to Yemen from exile until 1981.

Sánchez, Luis Alberto, Peruvian politician and author (b. Oct. 12, 1900, Lima, Peru—d. Feb. 6, 1994, Lima), was a prolific man of letters who wrote more than 70 volumes of history, biography, literary criticism, philosophy, fiction, poetry, and autobiography and was politically prominent as a longtime member of the centre-left American Popular Revolutionary Alliance (APRA), which was founded by Victor Raúl Haya de la Torre to combat imperialism in Latin America. Sánchez, an APRA loyalist, founded the party's newspaper, *Tribuna,* in 1931, the same year he was elected to Congress. The following year, however, he was imprisoned briefly by the military government of Luis Sánchez Cerro, and for the next 25 years he endured persecution and exile at the hands of successive military governments as a result of his APRA affiliation. Sánchez was elected to the Senate in 1963, 1980, and 1985, and he served as the chairman of the 1978–79 Constituent Assembly that drafted a new Peruvian constitution. When Alan García became the country's first APRA president in 1985, Sánchez was given the post of vice president, and he served briefly as prime minister in 1989, the year before García's term in office expired. Sánchez also served (1946–61) as rector of the National University of San Marcos, his alma mater.

Saraswati, Swamigal Chandrasekharendra, Indian religious leader (b. May 20, 1894, Viluppuram, Tamil Nadu, India—d. Jan. 8, 1994, Kanchipuram, Tamil Nadu), was a revered Hindu sage and a lifelong advocate of religious tolerance. Saraswati, the son of a Brahmin schoolteacher, originally was named Swaminathan. At the age of 13 he was chosen for a religious vocation and taken by a monk to a Hindu *math* (monastery) near Madras. Saraswati was a learned student of the sacred Vedic texts and devoted much of his life to the preservation and teaching of the dharma, the Hindu religious and moral law governing individual conduct. A devout and scholarly man, he spoke a dozen languages, including English, French, Swedish, and several Indian dialects. He also traveled throughout India on foot, visiting pilgrim centres, studying local customs, and preaching nonviolence and religious tolerance among Hindu castes and between India's Hindu majority and Muslim minority populations.

Savalas, Aristoteles ("TELLY"), U.S. actor (b. Jan. 21, 1924, Garden City, N.Y.—d. Jan. 22, 1994, Universal City, Calif.), specialized in portraying film villains before gaining international stardom as Lieut. Theo Kojak, television's bald-headed, lollipop-licking New York City detective who shielded a heart of gold under a gruff, wise-cracking exterior. As the Emmy award-winning star of the dramatic police series "Kojak" (1973–78), the hawk-nosed detective was renowned for sporting three-piece suits and for uttering his signature catchphrase, "Who loves ya, baby?" Savalas was an award-winning documentary producer at ABC News before he broke into acting (1959) as a stand-in. He was discovered by Burt Lancaster (*q.v.*), who featured him as a police detective in *The Young Savages* (1961) and then as a sadistic convict in *Birdman of Alcatraz* (1962). The latter role earned him an Academy Award nomination as best supporting actor. After first shaving his head for the role of Pontius Pilate in *The Greatest Story Ever Told* (1965), Savalas made his bald pate his trademark. Some of his other menacing roles were as a black marketeer in *Battle of the Bulge* (1965), a vicious Southern racist and rapist in *The Dirty Dozen* (1967), a renegade murderer in *The Scalphunters* (1968), the nemesis of James Bond in *On Her Majesty's Secret Service* (1969), and a sadistic bandit in *A Town Called Bastard* (1971). It was his portrayal as Kojak in the 1973 television

movie *The Marcus-Nelson Murders* that served as the springboard for the series. After "Kojak" was dropped in 1978, Savalas appeared in films, notably *Beyond the Poseidon Adventure* (1979), before reviving Kojak in 1989 for a few television episodes on "The ABC Saturday Mystery."

Scarry, Richard McClure, U.S. author and illustrator (b. June 5, 1919, Boston, Mass.—d. April 30, 1994, Gstaad, Switz.), captured the imagination of preschoolers with his oversized, highly detailed picture books, which featured a whimsical menagerie of characters, including such favourites as Huckle Cat, Sergeant Murphy, Mayor Fox, Farmer Goat, and especially Lowly Worm, a Tyrolean-hatted earthworm who slithered into numerous story lines. Scarry's 250 books appealed mainly to curious toddlers who were learning to talk and explore the world. Dog-eared and Scotch-taped copies of such best-sellers as *Richard Scarry's Best Word Book Ever* (1963), *Richard Scarry's Please & Thank You Book* (1973), and *Richard Scarry's Find Your ABC's* (1973) were tenderly preserved in homes and provided testimony to the enduring popularity of his works, which were translated into more than 30 languages. Scarry, a mediocre student who spent five years in high school, studied (1938–41) at the Boston Museum School before serving in the army (1941–46). He began illustrating books in 1947 and scored his first commercial success in 1963. Scarry's enticing books invited children to examine the minute details cluttered into many of his colourful illustrations, which were both informative and educational. His "busy" books and dictionaries sold more than 100 million copies worldwide, and in 1989 eight of his books made the list of the top 50 best-selling children's books of all time. In 1968 Scarry moved to Switzerland, where he continued to produce his delightful hardbacks. A cable-television animated series, "The Busy World of Richard Scarry," made its debut in 1994.

Schneerson, Menachem Mendel, Russian-born rabbi (b. April 14, 1902, Nikolayev, Russia [now in Ukraine]—d. June 12, 1994, New York, N.Y.), was a towering figure in Orthodox Judaism and for 44 years the charismatic spiritual leader of the New York-based Lubavitch Hasidic movement. He built a religious empire from the remnants of a Russian flock, whose numbers had been decimated to a few thousand by the Holocaust, into a powerful following of some 200,000 believers worldwide. Schneerson attracted members by using several strategies: converted campers (dubbed "mitzvah tanks") that served as recruitment centres canvassed New York City; toll-free telephone numbers, satellite television hookups, and faxes of

Talmudic disquisitions were made available; full-page newspaper advertisements were published; and Schneerson himself, a mesmeric figure with piercing blue eyes and a flowing white beard, dispensed blessings and a crisp new dollar bill to each Sunday morning visitor. A Sorbonne-educated scholar, Schneerson became the seventh Lubavitcher grand rabbi in 1950 following the death of his father-in-law. Schneerson, though he had not traveled beyond Crown Heights, Brooklyn, the site of the Lubavitch World Headquarters, in 37 years, had a strong influence on Israeli politics, both within the Knesset (parliament) and among the electorate. Because many of his followers revered Schneerson as the potential Messiah, his death caused great consternation, especially when his hoped-for resurrection failed to take place. He was childless and did not designate a successor.

Schubert, Max Edmund, Australian enologist (b. Feb. 9, 1915, Moculta, near Adelaide, Australia—d. March 6?, 1994, Adelaide), created Grange Hermitage, Australia's most internationally acclaimed red wine, and almost single-handedly changed the standard for the nation's wine industry. In 1930 Schubert took a menial job with the Penfolds winery, which followed the Australian tradition, producing mainly sweet sherry and port. He studied enology at night, was made an assistant winemaker in 1940, and was promoted to senior winemaker in 1947. While on a tour to study European winemaking techniques in 1950, he realized that the Shiraz, or Syrah, grape could be used to create an Australian claret similar to the great red Bordeaux and Rhône wines. Schubert's first attempts, aged in new American oak casks, were pronounced a dismal failure, and he was ordered to cease production. He persevered in secret, however, and his faith was rewarded when the 1955 vintage won a gold medal at the 1962 Sydney Wine Show. By 1994 Australian premium table wines were respected around the world, a bottle of the most recent vintage of Grange Hermitage was selling for around $A 100, and the previously much-maligned early vintages were commanding thousands of dollars a bottle. Schubert was made a Member of the Order of Australia in 1984.

Schwinger, Julian Seymour, U.S. physicist (b. Feb. 12, 1918, New York, N.Y.—d. July 16, 1994, Los Angeles, Calif.), was a brilliant theoretician whose studies helped define the basic principles of quantum electrodynamics, a theoretical description of the interaction of electrically charged particles with electromagnetic radiation; he won the 1965 Nobel Prize for Physics (with Richard P. Feynman of the U.S. and Tomonaga Shin'ichiro of Japan) for this important work. His mathematical formulations provided a vital link between quantum mechanics and Albert Einstein's special theory of relativity. A prodigy, Schwinger received (1939) a Ph.D. from Columbia University, New York City, at the age of 21 and began conducting research in the newly emerging field of nuclear physics under J. Robert Oppenheimer at the University of California at Berkeley. During World War II he helped develop radar at the Radiation Laboratory of the Massachusetts Institute of Technology. In 1945 he joined the faculty of Harvard University, where he began his work on quantum electrodynamics and became the first to calculate the anomalous magnetic property of the electron. His superb teaching methods were distinguished by scintillating lectures, and his mentorship of students resulted in dozens of them earning their Ph.D.'s under his guidance. Three of his pupils also later won Nobel Prizes. From 1972 to 1980 he served as professor of physics at the University of California at Los Angeles, and from 1980 until his death he was university professor there. Among his other honours were the first Albert Einstein Prize in 1951 (with Kurt Gödel) and the National Medal of Science in 1964.

Selvon, Samuel Dickson, Trinidadian-born Canadian author (b. May 20, 1923, Trinidad—d. April 16, 1994, Trinidad), was an important West Indian writer who, with V.S. Naipaul, was in the

vanguard of the Caribbean literary renaissance in London during the 1950s; he was best remembered for the 1956 classic novel *The Lonely Londoners,* a picaresque account of the initial exhilaration and excitement experienced by black West Indians living in post-World War II London tempered by discrimination, poverty, and a sense of exile. After serving (1940–45) in the Royal Navy Reserve as a wireless operator on patrol boats in the Caribbean Sea, Selvon worked as a reporter with the *Trinidad Guardian* newspaper while establishing a reputation as a gifted short-story writer. After moving to London (1950) he published his first book, *A Brighter Sun* (1952), which explored racial tensions between black Africans and Indians living in the West Indies. Selvon established a rich oral tradition in novels featuring painstaking attention to dialect, one of the hallmarks of his writing style. He was also praised for his vivid, if not ribald, descriptiveness and his colourful accounts of local life. His other important works include the short-story collection *Ways of Sunlight* (1957) and such novels as *I Hear Thunder* (1963), *The Housing Lark* (1965), *Moses Ascending* (1975), and *Moses Migrating* (1983). The latter two novels were sequels to *The Lonely Londoners.* In 1978 Selvon adopted Canada as his home, but he traveled to Trinidad in early 1994 to promote a reprinting of one of his books.

Senna, Ayrton, Brazilian race-car driver (b. March 21, 1960, São Paulo, Brazil—d. May 1, 1994, Imola, Italy), was a fierce competitor who was renowned for his ruthless and risky maneuvers on the Grand Prix circuit and dominated the sport with 41 Grand Prix titles and 3 circuit world championships (1988, 1990, and 1991). Senna was revered as a national hero in Brazil, and his death, from massive head injuries suffered when he smashed head-on into a concrete wall at some 300 km/h (186 mph) at the San Marino Grand Prix, plunged the country into mourning. At the age of four, Senna was already behind the wheel of a go-cart and demonstrating a determination to win. He joined the Formula One racing circuit in 1984 as one of the most promising new drivers, and he captured the coveted pole position a record 65 times for having the fastest race-qualifying times. An enigmatic figure who was deeply religious yet highly aggressive on the racetrack, Senna thrilled spectators and cowed competitors with his fearsome driving. He invited controversy over his long-standing rivalry with Frenchman Alain Prost, with 51 titles the most successful driver; the two collided during the final race of both the 1989 season, when Prost emerged victorious, and the 1990 season, when Senna captured the world crown. He reportedly earned more than $100 million during his career, which included an annual salary of some $10 million. Senna's death came one day after Austrian rookie Roland Ratzenberger was killed in a similar accident during qualifying trials. Both deaths renewed concerns about recent rule changes. The Fédération Internationale de l'Automobile banned electronics and other drivers' aids from Formula One cars, a move that many believed made the sport more dangerous.

Sharkey, Jack (JOSEPH PAUL ZUKAUSKAS), U.S. boxer (b. Oct. 26, 1902, Binghamton, N.Y.—d. Aug. 17, 1994, Beverly, Mass.), dethroned Max Schmeling as heavyweight champion of the world in a controversial 15-round split decision (June 21, 1932) but lost the title on June 29, 1933, when Primo Carnera knocked him out with a powerful uppercut in the sixth round of their bout. Sharkey, who named himself after pugilist Jack Dempsey and former heavyweight "Sailor" Tom Sharkey, was also a sailor before he entered the ring. His punishing body blows helped him defeat top-ranking boxers and earned him the chance to fight Dempsey on July 21, 1927. In that contest Sharkey led for the first seven rounds but was decked by Dempsey while complaining to the referee about a supposed low body blow. In his first attempt in 1930 at the heavyweight crown, Sharkey lost to Schmeling on a foul. Sharkey's subsequent 1932 victory over Schmeling was unpopular, and his loss to Carnera was questioned

because of Carnera's links to the underworld. During boxing's golden era Sharkey also fought Joe Lewis, who knocked him out in the third round. Sharkey was the only boxer ever to fight two sets of champions who had never faced each other in the ring—Dempsey and Schmeling and Dempsey and Lewis. Sharkey hung up his gloves after his loss to Lewis. Nicknamed "the Boston Cob," Sharkey had a career record that included 55 bouts, with 38 victories (14 by knockout), 13 losses, 3 draws, and 1 no-decision. He was inducted into the Boxing Hall of Fame in 1980 and the International Boxing Hall of Fame in 1994.

Shelepin, Aleksandr Nikolayevich, Soviet government official (b. Aug. 18, 1918, Voronezh, Russia—d. Oct. 24, 1994), was a ruthless, powerful member of the post-Stalin leadership of the Communist Party of the Soviet Union (CPSU) and at one time was thought to be in contention for his country's top position. Even though he gained power with the aid of Nikita S. Khrushchev and was chairman (1958–61) of the Committee for State Security (KGB) under him, he was thought to have played a major part in Khrushchev's overthrow (1964). Shelepin graduated (1939) from the Moscow Institute of History, Philosophy and Literature and then served with the Red Army during the war with Finland (1939–40). After joining the CPSU (1940), he rose rapidly through party and government ranks and by 1952 was director of the Komsomol (Young Communist League), a post he held until he became KGB head. As KGB chairman Shelepin was known to have been responsible for policies of political harassment, espionage, and assassinations. He gained even more power when he was named chairman of the Committee of Party and State Control (1962), and in 1964, after Khrushchev's ouster, he became a member of the party Presidium (later the Politburo). When Leonid Brezhnev assumed power, however, Shelepin gradually lost his prominence. After his 1975 trip to Britain as head of a trade union delegation provoked huge protest demonstrations because of his KGB activities, Shelepin was dismissed from the Politburo.

Shilts, Randy Martin, U.S. journalist and author (b. Aug. 8, 1951, Davenport, Iowa—d. Feb. 16, 1994, Guerneville, Calif.), was a top-notch investigative reporter who became the nation's first openly gay journalist to work on a major U.S. newspaper, the *San Francisco Chronicle.* He also was critically acclaimed for his weighty book *And the Band Played On* (1987), which chronicled the history of the AIDS epidemic in passionate yet unbiased prose. Because Shilts openly professed his homosexuality while he was attending

the University of Oregon, after graduation (1975) he found it difficult to secure employment and went to work for *The Advocate,* a San Francisco gay publication. Frustrated by his job prospects, Shilts penned a book on assassinated gay-rights activist Harvey Milk. *The Mayor of Castro Street: The Life and Times of Harvey Milk* (1982) appeared shortly after Shilts was offered a position at the *Chronicle.* There he covered the gay beat. He was struck by the growing number of young gay men who were afflicted with an uncommon cancer and succumbed to wasting ailments. The unknown syndrome was AIDS, first named Grid (Gay-Related Immunodeficiency Disorder), and Shilts was at the journalistic forefront of the story. He lambasted the scientific and government bureaucracies responsible for impeding the disclosure of vital information to the public and called for increased medical research funding. His stinging indictment of those agencies in *And the Band Played On,* which was made into a television movie in 1993, coupled with his warnings about casual sex and the dangers of the San Francisco gay bathhouses brought AIDS awareness into the limelight. Shilts, who was diagnosed HIV positive in 1987, published *Conduct Unbecoming* (1993), a history of homosexuals in the military, before AIDS took his life.

Shore, Frances Rose ("DINAH"), U.S. singer (b. March 1, 1917, Winchester, Tenn.—d. Feb. 24, 1994, Los Angeles, Calif.), projected a sunny disposition and exuded an effervescent Southern charm that, combined with her sultry contralto renditions of such favourites as "Blues in the Night," "I'll Walk Alone," and "Buttons and Bows," endeared her to record buyers and television audiences for some 40 years. Shore, who graduated from Vanderbilt University, Nashville, Tenn., with a degree in sociology, sang with newcomer Frank Sinatra on New York radio and was rejected as a vocalist by some of the top bandleaders of the 1930s before making a recording debut with Xavier Cugat's orchestra in 1939. Shore recorded 75 hits between 1940 and 1955, among them "Yes, My Darling Daughter," "Dear Hearts and Gentle People," and "The Anniversary Song." She starred on Eddie Cantor's radio show and made an unspectacular foray into films before finding her niche on television. In 1951 she debuted as the host of a 15-minute variety program, "The Dinah Shore Show." She followed this with "The Dinah Shore Chevy Show" (1956–63), on which she established the jingle "See the USA in Your Chevrolet" as her trademark along with a signature sign-off kiss for the audience. During her years on television, Shore garnered 10 Emmy awards, was repeatedly named one of America's

SUZIE BLEEDEN—GLOBE PHOTOS

most admired women, and continued to delight viewers as the host of "Dinah's Place" (1970–74), "Dinah" (1974–79), "Dinah and Friends" (1979–84), and "A Conversation with Dinah" (1989–91), which appeared on the Nashville Network. Shore was married twice, first to actor George Montgomery and then briefly to Maurice Smith. She raised eyebrows in the 1970s because of her romance with Burt Reynolds, who was almost 20 years her junior. She was an avid tennis player and golfer and the sponsor of a professional golf tournament.

Singh, Zail (JARNAIL SINGH), Indian politician (b. May 5, 1916, Sandhwan, Punjab, India—d. Dec. 25, 1994, Chandigarh, India), was India's seventh president (1982–87) and the first Sikh to hold that largely ceremonial office; he was an impotent bystander when government troops stormed (1984) the Golden Temple in Amritsar, the Sikhs' holiest shrine, in an effort to flush out militant Sikhs who were demanding independence for Punjab (an agriculturally rich state heavily populated by Sikhs). When he was barely 15, Singh became active in the politics of the Akali Dal, a Sikh organization that opposed British rule. Singh pursued traditional studies in Sikh holy books and earned the title Giani ("learned man") for his scholarly mastery of scriptures. In 1938 he established the Praja Mandal, a political organization allied to the Indian National Congress, in his home district of Faridkot. This insurrectionary act carried a five-year jail sentence. During his incarceration, he took the name Zail Singh. After India became independent in 1947, Singh served (1956–62) in parliament and was chief minister of Punjab (1972–77). When Prime Minister Indira Gandhi was voted out of power in 1977, Singh contined to support her. After returning to office in 1980, Gandhi rewarded his loyalty by naming Singh minister of home affairs. He held that post until 1982, when he was named the Congress (I) Party's presidential candidate. Many viewed Singh's easy elevation to the presidency as a way for Gandhi to appease extremist Sikhs in Punjab. Four months after Indian troops stormed the temple, Gandhi was assassinated by her Sikh bodyguards. Singh named Gandhi's son Rajiv to succeed her, but he soon fell out of favour with the new prime minister. Singh further inflamed the government by refusing to sign into law a 1987 bill permitting official censorship of private mail. He died after sustaining serious injuries in a car accident in November.

Smith, Arnold Cantwell, Canadian diplomat (b. Jan. 18, 1915, Toronto, Ont.—d. Feb. 7, 1994, Toronto), as the first secretary-general of the Commonwealth, organized and coordinated association activities but, more important, demonstrated aplomb while serving (1965–75) as a troubleshooter during several serious crises. During his two five-year terms in office, Smith expertly negotiated the storms that threatened to destroy the cohesion of the association, especially when the white-minority government in Rhodesia (now Zimbabwe) proclaimed independence from Britain in 1965, Britain proposed selling arms to South Africa in 1971, and Pakistan resigned from the Commonwealth in 1972. Smith, a Rhodes scholar, joined the diplomatic service in 1943 and was posted to the U.S.S.R. (1943–45) before serving in Brussels, New York City, Phnom Penh, and London. He was also ambassador to Cairo (1958–61) and Moscow (1961–63) before his appointment as secretary-general. In 1976 he was a cofounder of the North-South Institute in Ottawa, and he served as its chairman until 1991. Smith was made a Companion of Honour in 1975 and became an Officer of the Order of Canada in 1984. He published *Stitches in Time: The Commonwealth in World Politics* in 1981.

Smith, Hazel Brannon, U.S. publisher and editor (b. 1914?, Gadsden, Ala.—d. May 14, 1994, Cleveland, Tenn.), courageously crusaded for social reform and consistently promoted unpopular causes as the editor of four Mississippi newspapers—the Durant *News,* Lexington *Advertiser,* Flora *Banner County Outlook,* and Jackson *Northside Reporter.* Her thriving weeklies, however, were the targets of advertising boycotts when she became outspoken about civil rights abuses in her editorial column, "Through Hazel Eyes." After earning a B.A. in journalism from the University of Alabama in 1935, Smith purchased the *News* and boosted circulation by catering to local news and events rather than attempting to compete with larger papers. She was able to purchase three other weeklies in rapid succession. In 1954 she published a column calling for the resignation of a local Holmes county sheriff after he reportedly shot a black youth without provocation. As she focused more on civil rights, her papers continued to lose advertising, and Smith was forced to accept paid speaking engagements to keep her newspapers afloat. In Mississippi's "Freedom Summer" of 1964, when civil rights workers registered blacks to vote, the *Northside Reporter* was bombed. In that same year Smith became the first woman to win the Pulitzer Prize for editorial writing in recognition of her treatment of civil rights. She was also named 1964 Mississippi Woman of the Year. A documentary film, *An Independent Voice,* and a television movie, *A Passion for Justice,* chronicled her career.

Smith, John, British politician (b. Sept. 13, 1938, Dalmally, Argyll, Scotland—d. May 12, 1994, London, England), as the pragmatic leader of the British Labour Party from July 1992, was credited with moving the traditionally left-wing party to a more centrist, pro-European stance. It was widely believed that the revitalized party would be well positioned to challenge the ruling Conservatives after four consecutive election defeats, but Smith's sudden death from a heart attack threw the party into temporary disarray. Smith studied law at the University of Glasgow and was called to the bar in 1967 (he took silk in 1983). He was elected to Parliament in 1970 after unsuccessful efforts in 1963 and 1964. A man equally admired for his integrity and his debating skills, Smith held a succession of junior posts in the Energy Ministry and the Privy Council Office. He was named secretary of state for trade in 1978. When the Conservatives, led by Margaret Thatcher, ousted the Labour Party from power in 1979, Smith used his debating skills in the shadow cabinet as opposition spokesman on trade and prices (1979–82), energy (1982–83), employment (1983–84), and trade and industry (1984–87). In 1987 opposition leader Neil Kinnock appointed him the shadow chancellor of the Exchequer. After Kinnock resigned in the wake of Labour's disastrous 1992 election defeat, Smith was elected to succeed him by a massive 91% majority.

Smith, Oliver, U.S. set designer (b. Feb. 13, 1918, Waupun, Wis.—d. Jan. 23, 1994, Brooklyn Heights, N.Y.), used his imaginative painter's eye to create magnificent and visually striking set designs that served as centrepieces in some 250 theatre, dance, opera, and film productions and helped elevate Ballet Theater (now American Ballet Theater) to international renown while serving as its codirector (1945–80 and 1990–92). Smith, who graduated (1939) with a B.A. in architecture from Pennsylvania State University, was also an inspired painter. His works were displayed in such institutions as New York's Museum of Modern Art and the Art Institute of Chicago. He secured his first professional set design for the Ballet Russe's production of *Saratoga* (1941) and the following year made his Broadway bow with designs for *Rosalinda* (1942). His impressive list of credits, which showcased his versatility with colour and style, included Broadway sets for such musicals as *My Fair Lady, West Side Story, Camelot, Hello, Dolly!, Flower Drum Song,* and *Brigadoon*; for such ballets as Jerome Robbins' *Rodeo* and *Fancy Free,* Agnes deMille's *Fall River Legend,* Eliot Feld's *Harbinger,* and Martha Graham's *Gospel of Eve;* for such operas as *La Traviata* and *Martha;* and for such films as *Porgy and Bess, Oklahoma!,* and *The Sound of Music.* He both produced and provided the sets for *Gentlemen Prefer Blondes, No Exit,* and *On the Town.* Smith, the winner of seven Tony awards, was inducted into the Theatre Hall of Fame in 1981.

Somes, Michael, British ballet dancer (b. Sept. 28, 1917, Horsley, Gloucestershire, England—d. Nov. 18/19, 1994, London, England), was associated with the Royal Ballet for over 50 years and was considered the guardian of Sir Frederick Ashton's works, but he was best remembered for his 11-year partnership with Dame Margot Fonteyn. His affiliation with the Royal Ballet began when he was awarded (1934) the first scholarship ever given to a male by the school of the Vic-Wells Ballet, the company that—after first having changed its name to the Sadler's Wells Ballet—became (1956) the Royal Ballet. He joined the company in 1935. Somes possessed a musicality and sensitivity that soon took him from the corps to solo parts and, in 1938, to his first leading role—the Young Boy in Ashton's *Horoscope*—which was also his first partnership of Fonteyn. A serious injury during military service in World War II threatened his career, but he returned to the company and over the years created roles in some 30 ballets, including *Symphonic Variations* (1946), *Cinderella* (1948), *Daphnis and Chloë* (1951), and *Ondine* (1958). From 1950 to 1961 Somes was Fonteyn's official partner, his strength and noble sensitivity perfectly accompanying her precise characterizations and technique. He retired as premier danseur in 1961 but continued to perform in such character parts as Lord Capulet in *Romeo and Juliet,* the Emperor Franz Joseph in *Mayerling,* and, notably, Armand's father in *Marguerite and Armand,* which starred Fonteyn and Rudolf Nureyev. From 1963 to 1970 Somes was assistant director of the Royal Ballet, under Ashton's directorship, and until his retirement in 1984 he was the company's principal teacher. Somes was made a Commander of the Order of the British Empire in 1959 and in 1981 received the Queen Elizabeth II award from the Royal Academy of Dancing.

Spadolini, Giovanni, Italian politician (b. June 21, 1925, Florence, Italy—d. Aug. 4, 1994, Rome, Italy), was a prominent and respected elected official, editor, and author. Spadolini earned his law degree from the University of Florence, and at age 25 he joined the political science faculty there, eventually becoming professor of contemporary history. Concurrently, he served as a contributing author and political editor at several newspapers. In 1955 Spadolini was named editor of the Bologna daily *Il Resto del Carlino,* and in 1968 he moved to Milan to become the editor of the nation's largest circulation newspaper, the *Corriere della Sera.* In 1972 he embarked on a political career and was elected to the Senate as a member of the tiny Republican Party. Spadolini held several Cabinet positions in various coalition governments until 1979, when he gained leadership of the party. In 1981 a scandal centred on a powerful Freemasons lodge known as Propaganda Due led to the collapse of the government, and in June 1981 Spadolini put together the first of two five-party coalitions in which he would serve as prime minister. Spadolini, the first non-Christian Democrat to head the government in 35 years, held power until November 1982. He served as defense minister from 1983 to 1987 and was elected speaker of the Senate in 1987. Although he was one of the few veteran politicians to emerge unscathed from the political scandals that had rocked the system, Spadolini lost the speaker's post by one vote in April 1994 to a member of Prime Minister Silvio Berlusconi's party. While confined to the hospital, Spadolini completed the last of his more than 60 books, which spanned a range of topics. Several weeks before his death, he told an aide, "The sickness that afflicts me is called Italy."

Sperry, Roger Wolcott, U.S. neurobiologist (b. Aug. 20, 1913, Hartford, Conn.—d. April 17, 1994, Pasadena, Calif.), conducted fundamental studies on the left and right cerebral hemispheres of the brain and shared the 1981 Nobel Prize for Physiology or Medicine with David Hunter Hubel and Torsten Nils Wiesel for this work. Sperry was honoured for uncovering the function of the corpus callosum, a thick bundle of nerve fibres that passes information between the brain's hemispheres. Sperry earned a B.A. in literature and an M.A. in psychology from Oberlin (Ohio) College and a Ph.D. (1941) in zoology from the University of Chicago before serving as an associate of Karl Lashley, first at Harvard University and then at the Yerkes Laboratories of Primate Biology in Orange Park, Fla. He then joined the University of Chicago faculty before spending the remainder of his career (1954–84) at the California Institute of Technology. Beginning in the late 1940s, Sperry developed experimental and surgical techniques that dismantled previously held notions about the function of the brain and helped formulate a "map" that detailed various mental processes. During the latter part of his career, Sperry, who was hailed as a brilliant experimentalist, became fascinated with the mind and turned to psychology. He developed a controversial theory of consciousness and was in the process of formulating a new science based on ethical values. It was for this work that he wished to be remembered.

Spivak, Lawrence Edmund, U.S. broadcast journalist (b. June 11, 1900, Brooklyn, N.Y.—d. March 9, 1994, Washington, D.C.), was a founder of the pioneering radio and television show "Meet the Press," which set the standard for a generation of political interview programs. Spivak graduated from Harvard University cum laude in 1921 and went to work in the publishing business. In 1935 he purchased *American Mercury,* but he sold that magazine in 1950. In 1945, together with producer and moderator Martha Rountree, he launched "Meet the Press" as a radio program on the Mutual Broadcasting System. The show moved to NBC television three years later. Spivak developed the style of a moderated panel of journalists subjecting leading political figures to rigorous, direct questioning. Originally preferring to be a permanent panelist, Spivak took over as moderator of the program in 1960. A model of self-control and objectivity himself, he said that "if a man is honest and knows his stuff, he'll emerge with the proper stature. By the same token, so will a phony." The program rapidly won acclaim and attracted a stream of illustrious guests that included emperors, kings, presidents (including incumbent Pres. Gerald Ford on the occasion of Spivak's last regular show), chancellors, and senators. "Meet the Press" continued after Spivak's retirement in 1975 and in 1994 was the longest-running program on U.S. television.

Stewart, J(ohn) I(nnes) M(ackintosh), British novelist and literary critic (b. Sept. 30, 1906, Edinburgh, Scot.—d. Nov. 12, 1994, Coulsdon, Surrey, England), created the character of Inspector John Appleby, a British sleuth known for his suave humour, "raised eyebrow," and literary finesse. Stewart wrote such beloved murder mysteries as *Appleby's End* (1945), *The Journeying Boy* (1949), and *Operation Pax* (1951) under the pseudonym Michael Innes. Stewart was unique among fellow mystery writers of the day because he allowed his fictional inspector to grow older naturally, from a young man into middle age and finally into retirement. Stewart did not, however, set out to become a popular novelist. He was first an admired teacher and respected literary aficionado. While making a sea voyage from England to Australia to assume the post of Jury Professor of English Literature at the University of Adelaide (1935–45), Stewart began to write a mystery novel, *Death at the President's Lodging* (1936), the first of almost 50 novels and short stories written under his pseudonym. Upon publication the mystery was immediately recognized as unique within the genre because of its stylish wit. Other fictional works written under Stewart's name include *Mark Lambert's Supper* (1954), *The Guardians* (1955), *An Acre of Grass* (1965), and *A Villa in France* (1982). In addition to these novels, Stewart also wrote many scholarly books using his real name, including works on Shakespeare, Thomas Hardy, and Rudyard Kipling. He held academic posts at the University of Leeds in England (1930–35), Queen's University of Belfast (1946–48), and the University of Oxford (1969–73). His autobiography, *Myself and Michael Innes,* was published in 1987.

Styne, Jule (JULIUS KERWIN STEIN), U.S. songwriter (b. Dec. 31, 1905, London, England—d. Sept. 20, 1994, New York, N.Y.), composed more than 1,500 songs, many of them showcased in such smash Broadway hits as *High Button Shoes* (1947), *Gentlemen Prefer Blondes* (1949; filmed 1953), *Peter Pan* (1954), *Gypsy* (1959; filmed 1962), and *Funny Girl* (1964; filmed 1968), and counted among his prolific output at least 200 enduring songs, including "I Don't Want to Walk Without You," "Diamonds Are a Girl's Best Friend," "Everything's Coming Up Roses," and "People." Styne's musical genius was recognized by his parents, who arranged piano lessons and practice sessions on a rented instrument. Though Styne was a prodigy who studied from the age of eight at the Chicago College of Music and performed with the Chicago Symphony Orchestra, his career as a concert pianist was stymied because of his small hand span. He performed in burlesque and jazz clubs, and in 1926 he wrote his first song, "Sunday." He changed his name to avoid being confused with music executive Jules Stein and played with bands fronted by Charlie Spivak and Glenn Miller. After moving to New York City (1934) and then Hollywood (1937), he became a voice coach, notably for Shirley Temple. Styne was a songwriter for Gene Autry and Roy Rogers at Republic Pictures, where he teamed up with Sammy Cahn to compose a string of hits, including "I'll Walk Alone," "Five Minutes More," and "Three Coins in the Fountain," which won them an Academy Award. The two worked together on numerous stage musicals, and they created many songs for Frank Sinatra. Styne collaborated with Frank Loesser on *Sweater Girl* (1942). On Broadway he also scored hit songs written with lyricists Betty Comden and Adolf Green for such productions as *Two on the Aisle* (1951) and *Bells Are Ringing* (1956; filmed 1960). Following the success of his masterpiece, *Gypsy,* Styne had his last major success with *Funny Girl.* The Broadway production of *Sugar* (1972) had moderate success, but *The Red Shoes* (1993) closed in less than a week. Styne, whose melodies made stars of such leading talents as Carol Channing, Mary Martin, Judy Holliday, Ethel Merman, and Barbra Streisand, was honoured at the 1990 John F. Kennedy Center for the Performing Arts in Washington, D.C., and was the 1992 recipient of the New Dramatists Lifetime Achievement Award.

Sullivan, (Patrick Francis) Barry, U.S. actor (b. Aug. 29, 1912, New York, N.Y.—d. June 6, 1994, Sherman Oaks, Calif.), was a ruggedly handsome leading man who specialized in unsmiling roles, and his dour countenance was featured for more than four decades in thrillers, westerns, dramas, and gangster films. A one-time theatre usher and department store buyer, Sullivan made his Broadway debut in *I Want a Policeman* (1936). On the silver screen he secured his reputation after turning in a strong performance portraying a psychoanalyst in *Lady in the Dark* (1944). He returned to Broadway to replace Henry Fonda as the defense attorney in *The Caine Mutiny Court Martial* and reprised the role for the 1955 television adaptation. Often paired opposite strong-willed women on-screen, Sullivan costarred with Barbara Stanwyck in *Jeopardy* (1953), *The Maverick Queen* (1956), and *Forty Guns* (1957), Bette Davis in *Payment on Demand* (1951), and Joan Crawford in *Queen Bee* (1955). Other film credits include *The Gangster* (1947), *The Great Gatsby* (1949), *The Bad and the Beautiful* (1952), *Strategic Air Command* (1955), and *Earthquake* (1974). On television Sullivan was a regular on such series as "The Man Called X" (1956), "Harbourmaster" (1957–58), "The Tall Man" (1960–62), and "The Road West" (1966–67).

Swann, Donald Ibrahim, British entertainer and composer (b. Sept. 30, 1923, Llanelli, Wales—d. March 23, 1994, London, England), with his partner and lyricist, Michael Flanders, delighted audiences in England, Australia, the U.S., and Canada with satiric, often nonsensical songs and lively banter in their long-running two-man revues *At the Drop of a Hat* (1956–61) and *At the Drop of Another Hat* (1963–67). Swann, the son of a Russian-born doctor and his Muslim wife, was educated at Westminster School and Christ Church, Oxford. An accomplished pianist, he was in great demand for school musical revues. After serving in the Friends Ambulance Unit during World War II, he teamed up with his old schoolmate Flanders, by then confined to a wheelchair by polio, to write songs for such revues as *Penny Plain* (1951), *Airs on a Shoestring* (1953), and *Fresh Airs* (1956). *At the Drop of a Hat* opened in London in 1956, with the bespectacled Swann playing the piano with amateurish enthusiasm. The popularity of the team's songs, including "The Hippopotamus Song" (a paean to mud), "I'm a Gnu," "The Gas Man Cometh," and "Have Some Madeira, M'Dear," continued long after they retired from performing in 1967. Swann continued to compose after Flanders' death in 1975. He also wrote several books, including an autobiography, *Swann's Way* (1991).

Synge, Richard Laurence Millington, British biochemist (b. Oct. 28, 1914, Liverpool, England—d. Aug. 18, 1994, Norwich, Norfolk, England), shared the 1952 Nobel Prize for Chemistry with Archer J.P. Martin for their work in the development of partition chromatography, a sophisticated analytic technique by which samples of a mixture of closely related chemicals such as amino acids can be separated for identification and further study. In his most important individual research, Synge determined the sequence of amino acids that make up the antibiotic gramicidin S. Synge studied classics at Winchester College and then switched to the natural sciences at Trinity College, Cambridge (Ph.D., 1941). He spent his entire professional career as an active researcher, first with Martin under the auspices of the Wool Industries Research Association, Leeds (1941–43), and later on his own at the Lister Institute of Preventive Medicine, London (1943–48), the Rowett Research Institute, near Aberdeen, Scotland (1948–67), and the Food Research Institute, Norwich (1967–76). He was also an honorary professor at the University of East Anglia (1968–84). Synge was elected a fellow of the Royal Society in 1950.

Talhouni, Bahjat at-, Jordanian politician (b. 1913, Maʿan, vilayet of Syria, Ottoman Empire [now Maʿan, Jordan]—d. Jan. 30, 1994), was a loyal monarchist and close personal adviser to King Hussein of Jordan throughout a long career in public service; he was called upon to serve as prime minister four separate times between 1960 and 1970. Talhouni trained as a lawyer at the University of Damascus (LL.B.; 1936). He was appointed a judge in Kerak in 1938 and was elevated to president of the Court of Appeals in 1952. He joined the Cabinet as minister of the interior the next year. As chief of the Royal Diwan (secretariat) from 1954, he was Hussein's chief adviser. Talhouni was named prime minister for the first time in August 1960, after Prime Minister Hazzaʿ al-Majali's assassination, and served until January 1962. He was recalled to office three times (July 1964–February 1965, October 1967–March 1968, and August 1969–June 1970). Each time the self-effacing Talhouni was recalled during a period when Hussein wished to assert control over the Cabinet and present a moderate response to the question of Palestinian guerrillas based in Jordan, and each time he was removed when unpopular measures were deemed necessary. In 1974 Talhouni was named president of the Senate, of which he had been a member since 1962.

Tandy, Jessica, British-born U.S. actress (b. June 7, 1909, London, England—d. Sept. 11, 1994, Easton, Conn.), was a luminous stage, screen, and television star whose complex portrayals, including her original Tony award-winning performance as Blanche DuBois in Tennessee Williams' *A Streetcar Named Desire* (1947) and her best actress Academy Award-winning role as a dictatorial southern matron in *Driving Miss Daisy* (1989), highlighted a 67-year career. Besides earning solo acclaim, Tandy and her second husband, Hume Cronyn, worked together on radio and TV and made such motion pictures as *The Seventh Cross* (1944), *The Green Years* (1946), *The World*

REUTERS/BETTMANN

According to Garp (1982), *Cocoon* (1985) and its sequel, *Cocoon: The Return* (1988), and *Batteries Not Included* (1987). Their superb stage artistry—as evidenced in *The Fourposter* (1951), *Madame, Will You Walk* (1953), *The Honeys* (1955), *A Day by the Sea* (1955), *The Man in the Dog Suit* (1958), *A Delicate Balance* (1966), and *Noel Coward in Two Keys* (1974)—was likened to that of Alfred Lunt and Lynn Fontanne. Tandy, the daughter of a traveling salesman, grew up in London and studied acting at the Ben Greet Academy of Acting. She made her London stage debut in *The Rumour* (1929) and her Broadway bow in *The Matriarch* (1930). Her versatility onstage brought her roles ranging from light comedy to Shakespearean tragedy in both starring and supporting roles. After becoming a U.S. citizen in 1954, she garnered two other Tony awards for *The Gin Game* (1977) and *Foxfire* (1982), both with Cronyn; the couple also received the first-ever Tonys for Lifetime Achievement in 1994. Tandy's other film credits include *Dragonwyck* (1946), *The Desert Fox* (1951), *The Birds* (1963), *Fried Green Tomatoes* (1991), and *Used People* (1992).

Tchelistcheff, André, Russian-born U.S. enologist (b. 1901, Moscow, Russia—d. April 5, 1994, Napa, Calif.), was a pivotal figure in the revitalization of the California wine industry following Prohibition (1919–33) and used his Paris training in viticulture and wine making to pioneer such techniques as cold fermentation and the use of American oak barrels for aging. He was also an authority on the types of soil suitable for growing various grape varieties. Tchelistcheff, who served in the White Russian army during the Allied armies' retreat through the Crimea to Gallipoli, left the service in 1923, when he enrolled at the University of Brno, Czech., to study agronomy. He later continued his studies in Paris at the National Agronomy Institute and also worked in the champagne cellars of Moët & Chandon. A diminutive figure with a pronounced accent, Tchelistcheff was also distinguished by his Old World mannerisms and savoir faire. Hired by Georges de Latour, owner of the Beaulieu Vineyard in California's Napa Valley, where he worked from 1938 to 1973 and again from 1991 until his death, Tchelistcheff made Latour's Private Reserve Cabernet Sauvignon the best-selling wine of its kind in the United States.

Temin, Howard Martin, U.S. virologist (Dec. 10, 1934, Philadelphia, Pa.—Feb. 9, 1994, Madison, Wis.), won the 1975 Nobel Prize for Physiology or Medicine (with Renato Dulbecco and David Baltimore) for his role in discovering reverse transcriptase, an enzyme that transcribes RNA into DNA. Temin identified the enzyme while conducting research on a virus that causes cancer in chickens. Temin's groundbreaking finding dramatically illustrated the exception to one of the fundamental tenets of molecular biology—that the genetic instructions for protein synthesis flow uniquely from DNA to RNA. Temin's studies helped scientists determine that reverse transcriptase also has a role in the replication of such viruses as hepatitis B, cauliflower mosaic (a plant virus), and HIV, which causes AIDS. Temin's original 1964 theory that the DNA-into-RNA sequence could be reversed was derided in the scientific community, but he persevered for six years before proving his hypothesis. Temin graduated from Swarthmore (Pa.) College at the age of 18 and earned a Ph.D. (1959) at the California Institute of Technology. There, working under the tutelage of Dulbecco, he began his investigations into viruses and their role in animal cancers. Temin contended, however, that viruses probably did not play a central role in cancers in humans. An ardent antismoking crusader, he felt that the incidence of cancer could be reduced by the elimination of smoking. In 1960 Temin joined the staff of the University of Wisconsin, where he successively served as associate professor, full professor, Wisconsin Alumni Research Foundation professor of cancer research, and American Cancer Society professor of viral oncology and cell biology. Temin succumbed to lung cancer, but not a type associated with smoking.

Tinbergen, Jan, Dutch economist (b. April 12, 1903, The Hague, Neth.—d. June 9, 1994), shared the first Nobel Prize for Economic Science (1969) with Ragnar Frisch of Norway in recognition of their contributions to the development of econometrics, a method of measuring economic relationships through the systematic application of mathematical models and statistical techniques. This quantitative approach eventually formed the basis for modern economic forecasting. Tinbergen was particularly known for his revolutionary idea that a government cannot achieve a given number of economic policy objectives unless it applies an equal number of independent economic instruments. Late in his career he worked extensively on the problems of international aid to and economic reforms in less developed nations and on the principle of equitable income distribution. Tinbergen received a doctorate in mathematical physics from the University of Leiden (1929), with a dissertation on "Minimum Problems in Physics and Economics." He worked as a business-cycle statistician for the Dutch Central Bureau of Statistics from 1929 to 1945, except for a two-year stint (1936–38) with the League of Nations in Geneva. As director of the Netherlands Central Planning Bureau (1945–55), he applied his theories on the dynamics of the business cycle to the nation's post-World War II economic recovery. He resigned in 1955 to take a post as professor of economics at the Netherlands School of Economics (later part of Erasmus University), where he had taught part-time from 1933. He was professor of international cooperation at the University of Leiden from 1973 until he retired in 1975. Tinbergen's major books include *Statistical Testing of Business-Cycle Theories* (1939; 2 vols.), *Economic Policy: Principles and Design* (1956), and *Income Distribution* (1975).

Trilling, (Joshua) Ossia, Polish-born theatre critic (b. Sept. 22, 1913, Bialystok, Russian Empire [now Poland]—d. Sept. 13, 1994, London, England), as a London-based correspondent and magazine editor, tirelessly promoted European theatre for more than 50 years. Trilling moved with his family from Poland to Russia, Finland, and, finally, England. He was educated at St. Paul's School, London, and St. John's College, Oxford, where he joined the university dramatic society. In 1937 he codirected the British premieres of August Strindberg's *The Road to Damascus* and *Queen Christina.* After serving with the army intelligence corps during World War II, Trilling took up writing. He coedited *Theatre Newsletter* (1946–51) and *International Theatre;* founded the Theatre News Agency (1946); contributed on a regular basis to such publications as *Theatre World, The Stage, The Times, The Independent,* and the *Financial Times;* and did radio broadcasts for the BBC World Service. The multilingual Trilling traveled widely, covering drama from Scandinavia to Hungary to Israel and serving as an adviser for theatre companies from Belgium to Yugoslavia. He was also vice president of the International Association of Theatre Critics (1956–77). In 1980 he was made an Officer of the Royal Order of the North Star in recognition of his contributions to theatre in Sweden. Trilling was a regular contributor on the theatre to the *Britannica Book of the Year* from 1963 until 1990, when he suffered a stroke.

Turnbull, Colin Macmillan, British-born anthropologist (b. Nov. 23, 1924, Harrow, England—d. July 28, 1994, Kilmarnock, Va.), conducted extensive field studies in Africa among the Mbuti Pygmies in the Belgian Congo (now Zaire) and the Ik hunters of northern Uganda and recorded his experiences in two best-selling books, *The Forest People* (1961) and *The Mountain People* (1972). Turnbull earned a B.A. (1947) and an M.A. (1949) from Magdalen College, Oxford, and received degrees from Oxford in social anthropology (1956), literature (1957), and anthropology (D.Phil., 1964). During World War II he served in the Royal Navy. Turnbull was employed (1959–69) as a curator of African ethnology at the American Museum of Natural History, New York City, besides teaching anthropology at such universities as Hofstra University, Hempstead, N.Y. (1969–72); Virginia Commonwealth University (1972–75); and George Washington University, Washington, D.C. (1976 until his retirement in 1983). His anthropological field studies provided grist for such works as *The Lonely African* (1962); *Wayward Servants* (1965), another look at the Mbuti; *Tibet* (1968; with Thubten Jigme Norbu); *Man in Africa* (1976); and *The Human Cycle* (1983), which explored childhood to old age among various cultures. His classics *The Forest People,* an uplifting account of the resourceful Ituri Forest Pygmies, and *The Mountain People,* an exceedingly grisly portrayal of the often brutal customs of the hunger-starved Ik, secured his reputation. Turnbull spent the latter years of his life in Hawaii, Samoa, and India, where he became a Buddhist monk and adopted the name Lobsang Rigdol.

Vazgen I (LEVON GARABET BALJIAN), Armenian cleric (b. Oct. 3 [Sept. 20, Old Style], 1908, Bucharest, Rom.—d. Aug. 18, 1994, Yerevan, Armenia), as head of the Armenian Orthodox Church for nearly 40 years, was both the spiritual leader and the symbol of national unity for Armenians throughout the world. Levon Garabet Baljian graduated from the University of Bucharest's faculty of philosophy and literature (1936) and taught school for several years. He chose the religious name Vazgen when he was ordained in 1943. He was consecrated bishop of the diocese of Romania and Bulgaria in 1951, and in September 1955 the Church Assembly elected the scholarly, moderate Vazgen the 130th Patriarch of Echmiadzin and Catholicos of All Armenians. Vazgen was often criticized for his public accommodation with the officially atheist Soviet authorities and for his reluctance to endorse Armenian nationalism. On the other hand, he forged stronger ties with Armenian communities in the diaspora, gained government permission to accept funds donated by Armenians abroad, and established warm relations with leaders of other world churches. In 1970 he traveled to the Vatican for an historic meeting with Pope Paul VI. With the breakup of the U.S.S.R. (1991), he openly supported Armenian independence. He also worked for a peaceful solution to the dispute with Azerbaijan over the Nagorno-Karabakh enclave. Less than a month before his death Vazgen was named the first recipient of the title National Hero of Armenia.

Vines, (Henry) Ellsworth, Jr., U.S. tennis player and golfer (b. Sept. 28/29, 1911, Los Angeles, Calif.—d. March 17, 1994, La Quinta, Calif.), delivered blinding service aces and rapid-fire forehand shots that were marvels of precision and power, and he was hailed as one of the greatest tennis players of all time because of his hard-hitting accuracy and his ability to make sensational comebacks after teetering on the brink of defeat. Vines's lanky 1.88-m (6-ft 2-in), 65-kg (143-lb) frame belied his whipcordlike muscle strength. A versatile athlete, he attended the University of Southern California on a basketball scholarship before making his tennis debut on grass courts. He gained a reputation after beating Frank Shields and Frank Hunter twice each. In 1931 he won 11 tournaments, including the U.S. singles championship, and the following year he captured the title again and the Wimbledon singles in possibly the most one-sided final in the history of that event. Vines, who wore long trousers and favoured a small wooden racket, was an all-out player. In 1940 he abandoned tennis for amateur golf. Vines turned professional in 1942 and, though he never won a Professional Golfers Association tournament, usually ranked high among the money winners during his 15-year career. In 1962 Vines was inducted into the National Lawn (now International) Tennis Hall of Fame.

Volonté, Gian Maria, Italian actor (b. April 9, 1933, Milan, Italy—d. Dec. 6, 1994, Florina, Greece), epitomized, with his chiseled features, hooded eyes, and scowling demeanour, the classic tough guy in such films as Sergio Leone's *A Fistful of Dollars* (1964; under the stage name John Wells), *Investigation of a Citizen Above Suspicion* (1970), and *Lucky Luciano* (1973). Noted for his charisma and intensity, Volonté was called the Italian Laurence Olivier, although admittedly more for his bearing than for his dramatic skills. He was most popular as a heavy, but it was his role as a diligent journalist in the 1983 Swiss film *Death of Mario Ricci* that earned him his highest artistic honour—the Palme d'Or at the Cannes Film Festival. Other more sympathetic roles included Volonté's portrayal of antifascist Italian writer Carlo Levi in *Christ Stopped at Eboli* (1979), a good-hearted physician investigating a mysterious murder in *Chronicle of a Death Foretold* (1987), and an upstanding Sicilian judge in *Open Doors* (1990). Volonté's outspoken defense of militant leftist politics prompted him to refuse a lucrative Hollywood offer, declaring that his conscience would not allow him to accept such a large sum for work as an actor. Volonté began acting at the age of 17 with traveling theatre groups, and during the 1950s he appeared on television in adaptations of Dostoyevsky's *The Idiot,* Chekhov's *Uncle Vanya,* and Vittorio Alfieri's *Saul.* The actor was little known outside Europe. Volonté was on film location when he died in his hotel room after suffering a heart attack.

Wain, John Barrington, British writer (b. March 14, 1925, Stoke-on-Trent, Staffordshire, England—d. May 24, 1994, Oxford, England), was initially identified with the Angry Young Men, a generation of post-World War II writers who rejected the traditional middle-class strictures and stuffy literary conventions of the British establishment. Much of Wain's fiction, particularly his witty first novel, *Hurry On Down* (1953; U.S. title *Born in Captivity*), incorporated the antibourgeois realism and biting satire common to the movement. However, Wain, who felt equally comfortable writing fiction, poetry, plays, literary criticism, and the occasional biography, consistently refused to be categorized. He was educated at St. John's College, Oxford (B.A., 1946; M.A., 1950), where he was founding editor of the literary periodical *Mandrake.* He also became friends with Kingsley Amis and Philip Larkin, both of whom joined him in a series of poetry readings on BBC radio in 1953. Wain taught English literature at the University of Reading (1946–55); later he was a professor of poetry at Oxford (1973–78). His first poetry collection, *Mixed Feelings,* appeared in 1951. This was followed by more than a dozen volumes of verse, notably *Weep Before God* (1961), *Feng* (1975), and *Poems, 1949–1979* (1980). Other novels include *The Contenders* (1957), *A Winter in the Hills* (1970), *The Pardoner's Tale* (1978), and *Where the Rivers Meet* (1988). Wain's nonfiction

works include an award-winning 1974 biography of Samuel Johnson, a playgoer's guide to Shakespeare, and two volumes of memoirs. He was made Commander of the Order of the British Empire in 1983.

Walcott, Jersey Joe (ARNOLD RAYMOND CREAM), U.S. boxer (b. Jan. 31, 1914, Merchantville, N.J.—d. Feb. 25, 1994, Camden, N.J.), was crowned heavyweight champion of the world after knocking out Ezzard Charles in the seventh round of their July 18, 1951, bout and became, at the age of 37, the oldest fighter ever to win the title. Walcott, a precision technician, started fighting in 1930 but needed to supplement his meagre

UPI/BETTMANN

boxing purses by working as a shipyard labourer. Though Walcott knocked Joe Lewis down three times, twice during their Dec. 5, 1947, title fight, in which Lewis himself appeared stunned to win a 15-round split decision, he was never able to beat the champ. In their second match Walcott was knocked out by Lewis in the 11th round. Walcott twice challenged Charles for the title—in June 1949 and March 1951, being outpointed on both occasions—before finally winning the crown. He lost it 14 months later to Rocky Marciano, who knocked him out in the 13th round. In 1953, after Walcott unsuccessfully challenged Marciano and was knocked out in the first round, he hung up his gloves but stayed in the ring as a fight referee. Walcott, who fought in 69 matches and scored 30 knockouts among his 50 wins, competed in a record six heavyweight title bouts. He was inducted into the Boxing Hall of Fame in 1969. He later served as a New Jersey sheriff and athletic commissioner.

White, Terence de Vere, Irish author and editor (b. April 29, 1912, Dublin, Ireland—d. June 17, 1994, London, England), was the influential literary editor of the *Irish Times* (1961–77) and

the author of more than two dozen books. He was also a successful lawyer and a leading figure in the cultural life of Dublin for more than 30 years, with important positions on the boards of the National Gallery (from 1967), the National Library (1946–79), the Chester Beatty Library (1959–80), and the Gate Theatre (1969–81). The son of a Protestant solicitor (who died when White was a boy) and his Roman Catholic wife, he was apprenticed in a solicitor's office at age 15 and worked there full-time while studying law at Trinity College (B.A., 1931; LL.B., 1933). In 1946 White published *The Road of Excess.* This was followed by several more nonfiction works, but he kept his legal practice until the success of his first novel, *An Affair with the Moon* (1959), induced the *Irish Times* to offer him a job. Thereafter he wrote novels, short stories, criticism, histories, and biographies. White's novels include *Prenez Garde* (1961), *The March Hare* (1970), and *Chat Show* (1987), while his nonfiction works include *The Parents of Oscar Wilde* (1967) and *The Anglo-Irish* (1972). White was a member of the Irish Academy of Letters, a professor of literature at the Royal Hibernian Academy, and a fellow of the Royal Society of Literature.

Wigglesworth, Sir Vincent Brian, British entomologist (b. April 17, 1899, Kirkham, Lancashire, England—d. Feb. 11?, 1994, Cambridge, England), pioneered in the study of insect physiology; he was particularly respected for his research into the role of hormones in insect growth, metamorphosis, and reproduction and for his insights into simple mechanisms, such as how insects walk upside down. Wigglesworth was educated at Repton and at Gonville and Caius College, Cambridge. He received his medical qualification at St. Thomas' Hospital in London, but a research project into cockroaches (and later into other medically important insects) led him to change careers. Wigglesworth was lecturer in medical entomology at the London School of Hygiene and Tropical Medicine (1926–45), reader in entomology (1945–52) and later Quick professor of biology (1952–66) at Cambridge, and founding director of the Agricultural Research Council Unit of Insect Physiology (1943–67). He published some 300 papers and half a dozen books, most notably *Insect Physiology* (1934), *The Principles of Insect Physiology* (1939), *The Physiology of Insect Metamorphosis* (1954), and *Insect Hormones* (1970). He was elected to the Royal Society in 1939, made Commander of the Order of the British Empire in 1951, and knighted in 1964.

Wilkinson, Charles ("BUD"), U.S. football coach (b. April 23, 1916, Minneapolis, Minn.—d. Feb. 9, 1994, St. Louis, Mo.), led the University of Oklahoma Sooners to three national football championships (1950, 1955, and 1956), turned out 32 all-American players, and established a National Collegiate Athletic Association record for 47 consecutive victories between 1953 and 1957. The incredible string of wins was broken by a 7–0 loss to Notre Dame, but the record was never bettered. Wilkinson, a star athlete at the University of Minnesota, played football on three national championship teams and earned three letters for that sport besides three more for hockey. After graduating (1937) with a B.A. in English and briefly working in banking, Wilkinson coached football at the Universities of Syracuse, N.Y., and Minnesota. During World War II he served in the navy as a hangar deck officer, and he also coached the Iowa Pre-Flight team. He joined Oklahoma in 1946 as assistant coach and was elevated to head coach the following year. As a result of his coaching success—an impressive record of 145 wins, 29 losses, and 4 ties at Oklahoma, Wilkinson drew large audiences of fellow coaches, who flocked to his clinics on the split-T offense. Wilkinson was inducted into the National Football Foundation College Football Hall of Fame and retired from college coaching in 1964. He later served as a sports commentator, head of the President's Council on Physical Fitness, and head coach of the National Football League's St. Louis Cardinals from 1978 to 1979.

Williams, Marion, U.S. gospel singer (b. Aug. 29, 1927, Miami, Fla.—d. July 2, 1994, Philadelphia, Pa.), drew on blues, jazz, folk, and calypso music as inspirations for her innovative vocals, which included octave-spanning leaps from contralto to spine-tingling falsetto tones; her exceptional artistry was often compared to that of Mahalia Jackson. As a child Williams began singing with the congregation at her neighbourhood Church of God. Professional opportunities, however, had to be put off while she attended to her work as a laundress, which helped support the family. In 1947 Williams joined the Ward Singers, and she soon became the star of the group. Williams' solo interpretation of the song "Surely God Is Able" was the group's first recording to sell one million copies. After scoring such great hits as "Packin' Up" and "I'm Climbing Higher and Higher," she left the Ward Singers (1958) to form the Stars of Faith and pursue a solo career. Besides performing in *Black Nativity,* the first gospel musical, Williams gained exposure with her television-commercial rendition of "Standing Here Wondering Which Way to Go," 10 record albums, and singing appearances in the films *Fried Green Tomatoes* (1991) and *Mississippi Masala* (1992). In 1993 she was the first singer to receive a MacArthur Foundation "genius" grant.

Wörner, Manfred, German defense official (b. Sept. 24, 1934, Stuttgart, Germany—d. Aug. 13, 1994, Brussels, Belgium), was the first German to serve (1988–94) as secretary-general of NATO, and he worked vigorously to redefine the organization after the Cold War precept upon which it was founded crumbled away with the collapse of the Soviet Union. He sought to turn NATO into a stabilizing force when ethnic rivalries in Eastern Europe threatened to unbalance the region. From 1953 to 1957 Wörner studied law at the Universities of Heidelberg, Paris, and Munich, and he received his Ph.D. from the University of Munich in 1961. He had joined the Christian Democratic Union (CDU) in 1956 and, after serving as a civil servant for several years, was elected a member of the Bundestag in 1965, a seat he held until 1988. Wörner became increasingly knowledgeable about defense issues, and in 1976 he was named chairman of the Bundestag's committee on defense, serving in that post until 1980, when he was named deputy chairman of the party in the Bundestag. In 1982 the CDU gained power, and Wörner was named defense minister. He secured a reputation as an aggressive hawk, advocating a strong defense relationship with the U.S. He welcomed the deployment of U.S. Pershing and cruise missiles in Germany, despite much resistance, but also advocated the strengthening of NATO conventional forces, including increased participation by the German forces. These positions endeared him to the U.S. and the Reagan administration, which supported Wörner's election as secretary-general of NATO. Although he was diagnosed with cancer in 1992, Wörner worked through mid-1994 to negotiate peace in Bosnia and Herzegovina, where he had early called for the use of NATO forces.

Wright, William Ambrose ("BILLY"), British footballer (b. Feb. 6, 1924, Ironbridge, Shropshire, England—d. Sept. 3, 1994, London, England), was a mainstay of association football (soccer) in England for 13 years as a reliable defensive player and captain for the Wolverhampton Wanderers (1946–58) and as captain for 90 out of a then-record 105 appearances for England (1946–59). Wright joined the Wolverhampton grounds crew immediately after completing secondary school and tried out for the team in 1938. He played his first unofficial international match for England while serving his World War II tour of duty in the light infantry. Within two years of his return to professional football (1946), he had been named captain of both Wolverhampton and the national team. Wright's speed and brilliant defensive skills made him a valuable wing-half and (from 1954) centre-half. He led Wolves to the FA Cup title in 1949 and to the league championship in 1954, 1958, and 1959. He was named Footballer of the Year in 1952. After retiring as an active player in 1959, Wright tried his hand at managing Arsenal (1962–66), but he was deemed insufficiently ruthless. He had greater success as a television sportscaster and as an administrator with ATV Network (1966–81) and Central Independent Television (1982–89). Wright was made Commander of the Order of the British Empire in 1959.

Yang Dezhi (Yang Te-chih), Chinese military official (b. 1911, Zhuzhou (Chu-chou), Hunan province, China—d. Oct. 25, 1994, Beijing (Peking), China), joined the communist People's Liberation Army (PLA) at its creation and went on to serve in virtually every major Chinese military conflict for the next 50 years, eventually becoming the army's chief of staff. Yang was raised in a peasant family in an area that Mao Zedong (Mao Tse-Tung) heavily organized in the 1920s. Yang joined the PLA in 1927. He quickly rose through the ranks, commanding a vanguard regiment during the Long March (1934–36) and combat units during both the Sino-Japanese War (1937–45) and the struggle against the Nationalists (1945–49). Yang joined the Chinese People's Volunteers in 1951 after China decided to support North Korea, which was engaged in a blood conflict with UN forces. Yang was made commander of the Chinese forces in 1954. Upon his return to China in 1955 he was elevated to general. Yang, one of the few high-ranking officials to survive the Cultural Revolution (1966–76) with his reputation intact, was promoted to the party's Central Committee in 1967. His last post as a field officer was as deputy commander of the forces that invaded Vietnam in 1979. In 1980 he became the army's chief of staff, a position he held until his retirement in 1987. In 1989, several weeks before army tanks rolled into Tiananmen (T'ien-an-men) Square, Yang and six other retired military officials sent a letter to Premier Li Peng (Li P'eng) urging him not to allow the use of military force to crush the pro-democracy student demonstrations.

Yegorov, Boris Borisovich, Russian physician (b. Nov. 26, 1937, Moscow, U.S.S.R.—d. Sept. 12, 1994, Moscow, Russia), participated in the first spaceflight with more than one crew member and was the first practicing physician to soar into space. His flight was also the first in which the cosmonauts did not wear space suits. Yegorov graduated (1961) from the First Moscow Medical Institute, where he specialized in aviation and space medicine. He then worked in medical research institutions, studying medical telemetry data from Soviet missions, before beginning (1964) training for his flight. On Oct. 12–13, 1964—crowded with two other cosmonauts aboard Voskhod 1, a craft designed for one—Yegorov performed a number of tests on himself and the others during their 16 orbits. The information gained on the effects of radiation, confinement, and weightlessness helped scientists make advances in human adaptation to long journeys in space. After his flight, he earned (1965) a doctor of medicine degree from Humboldt University in East Berlin and went on to serve as head of several medical research institutions. Yegorov received a number of his country's highest awards, including the Order of Lenin.

Yoshiyuki, Junnosuke, Japanese novelist and short-story writer (b. April 1, 1923, Okayama, Japan—d. July 26, 1994, Tokyo, Japan), explored human sexuality and prostitution as a means of understanding human relationships. His prize-winning works include the short story "Shūu" (1954; "Sudden Shower," 1972), and the novels *Anshitsu* (1969: *The Dark Room,* 1975) and *Yugure made* (1978: "Until Evening"), the latter of which won the Noma Literary Prize. Yoshiyuki, a confessional writer in the Japanese genre "I novel," documented his own sexual adventures in wartime Tokyo in *Honoo no naka* (1956; "Among the Flames"). An asthmatic condition precluded military service during World War II, allowing him to write. Though he entered Tokyo University in 1945 and helped launch a small literary magazine, *Ashi* ("Reed"), Yoshiyuki ended his English literature studies to work for a scandal magazine. He found grist for his works by frequenting Tokyo's bars, cabarets, and gay quarters. He contracted tuberculosis in 1954 and during his hospitalization wrote "Shūu," which chronicled with detached objectivity his relationship with a prostitute. This first story won the Akutagawa Prize and secured his reputation. One of his novels, *Suna no ue no shokubutsugun* (1963; "Vegetable Garden in the Sand"), became a best-seller. At the time of his death, Yoshiyuki was working on a novel, *Medama* ("Eyeballs").

Zetterling, Mai Elisabeth, Swedish actress and director (b. May 24, 1925, Vasteras, Sweden—d. March 15?, 1994, London, England), was a popular stage and screen actress in post-World War II Britain; in the 1960s she became a successful film director. Zetterling grew up in poverty and was largely self-educated. Her stage debut at age 16 earned her an invitation to join the Royal Dramatic Theatre School in Stockholm. She gained international attention for her first major film, *Hets* (1945; "Frenzy"), and in 1947 she moved to England to star in Ealing Studio's *Frieda.* Other films include *Quartet* (1948), *Knock on Wood* (1954) opposite Danny Kaye, *Abandon Ship* (1957), and *Only Two Can Play* (1961) with Peter Sellers. She continued to appear onstage, with successful runs in *The Wild Duck, The Seagull, A Doll's House,* and *Hedda Gabler.* Dissatisfied with the movie roles being offered her, Zetterling turned to directing in 1960 and won a Golden Lion at the 1963 Venice Film Festival for a short documentary, *The War Game.* As a director she evinced a strong feminist perspective in films such as *Alskande par* (1964; *Loving Couples*), *Nattlek* (1966; *Night Games*), *Flikorna* (1968; *The Girls*), and *Scrubbers* (1983). She returned to the screen as an actress in *The Witches* (1989) and *Hidden Agenda* (1990). Zetterling also wrote novels and an autobiography, *All Those Tomorrows* (1985).

Events of 1994

Agriculture and Food Supplies

World agricultural production increased a little over 2% in 1994, according to preliminary estimates of the Food and Agriculture Organization (FAO) of the United Nations. The recovery of output in the developed countries, which fell 6% in 1993, was responsible for the bulk of the increase. Production in the less developed countries (LDCs) rose somewhat in excess of the 2% rate of population growth there. Output in the "countries in economic transition" in Eastern Europe and the former Soviet Union may have fallen 5% after increasing less than 1% in 1993.

INTERNATIONAL ISSUES

Food Emergencies. The most dramatic problems were those in Rwanda and in surrounding countries sheltering Rwandan refugees. After some 1 million people were reported killed in massacres by Hutu militiamen, 300,000 people fled to Tanzania and more than 1 million fled to Zaire. Both national and international relief organizations initially were overwhelmed by the speed and magnitude of these population movements before sufficient international assistance could arrive.

Famine conditions also existed in the Horn of Africa, and major food assistance was needed in Ethiopia, Eritrea,

Somalia, and The Sudan. Food supplies were critical for many subsistence farmers in Tanzania, and Uganda felt the impact of refugees fleeing Rwanda and The Sudan. Agriculture in Somalia was showing signs of recovery because of improved security conditions in the south that allowed some farmers to return to the land. The civil war intensified in southern Sudan in May 1994. The result was more displacement of people, disruption of agriculture, interference with relief operations, and reports of high rates of malnutrition for children under five. Ethiopia's food-aid needs remained exceptional because of the economic aftermath of three decades of civil war and an annual increase in population of nearly 3%. Burundi continued to feel the effects of the disruption of agriculture following the ethnic conflicts in October 1993.

Conditions generally improved in West Africa, but five years of civil war in Liberia had destroyed the country's capacity to import food commercially and increased its reliance on food aid. The breakdown of the 1993 peace agreement brought a resumption of fighting, impeding the commencement of normal agricultural activities and the distribution of food aid.

In southern Africa, Mozambique recorded another excellent grain harvest in 1994; the peace accords signed in 1992 encouraged farmers to return to their lands. Nonetheless, the country still faced the postwar problems of how to feed and resettle some 500,000 refugees and demobilized soldiers. The Angolan food-supply situation remained grave, with

Table I. Selected Indexes of World Agricultural and Food Production
(1979–81 = 100)

Region or country	Total agricultural production					Total food production					Per capita food production				
	1990	1991	1992	1993	1994	1990	1991	1992	1993	1994	1990	1991	1992	1993	1994
Developed countries	111	108	108	103	106	111	108	108	104	106	104	100	100	95	97
Canada	127	127	125	126	122	128	128	127	128	122	113	112	110	109	103
Europe	109	110	107	105	105	109	110	107	105	105	106	106	103	101	101
Japan	98	91	96	82	95	101	94	99	85	98	99	88	94	79	92
South Africa	103	106	86	100	108	104	106	86	103	112	82	82	64	76	80
United States	106	105	114	102	113	106	104	114	102	113	96	94	102	90	99
Former U.S.S.R.	121	105	94	94	88	123	106	96	96	89	113	97	88	87	81
Less developed countries	140	145	149	151	154	141	145	150	153	156	115	115	117	117	118
Argentina	109	112	116	110	115	109	112	116	112	116	94	95	98	94	98
Bangladesh	125	129	130	129	131	127	130	132	131	133	103	104	103	100	100
Brazil	130	133	141	141	150	134	137	147	148	157	109	110	116	114	119
China	159	166	171	175	178	158	163	170	176	178	136	139	143	147	147
Egypt	138	143	151	157	153	149	156	164	169	167	116	118	121	122	118
Former Ethiopia	112	112	116	113	113	113	114	118	116	115	86	85	85	81	78
India	147	152	158	160	165	149	154	160	162	167	121	122	124	124	125
Indonesia	162	166	177	182	186	166	170	182	187	192	138	138	145	147	149
Malaysia	184	198	204	223	224	224	244	255	284	286	173	184	187	204	200
Mexico	115	118	116	121	121	115	120	118	126	124	91	93	90	94	91
Nigeria	164	173	188	195	...	164	172	188	195	...	119	121	127	128	...
Philippines	117	116	117	118	121	117	116	117	119	123	93	90	89	89	90
Turkey	133	134	135	135	130	134	136	136	136	132	106	106	104	101	97
Venezuela	132	135	141	136	139	132	136	142	138	141	102	102	105	100	100
Vietnam	151	156	167	173	179	150	155	166	172	178	121	122	128	130	131
Zaire	138	143	147	151	146	136	143	148	152	147	100	100	100	100	94
World	126	127	128	128	130	126	126	129	128	131	106	105	105	103	104

Source: Food and Agriculture Organization of the United Nations, *FAO Quarterly Bulletin of Statistics.*

Table II. Shipment of Food Aid in Cereals
In 000-metric ton grain equivalent

Region and country	Average 1989–90, 1991–92	1992–93	1993–94	1994–95[1]
Australia	327	232	254	300
Canada	1,035	702	856	700
European Union	3,211	4,114	2,812	3,000
By members	884	926	1,110	...
By organizations	2,327	3,188	1,702	...
Japan	443	358	411	300
Norway	50	62	55	30
Sweden	97	168	134	80
Switzerland	62	60	65	30
United States	6,777	8,466	8,483	5,100
Others[2]	250	1,022	271	260
Total	12,252	15,184	13,341	9,800
To less developed countries	10,628	10,800	8,599	7,000
To LIFDC[3]	9,347	9,800	7,973	6,500
Sub Saharan Africa	3,450	5,227	3,706	...
To other countries	1,624	4,384	4,742	2,800

[1] Estimated.
[2] Includes Argentina, Austria, China, Finland, India, OPEC Special Fund, Saudi Arabia, Turkey, and World Food Program, but not necessarily for all years.
[3] Low-income food-deficit countries with per capita incomes under U.S. $1,305 in 1992.
Source: FAO, *Food Outlook*, November–December 1994.

starvation and severe malnutrition reported throughout the country because of massive displacement of the country's population following the resumption of intensive civil war in 1992 and the frequent interruption of food distribution by the fighting.

Swaziland, Yemen, and Kyrgyzstan were added to the FAO's list of countries requiring either exceptional or emergency food assistance. Food supplies remained difficult in Iraq, where the political dispute connected with the UN embargo continued to limit the country's ability to finance food imports. Armenia, Azerbaijan, Georgia, and Tajikistan faced exceptional or emergency food needs, while the availability of food supplies in Bosnia and Herzegovina waxed and waned with the military situation there.

In Asia the situation in Afghanistan deteriorated further because of renewed fighting and the needs of returning refugees adding to the displaced persons within the country. The small rice crop of Laos in 1993 placed some 10% of the population in need of emergency assistance. Food supplies were also tight in Cambodia and Mongolia. In Central America crops were seriously damaged by drought, and El Salvador, Honduras, and Nicaragua experienced acute food shortages requiring outside assistance.

Food Aid. In December the Food Aid Committee of the International Wheat Agreement approved and opened for signing an extension of the current Food Aid Convention (FAC), the international mechanism for guaranteeing minimum availability of food aid, which was due to expire in June 1995. FAC members were reportedly prepared to pledge to supply a minimum of 7,320,000 tons of grain (wheat equivalent) annually, a reduction of approximately 200,000 tons from the expiring agreement. The United States was said to be maintaining its long-standing pledge of a minimum of 4,470,000 tons annually. These minimums had previously applied to a list of poorer LDCs whose incomes fell under a level prescribed by the Organisation for Economic Co-operation and Development (OECD). The new convention was believed to add to the list some of the poorer countries of the former Soviet Union and Eastern Europe.

The FAO reported that the equivalent of about 13,340,-000 tons of food aid in cereals was provided in 1993–94. The last year in which the LDCs were virtually the sole recipients of food aid was 1988–89. During the three-year

period 1986–89, Africa on average was the recipient of 47% of such assistance, Asia 35%, and Latin America 18%. In 1993–94, however, LDCs received 64% of total assistance, while the former Soviet bloc became the top regional recipient, with 36% of total assistance. Among the LDCs, Africa commanded 31% of the total, Asia 21%, and Latin America 12%.

The availability of food aid in 1994–95 was reported down sharply from 1993–94. The final total, however, was likely to be larger because donors increasingly delayed their commitments in order to respond to evolving food emergencies. Budget cutbacks and high prices for wheat brought about by the worldwide reduction in grain stocks led to reduced food-aid commitments by several countries; the estimate for U.S. aid was the lowest since 1988–89.

AIDS and Agriculture. Particularly in Africa and parts of South America, AIDS was increasingly regarded as a serious obstacle to the economies of many LDCs. AIDS had initially been an urban disease, but more and more cases were being reported in rural areas. The impact was expected to be particularly severe because of the central role agriculture played in so many of the poorer countries and because the disease attacked the most economically productive age group—those roughly 15–45 years of age—in countries where the very young made up a large percentage of the population. In addition, infection rates for women were two and one-half times higher than for men, and women contributed the bulk of agricultural labour in Africa and in parts of Asia and Latin America. These facts suggested potential decimation of the rural labour force in some countries.

Table III. World Cereal Supply and Distribution
In 000,000 metric tons

	1991–92	1992–93	1993–94	1994–95[1]
Production				
Wheat	543	561	559	527
Coarse grains	803	863	787	866
Rice, milled	352	353	350	353
Total	1,698	1,777	1,696	1,746
Utilization				
Wheat	559	544	564	552
Coarse grains	806	834	830	851
Rice, milled	356	353	355	357
Total	1,721	1,731	1,749	1,750
Exports				
Wheat	109	113	99	96
Coarse grains	94	90	85	86
Rice, milled	14	15	16	15
Total	218	217	200	196
Ending stocks[2]				
Wheat	130	148	143	118
Coarse grains	138	167	124	139
Rice, milled	56	55	50	46
Total	323	370	317	303
Stocks as % of utilization				
Wheat	23.3%	27.2%	25.3%	21.4%
Coarse grains	17.1%	20.0%	15.0%	16.3%
Rice, milled	15.6%	15.5%	14.1%	13.0%
Total	18.8%	21.4%	18.1%	17.2%
Stocks held by U.S. in %				
Wheat	9.9%	9.7%	10.9%	11.9%
Coarse grains	24.7%	37.8%	22.1%	39.7%
Stocks held by EU in %				
Wheat	17.5%	15.6%	11.1%	11.6%
Coarse grains	14.1%	11.6%	13.0%	7.9%

[1] Forecast.
[2] Series includes estimates of Chinese and Russian stocks. Data not available for all countries, including parts of Eastern Europe and Asia.
Source: USDA, Foreign Agricultural Service, December 1994.

The stark economic problem for agriculture was how to invest in laboursaving technologies to compensate for the loss of able-bodied farm workers or to attract workers from other economic sectors. Subsidiary problems included how to adjust land-tenure arrangements and provide credit to accommodate the consolidation of farm holdings after the death of farmers. Another likely issue would be how to compensate for reduced domestic production of food through food imports, including food aid.

International Initiatives. A proposal by FAO Director-General Jacques Diouf to convene a World Food Summit in March 1996 in connection with the organization's 50th anniversary was endorsed by the FAO governing council in November. The aim was to develop a consensus among world leaders about the likely future direction of the world food situation and how to improve it. This would be the first meeting that heads of state had devoted to world food.

An international convention to combat desertification was signed in Paris in October. The document focused on Africa and called for the establishment of a process to combat land degradation. The convention, which was intended to establish a mechanism for linking planning with implementation and to coordinate local national activities with those of aid donors, would enter into force, probably sometime in 1996, upon ratification by a majority of the countries. The negotiators also approved a resolution calling for voluntary "Urgent Early Action for Africa" to start the process rolling before the convention formally came into force. The resolution was based on an OECD/Club du Sahel proposal to initiate partnership agreements between individual donors and individual countries.

Ecological and Technological Developments. International concern over the safe use of pesticides and other agricultural chemicals led to the establishment of a system by which nearly all developed exporting countries would voluntarily inform importing countries of safety issues related to agricultural chemicals traded internationally. The intent of these London Guidelines on International Trade, sponsored by the United Nations Environmental Program, was to give LDCs a means of protecting their populations from the effects of misuse of such chemicals. The FAO Council in November endorsed a proposal to initiate negotiations making this "prior informed consent" procedure formally part of an international agreement open to signature by all countries.

Technology and Food and Environmental Safety. Concerns about the effects of agricultural technologies received more attention in 1994, particularly in the U.S. The U.S. Food and Drug Administration (FDA) in May approved the first whole food developed through biotechnology for sale in the U.S. The Flavr Savr tomato was engineered by Calgene Inc. to delay the ripening process so that the tomato could be picked closer to full ripeness than most mass-marketed tomatoes, thus gaining more flavour while still retaining sufficient firmness to survive being shipped long distances. Calgene said it would label the product's origin, although the FDA said it was not necessary because the tomato had the essential characteristics of traditional tomatoes.

After lengthy hearings the U.S. Department of Agriculture (USDA) approved a genetically engineered yellow crookneck squash in December, ruling the squash was as safe as traditionally bred virus-resistant squash. Some ecologists and public-interest groups opposed the action, claiming the need for a more thorough examination of the potential risks from the escape of the genes into the wild, turning wild plants into weeds or forming new recombinant virus strains. Most plant pathologists and plant breeders saw no new risks.

The USDA also had granted field-testing permits for 57 plants in which virus resistance had been genetically engineered. They included corn (maize), cucumbers, melons, peanuts (groundnuts), potatoes, tobacco, lettuce, papayas, beets, barley, alfalfa, watermelons, and gladiolus. A virus-resistant tomato had been marketed in China for nearly two years, resistant potatoes were being tested in Mexico, and criollo melons were the subject of research in Costa Rica.

At the end of 1994, Agracetus, a U.S. company, was seeking a broad European patent based on the development of a key technology for insertion of genes into soybeans. In 1992 the company had obtained exclusive U.S. rights for genetically engineered cotton based on the same technique. A coalition of commercial and international public-interest groups argued that the patent was too broad and would have a chilling effect on research. The USDA also challenged the patent, saying the process was too important to be monopolized by one company and that other scientists, including some at USDA facilities, had also contributed. The company denied seeking a monopoly for cotton, saying it had licensed the process to others, including the USDA.

The U.S. Environmental Protection Agency (EPA) in October agreed to review and phase out the use of cer-

Table IV. World Production of Major Oilseeds and Products
In 000,000 metric tons

	1992–93	1993–94[1]	1994–95[2]
Production of oilseeds	227.3	226.9	251.3
Soybeans	117.1	116.6	132.9
U.S.	59.6	50.9	68.7
China	10.3	15.3	13.8
Argentina	11.4	11.7	12.4
Brazil	22.5	24.5	24.0
Cottonseed	31.6	29.5	32.8
U.S.	5.7	5.8	6.9
Former Soviet republics	3.7	3.8	3.8
China	7.7	6.4	7.7
Peanuts	23.1	24.0	24.5
U.S.	1.9	1.5	1.9
China	6.0	8.4	7.3
India	8.6	7.6	8.8
Sunflower seed	21.3	21.0	22.4
U.S.	1.2	1.2	2.1
Former Soviet republics	5.5	5.3	4.7
Argentina	3.1	3.8	3.7
European Union	4.1	3.4	4.2
Rapeseed	25.3	26.8	29.4
Canada	3.7	5.5	7.2
China	7.7	6.9	7.4
European Union	6.1	5.9	6.4
India	5.4	5.5	5.4
Copra	4.8	4.8	5.0
Palm kernel	4.0	4.3	4.3
Oilseeds crushed	183.6	186.8	197.6
Soybeans	96.2	99.7	104.9
Oilseed ending stocks	23.2	19.6	28.8
Soybeans	20.2	17.0	24.9
World production[3]			
Total fats and oils	...	...	...
Edible vegetable oils	59.6	61.2	64.4
Soybean oil	17.1	17.9	19.0
Palm oil	13.0	13.4	13.8
Animal fats	...	...	...
Marine oils	1.2	1.2	1.2
High-protein meals[4]	124.2	127.9	135.1
Soybean meal	75.8	76.9	83.0
Fish meal	5.9	6.2	6.4

[1] Preliminary.
[2] Forecast.
[3] Processing potential from crops in year indicated.
[4] Converted, based on product's protein content, to weight equivalent of soybeans of 44% protein content.

Source: USDA, Foreign Agricultural Service, December 1994.

tain cancer-causing chemicals on food as part of an out-of-court settlement with several consumer organizations. Some 85 pesticides were to be reviewed for compliance with the "Delaney Clause" of a federal law that prohibited the use of carcinogenic chemicals that concentrate during food processing. These chemicals were authorized to be used on a wide variety of fruits, vegetables, and field crops. Because not much use was made of Delaney chemicals on many crops and effective substitutes were available for others, however, the economic impact of the EPA action would likely vary from region to region.

The European Union (EU) in December approved the use of recombinant bovine somatotropin (BST) for restricted testing purposes but extended the moratorium on its commercial use, originally imposed in 1990, through 1999. This synthetic hormone, which promotes growth in cattle and increases milk output by supplementing the BST produced naturally by a cow, was approved in the United States in November 1993. The EU's resistance to its use was primarily economics; it was feared that increased production would swell existing government stocks of dairy products and put new pressure on costly subsidies to the industry. In the United States the use of the hormone was expected to increase per-cow milk yields by 2% in 1995 and perhaps 4% by 1999. The Canadian government in August decided to delay the introduction of BST until July 1, 1995.

Trade Issues. International agricultural trade issues were on the back burner in 1994 as countries prepared to implement the agreement reached in the multilateral trade negotiations under the General Agreement on Tariffs and Trade (GATT), which was concluded in December 1993. U.S. ratification of the agreement, which would become operational in 1995 under the new World Trade Organization, appeared assured with congressional acceptance of the agreement and passage of implementing legislation.

The agreement progressively reduced the level of specified agricultural subsidies but did not eliminate them. Countries were jockeying to make the most efficient use of those subsidies still permitted. For instance, to gain congressional support for GATT, the U.S. government announced that it would no longer use the export subsidies provided under its Export Enhancement Program and Dairy Export Incentive Program merely to combat other countries' unfair trade practices but would also use the programs for market expansion and promotion. The European Parliament approved the agreement and a $98-billion agricultural budget providing price supports and other subsidies under the EU's common agricultural policy (CAP). In December the United States was threatening retaliatory restrictions on European imports if the EU did not provide adequate compensation for U.S. exports lost because of tariffs raised in 1995 in connection with the enlargement of the EU from 12 to 15 members.

AGRICULTURAL COMMODITIES

Grains. World grain production overall was expected (in December) to increase in 1994–95, largely because of the recovery in U.S. corn production, which was devastated in 1993. Global wheat production was expected to be smaller because of a sharp reduction in output in the former Soviet Union and the effects of the most severe drought in 22 years in Australia. Even with an expected reduction in wheat consumption, world wheat stocks as a percentage of wheat use were likely to fall to the lowest level since the years leading up to the world food crisis in the early 1970s. EU policies pushed government-held "intervention stocks" into the EU domestic livestock market to help hold down

feed prices. The U.S., except for its Food Security Wheat Reserve of four million tons, had virtually eliminated its government-held wheat stocks.

A potential Canadian-U.S. trade war was averted in August when Canada agreed to limit wheat exports to the U.S. at the low rates permitted under the North American Free Trade Agreement (NAFTA). The U.S. had threatened unilateral restrictions under farm legislation that allowed curbs on imports when they interfered with U.S. price-support programs. Particularly irritating to Canadians and to U.S.

Table V. Livestock Inventories and Meat Production In Major Producing Countries

In 000,000 head and 000,000 metric tons (carcass weight)

Region and country	1993[1]	1994[2]	1993[1]	1994[2]
	Cattle and buffalo		Beef and veal	
World total	**1,034.3**	**1,039.0**	**44.19**	**44.76**
Canada	12.0	12.5	0.88	0.95
United States	101.7	103.4	10.58	11.12
Mexico	30.7	30.2	1.71	1.73
Argentina	54.9	54.7	2.55	2.48
Brazil	144.3	143.7	4.61	4.53
Uruguay	10.5	10.7	0.31	0.34
European Union	78.4	78.0	7.80	7.71
Other Western Europe[3]	6.0	6.1	0.49	0.52
Eastern Europe[4]	11.7	11.9	0.73	0.69
Former Soviet republics				
Kazakhstan	9.3	8.9	0.60	0.68
Russian Federation	48.9	48.5	3.36	3.20
Ukraine	21.6	20.9	1.39	1.30
Australia	26.8	26.6	1.81	1.82
India	272.7	274.2	0.95	1.05
China	113.2	119.0	2.34	2.70
	Hogs		Pork	
World total	**741.5**	**750.5**	**66.08**	**67.30**
Canada	11.2	11.7	1.19	1.25
United States	57.9	60.5	7.75	7.93
Mexico	12.1	12.4	0.87	0.92
European Union	110.2	109.8	14.64	14.63
Other Western Europe[3]	7.9	7.7	0.99	0.98
Eastern Europe[5]	34.4	35.5	2.71	2.28
Former Soviet republics				
Kazakhstan	2.4	2.2	0.24	0.22
Russian Federation	28.6	26.0	2.43	2.30
Ukraine	15.3	14.4	1.04	0.95
Japan	10.6	10.5	1.43	1.41
China	393.0	401.0	28.54	30.00
	Poultry		Poultry meat[6]	
World total	...	...	**39.32**	**41.56**
United States	...	...	12.40	13.15
Brazil	...	...	3.21	3.48
European Union	...	...	7.06	7.20
Eastern Europe[6]	...	...	0.77	0.83
Former Soviet republics				
Russia	...	...	1.28	1.20
Ukraine		...	0.42	0.40
Japan	...	...	1.37	1.32
China	...	...	5.30	6.10
	Sheep		Sheep, goat meat	
World total[7]	**896.0**	**889.1**	**6.30**	**6.28**
			All meat	
Total	...	...	**155.88**	**159.88**

[1] Preliminary livestock numbers at year's end. Countries included in totals but not shown include the most significant for trade in Latin America, Asia, and scattered coverage elsewhere.
[2] Forecast.
[3] Austria, Sweden, and Switzerland.
[4] Bulgaria, Poland, and Romania.
[5] Bulgaria, Hungary, Poland, and Romania.
[6] Ready-to-eat equivalent.
[7] Hungary, Poland, and Romania.
[8] Coverage includes China.
Source: USDA, Foreign Agricultural Service, October 1994.

producers was a subrestriction in NAFTA on imports of durum used to make pasta. They claimed that U.S. durum imports had increased mainly because U.S. export subsidies for durum had reduced domestic supplies, pushing up prices and attracting imports. The U.S. saw certain Canadian transportation subsidies as providing an unfair export advantage. An expert Joint Commission on Grains was due to make nonbinding recommendations by May 31, 1995.

World production of coarse grain was expected to increase more than 10% in 1994–95, largely because of a bumper U.S. corn crop. Aggregate output outside the U.S. was reduced because of the Australian drought's impact on barley, reduced yields in South Africa, smaller planted area in the former Soviet republics, and poor growing conditions for corn in Ukraine and the North Caucasus region of Russia. Only India, Eastern Europe, and China among the other major producers saw production increases. Decreased production, declining livestock inventories, and a limited ability to finance feed imports were pushing down coarse-grain consumption in the former Soviet Union. Australia, ordinarily a substantial exporter of coarse grains, was having to import large quantities to maintain its livestock industry.

Oilseeds. World oilseed production was expected (in December) to increase more than 10% in 1994–95 as a result of the recovery of the U.S. soybean crop from the 1993 drought and strong expansion in output of nearly all major oilseeds in response to strong prices in 1993–94 that carried over into 1994–95. Output lagged in the former Soviet Union, where sunflower-seed production fell to the lowest level in 10 years. Prices of soybeans peaked at an average of $282 per ton in January 1994 (c.i.f., Rotterdam, U.S. No. 2 yellow) and remained strong, averaging $259 per ton in 1993–94 (October–September). Prices fell rapidly when the prospect of a record-large U.S. crop in 1994–95 became clear, trading near $235 from July 1994.

Table VI. World Production of Milk
In 000,000 metric tons

Region and country	1992	1993[1]	1994[2]
Developed countries	**354.0**	**348.0**	**342.0**
United States	68.8	68.5	69.4
Canada	7.6	7.5	7.7
Europe	161.0	158.0	155.0
European Union	112.4	111.6	110.2
France	25.3	25.0	24.9
Germany	28.1	28.2	27.8
Italy	11.3	10.8	10.3
Netherlands, The	10.9	10.9	10.8
United Kingdom	14.4	14.5	14.4
Other Western Europe[3]	12.8	12.9	13.0
Eastern Europe			
Poland	13.1	12.7	12.5
Romania	3.8	3.5	3.5
Former Soviet republics			
Russian Federation	47.2	46.9	44.0
Ukraine	19.1	18.1	17.5
Australia/New Zealand[4]	15.5	16.6	17.9
Japan	8.6	8.6	8.5
Less developed countries	**172.0**	**177.0**	**181.0**
Latin America	44.0	45.0	46.0
Brazil	15.0	15.2	15.3
Africa	12.0	12.0	12.0
Asia	116.0	119.0	123.0
China	5.0	5.1	5.3
India	29.4	30.5	30.5
World total	**526.0**	**525.0**	**526.0**

[1] Preliminary.
[2] Forecast.
[3] Austria, Finland, Sweden, and Switzerland.
[4] Year ending June 30 for Australia and May 31 for New Zealand.
Sources: FAO, *Food Outlook*, November/December 1994; USDA, Foreign Agricultural Service, August 1994.

Global demand for protein meals for animal feed continued to grow more slowly than the demand for vegetable oils. The price of soybean meal slipped to $202 per ton (c.i.f., Rotterdam) in 1993–94, compared with $207 in 1992–93. Prices for most other protein meals were also either down or only a little higher than in the previous year. One reason for the lower prices was that the EU, with its large livestock industry, under CAP continued to price feed grains lower than protein meals to discourage the feeding of oilseed meal to animals. In Eastern Europe and the former Soviet Union the shortage of foreign exchange with which to purchase oilseed meal abroad was also a factor.

International prices of vegetable oil, which had been surging since 1993 as rising demand outpaced the growth of supplies, were much stronger in 1993–94. Soybean oil prices averaged $580 per ton (f.o.b., Rotterdam), compared with $453 in 1992–93. Despite record-large global oilseed output predicted in 1994–95, supplies of vegetable oil remained extremely tight. Soybean oil prices stood at $706 per ton in November, reflecting the fact that the vegetable oil stocks-to-use ratio was the lowest in 20 years. Helping keep vegetable oil supplies tight was the small expected increase in production of palm oil in 1994–95. Most of the gain was expected to come in Indonesia, where palm plantings had been increased sharply. Malaysian output was being restrained by the cyclical stress on trees that follows a bumper crop like the one in 1993, a shortage of labour to pick the fruit, and unfavourable weather late in 1994.

Livestock and Meat. The world cattle inventory grew modestly again in 1994. The most rapid gains continued to come in China, where rapid income growth was swelling the demand for meat and stimulating herd expansion. Expansion of the U.S. and Canadian economies was stimulating the demand for beef and leading to further strong growth of cattle herds there. The Australian drought necessitated the trucking of water into some towns and the temporary relocation of townspeople elsewhere. Both livestock and grain markets were disrupted, leading to increased slaughter of cattle (because of low feed supplies) and a halt to the expansion of cattle herds. Cattle herds in the former Soviet republics continued to decline.

The expansion of global hog inventories accelerated in 1994, mainly on the basis of strong growth in China and the United States. The steadily growing Chinese industry was obtaining higher carcass weights thanks in large part to the importation of semen and to higher slaughter rates that were the result of improved management practices. A shortage of feed in the former Soviet states was slowing production there. China and the United States were also responsible for most of the growth in world production of poultry meat in 1994. China, which nearly doubled its output in four years, made good use of imported breeding stock—some 60% of all broilers were raised from nonnative stock.

World sheep and goat inventories continued to decline and were down 10% from 1989–90. Falling wool prices and drought reduced the incentive for sheep production in Australia, as had the phaseout of the U.S. wool-support program, which was created to ensure supplies of wool for defense in World War II. Global wool production had declined every year since 1989–90.

Dairy. World milk output was forecast by the FAO (in December) to have fallen slightly in 1994, the fourth consecutive year of decline. Milk production overall in the developed countries was down about 2%, reflecting smaller output in the former Soviet Union, where modest growth in output on private farms was not enough to offset reductions in the former public sector. Milk output in the EU

Table VII. World Production of Centrifugal (Freed from Liquid) Sugar
In 000,000 metric tons raw value

Region and country	1992–93	1993–94	1994–95[1]
North America	**11.6**	**10.9**	**11.6**
United States	7.1	7.0	7.4
Mexico	4.3	3.8	4.0
Caribbean	**5.4**	**5.1**	**4.3**
Cuba	4.3	4.0	3.2
Central America	**2.3**	**2.5**	**2.5**
Guatemala	1.1	1.2	1.2
South America	**15.5**	**15.4**	**16.2**
Argentina	1.4	1.1	1.2
Brazil	9.8	9.9	10.5
Colombia	1.8	1.8	2.0
Europe	**21.6**	**22.3**	**19.9**
Western Europe	18.1	18.6	16.5
European Union	17.1	17.4	15.4
France	4.7	4.8	4.3
Germany	4.4	4.8	4.0
Eastern Europe	3.4	3.6	3.4
Poland	1.6	2.3	1.7
Former Soviet republics[2]	**7.1**	**7.5**	**6.3**
Russian Federation	2.5	2.7	2.0
Ukraine	4.0	4.2	3.8
Africa and Middle East	**10.0**	**9.8**	**10.8**
South Africa	1.6	1.7	2.1
Turkey	2.1	2.2	2.1
Asia	**33.7**	**31.9**	**35.4**
China	8.3	6.5	6.2
India	12.5	11.7	14.4
Indonesia	2.3	2.5	2.5
Pakistan	2.6	3.1	3.3
Philippines	2.1	1.8	2.0
Thailand	3.8	4.0	4.7
Oceania	**4.0**	**5.0**	**5.5**
Australia	4.4	4.5	5.0
Totals			
Beginning stocks	23.6	21.0	17.6
As % of consumption	20.6%	18.5%	15.4%
Production	112.0	110.2	112.6
Imports[3]	29.5	29.7	27.9
Consumption	114.6	113.7	116.8
Exports[3]	29.5	29.7	27.9

[1] Preliminary.
[2] Includes Estonia, Latvia, and Lithuania.
[3] Exports do not equal imports because "Totals" are a composite of slightly differing marketing years, not all beginning in the same months.
Source: USDA, Foreign Agricultural Service, November 1994.

was affected by adverse weather conditions and by Italian and Spanish attempts to bring production in line with EU quotas. Output was up as much as 3% in the LDCs, with the largest gains in Asia.

Australia and New Zealand were gaining importance in world dairy trade as output fell in the EU because of policy reform and as pressures increased to reduce export subsidies in Western European countries and the U.S. Subsidies were likely to increase with implementation of GATT. New Zealand, the largest exporter of butter, was investing in more output of whole-milk powder and cheese and less of butter and nonfat dry milk. The international butter market took on a two-tier character following the suspension of minimum prices for butter ($1,350 per metric ton f.o.b.) in May 1994 under the International Dairy Agreement.

Sugar. Global sugar output in 1993–94 proved to be smaller than anticipated because of shortfalls in the Indian and Chinese crops. Recovery of Indian sugar output and scattered gains elsewhere led to expectations (in November) of increased world production in 1994–95, despite the effects of drought in Western Europe, flooding in China, and another dismal performance by the Cuban sugar industry. Global sugar consumption was expected to exceed output

for the third year in a row. Sugar supplies around the world had been drawn down to their lowest levels in six years, and world prices for raw sugar by October 1994 had reached a four-year high of 14.4 cents per pound.

Sugar production in the former Soviet Union and Eastern Europe had declined during the difficult economic transition after the collapse of communism, and sugar consumption had fallen by some 20–25% in the past five years. Early in 1994 Russia and Cuba had agreed to an extension of their 1993–94 barter deal, under which Cuba would trade one million tons of sugar for 2.5 million tons of petroleum. By November Cuba had delivered half its quota but was reportedly behind schedule in deliveries. Cuba's growing inability to supply China's sugar needs was also making that country a major buyer on the open market. Having constituted about one-quarter of the world market in the 1970s, Cuba's share of world sugar exports had declined to only about 9%. It seemed likely that the Caribbean nation would be replaced in 1994–95 by Australia as the second largest exporter.

Coffee. Coffee prices shot upward in 1994, despite estimates (in December) of a modestly larger 1994–95 global coffee crop because of severe freezes in Brazil. Coffee prices began edging up early in 1994 on the basis of expectations that production would exceed consumption for the third year in a row, prefrost reductions in estimates of the 1994–95 Brazilian crop, and an announcement by members of the new World Association of Coffee Producing Nations that they would withhold coffee from the market under an export-retention scheme. The scheme replaced the expired International Coffee Agreement under the designation of the International Coffee Organization (ICO), to which both producing and consuming nations had belonged. The retention operation was barely under way when it was suspended after prices moved above 85 cents per pound.

Prices took off when a survey estimated that the freezes, followed uncharacteristically by drought, would cut the

Table VIII. World Green Coffee Production
In 000 60-kg bags

Region and country	1992–93	1993–94[1]	1994–95[2]
North America	**17,874**	**16,582**	**16,926**
Costa Rica	2,620	2,475	2,300
El Salvador	2,894	2,115	2,520
Guatemala	3,504	3,078	3,027
Honduras	1,981	2,060	2,060
Mexico	4,180	4,200	4,300
South America	**43,605**	**44,475**	**43,585**
Brazil	24,000	28,500	26,000
Colombia	14,950	11,400	12,500
Ecuador	1,560	1,850	1,910
Africa	**16,296**	**15,821**	**17,330**
Cameroon	837	1,250	1,300
Côte d'Ivoire	2,500	2,700	3,400
Ethiopia	2,800	3,000	3,500
Kenya	1,217	1,230	1,330
Uganda	2,800	2,700	3,000
Zaire	1,790	1,100	1,300
Asia and Oceania	**15,630**	**1,660**	**16,465**
India	2,700	3,450	3,000
Indonesia	7,350	7,400	7,000
Vietnam	2,250	2,500	3,100
Total production	93,405	93,538	94,306
Exportable[3]	72,471	70,019	72,061
Beginning stocks[4]	47,391	42,570	35,534
Exports	77,068	77,609	77,297

[1] Preliminary.
[2] Forecast.
[3] Production minus domestic use.
[4] In exporting countries.
Source: USDA, Foreign Agricultural Service, December 1994.

1995–96 Brazilian crop short by 9 million to 13 million bags from its 29 million-bag potential. The quantity of output from the 1994–95 crop was not affected, although its quality may have been reduced. Prices of green coffee, which had averaged about 62 cents per pound in 1993 (1979 ICO composite indicator), shot as high as $2.75 on the futures market in September but fell as low as $1.45 in early December. Retail prices of roasted coffee, which in the U.S. averaged $2.47 per pound in 1993, reached a plateau of a little under $4.50 in August–November 1994. Just before Christmas, producers in Colombia, Guatemala, Honduras, Nicaragua, Costa Rica, and El Salvador announced that they would withhold 20–22% of their exports beginning at the start of 1995, but traders speculated whether very much coffee was actually available to be withheld. It was forecast that U.S. imports of agricultural products in fiscal year 1995 would increase from $2 billion to $4 billion entirely because of higher coffee prices.

Cocoa. The new five-year International Cocoa Agreement established by the International Cocoa Organization (ICCO), concluded in September 1993, became operational provisionally in February 1994. The agreement attempted to influence international cocoa prices by the obligations of its individual members to control their own cocoa production. The old ICCO plan tried unsuccessfully to maintain cocoa prices within an agreed price band through operation of a buffer stock. The buffer stock continued to be liquidated gradually under a five-year schedule designed to recover some of the cost of the stock and to eliminate the potential price-depressing effects of its existence.

Stronger demand for cocoa generated by the economic upturn in the United States and Europe, together with the modest drawdown in cocoa stocks in recent years, helped strengthen prices. Futures prices (New York, nearest three-month average) for cocoa beans moved upward from a 20-year-low average of 46.7 cents per pound in 1993 to an average of 58.4 cents for 11 months of 1994. The higher prices were stimulating increased output in Africa in 1994–95. That, together with better weather in Brazil, was leading to expectations of a record-high global cocoa crop in 1994–95.

Bananas. The U.S. involved itself in a dispute between banana-exporting countries and the EU when in September it accepted a petition under Section 301 of the U.S. Trade Act by the Chiquita Banana Co. and the Hawaii Banana Industry Association. It alleged unfair trade practices by

Table IX. World Cocoa Bean Production
In 000 metric tons

Region and country	1992–93	1993–94	1994–95[1]
North and Central America	113	112	114
South America	496	444	475
Brazil	330	276	306
Ecuador	76	78	79
Africa	1,283	1,385	1,435
Cameroon	100	105	100
Côte d'Ivoire[2]	700	850	860
Ghana	312	260	315
Nigeria[3]	140	140	130
Asia and Oceania	525	547	522
Indonesia	240	280	260
Malaysia	225	210	200
Total production	2,417	2,488	2,545
Net production	2,393	2,463	2,520
Cocoa grindings	2,417	2,465	2,520
Change in stocks	−24	−2	0

[1] Forecast.
[2] Includes some cocoa marketed between Ghana and Côte d'Ivoire.
[3] Includes cocoa marketed through Benin.
Source: USDA, Foreign Agricultural Service, October 1994.

Table X. World Cotton Production and Consumption
In 000,000 480-lb bales

Region and country	1992–93	1993–94[1]	1994–95[1]
Production	82.7	76.9	85.8
Western Hemisphere	20.5	20.5	25.2
United States	16.2	16.1	19.6
Brazil	2.1	1.9	2.3
Europe	1.6	1.7	1.7
Former Soviet republics	9.4	9.6	9.5
Uzbekistan	6.0	6.2	6.0
Africa	6.0	5.8	6.2
Asia and Oceania[2]	54.5	49.0	52.7
China	20.7	17.2	20.7
India	10.9	9.6	10.0
Pakistan	7.1	6.3	6.3
Consumption	85.6	84.5	85.8
United States	10.3	10.4	11.0
China	21.5	20.9	21.2
India	9.8	10.0	10.2
Pakistan	6.6	6.5	6.3
European Union	5.0	5.1	5.1
Southeast Asia	4.4	4.6	4.8
Russia	2.2	2.0	1.8

[1] Estimate.
[2] Includes Middle East.
Source: USDA, Foreign Agricultural Service, December 1994.

the EU in establishing a new import regime in response to GATT. The EU previously had given preferential tariff treatment to imports of bananas from former European colonies in Africa and the Caribbean. Many Caribbean countries were heavily dependent on banana exports, and European preferences were important because the bananas they were importing were generally of lower quality and more expensive than Latin-American bananas. The new EU quota and licensing system continued to favour the importation of Caribbean over Latin-American bananas.

Two GATT panels—called at the behest of Colombia, Costa Rica, Ecuador, Nicaragua, and Venezuela, with U.S. support—ruled that the new system was not in conformity with GATT rules. Under a special "framework agreement," the EU proposed to increase its annual global tariff-rate import quota from 2 million to 2.2 million tons in 1995, to establish country subquotas based on historical level of exports to the EU, and to reduce the proposed tariffs on such within-quota imports.

Cotton. The sharp reduction in world cotton production in 1993–94, centred mainly in Asia, contributed to a widespread drawdown in cotton stocks by the beginning of 1994–95 that stimulated cotton prices in many countries. International prices (Northern European Cotlook Index "A"), which had fallen to an average of 57.7 cents per pound in 1992–93, climbed steadily to a peak of about 86 cents in May–June for an average of 70.7 cents in 1993–94. The result was the expectation (in December) of substantially larger global cotton output in 1994–95.

The recovery of production in China, where bollworm infestations were being brought under control, and a record-large U.S. crop were mainly responsible for the increase, although cotton plantings were expected to increase in most major producing countries. Economic recovery in the U.S., Japan, and Europe helped stimulate the demand for cotton textiles, although depressed use of cotton in the former Soviet bloc was holding down global use. Global output and use of cotton were expected to be roughly in balance following two years of substantial drawdown in global stocks.

(RICHARD M. KENNEDY)

See also Gardening; Business and Industry Review: *Textiles.*

This article updates the *Macropædia* article The History of AGRICULTURE.

FISHERIES

The total world harvest of fish and shellfish, including aquaculture, recovered during 1992, rising above the 1991 total by just under 1.1 million mt (metric tons), mainly because of a rise in the inland catch to a total of 98,112,800 mt. These figures, while above those of the previous two years, were still below those of the late 1980s. The UN Food and Agriculture Organization reported that the recent decline in the growth of the total catch represented a slowdown in growth of production that had been taking place almost continuously over the past four decades.

Production from inland fisheries grew steadily over the past few years, primarily because of the increase in aquaculture. Consistent with the pattern of increasing production over the past decade, the most productive areas were in Asia, where, for example, China reported an increase of 689,059 mt from inland fisheries. The leading freshwater species in terms of production were silver carp, grass carp, and common carp. The anchoveta became the leading maritime species, and the catch rose by 1,433,897 mt in 1992. Alaskan pollock, in second place, increased from 4,893,493 mt in 1991 to 4,992,289 mt in 1992 and had shown a steady decline in catch in recent years.

The top species landed in 1992 (in order of tonnage) were:

Species	metric tons
anchoveta	5,451,003
Alaskan pollock	4,992,269
Chilean Jack mackerel	3,390,263
South American pilchard	3,105,462
Japanese pilchard	2,488,533
caplin	2,109,459
silver carp	1,604,216
Atlantic herring	1,529,392
skipjack tuna	1,421,391
grass carp	1,254,383

These 10 species produced a combined total catch of 27,346,371 mt, compared with 27,716,381 mt in 1991. Other species with large increases included bighead carp, Japanese scallop, Japanese flying squid, Norway pout, South African anchovy, and mud carp. Species that exhibited a sharp decrease in catch included Argentine hake, Araucanian herring, Gulf menhaden, California pilchard, pink (humpback) salmon, European pilchard, and Atlantic cod.

China was again the leading producer, with a massive jump in its total catch for 1992, rising by 14.3% to 15,007,450 mt. Production of fish and shellfish by the rest of the world (excluding China) had fallen each year since 1989. Most of this decrease was a fall in production in the republics of the former U.S.S.R.—four million tons between 1989 and 1992—owing to a slump in marine fishing activity. Japan also showed a major drop. Chile, Norway, and Iceland showed increased catches in 1992, all by about 500,000 mt.

The problem of worldwide overfishing, dwindling fish stocks, and access to these stocks dominated the world fisheries agenda during 1994. Much publicity was given to the continuing work of the 1993 UN Conference on Straddling Fish Stocks and Highly Migratory Fish Stocks, where the world's fishing nations had begun resolving conflicts arising from commercial fish stocks that either straddle or, at some point during a migratory life cycle, pass through a country's 200-mi exclusive economic zone (EEZ) and out into international waters. One example of the problems was the situation faced by Canada and the commercial fisheries off the Maritime Provinces. Stocks of cod, redfish, flounder, American plaice, and turbot had dropped to record-low levels by 1992–93, and Canada instituted a two-year moratorium on the domestic fishing of cod along the northern coasts of Newfoundland and Labrador in 1992. Even the fishing of cod for personal use was stopped. The moratorium was later

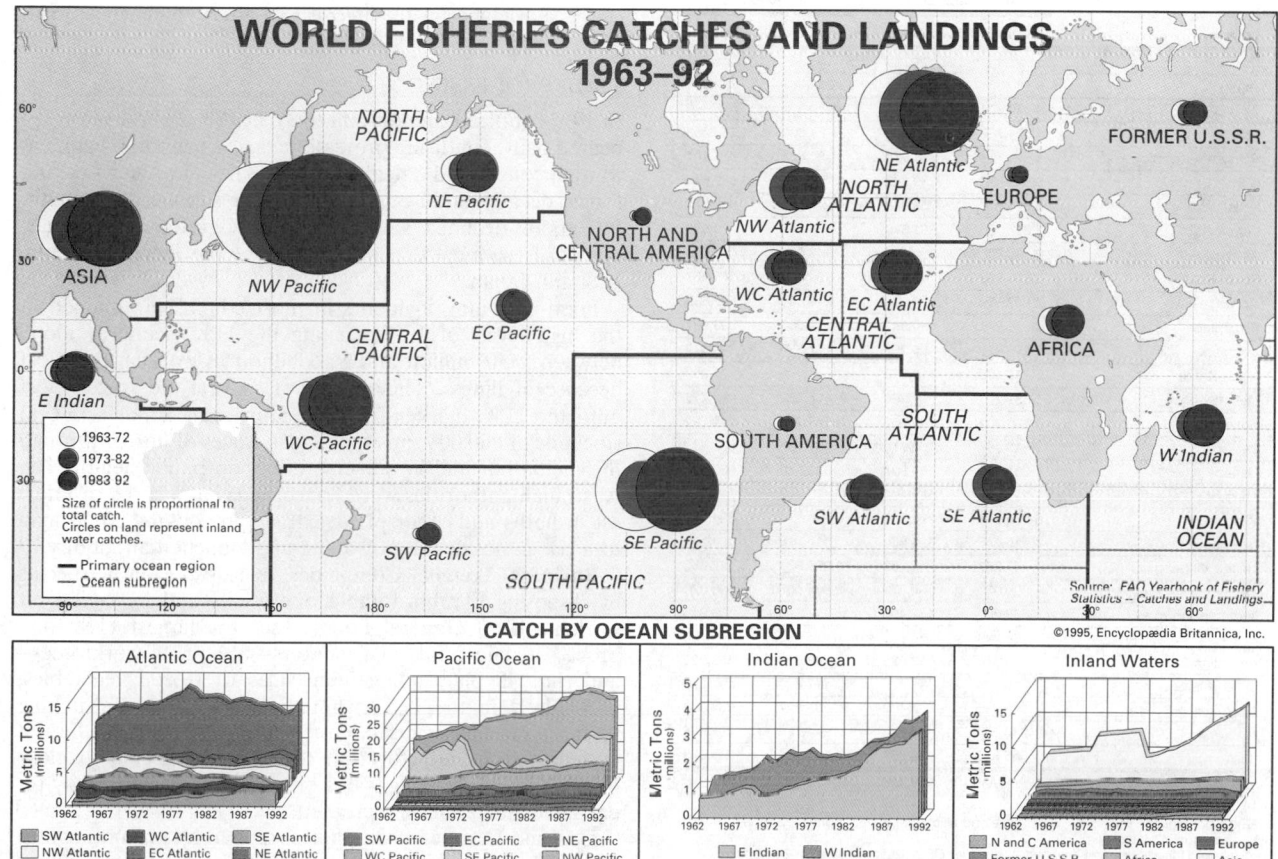

WORLD FISHERIES CATCHES AND LANDINGS 1963–92

Size of circle is proportional to total catch.
Circles on land represent inland water catches.

— Primary ocean region
— Ocean subregion

1963-72
1973-82
1983-92

Source: FAO Yearbook of Fishery Statistics – Catches and Landings

CATCH BY OCEAN SUBREGION

©1995, Encyclopædia Britannica, Inc.

extended and introduced for other species. The vital fishing industry in this region was decimated; upwards of 50,000 fishermen and fish-processing workers lost their livelihoods. The Canadians were infuriated by illegal operations by boats from the European Union (EU) and other countries operating on the Grand Banks in international waters outside Canada's 200-mi EEZ. These fishermen vastly exceeded agreed catch quotas for some species, sometimes by more than 16 times. (*See* LIFE SCIENCES: *Zoology.*)

Media attention in Western Europe was focused during the summer of 1994 on the tuna fishery in the Bay of Biscay off France and Spain. The long-standing tensions between Spanish traditional tuna "pole and line" fishermen and the French and British drift-net fishermen, who compete for bonito tuna during the short summer season, erupted into violence in July 1994. Spanish vessels surrounded French and British vessels and cut away their drift nets. The Spanish fishermen claimed that the drift-net vessels were using nets longer than the 2.5-km (1.6-mi) maximum allowed under EU legislation and were indiscriminately entrapping all bonito, including undersized fish. This, they claimed, was depleting spawning stocks and imperiling the shoals for future years. The French and British fishermen claimed that while the drift nets appeared to exceed the 2.5-km limit, they in fact consisted of lengths of net interspersed with large gaps to allow passage of marine mammals and, therefore, the total length of actual net sections did not exceed the legal limits. The real problem, however, was that the use of drift nets allowed French fishermen to capture three times as many tuna per boat as the traditional Spanish vessels while employing only half the crew.

Table XI. World Fisheries, 1992[1]

Country	Catch in 000 metric tons		Trade in $000,000	
	Total	Inland	Imports	Exports
China	15,007,450	6,217,185	680,844	1,559,961
Japan	8,460,324	187,169	12,831,762	792,369
Peru	6,842,700	29,532	960	470,900
Chile	6,501,767	12,492	21,892	1,252,363
Russian Federation	5,611,164	378,011	34,854	826,467
U.S.	5,602,876	339,369	6,024,064	3,582,545
India	4,175,112	1,702,061	—	615,377
Indonesia	3,357,700	861,570	56,145	1,178,552
Thailand	2,855,000	233,000	942,090	3,071,780
South Korea	2,695,630	45,038	504,853	1,365,867
Norway	2,549,130	580	346,048	2,436,832
Philippines	2,271,917	580,987	111,000	393,997
Denmark	1,995,025	36,287	1,197,370	2,319,917
North Korea	1,750,100	110,000	—	71,980
Iceland	1,557,207	866	14,232	1,252,713
Spain	1,330,000	29,550	2,898,232	712,729
Taiwan	1,313,987	160,710	489,176	1,803,399
Canada	1,251,018	64,907	686,876	2,085,495
Mexico	1,247,622	169,406	73,646	316,799
Vietnam	1,080,279	270,598	—	324,342
Bangladesh	966,727	686,600	60	151,200
United Kingdom	847,267	16,083	1,906,861	1,147,686
France	800,000	52,270	2,934,589	955,379
Myanmar (Burma)	800,000	182,400	—	33,915
Brazil	790,000	210,000	133,508	170,808
Argentina	705,316	13,029	48,173	559,029
South Africa	695,318	2,375	117,000	190,250
New Zealand	679,288	1,452	33,627	654,533
Malaysia	640,000	16,000	244,789	294,636
Italy	555,876	54,991	2,643,440	258,525
World Total	**98,112,800**	**15,578,600**	**45,451,914**	**40,275,588**

[1]Excludes aquatic mammals, crocodiles and alligators, pearls, corals, sponges, and aquatic plants.
Source: United Nations Food and Agriculture Organization, *Yearbook of Fishery Statistics*, vols. 74 and 75.

These examples only hint at the seriousness and global nature of the problem. During the year, Iceland sent gunboats against Norwegian trawlers in the latest outbreak of the North Atlantic "cod war." In a curious echo of the Cold War of the late 1950s, there were casualties as China and Taiwan disputed fishing rights off the island of Quemoy in the Taiwan Strait. The U.K. and Argentina were at it again over the Falkland Islands/Islas Malvinas, this time disputing squid-fishing rights. Even abject Somalia complained about EU fishermen taking one of its few remaining resources—lobsters—in the Gulf of Aden.

One country with a good opportunity to start afresh in the development and management of a sustainable fishing industry was Namibia. Following years of exploitation of the abundant fish stocks off its coast, with the attendant problems of overfishing and declining fish catches, Namibia at a stroke rid its fishing grounds of virtually all foreign fishing-vessel operators upon gaining independence in 1990. Since then the government had pursued a variety of strategic aims, including conserving stocks, maximizing local employment, and developing and diversifying the fishing industry in a coherent and rational manner.

Meeting in May, the International Whaling Commission voted to create a sanctuary free from commercial whaling in the waters south of Africa, South America, and Australia. Japan voted against the measure and also caused some consternation in November when it announced that it would sell some 65 tons of meat from minke whales caught for research purposes. Norway also continued its defiance of the 1987 international moratorium on whaling, announcing a quota of 301 minke for 1994. Finally, it was reported in February that the U.S.S.R. had consistently underreported its whaling catch by as much as one-half from the 1960s through the 1980s, which possibly would affect current estimates of the world whale population.   (MARTIN J. GILL)

This article updates the *Macropædia* article Commercial FISHING.

FOOD PROCESSING

In 1994 conflicting reports on food, health, and nutrition appeared daily, confusing professionals and consumers alike as to what constituted a healthful diet. Sales of reduced-calorie foods, decaffeinated coffee, and other supposedly "healthful" foods declined slightly in most developed countries; sales of fresh meat declined in Europe but increased in the U.S. and Japan.

Food-poisoning incidents in most countries remained at the high levels of 1993, costing the U.K. economy alone between $750 million and $1.5 billion in working days lost because of illness. The release of six-year-old frozen beef onto the U.K. market from the European Union's (EU's) stockpile of 860,000 tons sent shock waves of horror through the media but had no adverse effect on public health. The Australian authorities were concerned that a surge of interest in herbs and other plant extracts in cooking could lead to a rise in accidental poisoning and launched an inquiry.

Business Trends. Companies worldwide slashed costs by disposing of unprofitable operations and by laying off workers. Kraft General Foods, Inc., the largest U.S. food processor, laid off 14,000 workers—8% of its workforce—and shut 40 plants. Declining sales of frozen vegetables, particularly in the U.S., where consumers were switching to fresh produce, caused Green Giant, the second largest frozen-food manufacturer in the U.S., to decide to close four plants. Meanwhile, sales of chilled foods and ready-to-eat, shelf-stable meals increased.

U.S. and European companies stepped up promotions for children's products, often drawing criticism from consumer groups that claimed this encouraged unhealthful eating among children. Character merchandising, whereby companies acquired licenses to use popular film and cartoon characters in their brand logos, increased; for example, "dinosaur mania" swept global markets following the success in 1993 of the film *Jurassic Park*.

The conclusion of the General Agreement on Tariffs and Trade (GATT) negotiations promised increased opportunities for food and drink exporters. A cut in tariffs on a huge range of imports was likely to increase world income by more than $200 billion by the year 2000.

Manufacturers' profits in some countries were reduced by the increasing number of supermarkets' own-brand products and by the speed with which copycat products were brought onto the market. The Coca-Cola Co. prevailed upon the U.K.'s largest supermarket chain, Sainsbury's, to stop selling their cola in cans that resembled those of Coke. Sainsbury's look-alike instant coffee was in line for similar action by Nestlé. U.K. trademark protection was extended to cover the appearance of a package as well as the logo.

Sales of prepackaged nonalcoholic beverages surged on the European market, especially in Germany, boosted by increased demand for mineral waters and fruit juices. U.S. soft drink consumption remained static for the fourth consecutive year, although it exceeded that of all other beverages.

Major marketing changes took place in the British dairy industry as a result of the abolition of the Milk Marketing Board, which had fixed prices. Prices of milk and dairy products were expected to rise, a situation made worse by the EU's quota system for milk.

Technology. A new Japanese production method called single-cell technology involved using an enzyme to break down vegetables and fruits into cell units in order to produce liquid and powder ingredients of foods and beverages. A Japanese company, Single Cell Foods, started using the technology, which gained approval by the U.S. Food and Drug Administration.

By altering the structure of a natural enzyme used in cheese manufacture, two Japanese companies, NEC Corp. and Yakult Honsha, jointly developed an artificial enzyme potentially able to produce new types of food. Tetra Laval of Sweden launched Ovotherm, a system for processing and packaging liquid egg products that eliminated *Salmonella* and *Listeria* bacteria and reduced bacterial count to a level unattainable by other methods.

The U.K. government approved the use of a new genetically modified yeast that simplified brewing, improved beer quality, and cut costs. It was the first such new yeast strain to be approved for beer production. Roche Products of the U.K. developed a new method of refining fish oil that retained nutritive properties while removing taste, allowing food products to be nutritionally enhanced without affecting their flavour.

Air Products Co. of the U.K. launched a freezing process called zero adhesion technology (ZAT) based on the principle that nothing will stick to a surface that has been cooled to $-80°$ C ($-176°$ F) or below. The process allowed multilayer ice cream products of complex shape, such as realistic reproductions of popular characters, to be easily produced, a key factor in the market for children's products.

New Products and Ingredients. The first user of ZAT, Rowntree's of the U.K., launched Fruit Pastil-Lolly, a cross between a lollipop and an ice cream, the first sugar confectionery brand in the U.K. ice cream sector. White chocolate emerged as a global craze, particularly in the U.K., France, and Brazil.

Physicians in New Zealand claimed that honey derived from a tree growing there could eliminate certain bacteria from infected people and that it was cheaper than and just as effective in the treatment of some stomach disorders as antibiotics.

Packaging. After declining for two decades, glass containers began a comeback for food and drink applications, encouraged by the environmental friendliness of glass, its healthy image, and an increase in opportunities to recycle it.

AseptiCan, a cylindrical paperboard package for liquid foods, was launched in Europe jointly by United Paper Mills of the U.K., which made the paperboard, and Michael Höraul Maschinenfabrik of Germany, which made the forming machinery. Convenience, novel appearance, microwavability, and recyclability were its main advantages. The first customer was Finland's largest food packer, Valio Oy, which used the pack for juice drinks.

Company Developments. Grand Metropolitan, a U.K. food and drinks producer and owner of Pillsbury of the U.S., sold its U.S. pet food subsidiary Alpo to Nestlé for $510 million, at the same time engaging in a $420 million restructuring operation and shedding 4,000 jobs worldwide. In May Sandoz Ltd., a Swiss drug and chemicals firm, bought Gerber Products Co., the leading U.S. producer of baby foods, for $3.7 billion. Unilever, an Anglo-Dutch firm and the biggest spender on food research-and-development in the world, increased its research and development spending by 12%. Two major U.K. research organizations, Campden Food Research Association and the Flour Milling and Baking Research Association, announced that they planned to merge on Jan. 1, 1995.

Pfizer Food Science Group, part of the New York-based Pfizer Inc., opened its first European technical service laboratory, at Sandwich, England, and announced plans for two more labs, in France and Germany, adding to those already established in the U.S., Australia, and Japan. APV of the U.K. won a $24 million contract to equip a dairy plant in Harad, Saudi Arabia. The first of its kind in the country, it would be designed to process 375,000 litres (99,000 gal) of milk per day.

Coca-Cola announced plans to build a $26 million bottling plant in Qingdao (Tsingtao), China, bringing to 23 the number of its plants in the country. Kraft General Foods International Inc. announced in late 1993 a joint venture to build a $42 million dairy products plant in Beijing (Peking). Also in late 1993 Kraft's European subsidiary, Kraft Jacobs Suchard, bought a controlling interest in Kaunas Confectionery Co. of Lithuania, which produced 7,000 tons per year of confectionery products.

Antinori, one of Italy's oldest Chianti producers, bought Atlas Peak, a company in California's Napa Valley producing high-quality wines. It was one-third the size of Antinori's Italian holdings. After eight years of litigation, the Swedish Tetra Laval Group, the world's largest privately owned beverage and liquid foods packaging company, lost its appeal against the $45 million fine from the European Commission for breaking the EU's competition rules. This was the largest fine ever imposed by the commission.

Government Action. Food law continued to advance strongly in 1994, and so did efforts at deregulation and simplification. An attack on the growing complexity of EU draft food laws was made by the European Commission president, particularly in regard to novel and genetically modified foods. The European Commission was pressing for harmonization of national laws covering nearly 3,000 flavourings used by food companies, but discussions were likely to be contentious.

Fears about consumer confidence in milk and meat products prompted the European Commission to demand a seven-year extension of the European ban on the genetically engineered growth hormone bovine somatotropin (BST). Fears of a trade confrontation with the U.S., where the drug was developed, grew with the ending in September of a 15-month moratorium on the use of BST imposed by the U.S. Senate in June 1993.   (ANTHONY WOOLLEN)

See also Business and Industry Review: *Beverages; Tobacco;* Environment; Health and Disease.

This article updates the *Macropædia* article FOOD PROCESSING.

Anthropology

The discovery of fossil evidence in Ethiopia supporting the evolutionary divergence of humans and apes roughly 4.5 million to 6 million years ago, long predicted on the basis of molecular evidence, was announced in 1994. Consisting of teeth, jaw fragments, a skull base, and an arm, the fossils were classified as a new species of hominid, *Australopithecus ramidus*. The bones, which are both chimpanzee-like and humanlike, were securely dated at 4.4 million years, placing *A. ramidus* at or near the point at which the human ancestral line split from the apes (*see* Figure). Initial evidence indicated that the species may have been a bipedal woodland dweller. Given some of the arboreal anatomic features of more recent hominid fossils (including the *A. afarensis* fossil known as Lucy), it is possible that upright posture evolved quite some time before the specialized ground-dwelling, two-legged, striding gait of modern humans.

During 1993–94 new Ethiopian finds belonging to *A. afarensis* were announced. The hominids lived from nearly four million to three million years ago in both open-dry and open-wet forest environments. Some disagreement existed about the reason for the diversity in size seen in their skeletons (was it sexual dimorphism or the existence of separate species?) and about their bipedalism (could they really have made the footprints found at Laetoli?). The new discoveries—one being the first complete skull for the species (*see* Figure)—tended to support the argument that variation in size was due to male-female differences, but the issue of tree-climbing versus ground-walking ability remained unresolved.

New research on the human ancestor *Homo erectus* included the recovery of an almost complete skull from Java in 1993, tentatively dated as being 500,000 to 700,000 years old. Of greater significance was a 1994 report on a new age estimate, by means of a state-of-the-art technology called argon-argon dating, of the well-known *H. erectus* fossils from Mojokerto and Sangiran in Java. Originally estimated at 1,000,000

and 800,000 years old, respectively, the fossils yielded astonishing new ages of 1.8 million and 1.6 million years. It had been thought that *H. erectus* originated in Africa 1.8 million years ago and then migrated to Asia about a million years later. The new dates indicated that the species is apparently equally old on both continents or, if it first evolved in Africa (which was still believed to be the case), it migrated to Asia soon thereafter. An alternate explanation was that the African and Asian fossils represent different species. This seemed highly unlikely, however, since *H. habilis*, the presumed ancestor of *H. erectus*, had never been found in Asia (nor had any of the australopithecines).

Scientific debate continued over two, and possibly three, models for the origin of modern humans. What started it all was the discovery of anatomically modern human skulls of an unexpectedly early date (perhaps 120,000 years old) in South Africa and the analysis of a type of noncoding DNA, mitochondrial transfer DNA (mtDNA), gathered from living humans around the world, which indicated that the human populations with the most variable DNA sequences, and thus the oldest, were also African. Subsequent analysis of noncoding DNA sequences from cell nuclei yielded similar results. Furthermore, at least one case of replacement by an anatomically modern human population of, in this case, a

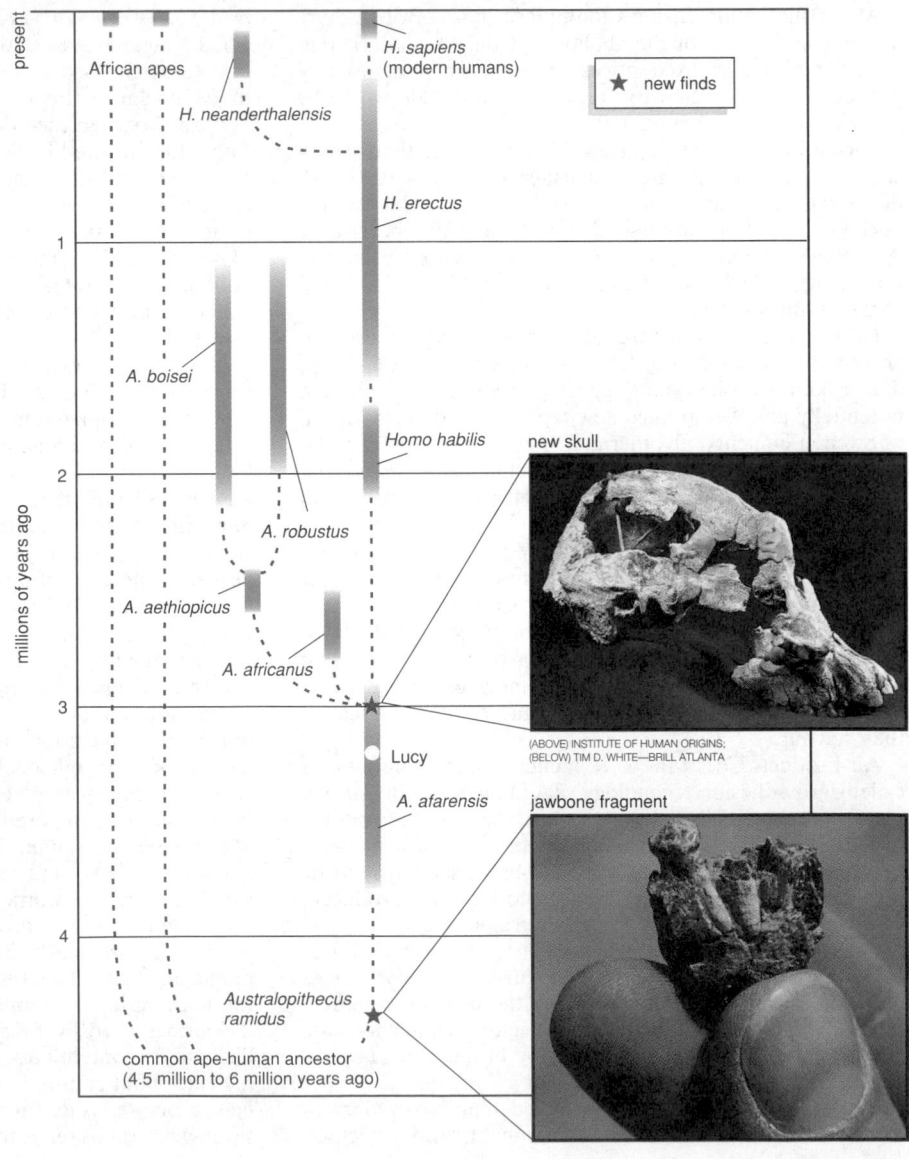

new skull

(ABOVE) INSTITUTE OF HUMAN ORIGINS;
(BELOW) TIM D. WHITE—BRILL ATLANTA

jawbone fragment

Neanderthal (*H. neanderthalensis*) population in Israel, was documented. Modern humans lived in the Levant while Neanderthals lived in Europe. Thus, when the latter traveled south to caves in Israel, modern humans already had been there thousands of years.

Although the interpretation of the evidence was debated, it was part of the "single-origin" model, which proposed that one early population of modern humans spread out of Africa and eventually replaced all less modern populations of *Homo* worldwide. Support for the opposing "regional-continuity" model was based primarily on evidence of gradual morphological change, mainly of the skull, from ancient to modern inhabitants in different areas of the world. The model seemed to work best with some Asian populations.

Recently a new model began attracting scientific interest. It suggested that about 65,000 years ago a large number of small groups of modern humans radiated out of Africa into Europe and Asia. Altogether only 100,000 migrants may have been involved. Survival was difficult, resulting in so-called genetic bottlenecks that caused the groups to become somewhat genetically distinct from one another over time. Nevertheless, by about 50,000 years ago, with the worst of the last Pleistocene ice age behind them, the groups dispersed all over the Old World and experienced population explosions. The peoples of the world today are the result of that process. The model is based on the historical demography and genetics of modern human populations. In both this model and the single-origin model, the genetic differences that exist today between the peoples of the world would not be very old. In the regional-continuity model, however, they would be quite old, reflecting differences that may have existed since the dispersal of *H. erectus* out of Africa.

The recent impetus for research into the origin and dispersion of modern humans came from the realization that noncoding DNA, both nuclear and mitochondrial, in human cells serves as a kind of historical document about the relationships between living people. Not only does the degree of similarity between DNA samples indicate the degree of shared heredity, but it also indicates how long ago any two groups diverged from a common ancestor. Only natural selection can interfere with this historical interpretation of DNA, but because all human populations today are far more similar genetically than they are different, most of their DNA differences must be due to limits on gene flow and genetic drift.

Thus, to understand human "genetic geography," one needs prehistoric and historic information, particularly about migrations and factors that affect population size. Since by the mid-1990s the amount of genetic information from all over the world was quite extensive and was usable in conjunction with archaeological, ethnohistorical, and linguistic data, a detailed picture of modern human evolution was beginning to emerge. Among some of the findings from this research to date: (1) linguistic differences between populations do parallel genetic differences; (2) craniometric differences (differences in the dimensions and proportions of the skull in different populations) also parallel genetic differences; (3) the spread of farming involved the spread of farmers, not just their technology; (4) the Ainu of Japan, long thought to have Caucasoid characteristics, are indeed northeastern Asians; (5) after the Lapps, the Scandinavians are genetically most divergent from other populations in Europe; (6) the Basques are the indigenous descendants of Paleolithic and Neolithic peoples; and (7) according to an analysis of mtDNA taken from ancient bones, the prehistoric inhabitants of Easter Island were of Polynesian origin.

The same broad-based research strategy, when applied to the question of the origin of American Indians, also led to some interesting and controversial findings. Analysis of mtDNA confirmed an Asian origin for American Indians, the speakers of Amerind-group languages having four kinds of Asian mtDNA and the speakers of Na-Dene–group languages having only one of the four. Whether this difference represents two separate migrations from Asia to North America or a loss of three mtDNA types from part of the descendants of a single migration (due to genetic drift) was debated. Moreover, the diversity that exists in the Amerind speakers indicated a much longer period of existence in the New World, as long as 42,000 years, compared with perhaps 12,500 years for the Na-Dene. The former date is very much earlier than was generally accepted.

A group of anthropologists and other scientists formed the Human Genome Diversity Project to address the problems of sampling the genetic diversity of the human species. Given the large number of populations globally and the rapid rate of disappearance of the smaller isolated populations, gathering a representative sample of human genetic diversity posed a real challenge. (HERMANN K. BLEIBTREU)

See also Archaeology.

This article updates the *Macropædia* article Human EVOLUTION.

Archaeology

Eastern Hemisphere. Old World archaeology suffered in 1994 from political circumstances in the Near East, in southeastern Europe, and in various parts of Africa and Asia, which understandably were not encouraging to field excavations. The number of yearly summaries on fieldwork given in the *American Journal of Archaeology* for some areas of Europe and for the Near East—but not, understandably, for countries such as Iran and Iraq—continued to increase.

Heinrich Schliemann recovered a spectacular amount of gold artifacts in the site of Troy in the late 1800s and presented the "gold of Troy" to a Berlin Museum. During World War II it disappeared, but it was recently reported to be safely stored in a Moscow museum. The Russians were considering returning it—but to whom? An international conference was scheduled in Moscow to discuss the matter. Troy is in Turkey, and the Turks requested the collection; Greece claimed it, believing Troy's antecedents were Greek; and Germany claimed it since the artifacts were Schliemann's gift to them.

The Institute of Paleolithic Culture in Japan reported the recovery of stone tools (hand axes, choppers, cleavers) of about 600,000 years ago. Given the region and the time, it was thought that these finds might relate to *Pithecanthropus* of Java. In northern Greece an impressive hand ax about 200,000 years old was recovered. Joint Russian and American work in the northwest Caucasus recovered sites of Mousterian hunters, while a French and American study was made of the faunal remains of the classic Mousterian cave sites at La Quina.

The lost half of a group of famous "Venus" figurines, about 18,000–25,000 years old, found in the Grimaldi cave in Italy in 1883, was recovered. The original finder, Louis Jullien, moved from France to Canada, apparently taking the missing pieces with him. A sculptor found the lost figurines in an antique shop in Montreal.

Knowledge of prehistoric art in Europe was enriched by two major finds. Archaeologists exploring a cave in the Ardèche River canyon in southern France discovered a gallery decorated with some 300 paintings of an astonishing variety of prehistoric animals, including bison, rhinoceroses, bears, horses, panthers, and owls. Thought to be 20,000 years old, the images were being compared to the world-famous cave art found at Lascaux, France, and Altamira, Spain. In northern Portugal a discovery of comparable age came to light: images of more than 60 animals such as bison, horses, ibexes, and deer chiseled with stone tools into the rock face along a deep gorge of the Côa River. The carvings, already partly covered by backed-up water from a dam on the Douro River, were being threatened with complete inundation by a second dam under construction in the region. News of the discovery came amid charges that knowledge of the prehistoric site's existence had been kept quiet for more than two years to allow building of the second dam to proceed.

To the extent that field work could be done in southwestern Asia, the attention to sites yielding evidence of agricultural beginnings continued. Particularly remarkable was the evidence for early pig domestication at Hallan Cemi in southeastern Turkey. Round or U-shaped house plans indicated year-round occupation around 10,500 years before the present. The site's early date and locality challenged the general current assumption that the beginnings of food production began only in the Levant (south and west Syria, Lebanon, Israel, and Jordan).

Excavations were especially active in southern Turkey and north-central Syria at sites yielding materials of the earlier urban periods. Public buildings with impressive wall paintings continued at the University of Rome's Arslantepe site near Malatya, and there were various other locations of interest farther south in the Euphrates valley in Turkey yielding further hints of Uruk (southern Mesopotamian) connections. There was also activity in northeastern Syria, where tributaries flow to the Euphrates. A Belgian expedition fueled the growing interest in the early literate range with a find of pre-Sargonid tablets at Tell Beidar. While many archaeologists working within the Euphrates drainage system might have preferred to work in southern Mesopotamia (Iraq), their enforced choices had nonetheless succeeded in opening a new area of considerable interest.

Excavations at sites of the historic ranges in Israel and Jordan were focused on sites in the later historic ranges, although work on the early village site of 'Ain Ghazal in Jordan continued. Many of the exposed Israeli sites appeared to have been of 1,000 BC or later, but interesting Chalcolithic materials appeared on Tell Shiqmim—a joint American, French, and Israeli excavation. Impressive Late Bronze Age architecture continued to appear on Tell Hazor. Several teams made new clearances at Petra, Jordan.

A variety of interesting excavations were reported north and west of the Tigris-Euphrates drainage—surely a reflection of the favourable prevailing circumstances for field work. At Troy a burned level discovered below Troy I, Schliemann's earliest excavations, demonstrated still earlier settlement, and broad later clearances (Troy II–VI) were made. More details of the tin mining and smelting at Goltepe-Kestel were recovered. Excavations on the long-worked sites of the later Bronze and Iron Age ranges and of Greco-Roman and Byzantine times continued.

The lack of field news from Egypt in 1994 reflected, to some degree, the prevailing political tension and perhaps the interest of some archaeologists there in not encouraging hordes of tourists. An Old Kingdom stone-paved road, about 12 km (7.5 mi) long, was cleared. It appeared to have facilitated the transportation of good stone for monumental use at Giza. In Sinai, near Egypt's border with Israel, a huge Roman fortress and large town were exposed in a region being cleared for a new agricultural development canal.

In early Europe continued study added to information about the life of "Ötzi," the 5,300-year-old "Iceman," whose frozen remains were found in the Ötz valley high in the Alps

in 1991. Both the body itself and more than 20 artifacts and clothing had aroused much interest. In southern Russia and Kazakhstan, an impressive amount of evidence concerning the very early development of wheels (on remains of chariots) was recovered. Vast areas being prepared for drainage for agriculture, in the fenlands of eastern England, yielded over 2,000 sites (7th millennium BC to medieval times).

In Greece much interest turned to the clearance and yield of the site of the battle of Actium, near Corinth. The identification of ash (from a datable ice core taken in Greenland) was believed to fix the date of the Santorini volcanic eruption that buried the Minoan colony there at about 1623 BC. The eruption may well have given rise to the Atlantis legend.

As the centre of Athens was laid partially bare in recent months for the construction of a subway, graves dated from the 5th century BC as well as materials of later Byzantine and Turkish times were being recovered. The general dearth of archaeological news from Greece might be ascribed to something of a xenophobic attitude on the part of the country's antiquity service or possibly to the tensions between successive Greek governments (for example, Melina Mercouri [see OBITUARIES], who served as minister of culture under the former Socialist government, was an energetic campaigner for the return of the Elgin Marbles to Greece).

In Lugnano, a town on the Tiber River 110 km (70 mi) north of Rome, a large 5th-century AD children's cemetery was being exposed—thus far, 49 skeletons had been recovered. Skeletal evidence pointed strongly to a plague of malaria mentioned in contemporary records. Attila the Hun may have cut short his invasion of Italy because of a fear of malaria. Similarly, a comparative study of the depictions of women on the Pompei frescoes with physical evidence from their skulls indicated hyperostosis frontalis interna, a hormonal disorder. At Suffolk, a Roman British site, 14,780 gold and silver coins, tableware, jewelry, and other ornaments were found and officially declared "treasure trove," thus the property of the Crown.

On the Chiang Jiang (Yangtze River) in China, where a new dam and flood plain was under construction, a government project began to recover a vast amount of archaeological materials spanning as much as 7,000 years. Many tombs and great quantities of pottery, porcelain, jade, and stoneware objects had already been recovered.

On a beach dune of Lake Victoria in New South Wales, Australia, a huge necropolis was located, with expected evidence of as many as 10,000 skeletons. The ancient people seem to have left their dead exposed on the sandy dunes, then bundled the disjointed bones for burial. The find suggested that far larger communities of hunter-gatherers existed before the arrival of Europeans than had been anticipated. (ROBERT J. BRAIDWOOD)

Western Hemisphere. New World archaeology in 1994 was marked by the announcement of important discoveries concerning the arrival and antiquity of humans in North America, the emergence of significant new evidence suggesting that the agricultural foundations of the Maya may have extended back to preceramic times, and the combining of traditional archaeological techniques with modern biotechnology to resolve a long-standing debate over the origins of tuberculosis in the New World.

It had been generally assumed that the first human immigrants to North America traveled from Siberia across a land bridge over the Bering Strait. They then moved from Alaska southward via an ice-free corridor through western Canada and down into the U.S. Southwest, where many artifacts of Paleo-Indians and extinct big game were first found. The early peoples were believed to have migrated

A figurine from a tomb in Mexico's Yucatán Peninsula resembles figures of goddesses associated with Teotihuacán. It was reported in 1994 that the investigation of two tombs in Mexico indicated classic Mayan cultural patterns to have been more widespread than previously thought.

JEANNE RANDALL—SELZ FOUNDATION YAXUNA PROJECT; SOUTHERN METHODIST UNIVERSITY

eastward from the Southwest to the Atlantic Coast several thousand years later. In the past year, however, the discovery of a mastodon tusk in deeply buried sediments below a river in Florida challenged the common wisdom about both the early migration routes and the causes for extinction of the mastodon, an early relative of the elephant, and other Late Pleistocene mammals.

A team led by David Webb of the University of Florida determined that the tusk, which showed clear signs of butchering by humans, is at least 12,200 years old, centuries older than similar documented activities in the Southwest. Well-preserved marks around the base of the bone tusk suggested that it had been cut off the carcass with sharp knifelike implements. Stone butchering tools were recovered at the site, including a razorlike stone flake for cutting and scraping, as were associated tools and weapons made of ivory and decorated with geometric designs. The Florida excavation now had to be considered the earliest butchering site in North America. The astonishing find supported a new scenario, one in which humans first migrated from Alaska across Canada and down the eastern seaboard, only later spreading to the Southwest. Likewise, the antiquity of the tusk—at least 1,000 years older than the dated human finds in the Southwest—suggested that instead of there having been a rapid killing off of big game through overhunting, mastodons and humans coexisted for at least a millennium.

The discovery of what may be the earliest evidence of Mayan culture, potentially pushing back the known origins of this ancient Mesoamerican civilization by some 1,500 years, was announced. Working in previously unstudied areas and deposits at the Colha site in northern Belize, a multidisciplinary team led by Thomas Hester of the University of Texas at Austin used radiocarbon dating of pollen cores, botanical identification of the contents of buried refuse pits,

and analysis of a set of agricultural tools to establish that the ancient inhabitants were actually engaged in land clearing and the cultivation of domestic crops as early as 2500 BC, long before the introduction of the distinctive Mayan ceramics that were traditionally interpreted as the initial indicators for the advent of settled society in Mesoamerica. Distinctive chipped and carved stone tools with hoelike or axlike edges were similar to those of the later classic Mayan sites, suggesting cultural continuity over time. In addition, shifts in the range and diversity of the natural plants were documented through pollen evidence and indicated that swamp areas bordering the site had been drained. Maize (corn) and manioc pollen identified in refuse-pit deposits suggested that the inhabitants were early agriculturists, present perhaps 1,500 years earlier than previous projections for the earliest manifestations of this culture.

The 1932 discovery by Alfonso Caso y Andrade of Tomb Seven at Monte Albán, Mexico, renowned for the whole gold mask and pectoral (chest piece) it contained, remains one of the most spectacular single discoveries in New World archaeology. Heated controversy over the site broke out in 1994 over a reinterpretation of the identity of the human skeletal remains in that tomb. Sharisse and Geoffrey McCafferty, associated with Brown University, Providence, R.I., announced that one of the skeletons, which had been thought to be that of a great king or priest, may in fact be that of a queen or priestess. The McCaffertys based their surprising reinterpretation on the fact that one of the original researchers at Monte Albán had belatedly included a female jawbone among the inventory of the contents of the tomb. Furthermore, the site contained a wide assortment of artifacts commonly taken as indicators of female activities—weaving batons, including an assortment of full size and miniature spinning tools, and small "spinning bowls" on which the base of a spindle is rested when it is twirled— as well as two miniature gold rings that the archaeologists suggested may have served as ritual thimbles. This reinterpretation could result in a radical shift away from the former predication of a predominantly male power structure in ancient Mesoamerican society. It could cause reexamination of artifacts from other early sites to see if they contain similar evidence of elevated status of women. The debate went into high gear when the McCaffertys' reassessment, which some perceived as long overdue, came under attack from others, notably Kent Flannery and Joyce Marcus of the University of Michigan, who charged that the McCaffertys, in the words of a *Science News* article, "parlayed a political concern about inequalities heaped upon women in ancient and modern societies . . . to promote a vision of once-powerful Mixtec woman."

The first successful use of genetic analysis techniques in the study of ancient disease was reported in 1994 in research into the origin and antiquity of tuberculosis in the New World. While not enjoying the broad media coverage that forensic DNA testing received in U.S. criminal court cases during the year, the study of DNA genetic structure in tissue samples from ancient South American mummies nonetheless proved to be an important new diagnostic tool for researchers.

The story began in 1990 with the excavation of some 600 pre-Inca burials near the village of Ilo in southern Peru. Archaeologists Jane Burikstra and Todd Holcomb of the University of Chicago investigated some 600 graves in 11 prehistoric cemeteries in the valley belonging to highland peoples who had migrated down to this lowland desert drainage on the coast about 1000 BC. These migrants, as evinced by their distinctive Andean pottery, apparently dominated the lowland valley for at least 2,000 years, until just before the arrival of the Inca empire. About 140 of the burials contained the well-preserved, naturally mummified remains of 700–1,000-year-old individuals.

The archaeologists enlisted paleopathologist Arthur C. Aufderheide and molecular biologist Wilmar L. Salo both from the University of Minnesota, Duluth. Together they identified and extracted tissue samples from what appeared to be tubercular lesions in desiccated lung and lymph node tissue from the body of a 40–50-year-old woman. They then used a modern genetic testing procedure called polymerase chain reaction (PCR), which amplifies traces of ancient DNA by an amount sufficient to permit the identification of particular DNA types—in this case the ancient "molecular fingerprints" of the tuberculosis-causing bacterium. This new tool of DNA analysis thus provided unequivocal evidence that tuberculosis existed in the New World at least 1,000 years before the arrival of the first Europeans and demonstrated that the disease probably evolved in the Americas independently of the European strains carried to the New World in the 15th century.

In addition to throwing new light on the antiquity of tuberculosis, an important disease worldwide, PCR also provided a new line of evidence for archaeologists to use in assessing such issues as the political and economic structure of the large pre-Inca settlements. Given the association of tuberculosis with poverty, crowded living conditions, and poor diet, it seemed probable that the ancient coastal population of Peru may have suffered under such conditions—a type of existence most people did not usually associate with societies predating the arrival of highly centralized empires and their expanded political and economic power.

(JOEL W. GROSSMAN)

See also Anthropology.

This article updates the *Macropædia* article The Study of History: *Archaeology*.

Architecture

Probably the most widely noted building of 1994 was the new home of the American Center, which opened in June on the Seine River in the Bercy neighbourhood of Paris. Designed by Los Angeles architect Frank O. Gehry (*see* BIOGRAPHIES), the centre contained stage and motion-picture theatres and a variety of other performance and exhibit spaces, as well as 26 apartments for resident scholars and artists.

Gehry employed the free-form tilting, curving, and colliding shapes that made him famous, but they seemed tamer than usual because of the traditional warm-toned limestone in which the entire building was clad. Many critics noted the appropriateness of the choice of Gehry, among the most innovative of contemporary U.S. architects, as designer of the American Center, which was founded in 1931 to promote French understanding of U.S. culture.

A more typically wacky Gehry design, the Frederick R. Weisman Art Museum, opened late in 1993 at the University of Minnesota. Known to students as "the Fred," it was a childlike jumble of shapes on a bluff overlooking the Mississippi River, with several facades clad in brushed stainless steel that reflected the sky and the sunset.

Awards. The Pritzker Architecture Prize, which bills itself as the equivalent of a Nobel Prize, retained its rank as the most prestigious architectural award despite a glut of rival $100,000-plus prizes. The 1994 Pritzker was awarded to Christian de Portzamparc, a French architect whose best-known work was the Cité de la Musique, a school for music and dance in Paris. The award ceremony was held in Columbus, Ind., as a way of honouring the town and its remarkable collection of works by modern architects. The Pritzker jury called Portzamparc "a powerful poet of forms and creator of eloquent spaces" and spoke of his "exuberant collage of contemporary architectural idioms, at once bold, colorful, and original."

Among other awards, the American Institute of Architects (AIA) gave its 1995 Gold Medal, its highest award for lifetime achievement, to Cesar Pelli. Pelli was born in Argentina, served as dean of the School of Architecture at Yale University from 1977 to 1984, and established a practice in New Haven, Conn. He was known for his buildings with a lightweight, almost tentlike, appearance, often surfaced in glass or thin stone veneer. Among his best-known works were the Pacific Design Center in Los Angeles, the World Financial Center in New York City, Herring Hall at Rice University, Houston, Texas, and Carnegie Hall Tower in New York City. The AIA named the Ford Foundation Headquarters in New York City as recipient of its 1995 Twenty-Five-Year Award, given to a building whose design has stood the test of time. The architect was Kevin Roche of Kevin Roche John Dinkeloo and Associates, with Dan Kiley as landscape architect. The AIA also named 17 buildings by U.S. architects as recipients of its annual Honor Awards for good design. Among the most prominent were Carnegie Hall Tower by Pelli, Oriole Park at Camden Yards baseball stadium in Baltimore, Md., by Hellmuth Obata & Kassabaum, and the United States Holocaust Memorial Museum in Washington, D.C., by James Ingo Freed, a New York City architect. The Gold Medal of the Royal Institute of British Architects went to Michael and Patty Hopkins, known for their marriage of high technology with tradition in such works as the new Glyndebourne opera house in England.

Civic Buildings. Of all types of buildings, it was those designed for transportation that dominated the world of architecture in 1994. The most spectacular was in Japan—the $14 billion Kansai International Airport, which opened in September. It was built on an island created from landfill in 18 m (59 ft) of water in Osaka Bay, connected to the mainland by a 3-km (1.85-mi)-long double-deck bridge. The building itself was 1.6 km (1 mi) long and four stories high under a single curving metal roof. The terminal's architect was Renzo Piano of Italy.

In France the Lyon airport railway station opened as a railroad station linked to an older airport, thus bringing users of cars, trains, and airplanes together beneath a structure of concrete ribs that resembled the skeleton of a vast whale. The architect was Santiago Calatrava of Spain.

In England a new Waterloo terminal, at the British end of the new Channel Tunnel, imitated the great glass-roofed railroad stations of the 19th century. Its architect was Nicholas Grimshaw. In the United States, Denver (Colo.) International Airport, the largest in the country, covered 137 sq km (53 sq mi) and included parking for 12,000 cars. Its main terminal, roofed in Teflon-coated tensile fabric, was the world's largest tent and looked, as one critic noted, like a Sioux encampment on the plain. The team of architects included August Perez and the firm of C.W. Fentress J.H. Bradburn & Associates. Designed and built with great speed in just over four years, the airport caused frustration when it failed to open on time because nobody could figure out how to get its $200 million automated baggage-handling system to work. Scheduled to open in late 1993, Denver was still not operational at the end of 1994, a delay that caused severe cost overruns.

In Washington, D.C., a new embassy for Finland by Mikko Heikkinen and Markku Komonen was an elegant collage of

Frank Gehry's new home for the American Center opened in Paris during the year. A playful structure using glass, zinc, and limestone among other materials, the building includes a theatre, a school, a bookstore, dance and visual arts studios, a restaurant, apartments, and parking.
ERICH KOYAMA

glass, copper, bronze, stainless steel, polished granite, and natural wood, held together by taut nautical detailing. It faced the street with a wall of leaves and flowers—a three-story bronze trellis planted with rose and clematis vines.

Cultural Buildings. A remarkable concentration of architectural energy occurred at Yerba Buena Gardens in San Francisco, just south of the city's downtown, where several internationally known architects created a cultural complex. Its core was a Center for the Arts designed by Fumihiko Maki of Japan and James Stewart Polshek of New York City. Maki's building contained a film and video theatre and a variety of exhibition and performance spaces and was surfaced on the outside with the architect's signature silver-toned finish. Polshek's building was a 755-seat theatre. Both structures stood atop the underground portion of a 185,000-sq m (2 million-sq ft) expansion of San Francisco's main convention facility, the Moscone Center; the expansion was designed by Freed.

Also part of the complex was an oval park, the Esplanade, by MGA Partners with Romaldo Giurgola. Scheduled to open in January 1995 across the street from Yerba Buena was a new San Francisco Museum of Modern Art by Swiss architect Mario Botta. It was a formal, symmetrical, blocky structure in red brick, topped by a huge elliptical skylight.

In Paris much attention surrounded the opening of the new Cartier building, which housed the company's headquarters as well as the Cartier Foundation for Contemporary Art. Designed by Jean Nouvel, the building contained exhibition spaces and was constructed of several transparent glass walls, one behind the other, creating elaborate depths and reflections.

In Santiago, Spain, a Galician Centre of Contemporary Art was under construction. Designed by Álvaro Siza, a Portuguese architect and winner of the Pritzker Prize, it was scheduled to open formally in 1995. The building, sited on a hillside and clad in gray granite, was to house a collection of regional art. Crisply modern, yet relaxed and angular, it

was already being hailed as a masterpiece. At the University of Wyoming, the Centennial Complex by Antoine Predock celebrated the Amerindian culture in a building shaped like a conical teepee.

In Managua, Nicaragua, a cathedral by Mexican architect Ricardo Legoretta replaced an earlier one destroyed by a 1972 earthquake. Built of raw concrete enlivened by bright colours, the cathedral was roofed by white bubblelike domes and featured a 34-m (111.5-ft) bell tower.

Exhibitions. The blockbuster architectural show of 1994 was "Frank Lloyd Wright: Architect," displayed at the Museum of Modern Art (MOMA) in New York City from February through May. It was the largest exhibit ever of the work of Wright, who lived from 1867 to 1959 and was usually regarded as the greatest U.S. architect. On view were over 450 drawings and photographs of famous Wright designs, from his early Prairie houses around Chicago to such later masterpieces as the vacation house "Fallingwater" in Pennsylvania and the Guggenheim Museum in New York City. The show included informative scale models of several of the buildings, including some that had been demolished or that were never built. For a time Manhattan—a place the car-loving, country-loving Wright always claimed he despised—seemed to have been turned over to the architect, as the Metropolitan Museum showed Wright's designs for furniture, ceramics, and textiles, while a number of art galleries displayed various other aspects of "Wrightiana."

MOMA was also host to "Bernard Tschumi: Architecture and Event." This exhibit featured the work of the controversial French-born architect Tschumi, the designer of the Parc de la Villette in Paris, who in 1994 was dean of the school of architecture at Columbia University, New York City.

In Montreal "Cities of Artificial Excavation: The Work of Peter Eisenman, 1978–1988" was on view from March through June at the Canadian Centre for Architecture. Eisenman, an avant-garde U.S. architect and teacher, designed the entire installation as a maze of twisting corridors

Swiss architect Mario Botta employs a number of basic geometric forms in his building for the San Francisco Museum of Modern Art. The museum, whose new building was completed in 1994, previously had been housed in cramped quarters in the War Memorial Veterans Building.
RICHARD BARNES

Industrial Revolution, especially in the U.S. Vast steel mills along the rivers of western Pennsylvania, as well as structures elsewhere such as grain elevators and bridges, attracted the interest of preservationists as those structures began to decay from abandonment. Once regarded as blighting scars on the landscape, the industrial relics were now viewed by some as powerful and haunting objects and important symbols of America's industrial past. Several "industrial heritage corridors" were proposed in different parts of the country.

In Paris the renovation of the Louvre Museum continued with the opening of the museum's Richelieu wing late in 1993. Part of a master plan for the museum by the U.S. architect I.M. Pei, the new wing, which once housed government offices, provided more than 12 ha (30 ac) of new space, most of it galleries for paintings and sculpture. (*See also* MUSEUMS.)

In Pittsburgh, Pa., the new Heinz Architectural Center at the Carnegie Museum of Art opened in November 1993 with plans for a series of thematic exhibitions. Already on permanent display was a complete suite of three rooms designed by Wright in 1951 as his San Francisco branch office.

Technology and Practice. A January earthquake in Los Angeles damaged some famous works of architecture and cultural history, including houses from the 1920s by Wright and the last surviving original "Golden Arch" McDonald's Restaurant, from 1953. The earthquake demonstrated the success of California's stringent building codes, which were upgraded in the 1970s and 1980s with earthquakes in mind. Little damage was suffered by buildings built or renovated in compliance with the codes, but it was noted that the 1994 quake had a modest magnitude of 6.7 and thus was no predictor of the performance of buildings in a future "big one"—the 8- or 9-point quake experts regarded as inevitable in Los Angeles.

In Chicago the prominent architect Stanley Tigerman and interior designer Eva Maddox opened a new school of architecture, which was to be called Archeworks. The school planned to combine design and research in an effort to develop socially conscious designs such as shelters for the homeless.

An unprecedented development boom in China was attracting the attention of architects around the globe. The world's most populous nation boasted the world's fastest-growing economy, a combination that created a need for buildings on a scale never before seen. The Ministry of Construction estimated that 1.4 billion sq m (15.1 billion sq ft) of new housing alone would be needed in just seven years—roughly the equivalent of building two new cities the size of the New York City metropolitan area. In Hong Kong, due to become part of China in 1997, more than 40,000 new apartments were built in 1994. U.S. and European architects were increasingly becoming associated with Chinese partners in the design of prominent commercial buildings. One

and tiny rooms, thus allowing the visitor to experience space as well as look at pictures and models of the architectural projects being displayed. Both the installation and the projects gave a sense of having been carved or quarried out of the earth, layer by layer, rather than constructed. Eisenman cited, as a source of his architecture, his personal experience of psychoanalysis, in which he dug into his own history and unconscious.

In Paris the Pompidou Centre held an exhibit of the lifetime work of the multifaceted Italian Ettore Sottsass. In the 1960s Sottsass designed modern-classic Olivetti typewriters. He later helped found an influential movement in Postmodern design that he called Memphis, and in 1994 he was an architect of houses.

Preservation. A major controversy erupted over a proposal by the Walt Disney Co. to build a new theme park on a 1,200-ha (3,000-ac) site in Virginia near Washington, D.C. "Disney's America" was to feature re-creations of events from U.S. history and was to be sited only 6.4 km (4 mi) from the Manassas National Battlefield Park in Virginia, a major Civil War memorial. The plan was opposed by both environmentalists and history buffs, and the Disney company abandoned the proposal.

A new concern in the field of architectural preservation was the fate of the disappearing monuments of the

of them, a proposed office and hotel tower in Chongqing (Chungking), by the U.S. firm Haines Lundberg Waehler, would be the tallest building in the world.

Deaths during 1994 included Pietro Belluschi in February. Italian-born, Belluschi gained a reputation for a gentle version of modernism, using wood and other natural materials, in the Portland, Ore., area in the 1940s. (*See* OBITUARIES.) Brazilian landscape architect Roberto Burle Marx, who combined abstract art with lush plantings in more than 3,000 gardens, died in June. (*See* OBITUARIES.) Friends of U.S. architect Charles Moore, who died in 1993, announced plans to acquire and preserve the house that was his last house and studio, in Austin, Texas.　　(ROBERT CAMPBELL)

See also Business and Industry Review: *Building and Construction;* Engineering Projects.

This article updates the *Macropædia* article The History of Western ARCHITECTURE.

Art Exhibitions

Venice, the incomparable Italian city of art, was both the subject and the venue of several of the outstanding art exhibitions of 1994. "The Glory of Venice, 1700–1800," at the Royal Academy in London in the autumn, was devoted to 18th-century Venetian art. It was a companion show to "The Genius of Venice, 1500–1600," which 10 years previously had centred on artists of the 16th century. The 60 artists represented included Giovanni Battista Piazzetta, Francesco Guardi, Canaletto, Bernardo Bellotto, Antonio Canova, and, of course, Giovanni Battista Tiepolo. A wide range of subject matter—religious scenes of Tiepolo, genre paintings of Pietro Longhi, and cityscapes of Canaletto and Bellotto—created a picture of life in the city in all its diversity. Prints, drawings, and sculptures as well as paintings were represented.

The year 1994 was the 400th anniversary of the death of the great Venetian painter Jacopo Tintoretto, and the occasion was marked by his home city, which designated itself Città del Tintoretto, an initiative that included the publication of various Tintoretto walks for visitors to enjoy. Associated were two exhibitions that, although not large, illustrated the extent of his talents. The shows were held at the church of San Bartolomeo ("Tintoretto: Sacred Representations in the Churches of Venice") and at the Accademia Gallery ("Jacopo Tintoretto: Portraits") and subsequently appeared in Vienna at the Kunsthistorisches Museum. There were 13 religious paintings drawn from various Venetian churches on view at San Bartolomeo and at the Accademia 41 portraits lent by European and American public collections. Many of Tintoretto's paintings hang in other public buildings in Venice, including the Ducal Palace, and at over 20 churches, and the two small exhibitions thus complemented the great permanent displays always present in the city. The exhibition at the Accademia was by far the largest such show ever devoted to the artist's work and comprised approximately 25% of his surviving portraits. The portraits were characterized by expressive heads, many of whose subjects were influential elderly men, painted for official purposes, but there were also several relaxed family portraits. A self-portrait of the artist from the Victoria and Albert Museum in London was loaned for inclusion in the show.

A major show devoted to the architecture of the Italian Renaissance was mounted at the Palazzo Grassi in Venice. Titled "The Renaissance from Brunelleschi to Michelangelo: The Representation of Architecture," it concentrated on exhibits that served to bring architecture alive. The im-

Preserving the World's Historical and Cultural Legacy

The continuing destruction of the architectural, artistic, and historical patrimony of the multicultural society in Bosnia and Herzegovina continued to shock and appall the world in 1994. While some of the damage to historic sites, religious structures, libraries, and archives might be classified as incidental to the general warfare, many significant cultural icons were deliberately targeted for destruction as part of "ethnic cleansing." All sides suffered, but Bosnian Muslim cultural objects were especially hard hit.

Such acts during hostilities are forbidden by an international treaty, the Convention for the Protection of Cultural Property in the Event of Armed Conflict, signed at The Hague in 1954 following disastrous losses of art and architectural treasures in Europe during World War II. The Convention was administered by the United Nations Educational, Scientific and Cultural Organization (UNESCO). Eighty-five nations were members, including Bosnia and Herzegovina, Croatia, and Yugoslavia. The treaty states that an enduring cultural heritage is a basic human right worthy of international collaborative respect and maintenance. Thus, responsibility for safeguarding manifestations of material culture transcends any particular ethnic group or nation.

Significant losses of cultural sites and monuments resulting from armed conflict during the past decade, the intentional nature of recent destruction in the Balkans, and the spectre of ethnic strife elsewhere in the world signaled the urgent need to strengthen international safeguards. Several major nations not yet party to the 1954 Hague Convention—including the United States and Canada—were considering ratification. UNESCO and the government of The Netherlands sponsored a series of meetings, one in 1993 and two in 1994, convening legal, military, and cultural resource-management experts to formulate recommendations for increasing the effectiveness of the convention to be presented for consideration by the signatories in 1995.

Other initiatives in 1994 supported protection, preservation, and reconstruction of cultural property in accordance with international humanitarian norms. A symposium at the Carnegie Endowment for International Peace in Washington, D.C., entitled "Destruction and Rebuilding of Architectural Treasures in Bosnia and Herzegovina," considered cultural damage and losses in the context of the 1954 Hague Convention and examined the scope and process of an investigation under the aegis of the UN by experts preparatory to action by the international war crimes tribunal. During the summer of 1994, the Research Centre for Islamic History, Art and Culture in Istanbul organized a pilot workshop on the reconstruction of Mostar, the historic Herzegovinian capital, with broad international support from educational institutions and professional organizations.

The International Council on Monuments and Sites, with national committees in 81 countries and headquarters in Paris, advocated improving preparation for protecting cultural heritage in the event of conflict or natural disaster. Approaches included identifying, inventorying, documenting, and marking cultural property worthy of protection and disseminating information about its worth among the military and civilian population.　　(ARLENE K. FLEMING)

mense show had as a centrepiece the massive wooden model of an unbuilt design for St. Peter's Basilica in Rome by Antonio da Sangallo the Younger, done in 1539–46, which stood some 4.5 m (15 ft) high. Newly restored, the model dominated the courtyard of the Palazzo Grassi, allowing visitors to walk around and view it from all angles. A smaller, partial model of Michelangelo's design for half of the drum and dome was suspended dramatically over the palace's main staircase, showing by contrast how he had simplified and monumentalized the design.

"The Man of the Woods and the Cat of the Mountains" was one of the works by R.B. Kitaj included in the 1994 retrospective at the Tate Gallery in London. Considered one of the early Pop artists in Britain, he also was influenced by Abstract Expressionism.

PRESENTED BY THE FRIENDS OF THE TATE GALLERY 1974

The show included a further 29 wooden models illustrating projects from the 15th and 16th centuries as well as drawings, documents, and portraits of architects. Many of the models could be appreciated as works of art in themselves. Ironically, the exhibition was not particularly comprehensive, focusing on surviving models, and Venetian architecture was virtually unrepresented, as was the work of Palladio. Three hundred examples of architectural drawings were included, however, and there was also a fascinating section devoted to templates used for carving decorative details ("modani"), a few of which had actually been used to reproduce moldings, cornices, and other ornamentation. The show filled 37 rooms, some devoted to general topics and others to single buildings. The exhibition comprised two distinct phases, with some of the exhibits being replaced at the halfway point by others, which was intended to protect the works on paper from too much light.

An exhibition devoted to Islamic works of art taken from Italian collections was shown at the Ducal Palace in Venice, an ideal venue because of the city's long history of Eastern connections. Despite shortcomings in the mounting of the exhibition and problems with loans being canceled at the last minute, the show generally offered much of interest. Objects on display included Persian pottery, Syrian silver work, and Egyptian textiles. Objects collected by the Medici, the Borgias, and the Estensi, including inlaid metalwork and hard-stone pieces, were notable. Ottoman textiles were especially well represented. Also at the Ducal Palace a large loan exhibition entitled "Normanni" surveyed Norman culture and its European and Middle Eastern conquests for the period 1030 to 1200. A charming exhibition in Florence at Fort Belvedere, entitled "Views of Florence," comprised views of that city as depicted by both foreign and Italian artists from the 14th to the 19th century, including photographs and representations of the city in the backgrounds of nonlandscape paintings.

An exhibition devoted to 20th-century art of the Low Countries appeared in the early summer at the Musée National d'Art Moderne in Paris. The survey divided its presentation of Dutch art into separate shows, one devoted to the earlier "historic" period and another to contemporary works, with the contemporary works actually being shown first. The subtitle of the exhibition ("From van Gogh to Mondrian") was slightly misleading, as some 19th-century Symbolist paintings were also included. The exhibition was theme-based and included landscape, portraiture, and abstraction. One room was devoted to architectural and design aspects of De Stijl and included studio photographs as well as decorative items. The star of the show was undoubtedly Mondrian, whose preeminent originality was unmistakable. The Belgian avant-garde was the subject of a show entitled "Impressionism and Post Impressionism in Belgium 1880–1900," which was devoted to that short, productive period. The two aesthetic groups Les Vingt and its successor La Libre Esthetique were represented. An exhibition at the Grand Palais in Paris explored the cultural links between France and Sweden in the 18th century and included among the items on display French paintings from Swedish collections, as well as works by French artists working at the Swedish court. Furniture and architecture were also represented. The title of the show was "The Sun and the North Star."

The work of Frank Lloyd Wright was celebrated by a major retrospective mounted at the Museum of Modern Art in New York City from February to May. A wide range of Wright's activity was covered by the exhibition, illustrating his technological innovations and his interest in the relationship between architecture and landscape. The exhibition comprised a well-chosen selection of models, photographs, drawings, and artifacts, along with several full-scale wall constructions. Wright's designs for New York's Guggenheim Museum formed the subject of a small show at that museum in the summer. (*See also* ARCHITECTURE.)

Another architectural exhibition was devoted to Augustus Pugin at the Victoria and Albert Museum. The show was entitled "Pugin: A Gothic Passion." Pugin, often considered the founder of the Gothic Revival, was best remembered for his work at Westminster Palace (Houses of Parliament), but he was a prolific architect, designing 6 cathedrals and over 40 churches and many other religious buildings, including convents, as well as major secular buildings. On display were many designs and objects, as well as drawings of architectural subjects, textiles, and wallpapers, along with examples of his writings. The exhibition was particularly rich in examples of furniture, church plate, ceramics, and jewelry, much of which had never before been on public view, and the various facets of his work were well shown in the analytic and scholarly show.

An exhibition devoted to the work of William Morris and his group, entitled "Morris and Co.: Pre-Raphaelites and the Arts and Crafts Movement in South Australia," was seen at the Art Gallery of South Australia in Adelaide in the spring. European and American enthusiasts of Morris may have been surprised to learn that from the early 1880s until the early 20th century, Adelaide was a major market for his works, owing to the interests and activities of the Barr-Smith family and their circle. Many of the furnishings and fabrics supplied to houses owned by the family had now been acquired by the Art Gallery of South Australia and formed the subject matter of this exhibition.

Several major exhibitions took the work of Pablo Picasso as their subject in 1994. "Picasso and the Weeping Women," comprising approximately 40 paintings and works on paper that depicted Marie-Thérèse Walter and Dora Maar between 1932 and 1942, was featured at the Los Angeles County Museum of Art and later at New York's Metropolitan Museum of Art. Sculpture was the subject of the exhibition at London's Tate Gallery entitled "Picasso: Sculptor/Painter." The exhibition focused on three-dimensional aspects of all of Picasso's work, including painting, and demonstrated as well the interactions between his painting and his sculpture. Picasso created nearly 1,000 sculptures in his life, using such diverse media as paper, metal, wood, plaster, and pottery, most of which he kept for himself and neither showed nor sold. Many of the items on display had been retained by the artist throughout his life and influenced his work at later stages. The show at the Tate Gallery included a variety of works in all media, including the 1909 "Head of a Woman (Fernande)" in the original plaster as well as in the bronze and painted iron ("Woman in a Hat") made from it in 1961–63. The influence of primitive sculpture and ethnographic objects on Picasso's paintings and sculpture were well illustrated, and his Spanish roots as a source of inspiration were also apparent. Many important items were lent by the Musée Picasso in Paris.

On a more contemporary theme, sculpture by the artist Richard Wentworth was seen at the Serpentine Gallery in London and also in Bristol, England, at the Arnolfini Gallery and later in the spring in 's-Hertogenbosch, Neth., and Calais, France. Wentworth assembled familiar objects in an unfamiliar manner; one "sculpture," for example, comprised a dictionary between the pages of which were interleaved candy-bar wrappers. An exhibit entitled "Mercator" featured overlapping corrugated iron sheets, a reference to the system of map projection, and an installation entitled "Drift" encouraged the viewer to move among floor-mounted cages in which various unrelated objects were to be seen, with mirrors and reflecting lenses giving the installation a series of reflections.

An exhibition entitled "Some Went Mad, Some Ran Away..." was selected by the English artist Damien Hirst to explore diverse themes of the past three decades. The work of 15 English, German, French, and U.S. artists was

"Winter Scene" is one of Francisco de Goya's smaller paintings, which were featured in a 1994 exhibition that traveled from the Prado Museum in Madrid to London and Chicago. The show included a number of works not usually available for public viewing.

included in the show, which was seen at the Serpentine Gallery, the Nordic Arts Centre in Helsinki, Fin., and the Kunstverein in Hanover, Germany, and which was due to travel early in 1995 to the Museum of Contemporary Art in Chicago. The exhibition included work in various media, including sculptures and photographs. One exhibit, entitled "Solomon Island Shark" by the American Ashley Bickerton, comprised a large black shark made of rubber, festooned with coconuts and bags of detergent, the whole being suspended from the ceiling of the gallery and being subject to numerous and diverse interpretations. An interest in the morbid combined with a perverse sense of humour seemed to unite a number of the works in the show.

A large exhibition devoted to the work of R.B. Kitaj, entitled "R.B. Kitaj: A Retrospective," was first shown at the Tate Gallery, then traveled to the Los Angeles County Museum of Art, and was scheduled to be shown in New York in 1995 at the Metropolitan Museum of Art. Kitaj (born in 1932), whose work was largely figurative, defied classification, but he was undoubtedly a major artist of the mid-20th century. The show was his first British retrospective and comprised a variety of paintings, pastels, and drawings, the installation of which was partially supervised by the artist.

It was one of three Kitaj exhibitions in London, the others being a print survey at the Victoria and Albert Museum and an exhibition of recent pictures at Marlborough Fine Arts.

In 1994 there were a number of exhibitions in London devoted to aspects of 19th-century art of German-speaking countries, a relatively little-known area in Britain. The British Museum mounted "German Printmaking in the Age of Goethe." The museum has a strong collection of German prints of the 19th and 20th centuries, which the organizers of the exhibition were able to draw on for the comprehensive show. The exhibition covered the period around 1800, a time of considerable importance for printmaking because of the emergence of a variety of new techniques. Both scholarly and visually exciting, the exhibition put the art and practice of printmaking in Germany into context and illustrated particularly the enormous scale of the industry in the late 18th and early 19th centuries. Leading centres of printmaking represented included Berlin, Munich, and Vienna, and themes covered both cultural and political subjects.

The influence of Goethe on the arts was also the subject of a show entitled "Goethe and Art," a major loan exhibition at the Staatliche Kunstsammlungen in Weimar, Germany, which concentrated on all aspects of the poet's influence on the arts from the 15th to the 19th century. The exhibition had previously been seen in Frankfurt am Main, Germany. "Printmaking in the Renaissance," an exhibition at the Rijksmuseum in Amsterdam, focused on early European printmaking and included works by Dürer and Mantegna.

A show entitled "Treasures from Heaven" was the first important exhibition devoted to illustrated and illuminated manuscripts of Armenia to be held in the United States. It was on display at the Pierpont Morgan Library in New York City in the summer and later at the Walters Art Gallery in Baltimore, Md. The 88 items on show were drawn entirely from public and private collections in North America and provided a chronological survey of the different periods and schools of the Armenian tradition. The items showed a

MICHEL BLOIT COLLECTION, NEUILLY

A porcelain jug, dating from the 1800s and honouring Napoléon Bonaparte, shows the French fascination with Egyptian art. The jug was among a collection of art and decorative items on display in "Egyptomania," seen in Paris, Ottawa, and Vienna.

variety of styles ranging over a period from 966 to the early 19th century. The rich and varied exhibition entitled "Egyptomania," which was seen at the National Gallery of Canada in Ottawa in the summer, had previously been on view at the Louvre in Paris and was also scheduled to be seen in Vienna. The show explored the influence of Egyptian art on the decorative and fine arts of Europe and North America from the mid-18th to the early 20th century.

The National Gallery in London mounted the major exhibition "Claude: The Poetic Landscape." Although small (28 paintings, 53 drawings) and with all but one drawn from British collections, it comprised a splendid survey of the artist's work and a fine introduction to the subject. Most of the pictures on display were drawn from the early part of Claude Lorrain's career, the 1630s and '40s. The interaction of subject and landscape was preeminent, and the exhibition focused on the narrative content of his landscapes and included drawings hung next to their connected or related paintings.

A show in the autumn at the Grand Palais in Paris was devoted to Claude's contemporary Nicolas Poussin and included almost all of his major works that were not considered too delicate to travel. The exhibition was an in-depth survey and was to be seen in a reduced version in London early in 1995. Associated shows were mounted at Chantilly, near Paris, at the Louvre, and at the Villa Medici in Rome.

The creativity of the artist was the main theme of a major exhibition devoted to the work of the Spaniard Francisco de Goya entitled "Goya: Truth and Fantasy," which was shown in the winter at the Prado Museum in Madrid and in the spring at the Royal Academy in London before traveling to the Art Institute of Chicago. This charming show offered visitors the chance to enjoy works rarely assembled or not usually publicly available; included were many portraits and miniatures.

"A Gift to America" was an assembly of 54 of the most important old-master pictures donated by merchant S.H. Kress and the Kress Foundation to public museums throughout the United States. The show included works by artists such as Titian, Goya, El Greco, and Van Dyck and toured a number of museums, including the North Carolina Museum of Art in Raleigh and museums in Houston, Texas, Seattle, Wash., and San Francisco.

"The Age of Rubens" was billed as the first U.S.-mounted international loan exhibition survey of Flemish Baroque painting, a subject not usually popular with U.S. audiences. The exhibition was seen at the Museum of Fine Arts in Boston and subsequently at the Toledo (Ohio) Museum of Art. Its aim was to enhance the appreciation of the subject among contemporary museum visitors, and as such the exhibition was a delight to the eye. Peter Paul Rubens was well represented by 33 canvases, approximately one-quarter of the total number on show. Other artists represented were Van Dyck, Jacob Jordaens, and Jan Bruegel the Elder. A particularly attractive group of oil sketches, studies for larger projects, were also included; some of them had never before been on public view.

Noteworthy exhibitions in Japan included, at the Metropolitan Teien Museum in Tokyo, the first of a series of shows that would assemble works from museums throughout the country. This first show concentrated on the introduction of oil painting to Japan and contrasted the medium as used by Japanese artists of the 20th century with its use by Western artists. "Scream Against the Sky" at the Yokohama Museum of Art surveyed Japanese art of the post-World War II period, with 180 exhibits representing the work of 60 artists. At the Fuji Art Museum in Tokyo, an exhibition commemorating the museum's 10th anniversary focused on Napoleon and his period and included works by the French artists Jean-Auguste-Dominique Ingres and Jacques-Louis David.   (SANDRA MILLIKIN)

PHOTOGRAPHY

A mood of looking back, summing up, and attempting to redefine both the photographic medium and the work of individual photographers who shaped it found expression in a number of impressive retrospective exhibitions in 1994.

In Washington, D.C., the National Gallery of Art opened "Robert Frank: Moving Out, 1944–94," a major overview of the work of the reclusive but influential photog-
rapher-cinematographer. The Swiss-born Frank, who moved to the U.S. in 1947, powerfully influenced post-war photography with the publication in 1958 of *The Americans*. In that seminal book Frank recorded with gritty, tilted-frame, snap-shot casualness a haunt-ing iconography of empty roads and lonely people and a bleakly pessimistic view of society. The ex-hibition displayed 150 of those and other Frank pho-tographs, many never be-fore shown. A program of

Robert Frank's "End of Dream, 1992" reflects on the breaking up of ice and the waiting for spring. The triptych was included in "Robert Frank: Moving Out, 1944–94," an exhibition at the National Gallery of Art, Washington, D.C., surveying the work of the photographer-cinematographer perhaps best known for *The Americans*.
© ROBERT FRANK—COLLECTION OF THE ARTIST

his innovative cinematic work included 21 films and videos and the premiere of his recently completed *Moving Pictures*.

Richard Avedon and his work, featured in a high-powered media blitz during 1993, continued to be energetically pro-moted in 1994 as the photographer pursued his monumental project of producing a series of major exhibitions and books. The keynote event was "Richard Avedon: Evidence 1944–1994," which opened at New York City's Whitney Museum of American Art. Covering the full range of Avedon's black-and-white photography over a half century, the exhibition revealed an astonishing versatility, a wildly innovative imag-ination, and a complexity of emotion that transcended the insouciant fashion work for which Avedon first became fa-mous. The collection included charming street photographs taken in New York and Italy during the late 1940s and '50s and heretofore unpublished harrowing images of Viet-namese women burned by napalm. His compelling but dis-turbing portraits of Isak Dinesen as—in the words of one reviewer—a "skull attached to a fur coat," Ezra Pound sunk in despairing madness, a half-naked beekeeper crawling with insects, and a ravaged, broken-toothed Oscar Levant raised questions about the status of photographic portraiture and the ethical relationship between photographer and subject.

Perhaps the most unusual exhibition of the year was "Talking Pictures: People Speak About the Photographs That Speak to Them" at New York's International Cen-ter of Photography, in which viewers listened to recorded comments from people both unknown and famous about the images being viewed. "André Kertész: A Centennial Tribute" at the J. Paul Getty Museum, Malibu, Calif., ex-hibited 50 pictures, including rare vintage prints made by the greatly admired Hungarian-born master. An exhibition at the San Francisco Museum of Modern Art, "Dorothea Lange: American Photographs," displayed 220 photographs, about one-fourth not previously shown, documenting the Great Depression, the internment of Japanese-Americans during World War II, and later photo essays.

News of one of the most amazing photographic finds of recent times was made public: the discovery of 143 paper-negative images taken in 1852 by German photographer Ernest Benecke during extensive travels in Africa and the Near East. Unlike most early travel photographers, who dwelled on landscapes and ancient ruins, Benecke frequently photographed people in a surprisingly modern, casual style, thereby qualifying as one of the first ethnographic pho-tographers. The collection, which was acquired by German collector Werner Bokelberg, was estimated to be worth $1 million.

The subject of controversy for 60 years, a blurred, grainy, and much reproduced photograph purporting to show the Loch Ness monster was revealed to be a fake. The prankster, 90-year-old Christian Spurling, confessed to Scottish re-searchers before he died. He shaped Nessie's plesiosaur-like neck and head out of a modeling compound applied to the conning tower of a small toy submarine, which he then photographed in the shallows of Loch Ness.

The 1994 Pulitzer Prize for spot news photography was awarded to Paul Watson of the *Toronto Star* for his pic-ture of a U.S. soldier being dragged through the streets in Somalia. Free-lance photojournalist Kevin Carter (*see* OBITUARIES) received the Pulitzer for feature photogra-phy for his picture of a starving Sudanese child under the patient gaze of a waiting vulture. At the 51st Pictures of the Year competition sponsored by the National Press Photographers Association and the University of Missouri School of Journalism, free-lancer Anthony Suau was named Magazine Photographer of the Year, while Lucian Perkins of the *Washington* (D.C.) *Post* took the title of Newspaper Photographer of the Year. At the 37th Annual World Press Photo contest, the Press Photo of the Year award was given to Larry Towell, a Canadian photographer associated with Magnum, for his photograph of "Children of the Intifada" in Gaza. The primary W. Eugene Smith Grant in Humanis-tic Photography went to Helen Binder for "Russia" and the secondary award to Viviane Moos for "The Girls of Brazil." Both recipients were New York-based free-lancers.

Robert Doisneau (*see* OBITUARIES) died at 81 in Paris, a city whose spirit he captured in many lighthearted and gently humorous images of its street life, parks, lovers, and children during the post-World War II years.

(ARTHUR GOLDSMITH)

See also Auctions and Collections; Motion Pictures; Museums.

This article updates the *Macropædia* articles THE HISTORY OF WESTERN PAINTING; The History of Western SCULPTURE; PHO-TOGRAPHY.

Astronomy

For astronomy 1994 was a particularly exciting year as astronomers and the general public thrilled to one of the most dramatic solar system encounters in memory, the crash of Comet Shoemaker-Levy 9 into the atmosphere of the giant planet Jupiter. (*See* Sidebar.) Sharp new images of a variety of astronomical objects were taken by the repaired Hubble Space Telescope (HST). The National Aeronautics and Space Administration's Extreme Ultraviolet Explorer (EUVE) satellite, launched in 1992, began making substantial contributions; with its sensitivity to the ultraviolet radiation normally absorbed by Earth's atmosphere, it, too, produced many new views of the cosmos. Japan's ASCA X-ray satellite kept unique observations of the sky pouring in at X-ray wavelengths. Astronomers had a field day using several large Earth-based telescopes (such as the Keck telescope in Hawaii) to provide fresh insights into objects ranging from the nearest asteroids to the most distant quasars.

Solar System. Without doubt the most exciting event in astronomy was the impact of Comet Shoemaker-Levy 9 with Jupiter, but studies of other small bodies in the solar system provided their own delights and surprises. Although the solar system is traditionally viewed as comprising the Sun, nine planets, their moons, and the asteroid belt between Mars and Jupiter, the discovery in the past few years of increasing numbers of small cometary or asteroid-like objects beyond the orbit of the planet Neptune was beginning to change that picture. In 1994 Jane X. Luu of Stanford University and David Jewitt of the University of Hawaii reported several more such trans-Neptunian bodies. The 17 objects found as of the end of 1994 orbit the Sun with periods of about 300 years, compared with the planet Pluto's 248-year orbital period. According to Brian Marsden of the Harvard-Smithsonian Center for Astrophysics, Cambridge, Mass., several of these distant objects, like Pluto, are locked into a so-called 3:2 resonance with the much more massive planet Neptune, meaning that they revolve twice about the Sun in stable orbits for each three revolutions of Neptune.

The Galileo spacecraft, launched in October 1989, continued to beam images to Earth of a variety of solar system objects as it moved closer to its rendezvous with Jupiter. Unfortunately, because its main radio antenna was not working, data had to be relayed to Earth very slowly through a smaller secondary antenna. Nonetheless, by the start of 1994 Galileo had already sent back a number of spectacular observations. In 1991, as the spacecraft passed near the asteroid Gaspra, it snapped the first close-up picture of an asteroid. Two years later it obtained a spectacular image of a second asteroid, 243 Ida, revealing it to be a heavily cratered, elongated body about 52 km across (1 km is about 0.62 mi). Then in early 1994 Galileo sent back an image that showed the presence of another asteroid, only about 1.5 km across, within 100 km of Ida. The chances that two asteroids would be this close together yet independent of each other were estimated to be less than one in a trillion. Therefore, the scientists from the Jet Propulsion Laboratory, Pasadena, Calif., who reported the observation concluded that Ida has a moon of its own, the first known asteroid-moon pair. The small moon, named Dactyl, has about a dozen craters more than 50 m (165 ft) in diameter, implying that it is at least 100 million years old but not as old as the solar system, since it would have been obliterated by repeated hits in less than a billion years. This information suggested that both Ida and Dactyl originated from a much larger asteroid, which itself broke up into a collection of pieces called the Koronis asteroid family.

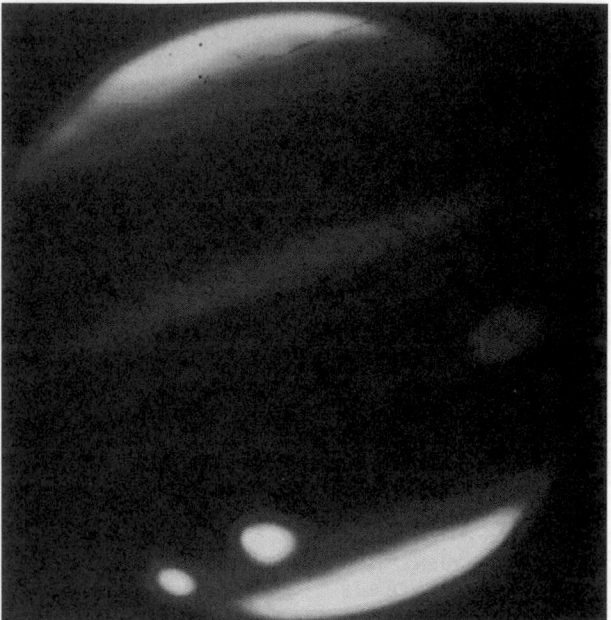

Impact sites of pieces of Comet Shoemaker-Levy 9 stand out in Jupiter's atmosphere as large oval regions near the planet's south pole. Telescopes on Earth and in space watched as 21 fragments of the comet bombarded the giant planet July 16–22, 1994.
DE PATER, GRAHAM, JERNIGAN—UNIVERSITY OF CALIFORNIA AT BERKELEY; W.M. KECK OBSERVATORY

Stars. In February 1987 observers on Earth witnessed the explosion of a star in the nearby Large Magellanic Cloud galaxy—the brightest supernova seen in more than three centuries. As Supernova 1987A became dimmer, astronomers detected an encircling ring of glowing gas about a light-year in radius. It was believed that the ring was composed of gas that had been ejected previously by the dying massive progenitor star and that was then stimulated to emit visible light by radiation from the supernova explosion. In 1994 Christopher Burrows of the Space Telescope Science Institute (STScI), Baltimore, Md., reported that sharp HST images showed two additional rings several light-years in diameter that appeared to intersect the central ring, producing a double-hoop pattern. The large rings were thought to lie in front of and behind the central ring, forming an hourglasslike arrangement in which the hoops outlined the end caps of the hourglass and the central ring outlined the neck. The new rings had not been predicted and were unique in all of astronomy. Scientists offered several possible explanations for the giant hoops. The most intriguing one involved the illumination of interstellar material by a neutron-star or black-hole remnant of the initial explosion. Such an object might emit fast-moving particle beams or jets that could hit the surrounding gas and cause it to glow.

The first well-established example of an extrasolar planetary system was reported during the year. Several years earlier astronomers had described two separate instances of a pulsar with one or more planets possibly in orbit around it. One of those reports proved erroneous, leaving the other also open to question. In 1994 Alexander Wolszczan of Pennsylvania State University presented data that confirmed the earlier evidence for at least two planets, and perhaps more, around the pulsar PSR B1257 + 12. A pulsar is a rapidly rotating neutron star whose spin period, as reflected in its pulse period, is normally extremely regular. The pulse period of PSR B1257 + 12, however, was observed to increase and decrease periodically above and below its average pulse period of 6.2 milliseconds. The variation was interpreted as due to motion of the pulsar toward and away from the Earth as one or more planet-sized objects orbit the pulsar, gravitationally tugging it to and fro. By measuring the increase and decrease in the pulsar arrival times, Wolszczan showed that at least two planets, each about three times the mass of the Earth, are revolving around the pulsar with orbital periods of roughly 67 and 98 days.

Galaxies and Cosmology. The Milky Way Galaxy, in which the solar system resides, was known to be surrounded by at least 10 small satellite galaxies. The nearest had been thought to be the Large Magellanic Cloud, which lies about 150,000 light-years from the Sun. During the year Rodrigo A. Ibata and Gerry Gilmore of the University of Cambridge and Mike Irwin of the Royal Greenwich Observatory, Hailsham, England, discovered a dwarf spheroidal galaxy only about 50,000 light-years from the Sun. The faint galaxy, which lies in the direction of the constellation Sagittarius, had remained undetected because of obscuration caused by stars and dust lying in the disk of the Milky Way. By starting with an image of the region under study and digitally subtracting the light from known foreground stars, the researchers were left with an image of the dwarf galaxy. It probably contains no more than 50 million stars, compared with some 200 billion for the Milky Way. From its elongated appearance, scientists speculated that the "Sagittarius dwarf" is destined to fall into the Milky Way within the next few hundred million years.

In an independent search for previously undetected galaxies, a Dutch group used a radio telescope to penetrate the Milky Way's obscuring disk of gas and dust. Using the Dwingeloo radio telescope in The Netherlands, Renee Kraan-Korteweg of the University of Groningen and collaborators from The Netherlands, the U.K., and the U.S. reported finding a spiral galaxy some 10 million light-years away. It is thus about five times farther than Andromeda, or M31, the nearest large galaxy. From its apparent size and rotational velocity, the galaxy was estimated to have about a quarter of the mass of the Milky Way.

New evidence was reported for a massive black hole at the heart of the giant elliptical galaxy M87. The galaxy is close to the Milky Way by cosmic standards, located about 50 million light-years away in the constellation Virgo, making it one of the best active galaxies for detailed study. Images of the centre of M87 captured by the repaired HST showed what seemed to be a tilted disk of hot, ionized gas only about 60 light-years in diameter. The study team, headed by Richard J. Harms of Applied Research Corp., Landover, Md., and Holland C. Ford of STScI, determined the velocity of the gas to be about 500 km per second. If the gas is orbiting a central object, the mass of the object must be about three billion times the mass of the Sun. Because the deduced mass occupies such a small region, it is possible that the central object is a massive black hole. The HST also obtained clear images of the bright jet that emanates from the centre of M87. This feature was thought to be radiation from a beam of electrons accelerated to nearly the speed of light as a result of processes occurring in or near the disk of material spiraling into the purported black hole. Many astronomers believed that the observational evidence, although still circumstantial, provided the best argument to date for the existence of black holes.

In some sense the study of cosmology is a search for two numbers: the age of the universe and its mass density. The first number is sought by means of attempts to determine the distances to certain types of stellar objects located in moderately distant galaxies. This can be done if one knows the absolute brightness, or luminosity, of these classes of stellar objects from their study within the Milky Way or relatively nearby galaxies. By finding what are believed to be the

---

Comet Shoemaker-Levy 9: A Spectacular Good-bye

In March 1993 a previously unknown comet caught the attention of veteran comet spotters Carolyn and Eugene Shoemaker and David Levy. (*See* BIOGRAPHIES.) Most unusual about Comet Shoemaker-Levy 9 was its appearance; it looked like a string of glowing pearls. An early image made with the Hubble Space Telescope (HST) revealed about 21 major separate cometary fragments strung out in a line. Calculations showed that the comet had broken up as the result of a near collision with the planet Jupiter in July 1992 and that the pieces would plunge into Jupiter's southern hemisphere between July 16 and July 22, 1994. The largest pieces, with diameters estimated at about four kilometres, were predicted to unleash an energy equivalent to several million megatons of TNT each during their plunge into Jupiter's atmosphere at speeds of 60 km per second (a kilometre is about 0.62 mi).

The comet's dazzling demise began right on time. It likely attracted more observations than any other astronomical event in history. Unfortunately, the impacts occurred, as predicted, a few degrees behind the darkened limb of Jupiter. Earth-bound telescopes and near-Earth satellites recorded the consequences as the impact sites were carried into view by Jupiter's 10-hour rotation shortly after the actual events occurred. The Galileo spacecraft, heading for Jupiter, had the only direct view of the show. The G-fragment impact, one of the largest, produced a set of dark rings in Jupiter's atmosphere resembling a black eye. Within hours it had swelled to twice the size of the Earth. Days later the site was the most prominent feature on Jupiter, upstaging even the famous Great Red Spot. Within months, however, the impact bruises were nearly gone, sheared into oblivion by Jupiter's violent winds.

Each of the impact sites appeared dark in ordinary optical images—a surprise in view of predictions that frozen water and ammonia, which were thought to be predominant components of comets, would show as white plumes above the impact sites as material splashed back into the upper atmosphere and cooled. More surprisingly, very little water was detected spectroscopically. Ultraviolet spectra from the HST did show the presence of ammonia, sulfur, and hydrogen sulfide, the latter two substances having never before been seen on Jupiter. Although some plumes rose 3,000 km above Jupiter, no evidence was found for excavated material of the type thought to lie deep in Jupiter's atmosphere. Apparently the cometary chunks did not penetrate as deeply into the atmosphere as expected.

Was Shoemaker-Levy 9 a typical comet, a "dirty snowball" composed of frozen ice and dust? Or was it more like an asteroid, made of rocky material? The comet tails seen in the early photos showed only dust, not gas. That detail and the impact results left scientists puzzling over the nature of the objects that had annihilated in Jupiter's clouds.   (KENNETH BRECHER)

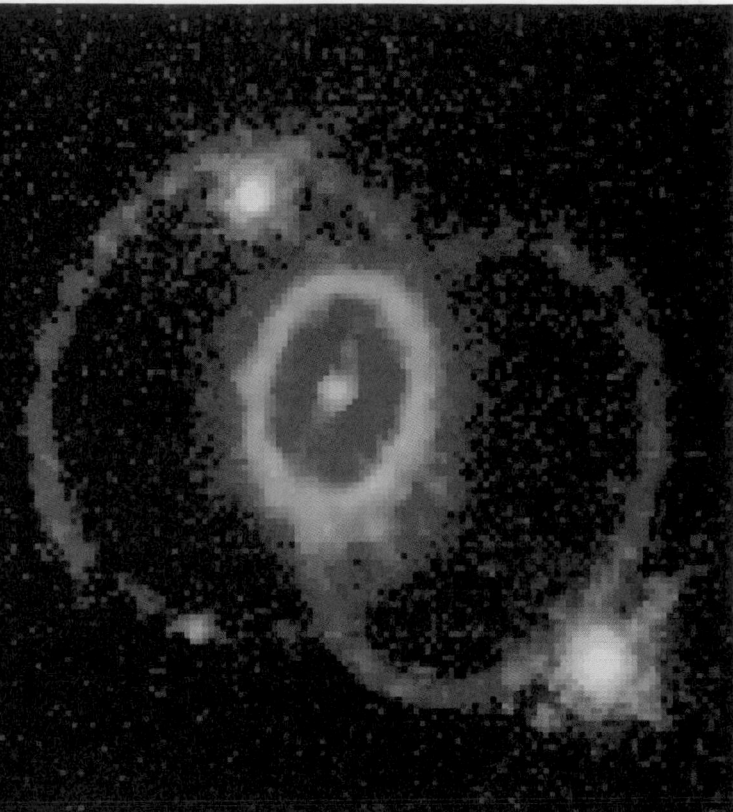

A Hubble Space Telescope image of the exploded star known as Supernova 1987A shows it to be encircled by a smaller inner ring, which in turn appears framed by a pair of larger, hoop-shaped outer rings. Discovered in 1994, the outer rings were unique in astronomy.

DR. CHRISTOPHER BURROWS (ESA/STSCI), NASA

Earth Perihelion and Aphelion, 1995

Jan. 4	Perihelion, 147,100,000 km (91,403,900 mi) from the Sun
July 4	Aphelion, 152,102,400 km (94,512,200 mi) from the Sun

Equinoxes and Solstices, 1995

March 21	Vernal equinox, 02:14[1]
June 20	Summer solstice, 20:34[1]
Sept. 23	Autumnal equinox, 12:13[1]
Dec. 22	Winter solstice, 08:17[1]

Eclipses, 1995

April 15	Moon, partial (begins 10:08[1]), the beginning visible in the western part of North America, Alaska, Hawaii, the southern tip of South America, Australia, New Zealand, eastern Asia, Antarctica, and the Pacific Ocean; the end visible in the western United States, Baja California, Alaska, Australia, eastern Asia, much of the Pacific Ocean, and the eastern Indian Ocean.
April 29	Sun, annular (begins 14:33[1]), the beginning visible south of French Polynesia in the southwestern Pacific Ocean, Peru (near Lima), northern Brazil, mouth of the Amazon; the end visible in the western Atlantic Ocean (near the Equator).
Oct. 8	Moon, penumbral (begins 16:43[1]), the beginning visible in the northwestern United States, western Canada, Alaska, Hawaii, Australia, eastern Asia, eastern Antarctica, the western Pacific Ocean, and the eastern Indian Ocean; the end visible in Europe, Asia, most of Africa, Australia, the western Pacific Ocean, and the Indian Ocean.
Oct. 24	Sun, total (begins 04:22[1]), the beginning visible south of the Caspian Sea (near Tehran), Afghanistan, Pakistan, India (near Calcutta), Myanmar (Burma), Thailand, Cambodia, southern Vietnam, South China Sea, south of the Philippines; the end visible in the western Pacific Ocean, near the Marshall Islands.

[1]Universal time.
Source: *The Astronomical Almanac for the Year 1995* (1994).

same types of objects in other galaxies and measuring their luminosities, astronomers can calculate galactic distances. Because galaxies appear to be receding from one another at velocities that vary with their distance from the point from which they are observed, by correlating the distances to galaxies with their measured velocities, astronomers can derive a relation, called the Hubble law, for determining the current rate of expansion of the universe. The resulting number, called Hubble's constant (H_0), then can be used to find the age of the universe. Actually, the age also depends on the mass density of the universe, which is not well known, so a range of ages results in which the value being sought is somewhere between ⅔ and 1 times the reciprocal of Hubble's constant ($1/H_0$).

In 1994 the controversy over the age of the universe gained new force. A group from the Harvard-Smithsonian Center for Astrophysics, headed by Robert Kirshner, reported an age for the universe of 9 billion to 14 billion years. Their work depended on calibrations of the brightness of exploding stars called type II supernovas. A group headed by Michael J. Pierce of Indiana University, along with five Canadian colleagues, used different types of stellar objects, Cepheid variable stars, to determine the distance to the Virgo cluster of galaxies. Their study led to an age estimate for the universe of 7 billion to 11 billion years. Finally, a group of astronomers using the HST and headed by Wendy Freedman of the Carnegie Observatories of California reported its findings for the distance to the galaxy M100, also using studies of Cepheid variable stars. The age of the universe according to their calculations was 8 billion to 12 billion years.

All this consistency may sound like good news; scientists at last know the age of the universe. Unfortunately, nearly half a century of studies of stars indicates that the oldest stars in the Milky Way are at least 16 billion years old. Therefore, (1) the recent determinations of the Hubble constant are in error, (2) the ages of the oldest stars are wrong, or (3) current cosmological models of the expanding universe need revision. Which of those options is correct was not known. Some astronomers, such as Alan Sandage of the Observatories of the Carnegie Institution of Washington, D.C., continued to report a Hubble constant (based on observations of type I supernovas) and an age of the universe consistent with that of the oldest stars. Given all the uncertainties involved in trying to determine the Hubble constant, at year's end the standard picture of an expanding universe still provided a satisfactory description of the history and age of the universe.   (KENNETH BRECHER)

See also Space Exploration.

This article updates the *Macropædia* articles The COSMOS; GALAXIES; The PHYSICAL SCIENCES: *Astronomy;* The SOLAR SYSTEM; STARS AND STAR CLUSTERS.

Auctions and Collections

ART AUCTIONS AND SALES

The 1993–94 auction season was dominated by the sales of celebrity collections and the exorbitant prices paid by admiring fans for artistic mementos. Princess Gloria von Thurn und Taxis of Germany, couturier Hubert de Givenchy, singer Barbra Streisand, and a 96-year-old former Chinese warlord, Zhang Xueliang (Chang Hsüeh-liang), were all delighted with the profits from the sales of their collections. The estates of U.S. millionaires Peter Sharp, famed for his Old Master collection, and Wendell Cherry, who favoured Impressionists and French furniture, also attracted feverish bidders. A buyer's market ensured that prices would not rise significantly. Many of the artworks offered for auction failed to sell. Auction houses, however, recorded a rise in seasonal turnover. Sotheby's turnover increased 19% and Christie's

14%. The Paris auction rooms recorded a 5.5% increase in turnover in the first six months of the year compared with the same period of 1993.

For once, profits were not dominated by prices for expensive pictures, whether Impressionists or Old Masters. For these works Sotheby's and Christie's reported level sales, although Impressionist paintings declined from the previous year. The decorative arts enjoyed buoyant sales, including strong performances for English and French furniture, European ceramics, and Chinese works of art, especially snuff bottles.

The growing number of private collectors buying directly from auction also increased. Traditionally, dealers bought at "wholesale" levels, but in recent years they had been joined at auction by private collectors who paid "retail" prices for furniture and pictures.

The first sensational auction of the season was Sotheby's 10-day sale of surplus furnishings from Schloss St. Emmeram, the Thurn and Taxis palace in Regensburg, Germany. The 6,596 lots sold for DM 31,417,712 (DM 1 = $0.65), some 60% over forecast. Other princely families, including the Liechtensteins, Württemburgs, and Wittelsbachs, attended the sale hoping to embellish the furnishings of their castles, but the wealthy bourgeoisie outbid the royalty. A walnut wardrobe of c. 1720 commanded DM 80,500, three times the original estimate. A French Empire hound with an ormolu clock in its mouth fetched DM 29,900, six times more than expected.

Christie's Givenchy sale in Monaco was a rousing success and made F 155,533,200 (F 1 = $0.19). The couturier had devoted 15 years to impeccably decorating his Paris apartment in 18th-century taste; he preferred the Baroque magnificence of the early years of the century and had acquired many pieces of royal provenance. It was the grandest furniture sale in many years and attracted acquisitive millionaires.

Muhammad Mahdi at-Tajir, former London ambassador of the United Arab Emirates and silver collector par excellence, paid F 19,980,000 for a silver chandelier designed in the 1730s by William Kent for King George II. It was a record price for silver. A Louis XIV library table by André Charles Boulle made F 18,870,000. The sale underscored a rise in the price for the best French furniture. A boulle bookcase, which was made by Étienne Levasseur in the 1780s and had sold at auction in 1982 for $209,000, made F 11.1 million, while a pair of Rococo ormolu candelabra supported by dragons made F 5.3 million after having sold in 1986 for $363,000.

The real connoisseurs' event in the field of 20th-century decorative arts was the sale of 143 pieces of furniture, designs, and drawings by Charles Rennie Mackintosh, the Scottish architect and designer. The items had been amassed over 50 years by Thomas Howarth, professor emeritus of architecture at the University of Toronto. A 1904 ebonized writing cabinet inlaid with mother-of-pearl brought £793,500 (£1 = $1.59), the highest auction price ever recorded for 20th-century furniture, while a high, oval-backed oak chair fetched £309,500. Howarth made £2,270,000.

In April a Sotheby auction of Chinese paintings in Taiwan demonstrated that Asian buyers were just as enamoured of celebrity offerings as Westerners. Sotheby's attempted to sell the collection anonymously, but news soon leaked out. The 700-odd paintings, dating from the 10th century to around 1980, had been collected by Zhang Xueliang, a famous Chinese warlord who was held under house arrest in Taiwan for almost 40 years after he attempted to arrest Chiang Kai-shek in 1936. Every lot sold, and the collection brought NT$132,895,500 ($5,035,000), three times Sotheby's

high estimate. A Sung dynasty painting of a spray of peach blossom made NT$16,550,000 ($627,000), four times the forecast price.

The widow of the U.S. millionaire Wendell Cherry, who founded the Humana hospital group and was one of the great art collectors of the 1980s, made Sotheby's summer by consigning paintings and furniture. Two of her Post-Impressionist paintings provided the top two picture prices—$11,662,500 for Gustav Klimt's "Lady with a Fan" and $7,592,500 for John Singer Sargent's "Spanish Dancer." The furnishings from Cherry's New York apartment, mainly French 18th century, made $13.7 million, including a Louis XIV boulle library table and filing cabinet, which commanded $2.2 million.

In the field of modern art, the best results were provided by a collection formed in the post-World War II years by H. Gates Lloyd and his wife, Lallie. One of David Smith's most famous sculptures, "Cubi V," made $4.1 million and Mondrian's "Composition No. 8" sold for $5.6 million. Both works made about double the projected estimate.

Specialty pieces and rarities also brought handsome profits. A 3,000-year-old Assyrian relief carving from the palace of Ashurnasirpal II at Nimrud sold for £7.7 million to Japanese dealer N. Horiuchi. The piece, which depicted a bearded divinity anointing a eunuch's back, had been rediscovered under a coat of whitewash in the tuckshop of an English public school. A Greek pottery water jar of the 6th century BC decorated with a scene of Hero battling the sea monster Ketos sold for £2.2 million; an Islamic bronze lion of the 11th or 12th century made £2 million; a 5.8-m (19-ft) Louis XV Savonnerie carpet, emblazoned with the royal arms of France, made £1,321,500 and established a record price for any carpet; and a blue-and-white Medici porcelain dish made around 1570–80 was sold for F 8.8 million, a new record for European porcelain.   (GERALDINE NORMAN)

BOOKS

The market for antiquarian books emerged from recession during 1993–94, but overall prices were flat, especially for major rarities. The most extraordinary transaction of the year was the exchange of roughly half a Persian manuscript for a Willem de Kooning painting, both valued at about £13 million. The heirs of Arthur Houghton, a book collector, inherited the remaining pages of the *Shah-nameh*, the celebrated work of Persian epic poet Ferdowsi. Though Houghton had sold off the best of the 256 illustrations in his lifetime, 118 miniatures, over 500 pages of text, a magnificent 16th-century binding, and an illuminated rosette remained. The Iranian government traded de Kooning's nude "Woman III" for the manuscript.

Two major collections of early printed books came on the market. Sotheby's sold some 400 books published before 1500 from the famous library of the Fürstenberg princes at Donaueschingen in southern Germany for £3.2 million, and a top price of £221,500 was paid for a tiny block book of c. 1465 titled *The Art of Dying*. Christie's sold a selection from the collection of Beriah Botfield (1807–63) for £3.8 million. Beres, a Paris dealer, paid a record £260,000 for a superb copy of Pierre Joseph Redouté's *Les Roses,* while the first Bible published in English—Miles Coverdale's translation printed in Antwerp in 1535—made £106,000. The British Library reportedly paid £1 million for one of the only two remaining copies of the New Testament translated by William Tyndale and published in 1526. A letter written by Abraham Lincoln sold for $728,500 at Christie's, and one by George Washington made a record $635,000 at Sotheby's. The Forbes family paid $321,500 for a map prepared by the lead pilot in the Japanese attack on Pearl Harbor.

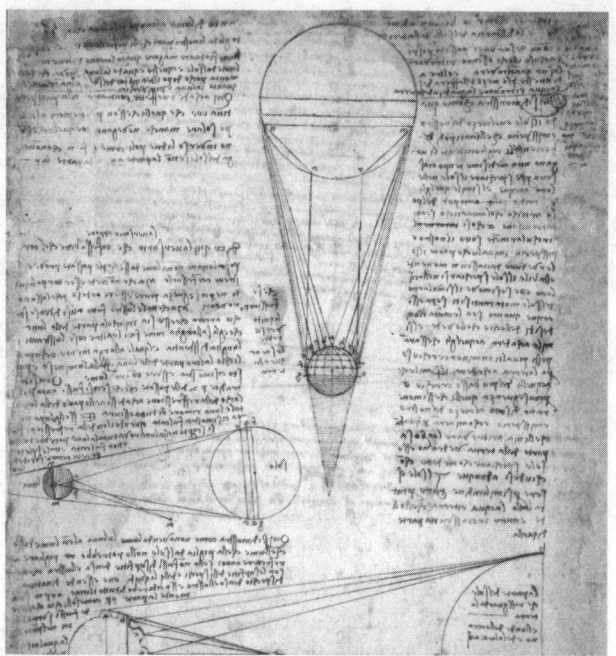

A page from Codex Hammer, one of Leonardo da Vinci's notebooks, shows notes and diagrams on astronomy. When the notebook was offered by Christie's, Bill Gates, chairman of Microsoft Corp., bought it for $30.8 million, the most ever paid for a manuscript sold at auction.

COURTESY OF THE ARMAND HAMMER COLLECTION, UCLA AT THE ARMAND HAMMER MUSEUM OF ART, LOS ANGELES, CALIFORNIA; PHOTOGRAPH, SETH JOEL

Children's books enjoyed buoyant sales, reflecting bulk buying by a single U.S. collector, Lloyd Cotsen. A first edition of Beatrix Potter's *The Tale of Peter Rabbit* commanded £63,250, and a pristine copy of the first Rupert bear annual, the 1936 *New Adventures of Rupert,* made £1,610.

The best collection of scientific books on the market for over 20 years, formed by Robert S. Dunham (1906–91), sparked fierce competition, with Newton's *Principia Mathematica* (1687) making $211,500 and Copernicus' *De revolutionibus* (1543) fetching $151,000. A record auction price, $30.8 million, for a manuscript was paid by Bill Gates of Microsoft Corp. for a notebook of Leonardo da Vinci's.

The sale of the last private copy of William Blake's *Jerusalem* was sold at Christie's for £617,500. Sotheby's sold both a rediscovered notebook containing the only known keyboard music written by Henry Purcell for £276,500 and the library of British double agent Kim Philby for £152,628.

(GERALDINE NORMAN)

PHILATELY

In 1994 the worldwide stamp market enjoyed brisk sales of both major single stamps and important, but not always large, collections. Postal authorities continued efforts to attract adolescent collectors, and the International Federation of Stamp Dealers' Associations instituted a new annual award, the Golden Globe, which honoured the national post office considered by the international stamp trade to have done the most to promote philately. The first award was bestowed on Britain's Royal Mail, with the U.S. Postal Service and the Australian Post Office close runners-up. An important factor in the Royal Mail's success was its reorganized Collectors' Club (the former Stamp Bug Club), which raised its membership to 70,000.

A new world record for a single philatelic item was established by David Feldman S.A. at the November 1993 auction in Zürich, Switz., of the Hiroyuki Kanai collection of classic Mauritius stamps. An 1847 cover addressed to a wine merchant in Bordeaux, France, the only known cover to bear both the 1*d.* red and the 2*d.* blue of the "Post Office" issue, made Sw F 5,750,000 ($3,840,000). A cover enclosing an invitation to the Government House ball from Lady Gomm, wife of the governor of Mauritius, fetched Sw F 1,610,000. Ian Ray's specialized collection of the Stock Exchange forgeries of the British Victorian 1*s.* green was sold intact for £57,000 by Sotheby's (London), and a miscellany of British postal history made £7,000 (estimate, £2,700). Sotheby's first stamp sale in Hong Kong, part of the firm's 250th anniversary celebrations (*see* Sidebar), included an 1883 Chinese 3-candarins red showing the error of an additional figure "3," a hitherto unknown variety. The stamp, which was found in a schoolboy's collection and estimated at HK$15,000, sold for HK$69,000 (approximately $9,000).

Phillips (London) marked its centenary as philatelic auctioneers with an outstanding sale of British stamps and postal history totaling £431,579; a first-day cover of the 1840 1*d.* black commanded £15,645. A Perkins Bacon archive document, bearing 20 examples of the 1840 "Rainbow" cancellation trials, brought £28,000. Phillips also sold Gordon Latto's British Commonwealth collection, with exceptional proofs and essays. The total sale amounted to £157,393, including £6,200 for a composite die proof of the 5*s.*, 10*s.*, and 20*s.* Australian Kangaroo (1913), valued before the sale at £1,000. Greg Manning Auctions Inc. of Montville, N.J., specialists in handling dealer stocks and accumulations, raised $3,618,000 in its record-breaking sale in June. A very successful international exhibition was held in Seoul, South Korea, under the patronage of the Fédération Internationale de Philatélie and a regional international exhibition in Hong Kong sponsored by the Federation of Inter-Asian Philately. The latter, four-day, event drew over 200,000 visitors.

Stanley Gibbons Ltd., London, acquired the bankrupt Bristol-based business of Urch Harris & Co. Ltd. for a reported £1 million and saved the firm's worldwide new-issue service. The Association of British Philatelic Societies was formally established on Jan. 1, 1994, replacing the defunct British Philatelic Federation. The annual congress was held in September at Chelmsford, Essex. Three prominent collectors signed the Roll of Distinguished Philatelists: Wolfgang C. Hellrigl of Italy, a leading expert on the stamps and postal history of Nepal; Juan Santa Maria of Colombia, an authority on Colombian philately; and Brig. Borje Carl-Gustav Wallberg of Sweden, a student of Far Eastern philately.

(KENNETH F. CHAPMAN)

NUMISMATICS

In July 1994 U.S. Treasury officials announced that the world's best-known currency, the U.S. "greenback," would be restyled in an attempt to prevent counterfeiting on high-tech equipment. The new money likely would include off-centre portraits, watermark images, and colour-shifting inks but would retain the size and feel of existing notes. The $100 bills, the denomination most favoured by counterfeiters, would be redesigned and introduced first, probably by 1996. Several other nations, including Belgium, Canada, France, Japan, and the U.K., produced currency with high-tech antiforgery devices. The Reserve Bank of Australia circulated $5, $10, and $20 notes made of plastic.

The U.S. Mint tried to keep up with increasing demand for U.S. coinage fueled by an improving economy. Merchants in several states reported spot shortages of one-cent coins, prompting the government to boost its 1994 mintage goal to at least 19 billion coins from the 15.8 billion made in 1993. One-cent pieces accounted for about 75% of the total. The U.S. Mint also worked on six commemorative coin programs authorized by Congress, including three coin types marking the 1994 World Cup soccer games played in nine U.S. cities. Several countries sold commemoratives honouring heroes or important events of World War II, notably the D-Day invasion of France on June 6, 1944.

U.S. Treasury Secretary Lloyd Bentsen called for a moratorium on the passage of new commemorative coin programs after several lawmakers introduced proposals in Congress. Collectors also complained that the market was saturated. In March, Mary Ellen Withrow became the 40th U.S. treasurer, with responsibility for overseeing the Bureau of Engraving and Printing (BEP) and the U.S. Mint. By midyear, series 1993 Federal Reserve notes with the facsimile signatures of Bentsen and Withrow had begun to circulate. Meanwhile, a BEP employee was arrested in June in connection with the theft of $1.7 million in $100 notes from the BEP facility in Washington, D.C.

Sales of investment-grade bullion coins slumped in the first half of 1994 as precious-metal prices remained static. In 1993 the U.S. American Eagle ranked as the world's most popular gold bullion coin (514,000 troy ounces sold) and silver bullion coin (5.9 million troy ounces sold). South Africa marketed its Krugerrand in the U.S. and elsewhere following the South African all-race elections in April. From the mid-1980s until 1991, several nations had banned its importation to protest South Africa's apartheid policy.

Almost all of the former Soviet republics issued their own money, often in large denominations to keep up with inflation. Ukraine circulated a 100,000-karbovanets coupon, and Lithuania printed litas-denominated notes. On July 1 Brazil introduced the real—its sixth currency in a decade—and pegged it to the U.S. dollar. The move greatly reduced Brazil's hyperinflation, which had been around 45% a month.

U.S. rare-coin prices slipped 0.5% in the 12 months ended August 31, according to a *Coin World* survey that monitored nearly 17,000 coin values. One of 15 known 1804 U.S. silver dollars, the Dexter specimen, reportedly traded hands in a private sale for more than $575,000. Merrill Lynch & Co. announced that 399 coins costing $3.3 million were missing from the NFA World Coin Fund limited partnership. In August Merrill said it would reimburse investors in the NFA fund for their initial purchase price and likewise would pay investors in its two other rare-coin partnerships, both of which had fallen in value. The moves cost Merrill up to $30 million.   (ROGER BOYE)

This article updates the *Macropædia* article COINS AND COINAGE.

ANTIQUES AND COLLECTIBLES

In 1994 such once-ignored "collectibles" as film memorabilia, advertising, bottles, and toys were featured at special auctions. The objects that interested most collectors and buyers were found, however, in shops, shows, flea markets, and garage sales and included cookie jars, Pez candy dispensers, bubble bath containers, Beatles memorabilia, artifacts used in spaceflight, gambling devices, toys and games, animation cels, advertising materials, and vintage clothing.

The biggest news in collectibles, however, was in sports. The baseball card market was returned to the collector as investment-oriented buyers turned to other items. Rarities still sold well, but common cards lost value. Golf clubs, baseball jerseys, baseball mitts, and player-endorsed advertisements sold for higher-than-expected prices. Babe Ruth's 1921 bat set a record at $63,000. Carved wooden duck calls dating from the early 1900s set several record prices; the highest was $16,500 for a Victor Glodo checkered call.

Buyers paid sizable amounts for the rarest pieces of 18th-century American and English furniture but found many bargains for middle-market examples. The sale of an important Pennsylvania German collection fetched strong prices,

Sotheby's Birthday

At precisely 12 noon on March 11, 1994, Sotheby's, the world's leading art auction house, invited each staff member to raise a glass of champagne to toast the firm's 250th birthday. During the company's first two centuries in business, Sotheby's had reigned exclusively as the world's largest seller of books by auction, and it was not until the 1950s that the firm seriously expanded into the realm of fine art, postage stamps, musical instruments, vintage cars, scientific instruments, wine, rock-and-roll memorabilia, toys and dolls, comic-book art, and film posters.

Sotheby's was established on March 11, 1744, when a London bookseller named Samuel Baker held his first book auction—a dispersal of "several Hundred scarce and valuable Books in all branches of Polite Literature" from the library of Sir John Stanley. He formed a partnership in 1767 with George Leigh, an experienced auctioneer. Upon Baker's death, his nephew John Sotheby and Leigh divided the estate. It was the Sotheby family, however, that played a leading role in the business for more than 80 years, a period that established the firm as the leading book auctioneer of the Western world. Sotheby's dispersed the libraries of Prince Talleyrand; the dukes of Devonshire, York, and Buckingham; and volumes amassed by Napoleon.

When the last Sotheby died in 1861, John Wilkinson, a senior accountant, took the helm and promoted cataloger Edward Hodge to help him manage the rechristened Sotheby, Wilkinson and Hodge. In 1907 Hodge's son, Tom, sold partnership rights to a new group, and in 1917 the firm moved to its permanent location at 34–35 New Bond Street. By this time Sotheby's had begun to auction coins, medals, prints, and a few antiquities as well as paintings, furniture, and works of art.

When Sotheby's began a spectacular international expansion during the 1950s, it usurped Christie's preeminent position as London's dominant art auctioneer since the 18th century. The move was masterminded by Peter Wilson, a brilliant connoisseur and businessman, who became Sotheby's chairman in 1958. In 1964 the concern took out a dangerously large loan to purchase the leading New York auctioneers, Parke-Bernet, an investment that proved hugely profitable. Wilson also oversaw the opening of Sotheby offices across Europe and began to organize sales in Geneva, Monaco, Florence, Amsterdam, and Hong Kong. The company's turnover increased from £1.7 million in 1955 to £241 million in 1980, when Wilson retired. Three troubled years followed before Sotheby's was acquired by U.S. industrialist A. Alfred Taubman. Under his guidance Sotheby's played a leading role in the art investment boom of the 1980s. The firm suffered a 50% reduction in turnover in 1991 but rebounded in 1994 with annual sales in excess of $1 billion.   (GERALDINE NORMAN)

including $43,700 for a painted poplar trinket chest. At the auction of the Nina Fletcher and Bertram K. Little collection of folk art, a curly maple dressing table and box brought $31,050. Though sales of ordinary "country" furniture lagged, Anglo-Indian furniture was rediscovered, Arts and Crafts furniture held steady, and Eclectic Revival Victorian pieces rose in price. The biggest surge of interest was in '50s furniture, notably styles lumped under the term *Modernism.* Renewed interest in the period also spurred prices for '50s pottery, glass, jewelry, silver, paintings, and bicycles.

Most 19th-century glass sold at average to lower prices, yet a Mt. Washington acid peachblow tankard pitcher decorated with flowers and a verse was auctioned at a record $26,950. Several important bottle collections were sold, and a dark amber Jenny Lind calabash flask sold for a record $12,430. Italian glass by name designers of the 1930s–'50s also increased in price. Depression glass prices remained steady, while the more formal glassware of the period, such as Heisey and Fostoria, went up slightly. Common Carnival glass patterns dropped in value, but rarities remained high.

The 19th-century English dinnerware and spatterware made for the American market found new competition from newer pieces, which brought high prices. Collectors also paid handsomely for Art Deco pieces by Clarice Cliff of England. A 20th-century Beswick figure made in England showing the Beatrix Potter character of the Duchess sold for a record $2,590, and a set of four Disney-character-head vases made in the '60s brought $2,000.

Entertainment memorabilia brought exceptional prices. The Academy Award won by Vivien Leigh for her role in *Gone with the Wind* (1939) sold for $563,500. The corset worn in a 1990 concert by singer Madonna auctioned for $18,150, a record for both Madonna clothing and for any corset. Elvis Presley's signed 1973 American Express card was auctioned for $41,400. Credit cards and telephone cards joined the ranks of collectibles, while animation cels and original comic art continued to set records. A Walt Disney storyboard for *When the Cat's Away* (1929) sold for $55,200. The original art from the March 1944 *Amazing Stories* brought $25,300.

Toys continued to sell well; a 1932 cast-iron Arcade Checker cab sold for $68,200. Dolls continued to rise in price. The Kammer & Reinhardt blue-eyed, strawberry-blond schoolgirl doll set a record at $282,750. A one-of-a-kind G.I. Joe fighter-pilot action figure sold for a record $5,750, and a Madame Alexander doll in the image of film star Kathryn Grayson brought $10,400. The 1908 stuffed blue Steiff teddy bear "Elliot" sold for $74,000. Glass marbles of the '20s went for up to $6,000 each.

Advertising collectibles, popular for over 25 years, continued to sell. Rare tobacco tins, labeled perfume bottles, talcum powder tins, and automobile related pieces found new collectors. An Aerio Gas Globe used in the '40s by the Gregory (N.D.) Independent Oil Co. sold for $9,350, a record price for the glass top of a gas pump. Labels for cigar boxes, fruit crates, or beer bottles rose in price. Lithographed tin signs commanded high prices, while paper signs made price strides. An Aunt Jemima die-cut hanging six-part paper sign showing pancakes and boxes sold for $5,170.   (RALPH AND TERRY KOVEL)

Botanical Gardens and Zoos

BOTANICAL GARDENS

Notable conservation initiatives marked 1994 as a year of further consolidation for botanical garden networks and the increasingly international nature of plant conservation.

In October 1994 the Toromiro Management Group met at the University of Bonn (Germany) Botanical Garden. This group included representatives of botanical gardens, researchers, and conservationists developing an integrated conservation strategy for the tree *Sophora toromiro,* now surviving only in botanical gardens following its extinction on Easter Island. This was one of the few international conservation programs for a threatened plant linking European collection managers with protected area managers and conservationists in the country of origin. The first experimental reintroductions were planned for 1995.

Other notable examples of international cooperation included the repatriation of the critically threatened Hawaiian endemic *Alsinidendron trinerve* from the Royal Botanic Gardens, Kew, near London. This species was close to extinction in the wild and was cultivated by the Waimea Arboretum and Botanical Garden, Haleiwa, Hawaii, as part of a recovery program that would involve reintroduction. Bulbs of the extinct Chilean blue crocus, *Tecophilaea cyanocrocus,* were sent from Kew to the Chilean national botanical garden at Viña del Mar as part of a collaborative conservation project.

In May 1994 staff from the Gibraltar Botanic Garden discovered the *Silene tomentosa,* long thought to be extinct. Seeds and propagation material were collected from the three plants found, and many hundreds of young plants were in cultivation in both Gibraltar and Kew. The Rio de Janeiro botanical garden was cultivating the threatened brazilwood, or pernambuco, tree, *Caesalpina echinata,* highly prized for its mahogany-like timber and particularly valued for its use in violin bridges. A strategy was being developed to create habitat reserves east of that Brazilian city.

National and regional conservation efforts continued to develop apace. The Indonesian Plant Conservation Network was launched at the Kebun Raya Indonesia, the botanical garden at Bogor, Java, in July 1994. The network was intended primarily to facilitate communication and cooperation among conservationists working in Indonesia.

Following a meeting in the Canary Islands, the European Network for Botanic Gardens was inaugurated in May. A parallel network for the United Kingdom and Ireland began work in October 1994 after a meeting at the Royal Botanic Gardens, Edinburgh. Botanic Gardens Conservation International opened a regional office at the Utrecht (Neth.) Botanic Garden, to support activities throughout Europe.

In recognition of the urgent need to develop regional and local training courses to strengthen the role of botanical gardens as major agents for plant conservation, such courses were being inaugurated in different regions of the world. In 1994, for the second year running, the Royal Botanic Gardens, Kew, held courses on plant-conservation techniques and botanical garden management. The Australian Network for Plant Conservation, in association with the Canberra Institute of Technology, initiated a new course on plant-conservation management. The Tropical Botanic Garden and Research Institute, Trivandrum, southern India, introduced a course entitled "Practical Horticulture and Conservation of Tropical Plants."

There were also happy surprises. In July it was announced that the New York Botanical Garden in the Bronx would receive a $15 million gift—its largest ever—from the Mary Flagler Cary Charitable Trust. A small stand of trees, called Wollemi pines, thought to have been extinct for 150 million years, was discovered in Australia. (*See* ENVIRONMENT: *Wildlife Conservation.*) And in Lesotho the world's smallest species of moss, the Cape pygmy moss, *Ephemerum capensi,* believed extinct, was rediscovered. The specimen was found in the flower beds of the National University of Lesotho's botanical garden!   (MICHAEL MAUNDER)

ZOOS

International coordination and cooperation between zoos has become critical to facilitation of long-term genetic and demographic management of animal collections to implement regional collection plans. In 1994 zoos continued to build the linkages through networks of national and international zoo associations. Comprehensive accreditation programs and codes of ethics were put in place or were under development in several countries.

The International Union of Directors of Zoological Gardens–the World Zoo Organization functioned as the umbrella organization and counted 48 nations, 129 institutions, and 11 regional zoo associations (August 1994) among its membership. The union's *World Zoo Conservation Strategy* (1992) was translated into eight languages to better communicate its stated aims and objectives internationally. At its annual conference in São Paulo, Brazil, Aug. 26–Sept. 1, 1994, the IUDZG established a permanent administrative office connected to the International Species Inventory System (ISIS) office at the Minnesota Zoo. The Committee on Inter-Regional Conservation Coordination was formed to organize officials of regional conservation programs, closely linked to the activities of the Conservation Breeding Specialist Groups (CBSG; formerly called Captive Breeding Specialist Group and renamed in September) of the Species Survival Commission of the World Conservation Union. The CBSG generated and recommended various strategic plans. One of these, the Global Captive Action Plan, in September was renamed Global Conservation Action Recommendation to better describe its role. A new Genome Resource Bank program was initiated to preserve sperm, ova, embryos, tissue, and blood.

The International Studbook added three more species: the Oriental white stork, the potto, and the Vietnamese sika deer; 142 studbooks were maintained. The Cincinnati (Ohio) Zoo hatched 18 Komodo dragons—a record number; the San Diego (Calif.) Zoo bred the open-billed stork, collared pigeon, carmine bee-eater, and Siberian musk deer; the Houston (Texas) Zoo bred the crowned hornbill; and the Honolulu Zoo reproduced the magnificent bird-of-paradise (all of these breedings are believed first occurrences in the U.S.). As part of a joint U.S.-Canadian program, Calgary (Alta.) Zoo hatched the first chick in its new whooping crane breeding facility.

New facilities opened in Nagoya, Japan (phase II of a new aquarium), Singapore ("Night Safari" exhibit), Moscow (new zoo bridge to connect the two exhibit areas), London (children's zoo), Wuppertal, Germany (South American aviary), and St. Louis, Mo. (research centre and veterinary hospital). Mexico City's Chapultepec Park Zoo reopened in May following $30 million in renovations. The Stanley Park Zoo in Vancouver, B.C., was designated to be phased out by city council decision, without replacement.

The quality of life for zoo animals remained a subject of much debate. Some, generally single-objective, interest groups targeted zoos and aquariums for closure. Zoo-Check of the Born Free Foundation called for public support to close facilities it deemed substandard. Zoos that had not been able to modernize experienced compounding effects of bad press, attention from antizoo activists, and political disfavour, which often led to reduced financial support. In July the World Society for the Protection of Animals and the Born Free Foundation produced a document called "The Zoo Inquiry" that proposed legislation for zoos and questioned the contribution of zoos to conservation action.

(PETER KARSTEN)

See also Environment; Gardening.

Business and Industry Review

The world recession finally ended in 1993 and, for the first time since 1990, output in all of the major economies advanced in the first quarter of 1994. By the end of the year, recovery was in progress across the industrialized world.

In the case of the G-7 economies (Group of Seven: the U.S., Japan, Germany, France, Italy, the U.K., and Canada), the economic cycle remained desynchronized. U.S. output had risen steadily since 1991; in the U.K. recovery began a year later. In continental Europe it was only at the end of 1993 that the turnaround definitely arrived; in Japan it was not until the second half of 1994 that recession finally came to an end. For the industrialized world as a whole, 1993 marked the fourth successive year in which the manufacturing industry had contracted.

The differing cyclical experience was reflected in the policy stance of the G-7 economies. In the U.S., where inflationary concerns were becoming more important than the need to support demand, the long period of monetary ease came to an end in 1994, starting with an upward move in interest rates in February. The U.K. followed with a severe fiscal tightening in April and an interest-rate hike in September. In Germany and across the core economies of the European exchange-rate mechanism (ERM), interest rates continued to fall. In Japan both fiscal and monetary policy eased.

Still, the U.S. dollar remained weak, falling in the course of 1994 to new post-World War II lows against the Japanese yen. Its weakness was exaggerated by the fall in world bond markets after the U.S. Federal Reserve Bank began to raise interest rates. While the U.S. authorities were happy to have a low dollar, since this improved the competitiveness of U.S. industry, it caused major problems for Japan, which traditionally relied upon exports to drive its economy forward. Japan was struggling to redirect demand away from exports in favour of domestic spending, especially consumption. Meanwhile in the U.S., domestic manufacturers reveled in the heightened competitiveness with the Japanese; nowhere was this more evident than in Detroit, Mich., where the U.S. automobile industry won back market share.

Table I. Annual Average Rates of Growth of Manufacturing Output, 1980–93

Percent

Area	1980–84	1985–89	1990	1991	1992	1993
World[1]	1.7	3.9	−0.5	−1.0	−0.9	0.3
Industrial countries	1.4	3.7	−1.3	−2.0	−1.7	−0.8
Less industrialized countries	3.5	5.1	4.5	4.0	3.8	6.0

[1] For definition, *see* Table IV.
Source: UN, *Monthly Bulletin of Statistics.*

Table II. Manufacturing Production in Eastern Europe and the Former Soviet Union[1]

1980 = 100

Country	1989	1990	1991	1992	1993	%[3]
Bulgaria[2]	139	116	90	76	...	−16
Former Czechoslovakia	125	121	89	74	...	−17
Hungary	111	101	76	63	65	3
Poland	109	80	70	71	77	8
Former Soviet Union	139	139	126	...	...	−9

[1] Romania not available.
[2] All industries.
[3] % change, latest year shown from previous year.
Source: UN, *Monthly Bulletin of Statistics.*

Table III. Pattern of Output, 1990–93
Percent change from previous year

	World[1] 1990	1991	1992	1993	Developed countries 1990	1991	1992	1993	Less developed countries 1990	1991	1992	1993
All manufacturing	0	−1	−1	0	−1	−2	−2	−1	5	4	4	6
Heavy industries	0	−1	−1	1	−1	−2	−2	0	6	4	5	8
Base metals	−2	−3	−2	0	−3	−4	−3	−2	4	3	2	7
Metal products	0	−2	−3	0	−1	−2	−3	−1	8	6	5	10
Building materials, etc.	−1	−2	0	0	−2	−5	−2	−1	3	6	4	4
Chemicals	−1	0	3	1	−2	−1	2	0	5	3	6	6
Light industries	−1	0	0	−1	−2	−1	0	−2	3	3	2	4
Food, drink, tobacco	1	2	1	1	0	1	0	−1	4	4	3	4
Textiles	−5	−2	−1	−2	−8	−4	−2	−4	2	1	1	3
Clothing, footwear	−6	−4	−3	−2	−7	−6	−4	−3	−1	1	0	2
Wood products	−1	−2	1	2	−2	−3	1	1	5	5	3	6
Paper, printing	2	1	0	−1	2	0	−1	−2	5	5	4	5

[1] Excluding Albania, China, North Korea, Vietnam, former Czechoslovakia, former Soviet Union, and former Yugoslavia.
Source: UN, *Monthly Bulletin of Statistics*.

Table IV. Index Numbers of Production, Employment, and Productivity in Manufacturing Industries
1980 = 100

Area	Relative importance[1] 1980	1993	Production 1992	1993	Employment 1992	1993	Productivity[2] 1992	1993
World[3]	1,000	1,000	126	126	...	...	...	...
Industrial countries	861	812	120	119	...	...	...	...
Less industrialized countries	139	188	164	174	...	...	...	...
North America[4]	282	303	130	136	...	...	...	...
Canada	22	21	115	120	...	...	...	...
United States	260	283	139	142	90	89	154	164
Latin America[5]	79	75	114	120	...	...	...	...
Brazil	26	21	93	103	...	...	...	...
Mexico	18	...	130	...	...	...	...	...
Asia[6]	183	252	172	173	...	...	...	...
India	11	...	210	...	...	...	...	...
Japan	131	140	141	135	122	121	116	112
South Korea	6	18	360	380	...	...	...	...

Area	Relative importance[1] 1980	1993	Production 1992	1993	Employment 1992	1993	Productivity[2] 1992	1993
Europe[7]	422	350	108	104	...	...	...	...
Austria	9	9	135	131	78	...	173	...
Belgium	13	12	122	118	...	...	...	...
Denmark	5	5	138	134	97	93	142	144
Finland	6	6	121	127	71	66	170	192
France	75	62	108	104	...	...	...	...
Former West Germany	114	105	125	116	...	...	...	...
Greece	4	3	100	97	...	...	...	...
Ireland	2	4	222	234	84	...	264	...
Netherlands, The	14	14	128	125	...	...	...	...
Norway	5	4	111	113	...	...	...	...
Portugal	3	3	142	135	...	...	...	...
Sweden	13	12	110	113	...	...	...	...
Switzerland	13	13	123	122	...	...	...	...
United Kingdom	58	54	116	117	...	...	...	...
Rest of the world[8]	34	...	...	...	...	...	...	...
Oceania	15	13	111	113	...	...	...	...
South Africa	8	6	98	98	...	...	...	...

[1] The 1980 weights are those applied by the UN Statistical Office.
[2] This is 100 times the production index divided by the employment index, giving a rough indication of changes in output per person employed.
[3] Excluding Albania, China, North Korea, Vietnam, former Czechoslovakia, former Soviet Union, and former Yugoslavia.
[4] Canada and the United States.
[5] South and Central America (including Mexico) and the Caribbean islands.
[6] Asian Middle East and East and Southeast Asia, including Japan, Israel, and Turkey.
[7] Excluding Albania, former Czechoslovakia, former Yugoslavia, and European countries of the former Soviet Union.
[8] Africa and Oceania.
Source: UN, *Monthly Bulletin of Statistics*.

Perhaps the major surprise in the world economy in 1994 was the speed with which continental Europe turned around. By midyear it was clear that recovery had begun and that exports were the main factor. German capital goods exporters in particular were taking advantage of the strength of the yen to steal the march on their Japanese competitors, especially in Far Eastern markets.

One reason why the U.S. government was so keen to secure a move away from export dependency in Japan was the way in which many Pacific Rim economies followed the Japanese strategy of export-led growth and developed rapidly as a result. The recession in the G-7 barely touched upon the dynamic Asian economies, which continued to record double-digit rates of growth in manufacturing output. In this they were helped not only by the strength of the yen—since many of these economies pegged their currency to the dollar—but also by the outflow of Japanese capital looking for more profitable opportunities in the low-wage economies elsewhere in Asia. Here the main development was the speed at which China was industrializing, especially in the provinces adjacent to Hong Kong.

The world economy was experiencing a major shift in the centre of gravity of industrial production—away from Europe and North America and toward the newly industrializing, dynamic economies of Southeast Asia. Vietnam, in particular, seemed to have begun the next great boom in the area. Newly privatized local industries were making an impressive turnaround, and foreign investors and aid agencies were lining up to assist. Coping with the competition from Asia was a key determinant of growth elsewhere in the world. One encouraging feature was that many of the economies of Latin America were responding well, throwing off their hyperinflationary past. (*See* WORLD AFFAIRS: *Spotlight:* Latin America's New Economic Strategy.)

For the former communist economies, now in transition to a market-based system, the challenge from Southeast Asia was an extra hurdle. So far the more reformist economies of Eastern Europe were meeting the challenge because they benefited from their proximity to main European markets and their low wage costs. For the less reform-minded and those economies farther from Western Europe, however, huge difficulties remained.

(GEOFFREY R. DICKS)

ADVERTISING

The advertising industry in 1994 saw a rebound in ad spending that made industry executives optimistic that the "lean and mean years" of the early 1990s were permanently in the past. Ad spending by the 100 leading national advertisers, which account for more than a quarter of all advertising in the U.S., reached $37.9 billion in 1993, up 5.2% from the previous year. The Procter & Gamble Co. retained its title as the nation's leading advertiser, with total 1993 ad outlays of $2,397,500,000, up 10.8% from 1992. Consumer products and tobacco giant Philip Morris Co. ranked second, and General Motors Corp. placed third.

Widespread recovery of ad spending elsewhere lagged somewhat behind the U.S. Worldwide ad spending in 1994 was expected by one analyst to be up 5.7% to $318.3 billion, with ad spending in the U.S. alone increasing 7.3% to $148 billion. Chief among the reasons for the renewed interest in advertising was a growing sense among corporations that brand-name products were their greatest long-term assets.

The annual brand value report issued by *Financial World* magazine rated Coca-Cola as the world's most valuable brand, with a value of $35,950,000,000. (*See* TABLE V.) The magazine made its valuations on the basis of each branded product's worldwide sales, profitability, and growth potential minus costs such as facilities, equipment, and taxes. A brand with huge manufacturing expenses and a big sales shortfall could slip into a negative valuation, as was the situation with computer giant International Business Machines Corp. (IBM), which ranked last on the list of 290 brands.

Concurrent with the increased ad spending and brand values, the big four television networks—CBS, NBC, ABC, and Fox—also posted record-setting gains. Advance sales of commercial time for the prime-time season, known as the upfront market, climbed 22% to a record high of $4.4 billion in the summer. The spending frenzy was led by new product introductions, and IBM alone spent at least $150 million in the last three months of 1994 to introduce the Aptiva personal computer.

Table V.

Most Valuable Brands Worldwide in 1993

1993 Rank (1992 Rank)	Brand Name	Brand Value
1 (2)	Coca-Cola	$35,950,000,000
2 (1)	Marlboro	$33,045,000,000
3 (4)	Nescafe	$11,549,000,000
4 (7)	Kodak	$10,020,000,000
5 (8)	Microsoft	$ 9,842,000,000
6 (5)	Budweiser	$ 9,724,000,000
7 (6)	Kellogg's	$ 9,372,000,000
8 (13)	Motorola	$ 9,293,000,000
9 (11)	Gillette	$ 8,218,000,000
10 (14)	Bacardi	$ 7,163,000,000
11 (16)	Hewlett-Packard	$ 6,996,000,000
12 (21)	Intel	$ 6,480,000,000
13 (18)	Frito-Lay	$ 5,907,000,000
14 (12)	Pampers	$ 5,732,000,000
15 (17)	GE	$ 5,710,000,000
16 (23)	Nintendo	$ 5,224,000,000
17 (20)	Levi's	$ 5,142,000,000
18 (19)	Pepsi	$ 4,939,000,000
19 (22)	Campbell's	$ 4,636,000,000
20 (9)	Newport	$ 4,287,000,000

Source: *Financial World*, Aug. 4, 1994.

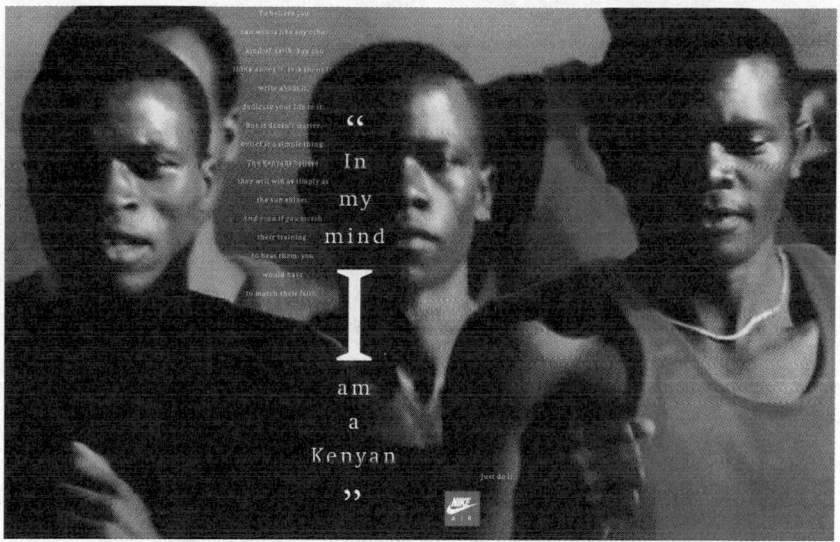

Kenyan runners, known throughout the world for their championship performances in track, appear in a Nike advertisement. Companies selling globally continued to search for advertising strategies that could be adapted effectively to different markets.
REPRINTED WITH PERMISSION OF NIKE, INC.

"Seinfeld," the NBC-TV megahit, commanded an average $390,000 per 30-second commercial, a 32% price increase over what it charged in 1993. In contrast, ABC's "Home Improvement," the number one rated show, charged only $350,000 a spot for the 1994–95 season. "Roseanne" (ABC) followed with $310,000; "Murphy Brown" (CBS) charged $290,000; and "Monday Night Football" (ABC) rounded out the top five, charging $285,000 per 30-second spot. The suspension of the major league baseball season and the delay in the National Hockey League schedule helped fuel prices for 30-second spots to air during the Super Bowl in January 1995 to more than $1 million, up from $950,000 during the 1994 Super Bowl. Advertisers usually avoided controversial programming, but the demand for advertising time was so strong in 1994 that even gavel-to-gavel television coverage of the O.J. Simpson hearings and trial generated plenty of paid advertising.

The advent of multimedia entertainment on CD-ROM and interactive, on-line media was much discussed in 1994. The opening to commercial users of the Internet global computer network, as well as commercial services such as CompuServe, Prodigy, and America Online, brought a rush of consumers interested in accessing information through their personal computers. Advertising was still in its infancy on the on-line services, with much debate taking place among advertisers and ad agencies as to how commercials should be presented.

Maurice Saatchi was forced out in December as chairman of Saatchi & Saatchi, the international advertising group he founded in 1970, under pressure from U.S. stockholders.

Regulatory agencies worldwide began placing restrictions, some of them outright bans or severe constraints, on the advertising of consumer products, particularly alcohol, tobacco, and children's toys and games. China, the world's largest cigarette market, in October banned all tobacco advertising, while Philip Morris took action against Australia and California for their strict limita-

tions on tobacco ads. In Australia, a country that many advertising executives regarded as a bellwether of social change worldwide, the government was considering tight regulation of advertising on children's media. Broadcasts of "The Mighty Morphin Power Rangers," an animated children's program, were banned in New Zealand after kindergarten teachers complained that children who watched the show were becoming increasingly aggressive and hard to discipline in the classroom. In late October, Greece prohibited toy commercials on TV between the hours of 7 AM and 10 PM. Consumer groups hailed the bill as a major step toward the "preservation of life quality" in Greece and said that it would help protect parents from being pestered by their children to buy the toys they saw advertised on TV. Investment spending in Vietnam by U.S. corporations sharply increased in 1994, led by dueling soft-drink giants Coca-Cola Co. and Pepsico. (LAURIE FREEMAN)

AEROSPACE

The Western aerospace manufacturing companies and airlines began to climb out of the worst-ever cyclical downturn in 1994, but often at savage cost to the social factors involved. Mergers, consolidations, and collaborative agreements continued apace throughout U.S., European, Russian, Indian, and Far Eastern companies in efforts to maintain or increase market share or merely to survive. In the U.S., airframe manufacturers continued to reduce the number of equipment suppliers in order to cut administrative costs and overheads. As a result of enforced slimming, many defense firms began to regain strength and stock prices started to rise.

The airlines also began a fragile recovery, and the International Air Transport Association predicted that 1994 would see a return to profitability and the end of a five-year slump for its 224 members. Reform of U.S. bankruptcy law was invoked to protect financially sound airlines against unfair competition from tottering operators, such as Eastern and TWA, whose health was being nursed prior to relaunch. In Europe, however, privatization stalled, and governments were still reluctant to liberalize controls and withdraw subsidies. Major examples were Air France and Germany's Lufthansa. The French government's efforts to bail out its national airline—Europe's biggest-ever financial rescue operation of a state-owned company—prompted threats to sue from the British government and seven European carriers.

The proposed merger between Lockheed Corp. and Martin Marietta showed how far U.S. industry was prepared to go to ensure global economic and technical ascendancy. The resulting Lockheed Martin Corp. was predicted to be the world's largest defense company and, after Boeing, the top Western aerospace company. Lockheed had previously acquired General Dynamics' Fort Worth division, builder of the top-selling F-16 military aircraft, while Martin had bought General Dynamics Space Systems (builders of Atlas) and GE Aerospace (Titan) space-launcher businesses to become the West's top rocket company.

Northrop Corp., meanwhile, bought out Grumman Corp., a leader in U.S. naval aviation, after an abortive bid by Martin Marietta only months before. In September Northrop Grumman Corp. announced layoffs of 9,000 employees. Later in the year, Northrop Grumman also moved to buy out Vought Aircraft Co.

Boeing continued as the world's ranking commercial aircraft builder, delivering about 260 aircraft during the year, although production rates generally declined. Boeing's 777 "big twin," a rival to the Airbus A330 that entered into service in 1993, made its first flight in June. The first airliner to be designed entirely on computer, it would also be—controversially—the first

aircraft to be certificated for long-range overwater operations from the date it entered into service.

With 1994 deliveries of around 130, Europe's Airbus Industrie remained the number two aircraft builder. During September the company claimed that it would eventually take 50% of the world's commercial aircraft market. U.S. Pres. Bill Clinton had earlier lobbied the Saudi Arabian royal family, however, and extracted a promise to buy Boeing and McDonnell Douglas aircraft. Aérospatiale, the French group that owned 37.9% of Airbus Industrie, received a $341 million subvention from the government in February.

McDonnell Douglas, almost bankrupt two years previously, was reborn back in business, a feat accomplished through the slashing of its workforce in half to reduce manufacturing costs. With just two families of airliners (the MD-80/90 series and the MD-11), however, it remained a niche player, and its future was still in doubt.

While demand for new airliners in the West remained sluggish, big industry growth was to be found among the Pacific Rim nations. Boeing and McDonnell Douglas both sought collaborative agreements with China to satisfy the requirements of the 400 airlines in the region. China's many airlines, already enjoying a growth rate of 25% a year over the past decade, increased that to about 30% in 1994. So phenomenal was the growth that airport capacity was predicted to be a limiting factor. Singapore Airlines took advantage of a still-depressed market to place orders and options for a staggering 52 Boeing 747-400 jumbo jets and Airbus A340-300Es worth in total $10.3 billion.

Both China and Russia experienced bad accident records. Some 320 operators sprang up in the Commonwealth of Inde-

pendent States after the breakup of the U.S.S.R.'s national carrier Aeroflot, and safety suffered. Most of the aircraft operated in the CIS had long exceeded their service lives, but deliveries of new aircraft produced locally, such as the Tupolev Tu-204 (with Rolls-Royce engines) and the larger Ilyushin Il-96, remained delayed.

The military aircraft industry was likewise a scene of struggle. Perceived lessening of world tensions, along with slashed national budgets, resulted in sharp downturns in new equipment purchases. The four-nation Eurofighter 2000 finally made its first flight, but because of development delays at least one customer—Spain—was facing the likelihood of having to acquire stopgap aircraft. The other major European project of immediate interest was the seven-nation Future Large Aircraft. Its sponsors proposed it as a replacement for the 40-year-old Lockheed C-130 Hercules. A bitter marketing struggle ensued with Lockheed to secure the business of the Royal Air Force, which would launch the project. The battle lines were drawn at the usual place: the trade-off of old but available, well-known, and inexpensive technology versus new and more expensive technology with likely development delays but with established European infrastructure. The RAF chose Lockheed on December 16, a $1.3 billion order.

Small, cheap unmanned aerial vehicles were used increasingly for clandestine surveillance of global trouble spots. The South African air force used them to watch that country's elections, while the CIA planned to introduce them over Croatia and join those already used over Bosnia and Herzegovina to monitor the progress of aid convoys and warn of ambushes.

Pentagon demands for new defense cuts put at risk such new programs as the V-22 Osprey tilt-wing transport, the F-22 fighter, and the RAH-66 attack helicopter and threatened cutbacks on the B-2 stealth bomber. Meanwhile, such impressive Russian fighters as the MiG-29 and Sukhoi-27, commercial and military threats to top Western fighters, continued to be flown with verve, imagination, and commercial success in search of customers at air shows. Russia completed its crucial deal with Malaysia for 18 MiG-29s.   (MICHAEL WILSON)

APPAREL

Clothing. In 1994 U.S. garment workers, already concerned about the competitive impact of the North American Free Trade Agreement (NAFTA), which went into effect on Jan. 1, 1994, were confronted with the news of the signing in April of the General Agreement on Tariffs and Trade (GATT), a global pact that could have even more far-reaching effects on job security.

The International Ladies' Garment Workers' Union, which boasted more than 1.2 million members at its peak in 1973, had its membership shrink to only 800,000 by June 1994.

Though apparel sales were stronger in 1994 than in 1993, they did not meet the expectation of retailers, who had overstocked inventories and were offering deeply discounted merchandise at year's end.

Simint, the Italian sportswear company that manufactured jeans for Italian designer Giorgio Armani, reported losses in 1994 of 226.5 billion lira. Armani, who held a 22.5% major stake in the concern, in-

RICH FRISHMAN

Workers complete assembly of the first Boeing 777-200, the world's largest twin-jet airliner. Designed entirely on computers and rolled out in 1994, the new airplane was intended to compete with wide-body craft from Airbus Industrie and McDonnell Douglas already in service.

fused it with 120 billion lira and placed his firm's financial director, Giorgio Gabbiani, at the helm of the troubled firm. As chairman, Gabbiani orchestrated the sale of the firm's U.S. subsidiary, Simint U.S.A., and its network A/X Armani Exchange stores. The Singaporean group of Ong Beng Seng purchased A/X Armani Exchange for $20 million in October but agreed to license the line under Armani's name.

Fruit of the Loom Inc., the largest supplier of blank T-shirts in the U.S., bought financially bankrupt jeans manufacturer Gitano Group Inc. Fruit of the Loom paid $100 million for the firm, which reportedly owed creditors $130 million. Particularly attractive to Fruit of the Loom was Gitano's high-profile, 96% name-recognition rate among consumers of jeans and the opportunity to offer Fruit of the Loom knit tops and other apparel to the Gitano line. U.S. designer Liz Claiborne expanded her clothing empire by establishing operations in Dubayy, United Arab Emirates.

Cross Colours, one of the hottest U.S. manufacturers of hip-hop clothing—apparel with a black urban attitude—nearly vanished from sight in 1994. Its parent company, Threads 4 Life Corp., had reported revenues of $89 million in 1992, up from $15 million in 1990. The Cross Colours factory on the edge of south-central Los Angeles was sold, and clothing production was farmed out to manufacturers through joint ventures and licensing agreements, after the Merry-Go-Round retail chain, which had accounted for some 60% of Cross Colours' revenues, filed for bankruptcy protection.

During the year some environmentally conscious manufacturers created recycled fabric by melting down clear plastic soft-drink bottles into raw polyester. The polyester was formed into fibres and spun into yarn to produce clothes or heavy-duty material suitable for jackets, hiking boots, backpacks, and shoes. This "green gear" carried the universal recycling symbol and cost a little more than its virgin counterpart.   (KAREN J. SPARKS)

Footwear. The catchword in footwear during 1994 was acquisitions. In the U.S., Nine West Group Inc. twice attempted to add U.S. Shoe Corp. to its empire. On July 27 Nine West offered $425 million to U.S. Shoe for its footwear division alone, which represented about 27% of the company's business. The offer was rebuffed by U.S. Shoe, but in December Nine West sweetened its bid by offering to pay $600 million in cash and warrants convertible into 1,850,000 shares of its own stock, approximately 80% of U.S. Shoe's market value. Investors urged U.S. Shoe to reconsider the deal, which, if completed, would create a nationwide, 800-store retail chain. The joint earnings of the combined companies were estimated at $1.4 billion, about twice Nine West's 1994 revenues.

Crédit Lyonnais, the distressed French banking company, announced in late December that it would sell its 19% stake in Adidas International Holding, which owned 95% of German sportswear giant Adidas AG, to an investment group headed by Robert Louis-Dreyfus, former senior executive of Saatchi & Saatchi PLC. The move left the state-owned Crédit Lyonnais with a 4% stake in Adidas AG, although it planned to sell that holding as well. Louis-Dreyfus controlled 28% of Adidas, which

had revolutionized the design of sneakers but faced increasingly strong competition from such rivals as Nike and Reebok. Adidas was expected to increase sales by 20% in 1994, however. In late December the French manufacturer Z Groupe Zannier sold its Kickers footwear brand to Flavio Briatore, director of the Benetton-Ford Formula One auto racing team.
                    (KAREN J. SPARKS)

Furs. Retail sales of fur apparel continued their upswing in 1994. Sales in the big United States market registered a third consecutive year of increase following five years of decline attributed to the recession that began in 1987. Estimates as the year ended were that U.S. fur sales would be up 10–15% to about $1.4 billion. Showing slower recovery, however, were the important Italian and Japanese markets. Still, 1993 found the supply-and-demand situation much more in balance. In fact, prices of mink and most other furs recovered sufficiently to cause ranchers and trappers to consider increasing production again. A major factor was the strong demand for pelts and apparel to supply not only rapidly growing markets in South Korea and Russia, which heretofore had been net exporters of furs, but also a new and potentially tremendous market in China.

Mink continued to be the dominant fur, by far, throughout the world, accounting for three-quarters of furs purchased by consumers in the U.S. About 20 million mink pelts were marketed internationally in 1994, and average prices of pelts climbed 43%.

Imports of manufactured fur apparel into the U.S. continued to rise in 1994, continuing the previous year's upward trend that followed a five-year decline. The increase reflected not only the uptrend in retail sales but also continued shrinkage in the U.S. fur-manufacturing industry, which paralleled declines in other apparel and related trades. Antifur activities appeared to subside somewhat.   (SANDY PARKER)

AUTOMOBILES

The automotive industry experienced significant structural changes in 1994, brought on by growing global competition. Automakers and suppliers alike were forced to undertake massive cost-cutting programs to remain competitive in their traditional, mature markets. At the same time, they were lured to the growth opportunities offered by the surging economies in many less developed nations.

Globalization. Ford Motor Co. announced a sweeping reorganization that combined its North American and European automotive operations under one umbrella. Instead of designing separate vehicles for different markets, the company would now develop common vehicle platforms and power trains to be sold worldwide. This was expected to slash costs by eliminating duplication of effort but would also result in hundreds if not thousands of employees being pushed into early retirement. Meanwhile in Japan, Honda was moving in the opposite direction by creating autonomous regional organizations in the Americas, Europe, Southeast Asia, and Japan, each with design and engineering as well as assembly responsibilities.

Germany's Bayerische Motoren Werke AG stunned the industry with its sudden $1.2 billion takeover of British automaker

Rover Group PLC that doubled the size of BMW overnight. The Munich-based manufacturer instantly joined in the low-priced market and the line of sport utility vehicles with the most upscale image in the industry: Land Rover. In late December it was announced that BMW would also collaborate with British Vickers on a new generation of Rolls-Royce and Bentley autos.

Daewoo in South Korea unveiled plans to double its capacity to two million units a year, which would vault it into the top 10 list of global manufacturers. It also announced a joint venture with a Romanian firm to build up to 200,000 cars by 1998. Samsung, the Korean electronics firm, announced it would enter the automaking business assembling cars in Korea with Nissan.

General Motors announced plans to use facilities in one place of the world to fill niches in another. Cadillac, for example, would sell a future model based on a platform built by Opel in Germany; Buick toyed with the idea of importing an Australian-built Opel; and Saturn was to get a new model based on the Opel Vectra. Meanwhile, GM's North American operations announced they would export vans to Opel in Europe and agreed on a plan to assemble pickup trucks with body panels made by GM do Brazil to be sold by Isuzu dealers in the U.S.

GM president Jack Smith announced that he would pull out of the day-to-day details of running North American operations to devote more time to increasing GM's global presence and overseeing its nonautomotive businesses. In a similar move, Louis Hughes was promoted to president of GM's international operations to devote more time to operations outside Europe.

During the year Detroit's big three automakers began taking advantage of the weak dollar to increase their sales in Japan. Not only did they lower prices, but they introduced several models with the steering wheel on the right-hand side, moves that critics had exhorted them to do for years. Ford bought the Autorama dealerships from Mazda and then announced plans to double sales in Japan every year for the next five years. Chrysler sold over 10,000 vehicles in Japan, small numbers by industry standards but a milestone in terms of the big three's efforts in the Japanese market. GM announced plans to sell 20,000 Chevrolet Cavaliers a year in Japan through Toyota dealers.

Not all the moves to globalize went well, however. Rumours of a split at Autolatina, the Ford-Volkswagen joint venture in South America, began to circulate about midyear. Though it seemed like a reasonable business deal in the mid-1980s when South America's highly protected markets suffered from few sales and exorbitant inflation rates, Autolatina floundered when South America's economies began to boom, and some of them opened the door a crack to imported vehicles. VW and Ford enviously watched as GM and Fiat racked up record sales in Brazil.

The joint-venture frenzy that began in the 1980s began to taper off. In Europe the AutoEuropa joint venture between VW and Ford to make minivans in Portugal hit a snag as VW reportedly cut its commitment to buy vans from the plant. Renault and Volvo officially broke off their attempt to merge.

China drew attention from automakers and suppliers as it unveiled a new five-year automotive plan to carry it into the 21st century. The Chinese government planned to attract two to three high-volume manufacturers and six to seven medium-sized ones by the end of the decade. Shortly after the turn of the century, three or four globally competitive companies would have survived the competition. The government engaged Chrysler and Mercedes-Benz in a race to see which would build minivans on a grand scale in China. The negotiations seesawed back and forth during the year. The government also encouraged automakers to establish parts-making operations in China, as it wanted a full-fledged automotive industry and not just a collection of assembly plants using parts made elsewhere.

The North American Free Trade Agreement focused tremendous attention on Mexico and opened the Mexican market to more imports. Exports of U.S.-made vehicles to Mexico increased ten-fold over 1993 levels even though Mexico struggled through a recession during the year. European and Japanese companies also laid plans to enter the Mexican market, knowing that in 10 years they would be able to export vehicles tax free into the U.S. and Canada. BMW, Honda, Fiat, and Volvo all announced plans to build assembly plants in Mexico.

Cutting Costs. Automakers came under increasing pressure to reduce prices, which, in turn, forced them to cut their costs to protect profit margins and market share. GM completed the sale of all its rear-wheel-drive axle manufacturing plants and sold its heavy-duty alternator and engine-starter business. VW attempted to reduce labour costs by adopting a four-day workweek in Germany. The trade unions accepted this measure only after VW threatened to lay off 30,000 workers. VW also announced it was cutting 43% of its U.S. workforce in a pitched effort to make its American operations profitable.

In a move that was quickly being emulated throughout the industry, VW announced it would develop all future cars from three basic platforms, down from the current more than a dozen. By increasing parts commonization, the company expected to increase economies of scale and cut costs.

Pressures were also passed down to the supplier industry. The automotive components groups at GM and Ford were given mandates to expand their sales to other car companies. GM's group was instructed to sell 50% of its components outside the corporation's North American operations, while Ford put plans in place to double its non-Ford business in components to 20% of sales. Chrysler announced that in the next five years it would slash the number of tier one suppliers (suppliers that deliver directly to the factory) it used to 150, down from the current 1,200. Many tier one suppliers announced they would reduce the number of suppliers they used, too.

GM announced a major reorganization of its North American operations, with an eye to reducing layers of management. GM also created a Small Car Group that included Saturn, ending that division's corporate autonomy, but tried to ensure that Saturn's unique culture was not completely lost by naming Saturn president Richard

G. ("Skip") LeFauve to run the Small Car Group. Despite previous attempts at efficiency, GM lost $328 million in North America during the third quarter, even though it was completely sold out of cars and trucks.

Marketing and Sales. Chrysler announced that its new Neon compact car would be priced at $8,975. Competitors recognized they could not profitably produce a vehicle at such a low price. Chrysler was thought to earn nearly $1,000 per vehicle. Showing its confidence in the future, the company announced it would boost capacity to 3.2 million units from 2.6 million by 1996.

U.S. automakers remained bullish throughout the year. Economists at the big three predicted the industry would enjoy strong sales through 1996. Chrysler, the most optimistic of the automakers, predicted the industry would achieve sales of about 17 million units a year by 1996, eclips-

ing the 16.3 million unit-a-year record set in 1986. Even so, suppliers cautioned there may not be enough manufacturing capacity to reach a 15.5 million sales rate, pointing to shortages in antilock brakes, iron castings, rear-wheel-drive axles, automatic transmissions, and V8 engines. On top of that, American steel companies began to run into capacity problems, which threatened to increase prices up to 10%. The industry also began to run into problems with heavy overtime schedules. Not only did this create labour problems in some places, but there was a growing feeling that the industry was simply working its people and machinery too hard. Gross pay for an average hourly worker in the U.S. reached $48,000 a year, with over $11,000 of that due to overtime pay.

As in 1993, trucks were the major force driving the increase in the U.S. market. Indeed, trucks (including minivans and sport utility vehicles) now represented 42% of all

sales. Chrysler, Ford Division, and Chevrolet were now selling more trucks than cars.

By midyear most Japanese automakers showed surprising resilience in the U.S. market, despite the strength of the yen, which forced them to raise prices several times. While this adversely affected earnings, they were able to increase their market share beginning in the second quarter and kept on gaining during the rest of the year, thanks to aggressive lease programs.

Japan's home market, however, struggled through its third year of recession. By year-end the first glimmers of a turnaround began to appear, but not before vehicle production sagged below that of the U.S. for the first time in 15 years.

The European market also continued to be extremely weak. With the hope that a stronger market was just over the horizon, Fiat, Lancia, Peugeot, and Citroën unveiled four new minivans that they produced jointly. Auto sales continued their

Welders work on a truck chassis at a Dana plant in Kentucky that supplied automotive components to General Motors. Although U.S. automakers were reducing the number of their suppliers, they tended to give even larger amounts of work to those remaining under contract.
FRITZ HOFFMANN—JB PICTURES

strong increase in South Korea, up 18.5% to two million units, and China, up 18.5% to 1,280,000 units. Sales increases in Latin America, though not in double-digit figures, continued at a robust rate.

Foreign Car Makers in the U.S. To escape the higher costs imposed by the rise of the yen, Japanese automakers announced they would increase their production in U.S. plants and buy more from U.S. suppliers. Honda, for example, announced plans to increase its North American capacity by 110,000 units a year and to make a new Acura luxury car in Ohio. Fuji announced it would begin assembling 2.2-litre engines for the Subaru Legacy in the U.S. in 1995. Toyota opened its second assembly plant in Kentucky, increasing its capacity in the U.S. by 200,000–250,000 units, and began laying plans to build a front-wheel-drive minivan at its new plant. On the other hand, the company bluntly warned its U.S. parts suppliers that their quality, response time, and costs were still not good enough. BMW hinted that production at its assembly plant in Spartanburg, S.C., would double to 150,000 units, and more models would get added than the company had originally announced.

Japanese automakers were irked by a U.S. content label law that was introduced in the fall for 1995 models. The label identified the percentages of U.S. and Canadian parts, the two countries that provided the most non-U.S./Canadian parts, the point of final assembly, the country source for the engine, and the country source for the transmission. The Japanese automakers objected to the label because it allowed the big three to count a component as 100% U.S. if it was sourced from one of their in-house suppliers—even if that component was made in Mexico. This deliberate provision in the law resulted in virtually identical cars built in the same plant exhibiting different levels of local content.

Research and Development. Major automakers poured millions of dollars into research and development of aluminum cars, spurred by fears of higher gasoline prices in the future and by concerns of stricter fuel economy and emission legislation. In the U.S. the big three and the federal government refined the goals of the government's Partnership for a New Generation Vehicle (PNGV), popularly known as the 80-mi-per-gal Super Car program. Almost all automakers continued to argue against the electric vehicle mandate in California, saying it would result in vehicles that had limited range and were very expensive to manufacture. California served notice that it would not back off the mandate, and 11 other states were considering analogous legislation.

The auto industry bullishly mobilized its marketing muscle behind navigation systems. These in-car guidance systems, which relied on either satellite positioning or an inertial guidance system, allowed motorists to follow computer directions to their destinations. The devices were already selling by the tens of thousands per month in Japan and promised to do the same in the U.S. and European markets. Oldsmobile was the first to offer a factory-installed navigation system in the U.S.—a $2,000 option available in the Eighty-Eight.

Sadly, one of the greatest growth markets for new automotive technology was theft deterrence. Antitheft devices were expected to create a $160 million-a-year market in North America by 2000—and a $1 billion market in Europe. (JOHN MCELROY)

BEVERAGES

Beer. Though brewers' main ingredients are hops, malt, yeast, and water, the leading beer marketers spent 1994 searching for a magic concoction that would spark sales for their beverages, as growth for the business in the United States and Europe remained sluggish, hovering in the 1% range.

The tonic of choice throughout the industry was ice beer. A second-year phenomenon now embraced by every major brewer, ice beer grew to represent 6% of the North American beer market and made inroads in Japan (where Anheuser-Busch was importing contract-brewed Kirin Ice from the U.S.). While such brands as Miller Lite Ice and Ice Draft from Budweiser left little doubt as to the identity of their mak-

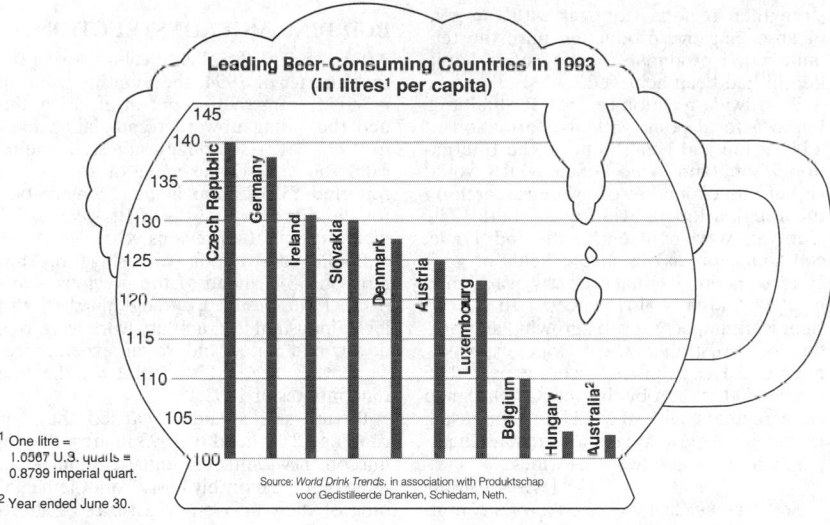

Leading Beer-Consuming Countries in 1993 (in litres[1] per capita)

[1] One litre = 1.0567 U.S. quarts = 0.8799 imperial quart.

[2] Year ended June 30.

Source: *World Drink Trends*, in association with Produktschap voor Gedistilleerde Dranken, Schiedam, Neth.

ers, brand names such as Red Dog and Red Wolf Lager were a little more mysterious. Nonetheless, both of these varieties came from the brewers of Miller and Budweiser, and each represented an effort to make these behemoths of brew seem a little more craft-oriented. Meanwhile, microbrewers, led by Boston Beer Co. and its Samuel Adams line, continued to set the fashion trend in the industry.

Brewers were not content to stick to their home turf in 1994 but restlessly prowled other markets. Anheuser-Busch continued to seek a greater presence in Europe, negotiating either to secure the Budejovicky Budvar name from its Czech owner, maker of the "other Budweiser," or to acquire a minority stake in the brewery. Among 1994's notable cross-border alliances were an agreement between Canada's John Labatt Ltd. and Mexico's Fomento Economico Mexicano, S.A. (Femsa), to provide imports for the U.S., and the entry of Japan's Asahi into the Canadian market through Molson. Vietnam sent its first-ever brew to the United States in the form of Hue Beer, while Stroh from the U.S. sought to return to Vietnam as the U.S. trade embargo was lifted. Nearby, Heineken made plans to begin brewing in Cambodia.

(GREG W. PRINCE)

Spirits. In the spirits industry, where growth in 1994 was disappointing (the sector struggled to keep pace with 1993 sales in both the U.S. and the U.K.), gains were made by flavoured spirits. Goldschläger Cinnamon Schnapps Liqueur and Finlandia Arctic Cranberry Vodka were in the vanguard of the new breed of spirits designed to tempt taste buds in the 21–35 age range. These brands succeeded on the strength of aggressive marketing and a lighter touch. Finlandia's cranberry offering kept the alcohol level down to 30% by volume, versus 40% for standard vodkas.

Vodka continued to be a spirited arena for all competitors. Boris Smirnov of Russia, grandson of Petr Smirnov, distiller to the tsar, won the latest round in a trademark war with Grand Metropolitan's Smirnoff's brand to sell in the homeland of the beverage. Longtime category leader Absolut vodka settled in with new distributor Seagram. Its former U.S. importer, Carillon, took on the Stolichnaya business from PepsiCo and created a flavoured line

of its own, featuring Stolichnaya Ohranj—an orange variety. There was also action in the tequila business, another place where younger drinkers were attracted. Led by mainstays like Jose Cuervo and comers including El Tesoro, the Mexican spirit continued enjoying 5%-plus growth.

More traditional spirits were not without their devotees in 1994, however. Scotch whisky celebrated its 500th anniversary in May. Distillers showed that an upscale-oriented marketing program could add lustre to established labels and cultivate the terrain for new "alternative" pours such as J.E.T., a product of the Paddington Corp. In response, the Isle of Arran in Scotland opened its first legal distillery in more than 150 years. In March Allied-Lyons, parent of Allied Distillers, a major player in the Scotch market, announced it was buying Spain's Pedro Domecq group for £739 million; the new concern, Allied Domecq, became the world's second largest spirits producer. Though not the U.S. force they were in the early 1990s, prepared cocktails showed that convenience could still be alluring to consumers in the U.K.—for example, a canned gin and tonic featuring Gordon's, the world's top-selling gin.

(GREG W. PRINCE)

Wine. World wine production fell 9% in 1993–94 compared with the previous season, reaching 260 million hl (hectolitres; 1 hl = 26.4 U.S. gallons). This was essentially attributable to a 17% fall in production in the countries of the European Union (EU). Italy remained the top producer, with 62.8 million hl, followed by France (54.8 million hl) and Spain (27.5 million hl). A slight recovery was noted in the United States, where production reached nearly 17 million hl.

Estimates of world exports showed an increase of 2%, to 46 million hl, of which nearly 90% represented trade within the EU. Imports fell in 1993 in both developed and less developed countries, with a worldwide drop of more than 2 million hl. The decline in global production in 1993–94 was generally more than offset by the fall in consumption, however. Wine reserves actually grew somewhat despite the uprooting of some 320,000 ha (768,000 ac) of vineyards in the EU between 1988 and 1993. A project to reform the EU market mechanism that was proposed in 1994 would strengthen regional controls with the goal of absorbing overproduction until the recommended production ceiling of 154 million hl had been achieved.

Worldwide reaction to "neo-Prohibition" found a focal point with the formation of a Nutrition and Health unit in the International Vine and Wine Office, which would gather and circulate worldwide research on the relationship of wine and health. The General Agreement on Tariffs and Trade, containing provisions in the fields of agriculture and intellectual property, was signed in 1994 and was also expected to have a significant impact on wine growing and production. Australia, whose wine exports—mainly to EU countries—were expected to reach $700 million by the year 2000, signed an agreement with the EU to stop using European geographic names such as Champagne and Burgundy for its wines.

(YANN JUBAN)

Soft Drinks. The global cola wars continued in 1994 as both Coca-Cola and Pepsi-Cola regained their beachheads in South Africa and Vietnam, which had been closed by political and trade barriers. Coca-Cola took its brand of refreshment to Uzbekistan, signing a joint venture agreement in March, and opened a new bottling plant in Albania in May.

Coca-Cola also persuaded the British grocery chain J. Sainsbury to redesign Coke-lookalike cans for its proprietary cola to avoid customer confusion. Even so the name-brand colas in the U.K. were gradually losing market share to the "supermarket" brands, which had won well over 30% of the market by December. These brands included Sainsbury's Classic, Safeway's Select, and Richard Branson's Virgin Cola—all produced by the Canadian firm, Cott's.

Pepsi introduced new consumer-readable "freshness dating" on its diet soft drinks in April. By admitting that low-calorie soda with aspartame tends to lose its taste over time (and being the first to offer "fresh" beverages), Pepsi hoped to revive sagging Diet Pepsi sales. Johnson & Johnson, meanwhile, introduced a new, more stable sweetener generically called sucralose. In the name of residual trademark recognition, Coca-Cola reinvented its hourglass-shaped bottle to fit plastic technologies of the 1990s. It also redesigned its Diet Coke can.

In the "sports drink" category, Quaker Oats Co. (maker of Gatorade) introduced fruit-flavoured, lightly caffeinated Sun Bolt in June. Meanwhile, Red Bull, the high-caffeine product of a tiny Austrian concern, captivated German youth and seemed poised to repeat its success elsewhere in Europe. Coca-Cola marketed its new OK Cola to young adults through a cool, "negative presence" campaign and introduced noncarbonated, fruit-juice-based Fruitopia through its Minute Maid subsidiary to fend off threats from the likes of New Age sensation Snapple. Coca-Cola and Nestlé announced that they were revamping their joint tea agreement after they placed a distant third behind Pepsico–Thomas J. Lipton and Snapple (which was sold to Quaker Oats in November) in that market. In 1994 the brand to watch seemed to be two-year-old Arizona Iced Tea. U.S. carbonated soft drink sales increased at about 5%, somewhat ahead of the rate in the U.K.

(GREG W. PRINCE)

BUILDING AND CONSTRUCTION

After shaking off a slight decline during the first quarter of 1994, the monthly value of new U.S. construction put in place continued the strong upward trend dating back to 1992. At a seasonally adjusted annual rate, the U.S. Department of Commerce reported $515 billion in new construction for the first nine months of the year, a 9% increase from the previous year.

Public construction was sluggish, running only 3% ahead of the previous year's pace. Educational spending matched this level, industrial and military work were well down, and water and sewer expenditures were well ahead of the total for the first nine months of 1993.

Private side spending carried the day, running 12% ahead of 1993 figures. Spending on new housing units continued to increase on a monthly basis from the beginning of the year, despite a series of short-

Studs and joists of steel are being used in the construction of this house in Pennsylvania. As the price of wood increased, the use of steel, which also could provide better protection against storms and earthquakes, increased in home building an estimated 150-fold between 1992 and 1994.

SAL DIMARCO—THE NEW YORK TIMES

term interest rate hikes by the Federal Reserve, which was trying to keep strong economic growth from fueling inflation. The Fed jumped the rate by $^{3}/_{4}$ of a point—to 5.5%—after the November elections, the largest increase since 1981 and the sixth during 1994. Fixed rates for 30-year residential mortgages, below 7% at the first of the year, had climbed to over 9%. Consequently, economists predicted that spending on new housing units would continue to fall off from the peak reached in May. Rising interest rates also slowed an upward trend in housing costs, according to the National Association of Home Builders. The median price during the second quarter of 1994 was $153,000, up from $148,000 for the second quarter in 1993.

In Canada the economic recovery strengthened, with a first-quarter growth rate of 4.2%. By June housing starts had hit 166,600 units, the highest level in 18 months and well above May's 158,400 units.

Unemployment fell to 10.3% in June, the lowest rate in almost three years. The growth in full-time employment was expected to boost consumption. But higher interest rates and expectations of a slowdown in U.S. economic growth led economists to lower predictions for real gross domestic product (GDP) growth to 3.7% for 1994 and 3.2% for 1995.

In the U.K. GDP growth continued above 1993's 2% level. It was running at an adjusted annual rate above 3%. By the end of the second quarter, the unemployment rate stood at 9.4%, down from the 1993 cumulative rate of 10.3%. Housing starts hit 50,800 for the second quarter, some 10% above the annualized rate from the previous year. House prices fell by 2% from March to September and stood below the level of September 1993, indicating low consumer confidence in the economy. Despite an absence of inflationary indicators, the authorities boosted interest rates by 50 basis points in September, the first increase in five years.

GDP growth in France pushed toward 2.2% for the year, thanks to improved private consumption and investment patterns. Employment growth was expected to offset any slowdown in consumption as government incentives expired and moderate wage and price inflation kept the recovery on a solid track. Germany came out of recession at a rapid pace during the first half of 1994. GDP growth predictions for the year were raised to 2.3%. Although exports were the main driver of the recovery, increased construction investment also played a role.

Japan's GDP growth rate for 1994 was running at a 1% level. Residential construction provided one exception to the bleak overall economic picture. Housing starts, stimulated by low interest rates and land prices, increased almost 12% in the second quarter from the 1993 level for the same period.

(ANDREW G. WRIGHT)

CERAMICS

In 1993 the ceramics industry showed both strong growth and significant change. The growth was due to the strengthening economy and the strength of the building, home appliance, and automotive industries. The change resulted from fluid markets, especially for advanced ceramics, with the reduction in defense spending having the most significant effect.

The defense sector had long been a major driver in the development of advanced ceramics because of their key role in modern military systems. With the decrease in U.S. government funding for research and development in this area, as well as a projected decrease in future military markets, ceramics-manufacturing companies found themselves downsizing in 1994 and trying to change their focus toward competing in civilian markets, which required lower-cost, higher-volume products.

Worldwide sales of ceramic materials and components in 1993 totaled over $90 billion, according to a survey by *Ceramic Industry*. This survey included captive production of ceramic materials and components, a growing percentage of total production, especially in advanced ceramics. Worldwide sales of advanced ceramics were over $18 billion in 1993, an increase of almost 25% over 1992, although this figure included some electronic devices based on electronic ceramics. Approximately one-third of these sales were capacitors, electronic substrates, and electronic packages, which continued to be the largest segment of the advanced ceramics market. Engineering ceramics now accounted for approximately 25% of the advanced ceramics market, however.

U.S. shipments of refractories in 1993 were estimated at $2.7 billion, which was well above the 1992 level of $1,950,000,000. Worldwide sales were about $6 billion in 1993. Orders and shipments in 1994 were running well above the 1993 levels because of strong steel production as well as increased capital spending in the glass industry and other thermal process industries.

Porcelain enamel sales showed a strong increase in 1993 due to increased appliance sales, which accounted for approximately 85% of porcelain enamel sales. Sales in 1994 were expected to increase at least 5% over the 1993 level of more than $6 billion.

U.S. sales of whiteware (including tile, dinnerware, sanitaryware, and electrical porcelain) increased in 1993. Tile was especially strong, with 8% growth in shipments, and another 10% growth was projected for 1994. Sanitaryware sales also showed strong growth. The increase in sales in both of these areas was primarily a result of the strong increase in residential and commercial construction.

Perhaps the top technical news of the year was the report that Hoechst CeramTec in Germany had developed a manufacturing process for silicon nitride valves for automobile engines. These ceramic valves could be processed at a cost equal to that of metal valves. The primary advantages of silicon nitride valves for passenger car engines were reduced noise (diesel engines) and improved fuel economy. Because of their lower density (about 35% of that of current metal valves), silicon nitride valves have been widely used in racing engines, but their cost had been too high for use in passenger cars. Now several European automobile manufacturers were planning to use silicon nitride valves. The significance of this development went beyond valves, since cost had been the major factor keeping silicon nitride and other structural ceramics from entering a number of other markets.

The Electrofuel Manufacturing Co. of Canada developed a diesel igniter based on silicon nitride. Because of their high cost and a life expectancy of only a few cold-weather start-ups, igniters were not often used for diesel buses in Canada; rather, the engines were kept running 24 hours a day during cold weather. With the new igniters, the engines could be cold started (at −40°) in 15 seconds. The lifetime of the igniter would be comparable to the life of the engines. A better fuel economy and reduced soot emissions would be obtained if the igniters were left on while the engine was running.   (DALE E. NIESZ)

CHEMICALS

Major product volumes were up in the world chemical industry in 1994—handsomely in the U.S. and encouragingly for European companies. Japan, too, was showing signs of recovery, although its chemical industry looked good only in comparison with other domestic industries. In the U.S., chemical plants as a group were operating at 90% of rated capacity. Generally, indications were that the boom would last through 1995—

most welcome news after several years of plant closings, huge corporate employment cutbacks, and company consolidations. Factors that encouraged industry leaders included the seemingly more stable world economy, successes in trade matters (the conclusion of the General Agreement on Tariffs and Trade and the formation of its successor, the World Trade Organization), and the stability of hydrocarbon products at moderate levels.

In financial terms the U.S. chemical industry had a fine year, easily the best in the past three, and companies reported outstanding profits. Production in 1993 was up 3%, with the gains in organic chemicals— the big petrochemicals—up 9%. The chemical units of E.I. du Pont de Nemours & Co. (which owns an oil company), the largest U.S. concern, for example, had third-quarter 1994 results 97% above 1993, and many others had reports nearly as good. Financial analysts were confident that overall, U.S. chemical company earnings would be 40% above the 1993 marks. Specialty chemicals (narrow use, relatively costly compounds) did well in 1994.

The commodities (lower-cost bulk items such as plastics, fibres, caustics, and sulfuric acid), partly because of their strong catch-up pace, enjoyed extraordinary growth that seemed probable to carry well into 1995. This pattern was likely to be followed in Europe and the Far East.

Europe's chemical producers recovered more slowly but nonetheless had a good year in 1994. The largest chemical company in the U.K., Imperial Chemical Industries PLC, saw its third-quarter profits up 59%. In March representatives of the chemical industry in several European countries met in Brussels and agreed on a program of collaboration in chemical research and development to help combat challenges from North American and Japanese industries.

The reunification of Germany wrought huge changes in its chemical industry, but there were complaints in that country that too much money had been poured into rehabilitating East German plants. Data from the European Chemical Industry Council showed that Germany's chemical workforce shrank by 46,100 in 1993 compared with that of 1992. In mid-October it was announced that the Dow Chemical Co. would obtain control of three large chemical complexes in former East Germany.

A more significant degree of rationalization was accomplished in Eastern Europe. Chemical production indexes in Bulgaria, Hungary, Poland, and Romania inched up in 1993 compared with the previous year's indexes but remained well below their marks of five years earlier, and job losses continued. Volume of sales in the Czech Republic and Slovakia dropped by about 10% in the period after their separation. Countries of the former U.S.S.R. saw their chemical industries still in turmoil, with Russia's 1992 chemical production index tumbling 21% and Ukraine's almost 25%.

The Far East—especially China— emerged as the region with the greatest growth potential for chemicals. Even hobbled by a shaky political outlook, aging leaders, severe inflation (27% in mid-1994), and an extraordinarily poor infrastructure, China nonetheless saw five years of success in moving toward industrialization. This boom reflected both the country's large

population and the government's willingness to encourage private enterprise.

Western chemical companies, following the lead of firms in Japan and Taiwan, initiated joint ventures with enterprising Chinese partners. By 1991 foreign cooperative industry (all types) had grown 55%, while state-owned company growth was 8.4%, and that at collectives was 16%. According to government figures, Chinese industry had reached a value of $18 billion in late 1994, 22% ahead of the output mark for 1993.

Japan in 1993 was in the depths of its recession, and its chemical production index dipped 1% compared with that of 1992 (not too bad, since the all-manufacturing figure slid 5% in 1993). South Korea, whose chemicals drive dogged Japan's producers, cranked up a 10% chemical production index gain (it was a 4% gain for all manufacturing). The value of its exports climbed 7%. Taiwan also managed a 7% 1993 gain in chemical production index, about three times that of its total manufacture picture.

The rising yen was part of Japan's economic trouble. In 1993, for example, its all-manufacturing category slipped 5%; chemicals did a bit better, with only a 1% dip in production index. Among Japan's problems were its dependence on foreign-produced oil and gas and its generally high-cost industrial structure. Japan's high-cost operations and small plants were exploited by Taiwan and South Korea, with the latter country's buildup in the key raw material ethylene particularly threatening.

Two Japanese giants, Mitsubishi Kasei Corp. and Mitsubishi Petrochemical Co. Ltd., merged to form Mitsubishi Chemical Corp., whose $10 billion-a-year sales would put it among the 15 largest chemical companies in the world.

India, despite some major political problems, built a chemical industry that far outpaced the rest of its industrial growth. In 1993 general manufacturing grew just 1%, but the chemical industry rose 5%. The chemical industry was India's largest (valued in 1988 at $1.2 billion), some 30% larger than textiles and 50–75% bigger than India's other most important industries.

On the world scene, performance of a handful of high-volume chemicals showed that this "mature" industry could be surprising. Polyester resins and fibres, for example, showed unexpected growth in 1994 and were expected to do so again in 1995. Polyester's hot growth area in Europe and the U.S. was its use in bottles. A cotton shortage in India and China in 1993 and 1994 imperiled their textile industries, and they turned to polyester fibres to keep mills turning.   (J. ROBERT WARREN)

ELECTRICAL

In North America and Great Britain, signs of a moderate recovery in the market for the electrical goods manufacturing industry began to appear in late 1993 and continued into 1994. Continental Europe was still in the grip of a recession, however. The electrical multinational Siemens reported that "during fiscal 1993, Germany slid into a severe recession, while growth in Western Europe and Japan ground to a halt. One of the few bright spots was the U.S., which continued its slow but perceptible recovery." In July Siemens warned that its 1994 profits would almost certainly be lower because of falling interest income (which accounted for one-third of net profit in 1993) and the continuing recession in Germany.

Siemens' views were echoed by Groupe Schneider, a new electrical multinational conglomerate formed by the pooling of the operations of two French companies, Merlin Gerin and Telemecanique, and the U.S.-based Square D.

Rebuilding the electrical industry in the former communist bloc was taking longer than expected. Siemens operated 29 joint ventures with Eastern European companies but did not expect a substantial expansion of business in the near or medium term because progress to a market-driven economy was proving slow. Percy Barnevik, president and CEO of Asea Brown Boveri (ABB), which had the majority share in 45 joint-venture companies in Central and Eastern Europe, saw the opening up of this market as "an historic opportunity, not as a threat to Western Europe."

For most electrical equipment manufacturers, the period of stagnation was not wasted. Managements learned how to rationalize operations and improve manufacturing efficiency. None fared better than General Electric (GE), where operating margins rose to a historic high of 12.5% in 1993 and a "stretch" target of 15% was set. ("Stretch" was the latest management idea devised by GE. It meant "using dreams to set business targets—with no real idea of how to get there. If you do know how to get there—it's not a stretch target.") The company also aimed at an inventory turnover of 10 times in a year (it was 4.7 in 1991, 5.3 in 1992, and 6 in 1993).

ABB set more modest targets. During 1993 ABB reported an increase of 6% in productivity, and its operating margin rose to 7.7% from the 1992 figure of 6.1%. ABB's target was a 10% operating margin and a 25% return on capital.

Electrical manufacturing revenue figures (excluding ancillary businesses) were $26,-499,000,000 for Siemens, $24,419,000,000 for ABB, and $23,592,000,000 for GE, followed by GEC Alsthom with $9,786,000,-000, Westinghouse with $7,407,000,000, and Groupe Schneider with $7,225,000,000.

The largest employer in the industry was also Siemens, with a total payroll at the end of 1993 of 391,000—down from 413,000 in 1992. ABB employed 206,490, down from 213,407 in the previous year. These figures hide radical changes that were taking place in the geographic distribution of the industry, however. For example, driven by weak growth in demand, major restructuring, and productivity gains, ABB's workforce fell in the industrialized world by some 47,000. At the same time, the company added 35,000 new personnel, chiefly in the Asia-Pacific region and Central and Eastern Europe, markets with good growth rates and lower costs.

Similarly, Siemens' president and CEO Heinrich von Pierer reported steady expansion in Southeast Asia, "a dynamic market for our products as well as an attractive production location for our global business activities." Siemens' annual reports were unusual in the amount of space devoted to employee affairs. The company invested DM 1.1 billion in basic and in-service training of its workforce in 1993. Siemens also had 15,000 young people worldwide undertaking industrial and commercial apprenticeships. During the year, 135,000 suggestions were made by the employees that benefited the company by DM 140 million.

Both Siemens and ABB were said to be interested in a new form of electric motor demonstrated at the 1994 Hanover (Germany) Fair by Reto Schob of the Swiss Federal Institute of Technology in Zürich. The motor had no bearings; the rotor was suspended magnetically, avoiding friction and the need for lubrication. The motor's potential was immense, notably in applications where bearing lubricants can cause contamination, such as blood pumps and devices for transporting food and pharmaceuticals. The bearingless motor could be built from standard motor parts with an additional winding and a few sensors.

(T.C.J. COGLE)

GAMES AND TOYS

Despite its commissioning of 33 manufacturing plants in locations as disparate as Thailand, Japan, Mexico, China, and Malaysia, Japanese toy company Bandai Co. still failed to meet massive global demand for the Mighty Morphin Power Rangers, its runaway hit toy of 1994. Power Rangers fever gripped the world and elevated the product to the all-time top five list—up with the likes of the Teenage Mutant Ninja Turtles and Cabbage Patch Kids. As 1995 approached, there was little sign that demand was slowing. In the U.S. alone, sales reached over $400 million, but they could have been much closer to $600 million if anyone had been able to predict just how obsessed children were going to become with the 10-year-old live-action TV series originating in Japan and repackaged with new U.S. footage based around five wholesome, all-American kids.

Supply and demand were very much the buzz words of the year in the games and toy business. In the U.S., demand for 16-bit video game machines such as Nintendo

GUY AROCH

A Power Ranger prepares to battle the enemy. "Mighty Morphin Power Rangers" was television's hottest show among U.S. children, creating an extraordinary demand for toys and other merchandise based on the series.

Co.'s Super Nintendo and Sega Enterprises' Genesis fell by as much as 30%, although this was viewed as a temporary stall in the popularity of TV gaming as people eagerly awaited the arrival in 1995 of new hardware platforms, such as Sony's PlayStation, Sega's Saturn, and Nintendo's Ultra 64, all of which were set to debut in Japan before going to Europe and the U.S.

In Europe the supply-and-demand debate centred around the European Union's vote in February to restrict imports of certain Chinese toys. Britain alone voted against a motion to impose quotas on three product categories (most noticeably soft toys and nonhuman figures) and found itself isolated as nations such as Spain and France showed their protectionist colours in the name of saving European jobs. The quotas were to damage the European toy business to the tune of $3 billion as local importers were granted licenses that allowed them to import far fewer toys than they needed to keep store shelves stocked. Rather than revitalize employment in the European toy industry, importers found ways around the quotas by switching their sources of supply to countries such as Macau and by recategorizing their products to avoid punitive restrictions. Ironically, Belgium's existing import license scheme took precedence under EU regulations, and the country became a major new route for Chinese imports.

Toys "Я" Us strengthened its global grip on the retail toy market in 1994 by entering Scandinavia and announcing its intentions to launch in the Middle East. Meanwhile, manufacturers Hasbro, Inc., and Mattel Inc. continued their dominance of the global toy industry in 1994. While Hasbro failed to reproduce its hit performance of 1994, when Barney and Jurassic Park generated massive revenues, the company still expanded with an international joint venture with the Connector Set Toy Co., producers of the successful K'NEX construction toy.

Mattel, meanwhile, was on a roll. Record revenues and profits came from increasing global sales of its "power brands" such as Barbie (who celebrated her 35th birthday in 1994; see BIOGRAPHIES), Fisher-Price, and Disney movie merchandise such as the all-conquering Lion King (the movie was re-released for the holidays in late 1994), and the company was again very active on the acquisition front, swallowing the Power Wheels electric ride-on brand and the Cabbage Patch Kids during the year.

Mattel was also triumphant in a hotly contested takeover battle with Hasbro for the little-known British games manufacturer J.W. Spear & Sons PLC, whose main claim to fame was the international rights to the game of Scrabble outside North America. Hasbro already owned 27.5% of Spear and seemed to have the company in the bag when it launched its long-awaited takeover pitch. Mattel responded with a bigger offer. Hasbro countered, but Mattel's hunger for a major games brand eventually won the day.

Having eaten, Mattel the Lion King, slept—on December 19 the company announced that it was eliminating about 1,000 jobs in a move that industry analysts saw as an effort to cut costs and raise efficiency after a few years of major acquisitions. In the meantime, Hasbro contented itself with acquiring the series of top board games from the British firm John Waddington for

£50 million. The games included the British version of Monopoly (Hasbro already had the U.S. Monopoly), Subbuteo, a football (soccer) game, and Cluedo (Clue in the U.S.). *The Guardian* speculated about how Colonel Mustard and Miss Scarlet would fare in the U.S. and wondered if the popular game's more genteel players might fear the appearance of serial killers blowing away their victims in the billiard room.

(JONATHAN M. SALISBURY)

GEMSTONES

The worldwide recession had forced companies, traditionally small in any case, to downsize or even to close, according to a report from Idar-Oberstein, European centre for gemstone marketing and cutting. By late 1994 gem trade in Europe was improving overall—but from a much lower base than for many years. As always, the highest section of the trade seemed to have been relatively unaffected by the recession. International salesroom prices remained high for exceptional stones, and major sales proceeded much as always. Nonetheless, consumer confidence was shaken—as well as unsettled by changing interest rates—and many buyers were disposed to save rather than spend.

New technology continued to cast a shadow over the industry. The prospect of synthetic gem diamonds' appearing on the market undetected had yet to cause serious anxiety in the trade, but the question of disclosure of artificial colour alteration or enhancement was a major topic at conferences where regulatory issues were discussed. No solution was formed in 1994, and in light of ever increasing degrees of sophistication in manufacture, a regulation, backed with sanctions, that would be binding on jewelers and stone dealers did not seem imminent. Many dealers seemed to be in general agreement that if the colour of a treated stone was known to be stable, disclosure was not necessary. Others regarded this as unethical, holding that all known treated stones (notably rubies, sapphires, and emeralds) should be advertised as such.

No new synthetic products were placed on the market, but the strength of cubic zirconia as the best diamond simulant yet known was established. India was the world's largest user.

Top salesroom news included Sw F 2,863,500 paid for the step-cut 40.46-carat Jonker II diamond found in 1934 as a 726-carat crystal; $6.4 million for the Archduke Joseph diamond, the largest D-colour (top colour) diamond with historical importance ever to come onto the market; and $1,050,-000 million for a fancy pink diamond of 6.32 carats ($165,000 per carat).

The General Electric Co., De Beers Centenary A.G., and two European businessmen were indicted in the U.S. in February on charges of price fixing in the industrial diamond industry; the case was thrown out in December. Russia, meanwhile, was reportedly reconsidering the deal it struck in 1990 with De Beers Consolidated Mines Ltd., under which it sold 95% of its uncut diamonds through the South African cartel.   (MICHAEL O'DONOGHUE)

GLASS

Increased competitiveness and a somewhat idle economy in industrialized countries still impeded glass manufacturers in 1994 and made long-term viability as challenging as ever. Production capacity overall continued to exceed demand in almost all areas. In the Americas and the Asia-Pacific region, composites growth was expected to lead the worldwide demand for fibreglass-reinforced composite materials in 1993–94. North American growth in this area was expected to increase by 7.2% in 1994, while sales were expected to grow 8% in the Asia-Pacific region, excluding Japan.

Japan had enjoyed steady market growth in the glass industry for the past 45 years but in 1993 suffered a slight setback, with sales declining. China, one of the largest glassmakers in the world, was hit hard by a three-year austerity program from 1989 to 1991, but now was enjoying unprecedented prosperity. Markets in Southeast Asia and South America continued to expand, with solid investment in new plant and technology. Glass container shipments in the U.S. exceeded expectations, rising 4% in 1993 and totaling over 300 million gross units.

The glass industry in the European Union (EU) produced 22.9 million tons in 1993, representing a decrease of nearly 2% from 1992. Employment levels increased slightly, by 1%, however, the first positive trend since 1989.

EU price levels were severely depressed (between 20% and 40%), according to the various sectors, and the foreign trade balance (especially imports from Eastern Europe) had a negative impact on the industry's overall situation. EU demand for flat glass remained relatively stable in the first half of 1992, the second half of the year showing a decline that continued in 1993, especially in the context of demand from the automotive sector. Exports by EU countries to the rest of the world increased by approximately 15% compared with 1992 and were expected to remain stable. The EU flat-glass industry had moved from high capacity utilization in 1988 (90%) to increased surplus capacity, lowering the utilization rate to nearly 81% in 1993. In the domestic tableware market, glassware sales from Eastern European suppliers fell slightly in 1993—about 7% to $127 million in 1993. Exports by the former Czechoslovakia amounted to $50 million for glassware in the EU countries in the first nine months of 1993, down from $55 million in the same period in 1992.

Container manufacturers worldwide continued efforts to reduce waste. In Europe some countries had over a 60% national recycling rate, with levels increasing every year. Weight reductions approaching 50% were achieved for many types of container; this trend, called "lightweighting," was set to continue. New coatings made containers stronger and made further lightweighting possible. In the U.K., the proposed Directive on Packaging and Packaging Waste gave rise to concern by container manufacturers because of the inclusion of regulations from the U.S. Coalition of North Eastern Governors to reduce or eliminate heavy metals in packaging and packaging materials.   (PETER N. SMITH)

HOME FURNISHINGS

Furniture. The furniture industry recorded its third successive year of improvement in 1994. Statistics provided by the American Furniture Manufacturers Association reported $17,985,000,000 in revenues, slightly higher than projected. The projection for 1994 took a big jump to $19,837,000,000. As of April, exports were up 6%, with over half of U.S. shipments going to Canada and Mexico and credit going to the North American Free Trade Agreement.

The lists of top manufacturers and retailers reported by *Furniture/Today* also reflected the movement upward. Each of the top three manufacturers posted significant gains in revenues over the previous year, with a net income increase of 70.3% for all manufacturers. In the same positions as last year, the top three companies were: Masco Home Furnishings ($1,698,000,000), Broyhill/Lane ($980.5 million), and La-Z-Boy ($762.2 million). Klaussner Furniture Industries moved into the fourth spot, knocking LADD Furniture down to fifth.

Retailers reported that revenues grew 13.5% and net income gain was up 38.2%. Fueling this change was significant expansion, led by Heilig-Meyers, which increased its number of stores by 196, putting it in the number two retailing position. Levitz Furniture ($985.6 million in revenues) was still in first place; Heilig-Meyers ($864 million) was followed by Pier 1 Imports ($663 million). Ethan Allen, dropping to 31st place, nonetheless seemed poised for a comeback under the leadership of CEO M. Farooq Kathwari and a new, modern look.

In U.S. design issues, Contemporary began to challenge the long dominance of Americana. Homespun styles were not gone, however, as evidenced by the introduction of a Norman Rockwell collection, Thomasville Furniture Industries' "American Revival," America Drew's "American Traveler Series," and an expansion of Lane's Museum of American Folk Art collection. On the Contemporary front, important introductions included Thayer Coggin's Retro Modern by Milo Baughman, Lane's "New Rhythms" by Dakota Jackson, Universal's "Home Colours" by Alexander Julian, and Directional's Larry Laslo collection. Most significant, however, was the initiation of cause-related groups. In April Masco introduced "Made with CARE," inspired by the many countries served by the humanitarian organization CARE. In October Lexington Furniture Industries introduced Bob Timberlake's environmentally conscious "Keep America Beautiful," tied to the national organization of the same name.

British retailer Courts (Furnishers) PLC was reporting success in its outlets throughout Southeast Asia and the Caribbean, while Swedish firm IKEA announced that it planned to open as many as 10 stores in China by the end of 1996.

Three design groups Council of Federal Interior Designs, Institute of Business Designers, and the International Society of Interior Designers—unified into one organization: International Interior Design Association. The American Furniture Hall of Fame inducted four: Robert George Culp, Sr., Gustav Stickley, Thomas Franklin Wrenn, and Rose Blumkin, its first woman member.   (ABBY CHAPPLE)

Housewares. Residential security was of great concern to U.S. consumers in 1994. The *New York Times* reported that a survey of 428 builders in February found that security systems were being installed in 13% of new houses and listed as options in 63%.

Staber Industries Inc. began production of a European-style horizontal-axis washing machine with a hexagonal, vertically mounted tub that reportedly saves both water and energy. In August the U.S. Department of Energy proposed new regulations on ranges, microwave ovens, and air-conditioning units to increase their energy efficiency. Manufacturers pointed out that production costs would increase and that new designs such as windowless oven doors would likely result in wasted energy.

Products using nonstick coatings such as Du Pont's Silverstone and Whitford Corp.'s Excalibur accounted for some 70% of cookware sold in the U.S. Embedded microchips were providing memory and control functions in appliances such as microwave ovens, coffeemakers, and exercise equipment.

Styles for housewares paralleled those for furniture and inclined toward early-20th-century nostalgia. Antique dealers reported great interest in early electric housewares, and new shops specializing in old-time appliances—the big item seemed to be toasters—popped up. Manufacturers such as Hamilton Beach, Sunbeam-Oster, and Waring were quick to introduce small appliance lines with what was termed "retro appeal."   (KAREN J. SPARKS)

INSURANCE

Land, sea, and air disasters shook the insurance world in 1994. The year started badly with a severe earthquake in California and widespread winter storm damage on the East Coast. Later, tragic airline crashes shocked Charlotte, N.C., Pittsburgh, Pa., and rural Indiana. Floods devastated parts of Texas, Italy, Egypt, India, and South America. One of the worst ferryboat sinkings in history left 900 dead in the Baltic Sea. These and other disasters meant uneven operating results for insurers, with revenues generally up but profits down.

U.S. property-liability insurance sales were up 5%, but profits plunged by 78% in the first half of 1994, largely owing to record catastrophe losses of $10 billion. Homeowners, particularly in California and eastern coastal states, faced restricted markets and sharply rising rates. Most life insurers continued the near-constant 3.5% operating gain of the past five years, with lower investment yields, higher taxes, and reduced general expenses.

The distinction between banks and alternative providers blurred. Some life insurers began to concentrate primarily on higher-income clients. Health insurance rates, increasing at an 8% rate in recent years, fell to about 5% in 1994. Annual U.S. marine insurance premiums hit $1 billion for the first time as rates began to increase.

Reported results in the U.K. were also mixed. General insurance and life insurers both earned a trading profit, but Lloyd's of London, on its three-year accounting system, suffered another heavy loss, exceeding £2 billion.

Advances of the new computer and communications age streamlined some insurance services. Cellular phones appeared in the cars of sales, claims, and management personnel. "Expert" systems for underwriting and other tasks remained high on the list of new cost controls. In the U.S., Continental Group experimented with an "electronic mall" for shopping through the CompuServe on-line network. Metropolitan Life Insurance began some sales in automated kiosks featuring video conferencing

Buildings in the Los Angeles area show the damage caused by a strong earthquake that struck on January 17. Although well under half of all homeowners carried earthquake insurance, industry officials estimated that the total for insured losses might be as high as $4 billion.
ALON REININGER—CONTACT PRESS IMAGES

with agents. Through employers' payroll-deduction plans, several insurers expanded group life-health options to include auto and homeowners insurance in "multichoice voluntary plans."

Some encouraging signs of growth appeared in the new unified European Union (EU) common market for insurance, although it remained competitive with few companies dominant in more than two countries. International prospects for U.S. insurers rose as the North American Free Trade Agreement aided entry into Mexico, and new trade bills promised access to Japan.

The merger trend continued in the EU and elsewhere as companies consolidated for distribution and financial benefits. Confederation Life Insurance, a Canadian company, collapsed on August 11 amid much confusion as to how U.S. trust funds and state guaranty plans protected policy values. Investors Equity Life of Hawaii faced liquidation proceedings. American International Group rescued earthquake-ravaged 20th Century Insurance from insolvency, thus gaining entry into automobile insurance markets. Metropolitan Life and Travelers Insurance merged their group health operations. American United Life and State Life formed a strategic alliance. Agreements to merge were also reached by Central Life Assurance and American Mutual Life, as well as by Kentucky Home Capital and Keystone State Life. Sales practices of two life insurance giants, Metropolitan Life and Prudential Securities, caused class-action lawsuits, but state regulators tabled action on model laws for policy illustrations. Enrollment in health maintenance organizations passed 45 million. Managed care plans increased cost controls. Two developments in liability insurance were significant: a multibillion-dollar worldwide proposal for settling breast-implant litigation and a $750 million settlement on behalf of six million homeowners who had had leak-prone plastic piping installed more than 10 years earlier.

In the U.K., life insurers and pension funds now accounted for more than half of all personal savings. Lloyd's of London's heavy property-liability losses, however, were compounded by continued litigation by hundreds of individual members suing underwriters and managing agents for negligence or fraud. One of the largest-ever preliminary cash awards in the U.K., £500 million, was won against the Gooda Walker agency.

Insurance CEOs listed the regulatory, legislative, and judicial environments as their top concerns in 1994. The U.S. news was highlighted by Pres. Bill Clinton's unrealized health care reform plan. General distrust and uncertain cost projections scuttled mandated care by employers. Proposals for increased insurer taxes for Superfund pollution cleanup also met strong resistance. A $36 million antitrust settlement with 20 states promised considerable changes in insurer controls of the Insurance Services Office and other rating agencies.

Bermuda proposed sweeping amendments to its 1978 act regulating insurance. The EU initiated free choice of insurers as of July 1, but some inconsistencies in taxes remained, to be leveled by such new laws as the first U.K. 2.5% premium tax. Also in the U.K., a new Personal Investment Authority replaced self-regulation of independent and affiliated financial institutions.   (DAVID L. BICKELHAUPT)

MACHINERY AND MACHINE TOOLS

Machine tools—generally categorized as either material-cutting machines or material-forming machines—are used to produce manufactured products directly or to produce other machines upon which manufactured components and products are made.

Japan was the leading world producer of machine tools, with 1993 production worth nearly $7 billion. It exported machine tools worth an estimated $3.7 billion, slightly more than the $3.6 billion in consumption recorded for the year. Production of metal-cutting machines ($5.3 billion) far exceeded that of metal-forming machines. Metal-forming machine-tool production had a value that totaled about $1.6 billion.

Germany's $5.4 billion in machine-tool production made it the world's second largest producer. Of that figure, $3.5 billion was for metal-cutting machines and $1.9 billion for metal-forming machines. Germany exported machines worth a total of $3.6 billion and imported $1.6 billion worth.

Ranking third, the U.S. produced metal-working machine tools worth a total of $3.1 billion and consumed metalworking machine tools worth a total of $4.3 billion in 1993. Imports were valued at $2 billion, exports at $800 million. After nine consecutive years of growth in U.S. machine-tool exports, such shipments declined in 1993, although export sales continued to grow at an annual rate of about 13% over the past 10 years. The major export markets were Canada, China, and Mexico. Exports to China more than doubled those of the previous year.

Machine-tool imports to the U.S., meanwhile, rose in 1993 after having fallen in each of the preceding three years. In 1993 Japan was again the major source of U.S. imports, accounting for about one-half the total value, followed by Germany, Switzerland, Taiwan, and Canada.

Other leading producers in 1993 were Italy ($2.3 billion), China ($1.8 billion), Switzerland ($1.4 billion), and Taiwan ($1.1 billion). Canada produced machine tools worth $340 million and put $550 million worth into production. Mexico produced machine tools worth $27 million but installed machines worth over 10 times that amount, an impressive $287 million.

(JOHN B. DEAM)

METALS AND MATERIALS

Iron and Steel. Given the improved general economic situation in 1994, world steel product consumption was expected to increase by over 2%, reaching nearly 630 million tons by year's end and over 650 million tons in 1995. North America's 1994 steel consumption (in product tons) would be more than 111 million tons, an increase over 1993 of almost 13% for Canada and 9% for the United States. The strong steel market, mainly led by the automotive industry, the building sector, and appliances sales, was likely to continue also in 1995. Steel consumption expanded further in Latin America in 1994, exceeding for the region as a whole the 30 million-ton mark. Most of the increase was in Argentina, Brazil, and Mexico.

Western European steel consumption was expected to rise from the low point of under 94 million product tons in 1993 to nearly 100 million tons in 1994 and further to 104 million tons in 1995. Steel demand was starting to rise in most of the Central European economies, albeit from a very low level; an increase by 6% in 1994 and some acceleration in the following year would bring steel product consumption back to more than 15 million tons in 1995. Use of steel in the former republics of the U.S.S.R. was expected to decline by 5 million tons in 1994, to 54 million tons; 1995 might bring stabilization at this level.

In Japan gross domestic product growth remained far below the long-term trend of the past 20 years. Steel consumption in the

country was depressed and in 1994 would see a low of 73 million tons, with little hope for improvement in 1995. Elsewhere in the Asia-Pacific region, steel consumption in 1995 was forecast to exceed 100 million tons. China was a powerful driving force for the area, and continued economic expansion would raise steel consumption to 100 million tons in 1995 from 95 million tons in 1994.

World crude steel production stood at 730 million tons in 1993, compared with 724 million tons in 1992. The year 1994 would be slightly less, reflecting further decline of output in the former Soviet Union although production in the Eastern European industries had all mostly begun to increase by late 1993 and 1994. Production of pig iron had risen marginally in 1993 to reach just over 500 million tons.

In one of the largest steel transactions in years, in December Norway awarded orders totaling about $1.2 billion for 1.5 million metric tons of natural gas pipe to producers in the U.K., Italy, France, Germany, and Japan.

(D.F. ANDERSON)

Light Metals. The end of the Cold War, combined with a worldwide recession, had

a negative impact on the light metals industry. The primary light metals titanium and aluminum suffered most owing to large excesses in world production capacity and the emergence of the countries of the former Soviet Union onto the market. World supply excesses led to a 20% decline in price for titanium and a 45% decline in revenues since 1990. This in turn resulted in plant closings and joint ventures (mergers). In the mid-1980s there were 11 titanium sponge plants worldwide. In 1994 there were only six, two each in the U.S., Japan, and the former Soviet Union.

Most major aluminum producers had also lost money during the past few years, with the primary metal exports from the former Soviet Union again the key factor. Most aluminum companies, including Alcan, Alcoa, Alusuisse-Lonza Holding Ltd., Kaiser, and Reynolds Metals Co., responded by reducing production in 1993–94 relative to 1992. Third-quarter 1994 profits were generally up.

Much of the decline in market demand for titanium was due to reduced military hardware procurement and a depressed aerospace market, which accounted for 50%

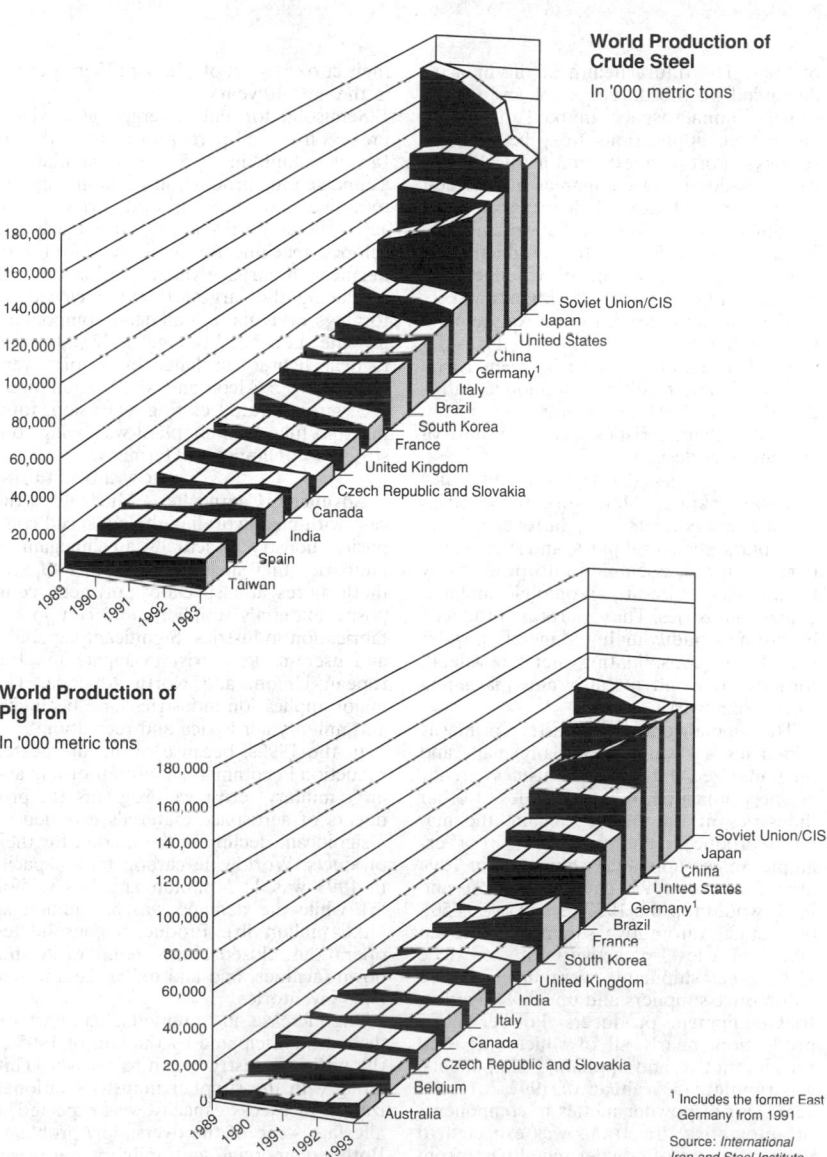

World Production of Crude Steel

In '000 metric tons

Soviet Union/CIS
Japan
United States
China
Germany[1]
Italy
Brazil
South Korea
France
United Kingdom
Czech Republic and Slovakia
Canada
India
Spain
Taiwan

World Production of Pig Iron

In '000 metric tons

Soviet Union/CIS
Japan
China
United States
Germany[1]
Brazil
France
South Korea
United Kingdom
India
Italy
Canada
Czech Republic and Slovakia
Belgium
Australia

[1] Includes the former East Germany from 1991

Source: *International Iron and Steel Institute*

Workers inspect aluminum at an Alcoa mill in Tennessee. After a period of declining demand and prices, in 1994 the aluminum industry began to see increased production and to realize solid profits, partly explained by new applications for the metal in automaking.

MICHAEL L. ABRAMSON

of sales. The future health of the industry depended on the development and expansion of nonaerospace markets, including automotive applications (*e.g.,* heavy truck springs), sporting goods, and medical applications. Aluminum companies also sought to develop and expand new markets. Although the aerospace market traditionally consumed only 5% of the production, it was a significant source of revenue. Numerous companies worked with automakers to develop new applications. An example was the aluminum spaceframe that was developed in a joint venture between Alcoa and Audi. The resulting automobile, introduced in late 1994, had stiffness and crash-durability characteristics exceeding those of current steel designs.

(EDGAR A. STARKE, JR.)

Metalworking. Metalworking industries provide components (*e.g.,* fasteners, drive-train parts, structural parts, and sheet metal parts) that are assembled into products by the appliance, aircraft, automobile, and machinery industries. These parts are produced by casting (solidifying liquid metal), powder metallurgy (consolidating metal powders), forming (of solid metals), and machining (metal removal).

The metalworking industry primarily comprises a diverse group of small- and medium-sized enterprises. Business trends are best indicated by the activities of other industries in the supplier chain, the material producers and parts users. For example, major appliance shipments in 1994 exceeded the 1993 pace by 11.5% and likely would top the 1987 record of 50,650,-000 units. Automotive shipments were up 10.5% to a level of activity not seen since 1979. Steel shipments were up 17.1% to automotive suppliers and up 9.6% to industrial equipment producers. Powder metal production, nearly all of which was used for automotive and appliance components, was running 15% ahead of 1993, a record year. Use of powder metals in components of automotive drivetrains was expected to double the use of powder metal parts from

their current level of 11.3 kg (25 lb) per car in the next 10 years.

Semisolid forming emerged as a viable process for small parts production. Alumax Inc. was building a $75 million plant in Tennessee for production of aluminum automotive parts by semisolid forming, and Japan Steel Works marketed a newly developed machine for semisolid forming of magnesium parts. Wyman-Gordon Co. was producing the largest titanium closed-die forgings ever made, bulkhead components for the Lockheed/Boeing F-22 advanced tactical fighter airplane. In a joint venture between Alcoa and VAW Aluminium AG, an integrated casting, extrusion, forging, and tube-forming plant was being constructed in Hannover, Germany.

(HOWARD A. KUHN)

Advanced Composites. Much like the case with metalworking, the advanced composite industry is actually an amalgam of industries that includes producers of synthetic fibres and specialty polymers, composite materials suppliers, and component fabrication industries. Significant capability and user markets exist in Japan, the European Union, and North America. The major application industries have been civil and military aerospace and recreation.

In the 1990s, because of an unexpected reduction in commercial aircraft orders and large military aerospace programs, the producers of aerospace materials experienced a significant decline in the market for their products. Worldwide carbon fibre capacity in 1993 was 11.3 million kg (24.9 million lb), while the demand was 6.2 million kg (13.6 million lb). Producers consolidated operations, closed plants, temporarily shut down facilities, and laid off workers to balance inventories.

An increase in commercial aircraft orders was anticipated by the end of 1995 as the airline industry began to recover. This, along with the supplier industry's rationalization of excess capacity, was expected to alleviate some of the oversupply problems. Both commercial and military aerospace

customers were placing great emphasis on affordability, however, so the life-cycle cost advantages of advanced composites might not justify their high material and manufacturing costs. In new applications the emphasis would be increasingly placed on automated processes such as resin transfer molding, automated tow placement, and pultrusion, as well as on design methods that optimize components for producibility and maintainability, rather than primarily for mechanical performance. Advanced composites should be able to find high-volume markets outside of aerospace: recreational applications, lightweight automotive structures, transportation, and civil infrastructure. In order to compete with existing technologies, producers would need to shift their emphasis substantially in order to lower costs of materials and processing methods.   (ROBERT E. SCHAFRIK;

THOMAS E. MUNNS)

MICROELECTRONICS

Because of increased demand for the chips used in personal and notebook computers, projected worldwide sales of semiconductors in 1994 rose by 29% to just under $100 billion, according to the Semiconductor Industry Association (SIA). North America again led the world's major semiconductor markets with 1994 shipments of $33.1 billion, a growth rate of 33.7%. The North American and Japanese markets supplied 62.1% of all semiconductors (33.1% and 29%, respectively). The Asia-Pacific market, including South Korea, Taiwan, and Singapore, with a growth rate of 32%, was expected to replace Europe as the third largest provider by 1997.

The SIA also expected the industry to invest more than $150 billion over the next few years on research and development to develop the technology to produce chips of 0.25 micron (micrometer) or below. (For comparison, Intel's Pentium chip was 0.8 micron.) New products and services such as interactive television, intelligent or "smart" automobiles, and wireless electronic devices were expected to increase the demand for microprocessors beyond the traditional computer-based applications.

Japanese semiconductor companies increased production capabilities in the U.S. in response to the strong Japanese yen, making production in the U.S. economically advantageous over the manufacture of chips in Japan. To keep pace with this increasing demand for smaller, faster, less power-hungry chips, modern plants would need to be built. Construction estimates for these new state-of-the-art plants ran as high as $1 billion or more each. Intel Corp. spent just under $2.5 billion for capital expenditures in 1993.

The joint venture of IBM Corp., Motorola, Inc., and Apple Computer, Inc., that produced the PowerPC microprocessor announced a new 64-bit version called the PowerPC 620. Among the anticipated uses of the 64-bit chips were new high-performance video games, due to arrive in the marketplace in 1995. In order to boost the sales of the PowerPC chip, Motorola reentered the computer-manufacturing business after an absence of a decade.

Neural-network and fuzzy-logic chips were being used in applications such as fingerprint recognition, antilock braking systems, voice recognition, and even a "smart" hair dryer that automatically adjusted its speed and temperature.

Digital signal processors (DSPs) were the leading-edge technology in microelectronics. These chips added functionality to personal computers, integrating data communications, telephony, audio, and multimedia capabilities. Texas Instruments, Inc., introduced the multimedia video processor chip, which incorporated four digital signal processors with a Reduced Instruction Set Computer (RISC) processor on a single chip. The chip's main uses would likely be in video processing and teleconferencing.

Augmenting the portable and laptop computers were the Personal Computer Memory Card International Association (PCMCIA) devices. These cards plug into portable computers to function as data/fax modems, local area network (LAN) adapters, audio cards, hard disks, and solid-state memory cards that replace or augment floppy disks and memory. The solid-state memory cards use SRAM (static RAM) chip or flash technology memory, a cheaper and smaller alternative. It was hoped that a new PCMCIA standard released in November would solve some of the compatibility problems of these products.

Digital Equipment Corp. (DEC) announced the Alpha AXP 21164, a new chip being added to its 64-bit RISC technology product line. This chip was capable of processing more than one billion instructions per second (BIPS), more than twice as fast as current designs provided in the Pentium and PowerPC chips. It contained over nine million transistors and would run at a speed of up to 300 MHz. Comparable products from Intel and PowerPC ran in the 150–160-MHz range. In November a flaw in Intel's Pentium chip was made public. (*See* INFORMATION PROCESSING AND INFORMATION SYSTEMS.)

Motorola and DEC announced embedded processor versions of their PowerPC and Alpha lines. These processors were to be installed in laser printers, telecommunications devices, and consumer products such as video games.

There was some movement in the court battles between industry giant Intel and Advanced Micro Devices, a rival chip manufacturer. On December 30 the California Supreme Court ruled that AMD was entitled to use Intel intellectual property in the manufacture of its 386-type microprocessors, reversing a lower court decision in October that had gone against AMD. Other suits between the two were still pending at year's end.

Motorola, IBM, and AT&T Corp. formed a joint venture with Loral Corp. to develop a new generation of computer chips using X-ray microlithography technology to make more circuits with finer lines. The venture was named the Proximity X-ray Collaborative Association. New devices called RDRAM (Rambus Dynamic Random Access Memory) were introduced by NEC Electronics, Inc. Able to transfer data at a rate of 500 megabytes per second, these devices would be used in graphics and multimedia workstations. (THOMAS E. KROLL)

PAINTS AND VARNISHES

Growth in the paint and varnish industry had largely been restored in North America by 1994, remained rampant in Asia Pacific, but stagnated in Europe and Japan. The U.S. reported an increase of 6.5% in volume shipments and of 8% in sales by June, thus promising to surpass the 1,090,000,000 gal ($12.9 billion) recorded for 1993 as a whole. At 4%, industrial factory-applied coatings showed the lowest growth, signifying perhaps a permanent loss in volume due to higher spray efficiency and lower solvent usage.

Markets in Europe remained largely static. Those for automotive coatings dipped, while coil and powder coatings offered one of the few bright spots. In Germany the decline in industrial and automotive paint demand was compensated by a building boom in its eastern states. The Japanese paint industry continued to stagnate; financial results of its top companies to March 1994 were particularly dire. Buoyant growth characterized the Asia-Pacific region, with paint production there now rivaling that of Europe. China had become the new focal point for Western investment and joint ventures. Other emergent areas of interest were Vietnam, India, Turkey, and Latin America.

Profitability remained a problem, especially in the wake of serious price increases for paint raw materials during the second half of the year. Prices of titanium dioxide and petrochemical precursors rose steeply in both Europe and North America.

Globalization strategies by the major players continued to dominate the corporate scene, especially a narrow specialization in a few key sectors and the divestment of noncore business areas. Both ICI and Akzo Nobel, the world's largest paint company, left the automotive original equipment manufacture market during the year. ICI disposed of its 50% interest in IDAC to DuPont, while Akzo sold its European business to PPG. American transactions included the acquisition of Rust-Oleum by RPM, Old Quaker Paint by Sherwin-Williams, Koch-PTI by HB Fuller, and Sinclair Paint by the Grow Group. Fuller also became a leading contender in the U.K. powder coatings market with the purchase of the Evode business from Laporte.

Reduction of volatile organic compounds (VOC) remained the prime target of environmental action, but under its newly proclaimed "common sense" approach, the U.S. Environmental Protection Agency shifted its focus from pollutants to industries. The U.K. cautiously moved toward a less-stringent compliance regime under its Environmental Protection Act by examining the extension of the deadline and the upward revision of the VOC limits for certain compliant coatings. The European Ecolabel, promised for 1994, reached deadlock.

(HELMA JOTISCHKY)

PHARMACEUTICALS

The U.S. pharmaceutical industry began 1994 with a good deal of trepidation, aware that it was likely to absorb much public criticism for prices and profiteering when Congress began considerations on a new health care bill. Drug manufacturers had been singled out as villains for being major contributors to the problem of health care costs, but intense lobbying, combined with briefings by drug executives of members of Congress and community leaders across the country, turned the tide.

Drug price pressure grew intense and was translated into still more downsizing, slashes in the workforce, and continued pressure to close nonprofitable or marginally profitable plants. Name-brand-drug companies moved more resolutely into the generic-drug business, sometimes by buying their generic competitors. The pace of conversion of prescription to over-the-counter (OTC) status for important drugs was accelerated, as a remedy for avoiding the inevitable slashing of prices that happened with expiration of patents. The year saw a flurry of acquisitions of pharmaceutical benefit management firms: SmithKline Beecham PLC bought Diversified Pharmaceutical Services and Eli Lilly & Co. agreed to buy PCS Health Systems. Among other mergers and acquisitions, unprecedented in number and size, was American Home Products Corp.'s $9.7 billion bid for American Cyanamid Co. and Roche Holding AG's $5.3 billion bid for Syntex Corp. Eastman Kodak, which bought Sterling Winthrop Inc. in 1988, began selling off the various parts in 1993: the prescription-drug business went to Sanofi SA, French pharmaceuticals/cosmetics giant, for $1,680,000,000, and the worldwide OTC drug business to SmithKline Beecham for $2,930,000,000—which in turn sold the North American OTC drug business to Bayer AG, Germany, for $1 billion. This put the German company back in control of the Bayer Aspirin trademark it had lost in a World War I takeover of German companies' possessions by the U.S. government.

Ivax Corp., which in January spent $440 million in stock to acquire McGaw, Inc., agreed to pay $593.7 million to buy Zenith Laboratories, Inc., one of the major generic-drug makers. Johnson & Johnson, which ranked first in worldwide sales of OTC drugs, said it would pay $924 million for Neutrogena Corp., a cosmetics company, thus reversing a 10-year trend that saw Eli Lilly, American Cyanamid, and SmithKline Beecham all sell off cosmetics properties.

There were signs that the industry's more aggressive stance on advertising and pricing was drawing regulatory attention. The Federal Trade Commission acknowledged that it was investigating discounting to hospitals and institutions, as well as possible reductions in competition when a brand-name drug company bought a generic manufacturer. The Community Retail Pharmacy Health Care Reform Coalition, a coalition of retail pharmacists, criticized drug makers for "arbitrary" pricing practices, probably with an eye toward getting Congress to hold hearings on special discounts not given to pharmacists. Bergen Brunswig Corp., a giant drug distributor, petitioned the Federal Trade Commission to halt Eli Lilly's bid to buy PCS Health Systems as anticompetitive. (DONALD A. DAVIS)

PHOTOGRAPHY

In 1994 the new head of Eastman Kodak, George M.C. Fisher, announced a major shift in the industry giant's direction: Kodak would sell its diversified nonphotographic operations and concentrate only on photography in both its traditional chemical-based and emerging electronic aspects. Kodak introduced a new digital camera for professional applications, the DCS 460, claimed to be the world's highest-resolution, single-shot colour device designed for studio and on-location use.

The most widespread advances in electronic photography, however, involved not image capture, which remained dominated by conventional photography, but the technology for processing, controlling, and outputting digitized images from conventional or electronic sources. (*See* Sidebar.) In what some observers called an "explosion of digital technologies," the photo lab business was experiencing its greatest transformation since the shift from black-and-white to colour.

Design changes in 35-mm single-lens-reflex (SLR) cameras were evolutionary rather than radically innovative. Canon introduced the hybrid EOS-1N, which combined the sturdy construction of the EOS-1 with advanced electronic features from the EOS A2. Its multitude of features included a five-sensor autofocusing system with two modes, a rewind claimed to be eight times quieter than that of the EOS-1, and a 16-zone evaluative metering system that also provided centre-weighted, 9% partial, spot, and fine spot metering. Nikon updated its top-of-the-line professional SLR, the N90, as the N90S with changes that included faster autofocus tracking, shutter-speed adjustments in increments of $\frac{1}{3}$, and increased weather resistance. Contax rekindled interest in 35-mm interchangeable-lens rangefinder cameras with its elegantly designed, titanium-finished G1, which married traditional values of unobtrusive compactness with electronic automation. Samsung's latest entry into the crowded field of point-and-shoot cameras was the ECX 1, whose unconventionally shaped Porsche-designed body made it the most unusual-looking new camera of 1994.

The fastest-growing segment of the camera market continued to be 35-mm preloaded single-use cameras as manufacturers strained to devise novel new features. Polaroid's talking SideKick had a "speech chip" that made such comments as "Smile and say cheese!" Lightning Bolt flash models were designed to provide red-eye reduction. A new Fuji Super Tele single-use camera (available only in Japan) used a mirror-path optical system to accommodate a 100-mm $f/9.5$ telephoto lens that did not protrude from the body.

Film manufacturers once again provided a bountiful harvest of new high-performance colour products. Kodak introduced Royal Gold, a line of premium-priced print films that claimed greater colour accuracy, higher saturation, and finer grain than Ektar or regular Gold films. (Ektar 25, widely recognized as the sharpest, finest-grain colour print film available, was repackaged as Royal Gold 25.) Fuji announced a professional line of Fujichrome Provia transparency films and an amateur series of Fujichrome Sensia transparency films. Agfa added an Agfacolor Optima 400 print film to its professional line and a new series of Agfacolor HDC print films for the amateur market. New Agfachrome CTx100 and 200 transparency films were described as having increased colour intensity and improved grain and sharpness.

The most persistent topic of speculation was the proposed Advanced Photo System being evolved by Kodak, Fuji, Canon, Nikon, and Minolta and scheduled to be launched in 1996. Leaks to the press in Japan and the U.S. indicated that it would include a new compact film cartridge (as slim as an AA battery) loaded with 24-mm film that had an ultrathin magnetic coating

for conveying important read-out information to the camera and photofinisher.

(ARTHUR GOLDSMITH)

PLASTICS

The recession in Europe ended in 1994. In Germany, by far the most important plastics market in the area, accounting for nearly a quarter of total usage, demand grew during the year by 3–4%, to around 5.4 million metric tons. This recovery followed a decline of the same order in 1993. The picture was similar in other European countries, resulting in critical supply shortages for all commodity thermoplastics by the autumn.

These shortages were quite unexpected and due to a number of reasons. With plastics demand in the Asia-Pacific region continuing its headlong expansion and sucking in imports, there was much less polymer available for other markets from usual exporters in such areas as the Middle East and Eastern Europe. U.S. domestic demand also remained very strong. There were also production problems in several parts of the world, ranging from a major explosion at an Exxon ethylene plant in the U.S. to climatic extremes in Japan, Taiwan, and Korea, and technical failures in Italy.

Processors hastily attempted to rebuild depleted inventories as the shortfalls became evident. Prices rose very sharply as suppliers seized the opportunity to recover some of the losses sustained during the recession. In short, the industry set off anew on the familiar and violent roller coaster of imbalanced supply and demand. It was generally felt, however, that despite short-term relief, the underlying malaise of huge overcapacity for polymer production—especially in Europe but also in the U.S.—had not been cured.

Two important new company names to appear in 1994 were Borealis, the merged petrochemicals and polyolefins interests of Neste of Finland and Statoil of Norway, and Montell Polyolefins, the joint venture between Royal Dutch/Shell and Montedison of Italy, which included the latter's Himont subsidiary. This new concern controlled polypropylene plants in 15 countries—making it easily the biggest world producer of what was still the fastest-growing large-tonnage polymer—as well as substantial polyethylene facilities. Shell Oil Co.'s polyolefins business in the U.S. and joint ventures in Germany, Singapore, and Japan were excluded, however.

Imperial Chemical Industries (ICI) in the U.K. and EniChem in Italy reviewed the future of EVC, their jointly owned subsidiary, which was the largest polyvinyl chloride producer in Europe. ICI expressed the intention to sell its stake in the business. Following the disposal of its polypropylene interests to BASF of Germany earlier in the year, when the sale was final, ICI's withdrawal from commodity-plastics manufacture would be complete. Union Carbide, which made a surprise exit from European (but not U.S.) polyethylene manufacture in 1978, decided to return to the area, however, with a large-scale joint venture with EniChem, using its updated Unipol technology.

Engineering plastics, which for the first time were as much affected by recession as were commodities, also began to recover in 1994. New applications continued to emerge steadily, not least in the automotive

sector, ranging from engine components to connectors in a multitude of electronic devices.

(ROBIN C. PENFOLD)

PRINTING

The world printing industry appeared to be moving out of the recession cycle in 1994. U.S. and British companies, as well as those in Southeast Asia, Mexico, South America, and Australia, undertook substantial capital investments, and China became an important market for equipment.

Major equipment sales were brisk. Twenty M-3000 "Sunday" gapless blanket extra-high-speed web offset presses were sold, three each to U.S., U.K., Germany, and Italian printers. "Tubeless" web presses were announced by MAN Roland and Mitsubishi.

Even before the official launch of its Speedmaster 74 series, Heidelberg Harris sold out production of 1,000 sheetfed units. Romania's Imprimerie Nationale ordered a printing line from Stevens Graphics Tricolor for the production of passports, stamps, share and bond certificates, and other security documents. Stevens had sold a simular system earlier to the Banque de France. The U.S. Bureau of Engraving and Printing, which used Stevens-Hamilton presses, ordered a second commercial security press.

Digital printing machines, notably from Indigo and Xeikon/Chromapress, entered short-run markets for colour. Competition was introduced by Xerox's launch of a new range of high-speed colour printers and aided by colour profile and management computer programs from Agfa and Electronics for Imaging. Stochastic (frequency-modulated random screening) took the world of prepress by storm.

Now active on five continents, industry giant R.R. Donnelley & Sons reported that $500 million of its sales derived from CD products. A fast short-run book print service using personal computers and Docutech presses targeted at customized textbooks and university course materials was inaugurated by Courier Epic in the U.S.

At the end of May, more than 400 of the world's leading printers and publishers met at Comprint in Cannes, France, to evaluate the changes brought about by the new customer-driven marketing strategies.

(W. PINCUS JASPERT)

RETAILING

The retail marketplace continued to undergo dramatic change in 1994 as competitors battled for supremacy in an increasingly global industry dominated by powerful chains. For many, international expansion was the preferred growth strategy, and the world's biggest retailer, Wal-Mart Stores, Inc., was certainly no exception. Seeking to conquer new territory outside the U.S. and Mexico, the huge discount chain pushed north by acquiring 122 Woolco stores in Canada from Woolworth Corp. Wal-Mart later announced expansion plans for Argentina, Brazil, Hong Kong, and China. The company, with about 2,700 discount stores, supercentres, and Sam's Club warehouse stores at year-end, was expected to report sales of $84 billion in 1994, up from $67 billion in 1993. Wal-Mart was poised to top the $100 billion sales mark in 1995.

Spurred by the North American Free Trade Agreement, the Home Depot, Inc., the Sports Authority, Inc., and several other U.S. chains followed Wal-Mart into Canada, which was viewed as a market ripe for competition. Mexico was another popular destination. Border hopping was not restricted to North America, however. With little room to grow in the U.K., where a price war was raging, supermarket operator J. Sainsbury PLC bought a 50% voting share of Giant Food Inc. of Landover, Md., complementing Sainsbury's previous acquisition of the Shaw's Supermarkets, Inc., chain in New England. Lidl & Schwarz GmbH of Germany, meanwhile, became the latest discounter to plant itself in the U.K., where it was expected to put further pressure on Sainsbury and other traditional grocers.

U.K.-based Body Shop International PLC also made headlines but for other reasons—amid allegations that its environmental record was not as squeaky clean as it would like customers to believe. The skincare products chain denied the charges, but its stock took a bath. The troubled Kmart Corp. announced store closings and layoffs in the U.S. as well as plans to sell its 21.5% stake in Coles Myer Ltd., the largest retailer in Australia.

In the U.S. another retail giant was created when R.H. Macy & Co., Inc., operating under bankruptcy court protection, agreed to a $4.1 billion merger with Federated Department Stores, Inc. The new company would have annual revenues of over $13 billion and control 330 department stores, including the prized Macy's and Bloomingdale's chains. Federated agreed to sell six stores in the New York City market to settle antitrust complaints. The merger looked set for approval late in 1994.

Big was not considered beautiful by everyone. Across the U.S. Wal-Mart met with opposition from small towns that feared that the retailer would disrupt their way of life. Wal-Mart reportedly dropped plans to build in some of these communities, but in Vermont, the only U.S. state it had not yet entered, it reached an agreement to locate in St. Johnsbury after promising to limit the store's size and to sell some local products.

As the economic recovery took hold, consumers in many countries appeared more willing to spend. U.S. retail sales, including automobiles, rose 6% in 1993 to $2,080,-000,000,000. Sales also rose in Canada and the U.K. but fell in Germany and Japan, which had slipped into recession later than North America. U.S. stores that specialized in building supplies, furniture, electronics, or sporting goods continued to post strong

---

Digitally Altered Photography: The New Image-Makers

Following football hero O.J. Simpson's arrest in June 1994 for the murder of his ex-wife and one of her friends, *Newsweek* and *Time* magazines ran the same police mug shot of Simpson on their covers. *Newsweek*'s version was a straight reproduction with normal tonality. *Time* electronically manipulated the photo to darken it and achieve a brooding, menacing quality that emphasized Simpson's unshaven cheeks and African-American skin tones. The alteration offended many readers and raised an increasingly familiar question: In an age of computer-controlled images, can anyone still trust a photograph?

Altering a digitized image, as *Time* did for its cover, has been one of the fastest-growing, most far-reaching, and most controversial techniques in contemporary photography. With this method a photograph is scanned, digitized (converted into a set of numeric values), and entered into a computer from which the operator can control the image virtually in any way imaginable: add, delete, or change the position of visual elements; modify tones and colours; create montages; combine photographs; and even create entirely imaginary scenes. The digitized image can be stored in a data base, outputted as a print or transparency, or converted for video-screen display from a CD-ROM or Photo CD.

Electronic image manipulation arrived in force in the 1980s with a pow-erful new breed of computers that cost on the order of $500,000 or more and occupied an entire room. More compact and far less expensive desktop systems soon proliferated. The necessary hardware and software for at least limited image control became available at chain-store prices.

The manipulation of photographs is not new. Long before electronic technology, photographs had been enhanced, edited, faked, and used to fabricate reality. In the latter 19th century, double exposures and darkroom trickery created ghostly "spirit" photographs that fooled even doctors and scientists, and in Stalin's era fallen leaders such as Trotsky were airbrushed out of group photos. Modern computer technology has vastly improved the ease, extent, and realistic results of such manipulations.

Electronic image control, which is applicable to both still images and full-motion video, has been welcomed enthusiastically as a new tool by graphic artists, art directors, producers of television commercials, and filmmakers in search of novel special effects, as witnessed by the startling realism of digitally fabricated scenes in the 1994 feature film *Forrest Gump*. However, what is acceptable in advertising and entertainment and as obvious satire and spoof causes concern when used to alter news, documentary, or other informational images.

The *Simpson* cover is but one example of a practice that has repeatedly stirred controversy. Similar criticism was leveled when *National Geographic* moved two of Egypt's Giza pyramids for a better cover composition, the *St. Louis (Mo.) Post-Dispatch* used a computer to excise a soft-drink can in a picture by a Pulitzer Prize-winning photographer, and *Newsweek* published an electronically altered picture of *Rain Man* costars Tom Cruise and Dustin Hoffman posing together when, in fact, they had been photographed separately in New York and Hawaii.

Responsible editors, photographers, picture agencies, and professional organizations have attempted to establish ethical codes regarding the use of electronic manipulation in news photography and to prevent copyright infringement by electronic means in commercial practice. Nevertheless, with digital technology so inexpensive and widely available, regulation has become increasingly difficult.

The ever rising flood of digitized visual information may not, as some critics fear, fatally subvert the certainty of photographic evidence. Yet many observers agree that both suppliers and consumers of photographic information must exercise greater care than ever before to distinguish fact from fabrication in the images they use.

(ARTHUR GOLDSMITH)

PHOTOGRAPH (RIGHT) GUY AROCH, PHOTOGRAPHS DIGITALLY MORPHED, JIM MCGRFAI

Through the use of digital technology, a photograph of a young boy is "morphed" into a portrait of a Mighty Morphin Power Ranger. The ability to alter images electronically troubled many people because it undermined the reliability of photographic evidence.

A customer of a Wal-Mart superstore in Mexico City loads purchases into his automobile. Like many other large retailing chains, Wal-Mart continued to grow by expanding outside its home base in the U.S. into such areas as Canada, Latin America, and Asia.
SERGIO DORANTES—SYGMA

sales gains in 1994, but clothing and grocery stores struggled in the face of stiff competition from discounters. Perhaps the biggest worry for supermarkets was the proliferation of supercentres. These hybrid retail outlets, which included a discount store and supermarket under one roof, were expected to be major engines of growth in the future for the big-three U.S. discounters, Wal-Mart, Kmart, and Dayton Hudson Corp.'s Target chain.

Companies were also lining up to catch the next wave in retailing: interactive home shopping. J.C. Penney Co., Inc., and Nordstrom, Inc., were among the numerous retailers that signed on to interactive services such as U S West Inc.'s "U.S. Avenue." Expected to debut by year's end in 1994, it allowed consumers to stroll through an electronic shopping mall and order merchandise by clicking their television remote controls.

Nordstrom also launched a 24-hour electronic-mail shopping service for computer users. In November 2Market and Contentware, two collections of multimedia mail-order catalogs on CD-ROM with connections to computer networks, made their debut. It was far too early to judge the impact of these new technologies on traditional retailing, but Americans had already demonstrated their enthusiasm for armchair shopping, having spent about $30 billion on mail-order purchases in 1994.

(JOHN HEINZL)

RUBBER

The rubber industry ended 1994 with the dilemma of rapidly rising material costs and its main customer, the automotive industry, demanding price cuts. It was the auto industry, however, that was fueling a strong demand for rubber as consumption

worldwide was up 2% over 1993 and was projected to reach 14.7 million metric tons. Most of the gain came from North America, where consumption rose nearly 4%. Rubber consumption in the U.S. was running at an eight-year high, even though the tire manufacturers were hit with several strikes.

Natural rubber prices dramatically increased during the year. Tapping was hindered in Thailand and Malaysia because it was too wet, but Indonesia was experiencing a drought that led to rubber plantation fires. The rapid rise in pricing put the International Natural Rubber Agreement (INRA) in jeopardy. INRA was ostensibly set up under UN auspices to guarantee a continuous supply of natural rubber and to stabilize prices. After years in which natural rubber was bought to bolster prices, however, the entire buffer stock was sold off during the summer of 1994, with little or no effect on the holding down of prices. Prices, which hovered around the 200-Malaysian/Singapore-cents-per-kilogram mark in October 1993, went over 330 cents in July, and by October 1994 they were at 280 cents. In the U.S., prices for ribbed smoke sheet were 45 cents a pound in January and 69 cents a pound in September.

Synthetic rubber prices also rose, with styrene-butadiene rubber (SBR), the major tire elastomer, experiencing five increases through October. Sharp price hikes for the major feedstocks, styrene and butadiene, plus shortages were the cause. Prices for SBR 1712 in the U.S. went from near 40 cents a pound in January to near 50 cents in September.

Tire shipments increased 9% in the first half of 1994 despite strikes at numerous tire-manufacturing facilities in the U.S. In August more than 8,000 United Rubber Workers (URW) members were on strike

at 10 different plants owned by four different companies. Agreements between Yokohama Tire and its 800 workers and Dunlop with its 1,500 employees were reached in the fall, but more than 4,000 at five Bridgestone/Firestone locations and 1,000 at two Pirelli Armstrong plants were still striking.

Having begun on July 12, the action at the Bridgestone/Firestone strike was the longest and most acrimonious. The URW accused the company of organizing a conspiracy to gain deep concessions and filed unfair labour charges with the U.S. National Labor Relations Board. Bridgestone/Firestone charged that the union had brought racism into the bargaining.

Numerous plans for expanding tire-production capacity were announced, particularly in Asia. In China, Shanghai Tyre said it would double tire output to 6 million units by 1995; Hualin Rubber Factory was constructing a 1.8 million-unit radial tire plant; Yunnan Tire planned a 2 million-unit-per-year passenger and light truck radial plant; Gulin was adding capacity for 1 million radial passenger/truck tires; and Goodyear, in a joint venture, announced it would build a factory with a capacity of 1 million tires per year. Goodyear also announced that its Indonesian plant would increase capacity from 7,000 to 11,000 tires daily. Pacific Dunlop said it was going to build a tire plant in Indonesia. In South Korea Hankook said it would build a factory with an annual capacity of five million units. Bridgestone announced plans for a new plant in Thailand, and Ceat said it would build a tire plant in Vietnam. Dunlop planned a new tire facility in the U.S., while Cooper Tire and Yokohama added significant U.S. capacity. Sumitomo bought Pneumant Reifen & Gummi Werke in East Germany for $35 million and planned to invest $65 million in its two factories. Continental of Austria was expanding tire capacity by 10%. Continental and Michelin each closed a truck tire plant in France, and Pirelli closed one in the U.K.

On the supplier side, Taiwan Synthetic Rubber (TSR) announced a joint-venture SBR plant in China to produce 100,000 metric tons per year; TSR also announced a major debottlenecking of a thermoplastic elastomer plant in Taiwan along with a 20% SBR expansion; Jilin Chemical planned to build the first ethylene-propylene plant in China; BASF formed a Chinese joint venture to build an SBR latex plant; Dinamika Erajaya was building an SBR plant in Indonesia; Hyundai Petrochemical said it would build a plant to produce polybutadiene, SBR, and nitrile in South Korea; and Yung Chemical was building two plants in Taiwan. Du Pont was increasing fluoroelastomer capacity, Dow Plastics increased thermoplastic polyurethane capacity, and Uniroyal announced plans for a new ethylene-propylene elastomer facility. Pirelli announced it would leave the U.S. farm tire market.   (DONALD SMITH)

SHIPBUILDING

According to *Merchant Shipbuilding Return* issued by Lloyd's Register, as of June 1994 there were 1,098 steamships and motorships being built around the world. They represented a gross tonnage of 15,844,647 gt (gross tons), up 149,823 gt from the previous quarter. There were also 1,050 ships that had been ordered but on which building had not yet started. If they were all built, their tonnage would amount to 24,997,199 gt, an increase of 1,621,252 gt over the previous quarter. These combined figures, 2,148 ships of 40,841,846 gt, constituted the total world order book, which was 1,600,081 gt more than the 1993 world order book. The principal types of ships in the order book were oil tankers (13,-151,800 gt), bulk carriers (13,756,934 gt), and general cargo vessels (7,291,487 gt). Of the total order book, tankers represented 32.2%, bulk carriers 33.7%, and general cargo ships 17.9%. The proportion of the order book tonnage that was to be registered in countries other than the country where it was built rose to 77.9% (31,819,-128 gt—an increase of 2,080,401 gt).

The major players in world shipbuilding were Japan, South Korea, and China (both the People's Republic and Taiwan). At June 1994 these countries together accounted for 64.38% of the world's shipping order book. European countries and Brazil also had significant percentages of the total.

In mid-July—after negotiations at the Organisation for Economic Co Operation and Development in Paris—Japan, South Korea, the European Union, the U.S., Finland, Norway, and Sweden agreed to halt subsidies for their shipyards. The move was expected to avert a new round of subsidy grants.

Competition from shipbuilders in South Korea and Europe forced Japanese builders to take drastic action to cut costs. Hitachi Zosen Corp. laid off 10% of its 2,000 workers, and NKK Corp. planned to reduce costs by 30% at its Tsu shipyard by amalgamating its design and construction departments. South Korean competition also forced Mitsubishi Heavy Industries, Ltd., to cut 900 jobs from its workforce of 7,000.

South Korea was not without its own labour problems, and Hyundai Heavy Industries Co. locked out 15,000 workers. The trade union was seeking a guaranteed monthly salary plus a series of improvements in working conditions. Demands amounted to a 13% increase, well above the government's 5% incomes-limit policy.

The sinking of the Baltic "roll-on, roll-off" ferry *Estonia,* with the loss of some 900 lives, revived concerns over the safety of this type of ship. Taken together with the loss of the *Herald of Free Enterprise* off Zeebrugge, Belgium, in 1987 with the loss of 188 lives, this incident caused serious doubts about a ship design that incorporated large open car decks. (*See* TRANSPORTATION.) Britain's Royal Institution of Naval Architects rebuked ferry operators for being slow to install stabilizers or watertight bulkheads on their ships. Losses of bulk carriers and oil tankers also continued despite some remedial action. A notable example was the loss with all 24 crew of the 93,355-deadweight ton bulk carrier *Iron Antonis* off South Africa. Some light was thrown on bulk carrier losses by the finding of the wreck of the *Derbyshire,* which had sunk in 1980 without trace. A remotely operated submersible provided evidence that the vessel broke apart at frame 65 and the aft accommodation section sank immediately. Photographs indicated that the bow fell off the carrier before the remainder of the vessel sank. This might suggest a previously unknown stress point at a quarter of the ship's length on this and other similar bulk carriers.   (EDWARD CROWLEY)

TELECOMMUNICATIONS

The year 1994, which marked the 10th anniversary of the breakup of the old Bell System, was also the year of partnerships and mergers among cellular, land-based telecommunications and cable companies. Among them was the $12.6 billion acquisition of McCaw Cellular Communications, Inc., by AT&T. Although announced in 1993, the merger was not completed until September 1994. After months of de-

bates and lawsuits over whether it violated the 1984 consent decree that broke up the Bell System, the Justice Department, U.S. District Court Judge Harold Green, and the Federal Communications Commission (FCC) all approved the merger. The new company, AT&T Wireless Services, was required to provide equal access to all long-distance carriers. Internationally, Sprint Corp. announced a joint venture with Deutsche Telekom and France Telecom. British Telecom invested $4.3 billion in MCI, and AT&T announced a $55 million venture with The Netherlands' Unisource NV. In November AT&T announced an alliance with Mexico's Grupo Industrial Alfa S.A. in order to provide long-distance telephone service in that country. In December the company received the go-ahead to provide full telephone services in the U.K. and also won a $1.2 billion contract to lay the "Fiberoptic Link Around the World," a cable running from the U.K. to Japan.

In anticipation of the personal communication services (PCS) license auction, a number of telephone and cable companies joined together. In June, Cox Enterprises Inc. and the Times Mirror Co. formed Cox Cable, a $2.3 billion venture that created the third largest cable company in the U.S., behind TCI and Time Warner. Also in June, Bell Atlantic Corp. and NYNEX Corp. agreed to combine their cellular companies; in July the $13.5 billion merger of U S West, Inc., with AirTouch Communications (formerly part of Pacific Telesis Group) formed the third largest U.S. cellular company. These four companies joined together to form the largest wireless communications network in the U.S. and entered the bidding for PCS licenses as PCS Primeco LP.

Sprint, along with its partners TCI, Comcast Corp., and Cox, formed the WirelessCo LP to also pursue PCS licenses. The joint venture also announced plans to provide local telephone service over cable. LDDS Communications Inc. became the nation's fourth largest long-distance carrier when it completed a $2.5 billion buyout of Wiltel Inc.'s fibre network.

A billboard in Ho Chi Minh City advertises cellular telephones. Vietnam, like a number of other countries with low per capita incomes, was emphasizing the development of a modern telecommunications infrastructure, seen as essential for economic growth.

Among the mergers that did not take place was the proposed largest buyout in U.S. history, a $32.5 billion purchase of TCI by Bell Atlantic Corp. A $4.9 billion agreement between Southwestern Bell and Cox Cable and a merger between MCI, Nextel, and Comcast Corp. that would have formed a $1.3 billion wireless network also fell through. This left MCI without a partner to enter the PCS bidding.

The FCC announced new cable rate regulations in May that would force cable companies to cut their rates an additional 7%. A 10% reduction, ordered in 1993, failed to reduce rates equitably, and about one-third of the cable customers actually paid more for their service. In November the FCC allowed cable companies to increase their rates about $18 a year over a three-year period to encourage the companies to expand the number of channels available as part of their basic services offering.

The much-awaited auction of airwaves for use in PCS, advanced paging services, and interactive television began in 1994. The FCC was surprised when the paging and interactive TV licenses netted the U.S. government more than $1.2 billion. The auction of the broadband PCS spectrum began in December and was expected to last a month or longer. Estimates ran as high as $15 billion for these 99 regional licenses, with every regional Bell operating company, cable company, and long-distance carrier except MCI depositing entry fees of up to $15 million per region. A separate auction for small businesses and women- and minority-owned businesses was to follow in 1995.

A new standard for modems developed by the International Telecommunications Union, called V.34, would double the current rate at which data could be transmitted to 28.8 Kbps—a rate approaching the theoretical maximum for transmission over voice-grade lines. RCA introduced the Digital Satellite System, a small 45.7-cm (18-in) dish that could be unobtrusively mounted on a rooftop. The system received 150 channels of high-quality digital video and audio.

AT&T announced it had changed the name of NCR, its computer division, to AT&T Global Information Solutions. Motorola announced it would build a $100 million cellular plant 105 km (65 mi) northwest of Chicago. Motorola also announced a pocket- or purse-sized wireless answering machine that would capture, store, and replay voice messages.   (THOMAS E. KROLL)

TEXTILES

Potentially profound changes for the world textile industry came with the signing of the North American Free Trade Agreement (NAFTA). Optimists in the U.S. saw NAFTA as a further step in the emergence of a world free-trade area and as an opportunity to establish production bases in Mexico, where manufacturing costs were likely to be very much lower than in the U.S. itself. The pessimists worried that there would now be a move into Mexico from the cotton fields of the Deep South, which would have a devastating effect on textile production and employment in that area. Rather than seeing NAFTA as a threshold to an enlarged total multinational market, U.S. textile manufacturers felt pressure from Mexico. Many U.S. companies saw an opportunity for business expansion and either set up manufacturing units there or entered into joint-venture agreements.

Elsewhere, there were more signs of a decline in textile manufacture in Europe and Japan, with a corresponding expansion in countries such as China, Vietnam, and Indonesia. Eastern Europe experienced many collapses of textile companies, although for some firms business remained good, if only because of low labour costs. Garment manufacture in Eastern Europe tended to remain competitive with that in the Far East because of road links with Western Europe.

Man-made fibres. World man-made fibre production was predicted to reach a total of 23,453,000 metric tons by 1995, compared with a 1994 level of 21,854,-000 tons. In 1994 strategic alliances were being forged between the various man-made fibre producers. U.S. and European companies established links with Japanese producers, and contacts were being made with countries such as India and Singapore. Huge market potential was seen to exist in China. The rate of growth in less developed countries suggested they eventually could overwhelm the commodity fibre makers elsewhere. Another trend was for some companies to withdraw completely from fibre production and dispose of their interests to companies still strong in the field. In order to distinguish between poorly performing fibre divisions and more lucrative chemical or plastics production, a number of companies, notably in Germany, created new fibre companies with responsibility for their own profitability. A number of the better fibre producers in Eastern Europe were taken over by Western interests, one example being nylon maker Silon, Slovakia, acquired by the French, possibly in order to locate facilities nearer Russia and Ukraine, expected to be growing markets for fibres.

Having started as a simulation of natural silk, the microfibres continued to gain in importance, particularly in the Far East. These were more than merely fashionable, as the fabrics made from them had a much-improved handle and were far softer than more conventional synthetics. These fibres required the highest-quality raw materials and more costly production, however, which should offer some protection for natural fibres in the immediate future.

(PETER LENNOX-KERR)

Wool. Wool prices sank in April 1993 to their lowest in 50 years in real terms. The Australian government appointed a review committee under Ross Garnaut, whose recommendations on disposal of the stockpile, which had built up to almost five million bales during the years of the reserve price scheme, were accepted. Prices showed signs of stabilizing in September 1993, and the market gathered pace rapidly. Despite periodic setbacks, the upward trend was clearly established and accepted by the beginning of 1994.

Rising prices were accompanied by a recovery in demand, associated with the general world economic recovery. China was by now a dominant buyer and played a major part in wool market recovery. The market indicator exceeded 800 cents (Australian) per kilogram (1 kg = 2.2 lb) by the end of October, equivalent to twice its lowest point 18 months before. An additional factor helping to raise wool prices was drought in Australia, which led to reduction in wool clip estimates from 750,000 to 735,000 met-ric tons after these had been raised from the lowest estimate of 690,000.

The stockpile-disposal method—a fixed monthly schedule with a doubled quarterly schedule from January 1995—was implemented with a smoothness that would have been unimaginable a year earlier. Forward sales were permitted, and in a rising market these were soon well ahead of the fixed schedule. With prices rising in 1994, the stockpile was no longer seen as a threat, though it still amounted to well over three million bales at the end of the year.

(H.M.F. MALLETT)

Cotton. Asian cotton crops suffered a disastrous year in 1994, with disease running rife through Pakistan, India, and China, all major producers. Prices rose steeply, and domestic industry requirements in many instances had to be made up by raw cotton imported from areas such as Central Asia. Pakistani producers also were affected by severe flooding and what they considered to be unnecessary obstructions by the government. Cotton production was booming in Brazil, however, and a world-class textile-production area in the northeast of that country was forecast by the year 2000.

In 1994 it was estimated that world consumption of all types of fibres was about 39.8 million metric tons, of which 19.1 million metric tons was cotton, so that roughly speaking cotton still represented around 48% of the world fibre market. New industry confidence was reflected in rising orders for new machinery, though the inflow of business was still well below previous peak levels. Early in the year there were predictions of increases in production from most countries, but with the disasters in Asia this resulted in shortages, and prices started to rise. This militated against the natural fibre and prompted textile makers to look toward synthetic alternatives—usually polyester—which tended to be more consistent in price. Genetic development of "coloured cottons"—fibres of specific shades caused by manipulation of the cotton pigmenting gene—continued. Other research was directed toward development of new types of cotton suitable for arid areas.

(PETER LENNOX-KERR)

Silk. The silk industry's mixed fortunes during 1993 could be characterized by poor prices for raw silk and poor business outside China, excellent sales of garments of Far Eastern origin in Europe and the U.S., and rapidly rising prices for silk noils and noil yarns, largely due to fashion. At the time of the International Silk Association Congress in Nanjing (Nanking), China, in November 1993, prices for raw silks were at their lowest, but over the following seven months they climbed by about 25%. Supplies were tight owing to poor weather conditions in China at the time the previous autumn cocoon crop was gathered.

Brazil's production increased, and much of it was sold to Japan, where import restrictions were being gradually relaxed. Such was the quality of Brazilian silk that certain suppliers could command higher prices than the Chinese.

The Chinese silk garment industry received a blow on March 13, 1994, when the European Commission imposed tight quotas—the 1992 levels minus 10%—to stem the flood of garment imports. Many complaints were made against the Commission for the way the quotas were introduced.

Early 1994 saw an improvement in confidence and a good demand for thrown silk, highly twisted yarns being particularly difficult to obtain. U.S. demand for European ties returned to levels last seen in 1988.

World silk production for 1993 was estimated at 100,175 metric tons. China remained the largest producer at 71,845 metric tons and overtook Japan as the largest consumer. Indian production was 14,000 metric tons and Brazilian 2,326 metric tons.

(ANTHONY H. GADDUM)

TOBACCO

Balance returned to the industry in 1994, with every major tobacco-growing country except Indonesia responding to the 1993 overproduction crisis by planting less. The 1994 harvest fell back to 6.8 billion kg (15 billion lb), resulting in free-market prices to farmers recovering from the previous season's distress levels. Production was slightly less than annual consumption, and quality was good, average yields being the highest on record. World consumption of tobacco products—overwhelmingly cigarettes—rose again to more than 5.3 trillion. While smoking fell in the U.S., Western Europe, and Australasia, it increased in Eastern Europe and the former Soviet Union as shortages were remedied, and it rose yet again in populous Asia and the Arab world. In the U.S., sales of mainline branded cigarettes recovered somewhat, but overall sales shrank again. Some signs suggested that the U.S.

A cigarette is tested in the laboratory for its nicotine content. A panel of experts reported to the Food and Drug Administration in 1994 that the nicotine found in cigarettes was addictive, which led to calls for further federal controls over the sale of tobacco products in the U.S.

STACEY PICK—STOCK, BOSTON

cigar market, the world's largest, was at last regaining vigour.

With a quarter of the Canadian cigarette market being contraband, the federal and provincial governments boldly slashed high tobacco taxes in February in order to beat the smugglers. The tax sacrifice worked—retail prices of many legal cigarettes dropped by more than half.

In India manufacturers launched microcigarettes to capture part of the vast market for bidis (cheap native products in which a type of bay leaf encloses scraps of rough tobacco), which had been outselling normal cigarettes by a 10-to-1 margin. The micros, which were made only 59 mm (2.3 in) long in order to qualify for a tax concession, sold for only slightly more than bidis. In Germany environmental awareness led to a movement to make all parts of cigarette packs recyclable alongside new efforts to make them totally biodegradable.

In April BAT Industries PLC, the owner of Brown & Williamson, bought American Tobacco (makers of Lucky Strike, Pall Mall, and other cigarettes) for $1 billion, raising its market share from 11% to 18%. While privatization of state tobacco monopolies inched ahead—Japan was progressing, with Poland and France next—private manufacturing conglomerates, once keen on diversification to blur their tobacco identity, regained faith and were reinvesting in core activities.

In some cases the big manufacturers also returned to the offensive against moves to ban or restrict smoking—even after a series of allegations in the spring that U.S. companies had suppressed adverse research data on the dangers of smoking and had manipulated the amount of nicotine in their products. A list of 599 substances that manufacturers used in cigarettes was also made public in April.   (MICHAEL F. BARFORD)

TOURISM

As the world economy climbed out of recession, prospects for tourism brightened. Despite rumours of heavy discounting, key hotels posted higher revenue levels and pointed to greater business confidence compared with 1993. Tour operators reported demand for traditional summer vacations buoyant, while carriers—despite recent heavy losses—saw passenger volume lifting again. Growth in international arrivals in 1994 was 3–4%.

Last puff postponed

The World Health Organization (WHO), seeing smoking as the most preventable cause of ill health worldwide, edged in 1994 a little closer to its objective of a smoke-free world, while it dropped the year 2000 as the target date. WHO predicted that if current trends continued unchecked, tobacco would eventually kill some 500 million people. In advanced countries, where persuasion was reinforced by ever tougher regulations, the message was thoroughly familiar, and the remaining smokers were perhaps irredeemable. The less developed two-thirds of the world presented huge obstacles to reformers—not least the 21 million people there who were employed by the tobacco industry.

Cigarette smoking continued to fall in the U.S. and in many other advanced countries. Often concerned that smoking among the young was a gateway into drug abuse, governments, with the press and broadcast media as allies, stepped up educational campaigns on the health risks of smoking. By 1994 health warnings appeared on most of the world's cigarette packs, and tides of legislation narrowly confined the public places where smokers could legally indulge their habit. Sharp rises in tobacco taxes, sanctified on public health grounds, yielded governments an estimated $125 billion in 1994.

Attempts to win over the world's 850 million smokers to healthier lifestyles were most dedicated where the antitobacco movement started—in North America and Western Europe. Europe was overtaking the New World in legislative restraints, with European Union limits on cigarette tar and nicotine contents. Countries that banned cigarette advertising sought to get others to do the same. What began as an anticigarette movement in Europe was broadened to condemn all forms of tobacco consumption. North America's main contribution to the quit-smoking campaign was its innovative forms of attack, including moves by U.S. government agencies to classify tobacco as a drug and to establish that "passive smoking" (exposure to other people's smoke) can cause cancer. Canada had a project requiring that cigarettes be sold in plain packs, without brand imagery. On both sides of the Atlantic, unrepentant smokers felt that campaigning had become a jihad, setting smoker against nonsmoker and stubbing out the mutual tolerance to which advanced nations are dedicated.

In the other two-thirds of the world, where most of the world's tobacco was consumed, virtually every country had an antismoking policy, with taxes on tobacco products and a patchwork of deterrent regulations varying from the determined—in Singapore and Australasia—to the well-intentioned but purely nominal. In large and populous Third World countries, where law enforcement was difficult or casual, the impact was high among the educated and prosperous classes but low among others. On balance, it looked like a long haul for any thoroughgoing reform of one of the world's favourite vices.

(MICHAEL F. BARFORD)

Men and women compete for space as they attempt to fish for salmon in an Alaskan river. A number of the most popular tourist areas in the U.S. were in danger of being overrun by the large numbers of visitors.
KEN GRAHAM

Canada's inbound tourism moved out of recession in 1994, with a 6% lift in arrivals. Island destinations such as The Bahamas and Bermuda showed tourism growing by 5% and 4%, respectively, while Jamaica posted only a 1% increase. Nicaragua's arrivals soared 28%, while those of Chile rose 17% and those of Paraguay 9%. The U.S. seemed headed for a turndown in arrivals, however, with half-year totals 4% below those of 1993.

Tourism to Finland and Norway was 13% ahead of 1993 levels. Countries with strong currencies, such as Austria, Germany, and Switzerland, experienced very nearly stationary tourism growth, however. Two of the giants of the European inbound travel industry, Italy and Spain, posted increases close to 10%, with the "full-up" sign appearing in Spanish resorts as early as Easter week, prompting tour operator fears about possible overbooking in popular destinations. Elsewhere in Europe, Bulgaria swung back into fashion with a 48% rise in arrivals, and Cyprus passed the two million-tourist mark for a 14% increase.

South Korea's tourism soared 18%, while in both Australia and New Zealand there were 12% more visitors than in 1993. Singapore lifted tourist arrivals 7%, while Sri Lanka (relatively peaceful as Tamil rebel violence subsided) and Thailand showed 5% increases. Hong Kong advanced 4%. Japan's rising yen and slow emergence from recession meant the world's third biggest tourism spender sustained a zero-growth year for inbound tourism.

Embattled Lebanon prepared a master plan to relaunch tourism, and Syria posted a 5% visitor increase. Tourism to Israel riding the optimism of the Israel-Jordan-Palestine accords, was 11% ahead of 1993, but Egypt's foreign tourism was hit sharply by the impact of fundamentalist violence.

Table VI. Leading International Tourist Destinations
Number of tourist arrivals from abroad

Destination	1992	1993[1]
France	59,590,000	61,300,000
United States	47,556,000	45,793,000
Spain	39,638,000	40,600,000
Italy	26,113,000	25,700,000
Hungary	20,118,000	22,800,000
China	16,512,000	19,452,000
United Kingdom	18,535,000	19,400,000
Austria	19,098,000	18,257,000
Mexico	17,271,000	16,860,000
Germany	15,147,000	15,200,000
Canada	14,741,000	15,021,000
Switzerland	12,800,000	12,750,000
Greece	9,331,000	9,384,000
Portugal	8,884,000	8,993,000
Hong Kong	6,986,000	7,896,000
Russian Federation[2]	6,900,000	7,869,000
Czech Republic	7,421,000	7,479,000
Malaysia	6,016,000	6,800,000
Turkey	6,549,000	6,432,000
Singapore	5,446,000	5,848,000

[1]1993 figures for some countries are provisional.
[2]Includes countries of the former U.S.S.R.
Source: World Tourism Organization, Madrid, 1994.

The democratic elections in South Africa helped the tourist industry there.

Tourism in 1994 was not without its setbacks, however. When a bomb rocked the Grand Bazaar in Istanbul during Easter week, Turkish tourism suffered along with the victims. The same was true when gunmen attacked a tourist bus in Nag Hammadi, Egypt, killing a Spanish boy and seriously injuring his father in August and when an American boy was killed by bandits while traveling in the family car in Calabria, Italy, in September. Crime was repeatedly a factor in the drop in Japanese tourism to California and European visitors choosing Florida as a holiday destination. In September the outbreak of pneumonic plague—spread by infected fleas—led Gulf states to ban flights to and from India, while the sinking of the ferry *Estonia* in the Baltic Sea with the loss of some 900 lives raised serious doubts about the safety of "roll-on, roll-off" ferries in extreme weather.

Many North American airlines were restructuring in 1994, and few European carriers were profitable. United Airlines became the largest U.S. airline to be owned by its employees. In Europe only British Airways, KLM Royal Dutch Airlines, and Swissair announced net profits for 1993. Others, such as Olympic Airlines (Greece), Air France, and Iberia (Spain), sought government aid to return to profitability, thereby raising questions of unfair competition for the European Union.

Following teething troubles, the Eurostar high-speed train began scheduled commercial service through the Channel Tunnel (Eurotunnel) in November 1994 between London's Waterloo station and the Gare du Nord in Paris. The journey took three hours, and a round-trip ticket cost around $300.

As ecotourism, or conservation-oriented tourism, continued to enjoy marketing success, there was steady growth in cruises to Antarctica. The XVIII Antarctic Treaty Consultative Meeting held in Kyoto, Japan, in April adopted "Guidance for Visitors and Those Organizing and Conducting Tours" intended for treaty states. In October, 20 countries gathered in Uzbekistan to sign the Samarkand Declaration on Silk Road Tourism to revive this 2000-year-old heritage route by easing visa and currency regulations for travelers.

The Walt Disney Co. announced cancellation of plans to open a history theme park near the U.S. Civil War battlefield at Manassas, Va., and welcomed a $500 million investment from Saudi Arabian Prince Walid (*see* BIOGRAPHIES) to help keep its Euro Disneyland (renamed Euro Disneyland Paris in the fall) afloat. News was better from Tokyo Disneyland, which reported soaring attendance and a $202 million pretax profit. Meanwhile, plans were announced for a $1.5 billion theme park at Osaka, Japan.

How much did it cost to attract a tourist in 1994? National promotional expenditure by the U.S. was, according to the World Tourism Organization, among the lowest in the world at $12 million, or just 28 cents per tourist. The WTO estimated that $1.4 billion was spent by national governments on tourism promotion.

(PETER SHACKLEFORD)

WOOD PRODUCTS

Global wood supplies tightened significantly in 1994, in part because of restrictions on federal lands in the U.S. Pacific Northwest related to environmental concerns, specifically the status of the spotted owl. Much of the federal timber in the region was restricted as a result of court actions. In December 1994, however, Pres. Bill Clinton's plan for managing Northwest forests was approved by a U.S. district court judge, allowing for harvests on federal lands in California, Oregon, and Washington at a rate of 4,520,000 cu m (1 cu m = 423.8 bd-ft) annually, less than one-quarter of the mid-1980s logging rate.

U.S. exports dropped from 6.6 million cu m between January and June 1993 to 5.3 million cu m during the same period in 1994. Use of engineered wood and nonwood products was up internationally. Japanese imports of oriented strand board jumped from 28,000 cu m in 1991 to 58,000 in 1993, mostly from Canada.

Wood from fast-growing plantations was expected to fill some of the supply gap. Already, plantation forests supplied approximately 10% of the world's industrial wood. Brazil, with its 5.2 million ha (12.8 million ac) in plantations, predominantly southern yellow pine and eucalyptus, had emerged as a major source. Other countries with plantation programs were Argentina, South Africa, Costa Rica, Australia, and China. With 57% of the world's softwood volume, Russia was also seen as a future source of wood, but environmentalists were concerned that imported Russian raw logs

could carry devastating pests and argued that Russia's forests had already seen too much clear-cutting.

Environmental groups argued that plantations failed to maintain biodiversity, but advocates countered that plantations—such as those in New Zealand and Chile, which covered 3.1 million ha (7.7 million ac)— could also relieve pressures to harvest native forests. The Convention on International Trade in Endangered Species attempted unsuccessfully to list mahogany in its appendix of endangered species.

The move to "certify" that timber came from sustainable forests gained momentum in 1994. Two commercial certification groups in the U.S. offered to study and approve forestry operations. Certification supporters hoped that consumers would begin choosing wood with this stamp of approval. Many producers opposed certification, saying the process was too costly and it was difficult to define *sustainable*.

According to the Food and Agriculture Organization of the United Nations, a global population growth rate of about 100 million people per year would result in a 77 million-cu m annual increase in wood consumption. After three years of decline, Europe generally increased its wood consumption. Germany, the major European wood market, however, focused less on the log trade and more on the manufacture of value-added products; it increased imports of hardwood veneers, mainly alder, from the U.S.

Housing starts were on the rise in the main European markets, Japan, and North America. Softwood lumber consumption in the U.S. was expected to reach 113 million cu m in 1994, an increase of 4.5 million cu m over 1993. Japan, which imported more wood than any other country in the world, increased imports of finished wood from the U.S. and expanded its supply sources to include northern Europe, South America, and Africa.   (ALEXANDRE BATTISTELLA)

Paper. The pulp and paper industry experienced another tough year in 1993, but 1994 looked to be a time for slow recovery for most convalescents in this industry. World paper and board production rose to 251.6 million metric tons in 1993, 1.6% above 1992. World pulp production fell to just over 163 million metric tons in 1993, from 165.6 million metric tons in 1992, mainly attributable to Eastern European production drops. On the other hand, world paper production increased because of increases in wastepaper recycling. Meanwhile, partly because of the large number of forest fires in North America, paper prices boomed. The chart, right, shows the production distribution in the industry in 1993.

Southeast Asian countries such as Malaysia and Thailand, small producers now, were poised for quick growth, and Vietnam and Laos with their large forest reserves were potential pulp producers. Major European and North American producers began to consider tailor-made, high value-added, environmentally sound paper, delivered just in time to the consumer. The industry could expect new tailor-made pulps to go with the new tailor-made papers.

Environmental pressure from tough governmental regulation was driving the development of totally chlorine-free (TCF) pulping and bleaching technologies, as well as various closed-cycle pulp and paper

Paper is loaded onto a ship in Vancouver, B.C., for export. After a period of weakness, the market for pulp and paper strengthened during 1994, partly because of the expanding economies in the U.S. and other countries.
DELORES BASWICK—FIRST LIGHT

End use of world paper and board output, 1993

19% 13%
- newsprint
- printing & publishing
- packaging
- other

38% 30%

Source: *Paper & Pulp International,* August 1994

mill concepts. Environmental-impact labeling requirements were forcing mills to reduce emissions. The estimated cost of the U.S. Environmental Protection Agency's proposed cluster rules ranged from $4 billion to more than $11 billion over three years, with TCF and zero discharge mandated for some pulp grades. If the cluster rules were implemented as proposed, 33 mills would close and 21,500 jobs would be lost.   (H.-CLAUDE LAVALLÉE)

This article updates the *Macropædia* articles BEVERAGE PRODUCTION; BUILDING CONSTRUCTION; DRESS AND ADORNMENT; ELECTRONICS; ENERGY CONVERSION; FORESTRY AND WOOD PRODUCTION; INDUSTRIAL GLASS AND CERAMICS; Chemical Process INDUSTRIES; Extraction and Processing INDUSTRIES; Manufacturing INDUSTRIES; Textile INDUSTRIES; INSURANCE; MARKETING AND MERCHANDISING; PHOTOGRAPHY; PRINTING, TYPOGRAPHY, AND PHOTOENGRAVING; TELECOMMUNICATIONS SYSTEMS; TOOLS.

Chemistry

Organic Chemistry. In an achievement regarded as a milestone in synthetic organic chemistry, two research groups in 1994 announced development of techniques for the total synthesis of the anticancer drug taxol. Originally isolated from the Pacific yew tree, taxol was regarded as a promising treatment for a variety of cancers, including those of the ovary, breast, and lung. At first, obtaining taxol in quantity had been expected to require the cutting and processing of thousands of trees, leading to concern about destruction of yew forests. The shortage in supply set off a worldwide race among organic chemists to obtain the molecule from other sources, yet its total synthesis from simple starting materials proved to be one of the most elusive goals of the past decade. The taxol molecule (*see* Figure) is large and complex, built from an unusual system of four rings extremely difficult to re-create in the laboratory.

The two techniques to taxol synthesis are different and were developed by separate research groups. Robert A. Holton and co-workers of Florida State University used ordinary camphor as a starting material and proceeded with a "linear" strategy to assemble each component of the molecule one piece after another. By contrast, K.C. Nicolaou and co-workers of the Scripps Research Institute, La Jolla, Calif., and the University of California at San Diego used a "convergent" strategy in which two large parts of the taxol molecule are synthesized separately and then joined.

Neither synthesis was expected to have an immediate impact on the commercial supply of taxol, which no longer was scarce. Taxol was being made in a semisynthetic process from chemical precursors collected from yew needles and twigs, which can be harvested without killing trees. But scientists said that the work could pave the way for a simpler total synthesis and that it had expanded knowledge about synthesizing complex molecular structures.

Natural gas, best known as a fuel for home heating and cooking, is typically 85–90% methane (CH_4). Researchers long have sought cheaper and better ways for exploiting the methane in natural gas as a raw material for making industrial chemicals that currently must be made from petroleum. Doing so has proved difficult because methane does not readily undergo the proper chemical reactions.

During the year Ayusman Sen and Minren Lin of Pennsylvania State University reported developing a single-step process that converts methane into acetic acid (CH_3COOH) under mild conditions. In addition to being the acid in vinegar, acetic acid is a key raw material of the chemical industry, used in the manufacture of plastics, pharmaceuticals, pesticides, dyes, and other products. Most industrial acetic acid has been obtained from petroleum. Sen and Lin's process requires only methane, carbon monoxide (CO), oxygen (O_2), and a catalyst, rhodium chloride ($RhCl_3$), which is dissolved in water to promote the conversion of methane. The reaction, which can be summarized as $CH_4 + CO + \frac{1}{2}O_2 \rightarrow CH_3COOH$, gives high yields and produces only methanol and formic acid as by-products. Importantly, the reactions require temperatures of only 100° C (212° F), the boiling point of water. By contrast, a process used for manufacturing acetic acid from methane requires three costly steps, consumes much energy, and requires hazardous organic solvents that must be contained or recycled. The researchers regarded the new process as an important first step toward exploiting the methane in natural gas.

Chemists were devoting increased research attention to molecular self-assembly, a phenomenon in which complex molecules form spontaneously from simple components.

Some scientists suggested that life on Earth originated in such a way, with simple chemical components spontaneously growing more complex and developing the ability to replicate. In an advance in the understanding of self-assembly, chemists at the University of Birmingham, England, announced discovery of a molecule that pieces itself together in a previously unrecognized way. J. Fraser Stoddart and David Amabilino synthesized the new molecule, which was dubbed olympiadane because its five interlinked molecular rings resemble the logo of the Olympic Games. Many organic compounds are formed from ringlike arrays of atoms that are attached by chemical bonds between atoms. Olympiadane's rings, however, are interlocked mechanically without bonds. Stoddart and Amabilino encouraged the self-assembly by careful control of temperature, pressure, and other conditions during synthesis. During assembly, chains of atoms thread together one inside the other, much like the links on a chain, ending with five interlocked rings.

Bleach additives in laundry detergent powders work by oxidizing fabric stains through the action of hydrogen peroxide. Laundry detergents usually contain a perborate compound that forms hydrogen peroxide when the detergent powder comes into contact with water. Hydrogen peroxide, even when aided by detergent additives that lower the water temperature needed for acceptable bleaching activity, does not bleach effectively unless the water temperature is above 40° C (104° F). Many consumers, however, want to do laundry in cooler water in order to conserve energy and avoid damaging modern fabrics. Chemists thus have searched for low-temperature oxidants that bleach in cooler water.

U.S. and Dutch chemists announced discovery of a family of manganese catalysts, derived from 1,4,7-trimethyl-1,4,7-triazacyclononane, that enhance hydrogen peroxide's bleaching action in cool water. Ronald Hage headed the research, which was carried out at the Unilever Research Laboratories, Vlaardingen, Neth., and Edgewater, N.J. Hage and co-workers reported that the catalysts work with hydrogen peroxide so that it begins bleaching at about 20° C (68° F).

Inorganic Chemistry. Most solid materials expand when heated as their chemical bonds lengthen and their atoms move farther apart. The tendency to expand creates serious problems for solids used in optical, electronic, and other applications. Even slight expansion of materials in telescope mirrors and lasers, for instance, can result in distortion and poor performance. Heat-related expansion is a major cause of premature failure of circuit boards in computers and other electronic devices.

Arthur Sleight and co-workers of Oregon State University announced discovery of a unique family of solid materials that could help solve such problems. The materials—typified by $ZrVPO_4$, an oxide of zirconium (Zr), vanadium (V), and phosphorus (P)—contract steadily when heated

taxol

between about 200° and 800° C (390° and 1,470° F). Sleight suggested that the unusual behaviour of the materials is due to their crystal structure, in which atoms of vanadium and phosphorus bond not to each other but to an intermediate atom of oxygen. When such a material is heated, the oxygen atom vibrates in a fashion that tends to physically pull the other atoms closer together. The behaviour differs from that of existing materials that resist expansion, such as those used in heat-resistant cookware. Those materials are made of small particles that, when heated, expand in some directions and contract in others, resulting in little net change in volume. But existing materials have disadvantages that limit their use in other applications. Sleight said that compounds such as $ZrVPO_4$ might be used as components in new polymer, graphite, or ceramic composites that would be more versatile yet highly resistant to heat-related failure.

Nuclear Chemistry. A commission of the International Union for Pure and Applied Chemistry (IUPAC) recommended names for nine chemical elements. The elements, which number 101 through 109 on the periodic table, long had gone without official names because of conflicting claims of discovery and the need for experimental confirmation. The problems were resolved in recent years. All of the elements are unstable and synthetic, having been made in accelerators by fusion of the nuclei of atoms of lighter elements. If approved by the full IUPAC at a meeting scheduled for 1995, the following names and symbols would become part of the periodic table: 101, mendelevium (Md); 102, nobelium (No); 103, lawrencium (Lr); 104, dubnium (Db); 105, joliotium (Jl); 106, rutherfordium (Rf); 107, bohrium (Bh); 108, hahnium (Hn); and 109, meitnerium (Mt). The recommendations caused intense controversy because the commission rejected several names proposed by the discoverers. Scientists who discover a new element traditionally have the right to name it. A stir arose, for instance, over rejection of the name seaborgium (Sg) proposed by the discoverers of element 106. The name would have honoured Nobel laureate Glenn T. Seaborg, the codiscoverer of plutonium and nine other transuranic elements.

In November Peter Armbruster and co-workers at the GSI (Heavy Ion Research Center), Darmstadt, Germany, announced the discovery of element 110. They created three atoms of the element by fusing nuclei of isotopes of nickel and lead in GSI's heavy-ion accelerator. The following month Armbruster's team announced that they had made element 111 by fusing nickel and bismuth nuclei.

Biochemistry. An enzyme called ATP synthase is the central energy-generating molecule in almost all forms of life. This protein promotes, or catalyzes, the synthesis of adenosine triphosphate (ATP), which stores chemical energy in a special bond, termed a high-energy phosphate bond. When the bond is broken, or hydrolyzed, thereby separating a phosphate group from the rest of the ATP molecule, the stored energy becomes instantly available. By means of additional chemical reactions, that energy can be transformed into energy needed, for example, to make muscle cells contract, assemble amino acids into proteins, or transmit signals along nerve fibres. In animals ATP is formed in cellular substructures termed mitochondria as nutrients are metabolized. Plants form ATP inside their chloroplasts as photosynthesis converts sunlight into chemical energy. Certain bacteria produce ATP in their cell membranes.

Many biochemists worldwide have studied ATP synthase's structure and function since it was first isolated in 1960. In an advance heralded as a landmark in those efforts, British biochemists in 1994 reported the deciphering of the atomic structure of a key portion of the ATP synthase molecule. John E. Walker of the Medical Research Council Labora-

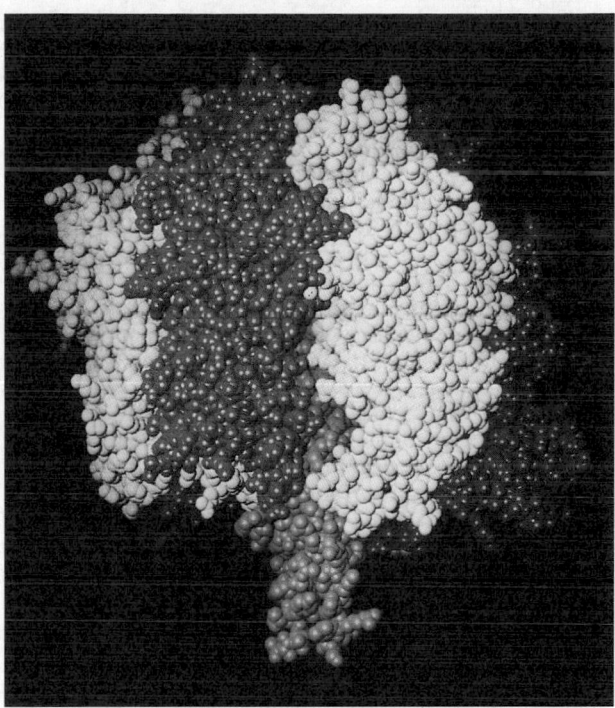

The detailed atomic structure of a key portion of the ATP synthase molecule was reported in 1994 and is shown in a computer model above. It consists of three of each of two kinds of subunits arrayed alternately, like the segments of an orange, around a central "stem."
LABORATORY OF MOLECULAR BIOLOGY, MEDICAL RESEARCH COUNCIL, CAMBRIDGE

tory of Molecular Biology, Cambridge, headed the research. Walker's group spent 12 years studying the biochemistry of ATP synthase and trying to grow high-quality crystals of the enzyme. Crystals were necessary for analyzing the enzyme's structure via X-ray diffraction techniques.

Researchers said the work would help answer many questions about the way living organisms produce energy. Walker also predicted that the structural determination would lead to new insights into the molecular basis of aging. Mitochondrial genes that direct the production of part of the ATP synthase molecule mutate at a much faster rate than conventional genes in a cell's nucleus. Walker and other scientists suspected that the mutations accumulate with time as an organism ages. The changes impair an organism's ability to produce energy and may be a key factor in Parkinson's disease, Alzheimer's disease, and other degenerative diseases of aging.   (MICHAEL WOODS)

This article updates the *Macropædia* articles BIOCHEMICAL COMPONENTS OF ORGANISMS; CHEMICAL COMPOUNDS; CHEMICAL ELEMENTS; CHEMICAL REACTIONS; The PHYSICAL SCIENCES: *Chemistry*.

Consumer Affairs

The signing of the General Agreement on Tariffs and Trade on April 15, 1994, was one of the year's most significant events for consumers everywhere. In theory, consumers stood to benefit from freer trade, in the form of more products and lower prices. The phaseout of quotas for clothing and textiles could be seen as a plus for less developed countries (LDCs). Consumers also stood to benefit from improvements in the procedures for settling disputes between countries. On the other hand, there were concerns that the agreement might lead to lower national food standards and higher drug prices in the LDCs. In 1962 the richest 20%

of the world population (most of whom lived in the North) had 30 times the income of the poorest 20%. In 1994 the gap was 60 times as great, and the role the new trade rules would play in shrinking that chasm was unclear.

Nowhere was this problem more clearly illustrated than in Africa, where consumers faced ongoing basic problems, such as poor service, a lack of awareness of consumer rights, and a shortage of funds. The move away from command economies that were heavily regulated and controlled by governments to more liberal open markets was welcome in many areas, but it also created new problems for consumers, such as huge and sudden price increases. In some African countries consumer organizations flourished, but more than a dozen of the poorest African countries still had no consumer movement. Overall, Africa in the 1990s was characterized by increased political tolerance, allowing the emergence of consumer and other movements. A model consumer protection law for Africa based on the 1985 UN Guidelines on Consumer Protection was due to be published in 1995. It was anticipated that this model would be used for lobbying across the continent at the regional and national level. The International Organization of Consumers Unions opened its first African office, in Harare, Zimbabwe, in March 1994. It signified the first attempt to bring the continent's diverse consumer organizations together under one pan-Africa umbrella.

Japanese consumers won greater protection through passage in 1994 of the country's first product liability law. India became one of the first LDCs to begin "ecolabeling"—letting customers know the environmental impact of the product they were buying. Eight of Asia's countries, however, including Bangladesh, Bhutan, and Cambodia, remained among the world's poorest nations, and many people continued to struggle to meet their most basic needs of clean water, adequate food, and shelter.

In the South Pacific, a fledgling consumer movement was fast-growing where Western-style consumerism had come quickly. In the Solomon Islands, for example, people who were moving away from their traditional healthful diet of coconut, tuna, and taro were facing new health conditions, including heart disease, obesity, and diabetes. Stories of people trading the fresh fish in their diet for canned Spam were common. Basic consumer education such as how to identify out-of-date packaged food was often needed.

In Latin America consumers breathed a sigh of relief in 1994 as the region emerged from the deep economic crisis of the previous decade. Governments pressed ahead with massive programs to liberalize trade, privatize public enterprises, and deregulate domestic markets. Economic gains had their ups and downs, and 40% of the region's population still earned less than a minimum wage and lacked sufficient access to basic consumer goods and services.

The lack of basic services for much of the world was highlighted by World Consumer Rights Day, held annually on March 15. The problems were everywhere; in Mexico the monopoly telephone company raised user costs by 160% over two years, and in El Salvador an estimated 30% of city dwellers and 80% of rural inhabitants had no access to piped water.

Perhaps the most dramatic changes in 1994 were felt in the former Soviet bloc countries, where consumers were grappling with the pluses and minuses of living in newly privatized economies. Throughout the republics of the former Soviet Union, the main issues were still the lack of available goods, poor quality, and fake and dangerous products, many of them imported. The breakdown of centralized structures continued, and problems with public services increased, particularly with medical services, housing, and transport.

Implementation of consumer protection legislation in these countries continued to be a major problem. Russian consumers could claim a victory in 1994, however; the courts ruled that services, as well as goods, should be included in the 1992 Law on the Protection of Consumers' Rights. The need for strict financial services legislation and better consumer education was demonstrated by the thousands of Russians who invested in a stock pyramid scheme and ended up losing their life savings. In Romania some four million people—50% of the population—took part in a pyramid investment scheme that collapsed in 1993.

A mother signs a petition demanding that milk be labeled if it comes from cows given a genetically engineered hormone. There were a number of similar protests in 1994 as food products using biotechnology were introduced to the marketplace.
RENATO ROTOLO—GAMMA LIAISON

Western European consumers in 1994 closely followed the changes in the European Union (EU) and expansion of its membership. Maintaining high health and safety standards in a single European market was the focus of much consumer concern. Many countries were afraid that membership in the EU would compromise their national health and safety standards. Consumer groups charged that the European Commission favoured industry concerns over consumer needs. In 1994, however, they managed to win a seven-year battle when the Commission agreed to regulate cross-border payments—when people send money from one country to another. Consumers would no longer have to pay double service charges to banks, and the Commission established bank liability on all payments.

At the end of the year, consumer groups everywhere were gearing up for the World Summit for Social Development, to be held in Copenhagen in March 1995. Organizers hoped it would be the people's equivalent of the 1992 "Earth Summit" in Rio de Janeiro. (ALINA TUGEND)

In 1994 the U.S. Food and Drug Administration (FDA) officially launched the most extensive renovation of food labels in 20 years. Mandated by the Nutrition Labeling and Education Act of 1990, the initiative imposed strict new standards for health, nutrition, and serving-size labeling claims from processors and manufacturers. For the first time, nutrition labels were required on most food packages, an estimated 90% of processed food sold in the marketplace—upwards of 285 billion items. Previously, only foods that made special claims or contained added nutrients had to carry labels, although processors labeled many other foods voluntarily.

Under the revised regulations, the FDA designed the new labels to provide consumers with a standard reference point, the "Daily Value," representing the average diet for a healthy adult (set at 2,000 calories). The listed amounts of a product's fat, cholesterol, sodium, fibre, and nutrients also had to be presented as a percentage of this Daily Value.

The Flavr Savr tomato became the first whole food produced by genetic engineering to reach the marketplace. Calgene Inc., of Davis, Calif., bred the tomato with a new version of a gene that affects the ripening process in tomatoes. The introduction of this gene allowed the Flavr Savr to remain firm longer than traditional tomatoes, increasing the time it could stay on the vine and ripen, thus allowing it to achieve better flavour than other commercially produced tomatoes. It was marketed amid heightened consumer concern over labeling and the safety of genetically engineered foods.

Biotechnology critics had sparked the controversy when the first milk produced with the aid of genetic engineering was marketed earlier in the year. Although that process had been approved by the relevant health agencies, critics said that as-yet-unknown risks could develop—if not in milk, then in other products slated for the market in coming years—and consumers would not be able to avoid them. Biotechnology proponents said such concerns stemmed from a misunderstanding of the science involved in genetic engineering. Half of all consumers surveyed said they would avoid genetically engineered products, according to the Wirthlin Group Inc., but such resistance would lessen if the technology resulted in consistently lower food prices.

Steps toward a major change in how consumers buy their electric power were taken by the California Public Utility Commission, which proposed fully opening electric power service to retail competition by the year 2002. Without utility monopolies, under which consumers were forced to purchase power at set rates from a local utility, business and residential consumers could shop among power companies for the best prices—much like people already shopped for long-distance telephone service. The proposed changes would allow consumers to tap into existing networks of electricity transmission that connect power companies nationwide.

Efforts to open the electricity market to consumers in California, New York, and other states were opposed by critics in the utility industry, who said open competition would cause stock values to plummet, and by some environmentalist groups, which held that cheaper power would increase electricity use and thus air pollution.

Despite the popularity and growing safety reputation among consumers, antilock brakes in automobiles were found to offer no clear advantage on the nation's roads. A study by the Highway Loss Data Institute found that antilock brakes were not reducing either the frequency or the cost of car crashes, including crashes on wet and slippery roads, where antilocks should have proved advantageous. The researchers said the problem was not the technology, which demonstrated clear benefits under test conditions, but drivers who did not know how to brake with antilocks properly. The Institute also cited studies showing that some drivers in cars equipped with antilock brakes drove less safely.   (PETER L. SPENCER)

See also Business and Industry Review: *Advertising; Retailing; Economic Affairs; Environment.*

Crime, Law Enforcement, and Penology

Terrorism. Peace talks continued in 1994 between Israel and its Arab neighbours despite a series of murderous incidents, while in Northern Ireland the Irish Republican Army, one of the world's most tenacious terrorist groups, announced in August that it was halting its 25-year campaign of violence immediately and unconditionally. Also in August the French government secured the arrest and extradition of Ilich Ramírez Sánchez, better known as Carlos or "the Jackal," one of the most feared and wanted international terrorists, who was tracked down in The Sudan.

These encouraging developments were overshadowed, however, by a number of bloody terrorist attacks linked to long-standing conflicts. On February 25 at Hebron in the Israeli-occupied Palestinian West Bank, about 30–40 Muslim worshipers were gunned down as they prayed at the Cave of the Patriarchs, a shrine venerated by both Arabs and Jews. An Israeli inquiry into the shooting subsequently laid sole blame for the carnage on Baruch Goldstein, a member of a group of Jewish settlers living in the West Bank. Goldstein was overpowered and beaten to death by survivors immediately after the massacre, which provoked widespread violence in the area and disrupted Israeli-Arab peace negotiations. These negotiations were again placed under severe duress in July when a wave of attacks against Jewish targets in a number of countries raised fears about the rapid spread and reach of Islamic terrorism. The worst attack occurred on July 18 in the Argentine capital of Buenos Aires, where a powerful car bomb destroyed a Jewish community centre, leaving 96 people dead and at least 140 injured. Later in the year, a bomb exploded on a crowded bus in Tel Aviv, Israel, on October 19, killing 22 and injuring 45, and a suicide bomber killed himself and wounded 13 people at a bus stop in Jerusalem on December 25. (*See* WORLD AFFAIRS: *Israel.*)

In Algeria a vicious terrorist campaign by Islamic extremists, aimed at toppling the country's ruling military regime, threatened to spill across the Mediterranean into France and other European nations with large North African immigrant and exile populations. During the year some 64 foreign nationals were murdered by terrorists, including at least 22 French citizens. As French authorities arrested numbers of Algerian exiles suspected of extremism and uncovered networks in France supporting Algerian-based terrorist groups, these groups promised violent reprisals against those responsible for the crackdown. On December 27, one day after French commandos killed four terrorists who had hijacked an airliner, executed three passengers, and held 173 others hostage, the Armed Islamic Group murdered four Roman Catholic priests in Algeria in retaliation. Meanwhile, in Iran, a nation widely viewed as one of the principal supporters of Islamic extremist violence in many parts of the world, a bomb exploded on June 20 in a crowded shrine in the Muslim holy city of Meshed, killing 70 people and wounding 114. The attack, which Iranian authorities blamed on the Mujahedin-e Khalq, an opposition group based in Iraq, was the worst terrorist incident in the country since the end of the 10-year Iran-Iraq war in 1990.

War Crimes. Amid mounting criticism of its lack of action and delay, the International Tribunal for the Prosecution of War Crimes in the former Yugoslavia announced in October that a Bosnian Serb, Dusan Tadic, was to be the subject of the first international investigation of this type since the Nürnberg and Tokyo trials after World War II. In July the tribunal appointed a South African judge, Richard Goldstone, as its principal prosecutor. Under the mandate given to the tribunal, persons found guilty of war crimes would not face the death penalty, but convicted defendants were likely to serve lengthy prison terms in countries that were prepared to accept them. The tribunal's critics continued to express concern that it would merely target minor offenders as scapegoats, and senior political leaders who should be held responsible for atrocities would evade punishment.

In March a long-suppressed U.S. Department of Justice report on the wartime activities of former UN secretary-general Kurt Waldheim was finally released. The 1987 report claimed that the Austrian was a key member of Nazi units responsible for executing prisoners, killing civilians, identifying Jews for deportation, and shipping prisoners to slave labour camps.

Drug Trafficking. With an estimated 2.7 million hard-core drug users on the street and with Americans spending $49 billion annually on illegal drugs, a progress report on U.S. national drug-control policy declared that action had to be taken. It called, among other things, for changes in the way international drug-control programs were viewed. For example, in countries that were major sources of drugs or through which drugs traveled, support for counternarcotics programs had to be an integral part of U.S. foreign policy.

Nowhere was this policy being more vigorously pursued than in Colombia, long the principal source for the lucrative international trade in cocaine. As Colombia's newly elected president, Ernesto Samper Pizano, was sworn into office in August, U.S. State Department officials expressed anxieties that the antidrug war would suffer a setback because he had received campaign funds from Colombia's powerful drug cartels. Denying these charges, Samper announced an array of measures to combat drug trafficking.

Murder and Other Violence. U.S. Pres. Bill Clinton fulfilled his campaign promise to get tough on crime by securing the passage through Congress in September of the Violent Crime Control and Law Enforcement Act of 1994. The new legislation provided funds for 100,000 new police and 100,000 new prison places and for crime-prevention programs. It also extended the federal death penalty from 2 to 60 crimes, including drive-by shootings and carjackings, and required mandatory life-imprisonment sentences for those convicted of a third felony involving violence. Against fierce opposition from the powerful U.S. gun lobby, the legislation incorporated a ban on 19 types of assault weapons. Sex-based violence was made a civil rights violation, thereby applying federal penalties to spousal abuse and stalking a woman across state boundaries.

The grim realities of domestic abuse in U.S. family life were graphically exposed in June when O.J. Simpson, a football hero and motion-picture star, was accused of stalking and slaying his ex-wife Nicole and her friend Ronald Goldman. They were found stabbed to death on June 12 outside Nicole Simpson's home in West Los Angeles. Simpson was arrested by Los Angeles police on June 17 following a bizarre low-speed chase along local freeways observed live by millions of television viewers in the U.S. and abroad. In the wake of Nicole Simpson's death, domestic violence hot lines across the U.S. reported a record surge in calls as many battered and abused women broke their silence and left violent homes for sanctuary in shelters.

In May a report by Pakistan's Human Rights Commission said that half of the victims of reported rapes in that country were juveniles. Very few rapes were reported and even fewer prosecuted. Under an Islamic ordinance in force in Pakistan since 1979, a woman had to present four witnesses in order to prove a case of sexual assault. In the U.S. a Justice Department study published in June covering 11 states and the District of Columbia found that about half the victims of rapes reported to the police in 1992 were girls younger than 18 and that about one in six was under 12. The study determined most of the rapes were committed by relatives or friends. In July the House of Lords created an offense of male rape for the first time in English legal history. The decision to change the legal definition of rape was taken

Photographs show three disguises used by Carlos "the Jackal," captured in The Sudan in August and extradited to France. Born Ilich Ramírez Sánchez in Venezuela and trained in Cuba and Moscow, Carlos was one of the most feared of international terrorists in the 1970s and '80s.

without a vote as part of a homosexual law reform package agreed upon by all parties in the British upper house.

The passions raised by international soccer resulted in the death of Colombian football star Andrés Escobar in July. On June 22 Escobar accidentally kicked a goal against his own team while playing in a World Cup match in Pasadena, Calif. On July 2, on his return home to Medellín, Escobar was accosted outside a bar by a number of persons who hurled abuse at him for his error and then shot him to death in what local police described as a planned execution. A few days later authorities arrested three Medellín men suspected of being involved in a murder that shocked a nation already traumatized during recent years by the deaths of thousands of citizens in drug-related violence.

In Mexico the assassination on March 23 of Luis Donaldo Colosio (*see* OBITUARIES), the presidential candidate of Mexico's Institutional Revolutionary Party, shook the foundations of the country and raised doubts about its long-term stability. Colosio, addressing a political rally in Tijuana at the time of his death, was shot in the head by an assailant who was then apprehended at the scene of the murder. (*See* WORLD AFFAIRS: *Mexico.*)

A series of incidents in the latter half of the year involved apparent or real attacks on the White House, including two cases in which bullets were fired into the U.S. presidential mansion and the crash of a small airplane onto the grounds. Motives were unclear in two apparently related firebombings in New York City's subway system in December that injured dozens of people.

Political Crime and Espionage. Italy's long-running corruption scandal claimed fresh victims during the year, including Paolo Berlusconi, the youngest brother of the nation's prime minister, billionaire Silvio Berlusconi. Spearheaded by a team of magistrates in Milan, the anticorruption inquiry, labeled Operation Clean Hands, extended its investigations to the prime minister's own business interests, and in December Berlusconi resigned from office. (*See* BIOGRAPHIES.)

In September the Greek Parliament voted to send to trial a former prime minister, Konstantinos Mitsotakis, for allegedly taking a bribe of $22.5 million in the 1992 sale of a

government-owned cement plant to an Italian company, but the case was dropped in December. In May Carlos Andrés Pérez, 71, a former president of Venezuela, was arrested and briefly jailed after the nation's Supreme Court ruled that he should be tried on charges of misappropriating part of $17 million in public funds. Following expressions of concern by foreign leaders, he was placed under house arrest. A series of trials took place in Indonesia during the year as the government sought to clean up the notoriously lax and corrupt state banking system. The most prominent of these prosecutions involved a multimillionaire entrepreneur, Eddy Tansil, who in September was sentenced to 17 years in jail for his part in a banking scandal involving the theft of $436 million.

The U.S. CIA announced in February that one of its most senior officers had been a spy for the Soviet Union and then Russia since 1985. Espionage charges were filed against Aldrich ("Rick") Ames, a 31-year career veteran and a past head of the CIA's counterintelligence division, and his wife, Maria del Rosario Casas Ames. In April both pleaded guilty to charges of conspiracy to commit espionage and tax fraud. Aldrich Ames was sentenced to life imprisonment without chance of parole, while his wife received a lesser sentence. Prosecutors said that Ames, motivated by greed, had caused the deaths, arrests, and disappearances of at least one East German and 10 Soviet double agents. The Ames affair was cited as a key factor in the resignation of CIA director James Woolsey in December.

White Collar Crime and Theft. Booming economic growth in China brought with it an unwelcome increase in economic crime. According to Chinese officials, 20,000 cases of embezzlement and corruption were reported in the first six months of 1994, an 81% increase from a year earlier. Communist Party leaders called for new vigour in the campaign to stamp out such crimes, including wider use of the death penalty.

The rapidly expanding worldwide market in mobile phones was reported to be producing an associated boom in theft and fraud. British mobile phone operating companies revealed that during the first half of 1994 the theft of handsets increased from 10,000 to 15,000 a month. In Ger-

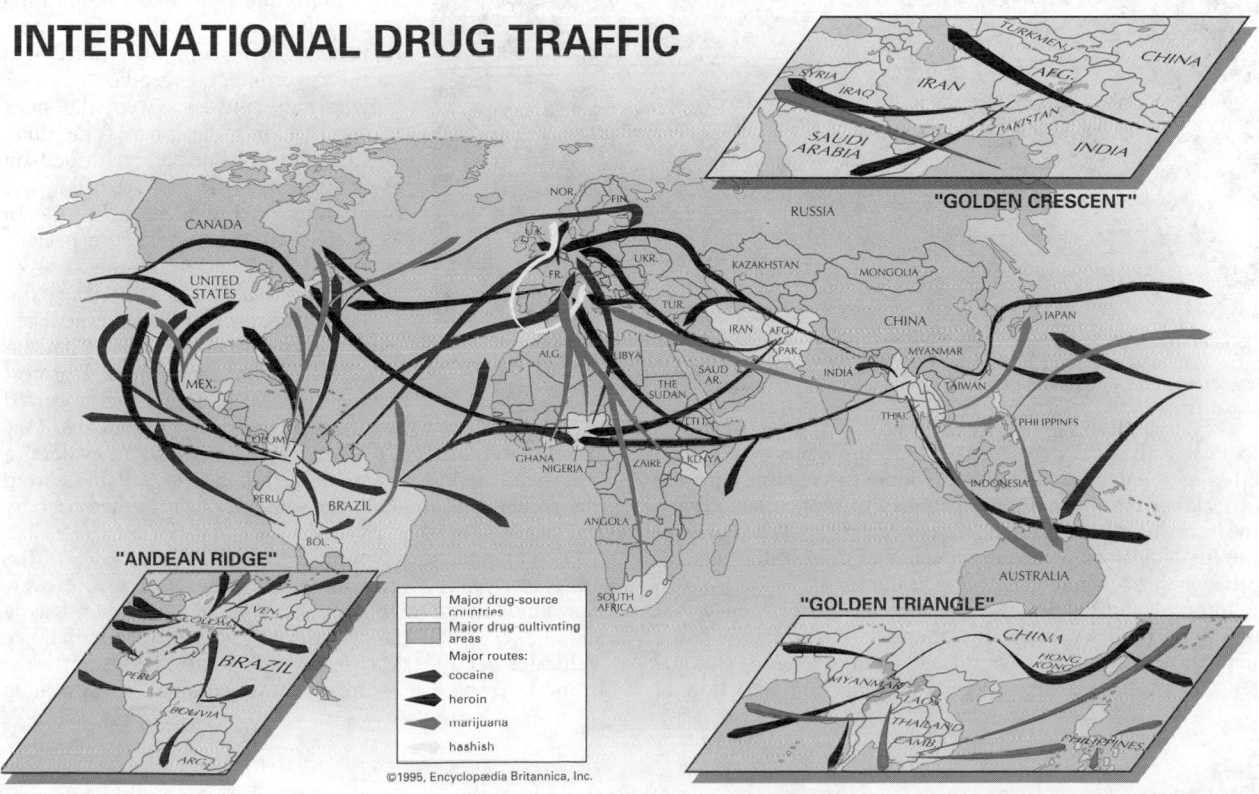

INTERNATIONAL DRUG TRAFFIC

"GOLDEN CRESCENT"

"ANDEAN RIDGE"

"GOLDEN TRIANGLE"

Major drug-source countries
Major drug cultivating areas
Major routes:
cocaine
heroin
marijuana
hashish

©1995, Encyclopædia Britannica, Inc.

many mobile phone service providers reported losses from fraud amounting to about 2% of their multimillion-dollar turnover. Most of this fraud was linked to the sophisticated Global System for Mobile Communications technology, which allows mobile phone subscribers in one country to use their phones to make calls on another network elsewhere in the world (known as "roaming"). Unscrupulous customers and mobile phone thieves used this "roaming" facility to amass large unpaid phone accounts, evading early detection because of delays in billing those calls to home networks.

Law Enforcement. Under the auspices of the UN, justice ministers from around the world gathered in Naples in November to discuss the growing problem of transnational organized crime. The meeting was prompted by concern that traditional law-enforcement techniques were failing to cope with newly emerging and sophisticated criminal groups operating with increasing impunity across the globe. Whether smuggling illegal immigrants into the U.S. from China, arms and icons from the former Soviet Union into Western Europe, or drugs from Latin America into North America, these groups represented a significant threat to the world community. A chilling portrayal of this threat emerged during the year in Germany, where law-enforcement officials seized four smuggled radioactive shipments in as many months. The shipments, three of which were of plutonium 239, an essential ingredient in the production of nuclear weapons, were said to have originated from poorly guarded installations in Russia.

The Naples meeting emphasized the importance of new forms of mutual assistance among nations to combat transnational organized crime. At present Italian, Chinese, Lebanese, Colombian, Russian, and other ethnically based criminal groups could all too easily exploit glaring structural weaknesses in law-enforcement agencies established mainly

Robert ("Yummy") Sandifer lies with his teddy bear in his coffin in Chicago. The 11-year-old, thought to have accidentally killed a 14-year-old girl during a gang-motivated shooting, apparently was murdered by members of his own gang to keep him from talking to the police.
REUTERS/BETTMANN

to deal with local or national crime problems rather than cross-national criminal activities. Some success was reported in tackling the international problem of money laundering, the term used to describe the concealing of the source of the funds derived from the proceeds of drug trafficking and other major revenue-generating crimes.

Interpol, the Paris-based international police agency, was asked in June to arrest the founder of the defunct and scandal-ridden Bank of Credit and Commerce International (BCCI), Agha Hassan Abedi, following his conviction of

fraud by an Abu Dhabi court. Abedi, who was said to be bedridden in Pakistan, was sentenced to an eight-year prison term, while 11 of his fellow BCCI executives also received prison terms and were fined a total of $9 billion. In the absence of an extradition treaty between Pakistan and Abu Dhabi, Interpol remained powerless to act unless Pakistan agreed voluntarily to hand over Abedi.

In London a surge in the number of stabbings and shootings of unarmed police resulted in May in further relaxation of the long-standing tradition for British police not to carry guns routinely. The commissioner of the Metropolitan Police, Paul Condon, said that officers in armed response vehicles would now carry weapons openly.

The development of new technology to assist law enforcement received a boost with the announcement in October that a British company had devised an electronic sniffer that could detect drugs and explosives, including the deadly Semtex favoured by terrorist bombers. The British Home Office said that the new device, called Itemiser, would be field-tested immediately in two maximum-security prisons. In Taiwan a new and highly sophisticated automatic fingerprint-verification system began to be released on the international market.   (DUNCAN CHAPPELL)

Prisons and Penology. The U.S. crime bill of 1994 called for a $30.2 billion expenditure by the federal government over the next six years, $9.9 billion of which was to be spent for prisons and "boot camps" (short-stay facilities run in military style). New powers for federal courts included the option of dealing with 13-year-olds as adults, and life imprisonment was mandated for a third violent felony. At the state level, California enacted a statute that enabled the courts to impose sentences of at least 25 years in prison without parole on persons convicted of a third felony. With opinion polls showing strong support for the slogan "three strikes and you're out," several other states were preparing to follow suit.

Strident postures on crime were also struck in Britain, where the home secretary, Michael Howard, unveiled a 27-point plan in October 1993. Tougher sentencing power for the courts in dealing with juveniles, electronic monitoring of offenders, and reductions in protections afforded to defendants were high on the government's agenda.

Even more intrusive were the steps taken in Delhi, India, where four young women had "pickpocket" tattooed on their foreheads, the first recorded case of branding in Indian legal history. In May considerable attention, especially in the U.S., focused on the case of Michael Fay, a young American convicted in Singapore of having vandalized parked cars with spray paint. The sentence that he be caned drew a protest from President Clinton but received the backing of many Americans. (*See* WORLD AFFAIRS: SPOTLIGHT: *Asian Values.*) Elsewhere, a UN special report on human rights in The Sudan asserted that recent legislation allowed crucifixion for armed robbery and stoning for adultery.

Prison populations continued to rise in many parts of the world, and there were widespread reports of severe overcrowding. According to a report issued in September, Russia and the U.S. had the world's largest prison populations, with rates per 100,000 citizens of 558 and 519, respectively. In the U.S. space pressures were exacerbated by worsening racial disparities, with African-Americans constituting 52% of state prison inmates, according to the Justice Department. Grim conditions also characterized prisons in South Africa, which, despite significant improvements since 1990, remained places of extreme violence.

Large-scale violent incidents were especially prevalent in South American prisons. In El Salvador a riot at San Francisco Gotera prison left 27 persons dead. An even more serious disturbance occurred in January at Sabaneta prison in Maracaibo, Venezuela; the death toll there was at least 122 prisoners. The prison, designed for 800, held 3,000 persons at the time of the riot. In Britain six prisoners who escaped in September from the top-security Whitemoor prison were quickly recaptured.

High rates of suicides, access to illegal drugs, and worsening health risks were among other problems associated with the increasingly crowded prison systems in many parts of the world. On a positive note, however, home-leave programs were vigorously pursued in Germany and Northern Ireland.

Death Penalty. The general trend throughout the world was toward an increased use of the death penalty. In February Amnesty International reported that 1,831 persons were known to have been executed in 32 countries during the previous year. China accounted for 77% of this recorded total. In the U.S. 31 people were executed during 1994 (7 fewer than in 1993).

Several countries acted to widen the scope of the death penalty, including Pakistan for drug trafficking, Lebanon for politically motivated murder, and Peru for terrorism. Elsewhere, demands for the death penalty by prosecutors in Turkey included a case involving Kurdish legislators charged with treason. In Trinidad and Tobago a man was hanged in July despite the fact that his case was before the court of appeal and the UN's International Rights Committee.

In Europe, however, the place of death penalty on the political agenda diminished. The British House of Commons in February voted by a majority of 244 votes not to restore capital punishment for murder and by 197 votes in the case of the murder of a police officer. These majorities occurred despite an opinion poll four months earlier showing 88% support for the death penalty.

Resort to capital punishment was reported in many countries, although it was not always officially acknowledged. For example, Amnesty International published reports of summary executions in Myanmar and also in Zaire, where it claimed that thousands of people had been put to death by the military authorities. Opponents of the regime in Iraq claimed that at least 1,000 people had been summarily executed at ar-Radwanieh prison camp in August 1993. By contrast, the Chinese authorities publicized (in some if not all cases) the frequent application of the death penalty. For example, in May after a mass sentencing in the southern province of Guangdong (Kwangtung), 33 car thieves were executed.

One aspect of the death penalty that continued to receive attention from human rights organizations was appalling conditions endured on death row, often over many years. For example, in May Amnesty International drew attention to the Oklahoma State Penitentiary in McAlester, constructed as an earth shelter, which held 400 persons on death row. Denied virtually all access to natural light or fresh air, prisoners were held in their cells for 23 hours per day during weekdays and for 24 hours on weekends.

(ANDREW RUTHERFORD)

See also Law

This article updates the *Macropædia* articles CRIME AND PUNISHMENT; POLICE.

Dance

North America. Preservation became something of a theme for dance in 1994. With basic funding, both private and public, on the low side and costs continuing on the high side, the dance world showed a pronounced focus on preserving its past. Nancy Reynolds, a former New York City Ballet (NYCB) dancer turned historian and writer, endowed a foundation furthering preservation of and education on the work of the late George Balanchine. This branch of the George Balanchine Foundation would augment the work of overseeing and disseminating Balanchine's legacy of teaching and choreography.

The Martha Graham Dance Company, marking what would have been Graham's 100th year, led off the Brooklyn Academy of Music's Next Wave Festival by featuring revivals of early Graham works for a season called "Radical Graham." A one-day symposium on Graham's history was held in New York City. In October a week of performances and symposia took place at the University of Michigan at Ann Arbor. The National Initiative to Preserve American Dance (NIPAD) announced inaugural grants to 12 organizations working to save selected elements from dance's past. The projects ranged from tap dancing to master teaching.

Similarly, company after company spent time looking toward the historical past. The Joffrey Ballet juggled touring its popular *Billboards* (including a stint in Canada) with performing its revival of Léonide Massine's 1933 *Les Présages.* This essentially turgid reading of Tchaikovsky's Fifth Symphony, a longtime curiosity in history books, became a living example of a precursor to the so-called abstract ballets that came to dominate 20th-century ballet making. American Ballet Theatre (ABT) revived *Echoing of Trumpets,* by its late mentor Antony Tudor. Thanks to the loving presence of its dancers, especially the luminous Julie Kent, this would-be dated and so-called antiwar ballet glowed on stage like a fiery filament in a naked lightbulb. The troupe's staging of the 102-year-old classic *The Nutcracker* fared less well, owing to its confused choreographic shaping and narrative reworking (the former by Kevin McKenzie and the latter by Wendy Wasserstein). Once more, however, ABT's dancers shone. Besides the ever remarkable Kent, the prodigious Paloma Herrera and the gifted Ashley Tuttle and Sandra Brown rose high above their uneven material. Brown also made the most of a nouveau revival, a restaging of the "ballet within the show" (by Lar Lubovitch, whose own modern dance troupe celebrated its 25th anniversary) from the defunct 1993 Broadway version of *The Red Shoes.*

San Francisco Ballet looked to the past by presenting Helgi Tomasson's new staging of the ever popular Prokofiev *Romeo and Juliet.* Praised more for its design (by Jens Jacob Worsaæ) and its narrative details than for its choreographic sweep, the production was the subject of a conference by the Dance Critics Association.

Pacific Northwest Ballet's Kent Stowell presented his Seattle, Wash., company in an original rendering of Prokofiev's other classic, *Cinderella.* Miami (Fla.) City Ballet's director Edward Villella chose a more recent classic in which to showcase his increasingly admired dancers—Balanchine's landmark plotless three-acter called *Jewels.* NYCB, which had accentuated its past in 1993 with an overly ambitious "Balanchine Celebration," began its 1994 spring season with a two-week run of Peter Martins' staging of *The Sleeping Beauty,* its hoped-for cash cow à la *The Nutcracker.* The keen interest seemingly stirred by the production's first season did not continue, however. The season proper included the biennial Diamond Project, a no-frills series of new bal-

Members of the Martha Graham Dance Company perform "Appalachian Spring," one of the choreographer's best-known works, at the Brooklyn Academy of Music's "Radical Graham" festival. The revival was part of the 100-year commemoration of Graham's birth.
LOIS GREENFIELD

lets. The 12 premiere dances, however, proved at best only somewhat interesting. Special dancer interest came largely from the male roster, with Ethan Stiefel, Peter Boal, Nikolaj Hübbe, Igor Zelensky, and Damian Woetzel standing out. On the female side, NYCB got its most stellar performances from guests; Britain's Darcey Bussell appeared in January, and Canada's Margaret Illman, formerly the star of Broadway's *The Red Shoes,* appeared in May.

International star Mikhail Baryshnikov also danced with NYCB in May, subsequent to the first New York City performances of his modern-dance-based ensemble, White Oak Dance Project (WODP), in March. Baryshnikov's appearances, still mostly sold-out occasions, were greatly distinguished by his presence (on both WODP and NYCB programs) in a new solo, *A Suite of Dances,* created for him by Jerome Robbins. Besides being inspired to return to the fold of active choreographers after a six-year hiatus, ballet's and Broadway's venerable Robbins also oversaw at NYCB the marking of the 50th anniversary of his *Fancy Free.* Farther along in his 75th year, he produced another new ballet. Created for the 60th anniversary of the School of American Ballet (NYCB's affiliate), *Two- and Three-Part Inventions* (named for the music by Bach) proved to be an enchantingly fresh, rich, and rigorous showcase for eight young, scrupulous ballet dancers. Robbins showed academic classical dancing as an evergreen medium of expression, and in his deft manipulation of its means, he put to shame the various attitudinizings of so many "new" ballets.

Dance Theatre of Harlem (DTH) celebrated its 25th anniversary in New York City with an odd repertoire. The relative absence of new works in the current financial climate was not strange, but there were no works by Balanchine, company founder Arthur Mitchell's foremost mentor. No official explanations were offered for the omissions, but the season did show Mitchell's continuing ability to inspire generous and remarkable dance performances. A gala program included pupils from the DTH school, repeating the homage the youngsters had paid Mitchell in Washington, D.C., when he was honoured at the John F. Kennedy Center for the Performing Arts. The Kennedy Center had a coup of its own when Britain's Royal Ballet chose to perform there the world premiere of its new production of *The Sleeping Beauty.* The staging by artistic director Anthony Dowell subsequently toured the United States, and with

its grandiose, eccentric, and handsome designs by Maria Bjørnson, the production proved controversial with the press and a hit with its audiences.

Along with creating two new works as usual, Paul Taylor initiated "The Paul Taylor Repertory Preservation Project," an activity funded by the National Endowment for the Arts to "preserve the core of Taylor's work, re-creating and restoring a significant number of earlier works, archiving company materials and videotaping dances for future generations." Merce Cunningham, who turned 75, presented two new dances (*Breakers,* which was cocreated for the Boston Ballet, and *CRWDSPCR*) in the United States and showed an even grander, bigger one (*Ocean*) abroad.

The Alvin Ailey American Dance Theater continued to shine through the radiant performing of its dancers even as it lost megastar dancer Desmond Richardson to a freelance career. The American Dance Festival honoured Katherine Dunham and the late Lester Horton, offering revivals of works by each choreographer as well as commissioning works from Eiko & Koma, Bill T. Jones/Arnie Zane Dance Company, and the Mark Morris Dance Group. Morris also completed a new dance, *The Office,* commissioned by Zivili, an Ohio-based folkloric company. In its enigmatic character, this modern folk work was read by some as a protest dance aimed at the war in Bosnia and Herzegovina.

The National Museum of Women in the Arts published *Isadora Duncan: The Dances,* a 532-page book of text and diagrammatic labanotation of more than 150 dances and exercises. With this volume, notation-literate dance students could relive and learn Duncan's art according to the teachings of her disciples.

The National Ballet of Canada (NBC) began 1994 with a new magnum opus by James Kudelka, *The Actress,* celebrating the 25-year career of beloved NBC ballerina Karen Kain. In the interests of repertory sharing, NBC called a "dance summit" with six American companies to discuss pooling efforts to acquire new works. Later in the year NBC hired Vladimir Malakhov, one of the former Soviet Union's most gifted dancers. A specially planned triple bill for Les Grands Ballets Canadiens by director Lawrence Rhodes focused on three works from the early 20th-century history of the Ballets Russes. Montreal's now annual Gala des Étoiles in 1994 included among its tutu-and-tights warhorses a number of nonballet contemporary dances, among them the work of Montrealer Margie Gillis.

Having won a NIPAD grant, the Erick Hawkins Dance Company lost its founder and director when Hawkins died in November. (*See* OBITUARIES.) Other deaths included those of dancer and teacher Klarna Pinska, dancer and teacher Igor Youskevitch, lighting designer Thomas Skelton, choreographer and director Michael Peters, and dancer Pearl Primus. (*See* OBITUARIES.)   (ROBERT J. GRESKOVIC)

Europe. In 1994 three long-established European dance companies changed direction and in doing so welcomed home favourite sons who had left the fold and enhanced their international reputations. At the Royal Danish Ballet (RDB), dancer, director, and producer Peter Schaufuss took over as director—returning to the company he had started with as a dancer—following high-profile periods as director of the English National Ballet (ENB) and the Berlin Ballet.

His first season in Copenhagen offered a span of work from classical to experimental and included a significant revival, Sir Frederick Ashton's *Romeo and Juliet*. The work had been created for the RDB in 1955, performed for a decade, and then somehow "lost"; it was Schaufuss who in 1985 had "found" it by persuading Ashton, three years before his death, to re-create it for the ENB.

In London Christopher Bruce became artistic director of Rambert Dance Company, returning to the organization where he too had made his debut as a dancer and where he had developed as a choreographer. His individual gifts coupled with his international experience helped change the look of Rambert, newly expanded to 25 dancers and to a different kind of content-based repertoire.

Also in London, Richard Alston became artistic director of the Contemporary Dance Trust, having previously held the same title with Rambert. He thus returned to the organization where in the late 1960s, during the formative years of the London Contemporary Dance Theatre (LCDT), he had produced his first choreography. A change in policy saw him heading a newly structured National Centre for Contemporary Dance, and he was charged with making more productive use of the trust's resources (including its theatre and school) while strengthening relationships nationally and elsewhere in Europe. LCDT, which had come to stand for solid modern values as opposed to dance at its "cutting edge," was adjudged to have outrun its useful life, and in the summer it closed, attracting a wealth of tributes for the achievement of 25 years. In November the trust launched the Richard Alston Dance Company, a smaller ensemble designed as a vehicle not only for Alston's choreography but for the development of other choreographers as well.

If modern dance was undergoing a sea change, in ballet the lack of change was cause for concern. At the Bolshoi Ballet there was widespread criticism at home and abroad of the artistic direction of Yury Grigorovich, who had led

NINA ALOVERT

Yulia Makhalina and Andris Liepa of the Mariinsky (Kirov) Ballet dance in Michel Fokine's *The Firebird*. It was the first time the work, created by the St. Petersburg native in 1910 for Sergey Diaghilev's Ballets Russes, had been performed in the city.

the company for 30 years but through whom it had become inward-looking and stale. A severe blow to the Bolshoi was cancellation—for lack of public response—of an English season optimistically called "The Grand Tour" and planned to take place in vast open spaces and arenas. Whether the problem was one of marketing or perception of a lost reputation was a matter for speculation, but the company had fallen from grace and morale was low. Grigorovich was not the only leader held to account, for at Germany's Stuttgart Ballet there was publicly aired bitterness about the regime that under Marcia Haydée had failed to move with the times. Change was promised, and Haydée signed a contract to direct the company until the year 2000.

Though unrest in both Moscow and Stuttgart was attributable to individual leadership styles, it could be seen as part of a bigger malaise about ballet's identity. Debate raged over artistic development and its relationship with social change, and ballet's strengths and weaknesses were highlighted through dependency on a glorious but inevitably conservative past. Proving the point, the legendary Ballets Russes continued to exert influence. *Till Eulenspiegel*, Vaslav Nijinsky's last ballet, which had not been seen since 1916–17, was reconstructed by Millicent Hodson and Kenneth Archer for the Paris Opéra Ballet and given on a triple bill with Nijinsky's *The Rite of Spring* and Michel Fokine's *Petrushka*. Reflecting changes on the wider political scene, two other Fokine ballets, *Schéhérazade* and *The Firebird*, both landmarks of Sergey Diaghilev's 1910 season in Paris, were performed for the first time in St. Petersburg by the Mariinsky (Kirov) Ballet. They were presented under the banner "Saison Russe," and the warmth of their reception acknowledged the history behind their performances and St. Petersburg's pride in having given birth to one of Russia's greatest exports.

The Firebird typified a wave of enthusiasm for the Diaghilev-Stravinsky ballets, as either revivals or radical new productions. Among the most innovative was *O* by Britain's Michael Clark, inspired by George Balanchine's *Apollo*. If proof was needed about dance's cyclical continuity, two American choreographers (Stephen Petronio from New York and Javier de Frutos from Venezuela) took iconoclastic but very different interpretations of *The Rite of Spring* to Britain's Dance Umbrella Festival.

These were postmodern experiments, however. In ballet only a few choreographers consciously developed form and widened conceptual thinking. Among them William Forsythe, the American leader of Germany's Frankfurt Ballet, upheld his reputation as one of the most radical and widely regarded choreographers. He continued to create new work that was paradoxical in content, and he pushed human plasticity and dynamism to extremes. Opinion generally regarded the Paris Opéra Ballet under Patrick Dupond as the most successful large-scale European ballet company because of the quality of its dancers and the balancing of tradition with experiment. Other European mainstream ballet companies frequently relied on a recycling of works, many of them not in the first league, and complained that a lack of cash was detrimental to artistic growth.

AIDS, which continued to take its toll of young professionals, was of increasing concern for the dance community, and organizations in Britain, France, and the U.S. widened the range of help available to sufferers. A gala at the London Coliseum in tribute to Rudolf Nureyev (who died of the disease in 1993) brought stars from around the world to honour him and to raise money for the cause. Nureyev, even from the grave, continued to haunt European stages and newspaper gossip columns. There were revivals of his productions of *La Bayadere*, *The Sleeping Beauty*, and *Swan Lake* (Paris Opéra Ballet); *The Sleeping Beauty* and *Raymonda* (Berlin State Opera Ballet); *Don Quixote* (Royal Swedish and Australian ballets); and *The Nutcracker* (Finnish National Ballet). *Nureyev: A Biography,* by Peter Watson, revealed hitherto undisclosed details about his private life. Nureyev's last wishes concerning his art collection and the funding of medical research and scholarships for dancers were the subject of protracted arguments between his family and the executors of his will.

Deaths during the year included the English artists Beatrice Appleyard, dancer, choreographer, and teacher; William Chappell, dancer, designer, director, and writer; Stanley Hall, dancer, director, and teacher; Michael Somes, dancer (*see* OBITUARIES); and Jack Spurgeon, dancer and teacher. Two Danish dancers and teachers, Fredbjørn Bjørnsson and Nina Stroganova, died, as did Jens Jacob Worsaæ, the Danish designer who worked in dance and the theatre. The Russians Kaleria Fedicheva, a dancer and teacher, and Nina Tarakanova, a dancer, actress, and revue artist, also died during the year. Two Italians connected with dance, the composer Vittorio Rieti (who was launched by Diaghilev) and the painter and stage designer Pier Luigi Samaritani, died, as did the South African dance teacher Dulcie Howes, the American dancer Traci-Kai Maier-Forsythe (who had been with the Frankfurt Ballet), and the Hungarian dancer and ballet master Viktor Rona.   (ANN NUGENT)

See also Music; Theatre.

This article updates the *Macropædia* article The History of Western DANCE.

Earth Sciences

GEOLOGY AND GEOCHEMISTRY

The astronomical display produced in July 1994 by the predicted explosive collisions of a string of fragments from a shattered comet with the atmosphere of Jupiter (*see* ASTRONOMY) ranked as the most spectacular planetary event of the year. It also drew attention to the role of asteroid and comet impacts in the Earth's history. The Jovian impacts followed by a few months a major scientific conference in Houston, Texas, devoted to the events associated with the boundary between the Cretaceous (K) and Tertiary (T) geologic periods, 65 million years ago, when dinosaurs and many other species became extinct. It was 15 years earlier that the U.S. physicist Luis Alvarez and his geologist son, Walter Alvarez, had proposed that the extinctions were the result of climatic disruptions caused by the impact of a massive asteroid or comet at the end of the Cretaceous. The initial evidence was an increased concentration of the trace element iridium (rare in asteroids but even rarer on Earth) discovered in a thin layer of sediment in rocks delineating the K-T boundary—an anomaly that proved to be global in extent.

The impact proposal was hotly debated because the idea that a catastrophic event could cause profound changes in the geologic record and the course of evolution is opposed to the venerable geologic doctrine of uniformitarianism—the idea that geologic changes and evolution occurred gradually through a progression of processes similar to those seen to be acting at present. Scientific doctrine is not easily overturned, but many earth scientists were converted following the discovery and investigation since 1992 of a giant 65 million-year-old impact crater, at least 180 km and perhaps 300 km in diameter (1 km is about 0.62 mi), at Chicxulub in Mexico's Yucatán Peninsula. Converts stretched the doctrine of uniformitarianism to include the occurrence of occasional impact events, such as that observed on Jupiter.

A crater about 35 km in diameter at Manson, Iowa, had previously been evaluated in connection with the K-T extinction and found to be too small. The observation of multiple impacts on Jupiter strengthened the proposal that the collisions that made the Manson and Chicxulub craters might have been part of a multiple event, although recent dating measurements indicated that the Manson crater may be older than 65 million years.

In 1994 there were few skeptics who doubted that a major collision with an extraterrestrial body occurred 65 million years ago. Some maintained, nevertheless, that the dinosaurs were already in decline and that the impact merely accelerated the mass extinction that was under way as a result of the climatic disruption caused by an enormous eruption of basalt—the flood basalts known today as the Deccan Traps—in India 65 million years ago. The argument was bolstered by the fact that only the K-T boundary is characterized by an iridium anomaly and that the several other mass extinctions that took place in the past 500 million years, therefore, must have had some other cause. At the Houston meeting Vincent Courtillot of the Institute of Physics of the Earth, Paris, presented evidence of a strong correlation between the ages of mass extinctions and of continental flood basalts, and he concluded that continental flood basalt volcanism is the main candidate for most extinction events. Interpretation of the evidence depends critically on accurate age measurements of both mass extinctions and flood basalt eruptions and their durations. Recent improvements in dating allowed researchers to confirm that most of the large flood basalt events lasted for less than one million years. Some uncertainties about the precise age of the Chicxulub crater could be resolved by a new drilling project, which would permit sampling of rocks in and under the crater.

Each continental flood basalt province represents a very large transfer of heat and material from within the Earth to its surface within a very short time. Recently a mechanism for the concentrated transfer was proposed that involved a modification of the concept of mantle plumes, cylinders of relatively hot rocks in the mantle (beneath the crust) that are rising slowly from perhaps as deep as the core-mantle boundary, 2,900 km down. Initially solid owing to the high pressure deep in the Earth, the plumes begin to melt as they approach the surface, yielding basaltic lavas. It was argued that "superplumes" sometimes developed and that the head of such a superplume grew in size by entraining rock from the surrounding mantle during its upward flow. When the large mushroom-shaped plume head approached the surface, it generated the enormous volumes of continental flood basalts. Subsequent plume activity from the thinner stem of the plume produced lesser volcanic activity, corresponding, for example, to that which formed the Hawaiian Islands.

Information about mantle plumes is based on fluid dynamics—*i.e.,* on interpretation of small-scale laboratory experiments with different fluids—and on interpretation of the geochemistry of basalts. During the year a drilling experiment under way on the island of Hawaii was beginning to reveal more about the mantle plume that feeds lava to the volcanoes. The successive lava flows on the island represent samples of successive portions of the rising plume, and the accessible lavas on the volcanoes thus represent only the most recent history. A drill hole near Hilo 1,100 m (3,600 ft) deep first traversed lavas from Mauna Loa and then passed into lavas from Mauna Kea. According to Donald Thomas of the University of Hawaii, Donald DePaolo of the University of California at Berkeley, and Edward Stolper of the California Institute of Technology, the frequency and ages of flows indicate that the volcanoes may be twice as old as previously thought. Detailed geochemical studies of the lava samples taken from the drilling were expected to provide information about variations along the rising mantle plume. The earlier stages of volcanic growth from these plume-derived lavas were being sampled in ocean-drilling studies of Loihi, the youngest Hawaiian volcano, which is growing on the submerged flanks of Kilauea.

Causal relationships have also been proposed between mantle plumes and the breakup of some continents, those having margins identified as having been created by volcanic rifting. It is widely believed that the northeastern Atlantic Ocean formed from a continental split that developed above a hot mantle plume, the ancestor of today's Iceland plume, and the possibility was explored during Leg 152 of the international Ocean Drilling Program in late 1993. Sites were drilled on the volcanically rifted margin of southeastern Greenland, and the first penetration through the volcanic cover into the underlying continental crust was achieved. Reports of results during 1994 revealed the tectonic and volcanic history of the continental breakup and confirmed the role of hot, buoyant mantle reaching fairly close to the surface in the rifting environment. Voluminous floodlike eruptions of basalt were in evidence. The upper series of lavas was richer in magnesium than normal oceanic basalts, indicating higher melting temperatures, but the trace-element geochemistry of the lavas was similar to that of normal mid-ocean ridge basalts, with no indication of basalts contributed from deep-seated mantle rocks, as would be expected if the lavas had been fed from a deep plume. Thus, a causal link between continental breakup and deep-seated mantle plumes was not yet established.

Basaltic volcanism causes the major chemical differentiation of the Earth; that is, the extraction of the components of the crust, hydrosphere, and atmosphere from the Earth's interior. But a more extreme differentiation is accomplished by geomorphic, weathering, and sedimentary processes at and near the Earth's surface. Sediments as diverse as limestone (calcium carbonate) and sandstone (silicon dioxide) derive from original basalts and other lavas. The weathering, transportation, and redeposition of rocks and soil form the differentiated sedimentary rocks, with many processes involving biological activity. The result is a modified landscape, the familiar scenery of the Earth's surface. The important effects of biological agents are limited in magnitude and time, but during the year Roger Hooke of the University of Minnesota emphasized that this generalization breaks down when human beings are considered.

The role of humans in landscape modification, although long recognized, had not been treated in textbooks of geomorphology. Hooke compared the efficacy of various geomorphic agents, humans included, on a global scale. The measure used was the mass of material moved from one location to another by unidirectional processes (the study thus excluded such processes as waves moving beach sand back and forth perpendicular to the shoreline and plows turning soil from furrow to ridge). According to Hooke, the amount of sediment moved by rivers is about 24 billion tons per year (24 Gt/yr), of which 10 Gt/yr is due to agriculture, while glaciers transport about 4.3 Gt/yr of material. Slope processes, wave action, and wind move only about 2.5 Gt/yr. Hooke estimated that the worldwide geomorphic activity of humans in earth moving, such as building excavations, mineral production, and highway construction, is about 30 Gt/yr, not including the 10 Gt/yr of river sediment due to agriculture. Humans were thus the most important geomorphic agent shaping the surface of the Earth.

(PETER JOHN WYLLIE)

GEOPHYSICS

On June 9, 1994, seismologist Waverly Person, cataloger and archiver for the U.S. Geological Survey's National Earthquake Information Center, Golden, Colo., was perplexed. The automated earthquake-location system had just located a great earthquake of magnitude 8.2 at latitude 13.2° S, longitude 67.6° W in Bolivia at a depth of 617 km (1 km is about 0.62 mi). Although the area experiences considerable seismic activity, the shock was exceptionally large considering its great depth. The location, depth, and magnitude were later found to be correct and, in any case, were not the cause of Person's concern. Shortly after the shock, people across a wide area of the U.S. began reporting that they had felt an earthquake. The suggestion was made that the reports were connected to the Bolivian earthquake, but Waverly was not convinced. After checking with many seismologists in areas from which "felt" reports had been received, however, and finding that no corresponding local shocks had been recorded, Pearson was forced to agree with his colleagues that an unprecedented phenomenon had occurred; people indeed had felt an earthquake whose focus was as much as 6,000 km distant.

Apparently only five people lost their lives in the earthquake; damage, though widespread, was minor, occurring in Peru and Brazil. As would be expected, the shock was felt in many parts of Bolivia, Brazil, Chile, Ecuador, and Peru; however, it was felt also in Puerto Rico, Dominica, several U.S. states from coast to coast, and Toronto. In the past 70 years many researchers had found evidence of certain layers in the crust that trap seismic energy as so-called channel waves and carry it, almost undiminished, for long distances and at comparatively slow speed, allowing it to escape slowly along its path. Such findings had been based on aberrant or anomalous seismic readings noted on instrumental records. The unique Bolivian shock finally furnished direct, dramatic evidence of such channel waves.

Seismic activity through much of 1994 was above average. In addition to the Bolivian shock, several other large

An overpass lies on the highway beneath it, destroyed in the earthquake that struck the Los Angeles area on January 17. In addition to causing widespread damage to houses and other structures, the quake, with a magnitude of 6.8, killed 61 people and injured thousands.

earthquakes of magnitude 7.0 or greater occurred around the globe, a number of them involving loss of life. One, of magnitude 7.2 (upgraded from 6.5), rocked the island of Sumatra, Indonesia, on February 16, killing at least 215 people. On June 3 a magnitude-7.7 earthquake (followed by another large shock the following day) struck off the south coast of Java, Indonesia, causing destructive tsunamis (seismic sea waves) and killing more than 200 people. On October 4 an undersea earthquake of magnitude 8.2, with an epicentre east of Hokkaido, Japan, and Russia's southernmost Kuril Islands, killed at least 16 people in the Kurils and caused damage and injuries in northern Japan.

Other earthquakes that resulted in fatalities include those of January 17 in southern California, where 61 deaths were recorded; June 6 in southwestern Colombia, where hundreds died; August 18 in northern Algeria, where at least

171 were killed; and November 15 in the vicinity of the Philippine island of Mindoro, where the shock and resulting tsunamis killed more than 60 people. The January 17 California quake, having a magnitude of 6.8 and an epicentre in the highly urbanized Northridge area of Los Angeles in the San Fernando Valley, followed four major shocks in 1993. It left more than 9,000 injured and an estimated 20,000 homeless and damaged more than 40,000 buildings. Overpasses collapsed in many places, closing several freeways.

The international Ocean Drilling Program (ODP) continued the exploration of the crust beneath the world's oceans by means of coring, extraction, and study of rock samples from below the seafloor. Among the more notable recent discoveries resulted from the exploration on ODP Leg 149 of the central portion of the Iberian Abyssal Plain. This ocean-continent transition zone, beneath the Atlantic off the

Mapmaking: Redrawing the Boundaries

Once considered a form of art, cartography is no longer limited to features of the Earth's surface drawn by hand on paper. Today mapmaking is being revolutionized by technologies that are advancing it into the Information Age, where the explosion of data and changing needs of scientists, policy makers, and commercial enterprise are remaking ideas of what maps are and what they can show. Three of the technologies that are transforming traditional cartography are geographic information systems (GIS), the Global Positioning System (GPS), and high-resolution satellite imagery.

GIS comprise software and hardware systems that relate and display collected data in terms of geographic, or spatial, location. The ability of GIS quickly to overlay new information on top of existing base data and to display it in colour on a computer screen is helping users conduct analyses and make decisions related to geology, ecology, land use, demographics, transportation, and other domains in ways never before possible. For example, in searching for a safe site for a landfill, a researcher may direct the computer to overlay a re-

gional elevation map with data on various types of soil. The soils data, in turn, can be removed or overlaid still further, say, with data on underground water.

Complementing GIS is GPS, a technology funded by the U.S. Department of Defense. Conceived for such applications as warship and aircraft navigation and missile guidance, GPS has become the foundation of modern mapmaking. GPS consists of a fleet of 24 satellites that transmit signals globally around the clock. In conjunction with receivers on Earth, GPS can quickly and accurately determine the latitude, longitude, and altitude of a point on or above the Earth's surface. A single GPS receiver costing as little as $250 can find its own position in seconds from GPS satellite signals with an accuracy of 50 m (165 ft). Accuracies of less than 10 cm (4 in) are possible if two (more expensive) receivers are used together. This capability has reduced the cost of acquiring the spatial data needed for making maps while increasing cartographic accuracy.

For decades the U.S. and the former Soviet Union have used high-resolution satellite imagery for military purposes. Only recently, however, has the civilian community in the U.S. been given permission to launch satellites that can resolve objects on the ground as little as a metre apart. Existing civilian satellites can obtain a 10-m (33-ft) ground resolution, and data from those satellites already have had an enormous impact on mapping, allowing the creation of specialized maps that can be used, for example, to predict crop yields, model optimal lumber harvests, or chart ever changing wetlands. With the higher resolution imagery expected to be available in 1995, along with GPS-controlled satellite positioning, mapmaking is certain to redraw its conceptual borders even more.

(JOHN D. BOSSLER)

NEXRAD IMAGE, EARTH SATELLITE CORPORATION; RADAR DATA PROVIDED BY UNISYS CORPORATION

NEXRAD (New Generation Weather Radar) data are overlaid on a geographic map of Alabama and Georgia by means of GIS technology to produce total precipitation estimates for the area from Tropical Storm Alberto. The storm brought severe flooding to the U.S. Southeast in July.

Iberian Peninsula, is one of a conjugate pair, its partner being that found off Newfoundland. They were created when the Iberian Peninsula and Newfoundland, once part of a single landmass, rifted and separated. The rifting apparently was nonvolcanic and resulted in crustal thinning. Magnetic and gravitational data agreed with this interpretation, but the six holes drilled on a west–east transect found not only a thinning crust but a ridge of mantle rocks 19 km wide. The latter discovery indicated that a break exists between the oceanic crust and the continental crust and that the edge of the latter lies a surprising 200 km west of the continental shelf. The findings suggested that the present models of the breakup of continents needed revision.

Leg 150, called the New Jersey Sea Level Transect, was designed to help earth scientists reliably recognize past worldwide sea-level changes in rocks formed of sediments laid down from the Oligocene to the Holocene epochs (from about 37 million years ago to the present). Studies of past sea-level changes were focusing on three major periods. These were colloquially dubbed the "Icehouse World" of the Oligocene to Holocene epochs, when ice sheets were known to have existed and to have affected sea levels; the ice free "Greenhouse World" that existed in the Cretaceous Period prior to 66 million years ago; and the "Doubthouse World" of the intermediate Paleocene and Eocene epochs, a time for which the existence of ice sheets was debated. The area off New Jersey was chosen because previous seismic profiles had shown it to be especially suitable for evaluating the effects of sea-level changes on sedimentation at a continental margin. Cores from four holes sampled sediments from both the Icehouse and Doubthouse periods and corroborated the profile data. Especially interesting was the discovery of a layer of microtektites (tiny glassy objects thought to be associated with meteorite impacts) in two of the cores. The finding correlated with one from a much-earlier deep-sea drilling study in the area and suggested the impact of an extraterrestrial body some 50 million years ago.

The Norwegian and Greenland seas, a relatively small area of the North Atlantic, have an inordinate influence on the weather patterns of the Northern Hemisphere, owing in large part to the interaction there of north-flowing warmer surface water from the North Atlantic and south-flowing water from the Arctic Ocean through the Fram Strait. Leg 151, which extended from a drilling site (Site 907) midway between Iceland and Jan Mayen Island north to the Yermak Plateau northwest of Spitsbergen, had the objective of determining the history of the Norwegian and Greenland seas, especially with respect to glaciation.

An interesting artifact that has helped to determine glaciation sequences are dropstones. When a glacier scours the land surface and then moves out to sea, it carries stones with it among the gravels and silt that it has picked up. Then, when it breaks off into floating rafts that eventually melt, the rafts drop their loads of stones, which become a signature of their passing. At Site 907 a 16 million-year sequence of glacial sediments was recovered. Dropstones were deposited as early as 6.4 million years ago, but their occurrence was rare from that time to the present. Sites 908 through 912 were concentrated at the northern end of the transect as far north as the 80th parallel, the most northern sites ever drilled by ODP researchers. Site 913 was located to the south on the oldest oceanic crust east of Greenland, where a penetration of 770 m (2,525 ft) brought up sediments dating back to the Eocene, the oldest obtained in this region. This site also produced an abundance of dropstones from about 2.5 million years ago, in agreement with finds throughout the North Atlantic and North Pacific indicating the beginning of major glaciation.   (RUTLAGE J. BRAZEE)

HYDROLOGY

Effects of the "great flood of 1993" that inundated much of the U.S. Midwest during the summer months of that year lingered through at least early 1994 as observers reported a freshwater "river" in the Atlantic Ocean off the coast of Florida. The flow, which measured 24 km (15 mi) wide and 18 m (60 ft) deep, was the result of the outpouring of the flooded Mississippi River into the Gulf of Mexico. Estimates varied for the length of time that the phenomenon would last, but no one believed that it would fade away before the end of 1994.

A report published during the year attributed a significant part of a decades-long annual rise of 1.5–2 mm (0.06–0.08 in) in sea level to the long-term accelerated drainage of aquifers, wetlands, and inland seas for human use. Researchers at Ohio State University suggested that as much as one-third of the rise could be due to human activities unassociated with global warming. Those activities included not only the increased drainage of water bodies but also the destruction of forests, which released enormous quantities of water from trees and soil, and the expansion of desert areas.

One of the Earth's rapidly shrinking bodies of water is the Aral Sea, which by the mid-1990s had lost two-thirds of the water volume that it possessed in 1960. Straddling the boundary between two Central Asian republics of the former Soviet Union, Kazakhstan to the north and Uzbekistan to the south, the Aral Sea was once the world's fourth largest inland body of water. Starved in recent decades by the diversion of its major inflowing rivers for purposes of irrigation, the sea was reduced in surface area to half that of three decades earlier; by the 1990s some one-time seaports were more than 50 km (31 mi) from the water. Five Central Asian countries whose activities affect the Aral Sea—the two aforementioned republics and Kyrgyzstan, Turkmenistan, and Tajikistan—agreed in 1994 to restoration and rehabilitation efforts, although they set no specific targets.

Another, much smaller body of water was given a new lease on life when court orders imposed a requirement on the city of Los Angeles to reduce its diversions from rivers feeding Mono Lake in California. Water-supply diversions for the city had reduced the volume of the lake to such a point that aquatic life was severely threatened.

Californians, who had hailed above-average rainfall in 1993 as the end of a six-year drought for the state, were disappointed with a light snowpack in the mountains over the winter of 1993–94. Although reservoirs were filled near capacity at the beginning of the water-use season, the light snowpack discouraged water managers from making confident predictions about the state of future water supplies. In spite of sober predictions, most California cities were reluctant to dust off rationing plans that had been developed during the 1987–92 years of shortage.

(N. EARL SPANGENBERG)

METEOROLOGY

A broad upper-level trough of low pressure over the central and eastern U.S. during January and early February 1994 brought bitterly cold conditions to those parts of the country. The mercury plunged to −37.8° C (−36° F) as far south as Indiana, and several locations across the Ohio Valley and central Appalachians established new all-time record-low temperatures. In sharp contrast, abnormally mild and dry weather prevailed across the Far West during the 1993–94 wet season, with some areas receiving less than 50% of normal precipitation. Snowpack, vital for adequate water supplies during the May–September dry season, ranged from 50% to 80% of normal across the region. During July and August hot, dry weather engendered numerous wildfires across the West. Beginning in late October, however, surplus precipitation fell on most of the Far West, easing concerns of a second straight subnormal wet season.

In early July Tropical Storm Alberto tracked inland over the Florida Panhandle and stalled over Georgia. As much as 615 mm (24 in) of rain generated widespread severe lowland and river flooding. In mid-November Tropical Storm Gordon pursued an erratic path that took it over Jamaica, Haiti, and Cuba; across southern Florida; and then into the Atlantic, where it looped westward, briefly menacing North Carolina's Outer Banks before drifting back toward Florida as it weakened. The storm killed several hundred people in Haiti and cost Florida an estimated $200 million in damage.

In South America, flooding claimed dozens of lives in Colombia and Peru in February and forced thousands of individuals to flee their homes. In late June and early July, winter temperatures dipped below freezing as far north as Brazil's Paraná state, damaging the coffee crop. In São Paulo state persistent dryness and heat from August to October cut into Brazil's orange production.

Frequent storms, heavy snows, and bitter cold afflicted much of Europe in January and February. Excessive precipitation plagued northern Europe through April, while unusually heavy rains also drenched the Middle East, where totals during March and early April were 600–850% of normal. Very dry conditions developed across southern Europe during March; by mid-July hot, dry conditions covered the entire continent. In late September and early October, storms battered the Baltics and southern Scandinavia. On September 28 more than 900 lives were lost when a ferryboat sank in rough waters of the Baltic Sea off Finland.

In February Cyclone Geralda slammed into the island of Madagascar. National officials declared it the "cyclone of the century," with 95% of the main commercial port of Toamasina reportedly destroyed. Geralda and Cyclone Daisy, which struck the island in January, combined to wipe out nearly 300,000 metric tons of the rice crop. In late March Cyclone Nadia crossed Madagascar before striking the African mainland. In Mozambique Nadia left almost 1.5 million people homeless and caused considerable damage to crops, including cashew trees, a major source of income for the nation. Across most of southeastern Africa, unusually wet conditions prevailed during January and February, contributing to an excellent fall harvest. Farther north, copious rains fell on most of the Sahel, resulting in the wettest growing season in 30 years.

Torrential rains spread across much of southeastern Asia during early April and persisted into early May. By contrast, unusually warm and dry weather developed across Korea, Japan, and northeastern China. Although tropical systems battered parts of Japan in late July and early August, prevailing hot and dry conditions severely depleted reservoirs and damaged crops in many parts of the country. Summer dryness in parts of central China was the worst since 1934, causing widespread crop stress. In July and August rains soaked much of south-central and southeastern China and Southeast Asia. Floods took at least 1,800 lives, nearly 1,000 of which, according to press reports, were lost as Typhoon Fred slammed into southeastern China in mid-August.

Following an exceptional midyear heat wave that claimed more than 400 lives, the 1994 Indian monsoon brought abundant rainfall, causing episodes of flooding in India and Pakistan. From January through early April, surplus rainfall was measured across most of Indonesia and southern Malaysia, generating periodic flooding in Sumatra and Java. By June, however, extremely dry conditions developed

across Indonesia; they persisted through November, abetting wildfires and crop damage across much of the archipelago.

In January, hot and dry conditions dominated Australia, setting the stage for extensive wildfires across New South Wales, but in February Tropical Storm Sadie brought heavy rains to the Cape York Peninsula, eastern Arnhem Land, and parts of Queensland. Widespread subnormal winter rains combined with early spring dryness to produce serious moisture shortages as the nation's primary agricultural season got under way. According to the Australian Bureau of Meteorology, portions of the southeastern quarter of the continent endured one of the driest April–August periods on record. At year's end large moisture deficits accumulated across eastern Australia.

In September El Niño conditions (a periodic appearance of abnormally warm surface waters in the tropical Pacific) developed, and by December they had entered the mature phase. The atmospheric and oceanic changes associated with an El Niño strongly influence temperature and precipitation patterns in various parts of the world. Some effects anticipated for 1994–95 included dryness over northern Australia (September–March), wetness in southeastern South America (November–February), warmth over southeastern Africa (October–April), and coolness along the U.S. Gulf Coast (October–March).   (ELBERT W. FRIDAY, JR.)

This article updates the *Macropædia* article CLIMATE AND WEATHER.

OCEANOGRAPHY

In June and October 1994 two major undersea earthquakes occurred, the first near Indonesia and the second near Japan. Both generated tsunamis, or seismic sea waves. In both cases reports of water running up onto land to heights of three to five metres were common (1 m is about 3.3 ft). In Indonesia many villages near river inlets were destroyed, and at least 200 people lost their lives. Tsunamis have been a recurring natural hazard throughout history. The Minoan civilization on Crete in the Mediterranean Sea was shaken by the combined effects of a volcanic eruption and a tsunami in the 2nd millennium BC, and Lisbon was devastated by a tsunami in 1755.

Tsunamis are particularly prevalent in the Pacific because of the seismic activity associated with the edges of the Pacific Ocean. Since the water wave of a tsunami travels across the ocean at about 200 m per second (450 mph) whereas seismic waves travel through the solid Earth roughly 20 times faster, tsunami warning systems in operation around the Pacific have been able to issue warnings hours before a tsunami's arrival at distant locations. On the other hand, the ability to predict in advance the actual run-up height or the pattern of sea-level fluctuations after the initial arrival has remained poor. Research in 1994 showed that previously puzzling resurgences of sea level, which sometimes occur many hours after the tsunami has arrived, are likely to be due either to the arrival of waves reflected from the coasts or to waves traveling along the coasts. Research also called attention to the importance of distinguishing between slow and rapid earthquakes. Earthquakes in which the seafloor deforms relatively slowly will not excite strong seismic waves, yet their potential for generating tsunamis may be great. Seismological measurements capable of resolving lower-frequency seismic waves were expected to help identify such earthquakes. The most difficult problem remained that of issuing useful tsunami warnings for locations close to the earthquake centre, where arrival times between earthquake and tsunami may be only a few minutes apart.

During the year oceanographers saw the beginning of near-real-time global observation of the circulation of the world's oceans. Meteorologists long had possessed the ability—by means of satellites and a worldwide system of observing stations—to visualize the state of the atmosphere at any time in detail sufficient to resolve major storms anywhere on the globe. By contrast, oceanographers generally had had to make do with partial pictures of the circulation reconstructed only months or years after the observations were made. It had been known that precise satellite-based altimetric measurements of sea level (to an accuracy of centimetres) had the potential to provide real-time pictures of the surface currents of the oceans. During the late 1980s the U.S. Navy's Geosat mission had collected more than four years of satellite altimetry, but in 1994 about two years of data with an accuracy 5–10 times better became available to oceanographers from the Topex/Poseidon satellite, which was launched in mid-1992. Using these data researchers observed major patterns of surface circulation over time in a way never before possible. Coastal winds appeared to generate theoretically predicted wavelike disturbances in both the middle latitudes and the tropics. The ability to observe such phenomena in a timely way was expected to lead to improved forecasting of the onset of El Niño, the appearance every few years of unusually warm water off the western coast of tropical South America.

The Topex/Poseidon system really makes two measurements. One, by radar, is of the instantaneous distance from satellite to sea surface. The other, based on knowledge of the Earth's gravity field gained from many years of satellite tracking, is of the distance from the satellite to the sea surface as it would be if the ocean were motionless. It is the difference between the two measurements that indicates the presence and strength of ocean currents. When the satellite crosses over strong currents such as the Gulf Stream, that difference may be as great as one metre, but for more gentle currents it is measured in centimetres. Consequently, ocean tides must be predicted and removed from the altimetric signal before currents can be recognized. That necessity resulted in 1994 in the formulation of global models of ocean tides that predict the world tide with an overall accuracy of a few centimetres.

Whereas tsunamis and ocean-current systems span ocean basins, it is small-scale water motion—currents that change over centimetres and seconds—that is important in the dilution of pollutants in the ocean or in the mixing of cold deep waters with warm surface waters to form water of an intermediate temperature. The effect of such small-scale motion on the diffusion of heat and salt in the ocean had long been studied theoretically and estimated indirectly, but in 1992 researchers began an experiment to look directly at the way in which a thin patch of an inert tracer substance injected in the eastern subtropical North Atlantic subsequently spread vertically and horizontally. By 1994 the patch had expanded vertically from its initial thickness of a few metres to about 80 m and had stretched from its initial horizontal size of a few kilometres to a sinuous streak several hundred kilometres long. Previous theoretical predictions of the rate of vertical diffusion proved to be accurate; further observation and analysis may give insight into what keeps the streak from getting ever narrower as it lengthens. Such studies of ocean diffusion were important for understanding pollutant dispersal and nutrient distribution in the oceans as well as the role of the oceans in global heat transport.

(MYRL C. HENDERSHOTT)

See also Disasters; Energy; Environment; Life Sciences; Mining; Space Exploration.

This article updates the *Macropædia* articles ATMOSPHERE; CLIMATE AND WEATHER; DINOSAURS; THE EARTH; THE EARTH SCIENCES; EARTHQUAKES; GEOCHRONOLOGY; THE HYDROSPHERE; OCEANS; PLATE TECTONICS; RIVERS; VOLCANISM.

Economic Affairs

World economic output recovered strongly during 1994 and headed for the fastest growth since 1989. According to estimates by the International Monetary Fund (IMF), global economic growth averaged 3.1%, compared with 2.3% in 1993. The pace of recovery was faster than had been expected. This bounce back was largely attributable to faster growth in the U.S., a well-established recovery in the U.K., an upturn in continental Europe, and the bottoming out of the recession in Japan.

Economic recovery in the developed countries as a group accelerated to 2.7%, twice as fast as the year before. Higher interest rates in the U.S.—and to a lesser extent in the U.K. and other European countries—which had been raised in a preemptive move to prevent inflationary forces from getting stronger, did not affect the outcome in 1994. Large budget deficits, a legacy of the recession and high social spending, and high unemployment (except in the U.S.) remained concerns of economic policy makers. These factors also explained why the "feel good" factor, which accompanied previous upswings, was missing this time around.

For the third year running, the less developed countries' (LDCs') economies continued to grow much faster than those of the industrialized countries. Economic output growth (close to 5.6%) was as great as the year before and exceeded population growth, leading to a slight increase in personal living standards. As in recent years, the main engine of growth remained Asia, especially China. Growth in Africa was slightly higher, but in Latin America and the Mediterranean region, output stagnated or fell.

Among the developed countries, growth in the U.S. accelerated to nearly 4% from 3.1% in 1993, despite higher interest rates, as improvement in consumer and corporate confidence led to higher consumption and investment. Canada, as a result of its close ties with the U.S., expanded by a similar rate. Australia and New Zealand also marked another year of good progress thanks to rapid growth in export markets in Asia and North America. The British economy enjoyed an investment- and export-led acceleration in recovery and grew by 4%. The speed of upturn in continental Europe was much faster than expected. Western Germany, the powerhouse of Europe, surprised forecasters as gross domestic product (GDP) growth bounced back to above 2% and reversed the 1.3% decline in 1993. In eastern Germany a 10% growth rate was achieved. The rest of Europe experienced average growth rates of between 1.7% and 2.5% during 1994. Most of the growth came from exports to rapidly growing North America and Asia, but a recovery in consumer spending and business confidence also contributed to the overall recovery.

Relaxation of the German Bundesbank's tough anti-inflationary policy in 1993, which allowed interest rates to fall, continued early in 1994. Lower interest rates were encouraged by low inflation and, more important, by stable exchange rates in Europe. By mid-1994 many of the currencies within the European exchange-rate mechanism (ERM) were back inside, or close to, their old narrow 2.25% divergence bands against the Deutsche Mark. Fears that the widening of the currency bands from 2.5% to 15% in August 1993 would create greater instability, keep interest rates high, and prolong the recession in Europe proved unfounded. The long recession came to an end in Japan thanks to the cumulative effect of four stimulatory economic packages of tax cuts and higher public spending introduced in 1993 and 1994. Despite the strength of the yen, a gradual pickup in exports also helped Japan's GDP grow by nearly 1%.

Among LDCs, economic growth in China remained very strong. Measures introduced in 1993 to control a very rapid economic boom were partly successful. In the rest of Asia, economic growth continued to be rapid, with many countries registering 8–9% growth. Economic growth in Latin America remained steady at 3–4%, but in Africa drought and civil war held back growth in many countries.

Most Central and Eastern European countries continued to make progress, and economic growth accelerated. Growth climbed to 4% in Poland, 2.5% in the Czech Republic, and more than 1% in Hungary. In the countries of the former Soviet Union, where economic reforms were still progressing slowly, economic decline held at around 10%, a slightly slower pace than in 1993.

Many components of demand strengthened as world economic growth gathered pace. In a number of countries, external demand, led by exports, grew more strongly than domestic demand (which depends on spending by households and businesses). Private consumption (which accounts for a large proportion of total private demand) expanded by nearly 2% in the developed world. There were wide regional differences, however, depending on each country's relative position in the recovery cycle. In the U.S. and Canada, where the recovery was well established, private consumption expanded by 3.6% and 5%, respectively. Retail sales were strong through most of the year, and investment outlays, both business and residential, surged ahead. In Western Europe, where households were still worried about job security and business confidence remained low, consumer spending was sluggish and business investment flat. Even in the U.K., where the recovery started earlier than in continental Europe, growth in retail sales and business investment was shallower than in previous upswings. At the same time, higher government spending or lower taxes contributed little to growth. Governments in North America and Europe were concerned with reducing their large budget deficits and either froze or scaled back public spending. Japan, unburdened by such constraints, continued to spend heavily on new public-works projects and cut income taxes. Thus, private consumption grew faster (2%, compared with 1% in 1993), while export growth slowed to below 3%. By contrast, Europe and North America enjoyed a boom in

Inflation Rate
Percentage change from December to December

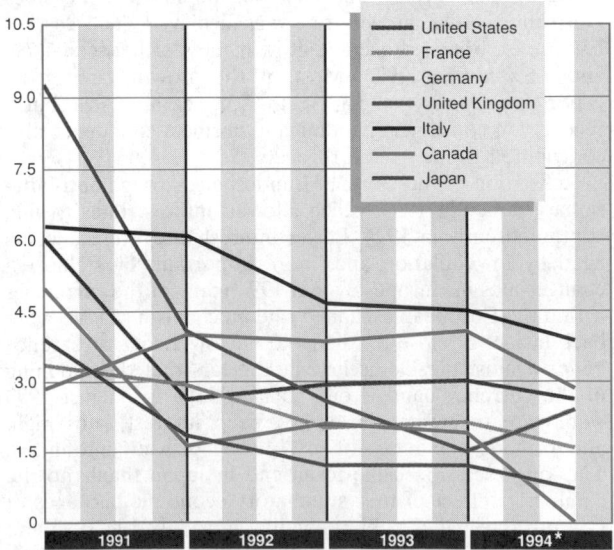

*Percentage change from October 1993 to October 1994.
Source: *The Economist*, Economic and Financial Indicators.

Industrial Production
semiannual averages; 1990 =100

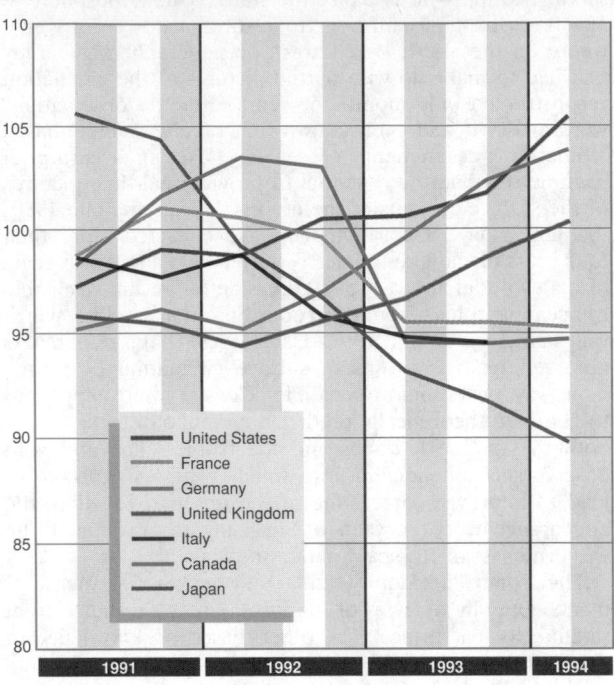

Source: International Monetary Fund, *International Financial Statistics*.

exports—7% in the U.S., 10% in the U.K., 5% in Germany, and 4% in France.

As new employment usually lags behind economic recovery, unemployment in the developed countries remained at historically high levels. In the 25 countries belonging to the Organisation for Economic Co-operation and Development (OECD)—which included the U.S., Canada, Japan, all Western European countries, Australia, and New Zealand—official unemployment rates averaged around 8%, compared with 7.8% in 1993. Some 35 million people were registered as unemployed in the OECD at the end of 1994. This figure excluded countless millions of workers who had withdrawn from the job market because they faced poor prospects, believed they were too old, or lacked necessary skills. The fastest job creation was in the U.S., where the unemployment rate fell to 5.4% from nearly 7% in 1993. In Japan the rate rose to 3% from 2.5%, but it was still low by most standards. The real problems were in Europe, where average unemployment within the European Union (EU) rose from 10.6% in 1993 to 11.5% in 1994. The highest unemployment was in Spain, Belgium, France, and Denmark (24%, 14%, 13%, and 12%, respectively). Those individuals with jobs also faced unsettling change and job insecurity as companies continually restructured and streamlined operations to become more efficient.

In Central and Eastern Europe, unemployment averaged around 20%. In Russia and other former Soviet bloc countries where output had fallen sharply, unemployment remained understated in the published statistics.

The long downward trend in interest rates came to an end in 1994, and in some countries the trend turned up, reflecting the strength of economic activity. In many industrialized countries real interest rates were regarded as historically high in relation to the comparatively low inflation rates. Despite inflation's being under control, the outlook for interest rates in 1995 was for continuing small increases in line with faster economic recovery. In the U.S.

the Federal Reserve Board (Fed) raised short-term interest rates for the first time in five years. The first move came in February (earlier than anticipated) and, together with subsequent rises, led to instability in the financial markets and an upward movement in long-term interest rates across the world. By year's end, after six successive rate increases, the Fed funds rate (the rate the banks pay when they borrow from each other's reserves held at the Fed) stood at 5.5%, compared with 3% at the beginning of the year. British rates went up by 0.5% in September, mimicking the preemptive moves in the U.S. Elsewhere in Europe interest rates followed Germany's lead. A series of small cuts in the spring reduced the discount rate in Germany from 5.75% to 4.5%. In France the intervention rate came down to 5% from 6.2%. In Denmark, Italy, Spain, and Portugal, similar small reductions occurred in the spring. In late summer, however, interest rates went up slightly in Italy, Sweden, and Spain. In Japan interest rates had been reduced to historically low levels by a 0.75% cut in September 1993, and no further reductions took place in 1994.

The decline in inflation rates in most countries continued in 1994. A few notable exceptions were found in Latin America and Eastern Europe. In the developed countries the outturn was better than expected, and inflation was ceasing to be a major issue. In OECD countries inflation dipped to around 2.5%, the lowest in more than two decades, but central banks remained vigilant and prepared to raise interest rates to prevent an upsurge in inflationary rates as economic recovery gathered pace. In the LDCs the median inflation rate rose slightly to 9%. Inflation remained relatively high in Latin America and Eastern Europe. Brazil's inflation accelerated to over 2,300% early in the year, but the introduction of a new, stronger currency, the real, brought monthly rates down to single digits, and at year's end annual inflation was under 1,100%. By contrast, it was only 3–8% in Argentina, Chile, and Mexico (despite the devaluation of the peso in December). In Central and Eastern Europe, ongoing economic reforms kept inflation relatively high. There was a dramatic slowdown in Russia from almost 1,000% in 1993 to around 300% in 1994. Inflation accelerated in Turkey, but in South Asia it was generally stable. In China inflation had doubled to 27%, despite measures taken to slow the pace of activity in the economy.

Economic policy makers remained concerned with reducing their budget deficits during 1994. In the developed world this meant tight control of government spending and few tax concessions. Fortunately, the faster-than-expected recovery had begun shrinking deficits by boosting tax revenue and reducing payouts to the unemployed. In the U.S. the budget deficit fell to $202 billion from $255 billion the year before and was heading for $168 billion in 1995. In the U.K. it came in at £34 billion. In 1993 it had been £45 billion, and

it was forecast to fall to £21 billion in 1995. In other EU countries, except Italy, and in Sweden, budget deficits as a proportion of GDP were expected to fall within a few years from the 1994 average of 6.5% to the less than 3% stipulated in the Maastricht Treaty as a convergence criterion for economic and monetary union. Japan was the only large economy where fiscal policy was stimulatory; significant tax cuts were accompanied by long-term plans to further boost government spending.

The IMF expected the external debt of the LDCs to rise by around 8% in 1994. This was similar to the increase seen the year before. Although in absolute terms the LDCs' debt continued to increase, as a proportion of exports of goods and services it was expected to be slightly down from the year before, with a further decline possible in 1995.

NATIONAL ECONOMIC POLICIES

United States. The pace of U.S. economic activity accelerated during 1994, and GDP grew by nearly 4%—the best performance in five years. At this level the economy was running close to full capacity, and the Fed repeatedly raised interest rates in an effort to keep inflationary pressures at bay and to prevent the economy from overheating. Despite charting an uneven course, economic growth during most of the year was at a rapid and unsustainable level. A blistering 6.3% rise in the final quarter of 1993 was followed by an abnormally slow 3.3% in the opening quarter of 1994, largely because of severe weather and an earthquake in California. Unsurprisingly, economic growth accelerated to 4.1% in the second quarter, but the pace eased a little to 3.9% in the third quarter, only to pick up again in the final quarter.

The economic expansion during 1994 was driven by fixed investment (including housing investment), export sales, and stronger consumer demand. Despite the increasing cost of borrowing, business investment rose by over 10%. Residential investment surged by a similar amount earlier in the year. Faced with a high capacity utilization and improved corporate profits, companies invested heavily, especially in information technology.

Responding to higher demand, production and capacity use rose further in 1994, and output reached record levels. Although the pace moderated somewhat after the summer, manufacturing output for the year grew by more than 6%, leading to tightness in manufacturing industries. The industrial-capacity utilization rate of 84.9% in October was a touch higher than the previous cyclical peak of 84.8%.

Consumers, encouraged by modest income growth and higher employment, increased their retail spending by 6% in real terms during the year, at a slightly faster pace than the year before. Spending on interest-rate-sensitive durable goods, including automobiles, furniture, and household goods, was strong during most of the year. Overall, retail sales were up 7.6%, but retailers reported a falling off in November and December.

In contrast to private spending, government spending fell by nearly 6% as a result of budget-reduction measures introduced in 1993 and earlier. Most of the decline was attributable to lower defense outlays. Nondefense spending also fell slightly, while expenditure at state and local levels picked up as a result of federal infrastructure projects. The U.S. economy showed robust growth, despite the faster-than-expected fall in government spending and a rapid contraction in the budget deficit. The budget deficit for fiscal year 1994, ended in September, was $202 billion, down from the previous year's $255 billion.

The robust economic recovery created new jobs at an average rate of 300,000 a month and reduced the unemployment rate to its lowest level since 1990. As in the previous

Table I. Real Gross Domestic Products of Selected OECD Countries
% annual change

Country	1990	1991	1992	1993	1994[1]
United States	1.2	−0.7	2.6	3.0	4.0
Japan	4.8	4.3	1.1	0.1	0.8
Germany[2]	5.7	4.5	2.1	−1.3	2.0
France	2.5	0.8	1.2	−0.9	1.8
United Kingdom	0.4	−2.2	−0.6	1.9	3.8
Canada	−0.2	−1.7	0.7	2.4	4.0
Italy	2.1	1.2	0.7	−0.7	2.0
All developed countries	2.5	0.8	1.7	1.2	2.7
Seven major countries above	2.4	0.8	1.7	1.3	2.8
European Union	3.0	1.5	1.0	−0.4	2.0

[1]Estimated. [2]From 1991, figures include former East Germany.
Sources: International Monetary Fund, OECD, The Economist.

10 years, most of the new jobs occurred in low-paid, part-time service sectors. Nevertheless, this strong job creation cut the unemployment rate to 5.4% in December from 6.7% in January.

A striking feature of the sustained economic growth in 1994 was the lack of inflationary pressures. Consumer prices rose 2.7%, less than generally expected, and the core inflation rate declined to 2.6% from 1993's average of 3%. Wages and salaries grew at a similar rate during the year, squeezing real (inflation-adjusted) take-home pay.

Exports performed better in 1994, stimulated by the decline in the external value of the dollar and by the worldwide economic recovery. Exports of goods and services rose by more than 7%, but export growth was once again outstripped by that of imports, reflecting the strength of domestic demand. Imports grew by around 12% but in the closing months slowed considerably. This was due to the weakness of the dollar, which made imports more expensive. Nevertheless, the U.S. was heading for a larger trade deficit of $150 billion, much higher than in 1993, which, at $116 billion, had been the worst since 1988. Likewise, the current-account deficit (including trade balances on invisibles and capital movements) widened.

Economic policy making during 1994 was characterized by the active use of monetary policy. The Fed reversed the five-year trend of falling or stable interest rates with six successive rate increases. The first move, in February, was seen as a preemptive strike to stop the economy from overheating. In August, when it raised the Fed funds rate for the fifth time, from 4.5% to 4.75%, the Fed indicated that it had almost attained its goal of neutral monetary policy. In November, however, the Fed raised interest rates by another 0.75%, higher than generally expected. Significantly, the Fed left the door open for further rises in 1995 to check inflation before it became a problem. In line with the upturn in the Fed funds rate, commercial banks raised their prime rates from 6% in January to 8.5% in August. As the year drew to a close, a lively debate continued among economists about whether the successive interest-rate increases had tightened policy sufficiently to cool the economy. The financial markets did not think so and were betting on another rise in the new year.

Japan. The stagnation in the world's second largest economy ended during the last quarter of 1993, but the recovery in 1994 was less robust than previous ones. After uneven progress in the first half of the year, the pace of economic activity picked up in the summer, giving a GDP growth of nearly 1% for the year as a whole. A pickup in consumer spending was largely responsible for this recovery. The sluggish upswing was explained by the fact that previous recoveries had been led by strong growth in capital investment and exports. In 1994 both of these factors were weak because of three structural weaknesses in the economy: surplus industrial capacity, deflation, and the weakness of the financial system.

Faced with a stagnant economy despite four spending packages totaling 45 trillion yen over the previous two years, the government introduced further measures in February to boost demand. These included tax cuts of 5,850,000,000,000 yen, with reductions in income, residential, and car sales taxes. These benefits were passed on as a tax rebate in the summer. Helped by a hot summer, lower-priced imports, and heavy retail discounting, consumer spending improved. In the three months to August, sales in department stores and supermarkets were 3.4% higher than a year earlier, compared with a 1.5% annual decrease in the previous three months. On the basis of partial data, total private consumption (a wider measure of spending) was estimated to have risen by 2%.

There was little contribution to demand from employment and rises in wages. The jobless total rose to more than two million, or about 3% of the workforce, in the final quarter of the year. At this level 20% more people were out of work than a year before. This was a large rise in an economy where layoffs were still taboo and employers accomplished reductions in workforce by curbing recruitment and encouraging early retirement. The immediate outlook was not too encouraging, as employment traditionally lags behind the economy. In an effort to safeguard jobs, employees were agreeing to lower increases, smaller bonuses, and reduced overtime. In the autumn industrial wages were down more than 1% from a year earlier.

Despite the hesitant recovery, industry made good progress in reducing its vast inventories of unsold goods. As private consumption growth boosted imported goods, industrial production was a late beneficiary. Industrial production picked up late in the year and in the third quarter was 1.6% higher than a year before. Because of a 2% decline in the first half, however, it was virtually flat for the year as a whole. Although there had been some improvement, Japanese industry still suffered from a large overhang of surplus capacity—a legacy of large capital investment during the halcyon days in the 1980s. During 1994 a decline in industrial capital investment eased to 4% from 8% the year before, giving rise to hopes that it might start rising in 1995.

The disinflationary effect of the yen's strength on the prices of imported goods, coupled with heavy price discounting by large retailers, pushed down the annual inflation rate of 0.2%. Earlier in the year the rate had been negative, but higher prices for seasonal foodstuffs in the summer pushed up inflation a little. This return to the previous low levels was good news for consumers, but there was a risk that it could squeeze the profits of manufacturers. It was feared this could further undermine manufacturers' confidence and cause them to delay or cancel investment decisions. A related problem was the continuing decline in the prices of land and commercial property. (Since the bubble burst

Table II. Consumer Prices in OECD Countries
% change from preceding year

Country	1990	1991	1992	1993	1994[1]
United States	5.4	4.2	3.0	3.0	2.9
Japan	3.1	3.3	1.7	1.3	0.0
Germany[2]	2.7	3.5	4.0	4.1	3.0
France	3.4	3.2	2.4	2.1	1.7
United Kingdom	9.5	5.9	3.7	1.6	2.4
Canada	4.8	5.6	1.5	1.8	0.2
Italy	6.1	6.5	5.3	4.2	3.7
Austria	3.3	3.3	4.0	3.6	3.2
Belgium	3.4	3.2	2.4	2.8	2.4
Denmark	2.7	2.4	2.1	1.3	2.2
Finland	6.1	4.3	2.9	2.2	1.9
Greece	20.4	19.5	15.9	14.4	11.1
Iceland	15.9	6.8	3.7	4.1	0.8
Ireland	3.3	3.2	3.1	1.4	2.7
Luxembourg	3.7	3.1	3.2	3.0	3.7
Netherlands, The	2.5	3.9	3.7	2.0	2.1
Norway	4.1	3.4	2.3	2.2	1.6
Portugal	13.4	11.4	8.9	5.8	4.8
Spain	6.7	5.9	5.9	4.6	4.8
Sweden	10.5	9.3	2.3	4.6	2.6
Switzerland	5.4	5.8	4.0	3.1	0.5
Turkey	60.3	66.0	70.1	66.1	107.5
Australia	7.3	3.2	1.0	1.8	1.7
New Zealand	6.1	2.6	1.0	1.3	1.1
OECD Total	5.8	5.2	4.0	3.6	4.2

[1]Twelve-month rate of change in August 1994. [2]Western Germany only.
Sources: International Monetary Fund, OECD, *The Economist*.

Using computer technology, traders at Chase Manhattan price the instruments known as derivatives, whose values are tied to other assets and financial indexes. In 1994 a number of companies, as well as pension funds and government agencies, suffered large losses from derivatives.
JOHN ABBOTT

in 1990, commercial property prices had fallen by nearly 50%.) This had increased the amount of nonperforming or bad debts, making the banks even more cautious about extending new loans. Thus, money-supply growth was sluggish and in the third quarter edged up by 1–2% year-on-year, well below the 5% annual growth considered necessary to fund a strong revival. Against this backdrop, the Bank of Japan's monetary policy remained accommodating. Short-term interest rates were unchanged during the year.

As a result of a surge in imports and a slowdown in exports (partly a reflection of the yen's appreciation), the trade surplus fell back to an estimated $130 billion from the previous year's record $142 billion. There was no corresponding reduction in the huge current-account surplus, estimated at $135 billion ($130 billion in 1993). Because only a part of this surplus was recycled, it maintained an upward pressure on the yen, but it was not enough to deflect from Japan's long-standing trade friction with the U.S. and the EU.

United Kingdom. During 1994 the U.K. economy enjoyed a favourable combination of rapid expansion, subdued inflation, relatively stable interest rates, booming exports, and falling unemployment. Nevertheless, this rosy economic picture had not translated into a "feel-good" factor or government popularity. A late upward revision to economic statistics indicated that GDP grew by nearly 4%. This better-than-expected performance was largely due to higher consumer spending, stronger export demand, and a recovery in investment, albeit from a low level.

Concerned that the rapid pace of economic growth might lead to faster inflation in the future and blow the economy off course, Chancellor of the Exchequer Norman Lamont and the governor of the Bank of England raised interest rates sooner than expected. A surprise 0.5% rise in the banks' base rates to 5.75% in early September mirrored similar preemptive moves by the Fed. The move marked the beginning of a shift toward neutral monetary policy, and higher interest rates were widely anticipated in 1995.

Despite better-than-expected progress in reducing the public-sector deficit, fiscal policy remained restrictive. For the second consecutive year, overall government spending was cut substantially and, as a result of phased tax increases introduced in 1993, the tax burden further increased. Arguing that "sound economics is good politics," Lamont opted to apply the revenue windfall arising from faster-than-expected economic growth and lower-than-projected inflation to reducing the public-sector deficit. Thus, voter-friendly tax cuts were deferred to a future date closer to the next general elections, which were not due before April 1997.

The engine that fueled growth until mid-1994 was the rise in consumer spending. The delayed impact of April tax increases, continuing fears about job security, and unease about the future direction of interest rates, however, caused the pace of consumer spending to slow. In the final quarter of the year, retail-sales volumes were barely 3% higher than those of 1993, compared with more than 4% earlier in the year. Car sales also lost momentum, particularly private (nonfleet) purchases.

As consumer spending faltered, export growth sustained the pace of economic activity. During 1994 export volumes were up by 10%, reflecting the global economic recovery. Improved competitiveness of British exports, thanks to low inflation and the relatively weak pound sterling, also con-

Table III. Standardized Unemployment Rates in Selected Developed Countries

% total labour force

Country	1990	1991	1992	1993	1994[1]
United States	5.4	6.6	7.3	6.7	5.8
Japan	2.1	2.1	2.2	2.5	3.0[2]
Germany[3]	4.8	4.2	4.6	5.8	8.2
France	8.9	9.4	10.4	11.6	12.7
United Kingdom	7.0	8.8	10.0	10.3	8.9
Canada	8.1	10.2	11.2	11.1	10.0
Italy	10.3	9.9	10.5	10.2	12.0[4]
All developed countries	6.1	6.8	7.5	7.8	7.9
Seven major countries above	8.1	10.2	11.2	11.1	6.9
European Union	8.4	8.7	9.5	10.6	11.5

[1]October, national definitions. [2]Western Germany only. [3]September. [4]August.
Sources: International Monetary Fund, OECD, *The Economist*.

tributed to export growth. Imports grew more strongly than in 1993, but the annual growth rate lagged well behind that of exports. As a result, both trade and current-account deficits were smaller than in 1993.

Investment in manufacturing, having fallen steeply since 1989, picked up in 1994, but its contribution to economic recovery was small. Total investment grew by more than 3% in 1994; it was mostly aimed at improving productivity and efficiency with only a small increase in capacity. Construction activity, including home building, also showed some recovery, again from a low base.

On the supply side, the pace of industrial production quickened, reflecting growth in demand. By late summer, however, a slowdown was evident. Manufacturing output in the third quarter stood 3.7% higher than a year earlier, having been 5.8% higher in the second quarter.

Historically, inflationary pressures had revived early when the British economy was coming out of a recession. During 1994, after more than two years of recovery, the various inflation indicators all remained at a low level. The headline rate of inflation in November was 2.4%, which was below the Bank of England's forecasts. Strong price competition between retailers and continuing productivity gains were the main reasons for slack inflationary pressures. Average earnings growth in the closing quarter was below 4% and steady, but because of efficiency gains, wage costs per unit of output fell slightly.

The modest increase in wage settlements reflected the general improvement in the labour market. Unemployment, having reached a peak of 2,960,000 in January 1993, dipped to under 2.5 million, or 8.9% of the workforce, in October. In addition to economic expansion, this better-than-expected reduction in joblessness was largely due to an increase in self-employment and a decrease in the number of people registering as available for work.

Germany. Economic activity in Germany exceeded expectations in 1994, and GDP in Germany as a whole expanded by almost 3% for the year. Growth in the western part of the country was around 2.5%, while in eastern Germany it was 10%. Although the eastern German economy was still heavily dependent on western Germany for transfer payments, it made progress toward self-sustained growth.

The economic upswing in western Germany was mainly supported by strong growth in exports, a rise in construction, and increased business investment activity. Boosted by stronger foreign demand, manufacturing output and capacity utilization both rose. Export volume grew by nearly 5% during 1994, reversing 1993's 10% decline. Apart from the faster pace of economic growth being enjoyed by Germany's main trading partners, this rise in exports was due to an increase in the competitiveness of German products. Moderate wage settlements, corporate restructuring, and substantial staff reductions were cited as the main elements behind this.

Gross capital investment rose by an estimated 2.5% in the west and 14% in the east, giving a pan-German increase of 4%. Investment in machinery and equipment was comparatively sluggish despite improved capacity utilization, suggesting that industrialists were in no hurry to expand capacity. Construction activity remained strong in eastern Germany, where housing construction complemented infrastructure improvements. Construction also expanded rapidly in western Germany, where demand for housing was stronger in response to lower interest rates and government incentives to ease housing bottlenecks caused by the high levels of immigration in recent years.

By contrast, consumer expenditure remained flat. A modest decline in the west was offset by a 1.3% gain in the east. Spending was depressed in the west by the introduction of higher taxes in January 1994 and by the virtual freeze on wages. Although inflation moderated, real disposable incomes in western Germany declined slightly.

Unemployment stabilized rather than improved, which was to be expected in the early stages of a recovery. Total unemployment stood at 3.6 million at year's end, nearly half a million above 1993 but below the spring peak. In western Germany the unemployment rate averaged 8%, compared with 15% in the east. The latter figures excluded disguised unemployment (early retirement, job creation, and training schemes), which stood at close to one million. Considerable progress was made in reducing the inflation rate; after three years of relatively high inflation in the east, prices moved broadly in line with those in western Germany. Consumer prices in October were 2.8% higher than a year before in western Germany and 3.2% in the east.

Against the backdrop of economic recovery, the government's fiscal policy remained one of tackling the deficits that had resulted from unification. Thus, the budget approved in July planned a nominal increase in federal government spending while holding the borrowing requirement broadly unchanged at DM 69 billion. The total deficit, however, including deficits of the Treuhandanstalt (privatization agency) and those of the states and municipalities, was much higher. Despite measures introduced in 1993 but not due to come into force until 1995 (such as reduced unemployment benefits and reintroduced solidarity surcharge), no early reduction in the deficit was projected. Monetary policy, on the other hand, was geared toward maintaining stable interest rates following a series of stepped reductions in the spring. These reduced the discount rate from 5.75% to 4.5% and the Lombard rate (the rate at which the Bundesbank offered emergency funding) from 6.75% to 6%. Despite the growth of the money stock outside the target range and weakness in the bond markets, which increased long-term interest rates, the Bundesbank opted for a policy of consistency and did not reverse the spring cuts in interest rates.

France. The modest economic recovery, which started in the summer of 1993, gathered pace during 1994. Compared with expectations of around 1% growth, GDP expanded by 2.7%. This strong upturn effectively negated the claims of those who argued during the 1993 currency crises that France's tough anti-inflationary stance and its policy of keeping interest rates tied to German rates would prolong the stagnation of the economy.

The recovery in 1994 was based on a mixture of stronger external demand, higher consumer spending at home, and a rise in investment. Consumer spending was stimulated early in the year by a F 5,000 government incentive to new-car buyers. Although the effect of this incentive tailed off by the autumn, consumer spending held up and rose by 1.5%. Improved external demand, however, came from economic recovery in Germany, France's most important trade part-

Table IV. Changes in Output in Less Developed Countries
% annual change in real gross domestic product

Area	1990	1991	1992	1993	1994[1]
All less developed countries	3.8	4.5	5.9	6.1	5.6
Oil-exporting countries	4.2	3.9	5.4	2.8	2.1
Non-oil-exporting countries	3.7	4.6	6.0	7.1	6.5
Africa	1.9	1.4	0.2	1.0	3.3
Asia	5.8	6.2	8.2	8.5	8.0
Middle East and Europe	4.0	1.9	7.0	4.8	1.4
Western Hemisphere	0.3	3.4	2.5	3.4	2.8

[1]Estimated.
Source: International Monetary Fund, *World Economic Outlook*, October 1994.

Interest Rates: Short-term
three-month money market rates

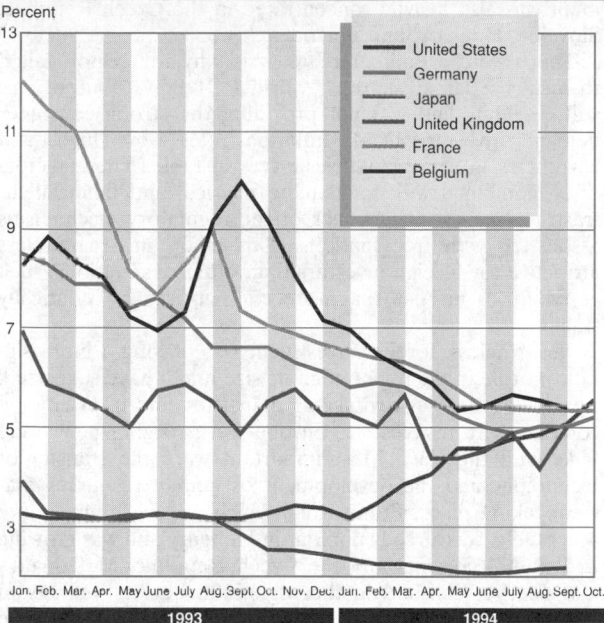

Source: International Monetary Fund, *International Financial Statistics.*

ner, and from the U.S. and the Far East. As domestic demand picked up during the year, the contribution of foreign trade to economic growth declined. Nevertheless, the trade balance was heading for a surplus of F 80 billion, only slightly down from F 83 billion in 1993 and well in excess of 1992's F 32 billion.

Business investment recovered in 1994 in response to a marked increase in capacity utilization, particularly in automobile and capital-goods sectors. The upturn in production, investment, and consumption had a marginal effect on the labour market. Thus, the total number of unemployed, at 3.3 million, was higher at year's end than at the beginning of 1994. At this level, the rate of unemployment stood at 12.6%, just below the post-World War II record level of 12.7% reached in May 1994. Not surprisingly, unemployment remained a major concern for the government, and several measures to fight unemployment were included in the September 1994 budget. These were aimed at reducing the cost of training less-qualified people and encouraging firms to hire young people.

Partly as a result of the gloomy employment market, wages and salaries grew at a subdued rate of 2.5% (2.8% in 1993). The downward drift in consumer prices also dampened the rise in earnings. Average inflation edged down to 1.7% from 2.1% in 1993. This outcome was in line with the Bank of France's objective of price stability. Despite greater freedom allowed by the 15% bands within the ERM, the value of the franc remained stable against the Deutsche Mark. This was achieved by keeping the French interest rates closely tied to German rates. The intervention rate, the floor for money market rates, was gradually reduced to 5% from 6.2% in the spring.

Fiscal policy in France remained focused on curbing the public-sector deficit in line with a five-year plan. With the aid of higher revenues from privatization and a freeze on real expenditure, the government aimed to cut the deficit in 1994 to F 330 billion—a reduction of F 16.5 billion. The target was to reduce the deficit by a further F 25 billion in 1995. With the approach of presidential elections in the spring of 1995, fiscal rigour would have been increasingly

difficult to maintain had it not been for the economic recovery.

The Former Centrally Planned Economies. The economic decline in the former centrally planned economies continued for the fourth consecutive year, but the rate slowed from the peak decline of 15.5% in 1992 to 9% in 1993 and 8.3% in 1994. The outlook was improving, with many countries beginning to expand, and output was expected to fall by only 1% in 1995.

The best-performing countries were those in Central Europe, where the reforms necessary to create a market economy had been put in place soon after the fall of communism, five years earlier. The overall output of Central and Eastern Europe (excluding Belarus and Ukraine) grew by 1.4% in 1994, compared with a decrease of 2.3% in 1993. Several countries were growing rapidly, with, for example, Hungary's output expected to increase by more than 4% because of strong investment and export performances.

Russia was still lagging behind, with output falling by 12% in 1994, as it had in 1993. Most of the former Soviet republics were also continuing to experience declines in output. Many had high rates of inflation that were causing social problems as well as acting as a deterrent to investment. Worst affected was Georgia, where prices in 1994 were expected to rise by 10,000%, followed by Azerbaijan with an increase of more than 5,000%.

Exceptional among the former Soviet states were the three small Baltic countries, Estonia, Latvia, and Lithuania, which all registered increases in output and had sharply falling inflation rates. All of them were asserting their economic independence from Russia and were anxious to become part of the EU, with which they were expected to negotiate association agreements in the near future.

Problems associated with restructuring continued. One of the most refractory was unemployment, of which the

Interest Rates: Long-term

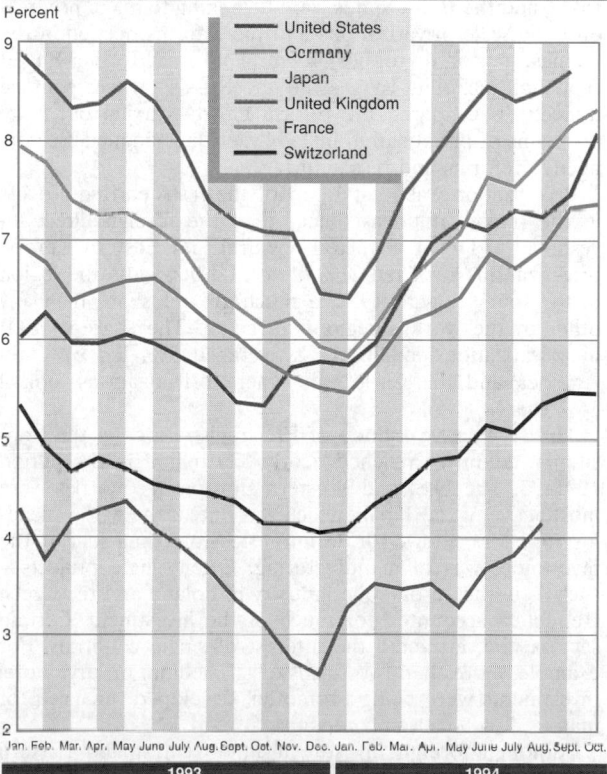

Source: International Monetary Fund, *International Financial Statistics.*

countries had had little experience under the old regimes. In many countries, as in Western Europe, early retirement was being used as a means of reducing labour forces. Welfare systems were able to offer little assistance, financial or otherwise. The numbers of unemployed were estimated to have risen in most countries in 1994. The situation was compounded by the lack of training or retraining facilities. There was a general lack of entrepreneurial skills and little knowledge or willingness to encourage them. People often needed more than one job to meet basic needs.

Open unemployment was greatest in the countries most advanced with economic reform, including Hungary, Poland, Albania, and the Baltic states, where the number of registered unemployed was equivalent to between 10% and 20% of the workforce. In some countries the rates exaggerated the true situation. The Czech Republic was exceptional among the more advanced countries because of its low unemployment rate of 4%. Although strict eligibility conditions applied to unemployment benefits, which may have influenced registrations, the many training programs under way, as well as the prospect of job opportunities in nearby Germany, contributed to the improved employment figures.

In the Transcaucasian and Central Asian countries, registered unemployment levels remained low, partly because of the stigma attached to being without a job but also because of the low or negligible benefits that were available. In Russia official unemployment stood at 1.5% of the labour force, but by international measuring standards the figure would be at least 6%, with as many again working short hours.

The privatization process was continuing in 1994 but was far from complete. In 9 of the 25 countries in the region, the private sector contributed over half of national GDP. The Czech Republic led in this respect, with private enterprise contributing 65% of GDP. Little headway was made in privatization of the agricultural sector, and land reforms were needed. The Czech Republic, Hungary, Poland, Slovakia, and the Baltic states were beginning to make progress on large-scale privatizations and the reforms needed in the financial sector to support them. The other former Soviet republics, including Kyrgyzstan and Russia—where political difficulties hampered the reform effort—carried out large programs of privatization in 1994, but their financial sectors needed reforms and restructuring.

Privatization was a vital part of the restructuring process in the region, not least because of the foreign direct investment (FDI) it attracted. Central and Eastern Europe privatizations attracted 67% of all FDI flows into the region in the four years to 1992, a much greater share than any other of the world's regions attracted. The share of FDI in privatizations in all LDCs averaged 5%, led by Latin America and the Caribbean, where privatizations took a 14% share.

The cumulative inflows of FDI registrations in the transitional countries reached nearly $20 billion in the period 1991–93. The U.S. and Western European countries were most active, while Japan, which was one of the world's leading investors, showed little interest. More than half of the investment was in manufacturing. Often single projects—such as in the automobile industry in Poland and the Czech Republic—accounted for much of the investment. Certain sectors, too, attracted the interest of single countries. For example, more than two-thirds of all medium or large hotel investments were being promoted, developed, financed, or managed by Austrian companies.

Although foreign investment into Central and Eastern Europe was increasing at a fast rate, it was from a very low base. In absolute terms, the amount was not so significant.

Between 1990 and 1993 total FDI into the region was less than the $15 billion received by Singapore alone. Investment was also heavily concentrated in the Czech Republic, Slovakia, Hungary, and Poland.

There were a number of reasons why the region failed to attract a larger share of world FDI flows. Output was still declining and was not providing the strong consumer demand investors liked. Inflation rates were high, and currencies in some countries were unstable. These factors often combined with inadequate physical and financial infrastructures and with a lack of the regulatory mechanisms associated with free markets. This made the region less attractive for foreign investors than other destinations, such as countries in Asia that were competitive and politically stable.

Nevertheless, foreign investment was playing a more significant role in the region than its size might have suggested. Foreign capital was revitalizing industries, and transnational companies from Western Europe were forging new trade links with the East. Most important were the transfer of technology and the development of human resources that were taking place. Franchising, which was becoming more acceptable, was already popular in Hungary and was growing in Poland, Slovakia, and the Czech Republic. McDonald's had been established in the region for several years, and other fast-food restaurants were making headway, as were print shops, hair salons, hotels, and computer centres.

Restructuring was having an adverse impact on tax revenues in the short term. High inflation eroded the value of tax collected, and the private sector, which was producing most of the economic output, was harder to tax. Taxation systems were being modified to be more compatible with a market system. Value-added taxes were replacing turnover taxes, and corporation taxes had become necessary. Tax administration needed to be improved and accounting skills learned. With falling revenues, governments were finding it difficult to meet the growing demand for social services, such as housing, education, and health care, which had often been provided by state enterprises in the past. The need to protect the most vulnerable members of society and provide for future pensioners was a growing concern.

Less Developed Countries. Economic growth in the LDCs, at 5.6%, remained largely unchanged from 1993. The main factors driving growth for the second year running were continuing benefits of economic reforms, low interest rates, and export growth. The latter was of strong benefit to countries in South Asia. Regionally, growth was strongest among the Asian countries, led by China. As a result of measures introduced in 1993 to control an unsustainable economic boom, GDP growth in China moderated to around 10% from over 13% in 1993. In many other Asian countries, economic growth remained strong. Singapore, Malaysia, South Korea, Thailand, and Vietnam all experienced economic growth rates of 8–9%. The economies of Hong Kong and Indonesia

Table V. Changes in Consumer Prices in Less Developed Countries

% change from preceding year

Area	1990	1991	1992	1993	1994[1]
All less developed countries	65.6	36.0	38.7	46.2	47.5
Oil-exporting countries	17.0	16.9	17.0	17.1	16.0
Non-oil-exporting countries	84.1	42.3	45.8	55.7	57.4
Africa	17.2	32.6	40.6	32.6	39.3
Asia	7.5	8.7	7.3	9.7	10.3
Middle East and Europe	24.6	24.7	24.2	24.7	27.0
Western Hemisphere	480.6	136.2	165.8	236.4	244.8

[1]Estimated.
Source: International Monetary Fund, *World Economic Outlook*, October 1994.

expanded relatively less strongly. The manufacture of electronic and consumer goods was an important element of economic activity in this region, and faster U.S. economic growth and an upturn in global economic activity stimulated their exports. The recovery in India accelerated a little to 4.5% as the economy continued to respond to liberalization. In Latin America, with the exception of Venezuela, economic growth remained largely unchanged at 3–4%. In Africa, despite a recovery in South Africa, drought, internal strife, and civil war induced stagnation or decline in other countries. In the Mediterranean region a financial crisis in Turkey and the effects of civil war in former Yugoslavia led to lower growth rates.

Although median inflation in LDCs moderated somewhat, it remained at a high level in many countries. Brazil had an annual inflation rate of close to 1,100%, but there were signs of easing. Venezuela's inflation increased to around 70%. Elsewhere in the region, however, inflation was below 10%. Economic reforms in Central and Eastern Europe kept inflation at 10–30%. In Russia there was a dramatic slowdown from almost 1,000% in 1993 to around 300% in 1994. Most of South Asia held steady at 3–9%, while China (27%), to the east, and Turkey (over 100%), to the west, rose rapidly. Across Africa inflation was generally stable at around 35%, but in South Africa it remained unchanged at around 9%.

There was no improvement in the external balances of the LDCs during 1994. IMF projections pointed to an expected current-account deficit of $106 billion. This was true despite the fact that exports from the LDCs increased slightly faster than imports. In Asia export volumes increased by 10%, two to three times as fast as in other regions of the world. Although the financing of the deficit was not problematic, the IMF expected the total external debt of the LDCs to rise by 8% to $1,675,000,000,000. Total debt as a proportion of exports and services continued to decline, however, and was expected to drop to 121% in 1994.

INTERNATIONAL TRADE

The volume of world trade grew by 7% in 1994, well above the long-term growth rate of 5%, according to IMF projections. Revisions to the previous year's figures indicated that the slowdown in world trade in 1993 was not as sharp as previously estimated. The revised estimates suggested that world trade grew by 4% in 1993—1.5 percentage points faster than earlier projections. (This revision was caused by distortions and delays in data collection within the EU since the abolition of customs controls.)

The upswing in world trade in 1994 was largely due to increased economic activity in developed countries, higher imports by the former communist countries in Europe, and continued rapid growth in LDCs. It was increased trade among the developed countries, however, that really buoyed world trade. Imports by the developed countries as a group grew by over 7% in 1994 from under 2% in 1993. By comparison, their exports expanded by 6%, up from 2.4% in 1993. Exports from the LDCs, on the other hand, improved marginally from 8.9% to 9.1%, while the volume of their imports dropped to 7% from the previous year's 9%.

Germany and the U.K. were the largest contributors to the surge in export volume in the developed world. Improved competitiveness, thanks to moderating inflation, corporate restructuring, and favourable currency movements against the dollar, boosted export growth in Germany (nearly 10% after a loss of 2% in 1993) and the U.K. (9% versus 2% in 1993). Despite the strength of domestic demand, exports from the U.S. gathered pace, thanks to the weaker dollar. By contrast, Italian exporters could not maintain the previ-

ous year's rapid growth rate, and export growth eased back to 6% from 8% in 1993. The appreciating yen and continuing trade hostility from the U.S. and Europe meant another year of slight decline in exports from Japan.

The growth in import volumes in developed countries was strongest among those at an advanced stage of recovery. Thus, the volume of import growth in the U.S., which was in its third year of recovery, swelled rapidly at 11.5%, well above the long-term average but not as fast as the previous year. In Europe economic recovery led to strong growth in imports by around 5%, more than making up for the 4% decline in 1993. There was a strong rise in imports into Japan, despite weak domestic demand. This was almost entirely due to the stronger yen, which made imported goods cheaper, but it was also in response to pressure on Japan to open its markets.

Many formerly communist countries looking for new export markets in the industrialized countries, particularly the EU and the U.S., found it difficult going. Their exports, which increased only by around 5%, were constrained by non-tariff barriers. Although a slower increase in import volumes prevented the trade balance from deteriorating, this group of countries continued to experience a fairly large current-account deficit.

The volume of exports from LDCs rose faster than imports owing to higher demand from manufacturers in the recovering developed countries as well as continuing rapid growth in Southeast Asia. Not surprisingly, Asia continued to increase its share of trade, with export volumes rising by 11% and imports by over 10%. Rapidly expanding domestic demand in China limited the resources available for exports and led to a surge in imports. In other regions export volumes in 1994 grew at the same rate as the year before (2–6%). Middle Eastern countries and Africa were at the lower end of this range, while Latin America experienced relatively faster growth in its exports. The volume of imports into LDCs grew more slowly for the second year in succession. The largest contributor to this slowdown was an actual drop in imports by Middle Eastern and European countries, but there was a slight slowdown in Asia and Latin America, too.

Although the LDCs earned more per unit of exports (partly because of currency movements and higher commodity prices), prices paid for imports rose faster. According to IMF estimates, their terms of trade declined by around 1.7%—slightly faster than the year before. The fuel-exporting countries were affected most, and their terms of trade fell by 8%, largely as a result of the weak dollar. In most developed countries, the terms of trade declined marginally, reflecting higher commodity prices. Japan, with its appreciating currency, went against the trend and experienced an 8.5% gain in its terms of trade.

The trade-liberalization process continued in 1994. The U.S.-Japan trade talks were successfully concluded in October but not without another cliffhanger reminiscent of the talks between the U.S. and the European Communities on the General Agreement on Tariffs and Trade (GATT) Uruguay round in December 1993. After 15 months of acrimonious talks, the U.S. and Japanese negotiators reached a partial agreement on trade just in time to avert U.S. sanctions against Japan. Two of the agreements opened up the Japanese telecommunications equipment market to foreign competition. The third deal was intended to make it easier for foreign companies to bid for Japanese government contracts to supply medical equipment. The fourth would classify regulations in Japan's insurance market. In one important area—automobiles and auto parts, which accounted for more than half of the U.S. trade deficit with Japan—

no agreement could be reached. The U.S. was to investigate this Japanese market under Section 301 of U.S. trade law and threatened to impose sanctions in 12–18 months' time.

Last-minute ratification by the U.S. Congress and the European Commission of the GATT Uruguay round agreement paved the way for the World Trade Organization to take over from GATT on Jan. 1, 1995. This followed a ceremonial signing of the Uruguay round in Marrakech, Morocco, in April by representatives of 120 governments. Once again the wrangling and brinksmanship delayed the ratification by the leading players until very close to the deadline of December 31.

The timetable was nearly wrecked by three unrelated developments. First, there was prolonged opposition from Republican protectionists in the U.S. Congress. This was overcome by a deal between Pres. Bill Clinton and Robert Dole, Republican leader in the Senate, after the November midterm elections ensured the Republicans majority control in Congress. Second, a power struggle broke out between the EU Council of Ministers (representatives of its 12 national governments) and the European Commission (unelected administration) on whether the Commission had the right to be the sole negotiator on trade matters. The dispute was resolved by a ruling by the European Court of Justice. The final delay was due to continuing political upheavals in Japan that disrupted the parliamentary calendar.

Despite huge uncertainties surrounding any estimates on economic benefits likely to arise from the Uruguay round, GATT economists in 1994 increased their estimates. If implemented by all 123 countries, by the year 2005 (the target date for full implementation of liberalization commitments), world income would rise by an estimated $510 billion a year (previous estimates had been $235 billion). The biggest gainer was the EU, with $164 billion a year by 2005. The annual gain for the U.S. was expected to be put at $122 billion, with Japan gaining $27 billion.

INTERNATIONAL EXCHANGE AND PAYMENTS

The year 1994 was characterized by large swings in foreign-exchange markets, largely driven by the weakness of the U.S. dollar and the strength of the Japanese yen. The most striking swing was in the Mexican peso, which fell 42% in 11 days after the newly elected government of Pres. Ernesto Zedillo Ponce de León (*see* BIOGRAPHIES) devalued the currency on December 20. The European currencies, however, did not exhibit the kind of instability feared following the widening of the ERM bands to 15% in August 1993.

The closing months of 1993 witnessed interest rates falling steadily in Europe, with hopes of more to come in the new year. The continuing weakness of the Japanese economy prompted expectations of a further interest-rate cut. By contrast, interest rates had been widely expected to rise in the U.S. as economic recovery moved into top gear. Sure enough, in early February the Fed raised its Fed funds rate by 0.25% to counter possible inflationary pressures arising from rapid economic growth. This was followed by another small rise in March. The tightening in policy was a shot in the arm for the dollar, and it moved up briskly to 113 yen and DM 1.76. Despite further interest-rate rises in April and May, however, sentiment turned against the dollar. New economic indicators pointed to continuing rapid economic recovery in the U.S., industries working at almost full capacity, and rising commodity prices. The financial markets became concerned with inflationary pressures building in the U.S. economy. This led to uncertainty on when and how far the Fed would have to raise interest rates to slow down the pace of activity. All this, together with the deadlock in its trade dispute with Japan and a continuing large U.S. trade

Demonstrators gather in Washington, D.C., to protest the U.S. Federal Reserve's hikes in interest rates. In an effort to dampen inflationary pressures by slowing the fast-growing U.S. economy, the Fed raised short-term rates six times during the year.
AFP

deficit, undermined the international investor's confidence in U.S. assets and resulted in capital outflows. In turn, this weakened the dollar in spite of widening short-term interest-rate differentials between the yen and Deutsche Mark. By June the dollar had breached the psychologically important 100-yen level and moved below DM 1.60.

The weakness of the dollar in early summer was amplified by signs of economic recovery in Germany and Japan. This led to expectations that short-term interest rates in Germany and other EU countries had reached their bottom during the current cycle. Likewise, a 1% growth in Japan during the first quarter made further interest-rate cuts unlikely and attracted international capital into yen-denominated financial assets. Failure of the large developed countries in the Group of Seven to take action in their July meeting to support the dollar sent the U.S. currency plunging to a post-1945 low of 96.9 yen and a 20-year low of DM 1.52. A brief period of relative stability followed, helped by three factors: reassuring statements by the U.S. administration that it did not want a weaker dollar, GDP data for the second quarter that were less strong than expected, and another increase in the Fed funds rate (the fifth) in August.

By September the financial market's fears of inflation were being reignited by new economic indicators signaling that economic activity was strengthening again. Consequently, for the next two months the U.S. bond market and the dollar came under pressure, despite a last-minute settlement of the U.S.-Japan trade talks, and hit new lows against the yen and the Deutsche Mark. The dollar rallied somewhat after the year's sixth and final rate increase by the Fed, in November. As the year drew to a close, the dollar was almost to 100 yen and DM 1.57, representing an effective decline of 7.5% against the Japanese and German currencies. On an effective exchange-rate basis, however, the decline was smaller. In December the effective exchange rate of the dollar stood at 62.8%, compared with 66.2% a year earlier, a decline of just over 5%. An unusual feature of the strength of the yen in 1994 was that it tended to reflect the weakness of the U.S. dollar. In 1992 and 1993 the yen's appreciation had been more general and not just against the dollar.

The global balance of payments position worsened slightly in 1994, reflecting economic recovery and pickup in trade generally. Despite a faster rate of economic activity among the developed countries, the improvement in their current-account balances continued in 1994. IMF estimates pointed to a surplus of $18 billion, a little less than the previous year's dramatically revised surplus of $19 billion. For the second consecutive year, most of the surplus was attributable to the EU. Many European countries were able

Effective Exchange Rates*
average rates, 1990 = 100

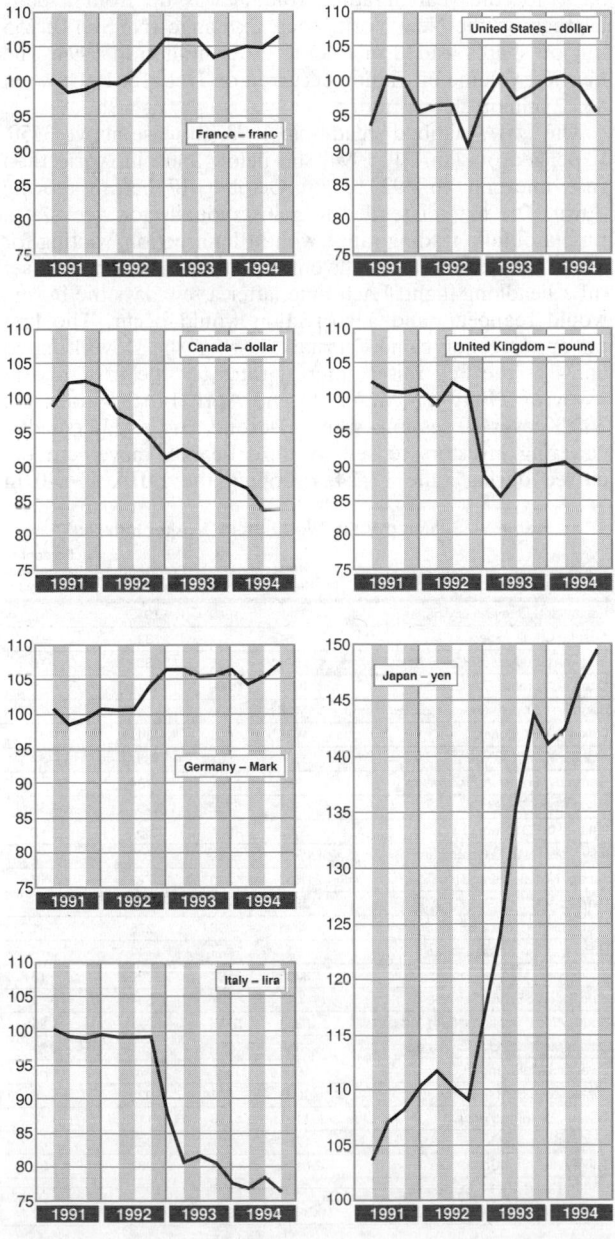

*Measure of a currency's value relative to a weighted average of the values of the currencies of the country's principal trading partners.

Source: International Monetary Fund, *International Financial Statistics*.

to take advantage of the buoyant export markets in the U.S. and Asia and increased their exports at a much faster rate than their imports. The U.S. absorbed more imports as the recovery strengthened and ran a smaller surplus on invisibles. Consequently, according to IMF projections, the U.S. was heading for a larger current-account deficit, $150 billion, compared with $103 billion the year before.

The relentless rise in Japan's current-account surplus continued in 1994, albeit more slowly. Despite a rise in the value of the yen, economic recovery in Europe, and buoyant export markets in the U.S. and Asia, Japan's surplus was heading for a record $136 billion, compared with $131 billion in 1993. If confirmed, this would be the lowest rate of increase since 1990, but it remained a source of friction with Japan's trading partners, particularly the U.S.

The current-account deficit of the LDCs as a whole was largely unchanged during 1994. IMF projections available in December pointed to an expected deficit of $105 billion, compared with $106 billion in 1993. In Asia the current-account deficit, which had expanded rapidly in recent years, stabilized at around $22 billion. Export growth from the dynamic, rapidly industrializing countries in the region were in line with imports of capital goods and raw materials. Some African countries benefited from higher commodity prices and improved their export earnings. As a region, however, Africa ran slightly larger trade and current-account deficits in 1994. In some Latin-American countries, an upsurge in foreign investments improved their capacity to finance higher imports and led to a widening of the trade and current-account deficit in the region.

The external debt of the LDCs was expected by the IMF to rise by around 8% in 1994 to $1,675,000,000,000. This was similar to the increase seen the year before. Although in absolute terms the LDCs' debt continued to increase, as a proportion of exports of goods and services it was expected to be slightly down from the year before, with a further decline possible in 1995. Asia and Latin America accounted for two-thirds of all debt.   (IEIS)

This article updates the *Macropædia* articles BANKS AND BANKING; ECONOMIC GROWTH AND PLANNING; GOVERNMENT FINANCE; INTERNATIONAL TRADE.

STOCK EXCHANGES

Whereas 1993 had been a year of spectacular gains, 1994 turned out to be a year of decline and volatility. Having entered the new year in sparkling form, most stock exchanges found the tide turned against them once the Federal Reserve began raising interest rates in the U.S. The *Financial Times* Actuaries (FT-A) World Index fell by 3% despite a relatively stronger performance in Japan. Wall Street also avoided an outright fall, and the Dow Jones industrial average (DJIA) ended the year roughly where it started. By contrast, Europe registered a 9% decline, according to the FT-A Europe Index of 708 leading shares. Likewise, most Asian stock markets fell sharply, reversing the steep gains of 1993.

As for the reasons behind the underperformance, equity markets were upset by the interest-rate environment, even though the economic news was positive. This was understandable, for falling interest rates had been the driving force behind the surge in share prices worldwide in 1993. In 1994, however, rising interest rates in the U.S. and stronger-than-expected economic growth introduced an element of uncertainty: how far would interest rates have to rise in the U.S. to prevent economic overheating? This uncertainty was mirrored in European and Asian markets.

Rising U.S. interest rates first upset government fixed-income securities (bonds), which in turn undermined equi-

New York Stock Exchange Common Stock Index Closing Prices
Stock prices (Dec. 31, 1965 = 50)

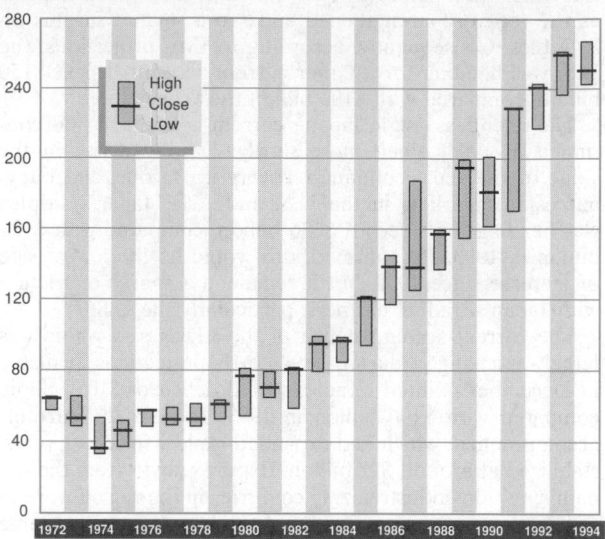

Number of shares sold
In millions of shares

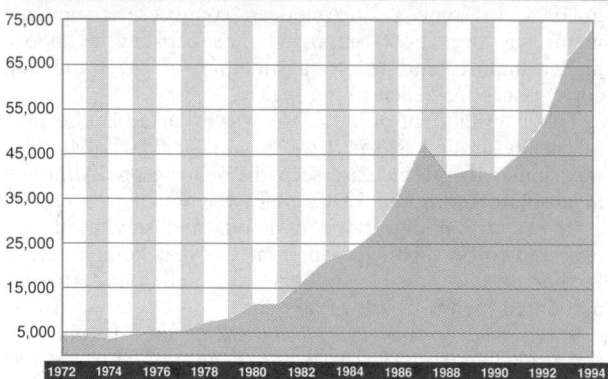

Source: *Barron's National Business and Financial Weekly; The Wall Street Journal.*

ties. The reason for the sharp fall in bond prices, in the face of a series of small rises in U.S. interest rates, was initially the surprise element. More important, the markets had expected the cheap-money policy to continue. As a result, speculative positions were held in bond markets through the use of borrowed funds. Realizing that this was the beginning of a policy tightening and that higher interest rates were on the way, bond funds scrambled to reduce their holdings. This pushed bond prices down and yields up, first in the U.S. and then across the world. As there is a direct relationship between bond prices and equity share prices, based on their respective yields, share markets in turn came under pressure. During the rest of the year, bond markets fell steadily and undermined share markets. Thus, investors in bond markets saw a negative return of 17% in the U.S. and over 15% in the U.K., in local currency terms, between January and November. Once a major uncertainty was out of the way with the sixth interest-rate rise in the U.S. in mid-November, relative calm returned to the bond and equity markets, but this was short-lived, and within a week the DJIA had plunged by 50 points, unsettling the rest of the world.

Many analysts viewed these adverse short-term developments in the share markets not as the beginning of a bear market but as a mid-cycle correction—a transition period between equity markets driven by falling interest rates and those driven by corporate profits. Fundamentally, global economic recovery was seen as a positive development as it improved corporate earnings, and once bond yields stabilized in 1995, growth in earnings and dividends were expected to push equity markets upward.   (IEIS)

United States. Investors were disappointed in 1994 as a result of a generally sluggish market in the U.S. Stock prices were relatively flat during the year. The range of index prices for the DJIA was an all-time high of 3978.36 to a low of 3593.35. At year's end it stood at 3834.44, an annual gain of a mere 2.14%. The Standard & Poor's (S&P) 500 stock index fluctuated between a high of 482 and a low of 438.92, ending the year at 459.27, an overall decline of 1.54%. The over-the-counter (OTC) stocks represented by the National Association of Security Dealers automated quotation (Nasdaq) composite index moved between a high of 803.93 and a low of 693.79 and closed at 751.96, down 3.2% for the year. Trading volume was up from a daily average on the New York Stock Exchange (NYSE) of 255 million shares traded in 1993 to 291.1 million in 1994. The heaviest volume of trading occurred on Dec. 16, 1994, when 483.2 million shares traded.

The DJIA climbed steadily in 1993, to close above 3750. It peaked on Jan. 31, 1994, slid below 3600 in April, then rose unevenly to 3923.93 on October 17 before moving down. The market tended to gain gradually for weeks at a time around a trading range with little direction, waiting for some bad news or an unfavourable trend, which would set off a headlong flight. Each time, after a few days the buyers would reappear, and a correction would occur. The first major correction came February 4, when the Dow dropped 96.24 as the Fed raised interest rates for the first time in five years. Between March 24 and April 14, the index fell 302.30 over 10 sessions when a second rate rise persuaded wavering investors to sell. A third bearish movement occurred during June 17–24, dropping the DJIA 174.40 in

Table VI. Selected Major World Stock Market Indexes[1]

country and index	1994 range[2] High	Low	Year-end close	Percent change from 12/31/93
Australia, Sydney All Ordinaries	2341	1842	1913	−12
Austria, Credit Aktien	461	377	395	−8
Belgium, Brussels BEL20	1543	1336	1390	−6
Canada, Toronto Composite	4610	3960	4214	−2
Denmark, Copenhagen Stock Exchange	416	336	349	−5
Finland, HEX General	1972	1601	1847	+17
France, Paris CAC 40	2356	1824	1881	−17
Germany, Frankfurt FAZ Aktien	859	742	784	−8
Hong Kong, Hang Seng	12,201	7708	8191	−31
Ireland, ISEQ Overall	2082	1694	1851	−2
Italy, Milan Banca Comm. Ital.	817	582	632	+2
Japan, Nikkei Average	21,553	17,370	19,723	+13
Mexico, IPC	2881	1957	2376	−9
Netherlands, The, CBS All Share	295	258	278	−1
Norway, Oslo Stock Exchange	1211	981	1142	+8
Philippines, Manilla Composite	3308	2507	2786	−13
Singapore, SES All-Singapore	642	507	534	−15
South Africa, Johannesburg Industrials	6984	5446	6977	+25
Spain, Madrid Stock Exchange	358	280	285	−121
Sweden, Affarsvarlden General	1604	1335	1471	+5
Switzerland, SBC General	1093	887	928	−8
Taiwan, Weighted Price	7191	5195	7111	+17
Thailand, Bangkok SET	1754	1197	1353	−20
Turkey, Istanbul Composite	29,145	12,981	27,257	+32
United Kingdom, FT-SE 100	3520	2877	3066	−10
United States, Dow Jones Industrials	3978	3593	3834	+2
World, MS Capital International	650	592	619	+3

[1] Index numbers are rounded.
[2] Based on daily closing price.
Source: *Financial Times.*

seven sessions. Sharply higher oil prices and a hard slide by the dollar depressed equity markets. Beginning November 17 the market fell 167.21 in four sessions.

The best-performing industry groups in the DJIA were: drug retailers, up 33.9%; footwear (1993's worst industry), up 32.58%; and computer software, up 30.59%. The worst performers were: home construction, down 32.62%; entertainment, down 30.24%; and airlines, down 30.11%.

The actions of the Fed—raising interest rates six times during the year to curb the risk of incipient inflation as the economy grew more rapidly than projected—depressed bond prices and restricted credit. The unemployment rate fell to a four-year low of 5.4%. Bond investors, particularly, feared that vigorous economic growth would lead to inflation that would erode the value of their fixed-income investments. Stock traders were concerned about the impact of recurrent inflation and the rise of interest rates. As the economy gained in strength, investor anxiety about inflation resulted in reluctance to support the bond market and discouraged stock buyers as well. Heavy use of computerized selling programs also depressed stock prices.

U.S. households owned about $2.8 trillion of stock directly in 1994, three times as much as their mutual funds, in both stocks and bonds. Individuals' direct holdings of Treasury, municipal, corporate, and mortgage bonds totaled another $1.6 trillion. With U.S. workers actively involved in the running of an additional $1.2 trillion of pension funds through 401(k) and other "defined contribution" plans, the universe of hands-on investors grew rapidly. It was also the biggest year for stock buybacks. The total authorized expenditure of companies buying back their stock reached $65.3 billion, shattering the old record of $61.9 billion set in 1989. General Electric announced its intention to buy back $5

Financial Times Industrial Ordinary Share Index
Annual averages, 1972–94

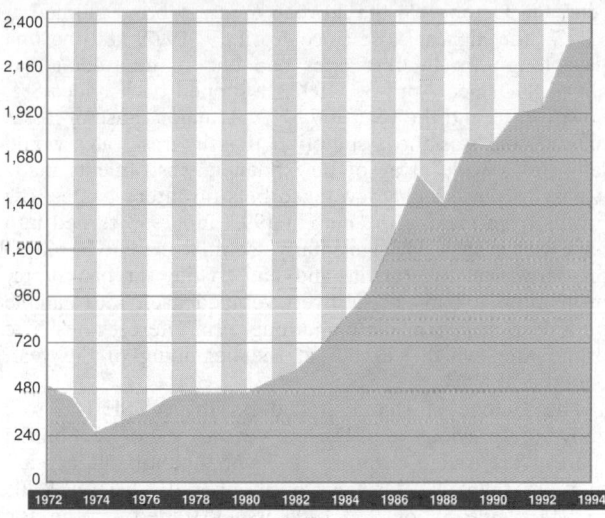

Source: Financial Times.

billion worth of shares. In a sluggish stock market, cash-rich companies favoured share buybacks as a means of boosting stock prices and strengthening stockholder confidence.

Merger and acquisition activity in 1994 was the highest in history, surpassing 1988, when $335.8 billion was reported. As of October 31, deals valued at $284.4 billion had been announced, but a flurry of activity late in the year raised the total to $339.4 billion. Among the most active industries were food, telecommunications, health care, and pharmaceuticals. About 8% were hostile takeovers, compared with 1–3% in the early 1990s. The dominant consideration in 1994 was large corporations seeking strategic alliances. Companies that slashed costs in the early 1990s were looking to increase their revenues, and acquisitions were an easy way to do it. Many of the buyers were foreign companies taking advantage of the weak dollar to make their expansion in the U.S. more affordable. The biggest deal completed during the year was AT&T's stock swap for McCaw Cellular Communications Inc. (valued at $18,920,000,000). In other big deals, American Cyanamid Co. was acquired by American Home Products Corp., a hostile tender offer ($9,270,000,-000), and Syntex was acquired by Roche Holding Ltd. in a friendly cash tender offer ($5,310,000,000). In much-publicized deals, Viacom Inc. acquired Paramount Communications ($9.6 billion) and Blockbuster Entertainment Corp. ($7,970,000,000). Through November, 1,298 publicly traded U.S. companies were involved in mergers and acquisitions, a record number.

The leading underwriters in domestic merger and acquisitions activity through mid-October on the basis of completed deals were Salomon Brothers ($44.8 billion), Lazard Freres & Co. ($42.1 billion), and Goldman Sachs & Co. ($38.8 billion). The top three firms in initial public offerings, excluding closed-end funds, were Goldman Sachs, $4,055,000; Merrill Lynch, $3,303,000; and Morgan Stanley, $2,328,000. Leaders in domestic corporate junk bonds, excluding split-rated issues, were Merrill Lynch, $3,953,000; Donaldson, Lufkin & Jenrette, $3,453,000; and Salomon Brothers, $3,374,000. The top three firms in domestic corporate investment-grade debt were Merrill Lynch, $29,261,000; Lehman Brothers, $23,032,000; and CS First Boston, $20,889,000.

Interest rates made headline news throughout 1994. After the yield on 30-year Treasury bonds sank to a low of

New York Stock Exchange Composite Index, 1994
Stock prices (Dec. 31, 1965 = 50)

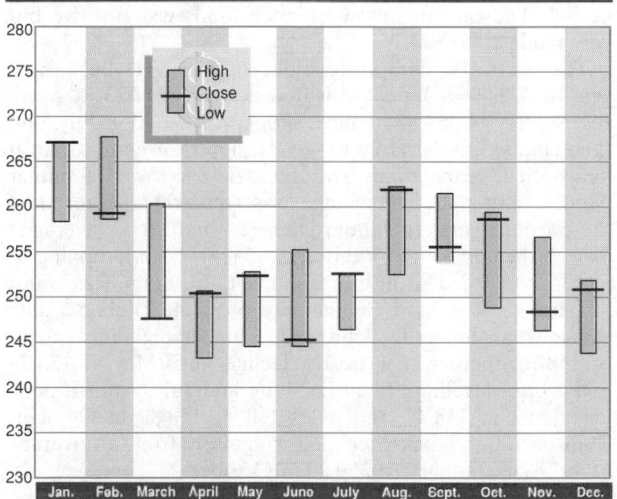

Average daily share volume
In thousands of shares

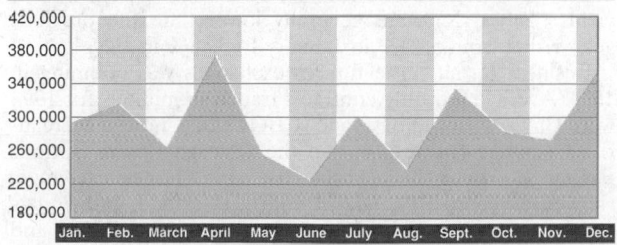

Sources: Barron's National Business and Financial Weekly; The Wall Street Journal.

5.78% on October 15, investors in Treasury securities suffered hundreds of billions of dollars in capital losses as the bond yield rose to the 8% level in the last quarter of the year. On October 24 the 30-year Treasury bond finished at 8.04%, the highest close since April 29, 1992, and the first time long-term interest rates had ended the trading day above 8% since April 30, 1992. It slipped back under 8%, however, to end the year at 7.87%. A major cause of losses to investors was the assumption that interest rates would fall, and a wide array of new financial instruments made it easy to place highly leveraged bets on interest rates. Big profits from making the bets in 1992 and 1993 turned into big losses in 1994. Orange county, Calif., lost some $2 billion on derivative investments and had to file for bankruptcy protection. It had grossly overleveraged itself in a gamble on a drop in intermediate and long-term interest rates. The prime rate, which was 6% at the beginning of the year, ended it at 8.5%.

The volume of shares traded on the NYSE was well above the previous year. For the year a total of 73.4 billion shares were traded, up from 1993's 66.9 billion, an increase of more than 9%. Declines outnumbered advances 2,405 to 944, while 57 of the 3,406 issues traded on the Big Board ended the year unchanged. The most active NYSE stocks were: Teléfonos de México (Telmex), with a volume of 1,048,663,100 shares traded; RJR Nabisco, 780,728,000;

General Motors, 702,171,600; Merck, 679,062,400; Wal-Mart, 661,180,000; and IBM, 600,784,900.

Bond volume on the NYSE was down substantially. As of December 16, bond volume was $6,983,845,000, a decrease of 26.4% from the year-earlier figure of $9,494,878,000. A seat on the Big Board sold in October for $825,000, down $5,000 from the price paid for the previous seat sold, on June 27. The bid price was $760,000 and the offering price was $830,000 in October. The record price for a seat was $1,150,000, paid in 1987.

Trading volume on the American Stock Exchange (Amex) was close to its 1993 level of 4.5 billion shares. By year-end, stock prices were down 10.67%, while bond volume had risen to $1,104,690,000, up more than 44% above the corresponding period of 1993. Of the 1,056 issues traded on the Amex, there were 720 declines, 321 advances, and only 15 unchanged. XCL Ltd. topped the active list as 236,738,900 shares changed hands.

Total sales on Nasdaq (6,274 issues) were 74.3 billion shares, with 1,576 issues advancing, 2,379 declining, and 79 left unchanged. All of the most active issues were computer-related companies. Intel Corp., with a volume of 1,184,213,-700 shares, led the way, followed by Cisco Systems, 1,007,-663,600; Microsoft, 841,901,800; and Novell, 836,291,700.

Many mutual fund investors were discouraged in 1994. The heavy flow of investments in bond mutual funds reversed course, causing the funds to liquidate their portfolios, thereby putting downside pressure on bonds and contributing to rising interest rates. Between October 1993 and August 1994, more than $30 billion was taken out of bond funds, according to the Investment Company Institute, a trade group. During the first nine months of 1994, net new investments in mutual funds plunged 53%. Stung by losses and lured by rising interest rates on much safer money market funds and certificates of deposit, investors pulled $26.8 billion out of bond funds in the March–September period. The rate of inflow in stock funds was positive but very modest.

The S&P 500 composite index (Table VII) began the year at 472.99 in January, drifted down to 447.23 in April, rose slightly to 454.83 in June, slipped to 451.40 in July, and then climbed moderately to 463.81, almost exactly where it had been a year earlier. The industrials followed a similar pattern, although the average was somewhat higher than the previous year. In January the S&P industrials averaged 550.53; they peaked in February at 551.04 before dipping to 520.36 in April. During the summer the average was about 525 before a rise in September to 551.48. Public utility stocks were generally depressed. From a high in January of 168.70, there was a steady decline until May at 153.74 and a brief leveling off during June and July. After a peak in August at 158.41, the index fell to 150.89 in October. Transportation stocks declined irregularly from an average of 441.47 in January to 359.20 in October.

U.S. government long-term bond yields (Table VIII) rose steadily during 1994, from 6.24% in January (contrasted with 7.17% a year earlier) to 7.47% by May, and remained above 7.5% from July to the year-end. U.S. corporate bond yields (Table IX) were generally lower than the previous year, rising from 5.14% in January to 5.88% in July.

Business on all three futures exchanges was booming in 1994. Average monthly contracts traded in millions for 1994 were Chicago Board of Trade (CBOT) 14, Chicago Mercantile Exchange (Merc) 14, and the Chicago Board Options Exchange 11. For the year the CBOT, the largest exchange, showed a record 219,504,074 contracts traded. Individuals accounted for less than 5% of turnover on the CBOT and the Merc, both of which asked the Commodity Futures

Table VII. U.S. Stock Market Prices

Month	Transportation (20 stocks) 1994	Transportation (20 stocks) 1993	Public utilities (40 stocks) 1994	Public utilities (40 stocks) 1993	Industrials (400 stocks) 1994	Industrials (400 stocks) 1993	Composite (500 stocks) 1994	Composite (500 stocks) 1993
January	441.47	374.27	168.70	159.79	550.53	504.96	472.99	435.23
February	437.50	379.57	164.41	166.41	551.04	508.91	471.58	441.70
March	417.97	376.22	160.97	170.48	543.71	517.24	463.81	450.16
April	393.29	390.85	157.57	172.27	520.36	505.00	447.23	443.08
May	386.73	386.40	153.74	167.52	526.27	513.68	450.90	445.25
June	391.89	374.77	155.41	171.65	528.76	515.73	454.83	448.06
July	385.53	379.98	155.09	176.50	525.88	508.10	451.40	447.29
August	382.73	400.98	158.41	180.06	542.48	514.17	464.24	454.13
September	371.67	397.25	152.02	186.76	551.48	517.37	466.96	459.24
October	359.20	...	150.89	175.43	551.09	...	463.81	463.90
November	...	...	...	173.43	...	...	...	462.89
December	...	...	...	...	...	...	...	465.95

Source: Prices, from Standard & Poor's, are monthly averages of daily closing prices, with 1941–43 = 10, except Transportation, 1982 = 100.

Table VIII. U.S. Government Long-Term Bond Yields

Month	Yield (%) 1994	Yield (%) 1993	Month	Yield (%) 1994	Yield (%) 1993
January	6.24	7.17	July	7.61	6.34
February	6.44	6.89	August	7.55	6.18
March	6.90	6.65	September	...	5.94
April	7.32	6.64	October	...	...
May	7.47	6.68	November	...	...
June	7.43	6.55	December	...	...

Source: Federal Reserve Board Bulletin. Yields are for U.S. Treasury bonds that are taxable and due or callable in 10 years or more.

Table IX. U.S. Corporate Bond Yields

Month	Yield (%) 1994	Yield (%) 1993	Month	Yield (%) 1994	Yield (%) 1993
January	5.14	7.91	July	5.88	7.17
February	5.06	7.71	August	5.88	6.85
March	5.29	7.58	September	...	6.66
April	5.44	7.46	October	...	...
May	5.62	7.43	November	...	...
June	5.76	7.33	December	...	5.18

Source: U.S. Department of Commerce, Survey of Current Business. Yields are based on Moody's Aaa domestic corporate bond index.

Trading Commission for broad regulatory exemptions for contracts used only by professional traders. They sought permission to create a new derivatives market that would offer a variety of simple swap arrangements for institutions.

The Securities and Exchange Commission (SEC) took steps to change the way bonds were traded in the municipal bond market. Three proposals required municipalities to provide more information about their financial health to the buyers of bonds, made bond dealers disclose more about their profits, and made it easier for buyers to get municipal bond prices. The SEC hoped that these measures would lead to more trading, improved information, better price data, and more buyers and sellers. In theory, the increased activity would lead to lower bond prices, making it more cost-effective for municipalities to borrow money and cheaper for investors to buy bonds. The SEC also called for new disclosure rules for municipalities, which would be required to publish annual reports. The Justice Department's antitrust investigation of the Nasdaq market focused on whether dealers set prices to wrest unfair profits from investors by fixing spreads on securities transactions. At year-end the SEC initiated an investigation of the Orange county financial municipal bond derivatives disaster.

Canada. Investors were bullish as the Canadian dollar strengthened and stock prices were close to their all-time highs. The fundamentals were good. Inflation and wage increases were the lowest among the most advanced industrialized countries, while growth in industrial production was strong. The market rallied in August as fears about the Quebec elections diminished. Canadian dollar fixed-income markets rallied after a downgrade of Quebec's debt rating in August, as investors were attracted to Canada with its high yield levels and low inflation pressures. The 10-year bond was 9.09% at mid-October, compared with 6.87% a year earlier.

The Canadian economy was strong, with robust sales and earnings as a result of the global business expansion. Major corporations such as Canadian Pacific Ltd., Bombardier, BCE, Inc., and Alcan Aluminum Ltd. did exceptionally well, particularly with exports. Canada reported a record trade surplus in July of Can$2.34 billion. While unemployment was a drag factor, at 10% GDP expanded at a rate of about 4% for the year. Canada also benefited from a sharp increase in foreign direct investment, as countries expanded there to gain access to a liberalized market arising from the North American Free Trade Agreement. Canadian interest rates of all maturities rose sharply in the first half of 1994 before leveling off toward year-end. The 10-year government bonds at 6.4% in January peaked at 9.2% in June at about the same level as the 20-year government bond. Short-term rates were more volatile.

The Toronto Stock Exchange (TSE), which handled 83% of Canadian stock transactions by value, compared with 12% on the Montreal Stock Exchange (MSE), was relatively flat throughout 1994. The TSE 300 composite price index began the year at 4400, climbed to 4470 in January, dipped to 4350 in February, climbed to a high of 4580 in March, and then dropped irregularly to a low of 3950 in June. It rallied in July, August, and September, when it reached 4400 before tapering off to 4200 in November. The TSE composite index closed the year at 4213.61.

Stock-exchange regulation was tightened up across Canada as the government took steps to conform more closely to the standards of the U.S. SEC. Listing requirements were strengthened, and an increasing number of companies were able to be listed on more than one exchange. Of the 579 companies on the MSE, 373 were also listed on the TSE and 28 on the NYSE.   (IRVING PFEFFER)

Western Europe. Most of the European stock exchanges performed poorly in 1994, losing money for investors. Encouraged by signs of an economic recovery, prospects of lower interest rates, and improved company profits, the European bourses entered the new year strongly and raced to new highs in February. However, the rise in U.S. interest rates, followed by the decline in U.S. and European bond prices, reversed the trend. A fall of nearly 10% from the February peak, as measured by Eurotrack Index, was exceeded by most markets. The worst performers were France with a 17% decline, Spain with a 12% drop, and the U.K. with a 10% drop; Austria and Germany were almost as weak, with falls of around 8%. Surprisingly, some smaller stock exchanges ended the year showing positive gains. The best performers were Finland and Portugal, with 17% and 11% gains, respectively.

The London Stock Exchange, being the largest and the most liquid in Europe, was an early casualty of the downward trend. The *Financial Times* Stock Exchange 100 (FT-SE 100) index peaked at 3520 in early February but fell rapidly to 3100 by the end of March. With the U.S. interest rates rising repeatedly during the spring and bond yields soaring, the psychologically important 3000 level was breached in May, and the index fell further in June—a drop of 16% from the peak. The second half of the year was characterized by some recovery but greater volatility. A summer rally was followed by a decline as the market reacted to a surprise 0.5% rise in British interest rates and then followed Wall Street's concern about strong U.S. economic growth data and fears of an imminent rise in interest rates. In the autumn a volatile Wall Street, frightened alternately by the prospects of higher interest rates and of a lower dollar, set the scene in London. Following short-lived calmer conditions after the 0.75% rise in the U.S. rates in mid-November, turbulence returned, and the FT-SE 100 index fluctuated around the 3050 mark to close at 3065.50.

With a strong economic recovery in Germany and further easing of interest rates in the spring, the German stock market proved less volatile and more resistant to the downward pressures. A modest decline in the spring, after the U.S. interest-rate increases, was followed by a sustained rally. The market was encouraged by a moderate wage agreement and by the favourable outlook for German interest rates. By the early summer, with the German economic recovery looking firmer and global bond yields nearly two points higher, prospects of early interest-rate cuts diminished. The market then fell under the influence of Wall Street, and by early October it was 12% below the summer peak. In the closing months, despite relative stability and a hesitant recovery, the FAZ Aktien Index closed the year below the 800 level with a loss of nearly 8%—a very different outturn from the previous year's 41% gain.

The Paris Bourse was among the worst performers in Europe, as the economy and company profits recovered hesitantly, and the French economy was perceived to be vulnerable to higher U.S. interest rates and political uncertainty at home. The CAC 40 Index followed London's pattern and by June was 20% below its January peak, canceling most of the previous year's gains. As in other European stock exchanges, an early summer rally gave way to further weakness and volatility, followed by relatively more settled conditions. By the year's end, the CAC 40 Index was more than 17% lower.

The Nordic block once again outperformed other European bourses generally, with a 17% gain in Finland, an 8% increase in Norway, and a 5% rise in Sweden, while Denmark registered a small decline. Economic recovery, continued corporate restructuring, and potential benefits of joining the EU in 1995 were some of the attractions of the bourses in these regions.

Southern European bourses were mixed. While the Madrid Stock Exchange could not hold on to early gains and ended the year 12% lower, Portugal and Italy bucked the trend with 11% and 2% gains, respectively. The election of media tycoon Silvio Berlusconi (*see* BIOGRAPHIES) as Italy's prime minister provided a boost to Italy, and the Milan Index soared by 36% between January and May. Under the weight of higher Italian interest rates, widespread protests against the proposed cuts in the generous pension scheme, and allegations about Berlusconi's unethical business dealings, the market fell steeply in the second half of the year and gave up its gains.

Other Countries. Stock markets in Asia, the highfliers of 1993, were impaled on higher U.S. interest rates, policy tightening in China, and recovery prospects in Tokyo. The flow of money from investors in the developed markets, particularly the U.S., seeking new opportunities slowed to a trickle as investors kept their money at home or switched to Tokyo. Although the export-driven economies of Pacific Rim countries continued to grow rapidly, the stock markets looked expensive after several years of heady growth. The FT Pacific Index, excluding Japan, registered a fall of 15% during 1994. Hong Kong (down 31%) and Malaysia (down 24%) performed worse than the regional average. The Philippines, Singapore, and Thailand fell by 13%, 15%, and 20%, respectively. South Korea, with a 28% gain, was the star performer of the region. Taiwan also went against the trend and ended the year in plus territory, up 17%.

Japan was one of the few large stock exchanges to buck the global decline and, together with the rise in the value of the yen, it returned good profits to overseas investors. Encouraged by hopes of economic recovery and improvement in corporate profits, foreign investors switched into Japanese shares at the start of the year and drove the market higher. The Nikkei 225 Index rose from the low of 17,370 in January to 21,553 by June—a gain of 24%. This marked a turning point, and the index fell steadily in the second half of the year to below 19,000. The downward trend was attributable to various economic and political factors, including uncertainty caused by the summer slowdown in the economy, arrival of a new, untried Socialist prime minister, the strength of the yen, and lack of progress in the trade talks with the U.S. The single most important factor, however, was lack of support from Japanese investors. Having been burned so many times since 1991 by poor market performance, Japanese investors remained on the sidelines. Against this lethargic second-half performance, foreign investment funds dried up, and the market ended the year drifting below the psychologically important 20,000 level but still showing gains of about 13%.

Australia, often seen as a global player on economic recovery and upswing on commodity prices, failed to reward investors in 1994. Despite the background of a 5% economic growth rate, low inflation, a stable political climate, and rising commodity prices, the collapse in world bond prices prompted by the Fed's interest-rate rises, put the skids under Australian shares. The All Ordinaries Index ended the year around the 1913 level, 12% below the start of the year, after having been as high as 2341 in early February.

The emerging markets, having burst into the big-time global investment scene in 1993 with phenomenal increases, consolidated their position in 1994. (*See* Special Report: *Emerging Equity Markets.*) After the early setbacks caused by the U.S. interest-rate rises, global emerging market indexes moved into positive territory. The Barings Emerging

(continued on page 174)

Special Report

Emerging Equity Markets

BY JOHN MULLIN

By the beginning of 1994, stock markets in less developed countries (LDCs)—known as emerging equity markets—had taken root in all corners of the globe. The most mature and prominent of these markets were concentrated in Asia and Latin America, with several notable exceptions, such as South Africa. Newer markets, however, were developing in Eastern Europe, Russia, Africa, and the Middle East. Markets had opened in such far-flung locales as Zambia, Malta, and Nepal. Many more countries, including Vietnam, Cameroon, and Uganda, were working to establish equity markets.

Rapid Growth of Emerging Markets. Equity markets in LDCs expanded rapidly during the first three quarters of 1994, despite a shift in U.S. monetary policy that left the more developed equity markets of Europe and the United States treading water. This growth marked the continuation of a trend, as the decade spanning 1983–93 had seen a 20-fold expansion in the total value of shares in the 25 emerging markets tracked by the World Bank's International Finance Corporation. Expansion had been particularly vigorous in 1993, when U.S. investors buoyed overseas bourses by purchasing record amounts of foreign-equity shares. The trend was interrupted in February and March 1994, when most of the world's stock markets suffered price declines following the U.S. Federal Reserve System's decision to increase the federal funds rate. Whereas most developed markets languished in the aftermath of the change in U.S. monetary policy, however, many emerging markets gained significant ground. In particular, Brazil's market capitalization increased more than 80% during the first three quarters of 1994. Overall, emerging-market capitalization (the total value of shares in emerging markets) increased from $1.4 trillion at the end of 1993 to $1.6 trillion by August 1994.

The resilience demonstrated by emerging equity markets in 1994 indicated that the dramatic growth of these markets in the previous several years had not been simply the product of an investment fad or speculative mania. Dramatic price gains in 1993, largely concentrated in the latter part of the year, had prompted many observers to question whether rapid increases in emerging market share prices constituted a "bubble." (In a bubble, investors shift their attention away from prospective income streams and increasingly speculate on further price increases.) Although bubbles may have existed in several emerging markets coming into 1994, the evidence strongly suggested that emerging market equity shares were not overpriced as an asset class. At the end of 1993, the composite emerging market price-to-earnings ratio (p/e) stood at 25.9, which meant that the total value of emerging market shares was 25.9 times 1993 corporate earnings. This multiple was very much in line with the composite developed market p/e, which stood at 28.6 at the end of 1993. In theory, emerging market shares probably

John Mullin is an analyst in the global asset allocation department at Smith Barney, Shearson, Inc.

should have had higher p/e's than developed market shares, given the emerging markets' outstanding growth prospects. Consequently, emerging market shares may well have been underpriced coming into 1993.

The Role of Emerging Markets. Starting in the late 1980s, emerging equity markets had begun to play a substantial role in channeling financing to firms located in LDCs. In this way the markets helped allocate the world's savings to areas where the potential returns on investment were greatest. Capital was scarce relative to labour in LDCs, and wage rates were generally low. Consequently, investments in plant and equipment in those economies could yield greater increases to income streams than similar investments in the developed economies of Western Europe, Japan, and the U.S. By helping to channel savings to the LDCs, emerging equity markets helped to improve the efficiency with which the world's savings were allocated.

Of course, capital had been scarce relative to labour in LDCs long before foreign portfolio equity investment became an important source of financing in the late 1980s. Key changes had taken place during the late 1980s and early 1990s, however, that helped free the flow of capital to LDCs. Among these changes were basic economic reforms. In Latin America far-reaching programs to eliminate government budget deficits and stabilize exchange rates and prices played a particularly important role, as did the restructuring of several Latin-American countries' commercial bank debt. Throughout the world, government policy makers increasingly began to promote market-oriented reform programs. A crucial element of these programs was privatization. LDCs in Latin America, Asia, and Eastern Europe sold shares of previously government-controlled enterprises. These stock offerings increased stock market depth and thereby increased the capacity of emerging equity markets to serve as sources of fresh capital for LDC firms.

The Effect of U.S. Investors. Emerging markets benefited from changes in developed economies. By 1994 U.S. institutional and individual investors had become committed to the notion that international portfolio diversification would enhance the performance of their investment portfolios. U.S. investors were attracted by the outstanding returns that emerging markets had registered historically. The stock markets of Argentina, Chile, and Malaysia in particular had registered annualized returns in excess of 30% between 1976 and 1993. Returns in Mexico, Taiwan, Thailand, and India exceeded 20% per year during the same period. These returns looked quite attractive relative to the annualized return of 14% achieved by the U.S. market during the same period. During 1993 and 1994, U.S. investors began to invest overseas aggressively. At the beginning of 1993, international assets accounted for only 2% of all mutual fund assets. By August 1994, however, the figure had increased to 6%. Purchases of emerging market equity shares contributed importantly to this increase.

The rapidly developing market for American Depository Receipts (ADRs) also continued to facilitate capital flows to emerging equity markets in 1994. ADRs were claims, issued by U.S. depository institutions, to underlying equity shares of foreign-based companies. Depository institutions held the underlying shares as custodians and thereby saved investors some of the costs and risks associated with settlement and clearance in foreign markets. The size of emerging market ADR programs had grown rapidly since Telmex, the Mexican telecommunications company, raised $1.2 billion in a successful ADR offering in May 1991.

Global Developments. Young markets in Russia, Eastern Europe, China, and Africa developed by fits and starts in 1994. Foreign and domestic investors were attracted to

shares in these relatively new markets by the prospect of buying stakes in potentially fast-growing companies at bargain prices and subsequently selling these shares at higher prices. Oftentimes the competition to acquire shares caused wide gyrations in share prices.

Shares of Russian firms yielded remarkable returns in 1994 for those investors brave enough to acquire them and tenacious enough to hold on to them. Share prices of the local telephone company in St. Petersburg increased 140-fold in the 12 months following the firm's 1993 privatization, and share prices of United Energy Systems—the world's largest electric utility—increased 50-fold during the first three quarters of 1994. Great opportunities in Russia, however, were accompanied by great problems. Investors found it extremely difficult to settle transactions and were unable to find suitable custodians to hold their shares for safekeeping. Foreign investors frequently had trouble obtaining satisfactory legal judgments from Russia's legal system because laws on capital gains were complicated and some of the country's larger companies did not recognize the rights of outside shareholders, foreign or domestic. Another basic problem in Russia was a lack of crucial information. In addition, accounting standards needed much improvement before relative share values could be measured with any degree of accuracy. Despite these problems, hedge funds and other risk takers brought large amounts of money into Russia during 1994. The country's privatization minister estimated that portfolio inflows reached $500 million per month during the summer.

Similar booms had already taken place in Eastern Europe. In the Czech Republic, Hungary, and Poland, stock markets had boomed in the second half of 1993 as domestic and foreign investors bid up the shares of recently privatized enterprises and speculated on future price increases. Despite volatile price swings in 1994, equity market capitalization in the three Eastern European economies grew rapidly during the first three quarters as governments continued to privatize firms through share issuance.

In Asia, too, markets continued to experience rapid capitalization growth in 1994 despite declining prices. Share prices in the Philippines and Indonesia, which had boomed in 1993, declined during the first three quarters of 1994. Nevertheless, market capitalization continued to grow. The value of shares in the Philippine market increased from $40 billion at the end of 1993 to $50 billion by the end of August 1994, while market capitalization in Indonesia increased from $33 billion to $40 billion. Equity market capitalization in China expanded at a similarly rapid pace during 1994.

Market capitalization in Africa remained modest in 1994 outside of South Africa, as only small numbers of firms were listed on national exchanges. Following a decade in which gross domestic product actually declined in many African countries, however, governments were becoming more reform-minded. Besides ASA Ltd., a closed-end fund that had specialized in South African precious metal stocks for years, there had been few investment funds concentrating on Africa. This changed in 1994, as several closed-end Africa funds came into existence with mandates to invest substantial amounts of capital in South Africa as well as other African countries. As in Latin America, Asia, and Eastern Europe, privatization began to play a critical role in equity market development. In March 1994 the Ghanaian government sold half of its 55% stake in Ashanti Goldfields Co., quadrupling the number of shares on the Accra exchange. Morocco planned to privatize $3 billion worth of state firms, and Zambia stated its intention to sell Zambia Consolidated Copper Mines within the next few years.

(continued from page 172)

Index, for instance, was nearly 3% above the previous year. This rise, however, masked huge regional and countrywide variations. While the European and Middle Eastern markets ended 1994 well below their highs achieved at the end of 1993, the Asian and Latin-American markets had more than reattained their highs. The best-performing individual markets, in U.S. dollar terms, included Brazil (70%), Chile (45%), and Hungary (2%), while the worst performers included Poland (−45%), Turkey (−40%), Venezuela (−30%), and the Czech Republic (−20%).

In Mexico the devaluation of the peso on December 20 triggered a sharp drop in the market there. The IPC index, which was already well below its February high of 2881, plunged more than 11.5% the next morning. It continued to be volatile but finished the year at 2375.66, down only 9%.

Commodity Prices. Commodity prices rose strongly during 1994, largely in response to global economic recovery and low interest rates. The activities of speculators were thought to be the main reason why the steep upturn in commodity prices occurred so soon in the global recovery cycle. (In November 1994 *The Economist* Index was less than 10% below its mid-1980s high). *The Economist* Commodity Price Index of spot prices for 28 internationally traded foodstuffs, nonfood agricultural products, and metals rose by 37% in U.S. dollar terms during the first 11 months of the year. In sterling terms the increase was slightly lower, at 29%.

The price of crude oil, which was not included in *The Economist* Index, rose by 10% to close to $17 per barrel in December, having been as low as $13 a barrel in February—a five-year low. A relatively mild winter in Europe and weak demand from the former Soviet Union were the main reasons for the weak oil prices in the spring. Recovery from this low point was steady, and oil prices reached a high for the year of $19.50 a barrel in early August as the market feared a politically motivated strike in Nigeria might reduce supplies. Following the collapse of this strike in early September, prices drifted back to the $16–$17-a-barrel level. This volatility left oil producers and consumers confused about the direction of oil prices. As the year drew to a close, oil prices were stable but poised to rise further. Supporting an upward trend was OPEC's decision in its November meeting to hold its output ceiling at 24.5 million bbl a day (in place since September 1993) and indications that Saudi Arabia, the world's largest exporter, was keen to see prices move up to $22 a barrel.

Both sectors of *The Economist* Index rose strongly in 1994. The Food Index rose by 30%, but the Industrials Index rose faster, by 47%. Copper, lead, and aluminum rose by nearly 50%, while nickel, tin, and zinc rose 5–30%. For most metals stronger industrial demand exceeded output and exports, reducing stock overhang and improving prices. Zinc and tin prices were held back by higher Chinese exports.

Food production was affected by drought, floods, and frosts. The wheat crop in Australia was cut back by a severe drought, while in Canada output fell as farmers switched to more profitable crops. Coffee prices soared in the summer to an eight-year high but fell from the July peak as frost damage in Brazil was less extensive than at first feared. Tea prices also improved in 1994 in sympathy with coffee prices. Nonfood agricultural products such as rubber rose by 50%; wool prices, responding to stronger demand, improved by 34%.

The gold price in 1994 was less volatile than in recent years and, although it moved in a fairly narrow range of $350–$390 per troy ounce, it ended the year 10% higher, close to the year's high.   (IEIS)

This article updates the *Macropædia* article MARKETS.

Education

Noteworthy concerns in education in 1994 included attention to academic performance levels, educational attainment in industrialized nations, problems of financing education, religion in the schools, and the expansion of women's educational rights. (*See also* 1995 BRITANNICA WORLD DATA: *Comparative National Statistics: Education.*)

Primary and Secondary Education. The educational program of the administration of U.S. Pres. Bill Clinton was called the Goals 2000: Educate America Act. Voluntary goals were proposed for the states: children entering school ready to learn; a 90% graduation rate; competence in basic subjects and in the arts; "world-class" instruction in mathematics and science; total adult literacy; drug- and violence-free schools; improved teacher education; and increased parental involvement in schooling. Meanwhile, the number of states contracting with private companies for the management of public schools continued to increase in 1994. During the year Massachusetts, for example, awarded contracts to private firms for the running of 15 new alternative schools. In November voters in California approved a referendum denying educational and other services to illegal immigrants.

The U.S. Congress reauthorized the Elementary and Secondary Education Act (ESEA) in 1994 to provide federal support for specific aspects of education. More than half of the expenditures were to provide local districts with resources to supplement the education of culturally disadvantaged students, served in 90% of the nation's schools. The act also provided for teacher-education and crime-reduction programs. The ESEA required a one-year expulsion of students who took guns into schools, and it prohibited the use of federal funds to promote either homosexual or heterosexual activity or to distribute condoms in schools. The five-year reauthorization, effective in fiscal year 1995, was for $12.7 billion. President Clinton also signed a reauthorization of the 29-year-old Head Start program. More admissions would be possible for infants and toddlers, and more all-day, all-year programs would be funded for poor children.

Simply disliking school continued to be the main reason U.S. students dropped out, according to the Department of Education's annual study. A quarter of female dropouts and 8% of males cited parenthood as the reason for ending their education. Eleven percent of the 16–24 age group—3.4 million people—were high-school dropouts, but overall the U.S. dropout rate had declined since 1970. Another national study found that students in small schools consistently did better on tests of performance. School size, which determined how well the staff knew and guided individual students, rather than racial homogeneity was found to be the critical factor.

Proposals for reforming U.S. welfare programs commonly included plans for encouraging teenage mothers to complete high school. Education was suggested as a way to increase the ability to get good jobs and to eliminate sliding into welfare cycles. An Ohio plan was lauded by federal officials as a model for the nation; incentives included cash bonuses, child care, transportation, and counseling by social workers. Education also was part of proposals to encourage welfare parents to keep their children in school on a regular basis, with penalties imposed on parents whose children's school-attendance patterns were unacceptable.

France and New Zealand continued to experiment with innovative school-attendance schedules aimed at enhancing students' academic progress, improving family life, and reducing stress for both students and teachers. In France a four-day school week (with Wednesday off for religious studies) was compared with a traditional five-day school week that included attendance on Saturday morning and Wednesday off. A survey revealed that 72% of teachers and 77% of parents with children in four-day programs preferred the arrangement. Parents reported that their children's schoolwork and health benefited under the four-day plan. In New Zealand 230 local boards of education chose to change from the established three-term school year to a four-term year that had proved successful when tried in six schools in 1993. The experimental schools reported that under the shorter (10-week) term, pupil-teacher interaction improved, pupils settled down to their studies more quickly after term breaks, and they stayed more motivated throughout the term. Officials estimated that the new plan would be instituted nationally by 1996.

Increasing numbers of parents in China engaged in prenatal teaching in order to maximize their children's educational opportunities early in life. The instructional procedure involved a pregnant woman, equipped with a cassette recorder, transmitting audiotaped lessons to her unborn child by means of a plastic speaker placed on her abdomen. Hospitals held training sessions in prenatal education for parents and sold them lesson tapes; newspapers and television stations cooperated by featuring information on prenatal instruction. In particular, the government's policy of one child per family stimulated parents' efforts to ensure that their one child would excel academically. In both China and Japan, programs of systematic instruction for children from the time of birth until they entered school grew in popularity. One Japanese version was the academic preschool to which parents sent toddlers at an average cost of $90 per 50 minute lesson, with such fees doubled or tripled for children in programs for the gifted. More than 100 of these early-learning centres in the Tokyo area prepared preschoolers to pass the tests required for admission to elite kindergartens.

Parents of an estimated one million of China's one-child families sent their children to summer camp in 1994 to experience the rigours of village life so as to toughen the youngsters physically and mentally. The growing summer-camp movement was designed to confront coddled city children with what their parents called "eating bitterness" (*chi ku*) as a means of inuring the young to frustrations they might face in the future. The number of campers in 1994 exceeded the 1993 total by several hundred thousand, and plans were set to expand the program in the years ahead.

Pressure exerted on children in Hong Kong to excel academically was held at least partly to blame for the colony's rising suicide rate among the young. A survey revealed that primary-school pupils in Hong Kong spent an average of three hours a day on homework, longer than pupils in any other Asian society. The study showed that homework began at age three, when kindergarten children took home the assignment of repeating Chinese characters an hour each day. Furthermore, pupils were found to suffer distress at the prospect of doing poorly on the examinations that dominated the schools' curricula. As an antidote to the pressure, the government issued a guidebook with ideas for teachers on how to make homework less onerous and involve less rote memorization.

To improve primary education in Mexico, a World Bank loan of $412 million was added to $204.7 million from the Mexican government for training teachers and administrators, reducing student dropout rates, and financing the development of reading materials in 17 regional dialects. The nation's new education secretary, Fernando Solana Morales, endorsed a plan to modernize the country's education system that included the transfer of decision making from federal to state authorities.

In Papua New Guinea a struggle over literacy programs ensued between proponents of indigenous languages on one side and a coalition of Western-trained teachers and fundamentalist Christians on the other. The teachers and Christians advocated literacy in English as a means of integrating the nation of more than 700 local tongues, a policy endorsed by the government's central department of education. In opposition, the nongovernmental "critical literacy" campaign that began in 1990 employed techniques created by Paulo Freire, the Brazilian educational revolutionary, to institute village-run reading, writing, and publishing programs in local languages for 1,500 rural communities. By 1994 teachers had provided evidence that children who already could read in their indigenous language upon entering the primary grades learned English more readily than those who entered without such training. In addition, more pupils whose literacy started with their local language completed primary school and passed tests for entry to high school. These results stimulated the government to introduce a major reform of elementary and secondary education that incorporated preschool literacy instruction.

A study by the Organisation for Economic Co-operation and Development (OECD) revealed that by the early 1990s more than half the adult population in most industrialized countries had completed secondary school. Educational attainment still varied among the OECD's 24 member nations, however. More than 30% of the adult population in Australia, Canada, and the United States, for example, had some higher education, while in Austria, Italy, Portugal, Spain, and Turkey the proportion was 10% or lower. The study also showed that earnings generally rose with an increase in educational attainment. For example, university graduates in the United States earned 64% more than high-school graduates.

During the UN-sponsored International Conference on Population and Development, increased accessibility to better education was offered as a justification for population control. Advocates suggested that better education would be available in smaller families. Better education for women was also advocated as an effective motivator of family planning. (*See* POPULATIONS AND POPULATION MOVEMENTS: *Sidebar.*)

UNICEF's *The Progress of Nations* study chided the United States and Europe for the levels of resources devoted to caring for women and children, saying that less developed nations do better. The UN report said, for example, that only 94% of U.S. children enter fifth grade, a low figure considering the nation's wealth.

In Russia the government's innovative noncommunist curriculum was introduced in the nation's schools. In contrast to curricula of the past, the plan was not mandatory, and it allowed a wide choice in course materials for public schools. Only one-third of the country's 67,000 schools adopted the new program during its first year, however, with the remaining two-thirds preferring to continue with traditional offerings. At the same time, hundreds of new private schools contributed to the growing diversity among institutions in terms of cost to parents, curriculum patterns, teaching methods, and quality of equipment. Observers were concerned that the advent of private schools catering to the rich was contributing to increased social-class distinctions in Russian society. In Uzbekistan hundreds of recently founded Islamic religious schools (madrasahs) posed a new form of competition for the existing secular public schools that had been based on Soviet models.

Authorities in Poland sought to alter the educational system's longtime emphasis on training workers for specific jobs in heavy industry, a curriculum that in the past had enrolled 70% of the nation's primary-school graduates. In 1994, under a reform plan, 60% of those leaving primary school would pursue broad academic studies that provided the basis for a wide range of occupational fields. As Poland emphasized academic programs, Australia moved in the opposite direction by increasing vocational offerings. Australia's Prime Minister Paul Keating announced that while his nation had established 17 new universities over the previous eight years, the rest of the 1990s would witness the rapid growth of postsecondary vocational programs. Educational planners in Australia sought to emulate Germany, which, compared with the size of its workforce, had four times as many apprentices as Australia and twice as many workers with nonuniversity postsecondary training.

The budget issued by South Africa's president, Nelson Mandela, increased spending on education by 11.5%. The plan also provided for supplying milk to schools as a means of alleviating malnutrition and illness among black children. An African National Congress proposal to redress social inequities and eliminate needless duplication in South Africa's educational system would unify the country's 14 different race-based education departments into a single Ministry of Education and Training. An expansion of education through correspondence and broadcast courses was also seen as an important aspect of educational provisions for the postapartheid era.

In Malawi, after three decades of dictatorship, voters in May brought to power a democratically elected government dedicated to free, universal primary education. The enthusiastic response of the populace was reflected in an increase in primary enrollment from 1.9 million children during the 1993–94 school year to more than 3 million as the new school year began in September 1994. Class sizes, already often as high as 200 pupils, were now expected to reach 300 in some districts.

Britain's Education Secretary John Patten courted widespread criticism for insisting that schools obey a law requiring all students to engage in daily collective worship "of a broadly Christian character." Not only did Patten's directive alienate those of non-Christian faiths, but the idea of daily worship was also opposed by the Church of England, by the nation's Office for Standards in Education, and by schools that lacked an auditorium in which to collect the entire student body. As a consequence, the directive was deemed unenforceable.

A U.S. federal judge held unconstitutional most of a Mississippi law that permitted prayer in public schools. The judge held that the law was too broad and vague to pass constitutional muster, but he did let stand a provision for student-initiated prayers at graduation ceremonies. The Mississippi law would have allowed students to incorporate prayers into almost any school situation. The case was one of many in which states sought a way around the 1962 and 1963 U.S. Supreme Court decisions outlawing prayers planned and led by school officials or religious leaders. A 1992 court appeal had opened the doors to student-led prayers at high-school commencement programs.

Expanded educational rights for women received attention in a variety of countries. World Bank studies of poverty in Latin America supported several conclusions: the less education people have, the more likely they will live in poverty; people of indigenous ancestry generally have less education and lower earnings than nonindigenous people; and indigenous women as a group have less education and lower earnings than indigenous men. Authors of the studies concluded that a key way for most Latin-American countries to improve their economies and to reduce poverty would be through the mounting of programs to raise the educational level of the large numbers of indigenous women in the labour force. The Andalucian education department in Spain launched a sex-discrimination investigation of the Opus Dei, a conservative organization of Roman Catholics, after that body organized a mathematics competition from which girls were excluded.

Higher Education. The successful record of the European Union (EU) in student and faculty exchanges between its 12 member nations since 1987 led to a planned $1,250,000,000 expansion of the effort for the period 1994–99. Two existing programs ("Erasmus" for one-year student exchanges and "Lingua" for foreign-language training abroad) would operate under a newly devised umbrella plan called "Socrates." Since Erasmus began in 1987, the number of participating students had grown 20% each year. In 1994 more than 100,000 students attended a European institution outside their own country through such programs. During the year the EU's experiment with facilitating the recognition of academic work abroad included 145 institutions in 18 countries.

A decade of major renovation in Denmark's system of higher education reached its final phase by 1994, after the architect of the reform, the minister of education and research, Bertel Haarder, left his post in 1993 to take a seat in the Folketing (parliament). During Haarder's tenure, the Education Ministry had returned decision-making powers to university rectors, linked the size of a university's budget to the number of degrees awarded, developed examinations for raising academic performance and eliminating weak students, and introduced internal and external monitoring procedures to foster academic quality. Enrollment in Sweden's colleges and universities reached a record of about 184,000 students in 1994, partly a result of funding policies that required each unit in the higher-education system to earn its annual budget by the number of students it enrolled and the number of academic credits they acquired. The policies were credited with motivating institutions to devise new ways of attracting and retaining students. To help cope with surging enrollments, the government authorized a second university for Stockholm, scheduled to open in 1995.

In its second year of operation, Japan's University of Aizu in 1994 enrolled 500 students taught by a multinational faculty—40% of the instructional staff from Japan and 60% from 14 other nations. The university was unique in offering only two curriculum choices—computer hardware and computer software. Its president, Tosiyasu I. Kunii, left his position as a prolific computer scientist at Tokyo University to establish the new university in an effort to stimulate creativity in computer design, which critics claimed had been missing among Japan's graduates in the past.

Pakistan's first independent think tank, the newly founded Sustainable Development Policy Institute, placed environmental concerns, social justice, and the quality of higher education as top-level issues for the immediate future. Among the initial projects was a plan to assist in founding a new private institution, Khaldunia University, which would emphasize the social sciences and humanities. The university was to be an elite institution open to talented youths from all social classes. Offerings would include a two-year master's degree program in environmental studies.

In many countries financial difficulties continued to frustrate university administrations and students alike. Faced with funding constraints and burgeoning enrollments, a growing number of German universities restricted the time students were permitted for pursuing an undergraduate degree. A law passed by the Berlin city government followed the lead of North Rhine-Westphalia in allowing no more than 9 semesters of attendance in most academic fields and 10 semesters in engineering and the natural sciences. At the same time, the federal government adopted stricter requirements for students receiving financial grants. The British government's new restrictions on the size of grants to institutions were expected to slow the sharp increase in university enrollments of recent years. Total enrollment during the fall term of 1994 reached a new high of over 1,140,000 students, 748,000 of whom attended full time. A survey revealed that more students than ever before had been forced to take jobs to help support themselves and pay for their education. At vocationally oriented universities up to one-third of the students were employed while pursuing their studies. Those attending Oxford and Cambridge were less likely to hold jobs.

Students in Portugal publicly protested what they viewed as weaknesses of the nation's institutions of higher education as compared with other European countries. Demonstrations by youths from the country's 11 universities and 13 polytechnics included campaigns against the ruling Social Democratic Party prior to midyear elections. The dissidents also condemned the government for linking fees to family income so that students from more affluent homes were now required to pay as much as $800 a year in tuition, compared with $8 two years earlier. The government of Ireland, on the other hand, planned to eliminate tuition in its seven universities within the next three years. During 1994, student fees ranged from about $2,250 to $3,300 a year, with only 40% of students receiving government aid. In Finland faculty members and students set aside a "Day of Outrage" to protest the government's 8% cut in the 1994 budget for the country's 20 colleges and universities, a decrease that extended funding reductions over the 1991–94 period to some 20%. The government announced that the economic recession was responsible for the cuts.

A 6% increase in four-year college tuitions in the United States in 1994, the smallest since 1989, brought the average annual cost at private colleges to $11,709 and at public institutions to $2,686. Private and public community colleges had smaller tuition increases, to $6,511 (up 5%) and $1,298 (4%), respectively.

A new approach to making college student loans in the United States went into effect during the year in 104 selected colleges. Some 1,000 institutions were expected to participate in the new plan in 1995. Touted as a way to save billions of dollars over time as fully implemented, the new procedure provided federal money directly to institutions, which in turn provided financial aid to students. In another economy move, a vigorous government drive resulted in a 15% drop in student-loan default rates. More than 440 institutions with high default rates for three consecutive years ran the risk of having their students become ineligible for loans, which could have a severe impact on those institutions' enrollments.

AmeriCorps also got under way in 1994. By 1996 the program would enable 100,000 volunteers to earn an average of $7,500 per year, plus child and health care if needed. Community service work could be done in areas such as education, social programs, environmental improvement, and public safety. Education vouchers for an additional $4,725 could be used both to pay off previous educational loans and for future expenses.

The German academic exchange service reported that foreign students were increasingly avoiding study opportunities in Germany because of that country's growing reputation for racist attacks on foreigners. Out of 800 overseas education grants allocated by the Turkish government in 1994,

for example, only 12 recipients chose to study in Germany, despite the country's large established population of Turks.

In Australia's institutions of higher education, women held only one-third of all faculty positions and one-tenth of posts at the rank of senior lecturer or above. To increase the number of women in senior positions, Edith Cowan University near Perth adopted a policy of awarding at least 40% of all 1994 faculty promotions to women. Kuwait University, newly restored from the damage inflicted by Iraqi military forces during the Gulf war of 1991, had broken with Islamic tradition in 1993 by appointing Faiza Muhammad al-Kharafi president, the first woman to hold such a post

A student at a for-profit school uses a computer to practice his basic skills. During the year private companies, which tended to rely more heavily on technology, continued to win contracts to run existing schools and to set up new schools in the U.S.
JEFFREY MACMILLAN—U.S. NEWS & WORLD REPORT

in an Arab nation. At Lucy Cavendish College for women in Britain's University of Cambridge, a clause in a contract for the construction of a dining hall forbade construction workers to whistle at, or otherwise harass, women students.

Former communist nations of Eastern Europe continued to renovate their systems of higher education. As a means of distancing themselves from Russian culture, all such institutions in Estonia and Latvia, for example, eliminated the practice of teaching many courses in Russian, as had been required during four decades of Soviet domination.

Institutions across the Arab world coped with a continuing anti-Western cultural campaign carried on by Islamic fundamentalist students and faculty members. Although Algerian authorities in the 1980s had given Islamists free rein in the universities, by 1994 they were banned from university campuses in order to prevent what authorities viewed as excessive interference with the proper conduct of education. The Egyptian government, in a similar move, expelled suspected fundamentalist radicals from university dormitories and began screening candidates for positions of student leadership. In such secular Arab states as Iraq, Libya, and Syria, tight government control over institutions of higher education prevented significant fundamentalist intrusion into university affairs.

A survey of 20,000 faculty members in 13 countries and Hong Kong revealed that a large proportion of scholars throughout the world thought their students came inade-

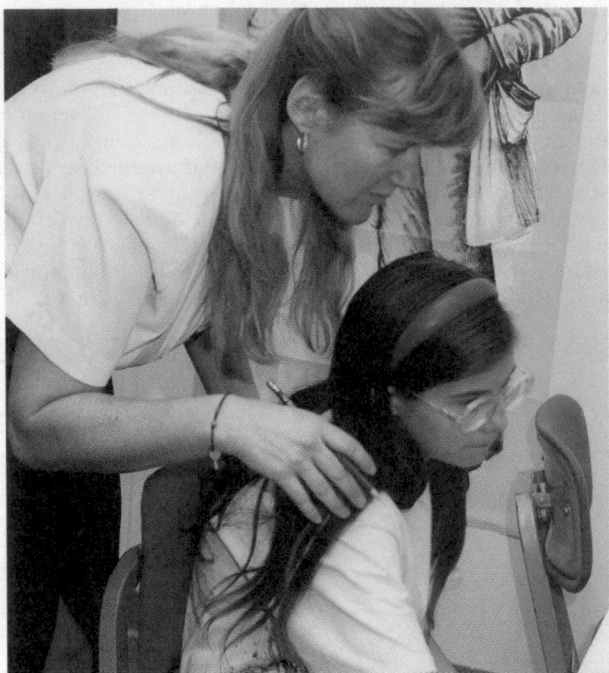

Sandra McBrayer, 1994 Teacher of the Year, helps a student in her self-contained classroom for grades 7–12 at the Homeless Outreach School in San Diego, Calif. The award is sponsored by Encyclopædia Britannica, Inc., and the Council of Chief State School Officers.

NATIONAL TEACHER OF THE YEAR PROGRAM; PHOTOGRAPH, BERT SEAL

quately prepared for university studies, their institution's administrators were often autocratic, their own salaries were inadequate, and respect for their profession was declining. The countries included Australia, Brazil, Chile, England, Germany, Israel, Japan, Mexico, The Netherlands, Russia, South Korea, Sweden, and the United States. While there was considerable agreement among scholars on some issues, marked differences between countries appeared on others. When asked about the freedom to pursue their own ideas, more than two-thirds of respondents in England, Japan, Sweden, and the United States said that they were satisfied, whereas fewer than 30% in Israel, Russia, and South Korea expressed such satisfaction. The proportion of participants rating the intellectual atmosphere at their institutions as "good" or "excellent" met or exceeded 60% in Brazil, The Netherlands, Russia, Sweden, and the United States but was under 40% in Chile, Japan, and South Korea. High ratings for the computer facilities at their institutions were given by at least 60% of respondents in Germany, Hong Kong, The Netherlands, Sweden, and the United States but by fewer than 30% in Brazil, Japan, Russia, and South Korea.

(JOEL L. BURDIN; ROBERT MURRAY THOMAS)

See also Law; Libraries.

This article updates the *Macropædia* articles History of EDU-CATION; TEACHING.

Energy

Petroleum. The price of oil was the dominant theme in the world energy sector in 1994. In February prices plummeted to five-year lows. The price of Brent Blend, a benchmark crude oil quoted on the London market, fell to just under $13 a barrel amid fears that an oil-price collapse was in the offing. At one stage some market analysts and oil traders were predicting that prices could fall to single-digit figures, something not seen since the oil-price collapse of 1986.

Prices, however, recovered steadily but slowly in the second and third quarters of the year. The Brent price reached its high for the year of about $19.40 a barrel during late July and early August, when strikes by oil workers led to a sharp cutback in exports from Nigeria. The average price for Brent Blend for the year was $15.86 per barrel, $1.15 below 1993's average. That put 1994 oil prices, on average, about the same in real terms as those before the first oil crisis in 1973.

The 12 members of OPEC tried to underpin prices by restricting their output. A production ceiling of 24,520,000 bbl a day had been set by OPEC oil ministers in September 1993. In meetings in March and June 1994, the ministers dropped their usual policy of trying to match OPEC output to short-term changes in worldwide oil demand. Instead, they agreed to freeze production in 1994 at the previously agreed-upon level in the hope that economic recovery in the main Western industrialized countries would result in higher oil demand.

In November OPEC decided to go along with the wishes of Saudi Arabia, its most influential member, and extend the production freeze for the whole of 1995, even though delegates admitted that such a course of action was unlikely to have any early impact on prices. A cut in production that might have boosted prices was never considered. OPEC ministers said they were reluctant to make any cuts in individual national quotas until Iraq, which was barred from exporting oil by UN sanctions, was readmitted to the production ceiling.

The inability of OPEC to exercise short-term influence over world oil markets was caused in large part by a surge in production from non-OPEC countries. The surge surprised OPEC officials, who were unable to agree on a strategy to counter its dampening effect on prices. The largest increases occurred in the Norwegian and British sectors of the North Sea, both of which set new production records during the year.

The surge in North Sea output reflected another trend that emerged in 1994—the growing ability of the oil industry to extend substantially the productive life of relatively mature oil provinces, such as the North Sea, or fields that had entered their decline, such as Prudhoe Bay in Alaska. Most industry experts had predicted that North Sea oil, first developed in the 1970s, would begin to run out by the mid-1990s. But the application of new technology enabled companies to get more oil out of individual fields and to tap smaller reservoirs that just a few years earlier had been thought to be uneconomic.

The technology, which had dramatically lowered production costs in a number of countries, included new three-dimensional seismic techniques that helped geologists to pick out the most promising areas in which to drill. Offshore wells could be drilled with horizontal sections several kilometres long. That eliminated the need to build additional platforms to tap small oil accumulations frequently found near bigger fields.

In the U.S. the new technology was enabling companies to explore beneath vast sheets of subsea salt, which until recently formed an impenetrable blanket over as much as 60% of the Gulf of Mexico, one of the richest U.S. oil- and natural gas-producing areas. In February a U.S. government auction of oil-exploration leases in the Gulf of Mexico resulted in record bids for "subsalt" acreage. Another rapidly developing technology allowed oil companies to exploit previously inaccessible oil deposits in very deep water far from shore. In April, Shell Oil Co. began producing oil from the Auger platform in 872 m (2,860 ft) of water in the Gulf of Mexico, a U.S. record.

In November the British government gave the go-ahead for the first development in a new oil province at the edge of the Atlantic Ocean, west of the Shetland Islands. Approval of the Foinaven field was likely to set off a flurry of interest in the region, which was thought to have reserves of about four billion barrels.

Much of the international interest was focused on promoting big projects in the former Soviet Union, despite continuing political uncertainty in the region. In December 46 countries signed the European Energy Charter, a treaty that established long-term ground rules for Western investment in the energy industries of the former Soviet Union and Eastern Europe. The U.S., however, declined to sign because it believed the charter failed to guarantee adequate protection for investors and fell below standards already obtained by the U.S. in bilateral and other multilateral investment agreements.

Projects in Russia announced during the year included a $9 billion plan by a consortium of Western oil companies to develop oil and gas deposits on the eastern side of Sakhalin Island. A Texaco-led consortium announced a 40-year, $40 billion project in the remote Timan Pechora Basin of Russia above the Arctic Circle. In September agreement was reached between a consortium led by British Petroleum and Amoco to develop three offshore oil fields in Azerbaijan's section of the Caspian Sea.

Few of the big Western projects in the former Soviet Union were proceeding smoothly. Those planned for Russia were held up by the lack of legislation establishing the legal rights of the Western partners. There were also officials within the Russian government who opposed large-scale Western participation in Russia's energy industries. But the Russian government did announce that foreigners would be able to buy shares in Lukoil, its biggest oil company, and Gazprom, the monopoly natural gas supplier that rivaled the Saudi Arabian state oil company as the world's largest producer of hydrocarbons.

Russia made it clear over the course of the year that it intended to participate in all big energy projects planned for the newly independent republics around the Caspian Sea. Lukoil took a 10% stake in the Azerbaijan project and was keen to participate in developments in Kazakhstan. Full development of the vast energy reserves of the Caspian Sea over the next few decades could alter the world pattern of energy trade.

Worldwide demand for oil increased by about one million barrels a day in 1994, but there was an important shift in world energy-consumption patterns. There was confirmation that China, one of the world's fastest-growing economies, had become a net oil importer for the first time since the early 1970s. Some analysts predicted that it would become a major oil importer by the year 2000, requiring as much as one million barrels a day of imported oil. A study published in April by the International Energy Agency and the Organisation for Economic Co-operation and Development (OECD) predicted that world consumption of energy in 2010 would be about 50% higher than in 1991 because of strong economic growth in China and elsewhere in Asia.

Environmental concerns and issues continued to play a large part in en-

ergy-sector development in 1994. Tough new rules imposing unlimited financial liability on oil tankers sailing into U.S. waters took effect at year's end. The new regulations were first proposed in the wake of the 1989 *Exxon Valdez* oil spill. Owners of tankers entering U.S. waters after December 28 would be required to show that they could provide unlimited compensation in the event of an oil spill.

An oil slick spilling from a pipeline near Usinsk in Russia's northern Komi Republic was the subject of widespread international publicity. It highlighted growing concerns that much of Russia's energy infrastructure, especially the pipelines that ran through environmentally sensitive areas such as the Arctic, were well below international standards. (*See also* WORLD AFFAIRS: *Arctic Regions.*)

U.S. oil companies spent much of the year preparing for the introduction on Jan. 1, 1995, of reformulated gasoline, the biggest change in motor-fuel specifications since unleaded gasoline was introduced in the 1970s. Only nine of the most polluted U.S. cities would be required to use the fuel, but a number of other metropolitan areas joined the program voluntarily. An estimated 90 million Americans lived in the areas where the fuel would be on sale.

In the European Union (EU) representatives from the European Commission, the executive branch of the organization, and the European oil and automobile industries began studying new fuel formulas and possible changes to car designs that might result in lower emissions of a wide variety of pollutants.

Natural Gas. Another major trend in 1994 was the emergence of natural gas as the world's fastest-growing fossil fuel. Gas was increasingly viewed as the least polluting fossil fuel and was one of the most efficient fuels for producing electricity when burned in combined cycle power plants. In the U.S. high natural gas prices at the beginning of the year caused a surge in production that helped offset the country's growing dependence on imported oil.

Elsewhere, a large number of new gas projects were put forward. In November Exxon announced a $40 billion plan to develop the giant Natuna field off Indonesia over the next 30 years. Other proposals made during the year included a plan to build an undersea pipeline to ship gas

DANIEL BELTRA—GAMMA LIAISON

Turbines whir on a large wind farm in Tarifa, Spain. Such farms were being increasingly used in Europe to generate electricity. Although the turbines produced no pollution, some people objected to them on the grounds that they were noisy, unsightly, and possibly dangerous to birds.

from Oman to India. Construction began on a new pipeline linking Algeria with Spain, and agreement was reached on the construction of a gas pipeline linking Britain with the continental European gas grid.

The British government also approved plans to introduce competition into the country's domestic gas market in one of the most ambitious public utility liberalization plans put forward by any industrialized country.   (ROBERT CORZINE)

Coal. World hard coal production in 1994 was estimated at 3,456,000,000 metric tons, about 30 million tons higher than in 1993. In the final months of 1994, the international coal industry saw its fortunes beginning to turn for the better. After years of depression and falling prices, an uptrend was apparent.

In the U.S., record production of 928.8 million metric tons (1,032,000,000 short tons) was projected. Coal's share of the U.S. power-generation market was expected to rise from 57% to 60% by the end of the century. Coal production in Canada also rebounded, while exports from the new producers in the hemisphere, Colombia and Venezuela, continued to grow. Australia continued as the world's leading coal exporter, shipping about 130 million tons in 1994, or 30% of the world market share. China, with 1,154,000,-000 tons of raw hard coal production in 1994, remained the world's leading producer—and consumer.

In Europe the decline of the coal industry continued unabated. In the U.K. the privatization of the British coal industry was completed with the sale of most of its remaining mines to RJB Mining. Hard coal production fell in all other EU countries and in former Soviet bloc states, with the exception of Poland.   (ROBERT J.M. WYLLIE)

Nuclear. Data for 1993, released by the International Atomic Energy Agency (IAEA) in 1994, showed that there were 430 nuclear power units in operation in 29 countries, with a total capacity of 330,651 MW. This was a net growth of 6 units, and a rise of 7,169 MW in total capacity, compared with the previous year. There were 55 units under construction in 18 countries, of which 6 began during the year. A total of 68 units were shut down, 19 units were suspended, and 65 projects were canceled. Worldwide, nuclear plants produced almost 2.1 billion MWh (megawatt hours) of electricity during 1993. Over half the national production of electricity was by nuclear power in Lithuania (87.2%), France (77.7%), Belgium (58.9%), and Slovakia (53.6%). The average nuclear power contribution in all the OECD countries was 24%.

Although Lithuania's dependence on nuclear power was the highest in the world in percentage terms, the total capacity was only 2,370 MW. This was very low compared with the 59,033 MW on-line in France. Electricité de France announced that no new nuclear plant orders would be placed for at least five years owing to the improved performance of existing plant and lower-than-expected growth in demand.

This announcement was another blow for the future of the French-German European pressurized-water reactor, the prototype for a new generation of plants in France and Germany. Germany, in the runup to its October general election, introduced legislation demanding that in any new nuclear project in the country, the effects of any accident create no dangers outside the site. While ostensibly keeping the option for new nuclear capacity active, proving a negative capability such as this was regarded as a virtual impossibility and would present a severe obstacle to the new design being introduced in Germany.

A similar impasse had arisen in the U.S. Continued delays in the designation of sites for disposal of nuclear waste led to lawsuits by groups of utilities and states against the U.S. Department of Energy, which would not be able to begin ac-

cepting irradiated nuclear fuel by January 1998, as required under the Nuclear Waste Policy Act. Only one disposal site was being considered—at Yucca Mountain, Nevada—but it could not possibly be ready by the 1998 date.

The best prospects for new nuclear projects were seen to be in the Far East. The Chinese market was increasingly important for the French nuclear industry. China entered a new agreement with the French firm Framatome on the joint design of a 600-MW unit. Construction of the first nuclear reactor in the world for district heating had already begun at Daqing (Ta-ch'ing) in northern China. Japan had one of the most rapidly growing nuclear power programs in the world, with an installed capacity of 38,029 MW at the beginning of the year that accounted for 31% of the national production of electricity in 1993. However, strong reaction, both at home and abroad, to plans for recycling plutonium from power reactors resulted in a revised long-term program by the country's Atomic Energy Commission. The Monju prototype fast-breeder reactor was set to reach full power late in 1995, but the start of construction of two demonstration commercial-scale fast-breeder prototypes had been put back some 10 years.

The Superphénix fast-breeder reactor in France began its return to power after a four-year shutdown following a failure of part of the liquid-sodium cooling system. This joint international project had been reclassified as a research reactor, but it would still produce and sell electricity to recoup some of the costs of the project. The reactor would be used to prove the viability of fast breeders and their use in the destruction of long-lived actinides, particularly plutonium, americium, and neptunium.

International pressure grew for a complete shutdown of all the Chernobyl units in Ukraine so that work could concentrate on repairing or replacing the sarcophagus on the destroyed Unit 4. An IAEA review of the Chernobyl station found numerous safety deficiencies in the two units in operation and continued deterioration in the Unit 4 sarcophagus. Despite these warnings, Ukraine, under the pressure of power shortages, insisted on continued operation and lifted the moratorium on the construction on other sites. (*See* WORLD AFFAIRS: *Ukraine.*)

India's government put nuclear energy expansion plans on hold as a result of the continuing long delays in construction. The Atomic Energy Corporation's Rs 80 billion expansion plan for Tarapur was among the projects deferred owing to lack of funds. Cost increases for the seven existing projects had been disastrous; the original Rs 30.2 billion estimate had risen beyond Rs 63.6 billion.

Nuclear Electric, the state-owned nuclear utility for England and Wales, published its best-ever annual results, including an 11% increase in output, a reduction in costs, and a 20% increase in operating profit. The company's chairman said that such results proved the company could compete with the privatized power companies and thus had earned the right to join them.   (RICHARD A. KNOX)

See also Business and Industry Review; Engineering Projects; Mining; Transportation.

This article updates the *Macropædia* articles ENERGY CONVERSION; FOSSIL FUELS.

Engineering Projects

BRIDGES

As the decade of the 1990s reached its midpoint, the limits to bridge design were being stretched both for main spans and for the total lengths of crossing. Multiple-span bridges of up to 60 km (1 km = 0.62 mi) in length were proposed for sea and estuary crossings, and several of about 20 km were under construction.

Nonetheless, it was in Europe, at France's Pont de Normandie, that the limits of engineering were challenged in 1994. When its central 856-m (1 m = 3.3 ft) cable-stayed span was completed in midyear, it increased by 40% the world record for this type of structure. The bridge was due to open to road traffic early in 1995, linking Le Havre westward along France's north coast over the Seine estuary.

Dramatic advances bring problems, and much-feared vibration effects were noted in the nearly completed bridge in steady wind conditions. Special spring dampers had already been necessary to stabilize the lightweight-steel central deck during the erection of its sections, and now permanent

Notable Engineering Projects
(in work or completed, 1994)

Name	Location	Year of completion	Notes
Airports		**Area**	
Chek Lap Kok	near Lantau Island, Hong Kong	1,248 ha	1997	Artificial island, terminal, bridge, tunnel links
Kansai/Kanku International Airport	Osaka, Japan		1994	Artificial island, terminal, rail terminal, bridge
Aqueduct		**Length (km)**	
Lesotho Highlands Water Project	Lesotho	82	2020	Supply water and power to South Africa
Bridges		**Length (m)**	
Akashi-Kaikyo	Kobe, Honshu, Japan	1,990	1998	World extreme (suspension)
Store Baelt (Great Belt)	Great Belt (Channel), Denmark	1,624	1996	World extreme (suspension)
Tsing Ma	Ma Wan-Tsing Yi islands, Hong Kong	1,377	1997	World extreme (double-deck)
Thai-Lao Friendship	Laos-Thailand	1,174	1994	First bridge over lower Mekong R.
Pont de Normandie	Le Havre, France	856	1995	World extreme (cable-stayed)
Trans-Tokyo Bay Highway Bridge	Kisarazu, Japan	590		Structure compl. Oct. 1994
Kap Shui Mun	Lantau-Ma Wan islands, Hong Kong	430	1997	Double-deck (road/rail)
Tagus II	Lisbon, Portugal	420	1998	Cable-stayed main span; 18-km approaches
Buildings		**Height (m)**	
Chongqing (Chungking) Tower	Chongqing, China	460	1997	World extreme; 114 stories
Petronas Towers (twin towers)	Kuala Lumpur, Malaysia	450	1996	Twin towers; 88 stories inhabitable space
Vegas World Stratosphere Tower	Las Vegas, Nev., U.S.	308	1995	Observation tower
Dams		**Crest length (m)**	
Yacyretá-Apipe	Paraná River, Argentina-Paraguay	69,600	1998	Hydroelectric power, navigation, irrigation
Gabcikovo (Hrusov-Dunakiliti)	Danube River, Hungary-Slovakia	31,500		Environmental controversy
Caruachi	Caroni River, Venezuela	4,320	2003	
Three Gorges	Chang Jiang (Yangtze River), China	1,983	2009	Flood control, 1,130,000 persons displaced
Sardar Sarovar	Narmada River, India	1,202	1994	100,000 persons to be displaced
Xingó	São Francisco River, Brazil	850	1994	Commercial power generation began Dec. 1994
Seven Oaks	Santa Ana River, U.S.	802		
Longtan	Hong Shui River, China	800		5,400 MW; flood control; navigation
Ertan	Yalong River, China	763	1998	2nd largest hydro power proj. in China
Katse	Malibamatso, Lesotho	700	1996	Part of Lesotho Highlands Water Project
Cipasang	Cimanuk River, Indonesia	640		
Highway		**Length (km)**	
Guangzhou-Shenzhen (Canton–Shen-chen)	China	120	1994	Expressway
Railways		**Length (km)**	
Konkan	Southwest coastal route, India	760	1995	83 tunnels, 143 major bridges
Guangzhou-Shenzhen	China	147	1994	China's first high-speed route
Subways		**Length (km)**	
Seoul Metro (extensions)	Seoul, South Korea	145	1997	
Taipei	Taipei, Taiwan	55	1995	
Pusan Metro (Line 2 extension)	Pusan, South Korea	39	1996	Phase 1: 22.4 km, phase 2: 16.7 km
Dallas	Dallas, Texas, U.S.	32	1996	Light Rail
Taegu Metro (Line 1)	Taegu, South Korea	28	1997	
Saint Petersburg Metro (extensions)	St. Petersburg, Russia	23		First part to open late 1994
Inchon Metro	Inchon, South Korea	23	1998	
Medellin Metro	Medellín, Colombia	23	1995	
Warsaw	Warsaw, Poland	23	1995	
Athens Metro (extensions)	Athens, Greece	18	1998	Red: 0.2 km, Blue: 8.4 km
Buenos Aires (Tren de la Costa)	Buenos Aires, Arg.	15	1995	Rehab of line closed in 1961
Tunnels		**Length (m)**	
NEAT (Saint Gotthard)	Switzerland	57,000		NEAT = Neue Eisenbahn Alpen Transversale
Channel Tunnel (Eurotunnel)	Sangatte-Cheriton, France-U.K.	50,000	1994	
NEAT (Bern-Lötschberg-Simplon)	Switzerland	38,000		NEAT = Neue Eisenbahn Alpen Transversale
Italy, north of Bolzano	near Bolzano, Italy	13,159	1994	
Trans-Tokyo Bay I	Tokyo, Japan	9,300	1997	World's widest undersea tunnels (14.1 m)
Trans-Tokyo Bay II	Tokyo, Japan	9,000	1997	World's widest undersea tunnels (14.1 m)
Store Baelt (twin)	Great Belt, Denmark	8,000	1995	Breakthrough Oct. 15, 1994
Saint Clair	Sarnia-Port Huron, Canada-U.S.	1,800		

A crew works in July to complete the final 2.7-m (9-ft) section of the Normandy Bridge across the estuary of the Seine River, shortening the southern coastal route to Le Havre, France. At 856 m (2,808 ft), the structure was the longest cable-stayed bridge in the world.
PETER REINA

shock absorbers were being fitted. These attached to the 24 longest cables to quell "ripple vibrations" visible along the cables in wind. There were also special cross-connecting wires between cables, another unusual feature of the bridge.

The Akashi-Kaikyo Bridge in Japan was beginning to show its enormous size as the 230-m-high twin steel towers were completed, dwarfing tankers and other vessels passing through the Akashi Strait. The diagonally braced towers were to start receiving the cables that would eventually suspend a 1,990-m-long central span, easily the longest in the world, upon the bridge's completion in 1998. The Store Bælt (Great Belt) suspension bridge, planned to have a world-record central span of 1,624 m, was part of a major rail and road bridge-and-tunnel link joining Denmark's islands to mainland Jutland. Huge concrete caissons sunk in the sea in 1993 between Zealand Island and a small island, Sprogo, were filled with concrete and by the end of 1994 supported the rising concrete shape of the main piers for the bridge as well as its anchor blocks. Cable spinning for the bridge was scheduled to begin in 1995.

Another world record was expected to be established earlier in Hong Kong, where the British were racing to finish a new airport on Landao (Lantau) Island before they handed Hong Kong back to China in 1997. Linking the airport to Hong Kong itself were to be two major bridges: the Kap Shui Mun, a 430-m cable-stayed main span with concrete piers that had begun to rise in 1994, and the Tsing Ma suspension bridge. Both were twin-decked, carrying a six-lane expressway above and a double-track rail link below, with additional road lanes, making the 1,377-m span of the Tsing Ma the longest double-deck bridge in the world. Designed to resist typhoon winds, it would also be the heaviest. Dramatic cable-spinning operations to form the 1.1-m-diameter cables were about half complete as 1994 ended.

China was the location of much bridge-building activity, with an 888-m suspension bridge going up across the Zhu Jiang (Pearl River) at Humen, a 400-m cable-stay bridge in central Wuhan across the Chang Jiang (Yangtze River), and a 900-m central span suspension bridge for the Three Gorges power-generation dam project, also across the Chang Jiang. The Yangpu Bridge, completed at the end of 1993 in Shanghai, at 602 m was the world's longest cable-stay.

Japan was also venturing into very long crossings, having already completed two multibridge links between the islands of Honshu and Shikoku, with the Akashi part of a third. Japan was also considering a 42-km structure across the La Perouse Strait from its northern island, Hokkaido, to Russia's Sakhalin Island. A second seven-kilometre bridge would link Sakhalin to the mainland.

Other major projects included Portugal's second Tagus River crossing at Lisbon. With three major viaducts and a central cable-stay bridge, it was to total 18 km in length. In Bangladesh work began on the 4.8-km Jamuna multipurpose cable bridge. In both these projects huge and very deep piles were required for coping with deep soft ground.

Wider bridges were also a feature of the 1990s. In Cologne, Germany, extra width was created for the 567-m-long Rodenkirchen suspension bridge. A third pier with a third cable was added to broaden the bridge from four road lanes to six plus two cycle lanes.   (ADRIAN LEE GREEMAN)

BUILDINGS

The new Kansai International Airport in Japan was opened in September 1994, marking the completion of one of the world's most ambitious construction projects. The airport complex was situated on a 4.5 x 2.5-km man-made island 5 km offshore in Osaka Bay. It included a railway station, shopping centre, and maintenance hangars, among other facilities, but it was the main terminal building for which the airport was best known. This building was commissioned on the basis of an international architectural competition held in 1988, and the result was a tribute to international cooperation. A central area comprising arrival and departure halls, baggage handling, and concessions measured 300 x 160 m. The aircraft were parked on either side of two 700-m-long fingers extending beyond the central area, giving a total length of 1.7 km. The most obvious feature of the terminal building was its roof, which stretched across the 160-m expanse and included an 80-m clear-span asymmetrical arch. The arch comprised triangular tubular trusses, supported on splayed column legs. The cladding envelope had strips of top glazing parallel to the trusses, and there were huge 20-m-high curved-glass facades facing the airside of the terminal.

The air-conditioning for the new airport terminal comprised a large-scale system for background climate control augmented by small systems around the check-in desks, waiting areas, and the like. The large system involved blowing air more than 80 m across the uninterrupted main span. In order for this to be achieved, the tendency of a jet of air to cling to a surface was utilized. The shape of the arched roof was especially designed to suit the path of the trajectory of air from a nozzle in free space and was intended to ensure the adequate mixing of cool and warm air without the forming of downdrafts.

Another interesting engineering feature concerned foundation conditions. The seabed was underlain by soft alluvial clay that consolidated under load by the gradual squeezing out of water from the weight of the island and its buildings. During the construction of the artificial island, vertical sand drains through the alluvial clay were formed to allow more rapid drainage and, therefore, accelerate the consolidation process. Nevertheless, long-term settlement was still expected, and for this reason the entire building was arranged to permit future adjustment of level by the jacking of each column position.

The world's tallest buildings in 1994 were being built in Asia. The Sears Tower in Chicago, at 443 m in height, was about to be exceeded by both the Petronas Towers in Kuala Lumpur, Malaysia, and the Chongqing Tower in Chongqing (Chungking), China, at 450 m and 460 m, respectively. The Petronas Towers project comprised two step-tapered towers clad in stainless steel and glass, circular in plan. The towers were to be linked to one another by a bridge at the 44th floor. The Chongqing project was a single 114-story building, partly offices and partly hotel. These two developments were planned for completion in 1996 and 1997, respectively.

At Manchester, England, a velodrome (cycle track) was completed, and construction of an associated arena with a seating capacity of 16,500 was well under way. This was being built on the site of the Victoria railway station, which formerly had 17 platforms and was the gateway to the north of England but had been converted to a commuter station with only four platforms. The station had to be remodeled to allow the arena to be built, and this work included the construction of a one-metre-thick transfer structure over the main station. This both protected the station during the construction and formed the base to one side of the arena structure.

Noise from the trains into the arena was limited by sound-attenuation measures in the structure, and the railway track was supported on rubber antivibration mountings. The arena was oval in plan, with seating in two tiers of 16 rows each, formed in precast concrete. The roof spanned the full 104-m width and took the form of a series of bowstring girders. These were lattice-framed girders having a horizontal bottom member and a circular-arc top member, with vertical and diagonal bracing members between them.

(GEOFFREY M. PINFOLD)

DAMS

Throughout the world more than 1,100 dams exceeding 15 m in height were under construction in 1994, with about 350 being completed annually. Countries with the most dam construction under way were: China 275, Turkey 164, Japan 149, South Korea 109, and the U.S. 46.

The construction of huge dams disrupts the natural surroundings. Not only do such dams affect the local river ecology, but their impact is much greater when they force thousands of river valley inhabitants to be relocated. In China the Three Gorges Dam on the Chang Jiang (Yangtze River) would require the dislocation of more than 750,000 people. China prepared a plan to mitigate the impact by spreading the relocation moves over a 20-year period. The flooded narrow valley would be on average 1.1 km wide, only twice the width of the original river channel, and would be 600 km long. When completed, it would eliminate the disastrous floods that had taken many lives, make water available where none previously existed, provide an expanding fishing industry, and expand industries that would provide new employment.

China's State Planning Committee announced the approval of 17 new hydroelectric projects, which were needed to add 20,000 MW to the industrial power network. Approximately 3,000 MW were added to the power system.

The resettlement issue at Sardar Sarovar Dam in India was being muted by the increased employment it provided and by the expectation of irrigation and power benefits. It was designed to ensure water supply to 5,614 villages and 130 small towns that had suffered water shortages. Because of the lack of water, the area experienced crop losses valued at $200 million.

In Ethiopia two dams were started to provide water for irrigation and to produce power to meet shortages. A dam on the Omo River was to be a 79-m-high rolled-compacted-concrete dam. Water would also be diverted through tunnels to another 80-m-high dam on the Den River. The project was designed to develop 270 MW of power.

In former East Germany, which had 72 dams, an intensive program of rehabilitation was initiated, and work was begun on the Schmalwasser embankment dam, which at 81 m high was the region's tallest. A five-year program involving 17 dams was adopted.

In Iran eight dams—Torog, Kardeh, Jiroft, Pishin, Chogakhov, Saveh, Khordad, and Barun—were completed under the five-year plan. These dams would furnish water for irrigation and supply the needs of cities. Twenty-two dams were under construction, and 19 were in the planning stage during the year.

In France the environmentalists scored a victory by persuading the government to demolish a dam at Maisons Rouges on the Vienne River to allow passage of migratory salmon. A second dam at St. Etienne du Vigan on the Allier River was also considered for demolition. Peruca Dam in Croatia, damaged during the Balkan conflict, was undergoing rehabilitation. The major work involved the reconstruction of both ends of the dam and reinforcement of the damaged portion of the tunnels.

The Vanch Dam in Tajikistan on the Pyandzh River failed after heavy rains, as did Belaya River Dam in Bashkortostan, a republic in the Russian Federation. The latter failed because the floodgates became inoperative and failed to release the incoming floodwaters. Some 55 people were reported missing, and about 150 houses were swept away. The dam was built in 1949. Several governments addressed the subject of dam safety by adopting regulations governing the design, construction, and maintenance of dams. Annual inspections required all floodgates to be operable and ready to release flood inflows when needed. Records of leakage were maintained, and many instruments were being added to monitor the dam behaviour in the interest of dam safety.

(T.W. MERMEL)

ROADS

The Jan. 17, 1994, earthquake that hit Los Angeles had a devastating effect on the highway network of the world's most motorized city. Three major highways were closed by the collapse of a number of elevated sections. These included the Santa Monica Freeway (Interstate 10), the busiest commuter road in the U.S., carrying more than 300,000 vehicles per day.

Rebuilding efforts began immediately, with the California Department of Transportation providing for substantial bonuses to be paid for early completion and similar penalties for delays. The result was that many rebuilding projects were completed weeks ahead of schedule, bringing relief to drivers and boosting profits of contractors. Officials stated soon after the earthquake that they hoped most roads would be reopened before the end of the year. In fact, the reconstruction was largely completed by the summer. The total repair bill was estimated at $1.4 billion.

New road-construction projects throughout the world were increasingly being financed and developed by private-sector companies instead of governments. A report by the International Bridge, Tunnel, and Turnpike Association stated that, worldwide, 45,000 km of toll highways valued at $120 billion were planned.

A new six-lane highway in Argentina, the Buenos Aires West Access toll road, was announced. The 23-km route would cost $115 million and would be scheduled to open in August 1996. This was one of many build-operate-transfer (BOT) road projects, which were to be constructed by private companies or consortia. The builders would then charge tolls for a concession period before handing ownership of the road over to the national government. BOT concessions typically lasted for 20–35 years.

The first BOT highway in China was opened in July. The Guangzhou–Shenzhen (Canton–Shen-chen) superhighway was 120 km long and was built in only two years by a Hong Kong-based developer. The highway linked two of the fastest-growing urban areas in China and was built largely on elevated structures. The developer was also granted rights to property development along the highway's corridor, which was expected to provide more revenue than the actual road tolls.

The contractual dispute that arose in 1993 between the government of Thailand and the Japanese-led consortium that had built an expressway in Bangkok was settled when the government took over the project. The experience led 23 international banks that had loaned $250 million to the project to withdraw their support and demand repayment of the money.

The growth in toll-road projects was mirrored by developments in toll-collection technology. In Germany and France trials were under way to test systems that would allow motorists to be charged for road use without stopping at a conventional toll booth. Most of these systems used stored-value "smart cards" containing a computer chip; these were mounted in a transmitter unit. These cards would communicate with roadside hardware at high speed, recording transactions. This technology would also allow "congestion pricing," whereby motorists were charged higher tolls at busier times. Germany and the United Kingdom were planning to convert their expressways from free use to tolls.

In response to growing congestion and pollution, the Swiss canton of Uri voted to ban all foreign truck traffic traveling through the Alps. Foreign trucks would be required to travel on railroad trains through the country.

In order to discourage private motoring, a U.K. Royal Commission on transportation recommended that the government's $30 billion road-building program be abandoned and the money spent on developing public transportation. It also recommended that fuel prices be doubled. The government had previously announced a reappraisal of its road-building plans.   (RUSS SWAN)

TUNNELS

Significant successes and serious setbacks characterized tunneling in 1994. Both of these situations were best illustrated on the troubled Store Bælt railway tunnel in Denmark, where the breakthrough of the first of the twin tube tunnels in October was overshadowed by a serious fire in the parallel tunnel in June. Fortunately, the fire did not cause any injury, but it did cause extensive damage to the tunnel-boring machine (TBM) as well as to a 10-m length of tunnel, particularly in the crown, where up to 300 mm (12 in) of the 400-mm (16-in)-thick precast concrete segmental lining was chipped away. The fire, suspected to have been caused by oil vapour escaping from a pinprick hole in a hydraulic hose, occurred when only 1% of the two 8-km tunnels remained to be bored and followed earlier problems, including mechanical difficulties, a devastating flood, and excessive wear of the cutting tools and TBM bodies. As a result, costs increased substantially, and completion was delayed by more than 12 months.

Serious tunnel collapses occurred on two projects using the New Austrian Tunneling Method (NATM) in soft ground and clay. In Munich, Germany, in September, two tunnel workers and a woman passenger died when a bus fell into a hole created when NATM tunneling beneath the road for a new section of the Munich subway collapsed. A few weeks later in London, the collapse of an NATM excavation for an underground station on the high-speed rail-link project between Heathrow Airport and London's Paddington Station caused subsidence damage to an airport building and left a large hole in a main airport access road.

After completion of only 480 m of the 1,800-m-long railway tunnel under the St. Clair River between Sarnia, Ont., and Port Huron, Mich., TBM excavation was halted so a bearing seal failure could be repaired before work under the river proceeded. The TBM was driven into a temporary shaft to remove the machine's cutting wheel and main bearing, causing a delay of a few months.

Meanwhile, major engineering successes were being celebrated. On May 6 Queen Elizabeth II of Great Britain and Pres. François Mitterrand of France inaugurated the Channel Tunnel (Eurotunnel or, more popularly, "Chunnel") under the English Channel. Tunnels, bridges, and other means of spanning the narrow body of water that separates (or joins—see SPECIAL REPORT: *Seafaring and History in the English Channel*) England and continental Europe had been dreamed about for centuries. Construction of the 50-km project took six years, and the final cost was over £10 billion in privately raised funds. Three tunnels, two for rail traffic and a central service tunnel, were bored at an average depth of 40 m through the chalk layer underlying the Channel. Whatever else may have delayed full operation of the Eurotunnel for more than a year and a half, it was not tunnel excavation. The removal of the almost 8 million cu m (282.5 million cu ft) of material to create the total 151.5 km of tunnel was completed in June 1991, slightly ahead of schedule.

In Lesotho the last of four TBMs working on the Lesotho Highlands Water Project broke through in October. More than 60 km of the total 82 km of five-metre-diameter tunneling required on the first phase of this massive project was completed by the four TBMs in Lesotho between February 1992 and October 1994. The project was designed to meet rapidly increasing demand for drinking water in the Johannesburg and Pretoria urban areas in South Africa.

Record speeds of advance were achieved in Australia when a 3.4-m-diameter Robbins Mk 12 TBM used to excavate the 13.4-km tunnel for the Blue Mountains Sewage Transfer project west of Sydney excavated a remarkable 2,300 m of tunnel in a production month.

Elsewhere, tunneling started beneath the centre of Paris to create the new Meteor Line of the Métro system. In Japan the first of eight huge 14.14-m-diameter soft-ground TBMs was launched on the Trans-Tokyo Bay Highway Project. In the U.S. tunneling continued on several projects, including the Los Angeles subway, the Dallas, Texas, light-rail system, the Boston Harbor sewer-tunnel project, and the Portland, Ore., light-rail system.   (SHANI WALLIS)

This article updates the *Macropædia* articles BUILDING CONSTRUCTION; PUBLIC WORKS.

Environment

INTERNATIONAL AND NATIONAL ACTIVITIES

International Cooperation. Efforts continued throughout 1994 to implement agreements made at the 1992 UN Conference on Environment and Development, or Earth Summit, held in Rio de Janeiro. The June 1994 deadline for drawing up the desertification treaty and action plan called for in Agenda 21 was not met, but the convention was agreed and signed in October. The UN General Assembly had agreed that priority should be given to Africa, but countries of Latin America and Asia refused to accept this, and the nations likely to provide most of the financing were uneasy about the open-ended nature of the plans being submitted.

At a meeting in December 1993, European Union (EU) environment ministers agreed to ratify the UN Convention on Climate Change after six members withdrew their objection that ratification would be hypocritical in the absence of a carbon and energy tax. The tax was opposed by the U.K., and at a meeting in Luxembourg on Oct. 5, 1994, the British secretary of state for the environment, John Gummer, reiterated his government's rejection of it, even though the chairman, Germany's Klaus Töpfer, suggested a compromise that would permit governments to raise existing fuel and energy taxes rather than introduce new ones.

An International Conference on Chemical Safety, held in Stockholm April 25–29 under UN auspices, was attended by delegations from 130 countries. Arising from Agenda 21, it aimed to find ways of policing the trade, use, and disposal of toxic substances. An International Forum on Chemical Safety was established as an instrument to integrate and consolidate efforts to promote chemical safety.

Countries participating in the Global Environment Facility (GEF) were presented with the recommendations of a study they had commissioned to evaluate its work at a meeting in Cartagena, Colombia, in December 1993. The study concluded that GEF activities should be suspended, control removed from the World Bank, and an independent secretariat appointed. The main criticism was of a lack of agreement between industrialized and less developed countries (LDCs) on the purpose and strategy of the GEF and the linking of projects to development schemes run by the same dominant institutions. The talks in Cartagena broke down over disagreements about the composition and chairmanship of the 30-member executive council. It was agreed to refresh GEF funds by $2 billion when negotiations were finally completed in March 1994.

Antarctica. In July François Goutorbe, director of the Institute for Polar Research and Study, told Greenpeace International that France had abandoned plans to build a landing strip near its Dumont d'Urville base on the Adélie Coast, on which about $22 million had already been spent, but it was considering renovating the small existing strip for the use of light aircraft. In January a large piece of the Astrolabe glacier had fallen into the sea, causing a huge wave that engulfed the 1,100-m (3,600-ft) runway, washed away a service road, and pushed boulders onto the runway. The area was important for wildlife.

United States. In October 1993 Pres. Bill Clinton published his 50-point plan to reduce U.S. emissions of greenhouse gases by 100 million tons. The plan relied on voluntary measures, such as greater energy efficiency in homes and electrical appliances, increased reliance on hydroelectric power, reduction of power-plant emissions, and tree planting. It made no attempt to reduce car emissions and was criticized by environmental groups for failing to set

targets. In July 1994 Carol Browner, Environmental Protection Agency (EPA) administrator, told a meeting of the President's Council on Sustainable Development that the EPA planned to allocate half its annual research budget to long-term research. This would direct more of its funds to universities and would improve standards of peer review.

In late July the House of Representatives joined the Senate in passing the California desert protection bill. The legislation, which was the largest U.S. land-conservation measure since 1980, had been debated for eight years. It was expected to protect some 3.2 million ha (8 million ac) of desert and more than 2,000 species of plants and animals.

Hearings relating to the 1989 *Exxon Valdez* oil spill in Prince William Sound commenced in Anchorage, Alaska, in May. The plaintiffs sought $1.5 billion in compensation from Exxon Corp. and the ship's captain, Joseph Hazelwood. In June the jury found in favour of the plaintiffs, and in September, in one of the largest awards in legal history, it ordered Exxon to pay $5 billion in punitive damages to a group of up to 34,000 fishermen, native Alaskans, and others for harm they had suffered. Hazelwood was also ordered to pay $5,000 in damages.

United Kingdom. During the early part of 1994, most environmental interest centred on the Thermal Oxide Reprocessing Plant (Thorp) for spent reactor fuel at Sellafield, Cumbria, England. It was reported in December 1993 that 63% of the 42,500 people who responded to a government request for comments on the desirability of the facility were opposed to it. Most objected to increased radioactive discharges and the lack of a fresh public inquiry. On December 15 Gummer announced in the House of Commons that permission had been granted for Thorp to commence operations and that the discharges permitted would not lead to unacceptable risks to human health or to the environment. Greenpeace and the Lancashire County Council applied in the High Court for orders that would block authorization of the plant, on the grounds that Gummer acted unlawfully and wholly unreasonably in failing to hold a public inquiry, but on March 4 their application was rejected. Thorp had already commenced operating on January 17. Following the High Court hearing, Thorp's operator, British Nuclear Fuels, Ltd., announced that reprocessing would start within one month.

Concern also grew over pollution caused by road traffic. In May the Expert Panel on Air Quality Standards recommended a maximum level for ozone of 50 ppb (parts per billion) measured over eight hours. Monitoring stations had recorded ozone levels exceeding the recommended limit on up to 83 days a year in southeastern England. For this target to be met, emissions of nitrogen oxides would have to be reduced by more than 95% and volatile organic compounds by 75–85%. The report of a two-year study by the Royal Commission on Environmental Pollution, published in September, concluded that the projected doubling of the number of cars over the next 30 years would cause unacceptable environmental damage.

The Inspectorate of Pollution received 524 complaints about industrial processes, a 60% increase, which its director, David Slater, welcomed as indicating that it was becoming better known. Following a U.S. report on health risks associated with dioxin, Slater announced a review of U.K. emissions and hinted that emission standards might have to be tightened.

Western Europe. Environment ministers from EU countries agreed to a directive on packaging waste on Dec. 16, 1993. Within five years of the directive's coming into force, probably by 2000, 25–45% of packaging waste would

(continued on page 187)

Save the Tiger

At the beginning of the 20th century, even though tigers had been hunted for at least a thousand years, there were still an estimated 100,000 of them living in the wild. As the century drew to a close, however, it was feared that there were only 5,000–7,500 left in the world. (*See* Map.) Until relatively recently tigers had been prized as trophies and as a source of skins for expensive coats. Tigers were also killed on the grounds that they posed a danger to humans. In the 1970s the sport of tiger hunting was banned in most countries where tigers ranged, and the trade in tiger skins was outlawed. Censuses of tigers in the 1980s showed their numbers to be increasing, and it appeared that conservation efforts had been successful and that there no longer was a threat of extinction.

Nonetheless, things were not as they seemed. Tiger parts—skulls, bones, whiskers, sinews, and blood—had long been used by Asian peoples, especially the Chinese, in medicines and potions used to treat rheumatism, rat bites, and various diseases; in the restoration of energy; and as aphrodisiacs. Until tiger hunting was banned, these body parts were never in short supply. In the late 1980s, however, stockpiles were becoming exhausted, and evidence that tigers were still being killed began to accumulate. New, more careful counts revealed that previous censuses had been inflated by officials who either were in connivance with poachers or were merely eager to impress their superiors. At the same time, reports of poaching were multiplying, and

the underground trade in tiger parts flourished as the dwindling supplies pushed prices ever higher. There were occasional highly publicized seizures and destruction of the confiscated parts, but little effort was really being put forth to stop the smugglers, and the potions remained available in Chinese apothecaries in several nations.

Pressure was put on governments to impose sanctions on countries that failed to take adequate measures to eliminate the trade in tiger parts. Conservationists, believing that only the threat of punitive measures by the U.S. would force any real change, urged Pres. Bill Clinton's administration to take action, and in April 1994 it did so, barring the importation of wildlife products from Taiwan, valued at about $25 million annually. Some governments were attempting to cooperate. In March India convened the first meeting of the 10-nation Global Tiger Forum in an organized attempt to save the species.

Nevertheless, it was feared that even if all poaching did cease, the threat to the tiger would not disappear. In India, where the largest number of tigers lived, the need of the rapidly growing human population for more territory was robbing the tiger of both its habitat and its food supply. Still, a true respect for nature continued to exist and, indeed, the country had already spent vast sums to help the tiger survive. There was hope that perhaps humans and tigers would yet find a way to continue to coexist.   (BARBARA WHITNEY)

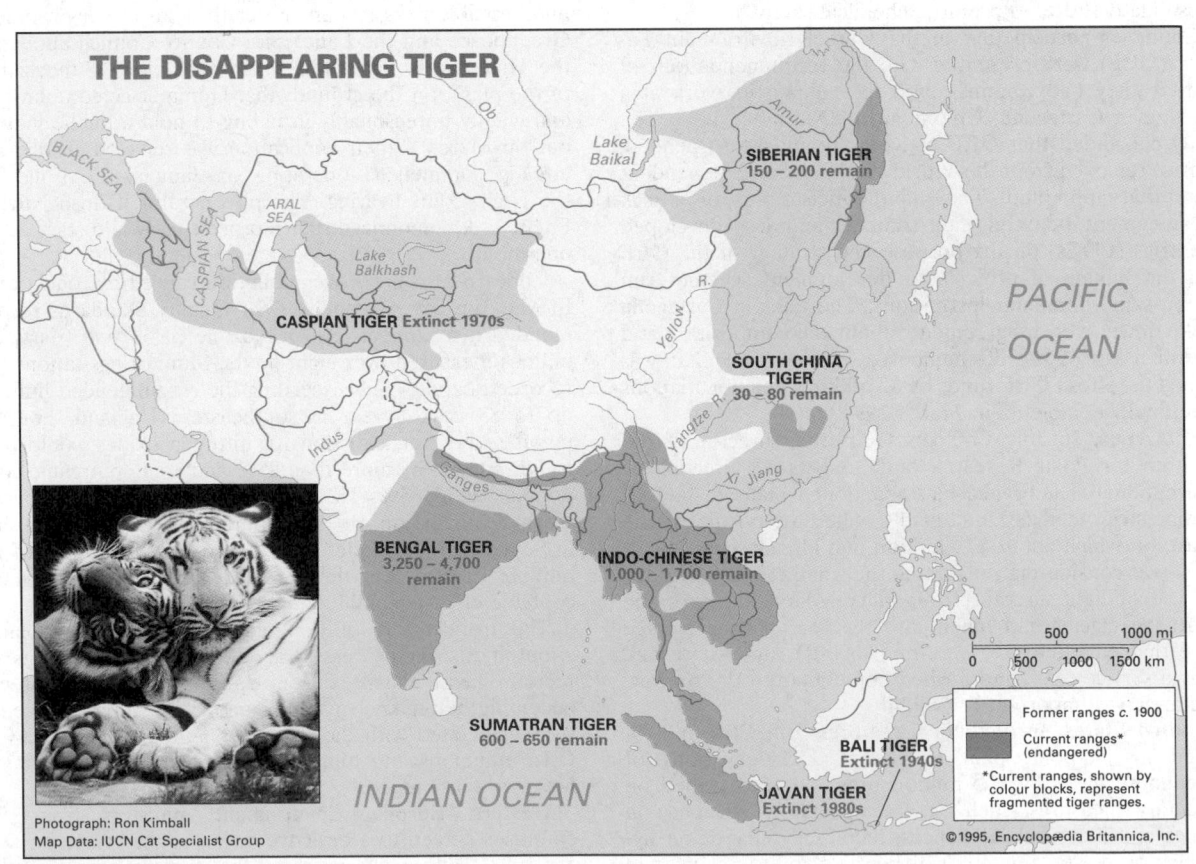

THE DISAPPEARING TIGER

SIBERIAN TIGER
150 – 200 remain

CASPIAN TIGER Extinct 1970s

SOUTH CHINA TIGER
30 – 80 remain

PACIFIC OCEAN

BENGAL TIGER
3,250 – 4,700 remain

INDO-CHINESE TIGER
1,000 – 1,700 remain

SUMATRAN TIGER
600 – 650 remain

BALI TIGER
Extinct 1940s

JAVAN TIGER
Extinct 1980s

INDIAN OCEAN

Former ranges *c.* 1900

Current ranges*
(endangered)

*Current ranges, shown by colour blocks, represent fragmented tiger ranges.

0   500   1000 mi
0   500   1000   1500 km

Photograph: Ron Kimball
Map Data: IUCN Cat Specialist Group

©1995, Encyclopædia Britannica, Inc.

(continued from page 185)

have to be recycled, either for reuse or for incineration to generate power. Different recycling targets were set for different materials, but none was below 15%. Greece, Ireland, and Portugal were allowed a longer implementation period. Germany, Denmark, and The Netherlands were permitted higher targets, provided the European Commission was persuaded they had sufficient recycling capacity to handle those targets without requiring the export of waste.

The Green parties, which fought the June elections for the European Parliament on a joint manifesto, maintained that economic growth should not continue regardless of its social and environmental costs. The German Greens held a congress in October 1993, while opinion polls showed their support holding steady at 8–10%. The dominant figure was Joschka Fischer, the environment minister in Hessen, who was influential in securing the merger with Alliance '90, the environmental and civil rights party from the former East Germany, and in broadening Green policies to include wealth redistribution. The Greens/Alliance '90 held a conference in Aachen in November 1993 at which old differences over the wisdom of power sharing reemerged, but at a later meeting of 700 delegates held in Mannheim on Feb. 26–27, 1994, the Greens pledged their readiness to share power. At the June elections earlier polls were confirmed as the Greens took 10% of the vote and 12 seats. Ireland's Green Party, which benefited from a protest vote and low poll, won two seats in the European Parliament.

The environment minister in the new Italian government, Altero Matteoli of the neofascist Italian Social Movement, said in May that he welcomed the idea of parks and specially protected areas (provided they were not off-limits to people or barred from possible economic use) and favoured nuclear energy. He also said he would revive plans for a major highway down the west coast from Livorno to Civitavecchia that had been shelved, largely because of environmental concerns. Environmentalists were outraged, and Prime Minister Silvio Berlusconi moved swiftly to placate them by appointing Roberto Lasagna—a former international director of the World Wildlife Fund and an opponent of nuclear power—as Matteoli's deputy.

On Dec. 1, 1993, Greenpeace protesters were evicted from the nuclear plant site at Cadarache, France, 50 km (31 mi) from Marseilles, after they climbed a chimney and unfurled a banner. They objected to an experimental meltdown that scientists studied by monitoring the movement of radionuclides through the reactor vessel. The experiment lasted five hours, and the meltdown went further than the 1979 Three Mile Island accident, with about 20% of the fuel melting. Fission products that escaped into the containment shield through safety valves in the pressure vessel were allowed to travel to different parts of the reactor for four days and then into an outer tank, where robots monitored them for three months.

Eastern Europe. Opposition to the Gabcikovo hydroelectric scheme in Slovakia weakened with the discovery, reported in July, that diversion of the Danube River might have actually proved environmentally beneficial by reviving wetlands and recharging underground aquifers. In response to environmental concerns, Slovakia had fed part of the diverted flow into wetlands, some of which had been largely dry for 30 years, apparently because dams built in Austria had altered the hydrology and caused the river to erode its bed. Until the flow was increased, there was less than one month each year when the water level rose high enough to enter the old arms of the river.

NIPSCO Industries, Inc., Wisconsin Electric Power Co., and Edison Development Co. agreed in May to contribute $200,000 each toward the $1.5 billion cost of converting the highly polluting Decin Bynov power plant in the Czech Republic from burning brown coal to burning natural gas and improving its efficiency. Carbon dioxide emissions would be reduced by 12,800 tons a year, more than 65%. The balance of the cost would be met by the city of Decin. The Czech government agreed to transfer to the U.S. 40% of the credits it earned for reducing emissions under the Convention on Climate Change. The U.S. companies hoped they would be allowed to offset this against cuts required in their own plants.

On September 26 the Greek High Court ruled that the government had acted illegally in proceeding with the EU-backed £1 billion scheme to divert the Achelous River without commissioning a full environmental-impact statement (EIS). The action was brought by three environmental groups—the Hellenic Ornithological Society, World Wildlife Fund Greece, and Elliniki Etaria—that feared the project would dry out wetlands and damage an important bird reserve. The judgment meant work had to cease on a 17.7-km (11-mi) tunnel through the Pindus Mountains and on a series of partially completed dams until the EIS was completed, which could take two years.

The World Health Organization (WHO) reported in October 1993 that the incidence of thyroid cancer among children in some areas of Belarus and Ukraine continued to rise following the nuclear accident at Chernobyl in Ukraine. Since 1989, 225 new cases had been identified in Belarus and 158 in Ukraine, against a normal incidence of 1–2 cases per million population. Thyroid cancer was also high among adults, with 2,039 cases registered in Belarus and more than 3,000 in Ukraine. Certain puzzling features remained unexplained. In Belarus more than half the cases were in Gomel oblast, with few reported from neighbouring Bryansk oblast in Russia, and in Ukraine the rise in cases was delayed and less pronounced than in Belarus. At a meeting in July the Group of Seven agreed to add $200 million to the $600 million already pledged to Ukraine by the EU, much of the additional funding coming from Europe, in the hope that the money would be used to close down the two remaining gas-graphite reactors at the Chernobyl plant. Ukraine also wanted to use the funds to complete five reactors that were under construction. Studies by the U.S. Department of Energy and the World Bank, however, found it would be cheaper to improve industrial efficiency than to build new reactors.

In March a group of Russian scientists and representatives of public interest groups announced the establishment of the Centre for Ecological Policy. The centre would be run by a board chaired by Aleksey Yablokov, a corresponding member of the Russian Academy of Sciences. Its aim was to influence government policy by offering novel solutions to urgent ecological problems, and it was expected to supply the environmental movement with objective scientific information and advice.

Asia and the Pacific. In Australia it was reported in November 1993 that the Tasmanian government had ordered the Mount Lyell Mining and Railway Co. to halt the revegetation of hills near Queenstown and to refrain from spraying fertilizer on native seedlings that were already planted. The hills had been denuded by acid rain caused by a copper smelter operated by the company, which was bound by legislation to revegetate the area. Opposition came from local people who preferred the hills to be left barren as a valuable tourist attraction and as part of the history and cultural heritage of the town. Most of the damage occurred between 1896 and 1904, when iron pyrite was used in the smelting process, but between 1904 and 1969, when smelting ended, the use of coal produced enough acid rain to prevent natural regeneration.

In May villagers living near the Ok Tedi River in Papua New Guinea lodged a $A 4 billion lawsuit against Australia's largest company, BHP. The action, started in Melbourne by Rex Dagi, leader of the Miripiki clan, was the largest civil claim ever lodged in Australia and was a representative action for about 7,500 villagers, with more writs expected to follow. The plaintiffs claimed that a copper and gold mine managed by BHP had destroyed their traditional way of life by discharging material into the river since 1984, clogging and polluting it with copper and cadmium. The plaintiffs claimed that the river was biologically dead and that villagers had had to move because they could no longer maintain market gardens.

ISSUES OF CONCERN

Air Pollution. Results of a study commissioned by the Swedish NGO Secretariat on Acid Rain, reported in July, identified 100 installations responsible for about 43% of Europe's sulfur dioxide emissions. Of the offenders, 95 were power plants, with 11 of them in Britain, but the biggest was the Maritsa plant in Bulgaria, which released 350,000 tons of sulfur dioxide a year. Three installations were metal smelters, two of them in the Russian Arctic; one was an oil refinery; and one was a blast furnace producing pig iron. EU figures released in May showed that in 1993 unleaded gasoline accounted for nearly 90% of sales in Germany, more than 75% in The Netherlands and Denmark, 52.6% in the U.K., and 20.9% in Portugal. The EU average was 53.3%. Results of a study of Antarctic snow, published in May, showed lead concentrations fell during the 1930s, declined overall between about 1920 and 1950, doubled by 1980 to six parts per billion, and declined again to five by 1986, probably because of the use of unleaded fuels in Brazil.

In March estimates by Joel Schwartz, an epidemiologist at the EPA, suggested that microscopic particulate emissions called PM10s could be causing up to 10,000 deaths a year in England and Wales, with vehicle emissions being the major source. This idea found support at a meeting on urban air pollution and public health held in London in September, when Jon Ayres of the Chest Research Institute at Birmingham (England) Heartlands Hospital reported that asthma attacks increased with rises in PM10 levels. Douglas Dockery of the Harvard School of Public Health said evidence that linked an increase of PM10s per cubic metre of air with a slight increase in deaths from heart attacks, respiratory illness, and asthma attacks was growing. He said these trends had been detected in 10 U.S. cities and in São Paulo, Brazil. Although PM10s were not known to be toxic, it was suspected they might carry toxins on their surfaces into the lungs. Medical researchers also found a link with gaseous pollutants. Ayres reported that patients with mild asthma caused by an allergy to house-dust mites had more severe symptoms if they inhaled nitrogen dioxide, which acted as a potentiating agent that made the respiratory tract more sensitive to allergens. Jagdish Devalia of St. Bartholomew's Hospital, London, reported studies that found nitrogen dioxide could inflame cells lining airways, preventing them from expelling allergens. Increased asthma was therefore linked to rising numbers of house mites, which thrive in centrally heated homes, and to rising emissions of nitrogen dioxide from vehicles and gas fires.

For four days in June an experiment in traffic control brought a marked improvement in air quality to Heilbronn, Germany. Cars were prevented from entering the town unless they had been fitted with three-way catalytic converters, and trucks were barred unless they had the most efficient diesel engines. At the same time, a 60-km/h (37-mph) speed limit was imposed on the nearby autobahn. Traffic within the town was reduced by 40%, and use of public

JIM WILSON—THE NEW YORK TIMES

Kelso Dunes in the Mojave Desert are part of some 3.8 million ha (9.4 million ac) of California desert that the U.S. Congress designated as national parks or preserves. Included were Death Valley and an area northeast of San Diego containing the world's largest forest of cactuslike Joshua trees.

transport increased 50%. Urban concentrations of nitrogen oxides decreased by 40%, and in the town centre benzene concentrations were halved. Results on the autobahn were inconclusive, although there was a reduction in traffic noise. In late July the state of Hessen introduced a 90-km/h (58-mph) speed limit on autobahns and an 80-km/h (50-mph) one on other roads in an attempt to curb tropospheric ozone levels, which reached record levels during a long spell of hot weather in Central Europe.

In June the U.S. government announced that alcohol made by fermentation of corn (maize) had to be added to gasoline sold in several cities in an effort to reduce carbon monoxide emissions. The decision required that by 1996 30% of the oxygen content in reformulated gasoline would have to come from renewable sources, mainly ethanol, which was made from corn. The remaining 70% would continue to come from methyl tertiary-butyl ether, made from methanol, which is derived from natural gas.

Ozone Layer. On October 4, scientists of the British Antarctic Survey reported a 65–70% depletion in stratospheric ozone over the Faraday base. This was similar to the depletion reported by the World Meteorological Organization (WMO) in October 1993, when ozone levels at three stations reached their lowest values in 30 years over a 22 million-sq km (8.5 million-sq mi) area extending across part of South America for two days in late September. Scientists believed the increased depletion was due to meteorologic conditions that produced record low stratospheric temperatures, possibly allowing polar stratospheric clouds to form at a higher altitude than usual.

It was reported in May that the WMO found springtime ozone levels over northern Europe more than 10% below the long term mean. A team from the US National Oceanic and Atmospheric Administration and the University of Colorado reported levels 12.6% below normal between January and April 1993 over the U.S., with reductions of up to 18% over Caribou, Maine, and Wallops Island, Virginia. Between May and August, levels at four sites were 8.5% below normal and 3.7% below the previous lowest levels for that time of year. Over Hawaii, summer levels were reduced by 5.5%. At a meeting of signatories to the Montreal Protocol held in Bangkok, Thailand, in November 1993, Elizabeth Dowdeswell, the executive director of the UN Environment Programme, said that while industrialized countries had reduced emissions of implicated substances by 45%, only nine LDCs had reduced their emissions. It was agreed to double the Interim Multilateral Fund to help LDCs phase out ozone-depleting chemicals.

Climate Change. At a meeting of the negotiating committee for the Convention on Climate Change, held in Geneva in August, it was agreed that the initial target of stabilizing greenhouse gas emissions at their 1990 levels was insufficient to prevent global warming. Germany suggested adding a clause to the convention requiring industrialized nations to make specified emission reductions by a target date after 2000. The committee failed to agree on new targets, although most industrialized countries agreed on the need for them.

In its 1994 report the Intergovernmental Panel on Climate Change (IPCC) endorsed the consensus reached in 1990 and repeated its conclusion that unless greenhouse gas emissions were reduced, average temperatures would rise 1.4°–4.5° C (2.5°–8.1° F) by 2100. Sir John Houghton, an IPCC working group chairman, suggested that a 20% reduction in emissions over 20 years would be appropriate and probably achievable for developed countries. The report revised upward the effect of methane and found that the upward trend in carbon dioxide and methane emissions

had slowed from 1991 to mid-1993, but by late 1993 carbon dioxide emissions were rising again. Two reports, published in June and August, found that atmospheric particles (aerosols), primarily of sulfuric acid and ammonium sulfate, were having a marked cooling effect—directly by increasing albedo and indirectly by nucleating the formation of small-droplet clouds. Taken together, direct and indirect aerosol effects were found to be equal to those due to greenhouse gases, but the climatic results were uncertain because of the concentration of aerosol emissions in particular regions.

In August the Japanese Environmental Agency reported that Japan was unlikely to reduce its total carbon dioxide emissions to the 1990 level by 2000, but it might be able to keep per capita emissions to the 1990 level. The per capita calculation allowed for a small increase in total emissions because of the increase in population. In the U.K. the department of applied ecology at the University of Cambridge said planned government action would easily meet the U.K. target of stabilizing greenhouse gas emissions by 2000 but would not make an adequate contribution to preventing global warming because the targets were well short of the required 60% reduction below 1990 levels.

Fresh Water. In October 1993 it was reported that a study of 40,000 people in Taiwan had found more than 400 cases of skin cancer among people exposed to water containing high levels of arsenic, some samples having up to 600 ppb, with a clear positive correlation between the number of cases and arsenic levels. A similar link had been found in Mexico and Germany. WHO planned to reduce its recommended limit for arsenic in tap water to 10 ppb, and the EPA was considering a 2-ppb limit in the U.S. Other scientists were skeptical, however, pointing out that there was no evidence of increased cancers in parts of Hungary with high arsenic levels.

In its fourth annual report, published in September, the National Rivers Authority said the number of pollution incidents in British rivers rose 8% in 1993, to 25,299, but the number of major incidents fell by 57, to 331. Some 25% of the incidents were caused by the sewage and water industries, especially from sewage overflows, a figure that was expected to fall over the next 10 years as investment programs were completed. Industrial sources accounted for 111 of the most serious incidents, diesel fuel being one of the most common pollutants.

Marine Pollution. On Nov. 12, 1993, the International Maritime Organization (IMO)—by a 37–0 vote with 5 abstentions (Belgium, the U.K., France, China, and Russia)—modified the London Dumping Convention by replacing the 10-year moratorium imposed in 1983 with a worldwide ban on the dumping of radioactive wastes at sea. Two weeks earlier Russian authorities had dumped 900 tons of radioactive cooling and cleaning water from submarine reactors into the Sea of Japan about 500 km (310 mi) from the Japanese coast. Following the outcry, Russia suspended plans to dump an additional 800 tons, and Japan abandoned its support for dumping radioactive waste. The IMO ban also covered the dumping of industrial waste and the incineration of industrial waste at sea.

A report by the North Sea Task Force, published in April, said pollution levels were falling in some parts of the sea but increasing in others, especially in inshore waters in the south. High cadmium and mercury levels were found in the kidneys and livers of seals and porpoises, cadmium in the livers of fish on the Dogger Bank, and lead on the coast of northeastern England and in the Dogger Bank and Norwegian Trench. Nutrients carried by rivers were causing algal blooms on Dogger and off Norway and Sweden, killing stock in fish nursery areas.

Toxic Wastes. On March 25, member countries of the Basel Convention on Hazardous Wastes—which had already prohibited dumping—agreed to ban from the end of 1997 all exports of toxic waste to LDCs for recycling, although the EU said it would continue to export substances it considered safe. In the U.S., on September 13 the EPA issued a draft of a report, to be finalized in September 1995, on the findings of a three-year review of the health effects of dioxins. The 2,000-page, six-volume report by more than 100 scientists affirmed a link between dioxins and cancer, a reduction in male sperm count, damage to fetuses and the immune system, and diminished IQ in children. The EPA concluded that there is no safe threshold for exposure. The main source of dioxins was found to be waste incinerators, which accounted for at least 95% of known emissions, and contaminated food and drink were the principal route by which humans encountered them. No immediate new controls were planned.

Radioactive Contamination. A report from the British Health and Safety Executive (HSE), published in October 1993, found that children who were born in Seascale, Cumbria, and whose fathers had worked at the Sellafield nuclear power plant prior to 1965 were 14 times more likely to develop leukemia or non-Hodgkin's lymphoma than the national average, but the incidence of these diseases was not raised among the 90% of Sellafield workers not living in Seascale. In a further report published in the *British Medical Journal* in August, the HSE said the methods used by Martin Gardner in his original study in 1990 had led to gaps and double counting in calculations of radiation doses, distorting his results. It found that there was no need to reduce the maximum permitted radiation dose for potential fathers, but the search for the cause of the cluster at Sellafield would continue.

In September a U.S. federal appeals court overturned an injunction brought by South Carolina Gov. Carroll Campbell, Jr., to prevent two ships carrying 153 spent fuel rods from entering U.S. waters. The rods, from European research reactors but originally produced in the U.S., contained highly enriched bomb-grade uranium.

Power Lines. In October 1993 the *British Medical Journal* reported conflicting findings from studies of the health effects of power lines. One, from a team led by Jorgen Olsen of the Danish Cancer Society, over 20 years examined 1,707 cases of various types of cancer in children under age 15 and found that the number living within 45 m (50 yd) of power lines was five times higher than expected. The other, a Finnish study of almost 135,000 children living within 500 m (550 yd) of power lines, found 140 cancer cases rather than the 145 expected and reported no increased cancer risk. A report by Britain's National Radiological Protection Board published on June 9 found no strong biological evidence for a general link between electromagnetic radiation and cancer but said some Scandinavian evidence suggested a possible link with childhood leukemia.

On August 25 the Institution of Electrical Engineers published the report of a two-year study that also found no clear evidence to link increased exposure to electromagnetic fields with cancer. The investigation analyzed 245 separate studies, none of which showed firm evidence of biological effects or identified any plausible mechanism by which such effects might occur. The Swedish study, it said, failed to take account of the length of time cancer patients had lived near power lines, and in Denmark, where electricity consumption had increased 30-fold since 1945, incidence of childhood cancers, including leukemia, had not changed significantly. It was reported in July that James Brewer, a former worker at the Kaiser Aluminum smelter in Tacoma, Wash., had won state workers' compensation for cancer, which he claimed was caused by exposure to electromagnetic fields while at work between 1969 and 1986 in a pot room where the metal was smelted. Brewer's claim was allowed because it was supported by his doctor, who said it was "more probable than not" that his cancer was due to workplace exposure to electromagnetic radiation.   (MICHAEL ALLABY)

WILDLIFE CONSERVATION

The Convention on Biological Diversity—the Rio Treaty—came into force on Dec. 29, 1993, 30 days after the 30th nation ratified it, and the first meeting of the signatories was held in December 1994 in The Bahamas. An Agreement on the Conservation of Bats in Europe (under the Bonn Convention) came into force on Jan. 16, 1994. It was the first international agreement to protect bats throughout Europe and aimed to provide cooperation on the protection of bats and their habitats, both in research and in the promotion of public awareness.

The flock of Siberian cranes (*Grus leucogeranus*) that once wintered in India's Bharatpur sanctuary was presumed extinct when no birds arrived in the winter of 1993–94. Numbers had been falling over the previous 30 years—probably owing to hunting along their migration route over Pakistan and Afghanistan. A survey for Queen Alexandra's birdwing (*Ornithoptera alexandrae*), the world's largest butterfly and the symbol of Papua New Guinea's Oro province, found that the butterfly's range was three times more extensive than previously known. Plans to extend oil palm plantations in the area threatened the butterfly's habitat, and a conservation program was being developed.

A survey of the Nam Theun National Biodiversity Conservation Area (NBCA) in Laos between January and April found 50 trophies of an undescribed species of muntjac deer. In March the survey team found an adult male of the new species in a private collection near the NBCA. The new deer was also found in the Vu Quang Nature Reserve in Vietnam, where the saola, or Vu Quang ox, had been discovered two years earlier. In May a new species of tree kangaroo was found in Irian Jaya, the Indonesian part of New Guinea. The black-and-white animal showed little fear of humans and was familiar to local people; in the western part of its known range it was protected by the Moni people, who revered it as an ancestor. Other new species described in 1994 included a bird—the chestnut-bellied cotinga (*Doliornis remseni*) from cloud forest in the Podocarpus National Park in the Andes of southern Ecuador—and a bat (*Lasiurus ebenus*) from southeastern Brazil.

Botanists were astonished by the discovery that a tree thought to have been extinct for 150 million years was still flourishing in a remote rain forest in New South Wales, Australia. Only 39 specimens of the tree, named the Wollemi pine, were found in the Wollemi National Park, about 200 km (125 mi) from Sydney. The largest was 40 m (130 ft) tall.

The world's tiger numbers continued to decline, and a Global Tiger Forum was established on March 4. It aimed to eliminate the use of tiger parts in traditional medicine in Asia. The demand for these products was causing heavy poaching of tigers in almost all range states. Particularly affected was the Amur, or Siberian, tiger in southeastern Russia and China; 20–25% of this population was lost to poachers between November 1993 and March 1994, leaving numbers as low as 150–200. (*See* Sidebar.)

In May a meeting of a the African Rhino Specialist group of IUCN-the World Conservation Union concluded that more than 2,550 black rhinos and 6,750 white rhinos survived in Africa. Black rhino numbers seemed stable, indicating in part that the sanctuary/intensive protection zone strategy in use in most countries appeared to be succeeding. In November several rhinos were found dead, apparently killed by elephants.

An oil slick from the *Apollo Sea,* which sank on June 20 off the west coast of South Africa, caused untold damage to colonies of breeding jackass penguins (*Spheniscus demersus*), which were found only off South Africa and Namibia. Penguins were airlifted from affected beaches to treatment centres, and on July 24, 1,400 of the 7,000 rescued birds were returned to their breeding islands. Bird experts predicted that there would be at least a 20% decrease in the population over the next 10 years.

The world's largest nesting ground for olive ridley turtles (*Lepidochelys olivacea*), located on Gahirmatha beach in Bhitarkanika sanctuary, Orissa state, India, was threatened by the construction of fishing quays and associated developments. The Orissa state government carried on with the work despite a ban by India's Ministry of Environment. The legal wing of the World Wide Fund for Nature sued the state and central government for gross violation of various environmental laws. In addition, the Indian army used one of Bhitarkanika's islands, another mass turtle nesting site, as a target for missile testing.

In July Namibia started its cull of Cape fur seals (*Arctocephalus pusillus*) despite the fact that 120,000 animals had already died in an unprecedented mass mortality. The cause was unknown, but tests were conducted to discover whether it was associated with a morbillivirus.

Almost the entire Antarctic Ocean, which was used by seven species of endangered whales, was declared a whale sanctuary by the International Whaling Commission at its meeting in Mexico on May 23–27. The meeting also acknowledged completion of the Revised Management Procedure, which would be used to calculate allowable catches of whales if the moratorium on commercial whaling was lifted in the future. On June 15 the California gray whale (*Eschrichtius robustus*) was removed from the U.S. endangered species list, the first time a marine animal had been removed from this category. There were now about 21,000 gray whales, compared with 2,000 just before the turn of the century, when heavy whaling brought numbers down. On June 30 the American bald eagle (*Haliaetus leucocephalus*) was reclassified from endangered to threatened in most of the U.S. because of successful recovery efforts.

(JACQUI M. MORRIS)

See also Agriculture and Food Supplies; Botanical Gardens and Zoos; Energy; Life Sciences.

This article updates the *Macropædia* article CONSERVATION OF NATURAL RESOURCES.

Fashion and Dress

Glamour became the style catchword of 1994 and summarized a look of being dressed up and made up. The new sophistication put an end to dressing down, the look popularized in 1993 by grunge and the style known as deconstruction, which featured clothes with unfinished seams, unironed cloth, and conspicuous stitching. For women, tailored trouser and skirt suits, short swingy dresses, brightly coloured clothes in rich lustrous fabrics, fake animal prints, red lipstick, and stiletto heels replaced 1993's looser, less constructed look. So enthusiastically were the new elements of style received that the fashion press christened the look "the new glamour."

The look, however, was not new. Fashion designers who made grunge clothes in 1993—mostly the young designers of Milan, Paris, and New York City—sent down the runways a style that was likened to the glam rock and disco-influenced fashions popular in the late 1970s. A more direct inspiration behind several collections from young designers, particularly those of Marc Jacobs and Anna Sui of the U.S., was Yves Saint Laurent's flashy coloured, slickly tailored clothes of the '70s. The short silver miniskirts and see-through plastic garments that many designers made to add a futuristic feel to their collections were reminiscent of the '60s designs by French couturier André Courreges.

The real news that came with glamour was the arrival of Nadja Auermann, a 23-year-old model from Berlin, who captured centre stage after hairdresser Julien D'Ys bleached her once dirty-blonde hair pure white. Auermann, standing at 1.8 m (5 ft 11 in), her lips painted an alarming red, and her platinum blonde hair hanging down her back, was the image of glamour personified. Dressed up in sheer plastics and shiny satin clothes, she became a futuristic depiction of an Amazon woman. The "Styles" section of the *New York Times* heralded Auermann's "On-the-cover coup" after she simultaneously graced the covers of the thick September issues of four major fashion magazines: English and American *Vogue, Harper's Bazaar,* and the British street-style magazine *The Face.*

But it was design elements—particularly the return of tailoring that flattered the female form, as well as colour-rich fabrics and accessories—that established glamour as the year's prevailing fashion mood. The length of skirts rose from the ankle to the knee (having not been seen since the 1940s, it was dubbed "the new length") or to just below or well above the thigh. Trousers, always paired with a man-tailored jacket, were slim and no longer flared at the ankle.

The dress made a major comeback. On the catwalk U.S. designer Donna Karan showed it as a staple to be worn to work by day paired with a jacket and worn alone in the evening. Other designers made dresses as fashion statements. The long, straight-to-the-floor singlets of rhinestones or velvet from the Italian design duo Dolce e Gabbana's autumn/winter collection, the bias-cut light-coloured long satin slip dresses designed by John Galliano, and Gianni Versace's slithering sheaths of silver metal mesh signified that it was indeed fashionable to dress up again.

The idea caught on. The baby-doll dress was promoted by U.S. designers Sui and Betsey Johnson for the spring and summer seasons. Supermodels and Courtney Love, a singer and the widow of Nirvana's lead singer Kurt Cobain (*see* OBITUARIES), were high-profile endorsers of the style. But the baby doll did not prove as popular as summer's ensemble—the short black slip dress worn over a basic white T-shirt. Dolce e Gabbana and U.S. designer Ralph Lauren put the look together first. It was later copied by chain stores.

Though glamour set the prevailing mood in 1994, the street continued to influence fashion. For his spring collection Jean-Paul Gaultier included T-shirts and leggings printed with tattoos. His male and female models appeared body pierced, sporting stud earrings above their eyebrows and hoops through their navels. Hoops also dangled from ears and were attached to noses with a chain. Popular fashions seen on urban streets were colourful suede sneakers and tight child-sized T-shirts worn by young women. The costume department of London's Victoria and Albert Museum also devoted an exhibition to the influence of the street on 20th-century fashion.

Punk, the popular '70s British street style, was Versace's influence for spring/summer. The clothes he unveiled, however, had little to do with the original punk designs—ripped T-shirts held together with safety pins, bondage trousers, and neon colours. Versace made his own safety pins to hype his new look, and he used punk as an excuse to use colour in such shockingly bright shades as hot pink, electric blue, orange, and yellow. Men's fashion offered a more genuine brand of punk style. Dolce e Gabbana paired authentic copies of bondage trousers with colourful mohair sweaters.

So popular was colour in the autumn/winter collections that it was difficult to distinguish whether the shades used were appropriate for cold winter months. Such items as short suede skirts came in acid-bright orange, as did long shearling coats. White, which was offered as an alternative to fashion's perennial basic colour, black, was also used to set off bright colours. White tights appeared with skirts, and white leather was popular for shoes and jackets.

For his autumn/winter collection, Versace's colour was so bright that it shined—thanks to his use of metallics and a special spray that lacquered his moiré and silk crepe. To achieve the same shiny effect, other designers used polyvinyl chloride to make trousers, skirts, tight tops, raincoats, and patches on sweaters. Patent leather and see-through plastic were popular materials for the sleek, spikey stiletto, the shoe that replaced the chunky platform.

Fake fur eclipsed real pelts in several designers' collections, appearing in rich gem-toned colours and such animal prints as leopard, pony skin, and zebra. Animal prints, particularly fake leopard, also debuted in the men's autumn/winter collections.

In 1994 the Washington, D.C.-based animal activists organization People for the Ethical Treatment of Animals stepped up its campaign to convince fashion industry professionals that it was morally objectionable to promote the use of fur. Such supermodels as Christy Turlington and Naomi Campbell went public, posing naked on billboards with the slogan "I'd Rather Go Naked than Wear Fur" emblazoned across their bare chests. U.S. designers Karan and Calvin Klein also went public with their decision not to design with fur.

Some questioned the practicality of the glamorous new styles. Women could not wear fishnet stockings, sequined miniskirts, and stilettos to the office. Some historians believed that the return of glamour was a reaction to the protracted economic slump. Department store buyers agreed and claimed that after six years of recession, customers had enough basics in their wardrobe. Women may not have adopted the entire look as it appeared on the runways, but they were shopping. *Women's Wear Daily* reported that in just one week at the end of the summer, Karan racked up $650,000 in sales at the New York City department store Bergdorf Goodman. In 10 days the U.S. department store Macy's sold 3,000 padded push-up bras manufactured by Wonderbra, a key glamour accessory. In the U.S. overall retail sales increased by a slim 7% compared with 1993.

Klein's prominence in the fashion industry seemed to strengthen as the year progressed. His perfume CK ONE was fashion's first official unisex scent, and it was also the first fragrance to be sold by the music chain Tower Records. Klein, like other designers, branched out globally. To strengthen business abroad, he opened offices in Japan and Milan. Karan also launched a Milan-based office to build up a European clientele. The Gap, a U.S. clothing chain, opened its first European boutique in Paris.

Men's fashion in 1994 offered something for every man, ranging from sober gray flannel suits to kilts, bright-coloured mohair sweaters, and powder blue biker jackets. Though wild elements were included in the 1994 collections, men's fashion returned to the traditional styles of tailoring. The dominant theme was classic tailoring taken from the traditional suit cuts of London's Savile Row tailors, and the clothes presented were suitable for a refined English gentleman.

The move in menswear in recent years had been toward relaxation. In 1994, however, the emphasis was on a put-together look. The focus was the suit, whether sharply tailored with a double-breasted jacket, soft-shouldered, three-piece with a waistcoat, or styled for the street with white shirt cuffs hanging loose and long from the sleeve. Wool suits were cut in basic colours, including black, as well as tweeds and tartans. Designs for young men had a strong theme of rebellion. Gaultier's kilt, now a permanent part of his collection, became a viable alternative to trousers. Men wore kilts on the street and to nightclubs. Berets, Doc Martens, and combat boots were other sartorial symbols of rebellion.

In September, just before the fall shows, the Italian fashion industry was saddened by the death of avant-garde designer Franco Moschino (*see* OBITUARIES) and shocked by revelations that such high-profile designers as Giorgio Armani and Gianfranco Ferre were accused of bribing tax inspectors. Santo Versace, Gianni's brother, was also implicated in the scandal. The industry was astounded to learn in December that French couturier Alix Grès had died in November 1993. (BRONWYN COSGRAVE)

See also Business and Industry Review: *Apparel.*

This article updates the *Macropædia* article DRESS AND ADORNMENT.

Star supermodel Nadja Auermann appears on the cover of *Harper's Bazaar* with her platinum blonde hair cut short. The tall German model, who had become a sensation for her striking long hair and red lipstick, epitomized the new glamorous look that was popular in 1994.

HARPER'S BAZAAR; PHOTOGRAPH, PATRICK DEMARCHELIER

Gardening

During 1994 plant suppliers offered home gardeners an enticing array of new flowers. Remarkable advances were made in the quality, colour, fragrance, and disease-resistance qualities of ornamental plants. Especially exciting was the summer arrival of Flower Carpet Roses to garden centres, nurseries, and home centres in the U.S. These fully disease-resistant pink landscape roses were high performers suitable for all climate zones and required no spraying or dusting to remain in top form. Already a sensation in Europe, New Zealand, and Australia, where one in 10 home gardens featured them, the flowers grew on a dense compact bush and were iridescent rose pink tinged with white. Blooms are of medium size, ranging between dish and cup shape, and had 15 to 20 petals. This blackspot- and mildew-resistant rose won three gold ADR awards from the world's toughest rose-performance test (All Deutschland Rose of Germany), in addition to top awards in France, England, The Netherlands, and Australia. Two flowers that received increased worldwide attention from breeders were sunflowers and delphiniums. Particular attention was paid to adapting sunflowers for cut-flower use, and both species were actively crossed to produce entirely new colours. Breeders predicted that within a very few seasons sunflowers and delphiniums would debut on the red-yellow end of the spectrum.

Four gold medals were awarded by Fleuroselect, the European-based seed-testing cooperative. New flower introductions were ranked on criteria of beauty, innovation, and performance. Of 16 possible points, an entrant had to score 12 or more points to receive a gold medal. Only 10 points were awarded on the basis of the various aspects of garden performance. Beauty and innovation were important factors in the selection of Fleuroselect winners. *Fuchsia* Florabelle scored mainly for innovation; it was the first small-flowered fuchsia grown from seed. The plants were 30–37.5 cm (12–15 in) across, were quite uniform, and branched freely without pinching. The 2.5-cm (1-in) red and purple flowers appeared only 14 weeks after sowing and were continuously blooming. *Papaver orientale* Pizzicato also won for innovation. It was the only gold-medal winner that was not a hybrid; the choice was a surprise because the organization had previously awarded medals to seed-grown flowers only.

Lobelia Fan Scarlet, a new addition to the fan series of tall (0.6–0.9-m [2–3-ft]) hybrid lobelias from Benary in Germany, also won a gold medal. Its most striking characteristic—copper-shaded, lance-shaped leaves—made a brilliant contrast to the bright 2.5-cm (1-in) scarlet blooms. Fan Scarlet looked best grouped in the annual border near blocks of neutral plants and, if given winter protection, might bloom a second year in areas where temperatures did not drop below −18° C (0° F).

The fourth medal was awarded to *Nicotiana* Havana Appleblossom, which added a new pastel combination of white and rose to one of the fastest-growing bedding plants. The plants grew about 45 cm (18 in) up and across and were covered with 5–7.5-cm (2–3-in) blooms that appeared continuously from June to frost in all but the hottest climates.

Another increasingly popular trend during the year was vegetative production of bedding plants and cut flowers. The advantage of vegetative production in bedding plants

Tulip Mania

In 1994, 400 years after the first Dutch tulip bloomed, The Netherlands staged celebrations to commemorate the introduction of this colourful flower, with which it has become indelibly identified.

Tulips, however, reportedly originated in south-central Asia, across a wide swath of territory from the Bosporus of western Turkey to the northern slopes of the Himalayan mountains. The bulbs, cultivated by the Turks as early as AD 1000, were taken to Europe in the mid-1500s by Augier Ghislain de Busbecq, Austria's ambassador to the Ottoman Empire.

The introduction of tulips to The Netherlands has been traced to Carolus Clusius, prefect of the Imperial Herb Gardens in Vienna, who took seeds and bulbs with him when he immigrated (1593) to The Netherlands to serve as head botanist of the newly established botanical garden at the University of Leiden. Clusius bred tulips primarily for medicinal purposes, but the plants became popular among the Dutch for their beauty as well.

As demand for these Asian rarities grew among the wealthy merchants and outstripped supply, parts of Clusius' collection were stolen. The illicit bulbs were propagated and were sold as ornamentals. A speculative frenzy, known as Tulip Mania, which began in the early 1600s and reached its height in 1633–37, seized many Dutch, from the aristocracy to the working class.

Though Holland's North Sea climate was ideal for the cultivation of tulips, propagation was slow, which caused tulip prices to soar. In 1924, for example, only a dozen bulbs of the variety *Semper Augustus* existed in the country, and each was worth about 1,200 guilders.

By the mid-1630s a single bulb of particular merit could command up to 4,000 guilders, a sum equivalent to the value of a ship filled with goods! At the height of the frenzy, even tradesmen and workers speculated in bulbs, which remained in the ground and were bought and sold over and over, on the basis of the future value of production. The business, which could blow away at any time, was dubbed the "Wind Trade."

When the tulip market crashed in 1637, those who had bought at the height of Tulip Mania went bankrupt. In 1994 high-quality Dutch tulip bulbs sold for less than a dollar each. (SHEPHERD OGDEN)

LARRY LEFEVER—GRANT HEILMAN

was increased uniformity. For cut flowers the advantage was the possibility of maintaining unusual but sterile plants that had resulted from large crossbreeding programs. Final production of such plants was carried out by means of tissue culture. A large program of this type was taking place in Taiwan under the joint auspices of Japanese, U.S., and Dutch companies.

In keeping with the popularity of vegetable gardens, large companies worldwide produced and sold more hybrids, primarily because of the influence of large commercial growers on the seed market. Smaller firms dedicated themselves to the production and distribution of vegetables, especially regional varieties and "heirlooms" (home garden favourites). More and more U.S. gardeners chose to grow their own produce because of the superior flavour of homegrown food. Relaxation, exercise, and the stress-relieving aspects of gardening were other often-mentioned reasons for growing vine-ripened fruits and vegetables.

Consolidation in the seed industry also continued apace during 1994. One of Europe's larger concerns, the Dutch company Royal Sluis, was acquired by the U.S. company Petoseed. Royal Sluis maintained both flower and vegetable programs, while Petoseed focused primarily on hybrid vegetable seed.

Labour-saving lawn and garden tools came under the close scrutiny of the U.S. Environmental Protection Agency during the year. The EPA proposed the first nationwide emissions standards for gasoline-powered lawn and garden equipment, including lawn mowers, garden tractors, chain saws, and weed trimmers. The move was aimed at protecting public health by reducing exhaust pollution. The EPA estimated that 10% of the nation's air pollution was generated by lawn and garden equipment. In addition, individual communities adopted noise-pollution ordinances outlawing or limiting the use of certain powered landscape tools. Power blowers operating at high-decibel levels were one of the chief offenders.

(SHEPHERD OGDEN; KAY MELCHISEDECH OLSON)

See also Agriculture and Food Supplies; Botanical Gardens and Zoos; Life Sciences.

This article updates the *Macropædia* article GARDENING AND HORTICULTURE.

Health and Disease

In 1994 scientists made major strides in understanding the genetic underpinnings of a number of conditions, including inherited forms of cancer, the skin disease psoriasis, dyslexia (a learning disorder), and even obesity. At the same time, public health authorities issued new warnings about the dangers of emerging and resurgent infectious diseases. Reversing a steady decline of nearly 40 years, tuberculosis deaths in Eastern Europe were again on the rise. An epidemic of pneumonic plague erupted in India, and cholera broke out among refugees fleeing the civil war in Rwanda. At an international meeting in Yokohama, Japan, AIDS researchers acknowledged that HIV was proving stubbornly resistant to their efforts.

Scientific reports published during the year challenged the conventional wisdom on several fronts. Two large studies questioned the value of vitamin supplements in preventing cancer. Researchers at Harvard Medical School suggested that, in the U.S. at least, popular procedures for treating coronary artery disease were being greatly overused. And an ongoing survey of nutrition and eating habits in the U.S. found that despite the health and fitness craze, more Americans were obese than ever before.

Genetics. The keenly contested race to identify genes associated with breast cancer susceptibility culminated in the isolation of one such gene, BRCA1, on chromosome 17, followed by the identification of another, BRCA2, located within a particular region of chromosome 13. Between them, mutations in these two genes may be responsible for most hereditary forms of the disease (which, in turn, account for 5–10% of all breast cancer cases).

The cloning of BRCA1, accomplished by researchers at the University of Utah Medical Center, Salt Lake City, and colleagues at other U.S. and Canadian institutions, was potentially highly significant for women with a strong family history of breast cancer. More than half of those who carried mutated forms of the gene would be diagnosed with breast cancer by age 50, and more than 85% would develop the disease by age 70.

Another gene race ended in a tie in March as two teams reported that they had independently isolated a second gene involved in a common form of colon cancer, hereditary nonpolyposis colorectal cancer (HNPCC). In December 1993 many of these same researchers had announced isolation of the first such colon cancer gene. Both genes were known to be involved in the repair of DNA. Together, defects in the two were thought to account for most cases of HNPCC. About one in 200 people carried an inherited mutation for this form of colon cancer, and the defective genes were also involved in uterine and ovarian cancers.

The pace of research in cancer genetics raised the prospect of widespread

BRIAN SMITH

At their home in Massachusetts, a young cancer patient and his mother use interactive technology to receive instructions on care. The use of computers in diagnosing diseases and in record keeping and other tasks could help reduce the cost of medical treatment and also improve the quality of care for patients.

Women in Surat, India, burn garbage in an attempt to halt the spread of pneumonic plague. There were outbreaks of the disease in several parts of India in 1994, and to prevent its spread to other countries, a number of governments imposed temporary travel restrictions.
AFP

testing to identify those who were susceptible to inherited forms of breast and colon cancer. In March a U.S. National Institutes of Health (NIH) advisory council warned that it was premature to offer DNA testing or screening for cancer predisposition outside of carefully controlled research projects.

Investigators in England, Wales, and The Netherlands succeeded in isolating the gene responsible for autosomal dominant polycystic kidney disease (ADPKD), one of the most common disorders attributed to a single abnormal gene. ADPKD causes progressive damage as fluid-filled cysts grow in the kidneys, leading to total kidney failure by the age of 60. About 10% of kidney transplant recipients in Europe and the U.S. suffered from ADPKD. The breakthrough would facilitate both understanding of the disease and earlier diagnosis, allowing complications such as hypertension (high blood pressure) and urinary tract infection to be treated more quickly.

The gene defect responsible for achondroplasia, the most common form of inherited dwarfism in most parts of the world, was identified by researchers at the University of California at Irvine. The gene, located on chromosome 4, codes for a protein that binds to growth factors. A tiny change in the amino acids that constitute the protein results in the characteristic skeletal deformations.

In other notable developments, an Australian team identified a single gene that has a significant influence on bone density and, by extension, risk of osteoporosis. Scientists studying families with a history of dyslexia found a characteristic defect within a particular region on chromosome 6, confirming the view that this learning disorder may have a biological basis. And investigators at the Howard Hughes Medical Institute, Rockefeller University, New York City, announced that they had cloned a gene that apparently regulates the size of the body's fat stores. In mice a mutation in this gene causes a severe hereditary form of obesity.

Cardiovascular Disease. Experts continued to debate the best treatment options for heart disease sufferers. Two separate clinical trials by U.S. and German researchers concluded that angioplasty was a reasonable alternative to coronary artery bypass surgery in treating some symptomatic heart patients with multiple blocked arteries. Their reports, published simultaneously in the *New England Journal of Medicine,* found that the two procedures had similar overall risks of complications and death in such patients. Those who underwent bypass surgery were initially hospitalized much longer and were more likely to have procedure-related heart attacks. On the other hand, those who underwent angioplasty, a simpler procedure in which a tiny balloon is inflated within a blocked artery, were far more likely to require repeat procedures within the next one to three years and to require medication for angina (chest pain). Heart disease specialists emphasized that treatment choices had to be made on an individual basis.

Health policy analysts at Harvard Medical School opined, however, that these treatments were being greatly overused. On the basis of a review of Medicare data on 200,000 elderly Americans hospitalized with heart attacks, the Harvard group concluded that invasive heart procedures, such as cardiac catheterization, angioplasty, and bypass surgery, could be reduced by more than 25% with no effect on death rates. They suggested that redirecting resources toward better emergency care of heart attack victims would do more to reduce mortality.

A meta-analysis of numerous trials of antiplatelet therapy (*i.e.,* treatment to inhibit blood clotting) confirmed that regular consumption of aspirin (75–325 mg per day) provided worthwhile protection against a subsequent heart attack or stroke and decreased the risk of death in individuals with circulatory and related conditions. There was, however, no clear evidence for recommending routine aspirin use among apparently healthy people with no history of cardiovascular problems.

Paralleling previous findings in the U.S., evidence from the U.K. established that men received better treatment than women for acute myocardial infarction (heart attack). One study in Nottingham showed that the survival chances of female patients both in the hospital and after discharge were poorer than those of males, in part because the women had longer delays in reaching the hospital, were less likely to be admitted to a coronary care unit, and were less likely to be given drugs to inhibit blood clotting. Research in London confirmed that female heart attack victims had an inferior prognosis over the first 30 days as a result of receiving less vigorous treatment than their male counterparts.

A formerly controversial surgical procedure received an endorsement in October when the directors of a multicentre U.S. and Canadian study reported their finding that the operation, called carotid endarterectomy, reduced by about half the projected risk of stroke in patients who had narrowed carotid arteries but no symptoms of incipient stroke. The carotid, a major artery in the neck, carries blood to the brain. Fatty deposits inside the artery can decrease blood flow and eventually cause a stroke. The investigators were puzzled by one result of the investigation: the risk reduction of women was considerably less than that of men.

A report presented in November at the annual meeting of the American Heart Association could have far-reaching implications for patients with coronary heart disease. Scandinavian scientists found that a cholesterol-lowering drug reduced the risk of death in such patients by 42%—the first "proof" that these medications have an impact on survival.

Cancer. An independent panel of experts assessed the U.S. government's war on cancer and found that, overall, cancer incidence had increased 18% and the death rate had risen by 7% since the effort was launched in 1971. While there had been progress in basic research and in treatments that keep patients alive longer, the panel concluded that more needed to be done to improve quality of life and access to care. The report noted that government policies subsidizing tobacco—the leading preventable cause of disability and death in the U.S. and many other countries—were undermining cancer-prevention efforts.

Throughout 1994 the U.S. Congress and the Food and Drug Administration (FDA) engaged in the first serious national inquiry over whether to regulate the nicotine in tobacco products as a drug. An FDA advisory committee concluded that nicotine in tobacco is indeed addictive. Congressional hearings were held, but the issue of tobacco regulation remained unresolved. (*See* BUSINESS AND INDUSTRY REVIEW: *Tobacco:* Sidebar.)

Two studies published in the *New England Journal of Medicine* cast doubt on the theory that antioxidant vitamin supplements can prevent cancer. In April a major trial of beta-carotene and vitamin E supplements, administered for five to eight years to more than 29,000 male smokers in Finland, found no significant protective effects against lung cancer. In July researchers at Dartmouth Medical School, Hanover, N.H., and five other U.S. medical centres said that administering beta-carotene, vitamin C, or vitamin E for four years did not reduce the development of new colon cancers in patients who had had a polyp removed before entering the study. Both studies were apparently at odds with the vast body of epidemiological evidence showing that people whose diets are rich in fruits and vegetables have reduced cancer risks. It was not clear whether the vitamins in these foods or some other protective substances were responsible for their anticancer properties. Longer-term studies now under way may shed light on the question.

Infectious Diseases. In 1994 leading authorities warned the public and the medical community that the international spread of drug-resistant organisms threatened to become a major health crisis by the end of the 20th century. Convening in Prague for the sixth International Congress for Infectious Diseases, U.S. microbiologist Alexander Tomasz and other government and academic experts observed that the world was entering an era in which some common disease-causing bacteria could become resistant to all available drug therapies. Few new antibiotics were being introduced, and an informal survey of large U.S. and Japanese pharmaceutical companies found that about half had reduced or phased out their antibacterial research programs, in part because of an erroneous assumption that bacterial diseases had already been brought under control.

Sensational headlines about flesh-eating "killer bugs" dominated the newspapers in the U.K. after several reports of serious invasive disease due to a particularly virulent strain of group A streptococcus. British public health authorities were quick to point out that such infections, although extremely grave, were not new and had not increased appreciably in recent years.

In the U.S. a number of events served as reminders of the persistence of microbial threats to health. Several hundred passengers on two cruise ships had to be evacuated as a result of outbreaks of Legionnaires' disease and shigellosis, and a 15-state salmonella epidemic was reported among customers of a Minnesota dairy. In response to a recent increase in foodborne disease attributed to a virulent strain of *Escherichia coli*—which can cause a fatal kidney condition—a group of medical, public health, and food industry experts suggested changes in the U.S. meat-inspection process and recommended that some ground beef be irradiated.

After a little more than a decade of controversy over the significance of the bacterium *Helicobacter pylori*—the so-called ulcer bug—several independent pieces of evidence confirmed the role of the organism as possibly the most important factor in the development of duodenal ulcers. Following earlier studies showing the effectiveness of a regimen of antibiotics plus acid-suppressing drugs, a clinical trial at the Prince of Wales Hospital, Hong Kong, demonstrated that in most ulcer patients antibiotics alone eradicated the bacterium and healed the ulcers. Longer-term research at the Royal Perth (Australia) Hospital and the University of Virginia confirmed that the reduction in ulcer recurrence following eradication of *H. pylori* persisted for at least seven years. Further, a survey in Stoke on Trent, England, showed that adults from crowded childhood homes were particularly likely to carry antibodies to *H. pylori*—an indication that the

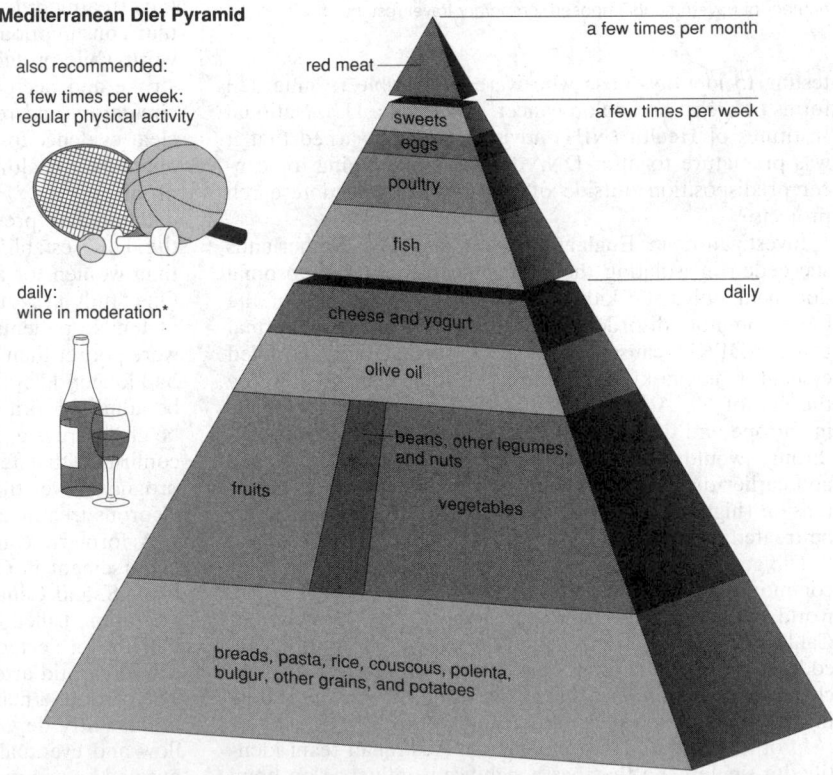

Mediterranean Diet Pyramid

also recommended:

a few times per week:
regular physical activity

daily:
wine in moderation*

red meat — a few times per month

sweets
eggs — a few times per week
poultry
fish

cheese and yogurt — daily

olive oil

beans, other legumes, and nuts

fruits   vegetables

breads, pasta, rice, couscous, polenta, bulgur, other grains, and potatoes

*avoid whenever consumption would put the individual or others at risk
Information provided by Oldways Preservation & Exchange Trust, the World Health Organization, and the Harvard School of Public Health

bacterium is transmitted directly from person to person and may be commonly acquired in early life. On the strength of these and other recent studies, an NIH panel issued an official statement endorsing antimicrobial drugs for the treatment of ulcers.

Diet and Nutrition. In October the U.S. National Task Force on the Prevention and Treatment of Obesity published a review of nearly 30 years of medical research on "yo-yo" dieting. Contrary to some individual studies, this overview found no convincing evidence that repeated loss and gain of weight carried significant health hazards. The task force concluded that obesity posed a far more serious medical problem than did dieting.

A panel of experts convened by the NIH concluded in June that a large percentage of Americans were not getting enough calcium. They noted that children and young adults must consume an adequate amount of calcium

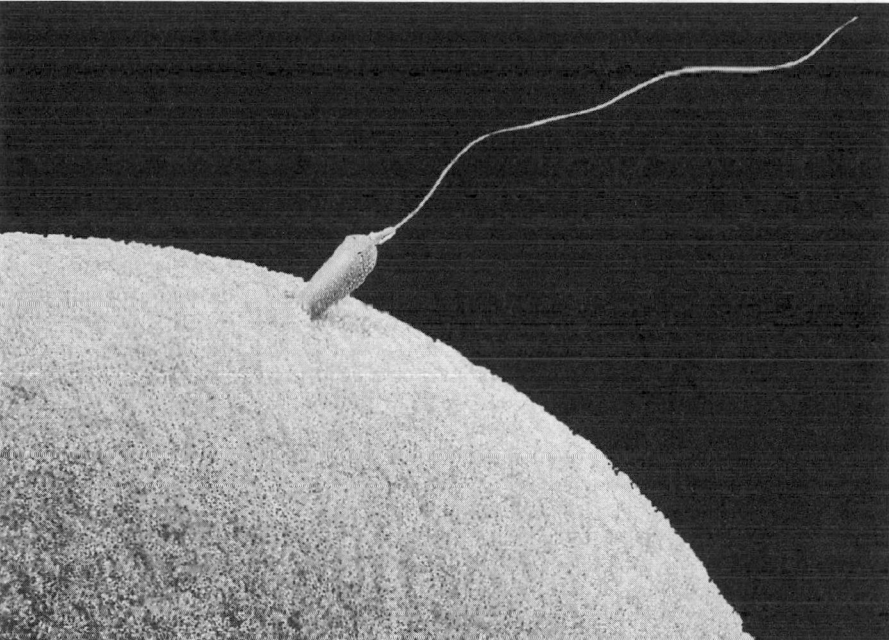

A human sperm fertilizes an egg. In October a U.S. panel recommended that the government fund certain kinds of embryo research. In December Pres. Bill Clinton, because of "profound ethical and moral questions," rejected support for studies using embryos created solely for research.
FRANCIS LEROY—BIOCOSMOS/SCIENCE PHOTO LIBRARY/PHOTO RESEARCHERS

if they are to reach their peak bone mass. Individuals who fail to achieve their peak are more vulnerable to the effects of bone loss in later life. The panel issued new recommendations for optimal daily calcium consumption. For several age groups the suggested levels were considerably higher than the recommended dietary allowances, or RDAs.

Clinicians in Cambridge, England, investigated the effect of milk consumption in childhood and early adulthood on the bone density of women aged 44 to 74. Their study showed that the frequent drinking of milk earlier in life had a favourable effect on the bone mass of the hip at the later age. The benefit was independent of factors such as body size, smoking, and hormone replacement therapy, which also influence bone density. Another study examined the purported relationship of coffee consumption and decreased bone density. The researchers, from the University of California at San Diego, found a positive correlation between caffeinated coffee intake and low bone mineral content, but they also determined that the harmful effects of coffee drinking on bone mass could be offset by regular consumption of milk.

Medical and nutrition professionals around the world continued to examine the health benefits of low-fat, high-fibre diets. One style of eating that was receiving a major share of attention was the diet of the Mediterranean region, where the population had traditionally enjoyed low rates of heart disease and some cancers. In 1994 an international group of experts interested in traditional eating patterns developed the Mediterranean diet pyramid as a model for healthful eating. The Mediterranean pyramid called for a largely plant-based diet. Cheese, yogurt, and olive oil were included with fruits, vegetables, and grains as foods that could be eaten daily, while red meat was to be consumed only a few times a month. Not all nutrition authorities were in favour of the concept. For one thing, the diet of the Mediterranean region derives more than 30% of its calories from fat, and current U.S. dietary recommendations call for limiting fat calories to 30% or less. For another, wine is a regular feature of meals in Mediterranean countries, and

many U.S. public health authorities hesitated to advocate a regimen that included alcohol as even an optional element.

Meanwhile, in France investigators from the Lyon Heart Study demonstrated that a Mediterranean-style diet was effective in reducing the risk of further heart problems in individuals who had already experienced a heart attack. Some 300 patients were encouraged to increase their consumption of grains, fruits, and vegetables and to eat less red meat and more poultry. The butter in their diet was replaced by a spread rich in alpha-linolenic acid, which some experts believed to have cardioprotective effects. During a follow-up, which averaged 27 months, there were three coronary deaths and five nonfatal heart attacks among those on the diet, compared with corresponding figures of 16 and 17 in a similar group that received no dietary advice.

The health benefits of a vegetarian diet were substantiated by the results of a 12-year survey conducted by nutritionists in London and Oxford, England. Comparing the fates of more than 5,000 British meat eaters with those of some 6,000 who were not meat eaters, the investigators reported a 40% lower rate of death from cancer among the vegetarians. Those who did not eat meat also had a markedly lower rate of atherosclerotic heart disease, though this was at least partly attributable to their much larger proportion of nonsmokers.

Other Developments. A major advance was reported in the treatment of Crohn's disease, a chronic inflammatory bowel disorder. Although corticosteroids had proved useful in the past, they sometimes produced potentially serious side effects. A multicentre Canadian study of the synthetic steroid budenoside showed not only that the drug was effective but also that those who received it had no greater incidence of adverse effects than patients who took a placebo.

A potentially significant finding about the etiology of amyotrophic lateral sclerosis (ALS), also known as Lou Gehrig's disease (and, in the U.K., as motor neurone disease), was reported from Scotland. Researchers in Glasgow, searching for possible signs of an infectious agent, found evidence of viral genetic material in spinal cord tissue from a high proportion of patients who had died of the disease but not in tissue samples from matched controls. The scientists cautioned that association of the virus—an enterovirus (a member of the family that includes the poliovirus)—with the disease did not prove a cause-and-effect relationship. In the meantime, there were cautiously optimistic claims from researchers in Paris that an experimental drug, riluzole, appeared to slow the progression of the inevitably fatal condition and to improve survival in certain patients. Perhaps the most promising development of the year, however, was the announcement by scientists in the U.S. that they had created a strain of mice genetically engineered to contract ALS. The existence of an animal model for the disease was expected to speed the search for effective therapies.

Evidence of the harmful effects of smoking continued to accumulate during 1994. Research conducted at the University of Melbourne, Australia, greatly strengthened the previously suspected link between smoking by women and an increased risk of osteoporosis. A study directed by investigators from the U.S. National Cancer Institute found that breast cancer patients who smoked had a 25% greater risk of dying from the disease than their nonsmoking counterparts. Scientists studying children and teens with high cholesterol levels found that those whose parents smoked had considerably lower levels of the so-called good cholesterol (believed to help prevent heart attacks) than the children from nonsmoking families. Since all other variables were the same, it seemed likely that exposure to secondhand smoke was responsible for the difference in the youngsters' cholesterol profiles. On the positive side, a multicentre U.S.-Canadian study published in November showed that smokers who already had chronic bronchitis and emphysema could effectively prevent further deterioration in lung function by quitting smoking.

A study from Sweden contributed to the ongoing disagreement as to whether radon gas, which was known to cause lung cancer in miners, was also responsible for the disease in people exposed to radon at home, albeit at much lower concentrations. Scientists from several Swedish environmental agencies and medical institutions studied 1,360 men and women with lung cancer and measured radon levels in nearly 9,000 buildings in which the individuals had lived in the past. A comparison with control subjects showed that the risk of lung cancer clearly increased in accordance with the level of radon exposure. The Swedish researchers concluded that residential exposure to radon was an important cause of lung cancer in the general population. U.S. and Canadian studies published during the year found just the opposite, however.

(BERNARD DIXON; CRISTINE RUSSELL)

MENTAL HEALTH

Paralleling the trend in other areas of medical research, advances were made in the understanding of the genetic basis of mental illness and the effects of abnormal genes on brain function. Researchers in Japan reported evidence that a variant of the gene that encodes one of the receptors for the neurotransmitter dopamine may be a risk factor for some types of schizophrenia. Comparing 156 schizophrenic patients with controls, they found that the frequency of the gene was significantly higher among patients, especially in those whose illness had begun before the age of 25 and those with a family history of the condition.

Fragile X syndrome—the most common form of mental retardation caused by a single gene defect—was also yielding some of its secrets. In 1991 molecular geneticists had discovered that the mutation responsible for the condition

(continued on page 200)

Special Report

Repressed Memories

BY MICHAEL D. YAPKO

In 1994 the mental health profession found itself deeply divided over an approach to psychotherapy known as "repressed memory therapy," or RMT. RMT relies on so-called memory-recovery techniques to help a patient "remember" or "recover" episodes, usually of sexual abuse, from childhood—episodes that presumably have been "forgotten." The abuse is assumed to be an underlying cause of the patient's current symptoms.

RMT is based on the theory that in order to cope with the trauma of being abused, the victim employed a psychological defense known as dissociation. Dissociation involves "splitting off" awareness so that the conscious mind is "elsewhere" when the abuse takes place. The result is repression, a self-protective memory loss, or amnesia. Despite the fact that the painful experiences are consciously forgotten, the repressed material can still cause severe symptoms; often these symptoms have no clear cause. The therapist's role in RMT is to help the patient recover the memories. Presumably, once the memories have been brought into awareness, the survivor's present problems can be effectively treated.

The professional controversy over RMT centres on questions such as: Why and under what conditions does an individual repress traumatic memories? Can one completely forget repeated episodes of childhood sexual abuse? Might the memories that are recovered have been "manufactured" to accommodate the expectations and suggestions of the therapist or to account for otherwise puzzling symptoms? Is it possible for a therapist to lead a patient to believe that he or she was sexually abused when no such event actually occurred? And perhaps most important, how should therapists conduct themselves when the answers to these questions remain unclear?

Mental health professionals generally agree that sexual abuse of children has been and is a widespread problem. They recognize that historically survivors of such abuse have been discounted owing to a "cultural denial" that has minimized both the scope and the seriousness of the offense. They know that creating a climate in which survivors can come forward, disclose what happened to them, and be believed is vital to their eventual recovery. Beyond this, however, opinions diverge.

On one side are those who believe that dissociation and repression are common responses to sexual abuse in childhood and that victims generally can be readily identifiable from a known list of symptoms. In their view, treatment should first lift the veil of repression through techniques such as hypnosis or "guided imagery." The therapist then must help the patient deal with the painful memories. Proponents of RMT are concerned that any disbelief in these assumptions on the part of therapists makes it more difficult for sexual abuse survivors to disclose their problems and easier for perpetrators to evade responsibility for their terrible deeds. They reject the notion that detailed trau-

Michael D. Yapko is a clinical psychologist in private practice in Solana Beach, Calif. He is the author of Suggestions of Abuse: True and False Memories of Childhood Sexual Abuse and Essentials of Hypnosis.

matic memories can arise merely on the basis of suggestion, contending that such memories need to be acknowledged as true before treatment can succeed.

On the other side of the controversy are those who view dissociation and repression as uncommon responses. They have grave doubts that anyone can suffer repeated trauma over a long period of time and repress all the memories, only to recover them many years or even many decades later under the influence of therapy (or some other suggestive source, such as a book or talk show). RMT opponents do not believe that victims can be identified on the basis of a "symptom checklist." Furthermore, they hold that it is unsound to hypothesize a history of abuse on the basis of symptoms that might be explained by other means. They recognize that some people may be particularly vulnerable in certain contexts—for example, psychotherapy—and thus may accept "evidence" that has no basis in fact. When therapists conclude that a patient has been sexually abused, they may lead that patient, intentionally or unintentionally, to reach the same conclusion. Consequently, appropriate treatment for that patient is delayed or even prevented. And finally, RMT opponents are concerned that innocent people will be falsely accused of perpetrating abuse, and their lives and families will be destroyed as a result.

Professionals on both sides of this controversy argue their points vehemently and intelligently, and both groups are motivated by a desire to help "victims" or potential victims.

In order to accommodate the theory of repressed memories, many U.S. states have passed laws allowing a "delayed discovery" to serve as the basis for civil suits. Otherwise, the statute of limitations in these cases would have expired. By the end of 1994, about 500 legal actions had been initiated—most often by a daughter against an allegedly abusive parent. Within the past two years, several cases have been highly publicized, bringing the RMT controversy before the public.

One such case involved Gary Ramona, a successful northern California winery executive, whose daughter Holly had sought psychotherapy for depression and bulimia (a severe eating disorder) when she was a college student. During her treatment in 1989–90, she began to recall scenes of sexual abuse from her childhood and came to believe they involved her father. In the process of therapy, she was given sodium amytal, the so-called truth serum, in an attempt to validate her conclusion that her father had abused her. While under the influence of the drug, she recounted specific instances of abuse by her father.

When Ramona was publicly accused of child sexual abuse, he vehemently denied it. Nonetheless, he lost his job, his wife left him, and his two other daughters cut off all contact with him. His reputation, family, and career thus ruined, Ramona filed an $8 million malpractice suit against Holly's former therapists and the medical centre at which they worked. He claimed they had planted inaccurate and damaging information in his daughter's mind and had used questionable techniques to do so. On May 13, 1994, the jury in the Napa county superior court where the case was tried awarded a judgment of $500,000 to Gary Ramona. The judgment was not based on the truth or falsity of Holly's memories but on how the memories were obtained. The jury believed the therapists had not conducted themselves appropriately in Holly's treatment.

This case was significant because it was the first repressed-memory case in the United States in which a third party was awarded damages. Normally, if a therapist is sued, it is by a patient. Previous "standard-of-care" cases had considered only the therapist's responsibility to his or her patients, not to the patients' relatives. Another interesting aspect of the Ramona case was that the patient, Holly, testified on behalf of her therapists and continued to maintain that the abuse took place even after the court's decision.

In another widely publicized case, 34-year-old Stephen Cook of Philadelphia filed a $10 million suit against Joseph Cardinal Bernardin of Chicago, claiming Bernardin had sexually abused him nearly two decades earlier when Cook was a seminary student. Cook had also accused another clergyman at the school of having molested him. Cook's memories of abuse by Bernardin came later and were obtained under hypnosis.

The cardinal quickly and convincingly denied the accusations, bringing Cook's credibility into question. Cook then consulted a psychologist to evaluate his "memories" and determine whether he might have been influenced by the hypnotist. Subsequently, Cook acknowledged publicly that his memories were "unreliable," and in early 1994 he withdrew his allegations against Bernardin. Cook's accusation and subsequent retraction raised many doubts in the public's mind about the validity of RMT. (Cook's case against the other priest was later settled out of court.)

In one of the most bizarre cases involving repressed memories, Paul Ingram, a former Washington state deputy sheriff, was accused by one of his daughters of sexual abuse. The charge stemmed from a memory that surfaced at a church retreat, where the subject of sexual abuse was discussed. Another of Ingram's daughters, who was at the same retreat, then claimed she, too, had been sexually abused by her father. Ingram's law-enforcement colleagues encouraged him to confess because that would help him "remember" the acts he must be repressing.

Although the daughters' allegations were improbable—expanding to include many of Ingram's fellow officers as accomplices and to involve satanic rituals and even human sacrifices (all charges for which no evidence was ever found)—the investigators in this case believed the abuses had occurred. They did not think such detailed stories could be entirely untrue. A deeply religious man, Ingram reasoned that his daughters would never make up such charges; despite having no such memories, he concluded that the accusations must be true. Believing that neither God nor his daughters would lead him to imagine unfounded guilt, Ingram confessed and went to prison. His intense religiosity led him to believe that any image he conjured up in his mind of having perpetrated abuse must have been placed there by God, thereby confirming his "guilt."

Without objective corroborating evidence—such as a photograph or videotape—how can a real memory of child sexual abuse be distinguished from an illusory one? At present, no reliable method exists for distinguishing truth from fiction in RMT cases. Clearly, the issues are complex, and courts have been asked to rule even in the absence of hard data. In 1990, for example, in the case in California of 30-year-old Eileen Franklin-Lipsker's recovered memories, the jury convicted her father, George Franklin, in the 1969 murder of one of her childhood friends after Franklin-Lipsker's testimony and that of child psychiatrist Lenore Terr convinced the jury beyond a reasonable doubt that Franklin was guilty. He was convicted of first-degree murder and sentenced to life in prison.

As pressure increases from within the field to approach these sensitive cases with extreme caution, undoubtedly more careful research will be conducted. And as legal rulings shape public perception and further define professional responsibilities, the intensity of the RMT controversy is likely to diminish. In the meantime, therapists must, as always, honour the Hippocratic oath: *Primum non nocere* ("Above all do no harm").

(continued from page 198)

consists of large numbers of repeated sequences of nucleotides (the subunits that constitute DNA). Now research has shown that carriers have "premutations"—smaller numbers of nucleotide repeats—that have the potential to increase as the gene is transmitted to subsequent generations. As well as accounting for the development of the disease, these discoveries have facilitated prenatal diagnosis.

Concurrent with developments of this sort, there was growing interest in the social context of mental illness. The relationship between mental disorders and unemployment was a matter of increasing concern in the U.K. Investigators based in Bristol, England, reported on a detailed analysis of the relationship between the occupancy of psychiatric hospital beds and the numbers of people out of work in different parts of their region. Their findings showed that unemployment was an extremely powerful indicator of the rate of serious mental illness requiring hospital treatment among individuals under 65.

Psychiatrists at the Clinical Research Centre, Harrow, England, and other U.K. centres published the results of a study that examined the social adjustment in childhood of people who developed psychiatric disorders as adults. The investigators consulted teachers' assessments of the social behaviour of 7- and 11-year-olds who by age 28 had been hospitalized for schizophrenia, affective psychoses (*e.g.,* major depression accompanied by hallucinations), or neurotic illness (*e.g.,* milder forms of depression). The results showed that whereas the individuals in the second category had differed little from normal controls at the younger ages, those later diagnosed as schizophrenic had all been rated at seven as manifesting more social maladjustment. This was more apparent in boys than in girls. By the age of 11 the preneurotic children, especially the girls, also had an increased rating of maladjustment.

Several studies carried out in different parts of the world provided encouraging evidence of the effectiveness of a new drug for the treatment of schizophrenia. The drug, risperidone, was introduced in the U.K. in 1993 and approved in the U.S. in 1994. Risperidone was reported to help patients who had failed to respond to other antipsychotic drugs and to have a beneficial effect on a wider range of symptoms than some of these existing alternatives. As was often the case with new drug compounds, however, it was considerably more expensive than the older agents.

Research at the University of California at San Diego clarified earlier claims from several European countries that low blood pressure was sometimes accompanied by an increased prevalence of weeping, fatigue, and psychological dysfunction. Psychiatrists in the U.S. and the U.K. had generally been skeptical about such reports. The new evidence came from a study of 594 male residents, aged 60–89, of Rancho Bernardo, Calif., who were categorized as having low, normal, or high blood pressure. The researchers observed a significant association between relatively low blood pressure and higher scores for both overt depression and symptoms of depression, irrespective of age or weight loss.

There was also progress in understanding the basis of the mental deterioration that often occurs in elderly people who are not suffering from Alzheimer's disease or other well-defined dementing disorders. One possible explanation was that a decline in cognitive function could be attributed to narrowing of the arteries that supply blood to the brain. Exploring the link between mental status and circulatory disease, researchers at Erasmus University Medical School, Rotterdam, Neth., examined some 5,000 subjects aged 55–94 for clinical signs of atherosclerosis and gave them tests of memory, attention, and other mental skills. The results were compatible with the view that impaired blood flow to the brain accounts for a considerable proportion of cognitive impairment among the elderly.   (BERNARD DIXON)

This article updates the *Macropædia* article MENTAL DISORDERS and Their Treatment.

VETERINARY MEDICINE

A major international symposium to assess the past and predict the future progress of the veterinary profession was held by the Royal College of Veterinary Surgeons in London. The event was the keynote of the 150th-anniversary celebrations marking the granting of a royal charter to the college by Queen Victoria in 1844. The charter had set the seal on the professional status of veterinarians in the U.K. and, by extension, it affected the development of veterinary practice throughout the English-speaking world. Speakers at the symposium reviewed the contemporary demands placed on the training of veterinarians and discussed issues in the care and welfare of animals, the production of livestock, and the safeguarding of public health. The symposium identified enormous potential benefits arising from biotechnology but also noted that such advances—for example, the use of bovine somatotrophin to increase milk production—raise serious ethical considerations.

HIV, the organism believed responsible for AIDS, is the best known of the lentiviruses (slow viruses), but others affect cats, horses, sheep, goats, and monkeys. Unlike other members of the group, all of which eventually cause disease in the host animal, bovine immunodeficiency virus (BIV), which affects cattle, could be carried for years without producing clinical signs. In 1994, however, this accepted view was challenged when BIV was discovered in a Cheshire, England, herd that was suffering from a mysterious wasting disease. Confirmation of the virus's role in causing the illness was hampered by the very slow development of the disease—a similar problem to that encountered in the study of bovine spongiform encephalopathy, a neurological disorder that affects cattle.

The practice of judging the age of a horse by the appearance of its teeth goes back well over 2,000 years, but there had never been any scientific validation of the method. J.D. Richardson and her colleagues at the Universities of Bristol, England, and London undertook a study to establish whether tooth wear is in fact an accurate measure of age. They examined the teeth of horses of known age and then compared estimated age, as indicated by the teeth, with the actual age. They found that up to the age of five the actual and estimated ages were similar. In older horses, however, the results were much less accurate. The pattern of wear was affected by diet, environment, and breed as well as by age. They concluded that while a horse's teeth could provide a convenient practical guide to its age, the result was more an informed guess than a precise answer.

Concern over the effects of high humidity on animals competing in the equine events at the 1996 Olympic Games in Atlanta, Ga., led the International Equestrian Federation to study the effects of high temperature and humidity on exercising horses. Work carried out at the Animal Health Trust in England involved treadmill exercises in an environment-controlled building. The tests demonstrated that high humidity, as might be encountered in Atlanta, could cause health problems resulting from increased fatigue. As a result, the rules of the three-day event might need to be changed to protect the horses' welfare.

(EDWARD BODEN)

See also Life Sciences: *Molecular Biology.*

This article updates the *Macropædia* articles DIAGNOSIS AND THERAPEUTICS; DISEASE; INFECTIOUS DISEASES; MEDICINE.

Information Processing and Information Systems

Sweeping change marked the U.S. computer industry in 1994 as longtime players exited the stage and rival systems struggled to dominate the next generation of personal computer (PC) operating systems and microprocessors. The industry also witnessed fundamental changes in technology as computers moved from desks to pockets and that old standby, the telephone line, was recast as the vehicle for carrying digital video images ranging from movies to computer graphics files.

In the marketplace a war was under way over which microprocessor would dominate as the brains of the latest generation of PCs. The battle involved some surprising alignments. On one side were former rivals Apple Computer, Inc., and IBM Corp., which introduced the new PowerPC family of microprocessors developed jointly with Motorola, Inc. On the other side were Intel Corp., which was once IBM's chief supplier of PC microprocessors, and Microsoft Corp., the world's largest producer of PC software and

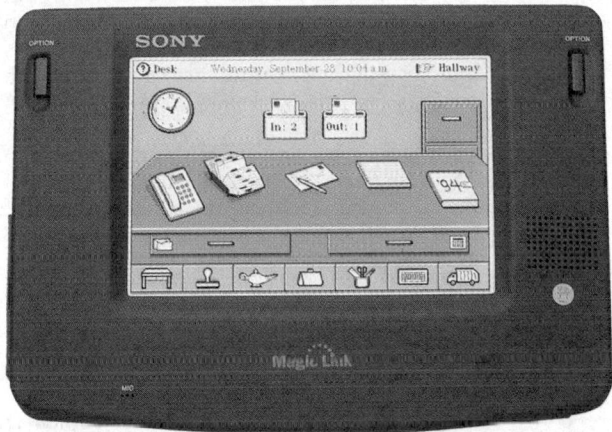

Sony's Magic Link allows users to send voice messages over E-mail. The company introduced the unit, which weighs less than half a kilogram (one pound) and sells for under $1,000, to compete in the growing market for personal digital assistants.
SONY

the supplier of both MS-DOS—the major Intel-based disk operating system (DOS)—and the popular Windows operating environment. Intel's fastest new chip, the Pentium, competed directly with PowerPC, but it did not have the speed edge of PowerPC's reduced instruction set computing (RISC) architecture. Intel competitors, including Advanced Micro Devices, Inc., and NexGen Software, would produce their own cheaper Pentium-class chips.

In March 1994 Apple released the first PowerPC-based hardware, the Power Macintosh (Power Mac) line of computers. Although the Power Macs used Apple's proprietary graphic operating system, Mac OS, they were capable of running both Apple and Windows-compatible software. In late 1994 it was uncertain who would emerge the victors in the Pentium-PowerPC battle. In November Apple, IBM, and Motorola disclosed plans for the joint development of a universal PowerPC capable of running multiple operating systems. It was expected to be available in 1996. Meanwhile, on December 19, IBM suspended sales of its personal computers that contained the Pentium chip, which had been found to contain a flaw that could affect calculations. Intel had stonewalled, insisting that problems would occur only

once in 27,000 years of normal use, but then, prompted by a precipitous drop in its stock, acknowledged its public relations blunder and offered free, no-questions-asked replacement of faulty chips.

The PC microprocessor war also sparked a battle over operating systems. Microsoft's as-yet unreleased Windows 95 (formerly code-named Chicago) faced IBM's new operating system, OS/2 Warp, and a new Mac OS, both of which could run several tasks at once. Windows 95 was expected to take advantage of the new Pentium chips' speed and to eliminate the need for DOS by incorporating an operating system with the Windows graphic interface. Windows 95, however, would require earlier Windows programs to be rewritten in order to take advantage of Windows 95 and, while Microsoft originally promised its new system for early 1994, in late December the company acknowledged that it would not arrive until August 1995.

A battle was also shaping up in a new line of hardware. In August 1993 Apple introduced Newton, the first personal digital assistant (PDA), a pocket-size computer with a write-on screen instead of a keyboard. Newton was immediately criticized for its poor handwriting recognition, and only about 80,000 units were sold. In 1994, however, the company introduced a new Newton with triple the memory and a $599 price tag, roughly $200 less than the original version. More important, Apple said that it had persuaded 2,400 software developers to write programs for Newton, something the machine had sorely lacked.

After Newton came Simon, a handheld cellular phone that could send and receive faxes, which was being sold by the regional phone company BellSouth for about $1,000. A similar product was Lingo, a Motorola-made unit that combined a wireless phone and pager. It sent and received text messages via a new two-way radio network being put together by Nextel. In 1994 the network serviced only Los Angeles, but full U.S. coverage was scheduled for 1996.

The biggest splash of all, though, came late in the year when Sony Corp. introduced the $995 Magic Link, a 0.45-kg (1-lb) unit that let users send voice messages throughout AT&T's national electronic mail (E-mail) network. Magic Link was introduced with one megabyte of memory and a 2,400-baud fax modem, but Sony said that memory and modem speed would be increased soon. Magic Link needed to connect with phone lines to communicate unless the customer bought a pager card that slipped into its side. Eventually, the PDA was to have two-way wireless connectivity.

With most PDAs selling at around $1,000 or less, there proved to be no room for AT&T's $3,600 EO Personal Communicator. That unit thus became the first casualty of the PDA wars and, taking notice, Compaq Computer Corp. said it would hold off releasing its PDA until at least the end of 1994.

The hubbub over PDAs, though, ignored the fact that their greatest benefits should eventually come from how they communicate over networks. To this end Magic Link's debut was accompanied by AT&T's announcement that it had incorporated "intelligent agent" software into its E-mail network. As a result, someone using the right PDA could order airline tickets by simply touching a pen against one or two of the images on the screen's "desktop" image. Instead of calling an airline or travel agent, the computer would connect with a special AT&T database, where the intelligent software would recognize the caller and arrange the ticket without further ado.

Among the industry's exiting players was John Sculley, who resigned in late 1993 after having taken Apple's annual earnings from $600 million to $8 billion during his 10 years as chief executive officer (CEO). When he quit, Apple was facing a challenge similar to the one he had been hired to solve: shifting to a new generation of computers while unloading a $1.5 billion inventory of existing machines.

In a major break with the past, Apple celebrated the 10th birthday of the Macintosh computer by announcing that it would soon license the Mac OS to other companies (mainly in Europe and Japan) and make possible the first Macintosh clones ever. The move was a strategy by Apple's new president and CEO, Michael Spindler, to increase the demand for Macintosh software and thus boost the variety of software available and the sale of all kinds of Mac-compatible computers. Some experts expected the move to boost Apple's market share in desktop computers from 10% to 30% in the coming three years.

At network software maker Novell, Inc., chairman Ray Noorda, a veteran of more than 10 years at the helm, stepped down—but not before he had the company spend $1,350,000,000 to acquire WordPerfect Corp. and $145 million to buy Borland International, Inc.'s Quattro Pro spreadsheet business. Novell had proposed a merger with rival Lotus Development Corp. in 1990.

The deal gave a much-needed cash infusion to Borland, where founder and longtime CEO Philippe Kahn saw his power slashed when the board put in place a new executive, Keith Maib, as chief operating officer. Maib's job was to get the company, which had been buffeted by three consecutive losing fiscal years, back on track and try to make a hit with the company's new Windows version of the dBASE database program, itself an aged PC workhorse.

Another merger of PC industry veterans had Adobe Systems Inc., maker of the Postscript printing language, buying Aldus Corp., producer of the PageMaker desktop publishing program, in a $525 million stock swap. With combined revenues of about $520 million and 1,200 employees, the new company—to be called Adobe Systems—would be the fourth largest PC software supplier in the U.S. As part of the deal, Aldus' high-end graphics application, FreeHand, which was in direct competition with Adobe Illustrator, reverted to its original developer, Altsys.

What was to have been the trendsetting merger of the year, the planned union of the regional phone company Bell Atlantic Corp. with cable television giant TCI, Inc., fell apart. Corporate differences also derailed a proposed "megamerger" between Electronic Data Systems Corp., the computer services company owned by General Motors Corp., and long-distance carrier Sprint Corp.

The TCI/Bell Atlantic breakdown highlighted the important role that regulators played in telecommunications and hence in the increasingly networked information processing sector. In 1994 landmark telecommunications reform legislation that would have allowed cable TV companies to offer phone service and phone companies to offer long-distance and cable TV service failed to pass the U.S. Senate after overwhelmingly passing the House of Representatives. Many analysts expected the fibre-optic phone networks to become the basis of a future national information highway that would integrate the computer and telecommunications industries.

The national standard proposed by U.S. Pres. Bill Clinton's administration for the encryption of data and voice transfers by telephone lines was attacked by privacy advocates and the information processing industry. The proposed Clipper encryption chip would contain a "key" that would give U.S. government agencies the ability to decode, or decrypt, private data sent over public phone lines. When a researcher on the project admitted that it might not work, the Clipper project was temporarily shelved. The Clinton administration was also criticized by many in the

PC software industry for ignoring its call for the freedom to export encryption programs, which were widely available worldwide.

In July the U.S. Justice Department settled an 11-month antitrust investigation of Microsoft by imposing minimal conditions on the company. The conditions would end Microsoft's practice of requiring PC makers to pay for one copy of MS-DOS for each PC that was shipped regardless of whether it was actually installed in the PC. The department, though, took no action regarding competitors' claims that Microsoft kept to itself special features in MS-DOS and its best-selling Windows, allowing only its own programmers to exploit them. Nor did it require Microsoft to pay damages to competitors or even admit guilt.

A month earlier a U.S. judge had ruled that Microsoft had infringed two patents on data-compression technology held by Stac Electronics, Inc. Microsoft appealed the ruling, which could affect millions of PCs, as well as the $120 million judgment.

IBM, in an effort to open new lines of business, and cash in on the boom in PDAs and the excitement over the PowerPC chip, signed two key deals with Japanese technology companies in 1994. One, a $100 million, 10-year licensing agreement with Hitachi, allowed the Japanese firm to build large computers based on the PowerPC chip and to sell IBM mainframe computers. The other deal, with Canon Inc., was a technology-sharing venture that would give birth to a PDA and to a PowerPC-based PC costing less than $4,000.

Canon's small role in the world PC business appeared to be about to change as Japan experienced what was expected to be a surge in PC buying perhaps matched only by that of the U.S. in the 1980s. Though a leader in the manufacture of laptop computers, Japan had few PCs in use in business, and only about one-fifth of those were networked, another major opportunity. In addition, only about 7% of Japanese households had computers, a quarter of the U.S. rate. A kanji version of Windows debuted in Japan in 1993, and big price cuts on PCs were expected.

As in years past, the big names of the U.S. computer industry did their usual rounds of layoffs in 1993–94, though many were done by healthy companies seeking to become smaller and more responsive. This category included IBM's plan to eliminate 35,000 jobs by the end of 1994, NCR's planned workforce reduction of 12–15%, and AT&T's plan to cut 14,000 to 15,000 jobs in its communications services operation over two years. Severe financial woes, however, did prompt the elimination of 20,000 jobs at Digital Equipment Corp. (DEC), leaving it with less than half its 1989 workforce of 137,000. DEC, thought to have hit bottom when it posted a $2.8 billion loss in 1992, was expected to post a 1994 loss of $1 billion.

Another PC industry veteran, DOS itself, seemed headed for the exit. Some evidence: WordPerfect introduced its magnum opus word processing application for DOS, WordPerfect 6.0, in 1993 but in 1994 said 6.0 was probably the end of the road. Microsoft also hinted there would be no improved versions of MS-DOS, which would be replaced by Windows 95 and the Windows NT network operating system. Quarterly sales of DOS-based applications plummeted by about $200 million from their $650 million level of the first quarter of 1992. The reason: computers running Windows were easier to use and apparently made their users more productive. The difference, according to one industry expert, was about $3,000 per computer.

(EDWARD S. WARNER)

This article updates the *Macropædia* articles COMPUTERS; INFORMATION PROCESSING AND INFORMATION SYSTEMS.

Labour-Management Relations

International Developments. For most of the industrialized market economies, the outlook brightened as 1994 progressed, and inflationary pressures proved manageable. Unemployment, however, was forecast to rise to 8.5% in the countries of the Organisation for Economic Co-operation and Development (OECD) by the end of the year. In June the OECD published the results of a two-year study of jobs, putting forward a number of recommendations that stressed the importance of technological know-how and of increasing the flexibility of working time, encouraging an entrepreneurial climate, making wages and labour costs more flexible, reforming restrictions on employment security, improving labour market policies and skills, and reforming unemployment benefit systems.

In the closing stages of the Uruguay round of international trade negotiations, the U.S., with support from others, proposed confining the advantages of the General Agreement on Tariffs and Trade (GATT) to countries observing fair labour standards. The proposal was strongly opposed by less developed countries, which saw it as protectionism on the part of rich countries and as likely to hurt their trade and their efforts to build an industrial base. The proposal was not accepted for inclusion in GATT, but it was agreed that it could be discussed in the committee charged with setting up the World Trade Organization.

Europe. In the European Union, action on labour matters was relatively low-key in 1994. The most notable event was the finalization of the long-discussed directive concerning establishment of European-level works councils, procedures under which management would discuss the progress and prospects of the company with workers' representatives at least once a year. The directive was approved by 11 of the 12 member states, the U.K. exercising its right to opt out. The European Commission issued a white paper on labour in July. It argued that Europe needed a broadly based, innovative, and forward-looking social policy to meet the challenges ahead. Defeating unemployment was given pride of place, but the Commission also stressed the importance of improving productivity, a high rate of investment in new technology, and promoting a well-educated, highly motivated, and adaptable working population.

In June the European Court of Justice issued two significant judgments against the U.K., one concerning a 1977 directive on the safeguarding of workers' rights in the transfer of a company and the other a 1975 directive on collective dismissals. In both cases the court found that U.K. law did not make adequate provision for workers' representatives to be consulted in reaching an agreement. Further, effective sanctions had not been provided against employers failing to inform and consult. In the 1977 case the U.K. had also wrongly excluded non-profit-making firms. In fact, the U.K. had anticipated nearly all the points covered by the rulings by amending its legislation. In September the court ruled on six British and Dutch cases concerning occupational pension plans. Notable aspects of the rulings dealt with the calculation of women's pensions, considering their longer life expectancy, and the right of part-time workers to be covered by an employer's plan.

The most prominent event in British labour-management relations during the year concerned railway signal personnel. Under the changes in the structure of railway operation, rail tracks, railway stations, and signaling became the responsibility of Railtrack, a state-owned company, while other enterprises were designated to run the trains. The Rail, Maritime and Transport Union lodged a claim, largely based on productivity improvements in recent years, for an 11% pay increase. In negotiations in early June the union understood the company to have proposed a 5.7% increase, but when the formal offer was made, it was for 2.5%. The government allegedly had intervened to stop the 5.7% offer. A strike ballot showed strong support for action, and a series of one- and two-day strikes were called, continuing into September. The strikes caused considerable disruption, though as time went by, the company made it possible for an appreciable proportion of normal services to operate on strike days. Agreement was reached at the end of September on a deal estimated to cost 3.7%, with a basic pay increase of 2.5%.

British union membership continued its 15 year decline, though polls suggested that unions were gaining favour in public opinion. The Trades Union Congress, under the leadership of John Monks, its new general secretary, embarked on its most radical internal reorganization in more than 70 years, replacing its network of committees with a tighter structure, reducing the frequency of its general meetings, and stepping up its campaigning and service activities.

In February a new, three-year central agreement was arrived at in Ireland, covering pay and social and economic issues for both the public and the private sector. The comprehensive agreement provided staged wage increases, over the three years, of 8% in the private and parallel increases in the public sector.

When the year started, German economic prospects appeared gloomy as the country coped not only with recession but also with the continuing high cost of helping the former communist sector. Unemployment, at around four million, was at a long-term high. Under these circumstances collective bargaining produced only moderate settlements, with wage increases that resulted in small reductions in real earnings and with provisions for increasing flexibility in working time. Thus, in the chemical industry an agreement reached in January provided a 2% pay rise, with newly hired workers being paid lower rates than those for existing workers. There could, by agreement between the employer and the works council, be a variation in working time, with a minimum of 35 hours a week and a maximum of 40 hours without payment of overtime, though the average of 37.5 hours had to apply over the course of a year. In the engineering industry an agreement gave a pay rise of 2% and restricted holiday pay and Christmas bonuses and also allowed shorter and more flexible working hours. A comprehensive law on working time came into force on July 1. While it retained restrictions on work on Sundays and public holidays for most employees, it also contained a number of provisions to increase flexibility. Legal vacation time was increased to 24 days a year (though in practice a majority of employees already enjoyed six weeks of vacation).

The French government launched a substantial and wide-ranging program aimed at encouraging employment. One of its provisions, allowing companies to take on certain workers under the age of 26 at 80% of the national minimum wage for a limited period, produced not only strong opposition from trade unions but also massive street demonstrations. In the end Prime Minister Édouard Balladur agreed to suspend the proposal (it was later withdrawn). In a postscript to the Air France strike of 1993, the new chairman of the company produced a restructuring plan, including job cuts, a wage freeze, and longer working hours. The plan was rejected by a majority of the unions, but when the chairman put it directly to the 40,000 workers concerned, 81% voted to accept it.

Teamsters picket in April during the union's 24-day strike (the longest in its history) against a group of freight-hauling companies. The union was successful in blocking the companies' plans to hire part-time employees, who would be paid lower wages, for certain types of work, but it gave in to the employers' wishes to be allowed to move more of their goods by rail.

BILL BURKE—IMPACT VISUALS

Pensions were the big issue in Italian industrial relations in 1994. It was apparent that the costs of the extravagant and much-abused national pension system (under which, for example, women in the public sector could retire on 80% of pay after 15 years of service) could no longer be afforded. The government's efforts to reduce the cost of pensions were strongly resisted by trade unions, and a four-hour stoppage on October 14 was supported by an estimated three million people. A general strike called for December 2 was canceled when the government made sufficient concessions to placate the unions. Among numerous disputes during the year, a proposal by Fiat, Italy's largest private employer, to dismiss up to 12,000 workers led to a series of strikes and demonstrations until agreement was reached on a restructuring plan with financial support from the government.

The Spanish government continued its efforts to reform the labour market against stiff union opposition marked by a general strike on January 27. The government's program included removing impediments to part-time employment, allowing unqualified people between the ages of 18 and 25 to work for a limited time at between 70% and 80% of the national minimum wage, facilitating layoffs for organizational and production or technical reasons, and replacing statutory ordinances made under the Franco dictatorship with collective agreements. In Portugal in June the prime minister mooted the idea of a social contract that would run to the end of the century, and discussions were started on the proposal.

A lengthy period of discussion between government, unions, and employers having failed to reach agreement in 1993, a Belgian royal decree authorized implementation of the government's plan for employment, competitiveness, and social security. With a few exceptions, until Jan. 23, 1995, there would be no pay increases, individual or collective, beyond those due under a system based on a price index excluding gasoline, cigarettes, and alcohol, with increases being triggered when the index reached a threshold figure. An employer breaching the rules would be liable to substantial penalties. On November 21 employers and unions reached agreement on proposals for a central agreement for 1995–96.

The United States. The Dunlop Commission on the Future of Worker-Management Relations issued a preliminary fact-finding report in June. The report concluded that a number of aspects of U.S. labour law were inadequate for present conditions. It also laid considerable stress on the value of employee participation. A bill to outlaw the permanent replacement of strikers—strongly backed by unions—was thrown out by the U.S. Senate in July when its backers failed to muster enough support to overcome a Republican filibuster.

The strike that attracted the most attention in the U.S. during the year was in baseball's major leagues. The players struck after the games of August 11, and the World Series was canceled. (*See* SPORTS AND GAMES: *Baseball:* Sidebar.)

Asia and Africa. In Japan there were signs in 1994 of recovery from the prolonged recession. Even so, unemployment was still high by Japanese standards (though it did not quite reach 3%), and many firms reduced their labour force. Japan's economic realities were reflected in the fact that wage increases averaged little more than 3%.

Not the least of the many problems facing the new South African government was how to satisfy the expectations of black South Africans for rapid improvement in living standards while retaining, and if possible increasing, competitiveness. In addition, the government placed high importance on reassuring the business community and offering investors a stable business environment and low inflation. Although the year passed without major labour problems, strike activity was high. (R.O. CLARKE)

See also Business and Industry; Economic Affairs: *World Economy.*

This article updates the *Macropædia* article WORK AND EMPLOYMENT.

Law

International Agreements. No clear pattern in regard to international law emerged during 1994. Instead, the significant events were scattered over a wide range of topics. One development, however, became so prominent as to constitute a trend: the proliferation of new international courts and the confirmation and extension of existing ones. It was as if the new world order, so uncertainly celebrated in the previous year or two by the development of the United Nations' peacemaking or peacekeeping role, had now matured enough to be crystallized in that ultimate symbol of civil society, the judges.

The most dramatic innovation was in the field of criminal law. Basing its action on the Nürnberg tribunal after World War II and on ideas for an international criminal court that had circulated in the early years of the United Nations, the UN Security Council had in 1993 set up an international tribunal to prosecute war crimes, genocide, crimes against humanity, and serious violations of international humanitarian law that had occurred in former Yugoslavia since 1991. The tribunal, with its seat at The Hague, comprised two judicial levels (trial and appellate) as well as a prosecutor.

At its second session in January and February 1994, the tribunal adopted its rules of procedure and evidence, and at its third session (April and May), it adopted rules governing the detention of accused persons. In August a South African judge, Richard Goldstone, took up his duties as the first prosecutor. The tribunal held its first public hearing on November 8, having the previous day issued its first formal indictment (and an arrest warrant), against a suspected Bosnian Serb prison camp commander, Dragan Nikolic. At the same time, the prosecutor was preparing to bring formal charges against Dusan Tadic, who, unlike Nikolic, was already in custody in Germany and would be transferred from the German penal system to the tribunal to become probably the first to be actually tried. A number of trials for war crimes in former Yugoslavia were also in preparation in the national court system of Germany, Denmark, and Austria. By the end of 1994 the Serb authorities in Bosnia and Herzegovina, Croatia, and Serbia had not recognized the authority of the tribunal but had begun their own proceedings against alleged war criminals there.

On the same day that the tribunal held its first public meeting, the UN Security Council voted to establish a second such tribunal to deal with genocide, war crimes, and crimes against humanity in Rwanda. It would have the same prosecutor as the Yugoslav tribunal, Richard Goldstone. Later in November the European Parliament urged that the UN prepare a convention setting up a permanent International Criminal Court. In this it was reinforcing the July report of the International Law Commission (ILC), which contained a draft statute for just such a court; it would comprise 18 judges divided into trial and appellate levels and would have its own prosecutor. It would cover not only war crimes and genocide but also hijacking, hostage taking, and apartheid.

The main event at the International Court of Justice, apart from acquiring in February a new president (Judge Muhammad Bedjaoui) and vice president (Judge Stephen Schwebel), was its judgment in the Libya-Chad boundary dispute over the Aouzou Strip. The court held that the 1955 treaty between Libya and France, combined with the 1919 treaty between France and the United Kingdom, was completely determinative of the issue. It was thus unnecessary to consider Libyan arguments of *uti possedetis* (effectiveness of occupation in the past), *terra nullius* (spheres of influence), the hinterland doctrine, or any others. The Libyan claim that would have changed the treaty boundary between the two nations was totally rejected. This judgment (in February) was followed by an agreement between Libya and Chad (April) for the withdrawal from the disputed territory of Libyan administration and forces and the establishment of joint teams both to delimit the boundary and to supervise the removal of antipersonnel mines on the main roads to Aouzou and around the Ermi wells. This was completed by the end of May.

The inclusion in the Libya-Chad treaty of a provision on removal of antipersonnel mines was consistent with a growing campaign to prohibit their use generally because of the destructive effect they have on civilians. It was estimated that there were some 100 million such mines lying around unmarked in about 60 countries worldwide. The concern expressed in the press and by welfare agencies pinpointed the ineffectiveness in this respect of the 1980 Geneva Convention on Inhumane Weapons, and some went so far as to propose that the use of such mines be treated as a crime

against humanity. An expert group was set up pursuant to a UN General Assembly resolution in December 1993 to examine the question and report by the end of 1994. Many countries, including France, The Netherlands, the United States, and South Africa, had imposed export bans; the U.K.'s regulations did not apply to so-called self-destruct mines. There was, however, resistance among the arms-manufacturing countries to an absolute ban on the use or manufacture of antipersonnel mines.

Other major judicial developments included the adoption of the 11th Protocol to the European Convention for the Protection of Human Rights and Fundamental Freedoms in May. When it came into force, it would abolish the European Commission of Human Rights and transfer some of its functions to the European Court of Human Rights. The Ninth Protocol, which allows complainants to have standing before the court, came into force in October. The change was necessitated by the growing caseload of the commission and the consequent need to alter the Convention's judicial structure from a part-time basis to a full-time professional court.

The European Free Trade Association (EFTA) Court of Justice, formed as part of the European Economic Area (EEA), moved into its premises in Geneva in January and began work using a structure and rules of procedure based on those of the European Court of Justice. It delivered its first judgment in the autumn, rejecting a complaint by a Slovenian couple resident in Austria that the refusal of a work permit was contrary to the rules on free movement of the EEA treaty.

By the end of the year, however, three EFTA members (Austria, Finland, and Sweden) had been accepted as new members of the European Union and would leave EFTA early in 1995. The EFTA court would then be reduced to only two judges (Iceland and Norway, with the possibility of Liechtenstein joining in). Thought was being given during December to the future viability of the EEA (including the EFTA court) and indeed even of EFTA itself, which would be reduced to four members (Iceland, Norway, Switzerland, and Liechtenstein; Slovenia had initiated a membership application).

Two other Geneva-based organizations also developed judicial sides to their activity. The World Intellectual Property Organization, which had been the driving force behind international harmonization of copyright, patent, and trademark laws for more than a century, opened its new Arbitration Centre (International Centre for the Resolution of Intellectual Disputes) in October. It would administer four dispute-settlement procedures—mediation, arbitration, expedited arbitration, and combined mediation and arbitration—and might be compared with the commercial arbitration service provided by the International Chamber of Commerce in Paris.

The judicial system of the new World Trade Organization, which forms Annex 2 (Understanding on Rules and Procedures Governing the Settlement of Disputes) of the General Agreement on Tariffs and Trade (GATT) Uruguay round package agreed upon at the end of 1993, was formally adopted at Marrakech, Morocco, in April 1994. It would replace the existing GATT panel system, which had depended on the voluntary cooperation of the "defendant" nation, with a more imperative procedure operated by the permanent Dispute Settlements Body. This had not yet been set up by the end of 1994.

Finally, mention should be made of the continuing work of the ILC on a far-reaching proposal. This stated that unilateral countermeasures by one nation allegedly wronged by another were prohibited if there were dispute-settlement procedures available. It arose in connection with the work on codification of the law on state responsibility and raised basic issues of international law and the rights of states that required careful examination.

The march toward regionalization of the world continued during the year. Although the European Union (EU) was experiencing increased nationalism in major member nations, the accession of Austria, Finland, Sweden, and Norway to the organization was successfully negotiated. The first three obtained positive votes in their popular referenda, but the vote in Norway was negative and, consequently, that country withdrew from the accession altogether. Ratification on the EU side was delayed by Spain, which made its consent to the expansion conditional on its receiving satisfactory arrangements for its fishing fleet in U.K. waters from January 1996, when the transitional period was to end. A compromise was worked out in late December, and the EU agreed (with the U.K. abstaining in the vote) that some Spanish vessels could fish in British waters. The way was clear for the three European nations in January 1995.

In the Western Hemisphere, at Buenos Aires, Arg., Mercosur (Argentina, Brazil, Paraguay, and Uruguay) signed an agreement in August to institute a common customs tariff except, temporarily, for high-technology goods. That paved the way for the signing on December 17 at Miami, Fla., of the Mercosur Customs Union Treaty, to create a common market as of 1995. In May the Andean Pact also agreed to a common external tariff to come into force in 1995.

U.S. implementation of the North American Free Trade Agreement (NAFTA) began under Executive Order 12889. Chile indicated its desire to join NAFTA and was invited to do so in December; others were seeking closer links. This culminated in a meeting in December of all nations in North and South America except Cuba. There it was agreed to establish a Free Trade Area of the Americas, which would embrace them all, hold biennial summit meetings, and aim to complete negotiations by the year 2005. Meanwhile, closer links were to be developed between NAFTA and the other regional groups: Mercosur, the Andean Pact, the Central American Common Market, and the Caribbean Community and Common Market.

Parallel with this, Mexico signed an agreement with Colombia and Venezuela to set up an economic area, signed a separate agreement with Costa Rica for a free-trade area, and cooperated with 24 other Caribbean nations (including Cuba) to form a new Association of Caribbean States. (*See* WORLD AFFAIRS: *Spotlight:* Latin America's New Economic Strategy and *Spotlight:* The New Caribbean Basin Identity.) Earlier, as a result of a U.S. initiative, the leaders of 18 Pacific nations met in a summit in Indonesia in November and agreed on the creation of an Asia-Pacific Economic Cooperation area, to be negotiated over the next 25 years.

The other major event of 1994 was the coming into force in November of the 1982 UN Convention on the Law of the Sea after having received its 60th ratification a year earlier. That, and the adoption by the UN General Assembly of an agreement on implementing the seabed provisions in Part XI of the Convention (those relating particularly to exploitation of mineral deposits, described originally as "manganese nodules"), cleared the way for the establishment of the International Seabed Authority and for ratification of the Convention by the major industrialized countries, particularly the U.S. and the U.K. As a result, maritime affairs were likely once more to figure more prominently in future international law developments.

(NEVILLE MARCH HUNNINGS)

Court Decisions. A number of important decisions were handed down by courts throughout the world in 1994. They ranged in subject matter from gender and sexual issues to drugs, the death penalty and other serious criminal sanctions, and the environment.

There was considerable concern in legal and business circles in the U.S. as to what kinds of conduct constitute sexual harassment so as to be actionable under civil or criminal law. During the year the U.S. Supreme Court did much to clarify the matter by handing down a sweeping decision establishing standards for sexual harassment. In *Harris* v. *Forklift Systems, Inc.,* the court held that Title VII of the Civil Rights Act of 1964, which prohibits sexual harassment, is violated when the workplace is permeated with discriminatory behaviour that is sufficiently severe or pervasive to create a hostile or abusive working environment. This standard, said the court, objectively requires an environment that a reasonable person would find hostile or abusive as well as the victim's subjective perception that the environment is abusive. Determination can be made only through investigation of all the circumstances, which may include the frequency of the discriminatory conduct, its severity— whether it is physically threatening or humiliating or a mere offensive utterance, and its unreasonable interference with an employee's work performance. The effect on the employee's psychological well-being is relevant in determining whether the employee actually found the environment abusive, but while psychological harm, like any other factor, may be taken into account, no single factor is required.

In *J.E.B.* v. *Alabama ex rel T.B.,* the Supreme Court held that the equal protection clause of the 14th Amendment to the Constitution forbade peremptory challenges by the state of Alabama to potential jurors on the basis of gender. This case was said to be an exemplification of the principle decided in 1986 in *Batson* v. *Kentucky,* which held that African-Americans could not be systematically excluded from juries by way of peremptory challenges. Prior to *Batson* it had been thought that each party to a lawsuit, including a criminal trial, could use its peremptory challenges to exclude a potential juror for any reason or for no reason at all. In the state and federal courts, each party has a specified number of peremptory challenges. After they are used, a party is required to furnish a reason why he or she thinks a particular person should not be allowed to serve on the jury. As a result of the Alabama decision, it was now often necessary for the state, in criminal cases at least, to give reasons why a black or a woman should not be seated on the jury.

The European Court of Justice held in *Office National de l'emploi* that national legislation providing exceptions to night work that were different for women and men infringed the European Community Treaty, which mandates equal treatment for men and women with respect to employment. Similarly, the European Court of Human Rights held that a German law requiring male residents to serve without pay in a fire brigade or, in lieu thereof, to pay a tax to support this service violated the European Convention on Human Rights because the same requirements were not imposed on women.

In France the Court of Appeal ruled that a contract under which a woman agreed to conceive and carry a child in order to give it up on birth to the other contracting party was invalid and unenforceable. The court viewed such a contract as a violation of the principle of the inalienability of the human body as well as of principles pertaining to the status of persons.

The U.S. Supreme Court ruled on two abortion-related cases during the year. In *National Organization for Women, Inc.* v. *Scheidler,* the women's organization, commonly known as NOW, won a significant victory when the court ruled that the Racketeer Influenced and Corrupt Organizations law (RICO) could be used to prosecute members of a conspiracy to shut down an abortion clinic. It had been thought by some legal scholars that RICO could be used only when economic interests were involved, but the court said that no economic motives were necessary in order for RICO to be applied.

NOW's victory was less conclusive in *Madsen* v. *Women's Health Center*. In that case a Florida state court had permanently prohibited protests from being made inside an 11-m (36-ft) buffer zone around an abortion clinic. This zone was necessary at the front of the clinic in order to permit access to it and was established at the rear of the clinic to curtail noise. The Supreme Court affirmed the Florida court with respect to the front of the clinic but reversed its ruling as to the rear. The court emphasized the privilege of the protesters to exercise their rights of free speech and assembly and stated that these rights could be suppressed only where absolutely necessary to permit traffic into and out of the clinic.

The Constitutional Court in Italy rendered an opinion on June 2 that no person who works in a health service and who deals with the care of others can refuse to be tested for AIDS. Homosexuals and others had succeeded in getting a statute enacted that excluded compulsory tests for the AIDS virus. The court held that this statute was unconstitutional because it abridged the fundamental right to health. This right, said the court, includes "the duty for the person (with the virus) not to put at risk, by his behaviour, the health of other persons."

Due process under the U.S. Constitution generally requires that individuals receive notice and an opportunity to be heard before they are deprived of property by government action. The federal government, however, contended that this principle does not apply to civil forfeiture action, which authorizes a civil taking of property that is used to commit or facilitate the commission of a drug offense. In *U.S.* v. *Good Real Property,* the Supreme Court disagreed with this contention and held that the federal government could not seize property pursuant to a drug forfeiture without prior notice and hearing.

Under California law, in order to sentence a defendant to death for first-degree murder, the jury must find the defendant guilty and then find one or more special circumstances to be true. The case then proceeds to the penalty phase, in which the jury must consider some factors specified in the statute. In *Tuilaepa* v. *California* the U.S. Supreme Court held this statute constitutional. The statute had been extensively reviewed by the news media in conjunction with the O.J. Simpson case, which involved the allegation that the famous football player and actor murdered his wife and another person. Simpson pleaded not guilty, and at the year's end the case had not yet been tried. Many seemed to feel that the statute was too vague to stand constitutional scrutiny. The matter became moot when the prosecution announced that it would not seek the death penalty if Simpson was convicted.

Italy and the U.K. apparently took different positions regarding the possibility of imposing severe criminal sanctions on minors. The Constitutional Court of Italy ruled that it is unconstitutional to sentence minors to life imprisonment. In the Italian system it is possible for a person sentenced to life to be released from prison if he or she has been rehabilitated, but this possibility did not deter the court from decreeing that a life sentence can never be imposed on a minor.

In the U.K., on the other hand, the Divisional Court abolished the rule that a child between the ages of 10 and 14 is presumed not to know that he or she has committed a crime. Under that rule the Crown was required to rebut the presumption by proving that the child, in fact, knew what he or she did was criminal. The court held that the old rule was necessary in earlier times because then the criminal law was much more severe. The court said that the old rule now had no utility in view of the complete change in the philosophy of crime and punishment. This change in the law, of course, did not mean that the U.K. would necessarily impose a heavy sentence on a minor convicted of a serious crime, nor did it mean that the Crown would necessarily, or even usually, prosecute a minor. It meant only that the Crown no longer had to overcome a presumption to be able to maintain such a prosecution if in its discretion it was indicated.

During the year the U.S. Supreme Court decided two important cases regarding environmental laws. The first, *City of Chicago* v. *Environmental Defense Fund,* denied a municipality an exemption from the operation of the Resource Conservation and Recovery Act of 1976 (RCRA). The RCRA is a comprehensive environmental statute that empowers the Environmental Protection Agency (EPA) to regulate hazardous waste in accordance with rigorous safeguards and

A teacher works with her students in a special education classroom at a Satmar Hasidic elementary school in Kiryas Joel, N.Y. In July the U.S. Supreme Court ruled that the public school district created especially for the unassimilated Orthodox Jewish sect was unconstitutional, thus making it ineligible to receive government funds for the education of handicapped students.

waste-management procedures. The city of Chicago owned and operated an incinerator that burned solid waste. The burning resulted in the creation of energy that was used by the city. It also left a residue of ash. The EPA filed an action claiming that the city had violated the RCRA in burning the solid waste and in handling the ash residue. The city contended that it was exempt from this law. Many legal scholars believed that such an exemption was provided for in the RCRA, and the federal district court found that to be the case. The Supreme Court, however, ruled that no such exemption exists. The case was believed to be important for many communities that considered themselves exempt from the RCRA.

Some cities in the U.S. adopted laws, often called "community development codes" or some similar title, that require an individual or entity seeking a building permit to dedicate portions of the land on which the building will be erected to the city for greenways, pedestrian walks, bicycle pathways, or the like. The city of Tigard, Ore., has such a law. A woman who owned a lot on which she operated a retail store applied to the city for a building permit to enlarge the store and its parking lot. The city granted the application subject to the conditions that she dedicate part of the lot for a greenway and another part for a pedestrian/bicycle pathway. The owner appealed this decision, claiming that the conditions, if enforced, would amount to a taking of her property without due process of law. The case finally reached the U.S. Supreme Court, and it agreed with the owner. The court acknowledged that governments must be able to engage in land-use planning and that "government could hardly go on if to some extent values incident to property could not be diminished without paying for every such change in general law." On the other hand, the Constitution bars the government "from forcing some people alone to bear public burdens which, in all fairness and justice, should be borne by the public as a whole." The task of the court is to strike a balance between these competing policies.

(WILLIAM D. HAWKLAND)

See also Crime, Law Enforcement, and Penology; World Affairs: *Multilateral Regional Organizations; United Nations.*

This article updates the *Macropædia* articles CONSTITUTIONAL LAW; INTERNATIONAL LAW.

Libraries

Violence—both man-made and natural—and the march of technology were the watchwords for libraries in 1994. After it was firebombed in 1993, the National Library of Bosnia and Herzegovina continued its valiant efforts to maintain its irreplaceable collections, including the richest assemblage of Arabic scientific and mathematical manuscripts in Europe and an invaluable collection of materials on the outbreak of World War I. In addition to rebuilding the catalog and trying to restore the library as a working tool for the people of Sarajevo, the 58 members of the staff still on the job were seeking to produce a retrospective bibliography of Bosnia and Herzegovina. International assistance was being sought through UNESCO and elsewhere. (*See* ARCHITECTURE: *Sidebar.*) In late July a truck bomb devastated the Jewish cultural centre and library in Buenos Aires, which served Argentina's 300,000 Jews, the Western Hemisphere's second largest community. Nearly 100 persons died, and half of the important collection of Judaica from Europe and South America was lost.

Natural disasters took their toll as well. Following the devastating January 17 earthquake, Los Angeles-area libraries struggled to recover from damage ranging from collapsed bookstacks to major structural damage. The library at California State University at Northridge, located at the quake's epicentre, was badly damaged, but the main portion of the facility was reopened in late August. Thirty-nine of the County of Los Angeles Public Library's 87 branches were initially closed owing to quake damage, but all but one had opened by mid-February. Forty-one of the Los Angeles Public Library's 64 branches reopened two days after the quake; in mid-October two still remained closed. Partly out of concern for potential earthquake damage, the University of California completed a $40 million renovation project that featured 84 km (52 mi) of underground shelves at its Berkeley campus.

In October the U.S. Library of Congress announced an ambitious plan to convert its most important holdings into digital form by the year 2000, creating a "virtual library" that would be accessible worldwide over computer networks. A Senate subcommittee held a hearing on "Libraries and Their Role in the Information Infrastructure" on April 19. In July Maryland launched a groundbreaking program to provide free Internet access to its residents through the state's public libraries.

Not everyone was enthralled with the march of technology, however. A long article by Nicholson Baker in the April 4 issue of *The New Yorker* described how the great libraries were discarding their card catalogs after replacing them with automated systems. Many U.S. libraries, notably those at Cornell University, Ithaca, N.Y., and Harvard, were doing this, as were a consortium of French libraries, the libraries of Queen's University, Belfast, Northern Ireland, and Waseda University, Tokyo, and the Royal Botanic Gardens, Kew, near London. Baker criticized this practice as shortsighted and anti-intellectual. It was true, he argued, that on-line catalogs made up-to-date processing of new acquisitions possible, they could not be vandalized as card catalogs had been, entries could not be torn out, and they were convenient to use and people could use them via a telephone modem without attending the library. Nevertheless, computerized card catalogs did not always answer the same questions that could be asked of a standard card catalog and they did not always include the "tracings" (comments made on the backs of the cards) and other notes. Where there was multiple input from many different catalogs (as in any large cooperative venture, such as the OCLC [On-line Computer Library Center] at Dublin, Ohio) uniform quality was difficult to maintain; countless new errors were being introduced. Card catalogs, Baker wrote, "currently do a better job of collocation [bringing like headings together] than on-line catalogues do."

Politics had its effect on library management in 1994. In England consideration was being given to removing control of libraries from the counties, where it had been since 1974, and returning it to the districts and boroughs. The reorganization would involve breaking up collections that had been developed over the past 20 years, not to mention the adverse impacts on staffs, services, and stocks.

Librarians pride themselves on catering to all sectors of the community, not excluding correctional facilities. At Wandsworth Prison in England, the "Escape with a Book" project, which used the library as a venue for exhibitions, talks, and discussion groups, won a community initiative award.

Ground was broken in late November for the $85 million George Bush Presidential Library at Texas A & M University at College Station. The 38.7-ha (90-ac) archival and educational centre was scheduled to open in 1997.

Public library circulation in the U.S. showed a modest decline of 3% in 1993, while expenditures rose by 8%, according to the annual University of Illinois survey. The U.K. reported 580 million library loans in 1993, with more than half the population using public libraries. Some £48 million was collected in overdue fines. The mission of public libraries was also seen to be changing. While a century earlier the principal aim had been to educate, inform, and entertain, that priority order had been reversed—now the aim was said to be to entertain, inform, and educate. A recent British Library Association list of the most stolen books indicated that the greatest interest was in sex, the occult, and tropical fish. Libraries were accordingly making great efforts to modernize and appeal to contemporary readers.

The long-feared closings of the graduate library schools at California's two largest universities, the University of California at Los Angeles and the University of California at Berkeley, were announced. Their library-education programs, however, were merged into two newly created schools.

The American Library Association's 113th annual conference drew 12,627 registrants to Miami, Fla., in June, a drop in attendance of some 4,500 from the previous year. U.S. Pres. Bill Clinton named attorney Jeanne Hurley Simon to chair the National Commission on Libraries and Information Science in late 1993. Mary Dempsey became Chicago's city library commissioner in January 1994. Gary Strong left the position of California state librarian to head the Queens Borough (N.Y.) Public Library in September. Scott Bennett became Yale University librarian on October 1.

(GORDON FLAGG; P. HAVARD-WILLIAMS)

This article updates the *Macropædia* article LIBRARIES AND LIBRARY SCIENCE.

Life Sciences

ZOOLOGY

Ecologically oriented research in zoology in 1994 revealed the potential sensitivities and responses of populations of animals to human-caused alterations in the environment. Wolves and Atlantic cod were at the focus of work that addressed the spatial ecology and movement patterns of animals. The fossil record provided further support for the evolution of whales from a terrestrial ancestry to the marine environment. New species of mammals were reported from Indonesia and Vietnam.

Andrew R. Blaustein and colleagues of Oregon State University conducted experiments to test the sensitivity of amphibian eggs to ultraviolet (UV) radiation. Scientists had suggested that increased UV radiation levels as a consequence of the destruction of the ozone layer in the Earth's upper atmosphere could be a reason for reported declines in amphibian populations in many regions of the world. In a study of the developing eggs of three species of frogs from the Cascade Range in Oregon, the investigators used a light-filtering apparatus to modify the amount of UV light to which eggs in experimental enclosures were exposed. Eggs of two of the species showed significantly greater hatching success in the treatments in which UV light had been blocked than did eggs receiving natural sunlight. Eggs of the frog species that appeared resistant to UV light were found to contain high levels of photolyase, an enzyme that repairs UV-damaged DNA. The findings supported a hypothesis that amphibian eggs are sensitive to UV light and that human-induced increases in levels of UV radiation were contributing to a decline in amphibian populations.

Michael C. Newman and Margaret Mulvey of the Savannah River Ecology Laboratory, Aiken, S.C., and colleagues provided evidence that snail populations that have been exposed to high levels of lead in the environment for long periods sequester the toxic metal differently from snails exposed for shorter periods. The investigators sampled populations of the common garden snail *Helix aspersa* in England and northern Wales and conducted laboratory analyses to determine the level of exposure of each population to lead. To estimate the duration of exposure, they used the isotopic signatures of lead (ratios of the isotopes making up the lead) to determine the proportion of the metal at a site that had been derived from recent human sources (*e.g.*, automobiles) compared with that from older mines and smelters. Thus, they were able to determine the time period over which a snail population had been exposed to high lead levels. In snail populations experiencing long-term exposure (as long as 2,000 years at sites mined since the Roman occupation), the proportion of lead in the shell compared with soft tissues was higher than that in populations experiencing shorter exposure periods (no more than a few decades). One implication of the study was that the sequestering of lead in biologically inert tissues (the shell) provided protection from a toxic material and had been enhanced owing to the continued exposure of the populations, through either genetic selection or physiological adaptation.

The importance of snails in the food web of a forest ecosystem was revealed by Jaap Graveland of the Netherlands Institute of Ecology, Heteren, and colleagues, who examined the ecological effect that acid precipitation on soils has had in parts of The Netherlands during the past several years. The eggshells of great tits (*Parus major*) have become increasingly thinner and more porous. Concomitantly, desertion of clutches by the birds has become more common. In the regions that they studied, the investigators documented declines in the species diversity and abundance of snails that are strongly correlated with acidification of the soil by acid rain. They further established that snail shells in the diet are critical for eggshell production in great tits and many other bird species owing to the need for calcium during egg production. High soil acidification in regions with poor soils could reduce bird populations by causing a decrease in reproductive success due to lack of snail shells.

The patterns in which animal species are spatially distributed are a complex of historical circumstance, response to environmental conditions, and intraspecific and interspecific interactions. George A. Rose of the Department of Fisheries and Oceans, St. John's, Newfoundland, used echo sounders to discover that Atlantic cod (*Gadus morhua*) migrating across the Newfoundland Shelf followed a deep highway of slightly warmer water (2°–2.5° C, or 35.6°–36.5° F) that flows under colder surrounding ocean water (less than 0° C, or 32° F). The investigator concluded that the fish, which sometimes numbered in the hundreds of millions over many kilometres, were led by larger, presumably older, scouts and that they veered from the narrow band of warm water when prey species were encountered. Midwater spawning above the warm oceanic highway was also observed. If the migration routes are learned by older fish and used annually, the recent decline in the numbers of Atlantic cod may turn out to have a disruptive effect on cod migration patterns.

Mark A. Lewis of the University of Utah and James D. Murray of the University of Washington used a simple, mechanistic mathematical model to explain the pattern of territoriality in gray wolves (*Canis lupus*) and the interactions between wolves and deer. Their model assumed that the direction and distance of wolf dispersal are mediated by the presence or absence of wolf scent markings characteristic of raised-leg urination. They demonstrated that a stable, steady-state condition is reached naturally among individuals and packs of wolves in their responses to scent marks. The model is based on assumptions that upon encountering a foreign scent mark, a wolf tends to increase its own scent marking and move toward the organizational centre of the pack. Thus, the levels of scent marking are greatest between adjacent packs, and buffer zones arise. Deer, and presumably other prey species, are most abundant in the buffer zones, where wolf densities are lowest. A significant feature of the study is that the seemingly complex formation of wolf territories can be reduced to a relatively simple formula involving scent marking.

Evidence was gathered on the evolutionary origin of swimming and an unusual adaptation for feeding in whales (order Cetacea). Two independent discoveries helped clarify and further define the evolutionary connection between the terrestrial ancestors of whales and their modern relatives. Two new fossil species were found in Eocene sediments (about 50 million years old) in Pakistan. One species, *Rodhocetus kasrani,* was described by Philip D. Gingerich of the University of Michigan and colleagues, and another, *Ambulocetus natans,* by J.G.M. Thewissen of the Northeastern Ohio Universities College of Medicine, S.T. Hussain of Howard University, Washington, D.C., and M. Arif of the Geological Survey of Pakistan, Islamabad. The structure of the pelvic and sacral regions of *R. kasrani* were intermediate between structures designed for terrestrial locomotion and for ocean swimming. Evidence of a terrestrial ancestry in *A. natans* included the termination of the toes in a convex hoof, the presence of a long tail, and presumably the absence of the tail fluke present in modern cetaceans. By determining the form and structure of the appendages, the investigators concluded that *A. natans* was able to walk on land in a manner similar to that of sea lions and could swim by moving its feet up and down like an otter.

The description of a toothed whale (Odontocete) in Lower Pliocene sediments (about five million years old) of southern Peru by Christian de Muizon of the French Institute for Andean Studies, Lima, Peru, provided evidence of evolutionary convergence and specialization in the feeding apparatus. The newly described fossil whale, *Odobenocetops peruvianus,* whose closest living relatives are the beluga whale and narwhal (family Monodontidae), had orbits (eye sockets) that faced dorsally (upward), possibly indicating binocular vision. The species apparently lacked the melon, a rounded organ in the head of some cetaceans that is used in echolocation. The structure of the anterior portion of the skull suggests that the species had a muscular upper lip, lacked teeth in its upper jaw, and presumably had an adaptation for feeding similar to that of walruses, which feed mainly on mollusks. These structural modifications for suction feeding are extreme among the cetaceans and suggest that *O. peruvianus* occupied an ecological niche previously unknown among toothed whales and comparable to ones occupied by Pliocene walruses in the Northern Hemisphere.

New species of large mammals came to the attention of zoologists during the year. Tim Flannery of the Australian Museum, Sydney, and a team of Australian and Indonesian colleagues described a marsupial previously unknown to science—a tree kangaroo found dwelling on a remote forested mountainside in central Irian Jaya, an Indonesian province on the island of New Guinea. The animal, about as large as a medium-sized dog, is thickly furred with unique black-and-white patterns. Scientists from the World Wildlife Fund and the Vietnamese Ministry of Forestry reported the discovery of a new species of muntjac, or barking deer, in a rain forest of the Vu Quang Nature Reserve in central Vietnam. The new species, which was identified by its remains rather than by means of a living specimen, is larger by half than any

other known muntjac species, weighs about 45 kg (100 lb), and has a red grizzled coat and long tusklike canine teeth. The animal was the second new species to be discovered in the Vu Quang reserve in recent years. In 1992 a large bovid, the Vu Quang ox (*Pseudoryx nghentinhensis*), also had been described from an examination of its remains. In June 1994 the World Wildlife Fund reported that after a two-year search, a living example of the Vu Quang ox had finally been located.   (J. WHITFIELD GIBBONS)

Entomology. During the year scientists employed wing patterns in insects as a means of understanding genetic development. The application of advanced technology gave insight into the mechanisms of prey capture by a predatory ant and the detection of magnetic fields by honeybees. A study involving butterflies that became dependent on human-caused changes to their habitats raised questions about the risks of even more rapid environmental change.

Sean B. Carroll of the University of Wisconsin and colleagues identified molecular processes involved in the developmental organization of wing patterns in butterflies. They examined the genes responsible for wing patterning in the butterfly *Precis coenia* and compared them with those of the fruit fly *Drosophila melanogaster,* about which the molecular events of early development are known better than for any other plant or animal. The investigators established that the organization of butterfly wing patterns is partitioned into two spatial coordinate systems. One comprises a regulatory network that provides information on positioning of elements with respect to the entire wing and operates in a manner similar to that found in fruit flies and possibly other insects. The second system involves some of the same genes and provides genetic instructions during development that elaborate specific elements of the pattern, such as eyespots, on the wing. This second system in butterflies appears to have been modified from one that governs development of other anatomic components and has no counterpart in fruit flies. A significant feature of the research is the prospect of identifying in one group of organisms a molecular process with a function that has evolved from a process with a separate function in another group.

Wulfila Gronenberg, Jürgen Tautz, and Bert Hölldobler of the Theodor Boveri Institute, Würzburg, Germany, reported that a trap-jaw mechanism used by a Neotropical ant (genus *Odontomachus*) when hunting prey may lead to a better understanding of the evolution of predator efficiency in prey capture. Using electrophysiological recordings, the researchers demonstrated that trigger hairs located on the inner edge of the ant's mandibles are associated with large sensory cells and function as mechanoreceptors, sensing mechanical stimuli. When prey animals touch the trigger hairs, the jaws close reflexively in less than 8 ms (milliseconds; thousandths of a second), and the actual jaw strike may take as little as 0.33 ms. The underlying neurons are among the thickest and fastest-conducting sensory cells in insects. Such rapid neuronal conduction supports one of the fastest known reflexes and thus leads to one of the fastest movements measured to date in an animal.

Honeybees are known to use the Earth's magnetic field for such activities as comb building and navigation. The existence of a magnetic-field receptor in the insects had been supported by the finding of magnetite (magnetic iron oxide crystals present in animals that can detect magnetic fields) in the abdomens of dried honeybees. Using high-resolution transmission electron microscopy, Hsu Chin-Yuan and Li Chia-Wei of the National Tsing Hua University, Hsinchu, Taiwan, found iron-containing granules located in the trophocytes, cells surrounding the abdominal segments, and examined their fine structure. The granules were seen to contain tiny magnetite particles, 10 nanometres (10 billionths of a metre) or less in diameter, leading the investigators to suggest that the granules are the magnetoreceptors of the honeybee. They also determined that trophocytes are innervated by the nervous system, thus providing a neural pathway for signals initiated in the bee's magnetoreceptors.

Michael C. Singer and Camille Parmesan of the University of Texas and Chris D. Thomas of the University of Birmingham, England, reported that two independent populations of a rare butterfly, *Euphydryas editha*, underwent rapid evolution in diet in response to human manipulation of habitats. At a California site the butterflies had fed primarily on a plant, *Pedicularis semibarbata*, that was killed as a result of logging operations. Following logging, another plant, *Collinsia torreyi*, became the preferred host plant for *E. editha*; during the 1980s the butterflies colonized this new host and rapidly evolved the habit of laying eggs on it. At a separate site in Nevada, a European weed, *Plantago lanceolata*, that had been introduced by cattle ranchers proved more suitable for *E. editha* than its traditional, native host plant, *Collinsia parviflora*. Whereas in 1983 most female butterflies preferred to lay eggs on the native plant, by 1990 most preferred the introduced weed. Experiments showed that this change was genetic and that the preferences in the insect population were evolving rapidly. By 1990 some butterflies refused to accept their traditional host, thus rendering themselves dependent on the modified habitat. If entire populations were to evolve a dependence on the continued existence of a habitat that had been changed by humans, still more human modification could result in elimination of those species in which evolution could not keep pace with the habitat changes. (ANNE R. GIBBONS)

This article updates the *Macropædia* article INSECTS.

Ornithology. Egg production in birds was the subject of a lecture given by C.M. Perrins of the University of Oxford at the 21st International Ornithological Congress, held in Vienna in August. Egg size can vary markedly within a species, and it is not uncommon for some birds to lay eggs that are 50% larger than those of others of the species. The differences in quantities of egg nutrients between small and large eggs appear to represent very small differences in a bird's daily energy budget. In a study of great tits (*Parus major*), larger eggs were found to be associated with warm weather, low breeding densities of great tits, and low densities of blue tits (*P. caeruleus*) occupying the same region. Each associated factor can be interpreted as a set of conditions in which food is likely to be more plentiful or in which the laying female is likely to need less food for her own bodily maintenance and so have more available for egg formation. Thus, although the differences in nutrient quantity between small and large eggs may appear tiny, it is possible that they result from responses of the birds to different feeding conditions. It is important for birds to lay large eggs. Larger eggs have a higher hatching success than small ones, a higher fledging success, and a higher weight for chicks that fledge, the increased weight improving the chances of survival. Hence, it remained to be understood why, if large eggs are so advantageous and require so little extra nutrients, birds lay small eggs under many circumstances.

The evolution of feathers remained an area of ongoing debate among researchers. Did feathers evolve originally for flight or for another purpose, such as heat regulation? Walter J. Bock of Columbia University, New York City, and Paul Bühler of Germany argued in support of the recent theory that feathers evolved for heat regulation, possibly initially to insulate the animal from the heat of the sun and secondarily to prevent the outward escape of body heat. Primitive feathers were most likely similar to contour

A tribesman holds a species of tree kangaroo (top) discovered in 1994 in the Indonesian province of Irian Jaya on New Guinea. The black-and-white animal, which is timid and lives both in trees and on the ground, was reported by Australian and Indonesian researchers. It had long been known to local people, some of whom regarded it as an ancestor. Danish scientists announced during the year that they had found a previously unknown partridgelike bird (bottom) in the Udzungwa Mountains of southern Tanzania. A new species belonging to a new genus, it was named *Xenoperdix udzungwensis* ("strange bird of Udzungwa").

feathers, not the specialized down feathers found in modern birds. Feathers are associated with obligatory homoiothermy (warm-bloodedness as a sole mode of life), which is energetically expensive; hence, the evolution of feathers must have been allied with important selective advantages. Moreover, the origin of homoiothermy in animals is believed to be connected with lethargic, rather than vigorous, activities. It was thus suggested that the evolution of homoiothermy, and thus of feathers, in the ancestors of birds was coupled with arboreal dwelling and incubation of eggs in a tree nest.

Bearded vultures (*Gypaetus barbatus*) that live in the wild have a strikingly rufous colour to the head, neck, and underparts. On the other hand, birds reared in captivity develop pure white plumage. David C. Houston of the University of Glasgow, Scotland, and colleagues reported that caged bearded vultures that were presented with intensely red damp soils became excited and enthusiastically rubbed their belly and head feathers in the soils, acquiring within an hour the characteristic rufous coloration of wild birds. The bearded vulture was the only bird species known to use cosmetic coloration from soils to such spectacular effect.

Sperm competition, a recently emerged and rapidly evolving concept in avian behavioral ecology, had changed in meaning, according to a report by T.R. Birkhead of the University of Sheffield, England. The term was used initially in a narrow sense to describe the events taking place in a female's reproductive tract following insemination by two or more males. Subsequently it came to encompass all the behaviours associated with copulation, including multiple mating and paternity guards (various means by which a male attempts to ensure that he will be the father of the resulting offspring). Since its inception the term *sperm competition* had emphasized the male, but with increasing attention being given to female-driven phenomena, such as the fact that females may control which sperm fertilize their eggs, the term could no longer be considered strictly accurate. Theories of selection advanced the idea that because of the fundamental differences between males and females, the interests of individuals of each sex differ, even within socially monogamous pairs, and, thus, so also will their attempts to maximize fitness.

Lars Dinesen and co-workers of the University of Copenhagen reported the discovery of a new genus and species of bird in Tanzania. Determined to be a distinctive kind of partridgelike bird and named *Xenoperdix udzungwensis,* the bird is a relict Afro-tropical form with Indo-Malayan affinities. An up-to-date count of the world's known birds, provided by Richard Howard and Alick Moore in their *Complete Checklist of the Birds of the World* (3rd ed., 1994), listed 9,522 species, subdivided into 26,898 races, in 1,916 genera.   (JEFFERY BOSWALL)

This article updates the *Macropædia* article BIRDS.

MARINE BIOLOGY

A study published during the year examined the effects of cleanup procedures on shore recovery following the *Exxon Valdez* tanker disaster of 1989, when some 38 million litres (240,000 bbl) of crude oil were spilled into Prince William Sound, Alaska. It was observed that although the addition of fertilizers significantly increased rates of oil degradation by naturally occurring microorganisms, the areas most intensively cleaned by this technique and by hot water sprayed at high pressure showed the slowest recovery of the brown alga *Fucus gardneri*. The finding confirmed earlier studies that intense cleaning of rocky shores after oil spills may not be justified environmentally.

After the accidental discharge in 1986 of some 15 million litres (95,000 bbl) of medium-weight crude oil into

fringing mangrove areas of Bahía Las Minas on the central Caribbean coast of Panama, mangrove muds in the region showed unexpected persistence of the full range of aromatic hydrocarbon residues. Researchers estimated a time scale of at least 20 years for catastrophic oil spills trapped in muddy coastal habitats to lose their toxicity.

The date mussel *Lithophaga lithophaga,* which bores into calcareous rocks, in recent years had been intensively harvested for human consumption by scuba divers in the Mediterranean Sea off the coast of southern Italy. Exploitation involved demolition of the rocky substratum, often with the help of underwater vehicles. As a result, the entire bottom-living community of animals disappeared, and tens of kilometres of coastline were "desertified."

Advanced very high-resolution radiometer (AVHRR) satellite images and simultaneous ship transects in the Baltic Sea revealed increased sunlight absorption at the surface by blooms of cyanobacteria (blue-green algae), raising water temperatures by as much as 1.5° C (2.7° F)—a rare quantified example of direct influence of a biological process on ocean physics. Scientists discovered that the noise and light emitted by remotely operated vehicles in the sea on scientific and exploratory missions adversely affected the behaviour of lobsters; the finding had clear implications for the future design of such vehicles for behavioral studies. Fibre-optic microprobes developed to measure the amount of light penetrating to various depths in sandy sediments permitted, for the first time, investigations of the interaction of light with the physiology of sediment microorganisms at a level comparable to that of open-sea phytoplankton (the plant and plantlike component of plankton).

Scientists characterized methane-seep habitats in sediments of the southern slope of the central Skagerrak off Denmark. In association with very high concentrations of methane gas and dissolved sulfide were found abundant populations of the pogonophoran worm *Siboglinum poseidoni* and the bivalve mollusk *Thyasira sarsi*. Each animal is dependent for food on internally living symbiotic bacteria, which, in the case of the worm, consume methane and, in the case of the mollusk, derive energy from the oxidation of sulfur. How such nutritionally restricted animals have crossed the vast distances between methane seeps and between related communities around hydrothermal vents to become dispersed around the world remained an unanswered question. The deep-diving research submersible *Alvin,* however, revealed similar communities associated with decaying whale skeletons at depth. It was concluded that "whale falls," which are widespread in the ocean, may nurture substantial sulfide-dependent communities on the deep seafloor and that some species may be dispersing to hydrothermal vents from whale-fall "habitat islands."

The effects on penguins of the flipper bands commonly used for marking the birds were quantified, and the use of the bands was questioned. Banded birds were shown to expend 24% more power than unbanded birds during swimming, with detrimental implications for performance and survival. In another study researchers attached transmitters to king penguins (*Aptenodytes patagonica*) near the Crozet Islands in the southwestern Indian Ocean and tracked the birds by satellite. Swimming distances ranged from 33 to 95 km (20 to 59 mi) daily, much greater than previously assumed. Late in the year observers reported a mysterious die-off of about 20,000 king penguin chicks on the island of South Georgia in the South Atlantic. Suspected causes included unseasonably heavy snow, which may have smothered the birds, and a food shortage.   (ERNEST NAYLOR)

This article updates the *Macropædia* articles CRUSTACEANS; FISHES; MOLLUSKS; etc.

BOTANY

Flowering plants exhibit a remarkable ability to sense different colours, or wavelengths, of visible light and then use the light energy that is absorbed by particular pigments in the plant to carry out specific processes. For example, photosynthesis is most effectively promoted by wavelengths that are absorbed by the pigment chlorophyll and include wavelengths in both the blue and red regions of the spectrum. The pigment phytochrome, which is used to signal a wide variety of developmental events, including flowering in some plants, absorbs most strongly in the red and far-red regions of the spectrum. Other light-influenced events such as phototropic bending—*i.e.*, bending toward a light source, as is observed in most plants—is most influenced by blue light. Additional responses to blue light include formation of chloroplasts, the cell organelles that serve as the sites of photosynthesis in green plants, and opening of stomata, or leaf pores. It has been difficult, however, to ascribe the signaling effect of blue light to a particular pigment.

During the year plant scientists reported on their search for the blue-light receptor pigment via an approach in which by various means they manipulated the amount of a suspected receptor, the carotene-like pigment zeaxanthin, in tips of maize (corn) seedlings. The seedlings that were rendered devoid of the pigment did not show phototropic bending, whereas those in which the pigment was present did bend. The scientists thus suggested that zeaxanthin may be a blue-light receptor for this response.

Introductory biology textbooks list a number of characteristics that distinguish a "typical" plant cell from a "typical" animal cell. Included is the fact that most mature, living plant cells possess a large, membrane-bound central space, called the vacuole, that is not present in animal cells. For many decades the vacuole, which often comprises more than 95% of the plant cell volume, had been considered simply a site for the accumulated waste products of cell metabolism. As early as the 1960s, however, reports that plant vacuoles function as protein storage centres began to appear. At that time it was pointed out that at certain stages of plant development, such as embryo formation and seed maturation, proteins accumulate in the storage vacuoles of certain cells in the cotyledons, or seed leaves. Later, when the seed begins to germinate, enzymes called proteases are made in the cytoplasm and then transported to the vacuoles. There they break down stored protein, their action resulting in the release of amino acids needed by the entire plant to make new proteins. Further, it was demonstrated that other molecules such as carbohydrates are also stored in the vacuoles of some cells.

An important question for plant cell biologists has been how plant cells are able to sort out specific proteins and other molecules to ensure their delivery to the vacuole. Several recent papers added to an understanding of the mechanism by which specific molecules such as proteins are targeted for delivery to a specific cell location. During the processing of these molecules in the Golgi apparatus, a complex organelle involved in molecular modification and transport, the molecules are packaged into membrane-bound vesicles, and specific chemical messages called targeting sequences are added. Functioning much like the zip code on a package, the targeting sequences allow the vesicle to recognize and bind to a docking molecule on the membrane of the vacuole. As a result, the molecules shipped to the vacuole for sequestering are specific rather than random ones. Included among proteins often found in the vacuoles are those involved in defense against leaf-eating insect predators. When the cell is damaged by an insect, the molecules are released from the vacuole and discourage further insect feeding.

A second distinguishing characteristic of a typical plant cell is its cell wall, which is composed mainly of polysaccharides—*i.e.*, polymers of sugar molecules, such as cellulose, hemicellulose, and pectin. Proteins are also present in plant cell walls and include molecules such as extensin, which confers some of the elastic properties of the wall. The walls provide mechanical support for cells but also are involved in other important processes, including cellular defense against disease-causing organisms, particularly fungi. The chemistry of cell-wall architecture is complex, and both the elucidation of pathways of molecular synthesis involved in the construction of cell walls and the listing of cell-wall composition have changed often in recent years.

During the year researchers seeking a better understanding of plant cell walls produced mutants of *Arabidopsis thaliana* (a small, fast-growing plant of the mustard family often used in genetics experiments) that lacked the sugar fucose as part of their cell-wall composition. Plants that lacked fucose, a component of both hemicellulose and pectin, were dwarfed compared with normal nonmutated plants and possessed cell walls more fragile than normal. The achievement suggested a useful approach for studying the synthesis, structure, and function of plant cell walls.

(PHILIP D. REID)

MOLECULAR BIOLOGY

Hyperthermophiles: Beneficial Relics of a Hotter Earth. Boiling as a means of sterilization is based on the expectation that heating to 100° C (212° F) kills virtually all microorganisms. Yet there are bacteria that not only survive exposure to such temperatures but also grow optimally at, or even above, 100° C. They are the extreme thermophiles, or hyperthermophiles, and many of their names—for example, *Pyrococcus furiosus* or *Methanothermus fervidus*—reflect the sense of amazement that they aroused in their discoverers. These organisms are usually found in naturally hot environments, such as hot springs or deep-sea hydrothermal vents, but they also occur in human-made environments, such as hot water tanks.

Hyperthermophiles are interesting for several reasons. First, there is the question of whether their adaptation to heat represents a primitive characteristic retained from their origin on a once hotter Earth or whether it is a recent adaptation to the limited hot environments that currently exist. Second, there is the question of how the organisms maintain the structural integrity of their components, particularly since protein, DNA, and RNA are generally considered to be quite heat-sensitive. Finally, there are the commercial advantages of the high-temperature stability, or thermostability, of the enzymes made by such organisms.

Evolutionary relationships between organisms are commonly deduced from features of form, function, or both that are observed in creatures living today or in fossils of extinct life. From such observations it is clear, for example, that whales evolved from land-dwelling animals. Direct observations of size and shape, however, are of little use in revealing relationships between microorganisms. Since the earliest inhabitants of Earth were microscopic, scientists had long been totally ignorant of the long course of evolution that preceded the appearance of larger, multicellular organisms.

In recent years methods for determining the precise sequences of the building blocks of protein, DNA, and RNA—the molecular carriers of genetic information—have opened a window on early evolution. The basic tenet is that evolutionary relatedness is revealed by similarity in sequence. If the sequences of, say, corresponding genes or RNA molecules taken from two different organisms are very similar, then the organisms are closely related. Conversely, great sequence differences reflect early evolutionary divergence. This relationship between sequence similarity and evolutionary relatedness is well-founded in theory and is in accord with a wealth of data, both molecular and traditional.

On the basis of such sequence data, all life on Earth can be grouped into three domains: the eubacteria, the archaea (or archaebacteria), and the eucarya (or eukaryotes). The more familiar kingdoms, such as the plants, fungi, and animals, are subdivisions of these domains. The hyperthermophiles are members of the archaea, and the sequence differences in their genetic material compared with that of the eubacteria and the eukaryotes suggest that they appeared early in the course of biological evolution. Their tolerance for heat thus likely represents a retained primitive characteristic.

Metabolism is another indicator of evolutionary history. The Earth contained little molecular oxygen prior to the advent of true photosynthesis carried out by cyanobacteria (blue-green algae), which occurred over a billion years ago. Hence, organisms that developed prior to the photosynthetic cyanobacteria must have been anaerobes—organisms that live in the absence of free oxygen. Significantly, hyperthermophiles are anaerobes. Volcanic vents and other environments heated by geologic processes are often rich in sulfur. The hyperthermophiles usually make heavy metabolic use of sulfur; most reduce sulfur to hydrogen sulfide, while others use nitrate to oxidize sulfur to sulfuric acid.

Enzymes are proteins that function to promote, or catalyze, biochemical reactions in living organisms. The enzymes that have been isolated from hyperthermophiles are remarkably thermostable, some retaining catalytic activity up to 140° C (284° F). Scientists had hoped that comparing heat-resistant proteins from hyperthermophiles with their heat-sensitive counterparts from mesophiles—organisms that live in moderate-temperature environments (such as *Escherichia coli* bacteria or human beings)—would reveal the structural basis for thermostability. Unfortunately, the situation proved more complex than expected. As of 1994, comparisons of proteins on the basis of their amino acid sequences had not revealed striking differences. On the other hand, comparisons of native three-dimensional structure, *i.e.*, the shape into which the amino acid chain folds to form the functional protein, did provide a clue.

The native conformation of a protein depends on a collection of many weak interactions, such as van der Waals interactions, hydrophobic bonding, hydrogen bonding, and electrostatic, or salt, bonding. The total effect of these weak bonds is a substantial net stabilization. However, once a few of the weak bonds are overcome, say, by the addition of heat energy, the entire structure can unfold and lose its functional properties, a phenomenon called denaturation. This explains why a small increase in temperature, above some critical value, can cause a large increase in the rate of denaturation of a protein. In research carried out in 1993, the structures of the enzymes called rubredoxins from mesophiles and hyperthermophiles were compared; the former enzyme was seen to contain an unattached amino terminal end, whereas the latter did not. It appears likely that the amino terminus is the Achilles' heel, the point of unfolding, of the mesophilic enzyme, whereas it is tied down by hydrogen bonding, and thus protected, in the thermophilic version.

Enzymes, nature's catalysts, are more efficient and more specific than any human-made catalysts devised to date. By the mid-1990s they had found use—and in the future may

become even more useful—in synthetic and analytic chemistry, biotechnology, food processing, and even laundering, to name a few applications. The problem of poor heat stability, an impediment to many possible applications, is solved by the enzymes in hyperthermophiles. For example, protein-containing food stains on clothing can be removed by enzymes called proteases, which digest protein. Such enzymes, however, must resist hot water and detergents. Proteases from hyperthermophiles do exhibit the necessary stability and were being studied for such use.

(IRWIN FRIDOVICH)

Fragile X and the Genetics of Anticipation. Most known genetic disorders, such as cystic fibrosis, exhibit traditional, or Mendelian, patterns of inheritance. Some are transmitted as recessive traits, so that two carrier parents, themselves unaffected, may produce an affected child; some as dominant traits, so that one affected parent may produce an affected child; and some as sex-linked traits, passed from either an affected father or an unaffected mother to sons but generally not to daughters. Numerous factors complicate the picture for certain diseases; *e.g.,* diseases that depend on the inheritance of more than one gene, that arise from new mutations, or that reflect a combination of genetic and environmental influences.

In marked contrast to the traditional patterns of inheritance, however, stand a growing list of serious human genetic disorders that exhibit patterns of inheritance far too complex to be explained in simple Mendelian terms. Examples include fragile X syndrome, the most common known form of inherited mental retardation, and myotonic dystrophy, the most common known form of adult-onset muscular dystrophy.

Fragile X syndrome affects about one in 1,500 males and one in 2,500 females. As the name implies, affected individuals almost always display, in addition to a collection of characteristic cognitive and physical traits, an unusual chromosomal constriction, known as a fragile site, which is visible microscopically under defined conditions on their X chromosomes. Although the gene associated with fragile X can be passed from one generation to the next by members of both sexes, the risk of someone in a subsequent generation being affected is much higher if the carrier parent is the mother rather than the father. Moreover, for any individual in a fragile X family, the risk of being affected depends not only on the degree of relatedness to any other known affected or carrier individual but also on one's position in the pedigree, or ancestral line. In brief, the farther down a pedigree a person is located, the greater is the risk of being affected. For example, the brothers of unaffected carrier males (dubbed NTMs, for normal transmitting males) run a low risk (about 9%) of being affected, while the grandsons and great-grandsons of NTMs run a much higher risk (about 40% and 50%, respectively). This unusual pattern of inheritance was first described by Stephanie Sherman of Emory University School of Medicine, Atlanta, Ga., in the mid-1980s and is named the Sherman paradox.

In 1991 a candidate gene associated with fragile X syndrome, called *FMR-1,* was identified and cloned as a result of work in the laboratories of several different investigators, including Stephen Warren, Emory University School of Medicine; C. Thomas Caskey, Baylor College of Medicine, Houston, Texas; and Ben Oostra, Erasmus University, Rotterdam, Neth. Subsequent studies of this gene region in normal and affected individuals in the laboratories of the researchers named above, as well as in those of Grant R. Sutherland, Adelaide (Australia) Children's Hospital, and Jean-Louis Mandel, National Institute for Health and Med-

(continued on page 216)

Prozac

BY RICHARD M. RESTAK

Prozac is at once a drug treatment for depression and a bellwether of contemporary attitudes toward the place of psychoactive chemicals in society. Since its introduction in the U.S. in 1987, this drug has revolutionized psychiatry's approach to the management of depression, inspired cover articles in countless newspapers and magazines, and prompted spirited discussions and debates on radio and television talk shows. So popular has Prozac become that many people who take it show no more reluctance to talk about the experience than they would to talk about taking medicines aimed at controlling blood pressure or other traditionally less stigmatizing illnesses.

Chemically, Prozac belongs to a class of antidepressants referred to as the selective serotonin reuptake inhibitors (SSRIs). Serotonin is one of the brain's neurotransmitters, chemical messengers that convey information from one neuron (nerve cell) to the other. This communication takes place by means of the release of a neurotransmitter from one neuron, the passage of the neurotransmitter across the synapse (the junction between neurons), and the attachment of the neurotransmitter to a specific receptor on the receiving neuron. This match between a neurotransmitter and a specific receptor is often compared to the fit of a key in a lock. Starting in the 1960s, researchers developed a series of antidepressant drugs that altered the dynamics of various neurotransmitters within the synapse. In all instances the drugs acted by increasing the amount of neurotransmitter in the synapse or prolonging its actions.

For reasons still not fully understood, increased availability of neurotransmitters within the synapse exerts an antidepressant effect on some depressed persons. Not all patients improve on these drugs, however; about 30% of sufferers fail to respond to any antidepressant drugs. The variability of response of different patients to the main classes of antidepressants—the SSRIs, tricyclics, and monoamine oxidase inhibitors—accounts for the large number of such drugs presently on the market.

A different kind of drug. Until the advent of Prozac, all of the available antidepressants influenced several neurotransmitters in a general, nonspecific manner. Prozac, synthesized by scientists at Eli Lilly & Co. in 1972 and marketed some 15 years later by Dista Products Co., a division of Eli Lilly, is different from the others in that it influences only the neurotransmitter serotonin. Prozac does not cause the characteristic side effects that made the earlier antidepressant drugs unacceptable to so many patients—dry mouth, blurred vision, daytime sleepiness, constipation, and weight gain, among the most troublesome. Prozac is generally considered safe and free of serious side effects if properly prescribed and monitored by a physician. An alleged association between the drug and an increased incidence of suicide did not hold up under careful scrutiny. Suicide rates are higher among depressed people, treated or otherwise,

Richard M. Restak is clinical professor of neurology, George Washington University School of Medicine and Health Sciences, Washington, D.C. He is the author of numerous books, including Receptors *(1994) and* The Modular Brain *(1994).*

than among those who are not depressed, and the incidence among patients taking Prozac did not appear to be any greater than that in individuals taking other antidepressants.

While Prozac has brought relief of symptoms to hundreds of thousands of depressed people, neither it nor any other antidepressant should be considered a "cure" for depression. Rather, as with hypertension, diabetes, or a host of other chronic medical conditions, the tendency toward depression often extends over a lifetime and requires continued or periodic use of a medication such as Prozac that helps control major symptoms. (In 1994 Prozac was also approved for use in obsessive-compulsive disorder.)

Since no one can be certain what neurochemical factors may turn out to be most important in explaining depression, the development of new classes of antidepressants remains a thriving industry. This should not be surprising. Depression is not a unitary illness with a single cause but the subjective and behavioral expression of varied neurochemical abnormalities. It is likely that different types of depression result from disturbances in different neurotransmitters acting alone or in concert.

Appropriate versus inappropriate uses. Recently the use of Prozac and other mood-altering drugs has been expanded beyond their traditional application to definable mental illnesses. Shyness, various forms of social inhibition, and a general feeling of dissatisfaction with one's life have been suggested as appropriate targets for psychopharmacological modification. In what may foreshadow a more liberal use of these agents, in 1994 Prozac (under the trade name Lovan) was under review by the U.S. Food and Drug Administration (FDA) for the treatment of obesity. Since obese persons are not necessarily depressed, some measure of concern seems appropriate in regard to employing a drug for weight loss that is known to exert a powerful influence on mood.

Many questions have been raised about the use, and potential *overuse,* of Prozac. What attitude should physicians take when patients request Prozac to relieve irritability, mild reclusiveness, hypersensitivity, or nothing more definable than a lack of contentment with their life and accomplishments? Such uses blur the distinctions between treatment and "personality engineering." And what does it portend when neuroscientists' ability to produce specific brain-altering drugs is far in advance of their understanding of how the brain works?

Such questions take on a special urgency in light of the favourable response to the drug shown by people afflicted with troubling personality traits (tactlessness, resentfulness, etc.) rather than depression. Indeed, every physician prescribing the drug has one or more stories of individuals "borrowing" some Prozac from a spouse or friend and reporting a generally increased sense of well-being. (Needless to say, such unorthodox uses of drugs do not meet with FDA approval.) Do such individuals represent cases of undiagnosed depression? Or are their experiences a measure of the drug's capacity to establish in those not suffering from an identifiable emotional illness what philosophers and seers have recommended for centuries: the achievement of a sense of detachment coupled with acceptance of the world as it is and one's place in it? Although the latter possibility is initially appealing, the long-term consequences of a chemically oriented approach to the emotions have yet to be carefully weighed. It is possible that the use of Prozac and other similar drugs for anything other than unequivocal depression may carry with it the danger of impairing one of the human species' most precious mental assets: the ability to employ inner feelings, especially the more uncomfortable ones, to stimulate efforts to effect positive changes in oneself and the world.

(continued form page 214)

ical Research, Strasbourg, France, revealed the molecular nature of the defect ostensibly responsible for the disease and provided a novel and unexpectedly intriguing resolution of the Sherman paradox.

A gene carries information for the synthesis of a specific protein in the sequence of building block molecules, called nucleotides (abbreviated A, G, C, and T, for the constituent bases adenine, guanine, cytosine, and thymine), that make up DNA. This sequence information is ultimately translated into information specifying the sequence of amino acids that form the protein. In fragile X syndrome the apparent molecular defect takes the form of an expansion, or amplification, of tandem repeats of the triplet base sequence CGG near the beginning of the *FMR-1* gene. Such a defect, in which the extra repeats range in number from one to more than 1,000, represented a novel form of mutation to be associated with human disease.

A molecular survey of the *FMR-1* CGG repeat regions in normal and fragile X families revealed a startling pattern. Normal individuals had on average about 29 repeats, spanning a range from 6 to 52 repeats, while unaffected carrier individuals had between 50 and greater than 200 repeats. Affected individuals could have as many as 1,000 repeats or more. Perhaps most striking, however, was the finding that of the *FMR-1* genes studied in families, those containing 46 repeats or fewer showed no instability, or tendency to change, when passed from parent to child, while those greater than 52 repeats showed complete instability. Genes carrying large numbers of repeats, *i.e.,* those associated with affected individuals, were so unstable that even different cells within a blood sample from a single individual could show different repeat sizes. In families having intermediate, or "premutation," numbers of repeats in the *FMR-1* gene, it was not uncommon to see expansion from, for example, 66 repeats in the mother to 80 repeats in one child, 73 in another child, and 110 in a third child.

Furthermore, the risk of expansion to a full mutation (greater than 230 repeats) on passage from mother to child increased with the number of repeats already present in the mother. For example, women with premutation numbers of repeats in the 60–69 range had about a 17% chance of transmitting a full mutation to a child, whereas women with premutation numbers of repeats greater than 90 had a 100% chance of transmitting a full mutation. Therefore, in a typical fragile X family one would often see repeats in the premutation range move from small to large numbers in one or two generations and then to full mutations in subsequent generations, thereby providing a molecular explanation for the Sherman paradox.

Among the early benefits to be realized from discovery of the *FMR-1* repeat expansion was a gain in the ease and reliability of diagnosing fragile X for both the affected and carrier states. Previously diagnosis could be confirmed only by an expensive, labour-intensive procedure specifically designed to visualize the fragile sites in the patient's X chromosomes. While this method reliably detects affected individuals, it does less well for carrier females, whose fragile sites are not always discernible. With the identification of the *FMR-1* gene and the discovery of the fragile X-associated repeat expansion came the prospect of diagnosing affected and carrier individuals with molecular methods, which were faster, cheaper, and in many cases more informative. Indeed, given the observed patterns of expansion risk as a function of premutation size, molecular methods could be used not only to distinguish probable carriers from probable noncarriers but also to distinguish particularly high-risk carriers from comparatively low-risk carriers.

Although the CGG triplet repeat expansion associated with fragile X syndrome was novel and unexpected when first identified, its discovery paved the way for similar discoveries about other disorders. For example, it was subsequently learned that myotonic dystrophy, an autosomal (non-sex-linked) dominant neuromuscular disease, also is associated with repeat expansion of a triplet base sequence located near one end of a newly identified gene for the enzyme myotonin kinase. Indeed, the discovery provided a molecular explanation for the unusual inheritance pattern, termed anticipation, observed earlier for myotonic dystrophy; namely, that although the disease is passed in an autosomal dominant manner, the age of onset decreases and severity of symptoms increases with each generation in an affected family. As with fragile X, the more severely the individual is affected with myotonic dystrophy, the larger the triplet repeat expansion appears to be. By 1994 a number of other disorders, many characterized by anticipation, also had been linked to triplet repeat expansions, and the list was expected to grow. Included were spinobulbar muscular atrophy, Huntington's disease, spinocerebellar ataxia type 1, and FRAXE mental retardation (a disorder resembling fragile X syndrome caused by a similar defect at a different site on the X chromosome).

The identification of triplet repeat expansion as a mechanism of mutation answered some important questions about human genetic disease, but it also raised some new ones. Why, for example, are some triplet repeat genes unstable and others not? If "normal-sized" triplet repeats are completely stable, where do the premutation sizes come from? What are the origins of repeat expansion? Is the observed instability perhaps a normal form of evolution, sometimes associated with disease but other times not? What mediates and controls the process in humans and other species? How does repeat size expansion cause the observed traits of the disorder?

Finally, what are the normal roles of the identified genes and gene products in healthy individuals? Recent work indicated that the product of the *FMR-1* gene is likely to be a protein that binds RNA. The gene product associated with spinobulbar muscular atrophy functions as a molecular receptor for androgen (male sex hormone). Genes and gene products associated with the other disorders were under study.

(JUDITH L. FRIDOVICH-KEIL)

PALEONTOLOGY

The origin of life, evolutionary time, and the nature of the early atmosphere and oceans are a direct concern of paleontology. The old model of the oceanic broth of organic "soup" as the birthplace of life has given way to speculation that life emerged in more limited, protected environments such as the systems of hydrothermal vents observed today on the ocean floor. There in geothermally heated, mineral-rich waters thrive hydrothermal bacteria, which together with the highly anaerobic methane-producing bacteria form a major division of extant life—the archaea. The way in which hydrothermal bacteria use chemical reactions to make the molecules needed for life, *i.e.,* their means of chemosynthesis, is considered to be the most primitive among organisms. In the March 1994 issue of *Geotimes,* Everett L. Shock of Washington University, St. Louis, Mo., supported the assumption that primordial chemosynthesis utilized elemental sulfur and hydrogen sulfide found at hot springs around deep oceanic trenches. (See *Molecular Biology,* above.)

Paleobotanists use microscopic fossil spores, pollen, and dinoflagellate cysts as indicators of past biogeography, floral diversity, and extinction. By means of such tools, Paul Colinvaux of the Smithsonian Tropical Research Institute,

Balboa, Panama, and his collaborators were reconstructing changes in global climate and the history of tropical Amazon Basin vegetation. It was believed that fossil plants lived under climatic restraints similar to those of recent plants and that detailed studies of stomata in fossil leaves could help determine past concentrations of gases in the atmosphere. Stomata, found on the underside of leaves, are openings through which gases such as carbon dioxide and oxygen can enter and leave a plant. Experiments with living plants had shown that such characteristics of stomata as their density on the leaf surface are influenced by the atmospheric concentration of carbon dioxide. Consequently, by charting the changes observed in the stomata of fossil leaves through time, researchers were attempting to build a picture of changing carbon dioxide levels over millions of years.

Invertebrate paleontologists, while still pursuing mass extinctions, were coming to recognize the existence of evolutionary stasis between extinctions. In other words, following a mass extinction and the subsequent few million years of recovery, which are marked by rapid evolutionary change and reorganization of living communities, ecological patterns stabilize for tens or hundreds of millions of years until the next mass extinction.

Researchers also began shifting their attention to the sudden, very rapid origination of animal species and higher groups in the Cambrian Period—the so-called Cambrian explosion or big bang of evolution that took place more than 500 million years ago. As observed in the Cambrian fossil record, animals emerged fully developed in a geologically "sudden" time as short as 5 million to 10 million years in duration. Unusually well-preserved and abundant fossil localities are windows to past life. Such windows were being reconstructed and interpreted: the Middle Cambrian Canadian Burgess Shale by the English paleontologists Matthew A. Wills and Derek E.G. Briggs of the University of Bristol, England, and Richard A. Fortey of the British Natural History Museum, London; the Swedish Upper Cambrian Orsten by the German scientist Dieter Walossek of the Rhenish Friedrich Wilhelm University, Bonn, Germany; and other Early Paleozoic localities by Jerzy Dzik of the Polish Academy of Sciences, Warsaw. Uranium-lead isotope dating of volcanic rocks from Siberia allowed Samuel A. Bowring and his co-workers from the Massachusetts Institute of Technology, Harvard University, and Yakutian Geoscience

Institute, Yakutsk, Russia, to place more exactly the beginning of the Cambrian at 544 million years ago, compared with the 570 million-year figure previously accepted. Many hypotheses for the sudden appearance of animals in the Cambrian were offered, among the more popular of which were those involving the oxygen level of the sea, climate, sea-level changes, biological "arms races," complexities regarding body forms and structures, and even sampling errors (*i.e.,* the Cambrian explosion is not real but an artifact of the way fossils have been collected and classified).

Adolf Seilacher of the University of Tübingen, Germany, and Yale University was the first paleontologist to receive the Crafoord Prize—the equivalent of the Nobel Prize for fields not covered by the traditional Nobels—from the Royal Swedish Academy of Sciences. A few years earlier Seilacher had proposed a fifth kingdom, Vendobionta, for the Precambrian Ediacaran fossils that had been classified originally among existing phyla and fitted into the general plan of such living animals as jellyfish, sea pens, worms, and certain problematic creatures. More recently he interpreted the Ediacaran fauna as an extinct animal phylum.

Among highlights in vertebrate paleontology, Paul C. Sereno of the University of Chicago reported on previously unknown species of carnivorous and herbivorous dinosaurs from the Early Cretaceous (about 130 million years ago) that he and colleagues discovered in the southern Sahara Desert. Strong similarities between the African dinosaurs and North American forms led Sereno to question accepted ideas about the way the supercontinent of Pangaea began fragmenting about 150 million years ago into the continents of today and to suggest that the land bridge that linked the two landmasses which would become the present-day northern and southern continents was maintained far longer than previously thought. In November Scott R. Woodward of Brigham Young University, Provo, Utah, reported that he and his co-workers had extracted DNA from 80 million-year-old fossil bone fragments, found in an underground coal mine, that he believed came from a dinosaur. Until other researchers could reproduce his results, however, both the ancientness of the DNA that he isolated and the proposed identity of its source would be regarded skeptically.

(MATTHEW H. NITECKI)

See also Botanical Gardens and Zoos; Chemistry; Earth Sciences; Environment.

This article updates the *Macropædia* articles BACTERIA; Animal BEHAVIOUR; BIOCHEMICAL COMPONENTS OF ORGANISMS; THE BIOLOGICAL SCIENCES; BIOSPHERE; CELLS; CONSERVATION OF NATURAL RESOURCES; DISEASE; The Theory of EVOLUTION; The Principles of GENETICS AND HEREDITY; GEOCHRONOLOGY; MAMMALS; PLANTS; REPRODUCTION AND REPRODUCTIVE SYSTEMS; SENSORY RECEPTION.

A new species of crested theropod dinosaur, *Cryolophosaurus ellioti,* is shown in a reconstruction based on fossils collected from Mt. Kirkpatrick in Antarctica. The bones of the carnivorous biped, a relative of *Tyrannosaurus,* were part of the first dinosaur fossils ever found on the Antarctic mainland. Their presence suggests that during the Early Jurassic (about 200 million years ago) a mild climate existed in the region, which at the time occupied a latitude at least 60° S and perhaps as high as 70° S.

ANDREW STARENKO

Literature

The 1994 Nobel Prize for Literature was awarded to the Japanese novelist Kenzaburō Ōe. (*See* NOBEL PRIZES.) The British professor Mark Morris congratulated the prize committee on "one of the bravest decisions in years," the only previous Japanese winner (in 1968) having been an easy choice, according to his view—much translated and presented as "exotic and quintessentially Japanese"—whereas there was "nothing comfortably Japanesey about Ōe's brand of grotesque realism." Ōe was a writer painfully conscious of his country's defeat and humiliation in World War II. His revulsion against nuclear weapons was first expressed in *Hiroshima nōto* (1965; *Hiroshima Notes,* 1981), begun after a visit to the bombed city. The birth of a son with severe brain damage became the basis for his most famous novel, *Kojinteki na taiken* (1964; *A Personal Matter,* 1968). Ōe's more recent works had not been widely translated. Japanese critics complained that his style was too "Westernized"—too precise, perhaps—and he seemed alien to the conservative spirit in Japan, where he was regarded as a spokesman for left-wing intellectuals.

The literature of Eastern Europe seemed to have lost its attraction for the rest of the world, which was generally reckoned to be a result of the collapse of the communist regimes there. Jasper Rees, in the *Daily Telegraph* (London), wrote wistfully of "the golden age of Czech fiction" and that nation's "grand old men of letters," Milan Kundera, Josef Škvorecký, and Ivan Klíma. Škvorecký, living in Canada, quoted a remark of Graham Greene—"The situation of a writer is incomparably better under communism than under capitalism"—and explained that "it's a ready-made drama if you live under the Nazis or the Stalinists." However, Škvorecký affirmed, "The *real* writers do not depend on that. . . . They survived the change of the regime." One such writer, Klíma, was applauded in Britain for his new novel, *Čekání na tmu, čekání na světlo* (1993; *Waiting for the Dark, Waiting for the Light,* 1995), which dealt with a disaffected television cameraman under the communist regime. The man dreams of freedom and works on an unpublishable screen drama, but when the "velvet revolution" comes, he remains disaffected, unmoved, and unpublished.

ENGLISH

United Kingdom. A disagreeable feature of the literary year in Britain was the attention paid to books that denigrated members of the royal family. Extracts, serializations, and ill-tempered review articles abounded in the generally conservative press. One long review in the *Daily Telegraph* was devoted to five books about Charles, Prince of Wales, his wife, Diana, their supposed adulteries, and his brother's father-in-law. The reviewer, Lynn Barber, said, "The most 'important' (I flatter him) book in this *galère* is Andrew Morton's *Diana: Her New Life,*" although she found it "not so jaw-droppingly sensational" as his previous book about the princess. Barber also sneered at the other bio books, which included *Princess in Love,* a romantic fantasy

about Diana's alleged adultery written by Anna Pasternak, a kinswoman of the celebrated Soviet dissident Boris Pasternak.

A dismissive attitude toward the royal house was apparent in Andrew Roberts' admired book *Eminent Churchillians*—seeming to invite comparison with Lytton Strachey's *Eminent Victorians,* as John Charmley pointed out in the *Times Literary Supplement,* and treating the political career of Winston Churchill as if it were a reign. The book comprised eight essays about some of Churchill's contemporaries. Included were essays on the royal family and their attitude toward the political policy of appeasing the Nazis and also a "wickedly funny and devastatingly cruel" essay on Lord Mountbatten, according to Charmley. He agreed with Roberts' verdict on the royal family that "they represented the most unprepossessing aspects of conventional wisdom, at precisely the time when it was proving dangerously mistaken." A milder form of iconoclasm was expressed in *The Oxbridge Conspiracy* by Walter Ellis, a denunciation of the Universities of Oxford and Cambridge and the power held by the graduates in the life of the nation; the book was reviewed widely but sneeringly by those very graduates.

Surprisingly well received was *Age of Extremes: The Short Twentieth Century, 1914–1991* by Eric Hobsbawm—surprisingly because Hobsbawm had long been a member of the Communist Party and still remained a Marxist. This was the fourth volume of his history of the modern world, the other three dealing with "the long 19th century"—from 1789 to 1914. The central argument, according to Niall Ferguson, was that the Russian Revolution of 1917 and the dictatorship of Stalin had served positively to preserve capitalism. Writing in a right-wing newspaper, Ferguson, an Oxford historian, urged his readers to ask, "Where is *our* Hobsbawm?" He went on: "No other living historian of whatever political affiliation has the intellectual firepower—the range and depth of knowledge, the analytical skill—to bring off a book like this."

As a relief from all the dismal commentaries on modern royal liaisons, Claire Tomalin offered *Mrs. Jordan's Profession,* a biography of the celebrated actress

Dorothea Jordan, who had been mistress to the Duke of Clarence, later King William IV. "A biography worthy of its subject," declared John Gross, appreciating the "remarkable woman" whose life had been recorded with such "penetrating analysis and narrative verve." Equally impressive was David Gilmour's biography *Curzon,* the story of the Marquess George Nathaniel Curzon, the ambitious politician and viceroy of India whose achievements had been long neglected, buried under humorous anecdotes.

The most noteworthy biographies, however, seemed to be accounts of two dead novelists who were sorely missed: Evelyn Waugh and Graham Greene. The latest biography of Waugh, by Selina Hastings, was described as "admirable and riveting" by Geoffrey Wheatcroft in *The Spectator.* According to the reviewer, she stressed Waugh's social unease (mixing with grandees, "he realised how inelegant and unsophisticated his own family were," said Wheatcroft), and she provided "more detail than ever before about Waugh's passionate homosexual affairs at Oxford." Hastings was equally sharp about Waugh's military career, his rudeness, and the failings of his friends. Her book seemed to be admired partly because it made Waugh pitiable.

Although Waugh's failings had already been much discussed, his friend Greene had remained rather mysterious. Four biographies of him appeared in 1994, however, attempting to shed light. Norman Sherry continued his own lengthy account with *The Life of Graham Greene, Volume Two: 1939–1955,* in a manner that was found to be "forbearing and deferential" by Karl Miller, the reviewer in the *Times Literary Supplement.* Miller, the former editor of the *London Review of Books,* also reviewed the other three biographies, and he noted the "adversarial case" made by Michael Shelden in *Graham Greene: The Man Within.* "Shelden's book is bold and unhesitating," said Miller. "If his criticisms are sometimes overdone, they are seldom misplaced. The anti-Semitism of the early fictions . . . is firmly documented." Other reviewers were more interested in other of Shelden's denigrations. David Lister, in the

James Kelman

Independent, for example, concentrated on Greene's habit of taking a toy bear on his travels, finding this a plausible support for Shelden's suspicion that Greene suffered from a homosexual tendency.

A third biography, *Graham Greene: Three Lives* by Anthony Mockler, was dismissed by Miller as "a fairly peculiar production." Mockler had displeased Greene, who then impeded the biographer's work. The fourth memoir, Leopoldo Durán's *Graham Greene: Friend and Brother,* was the work of the Spanish priest who had inspired Greene's novel *Monsignor Quixote* (1982). Durán was persuasive and compassionate about Greene's personality and his failed marriage, though he seemed to misunderstand the old dictum (said by George Orwell) that Greene was "our first Catholic fellow-traveller." He had welcomed Greene as a traveling companion and had not concerned himself with Greene's supposed sympathy for Soviet communism.

Kingsley Amis was perhaps the most successful of the established novelists publishing during 1994. His latest book, *You Can't Do Both,* was reckoned to be more autobiographical than the 20 other works that had preceded it—almost like a young man's "first novel." It told of a London boy's suburban adolescence in the 1930s, his oppressively supervisory father, his wartime military service, his marriage and adultery, and his job as a provincial university lecturer. Described by the publisher as "a precursor to *Lucky Jim,*" it was found, in general, to be far less funny than that success of 40 years ago. Martyn Harris in the *Sunday Telegraph* (London), however, was sympathetic to the novel, "with its bashful, shamefaced tenderness," and to the hero, with his sense of "having missed something important." He found the novel "excellent" and some of the scenes "hideously funny."

An element of autobiography was also apparent in V.S. Naipaul's unusual novel *A Way in the World,* which seemed to be trying to bridge the conventional gap between fact and fiction. The book began with the narrator, a Trinidadian youth (like Naipaul himself), waiting to take up a scholarship at Oxford; there followed an apparently true history of Uriah ("Buzz") Butler, who led an oil workers strike in 1937 and was jailed by the British authorities. Two intellectuals, one of them British, supported Butler and, many years later, met the narrator in London; though seemingly historical, the intellectuals were fictitious. There followed brief histories of Sir Walter Raleigh's discovery of Eldorado (1595) and, over two centuries later, of Francisco de Miranda's rebellion against Spanish rule in Venezuela. The histories were presented as "unwritten stories" from the narrator's bottom drawer, and the stories melded into a work that, in Abdulrazak Gurnah's view as expressed in the *Times Literary Supplement,* reflects Naipaul's tendency to "privilege Europe and European ways, and portray non-Europe (especially Africa and South America) with absurd malice." Interviewed in the *Times Literary Supplement* by Aamer Hussein, Naipaul explained his purpose in constructing "fiction" in such a manner and expressed his feeling that the "novel form has done its work."

John Bayley, the chairman of the Booker Prize jury, announced that reading the 130 novels submitted for the prize had been

V.S. Naipaul
DILIP MEHTA—CONTACT PRESS IMAGES

an "ordeal" and that the "new fiction is at best ambitious and at worst pretentious." Nevertheless, the Booker jury managed to select a shortlist of six novels that was generally respected, though without much enthusiasm.

In *Reef,* Romesh Gunesekera, a Sri Lankan settled in London, produced a story about a Sri Lankan boy working in the city. In *Paradise,* Gurnah, a university teacher of literature in England who was born in Zanzibar, told the story of an African boy's coming-of-age. Another candidate for the prize was *Knowledge of Angels* by Jill Paton Walsh, a writer best known for her children's books. In this, her third adult novel, she had imagined a medieval island where a child, reared by wolves, is discovered in the mountains; the girl is carefully secluded, without education or instruction, as a theological experiment to see if she will discover or invent a god. *Knowledge of Angels* was notable for having been rejected by 14 major London publishing houses, and the author, the only woman on the shortlist, had published the work herself. A novel about a gay man was contributed by Alan Hollinghurst, author of the successful *The Swimming-Pool Library;* his new novel, *The Folding Star,* concerned an English tutor in a Belgian city (resembling Bruges) who becomes obsessed with one of his adolescent pupils.

The two other novels on the shortlist came from Scotland. George Mackay Brown, a septuagenarian from the Orkney Islands, was an unexpected entrant—"much the bravest and most intriguing selection," according to David Robson, since "the veteran Orcadian novelist writes in a bardic, over-the-top style." His novel, *Beside the Ocean of Time,* consisted of eight stories of life on the fictitious island of Norday over a period of 1,000 years, the narrator being a crofter's son on the eve of World War II. However, the eventual winner of the prize was a different sort of Scottish writer, James Kelman, with *How Late It Was, How Late,* a painful story of poverty and the loss of eyesight, narrated by a hard-

drinking, hard-swearing, victim of modern life in the Glasgow underclass. The book was bitterly rebuked for its modern vernacular of foul language, but some critics noticed its literary roots in John Milton's *Samson Agonistes.*

Although the Booker Prize was intended for prose fiction, the jury was also asked to consider a poetry book, *History: The Home Movie* by Craig Raine, the most noticed new verse of the year. It had as its subject the family histories of the poet and his Russian wife—another kinswoman of Boris Pasternak. The scholarly novelist David Lodge said, "It is as absorbing, moving and amusing as a good novel, while achieving a lyric intensity that would look like straining for effect in prose fiction."

The novel *Theory of War* (1993) by Joan Brady, who was born in the U.S. but who had lived in England for about 30 years, won the Whitbread Book of the Year award in 1994. It was the first time the prize had been given to a woman. (D.A.N. JONES)

United States. For all of the moaning and groaning about the state of the literary arts in the United States—and from writers to editors to critics to booksellers to readers, all had done some of it—it had to be admitted that when people argued about books, and the quarrels made newspaper headlines, something valuable was taking place. In 1994 critic Harold Bloom stirred up the biggest hornet's nest in a long time by publishing *The Western Canon,* his book-length advertisement for the great books of the culture. Both a polemic against what he called "the recent politics of multiculturalism" and a persuasively argued answer to the question "What shall the individual who still desires to read attempt to read, this late in history?" Bloom's book took the high ground in the nearly decade-long debate on what books the university should teach.

Some of the country's best novelists meanwhile came out with new works, unmindful of the literary debate raging around the idea of the importance of the sociological component of their art. Jayne Anne Phillips' lyrical second novel, *Shelter,* was a story about innocence struggling with experience—and good wrestling with evil—against the backdrop of a summer camp for girls in the early 1960s in Appalachia. No less lyrical was Cormac McCarthy's *The Crossing,* the second novel in his "Border Trilogy," the first of which, *All the Pretty Horses,* had been a best-seller the year before. Also veering toward the lyric was Peter Taylor's masterly meditative novel about the early 20th-century South called *In the Tennessee Country.* Taylor died soon after its publication.

With *What I Lived For,* Joyce Carol Oates published her best novel in years. Set in a fictional upstate New York metropolis, resembling Buffalo, the book recounted one weekend—Memorial Day 1992—in the life of a 43-year-old American Everyman, Jerome ("Corky") Corcoran. He is a short fellow who demands the respect of men and the love of just about every woman he meets, and Oates brought him to life in all of his confused, bawdy reality and with a vigour and intelligence that few novelists, female or male, could muster on the subject. Another veteran novelist, Joseph Heller, brought out a new book with much less successful results. *Closing Time,* a sup-

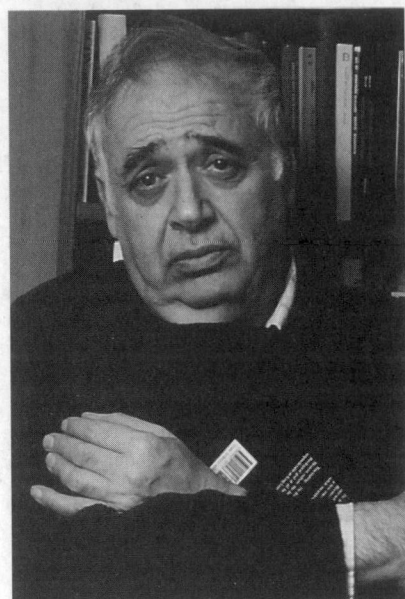

Harold Bloom
LUC NOVOVITCH—GAMMA LIAISON

posed sequel to Heller's 1960s cult classic *Catch-22*, delivered none of that first book's humour and none of its narrative drive. In *Mercy of a Rude Stream*, octogenarian novelist Henry Roth delivered the first of a new six-novel cycle about the education of a young Jewish New Yorker in the 1920s and '30s. Although not as memorable as his classic *Call It Sleep*, the new novel demonstrated some of that earlier book's lyrical strength and descriptive powers in its account of city life. With *The Waterworks*, E.L. Doctorow added another segment to his own continuing depiction of New York City, the novel taking the reader back to the mid-19th century and focusing on the mysterious disappearance of a post-Civil War mogul and his son's quest to find him.

Among younger writers who published novel-length fiction during 1994 were Joanne Meschery, with an engaging domestic narrative called *Home and Away* that was set in a community in California's High Sierra; Paul Russell, whose *Sea of Tranquility* told the story of an American astronaut and his struggle to come to terms with his son's homosexuality; and Beverly Lowry, with *The Track of Real Desires*, a ferocious portrait of a middle-class dinner party in a small Mississippi town. Howard Norman's *The Bird Artist* was nominated for a National Book Award and appeared to be a leap forward in his own evolution as an ethnographer turned fiction writer.

There were several striking debuts in 1994, particularly Maxine Clair's *Rattlebone*, a portrait in stories of a black Kansas City family; Susan Power's connected stories of Sioux history and life in *The Grass Dancer;* and David Guterson's memorable *Snow Falling on Cedars*, which told of the murder trial of a Japanese-American salmon fisherman in an island community on Puget Sound. Also worth noting was the first novel *Losing Absalom*, in which Alexs D. Pate focused on the death of a black Philadelphia patriarch and the effect of his demise on his estranged son.

Several veteran short-story writers came out with new collections: John Updike with

The Afterlife and Other Stories, T.C. Boyle with *Without a Hero*, and Richard Bausch with *Rare & Endangered Species*. Barry Lopez turned his narrative talent to stories in a new collection entitled *Field Notes*, and Louis Auchincloss brought out *The Collected Stories of Louis Auchincloss*. The PEN/Malamud Prize for Short Fiction went to Grace Paley for *The Collected Stories*.

American poets were enormously productive in 1994. The masterly Philip Levine, for example, published *The Simple Truth*, his 16th book, and Richard Howard's *Like Most Revelations* met with approving reviews. John Ashbery brought out *And the Stars Were Shining*, and John Wood produced a new volume entitled *In Primary Light*.

Several highly regarded poets offered new and selected poems, among them C.K. Williams, Kenneth Koch, Stephen Dunn, Heather McHugh, and Jack Gilbert. Carolyn Forché published her long-awaited *The Angel of History* and an impressively edited anthology entitled *The Poetry of Witness*.

E.L. Doctorow
SHONNA VALESKA—TIME MAGAZINE

Toward the end of the year, Robert Pinsky issued his new translation of Dante's *Inferno*. Rosellen Brown added to her verse saga of New Englander Cora Fry with *Cora Fry's Pillow Book*.

A number of gifted younger poets came out with new collections, including Edward Hirsch with *Earthly Measures* (which had the distinct honour of being one of the few recent volumes of poetry listed by Bloom in his portrait of the modern canon), Andrew Hudgins with *The Glass Hammer*, and Jane Hirshfield with *The October Palace*. Hirshfield also published a wonderful historical anthology, *Women in Praise of the Sacred*. Nearly 150 African-American poets were represented in the most beautifully produced anthology of the year, E. Ethelbert Miller's *In Search of Color Everywhere*.

Blackfoot novelist James Welch turned to nonfiction in *Killing Custer*, a meditative retelling from a Native American perspective of the U.S. cavalry incursions against indigenous tribes during the takeover of the West. Mixing autobiography with social

commentary, novelist John Edgar Wideman produced in *Fatheralong* what he dubbed "a meditation on fathers and sons, race and society." Tobias Wolff worked more in the direct vein of memoir in his chapterlike essays on his Vietnam service in *In Pharaoh's Army*. Another fine fiction writer, novelist Robb Forman Dew, published *The Family Heart*, a memoir of her family's response to the revelation of her older son's homosexuality. In the elegantly turned essays in *Last Watch of the Night*, Paul Monette portrayed his own illness and the life of the United States during the AIDS decades. Physician and fiction writer Abraham Verghese wrote a memorable account of his encounter with AIDS patients in small-town Tennessee in *My Own Country*.

Equally personal, and also with broader social resonance, was Lucy Grealy's finely composed *Autobiography of a Face*, the story of her childhood cancer and subsequent reconstructive surgery. In *Parallel Time* Brent Staples turned his journalistic style to autobiography and the pathology of racism. Novelist Reynolds Price put his storytelling gifts at the service of autobiography and an account of his difficult but rewarding battle with cancer in *A Whole New Life*. On the lighter side, novelist and story writer Bob Shacochis compiled a number of his magazine columns on home cooking under the title *Domesticity*.

Within the forms of history and biography, interesting and slightly unconventional work appeared. *London's Burning* by Peter Stansky and William Abraham treated the nexus of what they identified as "love, death, and art" during the period of World War II. Janet Malcolm, fresh from a libel trial in which she was exonerated of charges of character assassination made against her by the historian of psychoanalysis Jeffrey Masson, brought out a study of Sylvia Plath entitled *The Silent Woman*, in which the questions of the reliability of biographical sources and the biographer's own intentions come under as much scrutiny as the subject herself. John Demos focused in *The Unredeemed Captive* on a conventional early American captivity narrative and broadened his research to include questions of larger importance in colonial American family life.

Galileo, a biography of the great European thinker by James Reston, Jr., showed a freshness of style, if not approach. Shari Benstock's *No Gifts from Chance*, a biography of Edith Wharton, opened to public view previously veiled aspects of the New York novelist's private life. In the history of ideas, Page Smith's *Rediscovering Christianity* traced the relationship between modern democracy and the Christian ethic. David J. Garrow performed a similar labour in his massive *Liberty and Sexuality*. In the autobiography *Naturalist*, which treated both his life and the ideas in science that led him to fulfill it, sociobiologist Edward O. Wilson depicted the growth of an inquiring mind and the growth of a science. Scholarship was turned into fascinating narrative in Louise Levathes' study of the Chinese royal navy in the 15th century, *When China Ruled the Seas*.

For all of its intensity, Bloom's *The Western Canon* celebrated the works it touched on as much as it investigated them. In terms of analytic depth, moral reach, and practical use for the serious reader, the best book of literary criticism in 1994 was the posthumously published *A Critic's Notebook* by Irving Howe (edited by his son Nicholas). A study of the various aspects of the novel, *Notebook* offered full-blown essays on the function of character in modern fiction and the role of history in the novel and made a running argument with the new formalists who insisted, as Howe put it, that "if you are caught discussing a fictional character in the way that you might talk about a human being, you will probably be convicted of being a 'naive reader.' " Less analytic but just as entertaining were the numerous short essays—reflections on Proust, Fitzgerald, Wharton, and Pound, among others— in Auchincloss' *The Style's the Man.*

In poetry criticism Louise Glück, in her *Proofs & Theories,* put forward the notion that "within the discipline of criticism, nothing is more difficult than praise" and then elegantly disputed it with her pieces on George Oppen, John Berryman, Robinson Jeffers, and Stanley Kunitz. In a more conventional but valuable study of the work of Malcolm Lowry—*Forests of Symbols*— scholar Patrick A. McCarthy delved deep into the work of the often overlooked mid-20th-century modernist. Prizewinning essayist Arthur Danto published *Embodied Meaning: Critical Essays and Aesthetic Meditations.* Gerald Early covered issues from sports to race to literature in his collection *The Culture of Bruising,* and Saul Bellow collected a number of disparate essays in the sprightly volume *It All Adds Up.* As "cultural studies" programs advanced across the American academy, historian Daniel Boorstin came out with essays on various subjects from politics to literature under the title *Cleopatra's Nose,* in which he combined erudition and a rare clarity of style in order to illuminate the broader culture.

The Pulitzer Prize for Fiction was awarded to E. Annie Proulx (*see* BIOGRAPHIES) for her novel *The Shipping News,* and Yusef Komunyakaa won the poetry award for *Neon Vernacular.* In general nonfiction the winner was *Washington Post* reporter David Remnick for *Lenin's Tomb: The Last Days of the Soviet Empire.* Edward Albee

JERRY BAUER

Jayne Anne Phillips

won his third Pulitzer, for the play *Three Tall Women.*

The *Los Angeles Times* prize for poetry went to Forché for *The Angel of History.* The PEN/Faulkner Award for Fiction was won by Philip Roth for his novel *Operation Shylock.* Ernest J. Gaines took the National Book Critics Circle award in fiction for *A Lesson Before Dying.* The award in poetry went to Mark Doty's *My Alexandria. Genet,* by Edmund White, won in the category of biography, and in general nonfiction the prize was awarded to Alan Lomax for *The Land Where the Blues Began.*

The winners of the National Book Award were *A Frolic of His Own,* by William Gaddis, for fiction; *Worshipful Company of Fletchers,* by James Tate, for poetry; and *How We Die: Reflections on Life's Final Chapter,* by Sherwin B. Nuland, for nonfiction. The poet Gwendolyn Brooks received the National Book Foundation's medal for distinguished contributions to American letters.   (ALAN CHEUSE)

Gwendolyn Brooks
TOM HORAN

Canada. The output of fiction and poetry in 1994 perfectly mirrored the elusive Canadian identity—a mosaic, to be sure, but composed of amoebas, refusing to cohere in any one pattern for longer than a "nanolife," or the span of a longish novel. In *The Cunning Man,* Robertson Davies used the exceptional diagnostic talents of a doctor as a lens through which to examine the symptoms of contemporary life. Joan Clark's *Eiriksdottir: A Tale of Dreams and Luck* assembled the shards of legend and archaeology into an epic of survival on the coast of prehistoric Newfoundland. Charles Foran moved every which way through time in *Kitchen Music* as a Canadian man and his Vietnamese wife search for their parents and the redemption of a past they never knew. Contrariwise, in Alice Boissonneau's *A Sudden Brightness,* set in a mental hospital in British Columbia, both patients and staff try to find a tolerable future.

Poet Mary Di Michele turned to fiction to chart the multiple dimensions of fear in *Under My Skin,* a psychological thriller-

Alice Munro
ANDREW ECCLES—OUTLINE PRESS

within-a-thriller. Detective work of a historical kind was the focus of M.G. Vassanji's *The Book of Secrets,* based upon a diary that exposes the sins of earlier generations and confounds present ones. Among first novels were *Frog Moon* by Lola Lemire Tostevin, another poet venturing into prose, metaphors flashing; *The Cage* by Audrey Schulman, in which a small but feisty woman photographer faces down polar bears and human boars alike; and Paul William Roberts' *The Palace of Fears,* in which the better the good life gets, the worse the protagonist's dissatisfaction.

Alice Munro's latest collection, *Open Secrets,* ranged from the semicivilized hills of southern Ontario to the wilderness of Albanian mountains. In *Guerrilla Beach* former journalist Oakland Ross crafted stories from his years as a foreign correspondent in South America, while Hugh Hood bore witness to very strange country in *Around the Mountain: Scenes from Montreal Life.* Motherhood generated the action in Katherine Govier's *The Immaculate Conception Photography Gallery and Other Stories,* while absence informed the senses in Carole Giangrande's *Missing Persons* and artfulness played through Sky Lee's *Bellydancer: Stories.* The inhabitants of Bonnie Burnard's *Casino and Other Stories* are faced with more choices than they can deal with, while the characters in Gayla Reid's *To Be There with You* find that solitude and claustrophobia are much the same.

Notable among the outpourings of poetry in 1994 were Stephen Scobie's *Gospel,* in which the poet took on God's voice directly; *Hologram: A Book of Glosas,* in which P.K. Page paid homage to poets who had influenced her; Al Purdy's homage to life at large, *Naked with Summer in Your Mouth;* and Linda Rogers' *Hard Candy,* which included "Wrinkled Coloratura," winner of the new Stephen Leacock Award. Other distinguished works included Gary Geddes' *Girl by the Water,* mystery refracted through myriad voices; Susan Musgrave's first new collection since 1985, *Forcing the Narcissus;* Francis Sparshott's satirical tour called

The Hanging Gardens of Etobicoke; Cherie Geauvreau's first collection, *Even the Fawn Has Wings,* celebrating a logic of feeling rather than the mind; *Beds and Consenting Dreamers,* Joe Rosenblatt's playful revisionist parable of Marxist theory; Evelyn Lau's search for atonement through perversity in *In the House of Slaves;* and Ralph Gustafson's stately and startling *Tracks in the Snow.*

Rudy Wiebe won the 1994 Governor-General's Award for fiction for *A Discovery of Strangers,* a historical novel set in the Canadian north. The awards of the Canadian Authors Association went to Margaret Atwood, *The Robber Bride,* for fiction, and to Boyce Richardson, *The People of Terra Nullius: Betrayal and Rebirth in Aboriginal Canada,* for nonfiction. Winner of the new Giller Prize, established to honour the late popular Canadian journalist, Doris Giller, was Vassanji for *The Book of Secrets.*

(ELIZABETH WOODS)

Other Literature in English. Authors from the rich and variegated cultures of Australasia and central and southern Africa provided some of the finest literary works written anywhere in English in 1994. From Australia, for example, Thomas Keneally, author of *Schindler's List* (originally *Schindler's Ark*), continued his most productive career with perhaps his most complex and engaging novel to date, *Jacko: The Great Intruder.* Fiction writer Thea Astley brought out her 13th novel, *Coda,* a delightfully funny yet moving account of a woman's journey into old age. Peter Carey, winner of the 1988 Booker Prize, published *The Unusual Life of Tristan Smith,* a picaresque, tragicomic drama in which the world was boldly reimagined. Making its debut as well was *Albion's Story* (published as *Dark Places* in Australia and the United Kingdom), Kate Grenville's compelling tale of rape and incest told from the perpetrator's point of view. In a superb tribute befitting its subject, Hazel Rowley combined rich detail and thoughtful analysis in her literary biography *Christina Stead.*

In poetry Les Murray's *Translations from the Natural World* presented puns, verbal sound effects, and syntactic ambiguities among daring and frequently beautiful metaphors to evoke nature. David Rowthbaum, following a 13-year hiatus, offered *New and Selected Poems* (1945–93), which included selections from his Toowoomba childhood to more recent pieces on modern life and politics.

New Zealand writers demonstrated great diversity and high quality in a number of important new titles. *Deep River Talk,* for example, gathered 140 poems from 10 collections by Hone Tuwhare, the most internationally known contemporary Maori poet. Novelist Alan Duff depicted the sordid, violent despair of his characters and their milieu in *Once Were Warriors.* Bill Manhire's vision of New Zealand life was somewhat less bleak and often humorous in his short-story collection *South Pacific.*

Noteworthy among the year's literary contributions from sub-Saharan Africa were Abdulrazak Gurnah's *Paradise* (Tanzania) and Steve Chimombo's *Napolo and the Python* (Malawi). Author Wole Soyinka, the first African Nobel laureate in literature (1986), fled his homeland in November fearing that he would be arrested for criticizing Nigeria's military regime.

Thomas Keneally
JEFFREY MARKOWITZ—SYGMA

From South Africa came several outstanding offerings as well, including *None to Accompany Me,* the latest novel by the 1991 Nobel laureate Nadine Gordimer, which portrayed the lives of two couples—one black and the other white—during the confused and traumatic period just before the establishment of South African majority rule. Eighteenth-century South Africa was the setting of André Brink's 11th novel, *On the Contrary,* and veteran novelist J.M. Coetzee chose 19th-century Russia as his backdrop and Fyodor Dostoyevsky as his protagonist in *The Master of Petersburg.* The émigré writer Sheila Roberts examined exile and migration as recurring themes in her new collection, *Coming In and Other Stories.* Renowned poet Laurens van der Post unveiled his autobiographical anthology *Feather Fall,* a compilation of his verse from over 60 years.

In nonfiction two works of international interest appeared in 1994: *Nelson Mandela Speaks,* released in South Africa for the first time although previously published in the United States, and Nobel Peace Prize winner Archbishop Desmond Tutu's *The Rainbow People of God: The Making of a Peaceful Revolution.*

(DAVID DRAPER CLARK)

FRENCH

As in every year, there were a number of celebrations in 1994, including the 500th anniversary of the birth of François Rabelais and the 300th of Voltaire. There were not many major new works on Rabelais published during the year. Nevertheless, a short study by Jean-Yves Pouilloux (1993) appeared, and a number of important earlier works, including Lucien Febvre's *L'Incroyance au 16e siècle, la religion de Rabelais* and *Rabelais* (1988) by Gilles Henry, were reissued. Young writers such as François Bon, author of *La Folie Rabelais* (1990), reminded readers in newspaper articles of the radical originality of the work of Rabelais.

Voltaire—who wanted to be known as the "universal man" but who, with cruel irony, became the archetype of the engaged intellectual—was celebrated in 1994 as he should have been—with an avalanche of works. Noteworthy were *Dictionnaire Voltaire,* edited by Jacques Lemaire, Raymond Trousson, and Jeroom Vercruysse; *Voltaire et l'Europe* by Françoise Bléchet and Marie-Odile Germain; *Le Rire de Voltaire* by Pascal Debailly, Jean-Jacques Robrieux, and Jacques van den Heuvel; *Voltaire, l'affaire Calas et nous* by Gilbert Collard; and *Voltaire, le conquérant* by Pierre Lepape.

A number of works by and about Michel Foucault, who had died 10 years earlier, appeared in 1994. *Dits et écrits,* in four volumes, brought together various writings on philosophy. Didier Eribon, author of a biography of Foucault, published *Michel Foucault et ses contemporains,* which included treatment of Jean-Paul Sartre, Georges Dumézil, Roland Barthes, Jürgen Habermas, and Louis Althusser. *Michel Foucault, les jeux de la vérité et du pouvoir,* a collection of works edited by Alain Brossat, also appeared, along with *Michel Foucault, la clarté de la mort* by Jeannette Colombel, a friend of Foucault and Sartre.

During the year Jacques Derrida published two essays, *Politiques de l'amitié* and *Force de loi,* different in tone but both examining the notions of politics, justice, and the state. Marie-Anne Lescourret published the biography *Emmanuel Lévinas,* and Michel Serres *Atlas.* Edgar Morin published an important autobiographical work, *Mes Démons,* and Claude Lévi-Strauss published an album combining photographs and text, *Saudades do Brasil.* Alain Robbe-Grillet came out with *Les Derniers Jours de Corinthe,* which concluded his three-volume autobiography. In it he recalled, sometimes with humour, such colleagues as Claude Simon, Marguerite Duras, Barthes, Sartre, and his editor, Jérôme Lindon, the prestigious director of Éditions de Minuit.

The last, unfinished, autobiographical novel of Albert Camus was published in 1994, 34 years after the author's death. Although *Le Premier Homme* was an imperfect and incomplete work, it contained themes dear to the author of *L'Étranger* (Algeria, the maternal figure, injustice, absurdity, pleasure), and in it Camus revealed, for the first and only time, the inconsolable wounds of his childhood. A short work by Louis Aragon was also published posthumously; *Projet d'histoire littéraire contemporaine* on the one hand clarified his Dadaist period and the beginnings of Surrealism and on the other his relationship with his principal editor, Jean Paulhan. Volumes of the *Oeuvres* of Raymond Roussel appeared, accompanied by an essay by Annie Le Brun, "Vingt Mille Lieues sous les mots, Raymond Roussel." Finally, the newly discovered text of Jules Verne's *Paris au XXe siècle* was published for the first time in 1994. In this astonishing work of anticipation, the reader discovers the fervent advocate of progress making his first predictions.

Among the most notable novels of the year were *Du coeur et de l'affection* by Jacques Teboul, a book of reminiscences; *Comme des anges* by Frédéric Boyer, a lyrical portrayal of a family during the 1950s; *Le Fil* by Christophe Bourdin, a literary work on AIDS; *Un Mal imaginaire* by Maxime Montel, also with AIDS as a subject; and a humorous first novel on the world of work, *Extension du domaine de la lutte* by Michel Houellebecq. In poetry the collection of works by Philippe Jaccottet, *Après beaucoup d'années,* was notable.

Olivier Rolin received the Prix Fémina for his novel *Port-Soudan,* in which he succeeded in evoking a sad love story as well as the malaise of those who would have been 20 in May 1968. Didier Van Cauwelaert received the Prix Goncourt for *Un Aller simple,* which retraced the tragicomic voyage of a street Arab of Marseille deported by mistake to Morocco. Also recommended for the Goncourt was a novel by Paule Constant, *La Fille du Gobernator,* a dark and despairing book despite comical anecdotes in which the author recalled his childhood in Cayenne, French Guiana, where his father was governor of the prison. Guillaume Le Touze, a young writer of 26, received the Prix Renaudot for *Comme ton père,* and Yves Berger the Prix Médicis for *Immobile dans le courant du fleuve.*

(FRANÇOIS POIRIÉ)

Canada. In terms of popular appeal, the novel topped all other major literary genres in Quebec in 1994. Attention was focused mainly on *Va savoir* by Réjean Ducharme, an author whose aversion to the limelight was notorious but whose reclusive ways had not affected his productiveness (close to 10 novels published since 1966). Ducharme was esteemed for his creative handling of language and his poetic imagination, both of which appeared in nearly perfect balance in *Va savoir.* Michel Tremblay, the well-known author of *Les Belles-Soeurs* and of the chronicles of the Plateau Mont-Royal, also achieved success as a novelist in 1994. In *Un Ange cornu avec des ailes de tôle,* Tremblay transmuted his reminiscences into literature by exploring his youth from the standpoint of the books that had shaped it. Each of the chapters gave pride of place to a work of literature esteemed by Tremblay to have had a marked influence on his development as a writer.

Daniel Poliquin's novel, *L'Écureuil noir,* a tale of modern life that dexterously united elements of comedy and disillusionment, was hailed as the literary event of 1994 (of the decade by some). The seductive power of the novel was due to the simple way in which the hero, Calvin Winter, describes the events of his life. Finally, in *Ostende* the popular storyteller François Gravel provided a vividly written and richly textured account of the 1960s and '70s.

Poetry lovers were equally well served in 1994. Readers evinced a particular fondness for a book of poetry by Robert Mélançon called *L'Avant-printemps à Montréal.* One critic pointed out that the poet's special achievement was to make banal things seem luminous. Intent on precisely describing things such as the end of the day or the look of snow as it falls during the night, the poet created the kind of atmosphere wherein the reader experiences such things afresh. Another book of poetry that did well in 1994 was *L'Usage du temps* (1993) by Claude Beausoleil. This was poetry for readers not put off by obscurity, for Beausoleil gave them some 50 pages of quatrains unencumbered by punctuation.

(PIERRE HÉBERT)

GERMAN

The provocative question Is German literature boring? was posed in 1994 by the editor of the prestigious S. Fischer publishing house, Uwe Wittstock, who volunteered his own answer: Yes, German writers should learn to write more entertainingly and take Anglo-American authors as their model. His assessment was rejected by such highly regarded literary critics as Rolf Michaelis and Heinz Ludwig Arnold. In an effort to prove the existence of a lively and exciting contemporary German literature, Suhrkamp, the most important publisher of contemporary literature, issued the "Red Series," showcasing young writers of the past 10 years, Durs Grünbein and Ralf Rothmann, among others, being represented.

The year also saw the debut of promising new talent. One discovery was Guido Schmidt, whose magnificent story "Die Soldaten der Jungfrau" recounted the uprising of the Indians of the Chiapas region in southern Mexico at the end of the 16th century. In cool and detached prose, Schmidt depicted the merciless cruelty of the Inquisition and dissected in a sober and seemingly pitiless fashion the annihilation of the native peoples by the Spanish invaders. The German-Romanian author Herta Müller also wrote about persecution and terror in her poetic novel *Herztier.* Employing a prose at once forceful yet sensitive, she portrayed six German-Romanians who were destroyed by the Romanian dictatorship.

In *Tarzan am Prenzlauer Berg,* Adolf Endler recalled life under the East German dictatorship, specifically in the bohemian quarter of East Berlin. Laconic and rife with irony, his diary-styled text related the conflicting allegiances of writers and poets who on the one hand lived as if on a government-protected reservation and on the other hand were spied on by colleagues who betrayed them. Reiner Kunze likewise turned to the past in his journal *Am Sonnenhang,* citing from files in which the East German secret police had recorded his private life in detail. Kunze still felt as inwardly divided as he perceived the country to be outwardly riven. Similarly skeptical was Sarah Kirsch's *Das simple Leben,* which gathered together prose and verse from the

Christa Wolf

years 1991 to 1993. On the other hand, Christoph Hein's tales in *Exekution eines Kalbes* made it clear that there was no reason one should yearn for the old regime.

A more varied picture of the East German past emerged from the addresses, letters, prose texts, and journal entries that Christa Wolf published in October under the title *Auf dem Weg nach Tabou.* She raised a bristling defense against accusations of West German critics that she had not been critical enough of the communist regime yet admitted to errors and wrote openly of the wounds she had suffered before and after the fall of the Berlin Wall. Despite its political themes, *Auf dem Weg nach Tabou* remained first and foremost a work of poetry, full of strange images and a sensitive, suggestive language.

Contemporary German literature continued to reflect the differences that existed between Germans from the east and those from the west. While numerous eastern writers still struggled with the experience of life under the communist dictatorship, many young western writers were mapping new literary terrain. They were no longer beholden to the past—which for them meant the Nazi past of their forefathers—and they no longer saw themselves as writers forced to pay obeisance to their age.

Arnold Stadler traced his youth in his novel *Mein Hund, meine Sau, mein Leben,* and in so doing he revealed its essential loneliness. Stadler told his story oddly distanced, often even engaging in parody. In his novel *Wäldernacht,* Rothmann likewise had his protagonist returning to the period of his boyhood. Even more so than Stadler, Rothmann told of suffering and failure while using a pliant and realistic language. In two books the third writer of this young generation, Andreas Mand, spun tales of the "superfluous generation." The story *Peng* was written as the draft of a screenplay for a film that had young people failing miserably in order that they might grow closer to each other. By contrast, Mand's novel *Das rote Schiff* was a wonderfully light story about growing up in Germany and simultaneously a swan song to the culture of the 1970s and '80s. A member of an older generation, Reinhard Lettau, who for many years had taught in the United States, wrote one of the shortest (93 pages) and sharpest novels around, entitled *Flucht vor Gästen.* Hard-hitting, comic, and clever, this book about Lettau's homecoming was written in a prose style that read like poetry.

German lyric poetry continued to excite relatively little interest even among cognoscenti. A significant exception was the work of Grünbein, who responded to the situation in Germany after 1990 in *Falten und Fallen,* combining the words of an East German with the irony of his West German counterpart. Other important volumes of poetry were published by Jürgen Kolbe and Robert Gernhardt. An impressive biographical sketch of the late poet Ludwig Greve also appeared.

Several major diaries were published in 1994. Ninety-six years after the death of Theodor Fontane, his *Tagebücher—1852, 1855–1858, 1866 1882, 1884–1898* appeared, giving insight into the cultural life of Berlin in the second half of the 19th century. At the same time, the complete four-volume historical-critical edition of Franz

Kafka's diaries (1909–23) was published. They included passages originally excised by Kafka's literary executor, Max Brod, especially Kafka's uninhibited observations on sexuality. Also of historical import were the *Tagebücher, 1913–1917* of Gershom Scholem, relating his odyssey from Berlin to Palestine, and the *Tagebücher, 1910–1924* of the poet and revolutionary Erich Mühsam, who in 1934 was murdered by the Nazis.

(DANIEL HAUFLER)

NETHERLANDIC

Several established authors ventured outside their usual fields of expertise in 1994. A prominent existentialist writer of mostly World War II novels, W.F. Hermans published a book on photography, *Een foto uit eigen doos,* a valuable collectors' piece. Martin Hart received a literary prize for the most suspenseful novel of the year, *Het woeden der gehele wereld,* but he also wrote *Du holde kunst,* a series of essays on his favourite composers from Bach to the present day. Leo Vroman, the well-known poet, wrote *Warm, rood, nat en lief,* relating the impact on his poetry of his involvement in scientific research. J. Bernlef, a leading author since the 1950s and, like Hart, an amateur musician, published a collection of essays on music entitled *Schiet niet op de pianist.*

The established novelist Theun de Vries published *Terug uit Irkoetsk,* a historical work set in Russia. The promising young novelist Thomas Rosenboom published *Gewassen vlees,* about life in 18th-century Holland. Nelleke Noordervliet wrote the sociopsychological novel *De naam van de vader* and Hermine de Graaf the feminist novel *Vijf broden en drie vissen.* Important works came from the Flemish poet Hugo Claus, who issued *Gedichten 1948–1993;* Bernlef, *Vreemde wil;* Toon Tellegen, *Tijger onder de slakken;* and Leonard Nolens, *Honing en As.* (MARTINUS A. BAKKER)

SCANDINAVIAN

Denmark. The veteran writer Martha Christensen's *Her i nærheden* consisted of three novellas, the main one portraying a mother whose possessive love finally drives her son to murder. Gentler was Sten Kaalø's *Pilgrim i Paz,* about a midlife crisis in the chaos of Eastern Europe. Eastern Europe figured too in Janina Katz's *Heltens tykke kone,* both humorous and sad portrayals of exiled Jews after World War II. Peter Høeg produced *De måske egnede* (1993; *Borderliners,* 1994), about private schooling in Denmark and its traumatic effects on the pupils. He was chosen author of the year by *Time* and received the Danish Critics' Prize and the Golden Laurels of the Danish Booksellers' Association.

Already established as a young poet of character, Naja Marie Aidt published several idiosyncratic short stories, *Vandmærket,* on the surface banal, but in fact sophisticated, portraits of those on the edge of society. Also on the edge was one of the two main characters in Kirsten Thorup's 615-page *Elskede ukendte,* showing the meeting between a 22-year-old dropout and a religious fanatic. Even more depressing was Vagn Lundbye's *Udflugt med Billie,* about a half-Lapp Oslo girl who is left to fend for herself and who becomes alienated in the process. Lighter, but not without a serious perspective, was Svend Åge Madsen's

Peter Høeg
JO SELSING

Edens gave, centred on a discovery that allows unlimited enjoyment of food without weight gain and leads among other things to famine because of overconsumption by the rich.

Solvej Balle was a young writer making a name for herself. Her *Ifølge loven* was an experimental novel in the form of four interlinked short stories. Klaus Rifbjerg's *Vi blir jo ældre* was a volume of 18 short stories ranging from the playful to the profoundly moving but all reflecting the fact that Rifbjerg was aging. His *Synderegistret* was a series of reflections on the present day, overshadowed throughout by the spectre of Bosnia.

Ole Wivel published a new collection of poems, *Iris,* a mixture of erudition and tenderness showing his skill to be undiminished. With *Denne kommen og gåen,* Benny Andersen confirmed himself as a supreme master of play on language in poems that were both humorous and serious. Also linguistically brilliant were Lundbye's highly acclaimed poetical animal sketches, *Lundbyes dyrefabler.* Pia Tafdrup's intense *Territorialsang* centred on Jerusalem, reflecting both the city and the poet's search for community with it. (W. GLYN JONES)

Norway. A collection of 25 short stories by as many contemporary writers, *De beste norske novellene,* selected by Terje Holtet Larsen, underlined the strength of this genre in 1994. Among several new collections, pride of place went to Tor Ulven's *Vente og ikke se* for its original use of language and minimalistic brilliance. Øystein Lønn won the Norwegian Critics' Prize for his collection *Thranes metode.* In the novel, psychological complexities were unraveled with dramatic intensity in Ketil Bjørnstad's *Barnevakt.* In Finn Carling's *Gjenskinn* a man receives a book as a gift, which awakens in him painful memories of traumatic happenings in his own life. The cruel, sadistic world of a small group of 12-year-old boys was portrayed with humour, psychological insight, and linguistic mastery in Rolf Enger's *Solformøkelsen.* The atmosphere of Oslo in the 1950s was magnificently caught

in Bjørg Vik's *Elsi Lund,* with painful sexual awakening in teenage girls as one of its central themes. Johannes Heggland displayed his usual mastery as a narrator in the historical novel *Jordparadiset. Kunnskapstreet,* with action laid in the 18th century.

In Espen Haavardsholm's documentary novel *Ikke søkt av sol,* a portrayal of Norwegian intelligence during and after the German occupation was interwoven with an account of a retired agent's attempts to uncover the facts behind his cousin's mysterious death in Stockholm in 1945. The dramatic life of the Jewish-Russian psychiatrist Sabina Spielrein was re-created with great sensitivity in Karsten Alnæs's *Sabina,* from her sexual awakening as Carl Jung's young mistress to her tragic death during the German invasion of Russia in 1941.

Agnar Mykle died during the year, and in his highly personal biography, *Agnar Mykle—en dikterskjebne,* his son-in-law, Eystein Eggen, traced the tragic life of one of the most controversial figures in postwar Norwegian literature. Mykle's complete works were also published in seven volumes. As well as a biographical reevaluation, Yngvar Ustvedt's monumental *Henrik Wergeland. En biografi* provided fascinating insights into the cultural history of Norway in the first half of the 19th century. The profound influence exerted by Henrik Ibsen's dramas on Edvard Munch's art was thoroughly analyzed in Lars Roar Langslet's copiously illustrated *Henrik Ibsen—Edvard Munch,* with the text in English and Norwegian. The first of six planned volumes of Knut Hamsun letters, *Knut Hamsuns brev,* edited by Harald S. Næss, documented the trials and tribulations of Hamsun's life prior to his literary debut in 1890 marked by *Sult* (*Hunger,* 1899).

The Brague Prize went to Sigmund Mjelve for his poetry collection *Område aldri fastlagt* and an honorary Brague award to Halldis Moren Vesaas for her contributions to Danish literature. Deaths during the year included Rolf Jacobsen, a leading modernist poet. (TORBJØRN STØVERUD)

Sweden. Kerstin Ekman received the Nordic Council's literary prize in 1994 for her novel *Hemligheter kring vatten.* In Klas Östergren's novel *Under i september,* extramarital love is unexpectedly sidelined by the imperative to help illegal immigrants. Björn Ranelid's sprawling, chaotic *Synden* featured the struggle for love and survival of two young victims of adult moral turpitude. In the short story collection *Oskuld,* Robert Kangas presented a chilling world in which his protagonists shows no moral sensibilities or pity. Johan Lagerman's first novel, *Slumpen Lydia,* good-naturedly presented unglamorous, middle-aged friendship and incipient love between a prostitute and client. Helena Helsing's *Omständigheter* was a humorous first-person account of the traumas of pregnancy, while Mare Kandre's *Quinnan och Dr Dreuf* was a sparkling satire on Freud's view of women patients. In *Anna, Hanna och Johanna,* Marianne Fredriksson traced the lives of three women—grandmother, mother, and daughter—against the background of a century of social change, while Gerda Antti's *Bara lite roligt . . .* conveyed, through a female narrator, the aspirations and discontents of a group of country folk. Margareta Ekström wrote elegantly about the relationship between a cat and her female owner in *Olga om Olga*. Thus, the sociopolitical severity of the Vietnam years and their aftermath in Sweden had demonstrably been replaced by literature dealing with personal relationships.

Katarina Frostenson's *Tankarna*, Ann Jäderlund's *Mörker mörka mörkt kristaller*, and Arne Johnsson's *Fåglarnas eldhuvuden* were notable poetry collections. Per Olov Enquist published three plays in *Tre pjäser*, and astronomer Peter Nilson turned from the cosmos to describing humankind's home on Earth in *Hem till jorden*. Poet and scholar Lars Huldén published a monograph, *Carl Michael Bellman*, on the 18th-century poet. In *Jag bor i en annan värld men du bor ju i samma*, octogenarian Olof Lagercrantz recalled his friendship with the poet Gunnar Ekelöf.

Novelist Ulla Isaksson wrote a passionate account, much debated by readers, of how her aging husband, the distinguished literary scholar E.Hj. Linder, had "abandoned" her because of Alzheimer's disease. Poet and novelist Lars Gustafsson wrote informal memoirs in *Ett minnespalats. Vertikula memoarer*. Poet Ylva Eggehorn gave a suggestive account of her 1950s childhood in *Kvarteret Radiomottagaren*, while in *Svartenbrandt* Sweden's most notorious jailbreaker, Lars Ferm, described his violent criminal career and the peace he finally attained as a believer.   (KARIN PETHERICK)

ITALIAN

Audiences of all ages were captivated in 1994 by the weekly reading on television of Dante's *Inferno*. The cantos detailing punishments inflicted upon grafters, hypocrites, thieves, and fraudulent politicians proved to be especially popular. But, for once, television could not be blamed, either by publishers or by critics, for the fall in book sales—1994 being a World Cup year in which the president of the Milan association football (soccer) club, and owner of major national television channels, became prime minister. On the other hand, so many books were published and so many literary prizes were awarded that ordinary readers were right to feel totally overwhelmed by sheer quantity. Quality, however, was far from missing.

In the field of narrative the general trend was back toward formally traditional novels with a social and political conscience. An excellent example of the genre was the remarkable *Sostiene Pereira* by Antonio Tabucchi. Told in the slightly impersonal, but faintly unsettling, style of a witness's deposition and set in 1938 Lisbon with the Spanish Civil War, Italian Fascism, and German Nazism lurking in the background, it was the masterly psychological portrait of a journalist—a mature man, unhealthily fat, lonely, initially quite apolitical, but obsessed by the memory of his dead wife and by the thought of his own death—who is gradually forced by circumstances to take the path of decency and honour and to commit himself, weaknesses and all, to the cause of reason and humanity. A war was also the focus in *Attesa sul mare* by Francesco Biamonti, in which a sea captain is hired to take a shipload of arms to Bosnian partisans in former Yugoslavia and thus comes into contact with the cruelty of armed conflict and the sufferings of a disputed land, an experience that pushes him back to sea, searching for an all-too-elusive goodness.

A more direct concern for the country's moral and political crisis surfaced in such disparate novels as Andrea De Carlo's *Arcodamore* and Francesca Duranti's *Progetto Burlamacchi*. The former centred on a morbid and doomed love story that could be read as an allegory of contemporary Italy were it not for the fact that the country's predicament was itself raised in the book by the narrator's indignant voice. Duranti's novel was more ambitious in conception and execution, attempting to graft onto the present two historical examples of failed religious and moral reformation. Sebastiano Vassalli, the successful northern writer, caused a stir by attempting to complete his trilogy on the Italian character with a story about the Sicilian Mafia. His novel *Il Cigno*, set emblematically in 1893 Sicily, was highly praised for its structural qualities but ran into criticism for failing to understand and convincingly depict its Sicilian context.

A number of new young writers proved that the novel was alive and well. The most successful commercially was Susanna Tamaro's *Va' dove ti porta il cuore*, a diary in which an 80-year-old woman recounts to her granddaughter the story, largely painful, of three generations of Italian women. By coincidence, the compelling portrait of a grandmother was also the subject of Margaret Mazzantini's *Il catino di zinco*, which unconventionally and unsentimentally aimed to recover traditional female values that modern feminist thinking fought to discredit; the portrait was especially effective thanks to a firm and confident style that skillfully combined an almost precious linguistic sophistication with flashes of vernacular crudeness. Even more remarkable in stylistic range and structural conception was Alessandro Baricco's enigmatic *Oceano mare*, a series of disturbing encounters with a limitless sea that could be read, among other things, as historical thriller, prose poem, dramatic dialogue, "conte philosophique," and picaresque tale.

At the opposite end of the spectrum was Giuseppe Culicchia's minimalist *Tutti giú per terra*, a painfully realistic portrait of a contemporary antihero that rightly claimed to be a generational autobiography, with a young man who fails to live up to any of the television-induced expectations and myths of his family and social milieu as both narrator and protagonist.

Giuseppe Pontiggia published *Vite di uomini non illustri*, 18 fictional biographies of as many ordinary men and women of the 20th century. The secret of Pontiggia's writing was in his skillful application of the classical Plutarch-like biographical patterning of the lives of insignificant characters, a device that not only achieved ironic effects but also served to reveal how truly extraordinary every ordinary life was. In a category of its own was *Il dispatrio*, a kind of diary and essay in which, after several books devoted to his Italian upbringing, Luigi Meneghello attempted to recapture in characteristic plurilingual style what it was like for a young Italian intellectual—a recent graduate from both a civil war and a faculty of philosophy—to be living and working in an English academic environment from the late 1940s onward.

Among various literary polemics, there was much debate over *Notizie dalla crisi*, a collection of theoretical and applied literary essays in which Cesare Segre showed how effective a semiotic-philological approach to literary texts could continue to be after deconstruction and neohermeneutics had outlived their usefulness.   (LINO PERTILE)

SPANISH

Spain. In *El hermano pequeño*, Manuel Vázquez Montalbán gave Pepe Carvalho, the most famous detective in contemporary Spanish fiction, some easy warm-up assignments and then put him to the ultimate test in *Roldán, ni vivo ni muerto*: to step into reality and find Luis Roldán—who had riveted public attention, and deeply embarrassed the government, when he fled the country in April 1994 just before his impending arrest on charges of having embezzled a sizable fortune during his tenure (1986–93) as chief of the national Guardia Civil. At year's end the whereabouts of Spain's most infamous fugitive remained known only to Carvalho.

Life's peculiar symbiosis with literature also attracted two senior novelists. In Gonzalo Torrente Ballester's *La novela de Pepe Ansúrez*, a pathetic bank clerk attempts to write a roman à clef and gets a helping—or hindering—hand from everyone at work, and Camilo José Cela, silent since receiving the 1989 Nobel Prize for Literature, derived *El asesinato del perdedor* from the true story of a young man recently driven to suicide by a grotesque legal injustice. At a different, more hazardous intersection of fiction and reality, Cela himself got blindsided when his second novel of the year, *La cruz de San Andrés*, received the lucrative Planeta Prize, an award originally established to encourage young writers; prominent observers openly denounced the decision as a venal negotiation between the sponsoring publisher and the "prearranged" winner of the putatively blind annual competition.

In a year dominated by important new fiction, Carmen Martín Gaite—winner of the National Letters Prize—offered *La Reina de las Nieves*, full of literary cross-references and competing narrators; and Julio Llamazares published *Escenas de cine mudo*, an evocative reconstruction, from old photos, of childhood impressions and experiences in rural León. Strongly autobiographical elements also coloured *Malena es un nombre de tango*, Almudena Grandes' third novel; and the treacherous political climate of the final years of the Franco regime shaped *El dueño del secreto* by Antonio Muñoz Molina. Bernardo Atxaga won the Critic's Prize for his thriller *El hombre solo*, translated by the author from the Basque original. Widely praised were bestsellers by three exceptionally gifted writers: Luis Landero (*Caballeros de fortuna*), Rosa Regás (*Azul*, the Nadal Prize winner), and Javier Marías (*Mañana en la batalla piensa en mí*). The Peruvian novelist Mario Vargas Llosa, who became a citizen of Spain in 1993, won the highest award in Hispanic letters, the Cervantes Prize.

(ROGER L. UTT)

Latin America. The Mexican writer Carlos Fuentes was the most prominent novelist of Latin America to publish a book in 1994. It was a year of particular significance for Latin-American writers of Fuentes' generation as well as for earlier writers. Fuentes published the novel *Diana, o la cazadora solitaria*, part of his lifelong project "The Era of Time." The novel, set in the world of Mexican intellectuals during the 1960s, was a fictional account of Fuentes' experiences and dealt with an American actress who has an affair with a Mexican writer. In the work Fuentes asked the question What passions or ideals make human beings act in ways that carry them to their death?

Two writers belonging to the generation before Fuentes, Julio Cortázar and Juan Carlos Onetti, had works published posthumously in 1994. The *Cuentos completos* of Cortázar appeared in print 10 years after his death. In Mexico the University of Guadalajara established a permanent Julio Cortázar chair in October in honour of the Argentine writer. The chair was endowed by Fuentes and Gabriel García Márquez. The *Cuentos completos* of Onetti were also published during the year.

The Peruvian writer Julio Ramón Ribeyro received the Juan Rulfo Literary Prize, worth $100,000 and the major literary award in Latin America. Author of three novels, several volumes of short stories, and other assorted writings, Ribeyro had become one of the most respected of Latin-American writers and intellectuals, even though he was relatively unknown in the Anglo-American literary world. Ribeyro was a particularly accomplished craftsman of short fiction.

Major works of literature in Mexico were published by the novelists Carmen Boullosa, Homero Aridjis, Juan García Ponce, Francisco Rebolledo, and Federico Patán, as well as by the poets José Emilio Pacheco, Francisco Hernández, and Octavio Paz. Boullosa, who had become one of Mexico's leading female writers, considered gender issues in the colonial Hispanic world in her latest novel, *Duerme*. Aridjis published a historical novel set in the millennium, *El señor de los mil días*. García Ponce, who belonged to the generation of Fuentes, published a roman à clef about intellectuals in Mexico, *Pasado presente*. Rebolledo published an excellent first novel, *Rasero*, and Patán issued another fine anthology of short fiction, *El paseo*. Pacheco, who had become Mexico's major poet of the generation after Nobel laureate Paz, published the

Carlos Fuentes

collection *El silencio de la luna*. Hernández also published a notable book of poems, *El infierno es un decir*. The first volumes of Paz's complete works, entitled *Obras completas*, also began to appear in print. Poet Vicente Quirarte published an excellent literary essay, *Peces del aire altísimo*, which was awarded the essay prize at the National Autonomous University of Mexico.

In South America some of the most notable new fiction among young writers appeared in Colombia and Uruguay. The Colombian Héctor Abad Faciolince's first novel, *Asuntos de un hidalgo disoluto*, was a postmodern and digressive account of the narrator-protagonist, an elderly Colombian in Italy. The playful and irreverent work marked a new direction for Colombian fiction. Colombian Andrés Hoyos, author of two novels, published *Los viudos*, a volume of outstanding short fiction thematically similar to his previous nostalgic fiction. One of Uruguay's most innovative female writers, Teresa Porzecanski, published *Perfumes de Cartago;* she employed descriptions of perfume and other sensory stimuli to transport the reader to the Montevideo of the 1930s but also evoked the Orient. The Uruguayan Guillermo Degiovangelo, who had already written short fiction, published a well-received novel with a symphonic structure, *Descubrimiento de la melancolía.*   (RAYMOND LESLIE WILLIAMS)

PORTUGUESE

Portugal. The winner of the Great Prize for Fiction in 1994 was Vergílio Ferreira for his novel *Na tua face* (1993). It was the second time he had been awarded the distinction in his long career as a novelist and an author of nonfiction. Deeply concerned with the ravages of physical decay and the anguish of death, Ferreira told a moving story in a confessional tone that had the dreamlike qualities of stream of consciousness, with flashes of a surrealistic imagination. Divided between the woman he married and the elusive figure of the woman that he loved, the narrator is trapped in an existential predicament seen in the light of a dialogue with the tenets of the philosophical traditions of Western culture. In a subtle way the author reveals the futility of consolation and the fallacies of domesticity, to discover a redemption in beauty and in the memory of the dead that transcends the deceits of human existence.

The young people from the former Portuguese colonies in Africa and India who went to Lisbon after World War II for university studies were the subject of *Os netos de Norton,* an engaging and subtle novel by Orlando da Costa. Born and bred in the liberal and republican atmosphere, these young people were committed to a change of the regime and to the liberation of the colonies. Norton de Matos served as both a symbol for them and a presidential candidate to stand up to the dictatorship. Political vicissitudes, however, were only the framework for the beautifully written novel, in which a web of human relationships is tied up with self-discovery and the ills of a generation that seeks its emancipation through the labyrinths of eroticism, love, and art. The problem of art and the intensity of its expression occupies a large part of the novel, showing the changing values of a composition that gains its maturity in the warmth of human feeling and in the

melancholy that taints the hopes and fears of a fulfilled present.

A time of devastation and moral emptiness was how the distinguished poet Joaquim Manuel Magalhães saw the years preceding the end of the 20th century in his collection *A poeira levada pelo vento* (1993). His poems were admirable for their ideas, the pithiness of his metaphors, and the haunting desolation of the cities he described.   (L.S. REBELO)

Brazil. Perhaps owing to increasing national despondency over the political and economic future, Brazilian literature withdrew from its preoccupation with such matters in 1994. Notable works of fiction included Rubem Fonseca's *O selvagem da ópera,* about the life of the Brazilian opera composer Carlos Gomes, and Jorge Amado's *A descoberta da América pelos turcos,* which highlighted the Arab contribution to Brazilian civilization. There were other new works of fiction by Rachel de Queiroz and Luiz Antônio de Assis Brasil. In *Ah, é?* Dalton Trevisan wrote stories about the sexual preoccupations of banal people living in Curitiba, while Deonísio da Silva's *O assassinato do presidente* presented short tales of urban life.

The collected works of poets Murilo Mendes and Hélio Pellegrino were published posthumously. The essayist and short-fiction writer Marina Colasanti turned to poetry with *Rota da colisão* (1993), a collection of feminist views of womanhood in a macho Brazilian society. Several young poets, including Cláudia Roquette-Pinto, Alexei Bueno, and Rosane Serro, published new collections. João Cabral de Melo Neto, Brazil's preeminent poet, was awarded the Ibero-American Prize for Poetry by Queen Sophia of Spain.

It was a year for revivals in the theatre. Three of Nélson Rodrigues' most lauded works—*A falecida, Vestido de noiva,* and *Anjo negro*—were restaged. Works by Oduvaldo Viana Filho (Vianinha) and Plínio Marcos—major social dramatists of the 1960s and '70s—were also revived, as was Adélia Prado's *Dona Doida.* Among new theatrical productions were Geraldo Carneiro's *O eleito,* a parody on Brazilian politicians' cynicism, and Denise Stoklos' *Amanhã será tarde...,* about women and love. Miguel Fallabela, Maria Adelaide Santos de Amaral, and Beth Thomas also had new plays produced.

The *tropicalista* Paulo Coelho published yet another volume in his worldwide bestseller collection of pseudomystical self-help fiction, *Na margem do Rio Piedra eu sentei e chorei.* A study of the songs of Caetano Veloso, one of *tropicália*'s leading musical figures, was published in 1993 by Ivo Lucchesi and Gilda Korff Dieguez. Biographies of the Brazilian cultural entrepreneur Assis Chateaubriand and the poet Vinícius de Moraes appeared during the year. The illustrious novelists Antônio Callado and João Ubaldo Ribeiro were inducted into the Brazilian Academy of Letters. The distinguished American Brazilianist Raymond S. Sayers died in September.
    (IRWIN STERN)

RUSSIAN

Throughout the year Russian literature continued in a period of transition, in which many saw the myth of the Great Russian Writer slowly moving toward extinction.

Even the return of Aleksandr Solzhenitsyn to his homeland on May 27 did not revive the truly Russian institution of the writer as moral authority. Symbolically entering Russia from the east, Solzhenitsyn seemed like a prophet of the old times to some and an anachronism to others.

Most of the intellectuals who had played a part in the final years of the communist period stepped back from public view. The writers who had once occupied seats in the Soviet parliament and taken a lead in the press no longer dominated. "I think we are expecting too much from politics and politicians," commented Fazil Iskander, adding, "The spiritual life of a nation should be led by philosophers and poets." Other writers, such as Vasily Aksyonov, were openly worried about the place of the writer in the new Russia, especially at a time when publishers were intent on producing "commercial pulp from the West."

While there was no shortage of predictions that literature was dying and would soon expire in the flood of low-grade Western culture, there was a sense of exhilaration and power among the young. Self-proclaimed modernists and avant-gardists began to dominate the literary magazines and fill the vacuum created by the sense of stagnation in traditional literature. Dmitry Prigov remained the star of the avant-garde and the mentor to scores of younger writers. A recipient of literary awards and proclaimed a "living classic" by *Nezavisimaya gazeta,* Prigov combined words and performance, abolished the borders between genres, and cultivated the art of the happening. He claimed that a writer today had to be an actor as well as an artist and emphasized context over content, along with gesture and action. The works of the post-modernists—for example, Vyacheslav Kuritsyn and Vladimir Sorokin—were beginning to introduce questions of discourse and textual criticism that had not been fully explored in Russian literature before. A gay culture was also gaining in strength and found a classic in Yevgeny Kharitonov's *Pod domashnim arestom* ("Under House Arrest"). The fame of Kharitonov, who died in 1981, was only now beginning to peak.

The literary scene was dominated by discussions and controversy centring on the Russian Booker Prize. The 1994 award, valued at $15,000, was awarded in December to Bulat Okudzhava for his autobiographical novel *Uprazdnenny teatr* ("The Closed-Down Theatre"). Okudzhava, a poet and balladeer in addition to a prose writer, was reportedly ill and unable to attend the awards ceremony. Shortlisted for the Booker Prize were Pyotr Aleshkovsky's *Zhizneopisanie Khorka* ("Polecat's Biography"), Yury Buida's *Don domino* ("The Domino-Player"), Igor Dolinyak's *Mir trety* ("Another World"), Mikhail Levitin's *Sploshnoye neprilichiye* ("Total Indecency"), and Aleksey Slapovsky's *Pervoye i vtoroye prishestviye* ("The First and Second Coming"). Scholar Marina Ledkovsky, a member of the Booker jury, noted that the works submitted to the committee reflected the tendency of Russian literature to turn to the past. In addition, Slapovsky's novel marked the revival of a popularized religion that was at times vulgarized. Many of the works on the shortlist were united by the theme of childhood reminiscences. With the exception of Okudzhava's work, they

Aleksandr Solzhenitsyn
SICHOV—SIPA

depicted the darker side of life, focusing on the underground, criminal world. Many of them conveyed this world in coarse language, which some critics defined as a new aesthetics and others condemned as a sign of literary decline.

Other noteworthy works of fiction in 1994 included Lyudmila Petrushevskaya's cycle of fairy tales *Nu, mama nu* ("Tell Me, Mom"); Dina Rubina's short story "V vorotakh tvoikh" ("In Thy Gates"), a humourous story of an émigré in Jerusalem; and Irina Muraveva's *Kudryavy leytenant* ("The Curly-Haired Lieutenant"), a collection of short stories set in a modern-day Russia bewildered by changes and searching for a new path. Vladimir Sorokin's *Norma* ("A Norm") and Valeriya Narbikova's *Shepot shuma* ("The Whispers of Noise") received favourable reviews from several critics. Fridrikh Gorenshteyn published a novel entitled *Drezdenskiye strasti* ("Dresden's Passions"), and Anatoly Rybakov completed *Prakh i pepel* ("The Dust and Ashes"), the final part of his trilogy that began with *Deti Arbata* (1987; *Children of the Arbat,* 1988).

Joseph Brodsky published a cycle of poems entitled "Vozdukh s morya" ("Air from the Sea") and an essay on poetry in his introduction to Yevgeny Reyn's *Bella Akhmadulina.* Other noteworthy works in 1994 included a book of essays by artist Sergey Gollerbakh, *Moy dom* ("My Home"), and Dmitry Volkogonov's *Lenin,* a new biography that included documents previously unknown in Russia but partly published abroad—for example, in the émigré journal *Novy zhurnal.*

(EDWARD J. CZERWINSKI; AGNIESZKA PERLINSKA)

EASTERN EUROPEAN

The older generation of writers continued to dominate the literary scene in Poland in 1994. Tadeusz Różewicz's latest collection of poems, *Słowo po słowie* ("Word After Word"), contained newly published and revised poems and was, in many ways, a summing up for Poland's foremost poet. The same could be said for Urszula Kozioł's latest volume of poetry, *Postoje słowa* ("Stages of the Word"). Former exiles also returned to Poland. Edward Redliński's two novelettes, written during his stay in the United

States, presented a more urbane aspect of the writer. *Dolorado* included both the novelette of the same name, published in 1984, and *Tańcowały dwa Michały* ("Two Michaels Were Dancing," 1985). Folk humour, always a part of Redliński's works, was replaced by a worldly cynicism. *Dictionary of Polish Literature,* the first of its kind in English, edited by E.J. Czerwinski, was published in October.

In the Czech Republic and in Slovakia, both established and newly published writers dominated the literary market. Václav Havel was awarded the 1994 Philadelphia Liberty Medal for his writings about freedom and the individual. Martin M. Šimečka won the 1993 Pegasus Prize for Literature for his novel *Žabí rok* (1985; *The Year of the Frog,* 1993). According to Havel, who wrote the foreword to the novel, Šimečka had not distanced himself from his Czech roots, even though he had made "a conscious decision to become a Slovak writer." In Lubomír Martínek's *Mys dobré beznaděje* ("Cape of Good Hopelessness"), the hero embarked on a search for self-identity and the meaning of life. His travels took him to England and the Far East. The novel, however, was not simply a travelogue but also an exploration of the conscience of his generation. Martínek also published a collection of 20 essays, *Nomad's Land* (original title in English).

Alexandr v tramvaji ("Alexander in the Streetcar") was a collection of surrealistic and grotesque short stories by Pavel Řezníček, an original writer heretofore known for his poetry and translations. Ivan Diviš' *Jedná loď—Laura Blair* ("One Ship—Laura Blair") was a poetic parable of a ship's captain recollecting a tragic story; composed of 2,000 verses, the work was a meditation on the human desire for knowledge. Diviš' diary, *Teorie spolehlivosti* (1972; "Theory of Reliability"), covered 30 years of the writer's life and was considered one of the most remarkable texts in modern Czech literature. Karel Šiktanc's *Srdce sveho nejez* ("Don't Eat Your Heart Out") was a provocative collection of poetry that evoked the search for the secrets of human existence. Eda Kriseová's *Klíční kůstka netopýra* ("The Bat's Collarbone") consisted of three novellas, original tales filled with strong emotions and an intellectual approach to solving the country's moral problems. The Czech prime minister, Václav Klaus, also made a contribution to literature; his *Česká cesta* ("The Czech Road") was a compilation of speeches and articles that dissected his country's problems and value system.

In Romania Sorin Pârvu's *The Romanian Novel* was a notable critical attempt to introduce such novelists as Liviu Rebreanu, Cezar Petrescu, Mihail Sadoveanu, and Anton Holban to the English-speaking audience.

Since the death of Bulgaria's most important 20th-century poet, Elisaveta Bagryana, in 1991, her heir Blaga Dimitrova had gained a solid niche within the pantheon of Slavic poets. As a tribute to her mentor, Dimitrova (together with Iordan Vasilev) edited a collection of Bagryana's poetry, *Zhivota, koito iskakh da bude poema: izbrana poeziya* (1993; "Life, That Strives to Be a Poem: Selected Poems").

One of the most prolific and successful Serbian writers, Slobodan Selenić, had another best-seller with *Ubistvo s predumišljajem* (1993; "A Premeditated Murder"). The novel compared the present situation in Serbia with that of a half century ago in Yugoslavia. Two important Serbian poets in the diaspora published significant works in 1994: Sava Janković, *Putevima i prostorima* ("On Roads and Through Space"), his second collection of poetry; and Vasa Mihailović, *Na brisanom prostoru* ("In the Line of Fire"), his fifth volume of poetry. In both there was an unabashed lyricism and a love of homeland that permeated the poetry and underscored the ongoing tragic events. Written in the Bosnia and Herzegovinian capital but first published in its entirety in France, Zlata Filipović's *Zlata's Diary: A Child's Life in Sarajevo* reminded the world that the conflict continued unabated in former Yugoslavia.

In Hungary, Géza Ottlik's *Buda* (1993) (the old section of Budapest on the right bank of the Danube) was published posthumously, under the guidance of the novelist's friend Péter Lengyel. A continuation of Ottlik's first novel, *Iskola a határon* (1959; "School at the Frontier"), the book was a nostalgic retrospective of a time when loved ones were more important than material advantages. A conference dedicated to the life and works of Miklós Radnóti was organized by George Gömöri at the University of Cambridge. Literary life awakened in Hungary with recent works by highly regarded writers such as György Kardos G. (*Jutalomjáték;* "Benefit Performance"), György Spiró, Ákos Kertész, Zsuzsa Kapecz, and Judit Fenákel. The popular writer Péter Esterházy also had a new collection of political-literary essays, *Egy kékharisnya feljegyzesey* ("Notes from an Intelligent Whore").

(EDWARD J. CZERWINSKI; AGNIESZKA PERLINSKA)

JEWISH

Hebrew. Some of Israel's most prominent writers published new novels in 1994. Among them were A.B. Yehoshua's *Hashiva Mehodu* ("Return from India"), Amos Oz's *Al Tagidi Laila* ("Don't Pronounce It Night"), Aharon Appelfeld's *Laish,* and Meir Shalev's *Keyamim Aa'hadim* ("As a Few Days"). The novels created a vehement dispute among critics, some of them

arguing that the creativity and originality of the New Wave writers (notably Yehoshua and Oz) had dwindled severely. Indeed, the most powerful and intriguing novel of the year, *Am, Ma'akhal Melakhim* ("The People, Food Fit for a King"), by Yitzhak Laor, mocked the style and worldview of Oz and Yehoshua. Adopting postmodernist techniques and following Jacques Lacan's theories, Laor had become one of the main representatives of the younger Israeli generation.

Other noteworthy books in 1994 were David Grossman's *Yesh Yeladim Zigzag* ("The Zigzag Child"), Dan Tsalka's *Ananim* ("Clouds"), and Avraham Heffner's *Alelim* ("Alleles"). Among the most popular collections of short stories were the postmodern works of Etgar Errett (*Ga'agu'ai leKissinger;* "Missing Kissinger") and Orly Castel-Blum (*Sipurim Lo Retsoniim;* "Unvoluntary Stories"). First collections of short stories were published by the poet Shin Shifra (*Rehov haHol;* "The Sand Street"), Avner Shats (*Ma'agalim Mudpasim;* "Printed Circuits"), and Eyal Adar (*Hiyukho shel Na'ar haMa'alit;* "The Smile of the Bellboy").

Notable books by veteran poets included Aryeh Sivan's *Gevulot haHol* ("Borders of Sand"), Anadad Eldan's *Loheshet Hulshatah* ("Whispering Her Weakness"), Haim Gouri's *Haba Aa'harai* ("The One Who Comes After Me"), Maxim Ghilan's *Mipui* ("Mapping"), Roni Somek's *Bloody Mary,* Amir Or's *Pidyon haMet* ("Ransoming the Dead"), and the late Hezy Leskly's *Sotim Yekarim* ("Dear Perverts"). Efrat Mishori collected her poems in *Shirim, 1990–1994* ("Poems, 1990–1994").

Among the works of literary scholarship and criticism published during the year were Dan Miron's essays on modern Hebrew poetry (*Hadashot Me'ezor haKotev;* "News from the Polar Zone"), Hannan Hever's study of the rise of political Hebrew poetry (*Paitanim uViryonim;* "Poets and Zealots"), and Ruth Karton-Blum's discussion of Natan Alterman's *Hagigat Ka'yitz* (*Haletz vehaTzel;* "The Darkling Jester"). The novelist and poet Pinchas Sadeh died in 1994.

(AVRAHAM BALABAN)

Yiddish. Aleksander Beyderman published the small *Kaboles-Ponim* ("Welcoming Reception") in 1994. Rukhl Fishman's sophisticated and sensitive *Azoy yil ikh faln* (*I Want to Fall Like This,* 1994) celebrated nature with fresh images. A retrospective collection of modernist verse issued from the pen of H. Binyumin (pseudonym of Yale professor Binyumin Hrushovski), *Take oyf tshikaves* ("This Is Really Curious"). Boris Mogilner offered a unique perspective in his meditative *Like-Khame* ("Solar Eclipse"). A master of light verse, Beyle Schaechter-Gottesman produced *Lider* ("Poems") in a bilingual edition. Yankev Vorzoger made his debut with the reflective *Lider in shayer* ("Poems in a Barn").

Three novelists demonstrated remarkable range and depth. From Moscow, Hersh Polyanker's *Geven a mol a shtetl* ("There Was Once a Shtetl") chronicled Jewish life in Ukraine and in Birobidzhan, Russia. Boris Sandler re-created a sober and haunting world in *Der alter brunem* ("The Old Well"). Master wordsmith Eli Shekhtman concluded his epic lamentation for the courage of Belarussian Jews in Polesye (the Pripet Marshes area) in *Baym shkiye-aker* ("At the Twilight-Plowshare").

In collections of short stories, Gennady Estraykh penned the informative *Moskver Purim-shpiln* ("Moscow Purim Plays"). Dovid-Hirsh Katz created a unique voice in his *Der flakhershpits* ("The Flat Peak"). Yente Mash drew persuasive portraits of emigrant life in contemporary Israel in *Meshane mokim* ("Change of Place"). Meyer Yelin's *Di gliendike koyln* ("By the Glowing Coals") captured the fragile line that separated life from death for the inhabitants of Lithuania's Kaunas ghetto. Tsvi Kanar's belletristic *Ikh un Lemekh* ("Me and Lemech") was a masterly achievement.

Yisroel-Ber Alterman suggested philosophical analyses of writers, explored the craft of composition, and reflected on the work of specific authors in *Gerangl* ("Struggle"). Yankev-Tsvi Shargel scrutinized the Yiddish imagination in *Garbn in Elel* ("Sheaves in the Month of Elul"). Mordkhe Tsanin compiled a judiciously balanced and synthetic overview of a controversial theme in *Oyf di vegn fun yidishn goyrl: Der mytos goles* ("On the Paths of Jewish Fate: The Exile Myth").

(THOMAS E. BIRD)

TURKISH

Bilge Karasu, winner of the 1991 Pegasus Prize, had a U.S. reading tour in 1994 featuring his novel *Gece* (1984; *Night,* 1994). Aziz Nesin, the immensely popular satirist who at age 79 continued to be involved in one controversy after another, received a special prize in New York City from the Committee to Protect Journalists.

In a year when major authors—including the prolific Yaşar Kemal—published no novels, Orhan Pamuk's *Yeni hayat,* a scintillating literary mystery, broke all records, with 40 printings in four months, and his *Kara Kitap* was published in English as *The Black Book* in December. Adalet Ağaoğlu, the most prominent among Turkey's esteemed women novelists, was honoured as Writer of the Year at Istanbul's 13th annual Book Fair.

There was heated discussion in 1994 over the possibility of moving the remains of Nazım Hikmet, who had died in Moscow in 1963, from there to Istanbul. Two theatres staged dramatic renditions of his poetry. The first International Nazım Hikmet Poetry Prize went to the prominent Arab poet Adonis. Other major poetry prizes went to Ahmet Necdet, Abdülkadir Budak, and the popular poet-essayist Salah Birsel. Sulhi Dölek won the Yunus Nadi Prize for his short stories.

(TALAT S. HALMAN)

PERSIAN

Strict ideological censorship by the government continued in 1994 to be the background against which all discussions of the literary scene in Iran had to be conducted. In this regard the most sensational event of the year was the death, probably in November, of the noted essayist and satirist 'Ali Akbar Sa'idi Sirjani, who died in custody, under unexplained circumstances, after having been imprisoned and forced to "confess" his ideological errors. Women writers in Iran were flourishing as never before. Simin Daneshvar published a new novel, *Jazira-e Sargardani* ("The Island of Perplexity"), and many writers, including women, could now make their living solely from writing.

Communities of Persians living abroad supported the publication of Persian literature on a notable scale. The prominent woman novelist Shahrnush Parsipur published two works of fiction in Los Angeles: *Adab-e Sarf e Chai dar Hozur-e Gorg* ("Tea Ceremony in the Presence of the Wolf"), a collection of linked short stories in the mode of magical realism, and *'Aql-e Abi* ("Blue Logos"). In Stånga, Sweden, the publisher Nashr-e Baran issued the collected works of the poet Esma'il Kho'i.

(WILLIAM L. HANAWAY)

ARABIC

The attempt in October 1994 on the life of the Egyptian novelist Naguib Mahfouz, the only Arab to win the Nobel Prize for Literature (1988), demonstrated both the importance of literature and the predicament of writers in the Arab world. Mahfouz' assailant cited his 1959 novel *Awlād ḥāratinā* (*Children of Gebelawi,* 1981) and its treatment of religion as the reason for the attack.

Novels published in 1994 included Muḥammad al-Bisāṭī's *Ṣakhab al-buḥayrah* ("Clamoring of the Lake"), Badr ad-Dīb's *Ajāzat tafarrugh* ("Sabbatical Leave"), Muḥammad Nājī's *Khāfiyat qamar* ("Moon Song"), and Edwār al-Kharrāṭ's *Raqraqat al-aḥlām al-milḥiyyah* ("Glittering of Salty Dreams") in Egypt; Ḥannā Mīnah's *al-qamar fi 'l-maḥāq* ("Moon in Eclipse") and

Naguib Mahfouz
REUTERS/BETTMANN

the last two parts of Nabīl Sulaymān's quartet *Madārāt ash-Sharq* ("Orbits of the Orient") in Syria; Ilyās Khūrī's *Mujma' al-asrār* ("Record of Secrets") in Lebanon; al-Ḥabīb as-Sālimī's *Matāhat al-raml* ("Sand Maze") in Tunisia; and Muḥammad Zafzāf's *Al-Ḥayy al-khalfi* ("City Dregs") and Aḥmad al-Middīnī's *Ṭarīq as-saḥāb* ("Clouds' Path") in Morocco. Two novels by women stood out in 1994: by the Egyptian Raḍwā 'Āshūr (*Ghirnāṭah;* "Granada") and by the Palestinian Liyānah Badr (*Nujūm arīḥā;* "Gerico Stars"). Collections of short stories included *Nidā' Nūḥ* ("Noah's Summons") by the Syrian Zakariyyā Tāmir.

In poetry 1994 saw the publication of *Limādhā taraki al-ḥiṣān waḥīdā* ("Why Did You Leave the Horse Alone?") by the

Palestinian Maḥmūd Darwīsh, perhaps the most distinguished Arab poet. The Egyptian Muḥammad 'Afīfī Maṭar published two important collections, *Iqā'āt al-naml* ("Ants' Tempos/Rhythms") and *Iḥtifālīyāt al-mūmyā' al-mutawaḥḥishah* ("Festivities of the Wild Mummy"), in which he transformed his 1991 prison experience into a metaphor for the Egyptian, indeed Arab, condition.

(SABRY HAFEZ)

CHINESE

Two Chinese novels enjoyed a great succès de scandale in 1994. Ai Bei's crudely written *Jiao fuqin tai chenzhong* ("I Called Him Father"), which claims she was Zhou Enlai's illegitimate daughter, received both praise and blame for revealing the sordid private lives of China's highest leaders. The poet Gu Cheng's narcissistic novel *Ying Er,* the name of his mistress, gave rise to both sympathy and disgust. In the same vein was Li Zhisui's *The Private Life of Chairman Mao.* Better written and more authoritative than Ai Bei's novel, it painted a picture of Mao Zedong as a lecherous, cruel, egomaniacal tyrant, with Zhou his loyal sycophant.

Much of the best mainland fiction continued to be published in Taiwan. The year's top works included Yu Hua's highly acclaimed historical novel *Huozhe* ("Living"; the script of director Zhang Yimou's award-winning film was also published in Taiwan and Hong Kong); three books by Su Tong—the story collections *Lihun zhinan* ("A Guide to Divorce") and *Shiyi ji* ("Eleven Blows") and a historical novel about China's only ruling empress, *Wu Zetian* ("Empress Wu"); three novellas by Ye Zhaoyan entitled *Hong fangzi jiudian* ("The Red Room Tavern"); Wang Anyi's short novel *Xianggang qing yu ai* ("Love and Longing in Hong Kong"); and A Cheng's *Weinisi riji* ("Venice Diary"). Su Tong's novel *Chengbei didai* ("North of the City") was serialized in the Nanjing magazine *Zhongshan.*

A number of works were produced by established writers in their 30s. Ge Fei's *Bianyuan* ("On the Margins") came out in Taiwan in late 1993. In this historical novel of subtle pathos and often poetic narration, an unnamed first-person narrator in his 80s presented 60 years of Chinese history from the point of view of an anonymous, insignificant participant. Ge Fei also wrote several essays on literature, while Can Xue's novella *Gui tu* ("The Road Back") appeared in *Shanghai wenxue* and A Cheng contributed occasional short short stories to *Jiushi niandai,* published in Hong Kong. Taipei's Hungfan reissued six short stories by Mo Yan with the title *Mengjing yu zazhong* ("Dreams and Bastards"), a collection containing one of Mo's own favourites, "Ni de xingwei shi women kongju" ("Your Actions Terrify Us"), which was written on the eve of the Tiananmen Square massacre.

A newly emerging talent was the poet Hong Ying, author, under the pen name Lao Hong, of *Luowu dai* ("A Generation Dancing Naked"), a sexually explicit 1992 novel about the confused lives of youthful literary and artistic types after Tiananmen. In 1994 she published five short stories in *Zhongshan,* and her poems were the topic of a literary seminar.

Literature in Taiwan continued to be weak, but Ma Sen's experimental *M de lucheng* ("The Journey of M") linked a

series of nine previously published short stories in a collage of symbolic metamorphoses that related an anonymous narrator's quest for meaning and transcendence.

Noteworthy among English translations in 1994 were *Running Wild: New Chinese Writers* (an eccentric selection of stories); *Under-Sky, Underground* (translations of fiction, poetry, essays, and criticism); the poet Bei Dao's *Forms of Distance;* Wang Meng's *The Stubborn Porridge and Other Stories;* and *Death in a Cornfield and Other Stories from Contemporary Taiwan.*

(MICHAEL S. DUKE)

JAPANESE

For lovers of Japanese literature, 1994 was a year of rejoicing. Kenzaburō Ōe became the second Japanese to be awarded the Nobel Prize for Literature (*see* NOBEL PRIZES). After the prize was announced, the Japanese government said that Ōe would be given the Order of Merit Culture. Ōe shocked Japan, however, by rejecting this latter award, saying that he did not want to have anything to do with the establishment.

Ōe and Yukio Mishima had come to be regarded as a pair of literary prodigies, but their political and cultural stances were diametrically different. Whereas Mishima claimed to be a radical traditionalist, Ōe was a confirmed leftist. Although his themes were basically political, as when he wrote about Hiroshima and Okinawa, his novels and stories were also imaginative and modernist. His *Kojinteki na taiken* (1964; *A Personal Matter,* 1968) was largely autobiographical, and his *Man'en gannen no futtōbōru* (1967; *The Silent Cry,* 1974), telling the story of radical expatriate brothers struggling to return to and be reconciled with their native village in the deep woods of Shikoku island, used a highly involved and symbolic, even mythical, mode of narration.

Another major figure of the year was Rieko Matsuura, whose *Oya-yubi P no shūgyō jidai* ("The Study Period of Big Toe P") was awarded the Women Writers' Prize. It was a highly controversial, even sensational, novel, in which the central character, a student, is shocked to find that the big toe of her foot has turned into a penis.

Hiroyuki Agawa's *Shiga Naoya* was a remarkable literary biography, both detailed and readable. Shiga was considered to be one of the classic authors of modern Japan, and Agawa was successful in portraying his personality and the literary milieu that had enveloped him. Kazuko Ibuki's *Ware yori hoka ni: Tanizaki Jun'ichirō saigo no jūninen* ("Reminiscences of Tanizaki Jun'ichirō") was a highly evocative memoir of the novelist whose works include *Sasameyuki* (1943–48; *The Makioka Sisters,* 1957). Takashi Tsuji's *Niji no Misaki* ("Rainbow Promontory"), the Tanizaki Prize-winning novel of the year, was also biographical. Tsujii was the pen name of Seiji Tsutsumi, the well-known financial magnate.

In poetry there were two impressive collections, by Tetsuo Shimizu and Yasuo Irisawa. Shimizu's *Sekiyō ni Akai Ho* ("Red Sail in the Setting Sun") was successful in evoking the bittersweet taste of various memories through colloquial diction and was awarded the Sakutarō Hagiwara Prize. Irisawa's *Tadayou Fune* ("Drifting Ship") was an ambitious search for a "mythical" halo for a lost modern soul.

(SHOICHI SAEKI)

Mathematics

A year of ups and downs for mathematics, 1994 began with the awareness of a serious gap in Andrew Wiles's proof of Fermat's last theorem. In June 1993 Wiles, a Princeton University mathematician, had claimed a proof, by relating the problem to a deep conjecture in algebraic number theory, of Pierre de Fermat's famous 350-year-old assertion that $x^n + y^n = z^n$ has no solutions for which x, y, and z are whole numbers if n is three or more. The gap emerged in late 1993 in a review of the proof and lingered until October 1994, when Wiles sent colleagues a revised proof that he hoped would finally lay the problem to rest. At year's end the jury remained out on the validity of the new proof.

More encouraging news was the solution, by Krystyna Kuperberg of Auburn (Ala.) University, of the Seifert conjecture, a problem about the topology of dynamic systems. According to the celebrated hairy ball theorem, it is impossible to comb a hairy ball smoothly; somewhere at least one hair must stand up on end. The theorem is one of dynamics because such an arrangement of "hairs" is a description of the way the states of a system, represented by points on the sphere, change with time, or flow along the directions of the hairs. The hairy ball theorem was proved long ago, but its higher-dimensional cousins have been more elusive. The most notorious is a question asked in 1950 by Herbert Seifert of the University of Heidelberg, Germany, about a three-dimensional analogue of the surface of a sphere—a kind of curved space called a 3-sphere. If one defines a "flow" by filling the 3-sphere with curved lines that fit smoothly together like the flow lines of a fluid, most of the flow lines will wander around in a complicated way. Occasionally, however, one of them may close up into a loop. It is easy to find a flow with only two closed loops but, as Seifert asked, can one be found with no closed loops at all?

Kuperberg's surprising answer is "yes." All earlier approaches to the problem had used the same basic idea, that of inserting a "plug" into a given flow to change it and eradicate a selected closed loop. The plug is a small region of flow lines in which some of the lines that enter the region never exit but get trapped inside. Specifically, one starts with a known flow that has only two closed loops and then removes them both by inserting two plugs that trap the lines of the loops and render them no longer closed. The central difficulty is to ensure that no new loops are created inside the plugs themselves. Kuperberg succeeded with a seemingly outrageous idea; she made each plug "eat its own tail" like a snake so that closed loops get trapped in a kind of infinite regress. The solution is a geometric gem, and it changes forever mathematicians' most basic ideas about dynamics in three dimensions.

On the borderline with mathematical physics but clearly on the mathematical side came a fundamental breakthrough in the quantum mechanics of many-particle systems. According to quantum mechanics, the electrons of an atom can occupy only a discrete sequence of energy levels. In particular, there is a minimum energy level, the ground state, below which an atom cannot go. In effect, the ground state is a barrier that prevents atoms from evaporating. In 1981 the U.S. physicist Julian Schwinger (*see* OBITUARIES) devised an accurate approximation for the way in which the ground-state energy of an atom varies with atomic charge; *i.e.,* with the number of protons in the nucleus. His conjectured formula for the ground-state energy of an atom having charge Z is approximately $-aZ^{7/3} + \frac{1}{8} Z^2 - bZ^{5/3}$, in which a and b are particular constants. In the past year Schwinger's conjecture was given a rigorous proof by Charles Fefferman

of Princeton University and L.A. Seco of the University of Toronto. Their achievement represented an important step toward a more nearly complete understanding of the way in which chemistry derives from the laws of quantum mechanics. The next step would be to extend the work from atoms to molecules.

New mathematics does not have to be complicated and technical; it can also be based on very simple ideas. Near the end of the year, Charles Radin of the University of Texas at Austin published a very strange tiling of the plane: a finite set of tiles that can be assembled only in a highly complex way. Most simple tilings are periodic, repeating the same basic unit over again at regular intervals. In 1961, while investigating questions about decidability in mathematical logic, the philosopher Hao Wang introduced the idea of aperiodic tiles, which can cover the plane but not in any periodic way. Radin's tiles, which are based on an idea of John Horton Conway of Princeton, are aperiodic. In fact—and this is the great novelty—the tiles must appear in infinitely many orientations. Lying at the heart of this exotic tiling is a simple right triangle, formed from a domino cut in half along a diagonal.   (IAN STEWART)

This article updates the *Macropædia* articles ANALYSIS; ATOMS; GEOMETRY; NUMBER THEORY.

Military Affairs

In 1994 dignitaries and old soldiers, sailors, and airmen gathered at World War II battlegrounds from Monte Cassino in Italy to Leyte Gulf in the Philippines to recall the sacrifices of that global conflict. The largest such gathering was at Normandy, France, on June 6 to celebrate the 50th anniversary of D-Day, the Allied invasion of Nazi-occupied Europe. The failure to invite either Russian leaders or veterans to the D-Day ceremonies generated considerable bitterness in Russia.

On June 18 Berliners paid an emotional farewell to the U.S., British, and French troops who had defended their city during the Cold War. A week later the city held a separate and smaller parade for the departing Russian troops. Russia withdrew its remaining troops from Latvia, Estonia, and Germany on August 31 and from Poland on September 9, marking the end of a historic retreat. In the Middle East, Jordan became the second Arab country—the first was Egypt in 1979—to end its official state of war with Israel.

Suspicions that North Korea was building nuclear weapons flared when its government refused to allow International Atomic Energy Agency (IAEA) inspectors to monitor the refueling of a five-megawatt research reactor at its Yongbyon facility or inspect two suspected nuclear-waste sites. When the IAEA Board of Governors decided to cut off technical assistance, North Korea announced that it was withdrawing from the IAEA. Tensions were relieved somewhat during former president Jimmy Carter's visit to Pyongyang when North Korean leader Kim Il Sung agreed to freeze his nuclear program if the U.S. would agree to resume the stalled direct talks. The third round of these high-level talks began in Geneva on July 8, the day Kim Il Sung died. On October 21 the two countries signed an agreement under which North Korea would freeze its existing nuclear program, eventually dismantle its existing reactors, accept IAEA inspections, and allow, at an undetermined future date, inspection of the two controversial waste sites. In return the U.S. agreed to arrange for the international financing and supply of two modern nuclear reactors to North Korea. In an October agreement China said that it would accept the Missile Technology Control Regime rules and ban the export of missiles "inherently capable" of a range of 300 km (190 mi) with a payload of at least 500 kg (1,100 lb) in return for the lifting of the 1993 U.S. sanctions against China for the sale of M-11 missiles to Pakistan.

These positive developments were balanced by troubling indications that the former Soviet Union could become the source of nuclear weapons material sold to the highest bidder. Several incidents of attempted smuggling of nuclear materials were discovered, as when authorities at the Munich, Germany, airport seized 350 g of plutonium and some lithium 6 that had come from Moscow aboard an airliner.

United Nations forces remained heavily committed in peacekeeping and relief operations in such places as the Middle East and former Yugoslavia. The brutal civil war in Rwanda prompted France to deploy a 2,500-man force in a UN-mandated mercy mission to that country, while the U.S. initiated an airlift to help feed Rwandan refugees.

Russian troops, sometimes aided by token contributions from other members of the Commonwealth of Independent States (CIS), were involved in peacekeeping and peacemaking operations in Moldova, Georgia, Tajikistan, and Azerbaijan.

After having repeatedly warned Haiti's military rulers that they had to step down and allow the return of the democratically elected president, Jean-Bertrand Aristide, the U.S. mounted an invasion force to remove them from power. Once again, Carter was involved in a last-minute diplomatic solution. The U.S. forces went ashore in Haiti without opposition, and the small Haitian army was quickly disarmed of its heavy weapons. Iraq's Pres. Saddam Hussein moved several elite Republican Guard divisions to the border with Kuwait, threatening a replay of the 1991 invasion. U.S. Pres. Bill Clinton quickly responded by deploying air, naval, and ground forces to the Persian Gulf region, and the Iraqi leader promptly backed down and withdrew the divisions.

Arms Control and Disarmament. In January Clinton, Russian Pres. Boris Yeltsin, and Ukrainian Pres. Leonid Kravchuk signed a trilateral agreement in Moscow on the repatriation to Russia of the strategic nuclear weapons in Ukraine. After turning it down in February, the Ukrainian Rada (parliament) on November 16 agreed to accede to the Nuclear Non-proliferation Treaty (NPT) as a nonnuclear state. This removed the last stumbling block to implementing the Strategic Arms Reduction Talks treaties (START I and START II). On December 5, at the Budapest Conference on Security and Cooperation in Europe (CSCE) summit meeting, Belarus, Kazakhstan, and Ukraine formally acceded to the NPT, and START I entered into force, opening the way for the START II ratification process to proceed. Clinton and Yeltsin had pledged at their September Washington summit meeting that once START II had been ratified, their countries would dismantle their nuclear weapons more quickly than called for under the treaty.

In January the U.S. agreed to purchase some 500 tons of highly enriched uranium (HEU) from dismantled Russian nuclear weapons over a 20-year period. The HEU would first be diluted in Russia, and the subsequent low-enriched uranium (LEU) would be converted into reactor fuel rods in the United States. Russia also agreed to use some of the LEU to supply fuel rods for Ukrainian atomic power plants.

Formal negotiations to draft a comprehensive ban on all nuclear weapons tests resumed at the UN Conference on Disarmament in January. Even while declaring its support for such a ban, China conducted two nuclear tests in 1994, on June 10 and October 7. Hopes that the Chemical Weapon Convention eliminating chemical weapons would enter into force on Jan. 13, 1995—the earliest possibility— faded when only 10 of the 157 signatories had ratified the convention by mid-July. The convention would enter into force 180 days after 65 nations had ratified it. At the end of the year, the ratification count stood at 18.

The second reduction phase of the Conventional Armed Forces in Europe treaty ended on November 17. By that date the 30 participants (the members of NATO and the former members of the Warsaw Treaty Organization [WTO], including all the successor states of the U.S.S.R. except the three Baltic Republics) had destroyed 60% of the heavy weapons to be eliminated under the treaty. Russia and Ukraine were not satisfied with a provision of the treaty that placed limits on the numbers of weapons the former Soviet Union could deploy on what once were the northern and southern flanks of the WTO. The Russians argued that the parts of their country affected by these limits had been largely rear support areas of the Soviet Union but were now in Russia's first line of defense. In particular, they pointed to the conflicts in the Caucasus and the potential military threats in the south as justifications for wishing to

At ceremonies in August marking the final withdrawal of Russian forces from Germany, an honour guard stands at attention in Berlin's Treptow Park, where Soviet soldiers killed in World War II lie buried. Russia also completed troop withdrawals in Eastern Europe and the Baltic during the year.
DPA

have more heavy equipment than the treaty would allow in the Northern Caucasus military district. Most of the other signatories reacted coolly to these arguments, and by year's end the issue had not been resolved.

In other arms control developments, the Coordinating Committee for Multilateral Export Controls (COCOM), created in 1949 to prevent transfer of militarily useful technology to the communist world, was disbanded at a March 28–31 meeting in The Hague. The UN issued its second annual Register of Conventional Arms report, which aimed to contribute to transparency in world armaments by listing the imports and exports of major weaponry as reported by member governments. Although fewer than half of the UN members provided data, the report was believed to cover

Approximate Strengths of Selected Regular Armed Forces of the World

| Country | Military personnel in 000s | | | | Warships | | | | Combat aircraft[1] | | | Tanks[3] | Defense expenditure as % of 1993 GNP |
| | Total | Army | Navy | Air Force[2] | Submarines | | Aircraft carriers/ cruisers | Destroyers/ frigates | Bombers and fighter-ground attack | Fighters | Recon-nais-sance | | |
					Nuclear	Diesel							
I. NATO													
Belgium	63.0	48.0	2.9	12.1	—	—	—	2	85	48	—	334	1.8
Canada[4]	78.1	20.0	12.5	20.6	—	3	—	15	180	—	18	114	1.9
Denmark	27.0	16.3	4.6	6.1	—	5	—	3	63	—	—	452	2.0
France[4]	409.6	241.4	64.2[5]	89.8	11	7	3	40	678	82	108	1,047	3.4
Germany	367.3	254.3	30.1	82.9	—	20	—	12	494	24	18	2,855	2.1
Greece	159.3	113.0	19.5	26.8	—	8	—	14	247	80	28	2,722	5.5
Italy	322.3	205.0	44.0	73.3	—	9	2	27	256	112	18	1,210	2.0
Netherlands, The[4]	70.9	43.2	14.3[5]	9.0	—	6	—	18	164	—	21	740	2.2
Norway[4]	33.5	18.0	6.6	7.9	—	12	—	4	60	15	6	170	3.1
Portugal	50.7	27.2	12.5	11.0	—	3	—	11	77	—	6	209	2.8
Spain	206.5	145.0	33.1[5]	28.4	—	8	1	16	89	73	15	1,012	1.5
Turkey	503.8	393.0	54.0	56.8	—	15	—	21	458	51	67	4,919	4.1
United Kingdom	254.3	123.0	55.6[5]	75.7	15	2	3	35	393	134	49	921	3.6
United States	1,650.3	559.9	666.8[5]	433.8	110	—	87	97	4,460	1,008	364	14,795	4.7
II. NON-NATO EUROPE													
Albania	73.0	60.0	3.0	10.0	—	2	—	—	48	51	—	859	3.5
Armenia	32.7	32.7	—	—	—	—	—	—	5	1	—	120	3.6
Austria	51.3	44.0	—	7.3	—	—	—	—	30	24	—	169	0.9
Azerbaijan[4]	56.0	49.0	3.0	2.0	—	—	—	—	18	30	—	279	2.9
Belarus[4]	92.5	52.5	—	27.6	—	—	—	—	150	204	66	3,108	3.3
Bosnia and Herzegovina	110.0	110.0	—	—	—	—	—	—	—	—	—	40	48.7
Bulgaria	101.9	51.6	3.0	21.6	—	2	—	1	160	87	47	1,967	2.9
Croatia	105.0	99.6	1.1	4.3	—	1	—	—	20	—	—	173	5.9
Czech Republic	92.9	37.4	—	25.0	—	—	—	—	140	68	—	1,433	n.a.
Finland	31.2	25.7	2.5	3.0	—	—	—	—	—	110	—	230	2.0
Hungary	74.5	56.5	—	18.0	—	—	—	—	—	157	14	1,191	2.0
Ireland	13.0	11.2	1.0	0.8	—	—	—	—	15	—	3	—	1.1
Moldova	11.1	9.8	—	1.3	—	—	—	—	—	31	—	—	1.2
Poland	283.6	185.9	19.0	78.7	—	3	—	2	118	256	24	2,110	2.5
Romania[4]	230.5	160.5	19.0[5]	27.4	—	1	—	6	189	181	26	2,568	4.2
Slovakia	47.0	33.0	—	14.0	—	—	—	—	41	97	8	912	2.3
Sweden	64.0	43.5	9.0	11.5	—	12	—	—	149	191	51	627	2.3
Ukraine[4]	517.0	308.0	16.0	146.0	—	—	—	—	455	590	152	5,380	7.2
Yugoslavia	126.5	90.0	7.5	29.0	—	5	—	4	150	114	20	639	10.6
III. RUSSIA													
Russia[4]	1,714.0	780.0	295.0[5]	489.0[6]	48	72	27	134	1,733	1,985	400	20,460	7.0
IV. MIDDLE EAST AND NORTH AFRICA; SUB-SAHARAN AFRICA; LATIN AMERICA													
Algeria	121.7	105.0	6.7	10.0	—	2	—	3	50	140	3	960	2.5
Egypt	440.0	310.0	20.0	110.0	—	3	—	4	170	361	20	3,234	4.8
Iran[4]	513.0	345.0	18.0	30.0	—	2	—	5	170	125	14	1,245	4.3
Iraq	382.0	350.0	2.0	30.0	—	—	—	1	136	180	—	2,200	15.3
Israel	172.0	134.0	6.0	32.0	—	3	—	—	227	229	22	3,895	9.8
Jordan	98.6	90.0	0.6	8.0	—	—	—	—	70	32	—	1,141	9.4
Kuwait[4]	16.6	10.0	2.5	2.5	—	—	—	—	68	15	—	150	12.1
Lebanon	44.3	43.0	0.5	0.8	—	—	—	—	—	3	—	100	4.4
Libya	70.0	40.0	8.0	22.0	—	4	—	2	200	206	12	2,350	6.3
Morocco	195.5	175.0	7.0	13.5	—	—	—	1	84	15	2	224	3.8
Oman[4]	42.9	25.0	4.2	3.5	—	—	—	—	35	13	—	73	15.3
Saudi Arabia	104.0	70.0	12.0[5]	22.0	—	—	—	8	125	157	10	770	13.1
Sudan, The	118.5	115.0	0.5	3.0	—	—	—	—	40	23	2	320	11.6
Syria	408.0	300.0	8.0	100.0	—	1	—	2	255	330	6	4,500	8.6
Tunisia	35.5	27.0	5.0	3.5	—	—	—	—	32	—	—	84	3.5
United Arab Emirates	61.5	57.0	2.0	2.5	—	—	—	—	61	28	8	125	5.7
Yemen[7]	66.0	61.0	1.5	3.5	—	—	—	—	65	45	—	1,140	12.5

over 90% of the 1993 arms transfers in the seven categories covered by the register. Significant nonparticipants were Iran, North Korea, and Syria. United States efforts to develop the Theater High Altitude Area Defense (THAAD) system and other similar defenses against tactical ballistic missiles provoked a debate over the 1972 antiballistic missile treaty, with some arms control advocates arguing that THAAD would violate the treaty. U.S. and Russian negotiators on the Standing Consultative Commission tried unsuccessfully to reach agreement on a definition of anti-tactical ballistic missiles and their interceptors that could be accommodated within the treaty. At their September summit Presidents Clinton and Yeltsin agreed that the U.S. and Russia would conduct a joint exercise of theatre missile defenses and early warning. In his September 26 address to the UN General Assembly, Clinton called for a land mine control regime and the eventual elimination of antipersonnel land mines.

| Country | Military personnel in 000s | | | | Warships | | | | Combat aircraft[1] | | | Tanks[3] | Defense expenditure as % of 1993 GNP |
| | Total | Army | Navy | Air Force[2] | Submarines | | Aircraft carriers/ cruisers | Destroyers/ frigates | Bombers and fighter-ground attack | Fighters | Recon-nais-sance | | |
					Nuclear	Diesel							
Angola	82.0	75.0	1.5	5.5	—	—	—	—	58	21	3	200	32.4
Kenya	24.2	20.5	1.2	2.5	—	—	—	—	32	—	—	80	2.2
Madagascar	21.0	20.0	0.5	0.5	—	—	—	—	12	—	—	—	1.2
Mozambique	34.8	30.0	0.8	4.0	—	—	—	—	43	—	—	80	9.8
Nigeria	76.5	62.0	5.0	9.5	—	—	—	1	80	—	—	178	0.6
South Africa[4]	78.5	58.0	4.5	10.0	—	3	—	—	244	—	13	250	3.3
Tanzania	49.6	45.0	1.0	3.6	—	—	—	—	—	24	—	65	3.2
Zaire[4]	49.1	25.0	1.3[5]	1.8	—	—	—	—	22	—	—	60	3.0
Zimbabwe	46.9	42.9		4.0	—	—	—	—	32	14	8	40	3.9
Argentina	69.8	40.4	20.5[5]	8.9	—	2	—	13	252	0	9	266	2.4
Brazil	336.8	219.0	58.4[5]	59.4	—	4	1	20	256	16	64	—	1.0
Chile	93.0	54.0	25.0[5]	14.0	—	4	—	10	83	15	18	136	3.6
Colombia	146.4	121.0	18.1[5]	7.3	—	2	—	5	74	—	—	—	2.0
Cuba	106.0	85.0	6.0[5]	15.0	—	2	—	3	14	116	—	1,575	3.7
Ecuador	57.5	50.0	4.5[5]	3.0	—	2	—	—	70	14	—	—	3.8
El Salvador	30.7	28.0	0.7	2.0	—	—	—	—	27	—	—	—	2.7
Mexico	175.0	130.0	37.0[5]	8.0	—	—	—	5	90	11	19	—	0.5
Peru	115.0	75.0	25.0[5]	15.0	—	6	2	9	74	20	7	300	1.4
Uruguay	25.6	17.2	5.4[5]	3.0	—	—	—	3	24	—	7	—	1.8
Venezuela[4]	79.0	34.0	15.0[5]	7.0	—	2	—	6	119	—	4	70	2.4

V. SOUTH AND CENTRAL ASIA; EAST ASIA AND OCEANIA

Country	Total	Army	Navy	Air Force[2]	Nuclear	Diesel	Aircraft carriers/cruisers	Destroyers/frigates	Bombers and fighter-ground attack	Fighters	Recon-nais-sance	Tanks[3]	Defense expenditure %
Australia	61.6	28.6	14.8	18.2	—	4	—	12	132	—	23	103	2.4
Bangladesh	115.5	101.0	8.0	6.5	—	—	—	4	42	27	—	140	1.5
Cambodia[4]	88.5	36.0	2.0	0.5	—	—	—	—	—	21	—	150	5.4
China	2,930.0	2,200.0	260.0[5]	470.0[6]	6	43	—	55	1,225	4,600	60	8,000	5.4
India	1,265.0	1,100.0	55.0[5]	110.0	—	15	2	23	457	369	59	3,400	2.4
Indonesia	276.0	214.0	42.0[5]	20.0	—	2	—	13	65	14	28	—	1.4
Japan[4]	237.7	150.0	43.0	44.5	—	17	—	62	140	280	147	1,160	1.6
Kazakhstan	40.0	25.0	—	15.0	—	—	—	—	80	71	27	1,100	3.9
Korea, North	1,128.0	1,000.0	46.0	82.0	—	25	—	3	410	360	—	3,700	25.2
Korea, South	633.0	520.0	60.0[5]	53.0	—	2	—	40	321	96	43	1,900	4.2
Kyrgyzstan	12.0	12.0	—	—	—	—	—	—	199	—	—	204	1.7
Laos	37.0	33.0	0.5	3.5	—	—	—	—	31	—	—	—	8.3
Malaysia	114.5	90.0	12.0	12.5	—	—	—	4	74	13	12	—	4.4
Mongolia	21.2	20.0	—	1.2	—	—	—	—	15	—	—	650	6.9
Myanmar (Burma)	286.0	265.0	12.0[5]	9.0	—	—	—	—	55	36	—	56	10.5
New Zealand	10.0	4.5	2.2	3.3	—	—	—	4	37	—	6	—	1.5
Pakistan	587.0	520.0	22.0[5]	45.0	—	6	—	9	174	244	16	1,950	6.6
Philippines	106.5	68.0	23.0[5]	15.5	—	—	—	1	36	7	8	—	2.2
Singapore	54.0	45.0	3.0	6.0	—	—	—	—	109	38	16	—	5.2
Sri Lanka	126.0	105.0	10.3	10.7	—	—	—	—	27	—	6	25	4.7
Taiwan	425.0	289.0	68.0[5]	68.0	—	4	—	33	453	—	38	509	5.5
Thailand	256.0	150.0	63.0[5]	43.0	—	—	—	9	142	43	30	253	2.7
Turkmenistan	28.0	28.0	—	—	—	—	—	—	95	84	—	570	3.8
Uzbekistan	45.0	35.0	—	7.0	—	—	—	—	70	72	—	125	2.8
Vietnam	572.0	500.0	42.0[5]	30.0	—	—	—	7	65	125	4	1,300	4.3

Note: Data exclude most paramilitary, security, and irregular forces. Naval data exclude vessels of less than 100 tons standard displacement. Figures are for June 1994. Because of substantive changes in national forces and reassessments of evidence, data may not be comparable with previous editions.
[1]Includes combat aircraft from all services, including naval and air defense. Light strike/counterinsurgency aircraft are included in bomber/fighter-ground-attack category. Reconnaissance includes maritime reconnaissance, electronic warfare, and antisubmarine warfare aircraft.
[2]Includes air defense troops.
[3]Main battle tanks (MBT), weighing at least 16.5 metric tons with gun of at least 75-mm caliber.
[4]Some countries have staffs, centrally controlled units, support services, military police, regular armed forces not responsible to Ministry of Defense, and the like, which means total armed forces are greater than the sum of the three armed forces.
[5]Includes marines or naval infantry.
[6]Includes strategic missile forces.
[7]Does not reflect losses from 1991 civil war.
Source: International Institute for Strategic Studies, 23 Tavistock Street, London, The Military Balance 1994–1995.

United States. The deployment of some 15,000 troops and additional ships and aircraft to the Persian Gulf in response to Iraq's provocative moves against Kuwait and the deployment of 15,000 troops to Haiti in connection with the restoration to power of President Aristide were the major military events of the year for the United States. While it turned out that neither action was to involve combat operations, these simultaneous crises provoked a debate as to whether the country's armed forces could fight and win two major regional conflicts at nearly the same time, the assumption on which the administration's defense policy was based.

The Clinton administration's "don't ask, don't tell, don't pursue" policy on homosexuals in the military went into effect on February 28, but the "don't tell" element did not fare well in the courts. A federal district court ruled that Col. Margarethe Cammermeyer, a declared lesbian, had to be reinstated as the chief nurse in the Washington state

National Guard, and a federal appeals court decided that an admittedly gay sailor, Keith Meinhold, had to be reinstated in the navy. The 1991 "Tailhook affair" continued to have reverberations in 1994. While the navy and the Marine Corps, owing to a lack of evidence, dropped their efforts to court-martial officers accused of sexual assaults at the aviator's convention, a navy judge ruled that the chief of naval operations, Adm. Frank B. Kelso II, had misrepresented his role in the affair. Kelso denied the charge but then retired two months early; he was allowed to keep his four-star rank only after a heated Senate debate. Lieut. Paula Coughlin, who made the first complaints about the alleged misconduct at the convention, resigned from the navy in May. In October she was awarded $6.7 million in her lawsuit against the hotel that served as host for the convention. Lieut. Kara S. Hultgreen, the navy's first woman F-14 fighter pilot, was killed on October 25 when her jet crashed at sea during carrier operations.

President Clinton chose the deputy secretary of defense, William Perry, as secretary of defense. Marine Corps Lieut. Gen. John J. Sheehan was tapped to head the reshaped U.S. Atlantic Command (USACOM). The operation in Haiti was the first large-scale test of that command's new "adaptive joint force packaging" concept.

On May 13 President Clinton signed a directive on reforming multilateral peace operations. It established criteria for determining when the U.S. would vote for or participate in peacekeeping operations and called for what seemed to be the contradictory goals of enhancing and improving the UN's peacekeeping capabilities while cutting their cost. In addition to the operations in Haiti and the Persian Gulf, the U.S. continued to participate in the NATO effort to support the UN in former Yugoslavia. All U.S. forces had been withdrawn from Somalia by the end of March, and the short Rwandan relief effort ended in September. During their participation in Somalia, 30 U.S. service personnel were killed in combat and 175 wounded. On April 14, during missions to enforce the no-fly zone over the Kurdish area of northern Iraq, two U.S. Air Force F-15s shot down two army UH-60 helicopters after mistaking them for Iraqis; 26 international personnel were killed.

The 10-month-long Nuclear Policy Review, completed in September, detailed a number of unilateral reductions in both strategic and tactical nuclear forces to take place over the next seven years, although the cuts were more timid than many defense experts had expected. It was decided to retain 500 silo-based single-warhead Minuteman III intercontinental ballistic missiles (ICBM) in three locations. Air force B-1B bombers would no longer have a nuclear delivery capability. The chief role for the 20 planned B-2 bombers, and for the 66 B-52H bombers the air force planned to keep, would be to deliver conventional weapons, but these aircraft would retain a nuclear delivery capability. Instead of the previously planned 18 Trident ballistic missile submarines, the force would be capped at 14, each to be armed with 24 D-5 submarine-launched ballistic missiles (SLBM). Attack submarines would continue to be armed with Tomahawk nuclear cruise missiles, but the technical capability to carry nuclear weapons would be removed from all navy surface vessels and carrierborne aircraft.

U.S. defense spending for fiscal 1994 was $261.7 billion. The $263.8 billion fiscal 1995 defense authorization bill was signed by Clinton in September. It was characterized by a tendency to draw out expensive new weapons programs rather than cancel them and included money to build a new aircraft carrier, three Arleigh Burke guided-missile destroyers, six C-17 cargo aircraft, and 24 navy FA-18C and FA-18D fighter-attack aircraft. Continued research-and-devel-

opment funding was provided for the air force's F-22 fighter, a new attack submarine, the Marine Corps's controversial V-22 tilt-rotor aircraft, and the army's Comanche helicopter. Against the wishes of the Defense Department, Congress also inserted money to reactivate three SR-71 spy planes. In December Clinton announced that $25 billion would be added to the defense budget through 2001, and the Pentagon said that it would cut $7.7 billion in new weapons programs—both with an eye to redirecting funds to improve the combat readiness of U.S. forces.

With the government buying less military hardware in the post-Cold War era, many defense contractors looked to mergers to remain healthy. Northrop Corp. and Grumman merged in March and then acquired Vought Aircraft Co. in September. In August Lockheed Corp., already the world's largest defense contractor, and fourth-ranked Martin Marietta Corp. announced that they planned to merge.

NATO. The 16 NATO heads of state met in January in Brussels, where they formally invited the former members of the Warsaw Pact and the successor states of the Soviet Union to join with them in a "Partnership for Peace" (PfP). This program allowed the participating states to develop cooperative military relations with NATO, particularly in the area of joint planning and training for peacekeeping and humanitarian operations. Although falling far short of full or even associate membership in NATO, the alliance agreed to consult with any PfP participant if that state perceived a direct threat to its territorial integrity, political independence, or security. By the end of the year, Russia and all the other successor states of the Soviet Union except Belarus and Tajikistan had joined it, as had all the former Warsaw Pact members in Eastern Europe, including Albania. Members of the CSCE were also eligible for membership, and Finland, Slovenia, and Sweden joined. The first peacekeeping field exercises were held in Poland in September, and that same month ships from Lithuania, Poland, Russia, and Sweden joined those from 10 NATO nations in a joint naval exercise in the North Sea. Also in September, 250 American and 250 Russian troops took part in a joint peacekeeping exercise at the Totsk training ground in Russia's Urals region under a bilateral program of military cooperation.

Manfred Wörner, NATO's secretary-general since 1988, died on August 13. (*See* OBITUARIES.) He was succeeded in that post by Belgian Foreign Minister Willy Claes. (*See* BIOGRAPHIES.)

NATO continued to provide military support to the UN Protection Force (UNPROFOR) in former Yugoslavia. On February 28, NATO fighters shot down four Serbian jets violating the UN "no-fly" zone in Bosnia and Herzegovina, the first time forces under NATO command had ever been used in combat. On April 10 and 11, NATO aircraft provided close air support for UNPROFOR military observers under attack in the town of Gorazde. Additional support strikes occurred in August and September. Almost 4,500 personnel from 12 nations and nearly 170 aircraft participated in this NATO effort to enforce the "no-fly" zone, support UNPROFOR, and protect the UN-designated safe areas in Bosnia. The joint NATO-Western European Union (WEU) maritime Operation Sharp Guard continued to prevent all unauthorized shipping from entering the territorial waters of the Federal Republic of Yugoslavia (Serbia and Montenegro) or seaborne arms shipments from entering any state in former Yugoslavia. In July a new NATO command structure was introduced that eliminated the Allied Command Channel and left only two major military commands: Allied Command Europe and Allied Command Atlantic.

Germany, Italy, Spain, and the United Kingdom continued with development of the Eurofighter 2000, which had its first flight on March 24. Dogged by political and financial problems throughout its nine-year history, the program saw its costs continue to rise as the participating countries reduced or delayed their aircraft orders.

United Kingdom. Field Marshal Sir Peter Inge, who had headed the army, was appointed chief of the defense staff in March. The Royal Navy's first Trident submarine, HMS *Vanguard,* successfully fired an unarmed Trident missile in May, confirming that it was close to operational status. The four-year "Options for Change" program was completed in September. During this period the military strength of the armed forces had dropped from 306,000 to 254,000. In July the government announced the results of the seven-month Defence Costs Study. Also known as "Front Line First," it mandated a further manpower reduction of 11,600 military and 7,100 civil service jobs.

The unexpected peace initiatives in Northern Ireland raised the possibility that the British might be able to reduce their 16,500-man military presence in the troubled province, but no immediate cuts were in the offing. The army and the Royal Air Force continued to maintain more than 38,000 troops in Germany, while the army had some 3,700 personnel, under the command of Gen. Michael Rose (*see* BIOGRAPHIES), with UNPROFOR in Bosnia. Small British military contingents remained deployed in a number of other locations throughout the world, from Hong Kong to the Falkland Islands. The United Kingdom ended its military presence in Belize in 1994, withdrawing its 600-strong force and announced that its small naval base in Bermuda would close in 1995.

France. A defense White Paper published in February examined particularly France's ability to project military power overseas and established a requirement for the capability quickly to deploy up to two combat divisions and six fighter squadrons as far as 7,000 km (4,375 mi). The White Paper stated that France would maintain defense spending at current levels. In April, however, the six-year military spending program called for a 0.5% annual increase in spending beyond the rate of inflation. It also called for a slight shift in emphasis from nuclear to conventional programs. The M-5 SLBM program was endorsed, but its service entry date was postponed from 2005 to 2010. In May Pres. François Mitterrand revealed that France had approximately 500 nuclear warheads. On May 7 the nuclear-powered aircraft carrier *Charles De Gaulle* was "inaugurated," as the way in which the ship had been built prevented a traditional launching. The first nuclear-powered surface warship ever built in Western Europe, the *De Gaulle* was due to enter service in 1999.

A 15,000-strong armoured division was sent to Germany as part of the WEU's Eurocorps, and France maintained more than 30,000 military personnel in its colonies and former dependencies throughout the world, particularly in Africa. The French also remained major contributors to the UN forces in former Yugoslavia and in the NATO units supporting them. Cooperation between French and NATO military authorities was at the highest level since France withdrew from NATO's unified military structure in 1966.

Germany. In July the Federal Constitutional Court ruled that the country's basic law did not preclude German military forces from operating outside the NATO area, provided that the Bundestag (parliament) approved each such operation. The army completed its reorganization and now was made up of three corps headquarters—one of which was combined German-Dutch—with eight subordinate divisions. The division headquarters doubled as military district commands. An airborne division was under Army Headquarters command. The army's tank inventory dropped from 4,778 in 1993 to 2,855 in 1994 through the destruction of tanks once held by the East German army and through the transfer of equipment to other NATO members, particularly Turkey and Greece. This "cascading" of equipment in excess of its CFE limits had made Germany the second largest exporter of conventional weapons in 1993, and exports continued into 1994. Germany halted its arms transfers to Turkey on May 7 after charges were made that Turkey was breaking a pledge not to use German-supplied equipment in its fight against rebel Kurds. Shipments resumed one month later after no proof was evinced to support the charges.

Turkey. After the United States, Turkey fielded the largest armed forces in NATO, with 503,800 personnel under arms. This number would rise as the government extended the length of conscription service by five months to support army operations against the rebel Kurdistan Workers' Party (PKK) in the eastern part of the country. As Turkey was eager to modernize its military equipment, the Defense Ministry escaped most of the spending cuts imposed by the government in its austerity program, but inflation and currency devaluation forced the deferment of several procurement programs, such as the purchase of 50 Black Hawk helicopters. In 1993 Turkey became the first NATO country to purchase arms from Russia, and this relationship continued in 1994. Political instability in Russia and the ethnic conflicts in the Caucasus also threatened its security, however, and Turkey was one of the most vigorous opponents of Russia's efforts to alter the CFE treaty to permit more Russian forces near the Turkish border. An October dispute with Greece over the Aegean Sea once again illuminated the fragile cohesion on NATO's southern flank.

Commonwealth of Independent States (CIS). Russian efforts to transform the CIS into one "strategic space" along the lines of the U.S.S.R. met with little success. The attempt to create CIS joint armed forces proved a total failure, and in June the headquarters in Moscow was turned into a coordination cell. The Collective Security Treaty—not signed by all the members of the CIS—became a vehicle to legitimize Russian peacekeeping operations in Tajikistan and the Caucasus. On October 21 Moldova and Russia signed an agreement calling for the withdrawal of the Russian 14th Army from Moldova within three years. Ukraine and Russia remained unable to agree how to divide the former Soviet Black Sea Fleet, and the issue was complicated by the political unrest in the Crimea, where the bulk of the fleet was based.

The year was a difficult one for the Russian armed forces. Many in it felt humiliated by what they saw as a precipitous withdrawal from Eastern Europe and the Baltic States, with security and social considerations sacrificed to political expediency. Finding adequate housing for the returning officers became a top priority. By Russian accounts the strength of the armed forces fell from 2.2 million to 1.9 million during the year, although many foreign analysts suggested the real strength was far less. In October President Yeltsin issued a decree calling for a further reduction to 1.7 million by the end of 1995.

In December Russian troops invaded the republic of Chechnya in the northern Caucasus region to put down the republic's self-proclaimed independence. The Chechen capital, Grozny, was bombed and shelled, and at year's end pitched ground battles were reported. Russian Defense Minister Gen. Pavel Grachev was given direct responsibility for operations against the breakaway republic and its president, Dzhokhar Dudayev (*see* BIOGRAPHIES), himself a former Soviet air force general.

The military's financial problems dealt a severe blow to Russia's defense industry. With the Ministry of Defense unable to pay for many weapons ordered and already built, plant after plant furloughed workers without pay. Many also tried to replace domestic customers with foreign ones, with limited success. An official of the state-owned arms-exporting company indicated in November, however, that Russia would sell $4 billion worth of arms in 1994, nearly double the previous year's sales. Even greater profits were forecast once international sanctions had been removed from some of the Soviet Union's traditional overseas customers, such as Iraq and Libya.

During the year Ukraine transferred 180 strategic nuclear warheads to Russia and in return received fuel rods for its nuclear power plants. Ukrainian officials also confirmed that 30 of the 46 SS-24 ICBM in Ukraine had been disarmed, although Russian military authorities expressed concern that the nuclear weapons still in Ukraine were not being properly maintained. Pres. Leonid Kuchma (see BIOGRAPHIES) appointed a civilian, Valery Shmarov, as defense minister. Belarus' deputy foreign minister said in January that 34 of the 81 SS-25 mobile strategic missiles once deployed in Belarus had been returned to Russia. Other officials later said that five of the eight Russian strategic missile regiments in the country would be gone by the end of the year.

With all the various military groups active in the republics of the Transcaucasus, it was difficult to track all the former Soviet military equipment, complicating the task of those monitoring the CFE treaty reductions. Russian peacekeeping forces were deployed to the rebel Abkhazia and South Ossetia regions of Georgia and to Armenian-populated Nagorno-Karabakh in Azerbaijan. The CSCE's "Minsk Group" sought to mediate the conflict between Armenia and Azerbaijan over Nagorno-Karabakh, and President Yeltsin served as host for a meeting of the Armenian and Azerbaijani presidents in September. While Russia wished to build up the CSCE as an alternative to NATO, the Russians balked at the CSCE efforts in Nagorno-Karabakh, especially when Turkey showed itself eager and willing to contribute troops. At an October CSCE meeting in Vienna, Russia suggested that the CSCE should abdicate to Russia the responsibility for settling the conflict. In other regional developments, the Russian defense minister announced that Russia would establish three permanent military bases in Georgia, two in Armenia, and one at the ballistic-missile early-warning radar site in Azerbaijan. Late in the year a squadron of Russian jet fighters was deployed to Armenia to defend Armenian airspace.

Russia maintained the 8,500-strong 201st motorized rifle division in Tajikistan to prop up the neocommunist government, while Russian border troops guarded the Tajik-Afghan border. The 201st comprised virtually all of the CIS Collective Peacekeeping Forces in Tajikistan, the only operational command that remained in what were to have been the CIS joint armed forces. Lieut. Gen. Aleksandr Lebed, the outspoken commander of the Russian 14th Army in Moldova, turned down this command in Tajikistan in August when Moscow tried to ease him out of his Moldovan post. A flareup of fighting between the Tajik government and opposition forces in July made many fear a resumption of the 1992 civil war. Iran, Russia, and the UN brokered a temporary cease-fire in September, and 11 UN observers were sent to monitor it. The cease-fire was extended until Jan. 6, 1995, and the two groups exchanged some prisoners.

Turkmenistan's Pres. Saparmuryad Niyazov reminded the Military Council in January that Russia had strategic military interests in Turkmenistan that had to be respected. He indicated that the reorganization of the country's armed forces would not be completed until 1999, when they would number 37,000 men. During 1994 nearly all the officers in

the Turkmen armed forces were Russian, and they were not required to take an oath of allegiance to Turkmenistan. The Russian arms-exporting company Rosvooruzheniya agreed to supply military equipment in return for natural gas.

The last of the 40 strategic bombers that had been stationed in Kazakhstan flew to Russia in February. In March Pres. Nursultan Nazarbayev said that 12 of the 104 SS-18 ICBM stationed in Kazakhstan had been returned to Russia, although he indicated the warheads might still be in the country. That same month he signed an accord with Yeltsin giving Russia jurisdiction over the nuclear weapons in Kazakhstan. The Russians agreed to remove all the nuclear warheads within 18 months and destroy all the missiles and silos within three years. In November it was revealed that the U.S. had discovered and later negotiated the removal to the U.S. of a large cache of bomb-grade plutonium at Ust-Kamenogorsk. Russia and Kazakhstan also negotiated an agreement leasing the Baikonur cosmodrome to the Russian Space Forces for 20 years at a cost of $115 million per year. In October experts from 24 countries and several international organizations met in Almaty, Kazakhstan, to prepare for a Conference on Security and Measures of Confidence in Asia, a concept first proposed by Nazarbayev at the UN General Assembly in October 1992 and patterned on the CSCE.

The Rest of Europe. The war in Bosnia and Herzegovina continued sporadically throughout the year, with no permanent settlement in sight. The commander of the UN forces successfully negotiated a cease-fire around the capital, Sarajevo, in February coincident with the establishment by NATO of a heavy-weapons exclusion zone around the beleaguered city. Muslim and Bosnian Croat forces also agreed to a cease-fire in Mostar on March 18 as part of a broader accord calling for an eventual confederation with Croatia. With his people suffering from the UN embargo, Serbian Pres. Slobodan Milosevic stopped supporting the Bosnian Serbs in early August. The U.S. wished to see the UN arms embargo lifted for the Bosnian Muslims and in mid-November announced that it would act unilaterally. NATO also wished to loosen the rules of engagement and be given more flexibility in choosing targets when requested to assist UN forces. There was a "dual key" arrangement whereby each NATO strike had to be approved by both the UN and NATO authorities. In late October Bosnian government forces, after having been on the defensive for most of the war, won a decisive victory over the Bosnian Serbs with an offensive in the Bihac region. Combined Bosnian Serb and Bosnian Croat forces also made significant gains in the south. By late November, however, the Serbs had regained much lost ground; they surrounded Bihac and cut the city off from UN and NATO operations. Fighting eased somewhat in Croatia during the year, but the conflict was not resolved. A cease-fire came into effect on April 4, with UN troops separating the two sides. The Croatian parliament would extend the mandate for the UNPROFOR only until Jan. 6, 1995. There were signs that Milosevic might drop his support for the Serbs in the breakaway Croatian district of Krajina, as he had for the Bosnian Serbs.

In Poland Pres. Lech Walesa, the government, and the military were embroiled in a power struggle over control of the armed forces. Walesa, with support from many senior uniformed officers, wanted the chief of staff to report directly to the president rather than the minister of defense. In October Walesa asked Defense Minister Piotr Kolodziejczyk to resign, but the minister, with support from Prime Minister Waldemar Pawlak, held on until mid-November before succumbing. There was modest military cooperation between the four countries of the "Visegrad

Group"—the Czech Republic, Hungary, Poland, and Slovakia—but the cohesion of this fragile regional grouping was put to a severe test in January when the Czech minister of defense refused to attend a meeting to coordinate the group's efforts to join NATO. All four countries lacked the resources to modernize their armed forces and to make them compatible with NATO forces. All but Hungary had important but troubled defense industries, which they were trying to protect by seeking foreign customers. By the end of the year, the Hungarian air force had completed its program to install U.S.-built Identification-Friend-or-Foe (IFF) equipment in 109 of its aircraft, allowing them to be recognized by NATO air defense systems.

Neutrality had become less of an attractive option for some of Europe's traditionally neutral states after the Cold War. Sweden, Finland, and Austria were slated to join the European Union in 1995 (in some cases with special provisions to preserve some aspects of neutrality), while Sweden and Finland joined NATO's Partnership for Peace in 1994. Swedish naval forces participated in the PfP exercise Cooperative Venture 94 in September and October, the first time in modern history Sweden had taken part in joint military maneuvers other than peacekeeping outside its territory.

Middle East. In the volatile Middle East, 1994 brought a bitter civil war, the threat of another Gulf war, and encouraging progress toward Arab-Israeli peace. The shaky four-year old union of North and South Yemen broke apart in April when Northern units of the largely unintegrated armed forces conducted a preemptive strike on Southern troops garrisoned in the North. The struggle quickly escalated into a full-scale civil war with both sides using all the weapons at their disposal, including Scud surface-to-surface missiles. The North captured the Southern capital, Aden, on July 7, and the Southern leadership fled the country.

In June the UN Special Commission (UNSCOM) overseeing the destruction of Iraq's weapons of mass destruction announced that all its chemical weapons had been destroyed. In the two-year operation some 100 experts from 23 countries had destroyed 480,000 litres (130,000 gal) of chemical agent and 28,000 chemical munitions. UNSCOM also reported progress in constructing the long-term monitoring system that would verify Iraq's compliance with the ban on weapons of mass destruction and ballistic missiles. The Security Council, however, was not satisfied that Iraq was fully complying with all the other conditions called for in its resolutions of 1991 and repeatedly renewed the economic sanctions against Iraq.

In what was apparently a misguided effort to put pressure on the Security Council to lift these sanctions, Saddam Hussein, who had never recognized the independence of Kuwait or agreed on the border line, in early October sent 20,000 of his elite Republican Guards to join some 45,000 regular army troops near the Kuwaiti border. Clinton responded by immediately ordering troops, planes, and ships to the Gulf. The full-scale U.S. reinforcement was halted as Iraq quickly withdrew the two Republican Guards divisions well north of the border, but 12,000 U.S. troops remained in the region until the end of the year. The Iraqi feint prompted several Gulf states to agree to a long-standing U.S. request to station more military equipment in the region. Kuwait agreed to allow 24 A-10 attack aircraft as well as the equipment to support a full brigade to be permanently stationed on its territory. Equipment for a second brigade would be positioned in Qatar.

These October events sparked a critical reassessment of the 1991 Gulf war in the U.S., with many repeating earlier charges that the 100-hour-long ground phase had ended too soon, allowing far more Republican Guards to escape with their equipment than had been believed at the time. The greater regret was that the war had not toppled Saddam Hussein.

In May Israel turned control of Jericho and the Gaza Strip over to Yasir Arafat's Palestine Liberation Organization in accordance with the agreement reached in Washington the previous year. Israel's Prime Minister Yitzhak Rabin and King Hussein of Jordan met on July 25 in Washington, where they signed a declaration that the state of war between their two countries was over. On October 26, at a desolate border outpost called Arava Crossing, Israel and Jordan signed a formal peace treaty.

South and Central Asia. Afghanistan remained in a state of factionalism and near anarchy. In January the militia of Gen. 'Abd ar-Rashid Dostam, in alliance with Prime Minister Gulbuddin Hekmatyar, attacked and captured most of Kabul, only to be driven out of the capital in late June by forces loyal to Pres. Burhanuddin Rabbani. The bitter civil war in Sri Lanka showed no signs of being over. Myanmar (Burma) seemed to come out of its shell somewhat, acquiring jet fighters and ground-attack aircraft from China. The main strategic concern in the region, however, was the uneasy relationship between India and Pakistan. In February the U.S. administration repeated its belief that both countries could assemble a limited number of nuclear weapons in a relatively short time. Both possessed the means to deliver nuclear weapons as well. In addition to its Mirage attack aircraft, Pakistan deployed 18 Hatf-I short-range ballistic missiles. India had a number of different types of ballistic missiles. In February it conducted a successful test of the Agni-III intermediate-range ballistic missile. Russia agreed to supply India with cryogenic rocket engines for its space program but without transferring the related technology. In 1993 the U.S. had put pressure on Russia to block a similar deal, arguing that the technology transfer would violate the Missile Technology Control Regime. In addition, Russian companies signed contracts to modernize the Indian air force's large MiG-21 fleet, and the Indian defense minister

ALEX S. MACLEAN—LANDSLIDES

Rows of B-52s stand parked at Davis-Monthan Air Force Base in Tucson, Ariz., awaiting their destruction. The dismantling of the planes, which were then sold for scrap, was being carried out under START (Strategic Arms Reduction Talks) I.

made several shopping trips to Russia, looking at tanks, aircraft, and even one of Russia's "aircraft-carrying cruisers."

East and Southeast Asia, Oceania. Despite continued concerns about China's human rights record, the Clinton administration decided to resume military contacts with China, which had been suspended after 1989. Sino-U.S. arms control talks were also resumed after a six-year hiatus. The current series of nuclear tests was believed to be connected with the development of warheads for two new ballistic missiles, and the Chinese indicated that they would be willing to join a comprehensive nuclear test ban once these tests had been completed. China pressed its claim to a number of disputed islands in the South China Sea and in May launched the first of a new class of indigenously designed diesel-electric submarines.

The Korean peninsula remained a potential trouble spot. Following the breakdown in talks between North and South Korea in March, President Clinton announced that Patriot missiles would be deployed with U.S. forces in South Korea. Three Patriot batteries arrived by ship on April 18. Concerns about North Korea's nuclear weapons program eased following the October agreement between the U.S. and North Korea on freezing the program. As a result, the U.S. and South Korea canceled their annual "Team Spirit" joint military exercises. The North Korean conventional threat remained, however. The North's military was the fifth largest in the world, and two-thirds of its ground forces were deployed within about 100 km (60 mi) of the demilitarized zone dividing North from South Korea. An unarmed U.S. reconnaissance helicopter strayed into North Korea and was shot down on December 17, killing one of the pilots. North Korea elected to make it an incident, extracting a confession of wrongdoing from Bobby Hall, the surviving pilot, before releasing him on December 30.

Japan and Russia came no closer to resolving their dispute over the four small islands (one a group of islets) in the southern Kuril chain seized by Russia in the last week of World War II but claimed by Japan. Russian border forces fired on several Japanese fishing boats caught in waters around these disputed islands, causing some deaths, but the matter never escalated into a military confrontation. In a rare deployment of troops overseas, the first not made under a UN umbrella, Japan sent 260 soldiers to Zaire in September on a humanitarian mission to help Rwandan refugees, only to withdraw them in December.

Although one-third smaller than in the previous year, Vietnam's 572,000-strong armed forces remained larger than the militaries of Laos, Cambodia, Thailand, Malaysia, and Singapore combined. Russia maintained a military toe-hold in Southeast Asia with a small detachment at the former U.S. base at Cam Ranh Bay, Vietnam. Vietnamese-U.S. relations were the warmest in decades as the Vietnamese cooperated in trying to determine the fate of American servicemen missing in action following the Vietnam War, and President Clinton lifted the U.S. trade embargo in February. After nearly a year's negotiations, Malaysia finalized a deal to buy 18 MiG-29 jet fighters from Russia on June 7. The first aircraft was to be delivered in April 1995. The agreement represented a significant breakthrough for Russia's troubled defense industry and marked its first entry into the rapidly growing Southeast Asian arms market. In October Malaysia inaugurated a new rapid deployment force built around the 10th Parachute Brigade.

The Royal Cambodian Army had much success against the Khmer Rouge in an offensive that began in January. On March 25 the government captured the rebel stronghold at Pailin, and in October its troops overran a redoubt at Phnom Vour that had been under Khmer Rouge control since 1969.

Three Western hostages kidnapped by the Khmer Rouge in July were executed during the battle for Phnom Vour.

The U.S. restored some of the security ties with New Zealand that had been curbed in 1987 in retaliation for New Zealand's policy of denying port access to nuclear-powered or nuclear-armed ships. The U.S. did not resume its defense obligations to New Zealand contained in the ANZUS treaty, however.

Caribbean and Latin America. The U.S.-led multinational occupation of Haiti that began on September 19 was the most notable event in the Caribbean region in 1994. The leaders of the military junta that had ousted President Aristide were allowed to leave the country. The Haitian police force virtually evaporated, and the U.S. troops found it necessary to assume many police functions that they had expected to avoid. They hoped to turn over the Haitian operation to a 6,000-member UN Mission in Haiti early in 1995.

Cuba cut its armed forces in half as its economy continued to disintegrate. The U.S. Navy's base at Guantánamo Bay was used to house Haitian and Cuban boat people who had been picked up by U.S. Navy and Coast Guard ships as they tried to sail to Florida. Russia renewed a leasing agreement for the electronic intelligence-gathering station at Lourdes, near Havana. Cuba was the last significant holdout to the Treaty of Tlatelolco establishing a nuclear-weapons-free zone in Latin American and the Caribbean after Argentina, Brazil, and Chile formally ratified the treaty in early 1994. The Cubans announced that they would sign the treaty but with a reservation that they might later withdraw depending on future U.S. policy regarding Guantánamo Bay.

The armed forces of the region remained heavily involved in internal security operations as guerrilla and criminal activity continued to plague Central America, Colombia, and Peru. In Mexico the army was called out to battle an uprising in the southern province of Chiapas by the mainly indigenous Zapatista National Liberation Army.

Africa South of the Sahara. The brutal civil war in Rwanda was the most terrible of the troubles visiting the length and breadth of Africa. An August 1993 peace agreement had halted the struggle between the mainly Tutsi Rwandan Patriotic Front (FPR) and the Hutu-led government, but fighting resumed on April 6 after the presidents of Rwanda and Burundi were killed when their plane was shot down over Kigali, the Rwandan capital. The FPR quickly advanced on the capital, but the struggle degenerated into an unprecedented ethnic bloodbath between Hutu and Tutsi in which one million or more unarmed men, women, and children were slain. About two million more fled the country, overwhelming the resources of relief organizations and neighbouring Burundi, Tanzania, and Zaire. On July 4 the FPR seized most of the capital, and two weeks later it declared victory. Many units of the former government's army, however, with their weapons, remained intact in refugee camps outside Rwanda and threatened to renew the conflict.

Internal armed struggles of varying intensities continued in Djibouti, The Gambia, Liberia, Mali, Niger, Somalia, and The Sudan. The UN peacekeeping effort in Somalia began to wind down toward an ambiguous ending. In February the UN Security Council voted to reduce the force and to withdraw it entirely by the end of March 1995. The UN forces, which numbered around 15,000 at the year's end, no longer sought to disarm the contending factions. Angolan Pres. José Eduardo dos Santos and National Union for the Total Independence of Angola leader Jonas Savimbi initialed a peace accord in mid-November, providing some hope of ending nearly two decades of civil war.

Another bright spot in the region was South Africa. The republic's defense forces expelled a force of several thousand armed white right-wing extremists from Bophuthatswana in March, when the president of that homeland was deposed, and restored a degree of order in KwaZulu, where Pres. F.W. De Klerk declared a state of emergency in the same month. Integration of the South African defense forces and the armed wing of the African National Congress (ANC)—called Spear of the Nation—had begun even before the April elections, which swept the ANC to power. Pres. Nelson Mandela chose Joe Modise, the former commander of Spear of the Nation, as his first minister of defense.

New Technology. In January Israeli companies introduced Piano, a missile-warning system employing passive, electro-optic technology. The U.S. Army conducted a two-week-long Advanced Warfighting Experiment in April, testing an all-digitized combine-arms task force. More than 100 vehicles and aircraft were equipped with digital capability to relay commands and reports on the battlefield situation throughout the force. Another experiment, involving an entire brigade, was planned for 1997. In November a Russian company offered for international sale two air-defense systems supposedly able to detect aircraft and missiles employing radar-evading stealth technology. The radars operated in the very high-frequency band, a radar technology largely abandoned in the West following World War II, when higher frequencies became available.

(DOUGLAS L. CLARKE)

This article updates the *Macropædia* article The Technology of WAR.

Mining

Mining companies face challenges peculiar to their industry. Proximity to markets, infrastructure, and political risk all figure in investment decisions but, first and foremost, geology dictates the geographic location of mines. The resource begins to deplete as soon as mining commences. Because they are exploiting a depleting asset, mining companies cannot survive without committing investment in new projects. Judging the best time to invest in order to achieve the best rate of return is notoriously difficult. The more successful companies are those with the best timing—whether deliberate or fortuitous.

Few succeed completely. The mining industry has always been characterized by "feast or famine"—overproduction when demand is weak and underproduction when demand is strong. The former situation had prevailed for a few years, as witnessed by recent record stock for a number of metals and minerals. Now that demand was strengthening and prices for many raw materials had moved sharply higher, the temptation for many would be to restart idled capacity or invest in new capacity too quickly, thereby ensuring that the cycle continued.

As is usually the case, the health of the mining industry in 1994 was tied closely to overall economic activity. Although there were signs of economic improvement in the mature industrialized countries, the recovery was not synchronized; the U.S. was a strong performer, but the U.K. led only a fairly diffident recovery in Europe, while Japan remained in recession. Demand for metals and minerals in the industrialized economies continued to grow but at a far slower rate than incomes and output, and the world appeared to be witnessing a major geographic shift in terms of demand toward Asia.

As the principal source of foreign earnings, minerals were given priority by the new government of South Africa. Issues being debated included mineral rights and private versus state ownership, health and safety standards, small-scale mining, and the role of the industry in the government's development program. In the countries of the former Soviet Union, the slump in domestic consumption of metals and minerals continued, which ensured that exports of raw materials were maintained at a high level. The beginnings of economic recovery in the mature Western economies, however, meant that Russian exports did not weigh as heavily on the markets in 1994 as had been the case in 1993.

Exploration. In an analysis of exploration strategies by 151 companies accounting for some $2.1 billion of spending, approximately 80% of the world total, Metals Economics Group found that for the first time the largest share of funding was directed to South America (26%), followed by Australia (21%), the U.S. (16%), Canada (14%), and the Pacific region (8%).

For a number of reasons, gold in 1994 again proved to be the major attraction. The technology was at hand to exploit very low-grade deposits (as little as one gram per metric ton could be mined profitably), and the process to treat the ore and recover the gold was relatively simple. Most important of all, production costs could be very low, often less than half the price received for the gold. A successful gold project could therefore present a rapid and handsome return on the capital invested, and for a number of mining companies, it was profits from gold operations that helped them survive a prolonged period of low prices for their other products. The well-explored areas of North America continued to reveal new gold deposits, and the success of modern exploration techniques in Australia generated another exploration boom there. In South America the main focus was on Chile and Venezuela and, increasingly, on Peru, Argentina, and Bolivia. In the southwestern Pacific region, Papua New Guinea and Indonesia were front-runners. Elsewhere, West Africa was rapidly emerging as a major new area for gold exploration. Australian companies were already firmly established there, but the large South African mining houses, no longer restricted in their overseas activities, were quick to secure a presence, notably in Ghana. Promising new discoveries were also being made in Mali, Côte d'Ivoire, Burkina Faso, and Guinea.

In September, Ashton Mining, which operated the world's largest diamond mine, at Argyle in Western Australia, disclosed that it had discovered a diamond province in Finland. The worldwide search for diamonds over the past three years received much publicity as a result of a major discovery in Canada's Northwest Territories. The initial claim staking there rivaled the days of the Yukon gold rush, but excitement then moderated, and to date only one deposit seemed certain to develop into a major commercial mine. The project, a joint venture between Dia Met Minerals and Australia's Broken Hill Proprietary, could begin production in 1998. (*See also* WORLD AFFAIRS: Arctic Regions.) Improved technology and recovery techniques continued to make seabed diamond mining attractive, and several projects were launched, mainly off the coast of Namibia. Meanwhile, in November, De Beers Consolidated Mines, the South African diamond-mining giant, gave up its monopoly in Namibia in exchange for a guaranteed 25-year 50–50 stake with the Namibian government in a new firm, Namdeb Diamond Corp.

An estimated 80% of the world supply of rough (uncut) diamonds was controlled by De Beers through its Central Selling Organisation. The size of its stockpile was never disclosed, but over the past two years the CSO had been under pressure because of only moderate demand and because of a large increase in the supply of diamonds reaching the market independently. Relationships with Russia, a major producer, were also strained, with the diamond industry there calling for a major overhaul of the current sales agreement when it expired at the end of 1995.

Canada recorded some of the more significant base metals discoveries. Two of the biggest nickel producers, Falconbridge and Inco, delineated large, high-grade nickel/copper deposits at depths in excess of 2,000 m (6,560 ft) on the rim of the nickel-rich Sudbury basin in Ontario. Nickel discoveries were also made in Western Australia, but the deposits there were of a different type and the processing more energy-intensive; their development could begin once the construction of a gas pipeline, being laid primarily to provide the goldfields with cheaper fuel, had been completed.

Platinova, a junior explorer, ventured into uncharted territory for zinc and announced the discovery of a large near-surface deposit in Peary Land in northern Greenland. Mining in Arctic conditions was believed to be feasible, but concentrates would have to be shipped to Europe for smelting. Elsewhere, Peru was attracting considerable exploration for lead and zinc, and major successes were expected. Moves to privatize the state mining sector were going ahead, and in October Peru's second largest copper mine was sold to Magma Copper of the U.S. for $218 million.

The Andes Mountains were providing the world with an enormous copper "larder," and new discoveries were announced with almost monotonous regularity, mainly in Chile but also in Peru and Argentina. The technology was at hand for many deposits to be exploited by in situ leaching, in which the copper was extracted in solution and converted directly to copper cathode by electrolysis. The method was proving much cheaper than conventional processing and had significant environmental advantages—chiefly by obviating the need to smelt ore with the attendant release of sulfur dioxide. Outside South America, Indonesia had developed into a major copper producer, largely as a result of Freeport Indonesia's huge Grasberg deposit, a veritable copper mountain where exploration continued to expand reserves that were now the third largest in the world.

There was major exploration potential for several metals in the countries of the former Soviet Union, and a number of Western companies were active there. Thus far, however, poor infrastructure, doubts about ownership, and political uncertainty had discouraged major foreign investment in projects other than gold.

Commodities. On the London Metal Exchange (LME)—the world's principal terminal market for aluminum, copper, lead, nickel, zinc, and tin—stocks of metal at the start of 1994 were very high, supplies plentiful, and demand modest. Most producers were resigned to the prospect of another lean year, but this proved not to be the case when investment fund managers switched their interest to commodities, which were seen as having reached their price lows. When the huge volume of cash held by investment funds was moved into commodities, prices moved ahead despite weak supply-and-demand fundamentals. Later in the year, as demand began to strengthen, LME prices began to soar, and by mid-October the prices for copper, aluminum, and lead had risen 60%, 70%, and 80%, respectively, from their 1993 price lows.

Aluminum benefited further as a voluntary agreement reached in January by the European Union and leading producers, including Russia, to reduce output began to affect supply. High-cost European producers failed to agree on coordinated production cuts for zinc, which was the weakest performer on the LME. Nickel benefited from forecasts of strong growth in the stainless steel industry, its principal customer, and climbed to a two-year price peak.

The tin market remained weak despite the best efforts of producers to restrict supplies by voluntary export quotas. The seven-member Association of Tin Producing Countries welcomed China to its ranks, and Brazil agreed to join in 1995, which should give members control over more than 80% of the world's supply. The surplus of tin stocks was being reduced only slowly, however, and major new applications had not yet been developed to replace its diminished share of the can market lost to aluminum.

The world's two largest iron ore exporters, Brazil and China, had to settle for lower prices in their contracts with Japanese steelmakers in 1994 because of the weak Japanese economy, but the average price reduction was significantly less than the 10% cut some had feared. China emerged as the leading producer of iron ore, but its mines were still unable to keep pace with demand, and there were forecasts that it would have to import as much as 50 million tons per year by the end of the century. Australian producers stood to benefit most.

In the energy sector, world consumption, which had been flat since the peak demand reached in 1990, managed a slight improvement in 1993, and the trend appeared to have continued in 1994. The growth was generally in demand for natural gas, however, at the expense of coal, particularly in Europe. The coal industry in the U.K. was privatized in December, and some 30 British Coal mines were sold. RJB Mining, a relative newcomer to coal mining, bought 17, the largest number of any firm, for £815 million. In all, the selloff brought in almost £1 billion to the treasury. In the period that the pits were nationalized, 1946–94, the number of coal miners dropped from 700,000 to about 7,000. It was significant that two major U.K.-based companies, RTZ and Hanson, preferred to set their sights on the United States, where both expanded their interests by acquiring substantial low-sulfur coal deposits. In South Africa two large coal pro-

Indexes of Production, Mining and Mineral Commodities
(1980 = 100)

	1989	1990	1991	1992	1993
Mining (total)					
World[1]	99.9	99.6	97.1	101.1	106.5
Developed market economies[2]	106.2	105.3	105.5	105.5	105.2
North America[3]	94.7	96.2	95.5	94.2	93.0
European Economic Community[4]	96.3	90.7	90.9	89.3	87.2
Less developed market economies[5]	95.5	95.8	91.4	98.0	107.4
Coal					
World[1]	107.8	98.5	96.7	93.5	91.1
Developed market economies[2]	103.9	93.9	90.7	86.1	82.5
North America[3]	120.8	129.2	124.7	119.4	118.2
European Economic Community[4]	90.5	76.7	73.0	68.1	62.9
Less developed market economies[5]	175.5	181.5	203.0	224.2	244.1
Petroleum and natural gas					
World[1]	92.9	93.2	90.4	95.8	103.5
Developed market economies[2]	97.9	98.8	102.4	104.7	107.1
North America[3]	80.5	80.6	81.3	80.5	80.9
European Economic Community[4]	101.5	101.4	105.9	108.1	109.7
Less developed market economies[5]	91.0	91.0	85.6	92.4	102.1
Metals					
World[1]	129.8	134.4	134.4	135.8	135.8
Developed market economies[2]	138.0	144.3	143.5	145.1	144.7
North America[3]	138.7	139.8	142.3	143.9	139.0
European Economic Community[4]	70.6	72.0	69.2	65.8	51.8
Less developed market economies[5]	115.6	116.4	118.4	119.6	118.1
Manufacturing (total)	128.5	128.0	126.6	125.6	126.0

[1] Excluding Albania, China, former Czechoslovakia, North Korea, former U.S.S.R., Vietnam, and former Yugoslavia.
[2] Includes North America (Canada and the United States), Europe (excluding former Czechoslovakia and the European countries of the former U.S.S.R.), Australia, Israel, Japan, New Zealand, and South Africa.
[3] Canada and the United States.
[4] Now European Union; includes Belgium, Denmark, France, Germany, Greece, Ireland, Italy, Luxembourg, The Netherlands, Portugal, Spain, and the United Kingdom.
[5] Includes Caribbean nations, Central and South America, Africa (excluding South Africa), Asia (excluding China, North Korea, Israel, Japan, Vietnam, and Asian countries of the former U.S.S.R.), and Oceania (excluding Australia and New Zealand).

Built by the U.S. company Fluor and operated as a multinational joint venture, Escondida in Chile was the world's second largest copper mine. New copper discoveries were being made in the Andean countries, which continued to be the world's most important suppliers of the metal.
CARLOS GOLDIN—SABA

ducers, Randcoal and Trans-Natal Coal, announced merger plans involving assets worth R 4.3 billion. At nearly 60 million metric tons per year, the merged company would become the world's third largest privately owned hard coal producer.

Uranium producers suffered another year of low prices, and Canada reinforced its position as the major producing country. In Australia, which possessed huge uranium resources, development continued to be constrained by the government's three-mine policy.

Metallgesellschaft, one of Germany's largest industrial conglomerates with major metals interests, faced a grave liquidity crisis early in 1994 related to its exposure in U.S. oil-futures trading. Its share price collapsed, and Deutsche Bank, its dominant shareholder and creditor, staged a rescue operation to avoid bankruptcy proceedings.

In South Africa in July, Gencor reached an agreement with the Royal Dutch/Shell Group to acquire most of the oil giant's mineral assets held by its subsidiary, Billiton, for an estimated $1.2 billion. Substantial bauxite and aluminum interests were the main attraction. Gencor was a participant in a major new South African aluminum smelter and was seeking a secure source of raw materials. It would also benefit from Billiton's worldwide aluminum trading and marketing network.

Elsewhere, two of the largest aluminum producers, Aluminum Co. of America and Western Mining of Australia, announced plans in July for a merger of their worldwide alumina and bauxite-mining interests involving assets worth $A 7.5 billion. It would give the partners a 25% share of the world market for alumina. The proposed merger of two of the largest U.S. mining-equipment manufacturers, Harnischfeger Industries and Joy Technologies, was announced in August. The former already had a 75% share of the U.S. surface-mining-equipment market and the latter an 80% share of the underground-equipment market. The combined group would have a total market value of about $1 billion. In September, in a deal worth $A 740 million, it was announced that the Australian gold producer Normandy Poseidon and the French state-owned mineral and geologic agency Bureau de Recherches Geologiques et Minieres pro-posed forming a major new international mining company to be based in France. BRGM would contribute its international portfolio of mineral reserves and mining interests, and Normandy Poseidon would provide financial support and management experience.

Environment and Safety. As in 1993, concern continued about environmental damage caused by mining and smelting activities in the countries of the former Soviet Union. Although the importance of environmental protection was recognized by the governments involved and substantial efforts were being made to stem pollution, the task was enormous and was unlikely to be achieved without substantial financial assistance from Western countries.

In North America the industry had to contend with a vociferous antimining lobby and could ill afford the bad publicity resulting from the Summitville gold-mine disaster in Colorado, where cyanide and reactive sulfide waste material contaminated the groundwater and surrounding drainage system. The bankruptcy of the operator and the inadequacy of the financial surety for reclamation meant that the state of Colorado and the U.S. Environmental Protection Agency had to assume site management at a daily cost of some $40,000.

News that the Chinese government had ordered stricter enforcement of its mining safety law was a welcome development. An official decree called for better supervision at state mines and at thousands of small township mines, many of which were operating illegally without adequate safety measures. Government statistics indicated that as many as 10,000 miners had been killed each year as a result of mine collapses, explosions, and other accidents during the early 1990s, and the state radio reported that deaths had risen by 15% in the first eight months of 1994 alone. The main problem lay in the surge in development of small coal mines—about 120,000 such operations existed. Nearly one-third did not have operating licenses, and almost 75% failed to meet even basic safety standards.   (ROGER ELLIS)

See also Business and Industry Review: *Gemstones; Metals and Materials;* Earth Sciences; Energy.

This article updates the *Macropædia* article Extraction and Processing INDUSTRIES.

Motion Pictures

The overall picture of world cinema in 1994, on the eve of the 100th anniversary of motion pictures, was one of national cinemas throughout the world dwindling in face of the inevitable and irresistible domination of Hollywood production. (*See* Special Report.)

English-Speaking Cinema. The outstanding box-office successes of the year were the Disney animated feature *The Lion King,* directed by Roger Allers and Rob Minkoff, and Robert Zemeckis' *Forrest Gump,* a panorama of 30 years of U.S. history seen through the eyes of a charmed simpleminded man played by Tom Hanks (*see* BIOGRAPHIES). Other more predictable commercial hits included the resurrection of an old favourite theme in *Star Trek: Generations*

(directed by David Carson); Ivan Reitman's outrageous comedy *Junior,* in which a character played by Arnold Schwarzenegger becomes, for the sake of science, pregnant; and *The Flintstones,* a live-action version of a perennially popular animated cartoon series, directed by Brian Levant, with John Goodman as the Stone Age patriarch Fred Flintstone. Harrison Ford confirmed his stature as a box-office action hero in Philip Noyce's adaptation of Tom Clancy's quasi-political thriller, *Clear and Present Danger.*

The year's most controversial film was indisputably Oliver Stone's *Natural Born Killers,* which chronicled a mindless killing spree by a young couple and their subsequent lionization by the nation's media and public. The difficulty was to distinguish Stone's declared intention of indicting a degraded public taste and degrading media from a prurient exhilaration in the spectacle of violence for its own sake.

Selected Film Awards 1994

Golden Globes, awarded in Beverly Hills, Calif., in January 1994

Best drama	*Schindler's List* (U.S.; director, Steven Spielberg)
Best musical or comedy	*Mrs. Doubtfire* (U.S.; director, Chris Columbus)
Best director	Steven Spielberg (*Schindler's List,* U.S.)
Best actress, drama	Holly Hunter (*The Piano,* Australia)
Best actor, drama	Tom Hanks (*Philadelphia,* U.S.)
Best actress, musical or comedy	Angela Bassett (*What's Love Got to Do with It,* U.S.)
Best actor, musical or comedy	Robin Williams (*Mrs. Doubtfire,* U.S.)
Best foreign film	*Farewell My Concubine* (China; director, Chen Kaige)

Sundance Film Festival, awarded in Park City, Utah, in January 1994

Grand Jury Prize, dramatic film	*What Happened Was . . .* (U.S.; director, Tom Noonan)
Grand Jury Prize, documentary	*Freedom on My Mind* (U.S.; directors, Connie Field and Marilyn Mulford)
Audience Award, dramatic film	*Spanking the Monkey* (U.S.; director, David O. Russell)
Audience Award, documentary	*Hoop Dreams* (U.S.; directors, Peter Gilbert, Steve James, and Fred Marx)

Berlin International Film Festival, awarded in February 1994

Golden Bear	*In the Name of the Father* (U.K./U.S.; director, Jim Sheridan)
Special Jury Prize	*Fresa y chocolate* (Cuba/Mexico/Spain; directors, Tomás Gutiérrez Alea, Juan Carlos Tabio)
Best director	Krzysztof Kieslowski (*Trois Couleurs Blanc,* France/Poland/Switzerland)
Best actor	Tom Hanks (*Philadelphia,* U.S.)
Best actress	Crissy Rock (*Ladybird, Ladybird,* U.K.)

Césars (France), awarded in February 1994

Best film	*Smoking–No Smoking* (France; director, Alain Resnais)
Best director	Alain Resnais (*Smoking–No Smoking,* France)
Best actress	Juliette Binoche (*Trois Couleurs Bleu,* France)
Best actor	Pierre Arditi (*Smoking–No Smoking,* France)
Best first film	*The Scent of Green Papaya* (France/Vietnam; director, Tran Anh Hung)

Academy of Motion Picture Arts and Sciences (Oscars, U.S.), awarded in Los Angeles in March 1994

Best film	*Schindler's List* (U.S.; director, Steven Spielberg)
Best actor	Tom Hanks (*Philadelphia,* U.S.)
Best actress	Holly Hunter (*The Piano,* Australia)
Best supporting actor	Tommy Lee Jones (*The Fugitive,* U.S.)
Best supporting actress	Anna Paquin (*The Piano,* Australia)
Best director	Steven Spielberg (*Schindler's List,* U.S.)
Best foreign-language film	*Belle Époque* (Spain; director, Fernando Trueba)

British Academy of Film and Television Awards, awarded in April 1994

Outstanding British film of the year	*Shadowlands* (director, Richard Attenborough)
Best film	*Schindler's List* (U.S.; director, Steven Spielberg)
Best director	Steven Spielberg (*Schindler's List,* U.S.)
Best actress	Holly Hunter (*The Piano,* Australia)
Best actor	Anthony Hopkins (*The Remains of the Day,* U.K.)
Best supporting actress	Miriam Margolyes (*The Age of Innocence,* U.S.)
Best supporting actor	Ralph Fiennes (*Schindler's List,* U.S.)

Cannes International Film Festival, France, awarded in May 1994

Palme d'Or	*Pulp Fiction* (U.S.; director, Quentin Tarantino)
Jury Grand Prize	*Burnt by the Sun* (Russia/France; director, Nikita Mikhalkov) *To Live* (China/Hong Kong; director, Zhang Yimou)
Jury Prize	*La Reine Margot* (France; director, Patrice Chéreau)
Best director	Nanni Moretti (*Caro diario,* Italy)
Best script	Michel Blanc (*Grosse Fatigue,* France)
Best actor	Ge You (*To Live,* China/Hong Kong)
Best actress	Virna Lisi (*La Reine Margot,* France)
Caméra d'or for best first film	*Petits Arrangements avec les morts* (France; director, Pascal Ferran)
International Critics' Prizes	*Exotica* (Canada; director, Atom Egoyan) *Bab el-Oued City* (Algeria/France; director, Merzak Allouache)

Karlovy Vary International Film Festival, Czech Republic, awarded in July 1994

Grand Prix	*Mi hermano del alma* (Spain; director, Mariano Barroso)
Best director	Timur Bekmambetov, Gennady Kayumov (*Peshawar Waltz,* CIS)
Special Jury Prize	*Lekce Faust* (Czech Republic/France; director, Jan Svankmaer) *Przypadek pekoscinskiego* (Poland; director, Grzegorz Krolikiewicz)
Best actor	Max von Sydow (*Time Is Money,* France)
Best actress	Natasha Richardson (*Widows' Peak,* U.K.)

Venice Film Festival, Italy, awarded in September 1994

Golden Lion	*Before the Rain* (France/U.K./Macedonia; director, Milcho Manchevski) *Vive l'amour* (Taiwan; director, Tsai Ming-liang)
Special Jury Prize	*Natural Born Killers* (U.S.; director, Oliver Stone)
Silver Lion	*Heavenly Creatures* (New Zealand; director, Peter Jackson) *Little Odessa* (U.S.; director, James Gray) *The Bull* (Italy; director, Carlo Mazzacurati)
Volpi Cup, best actor	Xia Yu (*In the Heat of the Sun,* China)
Volpi Cup, best actress	Maria de Madeiros (*Três Irmãos,* Portugal)
Best director	Gianni Amelio (*Lamerica,* Italy)

San Sebastián International Film Festival, Spain, awarded in October 1994

Best film	*Dias contados* (Spain; director, Imanol Uribe)
Best director	Danny Boyle (*Shallow Grave,* U.K.)
Best actress	Ning Jing (*Red Firecracker, Green Firecracker,* China)
Best actor	Javier Bardem (*Dias contados, The Detective and Death,* Spain)
Special Jury Prize	*Von Lauter Feigheit gibt es kein Erbarman* (Germany; director, Andreas Gruber)

European Film Awards (Felix), awarded in Berlin in November 1994

Best European film of the year	*Lamerica* (Italy; director, Gianni Amelio)
Best young European film of the year	*Woyzeck* (Hungary; director, Janos Szasz) *Le Fils du requin* (France; director, Agnés Merlet)

1994 Tokyo International Film Festival, awarded in Kyoto, Japan, in October 1994

Grand Prix	*The Day the Sun Turned Cold* (Hong Kong; director, Ho Yim)
Special Jury Prize	*47 Ronin* (Japan; director, Kon Ichikawa)
Best director	Ho Yim (*The Day the Sun Turned Cold,* Hong Kong)
Best actress	Debra Winger (*A Dangerous Woman,* U.S.)
Best actor	Niu Zhenhua (*Back to Back, Face to Face,* China)

The original story was by Quentin Tarantino, whose own film *Pulp Fiction* certainly celebrated violence as a show, without any moral perspective. Winner of the grand prix of the Cannes Film Festival, the film's knowing combination of comedy, violence, and larger-than-life characters marked Tarantino as a considerable, if controversial, talent.

Much vaunted in advance, Kenneth Branagh's adaptation of *Mary Shelley's Frankenstein* demonstrated that fidelity to a literary original is small merit if the original in itself provides a bad screenplay. A modern horror story, Anne Rice's *Interview with the Vampire* also made a less-than-satisfying transition in Neil Jordan's film version.

There was a vogue for remakes of classic children's books; the Australian director Gillian Armstrong directed a new version of Louisa May Alcott's 1868–69 novel *Little Women*, Caroline Thompson a new *Black Beauty*, and Daniel Petrie *Lassie*. Richard Donner's witty comedy western *Maverick* was based on the popular television series of the late 1950s, while the long-ago popular *The Little Rascals* was adapted as a feature film, directed by Penelope Spheeris.

Comedy flourished on several levels. Peter Segal's *Naked Gun 33¹/₃: The Final Insult* returned to the proven formula of earlier films in the series. John Waters' anarchic *Serial Mom* featured Kathleen Turner as a respectable suburban housewife with a penchant for murder. Woody Allen's *Bullets over Broadway* was an enchanting comedy about a 1920s theatrical production whose embarrassing backer is a Prohibition-age gangster.

Notable films by African-Americans included Boaz Yakin's impressive debut with *Fresh,* about a 12-year-old boy learning the metaphorical lessons of the chess game and purposefully fending off the hazards of ghetto life. Charles Burnett's *The Glass Shield* was a passionate denunciation of a corrupt law-enforcement system. The first African-American woman to direct a Hollywood feature, Darnell Martin brought imagination and humour to issues of race and gender in *I Like It like That,* the story of a young black woman defying handicaps to make a career. Disorganized and raucous, Spike Lee's *Crooklyn* was nonetheless more authentically personal than some of the director's recent works. After observing and living in their Los Angeles neighbourhoods for many years, Allison Anders focused on the life of Hispanic girl gangs in *Mi vida loca*.

Notable directorial debuts included the actor Tom Noonan with *What Happened Was . . . ,* an intriguing and perceptive chamber piece about a date between two misfits. The coscreenwriter of *Mary Shelley's Frankenstein,* Frank Darabont, directed his own script, *The Shawshank Redemption,* an observant and unconventional study of two men in prison. Jan De Bont succeeded with the aptly named thriller *Speed.* And Steve James, Frederick Marx, and Peter Gilbert made *Hoop Dreams,* a powerful documentary about two African-American teenage boys from Chicago housing projects who play high-school basketball and dream of stardom in the National Basketball Association.

Several established figures chose unconventional themes. Robert Redford's *Quiz Show* re-created a national scandal of the 1950s in which Charles Van Doren, a brilliant scion of a distinguished academic family, was exposed as having colluded as a competitor in a fixed television quiz show. *Ed Wood,* Tim Burton's first film based on a true story, was an affectionate portrait of the director of 1950s camp movies. Disappointedly slight after his masterly *Short Cuts,* Robert Altman's *Ready to Wear (Prêt-à-porter)* was an informal entertainment set against the real-life world of the Paris fashion business. Robert Benton's adaptation of Richard Russo's novel *Nobody's Fool* was a delicate portrait of small-town life and character, notable for performances by Paul Newman and Jessica Tandy, who completed one more film, *Camilla,* before her death on September 11 (*see* OBITUARIES).

Louis Malle made an effective low-budget film, *Vanya on 42nd Street,* from André Gregory's exceptional theatre production of David Mamet's new version of Chekhov's play, with Wallace Shawn in the title role. Lawrence Kasdan retold the history of *Wyatt Earp* (played by Kevin Costner) with a concern for historical thoroughness that somewhat impaired its dramatic impact. In *Mrs. Parker and the Vicious Circle,* Alan Rudolph chronicled the lives of Dorothy Parker and her literary contemporaries. Jodie Foster coproduced and played the title role in *Nell,* a story of a young woman

Playing the title character in *Forrest Gump,* Tom Hanks (right) offers candy to strangers at a bus stop as he prepares to tell them the story of his life. The gentle, sentimental comedy of the experiences of a man with an IQ of 75 was one of the year's biggest hits with both audiences and critics.
EVERETT COLLECTION

who had been raised apart from civilization in backwoods North Carolina, directed by Michael Apted.

British cinema was impoverished by the death of two of its most influential directors, from different generations, Lindsay Anderson and Derek Jarman (*see* OBITUARIES). The final work of the latter, just before his death in February, was *Glitterbug,* an assembly of his early Super-8 home movies, some of them predating his professional film career, which provided an evocative picture of a quarter century of London artistic life.

In commercial terms the runaway British success of the year, making an instant international star of its leading actor, Hugh Grant, was *Four Weddings and a Funeral,* a modest film, at least in terms of its budget, that revealed the irresistible attractions of romantic comedy, given a clever, literate script (Richard Curtis), appreciative direction (Mike Newell), and elegant performances.

The work of other British feature directors showed a renewed interest in social themes. Suri Krishnamma's *Oh Mary This London* offered a rough and realistic view of the capital through the eyes of three young Irish people arriving to seek a new life there. Ken Loach's *Ladybird, Ladybird* focused on the battles of an unmarried mother against the too-intrusive social services. Antonia Bird's *Priest,* about the difficulties of a dedicated, homosexual Catholic priest, revealed a director of exceptional narrative sense. The extraordinary Amber Collective of Newcastle continued to make impressive low-budget films on the life of the region; *Eden Valley* told the story of a delinquent youth who finds a new life in a rural community.

Several young directors made creditable first features, often on very low budgets. Caleb Lindsay's *Chasing Dreams,* produced for £18,000, was a humorous, vital, sensitive, and finally optimistic story of dispossessed teenagers. Peter Mackenzie Litten directed a bright, intelligent, accessible

Arthur Agee, one of the subjects of the documentary film *Hoop Dreams,* grabs a rebound. The highly praised motion picture portrayed five years in the lives of two Chicago high-school basketball stars and their families, showing their successes and their crises.

comedy about homosexual life and love under the shadow of AIDS, *To Die For.* A former television director, Danny Boyle, made *Shallow Grave,* an uninhibited black comedy.

From Wales, Paul Turner's *Wild Justice* used a thriller about rape, murder, and revenge as a reflection on male violence against women. From Ireland, Mary McGuckian's *Words upon the Window Pane* adapted a play by W.B. Yeats about a séance conducted by a fraught spiritualist in a house once inhabited by Jonathan Swift's adored Stella, while Maurice O'Callaghan's *Broken Harvest* told the story of an Irish boyhood in the 1950s.

Australian production was vigorous and varied. The surprise international success of the year was Staphan Elliott's *The Adventures of Priscilla, Queen of the Desert,* a high-spirited road movie about three drag artists off to do a gig. P.J. Hogan's *Muriel's Wedding* related with telling humour its heroine's efforts to escape provincial boredom by seeking adventure and matrimony in Sydney.

Other original subjects were John Duigan's *Sirens,* a fictionalized comic incident from the life of the painter Norman Lindsay; Anne Turner's *Dallas Doll,* a sharply observed comedy about the intrusion of a disturbed and fraudulent American woman into an ordered middle-class family; John Ruane's adaptation of Tim Winton's mystical novel *That Eye, The Sky,* about another doubtful American stranger disrupting a troubled rural family; and Bill Bennett's *Spider and Rose,* a sinewy story about the cross-generational friendship of an elderly widow and an antisocial young man.

In New Zealand, Peter Jackson abandoned the low-budget, bad-taste shockers that had made his reputation to direct *Heavenly Creatures,* a stylish re-creation of a celebrated 1950s murder committed by two young schoolgirls. Made by a Maori cast and crew, Lee Tamahori's *Once Were Warriors* tellingly observed the social and cultural disintegration and also the resilience of aboriginal people living in urban ghettoes.

Out of an extensive production, the only Canadian film of the year to attract considerable international attention was Atom Egoyan's *Exotica,* the story of a tax man's entanglement with the people of a strange strip joint.

Continental Europe. Popular taste for expansively mounted adaptations of national classics seemed to be on the wane, and both Patrice Chéreau's toughly realistic interpretation of Dumas' *La Reine Margot* and Yves Angelo's adaptation of Balzac's *Le Colonel Chabert* proved commercial disappointments. Much more successful critically and commercially were the second and third parts of Krzysztof Kieslowski's *Trois Couleurs* trilogy, coproduced with Poland. *Blanc* (*White*) told of the breakup of an affair between a Polish man and a French woman and the man's return to postcommunist Poland; *Rouge* (*Red*), pursuing the unifying theme of coincidence and chance, was the story of a strange, edgy liaison between a young student and an embittered onetime judge. A very different box-office success was Luc Besson's stylized gangster story *Léon.*

In his two-part, six-hour *Jean la Pucelle,* Jacques Rivette retold, without adornment, the story of Joan of Arc, played touchingly by Sandrine Bonnaire. A coproduction with Italy and Belgium, Gérard Corbiau's *Farinelli Il Castrato* offered a finely staged and intriguing account of the career of the real-life 18th-century musical idol.

In *Grosse Fatigue,* one of the year's more notable comedies, Michel Blanc played a double role: his own real-life self and a double whose outrageous, even criminal behaviour becomes an increasing embarrassment. Marcel Ophuls, the undisputed master of the investigative documentary, completed the first of two parts on the media coverage and destructive folly of the wars in former Yugoslavia.

The Hollywood Conquest

BY DAVID ROBINSON

Hollywood did not set out to conquer the world. There was just no way of stopping it. The U.S. began its domination of the world's screens at the time of World War I, but only in the final decade of the century did Hollywood's hegemony reach such proportions that critics could talk seriously about the likelihood of extinction for many national film-production industries.

The reasons for this sudden crisis point are not entirely clear, though they are evidently linked to a changing industrial economy in Hollywood, whose success has come more and more to rely on a small annual group of productions that command phenomenal audience appeal and earnings counted in hundreds of millions of dollars. In 1993 and 1994 such films included *Jurassic Park, The Fugitive, Aladdin, The Lion King,* and *Forrest Gump.*

The universal appeal of such films as these had, by the mid-1990s, given the U.S. control of some 85% of the world film market—excluding India and China (although at the close of 1994, Hollywood distributors were making strenuous efforts to break into the huge Chinese market). In almost every country the box office was dominated week after week by U.S. titles. In Britain all 20 of the most successful films at the box office in 1993 were U.S., and American films earned some £300 million of the total British box-office earnings of £319 million. The situation was comparable in Denmark, Spain, and Sweden, and Hollywood films were increasingly taking over the screens of the former communist countries of Europe. Even in those countries with formerly strong national production, such as Japan, France, and Italy, as many as 8 out of the weekly top-10 films were regularly of U.S. origin. Until 1990 France was the only country in Europe to maintain a majority audience for its own product; by 1994 even that bastion had fallen, and it was estimated that French films accounted for no more than 30% of the national box office.

The historical explanation of Hollywood domination is geodemographic. Apart from China, the United States has the largest monolingual audience in the world. Thus, even the most expensive Hollywood film has the possibility of recouping its cost in the domestic theatrical market alone. Everything else, including television, video, and overseas distribution, is profit. This economy supports a level of production and marketing with which no other country can compete.

Hollywood films have an overwhelming attraction for a world audience because they are more opulent in production (in 1993 the average budget for a Hollywood film was $15 million, compared with $2 million for a British picture) and thus are more polished and assured in technique and more calculatedly popular in appeal. Moreover, the great vertically integrated Hollywood corporations, involved in both production and marketing, provide an incompara-

ble infrastructure for distribution, marketing, and publicity throughout the world. The economic self-sufficiency of U.S. cinema permits its film and television productions to be sold abroad at the most competitive prices.

Hollywood, too, has always had the means and perception to buy up talent from the rest of the world. During the past 30 years, 20% of the winners of Academy Awards have held British passports, though their work was for the most part performed on American-produced films. Successful foreign stars, from Pola Negri and Greta Garbo to Ingrid Bergman, Sophia Loren, Mel Gibson, Sean Connery, Liv Ullman, Daniel Day-Lewis, Max von Sydow, Joan Chen, and Emma Thompson, have constantly been recruited by the American cinema, impoverishing their native production at the same time as they enrich Hollywood's.

More than with other industries, this domination by one nation has enormous economic, industrial, and cultural implications. For generations the dreams of the impressionable, film-consuming young in every part of the world have been formed in the American image. Blue jeans, Coca-Cola, and McDonald's are universal. The German director Wim Wenders voiced this concern when he said, "People increasingly believe in what they see and they buy what they believe in. In the long run if we ever give up the European film industry as a pawn, then all the other European industries will suffer in the future. People use, drive, wear, eat and buy what they see in the movies."

Certainly, to crush indigenous film industries is neither in the American plan nor in the American interest. As the Italian director Bernardo Bertolucci pointed out, in the long run Hollywood itself would stand to lose by the collapse of European and other world cinemas: "Hollywood has absorbed a lot of European talent over the years. If European creative talent withers away from lack of financial resources, Hollywood will ultimately lack the oxygen it needs."

In Britain and Italy the survival of some level of film production has so far almost entirely been due to the film-production programs of television companies. The German and French cinemas, on the other hand, have depended upon a high level of financial support from the government. Europeans—particularly the French—fought fiercely to have these self-defensive measures exempted from the provisions of the 1993 General Agreement on Tariffs and Trade (GATT).

The effect of GATT as originally framed would have been to prohibit any future national policies designed to protect the indigenous product against foreign importations and to freeze any similar arrangements already in place. The final confrontation was between the Americans, who objected to any form of protectionism for national film and television industries, and the French, who resented the "industrial" tag and demanded a "cultural exception" that would exclude the audiovisual media from GATT regulations altogether. The Europeans eventually won their GATT point, and the U.S. seemed ready to recognize that the price of cultural freedom may sometimes be commercial control.

The GATT debate nevertheless stirred European filmmakers to ask if all the troubles of European cinema could be blamed wholly on Hollywood, or even the threat of GATT, or if there is not something inherently wrong with the European film itself. Audiences—U.S. as well as European—will go to see a European film—*Cyrano de Bergerac, The Crying Game, Four Weddings and a Funeral*—if it appeals to them. The trouble is that very few European pictures do make that appeal. The 1994 success of *Four Weddings and a Funeral,* however, made many begin to suspect that the surest way to compete with Hollywood is to make good pictures.

David Robinson is a film critic and historian in London and author of A History of World Cinema *and* Chaplin: His Life and Art.

One of 1994's undoubted masterworks in Italy was Gianni Amelio's *Lamerica,* which related the odyssey of an Italian in postcommunist Albania as he progresses from would-be exploiter to identification with the destroyed population, distracted by the impossible dream of emigration. Carlo Mazzacurati's *The Bull* also examined the fortunes of post-communist Europe, through the picaresque adventures of an Italian traveling from country to country, attempting to sell a stolen prize bull.

The most personal film of the year was Nanni Moretti's *Caro diario,* a series of musings on Rome, life, and his own troubled health. Mario Brenta's *Barnabo delle mantagne* was an austere yet richly textured study of a forest ranger, beset with moral anxieties, in the Dolomites in the 1920s.

In another lacklustre year, the most interesting German productions were Jan Schutte's *Auf Wiedersehen Amerika,* a charming, off-beat, melancholy, and beautifully played comedy about an elderly Jewish couple returning to Poland after 30 years in the U.S.; the actor Klaus Maria Brandauer's handsome, if somewhat remote, adaptation of Thomas Mann's novella *Mario und der Zauberer;* and Hans W. Geissendörfer's *Justice,* based on Friedrich Dürrenmatt's farce about a poor lawyer morally undone by a powerful client.

In Belgium the writer Jan Bacquoy made his directorial debut with *La Vie sexuelle des Belges,* a witty, unexpectedly charming recollection of a lifetime of sexual experience in the stifling moral atmosphere of his country as he sees it.

Finland's star filmmaker Aki Kaurismäki made a wryly comic road movie, *Take Care of Your Scarf, Tatjana,* about two dour Finns unwillingly involved with a pair of garrulous Russian women hitchhikers. The second film of the talented Veikko Aaltonen, *Pater Noster,* was an extraordinary composition of the past and present memories of a man returning to his home and the ghosts of his anxious childhood.

From Iceland, Fridrik Fridriksson's *Movie Days* was an evidently autobiographical reminiscence of a 1960s boyhood world, coloured by the excitements of the movie theatre. In *Beyond the Sky,* Berit Nesheim of Norway created a quirky and touching story about the friendship of a difficult teenage girl and a grumpy old teacher whom she helps to rediscover an ancient lost love.

The runaway commercial success of the year in Russia was Yury Mamin's neatly handled and human comedy *Window to Paris,* about a group of St. Petersburg citizens who discover a magical window in their awful apartment house that leads directly into the bewildering delights of the French capital. Several directors returned from working abroad. Andrey Konchalovsky's *Ryaba My Chicken* revisited the village where he shot his long-banned 1967 film *Asya's Happiness* to present a farcical view of the peasants' nonadjustment to the demise of communism. Konchalovsky's brother, Nikita Mikhalkov, played the main role in his own masterly *Burnt by the Sun,* which begins deceptively as a summer idyll at a dacha overflowing with an extended, Chekhovian family but then moves startlingly into the terror and betrayals of Joseph Stalin's 1930s. Mikhalkov also directed *Anna 6–18,* an assembly of home movies of his daughter. Boris Frumin, after 16 years of exile in the U.S., made *Viva, Castro!,* a reminiscence of the days of his own youth, and the confusions of farce and tragedy, cruelty and romance in the life of the early 1960s.

From Georgia came Eldar Shengelaya's mordant comedy *Information Express,* and from Kazakhstan, Talgat Temenov's enchanting lightweight romance *Love Station.*

Three Czech directors from Czechoslovakia's "new wave" of motion pictures in the 1960s returned to form— Jaromil Jires with a dark comedy-romance, *Helimadoe;* Karel Kachyna with a rural period drama, *The Cow;* and

Jiri Menzel with *The Life and Extraordinary Adventures of Private Ivan Chonkin,* a dated satire on the trials of a simple Russian soldier at the start of World War II. Also from the Czech Republic, Jan Sverak's science-fiction comedy about the power of television to suck the life force from humans, *Accumulator 1,* was rich in ingenious special effects.

From Poland, Dorota Kedzierzawska's *The Crow* was a small but exquisite study of a lonely little girl who runs away from home, taking with her a four-year-old whom she uses to fulfill her equivocal yearning to love and be loved, while Feliks Falk's *Summer of Love* was a sophisticated and elegant story of romance and manipulation in late Czarist Russia, based on an Ivan Bunin story.

Filmmakers in former Yugoslavia endeavoured to deal with the present reality. A collective of Bosnia and Herzegovinian directors exposed the anguish of their city in *MGM Sarajevo (Man, God, The Monster).* Boro Draskovic's *Vukovar Poste Restante* was a Romeo and Juliet fable about the love of a Croat woman and a Serbian man. A Serbian director, Zivojin Pavlovic, adapted Fyodor Dostoyevsky's "The Eternal Husband" to the conditions of present-day Serbia, centring the story on two friends caught up in the war in the devastated city of Vukovar.

Latin America. From Argentina, Luis César d'Angiolillo's *Matar al abuelito* subtly combined romantic mystery and black comedy in its story of an old gentleman rejuvenated by a young woman, to the annoyance of his prospective heirs. Gustavo Graef Marino's *Johnny Cien Pesos* from Chile was a striking political thriller, highlighting issues of crime and society in Latin America. Arturo Ripstein in Mexico chose to film the legend rather than the literal reality of the life of Lucha Reyes, a great popular singing star of the 1930s, *La reina de la noche.* In *Sin compasion,* Peru's most prominent filmmaker, Francisco J. Lombardi, updated Dostoyevsky's *Crime and Punishment* to present-day Lima.

A surprising and charming film from Cuba, *Fresa y chocolate,* directed by Tomás Gutiérrez Alea and Juan Carlos Tabio, provided a touching yet funny plea for human tolerance. It related the uneasy relationship and eventual friendship of a macho, naive, homophobic young Marxist idealist and an unrepentant homosexual.

North Africa and the Middle East. One of the best and most searching Arab films of the year, Nabil Maleh's *The Extras* used the encounter of a young couple to intimate the social and sexual oppression of young Syrians. In North Africa there was sporadic but lively activity. Yussef Chahine's attempt in Egypt to reconstruct the story of the biblical Joseph aroused fierce religious controversy. From Algeria, Merzak Allouache's *Bab el-Oued City* was a fine, moral drama generated out of the rise of religious intolerance. In Tunisia a woman director, Moufida Tlatli, directed the exquisite *The Silences of the Palace,* a story of the court life of the Tunisian beys early in the century and of a woman's revolt against the suppression and exploitation of her sex.

Iranian cinema continued to show sturdy renascence. Iran's outstanding film artist Abbas Kiarostami revisited the recently earthquake-devastated Koker region for *Through the Olive Trees,* a sweet story of an odd romance between two extras in a location film production. Kiyannush Ayyari's *The Abadanis* was an attractive experiment, updating the story of Vittorio de Sica's *Bicycle Thief* to the present reality of Abadani war refugees in Tehran.

In Israel, Claude Lanzmann made the third part of his trilogy on Jewish history, following *Pourquoi Israel?* and *Shoah. Tsahal* was an exploration of the history and ideological foundations of the Israeli army. The most attractive Israeli feature films were Dan Wohlman's *The Distance,* a sensitive

Irene Jacob plays Valentine, a woman who has a redeeming effect on a corrupt judge in the film *Red*, the final work in Polish director Krzysztof Kieslowski's trilogy *Three Colors*. The three films—*Blue, White,* and *Red*—were set, respectively, in France, Poland, and Switzerland.
EVERETT COLLECTION

analysis of the effect on family relationships of separation by emigration, and Rami Na'Aman's *The Flying Camel,* a comedy in which the encounter of a Jewish professor and an Arab garbageman bridges historical differences.

Asia. Alongside the continuing mass production of popular genre films, a few independent and idiosyncratic films stood out in India. They included poet-filmmaker Buddhadeb Dasgupta's *Shelter of the Wings,* an exquisite fable about a humble bird catcher who falls in love with his quarry, and Adoor Gopalakrishnan's *The Servile,* a polished and finely controlled portrait of a Kerala farmer's willing subjugation to a feudal village chief in 1960s Karnakata.

Chinese authorities introduced repressive new measures to control coproduction with neighbouring countries. The country's leading director, Zhang Yimou, was prevented from traveling after receiving international praise for his film *To Live,* which followed the fortunes of a little family battered by Chinese history from the 1940s to the Cultural Revolution. As the wife and mother, Gong Li (*see* BIOGRAPHIES) was especially outstanding.

Other filmmakers managed to coexist with the system. The new Chinese market economy provided the theme for Zhou Hiaowen's sinewy rustic comedy *Ermo,* about a peasant woman driven by a single-minded business sense. A coproduction with Hong Kong, Huang Jianxin's *Back to Back, Face to Face* provided a brisk satire on contemporary urban life and bureaucracy.

Hong Kong's superstar Jackie Chan enjoyed continuing success with *Drunken Master II,* directed by Lau Kar-leung—a sequel to the film that first established his fame. Wong Kar-wai's *Chungking Express,* with its vivid style and sound track and off-centre stories about the romantic distractions of two young cops, achieved the instant status of a cult film.

Taiwan moved into the forefront of Asian production. Tsai Ming-liang's *Vive l'amour*—a humorous and human study of the meeting of three lonely, nonconforming people in contemporary Taipei—shared the main prize at the Venice festival. Ang Lee, the director of *The Wedding Banquet,* showed again his gift for observing social and emotional subtleties in *Eat Drink Man Woman,* the story of a master chef and his relations with his three problematic daughters.

Cherd Songsri's literate and well-staged *Muen and Rid,* based on the life of a 19th-century advocate of women's rights, Amdang Muen, proved the most successful film in Thai cinema history. Rithy Panh's *Rice People* was an often poetic and finally tragic picture of the privations of peasant life in Cambodia's rice fields, forever at the mercy of the elements.

Africa. Few African films came to prominence during the year. Cheik Boukouré's *Le Ballon d'or,* from Guinea, used the story of a young boy's ambitions to become a world-class soccer player as an effective metaphor for central issues of the less developed nations. (DAVID ROBINSON)

Nontheatrical Films. Science, art, humour, and insightful fiction characterized nontheatrical award-winning films in 1994. *Blue Planet Theater,* a beautiful environmental science documentary about water, won recognition in four international festivals, including first place at Oeiras, Port. The producer was Bill Call of Scripps Institution of Oceanography, University of California at San Diego.

Behind the Scenes with Robert Gil De Montes, by Jane Garmey of Learning Designs of WNET in New York City, captured the grand prize plus Ministry of Foreign Affairs prize at the 20th Japan Prize Competition in Tokyo. De Montes, a painter, shows how colour can create moods or depth and even accentuate the dreamlike quality of the subject.

Three student films stood out, each winning a major award. *The Painter* by Noah Emmerich of New York University was the story of mistaken identity of a famous Italian painter; it won the Premi Extraordinari in Badalona, Spain. The Gold Monkey of Mons, Belgium, was shared by *The Roof,* a story of crisis among three generations of roofers, made by Paul Harris-Boardman of the University of Southern California, and *A Dollar and a Dream,* which spins the dilemma of an immigrant subway janitor who dreams of and wins a Ferrari but does not know how to drive, by Ian Corson of New York University. (THOMAS W. HOPE)

See also Art: *Photography;* Television and Radio.

This article updates the *Macropædia* article MOTION PICTURES.

Museums

Once again in 1994 France seemed to dominate new museum developments in Europe. The official opening of the Grand Louvre at the end of 1993 was quickly followed by the inauguration of a parallel commercial development, the Carrousel du Louvre. Architect I.M. Pei wittily created a mirror image of his glass "pyramid" descending from the ground level into an elegant underground multipurpose mall. Revenue from the development was to be retained for the benefit of the museum. London museums were considering a similar plan. The £100 million project announced in July for the remodeling of the British Museum after the British Library moved to its new site at St. Pancras, London (*see* LIBRARIES), was more traditional but called for a restoration of the great courtyard and retention of the famous circular reading room. The new Crown Jewels museum within the historic Tower of London included a travolator floor in front of the main display enabling the museum supervisor to control the viewing time of visitors. Madrid's Prado Museum, celebrating its 175th anniversary in 1994, also named a new director, José María Luzón Nogué, a university professor.

The Federal Museum of Contemporary German History opened amid controversy about both its Bonn location and its alleged bias against the former East Germany. An even greater outcry was heard over the opening of the new wing at the Peace Memorial Museum in Hiroshima, Japan. The emphasis of the museum shifted from presenting the Japanese as victims of the horrific first act of atomic warfare to drawing attention to Japanese militarism, Hiroshima's important role in the munitions industry, and the use of slave labour in the arms factories. Ironically, the Smithsonian Institution in Washington, D.C., also drew fire from veterans groups and some members of Congress over plans to exhibit portions of the *Enola Gay,* the airplane that dropped the atomic bomb on Hiroshima, in its National Air and Space Museum.

World War II in Europe surfaced again as further admissions were made in Russia—including from St. Petersburg's famed Hermitage—concerning the whereabouts of long-lost museum collections seized in Germany in 1945. The Hermitage had other problems as well, as it was reportedly struggling with claims from former republics of the U.S.S.R., the Russian Orthodox Church, and even the Russian government itself, which, some feared, might be eyeing art treasures as an easy source of foreign exchange. A major new study, *The Rape of Europa: The Fate of Europe's Treasures in the Third Reich and the Second World War* by Lynn H. Nicholas, included details about the intention of the U.S. Department of State and some leading U.S. museums in the late 1940s to acquire paintings from German museums as war reparations—a timely reminder that Joseph Stalin was not alone in coveting German collections.

It became clear that the national museum in Kabul, Afghanistan, had been looted of many outstanding archaeological artifacts and antiquities over recent years. Large-scale losses were reported at the 9th–15th century Angkor Wat complex in Cambodia (a World Heritage List site), while the whole of the rich historic jewelry collection and many world-class antiquities were found to be missing from the national museum in Phnom Penh, reportedly sold by or with connivance of the former Pol Pot regime.

Large-scale museum losses in Africa led to a conference in Bamako, Mali, of the International Council of Museums. The conference recommended the establishment in each country of an interagency authority for the rapid international dissemination of information about stolen cultural property. More conventional art crime in 1994 included the theft of Norwegian artist Edvard Munch's most famous work, *The Scream,* from the Oslo National Gallery on the eve of the Winter Olympics; the painting was eventually recovered. A burglary of the Museum of Modern Art in Stockholm later in the year seemed to follow an increasingly common pattern of "made-to-order" thefts of works of art.

Ground was broken on a number of large-scale museum projects around the world, including the long-planned National Museum in Wellington, N.Z., and two major new national science museums, one as part of the "Technopolis" development near Bangkok, Thailand, and another at "Science City" on the outskirts of Calcutta.

Government grants and private philanthropy supported U.S. museums handsomely in 1994. The Los Angeles County Museum of Art signed a 99-year contract with the county guaranteeing its funding at $14.2 million yearly; the museum itself had to provide matching funds for 80% of this public allocation. The museum also announced a large-scale expansion and launched a $5 million bond issue to fund a new sculpture garden. The Wight Art Gallery and the Grunwald Center for the Graphic Arts of the University of California at Los Angeles were to merge with, and move into the facilities of, the former Armand Hammer Museum. The San Diego Museum of Contemporary Art closed its original La Jolla facility for expansion, California State University at Long Beach planned to build a new museum facility, and the Newport Harbor Art Museum decided to double its gallery space.

In Pittsburgh, Pa., the Andy Warhol Museum was launched with 500 of its 3,000-work collection on display. The Carnegie Institution raised $15 million for the museum,

which rekindled controversy about the question of Warhol's importance in American art. Few questioned the importance of the National Museum of the American Indian, which debuted in the old Customs House in lower Manhattan in October. Plans called for construction of a permanent home for the one million-item collection in Washington, D.C., by the year 2001.

The Metropolitan Museum of Art in New York City opened two grand galleries: the Greek and Roman collections, through the gift of Robert and Renee Belfer, and its first permanent galleries given to Indian and Southeast Asian art, through a gift of Florence and Herbert Irving. The Brooklyn (N.Y.) Museum received the largest gift in its history, $5 million, from Morris A. Schapiro in honour of his brother, the well-known art historian Meyer Schapiro. New York City's Guggenheim Museum received two large gifts— $10 million from Ronald O. Perelman, with which the museum launched a $100 million capital campaign, and possibly as much as $10 million from Samuel J. and Ethel LeFrak. Having lost the sponsorship of the Guggenheim, the Massachusetts Museum of Contemporary Art in North Adams was reconstituted as a complex to support dance, music, theatre, and educational activities. The Detroit (Mich.) Institute of Arts completed its $24 million fund-raising drive. The Lila Wallace–Reader's Digest Fund continued to award large grants to various institutions, including the Walker Art Center, Minneapolis, Minn.; the Art Institute of Chicago; and the Hampton (Va.) University Museum.

Challenge grants from the U.S. National Endowment for the Arts, which required matching funds in the ratio of 3:1 from the institutions themselves, were awarded to the

THEO WESTENBERGER

Children's toys of 19th-century Plains Indians are part of the holdings of the George Gustav Heye Center in New York City. The centre, which opened in 1994, was the first of three facilities planned for the Smithsonian's National Museum of the American Indian.

Cincinnati (Ohio) Art Museum, the Jewish Museum in New York City, and the San Jose (Calif.) Museum of Art. The U.S. National Archives began a three-year move to a new satellite site on the campus of the University of Maryland at College Park.

For the first time in its history, the Smithsonian Institution chose a nonscientist as its director; I. Michael Heyman (*see* BIOGRAPHIES), a lawyer and management expert, replaced retiring Robert McC. Adams.

(PATRICK J. BOYLAN; JOSHUA KIND)

See also Art; Auctions and Collections.
This article updates the *Macropædia* article MUSEUMS.

Music

CLASSICAL

From "Encore! The Three Tenors" concert at Dodger Stadium in Los Angeles to the firing of Myung-Whun Chung from the Paris National Opéra, from pianist Van Cliburn's ill-starred 60th-birthday concert tour to soprano Kathleen Battle's dismissal from the Metropolitan Opera (*see* BIOGRAPHIES), the world of classical music scarcely lacked for headlines in 1994. There were happier developments, too, including the inauguration of Glyndebourne's opera house and Tanglewood's Seiji Ozawa Hall. Resignations from and appointments to major artistic posts also promised lively developments in years to come.

The prize for spilled ink almost certainly went to the "Three Tenors" extravaganza, internationally telecast and issued in both audio and video formats (by the pop label Atlantic). Backed by palm trees, 15-m (50-ft) waterfalls, giant classical columns, the Los Angeles Philharmonic, and the Los Angeles Opera Chorus, Luciano Pavarotti, Placido Domingo, and José Carreras thrilled the masses (some of whom paid as much as $1,000 for seats) and gave critics plenty to huff about. At least it was not the sad affair that Van Cliburn's 17-city U.S. tour, with the Moscow Philharmonic, became. Having spent most of 16 years in hibernation, the pianist planned a triumphant comeback with two concerti he had been most associated with in happier days: the Tchaikovsky First and the Rachmaninoff Third. When the Rachmaninoff came unglued in a preview performance, it was dropped in favour of solo pieces, and even the Tchaikovsky only occasionally hinted at past glories.

Just five years after Pierre Bergé had dismissed Daniel Barenboim as music director of the not-yet-open Bastille Opera and appointed dark horse Myung-Whun Chung, Chung himself got the ax from Bergé's successor, Hugues Gall. With the Paris Opéra losing more than $9 million a year, Gall wanted to renegotiate Chung's salary, set to reach $1.5 million by the year 2000; also at stake was control over artistic decisions. Dismissed during rehearsals for Verdi's *Simon Boccanegra*, Chung went to court and got a stay of execution; he was allowed to remain through the opening production, after which he left—with a buy-out reportedly worth $1.3 million. Financial and political complications also figured strongly at the Rome Opera in the sackings of superintendent Giampaolo Cresci (who was replaced by Giorgio Vidusso) and artistic director Gian Carlo Menotti. Kathleen Battle's much-reported dismissal from the Metropolitan Opera came after years of reports of temperamental behaviour.

Another relationship that went sour, although far less dramatically, was Franz Welser-Möst's with the London Philharmonic, but the announcement of his 1996 departure was tempered by his appointment as music director of the

Zürich (Switz.) Opera, effective in 1995. Giuseppe Sinopoli and London's Philharmonia Orchestra also agreed to part ways, their relationship a casualty, in part, of years of savage notices in the press. Citing a serious financial crunch, Matthew Epstein resigned as general director of the Welsh National Opera. Elaine Padmore left the plucky Wexford (Ireland) Festival to devote herself to the Royal Danish Opera; her Wexford successor was to be Luigi Ferrari. Pittsburgh, Pa., was hit by two high-visibility resignations: Lorin Maazel's from the music directorship of the Pittsburgh Symphony Orchestra (effective in 1996) and Tito Capobianco's as general director of the Pittsburgh Opera (in 1997).

There were two top-level appointments at the Kennedy Center in Washington, D.C.: Placido Domingo's as artistic director of the Washington Opera (effective in 1996) and Leonard Slatkin's as music director of the National Symphony Orchestra, succeeding Mstislav Rostropovich (in 1996). Domingo was also named artistic adviser and principal guest conductor of the Los Angeles Music Center Opera; Slatkin would leave the St. Louis (Mo.) Symphony Orchestra. Jukka-Pekka Saraste took up his duties as music director of the Toronto Symphony Orchestra, as did Andrew Litton with the Dallas (Texas) Symphony Orchestra; Eiji Oue was named music director of the Minnesota Orchestra, succeeding Edo de Waart.

In England, Glyndebourne's new 1,200-seat theatre, 400 seats larger than its predecessor, got good reviews for both looks and sound. So did the new Seiji Ozawa Hall, a 1,200-seat concert facility at Tanglewood, the Boston Symphony Orchestra's summer home in western Massachusetts. A fire destroyed the Gran Teatro del Liceo in Barcelona, the largest and most prestigious opera house in Spain, but a rebuilding project was immediately announced. The Paris Opéra announced a plan to renovate the venerable Garnier Opera House to accommodate approximately a third of the company's performances, and the Santa Fe (N.M.) Opera unveiled plans to rebuild its hillside amphitheatre, roofing over the hitherto exposed middle section of seating.

Awards included the Pulitzer Prize for Gunther Schuller's *Of Reminiscences and Reflections* (*see* BIOGRAPHIES) and the Grawemeyer Award, from the University of Louisville, Ky., for Toru Takemitsu's *Fantasma/Cantos*. Noncompetitive performance awards went to pianists Ralf Gothoni (the Gilmore Artist Award, presented by the Irving S. Gilmore International Keyboard Festival in Kalamazoo, Mich.) and Garrick Ohlsson (the Avery Fisher Prize). Deaths included those of composers Lejaren Hiller and Witold Lutoslawski (*see* OBITUARIES), conductor Norman Del Mar, pianists Artur Balsam, Rudolf Firkusny (*see* OBITUARIES), and György Cziffra, musical philanthropist Avery Fisher, and pianist-comedian Donald Swann (*see* OBITUARIES).

Opera. Germany and The Netherlands provided particularly fertile ground for new operas. Commissioned by Brussels' Théâtre de la Monnaie, Peter Schat's *Symposium*—based on the death of Tchaikovsky and the controversial theory that he committed suicide to avoid exposure as a homosexual—was premiered by the Netherlands Opera. The Holland Festival also saw the first performances of Guus Janssen's *Noach*, Guo Wenjing's *Wolf Cub Village*, and Xiao-Song Qua's *Death of Oedipus*. In Germany the Schwetzingen Festival offered the world premiere of Eckehard Mayer's *Sansibar*, a coproduction with the Bavarian State Opera in Munich, and the fourth Munich Biennale included new operas by Tania Leon, Robert Zuidam, Paul Engel, Benedict Mason, Nikolai Horndorf, and Jörg Widman, the last for marionettes. Other world premieres included Rodion Shchedrin's *Lolita* (Royal Opera, Stockholm), Judith Weir's *Blond Eckbert* (English National Opera, followed by the

Santa Fe Opera), Conrad Susa and Philip Littell's *Dangerous Liaisons* (San Francisco Opera), Dominick Argento's *The Dream of Valentino* (Washington Opera), Robert Moran's *The Dracula Diary* and Noa Ain's *The Outcast* (both Houston [Texas] Grand Opera), Bruce Saylor's *Orpheus Descending* (Lyric Opera of Chicago Center for American Artists), and Ilkka Kuusisto's *Miss Julie* (Vaasa Opera, Finland). A new Wagner *Ring* at the Bayreuth Festival—directed by Alfred Kirchner, designed by Rosalie, and conducted by James Levine—drew as many hisses as huzzahs.

In addition to brand-new works and repertory chestnuts, a number of recent operas and works off the beaten path showed up around the world. Among them were Clementi's *Carillon* (La Scala, Milan), Dvorak's *Dimitrij* (Bavarian State Opera), Delibes's *Lakmé* (New York City Opera), Massenet's *Hérodiade* (San Francisco Opera), Rimsky-Korsakov's *Kashchei the Immortal* and *The Maid of Pskov* (Kirov Opera, St. Petersburg), Rachmaninoff's *Aleko* and *The Miserly Knight* (Bolshoi Theater, Moscow), Rutland Boughton's *The Immortal Hour* (Juilliard Opera Center, New York City), Ingvar Lidholm's *Ett Droemspel* (Royal Opera, Stockholm), Hans Werner Henze's *The Bassarids* (Hamburg [Germany] State Opera), Aribert Reimann's *Das Schloss* (Deutsche Oper, Berlin), Philippe Boesmans' *La Ronde* (Chatelet, Paris) and *Reigen* (La Monnaie, Brussels), and Louis Andriessen's *Rosa* (Netherlands Opera). The Santa Fe Opera commissioned three new operas by American composers who had not previously essayed the form: David Lang, Tobias Picker, and Peter Lieberson.

Orchestras and Festivals. A series of major snowstorms early in the year played havoc with concert producers in the eastern United States. One storm made Philadelphia's Academy of Music inaccessible to many of the Philadelphia Orchestra's musicians, but with the soloists for the February 11 concert of Wagner opera excerpts housed in nearby hotels, music director Wolfgang Sawallisch decided to go ahead with the program. An audience of some 700 hardy souls was treated to the singing of soprano Deborah Voigt, tenor Heikki Siukola, and bass René Pape, with the maestro accompanying at the piano.

New concerti by living composers continued to figure prominently in orchestral programs. World premieres came from Krzysztof Penderecki (for clarinet, introduced by Sinfonia Varsovia at the Kissingen [Germany] Summer Festival), Rodion Shchedrin (for trumpet, Pittsburgh Symphony), John Adams (for violin, Minnesota Orchestra), Ned Rorem (English horn, New York Philharmonic), Richard Danielpour (for cello, San Francisco Symphony), and Christopher Rouse (for flute, Detroit Symphony). New second symphonies by Philip Glass and the late Stephen Albert were introduced by, respectively, the Brooklyn (N.Y.) Philharmonic and the New York Philharmonic. The latter orchestra also gave the world premiere of Alfred Schnittke's Seventh Symphony, while the National Symphony gave the first North American performance of his Sixth, introduced on a 1993 Russian tour. The Chicago Symphony Orchestra premiered major new works by Pierre Boulez (*Notations V–VIII*) and Elliott Carter (*Partita*). What might have seemed a passé medium, the oratorio, appeared to be alive and well to judge by new works by Edison Denisov (*St. Matthew Passion*, premiered at the Frankfurt [Germany] Festival), Paul Dessau (*Haggada*, Hamburg Music Festival), and Minas Alexiades (*Viva la Vida*, Frankfurt Festival).

Claudio Abbado signaled the new, post-Karajan era at the Salzburg (Austria) Easter Festival with a spectacular postmodern production of Mussorgsky's *Boris Godunov*.

The new theatre at Glyndebourne, which opened in 1994, sits among the hills of East Sussex, south of London. Replacing a smaller facility that dated to the opera festival's beginnings in 1934, the house was inaugurated with a production of Mozart's *The Marriage of Figaro*.

The Spoleto Festival USA, in Charleston, S.C., proved that it was quite capable of carrying on even after the contentious departure of founder Menotti. The Santa Fe Chamber Music Festival and the Aspen (Colo.) Festival honoured Schnittke's 60th birthday, but heart attacks kept the composer from attending. The Cardiff (Wales) Festival devoted attentions to works by female composers, while the Edinburgh Festival marked the centenary of Emmanuel Chabrier's death with stagings of *L'Étoile* and *Le Roi malgré lui,* plus a concert performance of the unfinished *Briséïs.*

Recordings. The record industry continued the trend toward huge boxed-set reissues of materials from its vaults. Without so much as an anniversary excuse, BMG came out with a 65-compact disc (CD) compilation of all of violinist Jascha Heifetz' RCA recordings, and Teldec issued a 60-CD repackaging of the pioneering period-instruments Bach cantata recordings of Nikolaus Harnoncourt and Gustav Leonhardt. From Koch Schwann came 24 double-disc releases of historic recordings from the Vienna State Opera. Philips produced a 21-CD Svyatoslav Richter compendium, and BMG honoured Pierre Monteux with a 15-CD collection. Among the most welcome of these megarepackagings was Deutsche Grammophon's (DG's) reissue of the Strauss opera recordings of Karl Böhm, whose collaborations with the composer lent a special authority to his interpretations.

Gramophone magazine's Record of the Year prize went to Krystian Zimerman's DG traversal of the Debussy preludes. Other notable new recordings included a Berlioz *Les Troyens* from Charles Dutoit and the Montreal Symphony (Decca/London), an extensive survey of Samuel Barber songs by Cheryl Studer and Thomas Hampson, with pianist John Browning (DG), and two more operas in Decca/London's "Entartete Musik" series: Berthold Goldschmidt's *Der gewaltige Hahnrei* and Viktor Ullmann's *Der Kaiser von Atlantis.* Among the most interesting books of the year were Frederic Spotts's exhaustively researched *Bayreuth: A History of the Wagner Festival* and Humphrey Burton's *Leonard Bernstein,* the latter a more measured consideration than the earlier—and hotly controversial—Joan Peyser biography. The most remarkable music-related release of all may have been François Girard's inventive—but also surprisingly penetrating—movie, *Thirty-two Short Films About Glenn Gould.*

(SCOTT CANTRELL)

JAZZ

In 1994 several pioneers of free improvisation were especially newsworthy. Anthony Braxton (*see* BIOGRAPHIES) was one of two jazz artists to receive a MacArthur Foundation fellowship during the year. Only a fraction of his music had been documented on recordings, so the appearance of *Composition No. 96* (Leo), played by an orchestra directed by Braxton, was welcome even if it was not a major work in his canon. What was indisputably major was *Duo (London) 1993* (Leo), free improvisations that found Braxton and fellow saxophone innovator Evan Parker alternating intensity, lyricism, and sly humour in exhilarating interplay. In a companion CD, *Trio (London) 1993* (Leo), Braxton and Parker were joined by trombone original Paul Rutherford.

Parker, a British artist, rarely played in the United States, but when a New York radio station devoted an entire week to playing nothing but Parker recordings, in honour of his 50th birthday, he offered a three-day improvisation festival in the city, including duets with Americans such as Braxton, trumpeter Paul Smoker, and tenor saxophonist Joe Lovano, and then embarked on a brief U.S. tour. Meanwhile, Parker's new recordings multiplied, including *Corner to Corner* with John Stevens (Ogun) and *Imaginary Values* (Maya) with bassist Barry Guy and drummer Paul Lytton.

The catalyst of the British free-improvisation scene was drummer John Stevens, who led a series of Spontaneous Music Ensembles ranging from duets to big bands; Stevens died in 1994, the year several of his early recordings, including *Karyobin* (Chronoscope), from 1968, were reissued. The most determinedly devoted of free improvisers, guitarist Derek Bailey, released the second volume of his *Guitar Improvisations* (Incus) and toured in the United States in 1994, including Chicago concerts where he duetted memorably with multiple saxophonist Roscoe Mitchell.

The battle lines between young jazz revivalists and their more exploratory elders continued to be entrenched. Trumpeter Wynton Marsalis, who increasingly wrote Ellington-like arrangements, introduced his extended tribute to African-American religious services, *In This House, on This Morning,* in concerts and on recording (Columbia), and the responses were typically enthusiastic or dismissive, depending on whether reviewers accepted Marsalis' own biases. Innovator Cecil Taylor, the most influential living jazz pianist, rented Lincoln Center's Alice Tully Hall for his 65th birthday concert, his first in New York City in two years; apart from its musical merits, the concert was an important symbolic gesture, since Taylor had been excluded from the official Jazz at Lincoln Center series, of which Marsalis was a founder. The most remarkable young lions to emerge in 1994 were from Los Angeles—the B Sharp Jazz Quartet, whose eponymous debut CD (Mama Foundation) introduced a sparkling hard-bop perspective and original repertoire.

Like Braxton, saxophonist Ornette Coleman received a MacArthur Foundation grant in 1994 and, perhaps more remarkably, formed a jazz quartet with outstanding musicians Geri Allen (piano), Charnett Moffett (bass), and Denardo Coleman (drums). Coleman was not quite ready to abandon his two-decades-long preoccupation with his free jazz-rock Prime Time band, however, and at the San Francisco Jazz Festival he offered a multimedia concert with both groups. He also announced the formation of Harmolodic Records, a cooperative venture with Verve, to document works by himself as well as by other artists. It was a coup by Verve, which was observing its 50th anniversary and which held an all-star concert at Carnegie Hall to celebrate.

The Louis Armstrong Archives, including music manuscripts and recordings, opened under the aegis of Queens College, New York. The collection was to be housed in a museum in Armstrong's home in Queens, and part of the collection was in a touring exhibit, "Louis Armstrong: A Cultural Legacy," sponsored by the college and the Smithsonian Institution. While Delmark was reissuing a near-classic, *Last Testament* with trumpeter Bunk Johnson, who claimed to have taught Armstrong and who was a key figure in the 1940s traditional jazz revival, Jazzology offered 44 discs, including no fewer than eight Johnsons, of New Orleans jazz from the pioneering American Music recording series.

For die-hard LP collectors, Blue Note rereleased 12 items from its 1960s catalog on limited-edition, heavy-duty LPs, and Michael Cuscuna's mail-order Mosaic label offered boxed sets by Benny Goodman's 1944–55 small groups, Serge Chaloff (the finest bop baritone saxophonist), Eddie Condon, and Jimmy Smith, among others, on LP as well as CD. There were boxed CD sets by two seminal instrumentalists, guitarist Django Reinhardt (Blue Note), including his 1930s Hot Club of France Quintet masterpieces, and pianist Bud Powell (Blue Note, Verve), including his early 1950s classics. Other recordings of note in 1994 included Peter Brötzmann's tribute to Albert Ayler, *Die like a Dog* (FMP); Ernest Dawkins' New Horizons Ensemble in *South Side Street Songs* (Silkheart); Damon Short's *All of the Above*

(Southport); and *Calling All Mothers* (Quinnah) by the NRG Ensemble. New issues recorded years earlier attracted special attention: Randy Weston Sextet, *Monterey '66* (Verve); Charlie Haden, *The Montreal Tapes* (Verve); and Fred Anderson-Steve McCall, *Vintage Duets* (Okka Disk).

Live jazz in 1994 included festivals ranging from the daringly programmed Vancouver (B.C.) Jazz Festival to New York City's cautious, conservative JVC Jazz Festival, where rival repertory bands, the Carnegie Hall Jazz Band and the Lincoln Center Jazz Orchestra, held a concert together. In Quebec the Victoriaville new music festival returned after a year's absence, and the Montreal Jazz Festival celebrated its 15th year with 350 concerts in 12 days. The Istanbul Jazz Festival went on in the face of fierce protests by Kurdish separatists and Islamic fundamentalists and included Okay Temiz' Magnetic Band, which joined jazz to traditional Turkish instruments and rhythms.

The year's deaths included critic Leonard Feather, bandleader and singer Cab Calloway, composer Antonio Carlos Jobim, singer Carmen McRae, trumpeter Red Rodney, and guitarist Joe Pass. (*See* OBITUARIES.) Among others who died were longtime Ellington clarinetist Jimmy Hamilton, drummer Connie Kay, trumpeter Max Kaminsky, guitarist Sonny Sharrock, bassist Ahmed Abdul-Malik, and West Coast bandleader Shorty Rogers.   (JOHN LITWEILER)

POPULAR

Major pop artists Pink Floyd, the Eagles, the Rolling Stones, Barbra Streisand, Billy Joel, and Elton John undertook tours in 1994, restoring the summer concert business to prosperity after several slow years. Pink Floyd toured in support of *The Division Bell,* the group's first studio album in seven years. Dramatic, sweeping, and laced with the sonorous guitar work of front man David Gilmour, the album received a warm welcome from fans, who bought 465,000 copies in its first week of release. The Rolling Stones also had a new album, *Voodoo Lounge,* ready for the public as they began their world tour. The album found the Stones in good form, relying again on the blues-influenced guitar work of Keith Richards and Ron Wood and the inimitable vocals of Mick Jagger. The album never topped the U.S. pop chart, however, but was held at number two by the motion-picture soundtrack of the Walt Disney film *The Lion King.* With music by Elton John, lyrics by Tim Rice, and three performances by John, the Disney album stayed at the top of the pop charts for nine weeks before yielding to the second album by the Philadelphia-based rhythm-and-blues quartet Boyz II Men. This group's success signaled the ongoing popularity of vocal-harmony groups in the rhythm-and-blues field.

The ballad "I Swear" (written by Nashville songwriters and a hit earlier for country singer John Michael Montgomery) was recorded by All-4-One, another harmony quartet, and stayed at number one on the pop charts for 11 weeks during the summer, tying Elvis Presley's "Don't Be Cruel"/"Hound Dog" as the third most successful single of the rock era. R. Kelly and Babyface dominated rhythm and blues during the year, Kelly with his lascivious "Bump n' Grind," Babyface with the sultry ballad "I'll Make Love to You," written and produced for Boyz II Men.

Soundgarden followed fellow Seattle, Wash., rock bands Nirvana, Pearl Jam (*see* BIOGRAPHIES), and Alice in Chains to the top of the pop album chart with *Superunknown,* the band's fourth album. The thriving Seattle rock scene was dealt a severe blow, however, when Kurt Cobain (*see* OBITUARIES), front man and creative force for Nirvana, died in April of a self-inflicted gunshot wound. Pearl Jam staged a hugely successful tour early in 1994, playing songs from

In Our Lives: 30th Anniversary of the Beatles' First U.S. Visit

The frenzied fandom known as Beatlemania was already in full swing in Britain when the Beatles (John Lennon, Paul McCartney, George Harrison, and Ringo Starr) landed on Feb. 7, 1964, at the New York City airport renamed for Pres. John F. Kennedy, whose November 1963 assassination the nation still mourned. The lovable mop tops from Liverpool, England, proved to be a sensation. Some 5,000 teenaged baby boomers greeted their arrival, but it was two nights later, when 73 million Americans watched the Beatles on "The Ed Sullivan Show," that an explosion in popular culture occurred that was still sending shock waves 30 years later.

Popular music had been in a pallid state. Elvis Presley had returned from the U.S. Army "tamed," Buddy Holly was dead, and wholesome white performers flourished with sanitized cover versions of rock-and-roll songs whose African-American originators were still mostly denied radio play. Rock and roll survived in Liverpool, however, and seamen brought in records from the U.S. The Beatles—influenced by Presley, Holly, Little Richard, Chuck Berry, and the Everly Brothers—claimed rock and roll as their own and reintroduced it to American teenagers, who had become a new social class with leisure time and money to spend.

By writing their own songs, the Beatles changed the role of pop performers. Initially, Lennon-McCartney and Harrison compositions were straightforward love songs, but in the "serious" folk songs of Bob Dylan the Beatles recognized new possibilities for the themes, language, and imagery of pop songs. Where once pop music had perhaps aimed principally to entertain, it increasingly became intimately involved in the most contentious political and social issues of the day.

In the process the Beatles became standard-bearers for a cultural revolution in which youth was the common denominator. From 1964 to their breakup in 1970, they seemed to be at the forefront of not just pop music, fashion, and film but also young people's politics and thought. Their albums were like messages from the front, somehow perfectly capturing the zeitgeist. Chameleon-like, the Beatles also appeared to lead the way toward higher consciousness, experimenting with hallucinogens, Eastern mysticism, and the politics of peace. Ultimately, whether they led or were just the most conspicuous followers is perhaps less important than their status as a symbol of their generation.

In 1994 the three remaining Beatles (Lennon was assassinated in 1980) collaborated on a 10–12-hour documentary of their history for British television. They also were recording together again, with—on at least one song—Lennon's voice provided by tracks made before his death. Moreover, *Live at the BBC,* a double CD featuring 56 songs the Beatles recorded for British radio between 1962 and 1965, and *Backbeat,* a feature film chronicling the band's early days, were released in 1994.   (JEFF WALLENFELDT)

Vs., their album released in late 1993. The band canceled plans for a summer tour when it became involved in a dispute over ticket prices and the service charges added by a national ticketing corporation.

Nine Inch Nails whose rock music had been described as industrial because it featured blasts of noise similar to those heard in foundries and factories—emerged from Woodstock '94 with a higher profile. The band members' spontaneous decision to cover themselves in mud, as many in the rain-soaked audience had done already, and the band's aggressive, futuristic stage show, in which front man Trent Reznor destroyed musical instruments and caromed about the stage, made Nine Inch Nails the most memorable performers of the highly touted festival. More than 500,000 attended the event in upstate New York marking the 25th anniversary of the original Woodstock festival. Among the artists who performed were veterans Joe Cocker, Aerosmith, Bob Dylan, and Crosby, Stills & Nash, along with newer acts Metallica, Porno for Pyros, Rollins Band, Candlebox, and Green Day.

Rolling Stones (from left) Mick Jagger, Ron Wood, and Keith Richards perform in Giants Stadium in New Jersey in a concert on their 1994 tour. The band was one of a number of veteran groups that toured during the summer, helping to revitalize the music concert business.
EBET ROBERTS

The San Francisco Bay-area punk-pop trio Green Day had a major-label debut album, *Dookie,* that sold more than two million copies and inspired a resurgence of punk bands. Driven by guitars and featuring edgy, disenchanted lyrics, Green Day also played throughout the summer at the alternative Lollapalooza festival. The Los Angeles-based record label Epitaph helped revitalize the punk movement with its roster of popular punk bands, including Offspring, Bad Religion, NOFX, and Rancid. Eric Clapton's collection of blues covers, *From the Cradle,* topped the pop charts, becoming the first blues album ever to reach the number one spot. Clapton included such favourites as Elmore James's "It Hurts Me Too" and Muddy Waters' "Hoochie Coochie Man." R.E.M., in recent years featuring a more acoustic sound, returned to hard-edged power pop with *Monster.* Among artists rising to prominence for the first time during 1994 were the angst-ridden, roots-oriented Counting Crows, a Berkeley, Calif., outfit; Seattle-based hard rockers Candlebox; Los Angeles-based session regular and singer-songwriter Sheryl Crow; and forthright hip-hop-influenced singer Me'Shell NdegéOcello.

In country music, Tim McGraw, a Louisiana native and son of former major league baseball star Tug McGraw, had the year's top-selling album, *Not a Moment Too Soon.* McGraw's hard country inflection and traditional instrumentation yielded the hits "Indian Outlaw," "Don't Take the Girl," and "Down on the Farm." Garth Brooks toured Australia and Europe but for the first time in his career did not release a new album during the year. The McDonald's restaurant chain sold two million copies of a collection of Brooks's earlier recordings. Johnny Cash received widespread critical acclaim for *American Recordings,* a new album featuring only Cash and his guitar.

Rock and Roll Hall of Fame inductees included Rod Stewart, Duane Eddy, the Grateful Dead, Bob Marley, Elton John, the Animals, the Band, and John Lennon for his post-Beatles work. Merle Haggard was chosen for the Country Music Hall of Fame.   (JAY ORR)

In Britain, as in the United States, the fragmentation of pop continued, and the diversity of musical styles could be judged from the nominees for the year's Mercury Prize, which had become the accepted barometer of British (and Irish) musical trends. In purely economic terms, the British pop industry continued to be dominated by dance music, particularly the electronics- and synthesizer-dominated house and techno styles that provided the soundtracks at discos and the controversial mass dance gatherings known as "rave" parties. The success of Manchester's M People and their *Elegant Slumming* album, the winner of the year's Mercury, was a reflection of the continued importance of dance music. The more soulful side of the new techno-pop was reflected by the success of Massive Attack, whose first album in three years, *Protection,* was a subtle blend of soul, funk, jazz, and reggae, with cool, sophisticated vocals from the Nigerian singer Nicollete. It was also an excellent year for Massive Attack's former singer, Shara Nelson, now a soloist specializing in atmospheric soulful ballads.

The influence of guitar-based pop—the predominant form from the 1960s to the 1980s—persisted, thanks to a handful of bands such as Oasis, Suede, and Blur. Blur's distinctively English album *Parklife* was a best-seller that revived memories of the Kinks and the Small Faces. Paul Weller, the onetime leader of punk-era heroes the Jam and then the more sophisticated Style Council, helped the new guitar-rock revival along with his *Wild Wood* and *Live Wood* albums, which echoed such 1960s and '70s heroes as Van Morrison and Traffic.

Veterans who had opted for lengthy periods of retirement returned in 1994 to find that their audience had not deserted them. Bryan Ferry produced a long-awaited selection of new songs on his *Mamouna* album, which was praised for sounding like his best latter-day work with Roxy Music—not that surprising since Ferry was helped by former Roxy members Brian Eno and Phil Manzanera. Other comebacks included Traffic, now reduced to just Steve Winwood (on keyboards) and Jim Capaldi (percussion) from the original band. Their new album, *Far from Home,* was less well received than their live shows, which included the Traffic trademark of extended improvised solos on almost every song. Those nostalgic for British pop from a later era applauded Elvis Costello's decision to team up once again with his original backing band, the Attractions. Their comeback album, *Brutal Youth,* marked Costello's return to snappy, clever pop styles and provided a stark contrast to his previous set, which had been recorded with a string quartet.

It was another excellent year for African music. South Africa's first multiracial elections and Nelson Mandela's election as president provided the opportunity for celebratory concerts inside and outside the country. The most ambitious such event, held in London, was the biggest-ever gathering of black South African musicians. It included Yvonne Chaka Chaka, a major success across Africa, reggae singer Lucky Dube, and those veterans of South Africa jazz and pop Hugh Masekela and his former wife, Miriam Makeba. The continent's best-known female singer after Makeba was Angelique Kidjo, born in Benin but living in Paris. Her new album, *Aye,* showed how international some African music had become. It was partly recorded in Minneapolis, Minn., with production work from Prince's engineer, and partly in London and Paris, and it succeeded because the Western funk and classy production work never swamped her majestic singing and energetic self-written songs.

Outstanding albums also originated in Third World trouble spots. Cecile Kayirebwa's *Rwanda*—recorded in exile—was a disconcertingly charming, relaxed set that provided a reminder of the beauty of the central African state before it was torn apart by civil war and genocide. Khaled's *N'ssi*—also recorded in exile—was a rousing demonstration of *rai* music, the Algerian pop style still hated by the country's fundamentalists (who murdered a rival *rai* star during the year). From Haiti came Boukman Eksperyans with *Kalfou Danjere,* an album that mixed harmonic chanting and echoes of African, blues and reggae styles with a political message. This "voodoo/political" band, which supported Jean-Bertrand Aristide, was none too popular with the country's military rulers, who threatened the band and banned its music from the radio.   (ROBIN DENSELOW)

See also Dance; Motion Pictures; Television and Radio; Theatre.
This article updates the *Macropædia* article The History of Western MUSIC.

Physics

Physicists in 1994 continued to be fascinated by the behaviour of matter on the largest and smallest scales. Both areas of interest were indulged by the announcement in June that a detector at the Los Alamos (N.M.) National Laboratory had monitored eight events that could represent the first direct evidence for a conjectured property of neutrinos called oscillation.

Neutrinos are extremely light particles—for decades they had been thought to be entirely massless—that are produced in abundance in nuclear reactions (as in the Sun). They travel through both space and solid matter at almost the speed of light. Neutrinos come in three types and, according to the oscillation theory, can change from one type to another as they go on their way. To make these transformations, however, neutrinos are required to have a tiny amount of mass. Apart from the intrinsic interest of observing such a curious phenomenon, physicists are intrigued by neutrino oscillation for two reasons. First, if neutrinos do oscillate, the phenomenon could explain why scientists detect fewer neutrinos coming from the Sun than theory

predicts. This so-called solar neutrino problem has persisted for more than two decades, since the first solar neutrino detectors were built. But the detectors designed to catch solar neutrinos passing through the Earth are sensitive to only one type of neutrino. If that type is produced inside the Sun as theory predicts but then oscillates into a mixture of types en route to Earth, the behaviour could explain the deficit measured for the original type.

The second reason for interest in neutrino oscillation is the requirement that neutrinos have mass. If they do, they exert gravitational effects and thus could account for at least some of the "dark matter" that is now thought to make up at least 90% of the mass of the universe. There is clear astronomical evidence, from the way that galaxies rotate and move about in clusters, that the bright stars and galaxies observable with telescopes or other instruments are embedded in much larger quantities of dark, or nonluminous, matter. The universe contains so many neutrinos—about a billion for every atom of ordinary matter—that even a small mass for each neutrino would add up to a lot of mass over the whole universe. Neutrinos, however, cannot be the only kind of dark matter in the universe. The year also brought further support of a finding announced in 1993 that galaxies like the Milky Way are embedded in dark halos made up of massive, comparatively small objects (dubbed MACHOs, for massive compact halo objects), rather like very faint stars or giant planets. The MACHOs were revealed by the way in which their gravitational influence magnified light from distant stars, making the stars flicker brightly as the MACHOs passed in front of them.

Particle physicists were cautiously optimistic that high-energy experiments at the Fermi National Accelerator Laboratory near Chicago had detected the long-sought top quark. The researchers would say only that the evidence was "persuasive," although it seemed to fit the last piece into the jigsaw puzzle of particle physics. Everyday matter is thought to be made up of just 12 types of particles in two families of six particles each. One family, the leptons, consists of the electron and its partner, the electron neutrino, together with two successively heavier equivalents of the electron, the muon and the tau particle, plus their own neutrino partners. The other family, the quarks, also consists of three pairs, dubbed up and down, charmed and strange, and top and bottom. All of these particles, except the top quark, have already been detected in particle accelerator experiments. The as-yet-tentative addition of the top quark completes the set and suggests that physicists' model of what matter is made of really is valid and complete.

The next task would be to use the completion of the particle puzzle to develop a better understanding of what went on during the conditions of extremely high density, pressure, and temperature that existed shortly after the birth of the universe, in the big bang itself. Physicists from several universities around the world were trying to re-create the conditions that existed in the big bang by smashing beams of heavy ions together head on at enormous speeds.

Ions are atoms given a positive charge by being stripped of one or more negatively charged electrons. The positive charge provides a "handle" by which the ions can be gripped in magnetic fields and accelerated to speeds that are a sizable fraction of the speed of light. The aim is to produce a transient sea of free-moving quarks and gluons called the quark-gluon plasma. (Gluons are the entities that carry the strong force that binds quarks together into particles such as protons and neutrons, in a way analogous to that in which an exchange of photons—quantum packets of electromagnetic energy—between charged particles generates the electromagnetic force between the particles.)

Preliminary experiments were under way at CERN (European Laboratory for Particle Physics) in Geneva and at Brookhaven National Laboratory, Upton, N.Y. To get a feel for the extreme conditions involved, one may consider what happens when the nucleus of an atom of gold that has been accelerated to 0.999957 the speed of light collides with another gold nucleus head on at the same speed. The greatest naturally occurring density of matter in the universe today is in the atomic nucleus. Albert Einstein's special theory of relativity shows, and many experiments have confirmed, that at this speed the mass of the nucleus is increased to 108 times the mass that it has when stationary. At the same time, it contracts to just $\frac{1}{108}$ of its rest length along the line of flight. In round terms the nucleus is 100 times heavier and 100 times smaller than when it is at rest, so it has increased in density 10,000 times. In the collision the two overlapping gold nuclei briefly create a density 20,000 times greater than that of an ordinary atomic nucleus.

Each nucleus is made up of protons and neutrons, and each proton and neutron is made up of three quarks. Under the extreme conditions generated in the collision—conditions that once existed in the big bang itself—the quarks from one nucleus interact directly with quarks from the other nucleus. The quarks are ripped from their nuclei, and new particles are created out of the pure kinetic energy associated with the collision, in line with Einstein's famous equation $E = mc^2$ (or, rather, $m = E/c^2$).

As of 1994, experimenters had gone an estimated one-fifth of the way toward reaching these extreme conditions, using collisions involving nuclei of sulfur instead of the heavier gold. The first, relatively low-energy, experiments with gold beams were carried out during the year. As particle physicists study successively bigger "little bangs" of this kind, they hope to unravel the secrets of how the universe exploded out of the big bang.

While experimental successes in understanding how the world works were made, 1994 also saw a revival of the debate about what it all means, reminiscent of the great debates of the quantum pioneers 60 years earlier. Quantum mechanics is the theory that describes the behaviour of matter on the very smallest scale. Among its many curious features, the theory says that an entity such as a photon or an electron can be described either as a solid particle, like a tiny billiard ball, or as a wave moving through space, like ripples on a pond. Einstein received his Nobel Prize for work demonstrating that photons of light exist as particles. Yet Geoff Jones, a British physicist, claimed in 1994 that it is "wrong and unnecessary" to describe light in terms of small, localized particles.

In a paper published in the *European Journal of Physics*, Jones showed a way in which the behaviour of light and other electromagnetic radiation can be explained entirely in terms of waves and claimed that the entity that physicists call a photon is simply the addition or extraction of one unit of energy from the electromagnetic field (the "pond") that the waves move through. On the other hand, Jones said that such entities as electrons really are particles and should not be treated as waves. Echoing once-unfashionable ideas of the quantum theorist David Bohm, Jones said that the apparent waviness of electrons is caused by a separate wave associated with electrons, which guides their behaviour.

All this might be just an esoteric curiosity for theorists and philosophers to debate were it confined to the world of electrons and photons. In 1994, however, researchers at the University of Paris-North, Villetaneuse, France, carried out experiments that seemed to show entire iodine molecules (I_2), each with a mass 254 times that of a neutron, behaving as waves. These were the largest objects for which the quan-

tum "wave-particle duality" was observed. With detectable quantum effects verging into the everyday world, the debate about the real meaning of quantum mechanics seemed set for a major revival at year's end.   (JOHN GRIBBIN)

This article updates the *Macropædia* articles ATOMS; The COSMOS; MECHANICS: *Quantum Mechanics;* Principles of PHYSICAL SCIENCE; SUBATOMIC PARTICLES; The PHYSICAL SCIENCES: *Physics.*

Populations and Population Movements

DEMOGRAPHY

At midyear 1994, world population stood at 5,607,000,000, according to estimates prepared by the Population Reference Bureau. The 1994 figure was 600 million higher than in 1987 and represented an increase of about 90 million over the previous year. The annual rate of increase declined to about 1.6% in 1994 from 1.64 in 1993, the result of birthrate declines in both less developed and industrialized nations. Each day world population increased by 245,000: 386,000 births and 141,000 deaths. Over 80% of the population growth in industrialized countries occurred in the United States. Data from recent censuses in 20 countries were reported to the United Nations in 1994. (*See* WORLD DATA: *Area and population.*)

Controlling population growth in the less developed countries (LDCs) was a major concern at the International Conference on Population and Development, sponsored by the UN in Cairo in September. (*See* Sidebar, page 257.) Worldwide, 57% of married couples reportedly used contraceptive methods of some type in 1994. Fully 49% were using a "modern" method such as clinically supplied contraceptives or sterilization. In LDCs 54% were practicing some form of family planning, and 48% were using a modern one. When China is excluded, however, only 34% of LDCs were using a modern method, the figure dropping to a low of 11% in sub-Saharan Africa.

Worldwide, 33% of the population was below the age of 15 in 1994, but the figure was 39% in LDCs besides China. In the more developed countries (MDCs), 20% were below age 15, a figure that dropped as low as 16% in Germany. Only 4% of the population in LDCs was over the age of 65, compared with 13% in the MDCs. Nearly half—43%—of world population in 1994 lived in urban areas. In the LDCs 35% of the population was classified as urban, although this was still low when compared with 74% in the MDCs. Among the world's least urbanized countries was Burundi, with only 6% urban in 1994.

Less Developed Countries. LDCs accounted for an ever larger share of world population growth in 1994. Of the 90 million people added annually, about 97% were in the world's poorer nations. Women in LDCs bore an average of about 3.6 children during their lifetime, slightly more than double that of the MDCs. In LDCs excluding the large statistical effect of China's 1.2 billion population, women averaged 4.2 children each. This was far from the "two-child family" essential to slowing population growth to zero and stabilizing world population size. Worldwide, life expectancy at birth was 63 years for males and 67 for females. In MDCs the same figures were 71 and 78 and in LDCs 61 and 64, respectively. The 1994 world infant mortality rate stood at 63 infant deaths per 1,000 live births—10 in the MDCs and 69 in the LDCs.

Birthrates were beginning to decline in sub-Saharan Africa for the first time in history. Demographic and Health Survey (DHS) data reported more drops in the total fertility rate (TFR). The TFR is the average number of children a woman would bear during her lifetime, assuming that the rate of childbearing in a given year remains constant. In Ghana the TFR fell to 5.5, from 6.0 previously, and Kenya's remarkable decrease continued, to 5.4 from about 8.0 in the 1980s. Botswana, prewar Rwanda, and Zimbabwe, among others, also reported drops. Nonetheless, new UN projections, released for the Cairo conference, showed that the population of Africa was expected to rise from 708 million in 1994 to 2.1 billion by 2050. Even this level of growth would occur only if the TFR dropped to about two children per woman by about 2040. In 1994 women in Africa still averaged about three times that number. In 1994 life expectancy was only 53 years for males and 56 for females in Africa, and the annual population growth rate was 2.9%.

Latin America's population stood at 470 million in 1994, with an annual growth rate of 2%. The TFR in this region remained a comparatively modest 3.2. The TFR in Latin America ranged from 5.4 in Guatemala to 1.8 in Cuba. Life expectancy stood at 65 for males and 71 for females in 1994.

Asia's population grew from 3.3 billion in 1993 to 3.4 billion in 1994, although it had the lowest growth rate of the less developed regions at 1.7%. Excluding China, however, the growth rate was 2%, the same as Latin America's. China's population, the world's largest, was 1,192,000,000; India was second with 912 million. China's birthrate remained at a low 18 births per 1,000 population, and its TFR was about 2 children per woman. India's TFR fell to 3.6, something of a milestone since fertility decline there was thought to have stalled closer to four children per woman. Life expectancy in Asia stood at 63 for males and 66 for females.

A number of countries—notably LDCs with low birthrates—were becoming concerned about shifts in the number of new labour-force entrants and aging populations. The East-West Center's Program on Population reported on such concerns among the "Asian tigers" as well; South Korea was said to be reducing public support for family-planning services, Taiwan now wished to raise its TFR from 1.7 to 2.1, Thailand was beginning to look at new policies

in the light of rapid birthrate decline, and Singapore had instituted programs to support couples with more than two children.

More Developed Countries. By 1994 Europe, with an annual growth rate of only 0.1%, had virtually reached zero population growth. In 1994 many of the republics of the former Soviet Union, including Russia's 148 million, were reclassified as European by the UN, raising Europe's population to 728 million. Fertility continued to plunge in Eastern Europe to the point where Bulgaria, Croatia, Estonia, Hungary, Latvia, Romania, Russia, and Ukraine now had natural decrease, or more deaths annually than births. According to data from Eurostat, the statistical agency of the European Union, Italy once again had the world's lowest TFR, 1.21, reclaiming that distinction from Spain, which had 1.24. Birthrates were also declining in France, with a TFR of 1.65, and in Ireland, with 2.03. Life expectancy in Europe stood at a high 69 for males and 77 for females, although the average was reduced by the addition of former republics of the Soviet Union to this region. Japan's life expectancy continued to set records at 76 for males and 82 for females.

United States. The population of the U.S. reached 260,-514,000 on May 1, 1994, up from 257,790,000 a year earlier. This represented an increase of 2,724,000, or 1.06%. The National Center for Health Statistics (NCHS) reported that during the 12 months ended in March 1994, natural increase—births minus deaths—amounted to 1,746,-000 (4,040,000 births and 2,294,000 deaths). The birthrate dropped to 15.6 births per 1,000 population, compared with 15.9 in the 12 months ended in March 1993. Preliminary estimates indicated that the U.S. TFR declined to 2.03 in 1993 from 2.08 in 1992 as the baby boomlet of the late 1980s and early 1990s had peaked. This was a significant trend because, were it not for immigration, a TFR below 2.0—the two-child family—would eventually result in population decline.

The age-adjusted death rate for the 12-month period ended February 1994 was 4% higher than for the same period in 1993, a fact attributed to more deaths associated with influenza outbreaks. The age-adjusted rate was 519.9 per 100,000 population, up from 501.5 for the same period one year earlier. The infant mortality rate for the period ended in March was 8.2 infant deaths per 1,000 live births, compared with 8.3 a year earlier. The NCHS reported that in 1992 life expectancy at birth rose to a new high, 75.7 years—79 for females and 72.3 for males. Life expectancy for white females approached 80 years, at 79.7, up from 79.6 a year earlier. Black males had a life expectancy of only 65.5 years in 1992. The 15 major causes of death accounted for 85% of all deaths in the year ended in February 1994, slightly less than one year earlier.

World's 25 Most Populous Urban Areas[1]

Rank	City and Country	City proper Population	Year	Metropolitan area Population	Year
1	Tokyo, Japan	8,082,286	1992 est.	29,200,000	1990 est.
2	New York City, U.S.	7,322,564	1990 cen.	18,087,251	1990 cen.
3	Seoul, South Korea	10,873,055	1991 est.	17,588,000	1989 est.
4	Osaka, Japan	3,288,464	1993 est.	16,210,000	1990 est.
5	São Paulo, Brazil	9,343,753	1991 cen.	15,416,416	1991 cen.
6	Mexico City, Mexico	9,815,795	1990 cen.	14,991,281	1990 cen.
7	Los Angeles, U.S.	3,607,700	1993 est.	14,531,529	1990 cen.
8	Shanghai, China	7,496,509	1990 cen.	13,341,896	1990 cen.
9	Moscow, Russia	8,789,200	1993 est.	13,150,000	1991 est.
10	Bombay, India	9,925,891	1991 cen.	12,596,243	1991 cen.
11	Buenos Aires, Arg.	2,960,976	1991 cen.	12,582,321	1991 cen.
12	London, U.K.	6,377,900	1991 cen.	12,275,600	1989 est.
13	Calcutta, India	4,399,819	1991 cen.	11,021,915	1991 cen.
14	Beijing, China	5,769,607	1990 cen.	10,819,407	1990 cen.
15	Rio de Janeiro, Brazil	5,473,909	1991 cen.	9,796,498	1991 cen.
16	Jakarta, Indonesia	8,259,266	1990 cen.	9,709,411	1990 cen.
17	Paris, France	2,156,766	1991 est.	9,319,000	1990 cen.
18	Tianjin, China	4,574,689	1990 cen.	8,785,402	1990 cen.
19	Cairo, Egypt	6,894,000	1994 est.	8,761,927	1986 cen.
20	Nagoya, Japan	2,158,713	1993 est.	8,432,000	1990 est.
21	Delhi, India	7,206,704	1991 cen.	8,419,084	1991 cen.
22	Chicago, U.S.	2,783,726	1990 cen.	8,065,633	1990 cen.
23	Manila, Philippines	1,876,194	1990 cen.	7,832,000	1990 cen.
24	Karachi, Pakistan	5,208,132	1981 cen.	7,702,000	1990 est.
25	Tehran, Iran	6,042,584	1991 cen.	6,773,000	1990 est.

[1]Ranked by population of metropolitan area.

Causes of death in the United States (year ended February 1994)	Estimated rate per 100,000 population
1. Diseases of the heart	290.4
2. Malignant neoplasms	207.2
3. Cerebrovascular diseases	58.9
4. Chronic obstructive pulmonary diseases	40.9
5. Accidents and adverse effects	34.1
6. Pneumonia and influenza	33.5
7. Diabetes mellitus	21.7
8. HIV infection	14.5
9. Suicide	11.7
10. Chronic liver disease and cirrhosis	9.7
11. Homicide and legal intervention	9.6
12. Nephritis, nephrotic syndrome, and nephrosis	9.6
13. Septicemia	8.0
14. Atherosclerosis	6.8
15. Certain conditions originating in the perinatal period	6.1

There were 2,329,000 marriages in the U.S. in the 12-month period ended in February 1994, down from 2,353,000 one year earlier. The marriage rate was 9 per 1,000 population, down from 9.2 in the previous 12-month period. The number of divorces dropped to 1,182,000 from 1,206,000 for the same two periods. A total of 880,014 immigrants were registered in 1993, compared with 810,635 in 1992. Including some remaining legalizations of illegals under immigration law, total fiscal year 1993 immigration amounted to 904,292. In 1994 immigration accounted for just over 30% of U.S. net population growth. (CARL V. HAUB)

See also World Data.

INTERNATIONAL MIGRATION

Pressures upon people in poor countries to migrate to escape civil wars, "ethnic cleansing," torture and murder, and economic dislocation as well as to find personal and economic security continued in 1994. So did the patterns of rich countries tightening refugee and immigration laws and procedures.

The governments of Switzerland and Germany signed an agreement in December 1993 providing that if it could be shown, within one year, that an asylum seeker or illegal immigrant had stayed in Germany or Switzerland before going to the second country, then he or she could be returned to the first country. The main Swiss political parties all backed the new "constraining measures" against asylum seekers announced by the government in December 1993. Germany more than doubled its expenditures on deportation in 1993. A Berlin court backed mass deportation of Vietnamese on the grounds that they were not threatened by political persecution at home and thus could be expelled under Germany's asylum laws. The Ministry of the Interior announced that more than 100,000 refugees from the rump Yugoslav areas of Serbia, Montenegro, and Kosovo should be deported. Pressure from Amnesty International (AI) forced the German government to extend the deadline for the repatriation of Croatian refugees to June 1995. Germany's commissioner for immigrants, Cornelia Schmalz-Jacobsen, expressed concern in October 1994 at the "rigorous deportation practices" that had been blamed for the deaths of 15 deportees since 1990.

French Interior Minister Charles Pasqua (*see* BIOGRAPHIES) set up a special police unit on January 15 to deal with immigration. Pasqua restated his intention to use chartered airplanes to deport illegals. Deportations of non-French nationals increased markedly after the new immigration laws of 1993 came into force. In one three-month period ended in June 1994, 2,666 people were deported, a 23% increase.

Pasqua announced in April that France would refuse to accept any more refugees fleeing Algeria in the event of the fundamentalist Islamic Salvation Front's taking power.

The government of The Netherlands introduced for the first time an Aliens Act that imposed carrier sanctions (fines for airlines and shipping companies that transported in undocumented or falsely documented passengers). The Dutch government continued negotiations with African governments to deploy military border police at their airports to assist in checking travel documents on flights to The Netherlands. Sweden led Europe in deporting asylum seekers, expelling a total of 16,861 in 1992–93. Between July and December 1993 more than £10 million was allocated to set up special police task forces charged with searching for and arresting refugees denied asylum.

In the United Kingdom many persons found that the 1993 Asylum and Immigration (Appeals) Act led to arbitrary and racist decision making on the part of immigration officials by removing rights of appeal against refusal of entry for visitors. In October AI issued a report, "Asylum-Seekers Detained in the United Kingdom," which found that "large numbers of vulnerable people are subjected to prolonged periods of incarceration, without adequate explanation and without an effective opportunity to challenge the basis on which they are held and seek their release, and often in conditions inappropriate to their status." By late 1994 the number of asylum seekers held in British prisons and immigration detention centres had doubled over the previous 18 months to more than 600. The High Court ruled in December 1993 that the Home Office could not ignore its own guidelines in deporting members of families established in Britain.

In the 1994 U.S. elections anti-immigrant feelings were sometimes encouraged by politicians and right-wing forces. California passed Proposition 187, the so-called Save Our State proposition, which would bar the estimated 1.7 million undocumented workers and their children living in California from receiving education and nonemergency medical care. Gov. Pete Wilson supported the proposition as a key issue in his reelection campaign. The measure ran into opposition immediately, and it seemed unlikely that it would withstand the certain court challenges. Operation Gatekeeper, a new program of the U.S. Border Patrol to staunch the stream of immigrants from Mexico, reported early successes in October.

On September 9 the U.S. and Cuban governments negotiated an end to the flood of Cuban refugees attempting

The Cairo Conference

World attention was focused on population issues as delegates from 175 countries gathered in Cairo on Sept. 5–13, 1994, for the International Conference on Population and Development. Previous population conferences had been held in Mexico City (1984) and Bucharest, Rom. (1974). The delegates in Cairo debated a 20-year Program of Action that had been drafted by the UN Population Fund, the conference organizers. Three provisions were considered essential to reducing fertility and holding the world population by the year 2050 to the "low" estimate of 7.8 billion (other projections ran as high as 12.5 billion): improved access to contraceptives, reduced child mortality, and promotion of women's rights to reproductive health. Language in the draft program favouring the empowerment of women

drew sharp attacks from fundamentalist regimes, and some Muslim countries boycotted the conference. Vatican City State promoted Pope John Paul II's crusade against abortion with a media campaign and pitched arguments against the contraception provisions. World leaders, however, including the conference host and chairman, Egyptian Pres. Hosni Mubarak, U.S. Vice Pres. Al Gore, and Norwegian Prime Minister Gro Harlem Brundtland, counterattacked with aggressive speeches supporting the conference goals. At the close most delegates enthusiastically endorsed the program, while the Vatican and some Latin-American countries voiced partial support, excepting those provisions that would legitimize abortion and sexual relations outside marriage. (CARL V. HAUB)

People demonstrate against Proposition 187, a ballot initiative in California barring illegal immigrants from receiving public education and social services. Voters approved the initiative by a comfortable margin, but it was immediately challenged in the courts.

TED SOQUI—SYGMA

to enter the United States on rafts and small boats. Cuba agreed to stop the outflow, and the U.S. agreed to grant entry rights to at least 20,000 Cubans a year. There was criticism of the continuing differential treatment of Cuban and Haitian boat people, with the former being generally welcomed as deserving political refugees and potential productive citizens while the latter were treated as economic migrants and future welfare recipients. In December U.S. authorities announced new measures to identify and process unqualified asylum seekers more quickly.

(LOUIS KUSHNICK)

REFUGEES

The year 1994 witnessed an enormous outpouring of refugees fleeing genocide in Rwanda, severely straining the emergency response capacity of the international community. Crises of displacement also persisted in the states of the former Soviet Union and former Yugoslavia. The Office of the United Nations High Commissioner for Refugees (UNHCR), responsible for approximately 23 million refugees, internally displaced persons, returnees, and other victims of war, undertook the challenge of assisting refugees to repatriate to and reintegrate within their countries of former residence.

Fresh on the heels of the 1993 exodus of some 580,000 Burundi refugees, the death of the Rwandan president on April 6, 1994, and the ensuing bloodbath led to the flight of more than two million Rwandans into neighbouring countries. The response to this emergency, which was ex-

acerbated by the emergence of multiple mortal epidemics, required a massive relief effort involving UNHCR and other UN agencies, national governments, and nongovernmental organizations. Elsewhere in Africa, the signing of a peace accord between Liberia's warring factions in 1993 was belied by the continuing state of war on the ground, which in turn forestalled the repatriation of the majority of the 700,000 Liberian refugees in the region. Sudanese refugees, numbering some 265,000 by early September, continued to stream into Uganda. Despite the signing of repatriation agreements between the concerned governments, troubles in Mali ensured the outflow of new refugees into Mauritania and Algeria. In southern Africa the repatriation of over 1.5 million Mozambicans dispersed in six countries proceeded, with over 240,000 assisted returns recorded by the end of September. This repatriation operation, the largest ever undertaken in Africa, encompassed an ambitious program to reintegrate returnees into their region of origin, notably by means of small-scale, quick-impact projects intended to bridge the gap between emergency relief and longer-term development. One serious obstacle to reintegration in Mozambique, as in numerous other countries of return that were emerging from war situations, was the presence of indiscriminately sown land mines.

The repatriation of some 250,000 Burmese Muslim refugees from Bangladesh entered a more active phase in July, and by the beginning of October about 71,000 refugees had returned to Myanmar. Some 85,000 Bhutanese refugees languished in Nepal despite numerous initiatives aimed at resolving their plight. Sri Lankan Tamils in southern India returned steadily, with some 87,000 having repatriated by October. The Comprehensive Plan of Action for Indo-Chinese Refugees stayed on course, seeking solutions for the remaining 56,000 Vietnamese and 23,000 Lao in camps in Southeast Asia and Hong Kong.

Confrontation lines and alliances shifted in former Yugoslavia, but the plight of the some 3.7 million refugees, internally displaced persons, and other war-affected victims remained, for the most part, unresolved. Warfare simmered in Transcaucasia, which by mid-1994 counted 2.5 million Armenian refugees and internally displaced persons (of a total national population of 3.5 million), 900,000 displaced Azerbaijanis, and some 300,000 displaced Georgians and Abkhazians.

At the start of 1994 well over three million Afghans remained in exile as internecine conflict within the country continued to undermine efforts to form a broad-based central government and clouded prospects for a full-scale repatriation. The vicious civil war in Tajikistan had resulted in the displacement of some 500,000 persons (or 10% of the total population) since 1992, 60,000 of whom sought refuge in Afghanistan to the south. Human rights monitoring and reconstruction assistance by UNHCR facilitated the return of some 90% of the internally displaced and 50% of the refugees to their places of origin in Tajikistan.

In the Americas two waves of boat people, from Haiti and then from Cuba, began appearing in the U.S. These outflows were resolved first through the use of temporary safe havens in the region and then on a bilateral basis between the U.S. and the concerned country. Progress on refugee issues in Latin America went hand in hand with the region's consolidation of peace and democracy. The situation in Chile merited the application by the High Commissioner of the cessation clauses of the UNHCR Statute of the Office and the 1951 Convention Relating to the Status of Refugees, thus recognizing the progress made in ensuring civil liberties. The International Conference on Central American Refugees concluded in June, leaving behind a

Rwandan children stand among the debris of a forlorn refugee camp. The plight of some two million Rwandan refugees living in such camps, located largely in neighbouring Tanzania and Zaire, was made even more grim by outbreaks of cholera and other infectious diseases.
JEAN-CLAUDE COUTAUSSE—CONTACT PRESS IMAGES

successful legacy and looking toward a constructive follow-up phase.   (UNHCR)

This article updates the *Macropædia* article POPULATION.

Publishing

Newspapers. In Britain 1994 was marked by an extraordinary bout of price cutting among the country's quality broadsheet newspapers, leading to the fiercest battle for readers since the 1930s. It embroiled the U.K.'s best-known titles—*The Times, Daily Telegraph,* and *Independent*—with the clear winner being Rupert Murdoch's *The Times,* which ended the year with sales up nearly 50%.

The battle had actually commenced in September 1993 when *The Times* declared war by cutting its price from 45 to 30 pence. When it became clear that circulation was being adversely affected, Conrad Black's *Daily Telegraph,* desperate to keep daily sales above one million, responded in June 1994 with a price cut from 48 to 30 pence. *The Times* reacted by undercutting further, to 20 pence. In August the *Independent,* trying to prop up its own falling sales, which had hit a low of 267,000, responded by cutting its price from 50 to 30 pence.

The new prices meant that newspapers, which were concentrated in London, were more dependent than ever before on advertising revenue and were looking hard at editorial costs. News International, controlled by Murdoch, attempted with partial success to raise its advertising rates by 15% in September to take advantage of the new readers it had attracted. The year ended, however, with analysts

questioning how long such artificially low cover prices could last, the consensus being that the participants had fought themselves to a standstill. Those newspapers that had not lowered prices were also facing up to the unpalatable fact that there was little opportunity for circulation growth.

One early sign of the pressures came in January 1994 when Newspaper Publishing, owners of the *Independent* and *Independent on Sunday,* announced a major restructuring, which led to Mirror Group Newspapers (MGN) and the *Irish Independent* becoming shareholders alongside the two main continental shareholders, *El País* of Spain and *La Repubblica* of Italy. The *Independent,* launched successfully with a brand of politically independent journalism and comment in 1986, subsequently moved into the Canary Wharf skyscraper, with MGN providing a range of services to save costs. As the year ended, however, it was still incurring large losses.

British newspapers spent the year critically examining their output. There had been a definite shift away from general-interest colour supplements by advertisers. A number of newspapers concluded that they had to attract more women readers, and the *Mail on Sunday* relaunched its market leader *You Magazine* in October to concentrate on lifestyle, fashion, beauty, and cookery, a move that was leading it and others to compete head-on with women's weeklies and monthly magazines. There was also renewed debate about journalistic standards during the year, with the government backing away from publishing a White Paper outlining new laws to restrict the use of photo lenses when people were on private property and of surveillance devices to tape conversations.

In France two daily newspapers, *InfoMatin* (backed by *Le Monde*) and *Aujourd'hui* (a sister title for the Amaury Group's Paris title *Le Parisien*), made their debuts in January. Given that only 50% of French people read daily papers, the two new ones had relatively successful launches and appeared to find niches. Hachette Filipacchi Presse also found success with a new weekly, *Infos du MONDE,* which relied on sensationalist journalism. In September the respected French daily tabloid *Liberation* was relaunched, doubling its size while retaining its cover price. *Le Monde,* the solid, sober afternoon paper started in 1944, promised a new, livelier format for 1995.

Although Russian journalists, a privileged group with perks and prestige under the old regime, had fallen on hard times, many found a way to supplement their reduced incomes. It was estimated that more than half of Moscow's journalists took money to write favourable stories. "Before, we advertised the Communist Party for free," said one newspaperman. "Now, we do the same for the commercial structure, only this time it's for money." There was even a name for it, *skritaya reklama,* "hidden advertising." In 1994 the Russian Journalists' Union established a code of professional ethics stating that such practices were unacceptable.

The *Los Angeles Times* helped publish the first English-language edition of *Oslobodjenje,* the only daily newspaper left in the besieged city of Sarajevo, capital of Bosnia and Herzegovina. The *Times* paid for a press run of 30,000 copies, which were distributed in Washington, D.C., and at college campuses and churches in selected cities. Bosnian relief activists in the U.S. did the translation.

In a survey of 732 U.S. editors, publishers, and advertising and marketing executives, only 25% of the respondents rated the newspaper industry as "very healthy." The survey, by the Foundation for American Communication, found the biggest threat to the industry to be declining readership, particularly among the young. In an ongoing effort to establish contact with the younger generation, newspapers continued to experiment with electronic media. The *New York Times,* for example, announced that it would begin a six-month test during which it would offer its help-wanted classified advertising on the Internet. The president of the newspaper's Information Services Group said that this was the latest effort to "explore new ways of delivering information and advertising." If successful, the on-line service could be expanded to include other types of advertisements. Earlier in the year, the *Times* had started offering stories about cultural and leisure activities on America Online.

The *Boston Globe* took another direction by joining with New England Cable News, a 24-hour all-news channel. The station set up a small studio in a corner of the *Globe's* newsroom, and at a specific time every hour, a *Globe* reporter, editor, or columnist was interviewed by a TV anchor. The paper expected more than half of its 450-member staff to get airtime by the end of the first year. The *Orange County* (Calif.) *Register* had a similar arrangement with a local channel, and other papers, including the *Philadelphia Inquirer,* were exploring the potential for partnerships between newspapers and television.

A similar experiment at the *Chicago Tribune,* started more than a year earlier, had flourished. The Tribune Company's cable news channel, ChicagoLand TV, was reaching 1.1 million homes, more than 90% of local households with cable TV. Appearances by *Tribune* staffers were scripted to fit their primary role as print journalists. "I don't ask anybody to come on this channel and provide analysis when they are reporters," said ChicagoLand's director of news and programming. "I ask them to come on and tell us what they know, not what they think."

One high-profile effort to reach the younger generation did not succeed. "Hip Replacement: New York Times Curbs Cool Section" was the headline in a *Wall Street Journal* story about the demise of the ill-fated Sunday section, Styles of the Times. Media critics had ridiculed the idea from the start for such front-page stories as "The Arm Fetish." The section, which reported on lifestyles, fashion, and social trends, was folded into the paper's Metro Report.

The *Wall Street Journal* unveiled two new weekly sections in 1994 devoted to regional business. Following on the Texas Journal, which was introduced in 1993, the Florida Journal and the Southeast Journal would feature four pages of locally reported business news. In addition, the Wall Street Journal Americas was launched. This two-page section of international business news would be published in the morning editions of eight Latin-American papers belonging to a federation of Spanish-language newspapers with a circulation of over one million. The *Wall Street Journal* also began its own weekly list of best-sellers. Unlike other fiction and nonfiction lists, this one would compare the relative sales of books in both categories.

The *Miami* (Fla.) *Herald,* which already had a Spanish-language edition, broadened its base by printing new features in Creole and Portuguese. With an estimated 200,000 Haitians living in the area, the *Herald* initiated a page of news capsules in Creole as a Sunday feature. To attract the 300,000 Brazilian tourists who visited Miami each year, the paper added a page of news in Portuguese.

A project called "Voices of Florida" linked six newspapers across the state in an innovative attempt to engage voters and find out what was on their mind. The *Miami Herald, Florida Times-Union, St. Petersburg Times, Tallahassee Democrat, Bradenton Herald,* and *Boca Raton News*—referred to as "the cartel" by critics—used phone banks, computer bulletin boards, town meetings, and polls and interviews to elicit information from voters. They then used the responses to question Florida's gubernatorial candidates. Not all the journalists involved were comfortable with a deal in which their papers had to share information and run one another's stories. The impetus for the project—the belief that traditional campaign journalism was failing the electorate—prodded other papers, such as the *Dallas* (Texas) *Morning News, Boston Globe,* and *San Francisco Chronicle,* to team up with National Public Radio affiliates and TV stations to elicit from voters their opinions on issues.

The *Akron* (Ohio) *Beacon Journal* won the 1994 Pulitzer Prize for Public Service for its examination of local race relations. Pulitzers were awarded to the *New York Times* (spot news reporting) for its staff coverage of the World Trade Center bombing; the *Providence* (R.I.) *Journal-Bulletin* (investigative reporting) for its coverage of corruption in the state court system, which led to the resignation of the chief justice of the state's Supreme Court; Ronald Kotulak of the *Chicago Tribune* (explanatory journalism) for two series on discoveries in the neurological sciences; Eric Freedman and Jim Mitzelfeld of the *Detroit* (Mich.) *News* (beat reporting) for coverage of spending abuses in the Michigan state legislature; *Albuquerque* (N.M.) *Tribune* (national reporting) for Eileen Welsome's stories on the effects of the U.S. government's radiation experiments on unsuspecting citizens in the 1940s; and Isabel Wilkerson of the *New York Times* (feature writing) for her reports on the floods in the Midwest and her profile of a 10-year-old boy living in a crime-infested area on the South Side of Chicago. The *Dallas Morning News* took the award for international reporting for team coverage of violence against women in different areas of the world. Other winners were the *Washington Post* (commentary) for William Raspberry's views on politics and society;

the *Boston Phoenix* (criticism) for Lloyd Schwartz's writings on classical music; Michael P. Ramirez of the *Commercial Appeal* of Memphis, Tenn. (editorial cartooning); the *Toronto Star* (spot news photography) for Paul Watson's picture of an American soldier being dragged through the streets of Mogadishu by Somali civilians; the *New York Times* (feature photography) for a picture of a vulture hovering nearby as a starving Sudanese girl collapsed taken by freelancer Kevin Carter (*see* OBITUARIES); and R. Bruce Dold's series in the *Chicago Tribune* (editorial writing) on the Illinois welfare system and the story of a three-year-old boy killed by his mother.

(MAGGIE BROWN; MELANIE ANNE COOPER)

Magazines. Overall, 1994 saw a sharp revival in new magazine launches in Britain as advertising revenue revived after four years of slowdown. The London-based *The Oldie* weekly magazine, devoted to those over 50, closed down in July, however, after circulation had plummeted from 100,-000 in 1992 to 20,000. It was restarted in September as a more modest monthly. Men were also being served; it was announced that the battle for their attention waged by the U.K. editions of *GQ* and *Esquire* would be joined in January 1995 by a British edition of the U.S. *Men's Health* magazine.

Pearson PLC, the international media and entertainment group that published the *Financial Times,* moved into the general magazine market for the first time in 1994 with the £52.5 million purchase of Future Publishing, which produced 30 consumer and computer magazines, including a new title on the Internet. Future Publishing, founded in 1985 by entrepreneur Chris Anderson, had grown rapidly from a humble £30,000 start.

In Poland the French publisher Hachette Filipacchi Presse launched an edition of *Elle* magazine in September with a print run of 250,000. The publisher was responding to the potential market of young and relatively well-educated Polish women eager for this type of magazine. It followed a more modest launch for *Elle* in the Czech Republic.

In Germany, where newsmagazines were a growing market (partly because there were no Sunday newspapers), publisher Gruner & Jahr launched the Berlin-based *Tango,* targeting 20- to 39-year-olds with a mix of news and celebrity gossip. This market was already being served by the influential *Der Spiegel,* founded after World War II, and *Stern,* owned by Gruner & Jahr, which together sold about two million copies weekly.

(MAGGIE BROWN)

Some U.S. publishers continued to be skeptical about a switch from print to on-line and CD-ROM formats, but by the end of 1994 many were changing their minds. For one thing, more and more computers were coming with built-in CD-ROM players. *Time,* along with a number of other magazines, joined *Newsweek* in offering a digital edition as part of the electronic newsstand. The real breakthrough, however, seemed to be in multimedia CD-ROMs, such as *Substance,* a pop music title. The first issue allowed the viewer not only to see and hear a heavy metal band but also to watch an interview with its leader and to read standard text about it and other groups. Similar multimedia magazines were promised on-line, particularly when the speed of sending pictures and sound increased enough to make it economical to use networks, such as the Internet, for transmission.

In lockstep with developments in personal computers, new magazines appeared in the U.S. in 1994 to meet the needs of not just the traditional computer buffs but also the whole family. Among the new entries were *Home PC,* a monthly catering to the estimated 15 million American households with personal computers; *Family Computing,* a quarterly from Scholastic Corp. that concentrated on the use of the computer for entertainment and education; and *FamilyPC,* a joint effort of Walt Disney Co. and Ziff-Davis Publishing Co. that featured reviews of CD-ROMs, including magazines, as well as advice on how to use the Internet and the new consumer networks.

For those who hated text and loved pictures, the new *Elle topModel* was a find in 1994. Primarily for young women, it was filled with little more than pictures of top models. Another new entry was *InStyle,* a primarily pictorial version of *People.* Time Inc. called it "celebrity journalism," which meant even more faces and little or no verbiage. (The wildly successful *People* celebrated its 20th anniversary in 1994.) Returning to words, Dell brought out a bimonthly, *Louis L'Amour Western Magazine,* which was filled with tales of the frontier.

At *New York* magazine a new editor was attempting to remodel the weekly on its earlier years. At *The New Yorker* editor Tina Brown continued her tailoring job to make what had been a literary delight look like *Vanity Fair.* (In a retrial, writer Janet Malcolm was found not guilty of libel for statements made in a 1983 *New Yorker* article.) The Library of Congress announced the publication of a new magazine called *Civilization;* it was to draw on the library's collection and offer a vari-

A mother sleeps with her child in the hallway of a building in Travnik, Bosnia and Herzegovina. The photograph was taken by Anthony Suau, who worked extensively in former Soviet bloc countries and who was named magazine photographer of the year by the National Press Photographers Association.

ety of material in the same popular format as *Smithsonian* and *Natural History.*

The advertising revenues of periodicals were up in 1994 even though newsstand sales were in a slump. Sales of leading magazines in supermarkets, airports, and drugstores declined sharply. The basic reason was increased reliance on subscription sales. Thus, when subscriptions failed, magazines closed. Among those publishing their last issues in 1994 was the six-year-old *Lear's,* a magazine for older women.

The National Magazine Awards in 1994 for feature writing, fiction, and essays and criticism went to *Harper's Magazine. Wired* was recognized for its contribution to rapidly evolving computer technology. *Health* took prizes for general excellence and best single-topic issue. The design award went to *Allure,* and *Fortune* won the personal service award.

(WILLIAM A. KATZ)

Books. Advocates of resale price maintenance (RPM) for books in the European Union (EU) suffered several setbacks in 1994. At the end of June, the advocate general of the European Court of Justice recommended that an appeal against prohibitions on RPM in respect of interstate trade be struck down. At the same time, the Competition Authority in Ireland refused to grant a license for the U.K.'s Net Book Agreement (NBA) to be introduced there. In addition, the U.K. Office of Fair Trading applied for a judicial review of the NBA. The review could take up to two years, but publishers appeared to be unwilling to finance a defense, given that the NBA continued to be undermined. Book Club Associates, for example, began looking for up to 50 additional retail outlets. In addition, a second warehouse club (Cargo Club, owned by Nurdin and Peacock) followed CostCo's example in challenging the NBA, although it conceded in May that discounted sales would be made only to trade customers. The issue of parallel imports also remained of concern, with pressure being exerted by U.K. publishers to expel U.S.-originated titles from other EU member states in order to prevent their indirect exportation to the U.K. It nevertheless remained unclear whether parallel imports were economic in practice.

As from July 1, 1995, copyright protection in the EU was to be extended to the author's lifetime plus 70 years. The protection would be extended to works by EU nationals and works first published in a member state. U.S. works that had not acquired EU origin or were not otherwise protected in a single member state would not benefit.

There were relatively few takeovers in European publishing in 1994. In March, Verlagsgruppe Georg von Holtzbrinck (VGH), based in Stuttgart, Germany, bought 20% of the multimedia publisher Voyager. In April, Baring Communications Equity bought the legal publisher Codex of Prague from the Hugo Grotius Foundation to add to a 30% stake in KJK of Hungary and to the purchase of Simon & Schuster's children's list. International Thompson Publishing bought the German book publisher IWT Verlag to add to its prior purchase of Wolfram Fachverlag. The trend to computer-linked acquisitions was also reflected in Paramount Publishing's purchase of the book and software operations of Markt & Technik of Germany.

Book publishing in the EU became more concentrated during 1994. In the U.K., for example, 49 publishers accounted for more than 50% of all turnover at trade prices. In 1994 Cassell and Pavilion were among those seeking stock exchange quotations in order to obtain capital for growth, indicating that current economic trends clearly were set to continue.

The U.K. experienced a major expansion of books onto supermarket shelves with specially tailored products from such publishers as HarperCollins and Dorling Kindersley. The emphasis was upon quality, and every title was expected at least to break even. Retail bookstores expressed alarm, but it remained unclear whether supermarket sales increased the overall size of the market or ate into sales elsewhere. The production of cheap versions of out-of-copyright classics in the U.K. expanded considerably with the introduction of Penguin Popular Classics. The higher reaches of literature clearly did not need to be either inaccessible or overpriced, although puzzle and quiz books were the most popular category of book. (PETER J. CURWEN)

The close of 1993 had the book-publishing industry in the U.S. in suspense as QVC Network Inc. and Viacom Inc. continued their heated battle to take over Paramount Communications Inc., the multimedia giant and parent company of Paramount Publishing, an umbrella title given to Simon & Schuster and its subsidiaries. At the same time, Paramount was setting a closing date for its $553 million purchase of Macmillan. In February Viacom emerged the winner, acquiring 51% of Paramount Communications. In May, Viacom announced that it was changing the name of Paramount Publishing back to Simon & Schuster, much to the approval of Paramount Publishing's chief executive officer, Richard E. Snyder.

If Snyder believed, however, that the name change signaled insurance for his position in the new company, the management of Viacom wasted no time in disabusing him of that notion. In an astonishing move that stunned the industry, Viacom dismissed Snyder, a 33-year veteran and industry legend, on June 14. Viacom paid Snyder a reported $10 million on the remaining four years of his contract.

Paris au XXe siècle, completed by Jules Verne in 1863, was first published (in French) in 1994. Critics noted many uncanny forecasts, including an automobile-like device, in this work.

COVER ILLUSTRATION BY FRANÇOIS SCHUITEN; © HACHETTE LIVRE, DÉPARTEMENT HACHETTE RÉFÉRENCE, EN COÉDITION AVEC LE CHERCHE MIDI ÉDITEUR, 1994

In his three decades with the company, Snyder had become famous for an aggressive, controversial, and confrontational style that turned a small trade house into a multibillion-dollar publishing giant. Industry insiders were shocked at the sudden move by Viacom because they feared the sudden loss of such a key publishing figure would have a destabilizing effect on trade publishing. Simon & Schuster's president and chief operating officer, Jonathan Newcomb, was named Snyder's successor. Under Newcomb's direction Simon & Schuster completed the integration of Macmillan.

There was good reason for the industry's concern over destabilization. In January, months before Snyder's dismissal, several trade houses folded or greatly reduced their literary imprints. Citing reasons of efficiency and cost cutting, Houghton Mifflin announced in January that it was eliminating Ticknor & Fields, a small but distinguished literary imprint. At the same time, Harcourt Brace cut its adult trade division drastically, firing half of the division's 24 New York-based employees and reducing the numbers of titles published. Harcourt General (the parent company of Harcourt Brace) called the move a "realignment." Another simultaneous development was the folding of Atheneum, Macmillan's esteemed literary

Under the aggressive leadership of Richard Snyder, Simon & Schuster had become a major U.S. publishing house. The company's new owner, Viacom, fired Snyder in midyear, however, creating an uproar among people in the trade publishing world.
ROBIN PLATZER—TWIN IMAGES

imprint, into the Scribner's line by Paramount Publishing, Macmillan's new corporate owner. The three events shook up literary agents and authors who found their projects orphaned or their futures with the houses unclear. Whether the moves were a death knell for quality publishing, as some claimed, or an intelligent way of streamlining money-losing propositions, as others countered, the result was illustrative of publishing's ages-old identity problem: was it a purveyor of culture and ideas or a commercial concern?

The competitive marketplace came under the spotlight again in May when the American Booksellers Association (ABA), an organization of independent retail booksellers, filed an antitrust suit against five publishers, claiming that they were offering illegal "secret" deals, prices, and promotions to various chain bookstores and discount outlets. The publishers named were Houghton Mifflin, Penguin USA, St. Martin's Press, Rutledge Hill Press, and Hugh Lauter Levin. The suit grew out of independent retailers' concern over publishers' preferential treatment of chain stores, discount outlets, and warehouse clubs and the independents' doubts over their ability to survive on such unequal terms. In accordance, the suit asked the court for an injunction that would force the publishers to offer their terms to all customers. Lawyers for the publishers filed a motion that argued that the suit should be dismissed since the ABA did not, as a trade organization, have the legal standing to file the lawsuit. (The ABA's counsel argued that the group had "associational standing.") Lawyers for the publishers also asked the court to stay the ABA action pending a resolution

of the Federal Trade Commission's 15-year investigation of six other publishers on similar charges.

Money did not seem to be a problem for three publishers who offered their authors multimillion-dollar deals. Harper-Collins signed best-selling author Jeffrey Archer to a new three-book deal, reportedly in the neighbourhood of $21 million. Alfred A. Knopf agreed to pay Pope John Paul II more than $6 million for English-language publishing rights to his book *Crossing the Threshold of Hope*. The money would be given to charity. Clive Cussler cashed in with a lucrative deal with Simon & Schuster—$14 million for two books, making him the publisher's highest-paid author.

The 1994 Pulitzer Prize for Fiction went to E. Annie Proulx (*see* BIOGRAPHIES), author of *The Shipping News* (Scribner's), which also had won the National Book Award in 1993. David Remnick won the prize for nonfiction for *Lenin's Tomb: The Last Days of the Soviet Empire* (Random House). Best-sellers for 1993, as reported by *Publishers Weekly*, were, in fiction, *The Bridges of Madison County* by Robert James Waller (4,362,352), *The Client* by John Grisham (2,927,376), and *Slow Waltz at Cedar Bend*, also by Waller, (1,978,342). In nonfiction the best-sellers were *See, I Told You So* by Rush Limbaugh (2,587,600), *Private Parts* by Howard Stern (1,228,298), and *Seinlanguage* by Jerry Seinfeld (1,106,000). Total book sales in the U.S. rose more than 6% in 1993, to over $18 billion.   (BETH S. LEVINE)

See also Literature.

This article updates the *Macropædia* article PUBLISHING.

Race and Ethnic Relations

Europe. Elections to the European Parliament in 1994 produced defeats for fascist parties in Germany and The Netherlands, with fascist or ultraright parties winning seats only in Belgium, France, and Italy. The elections did mark a decisive shift to the right and the triumph of nationalist politics, however, with mainstream right-wing parties moving farther to the right on issues of immigration and race.

The Campaign Against Racism and Fascism recorded 52 racist killings—41 connected to the far right—in Germany in 1993, double the figure for the previous year. On May 27, 1994, Manfred Kanther, the federal interior minister, admitted that there had been an increase in the number of violent anti-Semitic attacks, criminal damage to Jewish cemeteries, and neo-Nazi daubings of synagogues and of Jewish communal buildings and cemeteries—all representing an annual number of anti-Semitic incidents that was higher than the total number between 1926 and 1931. According to the annual 1993 report of the Verfassungsschutz, 42,500 right-wing extremists were operating in Germany; the report concluded that the number of crimes committed by right-wing extremists increased from 7,121 in 1992 to 8,109 in 1993.

In Britain the Institute of Manpower Studies at the University of Sussex, Brighton, calculated that racial discrimination in the workplace cost £18.7 billion a year. Discrimination against black soldiers, including racial abuse, led in 1994 to an investigation of the Ministry of Defence by the Commission for Racial Equality. A Law Society survey found that British-based white law students had a 47% chance of getting articles (the necessary work experience to become a practicing lawyer) with firms of solicitors, compared with 7% for black law students. An inquiry into allegations of racial discrimination at the Inns of Court concluded that blacks studying to become barristers suffered a "collapse of confidence" that contributed to an examination failure rate three times that of white students.

With the help of a trained dog, an Israeli worker searches the rubble of the Jewish community centre in Buenos Aires, Arg., which was destroyed in a bombing on July 18. It was alleged that Arab terrorists were responsible for the bombing, which killed 96 people.

AFP

The level of racial and ethnic violence in the U.K. increased. According to a report by the Institute of Jewish Affairs, anti-Jewish attacks rose by almost 20% to 346 in 1993 (the last year for which data were available). Complaints of racial harassment and abuse by police officers more than quadrupled in 1993—from 67 to 291—but only 4% of cases resulted in disciplinary action for racial abuse, compared with 10% of investigated complaints as a whole. Black and Asian Metropolitan Police officers announced in August 1994 the formation of their own pressure and support group that would highlight the treatment and experiences of ethnic minority officers within Britain's largest force.

In The Netherlands two researchers at the State University of Leiden in 1994 published a report saying that racist violence was more widespread than previously thought and many incidents were not recorded. The number of incidents rose from 4 in 1988 to 279 in 1993, with firebombings averaging three a month in 1992 and 1993. Attacks on asylum centres rose from 116 in 1992 to 123 in 1993. The authors concluded that the hardening of the political climate on migration and minorities could contribute to the occurrence of extreme right-wing violence.

In September 1994 the French education minister, François Bayrou, banned the wearing of the *hijab*, or Islamic head scarf, under new regulations banning all "ostentatious" religious symbols. A number of Muslim young women challenged the ruling by continuing to wear the *hijab*—seeing the ban as a violation of their rights and contending that the ruling was unfair by citing the unchallenged wearing of crosses by Roman Catholic students. In October a school in Lille expelled several young Muslim women—a decision described as a "parody of justice" by the women's lawyer, who said that he would take the case higher up the Education Ministry and into the courts. Later in the year there were expulsions from several schools in other parts of France. The attack on the wearing of head scarves was seen by many as part of a wider attack on the very concept of a multicultural society based on cultural diversity and religious tolerance.

In early 1994 the Consultative Commission for Human Rights published its fifth annual report into racism and xenophobia in France. According to official figures, between January 1980 and December 1993, 25 people were killed by racist violence and 323 people were injured in racist attacks.

Amnesty International issued a report on "Allegations of Ill-Treatment in Police Custody" in Switzerland that found that many of the cases of ill-treatment involved foreigners and Swiss citizens of non-European descent. In the September national referendum, 54.2% of the electorate voted in favour of a law making racial discrimination, racist propaganda, and denial of the Holocaust illegal.

Eastern Europe after the collapse of the Soviet bloc witnessed an upsurge in fascism and neo-Nazism. A particular target was the Roma (Gypsy) people. In the Czech Republic skinhead violence against Roma enjoyed the support of 22–37% of the people, depending on the region. Some 30% of Czechs supported deporting or isolating Roma. A law that came into effect on Jan. 1, 1993, excluded nearly half of the Czech Republic's estimated 200,000 Roma from citizenship and from the right to vote. Meanwhile, in Slovakia there was widespread scapegoating of Roma.

In Bosnia and Herzegovina the civil war between Serbs, Croats, and Muslims showed no real signs of ending. Late in

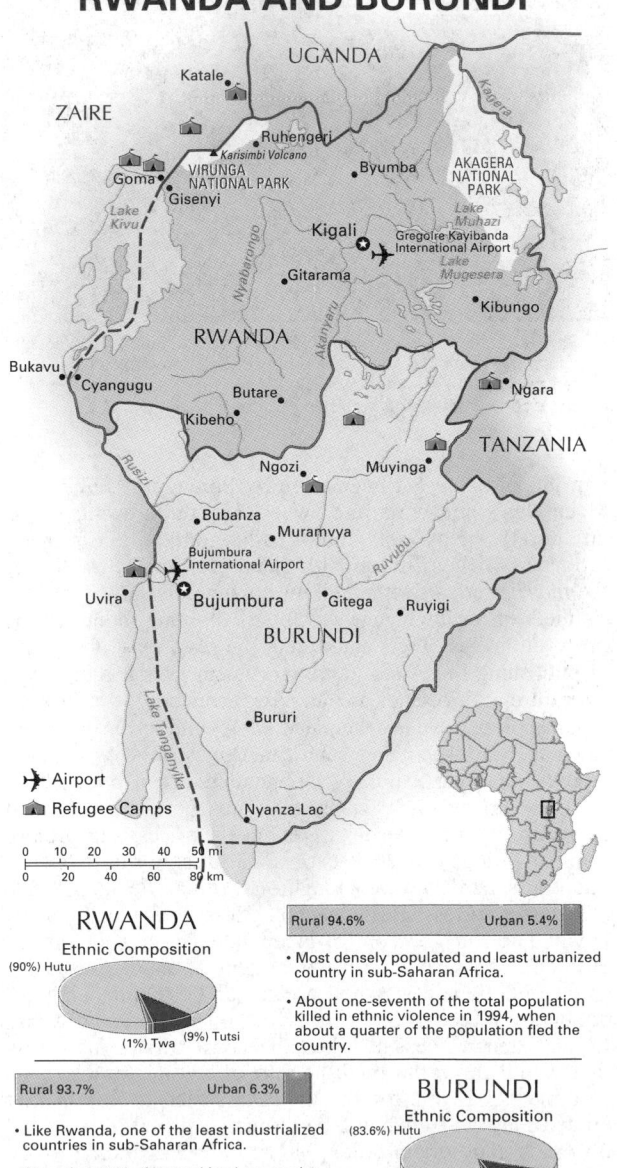

RWANDA AND BURUNDI

✈ Airport

🏚 Refugee Camps

0 10 20 30 40 50 mi
0 20 40 60 80 km

RWANDA

Ethnic Composition

(90%) Hutu
(1%) Twa   (9%) Tutsi

| Rural 94.6% | Urban 5.4% |

• Most densely populated and least urbanized country in sub-Saharan Africa.

• About one-seventh of the total population killed in ethnic violence in 1994, when about a quarter of the population fled the country.

| Rural 93.7% | Urban 6.3% |

• Like Rwanda, one of the least industrialized countries in sub-Saharan Africa.

• More than 50% of its total land area under cultivation, the highest figure for any African country.

BURUNDI

Ethnic Composition

(83.6%) Hutu
(1.6%) Other (1%) Twa (13.8%) Tutsi

©1995, Encyclopædia Britannica, Inc.

the year fighting broke out between Russian troops and the breakaway republic of Chechnya, led by Dzhokar Dudayev. (*See* BIOGRAPHIES.) The Chechens, a Muslim people of the northern Caucasus, had declared independence in 1991.

United States. In 1994 tensions rose within the African-American community, and relations also were strained between blacks and their longtime Jewish political allies, particularly in response to antiwhite, anti-Semitic, anti-Catholic statements made by Khalid Abdul Muhammad of the black nationalist group Nation of Islam. In February the Congressional Black Caucus voted to distance itself from the Nation of Islam and its controversial leader, Louis Farrakhan. Two months later Franklyn G. Jenifer resigned as president of predominantly black Howard University, Washington, D.C., amid widespread criticism for having allowed Muhammad to twice speak on campus. In August the Rev. Benjamin F. Chavis was ousted as executive director of the National Association for the Advancement of Colored People (NAACP). He had been accused of sexual harassment and questionable financial deals and had been criticized for seeking closer ties to the Nation of Islam. In October Chavis settled a wrongful dismissal lawsuit against the NAACP.

There were a number of contradictory federal court decisions on congressional districts created to ensure black representation in Congress. The Supreme Court's 1993 decision in *Shaw* v. *Reno* had questioned the constitutionality of oddly-shaped black-majority congressional districts. In 1994 lower federal courts in Louisiana, Texas, and Georgia held such districts to be unconstitutional, while a U.S. District Court in North Carolina upheld the constitutionality of a serpentine 257-km (160-mi)-long Congressional district on the grounds that it helped remedy past discrimination against blacks. A telephone survey of 3,800 adults by the Times Mirror Centre for the People and the Press revealed that 51% of white Americans thought equal rights had been pushed too far, up from 42% in 1992 and 16% in 1987.

Africa. Ethnic fighting between Hutu and Tutsi exploded in Rwanda after the plane in which Rwandan Pres. Juvénal Habyarimana (*see* OBITUARIES) and Burundian Pres. Cyprien Ntaryamira were flying was shot down on April 6. Underlying pressures between the two groups had been building for years (*see* Sidebar), and the fighting quickly escalated into genocide and mass slaughter by militia squads and civilian extremists. As many as one million people were killed, and another two million fled into exile, mainly into refugee camps in Zaire. At year's end there were indications that the violence was spreading into neighbouring Burundi, which had roughly the same ethnic makeup as Rwanda.

Rwanda's Complex Ethnic History

Historically, the geographic environment of the Great Lakes region of central Africa erected an effective barrier to all but the most determined intruders: neighbouring ethnic groups, slave traders, and, for a time, European invaders. Three immigrant groups, the Twa, the Hutu, and the Tutsi—known collectively as the Banyarwanda—established their homes there. While Rwanda's prehistory is not yet conclusive, the Twa (who now constitute less than 1% of the population of Rwanda) are believed to have been the first occupants of the region, arriving before the first millennium and followed shortly by the Hutu.

The origins of the Hutu are obscure. They exhibit the physical characteristics of other Bantu-speakers of central Africa as well as some Nilotic components stemming from their fusion with the Tutsi. Their language is Kinyarwanda, a branch of the Niger-Congo subfamily, and is spoken by the Twa and Tutsi as well, suggesting that these groups have lived together for centuries. Before the recent mass killings and population shifts, the Hutu made up 90% of the total population, although their distribution and density varied greatly from one region to the next. Hutu "toparchies" (small principalities) were situated principally in the northern and western regions of Rwanda. They farmed, bred cattle, raised goats and woolless sheep, chickens, and dogs, and typically lived in small fenced enclosures containing grain stores and ritual huts for ancestors.

The Tutsi represented about 9% of Rwanda's total population. Many authorities believe that they might earlier have inhabited the upper Nile valley. The date of their migration is not known, but they drifted southward onto the central plateau of Rwanda with their long-horned cattle in search of pastureland and sanctuary from cattle raiders. The Tutsi herds contribute little toward subsistence; milk production per cow is quite low, about a litre and a half per day in the good season. Rather, the Tutsi's cattle are a status symbol and sign of wealth. Before independence, elaborate rituals surrounded stockbreeding, and cattle figured prominently in royal rites as well as in literature. The Tutsi hunted but only for sport, to show their prowess and courage. Their daily life differed little from that of the Hutu, however; some farmed, others bred cattle, and many probably did a little of both.

These three groups lived in relative harmony and intermingled with relative equality until the Tutsi began to consolidate power and expand politically from their core area, centred on Kigali, in the 13th century. Social distinctions between the ethnic groups soon became a reality, however, enforced by consolidation or assimilation, custom, and ritual. The Tutsi invaded and colonized independent Hutu areas in the 16th and 17th centuries. The final phase of incorporation occurred in the late 19th century.

The German colonial government, begun in 1898 and continuing until 1916, pursued a policy of indirect rule that strengthened the hegemony of the Tutsi ruling class and the absolutism of its monarchy. Belgium took control of Ruanda-Urundi after World War I and administered the colony indirectly, under the tutelage of the League of Nations. The Belgians governed in concert with the Tutsi oligarchy, which had the effect of further enhancing Tutsi power in terms of access to educational opportunities and tenure of key civil and technical posts. Some Hutu began to demand equality and found sympathy from the Roman Catholic clergy and Belgian administrative personnel. The independence movement, which began in 1952, was often violent and convulsive. The mysterious death of King Mutara Rudahigwa III in July 1959 and the accession of King Kigeri V increased the ethnic violence and precipitated massacres and a mass exodus of Tutsi from the colony. After independence in 1962, unease between the two groups periodically led to mass killings and struggles.

(LEARTHEN DORSEY)

South Africa's first democratic elections, won by the African National Congress, were held April 26–29, 1994, and more than 19 million people voted, the majority newly enfranchised blacks. Racial divisions constructed and essential to the maintenance of the apartheid system were reflected in voting patterns and represented a continuing challenge to Pres. Nelson Mandela's new government. After more than 40 years of apartheid, seven million South Africans lived in squalor—often without formal housing, running water, electricity, health care, and proper employment. There was a 50% illiteracy rate, and almost all of the arable land was in the hands of whites. In September there were violent confrontations in a number of townships near Johannesburg between members of the Coloured (mixed-race) minority and the police.

Oceania. In November the Australian Parliament passed the Racial Hatred Bill, which would make incitement to racial hatred punishable by up to one year in jail. It was uncertain whether the bill would adequately protect minorities, and critics claimed that it would unduly restrict freedom of speech. Two weeks later Aborigines who had been displaced by and/or exposed to radiation from nuclear testing in the 1950s won a $A 13.5 million settlement against the British and Australian governments. In New Zealand, meanwhile, Maoris rejected as inadequate an offer of $NZ 1 billion compensation by the government.

(LOUIS KUSHNICK)

Religion

Theological justifications for violence were attempted on several fronts in 1994, even while new ground was broken in ecumenical and interfaith relations. Scholarly works on the life of Jesus and on the status of homosexuality in the early church drew attention and created controversy, and the news media acknowledged their deficiencies in covering the world of religion. Several religious bodies changed leaders during the year, and issues of feminism, sexuality, and church-state relations continued to engage faith groups.

Paul Hill, a defrocked minister of the Presbyterian Church in America, had defended the use of violence to stop abortion before he was arrested in July, charged, and convicted of the killing of an abortion doctor and his escort in Pensacola, Fla. The Rev. David C. Trosch, a Roman Catholic priest in Mobile, Ala., promoted the view that murdering doctors who performed abortions was "justifiable homicide." Trosch and Hill were among 25 people signing a declaration justifying the use of lethal force to defend "the lives of unborn children." Other incidents occurred later in the year, but the vast majority of abortion opponents denounced the use of such tactics.

Taslima Nasrin, a writer from Bangladesh, was threatened with death by Muslim extremists and was briefly targeted for arrest for criticizing certain teachings in the Koran. (See BIOGRAPHIES.) Her situation drew attention to the plight of other writers who had run afoul of fundamentalist Muslims, including 48 who had been executed by Iranian authorities since 1979 and 11 murdered by Muslim extremists in Egypt since 1990.

Rabbi Shlomo Goren (see OBITUARIES), former chief rabbi of Israel's Ashkenazic, or Western European, Jewish community, issued a religious ruling in June calling upon Jews to kill Palestine Liberation Organization leader Yasir Arafat. High-caste and low-caste Hindus rioted in January in India's Maharashtra state over that state government's decision to rename a university after Bhimrao Ramji Ambedkar, a cult figure for the lower castes. Two factions of normally pacifist Tibetan Buddhists engaged in a violent clash in New Delhi in March as part of a dispute over the identity of the reincarnation of their leader.

In October some 53 members of the "Order of the Solar Temple," a secretive mystical sect with alleged links to international arms-trafficking and money-laundering operations, were found dead in Switzerland and Quebec.

On the positive side, an international group of 60 religious leaders in Istanbul in February demanded an end to crimes against humanity in Bosnia, Armenia/Azerbaijan, Georgia, and Tajikistan. The participants—from Eastern Orthodox, Jewish, Muslim, and Roman Catholic traditions—rejected "any attempt to corrupt the basic tenets of our faith by means of false interpretation and unchecked nationalism." Leaders of the Evangelical Lutheran Church in America issued a declaration denouncing anti-Jewish statements made by Martin Luther, and officials of the National Conference of Catholic Bishops and the Synagogue Council of America urged educators to reject efforts to deny that the Holocaust ever occurred. In July the Vatican and Israel formally initiated diplomatic relations, a step that had been approved in December 1993. The Vatican joined with representatives of some Muslim countries in opposing abortion-rights sections of a document on population issues drafted at a United Nations conference in Cairo in September (see POPULATION AND POPULATION MOVEMENTS: Sidebar), but an interfaith gathering in Washington, D.C., stressed that abortion is "treated in different ways among and within religious communities."

A Vatican document issued in March criticized the fundamentalist approach to biblical interpretation as promoting "a kind of intellectual suicide." But later that month a group of evangelical Protestant and Roman Catholic leaders in the U.S. issued a 25-page statement in which they outlined common convictions and pledged to work together on such causes as opposing abortion and pornography while refraining from attempting to proselytize each other. Several Southern Baptists were among the signers, and the annual meeting of the Southern Baptist Convention in June formally endorsed Baptist-Catholic dialogues for the first time. The National Council of Churches in Australia was inaugurated in July by 13 churches, marking the first time the Roman Catholic Church had joined such a national ecumenical organization.

The Jesus Seminar, an organization of 74 biblical scholars formed in 1985 to seek the historical Jesus through scholarly means, stirred a controversy with the publication of The Five Gospels: The Search for the Authentic Words of Jesus. The volume concluded that 82% of the sayings attributed to Jesus in the Bible are inauthentic. Other scholarly works that differed with the scriptural accounts of the life of Jesus that drew attention during the year included Jesus: A Revolutionary Biography by John Dominic Crossan (see BIOGRAPHIES), The Lost Gospel by Burton L. Mack, Meeting Jesus Again for the First Time by Marcus J. Borg, and The Religion of Jesus the Jew by Geza Vermes. These works relied heavily on the Book of Q, a collection of sayings and aphorisms attributed to Jesus that the scholars in question believe were used as sources by Matthew and Luke. In June a conference on "Reclaiming the Bible for the Church," held in Northfield, Minn., drew theologians who charged that scholarly groups such as the Jesus Seminar were misinterpreting the Bible by removing it from its setting in the church community. Another academic volume on religion that made news in 1994 was Same-Sex Unions in Premodern Europe by Yale University historian John Boswell, who died of AIDS on December 23. The book asserted that from the 8th to the 18th century, the Catholic Church sanctioned same-sex unions and offered ceremonies for them. Several other scholars disputed Boswell's conclusions, pointing out that most of the rituals he cited were associated with early Eastern Orthodoxy rather than Western Christianity in Rome.

A number of research studies concluded that religion was being inadequately covered by the U.S. news media, an assertion echoed by such prominent broadcast journalists as Bill Moyers and Dan Rather. Signs in 1994 that some corrective steps were being taken included the purchase of the 60-year-old Religious News Service by the larger Newhouse News Service and the hiring of Peggy Wehmeyer by ABC News as the first full-time religious issues correspondent at a major television network.

The Chabad-Lubavitch, an ultra-Orthodox Jewish Hasidic movement based in Brooklyn, N.Y., found itself without a top spiritual leader when Rabbi Menachem Mendel Schneerson died in June without a successor or a procedure for selecting one. (See OBITUARIES.) Howard W. Hunter, an 86-year-old former corporate lawyer, succeeded Ezra Taft Benson as president and prophet of the Church of Jesus Christ of Latter-day Saints after Benson died at the age of 95. (See OBITUARIES.) The Rev. Henry Lyons of St. Petersburg, Fla., was elected president of the eight million-member National Baptist Convention, U.S.A., Inc., which claimed to be the world's largest black organization. The Rev. Jim Henry of Orlando, Fla., was elected president of the 15.4 million-member Southern Baptist Convention although he was not backed by most of the former presidents who had led SBC conservatives to victory since 1979. The Rev. Ishmael Noko of Zimbabwe was elected general secretary of the Lutheran World Federation in June, while Gen. Paul A. Rader, territorial commander for the Salvation Army U.S.A.'s western territory, became the first American to serve as top international leader of the London-based organization.

An ecumenical conference held in Minneapolis, Minn., in November 1993 sparked controversy during 1994 for its feminist theology as featured in worship using the name Sophia, or "Divine Wisdom" as personified in the book of Proverbs, and a ritual that featured milk and honey rather than bread and wine. The "RE-Imagining" conference drew 2,000 participants from 32 denominations and 27 countries and particularly rocked the Presbyterian Church (U.S.A.), one of its major sponsors. The denomination's General Assembly, meeting in June in Wichita, Kan., passed a resolution supporting efforts to improve and celebrate the status of women while saying the "RE-Imagining" conference went too far theologically.

The Church of England broke with 460 years of Anglican tradition when it ordained 32 women to the priesthood in March. The church allocated $4.5 million in pensions to compensate an estimated 200 male priests who were leaving because they disagreed with the action. The Scottish Episcopal Church voted in June to ordain women priests, leaving the Church in Wales the only Anglican denomination in the U.K. refusing to take the step. The Vatican criticized the Church of England's action, and Pope John Paul II issued an apostolic letter in May declaring that the church "has no authority whatsoever to confer priestly ordination on women and that this judgment is to be definitively held by all the church's faithful." But the Holy See broke with Catholic tradition in April by saying that girls may now assist priests during masses. The Christian Reformed Church voted at its synod in June in Grand Rapids, Mich., not to ratify a move taken a year earlier that would have permitted individual congregations to decide whether to ordain women.

A pastoral letter on sexuality issued by a commission of the Rabbinical Assembly of Conservative Judaism marked the first modern attempt to draft a sexual ethic by any branch of Judaism. The report said premarital sex "can embody a measure of morality" while affirming repeatedly that heterosexual marriage is the only proper setting for sexual relations. The document took no definitive stand on homosexuality. The Presbyterian Church (U.S.A.) barred clergy from blessing homosexual unions but declined to impose a celibacy requirement on clergy. The House of Bishops of the Episcopal Church decided not to have the denomination's General Convention in Indianapolis, Ind., in late August and early September consider resolutions to ban the blessing of same-sex unions, forbid sex outside marriage, or prohibit the ordination of anyone who had sex outside marriage. The 3.2 million-member Evangelical Lutheran Church in America announced in October that it was extending the time period for discussion of a proposed statement on human sexuality past the denomination's 1995 Churchwide Assembly. A draft of the statement had stirred criticism because of reports that it took permissive stances on masturbation, homosexual unions, and the use of condoms by teenagers to prevent disease. True Love Waits, a Southern Baptist-initiated campaign that encourages teenagers to abstain from sex before marriage, won support from several Protestant and Roman Catholic groups. More than 100,000 pledge cards were displayed outside the Southern Baptist Convention meeting in Orlando, and more than 200,000 were staked to the ground on the Mall in Washington, D.C., in July during a national Youth for Christ gathering.

In a 6–3 ruling the U.S. Supreme Court said the creation of a special school district in New York for children with disabilities in the Satmar Hasidic Jewish sect violated the First Amendment's separation of church and state. The court said creation of the district by the state legislature "singles out a particular religious sect for special treatment." The ruling disappointed several groups that had expected the court to use the case to modify the principles it established in 1971 to determine whether a government action benefiting religion is constitutionally permissible. A California appeals court ruled that the Boy Scouts could not exclude boys who do not believe in God. The 2–1 ruling found that the Orange County Council of the Boy Scouts was a business as defined by state law and therefore could not discriminate on the basis of religion. Another church-state battle ended with the U.S. Equal Employment Opportunity Commission's withdrawing proposed guidelines dealing with religious harassment in the workplace after protests from religious groups and a Senate resolution urging that they be withdrawn.

U.S. Pres. Bill Clinton continued to draw fire from several evangelical Christian groups. The National Religious Broadcasters refused to invite him to its Washington convention in January because of what it called his "policies and positions which are blatantly contrary to scriptural views." The Christian Life Commission of the Southern Baptist Convention, of which Clinton was a member, took issue with his health care reforms, including a proposal to finance abortions with tax money. The politically conservative Christian Coalition's opposition to the president's health care agenda was denounced by the ecumenical National Council of Churches, which called the coalition's stance "appalling" and "simply astonishing." In July a newly formed group called the Interfaith Alliance, made up of liberal Protestants, Roman Catholics, and Jews, challenged what it called the "extremist" and "intolerant" tactics of the Religious Right, saying they raised questions about religious liberty. The alliance also pointed out that the Religious Right represented only one segment of the U.S. religious community.

(DARRELL J. TURNER)

PROTESTANT CHURCHES

Anglican Communion. The Anglican Communion continued its 20-year struggle over sexual morality and women's ordination in 1994. The Church of England ordained its first women in March, and the Scottish Episcopal Church approved plans to ordain women, but in April the Anglican Church in Wales defeated a proposal to do so. By the end of the year, more than 1,100 women had been ordained to the priesthood of the Church of England. A number of clergymen had announced that they would join the Roman Catholic Church in protest.

The Anglican Church in Nigeria nullified the ordination of three women as deacons by one of its bishops in December 1993. The church's Standing Committee issued a communiqué in March saying, "The ministration of the women involved in that ordination is not acceptable in the Church of Nigeria." Meanwhile, in February the Anglican Church of Canada ordained its first woman bishop, Victoria Matthews, who was elected suffragan (assistant) bishop for the diocese of Toronto in November 1993. She became the Anglican Communion's fifth woman bishop; three were in the U.S. and one in New Zealand.

Debate over sexual morality galvanized the U.S. Episcopal Church, which reached a stalemate over the issue at its August convention in Indianapolis, Ind. By an 88–81 vote the House of Bishops passed a 76-page document on human sexuality drafted by one of its committees. Meanwhile, 101 bishops signed a more conservative "affirmation" of traditional sexual morality, while 55 bishops, led by John Spong of Newark N.J., signed a "declaration" affirming the acceptability of homosexual ordination and practice. Because of their disagreement, the bishops voted to call the document a "pastoral study document" instead of a "pastoral teaching," as it was proposed.

The Church of England rejected attempts to separate church from state when its July synod defeated a motion to remove state control over the appointment of diocesan bishops and over church legislation. The

issue of disestablishing the Church of England came to the fore after Prince Charles, in a televised interview earlier in the year, said he preferred to be regarded as the "defender of all faiths" rather than the defender of one faith.

The diocese of Sydney, Australia, became the communion's first to pass legislation allowing lay people and deacons to preside at Holy Communion, although final approval was still pending. The Church of England and Episcopal Church in the U.S. defeated similar proposals in 1994. Current practice allowed only priests and bishops to preside at Holy Communion services.

The Very Rev. John L. Peterson, dean of St. George's College, Jerusalem, was appointed secretary-general of the Anglican Communion and replaced the Rev. Samuel Van Culin upon his retirement. The secretariat's office is in London. The Rt. Rev. James Ottley, bishop of Panama, was appointed Anglican observer at the United Nations. He succeeded the Rt. Rev. Paul Reeves, who left the position to return to New Zealand.   (DAVID E. SUMNER)

Baptist Churches. The National Baptist Convention, U.S.A., at some eight million members the largest black organization of Baptists in America, moved in a newer direction with the election of an activist clergyman, the Rev. Henry J. Lyons, pastor of the Metropolitan Baptist Church of St. Petersburg, Fla. He was expected to move the body into the mainstream of civil rights, a role it avoided in the 1960s when it refused the plea of the Rev. Martin Luther King, Jr., to join in the battle.

The racially diverse American Baptist Churches USA, the oldest of the national Baptist groups, saw divisions over the ordination and acceptance of homosexuals. Both sides in the matter called upon Scripture to support their cases. The president of the 1.5 million-member denomination, Hector Gonzalez, noted sadly that whichever way the battle went, the Baptists stood to lose churches. Conservatives and evangelicals threatened to "disfellowship" churches supporting gay rights, while gay rights activists threatened to leave the denomination. On

a positive note, new church establishment was reported near the goal of "500 more in '94." Some 450 new church projects had been launched as of June 14, 1994.

The largest Protestant denomination in the U.S., the Southern Baptist Convention, continued its internecine warfare between conservatives and moderates. A new uproar was generated by the firing of the Rev. Russell H. Dilday, the popular president of Southwestern Baptist Theological Seminary, the largest theological school in the world. The fundamentalists' reaction was immediate and strong, giving further focus to the threat of the moderates to withdraw from the SBC to form their own denomination. The moderates' "fellowship" had added over 300 churches in 1993, bringing the total in 1994 to 1,201, with an expected income of $17 million for 1994. Southern Baptists, long opposing women in the ministry, nevertheless voted to leave the matter to local churches and not to "disfellowship" churches for supporting women ministers. In a departure from this tradition of local autonomy, however, support for gay rights or the ordination of homosexuals would lead to banishment of the local churches from the national body.

In Europe, Baptists planned to relocate their controversial seminary from Rüschlikon, Switz., to Prague. The 44-year-old seminary had been plagued by financial problems, most of them related to the reduction in funding by the conservatives in control of the Southern Baptists in the U.S. and to the difficulty foreign seminarians faced in obtaining Swiss visas for family members.   (NORMAN R. DE PUY)

Christian Church (Disciples of Christ). Mission and money issues dominated activities within the Christian Church (Disciples of Christ) during 1994. In July, at the urging of the general minister and president, Richard L. Hamm, the General Board backed a working set of mission imperatives calling for improved ministries with children, youth, and young adults; a focus on congregational renewal and establishment; and increased evangelism and outreach. The board approved the initiatives. Board members also affirmed the direction of a proposed mission-funding plan that would give congregations a more active role in deciding how to finance denominational ministries. Relations with the Disciples' "ecumenical partner," the United Church of Christ, advanced with the approval of a Common Global Ministries Board to direct their world mission arms.

The church stopped a building project in downtown Indianapolis, Ind., in February. In May church leaders signed a 10-year lease, relocating the international headquarters to existing downtown office space. The new "Disciples Center" would house nearly 200 employees. Disciples' membership totals dropped below one million for the first time in the 20th century. At the end of 1993 the church recorded 961,268 members in 3,995 congregations. Giving to denominational outreach dropped by 2% to $32,409,974.   (CLIFFORD L. WILLIS)

Churches of Christ. Over 13,000 assemblies of the Churches of Christ were operating in the U.S., in addition to several thousand around the world. Emphasis in 1994 was on worldwide evangelism, benevolence, and enriched public worship.

The most fertile mission field was East-

AFP

Deacons gathered at Bristol Cathedral on March 12 share their happiness as they await ordination as priests in the Church of England. Following two decades of debate, 32 women, the first in the history of the church to serve as priests, were ordained in the ceremony.

ern Europe, where 124 new churches were started. Programs in Barnaul, Siberia (Russia), Donetsk, Ukraine, and Prague were especially successful. A Russian children's Bible was published. Thousands of university students went in teams to every continent to strengthen churches. "Let's Start Talking" sent 34 evangelistic teams to 18 countries. India was the nation with the fastest growth in Churches of Christ. Teams of doctors served in Vietnam.

Among the 21 colleges and universities connected with Churches of Christ, International Christian University in Vienna opened a branch in Kiev, Ukraine. Pepperdine University, Malibu, Calif., launched a $300 million campaign for endowment. Oklahoma Christian University opened a new campus in Portland, Ore.

Two million dollars were sent to churches in California for earthquake and fire relief, and a similar amount went to states with flood damage. (M. NORVEL YOUNG)

Church of Christ, Scientist. In 1994 the Christian Science Church marked the centennial of two important events. On May 21, 1894, the cornerstone for the original edifice of the First Church of Christ, Scientist, in Boston was laid, and the building was completed on Dec. 31, 1894. In the early days of the church, personal preaching was a subject of great concern to church founder Mary Baker Eddy. On Dec. 19, 1894, she formally "ordained" the Bible and her book *Science and Health with Key to the Scriptures* as the church's impersonal "pastor."

The pastor was also the focus of the 1994 annual meeting held in Boston on June 6. Incoming church president Ruth Elizabeth Jenks of Chicago pointed out, "Generations of families are living witnesses not only to the immediate access to this pastor each one of us has as an individual, but also of the opportunity to share it with a yearning world." In response to growing public interest in books on spirituality and health, a new edition of *Science and Health with Key to the Scriptures* was published on October 1 and was available at bookstores and Christian Science Reading Rooms.

(M. VICTOR WESTBERG)

Church of Jesus Christ of Latter-day Saints. With approximately nine million members worldwide and membership continuing to grow rapidly, the church in 1994 faced challenges in administration, political unrest, and national and ethnic conflicts in many countries. In acknowledging cultural differences, officials and missionaries made valiant efforts to eliminate "Americanisms" from what was now a worldwide faith. The nearly 50,000 full-time missionaries in 131 countries baptized more than 310,000 new members in 1994, with spectacular growth recorded in Mexico, Brazil, the Philippines, and Eastern Europe. Almost a third of the missionaries were from outside the U.S. In addition to proselytizing missionaries, there were educational, health care, welfare, and humanitarian missions.

With the death of Ezra Taft Benson (*see* OBITUARIES), president of the church from 1985 to 1994, Howard W. Hunter, 86, was sustained as president. Born in Boise, Idaho, and a corporate attorney for many years in southern California, Hunter became an apostle in 1959.

New Temples were dedicated in Orlando, Fla., and Bountiful, Utah; temples were under construction in Hong Kong; Bogotá, Colombia; Preston, England; St. Louis, Mo.; and American Fork, Utah. Substantial welfare assistance was rendered to those suffering from the Mississippi River flood, fires and earthquake in southern California, and brushfires in Australia.

In a move to "preserve doctrinal purity," the church disciplined several persons who actively opposed church leaders and policies or published articles or books regarded as damaging to church interests.

(LEONARD J. ARRINGTON)

Jehovah's Witnesses. During the year, nearly five million Witnesses spent over one billion hours spreading Bible knowledge to their neighbours. This educational work was at the heart of the 80% growth in the number of the Witnesses during the past decade. Bible education or "Divine Teaching" was the theme of the 1993–94 worldwide series of conventions, attended by 7,802,996 persons, with 133,785 baptized. The 1,514 conventions were highlighted by eight international conventions with delegates attending from as many as 44 countries. "This convention showed," wrote a reporter in Kiev, Ukraine, "that the achievement of peace and harmony among people of different nationalities and from various countries is really possible." The 750-page book *Jehovah's Witnesses—Proclaimers of God's Kingdom* was released at these conventions. It provides an exhaustive and candid history of this educational work in 28 languages. Also in 1994 the *New World Translation* of the New Testament appeared in 10 additional languages: Greek, Indonesian, Korean, Polish, Cebuano, Iloko, Tagalog, Afrikaans, Yoruba, and Zulu. Bible study aids were being distributed in more than 200 languages.

(MILTON HENSCHEL)

Lutheran Communion. The Council of the Lutheran World Federation (LWF) met in Geneva in June 1994 and elected Ishmael Noko of Zimbabwe as general secretary to succeed Gunnar Staalsett of Norway. The first member of a church from the South to lead the LWF in this capacity, Noko would oversee the preparation for the next assembly, to be held in Hong Kong in 1997. The council passed resolutions supporting the International Year of the Family and the goals of the International Decade of the World's Indigenous People. Other resolutions deplored conflicts in Rwanda and Liberia but welcomed moves toward democracy in South Africa and El Salvador and the peace process in the Middle East. The Lutheran members of a new commission for Lutheran–Roman Catholic dialogue were appointed.

A consultation of LWF church leaders also convened in June. This unique event focused on the understanding of world Lutheranism as a communion with spiritual, human, and material gifts. The consultation affirmed the centrality of mission and evangelism for the churches and the struggle for justice and peace in several areas of the world.

A number of Nordic and Baltic Lutheran churches and several Anglican churches in the U.K. took steps toward the approval of the Porvoo Report, which recommended closer Anglican-Lutheran relations.

Several Lutheran churches in Germany and Eastern Europe elected new bishops, as a new generation of church leaders, edu-

cated during the communist era, came into place to face new problems. Leadership disputes continued within the Batak Church in Indonesia, while Lutheran church organizations in the Philippines were competing for resources and influence. The Lutheran Church of Tanzania concentrated on mission and evangelism in its context and on issues of democracy and women's rights. The Evangelical Church of the Lutheran Confession in Brazil struggled with the theme of ecclesiology and the question of what kind of church was appropriate for its Latin-American setting.

In 1994 the Evangelical Lutheran Church in America continued to confront the problem of declining resources. Although giving in congregations increased, fewer funds were available for the national church. Significant time and energy were devoted to proposed statements on human sexuality and peace. Ecumenical proposals for full communion with several Reformed churches and the Episcopal Church and for lifting condemnations against the Roman Catholic Church gained more attention. The Lutheran Church–Missouri Synod also experienced financial difficulties. During the year it developed a vision statement with a strong emphasis on mission.

(WILLIAM G. RUSCH)

Methodist Churches. The Executive Committee of the World Methodist Council met in Tallinn, Estonia, in September 1994 to coincide with the stonelaying of the new Baltic Mission Church Centre. Methodism was established in Estonia in 1907, and it was the only former Soviet bloc country in which Methodism had continued uninterrupted to the present day. The council welcomed the Free Methodist Church in Canada, the Methodist Church in Puerto Rico, and the United Methodist Church in Russia into membership, bringing the total number of member churches to 71. The Executive also received reports of continuing ecumenical conversations with Anglican, Orthodox, and Roman Catholic churches. In particular, the interim report of the Anglican-Methodist International Commission, entitled "Sharing in the Apostolic Communion," was being considered by member churches. A major part of the Executive Committee's work was planning the program of the next World Methodist Conference, to be held in Rio de Janeiro in 1996.

The 1994 World Methodist Peace Award was given to Father Elias Chacour, a Melchite Catholic priest and a Palestinian Israeli citizen from Galilee who founded the Prophet Elias Community College, in which Christians, Muslims, and Jews teach and learn together. In April the president of Zimbabwe, Robert Mugabe, formally opened the Africa University at Old Mutare, a project of the United Methodist Church and the first Methodist university in Africa. The fifth International Youth Conference was held in Hamburg, Germany, in August with nearly 1,000 representatives from 52 countries in attendance.

The "Connecting Congregations" initiative launched by the World Methodist Evangelism Institute in 1993 now included at least 65 churches from Eastern Europe. South America, Africa, and Indonesia were linked with churches in North America, Australia, Singapore, and Korea, which provided material and financial support.

The European Methodist Council meeting in September 1994 commended the report of conversations between the Methodist Church and the Churches (Lutheran and Reformed) of the Leuenberg Concord to member churches and urged its acceptance. The World Federation of Methodist Women issued a new statement of commitment during the year and commended it to all their members. A major activity of the federation over the year was the organizing of a worldwide campaign against the sexual exploitation of children. Considerable support was given as well to the United Nations Year of the Family.

(JOHN C.A. BARRETT)

Pentecostal Churches. On Oct. 19, 1994, the Pentecostal Fellowship of North America (PFNA), representing 21 white denominations, ended 46 years of racial separation by dissolving itself in favour of a new entity designed to be open to all ethnic groups. Black Pentecostals, who were not invited to join the PFNA in 1948, joined with white Pentecostals in creating a new fellowship called the Pentecostal/Charismatic Churches of North America. The two largest Pentecostal denominations represented were the Church of God in Christ (COGIC; predominantly black, 5.5 million members) and the Assemblies of God (white, 2.2 million members), which had established separate churches in 1914. Elected as the first chairman was Bishop Ithiel Clemmons of New York, a member of the General Board of COGIC.

Serving with Clemmons as cochairman was former PFNA chairman, Bishop B.E. Underwood of the predominately white International Pentecostal Holiness Church. The climax of the already emotional proceeding came when Bishop Charles Blake of California (COGIC) washed the feet of the Rev. Thomas Trask, general superintendent of the Assemblies of God. The first action of the new group was the adoption of a "Racial Reconciliation Manifesto," in which all 3,000 participants and observers pledged to "oppose racism prophetically in all its various manifestations."

Also in October the Assemblies of God conducted what was billed as the "world's largest prayer meeting" in Seoul, South Korea. Led by Korean pastor David Yonggi Cho, the meeting drew over one million worshipers from 134 nations to Yoido Plaza, site of Cho's church, which itself had 800,000 members.

In August the Church of God (Cleveland, Tenn.) conducted its biennial General Assembly in San Antonio, Texas, and elected Robert White as the new general overseer.

(VINSON SYNAN)

Reformed, Presbyterian, and Congregational Churches. The question of Reformed identity continued to preoccupy the World Alliance of Reformed Churches (WARC) in 1994. Dialogue with the Orthodox churches in Cyprus in January and with the Oriental Orthodox (non-Chalcedonian) churches in The Netherlands in September led to statements on how Jesus Christ was to be understood (Christology).

The main task facing the Alliance was preparing for its 23rd General Council, to be held in Debrecen, Hung., in 1997. The council would focus on the question of justice and especially on global economic justice. The gulf between North and South had concerned Reformed and other Chris-

tians for more than a generation. WARC wanted to ask if this chasm between rich and poor was not a "confessional" issue, challenging the integrity of its faith.

Apartheid in South Africa began in the church, with the development in the 19th century of separate Dutch Reformed churches divided on racial lines. It was fitting, then, that a year that witnessed the end of apartheid in the state should also see the beginning of the end of that separatist doctrine in the church. In April 1994 the black Dutch Reformed Church in Africa and the Coloured Dutch Reformed Mission Church came together to form the Uniting Reformed Church in Southern Africa. Deliberately it was "uniting" rather than "united," looking forward to a wider unity within and beyond the Dutch Reformed family.

Changes in Eastern Europe since 1989 continued to have an impact on Reformed churches. The disintegration of Yugoslavia led to the fragmentation there of the Reformed Christian Church. The Reformed Christian churches in Croatia and Slovenia were admitted to WARC membership in 1993 and 1994, respectively. WARC was meanwhile concerned with proposals from the Reformed Church of Hungary for a Universal Hungarian Reformed Synod, partly because "synod" was a misleading name for a consultative body but mainly because the proposed synod, in an already volatile region, was structured on ethnic lines.

Nine new churches were admitted to WARC membership in 1994: the Evangelical Church of the Republic of Niger, the Congregational Christian Church in American Samoa, the United Church of Christ in Mozambique, the Volkskerk van Afrika, the Evangelical Church of the Congo, the National Presbyterian Church (Chile), the Reformed Christian Church in Slovenia, the Presbyterian Reformed Church of Mexico, and the Uniting Reformed Church in Southern Africa. WARC now linked over 70 million Christians in 193 churches in 99 countries.

(PÁRAIC RÉAMONN)

Religious Society of Friends. Quakers from around the world met at Ghost Ranch, Abiquiu, N.M., on Aug. 15–24, 1994, for the 18th triennial meeting of the Friends World Committee for Consultation. Johan Maurer, general secretary of Friends United Meeting, gave the keynote address, in which he warned against the temptation to idolize traditions. The 270 representatives from over 70 autonomous national and regional Friends groups experienced the authenticity of different styles of Quaker worship and deliberated on issues of economic justice and the suffering of the poor, the inclusion of children in the life of the Friends Church, and a number of ways in which Friends are experiencing the Quaker peace testimony, as follows:

"We have heard about the far-ranging and devastating effects of the arms trade.... We should recognize our personal and corporate potential for being more effective peace builders.... We are encouraged to examine our personal lifestyle to see ways in which this may be contributing to the underlying causes of injustice and war. For many, it was clear that change to a more peaceful world would come about only through a personal change of heart and devotion to the Prince of Peace."

(THOMAS F. TAYLOR)

Salvation Army. The Salvation Army elected a new world leader, Gen. Paul A. Rader. In accepting the office during the International Year of the Family, General Rader focused on the importance of family values, emphasizing their central role in Salvation Army work around the world.

Civil war in Rwanda raged, tearing lives and communities apart. Working through UNICEF, the UN High Commissioner for Refugees, and Oxfam, the Salvation Army provided expert advice on irrigation and water purification. Involvement in the Rwandan relief program continued, with a successful initiative to supply 600 tons of essential clothing. Specialists in health, agriculture, and education formed a relief team, working to rehabilitate refugees, rebuild their communities, and restore their faith.

In the midst of other crises, natural calamities, and man-made disasters, the Salvation Army continued to provide practical aid and spiritual comfort. In 1994 the Army assisted victims of monsoons in the Philippines, flooding in China, tornadoes in the U.S., and an earthquake in Colombia. International endorsement of the need for the Salvation Army's services was underscored by its presence in 98 countries, including Bangladesh, Russia, and Zaire.

(CHARMAINE FLETCHER)

Seventh-day Adventist Church. Seventh-day Adventists trace their origin to the Millerite awakening of the 1830s and 1840s in North America. The year 1994 marked the 150th anniversary of Oct. 22, 1844, when the Millerites expected Jesus Christ to return. Throughout the year Adventists in many lands recalled their roots, celebrated God's leading in the church, and laid plans for the future.

The church continued its worldwide expansion. During the year membership passed eight million Adventists living in 209 countries. The church's rapid growth in the Third World, however, coupled with slower growth in the First World, led to increasing financial pressures.

The ordination of women to the gospel ministry again surfaced as a polarizing issue. Seventh-day Adventists permitted women to serve as unordained ministers of local churches; the church in North America in particular pressed for their ordination.

In a year of massive human disasters, Adventists, through the church's relief arm, Adventist Development and Relief Agency, provided help in Rwanda, Zaire, Somalia, and more than 100 other countries.

Although the church was not a member of the World Council of Churches, it engaged in dialogue with other Christian bodies. During 1994 it began conversations with the World Lutheran Alliance, the initial meeting convening in Darmstadt, Germany.

(WILLIAM G. JOHNSSON)

Unitarian (Universalist) Churches. Spared the divisiveness of theological controversy, Unitarian Universalists surged ahead happily on all fronts in 1994. The financial surpluses rung up by the Annual Program Fund and the Friends Program, accounting for 39% of the denomination's operating budget, increased the strength of ongoing and new social programs. Loans for building and remodeling church edifices stood at an unprecedented high. Congregations themselves were raising unusual amounts of money for building projects.

Approximately 400 persons were preparing themselves for a variety of ministries. Unfortunately, ministerial compensation and advancement were limited by the shortage of upper-level churches, while benefits were roughly one-half of those in other comparable religious bodies.

The movement was decentralizing its headquarters functions and turning toward greater district power and leadership. Paradoxically, a crucial debate on governance resulted in the rejection of moves that would have curtailed the president's power. The annual General Assembly of the Unitarian Universalist Association, June 23–28, 1994, attracted to Fort Worth, Texas, 2,204 registrants from all over North America. Critical social issues dealing with abuses of human rights and the development and dissemination of government, church, and individual resources to meet them occupied much attention.

New Unitarian fellowships were established in Bern, Switz., and Kaiserslautern, Germany. Transylvanian churches, and especially their rural village projects, received additional assistance, financial and otherwise. The Canadian Unitarian Council published a multigenerational curriculum on spiritual connection with the natural world. Its congregations nationwide engaged in public discussions of "Choice and the Act of Dying." British Unitarians called upon their government's secretary of state for education to ensure that state schools reflected the multifaith character of British society in moral and spiritual education, including all religious faiths and humanists on the basis of equal standing and respect.

(JOHN NICHOLLS BOOTH)

The United Church of Canada. National meetings held in Fergus, Ont., on August 19–28 were a focal point for the United Church of Canada in 1994. Laywoman Marion S. Best was elected moderator of Canada's largest Protestant denomination for a three-year term. Diaconal minister Virginia Coleman was appointed chief administrative officer. Delegates voted to continue to study restructuring from a four- to a three-tier system of government. The buildings that had housed the national offices since 1959 were sold, and the staff planned to relocate to rented facilities in Etobicoke (west Metropolitan Toronto) in 1995. In the last fiscal year, the denomination's two million known members and adherents raised Can$308,276,194 for all purposes. Contributions specifically to the church's national mission fund, however, remained static and had a restraining effect on program initiatives.

Work continued on a new denominational hymn book to be published in 1995; there was desire for a new liturgy resource as well. The United Church planned to establish a new body to support ethnic ministries within the denomination and also committed itself to greater funding for theological education through its 12 theological schools and centres. During 1994 the church released statements and reports on issues such as human rights in Mexico, democratic freedom in Haiti, the future of Canada and Quebec, and the Canadian economic crisis.

A covenant was signed to work in partnership with the United Church of Christ in the Philippines. This paralleled the 1992 covenant signed with the Evangelical Church of the Union in Germany. Reflecting its denominational heritage, the United Church of Canada continued its membership in the World Methodist Council and in the World Alliance of Reformed Churches.

As part of the national meetings, thousands of persons attended a daylong Church Fair '94. The harmony, goodwill, and hopefulness experienced at the event reflected the spirit of the meetings generally and the more peaceful temper of the denomination at large. (DOUGLAS L. FLANDERS)

United Church of Christ. For the United Church of Christ, 1994 marked the beginning of a season of churchwide theological reflection entitled "A Church Attentive to the Word." The season was based on the first of four marks of commitment in the "Statement of Commitment—Toward the 21st Century" (General Synod, 1993), in which church members were called upon to be attentive to the Word, inclusive of all people, responsive to God's call, and supportive of one another.

Work continued on proposed structural changes, particularly in the church's national setting, to be presented to the General Synod in 1995; a $30 million fund campaign in support of clergy, churches, and community, launched in 1993, reached its midpoint; and church-development and renewal efforts were intensified. The church lost a net total of 25,204 members in 1993; membership stood at 1,530,178 gathered in 6,225 congregations. Total church support in 1993 reached $621,894,219, compared with $595,096,785 in 1992.

Intensive work was done in 1994 to implement the 1993 pronouncement of General Synod 19 that the church become multiracial and multicultural. Health care reform was a major priority. A new curriculum, "The Word Among Us," was launched, as was a specialized curriculum in AIDS awareness and prevention and another entitled "Created in God's Image: A Human Sexuality Program for Ministry and Mission."

In July over 3,000 laypeople and clergy gathered at Purdue University, West Lafayette, Ind., for a second Faith Works celebration. The church continued its active involvement in the World Council of Churches, the National Council of the Churches of Christ in the U.S.A., and the World Alliance of Reformed Churches.

(PAUL H. SHERRY)

ROMAN CATHOLIC CHURCH

In April 1994 Pope John Paul II slipped while getting out of his bath and needed surgery to replace part of the thighbone. He had to walk with a cane and could no longer kneel to kiss the ground. The immediate result was a flurry of speculative succession stories about the next conclave. Frequently mentioned were Carlo Maria Cardinal Martini of Milan and Nigerian Francis J. Cardinal Arinze, since 1985 head of the Vatican's department for relations with non-Christian religions.

The pope soon resumed his active schedule. Fully expecting to lead the church into the year 2000, he called a June meeting of cardinals to discuss how to celebrate the anniversary. He proposed continental synods for North and South America, Asia, and the Far East. There was talk of a vast ecumenical celebration on Mt. Sinai.

Pope John Paul went to Zagreb, Croatia, September 11–12, ostensibly for the 900th anniversary of the diocese of Zagreb. His pleas for forgiveness were hard sayings for the nationalist Croats. The visit planned to Sarajevo, Bosnia and Herzegovina, for September 8 was canceled just 48 hours before, in part because the UN could not guarantee the security of the crowds and partly because local authorities might see such a visit as a provocation. The pope insisted his visit had been only postponed, not canceled. He had dearly wanted to visit what was left of the capital of Bosnia and Herzegovina to prove that Sarajevo, once an ecumenical haven for Catholics, Orthodox, Muslims, and Jews, had not been abandoned by the international community in its hour of need.

He had also planned to visit the United States in October for an address to the UN on United Nations Day and for a pastoral excursion to Newark, N.J., and Baltimore, Md. The visit was postponed in September because of renewed concerns over the pontiff's health.

Perhaps the most ecumenically positive document to emerge from the Vatican during the year was the report of the Pontifical Biblical Commission, released in January, on the use of the Bible. It reported that there was no specifically Catholic method of biblical research; Catholic scholars used the same methods as others. The difference lay in the approach, or "preunderstanding": "Catholic exegesis deliberately places itself within the living tradition of the Church, whose first concern is fidelity to the revelation attested by the Bible."

Less ecumenically welcome was the apostolic letter of Pentecost Sunday in late May, which declared that "the church has no authority whatsoever to confer priestly ordination on women, and that this judgment is to be definitively held by all the church's faithful." The papal argument was based on the fact that the 12 apostles were all men. Catholic theologians pointed out that "apostles" included many more than just those 12, that ministry was very fluid in the early church, and that women were certainly involved in it.

The archbishop of Canterbury was upset. The papal document looked like a direct response to the Church of England's ordination of more than a thousand women. (See *Anglican Communion,* above.) The pope declared the ordination of women "an obstacle to unity." A trickle of Anglican clergy continued to "go over to Rome" on this issue. Among them was the former bishop of London, Graham Leonard, who was "conditionally ordained" on April 23. (This meant his previous Anglican ordination was considered valid.) Some speculated that the ordination document was timed to preempt the deliberations of the October Roman Synod on Religious Life, at which 30 religious sisters were present. Its president was Benedictine Basil Cardinal Hume, archbishop of Westminster, London. For the first time, a woman, Sister Emilio Ehrlich, general of the Ursulines, acted as special secretary. The synod resolved that women should take their place in all the decision-making bodies of the church. Bishop Ernest Konbo suggested that women be made cardinals.

An earlier synod on the Church in Africa, which began in April, produced somewhat ambivalent results. African liturgy, complete with drums and dancing, was introduced

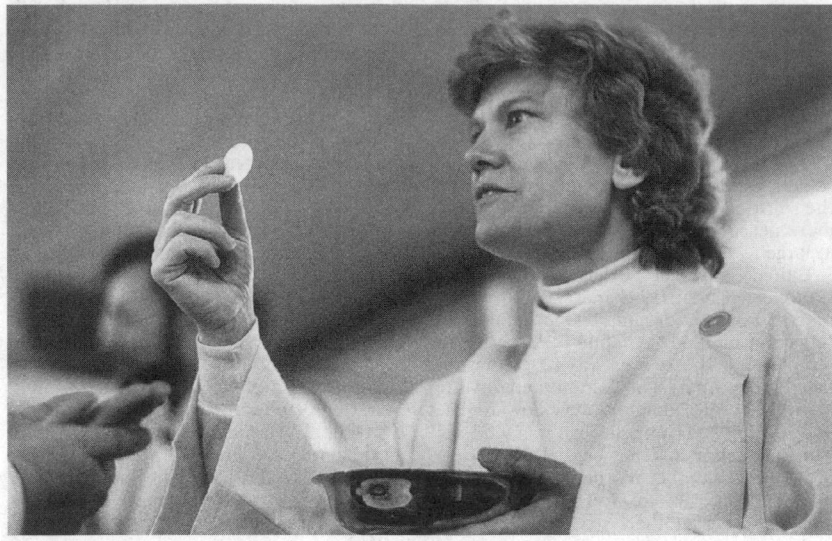

A Roman Catholic woman distributes communion hosts. Because of the shortage of priests in the United States, the church turned to women to assume some routine duties normally carried out by priests, but women continued to be prohibited from performing the sacraments.
ANGEL FRANCO—THE NEW YORK TIMES

into St. Peter's on a scale never seen before. The inability of the church to halt the killing in Rwanda, where some 70% of the population was Catholic, cast a shadow over the proceedings. "Tribal blood was thicker than the water of baptism," lamented one bishop. Some participants felt an African Synod should have been held in Africa and that they had been brought to Rome where they could be better controlled.

There was talk of a "holy alliance" between Christians and Muslims at the UN population conference in Cairo in September. (*See* POPULATIONS AND POPULATION MOVEMENTS: *Sidebar.*) Some delegates objected to the Vatican's fixation on excluding abortion as a method of population control. The Holy See also tried to unmask what it saw as the fudge implied in talking about "reproductive health" and the "empowerment" of women. The Vatican claimed victory and was able to sign the final text with reservations, but the price it paid was that the Holy See's reputation for subtle diplomacy suffered a grave blow.

On the other hand, the Fundamental Agreement signed with Israel on Dec. 30, 1993, contributed to the "peace process" in the Middle East. The denunciation of anti-Semitism and the pledge to work together on "pilgrim tourism" were crowned by the establishment of long-desired diplomatic relations. The first pro-nuncio to Israel, Archbishop Andrea Cordero, took up residence in Tel Aviv, and the first-ever Israeli ambassador to the Holy See, Shmuel Hadas, presented his credentials on Sept. 29, 1994.

The Catechism of the Catholic Church proved a best-seller in July. Two million copies had been in print. The English translation had been held up for several months so that the "inclusive language" used in the first U.S. translation could be eliminated. The pope's own book, *Crossing the Threshold of Hope,* published October 19, was an even bigger commercial success. (*See* PUBLISHING: *Books.*)

On October 30 Pope John Paul announced the creation of 30 new cardinals,

including two Americans and churchmen from the former communist countries of Albania, Belarus, Bosnia and Herzegovina, and the Czech Republic, as well as two— Cuba and Vietnam—still under authoritarian regimes.

See WORLD AFFAIRS: *Vatican City State.*

(PETER HEBBLETHWAITE)

THE ORTHODOX CHURCH

Ecumenical Patriarch Bartholomew I of Constantinople addressed the representatives of the 12 member states of the European Parliament on April 19, 1994, the first time an Orthodox clergyman had spoken to the body. Bartholomew emphasized the importance of human freedom, condemned fanaticism, and spoke of practical issues such as migration and unemployment. He asserted that the church contributes to unity by serving the spiritual needs of humanity.

In January Patriarch Pavle of Serbia called for an end to violence in former Yugoslavia in a communication to the World Council of Churches (WCC) Central Committee meeting in Johannesburg, South Africa. He expressed concern for all suffering because of violence "of whatever kind and by whomever it is used, regardless of religion or nation." Similar appeals for peace in southeastern Europe and the former Soviet republics were made by Bartholomew at the interdenominational Peace and Tolerance Conference, held in Istanbul in February and cosponsored by the patriarchate and the U.S.-based Appeal of Conscience Foundation.

On April 10 and on subsequent occasions, Archbishop Anastasios of Tiranë, head of the autocephalous Albanian Orthodox Church, issued appeals regarding the restrictions on religious freedom for the Orthodox in that primarily Muslim country, as well as in regard to Greek-Albanian ethnic conflicts involving the minority Greek-speaking Orthodox Albanian community. In a striking gesture, Aleksey II, patriarch of Moscow, in an address to the Hungarian parliament in April, sought forgiveness for the Soviet invasion of Hungary in 1956.

Arab Orthodox believers in Israel, Palestine, and Jordan protested policies of the Greek Orthodox patriarchate of Jerusalem in refusing to integrate Arabs into the hierarchy and property-management issues. The charges, expressed by the Arab Orthodox Initiative Committee, were rejected by Patriarch Diodoros I of Jerusalem.

The fourth official meeting of the Bilateral Orthodox–Reformed dialogue, begun in 1988, took place on Jan. 8–13, 1994, in Limassol, Cyprus. Participants judged that their doctrines on the Holy Trinity and the Incarnation of Jesus Christ were "not incompatible."

Early in the year, 5 of the 12 bishops who joined the Ukrainian Orthodox Church–Kiev patriarchate returned to the Autonomous Ukrainian Orthodox Church, which is loyal to the Moscow patriarchate. The Kiev patriarchate was formed in 1992, six months after Ukraine became an independent state.

In the U.S. a report was submitted on March 17 to Archbishop Iakovos seeking to end the financial scandal that developed when a former employee of the Greek Orthodox Archdiocese of North and South America used archdiocesan funds to pay private development bills in a joint real estate endeavour with the archdiocese. The agreement was challenged by the New York state attorney general on October 19. The Joint Committee of Orthodox–Roman Catholic Bishops met in Detroit, Mich., on March 8–10 for their 12th bilateral dialogue. The implications of "communion theology" and the "sister churches terminology" for the relations of the two church bodies were discussed, as were the relationships with the Oriental Orthodox churches.

The Orthodox Church in America celebrated its bicentennial in September, marking the arrival of Russian Orthodox monks on Sept. 24, 1794, in Alaska, then under Russian influence.   (STANLEY S. HARAKAS)

ORIENTAL ORTHODOX CHURCH

Armenian Patriarch-Catholicos Vazgen I died in Yerevan, Armenia, Aug. 18, 1994, at the age of 85. (*See* OBITUARIES.) He was a highly respected symbol of national unity in Armenia and for the Armenian diaspora and worked for peace in the Nagorno-Karabakh conflict.

Islamic fundamentalists were suspected of responsibility for the shootings of five members of Egypt's eight million-member Coptic Christian community on March 11, 1994, just outside the Muharraq Monastery, 30 km (19 mi) north of Asyut, a stronghold of the militant al-Jama'a al-Islamiya (Islamic Group). The action was protested by Pope Shenouda III, head of the Coptic Orthodox Church.

Aghan Baliozian, the archbishop of the Armenian Apostolic Church in Australia, was elected the first president of the National Council of Churches in Australia, established on July 3 in Syndey. Among the 13 member churches were the Armenian, Coptic, and Syrian orthodox churches.

In Addis Ababa, Eth., Abune Paulos, patriarch of the Ethiopian Orthodox Church, reopened the Holy Trinity Theological College, which had been closed by the communist government 17 years earlier. Faculty and students were recruited, and classes began in September 1994.

(STANLEY S. HARAKAS)

JUDAISM

For most Jews the past half century had been a struggle to create a secure political Jewish state in the Middle East and to disseminate worldwide knowledge about the destruction of European Jewry during the Holocaust. Both objectives were significantly advanced in 1993 and 1994 with the signing of an Israeli-Palestinian agreement and the opening (April 1993) of the U.S. Holocaust Memorial Museum in Washington, D.C. Indeed, the momentous steps toward peace between Israel and the Palestine Liberation Organization (PLO) now pushed the world's Jews to accept a new vision of Israel, one that did not necessarily include every square centimetre of land bequeathed to Abraham by God. In the U.S. the prospect of peace challenged the Jewish community to occupy itself with issues relating to hearth rather than to homeland. "There has to be more of a reason to be Jewish, a reason that's going to play itself out in . . . how you see yourself, how you relate to other people, how you live your life," said Conservative Rabbi Joel Zaiman of Baltimore, Md., in May.

Two of Judaism's four major denominations occupied themselves with discussions of sexual morality in 1994. Among the Reform rabbinate, which represents most of the world's Jews, an effort to prescribe a set of tenets for sexual behaviour for rabbis took shape, and the Conservative movement took on the issue of premarital sex, saying it must occur within the bounds of a committed relationship.

While the world's Jews dallied over such questions, however, one West Bank settler demonstrated the pathos of Jewish faith. On February 25, the holiday of Purim, when the Book of Esther is read, Baruch Goldstein burst into the Cave of the Patriarchs mosque in Hebron and killed about 30–40 Arab Muslims during their prayers. Goldstein, a religious Jew, had apparently taken literally the commandment in Esther to wipe out descendants of Haman, an enemy of ancient Persia's Jews. While

Goldstein was repudiated by most Jewish religious leaders, right-wing settlers in Israel's territories agreed he had followed God's commandment and said that making peace with their Arab enemies was tantamount to violating God's will. Goldstein's action seemed especially anachronistic as representatives of the two ancient religions were seeking new ways to live together in peace. (*See* CRIME, LAW ENFORCEMENT, AND PRISONS.)

The cost of underestimating religious sentiment was not limited to the understanding of extremist Jewish groups. Pope John Paul II's notable overtures toward Jews included recognition of Jews' right to live in Israel. He declared Jews "our elder brothers in the faith." The Vatican-Israeli agreement on diplomatic relations at the end of 1993 created a unique opportunity for Jews to engage in the first genuine dialogue with the Catholic Church in centuries. Some Israelis resisted the accord, however, because the Catholic Church wanted the Israeli representative to the Holy See to be a diplomat, not a rabbi. Representative of this view, for example, was former Israeli chief rabbi Shlomo Goren (*see* OBITUARIES), who at a large interfaith meeting in Jerusalem declared, "There is nothing for us to talk about with the goyim [gentiles]." He also opposed the accords with the PLO. Israel's Orthodox establishment boycotted the Jerusalem conference, which sought to discuss modern challenges to religions worldwide. By comparison, Roman Catholic Joseph Cardinal Ratzinger said Jews and Christians must accept each other "neither in disregard of their faith nor in its denial, but out of the depth of faith itself."

The community of Jews in Berlin saw the reopening of the New Synagogue, together with a Jewish cultural centre, late in 1994. The landmark building in the eastern part of the city was built in the 1860s and had been closed since it was burned by the Nazis on Kristallnacht in 1938.

The Lubavitch Hasidic movement mourned the loss of its leader of nearly a half century, Rabbi Menachem Mendel

Schneerson, who died on June 12, 1994, at the age of 92. (*See* OBITUARIES.) Schneerson built the Lubavitchers from a small band decimated in the Holocaust to a powerful, satellite-connected world organization with some 200,000 followers. Schneerson's influence extended widely, especially in Israel, where politics and religious doctrine bore his mark.　　　(NOAM NEUSNER)

BUDDHISM

Three peace marches dramatically asserted Cambodian Buddhism's political force during 1993–94. After escorting refugees to safety across Khmer Rouge-held territories, the Venerable Mahaghosananda's Dhammayetra Movement led thousands of Buddhists to Phnom Penh in March 1993, encouraging Cambodians to defy guerrilla threats against participating in subsequently successful national elections. Khmer Rouge shelling disrupted an April 1994 march for national reconciliation; one monk and one nun were killed. In June Prince Norodom Ranariddh welcomed Sri Lankan offers to retrain the Cambodian Buddhist Sangha and replace Buddhist scriptures destroyed by the Khmer Rouge. During June Sri Lankan Buddhist missionaries also began building a monastery at the Buddha's Nepalese birthplace, Lumbini, and presented gifts of sacred relics to Nepal.

Riots involving Hindu nationalists and refugee Tibetan Buddhists jarred Dharmshala in April 1994; leaflets threatened violence against Tibetans who remained after July. Most offices of Tibet's government-in-exile were shifted to Delhi, but local leaders persuaded the Dalai Lama to stay. Throughout the year protests continued against government oppression of opposition Buddhist groups in Vietnam.

In March 1994 a nephew of the 16th Karmapa, leader of the Black Hat (Kangyu) order of Tibetan Buddhism, challenged the November 1993 enthronement of his uncle's successor/reincarnation, sanctioned by China and the Dalai Lama, with a rival he supported as the true Karmapa. The ensuing violence in Delhi fulfilled the 5th Karmapa's prediction that the 17th Karmapa's succession would be conflict-ridden. In April the Rev. Suh Eui Hyun, leader of the Chogye order representing 80% of South Korean Buddhism, resigned after violent confrontations with reformist monks. The Reform Council took power, added women to the Chogye Assembly, and decentralized temple management nationwide, ending the government's assurance of official Buddhist support. Financial and sexual scandals in the spring involving several popular monks reverberated throughout Thailand as reports of monastic corruption flooded the popular press.

In May a Japanese monk, defining Buddhist temples as lucrative corporations with monks as employees, formed what may have been the world's first religious labour union. Wakyo Goda's union organized walkouts and sick-outs against temple superiors. In the same month, Western and Japanese musicians joined 100 chanting Buddhist monks for a rock concert at Nara's famous Todai Temple. Head priest Shinkai Shindoh defended the innovations as Buddhist attempts to make people happy and appeal to the Japanese youth.

The December 1993 unveiling of a 24-m (79-ft)-high Chinese-made bronze Buddha

Jews in Hebron, in the occupied West Bank, pray outside the Cave of the Patriarchs mosque, which was closed in February after a settler massacred Muslims worshiping there. The Israeli government reopened the shrine in November, after security had been improved.

image of Hong Kong design, facing China from Hong Kong's Lantau Island, was hailed as an important step toward forging new relations.   (JONATHAN S. WALTERS)

HINDUISM

Caste tension and strife within the Indian Hindu community continued in 1994. On March 11 the cause of the fundamentalist Bharatiya Janata Party (BJP)—a Hindu nation ("Hindutva")—suffered a major defeat. The Indian Supreme Court affirmed the constitutional principles of secular democracy and upheld the action of the central government in dismissing BJP governments in four states following the BJP-sanctioned demolition of a mosque in Ayodhya in 1992 by Hindu militants who believed the mosque desecrated the legendary birthplace of the god Rama. The ensuing Hindu-Muslim riots throughout the country led to the deaths of an estimated 2,000 people.

Undeterred by the high court's ruling, the BJP government of New Delhi enacted a law on March 31 imposing severe criminal penalties for the slaughter of cows, regarded by Hindus as sacred, and the sale or possession of beef. No bail would be allowed for those charged with the crime. The new law also established cow shelters throughout the city to accommodate an estimated 150,000 sick or old cows, which formerly could be slaughtered.

The political power of the BJP was openly challenged during the year by Hindu groups that regarded the BJP's agenda as reasserting the ancient domination of Indian society by the Brahmins and other upper castes. In May the 120-year-old reformist group Arya Samaj announced its intention to launch a political party to counter Hindu nationalism and promote liberal principles, including the political and economic emancipation of the lower castes, the abolition of child labour, and the full equality of women in Indian society.

Savouring newly found political power through a political coalition that defeated the BJP in state elections in Uttar Pradesh and Bihar, leaders of the Bahujan Samaj Party representing the untouchables (which make up more than 16% of India's population) and the Samajwadi Janata Party representing lower ("backward") castes publicly denounced 1994 celebrations of the 125th anniversary of Mohandas Gandhi's birthday. Although Gandhi sought the end of untouchability and called the untouchables Harijans, or children of God, the untouchables call themselves Dalits—"the oppressed"—and view Gandhi as a Brahmin elitist who sought to continue what one Dalit leader characterized in an April rally as "the divine slavery which the Hindu caste system has imposed on [Dalits]."

The bold assertion of political power by the Dalits brought retaliation from upper castes. During the year there were numerous reports of the burning of Dalit villages and murder of their inhabitants and the raping of Dalit women by upper-caste men. In January more than 4,000 were arrested in demonstrations when the Congress Party government in Maharashtra renamed a prestigious university in honour of the late B.R. Ambedkar, a leader of the untouchables who was the chief architect of the Indian constitution.

On January 8 Chandrasekharendra Saraswati, the revered Hindu leader, died.

(*See* OBITUARIES.) Throughout his life he had advocated religious tolerance in a land of great religious diversity and strife.
   (H. PATRICK SULLIVAN)

ISLAM

The struggle between conservative fundamentalist and moderate groups increased in intensity in many places in the Muslim world in 1994. The conclusion of the peace accords between Israel and the Palestine Liberation Organization brought new long-term consequences for Muslims. Religious questions involving the holy places in Jerusalem were not specifically addressed in the agreement, and when Israel indicated that Jordan (which had overseen restoration of the Dome of the Rock and contributed $6 million–$8 million to restoration activities) should take the lead, the PLO was concerned lest it lose influence in the holy city. There was widespread Muslim outrage at the terrorist shooting of Muslims in the Hebron mosque massacre in February.

P. BARTHOLOMEW—GAMMA LIAISON

Bangladeshi women demand the death of Taslima Nasrin. Muslims in Bangladesh forced the writer, who had expressed what fundamentalists considered blasphemous views, into hiding and, later, exile.

Elections in Turkey in March found the religious Welfare Party winning control in many localities, including the city governments of Ankara and Istanbul. Incidents occurred involving attacks or demonstrations against persons accused of behaving in ways considered un-Islamic. For two years Algeria had been under martial law while the military government tried to suppress widespread conservative fundamentalist violence. In Egypt foreign tourists continued to come under attack from Muslim terrorists. At the UN population conference in Cairo in September, some conservative Muslim groups joined with the Vatican in opposing the draft program promoting birth control. (*See* POPULATION AND POPULATION MOVEMENTS: *Sidebar*.)

Violence by and against Muslims was also reported in The Sudan, the Philippines, East Timor, Afghanistan, China, Malaysia, and Bosnia and Herzegovina, where fighting continued without great hope of a settlement. In Bangladesh a group calling itself the Council of Islamic Soldiers set a bounty for the death of a physician, Taslima Nasrin (*see* BIOGRAPHIES), because of her published writing. Tragedy occurred during the hajj to Mecca in May when some 270 pilgrims died in a stampede during the rite at Mina. About two and a half million Muslims went on pilgrimage during that period.

Grand Ayatollah Mohammad Ali Araki, *Marja al-Al'la*, the leading Shi'ite clergyman, died in late November in Tehran at the age of 105 or 106. In a blatant political move, the ruling Iranian mullahs pressed for Ayatollah Ali Khamenei to succeed Araki but, under pressure, Khamenei had to withdraw his candidacy.

Abu Dhabi announced construction of a large mosque to cover an area of more than 46,500 sq m (500,000 sq ft) at a cost estimated at $150 million. Meanwhile, plans for a mosque to be built in the outskirts of Moscow aroused controversy. Two prominent Western businesses apologized for inadvertently using passages of Islamic texts on their products—McDonald's on throwaway food bags and Chanel on clothing.

In the United States four Muslims were sentenced to life imprisonment for the bombing of the World Trade Center in 1993. In February Louis Farrakhan, leader of the separatist Nation of Islam, demoted his senior assistant, Khalid Abdul Muhammad, for anti-Jewish remarks made in November 1993. Controversy continued, however, because of Farrakhan's own statements at the time and later in the year. Muhammad was subsequently shot and wounded by a dissident after a speech in southern California in May. An experiment by the Chicago Housing Authority using members of the Nation of Islam's New Life, Inc., organization to patrol inner-city housing projects drew both praise and criticism. More than half a dozen Islamic finance companies in the U.S. began offering mortgages and investment opportunities that would avoid the use of interest, which is prohibited by Islamic law.   (REUBEN W. SMITH)

This article updates the *Macropædia* articles The Buddha and BUDDHISM; CHRISTIANITY; EASTERN ORTHODOXY; HINDUISM; Muhammad and the Religion of ISLAM; JUDAISM; PROTESTANTISM; The Study and Classification of RELIGIONS; ROMAN CATHOLICISM; and *Micropædia* entries on the various denominations.

Worldwide Adherents of All Religions by Seven Continental Areas, Mid-1994

	Africa	Asia	Europe	Latin America	Northern America	Oceania	Eurasia	World	%	Number of countries
Christians	351,682,000	304,887,000	422,159,000	422,140,000	246,319,000	23,240,000	109,747,000	**1,900,174,000**	33.6	260
Roman Catholics	132,102,000	132,053,000	267,972,000	411,514,000	100,386,000	8,427,000	5,615,000	**1,058,069,000**	18.7	249
Protestants	93,865,000	87,051,000	75,441,000	17,513,000	99,652,000	7,718,000	9,903,000	**391,143,000**	6.9	236
Orthodox	30,685,000	3,904,000	36,869,000	1,789,000	6,217,000	591,000	94,129,000	**174,184,000**	3.1	105
Anglicans	28,873,000	755,000	33,625,000	1,319,000	7,593,000	5,872,000	1,000	**78,038,000**	1.4	158
Other Christians	66,158,000	81,125,000	8,252,000	10,004,000	33,445,000	623,000	100,000	**199,707,000**	3.5	118
Muslims	293,993,000	675,297,000	13,194,000	1,395,000	5,500,000	107,000	43,967,000	**1,033,453,000**	18.3	184
Hindus	1,608,000	759,059,000	725,000	912,000	1,315,000	379,000	2,000	**764,000,000**	13.5	94
Buddhists	23,000	336,755,000	279,000	559,000	578,000	26,000	401,000	**338,621,000**	6.0	92
Chinese folk religionists	14,000	149,037,000	61,000	76,000	126,000	21,000	1,000	**149,336,000**	2.6	60
New-Religionists	23,000	126,869,000	51,000	548,000	1,473,000	10,000	1,000	**128,975,000**	2.3	27
Tribal religionists	69,872,000	28,197,000	1,000	967,000	42,000	71,000	0	**99,150,000**	1.8	104
Sikhs	29,000	19,557,000	237,000	8,000	363,000	9,000	1,000	**20,204,000**	0.4	21
Jews	128,000	4,289,000	1,761,000	458,000	5,907,000	95,000	813,000	**13,451,000**	0.2	134
Shamanists	1,000	10,754,000	2,000	1,000	1,000	1,000	250,000	**11,010,000**	0.2	11
Confucians	1,000	6,300,000	2,000	2,000	26,000	1,000	2,000	**6,334,000**	0.1	6
Baha'is	1,631,000	2,817,000	93,000	827,000	379,000	81,000	7,000	**5,835,000**	0.1	210
Jains	57,000	3,906,000	15,000	4,000	4,000	1,000	0	**3,987,000**	0.1	11
Shintoists	0	3,383,000	1,000	1,000	1,000	1,000	0	**3,387,000**	0.1	4
Other religionists	472,000	12,912,000	1,513,000	3,686,000	1,503,000	4,000	329,000	**20,419,000**	0.4	182
Nonreligious	2,936,000	733,740,000	58,199,000	19,327,000	23,884,000	3,756,000	82,236,000	**924,078,000**	16.3	226
Atheists	344,000	167,739,000	16,362,000	3,329,000	1,367,000	563,000	49,407,000	**239,111,000**	4.2	139
Total Population	**722,814,000**	**3,345,498,000**	**514,055,000**	**474,240,000**	**282,700,000**	**28,000,000**	**287,164,000**	**5,661,525,000**	**100.0**	**262**

Continents. These follow current UN demographic terminology. UN practice began in 1949 by dividing the world into 5 continents, then into 18 regions (1954), then into 8 major continental areas (called macro regions in 1987) and 24 regions (1963), and 7 major areas and 22 regions (1988). (*See* United Nations, *World Population Prospects: The 1992 Revision,* with populations of all continents, regions, and countries covering the period 1950–2025.) The table above therefore now combines its former columns "East Asia" and "South Asia" into one single continental area, "Asia" (which excludes Eurasia [or European Asia], our provisional new term for the former U.S.S.R.).
Countries. The last column enumerates sovereign and nonsovereign countries in which each religion or religious grouping has a significant following.
Rows. The list of religions is arranged basically by descending order of magnitude of global adherents in 1994; similarly for categories within "Christians."
Adherents. As defined and enumerated for each of the world's countries in *World Christian Encyclopedia* (1982), projected to mid-1994, adjusted for recent data.
Christians. Followers of Jesus Christ affiliated with churches (church members, including children: 1,759,289,000) plus persons professing in censuses or polls though not so affiliated.
Other Christians. Catholics (non-Roman), marginal Protestants, crypto-Christians, and adherents of African, Asian, black, and Latin-American indigenous churches.
Muslims. 83% Sunnites, 16% Shi'ites, 1% other schools. Up to 1990 the former ethnic Muslims in the U.S.S.R. who had embraced communism were not included as Muslims in this table. After the collapse of communism in 1990–91, these ethnic Muslims are once again enumerated as Muslims where they have returned to Islamic profession and practice.
Hindus. 70% Vaishnavites, 25% Shaivites, 2% neo-Hindus and reform Hindus.
Buddhists. 56% Mahayana, 38% Theravada (Hinayana), 6% Tantrayana (Lamaism).
Chinese folk-religionists. Followers of the traditional Chinese religion (local deities, ancestor veneration, Confucian ethics, Taoism, universism, divination, some Buddhist elements).
New-Religionists. Followers of Asian 20th-century New Religions, New Religious movements, radical new crisis religions, and non-Christian syncretistic mass religions, all founded since 1800 and most since 1945.
Jews. Adherents of Judaism. For detailed data on "core" Jewish population, *see* the annual "World Jewish Populations" article in the American Jewish Committee's *American Jewish Year Book.*
Confucians. Non-Chinese followers of Confucius and Confucianism, mostly Koreans in Korea.
Other religionists. Including 70 minor world religions and a large number of spiritist religions, New Age religions, quasi religions, pseudo religions, parareligions, religious or mystic systems, religious and semireligious brotherhoods of numerous varieties.
Nonreligious. Persons professing no religion, nonbelievers, agnostics, freethinkers, dereligionized secularists indifferent to all religion.
Atheists. Persons professing atheism, skepticism, disbelief, or irreligion, including antireligious (opposed to all religion).
Total Population. UN medium variant figures for mid-1994, as given in *World Population Prospects: The 1992 Revision* (New York: UN, 1993), pages 185–191. (DAVID B. BARRETT)

Religious Adherents in the United States of America, AD 1900–2000

Adherents	Year 1900	%	mid-1970	%	mid-1990	%	Annual change, 1990–95: Natural	Conversion	Total	Rate (%)	1995	%	2000	%
Christians	**73,270,000**	**96.4**	**186,121,000**	**90.8**	**214,979,000**	**86.0**	**2,264,100**	**–368,500**	**1,895,600**	**0.87**	**224,457,000**	**85.3**	**233,475,000**	**84.8**
Professing Christians	73,270,000	96.4	186,121,000	90.8	214,979,000	86.0	2,264,100	–368,500	1,895,600	0.87	224,457,000	85.3	233,475,000	84.8
Affiliated Christians	54,425,000	71.6	153,201,000	74.7	173,983,000	69.6	1,832,300	–526,300	1,306,000	0.74	180,513,000	68.6	186,670,000	67.8
Protestants	35,000,000	46.1	71,653,000	34.9	78,742,000	31.5	829,300	–442,100	387,200	0.49	80,678,000	30.7	82,670,000	30.0
Evangelicals	26,598,000	35.0	50,689,000	24.7	67,743,000	27.1	713,400	210,600,000	924,000	1.33	72,363,000	27.5	76,815,000	27.9
Roman Catholics	10,775,000	14.2	48,391,000	23.6	53,495,000	21.4	563,400	–210,600	352,800	0.65	55,259,000	21.0	56,441,000	20.5
Black Christians	5,750,000	7.6	19,679,000	9.6	23,998,000	9.6	252,700	–100	252,600	1.03	25,261,000	9.6	26,431,000	9.6
Black Evangelicals	5,320,000	7.0	13,551,000	6.6	17,248,000	6.9	181,600	52,800,000	234,400	1.32	18,420,000	7.0	19,548,000	7.1
Orthodox	400,000	0.5	3,387,000	1.7	4,999,000	2.0	52,600	73,800,000	126,400	2.41	5,631,000	2.1	6,260,000	2.3
Anglicans	1,600,000	2.1	3,234,000	1.6	2,500,000	1.0	26,300	–56,300	–30,000	–1.23	2,350,000	0.9	2,203,000	0.8
Catholics (non Roman)	100,000	0.1	472,000	0.2	500,000	0.2	5,300	–100	5,200	1.02	526,000	0.2	551,000	0.2
Other Christians	800,000	1.1	6,384,000	3.1	9,749,000	3.9	102,700	105,300	208,000	2.05	10,789,000	4.1	12,114,000	4.4
Unaffiliated Christians	18,845,000	24.8	32,920,000	16.1	40,996,000	16.4	431,800	157,800,000	589,600	1.40	43,944,000	16.7	46,805,000	17.0
Non-Christians	**2,725,000**	**3.6**	**18,930,000**	**9.2**	**34,996,000**	**14.0**	**368,500**	**368,500,000**	**737,000**	**2.02**	**38,681,000**	**14.7**	**41,849,000**	**15.2**
Jews	1,500,000	2.0	6,700,000	3.3	5,515,000	2.2	58,100	–40,700	17,400	0.31	5,602,000	2.1	5,702,000	2.1
Muslims	10,000	0.0	800,000	0.4	4,500,000	1.8	47,400	72,600,000	120,000	2.53	5,100,000	1.9	5,730,000	2.1
Black Muslims	0	0.0	200,000	0.1	1,250,000	0.5	13,200	16,800,000	30,000	2.29	1,400,000	0.5	1,650,000	0.6
New Religionists	0	0.0	110,000	0.1	750,000	0.3	7,900	31,500,000	39,400	4.78	947,000	0.4	1,074,000	0.4
Hindus	1,000	0.0	100,000	0.0	500,000	0.2	5,300	76,700,000	82,000	12.72	910,000	0.3	1,200,000	0.4
Baha'is	2,000	0.0	138,000	0.1	250,000	0.1	2,600	7,400,000	10,000	3.71	300,000	0.1	365,000	0.1
Buddhists	30,000	0.0	200,000	0.1	250,000	0.1	2,600	–6,200	–3,600	–1.48	232,000	0.1	200,000	0.1
Sikhs	0	0.0	1,000	0.0	150,000	0.1	1,600	6,400,000	8,000	4.84	190,000	0.1	240,000	0.1
Chinese folk-religionists	70,000	0.1	90,000	0.0	80,000	0.0	800	–1,600	–800	–1.02	76,000	0.0	70,000	0.0
Tribal religionists	100,000	0.1	70,000	0.0	45,000	0.0	500	–1,900	–1,400	–3.32	38,000	0.0	31,000	0.0
Other religionists	10,000	0.0	450,000	0.2	1,000,000	0.4	10,500	10,500,000	21,000	2.02	1,105,000	0.4	1,090,000	0.4
Nonreligious	1,000,000	1.3	10,071,000	4.9	21,206,000	8.5	223,300	197,700,000	421,000	1.91	23,311,000	8.9	25,157	9.1
Atheists	1,000	0.0	200,000	0.1	750,000	0.3	7,900	16,100,000	24,000	3.01	870,000	0.3	990,000	0.4
Total population	**75,995,000**	**100.0**	**205,051,000**	**100.0**	**249,975,000**	**100.0**	**2,632,600**	**0**	**2,632,600**	**1.03**	**263,138,000**	**100.0**	**275,324,000**	**100.0**

Methodology. This table extracts a microcosm of the world table above. It depicts the United States, the country with the largest number of adherents to Christianity, the world's largest religion. Statistics for five points in time across the 20th century are presented. Also analyzed is each religion's *Annual change* by: *Natural* increase (births minus deaths, plus immigrants minus emigrants) per year and *Conversion* (new converts minus new defectors), which together constitute the *Total* increase per year. *Rate* is then computed as percent per year.
Structure. Vertically the table lists 27 major religious categories. The 11 major religions (including nonreligion) in the U.S. are arrayed according to size in 1990, with largest (Christians) first; likewise Christianity's seven major ecclesiastico-cultural blocs are ranked by 1990 size. Indented names of groups in the "Adherents" column are subcategories of the groups above them and are also counted in these unindented totals, so they are not added into the column total. Figures for Christians in 1970 are built upon detailed head counts, then rounded to the nearest 1,000; 1990 figures are current estimates, also rounded. Because of the rounding, percentage calculations sometimes may not total 100%. Figures for AD 2000 are projections based on current long-term trends.
Christians. Professing Christians are all persons who profess publicly (in censuses or polls) to follow Jesus Christ as Lord and Saviour. This category is subdivided into **affiliated Christians** (church members) and **unaffiliated (nominal) Christians** (professing Christians not affiliated with any church).
Evangelicals, Protestant and Black. Churches, agencies, and individuals that call themselves by this term and/or emphasize five or more fundamental doctrines (salvation by faith, personal acceptance, verbal inspiration of Scripture, depravity of man, Virgin Birth, miracles of Christ, atonement, evangelism, Second Advent).
Black Christians. Members of denominations initiated by African-Americans.
Non-Christians. Followers of other, non-Christian religions or of no religion.
Other Christians. Members of denominations and churches regarding themselves as outside mainline Christianity.
Jews. Core Jewish population relating to Judaism, excluding Jewish persons professing a different religion but including immigrants from the former U.S.S.R., Eastern Europe, Israel, and other areas.
Other categories. Definitions as given above under the Worldwide Adherents table. (DAVID B. BARRETT)

Social Protection

In 1994 more emphasis than in previous years was given to private initiative and responsibility in devising social security reforms, especially in Western Europe, the U.S., and Canada. Against the background of economic stagnation and financial deficits in Western Europe, employment creation was favoured over income distribution. Though Central and Eastern European countries faced worse economic conditions than their Western neighbours, they forged ahead with social security reforms. Newly industrialized countries advanced social security systems in line with economic performance. In the less developed world individual countries introduced reforms but, on the whole, problems of inadequate social security coverage and financial imbalances predominated.

North America. In both the United States and Canada, 1994 was marked by reassessment and proposed reform of some basic social protection policies. The U.S. Congress and the Clinton administration wrestled with health care reform for most of the year before reaching a stalemate. The administration's proposal had been introduced near the end of 1993, after the Task Force on National Health Care Reform, headed by Hillary Rodham Clinton, had conducted months of meetings. At the heart of the plan was the promise of universal health insurance paid for largely by employers, with subsidized care for those who could not afford insurance and provisions to contain soaring health costs. The plan proposed to set up local quasi-governmental entities, known as health alliances, through which consumers would buy insurance and care providers would be paid.

Interest in reform was widespread. Health costs had been rising faster than inflation; they topped $900 billion in 1993 and were expected to exceed the trillion-dollar level in 1994. One estimate put the number of Americans without health insurance as high as 39.7 million in 1994, or 15.3% of the population. Despite these conditions and early public support, passage of reform bogged down. Partisan politics, questionable legislative strategy, the complexity of the issue, and lobbying efforts by various special-interest groups eroded the initial backing. Major issues included the cost of massive overhaul, the creation of a new bureaucracy, and the impact on patients' rights to choose their physicians. As Congress neared adjournment, attempts at compromise failed.

In the meantime, the spotlight shifted from Washington to the states. In September the federal government gave Florida permission to conduct a Medicaid experiment aimed at providing coverage for 1.1 million poor Floridians with no health insurance by enrolling them in some form of managed care. At least five states implemented programs to expand health coverage to hundreds of thousands of people not reached by Medicaid. A dozen others applied for federal waivers to allow such trials or were expected to ask for them. California, Florida, and Texas enrolled thousands of people in health insurance alliances that pooled the purchasing power of small businesses. Most states tightened insurance regulations, requiring insurers to sell coverage to small businesses and limiting the variation in rates. States were limited in what they could do, however. Federal law prevented them from regulating, taxing, or interfering with the health plans set up by companies that served as their own insurer.

The U.S. welfare system also had its problems. Aid to Families with Dependent Children grew to a record 14.3 million recipients in 1994, a 31% increase since the 1989 recession. The cost of running welfare programs was rising twice as fast as the number of people on the rolls. At the same time, welfare benefits had declined 40% over the past 20 years when adjusted for inflation. Following up on a campaign pledge to "end welfare as we know it," Pres. Bill Clinton in June unveiled a plan for welfare overhaul. The proposal was designed to get recipients off the dole by requiring them to take part in job-training, education, and placement programs; cutting off cash benefits to some mothers on welfare after two years; and providing subsidized jobs for persons who were unable to find other work after that time. The plan would also toughen enforcement of child-support laws and provide $400 million in grants to fight teenage pregnancy.

The cost of the Clinton plan was put at $9.3 billion

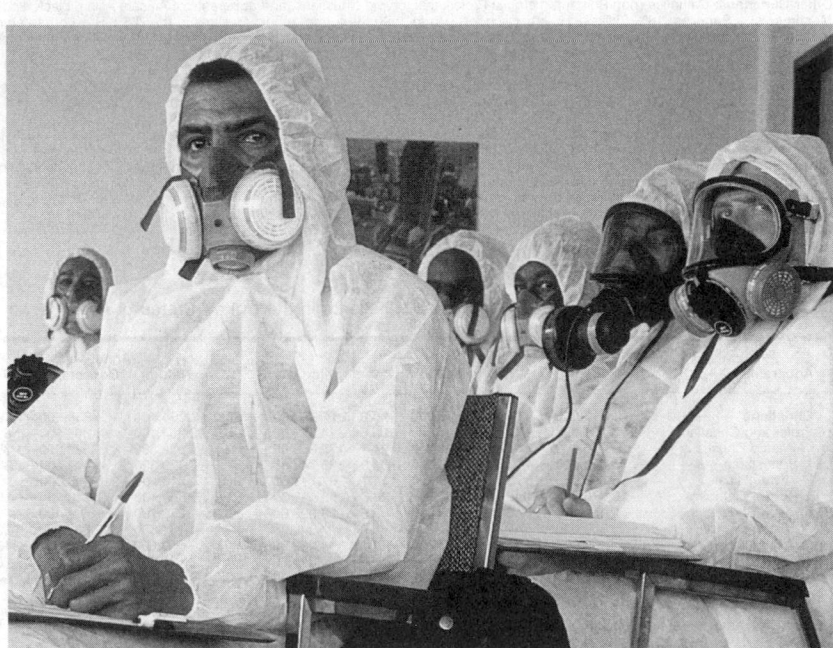

In preparation for their placement in jobs, men on welfare in Cleveland, Ohio, receive training in the removal of lead paint. This program was one of a number of new approaches being tried by various states in their efforts to reform the U.S. welfare system.
STEVE LISS—TIME MAGAZINE

over five years, with the bulk of the money to come from reducing other existing social programs, tightening and ending welfare eligibility for noncitizens, putting caps on state emergency welfare programs, limiting disability payments for drug and alcohol addicts, and reducing benefits to legal immigrants. The plan was greeted with criticism from both the left and the right, and welfare reform was put off by Congress to 1995.

In October the Census Bureau reported that the number of poor had risen in 1993 for the fourth year in a row; 39.3 million people, or 15.1% of the population, were below the official poverty line of $14,763 for a family of four. It was the highest level since 15.2% in 1983. The poverty rate dropped to 12.1% if noncash benefits, such as food stamps, school lunches, Medicare, and Medicaid, were included.

Reform measures were also pushed for social security. U.S. Rep. Daniel Rostenkowski, former chairman of the House Ways and Means Committee, sponsored a bill to raise taxes and reduce benefits enough to ensure that the system remained fiscally sound for the next 75 years. The measure was introduced after social security officials warned that the Medicare trust fund that paid hospital bills for the elderly would run out of money in 2001 and a separate trust fund that paid benefits to disabled workers would be bankrupt in 1995.

While Rostenkowski's bill failed to get out of committee, other changes were enacted in social security. Congress removed the Social Security Administration from the Department of Health and Human Services, making it a separate entity. The newly autonomous agency, to be administered by commissioners appointed by the president for six-year terms, would be one of the largest in the federal government. More than 40 million elderly and disabled received social security benefits, and 135 million paid into the funds in 1993. At the beginning of 1994, the trust fund balance was $365.9 billion. Congress also raised the earnings threshold above which an employer had to pay social security taxes for domestic workers from $50 to $1,000 annually.

Reform of social programs was also a major concern in Canada. After months of preparation, Human Resources Minister Lloyd Axworthy issued in October an 89-page discussion paper outlining radical reforms in $38.7 billion worth of government programs for welfare, unemployment insurance, and postsecondary education. The paper criticized the welfare system for trapping too many people in a cycle of dependency and offered several options for discussion. It suggested two possibilities for reforming unemployment insurance: an entirely new system that would differentiate between frequent and occasional users and tightening admissibility rules and reducing benefits. The paper concluded that the welfare system failed because of the high level of child poverty (40% of Canada's welfare recipients were children) and suggested replacing the shared-cost Canada Assistance Plan with block funding that would give provinces greater leeway in designing their own programs. For postsecondary education the government proposed to make $2.6 billion in loans directly to students (the money was currently distributed through the provinces). This would allow students to use the money for nonuniversity training.

While Canada's health care system was often cited as a model in the U.S. health debate, Canadians were engaged in their own reassessment of health care delivery. One concern was the growing privatization of health care. According to a study by the Canadian Medical Association, the private share of total health care spending rose from 25% to 28% between 1985 and 1991. In 1992 and 1993 every Canadian province except Prince Edward Island reduced or eliminated coverage that it had offered over and above the requirements of the law.

Western Europe. A major debate on social policy took place among the members of the European Union. EU institutions, governments of member states, workers' and employers' organizations, nongovernmental organizations, and individuals participated in the discussions. A European social model for the future was developed; outlined in a White Paper, it was published by the European Commission in July.

The objectives of an EU social policy were reconsidered. Rather than providing cash benefits through the redistribution of income, it placed a new emphasis on creating jobs and stimulating the economy. The 1994 outline for European social policy did not provide for a total harmonization of policies throughout the EU. Common objectives were to be defined and minimum standards respected, with a continuing aim to improve social standards for all EU members.

Human Rights: The Status of Women

The discrimination and violence experienced by women diverged significantly in 1994 from the vision of freedoms set out in the United Nations' 1948 *Universal Declaration of Human Rights*. The document called for such basic individual rights as freedom of conscience, freedom of expression and association, freedom from arbitrary arrest and detention, freedom from torture, the right to a fair trial, and freedom from extrajudicial execution.

During the 1990s groups such as Amnesty International took direct action to stop human rights violations against women in 50 countries around the world. Many of these women—including those imprisoned, in police custody, in areas of armed conflict, and attempting to flee government persecution—endured torture, rape, and such forms of sexual coercion as body-cavity and strip searches. Many governments, however, adamantly refused to recognize rape and sexual abuse by their agents as acts of torture and ill treatment for which the state bore responsibility.

Although Article Seven of the 1993 *UN Convention on the Elimination of All Forms of Discrimination Against Women* called upon governments to ensure women's full participation in the political and public life of their countries, women were often detained, harassed, intimidated, or tortured and killed because of their activities in groups that promoted civil, political, social, cultural, or economic rights. Among others, academics in China, journalists in Morocco, lawyers in the Philippines, judges in Colombia, political reformers in Myanmar (Burma), opposition leaders in Mozambique, environmentalists in Kenya, and feminists in Peru were threatened.

Women members of indigenous peoples and ethnic minorities, often marginalized by the dominant culture of their societies, were particularly vulnerable to human rights abuses. For example, the members of CONAVIGUA, the mainly indigenous Guatemalan widows' association organized to find relatives "disappeared" by the Guatemalan security forces, became victims of death threats, detentions, and assaults by the army. Similar abuses were reported in Peru, Brazil, and Mexico, as well as in Mauritania, The Sudan, Myanmar, India, and Bangladesh.

Family relationships could also trigger human rights violations. Women were frequently singled out for imprisonment, torture, or death because they were related to men suspected of opposing the government. Tunisian authorities arbitrarily detained and tortured the wives or relatives of men linked to illegal organizations, although most detainees were never charged or brought to trial. Similar practices were documented in Turkey, Syria, Guatemala, Iran, Senegal, Peru, and India.

(SUZANNE ROACH)

Street children in Moscow are sometimes victims of the tight housing market in Russia, which can lead parents to sell their homes to profiteers. It has been estimated that there are 100 million street children worldwide, with most in less developed countries.

YURI KOSYREV—KATZ/SABA

A new vision of the welfare state's role and capabilities was also reflected in concrete social security reforms, such as the passage of Germany's nursing care insurance and Sweden's pension reform.

New German legislation stipulated that a special benefit would be payable to persons requiring some form of non-medical personal care. Benefits were structured according to the extent of the individual's impediment, with a choice of cash benefits or a higher value of benefits in kind. A major goal was rehabilitation. Effective April 1, 1995, benefits would be granted to persons being cared for at home, while those in institutions would be paid benefits only from July 1, 1996. The role of the state was also diminished; everyone was encouraged to purchase additional private insurance to cover any difference between the statutory benefit and the actual cost of care. The state would not cover deficits associated with nursing care insurance but would subsidize investment in institutions providing nonmedical care.

In Sweden's Riksdag (parliament) agreement was reached on old-age-pension reform and the limitations of the welfare state's capabilities. Radical changes were dictated by economic realities. The national pension system would be reformed so that the size of an individual's pension would largely reflect the contributions paid on the income earned by that person. In the present system employees made no contributions; in the future half of the total contributions would be paid by the insured persons themselves and the rest by the employers. In this pay-as-you-go system, acquired pension credits, as well as the ceiling on pensionable income, would be indexed in accordance with general wage trends instead of on prices. The reform introduced a mechanism that provided for longer working lives as life expectancy rose; at retirement the yearly pension amount would be computed on the basis of the accumulated wage-indexed contributions and the pensioner's average life expectancy from age 61. Retirement age would be flexible—between the ages of 61 and 70. Because benefit payments would be linked to economic growth, negative adjustments were also possible. Years of child care, military service, and studies would carry pension rights. The system would re-

(continued on page 280)

Street Children

BY MARILYN E. ROCKY

An estimated 100 million children and youths between the ages of 5 and 18 spend the major part of their lives in the city streets of the less developed world. Most of these "street children," as they have come to be known, work "on" the street. They live at home but are forced into the streets to contribute to their families' meagre incomes in whatever way they can: by shining shoes, selling newspapers, hauling garbage, begging, and engaging in prostitution. The rest of these street children, called children "of" the street, live, work, and sleep on city streets and maintain minimal or no ties with their families.

In some parts of the world, the growing numbers of street children and their problems have been ignored. They constitute a population that does not show up in health or public education statistics or national censuses. The traditional response to this problem, in both less developed countries (LDCs) and industrialized ones, has been to institutionalize the children in state reform schools or isolated residential facilities.

In other cases street children have been ignored or treated as a public nuisance. In some countries "death squads" willfully torture and murder street children—their response to the growing street-crime statistics. During the past decade more than 5,000 Brazilian street children have been murdered by such vigilante groups. Human rights groups in Brazil claimed that private security forces were killing street children and other low-income youths as part of an effort to clean up the streets. Reports from South Africa, Colombia, Haiti, Guatemala, Thailand, and elsewhere point to similar trends of violence.

Underlying Causes. The two most commonly asked questions about street children are: Where do they come from, and why are there so many? Some suggested causes include rapid urbanization, national debt problems, economic stagnation, and drought, deforestation, and other forms of environmental degradation. Rapid population growth, unsustainable agricultural practices, and government policies that subsidize urban dwellers at the expense of rural farmers have caused increasing numbers of families and youths in the LDCs to move into cities in search of economic opportunities.

About one-third of the population of the LDCs now lives in urban areas. The United Nations estimates that within 15–20 years the LDCs will become predominantly urban, and the majority of urban dwellers will reside in low-income, marginal neighbourhoods. As more and more families settle in slum areas near large cities, they will lose the social and kinship networks found in rural areas. The side effects of this increasingly urban-based poverty are devastating: a lack of access to education, the breakup of families, malnutrition, inadequate health services, susceptibility to infectious diseases, vulnerability to AIDS and other sexually transmitted diseases (STDs), physical and sexual abuse, and drug abuse and prostitution. The children of poor urban dwellers are most directly affected, and increasing numbers of children

Marilyn E. Rocky is the director of CHILDHOPE.

are forced to contribute to their families' economic survival by turning to the streets.

In recent years the growth of the youth population and economic stagnation in LDCs have led to the growing participation of children and youths in the labour force. Worldwide estimates of the total number of working children—a term that includes both street children and children earning income in a variety of settings beyond ambulatory work in urban streets—range from 89 million (International Labour Organisation) to 145 million (UN).

Menial Labour. Work that street children can perform typically is the kind that requires few formal skills and produces relatively little income selling cigarettes, gum, candy, or newspapers; hauling garbage; washing cars or windshields; guarding cars; or carrying luggage for tourists. Less savoury sources of income include begging, theft, robbery, prostitution, and drug trafficking.

Working street children in LDCs range in age, although children as young as four can be found begging or selling on street corners or buses. Younger children are usually accompanied by their parents or siblings and work as part of family businesses.

A significant percentage of working street children are girls, many of them employed as street hawkers and peddlers. A Latin-American study found girls working both on and off the streets as vendors, maids, waitresses, dishwashers, and prostitutes. Other girls were involved in begging, stealing, scavenging in dumps, singing on street corners, carrying bags or luggage, or accepting other kinds of manual labour.

Most girls work either full- or part-time but continue to return home. Street girls are clearly subject to greater risk of sexual exploitation than boys, but they are also more susceptible to economic exploitation because of their gender. In a number of Latin-American countries, the lives of street girls and other working girls are characterized by early sexual initiation and abuse; exposure to STDs, including AIDS; and unwanted pregnancies. A significant number of girls work in brothels or on the streets as prostitutes, placing them at even higher risk of acquiring STDs.

Coping Strategies. While the work of street children is often risky or harmful to their own well-being, it is nonetheless crucial to the survival of millions of families in LDCs. In Jamaica 33% of the street children in one survey said that they were the only working member of their household, and 41% were from families with only one other working member. Similarly, in Lagos, Nigeria, studies found that children hawking goods on the street were able to sell between two and four times as much as adults. Most of the children surveyed reported that their mothers would have difficulty meeting the family's basic needs without the child's income.

Children are very resourceful, and those on the street find ways of adapting to the difficulties of their daily lives. Limited data suggest that a majority of children on the streets are regular drug users. In Guatemala as many as 9 of every 10 street children are thought to be addicted to paint thinner, cheap glue, or more potent drugs. Similarly, in Colombia it is estimated that on a daily basis more than 95% of Bogota's 12,000 street children use drugs.

Drugs also offer a means of escape and release from daily pressures of life and survival. Street children in Kenya said that they sniffed glue to enable themselves to eat the rotten food they needed in order to survive. Street children in Central America reported that the chief attraction of inhaling glue was that it took away their hunger. Because drugs offer street children an escape from difficult situations, they view them not as one of their problems but rather as part of the solution to their struggles.

Regular drug use by street children can have serious physical side effects. Industrial glue, when inhaled, produces light-headedness, occasional hallucinations, loss of appetite, and nausea. Long-term health problems can include lung, brain, or kidney damage; malnutrition; and a general decline in health. While there seems to be no physical addiction involved in the inhaling of glue, psychological withdrawal symptoms can be strong. Drug use among street children is closely related to other health issues, including prostitution and sexual exploitation, all of which have contributed to a growing incidence of AIDS among street children and youths.

Worldwide Response. During the past decade organizations and governments worldwide have begun to act to rescue this generation of children from exploitation, violence, and degradation. Benchmarks have been established, and several important steps have been taken by international nongovernmental organizations and by development organizations to create local, national, and international networks and movements to aid street children.

In 1986 CHILDHOPE was founded in response to UNICEF's search for an international nongovernmental organization that could serve as a partner. It was in this capacity that CHILDHOPE began to address the needs of both abandoned and street children and to serve as an international coordinator of services for street children.

Many other advocacy organizations have been formed to defend the rights of street children, provide them with appropriate services, and, most significantly, develop programs to meet their special and specific needs. The most successful have been noninstitutional street-based projects that are grounded in the understanding that the focus of a street child's life and activities, especially generating income, is the street. The most successful programs use street educators, specially trained individuals (often veterans of the street) who serve as a kind of "connective tissue" between the child and the community.

During the mid-1980s in Brazil, street children organized their own advocacy group. The National Movement for Street Boys and Girls has evolved into a major political and social force over the past decade and boasts a membership of more than 80,000 street children and youths throughout the country. The efforts of the movement have resulted in new legislation for the protection and well-being of all children in that country.

The U.S. government has earmarked money for street children in its foreign assistance budget over the past few years. Congress has appropriated funds to the U.S. Agency for International Development for use by local groups in Latin America and Eastern Europe.

The issue of street children became so compelling during the 1980s and the early 1990s that it finally moved leaders and governments to respond. It appears that the world has slowly begun to acknowledge that a large number of its youngest citizens the future of our planet—are living in unthinkable conditions, and the foundation for the mobilization of resources to aid this most vulnerable population has now been put in place.

The essence of the problem was eloquently stated by James Grant, executive director of UNICEF, at the second International Encounter of Street Children, held in Brazil in 1992. Grant called for the joining of forces among all sectors to combat the enormous problems confronting street children, including death squads, exploitation, and AIDS. He concluded that it was "personally unacceptable, ethically unthinkable, that on the eve of the 21st century, children and youth, by the tens of millions, should have to call the streets their home."

(continued from page 278)

main a compulsory national scheme with a basic protection for those with a previous low-income level. The new rules would be introduced gradually and primarily affect future retirees.

Central and Eastern Europe. Problems associated with the transition from a centrally planned economy to a market-oriented one led many countries to completely restructure their social security and pension systems. Most countries adopted a three-layer system, consisting of a means-tested flat-rate pension, a mandatory earnings-related pension, and an optional private (occupational) complementary scheme. High levels of inflation and unemployment posed difficulties in implementation, but reforms were made.

The Czech Republic and Hungary introduced the most notable changes during 1994. In the Czech Republic governmental contributions to approved private funds, including a bonus contribution during the first two years, provided incentives to individuals to contribute to a personal pension fund. Legislation to that effect was adopted in March 1994. In Hungary a law on voluntary mutual pension and savings funds took effect in January 1994. By September three funds had already been established.

Suggestions of raising the retirement age and equalizing the retirement age of men and women met with open hostility in all of the countries of Central and Eastern Europe where the issues were publicly debated.

Industrialized Asia and the Pacific. For members of the Organisation for Economic Co-operation and Development, support to families was the primary issue during the year. In Japan the increasing participation of women in the labour force and a declining birthrate were reflected in debates on social security reform as well as in legislation. An employer-financed Child Rearing Program was set up to support households in which both parents were employed. The law provided for flexible child-rearing services to be organized on a private basis. Proposals under discussion included a pension-contribution exemption and a benefit package for employees on child-care leave.

In Australia, where family allowances were financed from general revenues, measures were introduced to improve the distribution and equality of payments. In 1994 the income threshold in determining entitlement to these allowances was reduced, and overseas income was factored into the income level. Improved targeting for family support was also sought in New Zealand, which provided additional assistance to low-income families and launched pilot programs to facilitate single parents' entry into employment or training contracts.

Emerging and Less Developed Countries. High economic growth rates helped place the newly industrialized countries in a position to advance social security schemes in line with economic performance, and during 1994 almost all of them enhanced the levels of social protection. In South Korea the entire population was covered by health insurance, and more than half of them were enrolled in a pension plan. A proposal to extend compulsory coverage to farmers and fishermen by mid-1995 would cover 62% of the population in the old-age scheme.

Cambodia, Laos, and Vietnam all expressed interest in installing comprehensive social insurance schemes, financially autonomous from the state budget. Vietnam adopted a new Labour Code, and Mongolia passed legislation paving the way for the implementation of a 1995 integrated social insurance scheme. China's reform moved slowly, stymied by regional diversity and substantial internal labour migration. Argentina and Colombia adopted pension reforms inspired by a Chilean scheme. Zimbabwe's social security program

provided retirement, disability, survivors', and unemployment benefits. In South Africa 1994 marked the implementation of nondiscriminatory regulations adopted in 1993. Previously most benefits had differed according to the recipient's colour of skin. Whites, for example, had been paid 15% more than blacks in old-age benefits.

(DAVID M. MAZIE; CHRISTIANE KUPTSCH)

See also Business and Industry Review: *Insurance;* Education; Health and Disease.

This article updates the *Macropædia* article SOCIAL WELFARE.

Space Exploration

During 1994 the design of the international space station was established as the United States and Russia moved to combine forces in a single orbital facility. The DC-X launch vehicle program was revived, and Japan and Europe introduced new launch vehicles. In addition, an international campaign was begun to understand the effect of solar and space phenomena on the Earth.

Manned Flight. Only seven space shuttle missions were flown during 1994, two carrying the same Space Radar Laboratory to survey the Earth at different times of the year. Three missions studied materials and life sciences in space, and two continued detailed observations of the Earth's atmosphere.

The U.S. National Aeronautics and Space Administration (NASA) confirmed on January 13 that the repairs to the Hubble Space Telescope made in late 1993 were successful and that the Hubble's optics were working as planned. There was a marked increase in the sharpness of images taken by the wide-field camera.

On the first mission of the year, February 3–11, *Discovery* carried the Wake Shield Facility and Spacehab-02. The crew comprised commander Charles F. Bolden, Jr., pilot Kenneth S. Reightler, Jr., and mission specialists Franklin R. Chang-Diaz, N. Jan Davis, Ronald M. Sega, and Sergey K. Krikalev. The Wake Shield Facility was a satellite designed to be released by the shuttle and retrieved a few days later. As it orbited on its own, its wake would create a near-perfect vacuum in which high-quality semiconductor films could be grown. A problem with its guidance system, however, prevented the astronauts from releasing the facility. Six metal balls, from 5 to 15 cm (2 to 6 in) in diameter, were released for use as calibration targets by ground-based radar. Krikalev was the first Russian to be launched aboard a U.S. spacecraft as the two nations initiated their joint space station program.

Materials sciences were the focus of the mission of *Columbia* (March 4–18). The crew comprised commander John H. Casper, pilot Andrew M. Allen, and mission specialists Pierre J. Thuot, Charles D. Gemar, and Marsha S. Ivans. The U.S. Microgravity Payload comprised several automated devices for processing materials in the weightlessness of space. In one, a furnace processed samples of mercury cadmium telluride, an alloy that is valued as a detector of infrared radiation but that suffers from defects when fabricated on Earth. Another device observed how dendrites—branchlike structures—grow in transparent crystalline materials. *Columbia* also carried the Shuttle Solar Backscatter Ultraviolet instrument to measure ozone in the upper atmosphere. Inside *Columbia* the crew assembled scale models of solar array supports to measure vibration and stress.

The Earth was given a close examination by the Space Radar Laboratory (SRL), a special mapping radar flown twice by the shuttle *Endeavour.* On the first mission (April

9–20) the crew comprised commander Sidney M. Gutierrez, pilot Kevin P. Chilton, and mission specialists Linda M. Godwin, Jay Apt, Michael R. Clifford, and Thomas David Jones. On the second (September 30–October 11) the commander was Michael A. Baker, the pilot Terrence W. Wilcutt, and the mission specialists Thomas David Jones, Steven L. Smith, Peter J.K. Wisoff, and Daniel W. Bursch. The SRL uses synthetic aperture radar, which mathematically combines a series of radar echoes to generate an image that otherwise would require a single, larger antenna. SRL was the first space radar to use three bands of radio frequencies—C, L, and X—at once to obtain more detailed images. At some frequencies the radar penetrated the ground and revealed structures such as ancient streambeds.

A laser probed the atmosphere on the mission of *Discovery* (September 9–20). The crew comprised commander Richard N. Richards, pilot L. Blaine Hammond, Jr., and mission specialists Carl J. Meade, Mark C. Lee, Susan J. Helms, and Jerry M. Linenger. The Laser In-Flight Technology Experiment focused lasers on the Earth's atmosphere through a 1.5-m reflector telescope and then measured the return signal. This allowed scientists to measure the speed of aerosols and dust in atmospheric conditions that ranged from clear air to tropical storm Debby. *Discovery* also deployed and retrieved the Spartan 201-II satellite, which observed the Sun's corona. Lee and Meade tested a miniature backpack designed to rescue astronauts should they drift away from the space station, which would not be able to maneuver to retrieve them.

The second International Microgravity Laboratory on *Columbia* (July 8–23) carried life and materials sciences experiments provided by Japan's National Space Development Agency and the German Space Agency. The crew comprised commander Robert D. Cabana, pilot James D. Halsell, Jr., mission specialists Carl E. Waltz, Leroy Chiao, Richard J. Hieb, and Donald A. Thomas, and payload specialist Chiaki Naito-Mukai. In addition to tests on the crew, the life sciences experiments included observation of the hatching of newts and the behaviour of goldfish and carp, some with their balance organs removed. Materials experiments included the cooling of samples of molten metal alloys to below freezing while they were suspended in an electromagnetic field. Such experiments are limited on Earth.

Earth was surveyed yet again when *Atlantis* carried the third Atmospheric Laboratory for Applications and Space Science (ATLAS-3; November 3–14). The crew comprised commander Donald R. McMonagle, pilot Curtis L. Brown, and mission specialists Ellen E. Ochoa, Scott E. Parazynski, Joseph R. Tanner, and Jean-François Clervoy of the European Space Agency (ESA). ATLAS instruments observe the Sun as a source of energy for the Earth's atmosphere and as a light source whose changes reveal the presence of certain chemicals in the atmosphere.

Shuttle missions planned for 1995 were scheduled to carry the Astro cluster of ultraviolet telescopes on a new survey of the universe (January), rendezvous with the *Mir* space station (February) and then dock with it (May), recarry the Wake Shield Facility and launch a special Space Free-Flier Unit (October), launch the seventh Tracking and Data Relay Satellite (June), carry the second U.S. Microgravity Laboratory (September), and retrieve the Free-Flier Unit (September). The first woman pilot on a shuttle mission, Eileen Collins, was to fly the *Mir* rendezvous. The Microgravity Laboratory mission was planned to last a record 16 days.

NASA started plans to replace the shuttles' 1970s "green screen" electronic displays and 1960s electromechanical displays with high-resolution, full-colour liquid crystal displays (LCDs). Such "glass cockpits" would allow information to be displayed with much greater flexibility and detail. Each display would be driven by a powerful microcomputer.

Operations continued aboard Russia's *Mir* space station with the launch on January 8 of Soyuz TM-18, which carried Viktor Afanesyev, Yury Usacho, and Valery Polyakov to the station. Polyakov was scheduled to stay in space for 429 days. Soyuz TM-17 departed from *Mir* on January 14, returning with Vasily Tsibiliyev and Aleksandr Serebrov. On July 1, Soyuz TM-19 carried two cosmonauts to *Mir* and returned with Afanesyev and Usacho. On October 4 Ulf Merbold, a German astronaut from the ESA who had flown twice on the U.S. space shuttle, was launched aboard Soyuz TM-20 to spend 30 days aboard *Mir* as part of the Euro-Mir program. A second European astronaut was to begin a 135-day stay in August 1995.

NASA completed the redesign of its space station program by including the Russian Space Agency as a partner equal with the ESA, the Japanese National Space Agency, and the Canadian Space Agency. The new International Space Station Alpha was to be assembled during a five-year period beginning in 1997. Most of its design was based on earlier work on the Freedom program, which experienced severe cost overruns and was finally not funded further by the U.S. Congress.

Alpha was to have a wingspan of 110 m (328 ft) across its main truss, which would support the solar power panels that were to extend 88 m (289 ft) from tip to tip. Alpha's total weight in orbit was to be 377 metric tons. Its orbit would be at an altitude of about 352 km (218 mi) at an inclination of 51.6° to the Equator.

The program was to be developed in three phases, the first of which started with Krikalev's flight aboard the shuttle. The shuttle *Atlantis* was to rendezvous with *Mir* in May 1995 and then dock and exchange Russian and U.S. crew members in October 1995; nine more docking missions were planned. The second phase would assemble enough of Alpha during 1997–98 for a crew of three to operate aboard the station. Phase 3 would add more modules and round out the station's capabilities by June 2002.

Planetary Probes. During the Apollo 11 25th-anniversary year, the Moon was explored by Clementine, a modest spacecraft built by the U.S. Ballistic Missile Defense Organization (BMDO) and carrying an array of ultrasmall, lightweight sensors designed to detect and track missiles and warheads from space. Because budget and arms treaty concerns ruled out flying a special target vehicle, the BMDO decided to test Clementine around the Moon. It was launched on January 25 and, after some swing-by maneuvers, arrived in lunar orbit on February 19. Before its departure on May 1 for asteroid 1620 Geographos (later canceled by a computer failure), Clementine returned some 1.8 million images of the Earth and the Moon. It was able to map the Moon's polar regions and found a crater that is in perpetual darkness, an encouraging sign that water may be locked in the soil.

Ulysses, the international solar polar mission, sailed beneath the Sun's south pole during the summer. Ulysses recorded solar winds blowing at 3.2 million km/h (2 million mph).

The first two probes for NASA's new *Discovery* program to explore the planets with a series of low-cost missions were readied, and NASA sought proposals for at least one more. The first *Discovery* mission, to be launched in February 1996, was to be the Near Earth Asteroid Rendezvous (NEAR); the probe would rendezvous with asteroid 433 Eros, a 36-km (22-mi)-long block of silicate rock, in January 1999. Mars Pathfinder, to be launched in 1997, was to land a small probe on the surface of Mars and deploy a miniature rover to demonstrate technologies for a network of environmental survey probes.

Looking farther into the future, NASA and Carnegie Mellon University, Pittsburgh, Pa., successfully tested the Dante II robot on the slope of Mt. Spurr, a semiactive volcano 128 km (79 mi) west of Anchorage, Alaska. The 771-kg (1,696-lb), 3-m (9.8-ft)-tall robot had eight legs that moved in groups of four. It carried several TV cameras to let scientists view the terrain as the robot explored the volcano from July 29 to August 5. The robot eventually stumbled and fell, and a rock climber had to attach a harness to it so that a helicopter could retrieve it. NASA officials said that they were pleased with the results, however, and would continue development of the robot.

Investigators concluded that communication with the Mars Observer spacecraft was lost because of a slow leak that allowed fuel and oxidizer to mix and explode when the probe's thrusters were to be turned on just before it arrived at Mars in August 1993. The Magellan spacecraft ended its survey of Venus in a blaze of glory when engineers ordered the spacecraft to lower its orbit into the upper reaches of the planet's atmosphere. Magellan, orbiting Venus since 1990, was failing slowly and running out of attitude-control propellant. Its final experiment provided scientists with information about the density of the upper atmosphere.

Unmanned Satellites. The U.S. launched the second in a series of satellites designed to study Earth-Sun interactions such as the events that knocked out two Canadian communications satellites on January 20. NASA's Wind satellite was placed in orbit on November 1 as part of the International Solar-Terrestrial Physics (ISTP) program. The first satellite was Japan's Geotail probe, launched in July 1992 to study the tail of the Earth's geomagnetic field. The Earth is surrounded by belts of radiation trapped by its magnetic field. These, in turn, form a shield around which the solar wind must flow as it streams away from the Sun. The shield is not "bulletproof," as was demonstrated in January when a coronal mass ejection (CME) sprayed large quantities of charged particles from the Sun's corona into space. When these particles arrived at the Earth on January 20, the electronics on two Canadian communications satellites were knocked out of service for several hours; one was permanently damaged. A similar CME was spotted on April 14 by Japan's Yohkoh (Sunbeam) satellite. This allowed the Space Environment Laboratory in Boulder, Colo., to warn utility systems to take precautions against induced currents from a

geomagnetic storm that formed auroras visible as far south as Boulder. Three more satellites in the ISTP program were scheduled to be launched in 1995.

In a spectacular cosmic show observed by the Galileo spacecraft and the Hubble Space Telescope, Jupiter was pummeled by Comet Shoemaker-Levy 9 from July 16 to 22. (*See* ASTRONOMY: *Sidebar*). Also during the year astronauts learned that Earth is often pummeled by meteors. The U.S. Department of Defense revealed that several of its secret satellites had detected at least 136 meteor explosions in the Earth's upper atmosphere during 1975–92. The blasts had energies as great as the 15-kiloton atomic bomb that was dropped on Hiroshima, Japan.

GOES-8, the first of a new generation of Geostationary Operational Environmental Satellites, was launched on April 13 and soon started work. It had been delayed for several years because of design problems. The "GOES-NEXT" series, as it was known, would provide improved weather observations. The first of a new generation of military communications satellites, Milstar 1, was launched February 7. Critics claimed that it was unnecessary because it was designed to provide secure communications in case of a nuclear war.

Launch Vehicles. Japan introduced its new H-2 launch vehicle, Europe prepared to launch its first Ariane 5 in late 1995, and the U.S. finally pulled its revolutionary DC-X demonstrator from the brink of cancellation. Both the H-2 and Ariane 5 were designed to give their respective nations advanced space launch capabilities, including manned flight. The first H-2, launched on February 4 from Tanegashima, Japan, carried an Orbital Reentry Experiment to test a thermal protection system planned for the unmanned H-2 Orbital Plane Experiment to be flown in 1999. The first Ariane 5 launch was set for October or November 1995.

The DC-X, designed to demonstrate technologies for single-stage-to-orbit launches, flew missions on June 20 and June 27, thus demonstrating its capability to be reused quickly. However, the last (and fifth) flight resulted in a fire that damaged the vehicle but that also demonstrated its automated capability to abort its mission. NASA officials said that an orbital demonstrator could fly as early as 1999. NASA was also discussing a joint industry-government partnership for a similar vehicle to replace the space shuttle in the 21st century.

The last of an old reliable line of U.S. booster rockets, Scout, was launched May 9. Its capability was largely duplicated by the Pegasus air-launched rocket family. The U.S. government also decided to allow limited use of demobilized ballistic missiles as space launchers. Meanwhile, U.S. firms worked with new Russian companies to determine whether robust Russian rocket engines could be used to upgrade U.S. launch vehicles. Israel won permission to market its Shavit space launcher, which was derived from its Jericho ballistic missile. The U.S. government was concerned that sensitive U.S. missile technology might be improperly distributed through such sales.

(DAVE DOOLING)

See also Astronomy; Business and Industry Review: *Aerospace; Telecommunications;* Earth Sciences; Military Affairs; Television and Radio.

This article updates the *Macropædia* articles EXPLORATION: *Space Exploration;* TELESCOPES.

A dummy strapped upright in a sleeping bag, with curtains for privacy, illustrates the sleeping quarters in the habitation module of the Space Station Alpha. Designed by U.S. engineers, the module was part of the international effort to assemble a space station beginning in 1997.

Sports and Games

The sporting year in 1994 was dominated by Brazil, both in triumph and in tragedy. On May 1 the country was plunged into despair by the death of the three-time Formula One automobile racing world champion Ayrton Senna, a man who symbolized the heroism and struggle of a proud people (*see* OBITUARIES); then, on July 17, the mood was pure joy as the Brazilian soccer team beat Italy after a penalty shootout to win the World Cup for the first time since 1970.

In truth, the Cup final was a disappointment, but the success of the tournament had already been assured by the enthusiasm of the crowds, the strength of the organization, and the open, imaginative soccer played by the 24 finalists, including the host nation, the U.S., which surprised everyone, not least itself, by qualifying for the second stage of the competition. With referees ordered to punish foul play severely, such players as Romario of Brazil (*see* BIOGRAPHIES), Hristo Stoichkov of Bulgaria, and Gheorghe Hagi of Romania were able to express themselves to the full without the fear of physical injury that had been so prevalent in Italy four years earlier.

The only blemish on the tournament was the expulsion of Diego Maradona for taking drugs. The Argentine was subsequently banned from soccer for 18 months, effectively ending his career. The issue of drug taking also arose at the Commonwealth Games in Vancouver, B.C., in August, when five athletes, including two from England, were suspended, and later at the Asian Games, where positive tests on eight Chinese swimmers confirmed suspicions that the sudden emergence of a host of world-class swimmers and athletes from that nation had been based on a system of drug use similar to that employed by East Germany in the 1970s and '80s.

The baseball strike in the U.S., which began in mid-August and caused the cancellation of the World Series for the first time since 1904, showed no sign of ending as the year ended, with the players still refusing to accept the salary cap imposed on them by the club owners. In boxing, George Foreman's victory over Michael Moorer to become—at the age of 46—the oldest world heavyweight champion gave hope to everyone heading into middle age. Pete Sampras dominated the world of tennis, defending his Wimbledon title on the way, and Nick Price (*see* BIOGRAPHIES) of Zimbabwe was the year's supreme golfer, winning the British Open and the PGA championship, while Laura Davies of Britain was easily the outstanding woman golfer of the year. (ANDREW LONGMORE)

AUTOMOBILE RACING

Grand Prix Racing. International Formula One motor racing suffered tragedy in 1994. Ayrton Senna of Brazil, one of the sport's leading drivers, was killed in an accident when he slammed into a concrete wall while leading in the San Marino Grand Prix. (*See* OBITUARIES.) Only 24 hours earlier Roland Ratzenberger of Austria had died in a crash on the same course during a qualifying round.

Several new rules were made for the 1994 season. Refueling at the pits was permitted at the discretion of the entrants, but many protested because this appeared to involve a fire risk. This actually happened in the German Grand Prix, but fortunately the driver was not badly burned. The new regulations also required wooden skid plates to be attached to the undersides of the cars in order to slow them down. After the deaths at San Marino, a mechanism was introduced at the entries and exits to pit lanes to force cars to slow down. The season thus began with the rules disliked and often not

Colleagues Emerson Fittipaldi (left) and Gerhard Berger (right) are among the pallbearers in São Paulo for Brazilian auto racing hero Ayrton Senna, killed on May 1 in the San Marino Grand Prix. The 34-year-old Senna was world champion in 1988, 1990, and 1991.
EGBERTO NOGUEIRA—ABRIL IMAGENS

fully understood. The first event, over the Interlagos circuit in Brazil, was won by Michael Schumacher of Germany in a Benetton with a Cosworth-Ford Zetec engine, a lap ahead of Damon Hill's Williams-Renault. Accidents accounted for seven of the 14 retirements.

The competition then moved to Aida, Japan, for the Pacific Grand Prix, which Schumacher also won for Benetton. Gerhard Berger of Austria finished second in a Ferrari. The next race was on the Imola circuit at San Marino. It was there that Senna and Ratzenberger were killed. The race was won after the restart by Schumacher; Nicola Larini of Italy was second in a Ferrari.

The next race took place over the difficult and unique road circuit around Monaco. There Schumacher in the Benetton was again successful. Second place went to Martin Brundle of the U.K., for McLaren. At Barcelona for the Spanish Grand Prix, Schumacher suffered his first defeat when his Benetton became stuck in fifth gear, but even so he finished second to Hill's Williams-Renault. In Canada Schumacher scored an easy victory over Hill at Montreal.

In searing heat the French Grand Prix was contested at the Magny-Cours circuit. Untroubled, Schumacher defeated Hill by 12.642 sec. Silverstone served as host to the British Grand Prix, where Hill was a popular winner, 18.778 sec ahead of Schumacher. But because Schumacher had passed pole-sitter Hill on a warm-up lap and then failed for five laps to obey a black flag, he was excluded from the results and was banned from competing in the Italian and Portuguese Grand Prix. In the German Grand Prix at Hockenheim, Berger retrieved Ferrari fortunes, winning from the Ligier-Renault of French driver Olivier Panis. The Hungarian Grand Prix at Budapest was another Schumacher/Hill dual, with the German finishing 20.012 sec ahead of Hill.

Schumacher continued his top-class driving at Spa in the Belgian Grand Prix, beating Hill by 13.6 sec only to be disqualified because his Benetton had an "illegal" skidblock, giving it an aerodynamic advantage. Thus, Hill moved to first place. In the Italian Grand Prix at Monza, Hill won, and Berger finished second. The Williams-Renaults of Hill and newcomer David Coulthard of Scotland finished first and second at Estoril in the Portuguese Grand Prix.

Schumacher returned to racing at the European Grand Prix at Jerez de la Frontera, Spain, only one point ahead of Hill in the drivers' competition. The German won the race, and Hill finished second. Schumacher then led Hill by five points, but Hill narrowed the gap to one point with a close win over Schumacher in the Japanese Grand Prix. In the final event, the Australian Grand Prix at Adelaide, Schumacher hit a wall while leading Hill by a small margin; in attempting to pass, Hill collided with Schumacher, and both drivers had to retire. Schumacher thus won the drivers' championship. Nigel Mansell of the U.K., who had spent most of the year on the IndyCar circuit, won the race, and Berger was second.

The winter Monte Carlo Rally was won by a Ford Escort Cosworth, ahead of a Toyota and a Subaru, but a Toyota Celica took the Swedish Rally from a Mazda GTR and an Escort Cosworth RS. Toyotas won Portugal's TAP Rally, the Kenyan Safari Rally, and the Tour of Corsica. Didier Auriol of France won the drivers' championship, and Toyota took the manufacturers' championship. Paul Radisich won the touring car world championship with a Ford Mondeo after very close racing all season, with Alfa Romeo second. The Le Mans 24-hour race in France was a victory for Porsche, with a Toyota second.   (WILLIAM C. BODDY)

U.S. Racing.   The Indianapolis Motor Speedway in 1994 inaugurated a new era in U.S. automobile racing by putting its stamp of approval on stock cars. The traditional Indiana 500 on Memorial Day was now joined by National Association for Stock Car Auto Racing's (NASCAR's) Brickyard 400. The inaugural 400, held the first week of August, was won by an Indiana native, Jeff Gordon. Driving a Chevrolet Lumina, Gordon averaged 212.483 km/h (131.977 mph), beating Brett Bodine, Bill Elliott, and Rusty Wallace, all in Fords, in that order. He won $613,000 of the $3,213,849 purse, largest on the Winston Cup circuit.

The Indianapolis 500, the oldest and still the richest race in the world, witnessed the continued dominance of the Roger Penske team as that three-car entry drove cars more powerful than the rest of the field. Realizing that the rules gave stock-based engines an advantage for Indy only, Penske utilized Ilmor-modified Mercedes-Benz power plants. Penske's Al Unser, Jr., also the season CART champion, won the pole and the race, earning $1,373,815 of a purse of almost $8 million. His average speed was 259.004 km/h (160.872 mph). Teammate Emerson Fittipaldi had the fastest lap at 355.295 km/h (220.680 mph) but crashed late trying to lap Unser. Jacques Villeneuve in a Reynard-Ford, the only other car to complete the full 200 laps, finished second. The Penske trio switched to Ilmor-Chevrolet power

for the remainder of the season and won 12 of 16, finishing first, second, and third five times.

Dale Earnhardt made NASCAR history by tying now-retired Richard Petty with his seventh points championship for a season. Earnhardt's winnings totaled more than $3 million as he placed his Goodwrench Chevrolet Lumina into the victory lane four times and finished in the top five 20 times in 31 races. Runner-up Mark Martin in a Ford Thunderbird edged teammate Rusty Wallace for second by winning the final race at Atlanta, Ga. Ford won the manufacturers' crown.

The Daytona 500 was won by Sterling Marlin in a Chevrolet Lumina, with Ernie Irvan second in a Ford Thunderbird. Marlin averaged 252.659 km/h (156.931 mph) and won $253,575. Veteran Neil Bonnett and Rodney Orr were killed in one-car crashes while practicing for Daytona. NASCAR, meanwhile, announced another major variety of racing—full-sized pickup trucks with V-8 engines.

The International Motor Sports Association introduced its newest top class, World Sports Cars, which improved race by race in speed and durability and crowned Wayne Taylor (Mazda-Kudzu) its first champion. Scott Pruett, Paul Gentilozzi, Steve Millen, and Butch Leitzinger averaged 168.655 km/h (104.80 mph) to win the Daytona 24-hour race in a Nissan 300 ZX. Millen returned to win the Sebring 12-hour race, teamed with John Morton and Johnny O'Connell. Scott Kalitta won the National Hot Rod Association's Top Fuel season championship.   (ROBERT J. FENDELL)

BADMINTON

Indonesia rode the home-court advantage to domination of the badminton world in capturing 1994's Thomas and Uber cups. Contested in Jakarta, these biennial competitions featured (as always) three singles and two doubles matches for the men's Thomas Cup and the women's Uber Cup.

On the men's side Indonesia came through its preliminary round-robin group without losing a single match to either Finland, Sweden, or China, which finished second. In the other group Malaysia placed first, followed by South Korea, Denmark, and Thailand. The semifinals, following the cups' format, pitted Indonesia against South Korea and Malaysia against China. By twin scores of 4–1, Indonesia and defending champion (from 1992) Malaysia qualified for the final.

In the final Heryanto Arby started things off on the right foot for Indonesia by beating Rashid Sidek at first singles 15–6, 15–11. Bambang Suprianto and Gunawan at first doubles kept up the momentum and defeated Cheah Soon Kit and Soo Beng Kiang 15–10, 6–15, 15–8. Ardy Wiranata provided the decisive third point by beating Ong Ewe Hock 15–11, 15–5 in the second singles, at which time the stadium erupted into a near riot and the two final (and immaterial) matches were canceled. This was Indonesia's first Thomas Cup in 10 years.

In women's competition Indonesia came through on top of its group by beating Thailand, Denmark, and Sweden, which finished second. China won the other group, with South Korea second, followed by Japan and Russia. In the semifinals Indonesia defeated South Korea 4–1, and China beat Sweden 3–2. This Uber Cup came to a dramatic climax as Indonesia's 14-year-old third-singles player, Mia Audina, took the court against China's Zhang Ning. The match was tied at 2–2 after Susi Susanti defeated Ze Zhaoying 11–4, 12–10, Lili Tampi and Finarsih beat Chen Ying and Wu Yuhong 15–13, 17–16, Yuliani Santoso lost to Han Jingna 5–11, 5–11, and Eliza and Zellin fell to Ge Fei and Gu Jun 10–15, 8–15. Audina rose to the occasion and won 11–7, 10–12, 11–4 to bring the Uber Cup to Indonesia for the first time since 1975.   (WARREN K. EMERSON)

Formula One Grand Prix Race Results, 1994

Race	Driver	Average speed (km/h)	Car
Brazilian GP	M. Schumacher	192.363	Benetton B194-Ford Zetec V8
Pacific GP	M. Schumacher	173.975	Benetton B194-Ford Zetec V8
San Marino GP	M. Schumacher	198.333	Benetton B194-Ford Zetec V8
Monaco GP	M. Schumacher	141.751	Benetton B194-Ford Zetec V8
Spanish GP	D. Hill	192.765	Williams FW16-Renault V10
Canadian GP	M. Schumacher	188.088	Benetton B194-Ford Zetec V8
French GP	M. Schumacher	186.294	Benetton B194-Ford Zetec V8
British GP	D. Hill	202.216	Williams FW16-Renault V10
German GP	G. Berger	222.985	Ferrari 412 V12
Hungarian GP	M. Schumacher	169.807	Benetton B194-Ford Zetec V8
Belgian GP	D. Hill	208.253	Williams FW16-Renault V10
Italian GP	D. Hill	236.428	Williams FW16-Renault V10
Portuguese GP	D. Hill	185.665	Williams FW16-Renault V10
European GP	M. Schumacher	182.735	Benetton B194-Ford Zetec V8
Japanese GP	D. Hill	151.823	Williams FW16-Renault V10
Australian GP	N. Mansell	170.338	Williams FW16-Renault V10

WORLD DRIVERS' CHAMPIONSHIP: Schumacher 92 points, Hill 91 points, Berger 41 points.
MANUFACTURERS' WORLD CHAMPIONSHIP: Williams-Renault 118 points, Benetton-Ford 103 points, Ferrari 71 points.

BASEBALL

Regular Season. Until the Major League Baseball Players Association began its strike after the games of Aug. 11, 1994, baseball fans were enjoying an entertaining season that featured extraordinary individual performances and tight division races under a new system. Before the 1994 season, owners and players agreed to a revised alignment—the 14 teams in each league, the American and National, were placed in three divisions instead of two: the East, Central, and West. Thus, at the conclusion of the 162-game schedule on October 2, each league would produce three division champions. Also, there would be one wild-card team from each league to qualify for the postseason play-offs. That team would be the second-place team with the best record.

In previous seasons only four teams had participated in postseason competition—the American League East winner versus the American League West winner and the National League East winner versus the National League West winner—for the right to advance to the World Series. The new format would have doubled the number of teams eligible for postseason play. The premise was that by producing more champions baseball would create more interest during the latter stages of the regular season.

Baseball Strikes Out

On Sept. 14, 1994, acting commissioner Allan H. ("Bud") Selig announced that the remainder of the 1994 major league baseball season, including the World Series, would be canceled. The World Series had been contested every October since 1905, surviving cold snaps, two world wars, and the Great Depression. Fans throughout the U.S. and Canada mourned its loss.

But Selig, who was also chairman of the Milwaukee Brewers, said that the decision was unavoidable. The Major League Baseball Players Association called a strike after the games of August 11, and from then until the September announcement, management and the union failed to settle on a new basic agreement. Thus, Selig, with the support of 26 of 28 fellow owners, revealed what was deemed a foregone conclusion at a press conference in Milwaukee.

Because of the impasse, 669 regular-season games were canceled, not including the postseason play-offs and the World Series. Major league baseball, a $2 billion industry, thus entered what Selig termed "uncharted territory" as it headed toward an uncertain winter after revenue losses estimated at $800 million.

The work stoppage was baseball's eighth since 1972, because of either a strike or a lockout by the owners. The most serious interruption before 1994 occurred in 1981, when the union struck on June 12 and did not return until August 9. The disputes usually concerned issues such as free-agent compensation and salary arbitration, mechanisms that helped the union achieve leverage over owners.

The union gained power through two widely heralded events—Marvin Miller's appointment in 1966 as executive director of the Major League Baseball Players Association and, in 1975, arbitrator Peter Seitz's ruling that pitchers Andy Messersmith and Dave McNally were free agents, available to the highest bidder. Previously, management had tendered contracts containing a Reserve Clause, which bound players to one team in perpetuity.

Major league owners, led by Jerry Reinsdorf of the Chicago White Sox (*see* BIOGRAPHIES), held out for a salary cap to put a limit on team payrolls. Such caps were already being used in the National Football League and the National Basketball Association. Baseball owners, painting a dire picture for the future, insisted that a salary cap was imperative if disaster was to be averted. The union balked, claiming that the cap was an artificial restraint on earning power and a tool whereby players had to sacrifice to help the owners control their own free-spending ways.

Baseball fans express their opinion of the then impending strike by players, which began on August 12 and resulted in the first cancellation of the World Series ever. Money was at issue, principally the owners' attempt to institute a salary cap.
LUC NOVOVITCH—AP

Miller's successor as labour leader, Donald Fehr, discounted management's prediction of imminent doom. He also dismissed various reports that anywhere from 12 to 19 major league franchises were losing money. Richard Ravitch, representing management, decried the union's intransigence. The owners' original proposal provided a 50–50 split of revenue with players and guaranteed them $1 billion per year over a seven-year period even if revenues did not increase.

Several negotiating sessions were held between the time of the strike and the cancellation, but the mood was hostile and contentious. The owners had succumbed on previous occasions but were under no pressure from a commissioner to bend again. Fay Vincent, the previous commissioner, had resigned late in 1992 and not been replaced. Selig performed his duties, and that was another annoyance to the players, who felt that as an owner he had a conflict of interest.

Soon after Selig's announcement, U.S. Pres. Bill Clinton appointed William Usery to mediate the dispute. A veteran negotiator, Usery expressed confidence that there would be a settlement in time to start the 1995 baseball season, but the stalemate continued at year's end. On December 23 the owners implemented their salary cap, and the players prepared to mount legal challenges.   (ROBERT WILLIAM VERDI)

In the American League Central another lively race existed. The Chicago White Sox, at 67–46, were only one game ahead of the Cleveland Indians. In the American League East the New York Yankees were well ahead of the Baltimore Orioles, but the Orioles were still very much in contention for a wild-card berth. The Indians and Rangers opened new ballparks in April, to rave reviews.

In the National League the surprising Montreal Expos had posted the best record overall at 74–40, good enough for a six-game advantage over the highly favoured Atlanta Braves in the East. The Cincinnati Reds were only half a game ahead of the Houston Astros in the Central. In the West the Los Angeles Dodgers, though only two games above .500 at 58–56, were 3½ games ahead of the San Francisco Giants.

Individual Performances. Offense clearly dominated the abbreviated 1994 season. Matt Williams, third baseman for San Francisco, had 43 home runs through 115 games and was on a pace to challenge the single-season record of Roger Maris, who hit 61 home runs for the 1961 New York Yankees. Seattle's Ken Griffey, Jr., had collected 38 home runs through 112 games.

In the National League Houston first baseman Jeff Bagwell was making a serious bid to seize the Triple Crown—best batting average, most home runs, and most runs batted in. In the American League Frank Thomas of Chicago and Albert Belle of Cleveland were doing the same. Not since Carl Yastrzemski with the Boston Red Sox in 1967 had a player won the Triple Crown. Tony Gwynn, an outfielder for the San Diego Padres, had compiled a batting average of .394, the best mark since Ted Williams registered .406 with Boston in 1941.

Despite all the offense, however, a few pitchers had standout seasons. Kenny Rogers of Texas tossed a perfect game, while Atlanta's Kent Mercker and Scott Erickson of the Minnesota Twins threw no-hitters. Greg Maddux of the Braves, winner of the previous two National League Cy Young Awards for best pitcher, had crafted a splendid 1.56 earned run average per nine innings.

Thomas was voted the American League's Most Valuable Player, and Bagwell won the prize for the National League. Cy Young Awards for best pitcher went to David Cone of Kansas City in the American League and Maddux for the third straight year in the National. Rookies of the Year were Bob Hamelin of Kansas City in the American and the

Dodgers' Raul Mondesi in the National, and the top managers were the Yankees' Buck Showalter in the American and Felipe Alou of Montreal in the National.

Other Events. Ryne Sandberg, star second baseman for the Chicago Cubs, shocked the baseball world by retiring in June at the age of 34 because, he said, he had lost his desire to play. There were three inductees into the Hall of Fame at Cooperstown, N.Y.—Steve Carlton, a pitcher for the Philadelphia Phillies; Phil Rizzuto, shortstop for the Yankees; and Leo Durocher, who had managed several teams.

Little League. Venezuela defeated Northridge, Calif., 4–3 to win the Little League World Series at Williamsport, Pa., on August 28. Venezuela, the first Latin-American team to earn the title since 1958, ended a two-year reign by U.S. teams as Little League World Series champions.

(ROBERT WILLIAM VERDI)

Latin America. The Licey Tigers from the Dominican Republic dominated the 24th Caribbean Series, played February 2–9 in Puerto La Cruz, Venezuela. The Tigers won six straight games to gain the top championship of Latin-American baseball.

The San Juan Senators from Puerto Rico took second place. They were defeated twice by the Licey Tigers but beat their other two rivals. The Venezuelan team, the Magallanes Navigators, failed to capitalize on the advantage of playing at home and took third place. The Hermosillo Orange Growers from Mexico dropped six games in a row to finish last.

The controversy about allowing Cuba to compete in the Caribbean Series continued in 1994. Cuban teams had not been allowed to participate in the tournament because they were not formally professional, but it was widely acknowledged that their amateur teams would be able to compete successfully in the series. Cuba, in fact, continued to dominate world amateur baseball. In the 32nd world championship of amateur baseball, played in Nicaragua, the Cuban national team scored a series of easy wins and took the pennant, as it had done consistently for years, with a clear victory of 13–1 over Nicaragua in the final game. South Korea finished third and Japan fourth.

In the summer the Mexico City Red Devils won the AAA Mexican League pennant when they defeated the Monterrey Sultans in the seven-game final series. The Red Devils came from behind in the series and also in the final game to take their 11th Mexican championship.

(SERGIO SARMIENTO)

Japan. The Yomiuri Giants of Tokyo, champions of the Central League, defeated Tokorozawa's Seibu Lions of the Pacific League four games to two in the best-of-seven Japan Series. It was the Giants' first all-Japan title since 1989 and their 18th overall. The Lions, who had played in the fall classic 10 times in the past 12 years and won 8, including 3 against the Giants, got off to a good start and won the opener 11–0. For the remainder of the series, however, the Giants' pitchers dominated. They threw three complete games—one by Masumi Kuwata and two by Hiromi Makihara, who during the regular season completed a perfect game against the Hiroshima Carp. Makihara was voted the Most Valuable Player of the Series.

Before the 130th and final game of the season against the Chunichi Dragons in Nagoya, the Giants were tied with the Dragons. The Giants won the final game 6-3 to gain their first league championship in four years. Kuwata, a right-hander who won 14 games and struck out 185 batters, was voted the Most Valuable Player of the Central League. The Rookie of the Year award went to Osaka's Hanshin Tiger hurler Keiichi Yabu, who won nine games.

Final Major League Standings, 1994

AMERICAN LEAGUE
East Division

Club	W.	L.	G.B.
New York	70	43	–
Baltimore	63	49	6½
Toronto	55	60	16
Boston	54	61	17
Detroit	53	62	18

Central Division

Club	W.	L.	G.B.
Chicago	67	46	–
Cleveland	66	47	1
Kansas City	64	51	4
Minnesota	53	60	14
Milwaukee	53	62	15

West Division

Club	W.	L.	G.B.
Texas	52	62	–
Oakland	51	63	1
Seattle	49	63	2
California	47	68	5½

NATIONAL LEAGUE
East Division

Club	W.	L.	G.B.
Montreal	74	40	–
Atlanta	68	46	6
New York	55	58	18½
Philadelphia	54	61	20½
Florida	51	64	23½

Central Division

Club	W.	L.	G.B.
Cincinnati	66	48	–
Houston	66	49	½
Pittsburgh	53	61	13
St. Louis	53	61	13
Chicago	49	64	16½

West Division

Club	W.	L.	G.B.
Los Angeles	58	56	–
San Francisco	55	60	3½
Colorado	53	64	6½
San Diego	47	70	12½

Going into September the Pacific League competition was a four-way race between the Lions, Osaka's Kintetsu Buffaloes, Kobe's Orix Blue Wave, and Fukuoka's Daiei Hawks. The Lions then left the others behind, however, and finished the season 7½ games ahead of the Buffaloes and Blue Wave. The league's Most Valuable Player was Ichiro Suzuki, a 20-year-old outfielder for the Blue Wave, who became the first player in Japanese baseball history to collect more than 200 hits (210) and had a league-record batting average of .385. Hidekazu Watanabe, who won eight games for the Hawks, was the league's Rookie of the Year.

Sadaharu Oh, the Giants' great home-run hitter (868 in 22 years), was elected to the Japanese Hall of Fame in his first year of eligibility. He was joined by Wally Yonamine of the Giants, the first American so honoured.

(TOSHIHIKO SUZUKI)

BASKETBALL

United States. Duke University, a titan in the power-packed Atlantic Coast Conference (ACC), continued to prove that nothing succeeds like success in the National Collegiate Athletic Association (NCAA) basketball tournament. In 1994, for the fourth time in five years, the Blue Devils reached the championship game of the tourney. Under Coach Mike Krzyzewski they were appearing in the Final Four for the seventh time in nine years. Such a dominant stretch had not been equaled on the collegiate basketball scene since UCLA's unprecedented run of nine national championships in a 10-year dynasty (1964–73).

This time Duke's past success could not succeed against a coach and a team that refused to fail, however. Arkansas, fueled by the desire burning inside Coach Nolan Richardson, rallied in the final game to beat Duke 76–72 and capture its first NCAA title.

The poise of Duke's seniors seemed to be taking command early in the second half when a string of 11 straight points built a 48–38 lead for the Blue Devils. But the Razorbacks, from the tough Southeastern Conference, had been overcoming such adversity all season, despite the lack of a senior among the players Richardson relied on most.

Arkansas pulled ahead, then wilted briefly when Grant Hill's three-point basket pulled the Blue Devils into a 70–70 tie with just 1½ minutes remaining. At this crucial time Scotty Thurman of Arkansas responded with the crusher, a decisive three-pointer on the last tick of the 24-second shot clock. Only 50.7 seconds were left, and Duke could not recover from that knockout punch.

"Scotty made a tough shot even though I was right on him," said Duke's Antonio Lang, who led his team with 15 points. "I still don't know how it went in," Richardson said. "I'm not surprised that Thurman hit the biggest shot of his career when we needed it most," the victorious coach continued. "That's the way these kids have been picking each other up since our first game."

The Razorbacks, capping a 31–3 crusade orchestrated by Richardson's emotion, also proved they could handle the pressure of being ranked number one in the weekly polls for the last two months of the 1993–94 schedule. Their suffocating defense turned the tide in the championship clash, forcing Duke's tournament-tested veterans into an abnormally high total of 23 turnovers. Corliss Williamson, a tireless 2.01-m (6-ft 7-in) power forward, lived up to his "Big Nasty" nickname with a game-high 23 points. He was named Most Valuable Player of the tournament.

In women's basketball North Carolina's Charlotte Smith sank a three-point shot in the final second of the NCAA championship game to produce a stunning 60–59 upset over perennial power Louisiana Tech. Smith, a 1.83-m (6-ft) junior with the ability to dunk a basketball, found the range from outside to bring the nationally televised final to an exciting finish. Smith's heroics snapped a 25-game winning streak for Louisiana Tech (31–4). North Carolina won the title in its first trip to the Final Four.

The final duels were a fitting climax to an exciting college season. Not all of the action took place on the court, especially in mid-January when the Black Coaches Association (BCA) threatened a selective strike of Saturday

JOHN BIEVER—SPORTS ILLUSTRATED

Arkansas's Scotty Thurman gets off a shot against Duke in the final game of the National Collegiate Athletic Association tournament, which Arkansas won 76–72. It was Arkansas's first NCAA basketball title, and Nolan Richardson was named the Naismith Coach of the Year.

NBA Final Standings, 1993–94

EASTERN CONFERENCE			WESTERN CONFERENCE		
Team	Won	Lost	Team	Won	Lost
Atlantic Division			**Midwest Division**		
*New York	57	25	*Houston	58	24
*Orlando	50	32	*San Antonio	55	27
*New Jersey	45	37	*Utah	53	29
*Miami	42	40	*Denver	42	40
Boston	32	50	Minnesota	20	62
Philadelphia	25	57	Dallas	13	69
Washington	24	58			
Central Division			**Pacific Division**		
*Atlanta	57	25	*Seattle	63	19
*Chicago	55	27	*Phoenix	56	26
*Indiana	47	35	*Golden State	50	32
*Cleveland	47	35	*Portland	47	35
Charlotte	41	41	L.A. Lakers	33	49
Detroit	20	62	Sacramento	28	54
Milwaukee	20	62	L.A. Clippers	27	55

*Gained play-off berth.

games. Led by Richardson and John Thompson of Georgetown University, they were protesting new NCAA regulations aimed at tightening academic requirements for student athletes. The BCA coaches also were angered by a decision to cut the annual basketball scholarship limit from 15 to 13.

The walkout was avoided by last-minute negotiations. The underlying issues still ensured NCAA convention fireworks between the university presidents, who were determined to have a larger voice in athletic policy making, and their basketball coaches. Caught in the middle were the players, who faced harsh NCAA penalties, including the loss of their scholarships, if they elected to join the protest. With the aid of federal mediators, the two sides indicated that the issues might be settled without such drastic action. The university presidents stood firm on their insistence for higher standards but suggested that they could be implemented along with safeguards to avoid undue problems for minority students.

In professional competition life without Michael Jordan was both possible and profitable, as the National Basketball Association (NBA) discovered during the 1993–94 season. Somehow, though, without No. 23 of the Chicago Bulls soaring for one of his crowd-pleasing skywalks, it did not seem to be quite as much fun. Although Bulls fans were not expecting much without Jordan, their team made a strong showing throughout the 1993–94 campaign. The Bulls took the New York Knicks to the seven-game limit in an exciting Eastern Conference play-off semifinal before bowing out to snap their championship run at three straight.

The Knicks then defeated the Indiana Pacers to meet Western Conference champion Houston in the finals, setting up a struggle between two of the NBA's finest big men. It was 2.13-m, 116-kg (7-ft, 255-lb) Hakeem Olajuwon (*see* BIOGRAPHIES) of the Rockets against 2.13-m, 109-kg (7-ft, 240-lb) Patrick Ewing of the Knicks. Both centres, known around the league as consummate team players, hungered for their first taste of an NBA championship. But only one could satisfy his appetite and, in the end, it was Olajuwon, the league's Most Valuable Player for the season and series.

Ewing and the Knicks electrified New York by taking a 3–2 lead in the best-of-seven final play-off but needed one more victory in Houston to wrap it up. Olajuwon prevented that from happening on his home court by taking personal charge of both backboards. The veteran from Nigeria was a dominating force while the Rockets hung on to even the series with a pulse-pounding 86–84 decision in game 6.

That narrowed the whole season down to the June 22 climax. It was Olajuwon's night, with his 25 points and 10 rebounds powering Houston to a 90–84 victory and the NBA championship ring he had coveted for a decade.

A circle of competition also was closed by this confrontation. In 1984 Ewing had led Georgetown past Olajuwon and the University of Houston in the NCAA final. Instead of gloating, Olajuwon reached out to comfort the vanquished Ewing.　　　　(ROBERT G. LOGAN)

Charlotte Smith takes the game-winning shot in North Carolina's 60–59 victory over Louisiana Tech in the final game of the National Collegiate Athletic Association tournament. It was North Carolina's first women's national championship.

JIM GUND—ALLSPORT

International. The major events of the year in international basketball were the world championships for men and women, which were held in Toronto and Sydney, Australia, respectively. As expected, the United States won the men's championship for the third time, defeating Russia 137–91 in the final. Croatia beat Greece for third place. In the women's tournament Brazil won the title, defeating China 96–87 in the final. This was the first time in the history of the competition that a country other than the U.S. or the Soviet Union had finished first.

The second European championship for men 23 and under was held in Slovenia. In the final, Belarus, one of the nations in Europe formed by the division of the Soviet Union, defeated Italy 96–91. The European champions at the junior (under-18) level were Lithuania in the men's competition and Italy in the women's. Finishing second were Croatia and Spain, respectively.

The European Championship for Men's Clubs, the major club competition during the 1993–94 European season, was retained by Joventut Badalona (Spain), which defeated Olympiakos (Greece) 59–57 in a thrilling final in Tel Aviv, Israel. In the other European competitions, Olimpija Ljubljana (Slovenia) won the European Cup by beating Vitoria Álava (Spain), P.A.O.K. Salonica (Greece) defeated Trieste (Italy) to take the European Korac Cup, Como (Italy) won the Women's European Championships Cup with a victory over Dorna Valencia (Spain), and the Ronchetti Cup remained in Italy with Cesena defeating fellow Italian defending champions Primizie Parme.

In South America, Leite Moza from Brazil won the 10th South American Championship for Women's Clubs, defeating fellow Brazilians Unimed in the final. The 32nd men's championship was retained by Atenas (Argentina), which beat Olimpia, also from Argentina.

The fourth Commonwealth championship for men was held in Sungei Penang, Malaysia. Canada won the gold medal, with England taking silver and Nigeria bronze.

The international governing body of amateur basketball made some minor but important adjustments to the rules of the game. The four main changes included recognizing the front foot as the pivot when determining a traveling call, replacing the one-and-one rule with two free throws, taking an inbounds pass from wherever the ball leaves the court (previously, it could be taken from the baseline); and making the alley-oop a legal move.　　(MARK HANNEN)

BILLIARD GAMES

Carom Billiards. The 1993 World Billiard Association (BWA) three-cushion championship was won by an American for the first time in 40 years at the BWA's World Cup in Ghent, Belgium. Sang Chun Lee, a native South Korean who moved to New York City in 1987, won the crown despite lagging in cumulative tour scoring at the onset of the sixth and final tour stop. The 39-year-old Lee trailed both 21-time world titlist Raymond Ceulemans of Belgium and defending champion Torbjorn Blomdahl of Sweden in the standings. But an upset of three-time winner Blomdahl by Raimond Burgman of The Netherlands in the first round, coupled with Ceulemans' fall to his fellow Belgian Fredric Caudron in the second round, opened the door for Lee to claim his first world championship with a final match victory over Caudron. He did so with a powerful four-set win, 15–4, 6–15, 15–6, 15–8, averaging 1.457 points per inning (PPI). Blomdahl was the runner-up, and Ceulemans finished third.

Lee also played host and promoter of two World Open three-cushion tournaments in New York City. In the first, Caudron, ranked seventh in the world, averaged a somewhat modest 1.303 PPI but won key close matches to finish first with an 8–1 record. Lee was second with a sizzling 1.749 PPI average. The second event, won by Blomdahl with a 6–1 finish, saw these new records set: 50 points in 14 innings (U.S. record) by Semih Sayginer of Turkey; 60 points in 18 innings (world mark) by Blomdahl; 1.370-PPI field grand average for eight-player round-robin tournament (world); 82 points by two players, Sayginer and Lee, in 14 innings (world). Sayginer claimed second place with a 5–2 mark.

It was Lee in the winner's circle again at the U.S. national three-cushion championship in Chicago. The 24-player test was won for the fifth time by Lee in a play-off with Carlos Hallon of Miami, Fla., after both players finished round-robin play with 6–1 records.

Pocket Billiards. Pocket billiards in the U.S. continued to be the scene (and perhaps the victim) of unceasing turmoil and discontent as several groups and factions vied for control. At stake was control of the player groups that seemingly were the key to a long-awaited financial breakthrough for the sport. Several changes in leadership of the most prominent player and promotion groups again took place during 1994, some with alarming dispatch. The year ended with little apparent agreement between the parties in conflict and with many questions regarding the future of the professional tour still to be settled.

Meanwhile, however, play continued generally unabated. The final major event of the 1993 nine-ball tour year, the Professional Billiards Association 1993 Tour Championship in Bell Gardens, Calif., was won by Francisco Bustamante of the Philippines. At one of 1994's most prestigious events, the Professional Billiards Tour (PBT) Players' Championship in Valley Forge, Pa., Mike Sigel of Baltimore, Md., became the first winner of 100 professional pool tournaments with his 9–5 victory in the finals over Danny Harriman of Springfield, Mo. The Sands Regency XVIII title in Reno, Nev., went to 1993 Player of the Year Johnny Archer of Raleigh, N.C., while the Sands Regency XIX event was won by Tony Ellin of Hollywood, S.C.

The PBT's second annual World 9-Ball Championship in Las Vegas, Nev., featured live national television coverage of a U.S. pocket billiard tournament for the first time; the live feed was picked up in more than 50 countries. Earl Strickland of Greensboro, N.C., snared his fifth world title by whipping Efren Reyes of the Philippines 9–2 in the final. The competing World Pool-Billiard Association 9-Ball Championship in Arlington Heights, Ill., was won by Takeshi Okumura of Japan and, in a popular comeback, Ewa Mataya-Laurance. Earlier in the year Strickland had captured the 18th U.S. 9-Ball Open in Chesapeake, Va.

New York City was the site of the Billiard Congress of America (BCA) 16th Annual U.S. Open straight pool (14.1 continuous) championships. Germany's Oliver Ortmann won his second Open title, and Liu Hsin-mei of Taiwan took the women's crown.

The Women's Professional Billiard Association's 15th annual National 9-Ball Championship in San Francisco was won by the top-ranked Loree Jon Jones, while the year's richest first prize of $20,000 was rung up by Robin Bell with her victory in the $50,000 Gordon's 9-Ball (women's) Championship in Santa Monica, Calif. The top prize at the $32,000 Bicycle Club Women's Classic in Bell Gardens, Calif., was won by Vivian Villarreal.

The Association of College Unions–International national billiards championship for 1994 was held at Arizona State University, where defending champion Max Eberle, a senior at James Madison University, Harrisonburg, Va., became only the seventh man to win the title for two consecutive years. He defeated Randy Tate, a junior from Illinois State University, 7–5 in the final. The women's division was won by University of Washington senior Rachel Ross, who turned back University of Wyoming senior Dean Leath 6–4 in the championship match.

The BCA inducted pool stars "Cowboy" Jimmy Moore and Ray ("Cool Cat") Martin as player members of the BCA Hall of Fame at its 11th International Trade Expo in Las Vegas.   (BRUCE H. VENZKE)

Snooker. Stephen Hendry of Scotland retained the world professional snooker title in 1994 with a dramatic victory over Jimmy White of England by 18 frames to 17 in the final at Sheffield, England, in May, winning it for the fourth time in five years for a record prize of £180,000. In April Ronnie O'Sullivan of England won the British Open title at Plymouth with a 9–4 win over James Wattana of Thailand in the final. Ken Doherty from Ireland became Scottish Masters champion by defeating Hendry 9–7 in the final at Motherwell, Scotland, in September. Alan McManus of Scotland, earlier the winner of the Masters title at Wembley, England, in February, went on to win the Dubai Classic in October with a 9–6 victory over Peter Ebdon of England in the final. Former world champion Steve Davis of England secured both the Welsh Open and Irish Masters titles. Another Scot, John Higgins, won the Grand Prix in October at Derby, England, after defeating Dave Harold 9–6 in the final. Hendry regained the U.K. title with a 10–5 victory in the final over Doherty at Preston, England, in November.

(SYDNEY E. FRISKIN)

BOWLING

World Tenpins. The crown jewel among all international tenpin bowling tournaments of 1994 was the third world youth championships, held in Monterrey, Mexico, August 6–13. A record 29 countries sent their best young bowlers to Mexico to compete for world titles in boys' and girls' divisions. Stars of the tournament were Jaana Puhakka and Pasi Pöllänen of Finland, each of whom won two individual titles. In addition, Pöllänen won a gold medal in team competition and a silver in masters, and Puhakka took a silver in doubles. In girls' masters, Puhakka, the defending world champion from 1992, made bowling history by winning the title again. Her double was the first in the 40-year history of international bowling.

Champions in the girls' competition were: singles—Puhakka, Finland, 1,208; doubles—Australia 2,477; teams of four—Australia 4,626; all-events—Kelly Warren, Australia, 3,649; masters—Puhakka 394. Winners of the boys' events were: singles—Pöllänen, Finland, 1,285; doubles—U.S. 2,438; teams of four—Finland 4,710; all-events—Pöllänen 3,697; masters—Chiang An-Shan, Taiwan, 405. In competition for overall team performance, Finland easily won the Cojuangco Cup for men, and Australia took it for women.

At the 13th Asian zone championships in Guam, held July 1–10, women's winners were: singles—Shalin Zulkifli, Malaysia, 1,251; doubles—Australia 2,482; trios—Australia 3,550; five-person teams—Japan 5,767; all-events—

Cara Honeychurch, Australia, 4,883; masters—Honeychurch 3,390. Champions in men's competition were: singles—Muhammad Khalifa al-Qubaisi, United Arab Emirates, 1,367; doubles—Korea 2,467; trios—Qatar 3,736; five-person teams—Taiwan 6,320; all-events—Chen Yu-Chia, Taiwan, 5,027; masters—Paeng Nepomuceno, Philippines, 3,453.

The major tournament in Europe was the Team Cup, which took place in Scheveningen, Neth., May 30–June 5. Denmark won the men's competition, with Germany second and Sweden third. The Netherlands placed first in the women's competition, followed by Germany and the U.K.

(YRJÖ SARAHETE)

U.S. Tenpins. Bowling's oldest record was broken in 1994. The Hurst Bowling Supplies team of Wilkes-Barre, Pa., competing in the Empire Arcade Classic League in Luzerne, Pa., rolled a three-game score of 3,868, topping the 3,858 shot by the St. Louis (Mo.) Budweisers in 1958. Hurst's games were 1,351, 1,255, and 1,262.

When he won the General Tire Tournament of Champions in April, Norm Duke of Edmond, Okla., appeared to have assured himself of succeeding Walter Ray Williams, Jr., as Professional Bowlers Association (PBA) Player of the Year with only one-third of the year having elapsed. Duke had won three other PBA tournaments earlier. In the Tournament of Champions final, he defeated Eric Forkel of Chatsworth, Calif., 217–184 after Forkel followed a run of three strikes with a gutter ball in the eighth frame.

In the American Bowling Congress (ABC) Masters Tournament, in Mobile, Ala., Steve Fehr of Cincinnati, Ohio, took the $43,700 first prize by topping Steve Anderson of Colorado Springs, Colo., 224–206 in the final. The Regular Division winners in the tournament were: team, Bluemound Bowl No. 1, Milwaukee, Wis., 3,305; singles, John Weltzien, Boca Raton, Fla., 810; doubles, Dean Distin and Mike Tryniski, Fulton, N.Y., 1,468; all-events, Thomas Holt, Abilene, Texas, 2,190.

Anne Marie Duggan of Edmond, Okla., won the Women's International Bowling Congress (WIBC) Queens Tournament, defeating Aleta Sill of Dearborn, Mich., 238–218 in the title match. Duggan also was a member of the Strike Zone Pro Shop team of Rolling Meadows, Ill., which won the WIBC Classic Division team championship for the second consecutive year. The Strike Zones totaled 3,027. Both tournaments took place in Salt Lake City, Utah. Other WIBC winners included: singles, Vicki Fifield, El Paso, Texas, 716; doubles, Lucy Giovinco, Norcross, Ga., and Cindy Coburn-Carroll, Tonawanda, N.Y., tied with Rachel Perez, San Antonio, Texas, and Kim Straub, Beatrice, Neb., 1,307; all-events, Wendy Macpherson-Papanos, Las Vegas, Nev., 1,940.

(JOHN J. ARCHIBALD)

BOXING

One of the biggest upsets in world boxing history was recorded at Las Vegas, Nev., in November 1994 when 46-year-old George Foreman (U.S.) knocked out the World Boxing Association (WBA) and International Boxing Federation (IBF) heavyweight champion Michael Moorer (U.S.) in the 10th round. In his defeat of the 27-year-old and previously undefeated Moorer, Foreman thus became the oldest heavyweight ever to win the world crown. It was an extraordinary performance by a fighter who had first won the title by defeating Joe Frazier (U.S.) in Jamaica 21 years earlier only to be destroyed by a 32-year-old Muhammad Ali (U.S.) the following year. So humiliated was the young Foreman that he quit boxing for 10 years and became a Baptist preacher.

Adding to this almost unbelievable result was the fact that Foreman had not fought in a match for 17 months after he

George Foreman (left) jabs at Michael Moorer during their WBA/IBF title heavyweight fight. Twenty years after he had lost the undisputed heavyweight title to Muhammad Ali, the 46-year-old Foreman knocked out Moorer in the 10th round to become the oldest boxer ever to win a title.

HOLLY STEIN—ALLSPORT

was soundly outpointed by Tommy Morrison (U.S.) in a bid for the vacant World Boxing Organization (WBO) heavyweight title. Yet another bizarre situation in world heavyweight competition was that another former champion, 45-year-old Larry Holmes (U.S.), was scheduled to challenge Oliver McCall (U.S.) for the World Boxing Council (WBC) heavyweight championship early in 1995. If Holmes should win, a future bout with Foreman would match two grandfathers fighting for boxing's most lucrative prize.

Apart from the Moorer-Foreman upset, the heavyweight division went through another year of instability and unpredictable results. All the holders of WBC, WBA, IBF, and WBO versions lost titles in a series of upsets. Evander Holyfield (U.S.), who had regained the WBA/IBF crown, was surprisingly outpointed by Moorer, who had earlier relinquished the WBO version. More upsets followed when Michael Bentt (U.S.), who had shocked the experts by taking the WBO title with a first-round knockout of Morrison in late 1993, made his first defense against Herbie Hide (England) in London and was knocked out in the seventh round. After the fight, Bentt collapsed in his dressing room and spent a night in the hospital. It later emerged that he had had dizzy spells while in training and was reported to have blacked out on the plane back to New York. After a series of medical tests, the 29-year-old Bentt retired. He had taken part in only 13 professional contests, winning 11.

The heavyweight scene had to endure a complete fiasco. Hide had signed to make the first defense of the WBO title against Morrison in Hong Kong in October. It was to be the biggest boxing tournament ever staged in Hong Kong, also including several other fights for world championships. The promised financial backing never was obtained, however, and an angry press conference replaced the weigh-in only 17 hours before the tournament was scheduled to begin. Never before had a heavyweight championship been called off at such a late hour. Yet another upset took place when Lennox Lewis (England), having successfully defended the WBC title by defeating Phil Jackson (U.S.) in Atlantic City, N.J., was stopped in two rounds in London by McCall, the former sparring partner of Mike Tyson. Lewis' defeat by McCall brought back to prominence Don King, who had controlled the title for years when he managed Tyson and now handled McCall.

The outstanding fighter of the year was again Julio Cesar Chávez (Mexico), despite the big surprise when he lost the WBC junior welterweight (also called super lightweight) crown to Frankie Randall (U.S.). It was Chávez' first defeat in the 91 contests of his 14-year career. Randall, given his first shot at a championship after 11 years in boxing, was quoted as a 15–1 underdog but won the decision against an out-of-form Chávez at Las Vegas in January. In the return match in May, also at Las Vegas, Chávez regained the title with a controversial verdict following an accidental clash of heads in the eighth round that severely cut the Mexican. Under the rules the bout was stopped, and Chávez was awarded the decision on points. Many experts thought that Randall had been robbed and that the 31-year-old Mexican had seen his best days. But Chávez confounded the boxing world by coming back to demolish Meldrick Taylor (U.S.) at Las Vegas in September. Taylor, who had come close to defeating Chávez four years earlier, was leading when Chávez dug deep and with a savage attack finished off his challenger in the eighth round. Also fighting that night in Las Vegas, Randall gained consolation by surviving a knock-down and then defeating Juan Martin Coggi (Argentina) for the WBA junior welterweight crown.

Other outstanding champions of 1994 included Mike Mc-Callum (Jamaica), who at 37 won his third world title by defeating the WBC light heavyweight champion Jeff Harding (Australia). Orlando Canizales (U.S.) relinquished the IBF bantamweight crown after defending it for the 16th time. Virgil Hill (U.S.) remained the WBA light heavyweight king with only one defeat in 38 contests. Roy Jones (U.S.), IBF super middleweight, Ricardo López (Mexico), WBC mini-flyweight, and Pernell Whitaker (U.S.), WBC welterweight, were other impressive champions. In a tough fight against Jesse James Leija (U.S.), Azumah Nelson (Ghana), one of Africa's greatest fighters, lost the WBC junior lightweight title that he had held for six years. (For a complete list of world WBA, WBC, and IBF champions, *see* SPORTING RECORD, below.)

A tragedy took place in Britain in April when Bradley Stone (England) died after being defeated in 10 rounds by Richie Wenton (England) for the British junior featherweight championship, a weight division introduced in the U.K. in 1994. Another boxer, Robert Wangila Napunyl (Kenya), also died after being defeated at Las Vegas in July. Wangila had won an Olympic gold medal for Kenya at Seoul, South Korea, in 1988. (FRANK BUTLER)

CHESS

Rivalry between the world ruling body FIDE (Fédération Internationale des Échecs, founded 1924) and the Professional Chess Association (PCA, founded 1993) dominated competition in chess in 1994. The PCA ran a well-funded Grand Prix of quick-play events in Moscow, Munich, New York City, London, and Paris in which Garry Kasparov, PCA world champion, and his young Russian colleague, Vladimir Kramnik, tied for first. Kramnik had earlier won spectacular games against Kasparov, both at quick play and at the normal international tournament speed of 40 moves in two hours.

Both organizations issued rival rating lists. FIDE's list omitted Kasparov and Nigel Short of England, but these ratings were restored late in the year as part of the rapprochement between the two groups. Nevertheless, the lists did not coincide, as the ratings were computed on the basis of different tournaments.

Rival tournaments for qualifying for the world title were held throughout the year. In the PCA semifinals at Linares, Spain, in September, Short was eliminated by Gata Kamsky of New York City, and Michael Adams of England lost to Viswanathan Anand of India. Kamsky and Anand were scheduled to play one another in early 1995 for the right to challenge Kasparov later in the year.

Valery Salov, a Russian living in Spain, enhanced his reputation by winning the six-round knockout contest at Tilburg, Neth., for 112 leading players in September–October and the Sicilian Defense tournament in Buenos Aires, Arg., in October. In both contests he finished ahead of the FIDE world champion, Anatoly Karpov of Russia.

To many the event of the year was Kasparov's loss to a computer at the comparatively slow time limit of 25 minutes each for the game. Computers had beaten grandmasters quite often at quick time limits such as five minutes each for a game or 10 seconds for a move but were thought to be

At the Intel World Chess Grand Prix in London in August, chess champion Garry Kasparov (left) matches wits with a Pentium Plus processor loaded with a program called Genius 2. The program, created by English physicist Richard Lang, defeated its human opponent in the first round.

inferior at slower time limits. The epoch-making games took place at the end of August in London. In the first contest a program called Genius 2 won in 60 moves after Kasparov had held an early advantage. In the second game Kasparov was forced to agree to a draw in 56 moves. The computer then defeated Predrag Nikolic of Bosnia and Herzegovina 2–0 before being beaten by the same score by Anand.

Age records continued to be broken. Peter Leko of Hungary gained the grandmaster rank at the age of 14, emulating his compatriot Judit Polgar, who had achieved this high status at 15. Polgar was involved in one the year's most controversial incidents when she lost to Kasparov at Linares after the Russian took back a move; video evidence revealed that Kasparov let go of a knight for a split second before moving it to another square, an infraction of the rules.

Kasparov was impressive in two of the three strongest international tournaments of the year. At Novgorod, Russia, in mid-August, he scored 7 points out of a possible 10; Vasily Ivanchuk of Ukraine also had 7, while Kramnik scored 5, Short and Aleksey Shirov of Latvia 4, and Yevgeny Bareyev of Russia 3. At Horgen, Switz., just after his loss to Genius 2, Kasparov was the leading scorer, with 8.5 out of 11; Artur Yusupov, a Russian now representing Germany, and Shirov scored 7, while Viktor Korchnoi of Switzerland and Joel Lautier of France had 6.5. The Novgorod contest was noteworthy for its adoption of a first playing session of seven hours as opposed to the normal five or six.

Kasparov failed to win his expected first place in the prestigious Linares tournament for 14 players. There his archrival Karpov made the remarkable score of 11 points in 13 games, one of the greatest performances of the past few decades. Kasparov and Shirov trailed by 2.5 points in a tie for second place. Otherwise, Karpov was in indifferent form in 1994.

The last four months of the year brought dramatic developments for FIDE/PCA relationships. Long-serving FIDE Pres. Florencio Campomanes of the Philippines had given notice that he would not seek office again after his three four-year terms. An election to replace him was scheduled for mid-December in Greece, alongside the biennial World Chess Olympiad. On September 18 Campomanes announced that bidding was open again for the right to host the Olympiad, as the Greek authorities had neither confirmed their ability to host the event nor paid the subsidy due to FIDE. Amid hints that Campomanes might have to stay in office, Russia announced that it would arrange the Olympiad and the FIDE election on the dates previously agreed upon, November 30–December 15. This result turned out to be the decision taken after a bitter internal struggle in Moscow between two rival chess federations, each claiming that it exercised the legitimate authority to control the game in Russia.

The resolution of this impasse had serious implications and recalled for some observers the predominant position occupied in world chess and its decision-making body by the former Soviet Chess Federation. Kasparov was probably correct in claiming that the tensions were a mirror image of the complicated politics of Russia, with nationalists and conservatives battling against reformers and radicals. In the end, Campomanes did indeed reverse his decision to step down and, campaigning on a platform of FIDE-PCA reunification, was reelected.

Led by Kasparov, Russia won the Olympiad, which was held in Moscow and was attended by 120 nations. Russia's winning score was 37.5 points out of a possible 56. Bosnia and Herzegovina placed second with 35, and the Russian junior team and England tied for third with 34.5. The Russian juniors were awarded the bronze medal when they defeated England in a tiebreaker. The women's Olympiad, held at the same time in Moscow, was won by Georgia with 32 points. Hungary finished second with 31, and China and Romania tied for third with 27.   (BERNARD CAFFERTY)

CONTRACT BRIDGE

In 1994 bridge playing and exchanges of information about the game via computerized networks expanded rapidly. Many professionals began using the networks for coaching clients and for gaining match practice with other pros. Duplicate tournaments were open to all. The 1994 NEC world bridge championships were held in Albuquerque, N.M., from September 17 to October 1, and the tournament's official daily bulletin, the size of a small newspaper, was available worldwide via Internet.

In the championships the relatively small Polish contingent distinguished itself. In the open pairs two professionals, Marcin Lesniewski and Marek Szymanowski, narrowly outpointed the world's top-ranked player, Robert Hamman of Dallas, Texas, and his partner, Michael Rosenberg of New York City.

The world open team title was won by Seymon Deutsch (captain), Chip Martel, Lew Stansby, Gaylor Kasle, Roger Bates, and Rosenberg of the U.S. They defeated Poland's Erwin Otvosi, Marek Borewicz, Krzysztof Lasocki, Piotr Gawrys, Cezary Balicki, and Adam Zmudzinski by 141 international match points to 110.

The women's pairs victors were Bep Vriend and Carla Arnolds of The Netherlands over Veronique Bessis and Catherine Saul of France. The women's team title (the McConnell Cup) went to Marinesa Letizia, Sue Picus, Judi Radin, Rozanne Pollack, and Jillian Blanchard of the U.S. Radin became the first to win all four World Bridge Federation (WBF) women's events: the pairs in 1978, the team Olympiad in 1984, the Venice Cup team event in 1987, and the McConnell Cup.

The mixed pairs championship was won by Danuta Hocheker and Apolinare Kowalski of Poland from Sabine Zenkel of Germany and Hamman. The senior pairs winners were Hamish Bennett of Menlo Park, Calif., and Fred Hamilton of Encino, Calif., from Simon Kantor of Agawam, Mass., and Murray Melton of Las Vegas, Nev.

The 9th Worldwide Bridge Contest, the biggest official competitive event in any sport, was won by Albert Bouwer and John Ruddell of New Zealand playing at the Whangarei bridge club near Auckland, N.Z. For the first time, the Gen-

---

The International Bridge Press Association voted its Best-Played Hand of the Year award to Hervé Mouiel of France for this deal:

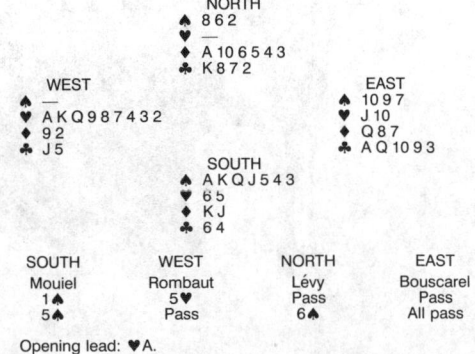

```
                        NORTH
                    ♠ 8 6 2
                    ♥ —
                    ♦ A 10 6 5 4 3
                    ♣ K 8 7 2
      WEST                              EAST
  ♠ —                              ♠ 10 9 7
  ♥ A K Q 9 8 7 4 3 2              ♥ J 10
  ♦ 9 2                            ♦ Q 8 7
  ♣ J 5                           ♣ A Q 10 9 3
                        SOUTH
                    ♠ A K Q J 5 4 3
                    ♥ 6 5
                    ♦ K J
                    ♣ 6 4
```

SOUTH	WEST	NORTH	EAST
Mouiel	Rombaut	Lévy	Bouscarel
1♠	5♥	Pass	Pass
5♠	Pass	6♠	All pass

Opening lead: ♥A.

After the heart lead Mouiel seemed to have only 11 tricks, even with a successful finesse against East's ♦Q. (A club lead sets the contract.) However, he ruffed in dummy, led a diamond, and finessed the jack. Then he trumped his last heart and played off his spades. On his last trump he threw the ♣8 from the dummy. Had East unguarded the ♦Q, South would have overtaken the ♦K with the dummy's ace, so East threw the ♣Q. Now the ♦K was cashed, and East, after winning with the ♣A, had to concede the last trick to dummy's ♦A.

erali World Masters Individual, organized by the European Bridge League and contested in Paris, included players from all WBF zones. Jon Baldursson of Iceland won the men's series, with Christian Mari of France second. Nicola Smith of Great Britain finished first in the women's series, and Pyttsi Flodquist of Sweden was second.

The executive board of the International Olympic Committee approved an application by the WBF for bridge to be recognized as an Olympic sport, subject to ratification by the IOC Congress in Budapest in 1995.

(ALBERT G. DORMER)

CRICKET

The emergence of Brian Lara (*see* BIOGRAPHIES), the West Indian left-hander, as potentially the greatest batsman of all time was the highlight of an intense season of Test cricket that saw the establishment of an independent panel of umpires for the first time; allegations of ball tampering against M.A. Atherton, the English captain; the retirement of A.R. Border, the Australian captain and the highest Test run scorer of all time; and a record number of Test wickets for Kapil Dev of India. Compared with Lara, much of the Test cricket was mediocre, though the return of South Africa as a force in world cricket—with two drawn series against Australia and one against England—added variety to a calendar still top-heavy with one-day internationals. The South Africans, sternly led by K.C. Wessels and with a fine pair of fast bowlers in A.A. Donald and P.S. de Villiers, proved more than a match for a combative Australian side. In both series, home and away, South Africa took the lead, and its victory by five runs in the second Test in Sydney, Australia, was a tribute to the South Africans' tenacity and team spirit. Needing just 117 runs to win, Australia had reached 51 for 1 before de Villiers took three wickets in five balls, and the last six Australian wickets went down for 48 runs to bring South Africa an unlikely but welcome victory on its first tour of Australia in 30 years. In the final Test, Australia turned the tables, thanks largely to a century by S.R. Waugh, who enjoyed a fine year.

After the second series against South Africa, Border retired from Test cricket with an incomparable record. In 156 Tests he scored 11,174 runs (average 56.56) with 27 centuries. He captained Australia a record 93 times, and it was sad that the end of a great career was marred by the insensitivity of administrators who seemed to be forcing Border from office. M.A. Taylor replaced Border as the Australian captain.

England's young captain, Atherton, had a year of contrasting fortune. As a batsman he went from strength to strength, scoring two centuries against the strong West Indian attack and often leading his team with imagination and drive. Having been comprehensively outplayed by the West Indies in the first three Tests, England fought back to inflict the West Indies' first defeat in Barbados in 59 years, with A.J. Stewart scoring a century in both innings, and A.R.C. Fraser taking eight wickets in the first innings. The most decisive bowler of the series was once again C.E.L. Ambrose, who belied rumours of tiredness by taking 26 wickets in the series at an average of 19.96. The West Indies also seemed to have unearthed another precocious talent in a young Guyanan, Shivnarine Chanderpaul.

Atherton returned to England with his reputation enhanced but, after a narrow victory over a poor New Zealand side in the first series of the summer, he was accused of rubbing an illegal substance onto the ball during the first Test against South Africa at Lord's. He compounded his error by withholding information about the incident when questioned by the International Cricket Council match ref-

Brian Lara of Trinidad displays the form that established him as one of the West Indies' greatest batsmen. The young cricketer made a Test-record 375 in the fifth Test against England in April and later scored a first-class record 501 not out for Warwickshire.
BEN RADFORD—ALLSPORT

eree, P. Burge. Atherton stoutly maintained that he was only rubbing dirt on his fingers to dry the ball and was not trying to alter the ball's condition—a sensitive issue in England after recent tampering allegations against the Pakistani side—but television pictures produced some powerful evidence to the contrary, and there were calls for his resignation. In the event, the England captain was heavily fined but escaped a suspension that would almost certainly have cost him the captaincy.

To compound the problem, South Africa marked its first Test in England in nearly 30 years with a handsome victory. It was not until the third Test at the Oval that England struck back. A devastating spell of fast bowling by D.E. Malcolm, whose 9 for 57 was the sixth best bowling performance in Test cricket, provided the platform for a comfortable win. Atherton, however, was in trouble once again and was fined half his match fee for showing dissent to the umpire when given out first ball.

Lara's feats rather overshadowed the performance of the Indian all-rounder Kapil Dev, who took his 432nd Test wicket in his 130th Test (against Sri Lanka in Ahmadabad, India, in February) to surpass Sir Richard Hadlee's total of 431. Hadlee took his wickets in 44 fewer Tests, but the fact that Kapil had missed only one Test since making his debut in 1979 was a tribute to his fitness and enthusiasm. Only Border had played more Tests. India won all three Tests of the series by an innings as Sri Lanka, thrashed also by Pakistan, struggled to justify its place as a Test-playing nation. Zimbabwe, the newest recruit to Test cricket, performed more creditably against Pakistan, though its batsmen had little answer for the pace of Waqar Younis, who took 27 wickets (average 13.7) in the three-match series. Spinners also enjoyed their moments of success. The Australian leg-

Test Series Results, September 1993–September 1994

Test	Host country	Ground	Date	Scores	Result
1st	Australia	Perth	Nov. 12–16	Australia 398 and 323 for 1 dec; New Zealand 419 and 166 for 4	Match drawn
2nd	Australia	Hobart	Nov. 26–29	Australia 544 for 6 dec; New Zealand 161 and 161	Australia won by an innings and 222 runs
3rd	Australia	Brisbane	Dec. 3–7	New Zealand 233 and 278; Australia 607 for 6 dec	Australia won by an innings and 96 runs
1st	Pakistan	Karachi	Dec. 1–6	Pakistan 423 and 131 for 3 dec; Zimbabwe 289 and 134	Pakistan won by 131 runs
2nd	Pakistan	Rawalpindi	Dec. 9–14	Pakistan 245 and 248; Zimbabwe 254 and 187	Pakistan won by 52 runs
3rd	Pakistan	Lahore	Dec. 16–21	Pakistan 147 and 174 for 1 dec; Zimbabwe 230	Match drawn
1st	Sri Lanka	Moratuwa	Dec. 9–13	Sri Lanka 190 and 43 for 2; West Indies 204	Match drawn (rain)
1st	Australia	Melbourne	Dec. 26–30	Australia 342 for 7 dec; South Africa 258 for 3	Match drawn (rain)
2nd	Australia	Sydney	Jan. 2–6	South Africa 169 and 239; Australia 292 and 111	South Africa won by 5 runs
3rd	Australia	Adelaide	Jan. 28–Feb. 1	Australia 469 for 7 dec and 124 for 6 dec; South Africa 273 and 129	Australia won by 191 runs
1st	India	Lucknow	Jan. 18–22	India 511; Sri Lanka 218 and 174	India won by an innings and 119 runs
2nd	India	Bangalore	Jan. 26–30	India 541; Sri Lanka 231 and 215	India won by an innings and 95 runs
3rd	India	Ahmedabad	Feb. 8–12	Sri Lanka 119 and 222; India 358	India won by an innings and 17 runs
1st	New Zealand	Auckland	Feb. 10–12	New Zealand 242 and 110; Pakistan 215 and 141 for 5	Pakistan won by 5 wkt
2nd	New Zealand	Wellington	Feb. 17–20	New Zealand 175 and 361; Pakistan 548 for 5 dec	Pakistan won by an innings and 12 runs
3rd	New Zealand	Christchurch	Feb. 24–28	Pakistan 344 and 179; New Zealand 200 and 324 for 5	New Zealand won by 5 wkt
1st	West Indies	Kingston	Feb. 19–24	England 234 and 267; West Indies 407 and 95 for 2	West Indies won by 8 wkt
2nd	West Indies	Georgetown	March 17–22	England 322 and 190; West Indies 556	West Indies won by an innings and 44 runs
3rd	West Indies	Port of Spain	March 25–30	West Indies 252 and 269; England 328 and 46	West Indies won by 147 runs
4th	West Indies	Bridgetown	April 8–13	England 355 and 394 for 7 dec; West Indies 304 and 237	England won by 208 runs
5th	West Indies	St. John's	April 16–21	West Indies 593 for 5 dec and 43 for 0; England 593	Match drawn
1st	South Africa	Johannesburg	March 4–8	South Africa 251 and 450 for 9 dec; Australia 248 and 256	South Africa won by 197 runs
2nd	South Africa	Cape Town	March 17–21	South Africa 361 and 164; Australia 435 and 92 for 1	Australia won by 9 wkt
3rd	South Africa	Durban	March 25–29	Australia 269 and 297 for 4; South Africa 422	Match drawn
1st	New Zealand	Hamilton	March 19–23	New Zealand 187 and 368 for 7 dec; India 246 and 177 for 3	Match drawn
1st	England	Nottingham	June 2–6	New Zealand 251 and 226; England 567 for 8 dec	England won by an innings and 90 runs
2nd	England	London (Lord's)	June 16–20	New Zealand 476 and 211 for 5 dec; England 281 and 254 for 8	Match drawn
3rd	England	Manchester	June 30–July 5	England 382; New Zealand 151 and 308 for 7	Match drawn
1st	England	London (Lord's)	July 21–24	South Africa 357 and 278 for 8 dec; England 180 and 99	South Africa won by 356 runs
2nd	England	Leeds	Aug. 4–8	England 477 and 267 for 5 dec; South Africa 447 and 116 for 3	Match drawn
3rd	England	London (Oval)	Aug. 18–21	South Africa 332 and 175; England 304 and 205 for 2	England won by 8 wkt
1st	Sri Lanka	Colombo	Aug. 9–13	Pakistan 390 and 318 for 4 dec; Sri Lanka 226 and 181	Pakistan won by 301 runs
2nd	Sri Lanka	Kandy	Aug. 26–28	Sri Lanka 71 and 234; Pakistan 357	Pakistan won by an innings and 52 runs

spinner S.K. Warne took 32 wickets in six Tests against South Africa, and A. Kumble of India had match figures of 11 for 128 in the first Test against Sri Lanka.

The year saw the setting up of an independent panel of Test umpires, with Tests controlled by one home umpire and one chosen from the panel. The experiment had its critics, but it worked well and certainly ended most of the accusations against biased umpiring. In domestic cricket Warwickshire (led by Lara's glorious hitting) completed a memorable treble in English county cricket by winning the county championship, the Benson and Hedges Cup, and the Sunday League. Had Worcestershire not beaten them in the final of the NatWest Trophy, Warwickshire would have swept the board. In Australia, New South Wales beat Tasmania to win the Sheffield Shield final. Unfashionable Orange Free State won the double of Castle Cup and Benson and Hedges night series in South Africa, and the Leeward Islands won the West Indies Red Stripe Cup.

(ANDREW LONGMORE)

CYCLING

A season that began on a low note ended in triumph for Miguel Indurain, who confirmed his position as the world's leading professional by winning the Tour de France, the premier event on the international calendar, for the fourth successive year and then capturing the world record for distance covered in one hour, 53.040 km, on the indoor track at Bordeaux, France. Injured in the early part of the season, the Spaniard failed in his attempt to win the Tour of Italy for the third year when he was beaten by Yevgeny Berzin of Russia, the first rider from Eastern Europe to win one of the sport's three major national tours.

The Tour de France began three weeks later in Lille, and Indurain took the overall lead after winning the ninth stage, a 64-km individual time trial from Périgueux to Bergerac. When the race ended in Paris after three weeks and 3,978 km, Indurain was 5 min 39 sec ahead of Piotr Ugrumov of Latvia and thus joined Jacques Anquetil (1961–64) and Eddy Merckx (1969–72) as the only riders to win the tour four years in a row. Three-time winner Greg LeMond, probably the finest cyclist the U.S. had produced, had to drop out of the Tour de France and, in early December, announced his retirement from professional cycle racing. Tony Rominger of Switzerland won the third major event, the Tour of Spain, for the third straight year.

The world championships were held in Sicily, Italy. Marty Nothstein of the U.S., who had broken a bone in his foot only two months earlier, was a double gold medalist on the track in Palermo, winning the sprint—the first U.S. success in the men's event since 1912—and keirin.

Graeme Obree of the U.K., the defending champion in the men's individual pursuit, was disqualified from the event when his tucked riding style, similar to the position of a downhill skier, was declared illegal under a ruling introduced by the governing body, the Union Cycliste Internationale (UCI), on the morning of the competition. He was succeeded as champion by fellow Briton Christopher Boardman, who also won the inaugural road time trial championship in Catania.

U.S.-born Marion Clignet, riding for France, won the women's pursuit, while Galina Yenyukhina of Russia, suspended for three months after testing positive for anabolic steroids at the 1993 championships, won the women's sprint. In the team pursuit the U.S. defeated defending champion Australia in the semifinals before losing to Germany, the 1992 Olympic champion.

1994 Cycling Champions

Event	Winner	Country
WORLD CHAMPIONS—TRACK		
Men		
Sprint	M. Nothstein	U.S.
Individual pursuit	C. Boardman	Britain
Kilometre time trial	F. Rousseau	France
40-km points	B. Risi	Switzerland
Team pursuit	A. Bach, G. Fulst,	Germany
	D. Hondo, J. Lehmann	
Keirin	M. Nothstein	U.S.
Motor paced	C. Podlesch	Germany
Tandem sprint	F. Colas, F. Magne	France
Women		
Sprint	G. Yenyukhina	Russia
Individual pursuit	M. Clignet	France
30-km points	I. Haringa	The Netherlands
WORLD CHAMPION—ROAD		
Individual time trial	C. Boardman	Britain
WORLD AMATEUR CHAMPIONS—ROAD		
Men		
Individual road race	A. Pedersen	Denmark
100 km team time trial	G. Colombo, D. Andriotto,	Italy
	G. Contri, C. Salvato	
Women		
Individual road race	M. Valvik	Norway
Individual time trial	K. Kurreck	U.S.
50-km team time trial	O. Sokolova, A. Iliaseva,	Russia
	S. Boubnenkova, V. Polhanova	
WORLD PROFESSIONAL CHAMPION—ROAD		
Individual road race	L. Leblanc	France
WORLD CHAMPION—CYCLO-CROSS		
	P. Herijgers	Belgium
MAJOR PROFESSIONAL ROAD-RACE WINNERS		
Tour de France	M. Indurain	Spain
Tour of Italy	Ye. Berzin	Russia
Tour of Spain	T. Rominger	Switzerland
Tour of Switzerland	P. Richard	Switzerland
Tour of Flanders	G. Bugno	Italy
Paris–Roubaix	A. Tchmil	Russia
Liège–Bastogne–Liège	Ye. Berzin	Russia
Leeds Classic	G. Bortolami	Italy
Championship of Zürich	G. Bortolami	Italy
San Sebastian Classic	A. De Las Cuevas	France
Paris–Nice	T. Rominger	Switzerland
Flèche Wallonne	M. Argentin	Italy
Dunkirk 4-Day	E. Seigneur	France
Grand Prix of Frankfurt	O. Ludwig	Germany
Tour of Britain	M. Fondriest	Italy
Tour DuPont	V. Yekimov	Russia

Luc Leblanc gave France its first win since 1980 in the professional road race championship held at Agrigento. Alex Pedersen of Denmark became the first reinstated amateur to win the road race title, at Capo d'Orlando, where Monica Valvik gave Norway its first title in 21 years by winning the women's road race.

(JOHN R. WILKINSON)

EQUESTRIAN SPORTS

Thoroughbred Racing. Holy Bull locked up honours as horse of the year and champion three-year-old colt for 1994 on Breeders' Cup day (November 5) at Churchill Downs in Louisville, Ky., without having to set foot outside of his stall. The Florida-bred colt, which was not nominated for the Breeders' Cup, earned his championship status with a record of 8 wins in 10 starts and earnings of $2,095,000. Holy Bull defeated older horses twice and won five Grade I stakes, including the Woodward in his final start of the year on September 17. He clinched his titles in absentia by virtue of Concern's upset victory in the $3 million Breeders' Cup Classic and Paradise Creek's loss in the $2 million Breeders' Cup Turf.

Concern's triumph in the Classic, a race that had evolved into a thoroughbred "kingmaker" in its 11-year history, was only the fourth career win for the colt, which had finished second or third in 15 of his 20 previous starts, and was his first victory since April. Three-year-olds dominated the Classic by finishing first through fourth in the 1¼-mi test. Six horses from Europe competed in the race, no doubt lured to the U.S. by Arcangues' stunning upset victory in 1993.

Concern, which defeated Preakness and Belmont Stakes winner Tabasco Cat by a neck, earned $1,560,000 for his Classic win to send his season's bankroll to $2,541,670. Because he was third to Holy Bull in the Haskell Invitational and second to him in the Travers, Concern was eliminated from staking a serious claim to the division title.

Holy Bull pulls away in the stretch to win the Woodward Stakes. Although the three-year-old failed to win the Kentucky Derby and did not run in the other Triple Crown races, he took 8 of 10 starts and was the favourite to be named horse of the year.

Boasting a record of eight wins in nine starts, including the Arlington Million and the Washington, D.C., International, Paradise Creek had the credentials to be the horse of the year, but all hopes for the crown were shattered when he finished third in the Breeders' Cup Turf. Victory in the race belonged to three-year-old Tikkanen, a son of Cozzene, winner of the Breeders' Cup Mile in 1985. Cozzene became the first winner of a Breeders' Cup race to sire another winner. Bred in the United States but based in Europe, Tikkanen had finished fifth in the Irish Derby earlier in 1994. He won the Turf Classic in his first start on U.S. soil just prior to the Breeders' Cup Turf.

Barathea made amends for his fifth-place finish in the Breeders' Cup Mile in 1993 by scoring an impressive three-length victory in the 1994 race. The Irish-bred four-year-old, trained by Luca Cumani, had won the Irish Two Thousand Guineas as a three-year-old. Barathea was sold to Rathbarry Stud in Ireland after his Breeders' Cup Mile victory. The colt completed his racing career with 5 wins in 16 starts and earnings of $1,236,367.

Lure, which won the Breeders' Cup Mile at Gulfstream Park, Fla., in 1992 and at Santa Anita, Calif., in 1993, was seeking to become the first horse ever to win three Breeders' Cup races. He finished ninth in the field of 14.

Although she finished second by a neck in the Breeders' Cup Distaff, Heavenly Prize probably clinched the three-year-old-filly championship with her game performance. Honours in the race went to 47–1 shot One Dreamer, which used a front-running performance to upset sixth-place finisher Hollywood Wildcat, which had won the race in 1993, and ninth-place Sky Beauty, which was undefeated in five starts in 1994 going into the event.

The six-furlong Breeders' Cup Sprint was captured by Cherokee Run, which prevailed by a head over the filly Soviet Problem, which had 9 wins and 3 seconds in 12 starts in 1994 going into the race. Cherokee Run, which improved his career record to 12 wins in 26 starts, was the 63rd stakes winner of the year for jockey Mike Smith, who broke the old record of 62 he set in 1993.

Timber Country left no doubt as to which was the top two-year-old colt in the U.S. in 1994 with his two-length triumph in the Breeders' Cup Juvenile. He was the 12th Breeders' Cup winner for trainer D. Wayne Lukas and the eighth Breeders' Cup winner for jockey Pat Day. Timber Country improved his record to four wins in seven starts and $927,025 in purse earnings.

Flanders wrapped up the two-year-old-filly crown with a gallant triumph in the Breeders' Cup Juvenile Fillies, but it may have been the final race of her undefeated five-start career. She pulled up lame after winning and was diagnosed with a fractured cannon bone and sesamoid bone in her right foreleg. Flanders won the race by a head over Serena's Song after the two fillies dueled the final 200 yd. Jockey Pat Day, who rode the winner, made the event his 100th career stakes victory over the Churchill Downs oval.

Go For Gin won the 1994 Kentucky Derby on the first Saturday in May, a race in which Holy Bull finished 12th. It was Holy Bull's only appearance in the Triple Crown races; Go For Gin went on to finish second to Tabasco Cat in both the Preakness and the Belmont Stakes.

In spite of his 11th place finish in the Breeders' Cup Classic, Devil His Due appeared destined to win the Eclipse Award for the best older male by virtue of his outstanding campaign until then, including a victory in the Grade I Suburban.

In August Steve Cauthen, age 34, became the youngest person ever inducted into the Racing Hall of Fame. Cauthen, who left the U.S. for Europe in 1979, was the only jockey to win the Kentucky, English, Irish, French, and Italian derbys.

Early in December Richard Duchossois, owner of the Arlington International Racecourse near Chicago, announced that he would not open the track for the 1995 season. He said that the track was losing money as a result of competition from riverboat casinos and that he could not survive financially unless he was also allowed to operate a casino. A week later a tentative plan was announced to have limited racing at the track in 1995.

In Canada's richest race, the Rothman Ltd. International, the French horse Raintrap won by a length from Alywow. Basqueian won the 135th running of the Queen's Plate for three-year-olds by seven lengths.   (JOHN G. BROKOPP)

Erhaab swept past King's Theatre and Colonel Collins well inside the final furlong to take the English Derby. He became the third consecutive winner of that race to be bought by the Japanese in the year of his victory.

The French-trained—but Japanese-owned and ridden—Ski Paradise was victorious in the newly opened Keio Hai Spring Cup at Tokyo Racecourse on April 23. She beat Zieten, from Dubayy, Sayyedati, from England, and another French horse, Dolphin Street. Horses that had raced outside Japan were allowed to compete in five events in 1994, up from three the previous year and two before that.

Zieten's fine performance in Tokyo was one of the first examples of the potential of Godolphin Racing, a new organization founded by Sheikh Muhammad al-Maktoum with the intention of wintering horses in Dubayy in order to gain an advantage when they returned to competition in Europe. Balanchine, bought from Robert Sangster after winning her two races in 1993, provided the greatest successes for Godolphin. Beaten by a head by the Irish-trained Las Meninas in the English One Thousand Guineas just days after her return from Dubayy, she went on to win the English Oaks and the Irish Derby but suffered an attack of colic a few weeks later (in mid-July) and was lucky to survive.

Her Irish Derby performance established Balanchine as the best in Europe. She beat King's Theatre and Colonel Collins, which finished second and third again, far more easily than Erhaab had in the English Derby. Four weeks later King's Theatre beat the best older horses, led by White Muzzle, Wagon Master, and Apple Tree, in the King George VI and Queen Elizabeth Diamond Stakes.

No colt could match Balanchine in midsummer, but one may have appeared in the autumn. He was Carnegie, the winner of the Prix de l'Arc de Triomphe and a son of Sadler's Wells and the 1980 Arc heroine, Detroit. He beat the 1993 Prix du Jockey-Club winner, Hernando, by a neck, with Apple Tree and Ezzoud a close third and fourth.

Carnegie, which was the first horse to imitate his dam by winning the Arc, belonged to Sheikh Muhammad. His owner's brother, Sheikh Hamdan al-Maktoum, won the English Derby with Erhaab and Australia's greatest race, the Melbourne Cup, with the British-bred Jeune, a horse that he had bought in England in late 1993. Twelve days before the Cup, Jeune had finished 13th of 14 behind the New Zealand-trained Solvit in the Cox Plate, the Southern Hemisphere's richest weight-for-age event. Vintage Crop, which had gained a second Irish St. Leger success at home in September, was favoured to repeat his 1993 triumph in the Melbourne Cup but finished seventh.

Coolmore Stud, the home of Europe's leading stallion, Sadler's Wells, successfully exploited many of its sires on double duty in Ireland and Australia. One of them, Last Tycoon, was the leading sire overall in the 1993–94 season in Australia, and another, Danehill, topped the sires of two-year-olds there. Paris Lane, conqueror of Jeune in the Mackinnon Stakes and second to him in the Melbourne Cup, was by a third Coolmore sire, the late Persian Heights.

One horse that covered mares in England and Australia in 1993 was Damister, which finished third in the English and Irish Derbys of 1985. Damister had sired many winners but none of great merit until the emergence of Celtic Swing. This colt was unbeaten in three races, the last a 12-length success in the Group 1 Racing Post Trophy.

Steeplechasing. The Fellow, whose previous attempts had resulted in two defeats by a head and then a fourth place, finally triumphed in a Cheltenham Gold Cup. The French-trained nine-year-old defeated the 1993 winner, Jodami, by 1½ lengths. However, he could not follow up in the Grand National, falling at the 24th of the 30 fences. The race, which was won by Miinnehoma, was run on muddy ground, and only 6 of the 36 runners completed the course. Ucello II won the Grand Steeple-Chase de Paris. Organizers were relieved when the National went off without a hitch after a disastrous double false start had forced them to void the race results in 1993. (ROBERT W. CARTER)

Harness Racing. Cam's Card Shark was retired in October 1994, heading for stud duty under syndication at Hanover Shoe Farms in Pennsylvania and regarded as a certainty as overall harness horse of the year. The son of Cam Fella, raced by Jeff Snyder and trained by Bill Robinson, numbered among his 1994 wins the $1 million North America Cup at Woodbine Raceway in Toronto in June and the Meadowlands Pace at the Meadowlands in New Jersey in July. By winning the James Dancer Memorial at Freehold, N.J., in September, Cam's Card Shark advanced his 1994 earnings to a single-season record of $2,264,714, surpassing the $2,222,168 won by Presidential Ball in 1993.

Victory Dream, owned by the F.A. Stable and Victory Dream Stable, N.Y., won the $1 million Hambletonian, the world's premier race for three-year-old trotters, at the Meadowlands on August 6. Trained by Ron Gurfein and driven by Mike Lachance, both of whom were savouring their first success in the prestigious event, Victory Dream cruised home in 1 min 54.2 sec after taking his $100,000 heat easily in 1 min 53.8 sec. With this triumph he had gained 10 wins and 2 second places in 14 starts and was the

Major Thoroughbred Race Winners, 1994

Race	Won by	Jockey	Race	Won by	Jockey
United States			**England**		
Acorn	Inside Information	M. Smith	One Thousand Guineas	Las Meninas	J. Reid
Arlington Million	Paradise Creek	P. Day	Two Thousand Guineas	Mister Baileys	J. Weaver
Beldame	Heavenly Prize	P. Day	Derby	Erhaab	W. Carson
Belmont	Tabasco Cat	P. Day	Oaks	Balanchine	L. Dettori
Breeders' Cup Juvenile	Timber Country	P. Day	St. Leger	Moonax	P. Eddery
Breeders' Cup Juvenile Fillies	Flanders	P. Day	Coronation Cup	Apple Tree	T. Jarnet
Breeders' Cup Sprint	Cherokee Run	M. Smith	Ascot Gold Cup	Arcadian Heights	M. Hills
Breeders' Cup Mile	Barathea	L. Dettori	Eclipse Stakes	Ezzoud	W. Swinburn
Breeders' Cup Distaff	One Dreamer	G. Stevens	King George VI and Queen Elizabeth Diamond Stakes	King's Theatre	M. Kinane
Breeders' Cup Turf	Tikkanen	M. Smith	Sussex Stakes	Distant View	P. Eddery
Breeders' Cup Classic	Concern	J. Bailey	International Stakes	Ezzoud	W. Swinburn
Champagne	Timber Country	P. Day	Dubayy Champion Stakes	Dernier Empereur	S. Guillot
Charles H. Strub Stakes	Diazo	L. Pinoay, Jr.			
Coaching Club American Oaks	Two Altazano	J. Santos	**France**		
Florida Derby	Holy Bull	M. Smith	Poule d'Essai des Poulains	Green Tune	O. Doleuze
Futurity	Montreal Red	J. Santos	Poule d'Essai des Pouliches	East of the Moon	C. Asmussen
Gulfstream Park Handicap	Scuffleburg	C. Perret	Prix du Jockey-Club	Celtic Arms	G. Mossa
Haskell Invitational	Holy Bull	M. Smith	Prix de Diane	East of the Moon	C. Asmussen
Hollywood Derby	River Flyer	C. Antley	Prix Royal-Oak	Moonax	P. Eddery
Hollywood Futurity	Afternoon Deelites	K. Desormeaux	Prix Ganay	Marildo	G. Guignard
Hollywood Gold Cup	Slew of Damascus	G. Stevens	Prix Lupin	Celtic Arms	G. Mosse
Hollywood Turf Cup	Frenchpark	C. Black	Grand Prix de Paris	Millkom	J. R. Dubooo
Hollywood Turf Handicap	Grand Flotilla	G. Stevens	Grand Prix de Saint-Cloud	Apple Tree	I. Jarnet
International	Paradise Creek	P. Day	Prix Vermeille	Sierra Madre	G. Mosse
Jockey Club Gold Cup	Colonial Affair	J. Santos	Prix de l'Arc de Triomphe	Carnegie	T. Jarnet
Kentucky Derby	Go For Gin	C. McCarron	Grand Critérium	Goldmark	S. Guillot
Kentucky Oaks	Sardula	E. Delahoussaye			
Man o' War	Royal Mountain Inn	J. Krone	**Ireland**		
Meadowlands Cup	Conveyor	M. Smith	Irish Two Thousand Guineas	Turtle Island	J. Reid
Metropolitan	Holy Bull	M. Smith	Irish One Thousand Guineas	Mehthaaf	W. Carson
Mother Goose	Lakeway	K. Desormeaux	Irish Derby	Balanchine	L. Dettori
Oak Tree Invitational	Sandpit	C. Nakatani	Irish Oaks	Bolas	P. Eddery
Pacific Classic	Tinners Way	E. Delahoussaye	Irish St. Leger	Vintage Crop	M. Kinane
Philip H. Iselin	Taking Risks	M. Johnston	Irish Champion Stakes	Cezanne	M. Kinane
Pimlico Special	As Indicated	R. Davis			
Preakness	Tabasco Cat	P. Day	**Italy**		
Santa Anita Derby	Brocco	G. Stevens	Derby Italiano	Time Star	T. Quirin
Santa Anita Handicap	Stuka	C. Antley	Gran Premio del Jockey-Club	Lando	M. Roberts
Spinster	Dispute	P. Day			
Suburban	Devil His Due	M. Smith	**Germany**		
Super Derby	Soul of the Matter	K. Desormeaux	Deutsches Derby	Laroche	S. Eccles
Travers	Holy Bull	M. Smith	Grosser Preis von Baden	Lando	P. Schiergen
Turf Classic	Tikkanen	C. Asmussen	Preis der Privatbankiers Merck, Finck & Co.	Sternkonig	A. Helfenbein
Whitney	Colonial Affair	J. Santos	Europa Preis	Monsun	A. Tylicki
Wood Memorial	Irgun	G. Stevens	**Australia**		
Woodward	Holy Bull	M. Smith	Melbourne Cup	Jeune	W. Harris

Antonacci family's fifth Hambletonian winner, after Lindy's Pride (1969), Speedy Crown (1971), Probe (1989), and Harmonious (1990).

Dontgetinmyway, a colt owned by the Guida Stables and Joan Goldsmith, powered to a 1-min 53.8-sec victory in the hands of John Campbell in the $774,750 Woodrow Wilson Pace for two-year-olds at the Meadowlands in August. At Woodbine in Toronto in July, the four-year-old Riyadh returned to the races after proving to be infertile and equaled the fastest mile in Canadian harness-racing history with a brilliant 1-min 50.8-sec win. The fastest trotting mile in history was recorded at the Meadowlands the same month when Beat The Wheel, a four-year-old daughter of Defiant Yankee, driven by Cat Manzi, upset world champion Pine Chip in 1 min 51.8 sec. Pine Chip, the four-year-old son of Arndon, lowered the world mark to 1 min 51 sec in a time trial in Lexington, Ky., in October. Soon afterward Pine Chip was retired to stud.

Magical Mike, North America's outstanding three-year-old pacer of 1994, with wins in the Little Brown Jug and Breeders' Crown, was slated to retire in October with earnings of $1,683,085. Trained by Tom Haughton for his owner-breeder David McDuffee and co-owner Tom Walsh, Jr., the colt ran a heat of the Tattersalls Pace in 1 min 50.8 sec.

U.S.-bred, German-owned Sea Cove, 1993 European Grand Circuit champion for Charles Grendel, avenged his 1993 Prix d'Amerique defeat by winning the 1994 edition at Vincennes, France, in February. But Sea Cove was no match for his Prix d'Amerique runner-up, Vourasie, in the Prix de France, also at Vincennes. A half-sister by Fakir du Vivier to former French champion Ourasie, Vourasie set a world-record mile rate of 1 min 56.3 sec for the 2,100-m race.

At Solvalla in Sweden in May, the Swedish-bred Copiad, driven by Erik Berglof, won the $230,000 Elitlopp in 1 min 55.6 sec over a wet track after a two-horse war with Pine Chip, which broke stride 50 m (165 ft) from the finish and was disqualified from second place. The Oslo Grand Prix

In the first polo match ever held between the two countries, England (light shirts) controls the ball in play against South Africa. The English team, made up entirely of professionals, defeated the South Africans 11–1 to take the Coronation Cup.

at Bjerke in Norway, which preceded the Elitlopp, also was won by Copiad. The Copenhagen Cup at Lunden in Denmark was taken by the Swedish horse Bolets Igor.

The retirement to stud of Peace Corps, harness racing's richest horse of all time, was announced in May in Sweden. The eight-year-old mare, with lifetime earnings of more than $5.7 million, was purchased by Bjorn Petterssen of Sweden from U.S. owner Lou Guida for $1.6 million in 1989 after being named U.S. trotter of the year.

At the 1994 Inter-Dominion Championships at Harold Park in Sydney, Australia, in March, local hope Weona Warrior, trained and driven by Brian Hancock, won the $250,000 Pacers' Grand Final from U.S. import Ultra Jet. New Zealand's Diamond Field, trained by Roy and Barry Purdon and driven by Tony Herlihy, won the Trotters' Final. The $150,000 New Zealand Trotting Cup at Addington on November 8 was taken by the five-year-old Bee Bee Cee in 4 min 1.5 sec for the 3,200 m.   (RONALD W. BISMAN)

Polo. In a rare year for the world's top-level polo competition, the Argentine Open, held in Palermo Stadium in Buenos Aires before a capacity crowd, Ellerstina won its first Open championship by defeating La Martina 19–15. The favourite and three-time defending champion, Indios Chapaleufu, was defeated before reaching the finals.

For the first time in 41 years, the U.S. Open returned to the New York City area. Competing were 11 teams, more than in the previous 16 years of the tournament. The brother combination of Memo and Carlos Gracida playing with Doug Matthews and "Tiger" Kneece as the Aspen team narrowly squeaked past Peter Brant's White Birch team to win 8–7 in an overtime chukker; the winning goal was scored on a penalty conversion. This was the 12th Open win for Memo Gracida, more than any other player in the tournament's history.

The U.S. Polo Association Rolex Gold Cup, at the Palm Beach (Fla.) Polo and Country Club in March, was a milestone for U.S. polo. The all-U.S. Team Michelob, led by Owen Rinehart, defeated Pegasus 10–7. Fort Lauderdale won the Royal Palm Polo Sports Club's International Gold Cup, upsetting JM Lexus 12–8. The highest level in U.S. competition, the World Cup, was also played at Palm Beach. Guy Wildenstein's Les Diables Bleus won the title for the first time by defeating Cellular One 12–8 in the final match.

The English season was again fully subscribed, with the maximum number of teams competing for the season's high-goal tournaments. Urs Schwarzenbach's Black Bears defeated Kerry Packer's Ellerston White 12–11 to win the Queen's Cup. Cowdray Park won the Prince of Wales Trophy, edging the Maple Leafs 10–9.

The British Open championship for the prestigious Gold Cup, played at Cowdray Park, was won for the first time by Jamie Packer's Ellerston Black from Australia in a 13–11 victory over Pegasus. England challenged South Africa's Springboks for the Coronation Cup at the Guards Polo Club in England. Unfortunately, it was not the most exciting game, with England winning by a lopsided 11–1 margin.

(ALLAN D. SCHERER)

Show Jumping and Dressage. German riders dominated the World Equestrian Games, held at The Hague in late July and early August. They won 7 of the 14 gold medals, while no other country claimed more than one. Franke Sloothaak, a Dutch-born German citizen, won the individual gold on the blue-eyed mare San Patrignano Weihaiwej and led the Germans to victory over France, Switzerland, and Brazil in the 20-team Nations Cup. Isabell Werth, on Gigolo, beat teammate Nicole Uphoff-Becker in the Grand Prix Special Dressage to lead Germany to victory over The Netherlands in the team event.   (ROBERT W. CARTER)

FIELD HOCKEY

After 14 years Pakistan regained the Champions Trophy in 1994 with a 3–2 victory over Germany in the final on a penalty shoot-out to break a 2–2 tie. The annual tournament for six nations was held at Lahore, Pak., in March. The Netherlands placed third, followed by Australia, Spain, and Great Britain. The Indira Gandhi Gold Cup was won by India at Lucknow, India, in February. South Africa finished second ahead of Egypt, Kenya, South Korea, and Japan. The Netherlands won a four-nation tournament at Madrid in June, prevailing over South Africa, England, and Spain, and had another success in July in a seven-nation tournament at Amstelveen, Neth., where Australia was second, followed by Pakistan, Germany, Argentina, South Africa, and Malaysia.

In August England won the Sultan Azlan Shah Cup in Penang, Malaysia, with a victory over Pakistan on a penalty shoot-out after a 2–2 tie in the final. Australia was third, Malaysia fourth, and South Africa fifth in the five-nation event. South Korea became Asian Games champion at Hiroshima, Japan, with a 3–2 victory over India in the final. Pakistan was third and Japan fourth, followed by Malaysia, Kazakhstan, Bangladesh, China, and Oman. Indoors, Germany retained the European Nations Cup at Bonn, Germany, in January, prevailing over England, Czech Republic, Austria, Spain, France, Denmark, and Russia. Pakistan recovered the World Cup at Sydney, Australia, in December with a victory on penalty strokes after a 1–1 tie in the final against The Netherlands.

In women's hockey Australia gained the World Cup for the first time with a 2–0 win over Argentina in the final of the quadrennial event at Dublin in July. The U.S. placed third and Germany fourth, followed by South Korea, The Netherlands, China, Spain, England, Canada, Ireland, and Russia. South Korea won the Indira Gandhi tournament at Chandigarh, India, in January, surpassing India, Italy, Uzbekistan, and Kazakhstan. In March the U.S. won a four-nation tournament in Dublin, where Ireland was second, Italy third, and Wales fourth. A five-nation tournament in Buenos Aires, Arg., in April was won by Australia, with Argentina in second place, followed by England, the U.S., and South Africa. (SYDNEY E. FRISKIN)

FOOTBALL

Association Football (Soccer). The Fédération Internationale de Football Association (FIFA), the world governing body of association football, celebrated its 90th anniversary with a record 191 members. At the 49th FIFA Congress in Chicago, 14 new members were added.

The Union des Associations Européenes de Football (UEFA) was forced to alter the format of its three major cup competitions. Among a record 159 entries, only Yugoslavia, which remained suspended from international activities, and San Marino did not enter teams for the 1994–95 season. The main innovation took place in the Champions' Cup, where the number of clubs eligible to participate was reduced. Past performances during the previous five years dictated whether the champions of a country either qualified for the UEFA Champions' Cup, competed in the qualifying round for the Cup, or were placed in the UEFA Cup.

For the 1993–94 UEFA competitions, drug tests were carried out on 150 players at 39 matches. None of the players violated the organization's doping regulations. The German association also revealed that its 500 doping tests among its top two divisions had also proved negative.

As a result of the bribery scandals in France, Marseille, the 1993 Champions' Cup winner, was not allowed to defend its title. It was also forcibly relegated to Division Two at the end of the 1993–94 season. Tbilisi Dynamo was fined and expelled from the Champions' Cup for attempted bribery of a referee, while the Latvian club RAF Jelgava was also expelled from the Cup-Winners' Cup for failing to make adequate travel arrangements in time for a match in the Faeroe Islands.

Corruption in Bulgaria also led to Yantra's being suspended after eight matches and its record's being expunged. Levski Sofia won a reduced competition of 28 matches by 17 points from CSKA Sofia. Despite having three points deducted for previous indiscretions, Legia Warsaw won the Polish League and also the Polish Cup, remaining unbeaten for six months. One of the most exciting finishes occurred in Spain, where Barcelona overtook longtime leader Deportivo La Coruna on the last day of the season.

The Rangers, which won their 44th championship in Scotland, signed Brian Laudrup from Fiorentina in Italy and Basile Boli from Marseille. For the 1994–95 season, the Scottish League added two new clubs and reshaped itself into four leagues of 10 teams each. Portugal won the European Under-18 championship; Italy retained its Under-21 title; and Nigeria, which qualified for the World Cup finals for the first time, won the African Nations Cup.

Two outstanding figures in British soccer died: Sir Matt Busby, probably the most renowned manager in the post-World War II era, and Billy Wright, the first Englishman to represent his country in internationals as many as 100 times. (*See* OBITUARIES.)

England's Arsenal deprived Italy of a hoped-for trio of European trophies, beating defending champion Parma 1–0 in the European Cup-Winners' Cup at Copenhagen on May 4. It was Arsenal's first European triumph since 1970. A

Players from Italy (dark shirts) and Brazil compete for the ball during the World Cup final played at the Rose Bowl in Pasadena, Calif., in July. Brazil won 3–2 in a penalty-kick shoot-out after 120 scoreless minutes, becoming the first country ever to win the tournament four times.

low-key final saw the well-organized Arsenal defense put a stranglehold on the Parma attack. Yet victory was won through the intervention of a goalpost at each end. After 14 minutes Gianfranco Zola's measured cross-field pass found Tomas Brolin striding purposefully onto the ball. His shot beat David Seaman in the Arsenal goal, only to bounce to safety off the inside of the upright. Unfortunately for Parma, five minutes later Lorenzo Minotti's acrobatic clearance was

snapped up by Alan Smith, who chested the ball down before scoring off the inside of goalkeeper Luca Bucci's left-hand post.

AC Milan of Italy produced one of the most memorable performances in the European Champions' Cup competition in recent years to defeat Barcelona of Spain decisively 4–0 in Athens on May 18. It was Milan's fifth success in the cup, yet the supremely confident Spaniards had gone into the match as firm favourites. Milan was thought to be weakened at the heart of its defense because of suspensions to centre-backs Franco Baresi and Alessandro Costacurta. Nevertheless, coach Fabio Capello decided to abandon the cautious approach and take the game to Barcelona, which was expected to threaten any sign of frailty in the Milan rear guard. The Italians grasped the initiative from the kickoff. Milan was quicker, more determined in every department, and showed impressive technical skill, and it seemed merely a matter of time before the team turned its superiority into goals. In the 22nd minute Dejan Savicevic emerged on the right, rounded Miguel Nadal, and chipped the ball to the far post, where Daniele Massaro scored with apparent ease. Massaro volleyed his second goal two minutes into injury time in the first half, after Roberto Donadoni had cut the ball back from the by-line. Any lingering hopes that Barcelona had of a recovery were dashed in the 47th minute, however, when Savicevic again had the better of a tangle with Nadal and lobbed the ball over Andoni Zubizarreta in the Spanish goal. Savicevic, the former Yugoslav international, almost scored again when he hit the post in the 58th minute, but after Barcelona failed to clear the danger, Demetrio Albertini passed to Marcel Desailly, who scored to make it 4–0.

Internazionale won the UEFA Cup for the second time in three years, edging Casino Salzburg, the first Austrian team to reach the final, 2–0 on aggregate scores. Italy thus gained its fifth win in six finals and the city of Milan its second European triumph in the season. In the first leg in Vienna on April 26, Nicola Berti's 35th-minute goal following a Ruben Sosa free kick put the Italians ahead. It was the first goal Salzburg had conceded in six international contests at home. Alessandro Bianchi was sent off for his second caution of the game in the 48th minute, but the 10-man Italian team held on comfortably to win. However, in the second leg on May 11 in Milan, the Austrians played a more spirited game, and only alert goalkeeping by Walter Zenga prevented them from scoring a goal. Internazionale survived and scored itself in the 63rd minute as Wim Jonk angled the ball over Otto Konrad into the Salzburg goal.

Optimism about the future of soccer in North America as a result of the U.S.'s serving as host to the World Cup may have been misplaced. A post-World Cup survey revealed that although 44% of U.S. adults watched at least one World Cup game on TV, 69% showed little interest in the launching of a new league. The Major League Soccer league planned to operate from April 1995, but as of the end of 1994 it had no actual teams or players.

(JACK ROLLIN)

Although Latin-American teams in general performed poorly in the World Cup, Brazil took the cup home for the first time since 1970. Later a team from Argentina became the unofficial club champion of the world, thus completing a Latin-American sweep of the top honours in soccer.

Colombia, which many experts had made a favourite to win the World Cup, was eliminated early and became the tournament's biggest disappointment. Argentina was eliminated in the first round amid a scandal when its star player, Diego Maradona, was found to have used illegal substances. Maradona later was banned from further com-

Table I. Association Football National Champions

Nation	League winners	Cup winners
Albania	Teuta Durres	SK Tirana
Argentina	Independiente	
Armenia	Ararat Yerevan	
Austria	Casino Salzburg	FK Austria
Belarus	Dynamo Minsk	Dynamo Minsk
Belgium	Anderlecht	Anderlecht
Bolivia	The Strongest (1993 title)	
Brazil	Palmpiras	
Bulgaria	Levski Sofia	Levski Sofia
Chile	Colo Colo	
Colombia	Nacional Medellín	
Costa Rica	Saprissa	
Croatia	Hajduk Split	Croatia Zagreb
Cyprus	Apollon Limassol	Omonia
Czech Republic	Sparta Prague	Viktoria Zizkov
Denmark	Silkeborg	Brondby
Ecuador	Emelec	
El Salvador	Alianza	
England	Manchester United	Manchester United
Estonia	Flora Tallinn	Norma Tallinn
Faeroe Islands	GI	B71 Sandur
Finland	FC Jazz Pori	TPS Turku
France	Paris St. Germain	Auxerre
Georgia	Tbilisi Dynamo	
Germany	Bayern Munich	Werder Bremen
Greece	AEK Athens	Panathinaikos
Guatemala	Municipal	
Honduras	Real Espana	
Hungary	Vac FC-Samsung	Ferencvaros
Iceland	IA Akranes	IA Akranes
Ireland	Shamrock Rovers	Sligo Rovers
Israel	Maccabi Haifa	
Italy	AC Milan	Sampdoria
Japan	Sanfrecce	
Latvia	Skonto Riga	
Lithuania	Romar Majeikai	Zalgiris
Luxembourg	Avenir Beggen	Avenir Beggen
Malta	Hibernians	Floriana
Mexico	Universidad Guadalajara	
Moldova	Zimbrul Chisinau	
Netherlands, The	Ajax Amsterdam	Feyenoord
Northern Ireland	Linfield	Linfield
Norway	Rosenborg	Bodo/Glimt
Paraguay	Cerro Porteño	
Peru	Universitario	
Poland	Legia Warsaw	Legia Warsaw
Portugal	Benfica	FC Porto
Romania	Steaua Bucharest	Gloria Bistrita
Russia	Spartak Moscow	Spartak Moscow
San Marino	Tre Fiori	
Scotland	Rangers	Dundee United
Slovakia	Slovan Bratislava	Slovan Bratislava
Slovenia	Olimpija Ljubljana	
Spain	Barcelona	Real Zaragoza
Sweden	IFK Gothenburg	IFK Norrkoping
Switzerland	Servette	Grasshopper
Turkey	Galatasaray	Besiktas
Ukraine	Dynamo Kiev	Odessa
Uruguay	Peñarol	
Venezuela	Caracas	
Wales	Bangor City	Barry Town
Yugoslavia (Serbia and Montenegro)	Partizan Belgrade	Partizan Belgrade

World Cup

Brazil became the first country to win the World Cup four times, defeating Italy 3–2 on penalty kicks in overtime in the final match at Pasadena, Calif., on July 17. Its previous victories were achieved in 1958, 1962, and 1970. There was no scoring in the 90 minutes of regulation play, and the extra half hour also failed to produce a goal. The drama was reserved for the shoot-out. Franco Baresi took the first kick for Italy but shot over the crossbar. For Brazil, Marcio Santos' effort was blocked by Gianluca Pagliuca. Demetrio Albertini then scored to give Italy a 1–0 lead. Romário (see BIOGRAPHIES) tied it at 1–1, and then Alberigo Evani restored Italy's advantage 2–1. Branco made it 2–2, but then Daniele Massaro had his shot blocked by Cláudio Taffarel in the Brazilian goal. Dunga scored to put Brazil 3–2 in the lead, and it was left to Roberto Baggio, the world player of the year, to salvage the situation for Italy. However, he shot over the crossbar.

The tournament as a whole, played in many cities in the U.S., attracted a total attendance of 3,567,415, a record for the World Cup. Despite pretournament misgivings, there were other pleasing aspects apart from the number of fans. For example, television ratings exceeded expectations. Some 8,760,000 U.S. households, representing a 9.3 rating, watched the second-round match between the U.S. and Brazil on ABC on July 4, and the final match was watched in 8,950,000 homes for a 9.5 rating.

Though 15 players were sent off and 227 were cautioned, the Fédération Internationale de Football Association's (FIFA's) insistence that referees enforce the rule outlawing the tackle from behind led to a more sporting attitude on the part of the players, who had all signed a pledge to promote fair play. Brazil deservedly won the Fair Play Award. It was also the most technically gifted team in the finals, completing more passing movements than any other nation. FIFA's other initiative of allowing players not interfering with play to be allowed to stay onside contributed to an increase in goal scoring. Goals per game averaged 2.71, compared with the all-time low of 2.21 in 1990.

Fan behaviour was generally disciplined, with a friendly atmosphere pervading the matches, and the plucky performance of the U.S. team captured the imagination of many American sports fans unfamiliar with soccer. There was tragedy, however. The assassination of the Colombian player Andrés Escobar back home near Medellín cast a shadow over the entire tournament. His crime: putting the ball into his own net in a defeat that cost Colombia dearly.

Favoured teams such as Germany and the South American trio of Colombia, Argentina, and Bolivia disappointed, while Sweden, Saudi Arabia, Romania, Bulgaria, and Nigeria did better than expected. Romário of Brazil was the outstanding performer, though he tired noticeably in the final. (JACK ROLLIN)

---

petition. Mexico tied with Bulgaria in the second round and was eliminated on penalty kicks.

The Brazilian national team was not up to the glory of its former championship years, when it had been overwhelmingly superior to the competition, but it always managed to make the necessary effort to beat its rivals in the tournament. The Brazilians tied the final game with Italy but took the cup on penalty kicks.

Vélez Sársfield, an Argentine team, put an end to the domination of the Libertadores de América Cup (South America's club championship) by Brazil's São Paulo. The Argentines edged the Brazilians 1–0 in Buenos Aires on August 25, but they lost by the same score in São Paulo on September 1. In a final match, consisting of penalty kicks, Vélez Sársfield won the series and the tournament.

Vélez Sársfield went on to win the Inter-Continental Cup, the unofficial world championship for clubs, when it defeated Italy's Milan in Tokyo in late December. This cup had been won by São Paulo two years in a row. São Paulo declined to play in the Inter-American Cup, in which the winner of the Libertadores de América Cup plays the champion of Concacaf (the North American, Central American, and Caribbean football organization). After dropping the first game in San José, Costa Rica, Chile's Catholic University took the Inter-American Cup by beating Costa Rica's Saprissa in overtime in Santiago.

Palmeiras won the Brazilian national championship in December after defeating Corinthians in the final play-off. Independiente won Argentina's closing tournament of the 1993–94 season, and River Plate triumphed in the opening tournament of the 1994–95 season. Guadalajara's Autonomous University won the Mexican League, and Peñarol became the 1994 Uruguayan champion.

(SERGIO SARMIENTO)

Rugby Football. As countries prepared for the 1995 Rugby Union World Cup, there was a great deal of touring activity in 1993–94. Early in the British season, for instance, New Zealand visited England, Scotland, and Wales between the end of October and the beginning of December 1993, winning 12 of its 13 matches. In the two international matches of the tour, New Zealand beat Scotland 51–15 at Murrayfield—the first time the Scots had ever conceded 50 points—but then lost 15–9 to England at Twickenham. At the same time of the year, Australia beat Canada 43–16 on the way to an eight-match tour of France. There the Australians were defeated by their hosts 16–13 at Bordeaux in the first of two internationals but won the second 24–3 in Paris.

The Five Nations Championship, held during the early months of 1994, ended in a bizarre fashion. In the final match—the 100th between the two countries—England defeated Wales 15–8 at Twickenham. This left those two countries at the top of the league table with three wins and one defeat each. It had been decreed that in the event of such a tie the difference between points scored and points conceded would decide first place. Wales had scored 78 points and conceded 51. England's figures were 60 and 49. Thus, although England had just defeated Wales, it was the Welsh captain who received the Five Nations Trophy. France finished in third place with two wins and two defeats; Ireland was fourth with a win, a draw, and two defeats; and Scotland finished last with one draw and three losses.

After the end of the European season, England played eight games in South Africa in May and June 1994. England surprised many people by winning the first of its two internationals 32–15 in Pretoria but was defeated 27–9 at Cape Town in the second. During the same time, Ireland played eight matches in Australia, winning only two and losing 33–13 at Brisbane in the first international and 32–18 at Sydney in the second. Wales made a less conventional tour, including internationals in Toronto against Canada (won 33–15), in Suva against Fiji (won 23–8), in Nuku'alofa against Tonga (won 18–9), and in Apia against Western Samoa (lost 34–9). Scotland toured Argentina, losing both internationals (16–15 and 19–17).

One of the most remarkable achievements was France's winning of both of its internationals in New Zealand, the first 22–8 at Christchurch and the second 23–20 at Auckland. On the way to New Zealand, the French were beaten 18–16 by Canada in Ottawa. New Zealand regained some self-respect by beating the touring South Africans 22–14 in Dunedin and 13–9 in Wellington and drawing the third and final international 18–18 in Auckland. It was beaten 20–16 in Sydney in the Bledisloe Cup match against Australia, however.

The main international event of the 1993–94 period for Rugby League was a tour of Great Britain by New Zealand in October and November 1993. The visitors played three test matches and lost all of them. Great Britain won the first 17–0 at Wembley, the second 29–12 at Wigan, and the third 29–10 at Headingley.   (DAVID FROST)

U.S. Football. Nebraska won the national championship of U.S. college football by defeating the University of Miami 24–17 in the Orange Bowl at Miami, Fla., on Jan. 1, 1995. The victory snapped a losing streak of seven bowl games for Big Eight champion Nebraska, which finished with a 13–0 won-lost record, and gained the first national crown for 22-year coach Tom Osborne.

Big Ten champion Penn State ranked second with a 12–0 record, the fourth of Joe Paterno's five undefeated teams to lose the vote for number one. Penn State gave Paterno his record 16th bowl game victory in 29 seasons 38–20 in the Rose Bowl over 9–4 Oregon, the Pacific Ten champion and home of Coach of the Year Rich Brooks.

Big Eight runner-up Colorado (11–1) beat unranked Notre Dame (6–5–1) 41–24 in the Fiesta Bowl to earn the number three ranking, followed in the coaches' poll by 12–1 Alabama, which was undefeated before losing the Southeastern Conference championship game to Florida (10–2–1). The writers' poll had Alabama behind Florida State, the Atlantic Coast Conference champion, which defeated seventh-ranked Florida 23–17 in the Sugar Bowl. Sixth-ranked Miami (10–2) won the Big East Conference. Rounding out the top 10 in the coaches' poll were 8th-ranked Utah (10–2) and 10th-ranked Brigham Young (10–3) of the Western Athletic Conference and 9th-ranked Ohio State (9–4) of the Big Ten and in the writers' poll, which included schools on probation, 8th-ranked Texas A&M, (10–0–1), 9th-ranked Auburn (9–1–1), and 10th-ranked Utah.

Southwest Conference champion Texas Tech (6–6) lost 55–14 to Southern California (8–3–1) in the Cotton Bowl. In the Citrus Bowl Alabama defeated Ohio State 24–17.

Colorado's Rashaan Salaam won the Heisman Trophy for the best player in Division I-A and the Doak Walker Award for the best running back. He led the country with 2,055 yd rushing, 2,349 all-purpose yards, and 24 touchdowns, all on the ground. Colorado's offense led the country with 6.2 yd per rushing attempt and ranked third in total and rushing offense and seventh in scoring. Quarterback Kordell Stewart threw only three interceptions to lead Division I-A with a percentage of .0127.

Penn State's Kerry Collins won the Maxwell Award, also honouring the best player of the year, and the Davey O'Brien Award for the best quarterback. Collins was the passing efficiency leader with 172.9 rating points, led the country with 10.1 yd per attempt, and connected 52 times with Bobby Engram, who won the Fred Biletnikoff Award as the best wide receiver. Penn State's offense led the country with 47.8 points and 520.2 total yards per game; Ki-Jana Carter's 7.8 yd per carry was best in the country, and Penn State led Kansas State with a national low of 11 turnovers lost.

Nebraska led the country with 340 yd rushing per game behind a line that featured Zach Wiegert, Outland Trophy winner as the best interior lineman. The Cornhuskers had unusual balance, ranking fifth in total offense, sixth in scoring offense, fourth in rushing defense, fourth in total defense, and second in points allowed, besides producing the Scholar-Athlete of the Year, Rob Zatechka.

Two other teams that excelled on both offense and defense were Florida State—fifth in scoring, fourth in total offense, and fourth in pass defense—and Florida—second in scoring, fourth in passing yards, and fifth in rushing defense.

Georgia had the best passing offense, with 338.3 yd per game, and Scott Milanovich's .688 completion percentage for Maryland led all passers. Brigham Young's John Walsh led with 3,712 yd passing; Nevada's Mike Maxwell ranked first with 3,498 yd total offense; and the two were coleaders with 29 touchdown passes apiece. The receiving leaders were Nevada's Alex Van Dyke with 98 catches, Florida's Jack Jackson with 15 touchdowns, Wyoming's Marcus Harris with 1,431 yd gained, and Michigan's Amani Toomer with 21.08 yd per catch on at least 40 catches.

Miami dominated Division I-A defenses, with defensive tackle Warren Sapp winning the Defensive Player of the Year award and the Vince Lombardi trophy, another top-lineman prize. The Hurricanes allowed national lows of 10.8 points, 220.9 yd, and 124.1 yd passing per game, and they had the best pass defense efficiency rating.

Virginia allowed the fewest rushing yards, 63.6 per game, and Southern Mississippi's defense led with 40 turnovers. Clemson had the best turnover differential, plus-17. West Virginia's Aaron Beasley was the interception leader with 10, Illinois' Dana Howard won the Dick Butkus Award as the best linebacker, and Chris Hudson of Colorado won the Jim Thorpe Award as the best defensive back.

Arizona's Steve McLaughlin won the Lou Groza Collegiate Place-Kicker Award with 23 field goals, one fewer than leader Remy Hamilton of Michigan. Southwestern Louisiana's Mike Shafer had the best field-goal percentage, 14 for 14. Other kicking-game leaders were West Virginia's Todd Sauerbrun with 48.4 yd per punt, Mississippi State's Eric Moulds with 32.8 yd per kickoff return, and Eastern Michigan's Steve Clay with 19.9 yd per punt return.

In Division I-AA Alcorn State quarterback Steve McNair was Player of the Year after breaking the all-division career record for total offense by more than 2,000 yd. He finished his collegiate career with 16,823 yd, and for the season he led his division with 5,799 yd total offense, 4,863 yd passing, 44 touchdown passes, 9.2 yd per pass attempt, 16 yd per completion, 530 pass attempts, and 304 completions. Youngstown State won its third Division I-AA championship in four years and finished 14–0–1 with a 28–14 victory over Big Sky champion Boise State (13–2). The only other undefeated I-AA team in the regular season was Ivy League champion Pennsylvania (9–0).

The national tournament champions in other divisions were North Alabama (13–1) 16–10 over Texas A&M–Kingsville (12–2) in Division II and Albion (13–0) 38–15 over Washington and Jefferson (11–2) in Division III. Other NCAA Players of the Year were Valdosta State quarterback Chris Hatcher in Division II and Coe running back Carey Bender in Division III.

In U.S. professional football the Buffalo Bills, having played in the last four Super Bowls, failed to repeat that feat for the National Football League (NFL) play-offs in 1994. They had lost their fourth consecutive Super Bowl on Jan. 30, 1994, in Atlanta, Ga., when the Dallas Cowboys won 30–13 and became the sixth team to win consecutive NFL championships.

During the 1994–95 season Dallas, with a won-lost record of 12–4, won its third consecutive championship of the Eastern Division in the National Football Conference (NFC). San Francisco, with a league-best record of 13–3, was the only other division champion to repeat, also for the third time, in the NFC Western Division. The other division champions all had won 1992 crowns: Minnesota in the NFC Central, Miami in the American Football Conference (AFC) Eastern, San Diego in the AFC Western, and Pittsburgh in the AFC Central with an AFC-leading record of 12–4.

The NFC Central became the first division ever to send four teams to the play-offs when wild cards Green Bay, Detroit, and Chicago qualified with the best runner-up records. Chicago was the only new NFC play-off team from 1993, after a two-year absence, while Miami, San Diego, New England, and Cleveland were new faces in the AFC. New England made the league's greatest improvement, five games, for its first play-off appearance in eight years, and Cleveland returned for the first time in five years.

Houston's record declined by 10 games and Buffalo's by five as they broke their play-off streaks of seven and six years, respectively. The other 1993 play-off teams that did not qualify were Denver, the Los Angeles Raiders, and the New York Giants.

The NFL took steps during the off-season to encourage more scoring and wound up with an average of 427 yd passing per game and 16 touchdowns on kickoff returns, both the most ever, as well as a record average attendance of 62,656. The scoring, 40.5 points per game, increased by 8.3% from 1993, while touchdowns increased by 12.6% and sacks decreased by 11.3%. The significant rule changes tightened pass-interference restrictions, pushed kickoffs back by five yards and required the kickers to use a shorter tee, and allowed teams to score two points after a touchdown by gaining two yards.

New England was the most prolific passing team, with 227.8 yd per game and with five receivers catching at least 50 balls, the first time that had happened in the NFL. Drew Bledsoe's 4,555 yd passing for New England led NFL quarterbacks, as did Joe Montana's .0183 interception percentage for Kansas City. Miami ranked second in passing yardage and first in total yards with 379.9.

San Francisco was the most efficient passing team, with quarterback Steve Young setting NFL records for both his 112.8 passer rating points and his fourth consecutive rating championship. Young also led the league with 8.61 yd per pass attempt, 35 touchdown passes, and percentages of .076 for touchdowns and .703 for completions. San Francisco led the NFL with 31.6 points per game and led the NFC with 378.8 total yards per game.

After only six seasons in the previous 30 years had seen a player have 100 or more receptions, three NFL receivers accomplished the feat in 1994. Cris Carter set an NFL record with 122 catches for Minnesota, which became the first team ever to produce 200 catches with two receivers, as Jake Reed chipped in for another 85. The other leaders were San Francisco's Jerry Rice with 112 and Atlanta's Terance Mathis with 111. Rice also led NFL receivers with 1,499 yd and set a league record with 139 touchdowns in his career. Other top receivers were Green Bay's Sterling Sharpe with 18 touchdowns and the Los Angeles Rams' Flipper Anderson with 20.5 yd per catch. The New York Jets' Art Monk set an NFL record with catches in 180 consecutive games, and Ben Coates' 96 catches for New England were the most ever by a tight end.

Pittsburgh had the league's best rushing offense with 136.3 yd per game, but the individual leader was Detroit's Barry Sanders (see BIOGRAPHIES), with league highs of 1,883 yd rushing, 5.7 yd per carry, and 2,166 total yards from scrimmage. Emmitt Smith of Dallas led the league with 22 touchdowns, 21 of them on runs.

Dallas had the league's best defense in terms of total yards allowed, 269.6 per game. The Cowboy's average passing yield of 172 also was an NFL low. Cleveland allowed the fewest points, 12.8 per game, and Minnesota's league-leading rushing defense allowed 68.1 yd per game. Pittsburgh's 55 sacks led the league and included 14 from individual leader Kevin Greene. The Steelers also had the AFC's best rushing defense.

New England forced the most turnovers, 40. Kansas City's 26 fumble recoveries led the league, and Miami, San Francisco, and Arizona tied for the league lead with 23 interceptions. The individual leaders in interceptions, with nine, were Arizona's Aeneas Williams and Cleveland's Eric Turner.

Pittsburgh led the NFL with 14 more take-aways than turnovers, relying on an offense that lost the fewest turnovers, 17, and tying Seattle with a league low of nine interceptions. Tampa Bay and the New York Giants each lost seven fumbles, best in the league.

Fuad Reveiz of Minnesota kicked 28 consecutive field goals, the most ever for a single season and one short of John Carney's record covering two seasons. Carney of San Diego led the league with 135 points, and Cleveland's Matt Stover had the highest field-goal percentage at .929 (26 for 28). The Rams' Sean Landeta led punters with 44.8 yd per kick.

Washington's Brian Mitchell led NFL punt returners with 14.1 yd per return and set a single-season record with 1,930 yd on kickoff and punt returns combined. Mel Gray of Detroit was the leading kickoff returner, with a 28.4 yd average, and he tied a league record with his ninth touchdown on kickoff and punt returns. Herschel Walker of Philadelphia was the first NFL player ever to have 90-yd plays on a run, pass reception, and kickoff return in the same season.

Table II. NFL Final Standings, 1994

AMERICAN CONFERENCE	W	L	T
Eastern Division			
*Miami	10	6	0
*New England	10	6	0
Indianapolis	8	8	0
Buffalo	7	9	0
New York Jets	6	10	0
Central Division			
*Pittsburgh	12	4	0
*Cleveland	11	5	0
Cincinnati	3	13	0
Houston	2	14	0
Western Division			
*San Diego	11	5	0
*Kansas City	9	7	0
Los Angeles Raiders	9	7	0
Denver	7	9	0
Seattle	6	10	0

NATIONAL CONFERENCE	W	L	T
Eastern Division			
*Dallas	12	4	0
New York Giants	9	7	0
Arizona	8	8	0
Philadelphia	7	9	0
Washington	3	13	0
Central Division			
*Minnesota	10	6	0
*Green Bay	9	7	0
*Detroit	9	7	0
*Chicago	9	7	0
Tampa Bay	6	10	0
Western Division			
*San Francisco	13	3	0
New Orleans	7	9	0
Atlanta	7	9	0
Los Angeles Rams	4	12	0

*Qualified for play-offs.

Canadian Football. The British Columbia Lions won the Grey Cup championship of the Canadian Football League (CFL) when Lui Passaglia's 38-yd field goal on the game's last play defeated Baltimore 26–23 at Vancouver, B.C., on November 27. British Columbia won 11, lost 6, and tied 1 in the regular season and then reached the Grey Cup game on a last-play victory over the Western Division champion Calgary Stampeders (15–3) in the play-offs. The Winnipeg Blue Bombers (13–5) won the Eastern Division but lost to 12–6 Baltimore in the play-offs.

Calgary led the league offensively, with 38.8 points and 443.6 yd per game, and defensively, with average yields of 19.7 points and 315 yd. Its individual league leaders included slotback Allen Pitts, who set league records with 126 catches, 2,036 yd receiving, and 21 touchdowns, and quarterback Doug Flutie, who set a record with 48 touchdown passes and led the league with 318.1 yd passing per game and a passer rating of 118.2. Flutie won a record fourth consecutive Most Outstanding Player award. Other Calgary league leaders were Tony Stewart with 14 rushing touchdowns and Will Johnson with 17 sacks.

Baltimore's Mike Pringle led the league with 1,972 yd rushing and 2,414 yd from scrimmage. Baltimore tackle Shar Pourdanesh was the Most Outstanding Lineman, and linebacker Matt Goodwin was the Most Outstanding Rookie. Slotback Gerald Wilcox of Winnipeg was the Most Outstanding Canadian Player, and linebacker Willie Pless of Edmonton was the Most Outstanding Defensive Player.

(KEVIN M. LAMB)

Australian Football. West Coast emerged the premier club in the Australian Football League in 1994 with a 20.23 (143)–8.15 (63) grand final match victory over Geelong at the Melbourne Cricket Ground. A total of 514,375 attended the nine finals matches, contested by eight clubs. The major awards for the season were: Brownlow Medal (for the best and fairest player in the home and away games), Greg Williams (Carlton); Coleman Medal (for most goals in home and away games), Gary Ablett (Geelong) 113; Norm Smith Medal (best player in the grand final), Dean Kemp (West Coast).

(GREG HOBBS)

GOLF

In 1994, for the first time, not one U.S. golfer won any of the world's four major championships. Nick Price of Zimbabwe (*see* BIOGRAPHIES) took both the British Open championship at Turnberry, Scotland, and the Professional Golfers' Association of America (PGA) championship at Tulsa, Okla. José-María Olazábal of Spain captured the Masters at Augusta, Ga., and Ernie Els of South Africa won the United States Open championship at Oakmont, Pa.

It was a notable season for Price. He led the Sony world rankings for the first time and was leading money winner on the American PGA tour for the second successive year, with earnings of $1,499,927, against the $1,330,307 won by Greg Norman of Australia. Price was also the first man since Tom Watson in 1982 to collect two consecutive major titles. Watson that year won both the U.S. and British Open championships.

It was not, however, a year bereft of U.S. success. Fred Couples and Davis Love won the World Cup at Dorado, P.R.—for the third successive year—with a record score of 536 (Couples 265, Love 271) for the 72 holes. This was 14 strokes ahead of Zimbabwe, which was represented by Mark McNulty and Tony Johnstone.

The U.S. also defeated the rest of the world in an inaugural President's Cup match played at Lake Manassas, Wash., along Ryder Cup lines but excluding players from Europe. The margin was a very comfortable 20–12. Additional success was gained by the U.S. women professionals, who regained the Solheim Cup from Europe 13–7 at the Greenbrier resort in West Virginia.

No individual approached the performance of Price, who gained seven victories during the year. In addition to the PGA, he won four other tournaments on the U.S. tour: the Honda Classic, the Southwestern Bell Colonial, the Motorola Western Open, and the Bell Canadian Open. Earlier in the year he had also taken the ICL International on the South African circuit.

Price had twice before come close to winning the British Open, losing a three-stroke lead to Watson at Royal Troon in 1982 and being beaten only by an exceptional last round by Severiano Ballesteros at Royal Lytham in 1988. The chances were that Price would suffer a similar fate at Turnberry, for Jesper Parnevik of Sweden, who was playing ahead of him, was three strokes ahead standing on the last tee. Price reduced the gap with a birdie three at the 16th, however, and, just after Parnevik had scored one over par on the 18th, the Zimbabwean sank a huge putt at the 17th for an eagle three. This gave him a lead that, this time, he held. Price had rounds of 69, 66, 67, 66 for a 72-hole total of 268, one shot ahead of Parnevik.

Price's victory in the PGA was much more conclusive. He played golf of the very highest standard and with rounds of 67, 65, 70, and 67 for a total of 269 finished six strokes ahead of Corey Pavin of the U.S.

Earlier in the year Olazábal, who had tended to live in the shadow of fellow Spaniard Ballesteros, at last realized one of his ambitions by winning the Masters. After an indifferent opening round of 74, he followed with scores of 67, 69, 69 for a total of 279. He finished two strokes ahead of Tom Lehman of the U.S., who had never won a tournament on the PGA tour. Lehman nonetheless summoned the bravest of challenges. He was particularly unlucky with a number of putts over the last few holes.

A star was born in Els. Though he had demonstrated precocious talent as an amateur, his victory in the U.S. Open was only his second outside his homeland, the other having been in the Japanese Dunlop Phoenix tournament in late 1993. His U.S. Open was achieved, however, only after a three-way play-off with Loren Roberts of the U.S. and Colin Montgomerie of Scotland.

The three of them tied after 72 holes with scores of 279, Els with rounds of 69, 71, 66, 73, Roberts with 76, 69, 64, 70, and Montgomerie with 71, 65, 73, 70. The unusual aspect of Els's victory in the play-off was that he dropped four strokes in the first two holes, taking a five at the first and a seven at the second. However, he finished the round in 74 to tie Roberts again, Montgomerie having been eliminated with a 78, and then won the championship at the second extra hole of a sudden-death play-off.

Later in the year Els also won the Toyota world match-play championship at Wentworth, Surrey, England, beating Montgomerie in the final by four and two. He also won the inaugural Gene Sarazen World Open in Atlanta, Ga.

Montgomerie's disappointment on both these occasions was compensated by the fact that for the second consecutive year he was leading money winner on the PGA European tour. He won three tournaments—the Peugeot Spanish Open, the Murphy's English Open, and the Volvo German Open—and was consistently in the top half dozen, so much so that his prize money of £762,719 set a record.

One of the surprises of the year was Canada's victory in the Alfred Dunhill Cup at St. Andrews, Scotland. Very much one of the outsiders, Canada defeated the U.S. 2–1 in the final. Dave Barr beat Tom Kite with a 70 to a 71, and Ray Stewart did the same to Fred Couples with a 71 to a

72. In the other game Rick Gibson lost to Curtis Strange, taking 74 against a 67.

If Price had an outstanding year, so too did Laura Davies, the first British woman professional to top the U.S. Ladies' Professional Golf Association (LPGA) money list. Her earnings totaled $687,201. She also finished the year far ahead in the world rankings. Her seven tournament victories included the Thailand Open; the Standard Register Ping tournament, the Sara Lee Classic, and the McDonald's LPGA championship in the U.S.; the Irish and Scottish opens in Europe; and the Itoen in Japan.

Davies' one disappointment was not to have helped Europe keep the Solheim Cup. But, after the honours were shared through the first two days, the U.S. women showed that they had the greater strength in the singles, in which they won 8 of the 10 matches. Including fourballs and foursomes, the final match result was U.S. 13, Europe 7.

Patty Sheehan, one of the members of that successful U.S. team, won the U.S. Women's Open championship. It was her second victory in three years, and her score of 277 at Indianwood Golf and Country Club in Lake Orion, Mich., for the 72 holes tied the championship record. She finished one stroke ahead of Tammie Green.

The British Open was won by Liselotte Neumann of Sweden. Her total of 280 at Woburn, Bedfordshire, England, was three strokes better than that of Dottie Mochrie, who played a considerable, if at times controversial, part in the Solheim Cup victory of the U.S., and Annika Sorenstam of Sweden. Neumann also topped the Women's Professional Golfers' European Tour with winnings of £102,750.

A very good future prospect may have emerged in Tiger Woods, the U.S. amateur, who won the U.S. amateur championship at Ponte Vedra Beach, Fla. At 18, he was the youngest champion and also the first African-American golfer to win the title. Moreover, he did it in the most thrilling manner, six down at one point, four down at lunch, and still four down with six holes to play. But he won each of those remaining holes to defeat Trip Kuehne by two up.

Woods was also a member of the team that ended five years of frustration for the U.S. by winning the world amateur team championship for the Eisenhower trophy at Paris. Woods, Allen Doyle, John Harris, and Todd Demsey had a four-round aggregate of 838.

The U.S.'s women amateurs also won the team championship in Paris. Sarah Ingram, Carol Thompson, and Wendy Ward scored 569 for the 54 holes. Ward had already become U.S. amateur champion by defeating Jill McGill by two and one at Hot Springs, Va.

The British women's amateur championship was won by Emma Duggleby, who defeated Cecilia Morgue d'Algue of France by three and one at Newport, Wales. Lee James of England took the British men's amateur championship, beating Gordon Sherry of Scotland by two and one at Nairn, Scotland.   (MICHAEL WILLIAMS)

GYMNASTICS

The world championships in gymnastics, held in Brisbane, Australia, April 19–24, 1994, were conducted under new rules of competition. First, there were no qualifications for the all-around competition; second, a separate team competition was held later in the year; third, there were no compulsory exercises; and, fourth, the top eight in a preliminary competition in the individual events advanced to the finals. This last change opened up the competition to specialists.

In women's competition Russia led in the medal count with one gold, one silver, and three bronze out of the 15 available. Romania also won five medals. For the United States Shannon Miller (*see* BIOGRAPHIES) won two golds; she retained her all-around title, the first back-to-back victory in that event since 1974, and triumphed in the balance beam. Other winners of more than one medal included Dina Kochetkova of Russia with a gold medal in the floor exercise and bronzes in the all-around and uneven parallel bars, Lovina Milosovici of Romania with silvers in the all-around and the floor exercise and a bronze in the vault, Svetlana Chorkina of Russia with silver medals in the vault and the uneven parallel bars, and Gina Gogean of Romania with a gold in the vault and a bronze in the floor exercise.

Although Vitaly Sherbo of Belarus yielded the all-around title in the men's competition to teammate Ivan Ivankov,

Stella Umeh performs on the balance beam at the Commonwealth Games, held in August in Victoria, B.C. The gymnast was Canada's biggest winner at the competition, with two silver and two gold medals, including the women's individual all-around title.
STEPHEN DUNN—ALLSPORT

he won gold medals in the vault, the floor exercise, and the horizontal bar and placed third in the all around. Thirteen nations shared the remaining 16 available medals. In addition to Sherbo, the champions in the individual events included Yuri Chechi of Italy, winner of the rings for the third straight year; Marius Urzica of Romania in the pommel horse; and China's Huang Liping in the parallel bars. Paul O'Neill of the U.S. placed second on the rings, the first time since 1979 that the U.S. had had a medal winner in the men's world championships.

Maria Petrova of Bulgaria was all-around champion in the world rhythmic championships in Paris in October. Russia won the group competition by a margin of 0.225 over Spain.

(CHARLES ROBERT PAUL, JR.)

ICE HOCKEY

North America. The National Hockey League's (NHL's) 1993–94 season was one of its most unusual. The New York Rangers won the Stanley Cup for the first time in 54 years. Then their coach, Mike Keenan, walked out after one year on the job to become coach and general manager of the St. Louis Blues and to gain the personnel control that he wanted. Mario Lemieux, the game's best player, decided to take off the 1994–95 season to recover from injury and illness. There were also labour problems. The NHL referees and linesmen struck for 17 days at the start of the 1993–94 season, and the league threatened to lock out the players from training camp before the 1994–95 campaign.

During the 1993–94 regular season, the changes started early. Under its new commissioner, Gary Bettman, the NHL discarded its historic conference names (Prince of Wales and Smythe) and division names in favour of geographic designations. The play-off format was also altered, giving automatic berths only to the four division winners.

The Minnesota North Stars moved to Dallas, Texas, and became the Dallas Stars. The Anaheim Mighty Ducks and the Miami-based Florida Panthers began play as expansion teams.

From October 1993 to April 1994, the 26 teams played 84 games each. The division champions were the Rangers (112 points), the Pittsburgh Penguins (101 points), the Detroit Red Wings (100), and the Calgary Flames (97).

In the first round of the Stanley Cup play-offs, the Boston Bruins eliminated the defending champion Montreal Canadiens 4 games to 3. The San Jose Sharks, a last-place team the year before, upset Detroit in the first round 4 games to 3 and took the Toronto Maple Leafs to the seventh game of the next round.

The Rangers won easily from the New York Islanders 4 games to 0 and the Washington Capitols 4 games to 1. Then they struggled past the New Jersey Devils, winning the decisive seventh game in double overtime.

That put the Rangers in the finals, where they had expected to be after their general manager, Neil Smith, at Keenan's urging, made late-season trades for such veterans as Glenn Anderson, Craig MacTavish, Stephane Matteau,

and Brian Noonan. To get them the Rangers gave up Mike Gartner and Tony Amonte.

Their surprising opponents in the finals were the Vancouver Canucks, whose regular-season record—41 victories, 40 losses, 3 ties—was only 14th best of the 16 teams in the play-offs. But Vancouver forced the best-of-seven finals to a seventh game on June 14 in New York City. The Rangers won it 3–2, and defenseman Brian Leetch was voted the Conn Smythe Trophy as the play-off's most valuable player.

In Keenan's previous coaching jobs, he had lost Stanley Cup finals with the Philadelphia Flyers in 1985 and 1987 and with the Chicago Black Hawks in 1992. On July 15, 1994, he resigned from the Rangers, saying that the team's management had breached his five-year contract by being a day late in paying a play-off bonus within 30 days of the last game. Two days later he signed with St. Louis.

On July 24 Bettman suspended Keenan for 60 days and ordered the Rangers to pay part of the bonus. He also fined St. Louis $250,000 for signing Keenan, Detroit $25,000 for approaching him about a coaching job, and the Rangers $25,000 for suing Keenan in federal court (even though the suit was later withdrawn).

In mid season centre Wayne Gretzky of the Los Angeles Kings broke Gordie Howe's NHL career record of 801 goals. He also became the season scoring champion with 130 points, ahead of centre Sergey Fedorov of Detroit, who had 120 points. In September 1993 Gretzky had agreed to the most lucrative contract in hockey history, $25.5 million over three years. Fedorov, a 24-year-old Russian, won the Hart Trophy as the NHL's most valuable player and the Selke Trophy as the outstanding defensive forward. Ray Bourque of the Boston Bruins won the Norris Trophy as the best defenseman for the fifth time, and Gretzky took the Lady Byng Memorial Trophy for gentlemanly play for the fourth time. The all-star team consisted of Dominik Hasek of the Buffalo Sabres in goal, Scott Stevens of New Jersey and Bourque on defense, Fedorov at centre, and Pavel Bure of Vancouver and Brendan Shanahan of St. Louis at wing.

The 28-year-old Lemieux, the Pittsburgh Penguin centre, worn down from four years of medical problems, announced that he would not play the 1994–95 season. He was in frequent pain from an old stress fracture of the spine, and he

In game six of the finals of the National Hockey League play-offs, Geoff Courtnall (centre) of the Vancouver Canucks slips the puck past goaltender Mike Richter of the New York Rangers despite the efforts of defenseman Doug Lidster. The Rangers won the Stanley Cup in the seventh game.

MIKE POWELL—ALLSPORT

developed anemia from radiation treatment for Hodgkin's disease, a cancer of the lymphatic system.

When the NHL's 58 referees and linesmen struck, they were replaced by 70 officials from minor and junior leagues. The strike ended with a four-year contract providing higher salaries and severance pay and other benefits. The club owners decided that they wanted to tie player salaries to team revenues, which would result in a salary cap. The players wanted no part of that, talks broke down in December, and the 1994–95 season was threatened. NHL players were allowed to play for European teams during the dispute.

(FRANK LITSKY)

International. Twice in 10 weeks Canada, able to field more top NHL players than usual, was featured in crucial penalty shoot-outs. It achieved its first world title in 33 years on May 8, 1994, after being denied an Olympic gold medal in an equally nail-biting final on February 27.

The 58th world championship was contested by a record 36 nations, requiring an enlarged two-section Pool C. The 12 title-contending countries in Pool A—staged at Bolzano, Canazei, and Milan, all in Italy—were split into two groups of six and provided surprisingly one-sided semifinals. The U.S., after gaining an upset 3–1 quarterfinal victory over defending champion Russia, lost to Finland 8–0, a margin due in no small measure to an early injury to the U.S. goalie, Guy Hebert, who had excelled against the Russians.

In the second semifinal Canada's hard checking, skillful skating, accurate passing, and lethal shooting overwhelmed Sweden 6–0. Sweden, the Olympic champion, defeated the U.S. 7–2 in the play-off for third place. Canada and Finland then provided a truly memorable final. The first two periods were goalless, and goalies Bill Ranford (Canada) and Jarmo Myllys (Finland) thus become recipients of player-of-the-match awards. The Finns at last ended the stalemate when talented passing between Janne Laukannen and Mika Nieminen enabled Esa Keskinen to slide the puck under Ranford. Less than five minutes before the end of the game, the Finns' dreams of gold were thwarted as Rod Brind'-Amour took a pass from Luc Robitaille to beat Myllys with a slap shot from 6 m (20 ft) out.

Ten minutes of sudden-death overtime failed to produce a score, moving the game to every goalkeeper's nightmare, the penalty shoot-out. Robitaille and Joe Sakic each found the net for Canada before goals from Jari Kurri and Mikko Makela evened the score at 2–2 after five shots apiece. Robitaille then netted and Nieminen missed, and the ice was quickly awash with jubilant, much-relieved Canadians.

Much interest centred on the return of Great Britain to Pool A after a 32-year absence but, despite the inclusion of 15 British passport-holding Canadians on the team, the glory was short-lived, ending in Britain's relegation to Pool B after it lost all six of its matches. After eight games apiece the tournament's three leading point scorers were Mats Sundin (Sweden) with 14, Paul Kariya (Canada) 12, and Saku Koivu (Finland) 11.

Promoted to replace Britain was Switzerland, which dropped only one point in an eight-team round-robin Pool B in Copenhagen. Latvia and Poland, second and third, respectively, were clearly stronger than the other five. China, without a win, was demoted. By winning Group 1 of Pool C, the host nation, Slovakia, gained promotion to Pool B. North Korea, at the bottom of Group 1, changed places with Estonia, the top nation in Group 2 of Pool C, contested in Barcelona, Spain. South Africa, finishing last in Group 2, was required to requalify for the season to follow.

The Olympic Games tournament, in February at Lillehammer, Norway, though dwarfed in importance by the world championships, enjoyed the usual wider public follow-ing through worldwide television coverage. Twelve nations competed. Finland defeated Russia 4–0 to gain the bronze medal, and then Canada and Sweden sweated out a title-deciding final as close as that in the world championship. Sweden went ahead early and, after a second session with no further score, the Canadians drew level 2–2 in a pulsating third period. Overtime failed to settle the issue, and Peter Forsberg netted for Sweden the goal that won the gold medal in another penalty shoot-out. In the final ranking fourth-place Russia was followed by the Czech Republic, Slovakia, Germany, and the United States.

TPS Turku of Finland won the 17th European Cup, contested by national club champions, by beating Dynamo Moscow of Russia 4–3 in the final at Düsseldorf, Germany. Malmö IF of Sweden, the defending champions, finished third by defeating Milan of Italy 4–3.

(HOWARD BASS)

Table I. NHL Final Standings, 1994

	Won	Lost	Tied	Points
EASTERN CONFERENCE				
Atlantic Division				
*New York Rangers	52	24	8	112
*New Jersey	47	25	12	106
*Washington	39	35	10	88
*New York Islanders	36	36	12	84
Florida	33	34	17	83
Philadelphia	35	39	10	80
Tampa Bay	30	43	11	71
Northeast Division				
*Pittsburgh	44	27	13	101
*Boston	42	29	13	97
*Montreal	41	29	14	96
*Buffalo	43	32	9	95
Quebec	34	42	8	76
Hartford	27	48	9	63
Ottawa	14	61	9	37
WESTERN CONFERENCE				
Central Division				
*Detroit	46	30	8	100
*Toronto	43	29	12	98
*Dallas	42	29	13	97
*St. Louis	40	33	11	91
*Chicago	39	36	9	87
Winnipeg	24	51	9	57
Pacific Division				
*Calgary	42	29	13	97
*Vancouver	41	40	3	85
*San Jose	33	35	16	82
Anaheim	33	46	5	71
Los Angeles	27	45	12	66
Edmonton	25	45	14	64

*Qualified for play-offs.

Table II. World Ice Hockey Championships, 1994

Pool A	Pool B	Pool C (1)	Pool C (2)
Canada	Switzerland	Slovakia	Estonia
Finland	Latvia	Belarus	Spain
Sweden	Poland	Ukraine	South Korea
United States	Japan	Kazakhstan	Croatia
Russia	Denmark	Slovenia	Belgium
Italy	The Netherlands	Hungary	Australia
Czech Republic	Romania	Bulgaria	Israel
Austria	China	North Korea	South Africa
Germany			
France			
Norway			
Great Britain			

The XVII Olympic Winter Games

BY MELINDA C. SHEPHERD

For 16 days in February 1994, Lillehammer, Norway (population 23,800), and five neighbouring towns welcomed 1,737 athletes (1,216 men and 521 women), 40,000 accredited officials, 8,000 media personnel, and an estimated 100,000 spectators per day to celebrate the XVII Olympic Winter Games. The Games were held only two years after the 1992 Winter Games in Albertville, France, and were the first scheduled in a different year from the Summer Games, due to take place in Atlanta, Ga., in 1996. Of the 67 national Olympic committees represented in Lillehammer, nine—Bermuda, Brazil, Cyprus, Fiji, Israel, Kyrgyzstan, Luxembourg, Mongolia, and Portugal—sent only one athlete apiece. Bosnia and Herzegovina was represented by four bobsledders (a Serb, a Croat, and two Muslims), who raced in a borrowed Dutch sled and were unable to return to their war-torn home after the Games. Nine former Soviet republics made their first appearances as independent nations. Medals were awarded in 61 events, with 22 nations recording at least one medal winner.

Norway topped the medal count (26), led by speed skater Johann Olav Koss (*see* BIOGRAPHIES), who won three gold medals in world-record times. Two other speed-skating favourites also triumphed. American Dan Jansen, who held the 500-m world record, finally won gold in the 1,000-m race after disastrous showings in the 1988 and 1992 Games. Jansen's teammate Bonnie Blair (*see* BIOGRAPHIES) once again dominated the short distances, winning her second consecutive gold medal in the 1,000-m race and her third in the 500 m. In cross-country skiing Lyubov Yegorova (*see* BIOGRAPHIES) of Russia, who won three gold medals in Albertville, captured three more to tie the Olympic record of six. Yegorova's record streak of nine consecutive first- or second-place finishes ended abruptly, however, as she was shut out of the 30-km race won by her Italian archrival, Manuela Di Centa, the overall leader of the 1994 Games, with five medals (two gold and three silver). Figure skating saw the return of several former medalists who had regained amateur status for the event, but only the Russian pairs team of Yekaterina Gordeyeva and Sergey Grinkov repeated their earlier success of striking gold.

Despite bitter cold temperatures weather conditions were generally good. Athletes and spectators alike were charmed by the warm Norwegian hospitality and by the high priority placed on environmental conservation at these "Green Games." Contractors were fined for cutting down too many trees; the ice hockey rink was set into the side of a mountain to conserve energy; bobsled and luge runs were chilled with environmentally safe coolant; bullets were automatically collected on the biathlon trails to prevent lead from leaching into the soil or poisoning local birds; and even the plates and utensils used for meals were made from recyclable or edible materials.

Melinda C. Shepherd is associate editor of Encyclopædia Britannica Yearbooks.

Olympic Champions, XVII Winter Games, Lillehammer

Alpine Skiing

Men

Downhill	T. Moe (U.S.)	1 min 45.75 sec
Slalom	T. Stangassinger (Austria)	2 min 2.02 sec
Giant slalom	M. Wasmeier (Ger.)	2 min 52.46 sec
Supergiant slalom	M. Wasmeier (Ger.)	1 min 32.53 sec
Combined event	L. Kjus (Nor.)	3 min 17.53 sec

Women

Downhill	K. Seizinger (Ger.)	1 min 35.93 sec
Slalom	V. Schneider (Switz.)	1 min 56.01 sec
Giant slalom	D. Compagnoni (Italy)	2 min 30.97 sec
Supergiant slalom	D. Roffe-Steinrotter (U.S.)	1 min 22.15 sec
Combined event	P. Wiberg (Swed.)	3 min 5.16 sec

Nordic Skiing

Men

10-km cross-country	B. Dæhlie (Nor.)	24 min 20.1 sec
15-km cross-country	B. Dæhlie (Nor.)	35 min 48.8 sec
30-km cross-country	T. Alsgaard (Nor.)	1 hr 12 min 26.4 sec
50-km cross-country	V. Smirnov (Kazakh.)	2 hr 7 min 20.3 sec
40-km ski relay	Italy	1 hr 41 min 15.0 sec
90-m ski jump	E. Bredesen (Nor.)	282.0 pt
120-m ski jump	J. Weissflog (Ger.)	274.5 pt
120-m team ski jump	Germany	970.1 pt
Nordic combined	F. Lundberg (Nor.)	247.0 pt/39 min 7.9 sec
Nordic team combined	Japan	733.5 pt/1 hr 22 min 51.8 sec

Nordic Skiing

Women

5-km cross-country	L. Yegorova (Rus.)	14 min 8.8 sec
10-km cross-country	L. Yegorova (Rus.)	41 min 38.1 sec
15-km cross-country	M. Di Centa (Italy)	39 min 44.5 sec
30-km cross-country	M. Di Centa (Italy)	1 hr 25 min 41.6 sec
20-km ski relay	Russia	57 min 12.5 sec

Biathlon

Men

10 km	S. Chepikov (Rus.)	28 min 7.0 sec
20 km	S. Tarasov (Rus.)	57 min 25.3 sec
30-km relay	Germany	1 hr 30 min 22.1 sec

Women

7.5 km	M. Bedard (Can.)	26 min 8.8 sec
15 km	M. Bedard (Can.)	52 min 6.6 sec
30-km relay	Russia	1 hr 47 min 10.5 sec

Freestyle Skiing

Men

Moguls	J.-L. Brassard (Can.)	27.24 pt
Aerials	A. Schönbächler (Switz.)	234.67 pt

Women

Moguls	S. Hattestad (Nor.)	25.97 pt
Aerials	L. Cheryazova (Uzbek.)	166.84 pt

Figure Skating

Men	A. Urmanov (Rus.)	1.5 pt
Women	O. Baiul (Ukr.)	2.0 pt
Pairs	Ye. Gordeyeva and S. Grinkov (Rus.)	1.5 pt
Ice dancing	O. Grichuk and Ye. Platov (Rus.)	3.4 pt

Speed Skating

Men

500 m	A. Golubev (Rus.)	36.33 sec[1]
1,000 m	D. Jansen (U.S.)	1 min 12.43 sec[2]
1,500 m	J. Koss (Nor.)	1 min 51.29 sec[2]
5,000 m	J. Koss (Nor.)	6 min 34.96 sec[2]
10,000 m	J. Koss (Nor.)	13 min 30.55 sec[2]

Women

500 m	B. Blair (U.S.)	39.25 sec
1,000 m	B. Blair (U.S.)	1 min 18.74 sec
1,500 m	E. Hunyady (Austria)	2 min 2.19 sec
3,000 m	S. Bazhanova (Rus.)	4 min 17.43 sec
5,000 m	C. Pechstein (Ger.)	7 min 14.37 sec

Short-Track Speed Skating

Men

500 m	Chae Ji Hoon (S. Kor.)	43.45 sec
1,000 m	Kim Ki Hoon (S. Kor.)	1 min 34.57 sec
5,000-m relay	Italy	7 min 11.74 sec[1]

Women

500 m	C. Turner (U.S.)	45.98 sec
1,000 m	Chun Lee Kyung (S. Kor.)	1 min 36.87 sec
3,000-m relay	South Korea	4 min 26.64 sec[1]

Ice Hockey

Winning team	Sweden	6–1–1

Bobsledding

Two man	Switzerland	3 min 30.81 sec
Four man	Germany	3 min 27.78 sec

Tobogganing (Luge)

Men (single)	G. Hackl (Ger.)	3 min 21.571 sec
Men (double)	K. Brugger and W. Huber (Italy)	1 min 36.720 sec
Women (single)	G. Weissensteiner (Italy)	3 min 15.517 sec

[1]Olympic record. [2]World record.

AL TIELEMANS—DUOMO

The XVII Olympic Winter Games opened with pageantry in February.

ICE SKATING

The first and probably last Olympic Winter Games to be contested only two seasons after its predecessor took place in Lillehammer, Norway, on Feb. 12–27, 1994. (*See* Special Report.) This once-only measure was taken because Olympic officials decided that the Winter and Summer Games would be more profitable if they were held two years apart rather than during the same year.

Figure Skating. Unprecedented interest was created in 1994 by the International Skating Union's selective reinstatement of ice-show professionals. Even so, the only such skaters to recapture an Olympic title were the immaculate Russian pair Yekaterina Gordeyeva and Sergey Grinkov, who repeated their 1988 success. They were, however, pressed hard by their compatriots Natalya Mishkutenok and Artur Dmitriyev, the defending Olympic champions. The Canadian world champions, Isabelle Brasseur and Lloyd Eisler, finished third despite some spectacularly high throws.

The men's contest was a triumph for another Russian, Aleksey Urmanov, who outjumped Elvis Stojko of Canada. Philippe Candeloro of France valiantly gained the bronze medal ahead of Viktor Petrenko of Ukraine, the champion of Europe. Oksana Baiul, a deceptively delicate-looking Ukrainian, followed her sensational 1993 world victory with another tremendous performance to take the Olympic women's crown. Nancy Kerrigan of the U.S. was a close runner-up, and Lu Chen of China placed third. Germany's two-time Olympic gold-medal winner, Katarina Witt, though only seventh in a much-heralded return, pleased the crowd with her elegant artistic presentation but could not match the jumping athleticism of her younger rivals. The presence of Tonya Harding of the U.S., who was permitted to skate only because of legal pressure following her subsequently admitted collusion in an earlier attempt to injure Kerrigan, was an unwanted distraction. Harding was later stripped of the 1994 U.S. title that she had won and was banned for life from the U.S. Figure Skating Association.

An exceptionally close finish was provided in the ice dancing, won by Oksana Grichuk and Yevgeny Platov of Russia over their world titleholder compatriots, Maya Usova and Aleksandr Zhulin. The crowd's favourites, Britain's Jayne Torvill and Christopher Dean, gained the bronze medal after a 10-year absence from competition and only weeks after defeating both Russian couples in the European championships.

In the world championships at Chiba, Japan, on March 22–26, the local favourite, Yuka Sato, was the women's victor, gaining a 5–4 decision over Surya Bonaly of France,

the four-time European champion. Both jumped six triples, but Sato had the edge on presentation. Brasseur and Eisler sought to retain their pairs title with justifiable optimism—until misfortune hit Brasseur. Skating amazingly well with a cracked rib, she and her partner somehow managed to secure the silver medal behind the new Russian victors, Yevgeniya Shishkova and Vadim Naumov. Grichuk and Platov added the world ice dance title to their Olympic success, surviving a rare fall to win from Sophie Moniotte and Pascal Lavanchy of France.

The men perhaps presented the most exciting event, in which Stojko became the new winner. He achieved seven perfect triple jumps and daringly added a highlight combination of quadruple and triple toe-loop jumps, though the second landing was flawed. For technique he received a 6 from the U.S. judge, the other eight each awarding 5.9. Candeloro, perhaps the season's most improved skater, finished second, with Vyacheslav Zagorodnyuk of Ukraine taking the bronze ahead of Olympic winner Urmanov.

Former world and Olympic figure skating champion John Curry died in April after a three-year battle with AIDS. (*See* Obituaries.)

Speed Skating. In a record-shattering season that left only two previous major world records intact, the most amazing new mark, an improvement of nearly 13 seconds, was the 13-min 30.55-sec triumph in the Olympic 10,000 m by Norway's Johann Olav Koss (*see* Biographies), whose three gold medals—the others were in the 1,500 m and 5,000 m—equaled the 1952 feat of his fellow countryman Hjalmar Andersen. The other Olympic men's winners were Aleksandr Golubev of Russia in the 500 m and Dan Jansen of the U.S. in the 1,000 m. Another U.S. skater, Bonnie Blair (*see* Biographies), was the outstanding woman sprinter, winning both the 500 m and 1,000 m. Blair's 500-m success made her the only speed skater of either sex to have won the event in three consecutive Olympics. The other speed-skating events were won by Emese Hunyady of Austria (1,500 m), Svetlana Bazhanova of Russia (3,000 m), and Claudia Pechstein of Germany (5,000 m).

Koss regained the overall title in the men's world championship at Göteborg, Sweden, on March 12–13, followed by two Dutchmen, Ids Postma and Rintje Ritsma. Hunyady captured the women's crown at Butte, Mont., on February 5–6, ahead of Ulrike Adeberg of Germany and Mihaela Dascalu of Romania.

In the separate world sprint championships at Calgary, Alta., on January 29–30, Jansen set a new world record of 35.76 sec in the 500 m. Blair won the women's 500 m in 39.12 sec.

The men's and women's world short-track overall titles were retained at Guildford, England, on March 31–April

At the Olympic Winter Games, held in Lillehammer, Norway, in February, Dan Jansen of the U.S. and his daughter celebrate his gold medal in the 1,000-m speed-skating race, in which he set a world record of 1 min 12.43 sec. Later in the year Jansen announced his retirement from competition.

CLIVE BRUNSKILL—ALLSPORT

2 by Marc Gagnon and Nathalie Lambert of Canada. The men's and women's team relays were won by Japan and Canada. Men's Olympic short-track events were won by South Korea's Chae Ji Hoon (500 m) and Kim Ki Hoon (1,000 m). Cathy Turner of the U.S. took the women's 500 m, and another South Korean, Chun Lee Kyung, won the 1,000 m. The relay events were won by Italy (men) and South Korea (women).   (HOWARD BASS)

JUDO

Most of the world's major international judo tournaments of 1994 were held in Japan, from the Shoriki Cup International University Judo Tournament in January to the Kano Cup in late November. Japan's three titles in the Shoriki Cup at Tokyo on January 8–9 were the fewest won by a host nation in the 11 years that the tourney had been held. Germany's Frank Moller, the European champion, won two titles—the open weights and the 95-kg (209-lb) classes.

In the Asian Games judo competition at Hiroshima in mid-October, Japan and South Korea split the 16 gold medals. Jun Konno, winner of the All-Japan Judo Championships on April 29, took the gold in the over-95-kg class. The Nakamura brothers each won his respective weight class, Yoshio taking the 86-kg (189-lb) division and Yukimasu winning the 65-kg (143-lb) class. South Korea's Yung Chung Hoon won the 71-kg (156-lb) title. Noriko Anno of Japan captured the women's open class, and world champion Ryoko Tamura won the women's 48-kg (106-lb) competition, but the South Korean women Jung Sun Yong and Hyun Sook took the 56-kg (123-lb) and 52-kg (114-lb) classes, respectively. Japan dominated the Kano Cup, held in Chiba prefecture on November 25–27, winning six of the eight classes.   (ANDY ADAMS)

LAWN BOWLS

Scottish bowlers had an outstanding year in individual international events in 1994, both outdoors on lawns and in indoor carpet play. Richard Corsie of Scotland won the singles title in the Commonwealth Games at Victoria, B.C., in August, defeating world outdoor champion Tony Allcock in the final.

Earlier, in March, Andy Thomson, who moved to England from Scotland in 1980, not only won the world indoor singles title played annually at Preston, England, but demonstrated his versatility in the Australian sunshine a few weeks later by outbowling Dave Stockham to win the Mazda International Jack High Tournament at Tweed Heads. Thomson just failed to complete a notably international triple triumph when he lost in the final of the Saga Open at Preston in September. He was outbowled by Mark McMahon, a Scot who had moved to Australia from Hong Kong, where he lived for some years. Yet another Scot, Jan Woodley, captured the women's world indoor title at Cumbernauld, Scotland, in April. At the Commonwealth Games, Scottish domination in the women's singles was halted by Margaret Johnston of Northern Ireland.

Twenty-two countries competed in the Commonwealth Games, and in the team events men's gold medals were won by Australia's Cameron Curtis and Rex Johnston in the pairs and by a South African team in the fours. In the women's events Scotland again gained success with Sarah Gourlay and Frances Whyte in the pairs. South Africa took the fours.   (DONALD J. NEWBY)

RODEO

Rodeo took on an international aspect in 1994 as two Canadians claimed Professional Rodeo Cowboys Association (PRCA) world titles and a Brazilian bull rider, Adriano Moraes of São Paulo, won the coveted $50,000 sudden-death bonus round July 17 at the Calgary (Alta.) Stampede. Moraes, the first Brazilian to compete at the season-ending National Finals Rodeo (NFR) on December 2–11 in Las Vegas, Nev., rode 10 bulls to win the Rodeo, only the third person to do so in NFR history.

Blaine Pederson of Amisk, Alta., clinched his first steer wrestling world title and the tournament's aggregate title on the final day of the $2.8 million NFR. The four-time Canadian champion battled from 12th place in the world standings to first place by the end of the 10-round NFR, concluding the season with earnings of $102,301. World championships in rodeo events—bareback riding, steer wrestling, calf roping, saddle bronc riding, team roping, steer roping, barrel racing, and bull riding—are based on earnings for the entire season.

Daryl Mills of Pink Mountain, B.C., claimed $54,481 at the NFR, the most of any bull rider, en route to his first world title with $105,178 in season earnings. Ty Murray of Stephenville, Texas, again dominated the world champion all-around cowboy title race with $246,170 in earnings in three events: bull riding, saddle bronc riding, and bareback riding. Murray joined Larry Mahan and Tom Ferguson as the only men to have garnered six all-around titles, awarded to the cowboy with the highest total earnings in two or more rodeo events.

Calf roper Herbert Theriot of Wiggins, Miss., edged five-time world champion Joe Beaver of Huntsville, Texas, for the world championship by $14.80—the smallest margin of victory in calf roping in the 49-year recorded history of the PRCA. Theriot concluded the season with $151,922, a new calf-roping record.

Charmayne Rodman's decade-long dominance in Women's Professional Rodeo Association barrel racing came to an end when Kristie Peterson of Elbert, Colo., claimed the world title. Rodman, of Galt, Calif., failed to win money at the NFR, opening the door for Peterson's $110,341 world-title victory.

Jake Barnes of Cave Creek, Ariz., and Clay O'Brien Cooper of Higley, Ariz., teamed for their seventh world title, a record in team roping. The pair snared 10 steers at the NFR in a record 59.1 sec, concluding the season with $94,461 each. At the National Finals Steer Roping, held November 25–26 in Guthrie, Okla., Guy Allen of Lovington, N.M., stretched his record to nine steer-roping world championships, with season earnings of $57,338.

Also winning 1994 world titles were Marvin Garrett of Belle Fourche, S.D., in bareback riding and Dan Mortensen of Manhattan, Mont., in saddle bronc riding. Garrett captured his third world championship with $124,001 in season earnings; Mortensen successfully defended his 1993 title with $177,664. Mortensen also won the NFR saddle-bronc-riding aggregate award with a record score of 791 points on 10 horses.   (GAVIN FORBES EHRINGER)

ROWING

Italy, winning four titles, was the most successful nation in world rowing during 1994. Germany and Great Britain each won three, and Denmark, Romania, and the United States took two apiece. Winners of the remaining championships were Austria, Canada, Croatia, France, The Netherlands, New Zealand, and Norway.

At the world championships at Indianapolis, Ind., in September, records fell in seven men's and women's events. Only seven of the reigning champions retained their titles in the 23 events. Nine of the winners had a victory margin of less than one second, and all three medalists finished within two seconds of one another in eight finals.

Italy took the honours in the men's events by winning the coxless fours in record time over France by 1.38 sec and breaking a second record with the defeat of Ukraine by 1.43 sec in quadruple sculls. However, a try for a third championship, in coxed pairs, was foiled narrowly by Croatia by 0.82 sec in another record time. Romania retained the coxed fours title by only 0.29 sec over the U.S., with The Netherlands 0.75 sec farther behind in the closest finish of the championships. Great Britain rowed Germany down to retain the coxless pairs by 1.10 sec in another record time. Germany was prominent in sculls, winning the singles but losing the doubles to Norway by 0.55 sec. The last men's record fell to the U.S., which mastered The Netherlands by just 0.60 sec for its first win in eights in seven years.

Italy won its last two titles in the men's lightweight coxless pairs and double sculls. In other lightweight competition Austria retained the quadruple sculls, Denmark took the coxless fours, and Great Britain completed a double triumph by successfully defending the single sculls title and producing the closest finish of the regatta in winning the eights by 0.36 sec over Denmark.

France and New Zealand retained, respectively, the coxless pairs title and the double sculls title in women's events, while The Netherlands beat the U.S. by 1.16 sec in coxless fours. Denmark took the single sculls in record time. Germany won quadruple sculls and a second title, in eights, by 0.82 sec at the expense of the U.S. In lightweight events the U.S. struck gold by defeating Great Britain, the defending champions, by 0.88 sec in coxless fours. Canada retained the double sculls, and Romania took the single sculls.

At the under-23 international championships in Paris, Germany won 6 of the 18 gold medals, Italy took 4, and 3 went to Denmark. The five other winners were Great Britain, Poland, Sweden, Switzerland, and the U.S.

Germany was once again the dominant nation in the world junior championships on home waters in Munich, winning 6 of the 14 titles. Romania and Switzerland won two each, while the other winners were Australia, France, Italy, and Russia.

At the Henley Royal Regatta in England, there were nine overseas winners. In eights competition the Grand, Thames, and Princess Elizabeth challenge cups along with the Ladies' Challenge Plate went to the U.S. Ireland triumphed in the Britannia Challenge Cup (coxed fours), and Hungary scored a first Henley win, in the Double Sculls Cup. The Queen Mother Challenge Cup (quadruple sculls) went to Germany and the Stewards' Challenge Cup (coxless fours) to France. Xeno Muller captured the Diamond Challenge Sculls for Switzerland. In the 140th University Boat Race, Cambridge decisively increased its lead in the series to 71—three more than Oxford.   (KEITH OSBORNE)

SAILING

The Whitbread Round-the-World event dominated large yacht competition for much of the first half of 1994. The new Whitbread-60 class demonstrated that these smaller yachts could match the much larger maxis in almost all conditions. In fact, the best maxi, *New Zealand Endeavour,* skippered by Grant Dalton, only just managed to keep its nose ahead of the leading pack of 60s.

Every leg of the race was remarkable for the fact that the leading five 60s were so closely matched for speed. That *Tokio,* skippered by Chris Dickson, held an edge over the others in most of the legs was almost certainly due to the skills of this very successful yachtsman. It was not until *Tokio*'s mast collapsed on the Uruguay-to-Fort Lauderdale, Fla., section that any other winner was even considered. When the wind conditions were strong from behind, Lawrie

1994 World Class Boat Champions

Class	Winner	Country
Contender	Graham Scott	United Kingdom
Enterprise	Ian Fisher	United Kingdom
Fireball	Ian Pinnell	United Kingdom
Flying 15	Roger Craddock	New Zealand
420 (women)	E. Pesle	Italy
420 (men)	John Merricks	United Kingdom
Fun	Claudio Costenaro	Italy
H boat	Vincent Hoesch	Germany
J-24	Ken Read	United States
OK	Leith Armit	New Zealand
Optimist	Martin Jenkins	Argentina
Solo	John Hunt	United Kingdom
Star	Ross McDonald	Canada
Tasar	Russell Ford	Australia
Tempest	Georg Rosch	Germany
Topper	Gordon Miller	United Kingdom
2.4 metre	Bo Hedensjo	Sweden

Smith in *Intrum Justitia* was able to show the fleet the way, recording 690 km (428.7 mi) in one 24-hour period in the South Atlantic. In very light winds Ross Field in *Yamaha* was the boat to beat, and it was *Yamaha* that sailed away from the fleet into Fort Lauderdale with a substantial lead after *Tokio*'s accident. The final leg, from Fort Lauderdale to Southampton, England, was again a close race, and at the end *New Zealand Endeavour* finished first with a time of 120 days 5 hr 9 min 23 sec. *Yamaha* won the 60s class with a time of 120 days 14 hr 55 min.

At the same time, two huge multihulls were seeking to win the Jules Verne Trophy for the fastest trip around the world under sail. *ENZA New Zealand,* with a New Zealand and British crew and recently lengthened to 28 m (92 ft), faced *Lyonnaise des Eaux Dumez* from France. *ENZA New Zealand* went ahead at the start of this 41,840-km (26,000-mi) race, recording the best 24-hour run under sail ever—838.3 km (520.9 mi), an average of 21.7 knots. After 74 days 22 hr 17 min, *ENZA New Zealand* arrived back off the coast of France with the French yacht 1,600 km (1,000 mi) astern. The time was a new record.

The Sydney-to-Hobart ocean race suffered from the worst storm since the Fastnet disaster in 1979. There were no fatalities on this occasion owing to the stringent safety rules now in force and also to some quite remarkable good fortune. John Quinn, the owner of the J35 *MEM,* was lost overboard from his yacht at the height of the storm. Given the fact that he spent 5½ hours in the water at night and without a proper life jacket, it was not far short of a miracle that he survived. Only 38 of the 105 starters finished the race, with Andrew Strachan's *Ninety Seven,* a Farr 47, taking the honours.

The Commodores' Cup, sailed far off Britain's south coast, was completely dominated by the U.S. "White" team, consisting of Donald Smith's Tripp 50 *Falcon,* Helmut Jahn's Farr 39 *Flash Gordon,* and David Clarke's Mumm 36 *Pigs in Space.* All three yachts had crack helmsmen—Peter Holmberg on *Falcon,* Terry Hutchinson on *Flash Gordon,* and Ken Read on *Pigs in Space.* This was also the first big international test of the new Mumm 36 class. *Pigs in Space,* the prototype of the class, seemed to have an extra burst of speed on many occasions.

On the 31st day out of Charleston, S.C., in the BOC Round-the-World solo race, Josh Hall's 60-ft *Gartmore Investment Managers* struck an underwater object and was disabled. Then in the Cape Town-to-Sydney leg, the sole woman participant, Isabelle Autissier, enjoying an unassailable five-day lead, was eliminated by a broken mast on her 60-ft *Ecureuil Poitou-Charentes 2.*   (ADRIAN JARDINE)

SKIING

An increasing share of Scandinavian honours in Alpine events combined with a greater prominence of non-Scandinavians in Nordic contests in 1994 to emphasize the trend toward greater regional equality in all phases of skiing. This was compounded by a growing North American and Far Eastern challenge. Although the Olympic Winter Games at Lillehammer, Norway, were a showpiece (*see* Special Report), with an estimated 10 billion TV viewers in 100 countries, the excitement the Games generated did not cloud the more serious regard for World Cup success, which truly reflected consistency of form in all disciplines throughout the winter. The season was initially marred by the death of Ulrike Maier of Austria, twice a world supergiant slalom (super G) champion, who broke her neck during a practice run in January.

Alpine Skiing. The supreme performers in the 28th Alpine World Cup series were Kjetil Andre Aamodt of Norway, who took the men's overall title ahead of Marc Girardelli, the five-time champion from Luxembourg, and the veteran from Switzerland, Vreni Schneider, who recaptured the women's crown by amassing seven slalom victories to outpoint her Swedish rival, Pernilla Wiberg. Girardelli was the top downhill scorer. The super G was won by Norway's Jan Einar Thorsen, the giant slalom by Austria's Christian Mayer, and the slalom by Alberto Tomba of Italy, who finished third overall. Katja Seizinger was third overall in the women's competition, leading the field in both the downhill and the super G. Schneider unsurprisingly won the slalom, and Anita Wachter of Austria was first in the giant slalom.

In the Olympic Winter Games, on February 12–27, Germany's Markus Wasmeier, aged 30, marked his final season as the only double gold medalist. By edging out Aamodt for the gold in the downhill, Tommy Moe won the first men's skiing medal for the U.S. in 10 years. Edi Podivinsky of Canada finished third. Wasmeier beat Switzerland's Urs Kaelin by only two-hundredths of a second in the giant slalom. His other success, in the super G, denied runner-up Moe a second win; Aamodt finished third. In the slalom Thomas Stangassinger gave Austria its only gold, narrowly defeating Tomba, with Jure Kosir of Slovenia third. Three Norwegians made a clean sweep of the medals in the combined event, Lasse Kjus outpacing Aamodt and Harald Nilsen.

Seizinger was impressive in winning the women's downhill, followed by Picabo Street of the U.S. and Isolde Kostner of Italy. Deborah Compagnoni gained the giant slalom gold medal for Italy, with Martina Ertl of Germany and Schneider second and third, respectively. In the slalom there was no holding Schneider, who was chased by Elfi Eder of Austria and Katja Koren of Slovenia. Diann Roffe-Steinrotter captured the super G for the U.S., with Svetlana Gladisheva of Russia second and Kostner third. Wiberg

Stine Hattestad executes a jump in the women's freestyle moguls at the Olympic Winter Games held in Lillehammer, Norway, in February. The Norwegian skier won the event, which is scored on a combination of marks for technique, speed, and execution of required jumps.
MARK BAKER—REUTERS/BETTMANN

survived a powerful second run from Schneider to take the gold in the women's combined, leaving Alenka Dovzan of Slovenia well behind in third.

Nordic Events. The 15th Nordic World Cup overall title for men's cross-country racing was clinched by Vladimir Smirnov of Kazakhstan, the previous season's runner-up. Defending champion Bjørn Dæhlie of Norway was second, and Jari Isometsae of Finland placed third. The women's crown was won by Manuela Di Centa of Italy, followed by two Russians, Lyubov Yegorova (*see* BIOGRAPHIES) and Yelena Vyalbe, the 1993 and 1992 winners, respectively. The separate Nordic Combined World Cup was retained by Kenji Ogiwara of Japan, and the Jumping World Cup was taken by Espen Bredesen of Norway.

At the Winter Games, Dæhlie, the winner of three world titles in 1993, claimed two gold medals, for the 10 km and 15 km. Thomas Alsgaard of Norway took the 30 km, and the stamina-sapping 50 km went to Smirnov. Italy was successful in the team relay. The winning jumpers were Germany's Jens Weissflog in the 120 m and Bredesen in the 90 m, with Germany winning the team event. The Nordic combined was won by Norway's Fred Borre Lundberg, with the team contest going to Japan. In the women's events Yegorova won both the shortest distances, the 5 km and the 10-km pursuit, and Di Centa was victor in the 15 km and 30 km; Russia took first in the team relay.

Freestyle Skiing. In the 15th Freestyle World Cup series, Sergey Shupletsov of Russia captured the men's combined title, ahead of David Belhumeur of Canada, with the defending champion, Trace Worthington of the U.S., third. The women's crown was gained by Kristean Porter of the U.S., ahead of Natalya Orekhova of Russia and Katherina Kubenk of Canada.

Two freestyle categories were contested at the winter Olympics. Jean-Luc Brassard of Canada won the men's moguls, with Shupletsov runner-up and Edgar Grospiron of France third. Andreas Schönbächler of Switzerland won the aerials, pursued by two Canadians, Philippe Laroche and Lloyd Langlois. The women's moguls went to Norway's Stine Hattestad, with Liz McIntyre of the U.S. and Yelizaveta Kozhevnikova of Russia claiming silver and bronze. Lina Cheryazova of Uzbekistan won the aerials, followed by Sweden's Marie Lindgren and Hilde Lid of Norway.

(HOWARD BASS)

SQUASH RACKETS

The dominance of Jansher Khan of Pakistan and Michelle Martin of Australia continued throughout 1994. Both retained their British Open titles in April and their world championships later in the year. Khan was untroubled throughout the men's World Open, staged in Barcelona, Spain, in September, and accumulated his fifth title when he beat Peter Marshall (England) 10–15, 15–11, 15–8, 15–5 in the final. Martin won her world championship in Guernsey, Channel Islands, where she comfortably beat England's Cassie Jackman 9–1 9–0 9–6. This was her second title.

Immediately after the women's World Open in Guernsey was the women's team championship. This was a contest between Australia and England, which were at the top of the world rankings. The final was one-sided in favour of the visiting team, Australia winning 3–0 to retain the crown gained in 1992 in Vancouver, B.C.

The other world title contested in 1994 was the men's junior. The favourite, Ahmad Barada of Egypt, triumphed 9–0, 7–9, 3–9, 9–3, 9–2 over fellow Egyptian Omar al-Borolosy and, not surprisingly, Egypt took the team title.

A notable new talent in 1994 was 21-year-old Peter Nicol from Scotland. In 12 months he rose from 44th in the world rankings to 5th. Spectacularly, he beat Khan in the second round of the Welsh Classic. Also rising during the year was Martin's brother Brett, who at the age of 31 rose to number two in the world rankings. His play was marked by a high level of consistency combined with hugely deceptive qualities. Meanwhile, the third of the Martin clan, Rodney (men's world champion in 1991), was sidelined for much of

the year with a hip condition. He returned in the autumn, however, and climbed back to seventh in the world rankings.

(ANDREW SHELLEY)

SWIMMING

In 1994, two years before the Olympic Games in Atlanta, Ga., swimming regained the peak it had achieved in previous Olympic years. Fourteen world records were set in 50-m pools: five by swimmers from China, five by Australians, and one each by competitors from Finland, Germany, Russia, and the United States.

Three major international competitions took place in 1994: the third Goodwill Games at St. Petersburg, July 23–24; the Commonwealth Games in Victoria, B.C., August 19–24; and the world championships in Rome, September 1–11.

Two world records were set prior to these international championships. On March 16 in Brisbane, Australia, Rebecca Brown of Australia lowered the 200-m breaststroke record by 0.59 sec to 2 min 24.76 sec. The previous record of 2 min 25.35 sec had been set in 1992 by Anita Nall of the U.S. On June 18 in Monaco, Aleksandr Popov of Russia lowered the six-year-old 100-m freestyle record by 0.21 sec to 48.21 sec. The previous record of 48.42 was held by Matt Biondi of the U.S.

At the Goodwill Games a malfunctioning filtering system in the newly renovated pool forced the organizers to combine two days of events into one. The cloudy condition of the pool ruled out the possibility of world-class times. Double gold medal winners in the men's individual events were Popov in the 50-m and 100-m freestyle and Martin López Zubero of Spain in the 100-m and 200-m backstroke.

World Swimming Records Set in 1994 in 50-m Pools

Event	Name	Country	Time
MEN			
100-m freestyle	Aleksandr Popov	Russia	48.21 sec
400-m freestyle	Kieren Perkins	Australia	3 min 48.80 sec
800-m freestyle	Kieren Perkins	Australia	7 min 46.00 sec
1,500-m freestyle	Kieren Perkins	Australia	14 min 41.66 sec
200-m individual medley	Jani Sievinen	Finland	1 min 58.16 sec
400-m individual medley	Tom Dolan	U.S.	4 min 12.30 sec
WOMEN			
50-m freestyle	Le Jingyi	China	24.51 sec
100-m freestyle	Le Jingyi	China	54.01 sec
200-m freestyle	Franziska van Almsick	Germany	1 min 56.78 sec
200-m individual medley	Lu Bin	China	2 min 11.57 sec
100-m breaststroke	Samantha Riley	Australia	1 min 07.69 sec
200-m breaststroke	Rebecca Brown	Australia	2 min 24.76 sec
100-m backstroke	He Cihong	China	1 min 00.16 sec
4 × 100-m freestyle relay	China national team (Le Jingyi, Shan Ying, Le Ying, Lu Bin)		3 min 37.91 sec
4 × 100-m medley relay	China national team (He Cihong, Dai Guohong, Liu Limin, Le Jingyi)		4 min 01.67 sec

World Swimming Records Set in 1994 in 25-m Pools

Event	Name	Country	Time
MEN			
50-m freestyle	Aleksandr Popov	Russia	21.50 sec
100-m freestyle	Aleksandr Popov	Russia	47.83 sec
100-m freestyle	Aleksandr Popov	Russia	47.82 sec
100-m freestyle	Aleksandr Popov	Russia	47.12 sec
100-m freestyle	Aleksandr Popov	Russia	46.74 sec
200-m butterfly	Franck Esposito	France	1 min 53.05 sec
200-m individual medley	Jani Sievinen	Finland	1 min 54.65 sec
WOMEN			
100-m butterfly	Yue Wei	China	58.71 sec

Le Jingyi of China celebrates her victory in the women's 50-m freestyle at the world swimming championships held in Rome in September. Her time, 24.51 sec, was 0.28 sec faster than the previous record, set by Chinese swimmer Yang Wenyi in the 1992 Olympic Games.

SHAUN BOTTERILL—ALLSPORT

Women's double gold medalists were Angel Martino of the U.S. in the 50-m and 100-m freestyle and Ren Xing of China in the 100-m and 200-m breaststroke. Russia won 15 medals in the men's events, of which 6 were gold, 3 silver, and 6 bronze. The U.S. gained seven medals: two gold, three silver, and two bronze. Spain won two golds, Germany three silvers and two bronzes, and Finland one silver and one bronze. In women's events the U.S. led with 10 medals: 4 gold, 4 silver, and 2 bronze. China totaled nine: five gold and four silver; Russia won five: one silver and four bronze; and Costa Rica took one gold and one silver.

At the Commonwealth Games on August 24 Kieren Perkins of Australia broke two world records in the same race. His time of 14 min 41.66 sec in the 1,500-m freestyle was more than a second faster than his world mark of 14 min 43.48 sec set at the 1992 Olympics. Perkins also broke his 800-m mark during the race, his 7 min 46.00 sec bettering by 0.06 sec the record of 7 min 46.60 sec set in Sydney, Australia, in 1992. Perkins also won the gold in the 200-m and 400-m freestyle and was a member of the winning 4 × 200-m freestyle relay. In addition to the world records, four Commonwealth and 15 championship records were achieved. In the 32 events Australia amassed 24 gold medals, 16 silvers, and 10 bronzes. Great Britain finished second with six golds, three silvers, and eight bronzes.

At the world championships 602 swimmers from 97 countries competed. China won 12 of 32 events, all by women, as compared with four in the 1991 world championships in Perth. Chinese women also added six silvers and one bronze for a total of 19 medals. The U.S., with 4 golds, compared with 13 won in Perth, added 10 silvers and 7 bronzes. Russia placed third with 11 medals, of which 4 were gold, 5 silver, and 2 bronze. Sixteen countries won at least one medal. The U.S. won the overall championship with 769 points, 381 from the men's events. Australia was second with 544, followed by Germany with 480 and China with 444, of which 440 were scored by women.

The outstanding achievement of the Chinese women was marred by widespread accusations that their performances were enhanced by the use of illegal drugs. Both the Chinese officials and swimmers denied the charges, and the drug tests all were negative. Later in September, however, Yang Aihua, winner of the 400-m freestyle at the world championships, tested positive for the muscle-building hormone testosterone and in November was suspended from all competition through Sept. 19, 1996. Lu Bin, winner of three gold medals and two silver medals at the world championships, also tested positive, along with six other swimmers.

Ten world records and 19 championship records were produced in seven days of swimming. In 16 events China's women set five of the world records and eight of the championship records. Le Jingyi's time of 24.51 sec lowered by 0.28 sec the 50-m freestyle world record set by Yang Wenyi in the 1992 Olympics. In the 100-m freestyle Le's 54.01 sec shattered by 0.47 sec the 1992 record set by Jenny Thompson at Indianapolis, Ind. In the 4 × 100-m freestyle relay, the quartet of Le Jingyi, Shan Ying, Le Ying, and Lu Bin was timed in 3 min 37.91 sec, taking 1.55 sec off the record set by the U.S. in the 1992 Olympics. In the 4 × 100-m medley relay, He Cihong and teammates Dai Guohong, Liu Limin, and Le Jingyi combined for the world record of 4 min 1.67 sec, erasing 0.87 sec off the mark set by U.S. in 1992. On the leadoff backstroke, he was timed in 1 min 0.16 sec, clipping 0.15 sec from the 1991 mark of Kristina Egerszegi of Hungary. In the 200-m freestyle Franziska van Almsick of Germany set a world record of 1 min 56.78 sec, taking 0.77 sec from the mark set by Heike Friedrich of East Germany in 1986. Samantha Riley of Australia won the 100-m breaststroke in 1 min. 7.69 sec, shaving 0.22 sec off the record set by Silke Horner of East Germany in 1987. Lu won three gold and two silver medals, and Le Jingyi won four gold medals, two silvers, and one bronze and earned the Politika Prize as the tournament's outstanding swimmer.

Three world records and seven championship records were set by men. Perkins was timed in 3 min 43.80 sec in the 400-m freestyle, lowering by 1.20 sec the previous mark set by Yevgeny Sadovy of the Unified Team in the 1992 Olympics. Perkins also won the 1,500-m freestyle. In the 200-m individual medley, Jani Sievinen of Finland in a time of 1 min 58.16 sec erased by 1.20 sec the world record set by Tamas Darnyi of Hungary in the 1991 world championships. Tom Dolan of Arlington, Va., won the 400-m individual medley in 4 min 12.30 sec. Double gold medal winners included Popov in the 50-m and 100-m freestyle, Norbert Rozsa of Hungary in the 100-m and 200-m breaststroke, and Perkins. The distribution of titles had never been so widespread; victors hailed from eight countries.

Diving. On June 5–7 at the 1994 China Open in Wuhan (Wu-han), divers achieved scores that broke previous records. In the women's platform China's Chi Bin scored 516.51 points to surpass the 508.65 scored by the Soviet Union's Yelena Miroshina at the 1987 International Springertag in Rostock, East Germany. China's Sun Shuwei, the 1992 Olympic platform gold medalist, won the men's 10-m platform competition with a score of 718.35, breaking the mark of 717.41 set by Greg Louganis of the U.S. in 1987. Other winners were Tan Shuping in the women's 1-m and 3-m springboard and Dmitry Sautin of Russia in the men's 1-m and 3-m springboard.

Russia and China dominated the Goodwill Games. Chen Lixia of China won the 1-m springboard, Vera Ilyina of Russia took the 3-m springboard, and Min Xiong of China won the 10 m platform. Chen Sheng of China won the men's 1-m springboard, Sautin the 3-m springboard, and Vladimir Timoshinin of Russia the 10-m platform.

In the world championships a record 138 divers from 36 countries competed in the diving events. Evan Stewart of Zimbabwe became the first African ever to win a diving event, triumphing in the 1-m springboard. Yu Zhuocheng of China led almost from the start and prevailed in the 3-m springboard with 655.44 points. In the 10-m platform Sautin scored 84.48 points on his final dive to win by more than four points, overtaking Sun 634.71 to 630.03. In the women's events China swept all three championships. Chen Lixia won the 1-m springboard with 279.30 points and Tan took the gold medal in the 3-m springboard with 548.49 points. The defending titlist and Olympic champion Fu Mingxia, needing to score more than 62 points on her final dive, produced a stunning inward 3½ somersault for 75.48 to snatch the gold in the platform from Chi 434.04 to 420.24.

Synchronized Swimming. In the Goodwill Games Olga Sedakova of Russia won the solo event gold medal over Becky Dyroen-Lancer of the U.S. 197.200 to 197.020. In the duet Dyroen-Lancer and Jill Sudduth of the U.S. scored 197.880 for the gold.

In the world championships 215 swimmers from 31 countries competed in three events. Dyroen-Lancer won the gold medal in solo, scoring 191.040 points. Dyroen-Lancer and Sudduth triumphed in the duet with 187.009. The team title was won by the U.S., with Canada second and Japan third.   (ALBERT SCHOENFIELD)

TABLE TENNIS

In the years between the biennial world championships, attention focused on regional events, the largest of which were the European championships. At the 19th staging of this tournament, in Birmingham, England, during March–April 1994, Jean-Michel Saive of Belgium became the new European men's singles champion by defeating Olympic gold medalist Jan-Ove Waldner of Sweden in the final. In the women's singles Marie Svensson of Sweden bested Gerdie Keen of The Netherlands.

The North American championships took place in Quebec in May. Winner of the men's title was Cheng Ying-hua,

1994 Table Tennis World Rankings

MEN	WOMEN
1. Jean-Michel Saive (Belgium)	1. Deng Yaping (China)
2. Jan-Ove Waldner (Sweden)	2. Qiao Hong (China)
3. Wang Tao (China)	3. Gao Jun (China)
4. Ma Wenge (China)	4. Chai Po Wa (Hong Kong)
5. Zoran Primorac (Croatia)	5. Chen Zihe (China)

who represented the U.S., and Geng Lijuan of Canada who triumphed in the women's competition.

As the year drew to a close, table tennis fans were looking forward to the 43rd world championships in Tianjin (Tientsin) in April 1995.   (TONY BROOKS)

TENNIS

The major prizes in tennis were distributed more liberally in 1994 than had been anticipated. The most unexpected triumph was that of the unseeded Andre Agassi in the United States Open in September. While continuing to be one of the sport's leading attractions with his designer-tramp appearance, confident gait, and potent ground strokes, Agassi had won only one Grand Slam title previously, his counterpunching style having succeeded on Wimbledon's grass in 1992.

At the outset it appeared that 1994 would be dominated by the excellence of the two players at the head of the respective world rankings, the men's events by Pete Sampras of the U.S. and the women's by Steffi Graf of Germany.

Martina Navratilova takes a few blades of grass before leaving Wimbledon, where she lost to Spain's Conchita Martínez 6–4, 3–6, 6–3. It was the last appearance in the All-England Championships for the U.S. star, who had won the event a record nine times, before her retirement.

BILL FRAKES—SPORTS ILLUSTRATED

This view was strengthened by the performances of the two players in winning the singles titles at the Australian Open in January, prompting discussion of their prospects of accomplishing a Grand Slam (a sweep of the Australian, French, Wimbledon, and U.S. singles championships within a calendar year).

Surprisingly, however, Graf did not add to her Grand Slam titles during the remainder of the year, and the women's game suddenly belonged to Spain. Arantxa Sánchez Vicario, emphatically beaten by Graf in the Australian final, went on to capture both the French and U.S. championships, and Conchita Martínez triumphed at Wimbledon; Martínez thus became the first Spanish woman to receive the singles trophy at the All-England Championships, winning a magnificent final against Martina Navratilova, who was marking her farewell to the grass courts. Sánchez Vicario and Martínez also made major contributions to Spain's successful defense of the Federation Cup, the women's premier international team competition, in Frankfurt, Germany, in July.

Spain also featured prominently in the men's game. Sergi Bruguera won the singles title at the French Open for the second consecutive year, on this occasion defeating a compatriot, Alberto Berasategui, in the final.

Sampras' prospects of adding a fourth consecutive Grand Slam title to his 1993 victories at Wimbledon and the United States Open and his successful opening in 1994 in Australia were ended in Paris. He was defeated in the quarterfinals of the French Open by Jim Courier of the U.S., the champion in 1991 and 1992. Sampras recovered his confidence, making a successful defense of the Wimbledon championship little more than a month later. But physical problems beset him during the U.S. Open, the title slipping away from him when he lost to Jaime Yzaga of Peru in the fourth round.

What Yzaga achieved by maneuvering a debilitated Sampras around the Stadium Court at Flushing Meadow, N.Y., an assertive young Russian had come close to accomplishing by driving impressive shots beyond Sampras in the second round of the Australian Open. Yevgeny Kafelnikov from the Black Sea resort of Sochi came within two points of eliminating Sampras before the American recovered to win 9–7 in the fifth set.

Australian Open. Sampras, so thoroughly shaken by Kafelnikov that he dropped a set 6–1 to the unseeded Frenchman Stephane Simian, required two tiebreakers before defeating Ivan Lendl (who retired later in the year) in straight sets and two more tiebreakers to discourage Magnus Gustafsson, the 10th seed from Sweden, in four sets. In the semifinals, however, Sampras was in such irresistible form that he was able to dispatch Courier, the champion for the previous two years, 6–3, 6–4, 6–4.

In the final Sampras played another fellow American, Todd Martin, the ninth seed, who had recovered from losing the first set of his semifinal against Stefan Edberg, the fourth seed, and defeated the Swede in three tiebreakers. Martin's prospects of causing an upset in his first Grand Slam final diminished after the opening set. Unable to convert any of six break points, he lost a tiebreaker in the first set 7–4, and Sampras took the title 7–6, 6–4, 6–4.

The most interesting feature of the women's singles as Graf and Sánchez Vicario advanced to meet as seeded in the final was the progress of Kimiko Date, the 10th seed. By defeating the third-seeded Martínez, Date became only the second Japanese woman to reach a Grand Slam semifinal. Her misfortune was to meet an overpowering Graf, who swept through Date's deep, flat shots, winning 6–3, 6–3. Sánchez Vicario's retrieving style was also treated with disdain in the final, and Graf won 6–0, 6–2 in 57 minutes.

French Open. At the French Open the chief issue was whether Sampras could successfully translate a smooth, attacking style, ideally suited to faster courts, to the slow clay of Paris, which favoured the ground stroke rallying of baseline players. The crux came in the quarterfinal match between Sampras and Courier. It was their first meeting on clay, and Courier's potent backcourt style flourished, bringing him victory in four sets.

Bruguera, who had beaten Courier in five sets in the 1993 final, required only four to defeat him in the 1994 semifinals. From the lower half of the draw, which after three rounds was bereft of all seeded players except Goran Ivanisevic of Croatia, Berasategui emerged to challenge Bruguera while their monarch, King Juan Carlos, waited to present the trophy. It went to Bruguera, who won the first-ever all-Spanish Grand Slam final 6–3, 7–5, 2–6, 6–1.

Sánchez Vicario had commanded the Centre Court less than four hours earlier, defeating Mary Pierce representing France 6–4, 6–4 to win the women's title. The match had begun under storm clouds the night before, and only 17 minutes of play were possible before rain intervened. Pierce, who had caused a sensation in the semifinals by bewildering Graf with the pace and accuracy of her strokes in winning 6–2, 6–2 in 77 minutes, was unable to reproduce her form against the scurrying Spaniard.

Wimbledon. Graf was under pressure at Wimbledon the moment the draw put her in an opening-round match against Lori McNeil, an experienced American with an attacking style suited to grass. Never before had a defending Wimbledon champion been eliminated in the first round of the women's singles, but the unseeded McNeil was the worthy winner 7–5, 7–6 of a contest that took an hour and 43 minutes spread over nearly five hours because of rain.

The defeat of the top player immediately caused an upturn in the expectations of the other contenders, notably Martínez and Navratilova, the third and fourth seeds, respectively. Navratilova sought a memorable finale to her long and glorious association with the All-England Championships, especially after losing in the first round of the French Open. Martínez and Navratilova advanced to the final and produced a showpiece, neither player allowing her game to be overwhelmed by the emotion of the occasion. The contrast in styles enhanced the match, Martínez brilliantly anticipating Navratilova's volleys and smashes and frequently bewildering the nine-time champion with the pace and variety of her passing shots. There was not the slightest indication that this was Martínez's first experience in a Grand Slam singles final as she dominated the final set to win 6–4, 3–6, 6–3 and become the first Spanish woman to gain the trophy.

Sampras performed at Wimbledon as if the Courier match in Paris had never happened. The defending champion conceded only one set in his seven matches and was two sets ahead when that occurred, against Martin in the semifinals. The final matched Sampras and Ivanisivec, two of the world's finest servers, and so it was inevitable that power would dominate at the expense of rallying. Sampras prevailed 7–6, 7–6, 6–0, with the concluding set requiring only 20 minutes.

U.S. Open. Doubts concerning the fitness of Sampras and Graf preceded the U.S. Open. Sampras was able to advance apparently stress-free to the third round, at which stage not a single seeded player remained in his quarter of the draw. He lost one set in the third round and then seemed to be on the verge of a physical collapse when taxed by Yzaga's ground strokes over five sets in the fourth round.

With Sampras gone, Michael Stich, the number four seed, took charge of the top half of the draw, but the German was unable to resist Agassi's inspired form in the final with any more conviction than had four other seeded players, Wayne Ferreira, Michael Chang, Thomas Muster, and Martin. Agassi defeated Stich 6–1, 7–6, 7–5 to become the first unseeded champion since Fred Stolle of Australia in 1966.

In an exciting women's final, Sánchez Vicario gave a characteristically spirited performance to defeat Graf 1–6, 7–6, 6–4. Graf began to experience problems with her lower back in the eighth game of the second set but did not offer the injury as an excuse.

Davis Cup. Kafelnikov, aided by compatriot Aleksandr Volkov, led Russia into and through the Davis Cup final for the first time, defeating Australia, the Czech Republic, and then defending champion Germany in the semifinals. Sweden traveled to Moscow in December to play the closely contested final. Volkov lost to Stefan Edberg and Kafelnikov to Magnus Larsson in the singles, both in five-set matches. Sweden's Jonas Bjorkman and Jan Apell beat Kafelnikov and Andrey Olkhovsky in the doubles, also in five sets. Kafelnikov's reverse singles victory over Edberg provided the Russians' only win.   (JOHN ROBERTS)

TRACK AND FIELD SPORTS

The even-numbered years between Olympic Games provide U.S. track and field athletes with a break from championship-level competition. Two years before the Olympics and with no world meets on the schedule, 1994 was such a respite year.

While U.S. athletes were free to focus on the series of high-powered invitational meetings that constitute Europe's Grand Prix circuit each summer season, Europeans aimed for the quadrennial European championships, staged in 1994 in Helsinki, Fin. In addition, athletes from nations composing the Commonwealth of Nations looked toward their own championships, held in Victoria, B.C.

Men's International Competition. The records set during 1994 could be summed up as "the short and long" of the sport. A U.S. sprinter lowered the world mark in the 100-m dash, while runners from three African nations achieved

Table I. 1994 World Outdoor Records—Men

Event	Competitor and country	Performance
100 m	Leroy Burrell (U.S.)	9.85 sec
3,000 m	Noureddine Morceli (Algeria)	7 min 25.11 sec
2 mi*	Moses Kiptanui (Kenya)	8 min 9.01 sec
5,000 m	Haile Gebresilasie (Ethiopia)	12 min 56.96 sec
10,000 m	William Sigei (Kenya)	26 min 52.23 sec
20,000-m walk	Bernardo Segura (Mexico)	1 hr 17 min 25.5 sec
50,000-m walk	René Piller (France)	3 hr 41 min 28.2 sec
4 × 200-m relay	Santa Monica Track Club (U.S.) (Marsh, Burrell, Heard, C. Lewis)	1 min 18.68 sec
Pole vault	Sergey Bubka (Ukraine)	6.14 m (20 ft 1¾ in)

Table II. 1994 World Outdoor Records—Women

Event	Competitor and country	Performance
2,000 m	Sonia O'Sullivan (Ireland)	5 min 25.36 sec
2,000-m steeplechase*	Marina Pluzhnikova (Russia)	6 min 11.84 sec

Table III. 1994 World Indoor Records—Men

Event	Competitor and country	Performance
60-m hurdles	Colin Jackson (U.K.)	7.30 sec
Triple jump†	Leonid Voloshin (Russia)†	17.77 m (58 ft 3¾ in)

Table IV. 1994 World Indoor Records—Women

Event	Competitor and country	Performance
50 m	Merlene Ottey (Jamaica)	6.00 sec
4 × 800-m relay	Russia (Zaltseva, Kusnyetsova, Afanyasyeva, Podkopayova)	4 min 2.94 sec
Triple jump	Inna Lasovskaya (Russia) Inna Lasovskaya (Russia)†	14.78 m (48 ft 5 in) 14.90 m (48 ft 9 in)

*Not an officially ratified record distance; best performance on record.
†Awaiting ratification.

record performances in the long distances. Leroy Burrell regained the 100-m record when he sped 9.85 sec in Lausanne, Switz. Burrell snipped the record from the 9.86 run in 1991 by Carl Lewis, his teammate on the Santa Monica (Calif.) Track Club. Lewis' effort in 1991 had bettered the 9.90 Burrell had run only two months earlier. In mid-April, Burrell and Lewis had helped set the season's first outdoor world record. The renowned pair joined their Santa Monica clubmates Michael Marsh and Floyd Heard to clock 1 min 18.68 sec in the 4 × 200-m relay, bettering the time of 1 min 19.11 sec run by the same quartet in 1992.

Both Burrell and Lewis, however, suffered early ends to their European summer seasons. A foot injury sidelined Burrell, while Lewis contracted a stomach virus from contaminated water. Both returned to their homes in Houston, Texas, and missed a number of major invitational meets at the height of the season.

The African distance runners all set their records in Europe. First to turn the trick was Haile Gebresilasie of Ethiopia in early June in Hengelo, Neth. The 1993 world champion at 10,000 m, Gebresilasie covered half that distance in a 5,000-m record time of 12 min 56.96 sec, eclipsing the mark of 12 min 58.39 sec run in 1987 by Morocco's Said Aouita. Some six weeks later in Oslo, Norway, Kenya's William Sigei—known more for his prowess in cross country—produced a surprising record in the 10,000 m. With his time of 26 min 52.23 sec, Sigei lowered the 1993 mark of 26 min 58.38 sec run on the same track by fellow Kenyan Yobes Ondicki—set in a race in which Sigei had placed second in his previous best time of 27 min 16.81 sec.

The third distance record, in the 3,000 m, was set in Monaco at the start of August by Algerian star Noureddine Morceli (see BIOGRAPHIES). Already the record holder at 1,500 m and one mile, Morceli clocked 7 min 25.11 sec to slash nearly four seconds off the 1992 mark of 7 min 28.96

sec established by Kenya's Moses Kiptanui. The 1994 campaign was the first season since 1978 in which world records were set at 3,000, 5,000, and 10,000 m. Kenya's Henry Rono had set the marks at all three distances in 1978.

Morceli later capped his season at the Grand Prix final in Paris. His victory in the 1,500 m gave him the highest point total in the season's overall Grand Prix standings—worth a total of $130,000. Even though Kiptanui lost his official 3,000-m record, he broke the record at an unofficial distance, covering two miles in 8 min 9.01 sec. The Kenyan trimmed more than three seconds off the old best of 8 min 12.17 sec, run in 1993 by Khalid Skah of Morocco.

The lone field event record setter was no newcomer to that level of achievement. The peerless Ukrainian pole vaulter Sergey Bubka set his 17th outdoor mark when he cleared 6.14 m (20 ft 1¾ in) in the helpful altitude of Sestriere in the Italian Alps. It was the 35th career record for Bubka, the other 18 having been set indoors. His highest indoor vault, in 1993, measured one centimetre higher at 6.15 m (20 ft 2 in).

At the European championships Linford Christie of Great Britain won his third consecutive title at 100 m, while countrymen Colin Jackson (110-m high hurdles) and Steve Backley (javelin) successfully defended their titles. Olympic champions Fermin Cacho of Spain (1,500 m) and Dieter Baumann of Germany (5,000 m) added European victories to their collection of titles. At the Commonwealth Games Christie and Backley (competing for England), as well as Jackson (representing Wales), retained the titles they had first won in 1990. Earlier in the year, during the winter indoor season, Jackson twice set records over the 60-m high hurdles (7.36 sec, then 7.30). Russia's Leonid Voloshin bounced to a triple-jump mark of 17.77 m (58 ft 3¾ in).

In race-walking events on the track outdoors, records for both official distances were set in the same Norwegian competition in early May. Mexico's Bernardo Segura covered 20 km in 1 hr 17 min 25.5 sec, while France's René Piller cut the best for 50 km to 3 hr 41 min 28.2 sec.

The outdoor track season concluded with the seventh staging of the World Cup, a team competition for national and continental squads. In London, two years after the previous World Cup in Havana. Africa's men's team retained its title, while an all-star team representing Europe won the women's crown. The U.S. teams produced the worst American placings in the meet's 17-year history—the men finishing sixth and the women eighth and last.

Women's International Competition. Frequent meetings among leading performers highlighted women's competition in 1994, just as it had the men's. The long jump produced repeated clashes between Jackie Joyner-Kersee of the U.S., the 1988 Olympic champion, and her career-long rival Germany's Heike Drechsler, who had won the 1992 Olympic title and the world championship in 1993.

Joyner-Kersee started her season in fine form in late May with a U.S. record leap of 7.49 m (24 ft 7 in), the second-longest women's jump in history, behind only the world record of 7.52 m (24 ft 8¼ in) set in 1988 by Galina Chistyakova of the Soviet Union. Joyner-Kersee then scored Grand Prix meet wins over Drechsler in Oslo; Brussels; Cologne, Germany; and finally at the Grand Prix final. Her total point score gave her the overall Grand Prix title and the $130,000 first prize. For good measure Joyner-Kersee matched her U.S. record distance of 7.49 m (24 ft 7 in) at the meet in Sestriere.

Despite her losses to Joyner-Kersee, Drechsler's season was not at all a failure. She won her third consecutive long-jump title at the European championships and then closed her season by competing in her first heptathlon since

1981. At the end of that two-day, seven-event discipline at Talence, France, in September, she had totaled 6,741 points, which was the highest score of the season. There now loomed the tantalizing prospect of a future meeting between Drechsler and the acknowledged master of the heptathlon, the world-record holder and two-time Olympic champion Joyner-Kersee.

On the track standout runners were Sonia O'Sullivan of Ireland and Maria Mutola of Mozambique. O'Sullivan produced the season's fastest times at 1,500 m (3 min 59.10 sec), one mile (4 min 17.25 sec), the infrequently contested 2,000 m (a world-record 5 min 25.36 sec), and the 3,000 m (8 min 21.64 sec).

The latter pair of efforts were contested against leading rival Yvonne Murray of Great Britain. O'Sullivan also became the first Irish athlete, man or woman, to win a European title when she outran Murray in Helsinki. Murray rebounded to win the 10,000 m at the Commonwealth Games for her native Scotland.

Mutola followed up her 800-m win at the 1993 world championships with an undefeated 1994 campaign and a best time of 1 min 55.19 sec at that distance. It was the fastest time ever for the 800 m by an athlete from outside the former communist Eastern European nations.

In addition to the European championship victories of Drechsler and O'Sullivan, another star in Helsinki was Russian sprinter Irina Privalova, the only woman to win two events as she sped to victories in the 100-m and 200-m dashes.

A number of clashes in Grand Prix meets between Privalova and U.S. rival Gwen Torrence presaged their meeting at the Grand Prix final. However, in that event they both were defeated over 100 m in an upset by 34-year-old Jamaican veteran Merlene Ottey, who had missed the first half of the summer season owing to a foot injury. Her time of 10.78 sec equaled the fastest of her career. Torrence finished second

to Ottey and lowered her career-best time to 10.82 sec. Early in the year Ottey set a new indoor world record in the 50 m of 6.00 sec.

Three other records were set in indoor competition. The Russian 4 × 800-m relay team established a new mark of 4 min 2.94 sec, and Russian triple jumper Inna Lasovskaya twice increased the distance in her specialty, to 14.78 m and then to 14.90 m. Sprinter Wilma Rudolph died in November (*see* OBITUARIES).

Cross Country and Marathon Running. Kenya's William Sigei successfully defended his men's title at the world cross country championships, while teammate Helen Chepngeno won the women's crown. Their nation emphasized its domination of the sport by winning team titles for senior and junior men and junior women.

The European championships marathon titles were won by Martin Fiz (2 hr 10 min 31 sec) as he led his Spanish teammates to a 1-2-3 finish and by Manuela Machado of Portugal (2 hr 29 min 54 sec). Commonwealth Games victories went to Steve Moneghetti of Australia (2 hr 11 min 49 sec) and Carole Rouillard of Canada (2 hr 30 min 41 sec).

The world half-marathon championship was won by Morocco's Khalid Skah. Winner of the 10,000 m at the 1992 Olympics, Skah covered the 21.1-km (13.1-mi) distance on the road in 1 hr 0 min 27 sec. South Africa's Elana Meyer won the women's title in 1 hour 8 min 36 sec. The team victories went to Kenya's men and Romania's women.

The men's and women's winners of other major marathons in 1994 were: Boston, Cosmas N'Deti (Kenya) 2 hr 7 min 15 sec and Uta Pippig (Germany) 2 hr 21 min 45 sec; Rotterdam, Neth., Vincent Rousseau (Belgium) 2 hr 7 min 51 sec and Miyoko Asahina (Japan) 2 hr 29 min 14 sec; London, Dionicio Ceron (Mexico) 2 hr 8 min 53 sec and Katrin Dörre (Germany) 2 hr 32 min 34 sec; New York, German Silva (Mexico) 2 hr 11 min 21 sec and Tegla Loroupe (Kenya) 2 hr 27 min 37 sec. (JON HENDERSHOTT)

RICHARD MARTIN—VANDYSTADT/ALLSPORT

Colin Jackson of Britain wins the 60-m hurdles in the European indoor championships held in Paris in March. He also won the 60-m sprint at that competition, and later in the year he won the 110-m hurdles at the European championships and at the Commonwealth Games.

VOLLEYBALL

At the 1994 men's world championships in Greece, the Italians reclaimed the top spot, adding to their first-place finish in the World League. The U.S. may have been the biggest surprise, however, capturing the bronze medal with victories over reigning Olympic champion Brazil and perennial power Cuba. Two-time Olympic medalist Bob Ctvrtlik, Scott Fortune, and Bryan Ivie appeared to have resurrected the U.S. as a world power in time for the 1996 Olympic Games. The $6 million World League was won by Italy, as the prize money doubled and the fan support increased. The Italians defeated Cuba in the finals, while Brazil placed third.

At the women's world championships in Brazil, Cuba continued to hold the top spot, winning the title with a triumph over an upstart Brazilian squad. The U.S. placed sixth after dropping matches to Cuba and bronze medalist Russia. In the $1.5 million world grand prix, held at various sites in Asia, Brazil won the championship. Cuba finished second and China was third.

In U.S. college competition Penn State won the men's championship by defeating the University of California at Los Angeles (UCLA). It was the first time in the 25-year history of the tournament that a college outside California had won the title. Stanford University beat UCLA 3–1 for the women's championship.

Beach volleyball continued to make its presence known as the Goodwill Games in St. Petersburg became the first multisport event to include it. Liz Masakayan and Karolyn Kirby of the U.S., the reigning world champions, won the gold medal, while all-world performer Sinjin Smith and Bruk Vandeweghe also collected a gold medal for the U.S. in the men's competition. (RICHARD S. WANNINGER)

WEIGHT LIFTING

In the 1994 world weight lifting championships at Istanbul in November, Russia, Turkey, and Bulgaria dominated the men's competition, and China won five titles in the women's events. After sweeping all nine classes in the Asian championships, China sent an entirely new team to the women's world championships.

In the men's competition there were 242 lifters from 52 nations, while 30 countries were represented among the 105

1994 World Weight Lifting Champions

Weight	Winner and country	Performance
MEN		
54 kg (118.8 lb)	H. Mutlu, Turkey	290 kg (638 lb)*
59 kg (130 lb)	N. Peshalov, Bulgaria	302.5 kg (665.5 lb)
64 kg (141 lb)	N. Suleymanoglu, Turkey	330 kg (726 lb)*
70 kg (154 lb)	F. Guler, Turkey	350 kg (770 lb)*
76 kg (167 lb)	P. Mara, Cuba	365.0 kg (803 lb)
83 kg (182.5 lb)	M. Muster, Germany	382.5 kg (841.5 lb)*
91 kg (200 lb)	A. Petrov, Russia	412.5 kg (907.5 lb)
99 kg (218 lb)	S. Syrtsov, Russia	417.5 kg (918.5 lb)
108 kg (238 lb)	T. Taimazov, Ukraine	435 kg (957 lb)*
+108 kg (+238 lb)	A. Kurlovich, Belarus	457.5 kg (1,006.5 lb)*
WOMEN		
46 kg (101 lb)	Y. Yun, China	180 kg (396 lb)
50 kg (110 lb)	R. Byrd, U.S.	175 kg (385 lb)
54 kg (118.8 lb)	S. Wang, China	197.5 kg (434.5 lb)
59 kg (130 lb)	F. Zou, China	220 kg (484 lb)
64 kg (141 lb)	H. Li, China	235 kg (517 lb)*
70 kg (154 lb)	M. Zhou, China	222.5 kg (489.5 lb)
76 kg (167 lb)	P. Antonopoulou, Greece	220 kg (484 lb)
83 kg (182.5 lb)	M. Urutia, Colombia	237.5 kg (522.5 lb)
+83 kg (+182.5 lb)	D. Li, China	242.5 kg (533.5 lb)

*World record.

athletes in the women's competition. Bulgaria won the most medals in the men's class with one gold, two silvers, and three bronzes. Turkey won three golds, and Russia earned two golds. Among the women China accounted for five golds, one silver, and one bronze in the nine classes. Taiwan captured two silvers and two bronzes.

Seven world records were set for total lifts in the 10 men's weight classes. The only record setter among the women was Hongyun Li of China in the 64-kg (141-lb) class. Two two-time Olympic champions were among the winners. Naim Suleymanoglu of Turkey won his sixth world title with a record total lift of 330 kg (726 lb) in the 64-kg (141-lb) class. Aleksandr Kurlovich, now representing Belarus, set a world mark of 457.5 kg (1,006.5 lb) in the super heavyweight class. (CHARLES R. PAUL, JR.)

WRESTLING

Freestyle and Greco-Roman. Turkey served as host for and won the 1994 freestyle wrestling world championships, held in Istanbul on August 25–28. Though Turkey tied Russia with 53 points, it was awarded the team championship by having won two gold medals and one silver. Russia gained one gold, one silver, and three bronze medals. Rounding out the top five finishers were Cuba and Iran with 50 points and Germany with 38. Bulgaria's Valentin Jordanov won the 52-kg (114.5-lb) match, his sixth world championship.

The Greco-Roman world championships took place in Tampere, Fin., on September 8–11. Russia won with 69 points and five gold medalists. Ukraine placed second with 50 points, followed by Poland with 44, Bulgaria with 35, and Germany with 30. Russian heavyweight Aleksandr Karelin claimed his fifth world title.

The freestyle World Cup took place in Edmonton, Alta., on March 25–26. The U.S. won this dual meet competition by defeating Iran in the final match 25–12 for a total of 10 team points. Iran had 8 points, Russia 6, Turkey 4, and Canada 2. The U.S. team won 45 of its 50 individual bouts, and U.S. heavyweight Bruce Baumgartner won his seventh World Cup.

The 64th U.S. collegiate championships were held in Chapel Hill, N.C., on March 17–19. With three individual champions Oklahoma State won the team title with 94.75 points. Winning an unprecedented fourth collegiate title was Oklahoma State's Pat Smith at 71.7 kg (158 lb). (JOHANNA SCHNEIDER)

Sumo. Sumo wrestling in 1994 was unexpectedly dominated by Takanohana, who won four of the six annual tournaments. He was promoted from *ozeki* to *yokozuna* (grand champion) after taking the *yusho* (tourney title) of the Kyushu *basho* (tournament) in November—the last tournament of the year—with his second consecutive perfect 15–0 record. The other two tournaments were won by two Hawaiians, *Yokozuna* Akebono in March and *Ozeki* Musashimaru in July.

The victory in November was Takanohana's seventh *yusho,* tying him with Akebono for most tourney titles by active *rikishi* (sumo wrestlers). It came on the heels of his first perfect record (15–0) in September, when most fans expected him to be elevated to sumo's top rank. But the Yokozuna Promotion Council (composed of 11 prominent, nonsumo citizens) voted only 6–5 in his favour, a two-thirds majority being necessary for promotion. After the November tournament, however, the council members unanimously recommended Takanohana for promotion to *yokozuna.* Takanohana also won Rikishi of the Year, awarded for most annual wins, when he chalked up a total of 80 victories in six tournaments—just two short of the record held by former *yokozuna* Kitanoumi. (ANDY ADAMS)

SPORTING RECORD

ARCHERY

FITA Outdoor World Target Archery Championships

year	men's individual		men's team		women's individual		women's team	
	winner	points	winner	points	winner	points	winner	points
1985	R. McKinney (U.S.)	2,601	South Korea	7,660	I. Soldatova (U.S.S.R.)	2,595	U.S.S.R.	7,721
1987	V. Esheyev (U.S.S.R.)	329	West Germany	891	Ma Xiangjun (China)	330	U.S.S.R.	884
1989	S. Zabrodsky (U.S.S.R.)	332	U.S.S.R.	985	Kim Soo Nyung (S.Kor.)	338	South Korea	995
1991	S. Fairweather (Austl.)	334	South Korea	998	Kim Soo Nyung (S.Kor.)	333	South Korea	1,030
1993	Park Kyung Mo (S.Kor.)	113	France	249	Kim Hyo Jung (S.Kor.)	104	South Korea	236

ATHLETICS

IAAF World Cup—men

	100 metre	200 metre	400 metre	800 metre	1,500 metre
1989	L. Christie (Gr.Brit.)	R. Caetano da Silva (Amer.)	R. Hernandez (Amer.)	T. McKean (Gr.Brit.)	A. Bile (Africa)
1992	L. Christie (Gr.Brit.)	R. Caetano da Silva (Amer.)	S. Bada (Africa)	D. Sharpe (U.K.)	M. Suleiman (Asia)
1994	**L. Christie (Gr.Brit.)**	**J. Regis (Gr.Brit.)**	**A. Pettigrew (U.S.)**	**M. Everett (U.S.)**	**N. Morceli (Africa)**

	5,000 metre	10,000 metre	Steeplechase	110-m hurdles	400-m hurdles
1989	S. Aouita (Africa)	S. Antibo (Europe)	J. Kariuki (Africa)	R. Kingdom (U.S.)	D. Patrick (U.S.)
1992	F. Bayesa (Africa)	A. Abebe (Africa)	P. Barkutwo (Africa)	C. Jackson (U.K.)	S. Matete (Africa)
1994	**B. Lahlafi (Africa)**	**K. Skah (Africa)**	**M. Kiptanui (Africa)**	**T. Jarrett (Gr.Brit.)**	**S. Matete (Africa)**

	4 × 100-m relays	4 × 400-m relays	Triple jump	High jump	Pole vault
1989	United States	Americas	M. Conley (U.S.)	P. Sjoberg (Europe)	P. Collet (Europe)
1992	United States	Africa	J. Edwards (U.K.)	Y. Sergeyenko (UT)	I. Potapovich (UT)
1994	**Great Britain**	**Great Britain**	**Y. Quesada (Amer.)**	**J. Sotomayor (Amer.)**	**O. Brits (Africa)**

	Long jump	Shot put	Discus throw	Hammer throw	Javelin throw
1989	L. Myricks (U.S.)	U. Timmermann (E.Ger.)	J. Schult (E.Ger.)	H. Weis (Europe)	S. Backley (Gr.Brit.)
1992	I. Pedroso (Amer.)	M. Stulce (U.S.)	T. Washington (U.S.)	T. Gécsek (Europe)	J. Zelezny (Europe)
1994	**F. Salle (Gr.Brit.)**	**C.J. Hunter (U.S.)**	**V. Dubrovshchik (Europe)**	**A. Abduvaliyev (Asia)**	**S. Backley (Gr.Brit.)**

	Team
1989	United States
1992	Africa
1994	**Africa**

IAAF World Cup—women

	100 metre	200 metre	400 metre
1989	S. Echols (U.S.)	S. Moller (E.Ger.)	A. Quirot (Amer.)
1992	N. Voronova (UT)	M.-J. Pérec (Europe)	J. Miles (U.S.)
1994	**I. Privalova (Europe)**	**M. Ottey (Amer.)**	**I. Privalova (Europe)**

	800 metre	1,500 metre	3,000 metre
1989	A. Quirot (Amer.)	P. Ivan (Europe)	Y. Murray (Europe)
1992	M. Mutola (Africa)	Y. Podkopayeva (UT)	D. Tulu (Africa)
1994	**M. Mutola (Africa)**	**H. Boulmerka (Africa)**	**Y. Murray (Gr.Brit.)**

	10,000 metre	100-m hurdles	400-m hurdles
1989	K. Ullrich (E.Ger.)	C. Oschkenat (E.Ger.)	S. Farmer-Patrick (U.S.)
1992	D. Tulu (Africa)	A. López (Amer.)	S. Farmer-Patrick (U.S.)
1994	**E. Meyer (Africa)**	**A. López (Amer.)**	**S. Gunnell (Gr.Brit.)**

	4 × 100-m relays	4 × 400-m relays	Triple Jump
1989	East Germany	Americas	
1992	Asia	Americas	
1994	**Africa**	**Great Britain**	**A. Biryukova (Europe)**

	High jump	Long jump	Shot put
1989	S. Costa (Amer.)	G. Chistyakova (U.S.S.R.)	Zhihong Huang (Asia)
1992	I. Quintero (Amer.)	H. Drechsler (Ger.)	B. Laza (Amer.)
1994	**B. Bilac (Europe)**	**I. Kravets (Europe)**	**Zhihong Huang (Asia)**

	Discus throw	Javelin throw	Team
1989	I. Wyludda (E.Ger.)	P. Felke (E.Ger.)	East Germany
1992	M. Marten (Amer.)	T. Sanderson (U.K.)	Unified Team
1994	**I. Wyludda (Europe)**	**T. Hattestad (Europe)**	**Europe**

World Marathon Cup

year	men	women
1985	A. Salah (Djib.)	K. Dörre (E.Ger.)
1987	A. Salah (Djib.)	Z. Ivanova (U.S.S.R.)
1989	K. Metaferia (Eth.)	S. Marchiano (U.S.)
1991	Y. Tolstikov (U.S.S.R.)	R. Mota (Port.)
1993	R. Nerurkar (U.K.)	Wang Junxia (China)

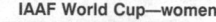

G. MORTIMORE—ALLSPORT

Maria Mutola: IAAF World Cup—women's 800-m (1994)

For records of previous years, *see* the entry SPORTING RECORD in the *Micropædia*.

World Track-and-Field Championships—men

event	1991	1993
100 m	C. Lewis (U.S.)	L. Christie (U.K.)
200 m	M. Johnson (U.S.)	F. Fredericks (Namib.)
400 m	A. Pettigrew (U.S.)	M. Johnson (U.S.)
800 m	B. Konchellah (Kenya)	P. Ruto (Kenya)
1,500 m	N. Morceli (Alg.)	N. Morceli (Alg.)
5,000 m	Y. Ondieki (Kenya)	I. Kirui (Kenya)
10,000 m	M. Tanui (Kenya)	H. Gebresilasie (Eth.)
steeplechase	M. Kiptanui (Kenya)	M. Kiptanui (Kenya)
110-m hurdles	G. Foster (U.S.)	C. Jackson (U.K.)
400-m hurdles	S. Matete (Zambia)	K. Young (U.S.)
marathon	H. Taniguchi (Japan)	M. Plaatjes (U.S.)
20-km walk	M. Damilano (Italy)	V. Massana (Spain)
50-km walk	A. Potashov (U.S.S.R.)	J.A. Garcia (Spain)
4 × 100-m relay	United States (A. Cason, L. Burrell, D. Mitchell, C. Lewis)	United States (J. Drummond, A. Cason, K. Mitchell, L. Burrell)
4 × 400-m relay	Great Britain (R. Black, D. Redmond, J. Regis, K. Akabusi)	United States (A. Valmon, Q. Watts, B. Reynolds, M. Johnson)
high jump	C. Austin (U.S.)	J. Sotomayor (Cuba)
pole vault	S. Bubka (U.S.S.R.)	S. Bubka (Ukr.)
long jump	M. Powell (U.S.)	M. Powell (U.S.)
triple jump	K. Harrison (U.S.)	M. Conley (U.S.)
shot put	W. Günthör (Switz.)	W. Günthör (Switz.)
discus throw	L. Riedel (Ger.)	L. Riedel (Ger.)
hammer throw	Y. Sedykh (U.S.S.R.)	A. Abduvaliyev (Tajik.)
javelin throw	K. Kinnunen (Fin.)	J. Zelezny (Cz.Rep.)
decathlon	D. O'Brien (U.S.)	D. O'Brien (U.S.)

World Track-and-Field Championships—women

event	1991	1993
100 m	K. Krabbe (Ger.)	G. Devers (U.S.)
200 m	K. Krabbe (Ger.)	M. Ottey (Jam.)
400 m	M.-J. Pérec (Fr.)	J. Miles (U.S.)
800 m	L. Nurutdinova (U.S.S.R.)	M. Mutola (Mozam.)
1,500 m	H. Boulmerka (Alg.)	Liu Dong (China)
3,000 m	T. Dorovskikh (U.S.S.R.)	Qu Yunxia (China)
10,000 m	L. McColgan (U.K.)	Wang Junxia (China)
100-m hurdles	L. Narozhilenko (U.S.S.R.)	G. Devers (U.S.)
400-m hurdles	T. Ledovskaya (U.S.S.R.)	S. Gunnell (U.K.)
marathon	W. Panfil (Pol.)	Asari Junko (Japan)
10-km walk	A. Ivanova (U.S.S.R.)	S. Essayeh (Fin.)
4 × 100-m relay	Jamaica (D. Duhaney, J. Cuthbert, B. McDonald, M. Ottey)	Russia (O. Bogoslovskaya, G. Malchugina, N. Voronova, I. Privalova)
4 × 400-m relay	U.S.S.R. (T. Ledovskaya, L. Dzhigalova, O. Nazarova, O. Bryzgina)	United States (G. Torrence, M. Malone, N. Kaiser-Brown, J. Miles)
high jump	H. Henkel (Ger.)	I. Quintero (Cuba)
long jump	J. Joyner-Kersee (U.S.)	H. Drechsler (Ger.)
shot put	Huang Zhihong (China)	Huang Zhihong (China)
discus throw	T. Khristova (Bulg.)	O. Burova (Russia)
javelin throw	Xu Demei (China)	T. Hattestad (Nor.)
heptathlon	S. Braun (Ger.)	J. Joyner-Kersee (U.S.)

Boston Marathon

year	men	h:min:s	women	h:min:s
1990	G. Bordin (Italy)	2:08:19	R. Mota (Port.)	2:25:23
1991	I. Hussein (Kenya)	2:11:06	W. Panfil (Pol.)	2:24:18
1992	I. Hussein (Kenya)	2:08:14	O. Markova (Russia)	2:23:43
1993	C. N'Deti (Kenya)	2:09:33	O. Markova (Russia)	2:25:27
1994	**C. N'Deti (Kenya)**	**2:07:15**	**U. Pippig (Ger.)**	**2:21:45**

New York City Marathon

year	men	h:min:s	women	h:min:s
1990	D. Wakiihuri (Kenya)	2:12:39	W. Panfil (Pol.)	2:30:45
1991	S. Garcia (Mex.)	2:09:28	L. McColgan (Scot.)	2:27:23
1992	W. Mtolo (S.Afr.)	2:09:29	L. Ondieki (Austl.)	2:24:40
1993	A. Espinosa (Mex.)	2:10:04	U. Pippig (Ger.)	2:26:24
1994	**G. Silva (Mex.)**	**2:11:21**	**T. Loroupe (Kenya)**	**2:27:37**

World Cross-Country Championship—men (12,000 m)

year	individual	team
1990	K. Shah (Mor.)	Kenya
1991	K. Shah (Mor.)	Kenya
1992	J. Ngugi (Kenya)	Kenya
1993	W. Sigei (Kenya)	Kenya
1994	**W. Sigei (Kenya)**	**Kenya**

World Cross-Country Championship—women (5,000 m)

year	individual	team
1990	L. Jennings (U.S.)	U.S.S.R.
1991	L. Jennings (U.S.)	Kenya
1992	L. Jennings (U.S.)	Kenya
1993	A. Dias (Port.)	Kenya
1994	**H. Chepngeno (Kenya)**	**Portugal**

AUTOMOBILE RACING

Indy Car Champions

year	driver
1989	E. Fittipaldi
1990	A. Unser, Jr.
1991	Mi. Andretti
1992	B. Rahal
1993	N. Mansell
1994	**A. Unser, Jr.**

Indianapolis 500

year	winner	avg. speed in mph
1990	A. Luyendyk	185.984
1991	R. Mears	176.457
1992	A. Unser, Jr.	134.479
1993	E. Fittipaldi	157.207
1994	**A. Unser, Jr.**	**160.872**

International Cup for Formula One Manufacturers

year	car	year	car
1989	McLaren/Honda	1992	Williams/Renault
1990	McLaren/Honda	1993	Williams/Renault
1991	McLaren/Honda	**1994**	**Williams/Renault**

Al Unser, Jr.: Indy Car Champion (1994)

World Championship of Drivers

year	winner	car
1990	A. Senna (Braz.)	McLaren/Honda
1991	A. Senna (Braz.)	McLaren/Honda
1992	N. Mansell (U.K.)	Williams/Renault
1993	A. Prost (Fr.)	Williams/Renault
1994	**M. Schumacher (Ger.)**	**Benetton/Ford**

Monte-Carlo Rally

year	car	driver, codriver
1990	Lancia	Auriol, Occelli
1991	Toyota Celica	Sainz, Moya
1992	Lancia Delta Integrale	Auriol, Occelli
1993	Toyota Celica	Auriol, Occelli
1994	**Ford Escort**	**Delecour, Grataloup**

Le Mans 24-hour Grand Prix d'Endurance

year	car	drivers
1990	Jaguar	J. Nielsen, P. Cobb, M. Brundle
1991	Mazda	V. Weidler, J. Herbert, B. Gachot
1992	Peugeot	Y. Dalmas, M. Blundell, D. Warwick
1993	Peugeot	G. Drabham, C. Bouchut, E. Helary
1994	**Dauer Porsche**	**Y. Dalmas, H. Haywood, M. Baldi**

National Association for Stock Car Auto Racing (NASCAR) Winston Cup Champions

year	winner	year	winner
1989	R. Wallace	1992	A. Kulwicki
1990	D. Earnhardt	1993	D. Earnhardt
1991	D. Earnhardt	**1994**	**D. Earnhardt**

BADMINTON

World Badminton Championships

year	men's singles	women's singles	men's doubles	women's doubles
1985	Han Jian (China)	Han Aiping (China)	Park Joo Bong, Kim Moon Soo (S.Kor.)	Han Aiping, Li Lingwei (China)
1987	Yang Yang (China)	Han Aiping (China)	Li Yongbo, Tian Bingyi (China)	Lin Ying, Guan Weizhen (China)
1989	Yang Yang (China)	Li Lingwei (China)	Li Yongbo, Tian Bingyi (China)	Lin Ying, Guan Weizhen (China)
1991	Zhao Jianhua (China)	Tang Jiuhong (China)	Park Joo Bong, Kim Moon Soo (S.Kor.)	Guan Weizhen, Nong Qunhua (China)
1993	J. Suprianto (Indon.)	S. Susanti (Indon.)	R. Subagja, R. Gunawan (Indon.)	Nong Qunhua, Zhou Lei (China)

All-England Championships—singles

year	men	women
1990	Zhao Jianhua (China)	S. Susanti (Indon.)
1991	A. Wiranata (Indon.)	S. Susanti (Indon.)
1992	Liu Jun (China)	Tang Jiuhong (China)
1993	H. Arbi (Indon.)	S. Susanti (Indon.)
1994	**H. Arbi (Indon.)**	**S. Susanti (Indon.)**

Uber Cup (women)

year	winner	runner-up
1985–86	China	Indonesia
1987–88	China	S.Korea
1989–90	China	S.Korea
1991–92	China	S.Korea
1993–94	**Indonesia**	**China**

Thomas Cup (men)

year	winner	runner-up
1985–86	China	Indonesia
1987–88	China	Malaysia
1989–90	China	Malaysia
1991–92	Malaysia	Indonesia
1993–94	**Indonesia**	**Malaysia**

BASEBALL

World Series*

year	winning team	losing team	results
1990	Cincinnati Reds (NL)	Oakland Athletics (AL)	4–0
1991	Minnesota Twins (AL)	Atlanta Braves (NL)	4–3
1992	Toronto Blue Jays (AL)	Atlanta Braves (NL)	4–2
1993	Toronto Blue Jays (AL)	Philadelphia Phillies (NL)	4–2
1994	**not held**		

*AL—American League; NL—National League.

Japan Series*

year	winning team	losing team	results
1990	Seibu Lions (PL)	Yomiuri Giants (CL)	4–0
1991	Seibu Lions (PL)	Hiroshima Tōyō Carp (CL)	4–3
1992	Seibu Lions (PL)	Yakult Swallows (CL)	4–3
1993	Yakult Swallows (CL)	Seibu Lions (PL)	4–3
1994	**Yomiuri Giants (CL)**	**Seibu Lions (PL)**	**4–2**

*CL—Central League; PL—Pacific League.

BASKETBALL

National Basketball Association (NBA) Championship

season	winner	runner-up	results
1989–90	Detroit Pistons	Portland Trail Blazers	4–1
1990–91	Chicago Bulls	Los Angeles Lakers	4–1
1991–92	Chicago Bulls	Portland Trail Blazers	4–2
1992–93	Chicago Bulls	Phoenix Suns	4–2
1993–94	**Houston Rockets**	**New York Knicks**	**4–3**

Division I National Collegiate Athletic Association (NCAA) Championship—men

year	winner	runner-up	score
1990	UNLV	Duke	103–73
1991	Duke	Kansas	72–65
1992	Duke	Michigan	71–51
1993	North Carolina	Michigan	77–71
1994	**Arkansas**	**Duke**	**76–72**

Division I National Collegiate Athletic Association (NCAA) Championship—women

year	winner	runner-up	score
1990	Stanford	Auburn	88–81
1991	Tennessee	Virginia	70–67
1992	Stanford	Western Kentucky	78–62
1993	Texas Tech	Ohio State	84–82
1994	**North Carolina**	**Louisiana Tech**	**60–59**

National Invitation Tournament (NIT) Championship

year	winner	runner-up	score
1990	Vanderbilt	St. Louis	74–72
1991	Stanford	Oklahoma	78–72
1992	Virginia	Notre Dame	81–76
1993	Minnesota	Georgetown	62–61
1994	**Villanova**	**Vanderbilt**	**80–73**

World Amateur Basketball Championship—men

year	winner	runner-up
1986	United States	U.S.S.R.
1988	U.S.S.R.	Yugoslavia
1990	Yugoslavia	U.S.S.R.
1992	United States	Croatia
1994	**United States**	**Russia**

World Amateur Basketball Championship—women

year	winner	runner-up
1986	United States	U.S.S.R.
1988	United States	Yugoslavia
1990	United States	Yugoslavia
1992	Unified Team	China
1994	**Brazil**	**China**

BILLIARDS

WPA World Nine-ball Championships

year	men's champion
1991	E. Strickland (U.S.)
1992	J. Archer (U.S.)
1993	Chao Feng-pang (Taiwan)
1994	**T. Okumura (Japan)**

year	women's champion
1991	R. Bell (U.S.)
1992	F. Stark (Ger.)
1993	L.J. Jones (U.S.)
1994	**E. Mataya-Laurance (U.S.)**

World Three-Cushion Championship

year	winner
1990	L. Dielis (Belg.)
1991	R. Ceulemans (Belg.)
1992	T. Blomdahl (Swed.)
1993	T. Blomdahl (Swed.)
1994	**Sang Lee (U.S.)**

World Professional Snooker Championships

year	winner
1990	S. Hendry
1991	J. Parrott
1992	S. Hendry
1993	S. Hendry
1994	**S. Hendry**

BOWLING

ABC Bowling Championships—Regular Division

year	singles	score	all-events	score
1990	R. Hochrein	791	M. Neumann	2,168
1991	E. Deines	826	T. Howery	2,216
1992	Blatchford, Youker (tie)	801	M. Tucker	2,158
1993	D. Bock	798	J. Nimke	2,254
1994	**J. Weltzien**	**810**	**T. Holt**	**2,190**

WIBC Bowling Championship—Open Division

year	singles	score	all-events	score
1990	Carter, Miller-Mackie (tie)	705	C. Norman	1,984
1991	D. Kuhn	773	D. Kuhn	2,036
1992	P. Ann	680	M. Tokimoto	1,928
1993	K. Collura, K. Murph (tie)	747	A.M. Duggan	1,990
1994	**V. Fifield**	**716**	**W. Macpherson-Papanos**	**1,940**

Professional Bowlers Association (PBA) Firestone Tournament of Champions

year	champion
1990	D. Ferraro
1991	D. Ozio
1992	M. McDowell
1993	G. Branham
1994	**N. Duke**

FIQ World Bowling Championship—men

year	singles	pairs	triples	fives
1979	G. Bugden (U.K.)	Australia	Malaysia	Australia
1983	T. Cariello (U.S.)	Australia	Sweden	Finland
1987	P. Rolland (Fr.)	Sweden	United States	Sweden
1991	Ying Chieh Ma (Taiwan)	United States	United States	Taiwan

FIQ World Bowling Championship—women

year	singles	pairs	triples	fives
1979	L. de la Rosa (Phil.)	Philippines	United States	United States
1983	L. Sulkanen (Swed.)	Denmark	West Germany	Sweden
1987	F. Piccini (Mex.)	United States	United States	United States
1991	M. Beckel (Ger.)	Japan	Canada	South Korea

BOWLS

World Lawn Bowls Championships

year	singles	pairs	triples	fours	team
1984	P. Bellis (N.Z.)	United States	Ireland	England	Scotland
1988	D. Bryant (Eng.)	New Zealand	New Zealand	Ireland	England
1992	T. Allcock (Eng.)	Scotland	Israel	Scotland	Scotland

BOXING

World heavyweight champions —no weight limit

WBA
Evander Holyfield (U.S.; 10/26/90)
Riddick Bowe (U.S.; 11/13/92)
Evander Holyfield (U.S.; 11/6/93)
Michael Moorer (U.S.; 4/22/94)
George Foreman (U.S.; 11/5/94)

WBC
Evander Holyfield (U.S.; 10/26/90)
Riddick Bowe (U.S.; 11/13/92)
 stripped of title in 1992
Lennox Lewis (U.K.; 12/14/92)
Oliver McCall (U.S.; 9/24/94)

IBF
Evander Holyfield (U.S.; 10/25/90)
Riddick Bowe (U.S.; 11/13/92)
Evander Holyfield (U.S.; 11/6/93)
Michael Moorer (U.S.; 4/22/94)
George Foreman (U.S.; 11/5/94)

World cruiserweight champions —top weight 195 pounds

WBA
Taoufik Belbouli (Fr.; 3/25/89)
 declared vacant in 1989
Robert Daniels (U.S.; 11/28/89)
Bobby Czyz (U.S.; 3/8/91)
 vacant
Orlin Norris (U.S.; 11/6/93)

WBC
Evander Holyfield (U.S.; 4/9/88)
 gave up title in 1988
Carlos de Léon (P.R.; 5/17/89)
Massimiliano Duran (Italy; 7/27/90)
Anaclet Wamba (Fr.; 7/20/91)

IBF
Glenn McCrory (U.K.; 6/3/89)
Jeff Lampkin (U.S.; 3/22/90)
 gave up title in 1991
James Warring (U.S.; 9/7/91)
Alfred Cole (U.S.; 7/30/92)

World light heavyweight champions —top weight 175 pounds

WBA
Virgil Hill (U.S.; 9/5/87)
Thomas Hearns (U.S.; 6/3/91)
Iran Barkley (U.S.; 3/21/92)
 gave up title in 1992
Virgil Hill (U.S.; 9/92)

WBC
Dennis Andries (U.K; 2/2/89)
Jeff Harding (Australia; 6/24/89)
Dennis Andries (U.K.; 7/28/90)
Jeff Harding (Australia; 9/11/91)
Mike McCallum (Jam.; 7/23/94)

IBF
Slobodan Kacar (Yugos.; 12/21/85)
Bobby Czyz (U.S.; 9/6/86)
Charles Williams (U.S.; 10/29/87)
Henry Maske (Ger.; 3/20/93)

World super middleweight champions —top weight 168 pounds

WBA
Baek In-chul (S.Kor.; 5/27/89)
Christophe Tiozzo (Fr.; 3/30/90)
Victor Cordoba (Pan.; 4/5/91)
Michael Nunn (U.S.; 9/12/92)
Steve Little (U.S.; 2/26/94)
Frank Liles (U.S.; 8/12/94)

WBC
Sugar Ray Leonard (U.S.; 11/7/88)
 gave up title in 1990
Mauro Galvano (Italy; 12/15/90)
Nigel Benn (U.K.; 10/3/92)

IBF
Lindell Holmes (U.S.; 1/27/90)
Darrin Van Horn (U.S.; 5/18/91)
Iran Barkley (U.S.; 1/10/92)
James Toney (U.S.; 2/13/93)
Roy Jones (U.S.; 11/18/94)

World middleweight champions —top weight 160 pounds

WBA
Mike McCallum (Jam.; 5/13/89)
 stripped of title in 1991
Reggie Johnson (U.S.; 4/22/92)
John David Jackson (U.S.; 10/2/93)
 stripped of title in 1994
Jorge Castro (Arg.; 8/12/94)

WBC
Iran Barkley (U.S.; 6/6/88)
Roberto Duran (Pan.; 2/24/89)
 stripped of title in 1990
Julian Jackson (U.S.; 11/24/90)
Gerald McClellan (U.S.; 5/8/93)

IBF
Michael Nunn (U.S.; 7/28/88)
James Toney (U.S.; 5/10/91)
 gave up title in 1993
Roy Jones (U.S.; 5/22/93)
 gave up title in 1994

World junior middleweight champions —top weight 154 pounds (also called super welterweight)

WBA
Gilbert Dele (Fr.; 2/23/91)
Vinny Pazienza (U.S.; 10/11/91)
 gave up title in 1992
Julio César Vásquez (Arg.; 12/22/92)

WBC
René Jacquot (Fr.; 2/11/89)
John Mugabi (Uganda; 7/8/89)
Terry Norris (U.S.; 3/31/90)
Simon Brown (U.S.; 12/18/93)
Terry Norris (U.S.; 5/7/94)
Luis Santana (Dom.Rep.; 11/12/94)

IBF
Matthew Hilton (Can.; 6/27/87)
Robert Hines (U.S.; 11/4/88)
Darrin Van Horn (U.S.; 2/4/89)
Gianfranco Rosi (Italy; 7/16/89)
Vincent Pettway (U.S.; 9/17/94)

Houston Rockets (Hakeem Olajuwon): NBA Championship (1994)

World welterweight champions —top weight 147 pounds

WBA
Mark Breland (U.S.; 2/4/89)
Aaron Davis (U.S.; 7/8/90)
Meldrick Taylor (U.S.; 1/19/91)
Crisanto España (Venez.; 10/31/92)
Ike Quartey (Ghana; 6/4/94)

WBC
Marlon Starling (U.S.; 2/4/89)
Maurice Blocker (U.S.; 8/19/90)
Simon Brown (Jam.; 3/18/91)
James McGirt (U.S.; 11/29/91)
Pernell Whitaker (U.S.; 3/6/93)

IBF
Simon Brown (Jam.; 4/23/88)
 gave up title in 1991
Maurice Blocker (U.S.; 10/4/91)
Felix Trinidad (P.R.; 6/19/93)

World junior welterweight champions —top weight 140 pounds (also called super lightweight)

WBA
Edwin Rosario (P.R.; 6/15/91)
Akinobu Hiranaka (Japan; 4/10/92)
Morris East (Phil.; 9/9/92)
Juan Martin Coggi (Arg.; 1/12/93)
Frankie Randall (U.S.; 9/17/94)

WBC
René Arrendondo (Mex.; 7/22/87)
Roger Mayweather (U.S.; 11/12/87)
Julio César Chávez (Mex.; 5/13/89)
Frankie Randall (U.S.; 1/29/94)
Julio César Chávez (Mex.; 5/7/94)

IBF
Rafael Pineda (Colom.; 12/7/91)
Pernell Whitaker (U.S.; 7/18/92)
 gave up title in 1993
Charles Murray (U.S.; 5/15/93)
Jake Rodriguez (P.R.; 2/13/94)

World lightweight champions —top weight 135 pounds

WBA
Pernell Whitaker (U.S.; 8/11/90)
 gave up title in 1992
Joey Gamache (U.S.; 6/13/92)
Tony Lopez (U.S.; 10/24/92)
Dingaan Thobela (S.Af.; 6/26/93)
Olzubek Nazarov (Russia; 10/30/93)

WBC
Julio César Chávez (Mex.; 10/29/88)
 gave up title in 1989
Pernell Whitaker (U.S.; 8/20/89)
 gave up title in 1992
Miguel González (Mex.; 8/24/92)

IBF
Greg Haugen (U.S.; 2/6/88)
Pernell Whitaker (U.S.; 2/20/89)
 gave up title in 1992
Fred Pendleton (U.S.; 1/10/93)
Rafael Ruelas (U.S.; 2/19/94)

World junior lightweight champions —top weight 130 pounds (also called super featherweight)

WBA
Brian Mitchell (S.Af.; 9/27/86)
 gave up title in 1991
Joey Gamache (U.S.; 6/28/91)
 gave up title in 1991
Genaro Hernandez (U.S.; 11/22/91)

WBC
Julio César Chávez (Mex.; 9/13/84)
 gave up title
Azumah Nelson (Ghana; 2/29/88)
Jesse James Leija (U.S.; 5/7/94)
Gabriel Ruelas (U.S.; 9/17/94)

IBF
Tony Lopez (U.S.; 5/20/90)
Brian Mitchell (S.Af.; 9/13/91)
 gave up title in 1992
Juan Molina (P.R.; 2/22/92)
vacant

World featherweight champions —top weight 126 pounds

WBA
Barry McGuigan (N.Ire.; 6/8/85)
Steve Cruz (U.S.; 6/23/86)
Antonio Esparragoza (Venez.; 3/6/87)
Park Yung Kyun (S.Kor.; 3/30/91)
Eloy Rojas (Venez.; 12/4/93)

WBC
Jeff Fenech (Australia; 3/7/88)
 gave up title in 1990
Marcos Villasana (Mex.; 6/2/90)
Paul Hodkinson (U.K.; 11/13/91)
Gregorio Vargas (Mex.; 4/28/93)
Kevin Kelley (U.S.; 12/4/93)

IBF
Jorge Paez (Mex.; 8/4/88)
 gave up title in 1991
Troy Dorsey (U.S.; 6/3/91)
Manuel Medina (Mex.; 8/12/91)
Tom Johnson (U.S.; 2/26/93)

Julio César Chávez (right): WBC junior welterweight champion (1994)

**World junior featherweight champions
—top weight 122 pounds
(also called super bantamweight)**

WBA
Jesus Salud (U.S.; 12/11/89)
 stripped of title in 1990
Luís Mendoza (Colom.; 9/11/90)
Raul Pérez (Mex.; 10/7/91)
Wilfredo Vásquez (P.R.; 3/27/92)

WBC
Kiyoshi Hatanaka (Japan; 2/3/91)
Daniel Zaragoza (Mex.; 6/14/91)
Thierry Jacob (Fr.; 3/20/92)
Tracy Patterson (U.S.; 6/23/92)
Hector Acero-Sánchez (U.S.; 8/26/94)

IBF
José Sanabria (Venez.; 5/21/88)
Fabrice Benichou (Fr.; 3/10/89)
Welcome Ncita (S.Af.; 3/10/90)
Kennedy McKinney (U.S.; 12/2/92)
Vuyani Bungu (S.Af.; 8/20/94)

**World flyweight champions
—top weight 112 pounds**

WBA
Leopard Tamakuma (Japan; 7/29/90)
Elvis Alvarez (Colom.; 3/14/91)
Kim Yong Kang (S.Kor.; 6/1/91)
Aquiles Guzmán (Venez.; 9/26/92)
David Griman (Venez.; 12/92)
San Sow Ploenchit (Thai.; 2/13/94)

WBC
Kim Young Kang (S.Kor.; 7/24/88)
Sot Chitalada (Thai.; 6/3/89)
Muangchai Kittlkasem (Thai.; 2/15/91)
Yury Arbachakov (Russia; 6/23/92)

IBF
Rolando Bohol (Phil.; 1/16/88)
Duke McKenzie (U.K.; 10/5/88)
Dave McAuley (U.K.; 6/7/89)
Rodolfo Blanco (Colom.; 6/11/92)
Phichit Sithbangprachan (Thai.; 11/29/92)

**World bantamweight champions
—top weight 118 pounds**

WBA
Israel Contreras (Venez.; 10/19/91)
Eddie Cook (U.S.; 3/15/92)
Ellecer Julio (Colom.; 10/10/92)
Junior Jones (U.S.; 10/23/93)
John Michael Johnson (U.S.; 4/22/94)
Daorung Chuvatana (Thai.; 7/16/94)

WBC
Joichiro Tatsuyoshi (Japan; 9/19/91)
 vacant
Victor Rabañales (Mex.; 3/30/92)
Byun Jong-Il (S.Kor.; 3/28/93)
Yasuei Yakushiji (Japan; 12/22/93)

IBF
Jeff Fenech (Austl.; 4/26/85)
 vacant
Kelvin Seabrooks (U.S.; 5/16/87)
Orlando Canizales (U.S.; 7/9/88)
gave up title in 1994

**World junior flyweight champions
—top weight 108 pounds**

WBA
Yuh Myung Woo (S.Kor.; 12/8/85)
Hiroki Ioka (Japan; 12/17/91)
Yuh Myung Woo (S.Kor.; 11/18/92)
 gave up title in 1993
Leo Gamez (Venez.; 10/21/93)

WBC
Humberto González (Mex.; 6/25/89)
Rolando Pascua (Phil.; 12/19/90)
Melchor Cob Castro (Mex.; 3/25/91)
Humberto González (Mex.; 6/4/91)
Michael Carbajal (U.S.; 3/13/93)
Chiquita Gonzalez (Mex.; 2/19/94)

IBF
Choi Chong Hwon (S.Kor.; 12/7/86)
Tacy Macalos (Phil.; 11/6/88)
Muangchai Kittikasem (Thai.; 5/2/89)
Michael Carbajal (U.S.; 7/29/90)
Chiquita Gonzalez (Mex.; 2/19/94)

**World junior bantamweight champions
—top weight 115 pounds
(also called super flyweight)**

WBA
Khaosai Galaxy (Thai.; 11/21/84)
 gave up title in 1991
Katsuya Onizuka (Japan; 4/10/92)
Lee Hyung Chul (S.Kor.; 9/18/94)

WBC
Jesús Rojas (Colom.; 8/9/87)
Gilberto Román (Mex.; 4/8/88)
Nana Konadu (Ghana; 11/7/89)
Moon Sung Kil (S.Kor.; 1/20/90)
José Luis Bueno (Mex.; 11/13/93)
Hiroshi Kawashima (Japan; 5/4/94)

IBF
Ellyas Pical (Indon.; 10/17/87)
Juan Polo Pérez (Colom.; 10/14/89)
Robert Quiroga (U.S.; 4/21/90)
Julio Borboa (Mex.; 1/16/93)
Harold Grey (Colom.; 8/29/94)

**World mini-flyweight champions
—top weight 105 pounds
(also called strawweight)**

WBA
Kim Bong Jun (S.Kor.; 4/16/89)
Choi Hi Yong (S.Kor.; 2/2/91)
Ohashi Hideyuki (Japan; 10/14/92)
Chana Porpaoin (Thai.; 2/10/93)

WBC
Napa Kiatwanchai (Thai.; 11/13/88)
Choi Jum Hwan (S.Kor.; 11/12/89)
Ohashi Hideyuki (Japan; 2/7/90)
Ricardo López (Mex.; 10/25/90)

IBF
Nico Thomas (Indon.; 6/17/89)
Eric Chavez (Phil.; 9/21/89)
Falan Lookmingkwan (Thai.; 2/21/90)
Manny Melchor (Phil.; 9/6/92)
Ratanapol Vorapin (Thai.; 12/10/92)

CHESS

World Chess Championships—men

year	winner	runner-up
1986	G. Kasparov (U.S.S.R.)	A. Karpov (U.S.S.R.)
1987	G. Kasparov (U.S.S.R.)	A. Karpov (U.S.S.R.)
1990	G. Kasparov (U.S.S.R.)	A. Karpov (U.S.S.R.)
1993	A. Karpov (Russia)	J. Timman (Neth.)

World Chess Championships—women

year	winner	runner-up
1986	M. Chiburdanidze (U.S.S.R.)	E. Akhmilovskaya (U.S.S.R.)
1988	M. Chiburdanidze (U.S.S.R.)	N. Ioseliani (U.S.S.R.)
1991	Xie Jun (China)	M. Chiburdanidze (U.S.S.R.)
1993	Xie Jun (China)	N. Ioseliani (Georgia)

Olympiads—men

year	winner	runner-up
1988	U.S.S.R.	United Kingdom
1989	U.S.S.R.	Yugoslavia
1992	Russia	Uzbekistan
1994	**Russia**	**Bosnia**

Olympiads—women

year	winner	runner-up
1986	U.S.S.R.	Hungary
1988	Hungary	U.S.S.R.
1992	Georgia	Ukraine
1994	**Georgia**	**Hungary**

CONTRACT BRIDGE

Bermuda Bowl

year	winner	runner-up
1987	United States	United Kingdom
1989	Brazil	United States
1991	Iceland	Poland
1993	Netherlands	Norway

World Contract Bridge Pair Championship

year	open winners	women's winners	mixed winners
1990	Marcelo Branco, Gabriel Chagas (Braz.)	Kerri Shuman, Karen McCallum (U.S.)	Peter Weichsel, Juanita Chambers (U.S.)
1994	**Marcin Lesniewski, Marek Szymanowski (Pol.)**	**Carla Arnolds, Bep Vriend (Neth.)**	**Danuta Hocheker, Apolinare Kowalski (Pol.)**

World Team Olympiad

year	open winner	open runner-up	women's winner	women's runner-up
1988	United States	Austria	Denmark	United Kingdom
1992	France	United States	Austria	United Kingdom

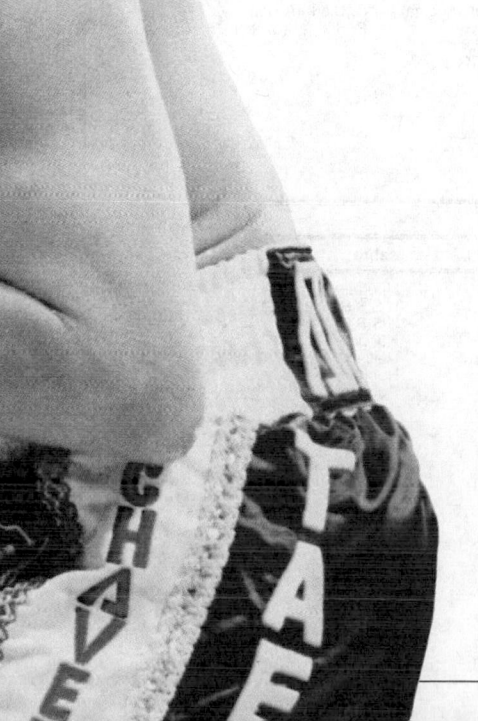

CRICKET

All-time First-class Test Cricket Standings (as of Sept. 30, 1994)

	England wins draws losses			Australia w d l			South Africa w d l			West Indies w d l			New Zealand w d l		
England v.	—	—	—	89	80	105	47	39	19	25	38	46	34	37	4
Australia v.	105	80	89	—	—	—	31	15	13	30	21*	26	13	11	7
South Africa v.	19	39	47	13	15	31	—	—	—	0	0	1	19	6	2
West Indies v.	46	38	25	26	21*	30	1	0	0	—	—	—	8	12	4
New Zealand v.	4	37	34	7	11	13	2	6	19	4	12	8	—	—	—
India v.	14	36	30	8	18*	24	0	3	1	6	30	26	12	14	6
Pakistan v.	7	31	14	9	13	12	†			7	12	12	16	16	4
Sri Lanka v.	1	1	3	0	3	4	0	2	1	0	1	0	1	6	1
Zimbabwe v.	†			†			†			†			0	1	1

	India w d l			Pakistan w d l			Sri Lanka w d l			Zimbabwe w d l		
England v.	30	36	14	14	31	7	3	1	1	†		
Australia v.	24	18*	8	12	13	9	4	3	0	†		
South Africa v.	1	3	0	†			1	2	0	†		
West Indies v.	26	30	6	12	12	7	0	1	0	†		
New Zealand v.	6	14	12	4	16	16	4	6	1	1	1	0
India v.	—	—	—	4	33	7	8	4	1	1	1	0
Pakistan v.	7	33	4	—	—	—	8	5	1	2	1	0
Sri Lanka v.	1	4	8	1	5	8	—	—	—	†		
Zimbabwe v.	0	1	1	0	1	2	†			—	—	—

*Including one tie. †No matches.

World Cup

year	result			
1975	West Indies	291–8	Australia	274
1979	West Indies	286–9	England	194
1983	India	183	West Indies	140
1987	Australia	253–5	England	246–8
1992	Pakistan	249–6	England	227

CYCLING

Tour de France

year	winner	km
1990	G. LeMond (U.S.)	3,399
1991	M. Indurain (Spain)	3,935
1992	M. Indurain (Spain)	3,983
1993	M. Indurain (Spain)	3,700
1994	**M. Indurain (Spain)**	**3,978**

Cycling World Track Championships—women (amateur)

year	sprint	3-km pursuit
1990	C. Young (U.S.)	J. Longo (Fr.)
1991	I. Haringa (Neth.)	P. Rossner (Ger.)
1992	E. Salumae (Est.)	P. Rossner (Ger.)
1993	T. Dubnicoff (Can.)	R. Twigg (U.S.)
1994	**G. Yenyukhina (Russia)**	**M. Clignet (Fr.)**

Cycling World Road-Racing Championships

year	men (amateur)	men (professional)	women (amateur)
1990	M. Gualdi (Italy)	R. Dhaenens (Belg.)	C. Marsal (Fr.)
1991	V. Pjaksinski (U.S.S.R.)	G. Bugno (Italy)	L. van Moorsel (Neth.)
1992	F. Casartelli (Italy)	G. Bugno (Italy)	K. Watt (Austl.)
1993	J. Ullrich (Ger.)	L. Armstrong (U.S.)	L. van Moorsel (Neth.)
1994	**A. Pedersen (Den.)**	**L. Leblanc (Fr.)**	**M. Valvik (Nor.)**

Cycling World Track Championships—men

year	sprint (amateur)	sprint (professional)	pursuit (amateur)	pursuit (professional)	motor-paced (amateur)	motor-paced (professional)
1991	J. Fiedler (Ger.)	not awarded	J. Lehmann (Ger.)	F. Moreau (Fr.)	R. Königshofer (Austria)	D. Clark (Austl.)
1992	not held	M. Hübner (Ger.)	not held	M. McCarthy (U.S.)	C. Podlesch (Ger.)	P. Steiger (Switz.)
1993*	G. Niewand (Austl.)		G. Obree (U.K.)		J. Veggerby (Den.)	
1994	**M. Nothstein (U.S.)**		**C. Boardman (U.K.)**		**C. Podlesch (Ger.)**	

*From 1993 professionals and amateurs competed in the same event.

FENCING

World Fencing Championships—men

year	individual			team		
	foil	épée	sabre	foil	épée	sabre
1988	S. Cerioni (Italy)	A. Schmitt (W.Ger.)	J.-F. Lamour (Fr.)	U.S.S.R.	France	Hungary
1989	A. Koch (W.Ger.)	M. Pereira (Spain)	G. Kirienko (U.S.S.R.)	U.S.S.R.	Italy	U.S.S.R.
1990	P. Omnès (Fr.)	T. Gerull (W.Ger.)	G. Nebald (Hung.)	Italy	Italy	U.S.S.R.
1991	I. Weissenborn (Ger.)	A. Shuvalov (U.S.S.R.)	G. Kirienko (U.S.S.R.)	Cuba	U.S.S.R.	Hungary
1992	P. Omnès (Fr.)	E. Srecki (Fr.)	B. Szabo (Hung.)	Germany	Germany	Unified Team
1993	A. Koch (Ger.)	P. Kolobkov (Russia)	G. Kirienko (Russia)	Germany	Italy	Hungary
1994	**R. Tucker (Cuba)**	**P. Kolobkov (Russia)**	**F. Becker (Ger.)**	**Germany**	**France**	**Russia**

World Fencing Championships—women

year	individual foil	team foil	individual épée	team épée
1989	O. Velitchko (U.S.S.R.)	West Germany	A. Straub (Switz.)	Hungary
1990	A. Fichtel (W.Ger.)	Italy	T. Chappe (Cuba)	West Germany
1991	G. Trillini (Italy)	Italy	M. Horvath (Hung.)	Hungary
1992	G. Trillini (Italy)	Italy	M. Horvath (Hung.)	Hungary
1993	F. Bortolozzi (Italy)	Germany	O. Jermakova (Est.)	Hungary
1994	**B. Szabo (Rom.)**	**Romania**	**L. Chiesa (Italy)**	**Spain**

CURLING

World Curling Championship—men

year	winner	runner-up
1990	Canada	Scotland
1991	Scotland	Canada
1992	Switzerland	Scotland
1993	Canada	Scotland
1994	**Canada**	**Sweden**

World Curling Championship—women

year	winner	runner-up
1990	Norway	Scotland
1991	Norway	Canada
1992	Sweden	United States
1993	Canada	Germany
1994	**Canada**	**Scotland**

FIELD HOCKEY

World Cup Field Hockey Championships—men

year	winner	runner-up
1986	Australia	England
1990	The Netherlands	Pakistan
1994	**Pakistan**	**The Netherlands**

World Cup Field Hockey Championships—women

year	winner	runner-up
1986	The Netherlands	West Germany
1990	The Netherlands	Australia
1994	**Australia**	**Argentina**

FOOTBALL

FIFA World Cup

year	result			
1986	Argentina	3	West Germany	2
1990	West Germany	1	Argentina	0
1994	**Brazil***	**0**	**Italy**	**0**

*Won on penalty kicks.

European Cup-Winners' Cup

season	result			
1989–90	Sampdoria (Italy)	2	Anderlecht (Belg.)	0
1990–91	Manchester United (Eng.)	2	Barcelona	1
1991–92	Werder Bremen (Ger.)	2	AS Monaco	0
1992–93	Parma (Italy)	3	Royal Antwerp	1
1993–94	**Arsenal (Eng.)**	**1**	**Parma (Italy)**	**0**

Libertadores de América Cup

year	winner (country)	runner-up (country)	scores
1990	Olímpia (Paraguay)	Barcelona (Ecuador)	2–0, 1–1
1991	Colo Colo (Chile)	Olímpia (Paraguay)	0–0, 3–0
1992	São Paulo (Braz.)	Newell's Old Boys (Arg.)	0–1, 1–0, 3–2*
1993	São Paulo (Braz.)	Universidad Catolica (Chile)	5–1, 0–2
1994	**Velez Sarsfield (Arg.)**	**São Paulo (Braz.)**	**1–0, 0–1, 5–3***

*Winner determined in penalty shootout after tiebreaking game.

The European Cup of Champion Clubs

season	result			
1989–90	AC Milan	1	Benfica (Port.)	0
1990–91	Red Star Belgrade*	0	Marseille	0
1991–92	Barcelona	1	Sampdoria (Italy)	0
1992–93	Olympique Marseille	1	AC Milan	0
1993–94	**AC Milan**	**4**	**Barcelona**	**0**

*Won on penalty kicks.

U.S. Football—professional

Super Bowl

	season	result			
XXIV	1989–90	San Francisco 49ers (NFC)	55	Denver Broncos (AFC)	10
XXV	1990–91	New York Giants (NFC)	20	Buffalo Bills (AFC)	19
XXVI	1991–92	Washington Redskins (NFC)	37	Buffalo Bills (AFC)	24
XXVII	1992–93	Dallas Cowboys (NFC)	52	Buffalo Bills (AFC)	17
XXVIII	**1993–94**	**Dallas Cowboys (NFC)**	**30**	**Buffalo Bills (AFC)**	**13**

Dallas Cowboys (Michael Irvin, with the ball): Super Bowl (1994)

JONATHAN DANIEL—ALLSPORT

U.S. Football—college

Rose Bowl

season	result			
1989–90	Southern California	17	Michigan	10
1990–91	Washington	46	Iowa	34
1991–92	Washington	34	Michigan	14
1992–93	Michigan	38	Washington	31
1993–94	Wisconsin	21	UCLA	16
1994–95	**Penn State**	**38**	**Oregon**	**20**

Sugar Bowl

season	result			
1989–90	Miami (Fla.)	33	Alabama	25
1990–91	Tennessee	23	Virginia	22
1991–92	Notre Dame	39	Florida	28
1992–93	Alabama	34	Miami (Fla.)	13
1993–94	Florida	41	West Virginia	7
1994–95	**Florida State**	**23**	**Florida**	**17**

Orange Bowl

season	result			
1989–90	Notre Dame	21	Colorado	6
1990–91	Colorado	10	Notre Dame	9
1991–92	Miami (Fla.)	22	Nebraska	0
1992–93	Florida St.	27	Nebraska	14
1993–94	Florida St.	18	Nebraska	16
1994–95	**Nebraska**	**24**	**Miami**	**17**

Cotton Bowl

season	result			
1989–90	Tennessee	31	Arkansas	27
1990–91	Miami (Fla.)	46	Texas	3
1991–92	Florida State	10	Texas A&M	2
1992–93	Notre Dame	28	Texas A&M	3
1993–94	Notre Dame	24	Texas A&M	21
1994–95	**Southern California**	**55**	**Texas Tech**	**14**

U.S. College Football National Champion

season	champion
1989–90	Miami (Fla.)
1990–91	Colorado*
	Georgia Tech*
1991–92	Miami (Fla.)*
	Washington*
1992–93	Alabama
1993–94	Florida St.
1994–95	**Nebraska**

*Tied.

Canadian football—professional

Grey Cup

year	result			
1989	Saskatchewan Roughriders (WFC)	43	Hamilton Tiger-Cats (EFC)	40
1990	Winnipeg Blue Bombers (EFC)	50	Edmonton Eskimos (WFC)	11
1991	Toronto Argonauts (EFC)	36	Calgary Stampeders (WFC)	21
1992	Calgary Stampeders (WFC)	24	Winnipeg Blue Bombers (EFC)	10
1993	Edmonton Eskimos (WFC)	33	Winnipeg Blue Bombers (EFC)	23
1994	**British Columbia Lions (WFC)**	**26**	**Baltimore (EFC)**	**23**

Rugby Union football

Record of International Test matches 1871 to Aug. 31, 1994

	England wins	draws	losses	Scotland wins	draws	losses	Ireland wins	draws	losses	Wales wins	draws	losses	British Isles wins	draws	losses
England *v.*				55	17	39	61	8	38	40	12	48	—	—	—
Scotland *v.*	39	17	55				55	5	45	42	2	54	—	—	—
Ireland *v.*	38	8	61	45	5	55				33	6	58	—	—	—
Wales *v.*	48	12	40	54	2	42	58	6	33				—	—	—
British Isles* *v.*															
South Africa *v.*	7	1	4	5	0	3	8	1	1	6	1	0	20	6	14
New Zealand *v.*	13	0	4	15	2	0	11	1	0	12	0	3	24	3	5
Australia *v.*	12	0	6	7	0	7	10	0	6	8	0	8	3	0	14
France *v.*	24	7	39	32	3	30	37	5	25	28	3	37			

	South Africa wins	draws	losses	New Zealand wins	draws	losses	Australia wins	draws	losses	France wins	draws	losses
England *v.*	4	1	7	4	0	13	6	0	12	39	7	24
Scotland *v.*	3	0	5	0	2	15	7	0	7	30	3	32
Ireland *v.*	1	1	8	0	1	11	6	0	10	25	5	37
Wales *v.*	0	1	6	3	0	12	8	0	8	37	3	28
British Isles* *v.*	14	6	20	5	3	24	14	0	3			
South Africa *v.*				20	3	18	22	0	10	13	5	5
New Zealand *v.*	18	3	20				66	5	27	23	0	7
Australia *v.*	10	0	22	27	5	66				10	2	13
France *v.*	5	5	13	7	0	23	13	2	10			

*The British Isles ("British Lions") is a combined team from the four "Home Unions" (England, Ireland, Scotland, and Wales).

Five Nations Championship

year	result
1990	Scotland*
1991	England*
1992	England*
1993	France
1994	**Wales**

*Grand Slam winner.

World Cup

year	result			
1987	New Zealand	29	France	9
1991	Australia	12	England	6

Rugby League football

World Cup

year	result			
1972	Great Britain	10*	Australia	10
1975†	Australia‡			
1977†	Australia	13	Great Britain	12
1988	Australia	25	New Zealand	12
1992	Australia	10	Great Britain	6

*Great Britain won on match points. †Called International Championship from 1975 to 1977. ‡Championships played without a grand final match; England was the runner-up.

GOLF

British Open Tournament—men

year	winner
1990	N. Faldo (U.K.)
1991	I. Baker-Finch (Austl.)
1992	N. Faldo (U.K.)
1993	G. Norman (Austl.)
1994	**N. Price (Zimb.)**

United States Open Championship—men

year	winner
1990	H. Irwin (U.S.)
1991	P. Stewart (U.S.)
1992	T. Kite (U.S.)
1993	L. Janzen (U.S.)
1994	**E. Els (S.Af.)**

Masters Tournament

year	winner
1990	N. Faldo (U.K.)
1991	I. Woosnam (U.K.)
1992	F. Couples (U.S.)
1993	B. Langer (Ger.)
1994	**J. Olazábal (Spain)**

U.S. Professional Golfers' Association (PGA) championship	
year	winner
1990	W. Grady (Austl.)
1991	J. Daly (U.S.)
1992	N. Price (Zimb.)
1993	P. Azinger (U.S.)
1994	**N. Price (Zimb.)**

British Amateur Championship—men	
year	winner
1990	R. Muntz (Neth.)
1991	R. Willison (U.K.)
1992	S. Dundas (U.K.)
1993	I. Pyman (U.K.)
1994	**L. James (U.K.)**

United States Amateur Championship—men	
year	winner
1990	P. Mickelson (U.S.)
1991	M. Voges (U.S.)
1992	J. Leonard (U.S.)
1993	J. Harris (U.S.)
1994	**T. Woods (U.S.)**

Women's British Open Championship	
year	winner
1990	H. Alfredsson (Swed.)
1991	P. Grice-Whittaker (U.K.)
1992	P. Sheehan (U.S.)
1993	K. Lunn (Austl.)
1994	**L. Neumann (Swed.)**

Ladies' British Amateur Championship	
year	winner
1990	J. Hall (U.K.)
1991	J. Morley (U.K.)
1992	P. Pedersen (Den.)
1993	C. Lambert (U.K.)
1994	**E. Duggleby (U.K.)**

United States Women's Open champions	
year	winner
1990	B. King (U.S.)
1991	M. Mallon (U.S.)
1992	P. Sheehan (U.S.)
1993	L. Merten (U.S.)
1994	**P. Sheehan (U.S.)**

United States Women's Amateur Championship	
year	winner
1990	P. Hurst (U.S.)
1991	A. Fruhwirth (U.S.)
1992	V. Goetze (U.S.)
1993	J. McGill (U.S.)
1994	**W. Ward (U.S.)**

Ladies' Professional Golf Association (LPGA) champions	
year	winner
1990	B. Daniel (U.S.)
1991	M. Mallon (U.S.)
1992	B. King (U.S.)
1993	P. Sheehan (U.S.)
1994	**L. Davies (U.K.)**

Team events

Walker Cup—men (amateur)	
year	result
1985	United States 13, Britain and Ireland 11
1987	United States 16½, Britain and Ireland 7½
1989	Britain and Ireland 12½, United States 11½
1991	United States 14, Britain and Ireland 10
1993	United States 19, Britain and Ireland 5

World Cup—men (professional)	
year	winner
1990	Germany (B. Langer and T. Giedeon)
1991	Sweden (A. Forsbrand and P.-U. Johansson)
1992	United States (F. Couples and D. Love III)
1993	United States (F. Couples and D. Love III)
1994	**United States (F. Couples and D. Love III)**

Ryder Cup—men (professional)	
year	result
1985	Europe 16½, United States 11½
1987	Europe 15, United States 13
1989	Europe 14, United States 14
1991	United States 14½, Europe 13½
1993	United States 15, Europe 13

Curtis Cup—women (amateur)	
year	result
1986	Britain and Ireland 13, United States 5
1988	Britain and Ireland 11, United States 7
1990	United States 14, Britain and Ireland 4
1992	Britain and Ireland 10, United States 8
1994	**Britain and Ireland 9, United States 9**

GYMNASTICS

World Gymnastics Championships—men

year	all-around team	all-around individual	horizontal bar
1991	U.S.S.R.	G. Misutin (U.S.S.R.)	R. Buechner (Ger.)* Li Chunyang (China)*
1992	not held	not held	G. Misutin (CIS)
1993	not held	V. Sherbo (Bela.)	S. Charkov (Russia)
1994	**China**	**I. Ivankov (Bela.)**	**V. Sherbo (Bela.)**

year	parallel bars	pommel horse
1991	Li Jing (China)	V. Belenky (U.S.S.R.)
1992	Li Jing (China)* V. Voropayev (CIS)*	Pae Gil Su (N.Kor.)* V. Sherbo (CIS)* Li Jing (China)*
1993	V. Sherbo (Bela.)	Pae Gil Su (N.Kor.)
1994	**Liping Huang (China)**	**M. Urzica (Rom.)**

year	rings	vault
1991	G. Misutin (U.S.S.R.)	You Ok Youl (S.Kor.)
1992	V. Sherbo (CIS)	You Ok Youl (S.Kor.)
1993	Y. Chechi (Italy)	V. Sherbo (Bela.)
1994	**Y. Chechi (Italy)**	**V. Sherbo (Bela.)**

year	floor exercise
1991	I. Korobchinsky (U.S.S.R.)
1992	I. Korobchinsky (CIS)
1993	G. Misutin (Ukr.)
1994	**V. Sherbo (Bela.)**

*Tied.

SIMON BRUTY—ALLSPORT

Nick Price: U.S. PGA championship (1994)

World Gymnastics Championships—women

year	all-around team	all-around individual	balance beam
1991	U.S.S.R.	K. Zmeskal (U.S.)	S. Boginskaya (U.S.S.R.)
1992	not held	not held	K. Zmeskal (U.S.)
1993	not held	S. Miller (U.S.)	L. Milosovici (Rom.)
1994	**Romania**	**S. Miller (U.S.)**	**S. Miller (U.S.)**

year	uneven parallel bars	vault	floor exercise
1991	Kim Gwang Suk (N.Kor.)	L. Milosovici (Rom.)	C. Bontas (Rom.)* O. Chusovitina (U.S.S.R.)*
1992	L. Milosovici (Rom.)	H. Onodi (Hung.)	K. Zmeskal (U.S.)
1993	S. Miller (U.S.)	Y. Piskun (Bela.)	S. Miller (U.S.)
1994	**Li Luo (China)**	**G. Gogean (Rom.)**	**D. Kochetkova (Russia)**

*Tied.

HORSE RACING

2,000 Guineas

year	horse	jockey
1990	Tirol	M. Kinane
1991	Mystiko	M. Roberts
1992	Rodrigo de Triano	L. Piggott
1993	Zafonic	P. Eddery
1994	**Mister Baileys**	**J. Weaver**

The Derby

year	horse	jockey
1990	Quest for Fame	P. Eddery
1991	Generous	A. Munro
1992	Dr Devious	J. Reid
1993	Commander in Chief	M. Kinane
1994	**Erhaab**	**W. Carson**

The St. Leger

year	horse	jockey
1990	Snurge	R. Quinn
1991	Toulon	P. Eddery
1992	User Friendly	G. Duffield
1993	Bob's Return	P. Robinson
1994	**Moonax**	**P. Eddery**

Triple Crown champions—British

year	winner
1915	Pommern
1917	Gay Crusader
1918	Gainsborough
1935	Bahram
1970	Nijinsky

The Kentucky Derby

year	horse	jockey
1990	Unbridled	C. Perret
1991	Strike the Gold	C. Antley
1992	Lil E. Tee	P. Day
1993	Sea Hero	J. Bailey
1994	**Go For Gin**	**C. McCarron**

The Preakness Stakes

year	horse	jockey
1990	Summer Squall	P. Day
1991	Hansel	J. Bailey
1992	Pine Bluff	C. McCarron
1993	Prairie Bayou	M. Smith
1994	**Tabasco Cat**	**P. Day**

The Belmont Stakes

year	horse	jockey
1990	Go and Go	M. Kinane
1991	Hansel	J. Bailey
1992	A.P. Indy	E. Delahoussaye
1993	Colonial Affair	J. Krone
1994	**Tabasco Cat**	**P. Day**

Triple Crown champions—U.S.

year	horse
1946	Assault
1948	Citation
1973	Secretariat
1977	Seattle Slew
1978	Affirmed

Harness racing

The Hambletonian Trot

year	horse	driver
1990	Harmonius	J. Campbell
1991	Giant Victory	J. Moiseyev
1992	Alf Palema	M. McNicholl
1993	American Winner	R. Pierce
1994	**Victory Dream**	**M. Lachance**

Australian Thoroughbred racing

Melbourne Cup

year	horse	jockey
1990	Kingston Rule	D. Beadman
1991	Let's Elope	S. King
1992	Subzero	G. Hall
1993	Vintage Crop	M. Kinane
1994	**Jeune**	**W. Harris**

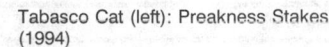

Tabasco Cat (left): Preakness Stakes (1994)

BILL FRAKES—SPORTS ILLUSTRATED

ICE HOCKEY

The Stanley Cup

season	winner	runner-up	games
1989–90	Edmonton Oilers	Boston Bruins	4–1
1990–91	Pittsburgh Penguins	Minnesota North Stars	4–2
1991–92	Pittsburgh Penguins	Chicago Black Hawks	4–0
1992–93	Montreal Canadiens	Los Angeles Kings	4–1
1993–94	**New York Rangers**	**Vancouver Canucks**	**4–3**

World Hockey Championships

year	winner
1990	Sweden
1991	Sweden
1992	Sweden
1993	Russia
1994	**Canada**

ICE SKATING

World figure skating champions—women

year	winner
1990	J. Trenary (U.S.)
1991	K. Yamaguchi (U.S.)
1992	K. Yamaguchi (U.S.)
1993	O. Baiul (Ukr.)
1994	**Y. Sato (Japan)**

World figure skating champions—men

year	winner
1990	K. Browning (Can.)
1991	K. Browning (Can.)
1992	V. Petrenko (UT)
1993	K. Browning (Can.)
1994	**E. Stojko (Can.)**

World figure skating champions—pairs

year	winners
1990	Ye. Gordeyeva, S. Grinkov (U.S.S.R.)
1991	N. Mishkutenok, A. Dmitriyev (U.S.S.R.)
1992	N. Mishkutenok, A. Dmitriyev (UT)
1993	I. Brasseur, L. Eisler (Can.)
1994	**Ye. Shishkova, V. Naumov (Russia)**

World ice dancing champions

year	winners
1990	M. Klimova, S. Ponomarenko (U.S.S.R.)
1991	I. Duchesnay, P. Duchesnay (Fr.)
1992	M. Klimova, S. Ponomarenko (UT)
1993	M. Usova, A. Zhulin (Russia)
1994	**O. Grichuk, Ye. Platov (Russia)**

World all-around speed-skating champions—men

year	winner
1990	J.O. Koss (Nor.)
1991	J.O. Koss (Nor.)
1992	R. Sighel (Italy)
1993	F. Zandstra (Neth.)
1994	**J.O. Koss (Nor.)**

World all-around speed-skating champions—women

year	winner
1990	J. Borner (E.Ger.)
1991	G. Kleeman (Ger.)
1992	G. Niemann (Ger.)
1993	G. Niemann (Ger.)
1994	**E. Hunyady (Austria)**

World Speed-skating Sprint Championships

year	men	women
1990	Ki Tae Bae (S.Kor.)	A. Hauck (E.Ger.)
1991	I. Zhelezovsky (U.S.S.R.)	M. Garbrecht (Ger.)
1992	I. Zhelezovsky (UT)	Ye Qiaobo (China)
1993	I. Zhelezovsky (Bela.)	Ye Qiaobo (China)
1994	**D. Jansen (U.S.)**	**B. Blair (U.S.)**

World Short-Track Speed-skating Championships—overall winners

year	men	women
1990	Lee Joon-ho (S.Kor.)	S. Daigle (Can.)
1991	W. O'Reilly (U.K.)	N. Lambert (Can.)
1992	Ki Hoon Kim (S.Kor.)	So He Kim (S.Kor.)
1993	M. Gagnon (Can.)	N. Lambert (Can.)
1994	**M. Gagnon (Can.)**	**N. Lambert (Can.)**

JUDO

World Judo Championships—men

year	open weights	60 kg	65 kg	71 kg
1985	Y. Masaki (Japan)	S. Hosokawa (Japan)	Y. Sokolov (U.S.S.R.)	Keun Ahn Byung (S.Kor.)
1987	N. Ogawa (Japan)	Kim Jae Yup (S.Kor.)	Y. Yamamoto (Japan)	M. Swain (U.S.)
1989	N. Ogawa (Japan)	A. Totikashvili (U.S.S.R.)	D. Becanovic (Yugos.)	T. Koga (Japan)
1991	N. Ogawa (Japan)	T. Koshino (Japan)	G. Quellmalz (Ger.)	T. Koga (Japan)
1993	R. Kubacki (Poland)	R. Sonada (Japan)	Y. Nakamura (Japan)	Yung Chung Hoon (S.Kor.)

year	78 kg	86 kg	95 kg	+ 95 kg
1985	N. Hikage (Japan)	P. Seisenbacher (Austria)	H. Sugai (Japan)	Chul Cho Yong (S.Kor.)
1987	H. Okada (Japan)	F. Canu (Fr.)	H. Sugai (Japan)	G. Verichev (U.S.S.R.)
1989	Kim Bying Ju (S.Kor.)	F. Canu (Fr.)	K. Kurtanidze (U.S.S.R.)	N. Ogawa (Japan)
1991	D. Lascau (Ger.)	H. Okada (Japan)	S. Traineau (Fr.)	S. Kosorotov (U.S.S.R.)
1993	Chun Ki Young (S.Kor.)	Y. Nakamura (Japan)	A. Kovacs (Hung.)	D. Douillet (Fr.)

World Judo Championships—women

year	open weights	48 kg	52 kg	56 kg
1986	I. Berghmans (Belg.)	K. Briggs (U.K.)	D. Brun (Fr.)	A. Hughes (U.K.)
1987	Fengliang Gao (China)	Zhang Yun Li (China)	S. Rendle (U.K.)	C. Arnaud (Fr.)
1989	E. Rodriguez (Cuba)	K. Briggs (U.K.)	S. Rendle (U.K.)	C. Arnaud (Fr.)
1991	Zhuang Xiaoyan (China)	C. Nowak (Fr.)	A. Giungi (Italy)	M. Blasco (Spain)
1993	B. Maksymow (Poland)	R. Tamura (Japan)	R. Verdecia (Cuba)	N. Fairbrother (U.K.)

year	61 kg	66 kg	72 kg	+72 kg
1986	D. Bell (U.K.)	B. Deydier (Fr.)	I. de Kok (Neth.)	Fengliang Gao (China)
1987	D. Bell (U.K.)	A. Schreiber (W.Ger.)	I. de Kok (Neth.)	Fengliang Gao (China)
1989	C. Fleury (Fr.)	E. Pierantozzi (Italy)	I. Berghmans (Belg.)	Fengliang Gao (China)
1991	F. Eickoff (Ger.)	E. Pierantozzi (Italy)	Kim Mi Jong (S.Kor.)	Moon Ji Yoon (S.Kor.)
1993	G. van de Cavaye (Belg.)	Cho Min Sun (S.Kor.)	Leng Chin Hui (China)	J. Hagn (Ger.)

RODEO

Men's World All-Around Rodeo Championship

year	winner	year	winner
1989	T. Murray	1992	T. Murray
1990	T. Murray	1993	T. Murray
1991	T. Murray	**1994**	**T. Murray**

ROWING

World Rowing Championship—men

year	single sculls	min:s	double sculls	min:s	coxed pairs	min:s
1990	Yu. Jensen (U.S.S.R.)	7:22.15	C. Zerbst, A. Jonke (Austria)	6:56.37	G. Abbagnale, C. Abbagnale (Italy)	6:48.30
1991	T. Lange (Ger.)	6:41.29	H.-J. Zwolle, N. Rienks (Neth.)	6:06.14	G. Abbagnale, C. Abbagnale (Italy)	7:34.39
1992	T. Lange (Ger.)	6:51.40	S. Hawkins, P. Antonie (Austl.)	6:17.32	J. Searle, G. Searle (U.K.)	6:49.83
1993	D. Porter (Can.)	6:59.03	Y. Lamarque, S. Barathay (Fr.)	6:24.69	J. Searle, G. Searle (U.K.)	7:01.50
1994	**A. Willims (Ger.)**	**6:46.33**	**R. Thorsen, L. Bjoenness (Nor.)**	**6:08.33**	**T. Frankovic, I. Boraska (Croatia)**	**6:42.16**

year	coxless pairs	min:s	coxed fours	min:s	coxless fours	min:s	eights	min:s
1990	T. Jung, U. Kellner (E.Ger.)	7:07.91	East Germany	6:46.73	Australia	5:52.20	West Germany	5:26.62
1991	S. Redgrave, M. Pinsent (U.K.)	6:21.35	Germany	5:58.96	Australia	6:29.69	Germany	5:50.98
1992	S. Redgrave, M. Pinsent (U.K.)	6:27.72	Romania	5:59.37	Australia	5:55.04	Canada	5:29.53
1993	S. Redgrave, M. Pinsent (U.K.)	6:37.11	Romania	6:14.64	France	6:04.54	Germany	5:37.08
1994	**S. Redgrave, M. Pinsent (U.K.)**	**6:18.65**	**Romania**	**6:06.69**	**Italy**	**5:48.44**	**United States**	**5:24.50**

World Rowing Championships—women

year	single sculls	min:s	double sculls	min:s	quadruple sculls	min:s
1990	B. Peter (E.Ger.)	7:24.10	K. Boron, B. Schramm (E.Ger.)	8:18.63	East Germany	6:14.08
1991	S. Laumann (Can.)	8:17.58	K. Boron, B. Schramm (Ger.)	6:44.71	Germany	6:55.85
1992	E. Lipa (Rom.)	7:25.54	K. Boron, K. Köppen (Ger.)	6:49.00	Germany	6:20.18
1993	J. Thieme (Ger.)	7:26.00	P. Baker, B. Lawson (N.Z.)	7:03.42	China	6:21.07
1994	**T. Hansen (Den.)**	**7:23.96**	**P. Baker, B. Lawson (N.Z.)**	**6:45.30**	**Germany**	**6:11.73**

year	coxless pairs	min:s	coxless fours	min:s	eights	min:s
1990	S. Werremeier, I. Althoff (W.Ger.)	8:28.37	Romania	7:51.68	Romania	5:59.26
1991	M. McBean, K. Heddle (Can.)	6:57.42	Canada	6:25.43	Canada	6:28.20
1992	M. McBean, K. Heddle (Can.)	7:06.22	Canada	6:30.85	Canada	6:02.62
1993	C. Gosse, H. Cortin (Fr.)	7:24.74	China	6:42.06	Romania	6:18.88
1994	**C. Gosse, H. Cortin (Fr.)**	**7:01.77**	**Netherlands**	**6:30.76**	**Germany**	**6:07.42**

The Diamond Challenge Sculls

year	winner	min:s
1990	EFM Verdonk (Koru, N.Z.)	8:21
1991	W. Van Belleghem (Belg.)	*
1992	R. Henderson (Leander R.C.)	7:44
1993	T. Lange (Ger.)	7:39
1994	**X. Muller (Grasshopper, Switz.)**	**7:35**

Grand Challenge Cup

year	winner	min:s
1990	Hansa Dortmund (W.Ger.)	6:36
1991	Leander and Star R.C.	6:22
1992	University of London	6:04
1993	Dortmund, Ger.	6:11
1994	**Charles River and San Diego**	**6:13**

*Not rowed out.

SKIING

World Nordic Skiing Championships—men

year	10-km	15-km	30-km	50-km	relay
1989		G. Svan (Swed.)	V. Smirnov (U.S.S.R.)	G. Svan (Swed.)	Sweden
1991	T. Langli (Nor.)	B. Daehlie (Nor.)	G. Svan (Swed.)	T. Mogren (Swed.)	Norway
1992	V. Ulvang (Nor.)	B. Daehlie (Nor.)	V. Ulvang (Nor.)	B. Daehlie (Nor.)	Norway
1993	S. Sivertsen (Nor.)	B. Daehlie (Nor.)	B. Daehlie (Nor.)	T. Mogren (Swed.)	Norway
1994	**B. Daehlie (Nor.)**	**B. Daehlie (Nor.)**	**T. Alsgaard (Nor.)**	**V. Smirnov (Kazakh.)**	**Italy**

World Nordic Skiing Championships—women

year	5-km	10-km	15-km	30-km	relay
1989	not held	E. Vialbe (U.S.S.R.)	M. Matikainen (Fin.)	E. Vialbe (U.S.S.R.)	Finland
1991	T. Dybendahl (Nor.)	E. Vialbe (U.S.S.R.)	E. Vialbe (U.S.S.R.)	L. Yegorova (U.S.S.R.)	U.S.S.R.
1992	M. Lukkarinen (Fin.)	E. Vialbe (U.S.S.R.)	L. Yegorova (UT)	S. Belmondo (Italy)	Unified Team
1993	L. Lazutina (Russia)	S. Belmondo (Italy)	E. Vialbe (Russia)	S. Belmondo (Italy)	Russia
1994	**L. Yegorova (Russia)**	**L. Yegorova (Russia)**	**M. Di Centa (Italy)**	**M. Di Centa (Italy)**	**Russia**

Katja Selzinger: World Alpine Skiing
champion—downhill (1994)

World Nordic Skiing Championships—ski jump

year	70-m hill	90-m hill	120-m hill	team jump	combined	team combined
1989	J. Weissflog (E.Ger.)	J. Puikkonen (Fin.)		Finland	T.E. Elden (Nor.)	Norway
1991	H. Kuttin (Austria)	F. Petek (Yugos.)		Austria	F.-B. Lundberg (Nor.)	Austria
1992		E. Vettori (Austria)	T. Nieminen (Fin.)	Finland	F. Guy (Fr.)	Japan
1993		M. Harada (Japan)	E. Bredeson (Nor.)	Norway	K. Ogiwara (Japan)	Japan
1994		**E. Bredesen (Nor.)**	**J. Weissflog (Ger.)**	**Germany**	**F.-B. Lundberg (Nor.)**	**Japan**

World Alpine Skiing Championships—slalom

year	men's slalom	men's giant slalom	men's supergiant	women's slalom	women's giant slalom	women's supergiant
1989	R. Nierlich (Austria)	R. Nierlich (Austria)	M. Hangl ((Switz.)	M. Svet (Yugos.)	V. Schneider (Switz.)	U. Maier (Austria)
1991	M. Girardelli (Lux.)	R. Nierlich (Austria)	S. Eberharter (Austria)	V. Schneider (Switz.)	P. Wiberg (Swed.)	U. Maier (Austria)
1992	F.C. Jagge (Nor.)	A. Tomba (Italy)	K.A. Aamodt (Nor.)	P. Kronberger (Austria)	P. Wiberg (Swed.)	D. Compagnoni (Italy)
1993	K.A. Aamodt (Nor.)	K.A. Aamodt (Nor.)	not held	K. Buder (Austria)	C. Merle (Fr.)	K. Seizinger (Ger.)
1994	**T. Stangassinger (Austria)**	**M. Wasmeier (Ger.)**	**M. Wasmeier (Ger.)**	**V. Schneider (Switz.)**	**D. Compagnoni (Italy)**	**D. Roffe-Steinrotter (U.S.)**

World Alpine Skiing Championships—downhill

year	men	women
1989	H. Tauscher (W.Ger.)	M. Walliser (Switz.)
1991	F. Heinzer (Switz.)	P. Kronberger (Austria)
1992	P. Ortlieb (Austria)	K. Lee-Gartner (Can.)
1993	U. Lehmann (Switz.)	K. Pace (Can.)
1994	**T. Moe (U.S.)**	**K. Seizinger (Ger.)**

World Alpine Skiing Championships—combined

year	men	women
1989	M. Girardelli (Lux.)	T. McKinney (U.S.)
1991	S. Eberharter (Austria)	C. Bournissen (Switz.)
1992	J. Polig (Italy)	P. Kronberger (Austria)
1993	L. Kjus (Nor.)	M. Vogt (Ger.)
1994	**L. Kjus (Nor.)**	**P. Wiberg (Swed.)**

Alpine World Cup

year	men	women
1990	P. Zurbriggen (Switz.)	P. Kronberger (Austria)
1991	M. Girardelli (Lux.)	P. Kronberger (Austria)
1992	P. Accola (Switz.)	P. Kronberger (Austria)
1993	M. Girardelli (Lux.)	A. Wachter (Austria)
1994	**K.A. Aamodt (Nor.)**	**V. Schneider (Switz.)**

Nordic World Cup

year	men	women
1990	V. Ulvang (Nor.)	L. Lazutina (U.S.S.R.)
1991	V. Smirnov (U.S.S.R.)	E. Vialbe (U.S.S.R.)
1992	B. Daehlie (Nor.)	E. Vialbe (Russia)
1993	B. Daehlie (Nor.)	L. Yegorova (Russia)
1994	**V. Smirnov (Kazakh.)**	**M. Di Centa (Italy)**

SQUASH RACKETS

British Open Championships—men		British Open Championships—women		World Open Championships—men		World Open Championships—women	
year	winner	year	winner	year	winner	year	winner
1989–90	Jah. Khan (Pak.)	1989–90	S. Devoy (N.Z.)	1990	Jan. Khan (Pak.)	1990	S. Devoy (N.Z.)
1990–91	Jan. Khan (Pak.)	1990–91	L. Opie (U.K.)	1991	R. Martin (Austl.)	1991	not held
1991–92	Jan. Khan (Pak.)	1991–92	S. Devoy (N.Z.)	1992	Jan. Khan (Pak.)	1992	S. Devoy (N.Z.)
1992–93	Jan. Khan (Pak.)	1992–93	M. Martin (Austl.)	1993	Jan. Khan (Pak.)	1993	M. Martin (Austl.)
1993–94	**Jan. Khan (Pak.)**	**1993–94**	**M. Martin (Austl.)**	**1994**	**Jan. Khan (Pak.)**	**1994**	**M. Martin (Austl.)**

SWIMMING

World Swimming Championships—men

freestyle

year	50 m	100 m	200 m	400 m	1,500 m
1982		J. Woithe (E.Ger.)	M. Gross (W.Ger.)	V. Salnikov (U.S.S.R.)	V. Salnikov (U.S.S.R.)
1986	T. Jager (U.S.)	M. Biondi (U.S.)	M. Gross (W.Ger.)	R. Henkel (W.Ger.)	R. Henkel (W.Ger.)
1991	T. Jager (U.S.)	M. Biondi (U.S.)	G. Lamberti (Italy)	J. Hoffmann (Ger.)	J. Hoffmann (Ger.)
1994	**A. Popov (Russia)**	**A. Popov (Russia)**	**A. Kasvio (Fin.)**	**K. Perkins (Austl.)**	**K. Perkins (Austl.)**

backstroke

year	100 m	200 m
1982	D. Richter (E.Ger.)	R. Carey (U.S.)
1986	I. Polyansky (U.S.S.R.)	I. Polyansky (U.S.S.R.)
1991	J. Rouse (U.S.)	M. López Zubero (Spain)
1994	**M. López Zubero (Spain)**	**V. Selkov (Russia)**

breaststroke

	100 m	200 m
1982	S. Lundquist (U.S.)	V. Davis (Can.)
1986	V. Davis (Can.)	J. Szabo (Hung.)
1991	N. Rozsa (Hung.)	M. Barrowman (U.S.)
1994	**N. Rozsa (Hung.)**	**N. Rozsa (Hung.)**

butterfly

	100 m	200 m
1982	M. Gribble (U.S.)	M. Gross (W.Ger.)
1986	P. Morales (U.S.)	M. Gross (W.Ger.)
1991	A. Nesty (Suriname)	M. Stewart (U.S.)
1994	**R. Szukala (Pol.)**	**D. Pankratov (Russia)**

individual medley

	200 m	400 m
1982	A. Sidorenko (U.S.S.R.)	R. Prado (Braz.)
1986	T. Darnyi (Hung.)	T. Darnyi (Hung.)
1991	T. Darnyi (Hung.)	T. Darnyi (Hung.)
1994	**J. Sievinen (Fin.)**	**T. Dolan (U.S.)**

team relays

	4 × 100-m freestyle	4 × 200-m freestyle
1982	United States	United States
1986	United States	East Germany
1991	United States	Germany
1994	**United States**	**Sweden**

year	4 × 100-m medley
1982	United States
1986	United States
1991	United States
1994	**United States**

diving

	1-m springboard	3-m springboard
1982		G. Louganis (U.S.)
1986		G. Louganis (U.S.)
1991	E. Jongejans (Neth.)	K. Ferguson (U.S.)
1994	**E. Stewart (Zimb.)**	**Yu Zhuocheng (China)**

platform

1982	G. Louganis (U.S.)	
1986	G. Louganis (U.S.)	
1991	Sun Shuwei (China)	
1994	**D. Sautin (Russia)**	

Andre Agassi: U.S. Open—men's singles (1994)

World Swimming Championships—women

freestyle

year	50 m	100 m	200 m	400 m	800 m
1982		B. Meineke (E.Ger.)	A. Verstappen (Neth.)	C. Schmidt (E.Ger.)	K. Linehan (U.S.)
1986	T. Costache (Rom.)	K. Otto (E.Ger.)	H. Friedrich (E.Ger.)	H. Friedrich (E.Ger.)	A. Strauss (E.Ger.)
1991	Zhuang Yong (China)	N. Haislett (U.S.)	H. Lewis (Austl.)	J. Evans (U.S.)	J. Evans (U.S.)
1994	**Le Jingyi (China)**	**Le Jingyi (China)**	**F. van Almsick (Ger.)**	**Yang Aihua (China)**	**J. Evans (U.S.)**

backstroke / breaststroke / butterfly

year	backstroke 100 m	backstroke 200 m	breaststroke 100 m	breaststroke 200 m	butterfly 100 m	butterfly 200 m
1982	K. Otto (E.Ger.)	C. Sirch (E.Ger.)	U. Geweniger (E.Ger.)	S. Varganova (U.S.S.R.)	M.T. Meagher (U.S.)	I. Geissler (E.Ger.)
1986	B. Mitchell (U.S.)	C. Sirch (E.Ger.)	S. Gerasch (E.Ger.)	S. Hörner (E.Ger.)	K. Gressler (E.Ger.)	M. Meagher (U.S.)
1991	K. Egerszegi (Hung.)	K. Egerszegi (Hung.)	L. Frame (Austl.)	F. Volkova (U.S.S.R.)	Qian Hong (China)	S. Sanders (U.S.)
1994	**He Cihong (China)**	**He Cihong (China)**	**S. Riley (Austl.)**	**S. Riley (Austl.)**	**Liu Limin (China)**	**Liu Limin (China)**

individual medley / team relays

year	individual medley 200 m	individual medley 400 m	team relays 4 × 100-m freestyle	4 × 200-m freestyle	4 × 100-m medley
1982	P. Schneider (E.Ger.)	P. Schneider (E.Ger.)	East Germany		East Germany
1986	K. Otto (E.Ger.)	K. Nord (E.Ger.)	East Germany	East Germany	East Germany
1991	Lin Li (China)	Lin Li (China)	United States	Germany	United States
1994	**Lu Bin (China)**	**Dai Guohong (China)**	**China**	**China**	**China**

diving

year	1-m springboard	3-m springboard	platform
1982		M. Neyer (U.S.)	W. Wyland (U.S.)
1986		Gao Min (China)	Chen Lin (China)
1991	Gao Min (China)	Gao Min (China)	Fu Mingxia (China)
1994	**Chen Lixia (China)**	**Tan Shuping (China)**	**Fu Mingxia (China)**

TABLE TENNIS

World Table Tennis Championships—men

year	St. Bride's Vase (singles)	Iran Cup (doubles)	Swaythling Cup (team)
1987	Jiang Jialiang (China)	Chen Longcan, Wei Qingguang (China)	China
1989	J.-O. Waldner (Swed.)	J. Rosskopf, S. Fetzner (W.Ger.)	Sweden
1991	J. Persson (Swed.)	P. Karlsson, T. Von Scheele (Swed.)	Sweden
1993	J.-P. Gatien (Fr.)	Wang Tao, Lu Lin (China)	Sweden

World Table Tennis Championships—women

year	G. Geist Prize (singles)	W.J. Pope Trophy (doubles)	Corbillon Cup (team)
1987	He Zhili (China)	Hyun Jung Hwa, Yang Young Ja (S.Kor.)	China
1989	Qiao Hong (China)	Qiao Hong, Deng Yaping (China)	China
1991	Deng Yaping (China)	Gao Jun, Chen Zihe (China)	Korea
1993	Hyun Jung Hwa (S.Kor.)	Liu Wei, Qiao Yunping (China)	China

World Table Tennis Championships—mixed

year	Heydusek Prize
1985	Cai Zhenhua, Cao Yanhua (China)
1987	Hui Jun, Geng Lijuan (China)
1989	Yoo Nam Kyu, Hyung Jung Hwa (S.Kor.)
1991	Wang Tao, Liu Wei (China)
1993	Wang Tao, Liu Wei (China)

Table Tennis World Cup

year	winner
1990	J.-O. Waldner (Swed.)
1991	J. Persson (Swed.)
1992	Ma Wenge (China)
1993	Z. Primorac (Croatia)
1994	**J.-P. Gatien (Fr.)**

TENNIS

United States Open Tennis Championships—singles

year	men	women
1990	P. Sampras (U.S.)	G. Sabatini (Arg.)
1991	S. Edberg (Swed.)	M. Seles (Yugos.)
1992	S. Edberg (Swed.)	M. Seles (Yugos.)
1993	P. Sampras (U.S.)	S. Graf (Ger.)
1994	**A. Agassi (U.S.)**	**A. Sánchez Vicario (Spain)**

United States Open Tennis Championships—doubles

year	men	women
1990	P. Aldrich, D. Visser	M. Navratilova, G. Fernandez
1991	J. Fitzgerald, A. Jarryd	P. Shriver, N. Zvereva
1992	J. Grabb, R. Reneberg	G. Fernandez, N. Zvereva
1993	K. Flach, R. Leach	A. Sánchez Vicario, H. Sukova
1994	**P. Haarhuis, J. Eltingh**	**A. Sánchez Vicario, J. Novotna**

All-England (Wimbledon) Tennis Championships—singles

year	men	women
1990	S. Edberg (Swed.)	M. Navratilova (U.S.)
1991	M. Stich (Ger.)	S. Graf (Ger.)
1992	A. Agassi (U.S.)	S. Graf (Ger.)
1993	P. Sampras (U.S.)	S. Graf (Ger.)
1994	**P. Sampras (U.S.)**	**C. Martinez (Spain)**

All-England (Wimbledon) Tennis Championships—doubles

year	men	women
1990	R. Leach, J. Pugh	J. Novotna, H. Sukova
1991	J. Fitzgerald, A. Jarryd	L. Savchenko, N. Zvereva
1992	J. McEnroe, M. Stich	G. Fernandez, N. Zvereva
1993	T. Woodbridge, M. Woodforde	G. Fernandez, N. Zvereva
1994	**T. Woodbridge, M. Woodforde**	**G. Fernandez, N. Zvereva**

Australian Open Tennis Championships—singles

year	men	women
1990	I. Lendl (Czech.)	S. Graf (W.Ger.)
1991	B. Becker (Ger.)	M. Seles (Yugos.)
1992	J. Courier (U.S.)	M. Seles (Yugos.)
1993	J. Courier (U.S.)	M. Seles (Yugos.)
1994	**P. Sampras (U.S.)**	**S. Graf (Ger.)**

Australian Open Tennis Championships—doubles

year	men	women
1990	P. Aldrich, D. Visser	J. Novotna, H. Sukova
1991	S. Davis, D. Pate	P. Fendick, M.J. Fernandez
1992	T. Woodbridge, M. Woodforde	A. Sánchez Vicario, H. Sukova
1993	D. Visser, L. Warder	G. Fernandez, N. Zvereva
1994	**P. Haarhuis, J. Eltingh**	**G. Fernandez, N. Zvereva**

French Open Tennis Championships—singles

year	men	women
1990	A. Gomez (Ecu.)	M. Seles (Yugos.)
1991	J. Courier (U.S.)	M. Seles (Yugos.)
1992	J. Courier (U.S.)	M. Seles (Yugos.)
1993	S. Bruguera (Spain)	S. Graf (Ger.)
1994	**S. Bruguera (Spain)**	**A. Sánchez Vicario (Spain)**

French Open Tennis Championships—doubles

year	men	women
1990	S. Casal, E. Sánchez	J. Novotna, H. Sukova
1991	J. Fitzgerald, A. Jarryd	G. Fernandez, J. Novotna
1992	J. Hlasek, M. Rosset	G. Fernandez, N. Zvereva
1993	L. Jensen, M. Jensen	G. Fernandez, N. Zvereva
1994	**B. Black, J. Stark**	**G. Fernandez, N. Zvereva**

Davis Cup

year	winner	runner-up	results
1990	United States	Australia	3–2
1991	France	United States	3–1
1992	United States	Switzerland	3–1
1993	Germany	Australia	4–1
1994	**Sweden**	**Russia**	**4–1**

Federation Cup

year	winner	runner-up	results
1990	United States	U.S.S.R.	2–1
1991	Spain	United States	2–1
1992	Germany	Spain	2–1
1993	Spain	Australia	3–0
1994	**Spain**	**United States**	**3–0**

VOLLEYBALL

World Volleyball Championships

year	men	women
1986	United States	China
1988	United States	U.S.S.R.
1990	Italy	U.S.S.R.
1992	Brazil	Cuba
1994	**Italy**	**Cuba**

WRESTLING

World Wrestling Championships—Freestyle

year	48 kg	52 kg	57 kg	62 kg	68 kg
1989	J. Kim (S.Kor.)	V. Jordanov (Bulg.)	S. Yeung (N.Kor.)	J. Smith (U.S.)	B. Bovdayev (U.S.S.R.)
1990	A. Martinez (Cuba)	M. Torkan (Iran)	A. Puerto (Cuba)	J. Smith (U.S.)	A. Fadzaev (U.S.S.R.)
1991	V. Orudzhev (U.S.S.R.)	Z. Jones (U.S.)	S. Smal (U.S.S.R.)	J. Smith (U.S.)	A. Fadzaev (U.S.S.R.)
1992	Park II (N.Kor.)	Li Hak (N.Kor.)	A. Puerto (Cuba)	J. Smith (U.S.)	A. Fadzaev (UT)
1993	A. Vila (Cuba)	V. Jordanov (Bulg.)	Terry Brands (U.S.)	Tom Brands (U.S.)	A.A. Fallah (Iran)
1994	**A. Vila (Cuba)**	**V. Jordanov (Bulg.)**	**A. Puerto (Cuba)**	**M. Azizov (Russia)**	**A. Leipold (Ger.)**

year	74 kg	82 kg	90 kg	100 kg	130 kg
1989	K. Monday (U.S.)	E. Jabraylov (U.S.S.R.)	M. Khadartsev (U.S.S.R.)	A. Atavov (U.S.S.R.)	A.R. Soleimani (Iran)
1990	R. Sofiyadi (Bulg.)	J. Lohyna (Czech.)	M. Khadartsev (U.S.S.R.)	L. Khabelov (U.S.S.R.)	D. Gobedzhishvili (U.S.S.R.)
1991	A. Khadem (Iran)	K. Jackson (U.S.)	M. Khadartsev (U.S.S.R.)	L. Khabelov (U.S.S.R.)	A. Schroder (Ger.)
1992	Park Jang (S.Kor.)	K. Jackson (U.S.)	M. Khadartsev (UT)	L. Khabelov (UT)	B. Baumgartner (U.S.)
1993	Park Jang (S.Kor.)	S. Ozturk (Tur.)	A. Jadidi (Iran)	L. Khabelov (Russia)	B. Baumgartner (U.S.)
1994	**T. Ceylan (Tur.)**	**L. Jabrailov (Moldova)**	**R. Khadem (Iran)**	**A. Sabejey (Ger.)**	**M. Demir (Tur.)**

World Wrestling Championships—Greco-Roman style

year	48 kg	52 kg	57 kg	62 kg	68 kg
1989	O. Kucherenko (U.S.S.R.)	A. Ignatenko (U.S.S.R.)	E. Iwanov (Bulg.)	K. Madzhidov (U.S.S.R.)	C. Passarelli (W.Ger.)
1990	O. Kucherenko (U.S.S.R.)	A. Ignatenko (U.S.S.R.)	R. Yildiz (Ger.)	M. Oliveras (Cuba)	I. Duguchiyev (U.S.S.R.)
1991	Duk Yong Gooun (S.Kor.)	R. Martínez (Cuba)	R. Yildiz (Ger.)	S. Martynov (U.S.S.R.)	I. Duguchiyev (U.S.S.R.)
1992	O. Kucherenko (UT)	J. Ronningen (Nor.)	An Han Bong (S.Kor.)	A. Pirim (Tur.)	A. Repka (Hung.)
1993	W. Sánchez (Cuba)	R. Martínez (Cuba)	A. Manukjan (Arm.)	S. Martynov (Russia)	I. Duguchiyev (Russia)
1994	**W. Sánchez (Cuba)**	**A. Mkrtchyan (Ger.)**	**J. Melnichenko (Kazakh.)**	**S. Martynov (Russia)**	**I. Duguchiyev (Russia)**

year	74 kg	82 kg	90 kg	100 kg	130 kg
1989	D. Turlykhanov (U.S.S.R.)	T. Komaromi (Hung.)	M. Bullmann (E.Ger.)	G. Himmel (W.Ger.)	A. Karelin (U.S.S.R.)
1990	M. Iskandarian (U.S.S.R.)	P. Farcas (Hung.)	M. Bullmann (Ger.)	S. Demiaschkievish (U.S.S.R.)	A. Karelin (U.S.S.R.)
1991	M. Iskandarian (U.S.S.R.)	P. Farcas (Hung.)	M. Bullmann (Ger.)	H. Milian (Cuba)	A. Karelin (U.S.S.R.)
1992	M. Iskandarian (UT)	P. Farcas (Hung.)	M. Bullmann (Ger.)	H. Milian (Cuba)	A. Karelin (UT)
1993	N. Alamanza (Cuba)	M. Yerlikaya (Tur.)	G. Koguchavili (Russia)	M. Ljungberg (Swed.)	A. Karelin (Russia)
1994	**M. Iskandarian (Russia)**	**T. Zander (Ger.)**	**G. Koguchavili (Russia)**	**A. Wronski (Pol.)**	**A. Karelin (Russia)**

YACHTING

America's Cup

year	winning yacht	owner	skipper	losing yacht	owner
1977	*Courageous* (U.S.)	Courageous syndicate	T. Turner	*Australia* (Australia)	A. Bond and syndicate
1980	*Freedom* (U.S.)	Maritime College at Fort Schuyler Foundation, Inc.	D. Conner	*Australia* (Australia)	A. Bond and syndicate
1983	*Australia II* (Australia)	A. Bond and syndicate	J. Bertrand	*Liberty* (U.S.)	Maritime College at Fort Schuyler Foundation, Inc.
1987	*Stars & Stripes* (U.S.)	Sail America syndicate	D. Conner	*Kookaburra III* (Australia)	K. Parry and syndicate
1988	*Stars & Stripes* (U.S.)	Sail America syndicate	D. Conner	*New Zealand* (New Zealand)	M. Fay
1992	*America³* (U.S.)	America³ Foundation	B. Koch	*Il Moro di Venezia* (Italy)	Compagnia della Vela di Venezia

Bermuda Race

year	winning yacht	owner
1986	*Silver Star* and *Puritan*	D. Clarke D. Robinson
1988	*Congere*	B. Koeppel
1990	*Denali*	L. Huntington
1992	*Constellation*	U.S. Naval Academy
1994	**Gaylark**	**K. Smith**

Transpacific Race

year	winning yacht	owner
1985	*Montgomery Street*	D. Denning
1987	*Merlin*	D. Campion
1989	*Silver Bullet*	J. DeLaura
1991	*Chance*	R. McNulty
1993	*Silver Bullet*	J. DeLaura

Admiral's Cup

year	winning team
1985	West Germany
1987	New Zealand
1989	United Kingdom
1991	France
1993	Germany

Television and Radio

Dominant trends in television and radio in 1994 included continuing globalization of services and programming and increased competition between cable and telephone companies. The industry's battle cry was expand or exit. Communications satellites in space, satellite dishes on rooftops, and underground fibreglass cables improved transmission between nations. Viewers, subscribers, and advertisers were offered increased coverage and choices. With the blurring of boundaries, the entire world became the battlefield for competition.

Organization. In the United States 1994 was supposed to be the year of convergence. Cable and local telephone companies would get together to create Vice Pres. Al Gore's "information superhighway"—a two-way, high-capacity network interconnecting homes and businesses for communications, TV, and multimedia entertainment and information. The $30 billion merger of Bell Atlantic Corp. and Tele-Communications, Inc. (TCI), one the biggest telephone companies and the largest cable company, announced in October 1993, was to have been the model that others would follow. The Bell Atlantic–TCI deal abruptly collapsed in February, however. Fingers were pointed at the U.S. Federal Communications Commission (FCC), which had recently restricted cable rates and made TCI and other cable companies less attractive assets.

In any event, convergence soon became divergence. Cable and telephone providers seemed intent on going their separate ways and getting into each other's core businesses—telephone into cable, cable into telephone. That homes and business might one day be able to choose between two providers of telephone and cable services became a real possibility.

In what they expected would be a year of peace and plenty, the big three broadcast networks—ABC, CBS, and NBC—found themselves in a scramble to secure affiliates in dozens of cities—something they had all taken more or less for granted. Affiliates are TV stations that agree to air the network programming for some of the advertising time in it and for hefty "network compensation" payments. The scramble was touched off by Fox, Rupert Murdoch's aggressive fourth network, which was determined to replace current ultra-high-frequency (UHF) affiliates with very high-frequency (VHF) affiliates. Since its inception Fox had been handicapped by an affiliate lineup laden with UHF TV stations, which broadcast only on channels 14 and above. UHF signals are weaker and afford poorer reception than VHF signals, channels 2 through 13.

In May Fox announced an affiliation agreement with New World Communications Group Inc. A dozen stations owned by New World would drop their affiliations with the big three networks and pick up Fox. That caused chaos in the 12 markets as the jilted Fox affiliates looked for a new network and the big three courted other VHF stations, hoping not to end up with UHF outlets. The chaos spread to other markets as the big three signed multistation affiliation agreements of their own. By autumn 1994 some 65 stations in 31 markets had made or were planning affiliation transfers.

In the aftermath of Fox's successful bid in 1993 for rights to the National Football Conference games of the National Football League (NFL), payments by the NFL's other TV outlets—ABC, NBC, ESPN, and Turner Network Television—were driven up. Altogether the contracts totaled nearly $4.5 billion over four years, a 21% increase over the previous deal.

Despite the turmoil, the broadcast TV business enjoyed one of its best years in recent memory. Audiences, advertising revenues, profits, and station values were all on the rise, deriving momentum from the healthy overall economy. Among the most telling facts was the rise of the broadcast networks' share of the TV audience for the 1993–94 prime-time season by one point to 61%. It was not much, but it marked a reversal in the 30-point slide that began in the late 1970s, when cable became a strong competitor.

The broadcast networks suddenly became desirable properties as their revenues and profits swelled. The most interested buyers were the major Hollywood film studios, which saw ownership of a network as a way of guaranteeing distribution of their prime-time TV productions and a way of keeping the networks out of their business. A series of decisions by the FCC and the federal courts between 1991 and 1993 eliminated the legal barriers to common ownership of a network and studio.

The number of broadcast stations in the U.S. inched upward. According to the FCC's October count, there were 1,520 TV stations, 1,157 commercial and 363 noncommercial. In addition, there were 11,701 radio stations, including 4,923 commercial AM, 5,070 commercial FM, and 1,708 noncommercial FM.

Times were not quite so cheery for cable TV, which was buffeted by tough federal rate regulations, the advent of competition, and the threat of more to come. Reed Hundt, whom U.S. Pres. Bill Clinton appointed to head the FCC in November 1993, began making his mark in February 1994 by tightening up cable rate regulations spawned by legislation in 1992. As a result, many cable subscribers across the country saw their monthly cable bills drop a dollar or two. Cable operators calculated that the regulations would cost them some $3 billion in revenues in 1994, 15% of the total. In November, however, the FCC ruled to allow cable companies to raise costs for new cable services, a move that was expected to bring in about the same revenue as had been lost in February. Some 58.8 million homes in the U.S. subscribed to cable in November.

Believing that what cable TV ultimately needed was competition, the FCC in October adopted final rules governing the entry of telephone companies into TV. The so-called video dial tone rules permitted local telephone companies such as Bell Atlantic and NYNEX Corp. to build video networks without having to submit to local regulations (and having to pay stiff local "franchise fees"), as cable operators did. But they also required telephone companies to make room on their networks for any video programmer prepared to pay for it.

Most big telephone companies intended to be programmers as well as operators of their video networks. They were helped toward that goal by a series of federal appeals court rulings striking down the federal statute prohibiting them from programming where they provided telephone service. Underscoring their interest, six of the Baby Bells found strategic partners to help them package and develop conventional and interactive TV programming. Bell Atlantic, NYNEX, and Pacific Telesis Group hooked up with the Creative Artists Agency, while Ameritech Corp., BellSouth Corp., and Southwestern Bell Corp. struck a deal with the Walt Disney Co.

The prospect of competition from telephone companies was not the only threat the cable operators had to worry about. After 15 years of development, high-powered satellite broadcasting finally was brought to fruition in the summer of 1994. DirecTV, a subsidiary of General Motors' Hughes Electronics, and Hubbard Broadcasting's United States Satellite Broadcasting (USSB) began beaming programming via satellite to subscribers with "dish" antennas 46 cm (18 in) in diameter.

The new satellite service was not cheap. Subscribers had to pay at least $700 for the RCA reception equipment and a monthly fee of $65 for the programming, which included all the popular cable services. For additional charges, they could choose pay-per-view movies scheduled with frequent start times and watch all the games of the NFL. Recognizing the threat posed by DirecTV and USSB, a group of the largest cable operators, led by TCI, countered with a similar service of their own. Primestar required a bigger dish (one metre [39.4 in]), but the cost of the reception equipment was included in the monthly subscription fee of approximately $35.

Satellite dishes decorate almost all of the houses on a street in Medan, Indonesia. With a potentially large, untapped audience waiting and with the capital for expansion readily available, a number of Western-based broadcasters were targeting Asia.

MUNSHI AHMED

STAR TV, Murdoch's Hong Kong-based satellite TV network, began officially beaming to India (where cable operators with satellite dishes pirated transmissions) after acquiring 49.9% of the Hindi-language Zee TV. Doordarshan, India's state-run network, stopped airing three of its five new channels, launched in 1993 to counteract STAR, owing to rampant criticisms of its programs. STAR's glowing success overseas was, however, tarnished by setbacks at home. After only five months of service, James Griffiths was replaced by Gary Davey, the fourth managing director in two and a half years. The pullout from the network of Taiwanese advertising agency Satellite Television Marketing (STM) prompted STAR to sue STM's parent company, United Communications Group. Another dispute erupted over failure to come to terms about channeling STAR programs through Wharf Cable, the exclusive licensee. Wharf's HK$5 billion pay-TV 20-channel system (with eight already operational) was a first in Hong Kong.

Murdoch's closest competitor, Turner International, launched TNT & Cartoon Network in Asia, the first 24-hour Hollywood film and cartoon service in the region. In the Philippines STAR's competitor, Sky Cable, extended its coverage throughout the nation. But the largest local TV network competed elsewhere; delivering the first trans-Pacific Asian program service via PanAmSat 2, ABS-CBN Broadcasting Corp. developed the Filipino Channel for some two million Filipino immigrants in the United States.

Similarly, Shaw Media Corp. of Hong Kong and the United Kingdom's Wilton Group set up the Chinese Channel, beamed via Astra satellite, for the 800,000 Chinese living in Europe. All programming—in Cantonese, Mandarin, and Vietnamese—for the subscription-only channel came from Hong Kong's Television Broadcast (TVB).

Competition intensified between Indonesian private networks after the government allowed stations to broadcast nationwide instead of being limited to certain cities. Elsewhere in Southeast Asia, Thai Sky TV and International Broadcasting Corp. were allowed by the government's Mass Communication Organization of Thailand to expand outside Bangkok in the face of strong competition from direct satellite operators. The existing situation of too many TV programmers and too few transponders, in fact, had experts predicting that orbiting satellites over Asia might soon be bumping into one another. (A transponder is a radio or radar set that, upon receiving a designated signal, emits a signal of its own.) For example, China-backed APT Satellite Co. launched Apstar 1 in a controversial orbital slot, risking disruption of its signal and that of two orbiting neighbours.

With capital for expansion, Asian private commercial media boomed. A second private station, TV 4, was opened in Malaysia. It was granted to a consortium of seven companies, including Metropolitan (M) Sdn. Bhd. (40%) and the largest Malay publishing group, Utusan Melayu (35%). In Indonesia problems were foreseen with Government Decree 20/1994, allowing foreign investments in media, telecommunications, shipping, railroads, and power supply. In joint ventures foreign partners could hold up to 95% equity, but Press Act 21/1982 stated explicitly that capital used to set up mass media companies must have originated from within Indonesia. In China as well, no foreign firms were allowed to set up or operate cable TV stations, not even as joint ventures.

Elsewhere, a U.S. partner, Continental Cablevision Inc., joined with Singapore CableVision in a S$500 million cable TV project to wire 116,000 Singaporean households by the end of 1995. Singapore's government, however, chose to keep a firm grip on Singapore Broadcasting Corp. (SBC).

Benefiting from these privatization trends was the new Asian satellite alliance of five of the world's leading TV networks: Turner Broadcasting System, Inc. (CNN), TVB International of Hong Kong, the Australian Broadcasting Corp., Home Box Office (HBO) Asia, and ESPN International. Leasing transponders on Palapa B2P and Apstar 1, the alliance served Malaysia, Singapore, Indonesia, Papua New Guinea, Thailand, the Philippines, Hong Kong, Laos, Cambodia, and Vietnam.

In Europe signals from the paging system Euro-Funkruf were interfering with German cable TV. A different kind of interference—in terms of viewership and advertising revenues—from (mainly U.S.) satellite and cable TV networks was met by a global strategic alliance between the BBC and British media conglomerate Pearson, which bought an interest in Thames TV, Britain's biggest independent producer. The Netherlands' biggest producer, Endemol, merged with Veronica, the largest broadcasting association. By the terms of the merger, Veronica gave up a government subsidy of up to 8 million guilders but hoped to cash in on increased revenues from advertisements and program sales.

Market positioning by European companies led to media concentration. Kirch Group, Bertelsmann AG, and Germany's telephone monopoly Telekom formed Media Service GmbH to provide video-on-demand and other interactive services soon to be available on pay-TV. Joachim Theye, a lawyer, claimed that as an international company, the new firm was not subject to the anticartel law. Consequently, the

German government planned on changing rules governing media to guard against media concentration and to restrict each network's televiewing share.

Italy had similar problems after electing as prime minister Silvio Berlusconi (*see* BIOGRAPHIES), owner of its second largest private company, Fininvest, which had interests in telecommunications, pension plans, insurance, and sports and owned the nation's largest publishing house, Mondadori. Berlusconi's national networks—Canale 5, Rete 4, and Italia 1—gained half of Italy's total TV ad revenues. As prime minister, he also had jurisdiction over the government networks RAI 1, RAI 2, and RAI 3, prompting calls to set up a "blind trust" for his company financial interests.

After elections in Russia, Pres. Boris Yeltsin replaced Vyacheslav Bragin, controller of two of four nationwide TV channels, with Aleksandr Yakovlev, the former chief of the Communist Party's Central Committee department for Soviet radio and TV. Next he replaced the two rivals for media control, the Ministry of Information and the unpopular Federal Information Centre, with a media-monitoring unit. Then he allowed NTV, Russia's first nationwide independent channel, to use the existing fourth channel's frequencies.

TV Programming. In the U.S. CBS dominated network TV through the 1993–94 season, finishing first in ratings in prime time, daytime, and late night—the first time that had happened since the rise of ABC in the early 1960s. In prime time, CBS pulled a 14.1 rating and 23 share, ABC 12.5/20, NBC 11.1/18, and Fox 7.2/11, according to the A.C. Nielsen Co. (A rating is the percentage of the 94.2 million homes with TVs; a share is the percentage of homes with their TVs on at the time of the program.)

CBS's strength came primarily from such perennials as "60 Minutes," "Murphy Brown," and "Murder, She Wrote." The other networks stayed competitive with successful new series. ABC's winning newcomers included "NYPD Blue" and "Grace Under Fire." NBC was able to partially fill the void created by the retirement of "Cheers" with "Frasier," a new series based on one of its characters. The good news of spring failed to sustain CBS in the fall, however. By mid-

November the network was in a virtual second-place tie with NBC behind ABC, which was riding high on the strength of its Tuesday- and Friday-night schedules. ABC's dominant lineup on Tuesday included "Home Improvement," "Grace Under Fire," and "NYPD Blue," which survived the loss of one of its lead actors, David Caruso. (*See* BIOGRAPHIES.) The season's big hit, however, was NBC's "ER," a fast-paced hospital drama.

At the 46th annual Emmy awards, CBS's "Picket Fences" won as best drama series for the second year in a row, and "Frasier" was named best comedy series. The British-made "Prime Suspect 3," starring Helen Mirren (*see* BIOGRAPHIES), won as best miniseries or special.

CBS's David Letterman solidly established himself as the funniest man in late-night TV, consistently outscoring NBC's Jay Leno in the ratings. After a five-year run, Paramount's "Arsenio Hall Show" slipped into late-night history.

One of the major events of the new season was Ken Burns' "Baseball," aired on PBS for 18½ hours in September. Produced in a style similar to Burns' "The Civil War," the series used a blend of action on the field, historic photographs, and commentary from baseball enthusiasts ranging from Walt Whitman to Mario Cuomo to evoke a sense of the sport's place in the life of the nation.

The European Union (EU) moved toward bolstering its film and TV industries by excluding an increased number of foreign films and broadcasts and by funding Europe-wide programming and distribution. The proposals were embodied in the "Green Paper," an EU Commission discussion document intended to lead to legislation.

The widening of Asian media's ownership base led to more specialty programming but also to abuses from all sides. Malaysia's Ministry of Information announced the amendment of the Broadcasting Act of 1988 to enable Malaysians to use a wider range of broadcasting facilities, "but there will be no open sky policy . . . no pollution of culture and values." It banned ads for rock concerts on TV because of "negative behaviour and activities" such as cigarette smoking and beer drinking by concert-watching youths. China's curb on foreign cable TV stations allowed

AL SCHABEN—LOS ANGELES TIMES

Inside this white Ford Bronco, O.J. Simpson, who was later charged with the murder of his former wife, holds a gun to his own head as he and the driver, his friend Al Cowlings, lead police on a slow "chase" along the freeways of Los Angeles. Millions watched the procession on TV.

only those foreign shows approved by central broadcast authorities to be aired. (*See* WORLD AFFAIRS: *Spotlight: Asian Values*.)

Japanese media, particularly the public television NHK, earned praise from disaster-prevention officials after Hokkaido was struck by a 7.9-magnitude earthquake on October 4. With the newly installed system linking Meteorological Agency seismographs to TV and radio stations, the quake automatically triggered warnings on the screen and voice-over announcements, helping to limit casualties.

Hong Kong's two broadcast stations and its cable provider came under fire from the Broadcasting Authority for breach of standards. TVB, ATV, and Wharf were reprimanded or fined for various offenses, including "inhumane" scenes of animals fighting, "vulgar and offensive" language, and "unsuitable" elements for children's viewing. TVB Pearl and ATV World were also rebuked for inaccurate news reporting.

The popular French show "Lovin' Fun" was canceled by the Superior Audiovisual Council for using earthy and brutal language in responding to questions about sex that were phoned in, mostly by young people. The youths' furious reaction caused the program to be restored.

Indonesia's educational TV channel, Televisi Pendidikan Indonesia, chose to become a family TV station without abandoning its original mission. The license change allowed it to compete for advertising revenues against fully commercial stations, which mostly broadcast U.S.-made action films. A cable TV channel for health professionals, Philippine Medical Television, was launched as a cooperative venture between the Philippine Medical Association and the American Medical TV Network, which was to supply 80% of the programming. Also in the Philippines, RJ TV 29, a music and home-shopping channel, signed up cable distributors for a new nationwide UHF TV channel. The program mix of the country's only video-marketing show was Filipino music and home TV shopping.

Germany's mail-order giants—Quelle, Otto, and Neckermann—introduced television shopping, already popular in North America, Italy, The Netherlands, and France. Otto could easily go into teleshopping because the son of its founder owned shares in two TV channels (Viva, Hamburg I), three radio stations (OK Radio, Hamburg; Delta Radio, Kiel; Kiss FM, Berlin), and, with partner Time Warner Inc., Catalog 1 home-shopping channel of the U.S.

In Britain the success of an adaptation of George Eliot's *Middlemarch* led to a renewed interest in adapting 19th-century novels. Later examples included Charles Dickens' *Hard Times* and *Martin Chuzzlewit*.

"La Chaine d'information," France's 24-hour, seven-day news and information service, began on private cable TV station TF1. Radio Television Brunei (RTB) started "RTB-Sukmaindera," a daily one-hour international satellite TV information service. For Malaysian commuters on the North and South expressways, Highway Radio provided information and entertainment, a joint venture of Time Engineering, the Ministry of Finance, and the privately owned Bernama (Malaysia News Agency). Japan's 250-channel Visual Information Radio allowed users to call up traffic information, news headlines, sports scores, or stock market data on a 60-character screen.

Radio. Radio also enjoyed a good year in the United States. According to the Radio Advertising Bureau, local and national ad revenues for the first nine months of 1994 were up 11% over the same period of 1993.

The news/talk format continued its resurgence in radio, claiming at midyear more than 900 stations. Listeners could tune into personalities for advice on health, money, and sex or for topical political commentary.

President Clinton's frustrations about the incessant criticism of his administration by conservative radio talk-show hosts boiled over during the summer. In an interview broadcast on KMOX (AM) St. Louis, Mo., he complained about the "unremitting drumbeat of negativism and cynicism."

A clampdown on six underground radio stations caused violent riots in Taiwan. Although relaxation of the broadcasting monopoly was part of the nation's overall political liberalization, stringent capital requirements allowed only the rich to own stations. Licenses for 13 new FM stations were approved. Buddhist Thailand gave the Roman Catholic Church an opportunity to air a TV program every other Sunday on Channel 9, alternating with a Protestant program. An Islamic program was aired every Friday, and Buddhist programs were broadcast on the other five days. Islamic missionary programs were broadcast from a Brunei-based radio station set up by Malaysia, Brunei, and Indonesia, which had a combined Muslim population of 220 million. By contrast, Radio Tanger was authorized in France by Interior Minister Charles Pasqua (*see* BIOGRAPHIES) to counter extremist Islamic propaganda.

In the Philippines, Kids Radio, a partnership between City Lite 88.3 FM and DWSS-AM Stereo, began broadcasting an array of programs for children, with a difference—the program hosts were children. Patterned after Radio AAHS in the U.S., it gave children a radio station to which they could relate. (RAMONA MONETTE S. FLORES; HARRY A. JESSELL; LAWRENCE B. TAISHOFF)

Amateur Radio. At the prompting of the American Radio Relay League, which represented 170,000 amateur (ham) radio operators, President Clinton on October 22 signed a congressional resolution recognizing the continuing importance of amateur radio and urging the FCC to permit the service to employ new technology and provide "reasonable accommodation" for its future growth. Although not binding on the agency, the resolution was expected to help the league in its fight to preserve two bands of microwave frequencies for amateur use. The U.S. Department of Commerce had proposed reallocating the bands from government to commercial use.

The number of ham licenses rose to 631,399, according to the FCC's May accounting. But officials believed that there were far fewer active operators, noting that the policy of granting 10-year licenses begun in 1983 made it difficult to calculate the number of active licensees.

(HARRY A. JESSELL; LAWRENCE B. TAISHOFF)

See also Business and Industry Review: *Advertising; Telecommunications;* Motion Pictures; Music.

This article updates the *Macropædia* article BROADCASTING.

Theatre

Great Britain and Ireland. In November 1994, 87 playwrights, including Harold Pinter, Arnold Wesker, and Peter Shaffer, wrote a letter to the artistic directors of subsidized theatres demanding a quota system of new plays—two or three a year—on their main stages. The writers expressed the feeling that the nation's theatre was slipping into "irrelevance and decline" because of a lack of opportunity for new work. Their argument was not exactly borne out by the abundance of good new plays that progressed from the regions and the fringe theatres into the West End of London. Touring companies, however, were feeling the pinch, and alarm signals sounded as, toward the end of the year, temporary closures were announced at the Salisbury Playhouse, Redgrave, Farnham, and Everyman in Cheltenham;

the latter proposed working in conjunction with its senior, and more prestigious, West Country neighbour, the Bristol Old Vic.

Although commercial success proved elusive, the stream of new plays was unprecedented. The West End welcomed Tim Firth's *Neville's Island* from the Nottingham Playhouse, with the young comedian Tony Slattery in an "Outward Bound" comic version of *The Lord of the Flies;* Maria Friedman in John Godber's *April in Paris,* a modest but tender piece originated by the Hull Truck touring company; Sue Townsend's *The Queen and I,* adapted from her own novel and presented by Max Stafford-Clark's new Out of Joint touring company in conjunction with the Leicester Haymarket and the Royal Court; and Jonathan Harvey's *Beautiful Thing,* a delightful and innocent comedy of a burgeoning homosexual friendship between two teenagers in South London, which was first produced by the tiny Bush Theatre in West London before moving into the Donmar Warehouse in Covent Garden and the Duke of York's Theatre.

In addition, Kay Mellor's entertaining *A Passionate Woman,* a play in the *Shirley Valentine* mode and mold, transferred from the West Yorkshire Playhouse in Leeds (with a stellar performance from Stephanie Cole, a popular television sitcom actress), and Wendy Wasserstein's Broadway comedy hit *The Sisters Rosensweig,* beautifully acted by Janet Suzman, Maureen Lipman, and Lynda Bellingham, crossed town from Greenwich to the Old Vic. The Old Vic also housed David Beaird's riotous *900 Oneonta,* which title signified the address of a plantation in Louisiana where, as one actor (Roger Allam) summed up on opening night, "*Dynasty* meets *The Munsters* meets the *Addams Family* meets Eugene O'Neill." There were less successful new plays: David Mamet's *The Cryptogram,* with Lindsay Duncan and Eddie Izzard (a brilliant transvestite comedian making his acting debut), failed to attract audiences, and Michael Palin's *The Weekend* was a crushing failure.

Nonetheless, Tom Stoppard's *Arcadia* sailed on unstoppably at the Haymarket, and Maggie Smith collected her fifth *Evening Standard* (ES) best actress award in Edward Albee's Pulitzer Prize-winning *Three Tall Women* (ES best play), which divided the critics. Audiences, however, flocked to Wyndham's Theatre to see Dame Maggie, who slew them in the aisles as a crabby, dilapidated nonagenarian before returning in the second half as a dignified, dominating 70-something. She was ably supported by Frances de la Tour and Anastasia Hille. The other big new writing hit of the year was Kevin Elyot's *My Night with Reg* (ES best comedy), first presented in the small Theatre Upstairs at the Royal Court, a subversive boulevard comedy in three movements about an enclave of homosexual friends devastated by AIDS. The unseen Reg was the promiscuous harbinger of death,

but the others battled on resiliently if apprehensively. The outstanding cast included John Sessions, David Bamber, Anthony Calf, and Roger Frost.

There was an interesting fuss over Deborah Warner's poetic production of Samuel Beckett's 20-minute *Footfalls.* The Beckett estate took issue with Warner's free interpretation of the stage directions and withdrew permission for the production (given just a few performances at the Garrick Theatre) to proceed to Paris. Fiona Shaw as the anguished monologuist swung between granite despair and flickering sensuality and bound the rhythms of the text to her own Irish identity. Another fleeting highlight was the

(From left) Anastasia Hille, Dame Maggie Smith, and Frances de la Tour appear in the London production of Edward Albee's *Three Tall Women.* Albee's work won the *Evening Standard* Award for the year's best play as well as the Pulitzer Prize for drama, and Smith took the *Evening Standard* Award for best actress.
CATHERINE ASHMORE

second shortest production of the year, Pinter's *Landscape,* a mere 38 minutes, which Ian Holm and Penelope Wilton played for 18 performances in the Royal National Theatre's (RNT's) Cottesloe auditorium after participating in the Pinter Festival at the Gate Theatre, Dublin, in May.

The West End celebrated Sir John Gielgud's 90th birthday by renaming the Globe the Gielgud. The actor beamed delightedly at a reception in his honour and revealed how confusing he had found it in recent years to wander along his beloved Shaftesbury Avenue and not recognize any names on the marquees; now at least, he said, there would be one name he could recognize.

As the new artistic director of the Royal Court, Stephen Daldry started tremendously with a revival of Wesker's early success *The Kitchen,* but the following new pieces—Howard Barker's *Hated Nightfall,* about the last days of the Romanov dynasty; Harvey's *Babies* (ES most promising new playwright award); and Meredith Oakes's *The Editing Process,* a feeble look at the absorption of small publishers in large conglomerates, which starred Alan Howard and Prunella Scales—failed to attract much critical favour. Upstairs, however, after *My Night with Reg*'s triumphant debut, there were promising first plays from Joe Penhall (*Some Voices*) and Nick Grosso (*Peaches*).

The RNT, too, had a mixed year, with so-so productions of Pinter's *The Birthday Party,* George Bernard Shaw's *The*

Devil's Disciple, and Anton Chekhov's *The Seagull* (Judi Dench as a blowzy Arkadina) and a couple of genuine catastrophes, both hastily withdrawn: Phyllida Lloyd's elaborate version of *Pericles* and Richard Eyre's unconvincing British premiere of Charles MacArthur's *Johnny on a Spot.* Eyre bounded back with a sumptuous revival of Tennessee Williams' *Sweet Bird of Youth.* Indeed, the RNT did well by the American repertoire all year, offering well-received productions of Arthur Miller's *Broken Glass* and Lillian Hellman's *The Children's Hour,* an initially creaking but finally moving period piece about an alleged lesbian relationship between two teachers. Harriet Walter and Claire Higgins (who also gave a knockout performance in the Williams) played these roles with considerable emotion and sensitivity. The RNT's other chief successes were Jonathan Kent's revival of Pierre Corneille's *Le Cid* and Sean Mathias' exotic gothic revival of Jean Cocteau's *Les Parents terribles* (with Sheila Gish, de la Tour, and Howard).

Mathias received the ES best director award for both this production and his subsequent Donmar Warehouse revival of Noël Coward's *Design for Living,* in which smoldering newcomer Rachel Weisz oscillated between the cool, frank sexual shenanigans of Clive Owen and Paul Rhys. The 1933 play suddenly seemed entirely contemporary. The small Donmar did as well as the RNT by American dramatists, repeating two of the RNT's successes of the early 1980s; Sam Mendes' new look at Mamet's *Glengarry Glen Ross* was a chilling confirmation of the play's status as a masterpiece, while Matthew Warchus directed Sam Shepard's *True West* (coproduced with the West Yorkshire Playhouse) as an actors' paradise for Mark Rylance and Michael Rudko, who alternated in the roles of the two brothers, and appeared to swap identities, in their mother's California house. Rylance, the previous year's West End Benedick in *Much Ado About Nothing,* gave what many considered to be a double-headed performance unmatched throughout the year. Tom Courtenay (ES best actor) played a short season at the Garrick as the alcoholic Russian layabout in *Moscow Stations,* the one-man show imported from the Traverse in Edinburgh.

Elsewhere in the West End, the Peter Hall Company offered one of the best productions of Georges Feydeau in living memory, *An Absolute Turkey* starring Felicity Kendal and Griff Rhys Jones (yet another young comedian in transition to the legitimate stage). Hall stuttered with a poorly received revival of Frederick Lonsdale's *On Approval* but recovered with a strong West End *Hamlet* in which Stephen Dillane, who made a great impression earlier in the year in the two parts of Tony Kushner's *Angels in America* (at the RNT), won critical acclaim as an ironic, detached, blackly modern prince of Denmark. Donald Sinden was a gruff and comical Polonius, and Michael Pennington a sepulchral, imposing ghost doubled with a sensual, deceitful Claudius.

Nicol Williamson returned with a great banging of the drum in his one-man show about John Barrymore, but he received lukewarm notices and poor audiences. Helen Mirren (*see* BIOGRAPHIES), another favourite who returned to the London stage too infrequently, scored a great success in Ivan Turgenev's *A Month in the Country,* paired with John Hurt (also in fine form) in Bill Bryden's bleakly funny production. David Suchet, television's Hercule Poirot, was well received as the drunken comedian Sid Field in a ribald, old-fashioned entertainment called *What a Performance!* and there was a gripping revival of Patrick Hamilton's *Rope.* Patricia Hodge, glacial and compelling, led a popular revival of *The Prime of Miss Jean Brodie* and survived all comparisons with such distinguished previous incumbents as Vanessa Redgrave (stage), Maggie Smith (film), and Geraldine McEwan (television).

It was a dire year for the musical theatre. *Hot Shoe Shuffle,* a feeble tap-dancing cabaret from Australia, came and went. *Once on This Island* proved a jolly but slight Broadway import with a few good but unoriginal songs. Topol trundled smugly back into the Palladium with a tatty touring version of *Fiddler on the Roof.* A much-touted Barry Manilow compilation, *Copacabana,* drew some praise for wholehearted tattiness and lack of pretension, while another compilation, *Only the Lonely* (which originated at the Liverpool Playhouse), using the songs of Roy Orbison, was sporadically entertaining but dramatically inept. A 40th anniversary production of Sandy Wilson's *The Boy Friend* emanated on tour from its first home, the Players' in Charing Cross, and proved as delightful as ever.

The Royal Shakespeare Company (RSC) maintained a good standard in London and Stratford-upon-Avon, though its metropolitan base was rocked by the unseemly disputes surrounding the allegedly authoritarian rule of the Barbican Centre's managing director, Detta O'Cathain, who vacated her position in mid-November. The Barbican highlights were Robert Stephens' *King Lear* (the actor struggled heroically through the run, though beset with illness) and *The Tempest* with Alec McCowen and Simon Russell Beale as Prospero and Ariel. There were two worthwhile events in the Barbican's smaller Pit: Euripides' rarely seen *Ion,* and *New England* by American Richard Nelson, a domestic drama following a suicide, with a sharp transatlantic tweak. It was Nelson's sixth play to be presented by the RSC.

In Stratford-upon-Avon there were two outstanding new pieces in the RSC's third auditorium, The Other Place: Anne Devlin's *After Easter,* charting a painful and hilarious homecoming to Belfast, and David Edgar's *Pentecost,* a confrontation with the events of Sarajevo—the action, set in an abandoned Byzantine church, weighed the sacrilegious destruction of a culturally significant mural against the plight of a mixed collection of stateless refugees. On the main Stratford stage, there was a seductively enjoyable *Twelfth Night,* a robust and nightmarish *A Midsummer Night's Dream,* and a powerful *Measure for Measure,* in which 50 supernumeraries swelled the stage for the public confrontation of the hypocritical deputy, Angelo, by the pleading Isabella of Stella Gonet. The production also contained a dark and brooding performance by Toby Stephens as Isabella's condemned brother, Claudio; Stephens (the younger son of Robert Stephens and Maggie Smith) had a fine summer, also playing an energetic Lysander in *A Midsummer Night's Dream* and knocking audiences dead in the title role of *Coriolanus* in the Elizabethan-style Swan Theatre.

A few miles from Stratford, the Birmingham Rep thrived under the new artistic directorship of former RSC associate Bill Alexander. Alexander's own production of *The Tempest* was a brave and bold companion in the repertoire to Anthony Clark's revival of Cyril Tourneur's rarely seen *The Atheist's Tragedy* and Philip Prowse's gloriously costumed and choreographed staging of Oscar Wilde's *Lady Windermere's Fan* (which moved into the West End, starring Francesca Annis as the woman with a past). Prowse was equally effective at his home theatre, the Glasgow (Scotland) Citizens', where he directed clever and appealing revivals of Coward's *Private Lives* and Williams' *The Milk Train Doesn't Stop Here Anymore.* Rupert Everett played Williams' Flora Goforth (the Tallulah Bankhead role) in glamorous drag, but the character's decline and isolation took on the grim resonance of AIDS-age mortality.

Manchester was the Arts Council's choice as City of Drama for the year, and the city responded with a full and attractive program. The highlights were undoubtedly the opening of a new venue, the Dancehouse, with the premiere of Theatre de Complicité's *The Three Lives of Lucie Cabrol,* a brilliant adaptation of a John Berger book, and the British premiere of Peter Brook's *The Man Who...* (*L'Homme qui...*), adapted from Oliver Sacks's neurological case studies, a meditation on pure methods of acting on a bare stage. In nearby Mold, Anthony Hopkins played the title role in Chekhov's *Uncle Vanya,* which he also filmed for Granada TV. The production transposed the action from Russia to Wales with limited success, but every ticket was sold.

Brian McMaster's third year in charge of the Edinburgh Festival attracted some of Europe's best directors to Britain: Peter Stein, with his momentous seven-hour production of Aeschylus' *Oresteia* performed in Russian; Peter Zadek, with his impassioned four-hour *Antony and Cleopatra* from Berlin; Luc Bondy, with his gorgeous, wordless 90-minute *The Hour We Knew Nothing of Each Other,* also from Berlin; Robert Lepage (*see* BIOGRAPHIES) with his first-draft version of a work-in-progress about Hiroshima, Japan, and photography, *The Seven Streams of the River Ota* from Montreal; and the new French wunderkind, Stéphane Braunschweig, with his grave and beautiful four-hour *The Winter's Tale* from Orléans. The splendid new Edinburgh Festival Theatre proved an ideal home for visiting dance and opera companies, and the sight of audiences spilling down the stairs behind the gleaming glass frontage only added to the sense of occasion and excitement.

For the first time in 30 years, the Abbey Theatre of Dublin performed in Edinburgh. Patrick Mason's production of J.M. Synge's *The Well of the Saints* proved a strange and potent parable of two blind, married beggars regaining their sight and promptly falling out of love with each other. Curiously, Brian Friel tackled almost the same theme in *Molly Sweeney,* his touching and poetic new play for the Gate Theatre in Dublin, later seen at the Almeida in London. Friel reverted to the tripartite monologue structure of his earlier *The Faith Healer,* and though the new play was less impressive, it marked a return to form after the previous year's slightly disappointing *Wonderful Tennessee.*

The 35th Dublin Theatre Festival featured *The Mai* by Marina Carr, a promising new playwright at the Abbey, and a misfired, expanded version of Jim Plunkett's *The Risen People,* about the Dublin lockouts in 1913 by the Sheridan brothers (playwright Peter and filmmaker Jim) at the Gaiety. Best of all was the visiting Romanian company from Rimnicu Vilcea in *Decameron 646,* a moving and sensuous distillation of Boccaccio by the outstanding young director Silviu Purcarete. The number in the title indicated the years that had passed since the Black Death in 1348, when Boccaccio's characters decamped to a Tuscan villa to tell each other 100 stories of sexual ingenuity and hilarity.

(MICHAEL COVENEY)

U.S. and Canada. Theatre in the U.S. in 1994 was vital but vexatious, a paradox reflecting Broadway's fading role in the overall picture, particularly in the realm of drama. The concept of Broadway as the national American theatre was fast losing credibility even while drama itself was not. The best dramatic work was being done either off-Broadway or in noncommercial, institutional theatres, whether in

New York City or elsewhere. By general consensus the best new play, produced off-Broadway, was Albee's *Three Tall Women,* a strikingly surreal drama of a woman's life and death as seen through three actresses playing her simultaneously in youth, the middle years, and old age. Beyond the value of the play itself, its success had personal resonances, partly because Albee had become the forgotten man of the American theatre. It had been 30 years since his youthful success with *Who's Afraid of Virginia Woolf?* and more than a decade since he had introduced a new play in a major theatre. With *Three Tall Women,* which won a Pulitzer, his reputation was instantly restored.

The mansion of a factory owner is central to Stephen Daldry's spectacular production of J.B. Priestley's 1946 mystery *An Inspector Calls.* The British production, which won rave reviews, moved to Broadway in 1994 and won the Tony for the best revival of the year.
MARC BRYAN—JOAN MARCUS

Albee's play, having been produced off-Broadway, was not eligible for the Tony, which was instead bestowed on *Perestroika,* the second half of Kushner's *Angels in America.* The first half, *Millennium Approaches,* had won the prize in 1993. By year's end, however, both Kushner plays had closed, and no other new dramas were running on Broadway. Indeed, the only play there was the brilliant British revival of J.B. Priestley's wartime melodrama *An Inspector Calls.*

Broadway apparently had lost its core audience of local theatregoers. The tourist audiences who paid its stiff prices (which in 1994 soared to $75) were not interested in mere dramas at such a cost. Thus, there was only the briefest of interest in such worthy new plays as Friel's heartfelt *Wonderful Tennessee;* Anne Deavere Smith's *Twilight: Los Angeles, 1992,* a brilliant collage about the post-Rodney King race riots; and Miller's perception of Jewish identity, *Broken Glass.* Indeed, even Neil Simon, the most popular playwright in Broadway history, announced that his next play (*London Suite*) would be produced off-Broadway. Thus was the death knell sounded for a Broadway dramatic theatre that had once nurtured the likes of O'Neill and Williams. Broadway was left a theatre of musicals.

At least musicals were popular. From the oldest (*Cats*) to the newest (*Sunset Boulevard*), in 1994 they attracted record audiences, despite a virtually unchanging lineup of long-run tourist attractions. The new hits were in that same blockbuster category—*Beauty and the Beast,* an adaptation of the popular animated Disney movie; *Sunset Boulevard,* the latest effort from Britain's Andrew Lloyd Webber; and a spectacular revival of the Jerome Kern-Oscar Hammerstein II classic, *Show Boat.* Each of these shows had merit as well as visual muscle, but only *Show Boat,* as directed by the masterful Harold Prince, had the pulse of living musical theatre.

The year's only other major new American musical was Stephen Sondheim's *Passion,* a rhapsodic examination of unending and utter love. As usual with this American artist, the work was artistically uncompromising as well as brilliant, beautiful, and brainy. Sondheim, beginning his fourth creative decade, remained the conscience as well as the genius of the American musical theatre, but despite his perennial winning of Tony awards (*Passion* was named the year's best musical), his esoteric shows had never been crowd-pleasing entertainments. This show was not able to attract full audiences to even a small theatre and, what was more depressing, Sondheim seemed to be the only regularly productive American writer of musicals.

The story was different among dead writers. Revivals of American musicals had grown to epidemic proportion in recent years, doubtless because they made money. In 1994 three more became hits—*Damn Yankees, Grease!,* and, in an innovative British production, Rodgers and Hammerstein's magnificently scored *Carousel.* Revivals were as important to the theatre as books to libraries, but an art form without new work was dead, and Broadway's producers apparently had lost confidence in their own taste, perhaps frightened by the staggering costs of production (*Sunset Boulevard* cost $13 million). It seemed safer to bet on an old favourite.

On the other hand, off-Broadway was alive with productivity during the year. The most significant of the hits was a show called *Stomp,* which was incomprehensible to nearly everyone except the youthful audiences who flocked to see it. A British import, *Stomp* was neither a musical, a drama, nor a comedy but 90 minutes with a small group of working-class youths who made rhythmic, percussive noises with a variety of props that ranged from garbage can lids to blocks of wood. What might be dismissed as illiterate noise was in fact an alert about the new languages of youth, languages perhaps inspired by a world of rock videos and computers and languages that had to be listened to. In fascinating contrast, another off-Broadway success was entirely about language, David Ives's four one-act plays entitled *All in the Timing.* Ranging from a playlet about a young man constantly testing and editing his flirtatious approach with a girl to a sketch about a new language altogether, the quartet was crisp, funny, and brainy. What both *Stomp* and *All in the Timing* suggested, different though they were, was that a modern theatre must embrace a wider range of genres than the old categories of musicals, dramas, and comedies.

Most vigorous of all, not only in New York City but across the United States, was the work in institutional theatres. At the Manhattan Theatre Club, for example, the emphasis was on well-crafted plays with social responsibilities. Terrence McNally seemed to be the resident playwright, providing the organization with *A Perfect Ganesh* early in the year and later with *Love! Valour! Compassion!* Both works were keyed to the AIDS crisis, with the first the more artistic. At Lincoln Center Theater, while *Carousel* was holding forth at the large Vivian Beaumont Theater, a series of exciting new American works were being presented in the studio theatre below (the Mitzi E. Newhouse). The most fascinating of these was *Hello Again,* written in its entirety (music, lyrics, libretto) by Michael John LaChiusa. This balletlike musical, a variation on Arthur Schnitzler's *La Ronde,* told its interconnecting love stories through songs that were operatic at one moment and ragtime the next and then as danceable as a Cole Porter tune. It was for exactly such work that LaChiusa was considered the most exciting newcomer in U.S. musical theatre.

Meantime, the Roundabout Theatre solidified its position as New York's hometown repertory theatre. Roundabout followed a sound and yet original formula, seldom venturing among playwrights older than Henrik Ibsen or Shaw

---

Toronto, Theatre's Third City

By the 1990s Toronto had quietly become the third-largest theatre centre in the English-speaking world, after New York City and London. With a population approaching four million in the metropolitan area, Toronto had come to serve as host to a wide range of theatrical activity, from fringe festivals in the summer to several midsize, not-for-profit theatres, national and international festivals, and, in 1994, four long-running, full-scale Broadway musicals. By 1994 there were more than 70 full-time theatrical venues in the city and an average of 75 productions every month. More than seven million tickets were sold during the year, half of them to tourists. The gross revenue for Toronto's commercial theatres was more than $200 million, accounting for 10% of all sales in North America, second only to New York, and the total economic impact on the Toronto economy was estimated at $1.2 billion.

Broadway musicals in Toronto in 1994 included *The Phantom of the Opera,* which had run for more than five years in the renovated Pantages Theatre. *Phantom*'s Toronto producer, Garth Drabinsky, was also responsible for the productions of the Hal Prince-directed *Kiss of the Spider Woman* and *Show Boat,* both of which had their premieres in Toronto before transferring to Broadway. The Toronto production of *Show Boat,* meanwhile, was scheduled to continue into 1995, after which it would make way for *Sunset Boulevard.* Ed and David Mirvish's productions of *Crazy for You* and *Miss Saigon*—the latter in the stunning, specially built Princess of Wales Theatre—continued to run profitably, and David Mirvish was set to present his own production of The Who's *Tommy* early in 1995. A Toronto production of the nostalgic musical *Forever Plaid* was into its third year, and the city consistently turned out for touring musicals in several large commercial venues. Other independent commercial productions running with various success included Stephen Sondheim's *Assassins* and Canadian John Roby's musical *The Old Man's Band.*

It was not all roses for commercial theatre in Toronto, however. The large-scale, independently produced Canadian musical *Napoleon* was neither a critical nor a box-office success, although it was seen by 60,000 people in nearly three months before it closed in May. Later, a production of George F. Walker's comedy-drama *Nothing Sacred* opened at the spacious Winter Garden Theatre, only to close after two and a half months of half-empty houses. Nonetheless, the fact that commercial productions could even get off the ground in Toronto spoke volumes, especially for such high-risk ventures as a new musical (the *Napoleon* budget was $5 million).　　　　　　　(H.J. KIRCHHOFF)

but, rather, concentrating on 20th-century works its public would enjoy. Its year of overflow business included excellent productions of Pinter's *No Man's Land* (with Jason Robards and Christopher Plummer), Friel's *Philadelphia, Here I Come!*, and William Inge's *Picnic*, as well as a glorious restaging of Williams' *The Glass Menagerie*. The latter showcased Julie Harris in the performance of her career. U.S. regional theatres likewise seemed to be thriving, but with a safe, standard repertoire of classics. In Cambridge, Mass., for instance, the American Repertory Theatre was doing Shakespeare's *Henry IV*, Chekhov's *The Cherry Orchard*, and O'Neill's *A Touch of the Poet*, while in Houston, Texas, the Alley Theatre was presenting Edmond Rostand's *Cyrano de Bergerac*, Williams' *Orpheus Descending*, and Molière's *Tartuffe*.

Canada's venerable Stratford (Ont.) Festival, with artistic director Richard Monette, brought back such familiar faces as director Michael Langham; actors Martha Henry, Marti Maraden, Nicholas Pennell, Roberta Maxwell, and Douglas Rain; designer Ming Cho Lee; and composers Louis Applebaum and Stanley Silverman, some of whom were in their third decades at Stratford. In 1994 the festival offered Shakespeare's *Hamlet, Twelfth Night, The Comedy of Errors*, and *Othello* along with O'Neill's *Long Day's Journey into Night* and Gilbert and Sullivan's *The Pirates of Penzance*.

(MARTIN GOTTFRIED)

See also Dance; Music.

This article updates the *Macropædia* article The History of Western THEATRE.

Transportation

As a result of subdued world trade, global passenger and freight traffic showed patchy growth in 1994. Key infrastructure projects continued to be promoted, most notably the much-delayed opening of the Channel Tunnel (Eurotunnel) to passengers on November 14. The most significant underlying trend, the change in emphasis from road to rail or public transport, was linked to both financial and environmental concerns. Russia was the only country with a significant reverse switch from rail to road transport.

Privatization of transport entities continued apace, although the nature, scale, and urgency of the timetable varied quite markedly. One common feature in transport operations was the increasing use of electronic means to provide better operational control and efficiency. The first world congress on intelligent transportation systems took place in Paris in December.   (JOHN H. EARP)

AVIATION

Helped by low jet-fuel prices, the world airline industry began in 1994 to emerge from the longest and most damaging period of financial losses in its 75-year history. A trend that began in July 1993 for traffic to grow faster than capacity continued strongly into the following year, and the International Air Transport Association (IATA) forecast a profit of $1 billion for its members as 1994 closed.

This was modest when viewed against the industry's future needs to finance debt, build reserves, and sustain investments in new aircraft and advanced technologies, such as satellite-based navigation systems. It was, however, a significant improvement over the disastrous record of $15.6 billion in losses on international scheduled services over the years 1990–93. These losses represented nearly 4% of revenue, whereas the airlines should have been making net profits of between 5% and 6% of revenue if they were to face their future commitments with confidence.

Pierre Jeanniot, IATA director-general, denied that the industry's malaise was a sign of decline or decadence, declaring that air transport was simply "reinventing itself." Jeanniot warned that the need for profitability was paramount. Without it, air transport would either die (as did maritime passenger transport) or become a political football in a game of subsidies (as with railroads). In the search for profitability, the attitude of governments was crucial. The industry was putting its own house in order, but the inaction, or wrong actions, of some governments was undermining its efforts, Jeanniot said, criticizing "inadequate infrastructure and misguided taxation, user charges, and environmental policies."

The airlines were certainly not short of advice on how to put their house in order. Committees of inquiry in the U.S., Europe, and Japan examined the industry and then advised it to liberalize, modernize, and become more consumer-conscious. In the U.S. a threat to the newly won profitability of the major airlines appeared in the shape of a rash of start-up companies offering cheap-fare, minimal-service, no-frills flights, while in Europe the big state-owned carriers continued to lay off thousands of employees as they pursued an often-painful course toward privatization.

In Europe a two-tiered airline industry began to emerge. One group was privately owned and financially successful, while the other was state-owned, relying on massive government handouts that were controversially sanctioned by the European Union (EU). Some major European airports—notably Heathrow, near London, and Frankfurt (Germany)—began to run out of takeoff and landing slots, making it difficult for new airlines spawned by EU liberalization to operate there. Modernization of the European air traffic control system continued on a national basis, with a campaign to have the system federalized within the EU gaining pace.

East Asia continued to outstrip the rest of the world in increases in numbers of passengers and tons of freight carried. New airlines emerging in the countries of the former Soviet bloc, as the previously monolithic civil aviation structure was dismantled and rebuilt, also did well—although from a much lower base and with worries in some cases over safety standards.

Overall, the world airline system carried almost 1.2 billion passengers in 1993 and nearly 18 million metric tons of cargo, according to the International Civil Aviation Organization, the UN aviation body. Within that total IATA airlines' international scheduled passenger traffic rose 6.4%, and freight traffic was up 7.3%. The IATA forecast annual growth of 6.6% for the years 1994–98 and predicted that northeastern Asia would overtake Western Europe in air traffic by 1998, with comparative growth rates of 12.1% and 6.7%, respectively.

Air safety came to the fore in the U.S. in 1994 as the airline industry had its worst year for accidents since 1988. In all, more than 250 people were killed in six crashes on major and regional carriers. Crashes and other incidents involving the turboprop ATR-72 led the U.S. Federal Aviation Administration to impose a ban on the planes in icy weather.   (ARTHUR REED)

SHIPPING AND PORTS

Two main problems continued to bedevil world shipping in 1994. The first was the increasing age of the world fleet, which promised to result in many more substandard ships unable to meet current shipping regulations. The second was the surplus of ships, which depressed freight rates below the point at which investment in new tonnage was a worthwhile option for shipowners.

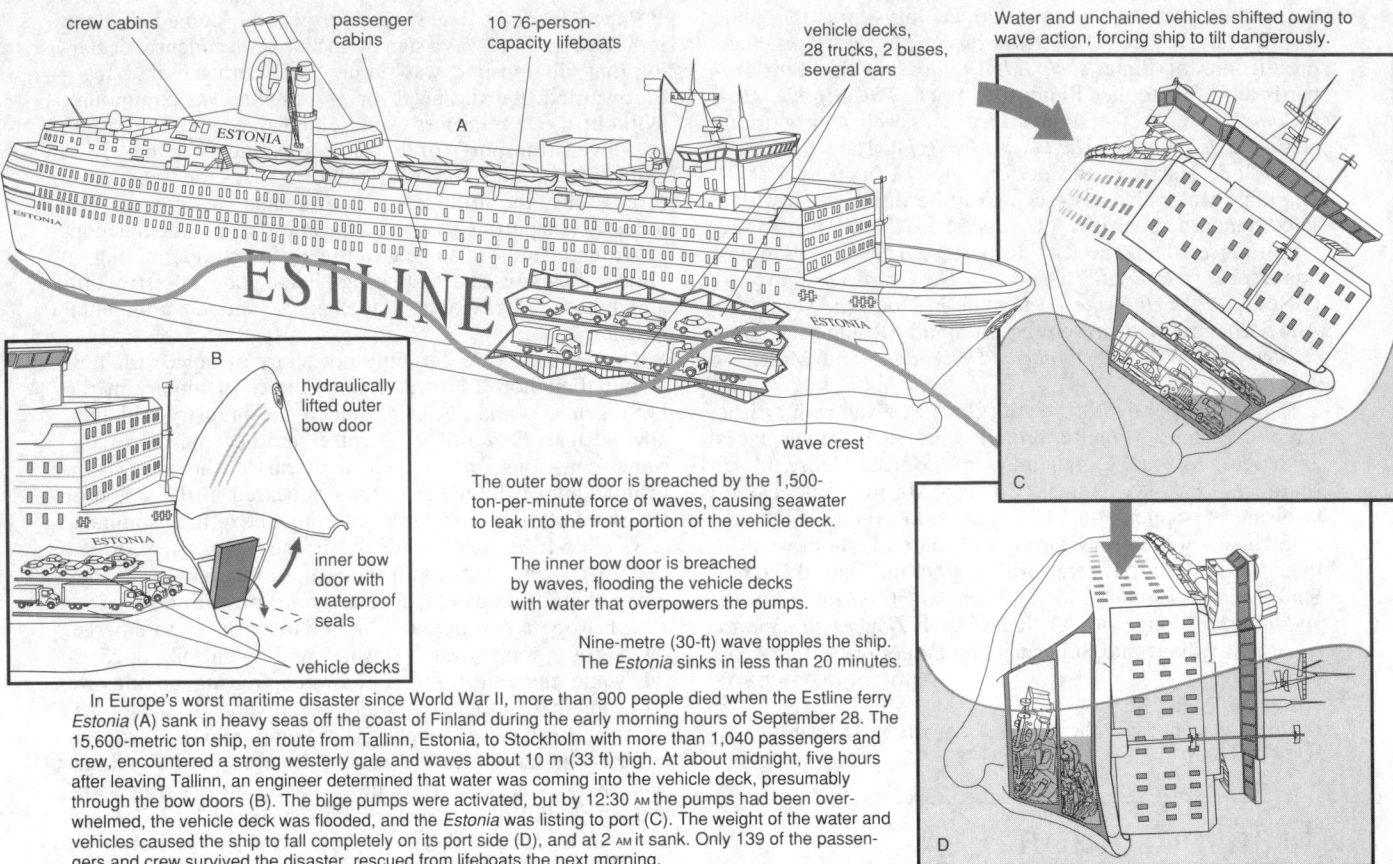

crew cabins

passenger cabins

10 76-person-capacity lifeboats

vehicle decks, 28 trucks, 2 buses, several cars

Water and unchained vehicles shifted owing to wave action, forcing ship to tilt dangerously.

hydraulically lifted outer bow door

inner bow door with waterproof seals

vehicle decks

wave crest

The outer bow door is breached by the 1,500-ton-per-minute force of waves, causing seawater to leak into the front portion of the vehicle deck.

The inner bow door is breached by waves, flooding the vehicle decks with water that overpowers the pumps.

Nine-metre (30-ft) wave topples the ship. The *Estonia* sinks in less than 20 minutes.

In Europe's worst maritime disaster since World War II, more than 900 people died when the Estline ferry *Estonia* (A) sank in heavy seas off the coast of Finland during the early morning hours of September 28. The 15,600-metric ton ship, en route from Tallinn, Estonia, to Stockholm with more than 1,040 passengers and crew, encountered a strong westerly gale and waves about 10 m (33 ft) high. At about midnight, five hours after leaving Tallinn, an engineer determined that water was coming into the vehicle deck, presumably through the bow doors (B). The bilge pumps were activated, but by 12:30 AM the pumps had been overwhelmed, the vehicle deck was flooded, and the *Estonia* was listing to port (C). The weight of the water and vehicles caused the ship to fall completely on its port side (D), and at 2 AM it sank. Only 139 of the passengers and crew survived the disaster, rescued from lifeboats the next morning.

The world fleet continued to increase, rising from 399 million gross tons (gt) in 1988 to 458 million gt in 1993. The world fleet expanded for the sixth consecutive year, although the expansion was a small one of 8.3 million gt. At the end of 1993, it consisted of 80,655 ships of 458 million gt, with an average age of 18 years. During 1993, 1,505 ships of 20 million gt were completed.

The 22.7 million gt of new ship orders received in 1993 represented the second highest level of annual new ordering in 10 years. The reason for the increased number of new orders was not clear-cut. It probably owed more to economic factors within the shipping industry, such as lower building costs and the increased average age of the world fleet, than to any dramatic improvement in world trade. Also highest since 1988 was the 1993 scrapping of 10.5 million gt. This was just over half the completion figure of 20 million gt.

The U.S. Oil Pollution Act of 1990 (OPA '90) continued to command the attention of shipowners who wanted to trade with the U.S. OPA '90 was applicable to vessels that stored, handled, or transported oil. The act was a direct result of the *Exxon Valdez* oil-spill disaster and imposed unlimited liability on shipowners trading with the U.S. for any oil-pollution incidents. During the year, $5 billion in punitive damages was assessed against Exxon for the disaster, in addition to the $3 billion already spent by the company on cleanup operations and settling court cases. This made shipping-industry calculations of the need for liability coverage of $2 billion per vessel look far too low.

On September 28 the "roll-on, roll-off" ferry *Estonia* sank in the Baltic Sea after a loading door was apparently ripped off by pounding waves. (*See* Figure.) The accident, in which more than 900 people died, raised questions about the safety of all such oceangoing ferries. Concerns over safety at sea were also an issue after the December 2 sinking of the cruise ship *Achille Lauro* in the Indian Ocean, although only two lives were lost.

Hong Kong remained the top container port, with a throughput in 1993 of 9,620,000 TEU (20-ft equivalent units). Singapore was next with 9,040,000 TEU; third was Kao-hsiung, Taiwan, with 4,249,250 TEU. An annual shipping review concluded that world seaborne trade would continue to benefit from Chinese industrialization.

(EDWARD CROWLEY)

FREIGHT AND PIPELINES

Despite the conclusion of the General Agreement on Tariffs and Trade, overall expansion of worldwide trade movements was not significant in 1994. The Pacific Rim continued to move ahead in terms of container activity, with container ships on order with capacities nudging the 5,000-TEU (20-ft equivalent units) mark. Ten of the 20 biggest container-carrying liners were Asian, offering over 50% of the slots. There was a similar pattern for container port traffic, with Hong Kong and Singapore outperforming all other ports in both absolute and percentage growth. Each handled more than 9 million TEU in 1993 and were headed toward 10 million in 1994. Kao-hsiung, Taiwan, which handled more than 4 million TEU, overtook Rotterdam, Neth., as the third busiest container port.

The use of special and/or non-International Organization for Standardization containers and the drive toward intermodalism were issues in 1994. Upsizing of containers was resisted in Japan through maximum-vehicle-weight legislation. In Europe increasing concern led to stronger legislation covering the use of hydrofluorocarbons in refrigerated containers. The new European Intermodal Association, in common with U.S. operators, placed greater emphasis on intermodal services to extract maximum flexibility.

New gas- and oil-pipeline development showed a decline from the 1992 high of 25,830 km (16,050 mi) to an estimated 23,650 km (14,700 mi) in 1994. The U.S. accounted for one-third of all new developments, although the gas-pipeline network expansion was held back pending clarification of federal and state regulatory procedures. Worldwide there was a new emphasis on long-term-storage facilities.

In Europe development centred on the $1.5 billion North Sea Europipe gas-line project. In the former U.S.S.R., after a number of years of underinvestment, the focus shifted to maintenance and rehabilitation, especially following the oil spill at Usinsk, Russia, in October, which was the third largest in history. The gas line connecting the China Sea Yacheng Field to Hong Kong was nearly complete, and the Maghreb-Europe line was begun. Major pipeline networks were under consideration in Oman, China, and South America.

ROADS AND TRAFFIC

Governments in 1994 faced with continued road-traffic demand, a lack of investment funding, and concern for the environment looked to traffic restraint and public transport in urban areas and to private funding and/or privatization for key interurban tolled facilities. California led the way in zero-emission legislation. The International Bridge, Tunnel, and Turnpike Association showed that some 45,000 km (27,960 mi) of toll roads were planned around the world. Poland planned 2,000 km (1,240 mi) of tollways, and Hungary was planning an M5 motorway similar to its successful M1-M15 project. Other tollroads included State Route 91 in Orange county, Calif.; the new expressway to Dulles International Airport near Washington, D.C.; the 58-km (36-mi) six-lane route in Toronto; and the Guangzhou (Canton)–Shenzhen (Shenchen) tolled superhighway in China. Mexico had a program for more than 6,000 km (3,730 mi) of toll roads.

Priority was generally given to water crossings or other natural barriers. The Danes made progress on the fixed link road/rail system traversing The Sound: 3,750 m (12,300 ft) of immersed tunnel, the 7,470-m (24,500-ft) Flinterenden bridge, and 4,210 m (13,810 ft) of connecting bridges. In Hong Kong the express highway being constructed from the Chinese border to the new Chek Lap Kok airport included the clear-span Tsing Ma suspension bridge, the cable-stay Kap Shiu Min bridge, and an immersed-tube tunnel. China was investigating the world's longest sea-crossing project: a $6.9 billion bridge/tunnel crossing of Bohai Haixia between Shandong (Shan-tung) and Liaoning. Pakistan, with help from Sweden, was reexamining the Lowari road-tunnel link to Tajikistan. Turkey was considering a third Bosphorus crossing comprising a twin-tube tunnel for road and rail traffic to supplement the existing suspension bridges.

INTERCITY RAIL

Most countries throughout the world were placing an ever greater emphasis on rail travel for passengers and freight movement in 1994. The use of rail in the countries of the former Soviet Union eclipsed the rest of the world, accounting for about half of all rail freight and, with over 400 billion passengers per kilometre, twice the total of passenger traffic in the U.K., France, Germany, and Italy combined. These countries, however, had a desperate need for economic restructuring and upgrading of rail maintenance and operations.

The most important rail development continued to be high-speed passenger trains. By 1994 Brussels, London, and Paris were linked by high-speed trains. With the inauguration of the Channel Tunnel (Eurotunnel) in May, followed by vehicle-carrying and passenger services later in the year,

England's land link to the continent finally came into being. (See Special Report.) The next step would be to extend through services in an ever widening network in Europe. The Belgian, Dutch, German, French, Italian, and Spanish railways all had active plans for network extension, with possible European Union funding of up to ECU 12 billion per year. Swiss and Austrian rail plans focused on new trans-Alpine tunnels. In October an agreement for funding Amtrak cleared the way for inviting bids for a 240-km/h (150-mph) train for the northeast corridor in the U.S. Russia made a start on its high-speed line linking St. Petersburg and Novgorod. China was planning a 1,300-km/h (800-mph) high-speed route linking Beijing (Peking) and Shanghai and was also to add 20,000 km (12,425 mi) to its overall rail network in the next decade.

Construction resumed on the 800-km (500-mi) privately financed line from Baikal to Yakutsk, Siberia. In South America, Ecuador and Colombia had ambitious plans to rehabilitate major positions of their rail networks, while in Argentina, despite the change in emphasis brought on by privatization, improved passenger services in the Pampas and Atlantic corridors achieved self-sufficient operations. New Zealand Rail also achieved operating profits (without receiving a subsidy except for commuter services to Wellington).

URBAN MASS TRANSIT

Development of urban transport systems continued its unprecedented growth. The main constraint lay in differing viewpoints of how to achieve the best overall result: economic viability against reduced congestion and pollution. Berlin, Paris, and Vienna led the way in providing strategic frameworks for totally integrated services. With more than 100 cities operating rapid transit systems around the world and planning to invest $13.8 billion during the year, unsatiated development looked certain.

A new metro system opened in Brasília, Brazil, as did extensions to existing systems in Calcutta; Madrid; Munich, Germany; Nagoya, Japan; Paris; Pusan, South Korea; and Washington, D.C. Metro construction was under way in Hanover, Germany; Kao-hsiung, Taiwan; Pasadena, Calif.; Santiago, Chile; and Toronto, with a go-ahead for planning systems in many locations, including three Chinese cities; Ho Chi Minh City, Vietnam; and a fourth line in São Paulo, Brazil. Metro extensions to airports were planned for Stockholm, Hong Kong, San Francisco, and Berlin.

Light transit systems were even more extensive. New schemes were opened in Denver, Colo.; Guadalajara, Mexico; Rouen and Strasbourg, France; Sheffield, England; and Valencia, Spain. Extensions were made in many other cities, including the Docklands Light Railway in London. Construction was authorized in numerous cities, including Izmir, Turkey; Saarbrucken, Germany; and San Juan, P.R., with detailed studies and planning being undertaken for Brisbane, Australia; Copenhagen; Johannesburg, South Africa; and Salt Lake City, Utah.

City authorities were also looking for solutions to connecting problems—especially using park-and-ride facilities—with a range of technologies from conventional rail (Chicago) to automated rail (Skytrain in Vancouver, B.C., and a second VAL line in Toulouse, France). They were also most interested in dual-mode vehicles (e.g., in Paris) and nonpolluting buses in a determined effort to combat vehicle-generated atmospheric pollution, which was increasingly being related to lung and heart diseases.

(JOHN H. EARP)

See also Business and Industry Review: Aerospace; Automobiles; Energy; Engineering Projects; Environment.

This article updates the Macropædia article TRANSPORTATION.

Seafaring and History in the English Channel

BY NIGEL CALDER

Queen Victoria welcomed an early proposal for a tunnel under the English Channel "in the name of all the ladies in England." Nearly 140 years later the tunnel is open, and its top selling point is still the gratifying lack of motion in the seabed rocks that envelop it. Off the coast of Normandy, on D-Day 1944, the roll and pitch of the landing craft in the Channel waters reduced many young heroes to green jelly. No wonder they hurried ashore to liberate Europe.

The English Channel's waves are not imposing. Surfers scorn them. They shrink in height by 50% from the wide Atlantic aperture to the narrow Strait of Dover, where most people cross the Channel. But tidal currents, shallow banks, and wave reflections from the cliffs all contribute to a disagreeable choppiness whenever the wind rises above 10 knots. That is why this most important strip of shallow water in the world belongs strictly to sailors. In Victoria's time women were always passengers, which explains her apparently sexist remark about the tunnel.

The sailors observe with good-humoured disdain those who cross the Channel by unorthodox means. It has been an inviting proving ground, from the first balloon crossing in 1785, through the first powered flight in 1909, to the pedal-powered aircraft of more recent times. Matthew Webb in 1875 was the first to swim the Channel, and now to do so is almost routine. People also cross by sailboard, canoe, water skis, and almost anything that floats.

The Island Mentality. Those who have written about the Channel must be mostly landlubbers. Otherwise, popular perceptions of the Channel, shared throughout the English-speaking world, could not be so wrongheaded. For example, landlubber Shakespeare had John of Gaunt describing England as "This precious stone set in the silver sea, / Which serves it in the office of a wall, / Or as a moat defensive to a house, / Against the envy of less happier lands." Many people believe that this moat has kept England safe from invasion since 1066, when the Normans landed.

Glorious isolation supposedly allowed English culture to diverge from mainland Europe's, with well-known consequences for Protestantism, science, and parliamentary democracy. Colonizers braving seasickness sailed off down-Channel to carry the English language and English ways to the ends of the Earth. But their libertarian ideals made their imperialism self-destruct. Retreating home, they had to find new partners, and the Channel Tunnel (Eurotunnel) symbolizes the islanders' reunion with mainland Europe.

The island mentality and its historical effects are not in dispute, and neither is the English Channel's contribution to this mentality. But to a sailor, any idea that such a narrow strip of water created the isolation is sheer nonsense. The Channel was no more than a conspicuous line chalked on the sidewalk to separate rival gangs. It was never a barrier to sailors. On the contrary, it was a convenient bridge linking the two shorelines. Except in long spells of adverse weather, travel by water was much quicker and easier than going the same distance overland. That did not change until the invention of steam trains in the 19th century.

Waves of Immigrants. People moved freely across the sea, and England was populated by wave after wave of peaceful settlers and warlike invaders. "From this amphibious ill-born mob began / That vain ill-natur'd thing, an Englishman." In saying so, Daniel Defoe showed a shrewder sense of maritime history than Shakespeare.

Hunter-gatherers strolled across the still-dry seabed as the last ice age ended, but the first farmers reached England 6,000 years ago on boats or rafts that had to accommodate cattle and sheep as well as people. Later immigrants came with plows and horses. Discoveries of Bronze Age shipwrecks by archaeologists reveal that traders were voyaging routinely across the wider parts of the English Channel more than 3,000 years ago.

During the century before Christ, Celtic ironworking people possessed both shores. Sturdy sailing vessels carried cargoes of Italian wine to England. They departed from Brittany, the tide-swept granite promontory of France that nurtured, then as now, some of the world's finest seamen. By rights they should have expunged Julius Caesar from the history books when he came to conquer them. Sadly, a rare calm left the Celts' battle fleet helpless while the Roman rowing galleys cut down their masts.

The written history of the Channel starts with Caesar, and a hundred years later the Roman legions were conquering England. The Celtic cousins in Gallia and Britannia then shared Roman rulers, in the first of three Channel-straddling empires. It lasted for four centuries, and no one ever complained about the lack of a tunnel.

A Roman fleet, the Classis Britannica, was based at Boulogne on the Gallic side of the Strait of Dover. It protected the Channel shores and the busy shipping routes against German pirates. They came from the sandy eastern shores of the North Sea with a variety of tribal names. The Angles gave theirs to England even though Saxons predominated on the island's Channel shore. The newcomers merged and modified their German dialects to produce Anglo-Saxon, the linguistic ancestor of English.

Romans had always regarded Britannia as the back of beyond, and their imperial relics were more impressive on the other side of the Channel. There the Franks from the Rhine River delta were the most successful invaders and so gave their name to France. They began to imitate Roman ways and to speak a form of Latin that would evolve into French. But cross-Channel linguistic divergence was interrupted by another wave of piratical cousins. The longships of the Vikings of Scandinavia became a fearsome sight on all the coasts and rivers of northwestern Europe. Danish Vikings subdued England but fumbled their grip on it. Vikings from Norway made inroads into France and cruised far up the Seine River, where they razed the Franks' stronghold of Paris. Taking possession of France's central Channel shore, these Northmen named it Normandy. In 1066 their longships took them to England, which became a colony in a Norman empire that spanned the Channel. The conquerors spoke French by that time, and their hearts remained rooted on the French side of the Channel. Nevertheless, they thought nothing of crossing over for an occasional binge or a murder.

Nigel Calder is an amateur sailor, an independent writer, and the author of many books about science and technology, including Spaceship Earth (1991) and Giotto to the Comets (1992).

A Channel shipwreck during a drunken onboard party drowned a Norman prince at Cap Barfleur. The ensuing war of succession produced a larger cross-Channel entity, the Angevin empire. This extended from the Spanish border in the south of France to the Scottish border in the north of England. Scotland and Ireland became satellites.

The Angevin empire appreciated its sailors and sea links. Its *rôles d'Oléron* codified maritime law for western Europe. It was not any difficulty with the cross-Channel shipping that caused the empire to crumble. The children of Queen Eleanor squabbled over their inheritance, and the chief beneficiaries were the Franks, whose enclave had been reduced to only one-tenth of the area of France.

England Versus France. The modern nations of France and England came into being in a 200-year struggle for territory and taxes between the heirs of the pirates from the Rhine and Norway. Early in the contest the Franks recaptured the Norman heartlands in France. Forced to regard England as their base, the Normans adopted the English language and sought to befriend their Anglo-Saxon subjects, whom they had treated severely at first.

So it was as the king of England—crying "God for Harry! England and Saint George!"—that Henry V invaded France. He compelled the French king, Charles VI, to name him as his heir instead of Charles' son, the dauphin. However, because Henry V died young, the fourth cross-Channel empire uniting England and France was not to be. The peasant girl Joan of Arc inspired the dispossessed dauphin to recover his kingdom and boot the Anglo-Normans out of France.

From that time onward, English identity was established through hatred of the French across the water. And vice versa. Did not Joan of Arc offer divine authority for killing Englishmen? France and England became the prototypes for the present division of the world into nation-states.

Nationalism was invented in the laboratory of the English Channel.

A Symbolic Role. The water's role was symbolic only. All through the medieval struggles, invading armies crossed in both directions and pounced on undefended beaches. Long after the Anglo-French sort-out was complete, Henry Tudor of Wales gathered French and Breton troops at the mouth of the Seine and sailed them to Wales. The invaders killed King Richard III of England in battle and gave his crown to Henry. As recently as 1688 the Dutchman William of Orange stepped ashore with a Dutch and German army in Devon, forced King James II to flee, and took the crown. This latter-day William the Conqueror had a wind from the east that carried his invasion fleet down-Channel while pinning the English navy in harbour.

With fighting men and favourable weather, the moat was defendable. Drake's long-cannoned squadrons defeated the Spanish Armada. A dogged British blockade kept Napoleon's invasion fleet at bay until he lost patience and gave up. And when the army of Adolf Hitler was preparing to cross the Channel in 1940, fighter aircraft denied him the prerequisite mastery of the sky.

Although 564 years have elapsed since the English caught Joan of Arc and burned her alive, the mutual scorn of the French and English remains ingrained in both populations. That a century of military, political, and economic cooperation has brought neither side to its senses astonishes their partners in the European Union and the Western alliance. Perhaps the myth of the English Channel as a formidable barrier is meant to excuse this gross irrationality, but the maritime history exposes it as a purely sociopsychological dividing line. When millions already cross the water by ferry or by air, why should anyone imagine that a slender tunnel under the seabed will change cross-Channel attitudes?

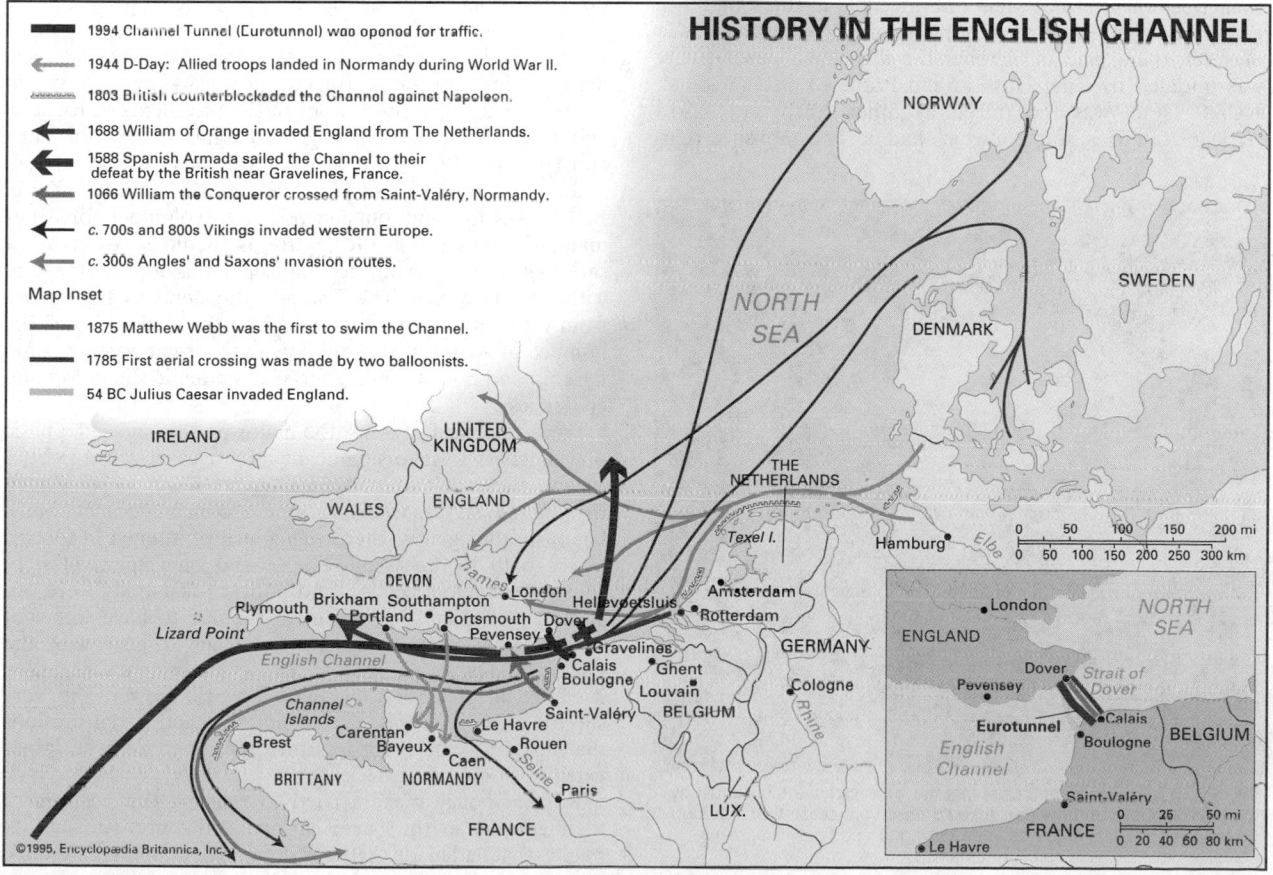

HISTORY IN THE ENGLISH CHANNEL

1994 Channel Tunnel (Eurotunnel) was opened for traffic.

1944 D-Day: Allied troops landed in Normandy during World War II.

1803 British counterblockaded the Channel against Napoleon.

1688 William of Orange invaded England from The Netherlands.

1588 Spanish Armada sailed the Channel to their defeat by the British near Gravelines, France.

1066 William the Conqueror crossed from Saint-Valéry, Normandy.

c. 700s and 800s Vikings invaded western Europe.

c. 300s Angles' and Saxons' invasion routes.

Map Inset

1875 Matthew Webb was the first to swim the Channel.

1785 First aerial crossing was made by two balloonists.

54 BC Julius Caesar invaded England.

©1995, Encyclopædia Britannica, Inc.

World Affairs

Relations between the major powers remained on an even keel in 1994, but bloody conflicts in various parts of the world acted as a reminder that a stable new world order had not yet emerged. It became equally clear that the ability of the major powers to act in unison to restore peace remained as limited as in the days of the Cold War.

The balance sheet was not all negative, however. The year witnessed the emergence of a free South Africa ruled by the majority. After the proclamation of a new constitution on Nov. 18, 1993, general elections took place in April 1994. While the National Party won in Western Cape province and the Inkatha Freedom Party in KwaZulu/Natal, the African National Congress (ANC) emerged as the overall winner, with 62% of the total vote. The ANC forces were incorporated into the South African army, and a new government under Nelson Mandela was installed. Another encouraging development was the armistice in Northern Ireland—after centuries of conflict and more than 20 years of acute terrorism.

Following months of secret talks, the Irish Republican Army expressed its wish in August 1994 to work for a political solution, and Protestants followed suit shortly thereafter. Jean-Bertrand Aristide, deposed president of Haiti, returned in October following massive pressure on the military junta exerted by the United Nations (the Security Council having authorized a military invasion in July 1994) and, above all, the United States. His return proceeded with little bloodshed.

There was spectacular progress in the Arab-Israeli peace process. In May 1994 Israeli forces withdrew from the Gaza Strip and Jericho, and Palestinians took control. While talks between Israel and Syria did not lead to immediate results, their positions did not seem unbridgeable in the long term. In July Jordan and Israel formally ended the state of war between them, and in October the draft of a peace treaty was initialed by King Hussein and Prime Minister Yitzhak Rabin. Israel was recognized by other Arab and North African countries, some of which had never established rela-

tions with the Jewish state and others of which had broken off relations at the time of the Six-Day War in 1967.

There was growing tension in 1994 as North Korea refused to allow international teams to inspect its nuclear facilities. When the United States and other countries threatened sanctions, the North Koreans announced that if they were imposed, Seoul, the capital of South Korea, would become "a sea of fire." The North Koreans had previously denied the possession of nuclear bombs, but this threat seemed to suggest otherwise. Most outside observers thought that North Korea possessed such devices but was willing to negotiate to improve its desperate economic situation. Shortly before Kim Il Sung, who had ruled the country for decades with an iron hand, died on July 8 (*see* OBITUARIES), former U.S. president Jimmy Carter went on an official peace mission to work out a new inspection plan that at least temporarily defused the dangerous situation.

The achievements of diplomacy in 1994 were by no means secure, however. It was not certain that the South African government would be able to live up to the high expectations that accompanied it, especially in the economic and social fields. The progress made between the Arabs and Israel was equally insecure; the peace process had powerful enemies, as a new terrorist campaign by radical Islamists (in Argentina and Britain as well as inside Israel) showed. The attacks weakened the Israeli government's willingness to proceed on the road of peace and also hurt Yasir Arafat, chairman of the Palestine Liberation Organization, and they made Arab governments less willing to take risks on the road to a rapprochement with Israel. Only a first, small step had been made toward peace in Ireland, and the armistices in Yugoslavia were only partly effective. There was constant danger that fighting would flare up again, even in parts of the Balkans such as Croatia and Macedonia, which had been relatively quiet in recent years. There was no certainty that the promises made by the North Koreans could be trusted.

Nor did diplomacy have much impact on what was perhaps the greatest single tragedy of 1994—the civil war in Rwanda. The apparent murder of the presidents of Rwanda and Burundi on April 6 triggered fighting between Tutsi and Hutu in which hundreds of thousands were murdered, and an equal number of Hutu fled to Tanzania and Zaire. France was the only outside power to volunteer for a humanitarian mission involving troops. It did so to create a safe haven and, having accomplished this limited mission, withdrew its forces. The Rwanda disaster was frightening from yet another point of view; given the general instability in much of Africa, it showed how easily tribal warfare could flare up and how it could aggravate endemic starvation and epidemics.

For a variety of reasons, the major powers showed a basic unwillingness to take significant initiatives in world politics except when their immediate interests were concerned. In the United States, where domestic policies loomed much larger on the agenda, there was a lack of interest in foreign affairs both in the White House and on Capitol Hill. In Japan economic recession and political instability were obstacles; no Japanese government seemed to have sufficient support, for example, to end the trade dispute with the United States. In China, which had traditionally regarded itself as an Asian rather than a world power, the very success of its economy caused inflation and social tensions that made its elderly leaders turn inward to an even larger extent.

Russian policy makers tried to reassert the position of their country in the "near abroad"—the non-Russian republics that had made up the former Soviet Union. Economic

Citizens of Northern Ireland celebrate the announcement in August by the Irish Republican Army that it would observe a cease-fire. Although Protestant groups later joined in promising to end hostilities, many obstacles to a political solution remained.

Changes to Flags of the World

Palau

South Africa

malaise—even greater in Ukraine and the other successor states than in Russia—and ethnic strife in the Caucasus and Central Asia assisted them. In several instances Russians were called in as peacemakers, in others to supervise truces that had been established. Russian armed forces were called in to reconquer Chechnya, a small region in the central Caucasus, which had seceded unilaterally from the Russian Federation. The troops encountered substantial resistance. The general trend toward the right (albeit not the extreme right) continued in Russian domestic politics. Although the government of Boris Yeltsin remained in power, equilibrium was not in sight, and many threats to the new system persisted.

Chancellor Helmut Kohl won the German elections in October with a reduced majority. He announced that he saw his main task as providing new impetus to the movement for political unity in Europe. Pres. François Mitterrand of France, in the last phase of his presidency and ill and politically weakened, was in no position to be of assistance. In Italy, in a political earthquake, the old system collapsed. Christian Democrats, who had ruled the country for most of the time since World War II, virtually disappeared, and the Socialists, likewise shaken by financial and other scandals, were decimated. A new right-wing coalition government was formed by media tsar Silvio Berlusconi, the Northern League, and the neo-Fascist National Alliance. The victors found it difficult to agree on common policies, however, and the weight of the investigation of scandals soon brought down the Berlusconi empire too.

It was the first time a neo-Fascist party had been represented in a major European government since the end of World War II, but there also was a strong showing of forces of the extreme right in other countries, most strikingly in Austria, where Jörg Haider's Freedom Party scored 22% in the elections of October 1994. Some of the components of this new movement in Europe belonged to the far right, others were neo-Fascists, some tended toward "revolutionary nationalism," and others advocated conservatism. The mainsprings were the crisis of the democratic system on the one hand (or, to be precise, the failures of the incumbents) and, on the other, the presence of the many immigrants who had arrived in recent years, some as "guest workers," others as asylum seekers. Their growing presence, especially in the big cities, generated tensions from which the extreme right benefited. In some cases there were acts of violence against foreigners and even murder. Although the violence was not remotely on the scale of the campaign of terror carried out by radical Islamists in countries such as Algeria and Egypt, against both foreigners and coreligionists, it was

still worrisome at a time when many thought that a more civilized political climate had prevailed.

(WALTER LAQUEUR)

This article updates the *Macropædia* article 20th-Century INTERNATIONAL RELATIONS.

UNITED NATIONS

The United Nations in 1994 fell victim to its members' uncertainty about their objectives and about the best way to use their resources in a post-Cold War world. Unclear goals led to disappointments, especially in Somalia, former Yugoslavia, and Rwanda. In other, nonmilitary endeavours, however, the UN made progress.

Somalia. Secretary-General Boutros Boutros-Ghali reported on January 6 that the international community was suffering "unmistakable signs of fatigue" in trying to assist Somalia. The Security Council on February 4 revised the mandate of the UN Operation in Somalia (UNOSOM II). It charged the peacekeepers—understrength at fewer than 19,000 after the U.S. withdrew its troops on March 25 and even weaker after the U.S. removed its remaining heavy equipment in the late summer—to assist the Somalis in disarming factional forces; protecting major ports, airports, and communications systems; supplying humanitarian relief to the needy; reorganizing the police and judicial systems; repatriating and resettling refugees and displaced persons; establishing a democratically elected government; protecting UN personnel, installations, and equipment; and guarding nongovernmental organizations (NGOs) providing food and fighting cholera. A Commission of Inquiry investigating armed attacks on mission personnel in Somalia noted on June 1 that member nations were unprepared "to accept substantial casualties for causes unrelated to their national interests," a position that severely limited international efforts to enforce peace.

The secretary-general cautioned on May 24 that the political and military situation continued to be unfavourable because of lagging cooperation by Somali leaders. Gen. Muhammad Farah Aydid, chairman of the Somali National Alliance, and Ali Mahdi Muhammad, spokesman of the "Group of 12" (the country's other factions), called for national reconciliation in the March 24 "Nairobi Declaration." On June 19, 19 Somali leaders signed a peace agreement at the Lower Juba Reconciliation Conference, but in October the parties failed to agree on how to establish an interim government. Factional fighting continued, and UNOSOM II forces, which suffered over 25 fatalities during the year, remained largely confined to fortified compounds in the capital, Mogadishu. On November 4 the Security Council decided to recall UNOSOM II on March 31, 1995, even without a political settlement. NGO personnel feared that the UN departure would lead to looting and violence that would destroy their relief programs.

Former Yugoslavia. Successive cease-fire agreements collapsed as the UN tried to end the conflict in former Yugoslavia. Meeting with top officials of NATO in Brussels on June 29, Yasushi Akashi, the secretary-general's special representative for Yugoslavia and chief of the UN Protection Force (UNPROFOR), reported "no large-scale offensives under way from either party." In October, however, Bosnian Muslim forces broke the Bosnian Serb siege of the city of Bihac, a UN-designated "safe area" in Bosnia and Herzegovina. Bosnian and Croatian Serbs counterattacked, even using napalm and cluster bombs, and resumed shelling Sarajevo.

Because of the attack on Bihac, NATO, with unanimous Security Council approval and at the request of UN commanders, sent 39 planes on November 21 to bomb the runway at Udbina, whence Serbs had launched their bombing run. The Serb offensive continued relentlessly, and by the end of November, Serb forces had surrounded Bihac and were holding as many as 450 UN personnel hostage against further air strikes. Boutros-Ghali flew to Sarajevo in hopes of arranging yet another cease-fire, but Bosnian Serb leader Radovan Karadjic refused to meet with him, and the mission failed.

In March the Security Council sought to send 10,000 additional peacekeeping troops to the region, but the U.S. blocked that effort, fearing that the U.S. Congress might not agree to pay its share of the extra cost. The Council then deployed only 3,500 additional troops. The U.S. consistently refused to supply troops unless the contending parties agreed to a truce. On April 25 Akashi criticized the U.S. for being "somewhat afraid . . . and tentative" after its Somalian experience.

On April 22, NATO Secretary-General Manfred Wörner (*see* OBITUARIES) informed Boutros-Ghali that NATO was prepared to launch air strikes to support UN efforts to protect Bihac and five other "safe areas" and to provide air support for UNPROFOR or other UN and relief agency personnel throughout Bosnia and Herzegovina if attacked by Bosnian Serb forces.

British Lieut. Gen. Sir Michael Rose (*see* BIOGRAPHIES), the UN commander in Bosnia, continued reluctant to retaliate, however, despite many Bosnian Serb provocations. He did authorize NATO forces to attack a Serbian tank on September 22 near Sarajevo after Serbs repeatedly violated a weapons ban and used machine guns and rockets against UN troops patrolling the city, wounding two French UNPROFOR soldiers. Criticized for ordering so mild a reprisal, Rose said that peacekeeping required "patience, persistence, and pressure," or the UN might find itself in a shooting war, as in Somalia. In December it was announced that Maj. Gen. Rupert Smith, who had been commander of the First British Armoured Division in the 1991 Gulf war, would assume command of the UN forces in Bosnia and Herzegovina when Rose's one-year term expired on Jan. 24, 1995.

NATO on October 10 formally requested the right to retaliate without warning against four targets at once in "robust and effective" fashion. On the other hand, UNPROFOR warned that the Bosnian Serbs, who controlled 70% of Bosnia, could lawfully ask UNPROFOR to leave. UNPROFOR would then be unable to supply three Muslim enclaves in eastern Bosnia. NATO and the UN consulted on mutually acceptable retaliatory standards and on October 27 agreed on unannounced air strikes only when little danger of

UN troops evacuate the wounded from Sarajevo. Late in the year, as Western governments failed to come to an agreement on a policy toward Bosnia and Herzegovina, Serb forces took several hundred UN soldiers hostage in Bihac, and the international mission was imperiled.
CHRISTOPHER MORRIS—BLACK STAR

civilian casualties existed. In August Serbian Pres. Slobodan Milosevic cut off arms and other supplies to Bosnian Serbs, and on September 24 the Security Council rewarded him by suspending (for 100 days) sanctions against Yugoslavia. It then imposed sanctions on the Bosnian Serbs for rejecting a peace that the "Contact Group" (France, Germany, Russia, the U.K., and the U.S.) had endorsed in July. The U.S. asked the Council on October 28 to lift the arms embargo against the Bosnian Muslim government by May 1995 and unilaterally stopped enforcing the embargo on November 12. Other Group members, fearing that the Bosnian Serbs might retaliate against their personnel, threatened to withdraw their troops from UNPROFOR if the embargo was lifted. Nonetheless, on November 3 the General Assembly recommended (97–0, with 61 abstentions) ending the embargo.

A UN commission of experts agreed in June that Bosnian Serbs had committed "crimes against humanity" and "genocide," engaged in "ethnic cleansing," and systematically raped Muslim and Croat women. It sent its report to the Yugoslav War Crimes Tribunal in The Hague for prosecution, and the tribunal indicted Dragan Nikolic on November 7 for killing eight Muslim prisoners, torturing seven others, and illegally imprisoning more than 500 Bosnian Muslims in 1992 in Susica camp.

Rwanda. On April 6 Rwandan Pres. Juvénal Habyarimana (*see* OBITUARIES) died in a plane crash that observers deemed suspicious. He was returning from a meeting at Dar es Salaam, Tanzania, where he purportedly agreed to surrender power to a broad-based transitional government. In the succeeding 10 weeks, Hutu militiamen, the army, and some Hutu civilians slaughtered at least one million mainly Tutsi men, women, and children, including the country's prime minister and leaders of six independent human rights organizations. As many as two million more were forced to leave their homes and seek refuge elsewhere.

On April 21, May 17, and June 8, the Security Council adjusted the mandate of the UN Assistance Mission for Rwanda (UNAMIR II), trying to make it a more effective instrument for protecting civilians and humanitarian operations. UN High Commissioner for Human Rights José Lasso visited Rwanda in early May and reported that the violence had exceeded any previous outbursts of hatred and intolerance between Hutus and Tutsis. On May 25 Boutros-Ghali condemned the killings as "genocide" and called the world's unwillingness to act speedily to stop it a "scandal." On November 8 the Security Council authorized an international tribunal to try persons accused of genocide and other serious crimes committed in 1994.

Many states, scarred by their Somalian and Bosnian experiences, proved reluctant to provide the UN with troops and matériel for Rwanda. The U.S. refused in May to sanction the immediate dispatch of 5,500 UN troops. Consequently, the Security Council accepted a French offer to send about 2,500 troops to Rwanda for one month to provide temporary security and humanitarian aid for hundreds of thousands of refugees.

On November 21 the secretary-general asked the Security Council to send 12,000 troops to stem growing violence in refugee camps in Zaire and Burundi and to protect private relief organization workers.

Iraq. Hoping to press the Security Council to lift sanctions against Iraq enacted in August 1990, Pres. Saddam Hussein moved troops close to the Kuwaiti border in October. The threat backfired, however, when the U.S. sent troops to guard Kuwait and the Security Council unanimously condemned the renewed threat to Kuwait and demanded that Iraq withdraw.

Rolf Ekeus, head of the special commission on Iraqi compliance with UN orders, reported on October 13 that the UN had created an effective arms-inspection system in the country, but he indicated later that Iraq was again threatening inspectors and not giving "straight and factual answers" about past suppliers of weapons material. France and Russia, eager to reestablish commerce with Iraq, favoured setting a timetable for lifting sanctions, but the Council refused on November 14 after the U.S. proved that Hussein had spent $500 million on palaces for himself and his family while Iraqis lacked food and medicine. A few days earlier, Iraq had met one Council requirement by formally recognizing Kuwait.

Haiti. On October 15 a UN force, mostly from the U.S., acting under a Security Council resolution adopted July 31 (authorizing "all necessary means" to restore democracy to the island) and an agreement made on September 18 with the Haitian military regime, returned Pres. Jean-Bertrand Aristide (see BIOGRAPHIES) to power. A joint mission from the Organization of American States and the UN, ordered out of the island on July 11 by the Haitian military authorities, resumed its work in October. The Security Council on October 16 lifted the trade embargo against Haiti imposed on May 6. On November 15 Secretary-General Boutros-Ghali arrived in Haiti to discuss the multinational force due to take over from U.S. troops in preparation for 1995 elections.

Economic and Social Matters. Political failures in Somalia, former Yugoslavia, and Rwanda tended to mask

successful UN humanitarian efforts. In Somalia UNOSOM II-trained civilian police secured airports and seaports for humanitarian-aid convoys and helped NGO personnel engaged in relief efforts to move safely, deployed a World Health Organization (WHO) task force supported by a Swiss disaster-relief team to coordinate the fight against a widespread cholera epidemic, and repatriated thousands of Somali refugees.

On July 3 the UN High Commissioner for Refugees (UNHCR) marked the second anniversary of the longest sustained humanitarian airlift in history, which averaged 14 flights a day and supplied Sarajevo's 300,000 people with more than 119,000 metric tons of goods, surpassing records set during the 1948–49 Berlin airlift. During the worst fighting, UNHCR supplied more than 95% of the assistance given to the besieged Bosnian capital. The World Food Program (WFP) appealed in January for $45 million in food and cash for thousands of needy refugees in Burundi, Rwanda, Tanzania, and Zaire. Although member nations were slow to respond, the WFP and the NGOs provided safe water, tons of food, and medical assistance.

An analysis by UNICEF on October 6 showed that in Central and Eastern Europe, the transition from communism to free-market democracies left the people there significantly poorer, less healthy, worse fed, and more prone to accidental death and homicide. More infectious diseases, stress, malnutrition, and alcoholism, already noted in Russia, were now affecting far wider areas.

The UN continued to ask member states to make peace-keeping troops available and announced that by April 12, 15 states had pledged at least 54,000 troops and specialists toward a UN inventory for future operations. On July 12, German courts ruled that German nationals might legally participate in UN operations. As of September 30, member states owed the UN $2.3 billion.

On October 26 the General Assembly adopted a resolution 101–2, with Israel and the U.S. opposed and 48 abstentions, calling on the U.S. to lift its embargo against Cuba. Supporters said that the embargo violated basic tenets of the UN Charter and ran counter to principles of international law, including freedom of trade and navigation.

On November 1 the U.S. notified the Trusteeship Council that Palau, the last remaining part of the Trust Territory of the Pacific Islands (itself the last UN trust territory), had opted for independence. Palau was admitted to the General Assembly as the UN's 185th member on December 15.

(RICHARD N. SWIFT)

This article updates the *Macropædia* article UNITED NATIONS.

COMMONWEALTH OF NATIONS

South Africa rejoined the Commonwealth on June 1, 1994, and became the 51st member. It had withdrawn 33 years earlier because other members had objected to its racial policies. In the ensuing years persistent pressure from the Commonwealth, including strong support for economic sanctions, played a major role in bringing change to South Africa. From time to time, differences over strategy, particularly over Britain's reluctance to support sanctions, threatened a Commonwealth breakup.

The return of South Africa to membership was seen as a considerable boost for the Commonwealth. One immediate manifestation of South Africa's return was its reappearance at the quadrennial Commonwealth Games at Victoria, B.C., in August.

Over a long period before the South African elections, the Commonwealth helped that nation make its transition in numerous ways. One successful contribution came from a team of police and legal experts who had been placed in violent areas (notably Natal) to resolve community conflict. For the election the Commonwealth sent 70 observers, led by former Jamaican prime minister Michael Manley. They found that the poll had been "a free and clear expression of the will of the South African people," but they also identified a number of irregularities.

The Commonwealth initiated the first international donors conference for South Africa. Held in Cape Town on October 26–28 and cosponsored by the UN, it sought support for the development of human resources, the subject of a special study by the Commonwealth in 1991 (*Beyond Apartheid*, published by the Commonwealth Secretariat).

In 1994 the Commonwealth chalked up both success and setbacks in its drive to improve the quality of democracy in member countries. In Malawi its observer group, headed by former deputy prime minister Datuk Musa Hitam of Malaysia, reported an "open and transparent" multiparty election that brought to power Bakili Muluzi of the United Democratic Front and led to the retirement after 30 years of Pres. Hastings Kamuzu Banda. In Lesotho, however, a few months after the multiparty election that ended military rule in 1993, rebellious soldiers generated a crisis lasting several months. Diplomats from the Commonwealth Secretariat mediated the conflict and finally helped the leaders of South Africa, Zimbabwe, and Botswana restore the civilian government.

In West Africa setbacks included the military coup in The Gambia on July 22 and the growing instability of the military government in Nigeria. The secretary-general of the Commonwealth, Chief Emeka Anyaoku, a Nigerian, visited Nigeria and talked with Gen. Sani Abacha, as well as MKO Abiola, apparent winner of the annulled 1993 elections, then under arrest. His mediation attempts, however, proved unsuccessful. When Anyaoku addressed the 40th Commonwealth Parliamentary Conference in Banff, Alta., on October 8, he said, "I believe . . . the day will not be far away when representatives of military regimes will find no welcome in the councils of the Commonwealth."

In September political leaders in Bangladesh asked the Commonwealth to help resolve deep differences between the prime minister, Khaleda Zia, and the leader of the opposition, Sheikh Hasina, that were leading to unrest in the country. Anyaoku visited Bangladesh and then sent Sir Ninian Stephen, a former governor-general of Australia, as his special envoy to discuss a three-point proposal to end the dispute. Such direct intervention by the Commonwealth in a domestic political dispute within a member country, although by agreement with the parties concerned, was unprecedented.   (DEREK INGRAM)

EUROPEAN UNION

The flagging course of the European Union (EU) showed signs of renewal in 1994. When he delivered a keynote speech in Brussels in January, U.S. Pres. Bill Clinton clearly spelled out that he thought Europe's future lay in closer unity. It was a theme that was to dominate the year, especially the autumn, when member-state governments began setting out their views for the forthcoming review of the Maastricht Treaty, scheduled for 1996. The promise of the talks was for a renewed advance toward monetary union, closer cooperation on defense and foreign policy, and sweeping reforms of the European institutions aimed at realigning their relationships and introducing greater levels of democratic control.

On the foreign policy front, the overriding crisis during the year continued to be the war in Bosnia and Herzegovina. As international forces struggled to keep aid convoys flowing, the EU became directly involved for the first time,

setting up an administration of Mostar, the divided capital of Herzegovina.

At their summit on the Greek island of Corfu in June, the heads of state and government of the EU signed cooperation agreements with Russia and Ukraine and gave their backing to NATO's Partnership for Peace agreements with former Soviet bloc countries. It was acknowledged that the agreements were no more than an interim step to full membership of NATO and the Western European Union (WEU), recognized as the defense arm of the EU. With Russia playing a full military role in the former Yugoslavia, European leaders also approved Moscow's admission to the Group of Seven.

NATO and the WEU also reached an agreement under which NATO forces might in future be earmarked for WEU operations not necessarily involving the U.S. The decisions reflected the debate toward the end of the year on what role defense might play in the EU's process of integration. The prime ministers of Poland, Hungary, the Czech Republic, Slovakia, Bulgaria, and Romania attended the EU summit in Essen, Germany, symbolizing the EU's commitment to enlarging its membership to countries in Eastern Europe.

The increasing confidence behind the EU's developing foreign and security policy began to be reflected on the economic front during 1994. Recession had been blamed for the weakening of some member governments' resolution to pursue closer integration in the face of public opposition. In fact, 1994 proved to be the year that Europe began to move out of economic recession while inflation continued at low levels. There was also evidence of remarkable currency stability despite the abandoning of the narrow band limits of the European exchange-rate mechanism in 1993.

Much hope for reinforcing economic recovery in Europe was pinned on the signing of the General Agreement on Tariffs and Trade (GATT) in Marrakech, Morocco, in April. The achievement of an agreement after eight years of difficult negotiations came despite some reservations, particularly in France. The only remaining question was whether the agreement would be ratified by national parliaments on both sides of the Atlantic.

Politically the year was dominated by the European Parliament elections in June, the first since the institution was given wider powers under the Maastricht Treaty. The members of the new European Parliament (MEPs) were elected in four days of voting across the EU. The results showed a low turnout, with the average voting figure down to 56.5% from 58.5% in 1989. This apparently reflected dissatisfaction among voters—but as much about their own national governments as about the status of the EU. Against a background of recession and political disagreement, opposition to integration appeared to be growing in Italy and France, and it continued unabated among sectors of political opinion in the U.K. In Germany polls showed that increasing numbers of citizens questioned the desirability of abandoning their strong Deutsche Mark in favour of a single European currency.

Two large groups, the Party of European Socialists and the centre-right Christian Democratic European People's Party, dominated the newly elected Parliament. Together with Liberals and Greens, the parties formed large new transnational political alliances. Huge gains by the Labour Party in the U.K. brought their numbers to almost one-third of the 198-strong Socialist grouping and gave the British their first opportunity to lead the Socialists in the Parliament.

Right-wing parties also made gains in Italy, France, and Belgium—most significantly the Forza Italia of Silvio Berlusconi. (*See* BIOGRAPHIES.) Although the extreme right failed to return any members in Germany, the French right-wing extremist Jean-Marie Le Pen was returned at the head of an 11-member European Parliament group that included three extreme-right MEPs from Belgium. The Italian neofascists, the National Alliance (formerly the Italian Social Movement), managed to win 11 seats.

Reflecting a growing disenchantment with European integration in France, the Other Europe party of Philippe de Villiers, which campaigned against GATT and the single market, joined with four Danish and two Dutch MEPs to form the "Europe of the Nations Group."

Although the signing of the Maastricht Treaty on political, economic, and monetary union had introduced the principle of subsidiarity, allowing member states greater control over their own affairs, an underlying suspicion of centralized government remained. Concerned that the public appeared not to have understood the increased powers of the European Parliament, the Commission launched a campaign to show that the Parliament would be closer to European citizens by having new instruments at its disposal, such as an ombudsman and the right of petition. Elected members would have to deal with the questions of integrating new member states into the EU beginning Jan. 1, 1995, and with establishing strong economic ties with the new democracies of Eastern and Central Europe.

The newly elected MEPs signaled at their first meeting in Strasbourg, France, that they should be actively involved in the preparation of the 1996 Intergovernmental Conference to reform the EU institutions and to review the Maastricht Treaty. In making their stand they clashed with the views of most member states that national governments should decide on any institutional changes.

On the eve of the European Council meeting in Corfu, the outgoing president of the European Commission, Jacques Delors, outlined the priorities facing Europe. He declared that governments would have to step up the fight against unemployment, promote economic growth, and prepare the EU for the next century. The European economy was at a crossroad between survival and decline. Government leaders would be focusing on four main areas: the Commission's White Paper on growth, competitiveness, and employment released earlier in the year; economic guidelines for the second stage of European economic and monetary union; Ukraine's nuclear power plants; and the establishment of the World Trade Organization as the successor to GATT.

Delors singled out six main elements of the White Paper for Council action: support for small firms, coordination of national research policies, a commitment to developing trans-European networks, a commitment to information technology, employment measures, and sustainable development.

The EU leaders took the White Paper as their main point under discussion in Corfu and pledged to pursue its recommendations vigorously. The Council stressed that improvements in Europe's economic situation should not be used as an excuse to slacken efforts to promote structural change but rather should serve as an incentive to introduce essential reforms, particularly in employment. Each member state was called upon to appoint a minister responsible for coordination of the Information Society, and the Council agreed on 11 major transport projects and 8 energy projects. In a deregulating mood, the Council gave its full backing to plans for a group of independent experts to look at the impact of both EU and national legislation on employment and competitiveness. This approach was confirmed by the Essen EU summit during December.

Britain's Prime Minister John Major, with support from German Chancellor Helmut Kohl (see BIOGRAPHIES) and others, welcomed references to labour-market deregulation and praised mention of private-sector funds to cofinance the construction of trans-European networks. The midyear summit meeting of the European Council reflected on the efforts of finance ministers to mobilize an additional ECU 8 billion ($9,660,000,000) a year in loans to help set up the trans-European networks, but they stressed that the funding should not run counter to efforts being made by member states to reduce public debt.

The talks on Europe's economic future were, however, overshadowed by the difficulty in agreeing on Delors's successor as president of the European Commission. Fol-

Jacques Santer (right), newly elected president of the European Commission, speaks at a press conference as outgoing president, Jacques Delors (left), and German Chancellor Helmut Kohl look on. The new president was the prime minister of Luxembourg.
DPA/PHOTOREPORTERS

lowing a meeting in Mulhouse, France, between Kohl and Pres. François Mitterrand of France, both announced that they preferred Belgian Prime Minister Jean-Luc Dehaene. Driven by vociferous and rebellious Euro-skeptic elements in his own Conservative Party, Major blamed what he called the arrogance of the Bonn/Paris axis and vetoed Dehaene's appointment. Britain stood alone among the 12 member states, but despite bitter European resentment, Major insisted on getting his way.

At a special summit in Brussels in July, it took only 20 minutes for the European leaders to agree on a new candidate. They chose the prime minister of Luxembourg, Jacques Santer (see BIOGRAPHIES), who would take office in 1995. After a long and bitter debate, the MEPs approved his nomination—but by only a 22-vote majority.

The ensuing battle over the appointments to Santer's team of commissioners demonstrated that the European Parliament was increasingly in the political driving seat of the EU. The democratically elected MEPs said they were determined to press on with essential democratic reforms and to ensure that the EU was representative of the will of the people of Europe.

The second half of the year saw the rekindling of the controversial debate about "a two-speed Europe." A policy paper published by the parliamentary faction of the German Christian Democratic Party advocated the creation of a possible "hard core" of EU countries committed to comprehensive economic political and defense integration. This provoked charges that the German and French governments were seeking to create a privileged inner core of EU states, leaving others outside.   (JOHN PALMER)

COMMONWEALTH OF INDEPENDENT STATES

Russian influence in the CIS continued to increase during 1994. CIS states owed Russia 3.5 trillion rubles at the end of 1993, 1.5 trillion of which was for products in the fuel and energy complex. During 1994 Russia cut back deliveries of oil and natural gas to CIS states, and this led to periodic confrontations with Ukraine.

At a summit in Moscow on April 15, Russia gained approval for its role as peacekeeper and guardian of CIS borders. The Central Asian states, as well as Armenia and Georgia, formally agreed that Russian troops should police their borders jointly with local forces. Ukraine and Moldova signed a memorandum that also moved in this direction. All states agreed that Russia should send troops to the breakaway Georgian region of Abkhazia and urged the UN to support this move. CIS forces, mainly Russian, remained in Tajikistan. Russia was less successful in getting CIS states to contribute to the costs of the peacekeeping forces. Russia won control of about 80% of the Black Sea Fleet from Ukraine. At the April meeting Ukraine became an associate member of the CIS economic union that was formed in September 1993. The planned economic union between Russia and Belarus, welcomed at this summit, did not materialize, however.

On September 9, 10 of the 12 CIS states agreed to form a payments union and an Interstate Economic Committee to deepen economic links. The union represented an attempt to settle payments between member states, many of whom did not have convertible currencies. Aleksandr Shokhin, the Russian deputy prime minister, described the Interstate Economic Committee as an embryonic European Commission. Its main task was to integrate economies and ensure that the multitude of agreements that had been signed by CIS states were implemented. Russia would control 50% of the votes in the committee, with 80% required for passage. Customs barriers were to be lowered, with the eventual goal of a customs union. Ukraine and Turkmenistan expressed reservations about the commitments, however, regarding them as a diminution of national sovereignty.

Leonid Kuchma (*see* BIOGRAPHIES), who had replaced Leonid Kravchuk as president of Ukraine in July, turned out to be less pro-Russian than expected, adopted a reformist stance, and did not commit Ukraine to the payments union, since it assumed the free convertibility of national currencies at market rates. With its limited associate membership in the CIS, Ukraine enjoyed limited status on the Interstate Economic Committee and participated only in certain discussions. Another CIS summit in October moved cautiously toward closer integration, and a proposed payments and customs union was initiated. Russia and Moldova agreed that Russian troops would leave Moldova by 1997.

(MARTIN MCCAULEY)

MULTINATIONAL AND REGIONAL ORGANIZATIONS

At the annual Association of Southeast Asian Nations (ASEAN) conference, which opened July 22, 1994, in Bangkok, Thailand's prime minister asked the members (Brunei, Indonesia, Malaysia, the Philippines, Singapore, and Thailand) to avert armed confrontation over resources and territory, especially in the Spratly Islands. Brunei, China, Malaysia, the Philippines, Taiwan, and Vietnam all claimed the islands and wished to exploit the adjacent seabed for oil. All the contenders except Brunei had troops stationed

in the archipelago. ASEAN members also discussed their growing commerce with Vietnamese industries since February, when the U.S. lifted its embargo on trade with that country. On July 25, ASEAN members and others (Canada, China, Japan, Laos, New Zealand, Papua New Guinea, Russia, South Korea, the U.S., and European Union representatives) met for the first time in an Asian Regional Forum to discuss security problems.

At a fifth summit meeting in Montevideo, Uruguay, on January 17, the Southern Cone Common Market (Mercosur) members (Argentina, Brazil, Paraguay, and Uruguay) authorized Bolivia to participate in its working groups. In March the Mercosur member states agreed to form a South American Free Trade Association, through which they planned to negotiate with other Latin-American countries. The goal was to abolish tariffs on 85% of their own trade and establish a common tariff against others. In August they signed a dozen agreements setting the preliminary terms for a common market to start on Jan. 1, 1995. On December 28 the presidents of the Mercosur countries approved revisions drafted at the sixth Mercosur summit (December 16–17, Ouro Preto, Brazil). The Organization of American States (OAS) and the UN condemned Haiti for expelling international human rights monitors on July 11. Since 1992 the mission had documented the military government's human rights abuses.

The U.S. Congress on July 14 proposed granting greater access to U.S. weapons by the Czech Republic, Hungary, and Poland, three of the four members of the "Visegrad Group." Slovakia, the fourth, immediately protested that excluding it would contribute to Eastern European instability. Foreign ministers from the countries of the Black Sea Economic Cooperation Project (principally the Black Sea littoral states) worked at establishing the Bank for Black Sea Trade and Development at Thessaloniki, Greece. The project had been agreed upon at Sofia, Bulg., on Dec. 9, 1993.   (RICHARD N. SWIFT)

DEPENDENT STATES

Europe and the Atlantic. Relations between Spain and the U.K. continued strained in 1994 as the two countries commemorated 10 years of attempted negotiations over the future status of Gibraltar. While Gibraltar Chief Minister Joe Bossano sought greater autonomy under British rule and eventual independence, Madrid demanded the colony's return to Spanish sovereignty under the terms of the 1713 Treaty of Utrecht, which ceded Gibraltar to Britain only as long as it remained a dependency. In June Spain issued a formal protest against alleged drug smuggling through Gibraltar. Late in the year Spain set up double checkpoints at the border, but these were lifted in late December when Britain agreed to joint measures against illegal trafficking.

Talks between the U.K. and Argentina over the disputed Falkland Islands/Islas Malvinas also showed little progress, although general relations improved. Fishing rights remained the most immediate issue, but the potential revenue from offshore oil reserves was also at stake. Islanders accepted an offer from Buenos Aires for help with disposal of land mines left behind after the 1982 Falkland Islands war. In October the Argentine government reportedly offered as much as $1.5 million to each Falkland Islands resident in exchange for repudiation of British citizenship. In November Argentine Pres. Carlos Menem's brother and the Duke of York, who served in the British navy during the war, exchanged official visits.

In the Faeroe Islands the opposition Union Party increased its share in the 32-seat Lagting (parliament) to 8 seats in the general election on July 7 and took over at the head of a four-party coalition. Edmund Joensen was sworn in as prime minister on September 15. The Faeroes authorized seismic studies to search for offshore oil in 1994. It was hoped that new oil discoveries could help the islands' economy, which had been hit hard by overfishing, the lowering of fish prices, and austerity measures imposed by Denmark in exchange for increased aid.

Caribbean and Bermuda. Anguilla gained new leadership in March 1994 when Hubert Hughes, the former opposition leader, was sworn in as head of a coalition government after the general election that month failed to produce a majority for any party. Hughes had led the Anguilla United Party in the election.

A new government took office also in Aruba following the general election in July. It was headed by Prime Minister Henny Eman of the Aruba People's Party (AVP), which won 10 of the 21 seats. The Aruban Liberal Organization, which obtained two seats, joined the AVP to give it a working majority.

In the Netherlands Antilles, Miguel Pourier of Curaçao was sworn in as federal prime minister on March 31. Pourier's Antillean Restructuring Party, which had won a majority in the February election, dominated the coalition. The new administration said at midyear that it would set up a fiscal fraud squad to combat tax evasion and other financial crimes. This followed the jailing of the leader of the St. Maarten's Democratic Party, Claude Wathey, for perjury and forgery in connection with expansion schemes at the international airport. In June the island governments on Curaçao and St. Maartens both collapsed. New lieutenant governors were appointed, effective from September 1. In October Bonaire, Saba, St. Eustatius, and St. Maartens followed Curaçao's example and voted to remain within the Netherlands Antilles federation.

It was confirmed during the year that both the foreign military installations in Bermuda would be closed, which posed a major threat to the economy. The British navy yard was to cease operations in April 1995, only five months before the U.S. government was due to withdraw funding from its naval air station. The Bermuda House of Assembly in May passed a motion rejecting a government proposal for a commission of inquiry into the issue of independence from Britain. This put a brake on the independence momentum for the time being.

The U.K. announced in March that it would enlarge the British Virgin Islands Legislative Council for the next election in February 1995, adding four new seats to the existing nine, to be voted for on a nonconstituency basis. Chief Minister Lavity Stoutt protested the lack of "consultation" with his government over the plan. In the Cayman Islands in February, constitutional changes came into effect under which executive council members became ministers, but there was no provision for a chief minister to be de facto head of government. Later in the year the Caymans sought British help in dealing with increasing numbers of Cuban refugees.

Guadeloupe was declared a disaster zone at the end of August following the worst drought in 30 years. The drought

Workers in Hong Kong fill in the harbour to create new land, the future site of office and residential buildings. The demand by Western companies for space in Hong Kong, where land is very scarce, pushed rents to extraordinarily high levels.
GREG GIRARD—CONTACT PRESS IMAGES

took a severe toll on the island's vital sugar and banana industries. The declaration would enable farmers to receive extensive financial assistance. Puerto Rico also announced a $2.4 billion water-development program to combat a severe shortage there. The program would be spread over seven years.

Pacific. Early in the year, Pres. François Mitterrand confirmed that France would undertake no further nuclear testing during his term of office. While the suspension of testing was welcomed by Pacific Islands leaders, it had serious implications for the economy of French Polynesia, where gross domestic product had dropped by 28%, the number of army personnel based on Mururoa had been halved to about 1,000, and army spending was down by 40%. The French government agreed to make compensatory payments of $118 million a year. There was tension between the territorial president, Gaston Flosse, and the French high commissioner in July when the latter boycotted anniversary celebrations of a decade of autonomy because the local flag and anthem were given precedence over the French national symbols. A major strike affecting fuel supplies seriously disrupted the economy in October.

In New Caledonia there was growing evidence that political parties across the spectrum favoured a negotiated constitutional settlement in 1998 rather than a simple referendum on independence. Despite these suggestions of accommodation political sparring continued, with anti-independence leader Jacques Lafleur being severely critical of financial arrangements for a ferry service run by the pro-independence Loyalty Islands provincial government.

Dependent States[1]

Australia	**Portugal**
Christmas Island	Macau
Cocos (Keeling) Islands	**United Kingdom**
Norfolk Island	Anguilla
Denmark	Bermuda
Faeroe Islands	British Virgin Islands
Greenland	Cayman Islands
France	Falkland Islands
French Guiana	Gibraltar
French Polynesia	Guernsey
Guadeloupe	Hong Kong
Martinique	Isle of Man
Mayotte	Jersey
New Caledonia	Montserrat
Réunion	Pitcairn Island
Saint Pierre and Miquelon	Saint Helena and Dependencies
Wallis and Futuna	Turks and Caicos Islands
Netherlands, The	**United States**
Aruba	American Samoa
Netherlands Antilles	Guam
New Zealand	Northern Mariana Islands
Cook Islands	Puerto Rico
Niue	Virgin Islands (of the U.S.)
Tokelau	
Norway	
Jan Mayen	
Svalbard	

[1]Excludes territories (1) to which Antarctic Treaty is applicable in whole or in part, (2) without permanent civilian population, (3) without internationally recognized civilian government (Western Sahara, Gaza Strip), or (4) representing unadjudicated unilateral or multilateral territorial claims.

In a March general election in the Cook Islands, the Cook Islands Party led by Sir Geoffrey Henry was returned to power in a landslide, winning 20 of the 25 seats in the Legislative Assembly. Voters also endorsed the status quo on the territory's name, national anthem, and flag. Henry's victory was achieved despite continuing controversy over a major tourist hotel development, which had suffered from serious financial and management difficulties, and from allegations that the tax-haven facilities of the Cook Islands had been misused to disguise mismanagement and tax evasion by New Zealand companies. Meanwhile, Niue legislated to provide a tax haven, though on a more modest scale. Niue, which had a resident population of 2,300 (with 14,400 Niueans living in New Zealand), hoped to make some $NZ 4 million a year to replace some New Zealand aid.

The most significant development in the U.S. Pacific dependencies was the independence of Palau following a referendum that allowed the Compact of Free Association to override Palau's antinuclear constitution. (See *Palau*, below.) Early in the year the U.S. passed legislation to allow the return to the Guam government of some 1,295 ha (3,200 ac) held by the federal government. The move was the first step toward the return of much larger holdings once the U.S. military bases on the island closed from April 1995. In the Northern Mariana Islands, the election of Democratic Gov. Froilan C. Tenorio brought early controversy when he instigated reforms to the local garment industry that depended on low-paid migrant labour, mostly from the Philippines. He also signaled a hiring freeze on government positions, measures to secure compliance with taxes and regulations, and checks on the misuse of government resources.

East Asia. Tension between the U.K. and China over Hong Kong grew worse in 1994. In June electoral reforms proposed by London-appointed Hong Kong Gov. Chris Patten two years earlier were passed 32–24 by the territory's Legislative Council. The measures included lowering the voting age to 18 and widening the franchise in legislative elections for "functional constituencies" based on professional groups. In response, China said that once it assumed sovereignty over Hong Kong in 1997, it would dismantle the three tiers of councils and hold new polls, thus abandoning the "through-train" concept by which those elected before 1997 would serve afterward. The Beijing (Peking)-appointed Preliminary Working Committee (PWC), set up to give advice on Hong Kong's post-1997 institutions, took a more prominent role. In December the PWC announced that China would appoint a provisional legislature to govern Hong Kong through the transition for up to a year.

The first elections under Patten's reformed system were held for neighbourhood-level district boards in September. Parties described as "pro-democracy" won 30% of the seats, compared with 19% for "pro-China" groupings. About half the posts went to independents.

In a speech in October, Patten said Britain and Hong Kong wanted to cooperate with China, but he continued to forbid formal contacts between civil servants and the PWC. He also proposed an ambitious but controversial social program that would increase spending on the elderly, the disabled, education, and housing.

In November China and Britain finally agreed on the financing of a new airport and connecting railway, already under construction. The Hong Kong government was to provide at least $7.7 billion in equity and borrow $3 billion to pay for the projects. Economic growth remained above 5%, while inflation stood just below 10%.

In September Macau Gov. Vasco Rocha Vieira paid an official visit to Beijing and won its agreement not to impose the death penalty in the Portuguese-run territory after it reverted to Chinese sovereignty in December 1999. In anticipation of completion of the territory's first airport in mid-1995, a Macau-based regional airline was set up.

(BARRIE MACDONALD; DAVID RENWICK; MELINDA C. SHEPHERD; BERTON WOODWARD)

This article updates the *Macropædia* articles HONG KONG; PACIFIC ISLANDS; THE WEST INDIES.

ANTARCTICA

Antarctica, as defined by the 42-nation Antarctic Treaty that entered into effect in 1961, comprises all lands and waters south of latitude 60° S. The land area is about 14.2 million sq km (5.3 million sq mi), principally the Antarctic continent itself and adjoining islands. There is no capital or permanent human habitation; scientific and support personnel, housed in some 40 year-round scientific stations, number about 4,100 in summer and about 1,000 in winter. Antarctica is effectively internationalized by the Antarctic Treaty, which places the territorial claims of seven countries (Argentina, Australia, Chile, France, New Zealand, Norway, and the United Kingdom) in abeyance for the duration of the treaty. The treaty also provides managerial mechanisms for regulating international affairs, scientific activity, environmental protection, and formal inspections to verify compliance.

The ozone hole in the stratosphere over Antarctica surprised scientists in 1994 by staying nearly as deep and wide as it had ever been. Ozone levels over South Pole Station dropped to 102 Dobson units in early October 1994, compared with 105 in 1992 and 108 in 1991. The average value before the ozone hole developed had been about 280 Dobson units.

The all-time record of 91 Dobson units was set on Oct. 12, 1993. In the journal *Geophysical Research Letters,* chemist D.J. Hofmann stated that the main reasons for this lowest-ever value were increased amounts of chlorine in the stratosphere, the prolonged presence of polar stratospheric clouds caused by unusually low temperatures, and sulfate aerosol from the 1991 eruption of Mt. Pinatubo in the Philippines. The aerosol had enlarged the ozone hole by providing surfaces for chlorine and bromine from industrial sources to react with ozone and destroy it. The investigators had expected something of a recovery in 1994 because most of the 20 million tons of Pinatubo debris had by then dropped out of the stratosphere.

Reporting 1994's bad news, *Science* magazine noted the discouraging possibility that the hole was being deepened and enlarged by the steady increase in the stratosphere of chlorine and bromine from synthetic chemicals. International controls on chlorofluorocarbons and bromine compounds were expected to halt their increases in the stratosphere by 1998, but in recent years chlorine levels had been rising by about 2% annually. These increases could extend the period of ozone destruction.

One argument regarding the ozone hole was that it occurred naturally in earlier decades of this century. If correct, this argument could relieve synthetic chemicals of their responsibility for the hole. A 1990 French report had said that spectrographic plates of the sky, the Moon, and two stars taken at the French Antarctic station suggested that ozone values were low in 1958, well before there were significant chlorofluorocarbon emissions. In 1994, however, a Goddard Space Flight Center scientist, Paul A. Newman, published a paper stating that there was no credible evidence for a 1958 Antarctic ozone hole. He said that the data on the French plates reflected "a large instrumental bias" and were inconsistent with other observations. This finding reinforced the increasingly widespread acknowledgment that synthetic chemicals cause the ozone hole.

Antarctic oceanographers made several noteworthy research cruises in 1994. The U.S. Coast Guard icebreaker *Polar Sea* on February 5 reached a new southernmost point on Earth accessible by surface ship—just 690.1 nautical miles from the South Pole—at the Ross Ice Shelf near Roosevelt Island. In 1987 an iceberg had broken away from the shelf's former Bay of Whales area, leaving a more southerly bay than Gould Bay on the Filchner Ice Shelf, the previous record holder.

The U.S. National Science Foundation's research icebreaker *Nathaniel B. Palmer* completed a winter cruise far into the Amundsen and Bellingshausen seas, the first since a Belgian expedition in the late 1800s; the ship managed to get into and out of Pine Island Bay, a place where few ships had been. The *Nathaniel B. Palmer* also spent two months in the central part of the seasonal ice pack in the Weddell Sea, studying winter heat flux. Water from the region plays a critical role in maintaining the character of deep water worldwide.

A huge wave caused by a glacier that was breaking apart severely damaged a new airstrip that was near completion at Dumont d'Urville, the French Antarctic station. The wave tore off a quarter of the runway and damaged a hangar. Then a storm removed all the gravel from the rest of the runway. France then decided that it would not rebuild the strip, dropping the project "because of the difficulty of maintaining it permanently and out of concern to protect the Antarctic environment." France agreed on a plan to stage Antarctic air operations out of Christchurch, N.Z., where U.S. Antarctic air operations also originated.

Vostok, Russia's Antarctic interior station, was closed for the Antarctic winter of 1994, breaking a record of continuous year-round operation that had lasted since 1957. The shutdown was necessary because tractor trains from the coast were not able to deliver enough fuel. The 1994 crew, already in Antarctica when the decision was made, wintered instead at Mirnyy, a coastal station, doing alternative research and readying the tractors for an October start. A ski-equipped U.S. LC-130 airplane flew Vostok's 1993–94 summer team to McMurdo, a U.S. station, to meet a Russian ship, and Americans were planning flights to help their Russian colleagues reopen Vostok. Vostok's research had included recording the world's lowest surface temperature, and the station supported deep ice-coring projects of great scientific importance.

Despite the vital importance of airplanes in much Antarctic research, few runways existed in Antarctica. The U.S. Antarctic Program, alone of the nations that operated in Antarctica, had large ski-equipped planes (C-130s), but it continued to depend on wheeled planes, particularly C-141s and C-5s, for intercontinental transport. Thus, completion in 1994 of a runway on glacier ice near McMurdo for wheeled planes was thought a significant achievement. The runway required years of grooming before the snow surface was hard enough to support the loads imposed by high-pressure airplane tires. Called Pegasus, the runway enabled larger loads to be flown between New Zealand and Antarctica and permitted winter operations.

In other developments, the discovery of the first dinosaur fossils from the Antarctic mainland was reported by William R. Hammer. The fossils, from a group of carnivorous bipeds called theropods, suggested that a mild climate existed at high latitudes during the Early Jurassic Period, nearly 200 million years ago. The find also revealed that dinosaurs lived on all the continents.

A total of 8,034 tourists from 42 countries visited Antarctica on 64 cruises by 10 ships during the 1993–94 summer season. Port Lockroy, the most popular destination, received 4,274 visitors. At least 42% of the tourists were American, 17% German, and 9% British.

Scientists continued to document and confirm the warming taking place in the Antarctic Peninsula region. The growing season was two weeks longer than it had been in 1964, according to the British Antarctic Survey. Average summer temperatures had risen 2° C (3.6° F), and one of Antarctica's two species of flowering plants increased on three islands from 700 in 1964 to 17,500 in 1990; the other species increased from 60 to 380. The Larsen Ice Shelf, on the east coast of the peninsula, had lost more than 30% of its area since 1975, and recession of up to 2.5 km (1.5 mi) per year continued in some places. (GUY G. GUTHRIDGE)

This article updates the *Macropædia* article ANTARCTICA.

ARCTIC REGIONS

The Arctic regions may be defined in physical terms (astronomical [north of the Arctic Circle, latitude 66° 30′ N], climatic [above the 10° C (50° F) July isotherm], or vegetational [above the northern limit of the tree line]) or human (the territory inhabited by the circumpolar cultures—Inuit, or Eskimo, and Aleut in North America; Saami, or Lapp, in northern Scandinavia; and, west to east, Uralic, Paleosiberian, Middle Asian, and Arctic peoples in northern Russia). No single national sovereignty or treaty regime governs the region, which includes portions of seven countries: Canada, the United States, Russia, Finland, Sweden, Norway, and Greenland (part of Denmark). The Arctic Ocean, 14,090,000 sq km (5,440,000 sq mi) in area, constitutes about two-thirds of the region, the remaining land area consisting of permanent ice cap, tundra, or taiga. Population (1994 est.) of peoples belonging to the circumpolar cultures, 1,240,000. International organizations concerned with the Arctic include: Arctic Environmental Protection Strategy, Council of the Euro-Arctic Region, International Arctic Committee, International Arctic Science Committee, and the Inuit Circumpolar Conference.

During 1994 the Inuit (Eskimos) of Alaska, Canada, Greenland, and Russia undertook a number of development and cultural projects, largely under the auspices of the Inuit Circumpolar Conference (ICC) and also in cooperation with various national and international governments and agencies. The inspiration for some of these initiatives evolved from the formation of the Inuit Business Development Council at the ICC General Assembly held in Inuvik, N.W.T., in 1992 and from the 1992 UN Conference on Economic Development. Both of these large international events provided encouragement for northern indigenous peoples to undertake joint ventures and to exchange ideas and information among themselves and also with indigenous peoples in the Southern Hemisphere. In June a delegation of Inuit from Arctic Quebec visited Greenland to explore the possibilities of cooperation and economic development projects. Representatives from the Canadian Arctic Resources Committee and the Inuit Circumpolar Conference initiated a cooperative program in July between the Inuit of Greenland, Canada, and the U.S. and the Saami people of Russia's Kola Peninsula. On the basis of their experience in their own homelands, the Inuit were exploring ways to assist the Saami in recovering rights to own and manage land, to fish in their traditional rivers, and to herd reindeer. Several Inuit organizations, including the ICC and the Inuit Women's Association, helped organize a meeting in April with representatives of Indian groups in Belize.

U.S. Pres. Bill Clinton held a historic meeting on the White House lawn in April with representatives of American Indian and Native Alaskan tribes to underscore their new status in dealing with the federal government. He became the first president to meet with leaders of the nearly 550 federally recognized tribes. The president called on his administration to treat the tribes with the same deference given to state governments.

In a July out-of-court settlement, Exxon Corp. agreed to pay $20 million to 3,500 Alaskan natives who claimed losses after the 1989 *Exxon Valdez* oil spill. The Alaskans asserted that the spill destroyed traditional food sources such as seals, kelp, and fish. The settlement did not resolve claims by the natives for alleged damage to their culture and economy. Earlier in the year the U.S. National Park Service had negotiated with the natives so that they could buy tens of thousands of hectares of wilderness within Kenai Fjords National Park. The shores of the park's spectacular glacier-field coastline were among the areas coated with oil from the *Exxon Valdez* spill, and the funds for purchasing land would come from the Exxon compensation settlement.

In September, as part of a separate judgment, the Exxon Corp. was ordered by a U.S. federal jury to pay $5 billion in damages to Alaskan natives, commercial fisherman, property owners, and others harmed by the spill. The jury earlier in June had found that the "reckless" actions of Exxon and the ship's captain had caused the oil tanker to run aground on a charted reef in Prince William Sound. In the class-action lawsuit an estimated 14,000 plaintiffs had asked for a $15 billion settlement as a result of damaged fishing and hunting grounds and reduced property values. Exxon argued that the company had learned its lesson after spending nearly $3 billion to clean up the spill and to settle lawsuits filed by Alaska and the U.S. government. In October the company petitioned the courts to overturn or reduce the verdicts in the case.

In April the *New York Times* reported that depressed oil prices and a declining supply of oil from Alaska's North Slope was threatening Alaska's state-subsidized lifestyle. The state, which depended on oil royalties for 85% of its budget, was facing a $600 million deficit and also had to reimburse nearly $1 billion taken from a reserve fund to cover the previous year's deficit. In the same month, a consortium of four companies, led by Texaco Inc., formed a new company,

Timan Pechora Corp., to continue exploring and possibly develop oil fields in the Timan Pechora Basin, a remote area in northwestern Russia near the Barents Sea. The area was reported to have reserves of two billion barrels of oil. To date, a regional Russian oil agency had drilled more than 130 test holes with a reported above-average success rate of 60%.

A major environmental disaster was reported in October as an oil pipeline near the town of Usinsk, just below the Arctic Circle in Russia's Komi Republic, failed, spilling some 15 million litres (about 95,000 bbl) of oil into the delicate ecosystem—this figure according to Russian government estimates (outside experts put the figure three or more times higher). The spill was being compared to the *Exxon Valdez* incident in magnitude and could be the largest ever recorded. The crude had been seeping from poorly made and often patched pipelines since February but had been contained by a 7.5-m (25-ft)-high dike until heavy rainstorms caused the dam to fail on October 1. Two tributaries of the Pechora, the Kolva and Usa rivers, were reportedly polluted. Environmental experts pointed out that cleanup would be extremely difficult if not impossible under the local permafrost conditions. Earlier in 1994 a commission from the Russian Academy of Sciences had recommended a 25-year moratorium on oil drilling because of the adverse effects on the environment.

In May reports from Canada's Northwest Territories indicated that Inuit and Dene hunters, who were attempting to follow a traditional way of life, appeared to be on a collision course with prospectors looking for diamonds. Since the discovery of diamonds in the area in 1991, an exploration boom had taken place. More than 150 mining companies, including some of the world's largest, reportedly spent hundreds of millions of dollars to explore areas staked over an area the size of Ireland. Because some of the richest discoveries were on land that the native peoples claimed as their hunting grounds, one of the key issues was how much of the diamond wealth would be distributed to the Inuit and

ROBERT WALLIS—SABA

Employees of U.S.-based Occidental Petroleum work at a well in a newly discovered field in the Russian Arctic. Despite political uncertainties, a number of international companies were investing in Russia in hopes of sharing in the exploitation of the country's petroleum and mineral wealth.

Dene. The native groups were negotiating for a share of the revenues, guarantees of jobs, and a role in determining how the land would be used for mining and for traditional purposes. (*See also* MINING.)

In April the Inuit in Arctic Quebec signed an agreement in principle with the government-owned utility Hydro-Quebec for compensation estimated by the Inuit to amount to $1 billion over a 50-year period. The agreement was conditional on regulatory approval of Hydro-Quebec's proposed $13.3 billion Great Whale hydroelectric project, which would generate an estimated 3,212 MW of power. In July the Inuit also signed a self-government agreement with the Quebec government that was expected to lead to an elected assembly with wide-ranging powers to govern the province north of latitude 55° N—more than a third of the province's land mass but home to fewer than 10,000 people. By the terms of the agreement, the Inuit would take over the administration of all or part of the justice, social, and education systems as early as 1995.

In March the 13th Arctic Winter Games took place in Slave Lake, Canada. A record number of approximately 1,400 athletes came from Alaska, the Northwest Territories, the Yukon Territory, Russia, Greenland, and northern Alberta to compete in 19 sports, including traditional winter events such as ice hockey and figure skating as well as uniquely northern sports such as snowshoeing and dogsledding.

In September a long-lost camp was found in the Canadian Arctic on the northwestern shore of King William Island, where at least four members of the 19th-century Franklin expedition to the Arctic had died. Also found nearby were remnants of wood and metal from a 10-m (33-ft) boat used to carry food and belongings ashore from the ships that had transported Sir John Franklin and 138 men from England in the ill-fated Royal Navy expedition of 1845–48.

During the summer two coast guard vessels, the USS *Polar Sea* and the Canadian *Louis S. St. Laurent,* became the first ships to traverse the Arctic via the North Pole, leaving Nome, Alaska, on July 24 and reaching the pole on August 22. On board were 70 researchers who discovered disturbing and unexplained evidence of warm water beneath the Arctic Ocean ice. It was speculated that the warm water may have displaced the colder, less salty Arctic waters being pushed along the coast of Greenland and down Canada's east coast, contributing to the dramatic decline in codfish stocks and other bottom-dwelling species.

(KENNETH DE LA BARRE)

This article updates the *Macropædia* article The ARCTIC.

POLITICAL PARTIES

The following table is a general guide to the principal political parties and coalitions of the world. All countries that were independent on Dec. 31, 1994, are included, except the Vatican City State. In most instances parties are included only if represented in elected parliaments (in the lower house in bicameral legislatures). Figures in the column "Parliamentary representation" indicate the number of seats obtained in the most recent general election (figures in parentheses are those of the penultimate one) and exclude nonelective seats and seats still undecided. If only a portion of the seats were at stake in the last general election, the figure given indicates the total number of seats held by each party after the election. The date of the most recent election follows the name of the country.

The capital letters in the column "Affiliation" show the relative positions of the parties within the political spectrum of each country. The key chosen is as follows: F-fascist; ER-extreme right; R-right; CR-centre right; C-centre; CL-centre left; SD-social democratic; S-socialist; L-non-Marxist left; K-Communist; and EL-extreme left. In addition, within some countries there are political organizations that exist chiefly to advance a special interest as distinct from a political orientation. These are represented by lower-case letters as follows: x-parties that have repudiated former Communist affiliation; c-parties based on distinct regional, ethnic, or linguistic identity; r religious fundamentalist; g-environmental, or Green; and p-parties based largely on personalities.

The numbers in the column "Voting strength" indicate proportions of the valid votes cast for the respective parties.

(MELINDA C. SHEPHERD)

Political Parties

Country Name of party	Affiliation	Voting strength (%)	Parliamentary representation	
Afghanistan				
Multifactional warfare from January 1993	…	…	…	
Albania (March 1992)				
Democratic Party	CR	62.1	92	(75)
Social Democratic Party	SD	4.4	7	—
Socialist Party	x	25.7	38	(169)
Other	—	7.8	3	(6)
Algeria				
Interim government since January 1992	—	—	—	
Andorra (December 1993)				
National Democratic Grouping and allies	…	…	15	
Others and independents	…	…	13	
Angola (September 1992)				
Popular Liberation Movement of Angola–Labour Party (MPLA–PT)	x	53.7	129	(203)
National Union for the Total Independence of Angola (UNITA)	—	34.1	70	—
Others	—	12.2	21	—
Antigua and Barbuda (March 1994)				
Antigua Labour Party	C	54.4	11	(15)
United Progressive Party	C	43.7	5	(1)
Barbuda People's Movement	e	1.4	1	(1)
Argentina (October 1993)				
Movement for Dignity and Independence	R	5.8	7	(3)
Union of the Democratic Centre	CR	2.6	5	(10)
Justicialist National Movement (Peronist)	—	42.3	126	(119)
Radical Civic Union	CL	30.0	83	(85)
Provincial parties	e	10.4	} 38	(19)
Others	—	8.9		(18)
Armenia (May–July 1990)				
Supreme Soviet	—	—	…	
Australia (March 1993)				
National	R	7.5	16	(14)
Liberal	C	36.8	49	(55)

Country Name of party	Affiliation	Voting strength (%)	Parliamentary representation	
Labor	L	44.9	80	(78)
Others and Independents	—	10.8	2	(1)
Austria (October 1994)				
Austrian Freedom Party	R	22.6	42	(33)
Austrian People's Party	C	27.7	52	(60)
Austrian Social Democratic Party	SD	35.2	65	(80)
Liberal Forum	L	5.7	11	(—)
Greens	Lg	7.0	13	(10)
Azerbaijan				
Interim parliament from May 1992	—	—	…	
Bahamas, The (August 1992)				
Progressive Liberal Party	C	44.7	15	(31)
Free National Movement	C	55.0	34	(16)
Others	—	0.3	0	(2)
Bahrain				
Consultative Council (advisory body)	—	—	—	
Bangladesh (February 1991)				
Bangladesh Nationalist Party	CR	31	166	(18)
National Party (coalition)	—	11	35	(251)
Awami League	SD	31	89	—
Islamic Assembly	r	12	21	(5)
Others	—	15	19	(25)
Barbados (September 1994)				
Democratic Labour Party	C	38.4	8	(18)
National Democratic Party	—	12.7	1	(0)
Barbados Labour Party	SD	48.3	19	(10)
Belarus (March 1990)				
Supreme Soviet	K	—	272	
Belgium (November 1991)				
Vlaams Blok	ERe	6.6	12	(2)
Volksunie	Re	5.9	10	(16)
Front Démocratique	Ro	1.5	3	(3)
Liberals { Flemish	CR	11.0	26	(25)
{ French	CR	8.2	20	(23)
Social Christians { Flemish	C	16.7	39	(43)
{ French	C	7.8	18	(19)

Country Name of party	Affiliation	Voting strength (%)	Parliamentary representation	
Socialists { Flemish	SD	12.0	28	(32)
{ French	SD	13.6	35	(40)
Greens { Flemish	g	4.9	7	(6)
{ French	g	5.1	10	(3)
Others	—	7.3	7	(3)
Belize (June 1993)				
United Democratic Party	R	48.8	16	(13)
People's United Party	C	51.2	13	(15)
Benin (February 1991)				
Union of the Forces of Progress (formerly sole party)	—	…	0	
21 other parties	—	…	64	
Bhutan				
National Assembly, no parties	—	—	105	
Bolivia (June 1993)				
Civic Solidarity Union	R	…	20	—
Nationalist Revolutionary Movement	CR	36	52	(40)
Patriotic Accord (coalition)	—	21	35	(71)
Conscience of the Fatherland	CL	…	13	(9)
Free Bolivia Movement	L	…	7	—
Others	—	…	3	(10)
Bosnia and Herzegovina (December 1990)				
Party of Democratic Action (Muslim)	e	…	86	
Serbian Democratic Party	e	…	72	
Croatian Democratic Union	e	…	44	
Democratic Party of Socialists	x	…	20	
Others	—	…	18	
Botswana (October 1994)				
Botswana Democratic Party	C	…	26	(31)
Botswana National Front	CL	…	13	(3)
Brazil (October 1994)				
Rightist parties	R	…	90	} (243)
Social Democracy and allies	C	…	175	
Democratic Movement and allies	CL	…	105	(146)
Workers Party and allies	L	…	77	(95)
Others	—	…	66	(14)
Brunei				
Legislative Council (nonelected)	—	—	—	

Political Parties

Country / Name of party	Affiliation	Voting strength (%)	Parliamentary representation
Bulgaria (December 1994)			
Union of Democratic Forces	CL	24	69 (110)
Bulgarian Socialist Party	x	44	125 (106)
Movement for Rights and Freedoms (Turkish)	e	...	46 (24)
Popular Union			(—)
Bulgarian Business Bloc			(—)
Burkina Faso (May 1992)			
Government coalition	...	...	84
Opposition parties	...	...	23
Burundi (June 1993)			
Burundi Democratic Front	—	72.6	65
Unity for National Progress	—	21.9	16
Cambodia (May 1993)			
Funcinpec	CR	45.5	58
Buddhist Liberal Democratic Party	L	3.8	10
Cambodian People's Party	x	38.2	51
Others	—	12.5	1
Cameroon (March 1992)			
People's Democratic Movement and allied party	—	...	94 (180)
Opposition parties	—	...	86 —
Canada (October 1993)			
Reform	R	18.1	52
Progressive Conservative	CR	16.1	2 (170)
Liberal	C	41.6	177 (82)
New Democratic	SD	6.6	9 (43)
Bloc Québécois	e	13.9	54 —
Others and independents		3.7	1 (0)
Cape Verde (January 1991)			
Movement for Democracy	—	68.5	56 —
African Party for the Independence of Cape Verde	—	31.5	23 (83)
Central African Republic (August–September 1993)			
Central African People's Liberation Party	—	...	34
Others			51
Chad			
Transitional government since March 1991	—	—	—
Chile (December 1993)			
Independent Democratic Union	ER	...	15 (11)
National Renovation and allied party	R	...	31 (29)
Centre-right independents	CR	...	4 (8)
Christian Democratic Party	C	...	37 (38)
Leftist parties and independent	CL–L	...	33 (34)
China (September 1992–March 1993)			
National People's Congress	K	...	2,978
Colombia (March 1994)			
Social Conservative Party	R	...	56 (15)
Other rightist parties	R	...	... (24)
Liberal Party	C	...	89 (86)
Democratic Alliance–April 19 Movement	L–EL	...	2 (15)
Patriotic Union	EL	...	... (2)
Others	—	...	... (19)
Comoros (December 1993)			
Government supporters	—	...	24 (17)
Opposition parties	—	...	18 (25)
Congo (May–October 1993)			
Presidential Coalition	—	...	63 (69)
Opposition Coalition	—	...	50 (49)
Others	—	...	4 (7)
Costa Rica (February 1994)			
Social Christian Unity Party	CR	...	25 (29)
National Liberation Party	CL	...	28 (25)
Others	—	...	4 (3)
Côte d'Ivoire (November 1990)			
Democratic Party	—	...	163 (175)
Popular Front	SD	...	9 —
Others and independents	—	...	3 —
Croatia (August 1992)			
Croatian Party of Rights	ERe	6.4	5
Croatian Democratic Union	e	41.5	85
Croatian People's Party	C	6.9	6
Croatian Social-Liberal Party	CL	18.3	14
Party of Democratic Changes	x	5.8	11
Others and independents	—	20.6	17
Cuba (February 1993)			
Communist Party	K	...	589 (499)
Cyprus			
Greek Zone (May 1991)			
Democratic Rally	R	35.8	20 (19)
Democratic Party (DIKO)	CR	19.5	11 (16)
Socialist Party (EDEK)	CL	10.9	7 (6)
Progressive Party of the Working People	K	30.6	18 (15)
Turkish Zone (December 1993)			
National Unity Party	CR	29.9	17
Democrat Party	—	29.2	15
Communal Liberation Party	CL	13.3	5
Republican Turkish Party	S	24.2	13
Czech Republic (June 1992)			
Association for the Republic–Czech Republican Party	ER	6.0	14
Governing coalition	R–CR	41.9	105
Czech Social Democratic Party	SD	6.5	16
Liberal Social Union (coalition)	L	6.5	16
Left Bloc	x	14.1	35
Moravia/Silesia regional party	e	5.9	14
Others	—	19.1	0
Denmark (September 1994)			
Progress	ER	6.4	11 (12)
Liberal	R	23.3	42 (29)
Conservative People's	R	15.0	27 (30)
Christian People's	CR	1.8	0 (4)
Centre Democrats	C	2.8	5 (9)
Radical Liberal	C	4.6	8 (7)
Social Democrats	SD	34.6	62 (69)
Socialist People's	S	7.3	13 (15)
Unity List	EL	3.1	6 (0)
Faeroe Islands and Greenland	—		4 (4)
Independents	—	1.0	1 (0)
Djibouti (December 1992)			
Popular Rally for Progress	—	74.6	65 (65)
New Democratic Party	—	25.4	0 —
Dominica (May 1990)			
Dominica Freedom Party	CR	49.4	11 (15)
Dominica United Workers' Party	C	23.5	6 —
Labour Party	L	26.9	4 (5)
Independents	—	...	0 (1)
Dominican Republic (May 1994)			
Social Christian Reformist Party	CR	...	51 (40)
Dominican Revolutionary Party and allies	L	...	57 (36)
Dominican Liberation Party	L	...	12 (44)
Ecuador (May 1994)			
Conservative Party	R	...	6 (6)
Republican Unity Party	CR	...	3 (12)
Social Christian Party	CR	...	25 (21)
Popular Democracy	C	...	8 (5)
Roldosist Party		...	11 (13)
Democratic Left	SD	...	8 (7)
Others	—	...	15 (13)
Egypt (November–December 1990)			
New Wafd Party	R	(Boycotted)	(35)
National Democratic Party	CR	79.6	348 (346)
Socialist Labour Party and allies	L	(Boycotted)	(60)
National Progressive Unionist	L	1.4	6 (0)
Independents	—	...	83 (7)
El Salvador (March 1994)			
Nationalist Republican Alliance (Arena)	R	45	39 (39)
National Conciliation Party	R	...	4 (9)
Christian Democratic Party	CR	16	18 (26)
Democratic Convergence	L	...	1 (8)
Farabundo Martí National Liberation Front	L	29	21 (—)
Others	—	...	1 (2)
Equatorial Guinea (November 1993)			
Democratic Party	—	...	68 (41)
Principal opposition parties	—	(Boycotted)	—
Others	—	...	12 —
Eritrea			
Transitional government from May 1993	—	—	—
Estonia (September 1992)			
Pro Patria coalition	CR	22.0	29
Estonian Popular Front	C	12.2	15 (43)
Estonian National Independence	C	8.8	10
Moderates	CL	9.7	12
Safe Haven	—	13.6	17
Others	—	33.7	18 (62)
Ethiopia			
Transitional government since July 1991	—	—	—
Fiji (February 1994)			
Ethnic Fijian seats	e	...	37 (37)
Ethnic Indian seats	e	...	27 (27)
Chinese/European seats	e	...	4 (4)
Multiracial seat	e	...	1 (1)
Rotuma Island	e	...	1 (1)
Finland (March 1991)			
National Coalition Party	R	19.0	40 (53)
Swedish People's	e	5.4	12 (12)
Centre Party	C	24.4	55 (40)
Christian Union	C	3.0	8 (5)
Rural Party	C	4.8	7 (9)
Social Democratic	L	21.7	48 (56)
Left-Wing Alliance	S	9.9	19 (20)
Green Union	g	6.7	10 (4)
Others	—	5.2	(1)
France (March 1993; 1st round %s)			
National Front	ER	12.4	0 (1)
Rally for the Republic (RPR)	R	20.4	247 (131)
Other right-wing parties	R	4.7	24 (16)
Union for French Democracy (UDF)	CR	19.1	213 (129)
Socialist Party	S	17.6	54 (260)
Other left-wing parties	L	4.5	16 (16)
Communist Party	K	9.2	23 (27)
Environmentalist parties	g	7.6	0
Other	—	4.5	0 (1)
Gabon (September 1990)			
Democratic Party	—	...	66 (111)
Progress Party	—	...	19 —
Rally of Woodcutters	—	...	17 —
Others	—	...	18 —
Gambia, The			
Military government since July 1994	—	—	—
Georgia (October 1992)			
Parliament	—	...	235
Germany (October 1994)			
Christian Social Union	R	7.3	50 (51)
Christian Democratic Union	CR	34.2	244 (268)
Free Democratic Party	C	6.9	47 (79)
Social Democratic Party	SD	36.4	252 (239)
Party of Democratic Socialism	x	4.4	30 (17)
Greens/Alliance '90	g	7.3	49 (8)
Others	—	3.5	0 (0)
Ghana (December 1992)			
National Democratic Congress	—	...	189
Others	—	...	11
Greece (October 1993)			
Political Spring	CR	4.9	10 —
New Democracy	CR	39.3	111 (152)
Panhellenic Socialist Movement (Pasok)	S	46.9	170 (124)
Progressive Left Coalition	L–K	2.9	9 (21)
Communist Party	K	4.5	
Others	—	1.5	0 (3)
Grenada (March 1990)			
Grenada United Labour Party	R	28.3	4 (1)
National Democratic Congress	C	34.6	7 (6)
National Party	C	17.4	2 (5)
New National Party	C	17.2	2 (3)
Guatemala (August 1994)			
National Advancement Party	R	25.3	24 (12)
Guatemalan Republican Front	R	32.2	32 (...)
Solidarity Action Movement	CR	3.2	0 (18)
Christian Democratic Party	C	12.1	13 (28)
National Centre Union	C	8.9	8 (41)
Others and independents	—	18.3	3 (17)
Guinea			
Transitional government since January 1991	—	—	—
Guinea-Bissau (July 1994)			
African Party for the Independence of Guinea and Cape Verde	—	...	62 (150)
Resistance Party	—	...	19 —
Other opposition parties	—	...	19 —
Guyana (October 1992)			
United Force	CR	1.2	1 (2)
People's National Congress	Se	43.6	31 (42)
People's Progressive Party	Se	52.3	32 (8)
Working Peoples Alliance	L	1.7	1 (1)
Haiti (December 1990–January 1991)			
National Front for Change and Democracy (coalition)	CL	...	27
Others	—	...	54
Honduras (November 1993)			
National Party	R	42	55 (71)
Liberal Party	CR	53	71 (55)
Others	—	5	2 (2)
Hungary (May 1994)			
Independent Smallholders	R	8.8	26 (43)
Hungarian Democratic Forum	CR	11.7	37 (165)
Christian Democratic People's Party	CR	7.1	22 (21)
Alliance of Free Democrats	CL	19.8	70 (92)
Federation of Young Democrats	L	7.0	20 (21)
Hungarian Socialist Party	x	33.0	209 (33)
Others and independents	—	12.6	2 (11)
Iceland (April 1991)			
Independence Party	R	38.6	26 (18)
Progressive (Farmers') Party	C	18.9	13 (13)
Social Democratic Party	SD	15.5	10 (10)
People's Alliance	x	14.4	9 (8)
Women's Alliance	—	8.3	5 (6)
Others	—	4.3	0 (8)
India (May 1991–February 1992)			
Bharatiya Janata	Rr	...	121 (88)
Congress (I)	C	...	245 (192)
Janata Dal	CL	...	58 (141)
Communist parties	K	...	49 (43)
Others	—	...	72 (59)
Indonesia (June 1992)			
Golkar (Functional Groups)	—	68	281 (299)
United Development Party	r	17	63 (61)
Indonesian Democratic Party	—	15	56 (40)
Iran (April–May 1992)			
Consultative Assembly, no parties since 1987	—	...	270

Political Parties

Country Name of party	Affili-ation	Voting strength (%)	Parlia-mentary represen-tation
Iraq (April 1989)			
Ba'th Party	—	64	} 250
Others	—	36	
Ireland (November 1992)			
Progressive Democrats	R	4.7	10 (5)
Fianna Fail (Republican)	C	39.1	68 (77)
Fine Gael (United Ireland)	C	24.5	45 (55)
Labour Party	SD	19.3	33 (16)
Democratic Left	S	2.8	4 (7)
Green Alliance	g	1.4	1 (1)
Others	—	8.2	5 (5)
Israel (June 1992)			
Moledet	ER	2.4	3 (2)
Tzomet	R	6.4	8 (2)
United Torah Judaism	r	3.3	4 (7)
Shas	Hr	4.9	6 (6)
Likud	R	24.9	32 (40)
National Religious (Mafdal)	CRr	5.0	6 (5)
Labour	SD	34.6	44 (39)
Meretz	SD	9.6	12 (10)
Arab (Democracy)	e	1.6	2 (1)
Hadash	K	2.4	3 (4)
Others	—	4.9	0 (4)
Italy (March 1994)			
National Alliance	F	13.5	(34)
Northern League	Re	8.4	} 366 (55)
Forza Italia	R	21.0	(—)
Centrist parties (formerly Christian Democratic Party)	C	15.7	46 (206)
Democratic Alliance/Italian Socialists	SD/L	3.4	(119)
The Network (anti-Mafia)	L	1.9	(12)
Democratic Party of the Left	x	20.4	213 (107)
Communist Refoundation Party	K	6.0	(35)
Green List	g	2.7	(16)
Others	—	7.0	5 (46)
Jamaica (March 1993)			
Jamaica Labour Party	CL	39	8 (15)
People's National Party	L	61	52 (45)
Japan (July 1993)			
Liberal-Democratic Party	R	36.7	225 (275)
Shinseito (Japan Renewal)	R	10.1	55 —
Japan New Party	R	8.1	36 —
New Party Sakigake	R	2.6	13 —
Komeito (Clean Government)	C	8.1	52 (45)
Democratic Socialist Party	SD	3.5	15 (14)
United Social Democratic Party	SD	0.7	4 (4)
Social Democratic Party	S	15.4	70 (136)
Japan Communist Party	L	7.7	15 (16)
Independents	—	7.1	27 (22)
Jordan (November 1993)			
Islamic Action Front	r	...	16 (20)
Independent Islamic fundamentalists	r	...	5 (12)
Tribal/traditional candidates	C	...	49 } (17)
Independent centrists	C	...	3
Leftists	L	...	7 (11)
Kazakhstan (March 1994)			
Presidential supporters	—	60	...
Others	—	40	...
Kenya (December 1992)			
Kenya African National Union	—	...	100 (188)
Forum for Restoration of Democracy (2 wings)	—	...	62 —
Democratic Party	—	...	23 —
Others	—	...	3
Kiribati (July 1994)			
House of Assembly	—	—	39
Korea, North (April 1990)			
Korean Workers' Party	K	99.8	687
Korea, South (March 1992)			
United People's Party	—	17.3	31
Democratic Liberal Party	—	38.5	149
Democratic Party	—	29.2	97
Others and independents	—	15.0	22
Kuwait (October 1992)			
Government supporters	—	...	19
Fundamental opposition	r	...	19
Liberal opposition	—	...	12
Kyrgyzstan (February 1990)			
Supreme Soviet	—	...	350
Laos (December 1992)			
Lao People's Revolutionary Party and allies	K	...	85 (79)
Latvia (June 1993)			
Ultranationalist parties	ER	18.8	21 —
Latvia's Way	CR	43.0	48 —
Latvian Farmers' Union		}	
Popular Front	—	2.6	0 (131)
Harmony for Latvia	CL	12.0	13 —
Equal Rights	CL	5.8	7 —
Communist Party	K	(banned)	(59)
Others	—	17.8	11 (11)
Lebanon (August–October 1992)			
Christian members	—	...	64
Muslim/Druze members	—	...	64

Country Name of party	Affili-ation	Voting strength (%)	Parlia-mentary represen-tation
Lesotho (March 1993)			
Basotho Congress Party	—	74.8	65
Basotho National Party	—	22.7	0
Liberia			
No effective government since December 1993	—	—	—
Libya			
Military government since Sept. 1, 1969	—	—	—
Liechtenstein (October 1993)			
Progressive Citizens' Party	CR	41.3	11 (12)
Fatherland Union	C	50.1	13 (11)
The Free List	g	8.5	1 (2)
Lithuania (October–November 1992)			
Christian Democrats and allies	R	12.9	18
Reform Movement (Sajudis)	CR	21.7	29
Social Democratic Party	SD	6.2	8
Democratic Labour Party	x	45.1	74
Others and independents	—	14.1	14
Luxembourg (June 1994)			
Christian Social People's Party	CR	29.3	21 (22)
Democratic Party	C	11.6	12 (11)
Socialist Workers' Party	S	33.5	17 (18)
Communist Party	K	2.8	0 (1)
Action Committee for Democracy and Justice	—	7.1	5 (4)
Green Alternative	g	10.2	5 (4)
Macedonia (October 1994)			
Alliance of Macedonia	x	...	95
Party of Democratic Prosperity (Albanian)	e	...	29
Others and independents	—	...	25
Madagascar (June 1993)			
Living Forces coalition	—	...	75
Others	—	...	59
Malawi (May 1994)			
United Democratic Front	e	...	84 (—)
Malawi Congress Party	e	...	55 (136)
Alliance for Democracy	e	...	36 (—)
Malaysia (October 1990)			
Muslim Unity Movement	CR	...	15 —
National Front (Barisan Nasional)			
United Malays National Organization	o	} 54.2	71 (83)
Allied parties	e		56 (65)
Democratic Action Party	SD	...	20 (24)
Others and independents	—	...	18 (5)
Maldives (December 1994)			
Citizens' Assembly	—	...	48
Mali (February–March 1992)			
Alliance for Democracy in Mali	—	48.4	76
Others	—	51.6	40
Malta (February 1992)			
Nationalist Party	R	51.8	34 (35)
Labour Party	SD	46.5	31 (34)
Marshall Islands (November 1991)			
House of Representatives	—	...	33
Mauritania (March 1992)			
Democratic and Social Republican Party	R	85	67
Others and independents	—	15	12
Mauritius (September 1991)			
Mauritian Social Movement and allies	CL	...	59 (49)
Opposition parties	CL	...	3 (13)
Mexico (August 1994)			
National Action Party (PAN)	CR	...	119 (89)
Institutional Revolutionary Party (PRI)	C	...	300 (320)
Democratic Revolutionary Party	L	...	71 (41)
Others	—	...	10 (50)
Micronesia (March 1993)			
Congress, no parties	—	...	14
Moldova (February 1994)			
Popular Front	Re	7.5	9
Peasants/Intellectuals bloc	Ce	9.2	11
Agrarian Democratic Party	C–x	43.2	56
Socialist/Unity bloc	xe	22.0	28
Others	—	18.1	0
Monaco (January 1993)			
National and Democratic Union	—	...	15 (18)
Others	—	...	3 (0)
Mongolia (June 1992)			
Mongolian People's Revolutionary Party	x	56.9	71 (33)
Others	—	43.1	5 (20)
Morocco (June–September 1993)			
Constitutional Union	CR	...	54 (83)
National Democratic Party	CR	...	24 (24)
Berber parties	CHe	...	76 (47)
National Assembly of Independents	C	...	41 (61)
Democratic Bloc	CL–EL	...	120 (85)
Others and independents	—	...	18 (6)

Country Name of party	Affili-ation	Voting strength (%)	Parlia-mentary represen-tation
Mozambique (October 1994)			
Mozambique Liberation Front (Frelimo)	K	44.3	129 (250)
Mozambique National Resistance (Renamo)	—	37.8	112
Democratic Union	—	5.2	9
Myanmar			
Military government since September 1988	—	—	—
Namibia (December 1994)			
Democratic Turnhalle Alliance	C	70	15 (21)
South West Africa People's Organization (SWAPO)	L	22	53 (41)
Others	—	8	4 (10)
Nauru (November 1992)			
Presidential supporters	p	—	9
Presidential opponents	p	—	9
Nepal (November 1994)			
National Democratic parties	R	...	20 (4)
Nepali Congress Party	C	...	83 (110)
Communist parties	K	...	88 (82)
Others and independents	—	...	14 (9)
Netherlands, The (May 1994)			
Christian Democratic Appeal	CR	22.2	34 (54)
People's Party for Freedom and Democracy	CR	19.9	31 (22)
Democrats 66	CL	15.5	24 (12)
Labour Party	SD	24.0	37 (49)
Green Left	g	3.5	5 (6)
Others	—	14.9	19 (7)
New Zealand (November 1993)			
New Zealand First	—	9.0	2 —
National Party	CR	35.2	50 (67)
Labour Party	CL	34.7	45 (29)
Alliance Party (coalition)	L	18.7	2 (1)
Nicaragua (February 1990)			
National Opposition Union	CR	54.7	51
Sandinista National Liberation Front	L	40.8	39
Others	—	4.5	2
Niger (February 1993)			
Government Coalition	—	...	50
Former government party	—	...	29
Others	—	...	4
Nigeria			
Military government since November 1993	—	—	—
Norway (September 1993)			
Progress Party	R	6.3	10 (22)
Conservative Party	R	16.9	28 (37)
Christian People's Party	CR	7.9	13 (14)
Centre (Agrarian) Party	CR	16.8	32 (11)
Labour Party	SD	37.0	67 (63)
Socialist Left	S	7.9	13 (17)
Others	—	7.2	2 (1)
Oman			
Consultative Council (advisory body)	—		
Pakistan (October 1993)			
Religious parties	Rr	...	10 (6)
Pakistan Muslim League (Nawaz)	—	41.0	72 } (105)
Pakistan Muslim League (Junejo)	—	...	6
Pakistan People's Party	—	38.0	86 (45)
Mohajir Qaumi Movement	e	(Boycotted)	(15)
Other and independents	—	...	27 (30)
Palau (November 1992)			
House of Delegates	—	—	14
Panama (May 1994)			
Democratic Revolutionary Party and allies	—	...	36
Opposition bloc	—	...	30
Papa Egoró	—	...	6
Papua New Guinea (June 1992)			
United Party (Pangu Pati)	p	...	22 (26)
People's Democratic Movement	p	...	15 (18)
Others	p	...	40 (41)
Independents	—	...	31 (21)
Paraguay (May 1993)			
Colorado Party	R	43.0	38 (48)
Authentic Radical Liberal Party	CL	35.1	33 (19)
National Encounter coalition	—	17.1	9 —
Others	—	4.8	0 (5)
Peru (November 1992)			
Christian Popular Party	R	7.5	8 }
Liberal Party	R	—	} (60)
Popular Action	CR	(Boycotted)	}
New Majority–Change 90	—	37.0	44 (32)
American Popular Revolutionary Alliance	CL	(Boycotted)	(52)
Others	—	55.5	28 (36)
Philippines (May 1992)			
National People's Coalition	R	...	48
Liberal Party	C	...	15
National Union of Christian Democrats	—	...	51
Democratic Filipino Struggle	—	...	87

Political Parties

Country / Name of party	Affiliation	Voting strength (%)	Parliamentary representation
Poland (September 1993)			
Confederation for an Independent Poland	R	5.8	22 (46)
Non-Party Bloc to Support Reform	R	5.4	16
Democratic Union	CL	10.6	74 (62)
Labour Union	L	7.3	41 (4)
Democratic Left Alliance	x	20.4	171 (60)
Polish Peasant Party	x	15.4	132 (48)
German minority organizations	e	0.5	4 (7)
Others	—	34.6	0 (233)
Portugal (October 1991)			
Social Democratic Party	C	50.4	135 (148)
Socialist Party	L	29.3	72 (60)
Communist alliance	K	8.8	17 (31)
Other parties	—	11.5	6 (11)
Qatar			
Consultative Council (advisory body)	—	—	—
Romania (September 1992)			
Romanian National Unity Party	ERe	7.7	30
Greater Romania	e	3.9	16
Democratic Convention of Romania	CR	20.0	82
Democratic National Salvation Front	x	27.7	117
National Salvation Front	x	10.2	43
Hungarian Democratic Union	r	7.5	27
Others	—	23.0	13
Russia (December 1993)			
Liberal Democratic Party	F	22.8	64
Russia's Choice	CR	15.4	58
Russian Party of Unity and Accord	CR	6.8	19
Yavlinsky–Boldyrev-Lukin bloc	C	7.8	22
Women of Russia	C	8.1	23
Democratic Party	C	5.5	15
Communist Party	K	12.3	48
Agrarian Union	K	7.9	33
Other parties	—	13.4	37
Independents elected from constituency lists	—	—	130
Rwanda			
Interim legislature from November 1994	—	—	—
Saint Kitts and Nevis (November 1993)			
People's Action Movement	CL	33.6	4 (6)
Nevis Reformation Party	CL	8.5	1 (2)
St Kitts–Nevis Labour Party	L	43.8	4 (2)
Concerned Citizens' Movement	—	10.9	2 (1)
Saint Lucia (April 1992)			
United Workers' Party	C	54.9	11 (9)
St. Lucia Labour Party	CL	41.9	6 (8)
Saint Vincent and the Grenadines (February 1994)			
New Democratic Party	C	54.5	12 (15)
St. Vincent Labour Party	L	43.7	3 (0)
Movement for National Unity			
San Marino (May 1993)			
Christian Democrats	CR	41.4	26 (27)
Socialist Party	S	23.7	14 (7)
Progressive Democratic Party	x	18.6	11 (18)
Popular Democratic Alliance	—	7.7	4
Other parties	—	8.6	5 (8)
São Tomé and Príncipe (October 1994)			
Party of Democratic Convergence	C	17	14 (33)
Movement for Liberation	L	43	27 (21)
Independent Democratic Action	—	26	14
Saudi Arabia			
Consultative Council (advisory body)	—	—	—
Senegal (May 1993)			
Socialist Party	SD	56.6	84 (103)
Senegalese Democratic Party	—	30.2	27 (17)
Let Us Unite Senegal	EL	4.9	3 —
Other parties	—	8.3	6 —
Seychelles (July 1993)			
People's Progressive Front	L	57.5	28 (23)
Others	—	42.5	5 —
Sierra Leone			
Military government since May 1992	—	—	—
Singapore (August 1991)			
People's Action Party	CR	61	77 (80)
Democratic Party	CL	12	3 (1)
Workers' Party	L	14	1 (0)
Slovakia (September–October 1994)			
Slovak National Party	Re	5.4	9 (15)
Christian Democratic Movement	CR	10.1	17 (18)
Movement for a Democratic Slovakia	—	35.0	61 (74)
Democratic Left	x	10.4	18 (29)
Hungarian minority coalition	e	10.2	17 (14)
Others	—	28.9	28 (0)
Slovenia (December 1992)			
Slovenian National Party	ER	10.2	12
Christian Democrats	CR	14.5	15
Slovenian People's Party	—	8.7	10
Associated List coalition	—	13.6	14
Democratic Party	C	5.1	6
Liberal Democratic Party	CL	23.5	22

Country / Name of party	Affiliation	Voting strength (%)	Parliamentary representation
Social Democratic Party	SD	3.3	4
Greens of Slovenia	g	3.7	5
Others	—	17.4	0
Solomon Islands (May 1993)			
Government Alliance	p	...	24
Opposition party	p	...	23
Somalia			
No effective government since January 1991	—	—	—
South Africa (April 1994)			
Freedom Front	ER	2.2	9
National Party	CR	20.4	82
Inkatha Freedom Party	e	10.5	43
Democratic Party	C	1.7	7
African National Congress	CL	62.7	252
Pan-Africanist Congress	EL	1.2	5
Others	—	1.3	2
Spain (June 1993)			
Popular Party	R	34.8	141 (107)
Democratic and Social Centre	C	1.7	0 (14)
Basque Nationalist Party	Ce	1.2	5 (5)
Canary Islands coalition	Ce	0.9	4 —
Convergence and Union (Catalan)	CLe	5.0	17 (18)
Socialist Workers' Party	S	38.7	159 (175)
United Left	L–K	9.6	18 (17)
Herri Batasuna (Basque radicals)	ELe	0.9	2 (4)
Others	—	7.2	4 (10)
Sri Lanka (August 1994)			
United National Party	SD	...	94 (125)
Muslim Congress	r	...	7 (4)
People's Alliance	—	...	105 } (96)
Others and independents	—	...	19 }
Sudan, The			
Transitional government since February 1992	—	—	—
Suriname (May 1991)			
National Democratic Party	—	21.8	12 (3)
Front for Democracy and Development (four-party coalition)	—	54.2	30 (42)
Democratic Alternative '91	—	16.7	9 —
Swaziland (September–October 1993)			
House of Assembly, no parties	—	...	55
Sweden (September 1994)			
New Democracy	R	1.2	0 (24)
Christian Democrats	R	4.1	14 (27)
Moderate (Conservative) Party	R	22.4	80 (80)
Centre (Agrarian) Party	CR	7.7	27 (31)
People's (Liberal) Party	C	7.2	25 (33)
Social Democrats	S	45.3	161 (138)
Left Party	x	6.2	22 (16)
Greens	g	5.0	18 (0)
Switzerland (October 1991)			
Christian Democrats	R	18.3	36 (42)
Liberal Party	R	3.0	10 (9)
Swiss People's	CR	11.9	25 (25)
Radical Democrats	C	21.0	44 (51)
Social Democrats	SD	18.5	41 (41)
Green Party	g	6.1	14 (9)
Others	—	21.2	30 (23)
Syria (August 1994)			
National Progressive Front			
Ba'th Party and allies	—	...	167 (166)
Independents	—	...	83 (84)
Taiwan (December 1992)			
Nationalist (Kuomintang)	—	53	94 (72)
Democratic Progressive Party	—	31	52 (21)
Others and Independents	—	16	15 (8)
Tajikistan (March 1990)			
Supreme Soviet	—	...	230
Tanzania (October 1990)			
Revolutionary Party of Tanzania (CCM)	—	...	204 (169)
Thailand (September 1992)			
Pro-military parties:			
Thai Nation	—	21.4	77
National Development	—	16.7	60
Others	—	1.1	4
Pro-democracy parties:			
Democrat	—	21.9	79
New Aspiration	—	14.2	51
Righteous Force	—	13.1	47
Solidarity	—	2.2	8
Others	—	9.4	34
Togo (February 1994)			
Rally of the Togolese People	—	...	38
Action Committee for Renewal	—	...	34
Union for Democracy	—	...	6
Others	—	...	3
Tonga (February 1993)			
Pro-Democracy Movement	—	...	6 (6)
Others	—	...	3 (3)
Trinidad and Tobago (December 1991)			
People's National Movement	C	45.1	21 (3)
National Alliance for Reconstruction (four parties)	C	24.4	2 (33)
United National Congress	L	29.1	13 —

Country / Name of party	Affiliation	Voting strength (%)	Parliamentary representation
Tunisia (March 1994)			
Government party	CL	97.7	144 (141)
Others	—	2.3	19 (0)
Turkey (October 1991)			
Nationalist Labour Party	ER }	16.4	19 —
Welfare Party	Rr }		43 (0)
True Path Party	CR	26.2	178 (59)
Motherland Party	CR	23.3	115 (292)
Social Democratic Populist	CL }	20.1	66 (99)
People's Labour Party	e }		22 —
Democratic Left Party	CL	10.4	7 (0)
Turkmenistan (December 1994)			
Assembly	—	—	50
Tuvalu (November 1993)			
Parliament, no parties	—	—	12
Uganda			
Military regime from July 1985	—	—	—
Ukraine (March–April 1994)			
Extreme nationalist parties	ERe	...	5
Less extreme nationalist parties	CRe	...	15
Ukrainian Popular Movement (Rukh)	Ce	...	20
Centrist parties	C	...	17
Communist Party and allies	K–EL	...	118
Unaffiliated members	—	...	163
United Arab Emirates			
Federal National Council (advisory body)	—	—	—
United Kingdom (April 1992)			
Democratic Unionists	Re	0.3	3 (3)
Conservative Party	CR	41.9	336 (375)
Liberal Democrats	CL	17.9	20 (22)
Labour Party	L	34.4	271 (229)
Scottish National Party	e	1.9	3 (3)
Plaid Cymru (Welsh Nationalists)	e	0.5	4 (3)
Ulster Unionists	—	0.8	9 (9)
Social Democratic and Labour Party (Northern Ireland)	CLe	0.6	4 (3)
Sinn Fein (Northern Ireland)	ELe	0.2	0 (1)
Other	—	1.5	1 (2)
United States (November 1994)			
Republican	CR	...	230 (175)
Democratic	C	...	204 (259)
Other	—	...	1 (1)
Uruguay (November 1994)			
National (Blanco) Party	C	31.4	31 (39)
Colorado Party	C	32.2	32 (30)
New Space	SD	5.1	4 (9)
Progressive Encounter	SD–EL	30.8	28 —
Broad Front	L	...	— (21)
Uzbekistan (December 1994)			
People's Democratic Party	x	...	205
National Progress Party	—	...	6
Vanuatu (December 1991)			
Union of Moderate Parties	CR	...	19 (20)
National United Party	CR	...	10 —
Vanua'aku Pati	—	...	12 (26)
Others	—	...	5 (0)
Venezuela (December 1993)			
COPEI (Social Christians)	CR	...	54 (67)
Democratic Action	SD	...	55 (97)
National Convergence	S }	...	50 —
Movement to Socialism	}		
The Cause R	EL	...	40 (3)
Others	—	...	0 (16)
Vietnam (July 1992)			
National Assembly	—	...	395
Western Samoa (April 1991)			
Human Rights Protection Party	—	...	30 (27)
National Development Party	—	...	14 (19)
Independents	—	...	3 (1)
Yemen (April 1993)			
Yemeni Alliance for Reform	Rr	...	62
General People's Congress	—	...	123
Yemeni Socialist Party	K	...	56
Others and independents	—	...	60
Yugoslavia (December 1992)			
Serbian Radical Party	Fe	24.4	34 (33)
Serbian Democratic Movement	C	18.7	20 —
Democratic Party	C	6.5	5 —
Socialist Party of Serbia	xe	34.2	47 (73)
Democratic Party of Socialists of Montenegro	xe	3.0	17 (23)
Democratic Community (Hungarian)	e	2.4	3 (2)
Others	—	10.8	12 (6)
Zaire			
Transitional government from April 1994	—	—	—
Zambia (October 1991)			
Movement for Multiparty Democracy	—	75.8	125
United National Independence	—	24.2	25 (125)
Zimbabwe (March 1990)			
Zimbabwe African National Union	S	75.4	117
Other parties	—	17.5	3

AFGHANISTAN

Afghanistan is a landlocked Islamic state in central Asia. Area: 652,225 sq km (251,825 sq mi). Pop. (1994 est.): 16,903,000 (excluding Afghan refugees estimated to number about 1.5 million in Pakistan and 1.8 million in Iran). Cap.: Kabul. Monetary unit: afghani, with (Oct. 7, 1994) a free rate of 2,605 afghanis to U.S. $1 (4,144 afghanis = £1 sterling). President in 1994, Burhanuddin Rabbani; prime minister to June 28, Gulbuddin Hekmatyar (term expired and not extended).

Destructive and inconclusive fighting between forces loyal to Prime Minister Gulbuddin Hekmatyar and troops loyal to Pres. Burhanuddin Rabbani in 1994 resulted in the disintegration of central state authority and weakened the cohesion of the multinational state.

On January 1 Hekmatyar's Hezb-i-Islami forces and those of Gen. 'Abd ar-Rashid Dostam coordinated an artillery and rocket assault on Kabul. The offensive represented a major realignment of forces vying for control of the government. Dostam had precipitated the surrender of Kabul to resistance forces in April 1992 by withdrawing his support from the Soviet-installed regime of Mohammad Najibullah. He placed the greater part of the communist army and air force under his command and assisted the new resistance government fighting Hekmatyar's forces. After intense but inconclusive fighting throughout the year, Kabul remained divided into zones controlled by rival groups. A blockade of Kabul led to fighting in northern Afghanistan over a tenuous road link to neighbouring Tajikistan. The prolonged bombardment reduced most of the Afghan capital to ruins and caused 75% of Kabul's population of two million to flee the area. Outside Kabul the central government's authority all but disappeared. Under the protection of Dostam, Mazar-i-Sharif, the largest industrial complex in Afghanistan, enjoyed relative stability. In Jalalabad local political groups and commanders cooperated to provide basic public services. In Kandahar local rivalries slowed reconstruction. Herat was generally peaceful and secure and began to reclaim its traditional role as commercial centre along trade routes with neighbouring Iran and Turkmenistan.

In March United Nations Secretary-General Boutros Boutros-Ghali appointed former Tunisian foreign minister Mahmoud Mestiri head of a special peace commission. He met leaders inside and outside Afghanistan, but no formal UN peace plan was announced. In July Hamid al-Ghabid, secretary-general of the Organization of the Islamic Conference, led a peace effort, but individual OIC member states were unable to agree on an appropriate solution.

Rabbani refused to relinquish the presidency when his term expired on June 28, and the Supreme Court in Kabul extended his term for an additional six months. General dissatisfaction over the unending power struggle led to renewed calls to convene a Loya Jirgah, or grand assembly. While many Afghans feared that a Loya Jirgah would serve to reinforce traditional social structures at the expense of social progress, there was movement nonetheless toward some form of assembly that could offer legitimate leadership. In July representatives from throughout Afghanistan and prominent Afghans living abroad met in Herat. Although the delegates endorsed Rabbani's continuance as president, they initiated measures aimed at organizing a Loya Jirgah to choose a new government.

International rivalries continued to agitate Afghanistan's divided society. The country's large Shi'ite minority and the 1.8 million Afghan refugees in neighbouring Iran automatically gave Tehran a role in Afghan affairs. Saudi Arabia became involved by supporting fractions it saw as a counter-

Afghanis gather wood amid the rubble of Kabul as a soldier (right) stands guard. During the year hundreds of thousands fled the capital city, where fighting between the forces of Pres. Burhanuddin Rabbani and Prime Minister Gulbuddin Hekmatyar caused extensive destruction.
AFP PHOTO

weight to Iranian influence. Dostam's military power and previous support of the communist regime ensured close relations between the general, an Afghan Uzbek, and the pro-Russian government of Uzbekistan. Pakistan's role was even more crucial. Not only did Pakistan give refuge to 1.5 million Afghan refugees, but it was permanent home to a section of the Pashtun ethnic group, which traditionally played a leading role in Afghan politics. India and China viewed the strengthening of Islamic fundamentalism in Afghanistan as a danger to their own authority in Kashmir and Sinkiang, respectively, while other countries throughout the world were concerned about terrorists trained by Afghanistan's warring factions and the country's expanding drug trafficking. Serious international attention to Afghanistan remained distracted, however, both by the apparent unwillingness of Afghan leaders to cooperate and by attention to international crises elsewhere.   (STEVE SEGO)

ALBANIA

A republic in the western Balkan Peninsula of southeastern Europe, Albania is situated on the Adriatic Sea. Area: 28,748 sq km (11,100 sq mi). Pop. (1994 est.): 3,374,000. Cap.: Tirana. Monetary unit: lek, with (Oct. 7, 1994) a free rate of 100.09 leks to U.S. $1 (159.20 leks = £1 sterling). President in 1994, Sali Berisha; prime minister, Aleksander Meksi.

During 1994 Albania's postcommunist recovery continued but with more progress in some areas than others. Greek-Albanian relations deteriorated, and Athens blocked European Union loans to Tirana, impeding Albania's much-needed integration into Europe.

Domestically, Albania not only halted economic decay but registered growth; gross domestic product grew by 8%, agricultural production increased an estimated 8% over 1993 levels, and inflation continued its downward spiral. Unemployment, however, remained the country's Achilles' heel; more than 300,000 workers were unemployed. Some $400 million sent home by Albanian emigrants played a vital role in boosting the domestic economy by increasing the volume of disposable income. For most, economic hardship and widespread poverty were the norm. Albania's foreign debt continued to soar and was expected to exceed $600 million.

The political climate was relatively stable, but hostility between ruling and opposition forces continued to surface. The Socialist Party of Albania (PSS) and other political groups accused Pres. Sali Berisha of becoming increasingly authoritarian. Berisha sought to end a constitutional impasse in October, however, when he called for a national referendum, the first of its kind. Surprisingly, the November vote went against Berisha, perpetuating the deadlock with the Socialists and likely delaying moves toward closer ties with Western Europe. The trials of PSS leader Fatos Nano and former communist leader Ramiz Alia resulted in prison terms of 12 and 9 years, respectively.

Albania made considerable progress in foreign affairs, although relations with some of its neighbours continued to be fraught with problems. The impasse in relations between Belgrade, Yugos., and Tirana persisted, but ties with Bulgaria, Turkey, Macedonia, and Italy further improved. Relations with Greece raised worries about a new Balkan flash point. Following a raid on an army training camp in which two Albanian conscripts were killed, Tirana arrested five ethnic Greeks, found them guilty of espionage and illegal possession of weapons, and sentenced them to between six and eight years in prison. Angered by the verdict, Athens reportedly expelled as many as 70,000 of the 300,000 Albanians living in Greece. (LOUIS ZANGA)

This article updates the *Macropædia* article BALKAN STATES: *Albania*.

ALGERIA

Algeria is a republic of North Africa on the Mediterranean Sea. Area: 2,381,741 sq km (919,595 sq mi). Pop. (1994 est.): 27,815,000. Cap.: Algiers. Monetary unit: Algerian dinar, with (Oct. 7, 1994) a controlled rate of 37.95 dinars to U.S. $1 (60.36 dinars = £1 sterling). Chairman of the High Committee of State in 1994, Ali Kafi until January 30; president from January 31, Liamine Zeroual; prime ministers, Redha Malek and, from April 11, Mokdad Sifi.

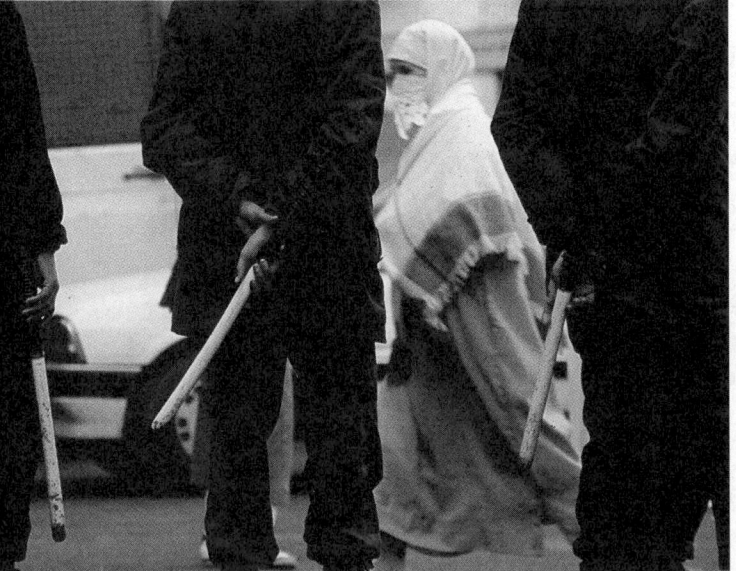

An Algerian woman in traditional dress passes in front of security forces. For the third year Algeria was beset by conflict between the government and the Islamic Salvation Front, which won a majority in the first round of voting in 1991 before the elections were canceled.

Algeria in 1994 was once again dominated by the conflict between the government and the banned Islamic Salvation Front (FIS). At the end of January the High Committee of State called a national meeting with the political parties in order to select a new president for the country. As all the major parties—except Hamas, the most moderate of Algeria's three Islamist parties—boycotted the meeting, the High Security Council, which was dominated by the army, appointed Liamine Zeroual, the defense minister and a former general, president for a three-year term.

In his first public address, on February 7, Zeroual, who came from the moderate wing of the government, promised a dialogue with the FIS. Two weeks later two leading FIS members, Abdelkader Boukhamkham and Ali Djeddi, were released from prison. In mid-September three more FIS leaders were released, and the two top leaders of the movement, Abbasi Madani and Ali BelHadj, were transferred from Blida prison, where they had been held since June 1991, to house arrest. These releases came in response to a letter from Madani to the president confirming that the FIS would respect a pluralistic political system in any future election. The anticipated dialogue was delayed, however, as the FIS was not prepared to accept government demands for an end to violence.

Violence, in fact, continued throughout the year at an intensified level as the government's security forces attempted to crush the Islamist opposition. The armed opposition split into two groups—the Armed Islamic Group (GIA) in and around Algiers and the Armed Islamic Movement in the east and west of the country. The deaths of more than 60 foreigners led to the withdrawal of their nationals by most countries and to intensified government action against the GIA. Incidents included an Islamist attack on Algeria's secure prison at Tazoult during which 1,000 detainees escaped, a GIA attack on the French embassy that resulted in five deaths, a French government decision to expel supporters of the FIS in France, the assassination of the military chief of Algiers in November, and an airline hijacking that resulted in the deaths of three passengers and four terrorists (and four priests in retaliation) in December.

Despite this violent background, the Algerian government continued to restructure the economy in accordance with International Monetary Fund (IMF) requirements. On April 10 the dinar was devalued by 40%, and an agreement was reached with the IMF to provide standby loan facilities worth $1,037,000,000. In June $5.3 billion of Algerian debt to the Paris Club of creditor nations was rescheduled, which significantly reduced the debt service burden on the country's $27 billion total of foreign debt. The IMF agreement was also marked by a change in government as Redha Malek, a well-known hard-liner, was replaced as prime minister by a technocrat, Mokdad Sifi, who was believed to be more prepared for dialogue with the Islamist opposition. (GEORGE JOFFÉ)

This article updates the *Macropædia* article NORTH AFRICA: *Algeria*.

ANDORRA

A landlocked parliamentary coprincipality of Europe, Andorra is in the Pyrenees Mountains between Spain and France. Area: 468 sq km (181 sq mi). Pop. (1994 est.): 62,400. Cap.: Andorra la Vella. Monetary units: French franc and Spanish peseta. Coprinces: the president of the French Republic and the bishop of Seu d'Urgell, Spain; head of the government in 1994, Oscar Ribas Reig.

A sovereign state after seven centuries of feudal rule, Andorra marked 1994 as its first year of democratic government. In the country's first general election under its new constitution, on Dec. 12, 1993, the National Democratic Grouping (AND), the party led by Oscar Ribas Reig, won the most seats (8) in the 28-seat legislature. On January 19 Ribas Reig, the outgoing president of the Executive Council, was reelected head of government by 15 of the 28 members of the legislature. On February 3 the new government, a coalition of AND members and independents, was sworn into office.

Ribas Reig announced that his government would concentrate on fiscal and tax reforms and the development of tourism. To enhance income from tourism, Andorra was considering opening its residential property market to foreigners. Sales of vacation homes in the country would be targeted at skiers. Ramon Sera, minister of social and cultural affairs, announced that if the ban against foreign ownership was lifted, priority would be given to citizens of the European Union and the European Free Trade Association "who can show that they are not reliant upon a job, will invest in residential property, and can meet defined status requirements." These included proof of external income, maintenance of an account in an Andorran bank, a good character reference, and information from Interpol that the applicant had not committed serious crimes.

(ANNE ROBY)

This article updates the *Micropædia* article ANDORRA.

ANGOLA

A republic, Angola is located on the Atlantic coast in southwestern Africa. The small exclave of Cabinda is separated from Angola by a strip of Zaire. Area: 1,246,700 sq km (481,354 sq mi). Pop. (1994 est.): 11,233,000. Cap.: Luanda. Monetary unit: new kwanza, with (Oct. 7, 1994) a controlled rate of 139,294 new kwanzas to U.S. $1 (free rate of 221,548 new kwanzas = £1 sterling). President in 1994, José Eduardo dos Santos; prime minister, Marcolino Moco.

Peace talks between the government and the rebel National Union for the Total Independence of Angola (UNITA), begun in Lusaka, Zambia, in November 1993, continued in 1994 under the chairmanship of the UN mediator, Alioune Blondin Beye, until UNITA withdrew in September without making it clear whether the withdrawal was permanent. From time to time it was announced that agreement had been reached on key issues. In May it was reported that the contending parties had agreed upon the method of conducting a second round of presidential elections. At other times it was said that both sides had committed themselves to the creation of a joint army and a joint police force. Also, although the government would not accede to UNITA's request for the portfolios of Defense, Finance, and the Interior, an agreement was said to have been reached regarding certain power-sharing proposals.

Decentralization and the allocation of governorships of provinces were also stumbling blocks. In spite of a number of suggestions by Pres. Frederick Chiluba of Zambia as to how the province of Huambo in particular might be administered, the government remained adamant that it would not acknowledge UNITA's claim to the province, which the rebels said was the heartland of the Ovimbundu people, from whom they drew much of their support. Accordingly, a treaty signed on November 20 did not seem to substantially alter the fighting or jockeying for position.

The growing despair of finding any solution to Angola's problems was reflected in the reluctance of foreign donors to provide assistance. By the beginning of the year, less than half the $227 million requested by the UN in June 1993 to provide aid for Angola had been subscribed. On March

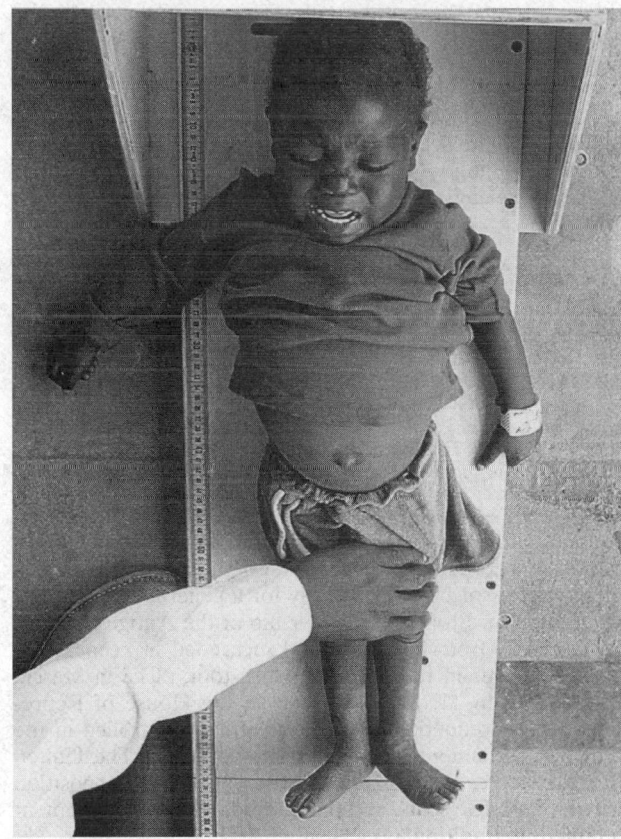

A malnourished Angolan orphan cries as he is measured. An upsurge in fighting between government troops and rebels, including the forces of UNITA (National Union for the Total Independence of Angola), during the year produced additional suffering among the people.

KEITH BERNSTEIN—GAMMA LIAISON

14 Pres. José Eduardo dos Santos seized the opportunity offered by the resignation of his finance minister to carry out a major Cabinet reshuffle. On the following day the new finance minister, Alvaro Craveiro, presented a budget in which spending on defense was still the largest component but that donor agencies agreed constituted a step in the direction of reform. Among other provisions, the budget set a target of the annual inflation rate of 260%, to be achieved by December 1994, in comparison with the annual rate registered in December 1993 of 1,840%.

Again and again, however, hopes of any improvement were shattered by recurrent outbreaks of fighting in different parts of the country. In February the minister of assistance and social integration lifted the ban on relief flights to areas under UNITA's military control in return for guarantees by UNITA that it would permit the World Food Program to conduct its operations in Kuito. On March 22, however, there were reports of major offensives by UNITA's forces in Benguela, Huila, and Bengo provinces, and in June the town of Kuito again came under heavy artillery and infantry attacks from UNITA troops, which resulted in many more civilian deaths. In the Cabinda exclave in August, a separatist movement calling itself the Front for the Liberation of Cabinda accused government troops of having carried out an attack on a village during which 100 civilians were killed. At the end of the month, government forces recaptured Belize district, and in September they conducted a successful operation against the rebels in Cunhinga in an attempt to free civilians held captive by UNITA.

It was the bombing of Huambo by government aircraft on August 31 that led to the withdrawal of UNITA's negotiating team from the Lusaka talks. This was followed by the arrival of James Jonah, a Sierra Leonean sent by the UN secretary-general to carry out an appraisal of the situation in Angola. His visit was widely believed to have been an indication that the UN was reluctant to commit further resources to the resolution of a conflict that neither side appeared willing to bring to an end.   (KENNETH INGHAM)

This article updates the *Macropædia* article SOUTHERN AFRICA: *Angola*.

ANTIGUA AND BARBUDA

A constitutional monarchy and member of the Commonwealth, Antigua and Barbuda comprises the islands of Antigua, Barbuda, and Redonda in the eastern Caribbean Sea. Area: 442 sq km (171 sq mi). Pop. (1994 est.): 66,000. Cap.: Saint John's. Monetary unit: Eastern Caribbean dollar, with (Oct. 7, 1994) a par value of EC$2.70 to U.S. $1 (free rate of EC$4.30 = £1 sterling). Queen, Elizabeth II; governor-general in 1994, James Carlisle; prime ministers, Vere Cornwall Bird and, from March 9, Lester Bird.

Antigua and Barbuda's veteran leader, Vere Cornwall Bird, retired in February after decades in politics, and the parliament was dissolved to make way for a general election. His son Lester Bird took over leadership of the Antigua Labour Party (ALP) from his father and succeeded in keeping the party in power in the election, which took place in March. The ALP won 11 of the 17 seats in the House of Representatives, a reduction from the 15 it had controlled in the previous parliament but a victory nonetheless. The United Progressive Party, an amalgam of three separate opposition parties, took five seats, and the Barbuda People's Movement retained its traditional one seat.

One of the ALP seats went to Vere Bird, Jr., Lester's older brother, who had been removed from the Cabinet by his father in 1990 after a commission of inquiry had recommended that he be disbarred from public office. He had been implicated in an illegal arms transshipment scandal involving the sending of Israeli weapons to Colombian drug barons. Bird had maintained his innocence, and the incident did not appear to affect his popularity with the electorate. He was, however, notably absent from the new Cabinet.

(DAVID RENWICK)

This article updates the *Macropædia* article The WEST INDIES: *Antigua and Barbuda*.

ARGENTINA

The federal republic of Argentina occupies the eastern section of the Southern Cone of South America, along the Atlantic Ocean. Area: 2,780,400 sq km (1,073,518 sq mi). Pop. (1994 est.): 33,880,000. Cap.: Buenos Aires. Monetary unit: peso, with (Oct. 7, 1994) an official (pegged) rate of 1 peso to U.S. $1 (1.59 pesos = £1 sterling). President in 1994, Carlos Saúl Menem.

The greater part of 1994 was dominated by Pres. Carlos Menem's efforts to change the 1853 constitution so that he could run for a second term in 1995. Elections for a 305-seat constituent assembly to oversee the revision process took place on April 10, with the ruling Justicialist National Movement (Peronist; PJ) winning the largest share of the vote, at about 38%. This was a significant reduction for the PJ from the 43% in the October 1993 congressional polls.

It was the main opposition Radical Civic Union (UCR) that fared worst, however, its share of the vote totaling 20%, compared with the 30% registered the previous October. The main beneficiary of the UCR's loss in support was the Frente Grande (or Broad Front) a coalition of left-leaning groups, including disenchanted members of the PJ, that polled 13.5% of the votes, compared with 3.7% in October

1993. More important, the Frente scored a decisive victory in Buenos Aires, with more than 35% of the vote, compared with 25% for the PJ and 15% for the UCR.

The constitutional revision began on May 25 and was to be completed within 90 days. This was done, and the document was promulgated on August 24. To achieve the main goal of changing the constitution so that he could run again in 1995, Menem had to cede significant powers currently available to the president. His ability to rule by decree was curtailed, and he had to obtain legislative approval for his appointment to the new office of Cabinet chief.

With an eye toward the 1995 election, Menem used his May 1 speech at the opening of the national legislature as an opportunity to announce new measures. A key provision was a boost of some $7 billion in the spending program for the country's poorest regions over the next three years. The emphasis would be on promoting public works projects (especially transportation, including rail and road links to Brazil and Chile) that would be designed to increase employment and exports. Provincial budgets (in the poorest regions of the country) were increased by up to $300 million above 1994 budget figures. Labour unions opposed to Menem's policies staged a one-day general strike on August 2. The bombing of the Jewish community centre in Buenos Aires on July 18, allegedly by Islamic extremists, caused the deaths of 96 people.

During 1994 Argentina continued to enjoy relative economic stability. Economy Minister Domingo Cavallo on September 29 indicated that real gross domestic product increased by 7% during the first half of 1994, with a 28% rise in investment. Manufacturing grew less robustly (4.1%) than the overall rate, while the agricultural sector fared poorly, with 0.7% expansion. Despite the strong growth performance, unemployment was 11%. Consumer price inflation declined to an annual rate of 3.4% at the end of October from 3.76% at the end of September. The annual result for 1994 was expected to be about 4%, well below the 7.4% in 1993 and a fraction of the totals in the previous two years.

In late October there was a revised official forecast that a budget deficit approaching $1 billion might be incurred for 1994. This contrasted with a target surplus of $4.6 billion originally agreed upon under the country's extended financing facility program with the International Monetary Fund (IMF). During September Cavallo indicated that the country would not be proceeding with the two final series of loans from the IMF (totaling more than $400 million); consequently, there was no need for compliance with the targets.

Overall, government spending during the first nine months outstripped government forecasts by close to $1.5 billion. In late October Cavallo requested legislative approval for an additional $1.3 billion for the social security budget to cover a deficit that was largely created by judicial rulings awarding retrospective pension increases to some 100,000 recipients.

Concerning the external accounts, the trade deficit was on a rising curve. The nine-month accumulated deficit stood at $4,340,000,000 (based on exports of about $11.2 billion and imports of $15.5 billion), compared with a deficit of $1,920,000,000 in the same period of 1993. The trade deficit for the whole of 1994 was expected to approach $6 billion, compared with $3,690,000,000 in 1993, while the current account deficit was projected at about $10 billion, compared with $7.6 billion in 1993.

Argentina's deficit on trade with its partners in the Mercosur common market (Brazil, Uruguay, and Paraguay) had increased by 42% at the end of August, to $727 million,

Retired workers in Buenos Aires protest the small size of their government pensions. Despite the grievances of some citizens, it was agreed that government reforms had produced dramatic benefits, including lower inflation and higher productivity, for the Argentine economy.

CARLOS CARRION—SYGMA

although Argentina's exports to those countries had risen by 13%. The deficit was expected to be reduced by the end of the year as a result of increased Argentine exports to Brazil.

On November 16 the Senate opened a debate on new patent and copyright legislation, which the U.S. government had been insisting upon for some time to update the existing 1864 law.   (SUSAN M. CUNNINGHAM)

ARMENIA

A landlocked republic of Transcaucasia, Armenia borders Georgia to the north, Azerbaijan to the east, Iran to the south, the Azerbaijani exclave of Nakhichevan to the southwest, and Turkey to the west. Area: 29,800 sq km (11,500 sq mi). Pop. (1994 est.) 3,553,000. Cap.: Yerevan. Armenia claims the predominantly Armenian-populated Nagorno-Karabakh region, which has been part of Azerbaijan since 1923. Monetary unit: dram, with (Oct. 3, 1994) a free rate of 356.68 dram = U.S. $1 (556.44 dram = £1 sterling). President in 1994, Levon Ter-Petrosyan; prime minister, Hrant Bagatyan.

The standoff between the unpopular leadership of Pres. Levon Ter-Petrosyan and Armenia's fractious opposition continued in 1994. In anticipation of parliamentary and presidential elections in 1995, several opposition parties (excluding the revitalized communists) formed a shadow cabinet in March and then a tentative alliance in September in order to intensify pressure on the ruling Armenian National Movement and to block the adoption of a new constitution. Former prime minister Vazgen Manukyan's National Democratic Union convened repeated protest demonstrations—at which former national security adviser Ashot Manucharyan accused the police of corruption and the leadership of the abuse of power. In late December Ter-Petrosyan suspended the activities of the opposition Dashnaktsyutyun party because of its suspected terrorist connections. Venerated patriarch Vazgen I died. (See OBITUARIES.)

After two years of stagnation, in 1994 the Armenian economy began to recover, but there was no tangible improvement in abysmal living standards although industrial production increased slightly, the monthly inflation rate fell from 82.5% in January to 9.1% in June, imports and exports increased, and the national currency exchange rate stabilized. In desperation an estimated 750,000 emigrated. The International Monetary Fund agreed to a $500 million loan to support economic reform contingent on price liberalization beginning in December.

Armenia emerged in 1994 from the international isolation that resulted from the Karabakh Armenians' occupation of much Azerbaijani territory in the autumn of 1993. Ter-Petrosyan's August visit to the U.S. at Pres. Bill Clinton's invitation signaled a warming in bilateral relations and resulted in promises of additional humanitarian aid, which in turn exacerbated relations with Turkey. In October Armenia joined NATO's Partnership for Peace program.

(ELIZABETH FULLER)

This article updates the *Macropædia* article TRANSCAUCASIA: *Armenia*.

AUSTRALIA

A federal parliamentary state (formally a constitutional monarchy) and member of the Commonwealth, Australia occupies the smallest continent and includes the island state of Tasmania. Area: 7,682,300 sq km (2,966,200 sq mi). Pop. (1994 est.): 17,875,000. Cap.: Canberra. Monetary unit: Australian dollar, with (Oct. 7, 1994) a free rate of $A 1.35 to U.S. $1 ($A 2.15 = £1 sterling). Queen, Elizabeth II; governor-general in 1994, Bill Hayden; prime minister, Paul Keating.

Domestic Affairs. In May 1994 the opposition Liberal Party dumped John Hewson as its leader and replaced him with Alexander Downer. (See BIOGRAPHIES.) Prime Minister Paul Keating's first attacks on Downer focused on his relatively privileged background. When Downer initially improved rather than fell in public opinion polls, Keating switched his attack to concentrate on Downer's support for the monarchy and opposition to the republic movement. This was a relatively successful tactic, as within Downer's party a split developed between monarchists and republicans. The initial split began when Andrew Parker, a member of Hewson's staff, organized a republican cell within the Liberal Party. Tony Abbott, the Liberal's most fervent monarchist, attacked both Parker and Hewson, accusing them of falling into Keating's hands. Hewson replied that it was ridiculous to say that people in the Liberal Party should not have a range of views on an issue such as the republic. Eventually Downer was forced to banish Hewson to the opposition back bench for disloyalty.

A *Time* magazine poll revealed that if an election had been held during the first two weeks of July, the opposition, with 52% support, would have defeated the ruling Australian Labor Party (ALP). Downer's popularity rose to 54%, while the approval rating of Prime Minister Keating remained steady at 38%. Keating dismissed the survey as irrelevant, and Downer agreed that recent history had shown that the only poll that counted was that on election day itself, the next still years in the future. Meanwhile, the minority Australian Democrats, led by Sen. Cheryl Kernot (see BIOGRAPHIES), sought to hold its pivotal centrist position in the Senate.

Former prime minister Bob Hawke was often in the headlines during 1994, much to the chagrin of the ALP, whose leaders believed, as Gough Whitlam put it, that Hawke should not have "fouled the nest" that nursed him. Hawke made a series of attacks on Keating, accusing him of describing Australia as "the arse-end of the world." Hawke also predicted that Downer would be the next prime minister of Australia. The most hurtful thrust by the former prime minister came with the publication of his memoirs, in which he repeated Keating's alleged derogatory remarks about Australia and Asia and claimed that Keating's supporters had been willing to see the ALP defeated at the general election in order to get rid of Hawke.

Australia's scandals were small by Italian standards, perhaps, but revenge was in the air in 1994. "Finally nailed him" was the popular verdict on a large number of failed political figures and businessmen who had flourished as entrepreneurs in the booming 1980s. Both the Labor and Liberal parties had representatives falling from grace.

Brian Burke, who had been ALP premier of Western Australia and Australian ambassador to Ireland and the Vatican City State, was jailed for two years for defrauding Western Australia. He was convicted of having abused his travel account, the judge saying that it was essential that public confidence in government and its officials be maintained. Nor were the conservatives free from litigation. John Elliott, former Elders IXL Ltd. chairman and former president of the Liberal Party, joked about football as he arrived at the Melbourne Magistrates Court to face trial on a charge of stealing $A 66.5 million. Elliott, accused of sham foreign-exchange deals, appeared far from concerned at facing one of the highest theft charges in Australian history.

The relationship between politics and business proved a fatal mix in many cases. One of Australia's richest men, Laurie Connell, was jailed after a nine-year investigation. His personal fortune of $A 30 million was gained from property investments during the 1980s. He donated hundreds of thousands of dollars to the ALP, entertained the U.K.'s Princess Anne during her visit to Australia for the 1987 America's Cup, and boasted that he often gambled $A 500,000 a week at horse races. However, in 1994 Connell was found guilty of conspiracy to pervert the course of justice by paying a jockey, Danny Hobby, to stay out of Australia and away from police. Fellow Western Australian Alan Bond was also charged. He was put on trial for fraud connected with his art collection. Bond, whose Dallhold company had assets of $A 2.4 billion in 1988, pleaded not guilty to deception, fraud, and dishonesty over the purchase and sale of Édouard Manet's painting *La Promenade*.

The most publicity, however, was generated by the case of fugitive property developer Christopher Skase, who fled from Queensland to Spain in 1990. Skase faced a trial in Australia on 32 charges arising from the collapse of his business empire. He refused to travel to Australia because he feared he would die on the journey as a result of a lung condition. He was arrested on an Australian warrant in January 1994 and held in a Majorca hospital while Spanish courts heard his extradition case.

In a bizarre comment on Australia's declining welfare services for the aging, Veterans' Affairs Minister Con Sciacca admitted that former servicemen were being "hunted" for war pensions. Some Filipinas were said to be marrying old men to obtain their health and pension benefits as their widows. The Federal Waste Watch Committee chairman, Sen. Paul Calvert, urged the Veterans' Affairs Department to warn veterans to be on the lookout for such women.

Australian Bureau of Migration figures in 1994 revealed a 23% decline in arrivals of new settlers to 34,957 in the six months to Jan. 1, 1994. To make matters worse, a low proportion of immigrants from the U.S., the U.K., and Malaysia wished to become Australian citizens.

In early January scores of savage firestorms, at least some of which appeared to have been the result of arson, swept

A firefighter battles a blaze in a suburb of Sydney. Scores of fires, some of them thought to have been caused by arson, burned along the southeastern coast of Australia in January, destroying homes and other buildings and forcing residents to flee.

through New South Wales. Fueled by temperatures as high as 40° C (104° F) and winds exceeding 70 km/h (43 mph), the fires came within 16 km (10 mi) of Sydney Harbour. Only four people died, but the fires laid waste to some 500,000 ha (1.2 million ac) and temporarily drove more than 20,000 residents from their homes. It was estimated that the cost could reach as high as $A 200 million.

The Economy. Good news remained the order of the day for the Australian economy in 1994. Low inflation was recorded for month after month against a background of debate between the governor of the Reserve Bank, Bernie Fraser, and money market dealers regarding the most appropriate time to increase interest rates. Fraser assured Japanese bankers that he would not hesitate to raise rates should the economy show signs of overheating. The first signs of renewed inflationary pressures occurred in July, when the number of vacancies for skilled workers in Australia rose to a three-year high. The building trades and the computing industry recorded vacancies that were 4–10% above the previous year's level. This, coupled with a dramatic rise in the number of home loans, led to warnings that the Reserve Bank ought to increase interest rates to nip in the bud any signs of boom.

Treasurer Ralph Willis delivered his first budget in May, promising a sustained recovery based on low inflation and a more competitive Australian economy. The budget was based on the optimistic expectation that a 14.5% surge in business investment, valued at $A 6.3 billion, would sustain further successive years of growth. The budget outlined new spending programs totaling more than $A 500 million in 1994–95 alone and set aside $A 1,460,000,000 over 10 years for a national land acquisition fund for Aborigines and Torres Strait Islanders; the Aborigines were also to receive a $A 499 million health-improvement program over a four-year period. This was to be used to provide basic infrastructure, such as housing, sewerage facilities, and water supplies. The increase followed a widespread debate about Aboriginal health, sparked by a visit to the outback by Sen. Graham Richardson. Richardson, who was appalled by what he saw, later resigned from Parliament, handing responsibilities for Aborigines over to Carmen Lawrence. Lawrence pointed out that Aborigines and Torres Strait Islanders had a life expectancy 17 years lower than that of other Australians and described the new funding as essential. Efforts to increase funding were defeated in the Senate in mid-November.

The major economic problem for Australia remained unemployment. Accordingly, the country increased its spending on labour-intensive projects by 15% in real terms in an attempt to cut unemployment. Critics said that the ALP planned to rely upon a statement called *Working Nation* as the blueprint for prosperity. This set up an agenda to help the long-term unemployed gain the skills and experience required for obtaining jobs. Key spending areas included $A 4 billion for expansion and improved delivery of employment subsidies and training programs. The government also planned to allocate $A 280 million to youth training for unemployed 15–17-year-olds. Major expenditure was also planned for defense. The government allocated $A 381 million for the Collins Class Submarine project in Adelaide and $A 441 million to launch frigates.

Asset sales reaping $A 2.4 billion were scheduled to pay for the new expenditures. The government planned to sell its remaining 75% equity in Qantas (the national airline), as well as its uranium stockpile, a substantial part of ANL Ltd., and all of Aerospace Technologies.

The government continued its policies of wage restraint, low interest rates, privatization, and a reliance on increased competition to generate economic growth. Keating forecast

in July that Australia could look forward to a "rolling recovery," with inflation under control, and also said that the nation was on the threshold of a new and exciting period of participation in world trade. Russia's Pacific region was particularly targeted as an area in which to place strategic investments; Australian companies invested in mining and fossil-fuel exploration and production, agriculture, and telecommunications. Indonesia was also viewed as a potentially valuable trading partner.

There was considerable public annoyance at the excessive and wasteful expense of paying for the travel and offices of former prime ministers. The bills run up by John Gorton, Whitlam, Malcolm Fraser, Hawke, and Dame Pattie Menzies (who as the widow of a former prime minister was eligible) totaled more than $A 1.2 million per year.

Foreign Affairs. Australia was busy building bridges—literally and metaphorically—in 1994, despite a continued rocky road in relations with Cambodia, North Korea, Vietnam, Indonesia, Malaysia, and China. In April Keating made visits to Laos, Thailand, and Vietnam, partly to help develop Australian links with those countries but mainly to open the Thai-Laos Friendship Bridge over the Mekong River. This bridge, which was designed to increase communications between Thailand and its neighbours, was built and financed by Australia as a showcase of engineering expertise. A dispute between Laos and Thailand over the exact position of the border between the two countries, however, overshadowed the celebrations surrounding the opening of the bridge. To make matters worse, on his continuing tour Keating made some undiplomatic remarks about Australia's Vietnam veterans that aroused anger at home. While in Thailand Keating attended a memorial for Australians who died in World War II, but he declined to do likewise for the Vietnam War. The opposition and the Returned Servicemen's League quickly attacked Keating. The president of the RSL, Maj. Gen. William ("Digger") James, said that the prime minister's comments were wrong, were sad, and showed a misunderstanding of the suffering endured by the Australian soldiers in Vietnam.

On July 2 the Australian construction minister, Sen. Chris Schacht, opened a second bridge in Laos. The 190-m (623-ft), three-span bridge over the Ngum River replaced a ferry service. Like the Friendship Bridge, said Senator Schacht, the Tha Ngon Bridge would serve as an example of the technologies that Australia could offer countries in the region.

Australia's relations with Vietnam were rougher than expected. After a successful visit by Keating, marked by a recognition of Australia's substantial role in the building up of the Vietnamese economy, a follow-up visit by a second delegation turned into a public relations disaster. One of the members of the proposed delegation, a former Vietnamese citizen, Quang Luu, wrecked the prospects of the trip by an interview he granted to the BBC on June 27, during which he criticized Vietnam's record on human rights. His behaviour was so potentially damaging that the Vietnamese government canceled his visa. In retaliation the Australian government scrapped the whole mission, complaining that Quang Luu's statement to the BBC was really no more than a description of the aspirations of one member of the delegation and should not have been made the justification for effectively aborting the entire process.

Keating continued to have difficulties in foreign relations with China, Malaysia, and Indonesia, and the Australian prime minister was unable to resist the temptation to comment on the internal affairs of those countries. They all deeply resented what they considered to be Keating's meddling, which usually came in response to questions by

(continued on page 375)

SPOTLIGHT: The South Pacific Forum by Barrie MacDonald

At the 25th South Pacific Forum meeting held in Brisbane, Australia, on July 31–Aug. 2, 1994, the designated theme was "managing our resources." This was something of a departure in that the annual summit—attended by the heads of governments of Australia, New Zealand, and 13 Pacific Islands nations—usually had a wide-ranging agenda but no overriding theme. The change reflected concern in some quarters that the Forum should be more than an informal gathering of leaders and that the region should confront the major issues facing its people. At the conclusion of the meeting, Australian Prime Minister Paul Keating praised the leaders' "willingness to grasp the nettle on big problems."

The context for this Forum meeting had been set in June by Gordon Bilney, Australia's minister of Pacific island affairs, who revisited his government's policy of "constructive commitment" to the region in light of post-Cold War era concerns and a turning away from the region by friendly powers, such as the U.K., that had traditionally taken an interest in it. He tried to look beyond the immediate political issues toward the longer-term future of the small countries of Oceania in the context of sustainable development and underlying economic structures. Bilney drew attention to slow economic growth in per capita terms (less than 1% per annum for the region as a whole), despite high levels of overseas development assistance, generally stable governments, sound management, and adequate infrastructure. Bilney's diagnosis was blunt and to the point:

> The lack of economic development, when combined with high population growth rates, unsustainable exploitation of natural resources and rapidly rising community expectations, has led to a growing range of social and economic problems, including permanent environmental degradation. Already, in some parts of the region, health and general living standards appear to be declining and community services are under strain. . . . No amount of regional and international assistance will bring about sustainable development in the South Pacific unless the countries of the region themselves play the leading role.

Bilney's analysis, though offered in the context of "constructive commitment," was not always well-received by Pacific leaders who saw Australia as adopting a "big brother" role in the region. With a small number of exceptions—for example, Nauru and Fiji—Pacific Islands countries relied on some form of overseas development assistance for at least one-third of their revenue. For some, notably Niue, the Cook Islands, France's overseas territories, and the former Trust Territories, the figure was two-thirds or more. It was a matter of speculation as to whether the recurrent costs of aid-financed capital development, together with rising expectations, would, in effect, commit these small nations to perpetual economic dependence and, as a consequence, strategic vulnerability.

These realities, though acknowledged readily enough, were seldom discussed openly. While acknowledging the need for development models that recognized traditional cultural values, Bilney pointed to customary resource-management practices, especially in forestry, that were destroying the prospect of future development. In some quarters Bilney's remarks were condemned as insensitive and bordering on interference in the internal affairs of other Forum members. Despite this, however, his comments, reinforced by the similarly strong position taken by Keating, gave a focus to discussions at the Brisbane summit.

The Forum decided to investigate the possibility of common protocols and legislative controls on logging and per-

ceived this as more of an issue for Papua New Guinea, Solomon Islands, and Vanuatu, in particular, where local benefits from logging were not large, a high percentage of logs were exported unsawn, and felling was well above sustainable levels. One study estimated that these three governments alone lost some U.S. $280 million in 1993 because of logging in excess of contracted levels and the understatement of actual yields by foreign logging companies. Fisheries were another area of concern, with the combined exclusive economic zones of Forum members accounting for one million tons of canning tuna annually, or about one-half of the world's supply. The countries involved had very small land areas and few resources, however, and the surveillance of fishing zones to detect unauthorized vessels and check on the actual catches taken by authorized vessels required regional cooperation even beyond that provided by the Forum Fisheries Agency. One estimate suggested that returns to island nations from this catch—with an annual commercial value of U.S. $1.6 billion—were no more than U.S. $60 million. Forum members also acknowledged that natural resources would have to be better managed if secondary industries, like tourism, were to have a long-term future. Here, too, the difficulties afflicting regional airlines were acknowledged, together with the need for stronger public-sector management.

These latter concerns were paralleled by the broader concerns of agencies such as the World Bank, which had focused its attention on "governance" and the gray area between insistence on high levels of managerial competence and public accountability as a condition for development assistance and interference in the domestic affairs of recipient nations.

Other environmental issues also attracted attention. Keating launched a strong attack on Greenpeace when it alleged that Australia was letting down its Pacific neighbours because of slow progress on reducing greenhouse gas emissions. These emissions were thought to be one of the major contributors to global warming, which, through rising sea levels, threatened the survival of atoll nations. Keating defended his government's record and accused Greenpeace of having little understanding of the realities of environmental protection.

The Forum welcomed the continuing suspension of nuclear testing by all major powers except China, but the other members were unable to persuade the Marshall Islands to drop plans for a feasibility study on the establishment of a nuclear-waste dump. According to Marshall Islands Pres. Amata Kabua, the dump would provide for "nuclear power countries of the northwestern Pacific rim to make nuclear materials shipments direct to a permanent disposal site in the Marshall Islands without infringing upon the territorial waters or 200-mile exclusive economic zones of other countries." Kabua said that his government was investigating the proposal in the hope that if it went ahead, it would provide revenue for the decontamination of the nuclear testing sites used by the U.S. in the 1940s and '50s.

While the economic and social challenges facing the small island countries of Oceania had changed little in the past year, in 1994 there was a noticeable change in the way that the issues were presented and discussed. And the South Pacific Forum, portrayed by some commentators as drifting and lacking purpose, showed that after 25 years it could still provide a focus for important regional debates.

Barrie MacDonald is professor of history at Massey University, Palmerston, N.Z.

(continued from page 373)
journalists about the Australian government's attitude toward current events in Asia. Typical of the prime minister's predicament was the question of how to deal with the decision of Indonesia to close three publications, *DeTik, Editor,* and *Tempo,* on the very eve of his departure for Jakarta. Keating commented on June 26 that while Australia was disappointed with the clampdown on the press in Indonesia, the links between the two countries remained strong.

On July 25 Keating announced that Australia would boost total humanitarian relief for Rwanda to $A 10 million. Medical personnel and water-purification equipment were dispatched to the refugee camps on the Rwanda-Zaire border. (A.R.G. GRIFFITHS)

See also *Dependent States.*

AUSTRIA

The federal republic of Austria is a landlocked state of Central Europe. Area: 83,859 sq km (32,378 sq mi). Pop. (1994 est.): 8,027,000. Cap.: Vienna. Monetary unit: Austrian Schilling, with (Oct. 7, 1994) a free rate of 10.85 Schillings to U.S. $1 (17.25 Schillings = £1 sterling). President in 1994, Thomas Klestil; chancellor, Franz Vranitzky.

In a referendum in June 1994, Austrians voted two to one in favour of joining the European Union (EU). This was the most significant development in Austrian history since 1955, when the state treaty that ended the post-World War II Allied occupation and restored Austrian sovereignty was signed. Accession to the EU, to take effect on Jan. 1, 1995, signified no compromise of the country's constitutionally mandated neutrality. As an EU member, Austria would not station foreign soldiers on its territory, take part in any war, or sign any military pact. The question of Austria's later participation in a European defense pact remained open.

In March elections were held to the regional parliaments in Kärnten, Tirol, and Salzburg. Losses by the Social Democrats (SPÖ) led to the resignations of the party leaders in Kärnten and Tirol. The Christian-democratic Austrian People's Party (ÖVP) lost in Salzburg and Tirol. The right-wing Austrian Freedom Party (FPÖ), under the leadership of millionaire Jörg Haider, registered gains. The Greens advanced, but the Liberal Forum scored no breakthrough and did not win representation in any regional parliament. Kärnten saw weeklong "political theatre" that ended in an electoral standoff; the state governor's job was retained by the chief of the ÖVP, the smallest faction in the Kärnten parliament.

A similar pattern emerged in the parliamentary elections in early October. The share of votes cast for the SPÖ fell from 42.8% in 1990 to 35.2% and that of the ÖVP dropped from 32% to 27.7%, while the FPÖ gained. (For tabulated results, see *Political Parties,* above.) For the first time, the two main parties lost their joint absolute majority in the parliament, which was required for the passage of laws, and would be forced to negotiate with the FPÖ. Several weeks after the elections, the partners in the shaky caretaker coalition still had not managed to sort out allocations of power and responsibility, notably on questions of who was to be in charge of Austria's European Union policy and if and how the government's economic-austerity program would be implemented.

Problems were caused anew by the influx of foreigners into Austria. By mid-1994 immigrants numbered 300,266, including some 150,000 from the former Yugoslavia and about 54,000 from Turkey. Besides these legal immigrants there were tens of thousands of "illegals," many of whom were prostitutes and criminals. Pressures on the housing market were immense (causing a housing shortfall of some 300,000 units), rents rose, and young people grew increasingly frustrated. The official policy established on the basis of the strict asylum law passed in 1992 was especially explosive. Assailed as too rigorous and inhumane, it was frequently cause for public criticism, even by the UN. The "invasion" of foreigners was unpopular, strengthened radicalism, and led in some cases to violence. A special unit of border defense troops to secure Austria's eastern borders—which, beginning in 1995, would be those of the EU as well—was being established.

The economic recession of 1993 played out somewhat more mildly than had been feared, thanks to government countermeasures. A new upturn began in 1994, and a growth rate of 2.5% for the year (rising to 3% in 1995) was projected, with between 18,000 and 27,000 new job openings. Industrial production and exports led the way as Austria enhanced its role as a major conduit for trade and investment between the EU and the emerging economies of Eastern Europe. On the downside were the budget deficit (66.4 billion Schillings in 1992, 100 billion Schillings in 1993, and at least the same level in 1994) and the national debt (projected to reach 1.2 billion Schillings by the end of 1994), burdened with an annual interest of 70 billion–80 billion Schillings. In addition, net payments of some 20 billion Schillings into the EU would begin in 1995.

A campaign poster for Jörg Haider has been altered to make him look like Adolf Hitler, with the slogan "Austria first!" changed to "Me first!" Haider, head of the Austrian Freedom Party, unsuccessfully campaigned against Austria's entry into the European Union.
REUTERS/BETTMANN

Environmentalists and citizens' groups had long been concerned about the nuclear power plant at Temelín, Czech Republic, near the Austrian border. With the help of a $300 million ExImBank loan, the plant, which many feared was technologically unsound, was to be completed in 1995. Strong representations by Austrian politicians in the Czech Republic and the U.S. proved futile.

(ELFRIEDE DIRNBACHER)

AZERBAIJAN

A republic of Transcaucasia, Azerbaijan borders Russia on the north, the Caspian Sea on the east, Iran on the south, Armenia on the west, and Georgia on the northwest. The 5,500-sq km exclave of Nakhichevan to the southwest is separated from Azerbaijan proper by a strip of Armenia. Area (including Nakhichevan): 86,600 sq km (33,400 sq mi). Pop. (1994 est.): 7,424,000. Cap.: Baku (Azerbaijani: Bakı). Monetary unit: manat, with (Sept. 27, 1994) a free rate (from May 24) of 1,632 manat to U.S. $1 (2,595 manat = £1 sterling). President in 1994, Heydar Aliyev; prime ministers, Surat Husseynov and, from October 6 (acting), Fuad Guliyev.

Chronic political instability forced the cancellation of a Turkic summit scheduled to take place in Baku in January and impeded progress toward democratization and economic reform. Throughout the year the Azerbaijani leadership implemented a systematic policy of repression; police intimidated journalists, detained opposition activists, raided the premises of several opposition parties, and forcibly prevented protest demonstrations. In early October Interior Ministry troops took the prosecutor-general hostage to protest the arrest of three security police officers in connection with the assassination of two close associates of Pres. Heydar Aliyev but later released him. On the following day, supporters of Prime Minister Surat Husseynov temporarily seized control of several provincial cities but were swiftly overpowered by government forces. The population of Baku took to the streets to demonstrate in support of Aliyev. Despite protestations of his innocence, Husseynov was fired and charged with treason; he later fled to Russia. Aliyev imposed a two-month state of emergency, arrested several government ministers suspected of complicity in the putsch, and purged numerous officials.

The economic situation continued to deteriorate faster than predicted. During the first six months, the gross national product fell by 25%, industrial production by 27%, and agricultural output by 13%. Annual inflation was estimated at 880%. The parliament failed to enact legislation on privatization. Oil-sector workers went on strike in August to protest a deterioration in living conditions.

The tension in relations with Turkey resulting from former president Abulfez Elchibey's ouster was dispelled in February when Aliyev traveled to Ankara to sign a 10-year treaty of friendship and cooperation and 15 other documents. Similar agreements were signed with Britain later that month. Azerbaijan joined NATO's Partnership for Peace in May and held talks on joining the Council of Europe.

In February Russia brokered a cease-fire in Nagorno-Karabakh that finally took effect in mid-May and was further extended in late July, thereby lending new impetus to the rival Conference on Security and Cooperation in Europe (CSCE) effort to mediate a settlement of the conflict. Despite intensive diplomatic activity by both Russia and the CSCE and an appeal by Aliyev to the UN General Assembly in August, progress toward a political settlement was obstructed by Azerbaijan's refusal to condone the deployment of predominantly Russian peacekeeping troops on its territory, its insistence on the withdrawal of Karabakh Armenian forces from all occupied Azerbaijani territory (about 20% of the country), and the inability of the CSCE to persuade Western governments to provide peacekeeping troops to monitor the cease-fire.

After protracted negotiations, in September Aliyev signed a $7.4 billion contract giving seven Western oil companies a 70% share in developing Azerbaijan's Caspian oil fields. Although Azerbaijan had earlier ceded 10% of its own 30%

share to the leading Russian oil company, Lukoil, the Russian government promptly denounced the contract, arguing that any decisions on exploitation of mineral reserves had to be coordinated with all Caspian littoral states. Azerbaijan ceded a further 5% of its share to Iran in November in exchange for considerable financial and technical assistance.

(ELIZABETH FULLER)

This article updates the *Macropædia* article TRANSCAUCASIA: *Azerbaijan*.

BAHAMAS, THE

A constitutional monarchy and member of the Commonwealth, The Bahamas comprises an archipelago of about 700 islands in the North Atlantic Ocean just southeast of the United States. Area: 13,939 sq km (5,382 sq mi). Pop. (1994 est.): 272,000. Cap.: Nassau. Monetary unit: Bahamian dollar, with (Oct. 7, 1994) a par value of B$1 to U.S. $1 (free rate of B$1.59 = £1 sterling). Queen, Elizabeth II; governor-general in 1994, Clifford Darling; prime minister, Hubert Ingraham.

Former prime minister Sir Lynden Pindling spent much of 1994 defending the conduct of the Bahamas Hotel Corporation (BHC), which he chaired during part of his tenure in office. The present Free National Movement government, led by Prime Minister Hubert Ingraham, set up the commission to investigate allegations of misconduct on Pindling's part. The latter strenuously denied that any BHC funds had been used to renovate his personal property or that he had benefited in any way from contracts awarded by the corporation.

The existence of the inquiry did not prevent the BHC from proceeding with its hotel privatization program during the year. It sold off, among others, the 400-room Ambassador Beach Hotel to Jamaican hotelier John Issa, the Winding Bay Hotel in Eleuthera to an Italian group, and the Lucayan Bay Hotel in Grand Bahama to the New Hope Holding Co.

In February one of the prominent Bahamas personalities from the Pindling era, lawyer Nigel Bowe, was sentenced in Miami, Fla., to 15 years in jail and fined $250,000 for conspiring to import cocaine into the United States. He was said to have provided protection for Colombian drug traffickers.

Ingraham presented a $756 million budget in May, designed to maintain the momentum of the nation's economic development. Projects announced during the year included a $31.8 million electricity supply system for Great Abaco Island and an $80 million container transshipment terminal at Freeport, sponsored in part by the Grand Bahama Port Authority.

(DAVID RENWICK)

This article updates the *Macropædia* article The WEST INDIES: *The Bahamas*.

BAHRAIN

The monarchy (emirate) of Bahrain consists of a group of islands in the Persian Gulf between the peninsula of Qatar and Saudi Arabia. Area: 694 sq km (268 sq mi). Pop. (1994 est.): 552,000. Cap.: Manama. Monetary unit: Bahrain dinar, with (Oct. 7, 1994) a free rate of 0.38 dinar to U.S. $1 (0.60 dinar = £1 sterling). Emir in 1994, Isa ibn Sulman al-Khalifah; prime minister, Khalifah ibn Sulman al-Khalifah.

The arrest of a leading Shi'ite cleric, Sheikh Ali Salman, in early December touched off antigovernment demonstrations in which two students and one policeman were killed. The disturbances, the worst in 20 years, took place just before the Gulf Cooperation Council summit meeting in Manama on December 19. Information Minister Tariq al-Mu'ayyid said that the demonstrators arrested in the clashes on December 12–13 would be brought to trial.

Sheikh Salman and 13 other community leaders apparently had signed a petition urging the restoration of the elected parliament, but other sources linked his arrest to inflammatory remarks made after Shi'ite villagers in northern Bahrain threw stones at women athletes taking part in a marathon in late November. On December 16 Emir Isa ibn Sulman al-Khalifah endorsed the work of the existing consultative council and appeared to rule out any early restoration of the former elected parliament.

On January 19, 20 people were arrested in disturbances in central Manama after a ceremony to mourn the death of a leading Iranian Shi'ite ayatollah. In June 200 youths were dispersed by baton-wielding police with tear gas outside the Labour Ministry after demonstrating against high unemployment.

As part of a drive to demonstrate Bahrain's "open door" to business, Israel's environment minister, Yossi Sarid, was officially received in Manama on October 25. This was the first public high-level contact between an Arab Gulf state and an Israeli minister. (JOHN WHELAN)

This article updates the *Macropædia* article ARABIA: *Bahrain*.

BANGLADESH

A republic and member of the Commonwealth, Bangladesh is in the northeastern part of the Indian subcontinent, on the Bay of Bengal. Area: 148,393 sq km (57,295 sq mi). Pop. (1994 est.): 117,404,000. Cap.: Dhaka. Monetary unit: taka, with (Oct. 7, 1994) an official rate of 39.50 taka to U.S. $1 (62.82 taka = £1 sterling). President in 1994, Abdur Rahman Biswas; prime minister, Khaleda Zia.

Bangladesh—a country routinely battered by storms, floods, and political violence—had a measure of good news in 1994. In 1991 some 130,000 people had died in a ferocious cyclone. When a similar cyclone battered the same southeastern coast in May, only 233 persons were killed, thanks to disaster defenses the government had built at a cost of millions of dollars.

On the political front, there were about a dozen antigovernment protests across the country. A general strike called to demand the resignation of Prime Minister Khaleda Zia shut down the capital, Dhaka, and four other cities for days. The main opposition parties—the Awami League, the Jatiya Party, and the Islamic fundamentalist Jamaat-e Islami accused the Zia government of mismanagement and demanded new elections. Zia, who had won a five-year term in 1991 in the first peaceful transition of power since Bangladesh became independent of Pakistan in 1971, rejected the demand as "unjustified and unconstitutional" and said that her party, which occupied a majority of the 330 seats in Parliament, would continue to govern until the scheduled March 1996 election. All 154 opposition legislators reacted by boycotting Parliament for most of the year.

Zia's government faced the people's wrath in September when nearly 9,000 doctors walked out of 1,850 state-run hospitals and rural health centres. They demanded that the government double its spending on health care and provide more medical facilities. The government insisted it could not afford to increase the $150 million national health care budget. There were sporadic strikes in November and a police mutiny in December.

Bangladesh attracted international attention during the year over the issue of freedom of expression. Taslima Nasrin (*see* BIOGRAPHIES), a 32-year-old physician turned author, first gained notoriety for her novel *Lajja* ("Shame"), which depicted the oppression of local Hindus and other minorities by Muslim extremists. A crisis developed when a newspaper reported that Nasrin was calling for a thorough revision of the Qur'an, Islam's sacred scripture. Nasrin denied ever having made such a sweeping statement. She did, however, acknowledge that she would like to see Islamic laws amended to give more rights to women.

When Nasrin was charged under a 19th-century law forbidding acts that offended religious sensibilities, the case was viewed by many in the context of Islamic fundamentalism, which seemed to be gaining favour among the predominantly Muslim population even though Bangladesh operated under a secular constitution. Those who were most

Khaleda Zia, prime minister of Bangladesh, addresses a political rally in Dhaka. During the year there were continued protests and strikes against the Zia government, primarily from Sheikh Hasina Wajed, head of the Awami League and Zia's main political opponent, but also from other parties.

uncompromising demanded that Bangladesh become an Islamic state and that it adopt the Muslim code of criminal justice. The most extreme segments of a society that denied equal rights to women demanded her execution. Nasrin was arrested, then released on bail pending her trial on charges of insulting Islam. The streets of the capital were filled with tens of thousands of religious fundamentalists demanding that Nasrin be put to death. Extremists offered $5,000 for her life. She eluded all the dangers she faced at home by fleeing to Sweden in September.   (DILIP GANGULY)

BARBADOS

The constitutional monarchy of Barbados, a member of the Commonwealth, occupies the most easterly island in the southern Caribbean Sea. Area: 430 sq km (166 sq mi). Pop. (1994 est.): 264,000. Cap.: Bridgetown. Monetary unit: Barbados dollar, with (Oct. 7, 1994) a par value of BDS$2.01 to U.S. $1 (free rate of BDS$3.20 = £1 sterling). Queen, Elizabeth II; governor-general in 1994, Dame Nita Barrow; prime ministers, Erskine Sandiford and, from September 7, Owen Arthur.

The government changed hands in Barbados during 1994, with the Barbados Labour Party (BLP) returning to office in September after defeating the incumbent Democratic Labour Party (DLP) by 19 seats to 8. One seat went to the National Democratic Party. The new prime minister was economist Owen Arthur.

When it successfully pushed a no-confidence motion against Prime Minister Erskine Sandiford through the House of Representatives in June, the BLP had maneuvered the DLP into a position where it had little choice but to call the election two years ahead of time. The motion was supported by several dissident DLP members. Sandiford managed to retain his own seat in the election.

The BLP was expected to maintain the DLP's main economic, social, and foreign policies. Privatization of government-owned assets was expected to continue. The DLP had completed the sale of the state's interests in the Heywoods Hotel and the Arawak Cement Co. before it left office. The new government planned to continue to give strong support to the tourist industry, which grew by 11.2% during the first half of 1994 after a successful season in 1993.

In regard to foreign affairs, the BLP honoured the DLP's commitment to supply Barbadian troops for UN-sanctioned activities in Haiti. In May Barbados served as host to the UN's first conference on the Sustainable Development of Small Island Developing States.   (DAVID RENWICK)

This article updates the *Macropædia* article The WEST INDIES: *Barbados*.

BELARUS

A landlocked republic of Eastern Europe, Belarus borders Latvia on the north, Russia on the north and east, Ukraine on the south, Poland on the west, and Lithuania on the northwest. Area: 207,595 sq km (80,153 sq mi). Pop. (1994 est.): 10,404,000. Cap.: Minsk. Monetary unit: Belarusian rubel, with (Oct. 7, 1994) a free rate of 5,854 rubels = U.S. $1 (9,312 rubels = £1 sterling). Chairmen of the Supreme Soviet in 1994, Stanislau Shushkevich and, from January 28, Myachaslau Hryb; president from July 20, Aleksandr Lukashenka; prime ministers, Vyachaslau Kebich and, from July 21, Mikhail Chyhir.

Relations with Russia, both political and economic, dominated 1994 in Belarus. On April 12 an agreement on a monetary union was reached by Prime Minister Vyachaslau F. Kebich and his Russian counterpart Viktor S. Chernomyrdin. The treaty encompassed a single pricing system and fixed exchange rate between the two currencies. Monetary union was opposed by the powerful chairman of the

Belarusian national bank, Stanislau Bahdankevich, and denounced by the Belarusian Popular Front (BPF) because of Russian recalcitrance and concerns about the emission of a single currency by the Russian central bank. By October the ailing Belarusian rubel (zaichik) had been declared the only legal tender in the republic.

The economy remained in crisis. From January to June gross domestic product dropped 31%, while inflation was about 30%. Several factories stopped work. In August prices were freed and rose to 10–30 times their former level. On August 12 the zaichik was devalued by a factor of 10, and wages were lowered accordingly. Privatization encompassed only 4% of all state enterprises by November. Though Belarus remained hopeful that an International Monetary Fund loan of $308 million would be forthcoming, a presidential decision to lower prices to the levels of November 1 and a huge budget deficit of $1.2 billion (one-third of which was owed to Russia for imports of gas) placed the loan in some doubt.

The republic experienced some dramatic political changes in 1994. The communist-dominated parliament, in January, established an anticorruption committee under the chairmanship of Aleksandr Lukashenka (*see* BIOGRAPHIES) that mounted sustained attacks on the republic's parliamentary chairman Stanislau Shushkevich and his supporters. On January 26 (shortly after the visit of U.S. Pres. Bill Clinton to Minsk), Shushkevich lost in a no-confidence vote in the parliament by 209–36. He was forced to resign and was replaced by Myachaslau Hryb. The pro-Communist prime minister, Vyachaslau Kebich, survived a similar vote.

Parliament adopted a new constitution in March that replaced the 1977 U.S.S.R. constitution and created a presidency with the main executive power and a 260-seat parliament. There followed a frenzied and bitter election campaign, with six candidates nominated by the May 15 deadline. Lukashenka received 45% of the vote on June 23, followed by Kebich, the favoured candidate, with 17%. In the run-off election on July 10, Lukashenka, whose campaign combined pro-Russian rhetoric with his anticorruption drive, took 80.1% of the vote.

The new president appointed a 45-year-old banker, Mikhail Chyhir, as his premier but retained some of Kebich's appointees. Lukashenka's relations with Russia, despite pre-election rhetoric, remained more distant than those of his predecessor, Kebich. In August he met with Russian Pres. Boris Yeltsin, and among issues discussed was the continued presence of 30,000 Russian troops in the republic guarding strategic missiles. In September Lukashenka established a National Security Council and phased out village councils, and in October he doubled the minimum wage to 20,000 rubels (around $3). On November 12, after his convalescence for spinal problems, Lukashenka declared a state of emergency to halt the drastic price rises that had occurred in his absence.   (DAVID R. MARPLES)

BELGIUM

A federal constitutional monarchy, Belgium is situated on the North Sea coast of northwestern Europe. Area: 30,528 sq km (11,787 sq mi). Pop. (1994 est.): 10,118,000. Cap.: Brussels. Monetary unit: Belgian franc, with (Oct. 7, 1994) a free rate of BF 31.70 to U.S. $1 (BF 50.42 = £1 sterling). King, Albert II; prime minister in 1994, Jean-Luc Dehaene.

After the failure of the social pact between employers and trade unions, in 1994 the Belgian government elaborated its own "global plan" to fight unemployment (9.8% in May), improve industrial competitiveness, and maintain social security levels. It also called for higher taxation. The plan was expected to create an extra 80,000 jobs over a three-to-four-year period. The Employers Federation regarded the lower labour costs as insufficient. After negotiations with the unions, they did offer more jobs in exchange for lower social welfare contributions and more flexible labour legislation.

Introduction of the new "eco-taxes" was delayed to provide manufacturers more time to conform to the legislation, but not without protest from the Green parties. Meanwhile, Parliament approved practical measures in pursuance of the so-called Saint-Michael agreements on the creation of a federal state. These dealt with the division of the still-bilingual central Brabant province into three new entities—Flemish-Brabant, Walloon-Brabant, and the Brussels-capital region—to become effective on Jan. 1, 1995. Starting with the municipal elections in October, restrictions were imposed on electoral expenditures. Parliament also approved legislation to provide for a minimal presence of women on the lists of candidates, agreed to the creation of a professional army (thus ending conscription), and endorsed closer cooperation between Dutch and Belgian naval forces within NATO.

Protests against the Flemish regional environment minister's plan to restrict the production and indiscriminate use of dung—as well as its relocation over all Flemish provinces—caused friction in the Flemish regional government. In addition, farmers unions rejected the scheme.

A bribery scandal involving three prominent French Socialist politicians, all members of either the federal or the regional governments, led to their resignations. All three were suspected of urging the Italian helicopter manufacturer Agusta to pay bribes to their party when the Belgian armed forces ordered 46 attack helicopters. Guy Coëme, who had been minister of defense at the time of the alleged bribes, resigned from his post as minister of communications, while Guy Spitaels, leader of the Walloon regional government, and Guy Mathot, regional minister of home affairs, budget, and public works, also resigned. Coëme was ordered to appear before the Supreme Court of Appeal. In March, after the mayor of Brussels, Michel Demaret, made an insulting statement aimed at Pope John Paul II, he was stripped of his powers and forced to step down from office. The defense minister, Leo Delcroix, denied allegations of impropriety in connection with the tax status of a house that he owned in the south of France but nonetheless resigned in December; he was replaced by Karel Pinxten.

The elections to the European Parliament confirmed the disaffection of the public toward the four government parties. Most pronounced was that of the French Socialists, with 30.4% of the vote, as against 38.5% in 1989. This was in spite of the huge personal score of their top candidate, José Happart, who captured 265,376 votes. The Flemish Liberal breakthrough did not materialize, despite the "enlargement" operation launched by the young party leader, Guy Verhofstadt. The Socialists were also the big losers in the local elections in October, in this case ceding seats to the far-right parties. The anti-immigrant Vlaams Blok, for example, took 18 of the 55 seats in Antwerp's city council, making it the largest party in that port city.

The murder in April of 10 Belgian members of the UN Assistance Mission to Rwanda and the hostile attitude of the authorities and the population toward the Belgians living in Rwanda prompted the repatriation of Belgian nationals, as well as the withdrawal of the Belgian UN contingent. Development aid to Rwanda was also suspended.

In July the last representative of the Belgian Surrealist school, Paul Delvaux, died in Veurne at the age of 96. (*See* OBITUARIES.) (JAN R. ENGELS)

BELIZE

A constitutional monarchy and member of the Commonwealth, Belize is on the Caribbean coast of Central America. Area: 22,965 sq km (8,867 sq mi). Pop. (1994 est.): 210,000. Cap.: Belmopan. Monetary unit: Belize dollar, with (Oct. 7, 1994) a par value of BZ$2 to U.S. $1 (free rate of BZ$3.18 = £1 sterling). Queen, Elizabeth II; governor-general in 1994, Colville Young; prime minister, Manuel Esquivel.

The governing United Democratic Party (UDP) won all seven of Belize's local councils in elections on March 8, 1994. The victory was 43 out of 49 seats. Previously, the UDP had controlled only two councils; in Orange Walk and in San Ignacio/Santa Elena. Voter turnout was 68.5%. After 30 years of involvement with the People's United Party, deputy leader Florencio Marin resigned in May.

The U.K. Defense Secretary Malcolm Rifkind visited in May for talks relating to the reduction of the British garrison in Belize. The Belizean government issued defense bonds to raise money for the expansion of the Belize Defence Force.

A national economic advisory task force of representatives from private and public organizations was formed in response to the ratification of the North American Free Trade Agreement. Among a variety of issues, the 11-member task force planned to study the development of a capital and securities market, establishment of one or more commercial-free zones, tax reform, and further development of tourism.

The economic citizenship program ended in June. This program was started in 1984 and gave Belizean citizenship to foreigners in return for substantial investment in the country. (INES T. BAPTIST)

This article updates the *Macropædia* article CENTRAL AMERICA: *Belize.*

BENIN

The republic of Benin is on the southern coast of West Africa, on the Gulf of Guinea. Area: 112,680 sq km (43,500 sq mi). Pop. (1994 est.): 5,235,000. Cap.: Porto-Novo (executive offices remain in Cotonou). Monetary unit: CFA franc, with (from Jan. 12, 1994) a par value of CFAF 100 to the French franc and (as of Oct. 7, 1994) a free rate of CFAF 526.67 to U.S. $1 (CFAF 837.67 = £1 sterling). President in 1994, Nicéphore Soglo.

The impact of the 50% devaluation of the CFA franc relative to the French franc, which went into effect on Jan. 12, 1994, was mixed. Economic growth continued at a rate of nearly 4% as exports of cotton, Benin's only important cash crop, rose. Fears of inflation mounted, however, as import prices virtually doubled. The government continued its structural adjustment program, concentrating on encouraging the private sector and reforming and reducing the size of the public sector. Major donor nations signaled their approval of Benin's economic program. Germany provided development aid of $51 million, and the European Community granted ECU 9.4 million for improvements in Benin's infrastructure. Little progress was made toward economic diversification and industrialization.

Pres. Nicéphore Soglo used executive powers to impose his own national budget, overriding that passed by the National Assembly in July on grounds that proposed increases in salaries and expenditures were economically unwise and politically motivated. In response, the Bureau of the National Assembly met in extraordinary session on August 2. Backed by a Supreme Court decision that Soglo's action was unconstitutional, the National Assembly passed a new budget on August 26. The struggle over the budget left vital development programs largely unfunded.

In July the president assumed leadership of the Benin Renaissance Party, founded by his wife, Rosine, in 1992. Soglo's strategy was seen as a means of trying to ensure a majority in the municipal and legislative elections scheduled for February 1995.   (NANCY ELLEN LAWLER)

This article updates the *Macropædia* article WESTERN AFRICA: *Benin*.

BHUTAN

The monarchy of Bhutan is a landlocked state situated in the eastern Himalayas between China and India. Area: 47,000 sq km (18,150 sq mi). Pop. (1994 est.): 800,000 (excluding Nepalese residents declared stateless by the Bhutanese government in late 1990, more than 100,000 of whom are now refugees in Nepal or India). Cap.: Thimphu. Monetary unit: ngultrum, at par with the Indian rupee (which is also in use), with (Oct. 7, 1994) a free rate of 31.37 ngultrums to U.S. $1 (49.89 ngultrums = £1 sterling). Druk gyalpo (king) in 1994, Jigme Singye Wangchuk.

In 1994 Bhutan, one of the world's most isolated kingdoms, failed to resolve a dispute over the issue of granting citizenship to settlers from neighbouring Nepal. The UN High Commissioner for Refugees criticized Bhutan because an estimated 100,000 settlers, mostly Nepalese, remained in refugee camps. A small Nepalese population in Bhutan dated back to at least the 1930s, but waves of immigrants from India and Nepal had swelled the number in the past three decades. Nepalese activists, who said they were waging a pro-democracy campaign against an absolute monarchy, claimed that 53% of Bhutan's residents were Nepalese. The government contended that barely a third were Nepalese and that many of those were illegal aliens.

Bhutanese Interior Minister Lyonpo Dago Tshering and two associates traveled to Nepal to discuss the refugee issue, but no progress was reported. The two sides, however, agreed to set up a joint committee to determine the citizenship of the refugees, but there was no agreement on how to start the identification work.

The nation printed the world's first three-dimensional postage stamp in 1994—a futuristic holographic issue commemorating the first U.S. moon landing 25 years earlier. The sale of stamps to foreign collectors had become one of Bhutan's most profitable enterprises. In a nation that depended on foreign aid for about half its budget and had only a handful of exports, the postal service brought in up to $485,000 a year from abroad.   (DILIP GANGULY)

BOLIVIA

Bolivia is a landlocked republic in central South America. Area: 1,098,581 sq km (424,164 sq mi). Pop. (1994 est.): 7,888,000. Administrative cap., La Paz; judicial cap., Sucre. Monetary unit: boliviano, with (Oct. 7, 1994) a free rate of 4.66 bolivianos to U.S. $1 (7.41 bolivianos = £1 sterling). President in 1994, Gonzalo Sánchez de Lozada Bustamente.

In January 1994 Pres. Gonzalo Sánchez de Lozada presented to Congress draft legislation for privatizing six state companies (electricity, telecommunications, the railways, an ironworks, the oil and gas corporation, and the national airline, Lloyd Aéreo Boliviano). The intention was to encourage private investment in up to half the equity of each company. The remaining shares would be given to the adult population to be deposited in private pension funds. It was hoped that the capitalization scheme would raise $3 billion in foreign investment over three years, cut unemployment, and increase gross domestic product threefold.

Although Congress passed the bill in March, the prospect of foreign involvement in state utilities and resources aroused fierce protests in February and again in April and May. A wave of strikes against privatization but linked to wage demands disrupted transportation, industry, and government. Contrary to its policies of reducing both the budget deficit and inflation, the government on May 7 conceded public-sector pay raises that were above the rate of inflation and increased the minimum urban salary. The cost of living was forecast to rise in 1994 by about 8%, roughly one percentage point below the 1993 increase.

During the protests tension was heightened by the force-feeding of hunger strikers and the deployment of the army. Military action against drug growers in the Chaparé region during the first half of the year was criticized as excessively violent. This was an effort to meet a September 30 deadline to destroy 5,000 ha (12,350 ac) of coca in order to qualify for a $40 million grant from the U.S. to promote alternative crops. Bolivia had failed to meet an original deadline of Dec. 31, 1993. The renewed assault on drug cultivation was accompanied by a new banking code of ethics designed to prevent the laundering of narcotics proceeds, although the Superintendency of Banking refused to lift secrecy laws.

Resentment against the U.S. influence on Bolivian drug policy was compounded by suggestions that the U.S. Drug Enforcement Administration helped prepare a report that accused former president Jaime Paz Zamora and several officials of his administration of involvement in the drug trade. While he admitted some misjudgments, Paz denied the charges but thereafter renounced politics. U.S. agents were also thought to be behind allegations of corruption that led to the impeachment of the Supreme Court's president and one of its judges.

After months of negotiation the governments of Bolivia and Brazil signed an accord in August approving a $2 billion natural gas pipeline. Bolivia would supply southern and southeastern Brazil with 8 million cu m (282 million cu ft) of gas per day from 1997. In September Bolivia and Mexico signed a free-trade pact, due to come into effect on Jan. 1, 1995.   (BEN BOX)

BOSNIA AND HERZEGOVINA

A republic of the western Balkans, Bosnia and Herzegovina borders Croatia on the north, southwest, and south, the Adriatic Sea on the south (via a narrow extension), and Yugoslavia on the east. Area: 51,129 sq km (19,741 sq mi). Pop. (1994 est. based on prewar projection): 4,447,000; (1994 de facto est.): 3.4 million. Cap.: Sarajevo. Monetary unit: no national currency. President in 1994, Alija Izetbegovic; prime minister, Haris Silajdzic.

In 1994 peace did not come to Bosnia and Herzegovina, the scene of a bitter war since early 1992. Military operations involving Muslim, Serb, and Croat forces as well as NATO troops continued throughout the year, with the exception of the period ushered in by a comprehensive cease-fire on December 23 that had been negotiated by former U.S. president Jimmy Carter.

Following a mortar bomb attack on the Sarajevo market on February 5, which killed about 68 people and injured some 200 others, NATO issued an ultimatum for Serb forces besieging the capital to cease their bombardment and pull back their heavy weapons from an exclusion zone around it. On February 6, UN Secretary-General Boutros Boutros-Ghali asked for NATO authorization to order future air strikes. By February 21 the Serbs had largely complied with the ultimatum in Sarajevo. On February 28, however, NATO jet planes on patrol over Bosnia and Herzegovina enforced the no-fly ban, which had been in existence since late 1992, for the first time by shooting down four Serb warplanes that had been bombing Sarajevo government forces' installations in the central Bosnia part of the republic.

In April NATO planes bombed Serb forces attacking Gorazde, a Muslim enclave in eastern Bosnia designated by the UN in 1993 as one of the six "safe areas." The NATO operations' lack of military impact was much criticized, notably in the United States. Leading Republican politicians continued to press for the lifting of the embargo on arms supplies to Bosnia and Herzegovina as the only effective means of pressure on the Serbs to give up occupied territories, allowing those driven out by the Serbs to return to their homes. Serb reprisals against UN and other foreign personnel in Bosnia and Herzegovina, including hostage taking on a large scale, led to talk of a pullout under NATO's protection of all UN personnel, but in December the decision was taken to carry on with the UN effort for the time being. Tensions between the U.S. government, which had throughout the war refused to commit U.S. ground forces to UN operations, and the British and French governments were somewhat alleviated in December after the U.S. stopped pressing for action against the Serbs.

The most important political event of the year was the signing in Washington on March 1 of the Muslim-Croat accord that ended the bitter fighting between the two former allies that had been going on since 1993—with the Serbs as the main beneficiaries. Under the Washington agreement it was decided to set up a Croat-Muslim federation as part

RACHEL COBB—SIPA

A young Bosnian girl in Sarajevo carries a plastic jug on her way to get water. Although, for the most part, Serbs had stopped shelling the city, Sarajevo was often without water and electricity, and residents continued to face grim living conditions.

of a Bosnia and Herzegovinian state entity to which the Serbs would be invited to accede. On May 31 Kresimir Zubak, a Croat, was elected president of the new Croat-Muslim federation. Ejup Ganic, a Muslim, was elected vice president and Haris Silajdzic as prime minister both of the Croat-Muslim federation and of Bosnia and Herzegovina as a whole.

In July the "contact group" (the U.K., France, Germany, Russia, and the U.S.) put forward a plan for dividing Bosnia and Herzegovina between a Serbian unit on one side with 49% of the land and the Croat-Muslim federation (with 51%) on the other. The Croats and the Muslims accepted the plan; the Serbs, who held about 70% of the republic's territory, rejected it following a referendum in the area under their control. Slobodan Milosevic, Serbia's president, urged Bosnia's Serbs to accept, and when they refused, he imposed an embargo on all trade except humanitarian and medical aid and other contacts.

On July 23 the European Union took over responsibility for running the divided city of Mostar, the Herzegovinian capital and the scene of some of the most bitter battles between Croats and Muslims in 1993, for two years. NATO aircraft were in action again in November in the Bihac region in northwestern Bosnia and Herzegovina, also designated in 1993 as a UN "safe area," but this time they extended their strikes also against targets in the Serb-occupied area in Croatia near the source of the attacks on Bihac.

Bosnia received many visitors in 1994, including Prime Ministers Benazir Bhutto of Pakistan and Tansu Ciller of Turkey and Croatian Pres. Franjo Tudjman. A planned visit to Sarajevo in September by Pope John Paul II had to be called off, however. (K.F. CVIIC)

This article updates the Macropædia article BALKAN STATES: Bosnia and Herzegovina.

BOTSWANA

A landlocked republic of southern Africa, Botswana is a member of the Commonwealth. Area: 581,730 sq km (224,607 sq mi). Pop. (1994 est.): 1,448,000. Cap.: Gaborone. Monetary unit: pula, with (Oct. 7, 1994) a free rate of 2.71 pula to U.S. $1 (4.32 pula = £1 sterling). President in 1994, Sir Ketumile Masire.

Botswana's generally sedate political profile was ruffled in April 1994 by a major scandal that rocked the ruling Botswana Democratic Party (BDP) with the disclosure that top Cabinet ministers, including Pres. Sir Ketumile Masire, owed the National Development Bank (NDB) 15 million pula. The president repaid his loan, but the other ministers did not; close to financial disaster, the NDB closed 15 district offices and sacked half its staff.

Elections for the National Assembly took place in October. The BDP retained power by winning 26 of the 40 contested seats, but this was a loss of 9 seats from the previous Assembly. The Botswana National Front (BNF) won 13 seats, a gain of 10. Voting was delayed for one seat because of the death of the BDP candidate. The BDP reaffirmed its hold on most of the rural population, while the BNF had the best returns in urban areas.

Although regarded as a more expensive area in which to do business than neighbouring South Africa, Botswana attracted a major investment during the year when Owens-Corning Fiberglas Corp. set up a plant in Botswana on the grounds that "political stability and Botswana's rapid economic growth and favourable geographic position won the day."

Owens-Corning planned to own 49% of the new company, with the Botswana Development Corp. owning 35%, and the balance being owned by private investors in Botswana.

The plant was to produce reinforced-plastic water pipes, for which there was substantial regional demand.

(GUY ARNOLD)

This article updates the *Macropædia* article SOUTHERN AFRICA: *Botswana*.

BRAZIL

Brazil is a federal republic in eastern South America on the Atlantic Ocean. Area: 8,511,996 sq km (3,286,500 sq mi). Pop. (1994 est.): 159 million. Cap.: Brasília. Monetary unit: real (introduced July 1 to replace the cruzeiro real at the rate of 1 real = 2,750 cruzeiros reais (a rate par to the U.S. $ on July 1), with (Oct. 7, 1994) a free rate of 0.89 real to U.S. $1 (1.34 reais = £1 sterling). President in 1994, Itamar Franco.

The year 1994 proved to be a complex one for Brazil. It was the final year of the term being served by Pres. Itamar Franco after Fernando Collor de Mello had to step down in the final quarter of 1992. (Collor was acquitted of

Fernando Henrique Cardoso speaks at a campaign rally in his successful bid to become president of Brazil. A former finance minister who was credited with dramatically slowing the country's ruinously high rate of inflation, Cardoso won a solid victory in the October voting.

PAULO FRIDMAN—SYGMA

bribery charges in December.) The year began with the final stages of a congressional inquiry (begun in October 1993) into allegations of impropriety by some two dozen senior political figures with respect to misappropriation of budget funds. "Budgetgate," as the episode was known, affected the progress of the constitutional revision, which also had begun in October 1993, and it contributed to delays in the legislature in approving the 1994 budget. During the year the budget was repeatedly revised, and it was not passed until late October. One important measure—the creation of a $15 billion emergency social fund—was approved in February, however.

A mid-March deadline for completion of the constitutional review had originally been set, but this was extended until May 31. Even so, few changes of major significance were approved, leaving such key proposals as fiscal reform, modifications to statutes governing state monopolies in telecommunications and oil, and the removal of discrimination against foreign mining concerns to be dealt with by the next government.

General elections for federal and state posts, including the president of the republic but excluding municipal positions, provided a central focus of attention during the year. They were scheduled for October 3 (with a second round on

November 15 when a candidate for an executive post failed to obtain a clear majority). At the end of March, Finance Minister Fernando Henrique Cardoso (*see* BIOGRAPHIES) of the Party of Brazilian Social Democracy (PSDB), who had been in that office since late May 1993, stepped down in order to run for president. His place was taken by Rubens Ricupero, a career diplomat, from April until early September, after which Ciro Gomes (a PSDB politician and former state governor) served.

Until late July Cardoso was trailing well behind Luis Inácio Lula da Silva ("Lula") of the Workers Party (PT), the top contender in all opinion polls over a prolonged period. During the remaining months before the election, however, Cardoso pulled sharply ahead of his main rival, boosted by the apparent success of an economic strategy—the Real Plan (so named after the new currency introduced from July 1) that he was instrumental in creating.

In the election Cardoso succeeded in winning the presidency in a single round, with some 54% of the vote against 27% for da Silva. This result also reflected the success of Cardoso's strategy of allying the PSDB in an electoral pact with two other parties, the Liberal Front (PFL) and the Labour Party (PTB). The congressional results were not as favourable for the Cardoso coalition, as it failed to secure a majority in either house. In the Chamber of Deputies the Cardoso grouping took some 36% of the 503 seats and in the Senate about 41% of the 81 seats.

Only 9 state governorships were decided on October 3, leaving 18 to be fought out on November 15. On the latter date there was also a rerun of legislative elections in the state of Rio de Janeiro, where investigations had shown that there had been widespread fraud. To avert a repeat of the fraud and to combat mounting criminal activity, heavy security was applied during the rerun, along with a military crackdown in the poorer favela (slum) districts, where drug traffickers had established a strong presence.

Having won only one governorship in the first-round poll (the state of Ceará), candidates from Cardoso's PSDB went on to win five more in November, including the three most economically important (São Paulo, Rio de Janeiro, and Minas Gerais) together with Pará and Sergipe in the northern and northeastern regions, respectively. By contrast, the PFL and PTB fared poorly, with the PFL in particular registering a decline in the number of states it controlled from nine to two.

The largest party—the Party of the Brazilian Democratic Movement (PMDB)—was able to improve its number of governorships from seven to nine, and the PT won two states (having held none previously). Leonel Brizola's Democratic Labour Party lost one of its three governors. During the second half of November, Cardoso was negotiating with the PMDB—which held some 28% of Senate seats and 22.5% of those in the Chamber of Deputies—in an effort to build majority congressional support. If constitutional reforms were to be pursued, however, a three-fifths majority would be required.

Increased crime in Rio de Janeiro caused President Franco in early November to order the Brazilian army to help the state and local police restore order in the city. In many of Rio's shantytowns, the police had been confronted with drug gangs firing automatic weapons and with residents burning buses and building street barricades. The army announced that its first effort would be to carry out arrest warrants against 300 suspected drug traffickers.

During his period in office as finance minister, Cardoso inaugurated policies for economic stabilization. The foundations for this were laid in the second half of 1993; on Aug. 2,

(continued on page 384)

SPOTLIGHT: Latin America's New Economic Strategy by John Sheahan

In the 1990s the great majority of Latin-American countries changed rapidly from the kind of economic strategy that many of them had been following since the Great Depression of the 1920s and '30s: away from state-led development behind high protective barriers and toward market-determined open economies. At the beginning of 1994 serious questions remained about the degree of public acceptance of this change in the two largest countries in the region, Mexico and Brazil. The doubts were answered positively in both cases. The change was incomplete and remained under active debate, but it moved a long way during the year.

On Jan. 1, 1994, the North American Free Trade Agreement (NAFTA) took effect, joining Mexico with Canada and the U.S. in a program that opened up free trade in many products, as well as in investment. The agreement allowed a long period of gradual adjustment for agriculture and some specific restrictions in other fields, but for Mexico it was a historic reversal of basic policies that had been in effect since the Mexican Revolution of 1910–20.

The major question at the beginning of the year was the depth of public opposition from groups that feared either loss of Mexican autonomy or damage to their economic interests. That question was raised in dramatic form by an armed uprising of peasants in the particularly poor state of Chiapas on January 1. The date was chosen to emphasize a connection to NAFTA, but the negotiations that followed came to focus instead on problems of democracy in Mexico, along with issues of land ownership and government neglect of local interests. Meanwhile, Cuauhtémoc Cárdenas, the main opponent of NAFTA in the Mexican presidential election, changed his position to one of questioning particular details rather than objecting to the agreement itself. It was a sign that public acceptance of a more open economy was recognized on all sides.

Brazil's position was questionable. It had taken steps toward liberalization of trade, but strong public opposition, plus a total breakdown of efforts to hold down the region's highest rate of inflation, made it seem unlikely that Brazil could continue to liberalize. That context changed after the government adopted a new stabilization program, linked by the minister of finance, Fernando Henrique Cardoso (*see* BIOGRAPHIES), to a commitment to liberalization. The program proved to have a surprisingly quick effect in cutting inflation and helped to elect Cardoso the new president.

The particular direction of liberalization emphasized by Cardoso for Brazil differed from that chosen by Mexico. Brazil aimed more at subregional agreements, intended to promote trade between Latin-American countries, than at a general opening to competition with industrialized countries. In August Brazil joined Argentina, Paraguay, and Uruguay in formally signing a customs union: the Southern Cone Common Market, known as Mercosur. In December Chile, the original leader of the movement toward economic liberalization, realized its desire to join this agreement. Meanwhile, Chile pursued the possibility of joining Mexico in an extended version of NAFTA. Bolivia, Colombia, Ecuador, Peru, and Venezuela also began discussions with Mercosur. Separately, Caribbean countries maintained their own association, the Caribbean Community and Common Market, and the Central American countries built on their low-tariff, export-oriented Central American Common Market.

In 1994 the strains of liberalization proved too great for Venezuela. As in other countries, an austerity program to reduce government deficits, restrain credit, and limit inflation was a vital part of the movement. In Venezuela the austerity program fed so much popular protest—against a government already unpopular for perceived corruption—that the president was forced out of office. The new government, facing many of the same strains, decided to repudiate the austerity program and back away from liberalization.

No other countries reversed the liberalization process in 1994, but two kinds of strain proved severe for many of them. Strong inflows of capital, in response to liberalization itself and to the high domestic interest rates associated with monetary restraint, often pushed up the value of national currencies. This made imports cheaper and exports more difficult than they would have been at exchange rates consistent with balanced trade. As a result, the region's exports failed to keep pace with the growth of its imports. This context could be regarded in a positive way; the richer countries were moving capital to Latin America, permitting higher rates of investment and consumption than would have been possible in the absence of the import surplus. It was also a problem for the future. External liabilities were increasing, and the region's exports were not developing in the way needed for sustainable long-term growth.

The social complications of liberalization were particularly evident in Bolivia, Mexico, and Peru, as they had been in Chile before them. The first years of austerity and liberalization, with intensified competition in previously sheltered industries, resulted in falling real wages, the failures of many firms, and increasing poverty. The distribution of income typically became more unequal. All these countries responded in varied ways to such social strains. Mexico negotiated a joint agreement between labour, business, and the government to restrain price increases while promoting limited but positive changes in real wages. Then it introduced its "Solidarity" program of social spending to generate employment and lessen poverty, financed by sales to private investors of previously state-owned firms. Chile used an alternative kind of negotiation; business was asked to agree to an increase of three percentage points in taxes on profits, to be used exclusively for a social program to provide direct help for the poor and to improve skills of low-income workers. Bolivia was helped by international financing agencies to create an extensive social program that increased employment in community-development programs. Peru, after three years of doing little to stop a rise in poverty, initiated a similar program in 1994.

More open economic systems were expected to help raise efficiency and incomes in the long run, but the impact in the first few years seemed to be so negative for lower income groups that the international financing agencies sought to accompany liberalization with large-scale social programs. Few people disagreed with the need for such programs, provided the financing could be made available. Intense disagreement continued over the question of whether governments should take direct measures to limit the negative effects of liberalization programs on the poor. Specific actions by governments to counteract effects of the movement toward open economies, however, could conceivably undermine the credibility of the basic strategy and, if mishandled, weaken the economies concerned. Or they could, if handled as well as in Chile, make the consequences of liberalization less unequal and continued public acceptance of the strategy more likely.

John Sheahan is professor of economics (emeritus) at Williams College, Williamstown, Mass., and the author of *Patterns of Development in Latin America: Poverty, Repression, and Economic Strategy.*

(continued from page 382)

1993, the cruzeiro became the cruzeiro real as a prelude to the launching of the real as a new stronger currency during 1994. The core of the Real Plan was developed during the first quarter of 1994 before Cardoso left office. An interim stage of the plan began on March 1 with the phasing in of a single exchange-rate-linked index for inflation—the unit of real value (or URV)—that was set daily by the central bank. Most prices, with the main exception of rents, had been converted to the new index by the end of June, reducing monthly rates of inflation as expressed in URVs. Expressed in terms of the cruzeiro real, however, monthly inflation in June was about 50%. This was reduced to the 5–8% range the following month (with a low 1–2% in September), after the introduction of the real on July 1, 1994.

A growth of more than 4% in gross domestic product was expected for the year. Fueled by an improvement in real incomes, consumption rose in the second half of the year, though a consumer boom was held in check by high interest rates and import liberalization. The trade surplus at the end of October stood at $11,880,000,000. The country's debt rescheduling, which had been negotiated with commercial bank creditors in 1993, was completed in mid-April. International reserves were buoyant at $40 billion.

Brazil and the world lost two enormously popular figures in 1994, race-car driver Ayrton Senna and songwriter and jazz musician Antônio Carlos Jobim. (*See* OBITUARIES.)

(SUSAN M. CUNNINGHAM)

BRUNEI

The sultanate of Brunei is located on the northern coast of the island of Borneo, on the South China Sea. Area: 5,765 sq km (2,226 sq mi). Pop. (1994 est.): 283,000. Cap.: Bandar Seri Begawan. Monetary unit: Brunei dollar, with (Oct. 7, 1994) a free rate of B$1.48 to U.S. $1 (B$2.36 = £1 sterling). Sultan and prime minister in 1994, Sir Muda Hassanal Bolkiah Mu'izzadin Waddaulah.

In March 1994 Brunei, the Philippines, Malaysia, and Indonesia created the East Asian Growth Area (EAGA). The regional economic market was patterned after the concept of international "growth triangles," which were becoming popular among the six members of the Association of Southeast Asian Nations (ASEAN). The latter also included Thailand and Singapore. In this "growth polygon" the four EAGA countries pledged to expand trade initially in four sectors: tourism, air transport, shipping, and fisheries. Brunei was to coordinate air transport. In May the sultanate established the Muara Export Zone in Bandar Seri Begawan, the capital. It would serve as the entry point for EAGA goods and as a regional transshipment centre.

In May the staunchly Muslim sultanate established ambassadorial-level relations with the Palestine Liberation Organization. In September, Foreign Minister Mohamed Bolkiah met for the first time with his Israeli counterpart, Shimon Peres, at the United Nations. The two countries hoped to establish diplomatic relations in the future. In April Brunei and Malaysia agreed to begin talks on resolving Brunei's claim to Limbang, the sliver of Malaysian territory on Borneo.

Oil-rich Brunei welcomed an initiative by Oman in January to coordinate oil prices among nonmembers of OPEC. The sultan visited Iran and three other Gulf countries in February. In October Brunei called for better regulation of world oil production because a glut had caused prices to hit a four-year low. (BERTON WOODWARD)

This article updates the *Macropædia* article SOUTHEAST ASIA: *Brunei.*

BULGARIA

The republic of Bulgaria is on the eastern Balkan Peninsula of southeastern Europe, along the Black Sea. Area: 110,994 sq km (42,855 sq mi). Pop. (1994 est.): 8,452,000. Cap.: Sofia. Monetary unit: lev, with (Oct. 7, 1994) a free rate of 62.84 leva to U.S. $1 (99.95 leva = £1 sterling). President in 1994, Zhelyu Zhelev; prime ministers, Lyuben Berov until September 8 and, from October 17, Reneta Indzhova.

In 1994 Bulgaria received substantial loans from the International Monetary Fund and succeeded in negotiating an almost 50% reduction in foreign debt obligations. Whatever benefits these agreements might have brought, few Bulgarians found cause for celebration in 1994. Political stagnation intensified, and when Prime Minister Lyuben Berov underwent heart surgery in March, few believed his administration could survive much longer. At the beginning of April, Pres. Zhelyu Zhelev announced that the Cabinet should broaden its parliamentary base or resign. Berov's weakness was further revealed on May 18 when Parliament rejected his revised Cabinet.

Berov, however, remained in office long enough to pass a privatization bill on June 28 and to see through its final stages the controversial Judiciary Bill. Its most important provision required legal officers to have been in office for at least five years before they could be promoted to a senior level; this in effect restricted the upper ranks of the judiciary to officials appointed during the communist regime.

On September 2 Berov submitted his resignation, which was accepted by Parliament on September 8. In accordance with constitutional requirements, President Zhelev allowed Parliament three attempts to form a new administration, and when it failed he dissolved Parliament, called new elections for December, and on October 17 appointed an interim Cabinet under Reneta Indzhova, the head of the Privatization Agency and the first woman to be prime minister of a Balkan nation.

The Socialists (former Communists) won a majority in the National Assembly in the December 18 elections, claiming 125 of the 240 seats in that body; the incumbent anticommunist Union of Democratic Forces won 69 seats. Even with their slight majority, the Socialists were expected to seek a coalition government, and their leader, 35-year-old Zhan Videnov, was poised to become prime minister.

For many Bulgarians, however, politics was becoming increasingly irrelevant in the face of corruption, crime, and rising prices. In January the minister of the interior, Viktor Mihailov, declared that the police were corrupt and incompetent, and few people had much faith in an anticrime package introduced by the government on August 30. On September 26 Mihailov admitted that Bulgarians needed to have the right to carry firearms to defend themselves because the government could no longer do so.

(RICHARD J. CRAMPTON)

This article updates the *Macropædia* article BALKAN STATES: *Bulgaria.*

BURKINA FASO

Burkina Faso is a landlocked country of West Africa. Area: 274,400 sq km (105,946 sq mi). Pop. (1994 est.): 10,044,000. Cap.: Ouagadougou. Monetary unit: CFA franc, with (from Jan. 12, 1994) a par value of CFAF 100 to the French franc and (as of Oct. 7, 1994) a free rate of CFAF 526.67 to U.S. $1 (CFAF 837.67 = £1 sterling). President (chairman) of the Popular Front in 1994, Capt. Blaise Compaoré; prime ministers, Youssouf Ouedraogo until March 17 and, from March 22, Marc-Christian Kaboré

The January devaluation of the CFA franc led to the resignation of Prime Minister Youssouf Ouedraogo in March. Having apparently lost the support of Pres. Blaise Compaoré, Ouedraogo's government was unable to meet widespread demands for higher wages, better working and living conditions, and a general reduction in prices. His replacement, Marc-Christian Kaboré, named a new 23-person Cabinet on March 22. The new government's inability to satisfy trade union demands for a 40–50% wage hike resulted in the National Labor Confederation's threat of a general strike on April 6.

At a National Production Meeting on June 2, President Compaoré announced an ambitious new social and economic program to 8,000 delegates throughout the nation. The six-point scheme focused on agricultural development, promotion of small businesses, environmental protection, unemployment, the status of women, and expansion of primary education. Funding was to be sought internationally. In July the National Assembly passed, over opposition protests, a law enabling the government to privatize 19 nationalized industries. Since adoption of a structural adjustment program in 1991, Burkina Faso had already privatized 14 state-owned companies. A Joint Cooperation Committee with Côte d'Ivoire, Burkina Faso's largest trading partner in Africa, was established in July. Its mission included the resolution of border disputes, revision of the 1966 trade agreement, and promotion of general cooperation between the two nations.   (NANCY ELLEN LAWLER)

This article updates the *Macropædia* article WESTERN AFRICA: *Burkina Faso*.

JIM DARNTON—THE NEW YORK TIMES

A woman works in a facility in Burkina Faso to mass-produce fermented corn flour, a staple that traditionally required intensive labour. It was hoped that the new method of production would lessen the growing dependence on rice and wheat, which had to be imported.

BURUNDI

Burundi is a landlocked republic of central Africa. Area: 27,816 sq km (10,740 sq mi). Pop. (1994 est.): 5,799,000 (including 800,000 Burundian refugees living mostly in Tanzania and Zaire). Cap.: Bujumbura. Monetary unit: Burundi franc, with (Oct. 7, 1994) a free rate of FBu 248.44 to U.S. $1 (FBu 395.15 = £1 sterling). Presidents in 1994, Cyprien Ntaryamira from February 7 to April 6 and, acting from April 8 and official from October 1, Sylvestre Ntibantunganya; prime ministers, Sylvie Kinigi and, from February 7, Anatole Kanyenkiko.

On Jan. 13, 1994, the National Assembly elected Cyprien Ntaryamira as president to succeed Melchior Ndadaye, who had been assassinated in October 1993. During the month, refugees who had fled the 1993 disturbances began to return. On February 3 the main political parties signed an agreement to allow the inauguration of Ntaryamira (a Hutu). In forming a government, Ntaryamira appointed a Tutsi, Anatole Kanyenkiko, as prime minister, while 60% of the Cabinet posts went to the Burundi Democratic Front (Frodebu) and 40% went to the Unity for National Progress and other parties. A report on the 1993 coup attempt revealed that the armed forces had been involved and that between 25,000 and 50,000 people had died.

On April 6 President Ntaryamira, along with Pres. Juvénal Habyarimana of Rwanda, was killed in an airplane crash near Kigali, Rwanda, setting off a major ethnic crisis. Two days later the speaker of the National Assembly, Sylvestre Ntibantunganya (a Hutu), became acting president. On April 19 violence erupted when members of the Tutsi-dominated army attacked Hutus, and six days later a number of Tutsis tried unsuccessfully to stage a coup. The violence continued in Bujumbura through May and increased during June; the resulting displacement of large numbers of people led to overcrowding and the outbreak of disease. As the slaughter escalated in neighbouring Rwanda, there were growing fears of copycat killings in Burundi. A power-sharing agreement was reached on July 12 under which Frodebu was to have control of nine provinces and the opposition parties would control seven. On that same day, the constitutional court extended for three months the mandate for the interim president while a search continued for a new president.

At the end of the year, the country was precariously poised on the edge of possible ethnic breakdown. Armed factions were killing hundreds of people every month, and the justice system had collapsed. The mainly Tutsi Unity for National Progress walked out of the parliament on December 2, after a Hutu was elected speaker, and left the government entirely on December 24.   (GUY ARNOLD)

See also RACE AND ETHNIC RELATIONS: *Sidebar*.

This article updates the *Macropædia* article CENTRAL AFRICA: *Burundi*.

CAMBODIA

A constitutional monarchy of Southeast Asia, Cambodia occupies the southwestern part of the Indochinese Peninsula, on the Gulf of Thailand. Area: 181,916 sq km (70,238 sq mi). Pop. (1994 est.): 9,525,000. Cap.: Phnom Penh. Monetary unit: riel, with (Oct. 7, 1994) an official rate of 2,587 riels to U.S. $1 (4,115 riels = £1 sterling). King, Norodom Sihanouk; first prime minister in 1994, Norodom Ranariddh, and second prime minister, Hun Sen.

Politics and security remained the key issues in Cambodia in 1994. King Norodom Sihanouk, who spent much of the year in China for treatment of cancer, failed to persuade the ruling coalition in June to form a government of national reconciliation that he would head. It would have included the Khmer Rouge. Both of the country's prime ministers, Prince Norodom Ranariddh (a son of Sihanouk) and Hun Sen, pushed through legislation in July declaring the rebel group illegal. In October the government ousted Sam Rainsy, an ally of the king, as finance minister. Prince Norodom Sereivut, half-brother to the king, resigned as foreign minister. Both supported Sihanouk's desire to bring the Khmer Rouge into the government.

Although the government agreed to talk with the Khmer Rouge in January, it still launched a military offensive. The army briefly had control of the rebels' base at Anlong Veng in February. It also took the Khmer Rouge's headquarters in Pailin in March, but the guerrillas recaptured the town the next month. Peace talks were held in May and June in response to an appeal by Sihanouk, but no agreement was reached. The Khmer Rouge proclaimed its own government after it was outlawed in July. Still led by the shadowy Pol Pot, the group remained in control of parts of the country's northwest, including remote areas bordering Thailand. It embarrassed the government by taking Westerners hostage in April and July. All six victims were killed.

The government faced another threat in July when Prince Norodom Chakrapong, Ranariddh's half-brother, and former interior minister Sin Song led an abortive coup. The prince then went into voluntary exile. Chakrapong, a member of Hun Sen's Cambodian People's Party (CPP), had also mounted a short-lived coup in 1993, but he was pardoned by Sihanouk. Sin Song and two other senior CPP officials were arrested. Sin Song, however, escaped from detention in September, but he was captured by Thai police outside Bangkok in November. He and Chakrapong were sentenced in absentia to 20 years in jail. The two other CPP leaders and nine Thai nationals were also found guilty of conspiracy.

The takeover attempt focused attention on factionalism within the CPP, the former communist party that had ruled Cambodia after Vietnam ousted the Khmer Rouge in 1979. Chakrapong and Sin Song hoped to put Sihanouk at the head of a government of national reconciliation that included the Khmer Rouge. There were rifts as well within Ranariddh's party, the royalist Funcinpec. When he resigned as foreign minister, party secretary-general Sereivut accused the government of disregarding Sihanouk's wishes. The Funcinpec-CPP coalition itself remained shaky. Many Funcinpec members resented the CPP's control of key government and military units despite the fact that Funcinpec held a plurality of seats in the National Assembly.

The political and security problems left the government with little time to attend to other problems. Ill-paid security forces turned to banditry and victimized citizens and foreigners. As finance minister, Rainsy pushed the centralization of revenue collection, discarding the previous system, which allowed individual ministries and provinces to collect and keep taxes. The government was under pressure to sack Rainsy, but he had the respect of Cambodians and international donors. In March Japan, the U.S., and others promised $777 million in aid for 1994 and 1995. A three-year economic plan was signed with the International Monetary Fund, which in May approved a $120 million loan.

Cambodia's relations with Thailand were strained because of suspicions that the Thais still had links with the Khmer Rouge. Bangkok served as the conduit for military aid to the Khmer Rouge and others in the anticommunist coalition that had fought the Vietnam-backed government in Phnom Penh. Ties with Vietnam suffered, too. Hanoi expressed concern that an immigration law passed in September threatened 140,000 ethnic Vietnamese residents and Cambodians of Vietnamese descent with deportation.

(CESAR BACANI)

This article updates the *Macropædia* article SOUTHEAST ASIA: *Cambodia*.

CAMEROON

A republic of western central Africa, Cameroon lies on the Gulf of Guinea. Area: 475,442 sq km (183,569 sq mi). Pop. (1994 est.): 12,905,000. Cap.: Yaoundé. Monetary unit: CFA franc, with (from Jan. 12, 1994) a par value of CFAF 100 to the French franc and (as of Oct. 7, 1994) a free rate of CFAF 526.67 to U.S. $1 (CFAF 837.67 = £1 sterling). President in 1994, Paul Biya; prime minister, Simon Achidi Achu.

The long-simmering border dispute over the oil-rich Bakassi peninsula boiled over on Jan. 3, 1994, when 500 Nigerian troops temporarily occupied Cameroon's Diamond and Djabane islands. After several months of diplomatic maneuvering, Pres. Paul Biya and Nigerian Pres. Sani Abacha met in Tunis during the June summit of the Organization of African Unity. Final resolution of the issue, however, remained stalled owing to political upheavals in Nigeria.

Biya felt strong enough to suspend the process of constitutional reform, begun in November 1992, for another year. On April 29 the second All Anglophone Conference

A group of Buddhist nuns and monks, numbering 1,000 in all, participate in a march in April to demonstrate their commitment to reconciliation between Cambodia's factions. The marchers were shelled by the Khmer Rouge, however; and a nun and a monk were killed.

was held. Deep divisions over the question of federalism and the composition of the anglophone (English-speaking) delegation to the constitutional conference emerged, thus weakening the support for opposition leader John Fru Ndi and his Social Democratic Front. Further cracks in the opposition emerged when Bello Bouba Maigari, president of the Union for Democracy and Progress (UNDP), demanded that his deputy, Hamadou Moustapha, resign from the government following a July 21 Cabinet reshuffle. Moustapha's refusal led to violence. On July 30 eight members of the UNDP died in factional fighting.

Despite opposition calls to leave the franc zone, Biya accepted the devaluation of the CFA franc, receiving promises of financial aid from France to offset the severe effects upon the economy. Cameroon was struggling with an enormous internal debt of unpaid back salaries for civil servants. Large cuts in current salaries led to a number of strikes during the year. The government sought funds from the World Bank, the International Monetary Fund, and the Paris Club, promising in return to cut 20,000 civil service jobs and to continue privatization of state-owned enterprises. Journalists continued to be a target of government harassment, and several were arrested for libel and failing to submit articles to the official censors. (NANCY ELLEN LAWLER)

This article updates the *Macropædia* article WESTERN AFRICA: *Cameroon.*

CANADA

Canada is a federal parliamentary state and member of the Commonwealth covering North America north of conterminous United States and east of Alaska. Area: 9,970,610 sq km (3,849,674 sq mi). Pop. (1994 est.): 29,107,000. Cap.: Ottawa. Monetary unit: Canadian dollar, with (Oct. 7, 1994) a free rate of Can$1.35 to U.S. $1 (Can$2.14 = £1 sterling). Queen, Elizabeth II; governor-general in 1994, Ramon Hnatyshyn; prime minister, Jean Chrétien.

Domestic Affairs. The possibility of the separation of Quebec from Canada was raised again in 1994 with the election of a provincial government in Quebec committed to independence. The event posed a serious challenge to the central government in Ottawa and promised to dominate public affairs in Canada in the coming months.

A separatist party, the Parti Québécois (PQ), had been organized in 1968 by the journalist René Lévesque, who appealed to the deep nationalist sentiments of generations of Quebeckers. The province represented a distinctive society in North America. The French language, spoken by 82% of Quebec's residents, stood isolated in a sea of English speakers, and its culture and law set it apart from the other Canadian provinces. Canada's federal system afforded Quebec self-government in local affairs as well as the advantages of an economic union with the other nine provinces. To Lévesque and his followers, however, this was not enough. Quebec needed outright independence if it was to fulfill its destiny as a French-speaking nation. Separatists believed that Quebec possessed the confidence, the resources, and the economic structure to stand on its own feet.

In 1976 the PQ was elected to office, and it governed Quebec until 1985. It put the question of independence to the Quebec people in a referendum held in 1980. The voters were asked not whether they preferred outright separation but whether they favoured "sovereignty-association"—more local autonomy for Quebec linked with a loose association with the rest of Canada. They rejected this proposition by a vote of 60% to 40%. Dejected by the result, Lévesque did not raise the question again during the remainder of his term in office.

The party that succeeded the PQ in government, the Liberal Party, was committed to the unity of Canada but demanded a "separate status" for Quebec. Its leader, Robert Bourassa, working with Brian Mulroney, the leader of the federal Progressive Conservative Party and prime minister of Canada from 1984 to 1993, attempted to amend Canada's constitution to reflect this conception. Two sets of suggested changes were turned down, the first (the Meech Lake accord) by two of the Canadian provinces in 1990 and the second (the Charlottetown accord) by the Canadian people in 1992.

These rejections were seen by many Quebeckers as humiliating and gave new momentum to the separatist cause. In opposition during the nine years of Liberal rule, the PQ came to be led by Jacques Parizeau, an economist who had been minister of finance in the Lévesque government. Although Parizeau stressed the need to strengthen Quebec's economy and reduce its 10% unemployment rate, he did not conceal the fact that his primary objective was independence. He promised that his party, if elected to office, would ask the legislature to approve a "solemn declaration" formally stating Quebec's desire to secede from Canada. Within 10 months it would go to the people and through a referendum gain popular support for secession.

In January 1994, after nine consecutive years in office, Bourassa resigned as premier. He was succeeded by a member of his Cabinet, Daniel Johnson. With a strong current demanding a change of government in the province, Johnson faced a daunting task in the election he called for September 12. Public opinion polls showed the PQ well ahead of the Liberals in support, although the polls indicated that the PQ's aim of sovereignty was still not the preferred option of a majority of Quebeckers.

The election gave the PQ the resounding win the polls had predicted. The party took 77 seats in the 125-seat National Assembly, compared with the 33 it had held at dissolution. The Liberals dropped from 78 to 47 seats. An additional seat was won by a splinter party advocating a gradual approach to independence. The PQ victory was won in French-speaking districts since most of the English-speaking and ethnic-minority vote went to the Liberals. Parizeau did not win the sweeping victory he had hoped for, however; the two parties each won 44% of the popular vote, being separated by less than one percentage point. The Liberals would still be a formidable force in the legislature, and Johnson could speak with authority for the federalist cause during the campaign for the forthcoming referendum.

Because the referendum would be decided by popular vote, the PQ faced the challenging task, in the months ahead, of convincing a majority of the electorate of the merits of sovereignty. Polls consistently showed that the 40% vote for sovereignty that had been recorded during the 1980 referendum still held in Quebec. In the recent election voters had cast their ballots for a change of government, not for separation. It would be misleading to see the situations in 1980 and 1994 as similar, however. In 1994 there was a separatist party in the federal Parliament, something that had not existed 14 years earlier. The election of 1993 had been responsible for sending to Parliament 54 members from Quebec who espoused the separatist cause. The Bloc Québécois (BQ), in fact, constituted the largest opposition group in the House of Commons, with its leader, Lucien Bouchard (see BIOGRAPHIES), holding the official position of leader of the opposition. The BQ was thus in a position to join with the PQ in harassing the federal government of Prime Minister Jean Chrétien. In 1994 there was also a harder attitude toward Quebec in the rest of Canada than there had been in 1980. There was no longer a readiness to make constitutional changes to meet Quebec's demands, and many Canadians believed that Quebec had to be content with the same position as the other provinces.

A new party that strongly held these attitudes had, in fact, entered Parliament in the 1993 election. The Western-based Reform Party, with 52 members, was convinced that the federal government paid too much attention to Quebec's wishes in governing the country. If the federal government moved to placate Quebec to head off separatism, the Reform Party would be certain to oppose the attempt.

The competing pressures of the BQ and the Reform Party posed a difficult challenge for the governing Liberals in Ottawa. Prime Minister Chrétien made it clear that his

Canadian Prime Minister Jean Chrétien (left) shakes hands with Li Peng, premier of China, after the signing of a nuclear cooperation agreement in Beijing in November. Chrétien headed a delegation of provincial premiers seeking economic agreements with China.
CANAPRESS

first duty was to maintain the unity of the country. Although he did not have a substantial bloc of French-speaking MPs behind him, his standing in the province of Quebec had improved since he became prime minister in November 1993. Polls showed that Chrétien's government enjoyed the support of 54% of Canadians, a 13% gain in popularity since it had taken office. Still, when Parizeau was sworn in as Quebec's 26th premier on September 26, a period of uncertainty was anticipated in Canadian affairs. The PQ government would do all it could to promote sovereignty in the period leading to the referendum. The Liberals would defend federalism by attempting to make it a more effective means of meeting Canadians' needs.

On December 6 the PQ tabled a draft bill in the National Assembly declaring Quebec "a sovereign country" that would draft its own constitution, maintain its present borders, and assume all the obligations and rights arising from current Canadian treaties. It would conclude an economic association with the rest of Canada, use the Canadian dollar as its currency, and permit its citizens to hold Canadian citizenship concurrently with its own. A public consultation would be held early in 1995, leading to a referendum later in the year in which Quebec voters would be asked to declare whether they were in favour of the act announcing the sovereignty of Quebec. If the voters approved the act, it would go into force a year later. Federalist groups in both Quebec and the rest of Canada, as well as the national opposition in Ottawa, branded the draft legislation as beyond the power of the province to enact and refused to participate in an allegedly "flawed" consultation process that shut out discussion of the federalist option for Quebec.

The Liberals, with a comfortable majority of 176 seats in the 295-seat House of Commons, carried out a modest legislative program during their first year in office. Only 35 bills were approved, most being of a routine nature. The government occupied itself with reviews of important areas marked out for future legislation. These included social assistance, unemployment insurance, health care, and foreign and defense policies. Its most solid achievement was an agreement, signed at a conference of first ministers (federal and provincial) in Ottawa on July 18, to eliminate or reduce interprovincial trade barriers. The barriers, which involved such areas as food products, government procurement, financial services, and labour mobility, were estimated to cost Canadians about $6.5 billion annually. The plan approved provided for dispute-settlement machinery similar to that found in the U.S.-Canadian and North American free-trade agreements.

The Economy. Exports slowly lifted the Canadian economy from the valley of the 1990 recession. A quickening demand in the United States led to substantial flows of forest products, fertilizers, and manufactured goods across the border, producing a record surplus in commodity trade in July. Economic growth for the year was estimated to be 3.7%. At the end of June, gross domestic product (GDP), on a seasonally adjusted basis at market prices, was calculated at $739.6 billion. Unemployment remained high, although a modest trend downward produced a November rate of 9.6%, the lowest level since the end of 1990. Most of the improvement occurred in Ontario and in the four provinces to the west. Inflation was not a concern, and in May the consumer price index actually fell 0.2% from the year before, a condition that had not occurred in 40 years. The partial elimination of taxes on tobacco by the federal government and five provinces contributed to this result, and in August, a more normal month, the rate of increase in the index stood at 0.2%.

Finance Minister Paul Martin presented his first budget on February 22. It imposed no new taxes or increases in tax rates. The deficit was to be reduced from $45.7 billion in fiscal year 1993–94 to an estimated $39.7 billion in 1994–95. With the deficit running at 5.4% of GDP, it was clear that stronger measures would have to be implemented to reach the 1996–97 goal (3% of GDP) the Liberals had proposed in their election campaign. Federal spending was held at $163.6 billion for 1994–95, an increase of only 2% over the previous year. Martin turned to defense expenditures for cuts, announcing a $7 billion reduction over the next five years. Four major bases—two in the Maritime Provinces and two in Ontario—were to be closed over the next three years, as were military colleges in British Columbia and Quebec, and 16 smaller installations were to be shut down or pared in size. More than 8,000 military personnel and 8,400 civilian employees would be laid off over the next four years, leaving an armed force of 66,700 men and women at the end of the process. Foreign aid was cut by 2%. The salary freeze instituted for 381,000 public employees by the previous government was extended for two more years, to 1997, and the salaries of members of Parliament were also frozen.

Tobacco taxes were cut by the federal government, Quebec, Ontario, and the three Maritime Provinces in an effort to stop the flood of smuggled cigarettes from the United States. Most of the contraband cigarettes moved through the Akwesasne Indian reserve straddling the borders between Quebec, Ontario, and New York state. The value of smuggled cigarettes was estimated to amount to at least $500 million a year. Not only had smuggling led to a loss of revenue for governments, but it also had contributed to a climate of lawlessness along the international section of the St. Lawrence River. In response to appeals from Premier Johnson of Quebec that the smuggling be curtailed, on February 8 the government in Ottawa reduced its tax on cigarettes by $5 a carton and offered to match any provincial tax cuts to a maximum of another $5. For Quebec the reductions meant that the price of cigarettes fell from $47 to $22.73 a carton.

Foreign Affairs. Prime Minister Chrétien, anxious to create a fresh image for his government in foreign affairs, resolved to take a more independent attitude toward U.S. policy than Mulroney had done. Relations with Cuba were a good example. Canada had never suspended diplomatic links with the government of Fidel Castro, and it now resumed aid, through nongovernmental organizations, that had been cut off in 1978 as a protest against Cuban involvement in Angola. Canada decided that it would not take part in the first phase of the U.S. intervention in Haiti, although it agreed to send 100 Royal Canadian Mounted Police and 500 soldiers later to help maintain law and order. The Canadian federal force also began training young Haitians for eventual police duties on the island. Canadian policy toward the fighting in Bosnia and Herzegovina also differed from the U.S. position, largely because of the presence of some 2,000 Canadian peacekeepers operating on the ground in Bosnia and Croatia. Chrétien agreed only reluctantly with the NATO decision to use air strikes in the area to force Serbian heavy guns to withdraw from the environs of Sarajevo. He insisted that air strikes be used only as a last resort and only upon the authority of the UN.

Canadian peacekeepers were active during the civil war in Rwanda before being relieved by a larger UN force in the summer. The original small UN force had been commanded by a Canadian general and operated a vital air link between Rwanda and neighbouring Kenya. It also provided a field hospital and a communications unit. One hundred and fifty Canadian soldiers, hemmed in by Bosnian Serb troops, guarded 40,000 Muslim refugees gathered around Srebrenica for a year before being relieved by Dutch forces in March. Altogether, 3,825 Canadian military personnel served under UN command in the Middle East, the Balkans, Africa, and Asia.

There was relief in Ottawa on May 17 when, during a visit to the capital, U.S. Secretary of Defense William Perry stated that the United States had no further need to test cruise missiles in Canadian airspace. The last U.S. military base in Canada, a submarine-detection facility in Newfoundland, closed in September.

In a controversial move, the government in November announced that it planned to reduce the number of immigrants admitted to Canada in 1995 and would henceforth put greater emphasis on applicants' skills and wealth and seek ways to reduce the financial burden on the state.

The flow of trade across the Canadian-U.S. border, the largest bilateral trade traffic in the world, saw a number of disputes in 1994. A dispute over durum wheat, which U.S. farmers claimed was being exported to the United States at unfair subsidized prices, threatened to lead to an agricultural trade war. Canada argued that floods in the Midwest in 1993 and U.S. wheat sales abroad under the Export Enhancement Program had made Canadian wheat imports necessary to meet the U.S. demand for pasta flour. Tough negotiations led to an agreement on Aug. 1, 1994, in which Canada would be allowed to export 300,000 metric tons of durum wheat to the United States during the following year. No trade sanctions would be applied by either country, and an independent binational commission would be set up to look into the merits of the dispute.

Another quarrel, one going back to 1982, was settled in Canada's favour. This dispute concerned the export of softwood lumber (spruce, pine, and fir), which had come to supply 30% of the U.S. market for these woods. U.S. lumber producers had claimed that the stumpage fees of certain Canadian provinces were set at a rate that constituted a form of subsidy, and the U.S. imposed tariffs on the Canadian lumber in 1991. A binational panel ruled in December 1993 that there was "no rational basis" for the tariffs. The U.S. referred the decision to an extraordinary-challenge committee, which in effect ratified the earlier decision. In a ruling delivered on August 3, the panel ordered the U.S. to return to Canadian lumber producers $800 million in duties collected under the tariff. It was the third extraordinary-challenge committee to be set up under the two countries' free-trade agreement of 1989.

Another dispute, this time over Pacific salmon, also emerged in 1994. Canada claimed that too many salmon spawned in the rivers of British Columbia had been taken by U.S. fishermen as the salmon made their way back to their spawning streams. The U.S.-Canadian Pacific Salmon Commission (PSC) estimated that in 1993 U.S. fishermen had netted 9 million Canadian salmon, while Canadians had caught only 3.7 million fish coming from U.S. rivers. When it proved impossible to renew an agreement specifying quotas on the number of salmon that could be caught, Canada took unilateral action by imposing a $1,500 fee on U.S. fishermen using the sheltered waters off the British Columbia coast to reach fishing grounds in Alaska. It also permitted its own fishermen to increase their catch in open waters so as to deny U.S. fishermen salmon from Canadian rivers.

Fishery policies in both countries were called into question when it was discovered that the number of salmon in the northeastern Pacific Ocean had been erroneously estimated by the PSC. By late September it was found that more than three million sockeye salmon had failed to appear in the lower reaches of the Fraser River, a major British Columbia salmon river. The reasons for the disappearance were unknown, but the consequences were apparent; fewer salmon than expected would lay eggs in 1994 to replenish fish stocks for the future. (*See also* Agriculture: *Fisheries.*)

(D.M.L. FARR)

CAPE VERDE

The republic of Cape Verde occupies an island group in the Atlantic Ocean about 620 km (385 mi) off the west coast of Africa. Area: 4,033 sq km (1,557 sq mi). Pop. (1994 est.): 355,000. Cap.: Praia. Monetary unit: Cape Verde escudo, with (Oct. 7, 1994) a free rate of 83.05 escudos to U.S. $1 (132.09 escudos = £1 sterling). President in 1994, Antonio Mascarenhas Monteiro; prime minister, Carlos Veiga.

The 1994 budget, presented in January, boosted public investment but also cut back on overall expenditure. The National People's Assembly approved an expenditure of $227 million, of which government spending would total $218 million; a deficit of $9 million would be made up by foreign aid. Public investment in 1994 was to be increased to $138 million (as compared with $80 million in 1993), with priority going to transportation, telecommunications, and various aspects of rural development. Fuel prices and taxes on alcohol and tobacco were raised to help pay for these proposed investments.

Following the resignation in February of Enrico Correia Monteiro, the minister of justice and labour, and his subsequent defection from the ruling party, the Movement for Democracy, to form a new party, Prime Minister Carlos Veiga was obliged to reshuffle his Cabinet. Pedro Monteiro

Freine de Andrade was appointed minister of justice and labour, and José Media was named minister of health.

(GUY ARNOLD)

This article updates the *Macropædia* article WESTERN AFRICA: *Cape Verde*.

CENTRAL AFRICAN REPUBLIC

The Central African Republic is a landlocked state in central Africa. Area: 622,436 sq km (240,324 sq mi). Pop. (1994 est.): 3,069,000. Cap.: Bangui. Monetary unit: CFA franc, with (Oct. 7, 1994) a par value of CFAF 100 to the French franc and a free rate of CFAF 526.67 to U.S. $1 (CFAF 837.67 = £1 sterling). President in 1994, Ange-Félix Patassé; prime minister, Jean-Luc Mandaba.

Pres. Ange-Félix Patassé spent much of 1994 trying to reestablish the Central African Republic's close ties with France. Twelve years earlier France had refused Patassé's bid for political asylum following an abortive coup against former Central African Republic leader Gen. André Kolingba, and in 1993 it had supported David Dacko in the presidential elections. Relations deteriorated further following a banking scandal in which a French associate of Patassé was arrested on January 19, charged with involvement in the disappearance of F 75 million in loan guarantees deposited with the Crédit Mutuel de Sud-Ouest. It was not until August that Patassé was able to arrange an official visit to French Pres. François Mitterrand, who had canceled two earlier meetings. Hints from Patassé that his government might close France's important military base in the Central African Republic apparently played a large part in Mitterrand's decision to welcome him to Paris.

The nation's economy remained extremely weak. The important mining industry was producing below capacity, and mineral revenues were further reduced by widespread smuggling. Civil servants were being paid but were still owed huge amounts in back pay. On August 3 legislators from Kuwait arrived in Bangui to express their gratitude for the nation's help during the Gulf war. It was anticipated that the Arab nation would continue to provide aid for road and school construction. (NANCY ELLEN LAWLER)

This article updates the *Macropædia* article CENTRAL AFRICA: *Central African Republic*.

CHAD

Chad is a landlocked republic of central Africa. Area: 1,284,000 sq km (495,755 sq mi). Pop. (1994 est.): 6,495,000. Cap.: N'Djamena. Monetary unit: CFA franc, with (from Jan. 12, 1994) a par value of CFAF 100 to the French franc and (as of Oct. 7, 1994) a free rate of CFAF 526.67 to U.S. $1 (CFAF 837.67 = £1 sterling). President in 1994, Col. Idriss Déby; prime minister, Delwa Kassire Koumakoye.

In January 1994 Prime Minister Delwa Kassire Koumakoye reshuffled his Cabinet; the most significant appointment was that of Abderamane Izo Miskine to the Ministry of the Interior and Security, which put him in charge of anti-rebel activities and national reconciliation. Two opposition groups—the Movement for Democracy and Development and the National Union for Democracy and Socialism—announced their decision to join in opposing the government of Pres. Idriss Déby, and they invited other groups to join them. There was increased violent activity by the Chadian National Front (FNT) in Abeche, where 31 deaths occurred (29 of them reportedly FNT members). The government signed a peace agreement with the rebels on October 12.

In March the International Monetary Fund approved a credit of SDR16,520,000 (about $23 million) to support a 12-month economic-growth program. Early in April the Higher Transitional Council extended by 12 months the transitional period before elections had to be held. President Déby carried out a major Cabinet reshuffle in May, dismissing nine ministers.

On February 3 the International Court of Justice ruled 16–1 in Chad's favour to confirm its sovereignty over the Aozou strip (114,000 sq km [44,000 sq mi]), which it had been contesting with Libya for 20 years; both nations had agreed at the outset to accept the ICJ ruling. On May 31 the Aozou strip was formally returned to Chad.

(GUY ARNOLD)

This article updates the *Macropædia* article WESTERN AFRICA: *Chad*.

CHILE

The republic of Chile extends along the Pacific coast of the Southern Cone of South America. Area: 756,626 sq km (292,135 sq mi), not including Chile's Antarctic claim. Pop. (1994 est.): 13,805,000. Cap.: Santiago (national); Valparaíso (legislative). Monetary unit: Chilean peso, with (Oct. 7, 1994) a free rate of 414.04 pesos to U.S. $1 (658.53 pesos = £1 sterling). Presidents in 1994, Patricio Aylwin Azócar and, from March 11, Eduardo Frei.

In the month prior to the inauguration of Pres. Eduardo Frei, the Chilean Congress in February 1994 reduced the presidential term of office from eight years to six. On taking office, Frei suggested further constitutional changes. In August he proposed to Congress the abolition of eight Senate seats appointed by the armed forces and the establishment of proportional representation. A third contentious issue, the president's inability to remove the chiefs of the armed forces, was not put before Congress. Frei hoped that this omission would help ensure his success in curtailing the disproportionate power of the right-wing opposition that had been written into the constitution by former president Augusto Pinochet.

The removal of military commanders, however, posed an immediate problem. In March Judge Milton Juica, who had sentenced three former police officers to life in prison for the 1985 murder of three communists, accused the police chief, Gen. Rodolfo Stange, of nonfulfillment of military duty. Following the accusation, Frei urged Stange to resign. Stange refused, and the impasse was not resolved until April, when Stange took leave until a military court decided if charges should be brought against him for covering up the 1985 murders.

Another erosion of the legacy of the Pinochet years was the appointment of four Socialists to the Cabinet, Germán Correa (Interior) and Ricardo Lagos (Public Works). While reflecting the Socialists' strong performance in the 1993 elections, it also eliminated the power of the military to veto the appointment of Socialists to senior public office.

The Frei administration announced reform of the public and private health care systems and the high priority of education, to be financed in part by privatization of government-owned enterprises. Roads, railroads, and ports were all earmarked for improvement, to keep pace with Chile's expanding exports.

On the trade front an agreement signed with the Southern Cone Common Market (Mercosur) was expected to lead to associate membership in the organization with Argentina, Brazil, Uruguay, and Paraguay. Discussions with the U.S. toward establishing a trade accord began in June, and in December Chile was invited to join the North American Free Trade Agreement. Prices for major exports in the first half of 1994 were better than expected, especially for copper, yielding a January–June trade surplus of $237 million, in contrast to a forecast annual deficit of $1 billion. Gross domestic product was predicted to grow 4–4.5%, compared with 6% in 1993 (according to the Chilean central bank), but it was feared that the government would not achieve its 11% target for inflation.

Early in the year it was revealed that the chief futures trader of Codelco, the state copper company, had lost the company more than $206 million in irregular transactions on the London Metal Exchange. The fiasco led to many resignations and major structural changes at the hands of a new Codelco president, Juan Villarzú. In May Codelco workers denounced as unconstitutional a bill that aimed to divide the company into autonomous units. Additional problems arose when Lac Minerals of Canada withdrew its share of a bid for a 51% stake in El Abra, a large, undeveloped copper deposit. Despite Codelco's difficulties, however, copper output from state and private mines surpassed two million metric tons in 1993. Together with new mines still to come into operation, Villarzú's modernization program aimed to increase production to more than three million metric tons by the year 2000. (BEN BOX)

CHINA

The People's Republic of China is situated in eastern Asia, with coastlines on the Yellow Sea and the East and South China seas. Area: 9,572,900 sq km (3,696,100 sq mi), including Tibet and excluding Taiwan. (See *Taiwan,* below.) Pop. (1994 est., excluding Taiwan): 1,192,300,000. Cap.: Beijing (Peking). Monetary unit: renminbi yuan, with (Oct. 7, 1994) an interbank rate of 8.53 yuan to U.S. $1 (13.57 yuan = £1 sterling). President in 1994, Jiang Zemin (Chiang Tse-min); premier, Li Peng (Li P'eng).

As contradictory political, economic, and social trends pulled China, a country of nearly 1.2 billion people, in opposite directions in 1994, it was difficult to discern a coherent pattern in the government's policies. At the beginning of the year, China's leaders proclaimed a period of comprehensive reforms, but these were nowhere in evidence at year's end apart from the introduction of a new tax system. Two conflicting images of China were unmistakable. The first was that of a rapidly developing economic powerhouse, playing an increasingly important international role and vigorously asserting its interests on the stage of Asian and world politics. The second was that of a country with decreasing internal cohesion, beset by intractable social and economic problems and indifferently governed by Communist Party veterans mainly interested in clinging to power. Ample evidence supported both of these images. China seemed to be a vessel adrift at high speed, its destination unknowable.

Domestic Affairs. This situation stemmed in part from the continuing deathwatch over senior leader Deng Xiaoping (Teng Hsiao-p'ing), which preoccupied the top leaders of the Communist Party of China (CPC), notably Pres. Jiang Zemin (Chiang Tse-min), Premier Li Peng (Li P'eng), and the chairman of the National People's Congress, Qiao Shi (Ch'iao Shih). (*See* BIOGRAPHIES.) Deng, who celebrated his 90th birthday on August 22, was reportedly suffering from Parkinson's disease and various other illnesses. He appeared in public just once, on television, at the Chinese New Year's reception in Shanghai.

In political as well as economic terms, Shanghai's star rose in 1994. Former mayor Jiang, chosen by Deng in 1989 as the core of China's new leadership, further strengthened his position as general secretary of the CPC, chairman of the Central Military Commission, and president. In September the fourth plenum of the 14th Central Committee elevated Shanghai Mayor Huang Ju (Huang Chü), a Jiang ally, to

Deng Nan (Teng Nan; left) supports her father, Deng Xiaoping (Teng Hsiao-p'ing), as another daughter, Deng Rong (Teng Jung), whispers in his ear. Because she served as the sole "interpreter" for the infirm Chinese leader, Deng Rong was in a position of enormous influence.

NEW CHINA PICTURES CO./CHINASTOCK

the Political Bureau of the CPC, and leading economic reformers Wu Bangguo (Wu Pang-kuo) and Jiang Chunyun (Chiang Ch'un-yün) to the Secretariat. Jiang continued to cultivate the military, promoting 19 generals in the course of the year. His greatest political asset, should he stumble badly, was that Deng was probably too feeble to dismiss him, as the senior leader had done to earlier designated successors Hu Yaobang (Hu Yao-pang) in 1987 and Zhao Ziyang (Chao Tzu-yang) in 1989.

Given its numerous problems, China could ill afford a post-Deng succession struggle. The collective leadership of Jiang, Li, and Qiao would probably work together, at least in the initial stage of the post-Deng period. Deng's generation was all but gone, and the reputation of the late Chairman Mao Zedong (Mao Tse-tung) was further tarnished with the publication in the West of *The Private Life of Chairman Mao.* These intimate memoirs by Mao's longtime personal physician, Li Zhisui (Li Chih-sui), portrayed the supposed exemplar of revolutionary virtue as a cruel and depraved monster, a despot who took pleasure in destroying his political adversaries, and a satyr with an insatiable appetite for young women. Estimates by respected scholars had suggested that as many as 60 million to 80 million Chinese may have died as a result of Mao's policies between 1949 and 1976. China's leaders, nonetheless, continued to honour Mao as a great patriot and national hero.

The results of the CPC's fourth plenum suggested disagreement within the leadership over how to tackle the nation's economic and social problems. The emphasis of the third plenum (November 1993) had been economic reform. The fourth plenum focused on ways to strengthen the influence of the CPC, which had been considerably attenuated by 15 years of capitalist-style reforms. "The Decision of the Central Committee of the Communist Party of China Concerning Some Major Issues on Strengthening Party Building" called for improving the system of "democratic centralism," choosing able and honest officials, and rebuilding the party's rural branches. Given the growing economic gap between urban and rural China, however, and the leadership's anxiety about the spectre of growing rural unrest, such a program was not difficult to understand. The party also sought to rekindle ideological fervour through a nationwide Program for Implementation of Education in Patriotism. In this connection Li Ruihuan (Li Jui-huan), fourth-ranking member of the Political Bureau Standing Committee, told an international conference on Confucianism that it was the duty of every Chinese to enhance the study of Confucianism. Having abandoned Karl Marx in all but name, the CPC sought moral salvation from the Chinese sage it had vilified not long before.

That Confucius was presented as an authoritarian taskmaster rather than the apostle of Chinese humanism was evident from the party's intolerance of political dissent. Even before international pressure eased on China, the government displayed a hard-edged attitude toward human rights and political opposition. The outspoken democratic activist Wei Jingsheng (Wei Ching-sheng), released in 1993 after serving nearly 15 years in prison, was rearrested in April 1994. U.S. Pres. Bill Clinton's decision in late May to delink U.S.-China trade from human rights considerations made China's democrats and dissenters vulnerable to intensified state repression. Among the many sentenced to labour camps were Yang Zhou (Yang Chou), spokesman for the Chinese Human Rights Association, and Shanghai democracy activists Bao Ge (Pao Ke) and Yang Qinheng (Yang Ch'in-heng). Journalists Xi Yang (Hsi Yang) and Gao Yu (Kao Yü) were among those imprisoned on spurious charges of publishing state secrets. Leaders of China's tiny Labour Alliance, an embryonic free-trade union, were arrested or forced underground, and 14 dissidents were tried in July, the largest number in a political trial since 1989. In December nine pro-democracy activists were jailed; three of the dissidents were sentenced to more than 15 years. Nonconforming religious leaders and worshipers were another target of state repression.

All these arrests were part of a systematic effort to implement the 1993 State Security Law, which, among other things, sought to sever ties between dissidents and their international supporters. Human Rights Watch/Asia, a human rights organization with excellent sources of information on China, reported that Chinese physicians were "harvesting" kidneys and other organs from condemned prisoners, sometimes under anesthesia before their actual execution, to use in organ transplants for high-ranking Chinese officials or for sale to foreigners; the going price for a kidney was $30,000. This report was confirmed by the on-site investigations of Harry Wu, a former prisoner in the Chinese gulag.

The Economy. CPC leaders, however, had reason to believe that their political sins would be overlooked by the outside world as long as the Chinese economy continued to grow and foreigners were given a piece of the action. In March, Li, fearing inflation and budgetary overruns, forecast a 9% gross domestic product (GDP) growth rate in 1994, down considerably from 1993's torrid 13.5%. This target proved too modest, however, because less than half of China's GDP was being produced by the state sector, and 9% growth was considered sluggish by booming coastal provinces such as Guangdong (Kuang-tung). In fact, the economy continued to expand at an 11.8% clip.

The most worrisome effect of high growth was an upwardly spiraling inflation rate. The consumer price index shot up 27.4% in the first three quarters of the year, with food responsible for about half the increase. (The average Chinese spent 50% of personal income on food.) Grain prices soared owing to sharp increases in the amount the state paid farmers for their grain, as well as disastrous floods, the imposition of a 17% value-added tax on goods, loose credit policies, the effects of price reforms in 1993, and excessive demand. Overall, increases in per capita income outpaced inflation, but the income gap between the urban nouveaux riches and the mass of ordinary workers and farmers continued to widen, with disturbing social consequences.

In the first half of 1994, crime soared 20% as new waves of rural migrants contributed to an accelerating breakdown of social order in the cities. Authorities cracked down on illegal firearms possession and struggled to control the activities of rapidly proliferating criminal gangs, many with international connections. In September the deadly rampage of a lone gunman in downtown Beijing (Peking) was a powerful symbol of growing lawlessness. Among the measures the authorities used to combat crime was the profligate application of the death penalty, making China responsible for more than 60% of the world's state-ordered executions. Officials estimated that there were 140 million "surplus labourers" in China—more than the entire population of Japan—a figure that could rise substantially as the shutdown of unprofitable state enterprises produced massive unemployment. During the first half of the year, 43% of state-run industries lost money. Any slowdown in urban and national infrastructure construction would further exacerbate a problem for which there appeared to be no solution other than long-term population control. The State Planning Commission and the Ministry of Foreign Trade and Economic Cooperation released a list of 210 major capital construction projects for the period 1993–2000. Concentrated in the fields of energy, transportation, and agriculture, they were intended to act as a magnet for foreign capital and facilitate the transformation of China into a modern industrial power.

The State Council announced a pilot program to provide one-time cash payments to workers who lost their jobs as a result of plant closings, but the absence of a comprehensive state system of social security, including unemployment insurance, caused government leaders to shy away from radical solutions to the problem. Yet pressure from insolvent enterprises for additional government subsidies made it difficult, if not impossible, to maintain the tight-credit policy needed to control inflation. The money supply grew by 37% in the first three quarters, rather than the planned 25% increase. China's foreign trade approached $234 billion in 1994, with exports up 30% to $120 billion and imports up 10% to $114 billion. The projected $6 billion surplus reversed the previous year's deficit. China's foreign-exchange reserves, bolstered by $22.7 billion from foreign direct investment in the first three quarters of the year, increased to $43.7 billion, more than double the level of a year earlier. Beijing's efforts to reenter the General Agreement on Tariffs and Trade (GATT) and become a founding member of the World Trade Organization (which was to replace GATT on Jan. 1, 1995) were blocked by the U.S. and European countries because of China's reluctance to fully open its domestic market to international competition. The U.S., irritated by China's slow crackdown on the rampant piracy of U.S. computer software and compact discs, temporarily suspended trade talks in December. At the beginning of the year, China abolished its dual currency system by withdrawing Foreign Exchange Certificates from circulation and moving toward a freely convertible yuan.

China was the largest borrower from the World Bank in 1994, with over $3 billion in loans. These included $925 million in soft loans from the International Development Association. In Hubei (Hu-pei) province ground was broken on Li's controversial pet project, the gargantuan Three Gorges Dam, scheduled for completion in the year 2009 at an official cost of $11.2 billion. It was designed to generate 84 billion kw-hr of electricity annually and to control flooding. China also unveiled plans for a huge North-South Water Diversion Project, which included a shift of water from the upper Chang Jiang (Yangtze River) to China's arid northwestern provinces. The World Bank and other international lenders shied away from such mammoth projects, however, because of doubts about their feasibility, efficacy, and human costs. Despite prevailing optimism about China's economic future, the difficulties many foreign companies faced in collecting hundreds of millions of dollars in loans that had been guaranteed by the government raised significant questions in the international business community about China's creditworthiness.

Nevertheless, numerous foreign companies vied for the privilege of coproducing with the Chinese automobile industry a "people's car" that would be within the financial reach of tens of millions of Chinese. The environmental impact of the "automobilization" of China would certainly be substantial.

Foreign Affairs. The question of whether the United States would extend China's most-favoured-nation (MFN) status, providing China normal access to the vital U.S. market, dominated the first half of the year. In May 1993 Clinton had threatened to withdraw China's MFN status if it failed to make substantial progress in the area of human rights. Gambling that pressure from U.S. business interests would force Clinton to back down, Chinese leaders called his bluff and won.

Continuing a policy initiated in September 1993, Clinton sent a stream of top officials to Beijing, including Secretary of State Warren Christopher, Secretary of Commerce Ron Brown, and Secretary of Defense William Perry. Christopher, preaching human rights prior to Clinton's MFN decision, was rebuffed. Brown and Perry, pursuing contracts and contacts after the MFN decision, were warmly greeted. However, Chinese leaders, angered that Washington had broken the long-standing taboo on direct contact between high-ranking U.S. and Taiwan officials, deferred a late-year trip by Secretary of Transportation Federico Peña, who had earlier visited Taipei. Clinton and Jiang met again at the Asia-Pacific Economic Cooperation summit in Bogor, Indon. Jiang outlined several principles for good U.S.-China relations, which Clinton endorsed. The Chinese angled for a prestigious presidential visit, but it seemed unlikely that Clinton, down on his political fortunes, would risk such a trip. In January the U.S. and China narrowly averted a confrontation over trade with an 11th-hour agreement on textile imports. In October China pledged once more to abide by the Missile Technology Control Regime and banned the sale or transfer of certain surface-to-surface missiles. In exchange the U.S. lifted sanctions that prohibited the export of certain U.S. high-technology satellites to China. Beijing supported Washington's efforts to settle the North Korean nuclear issue through peaceful means and endorsed the accord that obliged North Korea to abandon its nuclear program in return for modern nuclear power technology and financial incentives. Despite these efforts, an undercurrent of mutual suspicion continued to pervade official Chinese-U.S. relations, particularly after the U.S. announced in September that it would seek to upgrade official ties with Taiwan.

China's version of dollar diplomacy, successful vis-à-vis the U.S., worked elsewhere as well. Canadian Prime Minister Jean Chrétien visited China in November and returned with $6.6 billion in trade deals. The prime ministers of France, Japan, Australia, and Israel were among the many other influential figures who visited China.

Jiang and Li were active on the diplomatic front. Jiang visited Russia, Ukraine, and France in September. In Moscow he and Russian Pres. Boris Yeltsin signed military cooperation agreements. In Paris he dispensed $2.5 billion in commercial largesse, exacting in return a French pledge to engage in no further arms sales to Taiwan. In November Jiang visited Vietnam, Singapore, Indonesia, and Malaysia. In Hanoi he signed an agreement pledging peaceful negotiations with Vietnam over territorial issues and abstention from the threat or use of force.

Li ventured into Central Asia in April, visiting Turkmenistan, Kyrgyzstan, Mongolia, and Kazakhstan, where he signed a border-delimitation agreement with Pres. Nursultan Nazarbayev. In July Li visited Austria, Germany, and Romania. In Germany, China's largest European trading partner, he encountered hostile demonstrations because of his role

Unemployed men from the countryside congregate in front of a train station in Beijing (Peking). Growing unemployment was becoming one of the major problems faced by the Chinese government as it continued to develop a market economy.
JEFFREY AARONSON—NETWORK ASPEN

in the 1989 Tiananmen (T'ien-an-men) Square massacre. Chinese-South Korean relations, grounded in economic and security concerns, were bolstered by an exchange of visits between Li and Pres. Kim Young Sam. The death of long-time North Korean president Kim Il Sung in July deprived China of an irritating friend and elevated his enigmatic son Kim Jong Il to power. Because China sought stability in the Korean peninsula, it opposed North Korea's acquisition of nuclear weapons. (*See* SPOTLIGHT: *East Asia and the Transition in North Korea.*)

Brushing aside international criticism, China conducted two more nuclear tests in 1994 and announced it would continue testing until a comprehensive nuclear test ban treaty came into effect, possibly in 1996. Analysts believed the tests were designed to perfect China's submarine-launched ballistic missiles. Amphibious landing exercises by China's military and close-in naval patrols off the Taiwan coast raised anxieties in Taipei. Chinese media, however, argued that the country's low military expenditures disproved alarmist claims that China posed a military threat to its neighbours.

As the year drew to a close, the Chinese people, or at least many of those living in the booming coastal provinces, were more prosperous than before. Serious questions remained, however, as to whether the current leadership would be able to reawaken in the Chinese people concern for society as a whole and lessen their preoccupation with the individual and family moneymaking, which was dominating the last days of the Deng era.   (STEVEN I. LEVINE)

SPOTLIGHT: East Asia and the Transition in North Korea by Donald Morrison

The kingdom of Koguryo, the 7th-century equivalent of North Korea, had a distinctive way of dealing with outside enemies: avoid direct confrontation and maintain a formidable military capability inside fortified cities, including Pyongyang, the capital. For much of the post-World War II era, modern-day North Korea pursued a similar strategy. Contact with the outside world was severely limited; the armed forces were built up aggressively; and the nation was guided by the firm hand of a single leader, Kim Il Sung, whose guiding principle had been *juche* ("self-reliance"). One manifestation of that strategy was North Korea's energy program. To lessen dependence on foreign oil, the country launched a program to build two nuclear power plants—and, its neighbours feared, an unknown number of nuclear weapons. When North Korea in 1994 refused to allow international inspection of its atomic facilities, global tensions soared, and the worst suspicions about Kim's nuclear intentions seemed to be confirmed.

In the space of a few weeks, however, the course of North Korean history took an abrupt turn. First, the country began direct talks with the United States over the future of its nuclear program. Then Kim Il Sung died on July 8 at age 82, reportedly of a heart attack. After a long mourning period it appeared that his son, Kim Jong Il, would become North Korea's new leader. Finally, North Korea concluded a sweeping agreement with the U.S. to suspend its nuclear program in exchange for international energy assistance, diplomatic relations, and commercial ties. Under the deal an international consortium including the U.S., South Korea, and Japan would contribute $4 billion to build two light-water nuclear reactors for North Korea. Compared with the gas-graphite models they would replace, the new reactors would be safer and produce less plutonium, a key material in nuclear bombs. The consortium would also provide North Korea with 500,000 tons of heavy oil a year, or roughly the amount received from the Soviet Union before its breakup.

This international agreement predictably drew criticism for its vagueness and its reliance on North Korean goodwill. Nonetheless, the deal offered the distinct possibility that after four decades of isolation, North Korea might join the world community. Clearly, the country needed foreign investment to rebuild its crumbling roads, bridges, and other elements of infrastructure and to shore up an economy that had been shrinking by 5% a year. A more prosperous, less dangerous North Korea was an especially welcome prospect for the country's closest neighbours: South Korea, China, Russia, and Japan.

South Korea had perhaps the most to gain if North Korea were now to change its stripes. Since the end of the Korean War in 1953, the two countries had remained intensely hostile as they faced each other across the Demilitarized Zone, which separated them. Both sides maintained relatively large defense establishments; the North Korean military, with one million men under arms, was considered very much the equal of the less numerous but better equipped South Korean force. (In addition, the U.S. maintained 37,000 troops in the South.) To combat what it saw as North Korean subversion, authorities in South Korea had for years outlawed virtually all contact with the North and maintained tight controls over free expression and political activity. Although the South had become more democratic in recent years, any hint of ties with, or sympathy for, North Korea was still prohibited. After the nuclear deal with the U.S. was signed, the South Korean government of Pres. Kim Young Sam did its part to ease tensions by announcing that businessmen could make limited investments in the North,

thus ending a ban that had been in effect since the Korean War. Although Pyongyang immediately rejected the notion of South Korean investments, analysts expected that they would eventually be welcomed. Outside investment was in fact desperately needed, and the North had already been negotiating deals with a number of South Korean firms.

For China, North Korea's agreement with the U.S. solved a delicate problem. Beijing (Peking), which had remained Pyongyang's only major ally, found itself torn between loyalty to an eccentric friend and the need to increase trade with that friend's sworn enemies, the U.S. and South Korea. Only weeks after the accord with the U.S. was signed, Beijing felt free to initial its own agreement with Seoul for the construction of nuclear reactors in China.

For Russia, which shares a relatively short border with North Korea, the nuclear agreement was expected to have little immediate effect on a touchy issue: the occasional defections of North Korean workers from logging camps run by North Korea in Siberia. In the long run, though, it was expected that fewer North Koreans would want to flee their country if it became more prosperous and opened its doors to the outside world.

Japan remained wary of North Korea despite the evident lessening of nuclear tensions in the region. Tokyo did not follow the U.S. in moving to establish diplomatic relations with Pyongyang. One continuing problem was the presence of more than 100,000 North Koreans living in Japan. Many of them remained loyal to Kim Il Sung and sent considerable sums of money to their homeland. Japan presumed that many were involved in espionage and did not expect the situation to change as a result of the nuclear agreement. In addition, some Japanese officials said that they had learned a lesson from the international crisis that had preceded the nuclear agreement. Until then, Japan had relied heavily on U.S. intelligence about the region. But during the negotiations, they said, the U.S. had withheld key information from Japan, prompting the Japanese to begin developing their own intelligence capability.

The country with perhaps the biggest stake in fostering good relations between North Korea and other nations lay nearly half a world away. The U.S. had put its prestige on the line by signing an accord with a country that lacked experience in global diplomacy and was led by a man who came into power with virtually no experience. Kim Jong Il had been known to the outside world chiefly for his bouffant hairdo, elevator shoes, vast video collection, and taste for fine cognac. Some Westerners who had met him, however, reported that he was serious and intelligent. In any case, he had for years remained in the shadow of his father, who dominated the country and had attained cult status among its people. The younger Kim was unlikely to assume that mantle in the foreseeable future. Indeed, he was slow to take on all of his late father's titles and positions, and some analysts wondered whether his authority would be challenged by a rival family member or someone in the military. As the year drew to a close, however, Kim Jong Il appeared to have no serious challengers—and to be at least nominally in control of his country's destiny as it took steps to become part of a wider world that his father had barely known.

Donald Morrison, who has been at *Time* magazine since 1968, is currently the editor of the Asian edition of *Time International*. He was the coauthor and editor of *Mikhail S. Gorbachev* (1988), *Massacre in Beijing* (1989), and *The Winning of the White House, 1988* (1988).

COLOMBIA

A republic in northwestern South America, Colombia has coastlines on the Caribbean Sea and the Pacific Ocean. Area: 1,141,748 sq km (440,831 sq mi). Pop. (1994 est.): 34,520,000. Cap.: Santafé de Bogotá, D.C. Monetary unit: Colombian peso, with (Oct. 7, 1994) a free rate of 837 pesos to U.S. $1 (1,331 pesos = £1 sterling). Presidents in 1994, César Gaviria Trujillo and, from August 7, Ernesto Samper Pizano.

Colombians in 1994 voted for a continuation of Liberal Party government. In March the Liberals won a slightly reduced majority in the national legislature, and in June, after two rounds of voting, the Liberal candidate, Ernesto Samper Pizano, defeated the Social Conservative Party's Andrés Pastrana Arango for the presidency by a narrow margin. The Liberals owed their success in part to the popularity of outgoing Pres. César Gaviria Trujillo, who had presided over strong economic growth and some reduction in drug-related activity. In their campaigning the new president and the Liberal candidates for the legislature vowed to emphasize the alleviation of social problems, notably the gap between rich and poor.

The presidential election was briefly eclipsed by Colombia's participation in the soccer World Cup. The team's rapid exit from the competition was contrary to expectations, and the anger it engendered led to the murder, on his return to Medellín, of defender Andrés Escobar, who inadvertently scored in his own goal in Colombia's surprising loss to the U.S. The incident underlined the continuing problem of urban and rural violence. Before the elections, among several actions mainly by left-wing guerrillas, a National Liberation Army bomb almost killed Finance Minister Rudolf Hommes. In August the only senator of the left-wing Patriotic Union, Manuel Cepeda, was assassinated. Samper had hoped that through Cepeda dialogue could be renewed with the still-active left-wing guerrilla group, the Revolutionary Armed Forces of Colombia. Despite the surrender of a Marxist guerrilla group in April, neither the outgoing government's policies nor the new administration's proposals suggested an early end to violence. Consequently, those insurgents who were tempted to lay down arms could not be guaranteed immunity from assassination afterward by opponents.

Colombia's image abroad continued to be affected by both violence and narcotics. In May the Department of Administrative Security threatened to sue Amnesty International over a report that stated that the army and government disregarded human rights by endorsing the murder of political opponents. The accusations were strenuously denied.

Also in May the Supreme Court decriminalized the personal use of small amounts of drugs on the grounds that it was unconstitutional to limit personal freedom of choice. The ruling was condemned by President Gaviria, both presidential candidates, the police, and other authorities. During the recriminations after Samper's victory, both he and Pastrana were accused of accepting drug money to fund their campaigns, but in August the prosecutor-general found no proof of this. The allegation that the Cali drug cartel offered $3.6 million toward Samper's campaign prompted the rival Medellín cartel to threaten with death all prominent people rumoured to be supported by Cali. This gave the lie to the idea that the Medellín cartel had disbanded after the death of its leader, Pablo Escobar, in December 1993. On November 1 the government announced that it would modify the constitution to make drug consumption illegal. The government had planned to hold a nationwide referendum on the issue but, according to Vice Pres. Humberto de la

Thousands of Colombians accompany the funeral procession of association football (soccer) star Andrés Escobar, who was murdered in Medellín in July. Escobar had angered fans when in a World Cup match he accidentally deflected the ball into his own goal.
GUZMAN/PUNTOS DE VISTA—SIPA

Calle, it was decided that to do so would be too costly and might be seen as contemptuous of the court's ruling.

Gross domestic product was forecast to rise by about 5% in 1994 (a little less than in 1993), fueled in part by the repatriation of drug profits but also by domestic investment, healthy construction and services sectors, and high consumer spending. The economy also benefited from Colombia's ability to replace international shortages in coffee and sugar following weather damage to the crops of Brazil and Cuba, respectively. Coffee exports were also expected to reduce the trade deficit, expanding since 1993 because of a combination of soaring imports, declines in most traditional exports, and an overvalued peso.　　　　　(BEN BOX)

COMOROS

The Islamic republic of the Comoros is an island state in the Indian Ocean off the east coast of Africa. Area: 1,862 sq km (719 sq mi), excluding the island of Mayotte, which continued to be a de facto dependency of France. Pop. (1994 est.; excluding Mayotte): 527,000. Cap.: Moroni. Monetary unit: Comorian franc, with (from Jan. 12, 1994) a par value of CF 75 to the French franc and (as of Oct. 7, 1994) a free rate of CF 395.82 to U.S. $1 (CF 629.56 = £1 sterling). President in 1994, Said Mohamed Djohar; prime ministers, Mohamed Abdou Madi and, from October 14, Halifa Houmadi.

The early part of 1994 was dominated by political maneuvers as a consequence of the December 1993 legislative elections. These, in two rounds on December 12 and 20, had given Pres. Said Mohamed Djohar a clear victory, with his newly formed Rassemblement pour la Démocratie et le Renouveau (RDR) party taking 24 out of 42 seats while 18 went to opposition groups. Some violence and irregularities marred the second round; three people were killed on Anjouan Island, and voting was canceled (to be rerun) in seven constituencies.

On January 2 President Djohar appointed Mohamed Abdou Madi prime minister. Madi then named a Cabinet of 12. The opposition rejected the appointment of Madi and also continued to contest the validity of the elections. The later (January 7) appointment of Mohamed Said Abdallah

M'Changama (the president's son-in-law) as president of the National Assembly was also condemned by the opposition. On January 17 the 12 main opposition parties adopted a resolution denouncing the "brutal interruption of the transition to democracy" and called for Djohar's resignation. They agreed to form a Forum for National Recovery, and Abbas Djoussouf of the Popular Democratic Movement was elected its spokesman. M'Changama, viewed as the real power in the country, and Madi had a falling-out in October; another new government was named, and Madi was replaced as prime minister by Halifa Houmadi.

In March the International Monetary Fund provided a credit of SDR 1,350,000 (about $1.9 million) for a 12-month program to seek 0.7% growth while keeping inflation down to 15%. This was a consequence of the devaluation in January of the Comorian franc.   (GUY ARNOLD)

This article updates the *Micropædia* article COMOROS.

CONGO

A republic, Congo is in central Africa on the Atlantic Ocean. Area: 342,000 sq km (132,047 sq mi). Pop. (1994 est.): 2,856,000. Cap.: Brazzaville. Monetary unit: CFA franc, with (Oct. 7, 1994) a par value of CFAF 100 to the French franc and a free rate of CFAF 526.67 to U.S. $1 (CFAF 837.67 = £1 sterling). President in 1994, Pascal Lissouba; prime minister, Jacques Yhombi-Opango.

Clashes between supporters of the government and those opposed to it rocked Congo in 1994. Arising out of the opposition's challenge to the validity of the results of the 1993 legislative elections, the dispute escalated into armed confrontations. On January 14 soldiers in Brazzaville used artillery to counter machine-gun attacks by opposition militia. By the month's end more than 100 people had been reported killed in numerous encounters. In an attempt to control the situation, the army cordoned off two districts in the capital that were strongholds of Bernard Kolelas, the main opposition leader. A January 30 cease-fire agreement broke down.

In February an international arbitration committee that had earlier rejected opposition appeals to annul the election did invalidate the results of the contests for nine seats. Disorders, including the cutting of the main railway line, continued until mid-March, when the legislature signed a new cease-fire agreement. Although sporadic skirmishing occurred after the cease-fire, the election of Kolelas as mayor of Brazzaville on July 16 was taken as a peace gesture. On August 6 a national reconciliation ceremony was held in Brazzaville.

In February the government accepted International Monetary Fund terms for a resumption of structural adjustment aid, suspended in 1990 for nonpayment. The civil service was to be reduced by 9%. U.S., Italian, and British oil companies, eager to exploit Congo's reserves, agreed to increase royalties paid to Congo from 17% to 31% of profits, thereby pressuring the dominant French firm, Elf Oil, to offer the same terms.   (NANCY ELLEN LAWLER)

This article updates the *Macropædia* article CENTRAL AFRICA: *Congo*.

COSTA RICA

The Central American republic of Costa Rica has coastlines on the Caribbean Sea and the Pacific Ocean. Area: 51,100 sq km (19,730 sq mi). Pop. (1994 est.): 3,268,000. Cap.: San José. Monetary unit: Costa Rican colón, with (Oct. 7, 1994) a free rate of 159.70 colones to U.S. $1 (254.00 colones = £1 sterling). Presidents in 1994, Rafael Angel Calderón Fournier and, from May 8, José María Figueres Olsen.

José María Figueres Olsen of the National Liberation Party was elected president of Costa Rica on Feb. 6, 1994, with 49.6% of the vote against 47.5% for his rival, Miguel Angel Rodríguez of the ruling Social Christian Unity Party. The closely fought campaign contained little difference in the candidates' ideologies or platforms but was notable for the bitterness between the two camps. Figueres, 39, is the son of José ("Pepé") Figueres Ferrer, who founded the modern Costa Rican state and served three terms as president. The new president faced the challenge of maintaining the welfare state while continuing economic growth.

On August 1 the new administration presented its economic program, which differed only slightly from that of its predecessor. It aimed to keep inflation low, falling from 17% to a little over 14% by the end of 1994. The fiscal deficit was to be cut from 4.3% of gross domestic product (GDP) to 2.8% with the aid of a tax reform. Exports were to be promoted, and import growth was to be limited to 6%; as a result, the trade deficit was projected to fall to 4.9% of GDP in 1994 and to 3.2% in 1995. It was hoped that the economic goals contained in the plan would be adequate to release $250 million in structural adjustment loans from the Inter-American Development Bank and the World Bank.

After three years of negotiations, Mexico and Costa Rica reached a bilateral free-trade agreement, due to come into effect on Jan. 1, 1995. More than 8,300 products were to be traded tariff-free immediately, with others to be introduced over 10 years.   (SARAH CAMERON)

This article updates the *Macropædia* article CENTRAL AMERICA: *Costa Rica*.

CÔTE D'IVOIRE

A republic of West Africa, Côte d'Ivoire lies on the Gulf of Guinea. Area: 322,463 sq km (124,504 sq mi). Pop. (1994 est.): 13,845,000. Cap.: Abidjan; capital designate, Yamoussoukro. Monetary unit: CFA franc, with (Oct. 7, 1994) a par value of CFAF 100 to the French franc and a free rate of CFAF 526.67 to U.S. $1 (CFAF 837.67 = £1 sterling). President in 1994, Henri Konan Bédié; prime minister, Daniel Kablan Duncan.

The funeral of Félix Houphouët-Boigny, the first president of Côte d'Ivoire, took place on Feb. 7, 1994, in Yamoussoukro. In attendance were the presidents of France and Lebanon, 20 heads of African nations, and numerous high-level delegations from around the world.

Henri Konan Bédié, who as president of the National Assembly had succeeded Houphouët-Boigny, consolidated his hold on the ruling Democratic Party of Côte d'Ivoire (PDCI). Opposition parties charged that the extended period of mourning for Houphouët-Boigny (he did Dec. 7, 1993) had provided Bédié with an unfair political advantage. Former prime minister Alassane Ouattara returned from France and mounted an unsuccessful bid for the leadership of the PDCI. Bédié's election to that office in April was unanimous, and his popularity throughout the country made him a favourite for the 1995 presidential elections.

The government was able to resist widespread demands from the labour unions for relief from the effects of the 100% devaluation of the CFA franc in January. In what was interpreted as a reward for accepting devaluation, half the $10 billion debt owed to the Paris Club of creditor nations was canceled. Nevertheless, Côte d'Ivoire remained, on a per capita basis, the world's most indebted nation. Although prices rose sharply immediately after devaluation, Prime Minister Daniel Kablan Duncan announced in June that the nation's export economy was growing and the inflation rate moderating. Benefiting from its improved position in world markets, the government announced in September

The body of Félix Houphouët-Boigny is removed from the basilica in Yamoussoukro after funeral services on February 7, two months after his death. The founding president of Côte d'Ivoire, he was often credited with making his country one of the most stable in Africa.

PATRICK ROBERT—SYGMA

that prices paid to coffee and cocoa producers would be increased by 93% and 31%, respectively.

(NANCY ELLEN LAWLER)

This article updates the *Macropædia* article WESTERN AFRICA: *Côte d'Ivoire*.

CROATIA

A republic of the northwestern Balkans, Croatia is an elongated crescent-shaped country to the north, west, and southwest of Bosnia and Herzegovina. Its extensive Adriatic coastal region on the southwest includes nearly 1,200 islands and islets. Area: 56,538 sq km (21,829 sq mi). Pop. (1994 est.) 4,788,000. Cap.: Zagreb. Monetary unit: Kuna (introduced May 30) with (Oct. 7, 1994) a free rate of 5.68 kune to U.S. $1 (9.04 kune = £1 sterling). President in 1994, Franjo Tudjman; prime minister, Nikica Valentic.

In 1994 Croatia achieved an improvement in its international position as well as a measure of stability in its economy. Pope John Paul II's visit to Croatia on September 10–11 raised the country's international profile. It was under strong prompting from the Vatican and the United States that Croatia had agreed at the beginning of the year to underwrite the Croat-Muslim agreement signed in Washington, D.C., on March 1 that ended the fighting between the local Croats and the Muslims in Bosnia and Herzegovina and established a Croat-Muslim federation there.

In November Croatia and the United States signed a military-cooperation agreement. The U.S. also played a part in brokering a cease-fire on March 30 that ended several days' fighting between the Croat forces and those of a Serb-occupied region south of Zagreb. Lengthy talks between the rebel Serbs and the Zagreb government, sponsored by the U.S., Russia, and the European Union, led to an agreement on November 21 providing for the reopening of the Zagreb-Belgrade highway and the Adria pipeline and for the supply of water and electricity to Serbs in rebel-held territory. The attack by Croatian Serbs on Bihac in northwestern Bosnia and its spirited defense by Bosnian government troops caused new Croat-Serb tensions. The Croats responded by sending regular army units to help the Bosnian government forces in northwestern Bosnia. Relations with the government of rump Yugoslavia had been upgraded by the setting up of diplomatic missions in the spring, but full Croatian-Yugoslav mutual diplomatic recognition failed to materialize.

Opposition to Pres. Franjo Tudjman's authoritarian style and his Bosnia policy before the Washington agreement led to a split in the ruling Croatian Democratic Union and the creation of a moderate Independent Democrat Party led by Stipe Mesic and Josip Manolic, the respective chairmen of the lower and upper houses of the Croatian parliament. Subsequent protests against abuse of parliamentary procedure by the opposition parties led to a walkout lasting several months.

A visit to Zagreb by the German foreign minister, Klaus Kinkel, in October paved the way for the inclusion of Croatia in the European Union's technical and scientific aid program known as PHARE. In the wake of joint visits by Prime Minister Nikica Valentic and his Bosnian counterpart, Haris Silajdzic, to Malaysia, Pakistan, and Iran, Croatia obtained a $220 million order from Iran in October to build eight 22,000-ton ships in three years.

The Valentic government's economic-stabilization program, which had begun in 1993, remained on course. Croatia reported zero inflation in 1994. The Croatian national bank's gold and foreign-exchange reserves stood at $1,370,000 in November 1994. The number of foreign tourists increased by 55% in the first nine months of 1994 compared with the same period in 1993, but progress toward privatization continued to be slow. Industrial production fell by 9% in the first half of 1994, and the population's purchasing power dropped by 25% in that period. The unemployment rate stood at 20% during the year, which precipitated a steady increase in emigration by university graduates and skilled workers. In the first nine months of 1994, over 70,000 blue-collar workers emigrated to the West. The new currency, the kuna (initially valued at about $0.17), was introduced on May 30 amid some protests because this had been the name of Croatia's currency under the fascist Ustashi government in 1941–45.

(K.F. CVIIC)

This article updates the *Macropædia* article BALKAN STATES: *Croatia*.

CUBA

The socialist republic of Cuba comprises the island of Cuba and more than 1,600 smaller islands and cays in the Caribbean Sea. Area: 110,861 sq km (42,804 sq mi). Pop. (1994 est.): 10,994,000. Cap.: Havana. Monetary unit: Cuban peso, with (Oct. 7, 1994) an official rate of 1 peso to U.S. $1 (1.59 pesos = £1 sterling). President of the Councils of State and Ministers in 1994, Fidel Castro Ruz.

Emigration was a dominant issue in Cuba in 1994, as the dire state of the nation's economy persuaded many Cubans to seek their fortunes in the U.S. According to the 1984 immigration agreement, the U.S. could grant up to 20,000 immigrant visas per year; however, only 1,600 were issued in 1993, causing considerable resentment and frustration. Tempted by the Cuban Adjustment Law of 1966, which entitled Cubans to legal residence in the U.S. a year after arrival there, thousands of Cubans risked their lives in crossing the Straits of Florida on homemade craft. In 1993, 3,656 people reached Florida on rafts and other small vessels, compared with 2,557 in 1992 and 467 in 1990. It was thought that about half of all those who attempted the crossing perished at sea. In 1994 many more thousands attempted to leave, and crisis proportions were reached in August. Early in the month rioting broke out in Havana after the police prevented a ferry loaded with would-be emigrants from leaving the harbour.

Pres. Fidel Castro (*see* BIOGRAPHIES) declared on August 7 that if the U.S. did not take "quick and efficient measures to halt the promotion of illegal departures," the Cuban coast guard would be instructed not to prevent people from leaving. This unleashed a flotilla of small craft, which U.S. Pres. Bill Clinton sought to stem by announcing on August 19 that Cubans arriving in Florida would no longer be given automatic refugee status. By the next week, however, the U.S. Coast Guard was rescuing between 2,000 and 3,000 people each day in the Straits of Florida, depending on the weather.

Clinton banned remittances from the U.S. to Cuba, cut the number of charter flights from the U.S. to Cuba, and increased U.S. propaganda radio broadcasts. Cuban refugees were no longer allowed to stay in the U.S. but were returned to the U.S. naval base on Cuba at Guantánamo Bay, where a camp for 40,000 was made ready. In September, after a week of meetings, the U.S. and Cuba reached agreement to halt the flow of refugees. The U.S. agreed to admit at least 20,000 Cubans in 1994, in line with the existing quota, and could grant an additional 6,000 visas to Cubans already on the waiting list. In return, Cuba promised to restore patrols to prevent people from leaving the island by boat.

On March 17 the U.S. House of Representatives heard a bill for free trade with Cuba that was designed to end the 33-year-old embargo. The sponsor, Rep. Charles Rangel, argued that it made no sense to deal with China and Vietnam but not trade with Cuba. Various Cuban-American groups and U.S. business interests stepped up their efforts to ease travel restrictions and improve telephone service between Cuba and the U.S.

Neighbouring countries also called for the U.S. to relax its stance. At the 24th General Assembly of the Organization of American States (OAS) in Brazil, the foreign ministers of most OAS members called for the end of the U.S. embargo and the readmission of Cuba to the OAS. The presidents of the Rio Group of 11 Latin-American and Caribbean countries called in September for a peaceful transition to democracy in Cuba and the lifting of the U.S. embargo but did not directly link the two.

Investors from countries other than the U.S. showed interest in Cuba during the year. Tourism was buoyant, and Cuba was admitted to the Caribbean Hotel Association in January. French investors agreed to build a new hotel and renovate three others, while the German hotel subsidiary of the charter airline LTU took over the management of its fourth hotel on the island. In Cuba's first large-scale privatization since 1959, a Mexican investment group, Domos Internacional, announced plans to invest $1.4 billion in renovating Cuba's telephone system with a 49% purchase of the state telecommunications enterprise, ETEC.

The government introduced some reforms to modernize the administration and curb the rising budget deficit, estimated at 4.8 billion pesos, or one-third of total expenditure. Several committees and commissions were abolished, and six new economic ministries replaced them. The reorganization was aimed at superseding the cumbersome command economy with a more accountable and dynamic system of economic management. Steep price increases on a wide range of goods and services were announced, aimed at cutting the fiscal deficit and reducing money in circulation.

(SARAH CAMERON)

This article updates the *Macropædia* article The WEST INDIES: *Cuba*.

CYPRUS

An island republic and member of the Commonwealth, Cyprus is in the eastern Mediterranean Sea. Island area: 9,251 sq km (3,572 sq mi). Island pop. (1994 est.): 769,000. Area of the Turkish Republic of Northern Cyprus (TRNC), proclaimed unilaterally (1983) in the occupied northern third of the island (controlled by Turkish Cypriots since 1974): 3,355 sq km (1,295 sq mi); pop. (1994 est.): 155,000. Cap.: Nicosia. Monetary unit: Cyprus pound, with (Oct. 7, 1994) a free rate of £C 0.47 to U.S. $1 (£C 0.75 = £1 sterling). President in 1994, Glafcos Clerides. President of TRNC in 1994, Rauf Denktash.

In Cyprus 1994 was the 20th year of partition and the 30th year of UN peacekeeping. To some extent, the two uncelebrated anniversaries indicated the island's situation, for the tragic division into Greek and Turkish sectors separated by a UN buffer zone had become part of Cypriot life. The status of the British Sovereign Base Areas, dating from the independence of Cyprus in 1960, was challenged in Cypriot

Using a homemade raft, Cubans set sail bound for the United States. The governments of the two countries agreed in September that Cuba would curtail illegal emigration and that in return the U.S. would admit additional numbers of legal immigrants.

courts, but the legitimacy of British rule in the bases was upheld.

The year began optimistically, particularly since both Cypriot states had undergone significant political changes. A coalition government under the longtime president, Rauf Denktash, was installed in Turkish Cyprus in December 1993, while Glafcos Clerides had taken over the presidency of Greek Cyprus some six months previously. UN Secretary-General Boutros Boutros-Ghali continued to press for modest confidence-building accords, including a jointly run airport in Nicosia and the return of the border resort town of Varosha to the Greek Cypriots. Informal steps included a darts tournament between the island's communities, virtually the first personal contact between the two since partition. Intercommunal talks broke down, however. In June Boutros-Ghali blamed the Turkish Cypriots for the failure and proposed sanctions. The following month the European Court of Justice ordered an embargo on Turkish Cypriot exports, which consisted mostly of fruits and clothing shipped to Britain. Despite this setback, the situation generally remained nonviolent.

Greek Cyprus continued as a tourist mecca and a regional news-media listening post, and the number of offshore corporations increased. For example, Cyprus was home to some 2,000 Russian companies, with a reported billion dollars per month being transferred from Russia to Cypriot banks. The economy on the Turkish side of the line was troubled but was assisted somewhat by financial aid from Turkey. The export embargo threatened to hurt the small state and led to disorders and the closure of the one border crossing between the two parts of the island. (GEORGE H. KELLING)

CZECH REPUBLIC

The Czech Republic is a landlocked state of central Europe. Area: 78,864 sq km (30,450 sq mi). Pop. (1994 est.): 10,345,000. Cap.: Prague. Monetary unit: koruna, with (Oct. 7, 1994) a free rate of 27.80 koruny to U.S. $1 (44.22 koruny = £1 sterling). President in 1994, Vaclav Havel; prime minister, Vaclav Klaus.

By 1994 the Czech Republic's political system had settled down and appeared to be solidly based. The prime minister, Vaclav Klaus, commanded a clear majority in the legislature, and his popularity in the country was unchallenged. The opposition appeared cowed and proved rather ineffectual. The most important alternative voice was that of the country's president, Vaclav Havel, who continued to maintain that Czech politics had to include a moral component and that the country's democratic system had to be infused with the ethical values of individual responsibility. In terms of hard politics, however, Havel was not particularly influential, though he did enjoy considerable respect.

The system that Klaus built, for it was very much his system, consisted of his own dominance, which was highly personal, and a set of policies that looked contradictory at first sight but in reality appeared to be working well. The essence of this policy was that the privatization of large areas of the economy would go ahead except when it might bring into question the existence of outdated and inefficient industries.

In other postcommunist countries this formula had failed, but the Czech Republic possessed three assets on which Klaus's strategy was ultimately founded. First, there was the country's geographic proximity to Western Europe. This gave the Czech Republic a significant advantage over other Eastern European nations with a similar level of development. Second, unlike virtually all other postcommunist states, the Czech Republic had a low level of foreign indebtedness. It had avoided taking on foreign loans in the 1980s

and was reaping the benefits in the 1990s. The level of foreign investment in the republic continued at a fairly healthy rate, as investors appreciated the climate of political and economic security provided by Klaus. Not even the relatively primitive level of the economic infrastructure, especially in regard to banking and telecommunications, could act as a major deterrent in this respect.

This factor put the spotlight on the third asset—Prague. The city had quickly become one of the most popular tourist centres in Europe and thus became the goose that laid the golden eggs for the economy. There was virtually no unemployment in Prague, as any surplus labour was rapidly absorbed by the burgeoning service industry that grew up to supply tourists and the sizable international community that had moved there.

There were potential dangers lurking behind this seemingly successful strategy, however. In the first place, when viewed from a longer-term perspective, the absence of unemployment was a negative sign because it indicated that the problem of industrial restructuring had still to begin. In the parts of Prague not visited by tourists and elsewhere in the nation, there were the relics of communist-style massive industrial enterprises that could never be made profitable but could not be allowed to go bankrupt for fear of the social dislocation that would ensue. Indeed, in the spring a demonstration organized by the labour unions protesting against the erosion of the workers' standard of living was a signal that Klaus had much less leeway in this area than outsiders might have assumed. The level of unemployment in the republic was about 3.5%, most of it in the rundown industrial areas of northern Bohemia.

Although privatization had taken place and much of Czech industry was technically owned by private investors rather than the government, in reality the control of economic strategy was in the hands of investment funds, and those running the funds had yet to begin the process of reducing employment that was needed to make the enterprises profitable. The indirect influence of the government could not be discounted in this field. It was evident that the restructuring of the republic's heavy industry, a difficult and painful process for any country, would take many years, but for the time being the semblance of private ownership was sufficient to satisfy Czech public opinion.

The Czech Republic's foreign policy was similar to that of the other postcommunist countries—waiting for the West to begin the process of economic and political integration with Eastern Europe. For domestic consumption Klaus from time to time would insist that the Czech Republic had nothing in common with other postcommunist states and that it would be a member of the European Union within a few years, but as of the end of 1994 this seemed unlikely.

(GEORGE SCHÖPFLIN)

This article updates the *Macropædia* article CZECH AND SLOVAK REPUBLICS: *Czech Republic*.

DENMARK

A constitutional monarchy of north-central Europe, Denmark lies between the North and Baltic seas. Area: 43,094 sq km (16,639 sq mi), excluding the Faeroe Islands and Greenland. Pop. (1994 est.): 5,205,000. Cap.: Copenhagen. Monetary unit: Danish krone, with (Oct. 7, 1994) a free rate of 6.03 kroner to U.S. $1 (9.59 kroner = £1 sterling). Queen, Margrethe II; prime minister in 1994, Poul Nyrup Rasmussen.

National elections in September 1994 returned Social Democrat Prime Minister Poul Nyrup Rasmussen to power at the head of a new three-party centre-left minority coalition government. Rasmussen's first government, a four-party centre-left grouping with a one-seat majority in the 179-seat Folketing (parliament) was formed in January 1993 without elections being called when the 10-year-old Conservative-Liberal government fell because of a refugee scandal.

Gaining major advances in the election were the right-wing opposition Liberals of former foreign minister Uffe Ellemann-Jensen, who increased their representation in the Folketing to 42 from 29. They thus became Denmark's second biggest political party, after the Social Democrats, who lost seven seats for a total of 62. When combined with two small centrist parties, the Radical Liberals and the Centre Democrats, Rasmussen's Social Democrat-led coalition had 75 seats. Thus, it was able to continue in power only with the tacit support of two leftist opposition parties. These parties, the Socialist People's Party and the Unity List, held a total of 19 seats.

The most surprising winner was comedian Jacob Haugaard, who was elected as an independent on a campaign platform of shorter lines at supermarkets, better weather, nicer Christmas presents, a tailwind for cyclists, free kettles for old-age pensioners, and the right of men to be impotent. Haugaard, from the western city of Aarhus, won 23,000 personal votes to sweep into the house as Denmark's third independent ever to be elected to the Folketing.

With no burning issues, political controversies, or crises and Denmark's economic outlook bright, the election was a tame affair, with the main themes being the preservation of Denmark's cradle-to-grave welfare system and the ensuring of the momentum of the economic revival. Opening the Folketing in October, Rasmussen said that his government would seek consensus for a steady economic policy and a cautious approach in relations with the European Union. He was expected to seek economic and foreign policy deals with the mainstream opposition to the right, the Conservatives and the Liberals.

The Danish economic recovery continued apace, with a growth rate forecast for 1994 of 4.4% of gross domestic product, a strong currency, inflation of only about 2%, and solid trade and balance of payments surpluses. The budget deficit remained high, however, and unemployment stubbornly remained at around 12% of the workforce in defiance of government schemes, including elaborate job-rotation programs. (One such plan for the Copenhagen bus drivers, as reported by the *Financial Times,* involved, in addition to the normal paid vacation, one week of leave in every nine weeks on a rotation basis, during which period the drivers would receive 80% of the maximum Danish unemployment benefit.) With financial markets fearing that Denmark's economic boom would spark higher inflation, Rasmussen proposed a marginal fiscal tightening in his 1995 budget and further measures later if necessary to keep the country's economic upturn on track. Long-serving National Bank director Erik Hoffmeyer retired at the end of the year.

In international affairs Denmark continued to make a solid contribution to UN activities, with some 1,400 peacekeepers in former Yugoslavia. It also sent observer teams to the troubled West Bank town of Hebron as part of a 160-strong monitor force requested by the Palestine Liberation Organization.   (CHRISTOPHER FOLLETT)

DJIBOUTI

The republic of Djibouti is in the Horn of northeastern Africa on the Gulf of Aden. Area: 23,200 sq km (8,950 sq mi). Pop. (1994 est.): 569,000 (excluding about 60,000 Somali refugees). Cap.: Djibouti. Monetary unit: Djibouti franc, with (Oct. 7, 1994) a par value of DF 177.72 to U.S. $1 (free rate of DF 270.82 = £1 sterling). President in 1994, Hassan Gouled Aptidon; prime minister, Barkat Gourad Hamadou.

During March 1994 divisions surfaced in the rebel Front for the Restoration of Unity and Democracy (FRUD). The political bureau, led by Ahmad Dini Ahmad, was dissolved to be replaced by a 13-man "executive council" under Ahmad Ougoureh Kible, who was named the new commander-in-chief of the movement. In the communiqué the new leadership accused the deposed leaders of "unforgivable mistakes" and said they had paralyzed the movement for two years. FRUD then hinted at its readiness to negotiate with the government. In June negotiations between the government and FRUD led to a joint decision to end the 2½-year civil war, and FRUD was offered the prospect of participating in politics as a legal party. There were doubts, however, as to whether all the FRUD factions would obey the decision.

On June 5 the nation's security forces put down a demonstration by Afar residents of the Arhiba district of Djibouti, who were objecting to the bulldozing of their homes for "security" reasons. Four people were killed, 20 injured, and 300 arrested, including the president of the United Opposition Front, Muhammad Ahmad Issa.

An improvement in relations with France, which had been poor for four years, occurred in March when the French minister of cooperation, Michel Roussin, visited Djibouti to attend a meeting of the joint cooperation commission of the two countries. He announced a 1994 aid package of F 8.5 million to assist in Djibouti's budget and an additional F 11.5 million for reconstruction of the infrastructure destroyed in the conflict with FRUD.   (GUY ARNOLD)

This article updates the *Macropædia* article EASTERN AFRICA: *Djibouti.*

DOMINICA

An island republic within the Commonwealth, Dominica is in the eastern Caribbean Sea. Area: 750 sq km (290 sq mi). Pop. (1994 est.): 72,000. Cap.: Roseau. Monetary unit: Eastern Caribbean dollar, with (Oct. 7, 1994) a par value of EC$2.70 to U.S. $1 (free rate of EC$4.30 = £1 sterling). President in 1994, Crispin Sorhaindo; prime minister, Eugenia Charles.

An increase in vehicle license fees by the Dominica Freedom Party (DFP) government in April caused demonstrations by public transportation operators, which soon developed into disorder in downtown Roseau. The government was forced to impose a state of emergency and a curfew to deal with the situation. The emergency was lifted on May 6, and an agreement was reached that the increases would be scaled back to 35% instead of the 65% originally intended.

The opposition Dominica Labour Party successfully capitalized on the unrest to promote its own political interests, and its leader, Rosie Douglas, was spokesperson for the taxi and minibus drivers. For her part, Prime Minister Dame Eugenia Charles said that she regarded the disturbances as an attempt to force her from office a year ahead of time. The next general election was not due until 1995.

The 1994 budget set out policies that the DFP expected would help it win another election victory. Overall spending was set at EC$286.5 million. EC$110.9 million was devoted to capital development, with an emphasis on cruise tourism, which the government believed could provide many jobs. Dominica narrowly escaped being placed on a tourist boycott list by the International Wildlife Coalition—which would have been a major blow to the island's tourism-dependent economy—when it decided in May not to vote against a proposal by the International Whaling Commission to establish a whale sanctuary in Antarctic waters.

(DAVID RENWICK)

This article updates the *Macropædia* article The WEST INDIES: *Dominica.*

DOMINICAN REPUBLIC

The Dominican Republic covers the eastern two-thirds of the Caribbean island of Hispaniola, which it shares with Haiti. Area: 48,443 sq km (18,704 sq mi). Pop. (1994 est.): 7,803,000. Cap.: Santo Domingo. Monetary unit: Dominican peso, with (Oct. 7, 1994) a free rate of 13.94 pesos to U.S. $1 (22.18 pesos = £1 sterling). President in 1994, Joaquín Balaguer.

Presidential and legislative elections were held on May 16, 1994, but were marred by allegations of serious fraud. In the first count Pres. Joaquín Balaguer of the Social Christian Reformist Party (PRSC) was narrowly elected to his seventh term of office by about 30,000 votes over José Francisco Peña Gómez of the Dominican Revolutionary Party (PRD). The campaign had been bitterly fought, with opponents of Peña Gómez insinuating that his Haitian origins would lead him to merge the country with Haiti. There was considerable delay in announcing official election results, during which time tension mounted. Demonstrations took place, and hundreds of PRD supporters were detained.

The national electoral board, the Junta Central Electoral (JCE), appointed a revision committee composed of three JCE officials and two independent academic members. The committee reported that the JCE never knew the total number of registered voters and that voting lists sent to polling stations on the day of the election differed from those previously given to the political parties. The committee determined that about 200,000 citizens had been excluded.

Nevertheless, despite calls for new elections, President Balaguer was sworn in on August 16. The official results gave him a margin of only 22,281 votes. In an attempt to end the political crisis, Balaguer and Peña Gómez signed an agreement on August 10 for the new presidential term to run for only 18 months, with new elections to be held on Nov. 16, 1995. A PRSC alliance with the Dominican Liberation Party, however, ensured that the constitutional amendment later passed by the legislature gave Balaguer a two-year term, with the next elections to be held on May 16, 1996.   (SARAH CAMERON)

This article updates the *Macropædia* article The WEST INDIES: *Dominican Republic*.

AP/WIDE WORLD

Pres. Joaquín Balaguer (second from right) casts his ballot in the elections held on May 16. Despite evidence of extensive fraud, the nearly blind 87-year-old Balaguer was declared the winner, and in August he began his seventh term as president.

ECUADOR

The republic of Ecuador is in western South America, on the Pacific Ocean. Area: 272,045 sq km (105,037 sq mi), including the Galápagos Islands. Pop. (1994 est.): 11,221,000. Cap.: Quito. Monetary unit: sucre, with (Oct. 7, 1994) a free rate of 2,279 sucres to U.S. $1 (3,625 sucres = £1 sterling). President in 1994, Sixto Durán Ballén.

In the midterm elections of 1994, Pres. Sixto Durán Ballén's Republican Unity Party lost six seats, reducing its representation in the National Congress, in alliance with the Conservative Party, to only nine. The largest party, with 25 seats, was now the Social Christian Party, led by Jaime Nebot Saadi, and the president would have to forge alliances with it in order to ensure passage of his economic reform program. A referendum held at the end of August showed overwhelming support for political change. The electorate was faced with seven questions, including a proposal to end the disruptive midterm elections by increasing the congressional term to four years. A package of reforms was to be drawn up and discussed by Congress before it was submitted to a second referendum.

A forest fire on Isabela in the Galápagos Islands in April destroyed more than 6,000 ha (14,800 ac) of the islands' unique ecosystem and endangered the giant Galápagos tortoises. A state of emergency was declared, and experts arrived from the U.S. and Canada to help extinguish the fire and protect the animals. On September 28 the government issued a decree to protect the islands from the effects of tourist traffic, immigration, and illegal fishing for sharks (notably by the Japanese) and sea cucumbers.

A new agrarian law that took effect on June 13 allowed former estate owners to reclaim land that was occupied by tenants but not legally transferred under previous land-reform laws. All land, including that held in common, could now be broken up and freely traded. Tenants, many of them Indians, feared widespread repossessions, and there was massive resentment among them. They were concerned that a free land market would encourage environmental degradation because of intensive farming and mineral exploitation. Also, the Indians among them feared that their social and religious traditions would be destroyed by the loss of communal lands. Protests became increasingly violent, and roadblocks were set up to cut off several towns. On June 20 the president declared a state of emergency and deployed the army.

In October Ecuador signed an agreement to restructure $7.6 billion of foreign commercial debt with the use of bonds. Past-due interest of $2.5 billion accumulated since Ecuador ceased fully servicing its debt in 1987 was to be repaid with 30-year bonds.   (SARAH CAMERON)

EGYPT

A republic of North Africa, Egypt has coastlines on the Mediterranean and Red seas. Area: 997,739 sq km (385,229 sq mi). Pop. (1994 est.): 58,466,000. Cap.: Cairo. Monetary unit: Egyptian pound, with (Oct. 7, 1994) a free rate of LE 3.39 to U.S. $1 (LE 5.39 = £1 sterling). President in 1994, Hosni Mubarak; prime minister, Atef Sedki.

Political violence and attacks on tourists escalated in 1994 despite harsh government action against Islamic militants and the banned Muslim Brotherhood. Pres. Hosni Mubarak gained international prestige by serving as host to the signing of the accords on the Gaza Strip and Jericho between Israel and the Palestinians in Cairo on May 4, but on the economic front his government was still embroiled in

With pyramids in the distance, an Egyptian family gathers on the roof of its house to watch television. The struggle between the traditional and the modern and between Islamic fundamentalism and Western culture continued in Egypt and sometimes resulted in violence.
THOMAS HEGENBART—STERN/BLACK STAR

disputes with the International Monetary Fund (IMF) and faced criticism for moving too slowly in its program of opening up the economy to market forces.

In February Islamic militants opened another front by starting a wave of bombings against banks that charged interest, considered unacceptable by Muslim fundamentalists. The death in April of military commander Talaat Yasin Himam seemed to have little effect on al-Jama'a al-Islamiya, the principal terrorist group.

The government's security clampdown was extended in June to the officially banned Muslim Brotherhood, which government sources said was "at one" with the extremists. On May 21 a leading Brotherhood sheikh, Muhammad al-Ghazali, was barred from delivering a sermon to 30,000 worshipers for a religious feast. Meanwhile, the Education Ministry banned schoolgirls from wearing the veil before the age of 11, and only then with parental consent. On September 15, however, lawyers won a court ruling reversing the ban.

Egyptian lawyers protested against the unexplained death in police custody on April 27 of 'Abd al-Harith Madani, a defense attorney for Islamic militants. A week of mass rallies in Cairo culminated on May 17 in a general strike and an aborted march on the presidential palace. The reaction to the protests underlined the extent to which Islamic militants had come to dominate lawyers' professional associations.

After a brief lull, terrorist attacks on vacationers resumed in August to coincide with the new tourist season and preparation for the UN population conference in Cairo. In September, for the first time, foreign tourists were attacked at a beach resort, indicating that terrorists were now operating far from their strongholds in the Nile valley.

On October 14 Naguib Mahfouz, the 82-year-old novelist who in 1988 had won the Nobel Prize for Literature, was stabbed by Islamic militants in Cairo in a further escalation of violence against the secular establishment. Although police shot one of the attackers dead in a raid two days later, demonstrations of protest against the outrage were also quelled. By October the total number of people killed since March 1992, when Islamic groups stepped up their campaign to overthrow the government, had reached 460, with 800 injured. Seven foreign tourists were among the casualties, and there were 53 among the wounded. By late 1994 the government had sentenced 58 Islamic fundamentalists to death, of whom 41 had been executed, 16 were at large, and 1 was on death row.

The government angered many politicians when the People's Assembly on April 11 passed a new law abolishing local elections and allowing village mayors to be appointed by the Interior Ministry, but the cause of political pluralism was advanced in other ways. On May 29 President Mubarak formed a committee to organize a national dialogue between spokesmen for the ruling National Democratic Party and other public figures, including opposition leaders. In inaugurating the 40-member preparatory commission, the president nevertheless excluded communists and the Muslim Brotherhood as well as Coptic groups, although individual Copts were allowed. On July 7 the conference submitted a number of recommendations to the president for action, including a switch to a party system in parliamentary elections.

Egypt's political leadership was disappointed that its role in maintaining the momentum in the Middle East peace process had apparently been given scant recognition in the West. This went some way toward explaining Egypt's decision at the end of the year to apply for membership in the Arab Maghreb Union. The signing of the Israeli-Palestinian agreements went ahead only after intensive last-minute pressure by Egypt on Palestine Liberation Organization chairman Yasir Arafat, some of which took place in a side room during the ceremony.

The UN International Conference on Population and Development, attended by some 10,000 delegates from 156 countries in Cairo in September, was a showcase for the Egyptian government. (*See* POPULATIONS AND POPULATION MOVEMENTS: *Sidebar.*) The Muslim Brotherhood branded the conference un-Islamic for condoning abortion, and six countries boycotted the event, including Saudi Arabia. Although the conference passed without incident, Iran stated publicly that it would never have diplomatic relations with Egypt, and a row erupted over the continuation of female circumcision in rural Egypt. A proposed law to outlaw mutilation of the female genitalia was put on hold for two years for fear of driving the practice underground.

Talks between the Egyptian government and the IMF foundered over continued disagreement on the technical issues surrounding exchange-rate competitiveness and in particular the devaluation of the Egyptian pound. A meeting in early September between the president and the managing director of the IMF failed to break the deadlock. The dispute led to further delay in finalizing Egypt's debt-reduction program with its major creditors.

Relations with The Sudan reached their lowest ebb in several years. Early in September The Sudan alleged that Egypt had sent troops to the disputed border region and kidnapped a Sudanese officer. The Sudanese responded by impounding a passenger ferry. Egypt then seized a Sudanese minister's aircraft during a refueling stop in Cairo.

On May 31 Egypt served as host to the 111th ministerial conference on the Non-Aligned Movement, but it lost to Colombia in its bid to chair the organization. Egypt relinquished the chairmanship of the Organization of African Unity to Tunisia on June 14, and on June 24, freed from diplomatic constraints, it sent "observers" to join the French-led military mission to protect civilians in Rwanda. On May 10 Egypt resumed diplomatic relations with South Africa, interrupted 30 years previously to protest the policy of apartheid.   (JOHN WHELAN)

EL SALVADOR

The republic of El Salvador is situated on the Pacific coast of Central America. Area: 21,041 sq km (8,124 sq mi). Pop. (1994 est.): 5,642,000. Cap.: San Salvador. Monetary unit: Salvadoran colón, with (Oct. 7, 1994) a free rate of 8.77 colones to U.S. $1 (13.95 colones = £1 sterling). Presidents in 1994, Alfredo Cristiani and, from June 1, Armando Calderón Sol.

The first round of elections for the presidency of El Salvador was held on March 20, 1994, together with elections for the Legislative Assembly and the municipalities. Dubbed the "election of the century," it was the first time in more than 60 years that conservatives and communists had campaigned against each other. The campaign was marred by killings, however, particularly of former left-wing guerrilla leaders, and by accusations that the government had failed to implement fully the peace agreement signed with the guerrillas in January 1992 that ended the 12-year civil war. In rural areas most demobilized combatants from both sides had not been granted land; the corrupt judicial system had not been reformed; and deployment of a new civilian police force had been delayed.

The two main contestants for the presidency were Armando Calderón Sol, of the right-wing Nationalist Republican Alliance Party (Arena), and Rubén Zamora, leader of an alliance between the Democratic Convergence, a centre-left group, and the Farabundo Martí National Liberation Front, the former guerrilla organization. There were widespread claims of voting irregularities, and thousands of people were unable to vote because they were not on the electoral register. These problems were particularly bad in rural areas. Calderón narrowly failed to win the 50% of the vote needed to win outright, forcing a second round of elections on April 24. This he won with almost 70% of the vote, although less than half of the electorate turned out; he was sworn in as president on June 1. The front began to break up in December, when one of the main factions withdrew.

On August 18 the UN Observer Mission in El Salvador reported a decline in human rights violations between March 1 and June 30 but described the situation as precarious because of the growth of organized crime, abuses by the National Civilian Police, and illegal activity by members of the armed forces and National Police.   (SARAH CAMERON)

This article updates the *Macropædia* article CENTRAL AMERICA: *El Salvador.*

EQUATORIAL GUINEA

The republic of Equatorial Guinea consists of Río Muni, on the Atlantic coast of West Africa, and the offshore islands of Bioko and Annobon. Area: 28,051 sq km (10,831 sq mi). Pop. (1994 est.): 386,000. Cap.: Malabo. Monetary unit: CFA franc, with (from Jan. 12, 1994) a par value of CFAF 100 to the French franc and (as of Oct. 7, 1994) a free rate of CFAF 526.67 to U.S. $1 (CFAF 837.67 = £1 sterling). President in 1994, Brig. Gen. Teodoro Obiang Nguema Mbasogo; prime minister, Silvestre Siale Bileka.

Official figures for the elections at the end of 1993 gave the ruling Democratic Party of Equatorial Guinea (PDGE) 68 of the 80 seats in the House of Representatives and the three opposition parties the remaining 12. The election procedures were condemned by international observers, including the U.S. and Spanish governments. Pres. Teodoro Obiang Nguema Mbasogo reappointed Silvestre Siale Bileka prime minister, and a Cabinet of 38 was then appointed from the PDGE.

The expulsion of the Spanish consul general at Bata in December caused a breach with Spain, which announced that aid to Equatorial Guinea would be cut by half as of January 1994. With a debt of $210 million and gross national product of only $144 million, this was a major setback for the nation's economy.

On Dec. 30, 1993, the Ministry of State for Information and Communication registered the newspaper *El sol*, the first private newspaper to be recognized by the government. In March the final contingent of the Spanish air force, which had been in Equatorial Guinea for 14 years, was withdrawn by Spain.   (GUY ARNOLD)

This article updates the *Macropædia* article WESTERN AFRICA: *Equatorial Guinea.*

ERITREA

Eritrea is in the Horn of Africa, on the Red Sea. Area: 117,400 sq km (45,300 sq mi). Pop. (1994 est.): 3,779,000 (including about 500,000 refugees in The Sudan). Cap.: Asmera. Monetary unit: Ethiopian birr, with (Oct. 7, 1994) a free rate of 5.40 birr to U.S. $1 (free rate of 8.60 birr = £1 sterling). President in 1994, Isaias Afwerki.

The third congress of the Eritrean People's Liberation Front (EPLF) was held on Feb. 10–17, 1994, at Nakfa, symbolic centre of the long struggle that culminated in independence for Eritrea in May 1993. As part of the normalization of the political process, the EPLF converted itself from a national liberation front into a political party, called the People's Front for Democracy and Justice (PFDJ), and committed itself to an eventual multiparty system. For the present, however, the National Assembly was reconstituted to include 75 members of the PFDJ central committee and 75 popularly elected members.

Reintegration of former fighters into civilian life and repatriation of refugees from The Sudan continued to create problems, and relations with The Sudan began to deteriorate after Pres. Isaias Afwerki, in his January 1994 New Year message, referred to the attempted infiltration of Eritrea by a Muslim fundamentalist group associated with the National Islamic Front in The Sudan; all of its 20 members were reportedly killed. Eritrea broke off diplomatic relations in December. Relations with the Ethiopian government remained close.

Eritrea joined the International Monetary Fund and World Bank and was praised by bank officials for its realistic approach to development. Because of drought conditions and a pest infestation in 1993, the harvest amounted to only 20% of the nation's requirements, and most of the population remained dependent on relief food. Good rains in most of the country in 1994 permitted hopes of a greatly improved food situation in 1995.

(CHRISTOPHER S. CLAPHAM)

This article updates the *Micropædia* article ERITREA.

ESTONIA

A republic of northern Europe, Estonia borders the Baltic Sea on the west and north. Area: 45,227 sq km (17,462 sq mi). Pop. (1994 est.): 1,499,000. Cap.: Tallinn. Monetary unit: kroon, with (Oct. 7, 1994) a par value of 8 krooni to DM 1 (free rates of 12.32 krooni = U.S. $1 and 19.60 krooni = £1 sterling). President in 1994, Lennart Meri; prime ministers, Mart Laar and, from October 27, Andres Tarand.

With the withdrawal of Russian troops on Aug. 31, 1994, Estonia was free of foreign military forces for the first time since it was occupied in mid-1940. U.S. Pres. Bill Clinton's historic visit to Riga, Latvia, had facilitated the signing of the Estonian-Russian accords on July 26 in Moscow, yet the dispute over borders continued to sour bilateral relations. Estonia's "reintegration" with Europe was nevertheless proceeding rapidly, as evidenced by the country's active participation in the North Atlantic Cooperation Council and NATO's Partnership for Peace.

The year began with Pres. Lennart Meri's refusal to confirm Prime Minster Mart Laar's choice of several new ministers. A constitutional crisis was averted when Meri retreated before Parliament. In the spring, strife in Laar's own Pro Patria Party, the principal partner in his governing coalition, threatened to unseat him. Defectors from Laar's party joined the otherwise fragmented opposition in a vote of no confidence on September 26. Andres Tarand, Laar's minister of the environment, succeeded him as prime minister in October, but the composition of the Cabinet remained largely unchanged. At year's end Estonia was preparing for parliamentary elections. The number of parties had mushroomed, but many were expected to coalesce into electoral alliances with common lists.

The country was deeply shaken by the sinking of the ferry *Estonia* on stormy seas on September 28. (*See* TRANSPORTATION.) On October 31 the first postcommunist archbishop of the Evangelical Lutheran Church of Estonia was consecrated into office. To everyone's surprise, a former Communist Party secretary for ideology, Indrek Toome, was arrested on November 28 for bribery. During the year Estonians marked the 125th anniversary of their famed song festivals with separate events in Tallinn and Tartu.

(TÕNU PARMING)

This article updates the *Macropædia* article BALTIC STATES: *Estonia*.

ETHIOPIA

The landlocked republic of Ethiopia is in the Horn of northeastern Africa. Area: 1,133,882 sq km (437,794 sq mi). Pop. (1994 est.): 53,384,000. Cap.: Addis Ababa. Monetary unit: birr, with (Oct. 7, 1994) a free rate of 5.40 birr to U.S. $1 (8.60 birr = £1 sterling). Interim president in 1994, Meles Zenawi; acting prime minister, Tamirat Laynie.

The draft constitution for the "Federal Democratic Republic of Ethiopia" was approved by the transitional Council of Representatives in May 1994 for submission to the Constituent Assembly, which was elected in June. In keeping with the doctrine of ethnic federalism espoused by the ruling Ethiopian People's Revolutionary Democratic Front (EPRDF), it stated that "sovereignty resides in the nations, nationalities and peoples of Ethiopia" rather than in the people as a whole and granted each nation, nationality, or people rights of self-determination up to and including secession.

The Constituent Assembly elections were held on June 5 except in the Somali-inhabited Ogaden and Dire Dawa regions, where they were postponed. Despite attempts at mediation by the Carter Presidential Center in the U.S., the major opposition parties, notably including the All Amhara People's Organization (AAPO), the Oromo Liberation Front, and the Ogaden National Liberation Front (ONLF), boycotted the elections, leaving the field open for the numerous ethnically based parties affiliated with the EPRDF. In the Afar region the opposition Afar Liberation Front won two seats, but elsewhere EPRDF candidates won all the seats except for 14 that went to independents, 10 of them in Addis Ababa. According to government figures, between 60% and 80% of eligible voters registered in most regions, and between 81% and 94% of those voted; members of the formerly ruling Workers' Party of Ethiopia and of the armed forces under the previous regime were not permitted to participate. Although the conduct of the elections was generally peaceful and well-organized, the verdict of independent observers as to whether the results fairly represented the wishes of the Ethiopian people was expressed in guarded terms.

Human rights organizations, including Amnesty International, expressed increasing concern over conditions in the country. Beginning in January 1994 leading members of ONLF were arrested, and several of them were killed or died in military custody. In Addis Ababa several journalists disappeared or were detained, and several hundred demonstrators were arrested outside the High Court on September 20 while protesting against the imprisonment of AAPO leader Asrat Woldeyes. In the Oromo-inhabited area of western Ethiopia, a large number of people were arrested on September 6 while attending the funeral of an elderly businessman who had been killed by government forces. These incidents reinforced growing uncertainty both within the country and abroad over the sincerity of the government's commitment to opening a democratic government.

In mid-December the Supreme Court began proceedings against deposed dictator Lieut. Col. Mengistu Haile Mariam and 66 other former officials, 21 of whom, including Mengistu (who fled to Zimbabwe), would be tried in absentia. The charges included genocide and crimes against humanity and included allegations that the junta had ordered the murders of 1,905 persons, including Emperor Haile Selassie, who, the court said, was "strangled on Aug. 26, 1975, in his bed most cruelly." The Mengistu regime was said to have manipulated and withheld international famine-aid supplies in order to suppress dissent. Thousands of other ex-officials in the communist regime were expected to stand trial later on lesser charges.

Following poor rains and pest infestations in 1993, there were food shortages in much of the country and, although widespread famine did not occur, the government Relief and Rehabilitation Commission reported more than 5,000 famine-related deaths in southwestern Ethiopia in April and May, and by mid-June more than seven million people were dependent on relief food. The main July–September 1994 rains were good in most of the country, however, and indicated a likely improvement in the food situation after the December harvest. Other areas of the economy appeared to be improving in response to the encouragement of a free-market policy, and the World Bank announced a major commitment in support of the economic reform program in 1994–95.   (CHRISTOPHER S. CLAPHAM)

This article updates the *Macropædia* article EASTERN AFRICA: *Ethiopia.*

FIJI

The republic of Fiji occupies an island group in the South Pacific Ocean. Area: 18,274 sq km (7,056 sq mi). Pop. (1994 est.): 771,000. Cap.: Suva. Monetary unit: Fiji dollar, with (Oct. 7, 1994) a free rate of F$1.44 to U.S. $1 (F$2.30 = £1 sterling). President in 1994, Ratu Sir Kamisese Mara; prime minister, Sitiveni Rabuka.

In November 1993 six members of Prime Minister Sitiveni Rabuka's Fijian Political Party voted with the opposition against the 1994 budget, forcing a general election. Led by Josefata Kamikamica, a former deputy prime minister, the dissidents fought the February 1994 election under the banner of the Fijian Association. At the same time, the Fiji Labour Party (FLP), which had become increasingly dependent on Indo-Fijian support since the death of its former leader, Timoci Bavadra, lost ground to the National Federation Party (NFP), which had traditionally enjoyed strong Indo-Fijian support. Rabuka was returned to office, with the Fijian Political Party winning 31 of the 37 seats allotted to ethnic Fijians and also drawing the support of two independents and four members of the General Voters' Party. The Fijian Association won only five seats and was joined in opposition by the NFP with 20 seats and the FLP with 7.

The revised 1994 budget showed a projected income of F$694.9 million and expenditure of F$832.1 million; the deficit represented 2.9% of gross domestic product. Growth of 3.2% was projected for 1994. There were high returns from tourism and sugar, though the latter faced difficulty in the future because of planned changes in Fiji's access to the European Union.   (BARRIE MACDONALD)

This article updates the *Macropædia* article PACIFIC ISLANDS: *Fiji.*

FINLAND

The republic of Finland is in northern Europe, on the Gulf of Bothnia and the Gulf of Finland. Area: 338,145 sq km (130,559 sq mi). Pop. (1994 est.): 5,083,000. Cap.: Helsinki. Monetary unit: Finnish markka, with (Oct. 7, 1994) a free rate of 4.74 markkaa to U.S. $1 (7.53 markkaa = £1 sterling). Presidents in 1994, Mauno Koivisto and, from March 1, Martti Ahtisaari; prime minister, Esko Aho.

Finland elected Martti Ahtisaari of the Social Democratic Party as its president in February 1994 after Mauno Koivisto, also a Social Democrat, declined to run for reelection after two six-year terms. Ahtisaari, not previously active in domestic politics, defeated Elisabeth Rehn, the first woman

to serve as Finnish defense minister and the first to be a significant candidate for president. Ahtisaari had served for several years with the UN. He began his presidency with the traditional visits to the other Scandinavian countries and to Finland's eastern neighbour, Russia, and visited the U.S. as the guest of Pres. Bill Clinton.

During the year Ahtisaari became involved in a dispute with members of Parliament, including Prime Minister Esko Aho, about the powers of the presidency. The disagreements centred on who should represent the country at summit meetings of the European Union, which Finland was scheduled to join at the beginning of 1995. Ahtisaari said that the duty should fall to the president, possibly together with the prime minister as in France, while Parliament leaned strongly toward representation by the prime minister alone. The dispute was not resolved during the year.

In an advisory referendum on October 16, Finns voted 56.9% to 43.1% in favour of European Union (EU) membership. This was in line with government policy and was advocated by Ahtisaari. Some former communists rejected membership, however, as did the small Christian Union Party and several other groups. The most significant opposition came from members of the agrarian-based Centre Party, the biggest group in Parliament and in the ruling coalition government. They protested that accession to the EU and its inner market would subject the heavily subsidized Finnish farmers to unacceptable pressures in the form of competition from member countries where producer prices were much lower. The persisting division in the Centre Party over accession to the EU was accompanied by lower popularity ratings for it in opinion polls. The polls gave the top ratings to the Social Democratic Party, suggesting it would become the largest party in Parliament after the next elections, scheduled for March 1995.

By the end of 1994 the rate of unemployment in Finland had fallen slightly from the 20% recorded early in the year. Exports, led by products of the forestry and metalworking sectors, rose, and the country posted a trade surplus. Inflation fell to an annual rate of about 2%. The government continued to borrow to finance its deficit budgeting, and its debt was more than 60% of gross domestic product. In the private sector the nation's commercial banks continued to struggle with bad debts. Nokia, a manufacturer of electronic equipment, did increasingly well in the expanding world market for mobile telephones.

A group of researchers reported in *The New England Journal of Medicine* in late November that Finland had become the first country to eliminate indigenous cases of measles, German measles, and mumps.

(EDWARD M. SUMMERHILL)

FRANCE

A republic of western Europe, France includes the island of Corsica in the Mediterranean Sea and has coastlines on the English Channel, the Mediterranean, and the Atlantic Ocean. Area: 543,965 sq km (210,026 sq mi). Pop. (1994 est.): 57,982,000. Cap.: Paris. Monetary unit: franc, with (Oct. 7, 1994) a free rate of F 5.27 to U.S. $1 (F 8.38 = £1 sterling). President in 1994, François Mitterrand; prime minister, Édouard Balladur.

By all measurable indexes 1994 was a year of recovery for France. Gross domestic product grew by more than 2% after the 1993 recession. Unemployment ground to a halt at the still-high figure of 12.7% of the workforce, with approximately 3.4 million registered unemployed, a million of whom had been out of work for two years or more. The trade balance was in the black by F 100 billion. Car production grew by 14%. Inflation was the lowest since 1956, at

1.7%. The franc held its ground against the Deutsche Mark within the European Monetary System and appreciated by 18% against the dollar. Psychologically, however, '94 was still perceived by the French as one of the darkest years since 1945. An atmosphere of gloom dampened confidence; consumers stayed away from the shops, bosses put off hirings and capital investments, and fewer housing units were built than at any other time in the past 30 years.

This mood was caused partly by the aftereffects of the recession—homelessness became the first worry of the French, before unemployment and AIDS—and partly by a deleterious climate of corruption in political and business circles, leading to disenchantment with all politicians and most of the establishment figures. Hitherto timid French judges (who technically were under the authority of the minister of justice and therefore not completely independent) started charging and jailing politicians, top civil servants, and business leaders on corruption charges. Three ministers had to leave the Cabinet after having been charged with corruption; one was thrown in jail. Similarly, the bosses of some of France's largest corporations—including the electronics and engineering multinational Alcatel Alsthom, the water utilities Générale des Eaux and Lyonnaise des Eaux, the glassmakers Saint-Gobain—were the object of judicial inquiries.

Another cause for gloom was the disintegration of the French left following its resounding defeat in the European Parliament elections in June. Socialist Pres. François Mitterrand was weakened by illness as well as by revelations regarding his questionable past in collaborationist Vichy France during World War II. Prime Minister Édouard Balladur of the Gaullist Rally for the Republic (RPR) remained France's most popular politician by default, trusted more for his caution and conservatism than for any kind of political vision or élan. The European Commission president, Jacques Delors, a widely respected Socialist who repeatedly led in polls for the 1995 presidential election, eventually declined to run.

Domestic Affairs. The winter of 1994 saw Balladur demonstrate his political agility by weathering two crises caused by his government's proposed reforms. In December 1993 a bill had been introduced to enable local authorities to subsidize private schools above a hitherto limited 10% ceiling of total running costs. After a 750,000-strong demonstration in Paris in support of the state schooling system, the offending articles of the bill were quietly dropped. In February 1994 Balladur tried to pass measures to fight unemployment, enabling bosses to pay young people under 26 years old 80% of the $1,000 minimum monthly wage. Demonstrations by pupils and students throughout France in March eventually made Balladur cancel his decree. The prime minister's low-profile attitude paid off; in the first polls forecasting the outcome of the presidential election, he came out a strong favourite, with 52% of projected votes.

On February 25 Yann Piat, the right-wing deputy for the Var département on the Riviera, was shot dead in her car by two professional gunmen, the first assassination of a national representative since the war for Algerian independence in 1954–62. It was widely assumed that Piat was murdered because she opposed routine kickbacks and money laundering by some of the département's most prominent personalities. On March 8 the long-serving local centre-right senator, Maurice Arreckx, was first heard as a witness in the investigation, while two local men were held in remand under assassination charges. On August 1 Arreckx was jailed under three separate corruption charges.

After many delays the long-awaited trial of the Nazi collaborator Paul Touvier began on March 17. The first Frenchman ever to face trial for crimes against humanity, Touvier had been tried in absentia just after World War II, fled, and hid for 30 years in Roman Catholic convents. He was later pardoned, to general outrage, by Pres. Georges Pompidou in the name of "national reconciliation" but then was convicted of further crimes with new evidence. On April 20, after survivors and historians testified for several weeks that Touvier had assisted the Gestapo in the roundup and shooting of Jewish hostages, he was sentenced to life in prison.

Jacques Médecin, the former mayor of Nice who had been tried for corruption in absentia in 1992, finally returned to France in November. He had fled to Uruguay in 1990, but he was jailed there in 1993 and eventually was extradited.

It was a bad year for 78-year-old President Mitterrand, who underwent surgery and radiotherapy for prostate cancer. In the spring he became the target of several best-selling pamphlets when one of his closest aides, François de Grossouvre, committed suicide after having told journalists of the president's many favours to the corrupt businessman Roger-Patrice Pelat. In September the publication of two biographies of the young Mitterrand revealed that he had been a distinguished member of Marshall Philippe Pétain's collaborationist government until the end of 1943 and that until the late 1980s he had remained close to the notorious Vichy head of police, René Bousquet, who masterminded the massive roundups and deportation of French Jews to concentration camps. In November the weekly *Paris-Match* broke the traditional taboo against referring to politicians' private lives and published pictures of the president's adult daughter by his long-time mistress, whose existence had been widely known but never referred to in print.

The June European elections confirmed the rise of "Euroskepticism" in France, as the pro-Maastricht Treaty Gaullist-centrist list led by Toulouse Mayor Dominique Baudis managed to poll only 25.6% of the vote and the equally pro-Maastricht Socialist Party (PS) list led by former prime minister Michel Rocard polled an abysmal 14.5%, the worst results for the Socialists in any election since 1971. The shrilly anti-European right-wing list, lavishly bankrolled by French-British billionaire Sir James Goldsmith, won an unexpected 12.3% of the vote, while the pro-European populist businessman Bernard Tapie's supporters won approximately 12%. Rocard's poor results caused him to relinquish his job as PS first secretary and dashed his long-seated ambitions to run for the presidency as the left's candidate. Jean-Marie Le Pen's extreme-right National Front polled 10.5% of the vote; the Communists polled only 6.9%; and the two Green lists combined did not manage to poll 5% of the vote and thereby lost their nine seats in the European Parliament.

Tapie's success was the last piece of good news for the fallen tycoon, who was successively charged by four different magistrates with a series of serious accusations ranging from the fixing of the 1993 European association football (soccer) match between his club, Olympique Marseille, and Valenciennes to tax evasion, fraud, and the delay of personal bankruptcy proceedings while unable to reimburse some F 1.3 billion to the state-owned bank, Crédit Lyonnais. In July Tapie's antique furniture collection was seized by bailiffs, and expert estimates by Christie's and Sotheby's auction houses revealed the collection to have been grossly overvalued to be used as inflated collateral for Crédit Lyonnais loans. The estimated value fell from F 350 million to F 30 million–F 50 million. In November Tapie's parliamentary immunity was lifted, and in December a court started bankruptcy proceedings on two of his privately owned companies, which made him ineligible for any public office for five years.

Amid regular disclosures of financial impropriety by political leaders of both the RPR and the centre-right Union for French Democracy, as well as kickbacks by large corporations in exchange for public contracts, the French started favouring Delors as their dream candidate for the 1995 presidential election. Between September and December nine polls gave Delors as a clear winner against either former prime minister Jacques Chirac, leader of the RPR, or Balladur. Delors, who was about to step down from the European Union (EU) presidency he had held for two consecutive five-year mandates, was seen as a figure above the domestic fray and imbued with the aura of a statesman from his dealings on equal terms with all 12 EU heads of state. He was thought to be devoted to social equality and maintaining the welfare net, and nobody doubted this devout Roman Catholic's honesty and integrity. On December 11 Delors announced he would not run, pleading his age (69) as well as the lack of a left-wing majority to back him after his election. "It would be swindling the French to be a helpless president forced to condone policies contrary to my opinions," he said in what was read as a devastating indictment of Mitterrand's "cohabitation" compromises. By year's end Balladur was again the election's great favourite.

The Economy. On January 5 the Bank of France's new independence under the clauses of the Maastricht Treaty for the EU was formalized by the appointment of six outside members of the nine-strong Council for Monetary Policy (the other three being the bank's governor, Jean-Claude Trichet, and his two deputies). The councillors all agreed with Trichet to support the strong franc policy with perfectly orthodox monetary policies.

Crédit Lyonnais was revealed to have had some F 40 billion in losses over the past three years as a result of unwise real-estate speculations and bad investments in a series of companies. The bank's former chairman, Jean-Yves Haberer, was replaced by the Union des Assurances de Paris (UAP) insurance group chief, Jean Peyrelevade. A Swiss magistrate later charged Haberer with having had fraudulent dealings in Crédit Lyonnais's Swiss operations.

The Paris Bourse posted appalling results throughout 1994; the CAC 40 Index lost some 17% in value. The bond market was hit by the world bond crash but in more modest proportions. Most newly privatized companies, shares, including UAP, Elf Aquitaine, and Renault, fell below their privatization offering price. National health and unemployment benefits as well as pensions were reduced as once again France's comprehensive welfare system posted a huge deficit. The budget deficit grew to F 340 billion. The luxury-goods manufacturer LVMH posted profits up 16%, while shares of the companies involved in corruption scandals all took a two-digit fall.

Domestic airlines were deregulated in December, and the most profitable air routes (Paris–Marseilles, Paris–Toulouse) were opened to private and foreign competitors of Air Inter, the hitherto heavily protected domestic Air France subsidiary. Air France requested and obtained a F 20 billion recapitalization from the state, with the agreement of the European Commission, after it promised to privatize itself in 1995. The Eurolink started its shuttle train service between London, Paris, and Brussels via the Channel Tunnel (Eurotunnel) in November and was an instant success.

Foreign Affairs. On January 12 France broke with a 50-year-old tradition and agreed to devalue by 50% the CFA franc, the currency used by 14 French-speaking African countries, that had been traditionally pegged to the franc. While all economists agreed that the CFA franc was widely overvalued, its brutal devaluation had catastrophic effects on the affected countries' economies (all of them among the

REUTERS/BETTMANN

An image of Charles de Gaulle is projected onto a screen in front of City Hall in Paris on August 26 as citizens and government officials mark the 50th anniversary of the liberation of Paris from the Nazis. The observances were among a number of World War II commemorations held during the year.

world's poorest), which were suddenly unable to purchase more than half their needs of foreign staples, equipment, and oil.

France and French organizations were involved immediately and substantially in attempts to halt the disintegration of Rwanda during the year. French troops regularly stationed in Rwanda were evacuated from the country together with all French nationals after extremist Hutu militias began massacring minority Tutsis in April. By June 23, when France's humanitarian military expedition, code-named "Turquoise," entered Rwanda to try to stop the genocide, hundreds of thousands of Rwandans, mostly Tutsi, had been killed, and refugees were pouring into unprepared neighbouring Zaire, Uganda, and Burundi. France was accused of protecting the flight of many Hutu leaders and was held in defiance by the new provisional government set up in Kigali by exiled Tutsi. On French television screens, pictures of French-speaking victims telling genocide stories shocked the country into sending large but still inadequate amounts of aid, food, and money. The last French troops left Rwanda on August 21, to be replaced by African UN units, but teams of French humanitarian associations remained.

On August 3 five French citizens—three gendarmes and two consular employees—were killed by Islamic militants in Algiers. In retaliation Interior Minister Charles Pasqua (*see* BIOGRAPHIES) had 26 French-based known Islamic leaders arrested. Twenty of them were expelled from the country on August 31, triggering an escalation that culminated with the hijacking on Christmas Eve of a Paris-bound Air France Airbus with 239 passengers and crew by four Islamic terrorists. The hijackers released 63 passengers, killed 3, and held the plane for 54 hours before being killed in an assault by French antiterrorist special gendarmerie forces in Marseille airfield, where the plane had landed. Soon afterward Pasqua announced that the terrorists had intended to fly the plane over Paris and blow it and themselves up in a murderous kamikaze raid. The gendarmes' surprise attack and victory was a boon to Balladur's popularity but evidenced sharp differences between Foreign Minister Alain Juppé's and Pasqua's views on France's handling of the Algerian civil war. Juppé advocated negotiating with the more moderate Muslims who had won the 1992 elections, while Pasqua maintained that all Islamists were fanatics, to be fought with equal defiance by France. Meanwhile, Pasqua worked closely with Sudanese authorities in the capture and extradition to France of the international terrorist Carlos "the Jackal."

In December France prepared to take over the EU rotating presidency, but most observers predicted there would be practically no new initiatives as the Balladur government tried to keep the potentially damaging European issue from creating cross-party rifts during the presidential campaign. Defense Minister François Léotard several times threatened to withdraw France's 2,300 UN troops from war-torn Bosnia and Herzegovina, but he never acted on his threat since army studies showed the retreat to be very dangerous and costly, requiring first sending in 500 more soldiers in order to solve logistic problems.   (ANNE-ELISABETH MOUTET)

See also *Dependent States*.

GABON

Gabon is a republic of central Africa, on the Atlantic Ocean. Area: 267,667 sq km (103,347 sq mi). Pop. (1994 est.): 1,139,000. Cap.: Libreville. Monetary unit: CFA franc, with (Oct. 7, 1994) a par value of CFAF 100 to the French franc and a free rate of CFAF 526.67 to U.S. $1 (CFAF 837.67 = £1 sterling). President in 1994, Omar Bongo; prime ministers, Casimir Oyé-Mba and, from November 2, Paulin Obame-Nguema.

Government in Gabon virtually ground to a halt in 1994 as Pres. Omar Bongo spent much of the year trying to reassert his authority in the wake of his highly controversial victory in the December 1993 presidential elections. Opposition parties refused to accept the results. The government refused permission for nine opposition leaders, including two defeated presidential candidates, to leave for Paris in January. Although the travel ban was removed on January 26, Bongo justified the action as countering the opposition's announced plans to establish a rival government. Thirty people died in February during riots in Libreville, forcing Bongo to declare a state of siege on February 21. Adding to the government's woes was a strike by students at Omar Bongo University, Libreville, that began on May 26 and culminated in an attack on the university's rector and his deputy on June 14. The government closed the institution for three months.

Relations with France, which were already strained because of Bongo's strong objections to the devaluation of the CFA franc in January, cooled further after France disapproved of his harsh suppression of antigovernment demonstrators. Reports that some members of the army and the government were thinking of joining with the opposition may have prompted Bongo's decision to agree to participate in a peace conference in Paris between representatives of the government and opposition parties. The meetings, which began on September 9, lasted for two weeks and led to the formation of a coalition government that took office on November 2 and was to govern until new legislative elections could be held.

(NANCY ELLEN LAWLER)

This article updates the *Macropædia* article CENTRAL AFRICA: *Gabon*.

GAMBIA, THE

A republic and member of the Commonwealth, The Gambia extends from the Atlantic Ocean along the lower Gambia River in West Africa; it is surrounded by Senegal. Area: 10,689 sq km (4,127 sq mi). Pop. (1994 est.): 1,060,000. Cap.: Banjul. Monetary unit: dalasi, with (Oct. 7, 1994) a free rate of 9.53 dalasis to U.S. $1 (15.16 dalasis = £1 sterling). President in 1994, Sir Dawda Jawara until July 22; chairman of the Armed Forces Provisional Council from July 26, Lieut. Yahya Jammeh.

On July 22, 1994, an army coup toppled Pres. Dawda Jawara from power; he and his family were taken to asylum in Senegal by a U.S. warship that was on a courtesy visit to the country. The coup, led by Lieut. Yahya Jammeh, had begun as a rampage through the streets of Banjul by disgruntled soldiers claiming back pay for peacekeeping service in Liberia. There were no casualties. U.S. complicity in the coup was suggested, largely, it would seem, because of the coincidental presence of the U.S. warship at Banjul. Sir Dawda was the last head of state in Africa who had been in office since independence.

The new regime established an executive committee to run the daily affairs of the country and announced plans to merge the 800-strong army and 600-strong police force. On July 28 a new Cabinet was sworn in with Jammeh as chairman of the Armed Forces Provisional Council. One of the first decrees of the new regime empowered the vice-chairman, Lieut. S.B. Sabally, to arrest and detain members of the armed forces "in the interest of the security of Gambia," and another suspended all political activity. A reported coup attempt in November was put down.

(GUY ARNOLD)

This article updates the *Macropædia* article WESTERN AFRICA: *The Gambia*.

GEORGIA

A republic of Transcaucasia, Georgia borders Russia on the north and northeast, Azerbaijan on the southeast, Armenia and Turkey on the south, and the Black Sea on the west. Area: 69,700 sq km (26,900 sq mi). Pop. (1994 est.): 5,503,000. Cap.: Tbilisi. Monetary unit: Georgian coupon (transitional currency), with (Sept. 27, 1994) a free rate of 2,478,000 coupons = U.S. $1 (3,864,000 coupons = £1 sterling). De facto head of state and chairman of Parliament in 1994, Eduard A. Shevardnadze; prime minister, Otar Patsatsia.

Georgia remained chronically unstable in 1994, as evidenced by the assassinations of a deputy defense minister, Col. Nikolas Kekelidze, in early February and of opposition leader Giorgi Chanturia in November. Politics was dominated by the repercussions of the loss of jurisdiction in October 1993 over the breakaway region of Abkhazia, for which the radical opposition held Parliament Chairman Eduard A. Shevardnadze responsible, calling repeatedly for a no-confidence vote and convening public demonstrations to demand his resignation, but without success. Warning of the danger of an imminent coup, Shevardnadze initiated a Cabinet reshuffle in March that prompted Tbilisi police briefly to occupy the Parliament building to protest the appointment of a new interior minister. A former Soviet army general, Vardiko Nadibaidze, was named defense minister.

Economic collapse intensified. Over the first 10 months of 1994, Georgia registered a 42% drop in industrial output, the worst of any Commonwealth of Independent States (CIS) member; the October monthly inflation rate of 36% was similarly the highest in the CIS. The Georgian government's inability to pay its $500 million debt to Turkmenistan led to a drastic reduction in supplies of natural gas, Georgia's primary source of energy; by late November much of Tbilisi was without heating, electricity, or running water. Up to one million Georgians were estimated to have emigrated to escape impoverishment. Parliament failed to pass urgently needed legislation that would provide the foundation for radical economic reform. In November the International Monetary Fund criticized the Georgian government's failure to implement its minimum recommendations on price liberalization and reducing the state apparatus, on which credits were contingent.

The rapprochement with Russia that followed Georgia's entry into CIS membership in autumn 1993 continued with the signing during a visit to Tbilisi by Russian Pres. Boris Yeltsin in February of a major bilateral Treaty on Friendship and Cooperation (not yet ratified by the Russian parliament) plus two dozen related agreements, including one on the establishment in Georgia of three Russian military bases. In March Georgia joined NATO's Partnership for Peace program.

In early April Abkhazian, Georgian, UN, and Russian representatives signed an agreement stipulating conditions for the repatriation of Abkhazia's Georgian population, but UN Secretary-General Boutros Boutros-Ghali ruled out the dispatch of UN peacekeepers to oversee this operation. Five weeks later a formal cease-fire agreement was signed in Moscow, to the displeasure of the Georgian opposition. In mid-June the Russian parliament approved the dispatch to Abkhazia of a Russian peacekeeping force that was subsequently formally approved by the UN Security Council. A Russian attempt in September to expedite the return of the Georgian refugees, which had been repeatedly delayed by the Abkhazian authorities, failed after the latter warned of violent reprisals. Visiting Georgia in November, Boutros-Ghali pledged support for Georgia's territorial integrity but again refrained from pledging a UN peacekeeping presence.

The adoption by the Abkhazian Parliament in November of a new constitution designating Abkhazia an independent sovereign republic was denounced by both the Russian and Georgian governments. In November, former prime minister Tengiz Sigua and former defense minister Tengiz Kitovani announced they were recruiting volunteers for the military reconquest of Abkhazia. In South Ossetia the former Communist Party, restored to power in parliamentary elections in March, ceded to pressure from the radical parliamentary minority not to abandon the campaign begun by the latter for secession from Georgia. They sought unification with North Ossetia within the Russian Federation.

(ELIZABETH FULLER)

This article updates the *Macropædia* article TRANSCAUCASIA: *Georgia*.

GERMANY

Germany is in central Europe, on the North and Baltic seas. Area: 356,959 sq km (137,823 sq mi). Pop. (1994 est.): 81,966,-000. Cap. designate, Berlin; seat of government, Bonn. Monetary unit: Deutsche Mark, with (Oct. 7, 1994) a free rate of DM 1.54 to U.S. $1 (DM 2.45 = £1 sterling). President in 1994, Richard von Weizsäcker and, from July 1, Roman Herzog; chancellor, Helmut Kohl.

Germans limped into 1994 only to emerge from it with their confidence largely rebuilt. The worst recession since World War II had battered the country in 1993 and appeared still to be raging in the new year. Unemployment hit record heights, provoking widespread disenchantment with politics and with the government in particular. As Germans headed for a marathon series of 19 different elections, few gave Chancellor Helmut Kohl (*see* BIOGRAPHIES) much chance of winning a fourth term in the autumn.

By the spring, however, the economy was recovering much earlier and more vigorously than expected. Amid spreading optimism, the political mood of the country shifted markedly. Having trailed well behind in the opinion polls, Kohl watched his personal fortunes improve as his Christian Democratic Union (CDU) advanced, overtaking the Social Democratic Party (SPD) challengers. In October the recently written-off chancellor won the general election, but with a heavily reduced majority. Pledging continuity, the Kohl government set out to complete the unfinished business of unification and to push German support for the European Union (EU).

Domestic Affairs. Most Germans began 1994 expecting a change of government in Bonn at the general election on October 16. Opinion polls showed some three-quarters of the population had a negative view of the centre-right coalition government. After 12 years in power, Kohl was much less popular than the SPD leader, Rudolf Scharping. The ruling CDU with its Bavarian affiliate party, the Christian Social Union (CSU), held a bit more than 30% support in opinion polls, against some 40% for the SPD.

The electoral calendar was charged as never before, with 19 elections scheduled—at local, state, national, and European levels. Two new protest parties sought to exploit the spreading dissatisfaction. The anti-European Free Citizens' Federation focused mainly on the elections to the European Parliament in June and on German concerns about losing the Deutsche Mark to an eventual Eurocurrency. The anti-establishment Instead Party sought to expand from its local success in the city-state of Hamburg into a national force.

On January 24 the CDU/CSU nominated Roman Herzog (*see* BIOGRAPHIES), Germany's leading constitutional judge, to be its candidate to succeed Richard von Weizsäcker as the nation's president. The nomination to this sensitive post came after Kohl had suffered intense political embarrassment with his first nominee, the little known eastern German lawyer Steffen Heitmann, who withdrew amid controversy in late 1993.

On March 13, in the state of Lower Saxony in the first of the 19 electoral tests, Kohl's CDU suffered its worst performance in the region in 35 years, while the SPD narrowly won an absolute majority of seats in the state legislature. The liberal Free Democratic Party (FDP), Kohl's coalition ally in the federal government, fell below the 5% of votes needed to qualify for parliamentary representation. This was the beginning of a series of state defeats that was to rock this small but influential party in the run-up to the general election.

Shortly after this confidence-boosting start, Scharping made the first of three key blunders that were to undermine his challenge to Kohl. In announcing plans for an income tax surcharge to help pay for unification, Scharping confused the pay levels at which the tax would begin, exposing himself to government accusations that he did not understand economics.

An arson attack in late March on the synagogue in the city of Lübeck served as a reminder that right-wing violence was still present. Ignatz Bubis, head of the German Jewish community, said he had expected something similar for some time. The leader of the far-right Republicans, Franz Schönhuber, caused a furor by blaming Bubis for inciting people to anti-Semitic violence.

Scharping's tax confusion began rapidly to erode the SPD's popularity, while the CDU benefited from the multiplying signs of economic recovery. During April, opinion polls showed the gap between the rival main parties narrowing until, by the end of the month, the CDU/CSU had pulled equal with the SPD for the first time in 1994. Another poll showed over two-thirds of Germans seeing

German Chancellor Helmut Kohl (rear) appears with François Mitterrand, president of France, at a ceremony during the year. In voting on October 16, Kohl's coalition government was returned to power, despite recession in Germany and other problems.

improving economic trends. Controversy was provoked by a Federal Constitutional Court ruling that the possession of small quantities of marijuana and hashish was no longer a punishable offense.

On May 23 Herzog was chosen by a special electoral assembly to be Germany's next president, defeating the SPD challenger, Johannes Rau. The victory was an important political boost for Kohl. Scharping made his second big political error by publicly criticizing the outcome, thus being seen as a poor loser. In his victory speech, Herzog said he would represent Germany "as it really is: freedom-loving, tolerant, and open to the world."

By the end of May, opinion polls were showing the CDU comfortably ahead of the SPD and Kohl pulling away from Scharping. In particular, the chancellor's popularity in the east, only recently at a low ebb, was recovering strongly. The June 12 elections to the European Parliament provided further evidence of Kohl's comeback, as the CDU/CSU increased its vote share to 38.8%, and the SPD fell to 32.2%. A key psychological boost for Kohl, the outcome was most damaging to Scharping. The European elections confirmed the continuing weakness of the FDP, which again fell below the 5% barrier, as well as the popularity in the east of the former communists, renamed the Party of Democratic Socialism (PDS). The hopes of the anti-European protest parties, notably the Republicans and the new Free Citizens' Federation, failed to materialize.

At the state election in Saxony-Anhalt on June 26, the SPD just failed to beat the CDU. With an eye to the general election campaign, the SPD refused a left-right "grand coalition" with the CDU, forming instead a minority administration with the Greens/Alliance '90 that could survive only by being "tolerated" by the PDS. This was Scharping's third big strategic miscalculation, as it exposed the SPD to relentless accusations from the centre-right that it was collaborating with former communists. While the SPD's action provoked little controversy in eastern Germany, opinion polls showed it to be deeply unpopular in the much larger western sector. Scharping said that the SPD would not repeat the Saxony-Anhalt experience.

The SPD was by now on the defensive, as opinion polls showed declining popular confidence in the party's ability to solve Germany's main problems. The situation at the beginning of the year was reversed, with the CDU/CSU winning between 40% and 45% support in the opinion polls. On July 1 von Weizsäcker, after 10 years in office, stepped down as president amid enthusiastic tributes from all sides, and Herzog took over.

The political agony of the Free Democrats continued over the summer as they were ejected from one state parliament after another. This raised doubts about whether the chancellor would be able to reform his coalition government even if his own party emerged strongest from the general election. In the eastern states of Brandenburg and Saxony on September 11, the FDP dropped below the 5% barrier, while the strength of the PDS was confirmed. In the Bavarian state election on September 25, the CSU defended its absolute majority, while the FDP lost all its seats. At the Free Democrats' congress in Gera in December, party leader Klaus Kinkel was subjected to an almost unprecedented vote of confidence, which he barely survived.

The German general election on October 16 confirmed the extent of the turnabout in the political fortunes of the chancellor from his unpromising start to 1994. Although the centre-right coalition won, its majority was slashed from 134 to 10 in the 672-seat Bundestag (lower house of Parliament) in Bonn. The CDU/CSU was slightly down, with 41.5% of the vote; the SPD was up at 36.4%; the FDP succeeded nationally with 6.9% where it had failed at the state level; and the Greens/Alliance '90 returned to the Bundestag with 7.3%. The eastern German PDS won four directly elected seats, enough for them to be exempted from the 5% rule even though the party nationally captured only 4.4%. (For tabulated results, see *Political Parties,* above.)

The results of the general election became official on November 15 when Kohl was formally elected by the Bundestag—by one vote over the required majority. The narrowness of the new majority and the fact that the Bundesrat (upper house) was solidly under the control of the opposition SPD prompted speculation that governing Germany would be more difficult.

On May 29 Erich Honecker, the former communist leader of East Germany, who was forced to resign shortly before the fall of the Berlin Wall, died at the age of 81 in Santiago, Chile, after a long battle against liver cancer. (*See* OBITUARIES.)

The Economy. The year in Germany began on a sour economic note; unemployment broke the four million mark in January, while surveys showed a majority of firms intending to shed more labourers as they continued radical cost-cutting programs. The corporate community was still reeling from the shock of the near collapse at the turn of the year of Metallgesellschaft AG, one of Germany's biggest industrial conglomerates, after it ran into problems financing its huge oil-futures trading contracts in the United States. The need for a DM 3.4 billion rescue package sparked intense criticism of Germany's leading financial institution, Deutsche Bank AG, for not having spotted the impending problems earlier, in its role as head of Metallgesellschaft's supervisory board.

The corporate crisis fueled an energetic debate about the traditionally close links in Germany between banks and industry and whether these clubby boardroom contacts impeded the process of proper control and supervision of management. The damage to Deutsche Bank's image continued as the Metallgesellschaft affair dragged through the summer, marked mainly by criticism from prominent U.S. economists who argued that the German bank had mismanaged the crisis and was itself largely responsible for the huge losses suffered by Metallgesellschaft.

On January 11 the chemical workers' union set the stage for one of the most moderate pay rounds in the history of the Federal Republic. The settlement, which was well below inflation and contained important innovations on flexible working arrangements, marked a breakthrough, helping German companies' efforts to regain competitiveness after the cost explosion that occurred during the unification boom at the beginning of the 1990s. This first step was followed in early March by a momentous compromise deal by Germany's biggest trade union, IG Metall, which represented engineering workers. The pay deal, about half the expected rate of inflation, was struck just 48 hours before workers were due to strike and was hailed as proof of the resilience of Germany's industrial relations system based on consensus and compromise. For the first time, this pace-setting union agreed to reduce working time without full pay compensation and to give firms a flexible margin in working time arrangements. With unemployment rising at about 30,000 a month in the engineering sector, Klaus Zwickel, head of IG Metall, said, "We wanted job security and we were prepared to give up money for this."

Before Deutsche Bank had a chance to get over the worst of the Metallgesellschaft controversy, it found itself at the centre of another storm after one of Germany's leading private property developers, Jürgen Schneider, disappeared, leaving about DM 5 billion in debts. While an international

arrest warrant was issued, the bank, as Schneider's largest creditor, found itself under attack for having neglected its controlling duties. The influential role of the big banks in Germany came in for renewed criticism, while Kohl, with his eye on the election campaign, called upon the banks to look after the interests of hundreds of small businessmen facing ruin because of the Schneider empire's collapse.

Such scandals could not detract, however, from the increasing evidence of economic improvement as firms began to reap the fruits of recovery in their main export markets and made extensive efforts to improve production efficiency. After recording its first-ever loss in 1993, Daimler-Benz AG, Germany's leading industrial corporation, declared its fortunes to have turned. At the world's biggest industrial trade fair, in Hanover in late April, Kohl's hailing of an economic spring was supported by the heads of Germany's main industry associations, who agreed that the "leitmotiv of this year's fair is optimism." On April 26 Germany's six leading economic research institutes, presenting their spring

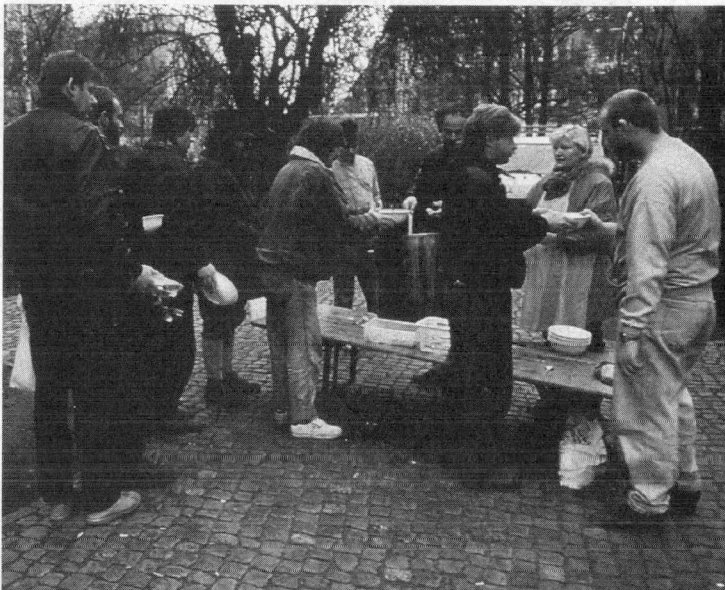

A food line forms in Berlin. Although there were signs that a strong economic recovery was beginning in Germany, unemployment remained extremely high, particularly in the former eastern sector, which had undergone extensive structural changes since reunification.
MARK SIMON—BLACK STAR

report, raised their forecast of national gross domestic product (GDP) growth to 1.5% in 1994, to reflect the improved conditions.

April also saw the first slight fall in unemployment, coming much sooner than most observers had expected. Subsequent job market data over the summer confirmed that the recovery was well under way, as unemployment began clearly to turn down, confounding gloomy predictions early in the year that it would continue rising toward 4.5 million. By June, in its most optimistic report for some time, the Deutsche Bundesbank, Germany's central bank, had declared the recession over and said economic growth was turning out to be surprisingly strong. Unemployment had dropped to 3.5 million by the autumn, and the six research institutes, in another report in October, raised their GDP growth forecast for 1994 to 2.5%, saying Germany was enjoying a robust recovery, amid signs that firms were beginning to invest strongly again in new machinery. The institutes' report warned, however, of the massive tax increases in the pipeline and said the priority of the new government had to be, primarily by cutting back public spending, to reduce the weight of the state in the economy, after it had expanded so much during unification.

Foreign Affairs. In his New Year's message, Kohl said Germany wanted to take a full part in UN peacekeeping and peacemaking missions, highlighting an issue that was to preoccupy the foreign policy debate for much of the year. German frustration was particularly acute over the Serbs in former Yugoslavia. The government in Bonn had to perform a delicate balancing act, supporting tougher military action against the Serbs while knowing its own constitution prevented Germany from taking any active role in such a policy.

There was also much anxiety at the growing influence of the Russian nationalist extremist Vladimir Zhirinovsky (*see* BIOGRAPHIES), dubbed the Russian Hitler by the German press. With his eye on the large numbers of Russian troops still in eastern Germany, Kohl said the extremist's success sent a warning to the West not to be lax in backing Russia's reform efforts.

At the NATO summit in January, Kohl argued strongly for eventual membership for the Eastern European countries, a theme that dominated the chancellor's visit to Washington, D.C., at the end of the month, when he emphasized to Pres. Bill Clinton the vital importance of a stable Eastern Europe. On a reciprocal visit to Germany in July, Clinton praised the "truly unique relationship" between Germany and the U.S.

The strains underlying the traditionally carefully presented relations between France and Germany suddenly broke to the surface in March when the French ambassador to Bonn was summoned to the Foreign Ministry to explain publicized remarks that demonstrated deep distrust about Germany's role in Europe and, notably, its leanings toward the east. This diplomatic row took place against a background of irritation in Bonn government circles that Kohl had not been invited, as a sign of reconciliation, to the D-Day celebrations to be held by the World War II allies in Normandy, France, in June.

In April the German government found itself embroiled in another sensitive diplomatic issue as Russia objected to plans for the final send-off of its troops from eastern Germany, saying it wanted to take part in the celebrations for the departure of the American, French, and British allied forces scheduled for September 8 in Berlin. Pres. Boris Yeltsin pressed the Russian case during a three-day visit, but Kohl refused to budge from his decision to have separate ceremonies. He agreed, however, to hold the Russian ceremony in Berlin on August 31 and to attend it himself with Yeltsin.

On May 18, in a two-year review of German foreign policy, Klaus Kinkel, the foreign minister, expressed shock at the "devastating image" of his country abroad, where the activities of the extreme right were given extensive coverage, notably in the U.S. In early July a visit by the Chinese premier, Li Peng (Li P'eng), provided much embarrassment, as the guest failed repeatedly to turn up at engagements and then cut short his trip, expressing anger at protests and references to China's human rights record.

On July 12 the Federal Constitutional Court made a historic judgment, permitting German troops to participate fully in international security missions for the first time since World War II. The only condition was that such operations had to have the backing of the Bundestag. In a significant gesture, German soldiers paraded down the Champs-Élysées in Paris during the Bastille Day celebrations on July 14. They were part of the recently formed Eurocorps, a combined force of German, French, Spanish, Belgian, and Luxembourgian troops. The gesture was partly meant to make up for Kohl's not having been invited to the D-Day anniversary.

On July 1 Germany assumed the rotating EU presidency for six months, setting its priorities as encouraging the opening to the east and easing the accession of new members due to join on Jan. 1, 1995. Later in the year a paper on European union by Kohl's CDU sparked controversy by calling for a hard core of countries, notably France and Germany, to push ahead with integration, regardless of whether other members could, or wanted to, keep up. Reflecting German determination to see the momentum of European integration maintained, the paper provoked much irritation among Germany's partners, notably Britain and Italy, who were deemed outside the hard core. In the autumn German and Polish troops took part in the first joint maneuvers as the German defense minister, Volker Rühe, said he expected Poland to be in NATO by the year 2000.

(JOHN EISENHAMMER)

GHANA

A republic of West Africa and member of the Commonwealth, Ghana lies on the Gulf of Guinea. Area: 238,533 sq km (92,098 sq mi). Pop. (1994 est.): 16,050,000. Cap.: Accra. Monetary unit: cedi, with (Oct. 7, 1994) a free rate of 996 cedis to U.S. $1 (1,585 cedis = £1 sterling). Chairman of the Provisional National Defense Council and president in 1994, Jerry John Rawlings.

In February 1994 Ghana witnessed some of the worst ethnic clashes since gaining independence. More than 1,000 people were killed and 150,000 displaced in ethnic clashes in the north between the Konkomba and Nanumba groups at Napayili. The Konkomba are migrants from Togo, and the clashes were over land rights. The government declared a state of emergency. On June 9 the groups that had been involved in the fighting signed an agreement in Accra under which they would settle land disputes peacefully. The government stationed a battalion of troops in the region, and the emergency was lifted in August.

In May, Pres. Jerry Rawlings reshuffled his Cabinet. To prevent officials from awarding themselves huge salaries, the government decided to establish a committee to fix the salaries of top management in state-owned enterprises. The nation planned to issue identity cards to voters for registration on the new electoral roll in September 1995. Early in 1994 the government announced plans to sell 25% of the Ashanti Goldfields Corp., reducing its share in the firm to 30%.

At the 17th annual summit of the Economic Community of West African States in Abuja, Nigeria, President Rawlings assumed the chairmanship; he said that Ghana was considering withdrawing its contingent from the Community's peacekeeping force in Liberia because it had its own ethnic problems to control and because of the cost.

(GUY ARNOLD)

This article updates the *Macropædia* article WESTERN AFRICA: *Ghana*.

GREECE

The republic of Greece occupies the southern part of the Balkan Peninsula and several adjoining island groups in southeastern Europe, in and between the Ionian and Aegean seas. Area: 131,957 sq km (50,949 sq mi). Pop. (1994 est.): 10,365,000. Cap.: Athens. Monetary unit: drachma, with (Oct. 7, 1994) a free rate of 235.24 drachmas to U.S. $1 (374.15 drachmas = £1 sterling). President in 1994, Konstantinos Karamanlis; prime minister, Andreas Papandreou.

During 1994 the government of Prime Minister Andreas Papandreou, whose Panhellenic Socialist Movement (Pasok) had regained power in October 1993, was unable to resolve the problems of the debt-ridden economy or to ease the strains in the country's relations with its Balkan neighbours. At the same time, persistent infighting bedeviled the main opposition party, the conservative New Democracy (ND). Its new leader, the 55-year-old Miltiadis Evert, who had been elected to succeed Konstantinos Mitsotakis, came under fire for being too bland in opposing the government. The loss of credibility by the two major parties was reflected in the results of the elections for the European Parliament, held on June 12. Pasok remained ahead, but its wings were severely clipped, and the ND suffered serious losses. Protest votes went to the smaller groups, the Political Spring party of Antonis Samaras and the two communist variants, the Communist Party and the Progressive Left Coalition.

As the problems piled up in 1994, public attention was deflected to a string of scandals allegedly implicating Mitsotakis, the former prime minister. In what looked like revenge for the indictment of Papandreou on corruption charges in 1991, the socialist majority in Parliament arraigned Mitsotakis on charges of tapping the telephones of friends and foes and of receiving bribes in the sale of a state-owned cement industry to an Italian company. Reports in December suggested that the case would be dropped, however.

The removal of the 76-year-old Mitsotakis from the ND leadership inevitably raised questions about the future of Papandreou, who was 75 and whose health clearly prevented him from exercising his duties in full. Papandreou's difficulties became more apparent at the beginning of the year, which coincided with the assumption by Greece of the rotating presidency of the European Union (EU). The Greek minister for European affairs, Theodoros Pangalos, skillfully turned the anticipated fiasco of the Greek tenure into a substantial success, however, and by the end of the six-month term, the EU was able to approve the admission of four new members, sign a pact with Russia, and give the green light to 11 public works projects to combat rising unemployment.

Pangalos' success, as well as his growing popularity within the party, made him a front-runner in the succession race, despite a serious setback in the October municipal elections when he was beaten by his conservative rival for the post of Athens mayor. Papandreou, despite his health problems, was widely assumed to want to succeed Konstantinos Karamanlis, whose term as president was due to end in May 1995. The strife within the party for the succession was so intensified by November, however, that Papandreou, fearing a breakup of Pasok, formally renounced his aspiration to become head of state, affirming that he would continue to serve as party leader.

Perennial deficits, enduring double-digit inflation, and rising unemployment forced the Pasok government to revise its stand against the privatization of debt-ridden state enterprises. A poorly prepared plan to float 25% of the stock of the state-owned Telecommunications Organization in November was aborted at the last moment, however, after signals from European stock markets that investors were uninterested. Efforts to limit tax evasion stumbled on the resistance of taxpayers such as doctors, lawyers, and taxi drivers. The drachma came under severe pressure in May in anticipation of its becoming freely convertible on July 1. The Bank of Greece skillfully rode out the storm, spending over $2 billion from its foreign-exchange reserves and overnight raising interest rates as high as 500%. Although the crisis abated, the underlying problems of the economy remained.

Greeks demonstrate in Thessaloniki over the issue of Macedonia. The dispute with the former Yugoslav republic over matters that included its name, flag, and constitution, along with quarrels with other Balkan neighbours, continued to influence Greek politics.
LAMBI PAPADOPOULOS—SYGMA

Papandreou set out on an arduous trip to the United States in April, but he failed to gain the unstinted support he sought from Pres. Bill Clinton over Greece's disputes with its Balkan neighbours. Throughout 1994 the EU also sent Greece angry messages over the imposition of sanctions against its neighbours, particularly as Greece used its EU prerogatives to put pressure on those states.

A crisis developed after a raid at the Albanian border post of Episkopi in April. The armed raiders were known to be seeking the annexation of a part of southern Albania where a Greek minority lived. In September Albanian leaders, eager to reassert their country's sovereignty, had five Greek minority leaders sentenced for high treason to terms of six to eight years, slightly reduced on appeal. Greece promptly recalled its ambassador, blocked EU aid to Albania, and deported some 50,000 Albanian economic refugees.

The feud over the name of the republic of Macedonia, temporarily known in the United Nations as The Former Yugoslav Republic of Macedonia, continued unabated. On February 15 Greece closed the port of Thessaloniki to all trade in and out of the Macedonian republic. The Macedonian government refused to negotiate until the trade embargo was lifted, and mediation efforts by the United States and the EU failed.

Tension built up throughout the year following a persistent Turkish campaign threatening war if Greece extended its territorial waters in the Aegean Sea to 12 mi from the present 6. The campaign was clearly launched in view of the entering into effect on November 16 of the Law of the Sea, a treaty opposed by Turkey, which made the 12-mi limit the international norm. Turkey argued that this would affect its Aegean coastline because of the number of Greek islands. Its reaction, however, was no doubt prompted by the prospect that such a move would extend Greek sovereignty to 90% of the oil-rich Aegean seabed. Strains reached a climax in May when Turkey officially accused Greece of training Kurdish separatist guerrillas in its territory, a charge the Greeks denied with vehemence. In July, Greek terrorists murdered a Turkish diplomat in Athens, the third such incident in recent years.　(MARIO MODIANO)

GRENADA

A constitutional monarchy within the Commonwealth, Grenada (with its dependency, the Southern Grenadines) is in the eastern Caribbean Sea. Area: 344 sq km (133 sq mi). Pop. (1994 est.): 91,800. Cap.: Saint George's. Monetary unit: Eastern Caribbean dollar, with (Oct. 7, 1994) a par value of EC$2.70 to U.S. $1 (free rate of EC$4.30 = £1 sterling). Queen, Elizabeth II; governor-general in 1994, Reginald Palmer; prime minister, Nicholas Brathwaite.

The National Democratic Congress (NDC) party learned in July 1994 that it would lose its leader, Prime Minister Nicholas Brathwaite, before the next general election, constitutionally due by March 1995. He announced that he would step down in the near future.

This was a further blow to the NDC, already unpopular after it reintroduced an income tax on individuals in its 1994 budget in January. The income tax had been abolished by a previous government in 1986, but successive administrations found that indirect taxation did not produce sufficient revenue to meet the country's needs. The new tax rates ranged from 10% to 30%, with the first EC$10,000 of income being tax exempt.

Some additional income did come the government's way in 1994 through asset sales. It concluded negotiations with Guinness Brewing Ltd. in March for the sale of a controlling interest in Grenada Breweries for EC$3.2 million.

Infrastructural improvements continued during the year. In February OPEC and the Kuwait development fund agreed to provide EC$27 million to upgrade Grenada's road and sea defense system.

In May the government reached what could prove to be a key agreement with Indonesia for informal collaboration in stabilizing the world price of nutmeg, one of Grenada's most important export earners. The two countries were the world's main nutmeg producers.　(DAVID RENWICK)

This article updates the *Macropædia* article THE WEST INDIES: *Grenada*.

GUATEMALA

A republic of Central America, Guatemala has coastlines on the Caribbean Sea and the Pacific Ocean. Area: 108,889 sq km (42,042 sq mi). Pop. (1994 est.): 10,322,000. Cap.: Guatemala City. Monetary unit: quetzal, with (Oct. 7, 1994) a free rate of 5.76 quetzales to U.S. $1 (9.17 quetzales = £1 sterling). President in 1994, Ramiro de León Carpio.

Frequent assassinations, bomb attacks, human rights abuses, land conflicts, labour disputes, and demonstrations marked 1994 as yet another violent year in Guatemala. The government of Pres. Ramiro de León Carpio faced one crisis after another and appeared increasingly impotent, although it moved forward on the political path to democracy.

In January the government and the Guatemalan National Revolutionary Unity agreed to resume peace negotiations (broken off in May 1993) and to sign a peace accord by the end of the year. Several subsidiary accords were signed during 1994; one of them involved the resettlement of people displaced by the armed conflict. There was no cease-fire, however, and insurgent activity continued.

Fewer than 20% of voters turned out for the January 30 referendum on constitutional change. Of those, 69% voted in favour of a new Congress and Supreme Court. Critics of the government pointed to the low turnout as evidence that the president had lost credibility, and there were rumours of coup attempts by the military. The Supreme Electoral Tribunal convened congressional elections for August 14. The number of deputies was reduced from 116 to 80, of which 64 were departmental and 16 nationwide. In another low turnout only 18.5% of the electorate cast valid votes, with high abstention rates in rural areas. The Guatemalan

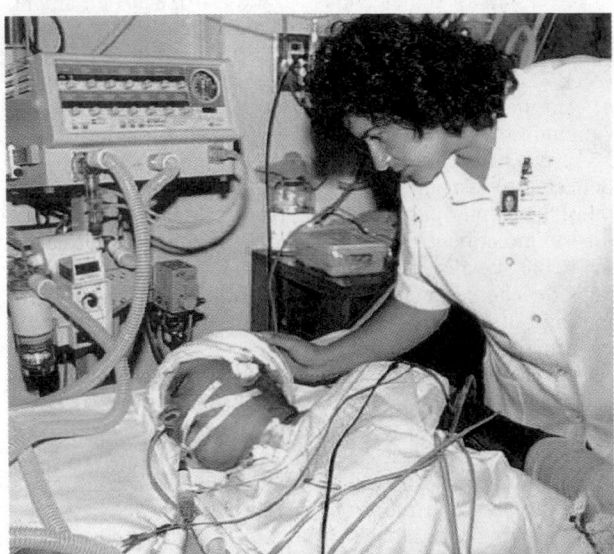

A U.S. journalist and tourist, June Weinstock, is treated in a hospital in Guatemala City after being beaten by a mob. She was one of several foreigners attacked by Guatemalans claiming that their children were being stolen for adoption or for trafficking in organs.

AFP

Republican Front, led by the fundamentalist evangelical former dictator Efraín Ríos Montt, won 32 seats, and another right-wing party, the National Advancement Party, won 24. (For tabulated results, see *Political Parties*, above.) The new Congress was inaugurated on September 13.

A massive police operation against alleged baby traffickers led to the discovery of several crib houses and arrests early in the year. In March a mob brutally beat a U.S. citizen, June Diane Weinstock, when it was rumoured that she had been trying to kidnap a child in San Cristóbal Verapaz. She was left unconscious and remained in a coma for weeks. There was speculation that the attack was instigated to destabilize the administration and thus justify greater military involvement in civilian policing. Another woman, Jennifer Harbury, who went on a 32-day hunger strike to force the government to release her husband, a leftist rebel who had been captured in 1992, faced legal action in November. The incidents had profound repercussions in the tourist industry, where cancellations caused lost revenue forecast at up to $100 million.　(SARAH CAMERON)

This article updates the *Macropædia* article CENTRAL AMERICA: *Guatemala*.

GUINEA

The republic of Guinea is located in West Africa, on the Atlantic Ocean. Area: 245,857 sq km (94,926 sq mi). Pop. (1994 est.): 6,501,000 (excluding 500,000–600,000 refugees from Liberia and Sierra Leone). Cap.: Conakry. Monetary unit: Guinean franc, with (Oct. 7, 1994) a free rate of GF 979 to U.S. $1 (GF 1,557 = £1 sterling). President in 1994, Gen. Lansana Conté.

Despite opposition charges of vote fraud, the Supreme Court of Guinea confirmed on Jan. 4, 1994, the election in December 1993 of Lansana Conté as the country's president. Violence continued, however, as supporters of defeated opposition candidate Alpha Condé repeatedly clashed with pro-government backers. Dozens of people reportedly died in riots on January 6 in Macenta, near the Liberian border.

On April 24 the main opposition group, the Rally of the Guinean People (RPG), gathered in Paris to plan a strategy for December's scheduled legislative elections. Chairman Condé called on the party to cooperate with the newly appointed independent electoral commission, which was to supervise the polls.

Eight high-ranking military officers, including the air force deputy chief of staff, were arrested on June 10 and accused of plotting to overthrow Conté. On June 16 the government released them, stating that there had been no intended coup and that the charges were without foundation. There was, however, more unrest. In August security forces broke up mass demonstrations by RPG supporters in Conakry. President Conté reshuffled his Cabinet on August 23, removing all opposition ministers who had remained in it.

(NANCY ELLEN LAWLER)

This article updates the *Macropædia* article WESTERN AFRICA: *Guinea*.

GUINEA-BISSAU

A republic of West Africa, Guinea-Bissau lies on the Atlantic Ocean. Area: 36,125 sq km (13,948 sq mi). Pop. (1994 est.): 1,050,000. Cap.: Bissau. Monetary unit: Guinea-Bissau peso, with (Oct. 7, 1994) a free rate of 12,484 pesos to U.S. $1 (19,856 pesos = £1 sterling). President in 1994, João Bernardo Vieira; prime minister, Carlos Correia.

On March 21, 1994, Pres. João Bernardo Vieira postponed the first multiparty presidential and legislative elections because of lack of money and delays in the registration of voters; later they were rescheduled for June 5. After further problems the elections were finally held on July 3, with 1,136 candidates vying for 100 seats in the National People's Assembly and 8 candidates, including Vieira, running for president. During the campaign the leader of the Party for Social Renovation, Kumba Iala, accused Vieira's African Party for the Independence of Guinea-Bissau and Cape Verde (PAIGC) of encouraging tribalism and racism.

Final results gave Vieira 46.2% of the vote (less than the 51% required for election) and Iala 21.88%, while the PAIGC won 64 out of the 100 seats in the Assembly. The opposition parties then decided to throw their weight behind Iala in the rerun of the presidential election. The runoff was a bitter contest between the two men; on August 20 Iala accepted defeat. According to the National Electoral Commission, Vieira polled 1,599,930 votes (52.02%), against 1,475,190 votes (47.98%) for Iala. Iala accused the PAIGC of buying votes and said that as a result he would not participate in a government of national unity.

(GUY ARNOLD)

This article updates the *Macropædia* article WESTERN AFRICA: *Guinea-Bissau*.

GUYANA

A republic and member of the Commonwealth, Guyana is situated in northeastern South America, on the Atlantic Ocean. Area: 215,083 sq km (83,044 sq mi). Pop. (1994 est.): 733,000. Cap.: Georgetown. Monetary unit: Guyana dollar, with (Oct. 7, 1994) an official rate of G$142.13 to U.S. $1 (G$226.06 = £1 sterling). President in 1994, Cheddi Jagan; prime minister, Sam Hinds.

After two years in power, the People's Progressive Party (PPP)/Civic alliance retained substantial support in 1994, judging by the results of local elections in August. The alliance achieved a sweeping victory, capturing 48 of the 65 Neighbourhood Democratic Councils. It also won in three of the six municipalities.

Only in Georgetown, the capital, did it fail to make headway, trailing both former prime minister Hamilton Green's group, named Good and Green for Georgetown, and the official opposition People's National Congress (PNC) party. Green won 12 seats, the PNC 10, and the PPP/Civic alliance 8.

Despite the PPP's roots in the labour movement, in May the government had to face a 10-day strike by workers in the public sector. The strike ended when the government agreed to pay a G$5,500 minimum monthly wage.

In July the government successfully concluded another Enhanced Structural Adjustment Facility with the International Monetary Fund, which required it to continue its market-liberalization measures. In return, the IMF promised $75 million in financial assistance over three years. The Caribbean Group for Cooperation in Economic Development offered Guyana $320 million in economic assistance during the same period.

(DAVID RENWICK)

HAITI

The republic of Haiti occupies the western one-third of the Caribbean island of Hispaniola, which it shares with the Dominican Republic. Area: 27,700 sq km (10,695 sq mi). Pop. (1994 est.): 6,491,000. Cap.: Port-au-Prince. Monetary unit: gourde, with (Oct. 7, 1994) a free rate of 19 gourdes to U.S. $1 (30.22 gourdes = £1 sterling). President in 1994, Jean-Bertrand Aristide (in exile until October 15); acting president from May 11 to October 12, Émile Jonassaint; head of military government until October 10, Lieut. Gen. Raoul Cédras; prime minister from November 8, Smarck Michel.

Throughout 1994 the U.S. government put pressure on the repressive Haitian military regime to resign and allow the elected president, Jean-Bertrand Aristide, to return to the country and restore democracy. On July 31 the UN Security Council called for all necessary means to be taken to oust the regime, authorizing the U.S. to invade Haiti. About 100 UN monitors went to the Dominican Republic-Haiti border in mid-August to stop oil smuggling, which was sustaining the Haitian military.

Within the United States there was opposition to a U.S. invasion, and no other country would agree to participate in anything other than a postinvasion force. Haiti judged that if the flow of boat people fleeing the nation ceased and there were no more massacres, there would be little reason for the U.S. to invade. The military regime's puppet president, Émile Jonassaint, declared a state of siege and accused the world of having "declared war on poor Haiti, which has harmed nobody." Throughout August the army and its paramilitary ally, the Front for the Advancement and Progress of Haiti, continued to murder Aristide supporters while organizing parades of "volunteers" to fight an invasion.

On September 18 a U.S. peace mission comprising former president Jimmy Carter, former chairman of the Joint Chiefs of Staff Gen. Colin Powell, and Sen. Sam Nunn successfully negotiated a compromise that averted an outright invasion to remove the regime. The army commander, Gen. Raoul Cédras; the army chief of staff, Gen. Philippe Biamby; and the police chief, Col. Joseph Michel François, agreed to step down by October. Subsequently, Colonel François fled to the Dominican Republic, while General Cédras and General Biamby left for Panama.

Haitians greet one of the U.S. soldiers sent to their country in September to prepare for the return of their deposed president, Jean-Bertrand Aristide. Troops went to Haiti after a negotiating team led by former U.S. president Jimmy Carter reached an accord with the nation's military government.

DAVID BURNETT—CONTACT PRESS IMAGES

On September 19 some 20,000 U.S. troops began landing in Haiti. Although it was originally intended that they would work alongside the Haitian military, after a few days U.S. soldiers were authorized to intervene to stop the savage street beatings of civilian demonstrators. U.S. Marines killed 10 Haitian policemen in Cap-Haitien on September 24, provoking delighted local people to tear down the barracks; pro-Aristide crowds took over other towns in the north, forcing troops and police to flee. In Port-au-Prince, U.S. troops took control of the parliament, allowing exiled legislators to return and debate a general amnesty; restored the elected mayor, Evans Paul; dismantled the Army Heavy Weapons Corps; seized police stations; and began street patrols. They worked with Haitians to find suspected army collaborators and other extremists who had previously terrorized the population. Late in October troops from the member nations of the Caribbean Community and Common Market arrived in Port-au-Prince, charged with maintaining security at the port.

Amid much celebration, President Aristide returned triumphantly to Haiti on October 15, three years after being ousted by the military coup. He spoke of reconciliation and set about arranging legislative elections for December (they were later postponed until March 1995 at the earliest). As prime minister, Aristide chose Smarck Michel, a businessman. His choices for other government posts favoured economics, and a technical and financial aid agreement was signed with the United States in mid-December.

(SARAH CAMERON)

This article updates the *Macropædia* article The WEST INDIES: *Haiti.*

HONDURAS

A republic of Central America, Honduras has coastlines on the Caribbean Sea and the Pacific Ocean. Area: 112,088 sq km (43,277 sq mi). Pop. (1994 est.): 5,302,000. Cap.: Tegucigalpa. Monetary unit: lempira, with (Oct. 7, 1994) a free rate of 8.91 lempiras to U.S. $1 (14.71 lempiras = £1 sterling). Presidents in 1994, Rafael Leonardo Callejas and, from January 27, Carlos Roberto Reina.

Carlos Roberto Reina of the Liberal Party was sworn in as president of Honduras on Jan. 27, 1994, pledging to promote economic growth, eradicate corruption, and respect human rights. A report by the National Human Rights Commission on the disappearances in the 1980s was published just before Reina's inauguration; it directly implicated the armed forces and attributed responsibility to the U.S. and Argentina. In March an autonomous and apolitical Public Ministry headed by an attorney general was created. The reform had been recommended by an ad hoc commission in 1993 in response to human rights abuses by the security forces and inadequacies in the justice system. The police special intelligence unit was replaced by a civilian Criminal Investigations Unit. The abolition of forced military recruitment was approved by Congress in May, but before it could be ratified, the president bowed to military pressure and gave his authorization to a temporary military recruitment drive.

In March President Reina outlined the difficult economic situation he had inherited and his plans for the future. The new administration aimed to increase tax collection and to cut spending by 10%; spending to fight poverty would account for 35% of the budget. The budget deficit was more than 11% of gross domestic product, and inflation for the first half of the year was over 20% as a result of the freeing of prices frozen by the previous government and the devaluation of the lempira. The government's economic program was unpopular with both business and labour; there were frequent labour disputes and demonstrations, some of which became violent, and isolated terrorist attacks.

In May the president ordered a three-month moratorium on logging while a policy was being formulated to reorganize the administration of state forests and to clarify the role of the private sector. The area covered by forest declined from 36% in 1980 to 28% in 1990, and the deforestation was causing erosion. Drought affected Honduras throughout 1994, and there were daily electricity blackouts.

(SARAH CAMERON)

This article updates the *Macropædia* article CENTRAL AMERICA: *Honduras.*

HUNGARY

A republic, Hungary is a landlocked state in central Europe. Area: 93,033 sq km (35,920 sq mi). Pop. (1994 est.): 10,257,000. Cap.: Budapest. Monetary unit: forint, with (Oct. 7, 1994) a free rate of 107.76 forints to U.S. $1 (171.39 forints = £1 sterling). President in 1994, Arpad Goncz; prime ministers, Peter Boross and, from July 15, Gyula Horn.

In 1994 Hungary underwent a major political change. The centre-right coalition led by the Hungarian Democratic Forum was severely defeated by the left, which then was able to form a new coalition with a two-thirds parliamentary majority. The elections were held in May—under Hungary's highly complex electoral law—and the Hungarian Socialist Party (HSP) gained an absolute majority of seats, taking 54% of the poll. The second largest party, the Alliance of Free Democrats, polled 18%. These two parties eventually put together a coalition. The opposition was in disarray, with the Forum down from 43% in 1990 to just under 10% in 1994. (For tabulated results, see *Political Parties,* above.)

The return of the HSP, put together from various elements of the Communist Party, which had ceded power in 1990, was viewed with dismay by some, and there were fears that some of the practices of communism would revive. In reality, the Forum-led coalition had been increasingly perceived as amateurish, bungling, and unconcerned with the needs of the average Hungarian. Crucially, it was seen as incapable of running the economy, as the standard of living was sliding and privatization, which had slowed to a crawl, was not producing growth in prosperity. It was also condemned as morally unfit to govern in light of the burgeoning corruption over which it presided.

The HSP benefited from the nostalgia factor, the memories that during the final years of the communist system the population had lived adequately and with a much higher sense of security than recently. The HSP was also effective in conveying an image of competence, convincing voters that it had considerable expertise at its disposal and that the amateurishness of its predecessors would be replaced by a modern, professional government. Finally, the HSP was the beneficiary of the disenchantment in Hungary with the nationalist sloganeering of the centre-right government. Hungarian opinion was increasingly neutral on the question of the ethnic Hungarians in neighbouring states, and many were irritated that the government seemed to be paying more attention to noncitizens of Hungary than to citizens. The extreme nationalist party led by the Forum dissident Istvan Csurka performed very badly at the polls, taking only 1.25% of the vote.

The overwhelming success of the HSP was a problem to the party leadership itself. The new prime minister, Gyula Horn, and his team came from the reform wing of the old Communist Party. They were uncertain whether some of the other left-wing deputies would be loyal when issues of economic restriction came on the agenda. To this end the HSP began negotiations with the Free Democrats, and after some weeks they put together a seemingly solid coalition.

The HSP leadership could be secure that with Free Democrat support it would be able to enact its program. There were also doubts as to how the West would react to a communist successor party with an absolute majority, and the Free Democrat participation in the government would provide a degree of international respectability. Furthermore, the construction of a coalition with a two-thirds majority would allow the government to introduce structural changes to the political system. The coalition was determined to oversee the formulation of a new constitution, a process that was expected to take about two years to complete. There were also plans to simplify the electoral law.

Once in office, however, the coalition seemed to become curiously torpid. Despite government promises of action and professionalism in the face of an urgent economic situation, very little was done during the coalition's first six months in office. In particular, the reform of the economic infrastructure was not tackled with the energy that had been expected. This was seen as all the more dangerous because without substantial improvement the country could easily find itself in a major balance of payments crisis.

In foreign policy the new government suffered from bad luck. Unlike its predecessor, it was eager to come to early arrangements with its neighbours. Unfortunately, it found itself without a negotiating partner as nationalists gained greater influence in both Slovakia and Romania. Hungary received the same reassurances at the European Union summit in December as did the other countries of the former Soviet bloc with which "Euroagreements" had been signed.

Local government elections were held as the year ended, and the dominance of the HSP was confirmed at this level, too. Although the majority of those elected as mayors were independents, the HSP gained about one-third of all elected councillors, while Gabor Demszky, the popular Free Democrat mayor of Budapest, was reelected.

(GEORGE SCHÖPFLIN)

ICELAND

Iceland is an island republic in the North Atlantic Ocean, near the Arctic Circle. Area: 102,819 sq km (39,699 sq mi). Pop. (1994 est.): 267,000. Cap.: Reykjavík. Monetary unit: Icelandic króna, with (Oct. 7, 1994) a free rate of 67.83 krónur to U.S. $1 (107.89 krónur = £1 sterling). President in 1994, Vigdís Finnbogadóttir; prime minister, David Oddsson.

During the spring and summer of 1994, a large number of Icelandic trawlers began fishing in a cod-rich area in the Barents Sea that lies outside the fishery limits of Norway and Russia. This caused considerable anger among Norwegian and Russian fishermen and authorities, who had done much in recent years to nurture the previously depleted fish stocks in that area back to health. Icelandic-Norwegian relations, which had always been close, cooled distinctly as a result of this dispute.

The prospective entry of Norway, Finland, and Sweden into the European Union at the beginning of 1995 generated considerable anxiety in Iceland, which feared that it would not be able to join the EU. Thus began a considerable debate on the merits of entering the EU. The Independence Party, the nation's largest, took the position that Iceland should remain outside the EU for the time being since it already had concluded an agreement with the European Economic Area. The Social Democrats, on the other hand, decided that Iceland should apply for membership in the EU as soon as possible.

On January 4 the governments of the United States and Iceland reached a new agreement concerning the continued U.S. and NATO military presence in Iceland. The U.S. government sought to reduce its military presence in the wake of reduced international tensions. The Icelandic authorities resisted this, partly because the air base was a large employer in an area with considerable unemployment. The two-year pact called for a gradual reduction in the number of F-15 jets stationed in Iceland from 12 to 4. It also provided for the possibility that the Icelandic authorities would take over the task of the search-and-rescue helicopter squadron stationed at the air base.

(continued on page 419)

SPOTLIGHT: Perils of Postcommunism in Eastern Europe by George Schöpflin

The pattern of postcommunist development may well have reached a kind of plateau in 1994. The high excitement associated with the collapse of communism and its aftermath, the construction of new political systems, was over. The systems were slowly crystallizing and acquiring features of their own, so it was no longer possible to put all the blame for systemic malfunctioning on the communists. However much they might be prisoners of their own past, the postcommunist actors were themselves responsible for their own errors.

By 1994 the private sector was producing over half of gross domestic product and employing over half the labour force in Poland, the Czech Republic, Hungary, and Slovenia, and Slovakia was not far behind. Privatization was much slower elsewhere, although it had not stalled completely anywhere. This expansion of the private sector was possibly the single most significant longer-term economic development in the region and was of considerable importance politically. The increase in the number of those with property meant that the nature, range, and intensity of property rights and the power to dispose of property grew correspondingly, and these people would gradually make an impact on the functioning of politics. Crucially, property owners were seen to have a greater stake in the enforcement of the law; there is a clear relationship between property ownership and democracy.

Despite the rise in the number of property owners, however, democracy would not follow automatically because the relationship between the two is a correlation, not a causation. This was where the problems arose in the postcommunist world; the other conditions that encouraged the development of democracy were still weak. In particular, the culture of an impersonal public sphere—a sense that the state, institutions, and civil society were neutral and not operating according to private interests—still had a long way to go. Correspondingly, trust in public institutions was low. Not least, the state was not trusted to enforce the law impartially, and many people were thus suspicious or dissatisfied with their status and inclined to blame the state or mysterious, uncontrollable forces for their losses. Conspiracy theories flourished, and those in turn gave nondemocratic options an opportunity.

Furthermore, the access to property on the part of some but not others was seen as unjust and was, therefore, rejected by many. The legacy of communism had produced a paradox; people wanted the prosperity of the market systems, but they were loath to abandon a certain commitment to the egalitarianism that they had learned under the former regime. The overall consequence was that suspicion of private enterprise increased, and the gulf between the haves and the have-nots deepened. Moreover, the nouveaux riches flaunted their newfound wealth and were disliked for doing so. The feelings of those who had not succeeded under the new system were those of envy and hope that the beneficiaries would be brought down to their level.

Because sizable sections of the population were very suspicious of democracy, there were serious implications for the construction of democratic systems. They saw democracy and markets as the means of enrichment for others and as responsible for their own impoverishment. Their readiness to move with the times was limited by their own inexperience and ignorance and by the sheer intellectual and cultural difficulty of transforming the habits of a lifetime from a dependent to an entrepreneurial culture.

These shortcomings of the social base helped to explain both the success of the successors to the communist parties in Poland, Hungary, Bulgaria, Lithuania, and elsewhere and equally the appeal of right-wing nationalist and populist movements, as in Slovakia and Romania. In former Yugoslavia the pattern was further complicated by war or the threat of war. These parties owed their electoral successes to the implicit promise that the shift to democracy interpreted as prosperity could be achieved relatively painlessly. In reality, they faced the near incompatible tasks of modernizing the political and economic infrastructures of their states and simultaneously satisfying the expectations of societies that were unprepared for the costs of transition. Should these parties fail to effect some qualitative change, the outlook would be decidedly poor.

Western governments were aware of the potential for instability in the region but were not in a position to do very much to help or, at any rate, perceived their options as limited. In particular, the two areas where the West could genuinely have given support—economics and international security—were both confused by contradictory Western interests and by unrealistic expectations on the part of the postcommunists. Observers were generally agreed that the postcommunist states would benefit substantially from an opening of Western markets to textiles, steel, and agricultural produce. Yet these were the very sectors that Western governments were most concerned to defend from competition. The members of the European Union (EU), with lobbies and vested interests of their own to contend with, had largely blocked Central and Eastern European imports, offering the postcommunist countries limited quotas.

As far as security was concerned, the West was impeded in any attempt to support the Central and Eastern European countries by their perceived need to placate Russia, a process that, if anything, intensified during the year. Russia had for all practical purposes vetoed any thought that NATO might be extended eastward, insisting that NATO membership for any of the former Warsaw Pact states was an infringement of its own security, something that the West was disinclined to challenge. This left Central and Eastern Europe in the same security vacuum with which they had been struggling from the end of communism. The EU, on the other hand, had embarked on a cautious process that would at some future date see six of the Central and Eastern European states integrated as full members. The essence of this process was that the states with which "Euroagreements" had been signed—Poland, the Czech Republic, Slovakia, Hungary, Romania, and Bulgaria—would ultimately be given membership. It was generally understood that Slovenia and the Baltic States—Estonia, Latvia, and Lithuania—could likewise look forward to membership.

The difficulty for the postcommunists was that there was no timetable attached to this process, and full EU membership was not likely to be attained until the end of the decade at the earliest. In this sense the invitation to the six Euroagreement states to attend the EU's summit in Essen, Germany, in December was an important symbolic step, but they were left lacking in concrete political achievement. It was generally understood that nothing would be done to define a timetable until after the conclusion of the EU intergovernmental summit in 1996. In all, the prospects of democracy and full integration into Western Europe for the countries of Central and Eastern Europe improved little during the year.

George Schöpflin is lecturer in Eastern European political institutions at the London School of Economics and the author of *Politics in Eastern Europe, 1945–1992* (1993).

(continued from page 417)

The Icelandic economy grew slowly in 1994. Gross domestic product (GDP), measured at constant prices, rose by an estimated 2%. Inflation was about 1% for the year, a record low for a nation that had been highly inflation-prone for decades. Unemployment averaged 4.8% in 1994, an increase of 0.5% from the previous year. The current account of the balance of payments was in deficit by less than 1% of GDP for the year.

Economic growth began to slow in 1987 because of a decline in fish stocks, the mainstay of the economy. The outlook for the cod stock, the most important species, continued to be bleak. A 23% reduction in the allowed cod catch was introduced for the fishery year begun in September 1994 in order to protect cod from continued overfishing. (*See* AGRICULTURE AND FOOD SUPPLIES: *Fisheries* and accompanying map.) All told, the value of the fish catch was expected to decline by 3% in 1995 following a 4% decline in 1994, both figures measured at constant prices.

(BJÖRN MATTHÍASSON)

INDIA

A federal republic of southern Asia and member of the Commonwealth, India is situated on a peninsula extending into the Indian Ocean, with the Arabian Sea to the west and the Bay of Bengal to the east. Area: 3,165,596 sq km (1,222,243 sq mi), including the Indian-administered portion of Jammu and Kashmir. Pop. (1994 est): 913.7 million, including Indian-administered Jammu and Kashmir. Cap.: New Delhi. Monetary unit: Indian rupee, with (Oct. 7, 1994) a free rate of Rs 31.37 to U.S. $1 (Rs 49.89 = £1 sterling). President in 1994, Shankar Dayal Sharma; prime minister, P.V. Narasimha Rao.

Domestic Affairs. Prime Minister P.V. Narasimha Rao's program of liberalization improved the economy in 1994. The government also achieved a majority in the Lok Sabha (House of the People) with the help of a faction of the Janata Dal headed by Ajit Singh. Congress (I) made a good showing in by-elections to Lok Sabha but was routed in three of four state assembly elections held late in the year. In Karnataka the Janata Dal won a majority, and in Andhra Pradesh and in Sikkim local parties came to power. Only in Goa did Congress (I) have success, where it emerged as the largest party.

In December three members of the Cabinet who had been accused of corruption resigned, two for their role in securities irregularities and the third named in a sugar scandal. At the same time, the prime minister's principal rival, Arjun Singh, also left the Cabinet, charging the government with corruption.

On October 25 the Supreme Court unanimously declined to give an opinion on whether any Hindu temple had existed at Ayodhya, where the Babri Mosque (built in 1528 and demolished by Hindu fundamentalists on Dec. 6, 1992) had stood. A reference by the president to such a temple was called superfluous and unnecessary. By a 3–2 majority the court upheld the legality of the acquisition by the union government of 27.4 ha (67.7 ac) of land around the disputed structure. The court also held that the former chief minister of Uttar Pradesh, Kalyan Singh, was guilty of contempt of court and in flagrant violation of an agreement that no permanent structure would be put up on the disputed land. Singh was symbolically sentenced to a day's imprisonment and a fine of Rs 2,000. The result of the judgment was that the issue would have to be resolved through adjudication by the Allahabad High Court or through negotiations.

New trouble arose in Uttar Pradesh when the people of the districts in the Himalayan region protested the policies of the state government and demanded the formation of a separate state of Uttarakhand. When the state police fired upon demonstrators proceeding to Delhi, reportedly killing 25 persons, the state Congress (I) threatened to withdraw its support of the chief minister.

The situation in Punjab moved toward normalcy. Elections were held to district and village councils, and Congress (I) emerged victorious. The various Akali factions combined into a single party and demanded autonomy for the state. Assam continued to be troubled by the militancy of Bodo tribesmen.

Workers in an Indian mill prepare rolls of denim fabric for shipment to the U.S. for use in making clothing. After decades of resistance to foreign investment, India continued to open up its economy, with one of the results being greatly expanded exports.

DILIP MEHTA—CONTACT

In Jammu and Kashmir the government claimed to have broken the back of the secessionist organizations, but attacks on police, military personnel, and civilians continued. In November, Prime Minister Rao took direct control of Kashmir's affairs.

The chief election commissioner announced a drive to reform the electoral process. He demanded that all states enforce a model election code and that they issue identity cards with photographs to all eligible voters in order to prevent fraud.

The Supreme Court delivered an important ruling in March on the scope of article 356 of the constitution and specified the conditions under which states could be brought under presidential rule. Declaring that state governments could be dismissed if they worked against secularism, a basic feature of the constitution, the court upheld the dismissals of the Bharatiya Janata Party governments in Madhya Pradesh, Rajasthan, and Himachal Pradesh in the wake of the Ayodhya incidents. The imposition of presidential rule in Nagaland in 1988, in Karnataka in 1989, and in Meghalaya in 1991 was held to be invalid, but no remedial action was decreed since elections had subsequently been held. In another judgment the court sustained the legality of the Terrorist and Disruptive Activities (Prevention) Act and the Terrorist Affected Areas (Special Courts) Act.

Hindu-Muslim riots in September in Bangalore, Karnataka, resulted in 27 deaths when the local television station telecast news bulletins in Urdu, which was considered to be the language of Muslims. In Nagpur in November, 128 were killed in a stampede when police dispersed a rally of tribal people demonstrating for job quotas outside the Maharashtra state assembly. Investigation into the blasts that occurred in Bombay in 1993 led to several arrests.

In September there was an outbreak of pneumonic plague in Delhi and in Surat, Gujarat, and an epidemic of bubonic plague in Bid, Maharahstra. The epidemic was controlled within three weeks, but it affected air travel to and from foreign countries and hurt tourism and exports.

The Tamil Nadu legislature passed an act reserving 69% of the posts in state government services to the Scheduled and Other Backward (lower) Castes. The act was incorporated into the constitution as an amendment. The Karnataka legislature adopted a bill fixing the level at 73%.

The Indian space program made notable advances with the success of a satellite launch vehicle in May and a polar satellite launch vehicle in October. The latter put an 804-kg (1,769-lb) remote-sensing communications satellite into orbit at an altitude of 820 km (510 mi). An intermediate-range ballistic missile and a multitarget surface-to-air missile were test-fired successfully earlier in the year.

Zail Singh (*see* OBITUARIES), the president of India from 1982 to 1987, died on December 25. He was the first Sikh to hold the office.

The Economy. There was a sizable increase in foreign-exchange reserves. At the end of September they stood at $18.8 billion, compared with $13 billion in February and a mere $2.2 billion in 1991. According to figures released in October, industrial production in the April–June quarter was 7.8% higher than in the corresponding period of the previous year. The growth in gross domestic product was estimated to be 4.2%. The annual rate of inflation fell slightly to less than 8.3% on October 1. Exports rose by 10.6% during April–August.

The budget of the union government for 1994–95 included concessions in income and corporate taxes as well as in excise and import and export duties, amounting to a revenue loss of Rs 40.8 billion. This was done to stimulate investment and industrial production, which had performed below expectations in the previous year. The prime interest rate was lowered from 15% to 14%. The rupee had been made fully convertible in 1993. The rise in foreign-exchange reserves enabled the government to repay loans from the International Monetary Fund a year in advance. The total revenue receipts were nearly Rs 861 billion, and capital receipts were slightly more than Rs 596 billion. A sum of Rs 40 billion was to be secured through sale of public-sector equity. The total expenditure was estimated at Rs 1.5 trillion. The provision for development was nearly Rs 465 billion and for defense Rs 230 billion, both marginally higher than in the previous year. The allocations for health, education, and employment and for rural development were increased. The uncovered revenue gap was Rs 60 billion, and the overall fiscal deficit was close to Rs 550 billion, which was 7.3% of the gap. The railway budget contained proposals for raising almost Rs 10 billion through increased fares and freight charges.

In September the government published a list of 27 leading public-sector undertakings allowed to offer shares to the public and delicensed 70 bulk drugs. Parliament permitted nationalized banks to raise capital from the market. A new telecommunications policy was announced by which private companies with minority foreign participation could operate domestic telephone services. Cable television was legalized.

The country signed the final act of the Uruguay round of the General Agreement on Tariffs and Trade, although there was spirited opposition to some of the GATT provisions. In December two presidential ordinances were issued amending earlier acts so as to meet the requirements of the World Trade Organization.

Foreign Affairs. Prime Minister Rao visited Switzerland, Germany, the U.K., the U.S., Russia, Vietnam, and Singapore. In Russia a joint statement was signed on terrorist threats to multiethnic states. The prime minister spoke about India's commitment to liberalization when he addressed the World Economic Forum at Davos, Switz., and the G-15 (nonaligned) nations in New Delhi. The president paid state visits to Bulgaria and Romania. Important foreign visitors included the presidents of Argentina, the Czech Republic, Egypt, Indonesia, Maldives, Mongolia, Nigeria, Poland, Senegal, Slovakia, Togo, Uzbekistan, and Zimbabwe, as well as the prime ministers of Malaysia and Singapore, the crown prince of Nepal, and the UN secretary-general.

Talks were held with China on the reduction of troops along the 4,000-km (2,500-mi)-long line of actual control between the two countries. Later the two countries signed an agreement to expand trade and travel. Relations with Pakistan continued to be uneasy. Pakistan closed its consulate in Bombay. A statement by Nawaz Sharif, former prime minister of Pakistan, that his country possessed nuclear weapons received a hostile response in India, but there was satisfaction at Pakistan's inability to get the UN Human Rights Commission to censure India. Delhi turned down suggestions for third-party mediation on Kashmir.

(H.Y. SHARADA PRASAD)

INDONESIA

A republic of Southeast Asia, Indonesia consists of the major islands of Sumatra, Java, Kalimantan (Indonesian Borneo), Celebes (Indonesian: Sulawesi), and Irian Jaya (West New Guinea) and more than 13,000 smaller islands and islets. Area: 1,919,317 sq km (741,052 sq mi). Pop. (1994 est.): 191,340,000. Cap.: Jakarta. Monetary unit: rupiah, with (Oct. 7, 1994) a free rate of 2,173 rupiah to U.S. $1 (3,456 rupiah = £1 sterling). President in 1994, Suharto.

Social tensions and political maneuvering intensified through much of 1994, partly fueled by President Suharto's statement in April that he did not expect to be in charge after his current term expired in 1998. Whereas the military, pro-Suharto technocrats and politicians, and Muslim leaders all sought to strengthen their political positions, labour groups, student activists, civil liberties advocates, and the press became more outspoken and assertive. But growing unrest led to a clampdown later in the year.

Many in the armed forces were unhappy with Research and Technology Minister B.J. Habibie. (*See* BIOGRAPHIES.) He had helped promote the children and allies of Suharto, in power since 1967, to top positions in the ruling Golkar organization by displacing former generals. He also spearheaded the purchase and refurbishing of 39 former East German naval vessels—a $900 million undertaking that the military resented as a costly encroachment on its prerogative. Leading generals, moreover, criticized the government's handling of labour unrest and emphasized the need for army involvement in running the country. Disaffected segments of the military helped Megawati Sukarnoputri—a daughter of Sukarno, the country's late founding father—become head of the fast-rising opposition Indonesian Democratic Party.

Muslims grumbled more loudly about their plight and the privileges enjoyed by rich ethnic Chinese and Christians. Their leaders also pressed for a greater say in matters affecting the nation's 164 million Muslims. In December 1993 a trial focused attention on unionist Marsinah, who had been murdered while campaigning for higher wages. In March the press reported a scandal involving defaulted government loans of $430 million to ethnic Chinese tycoon Eddy Tansil; he had been recommended to bank officials by a top minister. The following month workers rioted in Medan, Sumatra. In July a Muslim-backed newspaper criticized loans to Chinese businessman Sofyan Wanandi. After the U.S. told Indonesia early in the year to improve workers' treatment or lose trade preferences, the situation improved. The World Bank deplored Indonesia's monopolies and imprudent lending even as Finance Minister Mar'ie Muhammad disclosed that over one-fifth of state-bank loans might never be repaid. In July a factory owner and five of his staff were convicted in the Marsinah case. In August Tansil was given a 17-year jail term and fined $230 million for defaulting on improperly obtained government bank loans.

Many Indonesians, however, felt that key people were spared in both trials. In June the government closed the

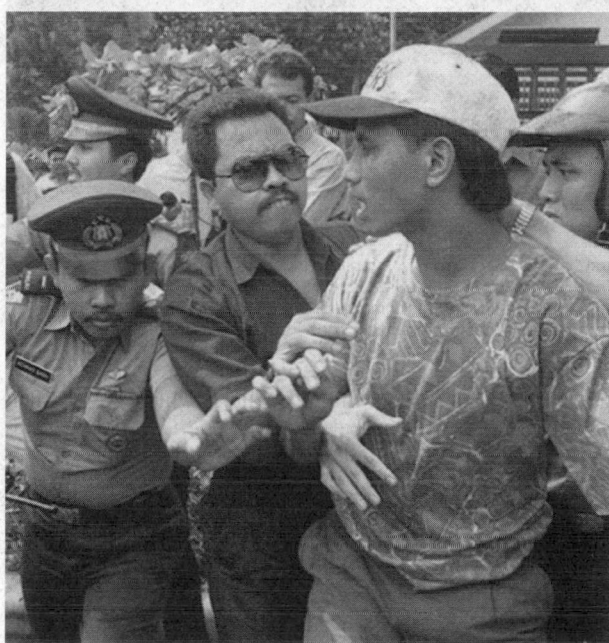

Indonesian riot police in Jakarta arrest a Timorese demonstrator outside the U.S. embassy during the Asia-Pacific Economic Cooperation meeting in November. Protesters used the meeting as an opportunity to call attention to the government's policies in the former East Timor.
AFP

tabloid *DeTik* (circulation 450,000) and the weeklies *Tempo* (200,000) and *Editor* (87,000). In August officials cautioned other publications to avoid sensitive subjects, and the government imposed tighter controls on such human rights groups as the Legal Aid Foundation. It also charged an independent union leader, Muchtar Pakpahan, with complicity in the Medan riots. Protests staged by artists and other intellectuals were not reported in the press. Even the military felt its clout diminished as capable officers were transferred to remote areas. To most observers President Suharto, who skipped the Cairo population conference owing to illness, had tightened the reins on political liberalization because it appeared to be fostering antigovernment sentiments.

Contentious politics did little to stanch economic growth, estimated at a robust 7%, even though export growth slowed to 12% from 31% in 1993. But with petroleum revenues and bank lending held back, the government had to promote foreign investment, down 20% to $8 billion in 1993. It had estimated capital needs, mainly for infrastructure, at $63 billion a year until 2000, twice the 1993 total. In midyear a presidential directive allowed 100% foreign ownership of local ventures and opened up the transport, communications, power, and media sectors. Approved foreign investments from January to September hit nearly $20 billion—almost double the 1992 record—with domestic outlays of another $20 billion, up 13.5% compared with all of 1993. But there

were fears of rising capital flight spurred by anti-Chinese unrest and political uncertainty. Two events highlighted Indonesian foreign affairs in 1994. The first was a May conference in the Philippines on East Timor, a former Portuguese colony annexed by Indonesia in 1976. Indonesian protests forced Filipino officials to bar foreigners from the conference, but the commotion only generated additional global interest in the event. The second event was the November summit of the Asia-Pacific Economic Cooperation forum in Bogor, near Jakarta. Despite domestic riots over East Timor, the summit was favourable to Jakarta, which sought a greater role on the international stage.

(RICARDO L. SALUDO)

IRAN

The Islamic Republic of Iran is in southwestern Asia on the Caspian and Arabian seas and the Persian Gulf. Area: 1,638,057 sq km (632,457 sq mi). Pop. (1994 est., excluding about 1.8 million Afghan refugees): 59,614,000. Cap.: Tehran. Monetary unit: Iranian rial, with (Oct. 7, 1994) an official floating rate of 1,732 rials to U.S. $1 (2,755 rials = £1 sterling). *Rahbar* (spiritual leader) in 1994, Ayatollah Sayyed Ali Khamenei; president, Hojatolislam Ali Akbar Hashemi Rafsanjani.

The government began 1994 facing deteriorating morale and disillusionment among much of the population. Pres. Ali Akbar Hashemi Rafsanjani conceded in February that the nation had severe domestic difficulties. In April a senior government adviser, Hossein Azimi, called publicly for "political reforms," including democratic local government and an end to suppression of political freedom, in order to enable the country to undergo economic regeneration.

In a test of nerves for the Islamic regime against the popular will, a ban was unsuccessfully attempted in September on the use of private satellite receiver dishes, which had become a widespread means of avoiding the censorship applied to domestic TV channels. The weakening political base of the regime was also symbolized on June 20 when a bomb exploded at the shrine of the Imam Reza in Mashhad, killing at least 24 persons and injuring at least another 70. The authorities blamed the outlawed Mujaheddin-e Khalq. An attempt on President Rafsanjani's life was reported in February. The city of Qazvin erupted in rioting in August.

Meanwhile, President Rafsanjani's government was becoming isolated and ineffectual in the face of opposition from Islamic hard-line factions. Further undermining of the regime was caused by widespread public apathy, intensified by falling living standards for most Iranians. The death in November of the Ayatollah Mohammad Ali Araki, the accepted source of Shi'ite emulation (*marja' at-taqlid*), left the regime embarrassed because the claims of the official spiritual guide, Ali Khamenei, to the succession were widely rejected.

Iran's foreign relations continued to be severely constrained. The U.S. did not have diplomatic representation in Iran, and the U.K. retained contacts only at the level of chargé d'affaires. U.S. policy emphasized Iran's outcast status, and in July U.S. Secretary of State Warren Christopher declared Iran an "outlaw nation." Western relations with Iran were governed by fears of Iranian aspirations for advanced weapons of mass destruction, Iran's assistance to international terrorism, Iranian subversion of other regional governments, and the lack of human rights inside Iran. A senior Iranian official was expelled from the U.K. in midyear, and a British diplomat was similarly expelled from Iran.

Disputes with the government of Saudi Arabia over Iranian participation in the annual pilgrimage to Mecca led to a deterioration in relations with that country. On July 18 an explosion at a Jewish cultural centre in Buenos Aires, Arg., was initially attributed to Iranian action and led to a diplomatic rupture with Argentina. Japan, however, maintained good relations with Iran and proposed, despite objections from the U.S., giving a $1 billion loan to aid a dam-construction project on the Karun River.

The Iranian economy fared badly in 1994. Oil revenue forecasts were severely reduced from $17.7 billion to $10.5 billion for the year March 1994–March 1995. Oil exports by volume averaged 3.7 million bbl per day in the first half of 1994, short of the official target of more than 4 million bbl per day. Inflation rose on the official index to more than 35%. Meanwhile, the value of the Iranian currency deteriorated rapidly on the free market to more than 3,000 rials to $1 by October against an official rate of 1,732 rials and an import rate of 2,340 rials to $1. In early October the government tried to control the activities of free-market currency dealers in order to stem the fall of the rial. The government also abandoned its subsidies on all but 23 items of food and medicine imports to limit its losses of foreign exchange on this account.

Symptomatic of the government's difficulties was a steady rise in foreign debt to more than $32 billion and a disinclination of overseas suppliers other than Japan to fund further credits. A second five-year plan adopted in March was based on an optimistic growth rate in gross domestic product of 5.4–6% annually in the period 1994–99.

(KEITH S. MCLACHLAN)

IRAQ

A republic of southwestern Asia, Iraq has a short coastline on the Persian Gulf. Area: 435,052 sq km (167,975 sq mi). Pop. (1994 est.): 19,869,000. Cap.: Baghdad. Monetary unit: Iraqi dinars, with (Oct. 1, 1994) an official rate of 500 dinar to U.S. $1 (795.25 dinars = £1 sterling). President in 1994, Saddam Hussein; prime ministers, Ahmad Husayn Khudayir as-Samarrai and, from May 29, Saddam Hussein.

UN sanctions were the dominant issue for Pres. Saddam Hussein in 1994, tempting him to take a desperate gamble by staging military maneuvers against Kuwait and to enforce harsh internal repression to retain his grip on power. In early October he dispatched two divisions of Republican Guards, along with tanks and armoured personnel carriers, to the border area with Kuwait. In addition, a contingent of bedouins (stateless Arabs)—described as members of the League of People with Rights but in reality Iraqi soldiers in disguise—were encamped on the border. In rapid response to the crisis, several thousand U.S. troops were sent to Kuwait within days.

Although describing the deployment as "an internal matter," Iraq had taken a chance on gaining international sympathy for its economic plight by staging the crisis, but even Saddam's erstwhile allies Palestine Liberation Organization leader Yasir Arafat and King Hussein of Jordan declined to back him. By October 11 Iraq had begun pulling back its units.

On November 10 the Iraqi parliament agreed to recognize Kuwait's sovereignty and the existing Iraq-Kuwait border as delineated by the UN. In early November Saddam also declared that his country was no longer at war with Israel. Despite these moves, which were clearly designed to improve Iraq's standing with the West, the UN Security Council on November 14 agreed to keep sanctions in place. The Western allies considered Iraq's recognition of Kuwait to be insufficient and doubted the regime's sincerity.

In late May Saddam abruptly sacked Prime Minister Ahmad Husayn Khudayir as-Samarrai, making him the scape-

Iraqi soldiers load military supplies and equipment in preparation for their withdrawal from the Iraq-Kuwait border. When the U.S. responded to an Iraqi buildup by sending troops to Kuwait, the Iraqis agreed to remove their most formidable forces from the border area.
AFP

goat for the collapse of the Iraqi dinar, which was by then valued on the black market at 510 to the U.S. dollar, compared with 54 to the dollar when the prime minister was appointed in September 1993. Saddam announced that he was taking over the post, and on November 27 he was also taking charge of foreign policy. Planning Minister Majid Faraj was demoted to minister of state without portfolio after his office issued a report estimating the annual rate of inflation at 24,000%.

In June Saddam declared that Islamic penalties of amputation would be applied to robbers, car thieves, and farmers who refused to sell their crops to the government. A ban on the public sale of alcohol was also decreed. In increasingly grandiose statements the president said that he would build the world's largest mosque, with a white dome and eight minarets, on one of the airport sites used in the Persian Gulf war. Lavish celebrations again marked Saddam's birthday in April.

The president's sons Uday and Qusai Hussein together with Ali Hassan al-Majid, a relative by marriage and the former governor of Kuwait, were adamantly opposed to compromise with the UN. Uday's views gained influence through his newspaper. On September 8 an antigovernment demonstration took place in Baghdad, which opposition sources said was dispersed by troops. The exiled Iraqi National Congress, the principal umbrella anti-Saddam grouping, tried repeatedly to negotiate an end to armed clashes between groups in the Kurdish-controlled northern enclave. A peace settlement was finally accepted in late November. In April U.S. missiles accidentally brought down two U.S. helicopters in the north, killing 26.

Conservationists, including the World Wildlife Fund (WWF), expressed growing alarm at the progress of Iraqi plans to drain the marshlands of southern Iraq in order to harass opponents of the regime. In late April work on the 108-km (70-mi) Umm al-Maarik (Mother of All Battles) Canal was completed. The WWF said that if the canal building program continued as scheduled, the marshes would disappear as a habitat in 10 to 20 years.

In early August Turkey reopened a border crossing with Iraq. Trade was to be limited to food and medicines, but reports persisted that violators were running other cargoes through the border post, while officials turned a blind eye. Iraq was accused by Lebanon of involvement in the assassination in Beirut of Sheikh Taleb Ali as-Suheil, an opposition leader normally based in London. As a result of unsatisfactory explanations from the Iraqis, Lebanon broke off diplomatic relations with Baghdad in late April.

(JOHN WHELAN)

IRELAND

The republic of Ireland, separated from Great Britain by the North Channel, the Irish Sea, and St. George's Channel, shares its island with Northern Ireland to the northeast. Area: 70,285 sq km (27,137 sq mi). Pop. (1994 est.): 3,512,000. Cap.: Dublin. Monetary unit: Irish pound (punt), with (Oct. 7, 1994) a free rate of £Ir 0.64 to U.S. $1 (£Ir 1.01 = £1 sterling). President in 1994, Mary Robinson; prime ministers, Albert Reynolds and, from December 15, John Bruton.

In November 1994 the coalition Labour/Fianna Fail government fell in highly dramatic circumstances. Difficulties had been growing between Prime Minister Albert Reynolds, leader of Fianna Fail, the larger party in the coalition, and the Labour leader, Dick Spring. Trust between the two broke down completely over the appointment of the attorney general as president of the High Court at a time when serious questions had been raised over his failure to extradite to Northern Ireland a priest under investigation for child molestation offenses. Reynolds went ahead with the appointment without the support of the Labour ministers, who immediately withdrew from the government. In attempts to salvage the administration, Reynolds withheld from members of Parliament a vital piece of information concerning the delay in extraditing the priest—who by then had been convicted—information that the leader of the Labour Party knew had been supplied by the new attorney general. On November 16 Spring announced his resignation as deputy prime minister and that of his ministers. The next day Reynolds announced his resignation as prime minister and that of his ministers, and the newly appointed president of the High Court also announced his resignation.

Now serving as acting prime minister, Reynolds did not ask the president to dissolve Parliament, and negotiations began almost immediately to form a new administration. Despite his belief that trust and accountability had been destroyed between the coalition partners, thus causing the collapse of the government, Spring opened a series of talks with the new leader of Fianna Fail, Bertie Ahern. On December 15, John Bruton, head of the Fine Gael party, was elected prime minister with the help of the Labour and Democratic Left parties, both of which would be members of the new coalition government.

A number of events during the year had heightened tensions within the Labour/Fianna Fail government. In June a passports-for-sale scandal erupted. It emerged that an Arab family had been given Irish passports in exchange for a large investment in the prime minister's family business. Further investigation revealed that this was not an isolated incident and that the process, personally supervised over a period of some years by Reynolds' predecessor, Charles Haughey, had not been subject to audit or control. The deputy prime minister called for an investigation and declared that if there had been wrongdoing he would resign. Subsequently he was shown documents connected with the granting of passports and declared himself satisfied.

Elections to the European Parliament, combined with two by-elections, took place on June 9, and public apathy was apparent from the turnout of only 50%. Government parties suffered a major setback, losing both by-elections and experiencing a collapse of the Labour vote in the European Parliament election. A major surprise was the election of two Green Alliance candidates.

In January the government dropped Section 31 of the Broadcasting Act, which had been introduced by the 1973–77 government. This had denied the nationalist party Sinn Fein access to the airwaves. The repeal was believed to have been part of an overall strategy to bring about a cessation of violence by the Irish Republican Army (IRA) following the historic agreement by the British and Irish prime ministers in December 1993. This important breakthrough was widely welcomed and was considered to offer Northern Ireland its best chance of peace in a quarter of a century.

Both governments held firm to the jointly declared positions of December 1993, and on August 31 the IRA announced the "cessation of military operations." It did not, however, include the word *permanent* in its statement. But the overall message soon became clear: the IRA, its long campaign of violence having failed to budge the British government, or change appreciably the political landscape in Northern Ireland, was prepared to adopt a new strategy involving democratic politics and debate.

Low and stable interest rates, improved consumer confidence, and rising disposable incomes all contributed to strong economic growth in Ireland in 1994, with the gross national product rising 5%. Inflation remained at 2.5%. But the introduction of a budget that provided government funds for economic development failed to expand the job market. Unemployment remained at 282,000. Two major industrial disputes—one in Irish Steel and the other in Team Aer Lingus—with more than 2,000 jobs hanging in the balance were finally resolved in the autumn.

(MAVIS ARNOLD)

See also *United Kingdom*.

ISRAEL

A republic of southwestern Asia, Israel is situated on the Mediterranean Sea. Area: 20,700 sq km (7,992 sq mi), not including territory occupied in the June 1967 war. Pop. (1994 est.): 5,331,000. Cap.: Jerusalem (but *see* Israel table in *World Data* section). Monetary unit: New (Israeli) sheqel, with (Oct. 7, 1994) a free rate of 3.01 sheqalim to U.S. $1 (4.79 sheqalim = £1 sterling). President in 1994, Ezer Weizman; prime minister, Yitzhak Rabin.

If 1993 was characterized by a general euphoria after the historic breakthrough with the Palestine Liberation Organization (PLO) in September, 1994 saw Israelis in a more sober mood. Important steps were taken during the year toward consolidation of the peace accords with the Palestinians, and a full peace treaty with Jordan was signed. The Syrian peace track remained deadlocked, however, and the immensity of the task of forging a stable peace with the Palestinians became clearer.

On February 25 a Jewish extremist almost shattered the brittle process of reconciliation. Dressed as an Israeli army officer, Baruch Goldstein, a U.S.-born doctor, gunned down at least 29 Muslim worshipers in the Cave of the Patriarchs in Hebron. Several more people, including Goldstein, died in the ensuing riot. There was an outcry in the Arab world, and the Palestinians, Jordan, Syria, and Lebanon broke off peace talks with Israel. In response, the Israeli government set up a judicial commission of inquiry, banned the militant anti-Arab Kach and Kahana Hai groups, which had hailed Goldstein's action, and agreed to a "temporary international presence in Hebron" to monitor Palestinian-settler relations.

Carrying a photograph of Yasir Arafat, leader of the Palestine Liberation Organization, Palestinian soldiers enter Rafah in the Gaza Strip to become policemen. Under an agreement with the Israelis, in May the Palestinians took civilian control of the Gaza Strip and of Jericho in the West Bank.

Within a month of the massacre, talks with the Palestinians restarted, and by the end of April a detailed agreement for Israeli withdrawal from the Gaza Strip and Jericho had been hammered out. Negotiations on the implementation of the "Gaza and Jericho first" peace deal, which were to have lasted two months, had dragged on for nearly seven months, exacerbating mutual suspicions. These came to the fore in embarrassingly public fashion when, at the signing ceremony in Cairo on May 4, PLO leader Yasir Arafat refused for several minutes to sign one of the maps because of a lingering dispute regarding the size of the Jericho area.

On May 17, 27 years of Israeli occupation in Gaza and Jericho came to an end. Palestinian flags were hoisted as the departing Israelis handed over all 38 civil administration departments and 9,000 armed Palestinian police moved in to take over internal security. The Israeli army redeployed around Jewish settlements in the Gaza and Jericho areas. Palestinian police and Israeli soldiers began joint patrols.

On July 1, after dismantling his PLO headquarters in Tunis, Arafat made a triumphal entry into Gaza, but he faced huge problems. He had to create new institutions from scratch and contend with widespread poverty. Although Western donor nations had promised $2.2 billion, they made transfer of funds dependent on the establishment of new accounting procedures. Arafat consequently was unable to do much to transform the quality of everyday life. The fundamentalist Hamas and Islamic Jihad spurred Palestinian opposition to the peace process and launched a campaign of terror against Israel. In the worst incident 22 people died when a suicide bomber blew himself up on a Tel Aviv bus on October 19.

Tensions between Arafat and his fundamentalist opponents came to a head in mid-November when Palestinian police shot dead 13 Hamas and Islamic Jihad demonstrators in Gaza. Israeli Arabs intervened to negotiate an uneasy truce. In what they called "early empowerment," the Israelis transferred to Palestinian control five areas of government—education, health, welfare, tourism, and tax collection. Palestinians wanted free elections and insisted that Israel withdraw from their population centres. For the Israelis the unresolved conundrum was how to redeploy troops while continuing to protect over 140 scattered Jewish settlements. In December it was revealed that Israeli authorities planned to build new highways in the West Bank, linking settlements. The year ended with Israeli and Palestinian negotiators deadlocked over how to extend Palestinian self-rule from Gaza and Jericho to the rest of the West Bank.

In October Arafat, Prime Minister Yitzhak Rabin, and Foreign Minister Shimon Peres were announced as the winners of the Nobel Prize for Peace. (*See* NOBEL PRIZES.) Although much still remained to be done, the three men were honoured for having laid the cornerstone on which a comprehensive Middle East peace could be built.

Indeed, the Israeli-Palestinian accommodation had led directly to a peace treaty with Jordan. On Sept. 14, 1993, the day after the historic Rabin-Arafat handshake that concluded the signing of the peace accords, the Jordanian government initialed a peace agenda with Israel they had been holding up for almost a year. It was not only a case of the Israeli-Palestinian accord legitimizing peacemaking with the Jewish state by other Arab parties. The Jordanians were also driven by a fear that if they were left out of the peace process, they could face the threat of rampant Palestinian nationalism spilling over onto the East Bank and destabilizing Jordan.

A series of secret meetings between Rabin and Jordan's King Hussein paved the way for the Israeli-Jordanian accord. In Washington, D.C., on July 25, they were able to announce an end to the state of belligerency, and in the Arava desert on October 26, with U.S. Pres. Bill Clinton as witness, they signed the full peace treaty.

For Jordan the economic benefits were immediate. The U.S. waived $696 million in foreign debt, while the U.K. forgave $92 million. In the longer term, Israel and Jordan planned major joint development. For Israel the importance of the peace deal was primarily strategic. It virtually spelled the end of the Israeli military planners' nightmare Cerberus of Syria, Iraq, and Jordan, racing across Jordanian territory to strike at Israel's narrow coastal plain.

Accommodation with Jordan further opened the way for Israel's integration into the Arab Middle East. On September 1 Morocco announced its readiness to establish diplomatic links with the Jewish state. In October Tunisia followed suit, and in December, after a lightning visit by Rabin to Muscat, Oman seemed next in line. On September 30 all six members of the Gulf Cooperation Council had lifted the secondary and tertiary elements of the Arab boycott of Israel. This meant that major companies throughout the world could trade with Israel without fear of Arab economic reprisal. From October 30 Morocco served as host to a three-day Middle East economic conference, the first to include Israeli participation.

Israel's diplomatic successes in 1994 went beyond the Middle East and included the establishment of full ties with Vatican City State on June 15. Israel's ambassador began work in the Vatican at the end of September. By year's end Israel had diplomatic relations with more than 130 countries, nearly half of which had renewed or established ties during the three years of Israeli-Arab peace talks.

The major disappointment of 1994 was the failure to make tangible progress in peace negotiations with Syria. Almost daily clashes between Israeli forces and the Syrian-backed Shi'ite fundamentalist Hezbollah in southern Lebanon took a heavy toll. On June 2 Israel bombed a Hezbollah training camp, killing about 40 guerrillas. In retaliation, fundamentalists blew up the Jewish community centre in Buenos Aires, Arg., on July 18, leaving 96 civilians dead. A week later they attacked the Israeli embassy and Zionist offices in London. In December, when the Israeli and Syrian chiefs of staff began discussing a new security regime to be established after Israeli withdrawal from the strategic Golan Heights, Israel insisted that containing the Hezbollah be part of any peace package.

The overall peacemaking climate helped to produce an economic boom as Israel led the industrialized world in 1994 with a growth rate of nearly 7%. Private consumption was up by 9.3%; exports topped the $24 billion mark; investments climbed by nearly 20%; and unemployment was slashed from 11% to 7.6%, despite the arrival of some 80,000 job-seeking immigrants from the former Soviet Union. On the down side, public-sector wages increased by 8.7%, inflation was running at about 15%, the balance of payments deficit increased by $3.1 billion, and the Tel Aviv stock market was down by close to 40%.

Ironically, the Rabin government ended the year looking extremely vulnerable. It was based on a minority coalition of 58 in the 120-member Knesset (parliament), with support from three communist members and two representatives from the Arab Democratic Party. At year's end Rabin was still seeking to reestablish a majority coalition by bringing back the ultraorthodox Shas Party.

The greatest threat to Rabin's government was the anarchy in his ruling Labor party (44 seats). In 1992 Labor had introduced a system of national primaries to select its Knesset candidates. No longer dependent on party bosses for their seats, Knesset members in 1994 regularly defied the party leadership as they vied to catch the public eye.

In February, Health Minister Haim Ramon was first off the block. He resigned over the Histadrut trade union federation's opposition to his national health bill and set up a breakaway list to challenge Labor in the May 10 Histadrut elections. He polled 47% to Labor's 33%, bringing to an end the party's almost 75-year-long domination of the giant trade union organization. The charismatic Ramon's victory was seen as part of a new personality-oriented politics in which party machines were losing much of their weight. The health bill over which Ramon had resigned was then passed in precisely the form he had submitted it.

Constitutional reform, however, foundered in 1994 as secular and religious parties clashed over the role of the Supreme Court. The court had ruled on a wide range of issues, from the right to import nonkosher meat to the legality of coalition agreements. Religious parties, wary of how court involvement on fundamental issues might affect the "religious status quo," balked at the idea of a secular Bill of Rights with a secular Supreme Court formally accorded powers of legal review. (LESLIE D. SUSSER)

A Palestinian youth slings stones at Israeli police in protest against a Jewish settler's attack on Muslim worshipers in the West Bank town of Hebron. In the Gaza Strip violence by Islamic militants and other opponents of Yasir Arafat threatened Palestinian rule.

ITALY

A republic of southern Europe, Italy occupies the Apennine Peninsula, Sicily, Sardinia, and a number of smaller islands in the Mediterranean Sea. Area: 301,303 sq km (116,334 sq mi). Pop. (1994 est.): 57,257,000. Cap.: Rome. Monetary unit: Italian lira, with (Oct. 7, 1994) a free rate of 1,569 lire to U.S. $1 (2,495 lire = £1 sterling). President in 1994, Oscar Luigi Scalfaro; prime ministers, Carlo Azeglio Ciampi and, from May 11, Silvio Berlusconi.

The sudden appearance of Silvio Berlusconi (*see* BIOGRA-PHIES), a rich and powerful businessman with no political experience, as prime minister dominated the news in Italy in 1994. Berlusconi was Europe's biggest media magnate and head of the second largest private conglomerate in Italy, after the automobile firm Fiat, and his assets included the lion's share of commercial television in the country. His advent marked a shift to the right in Italian politics as well as an end to a petrified system of government and patronage in place for 40 years. His fall from power was as abrupt as his rise, however, and at year's end he was forced to resign.

Berlusconi was swept into high office on a wave of disgust in the country over the profound corruption of the political class headed by the Christian Democrats (DC) and the Italian Socialist Party (PSI), in power for decades. Shown by hundreds of zealous magistrates in Milan and elsewhere as enmeshed in large-scale extortion, bribery, theft, swindling, and fraud, the old guard was evicted in general elections in March, called after the resignation in January of the "nonpolitical" caretaker prime minister, Carlo Azeglio Ciampi.

Berlusconi and his allies formed the so-called Alliance for Freedom and received from voters a strikingly clear mandate to sweep away the old regime and start afresh.

Adopting as his trademark a beaming grin learned from his early days as a crooner on cruise ships, Berlusconi had burst into the political arena only two months before the elections, with the avowed intent of thwarting a widely expected victory by the communist Democratic Party of the Left (PDS). He promised a new, efficient, clean Italy, scope for private enterprise, and an end to unemployment. His vehicle was a new political movement, Forza Italia (Go, Italy), a network of "clubs" hastily created by junior executives from his giant holding company, Fininvest, rooted in publishing, advertising, insurance, financial services, supermarkets, and the cinema, in addition to television. His main allies were the federalist Northern League of Umberto Bossi, which pursued greater autonomy for the industrial north, and the National Alliance (AN) of Gianfranco Fini, heir to the right-wing Italian Social Movement and generally considered to be neo-Fascist. The Alliance for Freedom romped home with an overall majority in the Chamber of Deputies, winning 366 of the 630 seats. The Northern League garnered the largest number—118 seats. The results spelled clear defeat for the PDS, which took only 115 seats. A rump of the once-dominant DC, retitled the Italian Popular Party in January, was reduced to 33 seats, while the corruption-weakened PSI took only 15. This pattern was repeated less decisively in the Senate.

Even so, the six weeks of haggling it took Berlusconi to form a 27-person Cabinet, announced in May, was for Italians remarkably reminiscent of the old days. After much

FRANCO ORIGLIA—SYGMA

Prime Minister Silvio Berlusconi sits alone in Parliament. The head of his own party, Forza Italia, and leader of a rightist coalition government, Berlusconi lost support during the year and was compelled to step down from office on December 20.

acrimony the Northern League wrested from Berlusconi the sensitive Interior Ministry, seen by Bossi as a key bastion from which to resist any threats to democracy. The unknown defense minister, Cesare Previti, came straight from a job as top lawyer in Fininvest. Most eyes, however, were on five new AN ministers, descendants of a party last in government at the time of the dictator Benito Mussolini. Fini said that there could be no return to that epoch and periodically during the year disowned thugs in the AN who were racist and observed the Fascist salute.

Berlusconi's initial popularity became more manifest in June when his alliance won a landslide victory in elections for the European Parliament. Forza Italia picked up 30.6% of the vote, AN 12.5%, and the Northern League 6.6%. It was a second defeat for the PDS, backed by only 19.1% of voters, and led to the resignation of its crestfallen leader, Achille Occhetto, for having botched party renewal. His stern second-in-command, Massimo D'Alema, took over.

Nevertheless, the Berlusconi Cabinet failed to sustain early support. First came sniping between the coalition partners, which was also all too familiar to Italians. The noisiest fire came from Bossi, who assumed the role of a rough-hewn democrat to whom dealings with a tycoon prime minister on the one hand and "fascists" on the other were repugnant. The squabbling halted government. Later in the year, relations between Berlusconi and the generally respected Pres. Oscar Luigi Scalfaro deteriorated. At one point the prime minister threatened to call new elections to resolve coalition disputes, but he was told by Scalfaro that he had no right to do so.

At the same time, a more significant confrontation developed between Berlusconi and the nation's loudly sung heroes, the small band, or "pool," of magistrates in Milan whose anticorruption Operation Clean Hands had brought down the old regime, paving the way for the newcomers. In July Berlusconi issued a surprise decree limiting the grounds for preventive detention. Almost overnight, 1,859 prisoners walked out of jail, including not only 180 suspected of corruption but also drug pushers, pimps, and car thieves as well. The Milan pool, including the popular magistrate Antonio Di Pietro, threatened on television to resign and, before an ensuing public outcry, the decree was withdrawn. Berlusconi explained his decree as an attempt to halt the transformation of Italy into a "police state." His enemies claimed that the aim was rather to neutralize Operation Clean Hands in order to forestall a rumoured investigation of Fininvest and to protect Paolo Berlusconi, his brother and business partner.

A week after the about-face, Berlusconi's brother was jailed in Milan. He later received a five-month suspended sentence. Paolo Berlusconi confessed to Di Pietro that he had sanctioned a secret slush fund of some $2 million so that the state Finance Police—who acted as tax inspectors and were usually regarded with awe—could be bribed into "forgetting" to check three Fininvest companies. Some 25 members of the Finance Police were jailed, and two committed suicide. In an interview in August, the prime minister confirmed the payments, though he dismissed them as being as insignificant as "a litre of water in the Mediterranean." The conflict came to a head again in October when the government claimed that it was being "persecuted" by the magistrates. It accused the head of the Milan pool, Francesco Saverio Borrelli, of "unconstitutionality" and reported him to President Scalfaro. The action was the result of a hint by Borrelli in an interview that Berlusconi himself might one day be investigated. The unmoved president referred Berlusconi's charge to the National Council of Judges, the judiciary's highest body, which voted to shelve the affair.

During the year Berlusconi repeatedly complained of hostile media attention, and in a move widely seen as an intended remedy, he began the revamp of the state television and radio network, RAI, whose three television channels rivaled his own three. RAI bosses were sacked and their successors nominated by the speakers of the Chamber of Deputies and the Senate, both chosen under Berlusconi. Parliament girded itself in October to plug a curious gap in Italian legislation by debating a proposal from three jurists for resolving the conflict of interest facing a businessman turned politician. The proposal was to entrust the entire Berlusconi empire to an Italian-style blind trust.

In the same month, Italy's three main trade unions began agitation, initially in the form of a half-day national strike, against the government's toughest initiative of the year, an unpopular budget that cut pensions and welfare spending and sought to improve the country's disastrous finances. Above all, the aim was to trim a mammoth national debt, which by autumn had reached 125% of the gross national product, the biggest in any of the Group of Seven countries. On the eve of the strike, Scalfaro told union leaders that he understood them, a reassurance felt by the government as a further pinprick in the relations between the prime minister and the president.

Berlusconi's troubles came to a head after Di Pietro resigned on December 6, claiming it was impossible to continue his investigation. The prime minister, who was questioned a week later for more than seven hours by Milanese magistrates, vowed to fight on, but the prospect of a no-confidence vote led by Bossi forced him to resign on December 22. Berlusconi remained at the head of a caretaker government at year-end.

In a new foreign-policy departure welcomed by nationalistic elements in the AN, Italy moved to block an application by Slovenia for associate membership in the European Union unless it granted property rights to the families of some 150,000 Italians who had fled the Istrian Peninsula when it was occupied by the partisans of the Yugoslav leader Marshal Tito at the end of the World War II. In October Italy publicly noted Slovenia's refusal and declared the speed of the membership process open to question.

Two former prime ministers stayed in the news in 1994. Bettino Craxi, former leader of the PSI, spent the year ensconced in his villa at al-Hammamat in Tunisia, leading a Milan court in July to declare him a fugitive. He was to have appeared as a defendant in a case centring on a giant swindle in 1990 involving Enimont, a joint enterprise between state and private business alleged to have collapsed because of payoffs to politicians. Another court in Milan sentenced Craxi to 8½ years in jail for his part in the fraudulent collapse 12 years earlier of the Banco Ambrosiano, one of the biggest financial scandals in postwar Italy. His deputy in the PSI, Claudio Martelli, former minister of justice, was jailed for the same term. Craxi faced 18 other investigations. The other former prime minister in the news was the DC veteran Giulio Andreotti, who had held the post seven times. In July judges in Palermo indicted him for criminal association with the Mafia, contending that while in office he knowingly furthered the organization's designs. He called the charge absurd, and no date for trial was set.

Italy reacted with dismay in the summer when the National Statistical Institute warned that the Italian race could die out in 150 years if the current zero growth rate continued. In 1993, for the first time, more Italians died than were born. The institute said that Italy had the world's lowest fertility rate, with Italian women having on average 1.2 children each, compared with a European average of 1.5.

(DEREK WILSON)

JAMAICA

A constitutional monarchy within the Commonwealth, Jamaica occupies an island in the Caribbean Sea. Area: 10,991 sq km (4,244 sq mi). Pop. (1994 est.): 2,497,000. Cap.: Kingston. Monetary unit: Jamaica dollar, with (Oct. 7, 1994) a free rate of J$32.53 to U.S. $1 (J$51.74 = £1 sterling). Queen, Elizabeth II; governor-general in 1994, Howard Cooke; prime minister, Percival J. Patterson.

The continuing refusal of the opposition Jamaica Labour Party (JLP) to participate in elections enabled the governing People's National Party to retain its hold on both the East Central St. Andrew and South St. Catherine constituencies during April and August 1994, respectively. Following its defeat in the 1993 general election, the JLP said that it would take no further part in elections of any kind until the polling process had been "reformed."

The JLP expected the electoral system to be improved in time for the 1998 general election, which probably explained why its 64-year-old leader, Edward Seaga, was showing no sign of wanting to retire. He said in April that he had no "immediate plans" to step down from the leadership position that he gained in 1974.

Prime Minister Percival J. Patterson signaled his belief during the year that the troubled Jamaican economy may finally have begun to recover. He said in May that the current Extended Fund Facility, which was to end in 1995, would be the last such arrangement with the International Monetary Fund. Jamaica had been dependent on IMF financing since 1977. The economy received an unexpected setback in June, however, when an explosion at the main power station destroyed 20% of Jamaica's generating capacity.

(DAVID RENWICK)

This article updates the *Macropædia* article The WEST INDIES: *Jamaica*.

JAPAN

A constitutional monarchy in the northwestern Pacific Ocean, Japan comprises an archipelago with four main islands (Hokkaido, Honshu, Kyushu, and Shikoku), the Ryukyus (including Okinawa), and lesser adjacent islands. Area: 377,750 sq km (145,850 sq mi). Pop. (1994 est.): 124,960,000. Cap.: Tokyo. Monetary unit: yen, with (Oct. 7, 1994) a free rate of 100.22 yen to U.S. $1 (159.40 yen = £1 sterling). Emperor, Akihito; prime ministers in 1994, Morihiro Hosokawa, Tsutomu Hata from April 25, and, from June 29, Tomiichi Murayama.

During 1994 Japan continued to experience turmoil in domestic politics as Tomiichi Murayama (*see* BIOGRAPHIES) became the third prime minister selected in one year. With electoral reform finally on the way to passage, it was doubtful that the three-party coalition led by Murayama's Social Democratic Party of Japan (SDPJ) could retain control of the government. Along with this uncertainty was a disturbing estimate that Japan's growth for 1994 would be 0.8%, the lowest rate among the Group of Seven advanced industrial democracies (G-7). Despite the ailing economy at home, Japan remained alone among the G-7 to display a towering current account surplus ($130 billion). In June the Finance Ministry reported that in 1993 Japan was the world's top creditor for the third straight year, net overseas assets having risen to a record $610.8 billion. The ever growing trade surplus was increasingly generating pressure on Tokyo, especially from the U.S.

Internal Affairs. In 1992 Morihiro Hosokawa had launched the Japan New Party (JNP), and in 1993 he headed a seven-party coalition dedicated to reform and corruption-free politics. In August 1993 he was elected prime minister.

Early in 1994 his coalition, with the support of the president of the Liberal-Democratic Party (LDP), revived and amended electoral reform bills. The package, which cleared both houses of the Diet (parliament) on January 29, would take effect in the autumn after a council had drawn new electoral districts.

The Public Office Election Law (with a parallel political funds control regulation) represented the biggest change in the electoral system since woman suffrage was enacted in 1945. Reduction in the number of seats in the (lower) House of Representatives to 500 was expected to free candidates from "money politics." Single-seat constituencies were increased to 300, and proportional representation in 11 regional blocs was to produce 200. Adoption of the laws proved to be the only major accomplishment of the Hosokawa regime. On April 8, eight months after he assumed office on a reform platform, Hosokawa announced his resignation to solve the Diet deadlock over charges that he had improperly profited from ties to a trucking company in the early 1980s.

Only hours after Tsutomu Hata, cofounder with Ichiro Ozawa of Shinseito (Japan Renewal Party) in 1993, was elected prime minister on April 25, the SDPJ withdrew from the new coalition. Angered by the formation of a parliamentary group that excluded the socialists, Murayama promised to cooperate in passing the long-stalled budget. On April 28 Hata formed the first administration in 39 years to lack majority support in both houses of the Diet. His coalition occupied only 14 of 20 posts in the new Cabinet. Aware of his low approval rating and facing a no-confidence motion, Hata consulted Ozawa and then decided on June 25 to step down. Before relinquishing power, the Hata Cabinet announced a program for promoting deregulation. Some 280 measures covered four main areas: reduction of land and housing costs; technological progress in communications; market access to increase imports and enhance consumer benefits; and support of innovations in finance, securities, and insurance. The package was designed to help reduce Japan's trade surplus and to relieve foreign pressure on Tokyo.

On June 29 Tomiichi Murayama became the first Socialist in 47 years to be elected prime minister. His SDPJ, the second largest party in the lower house, formed an astonishing alliance with its traditional rival, the LDP, and with New Party Sakigake. Murayama's Cabinet included 13 ministers from the LDP, the largest party in the lower house, and 5 from the SDPJ.

In his inaugural speech on July 18, Murayama pledged tax reform. He also promised that the next general election would be held under the new polling system. Until then the distribution of lower house seats (total 512) would be: LDP 200; the former coalition consisting of JNP, Shinseito, and the Democratic Socialist Party (DSP) 126; SDPJ 74; Komeito (Clean Government Party) 52; Sakigake 21; Japan Communist Party (JCP) 15; and independents and vacancies 24. In the upper house (total 252) the apportionment was: LDP 95, SDPJ 68, Komeito 24, JCP 11, and independents 54.

On August 11 a panel delivered to Murayama a new election map, which could produce further realignment of parties. The winner-take-all feature in the 300 single-seat constituencies favoured large parties and could enhance the role of LDP candidates, who had won the most seats in many districts. Moreover, on August 18 nine opposition groups, ousted by Murayama's three-party alliance, agreed on principles to establish a new party. Included were Shinseito, the JNP, Komeito, five smaller groups, and LDP dissidents. Hata predicted that 190–200 lower house members would join the New Frontier Party (Shinshinto), which was officially inaugurated in December.

Monju, Japan's first prototype fast-breeder reactor, located in Tsuruga, Fukui prefecture, achieved criticality on April 5. The facility was expected to supply commercial energy in 1995. Since such a reactor produced plutonium, which could be used for nuclear weapons, there were strong domestic and international protests. To offset criticism, Japan proposed an international agency to control disposition of the plutonium.

On August 29 a ceremony opening the new Kansai International Airport was held on a man-made island in Osaka Bay. The project, which took nearly eight years to build, cost about $14.4 billion. The 105-ha (260-ac) facility would eventually handle 390 round-trip international flights per week.

On October 4 a major earthquake with a magnitude of 7.9 shook Japan. The quake was centred on the ocean floor east of Hokkaido, where damage was reported, and south of the Kurils, where 16 people were reported killed. Another quake of similar magnitude (about 7.5) occurred off the northeast coast of Honshu on December 28, but damage was minimal.

The Economy. On February 15 the Hosokawa Cabinet added a $144 billion pump-priming package to fiscal 1993 expenditures and introduced an austere 1994 budget, showing only 1% growth. Finance Minister Hirohisa Fujii, however, expressed concern over an exchange rate that did not reflect fundamentals. The currency's steep rise to 103.2 yen to the U.S. dollar threatened to offset efforts to jumpstart the economy. The 1994 budget provided $731 billion in expenditures, including $409 billion in general account, $55 billion in income and residential tax reductions, and $89 billion in public works to revive the economy. Defense received somewhat more than $44 billion, just 0.95% of gross national product (GNP), the smallest increase in 34 years. Official development assistance rose 4.8% to $10 billion, but that was the lowest annual increase ever.

The March report of the Economic Planning Agency (EPA) described the economy as sluggish. Industrial output was lacklustre, and gross domestic product, which totaled $4 trillion, indicated an annual growth of less than 1%. The unemployment rate reached 2.9% in June, the third highest level on record.

In his inaugural speech as chairman of the Japan Federation of Economic Organizations (Keidanren), Shoichiro Toyoda called for drastic deregulation to revitalize the economy. He believed that a domestic-led recovery would increase imports and improve foreign trade relations. He favoured public subsidies of, and individual contributions to, political parties. Toyoda, head of the Toyota Motor Corp., was the first chairman of Keidanren to represent consumer interests, with automobiles accounting for 30% of GNP and 11% of total employment.

In July the chairman of the Japan Federation of Employers' Association denounced the government's freeze of rice prices as a "pretense" if subsidies to farmers were to rise 70% as planned. He believed that the purchase price of $1.24 per pound should come down to match the world level. This was especially important after the arrival of the first imported rice early in the year.

Also in July, Akira Yamagishi, head of Japan's largest union confederation, decried the SDPJ-LDP alliance, which had served to split organized labour. In a general election, he contended, the new constituency system would favour the LDP and serve to isolate both the SDPJ and the DSP, backed by different union groups.

Foreign Affairs. The Foreign Ministry's "blue book," covering diplomacy in 1993 and early 1994, indicated that

Laid-off Japanese managers look for jobs. The slowdown in the economy forced some companies to violate the traditional Japanese commitment to lifetime employment and to lay off at least small numbers of employees, particularly middle managers.
PHILIP JONES GRIFFITHS MAGNUM

trade with the U.S. was crucial to Japan and that it was "politically intolerable to leave the trade balance at current levels." In fiscal 1993 the total trade surplus reached a record $122 billion. The balance with the U.S. was $51 billion (up 12%), the third straight annual growth.

On January 23 U.S. Treasury Secretary Lloyd Bentsen warned Tokyo that Washington might reexamine the stalled "framework" negotiations if no agreement had been reached before scheduled talks in February. Japan continued to characterize U.S. efforts to set market shares as standards for progress as "managed trade."

In his meeting with Hosokawa on February 11, U.S. Pres. Bill Clinton demanded numerical targets as "objective criteria" for measuring the openness of Japanese markets. Hosokawa refused and expressed hope that the U.S. would not resort to unilateral action contravening the rules of the General Agreement on Tariffs and Trade. The meeting adjourned without a joint statement. Japanese editorials supported Hosokawa for saying "no" to the U.S. for the first time. Later, Hosokawa reacted calmly to Clinton's executive order reinstating Super 301 (a retaliatory trade law), saying that the measure did not mean immediate sanctions. In a phone call to Clinton on March 29, Hosokawa outlined steps to expand Japan's domestic demand and improve market access in the hope of resuming negotiations. On April 1, however, U.S. Trade Representative Mickey Kantor put Japan at the top of a list of nations with trade barriers, one step away from applying sanctions.

On June 1 Japan and the U.S. resumed "framework" talks in Tokyo. Foreign Minister Koji Kakizawa stated that the "Japan-U.S. gap has shrunk considerably," but he admitted that no sectorial targets had been reached. He was referring to Kantor's specific demands for gains in the areas of insurance, automobiles and auto parts, and government procurement of telecommunications and medical equipment. U.S. Ambassador Walter F. Mondale expressed hope that a cellular phone agreement involving Motorola, Inc., concluded in March, would become a model for negotiations. On June 19 he told Keidanren chairman Toyoda that deregulation should become Japan's tool for reducing the trade surplus.

Once again on the eve of a summit—the G-7 July meeting in Naples—Tokyo announced plans for a package of market-opening measures outlined in March. When the U.S. was informed that Murayama could not attend the talks because of illness, its skepticism over Tokyo's capacity to fulfill promises increased. On August 1 Murayama denied that negotiations had collapsed. Without agreement, however, the two parties moved steadily toward a U.S. deadline set for September 30. On October 1, after all-night negotiations in Washington, the two sides reached an agreement that was trumpeted on both sides as a "breakthrough." It gave the U.S. a victory with the opening up of Japanese markets for medical and telecommunications equipment, insurance, and plate glass. No guarantees of market shares or numerical targets were made, however, and the most important sector—autos and auto parts—was not resolved.

A Japanese woman tends a rice paddy. The U.S. government pressured Japan to accept rice imports, and despite protests by Japanese farmers, the first rice imported from the U.S. went on sale in Japanese supermarkets in February.
SYGMA

Limited Super 301 sanctions could still be applied after a 12–18-month period of further consultation.

There was no public evidence of tension during the 16-day whirlwind tour of the U.S. by Emperor Akihito and Empress Michiko. When they arrived in Washington on June 13, they were welcomed with a 21-gun salute. The emperor expressed Japan's gratitude for the "generosity of the support" offered by Americans after the Pacific war. Clinton responded: "Our commitment to common ideals is firm. Our determination to work with you is strong." Later the emperor and empress honoured the U.S. war dead by placing a wreath at the Tomb of the Unknowns in Arlington, Va. In the evening the Clintons served as host to a white-tie state dinner. On the return trip the royal couple visited the National Memorial Cemetery of the Pacific in Honolulu.

In 1991 Japan and North Korea met in China to begin discussing diplomatic relations, but the talks broke down in late 1992 over allegations that Korean terrorists had kidnapped a Japanese. North Korea thus remained the only Asian country that had no diplomatic ties with Japan. In 1993 both Tokyo and Washington became alarmed over Pyongyang's threat to withdraw from the Nuclear Nonproliferation Treaty and refusal to allow UN inspection of nuclear sites. Japan's Foreign Ministry stated that creation of nuclear weapons on the peninsula would be a "direct threat to Japan." In February 1994 North Korea, responding through the Korean Central News Agency (KCNA), accused Japan of pursuing a policy of "isolating and stifling" Pyongyang. Any consideration of UN sanctions, it said, would preclude a solution of the nuclear issue. In fact, the KCNA added, Japan's Monju reactor was evidence that Japan hoped to become a nuclear power.

In March Tokyo supported a U.S.-drafted statement by the UN Security Council urging North Korea to comply with international nuclear safeguards. The Japanese, however, hesitated to favour sanctions. For one thing, the constitution did not sanction the use of any force to back sanctions. Moreover, more than one-third of the roughly 680,000 Korean residents in Japan identified with Chongryun (a pro-Pyongyang association). Funds remitted annually by Koreans in Japan to the North were estimated at $575 million–$770 million, even though banks had begun to staunch the flow. Finally, Tokyo took Pyongyang's threats seriously; on April 5 the KCNA reported that the government had earmarked 11.6% of its 1994 budget for defense against Japan's "provocation." North Korea's Rodong 1 missile, which had been sent to a target in the Sea of Japan, was said to have a 960-km (600-mi) range, sufficient to hit U.S. bases at Sasebo and Iwakuni in Japan. At the Naples G-7 summit, Murayama expressed regrets over the death of Pres. Kim Il Sung (see OBITUARIES) and hoped that his passing would not have a negative impact on the peninsula.

Hosokawa had expressed remorse to Chinese leaders for past Japanese actions, including "aggression and colonial rule" on the continent, the first time a prime minister had used the terms abroad. He then noted that in 1993 Japan-China trade had grown to $38 billion, making China Japan's second largest trading partner (after the U.S., at $161 billion).

When Murayama visited Seoul in July, he made an explicit "apology" for Japanese actions in Korea. Until the visit his SDPJ had not recognized South Korea as a sovereign state. In late August Murayama made a tour of four nations in Southeast Asia. In the Philippines he pledged support for Manila's program of domestic reform. The visit was marred by demonstrations denouncing the Japanese military's use of Filipina "comfort women" during the Pacific war. In Vietnam Murayama offered grants-in-aid totaling $77 million. After a stop in Malaysia, he visited Singapore and offered aid through the Japan-Singapore Partnership program.

Although Japan had normalized relations with the U.S.S.R. in 1956, a formal peace treaty with its successor, Russia, continued to be blocked by a nagging territorial dispute over four small islands in the southern Kurils, occupied by Russia but claimed by Japan. No progress was made because Russian Pres. Boris Yeltsin was in a weak position to negotiate owing to pressure from extreme nationalists at home.

In March Hisashi Owada, Japan's senior career foreign service official and the father of Crown Princess Masako, was appointed ambassador to the UN. Political observers saw this as a quiet bid by Japan to win a permanent seat on the Security Council.   (ARDATH W. BURKS)

JORDAN

A constitutional monarchy, Jordan is located in southwestern Asia and has a short coastline on the Gulf of Aqaba. Area: 88,946 sq km (34,342 sq mi). Pop. (1994 est.): 4,224,000. Cap.: Amman. Monetary unit: Jordan dinar, with (Oct. 7, 1994) an official rate of 0.70 dinar to U.S. $1 (1.11 dinars = £1 sterling). King, Hussein I; prime minister in 1994, 'Abd as-Salam al-Majali.

Jordan's King Hussein and Israeli Prime Minister Yitzhak Rabin signed a bilateral peace treaty on Oct. 26, 1994, in the presence of U.S. Pres. Bill Clinton and 5,000 invited guests at an open-air ceremony along their border. The agreement evolved suddenly from negotiations that had appeared to be making only slow progress. Israel formally ceded 300 sq km (116 sq mi) of desert to Jordan, and the two countries delineated their mutual borders, but even greater significance was attached to key clauses on the relationship between King Hussein and the Islamic holy shrines in Jerusalem. Israel for the first time acknowledged King Hussein as "custodian" of the holy shrines and awarded him a "special role" as their guardian. This concession angered the Palestinians, for in September 1993 the Declaration of Principles signed by Israel and the Palestine Liberation Organization had left open the question of Jerusalem. By the end of 1994, Israel had opened an embassy in Amman and Jordan had established one in Tel Aviv.

The normalization of relations between Israel and Jordan had taken a step forward at a meeting of the Trilateral Commission in Washington, D.C., on October 3. The agenda included exchanges of technical and professional delegations, joint tourism initiatives, the possibility of a free zone embracing the Israeli Red Sea port of Elat and the neighbouring Jordanian port of al-'Aqabah, and two dams on the Jordan River.

In a significant move to quell speculation over the future of the Hashimite dynasty, King Hussein confirmed that his brother Hassan was the heir apparent but also said that a family council would determine Hassan's successor. Since 1978 it had been understood that Prince Ali, Hussein's only son by his third wife, Queen Alia, would succeed Crown Prince Hassan. On August 10, in a further move to boost his brother's status, King Hussein named Hassan head of a Royal Commission for Modernization and Development.

Prime Minister 'Abd as-Salam al-Majali reshuffled his Cabinet on June 8, appointing Dhouqar Hudauri as his deputy. Ten members of the parliament gained seats in the Cabinet, but no places were given to the Islamic Action Front, a party supported by the Muslim Brotherhood with 16 out of the 80 seats in the lower house. In a government move to satisfy Islamic feelings, a new Islamic University opened in the northern town of al-Mafraq in October, but authorities also announced a tough line on terrorists after the bombings on January 26 and February 1 of two cinemas in Amman and az-Zarqa', where pornographic films were allegedly being shown. In April some 72 Jordanian Islamic veterans of the Afghanistan war were arrested in Jordan and accused of involvement in terrorist attacks.

In July President Clinton announced that the U.S. would write off more than $700 million of Jordan's official debts, and the U.K. and France followed suit with smaller amounts. The International Monetary Fund in May approved a loan to support the government's structural adjustment program, which was followed by a rescheduling of more than $1.2 billion of Paris Club debts. The government made progress in improving relations with Saudi Arabia and Kuwait, which had been disrupted by Jordanian backing for Iraq in the Persian Gulf war. A new ambassador to Saudi Arabia was named, and a senior diplomat visited Kuwait in September for talks about the possible reopening of a Jordanian embassy. In March, Jordan and the Vatican established diplomatic relations. (JOHN WHELAN)

KAZAKHSTAN

A republic of Central Asia, Kazakhstan borders Russia on the west and north, China on the east, Kyrgyzstan on the southeast, Uzbekistan and the Aral Sea on the south, and Turkmenistan and the Caspian Sea on the southwest. Area: 2,717,300 sq km (1,049,200 sq mi). Pop. (1994 est.): 16,954,000. Cap.: Almaty (formerly Alma-Ata); capital-designate: Akmola (formerly Tselinograd). Monetary unit: tenge, with (Oct. 3, 1994) a free rate of 56.98 tenge − U.S. $1 (90.62 tenge = £1 sterling). President in 1994, Nursultan Nazarbayev; prime ministers, Sergey Tereshchenko and, from October 12, Arkezhan Kazhgeldin.

The first postindependence parliamentary elections dominated Kazakhstan's political life in the first two months of 1994. The new Supreme Council (Kenges), elected on March 7, included representatives of the most important political groups, although Kazakh nationalist groups and representatives of the Russian community did less well than the Socialist (former Communist) Party. The most successful party, the People's Unity Union, was supported by Pres. Nursultan Nazarbayev, who had assumed that the new legislature would be more supportive of his economic reforms than had its predecessor. At its first session, however, the new Supreme Soviet adopted a motion of no confidence in Prime Minister Sergey Tereshchenko's program to rescue the country from its post-Soviet economic malaise. Nazarbayev continued to support Tereshchenko, but after a series of corruption scandals involving government ministers and the failure of Tereshchenko's program to produce results by October, the president asked the government to resign. Arkezhan Kazhgeldin, the new prime minister, who had helped shape Nazarbayev's reform program in the former government, promised to accelerate, rather than slow down, market reforms.

The appointment of Kazhgeldin, a Kazakh, upset the ethnic balance that had prevailed when Tereshchenko, a Slav, held the post of prime minister. The increasing Kazakhization of the country contributed to the emigration of thousands of non-Kazakhs during 1994. Attempts by officials in the Russian Federation to persuade Kazakhstan's leadership to permit dual Kazakhstani-Russian citizenship were rejected. To lessen tensions between Kazakhs and Russians, journalist Boris Suprunyuk, a spokesman for the Russian community, was given a suspended sentence on a charge of fostering interethnic animosities.

The most ambitious privatization plan for any of the Central Asian states was launched in Kazakhstan at the end of April, with 3,500 enterprises, representing about 70% of the country's state-owned firms, slated for auction over a 15-month period. Popular anger over high inflation and falling living standards contributed to Tereshchenko's ouster, and in the autumn disturbances were reported over a rumoured increase in the price of bread and bread rationing.

In January Kazakhstan and Uzbekistan moved toward an economic union and began to dismantle customs and other barriers. In March Nazarbayev proposed a Eurasian Union embracing the former Soviet republics. It generated much discussion within the Commonwealth of Independent States, but only Russia reacted favourably. Frictions developed with Russia over the Baikonur space complex and its demand for a share in the development of Kazakhstan's gas and oil resources. (BESS BROWN)

This article updates the *Macropædia* article CENTRAL ASIA: *Kazakhstan*.

KENYA

A republic and member of the Commonwealth, Kenya is in eastern Africa, on the Indian Ocean. Area: 582,646 sq km (224,961 sq mi), including 11,230 sq km of inland water. Pop. (1994 est.): 27,450,000. Cap.: Nairobi. Monetary unit: Kenya shilling, with (Oct. 7, 1994) a free rate of 44.47 shillings to U.S. $1 (70.72 shillings = £1 sterling). President in 1994, Daniel arap Moi.

In November 1993 leading donor organizations lifted the boycott on aid to Kenya that they had imposed in order to force Pres. Daniel arap Moi to introduce a more democratic form of government. Their action was taken primarily in response to the efforts of Kenya's finance minister, Musalia Mudavadi, and the governor of the nation's central bank, Micah Cheserem, to root out corruption and to free trade from stultifying restrictions. This expression of goodwill was threatened in January 1994, however, when some prominent members of the ruling Kenya African National Union (KANU) began a campaign of vilification against Richard Leakey (see BIOGRAPHIES), head of the national wildlife service, and called for his resignation.

On a happier note, in January the government was able to reschedule $500 million of its debt to the Paris Club of creditor countries. This meant that Kenya's debt-servicing bill would be limited in 1994 to $240 million, equal to about 25% of the projected export earnings. In March Mudavadi also announced a further relaxation of exchange controls, which, he hoped, would encourage both local and overseas investors. Exporters were to be allowed to retain all export proceeds in foreign currency instead of only 50%, as had previously been the case. In May the currency was made fully convertible for nearly all transactions, the only area then remaining subject to controls being investment in stocks and government securities by foreigners.

These measures were a singular triumph for Mudavadi, who had fought hard against the opposition of some senior party members who feared that the relaxation of controls would undermine their powers. Moreover, his policy had the backing of President Moi, who stated in a speech read on his behalf at a conference in May that frank consultation between the government and the private sector was essential to economic progress and that it was important that those two groups, as well as the donor agencies, look upon their activities as a cooperative enterprise. The conference, he added, was one of a series of steps being taken by the government to make Kenya a more attractive area for foreign investment.

Mudavadi's path was not entirely smooth. On April 6 it was announced that the amount by which senior officials of the central bank and of the local exchange bank had successfully defrauded the central bank in 1993 was $210 million. Although action had already been taken in 1993 when the fraud was discovered, the report of the independent audit of the exchange bank was not made public, thereby encouraging the belief that senior politicians in KANU had benefited from the bank's dealings. The extent of the fraud only served to enhance the prevailing cynicism about the conduct of government. Donor agencies, while accepting the measures taken by the government, remained concerned that with inflation at 50% and with government expenditure scarcely under control, Mudavadi might be unable to maintain his objectives.

The majority of Kenyans relied on more immediate criteria by which to judge the government's performance, and drought, accompanied by food shortages, did little to increase their confidence. In March the government said it intended to distribute 126,385 bags of famine-relief food.

The Eastern and Rift Valley provinces would be the main beneficiaries, but other provinces would also receive help.

With the death of Oginga Odinga (see OBITUARIES) on January 20, Kenya lost not only its first vice president but also a courageous and outspoken statesman.

(KENNETH INGHAM)

This article updates the *Macropædia* article EASTERN AFRICA: *Kenya*.

KIRIBATI

A republic in the western Pacific Ocean and member of the Commonwealth, Kiribati comprises the former Gilbert Islands, Banaba (Ocean Island), the Line Islands, and the Phoenix Islands. Area: 811 sq km (313 sq mi). Pop. (1994 est.): 78,600. Cap.: Bairiki, on Tarawa. Monetary unit: Australian dollar, with (Oct. 7, 1994) a free rate of $A 1.35 to U.S. $1 ($A 2.15 = £1 sterling). Presidents (*beretitenti*) in 1994, Teatao Teannaki until May 24 and, from October 1, Teburoro Tito.

In May 1994 the government of Pres. Teatao Teannaki lost office when it was defeated narrowly in a no-confidence vote in the national legislature over the alleged misuse of government funds by Teannaki and his ministers. In the subsequent general election in July, Teannaki's National Progressive Party (a loose alliance of politicians rather than a mass organization), which had ruled Kiribati since independence in 1979, lost its majority to the Maneaba Te Mauri Party, a coalition of former opposition parties that combined to fight the September presidential election. Kiribati's new president, Teburoro Tito, a former teacher and the son of one of Kiribati's preindependence union leaders and politicians, won more votes than his three opponents combined.

The government proceeded during the year with a plan to privatize government-owned trading enterprises, including hotels and Kiritimati (Christmas Island) Marine Export Ltd., which sold fish and lobster to Hawaii. The government drew complaints from airlines when it closed its Bonriki International Airport for repairs for all except two half-days a week. Some politicians complained that the government had little control over the project, which was being undertaken by Chinese contractors as part of an aid project.

(BARRIE MACDONALD)

This article updates the *Macropædia* article PACIFIC ISLANDS: *Kiribati*.

KOREA, DEMOCRATIC PEOPLE'S REPUBLIC OF

A socialist republic of northeastern Asia on the northern half of the peninsula of Korea, the Democratic People's Republic of Korea (North Korea) borders the Sea of Japan, the Yellow Sea, and the Republic of Korea at roughly the 38th parallel. Area: 122,762 sq km (47,399 sq mi). Pop. (1994 est.): 23,067,000. Cap.: Pyongyang. Monetary unit: won, with (Oct. 7, 1994) a free rate of 2.15 won to U.S. $1 (3.42 won = £1 sterling). Presidents in 1994, Marshal Kim Il Sung and, from July 8, Kim Jong Il (designated); chairman of the Council of Ministers (premier), Kang Song San.

On July 8, 1994, Kim Il Sung, North Korea's only leader since the Stalinist state was founded in 1948, died at the age of 82. (See OBITUARIES.) The following day Radio Pyongyang informed the world that Kim had succumbed to a heart attack. The funeral was delayed until July 19 to permit mourners to arrive in time for the ceremony.

Kim's death came at a critical time. Pyongyang had been locked in a dispute with the International Atomic Energy Agency (IAEA), which had been denied access to North Korea's experimental nuclear facilities at Yongbyon, 100 km (60 mi) north of Pyongyang. The IAEA suspected that North Korea was diverting plutonium to build nuclear weapons.

After former U.S. president Jimmy Carter made a private visit to Pyongyang in mid-June, he announced that Kim Il Sung had pledged to temporarily freeze the country's nuclear program and allow IAEA inspectors to remain in the country. In return, the U.S. agreed to resume direct talks aimed at establishing formal ties. The two sides had begun negotiations in Geneva the day Kim Il Sung died. The talks were suspended, and the first face-to-face meeting between the presidents of North and South Korea, scheduled for late July, was indefinitely postponed. Meanwhile, Pyongyang was preoccupied with the transfer of power to Kim Il Sung's son Kim Jong Il. (*See* Biographies.)

Kim Jong Il had been the officially designated heir apparent since 1980. In 1991 he was named commander of the armed forces, and he was said to be in charge of day-to-day government operations. His succession, however, would not be complete until he secured two key posts: general secretary of the Communist Party and president of the republic.

Earlier in the year North Korea seemed ready to compromise over nuclear inspections. In February Pyongyang announced that it would allow IAEA inspectors to visit seven nuclear sites. In response, the U.S. and South Korea agreed to suspend their annual joint military exercises. IAEA inspectors were blocked from conducting key tests, however. On March 31 the UN Security Council urged North Korea to allow full inspections.

On June 3 the IAEA informed the UN that it could no longer verify the amount of plutonium North Korea might have produced. Shortly afterward North Korea said that it would "immediately withdraw from the IAEA and would no longer permit inspectors in the country."

Carter's mediation defused the crisis. The Geneva talks between North Korea and the U.S. resumed on August 5. On August 13 the North pledged to shut down its experimental graphite reactor, which produced significant amounts of plutonium, to halt construction of two other reactors, and to abide by the Nuclear Non-proliferation Treaty. In return, the U.S. agreed to arrange financing and construction of two light-water reactors for producing electrical power, at a cost of up to $4 billion. In late September, however, North Korea asked for an additional $7 billion and refused to accept nuclear technology from the South. The U.S. refused to accede to the North's new demands. Pyongyang finally relented, and an agreement was signed on October 21. It was almost derailed, however, when North Korea shot down a U.S. army helicopter that had violated Korean air space on December 17. The U.S. denied accusations that the crew had been on a spying mission. North Korea returned the body of the pilot who had died in the crash and, after 13 days of intense negotiations, released the surviving pilot, who had signed a statement admitting to an "illegal intrusion" into North Korean territory.   (JOSEPH L. NAGY)

This article updates the *Macropædia* article Korea: *North Korea.*

XINHUA/GAMMA LIAISON

North Koreans mourn their president, Kim Il Sung, who died on July 8. Head of the communist state since its founding in 1948, Kim was an authoritarian ruler who transformed North Korea into an austere, militaristic, and highly regimented society.

KOREA, REPUBLIC OF

A republic of northeastern Asia on the southern half of the peninsula of Korea, the Republic of Korea (South Korea) borders the Sea of Japan, the Korea Strait, the Yellow Sea, and the Democratic People's Republic of Korea at roughly the 38th parallel. Area: 99,274 sq km (38,330 sq mi). Pop. (1994 est.): 44,436,000. Cap.: Seoul. Monetary unit: won, with (Oct. 7, 1994) a free rate of 799 won to U.S. $1 (1,271 won = £1 sterling). President in 1994, Kim Young Sam; prime ministers, Lee Hoi Chang, Lee Yung Duk from April 22, and, from December 17, Lee Hong Koo.

The crisis over North Korea's nuclear program and the death of North Korean leader Kim Il Sung in July affected events in South Korea in 1994. At the truce village of Panmunjom in March, North and South Korea had begun talks to keep the peninsula free of nuclear weapons and set up a presidential summit. The negotiations collapsed, however, when the North threatened to turn Seoul into a "sea of fire" for supporting sanctions against Pyongyang. Seoul had backed U.S. efforts to seek a UN Security Council vote to force North Korea to allow inspections of all its nuclear facilities to determine whether it was diverting plutonium to the production of nuclear weapons. North Korea said that it would consider sanctions an act of war.

ASIAWEEK PICTURES

An effigy of Uncle Sam holding a missile appears on the street in Seoul. When the U.S. announced that it was sending Patriot missiles to South Korea, many South Koreans opposed the move, arguing that the action would only provoke already hostile North Korea.

As tensions on the peninsula mounted, U.S. Pres. Bill Clinton announced in late March that the U.S. would send Patriot antimissile batteries to South Korea. South Korean Pres. Kim Young Sam explained that they would be used to defend U.S. military bases. The first batch of missiles arrived in April. That month U.S. Defense Secretary William Perry visited Seoul to discuss plans to defend the South against North Korean aggression. The South Korean government agreed to modernize its forces by buying such sophisticated U.S. weapons as Apache attack helicopters and antitank missiles.

After months of escalating threats, North-South relations took an abrupt turn toward reconciliation. On June 28 both sides agreed to a date for a historic summit, the first ever between the presidents of North and South Korea. Kim Young Sam was to travel to Pyongyang on July 25 to meet his northern counterpart. This breakthrough came 10 days after former U.S. president Jimmy Carter visited Pyongyang. Carter's mediation also led to the reopening of talks between North Korea and the U.S. over the North's nuclear program. These negotiations put South Korea in the delicate position of being an observer of events that would directly affect its security. In April South Korea had made a major concession by dropping its demand for an exchange of special envoys with North Korea as a condition for approving direct U.S.-North Korean talks to resolve the nuclear crisis.

In his first public remarks on relations with North Korea following the death of Kim Il Sung, Kim Young Sam supported the Geneva accord. He also pledged to supply Pyongyang with nuclear power technology if it opened its nuclear facilities to international inspection. In further talks with the U.S., however, North Korea ruled out South Korea's participation in building the nuclear power plants. When the U.S. continued to insist that the South have a role in providing nuclear technology to the North, the talks were stalemated.

When news of Kim Il Sung's death was announced, the government in Seoul refused to send official condolences to Pyongyang. On the day of Kim's funeral, thousands of riot police took up positions across South Korea to prevent public mourning. Hundreds of defiant students were arrested.

In mid-August, militant students staged a reunification rally in Seoul to coincide with celebrations of Korea's liberation from Japan in 1945. Some 6,000 students battled riot police, who arrested more than 1,000 demonstrators. The rioting that continued the next day led to more arrests.

The government crackdown surprised many South Koreans. Kim Young Sam, a former dissident and the nation's first president in more than 30 years who had not had a military career, was criticized for using the harsh National Security Law to arrest student demonstrators, as former military governments had done.

During the crisis with North Korea, the president kept firm control over government policy. Prime Minister Lee Hoi Chang resigned on April 22 following a dispute with Kim over how to respond to the nuclear crisis. Lee had insisted on his right to approve all decisions made by a Cabinet group set up to coordinate government policy on North Korea. Lee himself had not been included in the group. Previously, the office of prime minister had been largely ceremonial. Lee, a former Supreme Court justice, sought to play a more direct role in policy making. The president replaced Lee with Lee Yung Duk, deputy premier and minister for reunification. In May the president initiated another shake-up in his administration by replacing seven vice-ministers, including the vice-minister of foreign affairs, who had publicly contradicted administration policy regarding North Korea. None of those replaced was given new assignments.

The government was drawn into a domestic controversy when hundreds of reformist monks staged demonstrations at the Chogye Temple complex in central Seoul to protest the reelection of Suh Eui Hyun as head of the nation's largest Buddhist order. After weeks of clashes between the reformists and Suh's supporters, riot police stormed the temple complex on April 11 and detained 134 monks. Suh was forced to resign. The reformists accused him of accepting $10 million from a local businessman and funneling the money to Kim Young Sam's 1992 election campaign.

The president was embarrassed by a corruption scandal in Inchon, one of South Korea's largest cities. Government prosecutors had arrested seven city officials for embezzling more than $1 million in tax revenues. In September the city's mayor, Choi Ki Son, a close associate of the president, resigned and took responsibility for the scandal. Kim Young Sam renewed his pledge to fight graft and corruption.

On October 29 the prosecutor's office in Seoul ruled that two former presidents, Chun Doo Hwan and Roh Tae Woo, had participated in "premeditated military rebellion"—the 1979 military coup that brought them to power. Many felt that the effects of a prosecution would have been so disruptive that the nation would be better served if no trials were held. The government's decision not to prosecute the men so angered Lee Ki Taek, leader of the opposition Democratic Party, that he disrupted the National Assembly proceedings for several weeks. After resigning his seat on November 25, he called upon other legislators to follow his lead and force new elections.

A bright spot for the government was the economy. For several years economic growth had slowed to between 5% and 6%—brisk for most countries but a decline for South Korea. The government predicted gross domestic product growth of 8.5% for 1994. The stock market index leaped some 10% in September, breaking the 1,000 mark to hit a record high. The Finance Ministry announced in October that the ceiling on foreign holdings in Korean companies would be raised from 8% to 10% by year's end and to 15% in 1995. The country's export growth rate averaged 14% during the first 10 months of the year, the highest it had been since 1988. This success was attributed to South Korea's restructuring of its industries, to the high value of the Japanese yen, and to economic recoveries in Europe, the U.S., and Japan. (JOSEPH L. NAGY)

This article updates the *Macropædia* article KOREA: *South Korea*.

KUWAIT

A constitutional monarchy (emirate), Kuwait is in the northeastern Arabian Peninsula, on the Persian Gulf. Area: 17,818 sq km (6,880 sq mi). Pop. (1994 est.): 1,469,000. Cap.: Kuwait City. Monetary unit: Kuwaiti dinar, with (Oct. 7, 1994) a free rate of 0.30 dinar to U.S. $1 (0.47 dinar = £1 sterling). Emir, Sheikh Jabir al-Ahmad al-Jabir as-Sabah; prime minister in 1994, Crown Prince Sheikh Saad al-Abdullah as-Salim as-Sabah.

Iraqi tanks and 50,000 of that nation's elite troops carried out threatening maneuvers against Kuwait in October 1994 in an area just north of the demilitarized zone between the two nations, raising fears of a new invasion. Iraq organized a mass demonstration by stateless nomads in the sensitive area but described its military action as "training exercises." The U.S. and the U.K. responded quickly to Kuwait's appeal for help with the deployment to the emirate of 40,000 U.S. troops, British marines, 600 aircraft, and a number of U.S. warships.

The deployment continued in late 1994 despite Iraqi withdrawal and a decree on November 10 recognizing Kuwaiti sovereignty. In a unanimous resolution the UN Security Council warned Iraq of UN retaliation if further provocative action was taken by Baghdad against its neighbours.

The invasion threat rekindled in Kuwait a spirit of national unity that had been fractured by internal wrangles between the government and the elected National Assembly. On June 29 the Constitutional Court in a procedural ruling declined jurisdiction over a corruption case brought by the Assembly against former finance minister Sheikh Ali Khalifah as-Sabah. Sheikh Ali accused the Assembly of pursuing the indictment to cover up its own lack of a coherent legislative program.

Thirteen terrorists were convicted on June 4 of having attempted to assassinate former U.S. president George Bush during a visit to Kuwait in April 1993. Five Iraqis and one Kuwaiti received death sentences, and others were jailed. Two days later 10 Jordanians, found guilty in May 1993 of having collaborated with Iraq during the 1990–91 invasion, had their death sentences commuted to prison terms by the Court of Appeal.

On April 13 the prime minister announced a Cabinet reshuffle; the principal casualty was outspoken Oil Minister Ali Ahmad al-Baghli, an elected assemblyman and lawyer. Baghli went without grace and launched a bitter attack on alleged corruption at the Kuwait Petroleum Corp.

(JOHN WHELAN)

This article updates the *Macropædia* article ARABIA: *Kuwait*.

KYRGYZSTAN

A landlocked republic of Central Asia, Kyrgyzstan borders Kazakhstan to the north, China to the southeast, Tajikistan to the south and west, and Uzbekistan to the west. Area: 198,500 sq km (76,600 sq mi). Pop. (1994 est.): 4,488,000. Cap.: Bishkek. Monetary unit: som, with (Oct. 3, 1994) a free rate of 10.20 som = U.S. $1 (16.22 som = £1 sterling). President in 1994, Askar Akayev; prime minister, Apas Dzhumagulov.

Kyrgyzstan's reputation as the most democratic state in Central Asia suffered as the result of clashes between the country's liberal president and the legislature, which was a holdover from the Soviet era. The economy progressively weakened as most industrial enterprises had to reduce production or close down for lack of materials from other Commonwealth of Independent States countries. Unemployment increased and living conditions worsened. Foreign investors were frightened off when the parliament raised charges of corruption against those involved in a Canadian-Kyrgyz venture that was to develop the country's gold resources.

In May local journalists charged that Soviet-style censorship had returned with the passage of a new law on state secrets. It prohibited media discussion of a wide range of topics, including price increases, livestock deaths, and the condition of roads. The same charge was raised in July after Pres. Askar Akayev charged that irresponsible media were stirring up political and interethnic conflict. Shortly thereafter a Bishkek court closed down the parliamentary daily. In the resulting crisis, more than half of the Supreme Soviet refused to attend a final session to set a date for parliamentary elections, and the government of Prime Minister Apas Dzhumagulov, which had been in power since Dec. 17, 1993, resigned. The election, originally scheduled by the president for December 25, was postponed to Feb. 5, 1995. Akayev warned that political turmoil would benefit only the Kyrgyz Communist Party. (BESS BROWN)

This article updates the *Macropædia* article CENTRAL ASIA: *Kyrgyzstan*.

LAOS

A landlocked republic, Laos is in the northern part of the Indochinese Peninsula. Area: 236,800 sq km (91,429 sq mi). Pop. (1994 est.): 4,743,000. Cap.: Vientiane. Monetary unit: kip, with (Oct. 7, 1994) an official rate of 720 kip to U.S. $1 (1,145 kip = £1 sterling). President in 1994, Nouhak Phoumsavan; prime minister, Gen. Khamtai Siphandon.

The defining event of 1994 was the opening on April 8 of the Thai-Laos Friendship Bridge, built with U.S. $30 million in aid from Australia. Laotian Pres. Nouhak Phoumsavan and King Bhumibol Adulyadej of Thailand jointly cut the ribbon in the presence of the prime ministers of Laos, Thailand, and Australia. The 1,170-m (3,840-ft) link across the Mekong River, 19 km (12 mi) downstream from Vientiane, not only opened the way for more trade and investment from Laos's richer southern neighbour but dramatically symbolized the swift realignment of Laos away from its colonial and Cold War ally Vietnam. The pace of reconciliation with Thailand, with which Laos shared a broad ethnic identity, approached cultural and economic absorption. Thai-owned banks, media companies, transport firms, and factories overwhelmingly dominated new investment in an economy that had shed virtually all its socialist principles.

On March 14 the National Assembly passed a foreign-investment law codifying rules for joint ventures and foreign-owned companies. It also eliminated business by contract, a vestige of the planned-economy system. It lowered corporate profit tax and reduced import duties on capital equipment from 5% to 1%. A new labour law guaranteed the rights of trade unions and established rules on workers' probation, dismissal, and overtime. The economy was expected to grow 7%. Prospects for large increases in export revenues from hydroelectricity and lumber worried some environmentalists. Tourism grew rapidly from a very modest base. The entire old royal city of Louangphrabang was declared a national heritage site to be preserved intact.

Political openness, however, had no place in this social reconstruction. The leadership in Vientiane, though committed to free-market forces, adhered resolutely to its communist identity. Poverty remained widespread. A poor 1993 rice harvest of 1.25 metric tons, down 17% from the previous year, caused serious 1994 food shortages. The European Union, Japan, and Australia purchased grain in Thailand for emergency relief. Only 33% of rural children were receiving five years or more of schooling. An ambitious program for upgrading teachers' qualifications got under way, with the goal of retraining 40% of educators by 1996.

(ROBERT WOODROW)

This article updates the *Macropædia* article SOUTHEAST ASIA: *Laos*.

LATVIA

A republic of northern Europe, Latvia is on the eastern shore of the Baltic Sea. Area: 64,610 sq km (24,946 sq mi). Pop. (1994 est.): 2,551,000. Cap.: Riga. Monetary unit: lats, with (Oct. 7, 1994) a free rate of 0.55 lats to U.S. $1 (0.87 lats = £1 sterling). President in 1994, Guntis Ulmanis; chairman of the Saeima (parliament), Anatolijs Gorbunovs; prime ministers, Valdis Birkavs until July 13 and, from September 15, Maris Gailis.

The internal political situation in Latvia in 1994 was rather turbulent. Prime Minister Valdis Birkavs was forced to resign on July 13 when the Latvian Farmers' Union (LZS) withdrew from its coalition with Latvia's Way in a dispute over import duties on food. After lengthy maneuvering, on September 15 Lativa's Way formed a new governing coalition headed by Maris Gailis. At the same time, the LZS joined three other right-of-centre parliamentary factions (known as the National Bloc) that had made a strong showing in the local elections on May 29—but had been unable

In a public demonstration in Riga, a Latvian nationalist brandishes a map showing areas of the former Soviet Union with Russian majorities. In 1994 Russia withdrew its remaining troops from Latvia, one of several newly-independent countries with large Russian communities.

to form a new state government in August—and formed a permanent council and secretariat to coordinate policy and have a greater effect on legislation.

Owing to the tight monetary policy of its central bank, Latvia had the lowest rate of inflation in 1994 among all former Soviet republics. Foreign investments in Latvia increased, but its economy remained dependent upon Russia for supplies of fuel and as its main export market. Economic reforms continued with greater privatization of state property, although budget and foreign-trade deficits remained sources of concern.

On August 31 Latvia achieved its main immediate foreign policy goal: the official withdrawal of Russian troops from its territory. In turn, Latvia allowed Russia to retain control of its radar station at Skrunda until Aug. 31, 1998 (with an additional 18 months for its dismantling), and granted various rights for Russian military retirees. The main stumbling block to Latvia's membership in the Council of Europe was removed on August 11 with the signing of a citizenship law, amended to remove a restrictive quota system as recommended by various international organizations. Latvia was to join the council in February 1995. Latvia joined NATO's Partnership for Peace program in February and expressed the wish to become a full member of NATO and the European Union.   (SAULIUS A. GIRNIUS)

This article updates the *Macropædia* article BALTIC STATES: *Latvia*.

LEBANON

A republic of southwestern Asia, Lebanon is situated on the Mediterranean Sea. Area: 10,230 sq km (3,950 sq mi). Pop. (1994 est.): 2,965,000 (including Palestinian refugees estimated to number nearly 350,000). Cap.: Beirut. Monetary unit: Lebanese pound, with (Oct. 7, 1994) a free rate of LL 1,664 to U.S. $1 (LL 2,647 = £1 sterling). President in 1994, Elias Hrawi; prime minister, Rafiq al-Hariri.

Political violence during the year continued to destabilize Lebanon and endanger both the consensus that characterized local political affairs and the wider issues that were involved as the Middle East moved slowly but deliberately toward a broad-based and lasting peace settlement. Four people were killed during fighting in southern Lebanon on December 22 when pro-Iranian Hezbollah guerrillas attacked fortified positions in Israel's "security zone" in revenge for a car bombing in Beirut a day earlier.

The car bomb casualties included Fuad Mughniyeh, a Hezbollah member and brother of Imad Mughniyeh, the reputed mastermind of the kidnapping of Western hostages in the 1980s. Prime Minister Rafiq al-Hariri said that the evidence of responsibility for the bombing pointed to Israel; by late December, 21 Israeli soldiers had been killed in 1994 in southern Lebanon.

Hariri resigned as prime minister on December 2 but on December 6 withdrew his resignation after assurances from Syria that it would not interfere with plans for the reconstruction of Lebanon. Throughout the year, however, Syria continued its long-term policy of exercising control over Lebanon, which had once been part of Syria. In early September, for example, Interior Minister Bishara Merhej was replaced by Deputy Prime Minister Michel al-Burr at the behest of the Syrians.

On May 21 Israeli commandos abducted Mustapha Dirani, a former member of the Islamic resistance, from his home in the al-Biqa' Valley, emphasizing Lebanon's vulnerability to its other powerful neighbour. The most serious terrorist incident of the year, however, had its roots in domestic politics. On February 27 in Junieh, 11 worshipers were killed

and 50 injured when a bomb was exploded in a church. Although no group claimed responsibility, the government blamed members of the Lebanese Forces, a Christian militia group, and on March 23 ordered disbandment. A visit by Pope John Paul II scheduled for late May was canceled.

In the aftermath of the bombing, the Lebanese Forces leader Samir Geagea was arrested and charged with complicity in the church killings. He went on trial on November 19 for this alleged crime and also for involvement in the 1990 killing of 11 Maronite Christians and the politician Dany Chamoun, his wife, and two sons. Geagea, considered one of the dominant personalities in Lebanese politics, was being defended at his trial by former central bank governor Edmond Naim and expressed confidence that he would be acquitted.

In March the government enacted a number of restrictive measures. Private radio and television services were ordered to close until a new audiovisual media law had been drafted. The government reintroduced the death penalty for assassinations and political crimes, and the first public executions since 1983 took place. On April 23 a child killer was hanged at Sidon, followed by two Syrians found guilty of shooting three police officers. On May 28 an alleged drug trafficker was shot by a firing squad.

Despite political turbulence, the economy continued its revival. Gross domestic product grew by an estimated 6% in 1994, with inflation at 8%. The Beirut property company Solidere, which was committed to a major role in the reconstruction of the city's centre, was successful in a $650 million share subscription. A number of banks from The Netherlands, the U.K., and France established offices in Beirut for the first time since civil war erupted in the mid-1970s.

Political differences were set aside on January 10 when the Cabinet agreed on two key diplomatic appointments. Riad Tabbara, a Sunni Muslim, was named ambassador to the U.S., and Samir Mubarak, a Maronite Christian, was made ambassador to the UN. Shi'ite Muslims on March 18 elected Sheikh Muhammad Mahdi Shamseddine president of the Higher Shi'ite Council.   (JOHN WHELAN)

LESOTHO

A constitutional monarchy of southern Africa and member of the Commonwealth, Lesotho forms a landlocked enclave within South Africa. Area: 30,355 sq km (11,720 sq mi). Pop. (1994 est.): 1,929,000. Cap.: Maseru. Monetary unit: loti (plural: maloti), at par with the South African rand, with (Oct. 7, 1994) a free rate of 3.57 maloti to U.S. $1 (5.68 maloti = £1 sterling). King, Letsie III; prime minister in 1994, Ntsu Mokhehle until August 17 and from September 14.

An unruly army and fears of coups caused 1994 to be a troubled year for Lesotho. In January fighting between rival military factions occurred in and around Maseru. Though low pay was the ostensible reason, the conflict was in fact caused by military resentment of the landslide victory of the Basotho Congress Party (BCP) in the 1993 elections. Fears of a coup receded when South Africa warned that it would seal the border should a coup be carried out. Under Commonwealth pressure the two groups laid down their arms at the beginning of February. In April, however, discontented soldiers kidnapped four ministers and killed Selometsi Baholo, the deputy prime minister and minister of finance. The government's plan to integrate the armed wing of the BCP, the Lesotho Liberation Army, into the army was a primary reason for the troubles.

In August King Letsie III, in what amounted to a royal coup, dissolved the government of Ntsu Mokhehle and the parliament. When crowds demonstrated in protest outside the palace, soldiers and police fired on them and killed at least four. The king then announced that he was suspending part of the constitution and calling new elections, but the government ignored his pronouncement and worked on. Opponents of the king now demanded that Lesotho become a republic, and five opposition parties petitioned the king to abdicate. Under pressure from other nations as well as from his own people, the king on September 14 officially restored Mokhehle and his government to power.

(GUY ARNOLD)

This article updates the *Macropædia* article SOUTHERN AFRICA: *Lesotho*.

LIBERIA

The republic of Liberia is located in West Africa, on the Atlantic Ocean. Area: 99,067 sq km (38,250 sq mi). Pop. (1994 est.): 2,377,000 (including Liberian refugees temporarily residing in surrounding countries estimated to number about 700,000). Cap.: Monrovia. Monetary unit: Liberian dollar, at par with the U.S. dollar, with a free rate (Oct. 7, 1994) of L$1.59 to £1 sterling. President of the interim government in 1994, Amos Sawyer until March 7; chairman of the Council of State from March 7, David Kpormakor.

During 1994 an uneasy semipeace prevailed in the aftermath of the civil war. In February the five-member Council of State elected David Kpormakor as chairman. The transition period began on March 7, when the Council of State and a

A Liberian woman carries her baby with her as she sows rice donated by a relief agency. With fighting between the country's political factions quiet during much of 1994, Liberia began to take steps toward the formation of a government lenient and toward economic recovery.

35-seat Transitional Legislative Assembly were inaugurated. Immediately afterward, however, there was a stalemate between the three principal political factions—Amos Sawyer's outgoing interim government, the National Patriotic Front of Liberia (NPFL), and the United Liberation Movement of Liberia for Democracy—concerning the allocation of Cabinet posts.

After much delay the three groups formed a government, which met on May 16 even as the UN Observer Mission complained that fighting among the factions was preventing the disarmament process. On July 19 Charles Taylor alleged that his NPFL forces had been attacked by ECOMOG (the peacekeeping forces of the Economic Community of West African States), resulting in a heavy loss of life. The NPFL held talks with Organization of African Unity and UN delegations at its Gbarnga headquarters, and on August 3 representatives of five warring factions, including the NPFL, agreed to "cease hostilities" and facilitate the deployment of ECOMOG and UN peacekeeping forces. However, in August renewed fighting occurred between the NPFL and the Liberian Peace Council. On September 15 Gen. Charles Julue, a commander in the army of slain dictator Samuel Doe, attempted a coup. He seized the presidential mansion but was captured the next day. On December 21 all seven warring factions agreed to a cease-fire, effective on December 28.

(GUY ARNOLD)

This article updates the *Macropædia* article WESTERN AFRICA: *Liberia*.

LIBYA

A socialist country of North Africa, Libya lies on the Mediterranean Sea. Area: 1,757,000 sq km (678,400 sq mi). Pop. (1994 est.): 5,225,000. Cap.: Tripoli (policy-making body meets in Surt). Monetary unit: Libyan dinar, with (Oct. 7, 1994) a free rate of 0.31 dinar to U.S. $1 (0.49 dinar = £1 sterling). De facto chief of state in 1994, Col. Muammar al-Qaddafi; secretary of the General People's Congress (nominal chief of state), Zentani Muhammad Zentani; secretaries of the General People's Committee (premiers), Abu Zaid Umar Dourda and, from January 29, 'Abd al-Majid al-Qa'ud.

Libya became increasingly isolated internationally during 1994. The UN had intensified its trade embargo in 1993, and its ban on international flights continued to impair the national economy severely. Despite efforts by the Libyan leadership, relations with the United States and European countries, especially Britain and France, did not improve. One of the most divisive issues involved the two Libyans suspected of planting the bomb that resulted in the deaths of 259 passengers aboard Pan Am flight 103 and 11 persons on the ground in December 1988. When they were handed over for trial in Libya, it was not in a court favoured by the U.S. and British governments.

The period of Libya's isolation, which began in 1988, was a significant proportion of the time during which Muammar al-Qaddafi had led the country. He came to power in 1969 and enjoyed a decade of running a cash-rich oil economy. But by the date of the celebrations on September 1 to mark the 25th anniversary of the 1969 revolution, Libya had endured a poor revolutionary economy longer than it had enjoyed a prosperous one. One would expect this to weaken Qaddafi politically, but the hard line taken against him by the international community tended to legitimize him at home because he persuasively projected Libya's difficulties as being caused by its old enemy, the U.S.

Economic management of Libya had changed during the past five years, with a significant reversal of the trend toward complete government control of all production and distribution. Retailing substantially reverted to a private-sector mode. Although the government remained careful in its overall national economic management, lower oil prices and the impact of UN sanctions forced it to devalue the dinar by 15% on November 3. Three weeks later a two-tier system was introduced, with a new rate of 1.019 dinars to U.S. $1 for use by local companies.

Long-term projects associated with water remained high on the list of priorities, although payment schedules and construction rates were delayed because of financial constraints. The Western Water Pipeline contract was signed after the promise of assistance from the African Development Bank. Such financing was a departure from the normal fiscal self-reliance of the Libyan government and was a measure both of the economic predicament of Libya and of the severity of the water crisis in the populous al-Jifarah Plain around Tripoli.

The central government faced internal problems during the year, stemming partly from the breakup of key relationships in Libya's domestic politics. Qaddafi's own tribe, the Quadaffa, was no longer aligned with the Maghara, of which 'Abd as-Salem Jalloud, Qaddafi's deputy since the 1969 revolution, was a member, or with the Warfalla, whose members precipitated the attempted coup in October 1993. The Libyan leader thus had to seek new alliances and did so in Libya's populous urban areas.

Relations in the southern region of Fezzan became tense after the decision in February by the International Court of Justice rejecting Libya's claim to the Aozou strip, which lies along Libya's southern border with Chad. The people of Fezzan were angry, as they had been deeply involved in the military struggle to establish Libya's claim to Aozou.

(J.A. ALLAN)

This article updates the *Macropædia* article NORTH AFRICA: *Libya*.

LIECHTENSTEIN

A landlocked constitutional monarchy of central Europe, Liechtenstein is united with Switzerland by a customs and monetary union. Area: 160 sq km (62 sq mi). Pop. (1994 est.): 30,500. Cap.: Vaduz. Monetary unit: Swiss franc, with (Oct. 7, 1994) a free rate of Sw F 1.28 to U.S. $1 (Sw F 2.03 = £1 sterling). Sovereign prince, Hans Adam II; head of government in 1994, Mario Frick.

The position of Liechtenstein within the framework of European integration dominated the country's foreign policy in 1994. The European Free Trade Association (EFTA), comprising Austria, Finland, Iceland, Liechtenstein, Norway, Sweden, and Switzerland, had negotiated a treaty with the European Community to create the European Economic Area (EEA). The voters of Liechtenstein ratified the treaty in mid-December 1993, but the citizens of Switzerland had already voted against it on December 6. Because of an existing customs treaty between Switzerland and Liechtenstein dating from 1923, the Swiss vote prevented the EEA treaty from automatically entering into force for Liechtenstein. Negotiations to adapt the EEA treaty and maintain the strong traditional links with Switzerland were successfully concluded in October. The fate of the revised treaty, which required the approval of the electorate, would be decided in the spring of 1995.

Negotiations continued between the Czech Republic and Liechtenstein over compensation for Czechoslovakia's 1945 confiscation of land and property of Liechtenstein citizens, including the ancestral home and estates of Prince Hans Adam II. The issue was still pending at year's end.

(ANNE ROBY)

This article updates the *Micropædia* article LIECHTENSTEIN.

LITHUANIA

A republic of northern Europe, Lithuania is on the southeastern shore of the Baltic Sea. Area: 65,301 sq km (25,213 sq mi). Pop. (1994 est.): 3,724,000. Cap.: Vilnius. Monetary unit: litas, with (Oct. 7, 1994) a par value (from April 1) of 4 litai to U.S. $1 (6.37 litai = £1 sterling). President in 1994, Algirdas Brazauskas; prime minister, Adolfas Slezevicius.

The domestic situation in Lithuania remained stable and relatively uneventful in 1994. The opposition Homeland Union challenged the ruling Lithuanian Democratic Labour Party (LDDP) by gathering more than 560,000 signatures to hold a referendum on compensation for savings lost to inflation and illegal privatization by the LDDP. Approval would have meant a renunciation of government economic policy, but the referendum failed because only 36.8% of eligible voters participated in the vote on August 27.

Although by midyear more than 60% of workers were employed by private firms, the economic situation in the country continued to worsen, albeit at a more moderate pace. By granting delays in tax payments, the government kept many large state-industrial enterprises from bankruptcy. In an effort to attract greater foreign investment and ensure a stable exchange rate, officials pegged the litas to the U.S. dollar at a rate of four to one beginning April 1. Internal interest rates remained very high, but inflation declined to less than one-quarter of the 1993 level of 188.3%. On October 24 the International Monetary Fund showed confidence by accepting the government's three-year economic memorandum and approving a $201 million loan.

The withdrawal of Russian troops from Lithuania in 1993 had little effect on the relations between the two countries in 1994. Lithuanian hopes for better ties did not bear fruit. Russia's parliament decided not to ratify the most-favoured-nation (MFN) trade agreement unless Lithuania acceded to an agreement on military transit to and from Russia's Baltic exclave of Kaliningrad. Without MFN status, Lithuania was forced to pay duties on goods exported to Russia at twice the normal rate. In January Lithuania joined NATO's Partnership for Peace program. It became an associate partner of the Western European Union on May 9 and continued to press for full NATO membership, despite Russian opposition.

(SAULIUS A. GIRNIUS)

This article updates the *Macropædia* article BALTIC STATES: *Lithuania*.

LUXEMBOURG

Luxembourg is a landlocked constitutional monarchy in western Europe. Area: 2,586 sq km (999 sq mi). Pop. (1994 est.): 398,000. Cap.: Luxembourg. Monetary unit: Luxembourg franc, at par with the Belgian franc, with (Oct. 7, 1994) a free rate of Lux F 31.70 to U.S. $1 (Lux F 50.42 = £1 sterling). Grand duke, Jean; prime minister in 1994, Jacques Santer.

Although 1994 began with Luxembourg focusing on domestic concerns, by year's end its prime minister had been chosen to lead the European Union, and so the nation found itself involved in European affairs. On July 15 Prime Minister Jacques Santer (*see* BIOGRAPHIES) was named to replace Jacques Delors as president of the European Commission on Jan. 1, 1995.

Santer was reelected Luxembourg's prime minister in a general election on June 12. The two largest parties, the Christian Social People's Party with 21 seats and the Socialist Workers' Party with 17 seats, retained a comfortable majority in the 60-seat legislature. The two parties had governed in coalition since 1984.

In elections to the European Parliament held on the same day, the coalition again maintained its majority. Of the six seats, the Christian Social won two, the Socialist Workers, two, the Democratic Party, one, and the Greens, one.

Earlier in the year domestic affairs were dominated by demands that immigration be curbed. Concern centred on the lack of jobs and the clash of cultures. Foreigners in 1994 made up 30% of the total population and more than 50% of the nation's workforce.   (ANNE ROBY)

MACEDONIA

A landlocked republic of the central Balkans, Macedonia borders Yugoslavia to the north, Bulgaria to the east, Greece to the south, and Albania to the west. Area: 25,713 sq km (9,928 sq mi). Pop. (1994 est.): 2,089,000. Cap.: Skopje. Monetary unit: denar, with (Aug. 1, 1994) a free rate of 41.95 denars to U.S. $1 (66.72 denars = £1 sterling). President in 1994, Kiro Gligorov; prime minister, Branko Crvenkovski.

In the presidential and parliamentary elections held on October 16, Kiro Giligorov was reelected president with a 52.4% share of the vote. Following the second round of parliamentary elections on October 30, the ruling Social Democratic Alliance of Macedonia (SDSM) led by Prime Minister Branko Crvenkovski formed a coalition government with the Liberals, the small Socialist Party, and the Party of Democratic Prosperity, the main ethnic Albanian party. The coalition was called the Alliance of Macedonia (SM). On November 13 a further election was held to decide who would occupy 10 unfilled seats. On November 28 the president ordered Crvenkovski to form still another government. Its members were expected to come from parties constituting the SM.

The results of the internationally monitored census announced on November 15 provoked claims of unfair manipulation from the Albanian and Serb minorities. Political tensions rose in December as a result of the Macedonian Albanians' decision to press for the foundation of an Albanian-language university in Tetovo.

Continuing its campaign against Macedonia, Greece on February 16 instituted a full economic blockade, barring its port of Thessaloniki and the entire northern border to traffic to and from Macedonia. Some 80% of Macedonia's trade and all of its oil went through Thessaloniki. On April 6 the European Commission took Greece to the European Court of Justice over the action, but Greece continued the blockade anyway.

In November Macedonian engineers completed the first section of an oil pipeline that would link the country to Serbia and thence to Russia. Also in November Macedonia concluded an agreement on military cooperation with the United States, which continued to maintain a small UN detachment on Macedonian territory.   (K.F. CVIIC)

This article updates the *Macropædia* article BALKAN STATES: *Macedonia*.

MADAGASCAR

The republic of Madagascar occupies the island of the same name and minor adjacent islands in the Indian Ocean off the southeast coast of Africa. Area: 587,041 sq km (226,658 sq mi). Pop. (1994 est.): 13,702,000. Cap.: Antananarivo. Monetary unit: Malagasy franc, with (Oct. 7, 1994) a free rate of FMG 3,343 to U.S. $1 (FMG 5,317 = £1 sterling). President in 1994, Albert Zafy; prime minister, Francisque Ravony.

In March 1994 the Council of Ministers introduced a set of austerity measures to deal with Madagascar's deteriorating economic situation. On March 13 Pres. Albert Zafy in-

formed the ministers that the International Monetary Fund and the World Bank demanded a wage freeze and a reduction in the size of the civil service. At the same time, as an austerity gesture, the ministers reduced their own salaries by 10%.

The state of the Madagascan economy—or its level of development—could be judged by a comparison of a series of figures over a 20-year period. Thus, between 1976 and 1992 the per capita income increased only from $200 to $230. In 1975 average life expectancy stood at 48, and in 1990 it had increased only to 55. Figures for adult literacy showed a better achievement, from 50% in 1970 to 80% in 1990. In what represented an absolute decline in basic welfare, however, the daily calorie supply as a percentage of requirements was 108% in 1964–66 but had dropped to 95% for 1988–90.

The new government expressed its desire to tackle economic development, and there were welcome signs that it was prepared to do so without reference to doctrine. At the same time, the country remained overwhelmingly dependent upon agriculture, which employed 78% of the workforce and accounted for most exports. The manufacturing sector, on the other hand, accounted for less than 12% of gross domestic product.

On January 27 Israel restored diplomatic relations with Madagascar. At the end of 1993 Madagascar was admitted to membership in the Preferential Trade Area for Eastern and Southern African States (PTA); 15 countries (of 16 present), including Madagascar, signed an agreement to establish the Common Market for Eastern and Southern Africa (COMESA).   (GUY ARNOLD)

MALAWI

A republic and member of the Commonwealth, Malawi is a landlocked state in eastern Africa. Area: 118,484 sq km (45,747 sq mi). Pop. (1994 est.): 9,732,000. Cap.: Lilongwe. Monetary unit: Malawi kwacha, with (Oct. 7, 1994) a free rate of 13.50 kwacha to U.S. $1 (21.48 kwacha = £1 sterling). Presidents in 1994, Hastings Kamuzu Banda and, from May 21, Bakili Muluzi.

On May 17, 1994, Malawi held its first multiparty elections for the office of president and for membership in the National Assembly. All citizens of the country who had reached the age of 18 by voting day were entitled to register as electors, and in spite of the fact that both the UN observer group and Malawi's own electoral commission reported intimidation, violence, bribery, and confiscation of registration cards—most of this attributed to the ruling Malawi Congress Party (MCP)—the UN group agreed that the freedom of the elections was not threatened. An attempt by the MCP to prevent Bakili Muluzi, the leader of the main opposition party, the United Democratic Front (UDF), from running for election as president because he had served a six-month prison sentence for petty theft was unsuccessful. Muluzi was duly elected president, ousting Hastings Kamuzu Banda, who had been stripped of his title of president for life in 1993.

The UDF failed to gain an overall majority in the assembly elections, winning 84 out of a total of 177 seats. Voting for the three main parties was almost entirely on a regional basis because of the absence of any marked differences in their economic or social policies. The Alliance for Democracy (Aford) won all 33 seats in the north and had a total of 36; the MCP held the rural seats in the central region and, though it lost some urban constituencies to its rivals, mustered 55 seats. Banda announced his retirement from politics in September, leaving the leadership of the MCP to Gwanda Chakuamba. An attempt to form

Mozambican refugees watch their house in Malawi burn as they prepare to return to their homeland. The government of Malawi, where thousands of people had gone to flee the civil war in Mozambique, required that refugees burn their homes on leaving to prevent others from moving in.
SEBASTIÃO SALGADO

a coalition between the UDF and Aford was unsuccessful because the ruling party would not accede to Aford's demands.

A more serious and immediate problem facing Malawi was a shortage of food. A severe drought early in the year had devastated crops and raised the spectre that one-third of the country's nine million inhabitants would be without sufficient food. Even so, the government was slow to respond. There was, moreover, no assurance that the government would be able to raise the $10 million it said was needed to buy food from Zimbabwe. All told, an estimated 183,000 metric tons of corn (maize) were needed to avert starvation, approximately half of which was promised by the World Food Programme.

(KENNETH INGHAM)

This article updates the *Macropædia* article SOUTHERN AFRICA: *Malawi*.

MALAYSIA

A federal constitutional monarchy of Southeast Asia and member of the Commonwealth, Malaysia consists of the former Federation of Malaya at the southern end of the Malay Peninsula (excluding Singapore) and Sabah and Sarawak on the northern part of the island of Borneo. Area: 330,442 sq km (127,584 sq mi). Pop. (1994 est.): 19,506,000. Cap.: Kuala Lumpur. Monetary unit: ringgit, with (Oct. 7, 1994) a free rate of 2.56 ringgit to U.S. $1 (4.08 ringgit = £1 sterling). Paramount rulers in 1994, with the title of *yang di-pertuan agong,* Tuanku Azlan Muhibbudin Shah ibni al-Marhum Yusuff Ghafarullahu-Lahu Shah and, from April 26, Tuanku Ja'afar ibni al-Marhum Tuanku Abdul Rahman; prime minister, Datuk Seri Mahathir bin Mohamad.

Prime Minister Datuk Seri Mahathir bin Mohamad marked his 13th year in office in 1994, becoming Malaysia's longest-serving leader. But the nation's attention was also focused on his heir apparent, Anwar Ibrahim, who had been promoted to deputy prime minister in December 1993. A month earlier Anwar had faced no competition when he was elected deputy president of the United Malays National Organization (UMNO), the senior partner in the ruling National Front coalition. His "Vision Team," comprising UMNO leaders in their 40s, also won key party posts.

Anwar was UMNO's chief strategist for the February elections in Sabah, the Borneo state long ruled by the opposition United Sabah Party. UMNO and its allies in the National Front won 23 state assembly seats, whittling PBS's legislative strength down to 25. Joseph Pairin Kitingan, Sabah's chief minister for nine years, was forced to dissolve the new assembly even before it could convene in March because almost all PBS legislators had defected. UMNO's Sakaran Dandai then became Sabah's chief minister.

In April, Tuanku Ja'afar ibni al-Marhum Tuanku Abdul Rahman, ruler of Negri Sembilan state, became king of Malaysia. (Under a unique system of constitutional monarchy, Malaysia's nine state rulers successively served five-year terms as king.) In May Parliament amended the constitution to make clear that the monarch was obliged to follow the government's advice at all times. Any bill not signed by the king within 30 days would automatically become law. The parliament also restructured the judiciary and made any breach of the judicial code of ethics grounds for impeachment. To guarantee the independence of the bench, the government agreed that judges should draft the code.

Controversy erupted in February when a London newspaper reported that a British contractor, bidding on a contract to build an aluminum smelter in 1985, was prepared to bribe Mahathir. The allegation came amid media stories that British aid to build the soon-to-be-finished Pergau Dam was part of a 1988 deal for Malaysia to buy British arms. The Malaysian Cabinet responded by banning all new government contracts with British companies, but it quietly reversed the decision in September. Another furor broke out in March when Bank Negara, Malaysia's central bank, revealed that it had lost $2.1 billion in foreign-exchange trading in 1993, in addition to the $3,570,-000,000 lost in 1992. The governor of the central bank resigned.

In August Malaysia's highest Islamic religious body forbade the influential al-Arqam sect to hold public meetings or disseminate its literature and videos. The government later arrested the group's founder, Ashaari Muhammad, under the Internal Security Act, which allowed imprisonment without trial. After his release in October, Ashaari announced the disbanding of al-Arqam.

The economy continued to perform strongly. Gross domestic product growth exceeded 8%, matching the previous year's robust expansion. The push for value-added manufacturing continued. Nine years after Proton produced its first highly successful automobile, state-backed Perodua unveiled its first subcompact model in August.

Mahathir made numerous state visits. By going to the Philippines, he confirmed that Malaysia no longer regarded Manila's territorial claim over Sabah as an insurmountable barrier to closer relations. Mahathir also paid a call on U.S. Pres. Bill Clinton. The prime minister had boycotted the 1993 Asia-Pacific Economic Cooperation (APEC) forum in Seattle, Wash., because Clinton did not endorse his proposed East Asian Economic Caucus. In November, however, Mahathir attended the second APEC summit in Indonesia.

(CESAR BACANI)

This article updates the *Macropædia* article SOUTHEAST ASIA: *Malaysia*.

MALDIVES

A republic and member of the Commonwealth in the Indian Ocean, Maldives consists of about 1,200 small islands southwest of the southern tip of India. Area: 298 sq km (115 sq mi). Pop. (1994 est.): 244,000. Cap.: Male. Monetary unit: rufiyaa, with (Oct. 7, 1994) a free rate of 11.83 rufiyaa to U.S. $1 (18.82 rufiyaa = £1 sterling). President in 1994, Maumoon Abdul Gayoom.

Following his landslide election victory in October 1993, Pres. Maumoon Abdul Gayoom began his fourth term in office by forming a new Cabinet of 23 members; he, however, continued to head the Ministries of Defense and National Security and of Finance. The budget for 1993–94, which was presented in December 1993, provided for a 1994 expenditure of 794 million rufiyaa, with a capital expenditure of 776.2 million rufiyaa. Social development—education, health, and welfare—absorbed 27% of budget expenditures; economic development was pegged at 30%, the largest portion of which (nearly 340 million rufiyaa) was allocated for the fisheries sector. Revenues for 1994 were estimated at 1,373,000,000 rufiyaa. Of that sum 835 million rufiyaa would be generated at home, 382 million rufiyaa from foreign loans, 136 million rufiyaa from an aid grant, and 20 million rufiyaa in food and financial aid. Although Maldives' debts were small by world standards— a mere $77.2 million—they represented nearly 75% of the gross national product, which stood at $114 million. The per

capita income had risen to $500. Maldives' small population accounted for a correspondingly small-scale economy and the intrinsic limits on economic performance. There was sound progress during the year and the country remained politically stable, but Maldives would continue to require aid on a more or less permanent basis.   (GUY ARNOLD)

This article updates the *Micropædia* article MALDIVES.

MALI

Mali is a landlocked republic of West Africa. Area: 1,248,574 sq km (482,077 sq mi). Pop. (1994 est.): 8,825,000. Cap.: Bamako. Monetary unit: CFA franc, with (Oct. 7, 1994) a par value of CFAF 100 to the French franc and a free rate of CFAF 526.67 to U.S. $1 (CFAF 837.67 = £1 sterling). President in 1994, Alpha Oumar Konaré; prime ministers, Abdoulaye Sekou Sow until February 2 and, from February 4, Ibrahima Boubacar Keita.

Massive student demonstrations against the government erupted in Bamako on Feb. 2, 1994. On the same day, Prime Minister Abdoulaye Sekou Sow resigned, citing differences with members of the ruling party, the Alliance for Democracy in Mali. He was the second prime minister to leave under pressure from the radical wing of the party. His replacement, Foreign Minister Ibrahima Boubacar Keita, immediately named a new Cabinet. The two main opposition parties withdrew from the coalition government on February 5 in protest against not being consulted about the Cabinet appointments. Following another bloody demonstration on February 15, all educational institutions above primary level were closed. An opposition radio station was also shut down. On May 6 the French Development Fund's Bamako offices were attacked by some 100 students, causing extensive damage. The students were apparently following a clandestine armed group's call for attacks on property belonging to Mali's main international donors.

An agreement was signed in June between the government and the powerful Tuareg Unified Movements and Fronts of Azaouad (MFUA). Integration of 1,500 former Tuareg rebels into the army and nearly 5,000 into other branches of government began in July despite continuing outbreaks of violence. Internal Tuareg conflicts were deemed responsible for the deaths of 30 members of the MFUA on June 10–12, while some 200 others, including women and children, were reported to have been killed by security forces in Gao and Beher during the same month.

Discussions over the repatriation of thousands of Tuareg refugees in Algeria and Mauritania continued. In the meantime, sporadic fighting occurred in a number of localities, including the Segou region, where 18 people died in the middle of July.

(NANCY ELLEN LAWLER)

This article updates the *Macropædia* article WESTERN AFRICA: *Mali*.

MALTA

The republic of Malta, a member of the Commonwealth, comprises the islands of Malta, Gozo, and Comino in the Mediterranean Sea between Sicily and Tunisia. Area: 316 sq km (122 sq mi). Pop. (1994 est.): 368,000. Cap.: Valletta. Monetary unit: Maltese lira, with (Oct. 7, 1994) an official rate of 0.37 lira to U.S. $1 (0.58 lira = £1 sterling). Presidents in 1994, Censu Tabone and, from April 4, Ugo Mifsud Bonnici; prime minister, Eddie Fenech Adami.

On April 4, 1994, Ugo Mifsud Bonnici, minister of education since 1987, was sworn in as president of Malta. Regarding the country's application to join the European Union, the Nationalist government welcomed the declaration of the

European Council that the next phase of expansion would involve Cyprus and Malta.

The continued growth of the Maltese economy was attributable to the service sector, with tourist arrivals expected to reach 1.2 million by the end of 1994. In July the parliament introduced a value-added tax (VAT) to supplant customs duties, effective Jan. 1, 1995. The Labour Party opposed the measure. The General Workers' Union maintained that the VAT would affect the cost of living and organized a general strike for October 24; it found support from an association of retailers. Other bodies approved of the VAT as essential for the control of tax evasion.

Under the fourth Italo-Maltese financial protocol, signed in March, Malta was to receive 60 million liri in grants between 1995 and 2000. Discussions took place with Tunisia on the issue of boundaries after an attempt to carry out a seismic survey in Maltese waters. The appointment of a U.S. ambassador to Malta after a long gap was followed by a visit of the prime minister to the U.S., where bilateral relations and international issues of mutual interest, including regional security, were discussed.   (ALBERT GANADO)

MARSHALL ISLANDS

A republic in the central Pacific Ocean, the Marshall Islands comprises two 1,300-km (800-mi)-long parallel chains of coral atolls. Area: 181 sq km (70 sq mi). Pop. (1994 est.): 54,100. Cap.: Majuro. Monetary unit: U.S. dollar, with (Oct. 7, 1994) a free rate of U.S. $1.59 to £1 sterling. President in 1994, Amata Kabua.

The Marshall Islands government became the focus of regional controversy in 1994 when it again contemplated providing a dumping facility for nuclear waste in the Islands. Under the proposal such islands as Bikini and Enewetak, which would be uninhabitable for 10,000 years because of contamination from nuclear weapons testing in the 1940s and 1950s, would be used to provide storage facilities. At home the controversy assumed great intensity because of revelations that Marshall Islanders had been used as unwitting subjects in experiments to test the effects of radiation on humans. Documents released by the U.S. government also revealed that, contrary to previous claims, the monitoring of radiation-related illnesses was carried out in the central and southern Marshall Islands, implying that the hazards of exposure were known, even though the population was not informed. The Marshall Islanders in 1994 had the greatest frequency of thyroid cancer in the world.

Relations with the U.S. were tested by these revelations and also by the funding of the Marshall Islands under the Compact of Free Association. The U.S. had agreed to pay $2 million as compensation for legal changes that removed preferential trade and tax provisions, while the compact provided for payments of up to $20 million. The government of the Marshall Islands claimed that the total damage to the economy amounted to $50 million.

During the year the government also established an office in Hong Kong to facilitate the sale of passports to Asians. The parliament set a limit of 3,000 passports, each of which would cost $33,000. Of that amount, $20,000 would go directly into government coffers; the balance would be invested in bonds that the purchaser could redeem after a period of 15 years. The World Bank advised the Islanders to structure their economy with an eye to the future, knowing that the day would come when the U.S. would begin to reduce the aid that the government had grown accustomed to receiving and to relying on.   (BARRIE MACDONALD)

This article updates the Macropædia article PACIFIC ISLANDS: Marshall Islands.

MAURITANIA

The republic of Mauritania is on the Atlantic coast of West Africa. Area: 1,030,700 sq km (398,000 sq mi). Pop. (1994 est.): 2,069,000. Cap.: Nouakchott. Monetary unit: ouguiya, with (Oct. 7, 1994) a free rate of 123.67 ouguiya to U.S. $1 (196.69 ouguiya = £1 sterling). President in 1994, Col. Maaouya Ould Sidi Ahmad Taya; prime minister, Sidi Mohamed Ould Boubacar.

The Interior Ministry reported on Jan. 20, 1994, only eight days before the local government elections were to be held, that the army had arrested dozens of people on charges of printing false voter identification cards. Those detained included members of the majority Democratic and Social Republican Party (PRDS) as well as officials of several opposition parties. Despite the scandal, PRDS candidates overwhelmed the opposition, winning control of 172 of Mauritania's 208 communes. A petition filed by the main opposition party, the Union of Democratic Forces–New Era (UFD–EN), to nullify the elections on grounds of vote fraud was ignored by the government. The opposition was further weakened by a split in the UFD–EN in June, when one faction withdrew to form a new alliance, the Movement of Independent Democrats.

On May 18, citing state security, police confiscated copies of the newspaper Le Calame, which had published a damaging report by the International Human Rights Association on the situation in the country. Negotiations over plans to transfer 15,000–20,000 Tuareg refugees to Mali in the near future were conducted in late July.

In October the government arrested 60 leaders of Islamic organizations, including former religious affairs minister Abu Bakr Ould Ahmad. They were charged with creating a "climate of fear" among Muslims and undermining national security by indoctrinating children into a new, underground organization. On October 19 the government ordered all militant Mauritanian Islamic organizations to suspend their activities.   (NANCY ELLEN LAWLER)

This article updates the Macropædia article WESTERN AFRICA: Mauritania.

MAURITIUS

The republic of Mauritius, a member of the Commonwealth, occupies an island in the Indian Ocean about 800 km (500 mi) east of Madagascar and includes the island dependencies of Rodrigues, Agalega, and Cargados Carajos Shoals. Area: 2,040 sq km (788 sq mi). Pop. (1994 est.): 1,120,000. Cap.: Port Louis. Monetary unit: Mauritian rupee, with (Oct. 7, 1994) a free rate of Mau Rs 17.70 to U.S. $1 (Mau Rs 28.15 = £1 sterling). President in 1994, Cassam Uteem; prime minister, Sir Anerood Jugnauth.

In August 1993 Prime Minister Anerood Jugnauth of the Mauritian Socialist Movement dismissed Foreign Minister Paul Berenger, a member of the Mauritian Militant Movement and a partner in the ruling coalition. When Berenger's two remaining supporters resigned their Cabinet posts in November, Jugnauth had to restructure his Cabinet. Early in 1994 Finance Minister Rama Sithanen called for an expansion of the Mauritius stock exchange, which, he claimed, needed to be more dynamic. The stock exchange had been launched in 1988 with five listed companies; by 1994 it had 28, with 4 others waiting to obtain a listing. The initial turnover of $330,000 in 1988 had increased to $1,750,000 in 1993. During that time a total of $63 million had been invested in the Mauritius free zone. The zone, however, still required foreign expertise for improving a number of its operations. A fund was scheduled to be established in October 1994 to assist companies seeking to hire foreign experts in such fields as computer assembly and the manufacture of leather goods. By mid-1994 the stock exchange was enjoying a boom, partly on expectations of a larger-than-predicted sugar crop (the island's main source of foreign exchange), and the index reached a record level of 366.92 points. Mauritius passed the midway point in its three-year development plan, which would cost Mau Rs 19 billion, covering 280 projects and 19 economic sectors. Its total foreign debt of $794 million represented only 25% of the gross national product, while its per capita income of $2,740 put Mauritius well into the World Bank's classification of upper-middle-income countries.   (GUY ARNOLD)

This article updates the *Micropædia* article MAURITIUS.

MEXICO

A federal republic of North America, Mexico has coastlines on the Pacific Ocean, the Gulf of Mexico, and the Caribbean Sea. Area: 1,958,201 sq km (756,066 sq mi). Pop. (1994 est.): 91,-840,000. Cap.: Mexico City. Monetary unit: Mexican new peso, with (Oct. 7, 1994) a free rate of 3.42 new pesos to U.S. $1 (5.44 new pesos = £1 sterling). Presidents in 1994, Carlos Salinas de Gortari and, from December 1, Ernesto Zedillo Ponce de León.

Various crises punctuated the election year of 1994 in Mexico. The first of these erupted on January 1 when a group, using the name Zapatista National Liberation Army (EZLN), launched a rebellion in the southern state of Chiapas. The rebels, who were fighting for the rights of indigenous Maya Indians and for greater democracy, called for the resignation of Pres. Carlos Salinas de Gortari, who had only 11 more months left in his six-year term. Salinas promptly appointed a peace negotiator and a local mediator. This put an end to the fighting, but it took until March to reach terms for a preliminary peace accord that had to be put to the indigenous people for approval. A series of political reforms, to be in place for the August 21 elections, were agreed upon by the ruling Institutional Revolutionary Party (PRI) and nine other parties, including members of the main opposition National Action Party (PAN) and the Democratic Revolutionary Party (PRD). Among the political reforms that had won approval was the appointment of independent electoral bodies to oversee elections and of a prosecutor to investigate allegations of fraud, as well as an end to the use of government funds to finance political parties. The reforms were enacted on March 24.

On March 23 the PRI's presidential candidate, Luis Donaldo Colosio, was assassinated after addressing a political rally in the border city of Tijuana. (*See* OBITUARIES.) A single gunman, Mario Aburto Martínez, was convicted in October, but it was also alleged that senior members of the PRI may also have been involved. Such allegations resurfaced in late September when José Francisco Ruiz Massieu, the PRI's secretary-general, was also murdered, and again in late November when his brother, Mario Ruiz Massieu, resigned as deputy attorney general, charging that party officials were obstructing the murder investigation. As a result of Colosio's assassination, the PRI announced on March 29 that Ernesto Zedillo Ponce de León, a former Cabinet member who had been running Colosio's campaign, would be its new presidential candidate. (*See* BIOGRAPHIES.)

On election day, Zedillo won by a clear margin of more than 20 percentage points ahead of his nearest rival, Diego Fernández de Cevallos of the PAN. His share of the votes was slightly smaller than that of his predecessor, Salinas. Soon after his election Zedillo invited his opponents to discuss the policies that his government would enact.

The PRI also retained its majorities in both the Chamber of Deputies (300 of 500 seats) and the Senate (95 of 128 seats), with the PAN winning 119 and 25, respectively, and the PRD 71 and 8. Zedillo took office on December 1. The Cabinet showed some continuity with the Salinas administration. The economic team was led by Jaime Serra Puche as minister of finance (formerly minister of trade and industry), and his deputy, Herminio Blanco, was pro-

LILIANA NIETO DEL RIO—JB PICTURES

As part of procedures to control fraud, a voter in the Mexican elections has his hand marked. Observers agreed that the voting, which gave Ernesto Zedillo Ponce de León of the ruling Institutional Revolutionary Party a comfortable victory, was generally honest.

moted to the trade and industry post. Former chief foreign debt negotiator José Angel Gurria Trevino was selected to head the foreign relations ministry. Three women were appointed: Norma Samaniego as controller, Silvia Hernández as minister of tourism, and Julia Carabias as minister of fisheries. A significant innovation was the appointment of PAN member Antonio Lozano García as attorney general, the first Cabinet member from an opposition party in 65 years of rule by the PRI.

A week after Zedillo took office, political turmoil again threatened Chiapas, where on December 8 the new state governor—Eduardo Robledo Rincón from the ruling PRI—took office. Because the EZLN alleged that Robledo's victory had been fraudulent, it installed its own governor, Amado Avendaño of the PRD. Zedillo ordered the army to continue to observe a cease-fire and rejected demands for a new election in Chiapas. Soon after he took office, Zedillo announced that he would "significantly intensify" efforts to solve the murders of Colosio and Massieu.

Despite Mexico's political difficulties, its economy remained on course for growth. Gross domestic product was projected to increase by 3.1% after a rise of 2.9% in the first nine months. Inflation was expected to be low, 6.9% for all of 1994 after monthly rates of about 0.5%. The combination of higher U.S. Treasury rates and Colosio's assassination pushed domestic interest rates up in the second quarter and temporarily checked expansion, but the situation improved in the third quarter, especially in manufacturing.

On September 24 the annual prices and wages pact between the government, business, and labour was renewed. Then, on December 20, faced with a rapid increase in the outflow of capital, the new government abandoned the nation's longtime policy of only gradually depreciating the peso. It devalued the currency about 14% against the dollar and on the following day allowed the peso to float freely. By the end of the year, the peso had fallen an additional 28%, bringing the 11-day loss to 42%. The collapse of the peso caused the stock market to plunge precipitously.

The accumulated trade deficit for the first nine months of 1994 stood at $13,730,000,000. This was already in excess of the $13.5 billion deficit at the end of 1993. With monthly deficits in the final quarter expected to rise to $1.5 billion, the annual deficit appeared likely to increase to well over $17 billion (a deficit of $17.5 billion was officially predicted), contributing to a current account deficit of $28.5 billion. The country's international reserves were eroded significantly during the year. The Banco de Mexico president, Miguel Mancera, announced on October 19 that on October 14 reserves stood at $17,190,000,000, the lowest figure since the end of 1991, when they were $17.5 billion. Reserves at the end of 1993 totaled $24.5 billion. The consequences of devaluation on the government's statistics had not yet been calculated.

Relations with the U.S. and Canada, the country's partners in the North American Free Trade Agreement (NAFTA), continued to strengthen. NAFTA became fully operational on January 1. Resentment, however, was expressed over California's approval of Proposition 187, which would deny educational and other benefits to illegal immigrants, many of whom were Mexican.   (SUSAN M. CUNNINGHAM)

MICRONESIA, FEDERATED STATES OF

A republic in the western Pacific Ocean, the Federated States of Micronesia comprises more than 600 islands and islets in the Caroline Islands archipelago. Area: 701 sq km (271 sq mi). Pop. (1994 est.): 104,000. Cap.: Palikir, on Pohnpei. Monetary unit: U.S. dollar, with (Oct. 7, 1994) a free rate of U.S. $1.59 to £1 sterling. President in 1994, Bailey Olter.

With the summoning of a state and national leadership conference in February 1994, Pres. Bailey Olter initiated a major reexamination of the economic situation and long-term future of the Federated States of Micronesia (FSM). The critical issues facing the country were identified as the lack of infrastructure and the need for joint-venture arrangements for large-scale fishing projects, interisland communication, freight and transport services, and manpower training and development. The nation faced particular difficulty because of its considerable dependence on U.S. aid under the Compact of Free Association and the scaling down and possible cessation of that aid. Under the compact, aid to the FSM was $60 million a year from 1987 to 1991, $50 million a year from 1992 to 1996, and $40 million a year from 1997 to 2001. While additional aid was expected beyond that date, it could not be guaranteed.

Compared with other components of the former Trust Territory of the Pacific Islands, the FSM lacked the U.S. military facilities in the Marshall Islands and the strategic importance of Palau, both of which were expected to earn long-term rental income from the U.S.

U.S. aid accounted for more than two-thirds of gross domestic product, and employment was heavily concentrated in the public sector. Agriculture and fisheries were in decline; there was little tourism; and the FSM had not yet developed a significant industrial capacity.

(BARRIE MACDONALD)

This article updates the *Macropædia* article PACIFIC ISLANDS: *Micronesia*.

MOLDOVA

A landlocked republic of the extreme northeastern Balkans, Moldova borders Ukraine on the north, northeast, and southeast and Romania on the west. Area: 33,700 sq km (13,000 sq mi). Pop. (1994 est.) 4,358,000. Cap.: Chisinau. Monetary unit: Moldovan leu, with (Sept. 27, 1994) a free rate of 4.21 lei = U.S. $1 (6.57 lei = £1 sterling). President in 1994, Mircea Snegur; prime minister, Andrei Sangheli.

Asserting its independence and nationhood was the top priority for Moldova in 1994. High points included the adoption of the constitution in July and the signing of an agreement in October on the eventual withdrawal of the Russian 14th Army from Moldovan territory. Talks with the breakaway "Dniester republic" continued through the year but yielded little progress. A border agreement was signed with Ukraine, but no state treaty with Romania proved possible. Moldova joined NATO's Partnership for Peace and pushed hard for membership in or ties with other European bodies.

The new constitution, which went into effect on August 27, defined Moldova as an independent, democratic, and unitary state; its official language was called Moldovan (*i.e.*, not Romanian) and was written in Latin script, but the use and development of other languages were guaranteed; the country would be neutral, and the stationing of foreign troops on Moldovan soil was banned; and provision was made for the autonomy of Transdniester and the Gagauz area. The constitution was championed by Prime Minister Andrei Sangheli and a legislature led by the nationalist (pro-Moldovan) Agrarian Democratic Party, which had decisively beaten the pro-Romanian Popular Front and Congress for Intellectuals in elections on February 27. The constitution dealt a blow to the Romanian government and the vocal pro-Romanians in Moldova, which viewed Moldova as a province temporarily separated from metropolitan Romania.

Negotiations about the future of Russia's 14th Army under the command of Lieut. Gen. Aleksandr Lebed, which was occupying the heavily Slavic-populated Transdniester area, continued. At first the size and responsibilities of the forces were to be reduced, and it looked as if Lebed would be removed, but Russian Pres. Boris Yeltsin changed tack and supported the continued role of the 14th Army in Transdniester. Nonetheless, the Moldovan-Russian agreement was signed on October 21. It required all Russian troops to depart within three years. Foreign Minister Mihai Popov, however, said that Russian officers would be welcome in Moldova's army.

Parliament ratified the charter of the Commonwealth of Independent States (CIS) in April but excluded Moldova from participation in CIS military pacts or the ruble zone. The sale of 30 MiG-29s was advertised in May, and four were sold to southern Yemen in September.   (EDITOR)

This article updates the *Macropædia* article BALKAN STATES: *Moldova*.

MONACO

A sovereign principality on the northern Mediterranean coast, Monaco is bounded on land by the French département of Alpes-Maritimes. Area: 1.95 sq km (0.75 sq mi). Pop. (1994 est.): 30,300. Monetary unit: French franc, with (Oct. 7, 1994) a free rate of F 5.27 to U.S. $1 (F 8.38 = £1 sterling). Chief of state, Prince Rainier III; minister of state in 1994, Jacques Dupont.

The economy of Monaco, driven by tourism, continued to thrive in 1994 despite the recession experienced by neighbouring countries. As the number of day visitors, particularly from Italy and France, declined, the more lucrative business conference sector burgeoned. Monaco served as host for large business conferences for the insurance and television industries as well as internal meetings and promotional events for many individual companies. Two major conference centres were in operation, and a huge new conference and cultural centre was under construction. The conference industry in 1994 accounted for almost a third of Monaco's foreign visitors.

The local economy expanded as work continued on such projects as the construction of a new jetty beside the present harbour and the creation of Fontvieille II, a complex of inexpensive housing for Monaco citizens. Both Fontvieille areas were built on land reclaimed from the sea. The planned reconstruction of the railroad station underground also promised to open up more land area.

Rumours of money laundering at the casino of Monte-Carlo prompted Prince Rainier to order an internal audit of the casino. Organized crime figures were said to have bought large quantities of chips for cash, played a few, and redeemed the remainder for a casino check. Jean Pastorelli, Monaco's finance councillor, denied the possibility of widespread laundering "because we know our main clients."

(ANNE ROBY)

This article updates the *Micropædia* article MONACO.

MONGOLIA

A landlocked republic between Russia and China in eastern Asia, Mongolia was formerly known as Outer Mongolia. Area: 1,566,500 sq km (604,800 sq mi). Pop. (1994 est.): 2,266,000. Cap.: Ulaanbaatar (Ulan Bator). Monetary unit: tugrik, with (Oct. 7, 1994) a free rate of 400 tugrik to U.S. $1 (636 tugrik = £1 sterling). President in 1994, Punsalmaagiyn Ochirbat; prime minister, Puntsagiyn Jasray.

Political events in 1994 continued to be dominated by the conflict between the Mongolian People's Revolutionary (Communist) Party (MPRP), which held 70 of the 76 seats in the Great Hural (assembly), and the opposition Mongolian National Democratic and Mongolian Social Democratic parties. Encouraged by the broad support for Pres. Punsalmaagiyn Ochirbat, their candidate in the 1993 presidential elections, the democrats launched street demonstrations and hunger strikes in the spring to broaden their protest against MPRP "corruption" and government monopoly of the media. Despite the MPRP's grudging agreement to cooperate on legislative procedure, tensions remained high. Ochirbat vetoed government bills, members of the Great Hural pursued political differences through the Constitutional Court, and one democrat was forced to resign following charges (later withdrawn) of disclosing "a state secret."

Former prime minister Dashiyn Byambasüren founded the Mongolian Democratic Renewal Party and was elected its chairman. He had resigned from the MPRP in 1992, claiming that it remained unreformed. During the autumn session of the Great Hural, the government came under attack from erstwhile MPRP supporters who worried that its lacklustre economic performance and the deepening crisis over poverty and unemployment would doom their hopes of reelection in 1996. With some 26.5% of the population living below the official minimum subsistence level, the government launched a 33.4 billion tugrik relief program to reduce the number of poor to 10% by the year 2000.

Mongolia was poised for positive growth for the first time since its transition to a market economy. Inflation control was on course to meet the International Monetary Fund's targets of 51.5% for 1994 and 12% for 1995. Industrial production, however, remained in the doldrums, threatening the IMF's predicted gross domestic product growth of 2.5% for 1994 and 3% for 1995. Foreign trade was in surplus in the first half of 1994, but turnover was much less than planned. The total foreign aid pledged in 1993 amounted to $238.9 million in grants and $532.7 million in credits.

(ALAN J.K. SANDERS)

MOROCCO

A constitutional monarchy of North Africa, Morocco has coastlines on the Atlantic Ocean and the Mediterranean Sea. Area: 458,730 sq km (177,117 sq mi). Pop. (1994 est.): 26,544,000. (Area and population figures refer to Morocco as constituted prior to the purported division of Western Sahara between Morocco and Mauritania and the subsequent Moroccan occupation of the Mauritanian zone in 1979.) Cap.: Rabat. Monetary unit: dirham, with (Oct. 7, 1994) a free rate of 8.83 dirhams to U.S. $1 (14.04 dirhams = £1 sterling). King, Hassan II; prime ministers in 1994, Muhammad Karim Lamrani and, from May 25, 'Abd al-Latif Filali.

The veteran Moroccan prime minister, Muhammad Karim Lamrani, stepped down on May 25, 1994, and was replaced by 'Abd al-Latif Filali, the foreign minister, who was linked by marriage to the royal family. The Cabinet remained unchanged, however, as Filali retained his Foreign Affairs portfolio. The new government was expected to preside over the building of a new political consensus in Morocco, with the political parties coalescing into two groups, the opposition Democratic Bloc and the pro-government Entente Nationale. In a surprising move in August, King Hassan called for the integration of Morocco's Berber languages and culture into national life.

In March UN Secretary-General Boutros Boutros-Ghali announced new proposals to resolve the Western Sahara crisis. They involved three choices: carrying out a referendum for self-determination there regardless of the attitudes of Morocco and the Polisario Front (the Western Saharan national liberation movement); withdrawing the UN presence in the region; or pursuing negotiations with a view to completing voter registration in order for a referendum to be held by the end of the year. The UN Security Council endorsed the third option, as did the political parties, but the Polisario Front voiced strong reservations. Voter registration did not begin until August because of Morocco's objections to Organization of African Unity participation. Nonetheless, Prime Minister Filali forecast in October that the referendum would finally be held in February or March 1995, but a later date appeared to be more likely.

Morocco took advantage of the expanding peace process in the Middle East to open low-level diplomatic relations with Israel in September. At the same time, it was announced that diplomatic representation was to be established in the Palestinian self-rule area in the Gaza Strip. The country's major industrial conglomerate, Omnium Nord Africain, was also seeking industrial and financial links with Israel.

Morocco's relations with its North African neighbours did not fare so well, however. Tensions with Algeria rose in August after Algerian Pres. Liamine Zeroual criticized the Moroccan presence in the Western Sahara. There was also growing anxiety over increasing influence of the Islamic Salvation Front in eastern Morocco. At the end of August two Spanish tourists were killed in a hotel in Marrakech by members of a combined Algerian-Moroccan Islamist group based in France. In response, Morocco imposed visas on all Algerians visiting the country. Algeria then closed its border with Morocco in protest against the Moroccan decision.

(GEORGE JOFFÉ)

This article updates the *Macropædia* article NORTH AFRICA: *Morocco.*

MOZAMBIQUE

The republic of Mozambique is located in eastern Africa, on the Indian Ocean. Area: 812,379 sq km (313,661 sq mi). Pop. (1994 est.): 17,346,000. Cap.: Maputo. Monetary unit: metical, with (Oct. 7, 1994) a free rate of 6,342 meticais to U.S. $1 (10,087 meticais = £1 sterling). President in 1994, Joaquim Chissano; prime minister, Mario da Graça Machungo.

Early in 1994 the UN called on Mozambique to hold national elections by November. Pres. Joaquim Chissano responded by announcing on April 11 that the country's first multiparty elections would take place on October 27–28. Afonso Dhlakama, the leader of the main opposition group, Renamo (Mozambique National Resistance), responded with a call for a government of national unity after the elections. His plea met with a mixed reaction from other opposition parties, and in July President Chissano made it clear that he had little sympathy for the proposal. Meanwhile, a National Elections Commission was appointed under the chairmanship of Brazão Mazula, and by mid-July 3.2 million voters had registered throughout the region under the government's control. The registration teams then turned their attention to those areas controlled by Renamo. While admitting that irregularities had occurred in the registration process, Mazula insisted that they were few in number and of no great significance.

In the weeks before the election, Dhlakama charged that Chissano and his party, Frelimo (Mozambique Liberation Front), were committing fraud by failing to register voters in Renamo areas. On October 27 Dhlakama announced that he and his party would boycott the election, but on the next day he changed his mind, voted, and urged his followers to do so. In the presidential vote he lost to Chissano 53.3–33.7%, while in the contests for the legislature Frelimo won 44.3% and Renamo 37.7%; the balance was won by smaller parties. After reviewing the election numbers, Dhlakama declared that Renamo would accept the results and strive to cooperate with the Chissano government.

The election was a considerable achievement in view of the continuing dispute over the confinement of government and Renamo troops in concentration centres in preparation for their demobilization. At the beginning of the year, the government was most strongly criticized by the UN, but in May the UN secretary-general's special representative in Mozambique, Aldo Ajello, said that no progress was being made by either party in either confining or demobilizing their forces. Nevertheless, on April 16 a number of agreements were signed by senior military officers of both the government and Renamo creating a command structure for the new Mozambique Defense Armed Forces (FADM).

Pres. Joaquim Chissano, head of the Mozambique Liberation Front (Frelimo), waves to supporters as he campaigns in his country's first multiparty elections. The president defeated Afonso Dhlakama, head of the Mozambique National Resistance (Renamo).
MANUEL MOURA—AGENCIA LUSA

By mid-August the government was claiming that its own forces had been dissolved and their command handed over to the FADM. Renamo said that its own troops had also been demobilized, but this was denied by a government spokesman, and in September a number of former Renamo guerrillas maintained that some of those said to have been demobilized by Renamo were, in fact, civilians who had never been soldiers.

Those working for peace and stability in the country could take encouragement from a variety of offers of external assistance. Early in January the U.K. agreed to reschedule £12.5 million of Mozambique's debt and to reduce drastically the interest on the remaining debt. Again, in March, Britain offered an additional £3 million to assist in the repatriation of Mozambican refugees from Malawi and other neighbouring countries. Later in the year the World Food Programme appealed for £7 million to feed those threatened with starvation in the aftermath of the civil war.

(KENNETH INGHAM)

This article updates the *Macropædia* article SOUTHERN AFRICA: *Mozambique.*

MYANMAR (BURMA)

Myanmar is a republic of Southeast Asia with coastlines on the Bay of Bengal and the Andaman Sea. Area: 676,577 sq km (261,228 sq mi). Pop. (1994 est.): 45,573,000. Cap.: Yangon (Rangoon). Monetary unit: kyat, with (Oct. 7, 1994) a free rate of 5.82 kyats to U.S. $1 (9.26 kyats = £1 sterling). Chairman of the State Law and Order Restoration Council in 1994, Gen. Than Shwe.

Myanmar's ruling junta met with opposition leader Aung San Suu Kyi on Sept. 20, 1994; it was their first face-to-face meeting since the Nobel Peace Prize laureate was put under house arrest in July 1989. After Suu Kyi's National League for Democracy won a landslide victory in the 1990 general election, the junta refused to allow the winners to take their seats in the National Assembly. Although the junta and Suu Kyi were reportedly eager for a reconciliation, there was no report of a rapprochement.

UN official Jehan Raheem (left) and U.S. Rep. Bill Richardson meet with Aung San Suu Kyi, under house arrest by Myanmar's military junta. The two men were the first outsiders to be allowed to visit the pro-democracy leader and Nobel laureate in more than four years.
KRAIPIT PHANVUT—THE NEW YORK TIMES

The draft of a new constitution adopted at a 700-member convention called for an executive president assisted by two vice presidents, all to be elected by an electoral college drawn from the parliament. The president's parents, children, and spouse could not be citizens of any foreign country or entitled to rights and privileges of another nation. The president also had to have resided in Myanmar for at least 20 consecutive years prior to the election. These provisions would disqualify Suu Kyi, who was married to a Briton and had spent most of her life abroad.

Amnesty International reported continued arrests of dissidents and severe restrictions on freedom of expression and assembly in 1994. Dissident writers and journalists were also subjected to long prison terms. Although about 2,000 prisoners had been released since a limited amnesty was announced in 1992, hundreds of political prisoners were still being held.

In July the 1,400-strong Kayan New Land Party formally halted its insurgency, the 12th rebel group to do so. Only two major rebel groups, from the Mon and Karen minorities, continued to fight. In August Myanmar and Cambodia restored diplomatic relations, which had been severed in 1975 when the communist Khmer Rouge took over Cambodia. (DILIP GANGULY)

This article updates the *Macropædia* article SOUTHEAST ASIA: *Myanmar*.

NAMIBIA

A republic and member of the Commonwealth, Namibia is in southern Africa, on the Atlantic Ocean. Area: 825,118 sq km (318,580 sq mi). Pop. (1994 est.): 1,596,000. Cap.: Windhoek. Monetary unit: Namibian dollar, at par with the commercial rate of the South African rand (also legal currency), with (Oct. 7, 1994) a rate of Nam$3.57 to U.S. $1 (Nam$5.68 = £1 sterling). President in 1994, Sam Nujoma; prime minister, Hage Geingob.

In December 1994 Namibia held its first national elections since becoming independent in 1990. As expected, Sam Nujoma was reelected president, defeating his only challenger, Mishake Muyongo of the Democratic Turnhalle Alliance, by a margin of 3–1. His popularity stemmed from his leadership of the South West Africa People's Organization (SWAPO) during the 23-year-old struggle to free the territory from South African domination. SWAPO also swept to victory in the parliamentary elections, winning more than 70% of the popular vote. Its huge majority meant it would have the decisive voice in rewriting the constitution.

Walvis Bay was handed over by South Africa to Namibia at midnight on February 28, and plans were set in motion to turn the area (1,124 sq km [434 sq mi]) into a free-trade zone. In June an inquest was completed and an announcement made that SWAPO advocate Anton Lubowski had been assassinated in 1989 by an Irish mercenary, Donald Acheson, at the behest of the South African Defense Force's Civil Cooperation Bureau. Four of Namibia's top white police officers, implicated in the assassination, were suspended from duty.

South African Pres. Nelson Mandela paid a visit to Namibia in August and announced the possible cancellation of all or part of the country's debt of Nam$1,330,000,000 to South Africa. In September Namibia introduced a Land Reform Bill forbidding foreign nationals to own rural freehold land without special permission and also giving the government powers of compulsory purchase and expropriation over such land. In discussion of the bill it was alleged that 75% of the land suitable for farming was controlled by less than 1% of the population. Allegations of corruption by government ministers were made.

Crop production improved dramatically, leading to a reduction of food aid. The growth in gross domestic product in 1993 was about 2%. The budget for 1994–95 anticipated spending of Nam$3,010,000,000, 23.8% on education and 17.1% on health. Inflation averaged 8.5% in 1993, down from 17.7% in 1992. (MARTIN LEGASSICK)

This article updates the *Macropædia* article SOUTHERN AFRICA: *Namibia*.

NAURU

An island republic within the Commonwealth, Nauru lies in the Pacific Ocean about 1,900 km (1,200 mi) east of New Guinea. Area: 21 sq km (8 sq mi). Pop. (1994 est.): 10,200. Cap.: Government offices in Yaren district. Monetary unit: Australian dollar, with (Oct. 7, 1994) a free rate of $A 1.35 to U.S. $1 ($A 2.15 = £1 sterling). President in 1994, Bernard Dowiyogo.

Nauru benefited in 1994 from the decision by the United Kingdom and New Zealand to help Australia pay $A 107 million as compensation for damage to the island caused by phosphate mining. For its part, Australia agreed to provide

$A 2.5 million annually to Nauru for 20 years. Recognizing that they shared with Australia the responsibility for the colonial exploitation of Nauru by the British Phosphate Commission, New Zealand and the U.K. agreed to contribute $A 12 million each to help repair the damage. This prevented further action by Nauru, which had been seeking compensation in the international courts.

A founding member of the Nauruan independence struggle, Buraro Detudamo, died in June. Detudamo was a member of the Nauruan delegation to Australia that led to the establishment of the republic.

On a lighter note, the smallest republic on Earth was proud to join the Olympic family, Nauru having succeeded in its bid to be recognized as a member country of the International Olympic Committee. The nation's most notable athlete was Marcus Stephen, who won a gold medal for weight lifting at the 1990 Commonwealth Games.

(A.R.G. GRIFFITHS)

This article updates the *Macropædia* article PACIFIC ISLANDS: *Nauru*.

NEPAL

A constitutional monarchy, Nepal is a landlocked country in the Himalayas between India and the Tibetan Autonomous Region of China. Area: 147,181 sq km (56,827 sq mi). Pop. (1994 est.): 19,525,000. Cap.: Kathmandu. Monetary unit: Nepalese rupee, with (Oct. 7, 1994) a free rate of NRs 49.40 to U.S. $1 (NRs 78.57 = £1 sterling). King, Birendra Bir Bikram Shah Dev; prime ministers in 1994, Girija Prasad Koirala and, from November 30, Man Mohan Adhikari.

As Nepal continued to adapt to the democratic form of government it adopted in 1990, the Himalayan nation showed an ability in 1994 to function relatively smoothly under a democratic administration.

Prime Minister Girija Prasad Koirala, Nepal's first democratically elected leader in three decades, resigned July 10 after losing a policy vote in Parliament. The dispute was rooted in factional fighting within Koirala's Nepali Congress Party (NCP). It also reflected frustration over his failure to make headway in overcoming Nepal's poverty and illiteracy and over his ineffective effort to stimulate development.

Koirala was forced to step down when Parliament rejected his annual policy statement. The motion lost 86–74 even though Koirala's NCP occupied 114 of the 205 seats in the legislature. The motion failed because 36 members of the NCP abstained during the voting. When new elections were held on November 15, the United Communist Party of Nepal won a plurality of 88 of the contested seats in the House of Representatives, and Koirala's NCP won only 83—a net loss of 27. On November 30 Man Mohan Adhikari was sworn in as prime minister.

Although Koirala took some measures to modernize and liberalize the economy, Nepal remained one of the world's poorest countries. It had an annual per capita income of $180 and an infant mortality rate of nearly 10%. Nearly three-quarters of the population could not read or write.

The communists in Nepal, who got ideological support from neighbouring China, led an anti-Koirala campaign that led to the deaths of 12 protesters when police fired at demonstrators in Kathmandu.

Nepal's relations with both China and India remained cordial. China agreed in August to let more foreign tourists travel to Tibet via Nepal to promote tourism in both countries. Every year 350,000 foreign tourists visited Nepal to view its stunning mountain scenery. China also gave Nepal a $10 million loan to hasten economic development.

(DILIP GANGULY)

NETHERLANDS, THE

A constitutional monarchy of northwestern Europe, The Netherlands, a Benelux country, is on the North Sea. Area: 41,526 sq km (16,033 sq mi). Pop. (1994 est.): 15,401,000. Cap., Amsterdam; seat of government, The Hague. Monetary unit: Netherlands guilder, with (Oct. 7, 1994) a free rate of 1.73 guilders to U.S. $1 (2.74 guilders = £1 sterling). Queen, Beatrix; prime ministers in 1994, Ruud Lubbers and, from August 22, Wim Kok.

The local elections held on March 2, 1994, resulted in severe losses for both parties of the government coalition—the Christian Democratic Appeal (CDA) and the Labour Party. The biggest winners were the centre-left Democrats 66 and the centre-right People's Party for Freedom and Democracy (VVD). The general parliamentary elections of May 3 confirmed the trend of the earlier voting, but with the losses being even more dramatic for the CDA. Labour was now the largest single party in Parliament, and small gains were made by xenophobic far-right parties and by parties representing the elderly. (For tabulated results, see *Political Parties*, above.) Never in Dutch history had a government coalition lost so much of its support, and analysts described the result as a historical turning point that marked the end of the Christian Democratic era. The main causes of the decline of the CDA were the difficult task the new party leader, Elco Brinkman, had in trying to succeed the popular Ruud Lubbers, who had held the post for 12 years before resigning to run for the presidency of the European Commission, and the clumsy maneuvering of the CDA leadership on social policy affecting elderly voters.

On August 22 Queen Beatrix appointed a new Cabinet. The new government was headed by Prime Minister Willem ("Wim") Kok, leader of the Labour Party, minister of finance in the previous Cabinet, and, earlier, the leader of the country's largest labour union. The Cabinet, composed of Labour and members from the VVD and Democrats 66, was called a "purple" cabinet, so named for the mix of the red and blue colours of the parties represented. It was the first time since 1918 that a Cabinet had been formed without any minister from a Christian Democratic party. Among the serious problems of the new government were high rates of unemployment and the soaring costs of social benefits. The Cabinet also intended to work to stimulate technological innovation in research and industry, to strengthen the quality and flexibility of primary and secondary education, and to continue the restructuring of the national army into a small and effective professional organization.

Meanwhile, on August 16 Brinkman had resigned as leader of the CDA. He was held responsible for the fact that the CDA did not take part in the negotiations for the forming of the new Cabinet. Two days later Enneus Heerma succeeded him as chairman of the parliamentary faction of the CDA. Heerma, a former secretary of state, had successfully initiated a privatization project in public housing.

Earlier, on May 27, the minister of justice, Ernst Hirsch Ballin, and the minister of internal affairs, Ed van Thijn, had been forced to resign their positions in the interim Cabinet. The scandal was caused by the way they had handled the liquidation of an interregional investigating team, made up of cooperating police forces, against organized crime. A parliamentary report concerning the affair concluded that their action was unnecessary and had ended a very effective operation. It also concluded that the liquidation was a struggle between political factions to discredit one another. Especially for van Thijn, the incident was a dramatic event in

An official checks the documents of a Nigerian passenger arriving at Amsterdam's Schiphol Airport. Traditionally known for its leniency toward immigrants, The Netherlands tightened restrictions in 1994, partly because it was flooded by refugees turned away by other European countries.
AD VAN DENDEREN

his political career. Formerly the highly successful mayor of Amsterdam, he had been appointed to the Cabinet post only in January on the unexpected death of Ien Dales, a popular personality and prominent representative of Labour. It was for van Thijn a return to national politics, for during the period 1973–78 he had been chairman of the parliamentary faction of Labour and he had served as minister of internal affairs once before, in 1981–82. Now, however, he stood in the impossible position of having to judge, in his position as minister, his own role in the affair as mayor of Amsterdam.

(KLAAS J. HOEKSEMA)

See also *Dependent States*.

NEW ZEALAND

New Zealand, a constitutional monarchy and member of the Commonwealth in the South Pacific Ocean, consists of North and South islands and Stewart, Chatham, and other minor islands. Area: 270,534 sq km (104,454 sq mi). Pop. (1994 est.): 3,525,000. Cap.: Wellington. Monetary unit: New Zealand dollar, with (Oct. 7, 1994) a free rate of $NZ 1.65 to U.S. $1 ($NZ 2.63 = £1 sterling). Queen, Elizabeth II; governor-general in 1994, Dame Catherine Tizard; prime minister, Jim Bolger.

Faced with the barest of parliamentary margins (50–49) after the November 1993 elections, New Zealand's conservative National Party (NP) government had no reason to welcome a by-election. It had one, however, in August 1994, following the resignation from Parliament of the deposed finance minister, Ruth Richardson. Richardson had been effective but not popular, and she was seen as a factor in the party's near defeat in 1993 and its vote-share erosion from 47.8% to 35.1%.

The major opposition Labour Party (with 45 seats) expressed its disappointment in the election by sacking leader Mike Moore and replacing him with former health minister Helen Clark in December 1993. To the dismay of traditionalist supporters, the new leader sanctioned agreement to the

nomination of Labour's Peter Tapsell as speaker, giving the NP a two-vote working majority. With this narrow control of the House, Prime Minister Jim Bolger negotiated legislative shoals, while members on all sides looked to possible new alliances in the looming era of mixed member proportional (MMP) representation—already approved by referendum in 1993. Finance Minister Bill Birch budgeted, at the end of June, for the first surplus ($NZ 527 million) since 1978. NP candidate David Carter took the August 13 by-election with 42.3% of the vote, to maintain a fluid status quo. Less than a month later, Ross Meurant, a junior Cabinet minister, quit the NP to form his own party, but he agreed to support the government until the next general election.

Through this trapeze politicking the most visible parliamentarian was Alliance leader Jim Anderton, whose New Labour Party had joined with the Democrat Party, the Greens, Mana Motuhake (a Maori grouping), and the Liberal Party to form the Alliance. Anderton topped personal polls; bolstered the government's confidence with assurances of support on supply; ensured that the Alliance candidate set the pace in the by-election, even displacing Labour as runner-up; and worked on a transactions-tax proposal based on 12 cents in every $NZ 100 withdrawn from a bank. On November 10 Anderton, 56, citing mainly personal reasons, resigned the Alliance leadership and announced that he would not stand for Parliament in the next term. Mana Motuhake's Sandra Lee, the first Maori woman elected to Parliament, was confirmed as Alliance leader.

Conclusion of the Uruguay round of the General Agreement on Tariffs and Trade (GATT) in Geneva was seen as offering huge opportunities for New Zealand exporters if they could reverse falling sheep numbers to keep meat available. Six months after the GATT negotiators' agreement, and in the ratification stage, a committee of farming, employee, and marketing representatives predicted that farm and forestry earnings would nearly double to $NZ 25.5 billion by the end of the century.

In December Bolger announced the government and the Tainui, a North Island Maori tribal federation, had reached agreement on compensation to settle claims arising from the confiscation of Maori lands and resources by British settlers in the mid-19th century. The land would not be returned because it was now in private hands or had been turned into national parks, but the Tainui would receive about $NZ 181 million. Other Maori claims awaited settlement.

In October the government recorded its first surplus in 17 years as strong economic growth supported a 7.3% increase in taxation revenue. Overheating became the complaint as gross domestic product rose 6.1% in the year to June, the dollar firmed, inflation moved to 1.8% for the year, and interest-rate rises caused home mortgages to inch up. Continued privatization of state services struggled for public support in making hospitals self-sufficient.

In the quarter to June 1994, registered unemployment fell from around 9% to a nearly four-year low of 8.4%. In six of nine industry groups surveyed, employment rose in the year, with manufacturing leading by 10%. For 15–19-year-olds unemployment was 20.4%; for 20–24-year-olds, 13%. Maori unemployment, always of concern, was measured at 19.8%; employment of Pacific Islanders resident in New Zealand was at 23.4%. (JOHN A. KELLEHER)

See also *Dependent States*.

NICARAGUA

A republic of Central America, Nicaragua has coastlines on the Caribbean Sea and the Pacific Ocean. Area: 131,670 sq km (50,838 sq mi). Pop. (1994 est.): 4,210,000. Cap.: Managua. Monetary unit: córdoba oro, with (Oct. 7, 1994) an official rate of 6.74 córdobas oro to U.S. $1 (10.71 córdobas oro = £1 sterling). President in 1994, Violeta Barrios de Chamorro.

The National Opposition Union (UNO) decided in January 1994 to end its 12-month boycott of the National Assembly after it was unable to mobilize support for a constituent assembly. Only 6 of the 14 parties that had formed UNO for the 1990 elections remained in the coalition. The others had joined with the Sandinista National Liberation Front to ensure passage of new laws.

In February a truce was negotiated with the rebels in the north known as the Northern Front 3-80. A disarmament accord that included their incorporation into the national police was signed. Violence continued in the countryside, where roving gangs of criminals competed with small groups of guerrillas, and the army launched a new offensive against all armed groups in the north in June.

Gen. Humberto Ortega confirmed in April that he would retire following approval of a new military code, and in August the National Assembly approved the Military Code of Organization, Jurisdiction, and Pension. The code aimed to depoliticize the Sandinista Popular Army and increase its accountability to civilian authority, but critics pointed to the lack of provision for a civilian defense minister and the appointment of the armed forces chief by a military council as evidence that the military was retaining its power.

The government signed a three-year agreement with the International Monetary Fund in April, releasing funds from other multilateral sources and paving the way for the renegotiation of official debt. Total external debt was estimated at $10 billion, which the country was unable to service. Unemployment was estimated at 43–60%, and per capita gross domestic product fell for the 11th consecutive year. A severe drought damaged the corn and bean crops, and food became scarce. (SARAH CAMERON)

This article updates the *Macropædia* article CENTRAL AMERICA: *Nicaragua*.

NIGER

Niger is a landlocked republic of West Africa. Area: 1,287,000 sq km (497,000 sq mi). Pop. (1994 est.): 8,813,000. Cap.: Niamey. Monetary unit: CFA franc, with (Oct. 7, 1994) a par value of CFAF 100 to the French franc and a free rate of CFAF 526.67 to U.S. $1 (CFAF 837.67 = £1 sterling). President in 1994, Mahamane Ousmane; prime ministers, Mahamadou Issoufou and, from September 28, Souley Abdoulaye.

Efforts to resolve the Tuareg rebellion in northern Niger dominated the year. In May 40 people died in clashes between rebels and government troops. The two sides finally met in June in Paris, where an agreement was reached to give the main Tuareg coalition, the Coordination of Armed Resistance (CRA), limited regional autonomy over an area to be reserved for an estimated 750,000 Tuaregs. Although another armed confrontation occurred on September 28, the government and the CRA signed the peace accord in Ouagadougou, Burkina Faso, on October 9.

Student unrest over unpaid grants and other issues erupted into violent demonstrations in March. The government arrested 91 members of the former ruling party, now in opposition as the National Movement for the Developing Society, on charges of inciting student violence. Another 25 were detained following further student protests on April 16, and 3 of them were sentenced on May 19 to two–three-year prison terms.

Pres. Mahamane Ousmane lost his parliamentary majority when the Nigerien Party for Democracy and Socialism (PNDS) withdrew from the nine-party ruling coalition. On September 28 Prime Minister Mahamadou Issoufou of the PNDS resigned and was replaced by Souley Abdoulaye. The new government resigned on October 16 after a vote of no confidence. Abdoulaye was almost immediately renamed prime minister, but because he reinstated his old government, which did not command a majority in the National Assembly, Ousmane was obliged to call new elections. The December 31 election was later postponed to Jan. 14, 1995. (NANCY ELLEN LAWLER)

This article updates the *Macropædia* article WESTERN AFRICA: *Niger*.

NIGERIA

A republic and member of the Commonwealth, Nigeria is located in West Africa, on the Gulf of Guinea. Area: 923,768 sq km (356,669 sq mi). Pop. (1994 est.): 93,471,000. Cap.: Abuja. Monetary unit: naira, with (Oct. 7, 1994) a free rate of 22.00 naira to U.S. $1 (34.99 naira = £1 sterling). Chairman of the Federal Executive Council in 1994, Gen. Sani Abacha.

On Jan. 10, 1994, Gen. Sani Abacha presented a budget in which he announced the abandonment of market reforms instituted in 1986. Interest rates were cut and foreign exchange controls imposed, while the exchange rate was fixed at 22 naira to the U.S. dollar. The measures ruled out a new agreement with the International Monetary Fund, whose previous agreement ended in 1992. Since then Nigeria had failed to service its international debts, adding $5 billion arrears of payments to $31 billion of previous debts. External debt servicing in 1994 (assuming debts were serviced) would cost $6 billion, equivalent to 97% of foreign exchange earnings. Industrial output stood at only 35% of capacity.

Resentment against the military government grew steadily during the early months of 1994. On April 22, following the establishment on April 16 of nonelected local government caretaker committees to replace the local administrations previously headed by state governors, the government announced details of its political transition program. May 28 was scheduled for the election of delegates to the constitutional conference to be held between June 27 and October 27. Then, on November 28, the draft constitution would be submitted to the Federal Executive Council. The second phase of transition was scheduled for January 1995, when the ban on political activity would be lifted.

On May 23 elections of delegates to the constitutional conference took place, but they were widely boycotted by the pro-democracy groups in action called for by the National Democratic Coalition. Abstentions were most frequent in the southwest and in Lagos. The boycott was part of a growing campaign to force the military to hand back power to Moshood ("MKO") Abiola, the presumed winner of the 1993 elections that the military had annulled. On May 31 the police issued a general statement to affirm that nongovernmental political activity was illegal, warning that the boycott was viewed by them as "designed to undermine the security of the government."

On June 11, before a crowd of about 3,000, Abiola declared himself president, army chief, and head of government. He then went into hiding, touching off a nationwide hunt for him by the military; he was arrested on June 23, by which time he was calling for a national uprising to force the military to relinquish power and recognize the 1993 election results. On June 24 more than 1,000 demonstrators in Lagos were teargassed by the police when they marched to demand Abiola's release. On June 27, opening the constitutional conference, General Abacha pledged to restore democracy, though he gave no date for a transfer of power.

By the beginning of July, the pro-democracy groups, supported by Nobel Prizewinning writer Wole Soyinka, had launched a war of attrition against the government. Abiola was charged with treason, and the High Court in Abuja refused him bail. The nation's oil workers then declared a 10-day strike in support of demands for Abiola's release. By

mid-July the oil strike was crippling the country's leading industry, which was responsible for 98% of Nigeria's export earnings. The currency meanwhile had slumped to the rate of 53 naira to the U.S. dollar. Riots flared in Lagos, and 20 people were killed as the oil strike entered its third week and other economic activity came to a halt. At this time the overwhelming support for Abiola remained in the western part of the nation, which was dominated by Abiola's fellow Yorubas. In Lagos, Soyinka led a protest march that was halted by the police, causing the writer to throw away his medal for "national merit," one of Nigeria's highest awards.

At the end of July, opponents of the government called for a general strike. On August 15 the military closed down the *Guardian,* Nigeria's leading newspaper, for suggesting that the military was divided on the issue of a return to civilian rule. Then the judge in the Abiola trial, Mohammed Mustapha, withdrew from the case. In a move to end the strike, the military fired the leaders of the two oil unions, the National Union of Petroleum and Natural Gas Workers (Nupeng) and Pengassan, as well as the National Labour Congress and replaced them with military appointments. By mid-August, with the oil strike in its sixth week, unrest was spreading to the northern and eastern parts of the country, where support for Abiola was increasing. Abacha sacked a number of high-ranking military deemed not to be loyal and followed this by firing the heads of all state companies and their boards.

A possible break in the opposition to the military came early in September when the sacked leaders of the oil unions decided to suspend the strike "in the interests of the suffering masses of Nigeria, the economy and the oil industry." On September 6 Abacha decreed that his regime had absolute power, denying the nation's courts any jurisdiction over his government. (GUY ARNOLD)

This article updates the *Macropædia* article WESTERN AFRICA: *Nigeria.*

Automobiles are lined up as drivers wait to buy gasoline during the strike by Nigeria's oil workers in support of the jailed "MKO" Abiola. The front-runner in the 1993 elections when they were suspended, Abiola continued his defiance of the country's military regime.

SPOTLIGHT: Africa's Second Liberation by Colin Legum

The first three decades of postcolonialism in Africa were characterized by the rise of single-party states and military regimes, but only four were dictatorships on the European or Soviet model—viz., Idi Amin in Uganda, Jean-Bédel Bokassa in the Central African Republic, Francisco Macías Nguema in Equatorial Guinea, and Mobutu Sese Seko in Zaire—and they were short-lived. The first generation of independence leaders, made up almost entirely of small modernizing elites, were principally engaged in consolidating their power, unifying their still nascent nation-states, striving for rapid economic growth, and experimenting in new forms of "African democracy" felt to be relevant to their cultures and resources. These varied from consensus politics (as in Tanzania) to socialism in "African dress" (e.g., Sékou Touré in Guinea).

The general outcome of these attempts was a highly centralized form of government and the creation of a network of state corporations that was used as a means of localizing the economy and for centralized planning. The absence of accountability on the periphery resulted in a form of state capitalism rather than socialism. The high priority given to rapid economic growth favoured urban society and often resulted in the neglect of the rural economy. Two of the prices paid for this lopsided development were a decline in food production and a growing concentration on export crops mercilessly dependent on fluctuating world market prices. Almost everywhere these policies failed to produce economic growth and, with a few notable exceptions, proved unsuccessful in the peaceful integration of the major tribal communities into the evolving nation-state.

Disillusionment with the policies of the first generation of independence leaders had spread throughout the continent by the mid-1980s. The demand for representative democracy spread from country to country like a bushfire. Flames were further fueled by the collapse of the Soviet Union. By the end of the 1980s, Africa had entered a new phase of its postcolonial experience, which came to be described as the Second Liberation Movement. The first was an anticolonial struggle against *alien* rule; the second was a struggle against *indigenous* undemocratic rule. The new battle cry was for multiparty democracy and respect for human rights.

The strength and passions of this pro-democratic upsurge, combined with the blatant failure of most of the postindependence governments, compelled the single-party and military regimes to concede, at least in principle, the need for radical political reform. The pressures of the democratic forces also produced a change in Western policies to favour these forces. Freed by the Soviet collapse from their Cold War concerns—which had led them to support any regime perceived as pro-Western, no matter how oppressive—Western governments now established criteria of "good governance" as a condition for economic aid. Regimes such as those in Zaire, Malawi, and Kenya were compelled to abandon their insistence on single-party rule.

By the beginning of the 1990s, sub-Saharan Africa had been plunged into turmoil as the established regimes engaged in rear-guard actions to prevent their total loss of power in the negotiations for democratic constitutions. Prolonged negotiations increased the frustrations and the militancy of the democratic forces, which resulted in the widespread breakdown of law and order. The spirit of the new age was highlighted by Pres. F.W. de Klerk's historic speech in February 1990 announcing the abandonment of apartheid in South Africa.

The immediate outcome of this first round in the struggle for a form of parliamentary democracy was mixed. Elections allowing for multiparty participation were held in some 31 of the 37 sub-Saharan states, but only 12 of the old regimes were defeated (Zambia, Cape Verde, São Tomé and Príncipe, Benin, Congo, Mali, Central African Republic, Burundi, Lesotho, Malawi, Madagascar, and, notably, South Africa). The conduct of elections in seven other countries (Mauritania, Djibouti, Cameroon, Togo, Equatorial Guinea, Gabon, and Kenya) was more or less flawed. The victory of four of the former ruling parties can be held to have been reasonably fair in four countries (Seychelles, Côte d'Ivoire, Ghana, and Guinea-Bissau). In addition, four of the practicing plural democratic countries (Mauritius, Botswana, Senegal, and The Gambia) saw the return of their governments. However, the results in The Gambia were nullified by a subsequent military coup—the first in the 1990s, a new record since the early 1970s. The election result in Nigeria was also vitiated when the military regime intervened to prevent the clear winner, MKO Abiola, from consummating his victory.

Apart from these two governments, military regimes are currently confined to Sierra Leone and The Sudan. Elections are pending in Tanzania, Namibia, Ethiopia, Zaire, and possibly also Angola. Only in one country, Uganda, does the regime still cling obstinately to the idea of a nonparty state.

There is strong encouragement to the hopes that democracy can strike its roots in African soil. The continuing success of the well-established pluralist political societies of Botswana, Mauritius, Senegal, and, until the recent setback, The Gambia and the electoral success in overturning 12 of the former governments are two examples. A third is the outstanding triumph of Eritrea, where a genuinely self-reliant, democratic government was established after 30 years of war. Other cases are those of South Africa and Burundi, where centuries-old ruling minorities agreed to surrender power in favour of majority rule.

The final success of the Second Liberation Movement depends more than anything else on the capacity of African countries to achieve economic recovery. The experience of the first round of multiparty elections shows that democracy is not yet fully understood; concentration on multipartyism as the criterion for a democratic constitution is misplaced since it is only one of a score of conditions required for the establishment of a democratic society. Without guarantees of other human and civil rights, concentration on multipartyism could lead to a dead end and the discrediting of the democratic process. The requirement of such a full range of principles involved in establishing a democratic constitution has so far been achieved only in the new South Africa.

The achievement of the conditions needed to establish a fully democratic society, as shown by the experience of Western and other democracies, takes not years but generations of struggle and political evolution. While it took several centuries for the Western democracies to reach their present state, modern conditions suggest that it need not take so long in Africa. Even so, it would be overoptimistic to suppose that fully fledged democratic states can be built in less developed countries within the lifetime of a single generation. Meanwhile, the proper test by which to judge whether African countries are moving toward democracy is to measure the incremental changes in the direction of what former president Julius Nyerere of Tanzania once described as acquiring "the habit of democracy."

Colin Legum is the editor of *Third World Reports* and consulting editor of the *Africa Contemporary Record*.

NORWAY

A constitutional monarchy of northern Europe, Norway occupies the western part of the Scandinavian Peninsula, with coastlines on the Skagerrak, the North Sea, the Norwegian Sea, and the Arctic Ocean. Area: 323,878 sq km (125,050 sq mi), excluding the Svalbard Archipelago and Jan Mayen Island. Pop. (1994 est.): 4,332,000. Cap.: Oslo. Monetary unit: Norwegian krone, with (Oct. 7, 1994) a free rate of 6.70 kroner to U.S. $1 (10.65 kroner = £1 sterling). King, Harald V; prime minister in 1994, Gro Harlem Brundtland.

Norwegians rejected membership in the European Union (EU) in an advisory referendum on Nov. 28, 1994. It was the second time in 22 years that Norway had voted against membership. The final outcome of the vote was 52.4% against and 47.6% in favour of joining. The percentage of Norwegians who opposed EU membership was the same as that of those in Sweden who had favoured it in a referendum about two weeks earlier. Nevertheless, one week after the referendum, Norway voted to support the General Agreement on Tariffs and Trade and the establishment of its successor, the World Trade Organization.

The referendum was an embarrassing defeat for Prime Minister Gro Harlem Brundtland, who had made winning over the country's skeptical electorate her central political goal of the 1990s. On the other hand, it was a major victory for Anne Enger Lahnstein, leader of the main opposition Centre Party, who announced that she would challenge Brundtland for the prime minister's office in the 1997 election.

The referendum was lost because of the failure by those favouring membership to win over the voters in the north and other outlying districts, who derived their livelihood from fishing and farming; these enterprises were supported by lavish subsidies that were among the highest in Europe. In many regions an even bigger majority than in 1972 voted "no." The EU advocates also failed to win support from women, who feared membership would undermine Norway's cradle-to-grave welfare system. In addition, many Norwegians feared the loss of sovereignty over the country's rich natural resources—fish, oil, gas, and light metals.

The Labour Party government said that because of the outcome of the referendum, the economy, among the strongest in Europe, faced new and demanding challenges, and it pledged to continue its stable course in economic policy to strengthen international confidence. The government said that it would unveil a package of measures worth between 10 billion kroner and 15 billion kroner to shore up business and industry against potential damaging effects of the vote against the EU and that it would continue to reduce the fiscal budget deficit.

In November Norway's average daily oil production reached a record-high 2.7 million bbl. Norway was Western Europe's biggest oil producer, but output was expected to decline sharply after 1996.

In 1994 the economy was strong, with an expected growth of 4.5%. The increase was forecast to weaken to 3% in 1995, and in the longer term a weak industrial base for employment was expected to lead to further problems. Unemployment fell to about 5% from 8% in 1993 and was expected to decline further in 1995 if Norwegian companies did not follow through on threats to relocate to EU countries. Norway's banks emerged from a persistent six-year banking crisis, the sector's worse since World War II. The business community suffered a jolt on December 13 when Erik Jarve, the well-respected president of the Oslo Stock Exchange, was found dead one day after he was dismissed for accepting bribes.

Norwegians continued to bask in the praise of the successful Olympic Winter Games held in February in Lillehammer, north of Oslo. Not only was the arrangement of this major winter event a huge success, but the Norwegians also walked off with a pocketful of medals: 10 gold, 11 silver, and 5 bronze. (KAREN L. FOSSLI)

See also *Dependent States.*

OMAN

The sultanate of Oman occupies the southeastern part of the Arabian Peninsula, facing the Persian Gulf, the Gulf of Oman, and the Arabian Sea. A small part of the country lies to the north and is separated from the rest of Oman by the United Arab Emirates. Area: 306,000 sq km (118,150 sq mi). Pop. (1994 est.): 2,048,000. Cap.: Muscat. Monetary unit: rial Omani, with (Oct. 7, 1994) a par value of 0.38 rial to U.S. $1 (free rate of 0.60 rial = £1 sterling). Sultan and prime minister in 1994, Qabus ibn Sa'id.

Sultan Qabus ibn Sa'id faced the first significant political upheaval of his reign since the end of the Dhofar war in 1975 when up to 500 dissidents, including high-ranking Omani civil servants and a prominent businessman, were arrested in the summer. Government sources initially failed to confirm the arrests in Muscat, the Dhofar area, al-Buraymi, and other towns, but in some cases heavily armed police and army units publicly seized dissidents from their offices.

A government statement in November referred to those arrested as "treacherous people intent on overthrowing the government while using Islam as a cover." Officials refused to confirm the number of people picked up but denied that there were as many as 500. On November 12 a separate statement announced that the sultan had commuted death sentences passed on "several people convicted by the state security court of conspiracy to foment sedition."

On July 6 the head of the self-proclaimed Democratic Republic of Yemen, Ali Salim al-Baidh, fled into exile in Oman with 9,000 armed followers and other refugees. During the Yemeni civil war, from May 5 to July 7, Oman urged other Persian Gulf states to recognize the breakaway southern republic. In subsequent negotiations with the victorious Yemen government, Baidh was permitted to stay in Oman provided he "retired" from politics.

Sultan Qabus announced in January that the Majlis ash-Shoura (consultative assembly) would be increased from 59 to 85 members in 1995. For the first time, women were allowed to run for office, and four were elected in the first round of voting in November. (JOHN WHELAN)

This article updates the *Macropædia* article ARABIA: *Oman.*

PAKISTAN

A federal republic and a member of the Commonwealth, Pakistan is in the northwestern part of the Indian subcontinent, on the Arabian Sea. Area: 796,095 sq km (307,374 sq mi), excluding the 83,716-sq km Pakistani-controlled section of Jammu and Kashmir. Pop. (1994 est., including nearly 1.5 million Afghan refugees and 3.4 million residents of Pakistani-controlled Jammu and Kashmir): 131,434,000. Cap.: Islamabad. Monetary unit: Pakistan rupee, with (Oct. 7, 1994) a free rate of PRs 30.62 to U.S. $1 (PRs 48.70 = £1 sterling). President in 1994, Farooq Ahmed Leghari; prime minister, Benazir Bhutto.

During 1994 Prime Minister Benazir Bhutto's government continued to face the daunting task of providing homes, schools, hospitals, food, gas, electricity, employment, and infrastructure to meet the needs of Pakistan's ever increasing population. Circumstances, however, forced Bhutto to abandon in great measure the ambitious social reforms she had not been able to implement during her first term (1988–90) as prime minister.

On a positive side, the coalition government led by her liberal Pakistan People's Party proved to be quite stable despite bitter public feuding with her mother, who argued that power should be held by her son, not her daughter. Bhutto kept coalition partners in line by doling out patronage, diluted tax reforms to appease business, and generally avoided direct confrontation with religious conservatives. Even so, Islamic fundamentalists created turmoil by accusing Iqbal Haider, the nation's minister of law and justice, of insulting Islam. Haider, who had a $40,000 price put on his head, was accused of betraying Islam by supporting a proposed amendment to Pakistan's blasphemy law that would make it a crime to falsely accuse anyone of blaspheming Islam. Of the hundreds of people jailed on charges of blasphemy, most belonged to the outlawed Ahmedi sect or professed Christianity.

Bhutto adhered to the financial diet prescribed by the International Monetary Fund (IMF) and moved to privatize inefficient state companies, but the economy remained stagnant on a continent where others were booming. Annual growth of about 3% with an equal rate of growth in population kept the per capita income at about $400.

Bhutto continued to make progress restoring democracy and many basic rights, but women were still generally treated as second-class citizens. In August, when unrest erupted in the southern city of Karachi, hundreds of political activists were arrested, and many were incarcerated without being formally charged with a crime. Political and ethnic violence continued in Karachi throughout the fall, leaving at least 135 people dead. Fierce clashes also broke out in the north, where Islamic fundamentalists demanded the introduction of Islamic law.

In foreign affairs Pakistan continued to support the Muslims in Kashmir, the Himalayan territory claimed by both Pakistan and India. Determined to keep the two-thirds of Kashmir that it controlled, India took steps to crush the Muslim rebellion. Pakistani support for the Muslims in the area merely escalated the bloodletting. Some 8,000 people, mostly civilians, had reportedly been killed over the previous five years, and many others, according to human rights groups, had been raped, tortured, and otherwise abused. Because tensions between India and Pakistan had led to three wars since they gained independence from the British in 1947, Pakistan had never felt it could trim military spending; as a result, military expenditures remained the largest item in the government's annual budget. The small increases in social spending were not large enough to affect a society that was 70% illiterate and had inadequate schools, housing, and medical care.

In February Bhutto imposed a tax on the country's landowners for the first time. Although the tax was small, the IMF and other financial institutions viewed the measure as a test of whether the government was serious about economic reform. The IMF wanted to see the new tax in place before deciding whether to approve a new $1.3 billion loan. Wealthy landowners dominated Pakistan's economy and its political system and had traditionally exempted themselves from taxes. Only one million of Pakistan's 130 million people paid taxes, and government officials conceded that no one had ever been prosecuted for tax evasion.

In a September drug bust, 10 tons of hashish were seized. The Federal Investigation Agency uncovered some of the hashish when a truck pulled into a customs post in the eastern city of Lahore. The narcotics, in small packages tucked inside cotton bales, were destined for Europe. The seizure was the largest ever in Pakistan, which in recent years had become a major exporter of illegal drugs.

(DILIP GANGULY)

PALAU

A republic in the Caroline Islands of the western Pacific Ocean, Palau comprises a 640-km (400-mi)-long chain of some 340 volcanic and coralline islands. The main islands of Babelthuap and Koror are situated about 900 km east of the Philippines. Area: 488 sq km (188 sq mi). Pop. (1994 est.): 16,600. Provisional cap.: Koror, on Koror; a site on Babelthuap was designated to be the eventual permanent capital. Monetary unit: U.S. dollar, with (Oct. 7, 1994) a free rate of $1.59 to £1 sterling. President in 1994, Kuniwo Nakamura.

Palau became a sovereign state on Oct. 1, 1994, when its Compact of Free Association with the U.S. became effective. Since 1991 it had been the only remaining dependent state constituting the U.S.-administered Trust Territory of the Pacific Islands, a trusteeship established under UN auspices after World War II to facilitate the transition to independence of the former Japanese colonial territory.

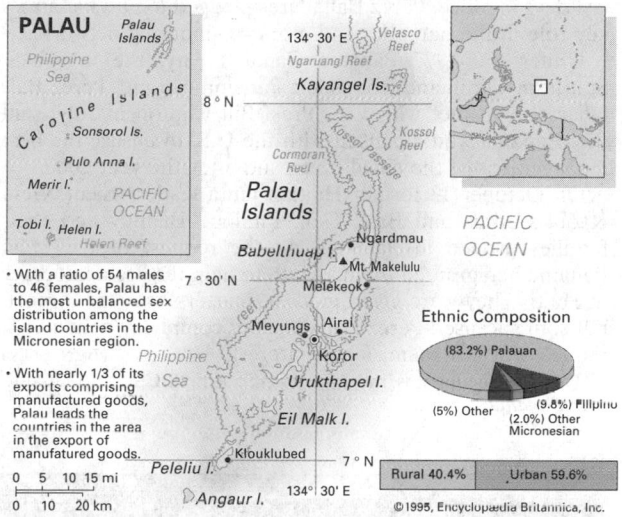

Palau's formal approval of the Compact of Free Association had been delayed by seven unsuccessful plebiscites between 1983 and 1990 (over the issue of disposal and storage of U.S. nuclear materials in Palau) that did not meet the 75% approval requirement of the Palau constitution. A 1992 constitutional amendment reducing the 75% to a simple majority ended the impasse with approval of the compact in the eighth plebiscite in November 1993 by an approval rate of 68%.

The compact recognized Palau's nearly complete autonomy in the conduct of domestic and foreign affairs but obligated it to avoid foreign policy initiatives that were contrary to U.S. interests as determined by joint consultations. The U.S. remained responsible for the defense of Palau for 50 years; Palau was required to grant the U.S. rights to existing military bases in Palau for that period of time.

The new nation applied to the United Nations in November and was admitted as the 185th member of the General Assembly on December 15.   (STEPHEN NEHER)

This article updates the *Macropædia* article PACIFIC ISLANDS: *Palau.*

PANAMA

A republic of Central America, Panama lies between the Caribbean Sea and the Pacific Ocean on the Isthmus of Panama. Area: 75,517 sq km (29,157 sq mi). Pop. (1994 est.): 2,583,000. Cap.: Panama City. Monetary unit: balboa, at par with the U.S. dollar, with a free rate (Oct. 7, 1994) of 1.59 balboas to £1 sterling. Presidents in 1994, Guillermo Endara Galimany and, from September 1, Ernesto Pérez Balladares.

Watched by 2,000 local and international observers, the May 1994 general elections were largely incident-free and were praised for their openness. The winner of the presidency was Ernesto Pérez Balladares of the Democratic Revolutionary Party, whose campaign invoked memories of the party's founder, Omar Torrijos, and successfully avoided links with its more recent, now discredited, leader, Manuel Noriega. In second place was Mireya Moscoso de Gruber of the Arnulfista Party, led by the outgoing president, Guillermo Endara Galimany. Third was salsa star and actor Rubén Blades (*see* BIOGRAPHIES), whose party, Papa Egoró (Mother Earth), in its electoral debut, won six seats in the legislature.

Despite economic improvements (rising international reserves, a forecast 4.6% growth of gross domestic product in 1994, and declining unemployment), Endara's administration failed to reduce poverty and an annual debt-service bill of about $900 million. Endara also failed to eliminate drug trafficking and corruption, accusations of which tainted his last days in office. Pérez Balladares pledged to end Panama's key role in the narcotics and money-laundering network.

Under the 1977 Panama Canal Treaty, the first U.S. Southern Command troops left Panama in June. Pérez Balladares, who met with U.S. Pres. Bill Clinton in July, said that Panama would consult with the U.S. to ensure the best management of the canal up to and after the year 2000.

On October 13 former Haitian junta leaders Lieut. Gen. Raoul Cédras and Brig. Gen. Philippe Biamby and their families arrived in Panama. At the request of the U.S., Panama had granted them asylum to help restore democracy in Haiti. They were given modest quarters near the airport, but some accused Pérez Balladares of complying with a U.S. request not in Panama's best interest.   (BEN BOX)

This article updates the *Macropædia* article CENTRAL AMERICA: *Panama.*

PAPUA NEW GUINEA

A constitutional monarchy and Commonwealth member, Papua New Guinea is situated in the southwestern Pacific Ocean and comprises the eastern part of the island of New Guinea, the islands of the Bismarck, Kiriwina (Trobriand), Louisiade, and D'Entrecasteaux groups, Muyua (Woodlark) Island, and parts of the Solomon Islands group, including Bougainville. Area: 462,840 sq km (178,704 sq mi). Pop. (1994 est.): 4,246,000. Cap.: Port Moresby. Monetary unit: kina, with (Oct. 7, 1994) a free rate of 1.09 kinas to U.S. $1 (1.73 kinas = £1 sterling). Queen, Elizabeth II; governor-general in 1994, Wiwa Korowi; prime ministers, Paias Wingti and, from August 30, Sir Julius Chan.

In September 1994 the Papua New Guinea government recaptured the Bougainville copper mine after the dwindling group of separatist guerrillas occupying it withdrew to the hills. No date was set for the reopening of the mine, but the government looked forward to achieving this as soon as worker access to the site could be secured on a daily basis. Even though the safety of the guerrilla leaders was guaranteed by the presence of a multinational peacekeeping force in the Pacific region, the government was not able to entice the leaders of the Bougainville Revolutionary Army from the hills to peace talks.

The good news in Bougainville was offset by disaster in the central highlands, where a massive explosion in a gold mine stopped production. The Porgera mine was one of the world's largest, producing 32,885,000 g (1,160,000 oz) of gold a year. Eleven miners, including five Australians, were killed in the blast in the mine's explosives area, and 48 were injured when two sealed containers of ammonium nitrate were ignited by a fire.   (A.R.G. GRIFFITHS)

This article updates the *Macropædia* article PACIFIC ISLANDS: *Papua New Guinea.*

Ernesto Pérez Balladares speaks to a crowd during his campaign for the presidency of Panama. Head of the Democratic Revolutionary Party, Balladares narrowly defeated Mireya Moscoso de Gruber of the Arnulfista Party and several minor candidates.

PARAGUAY

Paraguay is a landlocked republic of central South America. Area: 406,752 sq km (157,048 sq mi). Pop. (1994 est.): 4,732,000. Cap.: Asunción. Monetary unit: guaraní, with (Oct. 7, 1994) a free rate of 1,919 guaranies to U.S. $1 (3,053 guaranies = £1 sterling). President in 1994, Juan Carlos Wasmosy.

August 1994 marked the first anniversary of Paraguay's return to civilian leadership. The adjustment to multiparty democracy proved difficult for the ruling Colorado Party and its leader, Pres. Juan Carlos Wasmosy. He faced a legislature dominated by opposition parties determined to break the Colorado Party's relationship with the military. On May 28 Congress approved a law that would have banned members of the armed forces from political party membership and activity. The government and military high command immediately initiated legal proceedings to have the law declared unconstitutional. This caused the opposition, led by Domingo Laíno of the Authentic Radical Liberal Party, to withdraw from its cooperation pact with the Colorados.

Violent clashes between peasant farmers and police in February affected several regions of the country. Some 100 demonstrators blockading roads from the capital, Asunción, were injured when police opened fire with rubber bullets. The farmers were demanding government subsidies to compensate for losses due to low cotton prices. They gained widespread support from church organizations, labour unions, and opposition parties, but the government refused to relent. Ironically, international cotton prices rose by some 29% in 1994, but a 12% decline in Paraguay's cotton harvest prevented small farmers from reaping the benefits. An estimated 220,000 rural families depended on cotton for their livelihood. In order to stop deforestation through illegal exporting of wood products, mainly to Brazil, the government banned all exports of timber on December 14.

Labour unions and peasant organizations staged a general strike on May 2 to demand pay increases of up to 40% and land reform and to protest against the government's plans to privatize public-sector companies. The government conceded that the purchasing power of wages had fallen by 42% in the five years to June 1994 but offered pay increases of only 35%. Inflation remained under reasonable control in 1994 but was expected to end the year at 22%, slightly above the 19.5% recorded in 1993. (JANET KRENGEL)

PERU

The republic of Peru is located in western South America, on the Pacific Ocean. Area: 1,285,216 sq km (496,225 sq mi). Pop. (1994 est.): 23,383,000. Cap.: Lima. Monetary unit: nuevo sol, with (Oct. 7, 1994) a free rate of 2.25 nuevos soles to U.S. $1 (3.58 nuevos soles = £1 sterling). President in 1994, Alberto Fujimori; prime ministers, Alfonso Bustamente y Bustamente and, from February 17, Efrain Godenberg Schreiber.

In mid-1994 it appeared that Pres. Alberto Fujimori's only serious rival for the April 1995 elections would be former UN secretary-general Javier Pérez de Cuéllar. In August, however, Fujimori's estranged wife, Susana Higuchi, declared her intention to run against her husband, with the backing of a political movement called Harmony 21st Century. Her announcement was in direct contradiction to a law, passed by Fujimori, preventing a president's close relatives from running for office. She stated that the law was unconstitutional, but despite support for her claim from the Organization of American States, she was not permitted to run for president. In response to Higuchi's accusations of corruption throughout the government and criticisms of his failure to address Peru's acute poverty, Fujimori called her disloyal and stripped her of her duties as first lady. She moved out of the presidential palace, set up headquarters in a school her family owned, and vowed that she would run for Congress—and perhaps, later, higher office.

Fujimori himself delayed announcing his candidacy until October, a month after Pérez de Cuéllar launched his campaign. The latter allied himself to opposition figures who favoured the reestablishment of the democratic institutions that Fujimori had abolished. By October the list of candidates for the presidency was expected to exceed 20. They were drawn from a variety of new movements, reflecting the continuing mistrust (fostered by Fujimori) of the traditional parties, which would nevertheless be fielding their own candidates.

All those lining up against Fujimori would have to contend with his successful handling of a number of issues. The military offensive against the Sendero Luminoso (Shining Path) guerrillas was concentrated on the banks of the Río Huallaga, some 500 km (300 mi) northeast of Lima. A propaganda campaign succeeded in persuading many sympathizers to profess that they had renounced the Sendero cause, but armed actions were inconclusive in this and other regions. While the level of violence throughout the country declined, human rights organizations alleged that government forces killed, raped, and tortured innocent civilians in the drive to destroy the guerrillas.

The increased sense of security, especially in the Andean areas, allowed geologists and miners from other nations to investigate mineral deposits without interference. Joint ventures in gold and copper extraction and foreign investment in exploration revived the mining sector. Similar renewed interest in oil and gas promised to raise significantly the output of these fuels between 1994 and 2000. A program initiated in September gave Peruvian investors the opportunity to buy shares in companies that were to be privatized, the proceeds being used to finance the private pension fund system.

Economic growth continued to be strong: 8.5% in the first half of 1994, compared with 7% in 1993. Other positive economic indicators included an inflation rate of about 20% and record levels of international reserves. Multilateral lending resumed in earnest, mainly for infrastructure projects, but the government's inability to handle large amounts of funding for alleviating poverty and providing employment formed the main basis for opposition to Fujimori.

(BEN BOX)

PHILIPPINES

Situated in the western Pacific Ocean off the southeast coast of Asia, the republic of the Philippines consists of an archipelago of about 7,100 islands. Area: 300,076 sq km (115,860 sq mi). Pop. (1994 est.): 68,278,000. Cap.: Manila (lower house of the legislature meets in Quezon City). Monetary unit: Philippine peso, with (Oct. 7, 1994) a free rate of 25.60 pesos to U.S. $1 (40.72 pesos = £1 sterling). President in 1994, Fidel V. Ramos.

On Aug. 26, 1994, Pres. Fidel V. Ramos announced that he was forming a coalition with the Philippines' largest opposition party, Democratic Filipino Struggle (LDP), which had been obstructing legislation in the Congress. Agreement was reached on a common legislative program, but the main purpose of the coalition was to give each party six places on a common slate for the 12 Senate seats to be filled in the May 1995 elections. Whereas the LDP feared that it might fare poorly against Ramos' party, Ramos sought to end political confrontations that were hampering economic development.

The coalition took shape after a political squabble over taxes. Only 6% of workers paid direct taxes, so more indirect taxes were needed for the government to cope with its budget deficit and implement social programs. In September 1993 the government had imposed a levy of between 16% and 28% on petroleum products. The threat of nationwide demonstrations and a general strike on Feb. 9, 1994, forced Ramos to suspend the tax and then to rescind it on February 23. To make up for the lost revenues, Ramos persuaded Congress to pass a law in May that closed loopholes in a 10% value-added tax (VAT). Popular protests followed, and some LDP senators who had initially voted for it failed to support Ramos. The Supreme Court subsequently rejected challenges to the law.

Efforts to reduce the deficit by broadening the VAT were supported by the International Monetary Fund. After a delay of more than two years, the IMF endorsed the Philippines' economic program and on June 24 approved credits of $684 million. That triggered the rescheduling of debts and the granting of $5.6 billion in aid by various donor countries and agencies. In the first half of 1994 the economy grew 5.1%, more than double the rate of a year earlier. The improvement was due in part to increased electrical power, which industries sorely needed.

Ramos' domestic agenda included birth control programs to reduce the 2.5% annual increase in the country's population, which stood at 68 million. Ramos, the first Protestant president in a country that was 87.5% Roman Catholic, was challenged especially by the influential Jaime Cardinal Sin, who led a massive rally in downtown Manila against birth control programs. In January Ramos signed a law restoring the death penalty for 13 crimes, including murder, treason, kidnapping, and corruption. Vice Pres. Joseph Estrada led a campaign against widespread crime. More than 2% of the nation's policemen were dismissed for crimes, and an additional 5% were under investigation.

ASIAWEEK PICTURES

On Basilan Island in the southern Philippines, 20 hostages are led away after their release by a faction of the Moro National Liberation Front. The Muslim separatist group, which generally targeted Christians, killed 16 of those it had taken hostage.

The New People's Army (NPA), long a communist guerrilla threat to stability, continued to weaken. In March Ramos proclaimed a general amnesty for all rebels and for police and soldiers accused of crimes associated with the fighting. The NPA, torn by internal strife, assassinated a former leader planning to accept the amnesty; other leaders were captured in the Manila area and the central islands.

The Moro National Liberation Front (MNLF), an Islamic group fighting for a separate state in the southern Philippines, continued talks that had produced an interim cease-fire agreement on Nov. 7, 1993. During a September meeting in Indonesia, the government and the MNLF resolved several issues, including the right to use Islamic law in Muslim areas. A breakaway group that refused to accept the cease-fire continued to fight the army and to seize foreign hostages, however.

Indonesia put pressure on the Philippine government to prevent a privately sponsored conference on East Timor, a former Portuguese colony seized by Indonesia in 1975. Ramos prevented some foreigners from attending, but the conference opened in Manila on May 31. The government was widely criticized for obstructing free speech and yielding to foreign pressure. U.S. Pres. Bill Clinton visited on November 12–13, partly to help commemorate the anniversary of the liberation of the Philippines from the Japanese in World War II. A draft military agreement, due to be signed on December 15, was delayed by the Philippine side, however.   (HENRY S. BRADSHER)

POLAND

A republic of Eastern Europe, Poland is on the Baltic Sea. Area: 312,685 sq km (120,728 sq mi). Pop. (1994 est.): 38,653,000. Cap.: Warsaw. Monetary unit: zloty, with (Oct. 7, 1994) a free rate of 23,114 zlotys to U.S. $1 (36,763 zlotys = £1 sterling). President in 1994, Lech Walesa; prime minister, Waldemar Pawlak.

There were fears by late 1994 that the policies or lack of them espoused by Prime Minister Waldemar Pawlak and his ex-communist coalition, after more than one year in office, had brought Poland's dynamic reforms grinding to a halt. The economic statistics, though not exciting, did not appear to give undue cause for concern, however. Inflation dropped slightly to 30% per year, while unemployment continued at about three million, a rate of about 17%. Industrial growth increased 11%, largely through improved trade with Russia, while per capita gross domestic product (GDP) grew 4% and the trade deficit was significantly reduced. The budget deficit was 3.5% of GDP, and the zloty remained firm throughout the year, with only a gradual devaluation.

Instead, what set the alarm bells ringing for reformers was the commercialization rather than the privatization of state-owned enterprises. Under this formula, 50% of all industrial enterprises appeared set to remain in the government-owned sector for the foreseeable future. That this slowdown in privatization reflected a strong current in public opinion was to be expected, as the population was now more clearly divided into economic winners and losers.

Only after considerable delay did Prime Minister Pawlak sign the privatization bill, enabling 444 enterprises to be privatized through the National Investment Funds. Another 28 were sold into the private sector, compared with 39 in 1993. Only 32 companies were listed on the country's stock exchange, where the index kept just ahead of inflation.

Ailing and indebted state enterprises, especially the mining industry and inefficient farms, were receiving cheap credits and state subsidies and were defended by protectionist policies that were, in effect, creating a dual-sector economy. It was no surprise that such enterprises were among the major constituencies that supported the coalition government of Prime Minister Pawlak. The government also shied away from privatizing utilities such as telecommunications and transportation, while businesses that could be sold profitably, such as tobacco, oil refining, and banking enterprises, remained in state hands. The private sector, which produced all the economic growth, was burdened by high taxation and the increasing power of lobbies that were distorting the rules of the market.

As always, the political scene was punctuated by conflict between Pres. Lech Walesa and the coalition government. The battle was generally fought over the prerogative to fill key ministries, especially those considered to be within the scope of the president. This conflict was exemplified by Walesa's attempt to dismiss the minister of defense, Piotr Kolodziejczyk (he finally succeeded in November), which, along with the earlier confrontation between Andrzej Olechowski's Foreign Ministry and the legislature's Foreign Affairs Commission, made it obvious to an increasingly cynical population that the presidential campaign for 1995 was under way.

With a turnout as low as 28% in the towns and 38% in the countryside, the local government elections in June raised the political temperature only slightly. The coalition parties were seeking to repeat their general-election triumph at the local level. In this they were only partially successful and, in fact, the elections witnessed the rebirth of the political right, which captured seats in the poorer eastern parts of the country. The Roman Catholic Church, which had sought to distance itself from politics in the wake of the 1993 elections to the Sejm (parliament), found itself once again embroiled in conflict with the state over the concordat, which the legislature refused to ratify but chose to defer until the matter of the constitution had been settled.

The debate over the Polish constitution provided the backdrop for the country's politics since it not only would decide how secular Poland was to be but also would define the powers of the president and the legislature. Of the seven draft versions under consideration by the constitutional commission, it was the Solidarity draft backed by a campaign of more than one million signatures that attracted the most attention; it was notable for being accompanied by a rapprochement between Walesa and the Solidarity trade union after a period of estrangement.

Tensions within the ruling coalition of the Polish Peasant Party and the ex-communist Democratic Left Alliance (SLD) continued, as did the oft-repeated warnings of a major split in the opposition Democratic Union. The major candidates for president included Aleksandr Kwasniewski of the SLD; Jacek Kuron, regarded as the nation's most popular politician; Olechowski, who as foreign minister succeeded in staying above party politics; former prime ministers Hanna Suchocka and Tadeusz Mazowiecki, both of the Democratic Union; and President Walesa, who could never be discounted as a contender regardless of public opinion polls.

It seemed likely that for the first time foreign affairs could be as prominent as the perennial domestic issues of abortion and religious education in the political campaign. Poland's drive to gain membership in the European Union and NATO was given a significant boost by the visit of U.S. Pres. Bill Clinton in July; at that meeting any Russian veto of NATO's expansion into Eastern Europe was explicitly denied. Subsequent maneuvers held jointly with the Polish military and troops from NATO countries, on Polish territory, seemed to underline the Western commitment to the emerging democracies of Eastern Europe. On the other hand, the last-minute postponement of Russian Prime Minister Viktor Chernomyrdin's visit to Warsaw, where he was to sign important trade and energy agreements, ostensibly because of the ill-treatment of Russian citizens by Polish police, was followed by official Russian criticisms of the NATO extension into Eastern Europe. This move raised questions as to whether Poland was once again being defined as part of Russia's "legitimate sphere of influence."

(GEORGE KOLANKIEWICZ)

PORTUGAL

A republic of southwestern Europe, metropolitan Portugal is on the Atlantic coast of the Iberian Peninsula, which it shares with Spain. Area: 92,235 sq km (35,612 sq mi), including the Azores archipelago and Madeira Islands in the Atlantic. Pop. (1994 est.): 9,814,000. Cap.: Lisbon. Monetary unit: Portuguese escudo, with (Oct. 7, 1994) a free rate of 157.32 escudos to U.S. $1 (250.21 escudos = £1 sterling). President in 1994, Mário Soares; prime minister, Aníbal Cavaco Silva.

Prime Minister Aníbal Cavaco Silva and his Social Democratic Party (PSD) continued in power in 1994, though the government was shaken by a series of social and political problems that led to a decline in its popularity. Decisions to raise the tuition for public schools led to several months of sometimes violent and always noisy student protests and opened a more general debate on the declining quality of Portuguese schools. Cavaco Silva was also unable to reach an agreement with the leading labour unions on an increase in public workers' salaries. Negotiations continued, but it appeared that both sides had reached an insurmountable impasse. The labour troubles resulted in a variety of short-term strikes, notably among transport workers.

Most serious in terms of Cavaco Silva's public standing was the decision to raise tolls on Lisbon's April 25th bridge by 50%. That move, made in June just prior to the busy summer travel season, caused a week of commuter protest that culminated in a complete daylong blockade of the bridge by truckers. The government was forced to call in riot police to clear the bridge. The transport minister later backed off from the toll proposal, offering a free two-month grace period while new payment schemes were developed. Nonetheless, when the tolls came back in September with the increase still in place, the protests followed, and—while the constant blaring of horns and the sporadic blockades had tapered off—traffic on Lisbon's only bridge across the Tagus River remained problematic.

A major reason for the increase in tolls was a need for funds to build a second bridge across the river, from northeastern Lisbon to the suburb of Montijo. That bridge, a $1.2 billion project, was scheduled to be built and operating by 1998, when Lisbon was to act as host for the last world exposition of the 20th century.

Cavaco Silva's problems climaxed in late October when the tiny Democratic Social Centre Party (CDS), led by Manuel Monteiro, introduced a no-confidence motion in the Assembly of the Republic. While the PSD's absolute majority (135 votes to 95 in the 230-seat Assembly) removed any threat that the legislature would be dissolved, the ensuing two-day debate gave opposition parties a chance to air their frustrations. The opposition Socialist Party (PS), headed by António Guterres, criticized the PSD for "freezing economic reforms" and for failing to reach an agreement on the state workers' salary increase. The right-leaning CDS—which claimed just five votes in the Assembly—accused Cavaco Silva of waffling on European Union issues and undermining stability by shuffling key ministers, including those for education and finance. But while the no-confidence motion failed because of the PSD's majority, the opposition parties themselves were revealed to be splintered; Guterres' PS voted for the motion, as did the 17-seat Communist alliance, but both refused to align with the CDS and presented their own reasons for censuring Cavaco Silva.

A political modus vivendi had existed between Pres. Mário Soares, a Socialist, and Cavaco Silva of the centre-right PSD for several years, but Soares turned on the prime minister in December, saying that excessive powers had been placed in the hands of one man and warning of a drift toward a "dictatorship of the majority." Soares likely had his eye on the general election in October 1995 and the presidential election in early 1996. Cavaco Silva was expected to run again for prime minister or seek the presidency himself, but Soares was ineligible for a third term as president.

The draft budget for 1995, announced in October, was aimed at reducing the deficit and consolidating the economic recovery through a modest increase in spending and a rise in indirect tax rates. The government expected to take in 3.6 trillion escudos and to increase spending by 5% to 4,380,000,000,000 escudos, optimistically predicting economic growth at between 2.5% and 3.5% of gross domestic product, as compared with 1% in 1994. A one-percentage-point rise in the standard value-added tax and a continuing crackdown on tax evaders were planned to boost the government's revenue. Inflation dropped steadily throughout 1994, to an annualized 4.6% at the end of the third quarter, while unemployment for the same period rose to 6.7% from 5.5% at the end of 1993.   (ERIK BURNS)

See also *Dependent States.*

QATAR

A monarchy (emirate) on the Arabian Peninsula, Qatar occupies a desert peninsula and the nearby small Hawar Islands (also claimed by Bahrain) on the west coast of the Persian Gulf. Area (including Hawar Islands): 11,427 sq km (4,412 sq mi). Pop. (1994 est.): 552,000. Cap.: Doha. Monetary unit: Qatar riyal, with (Oct. 7, 1994) a free rate of 3.64 riyals to U.S. $1 (5.79 riyals = £1 sterling). Emir and prime minister in 1994, Sheikh Khalifah ibn Hamad ath-Thani.

In May 1994 an Israeli delegation invited to weapons-control talks in Doha along with representatives from 42 other countries caused controversy when other delegates attacked the Jewish state for its nuclear policy. The invitation to Israel emphasized Qatar's independent line in foreign policy. King Hussein I of Jordan, shunned by many of the other Arab Gulf states for his support of Iraq, visited Qatar in March, and other delegations were received from hard-line Arab states, including The Sudan (National Islamic Front) in February and Yemen in April. An Iraqi Information Ministry team visited Doha for a week.

The national budget provided for a 19.4% decline in revenues due to lower oil prices. Expenditure was cut to $3,250,000,000 from $3,590,000,000 in 1993, but the budget deficit was also slated to rise from $807 million in 1993 to $953 million in 1994. In a bid to replace oil income with other sources of wealth, new liquefied natural gas (LNG) contracts were negotiated with energy companies in East Asia. Qatar expected to export 24 million metric tons a year of LNG from its North Field by the year 2005.

On January 20 Qatar Airways, the Gulf's youngest airline, inaugurated its first scheduled passenger flight to the United Arab Emirates. The airline, which opened for business with two leased aircraft, had traffic rights for Dubayy, ash-Shariqah, and Khartoum in The Sudan.   (JOHN WHELAN)

This article updates the *Macropædia* article ARABIA: *Qatar.*

ROMANIA

A republic on the Balkan Peninsula in southeastern Europe, Romania has a coastline on the Black Sea. Area: 237,500 sq km (91,699 sq mi). Pop. (1994 est.): 22,740,000. Cap.: Bucharest. Monetary unit: leu, with (Oct. 7, 1994) a free rate of 1,746 lei to U.S. $1 (2,777 lei = £1 sterling). President in 1994, Ion Iliescu; prime minister, Nicolae Vacaroiu.

In January 1994 Romania became the first of 22 countries to sign the NATO Partnership for Peace agreement, and in July the Commission of the European Union (EU) recommended the expansion of its association agreement with Romania, signed on Feb. 1, 1993, to include wider commercial concessions. At the beginning of September the U.S. Congress accepted Pres. Bill Clinton's recommendation to extend Romania's most-favoured-nation trade status for another year.

Economic progress continued to be uneven. The inertia that characterized the government's approach to mass privatization in 1993 led to the shifting of the movement for reform to the International Monetary Fund. As a stimulus for reform the IMF approved a stand-by agreement for Romania on May 11 amounting to $700 million over the next 19 months. This triggered additional external assistance from international financial institutions, with the EU pledging ECU 90 million and the World Bank releasing part of its loan for privatization. In line with the IMF agreement, the government announced its Mass Privatization Plan (MPP) on July 22. The minister for economic reform said that almost 3,000 companies (the majority already profitable) would be privatized. Following the announcement the scheme was amended by the privatization commissions of the national legislature, and it was unlikely that the MPP would be implemented before early 1995.

Doubts about the government's ability to meet the privatization targets stemmed from its dependency for a parliamentary majority on the ultranationalist Romanian National Unity Party (PUNR) and the Greater Romania Party. Both of these parties opposed any significant privatization that involved foreign capital. Foreign companies continued to face legal difficulties in acquiring outright ownership of land, and there was still doubt as to whether even a Romanian-registered company could acquire such ownership. In 1994 more than 30% of the land confiscated by the communists in 1949 remained in the hands of the state. These restrictions, coupled with the continued inconsistency in fiscal legislation and its arbitrary application, kept foreign investment—largely restricted to joint ventures—at a modest level in comparison with that in most of the other former communist nations of Eastern Europe; in September it stood at $953 million.

Notable success was achieved in reducing inflation. Figures indicated that the government should meet its target of 75–80% inflation for 1994 (down from 300% in 1993). Exports for the first half of 1994 rose 41% compared with the same period in 1993. Unemployment, at 10.4% (1.2 million) in September 1994, was rising slowly.

On the political front the behaviour of the PUNR created problems for the government. The fourth largest party in the legislature since the September 1992 elections, the PUNR, under its leader Gheorghe Funar, exploited nationalist sensibilities among the mixed Romanian-Hungarian population in its Transylvanian stronghold of Cluj. One of Funar's most controversial acts was triggered by the collapse of the pyramid investment scheme Caritas, with which his party was closely linked. In an effort to distract attention from the scandal arising from this affair, Funar in July ordered excavations to begin in the town centre that might have resulted in the removal of a statue of the Hungarian King Matthias Corvinus, a native of Cluj regarded as a symbolic bridge between Hungarians and Romanians in Transylvania. In response, the Hungarian Democratic Union of Romania (HDUR) organized a protest rally in the city. The situation was defused as a result of government intervention, which led to the site of the excavation being moved.

Given the conflicts and tensions in the region, great emphasis was being placed by European governments on the need for Hungary and Romania to normalize their relations. Both countries received numerous signals from abroad to this effect, not least from the EU, which told all Eastern European governments that a resolution of outstanding minority and frontier issues was a precondition of integration into the organization.

Further complicating the situation, hard-liners in the HDUR were driving the party toward a radicalization of its policies. At the beginning of August the HDUR demanded special status for areas of Transylvania occupied by "compact Hungarian population," including greater control over education and culture. The HDUR also requested that Hungary include these demands in the proposed bilateral treaty with Romania. This announcement drew protests from all the major political parties in Romania.

(DENNIS J. DELETANT)

This article updates the *Macropædia* article BALKAN STATES: *Romania*.

RUSSIA

Russia is a federal republic occupying eastern and northeastern Europe and all of northern Asia. Area: 17,075,400 sq km (6,592,800 sq mi). Pop. (1994 est.): 148,174,000. Cap.: Moscow. Monetary unit: ruble, with (Oct. 7, 1994) a free rate of 2,927 rubles = U.S. $1 (4,656 rubles = £1 sterling). President in 1994, Boris Yeltsin; prime minister, Viktor Chernomyrdin.

Domestic Affairs. An uneasy truce prevailed during 1994 between Pres. Boris Yeltsin and the opposition, within the State Duma (lower house of parliament) and outside. In elections in December 1993 Yeltsin succeeded in getting a popular mandate for the new constitution, which conferred much greater powers on the president than Yeltsin had enjoyed under the 1978 (Soviet) constitution. The president had wanted the vote on the constitution to be a measure of the confidence of the electorate in him and his policies, but the low turnout (55%) and the fact that only 58.4% voted in favour of the constitution rather undermined the legitimacy of the president. Moreover, in May the results of an analysis of voting published in *Izvestiya* concluded that voter turnout had been only 46.1%; by these calculations the constitution had not been adopted. Both the president and the Duma ignored the report.

More bad news for Yeltsin was that the new Duma did not have a pro-reform majority. Twenty-one parties had applied to contest the election, but only 13 were permitted to do so. Here the pro-Yeltsin forces miscalculated. By banning some of the more extreme parties, they succeeded only in concentrating the antireform vote. Yeltsin, to the consternation of his supporters, refused to support Russia's Choice openly. As the main pro-reform party, Russia's Choice had confidently expected about a third of the vote but was shocked to discover that only 15.4% of voters chose it. With 22.8% of the vote, the clear winner, especially among businessmen, was the Liberal Democratic Party (in reality a right-wing nationalist party) of Vladimir Zhirinovsky (*see* BIOGRAPHIES), who promised to clamp down on crime and corruption and also to exclude Western

capital from the country. Moreover, many Russians were having second thoughts about the wisdom of breaking up the Soviet Union, and Zhirinovsky's promise to subordinate the U.S.S.R. successor states to Russia was very appealing.

This vote, however, in which the seats were allocated according to proportional representation, applied to only half of the 450 seats in the Duma. The other half were allocated according to the "first-past-the-post" principle, and here the pro-reformers did much better. Altogether, radical reformers (Russia's Choice and others) won 88 seats, moderate reformers (Russian Party of Unity and Accord and the Yavlinsky-Boldyrev-Lukin bloc) received 41 seats; centrists (New Regional Policy and Democratic Party), 80 seats; pro-communist (Agrarian Union, Women of Russia, and Communist Party), 104 seats; Russian nationalist (Russian Way), 25; and the extreme right (Liberal Democratic Party), 64. Ivan Rybkin of the Agrarian Union, a staunch communist, was elected speaker. Since much of the government's economic policy was opposed by the Yavlinsky-Boldyrev-Lukin bloc, there was little prospect that radical legislation would be passed. The tension that had existed between the

A woman waves a communist flag at a May Day rally in Moscow. Beset by severe economic hardships and a growing crime rate, many Russians were turning away from the development of a free market and closer ties to the West and turning toward a militant nationalism.
OTTO POHL

legislative (parliament) and the executive (president and government) continued under the new constitutional order.

In the Federation Council, the upper house of parliament, the situation was much more satisfactory from Yeltsin's point of view. Most of the 178 members were independents, but the pro-reform democrats had the largest group, 48 members. There were 23 moderate reformers. The Liberal Democratic Party was not formally represented. Vladimir Shumeyko, a Yeltsin supporter, was elected speaker.

Under the new constitution the president—not the parliament—proposed the prime minister and government. If the Duma rejected his nominees three times, he could dissolve the Duma. The constitution afforded the parliament, the president, the federal government, and the representative bodies of the subdivisions (republics, krays, oblasts) of the federation the right to initiate legislation. There were no legal or procedural means to prevent or mediate clashes between different types of legislation, however, one of the many instances that revealed that the constitution was drawn up in haste. On the other hand, it was extremely difficult to impeach the president; nothing short of a charge of treason or similar grave crime would suffice.

Although Yeltsin's attitude toward the Duma was conciliatory, the legislature was frustrated by its inability, under the constitution, to make the government accountable to it or even to obtain the information it sought. The opposition saw that the only recourse was to force a vote of no confidence in the government. Such a vote occurred in October, and the government came within 32 votes of losing.

From time to time the Duma openly challenged the president. For instance, in February the Duma granted an amnesty to the leaders of the attempted coup of August 1991, those responsible for attacks on the police at a Moscow demonstration on May Day 1993, and the leaders of the parliamentary revolt crushed by Yeltsin in October 1993 (including Yeltsin foes Ruslan Khasbulatov and Aleksandr Rutskoy). Yeltsin responded by phoning Prosecutor General Aleksey Kazannik and instructing him to find a legal device to block the amnesty. Kazannik refused to obey the "telephone law," declared that the amnesty was legal, and resigned.

The defeat of the pro-reform parties in the elections strengthened the hand of Prime Minister Viktor Chernomyrdin. Radical deputy prime ministers, except Anatoly Chubais (responsible for privatization), were replaced by more conservative men in order to appeal to the industrial, military-industrial, and agrarian lobbies. A major casualty was Yegor Gaydar, who stepped down as first deputy prime minister, whereupon Boris Fyodorov, the minister of finance, and Aleksandr Shokhin, the minister of economics, contended for the key reform post. Fyodorov threatened to resign from the Cabinet and demanded the resignation of Aleksandr Zaveryukha, deputy prime minister in charge of agriculture, and Viktor Gerashchenko, chairman of the Russian central bank. Fyodorov was also keen to succeed Gerashchenko. Chernomyrdin asked Fyodorov to withdraw his conditions and return as minister of finance. He refused, and the two main proponents of reform in the government, Gaydar and Fyodorov, were gone. Chernomyrdin also dismissed several of the government's pro-Western economic advisers and stressed that Russia was not going to adopt a Western economic model. He also pushed for closer ties (*i.e.*, more Russian influence) within the Commonwealth of Independent States (CIS).

Regional and local elections resulted in further defeats for the reformist movement and successes for the former communist elites. Many of the elections were declared invalid since less than 25% of the electorate went to the polls, revealing political apathy, which was partly due to the perception that local elected institutions were too weak to deal with pressing local problems.

In April the Civic Accord was signed by the president, representatives of the government and the parliament, and regional and republican leaders. Yeltsin had proposed the accord in February as a means for contentious political forces to work together to stabilize Russia's economic position. The draft had to be amended several times to satisfy the several participants, and the final version deleted provisions for sanctions against signatories who violated the accord. The Agrarian Union, the Communist Party, and the Yavlinsky-Boldyrev-Lukin bloc refused to sign.

In June Russia's Choice announced the formation of a new political party, Russia's Democratic Choice, headed by Gaydar. In October Zhirinovsky's Liberal Democrats boycotted the Duma in protest against what they called an official campaign of harassment against the party. They were joined by the Agrarian Union and the Communist Party,

and this led to the Duma's being deprived for a time of a working majority.

Matters took an alarming turn beginning in September when the currency began dropping in value; on October 11, dubbed Black Tuesday, the ruble lost over 20% against the U.S. dollar. The president dismissed the acting minister of finance, Sergey Dubinin, and demanded that the Duma remove Gerashchenko. When the Duma refused, he dismissed the central bank chairman himself, a violation of the constitution.

Chernomyrdin also lost face in the episode, and it appeared that the president might sacrifice him. On October 27 the prime minister narrowly survived a vote of no confidence. Only 54 deputies sided with the government, which revealed how thin support for the reform program was. Opposition was marshaled by the Communists, but the Agrarians were divided in their votes. Yeltsin dismissed the liberal minister of agriculture, Viktor Khlystun, and replaced him with the Agrarian Aleksandr Nazarchuk. This deal appeared to save the day for the government. The fallout from Black Tuesday permitted the president on November 4 to appoint Vladimir Panskov the new minister of finance and accept the resignation of Aleksandr Shokhin as deputy prime minister and minister of economics.

Pessimists thought that this meant a lurch to the right by Yeltsin, but he appointed Anatoly Chubais first deputy prime minister and Yevgeny Yasin, an academic who had worked on Mikhail Gorbachev's 500-day program, minister of economics. It appeared that the president's tactics were to include in his government all shades of opinion, from radical reformer Chubais to ex-Communist Nazarchuk. The Communist Party was offered a place in government, but it declined. Thus, three levels of executive power evolved: the president, the Security Council (which was concerned mainly with security, defense, and police affairs), and the government. Foreign affairs came directly under the president, while the government was mainly responsible for economic policy.

During the year Yeltsin distanced himself from all groups and attempted to placate pro-communists, nationalists, and reformers from time to time. He did not commit himself to a coherent policy of political or economic reform. The main information agencies remained under state control, and major initiatives were still launched by presidential decree. In some ways Yeltsin began to resemble Gorbachev in 1991.

A crisis of a different sort beset Yeltsin in the latter half of the year. Following the withdrawal of Russian troops from Eastern Europe and the Baltic states, Moscow signed an agreement with the government of Moldova on the eventual withdrawal of the Russian 14th Army from the territory of the self-declared "Dniester republic." At the same time, it also began to increase the support for a group in the southern oil-producing area of Chechnya that opposed that republic's nationalist president, Dzhokhar Dudayev (*see* BIOGRAPHIES), and his drive to take Chechnya out of the Russian Federation. Dudayev had declared Chechnya's independence in 1991.

Fighting between the Chechen government and the opposition escalated slowly throughout the fall, then intensified sharply at the end of November. On December 10 Yeltsin ordered the borders of Chechnya sealed, and the following day Russian troops entered the heavily Muslim-populated republic. They made slow, very costly progress toward Grozny, the capital, amid a growing chorus of criticism of Russian involvement—in Chechnya itself, among many Russian civilians and politicians, as well as some in the military, and almost universally abroad. Russian troops had not secured Grozny by year's end, and there seemed to be confusion among the leaders in Moscow about who was in charge.

The Economy. The economy appeared to be in free fall for most of the year. Gross national product declined by 27%, production by 28%, and investment by 27% during the first half of the year. Gross domestic product (GDP) was expected to fall 15% over the year. Agriculture suffered badly, with the private sector accounting for less than 10% of arable farming. Most food on sale in Moscow was imported. About 18% of the population lived below the poverty line. On the other hand, Russia enjoyed a balance of payments surplus, and by autumn about $500 million in venture capital was flowing in monthly. The service sector was booming, and privatization had resulted in about half the labour force working in the private sector. Small- and medium-scale privatization was almost completed, and Chubais envisaged 1995 as the year when large-scale privatization could really get under way.

Most conflict centred on the budget. The 1994 budget was passed by the parliament only in June, but the 1995 budget was already being hotly debated in November. This was an austerity budget, strongly backed by Chernomyrdin, and was tailored to please the International Monetary Fund (IMF) rather than the Duma. The draft abandoned the previous gradualist approach in the battle against inflation. There was to be a pegged exchange rate, strict rules against printing money to cover the budget deficit, and a planned $13 billion in Western aid. Tax revenues would most likely fail to meet targets, however (in 1994 tax revenues were only 11% of GDP). Spending cuts were implied, but the agrarian and military-industrial lobbies fought fiercely for large increases. Budget deficits would be financed by bond sales and help from outside. Demand for government bonds was weak in 1994, as there was little faith in the ruble. Half of all savings were being placed into foreign currencies.

Foreign policy. In December, at the Conference on Security and Cooperation in Europe session in Budapest, Yeltsin launched a blistering attack on NATO's plans to expand eastward and embrace the Eastern European states. He talked about the Cold War giving way to the Cold Peace. After some vacillation, in November Russia declined to join NATO's Partnership for Peace program, a rude shock for the U.S., which had doggedly stood behind Yeltsin throughout the year (Pres. Bill Clinton had visited Moscow in January). These moves signaled a toughening of the Russian position on relations with the West and made it clear that Moscow still regarded Eastern Europe as lying within its zone of influence.

In the area Russia had called the "near abroad," Moscow continued to expand its political, economic, and military influence as well. An Interstate Economic Committee was set up in the CIS (see COMMONWEALTH OF INDEPENDENT STATES), which pointed toward gradual economic integration. Russia also moved to improve relations with China and Japan, and a number of agreements were signed, but the key question of Russo-Japanese relations, the fate of the Kuril Islands, remained unsolved. Russia upgraded its relations with Iraq and sought to mediate in the Iraq-Kuwait conflict. Russia strongly opposed an expanded role for NATO in Bosnia and Herzegovina, although it did on occasion sanction NATO bombing of Serb positions and pressed for a negotiated settlement.

The conflict between Westernizers (those who favoured an Atlanticist foreign policy and close relations with the West) and nationalists (those who favoured a Eurasian and Russocentric foreign policy) appeared to be tipping in favour of the latter. Several influential scholars known for their Atlanticist position gradually moved toward the nationalists,

and in May author Aleksandr Solzhenitsyn returned to his homeland after 20 years in exile. Rumours about Yeltsin's health, his passion for vodka, and his fitness to rule were fueled by his failure to keep a date with Irish Prime Minister Albert Reynolds at Shannon Airport on September 30 on his way home from an official visit to the U.S. He was severely criticized in the Duma, and one deputy claimed that his behaviour had shamed Russia. Earlier, in Berlin for the withdrawal of the last Russian troops in August, Yeltsin had seized the bandleader's baton and delivered a rendition of a Russian folk song. His conspicuous absences and erratic decision making during the Chechen crisis led to speculation about the degree to which Yeltsin was in control of the country.   (MARTIN McCAULEY)

RWANDA

The landlocked republic of Rwanda is situated in central Africa. Area: 26,338 sq km (10,169 sq mi). Pop. (late August 1994 est.): 6.5 million to 7.2 million, including 2 million to 2.5 million refugees, of whom 1.5 million to 2 million are in Zaire. Cap.: Kigali. Monetary unit: Rwanda franc, with (Oct. 7, 1994) a free rate of RF 135.93 to U.S. $1 (RF 216.20 = £1 sterling). Presidents in 1994, Maj. Gen. Juvénal Habyarimana to April 6, Theodore Sindikubwabo from April 9, and, from July 19, Pasteur Bizimungu; prime ministers, Agathe Uwilingiyimana until April 7, Jean Kambanda from April 9 to July 19, and, from July 19, Faustin Twagiramungu.

The worst genocide and mass slaughter Africa had ever seen occurred in Rwanda from April to August 1994. The government had been stockpiling weapons for months and then passing them on to Hutu militias, and the uprising, despite the death in April of Pres. Juvénal Habyarimana that set it off, was not spontaneous but part of a planned massacre of the minority Tutsi. Moreover, those Hutu who favoured genuine democracy and were prepared to work with the Tutsi were targets of killer squads as much as were the Tutsi. Leaders of the opposition Social Democrat Party and Liberal Party were killed along with about 2,300 other people before the events of April 6. On that day Habyarimana and Burundi's Pres. Cyprien Ntaryarima were killed when the plane in which they were traveling was shot down near the Kigali airport (by Hutu extremists it seemed likely). The next day Prime Minister Agathe Uwilingiyimana, a Tutsi, was assassinated by Hutu soldiers. The months of horrific massacres that followed appeared to have had several objectives: to eliminate the Tutsi minority and opponents of the military regime established by Habyarimana and to ensure the absolute dominance of Hutu extremists.

As the conflict intensified, Kigali collapsed into chaos, though a transitional government was established under the speaker of the National Development Council, Theodore Sindikubwabo. The Rwandan Patriotic Front (FPR), which was dominated by Tutsi and had been fighting a civil war against the government since 1990, rejected his legitimacy and continued fighting; by April 12, FPR troops were invading the outskirts of Kigali. UN attempts to mediate a cease-fire were unsuccessful. On April 22, as the crisis deepened, the UN voted to reduce its presence in the country from 2,500 to 270. On May 17, however, the UN reversed its decision and voted to establish a force of 5,500 composed mainly of Africans (Europe and the U.S. refused to contribute troops). On June 23, with UN backing, France sent a military force into Rwanda to establish a safe zone; it was opposed by the FPR, which claimed that France had always supported the government and policies of President Habyarimana. By mid-August the French had withdrawn, but only a small number of African troops under UN auspices had arrived.

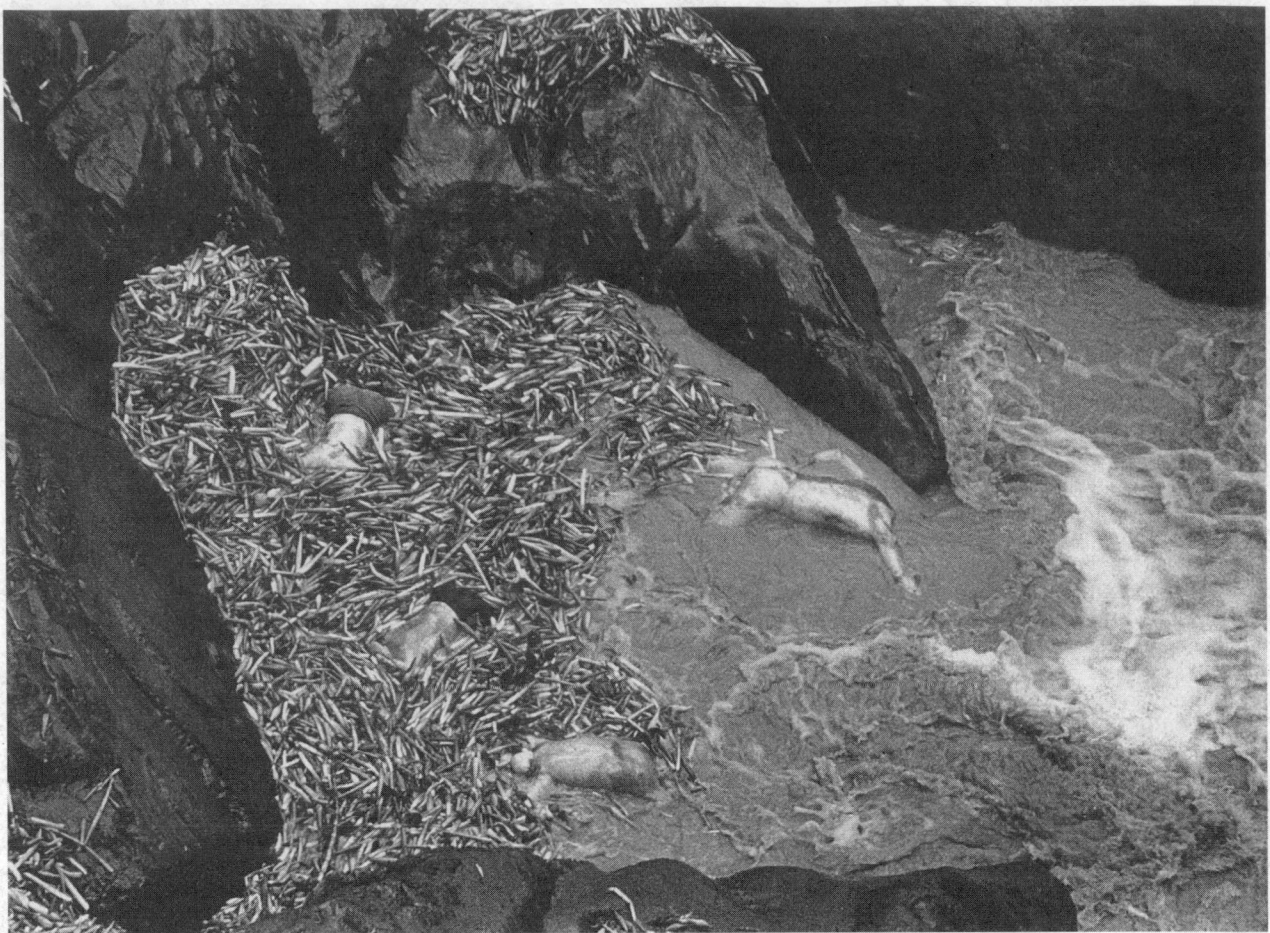

Bodies of massacred Rwandans lie amid debris in the Kagera River, along the border with Tanzania. Fighting between the Hutu and the Tutsi in 1994 led to enormous losses of life on both sides, and thousands also died in refugee camps in Tanzania and other neighbouring countries.

SEBASTIÃO SALGADO

During June and July the FPR continued to make gains on the battlefield, and by the end of August it had taken control of virtually all of Rwanda. One million or more were killed in the fighting from April to August. By September there were some 1.5 million to 2 million refugees, mostly Hutu, in camps in Zaire alone, and a virtual state of war existed between different groups there. An outbreak of cholera in the crowded camps killed thousands.

A few refugees began returning to Rwanda as early as July, although some Hutu, especially in rural areas, were reportedly victims of reprisals by the Tutsi-led FPR regime. After some vacillation the UN High Commissioner for Refugees agreed in December to provide assistance to refugees who wished to return. On November 8 the Security Council approved the establishment of an international court to examine charges of genocide.   (GUY ARNOLD)

See also Race and Ethnic Relations: *Sidebar.*

This article updates the *Macropædia* article CENTRAL AFRICA: *Rwanda.*

SAINT KITTS AND NEVIS

A constitutional monarchy and member of the Commonwealth, St. Kitts and Nevis comprises the islands of St. Kitts and Nevis in the eastern Caribbean Sea. Area: 269 sq km (104 sq mi). Pop. (1994 est.): 41,800. Cap.: Basseterre. Monetary unit: Eastern Caribbean dollar, with (Oct. 7, 1994) a par value of EC$2.70 to U.S. $1 (free rate of EC$4.30 = £1 sterling). Queen, Elizabeth II; governor-general in 1994, Sir Clement Arrindell; prime minister, Kennedy Alphonse Simmonds.

The dead heat between the incumbent People's Action Movement (PAM) and the St. Kitts-Nevis Labour Party (SKNLP) in the November 1993 general election created a climate of political and social instability that lasted well into 1994. The SKNLP did not take kindly to the fact that the governor-general had invited PAM to remain in office as a minority government. With the four seats it won and the support promised by the Nevis Reformation Party (NRP) with one seat, PAM could count on only five votes in the 11-seat National Assembly. The SKNLP, which also won four seats, insisted on new elections early in 1994, but that demand was rejected by the PAM leader, Prime Minister Kennedy Simmonds. Demonstrations by SKNLP supporters in the aftermath of the election forced the government to impose a state of emergency for 10 days. After being sworn in, SKNLP members boycotted all sittings of the Assembly, making it easier for the minority government to function.

Political disagreements did not seem to affect the economy, however, as the 1994 sugar harvest promised to reach 22,500 tons, compared with 21,258 tons in 1993. During the year the country "graduated" from World Bank concessionary lending because of its improved level of per capita national income. A prison riot and jailbreak in Basseterre in November after two sons of a prominent official received bail on charges related to drug and arms trafficking called attention to these problems, which were on the rise in the eastern Caribbean.   (DAVID RENWICK)

This article updates the *Macropædia* article The WEST INDIES: *Saint Kitts and Nevis.*

SAINT LUCIA

A constitutional monarchy and member of the Commonwealth, St. Lucia is the second largest of the Windward Islands in the eastern Caribbean Sea. Area: 617 sq km (238 sq mi). Pop. (1994 est.): 142,000. Cap.: Castries. Monetary unit: Eastern Caribbean dollar, with (Oct. 7, 1994) a par value of EC$2.70 to U.S. $1 (free rate of EC$4.30 = £1 sterling). Queen, Elizabeth II; governor-general in 1994, Stanislaus A. James; prime minister, John Compton.

Unrest in the banana industry continued as 1994 began, following a work stoppage by banana farmers in late 1993. The farmers were upset over low prices being paid by the St. Lucia Banana Growers Association (SLBGA). The protests turned violent at one stage, and two people were shot after clashes with the police. The United Workers' Party government, headed by Prime Minister John Compton, responded to the farmers' demands by sacking the entire SLBGA board and agreeing to raise prices for various grades of bananas, the island's main export crop.

The farmers' action was followed in February 1994 by that of the Seamen and Waterfront Workers' Trade Union. They struck in protest against new loading arrangements that resulted in 35–50% reductions in pay.

Britain announced during the year that it would provide another £4.3 million in development aid for the third phase of St. Lucia's west coast road-improvement project. Additional development funding also became available at midyear, with France offering a $2 million credit line to finance small infrastructural projects and the Caribbean Development Bank loaning $8.3 million for road construction to support the continued expansion of the tourism industry. In September Saint Lucia and the other Windward Islands suffered severe damage to agriculture, including the banana crop, and infrastructure from Tropical Storm Debbie.

(DAVID RENWICK)

This article updates the *Macropædia* article The WEST INDIES: *Saint Lucia.*

SAINT VINCENT AND THE GRENADINES

A constitutional monarchy within the Commonwealth, St. Vincent and the Grenadines comprises the islands of St. Vincent and the northern Grenadines in the eastern Caribbean Sea. Area: 389 sq km (150 sq mi). Pop. (1994 est.): 110,000. Cap.: Kingstown. Monetary unit: Eastern Caribbean dollar, with (Oct. 7, 1994) a par value of EC$2.70 to U.S. $1 (free rate of EC$4.30 = £1 sterling). Queen, Elizabeth II; governor-general in 1994, David Jack; prime minister, James Fitz-Allen Mitchell.

A preelection budget for 1994 promised EC$263.6 million in government spending. Income tax reductions amounting to more than EC$4 million were also announced.

A national election was called in February, earlier than constitutionally due, and the New Democratic Party (NDP), headed by Prime Minister James Mitchell, retained its hold on office but with a reduced majority. It won 12 of the 15 seats in the House of Assembly; the other 3 went to a coalition of opposition groups (the Movement for National Unity and the Saint Vincent Labour Party) led by Vincent Beache, who became official opposition leader in the Assembly. The election was marred by polling-eve clashes between supporters of both sides, during which more than 60 people were injured and a young NDP supporter died after being hit on the head with a stone.

The NDP government survived a no-confidence motion brought by the opposition in August, accusing it of failing to tackle economic problems, including a production decline in the banana industry. The decline to which the motion referred was evident during the first half of 1994, when banana exports dropped to 17,000 tons, compared with 30,000 tons in 1993.

Kuwait, OPEC, and the European Investment Bank agreed in July to help fund a new berth for cruise ships and to extend ferry facilities at the Kingstown port. The cost would be about $15 million. (DAVID RENWICK)

This article updates the *Macropædia* article The WEST INDIES: *Saint Vincent and the Grenadines.*

SAN MARINO

The republic of San Marino is a landlocked enclave in northeastern Italy. Area: 61 sq km (24 sq mi). Pop. (1994 est.): 24,500. Cap.: San Marino. Monetary unit: Italian lira, with (Oct. 7, 1994) a free rate of 1,569 lire to U.S. $1 (2,495 lire = £1 sterling). The republic is governed by two *capitani reggenti,* or coregents, appointed every six months by a popularly elected Great and General Council. Executive power rests with the Congress of State, headed by the coregents and composed of three secretaries of state and seven ministers.

In April 1994 the Great and General Council elected a schoolteacher and a state functionary as the new state leaders. Both coregents identified the family and the environment as the focal issues of 1994, the latter having been the subject of a recent treaty with Italy in which San Marino, landlocked though it was, expressed its commitment to share in the effort to protect the Adriatic Sea.

Earlier in the year Gabriele Gatti, the state secretary for foreign and political affairs, met with the Italian foreign minister to perfect legislative agreements intended to harmonize banking and financial procedures between the two countries while guarding against tax evasion and the illegal recycling of funds. Gatti also met in Brussels with the European Union (EU) commissioner for external economic affairs, Sir Leon Brittan, whose reassurances concerning trade between EU countries and San Marino induced Gatti to define the future economic prospects for the tiny republic as truly optimistic.

In 1994 San Marino received the credentials of a Russian ambassador for the first time. It also engaged in activities to aid people in former Yugoslavia through the agency of the national Red Cross. Further evidence of San Marino's commitment to world harmony was provided when one of its representatives traveled to Israel to participate with various European statesmen in discussions on the Arab-Israeli peace process. (GREGORY O. SMITH)

This article updates the *Micropædia* article SAN MARINO.

SÃO TOMÉ AND PRÍNCIPE

The republic of São Tomé and Príncipe comprises two main islands and several smaller islets that straddle the Equator in the Gulf of Guinea, off the west coast of Africa. Area: 1,001 sq km (386 sq mi). Pop. (1994 est.): 128,000. Cap.: São Tomé. Monetary unit: dobra, with (Oct. 7, 1994) a free rate of 811.68 dobras to U.S. $1 (1,291 dobras = £1 sterling). President in 1994, Miguel Trovoada; prime ministers, Norberto José d'Alva Costa Alegre until July 2, Evaristo Carvalho from July 7, and, from October 25, Carlos da Graça.

In July Pres. Miguel Trovoada dismissed the prime minister, Norberto Costa Alegre, and replaced him with Evaristo Carvalho. This caused the ruling Party of Democratic Convergence (PCD) to call for the president's resignation, for it was unhappy with Carvalho's appointment even though he was a member of the party. The crisis between Trovoada and the PCD led the former to dissolve the National Assembly on July 10 and to set a date for general elections on October 2.

In the elections the Movement for the Liberation of São Tomé and Príncipe–Social Democratic Party (MLSTP-PSD) won 27 seats in the 55-member National Assembly. The formerly Marxist party, which had at one time been the only legal party, thus came to power some three years after having been defeated in the country's first multiparty elections, in 1991. The PCD and Independent Democratic Action each took 14 seats. President Trovoada appointed Carlos da Graça, head of MLSTP–PSD, as prime minister.

In April 1994 the National Assembly began to examine draft legislation that would confer autonomy on the island of Príncipe, which lies about 150 km (90 mi) from the main São Tomé archipelago. The bill provided for the establishment of a regional assembly and a five-member government under a minister, who would be appointed by the president of the republic. In addition, Príncipe would be empowered to establish "bonds of cooperation" with nearby foreign powers.

The Supreme Court legalized two new political parties during the year: the Independent Democratic Action party, which was led by Gabriel Costa (an adviser to President Trovoada), and the People's Alliance. The National Assembly adopted a law that reinforced the rights of the parliamentary opposition; the government and president must consult all opposition parties on major political issues, including the budget, defense, the organization of elections, and foreign policy. The opposition was also to take part in controlling state media.   (GUY ARNOLD)

This article updates the *Macropædia* article CENTRAL AFRICA: *São Tomé and Príncipe*.

SAUDI ARABIA

The kingdom of Saudi Arabia occupies four-fifths of the Arabian Peninsula, with coastlines on the Red Sea and the Persian Gulf. Area: 2,240,000 sq km (865,000 sq mi). Pop. (1994 est.): 17,947,000. Cap.: Riyadh. Monetary unit: Saudi Arabian riyal, with (Oct. 7, 1994) an official rate of 3.75 riyals to U.S. $1 (5.97 riyals = £1 sterling). King and prime minister in 1994, Fahd.

Civil rights, religious issues, and demands for political and economic reform were dominant themes in Saudi Arabia in 1994 as the government faced an organized dissident movement for the first time since the seizure of the Grand Mosque in Mecca by young Muslim fundamentalists in 1979.

The Committee for the Defense of Legitimate Rights (CDLR), a broad coalition of Sunni Muslim academics and religious leaders opposed to the as-Sa'ud regime, moved its headquarters from Riyadh to London in April. Earlier in April Saudi special branch officers had arrested five teachers and clerics in the northern town of Ha'il and detained leading dissident Anwar Muhammad al-Masa'ari, son of the CDLR's leading spokesman, Muhammad ibn al-Masa'ari.

In September, during a much wider crackdown on dissidents, police arrested 157 men on charges of undermining security, although 130 were subsequently released. The fate of the remaining 27 detainees was not immediately clear. At the time of the arrests, Interior Ministry spokesmen said only 110 individuals had been detained.

Saudi Arabia also faced criticism from international human rights groups over the fate of 22,000 Iraqi refugees living at the Rafha camp in northern Saudi Arabia. The London-based human rights organization Amnesty International accused the Saudi authorities of gross mistreatment of the refugees. The Saudi embassy in London claimed that the United Nations High Commissioner for Refugees in Saudi Arabia had praised the Saudi government for its humane treatment of the Iraqi refugees, who fled their own country during the Gulf war. At the end of January, however, the International Committee of the Red Cross closed its Riyadh office in protest against the Saudi refusal to redesignate the Iraqi refugees as detainees.

While willing to embrace political and economic reform, King Fahd was keen to appease the religious right wing by announcing on March 10 a decree banning the use, manufacture, and importation of television satellite dishes. Some 150,000 satellite dishes were erected by private Saudi citizens during the Gulf war to satisfy their hunger for uncensored news and entertainment. The Ministry of Information declared that the Saudi authorities planned to install their own cable television network throughout the kingdom.

The first ordinary session of the all-male *majlis ash-shura* (Consultative Council) opened on January 22, following a formal address by the monarch some three weeks earlier in which King Fahd referred to the need for a "new framework" of consultation between the government and Saudi citizens. The assembly established committees covering Muslim affairs, foreign affairs, security, finance, society and health, culture and information services, and general utilities and administration. Meetings of the assembly and its committee were to take place behind closed doors, with no public access to the proceedings.

On May 9 King Fahd expressed concern at the low price of oil, which he said was damaging to both producers and consumers alike. He promised a privatization program to sell state assets to the public, which observers took to imply a commitment to sell shares in state utilities, such as the national airline and the telephone system. Despite official concern at the weak price of oil, Petroleum and Mineral Resources Minister Hisham Nazer said in November that there were no plans to expand oil-production capacity beyond its current 10 million bbl a day.

Ministers unveiled details of the sixth five-year plan (due to come into effect Jan. 1, 1995), which placed emphasis on the need for self-defense and an assertion of national consciousness, as well as for economic measures to privatize key industries, create jobs, and improve infrastructure. France and Saudi Arabia, meeting in Casablanca, Morocco, on November 19, signed an agreement for the supply of air-defense frigates and shore bases valued at $3.7 billion.

Relations with Iran were soured by bitter diplomatic exchanges over the hajj (pilgrimage). The Saudi government not only sought to limit the number of Iranian pilgrims to 60,000 instead of the 115,000 allowed in recent years but also tried to ban the Iranian contingent from staging an anti-American and anti-Israeli rally under the pretext of a "deliverance-from-infidels" ritual. When the rally took place, on May 23, some 270 were killed in a stampede. The Saudi Health Ministry said that overall 829 people died from natural causes during the hajj. Among the Muslim leaders taking part in the hajj in 1994 were Pakistan's Prime Minister Benazir Bhutto and Bosnia and Herzegovina's Pres. Alija Izetbegovic.

In foreign affairs Saudi Arabia showed strong support for the Middle East peace process and endorsed the May 4 agreement on Palestinian self-rule, describing it as a "practical step on the road to an overall settlement." Although still cool toward the Palestine Liberation Organization (PLO), the Saudi government expressed its willingness to support economic reconstruction in Jericho and the Gaza Strip, but only through the auspices of multilateral aid organizations. No subsidies were to be paid to the PLO. The Saudi government also welcomed the bilateral agreement between Israel and Jordan on October 26, although King Fahd declined to meet King Hussein of Jordan earlier in the year when he visited the holy places to perform *umra* (the minor pilgrimage).

In a move that suggested continuing border problems between Saudi Arabia and Qatar, the Doha authorities on November 26 boycotted a meeting in Riyadh of interior ministers from the Gulf states. The Saudi authorities denied Qatari claims that several border incidents had occurred, but persistent reports appeared to confirm that the diplomatic agreement of December 1992 had not ended conflict between the two states. (JOHN WHELAN)

This article updates the *Macropædia* article ARABIA: *Saudi Arabia.*

SENEGAL

The republic of Senegal is located in West Africa, on the Atlantic Ocean; it surrounds the country of The Gambia. Area: 196,712 sq km (75,951 sq mi). Pop. (1994 est.): 8,112,000. Cap.: Dakar. Monetary unit: CFA franc, with (Oct. 7, 1994) a par value of CFAF 100 to the French franc and a free rate of CFAF 526.67 to U.S. $1 (CFAF 837.67 = £1 sterling). President in 1994, Abdou Diouf; prime minister, Habib Thiam.

Senegal's reputation for tolerance and democracy was badly shaken during 1994. Violence on an unprecedented scale broke out on February 16 during a protest rally organized by the opposition coalition Coordination of Democratic Forces, in conjunction with various other groups. Speakers condemned the government both for its attempts to stifle dissent and for its failure to alleviate hardships caused by the January devaluation of the CFA franc. Militant demonstrators attacked security forces. Six police officers were killed, and dozens of people were injured.

Members of the opposition charged the government with provoking the violence. During the next week 179 persons, including opposition leaders Abdoulaye Wade and Landing Savané, were arrested for inciting the riot. Most were released on July 4. In September the courts found Wade and Savané innocent of involvement in the February riots. The government's handling of the situation brought condemnation from human rights organizations, the European Parliament, and the U.S. Congress.

Diplomatic relations with Iran were suspended in May, reflecting the government's anger at reports that Islamic fundamentalists were being funded by that country. Weeks of peaceful protests over proposed reforms in the university system ended when approximately 100 students rioted on June 6. (NANCY ELLEN LAWLER)

This article updates the *Macropædia* article WESTERN AFRICA: *Senegal.*

SEYCHELLES

A republic and member of the Commonwealth, the Seychelles consists of about 100 islands widely scattered over the western Indian Ocean. The main island of Mahé is 1,800 km (1,100 mi) from the east coast of the African continent. Area: 455 sq km (176 sq mi). Pop. (1994 est.): 71,800. Cap.: Victoria. Monetary unit: Seychelles rupee, with (Oct. 7, 1994) a free rate of SR 4.93 to U.S. $1 (SR 7.85 = £1 sterling). President in 1994, France-Albert René.

Following his landslide victory in the elections held in July 1993, Pres. France-Albert René and the Seychelles People's Progressive Front (FPPS) were able to concentrate on problems that were related to development. Of increasing importance to Seychelles was its membership in the Indian Ocean Commission, to which Comoros, Madagascar, and Mauritius also belonged. The commission received substantial aid from the European Union for its various regional activities. Among other things, it was responsible for coastal surveys and for protecting plant life and maintaining biodiversity.

In addition, the commission had a regional program to develop tourism, which included training programs, sales, promotion and marketing, and backup operations to assist the transfer of management know-how. Finally, there was an Indian Ocean program for automatization of telecommunications.

Tourism remained the largest source of income for Seychelles, with the annual number of visitors exceeding the total population. In 1993 receipts from tourism amounted to $118 million, but the number of visitors was down in 1994. Petroleum products (processed in the country's oil refinery) earned 53% of the country's foreign exchange and canned tuna an additional 30%.

Seychelles had a per capita gross national product (GNP) of $5,480, which placed it in the World Bank's upper-middle-income bracket. Its international debt of $154 million was approximately 40% of GNP. Other indicators of progress were an average life expectancy of 70 years, access to safe water for 99% of the population, and a daily caloric intake that satisfied all recommended requirements.

(GUY ARNOLD)

This article updates the *Micropædia* article SEYCHELLES.

SIERRA LEONE

A republic of West Africa and member of the Commonwealth, Sierra Leone lies on the Atlantic Ocean. Area: 71,740 sq km (27,699 sq mi). Pop. (1994 est.): 4,616,000. Cap.: Freetown. Monetary unit: leone, with (Oct. 7, 1994) a free rate of 585.55 leones to U.S. $1 (931.32 leones = £1 sterling). Chairman of the Supreme Council of State in 1994, Capt. Valentine E.M. Strasser; vice chairman (and head of government), Lieut. Julius Maada Bio.

In January 1994 the government claimed a series of successes against the Revolutionary United Front (RUF), the rebel movement that had been mounting attacks from bases in Liberia since 1991. Government forces recaptured rebel-held centres near Pujehun in southern Sierra Leone on January 11. Later in the month, however, it was reported that 100 civilians had been killed when the RUF razed several villages near Bo. On June 30 a rebel attack on the village of Telu led to the deaths of 58 civilians and 2 soldiers. The government launched a series of attacks on RUF positions near the diamond-mining centre of Kenema in August. In November the government called for a negotiated end to the fighting.

In December 1993 the government announced a schedule for the return to democracy and civilian rule, to take place by the end of 1995. The process was to begin with the creation of a National Electoral Commission that would oversee the registration of voters and defining of electoral boundaries. Work on a new constitution began in June 1994, and the finished document was to be put to a public referendum in May 1995. Presidential elections were to be held in November 1995 and general elections in December. In July Sierra Leone took part with Guinea and Liberia in talks on reactivating the largely defunct Mano River Union. The secretary-general of the Commonwealth, Chief Emeka Anyaoku, visited Sierra Leone during the year to discuss development problems and democracy.

Four Asian men from Britain were released in November as their trial on charges of treason began in Freetown. Accused of plotting to overthrow the government, the men had been held for more than a year. There were many baffling questions about the men and their activities, none of which was answered. (GUY ARNOLD)

This article updates the *Macropædia* article WESTERN AFRICA: *Sierra Leone.*

SPOTLIGHT: Asian Values by Berton Woodward

Is there such a thing as "Asian values"? If so, are they superior to Western values? For some time, Southeast Asian leaders, notably Lee Kuan Yew of Singapore and Malaysian Prime Minister Datuk Seri Mahathir bin Mohamad, had been highly critical of what they saw as a general moral and economic decline in the West. But as these and other Asian societies became more and more successful, more people in both Asia and the West seemed prepared to listen to what they had to say.

The case of American teenager Michael Fay, who was given four strokes of a rattan cane and imprisoned for nearly four months for spray painting cars in Singapore, was not the ideal focal point for an issue of such depth. Nonetheless, it served to spotlight many of the issues that were already being debated in Asia and the West. A Singaporean government spokesman remarked that tough laws had kept his nation relatively crime-free: "We don't have a situation where acts of vandalism are commonplace as in cities like New York." The Singaporean embassy in Washington, D.C., reported receiving strong support from Americans for its government's position in the Fay case.

To Singaporeans the issue hinged largely on their belief that their approach was creating a society that was better than those in the West, particularly in the U.S. In *Foreign Affairs* Samuel P. Huntington of Harvard University had published his essay "The Clash of Civilizations?" which suggested that in the post-Cold War world other cultures—notably those influenced by Islam and Confucianism—would challenge the West. Kishore Mahbubani, who later became permanent secretary of Singapore's Foreign Ministry, referred to "a fatal flaw that has recently developed in the Western mind: an inability to conceive that the West may have developed structural weaknesses in its core value systems and institutions."

To Mahbubani this explained "the recent rush to embrace the assumption that history has ended with the triumph of the Western ideal: individual freedom and democracy would always guarantee that Western civilization would stay ahead of the pack. Only hubris can explain why so many Western societies are trying to defy the economic laws of gravity." He pointed to a lack of budgetary discipline, low savings rates, an eroding work ethic, and uncompetitively high wages. He listed the soaring incidence of violent crime in the U.S., single-mother births, divorce rates, and children living in single-parent homes. He further remarked that "instead of traveling overseas with humility, Americans confidently preach the virtues of unfettered individual freedom, blithely ignoring the visible social consequences."

What then are Asian values? Commonly, they are considered to include strong family values, respect for authority, consensus in decision making, and supremacy of the community over the individual. In an article in the Paris-based *International Herald Tribune,* Singapore ambassador-at-large Tommy Koh listed 10 values he felt East Asia represented. Topping the list was the point that East Asians do not believe in the extreme form of individualism practiced in the West. Whatever they do or say, they must keep in mind the interests of others. He also mentioned a belief in strong families, education, saving and frugality, hard work, and national teamwork through labour-management cooperation. He pointed to a "social contract" between citizens and the state in which the government guarantees basic needs and law and order in exchange for respect for authority and self-reliance without welfarism. He also listed the promotion of private ownership, a morally wholesome environment, and a responsible press.

Although Koh's list reflected his Singaporean background, others in Malaysia, Indonesia, Thailand, and the Philippines have also articulated Asian alternatives to Western values. The Commission for a New Asia, a group of 18 respected thinkers from across the region, produced its first report in 1994, a vision of Asia in 2020. It called for a broad range of human and political rights but also noted that personal rights in most instances were relative, not absolute. It upheld democracy as by far the best form of government for all societies, but it also endorsed a strong and stable government that did not "sacrifice the public interest on the altar of reelection" and was not preoccupied with short-term considerations or vested interests. The group also saw virtue in consensual democracy. In all Asian societies, on many key issues, majoritarian democracy—decision making on the basis of the will of a simple majority—was viewed as clearly inadequate. On seriously divisive issues, the Asian emphasis on consensus building was, they believed, "clearly a superior form of democracy." As for the mass media, the group said that "the first duty of a free press in a productive democracy was to be responsible—and to be responsible to society."

Some analysts have defined Asian values as essentially Confucian. Singapore, for one, makes constant reference to the teachings of Confucius. But support for the concept of Asian values comes from cultures as disparate as those in predominately Hindu India and Islamic Malaysia and Indonesia. Anwar Ibrahim, Malaysia's deputy prime minister, pointed to harmony in society through good governance, the sanctity of the family, tolerance toward diversity, and compassion for the weak and unfortunate. Asians, he said, are "convinced of the efficacy of our ways because our cultures have survived largely intact for millennia." He also cautioned that Asia should not preach about its economic success without tackling such outstanding social problems as poverty.

One Western reaction to the concept of Asian values was expressed by Chris Patten, the British governor of Hong Kong: "Some Asian leaders and journalists define Asian values as a serene quartet—hard work, strong families, home ownership and morality. I happen to believe in all that myself." Others suggested that the values merely represented the Protestant work ethic in a new guise. The central point of departure, however, was the role of the individual in society. Whether or not the West suffered from excessive individual freedom and insufficient respect for authority, the Asian view puts the priority on the good of the group over that of a given individual. In this sense Asian values differ from the Western tradition and especially from America's Jeffersonian view.

Asian leaders continued to worry, however, that the pressures of affluence could lead to a more self-centred way of life. "Popular culture, TV, rock music, the buy-now-pay-later advertisements, conspicuous consumption, the desire for more material goods, all combine to erode the traditional virtues of hard work, thrift, personal responsibility and family togetherness," said Singapore's Prime Minister Goh Chok Tong in a National Day Rally speech. If these were lost, he said, "we will lose our vibrancy, and decline. This is the intangible factor in the success of East Asian economies." Indeed, maintaining what they see as a special cultural edge will be the challenge for these countries as they become ever wealthier.

Berton Woodward is assistant managing editor of *Asiaweek* magazine and is based in Hong Kong.

SINGAPORE

Singapore, a republic of Southeast Asia and member of the Commonwealth, consists of the island of Singapore and 58 nearby islets, at the southern extremity of the Malay Peninsula. Area: 641 sq km (247 sq mi). Pop. (1994 est.): 2,933,000. Monetary unit: Singapore dollar, with (Oct. 7, 1994) a free rate of S$1.48 to U.S. $1 (S$2.36 = £1 sterling). President in 1994, Ong Teng Cheong; prime minister, Goh Chok Tong.

Singapore became the centre of worldwide attention in 1994 as a result of the court ordered caning of American teenager Michael Fay. In October 1993 Fay and five other resident expatriate teenagers had been charged with vandalism. Fay initially faced 53 counts, mainly spray painting and otherwise damaging 18 vehicles over a 10-day period. Fay pleaded guilty to two counts of vandalism, two counts of mischief, and one count of possessing stolen property. In March 1994 he was sentenced to four months in jail and six strokes of a rattan cane and fined U.S. $2,200. The sentence provoked heated discussion in the United States, and Pres. Bill Clinton called the punishment "extreme" and asked Singapore to waive the caning. Singapore authorities responded that tough laws kept the nation relatively crime-free and that foreigners and Singaporeans should be treated equally under the law.

On May 5, following a recommendation of the Cabinet, Fay was subjected to only four strokes of the cane. A Hong Kong youth arrested with Fay received 6 rather than 12 strokes and had his prison time reduced from eight to six months.

AFP

U.S. teenager Michael Fay arrives at court in Singapore to appeal his sentence for vandalism, which included six strokes with a cane. Although the court rejected Fay's appeal, government officials later reduced the number of strokes to four.

Prime Minister Goh Chok Tong maintained Singapore's assertive approach to social issues in his National Day Rally speech in August, announcing that unwed mothers would no longer qualify for government-subsidized housing and that women civil servants would not gain medical benefits for their families. The latter decision, Goh said, upheld the principle that the husband was the "primary provider" according to his "pro-family" policies.

In September, over protests from The Hague, Dutch engineer Johannes van Damme was hanged for trafficking in heroin. He was the first Westerner executed under a law mandating death for persons dealing in illegal drugs. In March in another high-profile court case, a civil servant, two economists, and two journalists were convicted and fined for violating the Official Secrets Act. The crime involved the publication of quarterly economic growth estimates in the *Business Times* newspaper in 1992 before their official release. Singapore's gross domestic product continued to grow at an annual rate of about 9%. The Singapore dollar strengthened by more than 6% against the U.S. dollar. In April the government introduced a 3% tax on goods and services.   (BERTON WOODWARD)

This article updates the *Macropædia* article SOUTHEAST ASIA: *Singapore*.

SLOVAKIA

Slovakia is a landlocked state in central Europe. Area: 49,035 sq km (18,933 sq mi). Pop. (1994 est.): 5,352,000. Cap.: Bratislava. Monetary unit: Slovak koruna, with (Oct. 7, 1994) a free rate of 31.19 koruny to U.S. $1 (49.61 koruny = £1 sterling). President in 1994, Michal Kovac; prime ministers, Vladimir Meciar until March 11, Jozef Moravcik from March 16, and, from December 13, Meciar.

The stresses of implementing the democratic political system adopted by Slovakia on independence became acute in 1994. Throughout 1993 there had been unease about Prime Minister Vladimir Meciar's autocratic style of government, and this continued into 1994. Meciar persistently intervened in political and economic processes supposedly governed by law and was seen as undermining democracy.

Pres. Michal Kovac and others were concerned about Meciar's sometimes erratic policies, especially the slowing down of privatization and the international isolation toward which the policies seemed to be leading. Finally in March, exploiting a split in the party dominating the coalition, the Movement for a Democratic Slovakia (MDS), a parliamentary vote went against the prime minister, and Meciar had to resign.

Led by Jozef Moravcik, the new coalition that took over was shaky and unwieldy. It consisted of Christian Democrats, the Centre Union (refugees from Meciar's MDS), and the former communists, the Democratic Left. The main difficulty with the coalition was that it was united on only two broad strategic objectives—to keep Meciar out of power and to accept the general principles of European democracy. In practice this was too narrow a base for a long-term government, not least because there were major differences within the coalition that influenced its attitudes on such issues as the role of the state against the role of the market and the level of public spending.

General elections were held on September 30–October 1 and produced an unexpected and, from the Moravcik coalition's point of view, unwelcome result. Although the polls had forecast that Meciar's MDS would gain somewhere between 25% and 30% of the vote, in reality it polled nearly 35%. The Slovak National Party gained 5% and, rather surprisingly, the left-wing Association of Slovak Workers won

7%. All the coalition parties fared badly, with the Democratic Left suffering a serious loss. The Hungarian minority parties formed a coalition and emerged as the third largest party in the legislature.

After trying unsuccessfully to attract dissident deputies from other parties, Meciar accepted that he would have to govern with a simple majority. He immediately moved to reverse the privatization policies launched by his predecessor and reemphasized nationalism, much to the dismay of the Hungarian minority. (GEORGE SCHÖPFLIN)

This article updates the *Macropædia* article CZECH AND SLOVAK REPUBLICS: *Slovakia*.

SLOVENIA

A republic of the extreme northwestern Balkans, Slovenia borders Austria to the north, Hungary to the east, Croatia to the southeast and south, the Adriatic Sea to the southwest, and Italy to the west. Area: 20,256 sq km (7,821 sq mi). Pop. (1994 est.): 2,001,000. Cap.: Ljubljana. Monetary unit: tolar, with (Oct. 7, 1994) a free rate of 121.82 tolarji to U.S. $1 (193.75 tolarji = £1 sterling). President in 1994, Milan Kucan; prime minister, Janez Drnovsek.

Slovenia continued its economic and political advance on a broad front while maintaining its drive for membership in all important world institutions. On September 29 it became a full member of the General Agreement on Tariffs and Trade, which on Jan. 1, 1995, would be replaced by the World Trade Organization. Also in September, Slovenia's prime minister, Janez Drnovsek, was elected one of the

The large casino at Nova Gorica draws many of its customers from neighbouring Italy. Italians and Austrians are also able to buy cigarettes and alcohol duty-free across the border in Slovenia. The country's aggressive, freewheeling economy was one of the fastest-growing in all of Europe.

vice presidents of the Liberal International at its meeting in Reykjavík, Iceland. Slovenia's main goal of joining the European Union (EU), however, came no closer to being realized in 1994.

Italy obstructed Slovenia's attempt to obtain the EU's associate membership, demanding that Slovenia make concessions regarding the property of 160,000 former Italian citizens who left or were expelled from Slovenia after 1945. According to official Italian calculations, nearly 7,000 ha (17,300 ac) of land, 300 building plots, 21 companies, and 7,172 buildings belonging to Italians were nationalized between 1945 and 1972 by the Slovene authorities. An attempt to negotiate a compromise made by Slovenia's foreign minister, Lojze Peterle, and his Italian counterpart, Antonio Martino, in Aquilea, Italy, in October went awry when the government in Ljubljana repudiated its own foreign minister. Peterle, a Christian Democrat whose party was a coalition partner of the prime minister's Liberal Party, resigned. He had not been replaced by the end of 1994, and his ministry was temporarily taken over by the prime minister himself.

Relations with Croatia deteriorated during 1994. No solution was found in disputes over territorial rights in the Bay of Piran and sovereignty over certain inland villages. On October 3 the lower house of the Slovene National Assembly approved the assigning of disputed territory to a Slovene municipality. There was also no resolution of the dispute over savings deposited by Croats with the biggest Slovene bank, Ljubljanska Banka, before the breakup of former Yugoslavia.

Local elections held in December showed a swing toward the Christian Democrats, but that party maintained its coalition with the Liberals. In the first nine months of 1994, Slovenia reported a $250.5 million trade deficit. Its exports in that period increased by 8.1%, and imports grew by the same amount. About 60% of Slovene exports went to EU countries, and 5.7% of its imports came from there. Annual inflation was 19.9%. Privatization was slow, with 26,000 firms accounting for 77% of total output still in the public sector at the end of 1994. (K.F. CVIIC)

This article updates the *Macropædia* article BALKAN STATES: *Slovenia*.

SOLOMON ISLANDS

A constitutional monarchy and member of the Commonwealth, the Solomon Islands comprises a 1,450-km (900-mi) chain of islands and atolls in the western Pacific Ocean. Area: 28,370 sq km (10,954 sq mi). Pop. (1994 est.): 368,000. Cap.: Honiara. Monetary unit: Solomon Islands dollar, with (Oct. 7, 1994) a free rate of SI$3.27 to U.S. $1 (SI$5.20 = £1 sterling). Queen, Elizabeth II; governors-general in 1994, Sir George Lepping and, from June, Moses Pitakaka; prime ministers, Francis Billy Hilly until October 31 and, from November 7, Solomon Mamaloni.

The continuing rivalry between Prime Minister Francis Billy Hilly and his predecessor, Solomon Mamaloni, and their respective coalition parties dominated politics in 1994. Hilly's government survived a short budgetary session of Parliament in January but then remained in office without facing Parliament for several months. In October there was a constitutional crisis when the governor-general ruled that Hilly no longer had a parliamentary majority and tried to swear in Mamaloni as interim prime minister. The High Court held that only Parliament could decide the issue and gave Hilly until October 31 to resign. Hilly stepped down on October 31, and a week later Mamaloni was elected prime minister.

Despite the political turmoil, the government took steps to attack the country's economic problems with increases in indirect taxes and other measures to reduce inflation. Faced with the logging of its hardwood forests at twice the sustainable level, the government announced that the export of round logs would be banned beginning in 1997. Receipts from log exports had risen from SI$49 million in 1991 to SI$222 million in 1993, representing half of all export earnings. A moratorium was placed on the issue of new export licenses. With support from Japanese aid and joint ventures, steps were taken to expand local participation in the fishing industry. (BARRIE MACDONALD)

This article updates the *Macropædia* article PACIFIC ISLANDS: *Solomon Islands*.

SOMALIA

Situated in the Horn of northeastern Africa, Somalia lies on the Gulf of Aden and the Indian Ocean. Area: 637,000 sq km (246,000 sq mi). Pop. (1994 est.): 6,667,000 (excluding Somali refugees in neighbouring countries estimated to number about 600,000). Cap.: Mogadishu. Monetary unit: Somali shilling, with (Oct. 7, 1994) a free rate of 2,622 Somali shillings to U.S. $1 (4,171 Somali shillings = £1 sterling). Somalia had no functioning government in 1994.

In southern Somalia during 1994, a renewal of violence accompanied the phased withdrawal of UN troops. The principal contenders for power were two groupings of clan factions: Gen. Muhammad Farah Aydid at the head of the Somali National Alliance (SNA) and Ali Mahdi Muhammad with his "group of 12." In the northeast region, conditions were more stable, and the breakaway "Republic of Somaliland" in the northwest appeared successful in establishing order until violence broke out at the end of the year. In all parts of the country, the principal problem remained the disarmament of the militias and armed gangs that had controlled the nation since the ouster of Pres. Muhammad Siad Barre in 1991.

On February 4 the UN mandate in Somalia was revised by the Security Council. The UN was committed to promoting the establishment of the political process, but the military involvement of the UN Operation in Somalia (UNOSOM II) was to be reduced to the role of ensuring the security of communications and transportation. When the contingents of the U.S. and most of the European Union countries left Somalia on March 25, UNOSOM was reduced from a high of about 29,000 to about 19,000. The remaining troops were mostly from African countries and the Indian subcontinent.

Efforts to negotiate a peace agreement continued. On March 24 in Nairobi, Kenya, the principal opponents, Aydid and Ali Mahdi, pledged to form a government of national reconciliation. Neither this nor other local peace initiatives had any lasting effect, however. In May fighting broke out in Mogadishu when Aydid's forces captured the airport from the Hawadle clan. The southern port of Kismaayo was once again disputed between Aydid's ally Ahmad Omar Jess and his Ogaden clansmen and the militia of Muhammad "Morgan," the son-in-law of Barre. The conflict was sparked by an attempt by Aydid to ban the militia's lucrative export trade in scrap metal; this also fueled rebellion within his own SNA alliance. Although the UN force avoided intervention, 15 of its soldiers were killed in four incidents, as were several journalists.

In the northwest the breakaway "Republic of Somaliland" established a de facto autonomy and in the first part of the year appeared to be achieving stability, though its president, Muhammad Ibrahim Egal, did not succeed in his efforts to win international recognition for independence. Some groups in the region opposed secession, however. They were led by 'Abd ar-Rahman Ahmad Ali Tur, who in April told a press conference that the decision to secede had to be reversed. This was denounced by the breakaway government,

A U.S. medical team examines a Somalian child suspected of having cholera. Although a small UN peacekeeping force remained after the withdrawal of U.S. and most European forces in March, there was an increase in fighting between the country's warlords.
PATRICK ROBERT—SYGMA

and in October fighting broke out in the capital, Hargeysa, over the control of the airport. On December 19 fighting broke out again in Mogadishu between the forces of Aydid and those of Ali Mahdi. At least 20 persons were reported killed and more than 125 wounded, mostly civilians.

In October, as UNOSOM's mandate came up for renewal, another peace conference was held in Mogadishu. Tur and the antisecessionists from Somaliland took part; however, the conference was boycotted by the Ali Mahdi group, and by mid-November it appeared that each group was preparing to set up its own rival government. Meanwhile, the UNOSOM mandate was renewed until March 31, 1995.

(VIRGINIA R. LULING)

This article updates the *Macropædia* article EASTERN AFRICA: *Somalia*.

SOUTH AFRICA

South Africa, a member of the Commonwealth, occupies the southern tip of Africa, with the Atlantic Ocean to the west and the Indian Ocean to the east. The territory of South Africa in late 1994 excluded Walvis Bay (an exclave of Cape Province after 1910), which was jointly administered with Namibia 1992–94; it became part of Namibia on Feb. 28, 1994. South Africa included the former nominally independent, but not internationally recognized, republics of Bophuthatswana, Ciskei, Transkei, and Venda, which were reincorporated in March and April 1994. Area: 1,223,201 sq km (472,281 sq mi). Pop. (1994 est.): 41,749,000. Executive cap., Pretoria; judicial cap., Bloemfontein; legislative cap., Cape Town. Monetary unit: South African rand, with (Oct. 7, 1994) a financial rate of R 4.17 to U.S. $1 (R 6.64 = £1 sterling) and a commercial rate of R 3.57 to U.S. $1 (R 5.68 = £1 sterling). State presidents in 1994, Frederik W. de Klerk and, from May 10, Nelson Mandela.

Domestic Affairs. South Africa's first one-person one-vote election took place April 26–29, 1994. It was characterized by millions of people waiting patiently for hours in kilometre-long lines to vote for the first time in their lives. Held under rules set by a negotiated interim constitution, the election was won by the African National Congress (ANC), which gained nearly two-thirds of the vote. In a colourful and celebratory ceremony on May 10 attended by hosts of foreign dignitaries, under a new South African flag, ANC president Nelson Mandela, a political prisoner in South Africa for 27 years, was inaugurated as president of the republic and head of a government of national unity. "We pledge ourselves to liberate all our people from the continuing bondage of poverty, deprivation, suffering, gender and other discrimination," he said in his address. ANC chairman Thabo Mbeki (*see* BIOGRAPHIES) and former president F.W. de Klerk of the National Party (NP) became deputy presidents. U.S. Vice Pres. Al Gore remarked that "the nation that once was a pariah will now become a beacon of hope."

The election results were: ANC 62.7%; NP 20.4%; Inkatha Freedom Party (IFP) 10.5%; Freedom Front 2.2%; Democratic Party 1.7%; Pan Africanist Congress 1.2%; African Christian Democratic Party 0.5%. The election installed a National Assembly of 400 members and a Senate of 90 members, which would also function jointly as the body for writing a final constitution for the country. It also installed parliaments in nine regions. The ANC took office in all regions except the Western Cape, won by the NP, and KwaZulu/Natal, won by the IFP.

The postelection euphoria contrasted with the months leading up to the election. They were presided over by a Transitional Executive Council (TEC) in uneasy relationship with the NP government and were fraught with tension, ultraright sabotage, and threats of civil war and secession. A National Peacekeeping Force, which began training in January to police the election, failed dismally, being withdrawn within days of its first deployment in townships in April. It was subsequently dissolved.

The parties of the Freedom Alliance—the Afrikaner Volksfront (AVF), Chief Mangosuthu Gatsha Buthelezi's KwaZulu/Natal-based IFP, Lucas Mangope of the nominally independent Bophuthatswana, and Brig. Joshua Oupa Gqozo of the nominally independent Ciskei—had withdrawn from constitutional negotiations and declared an election boycott because of dissatisfaction with the insufficiently federal nature of the interim constitution. They threatened a nationwide passive-resistance campaign. Initial concessions made to them by the multiparty negotiating council included a double ballot paper (allowing separate national and regional votes), constitutional establishment of a *volkstaat* (people's state) council to consider possible self-determination for Afrikaners, and constitutional recognition of the name KwaZulu/Natal. These, however, did not appease the Alliance.

Events took a dramatic turn in mid-March when Mangope's government in Bophuthatswana was brought down as the result of strikes by public servants anxious about pension rights in a "new South Africa." The strikes precipitated a popular uprising joined by the Bophuthatswana police. An attempt by the white ultraright to deploy its forces in defense of the Mangope government failed, and the TEC appointed a temporary administration in the area. As many as 70 people were killed and 300 wounded in the course of these developments.

Angered by the role of the paramilitary, ultraright Afrikaner Weerstandsbeweging (AWB) in these events, Gen. Constand Viljoen split the AVF by registering a party for the elections named the Freedom Front, and he later signed an agreement with the NP and ANC on conditions for recognition of a *volkstaat*. Later in March, Gqozo, head of state in Ciskei, surrendered office to a TEC-appointed administration in the face of a police mutiny.

This left the IFP as the main party favouring a boycott (or postponement) of the election. Its opposition posed dangers of violence; during the preceding decade there had been 10,000–20,000 deaths from political violence in KwaZulu/Natal, with 2,145 deaths in 1993 alone (according to the Human Rights Commission). In speeches in January and

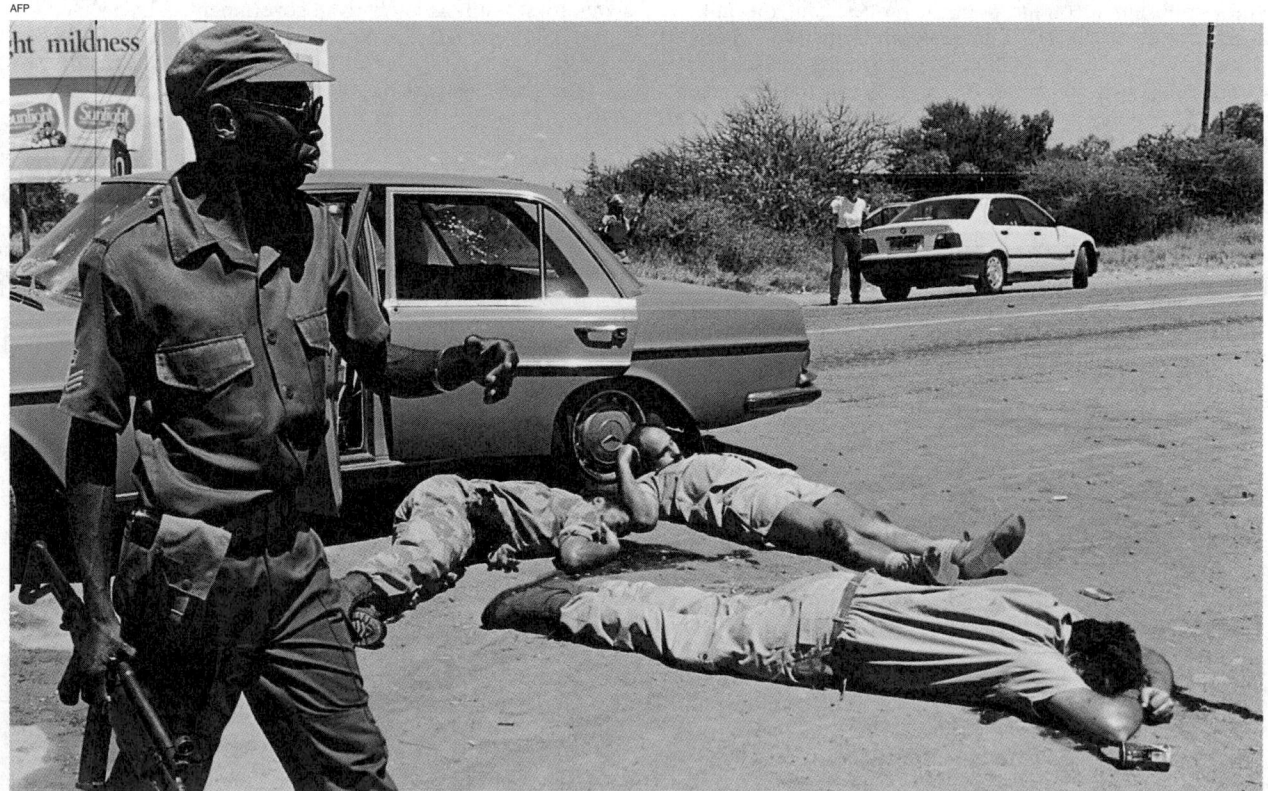

AFP

A black soldier in Bophuthatswana stands near three white neo-Nazis, two of whom had just been executed as a group of photographers looked on. Some 70 blacks and whites were killed, sometimes in racially motivated murders, during a period of government instability in March.

March, Zulu King Goodwill Zwelithini openly supported the IFP, declaring that the interim constitution was "deeply offensive" to the Zulu people, who had "never once been conquered in war." By proclaiming KwaZulu/Natal as a "sovereign entity," he appeared to threaten secession. The IFP organized "self-protection units" and occupied stadia in which the ANC was intending to hold election rallies. In a climate of increasing violence (with 311 deaths from political violence in Natal in March and 338 in April) and of demonstrations and counterdemonstrations, the ANC urged the TEC to appoint a new administration in KwaZulu/Natal to ensure free and fair elections.

On March 28 a large IFP demonstration in Johannesburg was fired on, resulting in 56 deaths and leaving some 400 people injured. A state of emergency was declared in 10 districts in the Transvaal and in KwaZulu/Natal. High-level talks in April between de Klerk, Mandela, Buthelezi, and King Zwelithini failed to resolve the matters in dispute, as did an attempt at mediation by Henry Kissinger of the U.S. and Lord Carrington of Britain. On April 19, however, a week before the election, an agreement was reached that achieved constitutional recognition of the Zulu monarchy and Zulu kingdom and promised further international mediation on any outstanding matters after the election. The IFP agreed to participate in the election, and arrangements were made for its name to be placed on stickers added to the ballots.

News emerged shortly after the election that de Klerk had also signed an act passed by the KwaZulu/Natal legislature transferring 1.2 million ha (2.9 million ac) of state-owned land to the sole trusteeship of King Zwelithini. The TEC and ANC claimed no knowledge of this transaction.

Despite a number of bombings in which 21 people were killed and 173 injured in the days leading up to it, the election, administered by the Independent Electoral Commission (IEC), took place under surprisingly peaceful conditions. On the second day of voting, police arrested 31 members of the ultra-right-wing AWB Ystergarde (Iron Guard) in connection with the bombings. There were numerous bungles, delays, and logistical failures by the IEC in the election process, and final results were not announced until a week after the final voting day. All political parties alleged widespread irregularities, particularly in KwaZulu/Natal. The result in that region, where the IFP received 50.3% and the ANC 32.2% of the vote, surprised many, as all opinion polls earlier in the year had placed the ANC ahead of the IFP. The elections were proclaimed free and fair by the IEC and the numerous international monitors, however.

The new ANC-dominated government of national unity included six Cabinet ministers from the NP and three from the IFP. Derek Keys, finance minister in the NP government, was reappointed to that post but later resigned for personal reasons and was replaced by the nonpartisan Chris Liebenberg in September. Parliament took on a less formal and more public character than under the old regime.

The ANC campaigned in the election on a Reconstruction and Development Program (RDP), pledging improved conditions for the majority—its election slogan was "a better life for all"—by providing jobs, housing, decent education, and health care. Jay Naidoo, former general secretary of the Congress of South African Trade Unions (COSATU), was appointed as minister responsible for implementing the RDP.

In his initial address to Parliament on May 24, Mandela pledged, as short-term measures, free medical care for children under six and pregnant mothers, a feeding program for primary-school children, electrification of 350,000 houses in

the next year, and the release from prison of many juveniles. Complexities of the transition delayed plans in a number of departments, but a national public works program to create 2.5 million jobs over five years was set in motion. Vigorous despite illness, Joe Slovo, Communist Party (SACP) chairman and minister of housing, launched a program to build 80,000 homes in 1994–95 and increase gradually to 300,000 a year by the end of the century. Tito Mboweni, minister of labour, promised a reform of workplace relations, including the reduction of the workweek to 40 hours.

The 1994–95 budget allocated R 2.5 billion to the RDP and added R 1.7 billion to it in September. A White Pa-

Nelson Mandela, head of the African National Congress, campaigns in Sasolburg, Orange Free State. Former political prisoner Mandela and the once-banned ANC won nearly two-thirds of the votes cast in South Africa's first one-person one-vote election, held in April.
REUTERS/BETTMANN

per produced in September repudiated nationalization as an instrument for implementing the RDP, mentioned the possible sale of state assets, and called for monetary and fiscal discipline. Mandela expressed concerns about high tax levels, the huge government debt and high level of borrowing, and sluggish investment by private companies.

In August, Archbishop Desmond Tutu of Cape Town criticized the high salaries awarded to legislators by the previous government's Melamet Commission. "They stopped the gravy train only long enough to get on. They have set a bad example," he said. Mandela called on legislators, as well as workers, to "tighten their belts."

Evidence of past government involvement in "death squad" activity continued to mount. In March the Goldstone Commission, investigating the causes of violence, accused three police generals of having sold arms to IFP members and organized violence in the hostels and on trains in what it called "a horrible network of criminal activity." The three, against their protests, were placed on compulsory leave. In June the reopened inquest into the murder of Matthew Goniwe and three others in 1985 concluded that they had been killed by security forces, but it could not name any specific persons responsible. Also in June, 17 members of the IFP were sentenced to terms of 10–18 years in prison for participating in the Boipatong massacre in 1992.

The government initiated a Truth and Reconciliation Commission to investigate political crimes by all parties between 1960 and December 1993. It would consider violations of human rights, amnesty, and reparations for and rehabilitation of victims. While the commission was widely supported, some people feared that it would reopen old wounds rather than foster reconciliation.

A wave of industrial strikes begun in July aroused anxiety and sparked some criticism. Wage increases had been delayed by the election, and workers were agitated by the slow pace of change. On two occasions Mandela called on workers to remember the five million unemployed and not to frighten away investment by their wage demands.

Integration of members of Umkhonto we Sizwe (MK; "Spear of the Nation"), the armed wing of the ANC, into the new South African National Defense Force proved difficult. In October at least 7,000 MK members went absent without leave from the defense force, complaining of racism, the slow pace of integration, and poor living conditions and demanding the presence of the president. Mandela responded by acknowledging their grievances but also calling for discipline.

Foreign Relations. Mandela's inauguration was attended by a large number of international leaders, including the Duke of Edinburgh from the U.K., Vice Pres. Gore and first lady Hillary Rodham Clinton from the U.S., PLO leader Yasir Arafat, and Cuban leader Fidel Castro. British Prime Minister John Major, French Pres. François Mitterrand, and Zimbabwean Pres. Robert Mugabe subsequently visited South Africa and addressed the National Assembly.

In October Mandela made a triumphant visit to the U.S., where he was praised by Pres. Bill Clinton and addressed the UN General Assembly. A U.S.-South Africa commission was established to promote cooperation and trade; the only other such U.S. commission was with Russia. After the election the UN Security Council lifted all remaining sanctions on South Africa, and the country was readmitted to the General Assembly after a 20-year absence. It was also readmitted to the Commonwealth (which it had left in 1961) and admitted to the Organization of African Unity (OAU) and the South African Development Community, where it declared its intention of promoting regional cooperation. Foreign Minister Alfred Nzo told the OAU that it "was a wonderful feeling to know that we are at last part of Africa." Mandela attended the OAU summit in June and was appointed second vice-chairman.

The new government resisted insistent demands to become involved in the resolution of foreign conflicts, arguing that this would detract from its priority of domestic reconstruction. It stated that its main aim was to capitalize on postelection goodwill, promote the RDP abroad, and gain foreign investment. It resisted pressure to send troops to Rwanda.

Nonetheless, Mandela persuaded Pres. Mobutu Sese Seko of Zaire to hold discussions with Pres. José Eduardo dos Santos of Angola regarding settlement of the Angolan civil war. Together with the presidents of Zimbabwe and Botswana, he was also instrumental in persuading the king of Lesotho to restore the government of Ntsu Mokhehle, which he had dismissed from office in August. Mandela visited Mozambique in July, and the two countries established a joint security commission to investigate illegal immigration and arms and drug smuggling.

White Settlement in South Africa

White settlement of South Africa began in 1652, when the Dutch East India Company established a station at Cape Town and soon introduced European settlers and black slaves. By the time Britain annexed the Cape Colony in 1814, white farmers had occupied much of the present-day Western and Eastern Cape. During the 19th century white settlement spread unevenly over much of present-day South Africa and beyond.

The 17th- and 18th-century settlers were mainly of Dutch and German origin, ancestors of the Afrikaners. In 1798 the white population was about 20,000, increasing to 43,000 by 1820. Some 5,000 British settlers were established in the Eastern Cape in 1820, and from the 1840s Natal attracted English immigrants. The discovery of diamonds in 1868 and gold shortly thereafter led to further white immigration, including miners from Australia and the United States and Jews from eastern Europe. In 1911 the white population of South Africa was 1,250,000 (to nearly 5 million blacks).

In 1899–1902 Britain defeated the South African Republic (Transvaal) and the Orange Free State in the South African (or Boer) War, paving the way for the unification of South Africa in 1910 with a constitution excluding the black majority from the vote (except in the Cape Colony, where there was a limited nonracial franchise, removed in the 1930s from blacks and in the 1950s from the mixed-race Coloureds).

In the 1930s, drawing on a legacy of enmity toward British imperialism, English-speaking capitalists, and African tribes and seeking to uplift impoverished whites, an exclusivist populist nationalism took shape among the Afrikaner majority of whites. Organized as the National Party (NP), it defeated the mildly reformist United Party government of Jan Smuts in 1948 and ruled South Africa until 1994.

The NP implemented the notorious system of racial apartheid, a rigid form of social engineering and repression of blacks that intensified the gap between white prosperity and black poverty. For this policy the NP gained increasing, though never unanimous, support among whites. Apartheid was fiercely resisted in the 1950s by the African National Congress (ANC), banned in 1960, and its allies.

Apartheid reached its peak in the early 1970s but then began to erode under its internal contradictions and challenges from below: the rise of a trade-union movement of black workers and the violent discontent of black youth.

In February 1990 Pres. F.W. de Klerk lifted the bans on the ANC and other organizations and released from jail ANC leader Nelson Mandela. The negotiations that followed established a constitution that for the first time in the country's history removed power from the white minority (now 5 million in a population of nearly 42 million) and gave a vote to all the people. The new freedoms and opportunities were welcomed by nearly all South Africans—black and white alike.

(MARTIN LEGASSICK)

The Economy. The recession that had begun in March 1989 leveled out in the first half of 1993, and recovery began in the third (8.6% growth in gross domestic product [GDP]) and fourth (6.4% growth) quarters. GDP growth in 1993 as a whole was 1.2%. (In 1992 it declined 2%.) During the first quarter of 1994, GDP fell 3.5%, but it recovered in the second quarter to grow by 1.9%, causing economists to lower their growth predictions for the year from 3% to 2–2.5%. The recovery was fueled by favourable weather and increased exports. Manufacturing and mining output, however, fell in the first two quarters of 1994.

From 1989 to the end of 1993, formal employment fell by 364,000 to 7,720,000, less than half the economically active population. Fixed investment, which began to decline in mid-1988, fell by 4% in 1993 but began to recover in the third quarter of 1993. It rose by 5.5% in the first quarter of 1994, 7% in the second quarter, and 4.5% in the year to June 1994. The new government's budget, except for R 2.5 billion raised for the RDP by cuts in department budgets, was largely a holding operation. The deficit before borrowing in 1993–94 was 6.9% of GDP and was projected at 6.6% for 1994–95.

The recovery led to a surge of capital-goods imports, leading to a deficit on the current account of the balance of payments by September of R 1 billion for the second month in a row. (In 1993 there was a surplus of R 5.9 billion on the current account.) For the first time in years, however, there was net capital inflow to compensate for the deficit (estimated at R 1 billion a month in August and September), and so foreign-exchange reserves rose. Cumulative net capital outflow since 1985 had amounted to R 58.5 billion to the end of 1993, with a net outflow of R 16.3 billion in 1993 and R 3.7 billion in the first six months of 1994.

The bank rate was increased by 1% to 13% in September. To calls for the lifting of foreign-exchange controls, the reserve bank governor, Chris Stals, responded that R 30 billion would first be required in reserves. There could be a gradual phasing out of controls on the basis of a healthy balance of payments, foreign reserves of R 15 billion, and an expansion of foreign debt to 40% of GDP.

(MARTIN LEGASSICK)

This article updates the *Macropædia* article SOUTHERN AFRICA: *South Africa*.

SPAIN

A constitutional monarchy of southwestern Europe with coastlines on the Bay of Biscay, the Atlantic Ocean, and the Mediterranean Sea, Spain shares the Iberian Peninsula with Portugal; it includes the Balearic and Canary island groups, in the Mediterranean and the Atlantic, respectively, and enclaves in northern Morocco. Area: 504,783 sq km (194,898 sq mi). Pop. (1994 est.): 39,193,000. Cap.: Madrid. Monetary unit: Spanish peseta, with (Oct. 7, 1994) a free rate of 127.62 pesetas to U.S. $1 (202.98 pesetas = £1 sterling). King, Juan Carlos I; prime minister in 1994, Felipe González Márquez.

The Socialist government of Prime Minister Felipe González Márquez survived major challenges to its economic policy and a wave of scandals in 1994. Despite widespread disenchantment, it held on to power thanks to the sustained support of the Catalan nationalist grouping Convergence and Union, which provided the minority Socialists with a working legislative majority.

Labour unions shut down much of the country in a general strike on January 27 to protest a loosening of labour laws that the Socialists described as essential to Spain's economic competitiveness. The legislature approved the reforms, which made it easier to hire, fire, and transfer workers, in several stages through June.

The first of several public figures closely linked to the Socialists came under scrutiny in April by a legislative commission investigating allegations of fraud. Mariano Rubio on April 15 denied that he had earned nearly $1 million from insider trading during his 1984–92 term as governor of the Bank of Spain and had failed to declare the earnings to tax authorities. He was subsequently jailed on those charges, along with former Madrid Stock Exchange chairman Manuel de la Concha, who ran an investment firm in which Rubio held an account.

In his April 19 state of the nation address, Prime Minister González vowed to fight corruption. He discussed allegations against Rubio and Luis Roldán, the Civil Guard chief accused of having made a fortune in kickbacks from construction contracts. Interior Minister Antoni Asunción resigned on April 30 after Roldán escaped arrest on embezzlement and tax fraud charges and fled Spain. Judge Juan Alberto Belloch was named Asunción's successor and also became minister of justice. Roldán's whereabouts remained unknown at the end of 1994.

The fall of the most prominent financier of Spain's late 1980s economic boom, Mario Conde, absorbed the attention of Spaniards in the early months of 1994 as the Bank of Spain supervised the restructuring and sale of Banco Español de Crédito (Banesto) after having removed Conde as chairman on Dec. 28, 1993. A legislative commission investigated possible wrongdoing by Conde's team in the spring. Conde was jailed on Dec. 23, 1994, on charges of fraud in the resale of Banesto subsidiaries and affiliated companies.

The arrest on October 18 of Javier de la Rosa, a man who had gained immense wealth representing Kuwaiti and other interests during the same boom period, led nearly all Spanish media and politicians to conclude that the country's "fast-buck culture" of the 1980s was finally over. De la Rosa stood accused of stealing the assets of his Grand Tibidabo real estate company. At the year's end he remained imprisoned without bond while awaiting trial.

The strongest challenge to González during his 12 years in power emerged in December as a judge reopened an inquiry into death squads that hunted down suspected Basque separatists from 1983 to 1987. González insisted that no proof would be uncovered to substantiate allegations that two Cabinet members knew that the Anti-Terrorist Liberation Groups, or GAL, had been run and funded by mid-level Interior Ministry officials. A former national security chief, Julián Sancristobal, and two other former officials were in jail at the end of the year, pending a possible trial on charges of running GAL. Opposition politicians called for González to resign and call early elections, but the government's key backers in the legislature maintained their support.

Yet another political scandal proved a challenge to the government in early November as González faced accusations that a business linked to his brother-in-law, Francisco Palomino Romero, was favoured in the awarding of public works contracts. González denied the charges.

Scandal reached into regional government as well. On November 5, two weeks after his conviction on corruption charges, the regional premier of Cantabria, Juan Hormachea, became the first head of one of Spain's 17 autonomous communities to resign from office.

The economy emerged more strongly than predicted from 1993's severe recession, with gross domestic product estimated to have risen by more than 2% for the year. Growth was fueled by a near-record tourist season and strong exports, both the result of several devaluations of the peseta in late 1993. Unemployment continued to rise slightly despite the recovery and at the year's end stood at more than

22%, the highest rate in the European Union. The government said that its labour-reform package, which included contracts designed to promote jobs for young people and the unskilled, was nevertheless meeting with success.

While private-sector firms showed improved results, labour conflict at the government-run Iberia Air Lines erupted in October as management announced plans for several thousand layoffs in order to avoid bankruptcy. The government appealed to the European Union to authorize a 130 billion-peseta bailout after unions and managements reached agreement on a restructuring plan in November.

The armed Basque separatist organization Euzkadi ta Azkatasuna (ETA) continued its campaign for independence of Spain's three Basque provinces throughout 1994, killing 12 people, mainly security force members and police. ETA's reputed number two leader, Felix Alberto López de la Calle, was arrested November 17 in southern France, which remained ETA's traditional haven despite growing cooperation between Spanish and French antiterrorism units. On December 24 Julián Sancristobal and two other former top police officials were arrested in connection with alleged involvement in Anti-Terrorist Liberation Groups in the Basque lands in the 1980s.

The Basque Nationalist Party, which had dominated the region's politics for a century, won a plurality in elections on October 23 and formed a coalition government in December with the Basque branch of the Socialist Party and a splinter Basque party, Eusko Alkartasuna. ETA's political arm, Herri Batasuna, won 11 seats in the 75-seat Basque parliament.

Algeria's civil war spilled over into Spain in the autumn with two hijackings of domestic Air Algerie flights to Algeria's nearest European neighbour. Hijackers surrendered peacefully in both incidents, in Palma de Mallorca and Alicante airports. (GARY ABRAMSON)

SRI LANKA

A republic and member of the Commonwealth, Sri Lanka occupies an island in the Indian Ocean off the southeast coast of peninsular India. Area: 65,610 sq km (25,332 sq mi). Pop. (1994 est.): 17,830,000. Legislative cap., Sri Jayawardenepura Kotte; administrative cap., Colombo. Monetary unit: Sri Lanka rupee, with (Oct. 7, 1994) a free rate of SL Rs 49.24 to U.S. $1 (SL Rs 78.32 = £1 sterling). Presidents in 1994, Dingiri Banda Wijetunga and, from November 12, Chandrika Kumaratunga; prime ministers, Ranil Wickremasinghe, Chandrika Kumaratunga from August 19, and, from November 14, Sirimavo Bandaranaike.

Sri Lanka underwent a change of government in 1994 and found reason to be optimistic that the change might foreshadow the end of a decade-old civil conflict with Tamil separatists. The fighting had already claimed some 34,000 lives.

In the August 16 general election, the People's Alliance—a coalition of nine left-leaning opposition parties headed by Chandrika Kumaratunga—won 105 of the 225 seats in Parliament. It was the first defeat in 17 years for the ruling United National Party (UNP), which captured only 94 seats. Sri Lankan law, however, did not require Pres. Dingiri Banda Wijetunga, the leader of the UNP, to step down. He was not even obliged to name a prime minister from the victorious People's Alliance. The post, however, was finally offered to Kumaratunga when outgoing Prime Minister Ranil Wickremasinghe indicated that he would oppose any effort by the UNP to form a new coalition government.

Kumaratunga quickly set to work to fulfill her pledge of unconditional negotiations with the Liberation Tigers of Tamil Eelam, a minority group of ethnic Indians who had been fighting to gain independence for the section of Sri Lanka they called their homeland. When the government partially lifted an embargo on goods entering the rebel-controlled Jaffna Peninsula in the north of the country, the insurgents released 10 policemen they had held captive for four years.

Tamil guerrillas invited Kumaratunga to Jaffna to hold peace talks, but wave after wave of violence diminished the prospects for peace. On September 9 at least 35 Tamil rebels were killed by government troops. Several weeks later 13 soldiers died in an ambush. In a retaliatory attack, the army killed 20 guerrillas. The Tamil rebels also attacked and sank the navy's largest ship, which went down with at least 22 sailors aboard. When opposition UNP leader Garnini Dissanayake was assassinated in October, peace talks were halted, but the rebels proposed a cease-fire in November, and talks resumed in late December.

During the campaign, Kumaratunga had also promised to support a free-market economy. At the same time, she planned to increase the welfare benefits of those who had not shared in the nation's growing prosperity. Sri Lanka could point to a sustained economic growth rate of between 5% and 7% in recent years. Soon after the new government assumed power, it reported that at least $700 million was missing from the national treasury. Kumaratunga, who also served as the country's finance minister, complained that so much was missing, "we cannot find the bottom of the well." The Justice Ministry also reported that it was being deluged with allegations of massive fraud, bribery, and corruption on the part of the previous regime. The treasury, moreover, had been seriously depleted by a sweeping welfare package that Wijetunga had approved two months before the parliamentary elections. His own political future would be decided by the November presidential election.

The discovery of financial irregularities forced the new government to suspend payments on all agreements signed by the previous regime, including a $72 million arms deal with Russia. The chaotic financial situation also forced Kumaratunga to postpone ratification of a $291 million deal for five Airbus Industrie A340 jetliners for Air Lanka, which was owned by the state. (DILIP GANGULY)

SUDAN, THE

A republic of North Africa, The Sudan has a coastline on the Red Sea. Area: 2,503,890 sq km (966,757 sq mi). Pop. (1994 est.): 25,699,000. Executive cap., Khartoum; legislative cap., Omdurman. Monetary units: Sudanese pound, with (Oct. 7, 1994) a free rate of Lsd 31.13 to U.S. $1 (Lsd 49.51 = £1 sterling), and (from May 1992) the Sudanese dinar (a new unit of currency circulating in parallel with the Sudanese pound at a rate of 1 dinar = Lsd 10). President of the Revolutionary Command Council for National Salvation, head of state, and prime minister in 1994, Lieut. Gen. Omar Hassan Ahmad al-Bashir.

The visit of George Carey, archbishop of Canterbury, to southern Sudan in December 1993 and January 1994 as guest of the Episcopal Church soured relations between the governments of The Sudan and the U.K., leading to the reciprocal expulsion of ambassadors. Carey had earlier canceled a visit to Khartoum, fearing that his movements there would be controlled by the Sudanese government. He did, however, meet Col. John Garang and Riak Machar, the leaders of the rival factions of the Sudan People's Liberation Army (SPLA), in Nairobi, Kenya, and shortly afterward Garang and Machar announced a cease-fire between their two groups. No progress was made, however, in negotiations between the Sudanese government and the SPLA, although a government representative was present in Nairobi.

On January 24 it was reported that the government was concentrating troops in the south, possibly with a view to cutting the relief routes from Kenya and Uganda. This conjecture was confirmed when, in early February and in spite of government denials, reliable sources stated that a large-scale operation had been launched against the rebels. Thousands of refugees from southern Sudan were soon on the move, many of them making their way into Uganda. On February 14 the UN issued an urgent appeal for humanitarian aid to meet the needs of an estimated 100,000 displaced persons.

On March 17 and again in May representatives of the government and the SPLA again assembled in Nairobi for meetings sponsored by the presidents of Kenya, Uganda, and Ethiopia and the foreign minister of Eritrea. Nothing positive resulted from these initiatives, and the plight of the homeless and starving people in southern Sudan steadily worsened while the despair of finding a peaceful solution dampened the enthusiasm of aid donors. Their disillusionment was compounded when the government declared a cease-fire in July only to find the offer rejected by the SPLA.

Two constitutional developments took place during the year. In February it was announced that the country would again be divided into 26 states instead of 9, with important new powers being given to some of the more remote districts. In April the president approved legislation to set up a presidentially appointed commission to supervise elections.

(KENNETH INGHAM)

SURINAME

The republic of Suriname is in northern South America, on the Atlantic Ocean. Area: 163,820 sq km (63,251 sq mi), not including a 17,635-sq km area disputed with Guyana. Pop. (1994 est.): 423,000. Cap.: Paramaribo. Monetary unit: Suriname guilder, with (Oct. 7, 1994) a floating rate (introduced July 11) of 183.49 guilders to U.S. $1 (291.85 guilders = £1 sterling). President in 1994, Ronald Venetiaan; prime minister, Jules Adjodhia.

On Jan. 3, 1994, a high-ranked officer of the army was arrested for suspicion of trafficking in cocaine. Two days later he was released for lack of proof. It was not the first indication of the involvement of the Suriname military with the cocaine trade. In May and June a Dutch antidrug team organized 81 house searches throughout the world in an effort to gain evidence of criminal activities by a former president of Suriname, Dési Bouterse. No action against Bouterse was initiated in Suriname because a treaty with The Netherlands had not been ratified by Suriname Pres. Ronald Venetiaan.

On March 21 rebels of unclear affiliation occupied the Afobaka Dam and threatened to destroy it. Destruction of the dam could cut off power to Paramaribo, housing half of the country's population. The occupation was generally considered a consequence of the desperately poor living conditions in the rural regions. The rebels demanded the resignation of the government, better education for the rural areas, and decentralization of power. On March 25 government troops drove the rebels from the dam.

(KLAAS J. HOEKSEMA)

SWAZILAND

Swaziland is a landlocked monarchy of southern Africa and a member of the Commonwealth. Area: 17,364 sq km (6,704 sq mi). Pop. (1994 est.): 883,000. Administrative cap., Mbabane; royal and legislative cap., Lobamba. Monetary unit: lilangeni (plural: emalangeni), at par with the South African rand, with (Oct. 7, 1994) a free rate of 3.57 emalangeni to U.S. $1 (5.68 emalangeni = £1 sterling). King, Mswati III; prime minister in 1994, Jameson Mbilini Dlamini.

Like other small countries on the periphery of South Africa, Swaziland in 1994 was reexamining its economic prospects in light of the democratic developments in its giant neighbour. In recent years Swaziland had been relatively untroubled politically and had done well economically. Yet despite the relative diversity of its economy—divided between agriculture and mining—the development indicators revealed some startling gaps. On the one hand, the nation enjoyed a per capita gross national product of $1,080, an average life expectancy of 57 years, and a daily calorie intake of 105% of requirements; on the other hand, only 30% of the people had access to safe water, and the mortality rate for live births until age five was a high 167 per 1,000.

During the 1993–94 fiscal year, Swaziland had a budget deficit for the first time since 1985. Approximately 90% of all imports came from South Africa, a rate of dependence that Swaziland sought to reduce. The nation's exports were led by sugar, which accounted for 33% of foreign exchange earnings, followed by wood and wood products.

In May Swaziland was host to a joint ministerial meeting of the European Union and African, Caribbean, and Pacific (ACP) states. Production and trade of ACP commodities were discussed. (GUY ARNOLD)

This article updates the *Macropædia* article SOUTHERN AFRICA: *Swaziland.*

SWEDEN

A constitutional monarchy of northern Europe, Sweden occupies the eastern side of the Scandinavian Peninsula, with coastlines on the North and Baltic seas and the Gulf of Bothnia. Area: 449,964 sq km (173,732 sq mi). Pop. (1994 est.): 8,773,000. Cap.: Stockholm. Monetary unit: Swedish krona, with (Oct. 7, 1994) a free rate of 7.32 kronor to U.S. $1 (11.64 kronor = £1 sterling). King, Carl XVI Gustaf; prime ministers in 1994, Carl Bildt until September 19 and, from October 7, Ingvar Carlsson.

Swedes made their most important decision since World War II when they voted to join the European Union (EU) in a referendum on Nov. 13, 1994. The move, which was due to take effect on Jan. 1, 1995, ended a long period during which Sweden deliberately distanced itself from mainstream Europe, cherishing its neutrality and championing the cause of small Third World countries.

The referendum endorsed EU entry by a margin of 52.2% to 46.9%. The political establishment and business leaders strongly advocated membership, but they faced determined opposition from left-wing groups and environmentalists. The country was also split along geographic lines, with southern urban areas broadly favouring membership while sparsely populated rural and Arctic communities opposed it.

Sweden's accession to the EU alongside its Nordic neighbour Finland would tilt the union's axis northward, countering the southern shift that took place in the 1980s when Spain, Portugal, and Greece joined. It also cleared the way for the next, eastward, phase of expansion that could bring such countries as Poland, Hungary, and the Czech Republic into the EU. Sweden was expected to be a net contributor to the EU budget. It believed that price was worth paying because of the influence it would gain in Europe's future political, economic, and military development.

The referendum result was a personal triumph for Prime Minister Ingvar Carlsson, who had led the Social Democrats back to power in September's general election after three years of rule by a centre-right coalition. The Social Democrats won 162 seats in the 349-seat Riksdag (parliament), 13 short of a majority. Carlsson decided to form a minority government rather than establish a formal coalition with left-wing or centrist parties.

The Social Democrats, who had governed Sweden for most of the past six decades, returned to power on hopes that they could achieve economic stability, substantially reduce unemployment, and preserve the welfare state. They also benefited from a reaction against some of the unpopular policies pursued by the previous government in the face of deep recession.

The Swedish economy remained weak. The good news was that the gross national product was positive for the first time since 1990, owing mainly to the success of the country's big exporters. They had an exceptional year because of the weak krona, productivity gains, and a recovery in most of their main markets. Inflation remained below 3%.

The legacy of the three recession years was a heavy one, however. The crisis manifested itself in the size of the Swedish budget deficit, which—at 13% of gross domestic product—was among the highest in the Western world, and in the rapid growth in the national debt.

The difficulties resulted in a turbulent year in the bond markets, with Swedish long-term interest rates among the highest in Europe. One leading Swedish insurer, Skandia, refused to buy any more state bonds until the government had put its finances in order.

In November the Social Democrats announced 57 billion kronor in tax increases and spending cuts in a drive to stabilize the growth of the national debt by 1998. They promised to announce a further 20 billion kronor package of measures in January 1995. Business leaders said that too much emphasis was being placed on tax increases, which could endanger the country's long-term competitiveness. The financial stock market remained convinced that tougher measures would have to be taken to prune the country's lavish cradle-to-grave welfare state.

Unemployment remained a serious problem for Sweden in 1994, although economic recovery brought the first indications that the problem was easing. Unemployment was about 13% of the workforce, including those in training

programs. The new government was particularly eager to reduce the number of long-term and young unemployed to prevent the problem from becoming entrenched at a permanently high level.   (CHRISTOPHER BROWN-HUMES)

SWITZERLAND

A landlocked federal state in west central Europe, Switzerland consists of a confederation of 26 cantons (6 of which are demi-cantons). Area: 41,284 sq km (15,940 sq mi). Pop. (1994 est.): 6,991,000. Administrative cap., Bern; judicial cap., Lausanne. Monetary unit: Swiss franc, with (Oct. 7, 1994) a free rate of Sw F 1.28 to U.S. $1 (Sw F 2.03 = £1 sterling). President in 1994, Otto Stich.

With political maneuvering for the next general elections—scheduled for Oct. 22, 1995—already apparent by late 1994, the year was a troubling one for those Swiss feeling themselves faced with fateful decisions. Judging by frequent opinion polls, views on the burning question of the country's relationship with the European Union (EU) remained about as evenly divided between for and against membership as in the Dec. 6, 1992, referendum. On that occasion the government's plans for entry into the European Economic Area—a stepping-stone to full Union membership—were blocked by the slimmest of margins, a mere 0.3% of the votes.

While bilateral discussions, started early in 1994, with the European Commission in Brussels on such issues as road transport regulations were unsatisfactory, the year closed with more hopeful prospects in a new round of negotiations whereby Switzerland could avoid increased political and economic isolation. As in previous negotiations, an evident stumbling block was the EU proviso on free movement of people to work anywhere in member nations, a concept on which the Swiss were markedly unenthusiastic.

Economic recession and industrial streamlining had increased the number of unemployed workers to just under 150,000, despite the return to their own countries of many

A chalet belonging to the religious cult Order of the Solar Temple burns in a mountainous resort area of southwestern Switzerland. Other homes nearby, as well as two in Canada, also burned, and investigators found the bodies of 53 cult members in all, including leader Luc Jouret.

thousands of foreign workers whose jobs also were lost. Swiss companies that moved some of their facilities to regions that had lower labour costs included the national airline, Swissair. It announced major savings by shifting its accounting department to Bombay, where it employed 250 Indians who were paid at less than a tenth of the Swiss rate.

It seemed for a time that the country might be retreating farther inside its neutralist shell when a June 12 national referendum rejected proposals for a 600-strong volunteer force to help in United Nations peacekeeping operations and for making it easier for resident foreigners to acquire Swiss nationality.

The government breathed a sigh of relief, however, when a September 25 referendum produced a 54.7% majority for its antiracism law penalizing racial and religious discrimination. Nonetheless, in a referendum on December 4 an almost 73% majority approved increased powers for the police to deal with foreigners who entered the country illegally and then broke the law. Critics said the measure violated both the Swiss constitution and the European Convention on Human Rights. (*See* POPULATION AND POPULATION MOVEMENTS: *International Migration.*)

The prevailing uncertainty, especially regarding the EU, was reflected in reported differences of opinion within the seven-member Federal Council (Cabinet), functioning on the collegiate system and by consensus. This, in turn, raised a question concerning the validity in changing circumstances of the "magic formula," devised by the legislature in 1959, in which the Radical Democrats, Christian Democrats, and Social Democrats had two seats each and the Swiss People's Party one.

Despite savings, Switzerland's 1995 budget showed a deficit of some Sw F 6 billion, making further cuts imperative, including a freeze on the pay of government officials. With the private sector similarly disposed, talk of strike action was in the air.

Attention continued to be focused on the country's serious drug problem, especially on the Letten, a disused railway station near the centre of Zürich that had become a centre for addicts. Several dealers died in shootouts there. The public was also aghast at the murders and suicides in Switzerland and Quebec during October 4–5 of 53 persons, women and children among them, who belonged to the Order of the Solar Temple, a quasi-religious sect.

(ALAN McGREGOR)

SYRIA

A republic of southwestern Asia, Syria is on the Mediterranean Sea. Area: 185,180 sq km (71,498 sq mi). Pop. (1994 est.): 13,853,000. Cap.: Damascus. Monetary unit: Syrian pound, with (Oct. 7, 1994) a par value (official rate) of LS 11.22 to U.S. $1 (LS 17.85 = £1 sterling) and a nonessential rate of LS 23 to U.S. $1 (LS 36.58 = £1 sterling). President in 1994, Gen. Hafez al-Assad; prime minister, Mahmoud Zuabi.

Although Syria remained aloof in 1994 from the mainstream moves toward peace with Israel, signs did emerge that Pres. Hafez al-Assad's aides were prepared to discuss mutual security arrangements with the Israelis at the highest levels. Nonetheless, neither side held out great hopes for an early breakthrough, largely because little progress had been made toward filling Syrian demands for a complete Israeli withdrawal from the occupied Golan Heights or Israel's insistence on early normalization of relations. Israel, however, appeared to be offering a three-year timetable for complete withdrawal amid indications that Egypt was urging Syria to adopt for the Golan Heights an arrangement similar to that which Egypt had accepted from Israel over the Sinai.

On January 16 President Assad met Pres. Bill Clinton in Geneva in what was only the fourth meeting between Assad and a U.S. president since 1970. Clinton followed up with a second meeting with Assad in Damascus on October 27, the first time in 20 years a U.S. president had traveled to the Syrian capital. Neither meeting resulted in breakthroughs, however.

Throughout most of 1994 Syria declined to negotiate directly with Israel in protest against the killing of some 29 Palestinians by an Israeli gunman at Hebron in late February. In September, however, Foreign Minister Farouk ash-Shara gave his first-ever interview to Israeli television, and in Washington, D.C., in December an unnamed Syrian general joined Israeli and Syrian diplomats and the Israeli chief of staff, Lieut. Gen. Ehud Barak, for talks. In October the jamming of Jordanian television was abandoned by the Syrian government, an apparent sign that the Syrians regarded the peace process as unstoppable.

A number of tangible benefits, nevertheless, accrued to Syria from the general move toward peace. On November 28, for example, apparently as a reward for not obstructing peace talks, the European Union lifted its eight-year embargo on sales of weapons by its member states to Syria. The move drew protests from Israel.

President Assad was forced to pay close attention to domestic political issues in 1994. On January 21 his eldest son, Basel al-Assad, who had been thought of as a possible successor, was killed at the age of 33 when his automobile, which he apparently was driving at a high rate of speed, crashed in thick fog near the Damascus airport. Assad, who had ruled Syria since taking power in a coup in 1970, seemed keen to groom Basel for high office, but his hopes for a smooth succession appeared dashed at his son's death. Basel had been head of the presidential security force and had been able to make some inroads against institutionalized corruption in the country. With Assad's estranged brother Rifaat, nominally vice president, apparently out of contention, attention switched to Assad's second son, Bashar, aged 28, as a likely successor to his father. A further shock for the elite was the sacking of special forces commander Brig. Gen. Ali Haider on allegations of drug trafficking and his replacement by the Persian Gulf war veteran Gen. Ali Habib.

The general election held on August 24–25 resulted in a victory for the ruling National Progressive Front and its allies, but with a low turnout of only 49% of the electorate. A Ba'thist, 'Abd al-Qadir Qaddoura, was elected speaker of the parliament, one-third of whose members were directly elected. The government budget, approved on June 8, provided for a 17.2% increase in spending to LS 144 billion. On November 14 Prime Minister Mahmoud Zuabi promised the new parliament that his government would introduce a program of economic reforms to implement changes to the banking system, unify exchange rates, and establish an export investment bank.

The Arab boycott of Israel, which was headquartered in Damascus and whose main supporter was the Syrian government, appeared to be crumbling in 1994. The six member Gulf Cooperation Council (GCC) decided in October to abandon the secondary and tertiary aspects of the boycott, thereby agreeing to do business with foreign companies that dealt with Israel as well as the Arab states. The April and October council meetings of the boycott members were canceled through lack of a quorum. Foreign ministers of the eight Damascus Declaration countries, the GCC plus Egypt and Syria, met in January and agreed to increase political and economic cooperation, but few tangible benefits emerged.

(JOHN WHELAN)

Carrying a banner reading "Murderer of Taiwanese," advocates of independence for Taiwan protest the arrival of Tang Shubei (T'ang Shu-pei) from China. Others in Taiwan, however, warmly welcomed the delegation, proclaiming that "blood is thicker than water."
AFP

TAIWAN

Taiwan, which consists of the island of Taiwan and surrounding islands off the coast of China, is the seat of the Republic of China (Nationalist China). Area: 36,179 sq km (13,969 sq mi), including the island of Taiwan and its 86 outlying islands, 22 in the Taiwan group and 64 in the Pescadores group. Pop. (1994 est.): 21,073,000. (Area and population figures include the Quemoy and Matsu groups, which are administered as an occupied part of Fujian [Fukien] province.) Cap.: Taipei. Monetary unit: New Taiwan dollar, with (Oct. 7, 1994) a free rate of NT$26.16 to U.S. $1 (NT$41.61 = £1 sterling). President in 1994, Lee Teng-hui; president of the Executive Yuan (premier), Lien Chan.

In December 1994 the Republic of China on Taiwan passed another milestone on its remarkable march toward full democracy. The results of the gubernatorial and mayoral elections, pitting the ruling Nationalist Party (KMT) against the Democratic Progressive Party (DPP), its main rival, and the upstart New Party, indicated that Taiwan's eight-year-old democracy was settling into what was basically a two-party system. Voters delivered a split verdict. DPP candidate Chen Shui-bian's election as mayor of Taipei gave his party its greatest electoral victory yet, but KMT incumbent Wu Tun-yi triumphed in Kao-hsiung, Taiwan's second-largest city. In the first election ever held for provincial governor of Taiwan, KMT incumbent James Soong was returned to office by a comfortable majority. The election also indicated that in media-saturated Taiwan, personality and image might be more important than party affiliation. The DPP's reaffirmation of its commitment to the formal independence of Taiwan elicited another warning from the government that Taiwan and the People's Republic on the mainland were juridically equal parts of a single China.

Taiwan's ongoing efforts to gain international political status and recognition commensurate with its economic strength were stymied by China's stubborn opposition. Taipei's bid to rejoin the UN again failed to get on the agenda. China,

moreover, pressured Japan to cancel an invitation to Pres. Lee Teng-hui to attend the Asian Games in Hiroshima, and at the APEC (Asia-Pacific Economic Cooperation) summit in Bogor, Indon., in November, Taiwan was represented by economic planning chief Vincent Siew rather than by the president. To Beijing's (Peking's) dismay, however, Lee's "vacation diplomacy" was quite successful. On unofficial visits he met with the leaders of Malaysia, Singapore, the Philippines, Thailand, and Indonesia. In addition, the Clinton administration responded to congressional pressure and eased some of the irksome restrictions placed on Taiwan's unofficial embassy in Washington, D.C.

The brutal murders in Zhejiang (Chekiang) province of 24 tourists from Taiwan on March 31 and the attempt at a cover-up by local authorities created an uproar. Taiwan's Straits Exchange Foundation suspended talks with China's Association for Relations Across the Taiwan Strait. Agreements, however, were later reached regarding air piracy, illegal immigration, and fishing disputes. Expanded trade made China Taiwan's second largest export market.

On April 26 a China Airlines Airbus A-300 crashed in flames at the Nagoya airport in Japan after an uneventful flight from Taipei. Only 7 of the 271 persons aboard survived. A minute before the crash, a pilot had informed the tower that he was aborting the landing and would make a second approach. Although the cause of the crash was not immediately known, Japanese police reported that both pilots had been drinking.

Taiwan's export-led economy slowly picked up steam in the second half of the year, expanding at an annual rate of just over 6%, a very respectable rate for a mature and developed national economy. Looking to the future, Lien Chan emphasized the need to rely on private-sector investment to achieve the nation's most important large-scale development goals. Despite considerable opposition from antinuclear activists and environmentalists, and over the objections of the DPP, the KMT majority in the Legislative Yuan approved construction of Taiwan's fourth nuclear power plant on the crowded and resource-poor island.

Unemployment in Taiwan hovered around 1.5%. The China External Trade Development Council pointed to a severe labour shortage, only partly relieved by foreign workers, as one of Taiwan's weaknesses in competing with such export rivals as South Korea, Hong Kong, and Singapore. To avoid U.S. sanctions, Taiwan took steps to ban trade in endangered species, including the elephant, rhinoceros, and tiger. For political rather than economic reasons, Taiwan's long-standing application to join the General Agreement on Tariffs and Trade (GATT) and become a founding member of the successor World Trade Organization was held hostage to China's own efforts to join GATT. Taiwan's sometimes volatile stock market finished the year quite strongly, up 17% from the beginning of the year. At midyear, the country's foreign exchange reserves stood at an impressive $90.1 billion. Once again Taiwan had demonstrated that political democratization was fully consistent with economic growth and social stability.   (STEVEN I. LEVINE)

TAJIKISTAN

A landlocked republic of Central Asia, Tajikistan borders Kyrgyzstan on the north, Uzbekistan on the north and west, Afghanistan on the south, and China on the east. Area: 143,100 sq km (55,300 sq mi). Pop. (1994 est.): 5,813,000. Cap.: Dushanbe. Monetary unit: Tajik ruble (introduced May 1994 as interim currency to replace the Russian ruble; in January 1994 Tajikistan had introduced the Russian ruble as its own currency to replace the pre-1993 Russian [or Soviet] ruble), with (Oct. 13, 1994) an official rate of 2,900 Tajik rubles to U.S. $1 (4,612 rubles = £1 sterling). Chief of state in 1994 (chairman of the National Assembly and president), Imomali Rakhmonov; prime ministers, Abdujalil Samadov (acting) and, from December 2, Dzamshed Karimov.

Throughout 1994 armed groups of the banned Tajik Islamic opposition and their Afghan supporters carried out almost daily attacks on Russian and Tajik border troops guarding the Tajik-Afghan frontier. Even though Tajikistan's neo-Communist regime was almost completely dependent on Russian military and economic assistance to remain in power, Russia had difficulty persuading the Tajik government to begin negotiations with the armed opposition to end the fighting that had dragged on since 1992. Although Russian forces were heavily engaged in protecting the border with Afghanistan, which Moscow viewed as the most important line of resistance against the spread of Muslim fundamentalism, Russia refused to become involved in Tajikistan's internal conflict. During the summer, when a number of journalists, government officials, and Russian officers assisting the Tajik Ministry of Defense were assassinated in Dushanbe, the opposition was accused of the murders. Foreign human rights activists protested when two prominent journalists were arrested for distributing an opposition Tajik-language newspaper that was printed in Moscow but never banned in Tajikistan. In July a group of armed oppositionists inside Tajikistan succeeded in seizing control of an important highway east of Dushanbe for several days; it was one of the most significant opposition successes since the restoration of the communists at the end of 1992.

In April Russian and UN officials brought together representatives of the Tajik leadership and the Islamic and democratic opposition-in-exile for talks in Moscow that, it was hoped, would lead to a cease-fire. Two rounds of talks ended inconclusively. In September, after the government met opposition demands for an amnesty for political prisoners, a temporary cease-fire under UN supervision was finally agreed to. A third round of talks to establish a permanent cease-fire was held in Islamabad, Pak., in late October. The talks began with an opposition charge, supported by Helsinki Watch, that the government had not fulfilled its promise to release a number of political prisoners.

In April the government released the draft of a new constitution, which was approved by the voters on November 6. In the presidential election held the same day, Imomali Rakhmonov, who had been acting president, was declared the victor despite charges of electoral fraud and voter intimidation. The Western-oriented Democratic Party broke with the rest of the opposition in accepting Rakhmonov's election, but the Islamic opposition refused to recognize it. Rakhmonov was formally installed in office on November 16. There was considerable criticism of the election both inside and outside Tajikistan because the two candidates, Rakhmonov and former prime minister Abdumalek Abdulajanov, represented only one region of Tajikistan. The election, therefore, was seen as further dividing the country. Officials of the Russian border guards in Tajikistan claimed that despite a cease-fire agreement, opposition forces were preparing a major offensive for the spring of 1995.

Tajikistan's government remained dependent on Russia not only to protect the border but also to support the country's economy, which had been weakened by two years of fighting. In January Tajikistan adopted the Russian ruble as the first step toward complete integration of the Tajik economy with that of Russia. Russian financial officials, however, were less than enthusiastic about the proposed monetary union, and Tajik pleas to speed up the planned union went unheeded.   (BESS BROWN)

This article updates the Macropædia article CENTRAL ASIA: Tajikistan.

TANZANIA

The republic of Tanzania, a member of the Commonwealth, consists of Tanganyika, on the east coast of Africa, and Zanzibar, just off the coast in the Indian Ocean, which includes Zanzibar Island, Pemba Island, and small islets. Area: 942,799 sq km (364,017 sq mi). Pop. (1994 est.): 27,296,000. Cap.: government in process of being transferred from Dar es Salaam; legislature meets in Dodoma, the new capital. Monetary unit: Tanzania shilling, with (Oct. 7, 1994) a free rate of 535 shillings to U.S. $1 (850.92 shillings = £1 sterling). President in 1994, Ali Hassan Mwinyi; prime ministers, John Malecela and, from December 7, Cleopa Msuya.

A World Bank report published on March 14, 1994, evaluated Tanzania's performance in carrying out its economic reform program as second only to Ghana's among 29 sub-Saharan African countries. This result had been achieved through close adherence to a stern structural-adjustment schedule, and in 1994 additional measures to curb expenditure and encourage production were introduced.

In February the charges for electricity supplied by the Tanzania Electric Supply Corporation to domestic users were increased by 68%, while charges for street lighting, paid for by town councils, municipalities, and districts, were raised by 233%. However, charges to industrial users were reduced. Hopes of cheaper electricity in the future were raised by the announcement that the government planned to construct a trial plant to produce methane by treating solid waste. The plant, costing $3.9 million, was to be financed by the Global Environment Facility, and if it proved successful other plants would be constructed in different parts of the country. The electricity generated would then be sold to the Tanzania Electric Supply Corporation.

As if to underscore the extent of Tanzania's problems, on January 11 Pres. Ali Hassan Mwinyi warned of the imminent danger of famine resulting from the prolonged drought from which the country had recently suffered, a warning reiterated in April by the Agency for International Development. Then, adding to the troubles caused by nature, a man-made catastrophe occurred when the violence that had burst out in Rwanda in April caused a flood of refugees to seek sanctuary in Tanzania. Although the government officially closed the border on May 1, within a 24-hour period some 250,000 Rwandan refugees occupied a camp near Ngara in northwestern Tanzania, making it the second most densely populated area in the country. An urgent appeal was made to the international community to assist in making provision for the refugees, a task that was beyond any resources immediately available in Tanzania itself.

The limitations that poverty imposed on the country were reflected in the decision, made reluctantly in June, to withdraw the Tanzanian contingent from the peacekeeping operation in Liberia. The UN, Tanzania complained, had failed to provide the funds needed to enable the troops to carry out their task effectively.

Yet not all was gloom. In March it was announced that the petroleum company Caltex had decided to use Zanzibar as its storage centre and distribution point for oil to be sold in eastern, central, and southern Africa. This, it was hoped, would cut the cost of petroleum products, and Zanzibar also anticipated that the beneficial effect on commodity prices would make the island more attractive to investors. Soon afterward five international investment corporations announced that they intended to fund three safari lodges on the mainland. In a Cabinet reshuffle in early December, Mwinyi reappointed former prime minister Cleopa Msuya.

(KENNETH INGHAM)

This article updates the *Macropædia* article EASTERN AFRICA: *Tanzania*.

THAILAND

Thailand is a constitutional monarchy in Southeast Asia, on the Andaman Sea and the Gulf of Thailand. Area: 513,115 sq km (198,115 sq mi). Pop. (1994 est.): 57,586,000. Cap.: Bangkok. Monetary unit: baht, with (Oct. 7, 1994) a free rate of 25.03 baht to U.S. $1 (39.81 baht = £1 sterling). King, Bhumibol Adulyadej; prime minister in 1994, Chuan Leekpai.

Internal differences within two of the five governing coalition parties repeatedly threatened political stability during 1994. While Prime Minister Chuan Leekpai's Democrat Party was free of dissension, the New Aspiration Party (NAP) headed by Interior Minister Chaovalit Yongchaiyuth was disrupted by factional rivalry. Even less united was the Righteous Force, led by Chamlong Srimuang, the pivotal figure in the overthrow of the autocratic regime in 1992. Chamlong, who entered the Cabinet as deputy prime minister only in October, insisted on replacing the foreign and communications ministers with unelected outsiders, causing much bitterness among parliamentarians.

For months the government was at odds with the opposition over a proposed revision of the constitution, which would reduce the size and power of the appointed Senate, lower the voting age to 18, and modify several clauses related to local government and parliamentary procedures. Though there were no substantial ideological differences involved, the opposition refused to endorse the Cabinet's draft bills. The impasse prompted democracy advocate Chalard Vorachat, who had been prominent in the 1992 turmoil, to go on a 68-day hunger strike outside the National Assembly. Chalard's protest was reported even by international media. Rallies in the provinces supporting Chalard and the army's

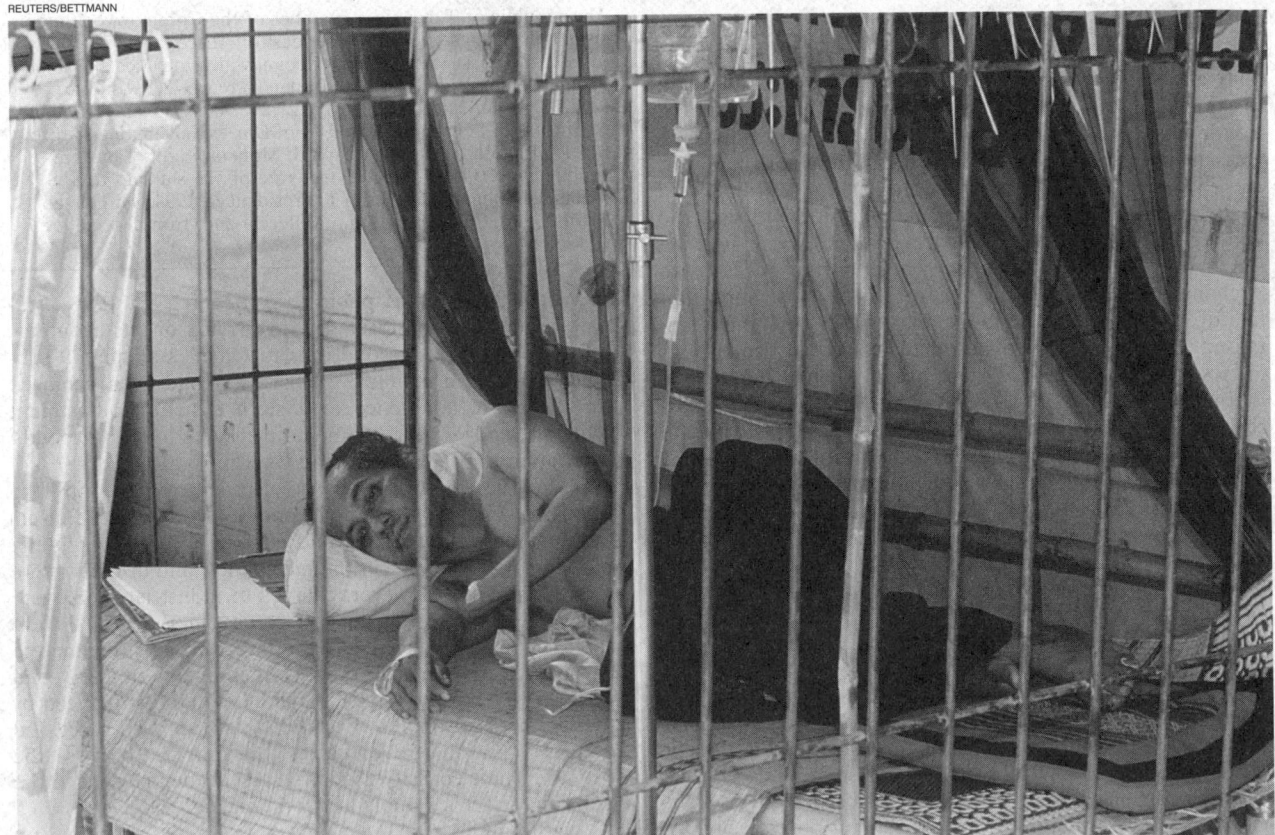

Chalard Vorachat, on a hunger strike over proposed changes to the Thai constitution, takes refuge inside a metal cage so that he cannot be taken to a hospital. When the pro-democracy activist went on a similar fast in 1992, his action fueled riots that brought down the government.

strong objections to the tactics he used raised the spectre of new unrest. The constitutional question had not been resolved by the beginning of December, despite numerous attempts at compromise. On December 9 Chaovalit pulled the NAP out of the coalition, thus increasing the likelihood of elections in early 1995.

The opposition Thai Nation was embarrassed when the U.S. Drug Enforcement Agency (DEA) identified one of its members as a coconspirator in drug-smuggling operations. Foreign Minister Prasong Sunsiri told the Cabinet that he believed 16 other members of the National Assembly were on an agency list. The furor was further fueled on June 30 when it was revealed that Thai Nation's deputy leader had been refused a U.S. entry visa on the recommendation of DEA officials. An even greater scandal erupted over the whereabouts of some 90 kg (198 lb) of jewelry, reportedly worth $20 million, that had been stolen from a Saudi prince's palace in 1989 by a Thai servant and shipped to Bangkok. The jewels had been recovered, but they disappeared while in the custody of police. After five years of investigation, Chuan, pressed by Saudi authorities, ordered investigators to report directly to him. Among those arrested were the current police chief, his predecessor, two police generals, and several civilians. Charges ranged from negligence to possession of stolen property and to the kidnapping and murder of the family of a key witness. It was taken for granted that senior politicians and civil servants were under investigation for possession of some of the jewels.

Another furious row brewed all year long over three proposed mass transit projects in Bangkok. The previous government had awarded rights to build elevated commuter railways to private consortia. Opponents charged that the tracks would be unsightly when finished and would disrupt Bangkok's already congested traffic during construction. In May international consultants hired by the government advised that inner-city lines be built underground. The Cabinet offered to pay the additional cost. In August, after a court validated one original contract, trees were felled on some of the city's finest avenues despite protests by environmentalists.

Thailand seemed set to record perhaps the world's best overall economic performance in 1994. With a modest 1.5% population increase, gross national product growth was forecast to be 9% and exports were expected to rise 16%, while inflation was steady at less than 5%. A clampdown on intellectual property infringements pleased the United States, but claims by Washington that the Thai military had broken a commitment to cut its links to Khmer Rouge guerrillas irked army commander Gen. Wimol Wongwanich. In April, Cambodian First Prime Minister Prince Norodom Ranariddh accused Thailand of helping "Pol Potists" escape government's troops. After a July coup attempt was foiled near Phnom Penh, some 14 Thais, including a police colonel, were accused of involvement. The U.S. Congress in October moved to cut $100 million in military aid.

(ROBERT WOODROW)

This article updates the *Macropædia* article SOUTHEAST ASIA: *Thailand*.

TOGO

A republic of West Africa, Togo is situated on the Bight of Benin. Area: 56,785 sq km (21,925 sq mi). Pop. (1994 est.): 3,922,000. Cap.: Lomé. Monetary unit: CFA franc, with (Oct. 7, 1994) a par value of CFAF 100 to the French franc and a free rate of CFAF 526.67 to U.S. $1 (CFAF 837.67 = £1 sterling). President in 1994, Gen. Gnassingbé Eyadéma; prime ministers, Joseph Kokou Koffigoh until March 21 and, from April 23, Edem Kodjo.

Gnassingbé Eyadéma's presidency survived another turbulent year in 1994. On the evening of January 5, approximately 100 armed men, possibly former commandos dismissed from the army in Eyadéma's 1993 purge, attacked the Toikin army barracks, where the president resided. The ensuing struggle with soldiers loyal to Eyadéma resulted in 67 deaths and dozens of injuries. The government accused the opposition of instigating the attack, which it regarded as an attempted coup.

After several postponements, elections to the national legislature were finally held on February 6 and 20. French observers were brought in to ensure the army's neutrality. Although the voting was generally calm and the elections judged to be fairly conducted, the process was overshadowed first by the abduction and murder of three opposition leaders, then by the firebombing of Eyadéma's ally, Communications Minister Benjamin Agbeka, and finally by the murder of Gaston Edeh, one of only 19 deputies to receive an outright majority in the first round of the elections.

Opposition parties won 43 of the 81 seats, but two months passed before Edem Kodjo was appointed prime minister by Eyadéma. Kodjo, however, was unable to form a coalition government until June 24. He allotted more than half the ministries to members of Eyadéma's Rally of the Togolese People and the pro-Eyadéma Union for Justice and Democracy. This led to bitter conflict, and in November members of the main opposition party, the Action Committee for Renewal, boycotted the legislature.

(NANCY ELLEN LAWLER)

This article updates the *Macropædia* article WESTERN AFRICA: *Togo*.

TONGA

A constitutional monarchy and member of the Commonwealth, Tonga comprises about 170 islands split into three main groups in the Pacific Ocean east of Fiji. Area: 750 sq km (290 sq mi). Pop. (1994 est.): 99,700. Cap.: Nuku'alofa. Monetary unit: pa'anga, with (Oct. 7, 1994) a free rate of 1.35 pa'anga (1$) to U.S. $1 (2.15 pa'anga = £1 sterling). King, Taufa'ahau Tupou IV; prime minister in 1994, Baron Vaea.

The continuing challenge to the government—largely controlled by the king, his nominees, and a small group of hereditary nobles—posed by the pro-democracy movement went a step farther in September 1994 with the formation of the Tonga Democratic Party. The new party's supporters controlled six of the nine people's (commoners') seats in the Legislative Assembly. 'Akilisi Pohiva, the movement's leader, remained under pressure from the government, losing a defamation action over allegations of improper payments within Tonga's highly profitable squash export industry. In 1993 squash exports to Japan reached 17,000 tons with a value of 15 million pa'anga, which represented Tonga's largest source of foreign exchange. Income from tourism (23,000 visitors) accounted for 11 million pa'anga.

In foreign affairs Tonga remained active in regional organizations. Late in 1993 the government announced a joint venture with the Malaysian Borneo Finance Bank, which opened a branch in Tonga; it was owned 51% by Asia Capital Corp., 25% by Crown Prince Tupouto'a, and 10% by Tongan business interests; the balance was offered to local investors. The king also announced a joint venture with Sarawak state in Malaysia, under which it was proposed that Tongans establish village settlements there to produce bananas and other crops for Malaysian consumption.

(BARRIE MACDONALD)

This article updates the *Macropædia* article PACIFIC ISLANDS: *Tonga*.

TRINIDAD AND TOBAGO

A republic and member of the Commonwealth, Trinidad and Tobago consists of two islands in the Caribbean Sea off the coast of Venezuela. Area: 5,128 sq km (1,980 sq mi). Pop. (1994 est.): 1,273,000. Cap.: Port of Spain. Monetary unit: Trinidad and Tobago dollar, with (Oct. 7, 1994) a free rate of TT$5.58 to U.S. $1 (TT$8.88 = £1 sterling). President in 1994, Noor Mohammad Hassanali; prime minister, Patrick Manning.

In legislative by-elections held in 1994 to replace three sitting members of the legislature who had died early in the year, the People's National Movement party lost two seats to the opposition. Prime Minister Patrick Manning, concerned over his party's losses, hinted that he might call elections in 1995, a year early.

Amoco Trinidad Oil Co. identified an additional 56.6 billion cu m (2 trillion cu ft) of natural gas in its east coast offshore fields in June and August. As a result, the company gained enough gas reserves to fulfill almost all the requirements of its proposed 12 million-cu m (425 million-cu ft)-per-day liquefied natural gas plant in Trinidad, which would be the first in the Western Hemisphere.

In July, against the background of a deteriorating crime situation, the government ended its self-imposed 15-year moratorium on hanging and executed convicted murderer Glen Ashby. The move drew international protests, in part because Ashby was put to death only minutes before the Privy Council in London agreed to a stay of execution on constitutional grounds.

The amnesty granted to the 114 members of the Jamaat-al-Muslimeen sect who had stormed the legislature in July 1990 and held Prime Minister A.N.R. Robinson and several of his ministers hostage for five days was declared invalid in September. The court, however, ruled that the group should not be rearrested or tried for the offenses they committed.

(DAVID RENWICK)

This article updates the *Macropædia* article The WEST INDIES: *Trinidad and Tobago.*

TUNISIA

A republic of North Africa, Tunisia lies on the Mediterranean Sea. Area: 164,150 sq km (63,378 sq mi). Pop. (1994 est.): 8,757,000. Cap.: Tunis. Monetary unit: Tunisian dinar, with (Oct. 7, 1994) a free rate of 0.98 dinar to U.S. $1 (1.56 dinars = £1 sterling). President in 1994, Gen. Zine al-Abidine Ben Ali; prime minister, Hamed Karoui.

During 1994 the Tunisian government had to deal with repeated attacks on its human rights record, beginning with a critical Amnesty International report in January. Most of the accusations focused on the issue of the government's attitude toward the major Islamic movement, the outlawed Nahda party, which, according to government sources, was implicated in violent opposition to the authorities. Tunisia reacted furiously to a British government decision to grant political asylum to Nahda leader Rachid Ghannouchi. It warned that Britain, together with the United States and Germany, did not understand the true nature of the Islamist threat to North Africa.

Needless to say, Nahda was not allowed to participate in the presidential and legislative elections that were held in March. All but 19 of the 163 seats in the Chamber of Deputies were won by the ruling Constitutional Democratic Assembly, with the opposition parties gaining only about 2.3% of the vote. The other 19 seats, reserved for the opposition as a result of a new electoral law, were distributed between four parties. In the wake of the elections, the president warned that now that there was an opposition presence in the legislature, unauthorized attempts to create new opposition groupings would not be permitted.

The presidential elections were marred by government irritation at attempts to contest them. Moncef Marzouki, a veteran human rights campaigner who resigned his post as head of the Tunisian human rights organization just before the election, warned that he intended to challenge the incumbent, Zine al-Abidine Ben Ali, in the election. However, Marzouki was not able to obtain the support of 30 parliamentary deputies or mayors, so his application as a candidate lapsed. Ben Ali, therefore, ran unopposed and obtained some 99.9% of the votes cast; about 95.5% of the electorate participated in the election.

The political tensions that had marked the election period bubbled to the surface immediately afterward. Marzouki was arrested for allegedly defamatory remarks he made to a Spanish newspaper after the election and released only some months later. Nearly three weeks after the elections, Hamma Hammami, the leader of the banned Communist Workers' Party, was sentenced to 9½ years in prison for trying to form an illegal opposition party.

In foreign affairs Tunisia continued to press for a regional approach. It handed over the presidency of the Maghreb Arab Union to Algeria in April, four months later than scheduled because of the unstable political situation there. One old foreign policy issue was resolved during the year when the Palestine Liberation Organization officially moved its headquarters from Tunis to the Gaza Strip on July 11.

(GEORGE JOFFÉ)

This article updates the *Macropædia* article NORTH AFRICA: *Tunisia.*

TURKEY

A republic of Asia Minor and southeastern Europe, Turkey has coastlines on the Aegean, Black, and Mediterranean seas. Area: 779,452 sq km (300,948 sq mi), including 23,764 sq km in Europe. Pop. (1994 est.): 61,183,000. Cap.: Ankara. Monetary unit: Turkish lira, with (Oct. 7, 1994) a free rate of 34,441 liras to U.S. $1 (54,779 liras = £1 sterling). President in 1994, Suleyman Demirel; prime minister, Tansu Ciller.

The coalition government of the centre-right True Path Party (DYP) and the centre-left Social Democratic Populist Party (SHP) had to contend with successive crises in 1994. A collapse in the value of the Turkish lira at the end of January forced Prime Minister Tansu Ciller to abandon her expansionary economic policy and introduce an austerity program on April 5. Bolstered by a standby agreement concluded with the International Monetary Fund in July, the government succeeded in cutting the public-sector deficit, moving into surplus in external payments and servicing its foreign debt. This was achieved, however, at the cost of a domestic recession, which reduced the gross national product by a record 11% in the second quarter of the year.

In local government elections on March 27, the DYP's share of the vote dropped to 22% and that of the SHP to 13%, while the Islamic-based Welfare Party (RP) advanced to 18% and won control of the Istanbul and Ankara metropolitan areas. The Motherland Party, representing the mainstream centre-right opposition, received 21% of the total vote.

Terrorists of the Kurdish Workers' Party (PKK) continued their attacks in southeastern Turkey and, to a lesser extent, in tourist resorts and cities outside the main Kurdish areas. The national security forces responded with an all-out offensive, which involved the forcible evacuation of hundreds of mountain villages as well as repeated attacks on PKK bases

A Turkish helicopter hovers in support of government troops assembling for an attack against Kurdish strongholds in the eastern part of the country. Turkish forces kept up their pressure on the Kurds throughout the year, entering Iraq for a short time in April in pursuit.

AFP

in northern Iraq. The conduct of the security forces, the decision made by the Grand National Assembly in March to revoke the parliamentary immunity of eight radical Kurdish deputies, the subsequent arrest of the deputies, who were sentenced to up to 15 years in prison on December 8, and the closing of the Democracy Party in June by order of the Constitutional Court strained relations with the West. The U.S. Congress decided that the disbursement of part of U.S. aid to Turkey should be made subject to improvements in human rights in Turkey and to progress in the dispute with Greece over Cyprus.

Within the government the two coalition partners found it difficult to work together. On August 5, when the Social Democratic leader, Deputy Prime Minister Murat Karayalcin, changed his party's ministers in the government, the Foreign Ministry was given to Mumtaz Soysal, until then a leading critic of the coalition's policies. A privatization law, earlier opposed by Soysal, was passed on November 24. Four days later Soysal resigned from the government.

Domestic preoccupations did not prevent Turkey from pursuing an active foreign policy. After visits to Ankara by leaders of the Turkic republics of the former Soviet Union, a Turkic summit was held in Istanbul on October 18. Later that month Pres. Suleyman Demirel visited Ashgabat, the capital of Turkmenistan, and took part in the inauguration of the construction of a pipeline to carry natural gas from Turkmenistan through Iran to Turkey.

Turkey's attempts at common action with the Turkic republics were ill-received in Russia, which had earlier ex-

pressed reservations about an agreement with a Western-led consortium to pipe oil from Azerbaijan through Turkey to the Mediterranean. Friction was also caused by the imposition of new rules on July 1 on commercial ships navigating the Turkish straits (the Bosporus and the Dardanelles). Although the case for better protection for the Istanbul metropolitan area had been demonstrated by the collision of two oil tankers at the northern entrance to the Bosporus in March, Russia argued that the new rules violated the 1936 Montreux Convention.

The first-ever visits by a president of Israel to Turkey, in January, and by the Turkish prime minister to Israel, in November, signaled closer Turkish involvement in the Middle Eastern peace process. At the same time, relations with Syria, already strained by the facilities afforded by the latter to the PKK terrorists, were further soured by the opening in November of the first tunnel to carry water from the newly built Ataturk dam on the Euphrates River to irrigate the Harran plain in Turkey, north of the Syrian frontier.

Turkey's role in the UN and NATO was highlighted by the dispatch of a Turkish peacekeeping contingent to Bosnia and Herzegovina in June, following a visit by Ciller to Sarajevo on February 2. This displeased Greece, with which Turkey's relations were strained by the continuing impasse over Cyprus, the murder of a Turkish diplomat in Athens on July 4, and the continuing dispute over territorial waters in the Aegean. (ANDREW MANGO)

TURKMENISTAN

A republic of Central Asia, Turkmenistan borders Uzbekistan on the northeast, Kazakhstan on the northwest, the Caspian Sea on the west, Iran on the southwest, and Afghanistan on the southeast. Area: 488,100 sq km (188,500 sq mi). Pop. (1994 est.): 4,044,000. Cap.: Ashgabat (formerly Ashkhabad). Monetary unit: manat, with (Oct. 7, 1994) an official rate of 10 manat to U.S. $1 (15.91 manat = £1 sterling). President in 1994, Saparmurad Niyazov.

There were no serious challenges to Pres. Saparmurad Niyazov's authoritarian rule in 1994, but his personality cult, which rivaled that of Joseph Stalin, suffered from a lack of visible improvement in the country's economy. In January 99.9% of Turkmenistan's voters approved a parliamentary proposal made by Niyazov's Democratic (formerly Communist) Party to exempt the president from facing reelection in 1997 so that he could oversee completion of a 10-year prosperity scheme. Political opponents of Niyazov were persecuted inside Turkmenistan, and in October the state prosecutor asked the Russian Federation to extradite Turkmen dissidents in exile in Moscow.

Turkmenistan, a major natural gas producer, put its own well-being before that of the Commonwealth of Independent States, turning off the supply to several of its neighbours to force them to pay their debts. Niyazov incurred the wrath of Western countries through his courtship of Iran, which promised financial support for a project to ship Turkmen natural gas across Iran to Turkey and Western Europe. Nonetheless, in May Turkmenistan became the first Central Asian state to join NATO's Partnership for Peace.

For a country with good economic prospects, Turkmenistan's currency, the manat, launched in November 1993, proved surprisingly unstable, declining from 2 to the dollar in late 1993 to 125 to the dollar a year later. In May Niyazov began the privatization of state-owned companies, starting with auctions of small enterprises, but the process moved very slowly. (BESS BROWN)

This article updates the *Macropædia* article CENTRAL ASIA: *Turkmenistan*.

SPOTLIGHT: The New Middle East by Robert D. Kaplan

Does the normalization of relations between Israel and its Arab neighbours constitute the *great change* that will allow the Middle East—as the storybooks say—to "live happily ever after"? Probably not. A wider Arab-Israeli peace could be just one of several epochal shifts about to transform the region in years and decades to come. Nor is it clear that the future Middle East will be any more stable than the Middle East to which the world has been accustomed since the end of World War II.

Important shifts could likely emanate from Iran and Turkey. In late 1994 Iran was being blamed for terrorist attacks on Israeli and Jewish installations in Latin America and Europe. There were also fears that it was trying to acquire a nuclear weapon. Iran thus appeared as a strategic threat to Israel, to its new friends in the Arab world, and to the West. However, that threat could evaporate upon political changes inside Iran itself, where the regime is increasingly weak and unpopular as it tries to satisfy a population that has grown from 35 million during the 1978–79 Iranian revolution to 65 million in 1994.

Whether it is the availability of hospital beds, the incidence of disease, or the memory of sons killed in the 1980–88 Iran-Iraq war, the revolution has brought hardship to the working poor it promised to uplift. Mosque attendance has dwindled. Tehranis have set up satellite dishes to watch American television shows such as "Baywatch" and the MTV network. Persian Americans have been returning to Iran in increasing numbers. In 1994 Iranian officials admitted that the United States was Iran's fourth biggest trading partner. Unofficially it may be the biggest, since U.S. goods often arrive in Iran by way of third countries. The so-called battle between East and West is being fought inside Iran itself.

The historical parentheses opened by the Iranian revolution in 1978 may be starting to close. Whatever the specific destiny of Iran's present clerical regime, to think that Iran's diplomatic estrangement from the U.S. (which has adversely affected Iran's ties to other Western countries) will continue indefinitely is to have no regard for history. In 1829 a crowd led by radical clerics stormed and destroyed the Russian embassy in Tehran, killing the ambassador. Russian-Iranian relations were later restored; the incident was forgotten. In the fullness of time, the 1979 siege of the U.S. embassy in Tehran, in which no American diplomats were killed or seriously wounded, will likely be similarly obscured.

Meanwhile, 1994 saw Turkey engaged in its ultimate crisis of identity as the nation grappled with the ethnic duality of its Anatolian land mass, which is both Turkish and Kurdish. The on-again, off-again war between the Turkish army and Kurdish guerrillas in southeastern Turkey stems ultimately from the inflexible border arrangements of the post-World War I Middle East peace treaties that denied the Kurds a state of their own and split them up among Turkey, Iran, Iraq, and Syria. Roughly half of the world's 20 million Kurds live in Turkey. Its ability, or inability, to solve the Kurdish problem will determine whether Turkey will be able to release its considerable dynamism—born of industrialization, a large middle class, an 81% literacy rate, and four decades of experience with democracy—upon the adjacent Arab world and Turkic Central Asia.

Turks led the House of Islam for nearly 850 years, from the Seljuq conquest of Anatolia in 1071 to the defeat of the Ottoman Empire in 1918. In a world of eroding borders, it goes against both history and geography not to expect Turkey to exert increasing influence upon the Middle East's Arab heartland especially as the one-man dictatorships governing Turkey's Arab neighbours, Iraq and Syria, must ultimately give way to more flexible, even chaotic regimes, whose ability to control the movement of people and ideas will be less.

Turkey and Iran are in the midst of crises that significant parts of the Arab world have yet to face. Syria, Iraq, and Jordan had their borders drawn by European colonialists. None of these states has ethnic boundaries that configure with official ones. Unlike Turkey or Israel, they have had little or no legitimizing, democratic tradition behind them. Their identity has been largely dependent upon two factors that are disappearing: the struggle with Israel, which created a siege mentality that fortified repressive regimes in Iraq and Syria, and a world of hard state borders controlled by military and economic elites.

These borders and elites are under slow siege. The Arab population is doubling about once every 22 years. In 1994 more than two-thirds of all Arabs were under the age of 25. Many Arab states have gross national products that are declining relative to population growth. Politicized Islam, which respects no state borders, is, on one very important level, a symptom of the demographic and economic stress that is experienced as it becomes harder for creaky, overly bureaucratized governments in places such as Cairo and Algiers to deliver such basic services as sanitation, electricity, and clean water to their populations. As populations increase yearly, the ability to control them centrally decreases. This is especially true in places where the regime is afforded little respect, whether because it is undemocratic or because it represents a hostile tribe or ethnic group.

Meanwhile, property prices have soared in Tel Aviv as greater Israel—in the sense of a regional economic magnet—comes into being. Israel, which has experienced just over a dozen democratic elections since its creation in 1948, without any riots or coup attempts, is a credible entity. But what of Jordan after King Hussein? What of Syria after Pres. Hafez al-Assad or Iraq after Pres. Saddam Hussein? What of Algeria and Egypt, whose populations continue to climb and whose secular governments become more repressive in the face of an Islamic resurgence?

From the standpoint of the period from 1945 to 1994, progress toward Arab-Israeli peace has been dramatic. But from the standpoint of future decades, the meeting in July in Washington, D.C., between Israeli Prime Minister Yitzhak Rabin and Jordan's King Hussein may symbolize no more than a tidying-up exercise left over from the Cold War—that idyllic time frame when policy-making elites in Washington, Europe, and elsewhere enjoyed more power to influence events than they ever would again.

Surprises beckon. Just consider: from antiquity through 1978 Iran maintained good ties with Jews in Palestine, using them as a lever against Arabs and others whom Iran always feared. The chances of a tectonic shift in Iran's political orientation appear more logical now than in the mid-1970s, prior to the Iranian revolution. A new Middle East, in which relatively coherent states such as Israel, Iran, and Turkey maintain close ties as a defense against an Arab world threatened by chaos, is easily imagined. So is the dissolution of Iran itself, if its regime collapses without a stable replacement and advantage is taken by Kurds and Turkic ethnics in Iran's border areas. So are other scenarios. The big, unimaginable surprise will be if things stay as they are, and the region lives "happily ever after." That would confound all the rules of history.

Robert D. Kaplan is a contributing editor of *The Atlantic Monthly* and author of *The Arabists* and *Balkan Ghosts*.

TUVALU

A constitutional monarchy within the Commonwealth, Tuvalu comprises nine main islands and their associated islets and reefs in the western Pacific Ocean. Area: 24.4 sq km (9.4 sq mi). Pop. (1994 est.): 9,300. Cap.: Fongafale, on Funafuti Atoll. Monetary unit: Australian dollar, with (Oct. 7, 1994) a free rate of $A 1.35 to U.S. $1 ($A 2.15 = £1 sterling). Queen, Elizabeth II; governors-general in 1994, Tomu Sione and, from June, Tulaga Manuella; prime minister, Kamuta Laatasi.

The government of Prime Minister Kamuta Laatasi dismissed Gov.-Gen. Tomu Sione, maintaining that he was a political appointee of the previous regime. The new governor-general was Tulaga Manuella, a former civil service accountant and secretary of the Tuvalu Christian Church and the Pacific Council of Churches.

As two of its major priorities, the Laatasi government declared its intention to reduce the number of government workers, which stood at approximately 500 in a total population of 9,300, and to decentralize government, with the Departments of Education and Health to be located on the island of Vaitupu and that of Fisheries on Nukufetau. The government was facing a shortage of land on the headquarters atoll of Funafuti, where some 43% of the population lived. One-third of the main islet was unusable for agriculture or settlement because of pits created by wartime excavations for the construction of the country's main airfield. Urbanization, resulting in the encroachment of settlement onto agricultural land, was being resisted by the indigenous people of Funafuti. The problem was likely to escalate in four to five years with the exhaustion of phosphate mining at Nauru and the consequent return home of some 700 Tuvaluans currently living there. To counter this, the government was seeking to expand work opportunities for Tuvaluans in Australia and New Zealand.

(BARRIE MACDONALD)

This article updates the *Macropædia* article PACIFIC ISLANDS: *Tuvalu*.

UGANDA

A landlocked republic and member of the Commonwealth, Uganda is located in eastern Africa. Area: 241,040 sq km (93,070 sq mi), including 44,000 sq km of inland water. Pop. (1994 est.): 18,194,000. Cap.: Kampala. Monetary unit: Uganda shilling, with (Oct. 7, 1994) a priority rate of 921 shillings to U.S. $1 (1,465 shillings − £1 sterling). President in 1994, Yoweri Museveni; prime ministers, George Cosmas Adyebo and, from November 18, Kintu Musoke.

Elections for members of a constituent assembly to consider a draft constitution were held on March 28, 1994, with some 1,500 candidates competing for 214 elected seats. In addition, Pres. Yoweri Museveni would nominate 10 members, and approximately 64 others would be appointed by special interest groups. Although the elections officially took place on a nonparty basis, voting was very much along party lines, as was implied, though unintentionally, by the official announcement that the president's supporters had won more than half the seats. Other observers were of the opinion that members of the Uganda People's Congress and the Democratic Party together outnumbered the president's supporters among the successful candidates. Nonetheless, even if the opposition parties had been prepared to cooperate, their majority was whittled away when the nominated and appointed members joined the assembly.

The president had no intention of encouraging the return of party politics to Uganda in the foreseeable future. The draft constitution before the assembly contemplated the suspension of all political party activity for at least five more years. Changing that would require a two-thirds majority in the assembly. In a Cabinet reshuffle on November 18, Museveni appointed a new prime minister, Kintu Musoke.

Assisted by fears of a marked decline in the production of coffee in South America, by the political instability in some other African coffee-producing countries, and by the plan to hold back exportable production introduced by a large number of coffee-growing countries in 1993, Uganda increased its exports of coffee in 1994. Thus, its main foreign-currency earner gave a strong boost to an economy that was already showing a marked upturn as a result of generous foreign aid and a strict adherence to a structural-reform program advocated by the International Monetary Fund. The main thrust of the program had been to establish a liberal economic environment that would encourage private enterprise while at the same time severely reducing government expenditure. Defense, which in 1993 accounted for 30% of the government's budget, was one obvious target, and in April 10,000 members of the armed forces were pensioned off, bringing the total reduction to 33,000, with more to follow. The number of civil servants also continued to be cut, and as a result of these initiatives, the value of the Uganda shilling rose steadily on the foreign-exchange market, reflecting the growing confidence in the country's economic performance. Nevertheless, much remained to be done to improve educational and health standards.

In February Museveni, with the support of their tribal elders, called upon Karamojong rebels in the northeast to hand in their arms in return for the promise of an amnesty. The rebels had harassed the region intermittently since the overthrow of Pres. Idi Amin in 1979. Trouble arose elsewhere in May when three districts on the shore of Lake Victoria had to be declared disaster areas because of the pollution caused by thousands of bodies floating down the Kagera River from neighbouring war-torn Rwanda. Farther north there was rejoicing among the Nyoro people when the office of *mukama* (king) was restored in June and the son of the previous *mukama* was crowned, though without the powers formerly enjoyed by the holder of that office.

(KENNETH INGHAM)

This article updates the *Macropædia* article EASTERN AFRICA: *Uganda*.

UKRAINE

A republic in eastern Europe, Ukraine borders Russia to the north and east, the Black Sea to the south, Romania and Moldova to the southwest, and Hungary, Slovakia, and Poland to the west. Area: 603,700 sq km (233,100 sq mi). Pop. (1994 est.): 52,304,000. Cap.: Kiev. Monetary unit: karbovanets (Ukrainian coupon), with (Oct. 7, 1994) a free rate of 30,028 karbovantsy = U.S. $1 (47,760 karbovantsy = £1 sterling). Presidents in 1994, Leonid Kravchuk and, from July 19, Leonid Kuchma; prime ministers, Yukhim Zvyahilsky (acting) and, from June 16, Vitaly Masol.

Politically, 1994 in Ukraine was dominated by election campaigns. The parliamentary elections of March 27 were indecisive because of the election law that required participation by at least 50% of the electorate and stipulated that a candidate had to receive over 50% of the vote to win a seat. In the Donetsk and Luhanske regions, the elections also saw referenda on the status of the Russian language, with heavy support for the adoption of the latter as a second state language. An attempt to attain the same provision for the whole country was defeated in the parliament after strong opposition from nationalists and several skirmishes between deputies. By April 11, 337 of 450 deputies had been elected, and by August the figure had risen to 393; most (219) of the deputies elected were nonaligned. The Communists, with 91 seats, maintained a plurality and formed a powerful faction with the Socialists and Agrarians. The democratic segment of the parliament was dominated by Rukh members, with some 30 seats; the remaining parties together elected some 20 deputies by the April runoffs.

A stalemate in the parliament led Pres. Leonid Kravchuk to try—unsuccessfully—to postpone the June 26 presidential elections. The incumbent president was defeated in the second round on July 10 by former prime minister Leonid Kuchma (*see* BIOGRAPHIES), who received 52.14% of the votes cast, compared with Kravchuk's 45.06%. The voting divided the country along the Dnieper River, with the eastern regions backing Kuchma and western Ukraine voting heavily in favour of Kravchuk. Kuchma acted quickly to subordinate the Cabinet of Ministers and local councils to his control. Visits to Canada and the U.S. (in October and November, respectively) raised his international profile significantly.

The volatile Crimean oblast elected a separatist pro-Russian president, Yury Meshkov, in a runoff election on January 30, and a series of constitutional disputes between Kiev and the autonomous oblast ensued. The Crimean parliament voted on May 20 to resurrect a 1992 constitution weakening its ties with Ukraine. The dispute also centred on the question of Ukrainian or Russian control of the Black Sea Fleet and the status of the city of Sevastopol, which declared itself a Russian city on August 23. The decision was rescinded immediately by the Ukrainian parliament, and Meshkov's impending revolt soon collapsed. On September 7 the parliament voted to curtail his powers and to institute a collective leadership. On October 6 Anatoliy Franchuk was appointed prime minister of Crimea. In the meantime, Kiev demanded that the Crimeans bring their constitution and laws into line with those of Ukraine by November 1. This was not carried out, and on November 17 the Ukrainian parliament rescinded a long list of laws adopted by Crimea.

Deep economic recession and shortages of power and heating plagued Ukrainians during 1994. Throughout the year Russia and Turkmenistan restricted fuel supplies to Ukraine because of the nonpayment of some $2 billion of debts. The gross national product in Ukraine fell by 18% in the first nine months of the year compared with the corresponding period in 1993. Industrial output dropped 31%, and there was a corresponding 24% fall in labour productivity. In the main, these dramatic figures reflected the decline in traditional heavy industries, such as metallurgy, machine building, chemicals, building materials, and light industry. In addition, coal industry production was expected to be down.

Ukraine's temporary currency, the karbovanets, plunged against the dollar, from 47,000 in May to around 140,000 in early December. By July only about 5% of all production was fully in private hands, and on July 29 the parliament resolved to postpone further privatization on the grounds that the shadow economy was in the hands of criminal elements. On October 11 the new president announced a new economic program based on the freeing of prices, the privatization of land and property, and a monetary reform that would see the belated introduction of a new currency, the hryvnya, and prompt payment of salaries. At the end of the year, however, the economic prognosis for the country remained gloomy.

On March 21 the director of the International Atomic Energy Agency, Hans Blix, declared that the Chernobyl nuclear power plant failed to meet international standards. The Ukrainian authorities were reluctant to close the plant, however, without alternative power sources and adequate compensation. The key question was the cost of shutting down Chernobyl and commissioning new reactors at the Khmelnytsky, Rivne, and Zaporizhzhya atomic stations. A referendum at the giant Zaporizhzhya nuclear station on June 26, however, rejected a proposal to add a sixth reactor and establish a nuclear-waste site there. By late November Ukrainian nuclear officials had agreed on the need to close down Chernobyl eventually but rejected what they perceived as the relatively paltry sums offered for assistance by the international community.

Ukraine also reached an agreement with the International Monetary Fund—conditional upon the introduction

Members of the Russian majority on the Crimean Peninsula, officially a part of Ukraine, demonstrate in favour of union with Russia. Annexed by Russia in 1783, Crimea was given to the former Ukrainian S.S.R. in 1954 by Soviet leader Nikita S. Khrushchev.

of market reforms and control over inflation and debts—for the receipt of $2 billion in loans over a three-year period. An initial loan of $360 million was granted on September 29. Both the U.S. and Canada pledged significant aid to Ukraine: $900 million on the part of the U.S. to support privatization and food and fuel imports, and $17.6 million in technical assistance from Canada. A further $5.5 billion was committed by a Group of Seven conference in Winnipeg, Man., on October 27 to assist Ukraine's reforms, shut down Chernobyl, and harness new nuclear reactors.

Ukraine made significant progress on disarmament when the parliament ratified the Strategic Arms Reduction Talks Treaty (START I) on February 3, decided to join NATO's Partnership for Peace Program on February 8, and ratified and signed on December 5 the Nuclear Non-proliferation Treaty.

The year was also notable for Kuchma's campaign against corruption, which resulted in the order for the arrest of former acting prime minister Yukhim Zvyahilsky in mid-November on charges of embezzlement. A horrific outbreak of cholera in southern Ukraine in September claimed at least 17 lives, with over 650 recorded cases.

(DAVID R. MARPLES)

UNITED ARAB EMIRATES

Consisting of Abu Dhabi, Ajman, Dubayy, al-Fujayrah, Ra's al-Khaymah, ash-Shariqah, and Umm al-Qaywayn, the United Arab Emirates is a federation of seven largely autonomous emirates located on the eastern Arabian Peninsula. Area: 83,600 sq km (32,280 sq mi). Pop. (1994 est.): 2,125,000. Cap.: Abu Dhabi. Monetary unit: United Arab Emirates dirham, with (Oct. 7, 1994) a free rate of 3.67 dirhams to U.S. $1 (5.84 dirhams = £1 sterling). President in 1994, Sheikh Zaid ibn Sultan an-Nahayan; prime minister, Sheikh Maktum ibn Rashid al-Maktum.

A call for dialogue between the United Arab Emirates and Iran over the future of Abu Musa and Greater and Lesser Tunb, islands located in the Persian Gulf between the two nations, was made by Egypt, Syria, and the other Gulf Cooperation Council states but to little avail. Iran appointed Hassan Rezai as the new governor of Abu Musa. In March Pres. Sheikh Zaid ibn Sultan an-Nahayan called for the matter to be settled by the International Court of Justice (ICJ). In December the government repeated its intention to refer the matter to the ICJ, but Iran still refused to negotiate.

On February 19 the minister for petroleum and mineral resources, Youssef Omair ibn Youssef, formerly a banker, resigned in protest against the federal Oil Ministry's lack of authority over the constituent emirates. Emphasizing its independence in oil policy, Dubayy established Emirates National Oil Co., a new holding company to carry out hydrocarbons projects.

An Abu Dhabi court sentenced former Bank of Credit and Commerce International (BCCI) founder Agha Hassan Abedi in his absence to eight years in prison on fraud charges in connection with the BCCI collapse. Creditors of the collapsed BCCI initially rejected a $1.8 billion settlement with Abu Dhabi but in November agreed in principle to the settlement.

In mid-February Sheikh Zaid agreed on legislation to make a wide range of crimes that were formerly tried in civil courts punishable by Islamic law. Included were murder, manslaughter, assault causing bodily harm, theft, adultery, and drug trafficking. The decree applied to all emirates and emphasized the president's concern about the rise of Islamic fundamentalism.

(JOHN WHELAN)

This article updates the Macropædia article ARABIA: *United Arab Emirates*.

UNITED KINGDOM

A constitutional monarchy in northwestern Europe and member of the Commonwealth, the United Kingdom comprises the island of Great Britain (England, Scotland, and Wales) and Northern Ireland, together with many small islands. Area: 244,110 sq km (94,251 sq mi), including 3,218 sq km of inland water but excluding the crown dependencies of the Channel Islands and Isle of Man. Pop. (1994 est.): 58,422,000. Cap.: London. Monetary unit: pound sterling, with (Oct. 7, 1994) a free rate of £0.63 to U.S. $1 (U.S. $1.59 = £1 sterling). Queen, Elizabeth II; prime minister in 1994, John Major.

Domestic Affairs. In two important respects the Conservative government of Prime Minister John Major could proclaim 1994 as a year of success. It presided over steady, noninflationary economic growth and brought peace to Northern Ireland. Yet these successes were more than offset by a series of problems that dented the government's reputation and saw the Conservatives slide in May to their worst defeat in any national election in the 20th century.

Much of the damage was done by a series of incidents that, cumulatively, provoked widespread criticism of government "sleaze." On January 5 Tim Yeo, who had previously endorsed Major's call for the Conservatives to be the party of "family values," resigned as a junior minister after having admitted being the father of his mistress's child. On February 7 a backbench Conservative MP, Stephen Milligan, was found dead at his London flat; he had apparently asphyxiated himself accidentally while performing a dangerous autoerotic act. In May the National Audit Office condemned the U.K.'s biggest overseas aid project—£234 million for the Pergau Dam in Malaysia—as a waste of money. On December 7 Foreign Secretary Douglas Hurd admitted that ministers had broken the law in agreeing to fund the dam from the U.K.'s overseas aid budget. In July Lord Archer (the novelist Jeffrey Archer and a close friend of Major) was subjected to an official inquiry into insider trading in a television company where his wife was a director. Archer, who was subsequently cleared of the charges, admitted he bought shares shortly before a takeover bid and sold them a few days later, thus making an £80,000 profit on behalf of a friend.

After each incident Major hoped that the "sleaze" factor would die away, but each time a new allegation soon emerged. On July 10 *The Sunday Times* reported that two backbench Conservative MPs had broken parliamentary rules by agreeing to accept money from a reporter (posing as a businessman) to present, or table, questions to ministers. The "cash for questions" row gained fresh impetus on October 20 when *The Guardian* disclosed that two junior ministers, Tim Smith and Neil Hamilton, had accepted payment in cash or hospitality for tabling parliamentary questions some years earlier (when both were backbenchers) on behalf of Mohamed al-Fayed, the owner of Harrods department store in London. Both Smith and Hamilton resigned their posts. On October 25 Major set up an independent inquiry to reconsider the rules governing standards of conduct by MPs, ministers, and civil servants. Few people were surprised when a Gallup Poll in late October found that 73% of those questioned considered the Conservatives "sleazy and disreputable."

Later the same month, the government feared that another backbench rebellion would defeat its European Communities (Finance) Bill, the main purpose of which was to sanction increases in the U.K.'s contribution to the European Union (EU). To minimize the rebellion, Major announced that he would regard the Commons vote as a vote of confidence, and if he lost, he would call an early general election. Major secured his immediate objective; the government won the vote on November 28 by 27 votes with the aid of Northern Ireland's Ulster Unionist MPs. Eight Conservative MPs abstained, however, and were promptly suspended from the party in Parliament. The following week the eight rebels retaliated by opposing the government's plans to increase the value-added tax on domestic fuel from 8% to 17.5%. This time the Ulster Unionists voted against the government, which lost by 319–311. The episode reinforced the image of a government unable to secure parliamentary approval for all its policies.

The Conservatives' problems caused the party to lose ground electorally. In the elections to the European Parliament in June, the party won only 28% support and held only 18 seats. Labour, with 44% of the vote, amassed 62 seats. The Liberal Democrats, with 17% support, won two seats—their first in the European Parliament. The Scottish Nationalists doubled their representation from one to two. By December opinion polls showed the Conservatives holding barely half the support that they had won in the 1992 general election. Their 22% rating was the lowest in their history. On December 15 they lost a by-election in Dudley West when Labour achieved a majority of 50%, compared with a Conservative majority of 8% in 1992. The shift in votes was the biggest between the two parties in modern times.

During the early months of 1994, the Conservatives' troubles had provoked speculation that Major might be replaced as party leader and prime minister. In the event, however, it was the opposition Labour Party that was forced to choose a new leader. On May 12 John Smith (*see* OBITUARIES) died of a heart attack. On July 21 Tony Blair was elected to succeed him. Blair obtained 57% of the vote of Labour MPs, party members, and trade unionists, defeating John Prescott (*see* BIOGRAPHIES), who took 24%, and Margaret Beckett (19%). In a parallel contest for the deputy leadership, Prescott (57%) defeated Beckett (43%), who had served as Smith's deputy.

Blair campaigned for the leadership on an uncompromising policy of reform. On October 4, in his first speech as party leader to Labour's annual conference, he announced a review of the party's constitution. This announcement signaled his intention to bury Labour's long-standing consti-

tutional commitment to work for "the common ownership of the means of production, exchange and distribution." That commitment—known as Clause IV from its position in Labour's constitution—had lasted since 1918. Blair argued that Labour needed to make clear its acceptance of the principles of a market economy.

Blair's strategy won wide public approval and posed a dilemma for the Conservatives: should they seek to fight Labour on the centre ground or move to the right and (in the words of Michael Portillo, one of Major's most right-wing Cabinet ministers) establish "clear blue water" between the parties? On October 14, in a speech to his party's annual conference, Major made clear his intention to disregard Portillo's advice. He announced that in the near future there would be no further big changes to two government services that had been through a series of recent upheavals: health and education.

Three significant social reforms were implemented in 1994. On February 21, MPs voted to reduce the age of homosexual consent to 18. This decision represented a compromise between those who wanted to keep the age of consent at 21 and those who wanted to reduce it to 16, in line with the age of heterosexual consent. On August 26 the Sunday Trading Act came into force. This allowed small shops in England and Wales to open at any time on Sunday and large shops to open for any six hours between 10 AM and 6 PM. The previous, far more restrictive, Sunday trading laws had been widely ignored. The third reform was enacted not by Parliament but by the General Synod of the Church of England, which voted on February 22 to allow women to be ordained as priests.

The monarchy had another turbulent year. Details surfaced of extramarital affairs by both the Prince and Princess of Wales prior to their separation in December 1992. Royal rumours and revelations filled the tabloid press and provided grist for the book-publishing industry as well. Prince Charles sought (with some success) to rebuild his reputation by cooperating with a two-hour television documentary about his life. During interviews given during the making of the film, which was shown in June, the prince insisted that he would become king (rather than allow the succession to pass straight to his elder son, Prince William) and that he wanted to create a more modest and open monarchy, with

Actor Sean Caffrey provides a voice-over for Gerry Adams, head of Sinn Fein, a way of skirting the British ban on broadcasting by the Irish Republican Army. In September, British Prime Minister John Major lifted the ban and also opened border crossings with Ireland.

fewer "minor royals" performing public functions. He also said that he wanted to be amend the coronation oath so that he would become "defender of faith" (meaning all religions) rather than just "defender of *the* faith," the traditional title accorded to the monarch as formal head of the Church of England.

Economic Affairs. The U.K.'s main economic indicators in 1994 told a story of steady progress. Gross domestic product grew by 3%; prices rose by only 2%; the value of sterling held steady; and unemployment fell by 300,000 to 2.5 million, or 9% of the workforce.

Throughout the year Kenneth Clarke sought to convince voters and investors alike that the United Kingdom was overcoming the problems of the early 1990s—recession, high inflation, a rising tax burden, and record levels of government borrowing. The public-sector borrowing requirement for the year to March 31, 1994, reached £46 billion. This exceeded the previous record, set in 1993, by £10 billion. Tax increases and higher-than-expected economic growth helped to reduce the level of borrowing during 1994, however. By the end of 1994 the rate of borrowing had fallen to £30 billion a year. Through the year Clarke and Eddie George, the governor of the Bank of England, stressed their determination to ensure that the U.K.'s recovery did not provoke higher inflation. On February 8 they reduced the bank's minimum lending rate to 5.25%, the lowest since 1977. On September 12, however, following the publication of data showing faster-than-expected economic growth, the rate was raised to 5.75%.

Some economic problems remained. Consumer confidence recovered only slowly. The housing market proved more fragile than the government either hoped or wanted. On average, house prices did not change through the year. Although this helped first-time buyers, it both reflected and reinforced consumer nervousness. One contributory cause was mounting insecurity in the labour market. Although the unemployment figures fell, so did the figures for the number of employees in full-time jobs.

Foreign Affairs. A brief but bitter dispute flared up in March between the U.K. and 10 of the other 11 members of the European Union (EU) over the enlargement of the Union. The dispute concerned the formula governing decisions taken by qualified majority voting (QMV) among the EU's Council of Ministers. The U.K. wanted to change the rules to increase the majority needed to adopt QMV decisions. On March 22, following an inconclusive meeting of the EU's foreign ministers, Major told the House of Commons that he would veto EU enlargement unless the QMV rules were changed. One week later, however, after a further meeting of foreign ministers, Major backed down, amid widespread criticism that he said one thing one week and did the opposite the next.

Major survived his next test rather better. On June 25 he vetoed the nomination of Belgian Prime Minister Jean-Luc Dehaene as the next president of the European Commission. Major considered Dehaene, who had the backing of the other 11 states, as too much of a European federalist. On this occasion Major stuck by his veto. Eventually, on July 15, the heads of government unanimously chose Jacques Santer (*see* BIOGRAPHIES), the prime minister of Luxembourg, as the next president of the commission.

During the year Major developed his belief that Europe should resist becoming a federal state. Instead, in a speech on May 31 during the European Parliament election campaign, he advocated a "multitrack, multispeed, multilayered" approach, in which the diverse interests of different member states would be recognized. On September 7, during a visit to Leiden, Neth., Major went farther and warned against

Germany, France, and the Benelux countries trying to create an inner group starting to construct a federal Europe regardless of the wishes of the rest. Major said, "I see a real danger in talk of a hard core, inner and outer circles, a two-tier Europe. . . . There is not, and should never be, an exclusive hard core either of countries or of policies."

A more tangible symbol of the U.K.'s links with the rest of Europe came when on May 6 the queen and French Pres. François Mitterrand officially opened the new Channel Tunnel (Eurotunnel), which was built to carry rail traffic between England and France. After overcoming some teething difficulties, the passenger service opened on November 14, allowing rail passengers to travel between London and Paris in three hours.

At the end of February, Major visited Washington, D.C., and sought to quell speculation that his relationship with U.S. Pres. Bill Clinton had been strained by reports that the Conservative Party had sought to help Pres. George Bush in his election campaign against Clinton in 1992. As a symbolic gesture, Clinton allowed Major to occupy the Lincoln bedroom at the White House—the first British leader to sleep there since Winston Churchill. Major and Clinton appeared to establish a good rapport, and later in the year Major acknowledged Clinton's supportive role in securing a cease-fire in Northern Ireland. The two leaders continued to disagree over policy in the former Yugoslavia, however, with Major opposing Clinton's call for the UN to lift its arms embargo on Bosnia and Herzegovina.

Northern Ireland. Hopes of an end to 25 years of violence rose dramatically in 1994 when the principal terrorist groups—both nationalist and unionist—announced cease-fires within seven weeks of each other. The Irish Republican Army (IRA) cease-fire came into effect on September 1 and that of the unionist groups on October 14.

The cease-fires followed months of intensive debate within the terrorist groups following a joint peace initiative in December 1993, when Major and Irish Prime Minister Albert Reynolds set out their common position on the future of Northern Ireland. The Downing Street Declaration (as the initiative came to be called) included an offer to include terrorist groups in political and constitutional negotiations within three months of a permanent end to violence.

During the nine months following the Downing Street Declaration, the IRA leadership came under considerable private pressure, both from Dublin and from the leadership of Northern Ireland's main (and nonviolent) nationalist party, the Social Democratic and Labour Party, to announce a cease-fire. On August 31 the IRA made its long-awaited announcement of "a complete cessation of military operations." Although the statement did not use the word "permanent," Reynolds immediately stated that he was satisfied with the IRA's wording.

Major's initial reaction was regret that the IRA had failed to commit itself to a permanent end to violence. He did, however, seek to maintain the momentum toward peace. On September 16, during a visit to Belfast, he lifted the broadcasting ban that had prevented the voices of terrorists and their supporters from being heard on British radio and television. The ban had been widely criticized for laying the U.K. government open to criticisms of censorship—without achieving its declared purpose of denying publicity to terrorist groups. During the six-year ban, broadcasters had employed Irish actors to speak the words that terrorists had used in speeches and interviews. The effect was akin to a badly dubbed foreign-language film.

Major also announced that the results of any negotiation over the future of Northern Ireland would be subject to a referendum in the province. This announcement was designed to satisfy unionists that Ulster would remain part of the U.K. as long as a majority of its electors so wished. Major's assurance helped to pave the way for the announcement by the main unionist (or "loyalist") terrorist groups on October 13 that they, too, would end "all operational hostilities" at midnight that day.

By October 21, with the IRA cease-fire 51 days old and holding firm, Major was able to state that he was making a "working assumption" that the IRA intended a permanent end to hostilities. During a visit to Belfast, the prime minister announced that government officials would seek exploratory talks with Sinn Fein, the political arm of the IRA, before the end of the year. In addition, Major lifted the exclusion orders that had prevented Sinn Fein's two most prominent members, Gerry Adams (*see* BIOGRAPHIES) and Martin McGuinness, from traveling to the British mainland.

The cease-fires followed 25 years of conflict, during which 3,169 people had been killed, including 2,224 civilians. The last major atrocity occurred on June 18, when six Roman Catholics watching the Ireland association football (soccer) team on television were killed by gunmen from the Ulster Volunteer Force (UVF). The UVF said the attack was in retaliation for the murder of one of their own prominent members the previous week.

The momentum for peace was strong enough to survive two awkward episodes in November: the fall of Reynolds' government in Ireland and the murder of a postal worker in Newry. The IRA claimed that its members had carried out the murder in violation of orders to observe the cease-fire. On December 9, British civil servants opened negotiations with leading members of Sinn Fein in Belfast. No government ministers were involved in the opening round of talks. Among the issues discussed was the government's insistence that the IRA surrender its weapons before full-scale political negotiations could begin. No progress was made on this issue by year-end.   (PETER KELLNER)

See also *Commonwealth of Nations*; *Dependent States*.

UNITED STATES

The United States of America is a federal republic composed of 50 states. Area: 9,372,571 sq km (3,618,770 sq mi), including 205,856 sq km of inland water but excluding the 156,492 sq km of the Great Lakes that lie within U.S. boundaries. Pop. (1994 est.): 260,967,000. Cap.: Washington, D.C. Monetary unit: U.S. dollar, with (Oct. 7, 1994) a free rate of U.S. $1.59 to £1 sterling. President in 1994, Bill Clinton.

U.S. Pres. Bill Clinton must have been hard pressed to discern much cause for cheer by the time 1994 wore to a close. Battered by allegations of sexual and financial misconduct—the latter focused as well on first lady Hillary Rodham Clinton—the president also saw the centrepiece of his legislative program, health care reform, die in Congress. Within the White House, a new chief of staff failed to bring much-needed discipline or prevent a steady string of resignations by top aides under attack for alleged improprieties or conflicts of interest. By the end of the year, the president was deemed anathema even by considerable numbers of fellow Democrats, who declined his campaign support during the November elections. Paradoxically enough, the man elected in 1992 to solve the nation's festering domestic problems could take solace as 1994 ended chiefly in a string of foreign policy successes and a hard-won victory in expanding the global free-market system.

For the first time since 1954, the Democrats lost control of both houses of Congress. (*See* Sidebar.) Newt Gingrich of Georgia, who would become the new speaker of the House,

Newt Gingrich speaks to reporters after the Republicans won control of both houses of Congress for the first time in 40 years. As the new speaker of the House of Representatives, Gingrich would attempt to enact the conservative policies set forth in his "Contract with America."
RICK REINHARD—IMPACT VISUALS

was hailed as the chief architect of the Republican triumph. The trend continued among the states, where Republicans had a net gain of 11 governorships, boosting their total to 30 and ousting such powerful figures as Mario Cuomo of New York and Ann Richards of Texas.

The Economy. The sentiment that seemed to motivate voters was not, on the surface, inspired by dire economic facts. The economic outlook in 1994 generally appeared to be good. The unemployment rate in December, 5.4%, was at a four-year low, down dramatically from a high of 7.8% two years earlier, and the economy was generating an average of some 275,000 new jobs every month, some 3.5 million for the year. The U.S. share of world manufactured exports, a time-honoured measure of national economic strength, was rising toward 16%, while those of Japan and Germany were in decline. Per capita disposable income was rising steadily, and so were corporate profits. General Motors, for example, the world's biggest industrial company, which had reported a titanic $4.9 billion loss in 1991, was showing a $2.8 billion profit by mid-1994, more than for all of 1993. A new wave of mergers and acquisitiveness gripped a number of U.S. business sectors, notably the telecommunications and health care industries. Inflation remained under control—the consumer price index rose 2.7% during the year—and price stability seemed more or less assured, at least for the short term.

There was, however, a steady ratcheting up of interest rates by the Federal Reserve Bank (Fed), from a short-term figure of 3% at the beginning of the year to 5.5% at year-end. Between February and November the Fed raised rates six times, and at one point it hiked its key interest rate twice in little more than a month. The main reason for the Fed's action was the feeling on the part of its chairman, Alan Greenspan, and a majority of the members of the Open Market Committee that the continuing economic expansion might lead to eventual overheating and supply bottlenecks, which would, in turn, refuel inflation. By making money more expensive and thereby slowing the rate of expansion, the Fed aimed to keep the underlying potential for inflation under control. The moves spread turmoil in the financial markets, however, always sensitive to interest-rate hikes, and early in the year there occurred the biggest single-day drop in the Dow Jones industrial average since 1991.

The effects were even more parlous in the bond markets, which had become highly dependent on mathematically complicated forms of futures contracts, known as derivatives, that offered substantial gains—and equally severe losses—depending on how successfully investors bet on the prevailing financial bellwethers. With the change in Fed policy, large numbers of institutional investors—from corporate treasurers to managers of college endowment funds—bet spectacularly wrong. In a move that rocked the municipal bond market, Orange county, in southern California, filed for bankruptcy protection after highly leveraged investments went sour and cost the county $2 billion. Lesser shocks were felt by millions of individual investors who had moved money out of traditional, low-interest forms of insured savings into mutual funds that held derivatives. The effect was to dispel some of the feeling of security and well-being that might have been inspired by the economic performance of goods, services, and jobs.

As is common in economic recoveries, U.S. productivity and profitability increased in important measure because workers stayed on the job for more overtime hours—more so in 1994 than in previous business cycles. In the third quarter of the year, for example, the factory workweek reached a near-record 42 hours, including almost 5 hours of overtime. Among debt-laden consumers, however, the resulting income gains were offset by hikes in the interest costs for credit card purchases, mortgages, and car payments. Too, despite the swelling number of available jobs, many corporations continued to cut payrolls to maintain their competitive advantage. Consumer spending remained strong through most of the year, with an annual rise of 7.6% in 1994, but retail sales unexpectedly slumped in December. Overall the improved economic picture was marred by a continuing, deep-rooted sense among individuals that all was not as well as it should have been or as secure as it had been in the past.

Health Care. It was just such a feeling of insecurity that Clinton had addressed during his successful 1992 election campaign and that his proposal for universal health care seemed designed to allay. At first the nation seemed willing to make the changes required for providing health coverage for the 37 million or more Americans said to be uninsured. At the same time, there was a strong feeling that the patchwork U.S. health care system—with its welter of private insurers, employer-sponsored insurance plans, private doctors and hospitals, plus a government subsidy system for the poor and elderly was far too expensive. Nonetheless, the plan the Clintons had unveiled in September 1993—with Mrs. Clinton as the overseer—ran into a minefield of opposition after it was presented to Congress. Its sheer complexity—the original document weighed in at 1,368 pages and included radical innovations such as national price controls, huge mandatory health care alliances, and government-mandated coverage by employers—brought together a broad array of opposition forces.

In fact, a number of dramatic changes had been occurring in the health care system. Spurred by the notion of widespread government intervention, private care providers had begun to rein in spiraling costs. More and more employers had enrolled workers in health maintenance organizations (HMOs)—networks of doctors and hospitals that closely monitored costs and rewarded caregivers for keeping them under control. The HMOs were sometimes bureaucratic and unwieldy, but their rapid expansion through start-ups, mergers, and acquisitions was one of the salient features of economic activity during the year. Further, the more large-scale employers began to get their costs under control, the less enthusiastic they became about endorsing enhanced government control. For example, the Business Roundtable, a group of 200 of the largest U.S. corporations, endorsed a rival congressional scheme that did not place emphasis on controlling prices or on universal coverage. There was also opposition from other groups, including small businesses, insurance companies, and the elderly.

At a rally in Lansing, Mich., against domestic violence, a woman remembers her granddaughter, who was killed by a boyfriend. The problem was one of many crime-related issues dealt with in legislation proposed by Pres. Bill Clinton and passed by Congress in August.

As the president faced an increasing number of opponents to the proposal, he frequently tried to be conciliatory to all sides at once, even while trying to talk Congress into doing his bidding on the issue. At various times he declared almost every aspect of the Clinton health care plan to be negotiable. Universal coverage itself, however, the president declared to be inviolable—until he eventually gave a nod to a competing proposal that would settle for 95% coverage over several years' time. Opponents came up with even more alternative schemes to bleed momentum from the reform movement, and at one point more than 150 different health care bills clogged the congressional system. Eventually none of the proposals picked up the legislative support necessary to force a bill through Congress.

Welfare Reform and Crime. In his state of the union address, Clinton also turned his attention to two other social issues of long-standing concern, welfare reform and crime. Welfare reform in particular was a notion that stirred enthusiasm across the country, where it was assumed to mean a cutback in support payments to the poor and near poor, including such programs as Medicaid and food stamps. Of particular concern in the public mind was Aid to Families with Dependent Children, a program that cost $16 billion annually—not much in the overall budget but symbolic to many of the culture of welfare dependency, involving unwed mothers, neglected children, and unemployed teenagers. Various states were already experimenting with "workfare" programs involving mandated employment when Clinton announced in his address that he would propose a similar scheme, including a welfare payment cutoff after two years coupled with aggressive programs of job training and retraining. Traditional constituencies within his party objected, however, and Congress took no action.

Even though various violent crime rates were still declining, Americans continued to see a growing threat to their way of life and to demand ever more draconian punishments. By 1994 the number of people sentenced to federal, state, and local prisons had far outstripped the nation's capacity to jail them. Federal and state prisons held some 925,000

inmates, about double the population of a decade earlier. Local jails held another 450,000, or triple the capacity 10 years earlier. The average cost of holding that population was $23,500 per inmate, yet the public demanded more: more police, more prisons, and more mandatory sentences.

Clinton's 1994 crime bill attempted to ride the law-and-order wave by endorsing the controversial proposal of mandatory life sentences for violent offenders found guilty of three consecutive offenses. It also included $28 billion for additional prisons and police, which Congress speedily bid up to $33.5 billion—and, after a series of horrifying massacres around the country, a proposal for the first time to ban outright 19 different so-called assault weapons, firearms capable of rapid, automatic fire. The ban was virulently opposed by the National Rifle Association but was supported by law-enforcement agencies, and it narrowly passed the House 216 to 214. It eventually became law separate from the crime bill. The overall bill, however, went down to defeat when Republicans attacked it for containing excessive amounts of pork-barrel funding. After lobbying by the White House, a slightly trimmed version became law.

Personnel and Personal Problems. Such near disasters only contributed to the Clinton White House's reputation for ill discipline, fecklessness, and lack of attention to the minutiae of pushing a program through Congress. The Clintons, loyal to the team of Arkansans and other friends they had brought to Washington, resolutely rejected the idea of a major administrative shake-up until the clamour grew too strong to ignore. The president in effect fired his boyhood chum, White House Chief of Staff Thomas ("Mac") McLarty, and replaced him with the head of the Office of Management and Budget, Leon Panetta. The anticipated broader shake-up failed to take place, however. Instead, the heads of top administration officials began to roll in connection with a variety of alleged scandals—none involving much hard evidence of wrongdoing—that had mostly been over long before the Clintons went to Washington and that were collectively known as the Whitewater affair.

The details of Whitewater rivaled, in their numbing complexity, the details of the Iran-contra scandal of the Reagan era but without the grave implications for the institution of the presidency, since most of the Whitewater action had taken place during 1978–91, while Clinton mainly occupied the attorney general's office and the governor's mansion in Little Rock, Ark. The finger-pointing mostly revolved around the Clintons' failed investment in a small-scale rural land development north of Little Rock in partnership with James McDougal, owner of the Madison Guaranty Savings and Loan. Madison Guaranty eventually went bankrupt, costing taxpayers $45 million, and McDougal was charged with, but eventually acquitted of, bank fraud. There was no evidence that the Clintons, who claimed to have lost almost $69,000 in the land deal, were aware of any wrongdoing, but critics made much of their association with McDougal at a time when Clinton was ultimately responsible for banking oversight in the state and when his wife, then an attorney with the Rose Law Firm in Little Rock, at one point performed minor legal work for Madison Guaranty.

The accusations of scandal had percolated without much result in 1993 until the apparent suicide that July of Vincent Foster, a Rose Law Firm partner who had gone to Washington as Clinton's personal counselor and the family lawyer. It was discovered that in the suicide's wake a number of top Clinton aides, including White House Counselor Bernard Nussbaum, had entered Foster's office and taken files related to the Clinton family's personal affairs. As critics cried cover-up, the Clintons spent much of 1994 in a determined effort to protect the privacy of their past deal-

A former CIA agent, Aldrich Ames, charged along with his wife with spying for the Soviet Union beginning in 1985, arrives at court. The case led to congressional hearings on the agency's security procedures and to the resignation of CIA director R. James Woolsey.

ings—which only convinced many, particularly in the press, that they had something to hide. The situation became even more difficult when a number of White House officials were subpoenaed to appear before Congress to explain their attempts to ride herd on the Whitewater scandal. Many of the officials suffered lapses of memory during their testimony, and one of them, Deputy Secretary of the Treasury Roger Altman, resigned after being accused of intentionally misleading Congress about his reports to the White House while serving as the acting head of the Resolution Trust Corporation, which was investigating the Madison Guaranty failure. An independent prosecutor continued investigation of Whitewater throughout the year.

Another matter that continued in the news was a series of investments in 1978 and 1979 by Mrs. Clinton in cattle futures, which netted a profit of about $100,000 on an investment of $1,000, less than the usual minimum for such high-risk trading. She had been advised in her moves by an attorney associated with the Tyson food-processing empire, Arkansas's largest private company and one regulated by both state and federal governments. The clamour went up that the investment was an apparent conflict of interest, and eventually the stain spread to include Secretary of Agriculture Mike Espy, who resigned after it was revealed that he had accepted favours from Tyson while in office.

On December 28 a federal district court judge ruled that a sexual harassment lawsuit filed against Clinton by a former Arkansas state employee should not proceed to trial until after the president left office.

Other Developments. One domestic triumph that stood out was the president's choice to replace Supreme Court Justice Harry Blackmun, who stepped down from the bench at age 85. In seeking a successor, Clinton first looked to Senate Majority Leader George Mitchell, who had decided to retire, but Mitchell declined. A month later Clinton named Boston federal appeals court judge Stephen Breyer (*see* BIOGRAPHIES) to the post. Breyer, a onetime chief counsel to the Senate Judiciary Committee, an antitrust specialist, and an expert on administrative law, was almost universally applauded for his intellect and his consensus-making skills.

On three occasions during 1994, the White House was the object of physical attacks. In September a small plane crash-landed on the grounds, killing the pilot. A month later a man, subsequently charged with several felonies, fired on the residence with a semiautomatic weapon. Near the end of the year, in December, shots were fired that reached the grounds and the White House itself, one bullet piercing a window in the State Dining Room. In none of them was the president injured or in immediate danger.

Foreign Affairs. In his first year in office, Clinton had gone to great lengths to avoid involvement in foreign affairs while pursuing his domestic agenda. In 1994, however, the sense of priorities was gradually reversed. The president began the year at a foreign policy summit, meeting with Russian Pres. Boris Yeltsin in Moscow in January and scoring a major national security triumph when the U.S. and Russia formally ended their mutual nuclear terror by agreeing to point their strategic missiles at empty oceans rather than at any country's territory. Ukrainian Pres. Leonid Kravchuk added further lustre to the trip when he agreed to dismantle about 175 former Soviet intercontinental ballistic missiles on his territory, along with their attendant 1,800 nuclear warheads, in exchange for $1 billion in aid. Soon thereafter, Clinton ended another decades-old enmity when he formally dropped the 19-year U.S. trade (and investment) embargo against Vietnam, citing the Hanoi government's cooperation in the search for U.S. servicemen still missing in action in Southeast Asia. Clinton then cauterized the

The 1994 Midterm Elections

Forty years of Democratic dominance in the U.S. Congress came to a stunning end on November 8, when the Republican Party rode a tidal wave of anti-incumbent sentiment to victory in the midterm elections. The Republicans took control of both houses of Congress for the first time since 1954 as voters delivered a strong rejection of Pres. Bill Clinton and his policies. The Republicans picked up a net gain of 53 seats in the House of Representatives and 7 in the Senate. The last time such carnage had been seen in Congress was in 1958, when Republicans lost 48 House and 13 Senate seats. Moreover, the Republicans won a majority of congressional seats from the South for the first time since the Civil War.

Not a single Republican incumbent was defeated, while 37 Democratic incumbents were denied reelection. The most prominent casualty was Rep. Thomas Foley of Washington, the first speaker of the House to lose since 1862. The election results underscored not only a shift in party control but an ideological and generational transformation as well. The Republican triumph was seen by many analysts as having been fueled by the "angry white male" vote, so-called because conservative white men, protesting higher taxes, affirmative action, and gun control and advocating tougher measures on crime, had voted in large numbers for the GOP. More than half of the new House would consist of members with four years of service or less.

The winds of change were most in evidence in the House, which had been continuously controlled by the Democrats since 1954 and for all but four years since the first term of Pres. Franklin D. Roosevelt in 1932. The new House would be composed of 230 Republicans, 204 Democrats, and 1 independent. In addition to Foley, other prominent Democrats who lost included 18-term veteran Dan Rostenkowski of Illinois, the former chairman of the powerful Ways and Means Committee who was under federal indictment, and, after a 42-year run, Jack Brooks of Texas, chairman of the Judiciary Committee.

The Senate reverted to Republican control for only the second time in 40 years. With the defection of Democratic Sen. Richard Shelby of Alabama one day after the election, the Republican majority stood at 53 to 47. Republicans won nine seats vacated by retiring senators and defeated Democratic incumbents in Tennessee, where 18-year veteran Jim Sasser lost to Bill Frist, a heart surgeon who had never held elective office, and in Pennsylvania, where Rep. Rick Santorum defeated Harris Wofford. A few prominent Democratic incumbents survived. Edward Kennedy of Massachusetts and Dianne Feinstein of California turned back well-financed challengers. In Virginia, Sen. Charles Robb defeated Oliver North, a former Reagan White House aide best known for his role in the 1986 Iran-contra scandal.   (MELANIE ANNE COOPER)

Chilean Pres. Eduardo Frei speaks at a news conference as (from left) U.S. Pres. Bill Clinton, Canadian Prime Minister Jean Chrétien, and Mexican Pres. Ernesto Zedillo Ponce de León look on. It was announced that Chile would begin talks on joining the North American free-trade zone.

AFP

embarrassment of the intervention in Somalia, undertaken by his predecessor, George Bush, by ordering U.S. troops out of the warlord-riddled country.

As much as possible, Clinton installed trade and economics rather than military and ideological considerations at the centre of his foreign policy. Among other things he scrapped almost all export controls on previously sensitive telecommunications devices and computers to Russia, Eastern Europe, and China. In the case of China, he ended the linkage between human rights and most-favoured-nation trading status. Later in the year he met again with the other leaders of the 18-nation Asia-Pacific Economic Cooperation forum, and he agreed to join in the creation of an enormous trans-Pacific free-trade zone by 2020. Similar action for the Western Hemisphere was taken at the 34-nation Summit of the Americas held in December. In the wake of the punishing midterm election results, the president successfully lobbied for passage by Congress of the General Agreement on Tariffs and Trade.

Throughout the year the administration kept up arduous and often frustrating negotiations with North Korea. (See SPOTLIGHT: *East Asia and the Transition in North Korea.*) The U.S. tried a wide variety of blandishments and threats to persuade the North Koreans to once again allow international inspections of their nuclear facilities. After Pres. Kim Il Sung died (see OBITUARIES) and was replaced by his son Kim Jong Il (see BIOGRAPHIES), former U.S. president Jimmy Carter resumed talks he had begun in June and successfully brokered an arrangement whereby North Korea would turn over outmoded equipment in exchange for less dangerous power reactors and agree to inspections in 10 years' time. In December, however, another crisis developed when a U.S. helicopter was downed on North Korean territory. One crew member was killed in the crash, while the other was released unharmed after 13 days of tense negotiations.

In the Middle East, long a focus of U.S. preoccupation, Clinton did not have a major role to play in 1994, yet for the second year in a row, he witnessed the signing of a historic peace accord. This time the pact was between

Jordan and Israel, and it left the issue of the Golan Heights and peace between Israel and Syria as the major unmet goal of diplomacy in the region. Clinton himself made a bid to move the process along at a meeting with Syrian Pres. Hafez al-Assad, but to little effect. Yet when it seemed appropriate to draw the sword in the Middle East, Clinton reacted with energy and dispatch. After Iraqi Pres. Saddam Hussein ordered 50,000 heavily armed troops toward the frontier with Kuwait, in October Clinton airlifted thousands of U.S. troops to the region, and the Iraqi dictator quickly backed away.

The same could not be said for the warring sides in the Balkans, who scoffed at half-hearted efforts by NATO forces to impose limits on the long-running war in Bosnia and Herzegovina through ineffectual air strikes at nearly valueless targets. The NATO effort reflected a deep split between the U.S. and its chief European allies, notably Britain and France, which had peacekeeping forces on the ground in Bosnia, as the U.S. did not. The rift deepened and even threatened the foundations of the North Atlantic alliance as the year wore on, and the U.S., prompted by sentiment in Congress, tried to redress the military balance between the beleaguered Bosnian Muslim forces and the Bosnian Serbs, who had essentially won the genocidal war. The U.S. unilaterally ended its own arms embargo against both sides (which meant effectively against the Muslims) and said that it would not help its allies to enforce their ban. Later, the U.S. pressed for NATO air strikes. Finally, however, Washington acknowledged that NATO solidarity was more important than the integrity of Bosnia and backed down amid admissions from Secretary of State Warren Christopher that the entire crisis had been bungled. At the invitation of the Bosnian Serbs, Carter went to the area in December to broker a tentative cease-fire.

The president was faced with equally thorny choices in defending U.S. borders from a flood of Cuban and Haitian refugees who took to the Caribbean in virtually anything that would float in order to escape conditions at home. In the case of the Cubans, Clinton at first hesitated and then reversed decades of U.S. policy that embraced such escapees automatically as legitimate seekers of political asylum. Some 30,000 were interned at U.S. bases at Guantánamo Bay and in Panama while the White House negotiated with the regime of Fidel Castro (see BIOGRAPHIES) to stanch the flow, to which the Cuban government had turned a blind eye. The two sides eventually agreed to an increase of 20,000 per year in the quota of Cubans allowed into the U.S. through proper channels.

The Haitian tide was harder to stem. Throughout much of the year, the Clinton administration hoped that an effective economic embargo of Haiti would cause the regime of Gen. Raoul Cédras, the Haitian army commander, to accept the return of ousted Pres. Jean-Bertrand Aristide (see BIOGRAPHIES). For his part, Aristide fumed that the U.S. did not object to Cédras' remaining in control. As thousands of boat people washed up on the coast of Florida, however, the administration came to the view that only military intervention would work. In September the U.S. assembled a fleet of 23 warships and 20,000 troops and set out for Port-au-Prince. Once again a last-minute intercession by Carter proved to be decisive. With U.S. warships in sight, Cédras and his cohorts agreed to allow the troops ashore. The U.S. soldiers quickly took control, ferried the top military leadership into exile, reinstalled Aristide, and began the longer-term, and more difficult, task of helping to rebuild the poorest country in the Western Hemisphere from the ground up.

(GEORGE RUSSELL)

See also *Dependent States.*

SPOTLIGHT: The New Caribbean Basin Identity by David Renwick

Traditionally, the English-speaking islands in the Caribbean Sea, the Spanish-speaking countries in Central America and northern South America, and the remnants of the Dutch and French empires in the region have gone their separate political and economic ways. In 1994, however, a "Caribbean Basin" approach to hemispheric and international affairs began to emerge.

The 13 English-speaking countries had grouped themselves into a Caribbean Community and Common Market (Caricom) to further their trading and economic interests. The Dutch territories had maintained varying relations with The Netherlands, ranging from internal self-government (the Netherlands Antilles) to full independence (Suriname). The French islands had remained a constitutional part of France. Five Central American nations had formed the Central American Common Market (CACM). Venezuela, Colombia, and Mexico, whose Yucatán Peninsula juts into the Caribbean, had organized themselves into the Group of Three.

There was loose cooperation among most of these countries within the Organization of American States (OAS), but no "Caribbean Basin identity" was apparent until recent months. The discovery of such an identity in 1994 served well the interests of the two main groups. For the Spanish-speaking countries, it strengthened their hand in international affairs to have the well-established democracies of the English-speaking part of the region in their camp. For the Caricom territories, the relationship added considerably to the potential regional market for their goods. It created a trading and economic bloc much larger than Caricom itself, at a time when the world was coalescing into such blocs and membership in one was rapidly becoming mandatory.

The new Caribbean Basin identity was formalized in Cartagena, Colombia, on July 24 with the signing of an agreement for an Association of Caribbean States (ACS). Caricom (which had taken the initiative in achieving the agreement), the Group of Three, the six Central American countries, the Dominican Republic, Suriname, Haiti, and Cuba all became part of the ACS.

The laying of the groundwork for the agreement included ministerial meetings between Caricom and Central American nations beginning in 1992, special trade and investment agreements with Venezuela and Colombia and one planned with Mexico, and a summit between the Group of Three presidents and Caricom leaders in Port of Spain, Trinidad, in October 1993.

The ACS secretariat was located in Port of Spain. This placed a Caricom country at the focal point of the movement and gave the English-speaking states the opportunity to have a major influence within the new bloc.

The Caribbean Basin approach achieved by the ACS was timely in light of issues facing the region that required a collective response. They included the threat to Caribbean Basin Initiative (CBI) privileges posed by the North American Free Trade Agreement (NAFTA) especially after a fourth state, Chile, was admitted in December, the ever simmering question of Cuba, and the crisis in Haiti.

The CBI, initiated by former U.S. president Ronald Reagan in the wake of the ousting of the Marxist regime in Grenada by U.S. troops in 1983, guaranteed duty-free entry into the U.S. market for such crucial Caribbean Basin exports as garments and textiles. It facilitated a 50% increase in Caribbean exports to the U.S. and helped create thousands of new jobs annually. Although the CBI was extended indefinitely in 1990, Mexico's entry into NAFTA was seen as posing powerful new competition for CBI products in the U.S. market. Jamaica was particularly eager to protect its annual $450 million garment trade with the U.S., on which 28,000 local jobs depended.

Under pressure from Caribbean Basin countries, the U.S. agreed to an Interim Trade Program (ITP), lasting for three years, during which CBI beneficiaries would continue to enjoy tariff parity with Mexico in the U.S. Mexico's involvement with the ACS ensured its support for the interim measure. Canada, which had its own free-trading arrangements with Caricom, also supported the ITP.

The Cuban question received new impetus with the advent of a Caribbean Basin viewpoint within the hemisphere. The paramount question, of course, was Cuba's role in the region under vastly changed circumstances. Would Cuba now join in regional initiatives? There were conflicting reports as to whether the U.S. government had attempted to keep Cuba out of the ACS. Caricom's secretary-general, Edwin Carrington, insisted that it had not and also stated that "Cuba is a Caribbean state and has a full right to membership in Caribbean institutions."

This was not a view with which the U.S. was sympathetic, although most observers believed that a U.S.-Cuban rapprochement was inevitable. Political and public opinion in the Caribbean Basin held to the view that the isolation of Cuba was a relic of "Cold War mentality" and should be abandoned.

Many English-speaking Caribbean countries became aware of the Cuban problem at a direct level for the first time during the year. Jamaica, The Bahamas, and the Cayman Islands, for example, were all unwilling hosts to Cuban refugees.

The Caricom-Cuba Mixed Commission, set up in 1993, was expected to hold its first formal meeting before the end of 1994 to advance political and economic relations within the framework of the Caribbean Basin system. The Caribbean Basin countries let it be known that while they would continue to press the U.S. to end its embargo of Cuba, they also expected Cuba to "take steps" toward "political liberalization" in the same way that it had tentatively begun to introduce some small market reforms.

The other point of divisiveness was Haiti and the U.S. plan to reinstate democracy, by force if need be. While the Caribbean Basin nations disagreed with the U.S. over Cuba and some voiced objections to plans to invade Haiti, they ultimately supported the U.S. position on Haiti and participated in postinvasion peacekeeping and rehabilitation activities. Even the Caribbean Congress of Labour (CCL), traditionally a critic of U.S. government policy in the region, agreed that "the circumstances in Haiti made the use of force legitimate." Caricom countries sent more than 300 soldiers and scores of policemen to Haiti. The Caricom troops were the first non-U.S. soldiers to arrive.

U.S. Secretary of State Warren Christopher praised the role played by the Caricom countries in helping restore to power Haitian Pres. Jean-Bertrand Aristide. (*See* BIOGRAPHIES.) Prior to the exodus of Haitian boat people, the English-speaking states within the OAS had been influential in transforming the Haitian crisis from a regional to an international concern by encouraging the UN Security Council to take up the matter.

The Caribbean Basin clearly flexed its muscles in 1994. It remained to be seen how it would apply its newfound collective will in the years to come.

David Renwick is editorial director of Daily News Ltd. in Trinidad and Tobago.

State and Local Affairs

The sweeping change wrought by voters in the 1994 midterm elections seemed to be a stark repudiation of U.S. Pres. Bill Clinton and of the Democratic Party. Voter rejection of Democrats did not stop in Washington, D.C., however, but filtered down to give state Republicans their biggest legislative victory in a generation as well as impressive gains in gubernatorial contests. Whether, as some pundits believed, the Republicans' victory presaged the eventual transfer of increased authority from Washington, the states continued in 1994 to be the real innovators in social policy.

Party Strengths. The political tidal wave that produced the Republican takeover of the U.S. Congress for the first time in 40 years produced a similar upheaval in the states. Republicans won control of a majority of state legislatures for the first time since the Eisenhower landslide in 1956, gaining 472 new legislative seats, compared with only 11 for the Democrats. They also captured a majority of the nation's governorships, with a net gain of 11. In all, Republicans made net gains in 45 of the 46 states holding elections in 1994. Legislative strength changed dramatically. Before the elections Democrats had a 24–8 lead in the control of state legislatures, with 17 others split. After the balloting Republicans controlled both chambers of 19 legislatures and Democrats controlled 18, with 12 others split. (Nebraska had a unicameral, nonpartisan legislature.) In 15 states Republicans controlled both the governorship and the legislature, compared with 7 for the Democrats.

In New York a relatively unknown Republican state senator, George Pataki, denied Mario Cuomo's bid for a fourth term as governor. Cuomo's opposition to the death penalty and his liberal philosophy benefited the challenger. In California incumbent Republican Gov. Pete Wilson handily defeated State Treasurer Kathleen Brown. In Texas, George W. Bush, son of the former president, rode a wave of anti-Clinton sentiment to victory against incumbent Ann Richards. Bush's brother Jeb was unsuccessful in Florida, where incumbent Democrat Lawton Chiles was reelected. Postelection results gave Republicans 25 statehouses to 23 for the Democrats, with one tied and one independent. Previously, Democrats had controlled 29 statehouses and Republicans 20, with one independent.

Government Structures and Powers. In those states where citizens were permitted to put initiatives on the ballot, they voted on a record 142 measures in November. Hot topics included taxes, term limits, gambling, and crime. The most heatedly discussed ballot initiative was California's Proposition 187, denying public services to illegal immigrants. The measure passed by 59% to 41%, but a federal court issued a restraining order to stop the state from implementing its provisions. If it survived court tests of its constitutionality, the measure would deny education, health, and social services to illegal aliens, and it would require people to report suspected illegals to federal and state authorities. Officials estimated that education, emergency health care, and prison expenses for illegal immigrants cost the state more than $2.5 billion a year, and California, as well as Florida

and New York, had sued the federal government for reimbursement for such costs.

By a slim margin Oregon voters approved the so-called death with dignity measure. The law gave terminally ill patients the right to get prescriptions for lethal drugs that would enable them to end their lives. Opponents, arguing that the law would encourage suicide for primarily financial reasons, initiated legal action.

The issue of term limits was prominent once again in 1994. Measures setting term limits passed in seven of the eight states where they were on the ballot. In Colorado, where the issue started in 1990, voters imposed term limits on local officeholders and toughened limits on members of its congressional delegation. Alaska, Maine, and Oklahoma put limits on federal lawmakers, and Idaho, Massachusetts, Nebraska, and Nevada passed limits on both state and federal officials. Only in Utah did a term-limits measure fail, but the failure might be partly explained by the fact that Utah was the first state in which legislators had passed a law limiting themselves to 12 consecutive years in office.

Voters were as tough on criminals as politicians. Georgians approved a "two-strikes" measure mandating life in prison without parole for a second violent felony, which gave that state the toughest sentencing law in the country. Oregon voters passed a measure that would toughen sentences for violent crimes and require state prison inmates to work full-time. Violent felons in Colorado would no longer be able to post bail while awaiting trial, and Ohio voters toughened death penalty appeals. Oklahoma and Wyoming passed constitutional amendments instructing their legislatures to crack down harder on crime. Lawmakers in Oklahoma would be able to set minimum prison terms with no parole for convicted felons. Wyoming voters limited the governor's power to commute death sentences and gave legislators the authority to create a sentence of life imprisonment without parole. Measures guaranteeing victims' rights passed in Alaska, Idaho, Maryland, Ohio, and Utah.

With voters, animals fared better than either politicians or criminals. Arizona eliminated leghold traps, and bears and cougars in Oregon could no longer be hunted with bait or dogs. Florida limited marine net fishing. In other issues, two wineries in Oklahoma got voter approval to use out-of-state grapes, and in Washington voters gave denture makers the right to sell false teeth directly to the public rather than through a dentist.

Finances. For the second consecutive year, once-embattled state governments breathed a little easier on finances. The continuing national economic recovery, combined with several years of state tax increases and spending cuts, resulted in a measure of stability not seen since the economic downturn in 1990. The National Conference of State Legislatures estimated that state tax changes would generate a net increase of $3.9 billion in fiscal year 1995, a modest 1.1% more than 1994. Net increases in 20 states and reductions in 15 others were a misleading measure of tax activity, however. Excluding a huge increase in Michigan, the net tax increase among the other 49 states was a paltry $800 million. Without the extension of some taxes

already in place, moreover, taxpayers would actually have seen their net liability drop by $1.3 billion.

Only six states levied significant tax increases. Michigan voters approved a major overhaul of state taxes in a March special election. As a result, local school property taxes were reduced by $4.5 billion, but a statewide property tax was enacted, and the sales tax increased by one-half, from 4% to 6%. The net effect was a $3.1 billion tax increase.

Although personal income taxes rose in 12 states and declined in 10, most of the changes were insignificant. In fact, for the first time in several years, no states increased personal income tax rates. New York, however, postponed a scheduled rate reduction, resulting in a whopping $800 million tax increase. Personal rates were reduced in Arizona, Michigan, New Mexico, and New Jersey, where the new governor, Christine Todd Whitman, redeemed a campaign pledge by signing a $480 million tax cut. Reductions in New Mexico and Pennsylvania were largely targeted to low-income taxpayers. Business tax activity was minor. Michigan and Pennsylvania reduced rates; Arizona, Minnesota, New York, and Wisconsin increased net business tax receipts.

The vast majority of net tax increases came as the result of higher sales and related taxes. Louisiana raised $410 million in revenues by continuing the suspension of an exemption for food, utilities, and other items from the sales tax. Maine increased its sales tax on automobile rentals, while Florida lowered the pari-mutuel tax on jai alai gambling by 28%. Oklahoma imposed a 1% entertainment tax (subject to voter approval), and South Dakota increased its video lottery tax. New York and Tennessee increased taxes on health care providers, and Kentucky made its health care tax permanent. Connecticut adopted its first health care provider tax and raised $300 million in revenues by extending its sales tax to medical services.

Taxes on cigarettes and tobacco products continued to rise, although not as drastically as in previous years. Only three states increased cigarette taxes, compared with 16 in 1993. The largest tax hikes were in Michigan, which imposed a new 16% tax on the wholesale price of tobacco products and tripled the cigarette tax from 25 to 75 cents per pack. Oregon, on the other hand, reduced the cigarette tax by 26%.

The downward trend in state taxation was expected to accelerate with the continuation of the taxpayers' revolt nationwide. Efforts to limit the power of state legislatures to raise taxes by such means as requiring a mandatory referendum on any tax hike or demanding a supermajority vote for tax-increase bills were growing in popularity.

Education. Changes in school financing continued in 1994. Although property taxes had traditionally been the mainstay of public-school financing, during the year more than two dozen states faced court challenges because of the inequities between wealthy districts and poor ones. In New York state, for example, the richest district spent almost $46,000 per student, while in New York City, the average was $6,644 per student. Michigan voters approved a constitutional amendment to replace property taxes as the method of financing school systems, choosing instead to raise the state sales tax and taxes on cigarettes. Although lawmakers in Colorado, Vermont, and Wisconsin advanced similar plans, no legislation was passed in 1994.

Education funding, which had been particularly hard hit in the preceding few years, showed signs of improvement in 1994. With the exception of California, state governments generally increased their funding by about 5%. The extra money came at a time when schools had seen an influx of Asian and Latin-American immigrants, resulting in eight consecutive years of enrollment increases. Texas enrolled more than 100,000 new public-school students in the early 1990s, and New Jersey, New York, Pennsylvania, Florida, Georgia, Louisiana, North Carolina, and Tennessee also had large numbers of new students. Total enrollment in public schools reached 42,550,000.

Declaring that in some school districts "the wrong combination of clothes can get you killed," California passed a bill giving public schools the authority to require students to wear uniforms. The new law, which came into force as a result of a petition drive started by an eighth grader, allowed all decisions about uniforms or dress codes to be made by local school officials and made provisions for those families who could not afford uniforms.

Health and Welfare. While the federal government's attempts to reform health care and welfare fell apart, the states continued their role as the real innovators in these areas. Many governors and state legislators, who viewed themselves as being on the front lines, had never really counted on Washington to solve their problems. With Washington's failure, however, the impetus to develop policy at the state level grew even more urgent.

Oregon began a five-year experiment extending Medicaid to 91,000 people who were not eligible for other medical programs; two-thirds were families with children. Tennessee's new plan, known as TennCare, included people with chronic illnesses, 803,000 former Medicaid recipients, and 335,000 people with no health insurance. The federal government gave permission for Florida to conduct a Medicaid experiment that officials hoped would provide coverage for 1.1 million uninsured Floridians. At least a dozen other states applied or had plans to apply for federal waivers of Medicaid law, enabling them to develop their own reforms.

With a record 15 million people on assistance, the eagerness with which states applied for federal waivers to deal with welfare reform was, if anything, even more intense. In all, more than 30 states had requested waivers, but plans for reform differed drastically. Oklahoma, for example, began a three-year pilot program to make children and teenage parents enrolled in the Aid to Families with Dependent Children (AFDC) program stay in school or have their benefits reduced. The state's Learnfare program followed several other state experiments to make welfare recipients stay in school or be properly immunized in order to keep their benefits.

Oregon received a federal waiver and launched a pilot welfare-reform program called Jobs Plus, designed to help welfare recipients work for their benefits. One thousand families in six counties would be affected. Participants were to receive cash in lieu of food stamps and would be expected to work for private employers for up to nine months at the minimum wage. Employers were to be reimbursed by the state with money that previously had been distributed as welfare benefits.

Jobs Plus participants who had not been hired after six months got one day a week to look for an unsubsidized job. If after nine months they were still not employed, they would be offered another government-funded job. In addition, a $1-per-hour educational fund was to be established for every worker to be used for community college classes or job training. Jobs Plus required employers to develop training programs and allowed welfare recipients to work without losing their health and child care benefits. Benefits would be reduced for anyone failing to participate or dropping out of the program.

Los Angeles county became the first place in the nation to require fingerprint checks for parents applying for welfare for their children. More than 850,000 people in the AFDC program would be affected. State officials estimated that first-year savings in Los Angeles county alone would be $4.2 million. If the program proved successful in combating welfare fraud, it would be implemented statewide, where savings could be as much as $750 million.

Laws and Justice. With crime the number one issue on voters' minds, punishment took top priority in many states. In just one year after voters in Washington state approved the Persistent Offender Act—commonly known as Three Strikes You're Out—about half of all the states had introduced similar legislation. Thirteen states—California, Colorado, Connecticut, Georgia, Indiana, Kansas, Louisiana, Maryland, New Mexico, North Carolina, Tennessee, Virginia, and Wisconsin—passed new "three-strikes" laws. In addition, seven others—Alaska, Illinois, New Jersey, Ohio, Pennsylvania, South Carolina, and Vermont—had legislation pending.

Although the basic premise was the same, there were variations in sentencing, prison terms, and the number and types of crimes to which the laws applied. Connecticut, Kansas, and Maryland, for example, permitted judicial discretion; elsewhere, courts were required to impose mandatory sentences as defined by statute. In Maryland and Virginia, prisoners 65 and older who had served a certain number of years were eligible for a "release mechanism." California, New Mexico, and Colorado offered parole eligibility after 25, 30, and 40 years, respectively, but other states had no provision for parole.

The perception that juvenile crime was not only on the rise but also more violent led to legislative action in several states. A Florida law created the Department of Juvenile Justice, as well as a basic-training program for youthful offenders in the Department of Corrections, including post-release plans and a recidivism-tracking system. North Carolina created a boot-camp-style program for 16- to 25-year-olds. A new Washington law established the Learning and Life Skills Program for juvenile offenders.

Lawmakers also showed a heightened awareness of and sensitivity to domestic violence, with several states increasing penalties for abusers. New York enacted the omnibus Family Protection and Domestic Violence Act, and Maryland passed three new domestic-violence laws. Colorado passed five domestic-violence bills, including one that mandated arrest for the violation of a restraining order and jail time for a second offense. Virginia passed a number of laws with stiffer penalties for domestic violence, while Michigan had 14 new laws that would help in prevention and prosecution.

Gun-control measures on the ballot in several cities failed to pass, but Alaskans voted to amend their constitution to allow citizens to bear arms, and Tennessee became the 18th state to permit adults to carry concealed handguns. Georgia and Utah joined at least 13 other states in making car jacking a crime. The death penalty was reinstated in Kansas as a possible sen-

Mexicans hoping to enter the United States wait at a fence along the border for the chance to cross over. Voters in California, home to more illegal immigrants than any other U.S. state, approved a resolution to deny public services to anyone found not to be a legal resident.

tence for anyone 18 or older convicted of capital murder.

Ethics. Judge Rolf Larsen became the first state Supreme Court justice ever to be impeached in Pennsylvania. By a two-thirds vote, the Senate also barred Larsen from holding public office again. One charge to which Larsen admitted was a scheme to have tranquilizers prescribed in the names of Supreme Court employees in an effort to conceal his own battle with depression. The judge said that he feared disclosure of his illness would destroy his career.

The former director of the Michigan House Fiscal Agency was convicted in both state and federal courts of embezzlement, conspiracy, racketeering, and tax evasion. John Morberg was sentenced to 6½ years in federal prison and 6–10 years in state prison. The federal court judge ordered Morberg to repay the state $406,200, but two days later a county judge ordered him to pay $834,000, saying, "You have destroyed something money cannot replace— public trust in government."

The results of a November 1993 state Senate election in Pennsylvania were invalidated by a federal court judge in February when evidence of vote fraud was uncovered. The court found that campaign workers for Democrat William G. Stinson had stolen the election from Bruce Marks by engaging in "massive absentee ballot fraud, deception, intimidation, harassment and forgery" in Philadelphia's 2nd Senatorial District. Stinson himself was later acquitted of election-law violations, despite his testimony that he had helped unlock voting machines and opened sealed absentee ballots. Pennsylvania's state Senate reverted to Republican control when Stinson was stripped of his seat.

Prisons. Total state appropriations for corrections grew 9.7% in fiscal year 1994, the biggest percentage increase in any spending category. In the decade from 1982, state corrections budgets went from $6 billion to $20 billion. As mandatory sentencing laws got tougher, the financial implications of lengthy or lifetime impris-

onment drew increased scrutiny. An aging prison population guaranteed higher health costs, for example, and in Connecticut part of the double-digit increase in the 1994 corrections budget went to pay for more health care facilities. Overcrowding also continued to plague the penal system. The U.S. Department of Justice reported that the average state-prison population exceeded institutional capacity by at least 18%.

Not content with longer, harsher sentences, politicians in at least nine states found additional ways to placate citizens' rage. In Wisconsin the governor ordered an end to prisoners' use of free weights and to their access to tennis. California gave prison officials the authority to bar inmates from receiving what were considered obscene publications, and Florida, Louisiana, New York, North Carolina, Ohio, and South Carolina proposed various measures banning amenities such as network television, cable television, basketball, weight rooms, boxing, and wrestling.

By far the worst place to get locked up was Mississippi, where Republican Gov. Kirk Fordice expressed the desire to make his state "the capital of capital punishment." In a special legislative session called to address prison overcrowding, debate centred on such punitive measures as caning. A law banning private television sets, radios, tape or compact disc players, computers, and weight-lifting equipment was passed. In a move reminiscent of the days of chain gangs, prisoners also were to be dressed in striped uniforms with the word "convict" written on the back.

Gambling. Gambling initiatives were on more state ballots than any other issue in 1994, but their luck in winning passage was mixed. Florida voters rejected the Proposition for Limited Casinos; off-track betting lost in Minnesota; and various other proposals were rejected in Colorado, Rhode Island, and Wyoming. In South Dakota voters revived the state's video lottery, which had been ruled illegal by the state Supreme Court. Missouri approved the use of slot machines on riverboat casinos, and New Mexico approved a state lottery and video gambling. State legislators in Connecticut overrode the governor's veto and gave themselves the final authority on gambling contracts between the state and Connecticut's Indian tribes.

Equal Rights. Ten states attempted to put antigay initiatives on their ballots during 1994. Most proposals were based on the measure that had passed two years earlier in Colorado prohibiting antidiscrimination laws protecting gays and lesbians, a measure that was subsequently declared unconstitutional. Only in Idaho and Oregon did the petition drives succeed. Backers in Arizona, Maine, Missouri, Nevada, Ohio, and Washington did not get the required number of signatures. In Florida the ballot language was ruled invalid, and in Michigan backers were forced to abandon their effort when it was determined that the measure contained the same language that had been declared unconstitutional in Colorado. In Idaho and Oregon voters rejected measures that would have restricted civil rights protection for homosexuals. Vermont became the first state to offer health insurance to domestic partners of state workers without regard to whether they were heterosexual or homosexual. (MELANIE ANNE COOPER)

Gay and lesbian marchers carry a mile-long "unity" flag through the streets of Manhattan in commemoration of the 25th anniversary of the Stonewall uprising. The 1969 New York City riot was seen by many as the beginning of the modern gay and lesbian rights movement.

URUGUAY

A republic of eastern South America, Uruguay lies on the Atlantic Ocean. Area: 176,215 sq km (68,037 sq mi). Pop. (1994 est.): 3,168,000. Cap.: Montevideo. Monetary unit: peso uruguayo, with (Oct. 7, 1994) a free rate of Ur$5.61 to U.S. $1 (Ur$8.92 = £1 sterling). President in 1994, Luis Alberto Lacalle.

The lack of a stable alliance with other parties continued to plague the outgoing administration of Pres. Luis Alberto Lacalle and his National (Blanco) Party in 1994, and little progress was made with economic reforms. In February the government faced a motion of censure against its industrial policies from opposition members in the Senate. The practice of delaying currency devaluation behind the rise in the rate of inflation was particularly criticized; it was deemed responsible for a doubling of the trade deficit to $590 million in 1993 and for a nearly 9% decline in manufacturing output. Manufacturing activity continued to decline in 1994, and by November unemployment reached 9.9%, compared with a level of 7.4% in 1993.

Fears that the impending implementation of Mercosur (the Southern Cone Common Market) would have a negative impact on Uruguay's economy prompted the national Chamber of Commerce and opposition parties to call for a pause in the implementation process in order to allow Uruguay a further five-year adjustment period. Their pleas were unsuccessful, but Uruguayan negotiators did manage to secure some minor concessions from Argentina and Brazil on bilateral trade agreements.

On August 28 the government called for, and lost, a national referendum on constitutional reform. A key proposal would have allowed voters to choose a multiparty slate when electing the president and congressional, municipal, and local legislators.

The opposition centre-right Colorado Party and its leading candidate, Julio María Sanguinetti Cairolo, won congressional and presidential elections held on November 27 by an exceptionally narrow margin. The Colorados gained 32.2% of the vote, compared with 31.4% for the Blancos and 30.8% for the left-wing Progressive Encounter (EP). Uruguay's three-way political split was emphasized by the fact that the EP's presidential candidate, Tabaré Vázquez of the leftist Broad Front, retained the key position of mayor of Montevideo for a second consecutive term. Sanguinetti, who had been president in 1985–90, was due to take office in March 1995.   (JANET KRENGEL)

UZBEKISTAN

A republic of Central Asia, Uzbekistan borders the Aral Sea to the north, Kazakhstan to the north and west, Turkmenistan to the southwest, Afghanistan to the south, and Tajikistan and Kyrgyzstan to the east. Area: 447,400 sq km (172,700 sq mi). Pop. (1994 est.): 22,382,000. Cap.: Tashkent (Uzbek: Toshkent). Monetary unit: sum (introduced July 1, 1994, to replace the sum-coupon at a rate of 1 sum to 1,000 sum-coupons; the sum-coupon had been introduced as an interim currency in November 1993 to replace the Russian ruble), with (Oct. 3, 1994) a free rate of 16 sumy to U.S. $1 (25.45 sumy = £1 sterling). President in 1994, Islam Karimov; prime minister, Abdulhashim Mutalov.

In late January 1994 Pres. Islam Karimov launched privatization with a decree authorizing auctions of small shops and service enterprises. Price increases of up to 300% for basic goods and energy were announced in May, together with wage and pension increases. The Uzbek authorities appeared to be trying to avoid provoking the kind of popular discontent and disturbances that had accompanied the first postindependence price rises in 1992. In July the country's new currency, the sum, went into circulation. It was later declared Uzbekistan's sole legal tender, effective October 15.

In April, Chinese Premier Li Peng (Li P'eng) discussed an exchange of Chinese consumer goods for Uzbek cotton and natural resources, but he complained that none of the existing Uzbek-Chinese joint ventures was succeeding because a Soviet-era bureaucracy still prevailed in Uzbekistan and its currency was weak. Karimov heard similar criticism in Japan.

Repression of the Uzbek democratic opposition continued throughout 1994. In May opposition leaders were arrested, and the National Security Committee attempted to kidnap five exiled oppositionists while they attended a human rights conference in Kazakhstan. In late June two members of the banned democratic opposition Erk (Freedom) Party were reported to have been seized in Almaty, Kazakhstan, by Uzbek law-enforcement officials and taken to Tashkent; in October six Erk activists were put on trial on charges of antigovernment activity. All genuine opposition groups were excluded from the parliamentary election on December 25; only Karimov's People's Democratic Party (PDP), formerly the Communist Party, and the National Progress Party, a grouping of government officials and intellectuals set up with Karimov's blessing, were permitted to nominate candidates. In the first round of voting, the PDP and its supporters took 205 of the 250 seats.

Uzbekistan continued to support the neocommunist regime in Tajikistan and was accused by Afghan officials of interfering in Afghanistan's internal affairs through active support of Uzbek Gen. 'Abd ar-Rashid Dostam, who was fighting the forces of Pres. Burhanuddin Rabbani. Although Uzbek authorities denied the charges, foreign journalists in northern Afghanistan confirmed the report.

In January the leaders of the Central Asian states met in Nukus, the capital of Karakalpakstan, to set up a five-year program to improve the environmental situation in the Aral Sea basin. Foreign experts were concerned that Uzbekistan's leaders were interested only in limiting the ecological damage resulting from the dessication of the sea. Uzbekistan needed the cotton grown with water from the Aral feeder rivers, however, and only a drastic reduction in irrigation could restore the sea.   (BESS BROWN)

This article updates the *Macropædia* article CENTRAL ASIA: *Uzbekistan*.

VANUATU

The republic of Vanuatu, a member of the Commonwealth, comprises 12 main islands and some 60 smaller ones in the southwestern Pacific Ocean. Area: 12,190 sq km (4,707 sq mi). Pop. (1994 est.): 164,000. Cap.: Vila. Monetary unit: vatu, with (Oct. 7, 1994) a free rate of 113.50 vatu to U.S. $1 (180.52 vatu = £1 sterling). Presidents in 1994, Fred Timakata, Alfred Masseng (acting) from January 31, and, from March 2, Jean-Marie Leye; prime minister, Maxime Carlot Korman.

Political instability remained throughout 1994, with difficulties within and between the government coalition partners—Prime Minister Maxime Carlot Korman's Union of Moderate Parties (UMP) and former prime minister Walter Lini's National United Party. When Lini withdrew from the coalition in April, three of his ministers remained and were expelled from the party. Led by Sethy Regenvanu, they formed the People's Democratic Party and joined in a new governing coalition with Carlot Korman.

In February an electoral college composed of 46 members of Parliament and 10 presidents of local government bodies failed on two occasions to elect a new president with the required two-thirds majority. On a third attempt, in March,

Jean-Marie Leye, Carlot Korman's nominee and a former vice president of the UMP, was elected.

In its 1994 budget the government announced a 5% increase in public service salaries and at the same time determined that more than 200 public service jobs would be eliminated. The number of public service workers had increased from 3,300 in 1985 to 4,800 in 1993. Government revenue for 1994 was estimated at 5,354,000,000 vatu, with the growth of gross domestic product projected at 2%.

(BARRIE MACDONALD)

This article updates the *Macropædia* article PACIFIC ISLANDS: *Vanuatu.*

VATICAN CITY STATE

The independent sovereignty of Vatican City State is surrounded by but is not part of Rome. As a state with territorial limits, it is properly distinguished from the Holy See, which constitutes the worldwide administrative and legislative body for the Roman Catholic Church. Area: 44 ha (109 ac). Pop. (1994 est.): 1,000. As sovereign pontiff, John Paul II is the chief of state. Vatican City is administered by a pontifical commission of five cardinals headed by the secretary of state, in 1994 Angelo Cardinal Sodano.

The intense round of activities required by international and domestic commitments placed heavy demands on the chief of state, Pope John Paul II, in 1994, especially after a fall in April incapacitated the pontiff for some weeks.

The Holy See reported that the previous financial year had closed with an income surplus, reversing the previous negative trend. This welcome achievement was attained in spite of continued expenditures of well over $1 million to aid the victims of human violence and natural disasters.

In January the pope received the mayor of Rome to discuss the Jubilee scheduled for the year 2000. Later he met with the provincial authorities of Rome and urged that they devote more attention to the housing needs of the urban poor. Farther afield, the Vatican City State continued its determined participation in world events, forging historic diplomatic ties with Israel, Jordan, and the Palestine Liberation Organization. The pontiff also received many international visitors, including Czech Pres. Vaclav Havel and U.S. Pres. Bill Clinton. The pope's only visit out of Italy during the year was a first-ever journey to Croatia for the Zagreb diocese's 900th anniversary; during the stay he addressed a crowd of almost a million and prayed for peace in the Balkans.

(GREGORY O. SMITH)

See also RELIGION: *Roman Catholic Church.*
This article updates the *Micropædia* article VATICAN CITY.

VENEZUELA

A republic of northern South America, Venezuela lies on the Caribbean Sea. Area: 912,050 sq km (352,144 sq mi). Pop. (1994 est.): 21,177,000. Cap.: Caracas. Monetary unit: bolívar, with (Oct. 7, 1994) a fixed rate of 170 bolívares to U.S. $1 (270.38 bolívares = £1 sterling). Presidents in 1994, Ramón José Velásquez (interim) and, from February 2, Rafael Caldera.

Pres. Rafael Caldera's first months in office were beset by serious economic problems. Even before he took office, in February 1994, the outlines of difficulties ahead were apparent, first with the imposition by the previous president, Ramón José Velásquez, of price controls on basic items and then with the collapse of Venezuela's second largest commercial bank, Banco Latino. A crisis in the financial community followed when many depositors made substantial withdrawals. By June it was apparent that government financial assistance was being misused; one finance house and seven banks were closed before the government took

effective control of the entire system by decree. Eight additional institutions were given temporary assistance in August. At the root of the financial problems was the central bank's policy of high interest rates, which had caused the banks to suffer from a shortage of liquidity. In order to reduce borrowing costs, and thus help cut inflation, the government lowered interest rates. This forced the resignation of the central bank president, Ruth de Krivoy, who maintained that high interest rates prevented capital flight and that government intervention compromised the bank's independence.

Unfortunately for Caldera, the efforts to solve the economic crisis postponed the plans that had won him the 1993 elections. His aim was to improve employment and living standards, but by midyear some austerity measures had to be introduced. Of chief concern was a rapid decline in the value of the bolívar against the dollar. From a rate of 106 bolívares to $1 at the end of 1993, it fell to 155 to $1 by the end of May. By June 23 the bolívar had fallen to 200 to the dollar. All foreign exchange trading was then suspended, to be partially restored in mid-July, when a new fixed exchange rate of 170 bolívares = $1 was set. Exports and imports were severely disrupted, threatening the chances for economic recovery.

To ease the budget deficit, new taxes on luxuries, wholesale trading, and debt transactions at banks were announced in April, along with a higher ceiling on income taxes for corporations and individuals. In September an economic recovery program for 1995 proposed a further increase in taxes and the raising of gasoline prices in order to convert the budget deficit from an estimated 3.5% of gross domestic product (GDP) in 1994 to a surplus in 1995 (not including the huge drain on finances to support the banking sector). GDP was forecast to grow by 0.5% in 1995, compared with a 3.3% decline in 1994, while the rate of inflation would be cut from 65% in 1994 to 25%.

In February Caldera assumed emergency powers in order to abolish the value-added tax. Congressional opposition was short-lived, and the administration was granted a month to draw up new tax measures. In June Caldera suspended constitutional guarantees concerning the seizure of assets and the possession and trading of property; he also imposed restrictions on foreign travel. In the face of strikes and demonstrations, the right to free assembly and immunity from arbitrary arrest were also suspended. The congress voted to restore all these rights on July 21, but Caldera reimposed them the next day to prevent capital flight and speculation in essential goods. He also offered to hold a national referendum on his actions, which the congress declined. On the other hand, the president's action did not inspire confidence in those foreign investors who would have preferred to enter a less controlled market. In this regard the failure to obtain a single offer to buy the Aeropostal airline prompted a Cabinet reshuffle, with a new head of the privatization program.

In March Caldera released from prison Hugo Chávez Frías, who had led the military rebellion against former president Carlos Andrés Pérez in February 1992. Chávez expressed his support for Caldera without actually joining his coalition. Both shared the opinion that economic deprivation was behind political unrest, but it was open to question how long Chávez and his military supporters would refrain from intervention should the austerity that Caldera was forced to impose continue for a prolonged period. In May, Pérez, who had been removed from office in 1993, was arrested and imprisoned on charges of embezzlement and misuse of public funds in 1989. Formal hearings into the case began in November.

(BEN BOX)

VIETNAM

The socialist republic of Vietnam occupies the eastern part of the Indochinese Peninsula in Southeast Asia and is bounded on the south and east by the South China Sea. Area: 331,041 sq km (127,816 sq mi). Pop. (1994 est.): 72,342,000. Cap.: Hanoi. Monetary unit: dong, with (Oct. 7, 1994) a free rate of 11,053 dong to U.S. $1 (17,581 dong = £1 sterling). President in 1994, Le Duc Anh; prime minister, Vo Van Kiet.

Two of Vietnam's major policies seemed in conflict in 1994. One was its push to reform and open up the economy, especially after the U.S. lifted its trade embargo in February. The other was the Communist Party's refusal to liberalize politics—a position it reiterated at conferences in January and July. Officials had long feared that ending the embargo would increase contacts with Westerners and returning émigrés. Even so, in August Prime Minister Vo Van Kiet urged officials to learn foreign languages, preferably English, because "in coming years contacts with foreigners will become more and more necessary and popular."

In January Do Muoi, general secretary of the Communist Party, stressed the importance of economic reforms and continued opposition to political pluralism. He warned of "hostile forces" advocating democracy and encouraged efforts to combat corruption and improve social services—two problems that could undermine popular support for the party. Only one of the four new members promoted to the Politburo had any reform experience. Nguyen Ha Phan, director of the party's economic commission and vice-chairman of the National Assembly, was viewed as a possible successor to Vo Van Kiet. Although he came from the enterprising south, he was not seen as an advocate of reform.

PepsiCo, Inc., and American Express were among the first companies to act when the United States ended its

GREG GIRARD—CONTACT PRESS IMAGES

A Vietnamese salesperson stands amid cartons of imported U.S. soft drinks. When the U.S. government lifted its trade embargo in February, U.S. companies immediately entered Vietnam in an attempt to compete with Asian and European firms in the country's potentially huge market.

embargo. Over 40 U.S. firms had set up local offices by mid-1994, many of which had earlier worked out deals for implementation as soon as the embargo ended. In March the U.S. Agency for International Development set up an orphanage and a training centre for disadvantaged children in Dalat. In April came the first postembargo shipment of Vietnamese rice to the U.S., and in May came the first U.S. commercial loan—Bank of America's $5 million share in a $100 million Thai-led syndication. There was no sudden surge in trade, however. Because the U.S. had not yet granted most-favoured-nation status to Vietnam, it was limiting big-ticket imports.

Hanoi took steps to remedy social ills and lessen its dependence on other nations. In February it jailed a corrupt former minister of energy. Later in the year Vo Van Kiet, who had called for tougher graft penalties in 1993, sacked two top officials in Ba Ria-Vung Tau. In July the government threatened civil servants with substantial fines and possible loss of jobs for gambling, drunkenness, or prostitution. An official report in October said corruption was rampant, but smuggling and tax evasion were also commonplace. In August regulations to curb the widespread use of U.S. dollars were announced, but many establishments ignored them. That same month party chief Do Muoi warned against excessive reliance on foreign capital.

Eight years after Vietnam had launched *doi moi* (economic renewal), it appeared to be repeating the progress China had experienced after adopting reforms in 1978. Overseas investment and a new north-south power line helped fuel Vietnam's overall economic expansion of 8.5%. The increase was 13% in industry and 20% in exports, but agriculture, which supported 80% of the population, grew only 3–4%. Some 90% of the poor, however, lived in rural areas, and two-thirds of the affluent resided in cities. For Do Muoi the key was to promote rural industry and ally "peasantry and intelligentsia." Two things helped: an inflation rate of less than 10% and a budget deficit down to 7% of the gross national product. Only food prices rose by double digits, and that increase was helpful to farmers.

In June Do Muoi confirmed that Vietnam was prepared to establish full diplomatic relations with the U.S.—but not with human rights conditions. In the following month, U.S. Assistant Secretary of State Winston Lord expressed appreciation in Hanoi for its cooperation in helping to determine the fate of U.S. military personnel still officially listed as missing in action. The prime ministers of Japan, South Korea, and Canada subsequently visited Hanoi. Late in the year Vietnam formally applied for membership in the Association of Southeast Asian Nations, with acceptance expected in 1995. China, which had fought a brief war with Vietnam in 1979, improved ties between the two countries in November with the visit of Pres. Jiang Zemin (Chiang Tse-min). (RICARDO L. SALUDO)

This article updates the *Macropædia* article SOUTHEAST ASIA: *Vietnam*.

WESTERN SAMOA

A constitutional monarchy and member of the Commonwealth, Western Samoa occupies an island group in the South Pacific Ocean. Area: 2,831 sq km (1,093 sq mi). Pop. (1994 est.): 164,000. Cap.: Apia. Monetary unit: Western Samoa tala, with (Oct. 7, 1994) a free rate of 2.54 tala to U.S. $1 (4.04 tala = £1 sterling). Head of state (*O le Ao o le Malo*) in 1994, Malietoa Tanumafili II; prime minister, Tofilau Eti Alesana.

Throughout 1994 the government of Prime Minister Tofilau Eti Alesana faced resistance to the value-added goods and service tax introduced at the beginning of the year.

Following public demonstrations in March, the government announced that as a compensatory measure it would eliminate import duties from a range of food items and drugs and reduce duties on other items by two-thirds. Despite this concession, public opposition continued.

Resistance to the new taxes was heightened by difficult economic conditions. Despite a partial recovery of agricultural exports after Cyclones Ofa (1991) and Val (1992), exports in 1993 totaled only half those of 1988. Exports of coconut products fell especially sharply, from 19 million tala in 1988 to 3.4 million tala in 1993. Exports of taro, the other major agricultural export, were reduced by a blight that could be eliminated only by the forgoing of an entire growing season. The export value of car parts assembled from imported components had increased in recent years, but even so, exports in 1994 were expected to pay for only 4% of imports (down from 20% in 1988). The deficit was covered by foreign aid and by remittances from Western Samoans working overseas.   (BARRIE MACDONALD)

This article updates the *Macropædia* article PACIFIC ISLANDS: *Western Samoa.*

YEMEN

A republic of the southwestern Arabian Peninsula, Yemen has coastlines on the Red Sea, the Gulf of Aden, and the Arabian Sea. Area: 531,869 sq km (205,356 sq mi), including 59,770 sq km of undemarcated area bordered by Saudi Arabia claimed by the former Yemen Arab Republic (North Yemen). Pop. (1994 est.): 12,961,000. Cap.: San'a'. Monetary unit: Yemen rial, with (Oct. 7, 1994) a par value of 12.01 rials to U.S. $1 (free rate of 19.10 rials = £1 sterling); a truer value of the rial was on the black market, where in October about 84 rials = U.S. $1 (about 134 rials = £1 sterling). President in 1994, Gen. Ali Abdallah Salih; prime ministers, Haidar Abu Bakr al-Attas, Muhammad Said al-Attar (acting) from May 9, and, from October 6, 'Abd al-Aziz al-Ghani.

Civil war erupted in Yemen on May 5, 1994, after weeks of skirmishes between troops from the south and the north. Southern secessionists, headed by Ali Salim al-Baidh of the Yemeni Socialist Party (YSP) and 'Abd ar-Rahman al-Jifri of the Sons of Yemen League, proclaimed the breakaway Democratic Republic of Yemen on May 21 and appealed to Saudi Arabia and the Persian Gulf states for diplomatic

Northern Yemeni troops advance on Aden, the stronghold of the opposing southern forces. Bitter fighting broke out during the year between northern groups, led by Pres. Ali Abdullah Salih, and those of the south, led by his former vice president, Ali Salim al-Baidh.

and moral support. On June 1 the UN, at the prompting of several Gulf states, adopted a resolution condemning the northern authorities and calling for an immediate cease-fire.

Despite southern forces' acquisition of MiG-29s from Moldova, northern forces drove the rebels back to their stronghold in Aden. With the oil fields at Masila in northern hands, on July 7 the cities of Aden and Mukallah surrendered. The leaders of the putative secessionist state had fled into exile in Saudi Arabia and Oman. Jifri vowed to fight on, but Baidh was said to have "retired from politics."

Northern leaders moved to heal the wounds of the civil war, which resulted in some 5,000 dead. On July 13 the council of ministers started a 10-day session, which adopted a reconciliation plan offering a general amnesty, compensation for losses, and a pledge to restore democracy and safeguard political pluralism. In a gesture to the south, the government proclaimed Aden the nation's economic capital. Subsequent talks between Planning and Development Minister 'Abd al-Karim al-Iryani and Haidar Abu Bakr al-Attas, prime minister of the rebel state, held in Geneva under UN auspices, failed to make progress.

In Cabinet changes announced in September, members of the YSP were dropped from the government. The Islamic fundamentalist party al-Islah gained six new seats in the Cabinet in what was seen as a sign of growing Islamic influence in the north. During a special session of the 301-seat Council of Representatives on September 28, all 235 delegates present approved a new constitution that abolished the presidential council and stipulated that the Shari'ah would henceforth be the source of all legislation in Yemen. Al-Islah was given credit for the change.   (JOHN WHELAN)

This article updates the *Macropædia* article ARABIA: *Yemen.*

YUGOSLAVIA

A federal republic comprising the republics of Serbia and Montenegro, Yugoslavia borders Hungary to the north, Romania to the northeast, Bulgaria to the southeast, Macedonia and Albania to the south, the Adriatic Sea to the southwest, and Croatia and Bosnia and Herzegovina to the west. Area: 102,173 sq km (39,449 sq mi). Pop. (1994 est.): 10,515,000. Cap.: Belgrade. Monetary unit: new dinar (second) or "super dinar," with (Sept. 26, 1994) a par value (from January 24) equal to the Deutsche Mark (free rates of 1.56 new dinars [second] = U.S. $1 and 2.47 new dinars [second] = £1 sterling); hyperinflation caused major ongoing devaluations in 1993, but inflation was close to zero in 1994. President in 1994, Zoran Lilic; prime minister, Radoje Kontic.

Slobodan Milosevic, the president of Serbia since 1989, strengthened his grip on power in Yugoslavia in 1994. Internationally, Milosevic, for so long condemned as a warmonger and even a war criminal, completed his truly breathtaking metamorphosis, begun in 1993, into a champion of peace in former Yugoslavia.

Although Milosevic's Socialist (former Communist) Party of Serbia had secured only 123 seats in the country's 250-seat single-chamber assembly in the December 1993 election, it managed to attract to its side eight opposition deputies. After lengthy negotiations, on March 15 the Socialists formed a government with Mirko Marjanovic, a Socialist deputy, as prime minister. The Socialists came under strong attack from their erstwhile ally, Vojislav Seselj, a Bosnian Serb and leader of the ultranationalist Serbian Radical Party. Following a fight with another deputy in the Belgrade assembly, Seselj was deprived of his parliamentary immunity, arrested, and charged with defaming the president of Serbia and incitement to disorder and unrest.

Several trials of Serbs charged with having committed atrocities while serving with Serb paramilitary units (including Seselj's) in Croatia in 1991 and Bosnia in 1992–93 were held as part of Milosevic's policy of distancing himself from those wars. This implied no relaxation of government control over the mass media. Purges were carried out in both state-controlled television and the Politika newspaper and magazine publishing house. Belgrade continued to keep a firm grip on Kosovo, the former autonomous province with an Albanian majority, reannexed to Serbia in 1989. In Sandzak, a Muslim-majority region in Serbia contiguous to Bosnia, 24 local members of the mainly Muslim Party of Democratic Action were sentenced on October 13 to jail terms of up to six years for "plotting to violate the territorial integrity of Yugoslavia."

Milosevic also succeeded in maintaining indirect political control over the Serbs in the occupied territories in Croatia and obtained the reelection of his man, Milan Martic, as president in January. Milosevic was, however, less successful in imposing his will on Radovan Karadzic, leader of the so-called Serbian Republic in Bosnia. Milosevic repeatedly appealed in July to Karadzic and his army commander, Gen. Ratko Mladic, to accept the plan for Bosnia prepared by the "contact group" (Britain, France, Germany, Russia, and the U.S.) that offered 49% of the republic's territory to the Serbs and 51% to the Muslim-Croat federation. Karadzic's rejection of the plan led to the imposition by Serbia on August 4 of an embargo on deliveries to Bosnian Serbs of all but essential medical and humanitarian supplies. Serbia's media links with the Bosnian Serbs were also cut. On September 24 the UN Security Council adopted Resolution 943, partially lifting for a period of 100 days sanctions originally imposed on Yugoslavia by the UN Security Council in May 1992 for its role in the war against Bosnia.

This diplomatic success for Milosevic helped increase his popularity at home. His stock had already risen after the introduction on January 24 of the economic plan prepared by Dragoslav Avramovic, a former official of the International Monetary Fund. The plan introduced a high degree of financial and fiscal responsibility and tempered Serbia's hyperinflation, which had reached an annual percentage rate of 313 million by January 1994. The "super dinar" (unofficially called "avram") pegged to the Deutsche Mark became Yugoslavia's new currency.

Yugoslavia's relations with Hungary improved following a visit to Belgrade in January by Geza Jeszenszky, Hungary's foreign minister. The slow thaw in the relations with Croatia continued with the establishment of diplomatic missions in Zagreb and Belgrade. Following elections on December 19, the Socialist Party of Serbia was three seats short of a majority in the parliament. Ethnic Hungarians, however, hesitated to join the government, fearing that their participation in a coalition would weaken their demand for autonomy in the province of Vojvodina.   (K.F. CVIIC)

This article updates the *Macropædia* article BALKAN STATES: *Yugoslavia*.

ZAIRE

The republic of Zaire is located in central Africa with a short coastline on the Atlantic Ocean. Area: 2,345,095 sq km (905,446 sq mi). Pop. (1994 est.): 43,775,000 (excluding 1.5 million to 2 million Rwandan refugees in late August). Cap.: Kinshasa. Monetary unit: new zaïre, with (Oct. 7, 1994) a free rate of 2,022 new zaïres to U.S. $1 (3,216 new zaïres = £1 sterling). President in 1994, Mobutu Sese Seko; first state commissioners (prime ministers), Faustin Birindwa until January 14 and, from July 6, Joseph Kengo Wa Dondo.

With the economy of Zaire plunging into ever deeper trouble in 1994, the struggle for political power continued unabated. On January 14 Pres. Mobutu Sese Seko announced that the National Assembly, which he himself had created, and the High Council of the Republic (HCR), the brainchild of the former national sovereign conference, would be reconstituted as a single body, the High Council of the Republic–Parliament of Transition (HCR-PT), and that the new body would choose either his own candidate, Mulumba Lukoji, or Étienne Tshisekedi, leader of one of the opposition parties, as prime minister. Tshisekedi opposed the announcement on two counts. The president, he said, had no authority to disband the HCR, and he himself was already prime minister, having been legally elected to that office by the national conference in August 1992. On the first count Tshisekedi had the backing of other opposition parties, and when he summoned an all-out one-day strike in Kinshasa for January 19, his call met with an almost total response.

Nevertheless, the HCR-PT met the same week and appointed Msgr. Laurent Monsengwo Pasinya, the former chairman of the HCR, as its president. After prolonged discussion a new Transitional Constitutional Act was endorsed on April 8 and was promulgated by Mobutu the following day. The act stated that the period of transition to a democracy should not exceed 15 months. During that time a constitutional referendum as well as presidential and legislative elections would take place, and the HCR-PT rather than the president would have control of the armed forces and the central bank. The HCR-PT also decided to call on all parties to submit the names of candidates for the office of prime minister. This latter proposal caused a split among the opposition groups constituting the Sacred Union coalition because Tshisekedi and his Union for Democracy and Social Progress were angered when other parties proposed their own candidates in opposition to him. However, Tshisekedi's candidacy was rejected by the HCR-PT because he had not applied to be a candidate for election but had sought reconfirmation as prime minister. The choice of a former prime minister, Joseph Kengo Wa Dondo, to hold office was vigorously challenged by opposition parties, which again organized a 24-hour strike, for July 8.

This was the political background to a series of economic disasters, outbreaks of unrest, and the invasion of the country by more than a million refugees from neighbouring Rwanda. In spite of the monetary reforms introduced in October 1993, the Bank of Zaire had to be closed to the public on January 31 because of a shortage of banknotes in its vaults. The governor of the bank, Buhendwa Bwa Mushaba, was dismissed by Mobutu the following day.

He was succeeded by Ndiang Kaboul, who was himself suspended by the government of Kengo Wa Dondo in July after millions of newly minted Zairean notes flooded the black market, reducing the value of the new zaïre, introduced in October 1993 at a rate of three to the U.S. dollar, to 1,300 to the dollar. As a countermeasure the government decided in September to cancel all currency-printing contracts and to suspend the printing of banknotes. The World Bank, despairing of any improvement in the government's handling of Zaire's economy, had already closed its office in Kinshasa on February 1, declaring the country insolvent.

Friction between the rebel Movement of Farmers and Workers and government troops in the eastern Kivu region led to a flight of refugees to Uganda in January. Meanwhile, ethnic warfare continued in Shaba province in the southeast, resulting in an additional movement of refugees to the Kasai region. Still worse was the influx of refugees from Rwanda, which began in July when supporters of the former Hutu government fled before the advance of their rivals, the Tutsi. Inadequate provision for the vast numbers involved led to an outbreak of cholera in the refugee camps.

Many relief agencies, finding it increasingly difficult to carry on their work, threatened to depart because Hutu soldiers were terrorizing fellow refugees, stealing supplies and forcibly recruiting young men to swell their ranks. In late November Zairean commandos moved into Katale camp after 19 Rwandans had been killed. The troops deported 37 Hutu to Rwanda, but the military force was too small to handle hundreds of thousands of refugees. The UN considered, then rejected, a plan to send peacekeepers to the camps, but it agreed to support Zaire's own personnel.

(KENNETH INGHAM)

This article updates the *Macropædia* article CENTRAL AFRICA: *Zaire*.

ZAMBIA

A landlocked republic and member of the Commonwealth, Zambia is in eastern Africa. Area: 752,614 sq km (290,586 sq mi). Pop. (1994 est.): 9,132,000. Cap.: Lusaka. Monetary unit: kwacha, with (Oct. 7, 1994) a free rate of 671 kwacha to U.S. $1 (1,067 kwacha = £1 sterling). President in 1994, Frederick Chiluba.

Faced with an inflation rate in 1993 of 140.6% and with a warning from the Paris Club of creditor nations that it would receive the full amount of aid requested only when it had dealt effectively with the drug trafficking for which the country was believed to be an important channel, the government pledged to continue its efforts to increase economic stability, to encourage the expansion of the private sector, and to improve basic services for the poor. As a demonstration of its good intentions, it proposed to make cuts amounting to 6 billion kwacha in its expenditure on the civil service, and an additional 63 government-owned companies were scheduled for privatization. In response to these efforts the Paris Club agreed in March to release the whole sum requested. Meanwhile, a number of ministers had resigned in order, they said, that false claims of their having been involved in drug trafficking could be thoroughly investigated.

On the agricultural front there were prospects of a good corn (maize) crop, and the government paid farmers 17 billion kwacha of the 27 billion owed them for their crops. But it issued a warning that no government buying agents would be appointed in the future and that corn imports would be unrestricted. The farmers, many of whom had already suffered because millers had been buying cheaper corn imported from South Africa, joined forces with manufacturers who had been complaining vigorously against unfair competition from subsidized foreign imports.

The copper-mining industry was also in a perilous state, the cost of production greatly exceeding the price offered on the world market. Drastic cuts in manpower seemed inevitable if the industry was to survive, and the question of privatization was carefully considered. In spite of pressure from external donors, however, the privatization program in general was not proving successful because potential foreign investors were wary of committing themselves to what they deemed to be unreliable ventures.

In April the University of Zambia was closed after 300 lecturers and research workers were dismissed for taking part in a strike to demand equality of pay with university lecturers and researchers from other countries. During the following month a local newspaper claimed that because of unpaid bills, acute shortages of teaching aids, and endless strikes by teachers for better pay, the education provided in government schools had deteriorated.

(KENNETH INGHAM)

This article updates the *Macropædia* article SOUTHERN AFRICA: *Zambia*.

ZIMBABWE

A republic and member of the Commonwealth, Zimbabwe is a landlocked state in eastern Africa. Area: 390,757 sq km (150,872 sq mi). Pop. (1994 est.): 10,971,000. Cap.: Harare. Monetary unit: Zimbabwe dollar, with (Oct. 7, 1994) a free rate of Z$8.36 to U.S. $1 (Z$13.30 = £1 sterling). President in 1994, Robert Mugabe.

On Jan. 1, 1994, Zimbabwe's currency was devalued by 17%. At the same time, it was announced that foreign companies that had invested in the country before independence and that had previously been allowed to remit 25% of pretax profits would now be permitted to remit 50%. Those that had invested after 1993 would be permitted to remit 100%. Although intended as a liberalizing reform, the change, favouring newcomers, was unlikely to please companies with a long-standing commitment to Zimbabwe. It did, however, provoke some of the reaction it was intended to stimulate because 67 new investment projects were approved in the first quarter of the year. A disappointing aspect of the growth in investment was its failure to generate new job opportunities on any significant scale, an issue of exceptional importance to a country with an unemployment rate of 30% and 200,000 students leaving school each year in search of work.

By linking a loan of $90 million in January to boost the country's energy output to a call for greater autonomy in the management of the Hwange power station and freedom to conduct its business on fully commercial lines, the World Bank indicated its interest in further reducing bureaucratic controls. This was a theme developed by Pres. Robert Mugabe during a visit in May to the United Kingdom, where he was seeking additional Western investment in Zimbabwe. His concern, already aroused by fears that the interest of potential Western investors was being diverted from Africa to Eastern Europe, was enhanced by the prospect that the democratic elections recently held in South Africa might have made that country more attractive to foreign investment than its less economically advanced neighbours. At the World Economic Forum held in Cape Town, South Africa, in June, Mugabe made it clear that the small African countries would not welcome domination by the economic power of South Africa.

There were indications during the year that Mugabe's attitude toward economic and political liberalization remained ambivalent. While pressure for reform was building up inside Zimbabwe, he insisted that his ruling party would continue to redefine its socialist ideology in a manner consistent with the country's culture and historical experience. His acquisition in June of 17 farms without any mention of compensation caused grave anxiety among the country's white commercial farmers. All the farms were fully productive, even though the 1992 law under which they were seized had stressed that only underused or derelict farms would be confiscated. Another victim of the government's policy was opposition leader Ndabaningi Sithole, who, along with 1,000 tenants, was forcibly evicted from his farm by riot police and government officials in October. This followed the earlier seizure of the 325-ha (800-ac) farm of another opposition politician, James Chikerema. Three white farmers who had been dispossessed and had taken their cases to court had their fears confirmed when the High Court ruled that the forcible seizure of their land for resettlement by landless blacks did not violate the nation's constitution.

(KENNETH INGHAM)

This article updates the *Macropædia* article SOUTHERN AFRICA: *Zimbabwe*.

Major Revisions from the 1995 *Macropædia*

This section of the *Britannica Book of the Year* consists of articles or parts of articles reprinted from the *Macropædia*. The articles appearing here have been selected from among those recently revised or rewritten and have been chosen for their general interest or their timeliness.

The section on the 20th century from the *Macropædia* article AMERICAN LITERATURE has been revised for the 1995 printing in light of current scholarship and trends. The latter part of this article, discussing developments after World War II, has been thoroughly updated. EASTERN AFRICA: *Eritrea,* the text of which is reprinted here in full, commemorates the birth in 1993 of that new country. The introductory section of the MARKETING AND MERCHANDISING article includes a new chapter on the marketing process, while the *Macropædia* discussion of the *Amazon River Basin,* from the SOUTH AMERICA article, has also been

brought up to date and now includes, for example, an important section on ecological concerns.

Past issues of the *Britannica Book of the Year* have included instructions for subscribers to order update sheets designed to be inserted into their encyclopædia to signal that a revision has been printed. This year we are including with the yearbook a single sheet that contains this update information for owners of the 14th and 15th editions and the various printings of *Encyclopædia Britannica*. The sheet is designed to be cut apart into strips that can be pasted into the appropriate pages in the *Macropædia* and thereby provide a reference to the updated article in the yearbook. If you did not receive this article update sheet with your 1995 yearbook, please write and request one from the editors at Yearbooks Department, Encyclopædia Britannica, Inc., 310 South Michigan Avenue, Chicago, IL 60604. There is no charge.

American Literature

The 20th century

WRITING FROM 1914 TO 1945

Important movements in drama, poetry, fiction, and criticism took form in the years before, during, and after World War I. The eventful period that followed the war left its imprint upon books of all kinds. Literary forms of the period were extraordinarily varied, and in drama, poetry, and fiction leading authors tended toward radical technical experiments.

Experiments in drama. Although drama had not been a major art form in the 19th century, no type of writing was more experimental than a new drama that arose in rebellion against the glib commercial stage. In the early years of the 20th century, Americans traveling in Europe encountered a vital, flourishing theatre; returning home, some of them became active in founding the Little Theatre movement throughout the country. Freed from commercial limitations, playwrights experimented with dramatic forms and methods of production, and in time producers, actors, and dramatists appeared who had been trained in college classrooms and community playhouses. Some Little Theatre groups became commercial producers; for example, the Washington Square Players, founded in 1915, which became the Theatre Guild (first production in 1919). The resulting drama was marked by a spirit of innovation and by a new seriousness and maturity.

Eugene O'Neill, the most admired dramatist of the pe-

riod, was a product of this movement. He worked with the Provincetown Players before his plays were commercially produced. His dramas were remarkable for their range. *Beyond the Horizon* (first performed 1920), *Anna Christie* (1921), *Desire Under the Elms* (1924), and *The Iceman Cometh* (1946) were naturalistic works, while *The Emperor Jones* (1920) and *The Hairy Ape* (1922) made use of the Expressionistic techniques developed in German drama in the period 1914–24. He also employed a stream-of-consciousness form in *Strange Interlude* (1928) and produced a work that combined myth, family drama, and psychological analysis in *Mourning Becomes Electra* (1931).

No other dramatist was as generally praised as O'Neill, but many others wrote plays that reflected the growth of a serious and varied drama, including Maxwell Anderson, whose verse dramas have dated badly, and Robert E. Sherwood, a Broadway professional who wrote both comedy (*Reunion in Vienna* [1931]) and tragedy (*There Shall Be No Night* [1940]). Marc Connelly wrote touching fantasy in a Negro folk biblical play, *The Green Pastures* (1930). Like O'Neill, Elmer Rice made use of both Expressionistic techniques (*The Adding Machine* [1923]) and naturalism (*Street Scene* [1929]). Lillian Hellman wrote powerful, well-crafted melodramas in *The Children's Hour* (1934) and *The Little Foxes* (1939). Radical theatre experiments included Marc Blitzstein's savagely satiric musical *The Cradle Will Rock* (1937) and the work of Orson Welles

The plays of Eugene O'Neill

507

and John Houseman for the government-sponsored Works Progress Administration (WPA) Federal Theatre Project. The premier radical theatre of the decade was the Group Theatre (1931–41) under Harold Clurman and Lee Strasberg, which became best known for presenting the work of Clifford Odets. In *Waiting for Lefty* (1935), a stirring plea for labour unionism, Odets roused the audience to an intense pitch of fervour, and in *Awake and Sing* (1935), perhaps the best play of the decade, he created a lyrical work of family conflict and youthful yearning. Other important plays by Odets for the Group Theatre were *Paradise Lost* (1935), *Golden Boy* (1937), and *Rocket to the Moon* (1938). Thornton Wilder used stylized settings and poetic dialogue in *Our Town* (1938) and turned to fantasy in *The Skin of Our Teeth* (1942). William Saroyan shifted his lighthearted, anarchic vision from fiction to drama with *My Heart's in the Highlands* and *The Time of Your Life* (both 1939).

The new poetry. Poetry ranged between traditional types of verse and experimental writing that departed radically from the established forms of the 19th century. Two New England poets, Edwin Arlington Robinson and Robert Frost, who were not noted for technical experimentation, won both critical and popular acclaim in this period. Robinson, whose first book appeared in 1896, found sonnets, ballad stanzas, and blank verse satisfactory to his thought. In the 1920s he won three Pulitzer Prizes—for his *Collected Poems* (published 1921), *The Man Who Died Twice* (1925), and *Tristram* (1927). Like Robinson, Frost used traditional stanzas and blank verse in volumes such as *A Boy's Will* (1913), his first book, and *North of Boston* (1914), *New Hampshire* (1923), *A Further Range* (1936), and *A Masque of Reason* (1945). The best-known poet of his generation, Frost, like Robinson, saw and commented upon the tragic aspects of life in poems such as "Design," "Directive," and "Provide, Provide."

Just as modern American drama had its beginnings in little theatres, modern American poetry took form in little magazines. Particularly important was *Poetry: A Magazine of Verse,* founded by Harriet Monroe in Chicago in 1912. The surrounding region soon became prominent as the home of three poets: Vachel Lindsay, Carl Sandburg, and Edgar Lee Masters. Lindsay's blend of legendary lore and native oratory in irregular odelike forms was well adapted to oral presentation, and his lively readings from his works contributed to the success of such books as *General William Booth Enters into Heaven, and Other Poems* (1913) and *The Congo, and Other Poems* (1914). Sandburg wrote of life on the prairies and in Midwestern cities in Whitmanesque free verse in such volumes as *Chicago Poems* (1916) and *The People, Yes* (1936). Masters' very popular *Spoon River Anthology* (1915) consisted of free-verse monologues by village men and women, most of whom spoke bitterly of their frustrated lives.

Writing traditional sonnets and brief, personal lyrics, Edna St. Vincent Millay and Sara Teasdale were innovative in being unusually frank (according to the standard of their time) for women poets. Three fine black poets—James Weldon Johnson, Langston Hughes, and Countee Cullen—also found old molds satisfactory for dealing with new subjects, specifically the problems of their race. While Conrad Aiken experimented with poetical imitations of symphonic forms often mingled with stream-of-consciousness techniques, e.e. cummings used typographical novelties to produce poems that had surprisingly fresh impact. Marianne Moore invented and brilliantly employed a kind of free verse that was marked by a wonderfully sharp and idiosyncratic focus on objects and details. Robinson Jeffers used violent imagery and modified free or blank verse to express perhaps the most bitter views voiced by a major poet in this period. Except for a period after World War II, when he was confined in St. Elizabeth's Hospital, Washington, D.C., Ezra Pound lived outside the United States after 1908. He had, nevertheless, a profound influence on 20th-century writing in English, both as a practitioner of verse and as a patron and impresario of other writers. His most controversial work remained *The Cantos,* the first installment of which appeared in 1926 and the latest in 1959 (*Thrones: 96–109 de los cantares*).

Like Pound, to whom he was much indebted, T.S. Eliot lived abroad most of his life, becoming a British subject in 1927. His first volume, *Prufrock and Other Observations,* was published in 1917. In 1922 appeared *The Waste Land,* the poem by which he first became famous. As a poet and critic, Eliot exercised a strong influence, especially in the period between World Wars I and II. In what some critics regard as his finest work, *Four Quartets* (1943), Eliot explored through images of great beauty and haunting power his own past, the past of the human race, and the meaning of human history.

Eliot was an acknowledged master of a varied group of poets whose work was indebted to 17th-century English Metaphysical poets, especially to John Donne. Eliot's influence was clear in the writings of Archibald MacLeish, whose earlier poems showed resemblances to *The Waste Land.* A number of Southern poets (who were also critics) were influenced by Eliot—John Crowe Ransom, Donald Davidson, and Allen Tate. Younger American Metaphysicals who emerged later included Louise Bogan, Léonie Adams, Muriel Rukeyser, Delmore Schwartz, and Karl Shapiro. But there were several major poets strongly opposed to Eliot's influence. Their style and subjects tended to be romantic and visionary. These included Hart Crane, whose long poem *The Bridge* (1930) aimed to create a Whitmanesque American epic, and Wallace Stevens, a lush and sensuous writer who made an astonishing literary debut with the poems collected in *Harmonium* (1923). Another opponent of Eliot was William Carlos Williams, who invested his experimental prose and magically simple lyrics—in works such as *Spring and All* (1923)—with the mundane details of American life and wrote about American myth and cultural history with great sweep in *In the American Grain* (1925).

Fiction. The little magazines that helped the growth of the poetry also contributed to a development of the fiction of the era. They printed daring or unconventional short stories and published attacks upon established writers. The *Dial* (1880–1929), the *Little Review* (1914–29), the *Seven Arts* (1916–17), and others encouraged modernist innovation. More potent were two magazines edited by the ferociously funny journalist-critic H.L. Mencken—*The Smart Set* (editorship 1914–23) and *American Mercury* (which he coedited between 1924 and 1933). A powerful influence and a scathing critic of puritanism, Mencken helped launch the new fiction.

Mencken's major enthusiasms included the fiction of Joseph Conrad and Theodore Dreiser, but he also promoted minor writers for their attacks on gentility, such as James Branch Cabell, or their revolt against the narrow, frustrated quality of life in rural communities, including Zona Gale and Ruth Suckow. The most distinguished of these writers was Sherwood Anderson. His *Winesburg, Ohio* (1919) and *Triumph of the Egg* (1921) were collections of short stories that showed villagers suffering from all sorts of phobias and suppressions. Anderson in time wrote several novels, the best being *Poor White* (1920).

In 1920 critics noticed that a new school of fiction had risen to prominence with the success of books such as F. Scott Fitzgerald's *This Side of Paradise* and Sinclair Lewis' *Main Street,* fictions that tended to be frankly psychological or modern in their unsparing portrayals of contemporary life. Novels of the 1920s were often lyrical and personal, but also, in the despairing mood that followed World War I, apt to express disillusionment. Novels of the 1930s inclined toward radical social criticism, in response to the miseries of the Great Depression, though some of the best, by writers such as William Faulkner, F. Scott Fitzgerald, Henry Roth, and Nathanael West, continued to explore the modernist vein of the previous decade.

Critics of society. F. Scott Fitzgerald's *This Side of Paradise* (1920) showed the disillusionment and moral disintegration of post-World War I America. The book initiated a career of great promise that found fruition in *The Great Gatsby* (1925), a spare but poignant novel about the promise and failure of the American Dream. Fitzgerald was to live out this theme himself. Though damaged by drink and by a failing marriage, he went on to do some of his best work in the 1930s, including numerous stories

Marginal notes:

Robinson and Frost

Pound, Eliot, and the influence of the 17th-century Metaphysical poets

The influence of the little magazines

and essays as well as his most ambitious novel, *Tender Is the Night* (1934). Unlike Fitzgerald, who was a lyric writer with real emotional intensity, Sinclair Lewis was best as a social critic. His onslaughts against the "village virus" (*Main Street* [1920]), average businessmen (*Babbitt* [1922]), materialistic scientists (*Arrowsmith* [1925]), and the racially prejudiced (*Kingsblood Royal* [1947]) were satirically sharp and thoroughly documented, though *Babbitt* is his only book that still stands up brilliantly at the end of the 20th century. Similar careful documentation, though little satire, characterized James T. Farrell's naturalistic *Studs Lonigan* trilogy (1932–35), which described the stifling effects of a lower-middle-class family and a street-corner milieu in the Chicago of the 1920s. The ironies of racial identity dominate the stories and novels produced by writers of the Harlem renaissance, including the portraits of the black middle class in Nella Larsen's *Quicksand* (1928) and *Passing* (1929) and the powerful stories of Langston Hughes in *The Ways of White Folks* (1934), as well as the varied literary materials—poetry, fiction, and drama—collected in Jean Toomer's *Cane* (1923). Richard Wright's books, including *Uncle Tom's Children* (1938), *Native Son* (1940), and *Black Boy* (1945), were works of burning social protest, Dostoyevskyan in their intensity, dealing boldly with the plight of American blacks especially in the urban ghetto. Zora Neale Hurston's training in anthropology and folklore contributed to *Their Eyes Were Watching God* (1937), her powerful feminist novel about the black Florida town in which she had grown up.

A number of authors wrote proletarian novels attacking capitalist exploitation, including several novels based on a 1929 strike in the textile mills in Gastonia, N.C., such as Fielding Burke's *Call Home the Heart* and Grace Lumpkin's *To Make My Bread* (both 1932). Other notable proletarian novels included Jack Conroy's *The Disinherited* (1933), Robert Cantwell's *The Land of Plenty* (1934), and Albert Halper's *Union Square* (1933), *The Foundry* (1934), and *The Chute* (1937), as well as some grim evocations of the drifters and "bottom dogs" of the depression era, such as Edward Anderson's *Hungry Men* and Tom Kromer's *Waiting For Nothing* (both 1935). The radical movement, combined with a nascent feminism, encouraged the talent of several politically committed women writers whose work was rediscovered later; they included Tillie Olsen, Meridel Le Sueur, and Josephine Herbst.

John Dos Passos Particularly admired as a protest writer was John Dos Passos, who first attracted attention with an anti-World War I novel, *Three Soldiers* (1921). His most sweeping indictments of the modern social and economic system, *Manhattan Transfer* (1925) and the *U.S.A.* trilogy (*The 42nd Parallel, 1919,* and *The Big Money* [1930–36]), employed various narrative innovations such as the "camera eye" and "newsreel" to attack society from the left. Nathanael West's novels, including *Miss Lonelyhearts* (1933), *A Cool Million* (1934), and *The Day of the Locust* (1939), used black comedy to create a bitter vision of an inhuman and brutal world. West evoked the tawdry but rich materials of mass culture and popular fantasy to mock the pathos of the American Dream, a frequent target during the depression years.

Hemingway, Faulkner, and Steinbeck. Three authors whose writings showed a shift from disillusionment were Ernest Hemingway, William Faulkner, and John Steinbeck. Hemingway's early short stories and his first novels, *The Sun Also Rises* (1926) and *A Farewell to Arms* (1929), were full of the existential disillusionment of the "lost generation" expatriates. The Spanish Civil War, however, led him to espouse the possibility of collective action to solve social problems, and his less effective novels, including *To Have and Have Not* (1937) and *For Whom the Bell Tolls* (1940), embodied this new belief. He regained some of his form in *The Old Man and The Sea* (1952) and his posthumously published memoir of Paris between the wars, *A Moveable Feast* (1964). Hemingway's great impact on other writers came from his deceptively simple, stripped-down prose, full of unspoken implication, and from his tough but vulnerable masculinity, which created a myth that imprisoned the author and haunted the World War II generation.

Hemingway's great rival as a stylist and mythmaker was William Faulkner, whose writing was as baroque as Hemingway's was spare. Influenced by Sherwood Anderson, Melville, and especially James Joyce, he combined stream-of-consciousness techniques with rich social history. Works such as *The Sound and the Fury* (1929), *As I Lay Dying* (1930), *Light in August* (1932), and *The Hamlet* (1940) were parts of the unfolding history of Yoknapatawpha County, a mythical Mississippi community, which depicted the transformation and the decadence of the South. Faulkner's work was dominated by a sense of guilt going back to the American Civil War and the appropriation of Indian lands. Though often comic, his work pictured the disintegration of the leading families and, in later books such as *Go Down, Moses* (1942) and *Intruder in the Dust* (1948), showed a growing concern with the troubled role of race in Southern life.

Steinbeck's career, marked by uneven achievements, began with a historical novel, *Cup of Gold* (1929), in which he voiced a distrust of society and glorified the anarchistic individualist typical of the rebellious 1920s. He showed his affinity for colourful outcasts, such as the *paisanos* of the Monterey area, in short novels like *Tortilla Flat* (1935), the fable *Of Mice and Men* (1937), and *Cannery Row* (1945). His best books were inspired by the social struggles of migrant farm workers during the Great Depression, including the simply written but ambiguous strike novel, *In Dubious Battle* (1936), and his flawed masterpiece, *The Grapes of Wrath* (1939). The latter, a protest novel interrupted by prose-poem interludes, tells the story of the migration of the Joads, an Oklahoma Dust Bowl family, to California. During their almost biblical journey, they learn the necessity for collective action among the poor and downtrodden to prevent them from being destroyed individually.

Lyric fictionists. An interesting development in fiction, abetted by modernism, was a shift from naturalistic to poetic writing. There was an increased tendency to select details and endow them with symbolic meaning, to set down the thought processes and emotions of the characters, and to make use of rhythmical prose. In varied ways, Crane, Norris, Cabell, Dos Passos, Hemingway, Steinbeck, and Faulkner all showed evidence of this—in passages, in short stories, and even in entire novels. Faulkner showed the tendency at its worst in *A Fable* (1954), which, ironically, won a Pulitzer Prize.

Willa Cather Lyricism was especially prominent in the writings of Willa Cather. *O Pioneers!* (1913), *The Song of the Lark* (1915), and *My Ántonia* (1918) contained poetic passages about the disappearing frontier and the creative efforts of frontier folk. *A Lost Lady* (1923) was elegiac in form and spare in style, though it also depicted a historic social transformation, and *Death Comes for the Archbishop* (1927) was an exaltation of the past and of spiritual pioneering. Katherine Anne Porter, whose works took the form of novelettes and stories, wrote more in the style of the Metaphysical poets. Her use of the stream-of-consciousness method in *Flowering Judas* (1930) as well as in *Pale Horse, Pale Rider* (1939) had the complexity, the irony, and the symbolic sophistication characteristic of these poets, whose work the modernists had brought into fashion.

Two of the most intensely lyrical works of the 1930s were autobiographical novels set in the Jewish ghetto of New York City's Lower East Side before World War I: Michael Gold's harsh *Jews Without Money* (1930) and Henry Roth's Proustian *Call It Sleep* (1934), one of the greatest novels of the decade. They followed in the footsteps of a prolific writer of the 1920s, Anzia Yezierska, whose passionate books about immigrant Jews, especially *Bread Givers* (1925), have been rediscovered by contemporary feminists.

Another lyrical and autobiographical writer, whose books have faded badly, was Thomas Wolfe, who put all his strivings, thoughts, and feelings into works such as *Look Homeward, Angel* (1929) and *Of Time and the River* (1935) before his early death in 1938. These Whitmanesque books, and posthumously edited ones such as *The Web and the Rock* (1939) and *You Can't Go Home*

Again (1940), dealt with a figure much like Wolfe—echoing the author's youth in the South, young manhood in the North, and eternal search to fulfill a vision. Though grandiose, they influenced many young writers, including Jack Kerouac.   (WALTER BLAIR/MORRIS DICKSTEIN)

AFTER WORLD WAR II

The literary historian Malcolm Cowley described the years between the two world wars as a "second flowering" of American writing. Certainly American literature attained a new maturity and a rich diversity in the 1920s and '30s, and significant works by several major figures from those decades were published after 1945. Faulkner, Hemingway, Steinbeck, and Katherine Anne Porter wrote memorable fiction; and Frost, Eliot, Wallace Stevens, Marianne Moore, e.e. cummings, William Carlos Williams, and Gwendolyn Brooks published important poetry. Eugene O'Neill's most distinguished play, *Long Day's Journey into Night,* appeared posthumously in 1956. Before and after World War II, Robert Penn Warren published influential fiction, poetry, and criticism. His *All the King's Men,* one of the best American political novels, won the 1947 Pulitzer Prize. Mary McCarthy became a widely read social satirist and essayist. Henry Miller's fiction, influential primarily because of its frank exploration of sexuality, first appeared in the United States in the 1960s. Still, impressive new novelists, poets, and playwrights emerged after the war. There was, in fact, a gradual changing of the guard.

Not only did a new generation emerge from the war, but its ethnic, regional, and social character was quite different from that of the preceding one. Among the younger writers were children of immigrants, many of them Jews; blacks, only a few generations away from slavery; and, eventually, women, who, with the rise of feminism, were to speak in a new voice. Though the social climate of the postwar years was conservative, even conformist, some of the most hotly discussed writers were homosexuals or bisexuals, including Tennessee Williams, Truman Capote, Gore Vidal, and James Baldwin, whose dark themes and experimental methods cleared a path for Beat writers like Allen Ginsberg and Jack Kerouac.

The novel and short story. Two distinct groups of novelists responded to the cultural impact, and especially the technological horror, of World War II. Norman Mailer's *The Naked and the Dead* (1948) and Irwin Shaw's *The Young Lions* (1948) were realistic war novels, though Mailer's book was also a novel of ideas, exploring fascist thinking and an obsession with power as elements of the military mind. James Jones, amassing a staggering quantity of closely observed detail, documented the war's human cost in an ambitious trilogy (*From Here to Eternity* [1951], *The Thin Red Line* [1962], and *Whistle* [1978]) that centred on loners who resisted adapting to military discipline. Younger novelists, profoundly shaken by the bombing of Hiroshima and the real threat of human annihilation, found the conventions of realism inadequate for treating the war's nightmarish implications. In *Catch-22* (1961) Joseph Heller satirized the military mentality with surreal black comedy but also injected a sense of Kafkaesque horror. A sequel, *Closing Time* (1994), was an elegy for the World War II generation. Kurt Vonnegut, Jr., in *Slaughterhouse-Five* (1969), described the Allied firebombing of the German city of Dresden with a mixture of dark fantasy and numb, loopy humour. Later this method was applied brilliantly to the portrayal of the Vietnam War—a conflict that seemed in itself surreal—by Tim O'Brien in *Going After Cacciato* (1978).

In part because of the atomic bomb, American writers turned increasingly to black humour and absurdist fantasy. Many found the naturalistic approach incapable of communicating the rapid pace and the sheer implausibility of contemporary life. A highly self-conscious fiction emerged, laying bare its own literary devices, questioning the nature of representation, and often imitating or parodying earlier fiction rather than social reality. Russian-born Vladimir Nabokov and the Argentine writer Jorge Luis Borges were strong influences on this new "metafiction." Nabokov, who became a U.S. citizen in 1945, pro-

duced a body of exquisitely wrought fiction distinguished by linguistic and formal innovation. Despite their artificiality, his best novels, written in English, have a strong emotional thread running through them, including *Lolita* (1955), *Pnin* (1957), and *Pale Fire* (1962).

Metafiction

In an important essay, "The Literature of Exhaustion" (1967), John Barth declared himself an American disciple of Nabokov and Borges. After dismissing realism as a "used up" tradition, Barth described his own work as "novels which imitate the form of the novel, by an author who imitates the role of Author." In fact, Barth's earliest fiction, *The Floating Opera* (1956) and *The End of the Road* (1958), fell partly within the realistic tradition, but in later, more ambitious works he simultaneously imitated and parodied conventional forms—the historical novel in *The Sot-Weed Factor* (1960), Greek and Christian myths in *Giles Goat-Boy* (1966), and the epistolary novel in *LETTERS* (1979). Similarly, Donald Barthelme mocked the fairy tale in *Snow White* (1967) and Freudian fiction in *The Dead Father* (1975). Barthelme was most successful in his short stories and parodies that solemnly caricatured contemporary styles, especially the richly suggestive pieces collected in *Unspeakable Practices, Unnatural Acts* (1968), *City Life* (1970), and *Guilty Pleasures* (1974).

Thomas Pynchon emerged as the major American practitioner of the absurdist fable. His novels and stories were elaborately plotted mixtures of historical information, comic-book fantasy, and countercultural suspicion. Using paranoia as a structuring device as well as a cast of mind, Pynchon worked out elaborate "conspiracies" in *V.* (1963), *The Crying of Lot 49* (1966), and *Gravity's Rainbow* (1973). The underlying assumption of Pynchon's fiction was the inevitability of entropy—*i.e.,* the disintegration of physical and moral energy. Pynchon's technique was later to influence writers as different as Don DeLillo and Paul Auster. In *Naked Lunch* (1959) and other novels, William S. Burroughs, abandoning plot and coherent characterization, used a drug addict's consciousness to depict a hideous modern landscape. Vonnegut, Terry Southern, and John Hawkes were also major practitioners of black humour and the absurdist fable. Other influential portraits of outsider figures included the Beat characters in Jack Kerouac's *On the Road* (1957), *The Dharma Bums* (1958), *Desolation Angels* (1965), and *Visions of Cody* (1972), the young Rabbit Angstrom in John Updike's *Rabbit, Run* (1960) and *Rabbit Redux* (1971), Holden Caulfield in J.D. Salinger's *Catcher in the Rye* (1951), and the troubling madman in Richard Yates's powerful novel of suburban life, *Revolutionary Road* (1961).

Though writers such as Barth, Barthelme, and Pynchon rejected the novel's traditional function as a mirror reflecting society, a significant number of contemporary novelists were reluctant to abandon Social Realism. In such novels as *The Victim* (1947), *The Adventures of Augie March* (1953), *Herzog* (1964), *Mr. Sammler's Planet* (1970), and *Humboldt's Gift* (1975), Saul Bellow tapped into the buoyant, manic energy and picaresque structure of black humour, while proclaiming the necessity of "being human." Though few contemporary writers saw the ugliness of urban life more clearly than Bellow, his central characters rejected the "Wasteland outlook" associated with modernism. A spiritual vision, derived from sources as diverse as Judaism, Transcendentalism, and Rudolph Steiner's cultish theosophy, found its way into Bellow's late novels, but he also wrote darker fictions like the novella *Seize the Day* (1956), a study in failure and blocked emotion that was perhaps his best work. Four other Jewish writers—Bernard Malamud, Grace Paley, Philip Roth, and Isaac Bashevis Singer—treated the human condition with humour and forgiveness. Malamud's gift for dark comedy and Hawthornean fable was especially evident in his short-story collections *The Magic Barrel* (1958) and *Idiots First* (1963). His first three novels, *The Natural* (1952), *The Assistant* (1957), and *A New Life* (1961), were also impressive works of fiction; *The Assistant* had the bleak moral intensity of his best stories. Grace Paley's stories combined an offbeat, whimsically poetic manner with a wry understanding of the ironies of family life and progressive politics. While Roth was known best for the wild satire and sex-

The novel of Social Realism

ual high jinks of *Portnoy's Complaint* (1969), a hilarious stand-up routine about ethnic stereotypes, his most lasting achievement may be his later novels built around the misadventures of a controversial Jewish novelist named Zuckerman, especially *The Ghost Writer* (1979), *The Anatomy Lesson* (1983), and, above all, *The Counterlife* (1987). Like all his later works, from *My Life as a Man* (1974) to *Operation Shylock* (1993), *The Counterlife* plays ingeniously on the relationship between autobiography and fiction. The Polish-born Singer won the Nobel Prize for Literature in 1978 for his stories, written originally in Yiddish. They evolved from fantastic tales of demons and angels to realistic fictions set in New York City's Upper West Side, showing him to be one of the great storytellers of modern times.

The sexual and moral confusion of the American middle class was the focus of the work of J.D. Salinger and Richard Yates, as well as John Updike's Rabbit series (four novels from *Rabbit, Run* [1960] to *Rabbit At Rest* [1990]), *Couples* (1968), and *Too Far to Go* (1979), a sequence of tales about the quiet disintegration of a civilized marriage. Updike's mentor, John Cheever, long associated with *The New Yorker* magazine, created in his short stories and novels a gallery of memorable eccentrics. He documented the anxieties of upper-middle-class New Yorkers and suburbanites in the relatively tranquil years after World War II. In sharp contrast, Nelson Algren (*The Man with the Golden Arm* [1949]) and Hubert Selby, Jr. (*Last Exit to Brooklyn* [1964]) documented lower-class urban life with brutal frankness. Similarly, John Rechy portrayed America's urban homosexual subculture in *City of Night* (1963). As literary and social mores were liberalized, Cheever himself dealt with homosexuality in his prison novel *Falconer* (1977) and even more explicitly in his personal journals, published posthumously in 1991.

Southern writers
Post-World War II Southern writers inherited Faulkner's rich legacy. Three women, specialists in the grotesque—Eudora Welty, Flannery O'Connor, and Carson McCullers—contributed greatly to Southern fiction. O'Connor, writing as a Roman Catholic in the Protestant South, created a high comedy of moral incongruity in her incomparable short stories. Welty, always a brilliant stylist, first came to prominence with her collections of short fiction, *A Curtain of Green* (1941) and *The Wide Net* (1943). Her career culminated with a large family novel, *Losing Battles* (1970), and a fine novella, *The Optimist's Daughter* (1972), which was awarded the 1973 Pulitzer Prize. Initially known for his lyrical portraits of Southern eccentrics (*Other Voices, Other Rooms* [1948]), Truman Capote published *In Cold Blood* (1966), a cold but impressive piece of documentary realism that contributed, along with the work of Tom Wolfe and Norman Mailer, to the emergence of a "new journalism" using many of the techniques of fiction. William Styron's overripe first novel, *Lie Down in Darkness* (1951), clearly revealed the influence of Faulkner. In two controversial later works Styron fictionalized the dark side of modern history: *The Confessions of Nat Turner* (1967) depicted an antebellum slave revolt and *Sophie's Choice* (1979) unsuccessfully sought to capture the full horror of the Holocaust. Inspired by Faulkner and Mark Twain, William Humphrey wrote two powerful novels set in Texas, *Home from the Hill* (1958) and *The Ordways* (1965). *The Moviegoer* (1961) and *The Last Gentleman* (1966) established Walker Percy as an important voice in Southern fiction. Their musing philosophical style broke sharply with the Gothic tradition, influencing later writers such as Richard Ford in *The Sportswriter* (1986). Equally impressive were the novels and stories of Peter Taylor, an impeccable Social Realist, raconteur, and genial novelist of manners, bringing back a bygone world in works such as "The Old Forest" (1985) and *A Summons to Memphis* (1986).

Black writers
Black writers of this period found alternatives to the Richard Wright tradition of social protest. James Baldwin and Ralph Ellison, both protégés of Wright, wrote polemical essays calling for a literature that reflected the full complexity of black life in the United States. In his first and best novel, *Go Tell It on the Mountain* (1953), Baldwin portrayed the Harlem world and the black church through his own adolescent religious experiences. Drawing on rural folktale, absurdist humour, and a picaresque realism, Ralph Ellison wrote a deeply resonant comic novel that dealt with the full range of black experience: rural sharecropping, segregated education, northward migration, ghetto hustling, and the lure of such competing ideologies as nationalism and communism. Many considered *Invisible Man* (1952) the best novel of the postwar years. Later two black women novelists published some of the most important post-World War II American fiction. In *The Bluest Eye* (1970), *Sula* (1973), *Song of Solomon* (1977), *Beloved* (1987), and *Jazz* (1992), Toni Morrison created a strikingly original fiction that sounded different notes from lyrical recollection to magic realism. Like Ellison, Morrison drew on diverse literary and folk influences and dealt with important phases of black history—*i.e.*, slavery in *Beloved* and the Harlem renaissance in *Jazz*. She was awarded the Nobel Prize for Literature in 1993. Alice Walker, after several volumes of poetry and an interesting novel dealing with the Civil Rights Movement (*Meridian* [1976]), received the 1983 Pulitzer Prize for her black feminist novel *The Color Purple*. Black male writers whose work gained attention during this period included Ishmael Reed, whose wild comic techniques resembled Ellison's, James Alan McPherson, a subtle short-story writer, Charles Johnson, whose novels, such as *The Oxherding Tale* (1982) and *The Middle Passage* (1990), showed a masterful historical imagination, and Randall Kenan, a gay writer with a strong folk imagination, whose style descended from both Ellison and Baldwin.

The horrors of World War II, the Cold War and the atomic bomb, the bizarre feast of consumer culture, and the cultural clashes of the 1960s prompted many writers to argue that reality had grown inaccessible, undermining the traditional social role of fiction. Writers of novels and short stories therefore were under unprecedented pressure to discover, or invent, new and viable kinds of fiction. One response was the postmodern novel of William Gaddis, John Barth, Donald Barthelme, Thomas Pynchon, Robert Coover, Paul Auster, and Don DeLillo—technically sophisticated and highly self-conscious about the construction of fiction and the fictive nature of "reality" itself. These writers dealt with themes such as imposture and paranoia; their novels drew attention to themselves as artifacts and often used realistic techniques ironically. Other responses involved a heightening of realism by means of intensifying violence, amassing documentation, or resorting to fantasy. A brief discussion of writers as different as Norman Mailer and Joyce Carol Oates may serve to illustrate these new directions.

The postmodern novel
In his 1948 World War II novel, *The Naked and the Dead*, Mailer wrote in the Dos Passos tradition of social protest. Feeling its limitations, he developed his own brand of surreal fantasy in fables such as *An American Dream* (1965) and *Why Are We in Vietnam?* (1967). As for many of the postmodern novelists, his subject was the nature of power, personal as well as political. However, it was only when he turned to "nonfiction fiction" or "fiction as history" in *The Armies of the Night* and *Miami and the Siege of Chicago* (both 1968) that Mailer discovered his true voice—grandiose yet personal, comic yet shrewdly intellectual. He refined this approach into a new objectivity in the 1980 Pulitzer Prize "true life novel" *The Executioner's Song*. When he returned to fiction, his work was of less interest. In her early work, especially *A Garden of Earthly Delights* (1967) and *them* (1969), Joyce Carol Oates worked naturalistically with violent urban materials, such as the Detroit riots. Incredibly prolific, she later experimented with surrealism in *Wonderland* (1971) and Gothic fantasy in *Bellefleur* (1980) before returning in works such as *Marya* (1986) to the bleak blue-collar world of her youth in upstate New York. While Mailer and Oates refused to surrender the novel's gift for capturing reality, both were compelled to search out new fictional modes to tap that power.

The surge of feminism in the 1970s gave impetus to many new women writers, including Erica Jong in her sexy and funny *Fear of Flying* (1974), Rita Mae Brown's exploration of lesbian life in *Rubyfruit Jungle* (1973), Ann

Beattie's account of the post-1960s generation in *Chilly Scenes of Winter* (1976) and many short stories, Gail Godwin's highly civilized *The Odd Woman* (1974), Mary Gordon's portraits of Irish Catholic life in *Final Payments* (1978), and the many social comedies of Alison Lurie and Anne Tyler. Perhaps the most influential fiction writer to emerge in the 1970s was Raymond Carver. He was another realist who dealt with blue-collar life, usually in the Pacific Northwest, in powerful collections of stories such as *What We Talk About When We Talk About Love* (1981) and *Cathedral* (1983). His self-destructive characters were life's losers, and his style, influenced by Hemingway and Samuel Beckett, was spare and flat but powerfully suggestive. It was imitated, often badly, by minimalists like Frederick Barthelme, Mary Robison, and Amy Hempel. More talented writers whose novels reflected the influence of Carver in their evocation of the downbeat world of the blue-collar male included Richard Ford (*Rock Springs* [1987]), Russell Banks (*Continental Drift* [1984] and *Affliction* [1989]), and Tobias Wolff (*The Barracks Thief* [1984] and *This Boy's Life* [1989]). Another strong male-oriented writer in a realist mode who emerged from the 1960s counterculture was Robert Stone. His *Dog Soldiers* (1974) was a grimly downbeat portrayal of the drugs-and-Vietnam generation, and *A Flag for Sunrise* (1981) was a bleak, Conradian political novel set in Central America.

New multi-cultural writing

Finally, the dramatic loosening of immigration restrictions in the mid-1960s set the stage for the rich multicultural writing of the 1970s and '80s. New Jewish voices were heard in the fiction of E.L. Doctorow, whose characters in *The Book of Daniel* (1971) were based on convicted spies Julius and Ethel Rosenberg and their family, and in the work of Cynthia Ozick, whose characters in her best story, "Envy; or Yiddish in America" (1969) were modeled on leading figures in Yiddish literature. David Leavitt introduced homosexual themes into his portrayal of middle-class life in *Family Dancing* (1984). Novels such as N. Scott Momaday's *House Made of Dawn*, which won the Pulitzer Prize in 1969, James Welch's *Winter in the Blood* (1974) and *Fools Crow* (1986), Leslie Marmon Silko's *Ceremony* (1977), and Louise Erdrich's *Love Medicine* (1984) and *The Beet Queen* (1986) were powerful and ambiguous explorations of Native American history and identity. Mexican-Americans were represented by works such as Rudolfo Anaya's *Bless Me, Ultima* (1972), Richard Rodriguez's autobiographical *Hunger of Memory* (1981), and Sandra Cisneros' *House on Mango Street* (1983).

Some of the best immigrant writers, while thoroughly assimilated, nonetheless had a subtle understanding of both the old and the new culture. These included the Cuban-American writers Oscar Hijuelos (*The Mambo Kings Play Songs of Love* [1989]) and Cristina Garcia (*Dreaming in Cuban* [1992]), and the prolific Jamaica Kincaid, the Antigua-born author of *Annie John* (1984) and *Lucy* (1990), whose work appeared frequently in *The New Yorker*. Chinese-Americans found an extraordinary voice in Maxine Hong Kingston's *The Woman Warrior* (1976) and *China Men* (1980), which blended old Chinese lore with fascinating family history. While many multicultural works were merely representative of their cultural milieu, some made remarkable contributions to a new American literature.

Poetry. The post-World War II years produced an abundance of strong poetry but no individual poet as dominant and accomplished as T.S. Eliot, Ezra Pound, Wallace Stevens, Robert Frost, or William Carlos Williams, whose long careers were coming to an end. The major poetry from 1945 to 1960 was modernist in its ironic texture yet formal in its insistence on regular rhyme and metre. Beginning in the late 1950s, however, there were a variety of poets and schools who rebelled against these constraints and experimented with more open forms and more colloquial styles.

The leading figure of the late 1940s was Robert Lowell, who, influenced by Eliot and such Metaphysical poets as John Donne and Gerard Manley Hopkins, explored his spiritual torments and family history in *Lord Weary's Castle* (1946). Other impressive formal poets included Theodore Roethke, influenced by William Butler Yeats, who revealed a genius for ironic lyricism and a profound empathy for the processes of nature in *The Lost Son and Other Poems* (1948), the masterfully elegant Richard Wilbur (*Things of This World* [1956]), two war poets, Karl Shapiro (*V-Letter and Other Poems* [1944]) and Randall Jarrell (*Losses* [1948]), and a group of young poets influenced by W.H. Auden, including James Merrill, W.S. Merwin, James Wright, Adrienne Rich, and John Hollander. Although they displayed brilliant technical skill, they lacked Auden's strong personal voice.

By the mid-1950s, however, a strong reaction developed. Poets began to turn away from Eliot and metaphysical poetry to more romantic or more prosaic models, including Walt Whitman, William Carlos Williams, Hart Crane, and D.H. Lawrence. A group of poets associated with Black Mountain College in western North Carolina, as, for example, Charles Olson, Robert Creeley, Robert Duncan, Edward Dorn, and Denise Levertov, treated the poem as an unfolding process rather than a containing form. Olson's *Maximus Poems* (1953–68) show a clear affinity with the jagged line and uneven flow of Pound's *Cantos* and Williams's *Paterson*. Allen Ginsberg's incantatory, prophetic "Howl" (1956) and his moving elegy for his mother, "Kaddish" (1961), gave powerful impetus to the Beat movement. Written with extraordinary intensity, these works were inspired by writers as diverse as the biblical prophets, William Blake, and Whitman, as well as by the dream-logic of the French Surrealists and the spontaneous jazz aesthetic of Ginsberg's friend, the novelist Jack Kerouac. Other Beat poets included Lawrence Ferlinghetti, Gregory Corso, and Gary Snyder, a student of Eastern religion, who, in *Turtle Island* (1974), continued the American tradition of nature poetry.

The Beat movement

The openness of Beat poetry and the prosaic directness of William Carlos Williams encouraged Lowell to develop a new autobiographical style in the laconic poetry and prose of *Life Studies* (1959) and *For the Union Dead* (1964). Lowell's new work influenced nearly all American poets but especially a group of "confessional" writers, some of them once students of his, including Anne Sexton in *To Bedlam and Part Way Back* (1960) and *All My Pretty Ones* (1962) and Sylvia Plath in the posthumously published *Ariel* (1965), who in her poetry joined an icy sarcasm to white-hot emotional intensity. Another poet influenced by Lowell was John Berryman, whose *Dream Songs* (1964, 1968) combine autobiographical fragments with minstrel-show motifs to create a zany style of self-projection and comic-tragic lament. Deeply troubled figures, Sexton, Plath, and Berryman all took their own lives.

Through his personal charisma and his magazine *The Fifties* (later *The Sixties* and the *The Seventies*), Robert Bly encouraged a number of poets whose work shifted toward the individual voice and open form, including Galway Kinnell, James Wright, David Ignatow, and, less directly, Louis Simpson, James Dickey, and Donald Hall. Sometimes called the "deep image" poets, Bly and his friends sought spiritual intensity and transcendence of the self rather than confessional immediacy. Their work was influenced by the poetry of Spanish and Latin American writers such as Federico García Lorca, Juan Ramón Jiménez, César Vallejo, and Pablo Neruda, especially their surreal association of images, as well as by the "Greenhouse poems" (1946–48) and the meditative poetry of the later Roethke, with its deep feeling for nature as a vehicle of spiritual transformation. Yet, like their Hispanic models, they were also political poets, instrumental in organizing protest and writing poems against the Vietnam war. Kinnell was a Lawrentian poet who, in poems such as "The Porcupine" and "The Bear," gave the brutality of nature the power of myth. His vatic sequence, *The Book of Nightmares* (1971), and the quieter poems in *Mortal Acts, Mortal Words* (1980) are among the most rhetorically effective works in contemporary poetry.

"Deep image" poets

James Wright was another writer whose style changed dramatically in the early 1960s. He abandoned his stiffly formal verse for the stripped-down, meditative lyricism of *The Branch Will Not Break* (1963) and *Shall We Gather at the River* (1968), which were more dependent on the emotional tenor of image than on metre, poetic diction, or rhyme. In books such as *Figures of the Human* (1964) and *Rescue the Dead* (1968), David Ignatow wrote brief but razor-sharp poems that made their effect through swiftness, deceptive simplicity, paradox, and personal immediacy. Another poet whose work ran the gamut from prosaic simplicity to Emersonian transcendence was A.R. Ammons. His *Briefings* (1971) were close to autobiographical jottings, small glimpses, and observations, but, like his longer poems, they turned the natural world into a source of vision. Like Ignatow, he made it a virtue to seem unliterary and found illumination in the pedestrian and the ordinary.

Both daily life and an exposure to French Surrealism helped inspire a group of New York poets, among them Frank O'Hara, Kenneth Koch, James Schuyler, and John Ashbery. Whether O'Hara was jotting down a sequence of ordinary moments or paying tribute to film stars, his poems had a breathless immediacy that was distinctive and unique. Koch's comic voice swung effortlessly from the trivial to the fantastic. Strongly influenced by Wallace Stevens, Ashbery's ruminative poems can seem random, discursive, and enigmatic. Avoiding poetic colour, they do their work by suggestion and association, exploring the interface between experience and perception.

Other impressive poets of the postwar years included Elizabeth Bishop, whose precise, loving attention to objects was reminiscent of her early mentor, Marianne Moore. Though she avoided the confessional mode of her friend Lowell, her sense of place, her heartbreaking decorum, and her keen powers of observation gave her work a strong personal cast. In *The Changing Light at Sandover* (1982), James Merrill, previously a polished lyric poet, made his mandarin style the vehicle of a lighthearted personal epic, in which he, with the help of a Ouija (trademark) board, called up the shades of all his dead friends, including the poet Auden. In a prolific career highlighted by such poems as *Reflections on Espionage* (1976), "Blue Wine" (1979), and *Powers of Thirteen* (1983), John Hollander, like Merrill, displayed enormous technical virtuosity. Richard Howard imagined witty monologues and dialogues for famous people of the past in poems collected in *Untitled Subjects* (1969) and *Two-Part Inventions* (1974). With the autobiographical knots and parables of *Reasons for Moving* (1968) and *Darker* (1970), Mark Strand's paradoxical language achieved a resonant simplicity.

Other strongly autobiographical poets working with subtle technique and intelligence in a variety of forms included Philip Levine, Charles Simic, Robert Pinsky, Louise Glück, and Sharon Olds. With the sinuous sentences and long flowing lines of *Tar* (1983) and *Flesh and Blood* (1987), C.K. Williams perfected a narrative technique founded on distinctive voice, sharply etched emotion, and cleanly observed detail. Adrienne Rich's work gained a burning immediacy from her lesbian feminism. *The Will to Change* (1971) and *Diving Into the Wreck* (1973) were turning points for women's poetry in the wake of the 1960s. That decade also enabled some older poets to become more loosely autobiographical and freshly imaginative, among them Stanley Kunitz, Robert Penn Warren, and W.S. Merwin. The 1960s invigorated gifted black poets such as Robert Hayden, Gwendolyn Brooks, and Michael S. Harper. It formed the background for the work of the younger poets of the 1980s, such as Edward Hirsch, Alan Shapiro, Jorie Graham, Cathy Song, and Rita Dove, whose sequence about her grandparents, *Thomas and Beulah*, was awarded the Pulitzer Prize in 1987.

Drama. Two post-World War II playwrights established reputations comparable to O'Neill's. Arthur Miller wrote eloquent essays defending his modern, democratic concept of tragedy; despite its abstract, allegorical quality and portentous language, *Death of a Salesman* (1949) came close to vindicating his views. Miller's intense family dramas were rooted in the works of the socially conscious ethnic dramatists of the 1930s, especially Clifford Odets, but he gave them a metaphysical turn. From *All My Sons* (1947) to *The Price* (1968), his work is at its strongest when he deals with father-son relationships, anchored in the harsh realities of the Great Depression. Yet Miller could also be an effective protest writer, as in *The Crucible* (1953), which used the Salem witch trials to attack the witch-hunt-

Arthur Miller

ing of the McCarthy era. Though his work was uneven, Tennessee Williams must be viewed as a more important playwright than Miller. Creating stellar roles for actors, especially women, Williams brought a passionate lyricism and a tragic Southern vision to such plays as *The Glass Menagerie* (1944), *A Streetcar Named Desire* (1947), *Cat on a Hot Tin Roof* (1955), and *The Night of the Iguana* (1961). He empathized with his characters' dreams and illusions and with the frustrations and defeats of their lives, and he wrote about his own dreams and disappointments in his beautifully etched short fiction, from which his plays were often adapted.

Miller and Williams dominated the post-World War II theatre until the 1960s, and few other playwrights emerged to challenge them. Then, in 1962, Edward Albee's reputation, based on short plays such as *The Zoo Story* (1959) and *The American Dream* (1960), was secured by the stunning power of *Who's Afraid of Virginia Woolf?*. A master of absurdist theatre who assimilated the influence of European playwrights like Samuel Beckett and Eugène Ionesco, Albee established himself as a major figure in American drama. His reputation with critics and audiences, however, began to decline with enigmatic plays such as *Tiny Alice* (1964) and *A Delicate Balance* (1966), but, like Eugene O'Neill, he eventually returned to favour with a complex autobiographical drama, *Three Tall Women*, which won the Pulitzer Prize in 1994.

When the centre of American drama shifted from Broadway to Off-Broadway and Off-Off-Broadway with works such as Jack Gelber's *The Connection* (1959), American playwrights, collaborating with the Living Theatre, the Open Theatre, and other adventurous new companies, were increasingly free to write radical and innovative plays. David Rabe's *The Basic Training of Pavlo Hummel* (1971) and *Sticks and Bones* (1972) satirized America's militaristic nationalism and cultural shallowness. David Mamet won a 1976–77 New York Drama Critics Award for *American Buffalo*. In plays such as *Glengarry Glen Ross* (1984) he showed brilliantly how men reveal their hopes and frustrations obliquely, through their language, and in *Oleanna* (1992) he fired a major salvo in the gender wars over sexual harassment.

The ascendancy of Off-Broadway

Imamu Amiri Baraka (LeRoi Jones) and Ed Bullins inspired an angry black nationalist theatre. Baraka's *Dutchman* and *The Slave* (1964) effectively dramatized racial confrontation, while Bullins' *In the Wine Time* (1968) made use of "street" lyricism. Maria Irene Fornes's *Fefu and Her Friends* (1977) proved remarkable in its exploration of women's relationships. A clear indication of Off-Broadway's ascendancy in American drama came in 1979 when Sam Shepard, a prolific and experimental playwright, won the Pulitzer Prize for *Buried Child*. Shepard's earlier work, such as *The Tooth of Crime* (1972), was rooted both in the rock scene and counterculture of the 1960s and in the mythic world of the American West. But he reached his peak with a series of offbeat family dramas including *Curse of the Starving Class* (1976), *True West* (1980), *Fool For Love* (1983), and *A Lie of the Mind* (1986). Other important new voices in American drama were the prolific Lanford Wilson, the 1980 Pulitzer winner for *Talley's Folly*, John Guare, who created serious farce in *The House of Blue Leaves* (1971) and fresh social drama in *Six Degrees of Separation* (1990), and Ntozake Shange, whose "choreopoem," *For Colored Girls Who Have Considered Suicide/When the Rainbow Is Enuf*, moved to Broadway in 1976. Other well-received women playwrights included Marsha Norman, Beth Henley, Tina Howe, and Wendy Wasserstein. In a series of plays that included *Ma Rainey's Black Bottom* (1984), *Fences* (Pulitzer Prize, 1987), and *Joe Turner's Come and Gone* (1986), August Wilson emerged as the most powerful black playwright of the 1980s. The anguish of the AIDS epidemic proved a dark inspiration to many gay playwrights, especially Tony Kushner, who had gained attention with *A Bright Room Called Day* (1991) and won Broadway fame with his epically ambitious two-part drama *Angels in America* (1993), which combined comedy with pain, symbolism with personal history, and invented characters with historical ones.

(JAMES R. GILES/MORRIS DICKSTEIN)

BIBLIOGRAPHY. Literary histories include ROBERT E. SPILLER et al. (eds.), *Literary History of the United States*, 4th ed., rev., 2 vol. (1974), a standard general work; MARCUS CUNLIFFE (ed.), *American Literature to 1900*, new ed. (1986, reissued 1993), and *American Literature Since 1900*, new ed. (1987, reissued 1993); VERNON LOUIS PARRINGTON, *Main Currents in American Thought: An Interpretation of American Literature from the Beginnings to 1920*, 3 vol. (1927–30, reissued 1987), essential background reading; and ALFRED KAZIN, *An American Procession* (1984), from Emerson to Fitzgerald. Since the 1980s, anthologies have shifted to a multicultural viewpoint with broad coverage of writing by women and minorities. The most controversial example has been PAUL LAUTER and RICHARD YARBOROUGH (eds.), *The Heath Anthology of American Literature*, 2nd ed., 2 vol. (1994). Recent full-scale literary histories representing the work of younger scholars include EMORY ELLIOTT et al. (eds.), *The Columbia Literary History of the United States* (1991); and SACVAN BERCOVITCH and CYRUS R.K. PATELL (eds.), *The Cambridge History of American Literature* (1994–).

Studies that focus on specific periods or trends of American literary history include the following: on the colonial era, PERRY MILLER, *The New England Mind: From Colony to Province* (1953, reprinted 1983), and *The New England Mind: The Seventeenth Century* (1939, reissued 1983), two authoritative works; SACVAN BERCOVITCH, *The American Jeremiad* (1978); and ANDREW DELBANCO, *The Puritan Ordeal* (1989); on the period of the American Revolution, closer to cultural history than criticism, KENNETH SILVERMAN, *A Cultural History of the American Revolution* (1976, reprinted 1987); and EMORY ELLIOTT, *Revolutionary Writers* (1982); on the period of the American Renaissance, F.O. MATTHIESSEN, *American Renaissance* (1941, reprinted 1980), a classic study of the great writers of the 1850s; and DAVID S. REYNOLDS, *Beneath the American Renaissance* (1988), a comprehensive view of the popular culture of the day; and, on the period from 1890 to 1940, ALFRED KAZIN, *On Native Grounds: An Interpretation of Modern American Prose Literature* (1942, reprinted 1982), a brilliantly written critical history.

Important studies of the pastoral and frontier traditions in American literature are HENRY NASH SMITH, *Virgin Land: The American West as Symbol and Myth* (1950, reissued 1978); LEO MARX, *The Machine in the Garden: Technology and the Pastoral Ideal in America* (1964, reprinted 1972); and, from a radically different viewpoint, RICHARD SLOTKIN, *Regeneration Through Violence: The Mythology of the American Frontier, 1600–1800* (1973), and *The Fatal Environment: The Myth of the Frontier in the Age of Industrialization, 1800–1890* (1985). Major work on the romance tradition in American fiction begins with D.H. LAWRENCE, *Studies in Classic American Literature* (1923, reissued 1977); and is developed in RICHARD CHASE, *The American Novel and Its Tradition* (1957, reprinted 1978); and LESLIE FIEDLER, *Love and Death in the American Novel*, rev. ed. (1966, reissued 1992). Among later studies on this subject, see MICHAEL DAVITT BELL, *The Development of American Romance* (1980). Recent work on American realism, stressing the social and historical context, includes ERIC J. SUNDQUIST (ed.), *American Realism: New Essays* (1982); and PHILIP FISHER, *Hard Facts: Setting and Form in the American Novel* (1985). The role of race in American literature is the ambitious subject of ERIC J. SUNDQUIST, *To Wake the Nations* (1993).

The wide range of neglected novels by 19th-century women has been mapped by NINA BAYM, *Woman's Fiction: A Guide to Novels By and About Women, 1820–70*, 2nd ed. (1993). Feminist criticism of American fiction can be found in JUDITH FETTERLEY, *The Resisting Reader* (1978). Radical and ethnic writing between the two world wars has been studied by MARCUS KLEIN, *Foreigners: The Making of American Literature, 1900–1940* (1981). The long history of African-American literature has been explored by ROBERT A. BONE, *The Negro Novel in America*, rev. ed. (1965); and HENRY LOUIS GATES, JR., *The Signifying Monkey* (1988).

Critical studies of post-World War II fiction include TONY TANNER, *City of Words* (1971), useful for understanding contemporary metafiction; MORRIS DICKSTEIN, *Gates of Eden: American Culture in the Sixties* (1977, reprinted 1989), which places postwar writers in their cultural context; and FREDERICK R. KARL, *American Fictions, 1940–1980* (1983), a comprehensive study. Studies of postwar poetry can be found in CHARLES MOLESWORTH, *The Fierce Embrace* (1979); and HELEN VENDLER, *Part of Nature, Part of Us: Modern American Poets* (1980). Studies of the period's drama include C.W.E. BIGSBY, *A Critical Introduction to Twentieth-Century American Drama*, 3 vol. (1982–85). Studies of 20th-century American critics can be found in FRANK LENTRICCHIA, *After the New Criticism* (1980); and MORRIS DICKSTEIN, *Double Agent: The Critic and Society* (1992). (WALTER BLAIR/JAMES R. GILES/MORRIS DICKSTEIN)

Eastern Africa

Eritrea

Eritrea (Tigrinya: Ertra) is a small country of the Horn of Africa, located on the Red Sea. Its 600 miles (1,000 kilometres) of coastline extend from Cape Kasar, in the north, to the Strait of Mandeb, separating the Red Sea from the Gulf of Aden in the south. It is bounded on the northwest by The Sudan, on the south by Ethiopia, and on the southeast by Djibouti. Total land area (including islands off the coast) is 45,300 square miles (117,400 square kilometres). Eritrea's capital and largest city is Asmera.

Eritrea's coastal location has long been important in its history and culture—a fact reflected in its name, which is an Italianized version of Mare Erythraeum, Latin for "Red Sea." The Red Sea was the route along which Christianity and Islām reached the area and took firm hold among the people, and it was an important trade route that such powers as Turkey, Egypt, and Italy hoped to dominate by seizing control of ports on the Eritrean coast. Those ports promised access to the gold, coffee, and slaves sold by traders in the Ethiopian highlands to the south, and in the second half of the 20th century Ethiopia became the power from which the Eritrean people had to free themselves in order to create their own state.

In 1993, after a war of independence that lasted nearly three decades, Eritrea became a sovereign country. During the long struggle, the people of Eritrea managed to forge a common national consciousness, but, with peace established, they now face the task of overcoming their ethnic and religious differences in order to raise the country from a poverty made worse by years of drought, neglect, and war.

PHYSICAL AND HUMAN GEOGRAPHY

The land. *Relief.* Eritrea's land is highly variegated. Running on a north-south axis through the middle of the country are the central highlands, a narrow strip of country some 6,500 feet (2,000 metres) above sea level that represents the northern reaches of the Ethiopian Plateau. Geologically, this plateau consists of a foundation of crystalline rock (*e.g.*, granite, gneiss, micaschist) that is overlain by sedimentary rock (limestone and sandstone) and then capped by basalt (rock of volcanic origin). The upper layers have been highly dissected by deep gorges and river channels, forming small steep-sided, flat-topped tablelands known as *amba*s. The highest point in the plateau is Mount Soira, at 9,885 feet (3,013 metres).

The central highlands

In the north of Eritrea the highlands narrow and then end in a system of hills, where erosion has cut down to the basement rock. To the east the plateau drops abruptly into a coastal plain. North of the Gulf of Zula, the plain is only 10 to 50 miles wide, but to the south it widens to include the Denakil Plain. This barren region contains a depression known as the Kobar Sink (more than 300 feet below sea level), the northern end of which extends into Eritrea. The coastal plain and the Denakil Plain are part of the East African Rift System and are sharply delimited on the west by the eastern escarpment of the plateau, which, although deeply eroded, presents a formidable obstacle to travelers from the coast.

The western flank of the central highlands is a broken

and undulating plain that slopes gradually toward the border with The Sudan. It lies at an average elevation of 1,500 feet. The vegetation is mostly savanna, consisting of scattered trees, shrubs, and seasonal grasses.

Off the coast in the Red Sea is the Dahlak Archipelago, a group of more than 100 small coral and reef-fringed islands. Only a few of these islands have a permanent population.

Drainage. The Eritrean highlands are drained by four major rivers and numerous streams. Two of the rivers, the Gash and the Tekeze, flow westward into The Sudan. The Tekeze River (also known as the Satit) is a major tributary of the Atbara River, which eventually joins the Nile. The Gash River reaches the Atbara only during flood season. As it crosses the western lowlands, the Tekeze forms part of Eritrea's border with Ethiopia, while the upper course of the Gash, known as the Mereb River, forms the border on the plateau.

The other two major rivers that drain the highlands of Eritrea are the Barka and the Anseba. Both of these rivers flow northward into a marshy area on the eastern coast of The Sudan and do not reach the Red Sea. Several seasonal streams that flow eastward from the plateau reach the sea on the Eritrean coast.

Climate. Eritrea has a wide variety of climatic conditions, produced mainly by differences in altitude. The effects of elevation are seen most clearly in the wide range of temperatures experienced throughout the country. On the coast, Mitsiwa has one of the highest averages in the world (86° F, or 30° C), while Asmera, only 40 miles away yet more than 7,500 feet higher on the plateau, averages 62° F (17° C).

Mean annual rainfall on the plateau is 16 to 20 inches (400 to 500 millimetres), while on the western plain it is less than 16 inches. In both the highlands and the western lowlands, rainfall comes in summer, carried on a southwesterly airstream that decreases in amount of precipitation and length of rainy season as it proceeds toward the northeastern extremes of the plateau. The eastern edges of the plateau and, to a lesser extent, the coastal fringes receive much smaller quantities of rain from a northeasterly airstream that arrives in winter and spring. The interior regions of the Denakil Plain are practically rainless.

Settlement patterns. The environment is a determining factor in the distribution of Eritrea's population. Although the plateau represents only one-quarter of the total land area, it is home to approximately one-half of the population, most of them sedentary agriculturalists. The lowlands on the east and west support a population mainly of pastoralists, although most of them also cultivate crops when and where weather conditions permit. As a rule, pastoralists follow various patterns of movement set by the seasons. Only the Rashaida, a small group in the northern hills, is truly nomadic.

Under Italian colonial rule from 1889 to 1941, Eritrea's urban sector flourished with the establishment of Asmera as the capital city, Aseb as a new port on the Red Sea, and a host of smaller towns on the plateau. In addition, Mitsiwa, an old and cosmopolitan port with strong links to Arabia, was expanded considerably. By the end of the colonial period, Eritrea had by far the highest urbanization rate in the Horn of Africa—approximately 15 percent— although a large part of the urban population was Italian nationals who eventually left the country. Subsequently, a population drift from the countryside to the towns was offset by emigration of Eritreans abroad, so that at the time of independence in 1993 the relative size of the urban sector remained unchanged.

The people. *Language groups.* Eritrea's population consists of several ethnic groups, each with its own language and cultural tradition. The Eritrean highlands are an extension of the Ethiopian Plateau to the south, and the bulk of the peasantry on the plateau belong to the Tigray, a group that also occupies the adjacent Ethiopian province of Tigray. The Tigrayan language, called Tigrinya, is spoken on both sides of the border and is the speech of nearly one-half of all Eritreans.

Inhabiting the northernmost part of the Eritrean plateau, as well as lowlands to the east and west, are people who speak the other major Eritrean language—Tigre. Tigre and Tigrinya are written in the same script and are descended from the same mother tongue (the ancient Semitic language of Ge'ez), but they are mutually unintelligible.

Also occupying the northern plateau are Bilin speakers, whose language belongs to the Cushitic family. The Rashaida are a group of Arabic-speaking nomads who traverse the northern hills.

On the southern part of the coastal region live Afar nomads, whose relatives live across the borders in Djibouti and Ethiopia; they are also called the Denakil, after the region that they inhabit. The coastal strip south of Mitsiwa, as well as the eastern flanks of the plateau, are occupied by Saho pastoralists. In the western plain, the dominant people are pastoralists of the Beja family, whose kin live across the border in The Sudan. Two small Nilotic groups, the Kunama and the Nara, also live in the west.

Religions. Historically, religion has been a prominent symbol of ethnic identity in the Horn of Africa. Christianity was established in the 4th century AD on the coast and appeared soon afterward in the plateau, where it was embraced by the Ethiopian highlanders. The Monophysite creed of the Ethiopian Orthodox church remains the faith of about half of the population of Eritrea, including nearly all the Tigray. Following the rise of Islām in Arabia, Muslim power flowed over the Red Sea coast, forcing the Ethiopians to retreat deep into their mountain fastness. Islām displaced other creeds in the lowlands of the Horn, and it remains the faith of nearly all the people inhabiting the eastern coast and the western plain of Eritrea, as well as the northernmost part of the plateau. Thus, while Islām claims nearly all pastoralists, Christianity is dominant among the peasant cultivators. (Muslims are significantly represented also in all towns of Eritrea, where they are prominent in trade.) In the perennial competition between cultivators and pastoralists over land, water, control of trade, and access to ports, religion has played an ideological role, and it remains a potent political force.

During the colonial period, Catholic and Protestant European missionaries introduced their own version of Christianity into Eritrea. They had considerable success among the small Kunama group, and they also attracted a few townspeople with the offer of modern education.

The economy. *Natural resources.* Salt mining, based on deposits in the Kobar Sink, is a traditional activity in Eritrea. Deposits of gold, copper, potash, and iron have been exploited at times in a minor way, and numerous other minerals have been identified, including zinc, feldspar, gypsum, asbestos, mica, and sulfur.

The area of cultivation is limited by climate and the uneven surface of the plateau, so that, of the 8 million acres (3.2 million hectares) of land considered cultivable, only 5 percent is being worked. There is room for expansion, however, especially if the country's considerable water resources are harnessed for irrigation.

In normal times, livestock is a valuable resource, and it has the potential to play a role in Eritrea's foreign trade. During the long war of independence, however, livestock was severely depleted. The fishing potential of the Red Sea is another underutilized resource.

Soil erosion, an age-old process, is particularly severe on the plateau. Encouraged by the steady expansion of cultivation, it has left few wooded areas and has created a shortage of fuel. The proximity of the oil-rich Arabian basin has occasionally raised expectations of discovering petroleum in Eritrea, but intermittent exploration since the days of Italian rule has failed to produce results.

Agriculture. Agriculture is by far the most important sector of the country's economy, providing a livelihood for about 80 percent of the population and normally accounting for the bulk of Eritrea's exports. Peasant cultivation and traditional pastoralism are the main forms of agricultural activity. These are not mutually exclusive occupations, since most peasants also keep animals and most pastoralists cultivate grains when possible. Both peasants and pastoralists produce primarily for their own subsistence, and only small surpluses are available for trade.

The staple grain products are an indigenous cereal named teff (*Eragostis abyssinica*) as well as corn (maize), wheat,

Marginal notes:

Christian highlanders and Muslim lowlanders

Highland agriculturalists and lowland pastoralists

barley, sorghum, and millet. Vegetables and fruit also are produced. Under Italian rule, modern irrigated plantations produced vegetables, fruit, cotton, sisal, bananas, tobacco, and coffee for the growing urban markets. This sector continued to operate under Ethiopian rule until it was disrupted by the long period of warfare.

Industry. A generation of war also damaged Eritrea's modest manufacturing sector, which also appeared during the Italian colonial period and provided many Eritrean workers with skills that enabled them later to find work abroad. Industry was based largely on the processing of agricultural products. Asmera was the main industrial centre, concerned with food products, beer, tobacco, textiles, and leather.

Red Sea
ports A petroleum refinery in the Red Sea port of Aseb, built by the Soviet Union for Ethiopia, is the prime industrial enterprise in Eritrea. Aseb also has a salt works, and there are a salt works and a cement works near the port of Mitsiwa.

Trade and transportation. Aseb and Mitsiwa have long been major ports of entry to Ethiopia, and that country, now landlocked, still has guarantees of access to the port facilities at Aseb. As a result, the bulk of Eritrea's trade is in the transit of goods to Ethiopia. A paved road links Aseb with Addis Ababa, and another paved road begins in Mitsiwa, climbs the plateau to Asmera, and continues south to the Ethiopian town of Adigrat. A railway was built by the Italians from Mitsiwa to Asmera, Keren, and Akordat, but it was rendered useless by the war of independence.

There are an international airport in Asmera and major airfields in Aseb and Mitsiwa.

Administration and social conditions. *Government.* After liberation from Ethiopia in May 1991, Eritrea was ruled by a provisional government that consisted essentially of the central committee of the Eritrean People's Liberation Front (EPLF). On May 19, 1993, shortly after a national referendum, this body proclaimed the Transitional Government of Eritrea, which was to rule for four years until the promulgation of a constitution and the election of a permanent government. The transitional government's legislative body, called the National Assembly, consisted of the original 30-member central committee of the EPLF augmented by 60 new members. At least 20 seats were to be reserved for women.

The National Assembly sets the policies of the government and elects the president. The president is assisted in implementing the government's policies by a State Council, containing cabinet ministers and the governors of Eritrea's provinces. In order to discourage ethnic rivalry, seats on the State Council are divided equally between Muslims and Christians, and political parties based on language or religion are banned.

Health and education. Chronic drought and decades of war have taken a toll on the health of Eritreans. The mortality rate at birth is 15 percent, and almost half of all infants die during their first year. The average life expectancy is about 50 years.

Only about 20 percent of Eritreans are literate, though the new government is intent on expanding education. Children are taught in their native languages, and in the higher grades they also are taught foreign languages, especially Arabic and English. There is a university in Asmera.

<u>HISTORY</u>

Precolonial Eritrea. *Rule from the highlands.* Beginning about 1000 BC, Semitic peoples from the South Arabian kingdom of Saba' (or Sheba) migrated across the Red Sea and absorbed the Cushitic inhabitants of the Eritrean coast and adjacent highlands. These Semitic invaders, possessing a well-developed culture, established the kingdom of Aksum, which, by the end of the 4th century AD, ruled the northern stretches of the Ethiopian Plateau and the eastern lowlands. An important trade route led from the port of Adulis, near modern Zula, to the city of Aksum, the capital, located in what is now the Ethiopian province of Tigray.

After extending its power at times as far afield as modern Egypt and Yemen, Aksum began to decline into obscurity

in the 6th century AD. Beginning in the 12th century, however, the Ethiopian Zagwe and Solomonid dynasties held sway to a fluctuating extent over the entire plateau and the Red Sea coast. Eritrea's central highlands, known as the *mereb melash* ("land beyond the Mereb River"), The "land
beyond the
Mereb" were the northern frontier region of the Ethiopian kingdoms and were ruled by a governor titled *bahr negash* ("lord of the sea"). The control exercised by the crown over this region was never firm, and it became even more tenuous as the centre of Ethiopian power moved steadily southward to Gonder and Shewa. Highland Eritrea became a vassal fiefdom of the lords of Tigray, who were seldom on good terms with the dominant Amhara branch of the Ethiopian family.

Contesting for the coastlands. Off the plateau, the pastoralist peoples in the west and north knew no foreign master until the early 19th century, when the Egyptians invaded the Sudan and raided deep into the Eritrean lowlands. The Red Sea coast, owing to its strategic and commercial importance, was contested by many powers. In the 16th century the Turks occupied the Dahlak Archipelago and then Mitsiwa, where they maintained, with occasional interruption, a garrison for more than three centuries. Also in the 16th century, Eritrea as well as Ethiopia were affected by the invasions of Aḥmad Grāñ, the Muslim leader of the sultanate of Adal. After the expulsion of Aḥmad's forces, the Turks temporarily occupied even more of Eritrea's coastal area. In 1865 the Egyptians obtained Mitsiwa from the Ottoman Porte. From there they pushed inland to the plateau, until in 1875 an Egyptian force that reached the Mereb River was annihilated by Ethiopian forces.

Meanwhile, the opening of the Suez Canal in 1869 had made the Red Sea a scene of rivalry among the world's most powerful states. Between 1869 and 1880 the Italian Rubattino Navigation company purchased from the local Afar sultan stretches of the Red Sea coast adjoining the village of Aseb. In 1882 these acquisitions were transferred to the Italian state, and in 1885 Italian troops landed at Mitsiwa, Aseb, and other locations. There was no resistance by the Egyptians at Mitsiwa, and protests made by the Turks and Ethiopians were ignored. Italian forces then systematically spread out from Mitsiwa toward the highlands. This expansion onto the plateau was initially opposed by Emperor Yohannes IV, the only Tigray to wear the Ethiopian crown in modern times, but Yohannes's successor, Menilek II, in return for weapons that he needed to fight possible rivals, acquiesced to Italian occupation of the region north of the Mereb. In the Treaty of Wichale, signed on May 2, 1889, Menilek recognized "Italian possessions in the Red Sea," and on Jan. 1, 1890, the Italian colony of Eritrea was officially proclaimed. From here, the Italians launched several incursions into Ethiopia, only to be decisively defeated by Menilek's army at the Battle of Adwa on March 1, 1896. Menilek did not pursue the defeated enemy across the Mereb. Soon afterward, he signed the Treaty of Addis Ababa, obtaining Italian recognition of Ethiopia's sovereignty in return for his recognition of Italian rule over Eritrea.

Colonial Eritrea. *Ruled by Italy.* In precolonial times there were no towns on the Eritrean plateau, urban centres being limited to the Red Sea coast. Under Italian rule, however, Eritrea's urban sector flourished. Tens of Economic
growth and
moderniza-
tion thousands of Italians arrived, bringing with them modern skills and a new lifestyle. Asmera grew into a charming city in Mediterranean style, the port of Mitsiwa was modernized and the port of Aseb improved, and a number of smaller towns appeared on the plateau. Road and rail construction linked the various regions of the colony, and a modest manufacturing sector also appeared, so that Eritreans acquired industrial skills.

At the same time, a sizable portion of Eritrea's best agricultural land was reserved for Italian farmers (although only a few actually settled on the land), and a small plantation sector was established to grow produce for the urban market. Eritrea's population grew rapidly during this period. Combined with the appropriation of land for Italian use, population growth created a shortage of land for the peasantry. This in turn stimulated a drift to the cities, which further expanded the urban population and produced an Eritrean working class.

Still, Eritrea had no valuable resources for exploitation and was not a wealth-producing colony for Italy. In fact, the colony was subsidized by the Italians, an extraneous factor that gave the local economy an artificial glow. Investment in education for Eritreans was negligible. There were very few schools for them, and even these were limited to the primary level. Also, Eritreans were not employed in the colonial service except as labourers and soldiers. As preparations for the invasion of Ethiopia got under way in the mid-1930s, several thousand Eritreans were recruited to serve in the invading army.

From Italian to Ethiopian rule. The invasion and occupation of Ethiopia beginning in 1935 marked the last chapter in Italian colonial history—a chapter that came to an end with the eviction of Italy from the Horn of Africa by the British in 1941. The following decade, during which Eritrea remained under British administration, was a period of intense political and diplomatic activity that shaped the future of Eritrea. Landlocked Ethiopia, coveting Eritrea's two seaports, launched an early campaign to annex the former colony, claiming that it had always been part of Ethiopia's domain. Lobbying of the Allied powers was carried out, and within Eritrea support for annexation was mobilized on the basis of religious loyalty by utilizing the services of Ethiopian Orthodox clergy. In order to promote the union of Eritrea with Ethiopia, a Unionist Party was formed in 1946; it was financed and guided from Addis Ababa.

Eritrea's Muslims had every good reason to oppose union with Ethiopia, where Christianity was the official religion and Muslims suffered discrimination in many areas of life. In order to counter Christian mobilization for union, a Muslim League was founded in 1947 to campaign for Eritrean independence. Thus, although there were some Christians who favoured independence and a few Muslims who were favourable to union with Ethiopia, the political division was drawn largely along sectarian lines.

Federation with Ethiopia. *Adoption of the federal scheme.* In 1950 the United Nations (UN), under the prompting of the United States, resolved to join Eritrea to Ethiopia within two years in a federation that would provide the former colony with autonomy under its own constitution and elected government. Elections to a new Eritrean Assembly in 1952 gave the Unionist Party the largest number of seats—but not a majority, so that it formed a government in coalition with a Muslim faction. The Eritrean constitution, prepared by the UN in consultation with Emperor Haile Selassie I of Ethiopia, was adopted by the Eritrean Assembly on July 10, 1952, and ratified by Haile Selassie on August 11. The act of federation was ratified by the emperor on September 11, and British authorities officially relinquished control on September 15.

Failure of the federal scheme. The federal scheme was short-lived, mainly because the imperial government in Addis Ababa was unwilling to abide by its provisions. First, the Eritrean constitution sought to establish an equilibrium between ethnic and religious groups. It made Tigrinya and Arabic the official languages of Eritrea, and it allowed local communities to choose the language of education for their children. In the spirit of the constitution, the practice evolved of ensuring parity between Christians and Muslims in appointment to state office. This delicate balance was destroyed by Ethiopian interference, and Muslims were the initial losers, as Arabic was eliminated from state education and Muslims were squeezed out of public employment. Furthermore, the Ethiopians were anxious to eliminate any traces of separatism in Eritrea, and to that end they harrassed the leaders of the independence movement until many of them fled abroad. With the collaboration of their Unionist allies and in express violation of the constitution, they also suppressed all attempts to form autonomous Eritrean organizations. Political parties were banned in 1955, trade unions were banned in 1958, and in 1959 the name Eritrean Government was changed to "Eritrean Administration" and Ethiopian law was imposed. Eventually, even Ethiopia's

Eritrean allies were alienated by crude intervention in the running of the Eritrean administration, financial disputes between Asmera and Addis Ababa, and mounting pressure on the Eritreans to renounce autonomy. The federation was already dead when, on Nov. 14, 1962, the Ethiopian parliament and Eritrean Assembly voted unanimously for the abolition of Eritrea's federal status, making Eritrea a simple province of the Ethiopian empire. Soon afterward, Tigrinya was banned in education; it was replaced by Amharic, the official language of Ethiopia.

The war of independence. *Beginning of armed revolt.* Muslims had been the first to suffer from Ethiopia's intervention in Eritrea, and it was they who formed the first opposition movement. In 1960, leaders of the defunct independence movement who were then living in exile announced the formation of the Eritrean Liberation Front (ELF). The founders, all Muslims, were led by Idris Mohammed Adam, a leading political figure in Eritrea in the 1940s. By the mid-1960s the ELF was able to field a small guerrilla force in the western plain of Eritrea, and thus began a war that was to last nearly three decades. In the early years, the ELF drew support from Muslim communities in the western and eastern lowlands as well as the northern hills. It also sought support from The Sudan, Syria, Iran, and other Islāmic states, used Arabic as its official language, and adopted Arab nomenclature in its organization. Ethiopian authorities portrayed the movement as an Arab tool and sought to rally Eritrean Christians to oppose it. Deteriorating economic and political conditions in Eritrea, however, combined to produce the opposite result.

During the 1930s and '40s the Eritrean economy had been stimulated by Italian colonial activity and by the special conditions created by World War II. After the war the local economy deflated, and it remained stagnant during the entire period of federation with Ethiopia. Many thousands of Eritreans were forced to emigrate to Ethiopia and the Middle East in search of employment. The suppression of the nascent trade-union movement further embittered this class, and many Eritrean workers— Muslims and Christians alike—rallied to the nationalist movement. In addition, the banning of Tigrinya in state education helped to turn an entire generation of Eritrean Christian students toward nationalism. Christians began to join the ELF in significant numbers at the end of the 1960s. Among them were students who had become politically radicalized in the Ethiopian student movement, which itself became a centre of opposition to the regime of Haile Selassie in the 1960s and '70s.

The spreading revolution. The ELF was now able to extend it operations to the central highlands of Eritrea— the home of the Tigray. However, the arrival of the radical students coincided with the emergence of a serious rift between the leadership of the ELF, which was permanently resident in Cairo, and the rank and file, which remained in the field. The newcomers joined the opposition to the leadership, and in 1972 several groups that had defected from the ELF joined forces to form the Eritrean Liberation Front–People's Liberation Forces (ELF–PLF). For several years the two rival organizations fought each other as well as the Ethiopians. After a series of splits and mergers, the ELF–PLF came under the control of former students, among whom Christians predominated, and was renamed the Eritrean People's Liberation Front (EPLF). Religion was of no concern to the EPLF, a highly committed and disciplined organization that adopted Marxism as its guide and proclaimed its intention to carry out a social as well as a national revolution in Eritrea.

The EPLF had made its presence felt by 1974, when the imperial regime in Ethiopia collapsed. While a power struggle for the succession was waged in Addis Ababa, the two Eritrean fronts liberated most of the territory and towns of Eritrea. By 1977 the nationalist revolution seemed on the verge of victory. It was not to be. A military dictatorship emerged in Addis Ababa, also espousing Marxism but finding a powerful new patron in the Soviet Union. Since World War II, the Red Sea had become a vital conduit through which oil from the Persian Gulf passed, and it thus became an object of intense competition between the

Suppression of Eritrean nationalism

Highlanders join the rebellion

United States and the Soviet Union. Neither superpower favoured Eritrean nationalism, and the United States had been the first to oppose it directly by assisting Ethiopia to build the largest army in sub-Saharan Africa in the 1960s. The United States now cut off its support, opening a gap that was quickly filled by the Soviets. Armed and assisted by the Soviet bloc, the new Ethiopian regime was able to regain most of Eritrea in 1978, and warfare on a scale unprecedented in black Africa raged for the next decade. The Ethiopians made enormous efforts with massive land attacks and heavy weaponry, but they had no success against the small and lightly armed guerrilla forces.

The violence of war and indiscriminate oppression in their homeland turned most Eritreans against Ethiopia, thereby producing a steady stream of young recruits for the nationalist movement. Throughout the 1980s the fighting was carried out by the EPLF, which by 1981 had succeeded in eliminating the ELF and had emerged as the unchallenged champion of Eritrean nationalism. In the latter part of the decade, the Soviet Union terminated its

military aid to Ethiopia. Unable to find another patron and faced with armed rebellion in other parts of the country, the regime in Addis Ababa began to falter. The final act occurred in 1991, when a rebel military offensive, led by the Tigray People's Liberation Front, swept toward the capital. The Ethiopian army disintegrated, and in May the EPLF assumed complete control of Eritrea.

Three decades of war had produced among Eritreans a sense of unity and solidarity that they had not known before. Indeed, an entire generation had come of age during the struggle for independence, which was now to become a reality. The new regime in Ethiopia supported Eritrea's independence, so that a separation was effected amicably. In a referendum held two years after liberation, on April 23–25, 1993, the overwhelming majority of Eritreans voted for independence. On May 21, Isaias Afwerki, the secretary-general of the EPLF, was made president of a transitional government, and on May 24 he proclaimed Eritrea officially independent.

Independence

(GEOFFREY CHARLES LAST/JOHN MARKAKIS)

Marketing and Merchandising

Marketing is a process whose principal function is to promote and facilitate exchange. Through marketing, individuals and groups obtain what they need and want by exchanging products and services with other parties. Such a process can occur only when there are at least two parties, each of whom has something to offer. In addition, exchange cannot occur unless the parties are able to communicate about and to deliver what they offer. Marketing is not a coercive process: all parties must be free to accept or reject what others are offering. So defined, marketing is distinguished from other modes of obtaining desired goods, such as through self-production, begging, theft, or force.

Marketing is not confined to any particular type of economy, because goods must be exchanged and therefore marketed in all economies and societies except perhaps in the most primitive. Furthermore, marketing is not a function that is limited to profit-oriented business; even such institutions as hospitals, schools, and museums engage in some forms of marketing. Within the broad scope of marketing, merchandising is concerned more specifically with promoting the sale of goods and services to consumers (*i.e.,* retailing) and hence is more characteristic of free-market economies.

Based on these criteria, marketing can take a variety of forms: it can be a set of functions, a department within an organization, a managerial process, a managerial philosophy, and a social process.

For coverage of related topics in the *Macropædia* and *Micropædia,* see the *Propædia,* sections 532 and 533, and the *Index.*

The evolving discipline of marketing

The marketing discipline had its origins in the early 20th century as an offspring of economics. Economic science had neglected the role of middlemen and the role of functions other than price in the determination of demand levels and characteristics. Early marketing economists examined agricultural and industrial markets and described them in greater detail than the classical economists. This examination resulted in the development of three approaches to the analysis of marketing activity: the commodity, the institution, and the function.

Commodity analysis studies the ways in which a product or product group is brought to market. A commodity analysis of milk, for example, traces the ways in which milk is collected at individual dairy farms, transported to and processed at local dairy cooperatives, and shipped to grocers and supermarkets for consumer purchase. In-

stitutional analysis describes the types of businesses that play a prevalent role in marketing, such as wholesale or retail institutions. For instance, an institutional analysis of clothing wholesalers examines the ongoing concerns that wholesalers face in order to ensure both the correct supply for their customers and the appropriate inventory and shipping capabilities. Finally, a functional analysis examines the general tasks that marketing performs. For example, any marketing effort must ensure that the product is transported from the supplier to the customer. In some industries, this transportation function may be handled by a truck, while in others it may be done by mail, facsimile, television signal, or airline. All these institutions perform the same function.

As the study of marketing became more prevalent throughout the 20th century, large companies—particularly mass consumer manufacturers—began to recognize the importance of market research, better product design, effective distribution, and sustained communication with consumers in the success of their brands. Marketing concepts and techniques later moved into the industrial-goods sector and subsequently into the services sector. It soon became apparent that organizations and individuals market not only goods and services but also ideas (social marketing), places (location marketing), personalities (celebrity marketing), events (event marketing), and even the organizations themselves (public relations).

Rise of marketing

Roles of marketing

As marketing developed, it took a variety of forms. It was noted above that marketing can be viewed as a set of functions in the sense that certain activities are traditionally associated with the exchange process. A common but incorrect view is that selling and advertising are the only marketing activities. Yet, in addition to promotion, marketing includes a much broader set of functions, including product development, packaging, pricing, distribution, and customer service.

Many organizations and businesses assign responsibility for these marketing functions to a specific group of individuals within the organization. In this respect, marketing is a unique and separate entity. Those who make up the marketing department may include brand and product managers, marketing researchers, sales representatives, advertising and promotion managers, pricing specialists, and customer service personnel.

As a managerial process, marketing is the way in which an organization determines its best opportunities in the marketplace, given its objectives and resources. The marketing process is divided into a strategic and a tactical phase. The strategic phase has three components—segmentation, targeting, and positioning (STP). The organization must distinguish among different groups of customers in the market (segmentation), choose which group(s) it can serve effectively (targeting), and communicate the central benefit it offers to that group (positioning). The marketing process includes designing and implementing various tactics, commonly referred to as the "marketing mix," or the "4 Ps": product, price, place (or distribution), and promotion. The marketing mix is followed by evaluating, controlling, and revising the marketing process to achieve the organization's objectives (see below the section *Marketing-mix planning*).

The managerial philosophy of marketing puts central emphasis on customer satisfaction as the means for gaining and keeping loyal customers. Marketers urge their organizations to carefully and continually gauge target customers' expectations and to consistently meet or exceed these expectations. In order to accomplish this, everyone in all areas of the organization must focus on understanding and serving customers; it will not succeed if all marketing occurs only in the marketing department. Marketing, consequently, is far too important to be done solely by the marketing department. Marketers also want their organizations to move from practicing transaction-oriented marketing, which focuses on individual exchanges, to relationship-driven marketing, which emphasizes serving the customer over the long term. Simply getting new customers and losing old ones will not help the organization achieve its objectives.

Finally, marketing is a social process that occurs in all economies, regardless of their political structure and orientation. It is the process by which a society organizes and distributes its resources to meet the material needs of its citizens. However, marketing activity is more pronounced under conditions of goods surpluses than goods shortages. When goods are in short supply, consumers are usually so desirous of goods that the exchange process does not require significant promotion or facilitation. In contrast, when there are more goods and services than consumers need or want, companies must work harder to convince customers to exchange with them.

Relation to supply and demand

The marketing process

The marketing process consists of four elements: strategic marketing analysis, marketing-mix planning, marketing implementation, and marketing control.

STRATEGIC MARKETING ANALYSIS

The aim of marketing in profit-oriented organizations is to meet needs profitably. Companies must therefore first define which needs—and whose needs—they can satisfy. For example, the personal transportation market consists of people who put different values on an automobile's cost, speed, safety, status, and styling. No single automobile can satisfy all these needs in a superior fashion; compromises have to be made. Furthermore, some individuals may wish to meet their personal transportation needs with something other than an automobile, such as a motorcycle, a bicycle, or a bus or other form of public transportation. Because of such variables, an automobile company must identify the different preference groups, or segments, of customers and decide which group(s) they can target profitably.

Segments can be divided into even smaller groups, called subsegments or niches. A niche is defined as a small target group that has special requirements. For example, a bank may specialize in serving the investment needs of not only senior citizens but also senior citizens with high incomes and perhaps even those with particular investment preferences. It is more likely that larger organizations will serve the larger market segments (mass marketing) and ignore niches. As a result, smaller companies typically emerge that are intimately familiar with a particular niche and specialize in serving its needs.

A growing number of companies are now trying to serve "segments of one." They attempt to adapt their offer and communication to each individual customer. This is understandable, for instance, with large industrial companies that have only a few major customers. For example, The Boeing Company (United States) designs its 747 planes differently for each major customer, such as United Airlines, Inc., or American Airlines, Inc. Serving individual customers is increasingly possible with the advent of database marketing, through which individual customer characteristics and purchase histories are retained in company information systems. Even mass-marketing companies, particularly large retailers and catalog houses, compile comprehensive data on individual customers and are able to customize their offerings and communications.

A key step in marketing strategy, known as positioning, involves creating and communicating a message that clearly establishes the company or brand in relation to competitors. Thus, Volvo Aktiebolaget (Sweden) has positioned its automobile as the "safest," and Daimler-Benz AG (Germany), manufacturer of Mercedes-Benz vehicles, has positioned its car as the best "engineered." Some products may be positioned as "outstanding" in two or more ways. However, claiming superiority along several dimensions may hurt a company's credibility because consumers will not believe that any one offering can excel in all dimensions. Furthermore, although the company may communicate a particular position, customers may perceive a different image of the company as a result of their actual experiences with the company's product or through word of mouth.

MARKETING-MIX PLANNING

Having developed a strategy, a company must then decide which tactics will be most effective in achieving strategy goals. Tactical marketing involves creating a marketing mix of four components—product, price, place, promotion—that fulfills the strategy for the targeted set of customer needs.

Product. The first marketing-mix element is the product, which refers to the offering or group of offerings that will be made available to customers. In the case of a physical product, such as a car, a company will gather information about the features and benefits desired by a target market. Before assembling a product, the marketer's role is to communicate customer desires to the engineers who design the product or service. This is in contrast to past practice, when engineers designed a product based on their own preferences, interests, or expertise and then expected marketers to find as many customers as possible to buy this product. Contemporary thinking calls for products to be designed based on customer input and not solely on engineers' ideas.

Consumer input in product development

In traditional economies, the goods produced and consumed often remain the same from one generation to the next—including food, clothing, and housing. As economies develop, the range of products available tends to expand, and the products themselves change. In contemporary industrialized societies, products, like people, go through life cycles: birth, growth, maturity, and decline. This constant replacement of existing products with new or altered products has significant consequences for professional marketers. The development of new products involves all aspects of a business—production, finance, research and development, and even personnel administration and public relations.

Packaging and branding are also substantial components in the marketing of a product. Packaging in some instances may be as simple as customers in France carrying long loaves of unwrapped bread or small produce dealers in Italy wrapping vegetables in newspapers or placing them in customers' string bags. In most industrialized countries, however, the packaging of merchandise has become a major part of the selling effort, as marketers now specify exactly the types of packaging that will be most appealing to prospective customers. The importance of packaging in the distribution of the product has increased with the spread of self-service purchases—in wholesaling as well as in retailing. Packaging is sometimes designed to facilitate the use of the product, as with aerosol containers for room deodorants. In Europe such condiments as mustard, mayonnaise, and ketchup are often packaged in tubes. Some packages are reusable, making them attractive to customers in poorer countries where metal containers, for instance, are often highly prized.

The same general marketing approach about the product applies to the development of service offerings as well. For example, a health maintenance organization (HMO) must design a contract for its members that describes which medical procedures will be covered, how much physician choice will be available, how out-of-town medical costs will be handled, and so forth. In creating a successful service mix, the HMO must choose features that are preferred and expected by target customers, or the service will not be valued in the marketplace.

Price. The second marketing-mix element is price. Ordinarily companies determine a price by gauging the quality or performance level of the offer and then selecting a price that reflects how the market values its level of quality. However, marketers also are aware that price can send a message to a customer about the product's presumed quality level. A Mercedes-Benz vehicle is generally considered to be a high-quality automobile, and it therefore can command a high price in the marketplace. But, even if the manufacturer could price its cars competitively with economy cars, it might not do so, knowing that the lower price might communicate lower quality. On the other hand, in order to gain market share, some companies have moved to "more for the same" or "the same for less" pricing, which means offering prices that are consistently lower than those of their competitors. This kind of discount pricing has caused firms in such industries as airlines and pharmaceuticals (which used to charge a price premium based on their past brand strength and reputation) to significantly reevaluate their marketing strategies.

Place. Place, or where the product is made available, is the third element of the marketing mix and is most commonly referred to as distribution. When a product moves along its path from producer to consumer, it is said to be following a channel of distribution. For example, the channel of distribution for many food products includes food-processing plants, warehouses, wholesalers, and supermarkets. By using this channel, a food manufacturer makes its products easily accessible by ensuring that they are in stores that are frequented by those in the target market. In another example, a mutual funds organization makes its investment products available by enlisting the assistance of brokerage houses and banks, which in turn establish relationships with particular customers. However, each channel participant can handle only a certain number of products: space at supermarkets is limited, and investment brokers can keep abreast of only a limited number of mutual funds. Because of this, some marketers may decide to skip steps in the channel and instead market directly to buyers through direct mail, telemarketing, door-to-door selling, shopping via television (a growing trend in the late 20th century), or factory outlets.

Promotion. Promotion, the fourth marketing-mix element, consists of several methods of communicating with and influencing customers. The major tools are sales force, advertising, sales promotion, and public relations.

Sales representatives are the most expensive means of promotion, because they require income, expenses, and supplementary benefits. Their ability to personalize the promotion process makes salespeople most effective at selling complex goods, big-ticket items, and highly personal goods—for example, those related to religion or insurance. Salespeople are trained to make presentations, answer objections, gain commitments to purchase, and manage account growth. Some companies have successfully reduced their sales-force costs by replacing certain functions (for example, finding new customers) with less expensive methods (such as direct mail and telemarketing).

Types of advertising   Advertising includes all forms of paid, nonpersonal communication and promotion of products, services, or ideas by a specified sponsor. Advertising appears in such media as print (newspapers, magazines, billboards, flyers) or broadcast (radio, television). Print advertisements typically consist of a picture, a headline, information about the product, and occasionally a response coupon. Broadcast advertisements consist of an audio or video narrative that can range from short 15-second spots to longer segments known as infomercials, which generally last 30 or 60 minutes.

While advertising presents a reason to buy a product, sales promotion offers a short-term incentive to purchase. Sales promotions often attract brand switchers (those who are not loyal to a specific brand) who are looking primarily for low price and good value. Thus, especially in markets where brands are highly similar, sales promotions can cause a short-term increase in sales but little permanent gain in market share. Alternatively, in markets where brands are quite dissimilar, sales promotions can alter market shares more permanently. The use of promotions has risen considerably during the late 20th century. This is due to a number of factors within companies, including an increased sophistication in sales promotion techniques and greater pressure to increase sales. Several market factors also have fostered this increase, including a rise in the number of brands (especially similar ones) and a decrease in the efficiency of traditional advertising due to increasingly fractionated consumer markets.

Public relations, in contrast to advertising and sales promotion, generally involves less commercialized modes of communication. Its primary purpose is to disseminate information and opinion to groups and individuals who have an actual or potential impact on a company's ability to achieve its objectives. In addition, public relations specialists are responsible for monitoring these individuals and groups and for maintaining good relationships with them. One of their key activities is to work with news and information media to ensure appropriate coverage of the company's activities and products. Public relations specialists create publicity by arranging press conferences, contests, meetings, and other events that will draw attention to a company's products or services. Another public relations responsibility is crisis management—that is, handling situations in which public awareness of a particular issue may dramatically and negatively impact the company's ability to achieve its goals. For example, when it was discovered that some bottles of Perrier sparkling water might have been tainted by a harmful chemical, Source Perrier, SA's public relations team had to ensure that the general consuming public did not thereafter automatically associate Perrier with tainted water. Other public relations activities include lobbying, advising management about public issues, and planning community events.

Because public relations does not always seek to impact sales or profitability directly, it is sometimes seen as serving a function that is separate from marketing. However, some companies recognize that public relations can work in conjunction with other marketing activities to facilitate the exchange process directly and indirectly. These organizations have established marketing public relations departments to directly support corporate and product promotion and image management.

(PHILIP KOTLER/KENT A. GRAYSON/JOHN D. HIBBARD)

MARKETING IMPLEMENTATION

Companies have typically hired different agencies to help in the development of advertising, sales promotion, and publicity ideas. However, this often results in a lack of coordination between elements of the promotion mix. When components of the mix are not all in harmony, a confusing message may be sent to consumers. For example, a print advertisement for an automobile may emphasize the car's exclusivity and luxury, while a television advertisement may stress rebates and sales, clashing with this image of exclusivity. Alternatively, by integrating the marketing elements, a company can more efficiently utilize its resources. Instead of individually managing four or five different promotion processes, the company manages only one. In addition, promotion expenditures are likely to be better allocated, because differences among promotion tools become more explicit. This reasoning has led to integrated marketing communications, in which all promotional tools are considered to be part of the same effort, and each tool receives full consideration in terms of its cost and effectiveness.

MARKETING EVALUATION AND CONTROL

No marketing process, even the most carefully developed, is guaranteed to result in maximum benefit for a company. In addition, because every market is changing constantly, a strategy that is effective today may not be effective in the future. It is important to evaluate a marketing program periodically to be sure that it is achieving its objectives. There are four types of marketing control, each of which has a different purpose: annual-plan control, profitability control, efficiency control, and strategic control.

The basis of annual-plan control is managerial objectives—that is to say, specific goals, such as sales and profitability, that are established on a monthly or quarterly basis. Organizations use five tools to monitor plan performance. The first is sales analysis, in which sales goals are compared with actual sales and discrepancies are explained or accounted for. A second tool is market-share analysis, which compares a company's sales with those of its competitors. Companies can express their market share in a number of ways, by comparing their own sales to total market sales, sales within the market segment, or sales of the segment's top competitors. Third, marketing expense-to-sales analysis gauges how much a company spends to achieve its sales goals. The ratio of marketing expenses to sales is expected to fluctuate, and companies usually establish an acceptable range for this ratio. In contrast, financial analysis estimates such expenses (along with others) from a corporate perspective. This includes a comparison of profits to sales (profit margin), sales to assets (asset turnover), profits to assets (return on assets), assets to worth (financial leverage), and, finally, profits to worth (return on net worth). Finally, companies measure customer satisfaction as a means of tracking goal achievement. Analyses of this kind are generally less quantitative than those described above and may include complaint and suggestion systems, customer satisfaction surveys, and careful analysis of reasons why customers switch to a competitor's product.

Profitability control and efficiency control allow a company to closely monitor its sales, profits, and expenditures. Profitability control demonstrates the relative profit-earning capacity of a company's different products and consumer groups. Companies are frequently surprised to find that a small percentage of their products and customers contribute to a large percentage of their profits. This knowledge helps a company allocate its resources and effort. Efficiency control involves micro-level analysis of the various elements of the marketing mix, including sales force, advertising, sales promotion, and distribution. For example, to understand its sales-force efficiency, a company may keep track of how many sales calls a representative makes each day, how long each call lasts, and how much each call costs and generates in revenue. This type of analysis highlights areas in which companies can manage their marketing efforts in a more productive and cost-effective manner.

Strategic control processes allow managers to evaluate a company's marketing program from a critical long-term perspective. This involves a detailed and objective analysis of a company's organization and its ability to maximize its strengths and market opportunities. Companies can use two types of strategic control tools. The first, which a company uses to evaluate itself, is called a marketing-effectiveness rating review. In order to rate its own marketing effectiveness, a company examines its customer philosophy, the adequacy of its marketing information, and the efficiency of its marketing operations. It will also closely evaluate the strength of its marketing strategy and the integration of its marketing tactics.

The second evaluation tool is known as a marketing audit. This is a comprehensive, systematic, independent, and periodic analysis that a company uses to examine its strengths in relation to its current and potential market(s). Such an analysis is comprehensive because it covers all aspects of the marketing climate (unlike a functional audit, which analyzes one marketing activity), looking at both macro-environment factors (demographic, economic, ecological, technological, political, and cultural) and micro- or task-environment factors (markets, customers, competitors, distributors, dealers, suppliers, facilitators, and publics). The audit includes analyses of the company's marketing strategy, marketing organization, marketing systems, and marketing productivity. It must be systematic in order to provide concrete conclusions based on these analyses. To ensure objectivity, a marketing audit is best done by a person, department, or organization that is independent of the company or marketing program. Marketing audits should be done not only when the value of a company's current marketing plan is in question; they must be done periodically in order to isolate and solve problems before they arise.

(KENT A. GRAYSON/JOHN D. HIBBARD/PHILIP KOTLER)

South America

AMAZON RIVER BASIN

The Amazon (Portuguese and Spanish: Amazonas) is the greatest river of South America and the largest drainage system in the world in terms of the volume of the river's flow and the area of its basin. The total length of this great river—measured from the headwaters of the Ucayali-Apurímac river system in Peru—is about 4,000 miles (6,400 kilometres), which is slightly shorter than the Nile River but still the equivalent of the distance from New York City to Rome. Its westernmost source is high in the Andes Mountains, within 100 miles of the Pacific Ocean, and its mouth is in the Atlantic Ocean.

The vast Amazon basin (Amazonia), the largest lowland in Latin America, has an area of about 2.3 million square miles (6 million square kilometres) and is nearly twice as large as that of the Congo River, the Earth's other great equatorial drainage system. Stretching some 1,725 miles from north to south at its widest point, the basin includes the greater part of Brazil and Peru, significant parts of Colombia, Ecuador, and Bolivia, and a small area of Venezuela; roughly two-thirds of the Amazon's main stream and by far the largest portion of its basin are within Brazil. The Tocantins-Araguaia catchment area in Pará state covers another 300,000 square miles. Although considered a part of Amazonia by the Brazilian government and in popular usage, it is technically a separate system. It is estimated that about one-fifth of all the water that runs off the Earth's surface is carried by the Amazon. The flood-stage discharge at the river's mouth is about 6,180,000 cubic feet (175,000 cubic metres) per second, which is four times that of the Congo and more than 10 times the amount carried by the Mississippi River. This immense volume of fresh water dilutes the ocean's saltiness for more than 100 miles from shore.

The extensive lowland areas bordering the main river and its tributaries, called *várzeas,* are subject to annual flooding, with consequent soil enrichment; however, most of the vast basin consists of upland, well above the inundations and known as *terra firme.* More than two-thirds of the basin is covered by an immense rain forest, which grades into dry forest and savanna on the higher northern and southern margins and into montane forest in the Andes to the west. The Amazon Rain Forest, which represents about half of the Earth's remaining rain forest, also constitutes its largest reserve of biological resources.

The first European to explore the Amazon, in 1541, was the Spanish soldier Francisco de Orellana, who is said to have given the river its name after reporting pitched battles with tribes of female warriors, whom he likened to the Amazons of Greek mythology. Although the name Amazon is conventionally employed for the entire river, in Peruvian and Brazilian nomenclature it properly is applied only to sections of it. In Peru the upper main stream (fed by numerous tributaries flowing from sources in the Andes) down to Iquitos (Peru) is called Marañón (Portuguese: Maranhão), and from there to the Atlantic it is called Amazonas. In Brazil the name Solimões is used from Iquitos to the mouth of the Negro River and Amazonas only from the Negro to the sea.

Physical features. *Landforms and drainage patterns.* The Amazon basin is a great structural depression, a subsidence trough that has been filling with immense quantities of sediment of Cenozoic age (*i.e.,* from the past 66.4 million years). This depression, which flares out to its greatest dimension in the Amazon's upper reaches, lies between two old and relatively low crystalline plateaus, the rugged Guiana Highlands to the north and the lower Brazilian Highlands (lying somewhat farther from the main river) to the south. The Amazon basin was occupied by a great freshwater sea during the Pliocene Epoch (5.3 to 1.6 million years ago). Sometime during the Pleistocene Epoch (1,600,000 to 10,000 years ago) an outlet to the Atlantic was established, and the great river and its tributaries became deeply entrenched into the former Pliocene seafloor.

The modern Amazon and its tributaries occupy a vast system of drowned valleys that have been filled with alluvium. With the rise in sea level that followed the melting of the Pleistocene glaciers, the steep-sided canyons that had been eroded into the Pliocene surface during the period of lower sea levels were gradually flooded. In the upper part of the valley—in eastern Colombia, Ecuador, Peru, and Bolivia—more recent outwash from the Andes has covered many of the older surfaces.

Physiography of the river course. The Amazon River has its main outlet north of Marajó Island, a lowland somewhat larger in size than Denmark, through a cluster of half-submerged islets and shallow sandbanks. Here the mouth of the river is 40 miles (64 kilometres) wide. The port city of Belém is on the deep water of the Pará River, an estuary marking the south side of Marajó, which is fed chiefly by the Tocantins River entering it southwest of Belém. The port city's link with the main Amazon channel is either north along the ocean frontage of Marajó or following the deep but narrow *furos* (channels) of Breves that bound the island on the southwest and link the Pará River with the Amazon. There are more than 1,000 tributaries of the Amazon that flow into it from the Guiana Highlands and from the Brazilian Highlands, as well as from the Andes. Seven of these tributaries—the Japurá (Caquetá in Colombia), Juruá, Madeira, Negro, Purus, Tocantins, and Xingu rivers—are more than 1,000 miles long; and one, the Madeira River, exceeds 2,000 miles from source to mouth. The largest oceangoing ships can ascend the river 1,000 miles to the city of Manaus, while lesser freight and passenger vessels reach Iquitos, Peru, 1,300 miles farther upstream, at any time of year.

The sedimentary axis of the Amazon basin comprises two distinct groups of landforms: the *várzea,* or floodplain of alluvium of Holocene age (*i.e.,* up to 10,000 years old), and the *terra firme,* or upland surfaces of Pliocene and Pleistocene materials (those from 10,000 to 5,300,000 years old) that lie well above the highest flood level. The floodplain of the main river is characteristically 12 to 30 miles wide. It is bounded irregularly by low bluffs 20 to 60 feet high, beyond which the older, undulating upland extends both north and south to the horizon. Occasionally these bluffs are undercut by the river as it swings to and fro across the alluvium, producing the *terra caída,* or "fallen land," so often described by Amazon travelers. At the city of Óbidos, where the river narrows to a width of 1.25 miles, a low range of relatively hard rock interrupts the otherwise continuous floodplain.

The streams that rise in the ancient crystalline highlands—the Jari, Trombetas, and Negro to the north and the Tocantins-Araguaia, Xingu, and Tapajós to the south—are so-called "blackwater" streams; they are acidic and rich in humus. Because these streams originate in

nutrient-poor, often sandy uplands, they carry little or no silt or dissolved solids. Where such blackwater tributaries enter the main river, they are sometimes blocked off to form funnel-shaped, freshwater lakes or estuaries, as at the mouth of the Tapajós.

In contrast, the Madeira River, which joins the Amazon some 50 miles downstream from Manaus, and its principal affluents—the Purus, Juruá, Ucayali, and Huallaga on the right or southern bank and the Japurá (Caquetá), Içá (Putumayo), and Napo from the northwest—have their source in the youthful and tectonically active Andes. There they pick up the heavy sediment loads that account for their "whitewater" designation. Where the silt-laden waters of the Amazon (Solimões in Brazil), derived from these streams, meet those of the Negro at Manaus, the darker and hence warmer and sediment-free waters of the latter tend to be overrun by those of the Amazon, creating a striking colour boundary which is erased by turbulence downstream.

The mother river, the Marañón above Iquitos, rises in the central Peruvian Andes at an elevation of 15,870 feet in a small lake in the Cordillera Huayhuash above Cerro de Pasco. The Huallaga and Ucayali, major right-bank affluents of the Marañón, originate considerably farther south. The headwaters of the deeply entrenched Apurímac and Urubamba, tributaries in turn of the Ucayali, reach to within 100 miles of Lake Titicaca (elevation 12,500 feet) on the Peru-Bolivia border, the farthest of any stream in the system from the great river's mouth.

The Negro River, the largest of all the Amazon tributaries, accounts for about one-fifth of the total discharge of the Amazon and 40 percent of its aggregate volume measured just below the confluence at Manaus. Its drainage area of 292,000 square miles includes that of the Branco, its major left-bank tributary, with its source in the Guiana Highlands. Another of the Negro's affluents, the Casiquiare, is a product of the bifurcation of the Orinoco River; it forms a link between the Amazon and the Orinoco's drainage system. The Branco watershed, approximately coincident with the state of Roraima, includes extensive tracts of sandy, leached soils that support a grassy and stunted arboreal cover (*campos*). Other tributaries of the Negro, such as the Vaupés and Guainía, drain eastward from the Colombian Oriente. The river traverses some of the least populous and least disturbed parts of the Amazon basin, including several national parks, national forests, or indigenous reserves. In its lower reaches it becomes broad and island-filled, in places reaching widths of 20 miles.

The Madeira River, second largest affluent of the Amazon, has a discharge of perhaps two-thirds that of the Negro. Silt from its turbid waters has choked its lower valley with sediments; where it joins the Amazon below Manaus, it has contributed to the formation of the 200-mile-long island of Tupinambarana. Beyond its first cataract 600 miles up the river, its three major affluents—the Madre de Dios, the Beni, and the Mamoré—gave easy access to the rubber-rich forests of the Bolivian Oriente, while the Mamoré's tributary, the Guaporé, opened the way to the goldfields of Mato Grosso. Even more important to the rubber tappers were the meandering Purus and Juruá rivers that flank the Madeira on the west.

Hydrology. Most of the estimated 1.3 million tons of sediment that the Amazon pours daily into the sea is transported northward by coastal currents to be deposited along the coasts of northern Brazil and Guiana. As a consequence, the river is not building a delta. Normally, the effect of the tide is felt as far upstream as Óbidos, 600 miles from the river's mouth. A tidal bore called the *pororoca* occurs at times in the estuary prior to spring tides. With an increasing roar it advances upstream at 10 to 15 miles per hour, forming a breaking wall of water from 5 to 12 feet high.

At the Óbidos narrows, the flow of the river has been measured at 216,000 cubic metres per second; its width is constricted to little more than a mile. Here the average depth of the channel below the mean watermark is more than 200 feet, well below sea level; in most of the Brazilian part of the river its depth exceeds 150 feet. Its gradient is extraordinarily slight. At the Peruvian border, some 2,000

Major tributaries

Blackwater rivers

The Negro River and its affluents

miles from the Atlantic, the elevation above sea level is less than 300 feet. The maximum free width (without islands) of the river's permanent bed is 8.5 miles, upstream from the mouth of the Xingu. During great floods, however, when the river completely fills the floodplain, it spreads out in a band 35 miles wide or more. The average velocity of the Amazon is about 1.5 miles per hour, a speed that increases considerably at flood time.

The Amazon floods

The rise and fall of the water is controlled by events external to the floodplain. The floods of the Amazon are not disasters but rather distinctive, anticipated events that define the calendar and the rhythm of life much as seasons do elsewhere. Their marked regularity and the gradualness of the change in water level are due to the enormous size of the basin, the gentle gradient, and the great temporary storage capacity of both the floodplain and the estuaries of the river's tributaries. The upper course of the Amazon has two annual floods, and the river is subject to the alternate influence of the tributaries that descend from the Peruvian Andes (where rains fall from October to January) and from the Ecuadorian Andes (where rains fall from March to July). This pattern of alternation disappears farther downstream, the two seasons of high flow gradually merging into a single one. Thus, the rise of the river progresses slowly downstream in a gigantic wave from November to June, and then the waters recede until the end of October. The flood levels are, in places, from 40 to 50 feet above low river.

Climate. The climate of Amazonia is warm, rainy, and humid. The length of day and night is equal on the Equator (which runs only slightly north of the river), and the usually clear nights favour relatively rapid radiation of the heat received from the sun during the 12-hour day. There is a greater difference between daytime and midnight temperatures than between the warmest and coolest months. Hence, night is the winter of the Amazon. At Manaus, the average daily temperature is 89° F (32° C) in September and 75° F (24° C) in April, but the humidity is consistently high and often oppressive. During the winter months of the Southern Hemisphere, a powerful south-polar air mass occasionally pours northward into the Amazon region, causing a sharp drop in temperature, known locally as a *friagem,* when the mercury may register as low as 57° F (14° C). At any time of the year, several days of heavy rain can be succeeded by clear, sunny days and fresh, cool nights with relatively low humidity. In the lower reaches of the river basin, cooling trade winds blow most of the year.

The main influx of atmospheric water vapour into the basin comes from the east. About half of the precipitation that falls originates from the Atlantic Ocean; the other half comes from evapotranspiration from the tropical forest and associated convectional storms. Rainfall in the lowlands typically ranges from 60 to 120 inches (1,500 to 3,000 millimetres) annually in the central Amazon basin (*e.g.,* Manaus). On the eastern and western margins of the

Rainfall

basin, rainfall occurs throughout the year, whereas in the central part there is a definite drier period, usually from June to November. Manaus has experienced as many as 60 consecutive days without rain, but such droughty periods are uncommon. The dry season is not sufficiently intense to arrest plant growth, but it may facilitate the onset and spread of fires, whether arsonous or natural. To the west the Andes form a natural barrier that prevents most of the water vapour from leaving the basin.

Along the southern margin of the Amazon basin the climate grades into that of west-central Brazil, with a distinct dry season during the Southern Hemispheric winter. As elevations increase in the Andes, temperatures fall significantly.

Soils. The vast Amazonian forest vegetation appears extremely lush, leading to the erroneous conclusion that the underlying soil must be extremely fertile. In fact, the nutrients in the system are locked up in the vegetation, including roots and surface litter, and are continuously recycled through leaf fall and decay. Generally, the soils above flood level are well-drained, porous, and of variable structure. Often they are sandy and of low natural fertility because of their lack of phosphate, nitrogen, and

potash and their high acidity. Small areas are underlain with basaltic and diabasic rocks, with reddish soils (*terra roxa*) of considerable natural fertility. The *terra preta dos Indios* ("black earth of the Indians") is another localized and superior soil type.

The agricultural potential of the annually flooded *várzea* areas is great. Their soils do not lack nutrients, since they are rejuvenated each year by the deposit of fertile silt left as the waters recede, but use for agricultural purposes is limited by the periodic inundations. It is estimated that these valuable soils occupy some 25,000 square miles.

Plant life. The overwhelmingly dominant feature of the Amazon basin is the tropical rain forest, or selva. From the air the Amazon forest appears to stretch unbroken to the horizon like a tufted green carpet. Closer inspection reveals its bewildering complexity and prodigious variety of trees; as many as 100 arboreal species have been counted on a single acre of forest with hardly any one of them occurring more than once.

The rain forest

The Amazon forest has a strikingly layered structure. The sun-loving giants of the uppermost story, the canopy, soar to as much as 120 feet above the ground; occasional individual trees, known as emergents, rise beyond the canopy, frequently attaining heights of 200 feet. Their straight, whitish trunks are splotched with lichens and fungus. A characteristic of these giant trees is the buttresses, or basal enlargements of their trunks, which presumably help stabilize the top-heavy trees during infrequent heavy winds. Further characteristics of the canopy trees are their narrow, downward-pointing "drip-tip" leaves that easily shed water and their cauliflory (the production of flowers directly from the trunks rather than from the branches). Flowers are inconspicuous. Among the canopy species, which capture most of the sunlight and conduct most of the photosynthesis, prominent members include the rubber tree (*Hevea brasiliensis*), the silk-cotton (*Ceiba pentandra*), the Brazil nut (*Bertholletia excelsa*), the sapucaia (*Lecythis*), and the sucupira (*Bowdichia*). Many creatures, including monkeys and sloths, spend their entire lives in this sunlit canopy. Below it are found two or three levels of shade-tolerant trees, including many species of palms, such as *Mauritia, Orbignya,* and *Euterpe.* Myrtles, laurels, bignonias, figs, Spanish cedars, mahogany, and rosewoods are also common. They support a myriad of epiphytes (plants living on other plants)—such as orchids, bromeliads, and cacti—as well as ferns and mosses. The entire system is laced together by a bewildering network of woody ropelike vines known as lianas.

In addition to the rain forests of the *terra firme,* there are two types of inundated rain forests, *várzea* and *igapó,* which constitute about 3 percent of the total Amazonian rain forest. *Várzea* forests can be found in the silt- and nutrient-rich floodplains of whitewater rivers such as the Madeira and the Amazon, with their ever-changing mosaic of lakes, marshes, sandbars, abandoned channels, and natural levees. They are generally not as high, diverse, or old as those of the *terra firme,* being subject to periodic destruction by floods and human manipulation. (The *várzea* and its flood-free margins are the principal rainforest habitat of human beings.) Wild cane (*Gynerium*) and aquatic herbs and grasses, as well as fast-growing pioneer tree species such as *Cecropia, Ficus,* and *Erythrina,* are conspicuous.

Igapó forests grow along the sandy floodplains of blackwater rivers such as the Negro, the Tapajós, and the Trombetas. Because human settlement is limited in these plains, there may be undisturbed, seasonally flooded forests that stand in water for up to half the year, the water reaching heights of up to 40 feet. A canoe can often be paddled between the trunks of trees adapted to such an aquatic environment.

The lowland rain forest on the Andean fringe grades into a discontinuous, tangled montane or cloud forest of misshapen trees cloaked with mosses, lichens, and bromeliads. Here one encounters the cinchona or fever-bark tree, once exploited for its antimalarial agent quinine. At still higher elevations is found the grass and shrub growth of the cold *puna* and *páramo* regions.

Along the drier, southern margin of the Amazon basin,

high forest gives way to the *cerrado* (savanna and scrub) and *caatinga* (heath forest). The latter is characteristic of parts of the Mato Grosso Plateau, where taller forest is restricted to the stream courses and swales (marshy depressions) that dissect the upland surface. On the sandy soils of the lower Negro and the Branco drainage areas and locally in Amapá, grassy savannas dotted with stunted trees replace the high forest.

Animal life.   To give a succinct overview of the complete fauna of the Amazon is as impossible as it is to adequately describe the great diversity of its flora; in part this is because many of the region's species have yet to be identified. The rivers and streams of the basin teem with life, and the forest canopy resonates with the cries of birds and monkeys and the whine of insects. There is a notable paucity of large terrestrial mammal species; indeed, many of the mammals are arboreal.

More than 8,000 species of insects alone have been collected and classified. Myriads of mosquitoes plague travelers and may transmit such diseases as malaria and yellow fever. Leaf-cutting ants (*Atta* and *Acromyrmex*) and other pests may torment the traveler. The most troublesome insects of all are the ubiquitous, small, black flies, called *piums,* whose bite can itch for days.

The Amazon and its tributaries, together with the bordering *várzea* lakes and flooded forests, constitute a vast sea of fresh water, much of it slowly flowing, which teems with fish life. About 1,500 fish species have been found within the Amazon system, but many more remain unidentified. Most fish are migratory, moving in great schools at spawning time. Fish represent a critical source of protein in the often meat-poor diet of the peasant (*caboclo*) population (the term *caboclo* is used for the peasant population of mixed Indian-European blood). Among the more important commercial species are the pirarucu (*Arapaima gigas*), one of the world's largest freshwater fish, and various giant catfish. The well-known, small, flesh-eating piranha generally feeds on other fish but may attack any animal, including humans, that enters the water; its razor-sharp teeth cut out chunks of flesh, stripping a carcass of its meat in a few minutes. The traffic in frozen and dried fish to urban markets has increased to such a degree that some stocks are locally threatened. With the rapid means of transport afforded by jet airplanes, a worldwide market has developed for tropical aquarium fish distinctive to the Amazon. Iquitos, Manaus, and the Colombian port of Leticia are centres of this trade.

Crocodiles are hunted for their skins; river turtles and their eggs are considered a delicacy; the giant sea cow, or manatee, is sought for its flesh and for oil. All are threatened by overhunting, and the manatee has been listed as an endangered species. Aquatic animals also include freshwater dolphins (*Inia geoffrensis*); the capybara, the largest rodent in the world (weighing up to 170 pounds); and the nutria, or coypu, valued especially for its pelt. Other common rodents are the paca, agouti, porcupine, and local species of squirrels, rats, and mice.

The tapir, the white-lipped peccary, and several species of deer are native to the Amazon basin and much sought for their meat. Water buffalo, introduced from Southeast Asia as work and dairy cattle, have run wild in the remote, swampy parts of Marajó Island.

Especially characteristic of the Amazon forest are several species of monkeys. Of note are the howler monkeys, which make the selva resound with their morning and evening choruses. The small, agile squirrel monkey, the most ubiquitous of Amazonia's monkeys, is used in laboratories, as is the larger spider monkey. Among a host of other primate species are woolly monkeys, capuchin monkeys, titis, sakis, and marmosets. All species are used for food and frequently are seen for sale in local markets. As the human population increases and the shotgun replaces the blowgun, pressure on the wild fauna is mounting.

Large cats, such as the jaguar and ocelot, are rare, although pumas may be found in larger numbers in the Andean fringe of the basin. Smaller carnivores include coati, grisons, and weasels. Countless bats inhabit the Amazonian night, including the blood-drinking vampire bat.

The Amazon basin is exceedingly rich in birdlife. Morn-

ing and evening, the parrots and macaws fly to and from their feeding grounds, their brilliant plumage flashing in the sunlight and their raucous voices calling out their presence. Through the day the caciques quarrel in trees where their hanging nests swing by the dozens. Hoatzins screech in noisy flocks from streamside brush, while solitary hawks and eagles scream from tree stumps. Everywhere is heard the twittering of small birds, the sound of woodpeckers, and the gutteral noises of such waterbirds as herons, cormorants, roseate spoonbills, and scarlet ibises. Parakeets, more common than sparrows in the United States, fly around in great flocks. At dusk, toucans cry a discordant plaint from the treetops and are joined by ground-dwelling tinamous and quail. The night air is filled with the cries of various species of nightjar.

The people.   *Early settlement patterns.*   At the time of the European conquest, the bottomlands and fringing upland surfaces of the Amazon River and its major tributaries supported relatively dense, sedentary populations of indigenous peoples who practiced intensive root-crop farming, supplemented by fishing and by hunting aquatic mammals and reptiles. The higher areas away from the rivers and their floodplains, were—and still are in some of the more remote sectors—inhabited by small, widely dispersed, seminomadic tribes of Indians. These groups traditionally have relied predominantly on hunting large and small animals and on gathering wild fruits, berries, and nuts, while practicing some small-patch agriculture of low yield. In the early 1990s the Indian population of the Amazon basin numbered about 600,000, of whom perhaps close to one-third live in Brazil and the rest in the Oriente of the four Andean countries.

The Amazonian Indians early devised means of making the poisonous bitter cassava (manioc) edible; the end product, called *farinha,* became a food staple widely used today in much of tropical America. Amazonian Indians perfected the use of quinine as a specific against malaria, extracted cocaine from the leaves of the coca tree, and collected the sap of the Brazilian rubber tree (*Hevea brasiliensis*). They were skilled navigators in their dugout canoes and sailing rafts (*jagandas*), and they invented the blowgun and the hammock. One of their ancient arrow poisons, curare (*Chondrodendron tomentosum*), has been used in modern times in the therapy of a host of paralyses and spastic disorders, such as multiple sclerosis.

The early European explorers of the Amazon provisioned themselves from the food supplies of the Indians they met and commandeered their canoes. Large numbers of Indians were taken into slavery, especially during the organized raids (*bandeiras*) of the 16th to 18th century; many others succumbed to such European diseases as influenza, measles, and smallpox. The result was a complete breakdown of native life and a precipitous decrease in the Indian population; survivors fled into increasingly inaccessible sections of the Amazon basin. As late as 1906 there were reports of the wholesale capture of Indians who were enslaved in order to tap rubber, which was plentiful and commanded a high price on the world market but which was difficult to exploit because rubber trees were sparsely scattered over a huge area.

Settlement by Europeans and mestizos (those of mixed Indian and European ancestry) did not occur to any appreciable degree until the 1870s and '80s, when victims of severe droughts in northeastern Brazil began to move into Amazonia to profit from the rubber boom. Another wave of immigration began at the end of World War II, spurred by the rapid economic development of the region.

Modern settlement patterns.   Its vast area notwithstanding, the Amazon basin, in the late 20th century, has a predominantly urban population. Almost one-third of the estimated nine million Brazilians living in the 1.9 million-square-mile area officially designated as Legal Amazonia are concentrated in Belém and Manaus, cities with more than one million inhabitants, and in Santarém. These cities, which are logistic bases of operations for cattle ranching, mining, timber, and agroforestry projects, are still growing rapidly, with modern residential towers and shantytowns standing side by side. Even frontier trading centres in the interior such as Marabá, Pôrto Velho, and

---

Margin notes:

Fish

Large cats

Indians

Decline of Indian culture

Rio Branco have 100,000 or more inhabitants. In the upper reaches of the drainage area, places such as Florencia in Colombia, Iquitos and Pucallpa in Peru, and Santa Cruz in Bolivia have become significant urban centres with most of the amenities of modern life. Air service effectively connects them with Andean and coastal metropolises and even with the more isolated settlements and mission stations of the Oriente.

The economy. *Development of the Amazon basin.* Since World War II the economic development of the Amazon basin has been high on the agenda of every country of which it is a part. From the mid-1940s onward, a number of "penetration roads" have been built from the populous highlands of Colombia, Ecuador, Peru, and Bolivia into the Oriente, which have funneled untold numbers of landless peasants into the lowlands. They also have served to facilitate development of major oil discoveries and timber resources. Tropical hardwoods, river fish, and, since the 1980s, clandestinely produced cocaine have been objects of commercial exploitation, along with Brahman-type livestock raised on pastures newly carved from the selva. Such activities have led to widespread displacement of indigenous groups, who were either forced onto new reserves or left to survive as best they could.

The opening of the Amazon basin has been pursued most aggressively in Brazil. In the mid-1950s the decision was made to refocus the country toward its interior by constructing a new inland capital, Brasília. One consequence of this decision was the initiation of a massive road-building program that aimed at integrating the North (consisting of the states of Amazonas, Acre, and Pará and the territories of Rondônia, Roraima, and Amapá) with the rest of Brazil while establishing an escape valve for the crowded and drought-stricken Northeast. A 1,100-mile-long highway linking Brasília with Belém, the trade centre at the mouth of the Amazon, was completed in 1964. Along with the even more ambitious 3,400-mile all-weather Transamazonian Highway from the Atlantic port of Recife to Cruzeiro do Sul on the Peruvian border—with extensions north to Santarém and Manaus (later to the Venezuelan border) and southward to Cuiabá (Mato Grosso) and Pôrto Velho (Rondônia)—it was to provide the frame for a network of nearly 20,000 miles of highways and feeder routes that was to supersede the traditional fluvial transport system.

The government had planned to settle about 100,000 families along the Transamazonian Highway, but this goal was not reached. Indeed, the majority of families who did come abandoned the *agrovilas* within a few years because of declining crop yields on the poor soils, weed invasions, plant diseases, lack of credit, and the distance to markets.

Disillusioned by the Transamazonian experience, the government shifted its emphasis to encouraging large-scale, capitalist enterprises. Cheap credit and tax breaks were offered to promote the creation of big cattle ranches within Legal Amazonia.

The completion of the Cuiabá–Pôrto Velho highway about 1970 facilitated movement between Mato Grosso and the Rondônia area along the Bolivian border with its more fertile *terra roxa* soils. It brought an unanticipated flood of immigrants from South Brazil, who had become displaced by the shift to large-scale commercial production of export crops (soybeans, citrus, cotton, and wheat). Between 1970 and 1990 the population of Rondônia increased from roughly 116,000 to more than 1,000,000, and that of Acre to the west reached 400,000 by 1990.

Agriculture and forestry. Upland rice, manioc (cassava), and, to a lesser extent, corn (maize) form the mainstay of smallholder agriculture, providing the carbohydrates for the *caboclo* diet. Jute, heart of palm (from *Euterpe oleracea*), and guarana (*Paullinia cupana,* for a favourite Brazilian soft drink) are all minor commercial crops. Black pepper, introduced from Southeast Asia, has become a specialty crop of Japanese colonists.

Cattle pasture by far dominates land use on the cleared parts of the Amazon basin, both in areas of large ranches, such as southern Pará and Mato Grosso, and in areas initially cut over by smallholders for annual crops, as along the Transamazonian Highway. Pasture is even dominant

(margin: Brazilian road-building program)

(margin: Cattle pasture)

in areas such as Rondônia, where government programs have promoted the cultivation of cacao, coffee, Brazil nuts, and other perennial crops for which a ready cash market exists.

Excellent timber is furnished by the mahogany (*Swietenia macrophylla* and *Swietenia humilis*), the Amazonian cedar (*Cedrela odorata*), the Brazilian rosewood (*Dalbergia nigra*), and many other species. Some types, however, are threatened by intensive exploitation. Other trees, such as the coumarou, or tonka bean (*Dipteryx odorata*), yield perfumes, flavourings, and pharmaceutical ingredients. The economic kings of trees, however, are the rubber tree and the Brazil nut. The rubber tree has been one of the most important objectives in the penetration and exploitation of the forest. It gave rise to a period of great but temporary prosperity, especially for the city of Manaus. The rubber gathered from both wild trees and those grown in small plantations continues to make a contribution to the Amazonian economy.

In Brazil areas within the remaining undisturbed forest have been designated for the use of rubber tappers and nut collectors. Yet the establishment of such "extractive reserve" lands has come into conflict with the claims of both squatters and speculators. The latter often have obtained titles by devious means, and their activities require close monitoring.

Corporate farming and agroforestry operations such as Fordlandia, Belterra, and Jari in eastern Brazil and Tournavista in Peru have had little success; the Jari enterprise, for example, was taken over by a consortium of Brazilian investors and the government in 1982. Transnational corporations investing in livestock operations, especially in southern Pará and Mato Grosso, included Volkswagen AG, Swift-Eckrich, Inc., King Ranch, Inc., and Liquigas Italiana. All have terminated their activities.

Mining and energy. The exploitation of the enormously rich mineral complex of the Serra dos Carajás area west of the boom town of Marabá (population 153,000 in 1991) on the Tocantins River has been highly profitable, but it has also had harmful effects on the environment. The site of one of the world's largest and richest iron ore deposits, the district also produces gold, copper, nickel, manganese, tin, and bauxite. The million-acre concession is run by the Companhia Vale do Rio Doce (CVRD), a partnership between private capital and the federal government. Plans for the local smelting of the iron ore could require the clearing of 490,000 acres (200,000 hectares) of forest annually to provide charcoal for producing pig iron. A rail line connects the Carajás development with the Atlantic coast.

Gold mining reached a feverish pitch in the 1980s, stimulated by high world prices of gold. At the height of the Amazon "gold rush," as many as a half million transient miners (*garimpeiros*) came equipped with picks, shovels, and sluice boxes to search for the mineral in the alluvial deposits of the Tocantins valley at Serra Pelada. Brazil's annual production peaked in 1987 at nearly 90 tons, declining thereafter. The mercury used in extracting the gold polluted waterways, causing the fish that are so important in the local diet to become inedible. On the Madeira River, teams operating from rafts pump up from the riverbed auriferous sediments, which have to be subjected to a similar treatment. Bauxite mining, both at Carajás and on the Trombetas River north of the Amazon, requires the use of large settling ponds to trap effluents.

The energy requirements of both the Carajás development and the city of Belém are met by the giant Tucuruí hydroelectric plant on the Tocantins (with a planned power capacity of 7,260 megawatts), the fifth-largest hydroelectric power station in the world. A more modest hydroelectric facility on a small river north of Manaus supplies that city with power. A growing sensitivity to the harmful consequences for both human beings and the environment of the construction of large dams has caused several ambitious projects to be placed on hold.

The principal oil developments within Amazonia have taken place in the Cordillera Oriental of the Andean countries. Oil pipelines lead from producing districts in both Colombia (the upper Putumayo) and Ecuador (Lago

(margin: Gold mining)

Agrio), as well as northeastern Peru, to export terminals on the Pacific coast. Within the Brazilian and Bolivian portions of the basin, developments have been of minimal consequence.

Ecological concerns. International concern about the ecological consequences of continuing deforestation has been growing and was underscored by the United Nations Conference on the Environment and Development ("Earth Summit") held in Rio de Janeiro in 1992. International calls for conservation are based on the view that the Amazon basin is a global resource, one that serves as a control mechanism for the world's climate and as a genetic repository for the future. The nations of the region, however, tend to look upon such calls as a challenge to "national sovereignty."

The extent and rate of deforestation have been subject to continuing controversy. The difficulty of distinguishing via satellite imagery between regenerating secondary vegetation and undisturbed forest as well as the persistence of cloud cover and sometimes smoke have frustrated investigators. The employment of radar has made investigations more precise. It has been suggested that by 1990 some 10 percent of the Amazon selva may have been cleared for pasture, crops, lumber, and firewood. In Brazil deforestation was initiated in Mato Grosso and southern Pará in the 1960s and became widespread over the next two decades in Rondônia and Acre. Already in 1988 Rondônia was estimated to have been deforested by 17 percent, and the process is continuing. In Colombia the upper Putumayo and Caquetá river areas, in Ecuador the province of Napo, and in Peru the Tingo Maria–Pucallpa district have been among the more notable foci of clearing. The cultivation of coca for illicit production of cocaine continues to stimulate such activities.

The consequences of continuing deforestation have been much discussed. Although the forest is an efficient absorber of carbon dioxide, scientists believe that the volume of gas released when substantial parts of the forest are cleared and burned may contribute to global warming through the greenhouse effect. Continued conversion of tropical forest to cropland, pasture, or second-growth forest (*capoeira*) may reduce the region's evapotranspiration, thereby interrupting the hydrologic cycle and the recycling of soil nutrients; a likely consequence is an increase in the amount of water running off the surface and greater extremes in water levels. The unique gene pool of the Amazon Rain Forest, with perhaps two-thirds of the known organisms of the world, is threatened by continuing deforestation. Particular emphasis has been placed on the threat to biodiversity and the possible loss of as yet unknown and unexploited pharmaceuticals contained in the forest. Finally, at stake is also the survival of many indigenous peoples who, through long residence, have become integrated into the ecosystem of the rain forest and have learned some of its many secrets.

Study and exploration. At the outset of the 19th century, the German explorer Alexander von Humboldt mapped the connection between the Amazon and Orinoco systems through the Casiquiare River. The English naturalist H.W. Bates spent the years from 1848 to 1859 along the Amazon, collecting thousands of species of animals and recording his notes of animals, local peoples, and natural phenomena in a charmingly objective manner. His book, *The Naturalist on the River Amazons,* originally published in two volumes in 1863, is still regarded as one of the great classics on the Amazon River. An official expedition was sent from the United States to Amazonia in the mid-19th century; in 1854 in Washington, D.C., William Lewis Herndon published as a public document the report that he and Lardner Gibbon—both lieutenants in the U.S. Navy—had made to Congress under the title of *Exploration of the Valley of the Amazon.*

The 20th century. The period since 1900 has been one of numerous exploratory and scientific expeditions. In 1913–14, the former U.S. president Theodore Roosevelt and Brazilian Colonel Cândido Rondon headed an expedition that explored a tributary of the Madeira and made natural history collections and observations. A party sponsored by Harvard University's Institute of Geographical Exploration did important scientific work in the years 1910–24. The American Geographical Society compiled data for and published detailed maps of this vast region.

Since World War II, the international scientific community has been increasingly attracted to Amazonia. British, French, German, Japanese, and North American groups have carried out detailed biophysical and cultural surveys; a large number of international workshops, conferences, and symposia on Amazonian problems have been held. Brazilian scientists have also contributed significant research on issues concerning the area. Particularly important has been the work of the National Institute of Amazonian Research (INPA) at Manaus and the Goeldi Museum in Belém. (RAYMOND E. CRIST/ ALARICH R. SCHULTZ/JAMES J. PARSONS)

International concern

Bibliography: Recent Books

The following list encompasses some 150 recent books in English that have been judged significant contributions to learning in their respective fields. Each citation includes a few lines of commentary to indicate the tenor of the work. The citations are organized by broad subject area, with the 10 parts of the *Propædia* as an outline.

Matter and Energy

Arthur I. Miller, *Early Quantum Electrodynamics: A Source Book* (1994), a collection of landmark papers by eminent physicists, with an introductory chapter on the history of scientific ideas that traces the development of theoretical nuclear physics.

Murray Gell-Mann, *The Quark and the Jaguar: Adventures in the Simple and the Complex* (1994), personal reflections of a Nobel laureate on the dynamic relationship between the simple (quark) and the complex (jaguar) and between fundamental laws of nature and chance.

Philip Ball, *Designing the Molecular World: Chemistry at the Frontier* (1994), a survey of recent developments in chemistry, including crystallography, spectroscopy, and such burgeoning fields as nanotechnology (molecular engineering) and fractals.

Ronald J. Gillespie, Donald R. Eaton, David A. Humphreys, and Edward A. Robinson, *Atoms, Molecules, and Reactions: An Introduction to Chemistry* (1994), a textbook that leads, step-by-step, through the processes, elements, and functions of chemistry.

Steven Vogel, *Life in Moving Fluids* (2nd ed., revised and expanded, 1994), an application of fluid mechanics to biological organisms, describing, in the terminology of physics, the relationship between the properties of fluids and biological form.

Sven Kullander and Börje Larsson, *Out of Sight! From Quarks to Living Cells* (1994), a study of the microworld and the chemical, physical, and biological forces that operate within it.

Michio Kaku, *Hyperspace: A Scientific Odyssey Through Parallel Universes, Time Warps, and the Tenth Dimension* (1994), an introduction to the 10 dimensions in which superstring theory predicts that the universe exists, a precursor to the unified theory sought by scientists.

Kip S. Thorne, *Black Holes and Time Warps: Einstein's Outrageous Legacy* (1994), a close look at black holes as a way of examining how scientists evaluate a theory and how the human mind grapples with complex cosmic questions.

Neil de Grasse Tyson, *Universe Down to Earth* (1994), an account of the universe—its population of constellations, their chemical composition, and brief "biographies" of selected elements.

Peter Cattermole, *Venus: The Geological Story* (1994), an account of Venus' atmosphere, topography, weathering, and more, all based on the high-resolution imagery beamed to Earth by the Magellan spacecraft.

The Earth

Stephen James O'Meara and Donna Donovan-O'Meara, *Volcanoes: Passion and Fury* (1994), photographs, apposite epigraphs, and text describing some 20 active volcanoes worldwide in various stages of quiescence or fury.

Yves Guéguen and Victor Palciauskas, *Introduction to the Physics of Rocks* (1994), a description of how the physical properties of rocks (*e.g.*, porosity, magnetism) of different types of rocks affect industrial technology (*e.g.*, well drilling, nuclear-waste disposal, and prospecting for geothermal energy).

David E. Fisher, *The Scariest Place on Earth: Eye to Eye with Hurricanes* (1994), accounts of hurricanes since the time of Genghis Khan, their genesis and composition, forecasting and warning systems, and the author's firsthand encounter with Hurricane Andrew in 1992.

E.C. Pielou, *A Naturalist's Guide to the Arctic* (1994), a comprehensive account of the Arctic environment—its climate and topography—and the wide array of plants and animals that have adapted their habits and structures in order to flourish there.

Donald R. Prothero, *The Eocene-Oligocene Transition: Paradise Lost* (1994), a review of the geologic events of the past 50 million–55 million years that obliterated the dinosaur, chilled the Earth, and culminated in conditions favourable to the emergence of early hominids.

Peter Ward, *The End of Evolution: On Mass Extinctions and the Preservation of Biodiversity* (1994), a paleoscholar's argument, using geologic and fossil evidence, that the present era marks the onset of the third great mass extinction.

Life on Earth

Karl J. Niklas, *Plant Allometry: The Scaling of Form and Process* (1994), an examination of how the interaction of size, form and structure, and metabolism can introduce evolutionary changes in plants.

Jonathan Weiner, *The Beak of the Finch: A Story of Evolution in Our Time* (1994), a study of 20 generations of Charles Darwin's Galápagos finches, using contemporary biochemical techniques to show how evolution can be a rapid-response phenomenon.

Benjamin Lewin, *Genes V* (1994), an up-to-date, occasionally technical review of gene research, noting that genetics is approaching a unified theory of its own.

Peter Wainwright and Stephen M. Reilly, eds., *Ecological Morphology: Integrated Organismal Biology* (1994), an exploration of the ways in which organisms are constructed to maximize their adaptive capacity and of the effect their form has on their place in the evolutionary and ecological scheme.

Steve Madge and Hillary Burn, *Crows and Jays: A Guide to the Crows, Jays, and Magpies of the World* (1994), a complete guide, both a field-identification manual and a concise natural history of the large and widely dispersed family Corvidae.

T.M. Caro, *Cheetahs of the Serengeti Plains: Group Living in an Asocial Species* (1994), a study that examines the normally solitary cheetah's occasional forays into group living and evaluates the causes and consequences of such altered behaviour.

Peter Steinhart, *Two Eagles/Dos Aguiles: The Natural World of the United States–Mexico Borderlands* (1994; photographs by Tupper Ansel Blake), a verbal and photographic pilgrimage through the desert border country of the Southwest, documenting the area's immense biological diversity.

Bert Hölldobler and Edward O. Wilson, *Journey to the Ants: A Story of Scientific Exploration* (1994), an in-depth observation of ant species, using the authors' lifelong study of ants as a model of how (and why) to pursue a scientific discipline.

Mark Jaffe, *And No Birds Sing: The Story of an Ecological Disaster in a Tropical Paradise* (1994), the story of a zoological calamity averted by a courageous and persistent biologist whose initially scorned evidence for the disappearance of the bird population of Guam was vindicated.

William Balée, *Footprints of the Forest: Ka'apor Ethnobotany—the Historical Ecology of Plant Utilization by an Amazonian People* (1994), an ethnographic account of the plant-centred culture of a group of Indians in the eastern Amazon region.

William H. MacLeish, *The Day Before America: Changing the Nature of a Continent* (1994), a biography of the North American continent from the end of the last ice age to the arrival of Columbus.

Human Life

Rod Caird, *Ape Man: The Story of Human Evolution* (1994), a richly illustrated history of human evolution that envisions the process as ongoing and that proposes possible future evolutionary directions for the human race.

Pat Shipman, *The Evolution of Racism: Human Differences and the Use and Abuse of Science* (1994), a paleoanthropological view of the volatile standoff between politics and science with respect to matters of evolution and the differences between human beings.

Robert Cook-Deegan, *The Gene Wars: Science, Politics and the Human Genome* (1994), an account of the Human Genome Project by a former participant, based on primary source documents and interviews with scientists currently involved.

Paul W. Ewald, *Evolution of Infectious Disease* (1994), a Darwinian approach to the evolution of pathogens that seeks to learn why some disease-causing organisms are virulent (cholera) while others remain relatively benign (the common cold).

Emily Martin, *Flexible Bodies: Tracking Immunity in American Culture from the Days of Polio to the Age of AIDS* (1994), an account of the changed view of what constitutes the body's immune system.

Mary Winkler and Letha B. Cole (eds.), *The Good Body: Asceticism in Contemporary Culture* (1994), the moral and clinical implications of Western culture's use of self-denial to achieve the perfect female (or male) body.

Harold J. Cook, *Trials of an Ordinary Doctor: Joannes Groenevelt in 17th-Century London* (1994), one of the early recorded malpractice cases—against a Dutch physician who challenged the authority of the medical establishment by prescribing experimental remedies.

Sheila M. Rothman, *Living in the Shadow of Death: Tuberculosis and the Experience of Illness in American History* (1994), firsthand accounts of patients' experience of "consumption," its impact on families and the wider community, and the changes in treatment that transformed the tubercular from "invalid" to "patient."

Karen Minden, *Bamboo Stones: Evolution of a Chinese Medical Elite* (1994), an account of the Western-style medical training offered to a select group of aspiring students in western China since the 19th century, with an evaluation of its success then and now.

Francis Crick, *The Astonishing Hypothesis: The Scientific Search for the Soul* (1994), a Nobel Prize-winning biophysicist's attempt to penetrate the "jungle of the brain sciences," concentrating on the mystery of consciousness, with particular emphasis on visual awareness.

Stanley Finger, *Origins of Neuroscience: A History of Exploration into Brain Function* (1994), a history of brain study, describing theories of brain function and discussing such brain-directed apparatuses as the intellect, the senses, and the emotions.

Clive Gamble, *Timewalkers: The Prehistory of Global Colonization* (1994), a hypothesis asserting that radical changes in behaviour were a cause, not a consequence, of the major migrations that dispersed the human race across the globe.

Vern L. Bullough, *Science in the Bedroom: A History of Sex Research* (1994), a defense of sexology as a respectable interdisciplinary science, showing how it synthesizes biology and the social sciences and provides worthwhile data for both laypeople and professionals.

John Boswell, *Same-Sex Unions in Premodern Europe* (1994), a history of European marriage rites from the time of the Greeks to the 14th century, especially those performed between men, with evidence that such ceremonies were widespread.

Stephen M. Kosslyn, *Image and Brain: The Resolution of the Imagery Debate* (1994), a study of the role of the "mind's eye" in the processing of information, showing how the disciplines of psychology, neuroscience, and cognitive studies collaborate in this field.

Jonathan Shay, *Achilles in Viet Nam: Combat Trauma and the Undoing of Character* (1994), a doctor's imaginative approach to posttraumatic stress disorder, using the concept to reveal how similarly soldiers in Homer's *Iliad* and those in Vietnam reacted to two wars 2,700 years apart.

Human Society

Peter Canby, *The Heart of the Sky: Travels Among the Maya* (1994), the account of a yearlong odyssey through the land of the Maya that reveals the transcendent vitality of their way of life.

Danah Zohar and Ian Marshall, *The Quantum Society: Mind, Physics, and a New Social Vision* (1994), a prescription for altering the way in which society functions, promoting pluralism and diversity, by using the approach of quantum physics.

Richard Scheinin, *Field of Screams: The Dark Underside of America's National Pastime* (1994), a history of the seamier side of baseball that redresses its sentimentality by revealing how the game faithfully mirrors American culture, warts and all.

Joel Davis, *Mother Tongue: How Humans Create Language* (1994), an attempt to answer several basic questions about the origin and history of language and about human cognition and linguistic memory.

J.E. Lighter (ed.), *Historical Dictionary of American Slang*, vol. 1: A–G (1994), the collected "underbelly language" of the United States, unflinchingly compiled, defined, and given full lexicographical treatment.

David Elkind, *Ties That Stress: The New Family Imbalance* (1994), a study tracing the development of the postmodern family, in which competence and autonomy are more evident than love and intuition.

Mary Ann Schwartz and BarBara Marliene Scott, *Marriages and Families: Diversity and Change* (1994), a textbook study of the institutions and activities connected to marriage and the family, with discussion of such family-related topics as race, class, sex and gender, divorce, and the elderly.

Thomas Sowell, *Race and Culture: A World View* (1994), a challenge to conventional assumptions about race and ethnicity, taking a historical perspective with emphasis on the history of culture.

Harry S. Ashmore, *Civil Rights and Wrongs: A Memoir of Race and Politics, 1944–1994* (1994), a sweeping view of race relations and civil rights issues from World War II to the present, by a veteran Southern journalist and civil rights activist.

W.K. Barger and Ernesto M. Reza, *The Farm Labor Movement in the Midwest: Social Change and Adaptation Among Migrant Farmers* (1994), an account of the rise of the Farm Labor Organizing Committee and its influence on the structure of agribusiness, with a description of the everyday life of the migrant family.

Anthony Downs, *New Visions for Metropolitan America* (1994), a description of the ills that beset metropolitan areas nationwide—traffic congestion, pollution, and concentration of poverty—with suggestions for solutions.

John Kenneth Galbraith, *A Journey Through Economic Time: A Firsthand View* (1994), a brief economic history from World War I and the Russian Revolution of 1917 through the Reagan years and the collapse of Soviet communism.

John Burnett, *Idle Hands: The Experience of Unemployment, 1790–1990* (1994), a historical study, based on firsthand accounts, of unemployment in Britain, portraying both its emotional and its economic cost.

Anne Digby, *Making a Medical Living: Doctors and Patients in the English Market for Medicine, 1770–1911* (1994), the economics of medicine in England, describing the difficulties of reconciling the art with the business of patient care.

Joseph Nocera, *A Piece of the Action: How the Middle Class Joined the Moneyed Class* (1994), a history of the "money revolution," showing how the middle class has taken control of its financial destiny with the credit card, the mutual fund, and discount brokerage.

Gary Dymski and Robert Pollin (eds.), *New Perspectives in Monetary Macroeconomics: Explorations in the Tradition of Hyman P. Minsky* (1994), a collection of essays taking the "Wall Street view" that, among other things, capitalist markets are inherently unstable and unemployment is the norm.

James Fallows, *Looking at the Sun: The Rise of the New East Asian Economic and Political System* (1994), observations on the effect of Western ignorance about Japan on that nation's growing economic dominance, suggesting ways to restore Western commercial vitality.

Donald A. Schön and Martin Rein, *Frame Reflection: Toward the Resolution of Intractable Policy Controversies* (1994), an exploration of possible approaches to insoluble public-policy controversies, using philosophical reflection as a way to begin promoting respect for differences.

Henry Kissinger, *Diplomacy* (1994), a history of the development of the concept of "nation" since the era of Richelieu and of the U.S. role in international affairs, with personal reminiscences illustrating the meaning and uses of diplomacy.

Frank M. Coffin, *On Appeal: Courts, Lawyering, and Judging* (1994), a close-up view of the appellate system by a senior appellate judge, who describes how judges study and analyze briefs and how lawyers argue cases.

Michael J. Perry, *The Constitution in the Courts: Law or Politics?* (1994), a study of the U.S. Supreme Court's role in resolving constitutional conflicts related to the Bill of Rights and the 14th Amendment.

Barry Murcombe and David F. Partlett, *Child Mental Health and the Law* (1994), the history of child mental health law: the rights of handicapped children, mental health clinicians as expert witnesses, custody disputes, and juvenile delinquency, inter alia.

Kim Hays, *Practicing Virtues: Traditions at Quaker and Military Boarding Schools* (1994), a comparison of two seemingly disparate types of schools, offering insights into their contrasting educational philosophies and the ideals they have in common.

Myra Sadker and David Sadker, *Failing at Fairness: How America's Schools Cheat Girls* (1994), an effort to expose and eliminate the gender disparity in school performance that preadolescent girls suffer as they lose their earlier testing advantage and with it their self-esteem.

George Roche, *The Fall of the Ivory Tower: Government Funding, Corruption, and the Bankrupting of American Higher Education* (1994), a critical look at U.S. colleges and universities, assigning the blame for their mismanagement and their failure as educators to government funding that places competition for grants ahead of the mission to teach.

James Moffett, *The Universal Schoolhouse: Spiritual Awakening Through Education* (1994), a holistic, user-driven approach to educational reform, promoting the importance of personal development, lifelong educational opportunity for all, and the separation of schools from government oversight.

Art

Hans Belting, *Likeness and Presence: A History of the Image Before the Era of Art* (1994), reflections on the visual image's loss of the mythic capacity to influence nature and embody the Christian saints' sacred power when it became an object to be viewed in a museum.

Barbara Stafford, *Artful Science: Enlightenment, Entertainment, and the Eclipse of Visual Education* (1994), a study of the blossoming and the withering of scientific entertainments in the 18th century, suggesting that 20th-century computer games and graphics are reincarnations of such pastimes.

Alex Potts, *Flesh and the Ideal: Winckelmann and the Origins of Art History* (1994), a penetrating reexamination of the writings of Johann Joachim Winckelmann, placing them in a modernist tradition that seeks the problematic and the perverse in classical Greek art.

Harold Bloom, *The Western Canon: The Books and School of the Ages* (1994), an argument for the continued study of the great writers of the Western world from Dante to Samuel Beckett, with a hierarchy of the greatest authors and lists of "essential" writers and books.

Sylvia Shorris and Marion Abbott Bundy, *Talking Pictures with the People Who Made Them* (1994), anecdotal interviews with nearly 40 people who conceive, write, produce, direct, act in, and edit motion pictures.

Paul F. Berliner, *Thinking in Jazz: The Infinite Art of Improvisation* (1994), an ethnomusicologist's analysis of what jazz is, what kind of musicianship it demands, and the training in technique that is implicit in improvisation, the heart of jazz.

Humphrey Burton, *Leonard Bernstein* (1994), an account of the career and personal life of one of the outstanding U.S. composers, who was also a prominent pianist and conductor.

Glenn Watkins, *Pyramids at the Louvre: Music, Culture, and Collage from Stravinsky to the Postmodernists* (1994), a juxtaposition of the visual component of collage with the aural component of music, illustrating an interaction that has revolutionized musical ideas and textures and introduced greater cultural pluralism.

John Milnes Baker, *American House Styles: A Concise Guide* (1994), a compendium of historical information on American architectural styles, with both exterior renderings and plans for the layout of interior spaces.

Jeffrey Chipps Smith, *German Sculpture in the Later Renaissance, c. 1520–1580: Art in an Age of Uncertainty* (1994), a study of the impact of the Reformation on German sculpture, showing how philosophical iconoclasm contributed to the expanding market for secular sculpture of all kinds.

John House et al., *Impressionism for England: Samuel Courtauld as Patron and Collector* (1994), a catalog of the modern French paintings in Samuel Courtauld's private collection, with a glance at cultural politics and the role of patronage as an arbiter of taste.

Philippe Perrot, *Fashioning the Bourgeois: A History of Clothing in the Nineteenth Century* (1994; originally published in French, 1981), a study of the "vestimentary landscape," exploring the role of dress in all its permutations as a marker for economic and social class.

Leonard Helfgott, *Ties That Bind: A Social History of the Iranian Carpet* (1994), a history of Iranian weavers and their products from the 15th century, when the carpet first became a commodity, to its present status, second only to oil as a major export to the West.

Technology

Elizabeth Wayland Barber, *Women's Work: The First 20,000 Years. Women, Cloth, and Society in Early Times* (1994), the origins of what may well be the first human technology—originally practiced by women—weaving and the fibre arts.

Richard L. Hills, *Power from Wind: A History of Windmill Technology* (1994), a history of wind-driven technology in Europe, Persia, and the Far East and of the uses of wind for locomotion in the sailing ships of antiquity.

Frances Gies and Joseph Gies, *Cathedral, Forge, and Water Wheel: Technology and Invention in the Middle Ages* (1994), a defense of medieval mechanical innovation, including evidence that the Middle Ages were not the Dark Ages of technology.

Robert Freidel, *Zipper: An Exploration in Novelty* (1994), a story of American ingenuity and persistent optimism: the invention and marketing of the zipper, with a cast of mountebanks, rubes, engineers, and more.

Joseph V. Rees, *Hostages of Each Other: The Transformation of Nuclear Safety Since Three Mile Island* (1994), the story of the Institute of Nuclear Power Operations (INPO), a powerful but little-known industry-created regulatory agency that was established following the Three Mile Island accident.

David Gelernter, *The Muse in the Machine: Computerizing the Poetry of Human Thought* (1994), an argument supporting the possibility that computers can be given minds through the direction of research in artificial intelligence toward creativity, the philosophy of the mind, and literary theory.

Steven R. Holtzman, *Digital Mantras: The Language of Abstract and Virtual Worlds* (1994), a forecast of one future direction for the computer: its own language in which it would create abstract and virtual worlds for exploring emotion and meaning.

Peter Katz, *The New Urbanism: Toward an Architecture of Community* (1994), a presentation of design ideas for buildings and communities, emphasizing compact, close-knit living patterns as an alternative to inner-city ills and suburban sprawl.

Ronald Florence, *The Perfect Machine: Building the Palomar Telescope* (1994), the story of the conception and construction of the 5-m (200-in) Palomar telescope in California, now superseded but still a favourite of astronomers.

Eric J. Chaisson, *The Hubble Wars: Astrophysics Meets Astropolitics in the Billion-Dollar Struggle over the Hubble Space Telescope* (1994), an account of the embarrassments and triumphs of the Hubble telescope, described by the author, an astrophysicist, as the best ever built.

Alan Shepard and Deke Slayton, *Moon Shot: The Inside Story of America's Race to the Moon* (1994), the story of the United States in space—from the first orbits around Earth to the Moon landing, told by two of the pioneer spacemen who were at Mission Control during the first Moon journey.

Religion

Roberto Calasso, *The Marriage of Cadmus and Harmony* (1993), an interweaving of Greek myths and legends that is a suggestive, imaginative, and scholarly history of the gods and their mortal cohorts.

Reginald A. Ray, *Buddhist Saints in India: A Study in Buddhist Values* (1994), an effort to restore the Buddhist saints of the forest—who are as old as Buddhism itself—to their rightful place in the pantheon.

Rabbi Joseph ben Abraham Gikatilla, *Sha'are Orah, Gates of Light* (1994), the first English translation of a 13th-century text in the Jewish mystical tradition known as the Kabbalah, regarded as a key to the secrets of the Torah.

John Shelby Spong, *Resurrection: Myth or Reality? A Bishop's Search for the Origins of Christianity* (1994), a study of the historical and social context of the Easter miracle for clues as to when some of the legends it spawned first surfaced and to reconstruct "what really happened."

Frank J. Tipler, *The Physics of Immortality: Modern Cosmology, God, and the Resurrection of the Dead* (1994), an argument by a cosmological scientist—and former atheist—claiming that the laws of physics appear to verify the eschatological claims of Judeo-Christian theology.

Jan Goodwin, *Price of Honor: Muslim Women Lift the Veil of Silence on the Islamic World* (1994), an account of the effect on Muslim women of the rising tide of religious fundamentalism in the principal Islamic nations, in contravention of the teachings of the Qur'an.

Yitzhak Nakash, *The Shi'is of Iraq* (1994), a history of the Iraqi Shi'ites that explains the difference between Persian (Iranian) Islam, a state religion, and the shrine-centred practices of the formerly nomadic Iraqi Shi'ites.

Steven Barboza, *American Jihad: Islam After Malcolm X* (1994), "portrait interviews" of representatives from American Muslim groups, not all native born or black, offering a more balanced view of Islam in the United States.

The History of Mankind

David Braund, *Georgia in Antiquity: A History of Colchis and Transcaucasian Iberia, 550 BC–AD 562* (1994), an introduction to recent archaeological findings in the "Greek periphery," locus of the Golden Fleece and of the Achaemenid and Seleucid empires.

Clifford Orwin, *The Humanity of Thucydides* (1994), a reevaluation of the *History of the Peloponnesian War* and its author by a political scientist who celebrates the little-recognized humanistic ethos in the most readable of classical Greek writers.

David M. Olster, *Roman Defeat, Christian Response, and the Literary Construction of the Jew* (1994), the uses of anti-Jewish literature as a Roman compensatory device when the Roman Empire was decaying and being replaced by Byzantine hegemony.

John E. Wills, Jr., *Mountain of Fame: Portraits in Chinese History* (1994), nearly 4,000 years of Chinese politics, civilization, and culture portrayed through the lives of 120 distinguished individuals from before Confucius to Mao Zedong (Mao Tse-tung).

Louise Levathes, *When China Ruled the Seas: The Treasure Fleet of the Dragon Throne, 1405–33* (1994), an account of the merchant fleet deployed by China in the Far East almost 90 years before Columbus.

Harold G. Marcus, *A History of Ethiopia* (1994), a history of the religions, languages, and cultures of Ethiopia since prehistoric times, offered as a pointed warning that without a restoration of the art of compromise, the people of the Horn of Africa are doomed.

J.D. Omer-Cooper, *History of Southern Africa* (2nd ed., 1994; originally published in 1987), the story of South Africa from the Iron Age to 1993, describing the collapse of apartheid, Nelson Mandela's release from prison, and the calling of the first free all-race elections.

Roger G. Kennedy, *Hidden Cities: The Discovery and Loss of Ancient North American Civilization* (1994), an account of a 6,000-year-old civilization of the Mississippi Valley, in whose excavation Thomas Jefferson took a scholarly interest.

Robert J. Sharer, *The Ancient Maya* (5th ed., 1994), a much-expanded history—the first revision since 1980—that includes new discoveries about Mayan history, language, and culture made in the past decade.

John Hale, *The Long Century: The Civilization of Europe in the Renaissance* (1994), an in-depth exploration of Renaissance thought, politics, science, religion, and society, emphasizing "what was then said and done."

Susan Dunn, *The Deaths of Louis XVI: Regicide and the French Political Imagination* (1994), a cautionary tale about what happens when idealistic ends collide with brutal means, using the example of an innocuous monarch's violent death and its indelible stain on French (and European) literature, philosophy, and politics.

Roger A. Mason (ed.), *Scots and Britons: Scottish Political Thought and the Union of 1603* (1994), insight from the Scottish point of view into the union with Britain, analyzing the events and political thinking in the formative 90-year period 1560–1650.

Steven Shapin, *A Social History of Truth: Civility and Science in 17th-Century England* (1994), a view of the practice of science that identifies the gentlemanly virtues of birth, wealth, and civility, personified by Francis Bacon and Robert Boyle, with the principled pursuit of scientific truth.

Peter N. Miller, *Defining the Common Good: Empire, Religion and Philosophy in Eighteenth-Century Britain* (1994), an analysis of changes in Britain's perception of "community" as the breakaway American colonies sought to establish their own rule of public good.

Michael Mason, *The Making of Victorian Sexuality* (1994), a reassessment of 19th-century sexual mores, suggesting that the stereotype of Victorian hypocrisy and prudery was exaggerated and that virtue lay in restraining the libido to prevent overpopulation.

C.I. Hamilton, *Anglo-French Naval Rivalry, 1840–1870* (1993), an account of the transformation from conflict to alliance in the Crimean War, thanks to such technological developments as the change from wooden sailing vessels to screw-propelled ironclads.

Kevin McAleer, *Dueling: The Cult of Honor in Fin-de-Siècle Germany* (1994), a description of one aspect of late 19th-century German culture that embodied national and personal ideals of courage, honour, and character and that foreshadowed their later perversion in the Third Reich.

Carolyn Johnston Pouncy (ed. and trans.), *The Domostroi: Rules for Russian Households in the Time of Ivan the Terrible* (1994), the rules by which noble Russian households were regulated in the 16th century, with an introduction that provides a scholarly and informative social history of Moscow during this period.

W. Bruce Lincoln, *The Conquest of a Continent: Siberia and the Russians* (1994), the story of the vast and little-known territory of Siberia, from the time of the Mongols through the 16th-century wars of Christians and Muslims and into the present.

Fernando Cervantes, *The Devil in the New World: The Impact of Diabolism in New Spain* (1994), a study of the devil in New World popular culture and of the unanticipated changes in life and conduct he inspired among the colonizers.

Thomas P. Lowry, *The Story the Soldiers Wouldn't Tell: Sex in the Civil War* (1994), a sampling of letters, diaries, and documents revealing the pure and the prurient in attitude and behaviour among the soldiers and those at home during the War Between the States.

Elizabeth D. Leonard, *Yankee Women: Gender Battles in the Civil War* (1994), narratives of the wartime work of three middle-class Northern women as field physician, public health activist, and battlefield nurse.

Joanne Punzo Waghorne, *The Raja's Magic Clothes: Re-Visioning Kingship and Divinity in England's India* (1994), a study of a South Indian state where, during the Victorian era, a prince's divinity was expressed through ornament, which exerted a significant influence on English style and culture in the mother country.

J.A.S. Grenville, *A History of the World in the 20th Century* (1994), an ambitious attempt to record, both geographically and chronologically, world events and personalities, and the social and economic forces associated with them, through 1993.

Gerhard L. Weinberg, *A World at Arms: A Global History of World War II* (1994), a massive history that weaves the several war theatres into a comprehensive entity and assesses the war's economic and human cost.

Ryszard Kapusinski, *Imperium* (1994), an account of the author's childhood in the Soviet Union, his later wanderings—often without official permission—throughout the country, and his experiences during the breakup of the U.S.S.R.

Thomas G. Paterson, *Contesting Castro: The United States and the Triumph of the Cuban Revolution* (1994), a history of the vexed relationship between Cuba and the United States that questions the U.S. failure to defeat Castro.

James Ridgeway, *The Haiti Files: Decoding the Crisis* (1994), a hastily assembled collection of documents that tell the story of Haiti after the emergence of Jean-Bertrand Aristide in 1990, depicting the tumultuous, often brutal events that continue to plague Haitian politics.

Han Suyin, *Eldest Son: Zhou Enlay and the Making of Modern China, 1898–1976* (1994), a history of 20th-century China and its communist revolution, portrayed through the biography, based on interviews, of one of China's most influential leaders.

Sidney Giffard, *Japan Among the Powers, 1890–1990* (1994), an account of Japan's launch into modern history, examining, from the Japanese viewpoint, the events and institutions that transformed it into a Great Power and a model of industrial success.

Marie Alexandrine Martin, *Cambodia: A Shattered Society* (1994; originally published in French, 1989), a review of the complex history of modern Cambodia, whose political and social chaos continued even after the end of Vietnam's 10-year occupation.

Milton Viorst, *Sandcastles: The Arabs in Search of the Modern World* (1994), a look at the people of the Arab world, 200 million strong, who, though they share language, experience, and religion, are still in search of their destiny after centuries of Ottoman rule.

Barry Rubin, *Revolution Until Victory? The Politics and History of the PLO* (1994), a political history of the Palestine Liberation Organization, its up-and-down fortunes, and its controversial leader, Yasir Arafat, emphasizing strategic triumphs and failures along the road to Middle Eastern peace.

William F.S. Miles, *Hausaland Divided: Colonialism and Independence in Nigeria and Niger* (1994), a former Peace Corps volunteer's view that their common language is helping the people compensate for the mistaken policy that has separated the Republic of Niger from the Federal Republic of Nigeria.

Mark Mathabane, *African Women: Three Generations* (1994), the lives, told in their own words, of the author's South African grandmother, mother, and sister and the story of their courage in overcoming violence, oppression, and apartheid.

The Branches of Knowledge

Jody Azzouni, *Metaphysical Myths, Mathematical Practice: The Ontology and Epistemology of the Exact Sciences* (1994), a detailed and technical approach to the philosophy of mathematics that grapples with the epistemological conundrum How does one know what one knows about an object?

William Dunham, *The Mathematical Universe: An Alphabetical Journey Through the Great Proofs, Problems, and Personalities* (1994), a collection of notable historic disputes, unsolved mysteries, and mathematical proofs from the time of the Greek geometers on.

Keith Devlin, *Mathematics: The Science of Patterns* (1994), a characterization of mathematics as a science of patterns that can be perceived in such functions as counting, shape, and position.

Ken Binmore, *Game Theory and the Social Contract, Vol. 1: Playing Fair* (1994), an application of game theory to politics, philosophy, and economics, using this mathematical theory to analyze the moral and ethical attitudes of politicians, philosophers, and economists.

Thomas Levenson, *Measure for Measure: A Musical History of Science* (1994), an explanation of the way science works by means of a comparison to music, taking as an example Pythagoras and the mathematically expressed harmony of the spheres.

George Saliba, *A History of Arabic Astronomy: Planetary Theories During the Golden Age of Islam* (1994), the history of non-Ptolemaic astronomy in Islam from the 11th to the 15th century, emphasizing its intellectual vigour in a period of so-called decline.

Raphael Patai, *The Jewish Alchemists: A History and Source Book* (1994), a chronology of the Jewish practitioners of the "Great Art" from Talmudic times to the 19th century, noting alchemy's influence on chemistry, medicine, and philosophy and its strikingly modern assertion that all substances are fundamentally one.

Hugh Thurston, *Early Astronomy* (1994), a world history of astronomy from the astronomers of megalithic Stonehenge to Johannes Kepler, including stargazers of Babylonia, India, China, Egypt, and pre-Columbian Central America, as well as the Arabs and Greeks.

Bruce Stephenson, *The Music of the Heavens: Kepler's Harmonic Astronomy* (1994), an analysis of astronomer Kepler's harmonic principles, a type of early unified theory that related the harmony of planetary orbits to the harmony of eternal geometric relationships.

Edward Speyer, *Six Roads from Newton: Great Discoveries in Physics* (1994), a history and philosophy of science that examines the six areas of inquiry that are either extensions, challenges, or descendants of the physics of Isaac Newton.

Philip Stehle, *Order, Chaos, Order: The Transition from Classical to Quantum Physics* (1994), a history of the second major revolution in the physical sciences, led by Max Planck, Albert Einstein, and others, which brought about a new, coherent theory of physics.

Jack Cohen and Ian Stewart, *The Collapse of Chaos: Discovering Simplicity in a Complex World* (1994), a study of the ways in which simplicity is the distillation of complexity and chaos, exemplified by the reduction of the complexity of DNA through a series of simplifying laws of physics.

Steven Pinker, *The Language Instinct: The New Science of Language and Mind* (1994), a panoramic study of the evolution, biology, and anthropology of language, its uniquely human design, and its almost limitless permutations and nuances.

Joyce Appleby, Lynn Hunt, and Margaret Jacob, *Telling the Truth About History* (1994), a history of historiography, pointing out that skepticism and relativism about truth have coloured society's attitudes toward science, politics, and history.

Martha C. Nussbaum, *The Therapy of Desire* (1994), an analysis of the relationship between emotion and belief, a distinction that originated with the Hellenistic philosophers.

Martin Heidegger, *Basic Questions of Philosophy: Selected "Problems" of Logic* (1994; originally published in German, 1984), a study of the relation of history to a system of philosophy and to the "essence of truth."

Paula Findlen, *Possessing Nature: Museums, Collecting, and the Scientific Culture in Early Modern Italy* (1994), a study of the beginnings of the museum in 17th-century Italy, where Aristotelianism and the scientific revolution collided.

(JEAN S. GOTTLIEB)

CONTRIBUTORS

Abramson, Gary. Reporter on Spain for *Businessweek*, the *Chicago Tribune*, and the *Associated Press*. • WORLD AFFAIRS: *Spain*

Adams, Andy. Editor and Publisher, *Sumo World*. Author of *Sumo* and *Sumo World Record Book*. • SPORTS AND GAMES: *Judo; Wrestling:* Sumo

Allaby, Michael. Writer and Lecturer. Author of *Ecology Facts; A Guide to Gaia*. • ENVIRONMENT: *International and National Activities; Issues of Concern*

Allan, J.A. Professor of Geography, School of Oriental and African Studies, University of London. • WORLD AFFAIRS: *Libya*

Anderson, D.F. Director, Department of Economic Affairs, International Iron & Steel Institute. Author of *Steel Demand Forecasting* and others. • BUSINESS AND INDUSTRY REVIEW: *Metals and Materials:* Iron and Steel

Archibald, John J. Retired Feature Writer, *St. Louis Post-Dispatch;* Adjunct Professor, Washington University; Member of Professional Bowlers Association Hall of Fame. • SPORTS AND GAMES: *Bowling:* U.S. Tenpins

Arnold, Guy. Freelance Writer. Author of *Modern Nigeria; Aid in Africa;* and others. • WORLD AFFAIRS: *Botswana; Burundi; Cape Verde; Chad; Comoros; Djibouti; Equatorial Guinea; Gambia, The; Ghana; Guinea-Bissau; Lesotho; Liberia; Madagascar; Maldives; Mauritius; Nigeria; Rwanda; São Tomé and Príncipe; Seychelles; Sierra Leone; Swaziland*

Arnold, Mavis. Freelance Journalist, Dublin. • WORLD AFFAIRS: *Ireland*

Arrington, Leonard J. Formerly Church Historian, Church of Jesus Christ of Latter-day Saints. • RELIGION: *Church of Jesus Christ of Latter-day Saints*

Bacani, Cesar. Associate Editor, *Asiaweek*. • WORLD AFFAIRS: *Cambodia; Malaysia*

Bakker, Martinus A. Professor of Germanic Languages, Calvin College. Editor of *Studies in Netherlandic Culture and Literature*. • LITERATURE: *Netherlandic*

Balaban, Avraham. Professor of Modern Hebrew Literature, University of Florida. Author of *Between God and Beast: An Examination of Amos Oz's Prose*. • LITERATURE: *Jewish:* Hebrew

Baptist, Ines T. Freelance Writer. • WORLD AFFAIRS: *Belize*

Barford, Michael F. Editor and Director, *Tabacosmos*. • BUSINESS AND INDUSTRY REVIEW: *Tobacco; Tobacco:* Sidebar

Barlow, Margaret. Freelance Writer. Associate Editor, *Women's Art Journal*. • BIOGRAPHIES *(in part);* NOBEL PRIZES *(in part)*

Barrett, David B. Hon. Research Adviser, United Bible Societies; Church Missionary Society, Church of England. Author of *Schism and Renewal in Africa*. • RELIGION: *Tables*

Barrett, John C.A. Headmaster, The Leys School; Secretary, British Committee, World Methodist Council. Author of *Family Worship in Theory and Practice*. • RELIGION: *Methodist Churches*

Bass, Howard. Journalist and Broadcaster; formerly Editor, *Winter Sports;* Ice Hockey Correspondent, *Daily Telegraph;* Skiing and Skating Correspondent, *Daily Mail*. Author of 16 books on winter sports. • BIOGRAPHIES *(in part);* SPORTS AND GAMES: *Ice Hockey:* International; *Ice Skating; Skiing*

Battistella, Alexandre. Information Specialist, World Forest Institute. • BUSINESS AND INDUSTRY REVIEW: *Wood Products:* Wood

Bickelhaupt, David L. Professor Emeritus, Faculty of Finance, College of Business, Ohio State University. • BUSINESS AND INDUSTRY REVIEW: *Insurance*

Bird, Thomas E. Director, Council for the Study of Ethics and Public Policy, Queens College, City University of New York. • LITERATURE: *Jewish:* Yiddish

Bisman, Ronald W. North Island Editor, *New Zealand Harness Racing Weekly*. Author of *Cardigan Bay; Salute to Trotting*. • SPORTS AND GAMES: *Equestrian Sports:* Harness Racing

Blair, Walter. Professor Emeritus of English, University of Chicago. Author of *Mark Twain;* Coauthor of *America's Humor: Poor Richard to Doonesbury*. • MACROPÆDIA: *American Literature (in part)*

Bleibtreu, Hermann K. Professor of Anthropology, University of Arizona. • ANTHROPOLOGY

Boddy, William C. Founder and Editor, *Motor Sport*. Full Member, Guild of Motoring Writers. • SPORTS AND GAMES: *Automobile Racing:* Grand Prix Racing

Boden, Edward. Publications Adviser, British Veterinary Association; formerly Editor, *Veterinary Record*. • HEALTH AND DISEASE: *Veterinary Medicine*

Booth, John Nicholls. Lecturer and Writer. Author of *The Quest for Preaching Power*. • RELIGION: *Unitarian (Universalist) Churches*

Bossler, John D. Director and Professor at the Center for Mapping, Ohio State University. • EARTH SCIENCES: Sidebar

Boswall, Jeffery. Senior Lecturer in Biological Imaging, University of Derby. • LIFE SCIENCES: *Ornithology*

Box, Ben. Editor, Trade and Travel Publications (*South American Handbook* and others). • WORLD AFFAIRS: *Bolivia; Chile; Colombia; Panama; Peru; Venezuela*

Boye, Roger. Formerly Coin Columnist, *Chicago Tribune*. • AUCTIONS AND COLLECTIONS: *Numismatics*

Boylan, Patrick J. Professor and Head, Department of Arts Policy and Management, City University, London. Author of *Museums 2000: Politics, People, Professionals and Profit* and others. • MUSEUMS *(international)*

Bradsher, Henry S. Foreign Affairs Writer. • WORLD AFFAIRS: *Philippines*

Braidwood, Robert J. Professor Emeritus of Old World Prehistory, Oriental Institute and Department of Anthropology, University of Chicago. Author of *Prehistoric Men*. • ARCHAEOLOGY: *Eastern Hemisphere*

Brazee, Rutlage J. Geophysical Consultant. • EARTH SCIENCES: *Geophysics*

Brecher, Kenneth. Professor of Astronomy and Physics, Boston University. Coauthor and coeditor of *Astronomy of the Ancients*. • ASTRONOMY; ASTRONOMY: Sidebar

Brokopp, John G. Specialist in publicity, public relations, and writing about horse racing. • SPORTS AND GAMES: *Equestrian Sports:* Thoroughbred Racing (U.S. and Canada)

Brooks, Tony. Retired Secretary-General, International Table Tennis Federation. • SPORTS AND GAMES: *Table Tennis*

Brown, Bess. Senior Research Analyst, Radio Free Europe/Radio Liberty Research Institute. • WORLD AFFAIRS: *Kazakhstan; Kyrgyzstan; Tajikistan; Turkmenistan; Uzbekistan*

Brown, Maggie. Media Editor, The Independent Newspapers. • PUBLISHING: *Magazines* (international); *Newspapers* (international)

Brown-Humes, Christopher. Stockholm Correspondent, *Financial Times*. • WORLD AFFAIRS: *Sweden*

Burdin, Joel L. Coordinator of Educational Administration, Frostburg State University. Author of *Diversity and Leadership in Education*. • EDUCATION (U.S.)

Burks, Ardath W. Professor Emeritus of Asian Studies, Rutgers University. Author of *Japan: A Postindustrial Power*. • WORLD AFFAIRS: *Japan*

Burns, Erik. Freelance Writer. • WORLD AFFAIRS: *Portugal*

Butler, Frank. Formerly Sports Editor, *News of the World*. Author of *The Good, the Bad and the Ugly: A Story of Boxing*. • SPORTS AND GAMES: *Boxing*

Cafferty, Bernard. Associate Editor, *British Chess Magazine;* Chess Columnist, *The Sunday Times*. • SPORTS AND GAMES: *Chess*

Calder, Nigel. Independent Science Writer. Author of *Spaceship Earth; Giotto to the Comets*. • SPECIAL REPORT: *Seafaring and History in the English Channel*

Cameron, Sarah. Freelance Writer and Editor, Trade and Travel Publications. • WORLD AFFAIRS: *Costa Rica; Cuba; Dominican Republic; Ecuador; El Salvador; Guatemala; Haiti; Honduras; Nicaragua*

Campbell, Robert. Architect and Architecture Critic. Author of *Cityscapes of Boston;* Coauthor of *American Architecture of the 1980s*. • ARCHITECTURE

Cantrell, Scott. Classical Music Editor, *Kansas City Star*. • MUSIC: *Classical*

Carter, Robert W. Journalist, London. • SPORTS AND GAMES: *Equestrian Sports:* Show Jumping and Dressage; Steeplechasing; Thoroughbred Racing (Europe and Australia)

Chapman, Kenneth F. Formerly Editor, *Stamp Collecting* and *Philatelic Magazine*. • AUCTIONS AND COLLECTIONS: *Philately*

Chappell, Duncan. Research Fellow, United Nations Interregional Crime and Justice Research Institute. • CRIME, LAW ENFORCEMENT, AND PENOLOGY: *Crime; Law Enforcement*

Chapple, Abby. Writer and Consultant, Consumer Communications (Annapolis, Md.) • BUSINESS AND INDUSTRY REVIEW: *Home Furnishings:* Furniture

Cheuse, Alan. Writing Faculty, English Department, George Mason University; Book Commentator, National Public Radio. Author of *The Light Possessed* and others. • LITERATURE: *English:* United States

Clapham, Christopher S. Professor of Politics and International Relations, University of Lancaster. Author of *Transformation and Continuity in Revolutionary Ethiopia*. • WORLD AFFAIRS: *Eritrea; Ethiopia*

Clark, David D. Managing Editor, *World Literature Today*. • LITERATURE: *English:* Other

Clarke, Douglas L. Captain, U.S. Navy (ret.). Military Analyst. Author of *The Missing Man: Politics and the MIA*. • MILITARY AFFAIRS

Clarke, R.O. Lecturer and Consultant on Industrial Relations, London. • LABOUR-MANAGEMENT RELATIONS

Cogle, T.C.J. Consultant, *Electrical Review*. • BUSINESS AND INDUSTRY REVIEW: *Electrical*

Collins, Cheryl L. Freelance Writer. • BIOGRAPHIES *(in part)*

Cooper, Melanie Anne. Senior Editorial Assistant, *Newsweek*. • PUBLISHING: *Newspapers* (U.S.); WORLD AFFAIRS: *United States:* State and Local Affairs; *United States:* Sidebar

Corzine, Robert. Oil and Gas Correspondent, *Financial Times*. • ENERGY: *Natural Gas; Petroleum*

Cosgrave, Bronwyn. Fashion Editor, *The European*. • FASHION AND DRESS

Coveney, Michael. Theatre Critic, *The Observer*. Author of *The Aisle Is Full of Noises* and others. • THEATRE: *Great Britain and Ireland*

Craine, Anthony G. Copy Editor, Encyclopædia Britannica. • BIOGRAPHIES *(in part)*

Crampton, Richard J. Fellow, St. Edmund Hall, Oxford, England; formerly Professor of East European History, University of Kent at Canterbury. Author of *Eastern Europe in the Twentieth Century* and others. • WORLD AFFAIRS: *Bulgaria*

Crist, Raymond E. Formerly Research Professor of Geography, University of Florida. Author of *The Cauca Valley, Colombia*. • MACROPÆDIA: *South America (in part)*

Crowley, Edward. Journalist; Director, Technical Writing Services, *Maritime Monitor*. • BUSINESS AND INDUSTRY REVIEW: *Shipbuilding;* TRANSPORTATION: *Shipping and Ports*

Cunningham, Susan M. Economic and Political Analyst; Freelance Writer. Author of *Latin America Since 1945* (in preparation). • WORLD AFFAIRS: *Argentina; Brazil; Mexico*

Curwen, Peter J. Reader in Business Policy, Sheffield Business School. Author of *The U.K. Publishing Industry* and others. • PUBLISHING: *Books* (international)

Cviic, K.F. East European Specialist, Royal Institute of International Affairs. • WORLD AFFAIRS: *Bosnia and Herzegovina; Croatia; Macedonia; Slovenia; Yugoslavia*

Czerwinski, Edward J. Professor Emeritus of Slavic and Comparative Literature, State University of New York at Stony Brook. Author of *A Dictionary of Polish Literature* and others. Area Editor, *Theater Companies of the World.* • LITERATURE: *Eastern European* (in part); *Russian* (in part)

Davis, Donald A. Editor, *Drug & Cosmetic Industry* and *Cosmetic Insider's Report.* • BUSINESS AND INDUSTRY REVIEW: *Pharmaceuticals*

Deam, John B. Retired Technical Director, AMT—The Association for Manufacturing Technology, McLean, Va. • BUSINESS AND INDUSTRY REVIEW: *Machinery and Machine Tools*

de la Barre, Kenneth. Director, Katimavik. • WORLD AFFAIRS: *Arctic Regions*

Deletant, Dennis J. Senior Lecturer in Romanian Studies, University of London. Author of *Studies in Romanian History; Colloquial Romanian* and others. • WORLD AFFAIRS: *Romania*

Denselow, Robin. Rock Music Critic, *The Guardian;* Current Affairs Reporter, BBC Television. Author of *When the Music's Over: The Politics of Pop.* • MUSIC: *Popular* (international)

de Puy, Norman R. Minister, American Baptist Churches; Editor and Publisher, *Cabbages and Kings* newsletter. • RELIGION: *Baptist Churches*

Dicks, Geoffrey R. U.K. Economist, NatWest Markets. Author of *Sources of World Financial and Banking Information.* • BUSINESS AND INDUSTRY REVIEW: (Introduction)

Dickstein, Morris. Director, Center for the Humanities; Professor of English, Queens College and Graduate School and University Center, City University of New York. Author of *Gates of Eden: American Culture in the Sixties* and others. • : *American Literature* (in part)

Dirnbacher, Elfriede. Austrian Civil Servant. • WORLD AFFAIRS: *Austria*

Dixon, Bernard. Science Writer; Consultant. European Editor, *Bio/Technology;* Editor, *Medical Science Research.* Author of *Health and the Human Body* and others. • HEALTH AND DISEASE: *Medicine* (international); *Mental Health*

Dooling, Dave. Consultant and Writer, D² Associates. • SPACE EXPLORATION

Dormer, Albert G. Bridge Correspondent, *The Times.* Coauthor of *Complete Book of Bridge* and others. • SPORTS AND GAMES: *Contract Bridge*

Dorsey, Learthen. Assistant Professor, Department of History, University of Nebraska. Author of *Historical Dictionary of Rwanda.* • RACE AND ETHNIC RELATIONS: Sidebar

Duke, Michael S. Professor of Chinese, University of British Columbia. Author of *Blooming and Contending the Iron House.* • LITERATURE: *Chinese*

Earp, John H. Director, Halcrow Fox and Associates. • TRANSPORTATION: *Introduction; Freight and Pipelines; Intercity Rail; Roads and Traffic; Urban Mass Transit*

Ehringer, Gavin Forbes. Rodeo Columnist, *Western Horseman.* • SPORTS AND GAMES: *Rodeo*

Eisenhammer, John. Chief Correspondent on Germany, *The Independent.* • WORLD AFFAIRS: *Germany*

Ellis, Roger. Editor, *Mining Journal.* • MINING

Emerson, Warren K. Writer and Photographer. • SPORTS AND GAMES: *Badminton*

Engels, Jan R. Retired Director, Centre Paul Hymans. • WORLD AFFAIRS: *Belgium*

Farr, D.M.L. Professor Emeritus of History, Carleton University. • WORLD AFFAIRS: *Canada*

Fendell, Robert J. Columnist, *Sport Scene Florida.* Author of *How to Make Your Car Last* and others. • SPORTS AND GAMES: *Automobile Racing:* U.S. Racing

Finkelstein, Ellen. Product Coordinator, Encyclopædia Britannica. • BIOGRAPHIES (in part)

Flagg, Gordon. Senior Editor, *American Libraries.* • LIBRARIES (U.S.)

Flanders, Douglas L. Director of Education and Information, The United Church of Canada. • RELIGION: *The United Church of Canada*

Fleming, Arlene K. Cultural Resource Management Consultant. Author of *Destruction of Cultural Heritage in Bosnia and Herzegovina 1992–94.* • ARCHITECTURE: Sidebar

Fletcher, Charmaine. Media and Press Officer, The Salvation Army. • RELIGION: *Salvation Army*

Flores, Ramona Monette S. Professor, University of the Philippines; Editorial Consultant, *Masks and Voices.* • TELEVISION AND RADIO (international)

Follett, Christopher. Denmark Correspondent, *The Times;* Danish Correspondent, Radio Sweden; Newscaster, Radio Denmark; Freelance Correspondent, Reuters. Author of *Fodspor paa Cypern.* • WORLD AFFAIRS: *Denmark*

Fossli, Karen L. Oslo Correspondent, *Financial Times.* • WORLD AFFAIRS: *Norway*

Freeman, Laurie. Freelance Writer and Editor. • BUSINESS AND INDUSTRY REVIEW: *Advertising*

Friday, Elbert W., Jr. Assistant Administrator for Weather Services, National Oceanic and Atmospheric Administration. • EARTH SCIENCES: *Meteorology*

Fridovich, Irwin. James B. Duke Professor of Biochemistry, Duke University Medical Center. • LIFE SCIENCES: *Molecular Biology* (in part)

Fridovich-Keil, Judith L. Assistant Professor, Department of Genetics and Molecular Medicine, Emory University School of Medicine. • LIFE SCIENCES: *Molecular Biology* (in part)

Friedrich, Mary Jane. Assistant Editor, Encyclopædia Britannica. • BIOGRAPHIES (in part)

Friskin, Sydney E. Hockey Correspondent, *The Times.* • SPORTS AND GAMES: *Billiard Games; Field Hockey; Snooker*

Frost, David. Formerly Rugby Union Writer, *The Guardian.* • SPORTS AND GAMES: *Football:* Rugby

Fuller, Amanda E. Assistant Editor, *The Great Ideas Today,* Encyclopædia Britannica. • BIOGRAPHIES (in part)

Fuller, Elizabeth. Senior Research Analyst, Radio Free Europe/Radio Liberty Research Institute. • BIOGRAPHIES (in part); WORLD AFFAIRS: *Armenia; Azerbaijan; Georgia*

Gaddum, Anthony H. Chairman, H. T. Gaddum and Company; Deputy Vice President, International Silk Association. • BUSINESS AND INDUSTRY REVIEW: *Textiles:* Silk

Ganado, Albert. Lawyer, Malta. Coauthor of *Malta in British and French Caricature 1798–1815.* • WORLD AFFAIRS: *Malta*

Ganguly, Dilip. Senior Correspondent, The Associated Press, South Asia Bureau (New Delhi). • WORLD AFFAIRS: *Bangladesh; Bhutan; Myanmar (Burma); Nepal; Pakistan; Sri Lanka*

Garland, Irene. Freelance Writer and Lecturer on Norwegian Matters. • BIOGRAPHIES (in part)

Gibbons, Anne R. Freelance Writer. • LIFE SCIENCES: *Entomology*

Gibbons, J. Whitfield. Professor of Zoology, Savannah River Ecology Laboratory, University of Georgia. Author of *Keeping All the Pieces.* • LIFE SCIENCES: *Zoology*

Giles, James R. Professor of English, Northern Illinois University. Author of *Confronting the Horror: The Novels of Nelson Algren* and others. • MACROPÆDIA: *American Literature* (in part)

Gill, Martin J. Editor, *World Fishing Magazine.* • AGRICULTURE AND FOOD SUPPLIES: *Fisheries*

Girnius, Saulius A. Senior Research Analyst, Open Media Research Institute. • WORLD AFFAIRS: *Latvia; Lithuania*

Goldsmith, Arthur. Editor-at-Large, *Popular Photography.* • ART: *Photography;* BUSINESS AND INDUSTRY REVIEW: *Photography; Photography:* Sidebar

Gottfried, Martin. Drama Critic, New York City. Author of *Sondheim; Nobody's Fool: The Lives of Danny Kaye;* and others. • THEATRE: *U.S. and Canada*

Gottlieb, Jean S. Freelance Editor; Historian of Science. Author of *A Checklist of the Newberry Library's Printed Books in Science, Medicine, Technology, and the Pseudosciences, ca. 1460–1750.* • BIBLIOGRAPHY

Grayson, Kent A. Assistant Professor of Marketing, London Business School. • MACROPÆDIA: *Marketing and Merchandising* (in part)

Greeman, Adrian Lee. Editor, *Civil Engineer International.* • ENGINEERING PROJECTS: *Bridges*

Green, Anthony L. Senior Copy Editor, Encyclopædia Britannica. • BIOGRAPHIES (in part)

Greskovic, Robert J. Dance Reviewer, *Arts & Entertainment Monthly;* Freelance Writer. • DANCE: North America

Gribbin, John. Visiting Fellow in Astronomy, University of Sussex. Author of *In the Beginning; In Search of the Edge of Time.* • PHYSICS

Griffiths, A.R.G. Senior Lecturer in History, Flinders University of South Australia. Author of *Contemporary Australia; Beautiful Lies.* • BIOGRAPHIES (in part); WORLD AFFAIRS: *Australia; Nauru; Papua New Guinea*

Grossman, Joel W. Archaeologist. • ARCHAEOLOGY: *Western Hemisphere*

Guthridge, Guy G. Manager, Polar Information Program, U.S. National Science Foundation. • WORLD AFFAIRS: *Polar Regions:* Antarctica

Hafez, Sabry. Professor of Modern Arabic, School of Oriental and African Studies, University of London. Author of *The Genesis of Arabic Narrative Discourse; Arabic Cinema.* • LITERATURE: *Arabic*

Halman, Talat S. Research Professor; Chairman, Department of Near Eastern Languages and Literatures, New York University. • LITERATURE: *Turkish*

Hanaway, William L. Associate Professor of Persian, University of Pennsylvania. Author of *Chapbook Publishing in Pakistan.* • LITERATURE: *Persian*

Hannen, Mark. Competitions Officer, English Basket Ball Association. • SPORTS AND GAMES: *Basketball:* International

Harakas, Stanley S. Archbishop Iakovos Professor of Orthodox Theology, Holy Cross Greek Orthodox School of Theology. Author of *Health and Medicine in the Eastern Orthodox Tradition* and others. • RELIGION: *Oriental Orthodox Church; The Orthodox Church*

Haub, Carl V. Demographer, Population Reference Bureau. Author of *The U.N. Long-Range Population Prosections: What They Tell Us.* • POPULATIONS AND POPULATION MOVEMENTS: *Demography;* POPULATIONS AND POPULATION MOVEMENTS: Sidebar

Haufler, Daniel A. Journalist, *Die Zeit.* • LITERATURE: *German*

Havard-Williams, P. Professor of Library and Information Studies, University of Botswana. Professor Emeritus, Loughborough University. • LIBRARIES (international)

Hawkland, William D. Chancellor Emeritus of Law and Boyd Professor, Louisiana State University. • LAW: *Court Decisions*

Hebblethwaite, Peter. Vatican Affairs Writer, *National Catholic Reporter.* Author of *Paul VI, The First Modern Pope.* • RELIGION: *Roman Catholic Church*

Hébert, Pierre. Professor *titulaire,* University of Sherbrooke. • LITERATURE: *French: Canada*

Heinzl, John. Business Reporter, *The Globe and Mail.* • BUSINESS AND INDUSTRY REVIEW: *Retailing*

Hendershott, Jon. Associate Editor, *Track & Field News.* Author of *Track's Greatest Women.* • SPORTS AND GAMES: *Track and Field Sports*

Hendershott, Myrl C. Professor of Oceanography, Scripps Institution of Oceanography. • EARTH SCIENCES: *Oceanography*

Hennelly, James. Researcher, Encyclopædia Britannica. • BIOGRAPHIES *(in part)*

Henschel, Milton. President, Watch Tower Bible and Tract Society. • RELIGION: *Jehovah's Witnesses*

Hibbard, Jonathan D. Assistant Professor of Marketing, Boston University. • MACROPÆDIA: *Marketing and Merchandising (in part)*

Hobbs, Greg. Editor, *The Football Record.* Author of 12 books on Australian Football. • SPORTS AND GAMES: *Football:* Australian

Hoeksema, Klaas J. Staff Member, Institute for Polytechnics, Amsterdam. • WORLD AFFAIRS: *Netherlands, The; Suriname*

Hope, Thomas W. Chairman, Hope Reports, Inc. • MOTION PICTURES: *Nontheatrical Films*

Hunnings, Neville March. Editor, *Encyclopedia of European Union Laws—Constitutional Texts.* • LAW: *International Agreements*

IEIS. International Economic Information Services. • ECONOMIC AFFAIRS: *World Economy; Stock Exchanges* (international)

Ingham, Kenneth. Professor Emeritus of History, University of Bristol. Author of *Politics in Modern Africa: The Uneven Tribal Dimension* and others. • WORLD AFFAIRS: *Angola; Kenya; Malawi; Mozambique; Sudan, The; Tanzania; Uganda; Zaire; Zambia; Zimbabwe*

Ingram, Derek. Consultant Editor, Gemini News Service. Author of *Commonwealth for a Colour-Blind World; The Imperfect Commonwealth.* • WORLD AFFAIRS: *Commonwealth of Nations*

Jardine, Adrian. Company Director. Member, Guild of Yachting Writers. • SPORTS AND GAMES: *Sailing*

Jaspert, W. Pincus. Technical and Editorial Consultant. International Editor, *American Printer* and *World-Wide Printer.* Author of *State of the Art* and others. • BUSINESS AND INDUSTRY REVIEW: *Printing*

Jessell, Harry A. Executive Editor, *Broadcasting and Cable.* • TELEVISION AND RADIO (U.S., *in part);* Amateur Radio *(in part)*

Joffé, George. Journalist and Writer on North African and Middle Eastern Affairs. • WORLD AFFAIRS: *Algeria; Morocco; Tunisia*

Johnsson, William G. Editor, *Adventist Review.* Author of *Behold His Glory* and others. • RELIGION: *Seventh-day Adventist Church*

Jones, D.A.N. Novelist and Critic. Author of *Parade in Pairs; Never Had It So Good.* • LITERATURE: *Introduction; English:* United Kingdom

Jones, W. Glyn. Professor Emeritus of Scandinavian Studies, University of East Anglia. Author of *Colloquial Danish* and others. • LITERATURE: *Danish*

Jotischky, Helma. Principal Research Officer, Paint Research Association. • BUSINESS AND INDUSTRY REVIEW: *Paints and Varnishes*

Juban, Yann. Jurist, International Wine and Vine Office. • BUSINESS AND INDUSTRY REVIEW: *Beverages:* Wine

Kaplan, Robert D. Contributing Editor, *The Atlantic Monthly.* Author of *The Arabists; Balkan Ghosts.* • WORLD AFFAIRS: *Spotlight:* The New Middle East

Karsten, Peter. Past President, IUDZG—The World Zoo Organization. • BOTANICAL GARDENS AND ZOOS: *Zoos*

Katz, William A. Professor, School of Information Science and Policy, State University of New York at Albany. • PUBLISHING: *Magazines* (U.S.)

Kelleher, J.A. Journalist, New Zealand. Formerly Editor, *The Dominion* and *Dominion Sunday Times* (Wellington). • WORLD AFFAIRS: *New Zealand*

Kelling, George H. Historian and Media Relations Officer, Wilford Hall Air Force Medical Center. Author of *Countdown to Rebellion: British Policy in Cyprus 1939–1955.* • WORLD AFFAIRS: *Cyprus*

Kellner, Peter. Political Commentator, BBC Television. Author of *The Civil Servants: An Inquiry into Britain's Ruling Class* and others. • BIOGRAPHIES *(in part);* WORLD AFFAIRS: *United Kingdom*

Kennedy, Richard M. Agricultural Economist, Agriculture and Trade Analysis Division, Economic Research Service, U.S. Department of Agriculture. • AGRICULTURE AND FOOD SUPPLIES; *International Issues; Agricultural Commodities*

Kind, Joshua B. Professor of Art History, Northern Illinois University. Author of *Rouault; Geometry as Abstract Art;* and others. • MUSEUMS (U.S.)

Kirchhoff, H.J. Theatre Critic, *The Globe and Mail.* • THEATRE: Sidebar

Knox, Richard A. Managing Editor, *Power Technology International* and *Power Generation Technology.* • ENERGY: *Nuclear*

Kolankiewicz, George. Lecturer in Sociology, University of Essex; Research Director, Research Programme on East-West Studies, U.K. Economic and Social Research Council. Coauthor of *Social Groups in Polish Society* and others. • WORLD AFFAIRS: *Poland*

Kotler, Philip. S.C. Johnson and Son Distinguished Professor of International Marketing, Northwestern University. Author of *Marketing Management: Analysis, Planning and Control* and others. • MACROPÆDIA: *Marketing and Merchandising (in part)*

Kovel, Ralph and Terry. Authors; Publishers. Authors of *Kovels' Antiques & Collectibles Price List 1995.* • AUCTIONS AND COLLECTIONS: *Antiques and Collectibles*

Krengel, Janet. Senior Economist, Kleinwort Benson Securities. • WORLD AFFAIRS: *Paraguay; Uruguay*

Kroll, Thomas E. Lecturer, Roosevelt University and Northwestern University; President, Thomas Kroll Associates. Author of *Introduction to Data Processing; C Language Programming.* • BUSINESS AND INDUSTRY REVIEW: *Microelectronics; Telecommunications*

Kuhn, Howard A. Vice President; Chief Technical Officer, Concurrent Technologies Corporation. Author of *Powder Forging; Powder Processing.* • BUSINESS AND INDUSTRY REVIEW: *Metals and Materials:* Metalworking

Kuptsch, Christiane. Research Officer, ISSA. • SOCIAL PROTECTION (international)

Kushnick, Louis. Senior Lecturer, Department of American Studies, University of Manchester, England. • POPULATIONS AND POPULATION MOVEMENTS: *International Migration;* RACE AND ETHNIC RELATIONS

Lamb, Kevin M. Special Projects Writer, *Dayton Daily News.* Author of *Quarterbacks, Nickelbacks & Other Loose Change.* • SPORTS AND GAMES: *Football:* Canadian, U.S.

Laqueur, Walter. Chairman, International Research Council, Center for Strategic & International Studies. Author of *Europe in Our Time* and others. • WORLD AFFAIRS: *Introduction*

Larsson, Gerd. Japan Correspondent, *Dagens Industri.* • BIOGRAPHIES *(in part)*

Laskey, Elizabeth. Formerly Senior Copy Editor, Encyclopædia Britannica. • BIOGRAPHIES *(in part)*

Last, Geoffrey C. Formerly Adviser, Imperial Ethiopian Ministry of Education and Fine Arts. • MACROPÆDIA: *Eastern Africa (in part)*

Latham, Arthur. Associate Editor, Encyclopædia Britannica. • CHRONOLOGY OF 1994

Lavallée, H.-Claude. Director, Pulp and Paper Research Centre, University of Quebec at Trois-Rivières. • BUSINESS AND INDUSTRY REVIEW: *Wood Products:* Paper

Lawler, Nancy Ellen. Professor of Economics, Oakton Community College. Author of *Soldiers of Misfortune* and others. • WORLD AFFAIRS: *Benin; Burkina Faso; Cameroon; Central African Republic; Congo; Côte d'Ivoire; Gabon; Guinea; Mali; Mauritania; Niger; Senegal; Togo*

Legassick, Martin. Professor, History Department, University of the Western Cape. • BIOGRAPHIES *(in part);* WORLD AFFAIRS: *Namibia; South Africa; South Africa:* Sidebar

Legum, Colin. Formerly Associate Editor, *The Observer;* Consultant Editor, *Africa Contemporary Record;* Editor, *Third World Reports.* Author of more than 20 books, mainly on Africa. • WORLD AFFAIRS: *Spotlight:* Africa's Second Liberation

Lennox-Kerr, Peter. Editor, *High Performance Textiles* and *OE Report & Fibre News;* European Editor, *Textile World.* Author of *World Fibres Book.* • BUSINESS AND INDUSTRY REVIEW: *Textiles:* Introduction; Cotton; Man-made Fibres

Lerner, Dietlind. Journalist. Author of television documentaries on German culture and politics. • BIOGRAPHIES *(in part)*

Levine, Beth S. Freelance Writer. Author of *Divorce: Young People Caught in the Middle* and others. • PUBLISHING: *Books* (U.S.)

Levine, Steven I. Director, Center for Slavic, Eurasian, and East European Studies, University of North Carolina. Author of *Anvil of Victory: The Communist Revolution in Manchuria* and others. • BIOGRAPHIES *(in part);* WORLD AFFAIRS: *China; Taiwan*

Litsky, Frank. Sportswriter, *New York Times.* • SPORTS AND GAMES: *Ice Hockey:* North America

Litweiler, John. Jazz Critic; Contributor to *Down Beat, Chicago Tribune,* and others. Author of *Ornette Coleman: A Harmolodic Life.* • BIOGRAPHIES *(in part);* MUSIC: *Jazz*

Logan, Robert G. Sportswriter, *Daily Herald* (Arlington Heights, Ill.). Author of *Cubs Win!* and others. • SPORTS AND GAMES: *Basketball* (U.S.)

Longmore, Andrew. Freelance Sportswriter, *The Times;* formerly Assistant Editor, *The Cricketer.* • BIOGRAPHIES *(in part);* SPORTS AND GAMES: *Cricket; Introduction*

Luling, Virginia R. Social Anthropologist. • WORLD AFFAIRS: *Somalia*

McCauley, Martin. Senior Lecturer in Politics, School of Slavonic and East European Studies, University of London. • WORLD AFFAIRS: *Commonwealth of Independent States; Russia*

Macdonald, Barrie. Professor of History, Massey University. • WORLD AFFAIRS: *Spotlight:* The South Pacific Forum; *Dependent States (Pacific); Fiji; Kiribati; Marshall Islands; Micronesia, Federated States of; Solomon Islands; Tonga; Tuvalu; Vanuatu; Western Samoa*

McElroy, John. Editor-in-Chief, *Automotive Industries.* • BUSINESS AND INDUSTRY REVIEW: *Automobiles*

McGregor, Alan. Freelance Contributor, *The Times; The Lancet;* Swiss Radio International; CBS Radio. • WORLD AFFAIRS: *Switzerland*

McLachlan, Keith S. Professor, School of Oriental and African Studies, University of London. Author of *Boundaries of Modern Iran.* • WORLD AFFAIRS: *Iran*

Mallett, H.M.F. Editor, *Wool Record Weekly Market Report.* • BUSINESS AND INDUSTRY REVIEW: *Textiles:* Wool

Mango, Andrew. Foreign Affairs Analyst. • WORLD AFFAIRS: *Turkey*

Markakis, John. Professor of African Studies, University of Crete. Author of *Ethiopia: Anatomy of a Traditional Polity* and others. • MACROPÆDIA: *Eastern Africa (in part)*

Marples, David R. Associate Professor of History, University of Alberta. Author of *Stalinism in Ukraine* and others. • BIOGRAPHIES (in part); WORLD AFFAIRS: *Belarus; Ukraine*

Martin, Marvin. Freelance Writer. • BIOGRAPHIES (in part)

Mathews, John H. Copy Editor, Encyclopædia Britannica. • BIOGRAPHIES (in part)

Matthíasson, Björn. Economist, Ministry of Finance, Iceland. • WORLD AFFAIRS: *Iceland*

Maunder, Michael. Head of Conservation Unit, Living Collections Department, Royal Botanic Gardens, Kew. • BOTANICAL GARDENS AND ZOOS: *Botanical Gardens*

Mazie, David M. Staff Writer, *Reader's Digest;* Freelance Writer. • SOCIAL PROTECTION (U.S.)

Mermel, T.W. Consultant; formerly Chairman, Committee on World Register of Dams, International Commission on Large Dams. • ENGINEERING PROJECTS: *Dams*

Michael, Tom. Writer, Encyclopædia Britannica. • BIOGRAPHIES (in part)

Millikin, Sandra. Architectural Historian. • ART: *Art Exhibitions*

Miwa, Takuji. Associate Professor, Daito College of Medical Technology; Director, International Health Evaluation Association. • BIOGRAPHIES (in part)

Modiano, Mario. Formerly Athens Correspondent, *The Times.* • WORLD AFFAIRS: *Greece*

Morris, Jacqui M. Editor, *Oryx.* • ENVIRONMENT: *Wildlife Conservation*

Morrison, Donald. Editor, *Time Asia.* • WORLD AFFAIRS: *Spotlight:* East Asia and the Transition in North Korea

Moutet, Anne-Elisabeth. Journalist, *The European.* • BIOGRAPHIES (in part); WORLD AFFAIRS: *France*

Mullin, John J. Analyst, Smith Barney. Author of *Emerging Equity Markets in the Global Economy.* • SPECIAL REPORT: *Emerging Equity Markets*

Munns, Thomas E. Senior Program Officer, National Materials Advisory Board, National Research Council. • BUSINESS AND INDUSTRY REVIEW: *Metals and Materials: Advanced Composites (in part)*

Nagy, Joseph L. Senior Editor, *Asiaweek.* • WORLD AFFAIRS: *Korea, Democratic People's Republic of; Korea, Republic of*

Naylor, Ernest. Lloyd Roberts Professor of Marine Zoology, University College of North Wales. • LIFE SCIENCES: *Marine Biology*

Neher, Stephen. Assistant Editor, Encyclopædia Britannica. • WORLD AFFAIRS: *Palau; Political Parties (in part)*

Neusner, Noam. Reporter, *Tampa Tribune.* Coauthor of *To Grow in Wisdom: An Anthology of Abraham J. Heschel.* • RELIGION: *Judaism*

Newby, Donald J. Bowls Correspondent, *Daily Telegraph;* formerly Editor, *World Bowls.* Author of various bowls publications. • SPORTS AND GAMES: *Lawn Bowls*

Niesz, Dale E. Director, Center for Ceramic Research, Rutgers University. • BUSINESS AND INDUSTRY REVIEW: *Ceramics*

Nitecki, Matthew H. Curator, Fossil Invertebrates, Field Museum of Natural History. Author of *Evolutionary Ethics; Evolutionary Innovations.* • LIFE SCIENCES: *Paleontology*

Norman, Geraldine. Art Market Correspondent, *The Independent.* Author of *Nineteenth Century Painters and Painting;* Coauthor of *The Fake's Progress.* • AUCTIONS AND COLLECTIONS: *Art Auctions and Sales; Books;* AUCTIONS AND COLLECTIONS: Sidebar

Nugent, Ann. Editor, *Dance Now;* Dance Critic, *The Stage.* Author of *Swan Lake: Stories of the Ballets.* • DANCE: Europe

O'Donoghue, Michael. Lecturer in Gemmology, London Guildhall University. • BUSINESS AND INDUSTRY REVIEW: *Gemstones*

Ogden, Shepherd. President, The Cook's Garden. Author of *Step by Step Organic Vegetable Gardening* and others. • GARDENING (international); GARDENING: Sidebar

Olson, Kay Melchisedech. Executive Editor, *Flower & Garden.* • GARDENING (U.S.)

Orr, Jay. Entertainment Writer, *Nashville Banner.* • MUSIC: *Popular* (U.S.)

Osborne, K.L. Editor, *British Rowing Almanack.* Author of *Boat Racing in Britain, 1715–1975.* • SPORTS AND GAMES: *Rowing*

Palmer, John. European Editor, *The Guardian.* • WORLD AFFAIRS: *European Union*

Parker, Sandy. Publisher, newsletter on fur industry; Copublisher, *Fur World.* • BUSINESS AND INDUSTRY REVIEW: *Apparel:* Furs

Parming, Tönu. President, Estonian Publishing Co. Author of *A Case Study of a Soviet Republic: The Estonian SSR.* • WORLD AFFAIRS: *Estonia*

Parsons, James J. Professor of Geography, University of California, Berkeley. Author of *Antioqueño Colonization in Western Colombia* and others. • MACROPÆDIA: *South America (in part)*

Paul, Charles Robert, Jr. Consultant, U.S. Olympic Committee. • SPORTS AND GAMES: *Gymnastics, Weight Lifting*

Penfold, Robin C. Freelance Writer on industrial topics. • BUSINESS AND INDUSTRY REVIEW: *Plastics*

Perlinska, Agnieszka. Ph.D. in Comparative Literature, New York University. • LITERATURE: *Eastern European (in part); Russian (in part)*

Pertile, Lino. Professor of Italian, University of Edinburgh. • LITERATURE: *Italian*

Petherick, Karin. Reader Emeritus in Swedish, University of London. • LITERATURE: *Swedish*

Pfeffer, Irving. Attorney. Author of *The Financing of Small Business.* • ECONOMIC AFFAIRS: *Stock Exchanges* (North America)

Pinfold, Geoffrey M. Director, NCL Stewart Scott. Author of *Reinforced Concrete Chimneys and Towers.* • ENGINEERING PROJECTS: *Buildings*

Poirié, François. Writer and Critic. Author of *La Passade légendaire; Ils dansent.* • LITERATURE: *French:* France

Polonsky, Naomi Bernards. Freelance Writer; Freelance Editor. • BIOGRAPHIES (in part)

Prasad, H.Y. Sharada. Formerly Information Adviser to the Prime Minister of India. • WORLD AFFAIRS: *India*

Prince, Greg W. Senior Editor, *Beverage World.* • BUSINESS AND INDUSTRY REVIEW: *Beverages:* Beer; Soft Drinks; Spirits

Rapp, Susan. Freelance Editor. • BIOGRAPHIES (in part)

Réamonn, Páraic. Communications Director, World Alliance of Reformed Churches. • RELIGION: *Reformed, Presbyterian, and Congregational Churches*

Rebelo, L.S. Reader Emeritus; Visiting Professor, Department of Portuguese Studies, King's College, University of London. • LITERATURE: *Portuguese:* Portugal

Reed, Arthur. Senior Editor, Europe, *Air Transport World.* Author of *Britain's Aircraft Industry;* Coauthor of *RAE Farnborough.* • TRANSPORTATION: *Aviation*

Reid, Philip D. Louise C. Harrington Professor of Biological Sciences, Smith College. • LIFE SCIENCES: *Botany*

Renwick, David. Editorial Director, *Daily News* (Trinidad). • WORLD AFFAIRS: *Spotlight:* The New Caribbean Basin Identity; *Antigua and Barbuda; Bahamas, The; Barbados; Dependent States (Caribbean and Bermuda); Dominica; Grenada; Guyana; Jamaica; Saint Kitts and Nevis; Saint Lucia; Saint Vincent and the Grenadines; Trinidad and Tobago*

Restak, Richard. Clinical Professor of Neurology, George Washington University Medical School. Author of *The Modular Brain.* • SPECIAL REPORT: *Prozac*

Reynaud, Bérénice. Faculty Member, California Institute of the Arts. • BIOGRAPHIES (in part)

Roach, Suzanne. Director, AIUSA Women's Human Rights Program. • SOCIAL PROTECTION: Sidebar

Roberts, John. Tennis Correspondent, *The Independent.* Author of *The Team That Wouldn't Die.* • SPORTS AND GAMES: *Tennis*

Robinson, David. Film Critic and Historian. Author of *A History of World Cinema; Chaplin: His Life and Art.* • SPECIAL REPORT: *The Hollywood Conquest;* MOTION PICTURES: General

Roby, Anne. Freelance Writer and Editor. • WORLD AFFAIRS: *Andorra; Liechtenstein; Luxembourg; Monaco*

Rocky, Marilyn E. Executive Director, CHILDHOPE. • SPECIAL REPORT: *Street Children*

Rollin, Jack. Association Football Columnist, *Sunday Telegraph.* Editor, *Rothmans Football Yearbook.* Author of *World Cup 1930–1990* and others. • BIOGRAPHIES (in part); SPORTS AND GAMES: *Football:* Association (Soccer); *Football:* Sidebar

Rusch, William G. Director, Department for Ecumenical Affairs, ELCA. Author of *Reception: An Ecumenical Opportunity.* • RELIGION: *Lutheran Communion*

Russell, Cristine. Freelance Science Writer and Special Health Correspondent, *The Washington Post.* • HEALTH AND DISEASE: *Medicine* (U.S.)

Russell, George. Senior Editor, *Time International.* Author of *Eyewitness: A History of Photojournalism.* • WORLD AFFAIRS: *United States*

Rutherford, Andrew. Reader, Faculty of Law, University of Southampton. Author of *Criminal Justice and the Pursuit of Decency* and others. • CRIME, LAW ENFORCEMENT, AND PENOLOGY: *Prisons and Penology*

Saeki, Shoichi. Professor Emeritus, Tokyo University. Author of *Japanese Autobiographies.* • LITERATURE: *Japanese*

Salisbury, Jonathan M. Publisher, *World Toy News.* • BUSINESS AND INDUSTRY REVIEW: *Games and Toys*

Saludo, Ricardo L. Senior Editor, *Asiaweek.* • BIOGRAPHIES (in part); WORLD AFFAIRS: *Indonesia; Vietnam*

Sanders, Alan J.K. Lecturer in Mongolian Studies, School of Oriental and African Studies, University of London. Author of *Mongolia: Politics, Economics and Society.* • WORLD AFFAIRS: *Mongolia*

Sarahete, Yrjö. General Secretary, Fédération Internationale des Quilleurs. • SPORTS AND GAMES: *Bowling:* World Tenpins

Sarmiento, Sergio. Editor in Chief, Encyclopædia Britannica Publishers, Inc. (Latin America). • SPORTS AND GAMES: *Baseball:* Latin America; *Football:* Association (Soccer): Latin America

Schafrik, Robert E. Director, National Materials Advisory Board, National Research Council. • BUSINESS AND INDUSTRY REVIEW: *Metals and Materials:* Advanced Composites (in part)

Scherer, Allan D. Director, United States Polo Association; Editor, *Polo Newsletter.* • SPORTS AND GAMES: *Equestrian Sports:* Polo

Schneider, Johanna. Assistant Editor, *Amateur Wrestling News.* • SPORTS AND GAMES: *Wrestling*

Schoenfield, Albert. Formerly Member, U.S. Swimming Olympic International Committee. Formerly Publisher, *Swimming World.* Honouree, International Swimming Hall of Fame. Author of *The Saga of the Exterminators Squadron.* • SPORTS AND GAMES: *Swimming*

Schöpflin, George. Lecturer in East European Political Institutions, London School of Economics and School of Slavonic and East European Studies, University of London. • WORLD AFFAIRS: *Spotlight:* Perils of Postcommunism in Eastern Europe; *Czech Republic; Hungary; Slovakia*

Schultz, Alarich R. Professor of Botany, Federal University of Rio Grande do Sul. Author of *Estudo Prático da Botânica Geral.* • MACROPÆDIA: *South America (in part)*

Sego, Steve. Formerly Director, Radio Free Afghanistan; Freelance Writer. • WORLD AFFAIRS: *Afghanistan*

Shackleford, Peter. Chief of Environment, Planning, and Finance, World Tourism Organization. • BUSINESS AND INDUSTRY REVIEW: *Tourism*

Sheahan, John. Professor Emeritus of Economics, Williams College. Author of *Patterns of Development in Latin America: Poverty, Repression, and Economic Strategy.* • WORLD AFFAIRS: *Spotlight:* Latin America's New Economic Strategy

Shelley, Andrew. Events Manager, Squash Rackets Association (England). • SPORTS AND GAMES: *Squash Rackets*

Shepherd, Melinda C. Associate Editor, Encyclopædia Britannica. • SPECIAL REPORT: *The XVII Olympic Winter Games;* OBITUARIES *(in part);* SPORTING RECORD; WORLD AFFAIRS: *Dependent States* (Europe and the Atlantic); *Political Parties (in part)*

Sherry, Paul H. President, United Church of Christ. • RELIGION: *United Church of Christ*

Smith, Donald. Editor, *Rubber World.* • BUSINESS AND INDUSTRY REVIEW: *Rubber*

Smith, Gregory O. Dean of Academic Affairs, American University of Rome. • WORLD AFFAIRS: *San Marino; Vatican City State*

Smith, Peter N. Information Officer, British Glass. • BUSINESS AND INDUSTRY REVIEW: *Glass*

Smith, Reuben W. Professor of History, University of the Pacific. • RELIGION: *Islam*

Spangenberg, N. Earl. Professor, College of Natural Resources, University of Wisconsin at Stevens Point. Editor, *HYDATA—News and Views.* • EARTH SCIENCES: *Hydrology*

Sparks, Karen J. Senior Editor, Encyclopædia Britannica. • BUSINESS AND INDUSTRY REVIEW: *Apparel:* Clothing; Footwear and Leather Goods; *Home Furnishings:* Housewares; DISASTERS; OBITUARIES *(in part)*

Spencer, Peter L. Editor, *Consumer's Research.* • CONSUMER AFFAIRS (U.S.)

Starke, Edgar A., Jr. Professor, University of Virginia. • BUSINESS AND INDUSTRY REVIEW: *Metals and Materials:* Light Metals

Stern, Irwin. Senior Lecturer in Portuguese, Columbia University. • LITERATURE: *Portuguese:* Brazil

Stewart, Ian. Professor of Mathematics, University of Warwick. Author of *Does God Play Dice?; The Collapse of Chaos.* • MATHEMATICS

Støverud, Torbjørn. Honorary Research Fellow, University College, London. • LITERATURE: *Norwegian*

Sullivan, H. Patrick. Dean Emeritus of the College and Professor of Religion, Vassar College. • RELIGION: *Hinduism*

Summerhill, Edward M. Part-Time Staff Member, Reuters; Freelance Writer, Finnish News Agency. • WORLD AFFAIRS: *Finland*

Sumner, David E. Columnist; Contributor to Episcopal Church periodicals. Author of *The Episcopal Church's History: 1945–1985.* • RELIGION: *Anglican Communion*

Susser, Leslie D. Diplomatic Correspondent, *The Jerusalem Report.* • WORLD AFFAIRS: *Israel*

Suzuki, Toshihiko. Senior Editor, Dobunshoin International. • SPORTS AND GAMES: *Baseball:* Japan

Swan, Russ. Editor, *World Highways.* • ENGINEERING PROJECTS: *Roads*

Swift, Richard N. Professor Emeritus of Politics, New York University. • WORLD AFFAIRS: *Multinational and Regional Organizations; United Nations*

Synan, Vinson. Dean, School of Divinity, Regent University. Author of *In the Latter Days; Pentecostal Churches.* • RELIGION: *Pentecostal Churches*

Taishoff, Lawrence B. Chairman, *Broadcasting and Cable;* Adviser, Cahners Consumer/ Entertainment Publishing Division. • TELEVISION AND RADIO (U.S. *in part); Amateur Radio (in part)*

Tateishi, Kay K. Freelance Writer and Translator, Tokyo. • BIOGRAPHIES *(in part)*

Taylor, Thomas F. General Secretary, Friends World Committee for Consultation. Formerly Editor, *Friends World News.* • RELIGION: *Religious Society of Friends*

Thomas, Robert Murray. Professor Emeritus of Education and Head, Program in International Education, University of California at Santa Barbara. Author of *International Comparative Education* and others. • EDUCATION (international)

Tugend, Alina. Press Officer, International Organisation of Consumers Unions. • CONSUMER AFFAIRS (international)

Turner, Darrell J. Writer on Religion; Formerly Editor and Writer, Religious News Service. • BIOGRAPHIES *(in part);* RELIGION: *Introduction*

UNHCR. The Office of the United Nations High Commissioner for Refugees. • POPULATIONS AND POPULATION MOVEMENTS: *Refugees*

Ustinov, Peter. Actor, Director, Author, Playwright, Commentator, and Chancellor of Durham University. • COMMENTARY: *Toward the Age of Common Sense*

Utt, Roger L. Editor, *Puerta del Sol;* formerly Assistant Professor of Spanish, Department of Romance Languages and Literatures, University of Chicago. • LITERATURE: *Spanish:* Spain

Venzke, Bruce H. Associate Editor, *Pool & Billiard Magazine.* Member, Statistics and Records Committee, Billiard Congress of America; Past President, Billiard Congress of Wisconsin. • SPORTS AND GAMES: *Billiard Games:* Carom Billiards; Pocket Billiards

Verdi, Robert William. Sports Columnist, *Chicago Tribune.* Author of *Once a Dodger, Always a Bum* and others. • SPORTS AND GAMES: *Baseball:* Little League; U.S.; *Baseball:* Sidebar

Wallenfeldt, Jeff. Copy Editor, Encyclopædia Britannica. • BIOGRAPHIES *(in part);* MUSIC: Sidebar

Wallis, Shani. Independent Technical Journalist. • ENGINEERING PROJECTS: *Tunnels*

Walters, Jonathan S. Assistant Professor of Religion, Whitman College. • RELIGION: *Buddhism*

Wanninger, Richard S. Director of External Affairs, Colorado Sports Council. • SPORTS AND GAMES: *Volleyball*

Warner, Edward S. Editor, *FCC Report,* Telecom Publishing Group. • INFORMATION PROCESSING AND INFORMATION SYSTEMS

Warren, J. Robert. Editor, Asia-Pacific Report, *Chemical Marketing Reporter.* • BUSINESS AND INDUSTRY REVIEW: *Chemicals*

Way, Diane Lois. Historical Researcher. • BIOGRAPHIES *(in part)*

Westberg, M. Victor. Manager, Committees on Publication, The First Church of Christ, Scientist, Boston. • RELIGION: *Church of Christ, Scientist*

Whelan, John. Editor, Waters Information Services. • WORLD AFFAIRS: *Bahrain; Egypt; Iraq; Jordan; Kuwait; Lebanon; Oman; Qatar; Saudi Arabia; Syria; United Arab Emirates; Yemen*

Whitney, Barbara. Copy Supervisor, Encyclopædia Britannica. • BIOGRAPHIES *(in part);* ENVIRONMENT: Sidebar

Wilkinson, John R. Sportswriter, Coventry Newspapers. • SPORTS AND GAMES: *Cycling*

Williams, Michael. Golf Correspondent, *Daily Telegraph.* Author of *Official History of the Ryder Cup.* • SPORTS AND GAMES: *Golf*

Williams, Raymond Leslie. Professor of Spanish, University of Colorado. Author of *The Colombian Novel, 1844–1987.* • LITERATURE: *Spanish:* Latin America

Willis, Clifford L. Director of News and Information, Office of Communication, Christian Church (Disciples of Christ). • RELIGION: *Christian Church (Disciples of Christ)*

Wilson, Derek. Correspondent, BBC, Rome. • WORLD AFFAIRS: *Italy*

Wilson, Michael. Freelance Aviation Writer and Consultant; Managing Editor, *Testimony.* • BUSINESS AND INDUSTRY REVIEW: *Aerospace*

Woodrow, Robert. Assistant Managing Editor, *Asiaweek.* • WORLD AFFAIRS: *Laos; Thailand*

Woods, Elizabeth. Writer. Author of *If Only Things Were Different (I): A Model for a Sustainable Society; Bird Salad;* and others. • LITERATURE: *English:* Canada

Woods, Michael. Science Editor, *Toledo Blade.* Author of *Science in Antarctica.* • CHEMISTRY; NOBEL PRIZES *(in part)*

Woodward, Berton. Assistant Managing Editor, *Asiaweek.* • WORLD AFFAIRS: *Spotlight:* Asian Values; *Brunei; Dependent States (East Asia); Singapore*

Woollen, Anthony. Formerly Editor, *Food Manufacture.* Editor, *Food Industries Manual.* • AGRICULTURE AND FOOD SUPPLIES: *Food Processing*

Wright, Andrew G. Associate Editor, *Engineering News-Record.* • BUSINESS AND INDUSTRY REVIEW: *Building and Construction*

Wyllie, Peter John. Professor, Division of Geological and Planetary Sciences, California Institute of Technology. Author of *The Dynamic Earth; The Way the Earth Works.* • EARTH SCIENCES: *Geology and Geochemistry*

Wyllie, Robert J.M. Editor, *Engineering & Mining Journal.* • ENERGY: *Coal*

Yapko, Michael D. Clinical Psychologist, private practice. Author of *Essentials of Clinical Hypnosis* and others. • SPECIAL REPORT: *Repressed Memories*

Young, M. Norvel. Chancellor Emeritus, Pepperdine University. Author of *Preachers of Today.* • RELIGION: *Churches of Christ*

Zanga, Louis. Analyst, Radio Free Europe/ Radio Liberty Research Institute. • WORLD AFFAIRS: *Albania*

1995
Britannica
World Data

Encyclopædia Britannica, Inc.
Chicago
Auckland/London/Madrid/Manila/Paris/Rome
Seoul/Sydney/Tokyo/Toronto

CONTENTS

539

INTRODUCTION

Britannica World Data provides a statistical portrait of some 216 countries and dependencies of the world, at a level appropriate to the size and importance of each. It contains 194 country statements (the "Nations of the World" section), ranging in length from one to four pages, and permits, in the 24 major thematic tables (the "Comparative National Statistics" section), simultaneous comparisons among all of these larger countries and 22 additional smaller dependent states.

Updated annually, *Britannica World Data* can be consulted as a separate work of reference developing a particular body of subject matter, but it is particularly intended as direct, structured support for many of Britannica's other reference works—encyclopaedias, yearbooks, atlases—at a level of detail that their editorial style or design do not permit.

Like the textual, graphic, or cartographic modes of expression of these other products, statistics possess their own inherent editorial virtues and weaknesses. Two principal goals in the creation of *Britannica World Data* were up-to-dateness and comparability, each possible to maximize separately, but not always possible to combine. If, for example, research on some subject is completed during a particular year (x), figures may be available for 100 countries for the preceding year ($x - 1$), for 140 countries for the year before that ($x - 2$), and for 180 countries for the year before that ($x - 3$).

Which year should be the basis of a thematic compilation for 220 countries so as to give the best combination of up-to-dateness and comparability? And, should $x - 1$ be adopted for the thematic table, ought up-to-dateness in the country table (for which year x is already available) be sacrificed for agreement with the thematic table? In general, the editors have opted for maximum up-to-dateness in the country statistical boxes and maximum comparability in the thematic tables, so as to take the best advantage of recent information.

Comparability, however, also resides in the meaning of the numbers compiled, which may differ greatly from country to country. The headnotes to the thematic tables explain many of these definitional problems; the Glossary serves the same purpose for the country statistical pages. Published data do not always provide the researcher or editor with a neat, unambiguous choice between a datum compiled on two different bases (say, railroad track length, or route length), one of which is wanted and the other not. More often a choice must be made among a variety of official, private, and external intergovernmental (UN, FAO, IMF) sources, each reporting its best data but each representing a set of problems: (1) of methodological variance from (or among) international conventions; (2) of analytical completeness (data for a single year may, successively, be projected [based on 10 months' data], preliminary [for 12 months], final, revised or adjusted, etc.); (3) of time frame, or accounting interval (data may represent a full Gregorian calendar year [preferred], a fiscal year, an Islamic or other national or religious year, a multiyear period or average [when a one-year statement would contain unrepresentative results]); (4) of continuity with previous data; and the like. Finally, published data on a particular subject may be complete and final but impossible to summarize in a simple manner. The education system of a single country may include, for example, public and private sectors; local, state, or national systems; varying grades, tracks, or forms within a single system; or opportunities for double-counting or fractional counting of a student, teacher, or institution. When no recent official data exist, the tables may show unofficial estimates, a range (of published opinion), analogous data, or no data at all. For certain subjects, especially population, the editors have prepared their own estimates.

The entrance of more than a score of newly independent countries onto the world stage since 1990 has displaced a number of smaller dependent states for which pages had been provided in past editions of *Britannica World Data*. These new countries, by virtue of their population, economic importance, and independent status, must, naturally, be assigned coverage commensurate with their importance, but, their present status being only recently acquired, most have not yet been assimilated by the information systems of international organizations like the UN. Thus, certain information provided must remain in the form published by the country itself, rather than the more-familiar international statistical presentations available for older states.

The published basis of the information compiled is the statistical collections of Encyclopædia Britannica, Inc., some of the principal elements of which are enumerated in the Bibliography. The information contained in those works is supplemented by unpublished data received in correspondence from the countries concerned. Usual holdings for a country with a well-developed statistical program may include any of the following kinds of documents: the national statistical abstract; the constitution; the most recent censuses of population; periodic or occasional reports on vital statistics, social indicators, agriculture, mining, labour, manufacturing, domestic and foreign trade, finance and banking, transportation, and communications.

The great majority of the social, economic, and financial data contained in this work should not be interpreted in isolation. Interpretive text of long perspective, such as that of the *Encyclopædia Britannica* itself; political, geographic, and topical maps, such as those in the *Britannica Atlas;* and recent analysis of political events and economic trends, such as that contained in the articles of the *Book of the Year,* will all help to supply balance, physical framework, and analytic focus that numbers alone cannot provide. By the same token, study of those sources will be made more concrete by use of *Britannica World Data* to supply up-to-date geographic, demographic, and economic data to illuminate the methodology of those works.

GLOSSARY

A number of terms that are used to classify and report data in the "Nations of the World" section require some explanation.

Those italicized terms that are used regularly in the country compilations to introduce specific categories of information (*e.g., birth rate, budget*) appear in this glossary in italic boldface type, followed by a description of the precise kind of information being offered and how it has been edited and presented.

All other terms are printed here in roman boldface type. Many terms have quite specific meanings in statistical reporting, and they are so defined here. Other terms have less specific application as they are used by different countries or organizations. Data in the country compilations based on definitions markedly different from those below will usually be footnoted.

Terms that appear in small capitals in certain definitions are themselves defined at their respective alphabetical locations.

Terms whose definitions are marked by an asterisk (*) refer to data supplied only in the larger two- to four-page country compilations.

access to services, a group of measures indicating a population's level of access to public services, including electrical power, treated public drinking water, sewage removal, and fire protection.*

activity rate, *see* participation/activity rates.

age breakdown, the distribution of a given population by age, usually reported here as percentages of total population in 15-year age brackets. When substantial numbers of persons do not know, or state, their exact age, distributions may not total 100.0%.

area, the total surface area of a country or its administrative subdivisions, including both land and inland (nontidal) water area. Land area is usually calculated from "mean low water" on a "plane table," or flat, basis.

area and population, a tabulation usually including the first-order administrative subdivisions of the country (such as the states of the United States), with capital (headquarters, or administrative seat), area, and population. When these subdivisions are especially numerous or, occasionally, nonexistent, a planning, electoral, census, or other nonadministrative scheme of regional subdivisions has been substituted.

associated state, *see* state.

atheist, in statements of religious affiliation, one who professes active opposition to religion; "nonreligious" refers to those professing only no religion, nonbelief, or doubt.

balance of payments, a financial statement for a country for a given period showing the balance among: (1) transactions in goods, services, and income between that country and the rest of the world, (2) changes in ownership or valuation of that country's monetary gold, SPECIAL DRAWING RIGHTS, and claims on and liabilities to the rest of the world, and (3) unrequited transfers and counterpart entries needed (in an accounting sense) to balance transactions and changes among any of the foregoing types of exchange that are not mutually offsetting. The *System of National Accounts* (SNA, published under the joint auspices of the UN, IMF, OECD, EEC, and World Bank) provides

a framework for international comparability in classifying such transactions, but detail of local law as to what constitutes a transaction, the basis of its valuation, and the size of a transaction visible to fiscal authorities all result in differences in the meaning of a particular national statement.*

balance of trade, the net value of all international goods trade of a country, usually excluding reexports (goods received only for transshipment), and the percentage that this net represents of total trade.

Balance of trade refers only to the "visible" international trade of goods as recorded by customs authorities and is thus a segment of a country's BALANCE OF PAYMENTS, which takes all visible and invisible trade with other countries into account. (Invisible trade refers to imports and exports of money, financial instruments, and services such as transport, tourism, and insurance.) A country has a favourable balance of trade when the value of exports exceeds that of imports.

barrel (bbl), a unit of liquid measure. The barrel conventionally used for reporting crude petroleum and petroleum products is equal to 42 U.S. gallons, or 159 litres. The number of barrels of crude petroleum per metric ton, ranging typically from 6.20 to 8.13, depends upon the specific gravity of the petroleum. The world average is roughly 7.33 barrels per ton.

birth rate, the number of live births annually per 1,000 of midyear population. Birth rates for individual countries may be compared with the estimated world annual average of 26.0 births per 1,000 population between 1990 and 1995.

budget, the annual receipts and expenditures—of a central government for its activities only;

Abbreviations

Measurements

cu m	cubic metre(s)
kg	kilogram(s)
km	kilometre(s)
kW	kilowatt(s)
kW-hr	kilowatt-hour(s)
metric ton-km	metric ton-kilometre(s)
mi	mile(s)
passenger-km	passenger-kilometre(s)
passenger-mi	passenger-mile(s)
short ton-mi	short ton-mile(s)
sq km	square kilometre(s)
sq m	square metre(s)
sq mi	square mile(s)
troy oz	troy ounce(s)
yr	year(s)

Political Units and International Organizations

CACM	Central American Common Market
Caricom	Caribbean Community and Common Market
CFA	Communauté Financière Africaine
CFP	Comptoirs Françaises du Pacifique
CIS	Commonwealth of Independent States
CUSA	Customs Union of Southern Africa
E.Ger.	East Germany
EEC	European Economic Community
EU	European Union
FAO	United Nations Food and Agriculture Organization
IMF	International Monetary Fund
OECS	Organization of Eastern Caribbean States
U.A.E.	United Arab Emirates
U.K.	United Kingdom
U.S.	United States
U.S.S.R.	Union of Soviet Socialist Republics
W.Ger.	West Germany

Months

Jan.	January	Oct.	October
Feb.	February	Nov.	November
Aug.	August	Dec.	December
Sept.	September		

Miscellaneous

AIDS	Acquired Immune Deficiency Syndrome
avg.	average
c.i.f.	cost, insurance, and freight
commun.	communications
CPI	consumer price index
est.	estimate(d)
excl.	excluding
f.o.b.	free on board
GDP	gross domestic product
GNP	gross national product
govt.	government
incl.	including
mo.	month(s)
n.a.	not available (in text)
n.e.s.	not elsewhere specified
NMP	net material product
no.	number
pl.	plural
pos.	position
pub. admin.	public administration
PVC	Polyvinyl Chloride
SDR	Special Drawing Right
SITC	Standard International Trade Classification
svcs.	services
teacher tr.	teacher training
transp.	transportation
voc.	vocational
$	dollar (of any currency area)
£	pound (of any currency area)
...	not available (in tables)
—	none, less than half the smallest unit shown, or not applicable (in tables)

541

does not include state, provincial, or local governments or semipublic (parastatal, quasi-nongovernmental) corporations unless otherwise specified. Figures for budgets are limited to ordinary (recurrent) receipts and expenditures, wherever possible, and exclude capital expenditures—*i.e.*, funds for development and other special projects originating as foreign-aid grants or loans.

When both a recurrent and a capital budget exist for a single country, the former is the budget funded entirely from national resources (taxes, duties, excises, etc.) that would recur (be generated by economic activity) every year. It funds the most basic governmental services, those least able to suffer interruption. The capital budget is usually funded by external aid and may change its size considerably from year to year.

capital, usually, the actual seat of government and administration of a state. When more than one capital exists, each is identified by kind; when interim arrangements exist during the creation or movement of a national capital, the de facto situation is described.

Anomalous cases are annotated, such as those in which (1) the de jure designation under the country's laws differs from actual local practice (*e.g.*, Benin's designation of one capital in constitutional law, but another in actual practice), (2) international recognition does not validate a country's claim (as with the proclamation by Israel of a capital on territory not fully recognized as part of Israel), or (3) both a state and a capital have been proclaimed on territory recognized as part of another state (as with the Turkish Republic of Northern Cyprus).

capital budget, *see* budget.

causes of death, as defined by the World Health Organization, "the disease or injury which initiated the train of morbid events leading directly to death, or the circumstances of accident or violence which produced the fatal injury." This principle, the "underlying cause of death," is the basis of the medical judgment as to cause; the statistical classification system according to which these causes are grouped and named is the *International List of Causes of Death,* the latest revision of which is the Tenth. Reporting is usually in terms of events per 100,000 population. When data on actual causes of death are unavailable, information on morbidity, or illness rate, usually given as reported cases per 100,000 of infectious diseases (notifiable to WHO as a matter of international agreement), may be substituted.

chief of state/head of government, paramount national governmental officer(s) exercising the highest executive and/or ceremonial roles of a country's government. In general usage, the chief of state is the formal head of a national state. The primary responsibilities of the chief of state may range from the purely ceremonial—convening legislatures and greeting foreign officials—to the exercise of complete national executive authority. The head of government, when this function exists separately, is the officer nominally charged (by the constitution) with the majority of actual executive powers, though they may not in practice be exercised, especially in military or single-party regimes in which effective power may reside entirely outside the executive governmental machinery provided by the constitution. A prime minister, for example, usually the actual head of government, may in practice exercise only cabinet-level authority.

In communist countries an official identified as the chief of state may be the chairman of the policy-making organ, and the official given as the head of government the chairman of the nominal administrative/executive organ.

c.i.f. (trade valuation): *see* imports.

colony, an area annexed to, or controlled by, an independent state but not an integral part of it; a non-self-governing territory. A colony has a charter and may have a degree of self-government. A crown colony is a colony originally chartered by the British government.

commonwealth (U.K. and U.S.), a self-governing political entity that has regard to the common weal, or good; usually associated with the United Kingdom or United States. Examples include the Commonwealth of Nations (composed of independent states [from 1931 onward]), Puerto Rico since 1952, and the Northern Marianas since 1979.

communications, collectively, the means available for the public transmission of information within a country. Data are provided for daily newspapers, their number and total circulation, and the per capita rate of circulation implied by that total; for radio, television, and telephone receivers, total numbers and rates of availability are supplied. Telephone receiver data refer to the number of sets (stations) having access to the public switched network. Data for a few countries refer to the number of "main lines" through which subscribers' equipment is connected to the network.

constant prices, an adjustment to the members of a financial time series to eliminate the effect of inflation year by year. It consists of referring all data in the series to a single year so that "real" change may be seen.

constitutional monarchy, *see* monarchy.

consumer price index (CPI), also known as the retail price index, or the cost-of-living index, a series of index numbers assigned to the price of a selected "basket," or assortment, of basic consumer goods and services in a country, region, or city to measure changes over time in prices paid by a typical household for those goods and services. Items included in the CPI are ordinarily determined by governmental surveys of typical household expenditures and are assigned weights relative to their proportion of those expenditures. Index values are period averages unless otherwise noted.

coprincipality, *see* monarchy.

current prices, the valuation of a financial aggregate as of the year reported.

daily per capita caloric intake (supply), the calories equivalent to the known average daily supply of foodstuffs for human consumption in a given country divided by the population of the country (and the proportion of that supply provided, respectively, by vegetable and animal sources). The daily per capita caloric intake of a country may be compared with the corresponding recommended minimum daily requirement. The latter is calculated by the Food and Agriculture Organization of the United Nations from the age and sex distributions, average body weights, and environmental temperatures in a given region to determine the calories needed to sustain a person there at normal levels of activity and health. The daily per capita caloric requirement ranges from 2,200 to 2,500.

de facto population, for a given area, the population composed of those actually present at a particular time, including temporary residents and visitors (such as immigrants not yet granted permanent status, "guest" or expatriate workers, refugees, or tourists), but excluding legal residents temporarily absent.

de jure population, for a given area, the population composed only of those legally resident at a particular time, excluding temporary residents and visitors (such as "guest" or expatriate workers, refugees, or tourists), but including legal residents temporarily absent.

deadweight tonnage, the maximum weight of cargo, fuel, fresh water, stores, and persons that may safely be carried by a ship. It is customarily measured in long tons of 2,240 pounds each, equivalent to 1.016 metric tons. Deadweight tonnage is the difference between the tonnage of a fully loaded ship and the fully unloaded tonnage of that ship.

See also gross ton.

death rate, the number of deaths annually per 1,000 of midyear population. Death rates for individual countries may be compared with the estimated world annual average of 9.2 deaths per 1,000 population between 1990 and 1995.

density (of population), usually, the DE FACTO POPULATION of a country divided by its total area. Special adjustment is made for large areas of inland water or other uninhabitable areas—*e.g.*, excluding the ice cap of Greenland.

department, a first-order civil administrative subdivision. The *overseas department* (France) is an overseas subdivision of the French Republic, almost equivalent to a department of

Dependent states[1]

Australia	Portugal
Christmas Island	Macau
Cocos (Keeling) Islands	**United Kingdom**
Norfolk Island	Anguilla
Denmark	Bermuda
Faeroe Islands	British Virgin Islands
Greenland	Cayman Islands
France	Falkland Islands
French Guiana	Gibraltar
French Polynesia	Guernsey
Guadeloupe	Hong Kong
Martinique	Isle of Man
Mayotte	Jersey
New Caledonia	Montserrat
Réunion	Pitcairn Island
Saint Pierre and Miquelon	Saint Helena and Dependencies
Wallis and Futuna	Turks and Caicos Islands
Netherlands, The	**United States**
Aruba	American Samoa
Netherlands Antilles	Guam
New Zealand	Northern Mariana Islands
Cook Islands	Puerto Rico
Niue	Virgin Islands (of the U.S.)
Tokelau	
Norway	
Jan Mayen	
Svalbard	

[1]Excludes territories (1) to which Antarctic Treaty is applicable in whole or in part, (2) without permanent civilian population, (3) without internationally recognized civilian government (Western Sahara, Gaza Strip), or (4) representing unadjudicated unilateral or multilateral territorial claims.

metropolitan France, with elected representation in the French Parliament.

dependent state, constitutionally or statutorily organized political entity outside of and under the jurisdiction of an independent state (or a federal element of such a state) but not formally annexed to it (*see* Table).

direct taxes, taxes levied directly on firms and individuals, such as taxes on income, profits, and capital gains. The *immediate* incidence, or burden, of direct taxes is on the firms and individuals thus taxed; direct taxes on firms may, however, be passed on to consumers and other economic units in the form of higher prices for goods and services, blurring the distinction between direct and indirect taxation.

distribution of income/wealth, the portion of personal income or wealth accruing to households or individuals constituting each respective decile (tenth) or quintile (fifth) of a country's households or individuals.*

divorce rate, the number of legal, civilly recognized divorces annually per 1,000 population.

doubling time, the number of complete years required for a country to double its population at its current rate of natural increase.

earnings index, a series of index numbers comparing average wages in a collective industrial sample for a country or region with the same industries at a previous period to measure changes over time in those wages. It is most commonly reported for wages paid on a daily, weekly, or monthly basis; annual figures represent averages of these shorter periods. The scope of the earnings index varies from country to country; the index is often limited to earnings in manufacturing industries. The index for each country applies to all wage earners in a designated group and ordinarily takes into account basic wages (overtime is normally distinguished), bonuses, cost-of-living allowances, and contributions toward social security. Some countries include payments in kind. Contributions toward social security by employers are usually excluded, as are social security benefits received by wage earners.

economically active population, *see* population economically active.

education, tabulation of the principal elements of a country's educational establishment, classified as far as possible according to the country's own system of primary, secondary, and higher levels (the usual age limits for these levels being identified in parentheses), with total number of schools (physical facilities) and of teachers and students (whether full- or part-time). The student-teacher ratio is calculated whenever available data permit.

educational attainment, the distribution of the population age 25 and over with completed educations by the highest level of formal education attained or completed; it must sometimes be reported, however, for age groups still in school or for the economically active only.

emirate, empire, *see* monarchy.

enterprise, a legal entity formed to conduct a business, which it may do from more than one establishment (place of business or service point).

ethnic/linguistic composition, ethnic, racial, or linguistic composition of a national population, reported here according to the most reliable breakdown available, whether published in official sources (such as a census) or in external analysis (when the subject is not addressed in national sources).

exchange rate, the value of one currency compared with another, or with a standardized unit of account such as the SPECIAL DRAWING RIGHT, or as mandated by local statute when one currency is "tied" by a par value to another. Rates given usually refer to free market values when the currency has no, or very limited, restrictions on its convertibility into other currencies.

exports, material goods legally leaving a country (or customs area) and subject to customs regulations. The total value and distribution by percentage of the major items (in preference to groups of goods) exported are given, together with the distribution of trade among major trading partners (usually single countries or trading blocs). Valuation of goods exported is free on board (f.o.b.) unless otherwise specified. The value of goods exported and imported f.o.b. is calculated from the cost of production and excludes the cost of transport.

external debt, public and publicly guaranteed debt with a maturity of more than one year owed to nonnationals of a country and repayable in foreign currency, goods, or services. The debt may be an obligation of a national or subnational governmental body (or an agency of either), of an autonomous public body, or of a private debtor that is guaranteed by a public entity. The debt is usually either outstanding (contracted) or disbursed (drawn).

external territory (Australia), *see* territory.

federal, consisting of first-order political subdivisions that are prior to and independent of the central government in certain functions.

federal republic, *see* republic.

federation, union of coequal, preexisting political entities that retain some degree of autonomy and (usually) right of secession within the union.

fertility rate, *see* total fertility rate.

financial aggregates, tabulation of seven-year time series, providing principal measures of the financial condition of a country, including: (1) the exchange rate of the national currency against the U.S. dollar, the pound sterling, and the International Monetary Fund's SPECIAL DRAWING RIGHT (SDR), (2) the amount and kind of international reserves (holdings of SDRs, gold, and foreign currencies) and reserve position of the country in the IMF, and (3) principal economic rates and prices (central bank discount rate, government bond yields, and industrial stock [share] prices). For BALANCE OF PAYMENTS, the origin in terms of component balance of trade items and balance of invisibles (net) is given.*

fish catch, the live-weight equivalent of the aquatic animals (including fish, crustaceans, mollusks, etc., but excluding whales, seals, and other aquatic mammals) caught in freshwater or marine areas by national fleets and landed in domestic or foreign harbours for commercial, industrial, or subsistence purposes.

f.o.b. (trade valuation): see exports.

food, see daily per capita caloric intake.

form of government/political status, the type of administration provided for in a country's constitution—whether or not suspended by extralegal military or civil action, although such de facto administrations are identified—together with the number of members (elected, appointed, and ex officio) for each legislative house, named according to its English rendering. Dependent states (*see* Table) are classified according to the status of their political association with the administering country.

global social product, *see* material product.

gross domestic product (GDP), the total value of the final goods and services produced by residents and nonresidents within a given country during a given year. The GDP excludes the value of net income earned abroad, which is included in the GROSS NATIONAL PRODUCT. Unless otherwise noted, the value is given in current prices of the year indicated.

gross national product (GNP), the total value of final goods and services produced both from within a given country *and* from external (foreign) transactions in a given year. Unless otherwise noted, the value is given in current prices of the year indicated. GNP is equal to GROSS DOMESTIC PRODUCT adjusted by net factor income from abroad, which is the income residents receive from abroad for factor services (labour, investment, and interest) less similar payments made to nonresidents who contribute to the domestic economy.

gross ton, volumetric unit of measure (equaling 100 cubic feet [2.83 cu m]) of the permanently enclosed volume of a ship, above and below decks available for cargo, stores, or passenger accommodation. Net, or register, tonnage exempts certain nonrevenue spaces—such as those devoted to machinery, bunkers, crew accommodations, and ballast—from the gross tonnage. *See also* deadweight tonnage.

head of government, see chief of state/head of government.

health, a group of measures including number of accredited physicians currently practicing or employed and their ratio to the total population; total hospital beds and their ratio; and INFANT MORTALITY RATE.

household, economically autonomous individual or group of individuals living in a single dwelling unit. A family household is one composed principally of individuals related by blood or marriage.

household income and expenditure, data for average size of a HOUSEHOLD (by number of individuals) and median household income. Sources of income and expenditures for major items of consumption are given as percentages.

In general, household income is the amount of funds, usually measured in monetary units, received by the members (generally those 14 years old and over) of a household in a given time period. The income can be derived from (1) wages or salaries, (2) nonfarm or farm SELF-EMPLOYMENT, (3) transfer payments, such as pensions, public assistance, unemployment benefits, etc., and (4) other income, including interest and dividends, rent, royalties, etc. The income of a household is expressed as a gross amount before deductions for taxes. Data on expenditure refer to consumption of personal or household goods and services; they normally exclude savings, taxes, and insurance; practice with regard to inclusion of credit purchases differs markedly.

immigration, usually, the number and origin of those immigrants admitted to a nation in a legal status that would eventually permit the granting of the right to settle permanently or to acquire citizenship.*

imports, material goods legally entering a country (or customs area) and subject to customs regulations; excludes financial movements. The total value and distribution by percentage of the major items (in preference to groups of goods) imported are given, together with the direction of trade among major trading partners (usually single countries), trading blocs (such as the European Union), or customs areas (such as Belgium-Luxembourg). The value of goods imported is given free on board (f.o.b.) unless otherwise specified; f.o.b. is defined above under EXPORTS.

The principal alternate basis for valuation of goods in international trade is that of cost, insurance, and freight (c.i.f.); its use is restricted to imports, as it comprises the principal charges needed to bring the goods to the customs house in the country of destination. Because it inflates the value of imports relative to exports, more countries have, latterly, been estimating imports on an f.o.b. basis as well.

incorporated territory (U.S.), see territory.

independent, of a state, autonomous and controlling both its internal and external affairs. Its date usually refers to the date from which the country was in effective control of these affairs within its present boundaries, rather than the date independence was proclaimed or the date recognized as a de jure act by the former administering power.

indirect taxes, taxes levied on sales or transfers of selected intermediate goods and services, including excises, value-added taxes, and tariffs, that are ordinarily passed on to the ultimate consumers of the goods and services. Figures given for individual countries are limited to indirect taxes levied by their respective central governments unless otherwise specified.

infant mortality rate, the number of children per 1,000 live births who die before their first birthday. Total infant mortality includes neonatal mortality, which is deaths of children within one month of birth.

invisibles (invisible trade), *see* balance of trade.

kingdom, *see* monarchy.

labour force, portion of the POPULATION ECONOMICALLY ACTIVE (PEA) comprising those most fully employed or attached to the labour market (the unemployed are considered to be "attached" in that they usually represent persons previously employed seeking to be re-employed), particularly as viewed from a short-term perspective. It normally includes those who are self-employed, employed by others (whether full-time, part-time, seasonally, or on some other less than full-time basis), and, as noted above, the unemployed (both those previously employed and those seeking work for the first time). In the "gross domestic product and labour force" table, the majority of the labour data provided refer to population economically active, since PEA represents the longer-term view of working population and, thus, subsumes more of the marginal workers who are often missed by shorter-term surveys.

land use, distribution by classes of vegetational cover or economic use of the land area only (excluding inland water, for example, but not marshland), reported as percentages.

leisure, the principal monetary expenditures, uses, or reported preferences in the use of the individual's free time for recreation, rest, or self-improvement.*

life expectancy, the number of years a person born within a particular population group (age cohort) would be expected to live, based on actuarial calculations.

literacy, the ability to read and write a language with some degree of competence; the precise degree constituting the basis of a particular national statement is usually defined by the national census and is often tested by the census enumerator. Elsewhere, particularly where much adult literacy may be the result of literacy campaigns rather than passage through a formal educational system, definition and testing of literacy may be better standardized.

major cities, usually the five largest cities proper whose population is at least one-tenth that of the primate (largest) city; fewer will be listed if the size disparity is very great or there are fewer urban localities in the country. For multipage tables, 10 or more will be listed without regard for the size of the primate city.* All populations will refer to the most specific administrative or demographically defined city proper, unless a municipality or METROPOLITAN AREA is specified.

manufacturing, mining, and construction enterprises/retail sales and service enterprises, a detailed tabulation of the principal industries in these sectors, showing for each industry the number of enterprises and employees, wages in that industry as a percentage of the general average wage, and the value of that industry's output in terms of value added or turnover.*

marriage rate, the number of legal, civilly recognized marriages annually per 1,000 population.

material (or social) product, in the national accounting systems of the socialist countries, the aggregate (sometimes "global") value of all "productive" economic activity, generally omitting personal (nonpublic) services, financial activities, and the like that in conventional Western national accounts would contribute to the GROSS DOMESTIC PRODUCT, a more comprehensive measure that includes not only material output but also every identifiable service element of a national economy. Socialist countries that are members of the International Monetary Fund have begun, however, to report gross domestic, and national, product according to the *System of National Accounts* that forms the basis of international standardization of national accounts.

material well-being, a group of measures indicating the percentage of households or dwellings possessing certain goods or appliances, including automobiles, telephones, television receivers, refrigerators, air conditioners, and washing machines.*

merchant marine, the privately or publicly owned ships registered with the maritime authority of a nation (limited to those in Lloyd's of London statistical reporting of 100 or more GROSS TONS) that are employed in commerce, whether or not owned or operated by nationals of the country.

metropolitan area, a city and the region of dense, predominantly urban, settlement around the city; the population of the whole usually has strong economic and cultural affinities with the central city.

military expenditure, the apparent value of all identifiable military expenditure by the central government on hardware, personnel, pensions, research and development, etc., reported here both as a percentage of the GNP, with a comparison to the world average, and as a per capita value in U.S. dollars.

military personnel, see total active duty personnel.

mobility, the rate at which individuals or households change dwellings, usually measured between censuses and including international as well as domestic migration.*

monarchy, a government in which the CHIEF OF STATE holds office, usually hereditarily and for life, but sometimes electively for a term. The state may be a coprincipality, emirate, empire, kingdom, principality, sheikhdom, or sultanate. The powers of the monarch may range from absolute (*i.e.,* the monarch both reigns and rules) through various degrees of limitation of authority to nominal, as in a constitutional monarchy, in which the titular monarch reigns but others, as elected officials, effectively rule.

monetary unit, currency of issue, or that in official use in a given country; name, spelling, and abbreviation in English according to International Monetary Fund recommendations or local practice; name of the lesser, usually decimal, monetary unit constituting the main currency; and valuation in U.S. dollars and U.K. pounds sterling, usually according to free-market or commercial rates.

See also exchange rate.

natural increase, also called natural growth, or the balance of births and deaths, the excess of births over deaths in a population; the rate of natural increase is the difference between the BIRTH RATE and the DEATH RATE of a given population. Natural increase is added to the balance of migration to calculate the total growth of that population.

net material product, *see* material product.

nonreligious, *see* atheist.

official language(s), that (or those) prescribed by the national constitution for day-to-day conduct and publication of a country's official business or, when no explicit constitutional provision exists, that of the constitution itself, the national gazette (record of legislative activity), or like official documents. Other languages may have local protection, may be permitted in parliamentary debate or legal action (such as a trial), or may be "national languages," for the protection of which special provisions have been made, but these are not deemed official.

official name, the local official form(s), short or long, of a country's legal name(s) taken from the country's constitution or from other official documents. The English-language form is usually the protocol form in use by the country, the U.S. Department of State, and the United Nations.

official religion, generally, any religion prescribed or given special status or protection by the constitution or legal system of a country. Identification as such is not confined to constitutional documents utilizing the term explicitly.

organized territory (U.S.), *see* territory.

overseas department (France), *see* department.

overseas territory (France), *see* territory.

parliamentary state, *see* state.

part of a realm, a dependent Dutch political entity with some degree of self-government and having a special status above that of a colony (*e.g.,* the prerogative of rejecting for local application any law enacted by The Netherlands).

participation/activity rates, measures defining differential rates of economic activity within a population. Participation rate refers to the percentage of those employed or economically active who possess a particular characteristic (sex, age, etc.); activity rate refers to the fraction of the total population who *are* economically active.

passenger-miles, or **passenger-kilometres,** aggregate measure of passenger carriage by a specified means of transportation, equal to the number of passengers carried multiplied by the number of miles (or kilometres) each is transported. Figures given for countries are often calculated from ticket sales and ordinarily exclude passengers carried free of charge.

people's republic, *see* republic.

place of birth/national origin, if the former, numbers of native- and foreign-born population of a country by actual place of birth; if the latter, any of several classifications, including those based on origin of passport at original admission to country, on cultural heritage of family name, on self-designated (often multiple) origin of (some) ancestors, and on other systems for assigning national origin.*

political status, see form of government/political status.

population, the number of persons present within a country or other civil entity at the date of a census of population, survey, cumulation of a civil register, or other enumeration. Unless otherwise specified, populations given are DE FACTO, referring to those actually present, rather than DE JURE, those legally resident but not necessarily present on the referent date. If a time series, noncensus year, or per capita ratio referring to a country's total population is cited, it will usually refer to midyear of the calendar year indicated. Populations for cities will usually refer to the city proper—*i.e.,* the legally bounded corporate entity, or the most compact, contiguous, demographically urban portion of the entity defined by the local authorities. Occasionally figures for METROPOLITAN AREAS are cited when the relevant civil entity at the core of a major agglomeration had an unrepresentatively small population.

population economically active, the total number of persons (above a set age for economic labour, usually 10–15 years) in all employment statuses—self-employed, wage- or salary-earning, part-time, seasonal, unemployed, etc. The International Labour Organisation defines the economically active as "all persons of either sex who furnish the supply of labour for the production of economic goods and services." National practices vary as regards the treatment of such groups as armed forces, inmates of institutions, persons seeking their first job, unpaid family workers, seasonal workers and persons engaged in part-time economic activities. In some countries, all or part of these groups may be included among the economically active, while in other countries the same groups may be treated as inactive. In general, however, the data on economically active population do not include students, persons occupied solely in family or household work, retired persons, persons living entirely on their own means, and persons wholly dependent upon others.

See also labour force.

population projection, the expected population in the years 2000 and 2010, embodying the country's own projections wherever possible. Estimates of the future size of a population are usually based on assumed levels of fertility, mortality, and migration. Projections in the tables, unless otherwise specified, are medium (*i.e.,* most likely) variants, whether based on external estimates by the United Nations, World Bank, or U.S. Department of Commerce or on those of the country itself.

price and earnings indexes, tabulation comparing the change in the CONSUMER PRICE INDEX over a period of seven years with the change in the general labour force's EARNINGS INDEX for the same period.

principality, *see* monarchy.

production, the physical quantity or monetary value of the output of an industry, usually tabulated here as the most important items or groups of items (depending on the available detail) of primary (extractive) and secondary (manufactured) production, including construction. When a single consistent measure of value, such as VALUE ADDED, can be obtained, this is given, ranked by value; otherwise, and more usually, quantity of production is given.

public debt, the current outstanding debt of all periods of maturity for which the central government and its organs are obligated. Publicly guaranteed private debt is excluded. For countries that report debt under the World Bank Debtor Reporting System (DRS), figures for outstanding, long-term EXTERNAL DEBT are given.

quality of working life, a group of measures including weekly hours of work (including overtime); rates per 100,000 for job-connected injury, illness, and mortality; coverage of labour force by insurance for injury, permanent disability, and death; workdays lost to labour strikes and stoppages; and commuting patterns (length of journey to work in minutes and usual method of transportation).*

railroads, mode of transportation by self-driven or locomotive-drawn cars over fixed rails. Length-of-track figures include all mainline and spurline running track but exclude switching sidings and yard track. Route length, when given, does not compound multiple running tracks laid on the same trackbed.

recurrent budget, *see* budget.

religious affiliation, distribution of nominal religionists, whether practicing or not, as a percentage of total population. This usually assigns to children the religion of their parents.

republic, a state with elected leaders and a centralized presidential form of government, local subdivisions being subordinate to the national government. A *federal republic* (as distinguished from a unitary republic) is a republic in which power is divided between the central government and the constituent subnational administrative divisions (*e.g.,* states, provinces, or cantons) in whom the central government itself is held to originate, the division of power being defined in a written constitution and jurisdictional disputes usually being settled in a court; sovereignty usually rests with the authority that has the power to amend the constitution. A *unitary republic* (as distinguished from a federal republic) is a republic in which power originates in a central authority and is not derived from constituent subdivisions. A *people's republic,* in the dialectics of Communism, is the first stage of development toward a communist state, the second stage being a *socialist republic.* An *Islamic republic* is structured around social,

ethical, and religious precepts central to the Islamic faith.

retail price index, *see* consumer price index.

retail sales and service enterprises, *see* manufacturing, mining, and construction enterprises/retail sales and service enterprises.

roundwood, wood obtained from removals from forests, felled or harvested (with or without bark), in all forms.

rural, see urban-rural.

self-employment, work in which income derives from direct employment in one's own business, trade, or profession, as opposed to work in which salary or wages are earned from an employer.

self-governing, of a state, in control of its internal affairs in degrees ranging from control of most internal affairs (though perhaps not of public order or of internal security) to complete control of all internal affairs (*i.e.,* the state is autonomous) but having no control of external affairs or defense. In this work the term self-governing refers to the final stage in the successive stages of increasing self-government that generally precede independence.

service/trade enterprises, see manufacturing, mining, and construction enterprises/retail sales and service enterprises.

sex distribution, ratios, calculated as percentages, of male and female population to total population.

sheikhdom, *see* monarchy.

social deviance, a group of measures, usually reported as rates per 100,000, for principal categories of socially deviant behaviour, including specified crimes, alcoholism, drug abuse, and suicide.*

social participation, a group of measures indicative of the degree of social engagement displayed by a particular population, including rates of participation in such activities as elections, voluntary work or memberships, trade unions, and religion.*

social security, public programs designed to protect individuals and families from loss of income owing to unemployment, old age, sickness or disability, or death and to provide other services such as medical care, health and welfare programs, or income maintenance.

socialist republic, *see* republic.

sources of income, *see* household income and expenditure.

Special Drawing Right (SDR), a unit of account utilized by the International Monetary Fund (IMF) to denominate monetary reserves available under a quota system to IMF members to maintain the value of their national currency unit in international transactions.*

state, in international law, a political entity possessing the attributes of: territory, permanent civilian population, government, and the capacity to conduct relations with other states. Though the term is sometimes limited in meaning to fully independent and internationally recognized states, the more general sense of an entity possessing a *preponderance* of these characteristics is intended here. It is, thus, also a first-order civil administrative subdivision, especially of a federated union. An *associated state* is an autonomous state in free association with another that conducts its external affairs and defense; the association may be terminated in full independence at the instance of the autonomous state in consultation with the administering power. A *parliamentary state* is an independent state of the Commonwealth that is governed by a parliament and that may recognize the British monarch as its titular head.

structure of gross domestic product and labour force, tabulation of the principal elements of the national economy, according to standard industrial categories, together with the corresponding distribution of the labour force (when possible POPULATION ECONOMICALLY ACTIVE) that generates the GROSS DOMESTIC PRODUCT.

sultanate, *see* monarchy.

territory, a noncategorized political dependency; a first-order administrative subdivision; a dependent political entity with some degree of self-government, but with fewer rights and less autonomy than a colony because there is no charter. An *external territory* (Australia) is a territory situated outside the area of the country. An *organized territory* (U.S.) is a territory for which a system of laws and a settled government have been provided by an act of the United States Congress. An *overseas territory* (France) is an overseas subdivision of the French Republic with elected representation in the French Parliament, having individual statutes, laws, and internal organization adapted to local conditions. An *unincorporated territory* (U.S.) is a dependency of the United States with limited self-government, whose inhabitants can claim the fundamental but not all of the procedural rights (*e.g.,* trial by jury) guaranteed by the United States Constitution.

ton-miles, or **ton-kilometres,** aggregate measure of freight hauled by a specified means of transportation, equal to tons of freight multiplied by the miles (or kilometres) each ton is transported. Figures are compiled from waybills (nationally) and ordinarily exclude mail, specie, passengers' baggage, the fuel and stores of the conveyance, and goods carried free.

total active duty personnel, full-time active duty military personnel (excluding militias and part-time, informal, or other paramilitary elements), with their distribution by percentages among the major services.

total fertility rate, the sum of the current age-specific birth rates for each of the child-bearing years (usually 15–49). It is the probable number of births, given present fertility data, that would occur during the lifetime of each woman should she live to the end of her child-bearing years.

tourism, service industry comprising activities connected with domestic and international travel for pleasure or recreation; confined here to international travel and reported as expenditures in U.S.$ by tourists of all nationalities visiting a particular country and, conversely, the estimated expenditures of that country's nationals in all countries of destination.

transfer payments, *see* household income and expenditure.

transport, all mechanical methods of moving persons or goods. Data reported for national establishments include: for railroads, length of track and volume of traffic for passengers and cargo (but excluding mail, etc.); for roads, length of network and numbers of passenger cars and of commercial vehicles (*i.e.,* trucks and buses); for merchant marine, the number of vessels of more than 100 gross tons and their total deadweight tonnage; for air transport, traffic data for passengers and cargo and the number of airports with scheduled flights.

unincorporated territory (U.S.), *see* territory.

unitary republic, *see* republic.

urban-rural, social characteristic of local or national populations, defined by predominant economic activities, "urban" referring to a group of largely nonagricultural pursuits, "rural" to agriculturally oriented employment patterns. The distinction is usually based on the country's own definition of urban, which may depend only upon the size (population) of a place or upon factors like employment, administrative status, density of housing, etc.

value added, also called value added by manufacture, the gross output value of a firm or industry minus the cost of inputs—raw materials, supplies, and payments to other firms—required to produce it. Value added is the portion of the sales value or gross output value that is actually created by the firm or industry. Value added generally includes labour costs, administrative costs, and operating profits.

The Nations of the World

Afghanistan

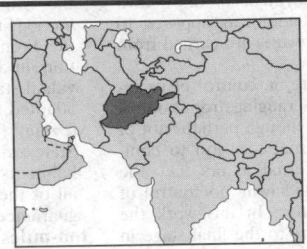

Official name: Islamic State of
  Afghanistan (Pashto and Dari
  [Persian] long-form names, n.a.).
Form of government[1]: Islamic state
  with an interim parliament[2] (250).
Chief of state: President.
Head of government: Prime Minister[3].
Capital: Kabul.
Official languages: Pashto; Dari
  (Persian).
Official religion: Islam.
Monetary unit: 1 afghani (Af) = 100
  puls (puli); valuation (Oct. 7, 1994)
  1 U.S.$ = Af 2,605; 1 £ = Af 4,144.

Area and population[4]

Regions	area		population
	sq mi	sq km	1988 estimate
Eastern	28,664	74,240	2,050,400
North-central	20,461	52,994	2,584,400
North-east	29,911	77,468	1,478,400
North-west	50,581	131,005	2,157,100
South-central	32,963	85,375	1,215,700
South-east	12,546	32,494	4,252,000
Western	76,699	198,649	1,666,400
TOTAL	251,825	652,225	15,404,400

Demography

Population (1994): 16,903,000[5].
Density (1994): persons per sq mi 67.1, persons per sq km 25.9.
Urban-rural (1993): urban 19.0%; rural 81.0%.
Sex distribution (1990): male 51.42%; female 48.58%.
Age breakdown (1990): under 15, 42.0%; 15–29, 27.3%; 30–44, 15.8%; 45–59, 10.1%; 60–74, 4.2%; 75 and over, 0.6%.
Population projection: (2000) 25,725,000; (2010) 32,889,000.
Doubling time: 25 years.
Ethnic composition (1983): Pashtun 52.3%; Tadzhik 20.3%; Uzbek 8.7%; Hazāra 8.7%; Chahar Aimak 2.9%; Turkmen 2.0%; Baluchi 1.0%; other 4.1%.
Religious affiliation (1990): Sunnī Muslim 84%; Shī'ī Muslim 15%; other 1%.
Major cities (1988): Kabul 700,000[6]; Kandahār (Qandahār) 225,500; Herāt 177,300; Mazār-e Sharīf 130,600.

Vital statistics

Birth rate per 1,000 population (1993): 51 (world avg. 26.0).
Death rate per 1,000 population (1993): 22 (world avg. 9.2).
Natural increase rate per 1,000 population (1993): 29 (world avg. 16.8).
Total fertility rate (avg. births per childbearing woman; 1993): 6.7.
Life expectancy at birth (1993): male 44.0 years; female 43.0 years.
Major causes of death per 100,000 population: n.a.; however, in the early 1990s, injuries and poisoning, infectious and parasitic diseases, and diseases of the respiratory system were the leading causes of death reported in hospitals.

National economy

Budget (1987–88). Revenue: Af 79,800,000,000 (1984–85; tax revenue 45.4%, nontax revenue 54.6%). Expenditures: Af 105,800,000,000 (1981–82; governmental ministries 50.0%, developmental budget 31.9%, debt service 13.9%).
Public debt (external, outstanding; 1991): U.S.$5,269,000,000.
Production (metric tons except as noted). Agriculture, forestry, fishing (1993): wheat 1,700,000, corn (maize) 350,000, grapes 330,000, rice 300,000, potatoes 228,000, barley 170,000; livestock (number of live animals) 14,200,000 sheep, 2,150,000 goats, 1,500,000 cattle, 1,180,000 asses, 320,000 horses, 265,000 camels, 7,000,000 chickens; roundwood (1992) 7,314,000 cu m; fish catch (1991) 1,500. Mining and quarrying (1992): salt 12,000; copper 5,000; gypsum 3,000[7]; barite 2,000. Manufacturing (by production value in Af '000,000,000; 1987–88): pharmaceutical products 462.5; food products 203.0; industrial chemicals (including fertilizers) 123.4; cement 104.0; textiles 15.6; salt 15.4. Construction (Af '000,000; 1985): 1,094. Energy production (consumption): electricity (kW-hr; 1992) 703,000,000 (834,000,000); coal (metric tons; 1992) 8,000 (8,000); petroleum products (metric tons; 1992) none (302,000); natural gas (cu m; 1992) 188,947,000 (188,947,000).
Population economically active (1989–90)[8]: total 6,009,000; activity rate of total population 38.0% (participation rates [1985]: ages 10–59, 43.1%; female 7.9%; unemployed 3.0%).

Price index (1990 = 100)

	1986	1987	1988	1989	1990	1991	1992[9]
Consumer price index	28.1	33.6	40.2	70.5	100.0	156.7	233.6

Tourism: receipts (1988) U.S.$1,000,000; expenditures (1987) U.S.$1,000,000.
Gross national product (1988): U.S.$3,100,000,000 (U.S.$220 per capita).

Structure of gross domestic product and labour force

	1989–90		1981–82	
	in value Af '000,000[10]	% of total value	labour force	% of labour force
Agriculture	65,600	52.6	2,194,770	57.3
Manufacturing, mining, and public utilities	35,600	28.5	466,860	12.2
Construction	7,200	5.8	48,880	1.3
Transp. and commun.	4,400	3.5	65,650	1.7
Trade	9,900	7.9	126,100	3.3
Public administration	} 2,000	} 1.6	79,260	2.1
Public services			204,940	5.3
Other			642,360	16.8
TOTAL	124,700	100.0[11]	3,828,820	100.0

Land use (1992): forested 2.9%; meadows and pastures 46.0%; agricultural and under permanent cultivation 12.4%; other 38.7%.

Foreign trade[12, 13]

Balance of trade (current prices)

	1986	1987	1988	1989	1990	1991
Af '000,000	−33,826	−17,917	−19,642	−24,217	−27,000	−17,600
% of total	37.8%	25.7%	33.0%	50.4%	53.2%	48.0%

Imports (1991): U.S.$616,400,000 (1989–90; machinery 37.7%, basic manufactures 18.3%, minerals and fuels 10.9%). *Major import sources* (1990): U.S.S.R. 56.3%; Japan 9.4%; Singapore 5.6%; India 2.9%; South Korea 2.2%.
Exports (1991): U.S.$188,200,000 (dried fruits and nuts 49.6%, carpets and rugs 23.6%, karakul wool and hides 6.7%, cotton 1.3%). *Major export destinations* (1990): U.S.S.R. 72.4%; Western Europe 11.0%; India 3.1%.

Transport and communications

Transport. Railroads (1988): length 10 km. Roads (1988): total length 19,200 km (paved 47%). Vehicles (1991): passenger cars 38,000; trucks and buses 35,000. Merchant marine: none. Air transport (1992): passenger-km 265,-000,000; metric ton-km cargo 11,000,000; airports (1994) 1.
Communications. Daily newspapers (1990): total number 14; total circulation 180,000; circulation per 1,000 population 11.3. Radio (1993): 1,500,000 receivers (1 per 14 persons). Television (1993): 100,000 receivers (1 per 203 persons). Telephones (1984): 31,200 (1 per 443 persons).

Education and health

Education (1988–89)

	schools	teachers	students	student/ teacher ratio
Primary	553	16,756	586,014	35.0
Secondary	819	5,715	271,000	47.4
Voc., teacher tr.	33	556	8,537	15.4
Higher	5	198	1,491	7.5

Educational attainment (1980). Percentage of population age 25 and over having: no formal schooling 88.5%; some primary education 6.8%; complete primary 0.3%; some secondary 1.2%; postsecondary 3.2%. *Literacy* (1990): percentage of total population age 15 and over literate 29.4%; males 44.1%; females 13.9%.
Health: physicians (1989–91) 2,233 (1 per 6,866 persons); hospital beds (1981–82) 6,875 (1 per 2,054 persons); infant mortality rate (1993) 161.
Food (1984–86): daily per capita caloric intake 2,290 (vegetable products 90%, animal products 10%); 91% of FAO recommended minimum requirement.

Military

Total active duty personnel (1993): no identifiable military units appear to represent the central government. *Military expenditure as percentage of GNP* (1984): 9.1% (world 5.6%); per capita expenditure U.S.$24.

---

[1]Central government in Kabul unites a number of Sunnī mujahedin guerrilla groups, who, following traditional deliberative and legislative models, have established a state, a parliament, and a constitution (through September 1993), though none is fully established in all of Afghanistan. But as of October 1994, there was no effective central authority. [2]Consisting of a nonelective body (named by the previous *Shura*, or constituent assembly), having the purpose of establishing a constitution and restoring civilian government. [3]Office vacant from June 1994. [4]In the early 1990s an administrative reorganization created 31 provinces (*wilayāh*), but detailed breakdown of area and population is unavailable. [5]Excluding Afghan refugees estimated to number about 1.5 million in Pakistan and 1.8 million in Iran. [6]1993 estimate. [7]1991. [8]Based on settled population only. [9]First quarter. [10]At prices of 1978–79. [11]Detail does not add to total given because of rounding. [12]Import figures are f.o.b. in balance of trade and c.i.f. in commodities and trading partners. [13]Trade figures are year ending March 20 of the following year.

Albania

Official name: Republika e Shqipërisë (Republic of Albania).
Form of government: unitary multiparty republic with one legislative house (People's Assembly [140])[1].
Chief of state: President.
Head of government: Prime Minister.
Capital: Tiranë.
Official language: Albanian.
Official religion: none.
Monetary unit: 1 lek = 100 qindars; valuation (Oct. 7, 1994) 1 U.S.$ = 100.09 leks; 1 £ = 159.20 leks.

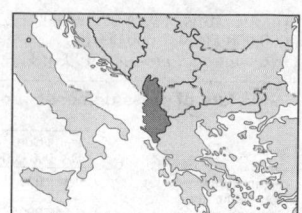

Area and population

Provinces	Capitals	area sq mi	area sq km	population 1990 estimate
Berat	Berat	396	1,027	180,489
Dibër	Peshkopi	605	1,568	153,775
Durrës	Durrës	327	848	251,029
Elbasan	Elbasan	572	1,481	248,676
Fier	Fier	454	1,175	251,115
Gjirokastër	Gjirokastër	439	1,137	67,392
Gramsh	Gramsh	268	695	44,791
Kolonjë	Ersekë	311	805	25,291
Korçë	Korçë	842	2,181	218,219
Krujë	Krujë	234	607	109,876
Kukës	Kukës	514	1,330	104,731
Lezhë	Lezhë	185	479	63,505
Librazhd	Librazhd	391	1,013	73,871
Lushnjë	Lushnjë	275	712	137,830
Mat	Burrel	397	1,028	78,754
Mirditë	Rrëshen	335	867	51,701
Përmet	Përmet	359	929	40,419
Pogradec	Pogradec	280	725	73,333
Pukë	Pukë	399	1,034	50,286
Sarandë	Sarandë	424	1,097	89,456
Shkodër	Shkodër	976	2,528	241,549
Skrapar	Çorovoda	299	775	47,605
Tepelenë	Tepelenë	315	817	51,022
Tiranë	Tiranë	478	1,238	374,483
Tropojë	Bajram	403	1,043	45,965
Vlorë	Vlorë	621	1,609	180,725
TOTAL		11,100[2]	28,748	3,255,891[2]

Demography

Population (1994): 3,374,000.
Density (1994): persons per sq mi 304.0, persons per sq km 117.4.
Urban-rural (1990): urban 36.1%; rural 63.9%.
Sex distribution (1990): male 51.40%; female 48.60%.
Age breakdown (1989): under 15, 33.0%; 15–29, 28.9%; 30–44, 18.5%; 45–59, 11.7%; 60–74, 5.9%; 75 and over, 2.0%.
Population projection: (2000) 3,610,000; (2010) 4,016,000.
Doubling time: 37 years.
Ethnic composition (1989): Albanian 98.0%; Greek 1.8%; Macedonian 0.1%; other 0.1%.
Religious affiliation (1992): a significant portion of the population are nonreligious; believers identify themselves as Muslim 65%, Orthodox 20%, Roman Catholic 13%, other 2%.
Major cities (1990): Tiranë 243,000; Durrës 85,400; Elbasan 83,300; Shkodër 81,800; Vlorë 73,800.

Vital statistics

Birth rate per 1,000 population (1991): 23.8 (world avg. 26.0).
Death rate per 1,000 population (1991): 5.4 (world avg. 9.2).
Natural increase rate per 1,000 population (1991): 18.4 (world avg. 16.8).
Total fertility rate (avg. births per childbearing woman; 1993): 2.9.
Marriage rate per 1,000 population (1990): 8.9.
Divorce rate per 1,000 population (1990): 0.8.
Life expectancy at birth (1993): male 70.0 years; female 76.2 years.
Major causes of death per 100,000 population: n.a.; however, in 1983 the leading causes of death were cardiovascular diseases, diseases of the respiratory system, malignant neoplasms (cancers), and injuries.

National economy

Budget (1993). Revenue: 31,599,000,000 leks (taxes 71.5%, of which turnover tax 15.8%, income tax 14.7%, excise tax 13.8%, enterprise profits tax 12.6%). Expenditures: 49,958,000,000 leks (economy 34.4%, transfer payments 19.3%, administration and defense 18.3%).
Public debt (1993): U.S.$861,000,000.
Tourism (1990): number of tourist arrivals 30,000; receipts from visitors, n.a.
Production (metric tons except as noted). Agriculture, forestry, fishing (1993): vegetables and melons 483,000, wheat 430,000, corn (maize) 110,000, sugar beets 70,000, grapes 67,000, potatoes 56,000, barley 30,000, sorghum 20,000, oats 15,000, sunflower seeds 14,000, tobacco 12,000, olives 8,000; livestock (number of live animals) 1,200,000 sheep, 750,000 goats, 450,000 cattle, 140,000 pigs, 105,000 horses, 76,000 mules and asses; roundwood (1991) 2,556,000 cu m; fish catch (1990) 11,961. Mining and quarrying (1993): chromite ore 282,000; copper ore 14,000; pyrite ore 7,300. Manufacturing (1991)[3]: cement 313,000; flour 311,000; phosphate fertilizers 43,000; sulfuric acid 21,000; caustic soda 11,000; soda ash 5,000; copper wire 2,000; soaps and detergents 1,000; cigarettes 1,703,000 units; television receivers 5,000 units. Construction (1990): 12,428 units. Energy production (consumption):

electricity (kW-hr; 1992) 3,357,000,000 (2,797,000,000); coal (metric tons; 1992) 676,000 (576,000); crude petroleum (barrels; 1992) 3,858,000 (7,596,000); petroleum products (metric tons; 1992) 506,000 (541,000); natural gas (cu m; 1992) 246,000,000 (246,000,000).
Gross national product (1993): U.S.$1,163,000,000 (U.S.$340 per capita).

Structure of net material product and labour force

	1990 value '000,000 leks	% of total value	labour force	% of labour force
Agriculture	4,705	35.9	674,000	47.0
Manufacturing, mining, public utilities	5,486	41.8	338,000	23.6
Construction	845	6.4	97,000	6.8
Transp. and commun.	435	3.3	29,000	2.0
Trade	1,333	10.1	26,000	1.8
Pub. admin., defense Services Other	318	2.5	209,000	10.0
TOTAL	13,122	100.0	1,433,000	100.0

Population economically active (1993): total 1,540,000; activity rate of total population 49.4% (participation rates: ages 15–64, 90.2%; female 49.0%; unemployed 17.5%).

Price and earnings indexes (1990 = 100)

	1987	1988	1989	1990	1991	1992	1993
Consumer price index	...	...	97.6	100.0	204.1	441.7	c. 176.7
Annual earnings index	96.0	96.4	97.2	100.0	117.1	...	...

Household income and expenditure. Average household size (1989) 4.7; income per household 14,505 leks (U.S.$ value, n.a.); sources of income: wages 80.2%, social insurance 13.0%; expenditure: n.a.
Land use (1992): forested 38.2%; meadows and pastures 14.8%; agricultural and under permanent cultivation 25.4%; other 21.6%.

Foreign trade

Balance of trade (current prices)

	1985	1986	1987	1988	1989	1990
'000,000 leks	−420	−175	−160	−668	−763	−1,522
% of total	9.1%	3.4%	3.1%	11.6%	11.2%	25.1%

Imports (1992): U.S.$671,000,000 (1990; machinery and transport equipment 30.9%; fuels, minerals, and metals 24.5%; organic raw materials 15.7%; food products 10.1%; chemical products 9.3%; consumer products 8.4%). *Major import sources:* Italy 23.8%; France 17.1%; South Korea 9.8%; Belgium-Luxembourg 7.9%; Greece 6.7%; United States 5.9%.
Exports (1992): U.S.$189,500,000 (1990; fuels, minerals, and metals 46.8%; food products 22.1%; organic raw materials 15.4%; consumer products 11.8%). *Major export destinations:* Italy 13.6%; France 8.5%; former Yugoslavia 7.9%; Germany 7.3%; Tunisia 6.1%.

Transport and communications

Transport. Railroads (1990): length 720 km; passenger-km 779,200,000; metric ton-km cargo 584,000,000. Roads (1990): total length 7,450 km (paved 38%). Vehicles (1991): passenger cars 16,000; trucks and buses 32,900. Merchant marine (1992): vessels (100 gross tons and over) 24; total deadweight tonnage 80,954. Air transport: passengers, n.a.; cargo, n.a.; airports (1994) with scheduled flights 1.
Communications. Daily newspapers (1990): total number 2; total circulation 135,000; circulation per 1,000 population 42. Radio (1991): 525,000 receivers (1 per 6.3 persons). Television (1989): 324,905[4] receivers (1 per 9.8 persons). Telephones (1992): 58,500 (1 per 57 persons).

Education and health

Education (1990)

	schools	teachers	students	student/teacher ratio
Primary (age 6–13)	1,726	28,798	557,000	19.3
Secondary (age 14–17)	47	2,318	68,000	29.3
Voc., teacher tr.	466	7,390	138,000	18.7
Higher	8	1,806	27,000	15.0

Educational attainment (1989). Percentage of population age 10 and over having: primary education 65.3%; secondary 29.1%; higher 5.6%. *Literacy* (1989)[5]: 91.8%; males 95.5%; females 88.0%.
Health (1990): physicians 5,566 (1 per 585 persons); hospital beds 19,000 (1 per 173 persons); infant mortality rate per 1,000 live births (1991) 32.9.
Food (1988–90): daily per capita caloric intake 2,585 (vegetable products 84%, animal products 16%); 97% of FAO recommended minimum requirement.

Military

Total active duty personnel (1994): 73,000 (army 82.2%, navy 4.1%, air force 13.7%). *Military expenditure as percentage of GNP* (1993): 8.2% (world, n.a.); per capita expenditure U.S.$28.

---

[1]A transitional constitution was adopted on April 29, 1991. The proposed text of a permanent constitution was rejected in a referendum on Nov. 6, 1994. [2]Detail does not add to total given because of rounding. [3]State sector only. [4]Families that had a television receiver. [5]Population age 10 years and older.

Algeria

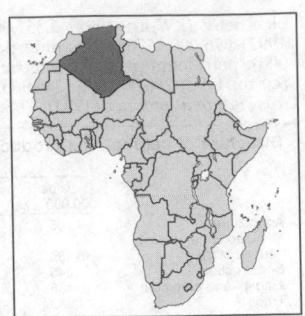

Official name: al-Jumhūrīyah al-Jazā'irīyah ad-Dīmuqrāṭīyah ash-Sha'bīyah (Arabic) (Democratic and Popular Republic of Algeria).
Form of government: military-backed regime with one interim legislative body (National Transition Council[1] [178[2]]).
Chief of state: President assisted by High Committee of State.
Head of government: Prime Minister.
Capital: Algiers.
Official language: Arabic.
Official religion: Islam.
Monetary unit: 1 Algerian dinar (DA) = 100 centimes; valuation (Oct. 7, 1994) 1 U.S.$ = DA 40.89; 1 £ = DA 65.04.

Population (1987 census)

Wilāyat	population	Wilāyat	population
Adrar	217,678	Médéa	652,863
Aïn Defla	537,256	Mila	511,605
Aïn Temouchent	274,990	Mostaganem	505,932
Alger	1,690,191	M'Sila	604,693
Annaba	455,888	Naâma	113,700
Batna	752,617	Oran	932,473
el-Bayadh	153,254	Ouargla	284,454
Béchar	185,346	el-Oued	376,909
Bejaïa	700,952	Oum el-Bouaghi	403,936
Biskra	430,202	Relizane	544,877
Blida	702,188	Saïda	235,494
Bordj Bou Arreridj	424,828	Sétif	1,000,694
Bouira	526,900	Sidi bel-Abbès	446,277
Boumerdes	650,975	Skikda	622,510
ech-Chleff	684,192	Souk Ahras	296,077
Constantine	664,303	Tamanrasset	95,822
Djelfa	494,494	et-Tarf	275,315
Ghardaïa	216,140	Tébessa	410,233
Guelma	353,309	Tiaret	575,794
Illizi	18,930	Tindouf	16,428
Jijel	472,312	Tipaza	620,151
Khenchela	246,541	Tissemsilt	228,120
Laghouat	212,388	Tizi Ouzou	936,948
Mascara	566,901	Tlemcen	714,862
		TOTAL	23,038,942[3]

Demography

Area: 919,595 sq mi, 2,381,741 sq km.
Population (1994): 27,815,000[4].
Density (1994): persons per sq mi 30.2, persons per sq km 11.7.
Urban-rural (1991): urban 52.0%; rural 48.0%.
Sex distribution (1990): male 49.86%; female 50.14%.
Age breakdown (1993): under 15, 42.3%; 15–29, 28.8%; 30–44, 15.1%; 45–59, 8.1%; 60–74, 4.3%; 75 and over, 1.4%.
Population projection: (2000) 32,693,000; (2010) 41,311,000.
Doubling time: 29 years.
Ethnic composition (1983): Arab 82.6%; Berber 17.0%; other 0.4%.
Religious affiliation (1990): Muslim 99.9%, of which Sunnī 99.5%, Ibāḍīyah 0.4%; Roman Catholic 0.1%.
Major cities (1987): Algiers 1,507,241; Oran 609,823; Constantine 440,842; Annaba 222,518; Batna 181,601.

Vital statistics

Birth rate per 1,000 population (1992): 30.3 (world avg. 26.0).
Death rate per 1,000 population (1992): 6.1 (world avg. 9.2).
Natural increase rate per 1,000 population (1992): 24.2 (world avg. 16.8).
Total fertility rate (avg. births per childbearing woman; 1993): 4.0.
Marriage rate per 1,000 population (1990): 5.9.
Divorce rate per 1,000 population (1985): 2.1.
Life expectancy at birth (1993): male 66.3 years; female 68.4 years.
Notified cases of infectious diseases per 100,000 population (1990): hepatitis 15.1; typhoid fever 11.3; measles 7.2; cholera 5.2; tuberculosis 4.8.

National economy

Budget (1994). Revenue: DA 410,000,000,000 (petroleum taxes 45.6%, turnover taxes 19.0%, direct taxes 11.6%). Expenditures: DA 535,300,000,000 (current expenditure 60.4%, development expenditure 39.6%).
Public debt (external, outstanding; 1992): U.S.$24,762,000,000.
Tourism (1992): receipts from visitors U.S.$75,000,000; expenditures by nationals abroad U.S.$163,000,000.
Production (metric tons except as noted). Agriculture, forestry, fishing (1992): wheat 1,750,000, barley 1,370,000, potatoes 900,000, tomatoes 500,000, grapes 260,000, onions 231,000, dates 210,000, oranges 192,000, olives 130,000; livestock (number of live animals) 18,600,000 sheep, 1,420,000 cattle; roundwood 2,307,000 cu m; fish catch 95,274. Mining and quarrying (1992): iron ore 2,350,000; phosphate rock 1,136,000; mercury 476,000 kilograms. Manufacturing (1992): cement 7,093,000; flour and semolina 2,540,000; bricks 1,776,000; crude steel 1,400,000; pig iron 900,000; edible oils 277,000; refined sugar 192,000; phosphate fertilizer 154,000; methanol 95,000. Construction: n.a. Energy production (consumption): electricity (kW-hr; 1992) 18,286,-000,000 (17,358,000,000); coal (metric tons; 1992) 15,000 (1,315,000); crude petroleum (barrels; 1992) 288,300,000 (168,600,000); petroleum products

(metric tons; 1992) 37,892,000 (9,341,000); natural gas (cu m; 1992) 55,032,-000,000 (19,922,000,000).
Gross national product (1993): U.S.$44,355,000,000 (U.S.$1,650 per capita).

Structure of gross domestic product and labour force

	1992		1990	
	in value DA '000,000	% of total value	labour force	% of labour force
Agriculture	118,800	12.2	907,490	15.9
Petroleum and natural gas	248,200[5]	25.5[5]	55,000	1.0
Other mining	2,300	0.2	...	...
Manufacturing	94,400[5]	9.7[5]	646,390	11.3
Public utilities	10,500	1.1 }	651,370	11.4
Construction	115,600	11.9		
Pub. admin., defense	130,100	13.3	1,318,370	23.1
Transp. and commun.			252,230	4.4
Trade	254,100	26.1	444,970	7.8
Other			1,435,180[6]	25.1[6]
TOTAL	974,000	100.0	5,711,000	100.0

Population economically active (1990): total 5,711,000; activity rate of population 22.8% (1987; participation rates: ages 15–64, 44.3%; female 9.2%; unemployed [1993] officially c. 20.0%, unofficially c. 40.0%).

Price and earnings indexes (1990 = 100)

	1987	1988	1989	1990	1991	1992	1993
Consumer price index	74.0	78.5	85.8	100.0	125.9	165.7	199.7
Earnings index	...	...	...	...	...	...	...

Household income and expenditure. Average household size (1987) 6.9; income per household: n.a.; sources of income: n.a.; expenditure (1988): food and beverages 52.3%, transportation and communications 12.0%, clothing and footwear 8.6%, housing and energy 6.7%, other 20.4%.
Land use (1991): forested 1.7%; meadows and pastures 13.0%; agricultural and under permanent cultivation 3.2%; other (mostly desert) 82.1%.

Foreign trade[7]

Balance of trade (current prices)

	1987	1988	1989	1990	1991	1992
U.S.$'000,000	+1,023	+702	−241	+1,757	+4,107	+4,140
% of total	6.8%	4.5%	1.3%	8.3%	21.1%	21.5%

Imports (1991): U.S.$7,683,000,000 ([8]capital goods 33.7%, agricultural products 25.0%, semimanufactures 24.0%). *Major import sources* (1992)[8]: France 29.0%; Italy 14.0%; U.S. 9.0%; Spain 9.0%; Germany 7.0%.
Exports (1991): U.S.$11,790,000,000 (petroleum and natural gas 96.6%, fertilizers 0.6%, wine 0.3%, dates 0.2%). *Major export destinations* (1992)[8]: Italy 21.0%; France 16.0%; U.S. 14.0%; Germany 13.0%; Spain 9.0%.

Transport and communications

Transport. Railroads (1992): route length 2,941 mi, 4,733 km; passenger-km 2,904,000,000; metric ton-km cargo 2,523,000,000. Roads (1992): total length 95,576 km (paved 66%). Vehicles (1992): passenger cars 800,000; trucks and buses 600,000. Merchant marine (1992): vessels (100 gross tons and over) 149; total deadweight tonnage 1,093,363. Air transport (1992)[9]: passenger-km 3,234,000,000; metric ton-km cargo 20,223,000; airports (1994) 11.
Communications. Daily newspapers (1992): total number 9; total circulation 1,412,000[10]; circulation per 1,000 population 54[10]. Radio (1993): 3,500,000 receivers (1 per 7.7 persons). Television (1993): 2,000,000 receivers (1 per 14 persons). Telephones (1992): 1,239,000 (1 per 21 persons).

Education and health

Education (1992–93)

	schools	teachers	students	student/ teacher ratio
Primary (age 6–11)	13,970	162,066	4,436,363	27.4
Secondary (age 12–18)	3,424	135,730	2,305,198	17.0
Voc., teacher tr.[11]	147	6,343	127,963	20.2
Higher	...	14,379	243,397	16.9

Educational attainment (1989). Percentage of economically active population age 16 and over having: no formal schooling 38.2%; Qur'anic education 0.9%; primary education 20.8%; secondary education 11.1%; vocational 19.7%; higher 9.3%. *Literacy* (1990): total population age 15 and over literate 8,090,000 (57.4%); males literate 4,840,000 (69.8%); females literate 3,250,000 (45.5%).
Health (1992): physicians 25,304 (1 per 1,041 persons); hospital beds 57,879 (1 per 455 persons); infant mortality rate per 1,000 live births (1993) 42.4.
Food (1988–90): daily per capita caloric intake 2,944 (vegetable products 89%, animal products 11%); 123% of FAO recommended minimum requirement.

Military

Total active duty personnel (1994): 121,700 (army 86.3%, navy 5.5%, air force 8.2%). *Military expenditure as percentage of GNP* (1991): 1.8% (world 4.2%); per capita expenditure U.S.$28.

[1]An advisory body, the National Consultative Council, appointed in April 1992, was replaced by an appointed interim legislature in May 1994. [2]Occupied seats in mid-1994; maximum number of seats is 200. [3]De facto population. [4]Excludes c. 2,500,-000 Algerians in France. [5]Petroleum and natural gas includes (and Manufacturing excludes) refined petroleum and manufacture of hydrocarbons. [6]Includes 1,141,278 unemployed, of whom 862,117 were not previously employed. [7]Imports c.i.f., exports f.o.b. [8]Estimated figures. [9]Air Algérie. [10]For seven newspapers only. [11]1991–92.

Andorra

Official name: Principat d'Andorra; (Principality of Andorra).
Form of government: parliamentary coprincipality[1] with one legislative house (General Council [28]).
Chiefs of state: President of France; Bishop of Seu d'Urgell, Spain.
Head of government: Head of the Government.
Capital: Andorra la Vella.
Official language: Catalan.
Official religion: none[2].
Monetary unit: There is no local currency of issue; the French franc and Spanish peseta are both in circulation. 1 franc (F) = 100 centimes; 1 peseta (Pta) = 100 céntimos. Valuation (Oct. 7, 1994) 1 U.S.$ = F 5.27, 1 £ = F 8.38; 1 U.S.$ = Ptas 127.62, 1 £ = Ptas 202.98.

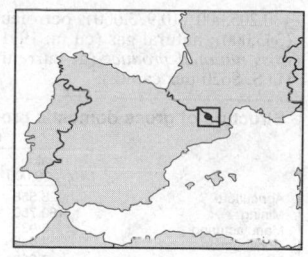

Area and population

Parishes	Capitals	area sq mi	area sq km	population 1993[3] estimate
Andorra la Vella	Andorra la Vella	49[4]	127[4]	22,387
Canillo	Canillo	74	191	2,193
Encamp	Encamp			9,654
La Massana	La Massana	25	65	5,302
Les Escaldes–Engordany	—	4	4	13,177
Ordino	Ordino	33	85	1,652
Sant Julià de Lòria	Sant Julià de Lòria	4	4	7,234
TOTAL		181	468	61,599

Demography

Population (1994): 62,400.
Density (1994): persons per sq mi 344.8, persons per sq km 133.3.
Urban-rural (1991): urban 66.2%; rural 33.8%.
Sex distribution (1993): male 53.14%; female 46.86%.
Age breakdown (1993): under 15, 16.3%; 15–29, 27.7%; 30–44, 27.2%; 45–59, 15.1%; 60–74, 9.9%; 75 and over, 3.8%.
Population projection: (2000) 66,000; (2010) 71,000.
Doubling time: 82 years.
Ethnic composition (by nationality; 1993): Spanish 46.4%; Andorran 28.3%; Portuguese 11.1%; French 7.6%; British 1.8%; German 0.5%; other 4.3%.
Religious affiliation (1991): Roman Catholic 90.0%; other 10.0%.
Major cities (1993): Andorra la Vella 22,387; Les Escaldes 13,177; Encamp 9,654.

Vital statistics

Birth rate per 1,000 population (1992): 12.1 (world avg. 26.0).
Death rate per 1,000 population (1992): 3.6 (world avg. 9.2).
Natural increase rate per 1,000 population (1992): 8.5 (world avg. 16.8).
Total fertility rate (avg. births per childbearing woman; 1993): 1.7.
Marriage rate per 1,000 population (1992): 2.2.
Divorce rate per 1,000 population: n.a.
Life expectancy at birth (1993): male 75.3 years; female 81.3 years.
Major causes of death per 100,000 population: n.a.; however, health problems are those of a developed country—cardiovascular disease, hypertension, malignant neoplasms (cancers).

National economy

Budget (1993). Revenue: Ptas 18,165,000,000 (excise taxes on imported consumer goods and gasoline 75.6%; nonspecific taxes 11.2%; concessions 3.7%). Expenditures: Ptas 23,220,000,000 (current expenditures 53.2%, of which education and culture 12.2%, general administration 9.2%, tourism and exports 7.5%, health, labour, and welfare 5.2%; development expenditures 46.8%).
Public debt (1992): U.S.$132,000,000.
Production (value of recorded exported products in Ptas '000 except as noted). Agriculture (1992): cattle 60,400, beef 15,800, horses and mules 4,200, flowers 1,000. Quarrying (1992): marble 11,800. Manufacturing (1992): wearing apparel 1,045,700; motor vehicles and parts 816,100, mineral water 343,100; furniture 213,300; newspapers and periodicals 204,700; electrical machinery and apparatus for industry 167,600. Construction (1984): 90 buildings totaling 83,834 sq m were authorized for construction. Energy production (consumption): electricity (kW-hr; 1989) 140,000,000 ([1990] 278,300,000[5]); coal, none (n.a.); crude petroleum, none (n.a.); petroleum products (metric tons; 1986) none (95,349); natural gas, none (n.a.).
Population economically active (1989): total 24,734; activity rate of total population 55.1% (participation rates: ages 15–64, 74.3%; female 45.6%; unemployed, n.a.).

Price and earnings indexes (1990 = 100)[6]

	1988	1989	1990	1991	1992	1993	1994[7]
Consumer price index	94.0	97.9	100.0	105.9	112.2	117.3	122.2
Earnings index	...	...	...	...	...	...	...

Gross national product (at current market prices; 1991): U.S.$999,000,000 (U.S.$17,600 per capita)[8].

Structure of labour force

	1989 labour force	1989 % of labour force
Agriculture	291	1.2
Mining	...	...
Manufacturing	2,719	11.0
Construction	2,914	11.8
Public utilities	...	...
Transportation and communications	...	...
Trade	5,984	24.2
Restaurants, hotels	4,698	18.9
Finance, real estate, insurance	1,331	5.4
Pub. admin., defense	2,553	10.3
Other	4,127	16.7
Unknown	117	0.5
TOTAL	24,704	100.0

Land use (1992): forested 22.2%; meadows and pastures 55.6%; agricultural and under permanent cultivation 2.2%; other 20.0%.
Household income and expenditure. Average household size: n.a.; income per household: n.a.; sources of income: n.a.; expenditure: n.a.
Tourism (1993): receipts have declined significantly since the mid-1980s; tourism nevertheless remains an important source of revenue, especially during the winter ski season.

Foreign trade

Balance of trade (current prices)

	1987	1988	1989	1990	1991	1992
Ptas '000,000	−73,200	−78,988	−89,007	−117,280	...	−112,177
% of total	93.8%	93.4%	94.2%	95.5%	...	93.0%

Imports (1992): Ptas 116,385,000,000 (wearing apparel 10.3%, electrical and electronic equipment 10.2%, transport equipment 8.8%, perfumes and cosmetics 5.5%, alcoholic beverages 5.3%, milk and related products 5.0%, nonelectrical machinery and equipment 4.7%). *Major import sources:* Spain 35.8%; France 35.1%; Japan 6.7%; Germany 5.6%; Italy 3.6%.
Exports (1992): Ptas 4,208,000,000 (wearing apparel 24.8%, motor vehicles and parts 19.4%, mineral water 8.2%, furniture 5.1%, newspapers and periodicals 4.9%). *Major export destinations:* Spain 59.3%; France 35.3%; Germany 1.9%; Italy 1.5%.

Transport and communications

Transport. Railroads: none; however, both French and Spanish railways stop near the border. Roads (1991): total length 167 mi, 269 km (paved 74%). Vehicles (1992): passenger cars 36,939; trucks and buses 4,382. Merchant marine: vessels (100 gross tons and over) none. Airports (1994) with scheduled flights: none.
Communications. Daily newspapers (1992): total number 1; circulation 3,000; circulation per 1,000 population 50. Radio (1993): total number of receivers 15,000 (1 per 4.1 persons). Television (1993): total number of receivers 4,000 (1 per 15 persons). Telephones (1992): 42,530 (1 per 1.4 persons).

Education and health

Education (1990–91)

	schools	teachers	students	student/ teacher ratio
Primary (age 6–11)	...	...	...	...
Lower secondary (age 11–14)	12	...	2,303	...
Voc., togchor tr.	6	...	1,455	...
Higher	...	...	802[9, 10]	...

Educational attainment (mid-1980s). Percentage of population age 15 and over having: no formal schooling 5.5%; primary education 47.3%; secondary education 21.6%; postsecondary education 24.9%; unknown 0.7%. *Literacy:* resident population is virtually 100% literate.
Health (1990): physicians 105 (1 per 502 persons); hospital beds 121 (1 per 435 persons); infant mortality rate per 1,000 live births (1991–92 avg.) 6.4.
Food (1988–90)[11]: daily per capita caloric intake 3,533 (vegetable products 64%, animal products 36%); 142% of FAO recommended minimum requirement.

Military

Total active duty personnel (1990): none. France and Spain are responsible for Andorra's external security; a 100-person police force maintains domestic security.

[1]First constitution of country went into effect May 4, 1993. [2]Roman Catholicism enjoys special recognition in accordance with Andorran tradition. [3]January 1. [4]Andorra la Vella includes Les Escaldes–Engordany and Sant Julià de Lòria. [5]Much electricity is imported from Spain. [6]In Spanish pesetas. [7]May. [8]Trade, tourism (including winter-season sports, fairs, and festivals), and the banking system (of some importance as a tax haven for foreign financial investment and transactions) are the primary sources of GNP. [9]Students attending universities in other countries. [10]1988–89. [11]Composite values derived from Spanish and French food data.

Angola

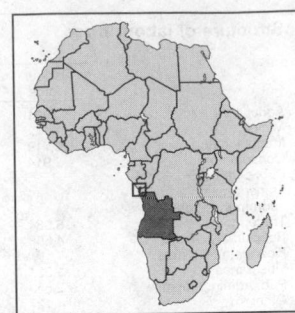

Official name: República de Angola (Republic of Angola).
Form of government: multiparty republic with one legislative house (National Assembly [220[1]]).
Head of state and government: President.
Capital: Luanda.
Official language: Portuguese.
Official religion: none.
Monetary unit: 1 new kwanza (NKz) = 100 lwei; valuation (Oct. 7, 1994) 1 U.S.$ = NKz 139,294; 1 £ = NKz 221,548.

Area and population		area		population
		sq mi	sq km	1994 estimate[2]
Provinces	**Capitals**			
Bengo	Caxito	12,112	31,371	178,000
Benguela	Benguela	12,273	31,788	686,000
Bié	Kuito	27,148	70,314	1,215,000
Cabinda	Cabinda	2,807	7,270	181,000
Cunene	N'Giva	34,495	89,342	242,000
Huambo	Huambo	13,233	34,274	1,644,000
Huíla	Lubango	28,958	75,002	926,000
Kuando Kubango	Menongue	76,853	199,049	136,000
Kuanza Norte	N'Dalatando	9,340	24,190	402,000
Kuanza Sul	Sumbe	21,490	55,660	679,000
Luanda	Luanda	934	2,418	1,892,000
Lunda Norte	Lucapa	39,685	102,783	307,000
Lunda Sul	Saurimo	17,625	45,649	158,000
Malanje	Malanje	37,684	97,602	953,000
Moxico	Lwena	86,110	223,023	341,000
Namibe	Namibe	22,447	58,137	129,000
Uíge	Uíge	22,663	58,698	921,000
Zaire	M'Banza Kongo	15,494	40,130	234,000
TOTAL		481,354[3]	1,246,700	11,233,000[3]

Demography

Population (1994): 11,233,000.
Density (1994): persons per sq mi 23.3, persons per sq km 9.0.
Urban-rural (1990): urban 28.3%; rural 71.7%.
Sex distribution (1991): male 48.80%; female 51.20%.
Age breakdown (1994): under 15, 45.0%; 15–29, 25.6%; 30–44, 15.1%; 45–59, 8.8%; 60 and over, 5.5%.
Population projection: (2000) 13,400,000; (2010) 18,082,000.
Doubling time: 22 years.
Ethnic composition (1983): Ovimbundu 37.2%; Mbundu 21.6%; Kongo 13.2%; Luimbe-Nganguela 5.4%; Nyaneka-Humbe 5.4%; Chokwe 4.2%; Luvale (Luena) 3.4%; Luchazi 2.4%; Ambo (Ovambo) 2.4%; Lunda 1.2%; Mbunda 1.2%; Portuguese 0.5%; mestizo 0.5%; other 0.4%.
Religious affiliation (1980): Christian 90.0%, of which Roman Catholic 68.7%; Protestant 19.8%; traditional beliefs 9.5%; other 0.5%.
Major cities: Luanda (1988) 1,134,000; Huambo (1983) 203,000; Benguela (1983) 155,000; Lobito (1983) 150,000; Lubango (1984) 105,000.

Vital statistics

Birth rate per 1,000 population (1990–95): 51.3 (world avg. 26.0).
Death rate per 1,000 population (1990–95): 19.2 (world avg. 9.2).
Natural increase rate per 1,000 population (1990–95): 32.1 (world avg. 16.8).
Total fertility rate (avg. births per childbearing woman; 1990–95): 7.2.
Marriage rate per 1,000 population (1972): 4.5.
Divorce rate per 1,000 population: n.a.
Life expectancy at birth (1990–95): male 44.9 years; female 48.1 years.
Major causes of death per 100,000 population (1973): accidents, poisoning, and violence 89.0; infectious and parasitic diseases 73.2; diseases of the respiratory system 24.6; diseases of the circulatory system 19.2; malignant neoplasms (cancers) 6.5.

National economy

Budget (1991). Revenue: NKz 186,383,000,000 (1989; tax revenue 82.8%, of which petroleum taxes 53.1%, income and property taxes 11.6%, domestic production taxes 9.5%, import duties 6.3%; nontax revenue 17.2%). Expenditures: NKz 275,468,000,000 (defense and internal security 36.9%; administration 23.9%; education 17.5%; health 7.5%; energy 3.6%; other 10.6%).
Public debt (external, outstanding; 1992): U.S.$7,628,000,000.
Tourism (1992): receipts from visitors, n.a.; expenditures by nationals abroad U.S.$75,000,000.
Production (metric tons except as noted). Agriculture, forestry, fishing (1993): cassava 1,870,000, sugarcane 290,000, bananas 280,000, corn (maize) 274,000, sweet potatoes 170,000, millet 40,000, palm oil 40,000, dry beans 36,000, peanuts (groundnuts) 18,000, coffee 5,000; livestock (number of live animals) 3,200,000 cattle, 1,550,000 goats, 810,000 pigs, 250,000 sheep, 6,000,000 chickens; roundwood (1992) 6,378,000 cu m; fish catch (1991) 75,062. Mining and quarrying (1992): diamonds 900,000 carats. Manufacturing (1990): fresh meat 93,000; bread 45,000; corn flour 35,000; wheat flour 22,000; laundry soap 7,556; sugar 3,190[4]; pasta 3,190[4]; leather shoes 132,000 pairs[4]; beer 410,000 hectolitres; soft drinks 69,050 hectolitres[4]; matches 6,357,000 boxes[4]. Construction (value in NKz '000,000; 1986): residential 1,977, nonresidential 1,977. Energy production (consumption): electricity (kW-hr; 1991) 1,840,000,000 (1,840,000,000); coal, none (none); crude petroleum (barrels; 1991

180,205,000 (10,973,000); petroleum products (metric tons; 1991) 1,309,000 (343,000); natural gas (cu m; 1991) 166,576,000 (166,576,000).
Gross national product (at current market prices; 1989): U.S.$6,010,000,000 (U.S. $620 per capita).

Structure of gross domestic product and labour force

	1991		1988	
	in value NKz '000,000[5]	% of total value	labour force	% of labour force
Agriculture	28,558	10.3	2,810,000	71.4
Mining	160,750	58.2		
Manufacturing	6,935	2.5		
Construction	5,235	1.9		
Finance	2,360	0.9	400,000	10.2
Trade	16,803	6.1		
Public utilities	818	0.3		
Transportation and communications	6,255	2.3		
Pub. admin., defense	48,391	17.5	726,000	18.4
Services				
Other	...	...		
TOTAL	276,105	100.0	3,936,000	100.0

Population economically active (1988): total 3,936,000; activity rate of total population 41.5% (participation rates [1985]: ages 15–64, 71.8%; female 39.7%; unemployed, n.a.).
Price and earnings indexes: n.a.
Household income and expenditure. Average household size (1980) 4.8; annual income per household: n.a.; sources of income: n.a.; expenditure: n.a.
Land use (1992): forested 41.6%; meadows and pastures 23.3%; agricultural and under permanent cultivation 2.8%; other 32.3%.

Foreign trade

Balance of trade (current prices)

	1987	1988	1989	1990	1991	1992
U.S.$'000,000	+953	+1,081	+1,191	+1,276	+2,080	+1,160.5
% of total	26.6%	28.1%	25.1%	25.1%	43.6%	19.0%

Imports (1991): U.S.$1,347,000,000 (current consumption goods 50.2%, capital goods 20.2%, intermediate consumption goods 18.9%, transport equipment 6.8%). *Major import sources:* Portugal 29.8%; United States 10.5%; France 9.7%; Japan 7.8%; Brazil 7.3%.
Exports (1991): U.S.$3,427,000,000 (mineral fuels 89.8%, diamonds 5.5%). *Major export destinations:* United States 56.6%; Germany 5.6%; Brazil 4.9%; The Netherlands 4.2%; United Kingdom 3.4%; Belgium-Luxembourg 3.3%.

Transport and communications

Transport. Railroads (1988): route length 1,739 mi, 2,798 km; passenger-mi 203,000,000, passenger-km 326,000,000; short ton-mi cargo 1,178,000,000, metric ton-km cargo 1,720,000,000. Roads (1992): total length 45,118 mi, 72,626 km (paved 25%). Vehicles (1991): passenger cars 120,000; trucks and buses 40,000. Merchant marine (1992): vessels (100 gross tons and over) 113; total deadweight tonnage 123,479. Air transport (1991)[6]: passenger-mi 771,000,000, passenger-km 1,241,000,000; short ton-mi cargo 28,000,000, metric ton-km cargo 42,000,000; airports (1994) with scheduled flights 17.
Communications. Daily newspapers (1993): total number 4; total circulation 84,500[7]; circulation per 1,000 population 7.7[7]. Radio (1993): total number of receivers 450,000 (1 per 24 persons). Television (1993): total number of receivers 50,500 (1 per 216 persons). Telephones (1991): 78,000 (1 per 132 persons).

Education and health

Education (1990–91)

	schools	teachers	students	student/ teacher ratio
Primary (age 7–10)	6,308[8]	31,062	990,155	31.9
Secondary (age 11–16)	5,276[8]	5,138[9]	166,812	...
Voc., teacher tr.	...	566[9]	19,687	...
Higher	1[8]	439	6,534	14.9

Educational attainment: n.a. Literacy (1990): percentage of population age 15 and over literate 41.7%; males literate 55.6%; females literate 28.5%.
Health (1990): physicians 662 (1 per 15,136 persons); hospital beds 11,857 (1 per 845 persons); infant mortality rate per 1,000 live births (1990–95) 127.0.
Food (1985): daily per capita caloric intake 1,969 ([1979–81] vegetable products 92%, animal products 8%); (1984) 84% of FAO recommended minimum requirement.

Military

Total active duty personnel (1994): 82,000 (army 91.5%, navy 1.8%, air force 6.7%). *Military expenditure as percentage of GNP* (1986): 23.9% (world 5.4%); per capita expenditure U.S.$173.

---

[1]Excludes 3 seats for Angolans abroad not filled at October 1992 elections. [2]Unified national estimates and projections based on sample surveys, partial censuses, and analysis of provincial vital statistics. [3]Detail does not add to total given because of rounding. [4]1989. [5]At official prices of 1980. [6]TAAG Airline only. [7]Circulation for three newspapers only. [8]1985–86. [9]1989–90.

Antigua and Barbuda

Official name: Antigua and Barbuda.
Form of government: constitutional
monarchy with two legislative
houses (Senate [17]; House of
Representatives [17]).
Chief of state: British Monarch
represented by Governor-General.
Head of government: Prime Minister.
Capital: Saint John's.
Official language: English.
Official religion: none.
Monetary unit: 1 East Caribbean dollar
(EC$) = 100 cents; valuation (Oct. 7,
1994) 1 U.S.$ = EC$2.70;
1 £ = EC$4.30.

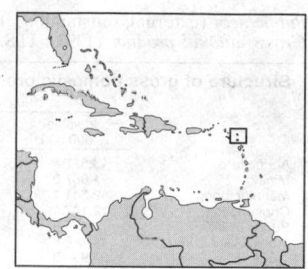

Area and population	area		population
Parishes[1]	sq mi	sq km	1991 census
Saint George	10.2	26.4	...
Saint John's	20.2	67.9	...
Saint Mary	25.1	65.0	...
Saint Paul	17.7	45.8	...
Saint Peter	12.8	33.2	...
Saint Phillip	16.0	41.4	...
Islands[1]			
Barbuda	62.0	160.6	1,400
Redonda	0.5	1.3	2
TOTAL	170.5	441.6	65,962

Demography

Population (1994): 66,000.
Density (1994): persons per sq mi 387.1, persons per sq km 149.5.
Urban-rural (1991): urban 31.0%; rural 69.0%.
Sex distribution (1985): male 48.00%; female 52.00%.
Age breakdown (1985): under 15, 37.2%; 15–29, 30.8%; 30–44, 12.8%; 45–59, 11.5%; 60–74, 6.4%; 75 and over, 1.3%.
Population projection: (2000) 66,000; (2010) 66,000.
Doubling time: 58 years.
Ethnic composition (1988): black 89.0%; mixed 10.0%; other (mostly British, Portuguese, and Lebanese) 1.0%.
Religious affiliation (1980): Anglican 44.5%; other Protestant (largely Moravian, Methodist, and Seventh-day Adventist) 41.6%; Roman Catholic 10.2%; Rastafarian 0.7%; other 3.0%.
Major cities (1986): Saint John's 36,000; Codrington 1,200[3].

Vital statistics

Birth rate per 1,000 population (1993): 17.5 (world avg. 26.0); (1988) legitimate 23.4%; illegitimate 76.6%.
Death rate per 1,000 population (1993): 5.5 (world avg. 9.2).
Natural increase rate per 1,000 population (1993): 12.0 (world avg. 16.8).
Total fertility rate (avg. births per childbearing woman; 1993): 1.7.
Marriage rate per 1,000 population (1988): 4.9.
Divorce rate per 1,000 population (1988): 0.2.
Life expectancy at birth (1993): male 70.8 years; female 74.9 years.
Major causes of death per 100,000 population (1988): diseases of the circulatory system 237.5; malignant neoplasms (cancers) 44.5; diseases of the respiratory system 44.5; endocrine and metabolic disorders 25.4; ill-defined conditions 68.6.

National economy

Budget (1992). Revenue: EC$259,700,000 (current revenue 94.7%, of which consumption taxes 26.0%, nontax revenue 17.3%, import duties 16.3%, taxes on goods and services 16.3%; grants 3.6%; development revenue 1.7%). Expenditures: EC$261,200,000 (current expenditures 93.8%; development expenditures 6.2%).
Production (metric tons except as noted). Agriculture, forestry, fishing (1993): vegetables 2,000, mangoes 2,000, cantaloupes and other melons 1,000, limes 249[4], sweet potatoes 219[4], "Antiguan Black" pineapples 126[4]; livestock (number of live animals) 16,000 cattle, 13,000 sheep; roundwood, n.a.; fish catch (1991) 2,300 (of which spiny lobster 200). Mining and quarrying: crushed stone for local use. Manufacturing (1988): rum 4,000 hectolitres; wine and vodka 2,000 hectolitres; other manufactures include bedding, paints, and furniture. Construction (1988): gross value of building applications EC$221,800,000. Energy production (consumption): electricity (kW-hr; 1992) 95,000,000 (95,000,000); coal, none (none); crude petroleum, none (none); petroleum products (metric tons; 1992) negligible (94,000); natural gas, none (none).
Population economically active (1985): total 32,254; activity rate of total population 42.6% (participation rates: over age 16 [1983] 56.2%; female 40.1%; unemployed, n.a.[5]).

Price and earnings indexes (1987 = 100)							
	1986	1987	1988	1989	1990	1991	1992
Consumer price index	96.5	100.0	103.4	108.9	117.3	119.7	...
Weekly earnings index[6]	...	100.0	110.0	122.1	122.1	122.1	134.9

Household income and expenditure. Average household size (1984) 3.5; income per household: n.a.; sources of income: n.a.; expenditure (1974)[7]: food and nonalcoholic beverages 42.9%, housing 23.3%, transportation 10.0%,

clothing and footwear 7.5%, energy 5.5%, alcoholic beverages and tobacco 3.6%, other 7.2%.
Gross national product (at current market prices; 1993): U.S.$428,000,000 (U.S.$6,390 per capita).

Structure of gross domestic product and labour force				
	1991[8]		1982	
	in value EC$'000,000	% of total value	labour force[9]	% of labour force[9]
Agriculture, fishing	39.0	4.1	2,090	9.0
Quarrying	18.0	1.9	00	0.3
Manufacturing	32.0	3.4	1,718	7.4
Construction	95.9	10.2	2,577	11.1
Public utilities	34.0	3.6	340	1.5
Transportation and communications	178.9	19.0	2,575	11.1
Trade, restaurants, and hotels	238.8	25.3	5,201	22.4
Finance, real estate	136.8	14.5	778	3.3
Pub. admin., defense	170.4	18.1	7,883	33.9
Services	63.7	6.7		
Other	−63.6[10]	−6.7[10]		
TOTAL	944.0[11]	100.0[11]	23,222	100.0

Land use (1992): forested 11.0%; meadows and pastures 9.0%; agricultural and under permanent cultivation 18.0%; other 62.0%.
Public debt (external, outstanding; end of 1993): U.S.$309,000,000.
Tourism (1992): receipts from visitors U.S.$329,000,000; expenditures by nationals abroad U.S.$19,000,000.

Foreign trade[12]

Balance of trade (current prices)						
	1988	1989	1990	1991	1992	1993
U.S.$'000,000	−280.0	−316.8	−325.0	−317.0	−364.0	−403.6
% of total	80.5%	83.4%	83.0%	83.2%	84.3%	84.9%

Imports (1992): U.S.$398,000,000 ([13]agricultural products 11.0%, unspecified 89.0%). *Major import sources* (1989)[13]: United States 27.0%; United Kingdom 16.0%; Canada 4.0%; OECS 3.0%; Italy 3.0%.
Exports (1992): U.S.$34,000,000 ([13]reexports [significantly, petroleum products] 82.0%, domestic exports 18.0%). *Major export destinations* (1989)[13]: United States 41.0%; United Kingdom 19.0%; Germany 19.0%.

Transport and communications

Transport. Railroads[14]. Roads (1990): total length 724 mi, 1,165 km (paved 33%). Vehicles (1992): passenger cars 13,500; trucks and buses 3,500. Merchant marine (1992): vessels (100 gross tons and over) 292; total deadweight tonnage 997,381. Air transport (1991): passenger-mi 121,000,000, passenger-km 195,000,000; short ton-mi cargo 137,000, metric ton-km cargo 200,000; airports (1994) with scheduled flights 2.
Communications. Daily newspapers: none[15]. Radio (1993): total number of receivers 75,000 (1 per 0.9 persons). Television (1993): total number of receivers 28,000 (1 per 2.4 persons). Telephones (1992): 19,390[16] (1 per 3.4 persons).

Education and health

Education (1991–92)	schools	teachers	students	student/ teacher ratio
Primary (age 5–10)	43	549	10,770	19.6
Secondary (age 11–16)	12	353	4,373	12.5
Higher	1	45	590	13.1

Educational attainment: n.a. *Literacy* (1985): total population age 15 and over literate 45,000 (90.0%).
Health: physicians (1991) 59 (1 per 1,119 persons); hospital beds (1987) 373 (1 per 207 persons); infant mortality rate per 1,000 live births (1993) 19.2.
Food (1988–90): daily per capita caloric intake 2,307 (vegetable products 64%, animal products 36%); 98% of FAO recommended minimum requirement.

Military

Total active duty personnel (1990): an almost 100-member defense force is part of the Eastern Caribbean regional security system. *Military expenditure as percentage of central government current expenditure* (1990–91): 1.4%[17].

[1]Community councils on Antigua and the local government council on Barbuda are the organs of local government. [2]Uninhabited. [3]1982. [4]1988. [5]In 1990–92 unemployment increased, particularly in the depressed construction sector. [6]Construction only. [7]Weights of consumer price index components. [8]At factor cost. [9]Wage earners and self-employed only. [10]Less imputed bank service charges. [11]Detail does not add to total given because of rounding. [12]Exports f.o.b.; imports c.i.f. [13]Estimated percentages. [14]Privately owned track are mostly nonoperative. [15]Three weekly newspapers and one twice-weekly newspaper had a total circulation of 12,200 in 1990. [16]Number of lines. [17]May not agree with military expenditure as percentage of GNP because of different bases used.

Argentina

Official name: República Argentina (Argentine Republic).
Form of government: federal republic with two legislative houses (Senate [48]; Chamber of Deputies [259]).
Head of state and government: President.
Capital: Buenos Aires.
Official language: Spanish.
Official religion: Roman Catholicism.
Monetary unit: 1 peso (pl. pesos)[1] (Ps) = 100 centavos; valuation (Oct. 7, 1994) 1 U.S.$ = Ps 1.00; 1 £ = Ps 1.59.

Area and population

Provinces	Capitals	area sq mi	area sq km	population 1991 census
Buenos Aires	La Plata	118,754	307,571	12,594,974
Catamarca	Catamarca	39,615	102,602	264,234
Chaco	Resistencia	38,469	99,633	839,677
Chubut	Rawson	86,752	224,686	357,189
Córdoba	Córdoba	63,831	165,321	2,766,683
Corrientes	Corrientes	34,054	88,199	795,594
Entre Ríos	Paraná	30,418	78,781	1,020,257
Formosa	Formosa	27,825	72,066	398,413
Jujuy	San Salvador de Jujuy	20,548	53,219	512,329
La Pampa	Santa Rosa	55,382	143,440	259,996
La Rioja	La Rioja	34,626	89,680	220,729
Mendoza	Mendoza	57,462	148,827	1,412,481
Misiones	Posadas	11,506	29,801	788,915
Neuquén	Neuquén	36,324	94,078	388,833
Río Negro	Viedma	78,384	203,013	506,772
Salta	Salta	60,034	155,488	866,153
San Juan	San Juan	34,614	89,651	528,715
San Luis	San Luis	29,633	76,748	286,458
Santa Cruz	Río Gallegos	94,187	243,943	159,839
Santa Fe	Santa Fe	51,354	133,007	2,798,422
Santiago del Estero	Santiago del Estero	52,645	136,351	671,988
Tierra del Fuego[2]	Ushuaia	8,329	21,571	69,369
Tucumán	San Miguel de Tucumán	8,697	22,524	1,142,105
Other federal entity				
Distrito Federal	Buenos Aires	77	200	2,965,403
TOTAL		1,073,518[3]	2,780,400	32,615,528

Demography

Population (1994): 33,880,000.
Density (1994): persons per sq mi 31.6, persons per sq km 12.2.
Urban-rural (1991): urban 86.9%; rural 13.1%.
Sex distribution (1991): male 48.90%; female 51.10%.
Age breakdown (1991): under 15, 30.6%; 15–29, 23.3%; 30–44, 19.3%; 45–59, 13.9%; 60–74, 9.6%; 75 and over, 3.3%.
Population projection: (2000) 36,239,000; (2010) 40,170,000.
Doubling time: 63 years.
Ethnic composition (1986): European 85%; mestizo, Amerindian, and other 15%.
Religious affiliation (1992): Roman Catholic 91.6%; other 8.4%.
Major cities (1991): Buenos Aires 2,960,976 (Greater Buenos Aires 12,582,-321); Córdoba 1,179,067; Rosario 1,078,374[4]; La Plata 542,567.

Vital statistics

Birth rate per 1,000 population (1994): 19.6 (world avg. 26.0); (1982) legitimate 67.5%; illegitimate 29.8%; unknown 2.7%.
Death rate per 1,000 population (1994): 8.6 (world avg. 9.2).
Natural increase rate per 1,000 population (1994): 11.0 (world avg. 16.8).
Total fertility rate (avg. births per childbearing woman; 1994): 2.7.
Marriage rate per 1,000 population (1990): 5.8.
Life expectancy at birth (1994): male 68.1 years; female 74.8 years.
Major causes of death per 100,000 population (1990): circulatory diseases 358.1; neoplasms (cancers) 142.5; accidents 51.5; respiratory diseases 50.8.

National economy

Budget (1993). Revenue: U.S.$51,885,200,000 (current revenue 97.2%, of which tax revenue 90.5%, nontax revenue 6.1%, other 0.6%; captial revenue 2.8%). Expenditure: U.S.$52,151,000,000 (1989; social security 35.3%; economic services 16.0%; education 9.9%; defense 9.9%; transportation and communications 8.8%; debt service 7.4%).
Land use (1992): forested 21.6%; meadows and pastures 51.9%; agricultural and under permanent cultivation 9.9%; other 16.6%.
Production (metric tons except as noted). Agriculture, forestry, fishing (1993): sugarcane 17,000,000, corn (maize) 10,897,000, soybeans 10,673,000, wheat 9,153,000, sunflower seeds 3,250,000, sorghum 2,860,000, potatoes 2,000,000, grapes 1,821,000, tomatoes 730,000; livestock (number of live animals) 50,-320,000 cattle, 24,500,000 sheep; roundwood (1992) 11,865,000 cu m; fish catch (1992) 692,110. Mining and quarrying (1992): silver 1,478,932 troy oz; gold 41,796 troy oz. Manufacturing (by value of production in U.S.$'000; 1990): petroleum and petroleum products 6,069,000; food products 4,695,-000; textiles 2,209,000; transport equipment 2,140,000; industrial chemicals 1,844,000; iron and steel 1,651,000; metal products 1,611,000. Construction (authorized; 1990): 7,750,600 sq m. Energy production (consumption): electricity (kW-hr; 1992) 56,273,000,000 (58,865,000,000); coal (metric tons; 1992) 215,000 (1,393,000); crude petroleum (barrels; 1992) 204,582,000 (182,-120,000); petroleum products (metric tons; 1992) 22,214,000 (18,035,000); natural gas (cu m; 1992) 25,876,000,000 (28,256,000,000).

Public debt (external, outstanding; 1992): U.S.$46,835,000,000.
Gross national product (1993): U.S.$244,091,000,000 (U.S.$7,290 per capita).

Structure of gross domestic product and labour force

	1992 in value A '000,000[1]	1992 % of total value	1980 labour force	1980 % of labour force
Agriculture	13,577.4	6.0	1,200,992	12.0
Mining	4,067.0	1.8	47,171	0.5
Manufacturing	49,541.1	21.9	1,985,995	19.9
Construction	12,107.4	5.3	1,003,175	10.1
Public utilities	3,825.8	1.7	103,256	1.0
Transp. and commun.	11,718.6	5.2	460,476	4.6
Trade	34,929.0	15.4	1,702,080	17.0
Finance	38,132.6	16.8	395,704	4.0
Pub. admin., defense Services	} 59,021.5	26.0	2,399,039	24.0
Other	−282.9[5]	−0.1[5]	691,302	6.9
TOTAL	226,637.6[3]	100.0	9,989,190	100.0

Population economically active (1990): total 12,305,346; activity rate of total population 38.1% (participation rates: ages 15–64, 59.6%; female 28.2%; unemployed [1989] 7.3%).

Price and earnings indexes (1990 = 100)[1]

	1990	1991	1992	1993
Consumer price index	100.0	272	339	375
Hourly earnings index	100.0	194.3	238.4	...

Household size and expenditure. Average household size (1991) 3.8; expenditure (1985–86): food 38.2%, transportation 11.6%, housing 9.3%, energy 9.0%, clothing and footwear 8.0%, health 7.9%, recreation and culture 7.5%, education 2.6%, other 5.9%.
Tourism (1992): receipts U.S.$3,090,000,000; expenditures U.S.$2,211,000,000.

Foreign trade[6]

Balance of trade (current prices)

	1988	1989	1990	1991	1992	1993
U.S.$'000,000	+4,051	+5,706	+8,627	+4,572	−1,388	−1,576
% of total	29.3%	42.5%	53.7%	23.6%	5.4%	5.7%

Imports (1992): U.S.$14,863,950,000 (machinery and transport equipment 47.8%, manufactured products 15.1%, chemical products 13.7%, food products and live animals 5.0%, petroleum and petroleum products 1.6%). *Major import sources:* Brazil 22.5%; U.S. 21.7%; Germany 7.3%; Italy 5.1%; Japan 4.7%; Chile 4.3%; France 3.9%.
Exports (1992): U.S.$12,234,949,000 (food products and live animals 44.1%, manufactured products 11.8%, vegetable and animal oils 9.0%, petroleum and petroleum products 8.5%, machinery and transport equipment 7.5%, chemical products 5.7%). *Major export destinations:* Brazil 13.7%; U.S. 11.0%; The Netherlands 9.9%; Germany 6.0%; Chile 4.7%; Italy 4.3%; Spain 4.1%; Japan 3.1%.

Transport and communications

Transport. Railroads (1992): route length (1990) 34,059 km; passenger-km 6,705,059,000; metric ton-km cargo 3,707,489,000. Roads (1986): total length 131,338 mi, 211,369 km (paved 27%). Vehicles (1992): passenger cars 4,417,-882; commercial vehicles and buses 1,552,893. Merchant marine (1992): vessels (100 gross tons and over) 423; total deadweight tonnage 1,173,105. Air transport (1993)[7]: passenger-km 7,751,369,000; metric ton-km cargo 176,407,000; airports (1994) 42.
Communications. Daily newspapers (1990): total number 159; total circulation 4,000,000; circulation per 1,000 population 124. Radio (1993): 21,582,456 receivers (1 per 1.6 persons). Television (1993): 7,165,000 receivers (1 per 4.7 persons). Telephones (1990): 4,622,360 (1 per 7.0 persons).

Education and health

Education (1991–92)

	schools	teachers	students	student/ teacher ratio
Primary (age 6–12)	21,703	259,579[8]	4,874,306	19.3[9]
Secondary (age 13–17)[8, 9]	7,224	262,000	1,862,000	7.1
Higher	1,540[10]	89,609	1,077,212	12.0

Educational attainment (1991). Percentage of population age 25 and over having: no formal schooling 5.7%; less than primary education 22.3%; primary 34.6%; incomplete secondary 12.5%; complete secondary 12.8%; higher 12.0%. *Literacy* (1990): percentage of total population age 15 and over literate 95.3%; males literate 95.5%; females literate 95.1%.
Health: physicians (1988) 96,000 (1 per 326 persons); hospital beds (1987) 150,000 (1 per 205 persons); infant mortality rate (1992) 34.0.
Food (1988–90): daily per capita caloric intake 3,068 (vegetable products 69%; animal products 31%); 131% of FAO recommended minimum requirement.

Military

Total active duty personnel (1994): 69,800 (army 57.9%, navy 29.4%, air force 12.7%). *Military expenditure as percentage of GNP* (1991): 1.9% (world 4.2%); per capita expenditure: U.S.$75.

---

[1]On Jan. 1, 1992, the austral was replaced by the peso at a ratio of 10,000 to 1. [2]Area of Tierra del Fuego (province since 1991) excludes claims to British-held islands in the South Atlantic Ocean. [3]Detail does not add to total given because of rounding. [4]*Municipio.* [5]Import duties. [6]Import figures are f.o.b. in balance of trade and c.i.f. in commodities and trading partners. [7]Aerolineas Argentina only. [8]1988–89. [9]Secondary includes vocational and teacher training. [10]1987.

Armenia

Official name: Hayastani Hanrape-
tut'yun (Republic of Armenia).
Form of government: unitary multiparty
republic with a single legislative body
(Supreme Council [185]).
Head of state: President.
Head of government: Prime Minister.
Capital: Yerevan.
Official language: Armenian.
Official religion: none.
Monetary unit[1]: 1 dram = 100 lumas;
valuation (Oct. 3, 1994) free rate,
1 U.S.$ = 356.68 dram;
1 £ = 562.06 dram.

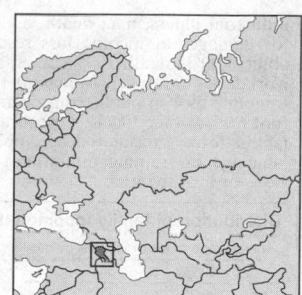

Area and population

Administrative subdivisions	Capitals	area sq mi	area sq km	population 1907 estimate
Cities[2]				
Gyumri	—	...	...	228,400
Kirovakan	—	...	...	169,400
Yerevan	—	...	...	1,184,500
Rural districts				
Abovyani	Abovyan	313	810	108,200
Akhuryani	Akhuryan	223	577	39,500
Amasiayi	Amasia	235	609	19,300
Anii	Maralik	166	429	19,700
Aparani	Aparan	228	591	19,900
Aragatsi	Tsaghkahovit	148	382	14,100
Ararati	Vedi	540	1,399	85,100
Artashati	Artashat	200	517	95,500
Art'iki	Art'ik	187	484	44,800
Ashtaraki	Ashtarak	267	692	36,400
Azizbekovi	Azizbekov	453	1,172	17,000
Baghramyani	Baghramyan	175	453	16,100
Ejmiadzini	Ejmiadzin	141	366	121,000
Ghap'ani	Ghap'an	529	1,371	61,500
Ghukasyani	Ghukasyan	211	547	9,800
Gorisi	Goris	290	752	38,000
Gugark'i	Gugark'	297	770	31,000
Hoktemberyani	Hoktemberyan	163	423	109,900
Hrazdani	Hrazdan	366	948	78,600
Ijevani	Ijevan	516	1,336	46,600
Kalininoyi	Kalinino	266	690	39,100
Kamoyi	Kamo	269	697	56,400
Krasnoselski	Krasnoselsk	269	697	27,900
Martunu	Martuni	458	1,185	67,900
Masisi	Masis	70	182	64,400
Meghru	Meghri	256	664	15,100
Nairii	Yeghvard	133	344	47,200
Noyemberyani	Noyemberyan	208	538	29,700
Sevani	Sevan	152	393	42,700
Shamshadini	Berd	318	824	34,200
Sisiani	Sisian	664	1,719	34,600
Spitaki	Spitak	212	549	46,300
Step'anavani	Step'anavan	246	637	36,500
T'alini	T'alin	421	1,091	35,100
T'umanyani	Alaverdi	433	1,121	58,200
Vardenisi	Vardenis	444	1,151	60,200
Yeghegnadzori	Yeghegnadzor	438	1,134	35,400
TOTAL		11,500[3]	29,800[3]	3,411,900[3]

Demography

Population (1994): 3,553,000[4].
Density (1994): persons per sq mi 309.0, persons per sq km 119.2.
Urban-rural (1991): urban 69.5%; rural 30.5%.
Sex distribution (1992): male 49.50%; female 50.50%.
Age breakdown (1990): under 15, 30.3%; 15–29, 25.7%; 30–44, 20.8%; 45–59, 13.6%; 60–69, 6.4%; 70 and over, 3.2%.
Population projection: (2000) 3,870,000; (2010) 4,463,000.
Doubling time: 54 years.
Ethnic composition (1989): Armenian 93.3%; Azerbaijani 2.6%; other 4.1%.
Religious affiliation: believers are predominantly Armenian Apostolic.
Major cities (1991): Yerevan 1,283,000; Gyumri 163,000[5]; Kirovakan 76,000[5].

Vital statistics

Birth rate per 1,000 population (1992): 20.7 (world avg. 26.0); (1989) legitimate 92.1%; illegitimate 7.9%.
Death rate per 1,000 population (1992): 7.3 (world avg. 9.2).
Natural increase rate per 1,000 population (1992): 13.4 (world avg. 16.8).
Total fertility rate (avg. births per childbearing woman; 1993): 3.3.
Marriage rate per 1,000 population (1992): 6.5.
Divorce rate per 1,000 population (1992): 0.9.
Life expectancy at birth (1993): male 68.4 years; female 75.4 years.
Major causes of death per 100,000 population (1990): circulatory diseases 305.9; cancers 98.3; accidents and violence 55.6; respiratory diseases 50.3.

National economy

Budget (1992). Revenue: 9,556,000,000 rubles (tax revenue 97.4%, of which value-added tax 49.2%, income tax 34.0%, excise taxes 10.5%; nontax revenue 2.6%). Expenditures: 10,746,000,000 rubles (education 29.9%, national economy 23.7%; health 18.3%; police 5.3%; defense 2.3%).
Production (metric tons except as noted). Agriculture, forestry, fishing (1993): vegetables (except potatoes) 413,000, potatoes 350,000, cereals 305,000, milk 200,000, wheat 165,000, grapes 100,000; livestock (number of live animals) 868,000 sheep and goats, 549,000 cattle, 243,000 pigs, 9,000,000 poultry; roundwood (1991) 44,100 cu m; fish catch (1992) 4,480. Manufacturing

(1992): cement 1,500,000; caustic soda 14,900; synthetic plastic 7,300; paper 4,400; chemical fibres 4,100; cotton fabrics 17,600,000 sq m; silk fabrics 9,300,000 sq m; wool fabrics 3,600,000 sq m; watches 2,200,000 pieces; car tires 900,000 units; metal-cutting equipment 7,100 units; automobiles 6,800 units; leather shoes 11,300,000 pairs. Construction (1991): 1,910,000 cu m. Energy production (consumption): electricity (kW-hr; 1992) 9,000,000,000 (9,000,000,000); coal (metric tons; 1992) none (141,000); petroleum products (metric tons; 1990) 292,000 (4,346,000); natural gas (cu m; 1992) none (1,860,000,000).
Gross national product (1993): U.S.$2,462,000,000 (U.S.$660 per capita).

Structure of gross domestic product and labour force

	1992 in value '000,000 rubles	1992 % of total value	1991 labour force	1991 % of labour force
Agriculture	20,360	39.9	389,000	20.5
Manufacturing, mining }	23,620	46.3	458,000	24.2
Public utilities			52,000	2.7
Construction	2,700	5.3	177,000	9.3
Transp. and commun.	842	1.6	80,000	4.2
Trade	2,923	5.7	101,000	5.3
Finance	—	—	8,000	0.4
Pub. admin., defense	—	—	25,000	1.3
Services			349,000	18.4
Other	605	1.2	257,000[6]	13.7[6]
TOTAL	51,050	100.0	1,896,000	100.0

Land use (1992): forest 9.5%; pasture 21.8%; agriculture 18.1%; other 50.6%.
Population economically active (1991): total 1,896,000; activity rate of total population 52.0% (participation rates: ages 16–59 [male], 16–54 [female] 94.5%; female [1990] 49.4%; unemployed [1990] 3.6%).

Price and earnings indexes (1990 = 100)

	1986	1987	1988	1989	1990	1991	1992
Consumer price index	102.0	103.0	103.0	104.0	100.0	274.1	2,271.5
Monthly earnings index	76.5	79.2	81.7	91.2	100.0	262.2	1,503.9

Household income and expenditure. Average household size (1989) 4.7; income per household (1990) 11,100 rubles; sources of income (1992): salaries and wages 55.8%, social benefits 31.9%, agricultural income 12.3%; expenditure (1992) 8,100 rubles: retail goods 70.5%, taxes 6.2%, services 16.2%.

Foreign trade

Balance of trade (current prices)

	1987	1988	1989	1990	1991	1992
'000,000 rubles	−135	−1,110	−1,207	−1,039	−1,808	−4,784
% of total	1.6%	12.8%	14.1%	12.7%	12.2%	4.8%

Imports (1992): 51,905,000,000 rubles (1991; basic manufactures 52.5%, light-industrial products 22.5%, machinery and transport equipment 11.8%, food products 4.6%, chemical products 2.3%). *Major import sources* (1990): Russia 30.0%; Ukraine 18.7%; Belarus 7.2%.
Exports (1992): 47,121,000,000 rubles (1991; basic manufactures 35.3%, machinery and transport equipment 18.9%, ferrous metals 11.2%, light-industrial products 10.6%, chemical products 6.3%). *Major export destinations* (1990): Russia 60.9%; Ukraine 12.2%; Kazakhstan 11.1%; Uzbekistan 4.1%; Turkmenistan 3.3%.

Transport and communications

Transport. Railroads (1991): length 823 km; (1990) passenger-km 316,000,000; metric ton-km cargo 4,884,000,000. Roads (1991): length 7,700 km (paved 99%). Vehicles (1988): passenger cars 230,100. Air transport (1990): passenger km 5,556,900,000; metric ton-km cargo 49,000,000; airports (1994) 2.
Communications. Daily newspapers (1991): total number 82; total circulation 1,678,000; circulation per 1,000 population 469. Radio (1992): 642,000 receivers (1 per 5.6 persons). Television (1992): 722,000 receivers (1 per 5.0 persons). Telephones (1991): 650,000 (1 per 5.3 persons).

Education and health

Education (1991–92)

	schools	teachers	students	student/ teacher ratio
Primary (age 6–13) } Secondary (age 14–17)	1,374	54,000	592,000	11.0
Voc., teacher tr.	69	...	40,600	...
Higher	14	...	66,100	...

Educational attainment (1989). Percentage of population age 25 and over having: primary education or no formal schooling 7.4%; some secondary 18.6%; completed secondary and some postsecondary 57.7%; higher 13.8%.
Health (1992): physicians 13,600 (1 per 254 persons); hospital beds (1990) 30,482 (1 per 117 persons); infant mortality rate (1992) 17.9.

Military

Total active duty personnel (1994)[7]: c. 32,700 (army 100%). About 9,000 Russian troops remained in Armenia in late 1994. *Military expenditure as percentage of GNP* (1992): 2.3%; per capita expenditure (1992): U.S.$20.

[1]The Armenian dram was introduced Nov. 22, 1993, to replace the Russian ruble, at a rate of 200 Russian rubles to 1 dram. [2]18 additional cities of republic jurisdiction exist. [3]Estimated total includes areas of Lake Sevan and cities and 86,700 persons not distributed by administrative subdivision. [4]De jure figure; 1994 de facto population is estimated to be 2,800,000 owing to displacement resulting from war with Azerbaijan. [5]1989; reduced in population by evacuation following Dec. 7, 1988, earthquake. [6]Includes self-employed and unemployed. [7]Total mobilization for war with Azerbaijan is not available; however, total reserve strength is 300,000.

Australia

Official name: Commonwealth of
Australia.
Form of government: federal
parliamentary state (formally a
constitutional monarchy) with two
legislative houses (Senate [76]; House
of Representatives [148]).
Chief of state: British Monarch
represented by Governor-General.
Head of government: Prime Minister.
Capital: Canberra.
Official language: English.
Official religion: none.
Monetary unit: 1 Australian dollar
($A) = 100 cents; valuation (Oct. 7,
1994) 1 U.S.$ = $A 1.35;
1 £ = $A 2.15.

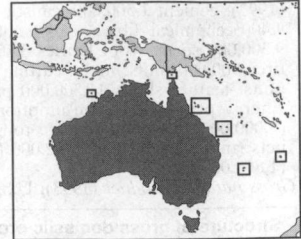

Area and population		area		population
		sq mi	sq km	1993[1] estimate
States	**Capitals**			
New South Wales	Sydney	309,500	801,600	6,041,300
Queensland	Brisbane	666,900	1,727,200	3,178,100
South Australia	Adelaide	379,900	984,000	1,468,600
Tasmania	Hobart	26,200	67,800	472,200
Victoria	Melbourne	87,900	227,600	4,473,600
Western Australia	Perth	975,100	2,525,500	1,695,700
Territories				
Australian Capital				
Territory	Canberra	900	2,400	300,300
Northern Territory	Darwin	519,800	1,346,200	170,800
TOTAL		2,966,200	7,682,300	17,800,600

Demography

Population (1994): 17,875,000.
Density (1994): persons per sq mi 6.0, persons per sq km 2.3.
Urban-rural (1986): urban 85.4%; rural 14.6%.
Sex distribution (1993): male 49.82%; female 50.18%.
Age breakdown (1993): under 15, 21.7%; 15–29, 23.3%; 30–44, 23.4%; 45–59,
16.0%; 60–74, 11.0%; 75 and over, 4.6%.
Population projection: (2000) 19,236,000; (2010) 21,598,000.
Doubling time: 87 years.
Ethnic composition (1986): white 95.2%; aboriginal 1.5%; Asian 1.3%; other
2.0%.
Religious affiliation (1991): Christian 74.0%, of which Roman Catholic 27.3%,
Anglican Church of Australia 23.8%, other Protestant 20.1% (Uniting
Church and Methodist 8.2%, Presbyterian 4.3%), Orthodox 2.8%; Muslim
0.9%; Buddhist 0.8%; Jewish 0.4%; Hindu 0.3%; no religion 12.9%; other
10.7%.
Major cities (1991): Sydney 3,538,900; Melbourne 3,022,200; Brisbane 1,334,-
700; Perth 1,143,300; Adelaide 1,023,600; Newcastle 427,703; Canberra 278,-
900; Wollongong 236,000; Hobart 181,800; Gold Coast 157,800.
Place of birth (1991): 77.3% native-born; 22.7% foreign-born, of which Europe 13.9% (United Kingdom 7.1%[2], Italy 1.5%, Yugoslavia 1.0%, Greece
0.8%, East and West Germany 0.7%, other Europe 1.9%), Asia and Middle
East 4.8%, New Zealand 1.7%, Africa and the Americas 1.5%, other 0.8%.
Mobility (1988). Population age 15 and over living in the same residence
as in 1987: 84.1%; different residence, same state 14.4%; different state
or territory 1.5%.
Households (1991–92). Total number of households 5,852,518. Average household size 3.0; (1986) 1 person 19.5%, 2–3 persons 47.1%, 4–5 persons 28.2%,
6 or more persons 5.2%. Family households (1992): 4,298,710 (74.5%);
nonfamily 1,553,808 (26.5%).
Immigration (1991): permanent immigrants admitted 116,650, from United
Kingdom and Ireland 16.2%, Hong Kong 12.4%, Vietnam 9.2%, New
Zealand 5.7%, Philippines 5.5%, India 5.0%, Malaysia 3.8%, China 2.9%,
Lebanon 2.0%. Refugee arrivals: 7,095.

Vital statistics

Birth rate per 1,000 population (1993): 14.7 (world avg. 26.0); (1992) legiti-
mate 76.0%; illegitimate 24.0%.
Death rate per 1,000 population (1993): 6.9 (world avg. 9.2).
Natural increase rate per 1,000 population (1993): 7.8 (world avg. 16.8).
Total fertility rate (avg. births per childbearing woman; 1993): 1.87.
Marriage rate per 1,000 population (1993): 6.4.
Divorce rate per 1,000 population (1993): 2.7.
Life expectancy at birth (1994): male 74.5 years; female 80.8 years.
Major causes of death per 100,000 population (1991): diseases of the cir-
culatory system 307.8; cancers 179.9; diseases of the respiratory system
56.8; accidents, poisoning, and violence 40.3; diseases of the digestive sys-
tem 22.0; diseases of the nervous system 14.9; endocrine, nutritional, and
metabolic diseases 13.5.

Social indicators

Educational attainment (1992). Percentage of population age 15 to 69 having: no formal schooling 0.3%; incomplete secondary education 41.3%;
completed secondary 14.8%[3]; postsecondary, technical, or other certificate/
diploma 34.0%; university 9.6%.
Quality of working life (1991–92). Average workweek: 40.1 hours (17%
overtime). Annual rate per 100,000 workers for: injury or accident, n.a.;

industrial illness, n.a.; death, n.a. Proportion of employed persons insured
for damages or income loss resulting from: injury 100%; permanent disability 100%; death 100%. Average days lost to labour stoppages per 1,000
workdays (1990): 0.5. Means of transportation to work (1986): private automobile 69.4%; public transportation 10.1%; motorcycle and bicycle 3.2%;
foot 6.6%; other 10.7%. Discouraged job seekers among persons not in the
labour force (considered by employers to be too young or too old, having
language or training limitations, or no vacancies in line of work; 1991):
1.5% of labour force.

Distribution of family income (1990[4])									
percentage of family income by decile									
1	2	3	4	5	6	7	8	9	10 (highest)
1.4%	3.1%	4.2%	5.5%	6.9%	8.6%	10.6%	13.3%	17.2%	29.2%

Access to services (1976). Proportion of dwellings having access to: electricity
99.5%; bathroom 96.0%; flush toilet 92.2%; kitchen 97.9%; public sewer
73.4%.
Social participation. Eligible voters participating in last national election
(1993): 95.3%; voting is compulsory. Population age 16 and over participating in voluntary work: n.a. Trade union membership in total workforce
(1992): 39.6%.
Social deviance (1988–89). Offense rate per 100,000 population for: murder
and attempted murder 4.2; sexual assault 53.3; assault 401.9; auto theft
760.4; burglary and housebreaking 1,969.4; fraud and forgery 760.4. Incidence per 100,000 in general population of: alcoholism, n.a.; drug offenses
(1985) 388.2; suicide (1990) 16.7.
Material well-being (1983). Households possessing: automobile 86.0%; telephone 85.0%; refrigerator 99.6%; air conditioner 32.3%; washing machine
91.7%; hot water 98.7%; central heating 3.9%; swimming pool 10.1%.

National economy

Gross national product (1993): U.S.$310,050,000,000 (U.S.$17,510 per capita).

Structure of gross domestic product and labour force				
	1992–93			
	in value $A '000,000	% of total value	labour force	% of labour force
Agriculture	12,869	3.2	398,000	4.6
Mining	17,315	4.3	91,600	1.1
Manufacturing	59,771	14.7	1,106,200	12.9
Construction	28,177	6.9	526,900	6.1
Public utilities	14,076	3.5	105,400	1.2
Transportation and communications	30,384	7.5	490,600	5.7
Trade	70,707	17.4	1,594,700	18.6
Finance	95,432	23.5	898,800	10.5
Pub. admin., defense	16,355	4.0	346,200	4.0
Services	70,735	17.4	2,120,900	24.7
Other	–9,961[5]	–2.4[5]	906,400[6]	10.6[6]
TOTAL	405,860	100.0	8,585,700	100.0

Budget (1993–94). Revenue: $A 99,100,000,000 (1991–92; income tax 68.9%,
of which individual 51.1%, corporate 17.8%; excise duties and sales tax
23.5%). Expenditures: $A 115,100,000,000 (1991–92; social security and wel-
fare 34.2%; transfers to state governments 25.2%; transfers to the nonbudget
sector 9.1%; interest on public debt 5.6%).
Public debt (1993): $A 80,948,000,000.
Tourism (1992): receipts from visitors U.S.$3,992,000,000; expenditures by
nationals abroad U.S.$3,994,000,000.

Manufacturing, mining, and construction enterprises (1991–92)[7]				
	no. of estab- lishments	no. of employees	Avg. annual wages[8] as a % of all wages	annual turnover ($A '000,000)
Manufacturing				
Food, beverages, and tobacco	4,228	166,000	91.7	35,768
Basic metal products	889	62,100	133.5	20,521
Machinery and equipment	5,910	114,200	99.3	15,902
Transport equipment	2,099	81,600	103.3	14,153
Chemical, petroleum, and coal products	1,213	50,500	126.8	23,462
Paper, printing, and publishing	4,913	100,300	106.0	14,332
Fabricated metal products	6,528	88,800	89.9	11,555
Miscellaneous manufacturing	3,843	58,200	92.0	8,402
Wood, wood products, and furniture	6,590	71,700	77.7	7,638
Nonmetallic mineral products	1,757	37,600	107.6	7,319
Clothing and footwear	2,574	49,800	74.8	4,847
Textiles	936	26,200	93.6	4,121
Mining[9]				
Coal, oil, and gas	257	34,111	191.8	16,901
Metallic minerals	269	31,667	163.9	11,985
Nonmetallic minerals	699	8,799	116.0	2,240
Construction	98,100	518,200	104.0[10]	34,407

Production (gross value in $A '000 except as noted). Agriculture, forestry,
fishing (1992–93): livestock slaughtered 6,074,700 (cattle 3,860,400, poultry
827,900, sheep and lambs 674,600, pigs 672,900); wool 2,604,400, wheat
2,139,900, sugarcane 803,200, cotton 744,400, barley 703,900, grapes 355,800,
potatoes 274,600, tomatoes 274,600, bananas 233,100, apples 168,700, oats
166,900, oranges 148,200, rice 137,200, pears 80,800, sorghum 71,500, carrots
65,700, tobacco 63,600, onions 54,100, pineapples 36,900, peaches 36,700,
cauliflower 33,700, corn (maize) 31,300; livestock (number of live animals)
138,102,000 sheep, 24,062,000 cattle, 2,646,000 pigs, 63,722,000 poultry; roundwood (1991) 19,315,000 cu m; fish catch (1992) 233,900 metric tons. Mining
and quarrying (metric tons [tons of contained metal]; 1992–93): iron ore

115,703,000; bauxite 40,946,000; copper 1,254,000; zinc 1,179,000; lead 856,000; tin 12,387; gold 275,331 kg; diamonds 40,000,000 carats. Manufacturing (metric tons except as noted; 1993–94): pig iron 7,209,000; cement 6,649,000; iron and steel slabs 2,246,000; beef and veal 1,824,500; sulfuric acid 833,000; lamb and mutton 642,200; pork 344,400; woven cotton cloth 48,992,000 sq m; textile floor coverings 45,918,000 sq m; woven woolen cloth 7,893,000 sq m; beer 22,660,000 hectolitres; electric motors 2,928,000 units; motor vehicles 298,000 units; colour television receivers 163,000 units. Construction (buildings completed, by value in $A '000; 1993–94): new dwellings 15,097,400; alterations and additions to dwellings 2,289,000; nonresidential 8,785,600.

Retail and service enterprises (1991–92)

	no. of establishments	no. of employees	total wages and salaries ($A '000,000)	annual turnover ($A '000,000)
Retail				
Motor vehicle dealers, gasoline and tire dealers	37,305	220,661	2,572[11]	44,954
Food stores	53,166	406,299	2,461[11]	40,811
Department and general stores	459	87,148	1,175[11]	9,880
Clothing, fabrics, and furniture stores	21,688	91,138	965[11]	8,495
Household appliances and hardware stores	14,268	75,355	629	12,012
Services[12]				
Real estate agents	5,741	42,106	835	2,201
Architectural services	4,534	17,717	354	1,030
Surveying services	1,104	6,872	116	309
Engineering and technical services	5,190	28,326	682	1,716
Legal services	6,459	55,363	500	3,069
Accounting services	6,048	49,479	503	2,334
Computing services	3,601	24,067	585	1,628
Advertising services	2,390	16,048	423	4,675
Debt collecting and credit reporting services	234	2,658	52	142
Pest control services	565	2,902	44	135
Cleaning services	4,181	44,322	330	622
Security/protection and business services	1,087	25,483	365	839

Energy production (consumption): electricity (kW-hr; 1992) 159,116,000,000 (159,116,000,000); coal (metric tons; 1992) 225,788,000 (103,406,000); crude petroleum (barrels; 1992) 196,429,000 (202,793,000); petroleum products (metric tons; 1992) 31,531,000 (31,906,000); natural gas (cu m; 1992) 23,089,000,000 (17,053,000,000).

Population economically active (1993–94): total 8,788,900; activity rate of total population 49.5% (participation rates: ages 15–64, 63.8%; female 42.5%; unemployed 9.3%).

Price and earnings indexes (1990 = 100)

	1988	1989	1990	1991	1992	1993	1994[13]
Consumer price index	86.7	93.2	100.0	103.2	104.2	106.1	107.8
Weekly earnings index	85.2	92.1	100.0	105.1	109.0	111.0	114.1

Household income and expenditure (1991–92). Average household size 3.0; average annual income per household $A 53,800 (U.S $41,157); sources of income (1992–93): wages and salaries 62.9%, transfer payments 17.4%, self-employment 7.0%, other 12.7%; expenditure (1992–93): housing 18.2%, transportation and communications 14.5%, food and beverages 14.4%, health 7.3%, household durable goods 6.6%, clothing and footwear 5.5%, education 5.0%, energy 2.2%, other 26.3%.

Financial aggregates

	1988	1989	1990	1991	1992	1993	1994[14]
Exchange rate, $A 1.00 per:							
U.S. dollar	0.78	0.79	0.78	0.78	0.69	0.68	0.74
£	0.44	0.48	0.44	0.44	0.45	0.46	0.47
SDR	0.64	0.60	0.54	0.53	0.50	0.49	0.50
International reserves (U.S.$)							
Total (excl. gold; '000,000)	13,598	13,780	16,264	16,534	11,208	11,102	11,894
SDRs ('000,000)	334	307	311	290	96	82	77
Reserve pos. in IMF ('000,000)	275	322	349	351	420	550	531
Foreign exchange ('000,000)	12,989	13,150	15,605	15,894	10,536	10,470	11,285
Gold ('000,000 fine troy oz)	7.93	7.93	7.93	7.93	7.93	7.90	7.90
% world reserves	0.8	0.8	0.8	0.8	0.8	0.9	0.9
Interest and prices							
Central bank discount (%)	13.20	17.23	15.24	11.0	6.25	5.83	5.75[13]
Govt. bond yield (%)	12.18	15.14	13.46	9.94	7.00	5.63	7.17[13]
Industrial share prices (1990 = 100)	93.4	97.6	100.0	96.4	100.3	104.9	110.8[13]
Balance of payments (U.S.$'000,000)							
Balance of visible trade	710	−3,436	+366	+3,611	+1,554	+12	−95
Imports, f.o.b.	33,892	40,329	38,966	38,494	40,820	42,362	10,759
Exports, f.o.b.	33,182	36,893	39,332	42,005	42,374	42,374	10,664
Balance of invisibles	−9,652	−14,231	−15,465	−13,782	−12,499	−10,792	−2,351
Balance of payments, current account	10,362	17,667	15,099	10,271	−10,945	−10,780	−2,256

Land use (1992): meadows and pastures 54.3%; agricultural and under permanent cultivation 6.7%; other 39.0%[15].

Foreign trade

Balance of trade (current prices)

	1988	1989	1990	1991	1992	1993
$A '000,000	−258	−4,100	1,194	4,141	2,898	−2,302
% of total	3.0%	4.1%	1.2%	4.0%	2.6%	2.0%

Imports (1992–93): $A 55,520,000,000 (machinery 25.8%, of which office machines and automatic data-processing equipment 6.7%; basic manufactures 14.2%, of which textile yarn and fabrics 3.5%, paper and paper products

2.4%, nonferrous metals 0.7%; transport equipment 13.0%, of which road motor vehicles 9.5%; chemicals and related products 9.0%; mineral fuels and lubricants 5.6%; food and live animals 3.6%; crude materials [inedible] excluding fuels 2.4%; beverages and tobacco 0.7%). *Major import sources:* U.S. 23.1%; Japan 17.6%; U.K. 6.3%; Germany 5.7%; New Zealand 4.2%; Taiwan 4.0%; France 2.7%; South Korea 2.7%; Italy 2.3%.

Exports (1992–93): $A 57,822,000,000 (mineral fuels and lubricants 17.0%, of which coal, coke, and briquettes 11.9%, petroleum, petroleum products, and natural gas 5.1%; crude materials excluding fuels 15.6%, of which metalliferous ores and metal scrap 7.1%, textile fibres and their waste 7.1%; food and live animals 15.4%, of which meat 6.0%, cereals 3.6%; machinery and transport equipment 9.2%; chemicals 2.8%). *Major export destinations:* Japan 24.6%; U.S. 10.9%; South Korea 5.8%; New Zealand 5.7%; U.K. 4.3%; Singapore 4.0%; Taiwan 3.3%; Indonesia 3.2%; Hong Kong 3.1%.

Trade by commodity group (1992–93)

SITC Group	imports U.S.$'000,000	imports %	exports U.S.$'000,000	exports %
00 Food and live animals	1,563	3.8	6,968	15.5
01 Beverages and tobacco	304	0.7	238	0.6
02 Crude materials, excluding fuels	1,035	2.4	7,052	15.7
03 Mineral fuels, lubricants, and related materials	2,392	5.6	7,674	17.0
04 Animal and vegetable oils, fat, and waxes	—	—	—	—
05 Chemicals and related products, n.e.s.	3,867	9.0	1,205	2.7
06 Basic manufactures	6,120	14.2	4,970	11.0
07 Machinery and transport equipment	16,997	39.7	4,146	9.2
08 Miscellaneous manufactured articles	6,247	14.6	1,271	2.8
09 Goods not classified by kind	4,296	10.0	11,504	25.5
TOTAL	42,821	100.0	45,028	100.0

Direction of trade (1992–93)

	imports U.S.$'000,000	imports %	exports U.S.$'000,000	exports %
Africa	171	0.4	675	1.5
Asia	16,230	37.9	24,270	53.9
Japan	7,536	17.6	11,122	24.7
South America	428	1.0	450	1.0
North and Central America	10,620	24.8	5,854	13.0
United States	9,892	23.1	4,908	10.9
Europe	11,133	26.0	7,024	15.6
EEC	9,078	21.2	6,259	13.9
former U.S.S.R.	...	...	...	...
Other Europe	2,055	4.8	765	1.7
Oceania	2,098	4.9	3,917	8.7
New Zealand	1,799	4.2	2,567	5.7
Other	2,141	5.0	2,838	6.3
TOTAL	42,821	100.0	45,028	100.0

Transport and communications

Transport. Railroads (1991)[16]: route length 23,174 mi, 37,295 km; passenger-mi 1,359,051,000[17], passenger-km 2,187,120,000[17]; short ton-mi cargo 36,414,000,000, metric ton-km cargo 53,163,000,000. Roads (1990): total length 503,474 mi, 810,264 km (paved 36%). Vehicles (1992): passenger cars 7,913,200; trucks and buses 2,041,300. Merchant marine (1992): vessels (100 gross tons and over) 695; total deadweight tonnage 3,857,271. Air transport (1990–91): passenger-mi 25,649,600,000, passenger-km 41,279,000; short ton-mi cargo 1,765,800,000, metric ton-km cargo 2,578,029,000; airports (1991) with scheduled flights 428.

Communications. Daily newspapers (1990): total number 62; total circulation 4,200,000; circulation per 1,000 population 249. Radio (1993): 20,000,000 receivers (1 per 0.9 persons). Television (1993): 8,000,000 receivers (1 per 2.2 persons). Telephones (1992): 8,540,000 (1 per 2.1 persons).

Education and health

Education (1993)

	schools	teachers	students	student/ teacher ratio
Primary (age 6–12) }	9,865	98,526	1,816,066	18.4
Secondary (age 13–17) }		103,385	1,282,300	12.4
Vocational[18]	234[19]	52,587[19]	985,942[20]	...
Higher[21]	95	25,916	420,640	16.2

Literacy (1980): percentage of total population age 15 and over literate 99.5%.
Health: physicians (1986) 38,527 (1 per 438 persons); hospital beds (1990) 86,036 (1 per 199 persons); infant mortality rate (1993) 6.1.
Food (1988–90): daily per capita caloric intake 3,302 (vegetable products 63%, animal products 37%); 124% of FAO recommended minimum requirement.

Military

Total active duty personnel (1994): 61,600 (army 46.4%, navy 24.0%, air force 29.6%). *Military expenditure as percentage of GNP* (1993): 2.4% (world, n.a.); per capita expenditure U.S.$408.

---

[1]March 31. [2]Includes both Northern Ireland and Republic of Ireland. [3]Completed highest level of secondary school available. [4]December. [5]Less imputed bank service charges. [6]Mostly unemployed. [7]Excludes operations of single-establishment enterprises employing fewer than four persons. [8]Excludes the drawings of working proprietors. [9]1990–91. [10]1985. [11]1985–86. [12]1987–88. [13]Second quarter. [14]September. [15]Urban areas, state forests and mining leases, unoccupied land (mainly desert). [16]Government railways only. [17]1978–79. [18]Includes special education. [19]1986. [20]1992. [21]1989.

Austria

Official name: Republik Österreich
(Republic of Austria).
Form of government: federal multi-
party republic with two legislative
houses (Federal Council [63];
National Council [183]).
Chief of state: President.
Head of government: Chancellor.
Capital: Vienna.
Official language: German.
Official religion: none.
Monetary unit: 1 Austrian Schilling
(S) = 100 Groschen; valuation
(Oct. 7, 1994) 1 U.S.$ = S 10.85;
1 £ = S 17.25.

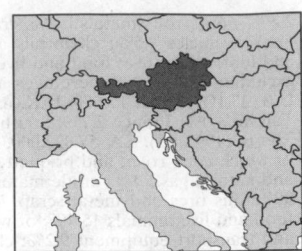

Area and population		area		population
		sq mi	sq km	1992 estimate
States	Capitals			
Burgenland	Eisenstadt	1,531	3,965	269,000
Kärnten	Klagenfurt	3,681	9,533	551,000
Niederösterreich	Sankt Pölten	7,403	19,174	1,479,000
Oberösterreich	Linz	4,626	11,980	1,342,000
Salzburg	Salzburg	2,762	7,154	490,000
Steiermark	Graz	6,327	16,388	1,188,000
Tirol	Innsbruck	4,883	12,648	637,000
Vorarlberg	Bregenz	1,004	2,601	338,000
Wien (Vienna)	—	160	415	1,568,000
TOTAL		32,378[1]	83,859[1]	7,863,000[1]

Demography

Population (1994): 8,027,000.
Density (1994): persons per sq mi 247.9, persons per sq km 95.7.
Urban-rural (1991): urban 64.5%; rural 35.5%.
Sex distribution (1991): male 48.15%; female 51.85%.
Age breakdown (1991): under 15, 17.4%; 15–29, 23.7%; 30–44, 21.6%; 45–59, 17.2%; 60–74, 13.4%; 75 and over, 6.7%.
Population projection: (2000) 8,181,000; (2010) 8,294,000.
Doubling time: not applicable; population is stable.
Ethnic composition (national origin; 1991): Austrian 93.4%; citizens of former Yugoslavia 2.5%; Turkish 1.5%; German 0.7%; other 1.9%.
Religious affiliation (1991): Roman Catholic 78.3%; nonreligious and athe-ist 8.3%; Reformed-Lutheran traditions 4.9%; Muslim 2.1%; Jewish 0.1%; other (mostly Christian) 2.8%; unknown 3.5%.
Major cities (1991): Vienna 1,539,848; Graz 237,810; Linz 203,044; Salzburg 143,978; Innsbruck 118,112.

Vital statistics

Birth rate per 1,000 population (1993): 11.8 (world avg. 26.0); (1991) legiti-mate 75.2%; illegitimate 24.8%.
Death rate per 1,000 population (1993): 10.3 (world avg. 9.2).
Natural increase rate per 1,000 population (1993): 1.5 (world avg. 16.8).
Total fertility rate (avg. births per childbearing woman; 1992): 1.6.
Marriage rate per 1,000 population (1992): 5.6.
Divorce rate per 1,000 population (1991): 2.1.
Life expectancy at birth (1992): male 72.9 years; female 79.4 years.
Major causes of death per 100,000 population (1992): diseases of the circu-latory system 555.3, of which ischemic heart diseases 211.3, cerebrovascular disease 134.8; malignant neoplasms (cancers) 246.1.

National economy

Budget (1993)[2]. Revenue: S 624,300,000,000 (social-security contributions 28.0%, direct taxes 27.5%, turnover taxes 19.5%, income from federal en-terprises 14.9%). Expenditures: S 688,400,000,000 (social affairs and health 25.8%, public debt 23.1%, federal enterprises 13.9%, education 8.4%, de-fense 2.8%).
National debt (end of year 1991): S 945,610,000,000.
Production (metric tons except as noted). Agriculture, forestry, fishing (1992): silage 4,252,000[3], sugar beets 2,265,000, barley 1,342,000, wheat 1,325,000, corn (maize) 1,118,000, potatoes 738,000, grapes 410,000, rye 278,000, ap-ples 233,000, turnips 173,000[3], rapeseed 115,000; livestock (number of live animals) 3,629,000 pigs, 2,532,000 cattle, 13,000,000 chickens; roundwood 13,875,000 cu m; fish catch (1991) 4,500. Mining and quarrying (1992): iron ore 1,632,000, magnesite 985,000, high-grade graphite 19,547, zinc ore 14,900. Manufacturing (value added in S '000,000,000; 1990): electrical machinery and apparatus 44.6; nonelectrical machinery and apparatus 37.4; fabricated metal products 28.8; food products 26.2; iron and steel 23.7; transport equipment 18.8; cement, bricks, and tile 16.7. Construction (completed; 1991): residential 3,981,000 sq m; nonresidential, n.a. Energy production (consumption): electricity (kW-hr; 1993) 52,656,000,000 ([1991] 52,249,000,-000); coal (metric tons; 1993) 1,788,000 ([1991] 6,926,000); crude petroleum (barrels; 1993) 8,194,000 ([1991] 61,101,000); petroleum products (metric tons; 1991) 7,750,000 (10,414,000); natural gas (cu m; 1993) 1,555,000,000 ([1991] 5,394,000,000).
Land use (1991): forested 39.0%; meadows and pastures 24.1%; agricultural and under permanent cultivation 18.4%; other 18.5%.
Tourism (1992): receipts from visitors U.S.$14,832,000,000; expenditures by nationals abroad U.S.$8,371,000,000.
Population economically active (1991): total 3,596,100; activity rate of total population 46.0% (participation rates: ages 15–64, 67.9%; female 41.0%; unemployed [1993] 6.8%).

Price and earnings indexes (1990 = 100)

	1988	1989	1990	1991	1992	1993	1994
Consumer price index	94.4	96.8	100.0	103.3	107.5	111.4	114.1[4]
Monthly earnings index	89.4	93.3	100.0	105.2	110.3	115.8[5]	...

Gross national product (at current market prices; 1992): U.S.$174,767,000,000 (U.S.$22,110 per capita).

Structure of gross domestic product and labour force

	1992		1991	
	in value S '000,000	% of total value	labour force	% of labour force
Agriculture	50,100	2.5	258,600	7.2
Mining	} 525,900	25.9	12,200	0.3
Manufacturing			966,400	26.9
Construction	153,600	7.6	312,200	8.7
Public utilities	55,600	2.7	40,400	1.1
Transportation and communications	126,300	6.2	228,200	6.3
Trade, restaurants	333,700	16.4	688,300	19.1
Finance, real estate	350,400	17.3	236,300	6.6
Pub. admin., defense	286,800	14.1	} 813,400	22.6
Services	86,400	4.3		
Other	59,800[6]	3.0[6]	40,200	1.0
TOTAL	2,028,600	100.0	3,596,100[1]	100.0[1]

Household income and expenditure. Average household size (1992) 2.6; net income per household[7] (1991) S 262,080 (U.S.$21,930); sources of income (1991): wages and salaries 55.6%, transfer payments 24.5%, other 19.9%; expenditure (1991): food and beverages 17.8%, transportation 16.9%, hous-ing 13.6%, cafe and hotel expenditures 10.8%, clothing and footwear 9.2%.

Foreign trade[8]

Balance of trade (current prices)

	1988	1989	1990	1991	1992	1993
S '000,000	−47,910	−62,180	−65,190	−86,300	−79,700	−72,500
% of total	5.9%	6.8%	6.5%	8.3%	7.6%	7.2%

Imports (1993): S 593,900,000,000 (machinery and transport equipment 39.5%, of which road vehicles 12.7%, electrical machinery and apparatus 6.3%; chemicals and related products 9.8%; clothing 4.8%; food products 4.5%).
Major import sources: Germany 42.9%; Italy 8.6%; Japan 4.7%; France 4.4%; Switzerland 4.0%; United States 3.9%.
Exports (1993): S 487,600,000,000 (machinery and transport equipment 38.9%, of which electrical machinery and apparatus 6.7%, road vehicles 6.5%, machine tools 5.9%; paper and paper products 5.9%; iron and steel 5.3%).
Major export destinations: Germany 39.8%; Italy 8.8%; Switzerland 5.9%; France 4.4%; United Kingdom 3.6%; Hungary 3.2%.

Transport and communications

Transport. Railroads (1993): length (1991) 4,136 mi, 6,657 km; passenger-mi 5,988,000,000[9], passenger-km 9,636,000,000[9]; short ton-mi cargo 8,080,-000,000[9], metric ton-km cargo 11,796,000,000[9]. Roads (1992): total length 68,400 mi, 110,000 km (paved 100%). Vehicles (1992): passenger cars 3,244,920; trucks and buses 278,643. Merchant marine (1992): vessels (100 gross tons and over) 26; total deadweight tonnage 208,504. Air transport[10] (1993): passenger-mi 4,328,000,000, passenger-km 6,965,000,000; short ton-mi cargo 89,970,000, metric ton-km cargo 131,354,000; airports (1994) with scheduled flights 6.
Communications. Daily newspapers (1992): total number 27; total circulation 3,108,357; circulation per 1,000 population 394. Radio (1993): total receivers 4,700,000 (1 per 1.7 persons). Television (1993): total receivers 2,706,000 (1 per 2.9 persons). Telephones (1992): 4,956,000 (1 per 1.6 persons).

Education and health

Education (1992–93)

	schools	teachers	students	student/ teacher ratio
Primary (age 6–10)	3,702	35,603	401,974	11.3
Secondary (age 11–18)	1,607	52,545	431,027	8.2
Voc., teacher tr.	1,318	24,607	315,376	12.8
Higher	94	14,809	216,765	14.6

Educational attainment (1991). Percentage of population age 25 and over having: lower-secondary education 38.2%; vocational education ending at secondary level 45.2%; completed upper secondary 5.4%; higher vocational 5.1%; higher 6.1%. *Literacy:* virtually 100%.
Health (1992): physicians 24,049 (1 per 327 persons); hospital beds 74,871 (1 per 105 persons); infant mortality rate per 1,000 live births 7.4.
Food (1988–90): daily per capita caloric intake 3,486 (vegetable products 64%, animal products 36%); 133% of FAO recommended minimum requirement.

Military

Total active duty personnel (1993): 52,000 (army 88.5%; navy, none; air force 11.5%). *Military expenditure as percentage of GNP* (1991): 1.0% (world 4.2%); per capita expenditure U.S.$213.

---

[1]Detail does not add to total given because of rounding. [2]Federal income and ex-penditure only. [3]1991. [4]March. [5]Average of 2nd and 3rd quarters. [6]Value-added tax plus import duties (S 184,500,000,000) less imputed bank service charges (S 124,700,-000,000). [7]Two-person households without children only. [8]Import figures are f.o.b. in balance of trade and c.i.f. in commodities and trading partners. [9]Federal railways only. [10]Austrian Airlines, Lauda Air, and Tyrolean Airways.

Azerbaijan

Official name: Azärbayjan Rcspublikasi
(Azerbaijani Republic).
Form of government: federal multiparty
republic with a single legislative body
(National Council [50]).
Head of state: President.
Head of government: Prime Minister.
Capital: Baku (Azerbaijani: Bakı).
Official language: Azerbaijani.
Official religion: none.
Monetary unit: 1 manat[1] = 100 gopik;
valuation (Oct. 7, 1994) free rate,
1 U.S.$ = 292.70 manat; 1 £ = 465.60
manat.

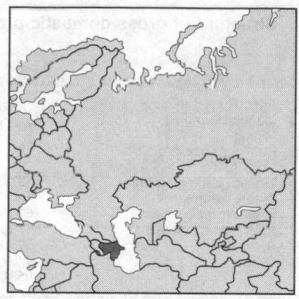

Area and population

Republics	Capitals	area		population
		sq mi	sq km	1991 estimate
Naxçıvan (Nakhichevan)	Naxçıvan (Nakhichevan)	2,100	5,500	305,700
Qarabağ[2] (Nagorno Karabakh)	Xankändi (Stepanakert)	1,700	4,400	193,300
Regions under republican jurisdiction	—	29,600	76,700	4,924,300
Cities				
Baku (Bakı)	—	...	...	1,713,300
TOTAL		33,400	86,600	7,136,600

Demography

Population (1994): 7,424,000.
Density (1994): persons per sq mi 222.3, persons per sq km 85.7.
Urban-rural (1992): urban 53.7%; rural 46.3%.
Sex distribution (1992): male 49.31%; female 50.69%.
Age breakdown (1989): under 15, 32.8%; 15–29, 29.7%; 30–44, 16.8%; 45–59, 12.8%; 60–74, 5.7%; 75 and over, 2.2%.
Population projection: (2000) 8,324,000; (2010) 9,445,000.
Doubling time: 37 years.
Ethnic composition (1989): Azerbaijani 82.7%; Russian 5.7%; Armenian 5.6%; Lezgin 2.4%; Avar 0.6%; Ukrainian 0.5%; Tatar 0.4%; other 2.1%.
Religious affiliation (1991): Shīʿī Muslim 70%; Sunnī Muslim 30%.
Major cities (1991): Baku 1,080,500; Gäncä (formerly Kirovabad) 282,200; Sumqayıt (Sumgait) 236,200; Mingacevir (Mingechaur) 90,900; Naxçıvan (Nakhichevan) 61,700.

Vital statistics

Birth rate per 1,000 population (1992): 25.6 (world avg. 26.0); (1989) legitimate 97.5%; illegitimate 2.5%.
Death rate per 1,000 population (1992): 7.1 (world avg. 9.2).
Natural increase rate per 1,000 population (1992): 18.5 (world avg. 16.8).
Total fertility rate (avg. births per childbearing woman; 1993): 2.8.
Marriage rate per 1,000 population (1992): 9.4.
Divorce rate per 1,000 population (1992): 1.3.
Life expectancy at birth (1993): male 66.7 years; female 74.6 years.
Major causes of death per 100,000 population (1989): diseases of the circulatory system 292.4; diseases of the respiratory system 88.9; malignant neoplasms (cancers) 72.1; accidents, poisoning, and violence 42.1; infectious and parasitic diseases 42.1; diseases of the digestive system 25.6; diseases of the nervous system 9.7; endocrine and metabolic disorders 8.6.

National economy

Budget (1993). Revenue: 61,549,000,000 manats (tax revenue 96%, of which value-added tax 23.1%, excise tax 21.0%, enterprise profits tax 19.7%, individual income tax 5.8%; nontax revenue 4.0%). Expenditures: 74,601,000,000 manats (1992: social welfare and culture 82.1%, of which education 27.3%, pensions 14.1%; health 11.2%; national economy 17.9%; defense 10.5%).
Public debt (external, outstanding): n.a.
Production (metric tons except as noted). Agriculture, forestry, fishing (1993): fruit (except grapes) 1,358,000, cereals 1,105,000, grapes 900,000, wheat 780,-000, vegetables (except potatoes) 700,000, cotton 336,000, potatoes 200,000, tobacco 70,000, tea 4,000; livestock (number of live animals) 5,255,000 sheep and goats, 1,570,000 cattle, 123,000 pigs, 33,000 horses, 26,000,000 poultry; roundwood (1993) 17,000 cu m; fish catch (1991) 39,700. Mining and quarrying (1989): iron ore 718,200. Manufacturing (1993): steel 236,000; steel pipes 146,000; sulfuric acid 141,000; pesticides 120,000; detergents and soaps 50,000; caustic soda 49,000; electric motors 1,355 units; air conditioners 179,000 units; pumps 161,000 units; drilling equipment 53,000 units; bicycles 51,000 units; radios 30,000 units. Construction (1991): 2,600,000 sq m. Energy production (consumption): electricity (kW-hr; 1992) 20,000,000,000 (20,000,-000,000); coal (metric tons; 1992) none (27,000); crude petroleum (barrels; 1992) 77,698,000 (91,273,000); petroleum products (metric tons; 1992) 400,000 (400,000); natural gas (cu m; 1992) 7,800,000,000 (11,553,000,000).
Household income and expenditure. Average household size (1989) 4.8; income per household: n.a.; sources of income (1992): salaries and wages 70.2%, social benefits 19.0%, agricultural income 10.8%; expenditure: retail goods 73.7%, services 7.4%, taxes 10.2%.
Gross national product (at current market prices; 1993): U.S.$5,428,000,000 (U.S.$730 per capita)[3].

Structure of net material product and labour force

	1993		1991	
	in value '000,000 manats	% of total value	labour force	% of labour force
Agriculture	34,802	29.4	978,000	26.6
Mining	} 53,985	} 45.6	459,000	12.4
Manufacturing				
Public utilities			110,000	3.0
Construction	10,247	10.7	240,000	6.7
Transportation and communications	9,111	7.7	213,000	5.8
Trade	2,595	2.2	174,000	4.7
Finance	—	—	10,000	0.3
Pub. admin., defense	—	—	53,000	1.4
Services	—	—	414,000	11.3
Other	1,655	1.4	1,021,000	27.8
TOTAL	118,395	100.0	3,678,000	100.0

Population economically active (1991): total 3,687,000; activity rate of total population 51.7% (participation rates: ages 16–59 [male], 16–54 [female] 92.1%; female [1989] 42.6%; unemployed [1991] 3.7%).

Price and earnings indexes (1990 = 100)

	1986	1987	1988	1989	1990	1991	1992
Consumer price index	...	...	...	...	100.0	211.8	2,463.7
Monthly earnings index	82.8	84.6	87.7	91.8	100.0	163.1	1,288.7

Tourism: receipts from visitors, n.a.; expenditures by nationals abroad, n.a.
Land use (1992): forest 21.9%; pasture 25.4%; agriculture 11.0%; other 41.7%.

Foreign trade

Balance of trade (current prices)

	1987	1988	1989	1990	1991	1992	1993
'000,000 rubles	1,209	1,110	1,933	678	2,502	78,818	3,838
% of total	...	...	...	...	12.3%	18.9%	1.7%

Imports (1993): 117,427,000,000 rubles (petroleum products 39.0%, ferrous metals 30.0%, textiles 10.6%, nonferrous metals 5.9%, chemical products 3.0%). *Major import sources:* Russia 24.7%; Turkey 12.8%; Turkmenistan 10.6%; Ukraine 10.4%; Iran 8.5%; Kazakhstan 6.8%.
Exports (1993): 113,589,000,000 rubles (food products 33.2%, machinery 20.1%, chemical products 16.1%, consumer products 16.0%, textiles 7.2%). *Major export destinations:* Iran 29.1%; Russia 26.9%; Turkey 9.1%; Ukraine 7.0%; Georgia 4.5%; Kazakhstan 4.4%.

Transport and communications

Transport. Railroads (1991): length 1,299 mi, 2,090 km; passenger-mi 3,025,-400,000, passenger-km 4,868,900,000; cargo traffic, n.a. Roads (1991): total length 22,800 mi, 36,700 km (paved 87%). Vehicles (1988): passenger cars 235,600; trucks and buses, n.a. Merchant marine: vessels (100 gross tons and over) n.a.; total deadweight tonnage, n.a. Air transport (1990): passenger-mi 3,025,400,000, passenger-km 4,868,900,000; cargo traffic, n.a.; airports (1994) with scheduled flights 1.
Communications. Daily newspapers (1990): total number 168; total circulation 520,000,000; circulation per 1,000 population 73. Radio (1992): total number of receivers 1,174,000 (1 per 6.1 persons). Television (1992): total number of receivers 1,522,000 (1 per 4.8 persons). Telephones (1991): 1,174,000 (1 per 6.1 persons).

Education and health

Education (1991–92)

	schools	teachers	students	student/ teacher ratio
Primary (age 6–13)	} 4,332	139,000	1,375,000	9.9
Secondary (age 14–17)				
Voc., teacher tr.	77	...	60,100	...
Higher	18	...	108,000	...

Educational attainment (1989). Percentage of population age 25 and over having: primary education or no formal schooling 12.2%; some secondary 19.2%; completed secondary and some postsecondary 58.1%; higher 10.5%.
Literacy (1989): percentage of total population 15 and over literate 97.3%; males literate 98.9%; females 95.9%.
Health (1992): physicians 29,100 (1 per 251 persons); hospital beds (1990) 72,700 (1 per 98 persons); infant mortality rate per 1,000 live births 25.0.

Military

Total active duty personnel (1994): 56,000[4] (army 87.4%, navy[5] 5.4%, air force 3.6%, CIS centrally controlled and other 3.6%). About 500 Russian troops remained in Azerbaijan in late 1994. *Military expenditure as percentage of GNP* (1992): c. 1.9% (world, n.a.); per capita expenditure (1992) U.S.$17.

---

[1]The manat was introduced Aug. 15, 1992, at a 10 to 1 ratio with the Russian ruble and circulated parallel with it; on June 20, 1993, the manat became the sole legal tender. [2]In November 1991 the Azerbaijan Supreme Soviet abolished Nagorno Karabakh's autonomous status. [3]Ruble-area GNP and exchange-rate data are very speculative. [4]Total mobilization data for war with Armenia is not available; however, total reserve strength is 560,000. [5]Azerbaijan shares a portion of the Caspian Flotilla.

Bahamas, The

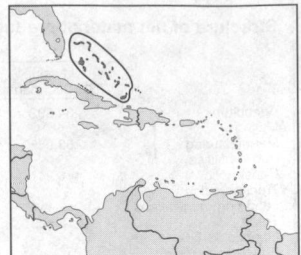

Official name: The Commonwealth of The Bahamas.
Form of government: constitutional monarchy with two legislative houses (Senate [16]; House of Assembly [49]).
Chief of state: British Monarch represented by Governor-General.
Head of government: Prime Minister.
Capital: Nassau.
Official language: English.
Official religion: none.
Monetary unit: 1 Bahamian dollar (B$) = 100 cents; valuation (Oct. 7, 1994) 1 U.S.$ = B$1; 1 £ = B$1.59.

Area and population	area[1]		population 1990 census
Islands and Island Groups[2]	sq mi	sq km	
Abaco, Great and Little	649	1,681	10,034
Acklins	192	497	405
Andros	2,300	5,957	8,187
Berry Islands	12	31	628
Bimini Islands	9	23	1,639
Cat Island	150	388	1,698
Crooked and Long Cay	93	241	412
Eleuthera	187	484	7,993
Exuma, Great, and Exuma Cays	112	290	3,556
Grand Bahama	530	1,373	40,898
Harbour Island	3	8	1,219
Inagua, Great and Little	599	1,551	985
Long Island	230	596	2,954
Mayaguana	110	285	312
New Providence	80	207	172,196
Ragged Island	14	36	89
Rum Cay	30	78	53
San Salvador	63	163	465
Spanish Wells	10	26	1,372
Other uninhabited cays and rocks	9	23	—
TOTAL	5,382	13,939[3]	255,095

Demography

Population (1994): 272,000.
Density (1994): persons per sq mi 50.5, persons per sq km 19.5.
Urban-rural (1990): urban 64.3%; rural 35.7%.
Sex distribution (1990): male 49.00%; female 51.00%.
Age breakdown (1990): under 15, 32.2%; 15–29, 30.8%; 30–44, 19.7%; 45–59, 10.5%; 60 and over, 6.8%.
Population projection: (2000) 295,000; (2010) 327,000.
Doubling time: 48 years.
Ethnic composition (1988): black 80.0%; mixed 10.0%; white 10.0%.
Religious affiliation (1980): non-Anglican Protestant 55.2%, of which Baptist 32.1%, Methodist 6.1%, Church of God (Anderson Ind.) 5.7%; Anglican 20.1%; Roman Catholic 18.8%; other 5.9%.
Major cities (1990): Nassau 172,196[4]; Freeport/Lucaya 26,574; Marsh Harbour 3,611; Bailey Town 1,490; Dunmore Town (Harbour Island) 1,219.

Vital statistics

Birth rate per 1,000 population (1992): 25.6 (world avg. 26.0); (1990) legitimate 42.8%, illegitimate 57.2%.
Death rate per 1,000 population (1992): 5.0 (world avg. 9.2).
Natural increase rate per 1,000 population (1992): 20.6 (world avg. 16.8).
Total fertility rate (avg. births per childbearing woman; 1992): 2.1.
Marriage rate per 1,000 population (1992): 9.1.
Divorce rate per 1,000 population (1992): 1.2.
Life expectancy at birth (1994): male 68.0 years; female 75.0 years.
Major causes of death per 100,000 population (1991): ischemic heart diseases 95.0; malignant neoplasms (cancers) 79.2; cerebrovascular disease 28.6; pneumonia 23.2.

National economy

Budget (1993–94). Revenue: B$568,700,000[5] (import taxes 47.1%, stamp taxes 15.6%, departure taxes 10.4%, fines and forfeits 7.0%, business and professional licenses 4.7%). Expenditures: B$638,300,000[6] (education 20.1%, health 13.4%, general administration 13.4%, interest on public debt 12.2%, public order 10.0%, tourism 5.9%, defense 2.9%).
National debt (March 1994): U.S.$1,401,000,000.
Production (value of production in B$'000 except as noted). Agriculture, forestry, fishing (1993): crayfish 45,200, other marine products (mostly sponges, groupers, conchs) 6,900, fruits and vegetables 22,800[7], poultry products 20,200; roundwood (1992) 115,000 cu m. Mining and quarrying (value of export production; 1993): salt 13,500; aragonite 4,800. Manufacturing (value of export production; 1993): pharmaceuticals and other chemical products 84,600; rum 12,600. Construction (gross value of buildings started in B$'000,000; 1993)[8]: residential 101; nonresidential 20. Energy production (consumption): electricity (kW-hr; 1991) 965,000,000 (965,000,000); coal, none (none); crude petroleum, none (none); petroleum products (metric tons; 1991) negligible (634,000); natural gas, none (none).
Tourism (1993): receipts from visitors U.S.$1,296,000,000; expenditures by nationals abroad U.S.$195,000,000.
Gross national product (1992): U.S.$3,161,000,000 (U.S.$12,020 per capita).

Structure of gross domestic product and labour force				
	1992		1993	
	in value B$'000,000	% of total value	labour force	% of labour force
Agriculture, fishing	89	2.9	6,435	4.7
Manufacturing	105	3.4	4,935	3.6
Mining			1,785	1.3
Public utilities	88	2.9		
Construction	91	3.0	7,730	5.6
Transp. and commun.	227	7.4	9,093	6.6
Trade, restaurants	705	23.0	36,711	26.8
Finance, real estate	610	19.9	11,201	8.2
Pub. admin., defense	179	5.8	40,543	29.6
Services	523	17.1		
Other	443[9]	14.5[9]	18,467[10]	13.5[10]
TOTAL	3,059[3]	100.0[3]	136,900	100.0[3]

Population economically active (1993): total 136,900; activity rate of total population 51.5% (participation rates: ages 15–64 [1990] 63.1%; female 47.5%; unemployed 13.1%).

Price and earnings indexes (1986 = 100)							
	1988	1989	1990	1991	1992	1993	1994
Consumer price index	110.4	116.4	121.8	130.5	138.0	141.6	143.0[11]
Annual earnings index[12]	105.6	146.2	...	146.6	165.3	171.3[13]	...

Household income and expenditure. Average household size (1993) 3.9; income per household (1993) B$26,373 (U.S.$26,373); sources of income: n.a.; expenditure (1988)[14]: food and beverages 19.8%, housing 19.2%, transportation and communications 18.9%, household furnishings 10.2%, education 7.8%.
Land use (1991): forested 32.4%; meadows and pastures 0.2%; agricultural and under permanent cultivation 1.0%; other 66.4%.

Foreign trade[15]

Balance of trade (current prices)						
	1986	1987	1988	1989	1990	1991
B$'000,000	−588	−309	−99	−534	−327	−284
% of total	9.8%	5.4%	2.4%	9.4%	5.9%	8.1%

Imports (1991): B$1,801,000,000 (petroleum for storage 34.3%, machinery and transport equipment 14.5%, food products 11.3%, chemicals and chemical products 9.1%). *Major import sources* (1990): Saudi Arabia 36.9%; United States 35.6%; United Kingdom 3.7%; Nigeria 3.1%; Iraq 2.8%.
Exports (1991): B$1,517,000,000 (chemicals [mostly pharmaceuticals] 50.8%, distillate fuels 24.4%, hormones 4.3%, crayfish 3.0%, rum 2.2%). *Major export destinations* (1990): United States 76.5%; Puerto Rico 17.3%; Belgium 1.0%; Canada 0.9%; United Kingdom 0.8%.

Transport and communications

Transport. Railroads: none. Roads (1990): total length 1,450 mi, 2,334 km (paved 56%). Vehicles (1992): passenger cars 66,696; trucks and buses 14,322. Merchant marine (1992): vessels (100 gross tons and over) 1,061; total deadweight tonnage 33,081,652. Air transport (1991): passenger-mi 215,000,000, passenger-km 346,000,000; short ton-mi cargo 205,000, metric ton-km cargo 300,000; airports (1994) with scheduled flights 24.
Communications. Daily newspapers (1991): total number 3; total circulation 35,000; circulation per 1,000 population 135. Radio (1993): total receivers 200,000 (1 per 1.3 persons). Television (1993): total receivers 60,000 (1 per 4.4 persons). Telephones (1991): 141,844 (1 per 1.8 persons).

Education and health

Education (1991–92)	schools	teachers	students	student/ teacher ratio
Primary/Secondary (age 5–16)	227	3,161	60,058	19.0
Higher[16]	1	300	3,201	10.7

Educational attainment: n.a. *Literacy* (1986): total population age 15 and over literate 139,000 (95.0%).
Health (1992): physicians 357 (1 per 714 persons); hospital beds 1,020 (1 per 250 persons); infant mortality rate per 1,000 live births (1991) 23.8.
Food (1988–90): daily per capita caloric intake 2,777 (vegetable products 66%, animal products 34%); 115% of FAO recommended minimum requirement.

Military

Total active duty personnel (1993): 850 (all paramilitary coast guard). *Military expenditure as percentage of GNP* (1992)[17]: 2.1% (world, n.a.); per capita expenditure U.S.$248.

[1]Land area only of individual islands or island groups. [2]Family (Out) Islands (all islands other than New Providence) are administered by commissioners assigned by the central government. Extent of commissioner districts varies from part of an island to island groups. [3]Detail does not add to total given because of rounding. [4]Population cited is for New Providence Island. [5]Current revenue only. [6]Of which current expenditure 92.5%, development expenditure 7.5%. [7]1990. [8]New Providence and Grand Bahama islands only. [9]Includes net indirect taxes (B$430,000,000) and statistical discrepancy (B$13,000,000). [10]Includes 517 not adequately defined and 17,950 unemployed. [11]March. [12]Annual mean household income. [13]May. [14]Domestic purchases by resident households only; data for expenditures in restaurants and hotels are not available. [15]Imports c.i.f.; exports f.o.b. [16]1992–93; College of The Bahamas only. [17]Includes police.

Bahrain

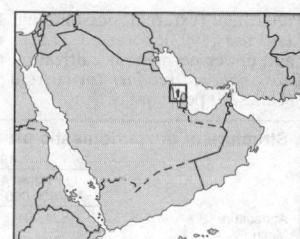

Official name: Dawlat al-Baḥrayn
(State of Bahrain).
Form of government: monarchy
(emirate) with an advisory
Consultative Council (30).
Chief of state: Emir.
Head of government: Prime Minister.
Capital: Manama.
Official language: Arabic.
Official religion: Islam.
Monetary unit: 1 Bahrain dinar
(BD) = 1,000 fils; valuation (Oct. 7,
1994) 1 BD = U.S.$2.63 = £1.67.

Area and population

Regions	area sq mi	area sq km	population 1991 census
al-Gharbīyah (Western)	60.3	156.1	22,034
al-Ḥadd	2.3	6.0	8,610
Jidd (Judd) Ḥafṣ	8.3	21.6	41,769
al-Manāmah	10.0	25.8	136,999
al-Muḥarraq	6.2	16.0	74,245
ar-Rifā'	112.6	291.6	49,752
ash-Shamālīyah (Northern)	14.2	36.8	33,763
ash-Sharqīyah (Eastern)	...	...	3,242
Sitrah	11.1	28.8	36,755
al-Wusṭā (Central)	13.6	35.2	34,304
Towns with special status			
Ḥammād	5.1	13.1	29,055
Madīnat 'Īsā	4.8	12.4	34,509
Islands			
Ḥawār and other	19.5	50.6	1
TOTAL	268.0[2]	694.2[2,3]	508,037

Demography

Population (1994): 552,000.
Density (1994): persons per sq mi 2,059.7, persons per sq km 795.2.
Urban-rural (1991): urban 88.4%; rural 11.6%.
Sex distribution (1993): male 56.99%; female 43.01%.
Age breakdown (1994): under 15, 36.5%; 15–29, 21.6%; 30–44, 25.8%; 45–59, 11.6%; 60–74, 3.9%; 75 and over, 0.6%.
Population projection: (2000) 653,000; (2010) 831,000.
Doubling time: 26 years.
Ethnic composition (1981): Bahraini Arab 68.0%; Persian, Indian, and Pakistani 24.7%; other Arab 4.1%; European 2.5%; other 0.7%.
Religious affiliation (1981): Muslim 85.0% (Shīʿī 60.0% and Sunnī 40.0%); Christian 7.3%; other 7.7%.
Major cities (1991): al-Manāmah 120,937; ar-Rifāʿ 45,956; al-Muḥarraq 45,337; Madīnat 'Īsā 34,509.

Vital statistics

Birth rate per 1,000 population (1992): 29.0 (world avg. 26.0); legitimate 100%.
Death rate per 1,000 population (1992): 4.8 (world avg. 9.2).
Natural increase rate per 1,000 population (1992): 24.2 (world avg. 16.8).
Total fertility rate (avg. births per childbearing woman; 1992): 3.7.
Marriage rate per 1,000 population (1991): 6.8.
Divorce rate per 1,000 population (1991): 1.3.
Life expectancy at birth (1992): male 68.7 years; female 72.8 years.
Major causes of death per 100,000 population (1991): diseases of the circulatory system 100.4; malignant neoplasms (cancers) 34.1; diseases of the respiratory system 29.7; accidents and violence 28.5; endocrine, nutritional, and metabolic diseases 17.4; congenital anomalies 13.8; diseases of the genitourinary system 13.4; diseases of the digestive system 10.7.

National economy

Budget (1993). Revenue: BD 580,000,000 (1991; petroleum company dividends and oil field receipts 59.8%, non-oil revenue including grants and loans 40.2%). Expenditures: BD 643,000,000 (1991; government services 30.7%, defense 17.8%, education 15.5%, transport and communication 11.8%, health 9.2%).
Public debt (external, outstanding; 1991): U.S.$1,810,000,000[4].
Population economically active (1991): total 226,448; activity rate of total population 44.6% (participation rates: ages 15–64, 66.1%; female 17.5%; unemployed 6.3%).

Price and earnings indexes (1990 = 100)

	1987	1988	1989	1990	1991	1992	1993[5]
Consumer price index	97.3	97.6	99.1	100.0	100.8	100.6	103.0
Earnings index	...	...	...	...	...	...	...

Production (metric tons except as noted). Agriculture, forestry, fishing (1993): fruit (excluding melons) 23,000, cow's milk 19,000, dates 19,000, tomatoes 4,000, hen's eggs 3,000, onions 1,000, cucumbers 1,000; livestock (number of live animals) 17,000 goats, 16,000 cattle, 9,000 sheep, 1,000 camels, 1,000,-000 chickens; fish catch (1991) 7,553. Manufacturing (barrels; 1992): gas oil 28,000,000; fuel oil 23,500,000; naphtha 12,263,000; kerosene 10,500,000; gasoline 7,900,000; jet fuel 7,500,000; heavy lubricant distillate 2,613,000[6]; petroleum bitumen 523,000; other manufactures include methanol, ammonia, aluminum metal and forms, plastics, and paper products. Construction (permits issued; 1991): residential 5,931; nonresidential 718. Energy produc-

tion (consumption): electricity (kW-hr; 1992) 3,510,000,000 (3,510,000,000); coal, none (n.a.); crude petroleum (barrels; 1992) 14,655,000 (94,501,000); petroleum products (metric tons; 1992) 10,705,000 (665,000); natural gas (cu m; 1992) 5,177,000,000 (5,177,000,000).
Gross national product (at current market prices; 1991): U.S.$6,910,000,000 (U.S.$6,310 per capita).

Structure of gross domestic product and labour force

	1992 value in BD '000,000[7]	1992 % of total value	1991 labour force	1991 % of labour force
Agriculture	15.1	0.9	5,108	2.3
Mining	293.2	17.9	3,638	1.6
Manufacturing	270.9	16.5	26,618	11.8
Construction	92.5	5.6	26,738	11.6
Public utilities	26.5	1.6	2,898	1.3
Transp. and commun.	211.0	12.9	13,789	6.1
Trade	173.4	10.6	29,961	13.2
Finance	280.0	17.1	17,256	7.6
Pub. admin., defense	330.0	20.1 }	83,944	37.1
Services	84.0	5.1 }		
Other	−135.7	−8.3	16,498	7.3
TOTAL	1,640.9	100.0	226,448	100.0[3]

Households. Average household size (1991) 5.8; income per household: n.a.; sources of income: n.a.; expenditure (1984): food and tobacco 33.3%, housing 21.2%, household durable goods 9.8%, transportation and communications 8.5%, recreation 6.4%, clothing and footwear 5.9%, education 2.7%, health 2.3%, energy and water 2.2%.
Land use (1992): meadows and pastures 5.9%; agricultural and under permanent cultivation 2.9%; built-on and wasteland (mostly sand plains and salt marshes) 91.2%.
Tourism (1992): receipts from visitors U.S.$177,000,000; expenditures by nationals abroad U.S.$141,000,000.

Foreign trade[8]

Balance of trade (current prices)

	1988	1989	1990	1991	1992	1993
BD '000,000	+28.2	+3.1	+156.7	−73.1	−119.0	+91.3
% of total	1.6%	1.4%	5.9%	2.7%	4.4%	3.4%

Imports (1992): U.S.$4,144,718,000 (crude petroleum products 36.5%, transport equipment and machines 26.0%, chemicals 7.0%, food and live animals 6.5%). Major import sources: United States 8.3%; United Kingdom 6.9%; Japan 6.6%; Germany 6.5%; Australia 3.9%; Saudi Arabia 3.6%.
Exports (1992): U.S.$3,417,315,000 (petroleum products 76.2%, basic manufactured goods 16.0%). Major export destinations: Saudi Arabia 4.2%; South Korea 2.9%; Japan 2.2%; United States 2.0%.

Transport and communications

Transport. Railroads: none. Roads (1992): total length 1,660 mi, 2,671 km (paved 75%). Vehicles (1992): passenger cars 107,657; trucks and buses 24,523. Merchant marine (1992): vessels (100 gross tons and over) 87; total deadweight tonnage 192,487. Air transport (1993)[9]: passenger-mi 1,089,000,-000, passenger-km 1,753,000,000; short ton-mi cargo 47,920,000, metric ton-km cargo 69,962,000; airports (1994) with scheduled flights 1.
Communications. Daily newspapers (1990): total number 2; total circulation 29,000; circulation per 1,000 population 60. Radio (1993): total number of receivers 320,000 (1 per 1.7 persons). Television (1993): total number of receivers 270,000 (1 per 2.0 persons). Telephones (1992): 182,520 (1 per 2.8 persons).

Education and health

Education (1991–92)

	schools	teachers	students	student/teacher ratio
Primary (age 6–11)	114	3,085	66,694	21.6
Secondary (age 12–17)	35[10]	2,118	42,435	20.0
Voc., teacher tr.	9[10]	809	6,165	7.6
Higher	4[10]	557[11]	6,868[11]	12.3[11]

Educational attainment (1991). Percentage of population age 10 and over having: no formal education 14.1%; knowledge of reading and writing 20.3%; primary education 31.6%; secondary 22.3%; higher 11.7%. *Literacy* (1991): percentage of population age 15 and over literate 69.7%; males literate 76.5%; females literate 58.6%.
Health (1991): physicians 542 (1 per 953 persons); hospital beds 1,187 (1 per 435 persons); infant mortality rate per 1,000 live births (1992) 24.5.
Food: n.a.

Military

Total active duty personnel (1994): 8,100 (army 84.0%, navy 7.4%, air force 8.6%). *Military expenditure as percentage of GNP* (1990): 6.5% (world 4.5%); per capita expenditure U.S.$389.

[1]Population of Ḥawār and other islands included with Eastern Region. [2]Total area includes numerous small uninhabited islands and dependencies of Bahrain. [3]Detail does not add to total given because of rounding. [4]Includes long-term private debt not guaranteed by the government. [5]Fourth quarter. [6]1991. [7]In purchasers' value at current prices. [8]Import figures are f.o.b. in balance of trade and c.i.f. for commodities and trading partners. [9]One fourth apportionment of international flights of Gulf Air (jointly administered by the governments of Bahrain, Oman, Qatar, and the United Arab Emirates). [10]1987–88. [11]1990–91.

Bangladesh

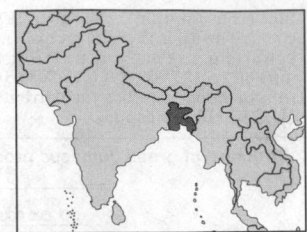

Official name: Gana Prajātantrī Bangladesh (People's Republic of Bangladesh).
Form of government: unitary multiparty republic with one legislative house (Parliament [330[1]]).
Chief of state: President.
Head of government: Prime Minister.
Capital: Dhākā.
Official language: Bengali.
Official religion: Islam.
Monetary unit: 1 Bangladesh taka (Tk) = 100 paisa; valuation (Oct. 7, 1994) 1 U.S.$ = Tk 39.50; 1 £ = Tk 62.82.

Area and population

Divisions[2]	Administrative centres	area sq mi	area sq km	population 1991 census[3]
Chittagong	Chittagong	18,153	47,016	28,811,446
Dhākā	Dhākā	12,038	31,178	33,593,103
Khulna	Khulna	13,800	35,742	20,804,515
Rājshāhi	Rājshāhi	13,304	34,457	26,667,913
TOTAL		57,295	148,393	109,876,977

Demography

Population (1994): 117,404,000.
Density (1994): persons per sq mi 2,049.1, persons per sq km 791.2.
Urban-rural (1989): urban 24.4%; rural 75.6%.
Sex distribution (1991): male 51.47%; female 48.53%.
Age breakdown (1991): under 15, 43.6%; 15–49, 45.0%; 50–64, 7.7%; 65 and over, 3.7%.
Population projection: (2000) 132,402,000; (2010) 161,775,000.
Doubling time: 29 years.
Ethnic composition (1983): Bengali 97.7%; tribal (Chakmā, Gāro, Khāsi, Santāl, etc.) 1.0%; other 1.3%.
Religious affiliation (1991): Muslim 86.8%; Hindu 11.9%; other 1.3%.
Major cities (1991)[4]: Dhākā 6,105,160; Chittagong 2,040,663; Khulna 877,388; Rājshāhi 517,136; Mymensingh 185,517[5].

Vital statistics

Birth rate per 1,000 population (1993): 35.4 (world avg. 26.0).
Death rate per 1,000 population (1993): 11.9 (world avg. 9.2).
Natural increase rate per 1,000 population (1993): 23.5 (world avg. 16.8).
Total fertility rate (avg. births per childbearing woman; 1993): 4.6.
Marriage rate per 1,000 population (1991): 11.0.
Divorce rate per 1,000 population (1981): 3.6.
Life expectancy at birth (1993): male 55.0 years; female 54.4 years.
Major causes of death (1990; percentage of recorded deaths): typhoid fever 19.8%; old age 14.8%; tetanus 10.1%; tuberculosis and other respiratory diseases 8.7%; diarrhea 6.4%; suicide, accidents, and poisoning 5.1%; high blood pressure and heart diseases 5.0%.

National economy

Budget (1991–92). Revenue: Tk 91,001,000,000 (customs duties 30.7%, sales tax 17.3%, excise duties 14.9%, dividends and profits from public enterprises 11.0%, business tax 10.2%, income taxes 3.8%). Expenditures: Tk 80,833,-000,000 (transfer payments 36.2%, employee compensation 33.6%, goods and services 27.8%, capital formation 2.4%).
Production (metric tons except as noted). Agriculture, forestry, fishing (1993): paddy rice 28,000,000, sugarcane 7,507,000, wheat 1,176,000, jute 898,000, bananas 640,000, pulses 517,000, oilseeds 378,000[6], condiments and spices 322,000[6], jackfruit 254,000[6], mangoes 184,000, pineapples 150,000, tea 49,000; livestock (number of live animals) 25,967,000 goats, 23,923,000 cattle, 989,000 sheep, 866,000 buffalo, 109,000,000 chickens, 14,000,000 ducks; roundwood (1992) 31,907,000 cu m; fish catch (1992) 966,727. Mining and quarrying (1991): marine salt 300,000; industrial limestone 42,484. Manufacturing (1992–93): chemical fertilizers 2,162,189; jute manufactures 445,500; sugar 187,464; food products 55,143; newsprint 44,830; paper 43,454; iron and steel 23,318; glass sheet 1,314,000 sq m; cotton yarn 324,000 bales; matches 12,-415,000 gross boxes. Construction: n.a. Energy production (consumption): electricity (kW-hr; 1992) 9,554,000,000 (9,554,000,000); coal (metric tons; 1992) none (338,000); crude petroleum (barrels; 1992) 224,000 (7,930,000); petroleum products (metric tons; 1992) 903,000 (2,048,000); natural gas (cu m; 1992) 5,570,000,000 (5,570,000,000).
Household income. Average household size (1991) 5.3; average annual income per household (1985–86) Tk 30,933 (U.S.$1,035); sources of income (1985–86): self-employment 50.8%, wages and salaries 26.1%, transfer payments 0.5%, other 22.6%; expenditure (1985–86): food and drink 63.3%, housing and rent 8.8%, fuel and light 8.4%, clothing and footwear 5.9%, other 13.6%.
Population economically active (1989): total 50,700,000; activity rate of total population 46.9% (participation rates: over age 10, 71.6%; female 41.4%; unemployed 1.2%[7]).

Price and earnings indexes (1985 = 100)

	1987	1988	1989	1990	1991	1992	1993
Consumer price index	121.6	133.0	146.3	158.1	169.5	176.8	176.7
Daily earnings index[8]	148.4	158.1	164.5	180.6	...	...	...

Public debt (external, outstanding; 1992): U.S.$12,226,000,000.
Land use (1992): forested 14.5%; meadows and pastures 4.6%; agricultural and under permanent cultivation 69.5%; other 11.4%.
Gross national product (at current market prices; 1993): U.S.$25,674,000,000 (U.S.$220 per capita).

Structure of gross domestic product and labour force

	1992–93 in value Tk '000,000	1992–93 % of total value	1989 labour force	1989 % of labour force
Agriculture	324,804	33.5	32,573,000	64.2
Mining	90,900	9.4	89,000	0.2
Manufacturing			6,977,000	13.8
Construction	56,758	5.8	662,000	1.3
Public utilities	16,650	1.7	17,000	—
Transp. and commun.	113,395	11.7	1,278,000	2.5
Trade	78,575	8.1	4,130,000	8.1
Finance	19,295	2.0	238,000	0.5
Public admin., defense	49,020	5.0	4,736,000	9.3
Services and other	220,795	22.8		
TOTAL	970,192	100.0	50,700,000	100.0[9]

Tourism (1992): receipts from visitors U.S.$8,000,000; expenditures by nationals abroad U.S.$111,000,000.

Foreign trade

Balance of trade (current prices)

	1988	1989	1990	1991	1992	1993
Tk '000,000	−39,386	−63,910	−55,550	−48,564	−55,276	−52,113
% of total	32.5%	43.1%	32.4%	28.2%	25.3%	22.5%

Imports (1992–93): Tk 156,010,000,000 (textile yarn, fabrics, and made-up articles 23.3%; machinery and transport equipment 9.3%; petroleum and petroleum products 8.9%; chemicals 4.7%; iron and steel 2.7%; dairy products and eggs 1.7%). *Major import sources* (1990–91): Japan 10.5%; South Korea 9.4%; United States 7.0%; Hong Kong 6.8%; Singapore 6.6%; India 6.3%; China 5.8%; Yemen 3.9%.
Exports (1992–93): Tk 83,710,000,000 (ready-made garments 57.4%; jute manufactures 12.5%; fish and prawns 9.5%; hides, skins, and leather 7.1%; raw jute 3.5%; tea 1.8%). *Major export destinations* (1990–91): United States 28.9%; West Germany 9.6%; United Kingdom 7.7%; Italy 5.5%; Belgium 4.5%; Singapore 3.8%; Japan 3.4%; The Netherlands 3.2%.

Transport and communications

Transport. Railroads (1991–92): route length 1,706 mi, 2,746 km; passenger-mi 3,323,000,000, passenger-km 5,348,000,000; short ton-mi cargo 492,000,000, metric ton-km cargo 718,000,000. Roads (1990): total length 120,100 mi, 193,283 km (paved 4%). Vehicles (1991): passenger cars 67,000; trucks and buses 63,000. Merchant marine (1992): vessels (100 gross tons and over) 301; total deadweight tonnage 566,775. Air transport (1992)[10]: passenger-mi 1,506,000,000, passenger-km 2,424,000,000; short ton-mi cargo 208,000,000, metric ton-km cargo 303,000,000; airports with scheduled flights (1994) 7.
Communications. Daily newspapers (1992): total number 51; total circulation 710,000; circulation per 1,000 population 6. Radio (1993): 4,500,000 receivers (1 per 26 persons). Television (1993): 350,000 receivers (1 per 329 persons). Telephones (1991): 261,738 (1 per 427 persons).

Education and health

Education (1990–91)

	schools	teachers	students	student/teacher ratio
Primary (age 6–10)	48,146	202,847	13,035,000	64.3
Secondary (age 11–17)	9,731	110,313	3,662,000	33.2
Voc., teacher tr.	153	1,440	27,891	19.4
Higher	997	23,332	767,385	32.9

Educational attainment (1981). Percentage of population age 25 and over having: no formal schooling 70.4%; primary education 24.1%; secondary 4.2%; postsecondary 1.3%. *Literacy* (1991): total population age 15 and over literate 34.8%; males literate 45.2%; females literate 23.7%.
Health (1991): physicians 21,004 (1 per 5,264 persons); hospital beds 34,353 (1 per 3,218 persons); infant mortality rate (1993) 109.2.
Food (1988–90): daily per capita caloric intake 2,037 (vegetable products 97%, animal products 3%); 88% of FAO recommended minimum requirement.

Military

Total active duty personnel (1994): 115,500 (army 87.5%, navy 6.9%, air force 5.6%). *Military expenditure as percentage of GNP* (1991): 1.4% (world 4.2%); per capita expenditure U.S.$3.

---

[1]Includes 30 seats reserved for women. [2]Geographic reorganization at the district level took place in 1984; each division is now divided into the following number of new districts: Chittagong 15, Dhākā 17, Khulna 16, and Rājshāhi 16. [3]Adjusted for underenumeration. [4]Metropolitan population. [5]Municipal population. [6]1989–90. [7]Excluding underemployment. [8]Skilled wage earnings in manufacturing. [9]Detail does not add to total given because of rounding. [10]Bangladesh Biman only.

Barbados

Official name: Barbados.
Form of government: constitutional
monarchy with two legislative
houses (Senate [21]; House of
Assembly [28]).
Chief of state: British Monarch
represented by Governor-General.
Head of government: Prime Minister.
Capital: Bridgetown.
Official language: English.
Official religion: none.
Monetary unit: 1 Barbados dollar
(BDS$) = 100 cents; valuation
(Oct. 7, 1994) 1 U.S.$ = BDS$2.01;
1 £ = BDS$3.20.

Area and population	area		population
			1990
Parishes[1]	sq mi	sq km	census
Christ Church	22	57	44,993
St. Andrew	14	36	6,426
St. George	17	44	18,390
St. James	12	31	20,827
St. John	13	34	10,206
St. Joseph	10	26	7,619
St. Lucy	14	36	9,454
St. Michael[2]	15	39	97,517
St. Peter	13	34	10,388
St. Philip	23	60	19,755
St. Thomas	13	34	11,508
TOTAL	166	430[3]	257,083

Demography

Population (1994): 264,000.
Density (1994): persons per sq mi 1,590, persons per sq km 615.
Urban-rural (1990): urban 37.9%; rural 62.1%.
Sex distribution (1993): male 47.89%; female 52.11%.
Age breakdown (1990): under 15, 24.1%; 15–29, 27.0%; 30–44, 22.1%; 45–59,
11.4%; 60 and over, 15.4%.
Population projection: (2000) 270,000; (2010) 279,000.
Doubling time: n.a.; doubling time exceeds 100 years.
Ethnic composition (1988): black 80.0%; mixed 16.0%; white 4.0%.
Religious affiliation (1980): Anglican 39.7%; other Protestant 25.6%, of which
Pentecostal 7.6%, Methodist 7.1%; nonreligious 17.5%; Roman Catholic
4.4%; not stated 2.7%; other 10.1%.
Major cities (1990): Bridgetown 6,070 (urban area 97,517); no other bounded
localities exist.

Vital statistics

Birth rate per 1,000 population (1993): 14.3 (world avg. 26.0); (1979) legiti-
mate 26.9%; illegitimate 73.1%.
Death rate per 1,000 population (1993): 9.1 (world avg. 9.2).
Natural increase rate per 1,000 population (1993): 5.2 (world avg. 16.8).
Total fertility rate (avg. births per childbearing woman; 1992): 1.8.
Marriage rate per 1,000 population (1989): 7.3.
Divorce rate per 1,000 population (1989): 1.6.
Life expectancy at birth (1990–95): male 72.9 years; female 77.9 years.
Major causes of death per 100,000 population (1988): diseases of the cir-
culatory system 338.9, of which cerebrovascular disease 103.9, ischemic
heart diseases 89.5; malignant neoplasms (cancers) 160.7; endocrine and
metabolic disorders 79.8.

National economy

Budget (1993–94). Revenue: BDS$1,006,259,000[4] (tax revenue 92.7%, of
which goods and services taxes 36.9%, personal income and company taxes
29.2%, import duties 7.5%; nontax revenue 7.3%). Expenditures: BDS$1,-
064,126,000 (current expenditure 89.7%, of which education 22.1%, general
public services 15.1%, health 13.1%, economic services 10.9%; development
expenditure 10.3%).
Production (metric tons except as noted). Agriculture, forestry, fishing (1993):
raw sugar 48,500, carrots 1,521, yams 1,152, sweet potatoes 773, cucumbers
599, onions 556, tomatoes 360; livestock (number of live animals) 66,000
sheep, 45,000 pigs, 38,000 goats, 33,000 cattle; roundwood, n.a.; fish catch
(1992) 2,852. Manufacturing (value added in BDS$'000; 1993): food, bev-
erages, and tobacco (mostly sugar, molasses, rum, beer, and cigarettes)
104,500; paper products, printing, and publishing 26,000; metal products and
assembly-type goods (mostly electronic components) 36,100; textiles and
wearing apparel 9,100. Construction (value added in BDS$; 1993): 116,300,-
000. Energy production (consumption): electricity (kW hr; 1992) 537,000,000
([1991] 527,000,000); coal, none (none); crude petroleum (barrels; 1991)
454,000 ([1991] 2,055,000); petroleum products (metric tons; 1990) 266,000
(265,000); natural gas (cu m; 1992) 22,000,000 ([1991] 23,000,000).
Population economically active (1993): total 126,300; activity rate of total population 48.5% (participation rates: ages 15 and over, 66.5%; female 59.8%;
unemployed 24.5%).

Price and earnings indexes (1985=100)							
	1987	1988	1989	1990	1991	1992	1993
Consumer price index	104.7	109.8	116.6	120.2	127.7	135.4	137.0
Hourly earnings index	106.0	113.8	116.9	122.7	...	...	...

Household income and expenditure. Average household size (1980) 3.7; income per household (1988) BDS$13,455 (U.S.$6,690); sources of income:
n.a.; expenditure (1978–79): food 43.2%, housing 13.1%, household operations 9.6%, alcohol and tobacco 8.4%, fuel and light 6.2%, clothing and
footwear 5.1%, transportation 4.6%, other 9.8%.
Gross national product (at current market prices; 1993): U.S.$1,622,000,000
(U.S.$6,240 per capita).

Structure of gross domestic product and labour force				
	1993		1992	
	in value BDS$'000,000	% of total value	labour force	% of labour force
Agriculture, fishing	146.7	4.5	6,000	4.8
Mining	15.2[5]	0.5[5]	...	...
Manufacturing	210.0	6.4	10,000	8.0
Construction	116.3	3.5	7,400	5.9
Public utilities	101.6[5]	3.1[5]	1,700	1.4
Transportation and communications	255.1	7.8	4,100	3.3
Trade, restaurants	868.7	26.5	14,200	11.4
Finance, real estate	437.1	13.3	4,100	-3.3
Pub. admin., defense	509.2	15.5 }	39,100	31.4
Services	110.6	3.4 }		
Other	509.9[6]	16.5[6]	38,100[7]	30.5[7]
TOTAL	3,280.6[3]	100.0	124,800[3]	100.0

Public debt (1992): U.S.$400,000,000.
Tourism (1992): receipts from visitors U.S.$463,000,000; expenditures by na-
tionals abroad U.S.$41,000,000.
Land use (1992): forested, negligible; meadows and pastures 4.7%; agricultural and under permanent cultivation 37.2%; other 58.1%.

Foreign trade[8]

Balance of trade (current prices)						
	1987	1988	1989	1990	1991	1992
BDS$'000,000	-631.2	-703.9	-856.7	-858.8	-984.6	-568.8
% of total	50.4%	49.8%	53.4%	50.5%	53.6%	42.6%

Imports (1993): BDS$1,153,881,000 (retained imports 92.0%, of which food
and beverages 17.3%, machinery 15.1%, construction materials 7.3%, chemicals 6.0%, fuels 4.7%; reexported imports 8.0%). *Major import sources*
(1992): United States 31.0%; Trinidad and Tobago 15.9%; Netherlands
Antilles 9.1%; United Kingdom 8.9%; Venezuela 7.0%; Canada 4.2%;
Germany 3.5%.
Exports (1993): BDS$363,982,000 (domestic exports 74.8%, of which sugar
13.1%, chemicals 11.6%, electrical components 13.4%, rum 4.3%, clothing
2.5%; reexports 25.2%). *Major export destinations* (1992): United Kingdom
17.0%; United States 13.0%; Trinidad and Tobago 8.4%; Canada 2.3%;
Dominica 1.9%; Jamaica 1.3%.

Transport and communications

Transport. Railroads: none. Roads (1989): total length 977 mi, 1,573 km
(paved 95%). Vehicles (1991): passenger cars 39,406; trucks and buses
9,318[9]. Merchant marine (1992): vessels (100 gross tons and over) 37; total
deadweight tonnage 84,000. Air transport (1992): passenger arrivals 584,-
900, passenger departures 590,300; cargo unloaded 7,261 metric tons, cargo
loaded 4,594 metric tons; airports (1994) with scheduled flights 1.
Communications. Daily newspapers (1992): total number 2; total circulation
41,008; circulation per 1,000 population 158. Radio (1993): total number
of receivers 200,000 (1 per 1.3 persons). Television (1993): total number
of receivers 69,350 (1 per 3.7 persons). Telephones (1991): 108,825 (1
per 2.4 persons).

Education and health

Education (1989–90)	schools	teachers	students	student/ teacher ratio
Primary (age 3–11)[10]	104	1,602	29,539	18.4
Secondary (age 12–16)	33	1,406	21,259	15.1
Vocational[11]	8	79	996	12.6
Higher[12]	1	153	1,314	8.6

Educational attainment (1980). Percentage of population age 25 and over having: no formal schooling 0.8%; primary education 63.5%; secondary 32.3%;
higher 3.3%. *Literacy* (1985): total population age 15 and over literate[13]
180,000 (98.0%).
Health: physicians (1986) 243 (1 per 1,042 persons); hospital beds (1987) 2,111
(1 per 121 persons); infant mortality rate per 1,000 live births (1993) 10.1.
Food (1988–90): daily per capita caloric intake 3,217 (vegetable products 73%,
animal products 27%); 133% of FAO recommended minimum requirement.

Military

Total active duty personnel (1989): 154 (paramilitary marine and coast guard
components only). *Military expenditure as percentage of GNP* (1988): 0.7%
(world 5.0%); per capita expenditure U.S.$41.

[1]Parishes and city of Bridgetown have no local administrative function. [2]Includes city
of Bridgetown. [3]Detail does not add to total given because of rounding. [4]Current
revenue only. [5]Mining excludes natural gas; Public utilities includes natural gas.
[6]Net indirect taxes. [7]Includes 28,700 unemployed persons. [8]Import figures are f.o.b.
in balance of trade and c.i.f. in commodities and trading partners. [9]Includes taxis.
[10]Includes preprimary. [11]1987–88. [12]University of the West Indies, Cave Hill campus.
[13]National literacy standard based solely on school attendance. Functional literacy
may be appreciably lower.

Belarus

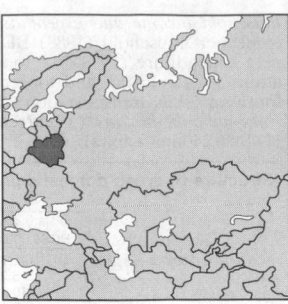

Official name: Respublika Belarus (Republic of Belarus).
Form of government: unitary multiparty republic with a single legislative body (Supreme Council [360[1]]).
Head of state and government: President.
Capital: Minsk.
Official language: Belarusian.
Official religion: none.
Monetary unit[2]: Belarusian rubel (plural rubli) valuation (Oct. 7, 1994) free rate, 1 U.S.$ = 5,854 rubli; 1 £ = 9,312 rubli.

Area and population

Provinces	Capitals	area sq mi	area sq km	population 1992[3] estimate
Brest	Brest	12,500	32,300	1,494,000
Homel (Gomel)	Homel	15,600	40,400	1,611,000
Hrodno (Grodno)	Hrodno	9,700	25,000	1,199,000
Mahilyoŭ (Mogilyov)	Mahilyoŭ	11,200	29,000	1,267,000
Minsk (Mensk)	Minsk	15,700	40,800	3,272,000
Vitebsk	Vitebsk	15,500	40,100	1,438,000
TOTAL		80,200[4]	207,600[4]	10,281,000

Demography

Population (1994): 10,404,000.
Density (1994): persons per sq mi 129.7, persons per sq km 50.1.
Urban-rural (1992): urban 70.0%; rural 30.0%.
Sex distribution (1992): male 47.00%; female 53.00%.
Age breakdown (1991): under 15, 23.2%; 15–29, 21.5%; 30–44, 22.1%; 45–59, 16.5%; 60–69, 10.1%; 70 and over, 6.6%.
Population projection: (2000) 10,634,000; (2010) 11,028,000.
Doubling time: not applicable; doubling time exceeds 100 years.
Ethnic composition (1991): Belarusian 77.9%; Russian 13.5%; Ukrainian 3.0%; Jewish 0.7%; other 4.9%.
Religious affiliation: believers are predominantly Belarusian Orthodox; there is a Roman Catholic minority.
Major cities (1992): Minsk 1,671,000; Homel 517,000; Vitebsk 373,000; Mahilyoŭ 364,000; Hrodno 291,000.

Vital Statistics

Birth rate per 1,000 population (1992): 12.4 (world avg. 26.0); (1990) legitimate 91.0%; illegitimate 9.0%.
Death rate per 1,000 population (1992): 11.3 (world avg. 9.2).
Natural increase rate per 1,000 population (1992): 1.1 (world avg. 16.8).
Total fertility rate (avg. births per childbearing woman; 1993): 1.9.
Marriage rate per 1,000 population (1992): 7.8
Divorce rate per 1,000 population (1992): 3.9.
Life expectancy at birth (1993): male 66.0 years; female 75.7 years.
Major causes of death per 100,000 population (1989): diseases of the circulatory system 563.7; malignant neoplasms (cancers) 167.6; accidents and violence 96.5; diseases of the respiratory system 79.8; diseases of the digestive system 21.3; diseases of the nervous system 7.8; infectious and parasitic diseases 7.5; endocrine and metabolic disorders 5.8.

National economy

Budget (1994). Revenue: 16,470,000,000,000 rubli (tax revenue 77.0%, of which enterprise profits tax 22.8%, excise tax 20.1%, value-added tax 19.3%; social security contributions 19.9%). Expenditures: 19,701,000,000,000 rubli (administration and defense 28.8%; national economy 22.3%; health 18.5%; education 10.3%).
Tourism: receipts from visitors, n.a.; expenditures by nationals abroad, n.a.
Land use (1992): forested 30.2%; meadows and pastures 15.1%; agricultural and under permanent cultivation 33.6%; other 21.1%.
Production (metric tons except as noted). Agriculture, forestry, fishing (1993): potatoes 11,600,000, grain 7,355,000, sugar beets 1,568,000, other vegetables 1,000,000, wheat 400,000, fruit 290,000; livestock (number of live animals) 6,221,000 cattle, 4,308,000 pigs, 380,000 sheep and goats, 215,000 horses, 47,000,000 poultry; roundwood (1991) 6,700,000 cu m; fish catch (1991) 15,500. Mining and quarrying (1992): dolomite 8,400,000; potash 3,900,000; salt 360,000. Manufacturing (1993): fertilizers 2,500,000; cement 1,908,000; steel 946,000; lime 939,000; synthetic fibres 293,000; cotton 35,200; electric motors 1,430,000 units; radio receivers 768,000 units; bicycles 603,000 units; cameras 495,000 units; light bulbs 180,000 units; motorcycles 128,000 units. Construction (1991): 5,395,000 sq m. Energy production (consumption): electricity (kW-hr; 1992) 37,600,000,000 (47,700,000,000); coal (1992) none (1,600,000); crude petroleum (barrels; 1992) 14,600,000 (158,300,000); petroleum products (1992) 18,320,000 (18,300,000); natural gas (cu m; 1992) 261,000,000 (15,900,000,000).
Population economically active (1992): 4,887,000; activity rate of total population 47.3% (participation rate: ages 16–59 [male], 16–54 [female] 81.6%; female [1991] 53.3%; unemployed 7.5%).

Price and earnings indexes (1990 = 100)

	1988	1989	1990	1991	1992	1993
Consumer price index	94.1	95.6	100.0	183.5	1,961.6	c. 25,200
Monthly earnings index	78.5	86.2	100.0	197.4	1,847.7	c. 22,200

Gross national product (at current market prices; 1993): U.S.$29,306,000,000 (U.S.$2,840 per capita).

Structure of net material product and labour force

	1992 in value '000,000 rubles[5]	1992 % of total value	1993 labour force	1993 % of labour force
Agriculture	186,579	23.9	945,000	19.8
Mining	}			
Manufacturing	364,268	46.7	1,364,000	28.6
Public utilities	}			
Construction	93,753	12.0	374,000	7.9
Transportation and commununications	28,940	3.7	308,000	6.5
Trade	50,586	6.5	271,000	5.7
Finance	—	—	34,000	0.7
Public administration, defense	—	—	157,500	3.3
Services	—	—	817,000	17.2
Other	55,923	7.2	489,500	10.3
TOTAL	780,049	100.0	4,760,000	100.0

Public debt (external, outstanding; 1993): U.S.$1,300,000,000.
Household income and expenditure. Average household size (1989) 3.2; income per household (1991) 8,000 rubles; sources of income (1992): wages and salaries 66.5%, transfers 23.6%, agricultural income 9.9%; expenditure (1992): retail goods 76.0%, services 5.6%, housing 1.1%, taxes 6.4%, other 10.9%.

Foreign trade

Balance of trade (current prices)

	1988	1989	1990	1991	1992	1993
'000,000,000 rubles	+2.1	+1.0	−0.8	−1.8	−3.7	+670.0
% of total	5.6%	2.5%	2.1%	2.3%	4.7%	5.3%

Imports (1993): 5,919,000,000,000 rublcs[5] (energy products 38.7%, machine building and metalworking machinery 18.5%, chemical and petrochemical products 13.8%, semimanufactured products 12.3%, ferrous metals 9.2%). *Major import sources:* Russia 56.6%; Ukraine 8.7%; Germany 8.1%; Kazakhstan 4.4%; U.S. 4.0%; Switzerland 2.3%.
Exports (1993): 6,589,000,000,000 rubles[5] (machine building and metalworking machinery 48.9%, light industry 12.7%, chemical and petrochemical products 12.2%, semimanufactured products 8.3%, energy products 4.6%). *Major export destinations:* Russia 33.3%; Ukraine 8.2%; Poland 4.3%; Germany 4.1%; Kazakhstan 2.3%; U.S. 1.6%.

Transport and communications

Transport. Railroads (1992): length 3,459 mi, 5,567 km; passenger-mi 9,815,000,000, passenger-km 15,795,000,000; short ton-mi cargo 44,974,000,000, metric ton-km cargo 65,551,000,000. Roads (1992): total length 30,600 mi, 49,300 km (paved 96%). Vehicles (1992): passenger cars 700,000; trucks and buses 46,200. Merchant marine (1992): vessels (100 gross tons and over) n.a.; total deadweight tonnage 18,373,000,000. Air transport (1992): passenger-mi 3,487,000,000, passenger-km 5,611,000,000; short ton-mi cargo 23,200,000, metric ton-km cargo 34,000,000; airports (1994) with scheduled flights 1.
Communications. Daily newspapers (1990): total number 28; total circulation 2,937,000; circulation per 1,000 population 286. Radio (1992): 8,755,000 receivers (1 per 1.2 persons). Television (1992): 3,538,000 receivers (1 per 2.9 persons). Telephones (1992): 1,862,000 (1 per 5.5 persons).

Education and health

Education (1991–92)

	schools	teachers	students	student/ teacher ratio
Primary (age 6–13)	} 5,187	123,300	1,488,500	12.1
Secondary (age 14–17)				
Voc., teacher tr.	148	...	139,000	...
Higher	33	...	184,600	...

Educational attainment (1989). Percentage of population age 25 and over having: primary education or no formal schooling 23.0%; some secondary 16.8%; completed secondary and some postsecondary 49.4%; higher 10.8%.
Literacy (1989): total population age 15 and over literate 7,690,000 (97.9%); males literate 3,661,000 (99.4%); females literate 4,029,000 (96.6%).
Health (1992): physicians 42,700 (1 per 242 persons); hospital beds 127,100 (1 per 81 persons); infant mortality rate (1992) per 1,000 live births 12.4.
Food: daily per capita caloric intake, n.a.

Military

Total active duty personnel (1994): 92,500 (57% army, 30% air force and air defense, 13% CIS controlled and other). About 35,000 Russian troops remained in Belarus in late 1994; they were scheduled to leave by the end of 1995. *Military expenditure as percentage of GNP* (1993): 1.8%; per capita expenditure U.S.$50.

---

[1]Includes 50 nonclective seats. The 1994 constitution established a new 260-member Supreme Soviet, elections to which had not been held by year-end 1994. [2]The Belarusian rubel was introduced May 25, 1992, at a rate of 1 rubel to 10 Russian rubles and circulated parallel with the Russian ruble; the fixed rates to the Russian ruble were adjusted on Aug. 15, 1993 (2 Belarusian rubli to 1 Russian ruble), and on Oct. 14, 1993 (3 Belarusian rubli to 1 Russian ruble). An April 12, 1994, agreement on monetary union between Belarus and Russia never went into effect. The Belarusian rubel was declared the sole legal tender in October 1994; it is unofficially known as the zaichik, or "hare." [3]January 1. [4]Rounded area figures; exact area figures are 80,153 sq mi (207,595 sq km). [5]Russian rubles.

Belgium

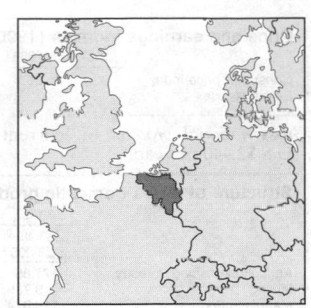

Official name: Koninkrijk België
(Dutch); Royaume de Belgique
(French) (Kingdom of Belgium).
Form of government: federal
constitutional monarchy with two
legislative houses (Senate [185[1]];
House of Representatives [212]).
Chief of state: Monarch.
Head of government: Prime Minister.
Capital: Brussels.
Official languages: Dutch; French;
German.
Official religion: none.
Monetary unit: 1 Belgian franc
(BF) = 100 centimes, valuation (Oct.
7, 1994) 1 U.S.$ = BF 31.70;
1 £ = BF 50.42.

Area and population		area		population
Regions[3]				1992[2]
Provinces	**Capitals**	sq mi	sq km	estimate
Brussels	—	62	162	951,217
Flanders		5,217[4]	13,511	5,794,857
Antwerp	Antwerp	1,107	2,867	1,610,695
Brabant[5]	—	813	2,106	976,956
East Flanders	Ghent	1,151	2,982	1,340,056
Limburg	Hasselt	935	2,422	755,593
West Flanders	Brugge	1,210	3,134	1,111,557
Wallonia		6,504[4]	16,845	3,275,923
Brabant[6]	—	421	1,091	325,621
Hainaut	Mons	1,461	3,786	1,283,252
Liège	Liège	1,491	3,862	1,006,081
Luxembourg	Arlon	1,714	4,440	234,664
Namur	Namur	1,416	3,666	426,305
TOTAL		11,783	30,518	10,021,997

Demography

Population (1994): 10,118,000.
Density (1994): persons per sq mi 858.7, persons per sq km 331.5.
Urban-rural (1992): urban 96.5%; rural 3.5%.
Sex distribution (1992[2]): male 48.88%; female 51.12%.
Age breakdown (1991): under 15, 18.1%; 15–29, 21.8%; 30–44, 22.5%; 45–59, 16.9%; 60–74, 14.1%; 75 and over, 6.6%.
Population projection: (2000) 10,338,000; (2010) 10,717,000.
Doubling time: not applicable; doubling time exceeds 100 years.
Nationality (1991): Belgian 91.0%; Italian 2.4%; Moroccan 1.4%; French 0.9%; Turkish 0.8%; Dutch 0.6%; other 2.9%.
Religious affiliation (1980): Roman Catholic 90.0%; Muslim 1.1%; Protestant 0.4%; nonreligious and atheist 7.5%; other 1.0%.
Major cities (1992[2]): Brussels 136,424[7] (951,217[8]); Antwerp 465,783; Ghent 230,232; Charleroi 206,903; Liège 196,303.

Vital statistics

Birth rate per 1,000 population (1993): 12.1 (world avg. 26.0); (1987) legitimate 90.8%; illegitimate 9.2%.
Death rate per 1,000 population (1993): 10.8 (world avg. 9.2).
Natural increase rate per 1,000 population (1993): 1.3 (world avg. 16.8).
Total fertility rate (avg. births per childbearing woman; 1990–95): 1.6.
Marriage rate per 1,000 population (1991): 6.1.
Divorce rate per 1,000 population (1991): 2.1.
Life expectancy at birth (1988–90): male 72.4 years; female 79.1 years.
Major causes of death per 100,000 population (1988): diseases of the circulatory system 414.1, of which cerebrovascular disease 102.6; malignant neoplasms (cancers) 275.5.

National economy

Budget (1992). Revenue: BF 1,981,428,000,000 (direct taxes 37.0%; value-added, stamp, and similar duties 10.3%; customs and excise duties 8.4%). Expenditures: BF 2,486,676,000,000 (public debt 27.3%; government departments 25.4%; pension 10.1%; defense 3.9%).
Public debt (1994[2]): U.S.$209,300,000,000.
Production (metric tons except as noted). Agriculture, forestry, fishing (1993)[9]: sugar beets 5,829,000, potatoes 2,100,000, wheat 1,415,000, apples 536,000, barley 530,000, tomatoes 345,000, corn (maize) 168,000, carrots 105,000, oats 80,000; livestock (number of live animals) 6,963,000 pigs, 3,303,000 cattle, 156,000 sheep, 21,000 horses; roundwood (1992) 4,730,000 cu m; fish catch (1991) 40,226, of which European plaice (flounder) 17,954, common sole 5,658, Atlantic cod 3,504. Mining and quarrying (1991): quartz 419,000; barite 35,000; marble 358 cu m. Manufacturing (value added in BF '000,000; 1990): metal products and machinery 422,238; chemical and plastic products 344,743; food, beverages, and tobacco 198,942; pig iron, steel, and nonferrous metals 136,244; paper, printing, and publishing 96,623; textiles 94,861; furniture and fixtures 61,626. Construction (1991): residential 29,050,100 cu m; nonresidential 54,044,400 cu m. Energy production (consumption): electricity (kW-hr; 1992) 72,259,000,000 (72,387,000,000); coal (metric tons; 1992) 1,197,000 (14,387,000); crude petroleum (barrels; 1992) none (211,646,000); petroleum products (metric tons; 1992) 26,311,000 (17,165,000); natural gas (cu m; 1992) 6,945,000 (13,230,000,000).
Household income and expenditure. Avg. household size (1991) 2.7; sources of income (1992): wages 49.6%, transfer payments 20.7%, property income 18.8%, self-employment 10.9%; expenditure (1990): food 22.0%, housing 16.1%, transp. 13.5%, health 11.5%, durable goods 9.4%, clothing 7.8%.

Gross national product (1992): U.S.$209,594,000,000 (U.S.$20,880 per capita).

Structure of gross domestic product and labour force				
	1991		1992	
	in value BF '000,000	% of total value	labour force	% of labour force
Agriculture	130,800	1.9	109,200	2.7
Mining	17,200	0.2	872,800	21.4
Manufacturing	1,462,600	21.3		
Construction	409,300	6.0	246,600	6.0
Public utilities	203,800	3.0	44,300	1.1
Transp. and commun.	562,900	8.2	269,100	6.6
Trade	1,439,800	20.9	670,800	16.4
Finance	1,160,000	17.0	327,500	8.0
Pub. admin., defense	867,700	12.6	1,232,300	30.1
Services	808,500	11.8		
Other	−194,400[10]	−2.8[10]	316,000[11]	7.7[11]
TOTAL	6,877,000	100.0[4]	4,088,600	100.0

Population economically active (1992): total 4,088,600; activity rate of total population 40.6% (participation rates: ages 14–64, 61.1%; female 40.7%; unemployed 7.7%).

Price and earnings indexes (1990 = 100)							
	1987	1988	1989	1990	1991	1992	1993
Consumer price index	92.7	93.8	96.7	100.0	103.2	105.7	108.6
Hourly earnings index	90.0	90.7	95.8	100.0	105.1	110.1	112.4

Land use (1992)[9]: forested 21.3%; meadows and pastures 20.9%; agricultural and under permanent cultivation 23.9%; other 33.9%.
Tourism (1992): receipts from visitors U.S.$4,053,000,000; expenditures by nationals abroad U.S.$6,603,000,000.

Foreign trade[9]

Balance of trade (current prices)						
	1987	1988	1989	1990	1991	1992
BF '000,000	+124,300	+96,400	+177,300	+61,200	+21,700	+65,200
% of total	2.0%	1.4%	2.3%	0.8%	0.3%	0.8%

Imports (1992): BF 4,023,293,000,000 (machinery and transport equipment 25.6%, of which road vehicles and parts 9.3%; chemicals and chemical products 11.9%; food and live animals 8.7%; mineral fuels and lubricants 7.6%, of which petroleum and petroleum products 5.4%; nonindustrial [gem] diamonds 5.9%). *Major import sources:* Germany 23.9%; The Netherlands 17.5%; France 16.5%; U.K. 7.7%; Italy 4.5%; U.S. 4.4%.
Exports (1992): BF 3,969,811,000,000 (machinery and transport equipment 27.0%, of which passenger cars 15.3%; chemicals 14.7%, of which plastics 5.1%; food and live animals 9.7%; iron and steel 6.3%; nonindustrial [gem] diamonds 6.2%; textiles 5.2%; petroleum and petroleum products 3.2%). *Major export destinations:* Germany 22.8%; France 19.2%; The Netherlands 13.7%; U.K. 7.8%; Italy 5.9%; U.S. 3.8%.

Transport and communications

Transport. Railroads (1992): route length 2,132 mi, 3,432 km; passenger-mi 4,224,000,000, passenger-km 6,798,000,000; short ton-mi cargo 5,540,000,000, metric ton-km cargo 8,089,000,000. Roads (1990[2]): total length 85,672 mi, 137,876 km (paved 97%). Vehicles (1993): passenger cars 4,109,601; trucks and buses 389,812. Merchant marine (1992): vessels (100 gross tons and over) 232; total deadweight tonnage 218,506. Air transport (1993): passenger-mi 4,026,000,000, passenger-km 6,480,000,000; short ton-mi cargo 287,440,000, metric ton-km cargo 419,650,000; airports (1994) with scheduled flights 2.
Communications. Daily newspapers (1991): total number 76; total circulation 3,609,000[12]; circulation per 1,000 population 361[12]. Radio (1993): 5,000,000 receivers (1 per 2.0 persons). Television (1993): 4,200,000 receivers (1 per 2.4 persons). Telephones (1992): 5,898,300 (1 per 1.7 persons).

Education and health

Education (1991–92)	schools	teachers[13]	students	student/ teacher ratio
Primary (age 6–12)	4,158	72,589[13]	711,521	...
Secondary (age 12–18)	2,055[14]	110,599	765,672	6.9
Voc., teacher tr.[14]	397	14,548[15]	137,175	...
Higher[14]	21	10,517[15]	111,845	...

Educational attainment (1981). Percentage of population age 15 and over having: less than secondary education 44.4%; lower secondary 26.5%; upper secondary 17.0%; vocational 2.9%; teacher's college 0.6%; university 3.5%.
Literacy (1991): virtually 100% literate.
Health (1993): physicians 36,178 (1 per 278 persons); hospital beds (1991) 80,549 (1 per 124 persons); infant mortality rate per 1,000 live births 8.0.
Food (1988–90): daily per capita caloric intake 3,925 (vegetable products 60%, animal products 40%); 149% of FAO recommended minimum requirement.

Military

Total active duty personnel (1994): 63,000 (army 76.2%, navy 4.6%, air force 19.2%). *Military expenditure as percentage of GNP* (1991): 2.4% (world 4.2%); per capita expenditure U.S.$463.

[1]Includes one ex officio member from the royal family. [2]January 1. [3]On May 8, 1993, the legislature approved constitutional establishment of federal regions. [4]Detail does not add to total given because of rounding. [5]Composed of Brabant districts Hal-Vilvorde and Louvaine. [6]Composed of Brabant district Nivelles. [7]1991. [8]Région Bruxelloise. [9]Includes Luxembourg. [10]Includes imputed bank service charges. [11]Unemployed. [12]For 40 newspapers only. [13]Includes preschool teachers. [14]1990–91. [15]1987–88.

Belize

Official name: Belize.
Form of government: constitutional monarchy with two legislative houses (Senate [9]; House of Representatives [29[1]]).
Chief of state: British Monarch represented by Governor-General.
Head of government: Prime Minister.
Capital: Belmopan.
Official language: English.
Official religion: none.
Monetary unit: 1 Belize dollar (BZ$) = 100 cents; valuation (Oct. 7, 1994) 1 U.S.$ = BZ$2.00[2]; 1 £ = BZ$3.18.

Area and population

Districts	Capitals	area sq mi	area sq km	population 1992 estimate
Belize	Belize City	1,663	4,307	58,504
Cayo	San Ignacio	2,006	5,196	39,346
Corozal	Corozal	718	1,860	30,617
Orange Walk	Orange Walk	1,790	4,636	32,867
Stann Creek	Dangriga	986	2,554	18,829
Toledo	Punta Gorda	1,704	4,413	18,837
TOTAL		8,867	22,965[3]	199,000

Demography

Population (1994): 210,000.
Density (1994): persons per sq mi 23.7, persons per sq km 9.1.
Urban-rural (1992): urban 46.6%; rural 53.4%.
Sex distribution (1992): male 50.75%; female 49.25%.
Age breakdown (1992): under 15, 43.9%; 15–29, 27.9%; 30–44, 14.9%; 45–59, 7.2%; 60–74, 4.5%; 75 and over, 1.6%.
Population projection: (2000) 235,000; (2010) 268,000.
Doubling time: 23 years.
Ethnic composition (1991): mestizo (Spanish-Indian) 43.6%; Creole (predominantly black) 29.8%; Mayan Indian 11.0%; Garifuna (black-Carib Indian) 6.7%; white 3.9%; East Indian 3.5%; other or not stated 1.5%.
Religious affiliation (1991): Roman Catholic 57.7%; Protestant 34.3%, of which Anglican 7.0%, Pentecostal 6.3%, Methodist 4.2%, Seventh-day Adventist 4.1%, Mennonite 4.0%; other Christian 1.7%; other 0.3%; none or not stated 6.0%.
Major cities (1992): Belize City 45,158; Orange Walk 11,728; San Ignacio/Santa Elena 9,533; Corozal 7,104; Belmopan 3,687.

Vital statistics

Birth rate per 1,000 population (1993): 35.7 (world avg. 26.0); (1991) legitimate 42.5%; illegitimate 57.5%.
Death rate per 1,000 population (1993): 6.1 (world avg. 9.2).
Natural increase rate per 1,000 population (1993): 29.6 (world avg. 16.8).
Total fertility rate (avg. births per childbearing woman; 1993): 4.5.
Marriage rate per 1,000 population (1991): 5.4.
Divorce rate per 1,000 population (1991): 0.5.
Life expectancy at birth (1991): male 67.0 years; female 72.0 years.
Major causes of death per 100,000 population (1990): accidents 92.6; ischemic heart diseases 84.7; diseases of the respiratory system 57.1; malignant neoplasms (cancers) 52.4; cerebrovascular disease 47.6; diabetes mellitus 37.0.

National economy

Budget (1993–94). Revenue: BZ$284,600,000 (current revenue 92.5%, of which taxes on international trade 41.0%, taxes on income and profits 20.5%, nontax revenue 18.6%, excise taxes 6.8%; grants 4.8%). Expenditures: BZ$350,-800,000 (current expenditures 53.0%; development expenditures 47.0%,· of which from foreign sources 28.0%).
Public debt (external, outstanding; 1992): U.S.$153,100,000.
Production (metric tons except as noted). Agriculture, forestry, fishing (1993): sugarcane 1,159,000, oranges 73,200, bananas 40,800, grapefruits 36,800, corn (maize) 27,200, rice 9,700, red kidney beans 3,600, coconuts 3,000, cocoa 72, honey 55; livestock (number of live animals) 58,000 cattle, 26,000 pigs, 1,000,000 chickens; roundwood (1992) 188,000 cu m; fish catch (1991) 1,639, of which lobsters 544, shrimp 447, freshwater and marine fish 415, conchs 229. Mining and quarrying (1992): limestone 300,000; sand and gravel 300,000. Manufacturing (1993): sugar 101,800; molasses 28,700; fertilizer 13,000; flour 12,300; orange concentrate 52,700 hectolitres; beer (1992) 36,-000 hectolitres; grapefruit concentrate 21,300 hectolitres; cigarettes (1992) 114,000,000 units; garments 4,276,000 units. Construction (publicly financed buildings under construction; 1991): residential 180 units; nonresidential, n.a. Energy production (consumption): electricity (kW-hr; 1992) 110,000,000 (110,000,000); coal, none (none); crude petroleum, none (none); petroleum products (metric tons; 1992) none (86,000); natural gas, none (none).
Household income and expenditure. Average household size (1991) 4.9; median annual income per employed person (1991) BZ$6,150[4] (U.S.$3,075[4]); sources of income: n.a.; expenditure (1980): food and beverages 51.5%, clothing and footwear 11.1%, household furnishings 10.1%, transportation and communications 6.5%, energy and water 6.0%, health care 3.4%, housing 2.3%, other 9.1%.
Population economically active (1991): total c. 65,000; activity rate of total population, c. 34.0% (participation rates: over age 15, c. 63.0%; female [1983–84] 32.5%; unemployed 19.6%).

Price and earnings indexes (1990 = 100)

	1987	1988	1989	1990	1991	1992	1993
Consumer price index	92.1	95.1	97.0	100.0	105.6	108.6	110.2
Earnings index	...	...	...	...	...	...	...

Gross national product (at current market prices; 1993): U.S.$500,000,000 (U.S.$2,440 per capita).

Structure of gross domestic product and labour force

	1993 in value BZ$'000[5]	1993 % of total value	1991 labour force[6]	1991 % of labour force[6]
Agriculture, fishing, forestry	171,866	19.4	18,256	17.6
Mining	9,786	1.1	326	0.3
Manufacturing	119,314	13.4	5,951	5.7
Construction	84,866	9.6	4,059	3.9
Public utilities	32,696	3.7	721	0.7
Transportation and communications	107,000	12.1	2,925	2.8
Trade, restaurants	145,001	16.3	10,013	9.7
Finance, real estate, insurance	93,549	10.5	1,771	1.7
Pub. admin., defense	108,343	12.2	5,352	5.2
Services	52,841	6.0	5,967	5.8
Other	−38,012[7]	−4.3[7]	48,226[8]	46.6[8]
TOTAL	887,250	100.0	103,567	100.0

Land use (1991): forested 44.4%; meadows and pastures 2.1%; agricultural and under permanent cultivation 2.5%; other 51.0%.
Tourism (1992): receipts from visitors U.S.$108,000,000; expenditures by nationals abroad U.S.$14,000,000.

Foreign trade[9]

Balance of trade (current prices)

	1988	1989	1990	1991	1992	1993
BZ$'000,000	−96.6	−143.1	−126.0	−203.9	−214.0	−247.6
% of total	17.2%	22.3%	19.6%	28.8%	27.5%	32.0%

Imports (1992): BZ$545,900,000 ([10]machinery and transport 25.3%; food and live animals 18.0%; manufactured goods 16.0%; mineral fuels 13.4%). Major import sources: United States 57.0%; Mexico 8.8%; United Kingdom 8.5%; The Netherlands 2.9%; Guatemala 2.3%.
Exports (1992)[11]: BZ$282,200,000 (domestic exports 77.0%, of which sugar 26.6%, orange concentrate 14.6%, garments 11.6%, bananas 7.3%, grapefruit concentrate 4.6%; reexports 23.0%). Major export destinations: United States 47.2%; United Kingdom 23.6%; Mexico 12.5%; Canada 4.4%; Germany 2.5%.

Transport and communications

Transport. Railroads: none. Roads (1991): total length 1,684 mi, 2,710 km (paved 18%). Vehicles (1991): passenger cars 12,075; trucks and buses 2,800. Merchant marine (1991): vessels (100 gross tons and over) 32; total deadweight tonnage 45,706. Air transport (1991)[12]: passenger arrivals 165,858, passenger departures 166,972; cargo loaded 304 metric tons, cargo unloaded 1,705 metric tons. Airports (1994) with scheduled flights 8.
Communications. Daily newspapers: none[13]. Radio (1993): total number of receivers 100,000 (1 per 2.0 persons). Television (1993): total number of receivers 27,048 (1 per 7.6 persons). Telephones (1992): 24,840[14] (1 per 8.0 persons).

Education and health

Education (1992–93)

	schools	teachers	students	student/ teacher ratio
Primary (age 5–14)	237	1,804	47,210	26.2
Secondary (age 14–18)	31	782	8,901	11.4
Voc., teacher tr. }	8[15]	...	1,726[15]	...
Higher				

Educational attainment (1991). Percentage of population age 25 and over having: no formal schooling 13.0%; primary education 64.3%; secondary 15.0%; higher (not university) 3.6%; university 3.0%; other/unknown 1.1%.
Literacy (1991): total population age 15 and over literate 99,000 (93%).
Health (1991): physicians 96 (1 per 2,021 persons); hospital beds 585 (1 per 332 persons); infant mortality rate per 1,000 live births (1993) 36.5.
Food (1988–90): daily per capita caloric intake 2,575 (vegetable products 70%, animal products 30%); 114% of FAO recommended minimum requirement.

Military

Total active duty personnel (1994): 950 (army 94.7%, maritime wing 3.7%, air wing 1.6%); British troops 600[16]. Military expenditure as percentage of GNP (1990): 2.6% (world 4.5%); per capita expenditure U.S.$51.

---

[1]Excludes speaker of the House of Representatives, who may be elected by the House from outside its elected membership. [2]The Belize dollar is officially pegged to the U.S. dollar. [3]Detail does not add to total given because of rounding. [4]Estimated figure for 36,346 employees. [5]At factor cost. [6]Data based on total population over age 15. [7]Less imputed bank service charges. [8]Includes not available and not stated. [9]Import figures are f.o.b. in balance of trade and c.i.f. in commodities and trading partners. [10]Based on imports through September only, totaling BZ$265,000,000. [11]Exports (1993): BZ$263,100,000 (domestic exports 86.9%, of which sugar 31.5%, garments 15.4%, orange and grapefruit concentrate 10.6%, marine products 9.9%, bananas 9.2%; reexports 13.1%). [12]Belize international airport only. [13]Four weekly newspapers had a total circulation in 1992 of 24,200. [14]Number of lines. [15]1991–92. [16]Most British troops are scheduled to withdraw in late 1994.

Benin

Official name: République du Bénin (Republic of Benin).
Form of government: multiparty republic with one legislative house (National Assembly [64]).
Head of state and government: President.
Capital[1]: Porto-Novo.
Official language: French.
Official religion: none.
Monetary unit: 1 CFA franc (CFAF) = 100 centimes; valuation (Oct. 7, 1994) 1 U.S.$ = CFAF 526.67; 1 £ = CFAF 837.67.

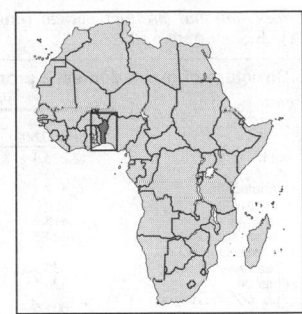

Area and population		area		population
Provinces	Capitals	sq mi	sq km	1992 census
Atacora	Natitingou	12,050	31,200	648,330
Atlantique	Cotonou	1,250	3,200	1,060,310
Borgou	Parakou	19,700	51,000	816,278
Mono	Lokossa	1,500	3,880	646,954
Ouémé	Porto-Novo	1,800	4,700	869,492
Zou	Abomey	7,200	18,700	813,985
TOTAL		43,500	112,680	4,855,349

Demography

Population (1994): 5,235,000.
Density (1994): persons per sq mi 120.3, persons per sq km 46.5.
Urban-rural (1992): urban 39.6%; rural 60.4%.
Sex distribution (1992): male 48.72%; female 51.28%.
Age breakdown (1990): under 15, 46.6%; 15–29, 25.7%; 30–44, 14.7%; 45–59, 8.4%; 60–74, 3.8%; 75 and over, 0.8%.
Population projection: (2000) 6,269,000; (2010) 8,357,000.
Doubling time: 24 years.
Ethnic composition (1982): Fon 25.0%; Yoruba (Nago) 13.5%; Goun 11.8%; Bariba 11.8%; Adjara 10.7%; Somba (Otomary) 7.0%; Aizo 4.4%; Mina 2.9%; Dendi 2.0%; other 10.9%.
Religious affiliation (1991): traditional beliefs 62.0%; Christian 23.3%, of which Roman Catholic 21.0%, Protestant 2.3%; Muslim 12.0%; other 2.7%.
Major cities (1992): Cotonou 533,212; Porto-Novo 177,660; Djougou 132,192; Abomey-Calavi 125,565; Parakou 106,708; Bohicon 81,121; Kandi 74,169; Abomey 65,725; Ouidah 64,068; Natitingou 57,535; Lokossa 52,909.

Vital statistics

Birth rate per 1,000 population (1992): 44.0 (world avg. 26.0).
Death rate per 1,000 population (1992): 15.0 (world avg. 9.2).
Natural increase rate per 1,000 population (1992): 29.0 (world avg. 16.8).
Total fertility rate (avg. births per childbearing woman; 1992): 6.2.
Marriage rate per 1,000 population (1980–85): 12.8.
Divorce rate per 1,000 population (1980–85): 0.8.
Life expectancy at birth (1992): male 49.0 years; female 52.0 years.
Major causes of death per 100,000 population (1986): n.a.; however, of the 184,310 reported cases of infectious diseases (notifiable to the World Health Organization): 82.0% were malaria, 4.2% dysentery, 4.0% measles, 2.6% pneumonia, 2.2% chicken pox, 1.4% mumps, 1.3% schistosomiasis.

National economy

Budget (1993). Revenue: CFAF 137,200,000,000 (current receipts 55.4%, of which fiscal receipts and customs duties 46.4%, other current receipts 9.0%; loans 28.7%; aid 13.7%). Expenditures: CFAF 155,200,000,000 (current expenditures 59.0%; public-investment program 30.1%; debt service 10.9%).
Public debt (external, outstanding; 1992): U.S.$1,322,000,000.
Production (metric tons except as noted). Agriculture, forestry, fishing (1993): yams 1,233,000, cassava 992,000, corn (maize) 550,000, seed cotton 146,000, sorghum 124,000, tomatoes 75,000, peanuts (groundnuts) 72,000, dry beans 52,000, millet 30,000, sweet potatoes 29,000, coconuts 20,000, bananas 13,000, mangoes 12,000, oranges 12,000, paddy rice 10,000, palm kernels 9,000, karité (a butter from the nut of the shea tree) 8,000[2], pineapples 3,000, coffee beans 1,000, cacao beans 900[3], tobacco 272[2]; livestock (number of live animals) 1,180,000 goats, 1,100,000 cattle, 940,000 sheep, 550,000 pigs, 26,000,000 chickens; roundwood (1992) 5,371,000 cu m; fish catch (1991) 11,000. Mining and quarrying (1993): limestone 500,000, marine salt 100. Manufacturing (1990): cement 275,000; meat 61,000; cotton fibre 58,025[5]; sugar 52,000[4]; palm oil and palm kernel oil 13,140. Construction: n.a. Energy production (consumption): electricity (kW-hr; 1992) 5,000,000 (203,000,000); coal, none (none); crude petroleum (barrels; 1992) 1,423,500 (negligible); petroleum products (metric tons; 1992) none (139,000); natural gas, none (none).
Tourism (1992): receipts from visitors U.S.$32,000,000; expenditures by nationals abroad U.S.$12,000,000.
Population economically active (1991): total 2,195,000; activity rate of total population 46.0% (participation rates: ages 15–64, 60.2%[4]; female 46.0%; unemployed, n.a.).

Price and earnings indexes (1990 = 100)							
	1985	1986	1987	1988	1989	1990	1991
Consumer price index[6]	...	...	...	...	...	...	...
Hourly earnings index[7]	100.0	100.0	100.0	100.0	100.0	100.0	100.0

Land use (1992): forested 30.7%; meadows and pastures 4.0%; agricultural and under permanent cultivation 17.0%; other 48.3%.
Gross national product (at current market prices; 1993): U.S.$2,182,000,000 (U.S.$420 per capita).

Structure of gross domestic product and labour force				
	1991			
	in value CFAF'000,000,000	% of total value	labour force	% of labour force
Agriculture	199.0	39.0	1,333,000	60.7
Mining and manufacturing	45.1	8.8	194,000	8.8
Public utilities	5.0	1.0		
Construction	17.6	3.4		
Trade and finance	153.3	30.0		
Transportation and communications	40.3	7.9	668,000	30.4
Pub. admin., defense	50.6	9.9		
TOTAL	510.9	100.0	2,195,000	100.0[8]

Household income and expenditure. Average household size (1979) 5.4; income per household (1983) U.S.$240; sources of income: self-employment 73.7%, wages and salaries 26.3%; expenditure: n.a.

Foreign trade[9]

Balance of trade (current prices)						
	1984	1985	1986	1987	1988	1989
CFAF '000,000	−81,830	−100.47	−98.23	−61.23	−80.84	−59.00
% of total	46.2%	42.9%	55.5%	13.3%	14.5%	40.7%

Imports (1991): U.S.$605,800,000 (1989; manufactured goods 30.7%, of which cotton yarn and fabric 16.9%; food products 19.4%, of which cereals 10.3%; machinery and transport equipment 14.5%, of which transport equipment 5.8%, nonelectrical equipment 5.3%, electrical equipment 3.4%; chemical products 7.1%; beverages and tobacco 7.1%). *Major import sources* (1989): India 23.4%; France 15.9%; The Netherlands 5.0%; Côte d'Ivoire 4.6%; Thailand 4.6%; United States 3.7%; West Germany 3.4%; Italy 3.2%; Taiwan 2.9%; Korea 2.7%.
Exports (1991): U.S.$350,300,000 (1989; cotton 63.7%; energy 21.3%; palm kernel oil and palm oil 4.6%; manufactured goods 4.4%). *Major export destinations* (1989): Portugal 15.2%; Italy 9.9%; Thailand 9.6%; Taiwan 9.0%; United States 7.4%; Niger 6.2%; France 6.1%.

Transport and communications

Transport. Railroads (1991): length[10] 359 mi, 578 km; passenger-mi 39,397,000, passenger-km 63,400,000; short ton-mi cargo 111,313,000, metric ton-km cargo 162,500,000. Roads (1992): total length 3,770 mi, 6,070 km (paved 20.0%). Vehicles (1991): passenger cars 25,000; trucks and buses 13,000. Merchant marine (1992): vessels (100 gross tons and over) 12; total deadweight tonnage 210. Air transport (1991)[11]: passenger-mi 126,000,000, passenger-km 203,000,000; short ton-mi cargo 11,000,000, metric ton-km cargo 16,000,000; airports (1994) with scheduled flights 1.
Communications. Daily newspapers (1990): total number 1; total circulation 12,000; circulation per 1,000 population 2.6. Radio (1993): total number of receivers 350,000 (1 per 14 persons). Television (1993): total number of receivers 20,000 (1 per 254 persons). Telephones (1992): 18,100 (1 per 272 persons).

Education and health

Education (1991)	schools	teachers	students	student/ teacher ratio
Primary	2,952	13,180[12]	505,970	34.7[12]
Secondary	151[13]	2,178	76,672	35.2
Voc., teacher tr.[13]	13	687	6,879	10.0
Higher[12]	13[13]	956	10,873	11.4

Educational attainment (1979). Percentage of population age 25 and over having: no formal schooling 89.2%; primary education 8.3%; some secondary 1.4%; secondary 0.8%; postsecondary 0.3%. *Literacy* (1990): total percentage of population age 15 and over literate 23.4%; males literate 31.7%; females literate 15.6%.
Health: physicians (1986) 363 (1 per 11,306 persons); hospital beds (1982) 4,902 (1 per 749 persons); infant mortality rate per 1,000 live births (1991) 119.0.
Food (1988–90): daily per capita caloric intake 2,383 (vegetable products 96%, animal products 4%); 104% of FAO recommended minimum requirement.

Military

Total active duty personnel (1994): 4,800 (army 93.8%, navy 3.1%, air force 3.1%). *Military expenditure as percentage of GNP* (1990): 2.0% (world 4.5%); per capita expenditure U.S.$8.

---

[1]Porto-Novo, the official capital established under the constitution, is the seat of the legislature, but the president and most government ministers reside in Cotonou. [2]1991–92. [3]1988–89. [4]1986. [5]Export figures. [6]No consumer price index is published, but inflation was estimated by the World Bank at an annual average of 8.0% during 1980–88. [7]January. [8]Detail does not add to total given because of rounding. [9]Figures do not include unaccountable reexports of black-market goods, which originate mainly in Nigeria and amounted to an estimated 90% of Benin's actual exports in 1981. [10]1993. [11]Air Afrique only. [12]1990. [13]1987–88.

Bhutan

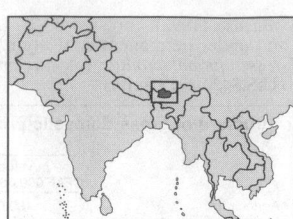

Official name: Druk-Yul (Kingdom of Bhutan).
Form of government: constitutional[1] monarchy with one legislative house (National Assembly [154[2]]).
Head of state and government: Monarch (*druk gyalpo*).
Capital: Thimphu.
Official language: Dzongkha (a Tibetan dialect).
Official religion: Mahāyāna Buddhism.
Monetary unit: 1 ngultrum[3] (Nu) = 100 chetrum; valuation (Oct. 7, 1994) 1 U.S.\$ = Nu 31.37; 1 £ = Nu 49.89.

Area and population

Districts	Capitals	area sq mi	area sq km	population 1994 estimate
Bumthang	Jakar	1,150	2,990	...
Chirang	Damphu	310	800	...
Chhukha	Chhukha	...	...	...
Dagana	Dagana	540	1,400	...
Gaylegphug	Gaylegphug	1,020	2,640	...
Ha	Ha	830	2,140	...
Lhuntshi	Lhuntshi	1,120	2,910	...
Mongar	Mongar	710	1,830	...
Paro	Paro	580	1,500	...
Pema Gatsel	Pema Gatsel	150	380	...
Punakha	Punakha	2,330	6,040	...
Samchi	Samchi	830	2,140	...
Samdrup Jongkhar	Samdrup Jongkhar	900	2,340	...
Shemgang	Shemgang	980	2,540	...
Tashigang	Tashigang	1,640	4,260	...
Thimphu	Thimphu	630	1,620	...
Tongsa	Tongsa	570	1,470	...
Wangdi Phodrang	Wangdi Phodrang	1,160	3,000	...
TOTAL		18,150[5,6]	47,000[5,6]	800,000[4]

Demography

Population (1994): 800,000[4].
Density (1994): persons per sq mi 44.1, persons per sq km 17.0.
Urban-rural (1985): urban 13.1%; rural 86.9%.
Sex distribution (1988): male 50.97%; female 49.03%.
Age breakdown (1988): under 15, 40.3%; 15–29, 26.4%; 30–44, 16.5%; 45–59, 10.5%; 60–74, 5.2%; 75 and over, 1.1%.
Population projection: (2000) 900,000; (2010) 1,100,000.
Doubling time: 30 years.
Ethnic composition (1993): Bhutiā (Ngalops) 50.0%; Nepalese (Gurung) 35.0%; Sharchops 15.0%.
Religious affiliation (1980): Buddhist 69.6%; Hindu 24.6%; Muslim 5.0%; other 0.8%.
Major cities (1985): Thimphu 20,000; Phuntsholing 10,000[7].

Vital statistics

Birth rate per 1,000 population (1993): 39.6 (world avg. 26.0); legitimate, n.a.; illegitimate, n.a.
Death rate per 1,000 population (1993): 16.3 (world avg. 9.2).
Natural increase rate per 1,000 population (1993): 23.3 (world avg. 16.8).
Total fertility rate (avg. births per childbearing woman; 1993): 5.5.
Marital status of population 15 years and over (1985): married 71.2%; single 19.7%; widowed 7.5%; divorced 1.6%.
Divorce rate per 1,000 population: n.a.
Life expectancy at birth (1993): male 50.7 years; female 49.6 years.
Major causes of death (percentage distribution; 1989): respiratory tract infections 19.5%; diarrhea/dysentery 15.2%; skin infections 12.2%; parasitic worm infestations 10.0%; malaria 9.4%.

National economy

Budget (1992–93). Revenue: Nu 2,919,000,000 (internal revenue 47.3%, grants from UN and other international agencies 33.1%, grants from government of India 19.6%). Expenditures: Nu 2,813,000,000 (capital expenditures 55.2%, current expenditures 44.8%).
Public debt (external, outstanding; 1992): U.S.\$82,700,000.
Production (metric tons except as noted). Agriculture, forestry, fishing (1993): oranges 58,000, rice 43,000, corn (maize) 40,000, potatoes 34,000, sugarcane 13,000, green peppers and chilies 8,000, millet 7,000, wheat 5,000, apples 5,000, barley 4,000, pulses 2,000; livestock (number of live animals) 429,000 cattle, 74,000 pigs, 54,000 sheep, 41,000 goats; roundwood (1992) 1,610,000 cu m; fish catch (1991) 1,000. Mining and quarrying (1992): limestone 190,000; dolomite 90,000; gypsum 20,000. Manufacturing (value in Nu; 1980–81): distillery products 47,000,000; cement 36,000,000; chemical products 19,000,000; processed food 14,000,000; forest products 3,000,000. Construction (number of buildings completed; 1977–78): residential 10; nonresidential (guest house) 1. Energy production (consumption): electricity (kW-hr; 1992) 1,627,000,000 (185,000,000); coal (metric tons; 1992) 2,000 (18,000); crude petroleum, none (n.a.); petroleum products (metric tons; 1992) none (27,000); natural gas, none (n.a.).
Household income and expenditure. Average household size (1980) 5.4[4]; income per household: n.a.; sources of income: n.a.; expenditure (1979): food 72.3%, clothing 21.2%, energy 3.7%, household durable goods 0.7%, personal effects and other 2.1%.

Gross national product (at current market prices; 1992): U.S.\$263,000,000 (U.S.\$340 per capita).

Structure of gross domestic product and labour force

	1991 in value Nu '000,000	1991 % of total value	1984 labour force	1984 % of labour force
Agriculture	2,326.4	42.7	580,000[8]	87.2
Mining	53.8	1.0		
Manufacturing	467.7	8.6		
Construction	456.5	8.4		
Trade	416.4	7.6	6,000[8]	0.9
Public utilities	404.5	7.4		
Transportation and communications	375.7	6.9		
Finance	426.1	7.8		
Pub. admin., defense	601.6	11.0	23,000[8]	3.4
Services			56,000[8]	8.5[9]
Other	−78.7[10]	−1.4[10]		
TOTAL	5,450.0	100.0	664,000	100.0

Population economically active (1984)[4]: total 664,000; activity rate of total population 52.7% (participation rates: ages 15–64, 94.8; female 55.0; unemployed 6.5).

Price and earnings indexes (1985 = 100)

	1986	1987	1988	1989	1990	1991	1992
Consumer price index	110.0	115.3	127.5	139.0	154.1	172.3	195.1
Earnings index	...	...	...	...	...	...	...

Land use (1992): forested 54.5%; meadows and pastures 5.8%; agricultural and under permanent cultivation 2.9%; other 36.8%.
Tourism (1992): receipts from visitors U.S.\$3,000,000; expenditures by nationals abroad, n.a.

Foreign trade[11]

Balance of trade (current prices)

	1986–87	1987–88	1988–89	1989–90	1990–91	1991–92
Nu '000,000	−908.4	−489.4	−833.8	−481.6	−583.5	−687.9
% of total	54.6%	25.8%	28.6%	17.5%	18.3%	17.4%

Imports (1991–92): Nu 2,319,910,000 (1989[12]; petroleum products 8.5%, rice 5.8%, motor vehicles and parts 5.7%, machinery parts 2.9%, iron and steel products 2.9%, fabrics 2.3%). *Major import source:* India 84.6%.
Exports (1991–92): Nu 1,632,010,000 (1989[12]; electricity 28.4%, minerals 18.5%, timber and wood manufactures 17.4%, cement 13.7%, fruit and vegetables 10.7%, alcoholic beverages 1.9%). *Major export destination:* India 90.2%.

Transport and communications

Transport. Railroads: none. Roads (1990): total length 1,600 mi, 2,500 km (paved 72%). Vehicles (1988): passenger cars 2,590; trucks and buses 1,367. Merchant marine: none. Air transport (1986): passenger-mi 2,722,000, passenger-km 4,381,000; metric ton-km cargo, n.a.; airports (1994) with scheduled flights 1.
Communications. Daily newspapers: none[13]. Radio (1993): total number of receivers 30,000 (1 per 26 persons). Television (1983): total number of receivers 200 (1 per 6,180 persons). Telephones (1989): 2,105 (1 per 669 persons).

Education and health

Education (1990)

	schools	teachers	students	student/ teacher ratio
Primary (age 7–11)	156	1,757	52,029	29.6
Secondary (age 12–16)	31	662	15,984	24.1
Voc., teacher tr.	8	149	1,822	12.2
Higher	2	57	519	9.1

Educational attainment: n.a. *Literacy* (1977): total population age 15 and over literate 124,000 (18.0%); males literate 98,000 (31.0%); females literate 26,000 (9.0%).
Health (1991): physicians 141 (1 per 5,335 persons); hospital beds 922 (1 per 816 persons); infant mortality rate per 1,000 live births (1993) 123.3.
Food (1975–77): daily per capita caloric intake 2,058 (vegetable products 98%, animal products 2%); 89% of FAO recommended minimum requirement.

Military

Total active duty personnel (1993): about 7,000 (army 100%).

[1]There is no formal constitution, but a form of constitutional monarchy is in place. [2]Includes 49 nonelective seats occupied by representatives of the King and religious groups. [3]Indian currency is also accepted legal tender; the ngultrum is at par with the Indian rupee. [4]The figure stated is an estimate based on recent reported figures resulting from the repudiation of the 1980 census by the King and from the existence of a large number of Nepalese refugees; as such the actual population could range from 800,000 to 1,600,000. [5]2,700 sq mi (7,000 sq km) are not included in the district area totals. [6]Includes Chhukha area. [7]1982. [8]Derived value. [9]Includes 6.5% with no occupation. [10]Imputed bank service charges. [11]Import figures are c.i.f. in balance of trade, commodities, and trading partners. [12]Trade data with India only. [13]A weekly newspaper is published from Thimphu in Dzongkha, Nepalese, and English, circulation (1989) 10,500.

Bolivia

Official name: República de Bolivia (Republic of Bolivia).
Form of government: unitary multiparty republic with two legislative houses (Chamber of Senators [27]; Chamber of Deputies [130]).
Head of state and government: President.
Capitals: La Paz (administrative); Sucre (judicial).
Official languages: Spanish, Aymara, Quechua.
Official religion: Roman Catholicism.
Monetary unit: 1 boliviano (Bs) = 100 centavos; valuation (Oct. 7, 1994) 1 U.S.$ = Bs 4.66; 1 £ = Bs 7.41.

Area and population

Departments	Capitals	area sq mi	area sq km	population 1992 census
Beni	Trinidad	82,458	213,564	276,174
Chuquisaca	Sucre	19,893	51,524	453,756
Cochabamba	Cochabamba	21,479	55,631	1,110,205
La Paz	La Paz	51,732	133,985	1,900,786
Oruro	Oruro	20,690	53,588	340,114
Pando	Cobija	24,644	63,827	38,072
Potosí	Potosí	45,644	118,218	645,889
Santa Cruz	Santa Cruz	143,098	370,621	1,364,389
Tarija	Tarija	14,526	37,623	291,407
TOTAL		424,164	1,098,581	6,420,792

Demography

Population (1994): 7,888,000.
Density (1994): persons per sq mi 18.6, persons per sq km 7.2.
Urban-rural (1992): urban 57.7%; rural 42.3%.
Sex distribution (1992): male 49.25%; female 50.75%.
Age breakdown (1992): under 15, 41.2%; 15–29, 26.6%; 30–44, 16.8%; 45–59, 8.9%; 60 and over, 6.5%.
Population projection: (2000) 9,038,000; (2010) 11,087,000.
Doubling time: 29 years.
Ethnic composition (1982): mestizo 31.2%; Quechua 25.4%; Aymara 16.9%; white 14.5%; other 12.0%.
Religious affiliation (1980): Roman Catholic 92.5%; Bahā'ī 2.6%; other 4.9%.
Major cities (1992): La Paz 711,036; Santa Cruz 694,616; El Alto 404,367; Cochabamba 404,102; Oruro 183,194; Sucre 130,952.

Vital statistics

Birth rate per 1,000 population (1993): 32.8 (world avg. 26.0).
Death rate per 1,000 population (1993): 8.6 (world avg. 9.2).
Natural increase rate per 1,000 population (1993): 24.2 (world avg. 16.8).
Total fertility rate (avg. births per childbearing woman; 1993): 4.3.
Marriage rate per 1,000 population (1980): 4.8.
Divorce rate per 1,000 population: n.a.
Life expectancy at birth (1993): male 60.3 years; female 65.3 years.
Major causes of death (percentage of total registered deaths; 1980–81): infectious and parasitic diseases 23.9%; diseases of the circulatory system 19.5%; diseases of the respiratory system 14.0%; accidents, homicides, and violence 9.8%; diseases of the digestive system 8.6%.

National economy

Budget (1992). Revenue: Bs 3,377,700,000 (taxes on goods and services 36.8%, income of government enterprises 28.7%, property taxes 8.7%, social-security contributions 8.4%, taxes on international trade 6.9%, income taxes 5.2%). Expenditures: Bs 4,460,600,000 (education 16.6%, public services 15.6%, social security 12.6%, transportation and communications 12.4%, defense 9.8%, health 8.2%, public order and safety 6.0%).
Public debt (external, outstanding; 1992): U.S.$3,694,000,000.
Production (metric tons except as noted). Agriculture, forestry, fishing (1992): sugarcane 3,306,798, potatoes 603,101, bananas and plantains 468,796, corn (maize) 405,469, soybeans 338,439, cassava 324,498, rice 209,292, wheat 95,726, coffee 26,828; livestock (number of live animals) 7,300,000 sheep, 5,779,000 cattle, 2,226,000 pigs, 1,440,000 goats, 634,000 asses, 323,000 horses; roundwood (1991) 1,632,000 cu m; fish catch (1991) 5,367. Mining and quarrying (metric tons of pure metal; 1993): zinc 122,640; lead 21,240; tin 18,624; silver 46,344 kg; gold 6,563 kg. Manufacturing (value added in Bs; 1989)[1]: food products 19,650,000; beverages 19,340,000; printing and publishing 3,770,000; wood products 3,160,000; nonferrous metals 2,760,000; textiles 2,740,000; drugs and medicines 2,710,000. Construction (1985)[2]: residential dwellings 226. Energy production (consumption): electricity (kW-hr; 1991) 2,150,000,000 (2,148,000,000); coal, none (none); crude petroleum (barrels; 1991) 8,110,000 (7,503,000); petroleum products (metric tons; 1991) 1,168,-000 (1,142,000); natural gas (cu m; 1991) 2,878,000,000 (699,000,000).
Population economically active (1992): total 2,530,409; activity rate of total population 33.6% (participation rates: ages 15–64, 63.6%; female 39.0%; unemployed [1990] 19.0%).

Price and earnings indexes (1985 = 100)

	1987	1988	1989	1990	1991	1992	1993
Consumer price index	431.2	500.1	575.2	674.7	819.4	918.3	996.7
Monthly earnings index[3]	255.8	366.9	432.8	525.4	608.6	637.3	...

Gross national product (at current market prices; 1992): U.S.$5,084,000,000 (U.S.$680 per capita).

Structure of gross domestic product and labour force

	1993 in value Bs '000[4]	1993 % of total value	1992 labour force[5]	1992 % of labour force[5]
Agriculture	2,400,446	17.0	984,407	38.9
Mining	1,092,737	7.7	52,623	2.1
Manufacturing	2,262,772	16.0	222,485	8.8
Construction	726,208	5.1	129,409	5.1
Public utilities	183,251	1.3	6,086	0.2
Transportation and communications	1,588,580	11.2	116,800	4.6
Trade	1,425,021	10.1	232,429	9.2
Finance	1,322,761	9.4	54,711	2.2
Pub. admin., defense	} 2,323,929	16.4	406,928	16.1
Services				
Other	821,699[6]	5.8[6]	324,531	12.8
TOTAL	14,147,404	100.0	2,530,409	100.0

Household income and expenditure. Average household size (1992): 3.8; average annual income per household: n.a.; sources of income: n.a.; expenditure (1988): food 35.5%, transportation and communications 17.7%, housing 14.8%, household durable goods 7.3%, clothing and footwear 5.1%, beverages and tobacco 4.5%, recreation 2.7%, health 2.1%, education 0.3%.
Tourism (1991): receipts from visitors U.S.$90,000,000; expenditures by nationals abroad U.S.$63,000,000.
Land use (1991): forested 51.2%; meadows and pastures 24.5%; agricultural and under permanent cultivation 2.2%; other 22.1%.

Foreign trade[7]

Balance of trade (current prices)

	1987	1988	1989	1990	1991	1992
U.S.$'000,000	−85.4	+99.2	+301.8	+326.6	+59.0	−294.4
% of total	7.0%	9.0%	22.5%	21.4%	3.6%	17.2%

Imports (1992): U.S.$543,100,000 (raw materials 47.4%, of which raw materials for industry 36.9%; capital goods 31.0%, of which capital goods for industry 19.2%, transport equipment 10.1%; consumer goods 21.0%, of which nondurable consumer goods 10.9%, durable consumer goods 10.1%). *Major import sources:* United States 26.0%; Brazil 14.3%; Japan 12.3%; Argentina 11.2%; Germany 8.4%; Chile 6.4%; Peru 2.2%.
Exports (1992): U.S.$340,100,000 (zinc 22.3%; natural gas 22.2%; tin 13.3%; soybeans 7.1%; silver 7.0%; timber 6.1%; sugar 4.1%; gold 3.6%; hides and skins 1.5%). *Major export destinations:* Argentina 25.3%; United Kingdom 17.2%; United States 13.3%; Belgium 12.0%; Peru 8.3%; Germany 5.9%; France 3.2%; Chile 2.2%.

Transport and communications

Transport. Railroads (1992): route length 2,264 mi, 3,643 km; passenger-mi 244,000,000, passenger-km 393,000,000; short ton-mi cargo 414,500,000, metric ton-km cargo 605,200,000. Roads (1991): total length 26,612 mi, 42,828 km (paved 4%). Vehicles (1991): passenger cars 265,000; trucks and buses 60,000. Merchant marine (1992): vessels (100 gross tons and over) 1; total deadweight tonnage 15,765. Air transport (1992): passenger-mi 739,000,000, passenger-km 1,190,000,000; short ton-mi cargo 99,927,000, metric ton-km cargo 145,891,000; airports (1994) with scheduled flights 21.
Communications. Daily newspapers (1990): total number 17; total circulation 400,000; circulation per 1,000 population 55. Radio (1993): total number of receivers 4,000,000 (1 per 1.9 persons). Television (1991): total number of receivers 610,000 (1 per 12 persons). Telephones (1991): 198,180 (1 per 38 persons).

Education and health

Education (1990–91)

	schools[8]	teachers	students	student/ teacher ratio
Primary (age 6–13)	9,758	51,763	1,278,775	24.7
Secondary (age 14–17)	724 }	12,434	219,232	17.6
Voc., teacher tr.	47			
Higher[9]	10	4,261	109,503	25.7

Educational attainment (1992). Percentage of population age 25 and over having: no formal schooling 23.3%; some primary 20.3%; primary education 21.7%; some secondary 9.0%; secondary 6.5%; some higher 5.0%; higher 4.8%; not specified 9.4%. *Literacy* (1990): total population age 15 and over literate 77.5%; males literate 84.7%; females literate 70.7%.
Health: physicians (1991) 2,868 (1 per 2,561 persons); hospital beds (1990) 6,190 (1 per 1,183 persons); infant mortality rate per 1,000 live births (1990–95) 75.1.
Food (1988–90): daily per capita caloric intake 2,013 (vegetable products 83%, animal products 17%); 84% of FAO recommended minimum requirement.

Military

Total active duty personnel (1993): 33,500 (army 74.6%, navy 13.4%, air force 12.0%). *Military expenditure as percentage of GNP* (1991): 2.4% (world 4.2%); per capita expenditure U.S.$16.

[1]Establishments with 20 or more employees. [2]National government sponsored only. [3]Private-sector earnings in La Paz. [4]In 1988 prices. [5]Population 7 years and over. [6]Net import duties. [7]Import figures are f.o.b. in balance of trade and c.i.f. for commodities and trading partners. [8]1986–87. [9]1991–92.

Bosnia and Herzegovina[1]

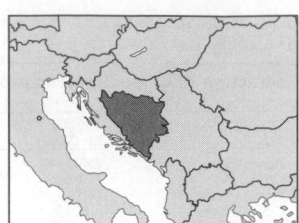

Official name: Republika Bosna i
  Hercegovina (Republic of Bosnia and
  Herzegovina).
Form of government: unitary multiparty
  republic with bicameral legislature
  (National Assembly [240[2]])[3].
Chief of state: President of collective
  presidency[3].
Head of government: Prime Minister[3].
Capital: Sarajevo.
Official language: Serbo-Croatian.
Official religion: none.
Monetary unit: [4].

Area and population (1991 census)

Districts	area sq km	population	Districts	area sq km	population
Banja Luka	1,232	195,139	Livno	994	39,526
Banovići	176	26,507	Ljubinje	326	4,162
Bihać	689	70,896	Ljubuški	289	27,182
Bijeljina	734	96,796	Lopare	429	32,400
Bileća	633	13,269	Lukavac	350	56,830
Bosanska Dubica	499	31,577	Maglaj	384	43,294
Bosanska Gradiška	762	60,062	Modriča	297	35,413
Bosanska Krupa	780	58,212	Mostar	1,300	126,067
Bosanski Brod	234	33,962	Mrkonjič Grad	679	27,379
Bosanski Novi	554	41,541	Neum	230	4,268
Bosanski Petrovac	853	15,552	Nevesinje	923	14,421
Bosanski Šamac	219	32,835	Odžak	205	30,651
Bosansko Grahovo	780	8,303	Olovo	408	16,901
Bratunac	793	33,575	Orašje	166	28,201
Brčko	493	87,332	Posušje	372	16,659
Breza	83	17,266	Prijedor	834	112,470
Bugojno	366	46,843	Prnjavor	631	46,894
Busovača	145	18,883	Prozor	477	19,601
Cajniče	275	8,919	Pucarevo	232	30,624
Capljina	249	27,852	Rogatica	664	21,812
Cazin	381	63,406	Rudo	344	11,572
Čelinac	365	18,666	Sanski Most	984	60,119
Citluk	181	14,709	Sarajevo	2,049	525,980
Derventa	516	56,328	Šekovići	195	9,639
Doboj	684	102,546	Sipovo	470	15,553
Donji Vakuf	338	24,232	Skender Vakuf	360	19,416
Foča	1,270	40,513	Sokolac	723	14,833
Fojnica	308	16,227	Srbac	447	21,660
Gacko	736	10,844	Srebrenica	527	37,211
Glamoč	1,096	12,421	Srebrenik	249	40,769
Goražde	383	37,505	Stolac	541	18,845
Gornji Vakuf	402	25,130	Tešanj	223	48,390
Gračanica	387	59,050	Teslič	846	59,632
Gradačac	405	56,378	Titov Drvar	950	17,079
Grude	218	15,976	Tomislavgrad	967	29,261
Han Pijesak	342	6,346	Travnik	563	70,402
Jablanica	289	12,664	Trebinje	1,205	30,879
Jajce	398	44,903	Tuzla	307	131,861
Kakanj	462	55,857	Ugljevik	199	25,641
Kalesija	272	41,795	Vareš	356	22,114
Kalinovik	732	4,657	Velika Kladuša	304	52,921
Kiseljak	165	24,081	Višegrad	448	21,202
Kladanj	325	16,028	Visoko	242	46,130
Ključ	850	37,233	Vitez	156	27,728
Konjic	1,101	43,636	Vlasenica	532	33,817
Kotor Varoš	574	36,670	Zavidovići	540	57,153
Kreševo	149	6,699	Zenica	500	145,577
Kupres	622	10,728	Žepče	210	22,840
Laktaši	387	29,910	Živinice	281	54,653
Ljištica	388	26,437	Zvornik	500	81,111
			TOTAL	51,129[5]	4,365,639

Demography

Population (1994): 4,447,000.
Density (1994): persons per sq mi 225.3, persons per sq km 87.0.
Urban-rural (1981): urban 36.2%; rural 63.8%.
Sex distribution (1981): male 49.73%; female 50.27%.
Age breakdown (1981): under 15, 27.5%; 15–29, 29.0%; 30–44, 19.2%; 45–59, 15.8%; 60–74, 6.3%; 75 and over, 1.9%.
Population projection: (2000) 4,601,000; (2010) 4,871,000.
Doubling time: 99 years.
Ethnic composition (1991): Muslim 49.2%; Serb 31.3%; Croat 17.3%.
Religious affiliation (1992): Muslim 40%; Serbian Orthodox 31%; Roman Catholic 15%; Protestant 4%; other 10%.
Major cities (1991): Sarajevo 415,631; Banja Luka 142,634; Zenica 96,238.

Vital statistics

Birth rate per 1,000 population (1993): 13.5 (world avg. 26.0).
Death rate per 1,000 population (1993): 6.4 (world avg. 9.2).
Natural increase rate per 1,000 population (1993): 7.7 (world avg. 16.8).
Total fertility rate (avg. births per childbearing woman; 1993): 1.6.
Life expectancy at birth (1993): male 72.1 years; female 77.7 years.
Major causes of death per 100,000 population (1989): circulatory diseases 344.1; malignant neoplasms (cancers) 122.6; accidents, violence, and poisoning 47.1; digestive system diseases 29.2.; respiratory diseases 29.0.

National economy

Tourism (1991): total tourist nights 2,360,000.
Production (metric tons except as noted). Agriculture, forestry, fishing (1993): corn (maize) 873,000, wheat 352,000, potatoes 296,000; livestock (head)

1,287,000 sheep, 826,000 cattle, 590,000 pigs, 8,000,000 poultry; roundwood (1990) 5,379,000 cu m; fish catch (1990) 3,606. Mining (1992): iron ore 500,000; bauxite 200,000; lead-zinc ore 50,000. Manufacturing (1990): crude steel 1,421,000; pig iron 1,284,000; cement 797,000, alumina 735,000; paper 281,000. Construction (residential units constructed; 1990): 26,568. Energy production (consumption): electricity (kW-hr; 1992) 13,000,000,000 (13,000,-000,000); coal (metric tons; 1992) 15,000,000 (15,000,000); crude petroleum (barrels; 1992) none (14,836,000); petroleum products (metric tons; 1992) 1,590,000 (1,590,000); natural gas (cu m; 1992) none (435,000,000).
Gross national product (1990): U.S.$10,667,000,000 (U.S.$2,454 per capita).

Structure of gross material product and labour force

	1989		1990	
	in value Din '000,000	% of total value	labour force[6]	% of labour force[6]
Agriculture	2,963	10.9	39,053	3.8
Manufacturing, mining	15,589	57.6	496,190	48.3
Construction	1,918	7.1	74,861	7.3
Public utilities	403	1.5	22,345	2.2
Transp. and commun.	1,600	5.9	68,798	6.7
Trade	3,777	13.9	130,914	12.8
Finance			38,686	3.8
Pub. admin., defense	834	3.1		
Services			155,411	15.1
Other				
TOTAL	27,084	100.0	1,026,258	100.0

Population economically active (1991): total 992,000; activity rate of total population 22.7% (participation rates: ages 15–64, n.a.; female [1990] 37.7%).

Price and earnings indexes (1985 = 100)

	1984	1985	1986	1987	1988	1989	1990[7]
Consumer price index	58	100	188	400	1,188	16,169	109,000
Monthly earnings index[8]	99	100	106	99	86	109	87

Land use (1990): forest 41.2%; pasture 19.6%; agricultural 18.4%; other 20.8%.
Household income and expenditure. Average household size (1991) 3.4; income per household (1990) Din 72,850 (U.S.$6,437); sources of income (1990): wages 53.2%, transfers 18.2%, self-employment 12.0%, other 16.6%; expenditure (1988): food 41.3%, clothing 8.3%, fuel and lighting 7.8%, housing 7.8%, transportation 6.0%, beverages and tobacco 5.7%, household durable goods 4.1%, education and entertainment 3.5%, health care 3.4%.

Foreign trade

Balance of trade (current prices)

	1985	1986	1987	1988	1989	1990
Din '000,000	−4	2	15	77	962	2,141
% of total	4.5%	1.2%	6.2%	9.2%	7.4%	4.8%

Imports (1990): Din 21,130,000,000 (fuels 31.6%; raw materials and semifinished goods 26.8%; basic manufactures 17.5%; consumer goods 13.3%).
Exports (1990): Din 23,271,000,000 (machinery 20.8%; chemicals 9.4%; clothing 9.2%; furniture 5.0%).

Transport and communications

Transport. Railroads (1990): length 646 mi, 1,039 km; passenger-mi 883,000,-000, passenger-km 1,421,000,000; short ton-mi cargo 3,205,000,000, metric ton-km cargo 4,679,000,000. Roads (1991): total length 13,153 mi, 21,168 km (paved 54%). Vehicles (1990): passenger cars 438,080; trucks and buses 50,578. Airports (1994) with scheduled flights 1.
Communications. Daily newspapers (1990): total number 4; circulation 165,-000; circulation per 1,000 population 37. Radio (1990): number of receivers 733,000 (1 per 5.9 persons). Television (1990): number of receivers 629,000 (1 per 6.9 persons). Telephones (1990): 727,316 (1 per 6.0 persons).

Education and health

Education (1990–91)

	schools	teachers	students	student/teacher ratio
Primary (age 7–14)	2,205	23,369	539,875	23.1
Secondary (age 15–18)	238	9,030	172,063	19.1
Higher	44	2,802	37,541	13.4

Educational attainment (1981). Percentage of population age 15 and over having: less than full primary education 49.5%; primary 24.2%; secondary 21.7%; postsecondary and higher 4.3%. *Literacy* (1981): total population age 10 and over literate 2,962,400 (85.5%); males 96.5%; females 76.6%.
Health: physicians (1989) 6,929 (1 per 624 persons); hospital beds (1990) 19,-858 (1 per 219 persons); infant mortality rate per 1,000 live births (1993) 13.2.

Military

Total active duty personnel (1994)[9]: 110,000 (army 100%).

[1]Data given refer to conditions prior to outbreak of civil war and subsequent de facto partition of Bosnia and Herzegovina. [2]161 seats occupied as of April 1994. [3]Government assumed interim status as of June 1994. [4]No national currency of issue exists. The principal currency in de facto use is the Yugoslav new dinar (Din), for which no exchange rate is offered, owing to persistent inflation since the late 1980s and to the current state of belligerency, in which extreme inflation, demonetization of transactions, barter, and use of external hard currencies prevent a simple characterization of the situation at year's end. [5]Detail adds to 554 sq km more than total given; the reason for the discrepancy is unknown. [6]Excludes 28,000 workers in the private sector. [7]On Jan. 1, 1990, the new dinar, equal to 10,000 old dinars, was introduced. [8]Based on worker real net personal income. [9]Excludes 130,000 foreign combatants and the 16,300-member UN protection force.

Botswana

Official name: Republic of Botswana.
Form of government: multiparty
  republic with one legislative body[1]
  (National Assembly [40[2]]).
Head of state and government:
  President.
Capital: Gaborone.
Official language: English[3].
Official religion: none.
Monetary unit: 1 pula (P) = 100 thebe;
  valuation (Oct. 7, 1994)
  1 U.S.$ = P 2.71; 1 £ = P 4.32.

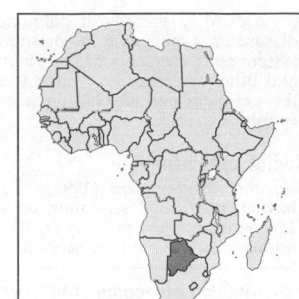

Area and population		area		population
		sq mi	sq km	1991 census[4]
Districts	**Capitals**			
Barolong	...	425	1,100	18,365
Central	Serowe	57,039[5]	147,730[5]	284,264
Ghanzi	Ghanzi	45,525	117,910	24,695
Kgalagadi	Tsabong	41,290	106,940	30,873
Kgatleng	Mochudi	3,073	7,900	57,160
Kweneng	Molepolole	13,857	35,890	169,835
North East	Masunga	1,977	5,120	43,361
North West				
Chobe	Kasane	8,031	20,800	14,186
Ngamiland	Maun	42,135	109,130	94,322
Ngwaketse	Kanye	10,568	27,370	129,474
Serowe/Palapye	...	[5]	[5]	111,300
South East	Ramotswa	687[5]	1,780[5]	31,101
Towns[6]				
Francistown	—	31	79	65,026
Gaborone	—	37	97	133,791
Jwaneng	—	39	100	11,199
Lobatse	—	12	30	25,992
Orapa	—	4	10	8,853
Palapye	—	8	21	17,131
Selebi-Pikwe	—	10	60	39,769
Sowa		...	...	2,220
Tlokweng	—	10	26	12,366
TOTAL		224,607	581,730	1,325,291

Demography

Population (1994): 1,448,000.
Density (1994): persons per sq mi 6.4, persons per sq km 2.5.
Urban-rural (1992): urban 27.3%; rural 72.7%.
Sex distribution (1990): male 47.70%; female 52.30%.
Age breakdown (1990): under 15, 46.1%; 15–29, 27.5%; 30–44, 14.1%; 45–59, 7.0%; 60–74, 4.0%; 75 and over, 1.3%.
Population projection: (2000) 1,713,000; (2010) 2,210,000.
Doubling time: 20 years.
Ethnic composition (1983): Tswana 75.5%; Shona 12.4%; San (Bushman) 3.4%; Khoikhoin (Hottentot) 2.5%; Ndebele 1.3%; other 4.9%.
Religious affiliation (1980): traditional beliefs 49.2%; Protestant 29.0%; African Christian 11.8%; Roman Catholic 9.4%; other 0.6%.
Major cities (1991): Gaborone 133,791; Francistown 65,026; Selebi-Pikwe 39,769; Molepolole 36,928; Kanye 31,341.

Vital statistics

Birth rate per 1,000 population (1990–95): 33.2 (world avg. 26.0); (1986) legitimate 28.8%[7]; illegitimate 71.2%[7].
Death rate per 1,000 population (1990–95): 5.7 (world avg. 9.2).
Natural increase rate per 1,000 population (1990–95): 27.5 (world avg. 16.8).
Total fertility rate (avg. births per childbearing woman; 1990–95): 4.3.
Marriage rate per 1,000 population (1986): 1.5.
Life expectancy at birth (1993): male 59.5 years; female 65.6 years.
Major causes of death (as percentage of total registered deaths; 1986): diseases of the circulatory system 17.3%; infectious and parasitic diseases 16.6%; malignant neoplasms (cancers) 13.4%; diseases of the respiratory system 12.2%; endocrine, nutritional, and metabolic diseases 6.1%.

National economy

Budget (1993–94). Revenue: P 3,907,000,000 (1992–93; mineral royalties 44.7%, customs and excise taxes 24.4%, nontax revenue 19.2%, other [nonmineral] income taxes 8.9%). Expenditures: P 4,294,000,000 (1992–93; recurrent expenditure 51.1%, development expenditure 34.9%, net lending 13.0%).
Population economically active (1991): total 443,455; activity rate of total population 33.4% (participation rates: ages 15–64, 59.6%; female 38.4%; unemployed 13.9%).

Price and earnings indexes (1990 = 100)							
	1987	1988	1989	1990	1991	1992	1993
Consumer price index	74.3	80.5	89.8	100.0	111.8	129.8	148.4
Earnings index[8]	76.1	81.5	90.2	100.0	...	...	...

Production (metric tons except as noted). Agriculture, forestry, fishing (1993): cereals 34,000 (of which sorghum 25,000, corn [maize] 7,000, millet 2,000), vegetables and melons 16,000, pulses 13,000, fruits 11,000, roots and tubers 9,000, seed cotton 3,000, cottonseed 2,000; livestock (number of live animals) 2,700,000 cattle, 2,300,000 goats, 325,000 sheep, 156,000 mules and asses, 34,000 horses; roundwood (1992) 1,398,000 cu m; fish catch (1991) 1,900. Mining and quarrying (1993): diamonds 14,726,000 carats; copper 20,197; nickel 17,808; cobalt 205. Manufacturing (value added in P '000,000; 1987–

88): food products 295.4; textiles 93.5; chemicals 68.6; paper and paper products 35.3; wood products 22.5. Construction (1985): residential 70,200 sq m; nonresidential 80,700 sq m. Energy production (consumption): electricity (kW-hr; 1991) 929,000,000 (929,000,000); coal (metric tons; 1992) 901,452 (n.a.); crude petroleum, none (n.a.).
Public debt (external, outstanding; 1992): U.S.$537,500,000.
Tourism (1991): receipts U.S.$79,000,000; expenditures U.S.$40,000,000.
Gross national product (1993): U.S.$3,631,000,000 (U.S.$2,590 per capita).

Structure of gross domestic product and labour force				
	1991–92		1991	
	in value P '000,000[9]	% of total value	labour force	% of labour force
Agriculture	219.9	5.2	100,446	22.7
Mining	1,550.0	36.6	13,287	3.0
Manufacturing	196.5	4.6	26,635	6.0
Construction	211.2	5.0	57,001	12.9
Public utilities	96.5	2.3	6,425	1.4
Transp. and commun.	150.1	3.5	10,094	2.3
Trade	642.5	15.2	34,322	7.7
Finance and business services	217.8	5.1	13,392	3.0
Pub. admin., defense	839.1	19.8 }	103,045	23.2
Services	116.4	2.7 }		
Other	...	...	78,808[10]	17.8[10]
TOTAL	4,240.0	100.0	443,455	100.0

Household income and expenditure (1985–86). Average household size 5.0; average annual income per household P 3,910 (U.S.$2,080); sources of income: wages and salaries 59.9%, transfers 30.8%, self-employment 9.3%; expenditure: food, beverages, and tobacco 39.4%, household durable goods 14.0%, rent and services 13.3%, transportation 13.1%, clothing 5.6%, health 2.3%.
Land use (1992): forested 19.2%; meadows and pastures 58.2%; agricultural and under permanent cultivation 2.1%; other 20.5%.

Foreign trade[11]

Balance of trade (current prices)						
	1988	1989	1990	1991	1992	1993
P '000,000	831.2	1,174.9	201.1	492.1	510.2	526.7
% of total	18.4%	18.6%	3.6%	5.0%	5.5%	6.7%

Imports (1992): P 3,958,000,000 (1990; transport equipment 19.2%; machinery and electrical goods 18.5%; food, beverages, and tobacco 14.1%; chemical and rubber products 8.5%; metal and metal products 8.4%; textiles and footwear 8.4%; mineral fuels 6.4%; wood and paper 4.3%). *Major import sources* (1988): Customs Union of Southern Africa 77.4%; European countries 10.2%, of which U.K. 6.1%; U.S. 2.3%.
Exports (1992): P 3,638,000,000 (diamonds 78.8%; copper-nickel matte 5.9%; beef products 5.4%). *Major export destinations* (1988): European countries 85.9%, of which U.K. 1.1%; African countries 13.5%; U.S. 0.3%.

Transport and communications

Transport. Railroads (1992): length 551 mi, 887 km; passenger-km 257,000,-000[12]; metric ton-km cargo 972,000,000. Roads (1991): total length 11,933 mi, 19,204 km (paved 13%). Vehicles (1990): passenger cars 17,399; trucks and buses 30,348. Merchant marine: none. Air transport (1992)[13]: passenger-km 84,000,000; metric ton-km cargo 648,000; airports (1994) 4.
Communications. Daily newspapers (1991): total number 1; total circulation 48,000; circulation per 1,000 population 27.5. Radio (1993): total receivers 1,100,000 (1 per 1.3 persons). Television (1993): total receivers 13,800 (1 per 102 persons). Telephones (1992): 66,100 (1 per 21 persons).

Education and health

Education (1992)	schools	teachers	students	student/teacher ratio
Primary (age 6–13)	654	9,708	308,840	31.8
Secondary (age 14–18)	169	3,743	68,137	18.2
Voc., teacher tr.	40	759	7,057	9.3
Higher	1	370	3,352	9.1

Educational attainment (1981). Percentage of population age 25 and over having: no formal schooling 54.7%; some primary education 31.0%; complete primary 9.4%; some secondary 3.1%; complete secondary 1.3%; postsecondary 0.5%. *Literacy* (1990): total population over age 15 literate 486,500 (73.6%); males literate 253,300 (83.7%); females literate 233,200 (65.1%).
Health (1990): physicians 240 (1 per 5,417 persons); hospital beds 3,212 (1 per 395 persons); infant mortality rate (1994) 39.0.
Food (1988–90): daily per capita caloric intake 2,260 (vegetable products 86%, animal products 14%); 97% of FAO recommended minimum requirement.

Military

Total active duty personnel (1994): 7,500 (army 93.3%, navy, none [landlocked], air force 6.7%). *Military expenditure as percentage of GNP* (1991): 4.9% (world 4.2%); per capita expenditure U.S.$126.

[1]In addition, the House of Chiefs, a 15-member body consisting of chiefs, subchiefs, and associated members, serves in an advisory capacity to the government. [2]Including four specially elected members and two nonelective seats. [3]Tswana is the national language. [4]Preliminary. [5]Areas for Central district and South East district include the area for Serowe/Palapye. [6]Areas are included with respective district totals; population figures are not included with district totals. [7]Registered births only. [8]Excludes government sector. [9]At 1985–86 prices. [10]Includes 61,638 unemployed. [11]Import figures are f.o.b. in balance of trade and c.i.f. in commodities and trading partners. [12]1986–87. [13]Air Botswana only.

Brazil

Official name: República Federativa
do Brasil (Federative Republic
of Brazil).
Form of government: multiparty
federal republic with 2 legislative
houses (Senate [81]; Chamber of
Deputies [513]).
Chief of state and government:
President.
Capital: Brasília.
Official language: Portuguese.
Official religion: none.
Monetary unit: 1 real[1] = 100 centavos;
valuation (Oct. 7, 1994)
1 U.S.$ = 0.89 real; 1 £ = 1.34 reais.

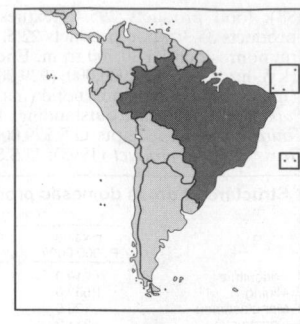

Area and population		area		population
				1991
States	Capitals	sq mi	sq km	census[2]
Acre	Rio Branco	59,132	153,150	417,165
Alagoas	Maceió	10,785	27,933	2,512,991
Amapá	Macapá	55,388	143,454	288,690
Amazonas	Manaus	609,200	1,577,820	2,102,901
Bahia	Salvador	219,034	567,295	11,855,157
Ceará	Fortaleza	56,505	146,348	6,362,620
Espírito Santo	Vitória	17,836	46,194	2,598,505
Goiás	Goiânia	131,772	341,289	4,012,562
Maranhão	São Luís	128,713	333,366	4,929,029
Mato Grosso	Cuiabá	350,120	906,807	2,022,524
Mato Grosso do Sul	Campo Grande	138,286	358,159	1,778,741
Minas Gerais	Belo Horizonte	227,176	588,384	15,731,961
Pará	Belém	483,850	1,253,165	5,181,570
Paraíba	João Pessoa	21,848	56,585	3,200,677
Paraná	Curitiba	77,108	199,709	8,443,299
Pernambuco	Recife	38,200	98,938	7,122,548
Piauí	Teresina	97,444	252,379	2,581,215
Rio de Janeiro	Rio de Janeiro	16,954	43,910	12,783,761
Rio Grande do Norte	Natal	20,582	53,307	2,414,121
Rio Grande do Sul	Pôrto Alegre	108,905	282,062	9,135,479
Rondônia	Pôrto Velho	92,090	238,513	1,130,874
Roraima	Boa Vista	86,918	225,116	215,950
Santa Catarina	Florianópolis	36,851	95,443	4,538,248
São Paulo	São Paulo	96,066	248,809	31,546,473
Sergipe	Aracaju	8,514	22,050	1,491,867
Tocantins	Palmas	107,499	278,421	920,116
Federal District				
Distrito Federal	Brasília	2,248	5,822	1,598,415
Disputed areas[3]		1,149	2,977	—
TOTAL		3,300,171[4,5]	8,547,404[4,5]	146,917,459

Demography

Population (1994): 159,000,000.
Density (1994): persons per sq mi 48.4, persons per sq km 18.7.
Urban-rural (1991): urban 75.5%; rural 24.5%.
Sex distribution (1991): male 49.37%; female 50.63%.
Age breakdown (1991): under 15, 34.7%; 15–29, 28.0%; 30–44, 19.2%; 45–59,
10.6%; 60–74, 5.7%; 75 and over, 1.7%; unknown 0.1%.
Population projection: (2000) 172,777,000; (2010) 194,002,000.
Doubling time: 42 years.
Ethnic composition (1990): white 54.0%, mulatto and mestizo 39.0%; black
and black/Amerindian 5.9%; Asian 0.9%; Amerindian 0.2%.
Religious affiliation (1990): Roman Catholic *c.* 76%[6]; evangelical Protestant
c. 11%; other *c.* 13%.
Major cities and metropolitan areas (1991)[2]: São Paulo 9,393,753 (15,416,-
416); Rio de Janeiro 5,473,909 (9,796,498); Salvador 2,070,296 (2,493,224);
Belo Horizonte 1,529,566 (3,431,755); Brasília[7] 1,492,542 (1,598,415[8]); Recife
1,296,995 (2,871,261); Pôrto Alegre 1,237,223 (3,026,029); Manaus[7] 1,005,634;
Goiânia[7] 912,136; Curitiba 841,882 (1,998,807); Belém 765,476 (1,332,723);
Campinas[7] 748,076; Fortaleza 743,335 (2,303,645).

Other principal cities (1991)[2]					
	population		population		population
Aracaju	401,676	Natal	459,827	São Bernardo	
Campo Grande	516,403	Niterói	400,586[9]	do Campo	550,030[10]
Guarulhos	544,698[10]	Nova Iguaçu	562,062[9]	São Jose dos	
João Pessoa	497,306	Osasco	566,949[10]	Campos	385,879
Juiz de Fora	377,538	Ribeirão Preto	416,186	Sorocaba	348,952
Londrina	355,062	Santo André	518,272[10]	Teresina	556,073
Maceió	554,727	Santos	415,554	Uberlândia	354,710

Place of birth/national origin: n.a.
Mobility: n.a.
Families (1990)[11]. Average family size 3.9; 1–2 persons 26.2%, 3 persons
21.3%, 4 persons 21.5%, 5–6 persons 22.3%, 7 or more persons 8.7%.
Immigration: n.a.

Vital statistics

Birth rate per 1,000 population (1991): 25.3 (world avg. 26.0).
Death rate per 1,000 population (1991): 6.6 (world avg. 9.2).
Natural increase rate per 1,000 population (1991): 18.7 (world avg. 16.8).
Total fertility rate (avg. births per childbearing woman; 1992): 2.8.
Marriage rate per 1,000 population (1990): 5.2.
Divorce rate per 1,000 population (1990): 0.5.
Life expectancy at birth (1990–95): male 63.5 years; female 69.1 years.
Major causes of death per 100,000 population (1989)[12]: diseases of the circu-
latory system 210.0, of which cerebrovascular disease 71.4, ischemic heart

diseases 61.8, diseases of pulmonary circulation and other forms of heart
disease 52.3; malignant neoplasms (cancers) 72.3; diseases of the respiratory
system 60.7; accidents 51.0; infectious and parasitic diseases 41.5; homicide
and other violence 39.2; birth trauma and other conditions originating in
the perinatal period 37.7; diseases of the digestive system 29.5; ill-defined
conditions 136.3.

Social indicators

Educational attainment (1990). Percentage of population age 10 and over
having: no formal schooling or less than one year of primary education
18.1%; incomplete primary 56.8%; complete primary 6.9%; incomplete secondary 12.4%; complete secondary or higher 5.7%; unknown 0.1%.

Distribution of income (1988)[11,13]									
percentage of national income by decile									
1	2	3	4	5	6	7	8	9	10 (highest)
0.7	1.7	2.2	3.4	3.9	5.0	6.8	9.9	15.9	50.5

Quality of working life. Average workweek (1986): 79.9% of the labour force
works 40 or more hours per week. Annual estimated rate per 100,000 insured workers (1990) for: on-the-job injury 2,032; industrial illness 17; death
4. Proportion of labour force participating in national social insurance system (1990): 50.1%. Proportion of formally employed population receiving
minimum wage (1993): 25.0%.
Access to services. Proportion of households having access to: electricity (1990)
87.8%, of which urban households having access (1989) 97.2%, rural households having access (1989) 53.2%; safe public (piped) water supply (1990)
73.3%, of which urban households having access (1986) 88.7%, rural households having access (1986) 11.6%; public refuse collection (1990) 64.5%.
Social participation. Eligible voters participating in last (October 1990) national election: *c.* 64%; although voting is mandatory, about 15% of the
electorate did not vote and about 25% of those who did spoiled their ballots
or cast blank votes. Trade union membership in total workforce (1989):
7,437,251. Practicing Roman Catholic population in total affiliated Roman
Catholic population (1990): 25%.
Social deviance (1990). The incidence of crime is not accurately reported.
Crimes resulting in imprisonment: 159,071, of which murder 7.3%, assault
11.0%, theft, burglary, and housebreaking 26.6%, robbery and extortion
12.2%, narcotics trafficking 6.3%, narcotics usage 4.5%. Suicide: 5,142.
Leisure. Favourite leisure activities include: playing soccer, rehearsing all year
in neighbourhood samba groups for celebrations of Carnival, and competing
in water sports, volleyball, and basketball.
Material well-being (1990)[11]. Households possessing: radio receiver 84.3%;
television receiver 73.7%; refrigerator 71.1%; stove 96.4%.

National economy

Gross national product (at current market prices; 1993): U.S.$470,511,000,000
(U.S.$3,010 per capita).

Structure of gross domestic product and labour force				
	1992		1990	
	in value Cr$'000,000,000[1,14]	% of total value	labour force[11]	% of labour force
Agriculture	182,639	11.1	14,180,519	22.0
Mining	25,899	1.6 }	860,453	1.3
Public utilities	58,821	3.6 }		
Manufacturing	377,680	22.9	9,410,712	14.6
Construction	120,472	7.3	3,823,154	5.9
Transportation and communications	93,321	5.7	2,439,920	3.8
Trade	111,563[15]	6.8[15]	7,975,670[15]	12.4[15]
Finance, real estate	418,578	25.4	1,715,598[16]	2.7[16]
Pub. admin., defense	168,627	10.2	3,117,005	4.8
Services	235,526[17]	14.3[17]	18,577,468[17]	28.8[17]
Other	−147,195[18]	−8.9[18]	2,367,482[19]	3.7[19]
TOTAL	1,645,931	100.0	64,467,981	100.0

Budget (1992). Revenue: Cr$478,409,000,000,000 (current receipts 48.9%, of
which social contributions 22.4% [including social security 12.2%], taxes
18.7% [including income taxes 10.1%]; development receipts 51.1%, of which
credits 44.0%). Expenditures: Cr$478,409,000,000,000 (current expenditures
41.9%; development expenditures 57.8%, of which amortization of domestic
debt 41.6%; contingency reserve 0.3%).
Public debt (external, outstanding; 1992): U.S.$86,251,000,000.
Production ('000 metric tons except as noted; 1993). Agriculture, forestry,
fishing: sugarcane 251,408, corn (maize) 29,967, soybeans 22,710, cassava
21,719, oranges 19,640[20], rice 10,193, bananas 5,650[20], coffee 2,550, dry beans
2,464, potatoes 2,365, tomatoes 2,314, wheat 2,201, papayas 1,400[20], seed
cotton 1,139, cottonseed 1,125[20], coconuts 878[20], pineapples 800[20], grapes
741[20], tobacco leaves 663, apples 611[20], cacao 346, peanuts (groundnuts)
150, cashews 97[20]; livestock (number of live animals; 1992) 153,000,000 cattle, 33,050,000 pigs, 19,500,000 sheep, 6,200,000 horses; roundwood (1992)
268,905,000 cu m; fish catch (1992) 790, of which freshwater fishes 210. Mining and quarrying (value of production in Cr$'000,000,000; 1990): iron ore
100.9; gold 100.7; granite 68.2; calcites 54.9; bauxite 22.6; natural phosphate
fertilizers 15.5; zinc ore 12.9; manganese 12.7; kaolin (clay) 12.6; diamonds
10.6. Manufacturing (value added in Cr$'000,000,000; 1991): food products
4,801; industrial chemicals 4,397; nonelectrical machinery 4,191; basic and
fabricated metals 4,152; electrical machinery 2,794; transport equipment
2,687; textiles 1,799; nonmetallic mineral products 1,565; paper and paper
products 1,456; clothing and footwear 1,372; printing and publishing 1,227.
Construction (authorized[21]; 1987): residential 20,090,000 sq m; nonresidential 8,180,000 sq m.
Land use (1991): forested 57.7%; meadows and pastures 22.1%; agricultural
and under permanent cultivation 7.0%; other 13.2%.

Manufacturing enterprises (1985)

	no. of enterprises	number of labourers	wages of labourers as a % of avg. of all mfg. wages	value added in producer's prices (in Cr$'000,000,000)[22]
Food products	43,034	733,199	68.4	4,801
Chemical products (excl. pharmaceuticals)	5,066	287,742	191.7	4,307
Nonelectrical machinery	11,088	552,163	146.5	4,191
Fabricated metals, iron and steel, and nonferrous metals	18,964	565,036	117.1	4,152
Electrical machinery	4,573	315,767	138.5	2,794
Transport equipment	4,184	341,621	154.8	2,687
Textiles	5,570	351,360	75.1	1,799
Nonmetallic mineral products	28,974	365,643	65.7	1,565
Paper and paper products	2,107	132,948	120.7	1,456
Clothing and footwear	23,200	655,234	49.6	1,372
Publishing and printing	9,053	164,523	100.1	1,227
Plastics	2,975	146,151	85.1	849
Beverages	2,798	77,167	...	782
Pharmaceuticals	930	49,048	173.7	680
Rubber products	1,421	71,656	136.3	472
Wood and wood products (excl. furniture)	17,129	218,059	48.4	406
Furniture	13,759	186,407	...	331

Population economically active (1990)[11]: total 64,467,981; activity rate of total population 43.8% (participation rates: ages 15–59, 68.5%; female 35.5%; unemployed [1993] 14.9%).

Price and earnings indexes (1988 = 100)

	1990	1991	1992	1993	1994
Consumer price index	100.0	541.3	6,002	134,800	2,670,500[23]
Monthly earnings index[24]	100.0	515.0	5,859	97,000	...

Tourism (1992): receipts from visitors U.S.$1,307,000,000; expenditures by nationals abroad U.S.$1,332,000,000.

Retail trade enterprises (1985)

	no. of enterprises	total no. of employees	annual wage as a % of all trade wages	annual values of sales in Cr$'000,000
Vehicles, new and used; parts	45,385	406,568	152.1	1,685
General merchandise stores (including food products)	10,180	368,590	116.7	1,324
Clothing, footwear, and apparel	147,671	634,713	94.7	1,124
Gas stations	24,881	211,689	106.0	1,067
Food, beverages, and tobacco	220,922	606,041	53.1	1,060
Hardware, appliances, and construction materials	57,577	338,519	99.1	775
Domestic goods, equipment, kitchenware, and antiques	28,636	202,146	115.3	567
Pharmaceutical and cosmetic products	49,435	213,118	79.9	377
Agricultural and industrial equipment and machinery	9,897	90,900	154.1	289
Books, magazines, newspapers	14,383	69,771	81.8	116

Family income and expenditure (1987–88)[25]. Average family size 4.0; annual income per family 516,528 (old) cruzados[1] (U.S.$1,233); sources of income: wages and salaries 54.3%, self-employed 27.3%, transfers 7.8%, other 10.6%; expenditure: n.a.

Financial aggregates[26]

	1989	1990	1991	1992	1993	1994[27]
Exchange rate, cruzeiros reais[1] per:						
U.S. dollar	.011	.177	1.07	12.39	326.11	913.35
£	.018	.341	2.00	18.73	483.03	1,353.76
SDR	.015	.252	1.53	17.03	447.92	1,290.19
International reserves (U.S.$)						
Total (excl. gold; '000,000)	7,535	7,441	8,033	22,521	30,604	36,672
SDRs ('000,000)	—	11	13	1	2	1
Reserve pos. in IMF ('000,000)	—	—	—	—	—	—
Foreign exchange ('000,000)	7,535	7,430	8,020	22,520	30,602	36,671
Gold ('000,000 fine troy oz)	2.98	4.57	2.02	2.23	2.93	3.36
% world reserves	0.32	0.49	0.21	0.24	0.32	0.37
Interest and prices						
Central bank discount (%)	38,341	1,083	2,494	1,489	5,757	9,610
Govt. bond yield (%)	...	...	...	...	...	...
Industrial share prices	...	...	...	...	...	...
Balance of payments (U.S.$'000,000)						
Balance of visible trade	+16,112	+10,747	+10,604	+15,610	...	...
Imports, f.o.b.	18,203	20,001	21,017	20,540	...	...
Exports, f.o.b.	34,375	31,408	31,621	36,150	...	...
Balance of invisibles	−15,087	−14,537	−10,994	−9,010	...	...
Balance of payments, current account	+1,025	−3,790	−390	+6,600	...	...

Energy production (consumption): electricity (kW-hr; 1993) 237,623,000,000 ([1992] 265,381,000,000); coal (metric tons; 1992) 4,728,000 ([1992] 16,-041,000); crude petroleum (barrels; 1993) 243,820,000 ([1992] 430,659,000); petroleum products (metric tons; 1992) 50,661,000 (51,754,000); natural gas (cu m; 1993) 3,924,000,000 ([1992] 3,731,000,000); carburant alcohol (cu m; 1992) 11,530,000 (8,052,000).

Foreign trade

Balance of trade (current prices)

	1988	1989	1990	1991	1992	1993
U.S.$'000,000	+19,168	+16,112	+10,747	+10,604	+15,239	+13,131
% of total	39.6%	30.6%	20.6%	20.1%	27.4%	20.4%

Imports (1992): U.S.$20,607,000,000 (crude petroleum and petroleum products 25.8%, nonelectrical machinery and apparatus 15.7%, electrical machinery and apparatus 8.9%, organic chemical products 6.6%, motor vehicles and parts 4.3%, professional goods and scientific equipment 4.0%). *Major import sources* (1993): United States 21.9%; Argentina 9.5%; Germany 8.2%; Japan 5.5%; Saudi Arabia 5.3%; Italy 3.6%; France 2.5%; Canada 2.4%; Switzerland 2.0%; United Kingdom 1.9%.

Exports (1993): U.S.$38,783,000,000 (machinery and equipment 11.9%, iron and steel fabricated products 10.3%, transport equipment 8.7%, iron ore 5.8%, footwear 5.0%, soya products 4.7%, textiles 3.6%, coffee beans 3.3%, crude aluminum 2.3%, wood and wood products 2.2%, orange juice 2.1%). *Major export destinations*: United States 20.3%; Argentina 9.4%; The Netherlands 6.4%; Japan 6.0%; Germany 4.7%; Italy 3.4%; Belgium-Luxembourg 3.0%; United Kingdom 2.9%; Chile 2.9%; Mexico 2.6%.

Transport and communications

Transport. Railroads: route length (1992) 18,816 mi, 30,282 km; passenger-mi 9,394,000,000, passenger-km 15,118,000,000; short ton-mi cargo 79,842,-000,000, metric ton-km cargo 116,567,000,000. Roads (1991): total length 934,566 mi, 1,504,041 km (paved 10%). Vehicles (1992): passenger cars 12,974,991; trucks and buses 1,371,127. Merchant marine (1992): vessels (100 gross tons and over) 635; total deadweight tonnage 9,348,339. Air transport (1993)[28]: passenger-mi 18,491,000,000, passenger-km 29,758,000,000; short ton-mi cargo 882,000,000, metric ton km cargo 1,288,000,000; airports (1993) with scheduled flights 110.

Communications. Daily newspapers (1992): total number 205; total circulation 7,815,400[29]; circulation per 1,000 population 51[29]. Radio (1993): total number of receivers 60,000,000 (1 per 2.6 persons). Television (1993): total number of receivers 30,000,000 (1 per 5.2 persons). Telephones (1991): 14,426,673 (1 per 11 persons).

Education and health

Education (1991)

	schools	teachers	students	student/ teacher ratio
Primary (age 7–14)	206,526	1,253,029	28,742,471	22.7
Secondary (age 15–18)	10,160[30]	248,705	3,558,946	14.3
Higher	918[30]	133,135	1,565,056	11.8

Literacy (1990)[31]: total population age 15 and over literate 79,100,000 (81.7%); males literate 38,500,000 (82.1%); females literate 40,600,000 (81.2%).
Health (1988): physicians 169,500 (1 per 848 persons); hospital beds 532,000 (1 per 270 persons); infant mortality rate per 1,000 live births (1994) 60.0.
Food (1988–90): daily per capita caloric intake 2,730 (vegetable products 84%, animal products 16%); 114% of FAO recommended minimum requirement.

Military

Total active duty personnel (1994): 336,800 (army 65.0%, navy 17.3%, air force 17.7%). *Military expenditure as percentage of GNP* (1991): 1.3% (world 4.2%); per capita expenditure U.S.$35.

[1]The real replaced the cruzeiro real on July 1, 1994, at a rate of 2,750 cruzeiros reais to 1 real (a rate par to the U.S.$ on that date). Previously, the cruzeiro real replaced the cruzeiro (Cr$) at a rate of 1,000 cruzeiros to 1 cruzeiro real on Aug. 2, 1993; the cruzeiro replaced the new cruzado (NCz$) at a rate of 1 to 1 on March 16, 1990; and the new cruzado replaced the (old) cruzado (Cz$) at a rate of 1,000 (old) to 1 new on Jan. 15, 1989. [2]Revised preliminary. [3]Area in dispute between Ceará and Piauí. [4]Detail does not add to total given because of rounding. [5]Land area excluding inland water is 3,265,076 sq mi (8,456,508 sq km). [6]Includes syncretic Afro-Catholic cults having Spiritist beliefs and rituals. [7]City has no officially designated metropolitan area. [8]Pop. of federal district. [9]Within Rio de Janeiro metropolitan area. [10]Within São Paulo metropolitan area. [11]Excludes rural economically active population of Acre, Amapá, Amazonas, Pará, Rondônia, and Roraima states. [12]Projected rates based on about 74% of total deaths. [13]As of 1992, 33,000,000 Brazilians lived in extreme poverty (more than half of whom lived in the nine states of the northeast). [14]At factor cost. [15]Excludes restaurants and hotels. [16]Includes classifications not adequately defined. [17]Includes restaurants and hotels. [18]Less imputed bank service charges. [19]Unemployed. [20]1992. [21]Urban construction only for 74 cities. [22]1991. [23]May. [24]Minimum wages. [25]Based on 3,888,185 families in São Paulo metropolitan area. [26]End-of-period figures. [27]March. [28]Brasil Central, Transbrasil, VARIG, and VASP airlines only. [29]184 newspapers only. [30]1990. [31]By official estimate; functional literacy, however, may be as low as 42% of total population over age 15.

Brunei

Official name: Negara Brunei
Darussalam (State of Brunei, Abode
of Peace).
Form of government: monarchy
(sultanate)[1].
Head of state and government: Sultan.
Capital: Bandar Seri Begawan.
Official language: Malay[2].
Official religion: Islam.
Monetary unit: 1 Brunei dollar
(B$) = 100 cents; valuation (Oct. 7,
1994) 1 U.S.$ = B$1.48;
1 £ = B$2.36.

Area and population

Districts	Capitals	area sq mi	area sq km	population 1991 census
Belait	Kuala Belait	1,052	2,724	52,957
Brunei and Muara	Bandar Seri Begawan	220	571	170,107
Temburong	Bangar	504	1,304	7,688
Tutong	Tutong	450	1,166	29,730
TOTAL		2,226	5,765	260,482

Demography

Population (1994): 283,000.
Density (1994): persons per sq mi 127.1, persons per sq km 49.1.
Urban-rural (1993): urban 90.0%; rural 10.0%.
Sex distribution (1992): male 52.76%; female 47.24%.
Age breakdown (1992): under 15, 34.5%; 15–29, 28.3%; 30–44, 24.7%; 45–59,
8.2%; 60–69, 2.5%; 70 and over, 1.8%.
Population projection: (2000) 334,000; (2010) 432,000.
Doubling time: 29 years.
Ethnic composition (1992): Malay 67.1%; Chinese 15.4%; other indigenous
6.0%; Indian and other 11.5%.
Religious affiliation (1991): Muslim 67.2%; Buddhist 12.8%; Christian 10.0%;
other religions and nonreligious 10.0%.
Major cities (1981): Bandar Seri Begawan 52,300[3]; Seria 23,511; Kuala Belait
19,281; Tutong 6,161.

Vital statistics

Birth rate per 1,000 population (1992): 27.2 (world avg. 26.0); (1982) legiti-
mate 99.6%; illegitimate 0.4%.
Death rate per 1,000 population (1992): 3.3 (world avg. 9.2).
Natural increase rate per 1,000 population (1992): 23.9 (world avg. 16.8).
Total fertility rate (avg. births per childbearing woman; 1992): 3.5.
Marriage rate per 1,000 population (1992): 6.7.
Divorce rate per 1,000 population (1987): 0.8.
Life expectancy at birth (1993): male 69.3 years; female 72.7 years.
Major causes of death per 100,000 population (1992): cardiovascular disease
55.3; malignant neoplasms (cancers) 37.3; accidents, poisoning, and violence
30.6; cerebrovascular diseases 19.0; pneumonia 12.3; hypertensive diseases
9.7; congenital anomalies 9.7.

National economy

Budget (1992). Revenue: B$2,729,570,000 (indirect taxes 47.3%; government
property 43.6%[4]; commercial receipts 8.9%). Expenditures: B$3,057,190,000
(current expenditure 69.9%, of which finance 15.5%, defense 13.4%, education 9.1%; development expenditure 15.1%; charged expenditure 15.0%).
Public debt (external, outstanding): none.
Tourism (1990): receipts from visitors U.S.$35,000,000; expenditures by na-
tionals abroad, n.a.
Production (metric tons except as noted). Agriculture, forestry, fishing (1992):
vegetables and melons 8,000, fruits (excluding melons) 5,000, eggs 3,000, rice
1,000, cassava 1,000, pineapples 1,000; livestock (number of live animals)
14,000 pigs, 10,000 buffalo, 1,000 cattle, 2,000,000 chickens; roundwood
(1991) 295,000 cu m; fish catch (1991) 1,652. Mining and quarrying (1992):
other than petroleum and natural gas (see below), none except sand and
gravel for construction. Manufacturing (1991): gasoline 152,000; diesel oils
109,000; jet fuels 41,000; naphtha 5,000; kerosene 3,000. Construction (number of buildings completed; 1984): residential 195; nonresidential 5. Energy
production (consumption): electricity (kW-hr; 1992) 1,257,000,000 (1,257,-
000,000); coal, none (none); crude petroleum (barrels; 1992) 58,470,000
(15,000); petroleum products (metric tons; 1992) 813,000 (808,000); natural
gas (cu m; 1992) 8,648,000,000 (2,207,000,000).
Population economically active (1991): total 111,955; activity rate of total
population 43.0% (participation rates: ages 15–64, 67.6%; female 32.9%;
unemployed 4.7%).

Price and earnings indexes (1985 = 100)

	1986	1987	1988	1989	1990	1991	1992
Consumer price index	101.8	103.1	104.3	105.7	107.9	109.6	111.0
Monthly earnings index[5]	87.9	88.8	87.5	...	...	76.9	87.5

Household income and expenditure. Average household size (1991) 5.8; income per household: n.a.; sources of income: n.a.; expenditure (1977):
food 45.1%, transportation and communications 17.2%, recreation, education, and cultural services 8.9%, household furnishings 8.3%, clothing and
footwear 6.1%, rent and utilities 5.0%.

Gross national product (at current market prices; 1992)[6]: U.S.$3,912,000,000
(U.S.$14,650 per capita).

Structure of gross domestic product and labour force

	1992 in value B$'000,000	1992 % of total value	1991 labour force	1991 % of labour force
Agriculture	191.5	3.0	2,162	1.9
Mining			9,397	8.4
Manufacturing }	2,654.4	41.7		
Construction	311.7	4.9	14,145	12.6
Public utilities	64.1	1.0	2,223	2.0
Transportation and communications	309.5	4.9	5,392	4.8
Trade	782.4	12.3	15,404	13.8
Finance	459.8	7.2	5,807	5.2
Services	1,754.8	27.5	52,121	46.6
Other	−156.2	−2.5	5,304[7]	4.7[7]
TOTAL	6,372.0	100.0	111,955	100.0

Land use (1991): forested 40.8%; meadows and pastures 1.1%; agricultural
and under permanent cultivation 1.3%; other 56.8%.

Foreign trade

Balance of trade (current prices)

	1987	1988	1989	1990	1991	1992
B$'000,000	+2,655	+1,939	+1,998	+2,197	+2,417	+1,946
% of total	49.6%	39.3%	37.4%	37.7%	39.2%	33.7%

Imports (1990): B$1,813,160,000 (machinery and transport equipment 34.4%,
manufactured goods 27.0%, food and live animals 15.3%, miscellaneous
manufactured articles 10.2%, chemicals 6.7%, beverages and tobacco 3.5%,
crude materials 1.3%, mineral fuels 0.9%). *Major import sources:* ASEAN
41.9%, of which Singapore 25.9%, Malaysia 10.3%; EEC 17.4%; United
States 15.3%; Japan 14.6%.
Exports (1990): B$4,010,150,000 (crude petroleum 50.9%, natural gas 40.0%,
petroleum products 5.6%, other 3.5%). *Major export destinations:* Japan
58.1%; South Korea 12.4%; ASEAN 20.9%, of which Thailand 7.7%, Singapore 7.1%, Philippines 4.9%.

Transport and communications

Transport. Railroads (1993)[8]: length 12 mi, 19 km. Roads (1992): total length
1,502 mi, 2,417 km (paved 51%). Vehicles (1992): passenger cars 122,104;
trucks and buses 13,658. Merchant marine (1992): vessels (100 gross tons
and over) 51; total deadweight tonnage 349,718. Marine transport (1992):
cargo loaded 20,411,000 metric tons, cargo unloaded 1,377,000 metric tons.
Air transport (1993): passenger-mi 1,008,000,000, passenger-km 1,623,000,-
000; short ton-mi cargo 44,394,000, metric ton-km cargo 64,814,000; airports
(1994) with scheduled flights 1.
Communications. Daily newspapers (1993): total number 1; total circulation
30,000; circulation per 1,000 population 9.2. Radio (1992): total number of
receivers 108,000 (1 per 2.5 persons). Television (1992): total number of
receivers 78,000 (1 per 3.4 persons). Telephones (1992): 67,293 (1 per 4.0
persons).

Education and health

Education (1992)

	schools	teachers	students	student/ teacher ratio
Primary (age 5–11)	161	3,047	50,434	16.6
Secondary (age 12–20)	23	1,939	25,309	13.1
Voc., teacher tr.	6	340	1,756	5.2
Higher	4	289	1,372	4.7

Educational attainment (1981). Percentage of population age 25 and over
having: no formal schooling 32.1%; primary education 28.3%; secondary
30.1%; postsecondary and higher 9.4%. *Literacy* (1986): total population age
15 and over literate 121,281 (85.1%); males literate 67,714 (90.9%); females
literate 53,567 (78.7%).
Health (1992): physicians 197 (1 per 1,359 persons); hospital beds 967 (1 per
277 persons); infant mortality rate per 1,000 live births 9.6.
Food (1988–90): daily per capita caloric intake 2,854 (vegetable products 80%,
animal products 20%); 128% of FAO recommended minimum requirement.

Military

Total active duty personnel (1993): 4,400[9] (army 77.3%, navy 15.9%, air force
6.8%). *Military expenditure as percentage of GNP* (1983): 5.8% (world 6.1%);
per capita expenditure U.S.$1,200.

[1]A nonelective 21-member body advises the sultan on legislative matters. [2]All official
documents that must be published by law in Malay are, however, also required to
be issued in an official English version as well. [3]1988 metropolitan area population
estimate. [4]In 1983 more than 98% of state revenue was derived from exports of oil
and gas. [5]Nonagricultural sectors only. [6]GDP data. [7]Mostly unemployed. [8]Privately
owned. [9]All services form part of the army.

Bulgaria

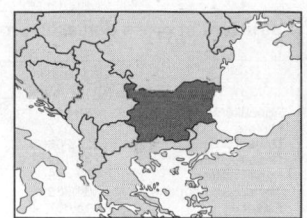

Official name: Republika Bŭlgaria
(Republic of Bulgaria).
Form of government: unitary multiparty
republic with one legislative body
(Parliament [240]).
Chief of state: President.
Head of government: Prime Minister.
Capital: Sofia.
Official language: Bulgarian.
Official religion: none[1].
Monetary unit: 1 lev (leva) = 100
stotinki; valuation (Oct. 7, 1994)
1 U.S.$ = 62.84 leva; 1 £ = 99.95 leva.

Area and population

| | | area | | population |
| | | | | 1994 |
Regions	Capitals	sq mi	sq km	estimate
Burgas	Burgas	5,659	14,657	850,003
Khaskovo	Khaskovo	5,364	13,892	903,928
Lovech	Lovech	5,849	15,150	1,009,196
Montana	Mikhaylovgrad	4,095	10,607	626,205
Plovdiv	Plovdiv	5,262	13,628	1,221,449
Ruse	Ruse	4,186	10,842	765,719
Sofiya	Sofia (Sofiya)	7,328	18,978	980,588
Varna	Varna	4,606	11,929	914,079
City Commune				
Sofiya	Sofia (Sofiya)	506	1,311	1,188,556
TOTAL		42,855	110,994	8,459,723

Demography

Population (1994): 8,452,000.
Density (1994): persons per sq mi 197.2, persons per sq km 76.1.
Urban-rural (1993): urban 67.6%; rural 32.4%.
Sex distribution (1993): male 49.07%; female 50.93%.
Age breakdown (1993): under 15, 18.6%; 15–29, 20.9%; 30–44, 20.9%; 45–59, 18.8%; 60–74, 16.3%; 75 and over, 4.5%.
Population projection: (2000) 8,361,000; (2010) 8,212,000.
Doubling time: not applicable; population is declining.
Ethnic composition (1992): Bulgarian 85.8%; Turkish 9.7%; Gypsy 3.4%; other 1.1%.
Religious affiliation (1992)[2]: Eastern Orthodox 87.0%; Muslim 12.7%; other 0.3%.
Major cities (1991): Sofia 1,140,795; Plovdiv 379,112; Varna 316,231; Burgas 211,579; Ruse 190,229.

Vital statistics

Birth rate per 1,000 population (1993): 10.0 (world avg. 26.0); (1990) legitimate 88.0%; illegitimate 12.0%.
Death rate per 1,000 population (1993): 11.8 (world avg. 9.2).
Natural increase rate per 1,000 population (1993): −1.8 (world avg. 16.8).
Total fertility rate (avg. births per childbearing woman; 1993): 1.7.
Marriage rate per 1,000 population (1993): 4.7.
Divorce rate per 1,000 population (1991): 12.3.
Life expectancy at birth (1993): male 69.6 years; female 76.3 years.
Major causes of death per 100,000 population (1992): diseases of the circulatory system 768.1; malignant neoplasms (cancers) 181.4; diseases of the respiratory system 70.7; accidents, poisoning, and violence 68.5; diseases of the digestive system 37.6; endocrine and metabolic disorders 22.3.

National economy

Budget (1991). Revenue: 62,967,000,000 leva (national economy 69.1%, taxes 29.9%). Expenditures: 70,476,500,000 leva (social security 28.2%, education and health 18.8%, economy 11.8%, administration and other 34.1%).
Public debt (external, outstanding; 1991): U.S.$11,923,000,000.
Tourism (1992): receipts from visitors U.S.$49,000,000; expenditures by nationals abroad U.S.$23,000,000.
Production (metric tons except as noted). Agriculture, forestry, fishing (1993): wheat 3,638,000, corn (maize) 1,038,000, barley 958,000, grapes 550,000, potatoes 500,000, tomatoes 444,000, sunflower seeds 378,000, apples 155,000; livestock (number of live animals; 1994) 4,293,000 sheep, 1,998,000 pigs, 673,000 cattle; roundwood (1993) 4,232,000 cu m; fish catch (1993) 27,000. Mining and quarrying (1992): iron ore 239,000; manganese 6,900. Manufacturing (1993): cement 2,006,000; crude steel 1,941,000; pig iron 1,027,000; fertilizers 315,200; paper 124,600; cotton fabrics 70,298,000 sq m; beer 4,226,000 hectolitres; wine 1,093,000 hectolitres; wearing apparel 6,333,000 pieces; refrigerators 81,300 units; television sets 19,800 units. Construction (1993): residential 836,000 sq m. Energy production (consumption): electricity (kW-hr; 1992) 35,587,000,000 (38,292,000,000); coal (metric tons; 1992) 30,340,000 (33,621,000); crude petroleum (barrels; 1992) 389,000 (17,736,-000); petroleum products (metric tons; 1992) 2,030,000 (4,655,000); natural gas (cu m; 1992) 7,543,000 (5,263,000,000).
Household income and expenditure (1992). Average household size (1992) 2.8; income per household (1993) 23,828 leva (U.S.$856); sources of income (1993): wages and salaries 42.9%, transfer payments 20.9%, self-employment in agriculture 20.2%; expenditure (1993): food 42.9%, clothing 8.1%, transportation 7.9%, household durable goods 4.7%, housing 4.2%, education and culture 3.5%, health care 2.5%.
Gross national product (1993): U.S.$9,812,000,000 (U.S.$1,160 per capita).

Structure of gross domestic product and labour force

| | 1993 | | | |
	in value '000,000 leva[3]	% of total value[3]	labour force	% of labour force
Agriculture	26,273	9.2	160,052	5.9
Manufacturing, mining	119,258	41.7	826,381	30.6
Construction			113,796	4.2
Transp. and commun.			192,879	7.1
Trade			123,040	4.6
Public utilities, housing	136,170	47.6	40,460	1.8
Pub. admin., defense			597,546	22.1
Services			...	...
Other	4,433	1.5	639,817	23.7
TOTAL	286,134	100.0	2,701,971	100.0

Population economically active (1993): total 2,701,971; activity rate of total population 31.9% (participation rates: ages 16–59 [male], 16–54 [female] 57.0%; female 47.4%; unemployed 23.2%).

Price and earnings indexes (1990 = 100)

	1987	1988	1989	1990	1991	1992	1993
Consumer price index	78.4	78.8	80.8	100.0	438.5	786.6	1,227.5
Monthly earnings index	65.0	70.0	75.9	100.0	267.7	541.6	831.9

Land use (1992): forested 35.0%; meadows and pastures 16.5%; agricultural and under permanent cultivation 39.2%; other 9.3%.

Foreign trade

Balance of trade (current prices)

	1988	1989	1990	1991	1992	1993
'000,000 leva	+489.4	+877.1	+244.6	+12,235.9	+1,049.1	−20,245
% of total	1.7%	3.3%	1.2%	11.9%	0.6%	9.3%

Imports (1993): 119,288,100,000 leva (1991; machinery and equipment 38.9%; fuels, mineral raw materials, and metals 15.8%; chemical products and rubber 5.1%; consumer goods 4.4%). *Major import sources:* C.I.S. 35.1%; Germany 6.1%; Italy 4.8%; Greece 3.7%; Ukraine 3.5%.
Exports (1993): 99,043,100,000 leva (1991; machinery and equipment 30.6%; consumer goods 22.3%; food and beverages 15.3%; chemicals and rubber 10.9%; fuels, minerals, and metals 10.5%). *Major export destinations:* C.I.S. 18.0%; Turkey 7.8%; Germany 6.9%; Greece 5.9%; Italy 5.8%.

Transport and communications

Transport. Railroads (1993): track length 4,073 mi, 6,556 km; passenger-mi 3,627,000,000, passenger-km 5,837,000,000; short ton-mi cargo 5,275,000,000, metric ton-km cargo 7,702,000,000. Roads (1993): length 22,943 mi, 36,922 km (paved 92%). Vehicles (1990): cars 1,300,000; trucks and buses 200,000. Merchant marine (1992): vessels (100 gross tons and over) 222; deadweight tonnage 1,962,345. Air transport (1993): passenger-mi 2,592,000,000, passenger-km 4,173,000,000; short ton-mi cargo 34,300,000, metric ton-km cargo 50,000,000; airports (1994) with scheduled flights 34.
Communications. Daily newspapers (1988): total number 17; total circulation 2,396,000; circulation per 1,000 population 267. Radio (1993): 2,917,000 receivers (1 per 2.9 persons). Television (1992): 3,127,000 receivers (1 per 2.7 persons). Telephones (1993): 2,838,800 (1 per 3.0 persons).

Education and health

Education (1993–94)

	schools	teachers	students	student/ teacher ratio
Primary (age 6–14) Secondary (age 15–17)	3,360	70,131	987,999	14.1
Voc., teacher tr.	494	18,991	214,558	11.3
Higher	87	21,148	203,601	9.6

Educational attainment (1992). Percentage of population age 7 and over having: incomplete primary education 24.6%; primary 30.4%; secondary 37.0%; higher 8.0%. *Literacy* (1980): total population age 15 and over literate 95.5%.
Health (1993): physicians 28,457 (1 per 298 persons); hospital beds 90,372 (1 per 93 persons); infant mortality rate per 1,000 live births 15.5.
Food (1988–90): daily per capita caloric intake 3,695 (vegetable products 75%, animal products 25%); 148% of FAO recommended minimum requirement.

Military

Total active duty personnel (1994): 101,900 (army 75.9%, navy 2.9%, air force 21.2%). *Military expenditure as percentage of GNP* (1993): 6.0% (world 5.0%); per capita expenditure U.S.$70.

---

[1]Bulgaria has no official religion; the 1991 constitution, however, refers to Eastern Orthodoxy as the "traditional" religion. [2]Census data reflect the traditional religious identity of Bulgaria but apparently disregard the nonreligious, who may exceed half the adult population. [3]Data are based on estimates. [4]International only; the number of domestic airports is not available.

Burkina Faso

Official name: Burkina Faso (Burkina Faso).
Form of government: multiparty republic with one legislative house (National Assembly [107])[1].
Chief of state: President.
Head of government: Prime Minister.
Capital: Ouagadougou.
Official language: French.
Official religion: none.
Monetary unit: 1 CFA franc (CFAF) = 100 centimes; valuation (Oct. 7, 1994) 1 U.S.$ = CFAF 526.67; 1 £ = CFAF 837.67.

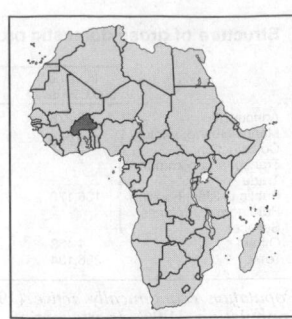

Area and population

Provinces	Capitals	area sq mi	area sq km	population 1991 estimate
Bam	Kongoussi	1,551	4,017	173,516
Bazéga	Kombissiri	2,051	5,313	352,104
Bougouriba	Diébougou	2,736	7,087	242,986
Boulgou	Tenkodogo	3,488	9,033	465,845
Boulkiemde	Koudougou	1,598	4,138	393,900
Comoé	Banfora	7,102	18,393	296,083
Ganzourgou	Zorgho	1,578	4,087	223,555
Gnagna	Bogandé	3,320	8,600	272,203
Gourma	Fada N'Gourma	10,275	26,613	350,336
Houet	Bobo-Dioulasso	6,438	16,672	724,803
Kadiogo	Ouagadougou	451	1,169	652,377
Kénédougou	Orodara	3,207	8,307	162,010
Kossi	Nouna	5,088	13,117	389,360
Kouritenga	Koupéla	628	1,627	227,060
Mouhoun	Dédougou	4,032	10,442	329,115
Nahouri	Pô	1,484	3,843	119,144
Namentenga	Boulsa	2,994	7,755	214,564
Oubritenga	Ziniaré	1,812	4,693	328,682
Oudalan	Gorom Gorom	3,879	10,046	123,495
Passoré	Yako	1,575	4,078	232,278
Poni	Gaoua	4,000	10,361	258,647
Sanguie	Réo	1,994	5,165	234,079
Sanmatenga	Kaya	3,557	9,213	404,563
Sèno	Dori	5,202	13,473	269,892
Sissili	Léo	5,303	13,736	297,598
Soum	Djibo	5,154	13,350	217,972
Sourou	Tougan	3,663	9,487	313,355
Tapoa	Diapaga	5,707	14,780	187,785
Yatenga	Ouahigouya	4,746	12,292	558,318
Zoundwéogo	Manga	1,333	3,453	175,166
TOTAL		105,946	274,400	9,190,791

Demography

Population (1994): 10,044,000.
Density (1994): persons per sq mi 94.8, persons per sq km 36.6.
Urban-rural (1991): urban 14.0%; rural 86.0%.
Sex distribution (1991): male 48.88%; female 51.12%.
Age breakdown (1990): under 15, 49.1%; 15–29, 23.6%; 30–44, 13.3%; 45–59, 8.3%; 60–74, 4.5%; 75 and over, 1.2%.
Population projection: (2000) 11,884,000; (2010) 15,549,000.
Doubling time: 24 years.
Ethnic composition (1983): Mossi 47.9%; Mande 8.8%; Fulani 8.3%; Lobi 6.9%; Bobo 6.8%; Senufo 5.3%; Grosi 5.1%; Gurma 4.8%; Tuareg 3.3%; other 2.8%.
Religious affiliation (1980): traditional beliefs 44.8%; Muslim 43.0%; Christian 12.2%, of which Roman Catholic 9.8%, Protestant 2.4%.
Major cities (1985): Ouagadougou 441,514; Bobo-Dioulasso 228,668; Koudougou 51,926; Ouahigouya 38,902; Banfora 35,319.

Vital statistics

Birth rate per 1,000 population (1990–95): 46.7 (world avg. 26.0).
Death rate per 1,000 population (1990–95): 17.6 (world avg. 9.2).
Natural increase rate per 1,000 population (1990–95): 29.1 (world avg. 16.8).
Total fertility rate (avg. births per childbearing woman; 1990–95): 6.5.
Life expectancy at birth (1990–95): male 46.6 years; female 49.9 years.
Major causes of morbidity (percentage of reported cases of infectious disease; 1984): measles 39.6%; malaria 12.4%; tetanus 5.7%; diarrheal diseases 5.3%.

National economy

Budget (1994). Revenue: CFAF 199,797,000,000 (1990; import duties 32.4%, sales taxes 26.7%, personal income taxes 11.1%, administrative fees 2.3%). Expenditures: CFAF 234,866,000,000 (1990; education 19.4%, defense 16.9%, debt service 16.6%, health 7.2%, agriculture 5.1%).
Production (metric tons except as noted). Agriculture, forestry, fishing (1992): sorghum 1,292,100, millet 783,500, corn (maize) 341,300, sugarcane 340,000, seed cotton 172,400, peanuts (groundnuts) 143,400, pulses 120,000, rice 46,-700, sweet potatoes 15,000, sesame 9,400, cassava 5,000; livestock (number of live animals) 6,860,000 goats, 5,350,000 sheep, 4,096,000 cattle, 18,000,000 chickens; roundwood (1991) 8,995,000 cu m; fish catch (1991) 7,012. Mining and quarrying (1992): gold 900 kg[2]; silver 100 kg. Manufacturing (1991): soap 25,611; wheat flour 21,402; cotton yarn 305; bicycle and motorcycle tires 29,674,000 units; motorcycles and bicycles 46,189 units; footwear 1,271,000 pairs; beer 393,681 hectolitres; soft drinks 99,307 hectolitres. Construction (value added in CFAF; 1992): 45,102,000,000. Energy production (consumption): electricity (kW-hr; 1991) 157,000,000 (157,000,000); crude petroleum, none (n.a.); petroleum products (metric tons; 1991) none (182,000).
Gross national product (1992): U.S.$2,908,000,000 (U.S.$290 per capita).

Structure of gross domestic product and labour force

	1992 in value CFAF '000,000	1992 % of total value	1985 labour force	1985 % of labour force
Agriculture	255,966	31.3	3,739,000	92.3
Mining	7,517	0.9		
Manufacturing	121,206	14.8	113,000	2.8
Construction	45,102	5.5		
Public utilities	7,415	0.9		
Transp. and commun.	34,789	4.3		
Finance	15,607	1.9		
Trade	124,610	15.3	199,000	4.9
Pub. admin., defense	84,086	10.3		
Services	94,868	11.6		
Other	25,871[3]	3.2[3]	...	...
TOTAL	817,037	100.0	4,051,000	100.0

Tourism: receipts (1992) U.S.$9,000,000; expenditures U.S.$36,000,000.
Public debt (external, outstanding; 1992): U.S.$994,000,000.
Population economically active: total (1985) 4,051,000; activity rate 51.0% (participation rates: over age 15, 83.0%; female 49.1%; unemployed 0.9%).

Price and earnings indexes (1985 = 100)

	1987	1988	1989	1990	1991	1992	1993
Consumer price index	94.8	98.6	98.8	97.8	102.5	100.5	101.1
Hourly earnings index[4]	100.0	114.0	114.6	114.6	114.6	114.6	...

Household income and expenditure. Average household size (1985) 6.2; average annual income per household CFAF 303,000 (U.S.$640); sources of income: n.a.; expenditure (1985)[5]: food 38.7%; transportation 18.6%; electricity and fuel 13.7%; beverages 9.0%; health 5.2%; housing 5.1%.
Land use (1991): forested 23.9%; meadows and pastures 36.5%; agricultural and under permanent cultivation 13.0%; other 26.6%.

Foreign trade

Balance of trade (current prices)

	1986	1987	1988	1989	1990	1991
CFAF '000,000	−80.25	−55.23	−63.31	−91.40	−78.70	−94.02
% of total	58.3%	37.2%	43.0%	39.9%	32.2%	61.1%

Imports (1991): CFAF 150,255,200,000 (machinery and transport equipment 22.9%, of which road transport equipment 7.2%, electrical machinery 7.0%; manufactured goods 20.4%; petroleum products 12.4%; chemicals 11.8%; cereals 9.9%; dairy products 3.8%; beverages and tobacco 2.3%; raw materials 2.0%). *Major import sources:* France 24.4%; Côte d'Ivoire 19.4%; United States 4.9%; Japan 4.2%; The Netherlands 4.0%; Nigeria 2.8%.
Exports (1991): CFAF 29,891,600,000 (raw cotton 62.7%; live animals 10.0%; manufactured goods 7.5%; hides and skins 4.0%). *Major export destinations:* Japan 20.3%; France 13.4%; Côte d'Ivoire 11.2%; Thailand 8.3%; Taiwan 6.2%; Togo 2.9%.

Transport and communications

Transport. Railroads (1984)[6]: route length[7] 308 mi, 495 km; passenger-km 679,790,000; metric ton-km cargo 469,675,000. Roads (1991): total length 8,161 mi, 13,134 km (paved 12%[8]). Vehicles (1990): passenger cars 12,000; trucks and buses 13,000. Merchant marine: none. Air transport (1991): passenger-km 235,000,000; metric ton-mi cargo 16,000,000; airports (1994) 2.
Communications. Daily newspapers (1992): total number 3; total circulation 17,000; circulation per 1,000 population 1.8. Radio (1993): 200,000 receivers (1 per 49 persons). Television (1993): 45,500 receivers (1 per 215 persons). Telephones (1988): 15,000 (1 per 569 persons).

Education and health

Education (1991–92)

	schools	teachers	students	student/teacher ratio
Primary	2,587	8,565	530,002	61.9
Secondary	173	2,419	60,629	25.1
Vocational	22	537	8,022	14.9
Higher	9	437	7,387	16.9

Educational attainment (1985). Percentage of population age 10 and over having: no formal schooling 86.1%; some primary 7.3%; general secondary 2.2%; specialized secondary and postsecondary 3.8%; other 0.6%. *Literacy* (1990): percentage of total population age 15 and over literate 18.2%; males 27.9%; females 8.9%.
Health (1991): physicians 341 (1 per 27,158 persons); hospital beds 5,041 (1 per 1,837 persons); infant mortality rate (1990–95) 118.0.
Food (1988–90): daily per capita caloric intake 2,219 (vegetable products 96%, animal products 4%); 94% of FAO recommended minimum requirement.

Military

Total active duty personnel (1993): 7,200 (army 97.2%, navy, none, air force 2.8%). *Military expenditure as percentage of GNP* (1991): 2.7% (world 4.2%); per capita expenditure U.S.$11.

---

[1]Ruling political party defeated a fragmented opposition (26 other political parties) at multiparty legislative elections of May 1992. [2]Officially marketed gold only; does not include substantial illegal production. [3]Includes indirect taxes less imputed bank service charges and subsidies. [4]January 1; index refers to the *S.M.I.G.* (*salaire minimum interprofessionnel garanti*), a form of minimum professional wage. [5]Weights of consumer price index components; Ouagadougou only. [6]Passenger-km and metric ton-km cargo figures are based on traffic between Abidjan, Côte d'Ivoire, and Ouagadougou. [7]1989. [8]1986.

Burundi

Official name: Republika y'u Burundi
(Rundi); République du Burundi
(French) (Republic of Burundi).
Form of government: unitary multiparty
republic[1] with one legislative house
(National Assembly [81]).
Head of state and government: Interim
president, assisted by Prime Minister.
Capital: Bujumbura.
Official languages: Rundi; French.
Official religion: none.
Monetary unit: 1 Burundi franc
(FBu) = 100 centimes; valuation (Oct.
7, 1994) 1 U.S.$ = FBu 248.44;
1 £ = FBu 395.15.

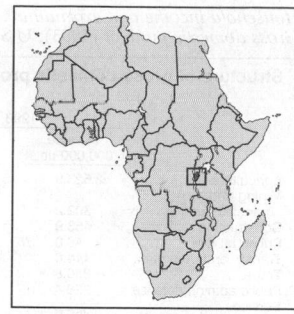

Area and population

		area		population
Provinces	**Capitals**	sq mi	sq km	1990 census
Bubanza	Bubanza	420	1,089	222,953
Bujumbura	Bujumbura	509	1,319	608,931
Bururi	Bururi	952	2,465	385,490
Cankuzo	Cankuzo	759	1,965	142,707
Cibitoke	Cibitoke	631	1,636	279,843
Gitega	Gitega	764	1,979	565,174
Karuzi	Karuzi	563	1,457	287,905
Kayanza	Kayanza	476	1,233	443,116
Kirundo	Kirundo	658	1,703	401,103
Makamba	Makamba	757	1,960	223,799
Muramvya	Muramvya	593	1,535	441,653
Muyinga	Muyinga	709	1,836	373,382
Ngozi	Ngozi	569	1,474	482,246
Rutana	Rutana	756	1,959	195,834
Ruyigi	Ruyigi	903	2,339	238,567
TOTAL LAND AREA		10,019	25,949	
INLAND WATER		721	1,867	
TOTAL		10,740	27,810	5,292,793[2]

Demography

Population (1994): 5,799,000[3].
Density (1994)[4]: persons per sq mi 578.8, persons per sq km 230.4.
Urban-rural (1990): urban 6.3%; rural 93.7%.
Sex distribution (1990): male 48.63%; female 51.37%.
Age breakdown (1990): under 15, 46.4%; 15–29, 25.3%; 30–44, 15.4%; 45–59, 7.0%; 60–74, 4.0%; 75 and over, 1.7%; not determined 0.2%.
Population projection: (2000) 6,674,000; (2010) 8,437,000.
Doubling time: 22 years.
Ethnic composition (1983): Rundi 97.4%, of which Hutu 81.9%, Tutsi 13.5%; Twa Pygmy 1.0%; other 1.6%.
Religious affiliation (1990): Roman Catholic 65.1%; nonreligious 18.6%; Protestant 13.8%; Muslim 1.6%; traditional beliefs 0.3%; other 0.6%.
Major cities (1990): Bujumbura 236,334; Gitega 20,708; Bururi 15,816; Ngozi 14,511; Cibitoke 8,280.

Vital statistics

Birth rate per 1,000 population (1991): 47.0 (world avg. 26.0).
Death rate per 1,000 population (1991): 15.0 (world avg. 9.2).
Natural increase rate per 1,000 population (1991): 32.0 (world avg. 16.8).
Total fertility rate (avg. births per childbearing woman; 1991): 6.9.
Marriage rate per 1,000 population: n.a.
Divorce rate per 1,000 population: n.a.
Life expectancy at birth (1991): male 50.0 years; female 54.0 years.
Major causes of death: n.a.; however, major health problems include malaria, influenza, diarrheal diseases, measles, and AIDS.

National economy

Budget (1993). Revenue: FBu 44,683,300,000 (excise duties 20.7%, customs duties 20.1%, taxes on goods and services 19.5%, income tax 14.2%, property tax 9.6%, administrative receipts 5.2%). Expenditures: FBu 46,609,700,-000 (goods and services 55.6%, subsidies and transfers 21.2%, public debt 10.9%).
Public debt (external, outstanding; 1992): U.S.$947,000,000.
Tourism (1992): receipts from visitors U.S.$4,000,000; expenditures by nationals abroad U.S.$21,000,000.
Production (metric tons except as noted). Agriculture, forestry, fishing (1992): bananas 1,625,600, sweet potatoes 697,600, cassavas 598,300, dry beans 345,900, corn (maize) 176,300, yams and taros 149,000, pumpkins 69,400, sorghum 66,800, potatoes 46,700, rice 40,400, coffee 37,100, palm kernels 14,900, peanuts (groundnuts) 14,200, millet 13,700, wheat 8,900, sugarcane 8,200; livestock (number of live animals) 932,000 goats, 440,000 cattle, 370,-000 sheep, 4,000,000 chickens; roundwood (1991) 4,343,000 cu m; fish catch (1991) 23,094. Mining and quarrying (1991): peat 10,026; kaolin clay 6,682; lime 86; gold 804 troy oz. Manufacturing (1993): beer 1,188,607 hectolitres; carbonated beverages 179,300 hectolitres; cigarettes 523,990,000 units; blankets 242,669 units; footwear 405,248 pairs. Construction: n.a. Energy production (consumption): electricity (kW-hr; 1992) 99,600,000 (142,500,000); coal, none (n.a.); crude petroleum, none (n.a.); petroleum products (metric tons; 1992) none (58,000); natural gas, none (n.a.); peat (metric tons; 1992) 12,000 (12,000).
Land use (1991): forested 2.6%; meadows and pastures 35.7%; agricultural and under permanent cultivation 52.6%; other 9.1%.

Gross national product (at current market prices; 1992): U.S.$1,193,000,000 (U.S.$210 per capita).

Structure of gross domestic product and labour force

	1991		1990	
	in value FBu '000,000[5]	% of total value	labour force	% of labour force
Agriculture	105,535.5	48.5	2,574,443	93.1
Mining	} 2,217.5	1.0	1,419	
Public utilities			1,672	0.1
Manufacturing	26,160.5	12.0	33,867	1.2
Construction	8,922.5	4.1	19,737	0.7
Transportation and communications	6,650.8	3.1	8,504	0.3
Trade	19,770.6	9.1	25,822	0.9
Finance	...	...	2,005	0.1
Pub. admin., defense	24,084.6	11.1 }	85,191	3.1
Services	3,844.4	1.8 }		
Other	20,302.4	9.3	13,270	0.5
TOTAL	217,548.8	100.0	2,765,945[2]	100.0

Population economically active (1991): total 2,779,777; activity rate of total population 52.9% (participation rates: ages 15–64, 91.4%; female 52.6%; unemployed, n.a.).

Price and earnings indexes (1985 = 100)

	1987	1988	1989	1990	1991	1992	1993
Consumer price index	109.3	114.0	127.3	136.3	148.5	155.2	170.3
Monthly earnings index[6]	101.8	...	...	...	...	...	...

Household income and expenditure. Average household size (1990) 4.6; income per household: n.a.; sources of income: n.a.; expenditure[7]: food 59.6%, clothing and footwear 11.1%, furniture and household goods 6.0%, energy and water 5.8%, housing 4.4%, other 13.1%.

Foreign trade[8]

Balance of trade (current prices)

	1987	1988	1989	1990	1991	1992
FBu '000,000	−12,273	−7,136	−13,719	−26,583	−28,144	−30,751
% of total	37.0%	16.6%	35.8%	51.0%	45.8%	50.0%

Imports (1992): FBu 46,105,700,000 (machinery and transport equipment 35.1%, food and food products 13.8%, mineral oil 10.2%, construction materials 6.2%). *Major import sources:* Belgium-Luxembourg 14.8%; France 11.1%; Tanzania 8.9%; Japan 8.1%; Germany 7.6%; United States 4.3%; China 3.7%.
Exports (1992): FBu 15,354,800,000 (coffee 65.3%, animal hides and skins 12.4%, cotton fabric 2.3%). *Major export destinations:* Germany 15.5%; United States 7.6%; Rwanda 7.6%; United Kingdom 5.8%; Kenya 4.9%; Zaire 3.4%; Switzerland 3.4%; France 2.8%; Zimbabwe 2.5%.

Transport and communications

Transport. Railroads: none. Roads (1991): total length 3,893 mi, 6,265 km (paved 16%). Vehicles (1992): passenger cars 14,483; trucks and other vehicles 14,914. Merchant marine (1979): vessels (100 gross tons and over) 1; total gross tonnage 385. Air transport (1992)[9]: passenger arrivals 33,176, departures 34,439; cargo loaded 1,780 short tons (1,615 metric tons), unloaded 4,151 short tons (3,766 metric tons); airports (1994) with scheduled flights 1.
Communications. Daily newspapers (1993): total number 1; total circulation 20,000; circulation per 1,000 population 3.5. Radio (1993): total number of receivers 500,000 (1 per 11 persons). Television (1993): total number of receivers 4,500 (1 per 1,259 persons). Telephones (1991): 10,857 (1 per 259 persons).

Education and health

Education (1991–92)

	schools[10]	teachers	students	student/ teacher ratio
Primary (age 6–11)	1,342	9,582	631,039	65.9
Secondary (age 12–18)	113	2,026[10]	46,508	21.8[10]
Higher	8	492	3,830	7.8

Educational attainment: n.a. *Literacy* (1990): percentage of total population age 7 and over literate 3,934,806 (74.3%); males literate 1,897,284 (73.7%); females literate 2,037,522 (74.9%).
Health (1990): physicians 168 (1 per 31,777 persons); hospital beds 10,370 (1 per 515 persons); infant mortality rate per 1,000 live births 111.0.
Food (1988–90): daily per capita caloric intake 1,948 (vegetable products 98%, animal products 2%); 84% of FAO recommended minimum requirement.

Military

Total active duty personnel (1993): 5,650 (army 97.3%, air force 2.7%). *Military expenditure as percentage of GNP* (1991): 2.4% (world 4.2%); per capita expenditure U.S.$5.

---

[1]A multiparty political system was approved by constitutional amendment of March 1992; presidential elections were held on June 1, 1993, and legislative elections on June 29, 1993. [2]Detail does not add to total given because of rounding. [3]Population is not adjusted for casualties or refugees of the recent civil war. [4]Based on land area. [5]Estimate. [6]Nonagricultural employees in Bujumbura only; includes family allowances. [7]Weights of consumer price index components. [8]Import figures are f.o.b. in balance of trade and c.i.f. in commodities and trading partners. [9]Figures for Bujumbura airport only. [10]1990–91.

Cambodia

Official name: Preah Reach Ana
Pak Kampuchea (Kingdom of
Cambodia)[1].
Form of government: constitutional
monarchy with one legislative house
(National Assembly [120]).
Chief of state: King.
Heads of government: First Prime
Minister assisted by Second Prime
Minister.
Capital: Phnom Penh.
Official language: Khmer.
Official religion: Buddhism.
Monetary unit: 1 riel = 100 sen;
valuation (Oct. 7, 1994)
1 U.S.$ = 2,587 riels; 1 £ = 4,115 riels.

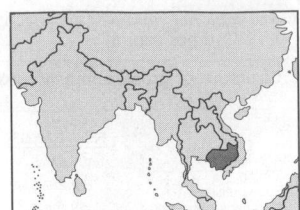

Area and population

Provinces	Capitals	area sq mi	area sq km	population 1987 estimate
Bântéay Méanchey	...	2	2	2
Bătdâmbâng	Bătdâmbâng	7,353[2]	19,044[2]	837,000[2]
Kâmpóng Cham	Kâmpóng Cham	4,053	10,498	1,244,000
Kâmpóng Chhnăng	Kâmpóng Chhnăng	2,131	5,520	257,000
Kâmpóng Saôm	Kâmpóng Saôm	27	69	61,000
Kâmpóng Spœ	Kâmpóng Spœ	2,709	7,016	396,000
Kâmpóng Thum	Kâmpóng Thum	4,730	12,251	441,000
Kâmpôt	Kâmpôt	3,808	9,862	412,000
Kândal	...	1,472	3,813	838,000
Kaôh Kŏng	Krŏng Kaôh Kŏng	4,301	11,140	30,000
Krâchéh	Krâchéh	4,283	11,094	182,000
Môndól Kiri	Senmonorom	5,517	14,288	18,000
Phnom Penh	Phnom Penh	18	46	564,000
Poŭthĭsăt	Poŭthĭsăt	4,900	12,692	204,000
Preăh Vihéar	Phnum Tbéng Meanchey	5,541	14,350	80,000
Prey Vêng	Prey Vêng	1,885	4,883	782,000
Rôtânôkiri	Lumphăt	4,163	10,782	52,000
Siĕmréab–Ŏtdâr Méanchey[3]	Siĕmréab	4,207	10,897	555,000
Stœng Trêng	Stœng Trêng	4,328	11,209	46,000
Svay Riĕng	Svay Riĕng	1,145	2,966	340,000
Takêv	Takêv	1,474	3,818	618,000
TOTAL LAND AREA		68,045	176,238	
INLAND WATER		2,192	5,678	
TOTAL		70,238[4]	181,916	7,957,000

Demography

Population (1994): 9,525,000.
Density (1994)[5]: persons per sq mi 140.0, persons per sq km 54.0.
Urban-rural (1991): urban 12.6%; rural 87.4%.
Sex distribution (1990): male 50%; female 50%.
Age breakdown (1990): under 15, 34.9%; 15–29, 29.6%; 30–44, 21.0%; 45–59, 9.6%; 60–74, 4.3%; 75 and over, 0.6%.
Population projection: (2000) 10,931,000; (2010) 13,357,000.
Ethnic composition (1979): Khmer 94.1%; Chinese 3.1%; Cham 2.3%; other (Thai, Lao, Kola, and Vietnamese) 0.5%.
Religious affiliation (1993): Buddhist 95%; Muslim 2%; other 3%.
Major cities (1987): Phnom Penh 900,000[6]; Bătdâmbâng 45,000; Kâmpóng Cham 33,000; Pursat 16,000; Kâmpóng Chhnăng 15,000.

Vital statistics

Birth rate per 1,000 population (1993): 40 (world avg. 26.0).
Death rate per 1,000 population (1993): 15 (world avg. 9.2).
Natural increase rate per 1,000 population (1993): 25 (world avg. 16.8).
Total fertility rate (avg. births per childbearing woman; 1993): 4.6.
Marriage rate per 1,000 population: n.a.
Divorce rate per 1,000 population: n.a.
Life expectancy at birth (1993): male 49 years; female 52 years.
Major causes of death per 100,000 population: n.a.; however, major health problems include tuberculosis, malaria, and pneumonia. Violence, acts of war, and unexploded military ordnance (especially mines) remain hazards.

National economy

Budget. Revenue (1993): 290,000,000,000 riels (customs duties 59.4%, state enterprises 23.3%, private enterprises 15.3%). Expenditures (1994): 890,-000,000,000 riels (public works and transport 19.2%, defense 18.4%, domestic affairs 9.7%, education and sports 8.6%, agriculture 7.8%, health 5.6%, postal and telecommunications services 3.8%, other 26.9%).
Public debt (external, outstanding; 1991): U.S.$1,564,000,000[7].
Tourism (1st quarter 1991): total number of tourist arrivals 8,989.
Production (metric tons except as noted). Agriculture, forestry, fishing (1993): rice 2,500,000, roots and tubers 227,000 (of which cassava 150,000, sweet potatoes 60,000), sugarcane 140,000, bananas 125,000, corn (maize) 60,000, rubber 40,000, soybeans 40,000, mangoes 25,000, pineapples 13,000, tobacco leaves 9,000; livestock (number of live animals) 2,468,000 cattle, 2,043,000 pigs, 804,000 buffalo, 14,000,000 poultry; roundwood (1992) 6,840,000 cu m (the Khmer Rouge market additional quantities to Thailand); fish catch (1991) 110,100. Mining and quarrying (1993): legal mining is confined to fertilizers, salt, and construction materials; smuggling of gemstones from Khmer Rouge-controlled areas is believed extensive. Manufacturing (value of production in '000,000 riels; 1988): cigarettes 1,064.5; food 116.9; chemical products (including rubber) 83.5; light industries (including textiles) 63.2; mechanical equipment and parts 46.8; building materials 4.5. Construction: n.a. Energy production (consumption): electricity (kW-hr; 1992) 150,000,000 (150,000,000); petroleum products (metric tons; 1992) none (155,000).

Household income and expenditure. Average household size (1980) 5.6.
Gross domestic product (1993): U.S.$1,580,000,000 (U.S.$170 per capita).

Structure of gross domestic product and labour force

	1993 in value '000,000 riels	1993 % of total value	Jan. 1992 labour force	Jan. 1992 % of labour force
Agriculture	2,623.9	47.3	2,495,000	69.4
Mining and manufacturing	302.2	5.4		
Construction	453.9	8.2		
Public utilities	46.0	0.8		
Transp. and commun.	114.8	2.1	1,100,000	30.6
Trade	930.8	16.8		
Public admin., defense	226.4	4.1		
Services	850.0	15.3		
Other				
TOTAL	5,548.0	100.0	3,595,000	100.0

Population economically active (1992): total 3,964,000; activity rate of total population 43.1% (participation rates: ages 16–60, 91.2%; female 55.7%).

Price and earnings indexes (1990 = 100)

	1989	1990	1991	1992	1993
Consumer price index	41.4	100.0	297.0	519.7	1,113.9
Earnings index	...	...	...	...	...

Land use (1992): forested 65.7%; meadows and pastures 11.3%; agricultural and under permanent cultivation 13.6%; other 9.4%.

Foreign trade[8]

Balance of trade (current prices)

	1988	1989	1990	1991	1992	1993
U.S.$'000,000	−124.5	−96.8	−77.7	−32.5	−86.2	−184.8
% of total	58.2%	37.9%	31.2%	7.1%	14.0%	29.7%

Imports (1993): U.S.$403,900,000 (cigarettes 14.1%, construction materials 12.1%, petroleum products 11.7%, electronics 8.2%). *Major import sources:* Singapore 24.3%; Vietnam 17.5%; Japan 8.2%; Australia 5.1%.
Exports (1993)[9]: U.S.$219,100,000 (felled and sawn timber 52.1%; rubber 22.5%; fish and fish products 4.5%; soybeans 1.1%). *Major export destinations*[9]: Singapore 65.8%; Japan 10.6%; Hong Kong 5.0%.

Transport and communications

Transport. Railroads (1988): length 403 mi, 649 km; passenger-mi 33,554,-000[10], passenger-km 54,000,000[10]; short ton-mi cargo 6,850,000[10], metric ton-km cargo 10,000,000[10]. Roads (1989): total length 9,200 mi, 14,800 km (paved 18%). Vehicles (1988): passenger cars 4,000; trucks and buses 7,100. Merchant marine (1992): vessels (100 gross tons and over) 3; total deadweight tonnage 3,839. Air transport (1977): passenger-mi 26,098,800, passenger-km 42,000,000; short ton-mi cargo 274,000, metric ton-km cargo 400,000; airports (1994) with scheduled flights 6.
Communications. Daily newspapers (1991): total number 1. Radio (1993): 1,000,000 receivers (1 per 9 persons). Television (1993): 70,000 receivers (1 per 133 persons). Telephones (1991): 5,500[11] (1 per 1,600 persons).

Education and health

Education (1992–93)

	schools	teachers	students	student/ teacher ratio
Primary (age 6–10)	4,539	42,405	1,465,958	34.6
Secondary (age 11–16)	440	19,540	239,363	12.2
Voc., teacher tr.	65	2,618	15,537	5.9
Higher	9	268	22,182	82.8

Educational attainment: n.a. *Literacy* (1987): total population age 15 and over literate 3,778,042 (74.3%); males literate 2,001,084 (85.0%); females literate 1,776,958 (65.0%).
Health: physicians (1990) 600 (1 per 14,300 persons); hospital beds (1988) 12,953[12] (1 per 632[12] persons); infant mortality rate per 1,000 live births (1993) 112.
Food (1986–88): daily per capita caloric intake 2,174 (vegetable products 95%, animal products 5%); 81% of FAO recommended minimum requirement.

Military

Total active duty personnel (1994): 88,500[13] (army 40.7%, navy 2.3%, air force 0.6%, provincial 56.4%). Armed Khmer Rouge guerrillas may number 10,000–12,000. About 22,000 UNTAC[1] troops were withdrawn after civilian government was reestablished in 1993.

[1]The United Nations Transitional Authority in Cambodia (UNTAC) assumed administrative responsibility for Cambodia in March 1992. Cambodian sovereignty, however, was retained by a Supreme National Council (SNC) until UN-supervised elections were held May 23–29, 1993. The Kingdom of Cambodia was proclaimed from Sept. 24, 1993. [2]Bântéay Méanchey included in Bătdâmbâng. [3]The province of Ŏtdâr Méanchey has been combined with Siĕmréab, and area and population figures reflect the change. [4]Detail does not add to total given because of rounding. [5]Based on land area. [6]1991. [7]Includes long-term debt not guaranteed by the government. [8]Trade statistics do not indicate whether imports are c.i.f. or f.o.b.; illegal or undeclared trade is not accounted for in the foreign-trade figures shown here. [9]Figures include reexports of U.S.$181,400,000 and direct exports of U.S.$37,700,000; percentage breakdowns are derived from direct exports and exclude reexports. [10]1981. [11]Number of telephone lines. [12]Public hospitals only. [13]Figures include provincial, and exclude paramilitary, forces.

Cameroon

Official name: République du Cameroun (French); Republic of Cameroon (English).
Form of government: unitary multiparty republic with one legislative house (National Assembly [180]).
Chief of state: President.
Head of government: Prime Minister.
Capital: Yaoundé.
Official languages: French; English.
Official religion: none.
Monetary unit: 1 CFA franc (CFAF) = 100 centimes; valuation (Oct. 7, 1994) 1 U.S.$ = CFAF 526.67; 1 £ = CFAF 837.67.

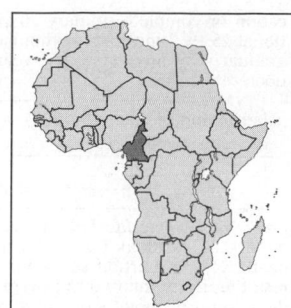

Area and population

Provinces	Capitals	area sq mi	area sq km	population 1987 census
Adamoua	Ngaoundéré	24,591	63,691	495,200
Centre	Yaoundé	26,613	68,926	1,661,600
Est	Bertoua	42,089	109,011	517,200
Extrême-Nord	Maroua	13,223	34,246	1,855,700
Littoral	Douala	7,814	20,239	1,354,800
Nord	Garoua	25,319	65,576	832,200
Nord-Ouest	Bamenda	6,877	17,810	1,237,400
Ouest	Bafoussam	5,356	13,872	1,339,800
Sud	Ebolowa	18,189	47,110	373,800
Sud-Ouest	Buea	9,448	24,471	838,000
LAND AREA		179,519	464,952	
INLAND WATER		4,051	10,492	
TOTAL		183,569[1]	475,442[1]	10,495,700

Demography

Population (1994): 12,905,000.
Density (1994)[2]: persons per sq mi 71.9, persons per sq km 27.7.
Urban-rural (1991): urban 41.2%; rural 58.8%.
Sex distribution (1991): male 49.88%; female 50.12%.
Age breakdown (1991): under 15, 46.4%; 15–29, 24.4%; 30–44, 15.1%; 45–59, 8.6%; 60 and over, 5.5%.
Population projection: (2000) 15,293,000; (2010) 20,225,000.
Doubling time: 25 years.
Ethnic composition (1983): Fang 19.6%; Bamileke and Bamum 18.5%; Duala, Luanda, and Basa 14.7%; Fulani 9.6%; Tikar 7.4%; Mandara 5.7%; Maka 4.9%; Chamba 2.4%; Mbum 1.3%; Hausa 1.2%; French 0.2%; other 14.5%.
Religious affiliation (1990): Roman Catholic 34.7%; animist 26.0%; Muslim 21.8%; Protestant 17.5%.
Major cities (1987): Douala 810,000; Yaoundé 649,000; Garoua 142,000; Maroua 123,000; Bafoussam 113,000.

Vital statistics

Birth rate per 1,000 population (1990–95): 40.7 (world avg. 26.0).
Death rate per 1,000 population (1990–95): 12.2 (world avg. 9.2).
Natural increase rate per 1,000 population (1990–95): 28.5 (world avg. 16.8).
Total fertility rate (avg. births per childbearing woman; 1990–95): 5.7.
Life expectancy at birth (1990–95): male 54.5 years; female 57.5 years.
Major causes of death per 100,000 population: n.a.; however, major health problems include measles, malaria, tuberculosis of respiratory system, anemias, meningitis, and intestinal obstruction and hernia.

National economy

Budget (1991–92). Revenue: CFAF 545,000,000,000 (direct taxes 36.0%; customs duties 28.3%; petroleum royalties 22.0%). Expenditures: CFAF 545,000,000,000 (current expenditure 69.4%, of which education 13.0%, defense 8.8%, administration 4.6%, health 4.5%, finance 3.1%).
Public debt (external, outstanding; 1992): U.S.$5,465,000,000.
Gross national product (at current market prices; 1993): U.S.$9,710,000,000 (U.S.$770 per capita).

Structure of gross domestic product and labour force

	1991 in value CFAF '000,000	1991 % of total value	1985 labour force	1985 % of labour force
Agriculture	740	23.9	2,900,871	74.0
Mining	406	12.9	1,793	0.1
Manufacturing	424	13.5	174,498	4.5
Construction	165	5.3	66,684	1.7
Public utilities	38	1.2	3,522	0.1
Transp. and commun.	195	6.2	51,688	1.3
Trade	368	11.7	154,014	3.9
Finance	417	13.3	8,009	0.2
Public admin., defense	310	9.9 }	292,922	7.5
Services	66	2.1 }		
Other	...	...	263,634	6.7
TOTAL	3,138	100.0	3,917,635	100.0

Household income and expenditure. Average household size (1980) 5.2; average annual income per household (1983)[3] U.S.$420; sources of income: n.a.; expenditure (1983)[3]: food 33.6%, clothing and footwear 16.3%, housing 14.6%, transportation and communications 10.5%, recreation 5.1%, health 5.0%.
Tourism: receipts from visitors (1992) U.S.$18,000,000; expenditures by nationals abroad (1991) U.S.$182,000,000.

Population economically active (1991): total 4,740,000; activity rate of total population 40.0% (participation rates [1985]: ages 15–69, 66.3%; female 38.5%; unemployed, n.a.).

Price and earnings indexes (1990 = 100)

	1987	1988	1989	1990	1991	1992
Consumer price index	98.7	93.2	98.3	100.0	101.9	103.3
Earnings index	...	...	...	...	...	...

Production (metric tons except as noted). Agriculture, forestry, fishing (1993): sugarcane 1,350,000, cassava 1,300,000, plantains 860,000, vegetables and melons 463,000, corn (maize) 430,000, sweet potatoes 165,000, palm oil 120,000, bananas 100,000, peanuts (groundnuts) 100,000, cacao 100,000, yams 93,000, rice 90,000, millet 60,000, palm kernels 54,000; livestock (number of live animals) 4,867,000 cattle, 3,770,000 sheep, 3,767,000 goats, 1,434,000 pigs; roundwood (1992) 14,600,000 cu m; fish catch (1991) 78,000. Mining and quarrying (1992): marble 200,000; pozzolana 130,000; aluminum 82,000; limestone 57,000; tin ore and concentrate 4. Manufacturing (1990): cement 781,000; wheat flour 49,000[4]; soap 31,000; footwear 1,567,000 pairs; sawn wood 489,000 cu m; beer 6,815,000 hectolitres; soft drinks 1,172,000 hectolitres[4]. Construction (1983): residential 230,400 sq m; nonresidential 51,100 sq m. Energy production (consumption): electricity (kW-hr; 1992) 2,720,000,000 (2,720,000,000); coal (metric tons; 1992) 1,000 (1,000); crude petroleum (barrels; 1992) 50,565,000 (5,007,000); petroleum products (metric tons; 1992) 618,000 (609,000); natural gas, none (n.a.).
Land use (1992): forested 52.3%; meadows and pastures 17.8%; agricultural and under permanent cultivation 15.1%; other 14.8%.

Foreign trade[5]

Balance of trade (current prices)

	1987	1988	1989	1990	1991	1992
CFAF '000,000,000	−228.3	−68.8	+40.3	+141.5	+198.6	+197.6
% of total	32.1%	11.1%	5.2%	14.8%	22.3%	25.9%

Imports (1991): CFAF 650,610,000,000 (machinery and transport equipment 27.2%, of which road vehicles 5.5%; chemical products 14.7%; food and live animals 13.6%; iron and steel 4.6%; paper and paper products 3.5%; textiles 3.5%; nonmetallic minerals 3.0%). *Major import sources:* France 27.3%; Germany 8.6%; United States 6.6%; Belgium-Luxembourg 5.1%; Guinea 4.7%; Italy 4.6%; Spain 3.8%.
Exports (1991): CFAF 815,994,000,000 (crude petroleum 47.4%; cocoa 12.5%; sawn wood and logs 5.3%; cotton 3.8%; coffee 3.0%). *Major export destinations:* The Netherlands 24.8%; France 16.8%; Italy 8.0%; Gibraltar 7.9%; Spain 6.3%; Morocco 5.1%; Gabon 3.5%; Germany 2.1%.

Transport and communications

Transport. Railroads (1990–91): route length 686 mi, 1,104 km; passenger-mi 268,000,000, passenger-km 431,000,000; short ton-mi cargo 401,000,000, metric ton-km cargo 585,000,000. Roads (1991): total length 30,074 mi, 48,400 km (paved 8%). Vehicles (1992): passenger cars 95,000; trucks and buses 80,000. Merchant marine (1992): vessels (100 gross tons and over) 47, total deadweight tonnage 39,797. Air transport (1991): passenger-mi 187,000,000, passenger-km 301,000,000; short ton-mi cargo 6,800,000, metric ton-km cargo 10,000,000; airports (1994) with scheduled flights 5.
Communications. Daily newspapers (1993): 1; total circulation 20,000; circulation per 1,000 population 1.6. Radio (1993): total number of receivers 2,000,000 (1 per 6.3 persons). Television (1993): total number of receivers 15,000 (1 per 836 persons). Telephones (1991): 53,000 (1 per 224 persons).

Education and health

Education (1990–91)

	schools	teachers	students	student/teacher ratio
Primary (age 6–14)	6,709	38,430	1,964,146	51.1
Secondary (age 15–24)	388[6]	11,400[7]	409,729	32.2[7]
Voc., teacher tr.	220[6]	6,267[7]	90,543	14.5[7]
Higher	5[6]	1,086	33,177	30.5

Educational attainment (1976). Percentage of population age 15 and over having: no schooling 51.1%; primary education 41.7%; some postprimary 0.2%; secondary 5.7%; some postsecondary 0.3%; higher 0.2%; other 0.8%.
Literacy (1990): percentage of total population age 15 and over literate 54.1%; males literate 66.3%; females literate 42.6%.
Health: physicians (1987) 888 (1 per 11,898 persons); hospital beds (1988) 29,285 (1 per 371 persons); infant mortality rate (1990–95) 86.0.
Food (1988–90): daily per capita caloric intake 2,208 (vegetable products 93%, animal products 7%); 95% of FAO recommended minimum requirement.

Military

Total active duty personnel (1994): 14,600 (army 89.0%, navy 8.9%, air force 2.1%). *Military expenditure as percentage of GNP* (1991): 1.6% (world 4.2%); per capita expenditure U.S.$14.

---

[1]Detail does not add to total given because of rounding. [2]Based on land area. [3]Capital city only. [4]1988. [5]Import figures are f.o.b. in balance of trade and c.i.f. for commodities and trading partners. [6]1986–87. [7]1989–90.

Canada

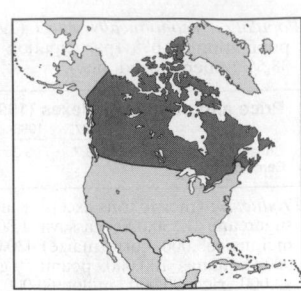

Official name: Canada.
Form of government: federal multiparty parliamentary state with two legislative houses (Senate [104]; House of Commons [295]).
Chief of state: Queen of Canada (British Monarch).
Representative of chief of state: Governor-General.
Head of government: Prime Minister.
Capital: Ottawa.
Official languages: English; French.
Official religion: none.
Monetary unit: 1 Canadian dollar (Can$) = 100 cents; valuation (Oct. 7, 1994) 1 U.S.$ = Can$1.35; 1 £ = Can$2.14.

Area and population

Provinces	Capitals	area sq mi	area sq km	population 1993 estimate
Alberta	Edmonton	255,287	661,190	2,662,000
British Columbia	Victoria	365,948	947,800	3,535,000
Manitoba	Winnipeg	250,947	649,950	1,116,000
New Brunswick	Fredericton	28,355	73,440	751,000
Newfoundland	St. John's	156,649	405,720	581,000
Nova Scotia	Halifax	21,425	55,490	923,000
Ontario	Toronto	412,581	1,068,580	10,746,000
Prince Edward Island	Charlottetown	2,185	5,660	132,000
Quebec	Quebec	594,860	1,540,680	7,209,000
Saskatchewan	Regina	251,866	652,330	1,003,000
Territories				
Northwest Territories	Yellowknife	1,322,910	3,426,320	63,000
Yukon Territory	Whitehorse	186,661	483,450	32,000
TOTAL		3,849,674	9,970,610	28,753,000

Demography

Population (1994): 29,107,000.
Density (1994)[1]: persons per sq mi 8.2, persons per sq km 3.2.
Urban-rural (1992): urban 77.5%; rural 22.5%.
Sex distribution (1993): male 49.54%; female 50.46%.
Age breakdown (1993): under 15, 20.7%; 15–29, 22.1%; 30–44, 25.3%; 45–59, 15.9%; 60–74, 11.2%; 75 and over, 4.8%.
Population projection: (2000) 31,325,000; (2010) 35,050,000.
Doubling time: 99 years.
Ethnic origin (1991): French 22.8%; British 20.8%; German 3.4%; Italian 2.8%; Chinese 2.2%; Amerindian and Inuktitut (Eskimo) 1.7%; Ukrainian 1.5%; Dutch 1.3%; multiple origin and other 43.5%[2].
Religious affiliation (1991): Roman Catholic 45.2%; Protestant 36.2%; Eastern Orthodox 1.5%; nonreligious 12.4%; other 4.7%.
Major metropolitan areas (1991): Toronto 3,893,046; Montreal 3,127,242; Vancouver 1,602,502; Ottawa-Hull 920,857; Edmonton 839,924; Calgary 754,033; Winnipeg 652,354; Quebec 645,550; Hamilton 599,760; London 381,522.

Other metropolitan areas (1991)

	population		population		population
Chicoutimi-		Regina	191,692	Sherbrooke	139,194
Jonquière	160,928	St. Catharines–		Sudbury	157,613
Halifax	320,501	Niagara	364,552	Trois Rivières	136,303
Kitchener	356,421	St. John's	171,859	Victoria	287,897
Oshawa	240,104	Saskatoon	210,023	Windsor	262,075

Place of birth (1986): 84.2% native-born; 15.8% foreign-born, of which United Kingdom 3.2%, other European 6.6%, Asian countries 3.2%, other 2.8%.
Mobility (1986). Population living in the same residence as in 1981: 56.3%; different residence, same municipality 24.2%; same province, different municipality 13.5%; different province 4.0%; different country 2.0%.
Households (1991). Total number of households 10,018,267. Average household size 2.7; (1985) 1 person 22.9%, 2 persons 31.4%, 3 persons 17.4%, 4 persons 17.6%, 5 persons 7.3%, 6 or more persons 3.4%. Family households: 7,356,168 (73.4%), nonfamily 2,662,099 (26.6%, of which 1 person 22.9%).
Immigration (1992): permanent immigrants admitted 248,200, from Hong Kong 15.2%, Indonesia 5.2%, India 5.1%, Poland 4.7%, China 4.1%, Vietnam 3.1%; United States 2.9%; refugee arrivals 28,699.

Vital statistics

Birth rate per 1,000 population (1992–93): 14.1 (world avg. 26.0); (1985) legitimate 83.8%; illegitimate 16.2%.
Death rate per 1,000 population (1992–93): 7.1 (world avg. 9.2).
Natural increase rate per 1,000 population (1992–93): 7.0 (world avg. 16.8).
Total fertility rate (avg. births per childbearing woman; 1992): 1.9.
Marriage rate per 1,000 population (1992–93): 4.5.
Divorce rate per 1,000 population (1992–93): 1.7.
Life expectancy at birth (1994): male 74.7 years; female 81.7 years.
Major causes of death per 100,000 population (1991): diseases of the circulatory system 278.6; malignant neoplasms (cancers) 197.7; diseases of the respiratory system 61.6; accidents and violence 48.5.

Social indicators

Educational attainment (1986). Percentage of population age 25 and over having: no formal schooling, negligible; less than complete primary education or complete primary 20.6%; secondary 35.0%; postsecondary vocational 25.1%; university without degree 8.3%; completed university 11.0%; graduates by level (1987): 4-year higher degree 101,960, master's 15,790, doctorate 2,385.

Distribution of income (1991)

percentage of national income by quintile

1	2	3	4	5 (highest)
5.3%	13.6%	19.7%	25.9%	35.5%

Quality of working life (1992). Average workweek: 38.3 hours. Annual rate per 100,000 workers for (1990): injury, accident, or industrial illness 7,543; death 5.1[3]. Proportion of labour force insured for damages or income loss resulting from: injury 99%; permanent disability 99%; death 99%. Average days lost to labour stoppages per 1,000 employee-workdays (1992): 0.4. Average duration of journey to work (1983): 23 minutes[4] (17.3% public transportation, 72.8% automobile, 9.9% other). Rate per 1,000 workers of discouraged (unemployed no longer seeking work; 1983): 10.5.
Access to services (1990). Proportion of households having access to: electricity 100.0%; public water supply 99.8%; public sewage collection 99.3%.
Social participation. Eligible voters participating in last national election (October 1993): 69.7%. Population over 18 years of age participating in voluntary work (1987): 27.0%. Union membership in total workforce (1992): 29.7%. Practicing religious population in total affiliated population (1991): 87.6%.
Social deviance (1991). Offense rate per 100,000 population for: violent crime 1,085, of which assault 8.8, sexual assault 111.0, homicide 2.8; property crime 6,316, of which auto theft 510, burglary and housebreaking 1,589. Incidence per 100,000 in general population of: alcoholism 2,285; drug and substance abuse 258; suicide (1990) 11.5.
Leisure (1992). Favourite leisure activities (hours weekly): television 15.3; social time 12.7; reading 3.5; sports and entertainment 0.9.
Material well-being (1988). Households possessing: automobile 88.3%, of which two or more 25.1%; telephone 98.5%[5]; radio 99.1%[5]; television receiver 99.0%[5]; refrigerator 99.6%; central air conditioner 24.6%[6]; automatic washing machine 77.0%; cable television 69.0%; videocassette recorder 58.8%[6]; microwave oven 63.4%[6].

National economy

Gross national product (1993): U.S.$574,936,000,000 (U.S.$20,670 per capita).

Structure of gross domestic product and labour force

	1993 in value Can$'000,000[7]	1993 % of total value	1994 labour force	1994 % of labour force
Agriculture	16,165	3.1	419,000	3.0
Mining	21,614	4.2	255,000	1.8
Manufacturing	92,431	17.9	1,820,000	12.9
Construction	27,624	5.3	655,000	4.7
Public utilities	16,316	3.2	928,000	6.6
Transportation and communications	44,087	8.5		
Trade	62,735	12.1	2,196,000	15.6
Finance	87,145	16.8	764,000	5.4
Pub. admin., defense	33,785	6.5	840,000	6.0
Services	115,494	22.3	4,620,000	32.9
Other	—	—	1,559,000[8]	11.1[8]
TOTAL	517,396[9]	100.0[10]	14,056,000	100.0

Budget (1992–93). Revenue: Can$140,981,000,000 (income taxes 54.3%, sales tax 21.0%, import duties 2.6%). Expenditures: Can$170,019,000,000 (public debt interest 23.3%, defense 7.0%, health 4.5%, education 2.6%, foreign assistance 2.2%).
National debt (1990–91): Can$443,278,000,000.
Tourism (1992): receipts from visitors U.S.$5,679,000,000; expenditures by nationals abroad U.S.$11,265,000,000.

Manufacturing, mining, and construction enterprises (1990)

	no. of establishments	no. of employees	hourly wages as a % of avg. of all mfg. wages	annual value added (Can$'000,000)
Manufacturing				
Food and beverages	3,657	222,000	91.3	18,260
Transport equipment	1,469	204,000	120.1	16,480
Chemicals and related products	1,629	101,000	115.0	12,910
Paper and related products	715	114,000	133.0	10,210
Printing, publishing, and related products	5,522	142,000	110.4	8,950
Machinery	4,694	148,000	96.0	8,840
Electrical and electronics products	1,378	123,000	97.2	8,710
Primary metals	493	97,000	150.8	7,530
Metal fabricating	3,913	135,000	94.1	7,530
Wood	2,672	104,000	100.9	5,210
Rubber and plastic	1,547	87,000	86.0	5,010
Clothing	2,994	110,000	59.2	3,880
Textiles	1,337	72,000	76.2	3,470
Nonmetallic mineral products	1,447	41,000	103.3	3,270
Furniture and fixtures	2,607	66,000	73.1	2,620
Petroleum and coal products	154	18,000	150.2	2,990
Tobacco products industries	18	5,000	...	1,140
Mining	1,232	113,000	149.3[11, 12]	29,650
Construction[13]	...	800,000	112.3[12]	28,182

Production (metric tons except as noted). Agriculture, forestry, fishing (1993): wheat 27,825,000, barley 13,342,000, corn (maize) 6,300,000, rapeseed 5,400,000, oats 3,615,000, potatoes 3,333,000, soybeans 1,900,000, vegetables 1,878,000 (of which tomatoes 475,000, carrots 310,000, onions 144,000, cabbage 135,000), sugar beets 1,050,000, linseed 620,000, hops 490,000, apples 482,000, rye 314,000, lentils 300,000, pelts (1992) 1,919,025 units; livestock (number of live animals) 11,786,000 cattle, 10,572,000 pigs, 662,000 sheep, 420,000 horses;

roundwood (1992) 186,049,000 cu m; fish catch (1993) 1,082,071. Mining and quarrying (1993): iron ore 31,720,000; zinc 998,234; copper 698,799; lead 187,554; nickel 180,763; molybdenum 10,006; uranium 9,015; silver 869; gold 4,905,400 troy oz. Manufacturing (value in Can$'000,000; 1992): transportation equipment 54,049; food and beverages 44,124; chemical products 21,963; paper products 20,797; electrical products 17,567; petroleum and coal products 16,995; metal products 14,976; printing and publishing 12,631; rubber and plastic products 8,467; clothing 5,993; textiles 5,693; furniture 3,937; tobacco products 2,251; leather products 912. Construction (value of building permits; 1993): residential Can$16,405,000,000; nonresidential Can$9,150,000,000.

Service enterprises (1988)

	no. of enter-prises	no. of employees[14]	weekly wages as a % of all wages	annual sales (Can$'000,000)
Retail trade				
Motor vehicle dealers	...	79,800	...	35,917
Food stores	...	213,400	...	35,187
Service stations	...	63,700	...	14,612
Department stores	...	[15]	...	13,271
Clothing stores	...	50,200	...	7,486
Pharmacies	...	52,400	...	7,459
Furniture and appliance stores	...	62,100	...	4,447
Automotive stores	...	31,500	...	3,767
General merchandise	...	231,700[15]	...	3,109
Sporting goods	...	...	...	2,669
General stores	...	[15]	...	2,415
Hardware stores	...	17,300	...	1,824
Shoe stores	...	18,400	...	1,599
Jewelry stores	...	14,000	...	1,215
Variety stores	...	45,100	...	1,057

Energy production (consumption): electricity (kW-hr; 1992) 520,857,000,000 (495,806,000,000); coal (metric tons; 1992) 65,362,000 (52,386,000); crude petroleum (barrels; 1992) 587,706,000 (468,503,000); petroleum products (metric tons; 1992) 80,718,000 (72,989,000); natural gas (cu m; 1992) 122,439,000,000 (69,413,000,000).
Population economically active (1994): total 14,056,000; activity rate of total population 48.3% (participation rates: ages 15–64, 75.2%[16]; female 45.0%; unemployed 11.1%).

Price and earnings indexes (1990 = 100)

	1987	1988	1989	1990	1991	1992	1993
Consumer price index	87.4	90.9	95.3	100.0	105.6	107.2	109.2
Hourly earnings index[17]	85.7	89.7	94.6	100.0	105.5	108.2	110.5

Household income and expenditure (1991). Average household size 2.8; average annual income per family Can$51,856 (U.S.$45,261); sources of income: wages and salaries 63.8%, transfer payments 16.6%, self-employment 6.6%, other 13.0%; expenditure: housing 24.4%[18], food 15.8%, transportation and communications 15.6%, household durable goods 9.0%, recreation 8.2%, clothing 5.2%, health 4.1%, education 3.0%.

Financial aggregates

	1988	1989	1990	1991	1992	1993	1994[19]
Exchange rate, Can$ per:							
U.S. dollar	1.23	1.18	1.17	1.14	1.21	1.29	1.35
£	2.18	1.94	2.08	2.03	2.14	1.94	2.12
SDR	1.60	1.52	1.65	1.65	1.75	1.82	1.97
International reserves (U.S.$)							
Total (excl. gold; '000,000)	15,391	16,055	17,845	16,252	11,431	12,481	15,589
SDRs ('000,000)	1,369	1,377	1,526	1,582	1,039	1,062	1,149
Reserve pos. in IMF ('000,000)	505	528	517	592	1,011	948	931
Foreign exchange ('000,000)	13,517	14,150	15,802	14,079	9,382	10,471	13,508
Gold ('000,000 fine troy oz)	17.14	16.10	14.76	12.96	9.94	6.05	4.20
% world reserves	1.81	1.71	1.56	1.38	1.07	0.65	0.45
Interest and prices							
Central bank discount (%)	11.17	12.47	11.78	7.67	7.36	4.11	6.00
Govt. bond yield (%)	10.22	9.92	10.85	9.76	8.77	8.75	9.04
Industrial share prices (1990 = 100)	96.5	111.1	100.0	101.4	99.5	114.1	127.3
Balance of payments (U.S.$'000,000)							
Balance of visible trade,	8,157	5,986	8,330	3,695	5,981	7,612	...
of which:							
Imports, f.o.b.	−107,274	−116,985	−120,108	122,308	126,370	136,418	...
Exports, f.o.b.	115,432	122,971	128,438	126,003	132,351	144,030	...
Balance of invisibles	−25,263	−28,714	−29,878	−27,747	−27,951	−31,481	...
Balance of payments, current account	−17,106	22,728	21,548	24,052	22,060	23,069	...

Land use (1992): forested 39.2%; meadows and pastures 3.0%; agricultural and under permanent cultivation 4.9%; built-on, wasteland, and other 52.9%.

Foreign trade

Balance of trade (current prices)

	1988	1989	1990	1991	1992	1993
Can$'000,000,000	8.2	6.0	8.8	5.2	8.2	12.1
% of total	3.7%	2.5%	3.5%	2.1%	3.2%	3.4%

Imports (1993): Can$169,316,000,000 (machinery and transport equipment 54.9%, of which motor vehicles 23.5%; food, feed, beverages, and tobacco 6.5%; petroleum and energy products 4.1%; forestry products 0.9%). *Major import sources* (1992): United States 65.1%; Japan 7.3%; United Kingdom 2.8%; Germany 2.4%; France 2.0%; Mexico 1.9%; China 1.7%; South Korea 1.4%; Italy 1.2%; Norway 1.1%.

Exports (1993): Can$181,026,000,000 (1992; machinery and transport equipment 37.5%, of which motor vehicles 22.1%; mineral fuels 10.3%, of which crude petroleum 4.1%, natural gas 2.9%; food 7.9%, of which wheat 2.9%; newsprint 3.5%; industrial machinery 3.3%; lumber 3.2%; wood pulp 3.1%; office equipment 2.5%; aluminum 2.0%; refined petroleum products 1.4%). *Major export destinations* (1992): United States 77.9%; Japan 4.7%; United Kingdom 1.9%; Germany 1.4%; China 1.4%; The Netherlands 0.9%; South Korea 0.9%; France 0.9%; Russia 0.8%; Italy 0.7%; Mexico 0.5%; Australia 0.5%.

Trade by commodities (1992)

SITC Group	imports U.S.$'000,000	imports %	exports U.S.$'000,000	exports %
00 Food and live animals	6,834.9	5.6	10,593.5	7.9
01 Beverages and tobacco	643.0	0.5	1,063.1	0.8
02 Crude materials, excluding fuels	3,885.2	3.2	15,713.8	11.7
03 Mineral fuels, lubricants, and related materials	5,364.1	4.4	13,808.8	10.3
04 Animal and vegetable oils, fats, and waxes	...	...	...	...
05 Chemicals and related products, n.e.s.	8,751.7	7.1	6,967.5	5.2
06 Basic manufactures	15,236.4	12.4	21,484.1	16.0
07 Machinery and transport equipment	61,848.9	50.5	50,304.6	37.5
08 Miscellaneous manufactured articles	15,302.6	12.5	5,672.2	4.2
09 Goods not classified by kind	4,455.4	3.6	8,284.0	6.2
TOTAL	122,475.3[10]	100.0[10]	134,165.7[10]	100.0[10]

Direction of trade (1993)

	imports Can$'000,000	imports %	exports Can$'000,000	exports %
Africa	1,345	0.8	826	0.5
Asia	23,347	14.3	15,442	9.1
Americas	112,444	69.0	141,552	83.2
United States	106,074	65.0	138,333	81.3
Mexico	3,543	2.2	724	0.4
South America	2,072	1.3	1,875	1.1
Other Americas	755	0.5	620	0.4
Europe	17,311	10.6	11,474	6.7
EEC	15,183	9.3	9,435	5.5
Russia	82	0.1	106	0.1
Other Europe	2,046	1.2	1,933	1.1
Oceania	1,226	0.8	826	0.5
TOTAL	163,070[20]	100.0[20]	170,122[21]	100.0

Transport and communications

Transport. Railroads (1992): length 53,166 mi[22], 85,563 km[22]; passenger-mi 851,900,000, passenger-km 1,371,000,000; short ton-mi cargo 166,057,000,000, metric ton-km cargo 242,439,000,000. Roads (1991): total length 527,794 mi, 849,404 km (paved 35%). Vehicles (1991): passenger cars 13,061,084; trucks and buses 3,744,012. Merchant marine (1992): vessels (100 gross tons and over) 1,185; total deadweight tonnage 2,896,830. Air transport (1992): passenger-mi 25,633,000,000, passenger-km 41,253,000,000; short ton-mi cargo 855,980,000, metric ton-km cargo 1,249,700,000; airports (1994) with scheduled flights 244.
Communications. Daily newspapers (1993): total number 108; total circulation 5,500,000; circulation per 1,000 population 195. Radio (1993): total number of receivers 22,600,000 (1 per 1.3 persons). Television (1993): total number of receivers 17,400,000 (1 per 1.6 persons). Telephones (1987): 20,126,490 (1 per 1.3 persons).

Education and health

Education (1993–94)

	schools	teachers	students	student/teacher ratio
Primary (age 6–14)[23]	16,231	300,797	5,360,900	17.8
Secondary (age 14–18)[23]	...	...	...	...
Postsecondary and higher	272	64,100	921,300	14.4

Literacy (1986): total population age 15 and over literate 18,745,000 (96.6%); males literate (1975) 8,003,000 (95.6%); females literate (1975) 8,182,000 (95.7%).
Health: physicians (1991) 60,559 (1 per 464 persons); hospital beds (1989) 183,775 (1 per 149 persons); infant mortality rate per 1,000 live births (1994) 6.9.
Food (1988–90): daily per capita caloric intake 3,242 (vegetable products 68%, animal products 32%); 122% of FAO recommended minimum requirement.

Military

Total active duty personnel (1994): 78,100 (army 25.6%, navy 16.0%, air force 26.4%, not identified by service 32.0%). *Military expenditure as percentage of GNP* (1991): 2.0% (world 4.2%); per capita expenditure U.S.$427.

[1]Based on land area of 3,558,096 sq mi (9,215,430 sq km). [2]Includes 4.0% who are of both French and British origin. [3]1987. [4]Urban areas. [5]1990. [6]1989. [7]At prices of 1986. [8]Unemployed. [9]GDP at current values in 1993 is Can$744,570,000,000. [10]Detail does not add to total given because of rounding. [11]1986. [12]Percentage of all wages. [13]1988. [14]1984. [15]Department and General stores included with General merchandise. [16]1992. [17]Manufacturing only. [18]Includes energy and utilities. [19]September. [20]Total for imports includes Can$7,364,000,000 (4.5% of total imports; mostly special transactions) not distributable by region. [21]Detail does not add to total given because of discrepancies in estimates. [22]1991. [23]Primary includes Secondary.

Cape Verde

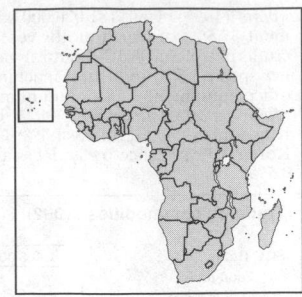

Official name: República de Cabo
Verde (Republic of Cape Verde).
Form of government: multiparty[1]
republic with one legislative house
(National People's Assembly [79]).
Chief of state: President.
Head of government: Prime Minister.
Capital: Praia.
Official language: Portuguese.
Official religion: none.
Monetary unit: 1 escudo (C.V.Esc.) =
100 centavos; valuation (Oct. 7, 1994)
1 U.S.$ = C.V.Esc. 83.05;
1 £ = C.V.Esc. 132.09.

Area and population

Island Groups Islands/Counties[2] Counties	Capitals	area sq mi	area sq km	population 1990 census
Leeward Islands		696[3]	1,803	221,537
Brava	Nova Sintra	26	67	6,975
Fogo	São Filipe	184	476	33,902
Maio	Porto Inglês	104	269	4,969
Santiago		383	991	175,691
Praia	Praia	153	396	82,802
Santa Catarina	Assomada	94	243	41,584
Santa Cruz	Pedra Badejo	58	149	25,892
Tarrafal	Tarrafal	78	203	25,413
Windward Islands		861[3]	2,230	119,954
Boa Vista	Sal Rei	239	620	3,452
Sal	Santa Maria	83	216	7,715
Santo Antão		300	779	43,845
Paúl	Pombas	21	54	8,121
Porto Novo	Porto Novo	215	558	14,873
Ribeira Grande	Ponta do Sol	64	167	20,851
São Nicolau	Ribeira Brava	150	388	13,665
São Vicente	Mindelo	88	227	51,277
TOTAL		1,557	4,033	341,491

Demography

Population (1994): 355,000.
Density (1994): persons per sq mi 227.9, persons per sq km 88.0.
Urban-rural (1990): urban 29.7%; rural 70.3%.
Sex distribution (1990): male 47.29%; female 52.71%.
Age breakdown (1990): under 15, 45.0%; 15–29, 27.3%; 30–44, 11.4%; 45–59, 7.9%; 60 and over, 8.4%.
Population projection: (2000) 383,000; (2010) 436,000.
Doubling time: 19 years.
Ethnic composition (1986): mixed 71%; black 28%; white 1%.
Religious affiliation (1991): Roman Catholic 93.2%; Protestant and other 6.8%.
Major cities (1990): Praia 61,644; Mindelo 47,109; São Filipe 5,616.

Vital statistics

Birth rate per 1,000 population (1993): 47.0 (world avg. 26.0); (1975) legitimate 55.2%; illegitimate 44.8%.
Death rate per 1,000 population (1993): 9.4 (world avg. 9.2).
Natural increase rate per 1,000 population (1993): 37.6 (world avg. 16.8).
Total fertility rate (avg. births per childbearing woman; 1990–95): 4.3.
Marriage rate per 1,000 population (1990): 4.5.
Divorce rate per 1,000 population: n.a.
Life expectancy at birth (1993): male 60.3 years; female 64.2 years.
Major causes of death per 100,000 population (1987): enteritis and other diarrheal diseases 97.4; heart disease 77.9; malignant neoplasms (cancers) 47.9; pneumonia 46.4; accidents, poisoning, and violence 44.0.

National economy

Budget. Revenue (1987): C.V.Esc. 3,428,939,000 (indirect taxes 38.2%, of which import duties 15.4%; direct taxes 21.2%, of which taxes from industry 7.2%; receipts from petroleum 3.1%). Expenditures (1986): C.V.Esc. 2,798,000,000 (current expenditure 90.8%, of which salaries 43.6%, transfer payments 26.8%; capital expenditure 9.2%).
Public debt (external, outstanding; 1992): U.S.$151,000,000.
Tourism: n.a.
Land use (1992): forested 0.2%; meadows and pastures 6.2%; agricultural and under permanent cultivation 11.2%; other 82.4%.
Production (metric tons except as noted). Agriculture, forestry, fishing (1993): sugarcane 19,000, fruits (except melons) 15,000, coconuts 10,000, vegetables (including melons) 8,000, bananas 6,000, sweet potatoes 4,000, potatoes 3,000, cassava 2,000; livestock (number of live animals) 128,000 goats, 105,000 pigs, 21,000 cattle; roundwood, n.a.; fish catch (1992) 8,500. Mining and quarrying (1992): salt 4,000. Manufacturing (C.V.Esc.; 1987): cigars 232,253,000; flour 176,677,000; cocoa powder 94,439,000[5]; canned fish 78,401,000; bread 35,530,000[5]; alcoholic beverages 25,972,000; soft drinks 7,419,000 litres. Construction (1982): residential C.V.Esc. 365,800,000; nonresidential C.V.Esc. 1,700,000. Energy production (consumption): electricity (kW-hr; 1992) 37,000,000 (37,000,000); coal, none (none); crude petroleum, none (none); petroleum products (metric tons; 1992) none (35,000); natural gas, none (none).
Gross national product (at current market prices; 1993): U.S.$346,000,000 (U.S.$870 per capita).

Structure of gross domestic product and labour force

	1988 in value C.V.Esc. '000,000	1988 % of total value	1990 labour force	1990 % of labour force
Agriculture	4,177	20.2	29,876	24.7
Manufacturing	1,113	5.4	5,520	4.6
Public utilities	208	1.0	883	0.7
Mining	127	0.6	410	0.3
Construction	2,238	10.8	22,722	18.9
Transportation and communications	2,595	12.6	6,138	5.1
Trade	5,123	24.8	12,747	10.6
Finance	1,846	8.9	821	0.7
Pub. admin., defense	2,026	9.8 }	17,358	14.4
Services	277	1.3 }		
Other	912[5]	4.4[5]	24,090	20.0
TOTAL	20,640[3]	100.0[3]	120,565	100.0

Population economically active (1990): total 120,565; activity rate of total population 35.3% (participation rates: ages 15–64, 64.3%; female 38.0%; unemployed, 25.8%).

Price and earnings indexes (1990 = 100)

	1988	1989	1990	1991	1992	1993
Consumer price index	86.0	90.0	100.0	110.0	113.0	125.0
Earnings index	...	...	...	...	...	...

Household income and expenditure. Average household size (1990) 5.1; income per household: n.a.; sources of income: n.a.; expenditure (1988): food 51.1%, housing, fuel and power 13.5%, beverages and tobacco 11.8%, transportation and communications 8.8%, household durable goods 6.9%, other 7.9%.

Foreign trade[6]

Balance of trade (current prices)

	1987	1988	1989	1990	1991	1992
C.V.Esc. '000,000	−6,714	−7,416	−8,179	−9,097	−10,031	−11,907
% of total	85.6%	93.8%	88.6%	92.0%	92.0%	94.8%

Imports (1990): C.V.Esc. 9,495,000,000 (foodstuffs and beverages 24.3%, transport equipment 19.9%, machinery and apparatus 10.9%, metal products 6.7%, nonmetallic mineral products 5.4%). *Major import sources:* Portugal 32.7%; The Netherlands 11.1%; Brazil 10.5%; Japan 5.8%; Germany 4.1%; Sweden 2.5%.
Exports (1990): C.V.Esc. 398,000,000 (petroleum and petroleum products 65.1%, fish and fish preparations 11.4%, machinery and transport equipment 11.1%, bananas and plantains [fresh or dried] 6.6%). *Major export destinations:* Portugal 8.3%; Algeria 6.4%; United Kingdom 1.5%; Germany 1.1%; France 0.6%; Italy 0.5%.

Transport and communications

Transport. Railroads: none. Roads (1987): total length 3,489 mi, 5,615 km (paved 29%). Vehicles (1991): passenger cars 10,000; trucks and buses 5,000. Merchant marine (1992): vessels (100 gross tons and over) 42; total deadweight tonnage 30,921. Air transport (1990): passenger-mi 100,000,000, passenger-km 161,000,000; short ton-mi cargo 685,000, metric ton-km cargo 1,000,000; airports (1994) with scheduled flights 9.
Communications. Daily newspapers: none. Radio (1993): total number of receivers 100,000 (1 per 3.5 persons). Television (1987): total number of receivers 5,000 (1 per 65 persons). Telephones (1992): 11,920 (1 per 29 persons).

Education and health

Education (1989–90)

	schools	teachers	students	student/ teacher ratio
Primary (age 7–12)	367	2,028	67,761	33.4
Secondary (age 13–17)	16[7]	238	7,114	29.9
Voc., teacher tr.	3[7]	56[8]	752	...
Higher	...	...	...	...

Educational attainment (1990). Percentage of population age 25 and over having: no formal schooling 47.9%; primary 40.9%; incomplete secondary 3.9%; complete secondary 1.4%; higher 1.5%; unknown 4.4%. *Literacy* (1990): total population age 15 and over literate 122,806 (65.3%); males literate 64,698 (52.7%); females literate 58,108 (47.3%).
Health (1987): physicians 77 (1 per 4,208 persons); hospital beds 625 (1 per 550 persons); infant mortality rate per 1,000 live births (1993) 59.6.
Food (1988–90): daily per capita caloric intake 2,778 (vegetable products 88%, animal products 12%); 118% of FAO recommended minimum requirement.

Military

Total active duty personnel (1993): 1,100 (army 90.9%, air force 9.1%). *Military expenditure as percentage of GNP* (1981): 12.1% (world 5.5%); per capita expenditure U.S.$43.

---

[1]Constitution revised Sept. 28, 1990, to adopt a multiparty system; first multiparty elections took place on Jan. 13, 1991. [2]Island/county areas are coterminous except Santiago and Santo Antão islands. [3]Detail does not add to total given because of rounding. [4]1986. [5]Less imputed bank service charges. [6]Imports are c.i.f. [7]1986–87. [8]Vocational teachers only.

Central African Republic

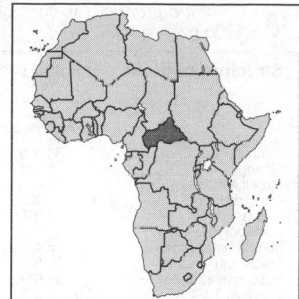

Official name: République Centrafricaine (Central African Republic).
Form of government: republic with a bicameral Congress that meets as two chambers, an upper (Economic and Regional Council[1]) and a lower (National Assembly [85]).
Chief of state: President.
Head of government: Prime Minister.
Capital: Bangui.
Official languages: French; Sango.
Official religion: none.
Monetary unit: 1 CFA franc (CFAF) = 100 centimes; valuation (Oct. 7, 1994) 1 U.S.$ = CFAF 526.67; 1 £ = CFAF 837.67.

Area and population		area		population
		sq mi	sq km	1988 census
Prefectures	**Capitals**			
Bamingui-Bangoran	Ndélé	22,471	58,200	28,643
Basse-Kotto	Mobaye	6,797	17,604	194,750
Haut-Mbomou	Obo	21,440	55,530	27,113
Haute-Kotto	Bria	33,456	86,650	58,838
Kemo	Sibut	6,642	17,204	82,884
Lobaye	Mbaïki	7,427	19,235	169,554
Mambéré-Kadéï	Berbérati	11,661	30,203	230,364
Mbomou	Bangassou	23,610	61,150	119,252
Nana-Gribizi	Kaga-Bandoro	7,721	19,996	95,497
Nana-Mambéré	Bouar	10,270	26,600	191,970
Ombella-M'poko	Boali	12,292	31,835	180,857
Ouaka	Bambari	19,266	49,900	208,332
Ouham	Bossangoa	19,402	50,250	262,950
Ouham Pondó	Bozoum	12,094	02,100	207,053
Sangha-Mbaéré	Nola	7,495	19,412	65,961
Vakaga	Birao	17,954	46,500	32,118
Autonomous commune				
Bangui	Bangui	26	67	451,690
TOTAL		240,324	622,436	2,688,426

Demography

Population (1994): 3,069,000.
Density (1994): persons per sq mi 12.8, persons per sq km 4.9.
Urban-rural (1992): urban 48.3%; rural 51.7%.
Sex distribution (1988): male 49.14%; female 50.86%.
Age breakdown (1988): under 15, 43.2%; 15–29, 27.5%; 30–44, 15.0%; 45–59, 9.2%; 60–74, 4.1%; 75 and over, 0.8%; unknown, 0.2%.
Population projection: (2000) 3,528,000; (2010) 4,449,000.
Doubling time: 32 years.
Ethnolinguistic composition (1988): Baya (Gbaya) 23.7%; Banda 23.4%; Mandjia 14.7%; Sara 6.5%; Mbum 6.3%; Mbaka 4.3%; Kare 2.4%; French 0.1%; other 18.6%.
Religious affiliation (1985): Protestant 40.0%; Roman Catholic 28.0%; traditional 24.0%; Muslim 8.0%.
Major cities (1988): Bangui 451,690; Berbérati 41,891; Bouar 39,676; Bambari 38,633; Bossangoa 31,502; Carnot 31,324; Bangassou 24,450; Kaga-Bandoro 24,249; Bria 22,735.

Vital statistics

Birth rate per 1,000 population (1994): 42.3 (world avg. 26.0); legitimate, n.a.; illegitimate, n.a.
Death rate per 1,000 population (1994): 20.7 (world avg. 9.2).
Natural increase rate per 1,000 population (1994): 21.6 (world avg. 16.8).
Total fertility rate (avg. births per childbearing woman; 1992): 5.8.
Marriage rate per 1,000 population: n.a.
Divorce rate per 1,000 population: n.a.
Life expectancy at birth (1990–95): male 44.7 years; female 49.4 years.
Morbidity (as percentage of reported cases of illness; 1984): malaria 13.3%; dysentery, enteritis, and other intestinal diseases 12.5%; respiratory diseases 9.9%, of which pneumonia 2.7%.

National economy

Budget (1994). Revenue: CFAF 49,210,000,000 (1993; fiscal receipts 93.4%; nonfiscal receipts 6.6%). Expenditures: CFAF 65,700,000,000 (1993; current expenditure 55.5%; capital expenditure 44.5%, of which grants from abroad 31.9%).
Tourism (1991): receipts U.S.$8,000,000; expenditures U.S.$42,000,000.
Public debt (external, outstanding; 1992): U.S.$807,200,000.
Production (metric tons except as noted). Agriculture, forestry, fishing (1993): cassava 610,000, yams 224,000, bananas 96,000, plantains 68,000, corn (maize) 55,000, peanuts (groundnuts) 43,000, seed cotton 20,000, oranges 17,000, pulses 16,000, sorghum 14,000, cottonseed 11,000, coffee 11,000, cotton lint 8,000, rice 7,000; livestock (number of live animals) 2,781,000 cattle, 1,334,000 goats, 474,000 pigs, 3,000,000 chickens; roundwood (1992) 3,448,000 cu m; fish catch (1991) 13,500. Mining and quarrying (1992): diamonds 429,734 carats[2]. Manufacturing (value of production in CFAF '000,000; 1991): food, beverages, and tobacco 17,146; textiles, wearing apparel, and leather products 8,354; wood products 7,069; chemical products 3,252; metal products 1,849. Construction (1992)[3]: residential 10,052 sq m; nonresidential 82,411 sq m. Energy production (consumption): electricity (kW-hr; 1992) 96,000,000

(96,000,000); coal, none (none); crude petroleum, none (none); petroleum products (metric tons; 1992) none (70,000); natural gas, none (none).
Land use (1992): forested 57.4%; meadows and pastures 4.8%; agricultural and under permanent cultivation 3.2%; other 34.6%.
Gross national product (at current market prices; 1993): U.S.$1,267,000,000 (U.S.$390 per capita).

Structure of gross domestic product and labour force				
	1991		1988	
	in value CFAF '000,000	% of total value	labour force	% of labour force
Agriculture	143,287	42.7	1,113,900	80.4
Mining	9,171	2.7	15,400	1.1
Manufacturing	23,975	7.1	22,400	1.6
Construction	9,397	2.8	7,000	0.5
Public utilities	1,606	0.5	1,500	0.1
Transp. and commun.	16,010	4.8	1,500	0.1
Trade	78,916	23.5	118,000	8.5
Finance, real estate	10,323	3.1	1,500	0.1
Pub. admin., defense	41,213	12.3	91,700	6.6
Services	1,601	0.5	...	...
Other	...	...	14,100	1.0
TOTAL	335,498[4]	100.0	1,387,000	100.0

Population economically active (1988): total 1,186,972; activity rate of total population 44.2% (participation rates: ages 15–64, 81.6%[5]; female 48.5%; unemployed 7.5%).

Price and earnings indexes (1990 = 100)							
	1987	1988	1989	1990	1991	1992	1993
Consumer price index	103.4	99.3	100.1	100.0	97.3	96.2	93.4
Earnings index	...	...	...	...	...	...	...

Household income and expenditure. Average household size (1988) 4.7; average annual income per household CFAF 91,985 (U.S.$435); sources of income: n.a.; expenditure (1991)[6]: food 70.5%, clothing 8.5%, other manufactured products 7.6%, energy 7.3%, services (including transportation and communications, recreation, and health) 6.1%.

Foreign trade

Balance of trade (current prices)						
	1987	1988	1989	1990	1991	1992
CFAF '000,000	−17,174	−18,346	−6,009	−10,917	−11,328	−14,916
% of total	18.0%	22.5%	6.3%	17.9%	17.8%	20.9%

Imports (1992). CFAF 43,211,000,000 (food products 22.2%, transportation equipment 16.6%, chemical products 13.7%, energy products 11.0%). *Major import sources:* Europe 62.4%, of which France 50.6%; Africa 13.1%, of which Cameroon 6.8%; Asia 7.9%, of which Japan 6.6%.
Exports (1992): CFAF 28,295,000,000 (diamonds 58.8%, wood 21.2%, cotton 18.9%[7], tobacco 12.3%, coffee 4.4%, gold 1.0%). *Major export destinations:* Belgium-Luxembourg 57.0%; France 9.8%; The Sudan 3.6%; Zaire 3.4%; Germany 0.6%.

Transport and communications

Transport. Railroads: none. Roads (1991): total length 14,750 mi, 23,738 km (paved 2%). Vehicles (1991): passenger cars 8,221; trucks and buses 8,541. Merchant marine: vessels (100 gross tons and over) none. Air transport (1991)[8]: passenger-mi 134,000,000, passenger-km 216,000,000; short ton-mi cargo 11,000,000, metric ton-km cargo 16,000,000; airports[9] (1994) with scheduled flights 1.
Communications. Daily newspapers (1990): total number 1; total circulation 2,000; circulation per 1,000 population 0.7. Radio (1993): 550,000 receivers (1 per 5.4 persons). Television (1993): 7,500 receivers (1 per 400 persons). Telephones (1991): 7,260 (1 per 413 persons).

Education and health

Education (1990–91)				
	schools	teachers	students	student/teacher ratio
Primary (age 6–11)	930	4,004	308,409	90.4
Secondary (age 12–18) } Vocational	46	845	46,989	55.6
Higher[10]	1	139	3,783	27.2

Educational attainment (1988). Percentage of population age 10 and over having: no formal schooling 59.3%; primary education 29.6%; lower secondary 7.5%; upper secondary 2.3%; higher 1.3%. *Literacy* (1988): total population age 15 and over literate 33.6%; males literate 48.0%; females literate 20.3%.
Health (1991): physicians (1992) 157 (1 per 18,660 persons); hospital beds 4,258 (1 per 672 persons); infant mortality rate per 1,000 live births 219.0.
Food (1988–90): daily per capita caloric intake 1,846 (vegetable products 88%, animal products 12%); 82% of FAO recommended minimum requirement.

Military

Total active duty personnel (1994): 2,650 (army 94.3%; navy, none; air force 5.7%). *Military expenditure as percentage of GNP* (1992): 2.2% (world [1991] 4.2%); per capita expenditure (1991) U.S.$8.

---

[1]Advisory body only; number of seats not available. [2]A similar amount is believed to be smuggled out of the country annually. [3]Bangui only. [4]Detail does not add to total given because of rounding. [5]January 1985. [6]Weights of consumer price index components. [7]1991. [8]Apportioned share of Air Afrique traffic, an airline shared by 10 West African countries. [9]International air service only. [10]University of Bangui only.

Chad

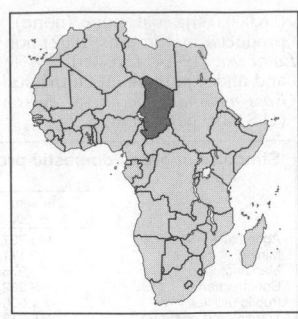

Official name: Jumhūrīyah Tshad
(Arabic); République du Tchad
(French) (Republic of Chad).
Form of government: transitional
regime with one legislative house
(Higher Transitional Council [57])[1].
Chief of state: President.
Head of government: Prime Minister.
Capital: N'Djamena.
Official languages: Arabic; French.
Official religion: none.
Monetary unit: 1 CFA franc
(CFAF) = 100 centimes; valuation
(Oct. 7, 1994) 1 U.S.$ = CFAF 526.67;
1 £ = CFAF 837.67.

Area and population

Préfectures	Capitals	area sq mi	area sq km	population 1992 estimate
Batha	Ati	34,285	88,800	470,900
Biltine	Biltine	18,090	46,850	238,400
Borkou-Ennedi-Tibesti	Faya Largeau	231,795	600,350	119,200
Chari-Baguirmi	N'Djamena	32,010	82,910	924,000
Guéra	Mongo	22,760	58,950	280,200
Kanem	Mao	44,215	114,520	268,200
Lac	Bol	8,620	22,320	178,800
Logone Occidental	Moundou	3,357	8,695	399,400
Logone Oriental	Doba	10,825	28,035	417,300
Mayo-Kebbi	Bongor	11,625	30,105	941,900
Moyen-Chari	Sarh	17,445	45,180	709,400
Ouaddaï	Abéché	29,436	76,240	465,000
Salamat	Am Timan	24,325	63,000	143,000
Tandjilé	Laï	6,965	18,045	405,300
TOTAL		495,755[2]	1,284,000	5,961,000

Demography

Population (1994): 6,495,000.
Density (1994): persons per sq mi 13.1, persons per sq km 5.1.
Urban-rural (1990): urban 32.0%; rural 68.0%.
Sex distribution (1990): male 49.31%; female 50.69%.
Age breakdown (1990): under 15, 42.8%; 15–29, 26.0%; 30–44, 15.9%; 45–59,
9.6%; 60–74, 4.8%; 75 and over, 0.9%.
Population projection: (2000) 7,647,000; (2010) 9,722,000.
Doubling time: 28 years.
Ethnic composition (1983): Sara, Bagirmi, and Kreish 30.5%; Sudanic Arab
26.1%; Teda (Tubu) 7.3%; Mbum 6.5%; Masalit, Maba, and Mimi 6.3%;
Tama 6.3%; Mubi 4.2%; Kanuri 2.3%; Hausa 2.3%; Masa 2.3%; Kotoko
2.1%; other 3.8%.
Religious affiliation (1989): Muslim 40.4%; Christian 33.0%; traditional beliefs
26.6%.
Major cities (1992): N'Djamena 687,800; Sarh 129,600; Moundou 117,500;
Abéché 95,800; Koumra 48,700.

Vital statistics

Birth rate per 1,000 population (1990–95): 43.3 (world avg. 26.0); legitimate,
n.a.; illegitimate, n.a.
Death rate per 1,000 population (1990–95): 17.9 (world avg. 9.2).
Natural increase rate per 1,000 population (1990–95): 25.4 (world avg. 16.8).
Total fertility rate (avg. births per childbearing woman; 1990): 6.0.
Marriage rate per 1,000 population: n.a.
Divorce rate per 1,000 population: n.a.
Life expectancy at birth (1990–95): male 45.9 years; female 49.1 years.
Major causes of death per 100,000 population: n.a.; however, major diseases in-
clude malaria, sleeping sickness, leprosy, venereal diseases, and tuberculosis.

National economy

Budget (1993)[3]. Revenue: CFAF 34,900,000,000 (1990; goods and services
tax 33.2%, customs duties 28.8%, income tax 28.0%). Expenditures: CFAF
46,700,000,000 (1990; administrative 65.0%, defense 23.9%).
Public debt (external, outstanding; 1992): U.S.$658,800,000.
Tourism (1992): receipts from visitors U.S.$21,000,000; expenditures by na-
tionals abroad U.S.$30,000,000.
Production (metric tons except as noted). Agriculture, forestry, fishing (1993):
sugarcane 400,000, cassava 339,000, yams 245,000, millet 234,000, peanuts
(groundnuts) 153,000, corn (maize) 100,000, seed cotton 85,000, sweet potatoes 47,000, pulses 36,000, rice 35,000, dates 32,000, mangoes 32,000, sesame
seeds 19,000, potatoes 18,000, onions 14,000; livestock (number of live
animals) 4,600,000 cattle, 3,100,000 goats, 2,100,000 sheep, 575,000 camels,
4,000,000 chickens; roundwood (1992) 4,158,000 cu m; fish catch (1992)
60,000. Mining and quarrying: clay, natron, tungsten, bauxite, and gold.
Manufacturing (1988): beef and veal 53,000; refined sugar 27,000; salted,
dried, or smoked fish 19,000[4]; goat meat 8,000; cattle hides 7,500; sheepskins
and goatskins 3,318; mutton and lamb 1,000; wheat flour 1,000[5]; woven cotton fabrics 6,000,000 metres; beer 116,000 hectolitres[6]; cigarettes 14,200,000
packets. Construction: n.a. Energy production (consumption): electricity
(kW-hr; 1992) 85,000,000 (85,000,000); coal, none (n.a.); crude petroleum,
none (n.a.); petroleum products (metric tons; 1992) none (83,000); natural
gas, none (n.a.).
Household income and expenditure (1980). Average household size 3.9; average annual income per household CFAF 96,806 (U.S.$458); sources of
income: n.a.; expenditure (1983)[7]: food 45.3%, health 11.9%, energy 5.8%,
clothing 3.3%.

Gross domestic product (at current market prices; 1993): U.S.$1,226,000,000
(U.S.$200 per capita).

Structure of gross domestic product and labour force

	1991 in value CFAF '000,000	1991 % of total value	1991 labour force	1991 % of labour force
Agriculture	134,609	44.0	1,489,000	73.9
Mining	1,411	0.5		
Manufacturing	27,886	9.1		
Construction	5,808	1.9	149,000	7.4
Public utilities	1,990	0.7		
Transportation and communications	5,499	1.8		
Trade and finance	93,833	30.7		
Pub. admin., defense	31,674	10.4	377,000	18.7
Services	2,912	0.9		
Other			...	...
TOTAL	305,622	100.0	2,016,000[2]	100.0

Population economically active (1992): total 1,993,000; activity rate of total
population 34.1% (participation rates [1987]: over age 10, 51.2%; female
21.6%; unemployed, n.a.).

Price and earnings indexes (1985 = 100)

	1986	1987	1988	1989	1990	1991	1992
Consumer price index	87.0	84.6	95.4	89.8	90.3	94.0	90.2
Earnings index	...	...	...	...	...	...	...

Land use (1992): forested 9.8%; meadows and pastures 35.0%; agricultural
and under permanent cultivation 2.5%; other 52.7%.

Foreign trade

Balance of trade (current prices)

	1986	1987	1988	1989	1990	1991
CFAF '000,000	− 20,253	− 17,400	− 7,470	− 6,060	+ 364	− 7,268
% of total	29.2%	20.9%	8.0%	5.8%	0.3%	6.2%

Imports (1991): CFAF 80,811,000,000 (1983; petroleum products 16.8%; cereal
products 16.8%; pharmaceutical products and chemicals 11.5%; machinery
and transport equipment 8.5%, of which transport equipment 7.3%; electrical equipment 5.7%; textiles 2.9%; raw and refined sugar 2.3%). *Major
import sources* (1989): France 36.2%; United States 20.4%; Cameroon 18.4%;
Italy 5.6%; West Germany 3.7%.
Exports (1991): CFAF 55,587,000,000 (1983; raw cotton 91.1%; live cattle
and frozen bovine meat 1.8%; hides and skins 0.4%). *Major export destinations* (1989): Portugal 21.0%; West Germany 16.9%; Japan 13.3%; France
9.9%; Spain 8.4%.

Transport and communications

Transport. Railroads: none. Roads (1983): total length 24,855 mi, 40,000
km (paved 1%). Vehicles (1992): passenger cars 9,000; trucks and buses
7,000. Merchant marine: vessels (100 gross tons and over) none. Air transport (1991): passenger-mi 144,044,000, passenger-km 232,329,000; short ton-
mi cargo 12,119,000, metric ton-km cargo 17,694,000; airports (1994) with
scheduled flights 4.
Communications. Daily newspapers (1990): total number 1; total circulation
2,000; circulation per 1,000 population 0.3. Radio (1993): total number of
receivers 1,260,000 (1 per 5.0 persons). Television (1987): total number of
receivers 5,000 (1 per 1,050 persons). Telephones (1992): 9,080 (1 per 678
persons).

Education and health

Education (1991)

	schools	teachers	students	student/ teacher ratio
Primary (age 6–12)	2,544	9,238	591,417	64.0
Secondary (age 13–19)	66[8]	2,062	72,641	35.2
Voc., teacher tr.	25[9]	285[8]	3,819[4]	15.1[8]
Higher[4]	4	59	2,969	50.3

Educational attainment: n.a. *Literacy* (1990): percentage of total population
age 15 and over literate 29.8%; males literate 42.2%; females literate 17.9%.
Health: physicians (1980) 94 (1 per 47,640 persons); hospital beds (1978) 3,553
(1 per 1,190 persons); infant mortality rate per 1,000 live births (1990–95)
122.
Food (1987–89): daily per capita caloric intake 1,791 (vegetable products 92%,
animal products 8%); 75% of FAO recommended minimum requirement.

Military

Total active duty personnel (1994): 25,350 (army 98.6%, navy, none, air force
1.4%). *Military expenditure as percentage of GNP* (1991): 5.2% (world 4.2%);
per capita expenditure U.S.$13.

---

[1]A 30-month national charter (transitional constitution) was adopted in February
1991. A new 12-month transitional charter was adopted in April 1993 by a broadly
representative National Council. The Council also elected a 57-member interim legislature, the Higher Transitional Council. [2]Detail does not add to total given because
of rounding. [3]In addition to the current revenues and expenditures shown, there is an
investment budget of CFAF 81,954,000,000, which is financed 57.9% by international
grants, 42.1% by loans. [4]1989. [5]1983. [6]1990. [7]Capital city only. [8]1988–89. [9]1987.

Chile

Official name: República de Chile (Republic of Chile).
Form of government: multiparty republic with two legislative houses (Senate [47[1]]; Chamber of Deputies [120]).
Head of state and government: President.
Capital: Santiago[2].
Official language: Spanish.
Official religion: none.
Monetary unit: 1 peso (Ch$) = 100 centavos; valuation (Oct. 7, 1994) 1 U.S.$ = Ch$414.04; 1 £ = Ch$658.53.

Structure of gross domestic product and labour force

| | 1992 | | | |
	in value Ch$'000,000[7]	% of total value	labour force	% of labour force
Agriculture	428,258	8.3	828,970	17.1
Mining	423,621	8.2	92,220	1.9
Manufacturing	916,556	17.7	776,210	16.0
Construction	277,927	5.4	331,150	6.8
Public utilities	148,564	2.7	25,200	0.5
Transp. and commun.	390,901	7.5	326,710	6.7
Trade	807,555	15.6	817,810	16.9
Finance			229,320	4.7
Pub. admin., defense	1,795,326	34.6	1,198,140	24.7
Services[8]				
Other			227,374[9]	4.7[9]
TOTAL	5,188,708	100.0	4,853,104	100.0

Population economically active (1991): total 4,794,100; activity rate of total population 36.6% (participation rates: ages 15–64, 56.7%; female 34.5%; unemployed 5.3%).

Price and earnings indexes (1985 = 100)

	1987	1988	1989	1990	1991	1992	1993
Consumer price index	143.2	164.3	192.2	242.0	295.0	341.0	384.0
Monthly earnings index	146.1	178.6	212.7	287.9	349.0	421.0	...

Household income and expenditure. Average household size (1992) 4.1; average annual income per family (household; 1985)[10] Ch$440,738 at June prices (U.S.$2,840); sources of income (1976): wages and salaries 40.8%, transfer payments 8.0%, self-employment and other 51.2%; expenditure (1989): food 27.9%, clothing 22.5%, housing 15.2%, transportation 6.4%.
Tourism (1992): receipts U.S.$706,000,000; expenditures U.S.$459,000,000.

Area and population[3]

| | | area | | population |
Regions	Capitals	sq mi	sq km	1993 estimate
Aisén del General Carlos Ibáñez del Campo	Coihaique	42,095	109,025	84,538
Antofagasta	Antofagasta	48,820	126,444	401,396
Araucanía	Temuco	12,300	31,858	823,103
Atacama	Copiapó	29,179	75,573	202,576
Bío-Bío	Concepción	14,258	36,929	1,722,577
Coquimbo	La Serena	15,697	40,656	505,916
Libertador General Bernardo O'Higgins	Rancagua	6,319	16,365	668,294
Los Lagos	Puerto Montt	25,868	66,997	945,525
Magallanes y la Antártica Chilena	Punta Arenas	50,979	132,034	171,059
Maule	Talca	11,700	30,302	880,005
Santiago, Región Metropolitana de	Santiago	5,926	15,349	5,569,605
Tarapacá	Iquique	22,663	58,698	385,647
Valparaíso	Valparaíso	6,331	16,396	1,452,998
TOTAL		292,135	756,626	13,813,239[4]

Foreign trade[11]

Balance of trade (current prices)

	1988	1989	1990	1991	1992	1993
U.S.$'000,000	+2,219	+1,578	+1,273	+1,575	+749	−979
% of total	18.7%	10.8%	8.3%	9.7%	3.9%	5.1%

Imports (1992): U.S.$9,670,200,000 (intermediate goods 53.5%; capital goods 26.6%; consumer goods 17.5%). Major import sources: U.S. 20.5%; Brazil 10.3%; Japan 10.0%; Argentina 6.6%; Germany 6.5%; Nigeria 3.4%; France 2.9%; Italy 2.8%.
Exports (1992): U.S.$10,125,500,000 (mining 46.7%; industrial products 40.9%, of which paper and paper products 6.8%, chemical and petroleum products 4.8%; fruits and vegetables 12.1%). Major export destinations: Japan 16.9%; U.S. 16.3%; Germany 6.0%; U.K. 5.6%; Taiwan 4.8%; Argentina 4.6%; Brazil 4.4%; France 3.9%.

Demography

Population (1994): 13,805,000.
Density (1994): persons per sq mi 47.3, persons per sq km 18.2.
Urban-rural (1993): urban 85.3%; rural 14.7%.
Sex distribution (1993): male 49.39%; female 50.61%.
Age breakdown (1993): under 15, 30.6%; 15–29, 26.4%; 30–44, 21.6%; 45–59, 12.3%; 60–74, 6.8%; 75 and over, 2.3%.
Population projection: (2000) 16,918,000; (2010) 15,037,000.
Doubling time: 41 years.
Ethnic composition (1983): mestizo 91.6%; Indian (mostly Araucanian) 6.8%; others (mainly European) 1.6%.
Religious affiliation (1982): Roman Catholic 80.7%; Protestant 6.1%; Jewish 0.2%; atheist and nonreligious 12.8%; other 0.2%.
Major cities (1993): Greater Santiago 4,628,320; Viña del Mar 319,440; Concepción 318,140; Valparaíso 301,677; Temuco 262,624; Talcahuano 257,767.

Vital statistics

Birth rate per 1,000 population (1991): 21.3 (world avg. 26.0); (1990): legitimate 65.7%; illegitimate 34.3%.
Death rate per 1,000 population (1991): 5.6 (world avg. 9.2).
Natural increase rate per 1,000 population (1991): 15.7 (world avg. 16.8).
Total fertility rate (avg. births per childbearing woman; 1990): 2.6.
Marriage rate per 1,000 population (1991): 6.9.
Divorce rate per 1,000 population (1987): 0.4.
Life expectancy at birth (1990–95): male 68.5 years; female 75.6 years.
Major causes of death per 100,000 population (1990): diseases of the circulatory system 163.7; malignant neoplasms (cancers) 107.5; diseases of the respiratory system 73.1; accidents and adverse effects 72.8.

National economy

Budget (1992). Revenue: Ch$4,289,975,000,000 (income from taxes 69.3%, nontax revenue 30.7%). Expenditures: Ch$3,717,455,000,000 (social security and welfare 24.4%, current transfers 20.1%, remunerations 15.4%, public-debt service 12.6%, goods and services 8.5%, real investment 10.4%).
Public debt (external, outstanding; 1992): U.S.$9,578,000,000.
Production (metric tons except as noted). Agriculture, forestry, fishing (1993): sugar beets 2,947,000, wheat 1,223,000, potatoes 926,000, tomatoes 924,000, corn (maize) 899,000, grapes 880,000, apples 840,000, onions (dry) 249,000, oats 202,000, rice 131,000, barley 84,000; livestock (number of live animals; 1992) 6,650,000 sheep, 3,300,000 cattle, 1,701,000 pigs; roundwood (1992) 28,348,000 cu m; fish catch (1992) 6,304,000. Mining (1993): iron 5,809,000; copper 2,065,219; zinc 29,435; molybdenum 14,899; silver 967,551 kg; gold 33,502 kg. Manufacturing (1991): cement 2,250,800; cellulose 798,000; refined sugar 353,300[5]; newsprint 172,900; noodles 55,200; carbonated drinks 7,197,000 hectolitres; tires 1,824,900 units; pressed-fibre panels 9,082,900 sq m; flat glass 5,730,300 sq m. Construction (1992)[6]: residential 6,876,562 sq m; nonresidential 2,577,190 sq m. Energy production (consumption): electricity (kW-hr; 1992) 22,146,000,000 ([1991] 19,961,000,000); coal (metric tons; 1991) 2,579,000 (3,057,000); crude petroleum (barrels; 1991) 5,667,000 (46,102,000); petroleum products (metric tons; 1991) 6,086,000 (6,610,000); natural gas (cu m; 1991) 4,067,200,000 (4,067,200,000).
Land use (1991): forested 11.8%; meadows and pastures 18.1%; agricultural and under permanent cultivation 5.8%; other 64.3%.
Gross national product (1992): U.S.$37,064,000,000 (U.S.$2,730 per capita).

Transport and communications

Transport. Railroads (1992): route length 2,778 mi, 4,470 km; passenger-km 1,141,926,000; metric ton-km cargo 2,694,133. Roads (1991): total length 49,457 mi, 79,593 km (paved 14%). Vehicles (1992): passenger cars 826,794; trucks and buses 437,520. Merchant marine (1992): vessels (100 gross tons and over) 392; total deadweight tonnage 854,850. Air transport (1992): passenger-km 3,619,654,000; metric ton-km cargo 862,456,000; airports (1994) with scheduled flights 18.
Communications. Daily newspapers (1993): total number 34; total circulation 868,300[12]; circulation per 1,000 population 63[12]. Radio (1993): 4,250,000 receivers (1 per 3.2 persons). Television (1993): 2,000,000 receivers (1 per 6.8 persons). Telephones (1992): 1,484,000 (1 per 9.0 persons).

Education and health

Education (1991)

	schools	teachers	students	student/ teacher ratio
Primary (age 6–13)	8,626	81,742	2,033,982	36.0
Secondary (age 14–17)	1,694[13]	...	436,892	...
Vocational	1,262[13]	...	262,563	...
Higher	201[13]	15,131[14]	286,962	...

Educational attainment (1982). Percentage of population age 25 and over having: no formal schooling 9.4%; primary education 56.6%; secondary 26.9%; higher 7.1%. Literacy (1990): total population age 15 and over literate 93.4%; males 93.5%; females 93.2%.
Health (1992): physicians 15,062 (1 per 889 persons); hospital beds 42,895 (1 per 312 persons); infant mortality rate per 1,000 live births (1991) 14.6.
Food (1988–90): daily per capita caloric intake 2,484 (vegetable products 82%, animal products 18%); 102% of FAO recommended minimum requirement.

Military

Total active duty personnel (1993): 91,800 (army 58.8%, navy 27.2%, air force 14.0%). Military expenditure as percentage of GNP (1991): 3.4% (world 4.2%); per capita expenditure U.S.$76.

[1]Includes 8 nonelective seats. [2]Legislative bodies meet in Valparaíso. [3]Excludes the 480,000-sq mi (1,250,000-sq km) section of Antarctica claimed by Chile (and administered as part of Magallanes y la Antártica Chilena region) and "inland" (actually tidal) water areas. The 1992 census population of Chilean-claimed Antarctica was 126. [4]Population projection based on 1982 census. Final 1992 census total is 13,348,401. [5]1989. [6]Construction approved and already begun only. [7]In constant prices of 1986. [8]Services includes restaurants and hotels. [9]Includes an estimated 226,694 unemployed persons. [10]Greater Santiago area. [11]Import figures are f.o.b. in balance of trade and c.i.f. for commodities and trading partners. [12]Circulation for 32 newspapers only. [13]1988. [14]1984.

China

Official name: Chung-hua Jen-min
Kung-ho-kuo (People's Republic
of China).
Form of government: single-party
people's republic with one legislative
house (National People's Congress
[2,978]).
Chief of state: President.
Head of government: Premier.
Capital: Peking (Beijing).
Official language: Mandarin Chinese.
Official religion: none.
Monetary unit: 1 Renminbi (yuan)
(Y) = 10 jiao = 100 fen; valuation (Oct.
7, 1994) 1 U.S.$ = Y 8.53;
1 £ = Y 13.57.

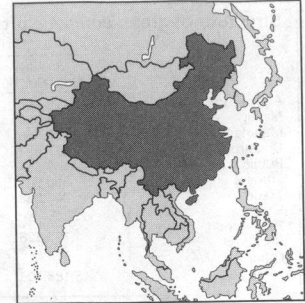

Area and population[1, 2]

Provinces	Capitals	area sq mi	area sq km	population 1993[3] estimate
Anhwei (Anhui)	Ho-fei (Hefei)	54,000	139,900	58,340,000
Chekiang (Zhejiang)	Hang-chou (Hangzhou)	39,300	101,800	42,360,000
Fukien (Fujian)	Fu-chou (Fuzhou)	47,500	123,100	31,160,000
Hainan (Hainan)	Hai-k'ou (Haikou)	13,200	34,300	6,860,000
Heilungkiang (Heilongjiang)	Harbin	179,000	463,600	36,080,000
Honan (Henan)	Cheng-chou (Zhengzhou)	64,500	167,000	88,610,000
Hopeh (Hebei)	Shih-chia-chuang (Shijiazhuang)	78,200	202,700	62,750,000
Hunan (Hunan)	Ch'ang-sha (Changsha)	81,300	210,500	62,670,000
Hupeh (Hubei)	Wu-han (Wuhan)	72,400	187,500	55,800,000
Kansu (Gansu)	Lan-chou (Lanzhou)	141,500	366,500	23,140,000
Kiangsi (Jiangxi)	Nan-ch'ang (Nanchang)	63,600	164,800	39,130,000
Kiangsu (Jiangsu)	Nanking (Nanjing)	39,600	102,600	69,110,000
Kirin (Jilin)	Ch'ang-ch'un (Changchun)	72,200	187,000	25,320,000
Kwangtung (Guangdong)	Canton (Guangzhou)	76,100	197,100	65,250,000
Kweichow (Guizhou)	Kuei-yang (Guiyang)	67,200	174,000	33,610,000
Liaoning (Liaoning)	Shen-yang (Shenyang)	58,300	151,000	40,160,000
Shansi (Shanxi)	T'ai-yüan (Taiyuan)	60,700	157,100	29,790,000
Shantung (Shandong)	Chi-nan (Jinan)	59,200	153,300	86,100,000
Shensi (Shaanxi)	Sian (Xi'an)	75,600	195,800	34,050,000
Szechwan (Sichuan)	Ch'eng-tu (Chengdu)	219,700	569,000	109,980,000
Tsinghai (Qinghai)	Hsi-ning (Xining)	278,400	721,000	4,610,000
Yunnan (Yunnan)	K'un-ming (Kunming)	168,400	436,200	38,320,000
Autonomous regions				
Inner Mongolia (Nei Monggol)	Hu-ho-hao-t'e (Hohhot)	454,600	1,177,500	22,070,000
Kwangsi Chuang (Guangxi Zhuang)	Nan-ning (Nanning)	85,100	220,400	43,800,000
Ningsia Hui (Ningxia Hui)	Yin-ch'uan (Yinchuan)	25,600	66,400	4,870,000
Sinkiang Uighur (Xinjiang Uygur)	Wu-lu-mu-c'hi (Urumqi)	635,900	1,646,900	15,810,000
Tibet (Xizang)	Lhasa	471,700	1,221,600	2,280,000
Municipalities				
Peking (Beijing)	—	6,500	16,800	11,020,000
Shanghai (Shanghai)	—	2,400	6,200	13,450,000
Tientsin (Tianjin)	—	4,400	11,300	9,200,000
TOTAL		3,696,100[4]	9,572,900[4]	1,171,710,000[5]

Demography

Population (1994): 1,192,300,000.
Density (1994): persons per sq mi 322.6, persons per sq km 124.5.
Urban-rural (1992): urban 27.6%; rural 72.4%.
Sex distribution (1992): male 51.05%; female 48.95%.
Age breakdown (1990): under 15, 27.7%; 15–29, 31.0%; 30–44, 20.7%; 45–59, 12.0%; 60–74, 6.9%; 75 and over, 1.7%.
Population projection: (2000) 1,276,200,000; (2010) 1,323,800,000.
Doubling time: 60 years.
Ethnic composition (1990): Han (Chinese) 91.96%; Chuang 1.37%; Manchu 0.87%; Hui 0.76%; Miao 0.65%; Uighur 0.64%; Yi 0.58%; Tuchia 0.50%; Mongolian 0.42%; Tibetan 0.41%; Puyi 0.23%; Tung 0.22%; Yao 0.18%; Korean 0.17%; Pai 0.14%; Hani 0.11%; Kazakh 0.10%; Tai 0.09%; Li 0.09%; other 0.51%.
Religious affiliation (1980): nonreligious 59.2%; Chinese folk-religionist 20.1%; atheist 12.0%; Buddhist 6.0%; Muslim 2.4%; Christian 0.2%; other 0.1%.
Major cities (1990): Shanghai 7,496,509; Peking 5,769,607; Tientsin 4,574,689; Shen-yang 3,603,712; Wu-han 3,284,229; Canton 2,914,281; Harbin 2,443,398; Chungking (Chongqing) 2,266,772; Nanking 2,090,204; Sian 1,959,044; Ta-lien (Dalian) 1,723,302; Ch'eng-tu 1,713,255; Ch'ang-ch'un 1,679,270; T'ai-yüan 1,533,884; Tsinan 1,480,915; Ch'ing-tao (Qingdao) 1,459,195; An-shan (Anshan) 1,203,986; Fu-shun 1,202,388; Lan-chou 1,194,640; Cheng-chou 1,159,679; Tzu-po (Zibo) 1,138,074; K'un-ming 1,127,411.
Households (1992). Average rural household size 4.7; urban household size 3.4. Family households (1990): 277,390,000 (99.4%); collective 1,671,000 (0.6%).

Vital statistics

Birth rate per 1,000 population (1992): 18.2 (world avg. 26.0).
Death rate per 1,000 population (1992): 6.6 (world avg. 9.2).
Natural increase rate per 1,000 population (1992): 11.6 (world avg. 16.8).
Total fertility rate (avg. births per childbearing woman; 1991): 2.3.
Marriage rate per 1,000 population (1992): 8.2.
Divorce rate per 1,000 population (1992): 0.7.
Life expectancy at birth (1990): male 68.6 years; female 71.8 years.

Major causes of death per 100,000 population (percentage distribution; 1992)[6]: malignant neoplasms (cancers) 21.7%; diseases of the circulatory system 21.1%; diseases of the respiratory system 16.8%; diseases of the heart 14.7%; injuries and poisoning 7.0%; digestive diseases 3.8%.

Social indicators

Educational attainment (1982). Percentage of population age 25 and over having: no schooling and incomplete primary 44.5%; completed primary 32.7%; completed junior secondary 16.1%; completed senior secondary 5.6%; postsecondary 1.1%.

Distribution of urban household income (1992)

avg. per capita income by quintile (avg. Y 2,032)

first quintile	second quintile	third quintile	fourth quintile	fifth quintile
Y 1,268	Y 1,665	Y 1,977	Y 2,330	Y 3,215

Quality of working life (1991). Average workweek: 48 hours. Annual rate per 100,000 workers for: injury or accident, n.a.; industrial illness, n.a.; death, n.a. Funds for pensions and social welfare relief (1992): Y 69,520,000,000. Average days lost to labour stoppages per 1,000 workdays: n.a. Average duration of journey to work: n.a. Method of transport: n.a. Rate per 1,000 workers of discouraged (unemployed no longer seeking work): n.a.
Access to services. Proportion of communes having access to electricity (1979) 87.1%. Percentage of urban population with: safe public water supply (1992) 92.5%; public sewage collection, n.a.; public fire protection, n.a.
Social participation. Eligible voters participating in last national election: n.a. Population participating in voluntary work: n.a. Trade union membership in total labour force (1988): 18.9%. Practicing religious population in total affiliated population: n.a.
Social deviance. Annual reported arrest rate per 100,000 population (1986) for: property violation 20.7; infringing personal rights 7.2; disruption of social administration 3.3; endangering public security[7] 1.0.
Leisure. Favourite leisure activities: n.a.
Material well-being (1992). Urban families possessing (number per family): wristwatches 2.7; bicycles 1.9; televisions 1.1; sewing machines 0.7; radios 0.4. Rural families possessing (number per family): wristwatches 1.9; bicycles 1.3; sewing machines 0.6; televisions 0.6.; radios 0.3.

National economy

Gross national product (at current market prices; 1992): U.S.$442,346,000,000 (U.S.$380 per capita).

Structure of gross national product and labour force

	1992 in value Y '000,000,000	1992 % of total value	1992 labour force ('000)[8]	1992 % of labour force
Agriculture	574.40	23.9	348,550	58.7
Mining			1,000	0.2
Manufacturing	1,012.84	42.1	102,190	17.2
Construction	144.68	6.0	27,020	4.5
Public utilities	...	...	...	...
Transp. and commun.	140.21	5.8	15,730	2.6
Trade	141.16	5.9	33,120	5.6
Finance	...	...	2,480	0.4
Pub. admin.	...	...	11,480	1.9
Services	388.73	16.2	29,620	5.0
Other	1.60	0.1	23,130	3.9
TOTAL	2,430.62	100.0	594,320	100.0

Budget (1993). Revenue: Y 427,187,000,000 (taxes 84.0%; funds collected for energy and transport projects 3.7%). Expenditures: Y 511,587,000,000 (capital construction 17.3%; culture, education, and public health 16.7%; government administration 8.7%; defense 8.3%; subsidies 7.3%).
Public debt (external, outstanding; 1992): U.S.$58,475,000,000.
Tourism: receipts from visitors (1992) U.S.$3,948,000,000; expenditures by nationals abroad U.S.$812,000,000.

Retail and service enterprises (1992)

	no. of enterprises	no. of employees	annual wage as a % of all wages	annual gross output value (Y '000,000)
Retail trade	10,063,000	24,345,000	...	...
Grocery stores	171,000	1,213,000		
Department stores	174,000	2,120,000		
Other food shops	120,000	824,000		
Agricultural supplies stores	100,000	508,000		
Electrical appliances stores	96,000	930,000		
Household supplies stores	71,000	377,000		
Grain and oil shops	81,000	783,000		
Textile stores	40,000	288,000		
Drugstores	32,000	251,000		
Bookstores	28,000	151,000		
Coal stores	16,000	200,000		
Service trade	1,842,000	4,522,000	...	...
Repair shops	742,000	1,110,000		
Barbershops	508,000	779,000		
Hotels	189,000	1,427,000		
Photo studios	98,000	225,000		

Production (metric tons except as noted). Agriculture, forestry, fishing (1992): grains—rice 188,150,000, wheat 101,003,000, corn (maize) 95,340,-000, sorghum 6,015,000, millet 5,001,000, barley 2,000,000; oilseeds—rapeseed 7,653,000, peanuts (groundnuts) 5,580,000, sunflower seeds 1,050,000; fruits and nuts—watermelons 6,530,000, oranges 5,090,000, apples 4,815,-000, cantaloupes 3,280,000, walnuts 160,000; other—sweet potatoes 109,-200,000, sugarcane 77,548,000, potatoes 33,937,000, sugar beets 15,010,000, seed cotton 13,584,000, soybeans 9,707,000, cabbage 8,303,000, tomatoes

5,620,000, cucumbers 4,315,000, tobacco leaves 3,178,000, eggplant 2,422,-000, tea 580,000; livestock (number of live animals) 379,739,000 pigs, 111,143,000 sheep, 95,032,000 goats, 82,760,000 cattle, 21,983,000 water buffalo, 11,200,000 asses, 10,201,000 horses, 2,179,000,000 chickens, 381,000,000 ducks; roundwood (1991) 282,334,000 cu m; fish catch (1991) 13,134,967. Mining and quarrying (1992): metal concentrates—copper 560,000, zinc 560,000, lead 330,000, tin 38,000, tungsten 25,000; metal ores—iron ore 197,-600,000, bauxite 3,000,000, manganese ore 1,600,000[9], silver 125,000[9], gold 90,000[9]; nonmetals—salt 28,100,000, gypsum 11,000,000, phosphates 4,100,-000[9], talc 2,650,000, barite 1,800,000, fluorite 1,600,000, asbestos 240,000, graphite 200,000[9]. Manufacturing (1993): cement 360,000,000; rolled steel 76,000,000; chemical fertilizer 20,160,000; paper and paperboard 18,200,-000; sulfuric acid 13,140,000; sugar 7,446,000; cotton yarn 5,020,000; cotton fabrics 19,100,000,000 m; cigarettes 33,670,000 cases; colour television sets 13,870,000 units; household washing machines 8,763,000 units; household refrigerators 6,220,000 units; motor vehicles 1,310,000 units. Construction (1992): residential 850,170,000 sq m; nonresidential 297,830,000 sq m. Distribution of industrial production (percentage of total value of output by sector; 1978 [1992]): state-operated enterprises 80.6% (48.1%); collectives 19.2% (38.0%); privately operated enterprises 0.2% (13.9%). Retail sales (percentage of total sales by sector; 1978 [1992]): state-operated enterprises 90.5% (41.3%); collectives 7.4% (27.9%); privately operated enterprises 2.1% (30.8%).

Manufacturing and mining enterprises (1992)

	no. of enter-prises	no. of employees[10]	annual wages as a % of avg. of all wages[11]	annual gross output value (Y '000,000)
Manufacturing				
Machinery, transport equipment, and basic manufactures,	102,995	18,240,000	96.7	736,407
of which,				
Industrial equipment	6,580	9,640,000	...	52,693
Transport equipment	11,238	2,400,000	...	154,401
Electronic goods	5,060	1,670,000	...	92,893
Measuring equipment	3,415	720,000	...	18,261
Textiles,	23,831	7,430,000	95.5	289,916
of which,				
Cotton	9,001	...	...	152,340
Foodstuffs,	36,605	4,750,000	87.5	167,191
of which,				
Grains and edible oils	10,930	...	...	45,808
Processed meat	...	...	...	...
Tobacco manufactures	340	...	...	64,652
Chemicals,	43,232	7,210,000	92.1	379,892
of which,				
Organic chemicals	7,180	...	...	60,961
Plastics	14,729	1,030,000	...	66,600
Building materials,	50,904	4,080,000	93.0	142,240
of which,				
Brick, tile, other	...	...	...	...
Cement (all forms)	5,336	856,000[12]	...	52,975
Secondary forest products (including paper and stationery)	29,816	2,400,000	96.1	76,429
Primary forest products	982	1,120,000	114.3	10,550
Mining				
Nonferrous and ferrous metals	4,015	920,000	107.6	18,500
Crude petroleum	41	830,000	...	61,122
Coal	9,215	5,550,000	119.8	61,234

Energy production (consumption): electricity (kW-hr; 1991) 677,550,000,000 (680,400,000,000); coal (metric tons; 1991) 1,087,406,000 (1,058,208,000); crude petroleum (barrels; 1991) 1,032,061,000 (905,111,000); petroleum products (metric tons; 1991) 95,311,000 (96,593,000); natural gas (cu m; 1991) 16,033,000,000 (16,033,000,000).

Financial aggregates[13]

	1987	1988	1989	1990	1991	1992	1993
Exchange rate, Y per:							
U.S. dollar	3.72	3.72	4.72	5.22	5.43	5.75	5.80
£	6.96	6.73	7.58	10.06	10.16	8.70	8.59
SDR	5.28	5.01	6.21	7.43	7.77	7.91	7.97
International reserves (U.S.$)							
Total (excl. gold; '000,000)	16,305	18,541	17,960	29,586	43,674	20,620	20,816[14]
SDRs ('000,000)	640	586	540	562	577	419	484
Reserve pos. in IMF ('000,000)	429	407	398	430	433	758	704
Foreign exchange	15,236	17,548	17,022	28,594	42,664	19,443	19,642[14]
Gold ('000,000 fine troy oz)	12.7	12.7	12.7	12.7	12.7	12.7	12.7[14]
% world reserves	1.3	1.3	1.4	1.4	1.4	1.4	1.4[14]
Interest and prices							
Central bank discount (%)	...	...	...	...	...	...	...
Govt. bond yield (%)	...	...	...	...	...	...	...
Industrial share prices	...	...	...	...	...	...	...
Balance of payments (U.S.$'000,000)							
Balance of visible trade,	−1,661	−5,315	−5,620	+9,165	+8,743	+5,183	...
of which:							
Imports, f.o.b.	−36,395	−46,369	−48,840	−42,354	−50,176	−64,385	...
Exports, f.o.b.	34,734	41,054	43,220	51,519	58,919	69,568	...
Balance of invisibles	+1,961	+1,513	+1,303	+2,833	+5,022	+1,218	...
Balance of payments, current account	300	−3,802	−4,317	+11,998	+13,765	+6,401	...

Household income and expenditure. Average household size (1992) 4.3; rural household 4.7, urban household 3.4. Average annual income per household Y 5,796; rural household Y 5,396, urban household Y 6,846. Sources of income: rural household (1992)—income from household businesses 82.1%, income from the collective 9.9%, rural new economic associations 0.3%, other 7.7%; urban household (1992)—wages 79.8%, business income 19.1%, other 1.1%. Expenditure (1992): rural household—food 56.8%, personal effects 11.8%, housing 10.3%, clothing 8.0%, fuel 4.4%, cultural activities

3.8%; urban household—food 52.9%, clothing 14.1%, health 8.8%, personal effects 8.4%, household materials 6.0%, cultural activities 5.1%, fuel 4.7%. *Population economically active* (1987): total 584,569,200; activity rate of total population 54.7% (participation rates: over age 15, 76.8%; female 49.7%; unemployed 2.0%[15]). Urban workforce by sector of employment, 1978 (1992): state-run enterprises 74,500,000 (108,890,000); collectives 20,000,000 (36,-210,000); self-employment or privately run enterprises 150,000 (11,197,000).

Price and earnings indexes (1985 = 100)

	1985	1986	1987	1988	1989	1990	1991
Consumer price index	100.0	107.0	116.4	140.5	163.4	165.7	174.1
Annual earnings index[16]	100.0	115.8	127.1	152.2	168.6	186.4	203.8

Land use (1991): forested 13.6%; meadows and pastures 42.9%; agricultural and under permanent cultivation 10.4%; other 33.1%.

Foreign trade[17]

Balance of trade (current prices)

	1987	1988	1989	1990	1991	1992
Y '000,000	−990	−11,810	−6,600	+62,570	+69,470	+57,730
% of total	0.3%	3.2%	1.7%	12.0%	10.2%	7.0%

Imports (1992): U.S.$80,610,000,000 (machinery and transport equipment 38.8%; products of textile industries, rubber and metal products 23.9%; chemical and related products 14.4%; inedible raw materials 7.2%; mineral fuels and lubricants 4.4%; food and live animals 3.9%). *Major import sources:* Hong Kong 25.5%; Japan 17.0%; United States 11.0%; Taiwan 7.3%; Germany 5.0%; Russia 4.4%; South Korea 3.3%; Canada 2.4%; Italy 2.2%; Australia 2.1%; Indonesia 1.9%.
Exports (1992): U.S.$84,998,000,000 (products of textile industries, rubber and metal products 19.0%; machinery and transport equipment 15.6%; food and live animals 9.8%; mineral fuels and lubricants 5.5%; chemicals and allied products 5.1%; inedible raw materials 3.7%). *Major export destinations:* Hong Kong 44.1%; Japan 13.8%; United States 10.1%; Germany 2.9%; South Korea 2.9%; Russia 2.7%; Singapore 2.4%; The Netherlands 1.4%; Italy 1.3%; Thailand 1.1%; United Kingdom 1.1%.

Transport and communications

Transport. Railroads (1992): length 42,564 mi, 68,500 km; (1993) passenger-mi 217,800,000,000, passenger-km 350,500,000,000; short ton-mi cargo 817,-548,000,000, metric ton-km cargo 1,193,600,000,000. Roads (1992): total length 656,606 mi, 1,056,707 km (paved 88%). Vehicles (1992): passenger cars 2,261,600; trucks and buses 4,655,800. Merchant marine (1992): vessels (100 gross tons and over) 2,390; total deadweight tonnage 20,657,996. Air transport (1993): passenger-mi 32,000,000,000, passenger-km 51,500,000,000; short ton-mi cargo 1,100,000,000, metric ton-km cargo 1,600,000,000; airports (1994) with scheduled flights 94.
Communications. Daily newspapers (1988): total number 78; total circulation 39,597,000[18]; circulation per 1,000 population 37[18]. Radio (1990): total number of receivers 209,500,000 (1 per 5.4 persons). Television (1990): total number of receivers 35,000,000 (1 per 32.4 persons). Telephones (1991): 14,989,800 (1 per 77 persons).

Education and health

Education (1992)

	schools	teachers	students	student/ teacher ratio
Primary (age 7–13)	885,479	6,342,000	146,295,000	23.1
Secondary (age 13–17)	84,021	3,141,000	47,708,000	15.2
Secondary specialized	13,763	483,000	5,836,000	12.1
Higher	1,053	388,000	2,184,000	5.6

Literacy (1990): total population age 15 and over literate 636,112,000 (77.7%); males literate 364,687,000 (87.0%); females literate 271,425,000 (68.0%).
Health (1992): physicians 1,808,000 (1 per 648 persons); hospital beds 3,049,-000 (1 per 382 persons); infant mortality rate per 1,000 live births (1993) 26.
Food (1988–90): daily per capita caloric intake 2,641 (vegetable products 89%, animal products 11%); 112% of FAO recommended minimum requirement.

Military

Total active duty personnel (1993): 3,030,000 (army 75.9%, navy 8.6%, air force 15.5%). *Military expenditure as percentage of GNP* (1991): 3.3% (world 4.2%); per capita expenditure U.S.$44.

[1]Names of the provinces, autonomous regions, and municipalities are stated in conventional form, followed by Pinyin transliteration; names of capitals are stated in conventional form or Wade-Giles transliteration, followed by Pinyin transliteration. [2]Data for Taiwan, Quemoy, and Matsu are excluded. [3]January 1. [4]Includes 4,600 sq mi (11,900 sq km) not shown separately. [5]Total includes servicemen not assigned to any political division. [6]Based on urban sample population. [7]Excludes arrests for anti-Communist activities. [8]Social labour force. [9]1989. [10]In state-owned and collective-owned industries only. [11]1979. [12]1984. [13]Exchange rates and international reserves are end-of-year figures. [14]End-of-November figures. [15]Rate of waiting for employment in cities and towns. [16]Average annual wage in industrial establishments in urban areas. [17]Imports and exports f.o.b. [18]Circulation data based on 58 dailies.

Colombia

Official name: República de Colombia (Republic of Colombia).
Form of government: unitary, multiparty republic with two legislative houses (Senate [102[1]]; House of Representatives [163[2]]).
Head of state and government: President.
Capital: Santafé de Bogotá, D.C.
Official language: Spanish.
Official religion: none.
Monetary unit: 1 peso (Col$) = 100 centavos; valuation (Oct. 7, 1994) 1 U.S.$ = Col$836.98; 1 £ = Col$1,331.

Area and population

Departments	Capitals	area sq mi	area sq km	population 1994 estimate
Amazonas	Leticia	42,342	109,665	57,107
Antioquia	Medellín	24,561	63,612	4,603,873
Arauca	Arauca	9,196	23,818	99,041
Atlántico	Barranquilla	1,308	3,388	1,779,491
Bolívar	Cartagena	10,030	25,978	1,506,813
Boyacá	Tunja	8,953	23,189	1,299,160
Caldas	Manizales	3,046	7,888	920,648
Caquetá	Florencia	34,349	88,965	324,950
Casanare	Yopal	17,236	44,640	186,508
Cauca	Popayán	11,316	29,308	959,693
Cesar	Valledupar	8,844	22,905	834,270
Chocó	Quibdó	17,965	46,530	363,617
Córdoba	Montería	9,660	25,020	1,149,887
Cundinamarca	Santafé de Bogotá, D.C.	8,735	22,623	1,722,009
Guainía	Puerto Inírida	27,891	72,238	13,294
Guaviare	Guaviare	16,342	42,327	69,580
Huila	Neiva	7,680	19,890	806,020
La Guajira	Riohacha	8,049	20,848	363,368
Magdalena	Santa Marta	8,953	23,188	1,010,150
Meta	Villavicencio	33,064	85,635	594,030
Nariño	Pasto	12,845	33,268	1,192,605
Norte de Santander	Cúcuta	8,362	21,658	1,039,112
Putumayo	Mocoa	9,608	24,885	238,029
Quindío	Armenia	712	1,845	422,116
Risaralda	Pereira	1,598	4,140	762,982
San Andrés y Providencia	San Andrés	17	44	43,247
Santander	Bucaramanga	11,790	30,537	1,688,124
Sucre	Sincelejo	4,215	10,917	628,738
Tolima	Ibagué	9,097	23,562	1,212,532
Valle	Cali	8,548	22,140	3,440,795
Vaupés	Mitú	25,200	65,268	37,241
Vichada	Puerto Carreño	38,703	100,242	19,573
Capital District				
Santafé de Bogotá, D.C.		613	1,587	5,131,582
TOTAL		440,831[3]	1,141,748	34,520,185

Demography

Population (1994): 34,520,000.
Density (1994): persons per sq mi 78.3, persons per sq km 30.2.
Urban-rural (1985): urban 67.2%; rural 32.8%.
Sex distribution (1992): male 49.60%; female 50.40%.
Age breakdown (1992): under 15, 34.4%; 15–29, 29.8%; 30–44, 20.0%; 45–59, 9.5%; 60–74, 4.9%; 75 and over, 1.4%.
Population projection: (2000) 37,822,000; (2010) 42,959,000.
Doubling time: 35 years.
Ethnic composition (1985): mestizo 58.0%; white 20.0%; mulatto 14.0%; black 4.0%; mixed black-Indian 3.0%; Amerindian 1.0%.
Religious affiliation (1993): Roman Catholic 93.1%; other 6.9%.
Major cities (1994): Santafé de Bogotá, D.C., 5,131,582; Cali 1,687,280; Medellín 1,608,379; Barranquilla 1,049,170; Cartagena 726,256.

Vital statistics

Birth rate per 1,000 population (1990–95): 25.8 (world avg. 26.0).
Death rate per 1,000 population (1990–95): 5.9 (world avg. 9.2).
Natural increase rate per 1,000 population (1990–95): 19.9 (world avg. 16.8).
Total fertility rate (avg. births per childbearing woman; 1981–86): 3.4.
Life expectancy at birth (1990–95): male 66.4 years; female 72.3 years.
Major causes of death per 100,000 population (1990)[4]: homicide with firearms 101.0; malignant neoplasms (cancers) 82.6; ischemic heart disease 70.4; accidents 49.0; infectious and parasitic diseases 25.5.

National economy

Budget (1992). Revenue: Col$7,349,538,000,000 (indirect taxes 26.1%, credit resources 24.1%, direct taxes 22.8%). Expenditures: Col$5,869,789,000,000 (finance and public credit 39.4%, education 18.9%, defense 8.8%, public works and transportation 6.1%, police 4.6%, health 4.5%).
Public debt (external, outstanding; 1992): U.S.$13,245,000,000.
Tourism (1992): receipts U.S.$705,000,000; expenditures U.S.$641,000,000.
Production (metric tons except as noted). Agriculture (1993): sugarcane 29,000,000, potatoes 2,860,000, plantains 2,573,000, bananas 1,950,000, rice 1,816,000, coffee (green) 1,362,000, corn (maize) 1,240,000, sorghum 676,- 000; livestock (number of live animals) 25,324,000 cattle, 3,708,000[5] vicuña, 2,635,000 pigs, 2,540,000 sheep; roundwood (1991) 19,702,000 cu m; fish catch (1991) 108,708. Mining and quarrying (1993): iron ore 657,210[6]; gold 895,204 troy oz; silver 240,712 troy oz; emeralds (1990) U.S.$116,700,000[7]. Manufacturing (value added in Col$'000,000; 1991): processed food 1,361,583; beverages 763,978; textiles and clothing 407,683; machinery and electrical

apparatus 256,286; transport equipment 193,554; pharmaceutical products 172,083; basic steel 168,330. Construction (1992)[8]: residential 9,436,277 sq m; nonresidential 2,180,763 sq m. Energy production (consumption): electricity (kW-hr; 1991) 37,000,000,000 (37,000,000,000); coal (metric tons; 1991) 24,000,000 (6,600,000); crude petroleum (barrels; 1991) 151,952,000 (91,632,- 000); petroleum products (metric tons; 1991) 11,411,000 (8,575,000); natural gas (cu m; 1991) 4,658,065,000 (4,658,065,000).
Gross national product (1992): U.S.$44,555,000,000 (U.S.$1,290 per capita).

Structure of gross domestic product and labour force

	1992 in value Col$'000,000	1992 % of total value	1980 labour force	1980 % of labour force
Agriculture	5,176,994	15.7	2,412,413	28.5
Mining	2,505,043	7.6	49,740	0.6
Manufacturing	6,545,605	19.8	1,136,735	13.4
Construction	1,640,860	5.0	242,191	2.9
Public utilities	845,743	2.5	44,233	0.5
Transp. and commun.	3,346,389	10.1	352,623	4.2
Trade			1,261,633	14.9
Finance			278,210	3.2
Pub. admin., defense	13,003,516	39.3	1,998,460	23.6
Services				
Other			690,762[9]	8.2[9]
TOTAL	33,064,150	100.0	8,467,000	100.0

Population economically active (1985): total 9,558,000; activity rate 34.3% (participation rates: over age 12, 49.4%; female 32.8%; unemployed 4.3%).

Price and earnings indexes (1990 = 100)

	1987	1988	1989	1990	1991	1992	1993
Consumer price index	48.0	61.5	77.4	100.0	130.4	165.6	203.1
Monthly earnings index[10]	50.0	62.5	79.4	100.0	126.1	158.9	198.7

Household income and expenditure. Avg. household size (1985) 4.7; sources of income (1991): wages 44.4%, self-employment 36.9%, transfer payments 11.3%; expenditure (1991): food 33.6%, transportation 17.9%, housing 8.2%, health care 6.6%, household durable goods 5.7%, clothing 4.7%.
Land use (1991): forest 48.1%; pasture 39.0%; agriculture 5.2%; other 7.7%.

Foreign trade[11]

Balance of trade (current prices)

	1987	1988	1989	1990	1991	1992
U.S.$'000,000	+735.0	+505.4	+729.9	+1,621.0	+2,720.1	+920.1
% of total	8.6%	5.3%	6.8%	13.6%	23.2%	7.1%

Imports (1992)[12]: U.S.$6,485,200,000 (machinery and transport equipment 34.6%, chemicals 24.4%, vegetable products 7.4%, metals 7.0%, petroleum 5.6%, textiles and leather products 4.3%). *Major import sources:* U.S. 38.4%; Japan 7.5%; Venezuela 6.7%; Germany 6.3%; Brazil 4.1%; France 3.0%.
Exports (1992)[12]: U.S.$7,263,200,000 (forestry and fisheries 32.4%, petroleum products 19.2%, coffee 17.3%, textiles and apparel 12.5%, chemicals 5.4%, food and tobacco 4.8%, paper and publishing 2.5%). *Major export destinations:* U.S. 39.2%; Germany 8.6%; Venezuela 8.5%; The Netherlands 4.0%.

Transport and communications

Transport. Railroads (1992): route length (1993) 3,230 km; passenger-km 15,- 524,000; metric ton-km cargo 242,917,000. Roads (1991): total length 107,377 km (paved 12%). Vehicles (1992): cars 854,160; trucks and buses 430,611. Merchant marine (1992): vessels (100 gross tons and over) 101; deadweight tonnage 403,047. Air transport (1992): passenger-km 4,582,132,000; metric ton-km cargo 956,177,000; airports (1994) 68.
Communications. Daily newspapers (1993): 27; circulation 1,358,800; circulation per 1,000 population 40. Radio (1993): 34,487,000 receivers (1 per 1.0 persons). Television (1993): 5,500,000 receivers (1 per 6.2 persons). Telephones (1991): 3,795,000 (1 per 8.7 persons).

Education and health

Education (1991)

	schools	teachers	students	student/ teacher ratio
Primary (6–10)	41,044	143,193	4,310,970	30.1
Secondary (11–16)[13]	6,134[14]	119,742	2,377,947	19.9
Higher	235[15]	51,725[16]	474,787[16]	9.2[16]

Educational attainment (1985). Percentage of population age 25 and over having: no schooling 15.3%; primary education 50.1%; secondary 25.4%; higher 6.8%; not stated 2.4%. Literacy (1990): population age 15 and over literate 86.7%; males literate 87.5%; females literate 85.9%.
Health (1989): physicians 29,498 (1 per 1,078 persons); hospital beds 45,888 (1 per 693 persons); infant mortality rate (1990–95) 37.0.
Food (1988–90): daily per capita caloric intake 2,453 (vegetable products 84%, animal products 16%); 106% of FAO recommended minimum requirement.

Military

Total active duty personnel (1993): 140,000 (army 85.7%, navy 9.3%, air force 5.0%). *Military expenditure as percentage of GNP* (1991): 2.6% (world 4.2%); per capita expenditure U.S.$31.

[1]Includes 2 nonelective seats. [2]Includes 2 nonelective seats from Amerindian communities and 2 from black communities. [3]Detail does not add to total given because of rounding. [4]Estimates based on about 75% of total deaths. [5]1991. [6]1992. [7]Value of foreign sales. [8]Construction permits issued for 11 urban centres. [9]Includes unemployed. [10]Minimum legal wages revised annually January 2. [11]Import figures are f.o.b. in balance of trade and c.i.f. in commodities and trading partners. [12]Estimate. [13]Secondary includes vocational and teacher training. [14]1988. [15]1987. [16]1989.

Comoros[1]

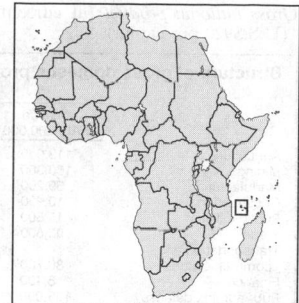

Official name: Jumhurīyat al-Qumur al-Ittihādīyah al-Islāmīyah (Arabic); République Fédérale Islamique des Comores (French) (Federal Islamic Republic of the Comoros).
Form of government: federal Islamic republic with one legislative house (Federal Assembly [42]).
Chief of state: President.
Head of government: Prime Minister.
Capital: Moroni.
Official languages: Comorian; Arabic; French.
Official religion: Islam.
Monetary unit: 1 Comorian franc (CF) = 100 centimes; valuation (Oct. 7, 1994) 1 U.S.$ = CF 395.82; 1 £ = CF 629.56.

Area and population

Islands[2,3]	Capitals	area sq mi	area sq km	population 1992 estimate
Mwali (Mohéli)	Fomboni	112	290	26,100
Ndzuwani (Anjouan)	Mutsamudu	164	424	205,400
Ngazidja (Grande-Comore)	Moroni	443	1,148	265,500
TOTAL		719	1,862	497,000[4]

Demography

Population (1994): 527,000.
Density (1994): persons per sq mi 733.0, persons per sq km 283.0.
Urban-rural (1990)[5]: urban 27.8%; rural 72.2%.
Sex distribution (1990)[5]: male 50.64%; female 49.36%.
Age breakdown (1990)[5]: under 15, 48.3%; 15–29, 26.3%; 30–44, 13.8%; 45–59, 7.7%; 60–74, 3.3%; 75 and over, 0.6%.
Population projection: (2000) 640,000; (2010) 883,000.
Doubling time: 20 years.
Ethnic composition (1980): Comorian (a mixture of Bantu, Arab, and Malagasy peoples) 96.9%; Makua (a Bantu people from East Africa) 1.6%; French 0.4%; other 1.1%.
Religious affiliation (1990): Sunnī Muslim 99.4%; Roman Catholic 0.6%.
Major cities (1990): Moroni 22,000; Mutsamudu 15,000; Domoni 8,000; Fomboni 5,600; Mitsamiouli 4,200.

Vital statistics

Birth rate per 1,000 population (1993): 46.7 (world avg. 26.0).
Death rate per 1,000 population (1993): 11.3 (world avg. 9.2).
Natural increase rate per 1,000 population (1993): 35.4 (world avg. 16.8).
Total fertility rate (avg. births per childbearing woman; 1993): 6.9.
Marriage rate per 1,000 population: n.a.[6]
Divorce rate per 1,000 population: n.a.
Life expectancy at birth (1993): male 55.2 years; female 59.5 years.
Major causes of death per 100,000 population: n.a.; however, major diseases include malaria (afflicts 80% of the adult population), tuberculosis, leprosy, and kwashiorkor (a nutritional deficiency disease).

National economy

Budget (1993). Revenue: CF 24,000,000,000 (grants 47.9%, tax revenue 44.6%, other 7.5%). Expenditures: CF 26,800,000,000 (current expenditures 58.2%; development expenditures 41.8%).
Production (metric tons except as noted). Agriculture, forestry, fishing (1993): bananas 55,400, coconuts 50,000[5], cassava 47,540, pulses 8,000[5], copra 5,000[5], corn (maize) 3,610, rice 3,030, cloves 1,566[7], vanilla 288[7], ylang-ylang 38[7], other export crops grown in small quantities include coffee, cinnamon, and tuberoses; livestock (number of live animals) 130,000 goats[5], 47,000 cattle[5], 15,000 sheep[5]; roundwood, n.a.; fish catch (1991) 6,455[5], of which tuna 3,205[5]. Mining and quarrying (1992): sand, gravel, and crushed stone from coral mining for local construction. Manufacturing: products include processed vanilla and ylang-ylang, cement, handicrafts, soaps, soft drinks, woodwork, and clothing. Construction: n.a. Energy production (consumption): electricity (kW-hr; 1993) 28,200,000 ([1992] 16,000,000); coal, none (none); crude petroleum, none (none); petroleum products (metric tons; 1992) none (21,000); natural gas, none (none).
Population economically active (1985): total 117,216; activity rate of total population 29.6% (participation rates: ages 15–64, 53.1%; female 26.2%; unemployed [1993]: unofficially more than 70%).

Price and earnings indexes (1985 = 100)

	1987	1988	1989	1990	1991	1992	1993
Consumer price index[8]	111.1	114.0	117.6	122.3	...	9	10
Earnings index	...	...	...	...	...	...	...

Tourism (1993): receipts from visitors U.S.$13,800,000; expenditures by nationals abroad U.S.$5,700,000.
Public debt (external, outstanding; 1992): U.S.$165,100,000.
Household income and expenditure. Average household size (1985) 5.6; income per household: n.a.; sources of income: n.a.; expenditure (1983)[11]: food and beverages 56.0%, energy 14.4%, clothing and footwear 10.0%, transportation and communications 6.6%, health care 5.0%, recreation 3.0%, tobacco 3.0%, other 2.0%.

Gross national product (at current market prices; 1993): U.S.$266,000,000 (U.S.$520 per capita).

Structure of gross domestic product and labour force

	1993 in value CF '000,000	1993 % of total value	1980 labour force[12]	1980 % of labour force
Agriculture, fishing	27,550	39.2	53,063	53.3
Mining	...	...	62	0.1
Manufacturing	3,161	4.5	3,946	4.0
Construction	3,897	5.6	3,267	3.3
Public utilities	995	1.4	129	0.1
Transportation and communications	3,197	4.6	2,118	2.1
Trade, restaurants, hotels	19,647	28.0	1,873	1.9
Finance, insurance	} 9,669	} 13.8	237	0.2
Public admin., defense			2,435	2.5
Services	2,093	3.0	4,646	4.7
Other	—	—	27,687[13]	27.8[13]
TOTAL	70,209	100.0[14]	99,463	100.0

Land use (1991)[5]: forested 15.7%; meadows and pastures 6.7%; agricultural and under permanent cultivation 44.9%; other 32.7%.

Foreign trade[15]

Balance of trade (current prices)

	1988	1989	1990	1991	1992	1993
CF '000,000,000	−9.2	−7.8	−9.2	−9.4	−12.3	−10.6
% of total	42.0%	40.1%	48.4%	40.0%	50.4%	46.2%

Imports (1993): CF 16,800,000,000 (petroleum products 10.7%, rice 9.8%, vehicles 9.0%, meat and fish 7.5%, cement 6.1%, iron and steel 3.7%, unspecified commodities 40.4%). Major import sources (1992)[16]: France 59.0%; Bahrain 5.0%; Singapore 5.0%; Japan 5.0%; India 4.0%.
Exports (1993): CF 6,200,000,000 (vanilla 77.5%, ylang-ylang 13.0%, cloves 4.3%). Major export destinations: United States 46.2%; France 41.7%; Germany 8.4%.

Transport and communications

Transport. Railroads: none. Roads (1992): total length 466 mi, 750 km (paved 28%). Vehicles (1989)[5]: passenger cars, 1,000; trucks and buses, 4,000. Merchant marine (1992): vessels (100 gross tons and over) 6; total deadweight tonnage 3,579. Air transport (1990): passenger-mi 1,900,000, passenger-km 3,000,000; short ton-mi cargo, n.a., metric ton-mi cargo, n.a.; airports (1994) with scheduled flights 4.
Communications. Daily newspapers: none[17]. Radio (1993): total number of receivers 50,000 (1 per 10 persons). Television: no local television broadcasting in 1992. Telephones (1993): 4,010[18] (1 per 128 persons).

Education and health

Education (1989–90)

	schools	teachers	students	student/teacher ratio
Primary (age 6–11)[19]	257	1,777	64,737	36.4
Secondary (age 12–18)	...	557	14,472	26.0
Higher	...	32	248	7.8

Educational attainment (1980). Percentage of population age 25 and over having: no formal schooling 56.7%; Qur'anic school education 8.3%; primary 3.6%; secondary 2.0%; higher 0.2%; not specified 29.2%. Literacy (1990): total population age 15 and over literate, about 125,000 (slightly more than 50%).
Health: physicians (1990) 57 (1 per 8,135 persons); hospital beds (1982) 813 (1 per 437 persons); infant mortality rate per 1,000 live births (1993) 81.8.
Food (1988–90)[5]: daily per capita caloric intake 1,760 (vegetable products 95%, animal products 5%); 75% of FAO recommended minimum requirement.

Military

Total active duty personnel (1993): 989[20]. Military expenditure as percentage of GNP (1987): 1.9% (world 5.3%); per capita expenditure U.S.$7.

Congo

Official name: République du Congo (Republic of the Congo).
Form of government: multiparty republic with two legislative houses (Senate [60]; National Assembly [125]).
Chief of state: President.
Head of government: Prime Minister.
Capital: Brazzaville.
Official language: French.
Official religion: none.
Monetary unit: 1 CFA franc (CFAF) = 100 centimes; valuation (Oct. 7, 1994) 1 U.S.\$ = CFAF 526.67; 1 £ = CFAF 837.67.

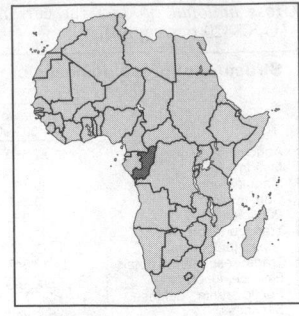

Area and population

Regions	Capitals	area sq mi	area sq km	population 1992 estimate
Bouenza	Madingou	4,733	12,258	177,357
Cuvette	Owando	28,900	74,850	151,839
Kouilou	Pointe-Noire	5,270	13,650	89,296
Lékoumou	Sibiti	8,089	20,950	74,420
Likouala	Impfondo	25,500	66,044	70,675
Niari	Loubomo	10,007[1]	25,918[1]	120,077
Plateaux	Djambala	14,826	38,400	119,722
Pool	Kinkala	13,110	33,955	182,671
Sangha	Ouesso	21,542[2]	55,795[2]	35,961
Communes				
Brazzaville	—	39	100	937,579
Loubomo	—	7	18	83,605
Mossendjo	—	2[1]	5[1]	16,405
Nkayi	—	3	8	42,465
Ouesso	—	2[2]	5[2]	16,171
Pointe-Noire	—	17	44	576,206
TOTAL		132,047	342,000	2,694,449

Demography

Population (1994): 2,856,000.
Density (1993): persons per sq mi 21.6, persons per sq km 8.4.
Urban-rural (1991): urban 41.1%; rural 58.9%.
Sex distribution (1990): male 49.27%; female 50.73%.
Age breakdown (1990): under 15, 46.1%; 15–29, 25.8%; 30–44, 14.4%; 45–59, 8.5%; 60–74, 4.2%; 75 and over, 1.0%.
Population projection: (2000) 3,374,000; (2010) 4,390,000.
Doubling time: 23 years.
Ethnic composition (1983): Kongo 51.5%; Teke 17.3%; Mboshi 11.5%; Mbete 4.8%; Punu 3.0%; Sango 2.7%; Maka 1.8%; Pygmy 1.5%; other 5.9%.
Religious affiliation (1980): Roman Catholic 53.9%; Protestant 24.9%; African Christian 14.2%; traditional beliefs 4.8%; other 2.2%.
Major cities (1992): Brazzaville 937,579; Pointe-Noire 576,206; Loubomo 83,605; Nkayi 42,465; Mossendjo 16,405.

Vital statistics

Birth rate per 1,000 population (1990–95): 44.7 (world avg. 26.0); legitimate, n.a.; illegitimate, n.a.
Death rate per 1,000 population (1990–95): 14.7 (world avg. 9.2).
Natural increase rate per 1,000 population (1990–95): 30.0 (world avg. 16.8).
Total fertility rate (avg. births per childbearing woman; 1990–95): 6.3.
Marriage rate per 1,000 population: n.a.
Divorce rate per 1,000 population: n.a.
Life expectancy at birth (1990–95): male 49.1 years; female 54.0 years.
Morbidity (reported cases of infectious disease per 100,000 population; 1988): diarrhea 1,144; malaria 874; gonorrhea 160; schistosomiasis 133; hookworm 69.5.

National economy

Budget (1992). Revenue: CFAF 175,000,000,000 (petroleum revenue 50.2%; nonpetroleum receipts 48.4%; aid 1.4%). Expenditures: CFAF 314,200,000,000 (current expenditure 85.1%, of which salaries 42.9%, transfers, subsidies, goods, and services 22.4%, interest 19.8%; restructuring expenditure 10.9%; capital expenditure 4.0%).
Tourism (1992): receipts from visitors U.S.\$6,000,000; expenditures by nationals abroad U.S.\$83,000,000.
Production (metric tons except as noted). Agriculture, forestry, fishing (1993): cassava 632,000, sugarcane 400,000, plantains 85,000, bananas 43,000, corn (maize) 28,000, peanuts (groundnuts) 25,000, avocados 24,000, palm oil 15,500, yams 13,000, pineapples 12,000, cacao beans 1,000, coffee 1,000; livestock (number of live animals) 305,000 goats, 111,000 sheep, 67,000 cattle; roundwood (1992) 3,624,000 cu m; fish catch (1991) 45,577. Mining and quarrying (1990): zinc concentrate 1,000; lead 1,000; gold 16 kg. Manufacturing (1990): distillate fuel oils 103,000, cement 58,000; raw sugar 36,000[3]; wheat flour 16,000[4]; soap 1,500[4]; cigarettes 1,000; beer 878,000 hectolitres; veneer sheets 60,000 cu m; plywood 2,000 cu m; footwear 171,000 pairs. Construction: n.a. Energy production (consumption): electricity (kW-hr; 1992) 428,000,000 (536,000,000); coal (metric tons; 1992) none (none); crude petroleum (barrels; 1992) 63,400,000 (9,160,000); petroleum products (metric tons; 1992) 527,000 (502,000); natural gas (cu m; 1992) 2,950,000 (2,950,000).
Land use (1992): forested 61.8%; meadows and pastures 29.2%; agricultural and under permanent cultivation 0.5%; other 8.5%.
Public debt (external, outstanding; 1992): U.S.\$3,878,000,000.

Gross national product (at current market prices; 1993): U.S.\$2,307,000,000 (U.S.\$920 per capita).

Structure of gross domestic product and labour force

	1991 in value CFAF '000,000[5]	% of total value	1991 labour force	% of labour force
Agriculture	113,000	14.8	471,000	59.1
Mining	160,300	21.0		
Manufacturing	69,200	9.1	101,000	12.7
Construction	10,900	1.4		
Public utilities	15,500	2.0		
Trade	93,800	12.3		
Transportation and communications	86,700	11.4	225,000	28.2
Finance	6,400	0.8		
Pub. admin., defense	133,000	17.5		
Services	73,200	9.6		
TOTAL	762,000	100.0[6]	797,000	100.0

Population economically active (1992): total 886,000; activity rate of total population 37.4% (participation rates [1984]: ages 15–64, 54.0%; female 45.6%; unemployed 2.3%[7]).

Price and earnings indexes (1985 = 100)

	1986	1987	1988	1989	1990	1991	1992
Consumer price index	102.4	104.0	109.0	113.1	113.4	117.5	120.0
Earnings index	...	...	...	...	...	...	...

Household income and expenditure. Average household size (1984) 5.2; income per household: n.a.; sources of income: n.a.; expenditure: n.a.

Foreign trade[8]

Balance of trade (current prices)

	1986	1987	1988	1989	1990	1991
CFAF '000,000,000	+64.8	+26.0	+87.2	+155.0	+105.4	+61.7
% of total	16.2%	9.1%	23.5%	36.3%	14.9%	10.9%

Imports (1991): CFAF 155,161,000,000 (machinery and transport equipment 38.0%, basic manufactures 27.4%, food and live animals 11.2%, chemicals and chemical products 8.4%, mineral fuels 3.2%, beverages and tobacco 2.3%). Major import sources (1990): France 48.1%; Cameroon 6.4%; Italy 6.1%; West Germany 4.2%; Zaire 4.1%; The Netherlands 3.9%.
Exports (1991): CFAF 225,688,000,000 (petroleum and petroleum products 90.6%, basic manufactures 4.4%, inedible crude materials 2.4%, food and live animals 1.9%). Major export destinations (1990): United States 42.9%; France 16.1%; Belgium-Luxembourg 8.3%; Italy 7.8%; The Netherlands 7.2%; Spain 6.2%.

Transport and communications

Transport. Railroads (1991): length 494 mi, 795 km; passenger-mi 340,000,000, passenger-km 547,000,000; short ton-mi cargo 273,000,000, metric ton-km cargo 399,000,000. Roads (1992): total length 7,920 mi, 12,745 km (paved 10%). Vehicles (1992): passenger cars 28,000; trucks and buses 17,418. Merchant marine (1992): vessels (100 gross tons and over) 22; total deadweight tonnage 10,840. Air transport: n.a.; airports (1994) with scheduled flights 3.
Communications. Daily newspapers (1990): total number 5; total circulation 17,000; circulation per 1,000 population 7.0. Radio (1993): total number of receivers 250,000 (1 per 11 persons). Television (1993): total number of receivers 8,500 (1 per 326 persons). Telephones (1989): 25,800 (1 per 85 persons).

Education and health

Education (1990)

	schools	teachers	students	student/teacher ratio
Primary (age 6–13)	1,655	7,626	502,918	65.9
Secondary (age 14–18)	238[9]	4,924	170,465	34.6
Voc., teacher tr.	60[9]	1,927	12,558	6.5
Higher	12[9]	1,112	10,671	9.6

Educational attainment (1984). Percentage of population age 25 and over having: no formal schooling 58.7%; some primary education 21.4%; secondary education 16.9%; postsecondary 3.0%. Literacy (1990): total population age 15 and over literate 56.6%; males literate 70.0%; females literate 43.9%.
Health (1989): physicians 567 (1 per 3,873 persons); hospital beds 4,817 (1 per 456 persons); infant mortality rate per 1,000 live births (1990–95) 65.
Food (1988–90): daily per capita caloric intake 2,295 (vegetable products 93%, animal products 7%); 103% of FAO recommended minimum requirement.

Military

Total active duty personnel (1994): 10,000 (army 80.0%, navy 8.0%, air force 12.0%). Military expenditure as percentage of GNP (1992): 3.8% (world [1991] 4.2%); per capita expenditure U.S.\$47.

---

[1]Mossendjo is included with Niari. [2]Ouesso is included with Sangha. [3]1993. [4]1988. [5]At current factor cost. [6]Detail does not add to total given because of rounding. [7]Previously employed only. [8]Import figures f.o.b. in balance of trade and trading partners, c.i.f. in commodities. [9]1989.

Costa Rica

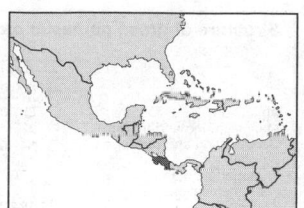

Official name: República de Costa Rica (Republic of Costa Rica).
Form of government: unitary multiparty republic with one legislative house (Legislative Assembly [57]).
Head of state and government: President.
Capital: San José.
Official language: Spanish.
Official religion: Roman Catholicism.
Monetary unit: 1 Costa Rican colón (₡) = 100 céntimos; valuation (Oct. 7, 1994) 1 U.S.$ = ₡159.70; 1 £ = ₡254.00.

Area and population

Provinces	Capitals	area sq mi	area sq km	population 1993 estimate
Alajuela	Alajuela	3,766	9,753	562,781
Cartago	Cartago	1,207	3,125	375,356
Guanacaste	Liberia	3,915	10,141	216,688
Heredia	Heredia	1,026	2,657	296,342
Limón	Limón	3,548	9,188	253,724
Puntarenas	Puntarenas	4,354	11,277	344,063
San José	San José	1,915	4,959	1,183,572
TOTAL		19,730[1]	51,100	3,232,526

Demography

Population (1994): 3,308,000.
Density (1994): persons per sq mi 165.6, persons per sq km 64.0.
Urban-rural (1993): urban 44.1%; rural 55.9%.
Sex distribution (1993): male 50.55%; female 49.45%.
Age breakdown (1993): under 15, 35.2%; 15–29, 27.5%; 30–44, 20.6%; 45–59, 10.0%; 60–74, 5.2%; 75 and over, 1.5%.
Population projection: (2000) 3,798,000; (2010) 4,534,000.
Doubling time: 32 years.
Ethnic composition (1990): white 85.0%; mestizo 8.0%; black/mulatto 3.0%; East Asian (mostly Chinese) 3.0%; Amerindian 1.0%.
Religious affiliation (1991): Roman Catholic 81.3%; other (mostly Protestant and nonreligious) 18.7%.
Major cities (1992): San José 280,613[2, 3] (metropolitan area 921,726[3]); Desamparados 54,668[4]; Limón 50,939[5]; Alajuela 45,442; Puntarenas 38,274.

Vital statistics

Birth rate per 1,000 population (1993): 25.7 (world avg. 26.0); (1984) legitimate 62.8%; illegitimate 37.2%.
Death rate per 1,000 population (1993): 4.2 (world avg. 9.2).
Natural increase rate per 1,000 population (1993): 21.5 (world avg. 16.8).
Total fertility rate (avg. births per childbearing woman; 1993): 3.1.
Marriage rate per 1,000 population (1993): 6.7.
Divorce rate per 1,000 population (1990): 1.1.
Life expectancy at birth (1990–95): male 71.9 years; female 77.5 years.
Major causes of death per 100,000 population (1991): diseases of the circulatory system 115.4; malignant neoplasms (cancers) 77.1; accidents, poisoning, and violence 41.0; diseases of the respiratory system 39.8; diseases of the digestive system 20.5.

National economy

Budget (1992)[6]. Revenue: ₡142,670,000,000 (customs duties 49.0%, general sales taxes 17.7%, income taxes 11.2%, consumption taxes 5.6%). Expenditures: ₡158,717,000,000 (current expenditure 89.8%, development expenditure 10.2%).
Public debt (external, outstanding; 1992): U.S.$3,207,000,000.
Gross national product (at current market prices; 1992): U.S.$6,261,000,000 (U.S.$2,000 per capita).

Structure of gross domestic product and labour force

	1993 In value U.S.$'000,000[7]	1993 % of total value[7]	1992 labour force	1992 % of labour force
Agriculture, forestry, fishing	1,159	15.3	259,052	23.8
Mining	...	...	1,554	0.1
Manufacturing	1,469	19.4	204,016	18.8
Construction	189	2.5	65,904	6.1
Public utilities	295	3.9	13,416	1.2
Transp. and commun.	424	5.6	50,205	4.6
Trade, restaurants	1,613	21.3	179,960	16.6
Finance, real estate	841	11.1	38,538	3.5
Public administration	1,045	13.8 }	258,370	23.8
Services	538	7.1 }		
Other	—	—	15,973	1.5
TOTAL	7,573	100.0	1,086,988	100.0

Production (metric tons except as noted) *Agriculture, forestry, fishing* (1992): sugarcane 2,840,000, bananas 1,633,000, rice 209,000, coffee 168,000, pineapples 154,000, oranges 134,000, plantains 86,000, palm oil 75,000, corn (maize) 40,000, dry beans 36,000, other products include other tropical fruits, cut flowers, and ornamental plants grown for export; livestock (number of live animals) 1,741,000 cattle, 224,000 pigs, 4,000,000 chickens; roundwood 4,306,000 cu m; fish catch (1991) 17,905, of which shrimps 3,492. *Mining and quarrying* (1992): limestone 1,300,000, gold 17,700 troy oz. *Manufacturing* (value added in ₡'000,000; 1990): food products 26,153; alcoholic and non-

alcoholic beverages 11,210; paper and paper products 3,940; plastic products 3,154; cement, cement products, bricks, and tiles 3,125; petroleum products 3,065; paints, varnishes, and soaps and other toiletries 2,986. *Construction* (completed; 1989): 1,914,000 sq m. *Energy production (consumption):* electricity (kW-hr; 1993) 4,385,000,000 (3,890,000,000); coal, none (none); crude petroleum (barrels; 1991) none (3,936,000); petroleum products (metric tons; 1992) 501,000 (1,116,000); natural gas, none (none).
Population economically active (1992): total 1,086,988; activity rate of total population 37.0% (participation rates: ages 15–69, 58.1%; female 29.9%; unemployed [1993] 4.1%).

Price and earnings indexes (1990 = 100)

	1988	1989	1990	1991	1992	1993	1994[8]
Consumer price index	72.1	84.0	100.0	128.7	156.8	172.1	187.3
Monthly earnings index[9]	70.7	84.3	100.0	116.8	144.5	...	...

Tourism (1993): receipts from visitors U.S.$577,000,000; expenditures by nationals abroad U.S.$266,000,000.
Family income and expenditure. Average household size (1993) 4.2; (1983) income per urban family ₡181,416 (U.S.$4,415), income per rural family ₡98,328 (U.S.$2,393); sources of income: n.a.; expenditure (1980–85): food and beverages 33.0%, household furnishings 9.0%, housing 8.0%, clothing and footwear 8.0%, education 8.0%, transportation 8.0%, other 26.0%.
Land use (1991): forested 32.1%; meadows and pastures 45.6%; agricultural and under permanent cultivation 10.4%; other 11.9%.

Foreign trade[10]

Balance of trade (current prices)

	1988	1989	1990	1991	1992	1993
U.S.$'000,000	−28.3	−136.4	−349.2	−97.5	−386.4	−540.7
% of total	1.1%	4.6%	10.8%	3.0%	9.5%	11.5%

Imports (1992): U.S.$2,441,500,000 ([11]basic manufactures for industry 38.0%; nondurable consumer goods 16.3%; capital goods for industry 15.1%; refined petroleum and derivatives 9.9%). *Major import sources:* United States 53.6%; Japan 6.7%; Venezuela 4.6%; Mexico 3.6%; Guatemala 3.4%.
Exports (1992): U.S.$1,828,900,000 (bananas 27.0%; coffee 11.1%; ornamental plants, leaves, and flowers 3.7%; pineapples 2.5%; fresh bovine meat 2.3%). *Major export destinations:* United States 55.2%; Germany 7.5%; Italy 5.3%; Canada 3.4%; Guatemala 3.1%.

Transport and communications

Transport. Railroads: route length (1992) 590 mi, 950 km; (1990) passenger-mi 26,500,000, passenger-km 42,600,000; (1987) short ton-mi cargo 102,700,000, metric ton-km cargo 150,000,000. Roads (1992): total length 22,096 mi, 35,560 km (paved 16%). Vehicles (1992): passenger cars 194,846; trucks and buses 100,356. Merchant marine (1992): vessels (100 gross tons and over) 24; total deadweight tonnage 8,368. Air transport (1993)[12]: passenger-mi 885,000,000, passenger-km 1,425,000,000; short-ton mi cargo 25,946,000, metric ton-km cargo 37,881,000; airports (1994) with scheduled flights 13.
Communications. Daily newspapers (1991): total number 4; total circulation 314,000; circulation per 1,000 population 102. Radio: n.a. Television (1993): total number of receivers 340,000 (1 per 9.4 persons). Telephones (1992): 485,680 (1 per 6.5 persons).

Education and health

Education (1991)

	schools	teachers	students	student/ teacher ratio
Primary (age 7–12)	3,317	14,078	453,297	32.2
Secondary (age 13–17)	179[13]	4,968	108,344	21.8
Vocational	77[13]	2,281	30,959	13.6
Higher[14, 15]	5	7,534	60,145	8.0

Educational attainment (1984). Percentage of economically active population age 25 and over having: no formal schooling 8.3%; incomplete primary education 28.6%; complete primary 26.3%; secondary 22.6%; postsecondary and higher 14.2%. *Literacy* (1990): total population age 15 and over literate 1,798,000 (92.8%); males literate 913,000 (92.6%); females literate 885,000 (93.1%).
Health (1993): physicians 3,362 (1 per 962 persons); hospital beds 6,126 (1 per 528 persons); infant mortality rate per 1,000 live births 13.7.
Food (1988–90): daily per capita caloric intake 2,711 (vegetable products 83%, animal products 17%); 121% of FAO recommended minimum requirement.

Military

Military expenditure as percentage of GNP (1991): 0.4% (world 4.2%); per capita expenditure U.S.$7. The army was officially abolished in 1948. Paramilitary and police forces had 7,500 members in 1993.

---

[1]Detail does not add to total given because of rounding. [2]Population of San José canton. [3]1993. [4]Within San José metropolitan area. [5]1991. [6]Excludes social security revenue and contributions. [7]Estimated figures. [8]April. [9]July wages only, for nonagricultural employees. [10]Import figures are f.o.b. in balance of trade and c.i.f. for commodities and trading partners. [11]Breakdown based on 1991 imports totaling U.S.$1,852,700,000. [12]Lacsa (Costa Rican Airlines) only. [13]1990. [14]Universities only. [15]1992.

Côte d'Ivoire

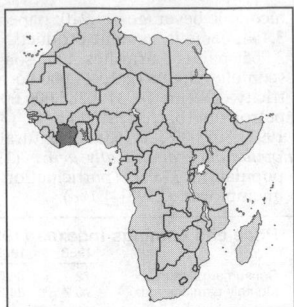

Official name: République de Côte d'Ivoire (Republic of Côte d'Ivoire [Ivory Coast][1]).
Form of government: multiparty republic with one legislative house (National Assembly [175]).
Chief of state: President.
Head of government: Prime Minister.
Capital: Abidjan (de facto; legislative).
  Capital designate: Yamoussoukro (de jure; administrative).
Official language: French.
Official religion: none.
Monetary unit: 1 CFA franc (CFAF) = 100 centimes; valuation (Oct. 7, 1994) 1 U.S.$ = CFAF 526.67; 1 £ = CFAF 837.67.

Area and population (1988 census)

Department	area sq km	population	Department	area sq km	population
Abengourou	5,200	216,058	Guiglo	11,220	170,321
Abidjan	8,550	2,485,847	Issia	3,590	195,663
Aboisso	6,250	225,895	Katiola	9,420	130,635
Adzopé	5,230	237,870	Korhogo	12,500	390,229
Agboville	3,850	203,493	Lakota	2,730	116,771
Agnibilékrou	1,700	84,349	Man	4,990	294,724
Bangolo	2,060	79,979	Mankono	10,660	123,362
Béoumi	2,820	90,327	M'bahiakro	5,460	102,531
Biankouma	4,950	98,236	Odiénné	20,600	169,764
Bondoukou	10,040	174,251	Oumé	2,400	141,268
Bongouanou	5,570	224,958	Sakassou	1,880	59,362
Bouaflé	3,980	165,822	San-Pédro	6,900	170,669
Bouaké	4,700	450,594	Sassandra	5,190	108,090
Bouna	21,470	135,813	Séguéla	11,240	121,235
Boundiali	7,895	127,847	Sinfra	1,690	121,903
Dabakala	9,670	81,820	Soubré	8,270	310,790
Daloa	5,450	359,753	Tabou	5,440	58,147
Danané	4,600	222,839	Tanda	6,490	204,070
Daoukro	3,610	86,494	Tengréla	2,200	54,847
Dimbokro	4,920	141,968	Tiassalé	3,370	133,708
Divo	7,920	387,106	Touba	8,720	107,886
Duékoué	2,930	102,168	Toumodi	2,780	80,802
Ferkessedougou	17,728	172,893	Vavoua	6,160	168,292
Gagnoa	4,500	276,217	Yamoussoukro	6,160	281,442
Grand-Lahou	2,280	52,559	Zuénoula	2,830	114,027
			TOTAL	320,763[2]	10,815,694

Demography

Population (1994): 13,895,000.
Density (1994): persons per sq mi 112.2, persons per sq km 43.3.
Urban-rural (1992): urban 42.0%; rural 58.0%.
Sex distribution (1988): male 51.10%; female 48.90%.
Age breakdown (1988): under 15, 46.8%; 15–29, 27.3%; 30–44, 15.0%; 45–59, 7.5%; 60–74, 2.8%; 75 and over 0.6%.
Population projection: (2000) 17,065,000; (2010) 23,657,000.
Ethnolinguistic composition[3] (1988): Akan 41.8%; Voltaic 16.3%; Malinke 15.9%; Kru 14.6%; Southern Mande 10.7%; other 0.7%.
Religious affiliation (1988): Muslim 38.7%; Catholic 20.8%; animist 17.0%; atheist 13.4%; Protestant 5.3%, excluding Harrism (1.4%), an indigenous form of Methodism; other 3.4%.
Major cities (1988): Abidjan 1,929,079[4]; Bouaké 329,850; Daloa 121,842; Korhogo 109,445; Yamoussoukro 106,786.

Vital statistics

Birth rate per 1,000 population (1990–95): 49.9 (world avg. 26.0).
Death rate per 1,000 population (1990–95): 14.7 (world avg. 9.2).
Natural increase rate per 1,000 population (1990–95): 35.2 (world avg. 16.8).
Total fertility rate (avg. births per childbearing woman; 1990–95): 7.4.
Life expectancy at birth (1988): male 53.6 years; female 57.2 years.
Major causes of death per 100,000 population: n.a.; however, the major infectious diseases include malaria, dysentery, yaws, pneumonia, leprosy.

National economy

Budget (1994). Revenue: CFAF 840,100,000,000 (current revenues 81.7%, of which duties 28.1%, taxes on income, goods, and services 16.8%). Expenditures: CFAF 789,800,000,000 (current expenses 79.1%; investments 20.9%).
Public debt (external, outstanding; 1992): U.S.$13,300,000,000.
Tourism (1992): receipts U.S.$53,000,000; expenditures U.S.$228,000,000.
Production (metric tons except as noted). Agriculture, forestry, fishing (1993): yams 2,480,000, sugarcane 1,450,000, cassava 1,388,000, plantains 1,199,000, cacao beans 775,000, rice 675,000, corn (maize) 540,000, coconuts 225,000, coffee 200,000; livestock (number of live animals) 1,219,000 sheep, 1,205,000 cattle, 940,000 goats; roundwood (1992) 13,302,000 cu m; fish catch (1992) 87,026. Mining and quarrying (1992): diamonds 15,000 carats. Manufacturing (1986): cement 770,000; beer 1,300,000 hectolitres; carbonated beverages 495,000 hectolitres; synthetic fibres 5,000,000 metres. Construction (in CFAF; 1984): 62,000,000,000. Energy production (consumption): electricity (kW-hr; 1992) 2,311,018,000 (1,946,170,000); coal, none (n.a.); crude petroleum (barrels; 1992) 2,382,000 (14,917,000); petroleum products (metric tons; 1992) 1,787,000 (1,763,000).
Land use (1992): forested 22.3%; meadows and pastures 40.9%; agricultural and under permanent cultivation 11.7%; other 25.1%.
Gross national product (1993): U.S.$8,416,000,000 (U.S.$630 per capita).

Structure of gross domestic product and labour force

	1993 in value CFAF '000,000,000	1993 % of total value	1988 labour force	1988 % of labour force
Agriculture	897.0	34.1	2,723,900	63.9
Manufacturing and mining			149,200	3.5
Construction and public utilities	542.0	20.6	89,500	2.1
Transportation and communications			123,600	2.9
Trade	1,194.0	45.3	558,400	13.1
Finance, pub. admin., defense, and services			618,100	14.5
TOTAL	2,633.0	100.0	4,262,700	100.0

Population economically active (1992): total 4,826,000; activity rate 37.4% (participation rates [1988]: ages 15–54, 66.4%; female 33.9%; unemployed 0.6%).

Price and earnings indexes (1985 = 100)

	1987	1988	1989	1990	1991	1992	1993
Consumer price index	114.3	122.3	123.5	122.5	124.5	128.9	132.7
Hourly earnings index[5]	100.0	100.0	100.0	100.0	100.0	100.0	...

Household income and expenditure. Average household size (1988) 5.4; average annual income per household (1980) CFAF 500,000; sources of income: self-employment 49.9%, wages 44.9%, transfers and other resources 5.2%; expenditure (1992)[6]: food 48.0%, clothing 10.1%, energy and water 8.5%, housing 7.8%, transportation 6.8%.

Foreign trade

Balance of trade (current prices)

	1987	1988	1989	1990	1991	1992
U.S.$'000,000	+1,118.3	+1,078.1	+1,067.4	+1,417.0	...	+657.0
% of total	23.4%	24.1%	23.5%	29.4%	...	11.5%

Imports (1993): CFAF 452,600,000,000 (1992; crude and refined petroleum 22.5%; machinery and transport equipment 21.2%; food and food products 16.6%; pharmaceuticals 5.7%; plastics 3.3%; paper and paper products 2.9%; chemicals 2.6%; iron 2.5%). *Major import sources* (1992): France 34.2%; Nigeria 18.7%; Japan 4.2%; Germany 3.9%; The Netherlands 3.9%.
Exports (1993): CFAF 755,600,000,000 (1992; food products 53.1%, of which cocoa beans and products 33.8%, coffee and coffee products 7.3%, fish products 3.4%; petroleum products 11.2%; wood and wood products 9.7%; cotton and cotton cloth 5.2%). *Major export destinations* (1992): France 15.0%; The Netherlands 11.5%; Germany 5.8%; Italy 5.6%; Burkina Faso 5.3%; Mali 4.5%; Nigeria 4.3%; Belgium-Luxembourg 4.3%; United States 4.2%.

Transport and communications

Transport. Railroads (1991): route length 660 km; passenger-km 1,210,000,000; metric ton-km cargo 680,000,000. Roads (1992): total length 42,250 mi, 68,000 km (paved 8%). Vehicles (1992): passenger cars 175,000; trucks and buses 95,000. Merchant marine (1992): vessels (100 gross tons and over) 51; total deadweight tonnage 98,618. Air transport (1991): passenger-km 286,000,000; metric ton-km cargo 16,000,000; airports (1994) 7.
Communications. Daily newspapers (1990): total number 1; total circulation 90,000; circulation per 1,000 population 8. Radio (1993): 1,500,000 receivers (1 per 8.9 persons). Television (1993): 810,000 receivers (1 per 17 persons). Telephones (1992): 206,610 (1 per 62 persons).

Education and health

Education (1992)

	schools	teachers	students	student/ teacher ratio
Primary (age 7–12)	6,844	39,237	1,447,785	36.9
Secondary (age 13–19)[7]	147	9,263	289,510	31.3
Voc., teacher tr.	15	1,947[8]	3,094	...
Higher	1[9]	1,204[10]	19,660[4]	...

Educational attainment (1988). Percentage of population age 6 and over having: no formal schooling 60.0%; Koranic school 3.6%; primary education 24.8%; secondary 10.7%; higher 0.9%. *Literacy* (1988): percentage of population age 15 and over literate 34.1%; males literate 44.4%; females literate 24.4%.
Health: physicians (1990) 1,020 (1 per 11,745 persons); hospital beds (1982) 10,062 (1 per 891 persons); infant mortality rate per 1,000 live births (1990–95) 91.
Food (1988–90): daily per capita caloric intake 2,568 (vegetable products 94%, animal products 6%); 111% of FAO recommended minimum requirement.

Military

Total active duty personnel (1994): 8,400 (army 81.0%, navy 10.7%, air force 8.3%). *Military expenditure as percentage of GNP* (1992): 0.8% (world avg. [1991] 4.2%); per capita expenditure U.S.$6.

---

[1]From 1986, Côte d'Ivoire has requested that the French version of the country's name be utilized as the official protocol version in all languages. [2]Total area per more recent survey is 322,463 sq km; area breakdown by department is not available. [3]"Ivoirian" nationals only, representing about 65% of the de facto population. [4]1990: 2,168,000. [5]January 1; index refers to the S.M.I.G. (*salaire minimum interprofessionel garanti*), a form of minimum professional wage. [6]Weights of consumer price index components for a worker's family living in the capital city. [7]Data do not include 208 private schools with 107,096 students. [8]1991. [9]1980. [10]1982.

Croatia

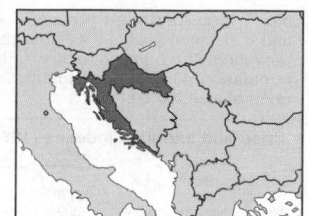

Official name: Republika Hrvatska (Republic of Croatia).
Form of government: multiparty republic with a two-chambered legislature (House of Counties [68[1]]; House of Representatives [138[2]]).
Head of state: President.
Head of government: Prime Minister.
Capital: Zagreb.
Official language: Croatian.
Official religion: none.
Monetary unit: 1 kuna (plural kune)[3] = 100 lipa; valuation (Oct. 7, 1994) 1 U.S.$ = 5.68 kune; 1 £ = 9.04 kune.

Area and population (1991 census)

Districts	population	Districts	population	Districts	population
Beli Manastir	54,265	Kaštela	32,286	Požega	71,745
Benkovac	33,378	Klanjec	10,917	Pregrada	16,939
Biograd na moru	17,661	Knin	42,954	Pula	85,326
Bjelovar	66,039	Koprivnica	61,052	Rab	9,205
Brač	13,824	Korčula	19,851	Rijeka	206,229
Buje	23,877	Kostajnica	14,851	Rovinj	19,727
Buzet	7,439	Krapina	26,382	Senj	9,205
Čabar	5,169	Križevci	39,248	Šibenik	85,002
Čakovec	119,866	Krk	16,402	Sinj	60,210
Cazma	15,263	Kutina	39,520	Sisak	84,348
Cres-Lošinj	11,796	Labin	25,983	Slavonski Brod	114,249
Crikvenica	19,154	Lastovo	1,228	Slunj	18,962
Đakovo	52,954	Ludbreg	21,848	Solin	27,402
Daruvar	30,092	Makarska	21,041	Split	207,147
Delnice	17,848	Metković	22,818	Sveti Ivan	
Donja Stubica	30,760	Našice	40,829	Zelina	17,152
Donji Lapac	8,054	Nova Gradiška	60,749	Titova Korenica	11,393
Donji Miholjac	20,365	Novi Marof	29,254	Trogir	22,168
Drniš	24,169	Novska	24,696	Valpovo	33,108
Dubrovnik	71,419	Obrovac	11,557	Varaždin	94,373
Duga Resa	30,485	Ogulin	29,095	Vinkovci	98,445
Đurđevac	40,901	Omiš	25,784	Virovitica	46,661
Dvor	14,555	Opatija	29,799	Vis	4,354
Garešnica	18,442	Orahovica	15,631	Vojnić	8,236
Glina	23,040	Osijek	165,253	Vrbovec	28,074
Gospić	29,049	Otočac	24,992	Vrbovsko	7,528
Gračac	10,434	Ozalj	14,787	Vrginmost	16,599
Grubišno Polje	14,206	Pag	7,969	Vrgorac	7,497
Hvar	11,459	Pakrac	27,589	Vukovar	84,189
Imotski	39,052	Pazin	19,006	Zabok	36,309
Ivanec	41,680	Petrinja	35,565	Zadar	136,572
Ivanić-Grad	25,592	Ploče	13,008	Zagreb	953,607
Jastrebarsko	32,422	Podravska Slatina	31,227	Zlatar	31,291
Karlovac	81,319	Poreč	22,988	Županja	49,026
				TOTAL	4,785,336

Demography

Population (1994): 4,788,000.
Density (1994): persons per sq mi 219.3, persons per sq km 84.7.
Urban-rural (1991): urban 50.8%; rural 49.2%.
Sex distribution (1991): male 48.46%; female 51.54%.
Age breakdown (1991): under 15, 19.4%; 15–29, 20.7%; 30–44, 22.7%; 45–59, 18.3%; 60–74, 12.9%; 75 and over, 4.5%; not stated 1.5%.
Population projection: (2000) 4,786,000; (2010) 4,782,000.
Doubling time: not applicable; population is declining.
Ethnic composition (1991): Croat 78.1%; Serb 12.2%; Bosnian 0.9%; Magyar 0.5%; Slovene 0.5%; other 7.8%.
Religious affiliation (1991): Roman Catholic 76.5%; Eastern Orthodox 11.1%; Muslim 1.2%; other 11.2%[4].
Major cities (1991): Zagreb 706,770; Split 189,388; Rijeka 167,964; Osijek 104,761; Zadar 76,343.

Vital statistics

Birth rate per 1,000 population (1992): 9.8 (world avg. 26.0); legitimate 92.4%; illegitimate 7.6%.
Death rate per 1,000 population (1992): 10.8 (world avg. 9.2).
Natural increase rate per 1,000 population (1992): −1.0 (world avg. 16.8).
Total fertility rate (avg. births per childbearing woman; 1991): 1.7.
Marriage rate per 1,000 population (1992): 4.6.
Divorce rate per 1,000 population (1992): 0.8.
Life expectancy at birth (1989–90): male 66.8 years; female 74.8 years.
Major causes of death per 100,000 population (1991): diseases of the circulatory system 571.8; malignant neoplasms (cancers) 226.1; accidents, violence, and poisoning 91.8; diseases of the digestive system 53.2.

National economy

Budget (1992). Revenue: HrD 651,518,000,000[3] (sales tax 48.6%, income tax 19.0%, import duties 15.3%). Expenditures: 649,336,000,000 (development 22.8%, social services 8.1%, education 2.5%, health 0.4%, defense 0.4%).
Production (metric tons except as noted). Agriculture, forestry, fishing (1992): corn (maize) 1,358,000, wheat 658,000, sugar beets 525,000, potatoes 480,-000, grapes 380,000, barley 107,000, plums 62,000; livestock (number of live animals) 1,182,000 pigs, 590,000 cattle, 539,000 sheep, 13,142,000 poultry; roundwood 3,244,000 cu m; fish catch 25,022, of which freshwater 6,246. Mining and quarrying (1992): lime 261,000; bauxite 6,878. Manufacturing (1992): ammonia 426,000; crude steel 102,000; aluminum 20,000; detergents 50,882; cotton fibre 12,132. Construction (1992): residential 623,000 sq m; nonresidential 1,081,000 sq m. Energy production (consumption): electricity (kW-hr; 1992) 8,860,000,000 (11,902,000,000); coal (metric tons; 1992)

120,000 (n.a.); crude petroleum (barrels; 1992) 12,775,000 (n.a.); petroleum products (metric tons; 1992) 2,997,000 (n.a.); natural gas (cu m; 1992) 1,820,000,000 (n.a.).
Gross national product (1991): U.S.$26,300,000,000 (U.S.$5,600 per capita).

Structure of gross domestic product and labour force

	1992			
	in value Din '000,000[3]	% of total value	labour force	% of labour force
Agriculture	784,986	14.2	54,003	3.5
Mining Manufacturing }	2,451,469	44.4	391,052	25.6
Construction	363,045	6.6	71,751	4.7
Public utilities	59,237	1.1	28,044	1.8
Transp. and commun.	520,125	9.4	93,890	6.2
Trade	1,113,900	20.2	195,767	12.8
Finance	176,512	3.2	49,350	3.2
Pub. admin., defense }			48,510	0.2
Services	51,329	0.9	184,758	12.1
Other			408,801[5]	26.9[5]
TOTAL	5,520,603	100.0	1,525,935	100.0

Population economically active (1992): total 1,525,935; activity rate of total population 31.8% (participation rates [1991]: ages 15–64, 57.1%; female 42.9%; unemployed 18.5%).

Price and earnings indexes (1990 = 100)

	1987	1988	1989	1990	1991	1992
Consumer price index	0.4	1	14	100	225	1,652
Annual earnings index[6]	95	98	120	100	75	43

Household income and expenditure. Average household size (1991) 3.1; income per household (1990) Din 165,813[3] (U.S.$14,650); sources (1990): self-employment 40.8%, wages 40.2%, transfers 12.1%, other 6.9%; expenditure (1988): food 34.2%, transportation 9.3%, clothing 8.6%, housing 8.3%, energy 7.6%, drink and tobacco 5.1%, durable goods 4.5%, health care 4.3%.
Land use (1990): forest 39.0%; pasture 24.1%; agricultural 18.2%; other 18.7%.

Foreign trade

Balance of trade (current prices)

	1987	1988	1989	1990	1991	1992
HrD '000,000[3]	−40	−34	−63	−91	−49	+21
% of total	8.5%	7.3%	11.5%	12.7%	7.8%	2.2%

Imports (1992): HrD 468,679,000[3] (basic manufactures 19.1%, chemicals 16.8%, machinery 16.6%, consumer goods 15.1%, food 12.0%). *Major import sources:* Germany 17.8%; Italy 16.7%; former U.S.S.R. 6.1%; Czech and Slovak republics 5.9%; Austria 4.6%.
Exports (1992): HrD 489,497,000[3] (consumer goods 20.8%, basic manufactures 19.2%, machinery 17.1%, chemicals 12.8%, food 12.0%). *Major export destinations:* Italy 20.1%; Germany 18.1%; Sweden 6.5%; China 2.6%; Austria 2.5%.

Transport and communications

Transport. Railroads (1993): length 1,676 mi, 2,699 km; passenger-km 981,000,-000; metric ton-km cargo 1,770,000,000. Roads (1993): total length 26,928 km (paved 81%). Vehicles (1993): passenger cars 669,761; trucks and buses 35,452. Merchant marine (1992): fishing vessels 315. Air transport (1992): passenger-km 145,000; metric ton-km cargo 1,261,000; airports (1994) with scheduled flights 4.
Communications. Daily newspapers (1990): 9; total circulation 715,000; circulation per 1,000 population 150. Radio (1992): 1,090,000 receivers (1 per 4.4 persons). Television (1992): 1,045,000 receivers (1 per 4.6 persons). Telephones (1992): 1,107,000 (1 per 4.3 persons).

Education and health

Education (1991–92)[7]

	schools	teachers	students	student/ teacher ratio
Primary (age 7–14)	1,906	22,785	418,586	18.4
Secondary (age 15–18)	485	11,893	174,588	14.7
Voc., teacher tr.[8]	3	104	2,326	22.4
Higher[8]	58	6,276	73,188	11.7

Educational attainment (1991). Percentage of population age 15 and over having: no schooling or unknown 10.1%; less than full primary education 21.2%; primary 23.4%; secondary 35.9%; postsecondary and higher 9.4%.
Literacy (1991): total population age 10 and over literate 3,734,000 (97.0%); males 98.8%; females 95.3%.
Health (1992): physicians 9,261 (1 per 517 persons); hospital beds 29,093 (1 per 165 persons); infant mortality rate per 1,000 live births 11.6.

Military

Total active duty personnel (1993): 103,300 (army 92.0%, navy 3.9%, air force and air defense 4.1%). *Military expenditure as percentage of GNP:* n.a.

[1]Includes 5 nonelective seats. [2]Includes 14 seats reserved for, and elected by, minority communities. [3]On Jan. 1, 1990, the Yugoslav new dinar (Din), equal to 10,000 Yugoslav old dinars (Din), was introduced. On Dec. 23, 1991, the Croatian dinar (HrD) was introduced at parity with the Yugoslav new dinar, which it replaced as Croatia's official currency. On May 30, 1994, the kuna, equal to 1,000 Croatian dinars, was introduced. [4]Includes a significant minority of adherents of the Croatian Old Catholic Church, as well as small communities of Protestant Christians and Jews. [5]Includes unemployed and private sector. [6]Based on worker real net personal income. [7]Data exclude private (combined) primary and secondary schools. [8]1992–1993.

Cuba

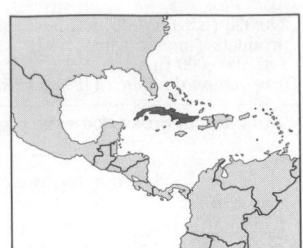

Official name: República de Cuba
(Republic of Cuba).
Form of government: unitary socialist
republic with one legislative house
(National Assembly of the People's
Power [589]).
Head of state and government:
President.
Capital: Havana.
Official language: Spanish.
Official religion: none.
Monetary unit: 1 Cuban peso (CUP) =
100 centavos; valuation (Oct. 7, 1994)
1 U.S.$ = 1.00 CUP[1];
1 £ = 1.59 CUP.

Area and population		area		population
		sq mi	sq km	1989[2] estimate
Provinces	**Capitals**			
Camagüey	Camagüey	6,174	15,990	732,056
Ciego de Avila	Ciego de Avila	2,668	6,910	358,059
Cienfuegos	Cienfuegos	1,613	4,178	358,589
Ciudad de la Habana[3]	—	281	727	2,077,938
Granma	Bayamo	3,232	8,372	781,331
Guantánamo	Guantánamo	2,388	6,186	491,422
Holguín	Holguín	3,591	9,301	982,722
La Habana[4]	Havana	2,213	5,731	636,889
Las Tunas	Las Tunas	2,544	6,589	485,136
Matanzas	Matanzas	4,625	11,978	602,996
Pinar del Río	Pinar del Río	4,218	10,925	684,725
Sancti Spíritus	Sancti Spíritus	2,604	6,744	424,243
Santiago de Cuba	Santiago de Cuba	2,382	6,170	980,002
Villa Clara	Santa Clara	3,345	8,662	801,456
Special municipality				
Isla de la Juventud	Nueva Gerona	926	2,398	71,097
TOTAL		42,804	110,861	10,468,661

Demography

Population (1994): 10,994,000.
Density (1994): persons per sq mi 256.8, persons per sq km 99.2.
Urban-rural (1990): urban 72.8%; rural 27.2%.
Sex distribution (1990): male 50.35%; female 49.65%.
Age breakdown (1989): under 15, 23.3%; 15–29, 31.7%; 30–44, 19.5%; 45–59,
13.7%; 60 and over, 11.8%.
Population projection: (2000) 11,502,000; (2010) 12,181,000.
Doubling time: 65 years.
Ethnic composition (1994): mixed 51.0%; white 37.0%; black 11.0%; other
1.0%.
Religious affiliation (1980): nonreligious 48.7%; Roman Catholic 39.6%; athe-
ist 6.4%; Protestant 3.3%; Afro-Cuban syncretist 1.6%; other 0.4%.
Major cities (1989[2]): Havana 2,077,938; Santiago de Cuba 397,024; Camagüey
278,958; Holguín 222,794; Guantánamo 197,868.

Vital statistics

Birth rate per 1,000 population (1990–95): 17.4 (world avg. 26.0).
Death rate per 1,000 population (1990–95): 6.7 (world avg. 9.2).
Natural increase rate per 1,000 population (1990–95): 10.7 (world avg. 16.8).
Total fertility rate (avg. births per childbearing woman; 1990–95): 1.9.
Marriage rate per 1,000 population (1992): 17.7.
Divorce rate per 1,000 population (1992): 4.2.
Life expectancy at birth (1990–95): male 73.9 years; female 77.6 years.
Major causes of death per 100,000 population (1989): diseases of the circula-
tory system 251.8; malignant neoplasms (cancers) 125.2; accidents, violence,
and suicide 69.4; diseases of the respiratory system 34.0; diabetes mellitus
20.6.

National economy

Budget (1990). Revenue: CUP 12,463,200,000. Expenditures: CUP 14,448,400,-
000 (capital investment 37.7%; education and public health 20.4%; social,
cultural, and scientific activities 17.3%; defense, internal security 9.5%;
housing, community services 6.0%).
Production (metric tons except as noted). Agriculture, forestry, fishing (1993):
sugarcane 44,000,000, oranges and tangerines 440,000, grapefruit 310,000,
bananas and plantains 295,000, cassava 290,000, potatoes 216,000, tomatoes
200,000, sweet potatoes 200,000, rice 186,000, tobacco leaves 44,000, coffee
beans 20,000; livestock (number of live animals) 4,500,000 cattle, 1,603,000
pigs, 25,000,000 chickens; roundwood (1992) 3,140,000 cu m; fish catch
(1991) 165,236. Mining and quarrying (1993): chromite 50,000; nickel (metal
content of ores) 36,500[5]. Manufacturing (value added in U.S.$'000,000;
1990): tobacco products 2,629; food products 1,033; beverages 358; chemical
products 354; transport equipment 225; nonelectrical machinery 176; textiles
(excluding ready-made clothing) 109; wearing apparel 88; rubber products
83. Construction (gross value of construction in CUP '000,000; 1989): residential 227; nonresidential 872. Energy production (consumption): electricity
(kW-hr; 1992) 12,492,000,000 (12,492,000,000); coal (metric tons; 1992) none
(151,000); crude petroleum (barrels; 1992) 6,036,000 (36,501,000); petroleum
products (metric tons; 1992) 4,557,000 (8,350,000); natural gas (cu m; 1992)
37,005,000 (37,005,000).
Household income and expenditure. Average household size (1990) 3.7; average annual income per household (1982) CUP 3,680 (U.S.$4,330); sources
of income (1982): wages and salaries 57.3%; bonuses and other payments
42.7%; personal consumption (1989): food 26.7%, other retail purchases

60.5%, transportation services 5.4%, energy 2.7%, value of self-produced
and consumed food 1.5%, household repairs 1.3%, other 1.9%.
Population economically active (1988): total 4,570,236; activity rate of total
population 43.7% (participation rates: over age 15, 56.9%; female 36.1%;
unemployed 6.0%).

Price and earnings indexes (1985 = 100)							
	1983	1984	1985	1986	1987	1988	1989
Implicit consumer price deflator index	94.9	98.0	100.0	101.4	102.8	103.1	...
Monthly earnings index[6]	95.9	99.0	100.0	100.1	98.1	99.6	100.0

Public debt (hard currency to the West; 1989): U.S.$6,800,000,000.
Tourism: receipts from visitors (1993) U.S.$216,000,000; expenditures by na-
tionals abroad (1990) U.S.$48,000,000.
Gross national product (at current market prices; 1991): U.S.$17,000,000,000
(U.S.$1,580 per capita).

Structure of global social product and labour force				
	1989			
	in value CUP '000,000	% of total value	labour force[6]	% of labour force
Agriculture	4,273	15.9	721,100	20.4
Mining[7]	1,039	3.9		
Manufacturing	10,617	39.4	767,500	21.8
Public utilities	733	2.7		
Construction	2,510	9.3	344,300	9.8
Transp. and commun.	2,151	8.0	235,900	6.7
Finance, insurance	—	—	21,700	0.6
Trade	5,401	20.1	395,300	11.2
Public administration			151,700	4.3
Services	—	—	835,700	23.7
Other	191	0.7	53,400	1.5
TOTAL	26,915	100.0	3,526,600	100.0

Land use (1992): forested 20.9%; meadows and pastures 27.0%; agricultural
and under permanent cultivation 30.4%; other 21.7%.

Foreign trade[8]

Balance of trade (current prices)						
	1984	1985	1986	1987	1988	1989
CUP '000,000	−1,751	−2,043	−2,275	−2,181	−2,062	−2,732
% of total	13.8%	14.6%	17.6%	16.8%	15.7%	20.2%

Imports (1989): CUP 8,124,200,000 (mineral fuels and lubricants 32.4%,
machinery and transport equipment 31.2%, food and live animals 11.4%,
basic manufactures 10.3%, chemicals 6.5%, inedible crude materials 3.8%).
Major import sources: U.S.S.R. 68.0%; East Germany 4.4%; China 3.1%;
Czechoslovakia 2.7%; Spain 2.3%; Argentina 2.2%.
Exports (1989): CUP 5,392,000,000 (sugar 73.2%, minerals and concentrates
9.2%, citrus and other agricultural products 3.9%, fish products 2.4%, raw
tobacco and tobacco products 1.6%). *Major export destinations:* U.S.S.R.
59.9%; East Germany 5.3%; China 4.0%; Bulgaria 3.3%; Czechoslovakia
2.5%.

Transport and communications

Transport. Railroads (1991): length 3,033 mi, 4,881 km; passenger-km 3,025,-
000,000; metric ton-km cargo 1,368,000,000. Roads (1986): total length
28,928 mi, 46,555 km (paved 27%). Vehicles (1988): passenger cars 241,300;
trucks and buses 208,400. Merchant marine (1992): vessels (100 gross tons
and over) 393; total deadweight tonnage 924,591. Air transport (1991):
passenger-km 3,070,000,000; metric ton-km cargo 34,794,000; airports with
scheduled flights (1994) 12.
Communications. Daily newspapers (1990): total number 17; total circulation
1,315,000; circulation per 1,000 population 124. Radio (1993): 2,140,000 receivers (1 per 5.1 persons). Television (1993): 2,500,000 receivers (1 per 4.4
persons). Telephones (1992): 614,220 (1 per 18 persons).

Education and health

Education (1991–92)				student/
	schools	teachers	students	teacher ratio
Primary (age 6–11)	9,346	74,354	917,889	12.3
Secondary (age 12–17)	2,175[9]	61,804	597,997	9.7
Voc., teacher tr.	618[9]	33,892	314,168	9.3
Higher	35[9]	24,668[10]	242,434[10]	9.8[10]

Educational attainment (1981). Percentage of population age 25 and over
having: no formal schooling or some primary education 39.6%; completed
primary 26.6%; secondary 29.6%; higher 4.2%. *Literacy* (1985): total population age 15 and over literate 7,200,000 (96.0%).
Health: physicians (1992) 46,860 (1 per 231 persons); hospital beds (1991) 79,-
997 (1 per 134 persons); infant mortality rate per 1,000 live births (1994) 9.4.
Food (1988–90): daily per capita caloric intake 3,129 (vegetable products 78%,
animal products 22%); 135% of FAO recommended minimum requirement.

Military

Total active duty personnel (1994): 106,000 (army 80.2%, navy 5.7%, air force
14.1%). *Military expenditure as percentage of GNP* (1990): 4.2% (world 4.5%);
per capita expenditure: U.S.$132.

---

[1]Official rate; the black-market rate is about 50 pesos (CUP) to U.S.$1. [2]January 1.
[3]Province coextensive with the city of Havana. [4]Province bordering the city of Havana
on the east, south, and west. [5]Includes cobalt. [6]State sector only; excludes military and
unemployed. [7]Mining includes metallurgy and refined petroleum products. [8]Imports
c.i.f.; exports f.o.b. [9]1989–90. [10]1990–91.

Cyprus

Island of Cyprus

Area: 3,572 sq mi, 9,251 sq km.
Population (1994): 769,000[1].

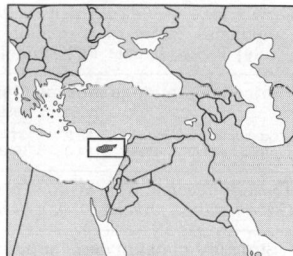

Two de facto states currently exist on the island of Cyprus: the Republic of Cyprus (ROC), predominantly Greek in character, occupying the southern two-thirds of the island, which is the original and still the internationally recognized de jure government of the whole island; and the Turkish Republic of Northern Cyprus (TRNC), proclaimed unilaterally Nov. 15, 1983, on territory originally secured for the Turkish Cypriot population by the July 20, 1974, intervention of Turkey. Only Turkey recognizes the TRNC, and the two ethnic communities have failed to reestablish a single state. Provision of separate data below does not imply recognition of either state's claims but is necessitated by the continuing lack of unified data.

Republic of Cyprus

Official name: Kipriakí Dimokratía (Greek); Kıbrıs Cumhuriyeti (Turkish) (Republic of Cyprus).
Form of government: unitary multiparty republic with a unicameral legislature (House of Representatives [80[2]]).
Head of state and government: President.
Capital: Nicosia.
Official languages: Greek; Turkish.
Monetary unit: 1 Cyprus pound (£C) = 100 cents; valuation (Oct. 7, 1994) 1 £C = U.S.$2.13 = £1.33.

Area and population

Districts	Capitals	area sq mi	area sq km	population[3] 1992[4] estimate
Famagusta	Famagusta	...	...	30,700
Larnaca	Larnaca	433	1,121	97,900
Limassol	Limassol	538	1,393	170,100
Nicosia	Nicosia	...	...	233,200
Paphos	Paphos	539	1,396	49,400
TOTAL		2,276[5]	5,896[5]	581,300[6]

Demography

Population (1994): 614,000[3].
Urban-rural (1992): urban 76.7%; rural 23.3%.
Age breakdown (1992): under 15, 26.1%; 15–29, 22.5%; 30–44, 22.5%; 45–59, 15.0%; 60–74, 9.8%; 75 and over, 4.1%.
Ethnic composition: Greek Cypriot *c.* 95%; other *c.* 5%.
Religious affiliation (1990): Cypriot Orthodox 82.0%; Maronite 1.5%; other 16.5%.
Major urban areas (1991): Nicosia 166,500; Limassol 129,700.

Vital statistics

Birth rate per 1,000 population (1992): 20.0 (world avg. 26.0).
Death rate per 1,000 population (1992): 8.9 (world avg. 9.2).
Natural increase rate per 1,000 population (1992): 11.1 (world avg. 16.8).
Life expectancy at birth (1987–91): male 74.1 years; female 78.6 years.

National economy

Budget (1992). Revenue: £C 874,900,000 (indirect taxes 38.1%, direct taxes 25.9%, social-security contributions 15.1%). Expenditures: £C 1,023,200,000 (current expenditures 88.6%, development expenditures 11.4%).
Tourism: receipts (1993) U.S.$1,400,000,000; expenditures (1992) U.S.$132,-000,000.
Household expenditure (1991): food, beverages, and expenditures in restaurants 26.9%, transportation and communications 17.7%.
Gross national product (1992): U.S.$6,946,000,000 (U.S.$11,860 per capita).

Structure of gross domestic product and labour force

	1993 in value £C '000,000	% of total value	labour force	% of labour force
Agriculture	183.5	5.7	35,000	12.1
Mining	9.3	0.3	700	0.2
Manufacturing	401.7	12.5	45,500	15.8
Construction	322.3	10.0	23,300	8.1
Public utilities	67.7	2.1	1,500	0.5
Transp. and commun.	267.1	8.3	16,200	5.6
Trade	621.7	19.3	67,800	23.5
Finance, insurance	516.4	16.0	19,400	6.7
Pub. admin., defense	418.0	13.0 }	57,800	19.9
Services	221.0	6.8 }		
Other	194.9	6.0	21,800[7]	7.6[7]
TOTAL	3,223.6	100.0	288,800	100.0

Production. Agriculture (value of production in £C '000,000; 1991): potatoes 31.4, milk 23.7, pork 18.2, poultry 16.3, sheep and goat meat 15.8, grapes 12.0. Manufacturing (value added in £C '000,000; 1991): wearing apparel

54.6; food 50.9; cement, bricks, and tiles 32.4; beverages 31.5; fabricated metals 27.9. Energy production: electricity (kW-hr; 1992) 2,404,000,000.

Foreign trade[8]

Imports (1993): £C 1,316,100,000 (consumer goods 26.4%; transport equipment 10.7%; capital goods 10.4%; mineral fuels 9.7%). *Major import sources:* U.K. 12.1%; Italy 10.0%; U.S. 8.9%; Greece 8.0%; Japan 7.8%.
Exports (1993): £C 431,500,000 (domestic exports 46.3%, of which clothing 11.8%, potatoes 4.7%; reexports 43.4%; ships' stores 10.3%). *Major export destinations:* U.K. 15.7%; Lebanon 12.8%; Greece 7.7%; Germany 5.2%.

Transport and communications

Transport. Roads (1992): total length 10,448 km (paved 55%). Vehicles (1992): cars 197,779; trucks and buses 84,326[9]. Merchant marine (1992): vessels 1,416; deadweight tonnage 36,198,083. Air transport (1993)[10]: passenger-km 2,541,000,000; metric ton-km cargo 33,336,000; airports (1994) 2.
Communications. Daily newspapers (1991): 10; total circulation 86,000; circulation per 1,000 population 150. Television (1993): 234,000 receivers (1 per 2.5 persons). Telephones (1991): 348,810 (1 per 1.6 persons).

Education and health

Education (1991–92)

	schools	teachers	students	student/teacher ratio
Primary (age 5–12)	390	3,257	63,454	19.5
Secondary (age 12–18) }	113	3,848	47,908	12.5
Vocational				
Higher	29	485	5,952	12.3

Educational attainment (1991). Percentage of population age 20 and over having: no formal schooling 6%; higher education 15%. *Literacy* (1991): population age 15 and over literate 94%; male 98%; female 90%.
Health (1991): physicians 1,265 (1 per 457 persons); hospital beds 3,391 (1 per 170 persons); infant mortality rate per 1,000 live births (1992) 11.0.

Turkish Republic of Northern Cyprus

Official name: Kuzey Kıbrıs Türk Cumhuriyeti (Turkish) (Turkish Republic of Northern Cyprus).
Capital: Lefkoşa (Nicosia).
Official language: Turkish.
Monetary unit: 1 Turkish lira (LT) = 100 kurush; valuation (Oct. 7, 1994) 1 U.S.$ = LT 34,441; 1 £ = LT 54,779.

Area and population

Districts	Administrative centres	area sq mi	area sq km	population[1] 1989 estimate
Lefkoşa (Nicosia)	Lefkoşa	...	...	78,772
Gazimağusa (Famagusta)	Gazimağusa			64,190
Girne (Kyrenia)	Girne	247	640	26,310
TOTAL		1,295	3,355	169,272

Population (1994): 155,000 (Lefkoşa 39,496[11]; Gazimağusa 20,516[11]).
Ethnic composition (1985): Turkish 98.7%; other 1.3%.

Structure of gross domestic product and labour force

	1992 in value LT '000,000,000	% of total value	labour force	% of labour force
Agriculture	427	11.5	18,690	25.2
Mining and manufacturing	307	10.7	7,000	9.4
Construction	265	7.1	7,862	10.6
Public utilities	65	1.7	1,231	1.7
Transp. and commun.	317	8.5	5,913	8.0
Trade, restaurants	779	20.9	7,185	9.7
Finance, real estate	310	8.3	2,092	2.8
Pub. admin.	721	19.3	16,267	22.0
Services	232	6.2	7,025	9.5
Other	217[12]	5.8[12]	800[13]	1.1[13]
TOTAL	3,730	100.0	74,065	100.0

Budget (1992). Revenue: LT 1,028,000,000 (tax revenue 70.9%, foreign aid 14.7%, other 14.4%). Expenditures: LT 1,323,000,000 (current expenditure 86.6%, development expenditure 7.0%, defense 6.4%).
Imports (1992): U.S.$371,400,000 (machinery and equipment 32.7%, petroleum [all forms] 9.2%). *Major import sources:* Turkey 48.1%; U.K. 12.3%.
Exports (1992): U.S.$54,600,000 (citrus fruits 40.7%). *Major export destinations:* U.K. 66.5%; Turkey 16.7%.

Education (1991–92)

	schools	teachers	students	student/teacher ratio
Primary (age 7–12)	155	849	19,400	22.9
Secondary (age 13–18)	28	963	16,719	17.4
Vocational	10	254	2,761	10.9
Higher	4	201[14]	6,145	26.1[14]

Health (1989): physicians 250 (1 per 677 persons); hospital beds 1,042 (1 per 162 persons); infant mortality rate per 1,000 live births (1987–89 avg.) 6.3.

---

[1]Includes "settlers" from Turkey in the TRNC; excludes 30,000 Turkish military in the TRNC, 4,100 British military in the Sovereign Base Areas in the ROC, and 1,200 UN peacekeeping forces. [2]Twenty-four seats reserved for Turkish Cypriots are not occupied. [3]Population excludes British and UN military forces. [4]January 1. [5]Area includes 99 sq mi (256 sq km) of British military Sovereign Base Areas and *c.* 107 sq mi (*c.* 278 sq km) of the UN Buffer Zone. [6]Population per October 1992 census is 602,025. [7]Includes 7,600 unemployed. [8]Imports c.i.f.; exports f.o.b. [9]1991. [10]Cyprus Airways. [11]1989. [12]Customs duties. [13]Unemployed. [14]1989–90.

Czech Republic

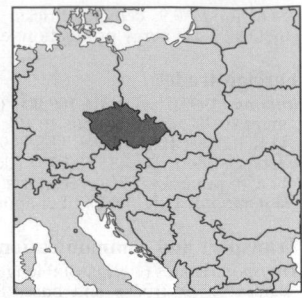

Official name: Česká Republika.
Form of government: unitary multiparty
republic with two legislative
houses (Senate [81[1]]; Chamber of
Deputies [200]).
Chief of state: President.
Head of government: Prime Minister.
Capital: Prague.
Official language: Czech.
Official religion: none.
Monetary unit[2]: 1 Czech koruna
(Kc) = 100 halura; valuation
(Oct. 7, 1994) 1 U.S.$ = 27.80 Kc;
1 £ = 44.22 Kc.

Area and population

Regions	Capitals	area sq mi	area sq km	population 1992[3] estimate
Jižní Čechy	České Budějovice	4,380	11,345	698,474
Jižní Morava	Brno	5,802	15,027	2,051,742
Severní Čechy	Ustí nad Labem	3,019	7,820	1,174,721
Severní Morava	Ostrava	4,273	11,067	1,964,288
Střední Čechy	Prague	4,245	10,994	1,111,244
Východní Čechy	Hradec Králové	4,340	11,240	1,234,566
Zapadní Čechy	Plzeň	4,199	10,875	860,624
Capital city				
Prague	—	192	496	1,216,889
TOTAL		30,450	78,864	10,312,548

Demography

Population (1994): 10,345,185.
Density (1994): persons per sq mi 339.7, persons per sq km 131.2.
Urban-rural: n.a.
Sex distribution (1992): male 48.55%; female 51.45%.
Age breakdown (1991): under 15, 21.2%; 15–29, 21.7%; 30–44, 22.8%; 45–59, 16.6%; 60–74, 12.5%; 75 and over, 5.2%.
Population projection: (2000) 10,449,000; (2010) 10,536,000.
Doubling time: not applicable; population growth is negligible.
Ethnic composition (1991): Czech 81.2%; Moravian 13.2%; Slovak 3.1%; Polish 0.6%; German 0.5%; Silesian 0.4%; Gypsy 0.3%; Hungarian 0.2%; Ukrainian 0.1%; other 0.4%.
Religious affiliation (1991): Roman Catholic 39.0%; Protestant 4.3%, of which Czechoslovak Brethren Reformed 2.0%, Czechoslovak Hussite 1.7%, Silesian Evangelical 0.3%; Eastern Orthodox 0.2%; Greek Catholic 0.1%; other Christian 0.3%; undenominational 39.9%; other 16.2%.
Major cities (1991): Prague 1,212,010; Brno 387,986; Ostrava 327,553; Plzeň 173,129; Olomouc 105,690.

Vital statistics

Birth rate per 1,000 population (1993): 11.7 (world avg. 26.0); (1991) legitimate 90.3%; illegitimate 9.7%.
Death rate per 1,000 population (1993): 11.5 (world avg. 9.2).
Natural increase rate per 1,000 population (1993): 0.2 (world avg. 16.8).
Total fertility rate (avg. births per childbearing woman; 1990): 1.9.
Marriage rate per 1,000 population (1993): 6.4.
Divorce rate per 1,000 population (1993): 2.9.
Life expectancy at birth (1992): male 68.5 years; female 76.1 years.
Major causes of death per 100,000 population (1991): diseases of the circulatory system 673.7; malignant neoplasms (cancers) 274.1; accidents, poisoning, and violence 85.2; diseases of the respiratory system 50.6; diseases of the digestive system 45.3; diseases of the genitourinary system 22.7; endocrine and metabolic disorders 18.1.

National economy

Budget (1994). Revenue: Kc 381,800,000 (taxes 62.2%, of which value-added taxes 39.8%, income taxes 32.6%, sales taxes 17.7%, other taxes 9.9%; other revenue 37.8%). Expenditures: Kc 381,800,000 (current expenditures 88.6%; capital expenditures 9.5%).
Public debt (external, outstanding; 1993): U.S.$6,580,000,000.
Production (metric tons except as noted). Agriculture, forestry, fishing (1992): cereals 6,565,000 (of which wheat 3,413,000, barley 2,512,000, corn [maize] 104,000, rye 240,000), sugar beets 3,874,000, potatoes 1,969,000; livestock (number of live animals; 1993) 4,052,000 pigs, 2,170,000 cattle (of which 830,000 dairy cows), 23,988,000 poultry; roundwood 9,850,000 cu m; fish catch (1992) 19,553. Mining and quarrying (1993): lead-zinc 180,000; iron ore 153,000. Manufacturing (1992): crude steel 7,334,000; cement 6,111,000; rolled steel 5,770,000; flour 722,000; plastics and resins 561,000; phosphate fertilizers 44,553; cotton fabrics 357,632,000 m; beer 18,564,000 hectolitres; other alcoholic beverages 999,170 hectolitres; bicycles 328,991 units; tractors 16,016 units; trucks 14,127 units. Construction (1992): residential 2,212,000 sq m. Energy production (consumption): electricity (kW-hr; 1992) 59,-132,000,000 (41,263,000,000); coal (1992) 68,084,000 (n.a.); crude petroleum (barrels; 1992) 549,000 (n.a.); petroleum products, n.a. (n.a.); natural gas (cu m; 1992) 1,552,000,000 (n.a.).
Household income and expenditure. Average household size (1992) 2.7; income per household (1992) Kčs 129,190[2] (U.S.$4,567); sources of income (1992): wages and salaries 49.8%, transfer payments 27.4%, other 22.8%; expenditure (1992): food and beverages 26.1%, taxes 13.4%, clothing and footwear 7.3%, housing and utilities 5.5%, household durable goods 4.5%, other 43.2%.

Population economically active (1993[3]): total 5,270,433; activity rate of total population 51.5% (participation rates: [1992] ages 15–59 [male], 15–54 [female] 86.3%; female 47.2%; unemployed 3.5%).

Price and earnings indexes (1990 = 100)

	1988	1989	1990	1991	1992	1993
Consumer price index	89.9	91.4	100.0	170.0	174.7	210.3
Annual earnings index	94.0	97.3	100.0	116.6	127.3	177.7

Tourism: receipts from visitors, n.a.; expenditures by nationals abroad, n.a.
Gross national product (1992): U.S.$25,313,000,000 (U.S.$2,440 per capita).

Structure of net material product and labour force

	1991 in value Kčs '000,000[2]	1991 % of total value	1992 labour force	1992 % of labour force
Agriculture	42,038	5.9	427,457	8.0
Mining and manufacturing	391,598	54.6	1,797,567	33.9
Construction	45,441	6.3	408,033	7.7
Public utilities	...	...	—	—
Transportation and communications	29,114	4.1	365,787	6.9
Trade	92,289	12.9	617,440	11.6
Finance	5,914	0.8	50,932	1.0
Pub. admin., defense	19,927	2.8	123,448	2.3
Services	78,568	11.0	1,136,472	21.4
Other	11,674	1.6	382,631[4]	7.2[4]
TOTAL	716,563	100.0	5,309,767	100.0

Land use (1991): forested 33.3%; meadows and pastures 11.0%; agricultural and under permanent cultivation 43.4%; other 12.3%.

Foreign trade

Balance of trade (current prices)

	1988	1989	1990	1991	1992	1993
Kc '000,000[2]	+18,310	+13,460	−14,410	+41,680	−60,368	+28,600
% of total	3.8%	2.8%	2.8%	5.9%	6.8%	2.8%

Imports (1993): Kc 366,359,000,000 (machinery and transport equipment 35.8%, manufactured goods 27.6%, chemicals 12.0%, fuels and lubricants 11.4%). *Major import sources:* Norway 25.1%; former U.S.S.R. 22.3%, of which Russia 9.9%; Slovakia 17.5%; Austria 7.7%.
Exports (1993): Kc 372,301,000,000 (manufactured goods 43.1%, machinery and transport equipment 27.4%, chemicals 9.3%, food and live animals 6.5%, fuels and lubricants 6.2%). *Major export destinations:* Norway 26.7%; Slovakia 20.0%; former U.S.S.R. 17.8%, of which Russia 4.2%; Austria 6.2%; Italy 5.1%.

Transport and communications

Transport. Railroads (1992): length 5,865 mi, 9,439 km; passenger-mi 6,694,-000,000, passenger-km 10,773,000,000; short ton-mi cargo 17,566,000,000, metric ton-km cargo 25,646,000,000. Roads (1992): total length 34,734 mi, 55,896 km (paved, n.a.). Vehicles (1992): passenger cars 2,522,369; trucks and buses 362,732. Merchant marine (1992): vessels (oceangoing) 17; total deadweight tonnage 402,462. Air transport (1992): passenger-mi 1,572,000, passenger-km 2,531,000; short ton-mi 52,475,000, metric ton-km 76,612,000; airports (1994) with scheduled flights 4.
Communications. Daily newspapers (1990): total number 17; total circulation 3,788,000; circulation per 1,000 population 368. Radio (1992): total number of receivers 2,883,000 (1 per 3.6 persons). Television (1992): total number of receivers 3,184,476 (1 per 3.2 persons). Telephones (1992): 3,238,051 (1 per 3.2 persons).

Education and health

Education (1992–93)

	schools	teachers	students	student/ teacher ratio
Primary (age 6–14)	4,142	65,186	1,115,027	17.1
Secondary (age 15–18)	285	8,574	117,765	13.7
Voc., teacher tr.	708	14,537	201,209	13.8
Higher	23	12,907	114,185	8.9

Educational attainment (1991). Percentage of adult population having: primary and incomplete secondary 33.1%; complete secondary 22.8%; higher 7.2%. *Literacy* (1990): total population age 15 and over literate 8,170,442 (100%); males literate 3,914,080 (100%); females literate 4,256,362 (100%).
Health (1992): physicians 31,935 (1 per 323 persons); hospital beds 105,412 (1 per 98 persons); infant mortality rate per 1,000 live births (1993) 8.5.
Food (1990): daily per capita caloric intake 3,303 (vegetable products 57%, animal products 43%); 134% of FAO recommended minimum requirement.

Military

Total active duty personnel (1993): 106,500 (army 66.6%, air force 33.4%). *Military expenditure as percentage of GNP:* n.a. Per capita expenditure: U.S.$77.

[1]Seats not yet occupied as of September 1994. [2]The Czech koruna (Kc) was introduced Feb. 8, 1993, at par with the former Czechoslovak koruna (Kčs), which it replaced. For settlement of obligations existing prior to February 8 between the Czech and Slovak republics, an interim currency, the clearing koruna (XCS) was introduced. [3]January 31. [4]Includes 134,788 unemployed and 247,843 women on maternity leave.

Denmark

Official name: Kongeriget Danmark (Kingdom of Denmark).
Form of government: parliamentary state and constitutional monarchy with one legislative house (Folketing [179]).
Chief of state: Danish Monarch.
Head of government: Prime Minister.
Capital: Copenhagen.
Official language: Danish.
Official religion: Evangelical Lutheran.
Monetary unit: 1 Danish krone (Dkr; plural kroner) = 100 øre; valuation (Oct. 7, 1994) 1 U.S.$ = Dkr 6.03; 1 £ = Dkr 9.59.

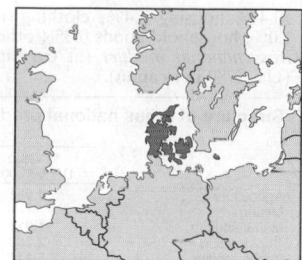

Area and population[1]

Counties	Capitals	area sq mi	area sq km	population 1993[2] estimate
Århus	Århus	1,761	4,561	609,890
Bornholm	Rønne	227	588	45,224
Frederiksborg	Hillerød	520	1,347	346,108
Fyn	Odense	1,346	3,486	465,239
København	—	203	526	603,883
Nordjylland	Ålborg	2,383	6,173	486,993
Ribe	Ribe	1,209	3,131	220,721
Ringkøbing	Ringkøbing	1,874	4,853	268,990
Roskilde	Roskilde	344	891	221,401
Sønderjylland	Åbenrå	1,520	3,938	251,306
Storstrøm	Nykøbing Falster	1,312	3,398	257,097
Vejle	Vejle	1,157	2,997	334,282
Vestsjælland	Sorø	1,152	2,984	286,290
Viborg	Viborg	1,592	4,122	229,888
Communes				
Copenhagen (København)	—	34	88	466,129
Frederiksberg	—	3	9	87,173
TOTAL		**16,639[3]**	**43,094[3]**	**5,180,614**

Demography

Population (1994): 5,205,000.
Density (1994): persons per sq mi 312.8, persons per sq km 120.8.
Urban-rural (1992): urban 84.9%; rural 15.1%.
Sex distribution (1993): male 49.31%; female 50.69%.
Age breakdown (1993): under 15, 17.0%; 15–29, 22.1%; 30–44, 21.7%; 45–59, 19.0%; 60–74, 13.2%; 75 and over, 7.0%.
Population projection: (2000) 5,303,000; (2010) 5,310,000.
Doubling time: not applicable; population is stable.
Ethnic composition (1993): Danish 96.5%; Asian 1.5%, of which Turkish 0.6%; other Scandinavian 0.5%; British 0.2%; German 0.2%; other 1.1%.
Religious affiliation (1992): Evangelical Lutheran 88.2%; other Christian 1.6%; Muslim 1.3%; other/nonreligious 8.9%.
Major cities (1992): Greater Copenhagen 1,342,679[4]; Århus 204,139; Odense 140,886; Ålborg 114,970; Frederiksberg 87,173[4,5].

Vital statistics

Birth rate per 1,000 population (1993): 13.0 (world avg. 26.0); (1992) legitimate 53.5%; illegitimate 46.5%.
Death rate per 1,000 population (1993): 12.1 (world avg. 9.2).
Natural increase rate per 1,000 population (1993): 0.9 (world avg. 16.8).
Total fertility rate (avg. births per childbearing woman; 1992): 1.8.
Marriage rate per 1,000 population (1992): 6.2.
Divorce rate per 1,000 population (1992): 2.5.
Life expectancy at birth (1991–92): male 72.4 years; female 77.8 years.
Major causes of death per 100,000 population (1992): malignant neoplasms (cancers) 292.2; ischemic heart disease 277.6; cerebrovascular disease 109.4.

National economy

Budget (1993)[6]. Revenue: Dkr 307,403,000,000 (income and property taxes 47.6%, customs and excise duties 41.1%, other 11.3%). Expenditures: Dkr 351,348,000,000 (social affairs 22.8%, education 6.3%, defense 4.1%, other/unspecified 66.8%).
National debt (end of year; 1992): Dkr 575,328,000,000.
Tourism (1992): receipts from visitors U.S.$3,784,000,000; expenditures by nationals abroad U.S.$3,779,000,000.
Population economically active (1991): total 2,912,428; activity rate of total population 56.6% (participation rates: ages 15–64, 82.4%; female 46.5%; unemployed [September 1993–August 1994] 12.5%).

Price and earnings indexes (1985 = 100)

	1988	1989	1990	1991	1992	1993	1994[7]
Consumer price index	93.0	97.4	100.0	102.4	104.5	105.9	107.9
Hourly earnings index	92.6	96.2	100.0	103.9	106.9	...	...

Household income and expenditure. Average household size (1993) 2.2; income per household (1988) Dkr 199,354 (U.S.$29,613); principal sources of income (1988)[8]: wages and salaries 48.2%, self employment 33.6%, transfers 18.2%; expenditure (1991): housing 22.2%, food and beverages 18.4%, transportation and communications 16.0%, recreation 8.4%, household furnishings 6.3%, cafe and hotel expenditures 5.8%.
Production (in Dkr '000,000 except as noted). Agriculture, forestry, fishing (value added; 1992): pork 17,299, milk 11,739, beef 4,422, wheat 3,550, barley 2,585, flowers and plants 2,583, furs 1,022, poultry 1,144; roundwood 2,300,-

000 cu m; fish catch 1,816,000 metric tons. Mining and quarrying (1992): sand and gravel 20,000,000 cu m; chalk 355,000 metric tons. Manufacturing (value added; 1992): food products 28,174; nonelectrical machinery and apparatus 19,609; chemicals and chemical products 17,300; metal products 12,210; printing and publishing 9,919; transport equipment 7,831; electrical machinery and apparatus 7,638. Construction (completed; 1992): residential 1,449,000 sq m; nonresidential 4,195,000 sq m. Energy production (consumption): electricity (kW-hr; 1993) 31,608,000,000 ([1992] 34,595,000,000); coal (metric tons; 1992) none (11,044,000); crude petroleum (barrels; 1992) 59,636,000 (64,272,000); petroleum products (metric tons; 1992) 8,310,000 (7,365,000); natural gas (cu m; 1992) 4,025,000,000 (2,284,000,000).
Gross national product (at current market prices; 1993): U.S.$137,613,000,000 (U.S.$26,510 per capita).

Structure of gross domestic product and labour force

	1992 in value Dkr '000,000[9]	1992 % of total value	1991 labour force	1991 % of labour force
Agriculture, fishing	26,393	3.5	160,647	5.5
Mining	6,377	0.9	3,183	0.1
Manufacturing	141,850	19.0	586,413	20.1
Construction	41,834	5.6	199,335	6.8
Public utilities	14,327	1.9	19,841	0.7
Transp. and commun.	67,522	9.1	194,596	6.7
Trade, restaurants	107,424	14.4	422,723	14.5
Finance, real estate	148,497	19.9	252,749	8.7
Pub. admin., defense	166,360	22.3 }	1,020,864	35.1
Services	45,965	6.2		
Other	−20,810[10]	−2.8[10]	51,659[11]	1.8[11]
TOTAL	745,739	100.0	2,912,010	100.0

Land use (1992): forested 10.5%; meadows and pastures 4.9%; agricultural and under permanent cultivation 60.0%; other 24.6%.

Foreign trade[12]

Balance of trade (current prices)

	1987	1988	1989	1990	1991	1992
Dkr '000,000	+8,891	+19,061	+18,764	+26,404	+32,060	+44,642
% of total	2.6%	5.4%	4.8%	6.5%	7.5%	10.3%

Imports (1992): Dkr 203,003,000,000 (intermediate goods for industries 44.6%, machinery 10.5%, food products 8.8%, transport equipment 6.7%). *Major import sources:* Germany 23.0%; Sweden 10.8%; United Kingdom 8.2%; United States 5.7%; France 5.6%; The Netherlands 5.5%.
Exports (1992): Dkr 238,718,000,000 (nonelectrical and electrical machinery 23.3%, chemical products 10.0%, fresh or frozen swine meat 6.6%, textiles and clothing 4.8%, furniture 4.3%). *Major export destinations:* Germany 23.6%; Sweden 10.5%; United Kingdom 10.1%; Norway 5.8%; France 5.7%; United States 4.9%.

Transport and communications

Transport. Railroads (1992): length (1991) 1,763 mi, 2,838 km; passenger-mi 2,858,000,000, passenger-km 4,600,000,000; short ton-mi cargo 1,281,000,000, metric ton-km cargo 1,870,000,000. Roads (1993): total length 44,186 mi, 71,-111 km (paved 100%). Vehicles (1993): passenger cars 1,674,939; trucks and buses 260,833. Merchant marine (1992): vessels (100 gross tons and over) 456; total deadweight tonnage 7,569,069. Air transport (1993)[13]: passenger-mi 2,714,000,000, passenger-km 4,368,000,000; short ton-mi cargo 91,243,000, metric ton-km cargo 133,212,000; airports (1994) with scheduled flights 12.
Communications. Daily newspapers (1992): total number 42; total circulation 1,710,000; circulation per 1,000 population 332. Radio (1993): 2,235,000 receivers (1 per 2.3 persons). Television (1993): 2,500,000 receivers (1 per 2.1 persons). Telephones (1992): 3,003,000[14] (1 per 1.7 persons).

Education and health

Education (1991–92)

	schools	teachers	students	student/teacher ratio
Primary/lower secondary (age 7–15)	2,127	59,800	613,329	10.3
Upper secondary (age 16–18)	154	7,500	74,000	9.9
Vocational	204	...	149,000	...
Higher	235	...	156,000	...

Educational attainment (1990). Percentage of population age 25–69 having: primary education 3.0%; completed lower secondary 23.4%; completed upper secondary or vocational 48.0%; advanced vocational 5.0%; undergraduate 7.4%; graduate 3.9%; unknown 9.3%. *Literacy:* virtually 100%.
Health: physicians (1990) 14,277 (1 per 360 persons); hospital beds (1991) 28,-072 (1 per 184 persons); infant mortality rate per 1,000 live births (1993) 5.7.
Food (1988–90): daily per capita caloric intake 3,639 (vegetable products 54%, animal products 46%); 135% of FAO recommended minimum requirement.

Military

Total active duty personnel (1994): 27,000 (army 60.4%, navy 17.0%, air force 22.6%). *Military expenditure as percentage of GNP* (1991): 2.1% (world 4.2%); per capita expenditure U.S.$518.

[1]Excludes the Faeroe Islands and Greenland. [2]January 1. [3]Detail does not add to total given because of rounding. [4]1993. [5]Within Greater Copenhagen. [6]Projections. [7]July. [8]Excludes interest and dividends. [9]At factor cost. [10]Imputed bank service charges less other producers. [11]Includes 42,933 activities not adequately defined. [12]Import figures are f.o.b. in balance of trade and c.i.f. in commodities and trading partners. [13]Danish share of Scandinavian Airlines System; scheduled air service only. [14]Number of lines.

Djibouti

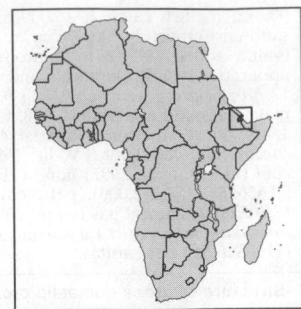

Official name: Jumhūrīyah Jībūtī (Arabic); République de Djibouti (French) (Republic of Djibouti).
Form of government: multiparty republic with one legislative house (National Assembly [65]).
Head of state and government: President.
Capital: Djibouti.
Official languages: Arabic; French.
Official religion: none.
Monetary unit: 1 Djibouti franc (DF) = 100 centimes; valuation (Oct. 7, 1994) 1 U.S.\$ = DF 177.89; 1 £ = DF 282.93.

Area and population

Districts	Capitals	area[1] sq mi	area[1] sq km	population 1982 estimate
'Alī Sabīḥ (Ali-Sabieh)	'Alī Sabīḥ	925	2,400	15,000
Dikhil	Dikhil	2,775	7,200	30,000
Djibouti	Djibouti	225	600	200,000
Obock	Obock	2,200	5,700	15,000
Tadjoura (Tadjourah)	Tadjoura	2,825	7,300	30,000
TOTAL		8,950	23,200	335,000[2]

Demography

Population (1994): 569,000[3].
Density (1994): persons per sq mi 64.1, persons per sq km 24.7.
Urban-rural (1991): urban 81.1%; rural 18.9%.
Sex distribution (1990): male 50.37%; female 49.63%.
Age breakdown (1990): under 15, 45.2%; 15–29, 24.9%; 30–44, 16.1%; 45–59, 9.0%; 60 and over, 4.8%.
Population projection: (2000) 680,000; (2010) 916,000.
Doubling time: 24 years.
Ethnic composition (1983): Somali 61.7%, of which Issa 33.4%, Gadaboursi 15.0%, Issaq 13.3%; Afar 20.0%; Arab (mostly Yemeni) 6.0%; European 4.0%; other (refugees) 8.3%.
Religious affiliation (1988): Sunnī Muslim 96%; Christian 4%, of which Roman Catholic 2%, Protestant 1%, Orthodox 1%.
Major city and towns (1989): Djibouti 450,000[4]; 'Alī Sabīḥ 4,000; Tadjoura 3,500; Dikhil 3,000.

Vital statistics

Birth rate per 1,000 population (1990–95): 45.8 (world avg. 26.0).
Death rate per 1,000 population (1990–95): 16.4 (world avg. 9.2).
Natural increase rate per 1,000 population (1990–95): 29.4 (world avg. 16.8).
Total fertility rate (avg. births per childbearing woman; 1990): 6.6.
Marriage rate per 1,000 population (1982): 6.7.
Divorce rate per 1,000 population (1982): 1.9.
Life expectancy at birth (1990–95): male 47.4 years; female 50.7 years.
Major causes of death (percentage of total deaths; 1984)[5]: diarrhea and acute dehydration 16.0%; malnutrition 16.0%; poisoning 11.0%; tuberculosis 6.0%; acute respiratory disease 6.0%; malaria 6.0%; anemia 6.0%; heart disease 2.0%; kidney disease 1.0%; other ailments 19.0%; no diagnosis 11.0%.

National economy

Budget (1993). Revenue: DF 29,011,000,000 (1990; current receipts 80.2%, of which indirect and direct taxes 72.9%, nontax revenue 7.3%; external development receipts 19.8%). Expenditures: DF 28,990,000,000 (defense 17.5%; education 9.4%; health 7.2%; debt service 5.2%; agriculture 1.6%; commerce 0.4%; industry 0.2%).
Public debt (external, outstanding; 1992): U.S.\$173,800,000.
Tourism: receipts from visitors (1990) U.S.\$6,000,000; expenditures by nationals abroad, n.a.
Production (metric tons except as noted). Agriculture, forestry, fishing (1993): vegetables and melons 22,000, of which tomatoes 1,000, eggplant (1985–86) 66; livestock (number of live animals) 507,000 goats, 470,000 sheep, 190,000 cattle, 62,000 camels, 8,000 asses; fish catch (1991) 380. Mining and quarrying: mineral production limited to locally used construction materials and evaporated salt. Manufacturing (1988): detail, n.a.; main items produced include furniture, nonalcoholic beverages, meat and hides, light electromechanical goods, and mineral water. Construction (1989): 53,900 sq m. Energy production (consumption): electricity (kW-hr; 1992) 180,000,000 (180,000,000); coal, none (n.a.); crude petroleum, none (n.a.); petroleum products (metric tons; 1992) none (424,000); natural gas, none (n.a.).
Population economically active (1991): total 282,000; activity rate of total population 54.2% (participation rates [1988]: over age 10, 67.0%; female 40.0%; unemployed [1987] c. 40–50%).

Price and earnings indexes (1988 = 100)

	1987	1988	1989	1990	1991	1992
Consumer price index	94.0	100.0	103.0	107.6	111.9	118.7
Earnings index	...	...	...	...	...	...

Household income and expenditure. Average household size[6] (1985) 7.2; income per household: n.a.; sources of income (1976): wages and salaries 51.6%, self-employment 36.0%, transfer payments 10.5%, other 1.9%; expenditure (expatriate households; 1984): food 50.3%, energy 13.1%, recreation

10.4%, housing 6.4%, clothing 1.7%, personal effects 1.4%, health care 1.0%, household goods 0.3%, other 15.4%.
Gross national product (at current market prices; 1993): U.S.\$448,000,000 (U.S.\$780 per capita).

Structure of gross national product and labour force

	1991 in value DF '000,000	1991 % of total value	labour force	% of labour force
Agriculture	1,281	2.4	212,000	75.2
Mining	—	—		
Manufacturing	1,911	3.6	31,000	11.0
Construction	2,588	4.8		
Public utilities	5,117	9.5		
Transportation and communications	10,896	20.3		
Trade	8,718	16.3	39,000	13.8
Finance	3,574	6.7		
Pub. admin., defense	17,620	32.9		
Services	1,903	3.5		
TOTAL	53,608	100.0	282,000	100.0

Land use (1992): forested 0.3%; meadows and pastures 8.6%; agricultural and under permanent cultivation[7]; built-on, wasteland, and other 91.1%.

Foreign trade[8]

Balance of trade (current prices)

	1989	1990	1991	1992	1993
DF '000,000	−27,624	−29,735	−31,509	−31,188	−30,669
% of total	35.0%	32.0%	32.9%	35.7%	34.1%

Imports (1991): DF 38,103,000,000 (food, beverages, and tobacco 32.7%; textiles and footwear 11.7%; fossil fuels 9.2%; machinery and electrical machinery 8.5%; transport equipment 7.1%; chemical products 6.2%; base metals and base metal products 6.2%). *Major import sources:* France 26.1%; Ethiopia 8.3%; Japan 7.2%; Italy 6.5%; Saudi Arabia 5.0%; United States 3.7%.
Exports (1991): DF 3,083,000,000 (unspecified special transactions 71.7%; live animals [including camels] 15.5%; food and food products 12.8%). *Major export destinations:* France 57.1%; Yemen 16.0%; Saudi Arabia 5.5%; Somalia 4.1%; Italy 3.2%.

Transport and communications

Transport. Railroads (1989): length 66 mi, 106 km; passenger-mi 182,000,000, passenger-km 293,000,000; short ton-mile cargo 81,700,000[9], metric ton-km cargo 119,300,000[9]. Roads (1991): total length 1,789 mi, 2,879 km (paved 13%). Vehicles (1992): passenger cars 13,000; trucks and buses 3,000. Merchant marine (1992): vessels (100 gross tons and over) 10; total deadweight tonnage 4,090. Air transport (1989)[10]: passenger arrivals 64,000, passenger departures 66,000; cargo loaded 1,100 metric tons, cargo unloaded 7,100 metric tons; airports (1994) with scheduled flights 1.
Communications. Weekly newspapers (1990): total number 1; total circulation 4,000; circulation per 1,000 population 7.6. Radio (1993): total number of receivers 30,000 (1 per 19 persons). Television (1993): total number of receivers 17,000 (1 per 33 persons). Telephones (1992): total number of receivers 14,000 (1 per 40 persons).

Education and health

Education (1991)

	schools	teachers	students	student/ teacher ratio
Primary (age 6–11)	69	737	31,926	43.3
Secondary (age 12–18) Voc., teacher tr.	26	362	9,363	28.6
Higher	1	13	108	8.3

Educational attainment: n.a. *Literacy* (1987): percentage of population age 20 and over literate 33.7%.
Health (1989): physicians 97 (1 per 5,258 persons); hospital beds[11] 1,383 (1 per 369 persons); infant mortality rate per 1,000 live births (1990–95) 112.
Food: n.a.

Military

Total active duty personnel (1994): 8,400[12] (army 95.2%, navy 2.4%, air force 2.4%). *Military expenditure as percentage of GNP* (1984): 9.0% (world 5.6%); per capita expenditure U.S.\$67.

---

[1]Original figures are those given in sq km; sq mi equivalent is rounded to appropriate level of generality. [2]Including 45,000 not distributed by district. [3]Excludes about 130,-000 Somali refugees. [4]Not including 20,000 people categorized as transients. [5]Infants and children to age 10, district of Djibouti only. [6]City of Djibouti only. [7]In 1988–89 only 1,005 acres (407 hectares) of land were cultivated. [8]The value of imports includes merchandise destined for Ethiopia and northern Somalia; that of exports excludes reexports coming from those areas. In 1980 the value of reexports from Ethiopia and northern Somalia was approximately five times greater than the value of domestic exports. Import figures are c.i.f. [9]Based on total weight of Ethiopian exports and imports transported to and from the port of Djibouti. [10]Djibouti International Airport only. [11]Public health facilities only. [12]Excludes 3,800 French troops.

Dominica

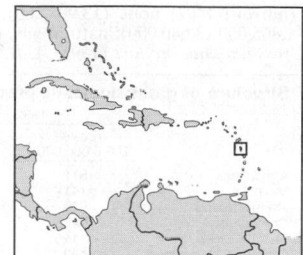

Official name: Commonwealth of
Dominica.
Form of government: multiparty
republic with one legislative house
(House of Assembly [31[1]]).
Chief of state: President.
Head of government: Prime Minister.
Capital: Roseau.
Official language: English.
Official religion: none.
Monetary unit: 1 East Caribbean
dollar (EC$) = 100 cents; valuation
(Oct. 7, 1994) 1 U.S.$ = EC$2.70;
1 £ = EC$4.30.

Area and population

Parishes[2]	area sq mi	area sq km	population 1991 census
St. Andrew	69	179	11,106
St. David	49	127	6,977
St. George	21	54	20,365
St. John	23	60	4,990
St. Joseph	46	119	6,183
St. Luke	4	10	1,552
St. Mark	4	10	1,943
St. Patrick	32	83	8,929
St. Paul	26	67	7,495
St. Peter	11	29	1,643
TOTAL	290[3, 4]	750[3, 4]	71,183[5]

Demography

Population (1994): 72,000.
Density (1994): persons per sq mi 248.3, persons per sq km 96.0.
Urban-rural: n.a.
Sex distribution (1991): male 50.04%; female 49.96%.
Age breakdown (1989): under 15, 35.1%; 15–29, 28.1%; 30–44, 14.5%; 45–59,
9.5%; 60 and over, 11.7%; unknown, 1.1%.
Population projection: (2000) 73,000; (2010) 74,000.
Doubling time: 45 years.
Ethnic composition (1981): black 91.2%; mixed race 6.0%; Amerindian 1.5%;
white 0.5%; not stated 0.6%; other 0.2%.
Religious affiliation (1992): Roman Catholic 79.2%; other 20.8%.
Major towns (1991): Roseau 15,853; Portsmouth 3,621; Marigot 2,919; Atkinson 2,518; Mahaut 2,372.

Vital statistics

Birth rate per 1,000 population (1993): 20.8 (world avg. 26.0).
Death rate per 1,000 population (1993): 5.1 (world avg. 9.2).
Natural increase rate per 1,000 population (1993): 15.7 (world avg. 16.8).
Total fertility rate (avg. births per childbearing woman; 1992): 2.5.
Marriage rate per 1,000 population (1990): 3.1.
Divorce rate per 1,000 population (1990): 0.4.
Life expectancy at birth (1993): male 73.9 years; female 79.7 years.
Major causes of death per 100,000 population (1990): diseases of the circulatory system 273.5, of which ischemic heart diseases 120.8, hypertensive
disease 88.8; malignant neoplasms (cancers) 116.6; endocrine, metabolic,
and nutritional disorders 51.4; diseases of the respiratory system 43.0; infectious and parasitic diseases 37.5.

National economy

Budget (1994–95). Revenue: EC$286,500,000 (current revenue 58.7%, external loans and sales of securities 22.9%, grants 15.1%, other 3.3%).
Expenditures: EC$286,500,000 (current expenditures 54.7%, development
expenditures 38.7%, debt repayment 3.5%, other 3.1%).
Public debt (external, outstanding; June 1993): U.S.$93,100,000.
Tourism (1992): receipts from visitors U.S.$25,000,000; expenditures by nationals abroad U.S.$6,000,000.
Gross national product (at current market prices; 1993): U.S.$193,000,000
(U.S.$2,680 per capita).

Structure of gross domestic product and labour force

	1992 in value EC$'000,000[6]	1992 % of total value	1989 labour force	1989 % of labour force
Agriculture	98.5	22.9	7,900	25.8
Mining	3.2	0.7	3,400	11.1
Manufacturing	31.3	7.3 }		
Construction	32.5	7.6	2,800	9.2
Public utilities	13.4	3.1	300	1.0
Transportation and communications	77.1	18.0	1,600	5.2
Trade, hotels, restaurants	58.2	13.6	3,700	12.1
Finance, real estate, insurance	69.4	16.2	800	2.6
Pub. admin., defense	79.1	18.4 }	5,800	19.0
Services	4.4	1.0 }		
Other	−37.9[7]	−8.8[7]	4,300[8]	14.1[8]
TOTAL	429.0[4]	100.0	30,600	100.0[4]

Population economically active (1989): total 30,600; activity rate of total
population 37.5% (participation rates: ages 15–64, 62.3%; female 41.8%;
unemployed [1992] 20.0%).

Price and earnings indexes (1990 = 100)

	1987	1988	1989	1990	1991	1992	1993
Consumer price index	88.1	90.7	96.9	100.0	105.5	111.1	113.1
Earnings index	...	...	...	...	...	...	...

Household income and expenditure. Average household size (1981) 4.3; income
per household: n.a.; expenditure (1984)[9]: food and nonalcoholic beverages
43.1%, housing and utilities 16.1%, clothing and footwear 6.5%, alcoholic
beverages and tobacco 2.0%, other 32.3%.
Production. Agriculture, forestry, fishing (value of production in EC$'000;
1991): bananas 39,600, root crops 32,800 (of which yams 9,800, dasheens
9,200, tanias 6,400, cassava 4,300), coconuts 4,600, plantains 3,700, grapefruit
3,500, oranges 3,300, cinnamon 2,400; livestock (number of live animals;
1993) 10,000 goats, 9,000 cattle, 8,000 sheep; roundwood, n.a.; fish catch
(1991) 590 metric tons. Mining and quarrying (1990): pumice and volcanic
ash 100,000 metric tons. Manufacturing (1990): coconut-based soaps 9,586
metric tons[10]; pasta products 156 metric tons; edible coconut oil 2,904
hectolitres; rum (1987) 2,614 hectolitres; bottled spring water 323,000 cases;
other products include garments, furniture, paint, and cardboard boxes.
Construction (value of starts; 1990): U.S.$29,800,000. Energy production
(consumption): electricity (kW-hr; 1992) 31,000,000 (31,000,000); coal, none
(none); crude petroleum, none (none); petroleum products (metric tons;
1992) none (19,000); natural gas, none (none).
Land use (1992): forested 41.0%; meadows and pastures 3.0%; agricultural
and under permanent cultivation 23.0%; other 33.0%.

Foreign trade[11]

Balance of trade (current prices)

	1987	1988	1989	1990	1991	1992
EC$'000,000	−49.6	−89.9	−167.3	−129.3	−110.5	−110.0
% of total	16.1%	23.5%	40.7%	29.9%	26.9%	26.3%

Imports (1992): EC$264,000,000 ([12]machinery and transport equipment 26.1%;
basic manufactures 24.5%; food 17.3%; chemicals and chemical products
11.1%). *Major import sources*[13]: United States 30.0%; United Kingdom
13.0%; China 6.0%; St. Lucia 5.0%; Italy 5.0%; France 5.0%.
Exports (1992): EC$154,000,000 (bananas 52.7%, coconut-based laundry and
toilet soaps 20.5%). *Major export destinations*[13]: United Kingdom 42.0%;
Jamaica 8.0%; Italy 7.0%; Taiwan 6.0%; Thailand 6.0%.

Transport and communications

Transport. Railroads: none. Roads (1990): total length 466 mi, 750 km (paved,
49%). Vehicles (1992): passenger cars 4,700, trucks and buses 5,500. Merchant marine (1992): vessels (100 gross tons and over) 7; total deadweight
tonnage 3,153. Air transport (1991): passenger arrivals 43,312, passenger
departures, n.a.; cargo unloaded 259 metric tons, cargo loaded 415 metric
tons; airports (1994) with scheduled flights 2.
Communications. Daily newspapers: none[14]. Radio (1993): 45,000 receivers
(1 per 1.6 persons). Television (1993): 5,200 receivers (1 per 14 persons).
Telephones (1992): 17,190 (1 per 4.2 persons).

Education and health

Education (1991–92)

	schools	teachers	students	student/ teacher ratio
Primary	65	605	12,120	20.0
Secondary	13[15]	199[15]	5,983	22.0[15]
Higher	2[15]	40	658	16.5

Educational attainment (1981). Percentage of population age 25 and over
having: no formal schooling 6.6%; primary education 80.6%; secondary
11.1%; higher 1.7%. *Literacy* (1986): total population age 15 and over literate, c. 49,000 (94.4%).
Health (1990): physicians (1991) 38 (1 per 1,889 persons); hospital beds 292
(1 per 247 persons); infant mortality rate per 1,000 live births 18.4.
Food (1988–90): daily per capita caloric intake 2,911 (vegetable products 79%,
animal products 21%); 120% of FAO recommended minimum requirement.

Military

Total active duty personnel (1990): none[16].

[1]Includes 10 nonelective seats. Nine of the 10 nonelective seats are potentially
elective according to the constitution. [2]Dominica is divided into 10 parishes for
statistical purposes only. Local government is based on city, town, or village councils.
[3]Includes inland water area. [4]Detail does not add to total given because of rounding. [5]Preliminary figure; excludes institutionalized population. [6]At factor cost. [7]Less
imputed service charges. [8]Activities not specified. [9]Weights of consumer price index
components. [10]Coconut-based soap products were the main contributor to total value
added of manufacturing sector in 1992. [11]Imports c.i.f.; exports f.o.b. [12]Based on 1990
imports totaling EC$318,400,000. [13]Estimated data. [14]Weekly newspapers (1991): total number 2; total circulation 5,050; circulation per 1,000 population 14. [15]1990–91.
[16]300-member police force includes a coast guard unit.

Dominican Republic

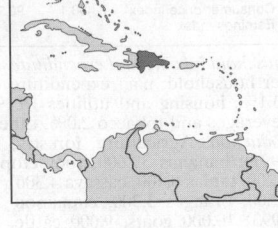

Official name: República Dominicana (Dominican Republic).
Form of government: multiparty republic with two legislative houses (Senate [30]; Chamber of Deputies [120]).
Head of state and government: President.
Capital: Santo Domingo.
Official language: Spanish.
Official religion: none[1].
Monetary unit: 1 Dominican peso (RD$) = 100 centavos; valuation (Oct. 7, 1994) 1 U.S.$ = RD$13.94; 1 £ = RD$22.18.

Area and population		area		population
				1990
Provinces	Capitals	sq mi	sq km	estimate
Azua	Azua	938	2,430	195,420
Bahoruco (Baoruco)	Neiba	531	1,376	87,376
Barahona	Barahona	976	2,528	152,405
Dajabón	Dajabón	344	890	64,123
Duarte	San Francisco de Macorís	499	1,292	261,725
El Seíbo	El Seíbo	641	1,659	97,590
Espaillat	Moca	386	1,000	182,248
Hato Mayor	Hato Mayor	514	1,330	77,823
Independencia	Jimaní	719	1,861	43,077
La Altagracia	Higüey	1,191	3,084	111,241
La Estrelleta	Elías Piña	690	1,788	72,651
La Romana	La Romana	209	541	169,223
La Vega	La Vega	916	2,373	303,047
María Trinidad Sánchez	Nagua	506	1,310	125,148
Monseñor Nouel	Bonao	388	1,004	124,794
Monte Cristi	Monte Cristi	768	1,989	92,678
Monte Plata	Monte Plata	841	2,179	174,799
Pedernales	Pedernales	373	967	18,896
Peravia	Baní	626	1,622	186,810
Puerto Plata	Puerto Plata	726	1,881	229,738
Salcedo	Salcedo	206	533	110,216
Samaná	Samaná	382	989	73,002
San Cristóbal	San Cristóbal	604	1,564	320,921
San Juan	San Juan	1,375	3,561	266,628
San Pedro de Macorís	San Pedro de Macorís	450	1,166	197,862
Sánchez Ramírez	Cotuí	453	1,174	140,635
Santiago	Santiago de los Caballeros	1,205	3,122	704,835
Santiago Rodríguez	Sabaneta	394	1,020	61,570
Santo Domingo[2]	—	570	1,477	2,411,895
Valverde	Mao	220	570	111,470
TOTAL		18,704[3]	48,443[3]	7,169,846[4]

Demography

Population (1994): 7,803,000[4].
Density (1994): persons per sq mi 417.2, persons per sq km 161.1.
Urban-rural (1990): urban 60.4%; rural 39.6%.
Sex distribution (1990): male 50.82%; female 49.18%.
Age breakdown (1990): under 15, 37.9%; 15–29, 29.9%; 30–44, 17.6%; 45–59, 9.1%; 60–74, 4.4%; 75 and over, 1.1%.
Population projection: (2000) 8,621,000; (2010) 9,903,000.
Doubling time: 36 years.
Ethnic composition (1990): mixed 70%; white 15%; black 15%.
Religious affiliation (1992): Roman Catholic 91.2%; other 8.8%.
Major urban centres (1993): Santo Domingo 2,100,000; Santiago de los Caballeros 690,000; La Vega 189,000[5]; San Pedro de Macorís 137,000[5].

Vital statistics

Birth rate per 1,000 population (1993): 25.7 (world avg. 26.0).
Death rate per 1,000 population (1993): 6.4 (world avg. 9.2).
Natural increase rate per 1,000 population (1993): 19.3 (world avg. 16.8).
Total fertility rate (avg. births per childbearing woman; 1993): 2.9.
Marriage rate per 1,000 population (1987): 2.3.
Life expectancy at birth (1993): male 65.9 years; female 70.2 years.
Major causes of death per 100,000 population (1985): diseases of the circulatory system 100.3; infectious and parasitic diseases 51.4; diseases of the respiratory system 35.4; accidents, poisoning, and violence 33.7.

National economy

Budget (1993). Revenue: RD$20,715,000,000 (tax revenue 87.0%, of which taxes on goods and services 38.7%, import duties 32.3%, income taxes 15.0%; nontax revenue 6.7%; grants and loans 6.3%). Expenditures: RD$20,257,-000,000 (development expenditure 58.4%; current expenditure 41.6%).
Public debt (external, outstanding; 1992): U.S.$3,761,000,000.
Tourism: receipts from visitors (1993) U.S.$1,223,000,000; expenditures by nationals abroad (1992) U.S.$115,000,000.
Production (metric tons except as noted). Agriculture, forestry, fishing (value of production in RD$'000,000; 1992): rice 3,020, beef 2,554, sugarcane 2,301, chicken meat 1,816, coffee 1,454, milk 1,307, plantains 1,036, eggs 755, beans 623, coconuts 493, cacao beans 410, bananas 343, cassava 317, tobacco 286, fish 92; roundwood 982,000 cu m. Mining (1993): ferronickel 35,400; gold 11,400 troy oz[6]. Manufacturing (1993)[7]: cement 1,271,000; refined sugar 102,800; beer 1,958,000 hectolitres; rum 441,000 hectolitres; cigarettes 218,-300,000 20-unit packs; cigars 65,000,000 units[8]. Construction (value of authorized construction in RD$'000,000; 1987): residential 352; nonresidential 253. Energy production (consumption): electricity (kW-hr; 1993) 4,926,000,-000 (3,321,000,000); coal (metric tons; 1992) none (58,000); crude petroleum

(barrels; 1992) none (13,993,000); petroleum products (metric tons; 1992) 1,865,000 (3,040,000); natural gas, none (none).
Gross national product (1993): U.S.$8,043,000,000 (U.S.$1,080 per capita).

Structure of gross domestic product and labour force				
	1992		1981	
	in value U.S.$'000,000[9]	% of total value	labour force	% of labour force
Agriculture	811	15.7	420,463	22.0
Mining	141	2.7	4,743	0.2
Manufacturing	929	17.9	224,437	11.7
Construction	542	10.5	80,850	4.3
Public utilities	111	2.1	13,891	0.7
Transp. and commun.	493	9.5	40,470	2.1
Trade	788	15.2	192,181	10.0
Finance, real estate	597	11.5	22,369	1.2
Pub. admin., defense	497	9.6 }	363,125	18.9
Services	275	5.3 }		
Other	—	—	552,859[10]	28.9
TOTAL	5,184	100.0	1,915,388	100.0

Population economically active (1991)[11]: total 2,758,000; activity rate of total population 37.6% (participation rates: age 10 and over, 50.3%; female 29.0%; unemployed [1994] 28.0%).

Price and earnings indexes (1990 = 100)							
	1987	1988	1989	1990	1991	1992	1993
Consumer price index	29.9	43.1	62.7	100.0	153.9	161.0	168.6
Monthly earnings index	39.7	50.2	64.1	100.0	125.3	150.8	...

Household income and expenditure. Average household size (1981) 5.1; average income: n.a.; sources of income: n.a.; expenditure (1980–85): food and beverages 46.0%, housing 10.0%, household goods 8.0%.
Land use (1991): forested 12.7%; meadows and pastures 43.2%; agricultural and under permanent cultivation 29.9%; other 14.2%.

Foreign trade[12]

Balance of trade (current prices)					
	1988	1989	1990	1991	1992	1993
U.S.$'000,000	−718	−1,039	−1,058	−1,071	−1,613	−1,588
% of total	28.8%	36.0%	41.9%	44.8%	58.9%	60.0%

Imports (1992): U.S.$2,175,000,000 (crude petroleum and petroleum products 22.4%; agricultural products 16.1%, of which cereals 5.2%; forest products 3.9%). *Major import sources:* U.S. 40.3%; Venezuela 11.0%; Japan 8.3%; Mexico 5.7%.
Exports (1992): U.S.$562,000,000[13] (ferronickel 31.9%; raw sugar 20.4%; cacao 6.3%; coffee 4.6%; gold alloy 4.3%). *Major export destinations:* U.S. 53.9%; The Netherlands 13.3%; Puerto Rico 7.1%; South Korea 4.5%.

Transport and communications

Transport. Railroads (1991)[14]: length 994 mi, 1,600 km. Roads (1990): total length 12,000 km (paved 48%). Vehicles (1992): passenger cars 150,000; trucks and buses 110,000. Merchant marine (1992): vessels (100 gross tons and over) 28; total deadweight tonnage 10,369. Air transport (1992): passenger-km 1,431,000,000; metric ton-km cargo 75,000,000; airports (1994) 5.
Communications. Daily newspapers (1990): total number 12; total circulation 230,000; circulation per 1,000 population 31. Radio (1993): 1,150,000 receivers (1 per 6.7 persons). Television (1993): 728,000 receivers (1 per 11 persons). Telephones (1992): 631,450 (1 per 12 persons).

Education and health

Education (1992–93)				
	schools	teachers	students	student/ teacher ratio
Primary (age 7–14)[15]	4,854	21,850	1,032,055	47.2
Secondary (age 15–18)[16]	...	9,963	426,962	42.9
Teacher tr.[16]	...	108	3,602	...
Higher[17]	7	5,041	68,301	13.5

Educational attainment (1981). Percentage of population age 25 and over having: no formal schooling 48.0%; incomplete primary education 31.7%; complete primary 4.0%; secondary 14.0%; higher 2.3%. *Literacy* (1990): total population age 15 and over literate, c. 3,710,000 (83.3%); males literate, c. 1,922,000 (84.8%); females literate, c. 1,788,000 (81.8%).
Health: physicians (1988) 7,332 (1 per 934 persons); hospital beds (1987) 13,169 (1 per 508 persons); infant mortality rate (1993) 53.6.
Food (1988–90): daily per capita caloric intake 2,310 (vegetable products 87%, animal products 13%); 102% of FAO recommended minimum.

Military

Total active duty personnel (1994): 24,500 (army 61.2%, navy 16.3%, air force 22.5%). *Military expenditure as percentage of GNP* (1991): 0.8% (world 4.2%); per capita expenditure U.S.$7.

[1]Roman Catholicism is the state religion per concordat with Vatican City. [2]National district. [3]Total includes 63 sq mi (163 sq km) of offshore islands not shown separately. [4]Preliminary 1993 census total released in late 1994 was 7,089,000. [5]1989. [6]Gold production was halted in early 1993 and resumed in mid-1994. [7]Excludes free-zone sector for reexport (mostly ready-made garments) employing (1994) 164,000; 1992 value added of free-zone sector equaled RD$3,800,000,000. [8]Export production for 1992. [9]At prices of 1988. [10]Not adequately defined (421,628) and those seeking work for first time (131,231). [11]Estimated figures. [12]Excludes free zones. [13]1992 reexports of free zones were estimated to equal U.S.$1,191,000,000. [14]Most track serves the sugar industry only, except for 65 mi (104 km) for public transport. [15]1989–90; public schools only. [16]1986–87. [17]Universities only.

Ecuador

Official name: República del Ecuador (Republic of Ecuador).
Form of government: unitary multiparty republic with one legislative house (National Congress [77]).
Head of state and government: President.
Capital: Quito.
Official language: Spanish.
Official religion: none.
Monetary unit: 1 Sucre (S/.) = 100 centavos; valuation (Oct. 7, 1994) 1 U.S.$ = S/. 2,201; 1 £ = S/. 3,501.

Area and population

Regions Provinces	Capitals	area sq mi	sq km	population 1990 census
Amazonica				
Morona-Santiago	Macas	13,100	33,930	84,216
Napo	Tena	9,918	25,690	103,387
Pastaza	Puyo	11,496	29,774	41,811
Sucumbíos	Nueva Loja	7,076	18,327	76,952
Zamora-Chinchipe	Zamora	8,923	23,111	66,167
Costa				
El Oro	Machala	2,259	5,850	412,572
Esmeraldas	Esmeraldas	5,884	15,239	306,628
Guayas	Guayaquil	7,916	20,503	2,515,146
Los Ríos	Babahoyo	2,770	7,175	527,559
Manabí	Portoviejo	7,289	18,879	1,031,927
Insular				
Galápagos	Puerto Baquerizo Moreno	3,093	8,010	9,785
Sierra				
Azuay	Cuenca	3,137	8,125	506,090
Bolívar	Guaranda	1,521	3,940	155,088
Cañar	Azogues	1,205	3,122	189,347
Carchi	Tulcán	1,392	3,605	141,482
Chimborazo	Riobamba	2,506	6,509	364,682
Cotopaxi	Latacunga	2,344	6,072	276,324
Imbabura	Ibarra	1,760	4,559	265,499
Loja	Loja	4,257	11,026	384,698
Pichincha	Quito	4,987	12,915	1,756,228
Tungurahua	Ambato	1,288	3,335	361,980
TOTAL		105,037[1,2]	272,045[2]	9,648,189[3]

Demography

Population (1994): 11,221,000.
Density (1994): persons per sq mi 106.8, persons per sq km 41.2.
Urban-rural (1990): urban 55.4%; rural 44.6%.
Sex distribution (1994): male 50.25%; female 49.75%.
Age breakdown (1994): under 15, 36.9%; 15–29, 29.0%; 30–44, 18.3%; 45–59, 9.4%; 60–74, 4.9%; 75 and over, 1.5%.
Population projection: (2000) 12,646,000; (2010) 14,899,000.
Doubling time: 34 years.
Ethnic composition (1989): Amerindian 40.0%; mestizo 40.0%; white 15.0%; black 5.0%.
Religious affiliation (1992): Roman Catholic 93.0%; other 7.0%.
Major cities (1990): Guayaquil 1,508,844; Quito 1,100,847; Cuenca 194,981; Machala 144,197; Portoviejo 132,937.

Vital statistics

Birth rate per 1,000 population (1993): 26.5[4] (world avg. 26.0); (1982) legitimate 67.9%; illegitimate 32.1%.
Death rate per 1,000 population (1993): 5.8[4] (world avg. 9.2).
Natural increase rate per 1,000 population (1993): 20.7[4] (world avg. 16.8).
Total fertility rate (avg. births per childbearing woman; 1993): 3.2.
Marriage rate per 1,000 population (1992): 6.4[4,5].
Divorce rate per 1,000 population (1992): 0.6[4,5].
Life expectancy at birth (1993): male 67.1 years; female 72.3 years.
Major causes of death per 100,000 population (1992): circulatory diseases 93.1; accidents, poisoning, and violence 66.7; infectious and parasitic diseases 52.0; neoplasms (cancers) 50.0; respiratory diseases 40.6.

National economy

Budget (1992). Revenue: S/. 3,008,560,000,000 (income from petroleum 51.1%, production and sales tax 22.7%, import duties 9.1%, income taxes 6.5%). Expenditures: S/. 3,102,440,000,000 (debt service 33.1%, public services 23.7%, education 19.5%, health 6.4%, transport and communications 4.1%).
Production (metric tons except as noted). Agriculture, forestry, fishing (1992): sugarcane 6,500,000, bananas 3,600,000, rice 981,000, plantains 930,000, corn (maize) 500,000, potatoes 375,000, soybeans 158,000, cacao 78,000; livestock (number of live animals) 4,665,000 cattle, 2,434,000 pigs, 1,511,000 sheep, 59,000,000 chickens; roundwood (1991) 7,762,000 cu m; fish catch (1991) 383,600. Mining and quarrying (1991): limestone 3,885,000; gold 96,900 troy oz. Manufacturing (value added in S/. '000,000; 1990): food products 175,126, of which beverages (including liquors) 25,606; textiles 72,554; chemical products 71,241; metal products 33,686. Construction (in S/.; 1992)[6]: residential 93,166,704,000; nonresidential 58,102,274,000. Energy production (consumption): electricity (kW-hr; 1991) 6,952,000,000 (6,952,000,000); crude petroleum (barrels; 1991) 111,506,000 (44,705,000); petroleum products (metric tons; 1991) 6,318,000 (5,034,000); natural gas (cu m; 1991) 91,350,000 (91,350,000).
Tourism (1992): receipts U.S.$192,000,000; expenditures U.S.$178,000,000.
Public debt (external, outstanding; 1992): U.S.$9,831,000,000.

Gross national product (1992): U.S.$11,843,000,000 (U.S.$1,070 per capita).

Structure of gross domestic product and labour force

	1992 in value U.S.$'000,000[7]	1992 % of total value	1990 labour force	1990 % of labour force
Agriculture	2,209	15.4	1,035,712	30.8
Mining	1,286	9.0	20,870	0.6
Manufacturing	2,807	19.6	370,338	11.0
Construction	523	3.6	196,716	5.9
Public utilities	10	0.1	12,660	0.4
Transp. and commun.	1,588	11.1	131,084	3.9
Trade	2,983	20.8	476,730	14.2
Finance	1,412	9.8	81,357	2.4
Pub. admin., defense	873	6.1	838,129	24.9
Services	654	4.6		
Other	...	...	196,171[8]	5.8[8]
TOTAL	14,344[1]	100.0[1]	3,359,767	100.0[1]

Population economically active (1990): total 3,359,767; activity rate of total population 34.8% (participation rates: ages 8 and over, 44.0%; female 26.4%; unemployed 1.3%).

Price and earnings indexes (1985 = 100)

	1987	1988	1989	1990	1991	1992	1993
Consumer price index	159.3	252.1	442.8	657.6	978.0	1,612.1	2,101.8
Hourly earnings index[9]	170.6	258.8	376.5	376.5	470.6	705.9	...

Household income and expenditure. Average household size (1990) 4.1; average annual income per household (1982) S/. 28,747 (U.S.$956); sources of income (1989): self-employment 74.9%, wages 17.4%, transfer payments 4.5%, interest, dividends, and rent 3.2%; expenditure (1991): food and tobacco 38.2%, transportation and communications 12.4%, clothing 10.4%, household furnishings 7.7%, housing and utilities 5.3%, health care 4.1%.
Land use (1991): forested 38.3%; meadows and pastures 18.7%; agricultural and under permanent cultivation 9.9%; other 33.1%.

Foreign trade[10]

Balance of trade (current prices)

	1987	1988	1989	1990	1991	1992
U.S.$'000,000	+232.2	+674.8	+719.7	+1,077.7	+736.0	+1,031.9
% of total	6.1%	18.2%	18.0%	24.7%	14.1%	20.7%

Imports (1992): U.S.$2,500,403,600 (industrial raw materials 33.4%, industrial capital goods 21.9%, transport equipment 13.9%, nondurable consumer goods 9.5%, durable consumer goods 9.2%). *Major import sources:* United States 32.5%; EEC 21.4%; Latin American Integration Association 19.3%; Japan 13.0%.
Exports (1992): U.S.$3,007,577,000 (crude petroleum 41.6%, bananas 21.7%, shrimp 17.5%, petroleum products 2.8%, coffee 2.7%, cocoa 2.5%). *Major export destinations:* United States 46.8%; EEC 15.5%; Latin American Integration Association 13.4%; Andean Group 5.8%; Taiwan 2.1%.

Transport and communications

Transport. Railroads (1990): route length (1992) 965 km; passenger-km 82,000,000; metric ton-km cargo 5,000,000. Roads (1991): total length 43,709 km (paved 12%). Vehicles (1991): passenger cars 335,903; trucks and buses 48,348. Merchant marine (1992): vessels (100 gross tons and over) 154; deadweight tonnage 504,127. Air transport (1992): passenger-km 948,393,000; metric ton-km cargo 146,376,000; airports (1994) 14.
Communications. Daily newspapers (1990): total number 25; total circulation 920,000; circulation per 1,000 population 87. Radio (1993): 3,000,000 receivers (1 per 3.7 persons). Television (1993): 900,000 receivers (1 per 12 persons). Telephones (1991): 540,533 (1 per 20 persons).

Education and health

Education (1989–90)

	schools[11]	teachers	students	student/ teacher ratio
Primary (age 4–12)	16,146	60,608	1,843,819	30.4
Secondary (age 12–18)[12,13]	2,207	36,730	504,481	13.7
Vocational[13]		16,838	260,850	15.5
Higher	21	12,856	206,541	16.1

Educational attainment (1990). Percentage of population age 25 and over having: no formal schooling 17.0%; primary 43.7%; secondary 22.6%; postsecondary 12.7%; not stated 4.0%. *Literacy* (1990): total population age 15 and over literate 5,217,543 (88.3%); males 2,616,192 (90.5%); females 2,601,351 (86.2%).
Health (1992): physicians 12,853 (1 per 836 persons); hospital beds 17,253 (1 per 623 persons); infant mortality rate per 1,000 live births 36.9.
Food (1988–90): daily per capita caloric intake 2,399 (vegetable products 85%, animal products 15%); 105% of FAO minimum requirement.

Military

Total active duty personnel (1993): 58,000 (army 86.2%, navy 7.8%, air force 6.0%). *Military expenditure as percentage of GNP* (1991): 2.1% (world 4.2%); per capita expenditure U.S.$22.

[1]Detail does not add to total given because of rounding. [2]Includes 884 sq mi (2,289 sq km) in nondelimited areas. [3]Total includes 70,621 persons in nondelimited areas. [4]Excluding nomadic Indian tribes. [5]Based on incomplete registration. [6]Authorized construction in Cuenca, Guayaquil, and Quito only. [7]At constant 1988 prices. [8]Includes unemployed persons not previously employed. [9]General minimum wage. [10]Import figures are f.o.b. in balance of trade and c.i.f. for commodities and trading partners. [11]1986–87. [12]Includes teacher training. [13]1987–88.

Egypt

Official name: Jumhūrīyah Miṣr al-'Arabīyah (Arab Republic of Egypt).
Form of government: republic with one legislative house (People's Assembly [454[1]]).
Chief of state: President.
Head of government: Prime Minister.
Capital: Cairo.
Official language: Arabic.
Official religion: Islam.
Monetary unit: 1 Egyptian pound (LE) = 100 piastres; valuation (Oct. 7, 1994) 1 U.S.$ = LE 3.39; 1 £ = LE 5.39.

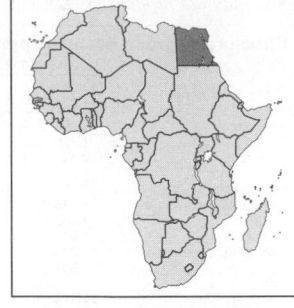

Area and population			area		population
Regions Governorates		Capitals	sq mi	sq km	1994[2] estimate
Frontier					
al-Baḥr al-Aḥmar		al-Ghurdaqah	78,643	203,685	111,000
Maṭrūḥ		Marsā Maṭrūḥ	81,897	212,112	179,000
Janūb Sīnā'		aṭ-Ṭūr	12,796	33,140	34,000
Shamāl Sīnā'		al-'Arīsh	10,646	27,574	213,000
al-Wādī al-Jadīd		al-Khārijah	145,369	376,505	134,000
Lower Egypt					
al-Buḥayrah		Damanhūr	3,911	10,130	3,895,000
ad-Daqahlīyah		al-Manṣūrah	1,340	3,471	4,144,000
Dumyāṭ		Dumyāṭ	227	589	879,000
al-Gharbīyah		Ṭanṭā	750	1,942	3,373,000
al-Ismā'īlīyah (Ismailia)		—	557	1,442	665,000
Kafr ash-Shaykh		Kafr ash-Shaykh	1,327	3,437	2,209,000
al-Minūfīyah		Shibīn al-Kawm	592	1,532	2,619,000
al-Qalyūbīyah		Banhā	387	1,001	2,983,000
ash-Sharqīyah		az-Zaqāzīq	1,614	4,180	4,125,000
Upper Egypt					
Aswān		Aswān	262	679	1,017,000
Asyūṭ		Asyūṭ	600	1,553	2,762,000
Banī Suwayf		Banī Suwayf	510	1,322	1,785,000
al-Fayyūm		al-Fayyūm	705	1,827	1,943,000
al-Jīzah		al-Jīzah	32,878	85,153	4,400,000
al-Minyā		al-Minyā	873	2,262	3,288,000
Qinā		Qinā	715[3]	1,851[3]	2,694,000
Sawhāj		Sawhāj	597	1,547	2,982,000
Urban					
Būr Sa'īd (Port Said)		—	28	72	460,000
al-Iskandarīyah (Alexandria)		—	1,034	2,679	3,382,000
al-Qāhirah (Cairo)		—	83	214	6,849,000
al-Uqṣur (Luxor)		—	...[3]	...[3]	155,000
as-Suways (Suez)		—	6,888	17,840	393,000
TOTAL			385,229	997,739	57,673,000

Demography

Population (1994): 58,466,000.
Density (1994): persons per sq mi 151.8, persons per sq km 58.6.
Urban-rural (1986): urban 43.9%; rural 56.1%.
Sex distribution (1992): male 51.76%; female 48.24%.
Age breakdown (1992): under 15, 38.7%; 15–29, 27.6%; 30–44, 17.7%; 45–59, 10.3%; 60–74, 4.8%; 75 and over, 0.9%.
Population projection: (2000) 65,556,000; (2010) 77,251,000.
Doubling time: 30 years.
Ethnic composition (1986): Egyptian 99.9%; other 0.1%.
Religious affiliation (1990): Sunnī Muslim c. 90%; Christian c. 10%[4].
Major cities (1994): Cairo 6,849,000; Alexandria 3,382,000; al-Jīzah 2,096,000[5].

Vital statistics

Birth rate per 1,000 population (1992): 30.4 (world avg. 26.0).
Death rate per 1,000 population (1992): 6.3 (world avg. 9.2).
Natural increase rate per 1,000 population (1992): 24.1 (world avg. 16.8).
Total fertility rate (avg. births per childbearing woman; 1992): 4.2.
Life expectancy at birth (1992): male 65.0 years; female 69.3 years.
Major causes of death per 100,000 population (1987): diseases of the circulatory system 314.4; diseases of the respiratory system 140.7; infectious and parasitic diseases 98.9; malignant neoplasms (cancers) 22.0.

National economy

Budget (1992–93). Revenue: LE 46,501,000,000 (general taxes 58.7%, of which sales taxes 15.5%, customs duties 10.8%; oil revenue 9.9%; Suez Canal fees 6.4%). Expenditures: LE 51,813,000,000 (debt servicing 26.3%; wages and salaries 18.9%; defense 10.8%; pensions and benefits 6.8%).
Public debt (external, outstanding; 1992): U.S.$35,724,000,000.
Production (metric tons except as noted). Agriculture, forestry, fishing (1993): sugarcane 11,800,000, corn (maize) 5,300,000, wheat 4,786,000, tomatoes 4,700,000, rice 3,800,000, oranges 1,650,000, sorghum 652,000, cotton (lint) 370,000; livestock (number of live animals) 3,707,000 sheep, 3,537,000 cattle[5], 3,017,000 goats, 2,527,000 buffalo[5], 37,000,000 chickens, 10,380,000 pigeons[5]; roundwood (1992) 2,352,000 cu m; fish catch (1991) 298,013. Mining and quarrying (1992[6]): iron ore 2,400,000; salt 890,000; clay 670,000. Manufacturing (1992–93): cement 16,000,000; nitrate fertilizers 5,437,000; reinforcing iron 1,650,000; sugar 1,074,000; phosphate fertilizers 970,000; cotton yarn 336,000; refrigerators 373,000 units; automobiles 6,800 units. Construction (1990–91): urban residential units 160,613. Energy production (consumption): electricity (kW-hr; 1993) 47,500,000,000 (39,320,000,000); coal (metric tons; 1992) n.a. (1,155,000); crude petroleum (barrels; 1993) 333,200,000 (178,300,000); petroleum products (metric tons; 1993) 24,209,000 (19,269,000); natural gas (cu m; 1993) 11,620,000,000 (11,620,000,000).

Gross national product (1993): U.S.$36,792,000,000 (U.S.$660 per capita).

Structure of gross domestic product and labour force				
	1992–93[7]		1989	
	in value LE '000,000	% of total value	labour force	% of labour force
Agriculture	22,300	16.6	6,335,200	39.5
Mining (petroleum)	13,536	10.1	43,300	0.3
Manufacturing	22,308[8]	16.7[8]	1,958,700	12.2
Construction	5,934	4.4	990,200	6.2
Public utilities	2,748	2.0	99,900	0.6
Transp. and commun.	15,427[9]	11.5[9]	780,200	4.9
Trade	24,655	18.4	1,340,000	8.4
Finance	7,253	5.4	255,300	1.6
Pub. admin., defense, services	9,745	7.3	3,115,500	19.4
Other	10,349	7.7	1,107,900[10]	6.9[10]
TOTAL	134,255	100.0[11]	16,033,600[12]	100.0[12]

Population economically active (1992–93): total 15,571,000; activity rate 27.6% (participation rates: ages 15–64, 48.7%; unemployed 10.0%).

Price and earnings indexes (1990 = 100)						
	1988	1989	1990	1991	1992	1993	1994[13]
Consumer price index	70.6	85.6	100.0	119.7	136.1	152.5	162.0
Annual earnings index[14]	73.6	91.0	100.0	120.3	137.6	...	...

Household income and expenditure. Average household size (1986) 4.9; expenditure (1986–87)[15]: food 55.7%, clothing 10.9%, housing 10.5%.
Tourism (1992): receipts U.S.$2,730,000; expenditures U.S.$918,000,000.
Land use (1991): agricultural 2.7%; other 97.3%.

Foreign trade

Balance of trade (current prices)[16]						
	1988	1989	1990	1991	1992	1993
U.S.$'000,000	−6,608	−5,933	−6,699	−5,975	−5,501	−7,315
% of total	54.4%	50.5%	48.2%	43.6%	44.7%	51.7%

Imports (1992–93)[17]: U.S.$10,731,800,000 (machinery and transport equipment 23.7%; foodstuffs 17.5%; chemical products 10.3%; base metals 8.5%). *Major import sources:* EEC 36.2%; U.S. 19.5%; other western European countries 10.4%; eastern Europe 3.3%.
Exports (1992–93): U.S.$3,417,300,000 (petroleum and petroleum products 52.8%; cotton yarn, textiles, and fabrics 13.2%; engineering and metallurgical goods 10.9%). *Major export destinations:* EEC 39.8%; Arab League 14.6%.

Transport and communications

Transport. Railroads (1990–91): length 8,831 km; passenger-km 43,185,000,000; metric ton-km cargo 3,162,000,000. Roads (1993): length 47,387 km (paved 73%). Vehicles (1993): passenger cars 1,119,727; trucks and buses 466,650. Merchant marine (1992): vessels (100 gross tons and over) 444; total deadweight tonnage 1,685,245. Inland water (1993): Suez Canal, number of transits 16,946; metric ton cargo 380,800,000. Air transport (1993)[18]: passenger-km 5,276,718,000; metric ton-km cargo 122,769,000; airports (1994) 9.
Communications. Daily newspapers (1990): total number 17; total circulation 3,307,100[18]; circulation per 1,000 population 62[19]. Radio (1993): 14,000,000 receivers (1 per 4.1 persons). Television (1993): 5,000,000 receivers (1 per 11.4 persons). Telephones (1991): 2,500,000 (1 per 22 persons).

Education and health

Education (1991–92)	schools	teachers	students	student/ teacher ratio
Primary (age 6–11)[20, 21]	16,481	279,315	6,964,306	24.9
Secondary (age 12–17)[20]	6,558[22]	155,941[23]	4,165,362	...
Vocational	...	79,167	1,110,184	14.0
Teacher training	519[24]	6,159	25,335	4.1
Higher[21]	12[25]	34,553[26]	600,680	...

Educational attainment (1986). Percentage of population age 15 and over having: no formal education 70.6%, of which literate 14.7%; primary and secondary 25.3%; higher 4.1%. *Literacy* (1990): total population age 15 and over literate 15,470,000 (48.4%); males 62.9%; females 33.8%.
Health: physicians (1990) 31,312 (1 per 1,698 persons); hospital beds (1991) 108,425 (1 per 504 persons); infant mortality rate (1992) 59.0.
Food (1988–90): daily per capita caloric intake 3,310 (vegetable products 92%, animal products 8%); 132% of FAO recommended minimum requirement.

Military

Total active duty personnel (1993): 430,000 (army 72.0%, navy 4.7%, air force [including air defense] 23.3%). *Military expenditure as percentage of GNP* (1992): 6.0% (world, n.a.); per capita expenditure U.S.$60.

[1]Includes 10 nonelective seats. [2]January 1. [3]The area of al-Uqṣur (Luxor) is included with Qinā governorate. [4]According to the 1986 census, the Christian population of Egypt was 5.9% of the total; this figure is considered by some external authorities to understate the Christian population by as much as 60%. [5]1991. [6]Year-end. [7]At factor cost. [8]Manufacturing includes mining but excludes petroleum. [9]Transportation includes earnings from traffic on the Suez Canal. [10]Unemployed and those seeking work for the first time. [11]Detail does not add to total given because of rounding. [12]Total includes 7,400 persons not classifiable by sector. [13]April. [14]Average nominal wages for each fiscal year (e.g., 1990–91). [15]Weight of consumer price components; urban households only. [16]Import figures are f.o.b. [17]Figures are c.i.f. [18]Egypt Air only. [19]Based on 12 dailies only. [20]Data exclude 1,399 primary and 1,290 secondary schools in the al-Azhar education system. [21]1990–91. [22]1989–90. [23]1987–88. [24]1983; includes vocational. [25]Universities only. [26]Excludes al-Azhar University.

El Salvador

Official name: República de El Salvador (Republic of El Salvador).
Form of government: republic with one legislative house (Legislative Assembly [84]).
Chief of state and government: President.
Capital: San Salvador.
Official language: Spanish.
Official religion: none.[1]
Monetary unit: 1 colón (₡) = 100 centavos; valuation (Oct. 7, 1994) 1 U.S.$ = ₡8.77; 1 £ = ₡13.95.

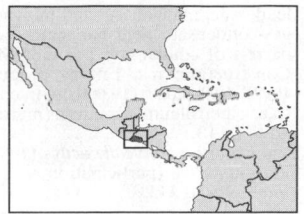

Area and population

Departments	Capitals	area sq mi	area sq km	population 1992 census[2]
Ahuachapán	Ahuachapán	479	1,240	260,563
Cabañas	Sensuntepeque	426	1,104	136,293
Chalatenango	Chalatenango	779	2,017	180,627
Cuscatlán	Cojutepeque	292	756	167,200
La Libertad	Nueva San Salvador	638	1,653	522,071
La Paz	Zacatecoluca	473	1,224	246,147
La Unión	La Unión	801	2,074	251,143
Morazán	San Francisco	559	1,447	166,772
San Miguel	San Miguel	802	2,077	380,442
San Salvador	San Salvador	342	886	1,477,766
San Vicente	San Vicente	457	1,184	135,471
Santa Ana	Santa Ana	781	2,023	451,620
Sonsonate	Sonsonate	473	1,226	354,641
Usulután	Usulután	822	2,130	317,079
TOTAL		8,124	21,041	5,047,925

Demography

Population (1994): 5,642,000.
Density (1994): persons per sq mi 694.5, persons per sq km 268.1.
Urban-rural (1992): urban 50.0%; rural 50.0%.
Sex distribution (1992): male 47.97%; female 52.03%.
Age breakdown (1991): under 15, 43.0%; 15–29, 28.5%; 30–44, 13.6%; 45–59, 9.0%; 60–74, 4.7%; 75 and over, 1.2%.
Population projection: (2000) 6,425,000; (2010) 7,772,000.
Doubling time: 26 years.
Ethnic composition (1990): mestizo (white and Indian) 90.0%; Indian 5.0%; white 5.0%.
Religious affiliation (1993): Roman Catholic 75.0%; other (mostly fundamentalist Protestant, Mormon, or Jehovah's Witness) 25.0%.
Major cities (1992)[3]: San Salvador 422,570 (metropolitan area 1,522,126); Soyapango 251,811[4]; Santa Ana 202,337; San Miguel 182,817, Mejicanos 145,000[4].

Vital statistics

Birth rate per 1,000 population (1994): 33.0 (world avg. 26.0); (1990) legitimate 30.6%; illegitimate 69.3%.
Death rate per 1,000 population (1994): 6.0 (world avg. 9.2).
Natural increase rate per 1,000 population (1994): 27.0 (world avg. 16.8).
Total fertility rate (avg. births per childbearing woman; 1994): 3.8.
Marriage rate per 1,000 population (1990): 4.3.
Divorce rate per 1,000 population (1990): 0.5.
Life expectancy at birth (1991): male 63.0 years; female 68.0 years.
Major causes of death per 100,000 population (1990)[5]: diseases of the circulatory system 120.1; violence 73.3; accidents 63.3; infectious and parasitic diseases 52.4; diseases of the respiratory system 49.1; ill-defined conditions 92.8.

National economy

Budget (1992). Revenue: U.S.$741,800,000 (current revenue 83.4%, of which stamp duties 30.3%, income taxes 15.9%, import duties 13.0%, consumption taxes 8.9%; other revenue 16.6%). Expenditures: U.S.$930,400,000 (defense and police 14.6%; education 11.7%; public works 8.9%; health and welfare 6.7%).
Production (value added in ₡'000,000 except as noted). Agriculture, forestry, fishing (1992): coffee 1,323, sugarcane 444, aviculture 363, fish catch 233, beans 216, *maicillo* (variety of millet) 208, rice 95, forest products 87, corn (maize) 82, tobacco 60, oranges 124,000 metric tons, bananas 68,000 metric tons; livestock (number of live animals; 1993) 1,345,000 cattle, 325,000 pigs. Mining and quarrying (1992): limestone 1,900,000 metric tons. Manufacturing (1992): food products 3,807; beverages 1,458; textiles 651; petroleum products 619; chemical products 564; nonmetallic mineral products 532; clothing and footwear 477; tobacco products 456. Construction (1992): private residential 694; private nonresidential 271; total public 619. Energy production (consumption): electricity (kW-hr; 1992) 2,316,000,000 (2,113,000,000); coal, none (none); crude petroleum (barrels; 1992) none (5,937,000); petroleum products (metric tons; 1992) 762,000 (1,017,000); natural gas, none (none).
Household income and expenditure. Average household size (1990) 4.9; income per household: n.a.; sources of income: n.a.; expenditure (1976–77)[6]: food and beverages 42.8%, housing 11.7%, education and recreation 8.7%, household furnishings 8.5%, clothing and footwear 8.4%.
Population economically active (1991)[7]: total 962,801; activity rate of total population 40.6% (participation rates: ages 15–64, 64.8%; female 45.1%; urban unemployed [1993] 8.1%).

Price and earnings indexes (1990 = 100)

	1988	1989	1990	1991	1992	1993	1994[8]
Consumer price index	68.6	80.7	100.0	114.4	127.2	150.9	166.0
Annual earnings index[9]	85.7	85.7	100.0	111.9	128.6	...	...

Public debt (external, outstanding; 1992): U.S.$2,016,000,000.
Gross national product (at current market prices; 1993): U.S.$7,230,000,000 (U.S.$1,320 per capita).

Structure of gross domestic product and labour force

	1992 In value ₡'000,000	1992 % of total value	1991 labour force[7]	1991 % of labour force[7]
Agriculture	5,244	9.6	100,451	10.4
Mining	99	0.2	863	0.1
Manufacturing	10,300	18.9	212,843	22.1
Construction	1,584	2.9	53,292	5.5
Public utilities	1,269	2.3	7,270	0.8
Transportation and communications	2,634	4.8	50,596	5.3
Trade	19,253	35.3	237,196	24.6
Finance, real estate	4,442	8.2	27,633	2.9
Public admin., defense	4,007	7.4 }	250,322	26.0
Services	5,666	10.4 }		
Other	—	—	22,335	2.3
TOTAL	54,498	100.0	962,801	100.0

Tourism: receipts (1992) U.S.$49,000,000; expenditures (1991) U.S.$57,000,000.
Land use (1992): forested 5.0%; meadows and pastures 29.5%; agricultural and under permanent cultivation 35.2%; other 30.3%.

Foreign trade[10]

Balance of trade (current prices)

	1988	1989	1990	1991	1992	1993
₡'000,000	−1,991	−3,717	−5,170	−6,560	−9,383	−10,379
% of total	24.6%	40.0%	36.9%	41.0%	48.0%	44.7%

Imports (1992): ₡14,475,000,000 (consumer goods 28.8%, capital goods 25.4%, crude petroleum 7.5%). *Major import sources:* United States 44.0%; Guatemala 9.7%; Mexico 7.0%; Japan 5.2%; Venezuela 5.1%.
Exports (1992): ₡5,092,000,000 (coffee 25.3%, raw sugar 7.5%, shrimp 3.3%, unspecified 63.6%). *Major export destinations:* United States 50.3%; Guatemala 16.1%; Costa Rica 6.7%; Germany 6.3%; Nicaragua 3.5%.

Transport and communications

Transport. Railroads (1992): route length 374 mi, 602 km; passenger-mi 3,900,000, passenger-km 6,300,000; short ton-mi cargo 26,200,000, metric ton-km cargo 38,200,000. Roads (1991): total length 9,371 mi, 15,081 km (paved 12%). Vehicles (1992): passenger cars 221,870; trucks and buses 33,229. Merchant marine (1992): vessels (100 gross tons and over) 15; total deadweight tonnage, n.a. Air transport (1992)[11]: passenger-mi 801,000,000, passenger-km 1,289,000,000; short ton-mi cargo 4,800,000, metric ton-km cargo 7,000,000; airports (1994) with scheduled flights 1.
Communications. Daily newspapers (1991): total number 6; total circulation 255,100; circulation per 1,000 population 48. Radio (1993): total number of receivers 1,935,000 (1 per 2.9 persons). Television (1993): total number of receivers 500,700 (1 per 11 persons). Telephones (1992): 296,910 (1 per 18 persons).

Education and health

Education (1991)

	schools	teachers	students	student/ teacher ratio
Primary (age 7–15)	3,516	22,622[12]	1,000,671	38.0[12]
Secondary (age 16–18) } Vocational	468[13]	...	84,100[14]	...
Higher[14]	...	4,216	78,211	18.6

Educational attainment (1990)[15]. Percentage of population over age 25 having: no formal schooling 13.9%; primary education 52.9%; secondary 19.7%; higher 13.5%. *Literacy* (1990): total population age 15 and over literate, c. 2,127,000 (73.0%); males literate, c. 1,048,000 (76.2%); females literate, c. 1,079,000 (70.0%).
Health (1991): physicians 2,483 (1 per 2,126 persons); hospital beds 5,726 (1 per 922 persons); infant mortality rate per 1,000 live births (1994) 41.0.
Food (1984–86): daily per capita caloric intake 2,152 (1979–81; vegetable products 88%, animal products 12%); 94% of FAO recommended minimum requirement.

Military

Total active duty personnel (1994): 30,700 (army 91.2%, navy 2.3%, air force 6.5%). *Military expenditure as percentage of GNP* (1991): 2.9% (world 4.2%); per capita expenditure U.S.$32.

---

[1]Roman Catholicism, although not official, enjoys special recognition in the constitution. [2]Preliminary figure. [3]Population of *municipios* (second-order administrative units). [4]Within San Salvador metropolitan area. [5]Projected rates based on about 75% of total deaths. [6]Based on middle-income urban families. [7]Urban areas only. [8]June. [9]Minimum wages in manufacturing and services in San Salvador metropolitan area. [10]Imports c.i.f., exports f.o.b. [11]TACA International Airlines. [12]Public schools only. [13]1989. [14]1990. [15]San Salvador metropolitan area only.

Equatorial Guinea

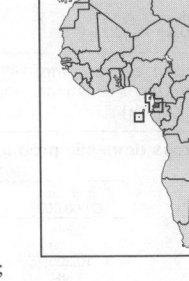

Official name: República de Guinea Ecuatorial (Republic of Equatorial Guinea).
Form of government: republic with one legislative house (Chamber of People's Representatives [80[1]]).
Chief of state: President.
Head of government: Prime Minister.
Capital: Malabo.
Official language: Spanish.
Official religion: none.
Monetary unit[2]: 1 CFA franc (CFAF) = 100 centimes; valuation (Oct. 7, 1994) 1 U.S.$ = CFAF 526.67; 1 £ = CFAF 837.67.

Area and population

	area		population
Regions	sq mi	sq km	1987 estimate
Provinces			
Insular	785[3]	2,034	70,280
Annobón	7	17	2,360
Bioko Norte	300	776	56,600
Bioko Sur	479	1,241	11,320
Continental	10,045[4]	26,017	259,950
Centro-Sur	3,834	9,931	55,970
Kie-Ntem	1,522	3,943	74,050
Litoral	2,573	6,665	75,640
Wele-Nzas	2,115	5,478	54,290
TOTAL	10,831[3]	28,051	330,230

Demography

Population (1994): 386,000.
Density (1994): persons per sq mi 35.6, persons per sq km 13.8.
Urban-rural (1991): urban 37.0%; rural 63.0%.
Sex distribution (1991): male 48.54%; female 51.46%.
Age breakdown (1990): under 15, 42.6%; 15–29, 26.4%; 30–44, 14.2%; 45–59, 10.5%; 60–74, 5.3%; 75 and over, 1.0%.
Population projection: (2000) 448,000; (2010) 573,000.
Doubling time: 27 years.
Ethnic composition (1983): Fang 82.9%; Bubi 9.6%; Ndowe 3.8%; Annobonés 1.5%; Bujeba 1.4%; other 0.8%.
Religious affiliation (1980): Christian (mostly Roman Catholic) 88.8%; traditional beliefs 4.6%; atheist 1.4%; Muslim 0.5%; other 0.2%; none 4.5%.
Major cities (1983): Malabo 30,418; Bata 24,308; Ela-Nguema 6,179; Campo Yaunde 5,199; Los Angeles 4,079.

Vital statistics

Birth rate per 1,000 population (1993): 41.1 (world avg. 26.0); legitimate, n.a.; illegitimate, n.a.
Death rate per 1,000 population (1993): 15.1 (world avg. 9.2).
Natural increase rate per 1,000 population (1993): 26.0 (world avg. 16.8).
Total fertility rate (avg. births per childbearing woman; 1993): 5.3.
Marriage rate per 1,000 population: n.a.
Divorce rate per 1,000 population: n.a.
Life expectancy at birth (1993): male 49.6 years; female 53.8 years.
Major causes of death per 100,000 population: n.a.; however, major diseases include malaria (affecting about 60% of the population), cholera, leprosy, trypanosomiasis (sleeping sickness), and waterborne (especially gastrointestinal) diseases.

National economy

Budget (1990). Revenue: CFAF 7,520,000,000 (fiscal receipts 68.4%; other receipts 31.6%). Expenditures: CFAF 8,105,000,000 (current expenditure 85.9%, of which interest 28.6%, salaries 26.1%; capital expenditure 14.1%).
Public debt (external, outstanding; 1992): U.S.$205,500,000.
Gross national product (at current market prices; 1993): U.S.$161,000,000 (U.S.$360 per capita).

Structure of gross domestic product and labour force

	1991		1983	
	in value CFAF '000,000	% of total value	labour force	% of labour force
Agriculture, forestry	23,328	50.2	59,390	57.9
Manufacturing, mining	597	1.3	1,616	1.6
Construction	1,299	2.8	1,929	1.9
Public utilities	1,358	2.9	224	0.2
Transportation and communications	855	1.8	1,752	1.7
Trade	3,319	7.1	3,059	3.0
Finance	1,005	2.2	409	0.4
Pub. admin., defense	6,354	13.7 }	8,377	8.2
Services	5,817	12.5 }		
Other	2,497	5.4	25,809	25.2
TOTAL	46,429	100.0[3]	102,565	100.0[3]

Production (metric tons except as noted). Agriculture, forestry, fishing (1993): roots and tubers 82,000 (of which cassava 47,000, sweet potatoes 35,000), bananas 17,000, coconuts 8,000, coffee 7,000, cacao beans 5,000, palm oil 5,000, palm kernels 3,000; livestock (number of live animals) 36,000 sheep, 8,000 goats, 5,000 pigs, 5,000 cattle; roundwood (1992) 613,000 cu m; fish catch (1991) 3,500. Mining and quarrying: details, n.a.; however, in addition to quarrying for construction materials, unexploited deposits of iron ore,

lead, zinc, manganese, and molybdenum are present; the new offshore Alba gas-condensate field has started commercial production at a rate of 4,500 barrels of condensate per day. Manufacturing (1992): veneer sheets 6,000. Construction: n.a. Energy production (consumption): electricity (kW-hr; 1992) 19,000,000 (19,000,000); coal, none (n.a.); crude petroleum[4], none (n.a.); petroleum products (metric tons; 1992) none (38,000); natural gas, none (n.a.).
Population economically active (1989): total 144,000; activity rate of total population 41.7% (participation rates [1983]: ages 15–64, 66.7%; female 35.7%; unemployed 24.2%).

Price and earnings indexes (1985 = 100)

	1986	1987	1988	1989	1990	1991	1992
Consumer price index	82.0	72.0	73.0	78.0	78.0	76.0	70.1
Earnings index	...	...	...	...	...	...	...

Household income and expenditure. Average household size (1980) 4.5; income per household: n.a.; sources of income: n.a.; expenditure: n.a.
Tourism: tourism is a government priority but remains undeveloped.
Land use (1992): forested 46.2%; meadows and pastures 3.7%; agricultural and under permanent cultivation 8.2%; built-on, wasteland, and other 41.9%.

Foreign trade

Balance of trade (current prices)

	1985	1986	1987	1988	1989	1990
CFAF '000,000	−3,819	−6,822	−3,426	−2,949	−4,083	−8,522
% of total	15.5%	22.2%	12.8%	9.5%	12.1%	29.7%

Imports (1990): U.S.$61,601,000 (machinery and transport equipment 58.2%; food, beverages, and tobacco 12.2%; fuels and lubricants 7.7%; basic manufactures 6.4%; chemicals 3.9%). *Major import sources* (1991): United States 29.4%; Cameroon 25.7%; Liberia 19.4%; Spain 10.3%; France 5.2%; Italy 2.6%; Japan 0.8%; Gabon 0.7%.
Exports (1990): U.S.$61,705,000 (machinery and transport equipment 39.8%; inedible crude materials 32.4%, of which cork and wood 20.8%; food and live animals 10.9%, of which cocoa 10.3%). *Major export destinations* (1991): Cameroon 54.8%; Spain 13.5%; Nigeria 10.4%; Gabon 2.8%; The Netherlands 2.4%; São Tomé and Príncipe 2.3%; Italy 1.9%; France 1.7%.

Transport and communications

Transport. Railroads: none. Roads (1989): total length 1,667 mi, 2,682 km (paved 19%). Vehicles (1991): passenger cars 5,500; trucks and buses 3,500. Merchant marine (1992): vessels (100 gross tons and over) 3; total deadweight tonnage 6,699. Air transport (1985): passenger-mi 4,000,000, passenger-km 7,000,000; short ton-mi cargo 700,000, metric ton-km cargo 1,000,000; airports (1994) with scheduled flights 1.
Communications. Daily newspapers (1990): total number 2; total circulation 2,000; circulation per 1,000 population 6.0. Radio (1993): total number of receivers 100,000 (1 per 3.8 persons). Television (1993): total number of receivers 2,500 (1 per 151 persons). Telephones (1987): 2,000 (1 per 163 persons).

Education and health

Education (1987–88)

	schools	teachers	students	student/ teacher ratio
Primary (age 6–11)	703	1,065	61,009	57.3
Secondary (age 12–17)	9	319	9,226	28.9
Voc., teacher tr.[5]	...	...	...	...
Higher	5	133	1,542	11.6

Educational attainment (1983). Percentage of population age 15 and over having: no schooling 35.4%; some primary education 46.6%; primary 13.0%; secondary 2.3%; postsecondary 1.1%; not specified 1.6%. *Literacy* (1983): percentage of total population age 15 and over literate 62.2%; males literate 77.8%; females literate 48.6%.
Health: physicians (1990) 99 (1 per 3,532 persons); hospital beds (1982) 3,200 (1 per 89 persons); infant mortality rate per 1,000 live births (1990–95) 117.
Food (latest): daily per capita caloric intake 2,230; 68% of FAO recommended minimum requirement.

Military

Total active duty personnel (1994): 1,320 (army 83.3%, navy 9.1%, air force 7.6%). *Military expenditure as percentage of GNP* (1981): 1.8% (world 5.8%); per capita expenditure U.S.$9.

---

[1]Conduct of November 1993 legislative elections was unacceptable to international observers. [2]As of Jan. 1, 1985, Equatorial Guinea became a member of the franc zone, substituting the CFA franc for the previous monetary unit, the ekwele; the CFA franc has a par value of 100 CFA francs to the French franc. [3]Detail does not add to total given because of rounding. [4]Equatorial Guinea's offshore prospective oil-lease areas total about 13,450 sq km. [5]Efforts are being undertaken to provide the training necessary to qualify nondegree teachers for service. Also, teacher-training schools are to be expanded in order to increase the number of primary-school teachers.

Eritrea

Official name: State of Eritrea.
Form of government: transitional regime[1] with one legislative house (National Assembly [60][2]).
Head of state and government: President assisted by State Council.
Capital: Asmara.
Official language: none.
Official religion: none.
Monetary unit: Ethiopian birr (Br) = 100 cents; valuation (Oct. 7, 1994) 1 U.S.$ = Br 5.41; 1 £ = Br 8.60.

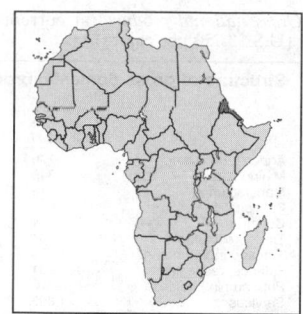

Area and population

Provinces	Capitals	area[3] sq mi	area[3] sq km	population 1994 estimate
Akele Guzai	Adi Qayeh	3,200	8,400	...
Asmara	Asmara (Asmera)	100	200	...
Barka	Agordat (Akordat)	10,700	27,800	...
Dankalia	Asseb (Aseb)	9,400	24,300	...
Gash and Setit	Barentu	7,200	18,600	...
Hamasien	...	1,000	2,700	...
Sahel	Nakfa	6,300	16,400	...
Semhar	Massawa (Mitsiwa)	2,400	6,300	...
Senhit	Keren	2,300	5,900	...
Seraye	Mendefera	2,600	6,800	...
TOTAL		45,300[4]	117,400	3,779,000

Demography

Population (1994): 3,779,000.
Density (1994): persons per sq mi 83.4, persons per sq km 32.2.
Urban-rural (1989): urban 15.4%; rural 84.6%.
Sex distribution (1992): male 49.90%; female 50.10%.
Age breakdown (1993): under 15, 46.0%; 15–29, 23.1%; 30–44, 16.0%; 45–59, 8.9%; 60–74, 4.4%; 75 and over, 1.6%.
Population projection: (2000) 4,523,000; (2010) 6,104,000.
Doubling time: 24 years.
Linguistic composition (1976): Tigrinya 47.9%; Tigré 31.0%; Afar 4.2%; Hedareb 3.9%; Bilen 3.1%; Saho 3.0%; Kunama 2.7%; Nara 2.1%; Amharic 1.7%; Rashaida 0.4%.
Religious affiliation (1993): believers are c. 50% Christian and c. 50% Muslim; there are also a few animists.
Major cities (1992): Asmara 400,000; Asseb 50,000; Keren 40,000; Massawa 40,000; Mendefera 14,833[5].

Vital statistics

Birth rate per 1,000 population (1992): 47.0 (world avg. 26.0).
Death rate per 1,000 population (1992): 18.0 (world avg. 9.2).
Natural increase rate per 1,000 population (1992): 29.0 (world avg. 16.8).
Total fertility rate (avg. births per childbearing woman; 1992): 6.8.
Marriage rate per 1,000 population (1992): 6.8.
Divorce rate per 1,000 population: n.a.
Life expectancy at birth (1992): 46 years.
Major causes of death per 100,000 population: n.a.; morbidity (principal causes of illness) arises mainly in malaria and other infectious diseases, parasitic infections, malnutrition, diarrheal diseases, and dysenteries.

National economy

Budget (1992). Revenue: Br 310,800,000. Expenditure: Br 350,200,000.
Public debt: n.a.
Tourism (1993): 12 major hotels.
Production (metric tons except as noted). Agriculture, forestry, fishing: (1993): roots and tubers 109,000, cereals 73,000, sorghum 51,000, vegetables and melons 25,000, pulses 13,000, millet 8,000, corn (maize) 6,000, barley 4,000, wheat 3,000; livestock (number of live animals) 1,550,000 cattle, 1,510,000 sheep, 1,400,000 goats, 69,000 camels; Red Sea fisheries landed c. 2,000 tons annually in the early 1990s, including lobster, prawns, sardines, sharks, anchovies, groupers, and snappers. Mining and quarrying: detail, n.a.; salt and sand and aggregate for construction are the principal minerals exploited; deposits of copper, zinc, mica, gold, iron, manganese, nickel, and lead exist but remain unexploited. Manufacturing (value added in Br '000; 1983–84): petroleum products 120,513; beverages 60,868, of which beer 54,275; food products 53,480; textiles 23,699, of which spinning and weaving 14,404, knitting products 5,816, rope and twine 3,479; chemical products 9,641; plastic products 9,423; tobacco products 6,262; nonmetallic mineral products 5,057; footwear 4,249; metal products 3,830; glass and glass products 3,258. Construction: reconstruction, after some 30 years of civil war, is a principal concern of the government. Energy production: energy resources include hydroelectricity, fossil fuels, geothermal power, coal, biogas, solar power, and wind; commercial electricity production for 1986–87 was 148,664,000 kW hr.
Persons economically active: n.a.

Price and earnings indexes (1985 = 100)

	1986	1987	1988	1989	1990	1991	1992
Consumer price index[6]	90.2	88.0	94.2	101.6	106.8	145.0	160.3
Earnings index	...	...	...	...	...	...	...

Gross national product (at current market prices; 1993): c. U.S.$393,415,000 (U.S.$115 per capita).

Manufacturing value added and employment (current prices)

	1983 84 in value '000 birr	% of total value	labour force	% of labour force
Apparel	4,275	1.4	796	5.2
Chemical products	9,641	3.1	531	3.4
Food and beverages	114,348	36.5	3,267	21.3
Metal products	3,830	1.2	611	4.0
Nonmetallic products	5,057	1.6	511	3.3
Petroleum products	120,513	38.4	1,070	7.0
Plastic products	9,423	3.0	813	5.3
Textiles	23,699	7.5	6,341	41.4
Other	22,818	7.3	1,370	8.9
TOTAL	313,604	100.0	15,310	100.0[4]

Household income and expenditure. Average household size (1984) 4.5; average annual income per household: n.a.; sources of income: n.a.; expenditure: n.a.
Land use (1993): forested 0.5%; woodland and scrubland 5.5%; agricultural and under permanent cultivation 3.5%; meadows and pastures 57.2%; other (predominantly barren land) 33.3%.

Foreign trade

Balance of trade (current prices): n.a.
Imports (1992): Br 367,000,000 (manufactured goods 58.0%, food products 31.0%, chemical products 9.0%, raw materials 2.0%). *Major import sources:* Saudi Arabia 49.0%[7]; Ethiopia 17.0%; United Arab Emirates 10.0%; Italy 8.0%.
Exports (1992): Br 46,000,000 (raw materials 75.0%, food products 14.0%, manufactured goods 10.0%, chemical products 1.0%). *Major export destinations:* Ethiopia 87.0%; Italy 7.0%; United Arab Emirates 1.0%; United Kingdom 1.0%.

Transport and communications

Transport. Railroads (1994): none; a 190-mi (306-km) rail line that formerly connected Massawa and Agordat is under reconstruction. Roads (1994): total length 621 mi, 1,000 km (paved, n.a.). Vehicles: n.a. Merchant marine: vessels (100 gross tons and over) n.a. Air transport (1993)[8]: passenger arrivals 47,645[9], passenger departures 42,548[9]; short ton cargo handled 25,907[10], metric ton cargo handled 28,557[10]; airports (1994) with scheduled flights 2.
Communications. Daily newspapers: none; (1994) 2 biweekly newspapers published; circulation c. 26,000[11]; circulation per 1,000 population 7.8[11]. Radio (1994): the government operates a station in Asmara. Television (1994): the government operates a station in Asmara. Telephones (1993): 13,356 (1 per 275 persons).

Education and health

Education (1992–93)

	schools	teachers	students	student/ teacher ratio
Primary (age 7–12)	447	4,954	184,492	37.2
Secondary (age 13–18)	86	1,759	59,962	34.1
Voc., teacher tr.	4	53	774	14.6
Higher[12]	1	144	2,032	14.1

Literacy (1993): total population literate c. 20%.
Health: physicians (1993) 69 (1 per 36,000 persons); hospital beds (1986–87): 2,449 (1 per 1,100 persons); infant mortality rate per 1,000 live births (1993) 135.
Food (1993): daily per capita caloric intake 1,750 (vegetable and animal products, n.a.); 93% of FAO recommended minimum requirement.

Military

Total active duty personnel (1994): estimated strength of Eritrean armed forces (predominantly former guerrillas) is some 42,000.

[1]Transitional regime (independent May 24, 1993) to govern for up to four years pending the drafting of a constitution and holding of multiparty elections. [2]Excludes members of the Central Council of the People's Front for Democracy and Justice, who are ex officio members of the Assembly. [3]Approximate figures. [4]Detail does not add to total given because of rounding. [5]1989. [6]Ethiopian CPI; no separate data available as yet. [7]Saudi Arabia is a transshipment point; not all goods included here are of Saudi Arabian origin. [8]Asmara airport only. [9]January to June only. [10]1987–88. [11]1992. [12]1993–94; full-time students only.

Estonia

Official name: Eesti Vabariik (Republic of Estonia).
Form of government: unitary multiparty republic with a single legislative body (Parliament [101]).
Chief of state: President.
Head of government: Prime Minister.
Capital: Tallinn.
Official language: Estonian.
Official religion: none.
Monetary unit: 1 kroon (EEK) = 100 senti; valuation (Oct. 7, 1994)
1 U.S.$ = EEK 12.32;
1 £ = EEK 19.60.

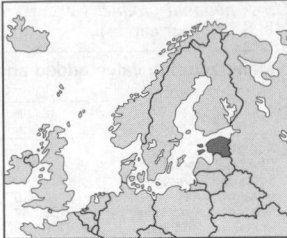

Area and population

Counties	Capitals	area sq mi	area sq km	population 1994[1] estimate
Harju	Tallinn	1,673	4,333	566,853
Hiiu	Kärdla	395	1,023	11,986
Ida-Viru	Jõhvi	1,299	3,364	209,827
Järva	Paide	1,013	2,623	43,746
Jõgeva	Jõgeva	1,005	2,604	42,549
Lääne	Haapsalu	920	2,383	32,756
Lääne-Viru	Rakvere	1,337	3,464	76,099
Pärnu	Pärnu	1,856	4,806	99,869
Põlva	Põlva	836	2,165	36,544
Rapla	Rapla	1,151	2,980	40,111
Saare	Kuressaare	1,128	2,922	40,822
Tartu	Tartu	1,193	3,089	155,568
Valga	Valga	790	2,047	40,342
Viljandi	Viljandi	1,386	3,589	64,793
Võru	Võru	890	2,305	45,062
TOTAL		17,462[2]	45,227[2,3]	1,506,927

Demography

Population (1994): 1,499,000.
Density (1994): persons per sq mi 85.8, persons per sq km 33.1.
Urban-rural (1994): urban 70.3%; rural 29.7%.
Sex distribution (1994): male 46.69%; female 53.31%.
Age breakdown (1994): under 15, 21.1%; 15–29, 20.9%; 30–44, 21.8%; 45–59, 17.8%; 60–74, 13.6%; 75 and over, 4.8%.
Population projection: (2000) 1,450,000; (2010) 1,450,000.
Ethnic composition (1989): Estonian 61.5%; Russian 30.3%; Ukrainian 3.1%; Belorussian 1.8%; Finnish 1.1%; other 2.2%.
Religious affiliation: believers are predominantly Evangelical Lutheran, with Orthodox and Baptist minorities.
Major cities (1994): Tallinn 442,679; Tartu 105,844; Narva 79,094; Pärnu 51,963; Kohtla-Järve 28,310[4].

Vital statistics

Birth rate per 1,000 population (1993): 10.2 (world avg. 26.0); (1992) legitimate 66.1%; illegitimate 33.9%.
Death rate per 1,000 population (1993): 14.0 (world avg. 9.2).
Natural increase rate per 1,000 population (1993): −3.8 (world avg. 16.8).
Total fertility rate (avg. births per childbearing woman; 1992): 1.8.
Marriage rate per 1,000 population (1993): 5.1.
Divorce rate per 1,000 population (1993): 3.8.
Life expectancy at birth (1994): male 65.0 years; female 75.0 years.
Major causes of death per 100,000 population (1990): diseases of the circulatory system, 746.7, of which ischemic heart diseases 465.9, cerebrovascular disease 233.4; malignant neoplasms (cancers) 194.2; accidents 90.4; suicide 26.8.

National economy

Budget (1992). Revenue: EEK 3,667,245,000 (sales taxes 24.6%, personal income taxes 23.4%, income taxes on enterprises 19.6%, subsidies 8.8%). Expenditures: EEK 3,667,245,000 (education 21.1%, housing 9.2%, social security 9.0%, subsidies 8.8%, transportation 6.6%, public health 2.7%, defense 1.7%).
Public debt (external, outstanding; 1992): U.S.$26,500,000.
Production (metric tons except as noted). Agriculture, forestry, fishing (1992): potatoes 669,100, hay 593,200, barley 300,800, rye 153,400, wheat 89,400, vegetables 78,400, fruits and berries 30,600; livestock (number of live animals) 615,000 cattle, 541,000 pigs; roundwood (1991) 1,653,000 cu m; fish catch (1991) 317,400. Mining and quarrying (value of production in EEK '000,000; 1992): oil shale 389, peat 34. Manufacturing (value of production in EEK '000,000; 1992): textiles, clothing, and footwear 1,388; chemicals and chemical products 891; meat 839; dairy products 788; furniture 532; nonmetallic mineral products 461; electrical machinery and components 454. Construction (completed; 1992): residential 239,700 sq m; nonresidential, n.a. Energy production (consumption): electricity (kW-hr; 1992) 11,831,-000,000 (5,916,000,000); oil shale (metric tons; 1992) 18,849,000 (20,502,000); coal and coke (metric tons; 1992) none (239,000); crude petroleum, none (n.a.); natural gas (cu m; 1992) none (890,000,000).
Household income and expenditure. Average household size (1994) 3.1; average annual income per household (1993) EEK 27,805 (U.S.$2,102); sources of income (1993): wages and salaries 66.0%, social security 9.0%, other 25.0%; expenditure (1992)[5]: food, beverages, and tobacco 47.3%, housing 13.8%, clothing and footwear 9.2%.

Gross national product (at current market prices; 1992): U.S.$4,297,000,000 (U.S.$2,750 per capita).

Structure of gross domestic product and labour force

	1992 in value EEK '000,000	1992 % of total value	1992 labour force[6]	1992 % of labour force
Agriculture, fishing	1,779	12.5	107,283	17.8
Mining	349	2.4	14,656	2.4
Manufacturing	4,019	28.2	158,008	26.3
Public utilities	614	4.3	15,377	2.6
Construction	654	4.6	37,551	6.2
Trade, restaurants	2,064	14.5	53,423	8.9
Transp. and commun.	1,698	11.9	57,438	9.5
Finance, real estate	581	4.1	25,699	4.3
Pub. admin., defense	279	2.0	110,824	18.4
Services	1,393	9.8	21,494	3.6
Other	817[7]	5.7[7]	—	—
TOTAL	14,247	100.0	601,753	100.0

Population economically active (1989): total 856,000; activity rate of total population 54.7% (participation rates: ages 15–64, 79.7%; female 50.0%; unemployed [April 1994] 2.3%).

Price and earnings indexes (1990 = 100)

	1988	1989	1990	1991	1992	1993	1994
Consumer price index	80	84	100	332	3,904	7,410	11,027[8]
Monthly earnings index[9]	...	...	100	218	1,340[10]	...	...

Tourism (1992): receipts from visitors U.S.$4,500,000; expenditures by nationals abroad U.S.$2,400,000.
Land use (1989): forested 42.6%; meadows and pastures, n.a.; agricultural and under permanent cultivation 32.5%; other 24.9%.

Foreign trade

Balance of trade (current prices)

	1991	1992	1993
EEK '000,000	+65	+421	−1,212
% of total	6.8%	3.9%	5.4%

Imports (1993): EEK 11,848,000,000 mineral fuels 15.1%, food products 15.0%, motor vehicles 12.8%, nonelectrical machinery 10.6%, textiles and clothing 10.5%). *Major import sources:* Finland 27.9%; Russia 17.2%; Germany 10.7%; Sweden 8.9%; Japan 4.2%; The Netherlands 3.6%; Lithuania 3.3%.
Exports (1993): EEK 10,636,000,000 (food products 23.5%, base metals 10.5%, motor vehicles 10.1%, wood and wood products 7.5%, mineral fuels 7.0%). *Major export destinations:* Russia 22.6%; Finland 20.7%; Sweden 9.5%; Latvia 8.6%; Germany 8.0%; The Netherlands 4.1%; Ukraine 3.6%.

Transport and communications

Transport. Railroads (1992): route length 633 mi, 1,018 km; passenger-mi 590,-000,000, passenger-km 950,000,000; short ton-mi cargo 2,497,000,000, metric ton-km cargo 3,646,000,000. Roads (1992): total length 9,194 mi, 14,797 km (paved 54%). Vehicles (1992): passenger cars 283,400; trucks and buses 83,-000. Merchant marine (1992): vessels (1,000 gross tons and over) 234; total deadweight tonnage 680,367. Air transport (1992): passenger-mi 118,700,000, passenger-km 191,100,000; short ton-mi cargo (1991) 4,100,000, metric ton-km cargo (1991) 6,000,000; airports (1994) with scheduled flights 1.
Communications. Daily newspapers: total number (1992) 7; total circulation 239,000; circulation per 1,000 population 155. Radio (1989): total number of receivers 926,000 (1 per 1.7 persons). Television (1992): total number of receivers 600,000 (1 per 2.6 persons). Telephones (1992): 386,000 (1 per 4.0 persons).

Education and health

Education (1992–93)

	schools	teachers	students	student/ teacher ratio
Primary } Secondary	715	15,783	216,427	13.7
Vocational	92	...	30,687	...
Higher	14	3,168[11]	24,464	8.2[11]

Educational attainment (1989). Percentage of persons age 25 and over having: no formal schooling 2.2%; primary education 39.7%; secondary 45.1%; higher 13.7%. Literacy (1989): 99.7%.
Health (1992): physicians 5,360 (1 per 288 persons); hospital beds 14,843 (1 per 103 persons); infant mortality rate per 1,000 live births 15.8.
Food: daily per capita caloric intake, n.a.

Military

Total active duty personnel (1993): 2,500[12]. *Military expenditure as a percentage of GNP:* n.a.

[1]January 1st. [2]Total includes 590 sq mi (1,528 sq km) not distributed by county, largely the Estonian portion of Lake Peipus. [3]Detail does not add to total given because of rounding. [4]1992. [5]Urban areas only. [6]Wage earners only. [7]Taxes on products less subsidies. [8]Average of June–July. [9]Manufacturing sector only. [10]Average of first three quarters. [11]1990–91. [12]The last Russian military personnel left Estonia in August 1994.

Ethiopia

Official name: Ītyop'iya (Ethiopia).
Form of government: transitional regime with one nonlegislative deliberative body (Constituent Assembly [545])[1].
Chief of state and government: President assisted by Prime Minister.
Capital: Addis Ababa.
Official Language: Amharic.
Official religion: none.
Monetary unit: 1 birr (Br) = 100 cents; valuation (Oct. 7, 1994) 1 U.S.$ = Br 5.41; 1 £ = Br 8.60.

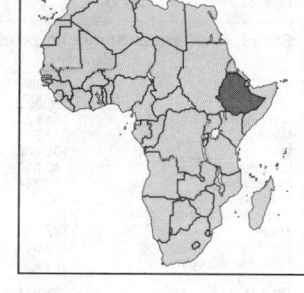

Area and population

Regions[2]	Capitals	area sq mi	area sq km	population 1993 estimate
Addis Ababa	...	2,003	5,188	2,657,559
Arsi	Asela	9,155	23,710	2,157,227
Asosa	...	8,906	23,067	570,910
Bale	Goba	25,996	67,330	1,063,382
Borena	...	36,301	94,018	723,746
Eastern Gojam	...	5,381	13,936	1,699,460
Eastern Harerge	...	34,981	90,600	2,774,346
Eastern Shewa	...	4,924	12,754	1,026,180
Gambela	...	10,064	26,065	195,023
Ilubabor	Mefa	12,905	35,059	3,117,220
Kefa	Jima	15,476	40,083	1,148,596
Metekel	...	11,768	30,481	416,380
Northern Gonder	...	23,946	62,020	2,038,164
Northern Omo	...	11,553	29,923	3,046,859
Northern Shewa	...	10,436	27,030	2,570,128
Northern Welo	...	11,906	30,835	1,621,520
Sidamo	Awasa	8,009	20,742	2,980,044
Southern Gonder	...	6,594	17,079	1,867,766
Southern Omo	...	8,494	22,000	269,197
Southern Shewa	...	6,486	16,799	3,235,768
Southern Welo	...	7,993	20,702	2,675,995
Wolega	Nekemte	10,400	42,632	2,673,652
Western Gojam	...	6,675	17,289	2,210,466
Western Harerge	...	12,814	33,188	1,482,628
Western Shewa	...	8,964	23,218	2,934,434
Autonomous regions				
Aseb[3]	...	17,786	46,065	246,373
Dire Dawa	...	11,291	29,244	521,691
Ogaden	...	69,239	179,327	906,632
Tigray	Mekele	20,656	53,498	2,999,948
TOTAL		437,794	1,133,882	51,831,290

Demography

Population (1994): 53,384,000.
Density (1994): persons per sq mi 121.9, persons per sq km 47.1.
Urban-rural (1993): urban 12.3%; rural 87.7%.
Sex distribution (1993): male 50.27%; female 49.73%.
Age breakdown (1993): under 15, 46.5%; 15–29, 22.8%; 30–44, 15.6%; 45–59, 8.9%; 60–74, 4.5%; 75 and over, 1.7%.
Population projection: (2000) 63,726,000; (2010) 85,605,000.
Ethnolinguistic composition (1983)[5]: Amhara 37.7%; Galla (Oromo) 35.3%; Tigrinya 8.6%; Gurage 3.3%; Ometo (Omotic) 2.7%; Sidamo 2.4%.
Religious affiliation (1980)[5]: Ethiopian Orthodox 52.5%; Muslim 31.4%; traditional beliefs 11.4%; other Christian 4.5%; other 0.2%.
Major cities (1988): Addis Ababa 1,673,060; Dire Dawa 117,734; Gonder 95,000; Nazret 90,975.

Vital statistics[5]

Birth rate per 1,000 population (1990–95): 49.1 (world avg. 26.0).
Death rate per 1,000 population (1990–95): 18.5 (world avg. 9.2).
Natural increase rate per 1,000 population (1990–95): 30.6 (world avg. 16.8).
Total fertility rate (avg. births per childbearing woman; 1990–95): 7.0.
Life expectancy at birth (1990–95): male 45.4 years; female 48.7 years.
Major causes of death (1987–88)[6]: infectious and parasitic diseases 33.1%; respiratory diseases 15.7%; digestive system diseases 10.7%.

National economy[5]

Budget (1991–92). Revenue: Br 2,176,100,000 (taxes 72.8%, of which income and profit tax 28.2%, sales tax 22.7%, import duties 19.5%, export duties 0.4%; nontax revenue 27.2%). Expenditures: Br 3,124,100,000 (general services 34.0%; social services 24.5%, of which education 15.5%, public health 4.4%; debt payment 9.7%).
Tourism: receipts (1992) U.S.$23,000,000; expenditures (1991) U.S.$7,000,000.
Production (metric tons except as noted). Agriculture, forestry, fishing (1993): corn (maize) 1,694,000, sugarcane 1,450,000, sorghum 950,000, barley 946,-000, wheat 897,000, pulses 802,000, potatoes 349,000, millet 262,000, yams 180,000, coffee 180,000, seed cotton 46,000; livestock (number of live animals) 29,450,000 cattle, 21,700,000 sheep, 16,700,000 goats, 8,580,000 horses, mules, and asses, 1,000,000 camels; roundwood (1992) 45,603,000 cu m; fish catch (1991) 4,500. Mining and quarrying (1992): cement 320,000; salt 110,000; limestone 100,000; gold 71,503 troy oz, platinum 16 troy oz. Manufacturing (gross value in Br '000[7]; 1991–92): food and beverages 555,800; textiles 251,400; leather and shoes 162,300; cigarettes 106,000; chemicals 53,-400. Construction (authorized; 1987–88)[8]: residential 260,251 sq m; nonresidential 63,346 sq m, of which commercial 16,994 sq m. Energy production (consumption): electricity (kW-hr; 1992) 1,257,000,000 (1,257,000,000); coal, none (n.a.); crude petroleum (barrels; 1992) n.a. (5,498,000); petroleum products (metric tons; 1992) 739,000 (893,000); natural gas, n.a. (n.a.).

Land use (1992): forest 24.4%; pasture 40.7%; agriculture 12.7%; other 22.2%.
Gross national product (1993): U.S.$5,329,000,000 (U.S.$100 per capita).

Structure of gross domestic product and labour force

	1991–92 in value Br '000,000	1991–92 % of total value	1991 labour force	1991 % of labour force
Agriculture	6,311.3	50.3	14,900,000	74.2
Manufacturing, mining	1,177.5	9.4	}	
Construction	346.2	2.8	} 2,065,000	10.3
Public utilities	163.4	1.3	}	
Transp. and commun.	678.5	5.4	}	
Trade	1,279.5	10.2	}	
Finance	414.2	3.3	}	
Pub. admin., defense	909.4	7.2	} 3,103,000	15.5
Services	960.2	7.7	}	
Other	303.3	2.4	}	
TOTAL	12,543.5	100.0	20,068,000	100.0

Public debt (external, outstanding; 1992): U.S.$4,168,000,000.
Population economically active (1992): total 23,518,000; activity rate of total population 41.3% (participation rates: ages 15–64, 70.1%; female 41.1%; unemployed [1990] 44.2%).

Price index (1990 = 100)

	1987	1988	1989	1990	1991	1992	1993
Consumer price index	82.4	88.2	95.1	100.0	135.7	150.0	155.3

Household income and expenditure. Average household size (1984) 4.5; income per household (1981–82) Br 1,728 (U.S.$835); sources of income (1981–82): self-employment 79.5%, wages and salaries 0.2%, other 20.3%; expenditure (1988): food 66.7%, fuel and power 15.9%, clothing and footwear 6.8%, health care 3.1%, education 2.5%, household goods 2.1%.

Foreign trade[5]

Balance of trade (current prices)

	1987	1988	1989	1990	1991	1992
Br '000,000	−1,121.7	−1,081.2	747.6	1,271.0	−433.1	−1,360.5
% of total	43.3%	60.8%	29.1%	50.8%	55.5%	60.3%

Imports (1991–92): Br 1,810,900,000 (petroleum products 10.7%, machinery [including aircraft] 10.5%, motor vehicles 9.9%, textiles 4.1%, metal wares 2.7%, pharmaceuticals 2.7%). *Major import sources:* U.S. 6.9%; Saudi Arabia 5.9%; Japan 5.1%; Germany 4.7%; Italy 4.6%; U.K. 4.2%.
Exports (1991–92): Br 318,400,000 (coffee 52.9%, hides 18.4%, gold 12.4%, petroleum products 5.9%). *Major export destinations:* Japan 24.6%; Germany 15.7%; Saudi Arabia 12.5%; Italy 7.3%; France 6.4%; U.K. 5.9%; U.S. 4.2%.

Transport and communications[5]

Transport. Railroads (1990–91)[9]: length 782 km; passenger-km 277,000,000; metric ton-km cargo 126,000,000. Roads (1991): total length 27,972 km (paved 15%). Vehicles (1992): passenger cars 37,799; trucks and buses 20,939. Merchant marine (1992): vessels (100 gross tons and over) 27; total deadweight tonnage 84,326. Air transport (1991): passenger-km 1,568,000,-000; metric ton-km cargo 79,000,000; airports (1994) 25.
Communications. Daily newspapers (1993): 3; circulation 107,000; circulation per 1,000 population 2.1. Radio (1993): 3,000,000 receivers (1 per 17.3 persons). Television (1993): 100,000 receivers (1 per 518 persons). Telephones (1992): 154,450 (1 per 326 persons).

Education and health

Education (1991)

	schools	teachers	students	student/ teacher ratio
Primary (age 7–12)	8,434	68,399	2,063,636	30.2
Secondary (age 13–18)	1,209[10]	23,110	775,211	33.5
Voc., teacher tr. [11]	...	763	8,243	10.8
Higher	11[12]	1,697	22,538	13.3

Educational attainment: n.a. *Literacy* (1984)[13]: total population age 15 and over literate 24.3%; males 32.7%; females 16.4%.
Health: physicians (1988) 1,466 (1 per 30,195 persons); hospital beds (1986–87) 11,745 (1 per 3,873 persons); infant mortality rate (1990–95) 122.0.
Food (1988–90): daily per capita caloric intake 1,699 (1979–81: vegetable products 93%, animal products 7%); (1984) 72% of FAO recommended minimum.

Military

Total active duty personnel (1994): following the independence of Eritrea in May 1993, the estimated strength of Ethiopian armed forces was some 120,-000. *Military expenditure as percentage of GNP* (1990): 21.9% (world 4.9%); per capita expenditure U.S.$28.

[1]Constitution of July 1991 created a formally transitional government and legislature (Council of Representatives). Elections were held June 5, 1994, for a nonlegislative Constituent Assembly, which replaced the Council of Representatives in June 1994. The Constituent Assembly has the sole purpose of drafting a permanent constitution. [2]In December 1991 the Council of Representatives established a regional administrative system comprising 13 ethnically based "national local administrations" and a single region made up of the towns of Addis Ababa and Harare. [3]Estimates adjusted to exclude the Eritrean portion of Aseb area. [4]Detail does not add to total given because of rounding. [5]Includes Eritrea. [6]Percentage of illnesses in a sample population of hospital outpatients. [7]At constant prices of 1978–79. [8]Addis Ababa only. [9]Includes 62 mi (100 km) of the Chemin de Fer Djibouti-Éthiopien (CDE) in Djibouti; excludes 190 mi (306 km) of Northern Ethiopia Railway, not in use since 1978. [10]1985–86. [11]1988. [12]1983–84. [13]Adult illiteracy was 37% in 1987.

Fiji

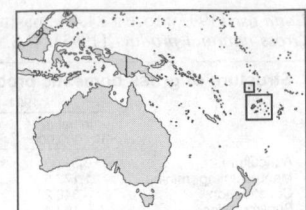

Official name: Sovereign Democratic
Republic of Fiji.
Form of government: republic with
two legislative houses (Senate [34[1]];
House of Representatives [70]).
Chief of state: President.
Head of government: Prime Minister.
Capital: Suva.
Official language: English.
Official religion: none.
Monetary unit: 1 Fiji dollar
(F$) = 100 cents; valuation (Oct. 7,
1994) 1 U.S.$ = F$1.44; 1 £ = F$2.30.

Area and population		area		population
Divisions				1986
Provinces	Capitals	sq mi	sq km	census
Central	Suva			
Naitasiri	—	643	1,666	100,227
Namosi	—	220	570	4,836
Rewa	—	105	272	97,442
Serua	—	320	830	13,356
Tailevu	—	369	955	44,249
Eastern	Levuka			
Kadavu	—	185	478	9,805
Lau	—	188	487	14,203
Lomaiviti	—	159	411	16,066
Rotuma	—	18	46	2,688
Northern	Labasa			
Bua	—	532	1,379	13,986
Cakaudrove	—	1,087	2,816	40,433
Macuata	—	774	2,004	74,735
Western	Lautoka			
Ba	—	1,017	2,634	197,633
Nadroga-Navosa	—	921	2,385	54,431
Ra	—	518	1,341	31,285
TOTAL		7,056	18,274	715,375

Demography

Population (1994): 771,000.
Density (1994): persons per sq mi 109.2, persons per sq km 42.2.
Urban-rural (1987): urban 38.7%; rural 61.3%.
Sex distribution (1990): male 50.65%; female 49.35%.
Age breakdown (1990): under 15, 37.3%; 15–29, 28.5%; 30–44, 18.7%; 45–59, 10.0%; 60–74, 4.1%; 75 and over, 1.4%.
Population projection: (2000) 826,000; (2010) 917,000.
Doubling time: 32 years.
Ethnic composition (1993): Fijian 48.5%; Indian 46.6%[2]; other 4.9%.
Religious affiliation (1986): Christian 52.9%; Hindu 38.1%; Muslim 7.8%; Sikh 0.7%; other 0.5%.
Major cities (1986): Suva 69,665; Lautoka 28,728; Lami 8,601; Nadi 7,679; Ba 6,518.

Vital statistics

Birth rate per 1,000 population (1993): 24.8 (world avg. 26.0); (1978) legitimate 82.7%; illegitimate 17.3%.
Death rate per 1,000 population (1993): 5.0 (world avg. 9.2).
Natural increase rate per 1,000 population (1993): 19.8 (world avg. 16.8).
Total fertility rate (avg. births per childbearing woman; 1990): 3.1.
Marriage rate per 1,000 population (1987): 8.4.
Divorce rate per 1,000 population (1979): 0.7.
Life expectancy at birth (1987): male 61.0 years; female 65.0 years.
Major causes of death per 100,000 population (1987): diseases of the circulatory system 153.4; malignant neoplasms (cancers) 35.5; accidents, poisoning, and violence 32.2; diseases of the respiratory system 31.7; diabetes mellitus 27.3; infectious and parasitic diseases 18.2; birth trauma 16.5.

National economy

Budget (1993). Revenue: F$642,687,000 (income taxes, estate taxes, and gift duties 53.8%; customs duties and port dues 27.9%; fees, royalties, and sales 8.7%). Expenditures: F$678,656,000 (departmental expenditure 73.6%; public-debt charges 22.5%; pensions and gratuities 3.9%).
Production (metric tons except as noted). Agriculture, forestry, fishing (1993): sugarcane 3,704,000; paddy rice 20,180, copra 10,688, ginger 4,068; livestock (number of live animals; 1992) 160,000 cattle, 124,000 goats, 15,000 pigs; roundwood (1992) 413,329 cu m; fish catch (1991) 31,089. Mining and quarrying (1993): gold 3,783 kg; silver 1,112 kg. Manufacturing (1993): refined sugar 442,000; cement 79,500; flour 33,314; stock feed 22,601; soap 7,002; coconut oil 6,231; beer 167,300 hectolitres; paint 27,950 hectolitres. Construction (1993): residential 64,000 sq m; nonresidential 33,000 sq m. Energy production (consumption): electricity (kW-hr; 1992) 477,000,000 (477,000,000); coal (metric tons; 1992) none (20,000); crude petroleum, none (n.a.); petroleum products (metric tons; 1992) none (200,000); natural gas, none (n.a.).
Population economically active (1986): total 241,160; activity rate of total population 33.7% (participation rates: ages 15–64, 56.0%; female 21.2%; unemployed [1990] 6.4%).

Price and earnings indexes (1985 = 100)						
	1987	1988	1989	1990	1991	1992	1993
Consumer price index	107.6	120.2	127.7	138.1	147.1	154.3	162.3
Daily earnings index	105.3	108.0	105.3	...	...	...	...

Gross national product (at current market prices; 1993): U.S.$1,510,000,000 (U.S.$2,010 per capita).

Structure of gross domestic product and labour force				
	1993		1986	
	in value F$'000[3]	% of total value	labour force	% of labour force
Agriculture	184,629	20.5	106,305	44.1
Mining	1,681	0.2	1,345	0.5
Manufacturing	108,002	12.0	18,106	7.5
Construction	42,557	4.7	11,786	4.9
Public utilities	12,334	1.4	2,154	0.9
Transportation and communications	131,606	14.6	13,151	5.4
Trade	183,157	20.4	26,010	10.8
Finance	119,981	13.3	6,016	2.5
Pub. admin., defense	} 151,581	16.9	36,619	15.2
Services				
Other	−35,951[4]	−4.0[4]	19,668[5]	8.2[5]
TOTAL	899,577	100.0	241,160	100.0

Public debt (external, outstanding; 1992): U.S.$306,000,000.
Household income and expenditure. Average household size (1986) 5.7; income per household (1980) F$2,837 (U.S.$3,546); sources of income (1973): wages and salaries 81.5%, self-employment 9.1%, other 9.4%; expenditure (1988): food 31.3%, housing and energy 11.9%, transportation and communications 11.3%, clothing and footwear 10.2%, household durable goods 7.8%.
Tourism (1992): receipts from visitors U.S.$223,000,000; expenditures by nationals abroad U.S.$44,000,000.
Land use (1991): forested 64.9%; agricultural and under permanent cultivation 13.2%; meadows and pastures 3.3%; other 18.6%.

Foreign trade

Balance of trade (current prices)						
	1988	1989	1990	1991	1992	1993
F$'000,000	−61.76	−253.87	−251.32	−279.57	−275.53	−521.42
% of total	5.6%	18.7%	14.1%	20.1%	20.9%	30.7%

Imports (1993): F$1,109,807,000 (machinery and transport equipment 27.6%; durable manufactures 22.7%; food, beverages, and tobacco 15.9%; mineral fuels 12.0%; miscellaneous manufactured consumer articles 11.4%; chemicals 7.4%). *Major import sources:* Australia 32.8%; New Zealand 19.2%; Japan 11.0%; United States 7.6%; Singapore 5.6%; Taiwan 3.4%; Hong Kong 3.3%; United Kingdom 3.1%.
Exports (1993)[6]: F$588,389,000 (sugar 39.2%; gold 11.3%; fish 5.3%; timber 5.3%; molasses 1.7%; coconut oil 0.6%). *Major export destinations*[7]: Australia 25.6%; United Kingdom 24.2%; United States 12.2%; Japan 8.6%; Canada 7.2%; Malaysia 6.4%; New Zealand 5.5%.

Transport and communications

Transport. Railroads (1990)[8]: length 370 mi, 595 km. Roads (1991): total length 2,996 mi, 4,821 km (paved 13%). Vehicles (1992): passenger cars 43,979; trucks and buses 30,899. Merchant marine (1992): vessels (100 gross tons and over) 64; total deadweight tonnage 60,444. Air transport (1992)[9]: passenger-mi 146,947,000, passenger-km 236,490,000; short ton-mi cargo 20,003,000, metric ton-km cargo 29,204,000; airports (1994) with scheduled flights 13.
Communications. Daily newspapers (1992): total number 1; total circulation 27,000; circulation per 1,000 population 36. Radio (1993): total number of receivers 450,000 (1 per 1.7 persons). Television (1990): total number of receivers 10,000 (1 per 73 persons). Telephones (1991): 77,718 (1 per 9.6 persons).

Education and health

Education (1991)	schools	teachers	students	student/ teacher ratio
Primary (age 5–15)	681[10]	4,664	144,924	31.1
Secondary (age 16–19)	140[11]	2,684[10]	55,622	19.6[10]
Voc., teacher tr.	44[11]	369[10]	5,992	8.9[10]
Higher	5[12]	277	7,908	28.5

Educational attainment (1986). Percentage of population age 25 and over having: no formal schooling 28.3%; primary only 19.1%; some secondary 44.1%; secondary 4.1%; postsecondary 3.3%; other 1.1%. *Literacy* (1986): total population age 15 and over literate 87.0%; males literate 90.0%; females literate 84.0%.
Health (1990): physicians 300 (1 per 2,438 persons); hospital beds 1,747 (1 per 413 persons); infant mortality rate per 1,000 live births (1990) 27.0.
Food (1988–90): daily per capita caloric intake 2,769 (vegetable products 85%, animal products 15%); 121% of FAO recommended minimum requirement.

Military

Total active duty personnel (1993): (army 92.3%, navy 7.7%, air force, none).
Military expenditure as percentage of GNP (1991): 2.2% (world 4.2%); per capita expenditure U.S.$44.

[1]All seats are appointed. [2]The emigration of Indian population after the coup in 1987 has resulted in the reemergence of a Fijian majority. [3]Constant 1977 prices. [4]Less imputed bank service charges. [5]Not stated and unemployed. [6]Excludes reexports, valued at F$104,013,000. [7]Based on exports of local products only. [8]Owned by the Fiji Sugar Corporation. [9]Air Pacific only. [10]1990. [11]1986. [12]1983.

Finland

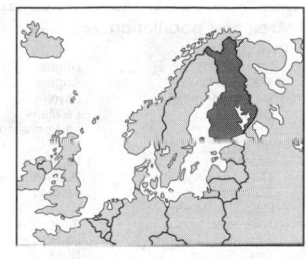

Official name: Suomen Tasavalta
 (Finnish); Republiken Finland
 (Swedish) (Republic of Finland).
Form of government: multiparty
 republic with one legislative house
 (Parliament [200]).
Chief of state: President.
Head of government: Prime Minister.
Capital: Helsinki.
Official languages: Finnish; Swedish
Official religion: none[1].
Monetary unit: 1 markka (Fmk) = 100
 penniä; valuation (Oct. 7, 1994)
 1 U.S.$ = Fmk 4.74; 1 £ = Fmk 7.53.

Area and population

Provinces	Capitals	land area sq mi	land area sq km	population 1993[2] estimate
Häme	Hämeenlinna	7,422	19,224	688,355
Keski-Suomi	Jyväskylä	6,274	16,249	255,879
Kuopio	Kuopio	6,375	16,510	258,712
Kymi	Kouvola	4,103	10,783	335,093
Lappi	Rovaniemi	35,930	93,057	202,434
Mikkeli	Mikkeli	6,302	16,323	207,875
Oulu	Oulu	21,957	56,868	445,632
Pohjois-Karjala	Joensuu	6,866	17,782	177,803
Turku ja Pori	Turku	7,705	19,955	731,792
Uusimaa	Helsinki	3,822	9,898	1,277,801
Vaasa	Vaasa	10,200	26,418	448,363
Autonomous Province				
Åland (Ahvenanmaa)	Mariehamn (Maarianhamina)	590	1,527	25,008
TOTAL LAND AREA		117,604[3]	304,593[3]	
INLAND WATER		12,954	33,551	
TOTAL		130,559[3]	338,145[3]	5,054,747

Demography

Population (1994): 5,083,000.
Density (1994)[4]: persons per sq mi 43.2, persons per sq km 16.7.
Urban-rural (1993): urban 62.5%; rural 37.5%.
Sex distribution (1993): male 48.61%; female 51.39%.
Age breakdown (1992): under 15, 19.2%; 15–29, 20.3%; 30–44, 24.2%; 45–59, 17.6%; 60–74, 13.0%; 75 and over, 5.7%.
Population projection: (2000) 5,159,000; (2010) 5,226,000.
Doubling time: not applicable; population is stable.
Linguistic composition (1992): Finnish 93.4%; Swedish 5.9%; other 0.7%.
Religious affiliation (1992): Evangelical Lutheran 87.3%; Finnish (Greek) Orthodox 1.1%; nonreligious 10.6%; other 1.0%.
Major cities (1993[2]): Helsinki 501,741 (urban area [1990]: 1,009,000); Espoo 178,899[5]; Tampere 175,202; Turku 160,320; Vantaa 159,462[5].

Vital statistics

Birth rate per 1,000 population (1992): 13.2 (world avg. 26.0); (1991) legitimate 72.6%; illegitimate 27.4%.
Death rate per 1,000 population (1992): 9.8 (world avg. 9.2).
Natural increase rate per 1,000 population (1992): 3.4 (world avg. 16.8).
Total fertility rate (avg. births per childbearing woman; 1992): 1.9.
Marriage rate per 1,000 population (1992): 4.6.
Divorce rate per 1,000 population (1992): 2.5.
Life expectancy at birth (1991): male 71.3 years; female 79.3 years.
Major causes of death per 100,000 population (1991): ischemic heart diseases 274.8; malignant neoplasms (cancers) 197.1; cerebrovascular disease 120.8; diseases of the respiratory system 68.8; accidents 55.7.

National economy

Budget (1993). Revenue: Fmk 175,277,000,000 (tax revenue 59.6%, of which sales taxes 22.9%, income and property taxes 15.8%, excise duties 12.7%; loans 27.7%). Expenditures: Fmk 175,275,000,000 (social security and health 29.5%; education 15.4%; state debt 7.8%; pensions 6.6%; agriculture 5.4%; transportation 5.2%; defense 5.1%).
Tourism (1993): receipts from visitors U.S.$1,239,000,000; expenditures by nationals abroad U.S.$1,617,000,000.
Production (metric tons except as noted). Agriculture, forestry, fishing (1992): silage 4,589,000, barley 1,331,000, sugar beets 1,049,000, oats 998,000, potatoes 673,000, peas 29,100; livestock (number of live animals) 1,273,000 pigs, 1,252,000 cattle, 215,000 reindeer; roundwood (1991) 34,091,000 cu m; fish catch (1991) 82,813. Mining and quarrying (1992): chromite concentrate 499,000; talc 371,000. Manufacturing (value added in Fmk '000,000; 1991): wood pulp, paper, and paperboard 11,076; nonelectrical machinery 9,984; food products 9,667; printing and publishing 7,548; electrical machinery 7,153; chemicals and chemical products 5,894; fabricated metal products 4,546. Construction (completed; 1992): residential 13,830,000 cu m; nonresidential 23,310,000 cu m. Energy production (consumption): electricity (kW-hr; 1992) 54,888,000,000 (60,270,000,000); coal (metric tons; 1991) none (5,626,000); crude petroleum (barrels; 1991) none (72,963,000); petroleum products (metric tons; 1991) 9,987,000 (8,870,000); natural gas (cu m; 1991) none (2,849,000,000).
Household income and expenditure. Average household size (1991) 2.3; available income per household Fmk 131,800 (U.S.$24,728); sources of gross income: wages and salaries 59.7%, transfer payments 24.1%, self-employment 11.1%, other 5.1%; expenditure (1991): food 17.9%, transportation and communications 17.0%, housing 15.8%, recreation and education 10.6%.

Gross national product (at current market prices; 1992): U.S.$116,309,000,000 (U.S.$22,980 per capita).

Structure of gross domestic product and labour force

	1992 in value Fmk '000,000	1992 % of total value	1992 labour force	1992 % of labour force
Agriculture, fishing	11,315	2.7 }	203,000	8.0
Forestry	9,567	2.3 }		
Mining	1,678	0.4	5,000	0.2
Manufacturing	92,432	22.3	488,000	19.3
Public utilities	11,172	2.7	27,000	1.1
Construction	26,016	6.3	208,000	8.2
Transp. and commun.	36,163	8.7	177,000	7.0
Trade, restaurants	50,574	12.2	357,000	14.1
Finance, real estate	74,645	18.0	206,000	8.2
Pub. admin., defense	90,851	21.9 }	797,000	31.6
Services	12,320	3.0 }		
Other	2,500	-0.8	58,000[6]	2.3[6]
TOTAL	414,225	100.0[3]	2,526,000	100.0

Population economically active (1992): total 2,526,000; activity rate of total population 50.1% (participation rates: ages 15–64, 74.2%; female 46.9%; unemployed [March 1993–February 1994] 18.3%).

Price and earnings indexes (1985 = 100)

	1987	1988	1989	1990	1991	1992	1993
Consumer price index	107.1	112.6	120.0	127.3	132.6	136.0	138.9
Annual earnings index	114.4	124.7	135.7	148.2	157.6	160.6	161.9

National debt (1992): Fmk 175,282,000,000.
Land use (1991): forested 76.2%; meadows and pastures 0.4%; agricultural and under permanent cultivation 8.3%; other 15.1%.

Foreign trade[7]

Balance of trade (current prices)

	1988	1989	1990	1991	1992	1983
Fmk '000,000	+784	-5,732	-1,700	+5,098	+12,516	+30,849
% of total	0.4%	2.8%	0.8%	2.8%	6.2%	13.0%

Imports (1993): Fmk 103,078,000,000 (raw materials 53.1%; consumer goods 20.4%; mineral fuels 10.6%). Major import sources: Germany 16.4%; Sweden 10.2%; United Kingdom 8.9%; Russia 7.6%; United States 7.3%; Japan 5.8%; Norway 4.9%.
Exports (1993): Fmk 133,927,000,000 (metal products and machinery 35.9%; paper, paper products, and publishing 27.9%; chemicals and chemical products 10.6%). Major export destinations: Germany 13.2%; Sweden 11.1%; United Kingdom 10.5%; United States 7.8%; France 5.3%; The Netherlands 5.0%; Russia 4.5%.

Transport and communications

Transport. Railroads: route length (1992) 3,637 mi, 5,853 km; passenger-mi 1,543,000,000, passenger-km 2,484,000,000; short ton-mi cargo 5,375,000,000, metric ton-km cargo 7,848,000,000. Roads (1993): total length[8] 47,693 mi, 76,755 km (paved 62%). Vehicles (1992): passenger cars 1,936,345; trucks and buses 271,230. Merchant marine (1992): vessels (100 gross tons and over) 263; total deadweight tonnage 989,270. Air transport (1992): passenger-mi 5,333,000,000, passenger-km 8,582,000,000; short ton-mi cargo 77,547,000, metric ton-km cargo 113,216,000; airports (1994) 25.
Communications. Daily newspapers (1992): total number 60; total circulation 2,640,381; circulation per 1,000 population 524. Radio (1993): 4,950,000 receivers (1 per 1.0 person). Television (1993): 1,900,000 receivers (1 per 2.7 persons). Telephones (1991): 3,800,000 (1 per 1.3 persons).

Education and health

Education (1991–92)

	schools	teachers	students	student/ teacher ratio
Primary (age 7–15)[9]	4,819	42,178	591,252	14.0
Secondary (age 16–18)[10]	465	6,262	106,511	17.0
Voc. (incl. higher)	541	...	180,019	...
Higher	20	7,802	115,358	14.8

Educational attainment (1992). Percentage of population age 25 and over having: incomplete upper-secondary education 48.3%; complete upper secondary or vocational 40.0%; some postsecondary 4.6%; undergraduate 2.2%; graduate 4.4%; postgraduate 0.5%. Literacy: virtually 100%.
Health (1991): physicians (1992) 12,929 (1 per 390 persons); hospital beds 61,752 (1 per 81 persons); infant mortality rate per 1,000 live births 5.9.
Food (1988–90): daily per capita caloric intake 3,066 (vegetable products 59%, animal products 41%); 113% of FAO recommended minimum requirement.

Military

Total active duty personnel (1993): 32,800 (army 83.2%, navy 7.6%, air force 9.2%). Military expenditure as percentage of GNP (1991): 2.0% (world 4.2%); per capita expenditure U.S.$492.

---

[1]The Evangelical Lutheran and Finnish (Greek) Orthodox churches have special recognition. [2]January 1. [3]Detail does not add to total given because of rounding. [4]Based on land area only. [5]Within Helsinki urban area. [6]Includes 51,000 unemployed persons not previously employed and 7,000 not adequately defined. [7]Imports c.i.f., exports f.o.b. [8]Excludes Åland Islands. [9]Includes lower secondary. [10]Excludes lower secondary.

France

Official name: République Française (French Republic).
Form of government: republic with two legislative houses (Parliament; Senate [321], National Assembly [577]).
Chief of state: President.
Head of government: Prime Minister.
Capital: Paris.
Official language: French.
Official religion: none.
Monetary unit: 1 franc (F) = 100 centimes; valuation (Oct. 7, 1994) 1 U.S.$ = F 5.27; 1 £ = F 8.38.

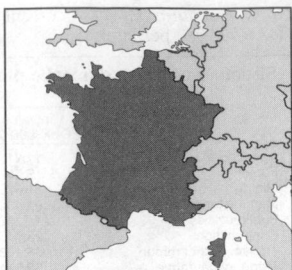

Area and population

Regions Departments	Capitals	area sq mi	area sq km	population 1992[1] estimate
Alsace				
Bas-Rhin	Strasbourg	1,836	4,755	961,020
Haut-Rhin	Colmar	1,361	3,525	681,443
Aquitaine				
Dordogne	Périgueux	3,498	9,060	388,669
Gironde	Bordeaux	3,861	10,000	1,234,434
Landes	Mont-de-Marsan	3,569	9,243	315,605
Lot-et-Garonne	Agen	2,070	5,361	305,945
Pyrénées-Atlantiques	Pau	2,952	7,645	589,415
Auvergne				
Allier	Moulins	2,834	7,340	355,438
Cantal	Aurillac	2,211	5,726	157,984
Haute-Loire	Le Puy	1,922	4,977	206,010
Puy-de-Dôme	Clermont-Ferrand	3,077	7,970	597,985
Basse-Normandie				
Calvados	Caen	2,142	5,548	625,665
Manche	Saint-Lô	2,293	5,938	482,457
Orne	Alençon	2,356	6,103	295,199
Bretagne				
Côtes-d'Armor	Saint-Brieuc	2,656	6,878	539,508
Finistère	Quimper	2,600	6,733	839,663
Ille-et-Vilaine	Rennes	2,616	6,775	816,111
Morbihan	Vannes	2,634	6,823	627,919
Bourgogne				
Côte-d'Or	Dijon	3,383	8,763	500,742
Nièvre	Nevers	2,632	6,817	231,826
Saône-et-Loire	Mâcon	3,311	8,575	557,316
Yonne	Auxerre	2,868	7,427	327,656
Centre				
Cher	Bourges	2,793	7,235	322,945
Eure-et-Loir	Chartres	2,270	5,880	400,317
Indre	Châteauroux	2,622	6,791	237,996
Indre-et-Loire	Tours	2,366	6,127	538,680
Loiret	Orléans	2,616	6,775	592,387
Loir-et-Cher	Blois	2,449	6,343	308,963
Champagne-Ardenne				
Ardennes	Charleville-Mézières	2,019	5,229	295,784
Aube	Troyes	2,318	6,004	292,066
Haute-Marne	Chaumont	2,398	6,211	202,636
Marne	Châlons-sur-Marne	3,151	8,162	559,974
Corse				
Corse-du-Sud	Ajaccio	1,550	4,014	119,427
Haute-Corse	Bastia	1,802	4,666	132,675
Franche-Comté				
Doubs	Besançon	2,021	5,234	490,637
Haute-Saône	Vesoul	2,070	5,360	229,790
Jura	Lons-le-Saunier	1,930	4,999	251,790
Territoire de Belfort	Belfort	235	609	136,111
Haute-Normandie				
Eure	Évreux	2,332	6,040	525,253
Seine-Maritime	Rouen	2,424	6,278	1,229,154
Île-de-France				
Essonne	Évry	696	1,804	1,117,764
Hauts-de-Seine	Nanterre	68	176	1,402,837
Paris	Paris	40	105	2,155,137
Seine-et-Marne	Melun	2,284	5,915	1,130,058
Seine-Saint-Denis	Bobigny	91	236	1,403,136
Val-de-Marne	Créteil	95	245	1,232,407
Val-d'Oise	Pontoise	481	1,246	1,080,938
Yvelines	Versailles	882	2,284	1,339,661
Languedoc-Roussillon				
Aude	Carcassonne	2,370	6,139	303,634
Gard	Nîmes	2,260	5,853	598,897
Hérault	Montpellier	2,356	6,101	823,589
Lozère	Mende	1,995	5,167	72,724
Pyrénées-Orientales	Perpignan	1,589	4,116	372,622
Limousin				
Corrèze	Tulle	2,261	5,857	236,744
Creuse	Guéret	2,149	5,565	128,729
Haute-Vienne	Limoges	2,131	5,520	353,070
Lorraine				
Meurthe-et-Moselle	Nancy	2,024	5,241	708,658
Meuse	Bar-le-Duc	2,400	6,216	194,713
Moselle	Metz	2,400	6,216	1,009,645
Vosges	Épinal	2,268	5,874	383,192
Midi-Pyrénées				
Ariège	Foix	1,888	4,890	136,867
Aveyron	Rodez	3,373	8,736	268,606
Gers	Auch	2,416	6,257	174,579
Haute-Garonne	Toulouse	2,436	6,309	955,113
Hautes-Pyrénées	Tarbes	1,724	4,464	225,256
Lot	Cahors	2,014	5,217	157,679
Tarn	Albi	2,223	5,758	340,899
Tarn-et-Garonne	Montauban	1,435	3,718	203,385
Nord-Pas-de-Calais				
Nord	Lille	2,217	5,742	2,540,359
Pas-de-Calais	Arras	2,576	6,671	1,438,839

Area and population (continued)

		area sq mi	area sq km	population 1992[1] estimate
Pays de la Loire				
Loire-Atlantique	Nantes	2,631	6,815	1,071,359
Maine-et Loire	Angers	2,767	7,166	713,790
Mayenne	Laval	1,998	5,175	281,277
Sarthe	Le Mans	2,396	6,206	518,117
Vendée	La Roche-sur-Yon	2,595	6,720	520,680
Picardie				
Aisne	Laon	2,845	7,369	540,247
Oise	Beauvais	2,263	5,860	748,150
Somme	Amiens	2,382	6,170	552,766
Poitou-Charentes				
Charente	Angoulême	2,300	5,956	342,301
Charente-Maritime	La Rochelle	2,650	6,864	538,607
Deux-Sèvres	Niort	2,316	5,999	346,228
Vienne	Poitiers	2,699	6,990	387,125
Provence–Alpes-Côte d'Azur				
Alpes-de-Haute-Provence	Digne	2,674	6,925	133,745
Alpes-Maritimes	Nice	1,660	4,299	994,940
Bouches-du-Rhône	Marseille	1,964	5,087	1,784,855
Hautes-Alpes	Gap	2,142	5,549	115,850
Var	Toulon	2,306	5,973	849,740
Vaucluse	Avignon	1,377	3,567	478,452
Rhône-Alpes				
Ain	Bourg-en-Bresse	2,225	5,762	487,431
Ardèche	Privas	2,135	5,529	279,793
Drôme	Valence	2,521	6,530	420,543
Haute-Savoie	Annecy	1,694	4,388	596,392
Isère	Grenoble	2,869	7,431	1,038,241
Loire	Saint-Étienne	1,846	4,781	748,003
Rhône	Lyon	1,254	3,249	1,527,264
Savoie	Chambéry	2,327	6,028	363,413
TOTAL		210,026	543,965	57,373,641

Demography

Population (1994): 57,982,000.
Density (1994): persons per sq mi 276.1, persons per sq km 106.6.
Urban-rural (1992): urban 72.7%; rural 27.3%.
Sex distribution (1993[1]): male 48.70%; female 51.30%.
Age breakdown (1993[1]): under 15, 19.9%; 15–29, 21.9%; 30–44, 22.5%; 45–59, 16.0%; 60–74, 13.4%; 75 and over, 6.3%.
Population projection: (2000) 59,908,000; (2010) 63,263,000.
Doubling time: not applicable; doubling time exceeds 100 years.
Ethnolinguistic composition (1990): French (mother tongue) 93.6%, of which fully or substantially bilingual in Occitan 2.7%, German (mostly Alsatian) 2.3%, Breton 1.0%, Catalan 0.4%; Arabic 2.5%; other 3.9%.
Religious affiliation (1980): Roman Catholic 76.4%; other Christian 3.7%; atheist 3.4%; Muslim 3.0%; other 13.5%.
Major cities (1990): Paris 2,152,423 (metropolitan area 9,060,257); Marseille 800,550 (1,231,082); Lyon 415,487 (1,262,223); Toulouse 358,688 (608,430); Nice 342,439 (475,507); Strasbourg 252,338 (338,483); Nantes 244,995 (492,-255); Bordeaux 210,336 (685,456); Montpellier 207,996 (236,788).
National origin (1990): French 93.6%, of which Martiniquais 0.2%, Guadeloupian 0.2%, Réunionese 0.2%; Portuguese 1.1%; Algerian 1.1%; Moroccan 1.0%; Italian 0.4%; Spanish 0.4%; Turkish 0.3%; other 2.1%.
Mobility (1990). Population living in same residence as in 1982: 51.4%; same region 89.0%; different region 8.8%; different country 2.2%.
Households (1990). Average household size 2.6; 1 person 27.1%, 2 persons 29.6%, 3 persons 17.7%, 4 persons 15.7%, 5 persons 6.7%, 6 persons or more 3.2%. Family households: 14,118,940 (72.1%); nonfamily 5,471,460 (27.9%, of which 1-person 24.6%).
Immigration (1991): permanent immigrants admitted 65,310 (Morocco 20.6%, Algeria 9.7%, Turkey 9.3%, Tunisia 5.1%, Portugal 1.4%, Yugoslavia 1.3%).

Vital statistics

Birth rate per 1,000 population (1993): 12.3 (world avg. 26.0); (1991) legitimate 68.2%; illegitimate 31.8%.
Death rate per 1,000 population (1993): 9.2 (world avg. 9.2).
Natural increase rate per 1,000 population (1993): 3.1 (world avg. 16.8).
Total fertility rate (avg. births per childbearing woman; 1992): 1.8.
Marriage rate per 1,000 population (1993): 4.4.
Divorce rate per 1,000 population (1991): 1.9.
Life expectancy at birth (1991): male 72.9 years; female 81.1 years.
Major causes of death per 100,000 population (1991): heart disease and other circulatory diseases 307.9; malignant neoplasms (cancers) 244.2; respiratory diseases 63.1; digestive-tract diseases 46.7.

Social indicators

Educational attainment (1990). Percentage of population age 25 and over having: primary 22.1%; lower secondary 7.8%; higher secondary and vocational 29.4%; postsecondary 11.6%; undeclared attainment 29.1%.

Distribution of income (1984)

percentage of household income by quintile				
1	2	3	4	5 (highest)
7.1%	12.3%	17.1%	23.2%	40.3%

Quality of working life. Average workweek (1993): 39.0 hours. Annual rate per 100,000 workers (1991) for: injury or accident 5,383 (deaths 7.4); accidents in transit to work 338 (deaths 3.1); industrial illness 16.6[2]; death 4.8[2]. Proportion of labour force insured for damages or income loss resulting from: injury, permanent disability, or death, n.a. Average days lost to labour stoppages per 1,000 workers (1992): 21.0. Average length of journey to work (1990)[3]: 8.7 mi (14 km).
Social deviance. Offense rate per 100,000 population (1991) for: murder 4.7; rape 8.9; other assault 93.1; theft (including burglary and housebreaking)

4,302.7. Incidence per 100,000 in general population of: alcoholism, n.a. (deaths related to alcoholism; 1991) 5.0; drug and substance abuse, n.a.; suicide (1991) 20.2.

Access to services (1990). Proportion of dwellings having: central heating 78.9%; piped water 99.7%; indoor plumbing 93.5%; natural gas (1982) 48.9%.

Social participation. Eligible voters participating in last (March 1993) national election: 78.0%. Population over 15 years of age participating in voluntary associations: 28.0%.

Leisure (1987–88). Participation rate for favourite leisure activities: watching television 82%; reading magazines 79%; listening to radio 75%; entertaining relatives 64%; visiting relatives 61%; attending fairs/expositions 56%.

Material well-being (1991). Households possessing: automobile 76.8%; television receiver 94.7%, of which colour 89.1%; videocassette recorder 37.1%; refrigerator 97.9%; washing machine 88.4%.

National economy

Gross national product (1993): U.S.$1,289,054,000 (U.S.$22,360 per capita).

Structure of gross domestic product and labour force

	1992			
	in value F '000,000	% of total value	labour force	% of labour force
Agriculture	197,326	2.8	1,311,000	5.3
Mining	52,563	0.8		
Manufacturing	1,413,399	20.2 }	4,726,000	10.0
Construction	367,476	5.3	1,639,000	6.6
Public utilities	164,269	2.4	...	...
Transp. and commun.	419,462	6.0	1,365,000	5.5
Trade	1,050,105	15.0	2,607,000	10.5
Finance	288,572	4.1	711,000	2.9
Pub. admin., defense	1,138,188	16.3	4,744,000	19.1
Services	1,643,067	23.5	5,228,000	21.1
Other	252,794[4]	3.6[4]	2,496,000[5]	10.0[5]
TOTAL	6,987,221	100.0	24,826,000	100.0

Budget (1993). Revenue: F 1,461,600,000 (value-added taxes 48.5%, direct contributions 40.3%, customs taxes 9.6%). Expenditure (1993): F 1,369,900,000 (current expenditures 86.0%, of which defense 17.9%; capital expenditure 14.0%).

Manufacturing enterprises (1991)

	no. of enterprises	no. of employees	annual salaries as a % of avg. of all salaries	annual value added (F '000,000)
Food products	55,197	569,100	87	190,443
Electrical machinery	15,620	453,400	118	156,885
Transport equipment	4,293	543,500	108	154,115
Mechanical equipment	32,134	437,900	104	122,101
Iron and steel	27,847	453,000	96	119,642
Petroleum refineries	180	51,400	174	112,454
Printing, publishing	30,359	238,800	125	78,109
Textiles and wearing apparel	29,701	340,900	78	68,417
Rubber products	5,875	210,600	94	55,748
Industrial chemicals	1,442	120,000	128	51,734
Paper and paper products	1,916	104,000	102	34,773
Metal products	442	90,400	103	34,331
Glass products	1,536	54,400	104	17,246
Footwear	4,236	69,500	75	13,877

Production (metric tons except as noted). Agriculture, forestry, fishing (1992): wheat 32,600,000, sugar beets 31,334,000, corn (maize) 14,613,000, barley 10,474,000, grapes 8,514,000, potatoes 6,495,000, apples 2,324,000, sunflower seeds 2,158,000, rapeseed 1,862,000, tomatoes 760,000, oats 690,000, sorghum 577,000, cauliflower 572,000, peaches 520,000, pears 394,000, rye 207,000, soybeans 77,000; livestock (number of live animals) 20,928,000 cattle, 12,384,000 pigs, 10,597,000 sheep, 1,221,000 goats; roundwood (1992) 44,840,000 cu m; fish catch (1991) 812,793. Mining and quarrying (1992): iron ore 1,066,000[6]; potash salts 950,000; zinc 13,800[6]; uranium 2,000[6]; gold 64,300 troy oz[6]. Manufacturing (1993): cement 19,320,000; crude steel 17,112,000; pig iron 13,056,000[7]; sulfuric acid 4,187,000[8]; aluminum 628,800[7]; rubber products 486,360, of which tires 62,520,000 units; automobiles 3,103,200 units. Construction (dwelling units completed; 1992) 248,400.

Retail trade enterprises (1990)

	no. of enterprises	no. of employees	weekly wages as a % of all wages	annual turnover (F '000,000)
Large food stores	4,454	401,091	...	576,722
Clothing stores	75,901	227,607	...	131,607
Small food stores	85,599	219,705	...	120,676
butcher shops	41,664	121,966	...	62,099
Pharmacies	23,557	125,635	...	100,685
Department stores	1,902	62,045	...	58,181
Furniture stores	6,531	55,930	...	52,688
Electrical and electronics stores	11,270	55,962	...	45,398
Publishing and paper	21,987	58,441	...	29,610
Gas, coal, and other energy products	2,995	12,599	...	19,918

Energy production (consumption)[9]: electricity (kW-hr; 1992) 462,263,000,000 (408,467,000,000); coal (metric tons; 1992) 11,056,000 (28,565,000); crude petroleum (barrels; 1992) 21,014,000 (543,301,000); petroleum products (metric tons; 1992) 69,773,000 (77,165,000); natural gas (cu m; 1992) 2,385,630,000 (33,750,289,000).

Household income and expenditure. Average household size (1991) 2.6; average annual income per household (1991) F 205,400 (U.S.$37,720). Sources of income (1991): wages and salaries 51.7%, social security 26.9%, self-employment 21.2%; expenditure (1992): housing 20.3%, food and tobacco 18.9%, transportation and communications 16.3%, health 10.0%, recreation 7.6%, clothing 6.2%.

Tourism (1992): receipts from visitors U.S.$25,000,000,000; expenditures by nationals abroad U.S.$13,910,000,000.

Population economically active (1992): total 24,826,000; activity rate of total population 43.2% (participation rates: ages 15–64, 66.9%[10]; female 43.3%; unemployed 10.0%).

Price and earnings indexes (1990=100)

	1987	1988	1989	1990	1991	1992	1993
Consumer price index	91.0	93.5	96.7	100.0	103.2	105.7	107.9
Hourly earnings index	91.2	94.1	98.5	100.0	104.2	108.0	...

Public debt (1992): F 2,070,100,000,000 (U.S.$351,130,000,000).

Financial aggregates

	1989	1990	1991	1992	1993	1994[11]
Exchange rate, F per:						
U.S. dollar	5.79	5.13	5.18	5.51	5.90	5.44
£	9.30	9.09	9.67	9.37	8.73	8.31
SDR	7.80	7.30	7.41	7.57	0.10	7.05
International reserves (U.S.$)						
Total (excl. gold; '000,000)	24,611	36,778	31,284	27,028	22,649	25,536[12]
SDRs ('000,000)	1,329	1,283	1,326	163	331	352
Reserve pos. in IMF ('000,000)	1,414	1,428	1,666	2,482	2,310	2,350
Foreign exchange	28,910	21,868	28,292	24,384	20,008	22,828[12]
Gold ('000,000 fine troy oz)	81.85	81.85	81.85	81.85	81.85	81.85[12]
% world reserves	8.7	8.7	8.7	8.7	8.7	8.7[12]
Interest and prices						
Central bank discount (%)	0.50	0.50	9.50	9.50	9.50	9.50
Govt. bond yield (%)	8.79	9.96	9.05	8.60	6.91	7.55
Industrial share prices (1990=100)	103.7	100.0	97.5	107.8	116.2	...
Balance of payments (U.S.$'000,000)						
Balance of visible trade	−10,651	−13,667	−10,139	1,661	8,418	...
Imports, f.o.b.	181,412	220,339	217,233	223,561	187,873	...
Exports, f.o.b.	170,761	206,672	207,084	225,222	196,291	...
Balance of invisibles	5,031	−105	3,991	1,819	3,503	...
Balance of payments, current account	−5,620	−13,772	−6,148	3,480	11,921	

Land use (1991): forested 27.0%; meadows and pastures 20.3%; agricultural and under permanent cultivation 35.0%; other 17.7%.

Foreign trade

Balance of trade (current prices)

	1988	1989	1990	1991	1992	1993
F '000,000,000	−32.8	−44.2	−51.3	−81.5	−31.1	+90.4
% of total	1.6%	1.9%	2.1%	3.2%	1.3%	4.0%

Imports (1993): F 1,142,748,000,000 (machinery 24.1%; agricultural products 12.2%; transport equipment 10.8%; fuels 8.8%). *Major import sources:* Germany 17.6%; Italy 10.0%; Belgium-Luxembourg 8.9%; U.S. 8.7%; U.K. 8.1%; Spain 5.5%; The Netherlands 5.1%; Japan 4.1%.

Exports (1993): F 1,173,948,000,000 (machinery 27.1%; agricultural products 16.8%; transport equipment 13.0%, of which automobiles 6.6%). *Major export destinations:* Germany 17.4%; Italy 9.4%; U.K. 9.4%; Belgium-Luxembourg 8.6%; U.S. 7.1%; Spain 6.6%; The Netherlands 4.8%.

Transport and communications

Transport. Railroads (1993): route length 34,074 km; passenger-km 58,380,000,000; metric ton-km cargo 45,864,000,000. Roads (1992): total length 811,200 km (paved [1985] 92%). Vehicles (1992): passenger cars 24,020,000; trucks and buses 5,040,000. Merchant marine (1992): vessels (100 gross tons and over) 729; total deadweight tonnage 4,981,027. Air transport (1992): passenger-km 43,082,000,000; metric ton-km cargo 7,801,300,000; airports (1994) with scheduled flights 63.

Communications. Daily newspapers (1993): number 116; circulation 10,096,000[13]; circulation per 1,000 population 175[13]. Radio (1993): 49,000,000 receivers (1 per 1.2 persons). Television (1993): 29,300,000 receivers (1 per 2.0 persons). Telephones (1992): 30,200,000 (1 per 1.9 persons).

Education and health

Education (1991–92)

	schools	teachers	students	student/teacher ratio
Primary (age 6–10)	44,131[14]	277,826[15]	4,068,000	14.6[14]
Secondary (age 11–18) }	11,325[14]	365,417	2,511,300 }	11.7
Voc., teacher tr. }			1,777,200 }	
Higher	1,062[16]	57,429	1,700,800	29.6

Literacy (1980): total population literate 41,112,000 (98.8%); males literate 19,933,000 (98.9%); females literate 21,179,000 (98.7%).

Health: physicians (1991) 152,096 (1 per 374 persons); hospital beds (1990) 702,184 (1 per 81 persons); infant mortality rate (1993) 6.4.

Food (1988–90): daily per capita caloric intake 3,593 (vegetable products 61%, animal products 39%); 143% of FAO recommended minimum requirement.

Military

Total active duty personnel (1994): 409,600 (army 58.9%, navy 15.7%, air force 21.9%, other 3.5%). *Military expenditure as percentage of GNP* (1991): 3.6% (world 4.2%); per capita expenditure U.S.$744.

---

[1]Annual average population; effective date would refer to early August. [2]1989. [3]Distance measured "as the bird flies." [4]Includes value-added taxes, customs duties, and imputed bank service charges. [5]Unemployed. [6]Metal content of ores. [7]1992. [8]1989. [9]All energy statistics include Monaco. [10]1991. [11]July, unless otherwise noted. [12]June. [13]For 90 newspapers only. [14]1990–91. [15]Includes preprimary teachers. [16]1988–89.

Gabon

Official name: République Gabonaise (Gabonese Republic).
Form of government: unitary multiparty republic with one legislative house (National Assembly [120]).
Chief of state: President.
Head of government: Prime Minister.
Capital: Libreville.
Official language: French.
Official religion: none.
Monetary unit: 1 CFA franc (CFAF) = 100 centimes; valuation (Oct. 7, 1994) 1 U.S.$ = CFAF 526.67; 1 £ = CFAF 837.67.

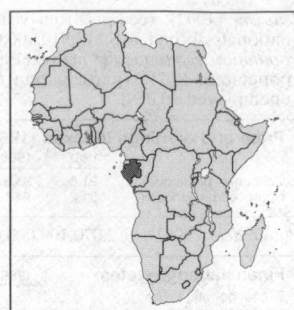

Area and population

Provinces	Capitals	area sq mi	area sq km	population 1978 estimate[1]
Estuaire	Libreville	8,008	20,740	359,000
Haut-Ogooué	Franceville	14,111	36,547	213,000
Moyen-Ogooué	Lambaréné	7,156	18,535	49,000
Ngounié	Mouila	14,575	37,750	118,000
Nyanga	Tchibanga	8,218	21,285	98,000
Ogooué-Ivindo	Makokou	17,790	46,075	53,000
Ogooué-Lolo	Koulamoutou	9,799	25,380	49,000
Ogooué-Maritime	Port-Gentil	8,838	22,890	194,000
Woleu-Ntem	Oyem	14,851	38,465	166,000
TOTAL		103,347[2]	267,667	1,300,000[2]

Demography

Population (1994)[3]: 1,139,000.
Density (1994)[3]: persons per sq mi 11.0, persons per sq km 4.3.
Urban-rural (1990): urban 45.7%; rural 54.3%.
Sex distribution (1990): male 49.23%; female 50.77%.
Age breakdown (1990): under 15, 32.5%; 15–29, 30.4%; 30–44, 15.3%; 45–59, 12.9%; 60–74, 7.3%; 75 and over, 1.6%.
Population projection[3]: (2000) 1,244,000; (2010) 1,445,000.
Doubling time: 41 years.
Ethnic composition (1983): Fang 35.5%; Mpongwe 15.1%; Mbete 14.2%; Punu 11.5%; other 23.7%.
Religious affiliation (1980): Christian 96.2%, of which Roman Catholic 65.2%, Protestant 18.8%; African indigenous 12.1%; traditional religion 2.9%; Muslim 0.8%; other 0.1%.
Major cities (1988): Libreville 352,000; Port-Gentil 164,000; Franceville 75,000.

Vital statistics

Birth rate per 1,000 population (1994): 28.5 (world avg. 26.0).
Death rate per 1,000 population (1994): 13.9 (world avg. 9.2).
Natural increase rate per 1,000 population (1990–95): 14.6 (world avg. 16.8).
Total fertility rate (avg. births per childbearing woman; 1994): 4.0.
Marriage rate per 1,000 population: n.a.
Divorce rate per 1,000 population: n.a.
Life expectancy at birth (1994): male 51.9 years; female 57.5 years.
Major causes of death per 100,000 population: n.a.; however, major diseases include malaria, measles, shigellosis (infection with dysentery), trypanosomiasis, and tuberculosis.

National economy

Budget (1993). Revenue: CFAF 398,500,000,000 (customs duties and other current revenues 46.0%; oil revenues 41.9%; loans and grants 12.1%). Expenditures: CFAF 398,500,000,000 (current expenditure 78.8%, of which running costs 58.7%, public debt 20.1%; capital expenditure 21.2%).
Public debt (external, outstanding; 1992): U.S.$2,998,000,000.
Tourism (1992): receipts from visitors U.S.$5,000,000; expenditures by nationals abroad U.S.$143,000,000.
Production (metric tons except as noted). Agriculture, forestry, fishing (1993): roots and tubers 381,000 (of which cassava 200,000, yams 115,000), sugarcane 260,000, plantains 245,000, corn (maize) 25,000, peanuts (groundnuts) 16,000, bananas 9,000, palm oil 5,000, cacao beans 1,000, coffee 1,000; livestock (number of live animals) 170,000 sheep, 165,000 pigs, 83,000 goats, 30,000 cattle, 3,000,000 chickens; roundwood (1992) 4,344,000 cu m; fish catch (1992) 21,000. Mining and quarrying (1991): manganese 1,600,000; uranium 680. Manufacturing (1990): cement 115,000; flour 36,000; refined sugar 18,000; beer 1,095,000 hectolitres; soft drinks 721,000 hectolitres; cigarettes 344,000,000 units; textiles CFAF 2,420,000,000[4]. Construction: n.a. Energy production (consumption) (kW-hr; 1992) 919,000,000 (919,000,000); crude petroleum (barrels; 1992) 107,802,000 (6,890,000); petroleum products (metric tons; 1992) 760,000 (620,000); natural gas (cu m; 1992) 50,700,000 (50,700,000); fuelwood (cu m; 1992) 2,711,000 (2,711,000).
Land use (1992): forested 74.2%; meadows and pastures 17.6%; agricultural and under permanent cultivation 1.7%; other 6.5%.
Population economically active (1992): total 534,000; activity rate of total population 43.2% (participation rates [1985]: ages 15–64, 68.2%; female 38.4%; unemployed, n.a.).

Price and earnings indexes (1985 = 100)

	1986	1987	1988	1989	1990	1991	1992
Consumer price index	102.3	104.6	109.7	103.2	111.1	118.7	100.8
Earnings index	...	...	...	...	...	...	...

Gross national product (at current market prices; 1993): U.S.$5,002,000,000 (U.S.$4,050 per capita).

Structure of gross domestic product and labour force

	1991 in value CFAF '000,000	1991 % of total value	1991 labour force	1991 % of labour force
Agriculture, forestry, fishing	85,920	8.8	338,000	67.1
Mining	297,880	30.6		
Manufacturing	71,730	7.4	71,000	14.1
Construction	90,410	9.3		
Public utilities	27,410	2.8		
Transportation and communications	61,500	6.3		
Trade	93,430	9.6		
Finance	73,900	7.6	95,000	18.8
Pub. admin., defense	156,770	16.1		
Services	15,530	1.6		
Other				
TOTAL	974,470[2]	100.0[2]	504,000	100.0

Household income and expenditure. Average household size (1980) 4.0; income per household: n.a.; sources of income (1983): private sector 73.4%, public sector 26.6%; expenditure (1983)[5]: food and tobacco 54.7%, clothing and footwear 17.5%, housing 13.0%, transportation and communications 6.3%.

Foreign trade

Balance of trade (current prices)

	1989	1990	1991	1992
CFAF '000,000	+279,000	+466,000	+397,000	+384,000
% of total	37.0%	52.6%	45.7%	45.5%

Imports (1992): CFAF 230,000,000,000 (1989; machinery and mechanical equipment 29.2%, food and agricultural products 14.6%, transport equipment 12.5%, manufactured products 12.1%, metal and metal products 11.2%, chemical products 5.4%, mining products 1.6%). *Major import sources:* France 50.0%; other EEC 22.0%; United States 9.0%; Japan 7.0%; Africa 5.0%.
Exports (1992): CFAF 614,000,000,000 (crude petroleum and petroleum products 80.0%, wood 9.0%, manganese ore and concentrate 7.0%, uranium ore and concentrate 2.0%). *Major export destinations* (1989): France 36.2%; United States 26.1%; The Netherlands 6.2%; Japan 3.3%; Côte d'Ivoire 2.9%; Italy 2.3%.

Transport and communications

Transport. Railroads (1993): length 414 mi, 668 km; passenger-mi 21,000,000[6], passenger-km 34,000,000[6]; short ton-mi cargo 126,000,000[6], metric ton-km cargo 184,000,000[6]. Roads (1991): total length 5,338 mi, 8,590 km (paved 8%). Vehicles (1992): passenger cars 23,000; trucks and buses 17,000. Merchant marine (1992): vessels (100 gross tons and over) 29; total deadweight tonnage 30,186. Air transport (1990)[7]: passenger-mi 276,679,000, passenger-km 445,273,000; short ton-mi cargo 17,863,000, metric ton-km cargo 26,079,000; airports (1994) with scheduled flights 16.
Communications. Daily newspapers (1990): total number 1; total circulation 20,000; circulation per 1,000 population 17. Radio (1993): total number of receivers 250,000 (1 per 4.5 persons). Television (1993): total number of receivers 40,000 (1 per 28 persons). Telephones (1990): 25,940 (1 per 42 persons).

Education and health

Education (1991)

	schools	teachers	students	student/teacher ratio
Primary	1,024	4,782	210,000	43.9
Secondary	51[8]	1,356[9]	42,871	...
Voc., teacher tr.	29[8]	760[9]	13,862	...
Higher[10]	2	299	3,000	10.0

Educational attainment: n.a. *Literacy* (1990): total population age 15 and over literate 60.7%; males literate 73.5%; females literate 48.5%.
Health: physicians (1989) 448 (1 per 2,337 persons); hospital beds (1984) 10,980 (1 per 103 persons); infant mortality rate per 1,000 live births (1994) 94.8.
Food (1984–86): daily per capita caloric intake 2,700 (vegetable products 88%, animal products 12%); (1984) 104% of FAO recommended minimum requirement.

Military

Total active duty personnel (1994): 4,700 (army 68.1%, navy 10.6%, air force 21.3%), not including 600 French troops. *Military expenditure as percentage of GNP* (1990): 3.6% (world 4.5%); per capita expenditure U.S.$143.

[1]Population distribution by province is based on a mid-1978 national estimate that is substantially higher than either the July 1993 preliminary census total of 1,011,710 or the current consensus of external analysts. [2]Detail does not add to total given because of rounding. [3]U.S. Bureau of the Census estimate. [4]1984. [5]Libreville only. [6]1987. [7]Air Gabon only. [8]1984–85. [9]Data refer to public schools only. [10]Universities only.

Gambia, The

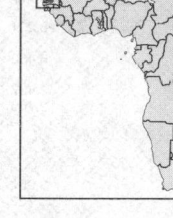

Official name: Republic of The Gambia.
Form of government: military regime[1].
Head of state and government:
Chairman of Armed Forces Provisional Ruling Council.
Capital: Banjul.
Official language: English.
Official religion: none.
Monetary unit: 1 dalasi (D) = 100 bututi;
valuation (Oct. 7, 1994)
1 U.S.$ = D 9.53; 1 £ = D 15.16.

Area and population

Divisions	Capitals	area sq mi	area sq km	population 1983 census[2]
Kombo St. Mary[3, 4]	Kanifing	29	76	101,504
Lower River	Mansakonko	625	1,618	55,263
MacCarthy Island	Kuntaur/Georgetown	1,117	2,894	126,004
North Bank	Kerewan	871	2,256	112,225
Upper River	Bacco	700	2,060	111,300
Western	Brikama	681	1,764	137,245
City				
Banjul[4]	—	5	12	44,188
TOTAL		4,127[5]	10,689[5]	687,817

Demography

Population (1994): 1,060,000.
Density (1994)[6]: persons per sq mi 318.8, persons per sq km 123.1.
Urban-rural (1988): urban 21.5%; rural 78.5%.
Sex distribution (1993): male 50.16%; female 49.84%.
Age breakdown (1990): under 15, 44.1%; 15–29, 24.8%; 30–44, 16.1%; 45–59, 10.1%; 60 and over, 4.9%.
Population projection: (2000) 1,227,000; (2010) 1,546,000.
Doubling time: 28 years.
Ethnic composition (1983): Malinke 40.4%; Fulani 18.7%; Wolof 14.6%; Dyola 10.3%; Soninke 8.2%; other 7.8%.
Religious affiliation (1983): Muslim 95.4%; Christian 3.7%; traditional beliefs and other 0.9%.
Major cities/urban areas (1986): Serekunda 102,600[3]; Banjul 44,188[4, 7] (Greater Banjul 145,692[4, 7]); Brikama 24,300; Bakau 23,600[3]; Faratenni 10,168[7].

Vital statistics

Birth rate per 1,000 population (1990–95): 44.1 (world avg. 26.0); legitimate, n.a.; illegitimate, n.a.
Death rate per 1,000 population (1990–95): 19.4 (world avg. 9.2).
Natural increase rate per 1,000 population (1990–95): 24.7 (world avg. 16.8).
Total fertility rate (avg. births per childbearing woman; 1990–95): 6.1.
Marriage rate per 1,000 population: n.a.
Divorce rate per 1,000 population: n.a.
Life expectancy at birth (1990–95): male 43.4 years; female 46.6 years.
Major causes of death per 100,000 population: n.a.; however, major infectious diseases include malaria, gastroenteritis and dysentery, pneumonia and bronchitis, measles, schistosomiasis, and whooping cough.

National economy

Budget (1992–93). Revenue: D 890,500,000 (tax revenue 78.9%, of which import duties and excises 37.4%, sales tax 27.8%, income taxes 13.7%; nontax revenue and grants 21.1%). Expenditures: D 847,800,000 (administrative expenses 19.0%; interest payments 15.6%; goods and services 14.6%; transportation and communications 13.2%; education and culture 5.4%; agriculture 3.2%; public services 2.6%).
Production (metric tons except as noted). Agriculture, forestry, fishing (1993): peanuts (groundnuts) 65,000, millet 53,000, corn (maize) 20,000, paddy rice 17,000, seed cotton 10,000, cassava 6,000, pulses (mostly beans) 4,000, palm oil 2,500, palm kernels 2,000; livestock (number of live animals) 400,000 cattle, 150,000 goats, 121,000 sheep; roundwood (1992) 946,000 cu m; fish catch (1992) 22,718, of which Atlantic Ocean 20,218, inland water 2,500. Mining and quarrying: sand and gravel are excavated for local use. Manufacturing (value of production in D '000; 1982): processed food, including peanut and palm-kernel oil 62,878; beverages 10,546; textiles 3,253; chemicals and related products 1,031; nonmetals 922; printing and publishing 358; leather 150. Construction: n.a. Energy production (consumption): electricity (kW-hr; 1992) 71,000,000 (71,000,000); coal, none (none); crude petroleum, none (none); petroleum products (metric tons; 1992) none (64,000); natural gas, none (none).
Population economically active (1983): total 325,623; activity rate of total population 47.3% (participation rates: ages 15–64, 78.2%; female 46.3%; unemployed, n.a.).

Price and earnings indexes (1985 = 100)

	1987	1988	1989	1990	1991	1992	1993
Consumer price index	193.4	216.0	233.9	262.5	285.0	312.1	332.2
Daily earnings index[8]	90.2	...	...	...	...	...	...

Tourism (1992): receipts from visitors U.S.$56,000,000; expenditures by nationals abroad U.S.$13,000,000.
Household income and expenditure. Average household size (1983) 8.3; income per household: n.a.; sources of income: n.a.; expenditure (1986)[9]:

food and beverages 58.0%, clothing and footwear 17.5%, energy and water 5.4%, housing 5.1%, education, health, transportation and communications, recreation, and other 14.0%.
Public debt (external, outstanding; 1992): U.S.$339,900,000.
Gross national product (at current market prices; 1993): U.S.$366,000,000 (U.S.$360 per capita).

Structure of gross domestic product and labour force

	1992–93[10] in value D'000,000	1992–93[10] % of total value	1983 labour force	1983 % of labour force
Agriculture	108.4	18.9	239,940	73.7
Mining	—	—	66	0.0
Manufacturing	33.3	5.8	8,144	2.5
Construction	34.4	6.0	4,373	1.3
Public utilities	3.5	0.6	1,233	0.4
Transportation and communications	93.7	16.4	8,014	2.5
Trade	111.5	19.5	16,551	5.1
Finance	34.2	6.0	4,577	1.4
Public administration	58.8	10.3	8,295	2.5
Services	18.0	3.1	9,381	2.9
Other	76.7[11]	13.4[11]	25,049[12]	7.7[12]
TOTAL	572.5	100.0	325,623	100.0

Land use (1992): forested 14.5%; meadows and pastures 9.0%; agricultural and under permanent cultivation 18.0%; built-on area, wasteland, and other 58.5%.

Foreign trade[13]

Balance of trade (current prices)

	1987	1988	1989	1990	1991	1992
D '000,000	−615.9	−530.7	−1,023.0	−1,195.3	−1,561.4	−1,675.9
% of total	52.3%	40.6%	72.1%	61.2%	67.8%	59.7%

Imports (1992–93): D 2,363,486,000 (food 29.1%; machinery and transport equipment 23.2%; basic manufactures 19.8%; mineral fuels and lubricants 5.9%; chemicals and related products 5.2%). *Major import sources* (1992): Hong Kong 16.0%; China 14.8%; United Kingdom 10.1%; Italy 7.1%; France 6.3%; Belgium-Luxembourg 5.7%.
Exports (1992–93): D 543,751,000 (domestic exports 53.5%, of which fish and fish preparations 4.4%; reexports 46.5%[14]). *Major export destinations* (1992): Belgium-Luxembourg 51.5%; Italy 19.7%; Japan 14.3%; Guinea 3.5%; Hong Kong 2.2%; United Kingdom 2.1%; Spain 2.0%.

Transport and communications

Transport. Railroads: none. Roads (1990): total length 1,483 mi, 2,386 km (paved 32%). Vehicles (1991): passenger cars 6,000; trucks and buses 2,500. Merchant marine (1992): vessels (100 gross tons and over) 11; total deadweight tonnage 2,029. Air transport (1990): passenger arrivals and departures 199,350; cargo 2,233 metric tons; airports (1994) with scheduled flights 1.
Communications. Daily newspapers (1992): total number 2; total circulation 2,000; circulation per 1,000 population 2.2. Radio (1993): total number of receivers 180,000 (1 per 5.7 persons). Television: none. Telephones (1991): 11,000 (1 per 80 persons).

Education and health

Education (1992)

	schools	teachers	students	student/teacher ratio
Primary (age 8–14)	245	3,193	97,262	30.5
Secondary (age 15–21)[15]	32	1,054	25,929	24.6
Postsecondary[16]	9	177	1,489	8.4

Educational attainment (1973). Percentage of population age 20 and over having: no formal schooling 90.8%; primary education 6.2%; secondary 2.6%; higher 0.4%. *Literacy* (1990): total population age 15 and over literate 27.2%; males literate 39.0%; females literate 16.0%.
Health (1990–91): physicians 61 (1 per 14,536 persons); hospital beds 601 (1 per 1,475 persons); infant mortality rate per 1,000 live births (1990–95) 132.
Food (1988–90): daily per capita caloric intake 2,290 (vegetable products 94%, animal products 6%); 96% of FAO recommended minimum requirement.

Military

Total active duty personnel (1994): 800. *Military expenditure as percentage of GNP* (1989): 0.7% (world 4.9%); per capita expenditure U.S.$1.

[1]Constitutional government overthrown July 22, 1994. [2]Preliminary. [3]Kombo St. Mary includes the urban areas of Serekunda and Bakau. [4]Kombo St. Mary and Banjul city make up Greater Banjul. [5]Includes inland water area of 2,077 sq km (802 sq mi). [6]Based on land area only. [7]1983. [8]December; nonagricultural employees only. [9]Low-income population in Banjul and Kombo St. Mary only; weights of consumer price index components. [10]At factor cost in constant prices of 1976–77. [11]Indirect taxes. [12]Not adequately defined. [13]Imports c.i.f.; exports f.o.b. [14]Mostly unofficial trade with Senegal. [15]Includes teacher training and vocational. [16]1984–85.

Georgia

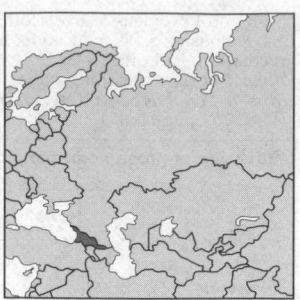

Official name: Sakartvelos Respublikis
(Republic of Georgia).
Form of government: unitary multiparty
republic with a single legislative body
(Parliament [222]).
Head of state: Chairman of Parliament.
Head of government: Prime Minister.
Capital: T'bilisi.
Official language: Georgian.
Official religion: none.
Monetary unit: Georgian coupon[1]
(decimal unit, n.a.); valuation (Sept.
27, 1994) free rate, 1 U.S.$ = 2,478,000
coupons; 1 £ = 3,864,000 coupons.

Area and population		area		population
Autonomous republics	**Capitals**	**sq mi**	**sq km**	**1991[2] estimate**
Abkhazia[3]	Sokhumi (Sukhumi)	3,300	8,600	533,800
Ajaria (Adzharia)	Bat'umi	1,200	3,000	381,500
Autonomous region				
South Ossetia[4]	Ts'khinvali	1,500	3,900	
Regions under republican jurisdiction		20,900	54,200	4,548,900
TOTAL		26,900	69,700	5,464,200

Demography

Population (1994): 5,503,000.
Density (1994): persons per sq mi 204.6, persons per sq km 80.0.
Urban-rural (1991): urban 55.8%; rural 44.2%.
Sex distribution (1991): male 47.6%; female 52.4%.
Age breakdown (1989): under 15, 24.8%; 15–29, 24.1%; 30–44, 19.2%; 45–59,
17.5%; 60–74, 10.8%; 75 and over, 3.6%.
Population projection: (2000) 5,569,000; (2010) 5,680,000.
Doubling time: 77 years.
Ethnic composition (1989): Georgian 70.1%; Armenian 8.1%; Russian 6.3%;
Azerbaijani 5.7%; Ossetian 3.0%; Greek 1.9%; Abkhazian 1.8%; other 3.1%.
Religious affiliation: believers are predominantly Georgian Orthodox (65%);
minorities include Muslims (11%), Russian Orthodox (10%), and Armenian
Orthodox (8%).
Major cities (1991): T'bilisi 1,283,000; K'ut'aisi 238,200; Rust'avi 161,900; Ba-
t'umi 137,500; Sokhumi (Sukhumi) 120,000.

Vital statistics

Birth rate per 1,000 population (1990): 17.0 (world avg. 27.0); (1989) legiti-
mate 82.3%; illegitimate 17.7%.
Death rate per 1,000 population (1990): 8.4 (world avg. 9.7).
Natural increase rate per 1,000 population (1990): 8.6 (world avg. 17.3).
Total fertility rate (avg. births per childbearing woman; 1993): 2.2.
Marriage rate per 1,000 population (1989): 7.2.
Divorce rate per 1,000 population (1989): 1.3.
Life expectancy at birth (1991): male 68.9 years; female 76.5 years.
Major causes of death per 100,000 population (1989): diseases of the cir-
culatory system 553.2; diseases of the respiratory system 513.0; malignant
neoplasms (cancers) 98.6; accidents, poisoning, and violence 58.2; diseases
of the digestive system 32.1; infectious and parasitic diseases 13.5; endocrine
and metabolic disorders 12.0; diseases of the nervous system 4.1.

National economy

Budget (1992). Revenue: 18,872,000,000 rubles (profit tax 37.6%, value-added
tax 26.3%, individual income tax 10.5%, turnover tax 4.5%). Expenditures:
42,672,000,000 rubles (national economy 48.7%, social and cultural affairs
28.8%, government administration 15.3%, other 6.9%).
Public debt (external; 1994): U.S.$1,000,000,000.
Land use (1992): forest 38.7%; pasture 28.7%; agriculture 14.8%; other 17.8%.
Production (metric tons except as noted). Agriculture, forestry, fishing (1993):
fruit (other than grapes) 1,267,000, vegetables (other than potatoes) 1,100,-
000, grapes 500,000, milk 400,000, corn (maize) 225,000, potatoes 190,000,
wheat 128,000, barley 35,000, sugarbeets 15,000, sunflower seeds 10,000, soybeans 6,000; livestock (number of live animals) 1,440,000 sheep and goats,
1,130,000 cattle, 688,000 pigs, 18,000,000 poultry; roundwood, n.a.; fish catch
(1991) 56,000. Mining and quarrying (1991): manganese ore 491,000. Manufacturing (1991): crude steel 961,700; rolled ferrous metals 818,100; rolled
steel 817,900; cast iron 500,800; steel tubes 452,800; canned food 385,300;
mineral fertilizers 134,500; meat and sausage 43,900; synthetic resins and
plastics 26,400; synthetic fibres 20,000; soap 6,900; bricks 170,600,000 pieces;
cement tiles 12,600,000 pieces; footwear 13,300,000 pairs; knitwear 24,300,-
000 units; colour television sets 39,200 units; machine tools 1,417 units;
prefabricated concrete structures 1,451,000 cu m; ceramic tiles 348,300 cu
m; silk fabrics 27,100,000 sq m; cotton fabrics 16,700,000 sq m; wool fabrics
6,100,000 sq m; carpets 500,000 sq m; grape wine 1,261,600 hectolitres; beer
600,100 hectolitres; cognac 146,000 hectolitres; vodka and liqueurs 77,400
hectolitres. Construction (1990): 1,313,000,000,000 rubles. Energy production (consumption): electricity (kW-hr; 1992) 9,300,000,000 (9,300,000,000);
coal (metric tons; 1992) 500,000 (736,000); crude petroleum (barrels; 1992)
733,000 (5,658,000); petroleum products (metric tons; 1991) 2,215,400 (n.a.);
natural gas (cu m; 1992) none (4,856,000,000).
Gross national product (1993): U.S.$3,055,000,000 (U.S.$560 per capita)[5].

Structure of net material product and labour force

	1992		1991	
	in value '000,000 rubles	% of total value	labour force	% of labour force
Agriculture	38,909	47.0	682,200	27.1
Mining		...	...	...
Manufacturing	} 28,201	} 34.1	487,700	19.4
Public utilities			110,100	4.4
Construction	6,452	7.8	224,800	9.0
Transportation and communications	2,457	3.0	103,500	4.1
Trade	2,766	3.3	227,000	9.0
Finance	—	—	12,000	0.5
Public administration, defense	—	—	48,100	1.9
Services	—	—	538,900	21.5
Other	3,967	4.8	79,700	3.1
TOTAL	82,752	100.0	2,514,000	100.0

Population economically active (1991): total 2,514,000; activity rate of total
population 45.9% (participation rates [1990]: ages 16–59 [male], 16–54 [fe-
male] 91.1%; female [1989] 45.9%; unemployed [1989] 3.5%).

Price and earnings indexes (1990 = 100)						
	1986	1987	1988	1989	1990	1991
Consumer price index	...	...	...	...	100.0	...
Monthly earnings index	70.5	73.2	77.1	87.5	100.0	143.1

Household income and expenditure. Average household size (1989) 4.1; income per household: n.a.; sources of income (1992): wages and salaries
68.1%, benefits 22.7%, agricultural income 9.2%; expenditure (1992): retail
goods 55.4%, savings 22.9%, services 12.1%, taxes 6.9%, housing 2.7%.

Foreign trade

Balance of trade (current prices)				
	1988	1989	1990	1991
'000,000 rubles	−592	−385	−855	−1,154
% of total	4.8%	3.1%	6.7%	8.6%

Imports (1991): 7,266,000,000 rubles (machinery and equipment 18.4%, light-
industry products 16.5%, food 14.6%, oil and gas 9.6%, chemicals 9.6%,
ferrous metals 4.1%, nonferrous metallurgical products 3.3%). *Major import
sources:* former Soviet republics 89.6%; other countries 10.4%.
Exports (1991): 6,112,000,000 rubles (food 34.5%, light-industry products
19.3%, machinery and metalworking equipment 13.7%, ferrous metallurgy
5.8%, chemicals 3.5%, building materials 1.1%). *Major export destinations:*
former Soviet republics 98.0%; other countries 2.0%.

Transport and communications

Transport. Railroads (1990): length 976 mi, 1,570 km; (1989) passenger-mi
10,600,000, passenger-km 17,000,000; cargo traffic, n.a. Roads (1989): length
21,000 mi, 33,900 km (paved 87%). Vehicles (1988): passenger cars 427,400;
trucks and buses, n.a. Merchant marine: vessels (1,000 gross tons and over)
54; total deadweight tonnage 1,108,068. Air transport (1989): passenger-mi
3,290,500,000, passenger-km 5,295,600,000; short ton-mi cargo, n.a., metric
ton-km cargo, n.a.; airports (1994) with scheduled flights 1.
Communications. Daily newspapers (1989): total number 147; total circulation 3,677,000; circulation per 1,000 population 671. Radio and television
(1990): total number of receivers 3,760,000 (1 per 1.5 persons). Telephones
(1992): 1,002,000 (1 per 5.5 persons).

Education and health

Education (1989–90)				
	schools	teachers	students	student/ teacher ratio
Primary (age 6–13) Secondary (age 14–17)	} 3,788	...	924,700	...
Voc., teacher tr.		...		...
Higher	19	...	93,100	...

Educational attainment (1989). Percentage of population age 25 and over
having: primary education or no formal schooling 12.3%; some secondary
15.2%; completed secondary and some postsecondary 57.4%; higher 15.1%.
Literacy (1989): percentage of total population age 15 and over literate
99.0%; males literate 99.5%; females literate 98.5%.
Health (1990): physicians 32,100 (1 per 170 persons); hospital beds 60,000 (1
per 90 persons); infant mortality rate per 1,000 live births 15.9.
Food: daily per capita caloric intake, n.a.

Military

Total active duty personnel (1994): 4,500 (army 95.5%, navy[6], air force 4.5%).
About 6,000 Russian troops remained in Georgia in late 1994. *Military expenditure as percentage of GNP* (1992): 1.5%; per capita expenditure U.S.$16.

[1]Georgian coupon introduced April 5, 1993, at par with Russian ruble and circulated
parallel with it; on Aug. 20, 1993, the coupon became sole legal tender, floating
against all currencies. The coupon is to function as an interim currency unit until
its eventual replacement by a new national currency, the lari, when the economic
situation has stabilized. [2]January 1. [3]Abkhazia adopted a constitution declaring it an
independent state on Nov. 26, 1994; Georgia has rejected its legality. [4]In December
1990 the Supreme Soviet of the Republic of Georgia abolished the South Ossetian
autonomous oblast. [5]Ruble-area GNP and exchange-rate data are very speculative.
[6]A portion of the former U.S.S.R. Black Sea Fleet has been allocated to Georgia.

Germany

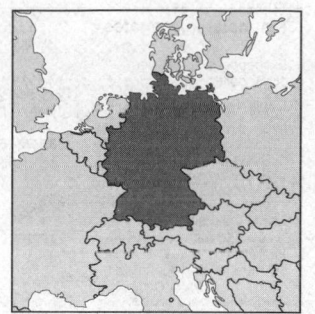

Official name: Bundesrepublik Deutschland (Federal Republic of Germany).
Form of government: federal multiparty republic with two legislative houses (Federal Council [68]; Federal Diet [672]).
Chief of state: President.
Head of government: Chancellor.
Seat of government: Bonn (Berlin is capital-designate).
Official language: German.
Official religion: none.
Monetary unit: 1 Deutsche Mark (DM) = 100 Pfennige; valuation (Oct. 7, 1994) 1 U.S.$ = DM 1.54; 1 £ = DM 2.45.

Area and population

States Administrative districts	Capitals	area sq mi	area sq km	population 1993 estimate
Baden-Württemberg	Stuttgart	13,804[1]	35,751[1]	10,148,700
Freiburg	Freiburg	3,613	9,357	2,041,100
Karlsruhe	Karlsruhe	2,671	6,919	2,612,800
Stuttgart	Stuttgart	4,076	10,558	3,807,400
Tübingen	Tübingen	3,443	8,918	1,687,400
Bayern	Munich	27,241	70,554[1]	11,770,400
Mittelfranken	Ansbach	2,798	7,246	1,641,300
Niederbayern	Landshut	3,989	10,331	1,109,200
Oberbayern	Munich	6,768	17,529	3,919,200
Oberfranken	Bayreuth	2,792	7,231	1,094,300
Oberpfalz	Regensburg	3,742	9,691	1,032,200
Schwaben	Augsburg	3,858	9,993	1,684,500
Unterfranken	Würzburg	3,294	8,532	1,289,700
Berlin	—	343	889	3,465,700
Brandenburg	Potsdam	11,219	29,053	2,542,700
Bremen	Bremen	156	404	686,800
Hamburg	Hamburg	292	755	1,688,800
Hessen	Wiesbaden	8,152[1]	21,114	5,922,600
Darmstadt	Darmstadt	2,875	7,445	3,649,600
Giessen	Giessen	2,078	5,381	1,032,100
Kassel	Kassel	3,200	8,288	1,240,900
Mecklenburg-Vorpommern	Schwerin	9,111	23,598	1,865,000
Niedersachsen	Hannover	18,287[1]	47,364[1]	7,577,500
Braunschweig	Braunschweig	3,126	8,097	1,670,200
Hannover	Hannover	3,493	9,048	2,108,600
Lüneburg	Lüneburg	5,891	15,260	1,535,500
Weser-Ems	Oldenburg	5,775	14,958	2,263,200
Nordrhein-Westfalen	Düsseldorf	13,155[1]	34,070	17,679,200
Arnsberg	Arnsberg	3,088	7,999	3,786,500
Detmold	Detmold	2,516	6,517	1,954,000
Düsseldorf	Düsseldorf	2,042	5,288	5,293,300
Köln	Köln	2,044	7,305	4,113,500
Münster	Münster	2,664	6,901	2,531,900
Rheinland-Pfalz	Mainz	7,664	19,846	3,881,100
Koblenz	Koblenz	3,125	8,093	1,445,100
Rheinhessen-Pfalz	Mainz	2,637	6,830	1,941,600
Trier	Trier	1,902	4,923	494,400
Saarland	Saarbrücken	992	2,570	1,084,000
Sachsen	Dresden	7,080	18,338	4,641,000
Sachsen-Anhalt	Magdeburg	7,893	20,443	2,797,000
Dessau	Dessau	1,642	4,254	586,700
Halle	Halle/Saale	1,880	4,869	997,300
Magdeburg	Magdeburg	4,371	11,320	1,213,000
Schleswig-Holstein	Kiel	6,074	15,731	2,679,600
Thüringen	Erfurt	6,275	16,251	2,545,800
TOTAL		137,735[1]	356,700[1]	80,974,900

Demography

Population (1994): 81,966,000.
Major cities (1992): Berlin 3,454,200; Hamburg 1,675,200; Munich 1,241,300; Cologne 958,600; Frankfurt am Main 660,800; Essen 627,800; Dortmund 600,700; Stuttgart 596,900; Düsseldorf 577,400; Duisburg 538,300; Hannover 520,900; Leipzig 500,000.

Other principal cities (1992)

	population		population		population
Aachen	244,600	Heilbronn	118,800	Oberhausen	225,300
Augsburg	261,900	Herne	179,600	Offenbach am	
Bergisch		Hildesheim	105,900	Main	116,600
Gladbach	104,600	Ingolstadt	107,700	Oldenburg	145,800
Bielefeld	323,300	Jena	100,200	Osnabrück	165,400
Bochum	399,800	Kaiserslautern	100,900	Paderborn	127,000
Bonn	297,400	Karlsruhe	279,900	Pforzheim	116,000
Bottrop	118,800	Kassel	197,900	Potsdam	138,700
Braunschweig	258,400	Kiel	248,000	Recklinghausen	126,200
Bremerhaven	131,100	Koblenz	109,600	Regensburg	123,700
Chemnitz	285,700	Krefeld	247,300	Remscheid	123,600
Cottbus	122,900	Leverkusen	161,700	Reutlingen	106,100
Darmstadt	140,900	Lübeck	216,500	Rostock	243,300
Dresden	483,400	Ludwigshafen		Saarbrücken	192,000
Erfurt	203,100	am Rhein	166,600	Salzgitter	116,000
Erlangen	102,600	Magdeburg	274,000	Schwerin	125,400
Freiburg		Mainz	183,300	Siegen	110,700
im Breisgau	194,700	Mannheim	316,900	Solingen	166,600
Furth	106,600	Moers	105,800	Ulm	113,000
Gelsenkirchen	294,700	Mönchenglad-		Wiesbaden	265,700
Gera	125,600	bach	263,900	Witten	105,400
Göttingen	127,200	Mülheim		Wolfsburg	129,100
Hagen	214,200	an der Ruhr	176,900	Wuppertal	386,600
Halle an der Saale	301,000	Münster	265,800	Würzburg	128,600
Hamm	180,700	Neuss	148,000	Zwickau	111,400
Heidelberg	139,900	Nürnberg	498,500		

Density (1994): persons per sq mi 595.1, persons per sq km 229.8.
Urban-rural (1990): urban 85.3%; rural 14.7%.
Population projection: (2000) 86,503,000; (2010) 93,324,000.
Sex distribution (1993): male 48.54%; female 51.46%.
Age breakdown (1993): under 15, 16.4%; 15–29, 21.2%; 30–44, 22.4%; 45–59, 19.7%; 60–74, 13.8%; 75 and over, 6.5%.
Doubling time: not applicable; doubling time exceeds 100 years.
Ethnic composition (by nationality; 1990): German 93.4%; Turkish 2.1%, of which Kurdish 0.5%; Yugoslav 0.8%; Italian 0.7%; Greek 0.4%; Polish 0.4%; Spanish 0.2%; other 2.0%.
Religious affiliation: (former West Germany; 1987) Roman Catholic 42.9%, Lutheran-Reformed and Lutheran traditions 41.6%, Muslim 2.7%, Reformed tradition 0.6%, Jewish 0.1%, other 12.1%; (former East Germany; 1990) Protestant 47.0%, Roman Catholic 7.0%, unaffiliated and other 46.0%.
Households (1992). Number of households 35,700,000; average household size 2.3; 1 person 33.7%, 2 persons 31.3%, 3 persons 16.9%, 4 persons 13.2%, 5 or more persons 4.9%.

Vital statistics

Birth rate per 1,000 population (1992): 10.4 (world avg. 26.0); legitimate 85.1%; illegitimate 14.9%.
Death rate per 1,000 population (1992): 11.3 (world avg. 9.2).
Natural increase rate per 1,000 population (1992): −0.9 (world avg. 16.8).
Total fertility rate (avg. births per childbearing woman; 1994): 1.5.
Marriage rate per 1,000 population (1992): 5.8.
Divorce rate per 1,000 population (1992): 1.7.
Life expectancy at birth (1994): male 73.20 years; female 79.80 years.
Major causes of death per 100,000 population (1992): diseases of the circulatory system 516.4; malignant neoplasms (cancers) 259.3, of which stomach, colon, and rectum 58.0, bronchial, lung, and tracheal 42.5; diseases of the respiratory system 60.2, of which pneumonia 18.9, chronic bronchitis 15.6; chronic liver disease and cirrhosis 23.3.

Social indicators

Educational attainment (1989)[2]. Percentage of population age 25 and over having: less than full primary education 0.9%; primary and lower (junior) secondary 67.2%; primary and intermediate secondary 17.7%; vocational postsecondary and certification for higher education 14.2%, of which postsecondary vocational degree 6.6%, university graduates (all levels) 5.7%.
Quality of working life. Average workweek (1993)[2]: 38.2 hours. Annual rate per 100,000 workers (1992) for: injuries or accidents at work 7,655; deaths, including commuting accidents, 10.5. Proportion of labour force insured for damages or income loss resulting from: injury, virtually 100%; permanent disability, virtually 100%; death, virtually 100%. Average days lost to labour stoppages per 1,000 workers (1993): 3.1.

Distribution of income (1984)[2]
percentage of household income by quintile

1	2	3	4	5 (highest)
6.8	12.7	17.8	24.0	38.7

Access to services. Proportion of dwellings (1992) having: electricity, virtually 100%; piped water supply, virtually 100%; flush sewage disposal 98.1%; public fire protection, virtually 100%.
Social participation. Eligible voters participating in last (October 1994) national election 79.1%. Trade union membership in total workforce (1993): 32.0%. Practicing religious population (1992): 7% of Protestants and 20% of Roman Catholics "regularly" attend religious services.
Social deviance (1991). Offense rate per 100,000 population for: murder and manslaughter 3; sexual abuse 53, of which child molestation 18, rape and forcible sexual assault 12; robbery 61; assault and battery 96; larceny 4,072. Incidence per 100,000 in general population (late 1970s) of: alcoholism 2,500 to 3,000; drug and substance abuse 650; suicide 16.5.
Material well-being (1993). Households possessing: automobile 73.6%; telephone 88.3%; colour television receiver 93.0%; refrigerator, 76.6%; washing machine 88.8%; home freezer 53.8%.

Recreational and leisure activities
(Monthly household expenditures, 1993; median income)[2]

Activity	DM	percentage
Vacations	203	26.9
Expenditures for motor vehicles	99	13.2
Sporting and camping equipment and sporting events	98	13.0
Televisions, radios, and their fees	88	11.7
Books, newspapers, and magazines	59	7.8
Gardening and pets	47	6.2
Games and toys	38	5.1
Photographic and moviemaking equipment and film	20	2.7
Visits to theatre and cinema	17	2.3
Tools	7	1.0
Other activities	76	10.1
TOTAL	752	100.0

National economy

Budget (1993). Revenue: DM 1,549,713,000,000 (taxes 84.8%). Expenditures: DM 1,682,186,000,000 (1991; consumption 43.5%, current transfers 40.1%, debt interest payments 6.1%).
Total national debt (1993[3]): DM 651,180,000,000.
Production (value of production in DM except as noted; 1992–93). Agriculture, forestry, fishing: cereal grains 7,227,000,000, fruits 4,038,000,000, flowers and ornamental plants 2,725,000,000, sugar beets 2,682,000,000, grapes for wine 2,085,000,000, vegetables 1,864,000,000, nurseries 1,610,000,-

000, potatoes 1,138,000,000, oilseed crops 738,000,000; livestock (number of live animals): 26,466,000,000 pigs, 16,200,000,000 cattle, 1,732,000,000 chicken eggs, 1,273,000,000 poultry; roundwood (1992) 27,759,000 cu m; fish catch (metric tons; 1992) 258,500. Mining and quarrying (metric tons; 1993): potash 30,434,000; iron ore 180,000; zinc 14,300; lead 2,100. Manufacturing (value added at factor cost in DM; 1992): capital equipment 319,988,000,-000, of which electrical equipment 85,418,000,000, machinery 81,338,000,000, transport equipment 79,522,000,000; chemicals (including pharmaceuticals) 57,581,000,000; food and beverages 39,411,000,000; calculators and computers 25,274,000,000; plastics and other synthetic products 20,029,000,000; furniture and other wood products 15,506,000,000; stone and ceramic products 14,370,000,000; printing and copy machines 12,811,000,000; iron founding 11,903,000,000; textiles 11,409,000,000; precision instruments 10,280,000,000; paper and cardboard products 8,919,000,000; office equipment 8,317,000,-000; clothing 7,433,000,000; musical instruments and toys 3,578,000,000; fine pottery and ceramic products 2,549,000,000. Construction (1992): residential 34,400,000 sq m; nonresidential 4,049,000 sq m.

Service enterprises (1991)

	no. of enterprises	no. of employees	weekly wage as a % of all wages	annual turnover (DM '000,000)
Gas	151	37,000	...	42,228
Water	183	40,000	...	3,443
Electrical power	462	296,000	...	147,076
Transport				
air	133	57,390	...	20,270
buses	6,054	192,869	...	12,586
rail	1	416,199	...	14,697
shipping	1,449	9,076	...	...
Communications				
press	2,452	240,075	...	31,096
film[4]	615	3,000	...	836
Postal services	17,616[5]	652,573	...	68,346
Hotels and restaurants	135,141	652,251	...	60,257
Wholesale trade	36,605[5]	1,214,000	...	1,015,984
Retail trade	152,629	2,241,000	...	605,755

Energy production (consumption): electricity (kW-hr; 1992) 537,134,000,-000 (531,814,000,000); hard coal (metric tons; 1992) 72,153,000 (82,000,-000); lignite (metric tons; 1991) 241,807,000 (245,500,000); crude petroleum (barrels; 1992) 23,763,000 (728,599,000); petroleum products (metric tons; 1992) 93,632,000 (117,119,000); natural gas (cu m; 1992) 16,144,000,000 (67,322,000,000).

Manufacturing, mining, and construction enterprises (1992)

	no. of enterprises	no. of tradesmen and professionals	wages as a % of avg. of all wages[2, 6]	annual gross production value (DM '000,000)
Manufacturing	44,788	8,082,000	101.1	2,037,084
of which				
Road motor vehicles	2,226	919,000	110.9	292,675
Machinery (nonelectric)	6,340	1,206,000	101.2	224,625
Machinery and appliances (electric)	3,555	1,179,000	91.9	242,287
Chemical	1,412	659,000	109.8	205,960
Food and beverages	4,701	601,000	95.1	218,691
Petroleum and natural gas	59	7	138.2	7
Calculators, computers	2,496	363,000	95.4	70,899
Plastics	2,642	293,000	96.2	85,248
Iron and steel	123	198,000	101.5	47,865
Textiles	1,335	217,000	81.0	40,387
Wood and wood products	5,554	481,000	91.7	109,293
Mining and quarrying	2,388	420,000	105.1	83,977
Construction	20,959	1,377,000	105.5	228,430

Gross national product (at current market prices; 1993): U.S.$1,908,570,000,-000 (U.S.$23,630 per capita).

Structure of gross domestic product and labour force

	1993			
	in value DM '000,000	% of total value	labour force[2]	% of labour force[2]
Agriculture	29,300	1.0	880,000	2.8
Public utilities, mining	74,140	2.6	441,000	1.4
Manufacturing	753,250	26.6	8,400,000	27.1
Construction	168,430	6.0	1,982,000	6.4
Transp. and commun.	155,770	5.5	1,630,000	5.3
Trade	230,120	8.1	3,965,000	12.8
Finance, real estate	394,480	13.9	951,000	3.1
Services	559,920	19.8	5,026,000	16.2
Pub. admin., defense	298,520	10.6	4,323,000	14.0
Other (productive)	29,270	1.0	3,387,300	10.9
Other (accounting)	138,800	4.9	—	—
TOTAL	2,832,000	100.0	30,985,300	100.0

Population economically active (1992): total 40,126,000; activity rate of total population 49.9% (participation rates: ages 15–64, 72.2%; female 41.2%; unemployed 6.6%).

Price and earnings indexes (1990 = 100)

	1987	1988	1989	1990	1991	1992	1993
Consumer price index	93.6	94.8	97.4	100.0	103.5	107.6	112.0
Hourly earnings index	87.6	91.0	94.9	100.0	107.2	114.8	121.7

Household income and expenditure. Average household size (1992) 2.3; average annual income per household (1993) DM 74,952 (U.S.$43,418); sources of take-home income (1993): wages 81.9%, self-employment 10.7%, transfer payments 7.4%; expenditure (1993): rent 21.8%, transportation 15.0%, food 14.4%, entertainment and education 11.1%, household operations and maintenance 8.2%, clothing and footwear 7.8%.
Land use (1991): forest 29.7%; pasture 15.3%; agriculture 33.8%; other 21.2%.

Financial aggregates[8]

	1988	1989	1990	1991	1992	1993	1994 (Aug.)
Exchange rate, DM per:							
U.S. dollar	1.7803	1.6978	1.4940	1.5160	1.6140	1.7263	1.5830
£	3.2215	2.7258	2.8804	2.8360	2.4404	2.1988	2.4283
SDR	2.3957	2.2312	2.1255	2.1685	2.2193	2.3712	2.2719
International reserves (U.S.$)							
Total (excl. gold; '000,000)	58,528	60,709	67,902	63,001	90,967	77,640	94,001
SDRs ('000,000)	1,857	1,804	1,880	1,917	841	962	1,096
Reserve pos. in IMF ('000,000)	3,346	3,043	3,056	3,567	4,239	3,951	4,022
Foreign exchange	53,324	55,862	62,967	57,517	85,877	72,727	88,883
Gold ('000,000 fine troy oz)	95.18	95.18	95.18	95.18	95.18	95.18	95.18
% world reserves	10.04	10.10	10.12	10.13	10.24	10.43	10.31
Interest and prices							
Central bank discount (%)	3.5	6.0	6.0	8.0	8.3	4.8	4.5[9]
Govt. bond yield (%)	6.1	7.1	8.9	8.6	7.7	6.3	7.3[9]
Industrial share prices (1990 = 100)[10]	68.3	87.3	100.0	89.1	86.2	87.8	106.8
Balance of payments (U.S.$'000,000,000)							
Balance of visible trade	+79.75	+77.71	+71.05	+23.23	+32.76	+44.54	+24.52[9]
Imports, f.o.b.	228.87	247.24	320.24	355.40	373.91	318.84	165.08
Exports, f.o.b.	308.62	324.95	391.29	378.63	406.66	363.38	189.60
Balance of invisibles	−28.97	−20.04	−24.81	−42.30	−54.91	−64.50	−34.13[9]
Balance of payments, current account	+50.78	+57.67	+46.24	+19.01	−22.15	−19.96	−9.61[9]

Tourism (1993): receipts from visitors U.S.$10,186,000,000; expenditures by nationals abroad U.S.$35,865,000,000.

Foreign trade

Balance of trade (current prices)[2]

	1987	1988	1989	1990	1991	1992	1993
DM '000,000,000	+127.88	+139.23	+147.85	+118.90	+15.31	+29.46	+59.13
% of total	13.8%	13.9%	13.0%	9.9%	1.2%	2.7%	5.2%

Imports (1993): DM 544,843,000,000 (machinery and transport equipment 34.5%, of which transport equipment 9.4%, electrical machinery other than office equipment 5.8%, office equipment 5.0%; chemicals and chemical products 8.3%, of which organic chemical products 1.9%, unfabricated plastics 1.6%; food and beverages 8.3%, of which fruits and vegetables 2.8%, meat and meat products 1.4%, milk and milk products 0.9%; mineral fuels 8.3%, of which crude petroleum and petroleum products 6.0%, natural gas 1.7%; clothing and wearing apparel 6.8%; thread, yarn, and finished spinning goods 3.0%; iron and steel 2.5%). *Major import sources:* France 11.2%; The Netherlands 8.3%; Italy 8.1%; United States 7.4%; Japan 6.3%; United Kingdom 6.0%; Belgium-Luxembourg 5.7%; Austria 4.8%; Switzerland 4.4%.
Exports (1993): DM 603,973,000,000 (machinery and transport equipment 49.5%, of which transport equipment 15.9%, electrical machinery other than office equipment 7.4%, office equipment 2.4%; chemicals and chemical products 13.1%, of which organic chemical products 2.6%, unfabricated plastics 2.1%, medical and pharmaceutical products 2.1%). *Major export destinations:* France 11.7%; United Kingdom 7.7%; United States 7.7%; The Netherlands 7.4%; Italy 7.2%; Belgium-Luxembourg 6.6%; Austria 6.2%; Switzerland 5.6%; Spain 2.6%; Japan 2.6%; Sweden 2.1%.

Transport and communications

Transport. Railroads (1992): length 56,813 mi, 91,432 km; passengers carried 1,564,000,000, passenger-mi 35,567,000,000, passenger-km 57,240,000,-000; short ton-mi cargo 46,254,000,000, metric ton-km cargo 72,848,000,000. Roads (1989)[2]: total length 308,614 mi, 496,652 km (paved 99%). Vehicles (1992): passenger cars 32,652,000; trucks and buses 1,752,000. Merchant marine (1992): vessels (100 gross tons and over) 1,574; total deadweight tonnage 5,636,000. Air transport (1992)[11]: passengers carried 71,000,000; passenger-mi 12,633,000,000, passenger-km 20,331,000,000; short ton-mi cargo 260,000,000, metric ton-km cargo 379,000,000; airports (1994) with scheduled flights 40.
Communications. Daily newspapers (1991)[2]: total number 352; total circulation 25,427,000; circulation per 1,000 population 402. Radio (1992): 35,302,-000 receivers (1 per 2.3 persons). Television (1992): 31,516,000[2, 12] receivers (1 per 2.5 persons). Telephones (1992): 45,711,000 (1 per 1.7 persons).

Education and health

Education (1992–93)

	schools	teachers	students	student/teacher ratio
Primary (age 6–10) } Secondary (age 10–19) }	43,941	656,809	9,345,162	14.2
Voc., teacher tr.	8,951	105,546	2,470,837	23.4
Higher	314	171,025[2, 13]	1,858,455	10.7[2, 13]

Health (1993): physicians 259,981 (1 per 313 persons); dentists 58,194 (1 per 1,397 persons); hospital beds 646,995 (1 per 126 persons); infant mortality rate per 1,000 live births 6.1.
Food (1988–90): daily per capita caloric intake 3,522 (vegetable products 65%, animal products 35%); 132% of FAO recommended minimum requirement.

Military

Total active duty personnel (1994): 367,300 (army 69.2%, navy 8.2%, air force 22.6%). *Military expenditure as percentage of GNP* (1992): 1.6% (world 5.0%); per capita expenditure U.S.$416.

[1]Detail does not add to total given because of rounding. [2]Former West Germany only. [3]August. [4]1984. [5]1990. [6]1993. [7]Data withheld for reasons of confidentiality. [8]End-of-period figures unless footnoted otherwise. [9]Through June. [10]Period averages. [11]Domestic service only. [12]Data include officially registered sets only. [13]1991.

Ghana

Official name: Republic of Ghana.
Form of government: unitary multiparty
republic with one legislative house
(House of Parliament [200]).
Head of state and government:
President.
Capital: Accra.
Official language: English.
Official religion: none.
Monetary unit: 1 cedi (₵) = 100
pesewas; valuation (Oct. 7, 1994)
1 U.S.$ = ₵996; 1 £ = ₵1,585.

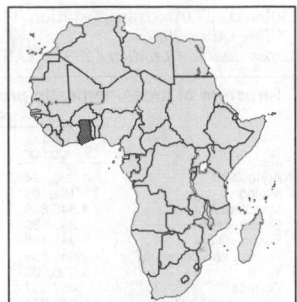

Area and population

Regions[2]	Capitals	area sq mi	area sq km	population 1991[1] estimate
Ashanti	Kumasi	9,417	24,389	2,485,766
Brong-Ahafo	Sunyani	15,273	39,557	1,432,971
Central	Cape Coast	3,794	9,826	1,359,861
Eastern	Koforidua	7,461	19,323	2,003,235
Greater Accra	Accra	1,250	3,245	1,090,170
Northern	Tamale	27,175	70,384	1,389,105
Upper East	Bolgatanga	3,414	8,842	921,196
Upper West	Wa	7,134	18,476	526,398
Volta	Ho	7,942	20,570	1,432,971
Western	Sekondi-Takoradi	9,236	23,921	1,374,483
TOTAL		92,098[3]	238,533	14,622,156

Demography

Population (1994): 16,050,000.
Density (1994): persons per sq mi 174.3, persons per sq km 67.3.
Urban-rural (1992): urban 34.9%; rural 65.1%.
Sex distribution (1990): male 49.64%; female 50.36%.
Age breakdown (1990): under 15, 46.8%; 15–29, 26.2%; 30–44, 14.4%; 45–59, 8.0%; 60–74, 3.8%; 75 and over, 0.8%.
Population projection: (2000) 18,749,000; (2010) 24,293,000.
Doubling time: 23 years.
Ethnolinguistic composition (1983): Akan 52.4%; Mossi 15.8%; Ewe 11.9%; Ga-Adangme 7.8%; Gurma 3.3%; Yoruba 1.3%; other 7.5%.
Religious affiliation (1980): Christian 62.6%, of which Protestant 27.9%, Roman Catholic 18.7%, African indigenous 16.0%; traditional beliefs 21.4%; Muslim 15.7%, of which Aḥmadīyah 7.9%; other 0.3%.
Major cities (1988[2]): Accra 949,100; Kumasi 385,200; Tamale 151,100; Tema 110,000; Sekondi-Takoradi 103,600.

Vital statistics

Birth rate per 1,000 population (1990–95): 43.2 (world avg. 26.0); legitimate, n.a.; illegitimate, n.a.
Death rate per 1,000 population (1990–95): 12.3 (world avg. 9.2).
Natural increase rate per 1,000 population (1990–95): 30.9 (world avg. 16.8).
Total fertility rate (avg. births per childbearing woman; 1990–95): 6.1.
Life expectancy at birth (1993): male 53.3 years; female 57.2 years.
Major causes of death per 100,000 population: n.a.; however, major infectious diseases include malaria, tuberculosis, leprosy, trypanosomiasis (sleeping sickness), and onchocerciasis (river blindness).

National economy

Budget (1992). Revenue: ₵396,143,200,000 (excise and value-added taxes 35.3%, of which petroleum tax 6.0%; import-export duties 31.1%; income and property taxes 18.4%; divestiture of government assets 9.2%). Expenditures: ₵498,813,000,000 (education 23.9%, debt service 12.2%, health 7.8%, social security and welfare 7.0%, defense 3.6%, transportation and communications 0.8%).
Production (metric tons except as noted). Agriculture, forestry, fishing (1993): roots and tubers 6,436,000 (of which cassava 4,200,000, taro 1,236,000, yams 1,000,000), cereals 1,645,000 (of which corn [maize] 961,000, sorghum 328,000, millet 198,000, rice 157,000), bananas and plantains 1,326,000, coconuts 220,000, cacao 215,000, green peppers 169,000, sugarcane 111,000, tomatoes 107,000, peanuts (groundnuts) 100,000, oranges 50,000, palm kernels 34,000, lemons and limes 30,000, pulses 20,000; livestock (number of live animals) 2,200,000 sheep, 2,200,000 goats, 1,200,000 cattle, 450,000 pigs, 12,000,000 chickens; roundwood (1992) 17,211,000 cu m; fish catch (1991) 364,959 (of which anchovies 74,668). Mining and quarrying (1993): bauxite 364,642; manganese ore 309,122; gold 38,224 kg; diamonds 590,821 carats. Manufacturing (1992): cement 1,023,900; kerosene, gasoline, and diesel fuel 806,600; wheat flour 121,000; soap 37,400; iron rods 26,200; cocoa cake, cocoa butter, and cocoa liquor 21,300; edible fats and oils 19,000; toothpaste 556; textiles 19,000,000 metres; soft drinks 3,300,000 hectolitres; beer 649,000 hectolitres; evaporated milk 231,000 hectolitres; ice cream 10,540 hectolitres; cigarettes 1,687,000,000 units. Construction (value added in ₵; 1992): 105,216,500,000. Energy production (consumption): electricity (kW-hr; 1992) 6,152,000,000 (5,870,000,000); coal (metric tons; 1992) 3,000 (3,000); crude petroleum (barrels; 1992) none (7,145,000); petroleum products (metric tons; 1992) 877,000 (1,037,000); natural gas, none (n.a.).
Household income and expenditure. Average household size (1983) 4.9; average annual income per household (1978) ₵9,600 (U.S.$[4]); sources of income: n.a.; expenditure (1978): food and beverages 57.4%, clothing and footwear 14.3%, housing and energy 11.5%, transportation and communications 3.3%, health care 1.3%.
Gross national product (1993): U.S.$6,992,000,000 (U.S.$430 per capita).

Structure of gross domestic product and labour force

	1992 in value ₵'000,000	1992 % of total value	1984 labour force	1984 % of labour force
Agriculture	1,461,005.1	48.6	3,310,967	59.4
Mining	57,117.5	1.9	26,828	0.5
Manufacturing	261,537.9	8.7	588,418	10.5
Construction	105,216.5	3.5	64,686	1.2
Public utilities	63,129.8	2.1	15,437	0.3
Transp. and commun.	132,272.1	4.4	122,806	2.2
Trade	550,131.5	18.3	792,147	14.2
Finance	108,222.6	3.6	27,475	0.5
Pub. admin., defense	225,463.8	7.5	97,548	1.7
Services	61,131.8	2.0	376,168	6.7
Other	−16,449.4[5]	−0.6[5]	157,624[6]	2.8[6]
TOTAL	3,008,779.2	100.0	5,580,104	100.0

Tourism (1992): receipts from visitors U.S.$167,000,000; expenditures by nationals abroad U.S.$17,000,000.
Population economically active (1984): total 5,580,104; activity rate of total population 45.4% (participation rates: over age 15, 82.5%; female 51.2%; unemployed 2.8%).

Price and earnings indexes (1989 = 100)

	1987	1988	1989	1990	1991	1992	1993
Consumer price index	60.8	79.9	100.0	137.2	162.0	178.3	222.6
Earnings index	43.4	56.9	100.0	...	...	...	...

Public debt (external, outstanding; 1992): U.S.$3,096,000,000.
Land use (1992): forested 34.9%; meadows and pastures 22.0%; agricultural and under permanent cultivation 12.0%; other 31.1%.

Foreign trade

Balance of trade (current prices)

	1984	1985	1986	1987	1988	1989
₵'000,000	+637.1	−4,070.0	+11,578.0	+7,594.0	+32,080	−49,087
% of total	1.6%	5.8%	8.1%	2.6%	8.5%	8.2%

Imports (1989): ₵346,218,000,000 (1987; machinery and transport equipment 28.1%; mineral fuels and lubricants 14.0%; chemicals 12.0%; food and live animals 5.2%; beverages and tobacco 0.4%). *Major import sources* (1987): United Kingdom 41.4%; Nigeria 13.2%; West Germany 11.5%; United States 11.1%; Japan 4.3%; France 3.8%.
Exports (1989): ₵274,784,000,000 (1986; food and live animals 60.4%, of which cocoa 53.9%; logs and sawn timber 17.9%; gold 15.5%; manganese ore 1.1%; industrial diamonds 0.7%). *Major export destinations* (1987): United Kingdom 27.0%; United States 18.6%; The Netherlands 13.5%; U.S.S.R. 9.2%; Japan 9.0%; West Germany 8.3%.

Transport and communications

Transport. Railroads (1992): route length 592 mi, 953 km; passenger-mi 839,500,000, passenger-km 135,100,000; short ton-mi cargo 74,380,000, metric ton-km cargo 108,600,000. Roads (1992): total length 22,800 mi, 36,700 km (paved 32%). Vehicles (1989): passenger cars 57,897; trucks and buses 30,125. Merchant marine (1992): vessels (100 gross tons and over) 155; total deadweight tonnage 130,977. Air transport (1991): passenger-mi 206,000,000, passenger-km 331,000,000; short ton-mi cargo 13,000,000, metric ton-km cargo 19,000,000; airports (1994) with scheduled flights 1.
Communications. Daily newspapers (1992): total number 3; total circulation 240,000; circulation per 1,000 population 23. Radio (1993): 4,000,000 receivers (1 per 3.8 persons). Television (1993): 250,000 receivers (1 per 61 persons). Telephones (1992): 81,340 (1 per 187 persons).

Education and health

Education (1991–92)

	schools	teachers	students	student/ teacher ratio
Primary (6–12)	11,056	66,068	1,796,490	27.2
Secondary (13–20)	5,513	43,349[7]	861,630[7]	19.9[7]
Voc., teacher tr.	57	422[7]	13,232[7]	31.4[7]
Higher	16	700[7]	9,274[7]	13.2[7]

Educational attainment (1984). Percentage of population age 25 and over having: no formal schooling 60.4%; primary education 7.1%; middle school 25.4%; secondary 3.5%; vocational and other postsecondary 2.9%; higher 0.6%. *Literacy* (1990): total population age 15 and over literate 4,960,000 (60.4%); males literate 2,835,000 (70.0%); females literate 2,125,000 (50.9%).
Health: physicians (1989) 678 (1 per 22,452 persons); hospital beds (1991) 18,477 (1 per 791 persons); infant mortality rate per 1,000 live births (1994) 83.
Food (1988–90): daily per capita caloric intake 2,144 (vegetable products 95%, animal products 5%); 93% of FAO minimum recommended requirement.

Military

Total active duty personnel (1994): 6,850 (army 73.0%, navy 12.4%, air force 14.6%). *Military expenditure as percentage of GNP* (1991): 0.6% (world 4.2%); per capita expenditure U.S.$2.

---

[1]January 1. [2]Government administration has been decentralized to the local level of 103 district assemblies, 4 municipal assemblies, and 3 metropolitan assemblies. [3]Detail does not add to total given because of rounding. [4]Unofficial 1978 exchange rate (7.5 to 9.9 times the official rate) does not permit meaningful conversion into other currencies. [5]Import duties and statistical adjustments less imputed bank service charges. [6]Unemployed only. [7]1989–90.

Greece

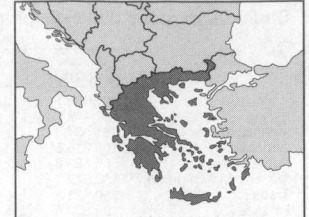

Official name: Ellinikí Dhimokratía
(Hellenic Republic).
Form of government: unitary multiparty
republic with one legislative house
(Greek Chamber of Deputies [300]).
Chief of state: President.
Head of government: Prime Minister.
Capital: Athens.
Official language: Greek.
Official religion: Eastern Orthodox.
Monetary unit: 1 drachma (Dr) = 100
lepta; valuation (Oct. 7, 1994)
1 U.S.$ = Dr 235.24; 1 £ = Dr 374.15.

Area and population		area		population
		sq mi	sq km	1991 census
Regions				
Anatolikí Makedonía	(Eastern Macedonia			
kaí Thráki	and Thrace)	5,466	14,157	570,261
Attikí	(Attica)	1,470	3,808	3,522,769
Dhytikí Ellás	(Western Greece)	4,382	11,350	702,027
Dhytikí Makedonía	(Western Macedonia)	3,649	9,451	292,751
Iónioi Nísoi	(Ionian Islands)	891	2,307	191,003
Ípiros	(Epirus)	3,553	9,203	339,210
Kedrikí Makedonía	(Central Macedonia)	7,393	19,147	1,737,623[1]
Kríti	(Crete)	3,218	8,336	536,980
Nótion Aiyaíon	(Southern Aegean)	2,041	5,286	257,522
Pelopónnisos	(Peloponnesos)	5,981	15,490	605,663
Stereá Ellás	(Central Greece)	6,004	15,549	578,876
Thessalía	(Thessaly)	5,420	14,037	731,230
Vóreion Aiyaíon	(Northern Aegean)	1,481	3,836	198,241
TOTAL		50,949	131,957	10,264,156

Demography

Population (1994): 10,365,000.
Density (1994): persons per sq mi 203.4, persons per sq km 78.5.
Urban-rural (1992): urban 63.5%; rural 36.5%.
Sex distribution (1991): male 49.26%; female 50.74%.
Age breakdown (1991): under 15, 18.5%; 15–29, 22.0%; 30–44, 20.6%; 45–59, 18.6%; 60–74, 14.0%; 75 and over, 6.3%.
Population projection: (2000) 10,493,000; (2010) 10,518,000.
Doubling time: not applicable; doubling time exceeds 100 years.
Ethnic composition (1983): Greek 95.5%; Macedonian 1.5%; Turkish 0.9%; Albanian 0.6%; other 1.5%.
Religious affiliation (1980): Christian 98.1%, of which Eastern Orthodox 97.6%, Roman Catholic 0.4%, Protestant 0.1%; Muslim 1.5%; other 0.4%.
Major cities (1991): Athens 748,110; Thessaloníki 377,951; Piraeus (Piraiévs) 169,622; Pátrai 155,180; Peristérion 145,854.

Vital statistics

Birth rate per 1,000 population (1993): 10.0 (world avg. 26.0); (1992) legitimate 96.1%; illegitimate 3.9%.
Death rate per 1,000 population (1993): 9.4 (world avg. 9.2).
Natural increase rate per 1,000 population (1993): 0.6 (world avg. 16.8).
Total fertility rate (avg. births per childbearing woman; 1992): 1.4.
Marriage rate per 1,000 population (1992): 5.1.
Divorce rate per 1,000 population (1990): 0.6.
Life expectancy at birth (1990): male 74.6 years; female 79.8 years.
Major causes of death per 100,000 population (1992): malignant neoplasms (cancers) 199.5; cerebrovascular disease 178.4; diseases of pulmonary circulation and other forms of heart disease 150.4; ischemic heart disease 121.1.

National economy

Budget (1992). Revenue: Dr 6,956,515,000,000[2] (indirect and excise taxes 41.5%, direct taxes 16.9%, European Community 1.2%). Expenditures: Dr 6,828,276,000,000 (1989; health and social insurance 20.4%, defense 10.2%, education and culture 9.0%, police and other sectors 2.6%).
Public debt (1992): U.S.$16,503,000,000.
Tourism (1992): receipts from visitors U.S.$3,268,000,000; expenditures by nationals abroad U.S.$1,186,000,000.
Production (metric tons except as noted). Agriculture, forestry, fishing (1993): sugar beets 2,989,000, wheat 2,143,000, olives 1,900,000, corn (maize) 2,099,000, tomatoes 1,886,000, grapes 1,400,000, potatoes 1,006,000, oranges 906,000, barley 415,000, cotton 320,000, tobacco 168,000, rice 146,000, onions 141,000; livestock (number of live animals) 9,659,000 sheep, 5,830,000 goats, 1,040,000 pigs, 631,000 cattle, 110,000 asses, 27,000,000 chickens; roundwood 2,546,000 cu m; fish catch (1991) 149,020. Mining and quarrying (1993): bauxite 2,200,000; nickel ore 1,300,000; zinc ore 42,000[3]; lead ore 37,000[3]; chromium ore 25,000[3]. Manufacturing (value added in Dr; 1992): food, beverages, and tobacco 492,276,000,000; chemicals 274,191,000,000; textiles 227,507,000,000; paper and printing 147,484,000,000; transport equipment 141,563,000,000; clothing and footwear 129,732,000,000. Construction (authorized; 1990): residential 46,434,236 cu m; nonresidential 12,535,570 cu m. Energy production (consumption): electricity (kW-hr; 1992) 37,410,-000,000 (38,015,000,000); coal (metric tons; 1992) 55,051,000 (56,424,000); crude petroleum (barrels; 1992) 4,687,000 (98,390,000); petroleum products (metric tons; 1992) 14,949,000 (14,352,000); natural gas (cu m; 1992) 147,-714,000 (147,714,000).
Household income and expenditure. Average household size (1988) 3.1; income per household (1982) Dr 252,300 (U.S.$3,777); sources of income (1991): property and entrepreneurial income 46.0%, wages and salaries 37.2%, transfer payments 16.8%; expenditure (1991): food, beverages, and tobacco 37.0%, transportation 14.9%, housing 9.8%, clothing and footwear 8.7%, other 29.6%.
Gross national product (1993): U.S.$76,679,000,000 (U.S.$7,390 per capita).

Structure of gross domestic product and labour force				
	1992		1991	
	in value Dr '000,000	% of total value	labour force	% of labour force
Agriculture	1,880,774	14.9	806,500	20.5
Mining	162,185	1.3	19,300	0.5
Manufacturing	1,940,848	15.4	699,000	17.8
Construction	849,180	6.7	245,700	6.2
Public utilities	338,480	2.7	36,600	0.9
Transp. and commun.	859,755	6.8	252,400	6.4
Trade	1,650,000	13.1	660,400	16.8
Finance	457,357	3.6	192,700	4.9
Pub. admin., defense	2,399,858	19.1 }	719,800	18.3
Services	1,111,173	8.8 }		
Other	946,159[4]	7.5[4]	301,100[5]	7.7[5]
TOTAL	12,595,768[6]	100.0[6]	3,933,500	100.0

Population economically active (1991): total 3,933,500; activity rate of total population 38.6% (participation rates: ages 15–64, 55.6%; female 35.7%; unemployed 7.7%).

Price and earnings indexes (1990 = 100)							
	1987	1988	1989	1990	1991	1992	1993
Consumer price index	64.3	73.0	83.1	100.0	119.5	138.4	158.4
Hourly earnings index	58.7	69.5	83.8	100.0	116.7	132.8	146.7

Land use (1992): forested 20.3%; meadows and pastures 40.8%; agricultural and under permanent cultivation 30.3%; other 8.6%.

Foreign trade

Balance of trade (current prices)					
	1987	1988	1989	1990	1991	1992
Dr '000,000,000	−688.4	−861.4	−1,199.2	−1,613.3	−1,886.1	−2,113.5
% of total	28.1%	33.8%	30.8%	44.3%	37.3%	36.8%

Imports (1992): Dr 4,441,848,500,000 (machinery and transport equipment 34.1%, of which automobiles 8.7%; food, beverages, and tobacco 11.7%, of which meat products 1.4%, dairy products 1.2%, coffee 0.3%; chemical products 10.6%, of which medicinal and pharmaceutical products 0.5%; crude petroleum 7.4%). *Major import sources:* Germany 20.2%; Italy 14.2%; France 7.8%; The Netherlands 6.9%; Japan 6.4%; United Kingdom 5.5%; United States 3.6%; Belgium-Luxembourg 3.5%.
Exports (1992): Dr 1,816,406,800,000 (food, beverages, and tobacco 27.8%, of which tobacco 6.7%, olive oil 5.2%, olives 1.1%; clothing 21.5%; petroleum products 4.9%; textiles 3.5%; furs and raw skins 1.0%). *Major export destinations:* Germany 23.1%; Italy 18.0%; France 7.2%; United Kingdom 7.0%; United States 4.0%; Cyprus 3.4%.

Transport and communications

Transport. Railroads (1992): route length 1,570 mi, 2,527 km; passenger-mi 1,245,000,000, passenger-km 2,004,000,000; short ton-mi cargo 386,000,000, metric ton-km cargo 563,000,000. Roads (1992): total length 72,170 mi, 116,-150 km (paved 92%). Vehicles (1993): passenger cars 1,958,544; trucks and buses 831,497. Merchant marine (1992): vessels (100 gross tons and over) 1,872; total deadweight tonnage 45,276,567. Air transport (1992): passenger-mi 4,512,624,000, passenger-km 7,262,379,000; short ton-mi cargo 73,294,000, metric ton-km cargo 107,008,000; airports (1994) with scheduled flights 34.
Communications. Daily newspapers (1993): total number 144; total circulation, n.a. Radio (1993): 4,085,492 receivers (1 per 2.5 persons). Television (1993): 2,300,000 receivers (1 per 4.5 persons). Telephones (1992): 5,289,560 (1 per 1.9 persons).

Education and health

Education (1992–93)	schools	teachers	students	student/ teacher ratio
Primary (age 6–12)	7,634	37,549	745,666	19.9
Secondary (age 12–18)	2,988	45,794	700,488	15.3
Voc., teacher tr.	695	14,319	190,443	13.3
Higher	17	13,007[7]	187,644[7]	14.4[7]

Educational attainment (1981). Percentage of population age 25 and over having: no formal schooling (illiterate) 11.4%; some primary education 16.8%; completed primary 44.1%; lower secondary 6.0%; higher secondary 13.5%; some postsecondary 2.5%; a degree from institution of higher education 4.9%. *Literacy* (1990): total population age 15 and over literate 7,550,000 (93.2%); males literate 3,925,000 (97.6%); females literate 3,625,000 (89.1%).
Health: physicians (1990) 34,336 (1 per 303 persons); hospital beds 51,329 (1 per 199 persons); infant mortality rate per 1,000 live births (1993) 8.5.
Food (1988–90): daily per capita caloric intake 3,775 (vegetable products 75%, animal products 25%); 142% of FAO recommended minimum requirement.

Military

Total active duty personnel (1994): 159,300 (army 70.9%, navy 12.3%, air force 16.8%). *Military expenditure as percentage of GNP* (1991): 5.5% (world 4.2%); per capita expenditure U.S.$379.

[1]Includes Mount Athos (Áyion Óros), an autonomous, self-governing monastic region; 1991 population 1,557. [2]Includes Dr 2,436,147,000,000 of domestic borrowing. [3]Metal content of ore. [4]Income from ownership of buildings. [5]Unemployed. [6]Detail does not add to total given because of rounding. [7]1988–89.

Grenada

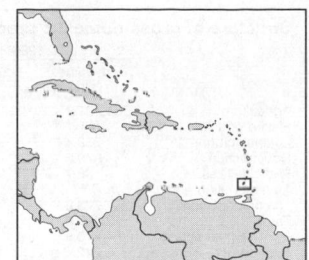

Official name: Grenada.
Form of government: constitutional monarchy with two legislative houses (Senate [13]; House of Representatives [15[1]]).
Chief of state: British Monarch represented by Governor-General.
Head of government: Prime Minister.
Capital: St. George's.
Official language: English.
Official religion: none.
Monetary unit: 1 East Caribbean dollar (EC$) = 100 cents; valuation (Oct. 7, 1994) 1 U.S.$ = EC$2.70; 1 £ = EC$4.30.

Area and population

Local Councils	Principal towns	area sq mi	area sq km	population 1991 census[2]
Carriacou	Hillsborough	10	26	4,595
Petite Martinique	...	3	8	720
St. Andrew	Grenville	38	99	23,531
St. David	...	17	44	10,703
St. George	...	25[3]	65[3]	24,719
St. John	Gouyave	14	35	8,547
St. Mark	Victoria	10	25	3,785
St. Patrick	Sauteurs	16	42	9,652
Town				
St. George's	—	3	3	4,439
TOTAL		133	344	90,691

Demography

Population (1994): 91,800.
Density (1994): persons per sq mi 690.2, persons per sq km 266.9.
Urban-rural (1991)[4]: urban 32.2%; rural 67.8%.
Sex distribution (1991): male 49.35%; female 50.65%.
Age breakdown (1988): under 15, 35.9%; 15–29, 28.5%; 30–44, 14.2%; 45–59, 8.5%; 60 and over, 11.3%; not stated, 1.6%.
Population projection: (2000) 93,000; (2010) 95,000.
Doubling time: 29 years.
Ethnic composition (1991): black 84.9%; mixed 11.0%; Indo-Pakistani 3.0%; other 1.1%.
Religious affiliation (1991): Roman Catholic 53.0%; Anglican 14.0%; Seventh-day Adventist 8.5%; Pentecostal 7.2%; other 17.3%.
Major localities (1991): St. George's 4,439; Gouyave 3,000[5]; Grenville 2,000[5].

Vital statistics

Birth rate per 1,000 population (1993): 30.8 (world avg. 26.0).
Death rate per 1,000 population (1993): 6.5 (world avg. 9.2).
Natural increase rate per 1,000 population (1993): 24.4 (world avg. 16.8).
Total fertility rate (avg. births per childbearing woman; 1992): 2.9.
Marriage rate per 1,000 population: n.a.
Divorce rate per 1,000 population: n.a.
Life expectancy at birth (1993): male 67.8 years; female 72.5 years.
Major causes of death per 100,000 population (1984): diseases of the circulatory system 290.3; malignant neoplasms (cancers) 90.5; endocrine and metabolic diseases 62.9; diseases of the respiratory system 54.1; accidents and violence 47.9; diseases of the digestive system 39.5.

National economy

Budget (1993). Revenue: EC$246,900,000 (current revenue 71.7%; development revenue 28.3%, of which foreign loans 13.0%, foreign grants 10.4%, special fund based on the sale of national assets 4.9%). Expenditures: EC$277,700,000 (current expenditures 70.2%; development expenditures 29.8%).
Public debt (external, outstanding; 1992): U.S.$97,700,000.
Tourism: receipts from visitors (1992) U.S.$38,000,000; expenditures by nationals abroad (1991) U.S.$5,000,000.
Gross national product (at current market prices; 1993): U.S.$219,000,000 (U.S.$2,410 per capita).

Structure of gross domestic product and labour force

	1992 in value EC$'000,000[6]	1992 % of total value	1988 labour force	1988 % of labour force
Agriculture	63.7	13.9	5,560	14.3
Quarrying	1.9	0.4	111	0.3
Manufacturing	25.5	5.6	2,835	7.3
Construction	48.0	10.5	3,531	9.1
Public utilities	16.0	3.5	389	1.0
Transportation and communications	69.8	15.3	1,696	4.4
Trade, restaurants	94.4	20.6	5,421	13.9
Finance, real estate	45.8	10.0	778	2.0
Pub. admin., defense	90.0	21.6 }	5,949	15.3
Services	13.0	2.9 }		
Other	−19.5[7]	−4.3[7]	12,650[8]	32.5[8]
TOTAL	457.5	100.0	38,920	100.0[9]

Production (metric tons except as noted). Agriculture, forestry, fishing (1993): bananas 10,000, coconuts 7,000, sugarcane 7,000, roots and tubers 4,000, nutmeg 2,235[10], mangoes 2,000, avocados 2,000, grapefruit 2,000, cacao

1,497[11], mace 136[10], other crops include soursop, sapodilla plums, cinnamon, cloves, and pimiento; livestock (number of live animals) 12,000 sheep, 11,000 goats, 4,000 cattle; roundwood, n.a.; fish catch (1991) 1,990. Mining and quarrying: excavation of gravel for local use. Manufacturing (1991): wheat flour 8,000[12]; beer 20,177 hectolitres; rum 3,345 hectolitres; malt 3,000 hectolitres[12]; cigarettes 20,000,000 units; clothing (1989) EC$3,800,000 in export sales; other products include edible coconut oil, paints, pharmaceutical products, and aerated beverages. Construction: n.a. Energy production (consumption): electricity (kW-hr; 1992) 62,000,000 (62,000,000); coal, none (none); crude petroleum, none (none); petroleum products (metric tons; 1992) none (39,000); natural gas, none (none).
Household income and expenditure. Average household size (1991) 3.7; income per household (1988) EC$7,097 (U.S.$2,629); sources of income: n.a.; expenditure (1987): food 38.7%, housing 11.9%, transportation 9.1%, personal effects and medical care 8.6%, household furnishings 8.3%, household operations 5.4%.
Population economically active (1988): total 38,920; activity rate of total population 39.9% (participation rates: ages 15–65, 72.7%; female 48.6%; unemployed [1994] 15.0%).

Price and earnings indexes (1990 = 100)

	1988	1989	1990	1991	1992	1993	1994
Consumer price index	92.2	97.3	100.0	102.7	106.5	109.5	112.4[13]
Annual earnings index[14]	...	...	100.0	108.0	118.8	...	...

Land use (1992): forested 9.0%; meadows and pastures 3.0%; agricultural and under permanent cultivation 32.0%; other 56.0%.

Foreign trade[15]

Balance of trade (current prices)

	1987	1988	1989	1990	1991	1992
U.S.$'000,000	−56.7	−59.4	−70.7	−79.7	−90.5	−83.2
% of total	47.1%	47.5%	55.5%	60.0%	66.1%	67.6%

Imports (1992): U.S.$103,200,000 ([16]machinery and transport equipment 24.2%; food 23.9%; basic manufactures 20.2%; chemicals and chemical products 8.5%). *Major import sources:* United States 26.6%; Trinidad and Tobago 23.7%; United Kingdom 10.9%; Germany 5.9%; Japan 4.1%.
Exports (1992): U.S.$20,000,000 (bananas 14.3%; nutmeg 11.1%; cocoa beans 13.2%; mace 3.0%; other exports include fresh fruit, electronic components, and pharmaceuticals). *Major export destinations:* United States 34.7%; United Kingdom 26.9%; St. Lucia 6.6%; Switzerland 4.8%.

Transport and communications

Transport. Railroads: none. Roads (1991): total length 700 mi, 1,127 km (paved 51%). Vehicles: n.a. Merchant marine (1992): vessels (100 gross tons and over) 3; total deadweight tonnage 484. Air transport (1991)[17]: passenger arrivals 101,694, passenger departures 104,695; cargo loaded 1,275 metric tons, cargo unloaded 457 metric tons; airports (1994) with scheduled flights 2.
Communications. Daily newspapers (1991): none[18]. Radio (1993): total number of receivers 80,000 (1 per 1.1 persons). Television (1993): total number of receivers 30,000 (1 per 3.1 persons). Telephones (1992): 24,300 (1 per 3.8 persons).

Education and health

Education (1993–94)

	schools	teachers	students	student/ teacher ratio
Primary (age 5–11)	57	781	21,311	27.3
Secondary (age 12–16)	19	352	6,939	19.7
Vocational	...	...	...	...
Higher	1	66	651	9.9

Educational attainment (1981). Percentage of population age 25 and over having: no formal schooling 2.2%; primary education 87.8%; secondary 8.5%; higher 1.5%. *Literacy* (1988): total population age 15 and over literate 49,000 (85.0%).
Health (1990): physicians 56 (1 per 1,617 persons); hospital beds 409 (1 per 222 persons); infant mortality rate per 1,000 live births (1993) 12.7.
Food (1988–90): daily per capita caloric intake 2,400 (vegetable products 77%, animal products 23%); 99% of FAO recommended minimum requirement.

Military

Total active duty personnel (1993): [19]. Military expenditure as percentage of GNP: n.a.; per capita expenditure, n.a.

[1]Excludes the speaker, who may be elected from outside its elected membership. [2]Preliminary; excludes 434 institutionalized residents and 33 Grenadians in foreign service. [3]St. George local council includes St. George's town. [4]Urban defined as St. George's town and St. George local council. [5]1987. [6]Current prices at factor cost. [7]Less imputed bank service charges. [8]Includes 1,752 persons in activities not adequately defined and 10,898 unemployed. [9]Detail does not add to total given because of rounding. [10]1992. [11]1993–94. [12]1990. [13]June. [14]Private sector only. [15]Imports c.i.f.; exports f.o.b. [16]Based on imports for 1991 equaling U.S.$117,200,000. [17]Point Salines airport. [18]Weekly newspapers (1993): 5. [19]The 750-member police force includes a paramilitary unit.

Guadeloupe

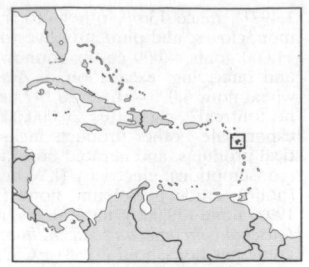

Official name: Département de la Guadeloupe (Department of Guadeloupe).
Political status: overseas department (France) with two legislative houses (General Council [42]; Regional Council [41]).
Chief of state: President of France.
Heads of government: Commissioner of the Republic (for France); President of the General Council (for Guadeloupe); President of the Regional Council (for Guadeloupe).
Capital: Basse-Terre.
Official language: French.
Official religion: none.
Monetary unit: 1 French franc (F) = 100 centimes; valuation (Oct. 7, 1994) 1 U.S.$ = F 5.27; 1 £ = F 8.38.

Area and population

Arrondissements	Capitals	area sq mi	area sq km	population 1990 census
Basse-Terre[1]	Basse-Terre	332	861	151,979
Pointe-à-Pitre[2]	Pointe-à-Pitre	297	769	192,643
Saint-Martin–Saint-Barthélemy[3]	Marigot	29	75	33,556
TOTAL		687[4]	1,780[4]	378,178[5]

Demography

Population (1994): 426,000.
Density (1994): persons per sq mi 620.1, persons per sq km 239.3.
Urban-rural (1990): urban 48.4%; rural 51.6%.
Sex distribution (1991): male 48.88%; female 51.12%.
Age breakdown (1991): under 15, 24.8%; 15–29, 29.5%; 30–44, 21.4%; 45–59, 12.5%; 60–74, 8.3%; 75 and over, 3.5%.
Population projection: (2000) 473,000; (2010) 541,000.
Doubling time: 58 years.
Ethnic composition (1991): Creole (mulatto) 77.0%; black 10.0%; Guadeloupe mestizo (French–East Asian) 10.0%; white 2.0%; other 1.0%.
Religious affiliation (1991[6]): Roman Catholic 88.1%; other 11.9%.
Major communes (1990): Les Abymes 62,605; Saint-Martin 28,518; Pointe-à-Pitre 26,029 (141,000[7, 8]); Le Gosier 20,708; Basse-Terre 14,000 (53,000[7]).

Vital statistics

Birth rate per 1,000 population (1992): 17.8 (world avg. 26.0); legitimate 39.3%; illegitimate 60.7%.
Death rate per 1,000 population (1992): 5.6 (world avg. 9.2).
Natural increase rate per 1,000 population (1992): 12.2 (world avg. 16.8).
Total fertility rate (avg. births per childbearing woman; 1990–95): 2.2.
Marriage rate per 1,000 population (1992): 4.7.
Divorce rate per 1,000 population (1992): 1.1.
Life expectancy at birth (1991): male 70.0 years; female 77.0 years.
Major causes of death per 100,000 population (1990): diseases of the circulatory system 186.8; malignant neoplasms (cancers) 121.2; accidents and violence 72.9; diseases of the respiratory system 30.5; diseases of the digestive system 29.7.

National economy

Budget (1992). Revenue: F 2,509,000,000 (1991; receipts from French central government and local administrative bodies 38.2%, new loans 21.5%, subsidies for investments 10.6%, taxes on motor fuels 7.4%). Expenditures: F 4,978,000,000 (1991; capital investments and works 30.8%, health and social services 23.1%, debt amortization 7.4%).
Public debt (external, outstanding; 1988[9]): U.S.$41,000,000.
Tourism (1992): receipts from visitors U.S.$269,000,000; expenditures by nationals abroad, n.a.
Production (metric tons except as noted). Agriculture, forestry, fishing (1992): sugarcane 516,000, bananas 148,300, yams 10,000, sweet potatoes 7,000, plantains 7,000, pineapples 4,400, tomatoes 4,000, melons 3,500, mangoes 2,000, limes 1,200, eggplants 1,000, foliage and plants 60[10, 11], cut flowers 29[10, 11]; livestock (number of live animals) 56,100 cattle, 47,500 pigs, 39,500 goats; roundwood (1991) 17,000 cu m; fish catch (1991) 8,444. Mining and quarrying (1988): pozzolana 240,000. Manufacturing (1993): cement 275,956; rum 65,921 hectolitres; raw sugar 50,084; other products include clothing, wooden furniture and posts, and metalware. Construction (buildings authorized; 1992): residential 358,474 sq m; nonresidential 160,084 sq m. Energy production (consumption): electricity (kW-hr; 1993) 958,700,000 (826,700,000); coal, none (none); crude petroleum, none (none); petroleum products (metric tons; 1992) none (341,000); natural gas, none (none).
Household income and expenditure. Average household size (1991) 3.4; income per household (1988) F 105,400 (U.S.$17,700); sources of income (1988): wages and salaries 78.9%, self employment 12.7%, transfer payments 8.4%; expenditure (1984–85): food and beverages 29.8%, housing, household furnishings, and energy 26.3%, transportation and communications 13.3%, clothing and footwear 8.2%, other 22.4%.
Gross national product (at current market prices; 1987): U.S.$1,170,000,000 (U.S.$3,200 per capita).

Structure of gross domestic product and labour force

	1989 in value F '000,000	1989 % of total value	1990 labour force	1990 % of labour force
Agriculture	1,177.4	9.2	8,391	4.9
Mining and manufacturing	758.4	5.9	9,630	5.6
Construction	949.3	7.4	13,976	8.2
Public utilities	38.7	0.3	...	...
Transportation and communications	773.3	6.1	6,950	4.1
Trade	2,499.6	19.6	15,020	8.8
Finance, real estate	848.8	6.6	26,533	15.5
Pub. admin., defense	4,242.4	33.2 }	37,025	21.6
Services	2,056.6	16.1 }		
Other	−563.3	−4.4[12]	53,500[13]	31.3[13]
TOTAL	12,781.2	100.0	171,025	100.0

Population economically active (1992): total 181,000; activity rate of total population 44.0% (participation rates [1990]: ages 15–64, 68.0%; female 45.5%; unemployed [1993] 22.2%).

Price and earnings indexes (1985 = 100)[14]

	1987	1988	1989	1990	1991	1992	1993
Consumer price index	104.9	106.9	109.9	114.0	116.0	117.6	119.8
Monthly earnings index[15]	102.0	105.0	107.0	112.2	114.4	115.8	117.6

Land use (1992): forested 38.9%; meadows and pastures 7.1%; agricultural and under permanent cultivation 18.1%; other 35.9%.

Foreign trade

Balance of trade (current prices)

	1988	1989	1990	1991	1992	1993
F '000,000	−6,260	−6,995	−8,439	−8,209	−7,505	−7,309
% of total	77.5%	83.8%	86.3%	79.8%	83.8%	83.2%

Imports (1993): F 8,044,223,000 (consumer goods 27.4%, food and agriculture products 23.4%, machinery and equipment 16.8%, transport vehicles and parts 11.3%). *Major import sources:* France 65.8%; other EEC 13.8%; United States 3.4%; Martinique 3.3%; Japan 2.5%.
Exports (1993): F 735,381,000 (agricultural products 74.7%, consumer goods 12.2%, machinery and equipment 6.4%, chemical products 2.2%). *Major export destinations:* France 78.0%; Martinique 14.1%; French Guiana 2.8%; other EEC 1.4%.

Transport and communications

Transport. Railroads: none. Roads (1992): total length 1,480 mi, 2,384 km (paved [1986] 80%). Vehicles (1985): passenger cars 95,962; trucks and buses 28,134. Merchant marine (1992): vessels (100 gross tons and over) 20; deadweight tonnage 4,430. Air transport (1992): passenger arrivals and departures 1,356,500; cargo loaded 8,677 metric tons, cargo unloaded 5,999 metric tons; airports (1994) with scheduled flights 6.
Communications. Daily newspapers (1993): total number 1; total circulation 25,000; circulation per 1,000 population 60. Radio (1993): total number of receivers 100,000 (1 per 4.2 persons). Television (1993): total number of receivers 150,000 (1 per 2.8 persons). Telephones (1992): 138,504 (1 per 3.0 persons).

Education and health

Education (1992–93)

	schools	teachers	students	student/teacher ratio
Primary (age 6–10)	340	3,135	39,075	12.5
Secondary (age 11–17) } Vocational	78	3,813	49,295	12.9
Higher[16]	1	310	4,296	13.9

Educational attainment (1982). Percentage of population age 25 and over having: no formal schooling 10.7%; primary education 54.6%; secondary 29.5%; higher 5.2%. *Literacy* (1982): total population age 15 and over literate 225,400 (90.1%); males literate 108,700 (89.7%); females literate 116,700 (90.5%).
Health (1991): physicians 590 (1 per 680 persons); hospital beds 3,230 (1 per 122 persons); infant mortality rate per 1,000 live births (1992) 10.4.
Food (1988–90): daily per capita caloric intake 2,777 (vegetable products 74%, animal products 26%); 115% of FAO recommended minimum requirement.

Military

Total active duty personnel (1992): 8,200 French troops[17].

---

[1]Comprises Basse-Terre 327 sq mi (848 sq km), pop. 149,943, and Îles des Saintes 5 sq mi (13 sq km), pop. 2,036. [2]Comprises Grande-Terre 228 sq mi (590 sq km), pop. 177,570; Marie-Galante 61 sq mi (158 sq km), pop. 13,463; La Désirade 8 sq mi (20 sq km), pop. 1,610; and the uninhabited Îles de la Petite-Terre. [3]Comprises the French part of Saint-Martin 20 sq mi (52 sq km), pop. 28,518; Saint-Barthélemy 8 sq mi (21 sq km), pop. 5,038; and the small, uninhabited island of Tintamarre. [4]Total area includes 29 sq mi (75 sq km) not allocated by arrondissement. [5]Preliminary; final 1990 census total was 386,987. [6]January 1. [7]Urban agglomeration. [8]Includes Les Abymes. [9]Includes external long-term private debt not guaranteed by the government. [10]1989. [11]Export only. [12]Less imputed bank service charges. [13]Unemployed. [14]Base and indexes are end of year unless footnoted. [15]Based on minimum-level wage of public employees. [16]University of Antilles–French Guiana, Guadeloupe campus. [17]Includes Martinique and French Guiana.

Guatemala

Official name: República de Guatemala (Republic of Guatemala).
Form of government: republic with one legislative house (Congress of the Republic [80]).
Head of state and government: President.
Capital: Guatemala City.
Official language: Spanish.
Official religion: none.
Monetary unit: 1 Guatemalan quetzal (Q) = 100 centavos; valuation (Oct. 7, 1994) 1 U.S.$ = Q 5.76; 1 £ = Q 9.17.

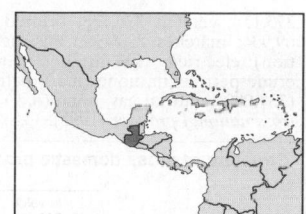

Area and population

Departments	Capitals	area sq mi	area sq km	population 1994 estimate[1]
Alta Verapaz	Cobán	3,354	8,686	650,127
Baja Verapaz	Salamá	1,206	3,124	200,019
Chimaltenango	Chimaltenango	764	1,979	374,898
Chiquimula	Chiquimula	017	2,376	260,079
El Progreso	Guastatoya (Progreso)	742	1,922	115,469
Escuintla	Escuintla	1,693	4,384	592,647
Guatemala	Guatemala City	821	2,126	2,188,652
Huehuetenango	Huehuetenango	2,857	7,400	790,183
Izabal	Puerto Barrios	3,490	9,038	359,056
Jalapa	Jalapa	797	2,063	206,355
Jutiapa	Jutiapa	1,243	3,219	378,661
Petén	Flores	13,843	35,854	295,169
Quetzaltenango	Quetzaltenango	753	1,951	606,556
Quiché	Santa Cruz del Quiché	3,235	8,378	631,785
Retalhuleu	Retalhuleu	717	1,856	261,136
Sacatepéquez	Antigua Guatemala	180	465	196,537
San Marcos	San Marcos	1,464	3,791	766,950
Santa Rosa	Cuilapa	1,141	2,955	285,456
Sololá	Sololá	410	1,061	265,902
Suchitepéquez	Mazatenango	969	2,510	392,703
Totonicapán	Totonicapán	410	1,061	324,225
Zacapa	Zacapa	1,039	2,690	171,146
TOTAL		42,042[2]	108,889	10,322,011

Demography

Population (1994): 10,322,000.
Density (1994): persons per sq mi 245.5, persons per sq km 94.8.
Urban-rural (1994): urban 38.5%; rural 61.5%.
Sex distribution (1990): male 50.52%; female 49.48%.
Age breakdown (1990): under 15, 45.4%; 15–29, 26.7%; 30–44, 14.6%; 45–59, 8.2%; 60–74, 4.1%; 75 and over, 1.0%.
Population projection: (2000) 12,222,000; (2010) 15,827,000.
Doubling time: 24 years.
Ethnic composition (1987): Amerindian 45%; Ladino (Hispanic/Amerindian) 45%; white 5%; black 2%; other mixed race and Chinese 3%.
Religious affiliation (1986): Roman Catholic c. 75%, of which Catholic/traditional syncretist c. 25%; Protestant (mostly fundamentalist) c. 25%.
Major cities (1994): Guatemala City 1,150,452; Mixco 413,002; Villa Nueva 154,508; Chinautla 59,349; Amatitlan 38,682.

Vital statistics

Birth rate per 1,000 population (1993): 36.2 (world avg. 26.0).
Death rate per 1,000 population (1993): 7.7 (world avg. 9.2).
Natural increase rate per 1,000 population (1993): 28.5 (world avg. 16.8).
Total fertility rate (avg. births per childbearing woman; 1993): 4.9.
Marriage rate per 1,000 population (1988): 5.4.
Divorce rate per 1,000 population (1988): 0.2.
Life expectancy at birth (1993): male 61.5 years; female 66.7 years.
Major causes of death per 100,000 population (1988): infectious and parasitic diseases 121.6; diseases of the respiratory system 110.8; perinatal causes 58.7; malnutrition 50.2; dehydration 18.5.

National economy

Budget (1992). Revenue: Q 5,524,000,000 (tax revenue 81.8%, of which taxes on goods and services 36.5%, customs duties 21.9%, income taxes 19.1%; nontax revenue 18.2%). Expenditures: Q 4,570,000,000 (1990: education 14.3%; defense 12.7%; transportation 8.2%; health 8.1%; agriculture 3.7%).
Tourism (1992): receipts from visitors U.S.$243,000,000; expenditures by nationals abroad U.S.$103,000,000.
Land use (1991): forested 33.8%; meadows and pastures 13.0%; agricultural and under permanent cultivation 17.4%; other 35.8%.
Production (metric tons except as noted). Agriculture, forestry, fishing (1992): sugarcane 9,788,000, corn (maize) 1,250,000, bananas 465,000, coffee 207,-000, tomatoes 140,000, dry beans 100,000, sorghum 80,000, plantains 56,000, seed cotton 55,000, cottonseed 29,000; livestock (number of live animals) 2,097,000 cattle, 1,110,000 pigs, 676,000 sheep; roundwood (1991) 8,409,000 cu m; fish catch (1991) 6,733. Mining and quarrying (1991): gypsum 51,519; iron ore 5,103; antimony ore 609. Manufacturing (value added in Q '000,000; 1989[3]): food products 138.0; beverages 66.2; clothing and footwear 47.6; textiles 43.2; metal products 30.2. Construction (value of buildings authorized in Q '000,000; 1991)[4]: residential 170.2; nonresidential 127.5. Energy production (consumption): electricity (kW-hr; 1991) 2,330,000,000 (2,330,000,000); crude petroleum (barrels; 1991) 1,226,000 (4,939,000); petroleum products (metric tons; 1991) 606,000 (973,000).
Gross national product (1993): U.S.$11,123,000,000 (U.S.$1,110 per capita).

Structure of gross domestic product and labour force

	1992 in value Q '000,000[3]	1992 % of total value	1990 labour force	1990 % of labour force
Agriculture	928.6	25.8	1,625,125	58.1
Mining	11.2	0.2	2,797	0.1
Manufacturing	537.1	14.9	380,408	13.6
Construction	74.1	2.0	114,682	4.1
Public utilities	101.1	2.5	8,391	0.3
Transp. and commun.	309.8	8.1	69,928	2.5
Trade	874.7	24.0	204,190	7.3
Finance, real estate	340.4	9.3	} 335,654	12.0
Pub. admin., defense	267.2	7.1		
Services	218.6	6.1		
Other	—	—	55,942[5]	2.0[5]
TOTAL	3,662.8	100.0	2,797,117	100.0

Public debt (external, outstanding; 1992): U.S.$2,104,000,000.
Population economically active (1990): total 2,797,117; activity rate of total population 31.4% (participation rates: ages 15–64, 46.5%; female [1989] 25.5%; unemployed 2.9%[6]).

Price and earnings indexes (1990 = 100)

	1987	1988	1989	1990	1991	1992	1993
Consumer price index	57.4	63.6	70.8	100.0	133.2	146.5	163.9
Annual earnings index[7]	54.7	73.3	86.9	100.0	126.6	162.1	...

Household income and expenditure. Average household size (1989) 5.4; income per household (1989) Q 4,306 (U.S.$1,529); sources of income: n.a.; expenditure (1981): food 64.4%, housing and energy 16.0%, transportation and communications 7.0%, household furnishings 5.0%, clothing 3.1%.

Foreign trade[8]

Balance of trade (current prices)

	1988	1989	1990	1991	1992	1993
U.S.$'000,000	−391.5	−389.2	−207.4	−197.3	−1,190.8	−1,096.2
% of total	16.1%	14.9%	8.0%	7.5%	35.7%	29.0%

Imports (1992): U.S.$2,462,757,400 (primary and intermediate materials for industry 41.5%, capital goods 22.4%, nondurable consumer goods 13.9%, petroleum 9.1%). *Major import sources:* United States 43.9%; Japan 6.0%; Mexico 5.8%; El Salvador 5.7%; Germany 4.6%; Venezuela 4.1%.
Exports (1992): U.S.$1,295,291,800 (coffee 19.2%, sugar 12.2%, bananas 8.0%, fish and other seafoods 3.5%, cardamon 2.5%). *Major export destinations:* United States 35.0%; El Salvador 14.1%; Costa Rica 6.9%; Nicaragua 4.8%; Honduras 4.7%; Mexico 4.3%.

Transport and communications

Transport. Railroads (1990)[9]: route length 570 mi, 917 km; passenger-km 10,099,000; metric ton-km cargo 42,700,000. Roads (1992): total length 7,477 mi, 12,033 km (paved 26%). Vehicles (1991): passenger cars 145,000; trucks and buses 105,000. Merchant marine (1992): vessels (100 gross tons and over) 8; total deadweight tonnage 353. Air transport (1991)[10]: passenger-km 230,000,000; metric ton-km cargo 9,200,000; airports (1994) 2.
Communications. Daily newspapers (1990): total number 5; total circulation 190,000; circulation per 1,000 population 21. Radio (1993): 400,000 receivers (1 per 25 persons). Television (1993): 475,000 receivers (1 per 21 persons). Telephones (1990): 250,000 (1 per 36 persons).

Education and health

Education (1991)

	schools	teachers	students	student/ teacher ratio
Primary (age 7–12)	9,362	36,757	1,249,413	34.0
Secondary (age 13–18)	1,274	13,588	207,935	15.3
Voc., teacher tr.	626	7,129	94,485	13.3
Higher[11]	5	4,346	69,532	16.0

Educational attainment (1989). Percentage of population age 25 and over having: no formal schooling 50.0%; incomplete primary education 21.6%; complete primary 16.2%; secondary 9.2%; higher 3.0%. *Literacy* (1989): total population age 15 and over literate 2,809,000 (60.3%); males literate 1,544,000 (69.7%); females literate 1,265,000 (51.7%).
Health (1987): physicians 3,579 (1 per 2,356 persons); hospital beds 13,667 (1 per 602 persons); infant mortality rate per 1,000 live births (1993) 55.6.
Food (1988–90): daily per capita caloric intake 2,254 (vegetable products 94%, animal products 6%); 103% of FAO recommended minimum requirement.

Military

Total active duty personnel (1993): 43,900 (army 95.7%, navy 2.7%, air force 1.6%). *Military expenditure as percentage of GNP* (1991): 1.0% (world 4.2%); per capita expenditure U.S.$9.

---

[1]Population of departments and cities taken from official projections based on 1973–81 intercensal growth rates and subsequent vital (birth and death) rates. [2]Detail does not add to total given because of rounding. [3]At prices of 1958. [4]Private construction in Guatemala City metropolitan area only. [5]Persons in activities not adequately defined. [6]Officially unemployed; 63% of economically active population is estimated to be underemployed. [7]Based on employees entitled to social security. [8]Import figures are f.o.b. in balance of trade and c.i.f. for commodities and trading partners. [9]Guatemala Railways only. [10]Aviateca Airlines only. [11]1989.

Guinea

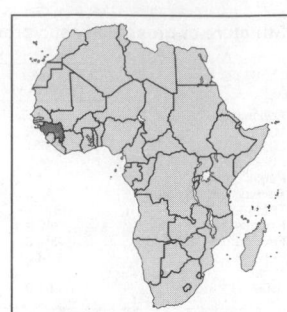

Official name: République de Guinée (Republic of Guinea).
Form of government: transitional government (composed of a 15-member Transitional Committee for National Recovery)[1].
Head of state and government: President[1].
Capital: Conakry.
Official language: French.
Official religion: none.
Monetary unit: 1 Guinean franc (GF) = 100 cauris; valuation (Oct. 7, 1994) 1 U.S.$ = GF 978.66; 1 £ = GF 1,557.

Area and population		area		population
				1983
Regions	Capitals	sq mi	sq km	census
Beyla	Beyla	6,738	17,452	161,347
Boffa	Boffa	1,932	5,003	141,719
Boké[2]	Boké	3,881	10,053	225,207
Conakry	Conakry	119	308	705,280
Coyah (Dubréka)	Coyah	2,153	5,576	134,190
Dabola	Dabola	2,317	6,000	97,986
Dalaba	Dalaba	1,313	3,400	132,802
Dinguiraye	Dinguiraye	4,247	11,000	133,502
Faranah[2]	Faranah	4,788	12,400	142,923
Forécariah	Forécariah	1,647	4,265	116,464
Fria	Fria	840	2,175	70,413
Gaoual	Gaoual	4,440	11,500	135,657
Guéckédou	Guéckédou	1,605	4,157	204,757
Kankan	Kankan	7,104	18,400	229,861
Kérouané	Kérouané	3,070	7,950	106,872
Kindia	Kindia	3,409	8,828	216,052
Kissidougou	Kissidougou	3,425	8,872	183,236
Koubia	Koubia	571	1,480	98,053
Koundara	Koundara	2,124	5,500	94,216
Kouroussa	Kouroussa	4,647	12,035	136,926
Labé	Labé	973	2,520	253,214
Lélouma	Lélouma	830	2,150	138,467
Lola	Lola	1,629	4,219	106,654
Macenta	Macenta	3,363	8,710	193,109
Mali	Mali	3,398	8,800	210,889
Mamou	Mamou	2,378	6,160	190,525
Mandiana	Mandiana	5,000	12,950	136,317
Nzérékoré	Nzérékoré	1,460	3,781	216,355
Pita	Pita	1,544	4,000	227,912
Siguiri	Siguiri	7,626	19,750	209,164
Télimélé	Télimélé	3,119	8,080	243,256
Tougué	Tougué	2,394	6,200	113,272
Yomou	Yomou	843	2,183	74,417
TOTAL		94,926[3]	245,857	5,781,014

Demography

Population (1994): 6,501,000.
Density (1994): persons per sq mi 68.5, persons per sq km 26.4.
Urban-rural (1990): urban 25.6%; rural 74.4%.
Sex distribution (1990): male 50.17%; female 49.83%.
Age breakdown (1990): under 15, 46.7%; 15–29, 25.9%; 30–44, 15.0%; 45–59, 8.0%; 60 and over, 4.4%.
Population projection: (2000) 8,879,000; (2010) 11,451,000.
Doubling time: 27 years.
Ethnic composition (1990): Fulani 40.3%; Malinke 25.8%; Susu 11.0%; Kissi 6.5%; Kpelle 4.8%; other 11.6%.
Religious affiliation (1988): Muslim 85.0%; traditional beliefs 5.0%; Christian 1.5%; other 8.5%.
Major cities (1983): Conakry 705,280; Kankan 88,760; Labé 65,439; Kindia 55,904.

Vital statistics

Birth rate per 1,000 population (1991): 47.0 (world avg. 26.0).
Death rate per 1,000 population (1991): 21.0 (world avg. 9.2).
Natural increase rate per 1,000 population (1991): 26.0 (world avg. 16.8).
Total fertility rate (avg. births per childbearing woman; 1990): 6.5.
Life expectancy at birth (1990–95): male 44.0 years; female 45.0 years.
Major causes of death per 100,000 population: n.a.; however, major diseases include malaria, venereal disease, tuberculosis, and measles.

National economy

Budget (1992). Revenue: GF 415,200,000,000 (mineral sector 46.3%; other 53.7%). Expenditures: GF 593,100,000,000 (capital spending 52.3%; current expenditure 47.7%, of which personnel 22.4%, services 14.7%).
Public debt (external, outstanding; 1992): U.S.$2,466,000,000.
Production (metric tons except as noted). Agriculture, forestry, fishing (1993): roots and tubers 997,000 (of which cassava 781,000, yams 73,000), rice 733,000, plantains 429,000, vegetables and melons 420,000, sugarcane 225,000, bananas 115,000, peanuts (groundnuts) 105,000, corn (maize) 95,000, pineapples 87,000, pulses 60,000, palm kernels 40,000, palm oil 40,000, coffee 29,000, coconuts 18,000, eggs 14,490; livestock (number of live animals) 1,650,000 cattle, 580,000 goats, 435,000 sheep, 33,000 pigs, 14,000,000 chickens; roundwood (1992) 4,235,000 cu m; fish catch (1991) 37,500. Mining and quarrying (1991): bauxite 17,800,000; alumina 640,000; diamonds 200,000 carats; gold 2,500 kg. Manufacturing (value of production in GF '000; 1985): corrugated and sheet iron 571,081; plastics 462,242; tobacco products

375,154; cement 326,138; printed matter 216,511; fruit juice 75,763; beer 69,934; matches 22,449. Construction: n.a. Energy production (consumption): electricity (kW-hr; 1992) 531,000,000 (531,000,000); coal, none (n.a.); crude petroleum, none (n.a.); petroleum products (metric tons; 1992) none (334,000); natural gas, none (n.a.).
Gross national product (1993): U.S.$3,260,000,000 (U.S.$520 per capita).

Structure of gross domestic product and labour force				
	1991		1983	
	in value GF '000,000,000	% of total value	labour force	% of labour force
Agriculture	506.38	23.2	1,423,615	78.2
Mining	480.74	22.0	12,241	0.7
Manufacturing	95.54	4.4	11,215	0.6
Construction	131.95	6.0	9,115	0.5
Public utilities	4.88	0.2	3,205	0.2
Transp. and commun.	107.78	4.9	29,496	1.6
Trade	518.30	23.8	37,309	2.0
Finance	110.97	5.1	3,556	0.2
Pub. admin., defense	192.60	8.8	137,600	7.5
Services	33.15	1.5		
Other			155,679	8.5
TOTAL	2,182.29	100.0[3]	1,823,031	100.0

Population economically active (1992): total 2,590,000; activity rate of total population 42.3% (participation rates [1983]: ages 15–64, 63.5%; female 39.4%; unemployed, n.a.).

Price index (1987 = 100)						
	1988	1989	1990	1991	1992	1993[4]
Consumer price index	129.6	163.3	194.2	233.1	...	...

Household income and expenditure. Average household size (1983) 6.7; average annual income per capita (1984) GS 7,660 (U.S.$305); sources of income: n.a.; expenditure (1985): food 61.5%, health care 11.2%, clothing and footwear 7.9%, housing and energy 7.3%, transportation 5.1%.
Land use (1992): forested 58.8%; meadows and pastures 22.4%; agricultural and under permanent cultivation 3.0%; other 15.8%.

Foreign trade[5]

Balance of trade (current prices)							
	1985	1986	1987	1988	1989	1990	1991
U.S.$'000,000	+111	+147	+120	+10	+146	+177	+33.2
% of total	11.0%	12.6%	9.6%	0.7%	10.6%	11.8%	2.7%

Imports (1990): U.S.$693,000,000 (1988; intermediate goods 33.7%, capital goods 13.1%, petroleum products 10.5%, food products 9.8%, consumer goods 9.7%). *Major import sources:* France 36.0%; U.S. 9.0%; Belgium-Luxembourg 9.0%; Germany 6.0%; Italy 5.0%.
Exports (1990): U.S.$788,000,000 (bauxite 56.9%, alumina 20.7%, diamonds 8.9%, gold 5.8%, coffee 4.5%, fish 1.8%). *Major export destinations:* U.S. 23.0%; France 14.0%; Germany 14.0%; Spain 13.0%; Ireland 9.0%.

Transport and communications

Transport. Railroads (1993): route length 411 mi, 662 km; (latest) passenger-mi 25,800,000, passenger-km 41,500,000; short ton-mi cargo 5,000,000, metric ton-km cargo 7,300,000. Roads (1992): total length 9,974 mi, 16,051 km (paved 4%). Vehicles (1992): passenger cars 23,155; trucks and buses 13,000. Merchant marine (1992): vessels (100 gross tons and over) 23; total deadweight tonnage 1,749. Air transport (1986): passenger-mi 17,873,000, passenger-km 28,764,000; short ton-mi cargo 1,684,000, metric ton-km cargo 2,458,000; airports (1994) with scheduled flights 2.
Communications. Daily newspapers (1988): 1; total circulation 13,000; circulation per 1,000 population 2.0. Radio (1993): 130,000 receivers (1 per 49 persons). Television (1993): 65,000 receivers (1 per 97 persons). Telephones (1991): 18,720 (1 per 317 persons).

Education and health

Education (1990)	schools	teachers	students	student/ teacher ratio
Primary (age 7–12)	2,476	8,699	346,807	39.9
Secondary (age 13–18)	225[6]	4,846	75,674	15.6
Voc., teacher tr.	35[6]	1,130	10,268	9.1
Higher	10[6]	805[7]	6,245[7]	7.8[7]

Educational attainment: n.a. *Literacy* (1990): percentage of total population age 15 and over literate 24.0%; males 34.9%; females 13.4%.
Health: physicians (1990) 773 (1 per 7,445 persons); hospital beds (1988) 3,382 (1 per 1,934 persons); infant mortality rate per 1,000 live births (1990–95) 134.
Food (1988–90): daily per capita caloric intake 2,242 (vegetable products 96%, animal products 4%); 97% of FAO recommended minimum requirement.

Military

Total active duty personnel (1994): 9,700 (army 87.6%, navy 4.1%, air force 8.3%). *Military expenditure as percentage of GNP* (1991): 1.3% (world 4.2%); per capita expenditure U.S.$5.

[1]Transitional government established January 1991 was to end with the advent of both the multiparty presidential elections held in December 1993 and legislative elections scheduled for December 1994. [2]The provinces of Boké and Faranah were abolished by presidential decree in January 1988. [3]Detail does not add to total given because of rounding. [4]Inflation, measured by the consumer price index, was 10.2% for the year ending March 31, 1993. [5]Imports c.i.f.; exports f.o.b. [6]1987–88. [7]Universities only.

Guinea-Bissau

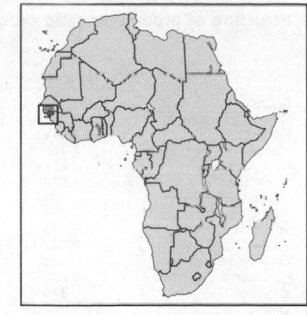

Official name: Répública da Guiné-Bissau (Republic of Guinea-Bissau).
Form of government: multiparty republic with one legislative house (National Assembly [100]).
Chief of state: President.
Head of government: Prime Minister.
Capital: Bissau.
Official language: Portuguese.
Official religion: none.
Monetary unit: 1 Guinea-Bissau peso (PG) = 100 centavos; valuation (Oct. 7, 1994) 1 U.S.$ = PG 12,484; 1 £ = PG 19,856.

Area and population

Regions	Capitals	area sq mi	area sq km	population 1979 census[1]
Bafatá	Bafatá	2,309	5,981	115,656
Biombo[2]	Bissau	324	840	51,796
Bolama	Bolama	1,013	2,624	25,449
Cacheu	Cacheu	1,998	5,175	127,514
Gabú	Gabú	3,533	9,150	103,683
Oio	Farim	2,086	5,403	131,271
Quinara	Fulacunda	1,212	3,138	35,567
Tombali	Catió	1,443	3,736	55,088
Autonomous Sector				
Bissau[2]	—	30	78	107,281
TOTAL		13,948	36,125	753,305

Demography

Population (1994): 1,050,000.
Density (1994): persons per sq mi 75.3, persons per sq km 29.1.
Urban-rural (1991): urban 20.3%; rural 79.7%.
Sex distribution (1990): male 49.17%; female 50.83%.
Age breakdown (1990): under 15, 40.9%; 15–29, 24.9%; 30–44, 16.7%; 45–59, 10.9%; 60–74, 5.6%; 75 and over, 1.0%.
Population projection: (2000) 1,192,000; (2010) 1,473,000.
Doubling time: 29 years.
Ethnic composition (1979): Balante 27.2%; Fulani 22.9%; Malinke 12.2%; Mandyako 10.6%; Pepel 10.0%; other 17.1%.
Religious affiliation (1992): traditional beliefs 54%; Muslim 38%; Christian 8%.
Major cities (1979): Bissau 125,000[3]; Bafatá 13,429; Gabú 7,803; Mansôa 5,390; Catió 5,179.

Vital statistics

Birth rate per 1,000 population (1991): 42.0 (world avg. 26.0); legitimate, n.a.; illegitimate, n.a.
Death rate per 1,000 population (1991): 18.0 (world avg. 9.2).
Natural increase rate per 1,000 population (1991): 24.0 (world avg. 16.8).
Total fertility rate (avg. births per childbearing woman; 1990): 6.0.
Marriage rate per 1,000 population: n.a.
Divorce rate per 1,000 population: n.a.
Life expectancy at birth (1990–95): male 41.9 years; female 45.1 years.
Major causes of death per 100,000 population: n.a.; however, major diseases include tuberculosis of the respiratory system, whooping cough, typhoid fever, cholera, bacillary dysentery and amebiasis, malaria, pneumonia, and meningococcal infections.

National economy

Budget (1989). Revenue: PG 42,740,000,000 (1988; tax revenue 43.7%, of which excise tax 15.4%, export duties 14.1%; grants from abroad 38.5%; nontax revenue 17.8%). Expenditures (1989): PG 190,431,000,000 (capital expenditures 61.4%[4]; current expenditures 38.6%).
Public debt (external, outstanding; 1992): U.S.$580,100,000.
Production (metric tons except as noted). Agriculture, forestry, fishing (1993): rice 126,000, fruits 66,000, roots and tubers (sweet potatoes and cassava) 65,000, plantains 34,000, cashews 30,000, millet 26,000, coconuts 25,000, vegetables 20,000, peanuts (groundnuts) 18,000, sorghum 14,000, corn (maize) 13,000, palm kernels 8,000, sugarcane 6,000, bananas 6,000, copra 5,000, palm oil 5,000, seed cotton 1,000; livestock (number of live animals) 475,000 cattle, 310,000 pigs, 270,000 goats, 255,000 sheep, 1,000,000 chickens; roundwood (1992) 572,000 cu m; fish catch (1991) 5,000. Mining and quarrying: extraction of construction materials only. Manufacturing (in PG '000,000; 1982): beverages 143.7, of which beer 122.3, orangeade and lemonade 14.5; clothing 14.0[5]; peanut oil 7.0; palm oil 2.4. Construction (value added in Esc[6]; 1987): 520,000,000. Energy production (consumption): electricity (kW-hr; 1992) 41,000,000 (41,000,000); coal, none (none); crude petroleum, none (none); petroleum products (metric tons; 1992) none (68,000); natural gas, none (none).
Population economically active (1992): total 461,000; activity rate of total population 45.8% (participation rates: ages 15–64 [1979] 41.0%; female 3.6%; unemployed, n.a.).

Price and earnings indexes (1990 = 100)

	1987	1988	1989	1990	1991	1992	1993
Consumer price index	25.9	41.6	75.2	100.0	157.6	267.3	395.8
Earnings index	...	...	...	...	...	...	...

Gross national product (at current market prices; 1993): U.S.$241,700,000 (U.S.$233 per capita).

Structure of gross domestic product and labour force

	1993 in value U.S.$'000,000	1993 % of total value	1991 labour force	1991 % of labour force
Agriculture	111.2	46.0	362,000	78.0
Mining	} 29.0	} 12.0	} 21,000	} 4.5
Manufacturing				
Construction				
Public utilities				
Transportation and communications				
Trade	} 101.5	} 42.0	} 81,000	} 17.5
Finance				
Pub. admin., defense				
Services				
Other				
TOTAL	241.7	100.0	464,000	100.0

Tourism: n.a.
Land use (1992): forested 38.1%; meadows and pastures 38.4%; agricultural and under permanent cultivation 12.1%; other 11.4%.
Household income and expenditure. Average household size (1981) 4.1; income per household: n.a.; sources of income: n.a.; expenditure: n.a.

Foreign trade

Balance of trade (current prices)

	1988	1989	1990	1991	1992	1993
PG'000,000	−46,297	−96,304	−120,821	−166,698	−530,592	−378,141
% of total	56.7%	65.2%	58.9%	52.7%	85.5%	54.0%

Imports (1991): U.S.$90,000,000 (1988; transport equipment 28.7%, building materials 17.9%, foodstuffs 8.6%, fuel and lubricants 8.6%, other 36.2%). *Major import sources* (1989): Italy 27.3%; Portugal 23.0%; Thailand 7.6%; The Netherlands 7.2%; France 4.3%; Senegal 4.2%; U.S.S.R. 3.0%.
Exports (1991): U.S.$23,000,000 (1988; cashews 52.8%, peanuts [groundnuts] 11.3%, frozen fish 3.1%). *Major export destinations* (1989): Portugal 34.4%; Spain 19.2%; France 18.1%; Japan 6.7%; The Netherlands 6.1%; Italy 6.0%; Belgium-Luxembourg 4.5%.

Transport and communications

Transport. Railroads: none. Roads (1991): total length 2,579 mi, 4,150 km (paved 9%). Vehicles (1992): passenger cars 3,500; trucks and buses 2,500. Merchant marine (1992): vessels (100 gross tons and over) 19; total deadweight tonnage 1,846. Air transport (1985): passenger-mi 6,000,000, passenger-km 9,000,000; short ton-mi cargo 700,000, metric ton-km cargo 1,000,000; airports (1994) with scheduled flights 2.
Communications. Daily newspapers (1990): total number 1; total circulation 6,000; circulation per 1,000 population 6. Radio (1993): total number of receivers 40,000 (1 per 26 persons). Television: n.a. Telephones (1991): 15,000 (1 per 67 persons).

Education and health

Education (1988)

	schools	teachers	students	student/ teacher ratio
Primary (age 7–13)	632[7]	3,065[7]	79,035	24.6[7]
Secondary (age 13–18)	12[8]	824[8]	5,505	7.8[8]
Voc., teacher tr.	4[7]	107	825	7.7

Educational attainment (1979). Percentage of population age 7 and over having: no formal schooling or knowledge of reading and writing 90.4%; primary education 7.9%; secondary 1.0%; technical 0.5%; higher 0.2%.
Literacy (1990): total population age 15 and over literate 211,200 (36.5%); males literate 138,800 (50.2%); females literate 72,400 (24.0%).
Health (1986): physicians 274 (1 per 3,263 persons); hospital beds 2,430 (1 per 368 persons); infant mortality rate per 1,000 live births (1990–95) 140.
Food (1984–86): daily per capita caloric intake 2,278 (vegetable products 93%, animal products 7%); 84% of FAO recommended minimum requirement.

Military

Total active duty personnel (1994): 7,250 (army 93.8%, navy 4.8%, air force 1.4%). *Military expenditure as percentage of GNP* (1987): 2.4% (world 5.4%); per capita expenditure U.S.$6.

---

[1]Preliminary. [2]Biombo region excludes Bissau city. [3]1988. [4]In 1987 capital expenditures were divided: economic affairs 40%, of which agriculture, forestry, and fishing 20.1%; general public services 25.5%; health 5.4%; education 5.2%; defense 4.4%. [5]Production figure for first three quarters only. [6]Esc is the abbreviation for Portuguese escudo. [7]1987. [8]1986.

Guyana

Official name: Co-operative Republic of Guyana.
Form of government: unitary multiparty republic with one legislative house (National Assembly [65[1]]).
Head of state and government: President.
Capital: Georgetown.
Official language: English.
Official religion: none.
Monetary unit: 1 Guyana dollar (G$) = 100 cents; valuation (Oct. 7, 1994) 1 U.S.$ = G$142.13; 1 £ = G$226.06.

Area and population

Administrative Regions	Capitals	area sq mi	area sq km	population 1986 estimate
Region 1 (Barima/Waini)	Mabaruma	7,853	20,339	18,516
Region 2 (Pomeroon/Supenaam)	Anna Regina	2,392	6,195	41,966
Region 3 (Essequibo Islands/West Demerara)	Vreed-en-Hoop	1,450	3,755	102,760
Region 4 (Demerara/Mahaica)	Paradise	862	2,233	310,758
Region 5 (Mahaica/Berbice)	Fort Wellington	1,610	4,170	55,556
Region 6 (East Berbice/Corentyne)	New Amsterdam	13,998	36,255	148,967
Region 7 (Cuyuni/Mazaruni)	Bartica	18,229	47,213	17,941
Region 8 (Potaro/Siparuni)	Mahdia	7,742	20,052	5,672
Region 9 (Upper Takutu/Upper Essequibo)	Lethem	22,313	57,790	15,338
Region 10 (Upper Demerara/Berbice)	Linden	6,595	17,081	38,598
TOTAL		83,044[2]	215,083[2]	756,072[3]

Demography

Population (1994): 733,000.
Density (1994)[4]: persons per sq mi 9.6, persons per sq km 3.7.
Urban-rural (1992–93): urban 31.0%; rural 69.0%.
Sex distribution (1990): male 49.50%; female 50.50%.
Age breakdown (1990): under 15, 33.4%; 15–29, 33.2%; 30–44, 18.8%; 45–59, 8.7%; 60–74, 4.6%; 75 and over, 1.3%.
Population projection: (2000) 710,000; (2010) 767,000.
Doubling time: 54 years[5].
Ethnic composition (1992–93): East Indian 49.4%; black (African Negro and Bush Negro) 35.6%; mixed 7.1%; Amerindian 6.8%; Portuguese 0.7%; Chinese 0.4%.
Religious affiliation (1990): Christian 52.0%, of which Protestant 34.0% (including Anglican 17.0%), Roman Catholic 18.0%; Hindu 34.0%; Muslim 9.0%; other 5.0%.
Major cities (1985): Georgetown 195,000; Linden 30,000; New Amsterdam 20,000.

Vital statistics

Birth rate per 1,000 population (1994): 20.0 (world avg. 26.0).
Death rate per 1,000 population (1994): 7.0 (world avg. 9.2).
Natural increase rate per 1,000 population (1994): 13.0 (world avg. 16.8).
Total fertility rate (avg. births per childbearing woman; 1992): 2.6.
Marriage rate per 1,000 population: n.a.
Divorce rate per 1,000 population: n.a.
Life expectancy at birth (1994): male 62.0 years; female 68.0 years.
Major causes of death per 100,000 population (1984): diseases of the circulatory system 202.5, of which cerebrovascular disease 79.0; diseases of the digestive system 74.0; accidents and violence 56.5; diseases of the respiratory system 39.8; malignant neoplasms (cancers) 37.1.

National economy

Budget (1993–94). Revenue: G$25,966,000,000 (current revenue 87.3%, of which consumption taxes 25.2%, income taxes on companies 17.0%, import duties 10.3%, personal income taxes 10.2%; development revenue 12.7%, of which external grants 4.9%). Expenditures: G$29,292,000,000 (current expenditure 74.3%, of which interest payments on debt 33.4%, personal emoluments 12.2%; development expenditure 25.7%).
Production (metric tons except as noted). Agriculture, forestry, fishing (1993): raw sugar 246,500, rice 210,200, coconuts 48,000, roots and tubers 32,000, plantains 23,000, bananas 21,000, oranges 15,000; livestock (number of live animals) 160,000 cattle, 130,000 sheep, 79,000 goats; roundwood 237,000 cu m; fish catch 37,100, of which shrimps and prawns 4,700. Mining and quarrying (1993): bauxite 897,300; gold 309,800 troy oz; diamonds 44,700 carats[6]. Manufacturing (1993): flour 35,800; rum 252,000 hectolitres; beer and stout 145,000 hectolitres; cigarettes 302,000,000 units; refrigerators 4,779 units; pharmaceuticals 11,700,000 tablets; other products include cotton cloth and dyed and printed fabrics. Construction: n.a. Energy production (consumption): electricity (kW-hr; 1992) 235,000,000 (235,000,000); coal, none (none); crude petroleum, none (none); petroleum products (metric tons; 1992) none (272,000); natural gas, none (none).
Tourism: receipts from visitors (1992) U.S.$31,000,000; expenditures by nationals abroad, n.a.
Household income and expenditure. Average household size (1980) 5.1; income per household: n.a.; sources of income: n.a.; expenditure (1970)[7]: food, beverages, and tobacco 42.5%, rent and water 21.4%, clothing and footwear 8.6%, education and recreation 6.4%, fuel and light 5.2%, other 15.9%.
Gross national product (at current market prices; 1993): U.S.$268,000,000[8] (U.S.$330[8] per capita).

Structure of gross domestic product and labour force

	1993 in value G$'000,000[9]	1993 % of total value	1980 labour force	1980 % of labour force
Sugar	11,139	23.6		
Other agriculture, forestry	7,203	15.3 }	50,316	20.4
Fishing	3,344	7.1		
Mining	8,150	17.3	9,669	3.9
Manufacturing	1,977[10]	4.2[10]	28,980	11.8
Construction	1,673	3.6	7,024	2.8
Public utilities	10	10	2,850	1.2
Transportation and communications	2,645	5.6	9,412	3.8
Trade	2,323	4.9	15,231	6.2
Finance, real estate	3,922	8.3	2,944	1.2
Pub. admin., defense	3,996	8.5	29,948	12.1
Services	746	1.6	29,295	11.9
Other	—	—	61,002[11]	24.7[11]
TOTAL	47,118	100.0	246,671	100.0

Public debt (external, outstanding; 1992): U.S.$1,665,000,000.
Population economically active (1987): total 270,074; activity rate of total population 35.7% (participation rates: ages 15–64, 60.4%; female 29.9%; unemployed [end of 1991] 13.5%).

Price and earnings indexes (1990 = 100)

	1987	1988	1989	1990	1991	1992
Consumer price index	66.3	92.7	96.4	100.0	102.3	104.9
Earnings index	...	...	...	...	...	...

Land use (1992): forested 83.2%; meadows and pastures 6.2%; agricultural and under permanent cultivation 2.5%; other 8.1%.

Foreign trade[12]

Balance of trade (current prices)

	1988	1989	1990	1991	1992	1993
G$'000,000	+197	−777	−1,691	−4,444	−7,623	−7,754
% of total	4.4%	5.9%	7.4%	6.9%	7.4%	7.4%

Imports (1993): G$61,376,000,000 (capital goods 35.0%, of which transportation 9.7%, agricultural 7.8%; consumer goods 21.3%; fuels and lubricants 16.7%). Major import sources (1992)[13]: United States 37.0%; Trinidad and Tobago 13.0%; United Kingdom 11.0%; Italy 8.0%; Japan 4.0%.
Exports (1993): G$53,622,000,000 (domestic exports 97.3%, of which sugar 27.6%, gold 23.8%, bauxite 21.5%, rice 7.7%, shrimps 2.7%, rum 2.2%; reexports 2.7%). Major export destinations (1992)[13]: United Kingdom 33.0%; United States 30.0%; Canada 9.0%; France 5.0%.

Transport and communications

Transport. Railroads: length (1991) 116 mi, 187 km. Roads (1993): total length 4,474 mi, 7,200 km (paved 10%). Vehicles (1991): passenger cars 24,000; trucks and buses 9,000. Merchant marine (1992): vessels (100 gross tons and over) 82; total deadweight tonnage 13,509. Air transport (1993): passenger-mi 229,000,000, passenger-km 369,000,000; short ton-mi cargo 1,900,000[14], metric ton-km cargo 2,800,000[14]; airports (1994) with scheduled flights 1[15].
Communications. Daily newspapers (1992): total number 2; total circulation 78,000; circulation per 1,000 population 106. Radio (1993): total number of receivers 310,000 (1 per 2.4 persons). Television (1993): total number of receivers 15,000 (1 per 49 persons). Telephones (1990): 16,003 (1 per 46 persons).

Education and health

Education (1989–90)

	schools	teachers	students	student/ teacher ratio
Primary (age 6–11)	423	4,010[16]	118,015[16]	...
Secondary (age 12–17)	93	...	72,096[16]	...
Voc., teacher tr.	8	176	5,388	30.6
Higher[17, 18]	1	220	2,297	10.4

Educational attainment (1980). Percentage of population age 25 and over having: no formal schooling 8.1%; primary education 72.8%; secondary 17.3%; higher 1.8%. Literacy (1990): total population age 15 and over literate, c. 490,000 (96.4%); males literate, c. 245,000 (97.5%); females literate, c. 245,000 (95.4%).
Health: physicians (1990) 286 (1 per 2,552 persons); hospital beds (1987) 2,204 (1 per 341 persons); infant mortality rate per 1,000 live births (1994) 49.0.
Food (1988–90): daily per capita caloric intake 2,495 (vegetable products 86%, animal products 14%); 110% of FAO recommended minimum requirement.

Military

Total active duty personnel (1994): 1,700 (army 82.3%, navy 11.8%, air force 5.9%). Military expenditure as percentage of GNP (1991): 1.1% (world 4.2%); per capita expenditure U.S.$4.

---

[1]Includes 12 indirectly elected seats. [2]Includes inland water area equaling c. 7,000 sq mi (c. 18,000 sq km). [3]Official estimate of June 1992 was 733,236. [4]Based on land area only. [5]Net migration nearly equals natural-increase rate. [6]1992. [7]Weights of consumer price index components for Georgetown, New Amsterdam, and Linden only. [8]Excludes considerable illegal and quasi-legal economic activity. [9]At factor cost. [10]Manufacturing includes Public utilities. [11]Represents "not stated." [12]Imports c.i.f.; exports f.o.b. [13]Estimated figures. [14]1991. [15]International only; domestic air service is provided on a charter basis. [16]1988–89. [17]University of Guyana only. [18]1992–93.

Haiti

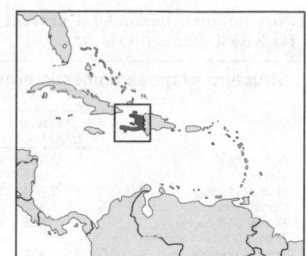

Official name: Repiblik Dayti (Haitian Creole); République d'Haïti (French) (Republic of Haiti).
Form of government: multiparty republic[1] with two legislative houses (Senate [27]; Chamber of Deputies [83])[2].
Chief of state: President.
Head of government: Prime Minister.
Capital: Port-au-Prince.
Official languages: Haitian Creole; French.
Official religion: none[3].
Monetary unit: 1 gourde (G) – 100 centimes; valuation (Oct. 7, 1994) 1 U.S.$ = G 19.02; 1 £ = G 30.25.

Area and population

Departements	Capitals	area[4] sq mi	area[4] sq km	population 1992 estimate
Artibonite	Gonaïves	1,924	4,984	961,447
Centre	Hinche	1,419	3,675	467,514
Grande Anse	Jérémie	1,278	3,310	616,151
Nord	Cap-Haïtien	813	2,106	724,084
Nord-Est	Fort-Liberté	697	1,805	239,734
Nord-Ouest	Port-de-Paix	840	2,176	395,442
Ouest	Port-au-Prince	1,864	4,827	2,285,044
Sud	Les Cayes	1,079	2,794	630,007
Sud-Est	Jacmel	781	2,023	444,323
TOTAL		10,695	27,700	6,763,746[5]

Demography

Population (1994): 6,491,000.
Density (1994): persons per sq mi 606.9, persons per sq km 234.3.
Urban-rural (1990): urban 30.3%; rural 69.7%.
Sex distribution (1990): male 49.03%; female 50.97%.
Age breakdown (1990): under 15, 40.2%; 15–29, 27.7%; 30–44, 16.3%; 45–59, 9.6%; 60–74, 4.9%; 75 and over, 1.3%.
Population projection: (2000) 7,102,000; (2010) 8,121,000.
Doubling time: 33 years.
Ethnic composition (1985): black 95.0%; mulatto 4.9%; white 0.1%.
Religious affiliation (1982): Roman Catholic 80.3%[6]; Protestant 15.8%, of which Baptist 9.7%, Pentecostal 3.6%; nonreligious 1.2%; other 2.7%.
Major cities (1992): Port-au-Prince 752,600 (metropolitan area 1,255,078); Carrefour 241,223[7]; Delmas 200,251[7]; Cap-Haïtien 92,122; Gonaïves 63,291.

Vital statistics

Birth rate per 1,000 population (1994): 40.0 (world avg. 26.0).
Death rate per 1,000 population (1994): 19.0 (world avg. 9.2).
Natural increase rate per 1,000 population (1994): 21.0 (world avg. 16.8).
Total fertility rate (avg. births per childbearing woman; 1992): 4.7.
Marriage rate per 1,000 population: n.a.
Divorce rate per 1,000 population: n.a.
Life expectancy at birth (1994): male 43.0 years; female 47.0 years.
Major causes of death per 100,000 population (1982)[8]: infectious and parasitic diseases 46.0; diseases of the circulatory system 11.9; diseases associated with malnutrition 8.5; diseases of the respiratory system 8.3; endocrine and metabolic disorders 8.0; ill-defined conditions 115.2.

National economy

Budget (1992). Revenue: G 1,106,200,000 (excises 17.0%; general sales taxes 16.7%; import duties 15.4%; income taxes 14.6%). Expenditures: G 1,835,700,000 (current expenditures 97.1%, of which extrabudgetary 40.5%; development expenditure 2.9%).
Tourism: receipts from visitors (1992) U.S.$46,000,000; expenditures by nationals abroad (1991–92) U.S.$21,000,000.
Production (metric tons except as noted). Agriculture, forestry, fishing (1993): sugarcane 2,250,000, plantains 270,000, mangoes 230,000, bananas 230,000, corn (maize) 200,000, sweet potatoes 190,000, rice 105,000, sorghum 80,000, dry beans 50,000, coffee 34,000, oranges 26,000, lemons and limes 22,000, sisal 8,000, cacao 3,000; livestock (number of live animals) 910,000 goats, 800,000 cattle, 200,000 pigs; roundwood (1992) 6,051,000 cu m; fish catch (1992) 5,000. Mining and quarrying (1992): limestone 220,000; marble 500 cu m. Manufacturing (1992–93): cement 84,000; essential oils (mostly amyris, neroli, and vetiver) 227; cigarettes 953,000,000 units; beer 4,300,000 units; articles assembled for reexport (export value in U.S.$'000,000) 104.4, of which garments 76.3, sports equipment and toys 9.9, electronic components 8.1, luggage and handbags 2.7. Construction: n.a. Energy production (consumption): electricity (kW·hr; 1992–93) 412,700,000 (227,700,000); coal, none (none); crude petroleum, none (none); petroleum products (metric tons; 1992) none (223,000); natural gas, none (none).
Population economically active (1990): total 2,679,140; activity rate of total population 41.1% (participation rates: ages 15–64, 64.8%; female 40.0%; unemployed [1993] unofficially 70.0%).

Price and earnings indexes (1985 = 100)

	1987	1988	1989	1990	1991	1992	1993
Consumer price index	91.5	95.2	101.8	123.7	142.8	162.3	207.2[9]
Annual earnings index	100.0	100.0	108.4	...	...	...	...

Household income and expenditure. Average household size (1982) 4.4; average annual income of wage earners (1984): urban (G 1,545 [U.S.$309]), rural (G 629 [U.S.$126]); expenditure (1986–87)[10]: food, beverages, and tobacco 51.1%, household furnishings 9.2%, clothing and footwear 8.7%, transportation and communications 7.6%.
Gross national product (1992): U.S.$2,479,000,000 (U.S.$370 per capita).

Structure of gross domestic product and labour force

	1992 in value G '000,000[11]	1992 % of total value	1990 labour force	1990 % of labour force
Agriculture	1,689	36.7	1,535,444	57.3
Mining	6	0.1	24,012	0.9
Manufacturing	504	11.0	151,387	5.6
Construction	208	4.5	28,001	1.0
Public utilities	40	0.9	2,577	0.1
Transp. and commun.	93	2.0	20,691	0.8
Trade, restaurants	747	16.2	352,970	13.2
Finance, real estate	341	7.4	5,057	0.2
Pub. admin., defense	774	16.8	} 155,347	5.8
Services	182	4.0		
Other	17[12]	0.4[12]	403,654[13]	15.1[13]
TOTAL	4,601	100.0	2,679,140	100.0

Public debt (external, outstanding; 1992): U.S.$625,900,000.
Land use (1992): forested 1.3%; meadows and pastures 18.0%; agricultural and under permanent cultivation 33.0%; other 47.7%.

Foreign trade[14, 15]

Balance of trade (current prices)

	1987–88	1988–89	1989–90	1990–91	1991–92	1992–93
U.S.$'000,000	– 201.4	– 162.9	– 172.4	– 156.1	– 221.1	– 192.0
% of total	42.2%	34.8%	33.8%	35.9%	43.9%	57.6%

Imports (1992–93): U.S.$262,200,000 (food and live animals 34.3%, mineral fuels 24.2%, basic manufactures 11.5%, chemicals and chemical products 8.7%). *Major import sources* (1992)[16]: United States 56.0%; Netherlands Antilles 7.0%; Malaysia 6.0%; France 4.0%; United Kingdom 3.0%.
Exports (1992–93): U.S.$70,200,000 (local manufactures—mostly processed foods, electrical equipment, textiles, and clothing—65.6%, coffee 10.4%, essential oils 7.8%, wood and sisal handicrafts 6.6%, sisal and twine 2.6%). *Major export destinations* (1992)[16]: United States 75.0%; France 7.0%; Italy 5.0%; Germany 4.0%.

Transport and communications

Transport. Railroad (1990)[17]: route length 25 mi, 40 km. Roads (1990): total length 2,485 mi, 4,000 km (paved 24%). Vehicles (1992): passenger cars 33,000; trucks and buses 22,000. Merchant marine (1992): vessels (100 gross tons and over) 4; total deadweight tonnage 429. Air transport (1991)[18]: passenger arrivals and departures 545,000; cargo unloaded and loaded 21,100 metric tons; airports (1994) with scheduled flights 1.
Communications. Daily newspapers (1992): total number 4; total circulation 45,000; circulation per 1,000 population 7.2. Radio (1993): total number of receivers 3,000,000 (1 per 2.1 persons). Television (1993): total number of receivers 25,000 (1 per 255 persons). Telephones (1990): 82,000 (1 per 79 persons).

Education and health

Education (1992–93)

	schools	teachers	students	student/ teacher ratio
Primary (age 6–12)	7,306[19]	27,607	787,553	28.5
Secondary (age 13–18) } Voc., teacher tr.	...	10,174	193,624	19.0
Higher[20]	2	554	6,678	12.1

Educational attainment (1982). Percentage of population age 25 and over having: no formal schooling 59.5%; primary education 27.6%; secondary 8.6%; vocational and teacher training 0.7%; higher 0.7%; unknown 2.9%.
Literacy (1990): total population age 15 and over literate 2,096,900 (53.0%); males literate 1,128,000 (59.1%); females literate 968,000 (47.4%).
Health (1992): physicians 623 (1 per 10,060 persons); hospital beds 5,192 (1 per 1,207 persons); infant mortality rate per 1,000 live births (1994) 109.0.
Food (1988–90): daily per capita caloric intake 2,005 (vegetable products 89%, animal products 11%); 89% of FAO recommended minimum requirement.

Military

Total active duty personnel (1994): 7,300 (army 95.8%, navy 2.1%, air force 2.1%). *Military expenditure as percentage of GNP* (1991): 2.0% (world 4.2%); per capita expenditure U.S.$8.

[1]UN-brokered agreement of July 1993 to end military rule (begun September 1991) was not put into effect until October 1994. [2]New legislative elections planned for March 1995. [3]Roman Catholicism has special recognition. [4]Estimated. [5]Official population projection based on 1982 census. [6]About 80% of all Roman Catholics also practice voodoo. [7]Within Port-au-Prince metropolitan area. [8]Public health facilities only. [9]July. [10]Based on nationwide sample survey of 3,120 households. [11]At prices of 1976. [12]Import duties. [13]Includes 63,975 not adequately defined and 339,679 officially unemployed. [14]The import and export value of preassembled and assembled U.S.-made components is excluded. Virtually all components used in the export assembly plants are imported. [15]Import figures c.i.f., export figures f.o.b. for fiscal year ending March 31. [16]Estimated figures. [17]The only railway is privately owned and used intermittently to haul sugarcane. [18]Port-au-Prince Airport only. [19]1990–91. [20]Port-au-Prince universities only.

Honduras

Official name: República de Honduras
(Republic of Honduras).
Form of government: multiparty
republic with one legislative house
(Congress [128]).
Head of state and government:
President.
Capital: Tegucigalpa[1].
Official language: Spanish.
Official religion: none.
Monetary unit: 1 Honduran lempira
(L) = 100 centavos; valuation (Oct. 7,
1994) 1 U.S.$ = L 8.91; 1 £ = L 14.17.

Area and population

Departments	Administrative centres	area sq mi	sq km	population 1991 estimate
Atlántida	La Ceiba	1,641	4,251	255,000
Choluteca	Choluteca	1,626	4,211	309,000
Colón	Trujillo	3,427	8,875	164,000
Comayagua	Comayagua	2,006	5,196	257,000
Copán	Santa Rosa de Copán	1,237	3,203	226,000
Cortés	San Pedro Sula	1,527	3,954	706,000
El Paraíso	Yuscarán	2,787	7,218	277,000
Francisco Morazán	Tegucigalpa	3,068	7,946	878,000
Gracias a Dios	Puerto Lempira	6,421	16,630	37,000
Intibucá	La Esperanza	1,186	3,072	130,000
Islas de la Bahía	Roatán	100	261	24,000
La Paz	La Paz	900	2,331	112,000
Lempira	Gracias	1,656	4,290	180,000
Ocotepeque	Nueva Ocotepeque	649	1,680	77,000
Olancho	Juticalpa	9,402	24,351	309,000
Santa Bárbara	Santa Bárbara	1,975	5,115	291,000
Valle	Nacaome	604	1,565	121,000
Yoro	Yoro	3,065	7,939	355,000
TOTAL		43,277	112,088	4,708,000

Demography

Population (1994): 5,302,000.
Density (1994): persons per sq mi 122.5, persons per sq km 47.3.
Urban-rural (1992): urban 41.7%; rural 58.3%.
Sex distribution (1990): male 50.07%; female 49.93%.
Age breakdown (1990): under 15, 44.6%; 15–29, 28.3%; 30–44, 14.4%; 45–59,
7.8%; 60–74, 3.9%; 75 and over, 1.0%.
Population projection: (2000) 6,251,000; (2010) 7,890,000.
Doubling time: 24 years.
Ethnic composition (1987): mestizo 89.9%; Amerindian 6.7%; black (including
Black Carib) 2.1%; white 1.3%.
Religious affiliation (1986): Roman Catholic 85.0%; Protestant (mostly fun-
damentalist, Moravian, and Methodist) 10.0%; other 5.0%.
Major cities (1992): Tegucigalpa 703,500[2]; San Pedro Sula 339,600; La Ceiba
79,900; El Progreso 73,600; Choluteca 66,200.

Vital statistics

Birth rate per 1,000 population (1993): 35.8 (world avg. 26.0); legitimate, n.a.;
illegitimate, n.a.
Death rate per 1,000 population (1993): 6.4 (world avg. 9.2).
Natural increase rate per 1,000 population (1993): 29.4 (world avg. 16.8).
Total fertility rate (avg. births per childbearing woman; 1993): 4.9.
Marriage rate per 1,000 population (1983): 4.9.
Divorce rate per 1,000 population (1983): 0.4.
Life expectancy at birth (1993): male 64.8 years; female 69.2 years.
Major causes of death per 100,000 population (1983): diseases of the cir-
culatory system 48.4; infectious and parasitic diseases 46.6; accidents and
violence 42.2; diseases of the respiratory system 26.3.

National economy

Budget (1992). Revenue: L 5,621,400,000 (current revenue 97.3%, of which
taxes on production and consumption 20.7%, income taxes 15.3%, import
duties 14.3%; capital revenue 2.7%). Expenditures: L 6,440,800,000 (current
expenditure 69.0%; capital expenditure 15.9%; public-debt service 15.1%).
Public debt (external, outstanding; 1992): U.S.$3,192,000,000.
Production (metric tons except as noted). Agriculture, forestry, fishing (1992):
sugarcane 3,004,000, bananas 1,086,000, corn (maize) 582,000, plantains
182,000, coffee 135,000, palm oil 78,000, sorghum 69,000, dry beans 46,000,
rice 41,000; livestock (number of live animals) 2,351,000 cattle, 750,000 pigs;
roundwood (1991) 6,288,000 cu m; fish catch (1991) 20,989. Mining and
quarrying (1991): zinc concentrate 38,280; lead (metal content) 8,719. Manufacturing (1992): cement 760,000; raw sugar 395,000; wheat flour 209,000;
beer 5,778,000 hectolitres; milk 594,000 hectolitres; cigarettes 2,145,000,000
units. Construction (value of private construction in L '000,000; 1992)[3]:
residential 151.4; nonresidential 126.3. Energy production (consumption):
electricity (kW-hr; 1991) 1,105,000,000 (1,273,000,000); coal, none (none);
crude petroleum (barrels; 1991) none (1,906,000); petroleum products (metric tons; 1991) 244,000 (512,000); natural gas, none (none).
Household income and expenditure. Average household size (1988) 5.4; income per household: n.a.; sources of income (1985): wages and salaries
58.8%, transfer payments 1.8%, other 39.4%; expenditure (1986): food
44.4%, utilities and housing 22.4%, clothing and footwear 9.0%, household
furnishings 8.3%, health care 7.0%, transportation and communications
3.0%, other 5.9%.

Gross national product (at current market prices; 1992): U.S.$3,142,000,000
(U.S.$580 per capita).

Structure of gross domestic product and labour force

	1992 in value L '000,000[4]	% of total value	labour force	% of labour force
Agriculture	3,491	22.0	718,100	45.3
Mining	302	1.9	4,100	0.3
Manufacturing	2,724	17.2	187,100	11.8
Construction	1,042	6.6	95,400	6.0
Public utilities	528	3.3	11,200	0.7
Transportation and communications	954	6.0	44,600	2.8
Trade	1,755	11.0	165,100	10.4
Finance, real estate	2,278	14.4	29,900	1.9
Public admin., defense	1,177	7.4 }		20.8
Services	1,612	10.2 }	330,900	
TOTAL	15,863	100.0	1,586,400	100.0

Population economically active (1992): total 1,586,400; activity rate of total
population 31.2% (participation rates: over age 15, 58.3%; female 31.7%;
unemployed [1990] 40.0%).

Price and earnings indexes (1985 = 100)

	1987	1988	1989	1990	1991	1992	1993
Consumer price index	106.9	111.8	122.8	151.4	202.8	220.6	244.3
Weekly earnings index[5]	100.0	100.0	100.0	100.0	132.9	151.1	...

Land use (1991): forested 28.4%; meadows and pastures 23.0%; agricultural
and under permanent cultivation 16.5%; other 32.1%.
Tourism (1991): receipts from visitors U.S.$31,000,000; expenditures by na-
tionals abroad U.S.$37,000,000.

Foreign trade[6]

Balance of trade (current prices)

	1987	1988	1989	1990	1991	1992
L '000,000	−99.0	−47.3	+5.4	−29.8	+11.9	−129.3
% of total	2.8%	1.3%	0.1%	0.8%	0.7%	7.5%

Imports (1992): U.S.$1,028,500,000 (machinery and transport equipment
21.8%, chemical products 16.9%, mineral fuels 16.5%, paper products 8.4%,
plastics and resins 7.8%). *Major import sources:* United States 52.1%; Mexico
8.8%; Guatemala 4.3%; Japan 3.8%; El Salvador 2.8%.
Exports (1992): U.S.$806,000,000 (bananas 35.5%, coffee 18.3%, shrimp and
lobsters 12.0%, lead and zinc 5.4%, frozen meats 4.4%). *Major export
destinations:* United States 53.9%; Germany 11.3%; Belgium 8.3%; United
Kingdom 4.7%; Italy 3.8%.

Transport and communications

Transport. Railroads (1989): length (1993) 488 mi, 785 km; passenger-km
7,700,000; metric ton-km cargo 30,200,000. Roads (1992): total length 8,825
mi, 14,203 km (paved 17%). Vehicles (1992): passenger cars 65,430; trucks
and buses 101,986. Merchant marine (1992): vessels (100 gross tons and over)
966; total deadweight tonnage 1,437,321. Air transport (1990): passenger-mi
321,000,000, passenger-km 516,000,000; short ton-mi cargo 2,000,000, metric
ton-km cargo 3,000,000; airports (1994) with scheduled flights 8.
Communications. Daily newspapers (1990): total number 5; total circulation
199,000; circulation per 1,000 population 39. Radio (1993): total number
of receivers 1,800,000 (1 per 2.9 persons). Television (1993): total number
of receivers 160,000 (1 per 32 persons). Telephones (1992): 104,559 (1
per 48 persons).

Education and health

Education (1992)

	schools	teachers	students	student/ teacher ratio
Primary (age 7–13)	8,074	26,420	959,466	36.3
Secondary (age 14–19)	590	9,708	144,456	14.9
Voc., teacher tr.	5[7]	581[7]	76,388	13.7[7]
Higher	5	2,512	36,870	14.7

Educational attainment (1988). Percentage of population age 10 and over
having: no formal schooling 33.4%; primary education 50.1%; secondary
education 13.4%; higher 3.1%. *Literacy* (1990): total population age 15 and
over literate 2,082,000 (73.1%); males literate 1,078,000 (75.5%); females
literate 1,004,000 (70.6%).
Health: physicians (1990) 2,900 (1 per 1,586 persons); hospital beds (1992)
5,544 (1 per 900 persons); infant mortality rate per 1,000 live births (1993)
47.2.
Food (1988–90): daily per capita caloric intake 2,210 (vegetable products
89%, animal products 11%); 98% of FAO recommended minimum.

Military

Total active duty personnel (1993): 16,800 (army 83.3%, navy 6.0%, air force
10.7%). *Military expenditure as percentage of GNP* (1991): 1.7% (world 4.2%);
per capita expenditure U.S.$10.

---

[1]Tegucigalpa and adjacent city of Comayagüela jointly form the capital according
to the constitution. [2]Population cited is for Central District (Tegucigalpa and Comayagüela). [3]Tegucigalpa, San Pedro Sula, and 10 other urban centres. [4]At factor
cost. [5]Official minimum wages in all sectors. Minimum wages were fixed from June
1981 to Jan. 1, 1990, when new minimum wages were introduced. [6]Import figures are
f.o.b. in balance of trade and c.i.f. for commodities and trading partners. [7]1989.

Hong Kong

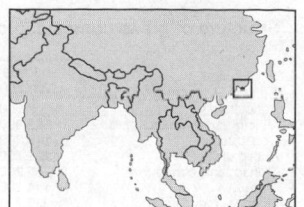

Official name: Hsiang Kang (Chinese); Hong Kong (English).
Political status: Crown Colony (United Kingdom)[1] with one legislative house (Legislative Council [60[2]]).
Chief of state: British Monarch.
Head of government: Governor.
Capital: none[3].
Official languages: Chinese; English.
Official religion: none.
Monetary unit: 1 Hong Kong dollar (HK$) = 100 cents; valuation (Oct. 7, 1994) 1 U.S.$ = HK$7.73; 1 £ = HK$12.29.

Area and population	area[4]		population
Area	sq mi	sq km	1991 census
Hong Kong Island	30.8	79.9	1,214,253
Kowloon and New Kowloon	16.5	42.7	1,975,265
New Territories	368.0	953.1	2,321,661
Marine	—	—	11,102
TOTAL	415.3	1,075.7	5,609,951[5]

Demography

Population (1994): 5,979,000.
Density (1994): persons per sq mi 14,396.0, persons per sq km 5,557.9.
Urban-rural (1993): urban 100.0%.
Sex distribution (1993): male 50.95%; female 49.05%.
Age breakdown (1993)[6]: under 15, 20.0%; 15–29, 24.2%; 30–44, 28.7%; 45–59, 13.9%; 60–74, 10.0%; 75 and over, 3.2%.
Population projection: (2000) 6,350,000; (2010) 7,020,000.
Doubling time: 87 years.
Linguistic composition (1991)[7]: Chinese 96.8%, of which Cantonese 88.7%; English 2.2%; other 1.0%.
Religious affiliation (1993): predominantly Buddhist and Taoist; however, there are about 258,000 Protestants, 249,000 Roman Catholics, 50,000 Muslims, and 12,000 Hindus.
Major cities: no bounded localities exist within Hong Kong.

Vital statistics

Birth rate per 1,000 population (1993): 12.0 (world avg. 26.0); legitimate (1985) 94.5%; illegitimate 5.5%.
Death rate per 1,000 population (1993): 5.1 (world avg. 9.2).
Natural increase rate per 1,000 population (1993): 6.9 (world avg. 16.8).
Total fertility rate (avg. births per childbearing woman; 1990): 1.2.
Marriage rate per 1,000 population (1992): 7.9.
Divorce rate per 1,000 population (1992): 1.0.
Life expectancy at birth (1993): male 75.1 years; female 80.8 years.
Major causes of death per 100,000 population (1993): malignant neoplasms (cancers) 157.2; diseases of the circulatory system 141.5; diseases of the respiratory system 93.9; accidents and poisoning 29.2; diseases of the digestive system 22.6; diseases of the genitourinary system 18.0.

National economy

Budget (1993–94). Revenue: HK$164,412,000,000 (earnings and profit taxes 39.4%; indirect taxes 28.0%, of which entertainment and stamp duties 17.7%, duties 4.3%; capital revenue 16.0%). Expenditures: HK$158,499,000,000 (education 15.8%; transportation and public works 14.9%; general services support 14.0%; health 11.7%; law and order 11.0%; housing 10.6%; social welfare 6.3%; culture and recreation 4.9%).
Public debt: n.a.
Gross domestic product (at current market prices; 1992): U.S.$89,274,000,000 (U.S.$15,380 per capita).

Structure of gross domestic product and labour force				
	1992			
	in value HK$'000,000	% of total value	labour force	% of labour force
Agriculture	1,468	0.2	19,000	0.7
Mining	236	—	400	—
Manufacturing	93,041	12.4	666,600	23.9
Construction	36,467	4.8	237,800	8.5
Public utilities	15,639	2.1	20,100	0.7
Transp. and commun.	67,599	9.0	299,600	10.7
Trade	187,241	24.9	762,600	27.3
Finance, insurance, and real estate	191,276	25.4	234,900	8.4
Pub. admin., defense, and services	110,729	14.7	546,100	19.6
Other	48,777[8]	6.5[8]	5,900	0.2
TOTAL	752,473	100.0	2,793,000	100.0

Production (metric tons except as noted). Agriculture, forestry, fishing (1993): vegetables 91,000, fruits and nuts 4,150, field crops 670, milk 520, eggs 47,800,000 units; livestock (number of live animals) 169,000 pigs[9], 410 cattle, 10,718,000 chickens; roundwood (1991) 193,000 cu m; fish catch 223,690. Mining and quarrying (1990): clay and kaolin 16,587; feldspar 3,820. Manufacturing (value added in HK$; 1991): wearing apparel 18,424,000,000; textiles 14,009,000,000; electrical and electronic products 11,464,000,000; publishing and printed material 7,049,000,000; basic metals and fabricated metal products 5,922,000,000; plastic products 5,238,000,000. Construction (1992):

residential 714,000 sq m; nonresidential 1,578,000 sq m. Energy production (consumption): electricity (kW-hr; 1991) 31,807,000,000 (28,746,000,000); coal (metric tons; 1991) none (9,635,000); petroleum products (metric tons; 1991) none (2,784,000); natural gas (cu m; 1990) none (385,800,000).
Population economically active (1992): total 2,793,000; activity rate of total population 48.1% (participation rates: over age 15, 62.3%; female 46.2%; unemployed 2.0%).

Price and earnings indexes (1985 = 100)							
	1987	1988	1989	1990	1991	1992	1993
Consumer price index	108.6	116.6	128.4	140.8	157.3	171.9	186.5
Daily earnings index[10]	115.0	125.1	139.8	157.0	173.3	190.6	209.1

Household income and expenditure (1991). Average household size 3.4; monthly income per household HK$9,964 (U.S.$1,282); sources of income: n.a.; expenditure (1989–90): food 34.2%, housing 25.6%, transportation and vehicles 7.6%, clothing and footwear 7.5%, durable goods 3.8%.
Tourism (1993): receipts from visitors U.S.$6,886,000,000; expenditures by nationals abroad, n.a.
Land use (1993): forested 20.4%; agricultural and under permanent cultivation 6.0%; fishponds 1.5%; built-on, scrublands, and other 72.1%.

Foreign trade

Balance of trade (current prices)						
	1988	1989	1990	1991	1992	1993
HK$'000,000	−5,717	+7,728	−2,656	−13,096	−30,342	−26,347
% of total	0.6%	0.7%	0.2%	0.1%	1.6%	1.2%

Imports (1993): HK$1,072,597,000,000 (machinery and transport equipment 35.2%, of which electrical machinery 10.8%, telecommunications equipment 8.7%; textile yarn and fabrics 9.2%; apparel and accessories 8.5%; chemicals and related products 6.2%; photographic apparatus, watches, and clocks 4.5%; food and live animals 4.0%). *Major import sources:* China 37.5%; Japan 16.6%; Taiwan 8.8%; United States 7.4%; South Korea 4.5%; Singapore 4.5%; Germany 2.3%; United Kingdom 2.0%.
Exports (1993): HK$223,027,000,000[11] (clothing accessories and apparel 32.2%; electrical machinery 10.2%; office and automatic data-processing machines 7.7%; watches and clocks 7.2%; textile fabrics 7.2%; telecommunications equipment 5.9%; metal products 2.7%; articles of artificial resins and plastics 2.1%; paper and paper products 1.3%). *Major export destinations:* China 28.4%; United States 27.0%; Germany 6.3%; Singapore 5.1%; United Kingdom 4.8%; Japan 4.3%; Taiwan 2.8%.

Transport and communications

Transport. Railroads (1992): route length 21 mi, 34 km; passenger-mi 1,939,000,000, passenger-km 3,120,000,000; short ton-mi cargo 41,000,000, metric ton-km cargo 60,000,000. Roads (1993): total length 1,010 mi, 1,625 km (paved 100%). Vehicles (1993): passenger cars 291,913; trucks and buses 159,891. Merchant marine (1992): vessels (100 gross tons and over) 387; total deadweight tonnage 11,688,605. Air transport (1993): passenger arrivals 9,339,000, passenger departures 9,492,000; airports (1994) with scheduled flights 1.
Communications. Daily newspapers (1993): total number 77; total circulation 2,951,000[12]; circulation per 1,000 population 498[12]. Radio (1993): total number of receivers 3,000,000 (1 per 2.0 persons). Television (1993): total number of receivers 1,749,000 (1 per 3.4 persons). Telephones (1992): 3,600,000 (1 per 1.6 persons).

Education and health

Education (1993–94)				
	schools	teachers[13]	students	student/ teacher ratio[13]
Primary (age 6–11)	633	19,346	485,061	26.7
Secondary (age 12–18)	489	20,360	472,200	22.5
Vocational	9	2,488[14]	53,604	18.5[14]
Higher	12	1,422[14]	70,426	32.4[14]

Educational attainment (1991). Percentage of population age 15 and over having: no formal schooling 12.8%; primary education 25.2%; secondary 45.8%; matriculation 4.9%; nondegree higher 5.4%; higher degree 5.9%.
Literacy (1985): total population age 15 and over literate 3,668,000 (88.1%); males literate 2,040,000 (94.7%); females literate 1,628,000 (80.9%).
Health (1993): physicians 7,625[15] (1 per 776 persons); hospital beds 27,389 (1 per 216 persons); infant mortality rate per 1,000 live births 4.7.
Food (1988–90): daily per capita caloric intake 2,860 (vegetable products 70%, animal products 30%); 125% of FAO recommended minimum requirement.

Military

Total active duty personnel (1993): 6,500[16] (army 87.7%, navy 7.7%, air force 4.6%). *Military expenditure as percentage of GNP* (1984): 0.6% (world 5.9%); per capita expenditure U.S.$39.

---

[1]On July 1, 1997, Hong Kong will revert to China as a Special Administrative Region in which the existing socioeconomic system would remain unchanged for a period of 50 years. [2]Includes 21 nonelective seats. [3]Victoria, for some time, had been regarded as the capital because it is the seat of the British administration of the Crown Colony. [4]Excludes the surface areas of reservoirs. [5]Includes 35,823 transients and 51,847 Vietnamese migrants not enumerated by area. [6]Excludes transients and Vietnamese refugees. [7]Excludes about 59,900 Vietnamese refugees, about 1% of the population. [8]Indirect taxes less subsidies. [9]Excludes local pigs not slaughtered in abattoirs. [10]September. [11]Excludes reexports valued at HK$823,224,000,000. [12]Thirty-two newspapers only. [13]1991–92. [14]1987–88. [15]Registered personnel; all may not be present and working in the country. [16]British forces with a few locally enlisted personnel.

Hungary

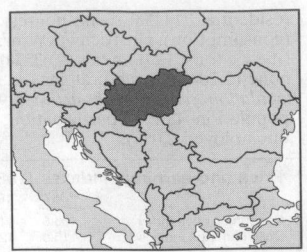

Official name: Magyar Köztársaság
(Republic of Hungary).
Form of government: unitary multi-
party republic with one legislative
house (National Assembly [394[1]]).
Chief of state: President.
Head of government: Prime Minister.
Capital: Budapest.
Official language: Hungarian.
Official religion: none.
Monetary unit: 1 forint (Ft) = 100
filler; valuation (Oct. 7, 1994)
1 U.S.\$ = Ft 107.76; 1 £ = Ft 171.39.

Area and population

Counties	Capitals	area sq mi	area sq km	population 1993[2] estimate
Bács-Kiskun	Kecskemét	3,229	8,362	541,000
Baranya	Pécs	1,732	4,487	417,000
Békés	Békéscsaba	2,175	5,632	404,000
Borsod-Abaúj-Zemplén	Miskolc	2,798	7,247	749,000
Csongrád	Szeged	1,646	4,263	438,000
Fejér	Székesfehérvár	1,688	4,373	422,000
Győr-Moson-Sopron	Győr	1,549	4,012	427,000
Hajdú-Bihar	Debrecen	2,398	6,211	550,000
Heves	Eger	1,404	3,637	330,000
Jász-Nagykun-Szolnok	Szolnok	2,165	5,607	421,000
Komárom-Esztergom	Tatabánya	869	2,251	313,000
Nógrád	Salgótarján	982	2,544	223,000
Pest	Budapest[3]	2,469	6,394	958,000
Somogy	Kaposvár	2,331	6,036	340,000
Szabolcs-Szatmár-Bereg	Nyíregyháza	2,293	5,938	564,000
Tolna	Szekszárd	1,430	3,704	251,000
Vas	Szombathely	1,288	3,337	274,000
Veszprém	Veszprém	1,810	4,689	378,000
Zala	Zalaegerszeg	1,461	3,784	303,000
Capital City				
Budapest[3]		203	525	2,009,000
TOTAL		35,920	93,033	10,312,000[4]

Demography

Population (1994): 10,257,000.
Density (1994): persons per sq mi 285.6, persons per sq km 110.3.
Urban-rural (1993): urban 63.2%; rural 36.8%.
Sex distribution (1993): male 47.95%; female 52.05%.
Age breakdown (1993): under 15, 19.0%; 15–29, 21.5%; 30–44, 22.2%; 45–59, 18.0%; 60–74, 14.3%; 75 and over, 5.0%.
Population projection: (2000) 10,170,000; (2010) 9,951,000. The population has declined at an average annual rate of 0.3% since 1980.
Ethnic composition (nationality; 1990): Magyar 97.8%; Gypsy 1.4%; German 0.3%; Croatian 0.1%; Romanian 0.1%; Slovak 0.1%.
Religious affiliation (1992): Christian 92.9%, of which Roman Catholic 67.8%; Protestant 25.1%; atheist and nonreligious 4.8%; other 2.3%.
Major cities (1993[2]): Budapest 2,008,546; Debrecen 217,287; Miskolc 191,005; Szeged 178,501; Pécs 171,562.

Vital statistics

Birth rate per 1,000 population (1993): 11.3 (world avg. 26.0); (1992) legitimate 81.5%; illegitimate 18.5%.
Death rate per 1,000 population (1993): 14.4 (world avg. 9.2).
Natural increase rate per 1,000 population (1993): −3.1 (world avg. 16.8).
Total fertility rate (avg. births per childbearing woman; 1992): 1.8.
Marriage rate per 1,000 population (1993): 5.2.
Divorce rate per 1,000 population (1992): 2.1.
Life expectancy at birth (1992): male 64.6 years; female 73.7 years.
Major causes of death per 100,000 population (1992): diseases of the circulatory system 738.7; malignant neoplasms (cancers) 316.5; accidents and self-inflicted injuries 126.8.

National economy

Budget (1993). Revenue: Ft 939,662,000,000 (value-added tax 28.4%, income tax 22.4%, payments by enterprises 22.1%, excise duties 15.8%). Expenditures: Ft 1,139,329,000,000 (social security 21.6%, health 15.9%, education 15.7%, defense 11.7%).
Production (metric tons except as noted). Agriculture, forestry, fishing (1992): corn (maize) 4,301,000, wheat 3,444,000, sugar beets 2,974,000, barley 1,723,000, potatoes 925,000, apples 819,000, sunflower seeds 757,000, grapes 607,000, rye 136,000; livestock (number of live animals; 1993) 5,001,000 pigs, 1,252,000 sheep, 999,000 cattle; roundwood (1993) 3,489,000 cu m; fish catch (1991) 29,378. Mining and quarrying (1992): limestone 3,703,000; bauxite 1,721,000; manganese ore 18,000. Manufacturing (1993): cement 2,533,000; rolled steel 1,835,000; crude steel 1,752,000; pig iron 1,407,000; alumina 548,000; fertilizers 201,630; cotton fabrics 91,942,000 sq m; leather footwear 11,963,000 pairs; buses 3,211 units. Construction (in Ft '000,000; 1992): residential 6,662[5]; nonresidential 51,837. Energy production (consumption): electricity (kW-hr; 1992) 31,396,000,000 (35,050,000,000); coal (metric tons; 1992) 15,943,000 (17,539,000); crude petroleum (barrels; 1991) 12,316,000 (49,465,000); petroleum products (metric tons; 1991) 6,711,000 (7,169,000); natural gas (cu m; 1992) 5,057,000,000 (9,870,000,000).
Tourism (1992): receipts from visitors U.S.\$1,260,800,000; expenditures by nationals abroad U.S.\$673,200,000.
Public debt (external, outstanding; 1992): U.S.\$19,152,000,000.
Gross national product (1992): U.S.\$30,894,000,000 (U.S.\$3,000 per capita).

Structure of gross domestic product and labour force

	1992 in value Ft '000,000	% of total value	labour force[2]	% of labour force[2]
Agriculture	207,900	7.4	588,900	12.7
Mining and manufacturing	653,300	23.3	1,286,200[6]	27.7[6]
Construction	149,300	5.3	272,800	5.9
Public utilities	121,700	4.3	[6]	[6]
Transp. and commun.	205,200	7.3	372,900	8.0
Trade	444,700	15.9 }	564,200	12.1
Finance, real estate	239,700	8.6 }		
Services	429,300	15.3	1,156,800	24.9
Other	354,000[7]	12.6[7]	406,100[8]	8.7[8]
TOTAL	2,805,100	100.0	4,647,900	100.0

Population economically active (1994[2]): total 4,552,200; activity rate of total population 44.3% (participation rates: working age 89.1%; female 47.4%; unemployed 10.9%).

Price and earnings indexes (1990 = 100)

	1987	1988	1989	1990	1991	1992	1993
Consumer price index	57.4	66.3	77.6	100	135.1	166.1	203.4
Monthly earnings index	51.9	66.7	78.6	100	133.4	165.8	201.6

Household income and expenditure. Average household size (1991) 2.8; income per household (1990) Ft 376,195 (U.S.\$5,900); sources of income (1992): wages 46.1%, social income 22.4%, self-employment 11.9%; expenditure (1991): food and beverages 38.1%, transportation and communications 15.1%, household durable goods 8.7%, clothing 7.4%, culture and recreation 5.9%, housing 5.7%.
Land use (1993): forested 18.9%; meadows and pastures 15.2%; agricultural and under permanent cultivation 50.7%; other 15.2%.

Foreign trade[9]

Balance of trade (current prices)

	1988	1989	1990	1991	1992	1993
Ft '000,000,000	+31.4	+47.8	+58.7	−91.4	−34.9	−342.6
% of total	3.3%	4.4%	5.1%	5.6%	2.0%	17.3%

Imports (1993): Ft 1,162,500,000,000 (intermediate industrial goods 33.4%, machinery and transport equipment 26.9%, industrial consumer goods 21.2%, fuels and electrical energy 12.6%, food and live animals 5.9%). *Major import sources:* former U.S.S.R. 22.2%; Germany 21.6%; Austria 11.6%; Italy 6.0%; Czech and Slovak republics 4.0%.
Exports (1993): Ft 819,900,000,000 (intermediate industrial goods 36.4%, industrial consumer goods 25.2%, food and live animals 21.4%, machinery and transport equipment 13.9%, fuels and electrical energy 3.4%). *Major export destinations:* Germany 26.6%; former U.S.S.R. 15.3%; Austria 10.1%; Italy 8.0%; U.S. 4.2%.

Transport and communications

Transport. Railroads (1992): length 8,200 mi, 13,200 km; passenger-mi 5,706,-000,000, passenger-km 9,183,000,000; short ton-mi cargo 6,860,000,000, metric ton-km cargo 10,015,000,000. Roads (1992): total length 18,610 mi, 29,950 km (paved 99%). Vehicles (1991): passenger cars 2,058,334; trucks and buses 229,191. Merchant marine (1992): vessels (100 gross tons and over) 15; total deadweight tonnage 93,204. Air transport (1992): passenger-mi 923,978, passenger-km 1,487,000; short ton-mi cargo 6,986,000, metric ton-km cargo 10,200,000; airports (1994) with scheduled flights 1.
Communications. Daily newspapers (1990): total number 29; total circulation 2,759,300; circulation per 1,000 population 266. Radio (1992): 6,000,000 (1 per 1.7 persons). Television (1992): 4,261,600 (1 per 2.4 persons). Telephones (1992): 2,052,210 (1 per 5.0 persons).

Education and health

Education (1992–93)

	schools	teachers	students	student/teacher ratio
Primary (age 6–13)	3,959	96,223	1,092,563	11.4
Secondary (age 14–17)	876	26,335	335,153	12.7
Vocational	343	6,624	212,932	32.2
Higher	91	17,743	119,828	6.8

Educational attainment (1990). Percentage of population age 10 and over having: no formal schooling 1.2%; primary education 78.1%; secondary 29.2%; higher 10.1%. *Literacy* (1984): total population age 15 and over literate 8,269,850 (98.9%); males literate 3,934,250 (99.2%); females literate 4,335,600 (98.6%).
Health (1992): physicians 40,869 (1 per 252 persons); hospital beds 101,809 (1 per 101 persons); infant mortality rate per 1,000 live births (1993) 14.0.
Food (1988–90): daily per capita caloric intake 3,608 (vegetable products 63%; animal products 37%); 137% of FAO recommended minimum.

Military

Total active duty personnel (1992): 80,800 (army 78.6%, air force 21.4%). *Military expenditure as percentage of GNP* (1989): 6.3% (world 4.9%); per capita expenditure U.S.\$391.

[1]Includes 8 nonelective seats. [2]January 1. [3]Budapest has separate county status. The area and population of the city are excluded from the larger county (Pest), which it administers. [4]Detail does not add to total given because of rounding. [5]Includes hotel construction. [6]Mining and manufacturing includes Public utilities. [7]Taxes on products. [8]Unemployed. [9]Import figures are f.o.b. in balance of trade and c.i.f. for commodities and trading partners.

Iceland

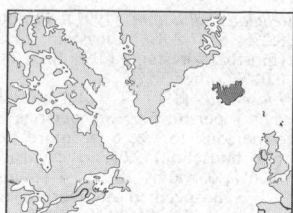

Official name: Lýdhveldidh Ísland (Republic of Iceland).
Form of government: unitary multiparty republic with one legislative house (Althing [63][1]).
Chief of state: President.
Head of government: Prime Minister.
Capital: Reykjavík.
Official language: Icelandic.
Official religion: Evangelical Lutheran.
Monetary unit: 1 króna (ISK) = 100 aurar; valuation (Oct. 7, 1994) 1 U.S.$ = ISK 67.83; 1 £ = ISK 107.89.

Area and population

Regions	Administrative centres	area sq mi	area sq km	population 1993[2] estimate
Austurland	Egilsstadhir	8,491	21,991	13,023
Höfudhborgarsvædhi	Reykjavík	765[3]	1,982[3]	154,268
Nordhurland eystra	Akureyri	8,636	22,368	26,751
Nordhurland vestra	Saudhárkrókur	5,055	13,093	10,442
Sudhurland	Selfoss	9,735	25,214	20,778
Sudhurnes	Keflavík	3	3	15,551
Vestfirdhir	Ísafjördhur	3,657	9,470	9,606
Vesturland	Borgarnes	3,360	8,701	14,503
TOTAL		39,699	102,819	264,922

Demography

Population (1994): 267,000.
Density (1994)[4]: persons per sq mi 29.1, persons per sq km 11.2.
Urban-rural (1993): urban 91.4%; rural 8.6%.
Sex distribution (1994): male 50.16%; female 49.84%.
Age breakdown (1994): under 15, 24.8%; 15–29, 23.7%; 30–44, 22.7%; 45–59, 13.9%; 60–74, 10.2%; 75 and over, 4.7%.
Population projection: (2000) 278,000; (2010) 294,000.
Doubling time: 63 years.
Ethnic composition (1993)[5]: Icelandic 96.1%; Danish 0.8%; Swedish 0.5%; persons born in the United States 0.5%; German 0.3%; other 1.8%.
Religious affiliation (1993): Protestant 96.3%, of which Evangelical Lutheran 92.0%, other Lutheran 3.2%; Roman Catholic 0.9%; nonreligious 1.4%; other 1.4%.
Major cities (1993): Reykjavík 101,855 (urban area 154,268); Kópavogur 17,176[6]; Hafnarfjördhur 16,787[6]; Akureyri 14,799; Keflavík 7,581.

Vital statistics

Birth rate per 1,000 population (1992): 17.6 (world avg. 26.0); legitimate 42.7%; illegitimate 57.3%.
Death rate per 1,000 population (1992): 6.6 (world avg. 9.2).
Natural increase rate per 1,000 population (1992): 11.0 (world avg. 16.8).
Total fertility rate (avg. births per childbearing woman; 1992): 2.2.
Marriage rate per 1,000 population (1992): 4.7.
Divorce rate per 1,000 population (1992): 2.0.
Life expectancy at birth (1991–92): male 75.7 years; female 80.9 years.
Major causes of death per 100,000 population (1992): diseases of the circulatory system 290.4, of which ischemic heart diseases 177.0, cerebrovascular disease 56.7; malignant neoplasms (cancers) 164.4; diseases of the respiratory system 91.2.

National economy

Budget (1993). Revenue: ISK 103,220,000,000 (sales tax 39.2%, income tax 19.3%, import duties 8.8%, taxes on alcohol and tobacco 6.0%). Expenditures: ISK 112,863,000,000 (health and welfare 47.0%, education 15.1%, general services 10.1%, communications 8.3%, agriculture 6.9%).
Public debt (external, outstanding; September 1993): U.S.$2,209,000,000.
Production (metric tons except as noted). Agriculture, forestry, fishing (1993): potatoes 3,900, dried hay 1,788,000 cu m, silage 1,069,000 cu m; livestock (number of live animals) 488,800 sheep, 76,700 horses, 73,900 cattle; fish catch (value in ISK '000,000; 1992) cod 18,474, redfish 6,391, shrimp 4,728, haddock 3,982. Mining and quarrying (1992): diatomite 20,000. Manufacturing (value added in ISK '000,000; 1990): food, beverages, and tobacco products 17,996; fabricated metal products 4,927; printing and publishing 4,904; nonmetallic mineral products 2,424; wood furniture 2,416. Construction (completed): residential (1992) 568,000 cu m; nonresidential (1991) 729,000 cu m. Energy production (consumption): electricity (kW-hr; 1993) 4,726,000,000 ([1992] 4,540,000,000); coal (metric tons; 1991) none (60,000); crude petroleum, none (none); petroleum products (metric tons; 1991) none (493,000); natural gas, none (none).
Land use (1991): forested 1.2%; meadows and pastures 22.7%; agricultural and under permanent cultivation 0.1%; other 76.0%.
Population economically active (November 1993): total 148,900; activity rate of total population 56.2% (participation rates: ages 16–74, 81.6%; female 45.9%; unemployed [May 1993–April 1994] 4.9%).

Price and earnings indexes (1990 = 100)

	1988	1989	1990	1991	1992	1993	1994[7]
Consumer price index	71.3	87.2	100.0	105.6	111.3	115.9	117.3
Hourly wages index	81.9	92.9	100.0	108.4	111.9	113.6	114.5

Tourism (1993): receipts from visitors U.S.$132,300,000; expenditures by nationals abroad U.S.$265,000,000.

Gross national product (at current market prices; 1992): U.S.$6,178,000,000 (U.S.$23,670 per capita).

Structure of gross national product and labour force

	1991 in value ISK '000,000[8]	1991 % of total value	1993 labour force[9]	1993 % of labour force
Agriculture	10,300	2.8	6,700	4.5
Fishing	33,000	9.2	7,400	5.0
Fish processing	18,400	5.0	8,800	5.9
Manufacturing	46,500	12.6	14,000	9.4
Construction	31,000	8.4	9,000	6.1
Public utilities	15,900	4.3	1,400	0.9
Transportation and communications	29,200	7.9	9,800	6.6
Trade	50,600	13.7	25,700	17.3
Finance, real estate	62,400	16.9	13,000	8.7
Public administration	60,200	16.3	8,200	5.5
Health, education, other services	22,900	6.2	37,000	24.9
Other	−12,200[10]	−3.3[10]	7,700[11]	5.2[11]
TOTAL	369,100[12]	100.0	148,700	100.0

Household income and expenditure. Average household size (1990)[13] 3.6; annual income per household (1990)[13] ISK 2,605,563 (U.S.$44,712); sources of income (1992): wages and salaries 72.5%, pensions 9.4%, self-employment 3.0%, other 15.1%; expenditure (1990): food 19.7%, transportation 17.5%, housing 11.2%, household furnishings 7.6%, recreation 7.4%, expenditures in restaurants and hotels and on package tours 6.9%.

Foreign trade

Balance of trade (current prices)

ISK '000,000	1988	1989	1990	1991	1992	1993
	−576	+6,943	+4,540	−3,253	302	+12,082
% of total	0.5%	4.5%	2.5%	1.7%	0.2%	6.8%

Imports (1993): ISK 82,576,000,000 (nonelectrical machinery and apparatus 12.1%; transport equipment 9.0%; food products 9.0%; crude petroleum and petroleum products 8.9%; electrical machinery and apparatus 8.9%). *Major import sources*[14]: Norway 12.4%; Germany 11.9%; Denmark 9.4%; United States 9.3%; United Kingdom 9.0%; Sweden 6.8%; The Netherlands 6.0%.
Exports (1993): ISK 94,658,000,000 (marine products 78.9%, of which frozen cod fillets 16.9%, frozen shrimp 9.0%, uncured salted fish 7.7%, fresh whole fish chilled or on ice 6.6%; aluminum 8.7%; ferrosilicon 2.5%). *Major export destinations:* United Kingdom 21.6%; United States 15.9%; Germany 11.1%; Japan 9.3%; France 8.2%; Denmark 5.6%.

Transport and communications

Transport. Railroads: none. Roads (1993): total length 7,067 mi, 11,373 km (paved 22%). Vehicles (1993): passenger cars 116,195; trucks and buses 15,644. Merchant marine (1992): vessels (100 gross tons and over) 394; total deadweight tonnage 114,851. Air transport (1993)[15]: passenger-mi 1,273,000,000, passenger-km 2,049,000,000; short ton-mi cargo 24,948,000, metric ton-km cargo 36,424,000; airports (1994) with scheduled flights 24.
Communications. Daily newspapers (1991): total number 6; total circulation 132,700; circulation per 1,000 population 514. Radio (1993): total number of receivers 155,000 (1 per 1.7 persons). Television (1993): total number of receivers 76,250 (1 per 3.5 persons). Telephones (1992): 140,031[16] (1 per 1.9 persons).

Education and health

Education (1991–92)

	schools	teachers	students	student/teacher ratio
Primary (age 7–12)	...	...	25,809	...
Secondary (age 13–20)	...	...	29,985	...
Higher	...	...	6,161	...

Educational attainment: n.a. *Literacy:* virtually 100%.
Health: physicians (1989) 715 (1 per 355 persons); hospital beds (1990) 3,204[17] (1 per 80 persons); infant mortality rate per 1,000 live births (1992) 4.8.
Food (1988–90): daily per capita caloric intake 3,473 (vegetable products 60%, animal products 40%); 131% of FAO recommended minimum requirement.

Military

Total active duty personnel (1993): 130 coast guard personnel; NATO-sponsored U.S. manned Iceland Defense Force (1993): 3,000 (navy 60.0%, air force 40.0%). *Military expenditure as percentage of GNP* (1991): none (world average 4.2%).

[1]Meets as single chamber since dissolution of the Upper House in May 1991. [2]December 1. [3]Höfudhborgarsvædhi includes Sudhurnes. [4]Population density calculated with reference to 9,191 sq mi (23,805 sq km) area free of glaciers, lava fields, and lakes. [5]By country of birth. [6]Within Reykjavík urban area. [7]May. [8]Data estimated from percentage distribution of sectors. [9]April. [10]Net of imputed bank service charges and income not classified elsewhere. [11]Unemployed. [12]GDP (1991) equals ISK 384,100,000,000. [13]Based on sample survey. [14]Import sources based on a c.i.f. total of ISK 91,307,000,000. [15]Icelandair only. [16]Number of subscribers. [17]Excludes nursing wards in old-age homes.

India

Official name: Bhārat (Hindī);
Republic of India (English).
Form of government: multiparty federal
republic with two legislative houses
(Council of States [245][1], House of
the People [545][2]).
Chief of state: President.
Head of government: Prime Minister.
Capital: New Delhi.
Official languages: Hindī; English.
Official religion: none.
Monetary unit: 1 Indian rupee
(Re, plural Rs) = 100 paise; valuation
(Oct. 7, 1994) 1 U.S.$ = Rs 31.37;
1 £ = Rs 49.89.

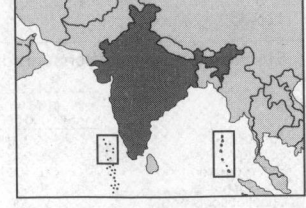

Area and population

States	Capitals	area sq mi	area sq km	population 1991 census
Andhra Pradesh	Hyderābād	106,204	275,068	66,508,008
Arunāchal Pradesh	Itānagar	32,333	83,743	864,558
Assam	Dispur	30,285	78,438	22,414,322
Bihār	Patna	67,134	173,877	86,374,465
Goa	Panaji	1,429	3,702	1,169,793
Gujarāt	Gāndhīnagar	75,685	196,024	41,309,582
Haryāna	Chandīgarh	17,070	44,212	16,463,648
Himāchal Pradesh	Shimla	21,495	55,673	5,170,877
Jammu and Kashmir	Srīnagar	38,830	100,569	7,718,700[3]
Karnātaka	Bangalore	74,051	191,791	44,977,201
Kerala	Trivandrum	15,005	38,863	29,098,518
Madhya Pradesh	Bhopāl	171,215	443,446	66,181,170
Mahārāshtra	Bombay	118,800	307,690	78,937,187
Manipur	Imphāl	8,621	22,327	1,837,149
Meghālaya	Shillong	8,660	22,429	1,774,778
Mizoram	Āīzawl	8,140	21,081	689,756
Nāgāland	Kohīma	6,401	16,579	1,209,546
Orissa	Bhubaneshwar	60,119	155,707	31,659,736
Punjab	Chandīgarh	19,445	50,362	20,281,969
Rājasthān	Jaipur	132,140	342,239	44,005,990
Sikkim	Gangtok	2,740	7,096	406,457
Tamil Nādu	Madras	50,216	130,058	55,858,946
Tripura	Agartala	4,049	10,486	2,757,205
Uttar Pradesh	Lucknow	113,673	294,411	139,112,287
West Bengal	Calcutta	34,267	88,752	68,077,965
Union Territories				
Andaman and Nicobar Islands	Port Blair	3,185	8,249	280,661
Chandīgarh	Chandīgarh	44	114	642,015
Dādra and Nagar Haveli	Silvassa	190	491	138,477
Damān and Diu	Damān	43	112	101,586
Delhi	Delhi	572	1,483	9,420,644
Lakshadweep	Kavaratti	12	32	51,707
Pondicherry	Pondicherry	190	492	807,785
TOTAL		1,222,243[4]	3,165,596[4]	846,302,688

Demography

Population (1994): 913,747,000.
Density (1993)[4]: persons per sq mi 747.0, persons per sq km 288.4.
Urban-rural (1991): urban 25.7%; rural 74.3%.
Sex distribution (1991): male 51.90%; female 48.10%.
Age breakdown (1990): under 15, 36.0%; 15–29, 27.7%; 30–44, 18.0%; 45–59, 11.2%; 60–74, 5.9%; 75 and over, 1.2%.
Population projection: (2000) 1,018,673,000; (2010) 1,189,396,000.
Doubling time: 36 years.
Linguistic composition (1981)[5]: Hindī (lingua franca) 45.00%; Hindī (including associated languages and dialects) 38.77%; Telugu 7.96%; Bengalī 7.56%; Marāṭhī 7.28%; Tamil 6.56%; Urdū 5.18%; Gujarātī 4.87%; Kannaḍa 3.95%; Malayālam 3.81%; Oṛiyā 3.36%; Punjābī 2.73%; English (lingua franca) 2.50%; Assamese 1.64%[6]; Bhīlī/Bhilodī 0.65%; Santhālī 0.62%; Kashmīrī 0.47%; Goṇḍī 0.29%; Sindhī 0.29%; Konkaṇī 0.23%; Dogrī 0.22%; Tulu 0.20%; Kurukh 0.19%; Nepālī 0.18%; Khandeshī 0.17%; Manipurī 0.13%; other 2.69%.
Place of birth (foreign born; 1981): other Asia 7,875,399, of which Bangladesh 4,170,524, Pakistan 2,736,038, Nepal 501,292, Sri Lanka 211,514, Myanmar 134,783; Africa 42,726; Europe 13,046; United States and Canada 5,923.
Major cities (urban agglomerations; 1991): Greater Bombay 9,925,891 (12,596,-243); Delhi 7,206,704 (8,419,084); Madras 3,841,396 (5,421,985); Bangalore 3,302,296 (4,130,288); Hyderābād 3,145,939 (4,253,759); Ahmadābād 2,954,526 (3,312,216); Kānpur 1,879,420 (2,029,889); Nāgpur 1,624,752 (1,664,006); Lucknow 1,619,115 (1,669,204); Pune 1,566,651 (2,493,987); New Delhi[7] 301,297.

Other principal cities (1991)

	population		population		population
Āgra	891,790	Indore	1,091,674	Rājkot	612,458
Allahābād	806,486	Jabalpur	764,586	Rānchi	599,306
Amritsar	708,835	Jaipur	1,458,183	Sholāpur	
Aurangābād	573,272	Jalandhar (Jullundur)	509,510	(Solāpur)	604,215
Bareilly	590,661	Jodhpur	666,279	Srīnagar	594,775[11]
Bhopāl	1,062,771	Kalyān[9]	1,014,557	Sūrat	1,505,872
Chandīgarh	510,565	Kota	537,371	Thāne (Thāna)[9]	803,389
Cochin (Kochi)	582,588	Ludhiāna	1,042,740	Trivandrum	699,872
Coimbatore	816,321	Madurai	940,989	Vadodara	
Farīdābād	617,717	Meerut	753,778	(Baroda)	1,061,598
Guwāhāti	584,342	Mysore	606,755	Vārānasi	
Gwalior	690,765	Nāshik (Nāsik)	656,925	(Benares)	932,399
Howrah (Hāora)[8]	950,435	Patna	917,243	Vijayawāda	701,827
Hubli-Dhārwād	648,298	Pimpri-Chinchwad[10]	517,083	Vishākhapatnam	752,037

Religious affiliation (1991): Hindu 80.3%; Muslim 11.0%, of which Sunnī 8.2%, Shī'ī 2.8%; Christian 2.4%, of which Roman Catholic 1.4%, other (mostly Protestant) 1.0%; Sikh 2.0%; Buddhist 0.7%; Jain 0.5%; Zoroastrian 0.01%; other 3.1%.
Households (1981)[12]. Total households 119,230,710. Average household size 5.6; 1 person 5.6%, 2 persons 8.3%, 3 persons 11.0%, 4 persons 14.6%, 5 persons 15.9%, 6 or more persons 44.6%. Average number of rooms per household 2.0; no exclusive room 0.6%, 1 room 44.7%, 2 rooms 28.6%, 3 rooms 12.2%, 4 rooms 6.3%, 5 rooms 2.7%, 6 or more rooms 3.1%, unspecified number of rooms 1.8%. Average number of persons per room 2.8. Shelterless (homeless) population estimated (1987) at more than 100,000,000.
Emigration (1987 estimation): persons living abroad 12,697,000 (accepting foreign citizenship 8,200,000), of which in Nepal (1980) 3,800,000 (2,388,-000); Malaysia 1,170,000 (1,029,000); Middle Eastern countries 1,064,000 (102,000); Sri Lanka 1,028,000 (457,000); South Africa 850,000 (850,000); United Kingdom 789,000 (395,000); Mauritius 701,000 (700,000); United States 500,000 (287,000); Trinidad and Tobago 430,000 (430,000); Fiji 339,-000 (339,000); Myanmar 330,000 (50,000); Canada 229,000 (129,000).

Vital statistics

Birth rate per 1,000 population (1991): 29.3 (world avg. 26.0).
Death rate per 1,000 population (1991): 9.8 (world avg. 9.2).
Natural increase rate per 1,000 population (1991): 19.5 (world avg. 16.8).
Total fertility rate (avg. births per childbearing woman; 1992): 3.9.
Marital status of male (female) population age 25 and over (1981): single 6.4% (1.1%); married 87.4% (79.4%); widowed 5.7% (18.8%); divorced or separated 0.5% (0.7%).
Life expectancy at birth (1992–93): male 60.4 years; female 61.2 years.
Major causes of death (rural areas only; 1991)[12]: senility 23.7%[13]; infectious and parasitic diseases 17.1%; diseases of the respiratory system 13.4%; causes peculiar to infancy 10.2%, of which prematurity 4.9%; diseases of the circulatory system 8.1%; accidents and injuries 6.7%; diseases of the digestive system 4.9%; diseases of the nervous system 4.4%; cancers 3.1%; anemias 3.0%; suicide 1.4%; diabetes 0.7%.

Social indicators

Educational attainment (1981)[14]. Percentage of population age 25 and over having: no formal schooling (illiterate) 64.8%; no formal schooling (literate) 1.0%; some primary education 7.1%; completed primary 10.9%; some secondary 6.2%; completed secondary 7.1%; higher vocational 0.4%; completed undergraduate degree 2.5%.

Distribution of expenditure (1989–90)

percentage of household expenditure by quintile				
1	2	3	4	5 (highest)
8.8%	12.5%	16.2%	21.3%	41.2%

Quality of working life. Average workweek (1989): 42 hours. Rate of fatal (nonfatal) injuries per 100,000 workers: industrial workers (1989) 17 (3,625); miners (1990) 32 (172); railway workers (1989) 15 (1,059). Employees covered under Employee's State Insurance Scheme (1991) 6,070,000; number of beneficiaries 26,749,000. Average days lost to labour stoppages per 1,000 workdays (1991): 6.
Access to services. Proportion of urban (rural) population having access to: electricity for lighting purposes (1988–89) 75.1% (26.9%); safe water supply (1992) 84.9% (78.4%); safe sewage disposal (1990) 46.0% (2.0%).
Social participation. Eligible voters participating in last (May/June 1991) national election: 53%. Trade union membership (1988): 5,079,000.
Social deviance (1986)[15]. Offense rate per 100,000 population for: murder 3.5; dacoity (gang robbery) 1.3; theft and housebreaking 57.9; riots 12.0. Rate of suicide per 100,000 population (1990): 6.9.
Availability of consumer durables. Local production in 1980 (1991): automobiles 31,000 (165,000); motorcycles 102,000 (431,000); black and white television receivers 369,000 (3,100,000); colour television receivers, none (880,000); refrigerators 278,000 (1,322,000); air conditioners 44,000 (80,000).

National economy

Public debt (external, outstanding; 1992): U.S.$76,980,000,000.
Gross national product (1993): U.S.$261,574,000,000 (U.S.$290 per capita).

Structure of gross domestic product and labour force

	1992–93[16] in value Rs '000,000,000	1992–93[16] % of total value	1981[14] labour force	1981[14] % of labour force
Agriculture	1,998	31.8	172,713,291	66.4
Mining	141	2.3	1,301,632	0.5
Manufacturing	1,098	17.5	26,554,517	10.2
Construction	347	5.5	3,864,104	1.5
Public utilities	137	2.2	989,490	0.3
Transp. and commun.	497	7.9	6,206,697	2.4
Trade, restaurants	796	12.7	12,638,204	4.9
Finance, real estate	514	8.2	1,822,229	0.7
Pub. admin., defense	360	5.7 }	18,514,810	7.1
Services	391	6.2 }		
Other	—	—	15,670,144[17]	6.0[17]
TOTAL	6,279	100.0	260,275,118	100.0

Budget (1993–94). Revenue: Rs 1,308,500,000,000 (tax revenue 59.8%, of which excise taxes 26.2%, customs duties 21.2%, corporation taxes 8.0%; nontax revenue 40.2%, of which economic services 22.4%, interest receipts 11.1%). Expenditures: Rs 1,484,800,000,000 (interest payments and debt servicing 25.6%; transportation 13.7%; grants to state governments 13.2%; defense 9.7%; communications 5.3%; agriculture 3.7%; social services 3.0%).

Production. Agriculture, forestry, fishing (value of production in Rs '000,000 except as noted; 1989–90): rice 239,120, wheat 115,270, sugarcane 78,760, peanuts (groundnuts) 53,950, kapoks 42,320, rapeseed and mustard 31,350, chick-peas 31,020, sorghum 27,140, corn (maize) 19,180, potatoes 19,140, coconuts 18,790, pigeon peas 18,210, bananas 13,230, pearl millet 12,330, tea 11,080, urd beans 10,670, mung beans 10,560, chilies 9,320, soybeans 8,470, tobacco 6,890, sesame seeds 6,740, finger millet 5,810, jute 5,790, rubber 4,650, betel nuts 4,420, red lentils 4,390, sunflower seeds 4,340, onions 4,270, tapioca 4,160, guar seeds 3,670, cashews 3,600, turmeric 3,600, coffee 3,600, safflower seeds 3,170, barley 3,110; livestock (number of live animals; 1992) 192,650,000 cattle, 117,000,000 goats, 78,550,000 water buffalo, 44,407,000 sheep; roundwood (1992) 282,359,000 cu m; fish catch (metric tons; 1991) 4,036,931, of which freshwater fish 1,700,800. Mining and quarrying (in '000 metric tons except as noted; 1992–93): limestone 70,000[18]; iron ore 57,600; bauxite 4,980; manganese 1,400[18]; chromite 1,000[18]; zinc ore 127; copper (metal content) 45; lead (primary metal) 39; gold 60,300 troy oz[19]; gem diamonds 15,000 carats[18]. Manufacturing (in '000 metric tons except as noted; 1992–93): cement 54,300; finished steel 14,330[18]; steel ingots 13,250; refined sugar 10,589; nitrogenous fertilizers 7,407; paper and paperboard 2,152; soda ash 1,391; jute manufactures 1,310; aluminum 483; nylon and polyester yarns 278; bicycles 6,963,000 units; motorcycles and scooters 1,496,000 units; power-driven pumps 525,000 units; passenger cars and jeeps 198,100 units; passenger buses and trucks 132,600 units; cotton cloth 13,054,000,000 metres; other important manufactured products include drugs and pharmaceuticals, computer software, gold jewelry, and silk goods. Construction (value of new construction in Rs; 1989–90): 563,670,000,000.

Manufacturing enterprises (1987–88)[20]

	no. of factories	no. of persons engaged	avg. wages as a % of avg. of all wages	annual value added (Rs '000,000)[16]
Chemicals and chemical products,	6,578	555,000	148.6	37,368
of which paints, soaps, etc.	3,171	215,000	92.7	10,487
drugs and medicine	1,497	135,000	170.0	8,631
industrial chemicals	1,049	84,000	166.7	7,429
fertilizers and pesticides	515	78,000	207.7	6,805
Textiles (excl. clothing)	12,029	1,414,000	87.8	28,581
Iron and steel	5,147	564,000	131.0	22,202
Food products	18,333	1,025,000	56.7	21,721
Electrical machinery/apparatus,	4,241	376,000	149.1	21,715
of which radios and televisions	1,070	109,000	130.8	5,131
Nonelectrical machinery/apparatus	7,584	447,000	129.1	19,455
Transport equipment,	3,318	485,000	147.9	18,810
of which motor vehicles	1,463	173,000	171.4	9,879
Refined petroleum	96	18,000	243.7	12,488
Bricks, tiles, cement	7,595	350,000	67.0	9,286
Metal products	6,390	209,000	100.2	7,147
Rubber products	1,762	94,000	120.8	5,333
Printing and publishing	3,187	164,000	117.1	4,828
Tobacco products	7,483	390,000	29.5	4,419
Paper and paper products	1,909	135,000	100.0	3,807
Nonferrous metals	1,037	60,000	148.1	3,508
Plastic products	2,023	66,000	84.5	2,568

Energy production (consumption): electricity (kW-hr; 1992–93) 300,972,000,000 ([1992] 329,340,000,000); coal (metric tons; 1992) 254,600,000 (256,750,000); crude petroleum (barrels; 1992–93) 205,000,000 ([1992] 389,000,000); petroleum products (metric tons; 1992) 42,217,000 (52,019,000); natural gas (cu m; 1992–93) 14,500,000,000 ([1992] 12,102,000,000).

Financial aggregates[21]

	1988	1989	1990	1991	1992	1993	1994[22]
Exchange rate, Rs per:							
U.S. dollar	14.95	17.03	18.07	25.83	26.20	31.38	31.37
£	27.05	27.35	34.84	48.33	39.61	46.48	47.35
SDR	20.12	22.39	25.71	36.95	36.02	43.10	44.59
International reserves (U.S.$)							
Total (excl. gold; '000,000)	4,899	3,859	1,521	3,627	5,757	10,199	15,436
SDRs ('000,000)	96	113	316	46	4	100	109
Reserve pos. in IMF ('000,000)	656	640	—	—	292	292	302
Foreign exchange ('000,000)	4,148	3,105	1,205	3,580	5,461	9,807	15,025
Gold ('000,000 fine troy oz)	10.449	10.449	10.692	11.282	11.348	11.457	11.800
% world reserves	1.1	1.1	1.1	1.2	1.2	1.3	1.3
Interest and prices							
Central bank discount (%)	10.0	10.0	10.0	12.0	12.0	12.0	12.0
Advance (prime) rate (%)	16.5	16.5	16.5	17.9	18.9	16.3	15.0
Industrial share prices (1990 = 100)[23]	47.7	72.1	100.0	134.8	247.3	202.9	200.5
Balance of payments (U.S.$'000,000)							
Balance of visible trade	−6,581	−6,110	−5,151	...	...	...	...
Imports, f.o.b.	20,091	22,254	23,437	...	...	...	...
Exports, f.o.b.	13,510	16,144	18,286	...	...	...	...
Balance of invisibles	−567	−716	−1,886	...	...	...	...
Balance of payments, current account	−7,148	−6,826	−7,037	...	...	...	...

Land use (1992): forested 23.0%; meadows and pastures 3.8%; agricultural and under permanent cultivation 57.1%; other 16.1%.
Population economically active (1991)[24]: total 314,903,642; activity rate of total population 37.6% (participation rates: over age 15 [1981] 60.7%; female 29.0%; unemployed[25] [December 1991] 13.5%).

Price and earnings indexes (1990 = 100)

	1988	1989	1990	1991	1992	1993	1994[22]
Consumer price index	86.4	91.8	100.0	113.9	127.3	135.4	144.4
Earnings index	...	...	...	...	...	...	...

Household income and expenditure. Average household size[26] (1981) 5.5; income per household: n.a.; sources of income (1984–85): salaries and wages 42.2%, self-employed 39.7%, interest 8.6%, profits and dividends 6.0%, rent 3.5%; expenditure (1990–91): food 50.8%, of which cereals and bread 14.7%;

transportation 9.9%, of which purchase of transport services 6.4%; clothing 9.1%; housing and water charges 6.1%; energy 4.7%.
Service enterprises (net value added at factor cost in Rs '000,000; 1989–90): wholesale and retail trade 468,450; community, social, and personal services 226,320; construction 211,520; finance and insurance 172,770; transport and storage 169,630; real estate and business services 115,140; communication 30,780; electricity, gas, and water 29,050; restaurants and hotels 25,390.
Tourism: receipts from visitors (1992) U.S.$1,540,000,000; expenditures by nationals abroad (1990) U.S.$425,000,000.

Foreign trade[27, 28]

Balance of trade (current prices)

	1987–88	1988–89	1989–90	1990–91	1991–92	1992–93
Rs '000,000	−43,326	−49,417	−40,249	−61,163	+12,031	−30,841
% of total	12.1%	10.0%	6.8%	11.4%	1.4%	2.8%

Imports (1992–93): Rs 633,750,000,000 (mineral fuels and lubricants 27.0%; machinery, transport equipment, and fabricated metals 20.7%; pearls and precious and semiprecious stones [mostly diamonds] 11.2%; industrial chemicals 6.5%; fertilizers 4.5%). *Major import sources:* U.S. 12.8%; Belgium 11.0%; Germany 10.0%; Saudi Arabia 9.0%; Japan 8.5%; U.K. 8.4%; Kuwait 5.8%; Australia 5.0%.
Exports (1992–93): Rs 536,880,000,000 (cut and polished diamonds and jewelery 16.6%; machinery, transport equipment, metal products, iron and steel, and electronic components 13.3%; ready-made garments 12.9%; chemicals and chemical products 7.4%; cotton yarn, fabrics, and thread 7.3%; leather and leather manufactures 6.9%; fish products 3.2%; oil cakes 2.9%). *Major export destinations:* U.S. 18.8%; Japan 7.7%; Germany 7.7%; U.K. 6.5%; Belgium 3.7%; former U.S.S.R. 3.2%; France 2.5%.

Transport and communications

Transport. Railroads (1992–93): route length 38,800 mi, 62,500 km; passenger-mi 186,500,000,000, passenger-km 300,100,000,000; short ton-mi cargo 176,100,000,000, metric ton-km cargo 257,100,000,000. Roads (1990–91): total length 1,266,000 mi, 2,037,000 km (paved 49%). Vehicles (1992): passenger cars 2,806,533; trucks and buses 2,396,738. Merchant marine (1992): vessels (100 gross tons and over) 888; total deadweight tonnage 10,365,939. Air transport (1993)[29]: passenger-mi 8,897,000,000, passenger-km 14,318,000,000; short ton-mi cargo 245,168,000, metric ton-km cargo 357,939,000; airports (1993) with scheduled flights 95.
Communications. Daily newspapers (1993): total number 3,805; total circulation 18,800,000; circulation per 1,000 population 21. Radio (1993): 55,000,000 receivers (1 per 16 persons). Television (1993): 20,000,000 receivers (1 per 45 persons). Telephones (1992): 6,705,600 (1 per 131 persons).

Education and health

Education (1992–93)

	schools	teachers	students	student/ teacher ratio
Primary (age 6–10)	572,541	1,681,970	105,370,216	62.6
Secondary (age 11–17)	235,793	2,435,293	59,255,258	24.3
Higher[18]	7,513	...	4,610,000	

Literacy (1991): total population age 7 and over literate 352,080,000 (52.1%); males literate 224,290,000 (63.9%); females literate 127,790,000 (39.4%).
Health: physicians (1991) 394,068 (1 per 2,189 persons); hospital beds (1992) 642,103 (1 per 1,357 persons); infant mortality rate (1990–95) 88.0.
Food (1988–90): daily per capita caloric intake 2,229 (vegetable products 93%, animal products 7%); 101% of FAO recommended minimum requirement.

Military

Total active duty personnel (1994): 1,265,000 (army 87.0%, navy 4.3%, air force 8.7%); personnel in paramilitary forces for internal or border security 442,500. *Military expenditure as percentage of GNP* (1991): 2.7% (world 4.2%); per capita expenditure U.S.$8.

[1]Council of States can have a maximum number of 250 members; a maximum of 12 of these members may be nominated by the president. [2]Includes 2 nonelective seats. [3]Census not conducted; population based on projection of 1989 official estimate. [4]Excludes 46,976 sq mi (121,667 sq km) of territory claimed by India as part of Jammu and Kashmir but occupied by Pakistan or China. [5]Mother tongue unless otherwise noted. [6]Percentage based on 1971 census. [7]Within Delhi urban agglomeration. [8]Within Calcutta urban agglomeration. [9]Within Greater Bombay urban agglomeration. [10]Within Pune urban agglomeration. [11]1981 census. [12]Percentage breakdown based on 22,629 deaths recorded at 1,303 nationally dispersed primary-health-centre villages. [13]Deceased over age 60 with no apparent sickness. [14]Excludes Assam. [15]Crimes reported to National Crime Records Bureau by police authorities of state governments. [16]At factor cost. [17]Not adequately defined. [18]1991–92. [19]1993. [20]Establishments with 10 or more workers using electrical power or 20 or more workers not using electrical power. [21]End-of-period unless otherwise noted. [22]April. [23]Annual average. [24]Based on preliminary census data. [25]Applicants registered at employment exchanges. [26]Excludes shelterless population. [27]Import figures are f.o.b. in balance of trade and c.i.f. in commodities and trading partners. [28]Fiscal year beginning April 1. [29]Air-India and Indian Airlines only.

Indonesia

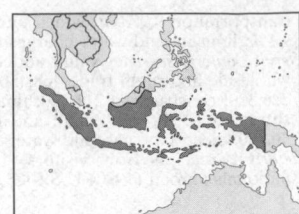

Official name: Republik Indonesia (Republic of Indonesia).
Form of government: unitary multiparty republic with two legislative houses (House of People's Representatives [500[1]]; People's Consultative Assembly [1,000[2]]).
Head of state and government: President.
Capital: Jakarta.
Official language: Bahasa Indonesia.
Official religion: monotheism.
Monetary unit: 1 Indonesian rupiah (Rp) = 100 sen; valuation (Oct. 7, 1994) 1 U.S.$ = Rp 2,173; 1 £ = Rp 3,456.

Area and population		area		population
		sq mi	sq km	1990 census
Metropolitan district	**Capitals**			
Jakarta Raya	Jakarta	228	590	8,259,266
Provinces				
Bali	Denpasar	2,147	5,561	2,777,811
Bengkulu	Bengkulu	8,173	21,168	1,179,122
Irian Jaya	Jayapura	162,928	421,981	1,648,708
Jambi	Jambi	17,297	44,800	2,020,568
Jawa Barat	Bandung	17,877	46,300	35,384,352
Jawa Tengah	Semarang	13,207	34,206	28,520,643
Jawa Timur	Surabaya	18,502	47,921	32,503,991
Kalimantan Barat	Pontianak	56,664	146,760	3,229,153
Kalimantan Selatan	Banjarmasin	14,541	37,660	2,597,572
Kalimantan Tengah	Palangkaraya	58,919	152,600	1,396,486
Kalimantan Timur	Samarinda	78,162	202,440	1,876,663
Lampung	Tanjung Karang	12,860	33,307	6,017,573
Maluku	Ambon	28,767	74,505	1,857,790
Nusa Tenggara Barat	Mataram	7,790	20,177	3,369,649
Nusa Tenggara Timur	Kupang	18,485	47,876	3,268,644
Riau	Pakanbaru	36,510	94,561	3,303,976
Sulawesi Selatan	Ujung Pandang	28,101	72,781	6,981,646
Sulawesi Tengah	Palu	26,921	69,726	1,711,327
Sulawesi Tenggara	Kendari	10,690	27,686	1,349,619
Sulawesi Utara	Menado	7,345	19,023	2,478,119
Sumatera Barat	Padang	19,219	49,778	4,000,207
Sumatera Selatan	Palembang	40,034	103,688	6,313,074
Sumatera Utara	Medan	27,331	70,787	10,256,027
Timor Timur[3]	Dili	5,743	14,874	747,750
Special autonomous districts				
Aceh	Banda Aceh	21,387	55,392	3,416,156
Yogyakarta	Yogyakarta	1,224	3,169	2,913,054
TOTAL		741,052	1,919,317	179,378,946

Demography

Population (1994): 191,340,000.
Density (1994): persons per sq mi 258.2, persons per sq km 99.7.
Urban-rural (1991): urban 31.4%; rural 68.6%.
Sex distribution (1990): male 49.88%; female 50.12%.
Age breakdown (1990): under 15, 36.5%; 15–29, 28.3%; 30–44, 18.1%; 45–59, 10.7%; 60–74, 5.3%; 75 and over, 1.1%.
Population projection: (2000) 210,625,000; (2010) 236,841,000.
Doubling time: 43 years.
Ethnolinguistic composition (1990): Javanese 39.4%; Sundanese 15.8%; Indonesian (Malay) 12.1%; Madurese 4.3%; Minang 2.4%; other 26.0%.
Religious affiliation (1990): Muslim 87.2%; Christian 9.6%, of which Roman Catholic 3.6%; Hindu 1.8%; Buddhist 1.0%; other 0.4%.
Major cities (1990): Jakarta 8,259,266; Surabaya 2,421,016; Bandung 2,026,893; Medan 1,685,972; Semarang 1,005,316.

Vital statistics

Birth rate per 1,000 population (1992): 25.2 (world avg. 26.0).
Death rate per 1,000 population (1992): 8.8 (world avg. 9.2).
Natural increase rate per 1,000 population (1992): 16.4 (world avg. 16.8).
Total fertility rate (avg. births per childbearing woman; 1991): 3.7.
Marriage rate per 1,000 population (1990–91): 8.5[4].
Divorce rate per 1,000 population (1990–91): 0.4[4].
Life expectancy at birth (1992): male 58.2 years; female 61.9 years.
Major causes of death: n.a.; however, major diseases include tuberculosis, malaria, dysentery, cholera, and plague.

National economy

Budget (1992–93). Revenue: Rp 58,168,000,000,000 (royalties from energy production 26.4%, income tax 20.5%, aid for development 18.4%, value-added tax 18.4%, nontax revenues 5.1%, import duties 4.6%). Expenditures: Rp 58,166,000,000,000 (development 41.5%, debt service 26.2%, civil service 16.3%, subsidies for autonomous regions 9.1%).
Public debt (external, outstanding; 1992): U.S.$49,289,000,000.
Tourism (1992): receipts U.S.$2,729,000,000; expenditures U.S.$1,166,000,000.
Production (metric tons except as noted). Agriculture, forestry, fishing (1992): rice 47,770,000, sugarcane 23,121,000, cassava 16,318,000, corn (maize) 7,987,000, palm oil 3,162,000, rubber 1,294,000, copra 1,135,000; livestock (number of live animals) 11,400,000 goats, 11,000,000 cattle, 5,900,000 sheep, 3,400,000 buffalo; roundwood 185,629,000 cu m; fish catch 3,314,366. Mining and quarrying (1993): nickel ore 1,970,000; bauxite 1,320,000; copper concentrate 928,189; iron sand 341,335; tin concentrate 28,585; silver 90,300 kg. Manufacturing (1990): cement 15,972,000; fertilizer 6,991,000; newsprint

157,000; cigarettes 148,000,000,000 units[5]. Energy production (consumption): electricity (kW-hr; 1992) 45,760,000,000 (45,760,000,000); coal (metric tons; 1992) 21,146,000 (5,520,000); crude petroleum (barrels; 1992) 557,266,000 (312,546,000); petroleum products (metric tons; 1992) 33,173,000 (26,684,-000); natural gas (cu m; 1992) 51,809,000,000 (20,623,000,000).
Gross national product (1993): U.S.$136,620,000,000 (U.S.$730 per capita).

Structure of gross domestic product and labour force				
	1992			
	in value Rp '000,000,000	% of total value	labour force	% of labour force
Agriculture	49,284.2	19.2	42,853,000	53.4
Mining	32,279.9	12.6	595,000	0.7
Manufacturing	53,894.9	21.0	7,848,000	9.8
Construction	15,393.2	6.0	2,363,000	3.0
Public utilities	1,887.4	0.7	173,000	0.2
Transp. and commun.	16,728.3	6.5	2,512,000	3.1
Trade	42,540.5	16.6	11,100,000	13.8
Finance, real estate	18,784.6	7.3	562,000	0.7
Pub. admin., defense	17,292.4	6.8 }	9,970,000	12.4
Services	8,422.6	3.3 }		
Other	...	...	2,323,000[6]	2.9[6]
TOTAL	256,508.0	100.0	80,299,000	100.0

Population economically active: total (1992) 80,299,000; activity rate 43.5% (participation rates: ages 15–64 [1989] 68.6%; female [1989] 39.9%; unemployed 2.7%).

Price and earnings indexes (1990 = 100)							
	1987	1988	1989	1990	1991	1992	1993
Consumer price index	80.7	87.2	92.8	100.0	109.4	117.7	128.5
Earnings index[7]	80.5	85.4	92.5	100.0	109.6	...	...

Household income and expenditure. Average household size (1990) 4.5; income per household: n.a.; sources of income (1976): wages 42.1%, self-employment 41.5%, transfer payments 2.5%; expenditure (1990): food 51.4%, housing and utilities 20.1%, clothing 5.5%, durable goods 2.9%.
Land use (1991): forested 60.3%; meadows and pastures 6.5%; agricultural and under permanent cultivation 12.3%; other 20.9%.

Foreign trade

Balance of trade (current prices)						
	1988	1989	1990	1991	1992	1993
U.S.$'000,000	+7,419	+7,229	+6,240	+6,075	+4,937	+8,872
% of total	23.5%	19.6%	13.8%	11.6%	9.2%	13.4%

Imports (1992): U.S.$27,279,600,000 (machinery and transport equipment 42.9%, chemicals 13.8%, crude materials 8.8%, mineral fuels 7.7%). *Major import sources:* Japan 22.0%; U.S. 14.0%; Germany 7.8%.
Exports (1992): U.S.$33,966,900,000 (crude petroleum 15.9%, natural gas 11.9%, plywood 9.5%, garments 9.4%, preparation rubber 3.2%). *Major export destinations:* Japan 31.7%; U.S. 13.0%; Singapore 9.8%.

Transport and communications

Transport. Railroads (1992): route length 6,583 km; passenger-km 10,532,000,-000; metric ton-km cargo 3,775,000,000. Roads (1990): length 283,516 km (paved 44%). Vehicles (1992): passenger cars 1,876,230; trucks and buses 1,666,195. Merchant marine (1992): vessels (100 gross tons and over) 2,014; deadweight tonnage 3,130,175. Air transport (1992): passenger-km 14,919,-000,000; metric ton-km cargo 460,220,000; airports (1994) 126.
Communications. Daily newspapers (1990): total number 64; total circulation 3,010,000; circulation per 1,000 population 28. Radio (1993): 22,000,000 receivers (1 per 8.5 persons). Television (1993): 11,000,000 receivers (1 per 17 persons). Telephones (1992): 1,621,650 (1 per 114 persons).

Education and health

Education (1990–91)[8]				
	schools	teachers	students	student/ teacher ratio
Primary (age 7–12)	147,064	1,331,993	26,308,423	19.8
Secondary (age 13–18)	28,834	707,987	8,236,018	11.6
Voc., teacher tr.	3,823	108,536	1,352,009	12.5
Higher	962	128,652	1,503,196	11.7

Educational attainment (1985). Percentage of population age 25 and over having: no schooling 30.3%; less than complete primary 32.2%; primary 22.8%; some secondary 6.4%; secondary 7.1%; higher 1.2%. *Literacy* (1987): total population age 15 and over literate 80,233,132 (77.6%); males literate 43,062,304 (85.6%); females literate 37,170,828 (70.0%).
Health: physicians (1989–90) 25,752 (1 per 6,861 persons); hospital beds (1991–92) 111,460 (1 per 1,643 persons); infant mortality rate per 1,000 live births (1992) 65.
Food (1988–90): daily per capita caloric intake 2,605 (vegetable products 97%, animal products 3%); 121% of FAO recommended minimum.

Military

Total active duty personnel (1993): 270,900 (army 74.9%, navy 16.2%, air force 8.9%). *Military expenditure as percentage of GNP* (1991): 1.6% (world 4.2%); per capita expenditure U.S.$10.

[1]Includes 100 nonelective seats reserved for the military. [2]Includes the 500 members of the House of People's Representatives plus 500 other delegates. [3]The legality of Indonesian administration of this province is disputed by the United Nations. [4]Muslim population only. [5]1989. [6]Includes unemployed. [7]Based on daily wage rate of production workers in manufacturing. [8]Refers to schools under the Department of Education and Culture only.

Iran

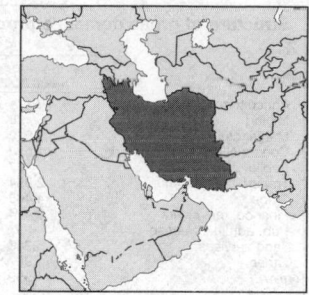

Official name: Jomhūrī-ye Eslāmī-ye Īrān (Islamic Republic of Iran).
Form of government: unitary Islamic republic with one legislative house (Islamic Consultative Assembly [270]).
Supreme leader: Rahbar (religious guide).
Head of state and government: President.
Capital: Tehrān.
Official language: Farsī (Persian).
Official religion: Islam.
Monetary unit: 1 rial (Rls); valuation (Oct. 7, 1994) 1 U.S.$ = Rls 1,732[1]; 1 £ = Rls 2,755[1].

Area and population

Provinces	Capitals	area sq mi	area sq km	population 1991 census
Āzārbāyjān-e Gharbī	Orūmīyeh	14,517	37,599	2,283,707
Āzārbāyjān-e Sharqī[2]	Tabrīz	25,421	65,842	4,390,303
Bākhtarān	Bākhtarān	9,121	23,622	1,600,568
Būshehr	Būshehr	9,792	25,360	692,211
Chahār Maḥāll va Bakhtīārī	Shahr Kord	5,722	14,820	722,504
Eṣfahān	Eṣfahān	40,852	105,805	3,657,040
Fārs	Shīrāz	46,334	120,005	3,480,112
Gīlān	Rasht	5,722	14,820	2,203,560
Hamadān	Hamadān	7,508	19,445	1,649,269
Hormozgān	Bandar 'Abbās	25,243	65,379	923,965
Īlām	Īlām	7,369	19,086	425,336
Kermān	Kermān	71,690	185,675	1,789,992
Khorāsān	Mashhad	121,007	315,687	5,997,468
Khūzestān	Ahvāz	25,688	66,532	3,155,453
Kohkīlūyeh va Būyer Aḥmadī	Yāsūj	5,289	13,699	476,564
Kordestān	Sanandaj	10,756	27,858	1,233,264
Lorestān	Khorramābād	11,027	28,560	1,470,524
Markazī	Arāk	11,402	20,530	1,102,611
Māzandarān	Sārī	18,010	46,645	3,792,772
Semnān	Semnān	35,345	91,544	458,125
Sīstān va Balūchestān	Zāhedān	70,066	181,471	1,440,251
Tehrān	Tehrān	10,896	28,221	9,981,878
Yazd	Yazd	26,875	69,605	691,067
Zanjān	Zanjān	14,047	36,382	1,774,645
TOTAL LAND AREA		630,578[3]	1,633,189[3]	
INLAND WATER		1,880[4]	4,868[4]	
TOTAL		632,457[3]	1,638,057	55,473,189[5]

Demography

Population (1994): 59,614,000[6].
Density (1994): persons per sq mi 94.3, persons per sq km 36.4.
Urban-rural (1991): urban 57.3%; rural 42.7%.
Sex distribution (1991): male 51.52%; female 48.48%.
Age breakdown (1991): under 15, 44.3%; 15–29, 26.6%; 30–44, 15.1%; 45–59, 8.2%; 60–74, 4.8%; 75 and over, 0.8%; unknown 0.2%.
Population projection: (2000) 68,329,000; (2010) 85,775,000.
Doubling time: 20 years.
Ethnic composition (1983): Persian 45.6%; Azerbaijani 16.8%; Kurdish 9.1%; Gīlakī 5.3%; Luri 4.3%; Māzandarānī 3.6%; Baluchi 2.3%; Arab 2.2%; Bakhtiari 1.7%; Turkmen 1.5%; Armenian 0.5%; other 7.1%.
Religious affiliation (1994): Muslim 99.1% (Shīʿī 93.4%; Sunnī 5.7%); Baháʾī 0.6%; Christian 0.1%; Zoroastrian 0.1%; Jewish 0.1%.
Major cities (1991): Tehran 6,475,527; Mashhad 1,759,155; Eṣfahān 1,127,030; Tabriz 1,088,985; Shīrāz 965,117; Ahvāz 724,653; Qom 681,253.

Vital statistics

Birth rate per 1,000 population (1993): 43.0 (world avg. 26.0).
Death rate per 1,000 population (1993): 8.1 (world avg. 9.2).
Natural increase rate per 1,000 population (1993): 34.9 (world avg. 16.8).
Total fertility rate (avg. births per childbearing woman; 1992): 6.1.
Marriage rate per 1,000 population (1991): 8.1.
Life expectancy at birth (1993): male 64.4 years; female 66.2 years.
Major causes of death per 100,000 population (1989)[7]: diseases of the circulatory system 249.2; accidents and violence 101.0; malignant neoplasms (cancers) 58.8; diseases of the respiratory system 48.9.

National economy

Budget (1994–95). Revenue: Rls 33,592,000,000,000 (oil revenue 65.8%, taxes 19.1%, other 15.1%). Expenditures: Rls 33,768,000,000,000 (current expenditure 62.6%, development expenditure 37.4%).
Production (metric tons except as noted). Agriculture, forestry, fishing (1992): wheat 10,800,000[8], sugar beets 5,800,000[8], barley 3,700,000, rice 2,600,000[8], grapes 1,650,000, sugarcane 1,600,000, apples 1,520,000, oranges 1,300,000, dates 635,000, pistachios 170,000; livestock (head) 45,000,000 sheep, 6,900,000 cattle; roundwood 6,840,000 cu m; fish catch (1991) 277,444. Mining and quarrying (1993): copper ore (concentrate) 10,800,000; iron ore (concentrate) 9,900,000. Manufacturing (value added, in Rls '000,000; 1989–90): textiles (excl. wearing apparel) 375,200; food products 235,700; bricks, tiles, and cement 211,500; nonelectrical machinery 160,000; iron and steel 133,200; nonindustrial chemical products 131,500. Construction (completed; 1990–91): residential 15,818,000 sq m. Energy production (consumption): electricity (kW-hr; 1992–93) 68,400,000,000 (49,175,000,000[9]); coal (metric tons; 1992) 1,500,000 (2,000,000); crude petroleum (barrels; 1992) 1,254,300,000 (340,500,000); petroleum products (metric tons; 1992) 42,246,000 (46,135,000); natural gas (cu m; 1992–93) 34,400,000,000 (33,900,000,000).

Public debt (external, outstanding; 1992): U.S.$3,065,000,000.
Gross national product (1992): U.S.$130,910,000,000 (U.S.$2,190 per capita).

Structure of gross domestic product and labour force

	1992–93 in value Rls '000,000,000[10]	1992–93 % of total value	1986 labour force	1986 % of labour force
Agriculture	15,392	23.3	3,208,613	25.0
Petroleum, natural gas	5,669	8.6 }	32,377	0.3
Other mining	362	0.5 }		
Manufacturing	9,218	14.0	1,460,132	11.4
Construction	2,619	4.0	1,207,459	9.4
Public utilities	834	1.3	91,064	0.7
Transp. and commun.	5,274	8.0	630,704	4.9
Trade, restaurants	11,308	17.1	875,919	6.8
Finance, real estate	8,095	12.3	114,302	0.9
Pub. admin., defense	6,505	9.9 }	3,050,943	23.7
Services	1,403	2.1 }		
Other	−674[11]	−1.0[11]	2,183,189[12]	17.0[12]
TOTAL	66,005	100.0[3]	12,854,702	100.0[3]

Tourism (1992–93): receipts U.S.$38,000,000[13]; expenditures U.S.$1,166,000,000.
Pop. economically active (1986): total 12,854,702; activity rate 26.0% (participation rates: ages 15–64, 46.8%; female 10.3%; unemployed [1993] 30%).

Price and earnings indexes (1987–88 = 100)

	1987–88	1988–89	1989–90	1990–91	1991–92	1992–93
Consumer price index	100.0	128.9	151.4	164.9	197.2	239.9
Daily earnings index[14]	100.0	121.9	144.0	157.5	181.2	216.9

Household income and expenditure. Average household size (1986) 5.1; income per urban household (1988) Rls 1,339,970 (U.S.$19,536); sources of urban income (1988): wages 37.4%, self-employment 30.5%, other 32.1%; expenditure (1990–91): food and hotels 46.0%, housing and energy 25.6%.
Land use (1991): forested 11.0%; meadows and pastures 26.9%; agricultural and under permanent cultivation 9.2%; other 52.9%.

Foreign trade

Balance of trade (current prices)

	1987–88	1988–89	1989–90	1990–91	1991–92[15]	1992–93[15]
U.S.$'000,000	−1,320	−810	−367	+975	−5,526	−1,871
% of total	5.2%	3.6%	1.4%	2.6%	13.0%	4.6%

Imports (1992–93)[15]: U.S.$21,150,000,000 ([16]motor vehicles and machinery 28.5%, iron and steel 15.0%, food and medicine 11.5%). *Major import sources* (1992): Germany 24.0%; Japan 13.0%; Italy 10.0%; U.A.E. 5.0%; U.K. 5.0%.
Exports (1992–93)[15]: U.S.$19,279,000,000 (petroleum and natural gas 84.8%, carpets 5.9%, pistachios 1.9%, copper bars 0.8%, leather 0.4%). *Major export destinations* (1992): Japan 15.0%; Italy 10.0%; The Netherlands 9.0%; Brazil 7.0%; France 6.0%; South Korea 6.0%.

Transport and communications

Transport. Railroads (1992): route length 2,838 mi, 4,567 km; (1991) passenger-km 4,584,000,000; metric ton-km cargo 7,704,000,000. Roads (1991): length 94,130 mi, 151,488 km (paved [1989] 34%). Vehicles (1992): passenger cars 1,557,000; trucks and buses 561,000. Merchant marine (1992): vessels (100 gross tons and over) 403; total deadweight tonnage 8,345,269. Air transport (1993)[17]: passenger-km 4,830,000,000; metric ton-km cargo 59,963,000; airports (1994) with scheduled flights 19.
Communications. Daily newspapers (1990): 21; circulation 1,500,000; circulation per 1,000 population 27. Radio (1993): 12,000,000 receivers (1 per 4.9 persons). Television (1993): 2,250,000 receivers (1 per 26 persons). Telephones (1993–94): 3,598,000 (1 per 16 persons).

Education and health

Education (1991–92)

	schools	teachers	students	student/ teacher ratio
Primary (age 7–11)	59,280[18]	312,273	9,787,593	31.3
Secondary (age 12–18)	...	199,451	5,311,988	26.6
Voc., teacher tr.	...	19,480	307,069	15.8
Higher	44[10, 19]	25,208	636,255	25.2

Educational attainment (1986). Percentage of population age 25 and over having: no formal schooling 12.8%; secondary education 38.0%; higher 7.8%.
Literacy (1990): total population age 15 and over literate 18,200,000 (54.0%); males literate 11,600,000 (64.5%); females literate 6,600,000 (43.3%).
Health (1993–94): physicians 29,000 (1 per 2,000 persons); hospital beds 90,000 (1 per 650 persons); infant mortality rate (1993) 62.1.
Food (1986–88): daily per capita caloric intake 3,317 (vegetable products 90%, animal products 10%); 130% of FAO recommended minimum requirement.

Military

Total active duty personnel (1993): 473,000 (revolutionary guard corps 25.4%, army 67.6%, navy 3.8%, air force 3.2%). *Military expenditure as percentage of GNP* (1991): 5.7% (world 4.2%); per capita expenditure U.S.$102.

[1]Official floating rate. [2]The former province of Āzārbāyjān-e Sharqi (East Azerbaijan) was divided into Ardabīl and Āzārbāyjān-e Markazī (Central Azerbaijan) provinces in 1993. [3]Detail does not add to total given because of rounding. [4]Area of Lake Urmia. [5]De jure figure. [6]De jure estimate excluding refugees. [7]Projected rates based on about 21% of total deaths. [8]1993. [9]1991–92. [10]At factor cost. [11]Less imputed bank service charge. [12]Includes 1,818,740 unemployed. [13]11 months only. [14]Construction sector only. [15]Estimated figures. [16]Based on 1991–92 imports equaling U.S.$23,941,000,000. [17]Iran Air. [18]1990–91. [19]Universities only.

Iraq

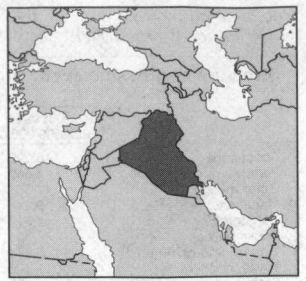

Official name: al-Jumhūrīyah
al-'Irāqīyah (Republic of Iraq).
Form of government: unitary
multiparty[1] republic with one
legislative house (National Assembly
[250]).
Head of state and government:
President.
Capital: Baghdad.
Official language: Arabic[2].
Official religion: Islam.
Monetary unit: 1 Iraqi dinar (ID) = 20
dirhams = 1,000 fils; valuation
(Oct. 1, 1994) 1 U.S.$ = 500 ID[3];
1 £ = 795.25 ID.

Area and population

Governorates	Capitals	area[4] sq mi	sq km	population 1991 estimate
al-Anbār	ar-Ramādī	53,208	137,808	865,500
Bābil	al-Ḥillah	2,163	5,603	1,221,100
Baghdād	Baghdad	1,572	4,071	3,910,900
al-Baṣrah[4]	Basra	7,363	19,070	1,168,800
Dhī Qār	an-Nāṣirīyah	4,981	12,900	1,030,900
Diyālā	Ba'qūbah	6,828	17,685	1,037,600
Karbalā'	Karbalā'	1,944	5,034	567,600
Maysān	al-'Amārah	6,205	16,072	524,200
al-Muthannā	as-Samāwah	19,977	51,740	350,000
an-Najaf	an-Najaf	11,129	28,824	666,400
Nīnawā	Mosul	14,410	37,323	1,618,700
al-Qādisiyah	ad-Dīwānīyah	3,148	8,153	595,600
Ṣalāḥ ad-Dīn	Tikrīt	9,407	24,363	772,200
at-Ta'mīm	Kirkūk	3,737	9,679	605,900
Wāsiṭ	al-Kūt	6,623	17,153	605,700
Kurdish Autonomous Region[5]				
Dahūk	Dahūk	2,530	6,553	309,300
Irbīl	Irbīl	5,820	15,074	928,400
as-Sulaymānīyah	as-Sulaymānīyah	6,573	17,023	1,124,200
LAND AREA		167,618	434,128	
OTHER[6]		357	924	
TOTAL		167,975	435,052	17,903,000

Demography

Population (1994): 19,869,000.
Density (1994): persons per sq mi 118.3, persons per sq km 45.7.
Urban-rural (1991): urban 70.4%; rural 29.6%.
Sex distribution (1992): male 50.59%; female 49.41%.
Age breakdown (1992): under 15, 44.6%; 15–29, 29.3%; 30–44, 14.0%; 45–59, 7.0%; 60–74, 3.8%; 75 and over, 1.3%.
Population projection: (2000) 23,521,000; (2010) 30,761,000.
Doubling time: 23 years.
Ethnic composition (1983): Arab 77.1%; Kurd 19.0%; Turkmen 1.4%; Persian 0.8%; Assyrian 0.8%; other 0.9%.
Religious affiliation (1993): Shī'ī Muslim 61.5%; Sunnī Muslim 34.0%; Christian 3.7%, of which Eastern-rite Roman Catholic 2.5%, Nestorian 0.8%, Orthodox 0.4%; Yazīdī syncretist 0.8%.
Major cities (1985): Baghdad (1990; urban agglomeration) 4,044,000; Basra 616,700; Mosul 570,926; Irbīl 333,903; as-Sulaymānīyah 279,424.

Vital statistics

Birth rate per 1,000 population (1992): 36.5 (world avg. 26.0).
Death rate per 1,000 population (1992)[7]: 6.5 (world avg. 9.2).
Natural increase rate per 1,000 population (1992): 30.0 (world avg. 16.8).
Total fertility rate (avg. births per childbearing woman; 1992): 5.8.
Marriage rate per 1,000 population (1992): 8.1.
Life expectancy at birth (1991)[8]: male 46.0 years; female 57.0 years.
Major causes of death (1993). Deprivation of medical care (because of acute medical supply shortages) and malnutrition.

National economy

Budget (1992). Revenue: ID 13,935,000,000. Expenditures: ID 13,935,000,000. Details of more recent proposed budgets were not released. Special emphasis was to be placed on the reconstruction of the infrastructure.
Tourism (1989): receipts U.S.$59,000,000; expenditures, n.a.
Public debt (external, outstanding; April 1991): U.S.$109,000,000,000.
Production (metric tons except as noted). Agriculture, forestry, fishing (1993): barley 1,562,000, wheat 1,187,000, dates 550,000, watermelons 490,000, tomatoes 460,000, grapes 450,000, cucumbers 350,000, corn (maize) 315,000, rice 215,000, oranges 180,000; livestock (number of live animals) 6,000,000 sheep, 1,200,000 cattle; roundwood (1992) 155,000 cu m; fish catch (1991) 12,100. Mining and quarrying (1992): phosphate rock 900,000; sulfur 600,000; gypsum 380,000. Manufacturing (value added in ID '000,000; 1990): petroleum products and chemical products 668; nonmetal mineral products 152; food 114; textiles 91; paper products, printing, and publishing 78; beverages 56; footwear 56; electrical machinery 54; nonelectrical machinery 53; tobacco products 53. Construction (authorized; 1991): residential 4,558,000 sq m; nonresidential 410,000 sq m. Energy production (consumption): electricity (kW-hr; 1992) 25,300,000,000 (25,300,000,000); coal, none (none); crude petroleum (barrels; 1992) 191,900,000 (156,000,000); petroleum products (metric tons; 1992) 16,020,000 (13,755,000); natural gas (cu m; 1992) 3,010,-000,000 (3,010,000,000).
Gross national product (1991): U.S.$12,640,000,000 (U.S.$710 per capita).

Structure of gross domestic product and labour force

	1991 in value ID '000,000[9]	1991 % of total value	1988 labour force	1988 % of labour force
Agriculture	6,171	28.1	477,264	11.6
Mining	98	0.4	60,701	1.5
Manufacturing	912	4.2	337,293	8.2
Construction	612	2.8	460,788	11.2
Public utilities	67	0.3	41,200	1.0
Transp. and commun.	2,854	13.0	266,233	6.4
Trade	4,465	20.3	281,877	6.8
Finance, real estate	3,414	15.6	41,532	1.0
Pub. admin., defense, and services	5,333	24.3	2,160,406	52.3
Other	−1,967	−9.0		
TOTAL	21,959	100.0	4,127,294	100.0

Population economically active (1988): total 4,127,294; activity rate of total population 24.7% (participation rates: ages 15–64, 45.3%; female 12.0%).

Price and earnings indexes (1988 = 100)

	1988	1989	1990	1991	1992[10]
Consumer price index	100.0	...	161.2	461.9	605.4
Earnings index	...	...	...	...	...

Household income and expenditure (1988). Average household size 8.9; sources of income: self-employment 33.9%, wages and salaries 23.9%, transfers 23.0%, rent 18.6%; expenditure: food and beverages 50.2%, housing and energy 19.9%, clothing and footwear 10.6%.
Land use (1992): forested 4.3%; meadows and pastures 9.1%; agricultural and under permanent cultivation 12.5%; built-on, wasteland, and other 74.1%.

Foreign trade[11, 12]

Balance of trade (current prices)

	1987	1988	1989	1990[13]	1991[13]	1992[13]
U.S.$'000,000	+7,662	+5,092	+7,644	+4,700	0	−800
% of total	49.9%	29.9%	35.5%	33.0%	0.0%	28.6%

Imports (1992): U.S.$1,800,000,000[13] (agricultural products 60.0%, of which cereals 26.0%; fish and forestry products 7.0%; unspecified 33.0%). *Major import sources*[14]: Australia 19.0%; Jordan 17.0%; Turkey 14.0%; United Kingdom 10.0%; Indonesia 7.0%.
Exports (1992): U.S.$1,000,000,000[13] (agricultural products 2.2%, of which dates 1.8%; other [mostly crude petroleum and petroleum products] 97.8%). *Major export destinations*[15]: Jordan 71.0%; Portugal 15.0%; Greece 13.0%.

Transport and communications

Transport. Railroads (1992): route length 1,493 mi, 2,403 km; passenger-mi 572,000,000, passenger-km 920,000,000; short ton-mi cargo 79,000,000, metric ton-km cargo 115,000,000. Roads (1989): total length 28,305 mi, 45,554 km (paved 84%). Vehicles (1992): passenger cars 672,000; trucks and buses 368,000. Merchant marine (1992): vessels (100 gross tons and over) 131; total deadweight tonnage 1,578,822. Air transport: [16].
Communications. Daily newspapers (1990): total number 6; total circulation 650,000; circulation per 1,000 population 37. Radio (1993): 3,500,000 receivers (1 per 5.5 persons). Television (1993): 1,000,000 receivers (1 per 19 persons). Telephones (1990): 712,109 (1 per 25 persons).

Education and health

Education (1991–92)

	schools	teachers	students	student/ teacher ratio
Primary (age 6–11)	8,875	127,578	3,316,036	26.0
Secondary (age 12–17)	2,746	43,937	1,084,715	24.7
Voc., teacher tr.	296	9,957	152,903	15.4
Higher	20	10,520	197,786	18.8

Educational attainment: n.a. Literacy (1990): total population age 15 and over literate 6,030,000 (59.7%); males literate 3,570,000 (69.8%); females literate 2,460,000 (49.3%).
Health: physicians (1991) 9,366 (1 per 1,922 persons); hospital beds (1990) 31,227 (1 per 568 persons); infant mortality rate per 1,000 live births (1992) 56.3.
Food (1991)[8]: daily per capita caloric intake 2,300–2,400; 93–97% of FAO recommended minimum requirement.

Military

Total active duty personnel (1994): 382,000 (army 91.6%, navy 0.5%, air force 7.9%). *Military expenditure as percentage of GNP* (1991): 74.9% (world 4.2%); per capita expenditure U.S.$528.

[1]Multipartyism authorized by a September 1991 law, but political power is in fact concentrated in a single-party apparatus. [2]Kurdish is official in the Kurdish Autonomous Region only. [3]Official rate per government announcement of Oct. 1, 1994; the black-market rate on the same date was about 600 Iraqi dinars per U.S.$. [4]Includes territory ceded to Kuwait as of Jan. 15, 1993, per UN resolution of May 1992. Iraq recognized Kuwait and its borders per official announcement of Nov. 10, 1994. [5]De facto self-government as of May 1992 elections. [6]Territorial water at the mouth of the Shaṭṭ al-'Arab. [7]Excludes c. 400,000 deaths (between 1990 and the end of 1993) caused by UN sanctions. [8]Postwar estimate. [9]At factor cost. [10]February. [11]Imports c.i.f.; exports f.o.b. [12]UN-imposed trade sanctions begun August 1990 continued through October 1994. [13]Estimated figure(s). [14]Based on estimated imports equaling U.S.$647,000,000. [15]Based on estimated exports equaling U.S.$557,000,000. [16]UN sanctions stopped international service from March 1991; lack of spare parts ended domestic service from June 1992.

Ireland

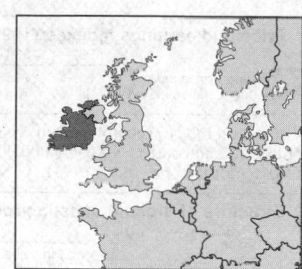

Official name: Éire (Irish); Ireland[1] (English).
Form of government: unitary multi-party republic with two legislative houses (Senate [60[2]]; House of Representatives [166]).
Chief of state: President.
Head of government: Prime Minister.
Capital: Dublin.
Official languages: Irish; English.
Official religion: none.
Monetary unit: 1 Irish pound (£Ir) = 100 new pence; valuation (Oct. 7, 1994) 1 £Ir − U.S.$1.56 = £0.99.

Area and population	area		population
Provinces Counties	sq mi	sq km	1991 census
Connacht	6,611	17,122	423,031
Galway[3]	2,293	5,940	180,364
Leitrim	501	1,525	25,301
Mayo	2,084	5,398	110,713
Roscommon	951	2,463	51,897
Sligo	693	1,796	54,756
Leinster	7,580	19,633	1,860,949
Carlow	346	896	40,942
Dublin[3]	356	922	1,025,304
Kildare	654	1,694	122,656
Kilkenny	796	2,062	73,635
Laoighis	664	1,719	52,314
Longford	403	1,044	30,296
Louth	318	823	90,724
Meath	902	2,336	105,370
Offaly	771	1,998	58,494
Westmeath	681	1,763	61,880
Wexford	908	2,351	102,069
Wicklow	782	2,025	97,265
Munster	9,315	24,127	1,009,533
Clare	1,231	3,188	90,918
Cork[3]	2,880	7,460	410,369
Kerry	1,815	4,701	121,894
Limerick[3]	1,037	2,686	161,956
Tipperary North Riding	771	1,996	57,854
Tipperary South Riding	872	2,258	74,918
Waterford[3]	710	1,838	91,624
Ulster	3,093	8,012	232,206
Cavan	730	1,891	52,796
Donegal	1,865	4,830	128,117
Monaghan	498	1,291	51,293
TOTAL LAND AREA	26,600	68,895[4]	
INLAND WATER	537	1,390	
TOTAL	27,137	70,285	3,525,719

Demography

Population (1994): 3,512,000.
Density (1994): persons per sq mi 129.4, persons per sq km 50.0.
Urban-rural (1991): urban 57.0%; rural 43.0%.
Sex distribution (1991): male 49.74%; female 50.26%.
Age breakdown (1991): under 15, 26.7%; 15–29, 24.1%; 30–44, 20.2%; 45–59, 13.8%; 60–74, 10.6%; 75 and over, 4.6%.
Population projection: (2000) 3,492,000; (2010) 3,458,000.
Doubling time: not applicable; doubling time exceeds 100 years.
Place of birth (1986): native born 93.7%; England and Wales 3.6%; Northern Ireland 1.0%; United States 0.4%; Scotland 0.4%; other 0.9%.
Religious affiliation (1981): Roman Catholic 93.1%; Church of Ireland (Anglican) 2.8%; Presbyterian 0.4%; other 3.7%.
Major cities (1991)[5]: Dublin 477,675; Cork 127,024; Limerick 52,040; Galway 50,842; Waterford 40,345.

Vital statistics

Birth rate per 1,000 population (1992): 14.6 (world avg. 26.0); legitimate 82.0%; illegitimate 18.0%.
Death rate per 1,000 population (1992): 8.7 (world avg. 9.2).
Natural increase rate per 1,000 population (1992): 5.9 (world avg. 16.8).
Total fertility rate (avg. births per childbearing woman; 1990–95): 2.1.
Life expectancy at birth (1985–87): male 71.0 years; female 76.7 years.
Major causes of death per 100,000 population (1992): heart and circulatory diseases 391.0, of which ischemic heart disease 216.7; malignant neoplasms (cancers) 210.1; respiratory disease 64.6, of which pneumonia 50.2.

National economy

Budget (1994). Revenue: £Ir 10,759,000,000 (income taxes 34.7%, value-added tax 23.6%, excise taxes 19.2%). Expenditures: £Ir 11,021,000,000 (1991; debt service 25.9%, social welfare 19.9%, health 14.8%, education 13.3%).
Public debt (1992): U.S.$46,262,000,000.
Tourism (1992): receipts U.S.$1,620,000,000; expenditures U.S.$1,361,000,000.
Production (metric tons except as noted). Agriculture, forestry, fishing (1992): sugar beets 1,397,000, barley 1,167,000, wheat 713,000, potatoes 642,000, oats 136,000, milk 52,270,000 hectolitres; livestock (number of live animals) 8,909,000 sheep, 6,976,000 cattle, 1,386,000 pigs; roundwood (1991) 1,677,000 cu m; fish catch (1991) 240,703. Mining and quarrying (1992): gypsum 343,-000; zinc ore 194,100[6]; lead ore 42,900[6]. Manufacturing (value added in £Ir; 1990): metals and engineering goods 3,237,500,000; food products 1,828,-300,000; chemical products 1,492,600,000; paper, printing, and publishing 452,900,000; nonmetallic mineral products 441,400,000; textiles 192,400,000. Construction (1992): residential 2,499,000 sq m; nonresidential 2,067,000

sq m. Energy production (consumption): electricity (kW-hr; 1991) 15,147,-000,000 (15,147,000,000); coal (metric tons; 1991) 1,000 (3,120,000); crude petroleum (barrels; 1991) none (13,106,000); petroleum products (metric tons; 1991) 1,728,000 (4,137,000); natural gas (cu m; 1991) 3,763,000,000 ([1990] 3,671,000,000).
Gross national product (1992): U.S.$42,798,000,000 (U.S.$12,100 per capita).

Structure of gross domestic product and labour force	1992			
	in value £Ir '000,000	% of total value	labour force	% of labour force
Agriculture	2,140	9.1	150,000	11.1
Mining			6,000	0.4
Manufacturing			223,000	16.5
Construction	9,043	38.6	74,000	5.5
Public utilities			13,000	1.0
Transp. and commun.			68,000	5.0
Trade	4,164	17.7	232,000[7]	17.2[7]
Pub. admin., defense	1,593	6.8	68,000	5.0
Services			291,000	21.6
Finance	6,514	27.8	[7]	[7]
Other			225,000[8]	16.7[8]
TOTAL	23,455[4]	100.0	1,350,000	100.0

Population economically active (1992): total 1,350,000; activity rate of total population 38.4% (participation rates: ages 15–64, 59.2%[9]; female 30.5%[9]; unemployed 15.5%[10]).

Price and earnings indexes (1985 = 100)						
	1987	1988	1989	1990	1991	1992	1993
Consumer price index	107.1	109.4	113.8	117.6	121.4	125.1	126.9
Weekly earnings index	113.0	118.3	123.1	127.8	133.4	138.8	179.2[11]

Household income and expenditure. Average household size (1983) 3.9; income per household: n.a.; sources of income (1987): wages and salaries 58.6%, self-employment 13.3%, interest and dividends 8.2%; expenditure (1992): food 27.2%, rent and household goods 11.6%, transportation 9.9%.
Land use (1991): forest 5.0%; pasture 68.1%; agricultural 13.5%; other 13.4%.

Foreign trade[12]

Balance of trade (current prices)						
	1987	1988	1989	1990	1991	1992
£Ir '000,000	2,004	2,574	2,880	2,458	2,784	4,062
% of total	10.3%	11.7%	11.0%	9.4%	10.2%	13.9%

Imports (1992): £Ir 13,195,019,000 (machinery and transport equipment 35.6%, manufactured goods 14.7%, chemicals 13.0%, food 9.7%, petroleum and petroleum products 5.2%, crude materials [inedible] 2.2%, beverages and tobacco 1.6%). *Major import sources:* U.K. 38.9%; U.S. 14.2%; Germany 8.4%; Japan 5.0%; The Netherlands 4.4%; France 4.4%.
Exports (1992): £Ir 16,628,836,000 (machinery and transport equipment 27.0%, food 22.1%, chemical products 19.3%, manufactured goods 7.6%). *Major export destinations:* U.K. 26.5%; Germany 12.8%; France 9.6%; U.S. 8.2%.

Transport and communications

Transport. Railroads (1992): length 2,814 km; passenger-km 1,225,600,000; metric ton-km cargo 663,300,000. Roads (1992): length 92,327 km (paved 94%). Vehicles (1992): passenger cars 858,498; trucks and buses 149,355. Merchant marine (1992): vessels (100 gross tons and over) 189; total deadweight tonnage 208,573. Air transport (1990): passenger-km 3,804,000,000; metric ton-km cargo 431,618,000; airports (1994) 10.
Communications. Daily newspapers (1992): 8; total circulation 652,350; circulation per 1,000 population 186. Radio (1993): 2,000,000 receivers (1 per 1.8 persons). Television (1993): 1,000,000 receivers (1 per 3.5 persons). Telephones (1990): 916,207 (1 per 3.8 persons).

Education and health

Education (1991–92)	schools	teachers	students	student/ teacher ratio
Primary (age 6–11)	3,425	20,430[13]	542,898	...
Secondary (age 12–18)	474	12,034	216,740	18.0
Voc., teacher tr.	317	9,004	132,117	14.7
Higher	48	3,934[14]	76,809	16.0[14]

Educational attainment (1981). Percentage of population age 25 and over having: primary education 52.3%; secondary 23.3%; some postsecondary 16.5%; university or like institution 7.9%. *Literacy* (1987): virtually 100% literate.
Health (1991): physicians (1984) 5,180 (1 per 681 persons); hospital beds 13,806[15] (1 per 255 persons); infant mortality rate 9.1.
Food (1988–90): daily per capita caloric intake 3,952 (vegetable products 62%, animal products 38%); 157% of FAO recommended minimum requirement.

Military

Total active duty personnel (1993): 13,000 (army 86.1%, navy 7.7%, air force 6.2%). *Military expenditure as percentage of GNP* (1991): 1.3% (world 4.2%); per capita expenditure U.S.$145.

[1]As provided by the constitution; the 1948 Republic of Ireland Act provides precedent for this longer formulation of the official name but, per official sources, "has not changed the usage *Ireland* as the name of the state in the English language." [2]Includes 11 nonelective seats. [3]Includes county borough(s). [4]Detail does not add to total given because of rounding. [5]County boroughs. [6]Metal content of ores. [7]Trade includes Finance. [8]Unemployed. [9]1988. [10]1991. [11]August. [12]Import figures are f.o.b. in balance of trade and c.i.f. for commodities and trading partners. [13]National schools only. [14]1988–89. [15]Acute-care public hospitals only.

Israel

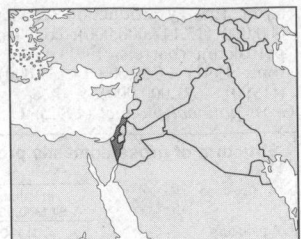

Official name: Medinat Yisra'el
(Hebrew); Isrā'īl (Arabic) (State
of Israel).
Form of government: multiparty
republic with one legislative house
(Knesset [120]).
Chief of state: President.
Head of government: Prime Minister.
Capital: Jerusalem is the proclaimed
capital of Israel (from Jan. 23, 1950)
and the actual seat of government,
but recognition of its status as capital
by the international community has
largely been withheld pending final
settlement of territorial and other
issues through peace talks between
Israel and the Arab parties
concerned.
Official languages: Hebrew; Arabic.
Official religion: none.
Monetary unit: 1 New (Israeli) sheqel
(NIS) = 100 agorot; valuation (Oct. 7,
1994) 1 U.S.$ = NIS 3.01;
1 £ = NIS 4.79.

Area and population

Districts	Capitals	area[1] sq mi	sq km	population 1993[2] estimate
Central (Ha Merkaz)	Ramla	479	1,242	1,112,300
Haifa (Hefa)	Haifa	330	854	691,000
Jerusalem (Yerushalayim)	Jerusalem	215	557	616,000
Northern (Ha Zafon)	Tiberias	1,347	3,490	877,400
Southern (Ha Darom)	Beersheba	5,555	14,387	651,700
Tel Aviv	Tel Aviv–Yafo	66	170	1,142,200
TOTAL		7,992	20,700	5,090,500[3, 4]

Demography

Population (1994): 5,331,000[3, 5].
Density (1994)[5, 6]: persons per sq mi 629.9, persons per sq km 243.2.
Urban-rural (1993): urban 90.4%; rural 9.6%.
Sex distribution (1992): male 49.6%; female 50.4%.
Age breakdown (1992): under 15, 30.2%; 15–29, 25.0%; 30–44, 20.2%; 45–59,
11.9%; 60–74, 8.8%; 75 and over, 3.8%.
Population projection: (2000) 5,990,000; (2010) 6,647,000.
Doubling time: 47 years.
Ethnic composition (1993): Jewish 81.3%; Arab and other 18.7%.
Religious affiliation (1993): Jewish 81.3%; Muslim (mostly Sunnī) 14.2%;
Christian 2.8%; Druze and other 1.7%.
Major cities (1993): Jerusalem 556,500; Tel Aviv–Yafo 356,900; Haifa 249,800;
Holon 162,800; Petah Tiqwa 150,900; Bat Yam 145,300.

Vital statistics

Birth rate per 1,000 population (1993): 21.3 (world avg. 26.0); (1990)[7] legiti-
mate 98.5%; illegitimate 1.5%.
Death rate per 1,000 population (1993): 6.3 (world avg. 9.2).
Natural increase rate per 1,000 population (1993): 15.0 (world avg. 16.8).
Total fertility rate (avg. births per childbearing woman; 1992): 2.9.
Marriage rate per 1,000 population (1992): 6.5.
Divorce rate per 1,000 population (1992): 1.3.
Life expectancy at birth (1992): male 75.1 years; female 78.5 years.
Major causes of death per 100,000 population (1990): diseases of the circu-
latory system 249.7; malignant neoplasms (cancers) 125.6; accidents 38.5;
diseases of the respiratory system 44.4.

National economy

Budget (1993). Revenue: NIS 102,447,000,000 (income tax and property tax
25.2%, value-added tax 18.1%, internal loans 18.0%, external loans 12.8%).
Expenditures: NIS 102,447,000,000 (defense 17.5%, debt 16.4%, interest on
loans 13.2%, labour and social welfare 10.2%, education and culture 8.8%).
Public debt (1991): U.S.$81,938,000,000.
Production (metric tons except as noted). Agriculture, forestry, fishing (1992):
fodder 1,391,000, grapefruit 378,000, tomatoes 328,000, wheat 180,000, potatoes 173,000, watermelons 110,200, seed cotton 34,000; livestock (number
of live animals) 360,000 sheep, 349,000 cattle, 111,000 goats, 23,000,000
chickens; roundwood (1992) 110,000 cu m; fish catch (1992) 19,200. Mining
and quarrying (1992): phosphate rock 2,372,000; potash 1,300,000; lime 208,-
000; bromine 135,000; bromine compounds 125,000. Manufacturing (1992):
cement 3,960,000; sulfuric acid 137,600; polyethylene 128,739; paper 98,702;
cardboard 92,072; chlorine 33,912; ammonium sulfate 12,444; wine 12,373,-
000 litres. Construction (1992): residential 7,620,000 sq m; nonresidential
1,450,000 sq m. Energy production (consumption): electricity (kW-hr; 1992)
24,475,000 (24,125,000); coal (metric tons; 1992) none (4,945,000); crude
petroleum (barrels; 1992) 65,000 (72,977,000); petroleum products (metric tons; 1992) 8,958,000 (8,178,000); natural gas (cu m; 1992) 23,320,000
(23,320,000).
Land use (1990): forested 5.5%; meadows and pastures 7.2%; agricultural
and under permanent cultivation 21.5%; other 65.8%.
Population economically active (1993)[8]: total 1,946,000; activity rate of total
population 36.7% (participation rates: over age 15, 52.8%; female 47.1%;
unemployed 10.0%).

Price and earnings indexes (1990 = 100)

	1987	1988	1989	1990	1991	1992	1993
Consumer price index	61	71	85	100	119	133	148
Monthly earnings index	58	70	85	100	116	130	144

Tourism (1992): receipts from visitors U.S.$1,891,000,000; expenditures by
nationals abroad U.S.$1,953,000,000.
Gross national product (1993): U.S.$72,667,000,000 (U.S.$13,760 per capita).

Structure of gross domestic product and labour force

	1991 in value NIS '000,000	1991 % of total value	1993 labour force	1993 % of labour force
Agriculture	2,398	2.3	62,000	3.2
Manufacturing, mining	21,488	20.9	371,300	19.1
Construction	7,777	7.6	118,300	6.1
Public utilities	2,299	2.2	17,500	0.9
Transp. and commun.	7,560	7.4	106,100	5.5
Trade	9,665	9.4	250,700	12.9
Finance	24,065	23.4	183,900	9.3
Public and community services	4,110	4.0	500,200	25.7
Services }	23,481	22.8	131,800	6.8
Other }			204,300[9]	10.5[9]
TOTAL	102,843	100.0	1,946,000[8]	100.0

Household income and expenditure (1992). Average household size 3.7;
monthly income per household[10] NIS 5,580 (U.S.$2,268); sources of income
(1992)[10]: salaries and wages 86.9%, allowances and assistance 10.6%, self-
employment 2.4%; expenditure (1992): food, beverages, and tobacco 25.1%,
housing 21.7%, household durable goods 6.7%, clothing 5.4%, transportation 4.3%, energy 4.2%.

Foreign trade

Balance of trade (current prices)

	1988	1989	1990	1991	1992	1993
U.S.$'000,000	−2,841.8	−2,358.1	−3,504.0	−5,473.3	−6,135.0	−5,692.1
% of total	13.1%	10.0%	13.1%	19.6%	19.8%	16.1%

Imports (1993): U.S.$20,517,600,000 (investment goods 17.4%; diamonds
17.2%; consumer goods 12.3%; fuel and lubricants 8.5%). *Major import
sources:* U.S. 17.7%; Belgium 12.2%; Germany 10.4%; U.K. 8.6%; Switzerland 7.5%; Italy 7.3%; Japan 5.1%; France 4.1%.
Exports (1993): U.S.$14,825,500,000 (machinery 34.0%; worked diamonds
19.2%; chemicals 12.7%; textiles 6.3%; food, beverages, and tobacco 3.7%;
rubber and plastic 3.2%). *Major export destinations:* U.S. 31.2%; U.K. 5.5%;
Belgium 5.4%; Germany 5.3%; Japan 5.2%; Hong Kong 4.9%; France 3.9%;
The Netherlands 3.7%; Italy 3.0%.

Transport and communications

Transport. Railroads (1992): route length 356 mi, 573 km; passenger-mi 123,-
000,000, passenger-km 198,000,000; short ton-mi cargo 751,000,000, metric
ton-km cargo 1,096,000,000. Roads (1992): total length 8,364 mi, 13,461 km
(paved 100%). Vehicles (1992): passenger cars 923,000; trucks and buses
186,000. Merchant marine (1992): vessels (100 gross tons and over) 58; total
deadweight tonnage 723,418. Air transport (1992)[11]: passenger-mi 5,332,-
000,000, passenger-km 8,581,000,000; short ton-mi cargo 534,832,000, metric
ton-km cargo 860,731,000; airports (1994) with scheduled flights 7.
Communications. Daily newspapers (1990): total number 30; total circulation
1,200,000; circulation per 1,000 population 261. Radio (1991): 2,250,000 receivers (1 per 2.2 persons). Television (1991): 1,200,000 receivers (1 per 4.1
persons). Telephones (1991): 2,545,000 (1 per 2.0 persons).

Education and health

Education (1992–93)

	schools	teachers	students	student/ teacher ratio
Primary (age 6–13)	1,735	51,321	661,063	12.9
Secondary (age 14–17)	816	50,392	449,407	8.9
Vocational	386	...	122,223	...
Higher	7	6,150[12]	84,990	...

Educational attainment (1991). Percentage of population age 25 and over
having: no formal schooling 6.7%; primary education 22.5%; secondary
39.6%; postsecondary, vocational, and higher 31.2%. *Literacy* (1992): total
population age 15 and over literate 3,390,027 (94.8%); males literate 1,698,-
696 (97.1%); females literate 1,692,331 (92.7%).
Health (1993): physicians (1987) 11,895 (1 per 345 persons); hospital beds
30,695 (1 per 177 persons); infant mortality rate per 1,000 live births 7.8.
Food (1988–90): daily per capita caloric intake 3,220 (vegetable products
79%, animal products 21%); 125% of FAO recommended minimum.

Military

Total active duty personnel (1993): 176,000 (army 76.1%, navy 5.7%, air force
18.2%). *Military expenditure as percentage of GNP* (1993): 9.4% ([1991] world
4.2%); per capita expenditure U.S.$1,337.

---

[1]Excluding West Bank (2,270 sq mi [5,879 sq km]), Gaza Strip (146 sq mi [378 sq
km]), Golan Heights (444 sq mi [1,150 sq km]), and East Jerusalem (27 sq mi [70 sq
km]). [2]January 1. [3]Includes population of Golan Heights (28,100) and East Jerusalem.
[4]Excludes Israelis in Jewish localities (pop. 105,400) in the West Bank and Gaza Strip.
[5]Includes Israelis in Jewish localities in the West Bank and Gaza Strip. [6]Includes
area and population of East Jerusalem and Golan Heights. [7]Jewish population only.
[8]Excludes armed forces; includes Israelis in occupied territories. [9]Mostly unemployed.
[10]Urban population only. [11]El Al only. [12]1991–92.

Italy

Official name: Repubblica Italiana (Italian Republic).
Form of government: republic with two legislative houses (Senate [326[1]]; Chamber of Deputies [630]).
Chief of state: President.
Head of government: Prime Minister.
Capital: Rome.
Official language: Italian.
Official religion: none.
Monetary unit: 1 lira (Lit, plural lire) = 100 centesimi; valuation (Oct. 7, 1994) 1 U.S.$ = Lit 1,569; 1 £ = Lit 2,495.

Area and population

Regions Provinces	Capitals	area sq mi	area sq km	population 1992[2] estimate[3]
Abruzzi	L'Aquila	4,168	10,794	1,249,156
Chieti	Chieti	999	2,587	382,034
L'Aquila	L'Aquila	1,944	5,034	297,832
Pescara	Pescara	473	1,225	289,355
Teramo	Teramo	752	1,948	279,935
Basilicata	Potenza	3,858	9,992	610,018
Matera	Matera	1,331	3,447	208,884
Potenza	Potenza	2,527	6,545	401,134
Calabria	Catanzaro	5,823	15,080	2,069,626
Catanzaro	Catanzaro	2,026	5,247	742,116
Cosenza	Cosenza	2,568	6,650	750,868
Reggio di Calabria	Reggio di Calabria	1,229	3,183	576,642
Campania	Naples	5,249	13,595	5,628,393
Avellino	Avellino	1,078	2,792	438,574
Benevento	Benevento	800	2,071	292,559
Caserta	Caserta	1,019	2,639	815,351
Napoli	Naples	452	1,171	3,015,195
Salerno	Salerno	1,900	4,922	1,066,714
Emilia-Romagna	Bologna	8,542	22,123	3,906,702
Bologna	Bologna	1,429	3,702	905,902
Ferrara	Ferrara	1,016	2,632	360,171
Forlì	Forlì	1,123	2,910	607,192
Modena	Modena	1,039	2,690	604,974
Parma	Parma	1,332	3,449	390,779
Piacenza	Piacenza	1,000	2,589	267,221
Ravenna	Ravenna	718	1,859	350,227
Reggio nell'Emilia	Reggio nell'Emilia	885	2,292	420,236
Friuli-Venezia Giulia	Trieste	3,029	7,845	1,196,494
Gorizia	Gorizia	180	467	138,076
Pordenone	Pordenone	878	2,273	275,147
Trieste	Trieste	82	212	261,353
Udine	Udine	1,889	4,893	521,918
Lazio	Rome	6,642	17,203	5,141,731
Frosinone	Frosinone	1,251	3,239	479,781
Latina	Latina	860	2,251	470,447
Rieti	Rieti	1,061	2,749	144,941
Roma	Rome	2,066	5,352	3,761,954
Viterbo	Viterbo	1,395	3,612	278,608
Liguria	Genoa	2,092	5,418	1,672,663
Genova	Genoa	709	1,836	948,012
Imperia	Imperia	446	1,155	213,617
La Spezia	La Spezia	341	882	226,725
Savona	Savona	596	1,545	284,309
Lombardia	Milan	9,211	23,857	8,853,461
Bergamo	Bergamo	1,066	2,760	932,370
Brescia	Brescia	1,846	4,782	1,044,699
Como	Como	798	2,067	795,756
Cremona	Cremona	684	1,771	327,784
Mantova	Mantova	903	2,339	369,314
Milano	Milan	1,066	2,762	3,920,626
Pavia	Pavia	1,145	2,965	490,478
Sondrio	Sondrio	1,240	3,212	175,453
Varese	Varese	463	1,199	796,981
Marche	Ancona	3,743	9,693	1,428,593
Ancona	Ancona	749	1,940	437,114
Ascoli Piceno	Ascoli Piceno	806	2,087	360,465
Macerata	Macerata	1,071	2,774	295,316
Pesaro e Urbino	Pesaro	1,117	2,892	335,698
Molise	Campobasso	1,713	4,438	330,806
Campobasso	Campobasso	1,123	2,909	238,925
Isernia	Isernia	590	1,529	91,881
Piemonte	Turin	9,807	25,399	4,299,912
Alessandria	Alessandria	1,375	3,560	437,794
Asti	Asti	583	1,511	208,174
Cuneo	Cuneo	2,665	6,903	547,020
Novara	Novara	1,388	3,594	496,272
Torino	Turin	2,637	6,830	2,235,826
Vercelli	Vercelli	1,159	3,001	374,826
Puglia	Bari	7,470	19,348	4,031,759
Bari	Bari	1,980	5,129	1,531,142
Brindisi	Brindisi	710	1,838	411,359
Foggia	Foggia	2,774	7,185	696,449
Lecce	Lecce	1,065	2,759	804,179
Taranto	Taranto	941	2,437	588,630
Sardegna	Cagliari	9,301	24,090	1,646,771
Cagliari	Cagliari	2,662	6,895	762,400
Nuoro	Nuoro	2,720	7,044	272,786
Oristano	Oristano	1,016	2,631	156,947
Sassari	Sassari	2,903	7,520	454,638
Sicilia (Sicily)	Palermo	9,926	25,709	4,966,118
Agrigento	Agrigento	1,175	3,042	476,083
Caltanissetta	Caltanissetta	822	2,128	278,252
Catania	Catania	1,371	3,552	1,036,063
Enna	Enna	989	2,562	186,112
Messina	Messina	1,254	3,248	646,854
Palermo	Palermo	1,927	4,992	1,224,083
Ragusa	Ragusa	623	1,614	289,768
Siracusa	Siracusa	814	2,109	402,034
Trapani	Trapani	951	2,462	426,869

Area and population (continued)

		sq mi	sq km	1992[2] estimate[3]
Toscana	Florence	8,877	22,992	3,526,752
Arezzo	Arezzo	1,248	3,232	314,330
Firenze	Florence	1,498	3,879	1,183,413
Grosseto	Grosseto	1,739	4,504	215,907
Livorno	Livorno	468	1,213	336,147
Lucca	Lucca	684	1,773	376,879
Massa-Carrara	Massa-Carrara	447	1,157	200,113
Pisa	Pisa	945	2,448	385,048
Pistoia	Pistoia	373	965	264,480
Siena	Siena	1,475	3,821	250,435
Trentino-Alto Adige	Bolzano	5,258	13,618	890,753
Bolzano-Bozen	Bolzano	2,857	7,400	440,727
Trento	Trento	2,401	6,218	450,026
Umbria	Perugia	3,265	8,456	811,638
Perugia	Perugia	2,446	6,334	588,687
Terni	Terni	819	2,122	222,951
Valle d'Aosta	Aosta	1,259	3,262	115,958
Veneto	Venice	7,090	18,364	4,379,932
Belluno	Belluno	1,420	3,670	211,925
Padova	Padova	827	2,142	820,530
Rovigo	Rovigo	691	1,789	247,801
Treviso	Treviso	956	2,477	744,025
Venezia	Venice	950	2,460	819,607
Verona	Verona	1,195	3,096	787,910
Vicenza	Vicenza	1,051	2,722	748,134
TOTAL		116,324	301,277	56,757,236

Demography

Population (1994): 57,313,000.
Density (1994): persons per sq mi 492.7, persons per sq km 190.2.
Urban-rural (1992[2]): urban 66.8%; rural 33.2%.
Sex distribution (1991): male 48.61%; female 51.39%.
Age breakdown (1988): under 15, 17.8%; 15–29, 24.1%; 30–44, 20.1%; 45–59, 18.6%; 60–74, 13.5%; 75 and over, 5.9%.
Population projection: (2000) 57,274,000; (2010) 56,270,000.
Doubling time: not applicable; population stable.
Ethnolinguistic composition (1983): Italian 94.1%; Sardinian 2.7%; Rhaetian 1.3%; other 1.9%.
Religious affiliation (1980): Roman Catholic 83.2%; nonreligious 13.6%; atheist 2.6%; other 0.6%.
Major cities (1992[2, 3]): Rome 2,773,889; Milan 1,367,733; Naples 1,068,927; Turin 961,512; Palermo 698,141; Genoa 676,069; Bologna 403,397; Florence 402,211; Bari 342,710; Catania 333,485; Venice 309,041.
National origin (1980): Italian 98.8%; foreign-born 1.2%, of which Austrian 0.4%, French 0.2%, Slovene 0.2%, Albanian 0.1%, other 0.3%.
Mobility (1981). Population living in the same residence as in 1976: 92.4%.
Households. Average household size (1990) 2.8; composition of households: 1 person 20.2%, 2 persons 23.9%, 3 persons 23.0%, 4 persons 22.9%, 5 or more persons 10.0%. Family households (1983): 15,205,000 (85.3%); non-family 2,617,000 (14.7%), of which 1-person 13.0%.
Immigration (1989): immigrants admitted 81,201, from Europe 48.2%, of which West Germany 16.2%, Switzerland 7.8%; Africa 14.0%; Argentina 9.3%; Asia 9.2%; U.S. 5.4%.

Vital statistics

Birth rate per 1,000 population (1993): 9.4 (world avg. 26.0); (1990) legitimate 93.7%; illegitimate 6.3%.
Death rate per 1,000 population (1993): 9.5 (world avg. 9.2).
Natural increase rate per 1,000 population (1993): 0.1 (world avg. 16.8).
Total fertility rate (avg. births per childbearing woman; 1992): 1.3.
Marriage rate per 1,000 population (1991): 5.4.
Divorce rate per 1,000 population: (1990): 0.4.
Life expectancy at birth (1990): male 73.6 years; female 80.2 years.
Major causes of death per 100,000 population (1991): diseases of the circulatory system 420.8; malignant neoplasms (cancers) 276.0; accidents and violence 68.8; diseases of the respiratory system 59.2; diseases of the digestive system 49.9.

Social indicators

Educational attainment (1981). Percentage of population age 25 and over having: no formal schooling 19.3%[4]; primary education 47.4%; lower secondary 18.0%; upper secondary 11.2%; higher 4.1%.

Distribution of income (1986)
percentage of household income by quintile

1	2	3	4	5 (highest)
6.8	12.0	16.7	23.5	41.0

Quality of working life. Average workweek (1985): 36.6 hours. Annual rate per 100,000 workers (1988) for: injury or accident 3,697; industrial illness 4055; death 5.7. Percentage of labour force insured for damages or income loss (1992) resulting from: injury 100%; permanent disability 100%; death 100%. Number of working days lost to labour stoppages per 1,000 workers (1991): 862. Average duration of journey to work: n.a. Rate per 1,000 workers of discouraged (unemployed no longer seeking work; 1990): 1.1.
Material well-being. Rate per 1,000 of population possessing (1991): telephone 579; automobile 494; television 299 (colour 188[6]). Households possessing (1979): television 72%; refrigerator 91%; washing machine 88%.
Social participation. Eligible voters participating in last national election (1992): 67.0%. Population participating in voluntary work: n.a. Trade union membership in total workforce (1990): c. 28%. Practicing Roman Catholic population in total affiliated population which attended church weekly (early 1990s) 25.0%.
Social deviance (1992). Offense rate per 100,000 population for: murder 2.9; rape 2.4; assault 240.5; theft, including burglary and housebreaking 2,958.

Access to services (1981). Proportion of dwellings having access to: electricity 99.5%; safe water supply 98.7%; toilet facilities 98.5%; bath facilities 86.4%.
Leisure (1988). Favourite leisure activities (as percentage of household spending on culture): sporting events 19.0%; cinema 18.5%; theatre 13.7%.

National economy
Gross national product (1993): U.S.$1,134,800,000,000 (U.S.$19,620 per capita).

Structure of gross domestic product and labour force

| | 1992 | | 1991 | |
	in value (Lit '000,000,000)	% of total value	labour force	% of labour force
Agriculture	46,369	3.1	1,823,000	7.5
Mining	} 305,100	20.2	227,000	1.0
Manufacturing			4,731,000	19.5
Construction	87,635	5.8	1,957,000	8.1
Public utilities	82,594	5.5	...	...
Transp. and commun.	90,949	6.0	1,149,000	4.8
Trade	277,814	18.4	4,660,000	19.2
Finance	200,450	13.3	1,003,000	4.1
Pub. admin., defense	194,081	12.9 }	6,042,000	24.9
Services	212,347	14.1 }		
Other	9,851[7]	0.7[7]	2,653,000[8]	10.9[8]
TOTAL	1,507,190	100.0	24,245,000	100.0

Budget (1991). Revenue: Lit 444,820,000,000,000 (1990; income taxes 37.7%, of which individual 30.9%, corporate 6.7%; value-added and excise taxes 30.0%; social-security taxes 29.5%; property taxes 1.4%). Expenditures: Lit 583,620,000,000,000 (1988; social security and welfare 39.7%; debt service 16.3%; health 11.8%; education and culture 9.7%; transportation 7.4%; defense 3.8%).
Public debt (1993): U.S.$1,038,200,000,000.
Tourism (1992): receipts U.S.$21,577,000,000; expenditures U.S.$16,617,000,000.

Manufacturing, mining, and construction enterprises (1989)

	no. of enterprises[9]	no. of employees[10]	hourly wages as a % of avg. of all wages[11]	annual value added (Lit '000,000,000)
Manufacturing				
Machinery (nonelectrical)	4,652	392,000	98.0	24,127
Transport equipment	899	319,000	117.7	18,090
Electrical machinery	1,742	267,000	112.1	16,422
Textiles	3,410	240,000	84.4	11,929
Iron and steel	1,027	151,000	122.6	10,706
Food products	1,762	160,000	92.2	10,062
Pottery, ceramics, and glass	1,847	153,000	...	10,027
Metal products	2,945	174,000	86.7	8,989
Industrial chemicals	848	146,000	119.7	8,168
Printing, publishing	1,062	86,000	103.2	7,009
Wearing apparel	2,921	163,000	75.0	5,983
Plastic products	1,474	93,000	84.4	5,299
Paper and paper products	719	63,000	102.2	4,201
Petroleum and gas	16	7,000	136.6	2,483
Mining and quarrying	343	18,000	...	1,022
Construction	326,000[12]	1,849,000[13]	...	53,465[13]

Production (metric tons except as noted). Agriculture, forestry, fishing (1992): sugar beets 14,960,000, grapes 10,538,000, wheat 9,037,000, corn (maize) 7,799,000, tomatoes 5,956,000, potatoes 2,736,000, olives 2,489,000, apples 2,469,000, barley 1,759,000, peaches 1,316,000, pears 1,189,000, soybeans 1,057,000; livestock (number of live animals) 10,435,000 sheep, 8,549,000 pigs, 8,004,000 cattle, 139,000,000 chickens; roundwood (1992) 8,423,000 cu m; fish catch 355,358. Mining and quarrying (1992): rock salt 3,365,946; potash 1,615,064; feldspar 1,387,968; barite 80,709; zinc 62,558; magnesium 35,565[14]; lead 27,475. Manufacturing (1992): cement 41,043,085; crude steel 25,100,622; pig iron 11,561,849; plastics 2,809,871; sulfuric acid 2,773,478; caustic soda 964,834; textiles 496,195[15]; wine 61,680,000 hectolitres[6]; beer 11,502,571 hectolitres[13]; olive oil 7,527,000 hectolitres[14]; 5,028,676 washing machines[14]; 4,155,481 refrigerators[14]; 2,653,952 motorized road vehicles[14], of which 1,631,943 automobiles[14], 775,884 motorcycles, scooters, and mopeds[14], 246,725 trucks and buses[14]; 2,434,484 televisions[14], of which 2,433,067 colour[14]. Construction (1991): residential 93,213,740 cu m; commercial, industrial, and other 103,628,468 cu m.

Service enterprises (1992)

	no. of enterprises[11]	no. of employees[15]	hourly wage as a % of all wages	annual value added (Lit '000,000,000)
Public utilities	1,398	230,000[6]	...	82,594
Transportation	} 132,164	1,146,000	...	90,949
Communications				
Finance	89,092	895,000	...	200,450
Wholesale and retail trade	1,495,702	4,537,000	...	277,814
Pub. admin., services	...	5,986,000	...	194,081

Energy production (consumption): electricity (kW-hr; 1992) 226,243,000,000 (261,543,000,000); coal (metric tons; 1992) 825,000 (18,389,000); crude petroleum (barrels; 1992) 30,694,000 (598,165,000); petroleum products (metric tons; 1992) 85,102,000 (92,982,000); natural gas (cu m; 1992) 17,996,000,000 (50,216,000,000).
Population economically active (1991): total 24,245,000; activity rate of total population 42.4% (participation rates: ages 14–64, 59.3%; female 37.1%; unemployed 10.9%).

Price and earnings indexes (1990 = 100)

	1987	1988	1989	1990	1991	1992	1993
Consumer price index	84.1	88.4	93.9	100.0	106.3	111.8	116.8
Earnings index	82.9	87.9	93.2	100.0	109.8	115.4	119.8

Household income and expenditure (1992). Average household size 2.7; average annual income per household (1984) Lit 19,692,000 (U.S.$11,208); sources of income (1991): salaries and wages 41.7%, property income and self-employment 38.0%, transfer payments 20.3%; expenditure (1991): food and beverages 20.2%, housing 15.4%, transportation and communications 12.1%, recreation and education 9.1%.

Financial aggregates

	1989	1990	1991	1992	1993	1994[16]
Exchange rate, Lit per:						
U.S. dollar	1,372.1	1,198.1	1,240.6	1,232.4	1,573.7	1,564.5
£	2,249.8	2,138.1	2,195.1	2,175.8	2,363.7	2,417.5
SDR	1,669.6	1,607.8	1,646.5	2,022.4	2,340.5	2,301.6
International reserves (U.S.$)						
Total (excl. gold; '000,000)	46,720	62,927	48,679	27,643	27,545	34,089
SDRs ('000,000)	998	1,037	930	238	241	120
Reserve pos. in IMF ('000,000)	1,444	1,714	2,255	2,439	2,164	2,133
Foreign exchange ('000,000)	44,278	60,176	45,495	24,966	25,140	31,836
Gold ('000,000 fine troy oz)	66.67	66.67	66.67	66.67	66.67	66.67
% world reserves	7.1	7.1	7.1	7.1	7.3	7.3
Interest and prices						
Central bank discount (%)	14.21	12.50	12.00	12.00	8.00	7.00[17]
Govt. bond yield (%)	11.61	11.87	11.37	11.99	9.60	8.92[17]
Industrial share prices (1990 = 100)	99.3	100.0	84.7	70.5	83.5	109.9[17]
Balance of payments (U.S.$'000,000)						
Balance of visible trade	−2,167	724	−895	3,088	...	...
Imports, f.o.b.	−142,285	−169,216	−169,701	−175,067	...	...
Exports, f.o.b.	140,118	169,940	168,806	178,155	...	...
Balance of invisibles	−8,719	−14,946	−20,556	−31,082	...	...
Balance of payments, current account	−10,886	−14,222	−21,451	−27,994	...	...

Land use (1990): forested 22.4%; meadows and pastures 16.2%; agricultural and under permanent cultivation 39.4%; other 22.0%.

Foreign trade

Balance of trade (current prices)

	1987	1988	1989	1990	1991	1992
Lit '000,000,000	−6,533	−1,012	−3,358	+724	−1,913	2,229
% of total	2.2%	0.3%	0.8%		0.5%	

Imports (1992): Lit 232,111,000,000,000 (machinery and transport equipment 34.1%, of which transport equipment 14.8%; precision machinery 6.1%; chemicals and chemical products 15.0%; metal and semiprocessed metal 8.0%; food and live animals 6.7%; crude petroleum 5.4%; textiles 3.8%). *Major import sources:* Germany 21.6%; France 14.5%; The Netherlands 5.9%; U.K. 5.7%; U.S. 5.2%; Switzerland 4.5%.
Exports (1992): Lit 219,436,000,000,000 (machinery and transport equipment 41.2%, of which electrical machinery 4.9%; automobiles 4.0%; precision machinery 3.8%; chemicals and chemical products 10.4%; textiles 8.8%; wearing apparel 7.7%, of which shoes 2.8%; metal and processed metal 6.3%). *Major export destinations:* Germany 20.4%; France 14.6%; U.S. 7.0%; U.K. 6.6%; Spain 5.1%.

Transport and communications
Transport. Railroads (1992): length 12,176 mi, 19,595 km; passenger-mi 30,050,000,000, passenger-km 48,361,000,000; short ton-mi cargo 15,091,000,000, metric ton-km cargo 22,033,000,000. Roads (1991): total length 188,597 mi, 303,518 km (paved 100%). Vehicles (1991): passenger cars 28,200,000; trucks and buses 2,521,000. Merchant marine (1992): vessels (100 gross tons and over) 1,636; total deadweight tonnage 10,940,065. Air transport (1993)[18]: passenger-mi 15,234,000,000, passenger-km 24,516,000,000; short ton-mi cargo 1,337,514,000, metric ton-km cargo 1,952,737,000; airports (1994) 32.
Communications. Daily newspapers (1991): total number 123; total circulation 8,838,200; circulation per 1,000 population 154. Radio (1993): 14,817,197 receivers (1 per 3.9 persons). Television (1993): 17,000,500 receivers (1 per 3.4 persons). Telephones (1991[2]): 32,945,122 (1 per 1.7 persons).

Education and health

Education (1992–93)

	schools	teachers	students	student/teacher ratio
Primary (age 6–10)	22,710	182,390	2,959,564	16.2
Secondary (age 11–18)	9,857	105,964	2,059,044	19.4
Voc., teacher tr.	7,930	133,685	2,833,150	21.2
Higher[19]	50	56,723	1,538,606	27.1

Literacy (1990): total population age 15 and over literate 47,507,000 (97.1%); males literate 22,832,000 (97.8%); females literate 24,675,000 (96.4%).
Health (1992): physicians 296,385 (1 per 193 persons); hospital beds (1991) 385,691 (1 per 148 persons); infant mortality rate per 1,000 live births (1993) 7.4.
Food (1988–90): daily per capita caloric intake 3,498 (vegetable products 74%, animal products 26%); 139% of FAO recommended minimum requirement.

Military
Total active duty personnel (1994): 322,300 (army 63.6%, navy 13.7%, air force 22.7%). *Military expenditure as percentage of GNP* (1991): 2.1% (world 4.2%); per capita expenditure U.S.$421.

[1]Includes 11 nonelective seats. [2]January 1. [3]Resident population only. [4]More than two-thirds are age 55 and over. [5]1978. [6]1988. [7]Imputed bank charges less duties on imports. [8]Unemployed. [9]Enterprises with 20 or more persons engaged. [10]Total number of persons engaged. [11]1981. [12]All enterprises (1982). [13]1987. [14]1991. [15]1990. [16]July. [17]June. [18]Alitalia only. [19]Universities only.

Jamaica

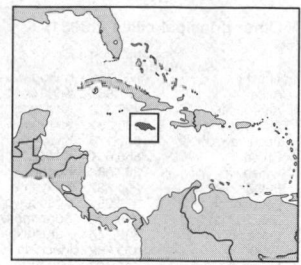

Official name: Jamaica.
Form of government: constitutional monarchy with two legislative houses (Senate [21]; House of Representatives [60]).
Chief of state: British Monarch represented by governor-general.
Head of government: Prime Minister.
Capital: Kingston.
Official language: English.
Official religion: none.
Monetary unit: 1 Jamaica dollar (J$) = 100 cents; valuation (Oct. 7, 1994) 1 U.S.$ = J$32.53; 1 £ = J$51.74.

Area and population		area		population
		sq mi	sq km	1992 estimate
Parishes	Capitals			
Clarendon	May Pen	462	1,196	219,400
Hanover	Lucea	174	450	66,000
Kingston	2	8	22	3
Manchester	Mandeville	321	830	167,900
Portland	Port Antonio	314	814	77,600
Saint Andrew	2	166	431	679,100[3]
Saint Ann	Saint Ann's Bay	468	1,213	151,700
Saint Catherine	Spanish Town	460	1,192	364,400
Saint Elizabeth	Black River	468	1,212	145,300
Saint James	Montego Bay	230	595	161,000
Saint Mary	Port Maria	236	611	113,000
Saint Thomas	Morant Bay	287	743	87,500
Trelawny	Falmouth	338	875	73,800
Westmoreland	Savanna-la-Mar	312	807	128,800
TOTAL		4,244	10,991	2,435,500

Demography

Population (1994): 2,497,000.
Density (1994): persons per sq mi 587.9, persons per sq km 227.0.
Urban-rural (1991): urban 50.2%; rural 49.8%.
Sex distribution (1993): male 49.98%; female 50.02%.
Age breakdown (1993): under 15, 31.9%; 15–29, 30.3%; 30–44, 18.1%; 45–59, 9.5%; 60 and over, 10.2%.
Population projection: (2000) 2,642,000; (2010) 2,907,000.
Doubling time: 38 years.
Ethnic composition (1982): black 74.7%; mixed black 12.8%; East Indian 1.3%; other 11.2%, of which not stated 9.5%.
Religious affiliation (1982): Protestant 55.9%, of which Church of God 18.4%, Baptist 10.0%, Anglican 7.1%, Seventh-day Adventist 6.9%, Pentecostal 5.2%; Roman Catholic 5.0%; nonreligious or atheist 17.7%; not stated 11.2%; other 10.2%, of which Rastafarian c. 5.0%.
Major cities (1991): Kingston 103,771[4] (metropolitan area 587,798); Spanish Town 92,383; Portmore 90,138; Montego Bay 83,446; May Pen 46,785.

Vital statistics

Birth rate per 1,000 population (1993): 23.9 (world avg. 26.0); (1987) legitimate 14.9%, illegitimate 85.1%.
Death rate per 1,000 population (1993): 5.6 (world avg. 9.2).
Natural increase rate per 1,000 population (1993): 18.3 (world avg. 16.8).
Total fertility rate (avg. births per childbearing woman; 1992): 2.6.
Marriage rate per 1,000 population (1992): 5.3.
Divorce rate per 1,000 population (1992): 0.6.
Life expectancy at birth (1990–95): male 71.4 years; female 75.8 years.
Major causes of death per 100,000 population (1985): diseases of the circulatory system 229.6; malignant neoplasms (cancers) 91.4; diseases of the respiratory system 36.8; endocrine and metabolic disorders 29.1.

National economy

Budget (1993–94). Revenue J$34,243,000,000 (tax revenue 85.0%, of which income taxes 32.5%, consumption taxes 30.6%, stamp duties 4.7%; nontax revenue 15.0%). Expenditures: J$41,256,900,000 (current expenditure 73.2%, of which debt interest 24.6%; development expenditure 26.8%).
Production (metric tons except as noted). Agriculture, forestry, fishing (1993): sugarcane 2,661,000, yams 221,900, vegetables 147,400, bananas 76,800, plantains 35,800, citrus fruits 27,700, coffee 12,300, legumes 11,100, cacao beans 6,300, pimientos 1,700; livestock (number of live animals; 1992) 440,000 goats, 320,000 cattle, 250,000 pigs, roundwood (1991) 180,000 cu m; fish catch (1991) 10,430. Mining and quarrying (1993): crude bauxite 3,938,600; alumina 2,989,400; gypsum 152,200. Manufacturing (1993): sugar 219,000; flour 147,800; molasses 102,500; beer and stout 781,200 hectolitres; rum 218,400 hectolitres; cigarettes 1,298,500,000 units. Construction (1992): residential units completed 5,286[5]; factory space completed 6,989 sq m[6]. Energy production (consumption): electricity (kW-hr; 1992) 2,735,000,000 (2,735,000,000); coal, none (none); crude petroleum (barrels; 1992) none (8,708,000); petroleum products (metric tons; 1992) 1,206,000 (1,028,000); natural gas, none (none).
Household income and expenditure. Average household size (1991) 4.2; average annual income per household (1988) J$8,356 (U.S.$1,525); sources of income (1989): wages and salaries 66.1%, self-employment 19.3%, transfers 14.6%; expenditure (1988)[7]: food and beverages 55.6%, housing 7.9%, fuel and other household supplies 7.4%, health care 7.0%, transportation 6.4%, clothing and footwear 5.1%, household furnishings 2.8%, other 7.8%.
Gross national product (at current market prices; 1992): U.S.$3,216,000,000 (U.S.$1,340 per capita).

Structure of gross domestic product and labour force				
	1993			
	in value J$'000,000	% of total value	labour force	% of labour force
Agriculture	8,043	8.4	220,800	20.4
Mining	6,961	7.3	7,800	0.7
Manufacturing	17,667	18.4	97,800	9.0
Construction	12,341	12.9	62,100	5.8
Public utilities	2,193	2.3	4,500	0.4
Transp. and commun.	7,630	8.0	40,100	3.7
Trade	22,707	23.7	191,100	17.7
Pub. admin., defense	9,063	9.5		
Finance, real estate	10,772	11.2	272,200	25.1
Services	4,343	4.5		
Other	−5,935[8]	−6.2[8]	186,600[9]	17.2[9]
TOTAL	95,785	100.0	1,083,000	100.0

Population economically active (1993): total 1,083,000; activity rate of total population 43.6% (participation rates: ages 14–64 [1990] 71.6%; female 48.0%; unemployed 16.3%).

Price and earnings indexes (1990 = 100)							
	1987	1988	1989	1990	1991	1992	1993
Consumer price index	66.2	71.7	82.0	100.0	151.1	267.8	327.0
Earnings index	...	...	...	...	...	...	...

Public debt (external, outstanding; 1992): U.S.$3,596,000,000.
Tourism (1992): receipts from visitors U.S.$858,000,000; expenditures by nationals abroad U.S.$64,000,000.
Land use (1991): forested 17.0%; meadows and pastures 17.5%; agricultural and under permanent cultivation 25.0%; other 40.5%.

Foreign trade[10]

Balance of trade (current prices)					
	1988	1989	1990	1991	1992	1993
U.S.$'000,000	−601	−873	−785	−654	−636	−1,121
% of total	26.5%	30.4%	25.3%	22.2%	23.2%	34.9%

Imports (1993): J$53,138,079,000 (raw materials 59.6%, of which fuels 15.5%; capital goods 20.3%, of which machinery and apparatus 7.1%; consumer goods 20.1%). *Major import sources* (1992): United States 55.9%; Venezuela 5.4%; United Kingdom 4.5%; Mexico 4.0%; Japan 3.6%; Netherlands Antilles 3.2%; Canada 3.1%; Hong Kong 2.8%.
Exports (1993): J$25,545,600,000 (alumina 42.1%; raw sugar 9.3%; bauxite 8.1%; bananas 3.4%; rum 2.1%; coffee 1.9%). *Major export destinations* (1992): United States 42.7%; United Kingdom 15.0%; Canada 10.4%; Norway 6.7%; Germany 3.7%; Ghana 3.3%.

Transport and communications

Transport. Railroads (1991): route length 129 mi, 208 km; passenger-mi 12,127,000[6], passenger-km 19,516,000[6]; short ton-mi cargo 1,700,000, metric ton-km cargo 2,482,000. Roads (1991): total length 10,212 mi, 16,435 km (paved 29%). Vehicles (1991): passenger cars 97,500; trucks and buses 18,000. Merchant marine (1992): vessels (100 gross tons and over) 12; total deadweight tonnage 16,207. Air transport (1992)[11]: passenger-mi 888,559,000, passenger-km 1,430,000,000; short ton-mi cargo 14,235,000, metric ton-km cargo 20,783,000; airports (1994) with scheduled flights 4.
Communications. Daily newspapers (1993): total number 3; total circulation 130,400[12]; circulation per 1,000 population 53[12]. Radio (1993): 1,500,000 receivers (1 per 1.6 persons). Television (1993): 484,000 receivers (1 per 5.1 persons). Telephones (1992): 278,872 (1 per 8.8 persons).

Education and health

Education (1992–93)[13]				
	schools	teachers	students	student/ teacher ratio
Primary (age 6–11)[14]	788[15]	10,147	386,688	38.1
Secondary (age 12–16)	126	7,927	152,367	19.2
Voc., teacher tr.	18	976	15,617	16.0
Higher	15[16]	1,047[17]	19,173[18]	17.9[17]

Educational attainment (1982). Percentage of population age 25 and over having: no formal schooling 3.2%; some primary education 79.8%; some secondary 15.0%; complete secondary and higher 2.0%. *Literacy* (1990): total population age 15 and over literate 1,630,000 (98.4%); males literate 800,000 (98.2%); females literate 830,000 (98.6%).
Health: physicians[19] (1993) 364 (1 per 6,791 persons); hospital beds (1992) 5,304 (1 per 462 persons); infant mortality rate per 1,000 live births (1989) 27.0.
Food (1988–90): daily per capita caloric intake 2,558 (vegetable products 83%, animal products 17%); 114% of FAO recommended minimum requirement.

Military

Total active duty personnel (1993): 3,320 (army 90.4%; coast guard 4.5%; air force 5.1%). *Military expenditure as percentage of GNP* (1991): 0.7% (world 4.2%); per capita expenditure U.S.$10.

[1]January 1. [2]The parishes of Kingston and Saint Andrew are jointly administered from the Half Way Tree section of Saint Andrew. [3]Kingston included with Saint Andrew. [4]City of Kingston is coextensive with Kingston parish. [5]51% public sector. [6]1990. [7]Weights of consumer price index components. [8]Less imputed service charges. [9]Includes 176,700 unemployed. [10]Import figures are c.i.f. [11]Air Jamaica only. [12]Circulation for 2 newspapers only. [13]Public schools only. [14]Includes lower-secondary students at all-age schools. [15]1991–92. [16]1988–89. [17]1987–88. [18]1989–90. [19]Public health only.

Japan

Official name: Nihon (Japan).
Form of government: constitutional monarchy with a National Diet consisting of two legislative houses (House of Councillors [252]; House of Representatives [511]).
Chief of state: Emperor.
Head of government: Prime Minister.
Capital: Tokyo.
Official language: Japanese.
Official religion: none.
Monetary unit: 1 yen (¥) = 100 sen; valuation (Oct. 7, 1994) 1 U.S.$ = ¥100.22; 1 £ = ¥159.40.

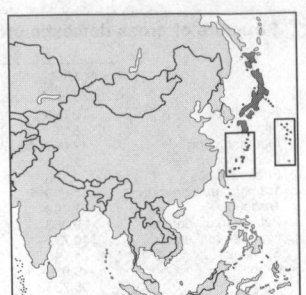

Area and population

Regions Prefectures	Capitals	area sq mi	area sq km	population 1993[1] estimate
Chūbu				
Aichi	Nagoya	1,984	5,139	6,795,000
Fukui	Fukui	1,619	4,192	825,000
Gifu	Gifu	4,091	10,596	2,085,000
Ishikawa	Kanazawa	1,621	4,198	1,171,000
Nagano	Nagano	5,245	13,585	2,170,000
Niigata	Niigata	4,857	12,579	2,478,000
Shizuoka	Shizuoka	3,001	7,773	3,712,000
Toyama	Toyama	1,642	4,252	1,121,000
Yamanashi	Kōfu	1,723	4,463	865,000
Chūgoku				
Hiroshima	Hiroshima	3,269	8,467	2,872,000
Okayama	Okayama	2,738	7,092	1,936,000
Shimane	Matsue	2,559[2]	6,629[2]	772,000
Tottori	Tottori	1,349[2]	3,494[2]	615,000
Yamaguchi	Yamaguchi	2,358	6,107	1,562,000
Hokkaidō				
Hokkaidō (Territory)	Sapporo	32,247	83,520	5,666,000
Kantō				
Chiba	Chiba	1,989	5,151	5,721,000
Gumma	Maebashi	2,454	6,356	1,988,000
Ibaraki	Mito	2,353	6,094	2,916,000
Kanagawa	Yokohama	928	2,403	8,149,000
Saitama	Urawa	1,467	3,799	6,632,000
Tochigi	Utsunomiya	2,476	6,414	1,966,000
Kinki				
Hyōgo	Kōbe	3,236	8,381	5,490,000
Mie	Tsu	2,231	5,778	1,818,000
Nara	Nara	1,425	3,692	1,413,000
Shiga	Ōtsu	1,551	4,016	1,258,000
Wakayama	Wakayama	1,824	4,725	1,079,000
Kyūshū				
Fukuoka	Fukuoka	1,916	4,963	4,875,000
Kagoshima	Kagoshima	3,539	9,167	1,786,000
Kumamoto	Kumamoto	2,860	7,408	1,847,000
Miyazaki	Miyazaki	2,986	7,735	1,170,000
Nagasaki	Nagasaki	1,588	4,113	1,550,000
Ōita	Ōita	2,447	6,338	1,232,000
Saga	Saga	942	2,440	879,000
Ryukyu				
Okinawa	Naha	871	2,255	1,247,000
Shikoku				
Ehime	Matsuyama	2,190	5,672	1,509,000
Kagawa	Takamatsu	727	1,883	1,025,000
Kōchi	Kōchi	2,744	7,107	815,000
Tokushima	Tokushima	1,601	4,146	830,000
Tohoku				
Akita	Akita	4,484[3]	11,613[3]	1,216,000
Aomori	Aomori	3,714[3]	9,619[3]	1,470,000
Fukushima	Fukushima	5,322	13,784	2,122,000
Iwate	Morioka	5,898	15,277	1,415,000
Miyagi	Sendai	2,815	7,292	2,290,000
Yamagata	Yamagata	3,601	9,327	1,253,000
Metropolis				
Tōkyō[4]	Tokyo	836	2,166	11,830,000
Urban prefectures				
Kyōto[5]	Kyōto	1,781	4,613	2,605,000
Ōsaka[5]	Ōsaka	722	1,869	8,723,000
TOTAL		145,883[6,7]	377,835[6,7]	124,764,000

Demography

Population (1994): 124,960,000.
Density (1994): persons per sq mi 856.6, persons per sq km 330.7.
Urban-rural (1992): urban 77.5%; rural 22.5%.
Sex distribution (1993[1]): male 49.08%; female 50.92%.
Age breakdown (1993[1]): under 15, 16.7%; 15–29, 22.1%; 30–44, 20.9%; 45–59, 21.0%; 60–74, 14.0%; 75 and over, 5.3%.
Population projection: (2000) 127,287,000; (2010) 130,344,000.
Doubling time: not applicable; doubling time exceeds 100 years.
Composition by nationality (1992): Japanese 99.0%; Korean 0.6%; Chinese 0.2%; other 0.2%.
Place of birth (1994): 99.2% native-born; 0.8% foreign-born (mainly Korean).
Immigration (1992): permanent immigrants/registered aliens admitted 1,281,644, from North and South Korea 53.7%, Taiwan, Hong Kong, and China 15.2%, Brazil 11.5%, Philippines 4.8%, United States 3.3%, Peru 2.4%, United Kingdom 0.9%, Thailand 0.8%, Vietnam 0.5%, Canada 0.5%, other 6.4%.
Major cities (1993[1]): Tokyo 8,080,286; Yokohama 3,288,464; Ōsaka 2,588,989; Nagoya 2,158,713; Sapporo 1,731,670; Kōbe 1,509,395; Kyōto 1,452,240; Fukuoka 1,268,626; Kawasaki 1,199,707; Hiroshima 1,102,047; Kita-Kyūshū 1,019,996.

Other principal cities (1993[1])

	population		population		population
Akashi	280,795	Kakogawa	249,390	Okayama	604,513
Akita	307,862	Kanazawa	446,325	Okazaki	318,983
Amagasaki	496,313	Kashiwa	316,725	Ōmiya	422,023
Aomori	288,291	Kasugai	273,116	Ōtsu	268,583
Asahikawa	362,176	Kawagoe	316,313	Sagamihara	560,366
Chiba	850,631	Kawaguchi	451,345	Sakai	806,263
Fujisawa	362,088	Kōchi	319,243	Sendai	950,893
Fukui	254,667	Koriyama	322,255	Shimonoseki	259,898
Fukushima	282,654	Koshigaya	294,966	Shizuoka	474,219
Fukuyama	370,873	Kumamoto	639,699	Suita	339,970
Funabashi	539,740	Kurashiki	418,450	Takamatsu	331,031
Gifu	409,558	Machida	358,891	Takatsuki	361,283
Hachiōji	488,187	Maebashi	287,912	Tokorozawa	315,517
Hakodate	304,286	Matsudo	463,517	Tokushima	265,243
Hamamatsu	560,660	Matsuyama	454,374	Toyama	324,073
Higashi-Ōsaka	515,375	Miyazaki	293,590	Toyohashi	349,590
Himeji	463,197	Morioka	283,398	Toyonaka	403,224
Hirakata	396,867	Nagano	352,378	Toyota	341,453
Hiratsuka	251,991	Nagasaki	441,308	Urawa	442,381
Ibaraki	255,500	Naha	301,679	Utsunomiya	434,029
Ichihara	270,332	Nara	355,869	Wakayama	395,496
Ichikawa	447,165	Neyagawa	257,137	Yamagata	251,354
Ichinomiya	266,648	Niigata	490,237	Yao	276,324
Iwaki	359,098	Nishinomiya	424,719	Yokkaichi	282,197
Kagoshima	539,911	Ōita	420,361	Yokosuka	435,383

Religious affiliation (1989): Shintō and related religions 39.5%; Buddhism 38.3%; Christian 3.9%; other 18.3%.
Households (1990). Total households 40,670,000; average household size 3.0; composition of households 1 person 23.1%, 2 persons 20.6%, 3 persons 18.1%, 4 persons 21.7%, 5 persons 9.3%, 6 or more persons 7.2%. Family households 31,204,000 (76.7%); nonfamily 9,466,000 (23.3%), of which 1 person 9,390,000 (23.1%).

Type of household (1988)

Total number of dwelling units: 37,413,000

	number of dwellings	percentage of total
by kind of dwelling		
exclusive entry (do not share bathroom or kitchen)	34,701,000	92.8
combined with nondwelling	2,712,000	7.3
detached house	23,311,000	62.3
apartment building	11,409,000	30.5
tenement (substandard or overcrowded building)	2,490,000	6.7
other	203,000	0.5
by legal tenure of householder		
owned	22,948,000	61.3
rented	14,015,000	37.5
other	450,000	1.2
by kind of amenities		
flush toilet	24,300,000	65.0
bathroom	34,126,000	91.2
by year of construction		
prior to 1945	2,701,000	7.3
1945–70	11,487,000	31.1
1971–80	13,543,000	36.8
1981–83	3,564,000	9.7
1984–88	5,556,000	15.1

Mobility (1980). Population living in same residence from birth 24.0%; different residence established prior to October 1975, 44.0%; different residence established after October 1975, 32.0%, of which: same prefecture 24.1%; different prefecture 7.7%.

Vital statistics

Birth rate per 1,000 population (1993): 9.6 (world avg. 26.0); (1985) legitimate 99.0%; illegitimate 1.0%.
Death rate per 1,000 population (1993): 7.0 (world avg. 9.2).
Natural increase rate per 1,000 population (1993): 2.6 (world avg. 16.8).
Total fertility rate (avg. births per childbearing woman; 1992): 1.5.
Marriage rate per 1,000 population (1992): 6.1; median age at first marriage (1987) men 28.3 years, women 25.6 years.
Divorce rate per 1,000 population (1992): 1.4.
Life expectancy at birth (1992): male 76.1 years; female 82.2 years.
Major causes of death per 100,000 population (1992): malignant neoplasms (cancers) 186.5; heart diseases 141.2; cerebrovascular diseases 95.0; pneumonia and bronchitis 64.6; accidents and adverse effects 27.9; senility without mention of psychosis 18.7; suicide 16.8; nephritis, nephrotic syndrome, and nephrosis 14.7; cirrhosis of the liver 13.8; diabetes mellitus 7.9.

Social indicators

Educational attainment (1990). Percentage of population age 25 years and over having: primary 34.3%; secondary education 44.5%; postsecondary 21.2%.

Distribution of income (1992)

percentage of average household income by quintile

1	2	3	4	5 (highest)
11.1	15.4	19.1	23.1	31.3

Quality of working life. Average workweek (1992): 39.4 hours. Annual rate of industrial deaths per 100,000 workers (1992): 2.8. Proportion of labour force insured for damages or income loss resulting from injury, permanent disability, and death (1991): 50.1%. Average man-days lost to labour stoppages per 1,000,000 workdays (1992): 14.1. Average duration of journey to work (1988)[8]: 26.8 minutes (1983; 26.7% private automobile, 67.4% public transportation, 5.5% taxi, 0.4% other). Rate per 1,000 workers of discouraged (unemployed no longer seeking work; 1987): 100.8.

Access to services (1989). Proportion of households having access to: gas supply 64.6%; safe public water supply 94.0%; public sewage collection 89.4%.

Social participation. Eligible voters participating in last national election (1993): 67.3%. Population 15 years and over participating in social-service activities on a voluntary basis (1987): 25.2%. Trade union membership in total workforce (1992): 24.4%.

Social deviance (1991). Offense rate per 100,000 population for: homicide 1.0; rape 1.3; robbery 1.5; larceny and theft 1,213.9. Incidence in general population of: alcoholism, n.a.; drug and substance abuse, n.a. Rate of suicide per 100,000 population: 16.0.

Leisure/use of personal time

Discretionary daily activities (1991)
(Population age 15 years and over)

	weekly average hrs./min.
Total discretionary daily time	5:56
of which	
Hobbies and amusements	0:36
Sports	0:11
Learning (except schoolwork)	0:12
Social activities	0:05
Associations	0:29
Radio, television, newspapers, and magazines	2:23
Rest and relaxation	1:21
Other activities	0:21

Major leisure activities (1991)
(Population age 15 years and over)

	percentage of participation		
	male	female	total
Hobbies and amusements	93.0	90.8	91.9
Sports	84.2	72.1	78.0
Light exercises	30.8	34.1	32.0
Swimming	27.1	20.8	23.8
Bowling	33.0	23.1	27.9
Learning (except schoolwork)	36.3	37.0	36.7
Travel			
Domestic	72.7	68.3	70.4
Foreign	10.4	7.6	9.0

Material well-being (1993). Households possessing: automobile 80.0%; telephone, virtually 100%; colour television receiver 99.3%; refrigerator 98.9%; air conditioner 72.3%; washing machine 99.4%; vacuum cleaner 98.7%; videocassette recorder 82.8%; camera 86.8%; microwave oven 81.3%; compact disc player 51.8%.

National economy

Gross national product (at current market prices; 1993): U.S.$3,926,375,000,000 (U.S.$31,450 per capita).

Structure of gross domestic product and labour force

	1992		1993	
	in value ¥'000,000,000[9]	% of total value	labour force	% of labour force
Agriculture, fishing	9,826	2.3	3,830,000	5.8
Mining	1,081	0.3	60,000	0.1
Manufacturing	130,992	31.1	15,300,000	23.1
Construction	36,972	8.8	6,400,000	9.7
Public utilities	15,214	3.6	350,000	0.5
Transportation and communications	26,299	6.2	3,940,000	6.0
Trade	58,986	14.0	14,480,000	21.9
Finance	65,855	15.7	2,600,000	3.9
Pub. admin., defense	14,613	3.5	2,090,000	3.2
Services	78,464	18.6	15,160,000	22.9
Other	−17,493[10]	−4.1[10]	1,950,000[11]	2.9
TOTAL	420,809[12]	100.0	66,160,000	100.0

Budget (1993). Revenue: ¥64,211,200,000,000 (income tax 42.0%; corporation tax 24.8%; value-added tax 8.5%; liquor and tobacco tax 4.8%; stamp duties 2.7%; customs duties 1.4%). Expenditures: ¥72,354,800,000,000 (transfers to local governments 21.6%; national debt 21.3%; social security 18.2%; public works 11.8%; culture, education, and science promotion 8.0%; national defense 6.4%; pensions 2.4%).

Public debt (1993): U.S.$1,624,500,000,000.

Population economically active (1993): total 66,160,000; activity rate of total population 53.1% (participation rates: age 15 and over, 63.8%; female 40.5%; unemployed 2.5%).

Price and earnings indexes (1990 = 100)

	1988	1989	1990	1991	1992	1993	1994[13]
Consumer price index	94.9	97.0	100.0	103.3	105.1	106.4	107.4
Monthly earnings index	93.4	96.3	100.0	103.4	105.6	107.8	109.4

Household income and expenditure (1991). Average household size 3.7; average annual income per household ¥6,585,200 (U.S.$48,900); sources of income: wages and salaries 58.5%, transfer payments 18.9%, self-employment 11.6%, other 11.0%; expenditure: food 19.3%, transportation 8.1%, reading and recreation 7.6%, clothing and footwear 5.7%, housing 4.2%, fuel, light, and water charges 4.1%, education 4.0%, furniture and household utensils 3.2%, medical care 2.0%.

Tourism (1992): receipts from visitors U.S.$3,588,000,000; expenditures by nationals abroad U.S.$26,837,000,000.

Land use (1991): forested 66.7%; meadows and pastures 1.7%; agricultural and under permanent cultivation 12.1%; other 19.5%.

Manufacturing and mining enterprises (1991)

	no. of establishments	avg. no. of persons engaged	annual wages as a % of avg. of all mfg. wages[14]	annual value added (¥'000,000,000)
Electrical machinery	35,657	1,875,000	94.9	20,936
Nonelectrical machinery	49,753	1,430,000	112.1	19,506
Transport equipment	15,129	969,000	113.1	14,119
Chemical products	5,390	406,000	131.6	12,669
Food, beverages, and tobacco	49,492	1,233,000	79.6	12,206
Fabricated metal products	52,367	917,000	97.6	10,116
Iron and steel	6,406	340,000	130.0	7,373
Printing and publishing	30,440	595,000	119.3	7,339
Ceramic, stone, and clay	20,614	457,000	100.8	5,732
Plastic products	21,840	476,000	92.2	4,953
Textiles	38,729	625,000	72.1	4,066
Paper and paper products	9,762	255,000	102.7	3,259
Lumber and wood products	25,758	295,000	85.5	2,078
Precision instruments	5,959	219,000	98.1	1,936
Apparel products	24,416	490,000	52.8	1,885
Rubber products	4,240	153,000	102.4	1,724
Nonferrous metal products	3,492	124,000	114.7	1,720
Furniture and fixtures	10,772	165,000	87.4	1,312
Petroleum and coal products	1,093	33,000	164.9	1,107
Leather products	4,036	79,000	76.1	516
Mining[15]	780	29,000	116.1	227

Energy production (consumption): electricity (kW-hr; 1992) 895,336,000,000 (895,336,000,000); coal (metric tons; 1992) 7,613,000 (116,813,000); crude petroleum (barrels; 1992) 6,243,000 (1,541,000,000); petroleum products (metric tons; 1992) 172,668,000, of which (by volume) diesel 29.7%, heavy fuel oil 22.6%, gasoline 18.1%, kerosene and jet fuel 13.8% (187,570,000); natural gas (cu m; 1992) 2,243,000,000 (56,363,000,000). Composition of energy supply by source (1992): crude oil and petroleum products 58.2%, coal 16.1%, natural gas 10.6%, nuclear power 10.0%, hydroelectric power 3.8%, other 1.3%. Domestic energy demand by end use (1990): mining and manufacturing 44.4%, residential and commercial 24.4%, transportation 23.1%, agriculture, forestry, and fisheries 3.7%, other 4.4%.

Financial aggregates

	1988	1989	1990	1991	1992	1993	1994[16]
Exchange rate[17], ¥ per:							
U.S. dollar	125.85	143.45	134.40	125.20	124.75	111.85	99.05
£	228.29	226.21	258.41	234.21	188.62	172.27	152.56
SDR	169.36	188.52	191.21	179.09	171.53	153.63	143.46
International reserves (U.S.$)							
Total (excl. gold; '000,000)	96,728	83,957	78,501	72,059	71,623	98,524	114,559
SDRs ('000,000)	2,036	2,447	3,042	2,579	1,094	1,543	1,793
Reserve pos. in IMF ('000,000)	3,278	3,518	5,971	7,722	8,641	8,261	8,579
Foreign exchange ('000,000)	90,514	77,992	69,487	61,758	61,888	88,720	104,187
Gold ('000,000 fine troy oz)	24.23	24.23	24.23	24.23	24.23	24.23	24.23
% world reserves	2.6	2.6	2.6	2.6	2.6	2.6	2.7
Interest and prices							
Central bank discount (%)[17]	2.50	4.25	6.00	4.50	3.25	1.75	1.75
Govt. bond yield (%)	4.27	5.05	7.36	6.53	4.94	3.69	3.67[18]
Industrial share prices (1990 = 100)	97.8	117.8	100.0	84.5	62.6	76.5	77.2
Balance of payments (U.S.$'000,000,000)							
Balance of visible trade	95.0	76.9	63.6	103.1	132.4	141.6	...
Imports, f.o.b.	164.8	192.7	216.8	203.5	198.5	209.7	...
Exports, f.o.b.	259.8	269.6	280.4	306.6	330.9	351.3	...
Balance of invisibles	−11.3	−15.6	−22.2	−17.7	−14.8	−10.1	...
Balance of payments, current account	131.5	79.6	57.0	35.9	72.9	131.5	...

Retail and wholesale trade and services (1991)

	no. of establishments	avg. no. of employees	annual sales (¥'000,000,000)
Retail trade	1,519,186	6,936,000	140,634
Food and beverages	622,751	2,542,000	41,453
Grocery	68,913	643,000	16,404
Liquors	106,650	315,000	6,323
General merchandise	4,347	440,000	19,898
Department stores	2,004	427,000	19,574
Motor vehicles and bicycles	93,230	566,000	18,934
Apparel and accessories	240,989	809,000	14,844
Furniture and home furnishings	158,104	587,000	11,987
Gasoline service stations	72,807	385,000	11,234
Books and stationery	76,730	600,000	4,722
Wholesale trade	475,967	4,773,000	572,982
Machinery and equipment	111,046	1,286,000	130,512
General machinery except electrical	54,612	577,000	47,910
Motor vehicles and parts	17,318	222,000	32,010
General merchandise	705	51,000	98,548
Minerals and metals	22,657	264,000	61,300
Farm, livestock, and fishery products	43,331	416,000	60,273
Food and beverages	56,656	561,000	47,677
Textiles, apparel, and accessories	44,748	506,000	38,517
Building materials	63,885	444,000	35,698
Chemicals	18,140	179,000	24,457
Drugs and toilet goods	21,319	291,000	19,783
Medical services[19]	171,986	2,026,000	...
Educational services[19]	84,512	2,065,000	...

Production (metric tons except as noted) Agriculture, forestry, fishing (1992): rice 13,255,000, sugar beets 3,823,000, potatoes 3,650,000, cabbages 2,500,000, sugarcane 1,863,000, mandarin oranges 1,400,000, sweet potatoes 1,300,000, onions 1,300,000, apples 1,025,000, raw sugar 987,000, cucumbers 870,000, wheat 800,000, tomatoes 740,000, watermelons 730,000, carrots 640,000, eggplants 500,000, pears 452,000, barley 340,000, grapes 276,000, pumpkins 265,000, strawberries 219,000, soybeans 197,000, peaches 192,000, dry beans 140,000, tea 85,000, green beans 80,000, to bacco leaves 77,000, green peas 50,000, cow's milk 8,300,000, hen's eggs 2,586,000; livestock (number of live animals) 10,966,000 pigs, 4,980,000 cattle (of which 42% dairy cows), 35,000 goats, 29,000 sheep, 26,000 horses, 337,000,000 poultry; roundwood (1992) 28,063,000 cu m; fish catch (1992) 9,266,000, of which sardines 2,224,000, Alaska pollack 499,000, squid 394,000, mackerel 269,000, oysters 245,000, crabs 59,000, river eels 36,000, carp 15,000. Mining and quarrying (1993): limestone 200,451,000; silica stone 18,854,000; dolomite 4,760,000; silica sand 3,884,000; pyrophyllite 730,000; pyrophyllite clay 298,000; zinc 118,599; lead 16,470; copper 10,277; tungsten 578[20]; silver 136,890 kg; gold 9,350 kg. Manufacturing (1992): crude steel 98,132,000; semifinished steel 102,727,000[21]; cement 95,820,000; hot-rolled steel products 87,982,000[21]; pig iron 73,144,000; paper pulp 11,199,900; sulfuric acid 7,100,000; plastic products 5,516,800[21]; compound fertilizers 3,186,000; spun yarn 939,100[21]; synthetic fabrics 2,591,760,000 sq m[21]; cotton fabrics 1,464,700,000 sq m; finished products (in number of units) 445,845,-000 watches and clocks, 69,371,000 electronic desk calculators[21], 26,058,000 videocassette recorders[21], 18,164,000 telephones[21], 14,478,000 cameras, 12,-024,000 television receivers, 9,378,700 passenger cars, 7,447,900 bicycles[21], 6,981,000 vacuum cleaners[21], 5,587,000 automatic washing machines[21], 5,212,000 electric refrigerators[21], 4,547,000 facsimile machines[21], 4,282,000 microwave ovens[21], 4,178,000 stereo recorders, 3,196,500 motorcycles, 2,654,-700 photocopy machines[21], 1,456,800 typewriters[21]. Construction (value in ¥ '000,000; 1992): residential 24,540,000; nonresidential 25,610,000.

Foreign trade[22]

Balance of trade (current prices)

	1988	1989	1990	1991	1992	1993
¥'000,000,000	+11,903	+11,235	+10,398	+13,093	+15,922	+15,591
% of total	21.3%	17.4%	14.3%	18.3%	22.7%	24.1%

Imports (1992): ¥29,527,000,000,000 (mineral fuels, lubricants, and related materials 22.6%, of which crude petroleum and petroleum products 15.6%; food, beverages, and tobacco 16.0%; machinery and transport equipment 14.1%, of which electrical equipment 5.5%, transport equipment 2.3%; chemicals and chemical products 7.4%). *Major import sources:* United States 22.4%; China 7.3%; Australia 5.3%; Indonesia 5.3%; South Korea 5.0%; Germany 4.6%; Saudi Arabia 4.4%; Taiwan 4.0%; Canada 3.3%; Malaysia 2.8%; Thailand 2.6%; France 2.3%.
Exports (1992): ¥43,011,000,000,000 (motor vehicles 17.8%; office machinery 7.5%; chemicals 5.6%, of which plastic materials 1.5%; scientific and optical equipment 4.0%; iron and steel products 3.9%; power-generating machinery 2.9%; textiles and allied products 2.5%; tape recorders 1.8%; metalworking machinery 1.1%; radio receivers 0.9%; television receivers 0.7%). *Major export destinations:* United States 28.2%; Taiwan 6.2%; Hong Kong 6.1%; Germany 6.0%; South Korea 5.2%; Singapore 3.8%; United Kingdom 3.6%; China 3.5%; Thailand 3.0%; Canada 2.1%; Australia 2.1%.

Trade by commodity group (1992)

		imports		exports	
SITC group		U.S.$'000,000	%	U.S.$'000,000	%
00	Food and live animals	37,289	16.0	1,765	0.5
01	Beverages and tobacco				
02	Crude materials, excluding fuels	23,326[23]	10.0[23]	2,116[23]	0.6[23]
03	Mineral fuels, lubricants, and related materials	52,739	22.6	1,720	0.5
04	Animal and vegetable oils, fats, and waxes	23	23	23	23
05	Chemicals and related products, n.e.s.	16,847	7.2	18,771	5.5
06	Basic manufactures	14,296	6.1	22,247	6.5
07	Machinery and transport equipment	32,801	14.1	172,186	50.7
08	Miscellaneous manufactured articles	34,615	14.8	85,309	25.1
09	Goods not classified by kind	21,108	9.1	35,536	10.5
	TOTAL	233,021	100.0[7]	339,650	100.0[7]

Direction of trade (1992)

	imports		exports	
	U.S.$'000,000	%	U.S.$'000,000	%
Africa	3,518	1.5	6,407	1.9
Asia	105,076	45.1	132,268	38.9
South America	6,446	2.8	5,173	1.5
North America and Central America	62,261	26.7	113,747	33.4
United States	52,693	22.6	96,716	28.4
other North and Central Am.	9,568	4.1	17,031	5.0
Europe	40,808	17.5	73,736	21.7[7]
EEC	31,399	13.5	62,921	18.5
U.S.S.R.[24]	2,507	1.0	1,164	0.3
other Europe	6,902	3.0	9,651	2.8
Oceania	14,848	6.4	8,780	2.6
TOTAL	232,947[7]	100.0	339,991[7]	100.0

Transport and communications

Transport. Railroads (1992): length 23,690 mi[21], 38,125 km[21]; rolling stock (1993[25]) locomotives 5,879, passenger cars 46,192[19], freight cars 40,951[19]; passengers carried 22,651,000,000; passenger-mi 249,947,000,000, passenger-km 402,252,000,000; short ton-mi cargo 18,263,000,000, metric ton-km cargo 26,664,000,000. Roads (1992): total length 691,488 mi, 1,112,844 km (paved 71%). Vehicles (1992): passenger cars 38,963,861; trucks 22,449,421; buses 248,624. Merchant marine (1992): vessels (100 gross tons and over) 10,091; total deadweight tonnage 37,815,779. Air transport (1992): passengers car-

ried 75,422,000; passenger-mi 65,699,000,000, passenger-km 105,732,000,000; short ton-mi cargo 4,914,300,000, metric ton-km cargo 7,174,700,000; airports (1994) with scheduled flights 75. Shares of domestic passenger traffic by mode of transportation (1991): automobiles and light motor vehicles 54.8%; railway 25.2%; buses 9.6%; ships 0.2%; airplanes 0.1%.

Distribution of traffic (1992)

	cargo carried ('000,000 tons)	% of national total	passengers carried ('000,000)	% of national total
Road	6,102.0	90.7	50,396.0	55.5
Rail (intercity)	82.0	1.2	22,694.0	25.0
Urban transport	—	—	17,445.0	19.2
road	—	—	8,445.0	9.3
rail	—	—	9,000.0	9.9
Inland water	540.0	8.0	158.0	0.2
Air	0.9	0.0	70.0	0.1
TOTAL	6,724.9	100.0[7]	90,763.0	100.0

Communications. Daily newspapers (1993): total number 122; total circulation 72,043,000; circulation per 1,000 population 579. Radio (1993): 97,000,000 receivers (1 per 1.3 persons). Television (1993): 100,000,000 receivers (1 per 1.2 persons). Telephones (1992): 57,652,000[26] (1 per 2.2 persons).

Other communications media (1992)

	titles		Electronic	traffic ('000)
Print				
Books (new)	45,595		Telegram	48,166
of which			Domestic	47,726
Social sciences	10,415		International	440
Fiction	9,332		Telex	14,250[21]
Engineering	3,597			
Arts	4,746			
Natural sciences	3,574			
History	2,989		**Post**	
Philosophy	2,237		Mail	24,166,000
Magazines/journals	3,851		Domestic	23,842,000
Weekly	107		International	324,000
Monthly	2,656		Parcels	431,500
			Domestic	426,000
Cinema			International	5,500
Feature films	617			
Domestic	240			
Foreign	377			

Radio and television broadcasting (1992): total radio stations 1,288, of which commercial 430; total television stations 14,229, of which commercial 7,307. Commercial broadcasting hours (by percentage of programs; 1991): reports—radio 13.2%, television 19.5%; education—radio 4.6%, television 12.1%; culture—radio 15.5%, television 24.4%; entertainment—radio 65.8%, television 41.9%. Advertisements (daily average; 1990): radio 168, television 290.

Education and health

Education (1993)

	schools	teachers	students	student/teacher ratio
Primary (age 6–11)	24,676	438,000	8,769,000	20.0
Secondary (age 12–17)	16,793	560,000	9,861,000	17.6
Higher	1,191	157,000	2,975,000	18.9

Literacy: total population age 15 and over literate, virtually 100%.
Health (1992): physicians 218,066 (1 per 570 persons); dentists 76,343 (1 per 1,628 persons); nurses 795,810 (1 per 156 persons); pharmacists 141,630 (1 per 878 persons); midwives (1987) 24,056 (1 per 5,082 persons); hospital beds 1,687,000 (1 per 74 persons), of which (1989) general 72.9%, mental 22.2%, tuberculosis 3.3%, other 1.6%; infant mortality rate per 1,000 live births 4.5.
Food (1988–90): daily per capita caloric intake 2,921 (vegetable products 79%, animal products 21%); 125% of FAO recommended minimum.

Military

Total active duty personnel (1994): 237,700 (army 63.1%, navy 18.1%, air force 18.8%). *Military expenditure as percentage of GNP* (1991): 1.0% (world 4.2%); per capita expenditure U.S.$263.

---

[1]October 1; preliminary. [2]Excludes Lake Naka (38 sq mi [98 sq km]), which is part of both Shimane and Tottori prefectures. [3]Excludes Lake Towada (23 sq mi [60 sq km]), which is part of both Akita and Aomori prefectures. [4]Part of Kantō geographic region. [5]Part of Kinki geographic region. [6]1987 survey; includes Lake Naka and Lake Towada. [7]Detail does not add to total given because of rounding. [8]Applies to passengers carried within metropolitan areas only. [9]At prices of 1985. [10]Import duties and statistical discrepancy less imputed bank service charge. [11]Includes 1,660,000 unemployed. [12]GDP in current values for 1992 is ¥463,850,000,000,000. [13]May. [14]1992. [15]1988. [16]July. [17]End of period. [18]June. [19]1985. [20]1992. [21]1991. [22]Import figures are f.o.b. in balance of trade and c.i.f. in commodities and trading partners. [23]Crude materials includes Animal and vegetable oils, fats, and waxes. [24]Data refer to U.S.S.R. as constituted prior to 1991. [25]January 1. [26]Number of subscribers.

Jordan

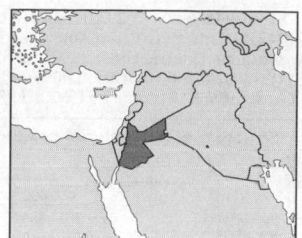

Official name: al-Mamlakah al-Urdunnīyah al-Hāshimīyah (al-Urdun) (Hashemite Kingdom of Jordan).
Form of government: constitutional monarchy[1] with a National Assembly comprising two legislative houses (Senate [40 appointed by king]; House of Deputies [80]).
Head of state and government: King assisted by Prime Minister.
Capital: Amman.
Official language: Arabic.
Official religion: Islam.
Monetary unit: 1 Jordan dinar (JD) = 1,000 fils; valuation (Oct. 7, 1994) JD 1.00 = U.S.$1.43 = £0.90.

Area and population

Governorates	Capitals	area		population
		sq mi	sq km	1993[2] estimate
'Ammān	Amman	4,097	10,612	1,625,000
al-Balqā'	aṣ-Ṣalt	425	1,100	245,000
Irbid	Irbid	985	2,551	979,000
al-Karak	al-Karak	1,548	4,010	169,000
Ma'ān	Ma'ān	13,954	36,141	148,000
al-Mafraq	al-Mafraq	10,475	27,129	160,000
aṭ-Ṭafīlah	aṭ-Ṭafīlah	850	2,202	64,000
az-Zarqā'	az-Zarqā'	2,008	5,201	622,000
TOTAL		34,342	88,946	4,012,000

Demography

Population (1994): 4,230,000.
Density (1994): persons per sq mi 123.2, persons per sq km 47.6.
Urban-rural (1993): urban 78.0%; rural 22.0%.
Sex distribution (1993): male 51.89%; female 48.11%.
Age breakdown (1993): under 15, 42.7%; 15–29, 32.2%; 30–44, 12.4%; 45–59, 8.4%; 60–74, 3.4%; 75 and over, 0.9%.
Population projection: (2000) 5,177,000; (2010) 7,572,000.
Doubling time: 20 years.
Ethnic composition (1983): Arab 99.2%, of which Palestinian *c.* 50.0%; Circassian 0.5%; Armenian 0.1%; Turk 0.1%; Kurd 0.1%.
Religious affiliation (1980): Sunnī Muslim 93.0%; Christian 4.9%; other 2.1%.
Major cities (1993): Amman 1,272,000; az-Zarqā' 605,000; Irbid 385,000; aṣ-Ṣalt 171,000; al-Mafraq 105,000.

Vital statistics

Birth rate per 1,000 population (1993): 38.8 (world avg. 26.0).
Death rate per 1,000 population (1993): 3.1 (world avg. 9.2).
Natural increase rate per 1,000 population (1993): 35.7 (world avg. 16.8).
Total fertility rate (avg. births per childbearing woman; 1993): 5.8.
Marriage rate per 1,000 population (1993): 9.3.
Divorce rate per 1,000 population (1993): 1.4.
Life expectancy at birth (1991): male 70.0 years; female 73.0 years.
Major causes of death per 100,000 population: n.a.; however, major diseases include tuberculosis, typhoid, paratyphoid fevers, salmonella, hepatitis, and dysentery; nonvenereal syphilis is widespread in the southern desert region.

National economy

Budget (1993). Revenue: JD 1,176,000,000 (direct and indirect taxes 55.2%, of which custom duties 38.2%; fees from telecommunication 10.9%). Expenditures: JD 1,623,000,000 (administration 49.4%, defense and security 20.1%, social welfare 13.6%, economic development 11.2%, transportation and communications 2.8%).
Public debt (external, outstanding; 1992): U.S.$6,914,000,000.
Production (metric tons except as noted). Agriculture, forestry, fishing (1993): tomatoes 490,000, oranges and tangerines 100,000, melons 90,300, olives 81,800, wheat 75,400, barley 68,900, lemons and lime 51,000, grapes 50,200, eggplants 49,400, cucumbers 33,500, cauliflower and cabbage 30,700, bananas 11,400; livestock (number of live animals; 1992) 2,000,000 sheep, 600,000 goats, 32,000 cattle, 18,000 camels, 55,000,000 chickens; roundwood (1992) 11,000 cu m; fish catch (1991) 22. Mining and quarrying (1993): phosphate ore 4,222,000; potash 1,511,000. Manufacturing (value added in JD '000; 1991): chemicals 69,449; nonmetallic mineral products 63,645; tobacco 53,187; food products 38,971; petroleum refining 35,083; basic metal products 21,054; beverages 20,195; paper and paper products 14,959; fabricated metal products, except machinery 14,814; textiles 14,327; furniture and wood products 13,309; plastic and plastic products 13,182; clothing 9,959; printing and publishing 9,601; nonelectrical machinery 8,516; electrical machinery 7,389. Construction (1993): 4,205,500 sq m. Energy production (consumption): electricity (kW-hr; 1992) 4,422,000,000 (4,422,000,000); coal, none (n.a.); crude petroleum (barrels; 1992) 21,600 (21,275,000); petroleum products (metric tons; 1992) 2,756,000 (3,349,000); natural gas, none (n.a.).
Land use (1991): forested 0.8%; meadows and pastures 8.9%; agricultural and under permanent cultivation 4.5%; wasteland (mostly desert), built-on, and other 85.8%.
Population economically active (1992): total 706,000; activity rate of total population 19.3% (participation rates: over age 15 [1986] 39.0%; female [1988] 10.9%; unemployed [1992] 15.0%).

Price and earnings indexes (1990 = 100)

	1987	1988	1989	1990	1991	1992	1993
Consumer price index	64.2	68.5	86.1	100.0	108.2	112.5	117.8
Daily earnings index	94.2	96.2	98.1	100.0	100.0	...	...

Household income and expenditure. Average household size (1991) 6.9; income per household (1979) JD 1,820 (U.S.$6,055); sources of income: n.a.; expenditure (1992): food and beverages 40.6%; housing and energy 26.9%; transportation 11.2%; clothing and footwear 8.2%; education 3.5%; health care 2.2%; other goods and services 7.4%.
Gross national product (at current market prices; 1993): U.S.$4,881,000,000 (U.S.$1,190 per capita).

Structure of gross domestic product and labour force

	1993		1992	
	in value JD '000,000[3]	% of total value	labour force	% of labour force
Agriculture	244.9	8.0	44,400	7.4
Mining	100.6	3.3	61,800	10.3
Manufacturing	451.4	14.7		
Construction	180.2	5.9	60,000	10.0
Public utilities	75.3	2.4	6,600	1.1
Transportation and communications	470.8	15.3	52,200	8.7
Trade	287.8	9.3	63,000	10.5
Finance	585.4	19.0	19,800	3.3
Pub. admin., defense	643.8	20.9	292,200	48.7
Services	111.4	3.6		
Other	−74.2[4]	−2.4[4]		
TOTAL	3,077.2	100.0	600,000	100.0

Tourism (1992): receipts from visitors U.S.$462,000,000; expenditures by nationals abroad U.S.$350,000,000.

Foreign trade

Balance of trade (current prices)[5]

	1988	1989	1990	1991	1992	1993
JD '000,000	−1,411	−773	−1,237	−1,173	−1,780	−1,899
% of total	41.2%	25.8%	36.8%	34.2%	42.2%	43.2%

Imports (1993): JD 2,453,600,000 (food and live animals 17.7%, of which cereals 3.9%; machinery and appliances 15.3%; mineral fuels 12.8%; transport [mainly equipment and parts] 11.6%; iron and steel 6.4%; clothing, textiles, and footwear 5.6%; pharmaceuticals 2.5%; plastics 2.5%). *Major import sources:* United States 12.7%; Iraq 12.5%; Germany 8.3%; Italy 5.5%; United Kingdom 5.2%; Japan 5.0%; France 4.0%; The Netherlands 2.6%.
Exports (1993): JD 691,282,000 (phosphate fertilizers 14.2%; potash 12.4%; pharmaceuticals 10.2%; fruits and vegetables 10.0%; fertilizers 8.0%; dairy products and eggs 5.5%; soap and detergents 5.2%; cement 2.5%). *Major export destinations:* Saudi Arabia 11.6%; Iraq 11.2%; India 9.5%; Indonesia 5.4%; United Arab Emirates 4.4%; Russia 3.7%; Syria 2.8%; Lebanon 2.5%.

Transport and communications

Transport. Railroads (1992): route length 490 mi, 789 km; passengers carried (1988) 31,304; short ton-mi cargo 542,000,000, metric ton-km cargo 791,000,000. Roads (1992): total length 3,958 mi, 6,370 km (paved 100%). Vehicles (1992): passenger cars 177,248; trucks and buses 44,209[6]. Merchant marine (1992): vessels (100 gross tons and over) 5; total deadweight tonnage 113,557. Air transport (1993): passenger-mi 2,487,800,000, passenger-km 4,003,700,000; short ton-mi cargo 146,228,000, metric ton-km cargo 213,590,000; airports (1994) with scheduled flights 2.
Communications. Daily newspapers (1990): total number 5; total circulation 230,000; circulation per 1,000 population 70. Radio (1993): 700,000 receivers (1 per 5.8 persons). Television (1993): 250,000 receivers (1 per 16.4 persons). Telephones (1991): 350,000 (1 per 10.5 persons).

Education and health

Education (1991–92)

	schools	teachers	students	student/ teacher ratio
Primary (age 6–14)	2,421	44,649	1,065,945	...
Secondary (age 15–17)	662			...
Voc., teacher tr.	49	2,105	26,175	12.4
Higher	55[7]	3,734[8]	83,777[8]	22.4

Educational attainment (1979). Percentage of population age 14 and over having: no formal schooling 47.9%; primary education 19.8%; secondary 26.4%; higher 5.9%. *Literacy* (1990): percentage of population age 15 and over literate 80.1%; males literate 89.3%; females literate 70.3%.
Health (1991): physicians 6,395 (1 per 574 persons); hospital beds (1992) 4,291 (1 per 920 persons); infant mortality rate per 1,000 live births (1992) 33.8.
Food (1988–90): daily per capita caloric intake 2,710 (vegetable products 89%, animal products 11%); 110% of FAO recommended minimum requirement.

Military

Total active duty personnel (1993): 100,600 (army 89.5%, navy 0.6%, air force 9.9%). *Military expenditure as percentage of GNP* (1991): 11.2% (world 4.2%); per capita expenditure U.S.$125.

---

[1]Political parties legalized July 1992; November 1993 legislative elections were multiparty. [2]January 1. [3]At factor cost. [4]Less imputed bank service charges. [5]Import figures are f.o.b. in balance of trade and c.i.f. in commodities and trading partners. [6]Includes vans. [7]1988–89. [8]Includes community colleges.

Kazakhstan

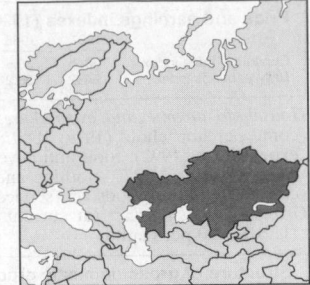

Official name: Qazaqstan Respublikasï
(Republic of Kazakhstan).
Form of government[1]: unitary
multiparty republic with a single
legislative body (Parliament [177]).
Head of state: President.
Head of government: Prime Minister.
Capital: Almaty (formerly Alma-Ata);
Akmola (formerly Tselinograd) is the
capital-designate[2].
Official language: Kazakh.
Official religion: none.
Monetary unit: tenge[3] (T; decimal unit,
n.a.); valuation (Oct. 3, 1994) free
rate, 1 U.S.$ = 56.98;
1 £ = 90.62 tenge.

Area and population		area		population
		sq mi	sq km	1991 estimate
Provinces[4]	**Capitals**			
Akmola	Akmola	35,600	92,100	885,400
Aktyubinsk	Aktyubinsk	115,300	298,700	752,900
Alma-Ata (Almaty)	Alma-Ata (Almaty)	40,600	105,100	2,153,700
Atyrau	Atyrau	43,800	113,500	447,100
Dzhambul	Auliye-Ata (Dzhambul)	55,700	144,200	1,056,400
Dzhezkazgan	Dzhezkazgan	121,000	313,400	496,200
East Kazakhstan	Ust-Kamenogorsk	37,600	97,300	949,000
Karaganda	Karaganda	45,500	117,900	1,339,900
Kokchetav	Kokchetav	30,200	78,100	669,400
Kustanay	Kustanay	44,200	114,500	1,074,400
Kzyl-Orda	Kzyl-Orda	88,100	228,100	664,900
Mangistau	Aktau	63,800	165,100	331,700
North Kazakhstan	Petropavlosk	17,100	44,300	610,400
Pavlodar	Pavlodar	49,200	127,500	956,900
Semipalatinsk	Semipalatinsk	69,300	179,600	841,900
South Kazakhstan	Chimkent	44,900	116,300	1,879,200
Taldy-Kurgan	Taldy-Kurgan	45,700	118,500	731,000
Turgay	Arkalyk	43,200	111,900	304,600
West Kazakhstan	Uralsk	58,400	151,200	648,000
TOTAL		1,049,200	2,717,300	16,793,100[5]

Demography

Population (1994): 16,954,000.
Density (1994): persons per sq mi 16.2, persons per sq km 6.2.
Urban-rural (1992): urban 57.5%; rural 42.5%.
Sex distribution (1992): male 48.52%; female 51.48%.
Age breakdown (1991): under 15, 31.4%; 15–29, 25.1%; 30–44, 21.3%; 45–59, 12.2%; 60–69, 6.1%; 70 and over, 3.9%.
Population projection: (2000) 17,312,000; (2010) 17,925,000.
Doubling time: 58 years.
Ethnic composition (1991): Kazakh 41.1%; Russian 37.3%; Ukrainian 5.3%; German 5.0%; Uzbek 2.1%; Tatar 2.0%; other 7.2%.
Religious affiliation: believers are predominantly Sunnī Muslims (Ḥanafīyah); there is a Christian minority (mainly Russian Orthodox and Baptist).
Major cities (1991): Alma-Ata (Almaty) 1,156,200; Karaganda 608,600; Chimkent 438,800; Semipalatinsk 344,700; Pavlodar 342,500.

Vital statistics

Birth rate per 1,000 population (1992): 19.9 (world avg. 26.0); (1991) legitimate 87.6%; illegitimate 12.4%.
Death rate per 1,000 population (1991): 8.1 (world avg. 9.2).
Natural increase rate per 1,000 population (1991): 11.8 (world avg. 16.8).
Total fertility rate (avg. births per childbearing woman; 1993): 2.5.
Marriage rate per 1,000 population (1992): 8.6.
Divorce rate per 1,000 population (1992): 2.9.
Life expectancy at birth (1993): male 63.2 years; female 72.7 years.
Major causes of death per 100,000 population (1991): diseases of the circulatory system 361.0; malignant neoplasms (cancers) 136.5; accidents, poisoning, and violence 107.3; diseases of the respiratory system 74.1; diseases of the digestive system (1989) 24.6; infectious and parasitic diseases 24.6; endocrine and metabolic disorders 6.3; diseases of the nervous system 6.1.

National economy

Budget (1994). Revenue: 67,500,000,000 tenge (1993; current revenue 96.8%, of which taxes on goods and services 29.2%, income and capital-gains taxes 26.8%, taxes on international trade 9.3%, other tax revenue 26.2%, nontax revenue 5.3%; grants 2.9%; capital revenue 0.3%). Expenditures: 87,700,-000,000 tenge (1993; national economy 16.7%; education 16.2%; defense and public safety 11.4%; foreign economic activity 11.0%; health care 8.3%; social security 6.4%).
Production (metric tons except as noted). Agriculture, forestry, fishing (1993): seed cotton 270,000,000, grain 21,500,000, wheat 18,500,000, corn 12,500,000, potatoes 2,300,000, sugar beets 1,300,000, oats 600,000, rye 400,000, rice 400,000, fruit (other than grapes) 230,000, sunflower seeds 192,000, grapes 85,000; livestock (number of live animals) 33,650,000 sheep and goats, 8,313,000 cattle, 2,459,000 pigs, 1,500,000 horses, 60,000 camels; roundwood (1991) 1,974,000 cu m. Mining and quarrying (1992): iron ore 23,000,-000; chrome 3,600,000; copper 200,000; manganese 130,000. Manufacturing (1992): steel 6,377,000; rolled ferrous metals 4,721,000; mineral fertilizers 1,516,000; textiles 249,100,000 sq m; carpets 2,048,000 sq m; shoes 34,100,000 pairs; bulldozers 11,280 units; metal-cutting machines 2,381 units; forge press machines 1,165 units; excavators 577 units. Construction (1991): residential 6,125,000 sq m. Energy production (consumption): electricity (kW-hr; 1992)

81,293,000,000 (81,293,000,000); coal (metric tons; 1992) 131,033,000 (91,-742); crude petroleum (barrels; 1992) 159,360,000 (110,780,000); petroleum products (metric tons; 1992) 5,683,000 (5,683,000); natural gas (cu m; 1992) 18,480,000,000 (8,113,000,000).
Gross national product (1993): U.S.$26,440,000,000 (U.S.$1,540 per capita)[6].

Structure of net material product and labour force				
	1992		1991	
	in value '000,000 rubles	% of total value	labour force[7]	% of labour force[7]
Agriculture	505,487	47.7	1,207,000	17.9
Manufacturing, mining }	430,360	40.6	1,385,000	20.5
Public utilities			260,000	3.9
Construction	62,402	6.0	674,000	10.0
Transp. and commun.	14,150	1.3	693,000	10.3
Trade	15,165	1.4	522,000	7.7
Finance	—	—	41,000	0.6
Public administration, defense	—	—	114,000	1.7
Services	—	—	1,845,000	27.4
Other	32,041	3.0	...	...
TOTAL	1,059,605	100.0	6,741,000	100.0

Population economically active (1992): total 7,450,000; activity rate of total population 43.8% (participation rates: ages 16–59 [male], 16–54 [female] 80.1%; female [1991] 60.0%; unemployed [1989] 2.2%).

Price and earnings indexes (1990 = 100)							
	1986	1987	1988	1989	1990	1991	1992
Consumer price index	82.6	84.0	84.0	84.4	100.0	155.2	1,200.4
Monthly earnings index	72.6	75.1	80.8	88.1	100.0	187.9	1,256.9

Land use (1989): forested 6.3%; meadows and pastures 68.7%; agricultural and under permanent cultivation 13.1%; other 11.9%.
Household income and expenditure. Average household size (1989) 4.0; income per household (1991) 5,290 rubles; sources of income (1992): salaries and wages 65.0%, social benefits 25.3%, agricultural income 8.0%, other 1.7%; expenditure (1992): retail goods 68.1%, services 9.3%, taxes 9.0%, housing 1.5%, other 12.1%.

Foreign trade

Balance of trade (current prices)			
	1990	1991	1992
U.S.$'000,000	−10,280	−3,160	−1,670
% of total	26.5%	13.4%	10.2%

Imports (1992): 781,770,000,000 rubles (1991; machinery and transport equipment 37.6%, food 10.8%, textiles 9.8%, minerals 9.1%, manufactured items 5.8%). *Major import sources:* China 43.6%; Austria 6.4%; Cuba 6.3%; Hungary 5.8%; Yugoslavia 5.7%.
Exports (1992): 618,283,000,000 rubles (1991; semifabricated metal 27.5%, chemical products 22.3%; manufactured items 16.9%, clothing 3.9%, textiles 2.0%). *Major export destinations:* China 15.4%; Sweden 11.8%; Germany 8.0%; Switzerland 6.8%; U.S. 6.3%.

Transport and communications

Transport. Railroads (1991): length 13,173 mi, 21,200 km; passenger-km 19,-400,000,000; metric ton-km cargo 374,200,000. Roads (1992): total length 102,464 mi, 164,900 km (paved 69%). Vehicles (1988): passenger cars 734,-800; trucks and buses, n.a. Air transport (1992): passenger-mi 7,800,000,-000, passenger-km 12,600,000,000; metric ton-km cargo 70,000,000; airports (1993) with scheduled flights 68[8].
Communications. Newspapers (1989): total number 450; total circulation 6,700,000; circulation per 1,000 population 405. Radio (1992): total number of receivers 4,188,000 (1 per 4.1 persons). Television (1992): total number of receivers 4,795,000 (1 per 3.6 persons). Telephones (1992): 2,209,000 (1 per 7.8 persons).

Education and health

Education (1991–92)	schools	teachers	students	student/ teacher ratio
Primary (age 7–13) }	8,841	262,600	3,226,400	12.3
Secondary (age 14–17)				
Voc., teacher tr.	3,115	...	1,091,600	...
Higher	61	...	288,000	...

Educational attainment (1989). Percentage of population age 25 and over having: primary education or no formal schooling 16.2%; some secondary 19.8%; completed secondary and some postsecondary 54.1%; higher 9.9%.
Health (1992): physicians[9] 69,100 (1 per 246 persons); hospital beds 225,600 (1 per 75 persons); infant mortality rate per 1,000 live births 26.1.

Military

Total active duty personnel (1994): about 40,000 (army forces include air forces). *Military expenditure as percentage of GNP* (1993): 2.6%; per capita expenditure U.S.$41.

[1]On Dec. 10, 1993, the Parliament voted to dissolve itself and called for elections on March 7, 1994. [2]Transition is to be completed by the year 2000. [3]The Kazakh tenge was introduced Nov. 18, 1993, to replace the Russian ruble, at a rate of 500 Russian rubles to 1 tenge; on Nov. 25, 1993, the Kazakh tenge became the sole legal tender. [4]Local government was directly subordinated to the president in January 1992. [5]Detail does not add to total given because of rounding. [6]Ruble-area GNP and exchange-rate data are very speculative. [7]State sector only. [8]International only; the number of domestic airports is not available. [9]Data include dentists.

Kenya

Official name: Jamhuri ya Kenya (Swahili); Republic of Kenya (English).
Form of government: unitary multiparty republic with one legislative house (National Assembly [202[1]]).
Head of state and government: President.
Capital: Nairobi.
Official languages: Swahili; English.
Official religion: none.
Monetary unit: 1 Kenya shilling[2] (K Sh) = 100 cents; valuation (Oct. 7, 1994) 1 U.S.$ = K Sh 44.47; 1 £ = K Sh 70.72.

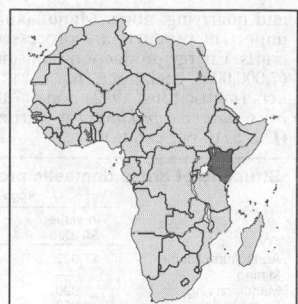

Area and population

Provinces	Provincial headquarters	area sq mi	area sq km	population 1990 estimate
Central	Nyori	5,087	13,176	3,601,700
Coast	Mombasa	32,279	83,603	2,150,400
Eastern	Embu	61,734	159,891	4,367,900
North Eastern	Garissa	48,997	126,902	640,600
Nyanza	Kisumu	6,240	16,162	4,322,700
Rift Valley	Nakuru	67,131	173,868	5,356,900
Western	Kakamega	3,228	8,360	2,836,700
Special area				
Nairobi	—	264	684	1,504,900
TOTAL		224,961[3]	582,646	24,871,800

Demography

Population (1994): 27,450,000[4].
Density (1994): persons per sq mi 122.0, persons per sq km 47.1.
Urban-rural (1991): urban 25.3%; rural 74.7%.
Sex distribution (1994): male 49.94%; female 50.04%.
Age breakdown (1994): under 15, 51.1%; 15–29, 26.6%; 30–44, 12.6%; 45–59, 6.4%; 60–74, 2.8%; 75 and over, 0.5%.
Population projection: (2000) 33,310,000; (2010) 44,850,000.
Doubling time: 21 years.
Ethnic composition (1989): Kikuyu 17.7%; Luhya 12.4%; Luo 10.6%; Kalenjin 9.8%; Kamba 9.8%; other 39.7%.
Religious affiliation (1987): Christian 73.0%, of which Roman Catholic 27.0%, Protestant 19.0%, other Christian (mostly African Indigenous, Anglican, and Eastern Orthodox) 27.0%; traditional beliefs 19.0%; Muslim 6.0%; other 2.0%.
Major cities (1984): Nairobi 1,504,900[5]; Mombasa 425,600; Kisumu 167,100; Nakuru 101,700; Machakos 92,300[6].

Vital statistics

Birth rate per 1,000 population (1990–95): 43.7 (world avg. 26.0).
Death rate per 1,000 population (1990–95): 10.3 (world avg. 9.2).
Natural increase rate per 1,000 population (1990–95): 33.4 (world avg. 16.8).
Total fertility rate (avg. births per childbearing woman; 1990–95): 6.3.
Life expectancy at birth (1990–95): male 57.1 years; female 60.8 years.
Major causes of death per 100,000 population: n.a.; however, major infectious diseases include AIDS, malaria, gastroenteritis, venereal diseases, diarrhea and dysentery, trachoma, amebiasis, and schistosomiasis.

National economy

Budget (1993–94). Revenue: K£4,551,140,000[2] (indirect taxes 61.5%, of which sales tax 31.2%, custom and excise duties 28.2%; direct taxes 27.3%; other 11.2%). Expenditures: K£7,763,450,000[2] (recurrent expenditure 84.9%; development expenditure 15.1%).
Production (metric tons except as noted). Agriculture, forestry, fishing (1993): sugarcane 4,210,000, corn (maize) 1,748,000, cassava 790,000, sweet potatoes 630,000, plantains 360,000, pineapple 270,000, potatoes 250,000, bananas 220,000, tea 211,000, pulses 200,000, wheat 150,000, sorghum 90,000, coffee 76,000, millet 58,000, coconuts 43,000, barley 37,000, sisal 34,000, tomatoes 32,000, seed cotton 16,000, cashew nuts 15,000, sunflower seeds 15,000, cotton seeds 11,000, copra 7,000; livestock (number of live animals) 11,000,000 cattle, 7,300,000 goats, 5,500,000 sheep; roundwood (1992) 37,311,000 cu m; fish catch 175,550, of which freshwater fish 95.7%. Mining and quarrying (1993): soda ash 216,890; fluorite 78,725; salt 74,669; limestone 30,349; garnet 127 kg[7]. Manufacturing (1990): cement 1,416,200; sugar 385,000; wheat flour 143,100; beer 3,492,000 hectolitres; mineral water 1,323,000 hectolitres; paint 47,000 hectolitres; alcoholic beverages 22,591 hectolitres. Construction (1986): residential 136,000 sq m; nonresidential 180,000 sq m. Energy production (consumption): electricity (kW-hr; 1993) 3,396,000,000 (3,074,000,000); coal (metric tons; 1992) none (110,000); crude petroleum (barrels; 1992) none (16,383,000); petroleum products (metric tons; 1992) 2,082,000 (1,393,000).
Public debt (external, outstanding; 1992): U.S.$4,635,000,000.
Household income and expenditure. Average household size (1980) 6.2; average annual income per household: n.a.; sources of income: n.a.; expenditure (1980): food 46.5%, housing 10.0%, furniture and utensils 9.4%, transportation 8.4%, clothing and footwear 7.7%, energy 2.6%, health 2.2%, education 1.0%.
Population economically active (1985): total 8,389,000; activity rate of total population 40.7% (participation rates: ages 15–64, 76.2%; female 40.9%; unemployed, n.a.).

Price and earnings indexes (1985 = 100)

	1987	1988	1989	1990	1991	1992	1993
Consumer price index	111.9	124.4	140.5	162.4	194.6	252.1	370.4
Monthly earnings index	116.3	133.1	141.4	154.1	168.4	...	...

Gross national product (at current market prices; 1993): U.S.$6,851,000,000 (U.S.$270 per capita).

Structure of gross domestic product and labour force

	1993 in value K£'000,000[2]	1993 % of total value	1993 labour force[8]	1993 % of labour force[8]
Agriculture	3,934.0	28.9	274,300	18.6
Mining	35.2	0.3	4,500	0.3
Manufacturing	1,419.7	10.4	193,600	13.1
Construction	759.2	5.6	72,600	4.9
Public utilities	174.8	1.3	22,100	1.5
Transp. and commun.	1,117.7	8.2	77,300	5.3
Trade	1,920.7	14.1	121,100	8.2
Finance	2,260.4	16.6	72,600	4.9
Pub. admin., defense	2,051.3	15.1 }	636,800	43.2
Services	177.3	1.3 }		
Other	−247.6[9]	−1.8[9]	—	—
TOTAL	13,602.7	100.0	1,474,900	100.0

Tourism (1992): receipts from visitors U.S.$442,000,000; expenditures by nationals abroad U.S.$29,000,000.
Land use (1992): forested 4.0%; meadows and pastures 66.9%; agricultural and under permanent cultivation 4.3%; other 24.8%.

Foreign trade[10]

Balance of trade (current prices)

	1988	1989	1990	1991	1992	1993
K Sh '000,000	−11,137	−18,131	−18,164	−11,890	−5,923	−5,938
% of total	22.6%	31.3%	27.7%	16.4%	6.2%	3.7%

Imports (1993): K£5,056,420,000[2] (machinery and transport equipment 19.5%, crude petroleum 18.7%, iron and steel products 6.0%, pharmaceuticals 5.4%, plastics and plastic products 3.9%). Major import sources: United Arab Emirates 15.0%; United Kingdom 11.9%; Japan 7.6%; Germany 7.1%; U.S. 5.8%; Saudi Arabia 4.6%; Italy 4.5%; France 4.2%; India 2.7%.
Exports (1993): K£3,678,250,000[2, 11] (tea 26.2%, coffee [not roasted] 15.5%, fruits and vegetables 11.0%, petroleum products 9.4%, cement 1.8%, soda ash 1.7%). Major export destinations: United Kingdom 16.0%; Uganda 8.7%; Tanzania 7.4%; Germany 7.3%; The Netherlands 4.0%; U.S. 3.7%.

Transport and communications

Transport. Railroads (1993): route length 1,885 mi, 3,034 km; passenger-mi 288,000,000, passenger-km 464,000,000; short ton-mi cargo 898,600,000, metric ton-km cargo 1,312,000,000. Roads (1993): total length 39,400 mi, 63,400 km (paved 14%). Vehicles (1990): passenger cars 157,166; trucks and buses 172,023. Merchant marine (1992): vessels (100 gross tons and over) 29; total deadweight tonnage 11,649. Air transport (1992)[12]: passenger-mi 828,062,-000, passenger-km 1,332,639,000; short ton-mi cargo 82,950,000, metric ton-km cargo 121,105,000; airports (1994) with scheduled flights 14.
Communications. Daily newspapers: total number (1992) 5; total circulation 328,000[13]; circulation per 1,000 population 12[13]. Radio (1993): 4,200,000 receivers (1 per 6.3 persons). Television (1993): 260,000 receivers (1 per 102 persons). Telephones (1992): 420,570 (1 per 61 persons).

Education and health

Education (1993)

	schools	teachers	students	student/teacher ratio
Primary (age 5–11)	15,804	173,002	5,428,600	31.4
Secondary (age 12–17)	2,639	31,657	517,577	16.3
Voc., teacher tr.	63	1,332[14]	29,593	13.4[14]
Higher	14	4,392[15]	88,180	8.1[15]

Educational attainment (1979). Percentage of population over age 25 having: no formal schooling 58.6%; primary education 32.2%; some secondary 7.9%; complete secondary and higher 1.3%. Literacy (1990): total population over age 15 literate 69.0%; males literate 79.8%; females literate 58.5%.
Health (1993): physicians 3,794 (1 per 7,410 persons); hospital beds 38,137 (1 per 737 persons); infant mortality rate per 1,000 live births (1990–95): 66.0.
Food (1988–90): daily per capita caloric intake 2,064 (vegetable products 86%, animal products 14%); 89% of FAO recommended minimum requirement.

Military

Total active duty personnel (1994): 24,200 (army 84.7%, navy 5.0%, air force 10.3%). Military expenditure as percentage of GNP (1991): 2.8% (world 4.2%); per capita expenditure U.S.$9.

---

[1]Includes 14 nonelective seats. [2]Kenya pound (K£) as a unit of account equals 20 K Sh. [3]Detail does not add to total given because of rounding. [4]Excludes a reported 402,000 refugees. [5]1990. [6]1983. [7]1989. [8]Employed persons only. [9]Indirect taxes less subsidies and imputed bank service charges. [10]Import figures are f.o.b. in balance of trade and c.i.f. in commodities and trading partners. [11]Includes K£53,040,000 in reexports. [12]Kenya Airways only. [13]Circulation for four newspapers only. [14]1987–88; teacher training only. [15]Universities only; 1990–91.

Kiribati

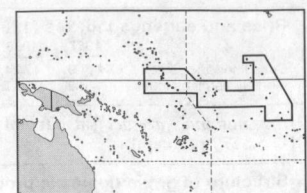

Official name: Republic of Kiribati.
Form of government: unitary republic with one legislature (House of Assembly [41[1]]).
Head of state and government: President.
Capital: Bairiki, on Tarawa Atoll.
Official language: English.
Official religion: none.
Monetary unit: 1 Australian Dollar ($A) = 100 cents; valuation (Oct. 7, 1994) 1 U.S.$ = $A 1.35; 1 £ = $A 2.15.

Area and population		area[2]		population
Island Groups Islands	Capitals	sq mi	sq km	1990 census
Gilberts Group	Bairiki Islet	110	286[3]	67,508
Abaiang	Tuarabu	7	18	5,233
Abemama	Kariatebike	11	27	3,218
Aranuka	Takaeang	5	12	1,002
Arorae	Roreti	3	9	1,440
Banaba	Anteeren	2	6	284
Beru	Taubukinberu	7	18	2,909
Butaritari	Butaritari	5	13	3,774
Kuria	Tabontebike	6	16	990
Maiana	Tebangetua	6	17	2,180
Makin	Makin	3	8	1,762
Marakei	Rawannawi	5	14	2,863
Nikunau	Rungata	7	19	1,994
Nonouti	Teuabu	8	20	2,814
Onotoa	Buariki	6	16	2,100
Tabiteuea North	Utiroa	10	26	3,201
Tabiteuea South	Buariki	5	12	1,331
Tamana	Bakaka	2	5	1,385
Tarawa North	Abaokoro	6	15	3,648
Tarawa South	Bairiki	6	16	25,380
Line Group	Kiritimati	192	496	4,782
Northern		167	432	
Kiritimati (Christmas)	London	150	388	2,537
Tabuaeran (Fanning)	Paelau	13	34	1,309
Teraina (Washington)	Washington	4	10	936
Southern (Caroline, Flint, Malden, Starbuck, Vostok)		25	64	—
Phoenix Group (Birnie, Enderbury, Kanton [Canton], McKean, Manra [Sydney], Nikumaroro [Gardner], Orona [Hull], Rawaki [Phoenix])	Kanton	11	29	45
TOTAL		313	811	72,335

Demography

Population (1994): 78,600.
Density (1993)[4]: persons per sq mi 280.7, persons per sq km 108.3.
Urban-rural (1990): urban 34.8%; rural 65.2%.
Sex distribution (1990): male 49.45%; female 50.55%.
Age breakdown (1990): under 15, 40.3%; 15–29, 27.5%; 30–44, 17.3%; 45–59, 9.2%; 60–74, 4.8%; 75 and over, 0.9%.
Population projection: (2000) 87,700; (2010) 106,000.
Doubling time: 35 years.
Ethnic composition (1990): I-Kiribati 97.4%; mixed (part I-Kiribati and other) 1.5%; Tuvaluan 0.5%; European 0.2%; other 0.4%.
Religious affiliation (1990): Roman Catholic 53.4%; Kiribati Protestant (Congregational) 39.2%; Bahā'ī 2.4%; Seventh-day Adventist 1.9%; Mormon 1.6%; other 1.5%.
Major cities (1990): Urban Tarawa 25,154.

Vital statistics

Birth rate per 1,000 population (1993): 32.0 (world avg. 26.0); legitimate, n.a.; illegitimate, n.a.
Death rate per 1,000 population (1993): 12.3 (world avg. 9.2).
Natural increase rate per 1,000 population (1993): 19.7 (world avg. 16.8).
Total fertility rate (avg. births per childbearing woman; 1993): 3.8.
Marriage rate per 1,000 population (1988): 5.2.
Divorce rate per 1,000 population: n.a.
Life expectancy at birth (1993): male 52.6 years; female 55.8 years.
Major causes of death per 100,000 population (1990): infectious intestinal diseases 79.4; certain conditions originating in the perinatal period 38.2; pneumonia 26.5; cerebrovascular disease 23.5; tuberculosis 20.6; chronic liver disease and cirrhosis 20.6; meningitis 19.2.

National economy

Budget (1991). Revenue: $A 22,800,000 (1988; nontax revenue 46.0%, of which reserve fund drawdown 32.1%, fishing licenses 9.8%; tax revenue 28.4%, of which import duties 9.4%, income tax 4.9%; development revenue 25.6%). Expenditures: $A 22,800,000 (1988; education 16.1%; development 15.9%; health 13.0%; natural resources 7.3%; communications 7.0%; public works 6.6%).
Production (metric tons except as noted). Agriculture, forestry, fishing (1993): coconuts 65,000, roots and tubers 8,000 (of which taro 1,000), copra 8,000, vegetables and melons 5,000, bananas 4,000; livestock (number of live animals) 9,000 pigs, 191,000 chickens[5]; fish catch (1991) 30,000. Mining

and quarrying: none. Manufacturing (1988): processed copra 14,406; other important products are processed fish, baked goods, clothing, and handicrafts. Energy production (consumption): electricity (kW-hr; 1992) 7,000,000 (7,000,000); coal, none (n.a.); crude petroleum, none (n.a.); petroleum products (metric tons; 1992) none (7,000); natural gas, none (n.a.).
Gross national product (at current market prices; 1993): U.S.$54,000,000 (U.S.$710 per capita).

Structure of gross domestic product and labour force	1992		1990	
	in value $A '000	% of total value	labour force	% of labour force
Agriculture, fishing	11,022	23.8	23,137[6]	71.0[6]
Mining	—	—		
Manufacturing	920	2.0	622	1.9
Construction	2,300	5.0	339	1.0
Public utilities	800	1.7	301	0.9
Transp. and commun.	7,130	15.4	921	2.8
Trade	6,530	14.1	1,341	4.1
Finance	3,210	6.9	441	1.4
Pub. admin., defense }	11,935	25.8	2,123	6.5
Services			2,286	7.0
Other	2,413	5.2	1,099[7]	3.4[7]
TOTAL	46,260	100.0[3]	32,610	100.0

Public debt (external, outstanding; 1989): U.S.$16,000,000.
Population economically active (1990): total 32,610; activity rate of total population 45.1% (participation rates: over age 15, 75.6%; female 46.4%; unemployed 2.8%).

Price and earnings indexes (1985 = 100)							
	1987	1988	1989	1990	1991	1992	1993
Consumer price index	111.8	113.8	120.8	126.9	131.7	138.3	148.0
Earnings index	...	...	...	...	...	...	...

Household income and expenditure. Average household size (1990) 6.6; income per household: n.a.; sources of income (1978): wages 69.7%, self-employment 21.4%, transfer payments 6.0%, other 2.9%; expenditure (1982): food 50.0%, tobacco and alcohol 14.0%, clothing 8.0%, transportation 8.0%, housing, energy, and household operation 7.5%.
Tourism (1992): receipts from visitors U.S.$2,000,000; expenditures by nationals abroad, n.a.
Land use (1992): forested 2.7%; agricultural and under permanent cultivation 50.7%; other 46.6%.

Foreign trade

Balance of trade (current prices)						
	1988	1989	1990	1991	1992	1993
$A '000	−21,515	−22,161	−30,765	−29,529	−44,017	−29,478
% of total	61.7%	63.3%	80.7%	80.0%	77.2%	73.8%

Imports (1992): $A 50,530,000 (machinery and transport equipment 47.3%; food 21.1%; manufactured goods 8.0%; mineral fuels 7.8%; beverages and tobacco 5.0%; chemicals 3.5%; crude materials 1.2%). *Major import sources:* Australia 38.4%; Japan 22.7%; Fiji 11.3%; New Zealand 5.4%; China 3.3%; United States 2.9%; Hong Kong 1.0%.
Exports (1992): $A 6,513,000 (domestic exports 86.7%, of which copra 66.8%, fish and fish preparations 11.3%; reexports 13.3%). *Major export destinations:* United States 12.3%; Australia 4.8%; Denmark 4.5%; Fiji 4.1%; New Zealand 1.6%; United Kingdom 0.9%.

Transport and communications

Transport. Roads (1991): total length 398 mi, 640 km (paved 5%). Vehicles (1982): passenger cars 307; trucks and buses 130. Merchant marine (1992): vessels (100 gross tons and over) 7; total deadweight tonnage 2,685. Air transport (1990): passenger-mi 5,331,000, passenger-km 8,579,000; short ton-mi cargo 514,000, metric ton-km cargo 750,000; airports (1994) with scheduled flights 18.
Communications. Daily newspapers: none. Radio (1993): total number of receivers 10,000 (1 per 7.7 persons). Television: none. Telephones (1992): 1,600 (1 per 47 persons).

Education and health

Education (1992)	schools	teachers	students	student/ teacher ratio
Primary (age 6–13)	95	545	16,020	29.4
Secondary (age 14–18)	9[8]	194	3,069	15.8
Voc., teacher tr.	6[8]	43	288	6.7
Higher[9]	—	—	—	—

Educational attainment (1990)[10]. Percentage of population age 15 and over having: no schooling 6.9%; primary 67.8%; secondary 24.5%; higher 0.6%; not stated 0.2%. *Literacy* (1985): total population age 15 and over literate 90%.
Health (1990): physicians 16 (1 per 4,483 persons); hospital beds 283 (1 per 253 persons); infant mortality rate per 1,000 live births (1993) 98.4.
Food (1988–90): daily per capita caloric intake 2,517 (vegetable products 89%, animal products 11%); 110% of FAO recommended minimum requirement.

---

[1]Includes two nonelective members. [2]Includes uninhabited islands. [3]Detail does not add to total given because of rounding. [4]Density based on inhabited island areas (280 sq mi, 726 sq km) only. [5]1982. [6]Includes 20,568 persons engaged in "village work" (subsistence agriculture or fishing). [7]Includes 900 unemployed. [8]1990. [9]54 students overseas. [10]For indigenous population.

Korea, North

Official name: Chosŏn Minjujuŭi
In'min Konghwaguk (Democratic
People's Republic of Korea).
Form of government: unitary
single-party republic with one
legislative house (Supreme People's
Assembly [687]).
Chief of state: President.
Head of government: Premier.
Capital: P'yŏngyang.
Official language: Korean.
Official religion: none.
Monetary unit: 1 won = 100
chŏn; valuation (Oct. 7, 1994)
1 U.S.$ = 2.15 won; 1 £ = 3.42 won.

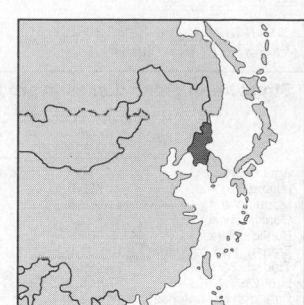

Area and population		area		population[1]
				1987
Provinces	Capitals	sq mi	sq km	estimate
Chagang-do	Kanggye	6,551	16,968	1,156,000
Hamgyŏng-namdo	Hamhŭng	7,324	18,970	2,547,000
Hamgyŏng-pukto	Ch'ŏngjin	6,784	17,570	2,003,000
Hwanghae-namdo	Haeju	3,090	8,002	1,914,000
Hwanghae-pukto	Sariwŏn	3,092	8,007	1,409,000
Kangwŏn-do	Wŏnsan	4,306	11,152	1,227,000
P'yŏngan-namdo	P'yŏngsan	4,470	11,577	2,653,000
P'yŏngan-pukto	Sinŭiju	4,707[2]	12,191[2]	2,380,000
Yanggang-do	Hyesan	5,528	14,317	628,000
Special cities				
Kaesŏng	—	485	1,255	331,000
Namp'o	—	291	753	715,000
P'yŏngyang	—	772	2,000	2,355,000
Special district				
Hyangsan-chigu	—	2	2	28,000
TOTAL		47,300[3]	122,762	10,346,000

Demography

Population (1994): 23,067,000.
Density (1994): persons per sq mi 486.7, persons per sq km 187.9.
Urban-rural (1993): urban 60.0%; rural 40.0%.
Sex distribution (1992): male 49.36%; female 50.64%.
Age breakdown (1990): under 15, 29.4%; 15–29, 33.8%; 30–44, 20.4%; 45–59, 10.6%; 60–74, 4.7%; 75 and over, 1.1%.
Population projection: (2000) 25,491,000; (2010) 28,491,000.
Doubling time: 37 years.
Ethnic composition (1989): Korean 99.8%; Chinese 0.2%.
Religious affiliation (1980): atheist or nonreligious 67.9%; traditional beliefs 15.6%; Ch'ŏndogyo 13.9%; Buddhist 1.7%; Christian 0.9%.
Major cities (1987): P'yŏngyang 2,355,000; Hamhŭng 701,000; Ch'ŏngjin 520,000; Namp'o 370,000; Sunch'ŏn 356,000.

Vital statistics

Birth rate per 1,000 population (1993): 23 (world avg. 26.0).
Death rate per 1,000 population (1993): 5 (world avg. 9.2).
Natural increase rate per 1,000 population (1993): 18 (world avg. 16.8).
Total fertility rate (avg. births per childbearing woman; 1993): 2.4.
Marriage rate per 1,000 population (1987): 9.3.
Divorce rate per 1,000 population (1987): 0.2.
Life expectancy at birth (1993): male 68 years; female 74 years.
Major causes of death per 100,000 population (1986): diseases of the circulatory system 224.9; malignant neoplasms (cancers) 69.0; diseases of the digestive system 51.6; diseases of the respiratory system 46.7; injuries and poisoning 38.2; infectious and parasitic diseases 19.4.

National economy

Budget (1993). Revenue: 40,449,900,000 won (1984; turnover tax 55.0%, payments by state enterprises 30.0%). Expenditures: 40,449,900,000 won (national economy 67.8%, social and cultural affairs 19.2%, defense 11.6%, administration 1.4%).
Public debt (external, outstanding; 1992): U.S.$8,000,000,000.
Tourism (1986): total number of tourist arrivals 85,000.
Population economically active (1987)[4]: total 12,517,000; activity rate of total population 61.7% (participation rates: ages 15–64, n.a.; female, n.a.; unemployed, n.a.).
Price and earnings indexes: n.a.
Production (metric tons except as noted). Agriculture, forestry, fishing (1992): corn (maize) 3,800,000[5], rice 2,940,000[5], potatoes 1,975,000, cabbages 850,000, sweet potatoes 500,000, soybeans 400,000, wheat 150,000[5], pears 122,000, barley 120,000[5], peaches 105,000, watermelons 104,000, tomatoes 70,000, cucumbers and gherkins 70,000, tobacco leaves 67,000, millet 60,000, oats 56,000; livestock (number of live animals) 3,300,000 pigs, 1,300,000 cattle, 390,000 sheep, 300,000 goats, 44,000,000 chickens; roundwood (1992) 4,783,000 cu m; fish catch (1991) 1,700,100. Mining and quarrying (1992): iron ore 10,500,000; magnesite (metal content) 1,600,000; phosphate rock 500,000; sulfur 240,000; zinc 200,000; lead (metal content) 75,000; fluorspar 41,000; graphite 38,000; copper 16,000; gold 5,000 kg; silver 50. Manufacturing (1992): cement 17,000,000; crude steel 8,100,000; pig iron 6,600,000; steel semimanufactures 3,200,000[6]; coke 3,000,000; chemical fertilizers 3,000,000[7]; gasoline 1,130,500; meat 220,000[6]; textile fabrics 210,000,000 m[6]. Construc-

tion: n.a. Energy production (consumption): electricity (kW-hr; 1992) 38,000,000 (38,000,000); coal (metric tons; 1992) 70,000,000 (72,050,000); crude petroleum (barrels; 1992) none (18,325,000); petroleum products (metric tons; 1992) 2,965,000 (4,505,000); natural gas, none (n.a.).
Household income and expenditure. Average household size (1987) 4.8; average annual income per household (1980) 3,677 won (U.S.$4,275); sources of income: n.a.; expenditure (1984)[8]: food 46.5%, clothing 29.9%, furniture 3.8%, energy 3.3%, housing 0.6%.
Gross national product (1992): U.S.$22,000,000,000 (U.S.$990 per capita).

Structure of gross domestic product and labour force				
	1982			
	in value '000,000 won	% of total value	labour force	% of labour force
Agriculture	...	...	3,726,000	44.1
Mining and manufacturing	...	...	} 2,790,000	} 33.0
Construction	...	...		
Public utilities	...	...		
Transportation and communications	...	...	418,000	4.9
Trade	...	...		
Finance	...	...		
Pub. admin., defense	...	...	} 1,521,000	} 18.0
Services	...	...		
Other	...	...		
TOTAL	11,000	100.0	8,455,000	100.0

Land use (1991): forested 74.5%; meadows and pastures 0.4%; agricultural and under permanent cultivation 16.7%; other 8.4%.

Foreign trade[9]

Balance of trade (current prices)						
	1987	1988	1989	1990	1991	1992
U.S.$'000,000	−391.7	−315.2	−433.9	−420.5	−764.7	−600.0
% of total	20.0%	14.1%	21.0%	21.0%	35.6%	18.8%

Imports (1992): U.S.$1,900,000,000 (crude petroleum, coal and coke, industrial machinery and transport equipment [including trucks], industrial chemicals, textile yarn and fabrics, and grain are among the major imports). *Major import sources:* Russia 37.6%; China 23.0%; Japan 9.8%; Hong Kong 5.4%.
Exports (1992): U.S.$1,300,000,000 (minerals [including lead, magnesite, zinc], metallurgical products [iron and steel, nonferrous metals], cement, agricultural products [including fish, grain, fruit and vegetables, tobacco], and manufactured goods [textile fabrics, clothing] are among the major exports). *Major export destinations:* Russia 45.4%; Japan 22.9%; China 6.8%; Germany 5.8%; Hong Kong 3.2%.

Transport and communications

Transport. Railroads (1990): length 5,302 mi, 8,533 km; (latest) passenger-mi 2,100,000,000, passenger-km 3,400,000,000; (latest) short ton-mi cargo 5,100,000,000, metric ton km cargo 9,100,000,000. Roads (1991): total length 18,600 mi, 30,000 km (paved 7.5%). Vehicles (1990): passenger cars 248,000. Merchant marine (1992): vessels (100 gross tons and over) 100; total deadweight tonnage 951,222. Air transport (1994): passenger-mi 52,200,000, passenger-km 84,000,000; short ton-mi cargo 1,370,000, metric ton-km cargo 2,000,000; airports (1994) with scheduled flights 1.
Communications. Daily newspapers (1990): total number 11; total circulation 5,000,000; circulation per 1,000 population 230. Radio (1993): total number of receivers 4,700,000 (1 per 4.8 persons). Television (1993): total number of receivers 338,000 (1 per 67 persons). Telephones (1992): 1,089,300[10] (1 per 20 persons).

Education and health

Education (1987)	schools	teachers	students	student/ teacher ratio
Primary (age 6–9)	6,122	138,945	1,543,000	11.1
Secondary (age 10–15)	...	111,000	2,468,000	22.2
Voc., teacher tr.	473[11]	...	220,000	...
Higher	281	27,000	390,000	14.4

Educational attainment (1987–88). Percentage of population age 16 and over having attended or graduated from postsecondary-level school: 13.7%. *Literacy* (1984): 99%.
Health (1989): physicians 57,690 (1 per 370 persons); hospital beds 290,590 (1 per 74 persons); infant mortality rate per 1,000 live births (1993) 24.
Food (1988–90): daily per capita caloric intake 2,843 (vegetable products 92%, animal products 8%); 121% of FAO recommended minimum requirement.

Military

Total active duty personnel (1994): 1,128,000 (army 88.6%, navy 4.1%, air force 7.3%). *Military expenditure as percentage of GNP* (1993): 25.5% (world [1992] 4.0%); per capita expenditure U.S.$234.

---

[1]Civilian population only. [2]P'yŏngan-pukto includes special district of Hyangsan-chigu. [3]Detail does not add to total given because of rounding. [4]The Democratic People's Republic of Korea categorizes economically active as including students in higher education, retirees, and heads of households, as well as those in the civilian labour force. [5]1993. [6]1990. [7]1991. [8]Workers and clerical workers only. [9]Imports are f.o.b. [10]Number of telephone stations. [11]1986.

Korea, South

Official name: Taehan Min'guk
 (Republic of Korea).
Form of government: unitary multiparty
 republic with a National Assembly
 (299 members).
Chief of state: President.
Head of government: Prime Minister.
Capital: Seoul.
Official language: Korean.
Official religion: none.
Monetary unit: 1 won (W) = 100 chon;
 valuation (Oct. 7, 1994)
 1 U.S.$ = W 798; 1 £ = W 1,271.

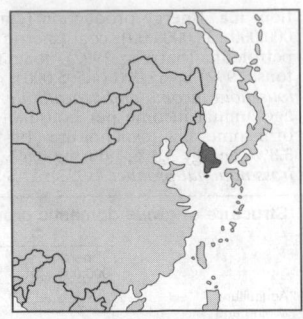

Gross national product (at current market prices; 1993): U.S.$337,910,000,000
 (U.S.$7,670 per capita).

Structure of gross domestic product and labour force

| | 1993 | | | |
	in value W '000,000,000[3]	% of total value	labour force	% of labour force
Agriculture	16,210.7	7.5	2,845,000	14.4
Mining	885.0	0.4	54,000	0.3
Manufacturing	62,997.3	29.0	4,584,000	23.2
Construction	24,901.7	11.5	1,680,000	8.5
Public utilities	5,069.9	2.3	65,000	0.3
Transp. and commun.	15,961.8	7.3	1,008,000	5.1
Trade	27,486.8	12.7	4,831,000	24.5
Finance	37,505.1	17.3	1,355,000	6.9
Pub. admin., defense	14,458.0	6.7 }	2,784,000	14.1
Services	12,860.2	5.9		
Other	−1,097.3[4]	−0.5[4]	551,000[5]	2.8[5]
TOTAL	217,239.2	100.0[6]	19,754,000[6]	100.0[6]

Population economically active (1993): total 19,754,000; activity rate 44.8%
 (participation rates: ages 15 and over, 61.0%; female 39.9%; unemployed
 2.8%).

Price and earnings indexes (1990 = 100)

	1987	1988	1989	1990	1991	1992	1993
Consumer price index	81.3	87.1	92.1	100.0	109.3	116.1	121.7
Monthly earnings index	55.6	66.5	83.2	100.0	116.9	135.2	149.9

Tourism (1992): receipts from visitors U.S.$3,272,000,000; expenditures by
 nationals abroad U.S.$3,794,000,000.
Land use (1992): forested 65.5%; meadows and pastureland 0.9%; agricultural and under permanent cultivation 21.0%; other 12.6%.

Foreign trade

Balance of trade (current prices)

	1988	1989	1990	1991	1992	1993
U.S.$'000,000	+8,510	+2,875	−701	−3,968	−588	+2,880
% of total	10.6%	3.6%	0.8%	3.6%	0.4%	1.8%

Imports (1993): U.S.$83,800,100,000 (machinery and transport equipment
 33.9%, mineral fuels and lubricants 18.0%, manufactured goods 14.4%, inedible crude materials 10.6%, chemicals 9.8%). *Major import sources:* Japan
 23.9%; United States 21.4%; Germany 4.7%; Saudi Arabia 4.5%; Australia
 4.0%; Indonesia 3.1%; Malaysia 2.3%, Canada 2.0%.; Singapore 1.8%.
Exports (1993): U.S.$82,235,900,000 (machinery and transport equipment
 44.9%, manufactured goods 25.2%, chemicals 6.0%, food and live animals
 2.5%, mineral fuels 2.2%). *Major export destinations:* United States 22.1%;
 Japan 14.1%; Hong Kong 7.8%; Germany 4.4%; Singapore 3.8%; Taiwan
 2.8%; Indonesia 2.5%; India 2.2%.

Transport and communications

Transport. Railroads (1992): length 4,049 mi[7], 6,517 km[7]; passenger-km 34,-
 787,000,000; metric ton-km cargo 14,256,000,000. Roads (1989): total length
 34,659 mi, 55,778 km (paved 61%). Vehicles (1992): passenger cars 3,461,-
 057; trucks and buses 1,745,097. Merchant marine (1992): vessels (100 gross
 tons and over) 2,138; total deadweight tonnage 11,724,942. Air transport
 (1991): passenger-km 19,957,000,000; metric ton-km cargo 2,664,000,000;
 airports (1994) with scheduled flights 13.
Communications. Daily newspapers (1993): total number 63; total circulation
 9,736,000[8]; circulation per 1,000 population 221[8]. Radio (1993): 42,000,000
 receivers (1 per 1.0 persons). Television (1993): 9,101,000 receivers (1 per
 4.8 persons). Telephones (1992): 19,021,000 (1 per 2.3 persons).

Education and health

Education (1993)

	schools	teachers	students	student/ teacher ratio
Primary (age 6–13)	6,057	139,159	4,336,252	31.2
Secondary (age 14–19) } Vocational	4,358	194,565	4,497,242	23.1
Higher	605	48,535	1,652,665	34.0

Educational attainment (1990). Percentage of population age 6 and over having: primary education or less 33.7%, of which no formal schooling (1985)
 14.3%; some secondary and secondary 52.1%; postsecondary 14.2%. *Literacy*
 (1990): total population age 15 and over literate 96.3%; males literate 99.1%;
 females literate 93.5%.
Health (1992): physicians 48,390 (1 per 902 persons); hospital beds 115,140 (1
 per 379 persons); infant mortality rate per 1,000 live births (1994) 15.0.
Food (1988–90): daily per capita caloric intake 2,826 (vegetable products 87%,
 animal products 13%); 120% of FAO recommended minimum requirement.

Military

Total active duty personnel (1994): 633,000 (army 82.1%, navy 9.5%, air force
 8.4%). *Military expenditure as percentage of GNP* (1991): 3.8% (world 4.2%);
 per capita expenditure: U.S.$244.

Area and population

| | | area | | population |
Provinces	Capitals	sq mi	sq km	1990 census
Cheju-do	Cheju	705	1,826	514,605
Chŏlla-namdo	Kwangju	4,561	11,814	2,507,439
Chŏlla-pukto	Chŏnju	3,106	8,043	2,069,960
Ch'ungch'ŏng-namdo	Taejŏn	3,212	8,318	2,013,926
Ch'ungch'ŏng-pukto	Ch'ŏngju	2,871	7,436	1,389,686
Kangwŏn-do	Ch'unch'ŏn'	6,524	16,898	1,580,430
Kyŏnggi-do	Suwŏn	4,160	10,773	6,155,632
Kyŏngsang-namdo	Masan	4,546	11,774	3,672,396
Kyŏngsang-pukto	Taegu	7,509	19,447	2,860,595
Special cities				
Inch'ŏn-si	Inch'ŏn	122	317	1,817,919
Kwangju-si	Kwangju	193	501	1,139,003
Pusan-si	Pusan	204	529	3,798,113
Sŏul-t'ŭkpyŏlsi	Seoul	234	605	10,612,577
Taegu-si	Taegu	176	456	2,229,040
Taejŏn-si	Taejŏn	207	537	1,049,578
TOTAL		38,330	99,274	43,410,899

Demography

Population (1994): 44,436,000.
Density (1994): persons per sq mi 1,159.3, persons per sq km 447.6.
Urban-rural (1990): urban 74.4%; rural 25.6%.
Sex distribution (1992): male 50.34%; female 49.66%.
Age breakdown (1992): under 15, 24.8%; 15–29, 29.3%; 30–44, 23.8%; 45–59,
 14.0%; 60–74, 6.5%; 75 and over, 1.6%.
Population projection: (2000) 46,789,000; (2010) 49,683,000.
Doubling time: 77 years.
Ethnic composition (1990): Korean 99.9%; other 0.1%.
Religious affiliation (1991): religious[1] 54.0%, of which Buddhist 27.6%, Protes-
 tant 18.6%, Roman Catholic 5.7%, Confucian 1.0%, Wonbulgyo 0.3%,
 Ch'ondogyo 0.2%, other 0.6%; nonreligious 46.0%.
Major cities (1990): Seoul 10,612,577; Pusan 3,798,113; Taegu 2,229,040; In-
 ch'ŏn 1,817,919; Kwangju 1,139,003.

Vital statistics

Birth rate per 1,000 population (1994): 15.0 (world avg. 26.0).
Death rate per 1,000 population (1994): 6.0 (world avg. 9.2).
Natural increase rate per 1,000 population (1994): 9.0 (world avg. 16.8).
Total fertility rate (avg. births per childbearing woman; 1994): 1.6.
Marriage rate per 1,000 population (1992): 7.5.
Divorce rate per 1,000 population (1989): 1.1.
Life expectancy at birth (1994): male 69.0 years; female 76.0 years.
Major causes of death per 100,000 population (1991): diseases of the circula-
 tory system 166.3; malignant neoplasms (cancers) 111.4; accidents, poison-
 ing, and violence 90.2; diseases of the digestive system 45.1; diseases of the
 respiratory system 22.6.

National economy

Budget (1993). Revenue: W 53,127,900,000,000 (taxes on goods and services
 34.7%, income taxes 28.8%, nontax revenue 27.8%, customs duties 5.4%).
 Expenditures: W 52,869,700,000,000 (general expenses 51.0%, defense 17.6%,
 economic development 5.5%).
Public debt (external, outstanding; 1992): U.S.$23,919,000,000.
Production (metric tons except as noted). Agriculture, forestry, fishing (1993):
 rice 6,597,000, cabbages 2,600,000, dry onions 1,000,000, apples 700,000,
 tangerines 619,000, garlic 450,000, barley 400,000, soybeans 160,000; livestock (number of live animals) 5,928,000 pigs, 2,814,000 cattle, 78,000,000
 chickens; roundwood (1992) 6,485,000 cu m; fish catch (1992) 3,289,200.
 Mining and quarrying (1993): copper ore 221,570; iron ore 218,663; zinc
 concentrate 27,616; lead concentrate 14,818. Manufacturing (1993): cement
 47,313,000; pig iron 21,870,000; urea fertilizers 831,066; newsprint 742,327;
 caustic soda 506,794; synthetic fabrics 2,459,299,000 sq m; television receivers
 15,956,000 units; passenger cars 1,527,753 units. Construction (1993): residential 69,300,000 sq m; nonresidential 48,487,000 sq m. Energy production
 (consumption): electricity (kW-hr; 1992) 147,843,000,000 (147,843,000,000);
 coal (metric tons; 1992) 11,970,000 (39,814,000); crude petroleum (barrels;
 1992) none (511,319,000); petroleum products (metric tons; 1992) 59,726,000
 (54,103,000); natural gas (cu m; 1992) none (4,915,000,000).
Household income and expenditure (1993)[2]. Average household size (1990)
 3.8; income per household W 27,470,000 (U.S.$34,223); sources of income:
 wages 55.7%, other 44.3%; expenditure: food and beverages 29.3%, education and recreation 13.5%, transportation and communications 10.2%,
 clothing and footwear 7.7%, health care 5.4%, household durable goods
 5.2%, housing 4.4%, energy 4.3%, other 20.0%.

---

[1]Refers to persons who have received commandments, accepted baptism, or entered
a faith and who participate in a religious function regularly or put the religious idea
less imputed bank service charges. [5]Unemployed. [6]Detail does not add to total given
into practice. [2]Excludes farm households. [3]At 1990 constant prices. [4]Import duties
because of rounding. [7]1993. [8]Circulation for 20 newspapers only.

Kuwait

Official name: Dawlat al-Kuwayt (State of Kuwait).
Form of government: Constitutional monarchy with one legislative body (National Assembly [50]).
Head of state and government: Emir[1].
Capital: Kuwait City.
Official language: Arabic.
Official religion: Islam.
Monetary unit: 1 Kuwaiti dinar (KD) = 1,000 fils; valuation (Oct. 7, 1994) 1 KD = U.S.$3.33 = £2.13.

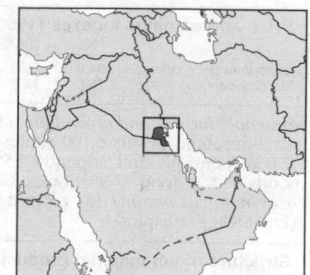

Area and population[2]

Governorates[3]	Capitals	area sq mi	area sq km	population 1993 estimate
al-Ahmadī	al-Ahmadī	1,984	5,138	266,400
al-Farwānīyah	al-Farwānīyah	...	...	363,300
al-Jahrā'	al-Jahrā'	4,372	11,324	178,700
Capital	Kuwait City	38	98	237,900
Hawallī	Hawallī	138	358	387,000
Islands[4]	—	347	900	...
TOTAL		6,880[5]	17,818	1,433,300

Demography

Population (1994): 1,469,000.
Density (1994): persons per sq mi 213.5, persons per sq km 82.4.
Urban-rural (1992): urban 96.3%; rural 3.7%.
Sex distribution (1994): male 57.07%; female 42.93%.
Age breakdown (1992): under 15, 43.0%; 15–29, 26.1%; 30–44, 18.4%; 45–59, 9.0%; 60–74, 2.9%; 75 and over, 0.6%.
Population projection: (2000) 1,702,000; (2010) 2,177,000.
Doubling time (1992): 16 years.
Ethnic composition (by nationality; 1994): Kuwaiti 43.6%; non-Kuwaiti (including other Arab, South Asian, Palestinian, and Badoun [stateless immigrants]) 56.4%.
Religious affiliation (1986): Muslim 90.0%, of which Sunnī 63.0%, Shīʿah 27.0%; Christian 8.0%; Hindu 2.0%.
Major cities (1985): as-Sālimīyah 153,220; Hawallī 145,215; al-Jahrā' 111,165; al-Farwānīyah 68,665; Kuwait City 44,224.

Vital statistics

Birth rate per 1,000 population (1992): 24.5 (world avg. 26.0); legitimate, n.a.; illegitimate, n.a.
Death rate per 1,000 population (1992): 2.2 (world avg. 9.2).
Natural increase rate per 1,000 population (1992): 22.3 (world avg. 16.8).
Total fertility rate (avg. births per childbearing woman; 1992): 4.9.
Marriage rate per 1,000 population (1989): 5.4.
Divorce rate per 1,000 population (1989): 1.5.
Life expectancy at birth (1992): male 74.3 years; female 78.1 years.
Major causes of death per 100,000 population (1992): circulatory diseases 79.8; accidents, poisoning, and violence 40.3; malignant neoplasms (cancers) 22.6; respiratory diseases 17.1; congenital anomalies 9.2; endocrine, nutritional, and metabolic diseases 8.4; diseases of the nervous system 7.4; infectious and parasitic diseases 5.7; diseases of the digestive system 4.4.

National economy

Budget (1994–95). Revenue: KD 2,537,000,000 (oil revenue 88.1%). Expenditures[6]: KD 4,000,000,000 (1993–94; defense 30.7%; education 11.9%; health 9.9%; electricity, water, and public utilities 6.1%; administrative services 5.9%; transportation and communications 3.0%).
Public debt (external, outstanding; 1991): U.S.$792,000,000[7].
Tourism (1992): receipts from visitors U.S.$273,000,000; expenditures by nationals abroad U.S.$1,705,000,000.
Gross national product (at current market prices; 1993): U.S.$28,486,000,000 (U.S.$19,875 per capita).

Structure of gross domestic product and labour force

	1993 in value KD '000,000	% of total value	labour force	% of labour force
Agriculture	33.1	0.5	9,150	1.2
Mining (oil sector)	2,968.8	43.4	6,025	0.8
Manufacturing	586.5	8.6	51,948	7.1
Construction	217.2	3.2	79,709	10.8
Public utilities	−63.9	−0.9	5,956	0.8
Transportation and communications	236.8	3.5	28,388	3.9
Trade	377.2	5.5	132,190[8]	18.0[8]
Finance and business services	760.6	11.1	28,397	3.9
Pub. admin., defense Services	} 1,723.0	25.2	364,123	49.5
Other	—		29,790	4.0
TOTAL	6,839.3	100.0[5]	735,676	100.0

Production (metric tons except as noted). Agriculture, forestry, fishing (1993): tomatoes 35,000, cucumbers and gherkins 17,000, onions 16,000, eggplants 2,000, garlic 1,000; livestock (number of live animals) 150,000 sheep, 15,000 goats, 12,000 cattle, 1,000 camels, 10,000,000 chickens; fish catch 8,000. Mining and quarrying (1992): sulfur 150,000; lime 5,000. Manufacturing (1992): cement 533,500; ammonia (urea) 257,300; flour 104,900; bread 63,500; bran

34,100; concrete pipes 12,800; liquefied caustic soda 12,200; chlorine gas 10,800; biscuits 1,300; detergents 700; hydrochloric acid 1,427,900 gallons; concrete slabs 695,700 sq m; sodium hydrochloride 7,560 cu m. Construction (floor area approved for construction; 1989): residential 2,563,000 sq m; nonresidential 416,000 sq m. Energy production (consumption): electricity (kW-hr; 1992) 16,885,000,000 (14,209,000,000); coal, none (none); crude petroleum (barrels; 1992) 388,700,000 (117,400,000); petroleum products (metric tons; 1992) 16,059,000 (3,064,000); natural gas (cu m; 1992) 2,619,-800,000 (2,619,800,000).
Population economically active (1990): total 722,495; activity rate of total population 37.2% (participation rates [1988]: ages 15–64, 56.1%; female 18.8%; unemployed 1.9%).

Price and earnings indexes (1990 = 100)

	1987	1988	1989	1990[9]	1991[10]	1992	1993[11]
Consumer price index	93.5	94.8	98.1	100.0	110.0	110.7	110.8
Earnings index	...	...	...	...	...	...	...

Household income and expenditure. Average household size (1986) 7.4; annual income per household (1973)[12] KD 4,246 (U.S.$12,907); sources of income: wages and salaries 53.8%, self-employment 20.8%, other 25.4%; expenditure (1986–87): food, beverages, and tobacco 28.1%, housing and energy 15.5%, transportation 13.7%, household appliances and services 11.2%, clothing and footwear 8.1%, education and recreation 5.2%, health 0.7%.
Land use (1992): forested 0.1%; meadows and pastures 7.7%; agricultural and under permanent cultivation 0.3%; other, built-up, and wasteland 91.9%.

Foreign trade[13]

Balance of trade (current prices)

	1988	1989	1990	1991	1992	1993
KD '000,000	+452	+1,529	+886	−1,045	−198	+1,194
% of total	11.6%	29.2%	27.9%	62.8%	4.9%	23.1%

Imports (1993): KD 1,986,000,000 (machinery and transport equipment 37.6%, manufactured goods 20.3%, miscellaneous manufactured articles 16.4%, food and live animals 14.3%, chemical products 6.8%, beverages and tobacco 1.5%). *Major import sources:* United States 16.2%; Japan 13.8%; West Germany 8.4%; United Kingdom 7.2%; Italy 6.3%; Saudi Arabia 5.3%; South Korea 4.3%; France 4.2%.
Exports (1993)[14]: KD 3,180,500,000 (crude petroleum and petroleum products 94.9%). *Major export destinations:* Saudi Arabia 20.8%; United Arab Emirates 18.1%; India 12.1%; Oman 3.0%; Egypt 2.9%; Syria 2.7%; Singapore 2.5%.

Transport and communications

Transport. Railroads: none. Roads (1990): total length 2,655 mi, 4,273 km (paved 100%). Vehicles (1992): passenger cars 579,841; trucks and buses 126,754. Merchant marine (1992): vessels (100 gross tons and over) 209; total deadweight tonnage 3,188,526. Air transport (1993)[15]: passenger-mi 2,518,801,000, passenger-km 4,053,626,000; short ton-mi cargo 174,042,000, metric ton-km cargo 254,097,000; airports (1994) with scheduled flights 1.
Communications. Daily newspapers (1992): total number 9; total circulation 655,000; circulation per 1,000 population 550. Radio (1993): total number of receivers 1,000,000 (1 per 1.4 persons). Television (1993): total number of receivers 800,000 (1 per 1.8 persons). Telephones (1992): 345,580 (1 per 4.0 persons).

Education and health

Education (1993–94)

	schools	teachers	students	student/ teacher ratio
Primary (age 6–9)	239	8,217	130,877	15.9
Secondary (age 10–17)	390	17,340	188,399	10.9
Voc., teacher tr.	36	650	2,524	3.9
Higher[16]	1	927[17]	11,284	...

Educational attainment (1988). Percentage of population age 25 and over having: no formal schooling 44.8%; primary education 8.6%; some secondary 15.1%; complete secondary 15.1%; higher 16.4%. *Literacy* (1988): total population age 15 and over literate 961,880 (79.7%); males literate 574,739 (83.3%); females literate 387,141 (74.9%).
Health (1992): physicians 2,215 (1 per 515 persons); hospital beds 4,039[18] (1 per 347 persons); infant mortality rate per 1,000 live births 16.4.
Food (1987–89): daily per capita caloric intake 3,146 (vegetable products 75%, animal products 25%); 130% of FAO recommended minimum requirement.

Military

Total active duty personnel (1994): 16,600 (army [including central staff] 69.8%, navy 15.1%, air force 15.1%). *Military expenditure as percentage of GNP* (1990): 5.5% (world 4.5%); per capita expenditure U.S.$782.

---

[1]Assisted by prime minister. [2]Area of governorates reflects situation prior to Amiri Decree No. 156 of 1988, which established al-Farwānīyah governorate; but population estimate accounts for the reorganization. [3]Governorates have no administrative function. [4]Bubian Island 333 sq mi (863 sq km) and Warba Island 14 sq mi (37 sq km). [5]Detail does not add to total given because of rounding. [6]Total includes current and capital expenditure, but 1993–94 breakdown is derived from current expenditure. [7]Includes external long-term debt not guaranteed by the government. [8]Trade includes restaurants and hotels. [9]May. [10]Fourth quarter. [11]Third quarter. [12]Kuwaiti households only. [13]Imports c.i.f.; exports f.o.b. [14]Total expenditure includes oil and non-oil, but breakdown by products and destinations is derived from non-oil exports. [15]Kuwait Airways only. [16]1992–93. [17]1989–90. [18]Public hospitals only.

Kyrgyzstan

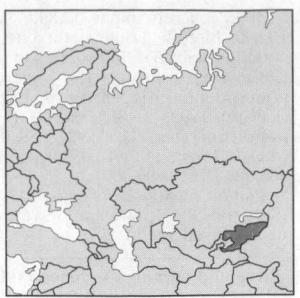

Official name: Kyrgyzstan Respublikasy (Republic of Kyrgyzstan).
Form of government: unitary multiparty republic with a bicameral legislative body (Supreme Council, comprising a Legislative Assembly [35] and an Assembly of People's Representatives [70][1]).
Head of state: President.
Head of government: Prime Minister.
Capital: Bishkek (formerly Frunze).
Official languages: Kyrgyz; Russian.
Official religion: none.
Monetary unit: 1 som = 100 tiyin;
valuation (Oct. 3, 1994) free rate,
1 U.S.$ = 10.20 som; 1 £ = 16.22 som.

Area and population		area		population
		sq mi	sq km	1993[2] estimate
Provinces	**Capitals**			
Chu	Kara-Balta	7,200	18,700	774,000
Dzhalal-Abad	Dzhalal-Abad	15,200	39,500	812,800
Issyk-Kul	Issyk-Kul	16,800	43,500	429,300
Naryn	Naryn	18,300	47,300	267,900
Osh	Osh	14,700	38,100	1,360,900
Talas	Talas	4,400	11,400	203,000
City of republic subordination				
Bishkek (Frunze)	—	...	...	634,100
TOTAL		76,600	198,500	4,482,000

Demography

Population (1994): 4,488,000.
Density (1994): persons per sq mi 58.6, persons per sq km 22.6.
Urban-rural (1992): urban 37.8%; rural 62.2%.
Sex distribution (1991): male 49.10%; female 50.90%.
Age breakdown (1989): under 15, 37.5%; 15–29, 27.0%; 30–44, 16.3%; 45–59, 10.9%; 60–74, 6.2%; 75 and over, 2.1%.
Population projection: (2000) 4,653,000; (2010) 4,944,000.
Doubling time: 33 years.
Ethnic composition (1989): Kyrgyz 52.4%; Russian 21.5%; Uzbek 12.9%; Ukrainian 2.5%; German 2.4%; Tatar 1.6%; other 6.7%.
Religious affiliation: believers are predominantly Sunnī Muslim (Ḥanafīyah).
Major cities (1991): Bishkek (Frunze) 631,300; Osh 218,700; Dzhalal-Abad 74,200; Tokmak 71,200; Przhevalsk 64,300.

Vital statistics

Birth rate per 1,000 population (1992): 28.5 (world avg. 26.0); (1990) legitimate 87.0%; illegitimate 13.0%.
Death rate per 1,000 population (1992): 7.1 (world avg. 9.0).
Natural increase rate per 1,000 population (1992): 21.4 (world avg. 16.8).
Total fertility rate (avg. births per childbearing woman; 1992): 4.0.
Marriage rate per 1,000 population (1992): 9.1.
Divorce rate per 1,000 population (1992): 1.8.
Life expectancy at birth (1991): male 64.6 years; female 72.7 years.
Major causes of death per 100,000 population (1992): diseases of the circulatory system 281.4; diseases of the respiratory system 114.3; accidents, poisoning, and violence 81.9; malignant neoplasms (cancers) 78.9; infectious and parasitic diseases 30.6; diseases of the digestive system (1989) 28.7; diseases of the nervous system (1989) 7.9; endocrine and metabolic disorders (1989) 5.3.

National economy

Budget (1993). Revenue: 601,800,000 som (development grants 50.4%[3]; tax revenue 39.5%, of which sales tax 17.6%, value-added tax 14.1%, enterprise profits tax 12.4%, excise duties 3.5%, individual income tax 5.8%; nontax revenue 10.1%). Expenditures: 869,600,000 som (current expenditure 76.5%, of which national economy 14.8%; lending to state enterprises 19.4%; education 8.1%; health 4.6%).
Tourism: receipts from visitors, n.a.; expenditures by nationals abroad, n.a.
Production (metric tons except as noted). Agriculture, forestry, fishing (1993): grain 1,603,000, vegetables (other than potatoes) 305,000, potatoes 300,000, fruit (other than grapes) 136,000, seed cotton 58,000, grapes 30,000; livestock (number of live animals) 9,300,000 sheep and goats, 1,002,000 cattle, 310,000 horses, 264,000 pigs; roundwood (1990) 6,000 cu m; fish catch 1,000. Mining and quarrying (1992): detail not available; however, antimony, gold, and mercury are mined. Manufacturing (1992): cement 1,100,000; light bulbs 319,700,000 units; roofing tiles 176,300,000 units; knitted fabrics 22,749,000 units; electrical engines 172,000 units; washing machines 94,000 units; centrifugal pumps 43,100 units; trucks 14,800 units; hay-baling machines 11,900 units; metal-cutting machines 789 units; forge-press machines 245 units; textiles 121,284,000 sq m; rugs 1,701,000 sq m; window glass 7,700,000 sq m. Construction (1992): residential 1,232,000 sq m. Energy production (consumption): electricity (kW-hr; 1992) 11,892,000,000 (9,804,000,000); coal (metric tons; 1992) 3,262,000 (3,577,000); crude petroleum (barrels; 1992) 828,300 (198,000); petroleum products (metric tons; 1992) 1,000 (1,471,000); natural gas (cu m; 1992) 72,000,000 (1,876,000,000).
Population economically active (1992): total 1,764,900; activity rate of total population 39.4% (participation rates: ages 16–59 [male], 16–54 [female] 82.9%; female [1990] 49.5%; unemployed [1989] 2.6%).

Price and earnings indexes (1990 = 100)							
	1986	1987	1988	1989	1990	1991	1992
Consumer price index	94.3	95.2	95.2	97.1	100.0	279.1	3,792.3
Monthly earnings index	76.6	78.9	84.5	90.9	100.0	137.3	252.2

Household income and expenditure (1990). Average household size 4.7; income per household (1989) 6,100 rubles[4]; sources of income: wages and salaries 72.0%, pensions and stipends 7.5%, other 20.5%; expenditure: consumer goods 33.5%, food 32.9%, taxes 8.2%, alcohol 2.8%, housing 2.0%.
Gross national product (at current market prices; 1993): U.S.$3,745,000,000 (U.S.$830 per capita)[5].

Structure of net material product and labour force				
	1992		1991	
	in value '000,000 rubles[4]	% of total value	labour force[6]	% of labour force[6]
Agriculture	58,169.0	42.5	622,700	35.5
Mining	}			
Manufacturing	51,799.0	37.8	318,700	18.2
Public utilities	}			
Construction	8,084.3	5.9	147,000	8.4
Transportation and communications	3,852.5	2.8	93,500	5.4
Trade	4,102.5	3.0	87,900	5.0
Finance	—	—	7,200	0.4
Public administration, defense	—	—	36,600	2.1
Services	2,769.1	2.0	383,400	21.7
Other	8,196.3	6.0	57,100	3.3
TOTAL	136,972.7	100.0	1,754,100	100.0

Public debt (external, outstanding; October 1991): U.S.$760,000,000.
Land use (1992): forested 3.5%; meadows and pastures 45.3%; agricultural and under permanent cultivation 6.7%; other 44.5%.

Foreign trade

Balance of trade (current prices)						
	1987	1988	1989	1990	1991	1992
'000,000 rubles	−458	−435	−813	−417	−958	−17,800
% of total	9.9%	7.9%	13.8%	7.9%	8.2%	14.4%

Imports (1992): 70,586,200,000 rubles[4] (oil and gas 27.8%, machine-building equipment 24.1%, chemicals 11.0%, light industrial products 7.3%, ferrous metals 6.1%, food products 6.0%). *Major import sources:* Russian Federation 49.0%; Kazakhstan 23.2%; Uzbekistan 9.1%; Ukraine 8.1%; Turkmenistan 6.1%.
Exports (1992): 52,785,700,000 rubles[4] (machine-building equipment 40.7%, light industrial products 24.1%, nonferrous metals 10.7%, food products 7.1%, electricity 5.8%). *Major export destinations:* Russian Federation 39.1%; Kazakhstan 22.4%; Ukraine 17.3%; Uzbekistan 10.4%; Belarus 3.0%.

Transport and communications

Transport. Railroads (1992): length 490 mi[7], 789 km[7]; passenger-mi 81,500,000, passenger-km 131,200,000; short ton-mi cargo 987,000,000, metric ton-km 1,588,900,000. Roads (1990): total length 11,900 mi, 19,100 km (paved 86%). Vehicles (1988): passenger cars 173,800; trucks and buses, n.a. Merchant marine: vessels (100 gross tons and over) n.a.; total deadweight tonnage, n.a. Air transport (1992): passenger-mi 1,601,800,000, passenger-km 2,577,800,000; short ton-mi cargo 144,100,000; metric ton-km cargo 231,900,000; airports (1994) with scheduled flights 1.
Communications. Daily newspapers (1990): total number 128; total circulation 1,622,000; circulation per 1,000 population 367. Radio (1991): 825,000 receivers (1 per 18.5 persons). Television (1991): 875,000 receivers (1 per 19.6 persons). Telephones (1992): 352,000 (1 per 12.8 persons).

Education and health

Education (1992–93)				
	schools	teachers	students	student/ teacher ratio
Primary (age 6–13)	1,862 }	76,300	954,700	12.5
Secondary (age 14–17)	1,472 }			
Voc., teacher tr.	37	...	40,922	...
Higher	12	...	53,670	...

Educational attainment (1989). Percentage of population age 19 and over having: primary education 4.7%; some secondary 20.9%; completed secondary 44.4%; some postsecondary 19.3%; higher 10.7%. *Literacy:* total population age 15 and over literate, n.a.; males literate, n.a.; females literate, n.a.
Health (1993): physicians[8] 15,758 (1 per 283 persons); hospital beds 52,285 (1 per 85 persons); infant mortality rate per 1,000 live births (1992) 21.4.
Food: daily per capita caloric intake, n.a.

Military

Total active duty personnel (1994): 12,000 (army 100%). *Military expenditure as percentage of GNP* (1993): 1.4% (world, n.a.); per capita expenditure U.S.$108.

---

[1]On Oct. 22, 1994, the Great Council was dissolved by referendum and a new legislative body, the Supreme Council, was created, elections to which were to be held Dec. 24, 1994. [2]January. [3]Primarily food and medical aid from the United States. [4]The value of the ruble during 1989–92 ranged from an official 1.61 rubles to more than 300 rubles per 1 U.S.$. [5]Ruble-area GNP and exchange-rate data are very speculative. [6]State sector only. [7]1990. [8]Data include dentists.

Laos

Official name: Sathalanalat
Paxathipatai Paxaxôn Lao (Lao
People's Democratic Republic).
Form of government: unitary
single-party people's republic with
one legislative house (National
Assembly[1] [85]).
Chief of state: President.
Head of government: Prime Minister.
Capital: Vientiane.
Official language: Lao.
Official religion: none.
Monetary unit: 1 kip (KN) = 100 at;
valuation (Oct. 7, 1994)
1 U.S.$ = KN 720; 1 £ = KN 1,146.

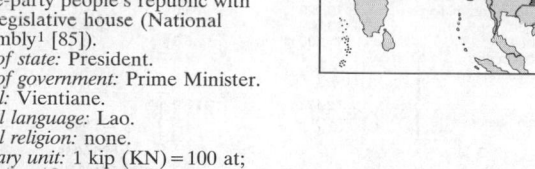

Area and population

Provinces	Capitals	area sq mi	area sq km	population 1990 estimate
Attapu	Attapu	3,985	10,320	80,000
Bokeo	Houayxay	1,919	4,970	64,000
Bolikhamxay	Pakxan	6,359	16,470	145,000
Champasak	Pakxé	5,952	15,415	469,000
Houaphan	Xam Nua	6,371	16,500	243,000
Khammouan	Thakhek	6,299	16,315	249,000
Louang Namtha	Louang Namtha	3,600	9,325	114,000
Louangphrabang	Louangphrabang	6,515	16,875	339,000
Oudomxay	Xay	8,182	21,190	291,000
Phôngsali	Phôngsali	6,282	16,270	142,000
Saravan	Saravan	4,010	10,385	211,000
Savannakhét	Savannakhét	8,525	22,000	640,000
Vientiane	Vientiane	7,718	19,990	312,000
Xaignabouri	Xaignabouri	4,554	11,795	182,000
Xékong	Thong	2,959	7,665	58,000
Xiangkhoang	Phônsavan	6,685	17,315	189,000
Municipalities				
Vientiane		1,514	3,920	442,000
TOTAL		91,429	236,800	4,170,000

Demography

Population (1994): 4,743,000.
Density (1994): persons per sq mi 51.9, persons per sq km 20.0.
Urban-rural (1993): urban 19.0%; rural 81.0%.
Sex distribution (1990): male 50.25%; female 49.75%.
Age breakdown (1990): under 15, 43.7%; 15–29, 26.0%; 30–44, 16.2%; 45–59, 9.2%; 60–74, 4.2%; 75 and over, 0.7%.
Population projection: (2000) 5,592,000; (2010) 7,119,000.
Doubling time: 25 years.
Ethnic composition (1983): Lao-Lum (Lao) 67.0%; Lao-Theung (Mon-Khmer) 16.5%; Lao-Tai (Tai) 7.8%; Lao-Soung (Miao [Hmong] and Man [Yao]) 5.2%; other 3.5%.
Religious affiliation (1980): Buddhist 57.8%; tribal religionist 33.6%; Christian 1.8%, of which Roman Catholic 0.8%, Protestant 0.2%; Muslim 1.0%; atheist 1.0%; Chinese folk-religionist 0.9%; none 3.8%; other 0.1%.
Major cities (1985): Vientiane 178,203; Savannakhét 96,652; Louangphrabang 68,399; Pakxé 47,323.

Vital statistics

Birth rate per 1,000 population (1994): 43.0 (world avg. 26.0).
Death rate per 1,000 population (1994): 15.0 (world avg. 9.2).
Natural increase rate per 1,000 population (1994): 28.0 (world avg. 16.8).
Total fertility rate (avg. births per childbearing woman; 1994): 6.4.
Marriage rate per 1,000 population: n.a.
Divorce rate per 1,000 population: n.a.
Life expectancy at birth (1994): male 50.0 years; female 53.0 years.
Major causes of death per 100,000 population (incomplete, 1990): malaria 7.6; pneumonia 3.0; meningitis 1.5; diarrhea 1.2; tuberculosis 0.8.

National economy

Budget (1991). Revenue: KN 79,022,000,000 (1990; taxes 76.0%, nontax revenue 24.0%). Expenditures: KN 147,895,000,000 (current expenditure 55.4%, capital expenditure 44.6%).
Public debt (external, outstanding; 1992): U.S.$1,891,000,000.
Tourism (1991): total number of tourist arrivals 20,614.
Population economically active (1989): total 1,888,000; activity rate of total population 49.0% (participation rates [1985]: ages 15–64, 84.2%; female 45.3%; unemployed 3.0%).

Price and earnings indexes (1985 = 100)

	1987	1988	1989	1990	1991	1992	1993
Consumer price index	143.9	165.2	263.5	357.0	405.5	445.2	476.4
Earnings index	...	...	...	...	...	...	...

Production (metric tons except as noted). Agriculture, forestry, fishing (1993): rice 1,251,000, sweet potatoes 113,000, sugarcane 90,000, cassava 68,000, corn (maize) 48,000, onions 44,000, potatoes 34,000, pineapples 34,000, melons 33,000, oranges 22,000, bananas 20,000; livestock (number of live animals) 1,561,000 pigs, 1,131,000 water buffalo, 993,000 cattle, 104,000 goats, 29,000 horses, 9,000,000 chickens; roundwood (1992) 4,398,000 cu m; fish catch (1991) 20,000. Mining and quarrying (1992): gypsum 79,863; rock salt 8,000; tin (metal content) 300; gemstones (mainly sapphires) 35,000 carats. Man-

ufacturing (1991): detergent 566,000; soap 481,300; plastic products 85,000; nails 55,000; clothing 882,500 pieces; cigarettes 29,600,000 packets; plywood 346,600 sheets; electrical wire 101,000 metres; soft drinks 59,800 hectolitres; beer 68,900 bottles. Construction: n.a. Energy production (consumption): electricity (kW-hr; 1992) 910,000,000 (298,000,000); coal (metric tons; 1992) 1,000 (1,000); crude petroleum, n.a. (n.a.); petroleum products (metric tons; 1992) none (88,000); natural gas, n.a. (n.a.).
Gross national product (at current market prices; 1993): U.S.$1,308,000,000 (U.S.$290 per capita).

Structure of gross domestic product and labour force

	1992 in value KN '000,000[2]	1992 % of total value	1989 labour force	1989 % of labour force
Agriculture	395,537	58.0	1,359,000	72.0
Manufacturing	85,766	12.6		
Mining	932	0.1		
Construction	19,055	3.0		
Public utilities	7,825	1.1		
Transportation and communications	34,333	5.0	529,000	28.0
Trade	49,415	7.2		
Finance	57,735	8.5		
Pub. admin., defense				
Services	31,044	4.6		
Other				
TOTAL	681,642	100.0[3]	1,888,000	100.0

Household income and expenditure. Average household size (1985) 6.0; average annual income per household KN 3,710 (U.S.$371); sources of income: n.a.; expenditure: n.a.
Land use (1992): forested 54.2%; meadows and pastures 3.5%; agricultural and under permanent cultivation 3.5%; other 38.8%.

Foreign trade[4]

Balance of trade (current prices)

	1987	1988	1989	1990	1991	1992
U.S.$'000,000	−154.0	−125.0	−162.0	−127.8	−131.7	−133.0
% of total	55.4%	49.8%	58.7%	46.4%	45.8%	33.3%

Imports (1991): U.S.$209,600,000 (1989; major imports include cereals, other food products, petroleum products, agricultural and general machinery, and transport equipment). *Major import sources* (1990): Thailand 51.9%; Japan 15.3%; China 8.1%; Hong Kong 0.9%.
Exports (1991): U.S.$77,900,000 (1989; wood 33.3%, electricity 23.8%, coffee 14.3%, tin 3.2%). *Major export destinations* (1990). Thailand 34.1%, China 6.4%; Japan 3.9%; Malaysia 0.1%.

Transport and communications

Transport. Railroads: none. Roads (1992): total length 8,780 mi, 14,130 km (paved 16%). Vehicles (1992): passenger cars 20,233; trucks and buses 12,987. Merchant marine (1992): vessels (100 gross tons and over) 1; total deadweight tonnage 1,469. Air transport (1989): passenger-mi 27,000,000, passenger-km 44,000,000; short ton-mi cargo 3,000,000, metric ton-km cargo 5,000,000; airports (1994) with scheduled flights 11.
Communications. Daily newspapers (1990): total number 3; total circulation 14,000; circulation per 1,000 population 3.0. Radio (1993): total number of receivers 425,000 (1 per 11 persons). Television (1993): total number of receivers 80,000 (1 per 58 persons). Telephones (1992): 8,230 (1 per 543 persons).

Education and health

Education (1991–92)

	schools	teachers	students	student/teacher ratio
Primary (age 6–10)	7,140	21,036	580,792	27.6
Secondary (age 11–16)	750[5]	8,936	117,504	13.1
Voc., teacher tr.	139[6]	1,262	8,198	6.5
Higher[5]	9	698	4,730	6.8

Educational attainment (1985). Percentage of population age 6 and over having: no schooling 49.3%; primary 41.2%; secondary 9.1%; higher 0.4%.
Literacy (1985): total population age 15 and over literate 83.9%; males literate 92.0%; females literate 75.8%.
Health (1990): physicians 1,173 (1 per 3,555 persons); hospital beds 10,364 (1 per 402 persons); infant mortality rate per 1,000 live births (1994) 94.
Food (1984–86): daily per capita caloric intake 2,190 (vegetable products 90%, animal products 10%); 101% of FAO recommended minimum requirement.

Military

Total active duty personnel (1994): 37,000 (army 89.2%, navy 1.4%, air force 9.4%). *Military expenditure as percent of GNP* (1984): 10.5% (world 5.7%); per capita expenditure U.S.$16.

---

[1]Formerly known as the Supreme People's Assembly. [2]At constant 1990 prices. [3]Detail does not add to total given because of rounding. [4]Import figures are c.i.f. in balance of trade and commodities. [5]1989–90. [6]1988–89.

Latvia

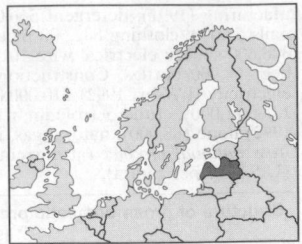

Official name: Latvijas Republika (Republic of Latvia).
Form of government: unitary multiparty republic with a single legislative body (Supreme Council [100]).
Chief of state: President.
Head of government: Prime Minister.
Capital: Rīga.
Official language: Latvian.
Official religion: none.
Monetary unit: 1 lats[1] (plural lati) = 10 santimi; valuation (Oct. 7, 1994) 1 U.S.$ = 0.55 lats; 1 £ = 0.87 lats.

Area and population	area	population		area	population
		1992[2]			1992[2]
Cities of republic jurisdiction	sq km[3]	estimate	**Rural districts**	sq km[3]	estimate
Daugavpils	72	127,279	Jelgava	1,613	39,137
Jelgava	60	73,917	Krāslava	2,288	41,019
Jūrmala	100	60,901	Kuldīga	2,503	41,361
Liepāja	60	113,815	Liepāja	3,589	54,475
Rēzekne	17	43,073	Limbaži	2,602	41,436
Rīga	295	897,078	Ludza	2,566	41,747
Ventspils	46	50,435	Madona	3,348	49,953
			Ogre	1,816	66,040
Rural districts			Preiļi	2,042	45,342
Aizkraukle	2,558	45,093	Rēzekne	2,654	42,899
Alūksne	2,246	28,631	Rīga	3,094	152,070
Balvi	2,384	33,576	Saldus	2,134	40,235
Bauska	1,884	55,612	Talsi	2,748	50,603
Cēsis	3,062	63,820	Tukums	2,457	59,069
Daugavpils	2,526	46,329	Valka	2,444	37,119
Dobele	1,680	44,749	Valmiera	2,377	63,067
Gulbene	1,876	30,243	Ventspils	2,471	15,400
Jēkabpils	2,998	61,435	TOTAL	64,610	2,656,958

Demography

Population (1994): 2,551,000.
Density (1994): persons per sq mi 102.3, persons per sq km 39.5.
Urban-rural (1992): urban 68.7%; rural 31.3%.
Sex distribution (1992): male 46.46%; female 53.54%.
Age breakdown (1992[2]): under 15, 21.4%; 15–29, 20.7%; 30–44, 21.4%; 45–59, 18.3%; 60–74, 13.1%; 75 and over, 5.1%.
Population projection: (2000) 2,602,000; (2010) 2,681,000.
Ethnic composition (1994[2]): Latvian 54.2%; Russian 33.1%; Belarusian 4.1%; Ukrainian 3.1%; Polish 2.2%; Lithuanian 1.3%; Jewish 0.5%; other 1.5%.
Religious affiliation: believers are predominantly Evangelical Lutheran, Russian Orthodox, or Roman Catholic.
Major cities (1993[2]): Rīga 874,000; Daugavpils 125,000; Liepāja 108,000; Jelgava 72,000; Jūrmala 60,000.

Vital statistics

Birth rate per 1,000 population (1993): 12.1 (world avg. 26.0); (1991) legitimate 81.6%; illegitimate 18.4%.
Death rate per 1,000 population (1993): 13.6 (world avg. 9.2).
Natural increase rate per 1,000 population (1993): −1.5 (world avg. 16.8).
Total fertility rate (avg. births per childbearing woman; 1993): 2.2.
Marriage rate per 1,000 population (1993): 7.2.
Divorce rate per 1,000 population (1993): 5.6.
Life expectancy at birth (1993): male 64.2 years; female 74.6 years.
Major causes of death per 100,000 population (1990): diseases of the circulatory system 756.5; malignant neoplasms (cancers) 204.9; accidents, poisoning, and violence 138.9; diseases of the respiratory system 49.6.

National economy

Budget (1993). Revenue: 81,143,000,000 Latvian rubles (social-security taxes 43.6%; value-added taxes 14.9%; profit tax 10.7%; income tax 7.8%; customs duties 6.7%). Expenditures: 80,724,000,000 Latvian rubles (1991; economic affairs 46.8%; social affairs 28.6%, of which education and science 11.1%, social security 11.1%, health 6.1%).
Production (metric tons except as noted). Agriculture, forestry, fishing (1993): potatoes 1,272,000, barley 446,000, wheat 305,000, sugar beets 298,000, vegetables 226,000, fruits and berries 85,000; livestock (number of live animals) 1,144,000 cattle, 867,000 pigs, 170,000 sheep, 4,000,000 poultry; roundwood (1991) 1,421,000 cu m; fish catch (1991) 369,900. Mining and quarrying (1992): peat 3,500,000; gypsum 350,000. Manufacturing (1992): steel 800,-000[4]; cement 720,000[4]; processed milk 609,600[4]; processed meats 253,000; synthetic fibre 39,300; fertilizers 31,000; telephones 885,000 units; diesel engines 60,000 units; buses 15,100 units; rail passenger cars 263 units; beer 900,000 hectolitres[4]; vodka 220,000 hectolitres[4]; textiles 44,200,000 sq m. Construction (1992): new residential 312,000 sq m. Energy production (consumption): electricity (kW-hr; 1992) 3,800,000,000 (7,900,000,000); coal (1992) none (663,000); crude petroleum, none (n.a.); petroleum products 3,057,000 (2,488,000); natural gas (1992) none (2,700,000,000).
Population economically active (1991): total 1,461,900; activity rate of total population 54.8% (participation rates: ages 16–59/55[5] [1990] 93.4%; female, n.a.; unemployed [1993] 6.0%).

Price and earnings indexes (1990 = 100)							
	1986	1987	1988	1989	1990	1991	1992
Consumer price index	66.0	68.9	71.4	74.7	100.0	272.0	2,861
Monthly earnings index	67.3	69.2	71.8	78.4	100.0	193.0	...

Gross national product (1993): U.S.$5,254,000,000 (U.S.$2,030 per capita).

Structure of net material product and labour force				
	1992		1991	
	in value '000,000 Latvian rubles	% of total value	labour force	% of labour force
Agriculture	45,221	24.8	83,000	5.7
Manufacturing and mining	70,029	38.5	351,400	24.0
Construction	13,049	7.2	82,200	5.6
Public utilities	11,530	6.3	...	...
Transportation and communications	} 42,173	} 23.2	103,700	7.1
Trade			119,600	8.2
Finance				
Pub. admin., defense			194,000	13.3
Services				
Other			528,000[6]	36.1[6]
TOTAL	182,002	100.0	1,461,900	100.0

Household income and expenditure. Average household size (1989) 3.1; average annual income per household: n.a.; sources of income (1991): wages and salaries 63.2%, pensions and transfers 16.6%, self-employment 5.3%, other 14.9%; expenditure (1991): food and alcohol 45.2%, consumer goods 34.8%, rent and social services 7.1%.
Land use (1992): forested 43.6%; meadows and pastures 12.7%; agricultural and permanent cultivation 26.5%; other 17.2%.

Foreign trade

Balance of trade (current prices)					
	1988	1989	1990	1991	1992
'000,000 rubles	−700	−617	−784	+1,396	+6,707
% of total	6.7%	5.4%	6.5%	10.0%	3.0%

Imports (1992): 108,668,000,000 rubles (1991; textiles 22.0%, chemical products 14.4%, machinery and equipment 13.7%, food and agricultural products 13.6%, fuels 8.8%). *Major import sources:* Russia 27.8%; Germany 14.9%; Estonia 6.4%; Sweden 3.8%; Belarus 3.7%.
Exports (1992): 115,375,000,000 rubles (1991; machinery and equipment 24.8%, food and agricultural products 21.7%, textiles 12.9%, chemical products 8.2%, forestry products 5.4%). *Major export destinations:* Russia 25.8%; Ukraine 8.2%; Germany 7.9%; The Netherlands 7.4%; Belgium 5.6%.

Transport and communications

Transport. Railroads (1993): length (1991) 2,397 km; passenger-km 2,388,000,-000; metric-km cargo 9,828,000,000. Roads (1991): total length 60,224 km (paved 55%). Vehicles (1992): passenger cars 340,000; trucks and buses 87,-000. Merchant marine (1992): cargo vessels 261; total deadweight tonnage 1,436,899. Air transport (1991): passenger-km 2,999,000,000; metric ton-km cargo 22,000,000[7]; airports with scheduled flights (1994) 1.
Communications. Total newspapers (1991): total number 188; total circulation 3,676,000; circulation per 1,000 population 1,377. Radio (1991): 1,396,000 receivers (1 per 1.9 persons). Television (1991): 1,126,000 receivers (1 per 2.4 persons). Telephones (1991): 746,000 (1 per 3.6 persons).

Education and health

Education (1991–92)	schools	teachers	students	student/ teacher ratio
Primary Secondary }	943	33,712[7]	330,468	9.8
Voc., teacher tr.[8]	57	...	36,100	...
Higher	14	...	46,279	...

Educational attainment (1989). Percentage of persons age 15 and over having: primary or less 18.7%; incomplete secondary 23.4%; complete secondary 46.4%; some higher 11.5%. *Literacy* (1989): percentage of total population age 15 and over literate 99.5%; males literate 99.8%; females literate 99.2%.
Health (1992): physicians 10,700 (1 per 245.9 persons); hospital beds 33,800 (1 per 77.9 persons); infant mortality rate per 1,000 live births 17.4.

Military

Total active duty personnel (1994): 2,550 (army 58.8%, navy 35.3%, air force 5.9%). *Military expenditure as percentage of GNP:* 0.9%; per capita expenditure U.S.$18. Until 1991, the U.S.S.R. was responsible for Latvia's external security; final withdrawal of its military personnel was completed on Aug. 31, 1994.

[1]The lats (pre-World War II Latvian currency), reintroduced in parallel with the Latvian ruble (LR; at 200 LR per lats) on March 5, 1993, became the sole official currency Oct. 18, 1993. From May 7, 1992, LR circulated in parallel at par with the Soviet ruble, serving temporarily as the sole legal tender until introduction of the lats on March 5, 1993. [2]January 1. [3]One sq km is equal to approximately 0.3861 sq mi. [4]1991. [5]Males retire at age 59, females at 55. [6]Includes 313,600 employed outside the state sector, 65,000 unemployed, and 149,300 not allocated by sector. [7]Includes part-time teachers. [8]1990–91.

Lebanon

Official name: al-Jumhūrīyah al-Lubnānīyah (Republic of Lebanon).
Form of government: unitary multiparty republic with one legislative house (National Assembly [128])[1].
Chief of state: President.
Head of government: Prime Minister.
Capital: Beirut.
Official language: Arabic.
Official religion: none.
Monetary unit: 1 Lebanese pound (LL) = 100 piastres; valuation (Oct. 7, 1994) 1 U.S.$ = LL 1,664; 1 £ = LL 2,647.

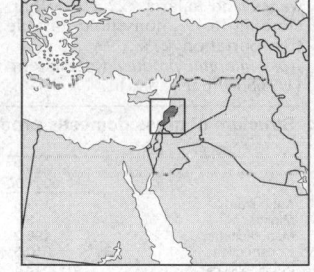

Area and population

Governorates	Capitals	area sq mi	area sq km	population 1970 estimate
Bayrūt	Beirut (Bayrūt)	7	18	474,870
al-Biqā'	Zahlah	1,653	4,280	203,520
Jabal Lubnān	B'abdā	753	1,950	833,055
al-Janūb	Sidon (Şaydā)	772	2,001	249,945
ash-Shamāl	Tripoli (Ṭarābulus)	765	1,981	364,935
TOTAL		3,950	10,230	2,126,325

Demography

Population (1994): 2,965,000.
Density (1994): persons per sq mi 750.6, persons per sq km 289.8.
Urban-rural (1990): urban 83.7%; rural 16.3%.
Sex distribution (1992): male 50.37%; female 49.63%.
Age breakdown (1992): under 15, 33.1%; 15–29, 30.8%; 30–44, 17.4%; 45–59, 11.4%; 60–74, 5.9%; 75 and over, 1.4%.
Population projection: (2000) 3,312,000; (2010) 3,777,000.
Doubling time: during the 1970–75 prewar period the average growth rate was 2.6%; however, the dislocation of the population by the civil war between 1976 and 1991 rendered both the absolute size and principal components of population change (births, deaths, migration) highly problematic.
Ethnic composition (1993): Lebanese, c. 80%; Palestinian 12%; Armenian 5%; Syrian, Kurd, and other 3%.
Religious affiliation: no official data exist subsequent to the 1932 census, when Christians (predominantly Maronite Roman Catholic) were a slight majority; it is thought that Muslims today constitute the majority, but by what margin is highly uncertain. Unofficial and CIA estimates (1984/1986) indicated the main religious groups as follows: Shī'ī Muslim 32/41%; Maronite Christian 24.5/16%; Sunnī Muslim 21/27%; Druze 7/7%; Greek Orthodox 6.5/5%; Greek Catholic 4/3%; Armenian Christian 4%/n.a.; other 1/1%.
Major cities (1990): Beirut 1,500,000; Tripoli 160,000; Zahlah 45,000; Sidon (Şaydā) 38,000; Tyre 14,000.

Vital statistics

Birth rate per 1,000 population (1992): 25.2 (world avg. 26.0).
Death rate per 1,000 population (1992): 4.5 (world avg. 9.2).
Natural increase rate per 1,000 population (1992): 20.7 (world avg. 16.8).
Total fertility rate (avg. births per childbearing woman; 1992): 2.9.
Life expectancy at birth (1992): male 72.5 years; female 77.9 years.
Major causes of death: normally, cardiovascular and gastrointestinal diseases, including typhoid fever and dysentery; but violence and acts of war were also among the principal causes of mortality between 1975 and 1991.

National economy

Budget (1994). Revenue: LL 2,195,795,000,000 (almost entirely taxation, direct and indirect). Expenditures: LL 4,206,705,000,000 (debt service 35%, government salaries 32%, defense 22%, education 10%).
Production (metric tons except as noted). Agriculture, forestry, fishing (1993): grapes 365,000, potatoes 280,000, oranges 270,000, tomatoes 235,000, apples 160,000, cucumbers 155,000, lemons and limes 94,000, onions 68,000, olives 50,000; opium poppies and marijuana were important cash crops in the late 1980s and early 1990s but were reportedly eradicated in 1993; livestock (number of live animals) 450,000 goats, 250,000 sheep, 77,000 cattle, 24,000,000 chickens; roundwood (1992) 488,000 cu m; fish catch (1991) 1,800. Mining and quarrying (1992): lime 15,000; salt 3,000; gypsum 2,000. Manufacturing (1991): cement 907,000; paper 36,000; cigarettes 4,000,000,000 units; petroleum refining, dairying, curing of leather, meat cutting, and milling of flour are also significant. Construction (1987): 4,938,000 sq m. Energy production (consumption): electricity (kW-hr; 1992) 2,500,000,000 (2,540,000,000); coal, n.a. (none); crude petroleum (barrels; 1992 none (2,565,000); petroleum products (metric tons; 1992) 317,000 (3,422,000).
Public debt (external, outstanding; 1992): U.S.$304,000,000.
Household income and expenditure. Average household size (1987) 5.0; average annual income per household (1985) LL 120,000 (U.S.$6,630; in constant prices, about 75% of 1966 income levels); sources of income (1974): wages and salaries 27.9%, transfers 3.0%, other 69.1%; expenditure (1966)[2]: food 42.8%, housing 16.8%, clothing 8.6%, health care 7.2%.
Land use (1992): forested 7.8%; meadows and pastures 1.0%; agricultural and under permanent cultivation 29.9%; wasteland and other areas 61.3%.
Population economically active (1988): total 904,000; activity rate of total population 26.5% (participation rates: over age 15, 44%; female 16.6%; unemployed [1991] reported by the national trade union at 30% but perhaps as low as 7–8% according to a 1987 study of 60,000 households).

Consumer price index (1990 = 100)

	1986	1987	1988	1989	1990	1991	1992
Consumer price index[3]	99.7	52.4	74.5	82.6	100.0	112.0	168.0

Gross domestic product (at current market prices; 1992): estimated at U.S.$3,500,000,000–4,000,000,000 (U.S.$1,250–1,425 per capita).

Structure of gross domestic product and labour force

	1992 in value[4] LL '000,000[5]	1992 % of total value	1986 labour force	1986 % of labour force
Agriculture	575,800	8.8	132,211	19.1
Mining	—	—	694	0.1
Manufacturing	823,700	12.6	123,647	17.8
Construction	216,300	3.3	43,357	6.2
Public utilities	343,600	5.3	6,668	1.0
Transp. and commun.	246,000	3.8	48,242	7.0
Trade	1,853,200	28.4	114,706	16.5
Finance	503,600	7.7	24,224	3.5
Real estate and business services	583,500	9.0	} 200,063	} 28.8
Services	703,900	10.8		
Pub. admin., defense	667,400	10.2		
TOTAL	6,517,000	100.0[6]	693,812	100.0

Tourism (1980): number of tourist arrivals 135,548[7].

Foreign trade

Balance of trade (current prices)

	1988	1989	1990	1991	1992	1993
U.S.$'000,000	−716	−874	−1,419	−2,983	−6,182	−7,100
% of total	58.6%	64.9%	67.8%	75.2%	76.7%	76.6%

Imports (1993): LL 8,191,000,000,000 (1982; consumer goods 40.0%, machinery and transport equipment 35.0%, petroleum products 20.0%). *Major import sources* (1991): Italy 14.0%; France 12.0%; U.S. 6.0%; Turkey 5.0%.
Exports (1993): LL 1,091,000,000,000 (1985; jewelry 10.2%, clothing 5.2%, pharmaceutical products 4.9%, metal products 4.8%). *Major export destinations* (1991): Saudi Arabia 21.0%; Kuwait 12.0%; Switzerland 9.5%.

Transport and communications

Transport. Railroads (1982)[8]: length (1986) 417 km; passenger-km 8,570,000; metric ton-km cargo 42,010,000. Roads (1987): total length 7,370 km (paved 85%). Vehicles (1985): passenger cars 300,000; trucks and buses 49,560. Merchant marine (1992): vessels (100 gross tons and over) 163; total deadweight tonnage 438,165. Air transport (1992)[9]: passenger-km 1,285,197,000; metric ton-km cargo 37,192,000; airports (1994) with scheduled flights 1.
Communications. Daily newspapers (1986): total number 39; total circulation 572,734[10]; circulation per 1,000 population 212[10]. Radio (1993): 2,150,000 receivers (1 per 1.3 persons). Television (1993): 1,100,000 receivers (1 per 2.6 persons). Telephones (1993): 351,000 (1 per 8.3 persons).

Education and health

Education (1988–89)

	schools	teachers	students	student/ teacher ratio
Primary (age 5–9)	2,130[11]	22,810[12]	346,534	...
Secondary (age 10–16)	1,405[12]	21,344[12]	241,964	...
Voc., teacher tr.	181[12]	4,792	32,708	6.8
Higher	18[12]	5,400[13]	85,495[13]	15.8[13]

Educational attainment (1970). Percentage of population age 25 and over having: no formal schooling 45.6%, of which, ability to read and write 35.6%; incomplete primary education 28.5%; complete primary 10.8%; incomplete secondary 7.1%; complete secondary 4.9%; higher 3.1%. *Literacy* (1990): total population age 15 and over literate, c. 1,538,800 (80.1%); males literate, c. 798,100 (87.8%); females literate, c. 739,100 (73.1%).
Health: physicians (1989–91) 6,638 (1 per 407 persons); hospital beds (1982) 11,400 (1 per 263 persons); infant mortality rate per 1,000 live births (1992) 28.0.
Food (1979–81): daily per capita caloric intake 2,995 (vegetable products 84%, animal products 16%); 120% of FAO recommended minimum requirement.

Military

Total active duty personnel (1994): Lebanese national armed forces 44,300 (army 97.1%, navy 1.1%, air force 1.8%). External regular military forces include: UN peacekeeping force in Lebanon 5,200; Syrian army 30,000. Most civilian militias were progressively disbanded after the civil war ended in 1991. According to external analysts, however, only two factions were still active in 1994, though on a much-reduced scale[14]: Shī'ī Muslim (pro-Iran Hezbollah [Party of God]) 3,000; Maronite Christian (Lebanese Forces [Phalange]) 2,500. *Military expenditure as percentage of GDP* (1993): 4.4% (world, n.a.); per capita expenditure: U.S.$95.

[1]The current legislature was elected between August and October 1992; one-half of its membership is Christian and one-half Muslim/Druze. [2]Weights based on consumer price index components. For capital city only. [3]UN estimate; for Beirut only. [4]In purchasers' value at current prices. [5]The domestic economy reportedly became increasingly "dollarized" as more transactions were quoted or paid in dollars during the late 1980s and early '90s. By 1993, however, the pound had once again stabilized against the dollar. [6]Detail does not add to total given because of rounding. [7]Approximately one-fourth the annual prewar rates of the early 1970s. [8]Apart from a 14-mi (23-km) section delivering oil from the Zahrani refinery to a thermal power station serving Beirut, no passenger or general cargo track is currently in use. [9]MEA-Airliban international flights only. [10]For 20 newspapers only. [11]1984–85. [12]1981–82. [13]1991–92. [14]Active personnel.

Lesotho

Official name: Lesotho (Sotho); Kingdom of Lesotho (English).
Form of government: multiparty republic[1] with 2 legislative houses (National Assembly [65]; Senate [33[2]]).
Chief of state: King.
Head of government: Prime Minister.
Capital: Maseru.
Official languages: Sotho; English.
Official religion: Christianity.
Monetary unit: 1 loti (plural maloti [M]) = 100 lisente; valuation (Oct. 7, 1994) 1 U.S.$ = M 3.57; 1 £ = M 5.68.

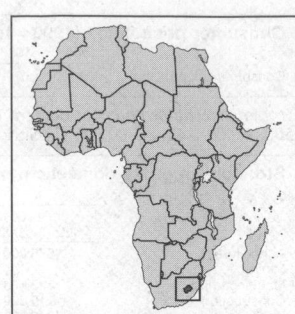

Area and population

Districts	Capitals	area sq mi	area sq km	population 1987 estimate
Berea	Teyateyaneng	858	2,222	199,600
Butha-Buthe	Butha-Buthe	682	1,767	103,000
Leribe	Hlotse	1,092	2,828	264,600
Mafeteng	Mafeteng	818	2,119	200,600
Maseru	Maseru	1,652	4,279	319,100
Mohale's Hoek	Mohale's Hoek	1,363	3,530	168,600
Mokhotlong	Mokhotlong	1,573	4,075	76,600
Qacha's Nek	Qacha's Nek	907	2,349	65,600
Quthing	Quthing	1,126	2,916	113,200
Thaba-Tseka	Thaba-Tseka	1,649	4,270	106,800
TOTAL		11,720	30,355	1,617,700

Demography

Population (1994): 1,929,000.
Density (1994): persons per sq mi 164.6, persons per sq km 63.5.
Urban-rural (1992): urban 20.9%; rural 79.1%.
Sex distribution (1990): male 48.08%; female 51.92%.
Age breakdown (1990): under 15, 43.1%; 15–29, 25.6%; 30–44, 15.7%; 45–59, 9.8%; 60 and over, 5.8%.
Population projection: (2000) 2,233,000; (2010) 2,821,000.
Doubling time: 28 years.
Ethnic composition (1986): Sotho 85.0%; Zulu 15.0%.
Religious affiliation (1980): Roman Catholic 43.5%; Protestant (mostly Lesotho Evangelical) 29.8%; Anglican 11.5%; other Christian 8.0%; traditional beliefs 6.2%; other 1.0%.
Major urban centres (1986): Maseru 109,382; Maputsoe 20,000; Teyateyaneng 14,251; Mafeteng 12,667; Hlotse 9,595.

Vital statistics

Birth rate per 1,000 population (1993): 34.6 (world avg. 26.0); legitimate, n.a.; illegitimate, n.a.
Death rate per 1,000 population (1993): 9.4 (world avg. 9.2).
Natural increase rate per 1,000 population (1993): 25.2 (world avg. 16.8).
Total fertility rate (avg. births per childbearing woman; 1993): 4.6.
Marriage rate per 1,000 population: n.a.
Divorce rate per 1,000 population: n.a.
Life expectancy at birth (1990–95): male 54.0 years; female 63.0 years.
Major causes of death per 100,000 population: n.a.; however, major diseases include malaria, typhoid fever, and infectious and parasitic diseases.

National economy

Budget (1994–95). Revenue: M 1,400,000,000 (1991–92; tax revenue 74.7%, of which customs receipts 46.2%[3], sales tax 11.0%, income tax 8.0%, company tax 6.2%; grants and other nontax revenue 25.3%). Expenditures: M 1,590,-000,000 (recurrent expenditure 67.3%, of which education 20.9%, public works 12.8%, health 7.8%, defense 5.7%; capital expenditure 32.7%).
Production (metric tons except as noted). Agriculture, forestry, fishing (1993): corn (maize) 92,000, sorghum 52,000, fruit 18,000, roots and tubers 8,000, peas 2,000, beans 1,000; livestock (number of live animals) 1,665,000 sheep, 1,010,000 goats, 650,000 cattle, 162,000 asses, 123,000 horses, 76,000 pigs, 1,000,000 chickens; roundwood (1992) 635,000 cu m; fish catch (1991) 15. Mining and quarrying (1988): sand and gravel 50,000 cu m. Manufacturing (total value added; 1991): M 193,800,000, of which (1990) food and beverages 47.2%, textiles, apparel, and leather 39.8%, chemical products 2.1%, printing and publishing 2.0%, iron and steel products 1.6%, furniture and fixtures 1.2%. Construction (total value added; 1991): M 310,500. Energy production (consumption): electricity (kW-hr; 1988) 1,000,000 (n.a.); coal, none (n.a.); petroleum, none (n.a.); natural gas, none (n.a.).
Public debt (external, outstanding; 1992): U.S.$441,800,000.
Tourism (1992): receipts from visitors U.S.$19,000,000; expenditures by nationals abroad U.S.$11,000,000.
Population economically active (1986): total 716,270; activity rate of total population 45.7% (participation rates: ages 15–64, 79.8%; female 45.5%; unemployed [1988] 23%).

Price and earnings indexes (1990 = 100)

	1987	1988	1989	1990	1991	1992	1993
Consumer price index	70.1	78.1	89.6	100.0	117.7	137.9	157.0
Earnings index	...	...	...	...	...	...	...

Household income and expenditure. Average household size (1986) 4.8; average annual income per household (1986–87) M 2,832 (U.S.$1,297); sources of income (1986–87): transfer payments 44.7%, self-employment 27.8%,

wages and salaries 22.4%, other 5.1%; expenditure (1989): food 48.0%, clothing 16.4%, household durable goods 11.9%, housing and energy 10.1%, transportation 4.7%.
Gross national product (at current market prices; 1993): U.S.$1,253,000,000 (U.S.$660 per capita).

Structure of gross domestic product and labour force

	1991 in value M '000,000	1991 % of total value	1986 labour force	1986 % of labour force
Agriculture	193.8	11.8	474,171	66.2
Mining	3.7	0.2	6,446	0.9
Manufacturing	198.2	12.1	19,339	2.7
Construction	310.5	18.9	31,516	4.4
Public utilities	19.3	1.2	1,433	0.2
Transp. and commun.	53.7	3.3	5,014	0.7
Trade	127.2	7.7	22,204	3.1
Finance	89.1	5.4	3,581	0.5
Pub. admin., defense	259.1	15.8	17,907	2.5
Services	139.3	8.5	126,780	17.7
Other	249.7[4]	15.2[4]	7,879	1.1
TOTAL	1,643.8[5]	100.0[5]	716,270[6]	100.0[6]

Land use (1992): meadows and pastures 65.9%; agricultural and under permanent cultivation 10.5%; other 23.6%.

Foreign trade[7]

Balance of trade (current prices)

	1987	1988	1989	1990	1991	1992
M '000,000	−830.5	−1,106.3	−1,072.1	−1,517.0	−1,992.9	−2,720.8
% of total	81.4%	79.2%	75.8%	83.2%	84.3%	88.0%

Imports (1991): M 2,259,690,000 (1990; manufactured goods [excluding chemicals, machinery, and transport equipment] 42.5%; food and live animals 19.1%; machinery and transport equipment 15.3%; petroleum products 8.6%). *Major import sources:* Customs Union of Southern Africa 94.1%; Asia 3.4%; Europe 1.4%, of which European Economic Community 1.3%; the Americas 0.3%.
Exports (1991): M 186,165,000 (manufactured goods 83.1%, of which machinery and transport equipment 2.8%; food and live animals 11.6%, of which preserved vegetables 4.3%, cornmeal 1.6%, wheat flour 1.2%; crude materials 3.7%, of which mohair 2.4%, wool 1.1%; chemicals 1.6%). *Major export destinations:* Customs Union of Southern Africa 42.1%; Europe 30.0%, of which European Economic Community 27.9%; the Americas 25.4%; Asia 0.4%.

Transport and communications

Transport. Railroads (1993): length 1.6 mi, 2.6 km. Roads (1993): total length 3,257 mi, 5,242 km (paved 16%). Vehicles (1991): passenger cars 6,000; trucks and buses 14,000. Merchant marine: vessels (100 gross tons and over) none. Air transport (1992)[8]: passenger-mi 4,767,000, passenger-km 7,671,000; ton-mi cargo 21,200, metric ton-km cargo 31,000; airports (1994) with scheduled flights 1.
Communications. Daily newspapers (1993): total number 6; total circulation 36,000; circulation per 1,000 population 19. Radio (1993): total number of receivers 425,000 (1 per 4.4 persons). Television (1993): total number of receivers 50,000 (1 per 38 persons). Telephones (1992): 22,420 (1 per 82 persons).

Education and health

Education (1991–92)

	schools	teachers	students	student/ teacher ratio
Primary (age 6–12)	1,198	6,685	361,144	54.0
Secondary (age 13–17)	179	2,407	46,572	19.3
Voc., teacher tr.	10	227	2,167	9.5
Higher	1	204	1,421	7.0

Educational attainment (1986–87). Percentage of population age 10 and over having: no formal education 22.9%; primary 52.8%; secondary 23.2%; higher 0.6%. *Literacy* (1985): total population age 15 and over literate 655,400 (73.6%); males literate 273,800 (62.4%); females literate 381,600 (84.5%).
Health (1992): physicians 139 (1 per 13,209 persons); hospital beds 2,400 (1 per 765 persons); infant mortality rate per 1,000 live births (1993) 71.5.
Food (1988–90): daily per capita caloric intake 2,121 (vegetable products 93%, animal products 7%); 93% of FAO recommended minimum requirement.

Military

Total active duty personnel (1994): 2,000[9]. *Military expenditure as percentage of GNP* (1990): 3.8% (world 4.5%); per capita expenditure U.S.$33.

[1]New constitution, effective April 1993, ended seven years of military rule. [2]Composed of 22 chiefs and 11 nominated members. [3]Lesotho's share of customs revenue from the Southern African Customs Union accounted for 60% of 1994–95 revenue. [4]Indirect taxes less imputed bank service charges. [5]Detail does not add to total given because of rounding. [6]Approximately 110,000 to 120,000 persons (45% of Lesotho's adult male labour force) were employed in South Africa in 1987. [7]Import figures are f.o.b. in balance of trade and c.i.f. in commodities and trading partners. [8]Lesotho Airways only. [9]Royal Lesotho Defence Force.

Liberia

Official name: Republic of Liberia.
Form of government: republic.
Head of state and government: none[1].
Capital: Monrovia.
Official language: English.
Official religion: none.
Monetary unit: 1 Liberian dollar
(L$) = 100 cents; valuation (Oct. 7,
1994) 1 U.S.$ = L$1.00; 1 £ = L$1.59.

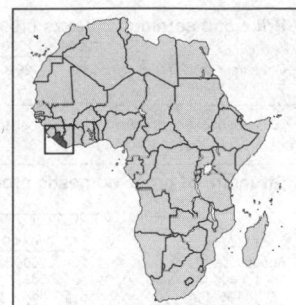

Area and population

Counties	Capitals	area sq mi	area sq km	population 1986 estimate
Bomi	Tubmanburg	755	1,955	67,300
Bong	Gbarnga	3,127	8,099	268,100
Grand Bassa	Buchanan	3,382	8,759	166,900
Grand Cape Mount	Robertsport	2,250	5,827	83,900
Grand Gedeh	Zwedru	6,575	17,029	109,000
Grand Kru[2]	Barclayville	3	3	3
Lofa	Voinjama	7,475	19,360	261,000
Margibi[4]	Kakata	1,260	3,263	104,000
Maryland	Harper	2,066[3]	5,351[3]	137,700[3]
Montserrado	Bensonville	1,058	2,740	582,400
Nimba	Sanniquellie	4,650	12,043	325,700
Rivercess	Rivercess City	1,693	4,385	39,900
Sinoe	Greenville	3,959	10,254	65,400
TOTAL		38,250	99,067[5]	2,221,300[6]

Demography

Population (1994): 2,377,000[7].
Density (1994): persons per sq mi 62.1[7], persons per sq km 24.0[7].
Urban-rural (1992): urban 47.5%; rural 52.5%.
Sex distribution (1990): male 50.60%; female 49.40%.
Age breakdown (1990): under 15, 45.3%; 15–29, 25.8%; 30–44, 14.8%; 45–59, 8.7%; 60 and over, 5.4%.
Population projection: (2000) 2,785,000; (2010) 3,755,000.
Doubling time: 22 years.
Ethnic composition (1984): Kpelle 19.4%; Bassa 13.8%; Grebo 9.0%; Gio 7.8%; Kru 7.3%; Mano 7.1%; other 35.6%.
Religious affiliation (1984): Christian 67.7%; Muslim 13.8%[8]; traditional beliefs and other 18.5%.
Major cities (1974): Monrovia 421,058[9]; Buchanan 23,999; Congo Town 21,495; Yekepa 14,189; Tubmanburg 14,089.

Vital statistics

Birth rate per 1,000 population (1993): 43.9 (world avg. 26.0).
Death rate per 1,000 population (1993): 12.4 (world avg. 9.2).
Natural increase rate per 1,000 population (1993): 31.5 (world avg. 16.8).
Total fertility rate (avg. births per childbearing woman; 1993): 6.4.
Marriage rate per 1,000 population: n.a.
Divorce rate per 1,000 population: n.a.
Life expectancy at birth (1990–95): male 54.0 years; female 57.0 years.
Major causes of death per 100,000 population (1985)[10]: complications during pregnancy 632.6[9]; malaria 79.8; pneumonia 64.2; anemia 50.2; malnutrition 23.4; measles 12.7. Violence and acts of war were major causes of both morbidity and mortality from 1990 onward.

National economy

Budget (1993). Revenue: L$249,825,000 (1989; income and profits taxes 33.9%; import duties and consular fees 29.6%; excise tax 12.7%; property taxes 1.9%). Expenditures: L$273,930,000 (1988; current expenditure 91.1%, of which wages and salaries 34.1%, interest on public debt 13.1%, goods and services 7.8%, subsidies and grants 5.1%; development expenditure 8.9%).
Public debt (external, outstanding; 1992): U.S.$1,101,000,000.
Tourism: receipts from visitors (1986) U.S.$6,000,000; expenditures by nationals abroad, n.a.
Population economically active (1984): total 704,321; activity rate 33.5% (participation rates: ages 15–64, 56.3%; female 41.0%; unemployed 12.5%).

Price and earnings indexes (1985 = 100)

	1984	1985	1986	1987	1988	1989	1990[11]
Consumer price index	100.6	100.0	103.6	108.8	119.3	130.6	139.4
Earnings index	...	...	...	...	...	...	...

Production (metric tons except as noted). Agriculture, forestry, fishing (1993): cassava 310,000, sugarcane 234,000, bananas 80,000, rice 71,000, plantains 33,000, sweet potatoes 18,000, yams 15,000, natural rubber 10,000, oranges 7,000, pineapples 7,000, cacao beans 2,000; livestock (number of live animals) 220,000 goats, 210,000 sheep, 120,000 pigs, 36,000 cattle, 4,000,000 chickens; roundwood (1992) 6,099,000 cu m; fish catch (1991) 9,620. Mining and quarrying (1992): iron ore 6,590,000[12]; diamonds 150,000 carats; gold 22,500 troy oz. Manufacturing (1990): cement 50,000; palm oil 30,000; cigarettes 22,000,000 units; soft drinks 171,000 hectolitres[13]; beer 158,000 hectolitres[13]. Construction: n.a. Energy production (consumption): electricity (kW-hr; 1992) 460,000,000 (460,000,000); coal, none (n.a.); crude petroleum, none (n.a.); petroleum products (metric tons; 1992) none (90,000); natural gas, none (n.a.).

Household income and expenditure. Average household size (1983) 4.3; income per household: n.a.; sources of income: n.a.; expenditure (1963)[14]: food 34.4%, rent 14.9%, clothing and footwear 13.8%, household goods and services 6.1%, beverages and tobacco 5.7%, fuel and light 5.0%.
Gross national product (1990): U.S.$1,178,000,000 (U.S.$498 per capita).

Structure of gross domestic product and labour force

	1989 in value L$'000,000	1989 % of total value	1984 labour force	1984 % of labour force
Agriculture	410.7	34.4	481,177	68.3
Mining	122.3	10.2	17,500	2.5
Manufacturing	81.6	6.8	10,699	1.5
Construction	26.3	2.2	4,072	0.6
Public utilities	19.0	1.6	2,878	0.4
Transp. and commun.	79.1	6.6	13,986	2.0
Trade	63.3	5.3	46,850	6.6
Finance	141.8	11.9	2,117	0.3
Pub. admin., defense	139.4	11.7 }	61,168	8.7
Services	35.5	3.0 }		
Other	74.8[15]	6.3[15]	63,874[16]	9.1[16]
TOTAL	1,193.6[5]	100.0	704,321	100.0

Land use (1992): forested 17.6%; meadows and pastures 58.9%; agricultural and under permanent cultivation 3.9%; other 19.6%.

Foreign trade

Balance of trade (current prices)

	1983	1984	1985	1986	1987	1988
L$'000,000	+73.8	+137.6	+189.4	+184.1	+115.9	+160.6
% of total	9.4%	17.1%	27.0%	29.1%	17.9%	25.4%

Imports (1990): L$294,000,000 (machinery and transport equipment 26.9%, petroleum and petroleum products 23.5%, food and live animals 21.1%, basic manufactures 13.9%, chemicals 5.8%). *Major import sources* (1988): United States 21.0%; West Germany 14.5%; United Kingdom 4.7%; Japan 4.4%; China 1.8%; France 1.7%.
Exports (1990): L$365,000,000 (1988; iron ore 55.1%, rubber 28.0%, logs and timber 8.4%, diamonds 2.1%, gold 1.8%, coffee 1.5%). *Major export destinations* (1988): West Germany 27.3%; United States 18.8%; France 8.4%; United Kingdom 1.6%; Japan 1.2%.

Transport and communications

Transport. Railroads (1991)[17]: route length 306 mi, 493 km; short ton-mi cargo 1,746,000,000[13, 18], metric ton-km cargo 2,549,000,000[13, 18]. Roads (1991): total length 3,787 mi, 6,095 km (paved 39%). Vehicles (1991): passenger cars 22,000; trucks and buses 18,000. Merchant marine (1992): vessels (100 gross tons and over) 1,672; total deadweight tonnage 97,373,965. Air transport (1990): passenger-mi 10,600,000; passenger-km 17,000,000; short ton-mi cargo 68,000, metric ton-km cargo 100,000; airports (1994) 2.
Communications. Daily newspapers (1990): total number 8; total circulation 35,000; circulation per 1,000 population 13.6. Radio (1993): 600,000 receivers (1 per 3.9 persons). Television (1993): 45,000 receivers (1 per 53 persons). Telephones (1991): 9,380 (1 per 252 persons).

Education and health

Education (1980)

	schools	teachers	students	student/ teacher ratio
Primary (age 6–12)	1,651	9,099	227,431	25.0
Secondary (age 13–18)	419	1,129	51,666	45.8
Voc., teacher tr.	6	63	2,322	36.9
Higher	3	472[19]	5,095[19]	10.8[19]

Educational attainment (1974). Percentage of population age 25 and over having: no grade completed 87.1%; some primary education 4.8%; complete primary 1.5%; some secondary 5.1%; higher 1.5%. *Literacy* (1990): total population age 15 and over literate 547,800 (39.5%); males literate 350,200 (49.8%); females literate 197,600 (28.8%).
Health: physicians (1985) 227 (1 per 9,687 persons); hospital beds (1981) 3,000 (1 per 653 persons); infant mortality rate (1993) 115.9.
Food (1988–90): daily per capita caloric intake 2,259 (vegetable products 96%, animal products 4%); 98% of FAO recommended minimum requirement.

Military

Total active duty personnel: as a result of the civil war, the Armed Forces of Liberia (AFL) has ceased to exist. *Military expenditure as percentage of GNP* (1988): 4.4% (world 5.0%); per capita expenditure U.S.$21.

[1]No effective nationwide executive leadership existed in 1994. The transitional government established in 1993 had no power outside of Monrovia. [2]New county created from Kru Coast and Sasstown territories and part of Maryland county. [3]Figures for Grand Kru included in Maryland. [4]New county created from Marshall and Gibi territories. [5]Detail does not add to total given because of rounding. [6]Includes 10,000 persons not accounted for. [7]Includes Liberian refugees residing in surrounding countries, estimated to number about 700,000. [8]Some external sources estimate the Muslim population to exceed 30%. [9]1984. [10]Hospital inpatient morbidity rates. [11]July 1. [12]1990. [13]1988. [14]Monrovia only. [15]Import duties less imputed bank service charges. [16]Includes 34,991 unemployed. [17]For iron-ore transport only. [18]Lamco and Bong Mining Company railroads only. [19]1987.

Libya

Official name: al-Jamāhīrīyah al-'Arabīyah al-Lībīyah ash-Sha'bīyah al-Ishtirākīyah (Socialist People's Libyan Arab Jamahiriya).
Form of government: socialist state with one policy-making body (General People's Congress [750]).
Chief of state: Muammar al-Qaddafi (de facto)[1]; Secretary of General People's Congress (de jure).
Head of government: Secretary of the General People's Committee (prime minister).
Capital: Tripoli[2].
Official language: Arabic.
Official religion: Islam.
Monetary unit: 1 Libyan dinar (LD) = 1,000 dirhams; valuation (Oct. 7, 1994) 1 Libyan dinar = U.S.$3.23 = £2.04.

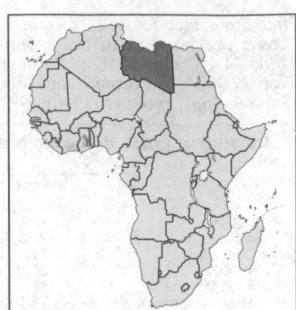

Area and population

Baladīyāt	Capitals	area sq mi	area sq km	population 1988 estimate
Banghāzī	Banghāzī	5,800	15,000	512,200
al-Jabal al-Akhḍar	al-Baydā'	14,300	37,000	308,300
al-Jabal al-Gharbī	Gharyān	33,600	87,000	204,300
Khalīj Surt	Surt	145,200	376,000	382,100
al-Kufrah	al-Kufrah	186,900	484,000	23,800
Margib	al-Khums	11,200	29,000	408,900
Marzūq	Marzūq	135,100	350,000	45,200
Nikāt al-Khums	Zuwārah	39,000	101,000	196,000
Sabhā	Sabhā	31,700	82,000	121,700
Ṭarābulus	Tripoli (Ṭarābulus)	1,200	3,000	1,083,100
Ṭubruq	Ṭubruq	32,400	84,000	110,900
Wādī al-Ha'iṭ	Awbārī	40,500	105,000	49,600
az-Zāwiyah	az-Zāwiyah	1,500	4,000	326,500
TOTAL		678,400	1,757,000	3,772,600

Demography

Population (1994): 5,225,000.
Density (1994): persons per sq mi 7.7, persons per sq km 3.0.
Urban-rural (1990): urban 82.4%; rural 17.6%.
Sex distribution (1990): male 52.41%; female 47.59%.
Age breakdown (1990): under 15, 45.8%; 15–29, 25.6%; 30–44, 15.6%; 45–59, 8.8%; 60–74, 3.5%; 75 and over, 0.6%.
Population projection: (2000) 6,386,000; (2010) 8,720,000.
Doubling time: 20 years.
Ethnic composition (1984): Libyan Arab and Berber 89.0%; other 11.0%.
Religious affiliation (1992): Sunnī Muslim 97.0%; other 3.0%.
Major cities (1988): Tripoli 591,100; Banghāzī 446,250; Miṣrātah 121,700; az-Zāwiyah 89,338.

Vital statistics

Birth rate per 1,000 population (1990–95): 43.4 (world avg. 26.0).
Death rate per 1,000 population (1990–95): 8.2 (world avg. 9.2).
Natural increase rate per 1,000 population (1990–95): 35.2 (world avg. 16.8).
Total fertility rate (avg. births per childbearing woman; 1990–95): 6.7.
Marriage rate per 1,000 population (1988): 4.5[3].
Divorce rate per 1,000 population (1988): 0.6[3].
Life expectancy at birth (1990–95): male 61.6 years; female 65.0 years.
Major causes of death per 100,000 population: n.a.; however, the major causes of death in the early 1990s were pneumonia, dysentery and diarrhea, cardiovascular disease, accidents, and malignant neoplasms (cancers).

National economy

Budget (1990–91). Revenue: LD 2,640,000,000 (current revenue 55.7%, of which oil revenues 17.7%, income taxes 13.7%, customs duties 9.7%, stamp duties 2.4%; capital revenue 44.3%). Expenditures: LD 2,640,000,000 (current expenditures 55.7%, of which allocations to municipal people's committees 39.4%, education and scientific research 4.3%, health 2.7%; capital expenditures 44.3%, of which agriculture and land reclamation 13.6%, industry 5.3%).
Public debt (long-term debt; 1991): U.S.$3,500,000,000.
Production (metric tons except as noted). Agriculture, forestry, fishing (1993): watermelons 220,000, tomatoes 175,000, potatoes 155,000, wheat 150,000, barley 150,000, oranges 100,000, onions 90,000, dates 77,000, olives 73,000, almonds 35,000, lemons and limes 4,000; livestock (number of live animals) 5,650,000 sheep, 1,260,000 goats, 160,000 camels, 135,000 cattle, 26,000,000 chickens; roundwood (1992) 646,000 cu m; fish catch (1991) 7,833. Mining and quarrying (1992): lime 260,000; gypsum 180,000; salt 12,000. Manufacturing (1992): distillate fuel 3,992,000; cement 2,300,000; jet fuel 1,730,000; gasoline 1,464,000; crude steel 822,000; meat 137,000[4]. Construction (gross value in LD; 1982): residential 127,051,000; nonresidential 200,877,000. Energy production (consumption): electricity (kW-hr; 1992) 16,950,000,000 (16,950,000,000); coal (metric tons; 1992) none (5,000); crude petroleum (barrels; 1992) 519,400,000 (113,500,000); petroleum products (metric tons; 1992) 13,002,000 (6,555,000); natural gas (cu m; 1992) 6,770,000,000 (5,470,000,000).
Population economically active (1991): total 1,169,000; activity rate of total population 24.9% (participation rates: ages 10 and over, n.a.; female 9.3%; unemployed, n.a.).

Price and earnings indexes (1990 = 100)

	1985	1986	1987	1988	1989	1990	1991
Consumer price index	23.8	29.8	44.3	58.8	96.2	100.0	109.0
Earnings index	...	...	...	...	...	...	...

Gross domestic product (at current market prices; 1993): U.S.$32,000,000,000 (U.S.$6,600 per capita).

Structure of gross domestic product and labour force

	1991 in value LD '000,000	1991 % of total value	1992 labour force	1992 % of labour force
Agriculture	768	7.5	191,600	19.2
Mining and quarrying	2,681	26.3	23,700	2.4
Manufacturing	809	7.9	92,200	9.3
Construction	1,209	11.8	156,300	15.7
Public utilities	231	2.3	28,500	2.9
Transportation and communications	644	6.3	78,500	7.9
Trade	896	8.8	52,800	5.3
Finance, insurance	1,162	11.4	15,000	1.5
Pub. admin., defense	1,079	10.6	308,000	31.0
Services	724	7.1	48,300	4.8
TOTAL	10,203	100.0	994,900	100.0

Household income and expenditure. Average household size (1980) 5.1; income per household: n.a.; sources of income: n.a.; expenditure (1977): food 37.2%, housing and energy 32.2%, transportation 9.4%, education and recreation 8.5%, clothing 6.9%, health care 3.3%.
Land use (1992): forested 0.4%; meadows and pastures 7.6%; agricultural and under permanent cultivation 1.0%; desert and built-up areas 91.0%.
Tourism (1992): receipts from visitors U.S.$6,000,000; expenditures by nationals abroad U.S.$154,000,000.

Foreign trade[5]

Balance of trade (current prices)

	1988	1989	1990	1991	1992	1993[6]
U.S.$'000,000	+2,633	+4,244	+5,212	+4,763	+4,447	−560
% of total	23.5%	32.5%	31.9%	28.8%	29.6%	3.5%

Imports (1993): U.S.$8,260,000,000[6] (1991; manufactured goods 78.3%, agricultural goods 20.3%). *Major import sources* (1990)[6]: Italy 13.3%; Germany 8.6%; United Kingdom 5.0%; France 4.3%.
Exports (1993): U.S.$7,700,000,000 (1991; crude petroleum 99.8%). *Major export destinations* (1990): Italy 49.2%; Germany 21.7%; Spain 11.4%; France 7.5%; United Kingdom 2.5%.

Transport and communications

Transport. Railroads: none. Roads (1992): total length 12,000 mi, 19,300 km (paved 56%). Vehicles (1991): passenger cars 450,000; trucks and buses 330,000. Merchant marine (1992): vessels (100 gross tons and over) 150; total deadweight tonnage 1,223,589. Air transport (1992)[7]: passenger-mi 693,230,000, passenger-km 1,115,616,000; short ton-mi cargo 2,610,000, metric ton-km cargo 3,810,000; airports (1994) with scheduled flights 12.
Communications. Daily newspapers (1992): total number 1; circulation 40,000; circulation per 1,000 population 8.2. Radio (1993): total number of receivers 1,000,000 (1 per 5.0 persons). Television (1993): total number of receivers 500,000 (1 per 10.1 persons). Telephones (1991)[8]: 270,000 (1 per 17.4 persons).

Education and health

Education (1991–92)

	schools	teachers	students	student/ teacher ratio
Primary (age 6–12)	2,744[9]	99,623	1,238,986	12.4
Secondary (age 13–18)	1,555[9]	11,429	138,860	12.1
Voc., teacher tr.	195[9]	7,072	76,648	10.8
Higher[10]	10	...	47,300	...

Educational attainment (1973). Percentage of population age 25 and over having: no formal schooling (illiterate) 72.7%; incomplete primary education 18.8%; complete primary 3.5%; secondary 4.0%; higher 1.0%. *Literacy* (1990): percentage of total population age 15 and over literate 63.8%; males literate 75.4%; females literate 50.4%.
Health: physicians (1989–91) 4,749 (1 per 948 persons); hospital beds (1982) 16,051 (1 per 207 persons); infant mortality rate per 1,000 live births (1990–95) 68.0.
Food (1988–90): daily per capita caloric intake 3,293 (vegetable products 86%, animal products 14%); 140% of FAO recommended minimum requirement.

Military

Total active duty personnel (1994): 70,000 (army 57.2%, navy 11.4%, air force 31.4%). *Military expenditure as percentage of GNP* (1989): 14.9% (world 4.9%); per capita expenditure U.S.$808.

[1]No formal titled office exists. [2]Policy-making body (General People's Congress) meets in Surt. [3]Registered events; incomplete to some degree. [4]1993. [5]Dollar values based on IMF Direction of Trade Statistics (DOTS), which are compiled from available reports of trading partners (not the subject country's reports) and may, thus, be substantially incomplete. [6]Import figures are f.o.b. [7]Libyan Arab Airlines. [8]Main telephone lines. [9]1982–83. [10]1988–89.

Liechtenstein

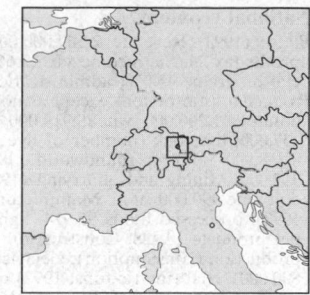

Official name: Fürstentum Liechtenstein (Principality of Liechtenstein).
Form of government: constitutional monarchy with one legislative house (Diet [25]).
Chief of state: Prince.
Head of government: Head of the Government.
Capital: Vaduz.
Official language: German.
Official religion: none.
Monetary unit: 1 Swiss franc (Sw F) = 100 centimes; valuation (Oct. 7, 1994) 1 U.S.$ = Sw F 1.28; 1 £ = Sw F 2.03.

Area and population

Communes	area sq mi	area sq km	population 1994[1] estimate
Balzers	7.6	19.6	3,841
Eschen	4.0	10.3	3,336
Gamprin	2.4	6.1	1,085
Mauren	2.9	7.5	2,938
Planken	2.0	5.3	317
Ruggell	2.9	7.4	1,529
Schaan	10.3	26.8	5,129
Schellenberg	1.4	3.5	881
Triesen	10.2	26.4	3,776
Triesenberg	11.5	29.8	2,406
Vaduz	6.7	17.3	5,072
TOTAL	61.8[2]	160.0	30,310

Demography

Population (1994): 30,500.
Density (1994): persons per sq mi 493.7, persons per sq km 190.6.
Urban-rural: n.a.
Sex distribution (1993): male 48.74%; female 51.26%.
Age breakdown (1993): under 15, 19.3%; 15–29, 23.7%; 30–44, 25.2%; 45–59, 17.8%; 60–74, 9.7%; 75 and over, 4.3%.
Population projection: (2000) 33,400; (2010) 38,900.
Doubling time: n.a.; doubling time exceeds 100 years.
National composition (1993): Liechtensteiner 61.7%; Swiss 15.7%; Austrian 7.4%; German 3.7%; other 11.5%.
Religious affiliation (1993): Roman Catholic 81.0%; Protestant 7.3%; other 4.4%; not stated 7.3%.
Major cities (1993): Schaan 5,129; Vaduz 5,072.

Vital statistics

Birth rate per 1,000 population (1992): 12.6 (world avg. 26.0); legitimate 85.3%; illegitimate 14.7%.
Death rate per 1,000 population (1992): 6.0 (world avg. 9.2).
Natural increase rate per 1,000 population (1992): 6.6 (world avg. 16.8).
Total fertility rate (avg. births per childbearing woman; 1993): 1.5.
Marriage rate per 1,000 population (1992): 6.8.
Divorce rate per 1,000 population (1991): 1.2.
Life expectancy at birth (1993): male 73.7 years; female 80.9 years.
Major causes of death per 100,000 population (1992): diseases of the circulatory system 160.7, of which heart disease 120.5 (including ischemic heart disease 50.2); malignant neoplasms (cancers) 144.0; diseases of the respiratory system 33.5; accidents, poisoning, and acts of violence 20.1 (including suicide 3.3).

National economy

Budget (1992). Revenue: Sw F 471,342,000 (taxes and interest 68.3%; post, telephone, and telegraph 15.1%; other revenue sources include real estate capital-gains taxes and death and estate taxes). Expenditures: Sw F 448,702,000 (financial affairs 37.9%; education 15.3%; post, telephone, and telegraph 12.6%; social affairs 12.6%).
Public debt: none.
Tourism (1993): 148,218 tourist arrivals; receipts from visitors, n.a.; expenditures by nationals abroad, n.a.
Population economically active (1993[3]): total 15,149; activity rate of total population 49.9% (participation rates: ages 15–64, 70.5%; female 37.7%; unemployed 1.9%).

Price and earnings indexes (1990 = 100)

	1987	1988	1989	1990	1991	1992	1993
Consumer price index[4]	90.3	91.9	94.9	100.0	105.8	110.2	113.7
Earnings index	...	...	...	...	...	...	...

Household income and expenditure. Average household size (1980) 3.0; income per household: n.a.; sources of earned income (1987): wages and salaries 92.9%, self-employment 7.1%; expenditure (1990)[5]: rent 20.9%, food 17.7%, transportation 11.0%, education and self-improvement 9.7%, clothing 7.0%, health 4.7%.
Production (metric tons except as noted). Agriculture, forestry, fishing (1992): silo corn (maize) 27,880[6], milk 12,871, potatoes 1,040[6], wheat 460[6], barley 416[6]; livestock (number of live animals) 6,650 cattle, 2,970 pigs, 2,614 sheep; commercial timber 16,853 cu m. Mining and quarrying: n.a. Manufacturing

(1992): whipped cream 1,626; yogurt 74; cheese 5; wine 1,151.3 hectolitres; small-scale precision manufacturing includes optical lenses, electron microscopes, electronic equipment, and high-vacuum pumps; metal manufacturing, construction machinery, and ceramics are also important. Construction (1992): residential 299,128 cu m; nonresidential 193,306 cu m. Energy production (consumption): electricity (kW-hr; 1992) 59,655,000 (223,000,000); coal (metric tons; 1992) none (42); petroleum products (metric tons; 1992) none (56,328); natural gas (cu m; 1992) none (21,475,000).
Gross national product (at current market prices; 1991): c. U.S.$978,000,000 (U.S.$33,510 per capita).

Structure of gross domestic product and labour force

	1988 in value Sw F '000	1988 % of total value	1993 labour force	1993 % of labour force
Agriculture	...	...	335	2.2
Mining	...	...	0	—
Manufacturing	...	...	4,713	31.1
Construction	...	...	1,172	7.7
Public utilities	...	...	158	1.1
Transportation and communications	...	...	467	3.1
Trade	...	...	2,071	13.7
Finance, insurance, real estate	...	...	1,128	7.5
Pub. admin., defense	...	...	914	6.0
Services	...	...	3,730	24.6
Other	...	...	455[7]	3.0[7]
TOTAL	1,700,000	100.0	15,149	100.0[2]

Land use (latest): forested 34.8%; meadows and pastures 15.7%; agricultural and under permanent cultivation 24.3%; other 25.2%.

Foreign trade

Balance of trade (current prices)

	1987	1988	1989	1990	1991	1992
Sw F '000,000	+737.6	+745.2	+742.8	+757.1	+822.8	+947.1
% of total	42.0%	37.3%	29.8%	27.8%	31.4%	30.6%

Imports (1992): Sw F 1,074,566 (machinery and transport equipment 28.9%; other finished goods 28.8%; limestone, cement, and other building materials 15.5%; metal products 11.5%; unrefined and semifabricated metal 5.5%; chemical products 5.2%). *Major import sources:* n.a.
Exports (1992): Sw F 2,021,711 (machinery and transport equipment 45.1%; metal products 17.6%; other finished goods 13.8%; limestone, cement, and other building materials 9.4%; chemical products 5.2%). *Major export destinations:* European Economic Community countries 44.9%; other European Free Trade Association countries 18.9%; Switzerland 13.4%.

Transport and communications

Transport. Railroads (1992): length 11.5 mi, 18.5 km; passenger and cargo traffic, n.a. Roads (1992): total length 201 mi, 323 km. Vehicles (1992): passenger cars 17,697; trucks and buses 1,787. Merchant marine: none. Air transport: none.
Communications. Daily newspapers (1992): total number 2; total circulation 17,739; circulation per 1,000 population 611. Radio (1992): total number of receivers 10,831 (1 per 2.7 persons). Television (1992): total number of receivers 10,445 (1 per 2.8 persons). Telephones (1992): 18,455 (1 per 1.6 persons).

Education and health

Education (1992–93)

	schools	teachers	students	student/teacher ratio
Primary (age 7–12)	14	118	1,912	16.2
Secondary (age 13–19)	8	74	1,161	15.7
Vocational	1	163[8]	214	1.3

Educational attainment (1980). Percentage of population age 25 and over having: no formal schooling 0.2%; primary and lower secondary education 47.6%; higher secondary and vocational 41.0%; some postsecondary 6.6%; university 4.6%. *Literacy:* virtually 100%.
Health: physicians (1992) 31 (1 per 956 persons); hospital beds[9] (1985) 100 (1 per 269 persons); infant mortality rate per 1,000 live births (1993) 5.3.
Food (1987–89)[10]: daily per capita caloric intake 3,530 (vegetable products 62%, animal products 38%); 133% of FAO recommended minimum requirement.

Military

Total active duty personnel: none. *Military expenditure as percentage of GNP:* none.

---

[1]January 1. [2]Detail does not add to total given because of rounding. [3]December 31. [4]The index is for Switzerland, which is united with Liechtenstein in a customs and monetary union. [5]Household expenditures are taken from a 1986 Swiss sample survey; a similarity of consumption patterns is assumed. [6]1987. [7]Includes 156 unclassifiable and 298 unemployed persons. [8]Part-time teachers only. [9]Liechtenstein has one hospital. Agreements with the Swiss cantons of St. Gallen and Graubünden and the Austrian Federal State of Vorarlberg allow use of certain hospitals. [10]Figures are derived from statistics for Switzerland and Austria.

Lithuania

Official name: Lietuvos Respublika
(Republic of Lithuania).
Form of government: unitary multi-
party republic with a single legislative
body, the Seimas (141).
Head of state: President[1].
Head of government: Prime Minister.
Capital: Vilnius.
Official language: Lithuanian.
Official religion: none.
Monetary unit[2]: 1 litas (plural litai) =
100 centai; valuation (Oct. 7, 1994)
1 U.S.$ = 4.00 litai; 1 £ = 6.37 litai.

Area and population

Cities of republic jurisdiction		area sq mi	area sq km	population 1989 estimate
Alytus	—		1	3	73,100
Birštonas	—	5	12	4,100
Druskininkai	—	8	22	22,500
Kaunas	—	46	120	422,600
Klaipėda	—	27	71	204,000
Marijampolė	—	8	20	50,500
Neringa	—	35	90	2,500
Palanga	—	27	69	19,400
Panevėžys	—	12	30	126,500
Šiauliai	—	27	69	145,000
Vilnius	—	110	286	582,400
Regions	**Capitals**			
Akmenė	Naujoji Akmenė	407	1,055	37,800
Alytus	Alytus	545	1,411	32,700
Anykščiai	Anykščiai	681	1,765	38,300
Biržai	Biržai	570	1,476	38,600
Ignalina	Ignalina	581	1,505	59,000
Jonava	Jonava	364	944	54,000
Joniškis	Joniškis	445	1,152	32,900
Jurbarkas	Jurbarkas	582	1,507	40,200
Kaišiadorys	Kaišiadorys	451	1,169	40,200
Kaunas	Kaunas	588	1,522	85,500
Kėdainiai	Kėdainiai	647	1,677	69,400
Kelmė	Kelmė	660	1,710	42,900
Klaipėda	Gargždai	527	1,366	45,000
Kretinga	Kretinga	385	997	44,100
Kupiškis	Kupiškis	417	1,080	25,900
Lazdijai	Lazdijai	595	1,542	33,400
Marijampolė	Marijampolė	599	1,551	49,200
Mažeikiai	Mažeikiai	390	1,009	61,200
Molėtai	Molėtai	528	1,368	27,300
Pakruojis	Pakruojis	508	1,316	30,700
Panevėžys	Panevėžys	849	2,199	41,900
Pasvalys	Pasvalys	498	1,289	36,800
Plungė	Plungė	653	1,691	53,900
Prienai	Prienai	443	1,148	39,500
Radviliškis	Radviliškis	631	1,635	54,800
Raseiniai	Raseiniai	607	1,573	46,100
Rokiškis	Rokiškis	697	1,806	47,800
Šakiai	Šakiai	623	1,613	41,600
Šalčininkai	Šalčininkai	578	1,498	41,500
Šiauliai	Šiauliai	701	1,815	49,900
Šilalė	Šilalė	459	1,188	31,700
Šilutė	Šilutė	866	2,243	69,000
Širvintos	Širvintos	350	906	21,500
Škuodas	Škuodas	352	911	26,600
Švenčionys	Švenčionys	653	1,692	37,800
Tauragė	Tauragė	455	1,179	52,600
Telšiai	Telšiai	556	1,439	59,200
Trakai	Trakai	640	1,657	81,700
Ukmergė	Ukmergė	539	1,395	52,500
Utena	Utena	475	1,229	52,300
Varėna	Varėna	933	2,416	38,500
Vilkaviškis	Vilkaviškis	497	1,286	52,200
Vilnius	Vilnius	855	2,215	93,800
Zarasai	Zarasai	515	1,334	25,900
TOTAL		**25,213**[3]	**65,301**[3]	**3,690,000**

Demography

Population (1994): 3,724,000.
Density (1994): persons per sq mi 147.7, persons per sq km 57.0.
Urban-rural (1993): urban 68.5%; rural 31.5%.
Sex distribution (1993): male 47.33%; female 52.67%.
Age breakdown (1991): under 15, 22.6%; 15–29, 22.8%; 30–44, 20.9%; 45–59, 17.4%; 60–74, 11.5%; 75 and over, 4.8%.
Population projection: (2000) 3,725,000; (2010) 3,727,000.
Doubling time: not applicable; doubling time exceeds 100 years.
Ethnic composition (1994): Lithuanian 81.1%; Russian 8.5%; Polish 7.0%; Belorussian 1.5%; Ukrainian 1.0%; other 0.9%.
Religious affiliation (1990): Roman Catholic, about 80%; Russian Orthodox, Old Believer, Evangelical Lutheran, and nonreligious minorities.
Major cities (1993): Vilnius 590,100; Kaunas 429,000; Klaipėda 206,400.

Vital statistics

Birth rate per 1,000 population (1993): 12.5 (world avg. 26.0).
Death rate per 1,000 population (1993): 12.4 (world avg. 9.2).
Natural increase rate per 1,000 population (1993): 0.1 (world avg. 16.8).
Total fertility rate (avg. births per childbearing woman; 1989): 2.0.
Marriage rate per 1,000 population (1991): 9.2.
Divorce rate per 1,000 population (1991): 4.1.
Life expectancy at birth (1991): male 65.3 years; female 76.1 years.
Major causes of death per 100,000 population (1992): circulatory diseases 594; cancers 196; accidents 139; respiratory diseases 41.

National economy

Budget (1993). Revenue: 2,569,000,000 litai (value-added tax 29.3%, enterprise profits tax 24.6%, income tax 23.6%). Expenditures: 2,511,000,000 litai (social programs 45.0%, administration and defense 14.5%, economy 14.0%).
Production (metric tons except as noted). Agriculture, forestry, fishing (1993): potatoes 1,200,000, wheat 919,000, barley 842,000, sugar beets 700,000, rye 437,000; livestock (number of live animals) 1,701,000 cattle, 1,359,800 pigs, 8,258,900 poultry; roundwood (1991) 1,443,000 cu m; fish catch (1991) 317,000. Mining and quarrying (1991): limestone 6,370,000; sand 3,390,000; dolomite 990,000 cu m. Manufacturing (value of production, '000,000 rubles; 1992): processed foods 95,914; light industry 56,142; machinery 54,266; paper products 19,428. Construction (1992): residential 872,000 sq m. Energy production (consumption): electricity (kW-hr; 1992) 18,707,000,000 (13,403,-800,000); coal (metric tons; 1992) none (657,000); crude petroleum (barrels; 1992) 469,000 (30,000,000); petroleum products (metric tons; 1992) 3,591,000 (3,825,000); natural gas (cu m; 1992) none (3,437,000,000).
Gross national product (1993): U.S.$4,909,000,000 (U.S.$1,310 per capita).

Structure of gross national product and labour force

	1992 in value '000,000 rubles	1992 % of total value	1992 labour force	1992 % of labour force
Agriculture, forestry	836.8	25.6	343,200	18.6
Manufacturing, mining	611.2	18.7	535,300	29.0
Construction	290.9	8.9	169,400	9.2
Public utilities	281.1	8.6	...	...
Transp. and commun.	421.7	12.9	124,000	6.7
Trade	441.3	13.5	227,400	12.3
Finance	29.4	0.9	14,000	0.8
Pub admin., defense	258.2	7.9	26,000	1.4
Services	317.1	9.7	344,700	18.6
Other	−219.1	−6.7	64,400	3.5
TOTAL	3,268.6	100.0	1,848,400	100.0[4]

Population economically active (1993): total 1,841,000; activity rate of total population 49.4% (participation rates: ages 16–60/55[6], 91.4%; female [1992] 48.4%; unemployed [1993] 4.2%).

Price and earnings indexes (1985 = 100)

	1987	1988	1989	1990	1991	1992	1993
Consumer price index[7]	...	...	...	100.0	216.4	2,207.3	9,054.3
Monthly earnings index	107.4	117.4	128.4	149.2	387.9	2,995.3	3,321.8

Household income and expenditure (1992). Avg. household size (1989) 3.2; sources of income: wages 66.4%, pensions and grants 18.7%, self-employment in agriculture 9.7%, other 5.2%; expenditures: food 50.3%, nonfood goods 23.2%, taxes 9.6%, services 8.4%, agricultural expenses 4.2%.
Land use (1992): forest 30.2%; pasture 7.1%; agricultural 47.0%; other 15.7%.

Foreign trade

Imports (1993): U.S.$1,054,400,000 (1992; from Commonwealth of Independent States [CIS]: petroleum and gas 48.9%, machinery 13.3%, chemicals 9.8%, light industry 6.0%, coal 4.6%). *Major import sources:* CIS-member countries 84.1%; developed market economies 11.7%; Baltic states 1.5%.
Exports (1993): U.S.$1,176,100,000 (1992; to CIS: machinery 29.2%, light industry 20.9%, food products 13.5%). *Major export destinations:* CIS countries 62.8%; developed market economies 18.9%; Baltic states 12.8%.

Transport and communications

Transport. Railroads (1992): length 2,996 km; passenger-km 2,740,000,000; metric ton-km cargo 11,337,000,000. Roads (1991): total length 44,500 km (paved 80%). Vehicles (1992): passenger cars 565,320; trucks and buses 92,056. Merchant marine (1992): vessels (100 gross tons and over) 52; total deadweight tonnage 373,911. Air transport (1992): passenger-km 917,000,-000; metric ton-km cargo 5,253,000; airports (1994) 3.
Communications. Daily newspapers (1983): 12; circulation (1990) all newspapers 5,780,000; circulation per 1,000 population 1,547. Radio (1993): 1,420,000 receivers (1 per 2.6 persons). Television (1993): 1,400,000 receivers (1 per 2.7 persons). Telephones (1992): 886,300 (1 per 4.3 persons).

Education and health

Education (1992–93)

	schools	teachers	students	student/ teacher ratio
Primary and secondary	2,219	43,900	512,400	11.7
Voc., teacher tr.	104	4,638	42,000	9.1
Higher	17	9,003[8]	55,000	7.3[8]

Educational attainment (1989). Percentage of population age 25 and over having: no schooling 9.1%; complete primary 21.3%; incomplete secondary 57.0%; postsecondary 12.6%. *Literacy* (1989): total population age 15 and over literate 98.4%; males literate 99.2%; females literate 97.8%.
Health (1992): physicians 13,764 (1 per 274 persons); hospital beds 44,500 (1 per 85 persons); infant mortality rate (1993) 16.0.

Military

Total active duty personnel (1994): 8,900 (army 93.3%, navy 3.9%, air force 2.8%). Russia withdrew its last military personnel in August 1993.

---

[1]The constitution adopted by referendum on Oct. 25, 1992, provided for a presidential form of government. [2]The litas was established as the official currency on July 20, 1993, and pegged to the U.S. dollar at a rate of 4 to 1 on April 1, 1994. [3]Total includes 12 sq mi (30 sq km) not distributed by administrative subdivision. [4]Detail does not add to total given because of rounding. [5]Males retire at age 60, females at 55. [6]1990 = 100. [7]1987–88.

Luxembourg

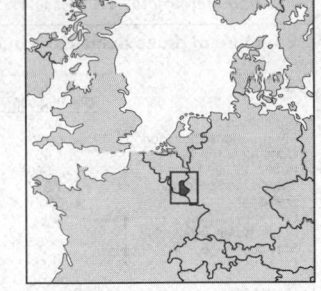

Official name: Groussherzogtum Lëtzebuerg (Luxemburgian); Grand-Duché de Luxembourg (French); Grossherzogtum Luxemburg (German) (Grand Duchy of Luxembourg).
Form of government: constitutional monarchy with two legislative houses (Council of State [21][1]; Chamber of Deputies [60]).
Chief of state: Grand Duke.
Head of government: Prime Minister.
Capital: Luxembourg.
Official language: none; Luxemburgian (national); French (used for most official purposes); German (lingua franca).
Official religion: none.
Monetary unit: 1 Luxembourg franc (Lux F) = 100 centimes; valuation (Oct. 7, 1994) 1 U.S.$ = Lux F 31.70; 1 £ = Lux F 50.42.

Area and population	area		population
Districts Cantons	sq mi	sq km	1991 census
Diekirch	447	1,157	56,896
Clervaux	128	332	10,263
Diekirch	92	239	23,258
Redange	103	267	11,073
Vianden	21	54	2,720
Wiltz	102	265	9,582
Grevenmacher	203	525	42,837
Echternach	72	186	11,726
Grevenmacher	82	211	18,113
Remich	49	128	12,998
Luxembourg	349	904	284,329
Capellen	77	199	31,817
Esch	94	243	116,389
Luxembourg (Ville et Campagne)	92	238	116,988
Mersch	86	224	19,135
TOTAL	999	2,586	384,062

Demography

Population (1994): 398,000.
Density (1993): persons per sq mi 398.4, persons per sq km 153.9.
Urban-rural (1991): urban 85.9%; rural 14.1%.
Sex distribution (1993[2]): male 49.11%; female 50.89%.
Age breakdown (1991): under 15, 17.3%; 15–29, 21.5%; 30–44, 23.8%; 45–59, 17.5%; 60–74, 12.8%; 75 and over, 7.1%.
Population projection: (2000) 407,000; (2010) 415,000.
Doubling time: not applicable; population stable.
Ethnic composition (nationality; 1993): Luxemburger 69.7%; Portuguese 10.8%; Italian 5.0%; French 3.4%; Belgian 2.5%; German 2.2%; other 6.4%.
Religious affiliation (1990): Roman Catholic 94.9%; Protestant 1.1%; other 4.0%.
Major cities (1991): Luxembourg 75,377; Esch-sur-Alzette 24,012; Dudelange 14,677; Differdange 8,489; Schifflange 6,859.

Vital statistics

Birth rate per 1,000 population (1992): 13.1 (world avg. 26.0); legitimate 87.3%; illegitimate 12.7%.
Death rate per 1,000 population (1992): 10.2 (world avg. 9.2).
Natural increase rate per 1,000 population (1992): 2.9 (world avg. 16.8).
Total fertility rate (avg. births per childbearing woman; 1992): 1.7.
Marriage rate per 1,000 population (1992): 6.4.
Divorce rate per 1,000 population (1992): 1.8.
Life expectancy at birth (1990–92): male 72.6 years; female 79.1 years.
Major causes of death per 100,000 population (1990): circulatory diseases 432.3, of which cerebrovascular disease 140.0, ischemic heart disease and myocardial infarction 131.8; malignant neoplasms (cancers) 255.4; accidents and suicide 69.2, of which suicide 15.1.

National economy

Budget (1994). Revenue: Lux F 132,967,000,000 (income and excise taxes 54.3%, customs taxes 17.7%). Expenditures: Lux F 134,911,600,000 (social security 22.8%, education 13.3%, transportation 9.7%, administration 8.5%, defense 2.4%, debt service 1.4%).
Public debt (1992): U.S.$227,387,000.
Production (metric tons except as noted). Agriculture, forestry, fishing (1992): barley 70,000, wheat 46,200, potatoes 26,100, rye 19,200, oats 17,600, apples 10,200; livestock (number of live animals; 1993) 205,161 cattle, 71,681 pigs; roundwood (1990) 706,000 cu m. Mining and quarrying (1987): metal ores, none; sand and gravel 956,810; gypsum 420,000; crushed stone 344,841. Manufacturing (1992): steel ingots and castings 3,264,000; pig iron 2,255,000; milk 265,100; beef and pork 22,500; wine 271,200 hectolitres. Construction (1991): residential and semiresidential 540,038 sq m; nonresidential 177,767 sq m. Energy production (consumption): electricity (kW-hr; 1990) 1,374,000,000 (5,242,000,000); coal (metric tons; 1990) none (197,000); crude petroleum, none (n.a.); petroleum products (metric tons; 1990) none (1,462,000); natural gas (cu m; 1990) none (461,286,000).

Gross national product (at current market prices; 1992): U.S.$13,716,000,000 (U.S.$35,260 per capita).

Structure of gross domestic product and labour force				
	1991			
	in value Lux F '000,000	% of total value	labour force	% of labour force
Agriculture	4,477	1.4	5,631	3.4
Mining	997	0.3	34	0.1
Manufacturing	77,303	24.3	29,711	18.0
Construction	23,905	7.5	15,347	9.3
Public utilities	5,264	1.6	1,876	1.1
Transp. and commun.	22,130	6.0	11,319	6.9
Trade	52,285	16.4	32,462	19.7
Finance	44,236	13.9	21,137	12.8
Pub. admin., defense	46,800	14.7 }	44,756	27.2
Services	48,656	15.3 }		
Other	−7,258[3]	−2.3[3]	2,441[4]	1.5[4]
TOTAL	318,804	100.0	104,713[5]	100.0

Population economically active (1991): total 164,713; activity rate of total population 42.8% (participation rates: ages 15–64, 61.6%; female 35.9%; unemployed 1.5%).

Price and earnings indexes (1990 = 100)						
	1987	1988	1989	1990	1991	1992
Consumer price index	91.9	93.3	96.4	100.0	103.1	106.4
Hourly earnings index	89.9	92.0	96.8	100.0	...	...

Household income and expenditure. Average household size (1991) 2.6; income per household (1987) Lux F 1,113,000 (U.S.$29,800); sources of income (1987): wages and salaries 88.6%, self-employment 9.1%, transfer payments 2.3%; expenditure (1990): transportation and communications 17.9%, food and beverages 14.2%, housing 14.1%, household goods and furniture 10.3%, health 7.6%, clothing and footwear 6.4%.
Tourism (1989): receipts from visitors U.S.$286,000,000.
Land use (1992): forested 34.2%; meadows and pastures 25.6%; agricultural and under permanent cultivation 23.2%; other 17.0%.

Foreign trade

Balance of trade (current prices)						
	1987	1988	1989	1990	1991	1992
Lux F '000,000	−24,530	−20,549	−31,900	−43,100	−60,500	−57,000
% of total	7.0%	5.2%	6.8%	9.3%	12.4%	12.0%

Imports (1992). Lux F 265,180,000,000 (metal products, machinery, and transport equipment 46.9%, of which transport equipment 12.2%; mineral products 11.5%; food, beverages, and tobacco 10.6%; chemical products 8.0%). *Major import sources:* Belgium 38.7%; Germany 31.4%; France 11.5%; The Netherlands 4.5%; U.S. 2.1%; Italy 2.0%.
Exports (1992): Lux F 208,128,000,000 (metal products, machinery, and transport equipment 54.7%, of which transport equipment 5.9%; plastic materials and rubber manufactures 13.2%; textile yarn, fabrics, and related products 7.1%; food, beverages, and tobacco 6.4%; chemical products 4.8%). *Major export destinations:* Germany 29.2%; France 16.8%; Belgium 16.2%; U.K. 5.7%; Italy 5.6%; The Netherlands 5.1%; U.S. 3.7%.

Transport and communications

Transport. Railroads (1992): route length 171 mi, 275 km; passenger-mi 175,000,000[6], passenger-km 282,000,000[6]; short ton-mi cargo 460,271,000, metric ton-km cargo 671,985,000. Roads (1991): total length 3,163 mi, 5,091 km (paved 99%). Vehicles (1993): passenger cars 209,006; trucks and buses 21,649. Merchant marine (1992): vessels (100 gross tons and over) 54; total deadweight tonnage 2,603,611. Air transport (1992): passenger arrivals 529,684, departures 531,436; short ton-mi cargo 606,902,000[7], metric ton-km cargo 886,062,000[7]; airports (1994) with scheduled flights 1.
Communications. Daily newspapers (1992): total number 5; total circulation 149,000; circulation per 1,000 population 382. Radio (1992): 230,000 receivers (1 per 1.7 persons). Television (1991): 134,845 receivers (1 per 2.9 persons). Telephones (1992): 206,502 (1 per 1.9 persons).

Education and health

Education (1991–92)	schools	teachers	students	student/ teacher ratio
Primary (age 6–11)[8]	...	2,032	26,197	12.9
Secondary (age 12–18)	...	} 1,953	8,465	...
Voc., teacher tr.	...		11,877	6.1
Higher	...		4,957[9]	...

Educational attainment: n.a. *Literacy* (1990): virtually 100% literate.
Health (1993[2]): physicians 814 (1 per 486 persons); hospital beds (1992) 4,438 (1 per 87 persons); infant mortality rate per 1,000 live births (1992) 8.6.
Food (1988–90): daily per capita caloric intake 3,925 (vegetable products 60%, animal products 40%); 149% of FAO recommended minimum.

Military

Total active duty personnel (1994): 800 (army 100.0%). *Military expenditure as percentage of GNP* (1991): 0.8% (world 4.2%); per capita expenditure U.S.$277.

[1]Has limited legislative authority. [2]January 1. [3]Imputed bank service charges. [4]Unemployed. [5]Detail does not add to total given because of rounding. [6]1991. [7]1987. [8]Public schools only. [9]1990–91.

Macedonia

Official name[1]: Republika Makedonija (Republic of Macedonia).
Form of government: unitary multiparty republic with a unicameral legislature (Assembly [120]).
Head of state: President.
Head of government: Prime Minister.
Capital: Skopje.
Official language: Macedonian.
Official religion: none.
Monetary unit[2]: denar; valuation (Aug. 1, 1994) 1 U.S.$ = denar 82.00; 1 £ = denar 126.17.

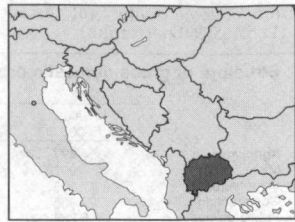

Area and population (1991 census)

Districts	area sq km[3]	population	Districts	area sq km[3]	population
Berovo	806	20,395	Negotino	734	23,246
Bitolj	1,798	122,173	Ohrid	1,069	65,531
Brod	924	11,671	Prilep	1,675	98,327
Debar	274	26,266	Probištip	326	16,556
Delčevo	589	25,531	Radoviš	735	30,975
Demir Hisar	443	12,078	Resen	739	23,203
Gevgelija	757	35,055	Škopje	1,818	563,301
Gostivar	1,341	116,107	Stip	815	51,947
Kavadarci	1,132	41,852	Struga	507	62,950
Kičevo	854	55,157	Strumica	952	94,517
Kočani	570	50,122	Sveti Nikole	649	21,569
Kratovo	376	11,329	Tetovo	1,080	180,654
Kriva Palanka	720	25,601	Titov Veles	1,536	67,535
Kruševo	239	12,620	Valandovo	331	12,264
Kumanovo	1,212	135,529	Vinica	432	19,903
			TOTAL	25,713[4]	2,033,964

Demography

Population (1994): 2,089,000.
Density (1994): persons per sq mi 210.4, persons per sq km 81.2.
Urban-rural (1991): urban 58.1%; rural 41.9%.
Sex distribution (1993): male 50.48%; female 49.52%.
Age breakdown (1981): under 15, 29.1%; 15–29, 27.1%; 30–44, 19.6%; 45–59, 14.8%; 60–74, 7.1%; 75 and over, 2.3%.
Population projection: (2000) 2,185,000; (2010) 2,356,000.
Doubling time: 70 years.
Ethnic composition (1991): Macedonian 64.6%; Albanian 21.0%; Turkish 4.8%; Romanian 2.7%; Serb 2.2%; other 4.7%.
Religious affiliation (1991): most believers are Christians, predominantly of the Eastern Orthodox Church; other Christians include members of the Macedonian Orthodox Church and the Roman Catholic Church; there are also a substantial Islamic community and a small Jewish community.
Major cities (1991)[5]: Skopje 563,301 (408,143[6]); Tetovo 180,654 (46,523[6]); Kumanovo 135,529 (60,842[6]); Bitolj (Bitola) 122,173 (78,507[6]).

Vital statistics

Birth rate per 1,000 population (1993): 15.2 (world avg. 26.0).
Death rate per 1,000 population (1993): 7.5 (world avg. 9.2).
Natural increase rate per 1,000 population (1993): 7.7 (world avg. 16.8).
Total fertility rate (avg. births per childbearing woman; 1993): 2.0.
Marriage rate per 1,000 population (1989): 7.9.
Divorce rate per 1,000 population (1989): 0.5.
Life expectancy at birth (1993): male 71.2 years; female 75.4 years.
Major causes of death per 100,000 population (1989): diseases of the circulatory system 346.2; malignant neoplasms (cancers) 102.4; diseases of the respiratory system 49.8; accidents, violence, and poisoning 34.5; diseases of the digestive system 18.2.

National economy

Budget (1992). Revenue: 122,895,000 denar. Expenditures: 122,895,000 denar.
External debt (1993): U.S.$842,000,000.
Production (metric tons except as noted). Agriculture, forestry, fishing (1993): wheat 384,000, grapes 205,000, corn (maize) 110,000, potatoes 90,000, plums 16,000; livestock (number of live animals) 2,351,000 sheep, 285,000 cattle, 173,000 pigs, 22,000,000 poultry; roundwood 830,362 cu m; fish catch (1990) 1,572 (all freshwater). Mining and quarrying (1992): copper ore 3,000,000; lead-zinc ore 400,000; gypsum 30,000; lime 20,000; iron ore 20,000; refined silver 10,000. Manufacturing (1990): rolled zinc products 6,907,000; hot rolled iron slabs 619,000; steel plates 507,000; crude steel 247,000; fermented tobacco 26,481; hydrochloric acid 24,000; detergents 21,000; cotton yarn 15,000; household ceramics 8,872; fancy candies 7,392; woolen yarn 5,000; chocolate products 2,903; glues 2,700; cosmetics 2,225; rubber goods 348; cotton fabric 40,000,000 sq m; ready-made underwear 30,000,000 sq m; ready-made outerwear 20,000,000 sq m; woolen fabric 9,000,000 sq m; silk fabric 5,900,000 sq m; upper shoe leather 2,259,000 sq m; domestic animal fur 851,000 sq m; carpets 555,000 sq m; leather outerwear 446,000 sq m; wine 634,000 hectolitres; brandy 39,000 hectolitres; leather footwear 6,638,000 pairs; jewelry 994 kg; refrigerators 156,000 units; toys 85,000 units; buses 953 units. Construction (residential units constructed; 1992): 6,583. Energy production (consumption): electricity (kW-hr; 1992) 5,100,000,000 (5,100,000,000); coal (metric tons; 1992) 5,000,000 (n.a.); crude petroleum (barrels; 1992) none (8,160,000); petroleum products (metric tons; 1992) 1,120,000 (1,120,000); natural gas (cu m; 1992) none (256,000,000).
Land use (1992): forested 39.5%; meadows and pastures 27.6%; agricultural and under permanent cultivation 23.8%; other 9.1%.

Gross national product (1993): U.S.$1,709,000,000 (U.S.$780 per capita).

Structure of gross domestic product and labour force

	1992		1993	
	in value Din '000,000	% of total value	labour force	% of labour force
Agriculture	2,835	17.7	34,212	5.4
Mining and manufacturing	6,743	42.1	170,221	26.9
Construction	1,057	6.6	36,513	5.8
Public utilities	528	3.3		
Transp. and commun.	977	6.1		
Trade	3,171	19.8	180,082	28.5
Finance				
Public admin., defense	705	4.4		
Services				
Other			211,035	33.4
TOTAL	16,016	100.0	632,063	100.0

Population economically active (1993): total 632,063; activity rate of total population 30.6% (participation rates: ages 15–64, n.a.; female [1990] 37.7%; unemployed 27.6%).

Price and earnings indexes (1990 = 100)

	1990	1991	1992	1993
Consumer price index	100.0	310.8	5,319	29,891
Earnings index[7]	100.0	284.3	3,358	23,359

Tourism (1993): total tourist nights 2,706,000.
Household income and expenditure. Average household size (1991) 3.9; income per household (1990) Din 75,556 (U.S.$6,676); sources of income (1990): wages and salaries 57.7%, self-employment 17.1%, transfer payments 16.2%, other 9.0%; expenditure (1992): food 43.7%, clothing and footwear 7.9%, drink and tobacco 6.8%, transportation and communications 6.6%, fuel and lighting 6.3%, health care 4.8%, education and entertainment 2.8%.

Foreign trade

Balance of trade (current prices)

	1988	1989	1990	1991	1992	1993
U.S.$'000,000	−205	−280	−551	−416	−74	−144
% of total	13.4%	17.6%	32.3%	24.3%	4.0%	6.4%

Imports (1993): U.S.$1,199,000,000 (1990; raw materials and semifinished goods 33.2%; consumer goods 28.4%, of which food, beverages, and tobacco 14.8%, clothing and footwear 4.9%, medicine and pharmaceuticals 0.6%; mineral fuels 19.1%; basic manufactures 10.7%; machinery 6.7%, of which electrical motors 1.0%). *Major import sources:* n.a.
Exports (1993): U.S.$1,055,000,000 (1990; clothing 20.7%; machinery and transport equipment 14.2%, of which transport equipment 1.3%; chemicals 4.6%; food 3.6%; textiles 2.2%; pharmaceuticals 0.8%; furniture 0.5%). *Major export destinations:* n.a.

Transport and communications

Transport. Railroads (1992): length 922 km; passengers transported 1,804,000; cargo transported 3,995,000 tons. Roads (1991): total length 10,591 km (paved 48%). Vehicles (1992): passenger cars 279,861; trucks and buses (1990) 22,594. Merchant marine: n.a. Air transport (1993[8]): passenger-km 292,372,000; metric tons cargo transported 625; airports (1994) with scheduled flights 1.
Communications. Daily newspapers (1990): total number 2; total circulation 52,000; circulation per 1,000 population 26. Radio (1989): 449,000 receivers (1 per 4.5 persons). Television (1989): 385,000 receivers (1 per 5.2 persons). Telephones (1990): 356,837 (1 per 5.7 persons).

Education and health

Education (1990–91)

	schools	teachers	students	student/ teacher ratio
Primary (age 7–14)	1,067	12,976	266,813	20.6
Secondary (age 15–18)	90	4,227	70,696	16.7
Higher	27	2,101	26,413	12.6

Educational attainment (1981). Percentage of population age 15 and over having: less than full primary education 45.3%; primary 28.1%; secondary 21.2%; postsecondary and higher 5.1%; unknown 0.3%. *Literacy* (1981): total population age 10 and over literate 1,365,000 (89.1%); males literate 729,000 (94.2%); females literate 636,000 (83.8%).
Health: physicians (1989) 4,331 (1 per 464 persons); hospital beds (1990) 11,-804 (1 per 171 persons); infant mortality rate (1993) per 1,000 live births 24.4.

Military

Total active duty personnel (1994): 10,400 (army 100%). *Military expenditure as percentage of GNP* (1993): 1.8% per capita expenditure U.S.$14.

[1]Member of the United Nations under the name Former Yugoslav Republic of Macedonia. [2]Macedonia, as part of Yugoslavia, utilized the Yugoslav (old) dinar (Din) until Jan. 1, 1990, when it was replaced by the Yugoslav (new) dinar (Din) at a rate of 10,000 old for 1 new. Macedonia left the Yugoslav currency area in September 1991, utilizing a local coupon alone until May 1992, when a transitional local currency, the denar, was introduced. The denar (valued initially at denar 255 = 1 U.S.$) was established at par with the Yugoslav (new) dinar but circulated in parallel with the coupon until May 1993, when a differently defined denar was introduced, replacing both the transitional denar and the coupon. [3]One sq km is equal to approximately 0.3861 sq mi. [4]Total includes 280 sq km of inland water not distributed by district. [5]Populations refer to municipal areas, not cities proper. [6]City proper, 1981 census. [7]Based on nominal net wages per worker. [8]Palair Macedonian airline only.

Madagascar

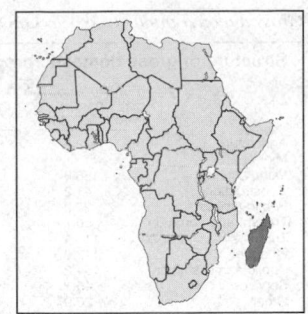

Official name: Repoblikan'i
Madagasikara (Malagasy);
République de Madagascar
(French) (Republic of Madagascar).
Form of government: unitary
multiparty republic with one
legislative house (National Assembly
[138]).
Chief of state: President.
Head of government: Prime Minister.
Capital: Antananarivo.
Official languages: Malagasy; French.
Official religion: none.
Monetary unit: 1 Malagasy franc
(FMG) = 100 centimes; valuation
(Oct. 7, 1994) 1 U.S.$ = FMG 3,343;
1 £ = FMG 5,317.

Area and population

Provinces	Capitals	area sq mi	area sq km	population 1993 census[1]
Antananarivo	Antananarivo	22,503	58,283	3,483,236
Antsirañana	Antsirañana	16,620	43,046	942,410
Fianarantsoa	Fianarantsoa	39,526	102,373	2,671,150
Mahajanga	Mahajanga	57,924	150,023	1,330,612
Toamasina	Toamasina	27,765	71,911	1,935,330
Toliary	Toliary	62,319	161,405	1,729,419
TOTAL		226,658	587,041	12,092,157

Demography

Population (1994): 13,702,000.
Density (1994): persons per sq mi 60.5, persons per sq km 23.3.
Urban-rural (1991): urban 24.4%; rural 75.6%.
Sex distribution (1993): male 49.55%; female 50.45%.
Age breakdown (1990): under 15, 45.6%; 15–29, 26.7%; 30–44, 15.0%; 45–59, 7.7%; 60–69, 3.3%; 70 and over, 1.7%.
Population projection: (2000) 16,579,000; (2010) 22,431,000.
Doubling time: 22 years.
Ethnic composition (1983): Malagasy 98.9%, of which Merina 26.6%, Betsimisaraka 14.9%, Betsileo 11.7%, Tsimihety 7.4%, Sakalava 6.4%, Antandroy 5.3%; Comorian 0.3%; Indian and Pakistani 0.2%; French 0.2%; Chinese 0.1%; other 0.3%.
Religious affiliation (1980): Christian 51.0%, of which Roman Catholic 26.0%, Protestant 22.8%; traditional beliefs 47.0%; Muslim 1.7%; other 0.3%.
Major cities (1993): Antananarivo 1,052,835; Toamasina 127,441; Antsirabe 120,239; Mahajanga 100,807; Fianarantsoa 99,005.

Vital statistics

Birth rate per 1,000 population (1990–95): 44.9 (world avg. 26.0); legitimate, n.a.; illegitimate, n.a.
Death rate per 1,000 population (1990–95): 12.6 (world avg. 9.2).
Natural increase rate per 1,000 population (1990–95): 32.3 (world avg. 16.8).
Total fertility rate (avg. births per childbearing woman; 1993): 6.1.
Marriage rate per 1,000 population: n.a.
Divorce rate per 1,000 population: n.a.
Life expectancy at birth (1990–95): male 54.0 years; female 57.0 years.
Major causes of death per 100,000 population: n.a.; however, major causes of death include communicable diseases and respiratory diseases.

National economy

Budget (1993). Revenue: FMG 1,470,548,000,000 (1987; taxes 80.2%, of which import duties 14.9%, excises 14.8%, income tax 12.5%; other receipts 19.8%). Expenditures: FMG 2,457,749,000,000 (1987; current expenditure 77.3%, of which education 12.3%, defense 7.5%, health 4.2%, agriculture 1.8%, public works 0.7%).
Tourism (1992): receipts from visitors U.S.$39,000,000; expenditures by nationals abroad U.S.$37,000,000.
Production (metric tons except as noted). Agriculture, forestry, fishing (1993): rice 2,550,000, cassava 2,350,000, sugarcane 1,980,000, sweet potatoes 498,000, potatoes 278,000, bananas 230,000, mangoes 205,000, corn (maize) 180,000, taro 125,000, coffee 88,000, oranges 86,000, coconuts 86,000, dry beans 52,000, pineapples 50,000, peanuts (groundnuts) 32,000, seed cotton 27,000; livestock (number of live animals) 10,280,000 cattle, 1,495,000 pigs, 1,270,000 goats, 735,000 sheep, 22,000,000 chickens; roundwood (1992) 8,597,000 cu m; fish catch (1992) 120,000. Mining and quarrying (1992): chromite concentrate 69,123; salt 30,000; graphite 8,910; mica 798; gold 200 kg; in addition, a wide variety of semiprecious stones and gemstones are produced. Manufacturing (1990): raw sugar 111,000; cement 20,000; soap 14,900; palm oil 3,800; paint 2,400; cigarettes 1,955; beer 298,000 hectolitres. Construction (1986)[2]: residential 19,700 sq m; nonresidential 5,700 sq m. Energy production (consumption): electricity (kW-hr; 1992) 569,000,000 (569,000,000); coal (metric tons; 1991) none (13,000); crude petroleum (barrels; 1992) none (1,356,000); petroleum products (metric tons; 1992) 176,000 (296,000); natural gas, none (n.a.).
Household income and expenditure. Average household size (1993) 4.6[3]; average annual income per household: n.a.; sources of income (1975)[4]: wages and salaries 58.8%, self-employment 14.1%, other 27.1%; expenditure (1983)[5]: food 60.4%, fuel and light 9.1%, clothing and footwear 8.6%, household goods and utensils 2.4%.

Gross national product (at current market prices; 1993): U.S.$3,055,000,000 (U.S.$240 per capita).

Structure of gross domestic product and labour force

	1991 in value FMG '000,000[6]	1991 % of total value	1991 labour force	1991 % of labour force
Agriculture	1,488,350	32.6	4,043,000	76.1
Manufacturing	530,560	11.6		
Mining	14,800	0.3	632,000	11.9
Construction	52,600	1.2		
Public utilities	86,950	1.9		
Transportation and communications	747,920	16.4		
Trade	497,990	10.9		
Finance	70,020	1.5	636,000	12.0
Services	791,890	17.4		
Pub. admin., defense	204,430	6.2		
TOTAL	4,666,510	100.0	5,311,000	100.0

Population economically active (1991): total 5,311,000; activity rate of total population 42.8% (participation rates [1985]: ages 15–64, 74.9%; female 39.3%; unemployed [1982] 0.6%).

Price and earnings indexes (1990 = 100)

	1987	1988	1989	1990	1991	1992	1993
Consumer price index	64.7	82.1	89.5	100.0	108.6	124.4	136.8
Earnings index	...	...	...	...	...	...	...

Public debt (external, outstanding; 1992): U.S.$3,805,000,000.
Land use (1992): forested 26.6%; meadows and pastures 58.5%; agricultural and under permanent cultivation 5.3%; other 9.6%.

Foreign trade

Balance of trade

	1986	1987	1988	1989	1990	1991
FMG '000,000,000	+14.8	+85.9	−39.9	+50.8	−244.5	−93.0
% of total	3.6%	13.8%	4.9%	5.3%	21.0%	7.7%

Imports (1992): FMG 844,935,600,000 (chemical products 13.7%, crude petroleum 11.3%, machinery 10.4%, vehicles and parts 9.6%, electrical equipment 7.2%, metal products 7.1%, textiles 1.5%). *Major import sources:* France 30.3%; Germany 6.1%; United States 5.9%; Japan 5.8%; United Kingdom 5.0%; Italy 2.9%; The Netherlands 2.2%.
Exports (1992): FMG 499,805,900,000 (vanilla 19.1%, shrimp 14.1%, coffee 11.8%, cloves and clove oil 4.2%, cotton fabrics 3.5%, sugar 3.4%). *Major export destinations:* France 26.6%; United States 15.5%; Germany 9.9%; Japan 8.6%; Belgium-Luxembourg 3.3%; Italy 3.1%; United Kingdom 2.6%; The Netherlands 2.2%.

Transport and communications

Transport. Railroads (1991): route length 640 mi, 1,030 km; passenger-mi 152,000,000, passenger-km 245,000,000; short ton-mi cargo 90,000,000, metric ton-km cargo 132,000,000. Roads (1991): total length 21,593 mi, 34,750 km (paved 15%). Vehicles (1992): passenger cars 50,000; trucks and buses 35,000. Merchant marine (1992): vessels (100 gross tons and over) 85; total deadweight tonnage 82,077. Air transport (1992): passenger-mi 268,221,000, passenger-km 431,660,000; short ton-mi cargo 45,245,000, metric ton-km cargo 66,057,000; airports (1994) with scheduled flights 18.
Communications. Daily newspapers (1990): total number 5; total circulation 53,000[7]; circulation per 1,000 population 4[7]. Radio (1993): total number of receivers 1,500,000 (1 per 8.8 persons). Television (1993): total number of receivers 130,000 (1 per 102 persons). Telephones (1992): 67,690 (1 per 189 persons).

Education and health

Education (1990–91)

	schools	teachers	students	student/ teacher ratio
Primary (age 6–13)	13,791	38,933	1,570,721	40.3
Secondary (14–18)	1,142[8]	14,856	322,772	21.7
Voc., teacher tr.	61[9]	1,484	17,419	11.7
Higher	5[8]	939	35,824	38.2

Educational attainment: n.a. *Literacy* (1990): percentage of total population age 15 and over literate 80.2%; males literate 87.7%; females literate 72.9%.
Health: physicians (1990) 1,392 (1 per 8,628 persons); hospital beds (1989) 10,900 (1 per 1,067 persons); infant mortality rate per 1,000 live births (1990–95) 110.
Food (1988–90): daily per capita caloric intake 2,156 (vegetable products 89%, animal products 11%); 95% of FAO recommended minimum requirement.

Military

Total active duty personnel (1994): 21,000 (army 95.2%, navy 2.4%, air force 2.4%). *Military expenditure as percentage of GNP* (1991): 1.2% (world 4.2%); per capita expenditure U.S.$2.

[1]Preliminary. [2]Capital city only. [3]Antananarivo only. [4]Malagasy households only. [5]Weights of consumer price index components in Antananarivo only; housing not included. [6]At factor cost. [7]For four newspapers only. [8]1988–89. [9]1987–88.

Malaŵi

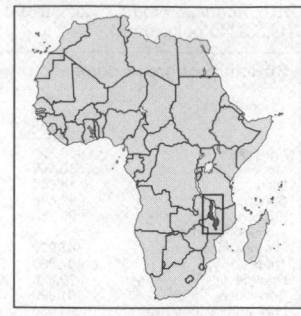

Official name: Republic of Malaŵi.
Form of government: multiparty
 republic with one legislative house
 (National Assembly [177]).
Head of state and government:
 President.
Capital: Lilongwe.
Official language: English[1].
Official religion: none.
Monetary unit: 1 Malaŵi kwacha
 (MK) = 100 tambala; valuation
 (Oct. 7, 1994) 1 U.S.\$ = MK 13.50;
 1 £ = MK 21.48.

Area and population		area		population
Regions				1987
Districts	Capitals	sq mi	sq km	census
Central	Lilongwe	13,742	35,592	3,110,986
Dedza	Dedza	1,399	3,624	411,787
Dowa	Dowa	1,174	3,041	322,432
Kasungu	Kasungu	3,042	7,878	323,453
Lilongwe	Lilongwe	2,378	6,159	976,627
Mchinji	Mchinji	1,296	3,356	249,843
Nkhotakota	Nkhotakota	1,644	4,259	158,044
Ntcheu	Ntcheu	1,322	3,424	358,767
Ntchisi	Ntchisi	639	1,655	120,860
Salima	Salima	848	2,196	189,173
Northern	Mzuzu	10,398	26,931	911,787
Chitipa	Chitipa	1,353	3,504	96,794
Karonga	Karonga	1,141	2,955	148,014
Mzimba	Mzimba	4,027	10,430	433,696
Nkhata Bay	Nkhata Bay	1,579	4,090	138,381
Rumphi	Rumphi	2,298	5,952	94,902
Southern	Blantyre	12,260	31,753	3,965,734
Blantyre	Blantyre	777	2,012	589,525
Chikwawa	Chikwawa	1,836	4,755	316,733
Chiradzulu	Chiradzulu	296	767	210,912
Machinga	Machinga	2,303	5,964	515,265
Mangochi	Mangochi	2,422	6,272	496,578
Mulanje	Mulanje	1,332	3,450	638,062
Mwanza	Mwanza	886	2,295	121,513
Nsanje	Nsanje	750	1,942	204,374
Thyolo	Thyolo	662	1,715	431,157
Zomba	Zomba	996	2,580	441,615
TOTAL LAND AREA		36,400	94,276[2]	
INLAND WATER		9,347	24,208	
TOTAL		45,747	118,484	7,988,507

Demography

Population (1994): 9,732,000.
Density (1994)[3]: persons per sq mi 267.4, persons per sq km 103.2.
Urban-rural (1987): urban 10.7%; rural 89.3%.
Sex distribution (1987): male 48.40%; female 51.60%.
Age breakdown (1987): under 15, 46.0%; 15–29, 25.4%; 30–44, 14.5%; 45–59,
 8.1%; 60 and over, 6.0%.
Population projection: (2000) 11,045,000; (2010) 13,233,000.
Doubling time: 20 years.
Ethnic composition (1983): Maravi (including Nyanja, Chewa, Tonga, and
 Tumbuka) 58.3%; Lomwe 18.4%; Yao 13.2%; Ngoni 6.7%; other 3.4%.
Religious affiliation (1980): Christian 64.5%, of which Protestant 33.7%, Ro-
 man Catholic 27.6%; traditional beliefs 19.0%; Muslim 16.2%; other 0.3%.
Major cities (1987): Blantyre 333,120; Lilongwe 223,318; Mzuzu 44,217.

Vital statistics

Birth rate per 1,000 population (1990–95): 54.5 (world avg. 26.0).
Death rate per 1,000 population (1990–95): 21.5 (world avg. 9.2).
Natural increase rate per 1,000 population (1990–95): 33.0 (world avg. 16.8).
Total fertility rate (avg. births per childbearing woman; 1990–95): 7.6.
Marriage rate per 1,000 population (1987): 4.4.
Divorce rate per 1,000 population (1977): 1.4.
Life expectancy at birth (1990–95): male 43.2 years; female 44.9 years.
Major causes of death per 100,000 population (1986)[4]: infectious and parasitic
 diseases 711, of which malaria 270, diarrheal diseases 148, measles 128;
 malnutrition 267; diseases of the respiratory system 265.

National economy

Budget (1993). Revenue: MK 1,549,000,000 (recurrent revenue 79.7%, of
 which surtax 27.4%, import duties 15.6%). Expenditures: MK 2,343,700,000
 (wages and salaries 21.7%; debt service 12.0%).
Public debt (external, outstanding; 1992): U.S.\$1,557,000,000.
Production (metric tons except as noted). Agriculture (1992) sugarcane
 2,100,000, corn (maize) 2,034,000, potatoes 370,000, cassava 216,000, plantains 195,000, tobacco 136,000, bananas 90,000, dry beans 80,000, peanuts
 (groundnuts) 59,000, tea 40,000, sorghum 22,000; livestock (number of live
 animals) 970,000 cattle, 888,000 goats, 240,000 pigs, 195,000 sheep; roundwood (1992) 9,706,000 cu m; fish catch (1991) 63,726. Mining and quarrying
 (1992): limestone 175,000; cement 120,000. Manufacturing (value added in
 MK '000; 1986): chemicals 30,805; textiles 19,630; food products 11,988;
 beverages 11,988; tobacco 9,480; printing and publishing 9,250. Construction (value in MK; 1993): 24,100,000[5]. Energy production (consumption):
 electricity (kW-hr; 1992) 792,000,000 (792,000,000); coal (metric tons; 1992)
 none (12,000); petroleum products (metric tons; 1992) none (183,000).
Land use (1992): forested 36.2%; meadows and pastures 19.6%; agricultural
 and under permanent cultivation 18.1%; other 26.1%.

Gross national product (1993): U.S.\$2,046,000,000 (U.S.\$220 per capita).

Structure of gross domestic product and labour force				
	1993		1987	
	in value MK '000,000[6]	% of total value	labour force	% of labour force
Agriculture	422.2	39.2	2,967,933	85.8
Mining	...	...	7,164	0.2
Manufacturing	126.8	11.8	97,776	2.8
Construction	41.2	3.8	46,875	1.4
Public utilities	27.2	2.5	8,833	0.2
Transp. and commun.	56.7	5.3	24,863	0.7
Trade	118.4	11.0	94,445	2.7
Finance	112.2	10.4	5,590	0.3
Public administration	154.2	14.3 }		
Services	45.1	4.2 }	147,039	4.3
Other	−26.9[7]	−2.5[7]	57,235	1.6
TOTAL	1,077.1	100.0	3,457,753	100.0

Population economically active (1987): total 3,457,753; activity rate 43.3%
 (participation rates: ages 15–64, 84.6%; female 51.5%; unemployed 5.4%).

Price and earnings indexes (1990 = 100)							
	1987	1988	1989	1990	1991	1992	1993
Consumer price index	59.4	79.5	89.4	100.0	112.6	138.2	163.7
Monthly earnings index	61.8	70.1	81.6	100.0	...	...	...

Household income and expenditure (1979–80). Average household size (1987)
 4.3; income per household MK 1,934 (U.S.\$2,419); sources of income:
 wages 83.3%, household enterprise 6.0%; expenditure (1990)[8]: food 55.5%,
 clothing and footwear 11.7%, housing 9.6%, household durable goods 8.4%,
 transportation 6.5%.
Tourism: receipts (1991) U.S.\$13,000,000; expenditures (1990) U.S.\$13,000,000.

Foreign trade[9]

Balance of trade (current prices)					
	1988	1989	1990	1991	1992	1993
MK '000,000	+139.4	−96.1	+180.1	+140.9	−103.4	−29.0
% of total	10.1%	6.1%	8.7%	5.6%	3.4%	1.0%

Imports (1993): MK 2,404,844,000 (1989; basic manufactures 40.6%, machinery and equipment 14.9%, transport equipment 14.3%, consumer goods
 11.1%, building and construction materials 5.7%). *Major import sources*
 (1989): South Africa 36.8%; U.K. 17.1%; W.Ger. 6.3%; Japan 6.3%.
Exports (1993): MK 1,370,661,000 (tobacco 68.4%, tea 11.4%, sugar 5.0%,
 cotton 0.7%). *Major export destinations* (1989): U.K. 21.0%; U.S. 12.8%;
 W.Ger. 10.5%; South Africa 9.7%.

Transport and communications

Transport. Railroads (1991): route length 495 mi, 797 km; passenger-km
 91,680,000; metric ton-km cargo 59,147,000. Roads (1989): total length 7,590
 mi, 12,215 km (paved 22%). Vehicles (1989): passenger cars 16,118; trucks
 and buses 17,394. Merchant marine (1991): vessels (100 gross tons and
 over) 1; total deadweight tonnage 300. Air transport (1992)[10]: passenger-
 km 53,410,000; metric ton-km cargo 2,256,000; airports (1994) 6.
Communications. Daily newspapers (1993): total number 1; total circulation
 20,000; circulation per 1,000 population 1.9. Radio (1993): total number of
 receivers 1,100,000 (1 per 9.7 persons). Television (1993): total number of
 receivers, n.a. Telephones (1992): 56,820 (1 per 180 persons).

Education and health

Education (1989–90)				
	schools	teachers	students	student/ teacher ratio
Primary (age 6–13)	2,624	20,580	1,325,453	64.4
Secondary (age 14–18)	94	1,096	29,326	26.8
Teacher tr., voc.	13	250	3,679	14.7
Higher	4	235	2,685	11.4

Educational attainment (1987). Percentage of population age 5 and over
 having: no formal education 54.9%; primary education 41.7%; secondary
 and higher 3.4%. *Literacy* (1987): total population age 5 and over literate 2,746,143 (41.6%); males literate 1,665,559 (52.4%); females literate
 1,080,584 (31.6%).
Health (1987): physicians (1984) 262 (1 per 27,094 persons); hospital beds
 12,617 (1 per 627 persons); infant mortality rate per 1,000 live births
 (1990–95) 142.0.
Food (1988–90): daily per capita caloric intake 2,049 (vegetable products 97%,
 animal products 3%); 88% of FAO recommended minimum requirement.

Military

Total active duty personnel (1994): 10,400 (army 96.2%, marines 1.9%, air
 force 1.9%). *Military expenditure as percentage of GNP* (1991): 1.1% (world
 4.2%); per capita expenditure U.S.\$3.

---

[1]Chewa is the national language. [2]Detail does not add to total given because of
rounding. [3]Based on land area. [4]Estimates based on reported inpatient deaths in
hospitals, constituting an estimated 8% of total deaths. [5]Cities of Blantyre, Lilongwe,
and Mzuzu only. [6]At constant prices of 1978. [7]Less imputed bank service charges.
[8]Weights of consumer price index components, cities of Blantyre and Lilongwe only.
[9]Import figures are f.o.b. in balance of trade and c.i.f. in commodities and trading
partners. Reexports included in balance of trade, excluded from commodities and
trading partners. [10]Air Malaŵi only.

Malaysia

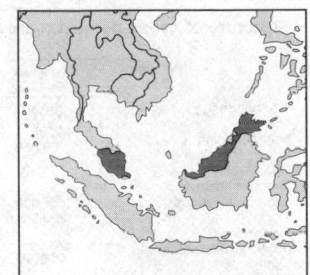

Official name: Malaysia.
Form of government: federal constitutional monarchy with two legislative houses (Senate [69[1]]; House of Representatives [180]).
Chief of state: Yang di-Pertuan Agong (Paramount Ruler).
Head of government: Prime Minister.
Capital: Kuala Lumpur.
Official language: Malay.
Official religion: Islam.
Monetary unit: 1 ringgit, or Malaysian dollar (M$) = 100 cents; valuation (Oct. 7, 1994) 1 U.S.$ = M$2.56; 1 £ = M$4.08.

Area and population

Regions States	Capitals	area sq mi	area sq km	population 1991 census[2]
East Malaysia				
Sabah	Kota Kinabalu	28,425	73,620	1,706,002
Sarawak	Kuching	48,050	124,449	1,648,217
West Malaysia				
Johor	Johor Baharu	7,331	18,986	2,074,297
Kedah	Alor Setar	3,639	9,426	1,304,800
Kelantan	Kota Baharu	5,769	14,943	1,181,680
Melaka	Melaka	637	1,650	504,502
Negeri Sembilan	Seremban	2,565	6,643	691,150
Pahang	Kuantan	13,886	35,965	1,036,724
Perak	Ipoh	8,110	21,005	1,880,016
Perlis	Kangar	307	795	184,070
Pulau Pinang	George Town	398	1,031	1,065,075
Selangor	Shah Alam	3,072	7,956	2,289,236
Terengganu	Kuala Terengganu	5,002	12,955	770,931
Federal Territories				
Kuala Lumpur	—	94	243	1,145,075
Labuan	—	35	91	54,307
TOTAL LAND AREA		127,320	329,758	
INLAND WATER		264	684	
TOTAL		127,584	330,442	17,566,982

Demography

Population (1994): 19,506,000.
Density (1994): persons per sq mi 152.9, persons per sq km 59.0.
Urban-rural (1993): urban 43.0%; rural 57.0%.
Sex distribution (1992): male 50.41%; female 49.59%.
Age breakdown (1992): under 15, 36.4%; 15–29, 28.1%; 30–44, 19.3%; 45–59, 10.1%; 60 and over, 6.1%.
Population projection: (2000) 21,592,000; (2010) 24,280,000.
Doubling time: 30 years.
Ethnic composition (1990): Malay and other indigenous (Orang Asli, or Bumiputera) 61.7%; Chinese 29.7%; Indian 8.1%; other nonindigenous 0.5%.
Religious affiliation (1980): Muslim 52.9%; Buddhist 17.3%; Chinese folk-religionist 11.6%; Hindu 7.0%; Christian 6.4%; other 4.8%.
Major cities (1991): Kuala Lumpur 1,145,075; Ipoh 382,633; Johor Baharu 328,646; Melaka 295,999; Petaling Jaya 254,849.

Vital statistics

Birth rate per 1,000 population (1994): 28.0 (world avg. 26.0).
Death rate per 1,000 population (1994): 5.0 (world avg. 9.2).
Natural increase rate per 1,000 population (1994): 23.0 (world avg. 16.8).
Total fertility rate (avg. births per childbearing woman; 1994): 3.5.
Marriage rate per 1,000 population (1979): 1.7.
Divorce rate per 1,000 population (1979): 0.02.
Life expectancy at birth (1994): male 69.0 years; female 73.0 years.
Major causes of death per 100,000 population (1990): diseases of the circulatory system 37.2; malignant neoplasms (cancers) 20.2; infectious and parasitic diseases 8.8; diseases of the digestive system 8.4; diseases of the respiratory system 7.8; accidents, homicide, and other violence 7.8.

National economy

Budget (1994). Revenue: M$44,730,000,000 (income tax 43.0%, nontax revenue 21.6%, import duties 12.1%, sales taxes 8.5%). Expenditures: M$33,285,000,000 (social services 33.9%, security 15.2%, administration 10.5%, economic services 8.4%).
Tourism (1992): receipts from visitors U.S.$1,768,000,000; expenditures by nationals abroad U.S.$1,740,000,000.
Production (metric tons except as noted). Agriculture, forestry, fishing (1992): palm oil 6,374,000, rice 1,860,000, rubber 1,218,000, bananas 510,000, cacao beans 217,000, pineapples 189,000; livestock (number of live animals) 2,491,000 pigs, 719,000 cattle, 347,000 goats, 310,000 sheep, 184,000 buffalo, 155,000,000 chickens; roundwood 54,008,000 cu m; fish catch (1991) 620,000. Mining and quarrying (1993): iron ore 222,848; copper concentrates 100,129; bauxite 68,824; tin concentrates 10,384. Manufacturing (1992): cement 8,366,000; refined sugar 951,000; wheat flour 602,000; fertilizer 325,000; plywood 1,664,000 cu m; radio receivers 31,360,000 units; automotive tires 8,540,000 units. Construction (completed; 1986)[3]: residential 8,809,100 sq m; nonresidential 959,900 sq m. Energy production (consumption): electricity (kW-hr; 1992) 32,082,000,000 (32,066,000,000,000); coal (metric tons; 1992) 190,000 (2,225,000); crude petroleum (barrels; 1992) 239,102,000 (73,109,000); petroleum products (metric tons; 1992) 9,919,000 (14,309,000); natural gas (cu m; 1992) 20,065,000,000 (7,507,000,000).
Gross national product (1993): U.S.$60,141,000,000 (U.S.$3,160 per capita).

Structure of gross domestic product and labour force

	1993 in value M$'000,000[4]	% of total value	labour force	% of labour force
Agriculture	15,895	15.8	1,580,000	20.7
Mining	7,991	8.0	35,000	0.4
Manufacturing	30,216	30.1	1,766,000	23.1
Construction	4,013	4.0	550,000	7.2
Public utilities	2,153	2.1	...	...
Transp. and commun.	7,132	7.1	342,000	4.5
Trade	12,315	12.3	...	...
Finance	10,664	10.6	315,000	4.1
Pub. admin., defense	9,092	0.8	862,000	11.3
Services	2,125	2.1	1,920,000[5]	25.1[5]
Other	−1,921[6]	−1.9[6]	276,000	3.6
TOTAL	100,475	100.0	7,646,000	100.0

Public debt (external, outstanding; 1992): U.S.$13,346,000,000
Population economically active (1993): total 7,646,000; activity rate 40.1% (participation rates: ages 15–64 [1990] 66.5%; female [1990] 35.5%; unemployed 3.6%).

Price index (1990 = 100)

	1987	1988	1989	1990	1991	1992	1993
Consumer price index	92.4	94.8	97.4	100.0	104.4	109.3	113.2

Household income and expenditure. Average household size (1980) 5.2; annual income per household (1987) M$12,890 (U.S.$5,120); sources of income: n.a.; expenditure (1983): food 28.7%, transportation 20.9%, recreation and education 11.0%, housing 10.2%, household durable goods 7.7%, clothing and footwear 4.3%, health 2.5%.
Land use (1991): forested 57.8%; meadows and pastures 0.1%; agricultural and under permanent cultivation 14.9%; other 27.2%.

Foreign trade[7]

Balance of trade (current prices)

	1988	1989	1990	1991	1992	1993
M$'000,000	+16,048	+12,725	+7,947	+3,165	+11,446	+15,095
% of total	17.0%	10.3%	5.3%	1.7%	5.9%	6.6%

Imports (1992): M$101,440,000,000 (machinery and transport equipment 54.9%; basic manufactured goods 16.0%; chemicals 8.0%; food 5.4%; mineral fuels 4.2%; inedible crude materials 2.6%). *Major import sources:* Japan 26.0%; U.S. 15.8%; Singapore 15.7%; Taiwan 5.7%; Germany 4.2%; U.K. 3.4%; South Korea 3.1%; Australia 2.7%.
Exports (1992): M$103,657,000,000 (machinery and transport equipment 43.8%; mineral fuels 12.9%; inedible crude materials 10.7%; basic manufactures 8.5%; animal and vegetable oils 6.6%; food, beverages, and tobacco 3.8%). *Major export destinations:* Singapore 23.0%; U.S. 18.6%; Japan 13.4%; U.K. 4.0%; Germany 4.0%; Hong Kong 3.8%; Thailand 3.7%.

Transport and communications

Transport. Railroads (1993): track length 2,222 km; passenger km 1,848,000,000[8]; metric ton-km cargo 1,380,000,000[8]. Roads (1992): total length 92,545 km (paved 75%). Vehicles (1992): passenger cars 2,147,974; trucks and buses 472,414. Merchant marine (1992): vessels (100 gross tons and over) 552; total deadweight tonnage 2,916,315. Air transport (1993): passenger-km 15,001,000,000; metric ton km cargo 585,130,000; airports (1994) 40.
Communications. Daily newspapers (1990): total number 45; circulation 2,500,000; circulation per 1,000 population 140. Radio (1993): 3,500,000 receivers (1 per 5.4 persons). Television (1993): 2,000,000 receivers (1 per 9.5 persons). Telephones (1992): 2,091,580 (1 per 8.9 persons).

Education and health

Education (1992)

	schools	teachers	students	student/ teacher ratio
Primary (age 7–12)	6,891	125,916	2,641,000	21.0
Secondary (age 13–19)	1,336	77,149	1,400,000	18.1
Voc., teacher tr.	75	3,489	33,000	9.5
Higher	54	11,471[9]	136,000[9]	11.9[9]

Educational attainment (1980). Percentage of population age 25 and over having: no formal schooling 36.6%; primary education 42.1%; secondary 19.4%; higher 1.9%. *Literacy* (1990 est.): total population age 15 and over literate 78.4%; males literate 86.5%; females literate 70.4%.
Health (1992): physicians 7,719 (1 per 2,412 persons); hospital beds 38,662 (1 per 482 persons); infant mortality rate per 1,000 live births (1994) 14.
Food (1988–90): daily per capita caloric intake 2,671 (vegetable products 85%, animal products 15%); 120% of FAO recommended minimum.

Military

Total active duty personnel (1994): 114,500 (army 78.6%, navy 10.5%, air force 10.9%). *Military expenditure as percentage of GNP* (1991): 3.7% (world 4.2%); per capita expenditure U.S.$91.

---

[1]Includes 43 appointees of the paramount ruler; the remaining 26 are indirectly elected at different times. [2]Preliminary results. [3]Results of the Central Bank Survey of four major towns: Kuala Lumpur, Shah Alam, Kelang, and Seberang Prai. [4]At constant prices of 1978. [5]Includes data for Public utilities and Trade. [6]Net bank service charges. [7]Import figures are f.o.b. in balance of trade. [8]Peninsular Malaysia and Singapore. [9]1991.

Maldives

Official name: Divehi Jumhuriyya (Republic of Maldives).
Form of government: republic with one legislative house (People's Council [48[1]]).
Head of state and government: President.
Capital: Male'.
Official language: Divehi.
Official religion: Islam.
Monetary unit: 1 Maldivian Rufiyaa (Rf) = 100 laari; valuation (Oct. 7, 1994) 1 U.S.$ = Rf 11.83; 1 £ = Rf 18.82.

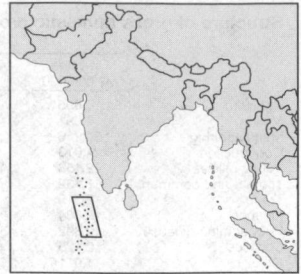

Structure of gross domestic product and labour force

	1992		1990	
	in value Rf '000[5]	% of total value	labour force	% of labour force
Agriculture[6]	264,300	23.6	14,117	25.0
Mining	20,900	1.9	496	0.9
Manufacturing }	66,300	5.9	8,441	15.0
Public utilities }			445	0.8
Construction	100,300	8.9	3,151	5.6
Transportation and communications	67,400	6.0	5,321	9.4
Trade	200,300	17.9	8,884	15.7
Finance			1,058	1.9
Public administration, defense } Services }	401,600	35.8 }	11,848	21.0
Other	...	...	2,674	4.7
TOTAL	1,121,100	100.0	56,435	100.0

Population economically active (1990): total 56,435; activity rate of total population 26.5% (participation rates: ages 15–64, 50.2%; female 19.9%; unemployed 0.9%).
Land use (1991): forested 3.3%; meadows and pastures 3.3%; agricultural and under permanent cultivation 10.0%; built-on, wasteland, and other 83.4%.

Area and population[2]

Administrative atolls	Capitals	area sq mi	area sq km	population 1990 census
North Thiladhunmathi (Haa-Alifu)	Dhidhdhoo	...	...	12,031
South Thiladhunmathi (Haa-Dhaalu)	Nolhivaranfaru	...	...	12,890
North Miladhunmadulu (Shaviyani)	Farukolhu-funadhoo	...	...	9,022
South Miladhunmadulu (Noonu)	Manadhoo	...	...	8,437
North Maalhosmadulu (Raa)	Ugoofaaru	...	...	11,303
South Maalhosmadulu (Baa)	Eydhafushi	...	...	7,716
Faadhippolhu (Lhaviyani)	Naifaru	...	...	7,224
Male' (Kaafu)	Thulusdhoo	...	...	6,726
Ari Atoll Uthuru Gofi (Alifu)	Rasdhoo	...	...	3,998
Ari Atoll Dhekunu Gofi (Alifu)	Mahibadhoo	...	...	5,029
Felidhu Atoll (Vaavu)	Felidhoo	...	...	1,579
Mulakatholhu (Meemu)	Muli	...	...	4,186
North Nilandhe Atoll (Faafu)	Magoodhoo	...	...	2,614
South Nilandhe Atoll (Dhaalu)	Kudahuvadhoo	...	...	4,199
Kolhumadulu (Thaa)	Veymandoo	...	...	8,189
Hadhdhunmathi (Laamu)	Hithadhoo	...	...	9,101
North Huvadhu Atoll (Gaafu-Alifu)	Viligili	...	...	7,295
South Huvadhu Atoll (Gaafu-Dhaalu)	Thinadhoo	...	...	10,417
Foammulah (Gnyaviyani)	Foahmulah	...	...	6,160
Addu Atoll (Seenu)	Hithadhoo	...	...	15,177
Male'				55,130
TOTAL		115	298	213,215[3]

Demography

Population (1994): 244,000.
Density (1994): persons per sq mi 2,121.7, persons per sq km 818.8.
Urban-rural (1993): urban 30.0%; rural 70.0%.
Sex distribution (1990): male 51.28%; female 48.72%.
Age breakdown (1990): under 15, 46.9%; 15–29, 26.7%; 30–44, 12.3%; 45–59, 9.0%; 60–74, 4.0%; 75 and over, 0.8%; not stated, 0.3%.
Population projection: (2000) 286,000; (2010) 369,000.
Doubling time: 23 years.
Ethnic composition: the majority is principally of Sinhalese and Dravidian extraction; Arab, African, and Negrito influences are also present.
Religious affiliation: virtually 100% Sunnī Muslim.
Major cities (1990): Male' 55,130.

Vital statistics

Birth rate per 1,000 population (1993): 38.0 (world avg. 26.0); legitimate, n.a.; illegitimate, n.a.
Death rate per 1,000 population (1993): 8.0 (world avg. 9.2).
Natural increase rate per 1,000 population (1993): 30.0 (world avg. 16.8).
Total fertility rate (avg. births per childbearing woman; 1993): 6.1.
Marriage rate per 1,000 population (1990): 10.6.
Divorce rate per 1,000 population (1990): 7.9.
Life expectancy at birth (1993): male 65.0 years; female 62.0 years.
Major causes of death per 100,000 population (1988): rheumatic fever 106.0; ischemic heart diseases 65.0; bronchitis, emphysema, and asthma 61.0; tetanus 23.5; tuberculosis 13.0; accidents and suicide 10.0.

National economy

Budget (1992). Revenue: Rf 1,021,000,000 (1990; nontax revenue 34.8%, import duties 25.5%, foreign grants 18.2%, tourism tax 15.3%). Expenditures: Rf 1,512,400,000 (economic development 23.9%, atoll development 21.6%, education 14.7%, public order and safety 7.7%, health 7.3%).
Public debt (external, outstanding; 1992): U.S.$92,600,000.
Production (metric tons except as noted). Agriculture, forestry, fishing (1993): vegetables and melons 19,000, coconuts 13,000, fruits (excluding melons) 10,000, roots and tubers (including cassava, sweet potatoes, and yams) 8,000, copra 2,000; fish catch (1991) 80,713. Mining and quarrying: coral for construction materials. Manufacturing: details, n.a.; however, major industries include boat building and repairing, coir yarn and mat weaving, coconut and fish processing, lacquerwork, garment manufacturing, and handicrafts. Construction: n.a. Energy production (consumption): electricity (kW-hr; 1991) 28,000,000 (28,000,000); coal, none (n.a.); petroleum products (metric tons; 1991) none (31,000); natural gas, none (n.a.).
Tourism (1992): receipts from visitors U.S.$113,000,000; expenditures by nationals abroad U.S.$22,000,000.
Household income and expenditure. Average household size (1990) 7.1; income per household: n.a.; sources of income: n.a.; expenditure (1981)[4]: food and beverages 61.8%, housing equipment 17.0%, clothing 8.0%, recreation and education 5.9%, transportation 2.6%, health 2.5%, rent 1.6%.
Gross national product (at current market prices; 1992): U.S.$114,000,000 (U.S.$500 per capita).

Foreign trade[7]

Balance of trade (current prices)

	1987	1988	1989	1990	1991	1992	1993
U.S.$'000,000	−42.9	−41.7	−51.0	−65.0	−83.3	−126.6	−133.7
% of total	41.1%	34.2%	36.3%	38.4%	43.7%	61.3%	65.9%

Imports (1992): Rf 2,001,400,000 (consumer products 49.8%; intermediate and capital goods 38.1%; petroleum products 12.1%). *Major import sources* (1991): India 7.7%; Sri Lanka 7.6%; United Kingdom 5.8%; Singapore 5.7%; Japan 4.0%; Thailand 2.8%.
Exports (1992): Rf 403,300,000 (canned tuna 40.1%; apparel and clothing 20.9%; dried skipjack tuna 18.1%; frozen skipjack tuna 8.9%). *Major export destinations* (1991): United Kingdom 24.6%; United States 22.8%; Sri Lanka 18.9%; Thailand 10.8%; Germany 6.5%; Singapore 5.1%.

Transport and communications

Transport. Railroads: none. Roads: total length, n.a. Vehicles (1992): passenger cars 804; trucks and buses 1,114. Merchant marine (1992): vessels (100 gross tons and over) 44; total deadweight tonnage 78,994. Air transport (1990): passenger arrivals 217,953, passenger departures 217,841; cargo loaded 2,263 metric tons, cargo unloaded 7,711 metric tons; airports (1994) with scheduled flights 1.
Communications. Daily newspapers (1993): total number 2; total circulation 4,300; circulation per 1,000 population 18. Radio (1993): total number of receivers 25,000 (1 per 9.5 persons). Television (1993): total number of receivers 4,750 (1 per 50 persons). Telephones (1992): 8,523 (1 per 27 persons).

Education and health

Education (1986)

	schools	teachers	students	student/teacher ratio
Primary (age 6–11)	243	1,138	41,812	36.7
Secondary (age 11–18)	9	291	3,581	12.3
Voc., teacher tr.	10	52	462	8.9
Higher	—	—	—	

Educational attainment (1990). Percentage of population age 15 and over having: no standard passed 25.6%; primary standard 37.2%; middle standard 25.9%; secondary standard 6.3%; preuniversity 3.4%; higher 0.4%; not stated 1.2%. *Literacy* (1985): total population age 15 and over literate 90,189 (90.4%); males literate 47,412 (90.6%); females literate 42,777 (90.1%).
Health (1992): physicians 35 (1 per 6,560 persons); hospital beds[8] 174 (1 per 1,320 persons); infant mortality rate per 1,000 live births (1993) 53.
Food (1984–86): daily per capita caloric intake 2,033 (vegetable products 91%, animal products 9%); 92% of FAO recommended minimum requirement.

Military

Total active duty personnel: Maldives maintains a single security force numbering about 700–1,000; it performs both army and police functions.

---

[1]Includes 8 nonelective seats. [2]Maldives is divided into 20 administrative districts corresponding to atoll groups; arrangement shown here is from north to south. Total area excludes 34,634 sq mi (89,702 sq km) of tidal waters. [3]Includes 4,792 people in resort and industrial islands. [4]Weights of consumer price index components. [5]At 1985 prices. [6]Primarily fishing. [7]Import figures are f.o.b. in balance of trade and c.i.f. for commodities and trading partners. [8]In government establishments only.

Mali

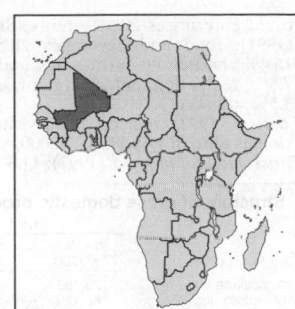

Official name: République du Mali (Republic of Mali).
Form of government: multiparty[1] republic with one legislative house (National Assembly [116]).
Chief of state: President.
Head of government: Prime Minister.
Capital: Bamako.
Official language: French.
Official religion: none.
Monetary unit: 1 CFA franc (CFAF) = 100 centimes; valuation (Oct. 7, 1994) 1 U.S.$ = CFAF 526.67; 1 £ = CFAF 837.67.

Area and population

Regions[2]	Capitals	area sq mi	area sq km	population 1994 estimate
Gao	Gao	124,326	322,002	399,000
Kayes	Kayes	46,233	119,743	1,219,000
Koulikoro	Koulikoro	37,007	95,848	1,432,000
Mopti	Mopti	30,508	79,017	1,394,000
Ségou	Ségou	25,028	64,821	1,546,000
Sikasso	Sikasso	27,135	70,280	1,489,000
Tombouctou	Timbuktu (Tombouctou)	191,743	496,611	452,000
District				
Bamako	Bamako	97	252	894,000
TOTAL		482,077	1,248,574	8,825,000

Demography

Population (1994): 8,825,000.
Density (1994): persons per sq mi 18.3, persons per sq km 7.1.
Urban-rural (1994): urban 26.1%; rural 73.9%.
Sex distribution (1994): male 48.87%; female 51.13%.
Age breakdown (1991): under 15, 48.3%; 15–29, 22.5%; 30–44, 14.3%; 45–59, 8.8%; 60–74, 4.9%; 75 and over, 1.2%.
Population projection: (2000) 9,980,000; (2010) 12,252,000.
Doubling time: 23 years.
Linguistic composition (1987): Bambara-Malinké-Dyula (-Dioula) 50.3%; Fulani (Peulh-Foulfoulbe) 10.7%; Dogon-Kado 6.9%; Songhai-Djerma 6.3%; Soninké-Marka 6.3%; Tamashek-Bella (Berber) 4.2%; Minianka 3.9%; Senufo 2.4%; Bwa- (Bobo-) Dafing 2.3%; Bozo-Somono 2.0%; other 4.7%.
Religious affiliation (1983): Muslim 90%; traditional beliefs 9%; Christian 1%.
Major cities (1987): Bamako 646,163; Ségou 88,877; Mopti 73,979; Sikasso 73,050; Gao 54,874.

Vital statistics

Birth rate per 1,000 population (1993): 51.7 (world avg. 26.0); legitimate, n.a.; illegitimate, n.a.
Death rate per 1,000 population (1993): 20.8 (world avg. 9.2).
Natural increase rate per 1,000 population (1993): 30.9 (world avg. 16.8).
Total fertility rate (avg. births per childbearing woman; 1993): 7.3.
Marriage rate per 1,000 population (1990)[3]: 0.4.
Divorce rate per 1,000 population: n.a.
Life expectancy at birth (1987): male 54.7 years; female 58.2 years.
Major causes of death per 100,000 population: n.a.; morbidity ([notified cases of illness] by cause as a percentage of all reported infectious disease; 1985): malaria 62.1%; measles 10.3%; amebiasis 10.3%; syphilis and gonococcal infections 6.0%; influenza 4.9%; other principal causes in 1989 included polio and conditions originating in the perinatal period.

National economy

Budget (1993). Revenue: CFAF 188,300,000,000 (fiscal receipts 60.1%, nonfiscal receipts 4.6%). Expenditures: CFAF 192,400,000,000 (capital expenditure 50.8%, current expenditure 38.3%).
Public debt (external, outstanding; 1992): U.S.$2,472,000,000.
Tourism (1992): receipts from visitors U.S.$45,000,000; expenditures by nationals abroad U.S.$68,000,000.
Population economically active (1987): total 3,437,489; activity rate of total population 44.7% (participation rates: ages 15–64, 67.4%; female 37.4%; unemployed 0.8%).

Price and earnings indexes (1990 = 100)

	1987	1988	1989	1990	1991	1992	1993
Consumer price index	...	99.5	99.4	100.0	101.8	95.4	95.2
Hourly earnings index[4]	100.0	100.0	100.0	100.0	100.0	127.9	...

Production (metric tons except as noted). Agriculture, forestry, fishing (1993): sorghum 694,000, millet 691,000, rice 388,000, seed cotton 317,000, corn (maize) 275,000, peanuts (groundnuts) 135,000, cassava 73,000, sweet potatoes 55,000; livestock (number of live animals) 13,942,000 goats and sheep, 5,554,000 cattle, 610,000 asses, 250,000 camels, 87,000 horses, 84,000 pigs; roundwood (1992) 5,953,000 cu m; fish catch (1991) 60,031. Mining and quarrying (1991): limestone 100,000[5]; phosphate 8,000; gold 5,352 kg. Manufacturing (1991): cotton fibre 46,396; sugar 29,040; cement 10,953; soft drinks 64,750 hectolitres; beer 37,754 hectolitres; shoes 127,000 pairs; cigarettes 141,757 cartons. Construction: n.a. Energy production (consumption): electricity (kW-hr; 1992) 313,000,000 (313,000,000); coal, none (n.a.);

crude petroleum, none (n.a.); petroleum products (metric tons; 1992) none (141,000); natural gas, none (n.a.).
Gross national product (at current market prices; 1993): U.S.$2,770,000,000 (U.S.$300 per capita).

Structure of gross domestic product and labour force

	1991 in value CFAF '000,000	1991 % of total value	1987 labour force	1987 % of labour force
Agriculture	320,169	45.6	2,802,722	82.2
Mining	10,326	1.5	1,524	—
Manufacturing	48,260	6.8	186,243	5.5
Construction	27,920	4.0	13,065	0.4
Public utilities	9,432	1.3	3,157	0.1
Transp. and commun.	30,974	4.4	6,174	0.2
Trade	109,131	15.5	158,892	4.7
Finance	8,202	1.2	320	—
Pub. admin., defense Services	} 105,185	15.0	168,701	4.6
Other	33,026[6]	4.7[6]	78,470	2.3
TOTAL	702,625	100.0	3,409,271	100.0

Household income and expenditure. Average household size (1987) 5.6; average annual income per household: n.a.; sources of income: n.a.; expenditure (1986–87)[3, 7]: food 54.6%, clothing 14.2%, transportation and communications 11.9%, housing and energy 8.7%, household durable goods 4.2%.
Land use (1992): forested 5.7%; meadows and pastures 24.6%; agricultural and under permanent cultivation 1.8%; other 67.9%.

Foreign trade[8]

Balance of trade (current prices)

	1985	1986	1987	1988	1989	1990
CFAF '000,000,000	−38.6	−34.2	−24.9	−41.2	−2.9	−17.1
% of total	25.8%	18.9%	18.8%	24.4%	1.4%	8.0%

Imports (1990): CFAF 187,735,000,000 (machinery, appliances, and transport equipment 29.3%; food products 12.7%; chemicals 9.2%; petroleum products 9.1%). *Major import sources:* France 27.2%; Côte d'Ivoire 18.8%; Senegal 5.8%; Germany 5.6%; The Netherlands 4.8%; U.S.S.R. 4.8%; Belgium-Luxembourg 4.0%; Italy 3.3%; Saudi Arabia 3.0%; United Kingdom 2.7%; Guinea 2.6%; Hong Kong 2.4%; Spain 1.9%; United States 1.7%.
Exports (1990): CFAF 101,920,000,000 (raw cotton and cotton products 44.9%; live animals 24.0%; gold and diamonds 12.5%). *Major export destinations:* U.S.S.R. 12.5%; Algeria 11.6%; Taiwan 10.5%; Belgium-Luxembourg 9.1%; France 7.1%; China 5.2%; Canada 4.9%; Germany 4.4%; Morocco 4.4%.

Transport and communications

Transport. Railroads (1990): route length 399 mi, 642 km; passenger-mi 304,155,000, passenger-km 489,491,000; short ton-mi cargo 187,176,000, metric ton-km cargo 273,273,000. Roads (1987): total length 11,185 mi, 18,000 km (paved 8%). Vehicles (1992): passenger cars 23,000, trucks and buses 10,000. Merchant marine: vessels (100 gross tons and over) none. Air transport (1983): passenger-mi 68,000,000, passenger-km 110,000,000; short ton-mi cargo 411,000, metric ton-km cargo 600,000; airports (1994) with scheduled flights 1.
Communications. Daily newspapers (1993): total number 1; total circulation 40,000; circulation per 1,000 population 4.6. Radio (1993): total number of receivers 150,000 (1 per 58 persons). Television (1993): total number of receivers 10,000 (1 per 865 persons). Telephones (1990): 11,165 (1 per 730 persons).

Education and health

Education (1991–92)

	schools	teachers	students	student/teacher ratio
Primary (age 6–14)	1,514	7,963	375,131	47.1
Secondary (age 15–17)	307[9]	5,883[10]	88,529	...
Higher	7[10]	701	6,703	9.6

Educational attainment (1987). Percentage of population age 6 and over having: no formal schooling 86.0%; primary education 12.5%; secondary 1.2%; postsecondary and higher 0.3%. *Literacy* (1987): percentage of total population age 6 and over literate 1,116,019 (18.8%); males literate 767,981 (26.7%); females literate 348,038 (11.4%).
Health (1987): physicians 114 (1 per 67,789 persons); hospital beds 3,430 (1 per 2,253 persons); infant mortality rate per 1,000 live births (1993) 108.
Food (1988–90): daily per capita caloric intake 2,259 (vegetable products 91%, animal products 9%); 96% of FAO recommended minimum requirement.

Military

Total active duty personnel (1994): 7,350 (army 93.9%, navy 0.7%, air force 5.4%). *Military expenditure as percentage of GNP* (1989): 2.0% (world 4.9%); per capita expenditure U.S.$5.

[1]Multiparty legislative elections of February–March 1992 were boycotted by most opposition parties. [2]Kidal region established on May 15, 1991. Separate data not available. [3]Bamako only. [4]Minimum hourly wages of industrial workers. [5]1990. [6]Less imputed bank service charges. [7]Weights of consumer price index components. [8]Imports c.i.f. [9]Excludes vocational. [10]1990–91.

Malta

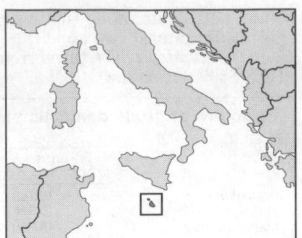

Official name: Malta (Maltese); Malta (English).
Form of government: unitary multiparty republic with one legislative house (House of Representatives [65]).
Chief of state: President.
Head of government: Prime Minister.
Capital: Valletta.
Official languages: Maltese; English.
Official religion: Roman Catholicism.
Monetary unit: 1 Maltese lira (Lm) = 100 cents = 1,000 mils; valuation[1] (Oct. 7, 1994) 1 U.S.$ = Lm 0.37; 1 £ = Lm 0.58.

Area and population	area		population
Census regions[2]	sq mi	sq km	1994 estimate[3]
Gozo and Comino	27	70	27,258
Inner Harbour	6	15	102,394
Northern	30	78	35,787
Outer Harbour	12	32	106,312
South Eastern	20	53	46,884
Western	27	69	47,796
TOTAL	122	316[4]	366,431

Demography

Population (1994): 368,000.
Density (1994): persons per sq mi 3,016.0, persons per sq km 1,164.2.
Urban-rural (1992): urban 85.3%; rural 14.7%.
Sex distribution (1994[3]): male 49.46%; female 50.54%.
Age breakdown (1994[3]): under 15, 22.4%; 15–29, 21.2%; 30–44, 23.4%; 45–59, 17.8%; 60–74, 11.4%; 75 and over, 3.8%.
Population projection: (2000) 378,000; (2010) 394,000.
Doubling time: 104 years.
Ethnic composition (by nationality; 1980): Maltese 95.7%; British 2.1%; other 2.2%.
Religious affiliation (1992): Roman Catholic 98.6%; other 1.4%.
Major cities (1994[3]): Birkirkara 21,770; Qormi 19,904; Hamrun 13,654; Sliema 13,514; Valletta 9,144.

Vital statistics

Birth rate per 1,000 population (1993): 14.0 (world avg. 26.0); legitimate 97.7%; illegitimate 2.3%.
Death rate per 1,000 population (1993): 7.3 (world avg. 9.2).
Natural increase rate per 1,000 population (1993): 6.7 (world avg. 16.8).
Total fertility rate (avg. births per childbearing woman; 1992): 2.1.
Marriage rate per 1,000 population (1993): 6.8.
Divorce rate per 1,000 population: n.a.
Life expectancy at birth (1992): male 73.0 years; female 77.8 years.
Major causes of death per 100,000 population (1992): diseases of the circulatory system 362.0; malignant neoplasms (cancers) 179.4; diseases of the respiratory system 68.6; endocrine, nutritional, and metabolic diseases of the blood and blood-forming organs 46.3; accidents, poisoning, and violence 31.1; diseases of the digestive system 22.6.

National economy

Budget (1994). Revenue: Lm 426,929,000 (1992; customs and excise taxes 23.6%, national insurance and Central Bank contributions 20.6%, income tax 19.2%, Central Bank profits 5.1%). Expenditures: Lm 407,303,000 (1992; national insurance benefits 41.1%, education 12.3%, health 9.8%, debt service 4.7%).
Public debt (1993): U.S.$882,900,000.
Production (wholesale value in Lm except where noted). Agriculture, forestry, fishing (1992): vegetables 4,589,043 (of which tomatoes 798,617, melons 643,126, cauliflower 377,532, carrots 288,643, onions 133,864), fruits 985,225 (of which peaches 219,120, grapes 160,864), potatoes 580,549; livestock (number of live animals; 1992) 107,000 pigs, 23,000 cattle, 6,000 sheep, 5,000 goats, 1,000,000 chickens; fish catch (1992) 745,956. Quarrying (1990): 2,853,000. Manufacturing (value of sales in Lm; 1993): machinery and transport equipment 283,488,000, of which transport equipment 5,306,000; food and beverages 97,050,000; textiles and wearing apparel 82,173,000; paper and publishing 37,934,000; chemicals 28,897,000; metal manufacture 14,771,000. Construction (buildings completed; 1993): residential 4,605[5]; nonresidential 2,024. Energy production (consumption): electricity (kW-hr; 1991) 1,278,502,000 (954,804,000); coal (metric tons; 1991) none (297,000); crude petroleum, none (n.a.); petroleum products (metric tons; 1991) none (320,000); natural gas, none (n.a.).
Population economically active (1993): total 139,868; activity rate of total population 38.2% (participation rates: ages 15–64 [1985] 45.9%; female 32.7%; unemployed 4.2%).

Price and earnings indexes (1987 = 100)							
	1987	1988	1989	1990	1991	1992	1993
Consumer price index	100.0	100.9	101.8	104.8	107.4	109.2	113.7
Annual earnings index	100.0	103.8	106.9	108.6	117.8	121.4	...

Household income and expenditure. Average household size (1985) 3.3; average annual income per household (1982) Lm 4,736 (U.S.$11,399); sources of income (1991): wages and salaries 62.4%, professional and unincorpo-

rated enterprises 20.1%, rents, dividends, and interest 17.5%; expenditure (1991): food and beverages 28.5%, transportation and communications 16.4%, household furnishings and operations 9.9%, clothing and footwear 7.6%, recreation, entertainment, and education 7.5%, housing 5.5%, health 3.5%, tobacco 2.7%.
Tourism (1992): receipts from visitors U.S.$568,000,000; expenditures by nationals abroad U.S.$138,000,000.
Gross national product (1992): U.S.$2,606,000,000 (U.S.$7,210 per capita).

Structure of gross domestic product and labour force				
	1991		1993	
	in value Lm '000	% of total value	labour force	% of labour force
Agriculture	23,439	3.3	2,768	2.0
Manufacturing	188,129	26.5 }	34,198	24.4
Mining	26,511	3.7 }	5,491	3.9
Construction				
Public utilities	[6]	[6]	[6]	[6]
Transportation and communications	41,845	5.9	10,949	7.8
Trade	101,374	14.3	13,981	10.0
Finance	101,033[7]	14.2[7]	3,643	2.6
Pub. admin., defense	162,396[6]	22.9[6]	40,922[6]	29.3[6]
Services	65,129	9.2	15,590	11.2
Other	...	...	12,326[8]	8.8[8]
TOTAL	709,856	100.0	139,868	100.0

Land use (1991): agricultural and under permanent cultivation 40.6%; other (infertile clay soil with underlying limestone) 59.4%.

Foreign trade[9]

Balance of trade (current prices)						
	1988	1989	1990	1991	1992	1993
Lm '000,000	−168.1	−169.0	−172.8	−214.5	−182.9	−229.5
% of total	26.3%	22.3%	18.3%	21.1%	15.7%	18.2%

Imports (1992): Lm 747,770,000 (machinery and transport equipment 48.4%, semimanufactured goods 17.0%, food and live animals 8.9%, chemicals and chemical products 6.8%, mineral fuels 4.7%, nonfuel materials 1.8%, beverages and tobacco 1.0%). *Major import sources:* Italy 37.7%; U.K. 12.9%; Germany 10.7%; France 6.3%; U.S. 3.2%.
Exports (1992): Lm 490,903,000 (machinery and transport equipment 55.9%, clothing and footwear 11.3%, reexports 8.0%, semimanufactured goods 6.4%, food and live animals 1.6%, beverages and tobacco 0.4%). *Major export destinations:* Italy 43.6%; Germany 14.6%; France 9.2%; U.S. 6.0%; U.K. 5.4%; Libya 4.0%; The Netherlands 1.8%.

Transport and communications

Transport. Railroads: none. Roads (1992): total length 988 mi, 1,588 km (paved 92%). Vehicles (1992): passenger cars 120,320; trucks and buses 27,978. Merchant marine (1992): vessels (100 gross tons and over) 889; total deadweight tonnage 17,073,207. Air transport (1991): passenger-mi 630,197,000, passenger-km 1,014,205,000; short ton-mi cargo 3,840,000, metric ton-km cargo 5,607,000; airports (1994) with scheduled flights 1.
Communications. Daily newspapers (1992): total number 3; total circulation 68,000; circulation per 1,000 population 192. Radio (1993): 90,000 receivers (1 per 4.0 persons). Television (1993): 146,107 receivers (1 per 2.5 persons). Telephones (1992): 201,780 (1 per 1.8 persons).

Education and health

Education (1991–92)				
	schools	teachers	students	student/ teacher ratio
Primary (age 5–10)	168	1,455[10]	35,626	25.4[10]
Secondary (age 11–17)	46	1,594[10]	24,462	16.2[10]
Voc., teacher tr.	31	738	7,093	9.6
Higher	1	320	3,150	9.8

Educational attainment (1967). Percentage of economically active population having: no formal schooling 10.8%; primary education 60.4%; lower secondary 3.4%; upper secondary 17.6%; technical secondary 3.9%; postsecondary and higher 3.9%. *Literacy* (1985): total population age 15 and over literate 250,419 (96.0%); males literate 121,899 (96.2%); females literate 128,520 (95.9%).
Health (1993): physicians 860 (1 per 424 persons); hospital beds (1991) 3,326 (1 per 107 persons); infant mortality rate per 1,000 live births (1992) 10.3.
Food (1988–90): daily per capita caloric intake 3,169 (vegetable products 72%, animal products 28%); 128% of FAO recommended minimum requirement.

Military

Total active duty personnel (1993): 1,650 (army 100%). *Military expenditure as percentage of GNP* (1991): 0.8% (world 4.2%); per capita expenditure U.S.$61.

---

[1]The Maltese lira is tied to the currencies of several principal trading partners. [2]Data are reported according to census regions as of January 1993; in late 1993 new administrative districts (Local Councils) were created. [3]January 1. [4]Detail does not add to total given because of rounding. [5]Dwellings completed. [6]Pub. admin., defense includes Public utilities. [7]Finance includes income from property. [8]Includes 5,816 unemployed. [9]Import figures are f.o.b. in balance of trade and c.i.f. for commodities and trading partners. [10]1990–91.

Marshall Islands

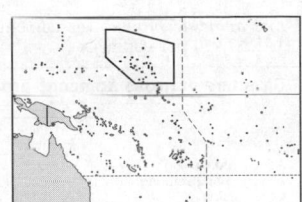

Official name: Majōl (Marshallese); Republic of the Marshall Islands (English).
Form of government: unitary republic with two legislative houses (Council of Iroij [12][1]; Nitijela [33]).
Head of state and government: President.
Capital. Majuro.
Official languages: Marshallese (Kajin-Majōl); English.
Official religion: none.
Monetary unit: 1 U.S. dollar (U.S.$) = 100 cents; valuation (Oct. 7, 1994) 1 £ = U.S.$1.59.

Area and population

Election districts	area sq mi	sq km	population 1988 census
Ailinglaplap	5.67	14.69	1,715
Ailuk	2.07	5.36	488
Arno	5.00	12.95	1,656
Aur	2.17	5.62	438
Bikini	2.32	6.00	10
Ebon	2.22	5.75	741
Enewotak and Ujelang	2.93	7.59	715
Jabat	0.22	0.57	112
Jaluit	4.38	11.34	1,709
Kili	0.36	0.93	602
Kwajalein	6.33	16.39	9,311
Lae	0.56	1.45	319
Lib	0.36	0.93	115
Likiep	3.97	10.28	482
Majuro	3.75	9.71	19,664
Maloelap	3.79	9.82	796
Mejit	0.72	1.86	445
Mili	6.15	15.93	854
Namorik	1.07	2.77	814
Namu	2.42	6.27	801
Rongelap	3.07	7.95	0
Ujae	0.72	1.86	448
Utrik	0.94	2.43	409
Wotho	1.67	4.32	90
Wotje	3.16	8.18	646
Other atolls	4.05	10.49	0
TOTAL	70.07	181.48[2]	43,380

Demography
Population (1994): 54,000.
Density (1994): persons per sq mi 770.7, persons per sq km 297.6.
Urban-rural (1988): urban 64.5%; rural 35.5%.
Sex distribution (1994): male 51.01%; female 48.99%.
Age breakdown (1994): under 15, 50.4%; 15–29, 25.4%; 30–44, 14.2%; 45–59, 6.2%; 60–74, 3.0%; 75 and over, 0.8%.
Population projection: (2000) 68,400; (2010) 100,000.
Doubling time: 18 years.
Ethnic composition (nationality; 1988): Marshallese 96.9%; other Pacific islanders 1.7%; Filipino 0.5%; all other 0.9%.
Religious affiliation (1973): Protestant 90.1%; Roman Catholic 8.5%; other 1.4%.
Major cities (1988): Dalap-Uliga-Darrit 14,649; Ebeye 8,324; no other urban localities.

Vital statistics
Birth rate per 1,000 population (1993): 46.6 (world avg. 26.0).
Death rate per 1,000 population (1993): 7.9 (world avg. 9.2).
Natural increase rate per 1,000 population (1993): 38.7 (world avg. 16.8).
Total fertility rate (avg. births per childbearing woman; 1993): 7.0.
Marriage rate per 1,000 population: n.a.
Divorce rate per 1,000 population: n.a.
Life expectancy at birth (1993): male 61.3 years; female 64.4 years.
Major causes of death per 100,000 population (1988–91)[3]: circulatory diseases 87.6; infectious and parasitic diseases 74.4; respiratory diseases 62.8; accidents, injuries, and violence 37.5; digestive diseases 37.5; malignant neoplasms (cancers) 27.6.

National economy
Budget (1990–91). Revenue: U.S.$34,704,774 (U.S. government grants 35.3%, income tax 21.4%, import tax 17.0%, fishing rights 5.3%, fuel taxes 1.5%). Expenditures: U.S.$44,128,786 (health services 18.9%, education 17.5%, public works and social programs 12.5%, transportation and communications 4.4%, internal security 3.4%).
Production (metric tons except as noted). Agriculture, forestry, fishing (1991): copra 5,545, fruits 1,809 (of which pandanus 836, breadfruit 645, bananas 264, papaya 64), tubers 1,500 (of which taro 1,300, sweet potatoes 182), vegetables 136 (of which cabbage 36, pumpkins 36); livestock consists mostly of swine and poultry; roundwood, n.a.; fish catch (1989) 12,193[4]. Mining and quarrying: high-grade phosphate mining on Ailinglaplap Atoll, quarrying of sand and aggregate for local construction only. Manufacturing: n.a.; however, coconut oil and processed (mostly frozen) fish are the most important products; the manufacture of handicrafts and personal items (clothing, mats, boats, etc.) by individuals is also important. Construction: n.a. Energy production (consumption): electricity (kW-hr; 1991) 45,759,000

(45,759,000); coal, none (n.a.); gasoline, oil, and lubricants (barrels; 1988)[5] n.a. (84,588); natural gas, none (n.a.).
Public debt (external, outstanding): n.a.
Gross domestic product (1991): U.S.$75,694,000 (U.S.$1,577 per capita).

Structure of private (nongovernmental) gross sales and labour force

	1981 in value U.S.$'000	% of total value	1988 labour force	% of labour force
Agriculture	32.5	0.1	2,150	18.7
Mining	...	...	2	—
Manufacturing	155.3	0.5	945	8.2
Public utilities	—	—	82	0.7
Construction	2,235.6	7.5	1,076	9.4
Transportation and communications	1,682.7	5.6	537	4.7
Trade, restaurants, hotels	25,150.6	83.8	1,394	12.1
Finance, insurance, real estate	510.5	1.7	833	7.3
Public administration	}	}	3,035	26.4
Services	235.9	0.8		
Other			1,434[6]	12.5[6]
TOTAL	30,003.1	100.0	11,488	100.0

Land use (1989)[7]: forested 22.5%; meadows and pastures 13.5%; agricultural and under permanent cultivation 33.1%; other 30.9%.
Household income and expenditure. Average household size (1988) 8.7; income per household (1979) U.S.$3,366; sources of income: n.a.; expenditure (1982): food 57.7%, housing 15.6%, clothing 12.0%, personal effects and other 14.7%.
Population economically active (1988): total 11,488; activity rate of total population 26.5% (participation rates: over age 14, 54.1%; female 30.1%; unemployed 12.5%).

Price and earnings indexes (1990 = 100)

	1987	1988	1989	1990	1991	1992	1993
Consumer price index	93.6	97.1	99.4	100.0	103.4	116.8	119.5
Earnings index	...	...	...	...	...	...	...

Tourism (1992): receipts from visitors U.S.$4,000,000; expenditures by nationals abroad, n.a.

Foreign trade

Balance of trade (current prices)

	1986	1987	1988	1989	1990	1991
U.S.$'000,000	−29.4	−31.6	−31.7	−41.9	−53.9	−53.5
% of total	92.7%	89.2%	88.3%	89.4%	94.0%	90.3%

Imports (1991): U.S.$56,442,000 (food and live animals 24.3%, machinery and transport equipment 16.2%, mineral fuels and lubricants 11.1%, beverages and tobacco 9.9%, manufactured goods 9.7%). *Major import sources.* United States 58.5%; Guam 16.3%; Japan 9.6%; Australia 1.6%.
Exports (1991): U.S.$2,890,000 (crude coconut oil 48.3%, frozen fish 27.0%, live animals 17.9%, trochus shells 6.1%). *Major export destinations* (1983): United States 79.4%; other 20.6%.

Transport and communications
Transport. Railroads: none. Roads: n.a. Vehicles (1991): passenger cars 1,332; trucks and buses 75. Merchant marine (1992): vessels (100 gross tons and over) 35; total deadweight tonnage 4,182,356. Air transport (1990): passenger-km 52,000,000; metric ton-km cargo 3,000; airports (1994) with scheduled flights 23.
Communications. Daily newspapers (1993): there are no dailies, only weeklies, of which there are two with a total circulation of over 10,000. Radio (1990): n.a.; but there are two radio stations. Television (1990): n.a.; but there are two television stations. Telephones (1992): 980 (1 per 51 persons).

Education and health

Education (1991–92)

	schools	teachers	students	student/ teacher ratio
Primary (age 6–14)	102	515	12,248	23.8
Secondary (age 15–18)	8[8]	137	2,215	16.2
Voc., teacher tr.	...	...	...	...
Higher	...	...	...	...

Educational attainment (1988). Percentage of population age 25 and over having: no grade completed 5.1%; elementary education 43.2%; secondary 39.7%; higher 11.4%; not stated 0.6%. *Literacy* (latest): total population age 15 and over literate 19,377 (91.2%); males literate 9,993 (92.4%); females literate 9,384 (90.0%).
Health: physicians (1987) 19 (1 per 2,207 persons); hospital beds (1985) 54 (1 per 698 persons); infant mortality rate per 1,000 live births (1991) 53.0.
Food: daily per capita caloric intake, n.a.

Military
Under the 1984 Compact of Free Association, the United States provides for the defense of the Republic of the Marshall Islands.

[1]Council of Iroij is an advisory body only. [2]Detail does not add to total given because of rounding. [3]Registered deaths only. [4]Total for foreign vessels only, including 6,762 metric tons caught by Japanese vessels. [5]Imports only. [6]Includes 1,432 unemployed. [7]Data are for the former Trust Territory of the Pacific Islands. [8]1986–87.

Martinique

Official name: Département de
la Martinique (Department of
Martinique).
Political status: overseas department
(France) with two legislative houses
(General Council [45]; Regional
Council [41]).
Chief of state: President of France.
Heads of government: Commissioner
of the Republic (for France);
President of the General Council
(for Martinique); President of the
Regional Council (for Martinique).
Capital: Fort-de-France.
Official language: French.
Official religion: none.
Monetary unit: 1 French franc (F) = 100
centimes; valuation (Oct. 7, 1994)
1 U.S.$ = F 5.27; 1 £ = F 8.38.

Area and population

Arrondissements	Capitals	area		population
		sq mi	sq km	1990 census
Fort-de-France	Fort-de-France	147	381	187,275
Le Marin	Le Marin	158	409	93,411
La Trinité	La Trinité	131	338	78,893
TOTAL		436	1,128	359,579

Demography

Population (1994): 381,000.
Density (1994): persons per sq mi 873.8, persons per sq km 338.4.
Urban-rural (1990): urban 80.5%; rural 19.5%.
Sex distribution (1990): male 48.36%; female 51.64%.
Age breakdown (1990): under 15, 23.1%; 15–29, 28.9%; 30–44, 20.5%; 45–59,
13.5%; 60–74, 9.7%; 75 and over, 4.3%.
Population projection: (2000) 415,000; (2010) 458,000.
Doubling time: 62 years.
Ethnic composition (1983): mulatto 93.7%; French (metropolitan and Mar-
tinique white) 2.6%; East Indian 1.7%; other 2.0%.
Religious affiliation (1993): Roman Catholic 84.6%; other (mostly Seventh-day
Adventist, Jehovah's Witness, Hindu, syncretist, and nonreligious) 15.4%.
Major urban areas (1990): Fort-de-France 100,072; Le Lamentin 30,026;
Schoelcher 19,825; Sainte-Marie 19,683; Le Robert 17,675.

Vital statistics

Birth rate per 1,000 population (1993): 15.8 (world avg. 26.0); (1992) legiti-
mate 34.1%; illegitimate 65.9%.
Death rate per 1,000 population (1993): 6.0 (world avg. 9.2).
Natural increase rate per 1,000 population (1993): 9.8 (world avg. 16.8).
Total fertility rate (avg. births per childbearing woman; 1993): 1.9.
Marriage rate per 1,000 population (1993): 4.2.
Divorce rate per 1,000 population (1993): 0.9.
Life expectancy at birth (1993): male 74.7 years; female 81.0 years.
Major causes of death per 100,000 population (1990): diseases of the circula-
tory system 208.0; malignant neoplasms (cancers) 135.5; accidents, poison-
ing, and violence 54.8; diseases of the digestive system 31.3; endocrine and
metabolic disorders 30.7.

National economy

Budget (1991). Revenue: F 1,755,000,000 (general receipts from French central government and local administrative bodies 49.2%, tax receipts 29.2%,
new loans 11.6%, public-works subsidies 6.0%). Expenditures: F 1,755,000,-
000 (health and social assistance 35.0%, improvements to public works
and property 34.0%, other administrative services 16.2%, debt amortization
3.3%).
Public debt (external, outstanding; 1987)[1]: U.S.$30,000,000.
Production (metric tons except as noted). Agriculture, forestry, fishing (1992):
bananas 255,000, sugarcane 98,443, pineapples 16,182, plantains 10,000,
yams 9,000, cucumbers 4,000, sweet potatoes 3,000, tomatoes 3,000, melons
2,300, avocados 1,000, limes 576, flowers and foliage 139[2], pimientos 170[2,3];
livestock (number of live animals) 63,000 sheep, 49,000 pigs, 35,000 cattle;
roundwood (1991) 12,000 cu m; fish catch 4,553. Mining and quarrying
(1992): pumice 140,000; sand and gravel for local construction. Manufacturing (1993): cement 233,653; processed pineapples 17,276; sugar 6,980; rum
99,001 hectolitres; other products include clothing, fabricated metals, and
yawls and sails. Construction (buildings authorized; 1993): residential permits 5,713; nonresidential 85,279 sq m. Energy production (consumption):
electricity (kW-hr; 1992) 762,000,000 (700,000,000); coal, none (none); crude
petroleum (barrels; 1992) none (5,409,000); petroleum products (metric
tons; 1992) 493,180 (493,180); natural gas, none (none).
Household income and expenditure. Average household size (1990) 3.3; income per household (1989) F 147,150 (U.S.$24,525); sources of income
(1989): wages and salaries 80%, other 20%; expenditure (1993): food and
beverages 32.1%, transportation and communications 20.7%, housing and
energy 10.6%, household durable goods 9.4%, clothing and footwear 8.0%,
education and recreation 5.4%, health care 5.2%, other 8.6%.
Tourism (1992): receipts from visitors U.S.$282,000,000; expenditures by na-
tionals abroad, n.a.

Gross domestic product (at current market prices; 1989): U.S.$2,835,000,000
(U.S.$7,970 per capita).

Structure of gross domestic product and labour force

	1989		1990	
	in value F '000,000	% of total value	labour force	% of labour force
Agriculture, fishing	1,063	6.3	8,445	5.2
Mining, manufacturing	1,337	8.0	9,706	6.0
Construction	817	4.9	9,298	5.7
Public utilities	475	2.8		
Transportation and communications	1,008	6.0	6,673	4.1
Trade, restaurants, hotels	3,463	20.7	13,965	8.6
Finance, real estate, insurance	891	5.3	26,489	16.2
Pub. admin. and defense	4,922	29.4	35,541	21.8
Services	2,873	17.2		
Other	−110[4]	−0.7[4]	52,900[5]	32.4[5]
TOTAL	16,738[6]	100.0[6]	163,017	100.0

Population economically active (1990): total 164,870[7]; activity rate of total
population 45.9% (participation rates: ages 15–64 68.1%; female 47.5%;
unemployed 32.1%).

Price and earnings indexes (1985 = 100)

	1987	1988	1989	1990	1991	1992	1993
Consumer price index[8]	106.3	108.8	112.4	116.8	118.3	126.6	131.0
Monthly earnings index[9]	105.2	108.0	111.0	115.9	118.8	122.8	128.3

Land use (1991): forested 44.3%; meadows and pastures 17.9%; agricultural
and under permanent cultivation 18.9%; other 18.9%.

Foreign trade[10]

Balance of trade (current prices)

	1988	1989	1990	1991	1992	1993
F '000,000	−6,551	−6,732	−7,970	−7,934	−7,982	−7,744
% of total	73.7%	73.5%	72.7%	78.4%	75.6%	78.0%

Imports (1993): F 8,814,145,000 (food products 21.4%, machinery 15.8%,
chemical products 11.6%, transport equipment 11.6%, metal manufactures
5.8%). *Major import sources:* France 61.6%; United States 2.9%; Venezuela
1.1%; Guadeloupe 1.1%; other Caribbean 1.8%.
Exports (1993): F 1,081,644,000 (food products 59.0%, refined petroleum
19.5%, machinery 6.3%, chemical products 4.0%). *Major export destinations:*
France 65.1%; Guadeloupe 28.6%; French Guiana 2.6%.

Transport and communications

Transport. Railroads: none. Roads (1992): total length 1,286 mi, 2,069 km
(paved [1988] 75%). Vehicles (1985): passenger cars 135,269; trucks and
buses 7,328. Merchant marine (1992): vessels (100 gross tons and over) 6;
total deadweight tonnage 1,121. Air transport (1993): passenger arrivals and
departures 1,506,730; cargo unloaded 7,635 metric tons, cargo loaded 5,809
metric tons; airports (1994) with scheduled flights 2.
Communications. Daily newspapers (1990): total number 1; total circulation
32,000; circulation per 1,000 population 88. Radio (1993): total number
of receivers 60,000 (1 per 6.3 persons). Television (1993): total number
of receivers 65,000 (1 per 5.8 persons). Telephones (1992): 140,752[11] (1
per 2.6 persons).

Education and health

Education (1992–93)

	schools	teachers	students	student/ teacher ratio
Primary (age 6–11)	282	2,711	33,170	12.2
Secondary (age 12–18)	79	3,830	47,295	12.3
Vocational				
Higher	1	71	3,670	51.7

Educational attainment (1982). Percentage of population age 25 and over having: no formal schooling 9.8%; primary education 62.7%; secondary 21.2%;
higher 6.3%. *Literacy* (1982): total population age 15 and over literate 206,-
807 (92.5%); males literate 97,538 (91.8%); females literate 109,269 (93.2%).
Health (1991): physicians 625 (1 per 584 persons); hospital beds 3,747 (1 per
97 persons); infant mortality rate per 1,000 live births (1992) 6.2.
Food (1988–90): daily per capita caloric intake 2,768 (vegetable products 75%,
animal products 25%); 114% of FAO recommended minimum requirement.

Military

Total active duty personnel (1992): 8,200 French troops[12].

---

[1]Includes external long-term private debt not guaranteed by the government.
[2]Production for export only. [3]1990. [4]Imputed bank service charges less other items.
[5]Unemployed. [6]Detail does not add to total given because of rounding. [7]Includes military reserve personnel. [8]Figures are end-of-year unless otherwise footnoted. [9]Based
on monthly salaries of employees in commerce, banking, and government services.
[10]Imports c.i.f.; exports f.o.b. [11]Telephone lines. [12]Includes troops stationed in Guadeloupe and French Guiana.

Mauritania

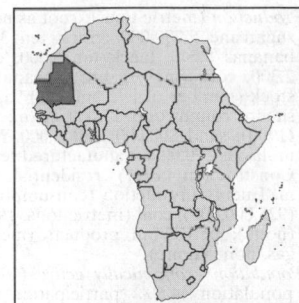

Official name: al-Jumhūrīyah al-Islāmīyah al-Mūrītānīyah (Arabic) (Islamic Republic of Mauritania).
Form of government: unitary multiparty republic with two legislative houses (Senate [56]; National Assembly [79]).
Head of state and government: President.
Capital: Nouakchott.
Official languages: Arabic[1].
Official religion: Islam.
Monetary unit: 1 ouguiya (UM) = 5 khoums; valuation (Oct. 7, 1994) 1 U.S.$ = UM 125.67; 1 £ = UM 196.69.

Area and population

Regions	Capitals	area sq mi	area sq km	population 1992 estimate
el-'Açâba	Kiffa	13,900	36,000	185,574
Adrar	Atar	83,100	215,300	62,906
Brakna	Aleg	14,000	37,100	207,590
Dakhlet Nouadhibou	Nouadhibou	11,600	30,000	83,246
Gorgol	Kaédi	5,400	14,000	201,301
Guidimaka	Sélibaby	4,000	10,000	129,797
Hodh ech-Chargui	Néma	64,000	166,000	234,011
Hodh el-Gharbi	'Ayoûn el-'Atroûs	22,000	57,000	175,089
Inchiri	Akjoujt	19,000	49,000	13,630
Tagant	Tidjikdja	36,000	93,000	67,939
Tiris Zemmour	Zouérate	98,600	255,300	37,534
Trarza	Rosso	26,000	67,000	217,867
District				
Nouakchott	Nouakchott	400	1,000	324,037
TOTAL		398,000	1,030,700	1,940,521

Demography

Population (1994): 2,069,000.
Density (1994): persons per sq mi 5.2, persons per sq km 2.0.
Urban-rural (1988): urban 39.1%; rural 60.9%.
Sex distribution (1990): male 49.41%; female 50.59%.
Age breakdown (1990): under 15, 44.6%; 15–29, 25.8%; 30–44, 15.5%; 45–59, 9.1%; 60–74, 4.2%; 75 and over, 0.7%.
Population projection: (2000) 2,467,000; (2010) 3,307,000.
Doubling time: 22 years.
Ethnic composition (1993): Moor 70.0% (of which about 40% "black" Moor [Haratin, or African Sudanic] and about 30% "white" Moor [Bidan, or Arab-Berber]); other black African 30.0% (including [1983] Wolof 6.8%, Tukulor 5.3%, Soninke 2.8%, Fulani 1.1%, other 2.5%).
Religious affiliation (1980): Muslim 99.4%; Christian 0.4%; other 0.2%.
Major cities (1992): Nouakchott 480,408; Nouadhibou 72,305; Kaédi 35,241; Kiffa 29,292[2]; Rosso 27,783[2].

Vital statistics

Birth rate per 1,000 population (1994): 48.0 (world avg. 26.0); legitimate, n.a.; illegitimate, n.a.
Death rate per 1,000 population (1994): 16.0 (world avg. 9.2).
Natural increase rate per 1,000 population (1994): 32.0 (world avg. 16.8).
Total fertility rate (avg. births per childbearing woman; 1994): 7.0.
Marriage rate per 1,000 population: n.a.
Divorce rate per 1,000 population: n.a.
Life expectancy at birth (1994): male 45.0 years; female 51.0 years.
Morbidity (notified cases of infectious disease per 100,000 population; 1984): enteritis and diarrhea 10,566; conjunctivitis 7,080; malaria 2,897; scarlet fever 2,476; measles 714.0; chicken pox 306.4.

National economy

Budget (1993). Revenue: UM 32,000,000,000 (1992; tax revenue 77.0%, of which import and export duties 35.7%, value-added tax 26.8%, excise tax 13.1%). Expenditures: UM 32,200,000,000 (1992; administrative expenses 26.1%; defense 15.0%; interest on debt 9.0%).
Tourism: receipts from visitors (1991) U.S.$13,000,000; expenditures by nationals abroad (1988) U.S.$27,000,000.
Land use (1991): forested 4.2%; meadows and pastures 38.3%; agricultural and under permanent cultivation 0.2%; desert 57.3%.
Production (metric tons except as noted). Agriculture, forestry, fishing (1992): sorghum 50,000, pulses 19,000, rice 18,000, dates 12,000, vegetables (including melons) 11,000, roots and tubers 6,000 (of which sweet potatoes 3,000, yams 3,000), millet 3,000, corn (maize) 2,000; livestock (number of live animals) 5,400,000 sheep, 3,600,000 goats, 1,400,000 cattle, 990,000 camels, 154,000 asses, 18,000 horses, 4,000,000 chickens; roundwood (1991) 13,000 cu m; fish catch (1992) 100,700. Mining and quarrying (1993): iron ore (gross weight) 9,362,000; gypsum 3,240. Manufacturing (1990): cow's milk 97,000; meat 44,000, of which fresh beef and veal 17,000, fresh mutton and lamb 6,000, goat meat 5,000; hides and skins 4,720; cheese 1,841; butter 680. Construction (1984): 42,478 sq m. Energy production (consumption): electricity (kW-hr; 1992) 146,000,000 (146,000,000); coal (metric tons; 1992) none (6,000); crude petroleum (barrels; 1992) none (6,802,000); petroleum products (metric tons; 1992) 825,000 (907,000); natural gas, none (n.a.).
Household income and expenditure. Average household size (1980) 5.0; income per household: n.a.; sources of income: n.a.; expenditure (1990): food

and beverages 74.5%, housing 9.2%, clothing and footwear 7.6%, health 0.8%, education 0.3%, other 7.6%.
Gross national product (at current market prices; 1992): U.S.$1,109,000,000 (U.S.$530 per capita).

Structure of gross domestic product and labour force

	1992 in value UM '000,000	1992 % of total value	1988 labour force	1988 % of labour force
Agriculture	26,240	26.2	225,238	38.5
Mining	10,625	10.6	6,322	1.1
Manufacturing	8,869	8.8	5,630	1.0
Public utilities	6,165	6.2	1,326	0.2
Construction			12,291	2.1
Transportation and communications	6,255	6.2	8,378	1.4
Trade and finance	13,860	13.8	73,451	12.5
Services	6,112	6.1	86,807	14.8
Pub. admin., defense	12,412	12.4		
Other (indirect taxes net of subsidies)	9,682	9.7	166,366[3]	28.4[3]
TOTAL	100,220	100.0	585,809	100.0

Population economically active (1990): total 678,000; activity rate of total population 33.5% (participation rates: over age 10, 49.7%; female 22.1%; unemployed [1988] 50.0%).

Price and earnings indexes (1990 = 100)

	1987	1988	1989	1990	1991	1992	1993
Consumer price index	82.0	83.1	93.8	100.0	105.6	116.3	127.2
Earnings index	...	...	...	...	...	...	...

Public debt (external, outstanding; 1992): U.S.$1,855,000,000.

Foreign trade[4]

Balance of trade (current prices)

	1987	1988	1989	1990	1991	1992
UM '000,000	+3,395	+4,576	+8,277	+3,838	+1,272	+1,657
% of total	5.7%	6.4%	12.4%	5.8%	1.8%	2.3%

Imports (1992): UM 35,362,000,000 (crude petroleum and petroleum products 10.7%, milk and dairy products 5.3%, sugar 5.2%, tea 4.2%, rice 3.9%, cement 1.9%). *Major import sources* (1990): France 45.7%; Belgium 9.8%; West Germany 9.1%; United States 7.4%; Spain 7.3%; Algeria 6.0%; China 5.9%; The Netherlands 4.1%; Japan 2.8%; Thailand 1.9%.
Exports (1992). UM 37,019,000,000 (1991; iron ore 50.6%, fish 49.4%). *Major export destinations* (1991): Japan 24.2%; Italy 16.4%; U.S.S.R. 11.5%; Belgium 10.5%; France 9.9%; Spain 8.6%; United Kingdom 5.2%; Côte d'Ivoire 3.1%; United States 2.3%; Cameroon 1.9%.

Transport and communications

Transport. Railroads (1992): route length 416 mi, 670 km; passenger-mi 4,350,000[5], passenger-km 7,000,000[5]; short ton-mi cargo 3,860,000,000, metric ton-km cargo 5,635,000,000. Roads (1992): total length 4,683 mi, 7,536 km (paved 24%). Vehicles (1991): passenger cars 10,000; trucks and buses 5,000. Merchant marine (1992): vessels (100 gross tons and over) 126; total deadweight tonnage 23,875. Air transport (1991)[6]: passenger-mi 173,000,000, passenger-km 278,000,000; short ton-mi cargo 11,000,000, metric ton-km cargo 16,000,000; airports (1994) with scheduled flights 10.
Communications. Daily newspapers (1993): total number 1; total circulation, n.a. Radio (1993): total number of receivers 300,000 (1 per 7.2 persons). Television (1993): total number of receivers 1,100 (1 per 1,974 persons). Telephones (1991): 17,000 (1 per 120 persons).

Education and health

Education (1991–92)

	schools	teachers	students	student/ teacher ratio
Primary (age 6–11)	1,309	3,967	187,202	47.2
Secondary (age 12–17)	56	1,905	36,882	19.4
Voc., teacher tr.	5	169	1,782	10.5
Higher	4	176	5,850	33.2

Educational attainment (1988): Percentage of population age 10 and over having: no formal schooling 60.9%; primary and incomplete secondary 30.9%; secondary 4.0%; higher 1.4%; other 2.8%. *Literacy* (1990): percentage of total population age 15 and over literate 34.0%; males literate 47.1%; females literate 21.4%.
Health: physicians (1991) 135 (1 per 14,259 persons); hospital beds (1988) 1,556 (1 per 1,217 persons); infant mortality rate per 1,000 live births (1994) 85.
Food (1988–90): daily per capita caloric intake 2,447 (vegetable products 81%, animal products 19%); 106% of FAO recommended minimum requirement.

Military

Total active duty personnel (1993): 15,600 (army 96.2%, navy 2.6%, air force 1.2%). *Military expenditure as percentage of GNP* (1992): 3.1% (world 4.9%); per capita expenditure U.S.$17.

---

[1]The 1991 constitution names Arabic as the official language and the following as national languages: Arabic, Fulani, Soninke, and Wolof. [2]1988. [3]Mostly unemployed. [4]Import figures are c.i.f. [5]1984. [6]Air Afrique traffic only.

Mauritius

Official name: Republic of Mauritius.
Form of government: republic with
  one legislative house (Legislative
  Assembly [70[1]]).
Chief of state: President.
Head of government: Prime Minister.
Capital: Port Louis.
Official language: English.
Official religion: none.
Monetary unit: 1 Mauritian rupee (Mau
  Re; plural Mau Rs) = 100 cents;
  valuation (Oct. 7, 1994) 1 U.S.$ = Mau
  Rs 17.70; 1 £ = Mau Rs 28.15.

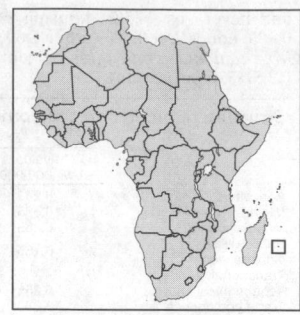

Area and population

Islands Districts/Dependencies	area sq mi	area sq km	population 1992[2] estimate
Mauritius			
Black River	720	1,865	1,043,294
Flacq	100	259	45,559
Grand Port	115	298	114,670
Moka	100	260	98,530
Pamplemousses	89	231	66,743
Plaines Wilhems	69	179	104,495
Port Louis	78	203	328,625
Rivière du Rempart	17	43	134,018
Savanne	57	148	88,691
	95	245	61,963
Mauritian dependencies			
Agalega[3]			
Cargados Carajos Shoals (Saint Brandon)[3]	27	71	170
Rodrigues[4]	40	104	34,379
TOTAL	788[5]	2,040[5]	1,077,843

Demography

Population (1994)[6]: 1,120,000.
Density (1994): persons per sq mi 1,421.7, persons per sq km 549.2.
Urban-rural (1991)[7]: urban 40.7%; rural 59.3%.
Sex distribution (1991): male 49.80%; female 50.20%.
Age breakdown (1991)[8]: under 15, 29.6%; 15–29, 28.5%; 30–44, 22.8%; 45–59, 10.9%; 60–74, 6.5%; 75 and over, 1.7%.
Population projection[6]: (2000) 1,207,000; (2010) 1,365,000.
Doubling time: 48 years.
Ethnic composition (1992): Indo-Pakistani 68.0%; Creole (mixed Caucasian, Indo-Pakistani, and African) 27.0%; Chinese 3.0%; white 2.0%.
Religious affiliation (1990): Hindu 50.6%; Roman Catholic 27.2%; Muslim 16.3%; Protestant 5.2%; Buddhist 0.3%; other 0.4%.
Major cities (1992): Port Louis 142,850; Beau Bassin–Rose Hill 94,299; Vacoas-Phoenix 92,072; Curepipe 74,738; Quatre Bornes 71,534.

Vital statistics

Birth rate per 1,000 population (1992): 21.1 (world avg. 26.0); (1985) legitimate 72.8%; illegitimate 27.2%.
Death rate per 1,000 population (1992): 6.5 (world avg. 9.2).
Natural increase rate per 1,000 population (1992): 14.6 (world avg. 16.8).
Total fertility rate (avg. births per childbearing woman; 1991): 2.3.
Marriage rate per 1,000 population (1992): 10.5.
Divorce rate per 1,000 population (1992)[7]: 0.7.
Life expectancy at birth (1989–91): male 65.6 years; female 73.4 years.
Major causes of death per 100,000 population (1992)[7]: diseases of the circulatory system 279.5; diseases of the respiratory system 67.0; malignant neoplasms (cancers) 62.5; homicide, suicide, and accidents 45.5.

National economy

Budget (1993–94). Revenue: Mau Rs 12,860,000,000 (tax revenue 89.0%, of which import and stamp duties 40.6%, income tax 13.2%, sales tax 9.3%). Expenditures: Mau Rs 12,730,000,000 (social services 35.6%, of which education, art, and culture 14.6%, social security 10.9%, health 8.2%; public-debt service 27.7%).
Tourism (1992): receipts from visitors U.S.$299,000,000; expenditures by nationals abroad U.S.$142,000,000.
Public debt (external, outstanding; 1992): U.S.$742,000,000.
Gross national product (at current market prices; 1993): U.S.$3,311,000,000 (U.S.$2,980 per capita).

Structure of gross domestic product and labour force

	1993 in value Mau Rs '000,000[9]	1993 % of total value	1993 labour force[10, 11]	1993 % of labour force[10, 11]
Agriculture	4,460	9.9	42,900	14.9
Mining	55	0.1	200	0.1
Manufacturing	10,005	22.3	107,000	37.1
Construction	3,505	7.8	14,000	4.8
Public utilities	1,180	2.6	3,600	1.2
Transportation and communications	5,430	12.1	13,800	4.8
Trade	7,805	17.4	19,800	6.9
Finance	5,415	12.1	...	...
Pub. admin., defense	4,515	10.1	73,800	25.6
Services	2,530	5.6		
Other	...	...	13,500	4.7
TOTAL	44,900	100.0	288,600	100.0[5]

Production (metric tons except as noted). Agriculture, forestry, fishing (1992): sugarcane 5,780,000, green tea 30,162, potatoes 19,155, tomatoes 10,275, bananas 8,540, black tea 6,000, cabbages 3,320, onions 3,240, pineapples 2,300, corn (maize) 1,850, peanuts (groundnuts) 1,190, tobacco 970; livestock (number of live animals) 95,000 goats, 34,000 cattle, 10,000 pigs, 7,000 sheep; roundwood 17,000 cu m; fish catch 18,200. Mining and quarrying (1990): sand 800,000, salt 3,000. Manufacturing (1991): raw sugar 611,340; molasses 170,000; manufactured tea 5,934; beer and stout 291,453 hectolitres. Construction (1991): residential 921,103 sq m; nonresidential 296,755 sq m. Energy production (consumption): electricity (kW-hr; 1992) 925,000,000 (925,000,000); coal (metric tons; 1992) none (62,000); crude petroleum, none (none); petroleum products (metric tons; 1992) none (388,000); natural gas, none (none).
Population economically active (1991)[7]: total 462,600; activity rate of total population 44.5% (participation rates: ages 15–64, 68.0%; female 34.9%; unemployed 10.6%).

Price and earnings indexes (1990 = 100)

	1987	1988	1989	1990	1991	1992	1993
Consumer price index	71.6	78.2	88.1	100.0	107.0	112.0	123.7
Monthly earnings index[11]	59.2	79.9	94.6	100.0	115.8	128.5	127.3

Household income and expenditure. Average household size (1990) 4.5[7]; income per household (1979) Mau Rs 15,540 (U.S.$2,430); sources of income (1990): salaries and wages 48.4%, entrepreneurial income 41.2%, transfer payments 10.4%; expenditure (1986–87)[12]: food, beverages, and tobacco 49.1%, housing 13.5%, transportation 9.3%, clothing and footwear 8.4%, recreation, entertainment, education and cultural services 6.0%, energy 5.7%, health care 3.0%, other 5.0%.
Land use (1991): forested 28.1%; meadows and pastures 3.4%; agricultural and under permanent cultivation 52.2%; other 16.3%.

Foreign trade[13]

Balance of trade (current prices)

	1988	1989	1990	1991	1992	1993
U.S.$'000,000	−167.8	−211.1	−280.0	−222.6	−170.8	−254.2
% of total	7.7%	9.6%	10.6%	8.4%	6.2%	8.9%

Imports (1992): Mau Rs 25,313,000,000 (manufactured goods classified chiefly by material 36.1%, machinery and transport equipment 22.6%, food 11.6%, mineral fuels and lubricants 7.6%, chemicals 7.5%, inedible crude materials excluding fuels 3.0%, animal and vegetable oils and fats 1.1%). *Major import sources:* France 13.3%; South Africa 12.9%; Japan 8.6%; United Kingdom 7.0%; Germany 5.4%; India 4.4%; Taiwan 4.4%; Hong Kong 4.2%.
Exports (1992): Mau Rs 20,072,000,000 (clothing and textiles 52.2%, sugar 28.2%, yarn 2.5%, diamonds and synthetic stones 1.6%). *Major export destinations:* United Kingdom 34.8%; France 21.0%; United States 12.5%; Germany 8.9%; Italy 4.7%.

Transport and communications

Transport. Railroads: none. Roads (1991): total length 1,138 mi, 1,831 km (paved 93%). Vehicles (1992): passenger cars 32,751; buses 2,097. Merchant marine (1992): vessels (100 gross tons and over) 35; total deadweight tonnage 152,197. Air transport (1993)[14]: passenger-mi 1,658,998,000, passenger-km 2,669,903,000; short ton-mi cargo 63,903,000, metric ton-km cargo 93,337,000; airports (1994) with scheduled flights 1.
Communications. Daily newspapers (1993): total number 7; total circulation 96,000; circulation per 1,000 population 87. Radio (1993): 250,000 receivers (1 per 4.4 persons). Television 156,850 receivers (1 per 7.1 persons). Telephones (1992): 100,200 (1 per 11 persons).

Education and health

Education (1992)

	schools	teachers[15]	students	student/ teacher ratio[15]
Primary (age 5–12)	283	6,389	129,738	20.2
Secondary (age 12–20)	122	3,949	83,784	20.5
Voc., teacher tr.	19	69[16]	2,052	...
Higher	2	382[17]	2,159	5.7[17]

Educational attainment (1990). Percentage of population age 25 and over having: no formal education 18.3%; incomplete primary 42.6%; primary 6.1%; incomplete secondary 18.0%; secondary 13.1%; higher 1.9%. *Literacy* (1990): percentage of total population age 15 and over literate 79.9%; males literate 85.2%; females literate 74.7%.
Health (1991): physicians 990 (1 per 1,098 persons); hospital beds 3,094 (1 per 351 persons); infant mortality rate per 1,000 live births 18.6.
Food (1988–90): daily per capita caloric intake 2,897 (vegetable products 87%, animal products 13%); 128% of FAO recommended minimum requirement.

Military

Total active duty personnel: none; however, a special 1,300-person paramilitary force ensures internal security. *Military expenditure as percentage of GNP* (1991): 0.4% (world 4.2%); per capita expenditure U.S.$9.

---

[1]Includes 8 nonelective seats. [2]January 1. [3]Administered directly from Port Louis. [4]Administered by resident commissioner assisted by local council. [5]Detail does not add to total given because of rounding. [6]Based on 1990 census figures. [7]Island of Mauritius only. [8]Excludes Agalega and Cargados Carajos Shoals. [9]At factor cost. [10]Employed persons in establishments employing 10 or more persons. [11]March. [12]Current weights of CPI components; Island of Mauritius only. [13]Import figures are f.o.b. in balance of trade and c.i.f. for commodities and trading partners. [14]Air Mauritius only. [15]1991. [16]1982. [17]1989.

Mexico

Official name: Estados Unidos
 Mexicanos (United Mexican States).
Form of government: federal republic
 with two legislative houses (Senate
 [128]; Chamber of Deputies [500]).
Chief of state and head of government:
 President.
Capital: Mexico City.
Official language: Spanish.
Official religion: none.
Monetary unit: 1 new peso[1] (Mex$) =
 100 centavos; valuation (Oct. 7, 1994)
 1 U.S.$ = Mex$3.42; 1 £ = Mex$5.44.

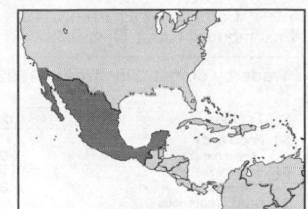

Area and population

States	Capitals	area sq mi	area sq km	population 1990 census
Aguascalientes	Aguascalientes	2,112	5,471	719,659
Baja California Norte	Mexicali	26,997	69,921	1,660,855
Baja California Sur	La Paz	28,369	73,475	317,764
Campeche	Campeche	19,619	50,812	535,185
Chiapas	Tuxtla Gutiérrez	28,653	74,211	3,210,496
Chihuahua	Chihuahua	94,571	244,938	2,441,873
Coahuila	Saltillo	57,908	149,982	1,972,340
Colima	Colima	2,004	5,191	428,510
Durango	Durango	47,560	123,181	1,349,378
Guanajuato	Guanajuato	11,773	30,491	3,982,593
Guerrero	Chilpancingo	24,819	64,281	2,620,637
Hidalgo	Pachuca	8,036	20,813	1,888,366
Jalisco	Guadalajara	31,211	80,836	5,302,689
México	Toluca	8,245	21,355	9,815,795
Michoacán	Morelia	23,138	59,928	3,548,199
Morelos	Cuernavaca	1,911	4,950	1,195,059
Nayarit	Tepic	10,417	26,979	824,643
Nuevo León	Monterrey	25,067	64,924	3,098,736
Oaxaca	Oaxaca	36,275	93,952	3,019,560
Puebla	Puebla	13,090	33,902	4,126,101
Querétaro	Querétaro	4,420	11,449	1,051,235
Quintana Roo	Chetumal	19,387	50,212	493,277
San Luis Potosí	San Luis Potosí	24,351	63,068	2,003,187
Sinaloa	Culiacán	22,521	58,328	2,204,054
Sonora	Hermosillo	70,291	182,052	1,823,606
Tabasco	Villahermosa	9,756	25,267	1,501,744
Tamaulipas	Ciudad Victoria	30,650	79,384	2,249,581
Tlaxcala	Tlaxcala	1,551	4,016	761,277
Veracruz	Jalapa (Xalapa)	27,683	71,699	6,228,239
Yucatán	Mérida	14,827	38,402	1,362,940
Zacatecas	Zacatecas	28,283	73,252	1,276,323
Federal District				
Distrito Federal	—	571	1,479	8,235,744
TOTAL		756,066	1,958,201	81,249,645

Demography

Population (1994): 89,998,000.
Density (1994): persons per sq mi 119.0, persons per sq km 46.0.
Urban-rural (1990): urban 71.3%; rural 28.7%.
Sex distribution (1992): male 48.77%; female 51.23%.
Age breakdown (1992): under 15, 37.8%; 15–29, 28.5%; 30–44, 18.2%; 45–59,
 8.9%; 60 and over, 6.6%.
Population projection: (2000) 102,555,000; (2010) 118,455,000.
Doubling time: 26 years.
Ethnic composition (1990): mestizo 60.0%; Amerindian 30.0%; Caucasian
 9.0%; other 1.0%.
Religious affiliation (1990): Roman Catholic 89.7%; Protestant (including
 Evangelical) 4.9%; Jewish 0.1%; other 2.1%; none 3.2%.
Major cities (1990): Mexico City 9,815,795; Guadalajara 1,650,042; Ciudad
 Netzahualcóyotl 1,255,456; Monterrey 1,068,996; Puebla 1,007,170; Juarez
 789,522; León 758,279; Tijuana 698,752; Mérida 523,422; Chihuahua 516,153.
Place of birth (1990): 93.1% native-born; 6.9% foreign-born and unknown.
Mobility (1990). Population 5 years and older living in the same state as in
 1985: 94.3%; different state 4.9%; unspecified 0.8%.
Households. Total households (1992) 17,152,000; distribution by size (1990):
 1 person 1.0%, 2 persons 4.3%, 3 persons 8.9%, 4 persons 14.9%, 5 persons
 17.4%, 6 persons 15.3%, 7 or more persons 38.2%. Family households (1990):
 17,064,507 (98.4%); nonfamily 1,039,738 (1.3%); unspecified 256,554 (0.3%).
Immigration (1987): permanent immigrants admitted 72,649.
Emigration (1992): legal immigrants into the United States 213,800.

Vital statistics

Birth rate per 1,000 population (1992): 31.7 (world avg. 26.0); (1983) legiti-
 mate 72.5%; illegitimate 27.5%.
Death rate per 1,000 population (1992): 4.6 (world avg. 9.2).
Natural increase rate per 1,000 population (1992): 27.1 (world avg. 16.8).
Total fertility rate (avg. births per childbearing woman; 1990): 3.7.
Marriage rate per 1,000 population (1992): 7.6.
Divorce rate per 1,000 population (1992): 0.6.
Life expectancy at birth (1990): male 66.5 years; female 73.1 years.
Major causes of death per 100,000 population (1992): diseases of the circu-
 latory system 99.1; accidents 68.2; endocrine and metabolic disorders 53.3;
 malignant neoplasms (cancers) 51.3; diseases of the respiratory system 44.9;
 diseases of the digestive system 39.8; infectious and parasitic diseases 27.9.

Social indicators

Access to services (1992). Proportion of dwellings having: electricity 89.3%;
 piped water supply 81.0%; drained sewage 66.1%.

Educational attainment (1992). Percentage of population age 15 and over
 having: no primary education 14.1%; some primary 22.3%; completed
 primary 20.7%; incomplete secondary 10.4%; complete secondary 24.2%;
 higher 8.3%.

Distribution of income (1983)

percentage of household income by quintile

1	2	3	4	5 (highest)
4.0	8.8	14.2	22.4	50.6

Quality of working life. Average workweek (1992): 45.7[2] hours. Annual rate
 (1992) per 100,000 insured workers for: temporary disability 6,426; indemni-
 fication for permanent injury 239; death 18. Labour stoppages (1992): 156,
 involving 91,424 workers. Average duration of journey to work: n.a. Method
 of transport: n.a. Rate per 1,000 workers of discouraged (unemployed no
 longer seeking work): n.a.
Social participation. Eligible voters participating in last national election
 (1991): c. 60%. Population participating in voluntary work: n.a. Trade union
 membership in total workforce: n.a. Practicing religious population in total
 affiliated population: national average of weekly attendance (1993) 11%;
 (1970) weekly 10% of urban dwellers, 25% of rural dwellers; yearly 55% of
 urban dwellers, 73% of rural dwellers.
Social deviance (1991). Criminal cases tried by local authorities per 100,000
 population for: murder 60.3; rape 22.4; other assault 301.0; theft 703.8.
 Incidence per 100,000 in general population of: alcoholism, n.a.; drug and
 substance abuse, n.a.[3]; suicide 1.72.
Leisure (1985). Favourite leisure activities (average daily paid attendance):
 cinema 582,416; sporting events 31,518; live theatre 16,400; museums and
 archaeological sites 12,169; bullfights 3,049.
Material well-being (1985). Households possessing: radio 96%; television 73%;
 washing machine 33%; automobile 29%; telephone 27%; refrigerator 23%.

National economy

Gross national product (1993): U.S.$325,170,000,000 (U.S.$3,750 per capita).

Structure of gross domestic product and labour force

	1993 in value Mex$'000,000[1, 4]	1993 % of total value	1992 labour force	1992 % of labour force
Agriculture	419.9	7.4	6,380,101	21.1
Mining	195.0	3.5	244,366	0.8
Manufacturing	1,261.7	22.4	5,441,899	18.0
Construction	304.7	5.4	2,294,208	7.6
Public utilities	86.5	1.5	138,544	0.5
Transportation and communications	404.2	7.2	1,129,780	3.7
Trade	1,447.0	25.6	6,215,741	20.5
Finance	642.5	11.4	1,128,511	3.7
Pub. admin., defense } Services	978.6	17.3	3,231,842 2,913,180	10.7 9.6
Other	−95.6[5]	−1.7[5]	1,143,428[6]	3.8[6]
TOTAL	5,644.5	100.0	30,261,606	100.0

Budget (1992). Revenue: Mex$180,170,000,000[1] (petroleum revenues 28.3%).
 Expenditures: Mex$164,211,000,000[1] (transfers 35.6%, wages and salaries
 26.5%, interest on public debt 22.2%).
Public debt (external, outstanding; 1992): U.S.$76,087,100,000.
Tourism (1992): receipts from visitors U.S.$6,641,000,000; expenditures by
 nationals abroad U.S.$3,964,700,000.

Manufacturing, mining, and construction enterprises (1988)

	no. of enter- prises	no. of employees ('000)	yearly wages as a % of avg. of all wages	value added (Mex$'000,000[1])
Manufacturing	138,835	2,640.5	97.5	20,950,900
Metal products	26,414	759.3	114.2	6,605,300
Chemicals	4,948	354.9	152.3	4,228,000
Food, beverages, and tobacco	50,454	543.7	86.4	3,378,700
Textiles and apparel	16,621	423.3	80.0	2,414,800
Iron and steel	871	100.4	128.2	1,332,400
Nonmetallic mineral products	14,343	150.9	98.6	1,177,700
Paper and printing	7,762	141.4	100.0	1,127,900
Wood and wood products	15,951	135.4	62.8	497,000
Nonelectrical machinery and transport equipment	7	7	...	7
Electrical machinery	7	7	...	7
Other manufactures	1,471	31.1	...	189,200
Mining	2,073	153.0	161.0	1,643,800
Construction	5,308	342.4	62.1	1,414,800

Production (metric tons except as noted). Agriculture, forestry, fishing (1993):
 sugarcane 41,652,000, corn (maize) 18,600,000, wheat 3,622,000, sorghum
 2,602,000, oranges 2,530,000, bananas 1,650,000, mangoes 1,130,000, avocados 786,000, dry beans 700,000, lemons 700,000, cantaloupes 647,000, apples
 580,000, barley 525,000, grapes 525,000, soybeans 520,000, rice 325,000,
 pineapples 300,000, strawberries 67,000, cottonseed 40,000, walnuts 23,000;
 livestock (number of live animals) 30,649,000 cattle, 16,832,000 pigs, 11,-
 066,000 goats, 6,185,000 horses, 6,000,000 turkeys, 5,816,000 sheep, 3,210,000
 mules, 3,190,000 asses, 285,000,000 chickens; roundwood (1992) 22,966,000
 cu m; fish catch (1992) 1,125,756, of which sardines 323,832. Mining and
 quarrying (metal content of ores; 1993): iron ore 5,850,414; zinc 328,223;
 copper 293,401; lead 196,337; manganese 121,226; silver 2,288; gold 10.23;
 (nonmetals; 1993) salt 7,395,152[8]; gypsum 2,960,126[8]; sulfur 884,830; fluorite 301,615; barite 149,647. Manufacturing (gross value of production in
 Mex$'000[1]; 1992): machinery and equipment 74,385,052; food, beverages,
 and tobacco products 52,423,025; chemical products 43,431,256; metal products 21,692,652; mineral products 13,719,891; paper and paper products
 8,813,992; textiles 8,609,539. Construction (gross value of new construction,
 in Mex$'000,000[1]; 1985): residential 154,835; nonresidential 168,096.

Trade and service enterprises (1988)

	no. of establish-ments	no. of employees	yearly wage as a % of avg. of all wages[9]	annual income (Mex$'000,000[1])
Trade	749,827	2,087,945	...	143,925,445
Wholesale	39,162	401,137	...	54,068,677
Retail	710,665	1,686,808	...	89,856,768
Boutiques (excluding food products)	270,137	712,130	...	33,492,036
Food and tobacco speciality stores	410,111	686,177	...	20,249,541
Automobile, tire, and auto parts dealers	21,222	117,649	...	15,159,881
Small supermarkets and grocery stores	5,832	100,167	...	10,298,664
Gasoline stations	2,458	26,588	...	6,279,858
Other	905	44,097	...	4,376,788
Services	410,214	1,701,784	85.2	34,040,415
Professional services	27,731	276,451	77.9	7,447,871
Food and beverage services	116,628	381,251	...	6,108,983
Transp. and travel agencies	2,985	22,012	133.4	939,798
Lodging	7,671	125,614	...	2,886,551
Automotive repair	65,839	174,738	...	2,309,821
Educational services (private)	10,913	153,034	134.3	1,810,869
Medical and social assistance	46,205	110,215	206.4	1,681,172
Amusement services (cinemas and theatres)	4,029	36,006	148.9	2,431,861
Recreation	8,262	40,418	...	584,315
Other repair	47,767	80,068	...	682,882
Commercial and professional organizations	4,753	44,588	77.9	624,443
Other	67,431	257,389	49.9	6,541,849

Energy production (consumption): electricity (kW-hr; 1992) 131,501,000,-000 (120,709,000,000); coal (metric tons; 1992) 6,539,000 (6,932,000); crude petroleum (barrels; 1992) 975,000,000 (968,000,000); petroleum products (metric tons; 1992) 74,844,000 (80,275,000); natural gas (cu m; 1992) 21,826,-000,000 (24,109,000,000).

Population economically active (1992): total 30,261,606; activity rate of total population 35.9% (participation rates: ages 12 and over, 51.6%; female 29.4%; unemployed 2.0%).

Price and earnings indexes (1990 = 100)

	1987	1988	1989	1990	1991	1992	1993
Consumer price index	30.7	65.8	79.0	100.0	122.7	141.7	155.5
Monthly earnings index	27.0	57.3	76.6	100.0	129.1	292.9	164.7

Household income and expenditure. Average household size (1992) 4.8; income per household (1989) Mex$3,461[1] (U.S.$1,384); sources of income (1992): wages and salaries 61.5%, property and entrepreneurship 29.1%, transfer payments 7.8%, other 1.6%; expenditure (1991): food, beverages, and tobacco 34.9%, housing (includes household furnishings) 23.3%, transportation and communications 11.5%, clothing and footwear 7.3%, recreation and entertainment 4.9%, health and medical services 4.1%.

Financial aggregates[1, 10]

	1988	1989	1990	1991	1992	1993	1994 (8 mo.)
Exchange rate, Mex$ per:							
U.S. dollar	2.273	2.462	2.813	3.018	3.095	3.116	3.401
£	4.049	4.036	5.020	5.114	5.464	4.680	5.255
SDR	3.070	3.471	4.190	4.393	4.284	4.266	4.910
International reserves (U.S.$)							
Total (excl. gold; '000,000)	5,279	6,329	9,863	17,726	18,942	25,110	25,855[11]
SDRs ('000,000)	394	383	417	586	548	223	113
Reserve pos. in IMF ('000,000)	—	—	—	—	—	—	—
Foreign exchange	4,885	5,946	9,446	17,140	18,394	24,886	25,720[11]
Gold ('000,000 fine troy oz)	2.56	1.03	0.92	0.92	0.69	0.48	0.47[11]
% world reserves	0.27	0.11	0.10	0.10	0.07	0.05	0.05[11]
Interest and prices							
Treasury bill rate	61.95	45.01	34.76	19.28	15.62	15.03	17.07
Balance of payments (U.S.$'000,000)							
Balance of visible trade, of which:	+1,752	−645	−4,433	−11,063	−20,677	−18,891	...
Imports, f.o.b.	−18,905	−23,410	−31,271	−38,184	−48,193	−48,924	...
Exports, f.o.b.	20,657	22,765	26,838	27,121	27,516	30,033	...
Balance of invisibles	−691	−4,603	−16,153	−24,346	−43,488	−42,281	...
Balance of payments, current account	−2,443	−3,958	−7,117	−13,283	−22,811	−23,390	...

Land use (1992): forested 21.5%; meadows and pastures 39.0%; agricultural and under permanent cultivation 13.0%; other 26.5%.

Foreign trade

Balance of trade (current prices)

	1988	1989	1990	1991	1992	1993
Mex$'000,000,000	+4,635.0	−863.8	−7,494.0	−27,746	−57,138	−53,615
% of total	5.2%	6.0%	4.7%	14.4%	25.1%	22.2%

Imports (1992): U.S.$62,129,400,000 (metallic products, machinery, and equipment 54.3%; chemical products 7.1%; iron and steel 5.6%; food, beverages, and tobacco 5.4%; textiles and clothing 4.7%). *Major import sources:* U.S. 71.4%; Japan 4.9%; Germany 4.0%; France 2.1%; Brazil 1.8%; Canada 1.7%; Italy 1.6%; Spain 1.4%.
Exports (1992): U.S.$46,195,600,000 (metallic products, machinery, and equipment 51.3%, of which machinery and electrical 33.4%, automobile 8.6%; crude petroleum 16.1%; chemical products 5.0%; processed food and beverages 3.0%). *Major export destinations:* U.S. 81.3%; Spain 2.6%; Japan

1.9%; Canada 1.7%; France 1.2%; Germany 1.1%; Brazil 0.9%; Belgium-Luxembourg 0.6%; U.K. 0.5%.

Trade by commodity group (1992)

SITC group	imports U.S.$'000,000	%	exports U.S.$'000,000	%
00 Food and live animals	4,096	8.6	2,681	9.8
01 Beverages and tobacco	315	0.6	331	1.2
02 Crude materials, excluding fuels	2,431	5.1	1,052	3.9
03 Mineral fuels, lubricants, and related materials	1,675	3.5	8,114	29.8
04 Animal and vegetable oils, fats, and waxes	383	0.8	—	—
05 Chemicals and related products, n.e.s.	4,397	9.2	2,079	7.6
06 Basic manufactures	6,655	13.9	3,105	11.4
07 Machinery and transport equipment	23,012	48.1	8,604	31.6
08 Miscellaneous manufactured articles	4,870	10.1	1,152	4.2
09 Goods not classified by kind	44	0.1	58	0.2
TOTAL[12]	47,878	100.0	27,207[13]	100.0[13]

Direction of trade (1992)

	imports U.S.$'000,000	%	exports U.S.$'000,000	%
Western Hemisphere	43,433	74.2	36,905	86.4
United States	40,598	69.3	32,624	76.4
Latin America and the Caribbean	2,222	3.8	2,074	4.8
Canada	613	1.1	2,207	5.2
Europe	8,305	14.2	3,557	8.3
EEC	7,305	12.5	3,340	7.8
EFTA	907	1.6	159	0.4
U.S.S.R.	22	—	24	—
Other Europe	71	0.1	34	0.1
Asia	6,438	11.0	1,924	4.5
Japan	3,805	6.5	1,130	2.6
Africa	121	0.2	55	0.2
Other	248	0.4	250	0.6
TOTAL	58,545	100.0	42,700[13]	100.0

Transport and communications

Transport. Railroads (1993): route length 12,747 mi, 20,515 km; passenger-mi 2,408,000,000, passenger-km 3,875,000,000; short ton-mi cargo 23,973,000,000, metric ton-km cargo 35,001,000,000. Roads (1992): total length 151,309 mi, 243,509 km (paved 35%[14]). Vehicles (1992): passenger cars 7,497,128; trucks and buses 3,607,282. Merchant marine (1992): vessels (100 gross tons and over) 635; total deadweight tonnage 1,495,311. Air transport (1992)[15]: passenger-mi 11,901,700,000, passenger-km 19,154,000,000; short ton-mi cargo 1,240,982,000, metric ton-km cargo 1,811,802,000; airports (1994) 57.
Communications. Daily newspapers (1990): total number 285; total circulation 11,256,000[16]; circulation per 1,000 population 142[16]. Radio (1993): 16,325,-000 receivers (1 per 5.5 persons). Television (1991): 12,350,000 receivers (1 per 6.7 persons). Telephones (1992): 11,128,000 (1 per 7.6 persons).

Education and health

Education (1992–93)

	schools	teachers	students	student/teacher ratio
Primary (age 6–12)	86,636	481,466	14,500,000	30.1
Secondary (age 12–18)	25,131	352,865	5,980,000	16.9
Voc., teacher tr.	6,571	77,347	1,076,700	13.9
Higher	1,832	128,212	1,256,100	9.8

Literacy (1992): total population age 15 and over literate 45,050,633 (85.9%); males literate 22,181,999 (88.7%); females literate 22,868,634 (83.5%).
Health (1991): physicians 97,506 (1 per 885 persons); hospital beds 63,103 (1 per 1,367 persons); infant mortality rate per 1,000 live births (1992) 41.0.
Food (1988–90): daily per capita caloric intake 3,062 (vegetable products 82%, animal products 18%); 131% of FAO recommended minimum requirement.

Military

Total active duty personnel (1994): 175,000 (army 74.3%, navy 21.1%, air force 4.6%). *Military expenditure as percentage of GNP* (1991): 0.4% (world 4.2%); per capita expenditure U.S.$13.

[11] new peso = 1,000 (old) pesos; the (old) peso was withdrawn at the beginning of 1995. [2]Manufacturing only. [3]Through 1982, cannabis remained the most abused drug. [4]In constant 1980 prices. [5]Imputed bank service charge. [6]Unemployed. [7]Included in Metal products. [8]1992. [9]1984. [10]Exchange rates and treasury bill rates are expressed in period averages; international reserves are expressed in end-of-period rates. [11]End of March. [12]Totals include adjustments of unspecified nature. [13]Detail does not add to total given because of rounding. [14]1989. [15]All scheduled traffic of Mexicana and AeroMexico airlines. [16]1986.

Micronesia, Federated States of

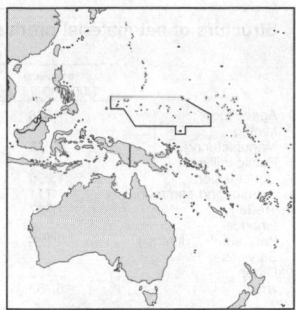

Official name: Federated States of Micronesia.
Political status: federal republic in free association with the United States with one legislative house (National Congress [14])[1].
Head of state and government: President.
Capital: Palikir, on Pohnpei.
Official language: none.
Official religion: none.
Monetary unit: 1 U.S. dollar (U.S.$) = 100 cents; valuation (Oct. 7, 1994) 1 £ = U.S.$1.59.

Area and population

States Major Islands	area		population
	sq mi	sq km	1991 census
Chuuk (Truk)	49.1	127.2	48,853
Weno (Moen) Islands	7.0	18.1	15,253[2]
Kosrae	42.3	109.6	7,435
Kosrae Island	42.3	109.6	7,435
Pohnpei	133.3	345.2	33,346
Pohnpei Island	129.0	334.1	33,346
Yap	45.9	118.9	10,886
Yap Island	38.7	100.2	6,650[3]
TOTAL	270.8[3]	701.4[4]	100,520

Demography

Population (1994): 104,000.
Density (1994): persons per sq mi 384.0, persons per sq km 148.3.
Urban-rural (1992): urban 26.0%; rural 74.0%.
Sex distribution (1990): male 50.73%; female 49.27%.
Age breakdown (1980): under 15, 46.4%; 15–29, 26.8%; 30–44, 12.6%; 45–59, 8.5%; 60–74, 4.5%; 75 and over, 1.2%.
Population projection: (2000) 110,000; (2010) 120,000.
Doubling time: 24 years.
Ethnic composition (1980): Trukese 41.1%; Pohnpeian 25.9%; Mortlockese 8.3%; Kosraean 7.4%; Yapese 6.0%; Ulithian, or Woleaian, 4.0%; Pingelapese, or Mokilese, 1.2%; Western Trukese 1.0%; Palauan 0.4%; Filipino 0.2%; other 4.5%.
Religious affiliation (1980): Christianity is the predominant religious tradition, with the Kosraeans, Pohnpeians, and Trukese being mostly Protestant and the Yapese mostly Roman Catholic.
Major cities (1989): Weno (Moen) 15,253; Tol 6,705[5]; Kolonia 6,169.

Vital statistics

Birth rate per 1,000 population (1992): 36.7 (world avg. 26.0); legitimate, n.a.; illegitimate, n.a.
Death rate per 1,000 population (1992): 7.8 (world avg. 9.2).
Natural increase rate per 1,000 population (1991): 28.9 (world avg. 16.8).
Total fertility rate (avg. births per childbearing woman; 1985–89): 5.6.
Marriage rate per 1,000 population: n.a.
Divorce rate per 1,000 population: n.a.
Life expectancy at birth (1991)[6]: male 70.6 years; female 77.3 years.
Major causes of death per 100,000 population (1991)[6]: diseases of the cerebrovascular system 89.6; diseases of the respiratory system 42.8, of which tuberculosis 8.9; malignant neoplasms (cancers) 38.8; homicide, suicide, and accidents 30.8; infectious and parasitic diseases 22.9.

National economy

Budget (1990). Revenue: U.S.$161,988,000 (external grants 73.2%; tax revenue 8.5%; fishing rights fees 7.8%). Expenditures: U.S.$127,779,000 (current expenditures 79.4%, of which education 18.2%, health 11.8%, public works 10.2%, transportation 2.7%, public safety 2.6%; capital expenditure 20.6%).
Public debt (external, outstanding): n.a.
Tourism (1990): number of visitors 23,171.
Production (metric tons except as noted). Agriculture, forestry, fishing: n.a.; however, Micronesia's major crops include coconuts (which provide annually more than 4,000 tons of copra), breadfruit, cassava, sweet potatoes, and a variety of tropical fruits (including bananas); livestock comprises mostly pigs and poultry; fish catch (1991) 1,411, of which skipjack tuna 400. Mining and quarrying: quarrying of sand and aggregate for local construction only. Manufacturing: n.a.; however, copra and coconut oil, traditionally important products, are being displaced by garment production; the manufacture of handicrafts and personal items (clothing, mats, boats, etc.) by individuals is also important. Construction: n.a. Energy production (consumption): electricity (kW-hr; 1990) 40,000,000 (40,000,000); coal, none (n.a.); crude petroleum, none (n.a.); petroleum products[7] (metric tons; 1992) none (77,000); natural gas, none (n.a.).
Household income and expenditure. Average household size (1988–89) 8.5; annual income per household (1989) U.S.$3,435; sources of income: wages and salaries 67.2%, self-employment 18.0%, operating surplus 14.8%; expenditure (1985): food and beverages 73.5%.
Land use (1984)[7]: forested 22.5%; meadows and pastures 13.5%; agricultural and under permanent cultivation 33.5%; other 30.5%.
Gross national product (at current market prices; 1989): U.S.$157,400,000 (U.S.$1,595 per capita).

Structure of gross domestic product and labour force

	1983		1990	
	in value U.S.$'000,000	% of total value	labour force	% of labour force
Agriculture and fishing	44.9	42.2	12,700	41.6
Trade	12.7	11.9	[8]	[8]
Public administration	31.5	29.6	6,300	20.7
Manufacturing			1,600	5.2
Construction			1,900	6.2
Transportation, communications, and public utilities	17.4	16.3	...	...
Finance			...	...
Services			3,700[8]	12.1[8]
Other			4,400[9]	14.4[9]
TOTAL	106.5	100.0	30,500[4]	100.0[4]

Population economically active (1990): total 30,500; activity rate of total population 60.6% (participation rates: ages 15–64, 60.6%; female 46.9%; unemployed 13.5%).
Price and earnings indexes: n.a.

Foreign trade

Balance of trade (current prices)

	1987	1988	1989	1990	1991	1992
U.S.$'000,000	−41.0	−52.7	−55.4	−62.2	−59.9	−57.3
% of total	95.6%	63.7%	61.6%	58.9%	51.0%	40.8%

Imports (1992): U.S.$98,796,385 (food, beverages, and tobacco 28.1%; manufactured goods 21.8%; mineral fuels 17.1%; machinery and transport equipment 17.0%; chemicals 4.5%). *Major import sources:* United States 40.3%; Guam 29.2%; Japan 20.0%; Australia 3.2%.
Exports (1992): U.S.$23,319,264 (marine products 86.2%; clothing and textiles 8.8%; agricultural products 4.1%, of which bananas 1.2%, copra 1.1%). *Major export destinations:* Japan 80.0%; United States 9.3%; Guam 8.3%; South Pacific Region 2.4%.

Transport and communications

Transport. Railroads: none. Roads (1990): total length 140 mi, 226 km (paved 17%). Vehicles: passenger cars, trucks, and buses, n.a. Merchant marine (1992): vessels (100 gross tons and over) 17; deadweight tonnage 6,863. Air transport: n.a.; airports (1994) with scheduled flights 4.
Communications. Daily newspapers: there are no private newspapers. Radio (1993): total number of receivers 70,000 (1 per 1.5 persons). Television (1993): total number of receivers 7,000 (1 per 15 persons). Telephones (1992): 5,730 (1 per 18 persons).

Education and health

Education (1987–88)

	schools	teachers	students	student/ teacher ratio
Elementary (age 6–12)	177	1,051[10]	25,139	22.2[10]
Secondary (age 13–18)	16	314[10]	5,385	13.2[10]
College[11]	1	...	[12]	...

Educational attainment (1980). Percentage of population age 25 and over having: no formal schooling 24.8%; some primary education 38.2%; primary 11.7%; some secondary 7.7%; secondary 9.6%; higher 8.0%. *Literacy* (1980): total population age 15 and over literate 30,074 (76.7%); males literate 13,710 (67.0%); females literate 16,364 (87.2%).
Health: physicians (1992) 46 (1 per 2,227 persons); hospital beds (1989) 319 (1 per 309 persons); infant mortality rate per 1,000 live births (1990) 52.2.
Food: daily per capita caloric intake, n.a.

Military

External security is provided by the United States.

[1]On Nov. 3, 1986, the United States unilaterally terminated the UN trusteeship it held over the Federated States of Micronesia (FSM), thus formally initiating their free-association political status. On Dec. 22, 1990, the United Nations Security Council joined the Trusteeship Council, which had endorsed the termination of the trusteeship in May 1986. [2]1989. [3]1987. [4]Detail does not add to total given because of rounding. [5]1980. [6]Registered deaths only. [7]Includes all areas formerly constituting the U.S. Trust Territory of the Pacific Islands. [8]Services includes Trade. [9]Includes 4,100 unemployed. [10]1983–84. [11]In 1985, 1,200 students were enrolled in colleges and universities in the United States. [12]In 1989, fewer than 300 students were enrolled in the College of Micronesia.

Moldova

Official name: Republica Moldova (Republic of Moldova).
Form of government: unitary multiparty republic with a single legislative body (Parliament [104]).
Head of state: President.
Head of government: Prime Minister.
Capital: Chişinău.
Official language: Romanian.
Official religion: none.
Monetary unit[1]: 1 Moldovan leu (plural lei) = 100 bani; valuation (Sept. 27, 1994) free rate, 1 U.S.$ = 4.21 Moldovan lei; 1 £ = 6.69 Moldovan lei.

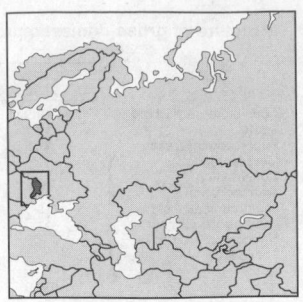

Area

Administrative subdivisions

Cities	area sq km[2]	Rural districts	area sq km[2]	Rural districts	area sq km[2]
Bălţi	...	Anenii Noi	830	Hânceşti	
Cahul	...	Basarabeasca	660	(Kotovsk)	1,350
Chişinău	160	Brinceni	810	Ialoveni	...
Dubăsari	...	Cahul	800	Leova	720
Orhei	...	Cainari	...	Nisporeni	760
Râbniţa	...	Călăraş	760	Ocniţa	660
Soroca	...	Camenca	820	Orhei	1,100
Tighina (Bendery)	...	Cantemir	860	Râbniţa	850
Tiraspol	...	Căuşeni	1,120	Rezina	670
Ungheni	...	Ciadâr-Lunga	720	Rişcani	1,000
		Cimişlia	1,170	Sângerei	...
		Comrat	840	Slobozia	960
		Criuleni	850	Şoldăneşti	...
		Donduşeni	890	Soroca	870
		Drochia	780	Ştefan-Vodă	
		Dubăsari	670	(Suvorovo)	1,030
		Edineţ	860	Străşeni	760
		Făleşti	1,070	Taraclia	...
		Floreşti	830	Teleneşti	860
		Glodeni	760	Ungheni	1,070
		Grigoriopol	820	Vulcăneşti	930
				TOTAL	33,700[3]

Demography

Population (1994): 4,358,000.
Density (1994): persons per sq mi 334.9, persons per sq km 129.3.
Urban-rural (1992): urban 46.6%; rural 53.4%.
Sex distribution (1992): male 47.08%; female 52.92%.
Age breakdown (1989): under 15, 27.9%; 15–29, 22.9%; 30–44, 21.0%; 45–59, 15.6%; 60–74, 9.7%; 75 and over, 2.9%.
Population projection: (2000) 4,381,000; (2010) 4,420,000.
Doubling time: not applicable; doubling time exceeds 100 years.
Ethnic composition (1989): Moldovan 64.5%; Ukrainian 13.8%; Russian 13.0%; Gagauz 3.5%; Jewish 2.0%; Bulgarian 1.5%; other 1.7%.
Religious affiliation: believers are predominantly Moldovan Orthodox.
Major cities (1991): Chişinău 753,500; Tiraspol 186,000; Bălţi 164,900; Tighina (Bendery) 141,500; Râbniţa 62,900.

Vital statistics

Birth rate per 1,000 population (1992): 15.9 (world avg. 26.0); (1989) legitimate 89.6%; illegitimate 10.4%.
Death rate per 1,000 population (1992): 10.2 (world avg. 9.2).
Natural increase rate per 1,000 population (1992): 5.7 (world avg. 16.8).
Total fertility rate (avg. births per childbearing woman; 1993): 2.5.
Marriage rate per 1,000 population (1990): 9.1.
Divorce rate per 1,000 population (1991): 3.2.
Life expectancy at birth (1993): male 67.9 years; female 71.5 years.
Major causes of death per 100,000 population (1989): diseases of the circulatory system 452.2; malignant neoplasms (cancers) 131.6; accidents and violence 105.3; diseases of the digestive system 85.4; diseases of the respiratory system 64.2; infectious and parasitic diseases 12.4; endocrine and metabolic disorders 8.3; diseases of the nervous system 8.2.

National economy

Budget (1995). Revenue: 1,947,400,000 lei (enterprise profits tax 22.1%; value-added tax 19.5%; property tax 14.1%; income tax 7.7%; excise duties 5.1%). Expenditures: 2,247,400,000 lei (social welfare, health, and culture 44.3%, of which education 20.0%, health services 14.0%, social insurance 6.0%; capital construction 14.3%; domestic debt service 10.4%; national economy 4.6%; foreign debt service 3.6%).
Production (metric tons except as noted). Agriculture, forestry, fishing (1993): sugar beets 1,900,000, grain 1,862,000, fruit (except grapes) 1,430,000, vegetables (except potatoes) 1,430,000, wheat 1,394,000, grapes 730,000, potatoes 300,000; livestock (number of live animals) 1,600,000 pigs, 1,130,000 sheep, 909,000 cattle, 22,000,000 poultry; roundwood (1991) 125,000 cu m; fish catch (1991) 5,200. Mining and quarrying (1992): limestone 1,500,000, clay 400,000, gypsum 300,000. Manufacturing ('000,000 rubles; 1991): food 3,244; machinery 2,435; textiles 2,400; building materials 397; wood products 389; chemicals 272; ferrous metals 110. Construction (1990): 433,400,000 rubles. Energy production (consumption): electricity (kW-hr; 1992) 11,248,000,000 (11,221,000,000); coal (metric tons; 1992) none (2,409,000); crude petroleum (barrels; 1990) none (51,625,000); petroleum products (metric tons; 1992) none (393,000); natural gas (cu m; 1992) none (3,643,000,000).
Gross national product (1993): U.S.$5,140,100,000 (U.S.$1,180 per capita)[4].

Structure of net material product and labour force

	1991		1992	
	in value '000,000 rubles	% of total value	labour force	% of labour force
Agriculture	7,836	41.8	820,000	40.0
Mining	} 7,048	37.6	408,000	19.9
Manufacturing				
Public utilities				
Construction	1,296	6.9	120,000	5.9
Transp. and commun.	711	3.8	102,000	5.0
Trade	1,757	9.4	111,000	5.4
Finance	—	—	9,000	0.4
Pub. admin., defense	—	— }	422,000	20.6
Services				
Other	105	0.5	58,000[5]	2.8[5]
TOTAL	18,753	100.0	2,050,000	100.0

Population economically active (1992): total 2,050,000; activity rate of total population 47.1% (participation rates [1991]: ages 16–59 [male], 16–54 [female] 84.0%; female [1989] 50.0%; unemployed [1991] 4.2%).
Land use (1992): forested 12.8%; meadows and pastures 10.9%; agricultural and under permanent cultivation 66.8%; other 9.5%.
Household income and expenditure. Average household size (1989) 3.4; income per household (1990) 4,000 rubles; sources of income (1992): wages and salaries 64.7%, agricultural income 18.6%, social benefits 15.8%, other 0.9%; expenditure (1992): retail goods 76.5%, services 6.6%, taxes 2.7%, housing 1.2%.

Foreign trade

Balance of trade (current prices)

	1987	1988	1989	1990
'000,000 rubles	−287.2	−1,023	−1,155	−284.7
% of total	2.6%	9.2%	9.6%	2.3%

Imports (1990): 6,461,400,000 rubles (machinery and equipment 39.2%, basic manufactures 12.1%, food products 11.4%, textiles 7.4%, chemicals 5.0%). *Major import sources* (1990): Russia 38.7%; Ukraine 17.2%; Belarus 8.6%; Uzbekistan 5.3%; Lithuania 2.7%.
Exports (1990): 6,176,700,000 rubles (basic manufactures 34.4%, food products 23.1%, machinery and equipment 10.9%, chemical products 9.4%, textiles 8.9%). *Major export destinations* (1990): Russia 61.6%; Ukraine 14.1%; Belarus 7.2%; Uzbekistan 3.4%; Kazakhstan 2.9%.

Transport and communications

Transport. Railroads (1991): length 1,150 km; passenger-km 8,875,000,000; metric ton-km cargo 15,007,000,000. Roads (1991): total length 10,300 km (paved 94%). Vehicles (1992): passenger cars 221,883. Air transport (1990): passenger-km 2,352,000,000; metric ton-km cargo 19,000,000; airports (1994) with scheduled flights 1.
Communications. Daily newspapers (1990): total number 240; total circulation 309,000,000; circulation per 1,000 population 71. Radio (1991): 1,421,000 receivers (1 per 3.1 persons). Television (1991): 1,264,000 receivers (1 per 3.4 persons). Telephones (1992): 553,000 (1 per 7.9 persons).

Education and health

Education (1991–92)

	schools	teachers	students	student/ teacher ratio
Primary (age 7–13) }	1,654	53,000	725,000	13.7
Secondary (age 14–17)				
Voc., teacher tr.	53	...	47,200	...
Higher	11	...	52,200	...

Educational attainment (1989). Percentage of population age 15 and over having: no formal schooling or some primary education 24.5%; some secondary 20.4%; secondary or some postsecondary 46.4%; higher 8.7%. *Literacy* (1989): percentage of total population age 15 and over literate 96.4%; males literate 98.6%; females literate 94.4%.
Health (1991): physicians 17,400 (1 per 251 persons); hospital beds 56,400 (1 per 77 persons); infant mortality rate per 1,000 live births (1992) 19.8.

Military

Total active duty personnel (1994): 11,100 (army 88.3%, air force 11.7%). About 7,000 Russian troops remained in Moldova in late 1994. *Military expenditure as percentage of GNP* (1992): 0.8% (world, n.a.); per capita expenditure U.S.$10.

[1]On Sept. 22, 1993, the Moldovan coupon was introduced to permit replacement of the Russian ruble by new national currency, the leu. On Nov. 30, 1993, the leu was introduced at a 1,000-to-1 ratio with the Moldovan coupon and circulates parallel with it. [2]One sq km is equal to approximately 0.3861 sq mi. [3]Total includes 3,190 sq km (1,230 sq mi) not distributable by administrative subdivision. [4]Ruble-area GNP and exchange-rate data are very speculative. [5]Includes film, media, forestry, and computer services.

Mongolia

Official name: Mongol Uls
(Mongolia).
Form of government: unitary multiparty
republic with one legislative house
(State Great Hural [76]).
Chief of state: President.
Head of government: Prime Minister.
Capital: Ulaanbaatar (Ulan Bator).
Official language: Khalkha Mongolian.
Official religion: none.
Monetary unit: 1 tugrik (Tug) = 100
möngö; valuation (Oct. 7, 1994) 1
U.S.$ = Tug 400.38; 1 £ = Tug 636.80.

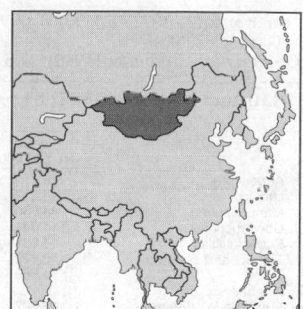

Area and population

Provinces	Capitals	area sq mi	area sq km	population 1991 estimate
Arhangay	Tsetserleg	21,000	55,000	89,200
Bayan-Ölgiy	Ölgiy	18,000	46,000	99,300
Bayanhongor	Bayanhongor	45,000	116,000	78,700
Bulgan	Bulgan	19,000	49,000	56,700
Dornod	Choybalsan	47,700	123,500	82,600
Dornogovĭ	Saynshand	43,000	111,000	58,600
Dundgovĭ	Mandalgovi	30,000	78,000	51,900
Dzavhan	Uliastay	32,000	82,000	93,600
Govĭ-Altay	Altay	55,000	142,000	65,100
Hentiy	Öndörhaan	32,000	82,000	76,700
Hovd	Hovd	29,000	76,000	81,100
Hövsgöl	Mörön	39,000	101,000	106,900
Ömnögovĭ	Dalandzadgad	64,000	165,000	43,500
Övörhangay	Arvayheer	24,000	63,000	100,400
Selenge	Sühbaatar	16,000	42,000	92,000
Sühbaatar	Baruun-Urt	32,000	82,000	53,500
Töv	Dzüünmod	31,000	81,000	105,900
Uvs	Ulaangom	27,000	69,000	91,800
Autonomous municipalities				
Darhan	—	100	200	88,600
Erdenet	—	300	800	58,200
Ulaanbaatar	—	800	2,000	575,000
TOTAL		604,800[1]	1,566,500	2,149,300

Demography

Population (1994): 2,266,000.
Density (1994): persons per sq mi 3.8, persons per sq km 1.5.
Urban-rural (1994): urban 59.0%; rural 41.0%.
Sex distribution (1991): male 49.89%; female 51.11%.
Age breakdown (1989): under 15, 41.9%; 15–29, 29.2%; 30–44, 14.6%; 45–59, 8.5%; 60 and over, 5.8%.
Population projection: (2000) 2,525,000; (2010) 3,025,000.
Doubling time: 27 years.
Ethnic composition (1989): Khalkha Mongol 78.8%; Kazakh 5.9%; Dörbed Mongol 2.7%; Bayad 1.9%; Buryat Mongol 1.7%; Dariganga Mongol 1.4%; other 7.6%.
Religious affiliation: although formal freedom of worship exists, all traditional forms of religious practice (lamaistic Buddhism, shamanism, Islam, and others) have been greatly reduced during the 20th century; reliable data on the current situation do not exist.
Major cities (1991): Ulaanbaatar (Ulan Bator) 536,600; Darhan 80,100; Erdenet 48,500; Choybalsan 38,600; Ölgiy 29,400.

Vital statistics

Birth rate per 1,000 population (1992): 34.2 (world avg. 26.0); legitimate, n.a.; illegitimate, n.a.
Death rate per 1,000 population (1992): 7.9 (world avg. 9.2).
Natural increase rate per 1,000 population (1992): 26.3 (world avg. 16.8).
Total fertility rate (avg. births per childbearing woman; 1993): 4.6.
Marriage rate per 1,000 population (1989): 7.8.
Divorce rate per 1,000 population (1989): 0.5.
Life expectancy at birth (1993): male 63 years; female 65 years.
Major causes of death per 100,000 population: n.a.; however, in the 1980s, major causes of mortality included diseases of the respiratory system, diseases of the cardiovascular system, malignant neoplasms (cancers), diseases of the digestive system, and injuries, accidents, and poisoning.

National economy

Budget (1994). Revenue: Tug 63,304,800,000 (taxes 67.2%, of which income tax 24.1%, deductions from profits 19.8%, turnover tax 17.6%, other taxes 5.7%; nontax revenue 32.8%, of which social insurance contributions 7.4%). Expenditures: Tug 78,468,100,000 (social and cultural services 69.9%, of which education 22.2%, health 16.7%, social security 13.2%; defense 9.2%; administration and other 6.6%).
Public debt (external; 1991): U.S.$16,800,000,000.
Tourism (1990): number of international arrivals 147,200.
Production (metric tons except as noted). Agriculture, forestry, fishing (1993): cereals 510,000 (of which wheat 480,000), potatoes 74,000, vegetables 15,000; livestock (number of live animals) 14,657,000 sheep, 5,603,000 goats, 2,819,-000 cattle, 2,200,000 horses, 415,000 camels, 49,000 pigs; roundwood (1991) 2,390,000 cu m; fish catch (1991) 100. Mining and quarrying (1992): copper 105,100; molybdenum 1,522; silver 18,000 kg; gold 900 kg. Manufacturing (value added by manufacturing, Tug '000,000; 1990): food products 691.1; textiles 429.8; leather and hides 302.6; construction materials 153.5; clothing and apparel 140.2; wood products 131.0; chemicals 127.3; printing and publishing 44.4; glass and ceramics 12.2. Construction (1991): residential

112,000 sq m; nonresidential, n.a. Energy production (consumption): electricity (kW-hr; 1992) 3,300,000,000 (3,370,000,000); coal (metric tons; 1992) 7,535,000 (7,035,000); crude petroleum, none (n.a.); petroleum products (metric tons; 1992) none (605,000); natural gas, none (n.a.).
Gross national product (1993): U.S.$984,800,000 (U.S.$400 per capita).

Structure of gross domestic product and labour force

	1989 in value Tug '000,000	1989 % of total value	1990 labour force	1990 % of labour force
Agriculture	1,722.9	16.1	191,500	27.6
Manufacturing and mining	2,919.8	27.2	123,400	17.8
Construction	617.2	5.8	44,600	6.4
Transp. and commun.	903.8	8.4	55,000	7.9
Trade	2,327.4	21.7	49,200	7.1
Services[2]	1,285.4	12.0	185,000	26.6
Other	954.4[3]	8.9[3]	45,700[4]	6.6[4]
TOTAL	10,700.0	100.0[1]	604,400	100.0

Population economically active (1990): total 694,400; activity rate of total population 32.3% (participation rates: ages 15–64 [1985] 82.2%; female [1992] 46.0%; unemployed 6.6%).

Price and earnings indexes (1990 = 100)

	1985	1986	1987	1988	1989	1990	1991[5]
Consumer price index	46.8	46.4	46.4	46.4	46.4	100.0	119.3
Monthly earnings index	96.9	97.3	97.9	98.2	99.7	100.0	...

Household income and expenditure. Average family size (1989) 4.8; income per household (1992)[6] Tug 5,500 (U.S.$140); sources of income (1990): wages and salaries 74.4%[7], transfer payments 13.5%, self-employment 3.3%, other 8.8%; expenditure (1990): products 82.1%, services 17.9%.
Land use (1992): forested 8.9%; meadows and pastures 79.7%; agricultural and under permanent cultivation 0.9%; other 10.5%.

Foreign trade

Balance of trade (current prices)[8]

	1987	1988	1989	1990	1991	1992
U.S.$'000,000	−542	−629	−744	−314	−80	−35
% of total	24.9%	27.5%	31.8%	26.1%	10.3%	6.5%

Imports (1992): U.S.$285,000,000 (1990; machinery and transport equipment 31.1%; fuels, minerals, and metals 27.2%; consumer goods 21.6%; food products 8.8%; chemical products and rubber 5.3%). *Major import sources* (1990): U.S.S.R. 71.5%; Germany 4.1%; Czechoslovakia 3.7%; China 2.4%; Hungary 2.2%.
Exports (1992): U.S.$250,000,000 (1990; minerals and metals 48.1%; raw materials and food products 27.3%; consumer goods 20.1%; construction materials 3.9%). *Major export destinations* (1990): U.S.S.R. 78.3%; Czechoslovakia 4.5%; Bulgaria 2.5%; Hungary 2.1%.

Transport and communications

Transport. Railroads (1990): length (1991) 1,445 mi, 2,325 km; passenger-km 524,100,000; metric ton-km cargo 5,087,800,000. Roads (1988): total length 30,600 mi, 49,200 km (paved 2%). Vehicles (1989): passenger cars 5,660; trucks and buses 29,794. Merchant marine: vessels (100 gross tons and over) none. Air transport (1992): passenger-km 286,000,000; metric ton-km cargo 3,100,000; airports (1994) with scheduled flights 1.
Communications. Daily newspapers (1990): total number 2; total circulation 222,000; circulation per 1,000 population 106. Radio (1992): total number of receivers 275,000 (1 per 7.8 persons). Television (1992): total number of receivers 120,000 (1 per 18 persons). Telephones (1991): 68,480 (1 per 31 persons).

Education and health

Education (1990–91)

	schools	teachers	students	student/teacher ratio
Primary and secondary (age 8–18)	634	20,600	440,900	21.4
Vocational	75	2,500	47,600	19.0
Higher	9	1,465	13,829	9.4

Educational attainment (1989). Percentage of population age 10 and over having: primary education 33.7%; some secondary 31.9%; complete secondary 16.9%; vocational secondary 9.4%; some higher and complete higher 8.1%.
Literacy (1989): total population age 10 and over literate 97.9%.
Health (1991): physicians 6,318 (1 per 340 persons), hospital beds 26,350 (1 per 83 persons); infant mortality rate per 1,000 live births 64.0.
Food (1988–90): daily per capita caloric intake 2,361[9] (vegetable products 61%, animal products 39%); 97% of FAO recommended minimum requirement.

Military

Total active duty personnel (1994): 21,250 (army 93.0%; navy, none; air force 7.0%). *Military expenditure as percentage of GNP* (1993): 2.4%; per capita expenditure (1993) U.S.$10.

---

[1]Detail does not add to total given because of rounding. [2]Services includes finance, public administration, and defense. [3]Other includes depreciation of fixed capital. [4]Unemployed. [5]April. [6]Urban households. [7]Includes income from agricultural cooperatives. [8]Trade in convertible currencies. [9]FAO estimate; alternate 1988–90 data reported by World Bank: 2,578 calories. According to Mongolian sources, November 1992 consumption was 1,875 calories (urban) and 2,092 (rural).

Morocco

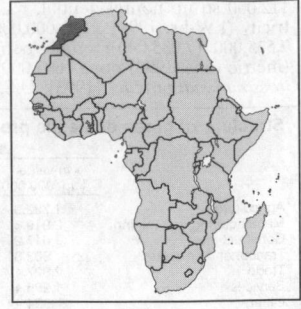

Official name: al-Mamlakah
al-Maghribīyah (Kingdom of
Morocco).
Form of government: constitutional
monarchy with one legislative house
(Chamber of Representatives [333]).
Chief of state: King.
Head of government: King assisted by
Prime Minister.
Capital: Rabat.
Official language: Arabic.
Official religion: Islam.
Monetary unit: 1 Moroccan dirham
(DH) = 100 Moroccan francs;
valuation (Oct. 7, 1994)
1 U.S.$ = DH 8.83; 1 £ = DH 14.04.

Area and population (1992 est.)

Provinces[1]	area sq km[2]	population	Provinces[1]	area sq km[2]	population
Agadir	5,910	807,000	Safi	7,285	848,000
Azilal	10,050	419,000	Settat	9,750	790,000
Ben Slimane	2,760	204,000	Sidi Kacem	4,060	602,000
Béni Mellal	7,075	936,000	Tan-Tan	17,295	55,000
Boulemane	14,395	156,000	Tangier	1,195	566,000
Chaouen			Taounate	5,585	603,000
(Chefchaouen)	4,350	363,000	Taroudannt	16,460	658,000
Essaouira	6,335	428,000	Tata	25,925	107,000
Fès	5,400	1,029,000	Taza	15,020	715,000
Figuig	55,990	108,000	Tétouan	6,025	864,000
Guelmim	28,750	168,000	Tiznit	6,960	381,000
al-Hoceima	3,550	371,000			
Ifrane	3,310	116,000	**Prefectures**		
el-Jadida	6,000	928,000	Ain Chok–		
el-Kelaa des Srarhna	10,070	684,000	Hay Hassani		452,000
Kénitra	4,745	920,000	Ain Sebaa–		
Khémisset	8,305	473,000	Hay Mohammadi		587,000
Khénifra	12,320	442,000	Ben Msik–		
Khouribga	4,250	547,000	Sidi Othmane	1,615	984,000
Larache[3]	...	...	Casablanca-Anfa		1,069,000
Marrakech	14,755	1,525,000	Mohammadia–		
Meknès	3,995	753,000	Znata		219,000
Nador	6,130	796,000	Rabat		690,000
Ouarzazate	41,550	649,000	Salé	1,275	656,000
Oujda	20,700	974,000	Skhirate-Temara		199,000
er-Rachidia	59,585	503,000	**TOTAL**	458,730	25,344,000

Demography

Population (1994): 26,544,000.
Density (1994): persons per sq mi 149.9, persons per sq km 57.9.
Urban-rural (1992): urban 49.5%; rural 50.5%.
Sex distribution (1991): male 49.02%; female 50.98%.
Age breakdown (1991): under 15, 40.5%; 15–29, 28.3%; 30–44, 16.8%; 45–59,
8.4%; 60–74, 4.8%; 75 and over, 1.2%.
Population projection: (2000) 30,351,000; (2010) 37,949,000.
Doubling time: 30 years.
Ethnic composition (1986): Arab 70%; Berber 30%; other, less than 1%.
Religious affiliation (1982): Muslim (mostly Sunnī) 98.7%; Christian 1.1%.
Major cities (1982): Casablanca 2,139,204; Rabat 518,616; Fès 448,823.

Vital statistics

Birth rate per 1,000 population (1994): 28.6 (world avg. 26.0).
Death rate per 1,000 population (1994): 6.3 (world avg. 9.2).
Natural increase rate per 1,000 population (1994): 22.3 (world avg. 16.8).
Total fertility rate (avg. births per childbearing woman; 1994): 3.8.
Life expectancy at birth (1994): male 66.4 years; female 70.2 years.
Major causes of death (1989)[4]: childhood diseases 22.9%; circulatory diseases
15.4%; accidents 7.3%; infectious and parasitic diseases 6.3%; neoplasms
(cancers) 5.6%.

National economy

Budget. Revenue (1993): DH 77,227,000,000 (indirect taxes 27.1%; customs
duties 20.4%; stamp duties 3.8%). Expenditures (1993): DH 80,117,000,000
(current expenditure 81.1%, of which debt payments 28.9%; investment
expenditure 18.8%).
Public debt (external, outstanding; 1992): U.S.$20,974,000,000.
Land use (1992): forested 17.7%; meadows 46.8%; agricultural 22.1%; built-
on, wasteland, and other 13.4%.
Tourism (1992): receipts from visitors U.S.$1,360,000,000; expenditures by
nationals abroad U.S.$242,000,000.
Production (metric tons except as noted). Agriculture, forestry, fishing (1993):
sugar beets 3,162,000, wheat 1,573,000, barley 1,027,000, sugarcane 946,000,
tomatoes 917,000, potatoes 869,000, oranges 860,000, olives 550,000, dates
111,000; livestock (number of live animals) 16,302,000 sheep, 4,773,000
goats, 2,924,000 cattle, 78,000,000 chickens; roundwood (1992) 2,356,000 cu
m; fish catch (1993) 607,000. Mining and quarrying (value of production
in DH '000,000; 1993): phosphate rock 3,551.2; mineral water 217.1; zinc
166.4; copper 137.8; lead 127.4; manganese 75.5; fluorspar 47.2; barite 41.3;
iron ore 3.1. Manufacturing (1992): cement 6,036,000; refined sugar 520,-
000[5]; olive oil 53,000[5]; wine 435 hectolitres; passenger automobiles and
commercial vehicles 20,150[6] units. Construction (value added in DH; 1991):
8,821,700. Energy production (consumption): electricity (kW-hr; 1992) 10,-
325,000,000 (11,257,000,000); coal (metric tons; 1992) 576,000 (1,791,000);
crude petroleum (barrels; 1992) 83,600 (47,500,000); petroleum products

(metric tons; 1992) 5,111,000 (5,907,000); natural gas (cu m; 1992) 23,987,-
000 (23,987,000).
Gross national product (1993): U.S.$26,736,000,000 (U.S.$1,030 per capita).

Structure of gross domestic product and labour force

	1993 in value DH '000,000	1993 % of total value	1982 labour force	1982 % of labour force
Agriculture	35,419	14.3	2,351,629	39.2
Mining	4,872	2.0	63,360	1.1
Manufacturing	44,636	18.0	930,615	15.5
Construction	11,641	4.7	437,464	7.3
Public utilities	18,994	7.7	22,465	0.4
Transp. and commun.	16,622	6.7	140,981	2.3
Trade	51,659	20.9 }	498,130	8.3
Finance	...			
Pub. admin., defense	32,507	13.1	532,803	8.9
Services }	31,333	12.6	474,109	7.9
Other }			547,704[7]	9.1[7]
TOTAL	247,683	100.0	5,999,260	100.0

Population economically active (1991)[8]: total 4,095,393; activity rate 33.0%
(participation rates: over age 15, 49.7%; female 25.5%; unemployed [1993]
16.0%).

Price index (1990 = 100)

	1988	1989	1990	1991	1992	1993	1994[9]
Consumer price index	90.7	93.5	100.0	108.0	114.2	120.1	125.1
Earnings index[10]	72.0	79.2	100.0				

Household income and expenditure. Average household size (1982) 5.8; expenditure (1993)[11]: food 45.2%, housing 12.5%, transportation 7.6%, clothing
7.5%.

Foreign trade[12]

Balance of trade (current prices)

	1988	1989	1990	1991	1992	1993
DH '000,000	−5,853	−14,130	−16,755	−13,576	−23,192	−28,740
% of total	9.0%	20.0%	19.3%	15.4%	25.5%	31.1%

Imports (1993): DH 61,798,000,000 (capital goods 27.6%; food, beverages,
and tobacco 14.5%, of which wheat 5.3%; consumer goods 10.9%; crude oil
10.8%). *Major import sources:* France 23.0%; Spain 10.5%; U.S. 10.1%; Italy
6.3%; Germany 5.9%; U.K. 2.7%; Iran 2.5%.
Exports (1993): DH 34,266,000,000 (consumer goods 28.8%, of which clothing
11.7%; food 26.1%, of which fresh, canned, and frozen fish 14.4%; minerals
10.2%, of which phosphates 7.0%). *Major export destinations:* France 33.3%;
Spain 8.8%; Japan 5.6%; Italy 5.2%; Germany 4.4%; India 3.9%; U.K. 3.6%.

Transport and communications

Transport. Railroads (1993): route length 1,768 km[6]; passenger-km 1,908,000,-
000; metric ton-km cargo 4,416,000,000. Roads (1992): total length 59,474
km (paved 50%). Vehicles (1992): passenger cars 811,896; trucks and buses
291,973. Merchant marine (1992): vessels (100 gross tons and over) 492;
total deadweight tonnage 586,221. Air transport (1992)[13]: passenger-km
4,395,185,000; metric ton-km cargo 53,252,000; airports (1994) 16.
Communications. Daily newspapers (1990): total number 13; total circulation
320,000[14]; circulation per 1,000 population 13[14]. Radio (1993): 4,500,000
receivers (1 per 5.8 persons). Television (1993): 1,210,000 receivers (1 per
21.4 persons). Telephones (1992): 714,210 (1 per 35 persons).

Education and health

Education (1991–92)

	schools[15]	teachers	students	student/ teacher ratio
Primary (age 7–12)	4,052	95,206	2,578,566	27.1
Secondary (age 13–17)[16]	1,080	75,708[15]	1,151,771	...
Vocational[17]	562	1,191[15]	17,147	...
Higher[15]	35	7,713	225,001	29.2

Educational attainment (1982). Percentage of population age 25 and over
having: no formal education 47.8%; some primary education 47.8%; some
secondary 3.8%; higher 0.6%. *Literacy* (1990): total population over age 15
literate 49.5%; males 61.3%; females literate 38.0%.
Health: physicians (1992) 6,120 (1 per 4,148 persons); hospital beds[18] (1991)
26,505 (1 per 937 persons); infant mortality rate (1994) 49.6.
Food (1988–90): daily per capita caloric intake 3,031 (vegetable products 94%,
animal products 6%); 125% of FAO recommended minimum requirement.

Military

Total active duty personnel (1994): 195,500 (army 89.5%, navy 3.6%, air force
6.9%). *Military expenditure as percentage of GNP* (1990): 5.2% (world 4.5%);
per capita expenditure U.S.$62.

---

[1]Provincial capitals have same name as province. [2]One sq km is approximately equal
to 0.3861 sq mi. [3]Area and population figures included with Tétouan province.
[4]Registered deaths of urban population only. [5]1993. [6]1991. [7]Unemployed, not previously employed only. [8]Urban labour force only, representing the total urban employed
and unemployed. [9]July. [10]Based on minimum hourly wage of workers 18 years of
age and older; values reflect adjustments made to the minimum wage during the
year. [11]Weights of consumer price index components. [12]Import figures are f.o.b. in
balance of trade and c.i.f. for commodities and trading partners. [13]Royal Air Maroc
only. [14]Partial data. [15]1990–91. [16]Public institutions only. [17]Excludes teacher training. [18]Public only.

Mozambique

Official name: República de Moçambique (Republic of Mozambique).
Form of government: multiparty republic[1] with a single legislative house (Assembly of the Republic [250]).
Chief of state and head of government: President.
Capital: Maputo.
Official language: Portuguese.
Official religion: none.
Monetary unit: 1 metical (Mt.; plural meticais) = 100 centavos; valuation (Oct. 7, 1994) 1 U.S.$ = Mt. 6,342; 1 £ = Mt. 10,087.

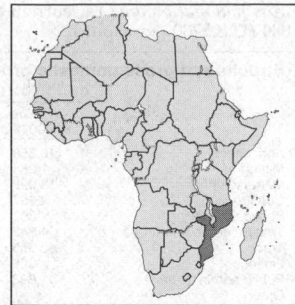

Area and population

Provinces	Capitals	area sq mi	area sq km	population 1991 estimate
Cabo Delgado	Pemba	31,902	82,625	1,202,221
Gaza	Xai-Xai	29,231	75,709	1,401,485
Inhambane	Inhambane	26,492	68,615	1,156,958
Manica	Chimoio	23,807	61,661	609,512
Maputo	Maputo	9,944	25,756	840,757
Nampula	Nampula	31,508	81,606	2,841,416
Niassa	Lichinga	49,828	129,055	686,650
Sofala	Beira	26,262	68,018	1,427,493
Tete	Tete	38,890	100,724	734,561
Zambézia	Quelimane	40,544	105,008	2,619,281
City				
Maputo	—	232	602	931,591
TOTAL LAND AREA		308,642[2]	799,379	
INLAND WATER		5,019	13,000	
TOTAL		313,661	812,379	14,451,925[3]

Demography

Population (1994): 17,346,000.
Density (1994)[4]: persons per sq mi 56.2, persons per sq km 21.7.
Urban-rural (1991): urban 28.1%; rural 71.9%.
Sex distribution (1990)[5]: male 49.32%; female 50.68%.
Age breakdown (1990)[5]: under 15, 44.0%; 15–29, 26.2%; 30–44, 15.4%; 45–59, 9.2%; 60–74, 4.4%; 75 and over, 0.8%.
Population projection: (2000) 20,868,000; (2010) 27,381,000.
Doubling time: 26 years.
Ethnolinguistic composition (1983): Makua 47.3%; Tsonga 23.3%; Malawi 12.0%; Shona 11.3%; Yao 3.8%; Swahili 0.8%; Makonde 0.6%; Portuguese 0.2%; other 0.7%.
Religious affiliation (1980): traditional beliefs 47.8%; Christian 38.9%, of which Roman Catholic 31.4%; Muslim 13.0%; other 0.3%.
Major cities (1991): Maputo 931,591; Beira 298,847; Nampula 250,473.

Vital statistics

Birth rate per 1,000 population (1990–95): 45.1 (world avg. 26.0).
Death rate per 1,000 population (1990–95): 18.2 (world avg. 9.2).
Natural increase rate per 1,000 population (1990–95): 26.9 (world avg. 16.8).
Total fertility rate (avg. births per childbearing woman; 1990–95): 6.5.
Marriage rate per 1,000 population (1974): 0.7.
Divorce rate per 1,000 population (1973): 0.01.
Life expectancy at birth (1990–95): male 45.2 years; female 48.4 years.
Major infectious diseases (certified cases per 100,000 population; 1980): measles 227.4; pulmonary tuberculosis 55.9; viral hepatitis 19.2; leprosy 13.8; cholera 4.6; tetanus 4.5.

National economy

Budget (1992). Revenue: Mt. 660,800,000 (sales tax 42.6%, customs taxes 25.5%, individual income tax 15.6%). Expenditures: Mt. 1,490,100,000 (defense and security 17.4%, wages and salaries 9.6%).
Production (metric tons except as noted). Agriculture, forestry, fishing (1993): cassava 3,511,000, corn (maize) 533,000, coconuts 425,000, sugarcane 330,000, sorghum 143,000, peanuts (groundnuts) 84,000, bananas 80,000; livestock (number of live animals) 1,250,000 cattle, 385,000 goats, 170,000 pigs, 118,000 sheep, 22,000,000 chickens; roundwood (1992) 15,993,000 cu m; fish catch (1991) 34,000. Mining and quarrying (1992). marine salt 40,000, bauxite 8,340; copper 133[6,7]; garnet 1,500 kg; gemstones 8,447 carats. Manufacturing (1992): cement 76,767; wheat flour 49,368; raw sugar 33,141; soap 8,843; cotton threads 4,676; beer 352,900 hectolitres; cigarettes 414,000,000 units; poplin 3,664,000 sq m. Construction (1974): residential 247,000 sq m; nonresidential 121,000 sq m. Energy production (consumption): electricity (kW-hr; 1992) 490,000,000 (815,000,000); coal (metric tons; 1992) 40,000 (60,000); crude petroleum (1992) none (none[8]); petroleum products (metric tons; 1992) none[8] (268,000); natural gas, none (none).
Population economically active (1980): total 5,671,290; activity rate of total population 48.6% (participation rates: over age 15, 87.3%; female 52.4%; unemployed 1.7%).

Price and earnings indexes (1990 = 100)

	1987	1988	1989	1990	1991	1992	1993
Consumer price index	32.3	48.5	68.0	100.0	132.9	193.4	275.0
Earnings index	...	...	...	...	...	...	...

Public debt (external, outstanding; 1992): U.S.$4,136,000,000.
Household income and expenditure. Average household size (1980) 4.2; income per household: n.a.; sources of income: n.a.; expenditure: n.a.
Gross national product (at current market prices; 1993): U.S.$1,353,280,000 (U.S.$80 per capita).

Structure of gross domestic product and labour force

	1991 in value Mt. '000,000	1991 % of total value	1980 labour force	1980 % of labour force
Agriculture	801,780	39.1	4,754,831	83.8
Mining	4,320	0.2	73,425	1.3
Manufacturing	504,840	24.6	273,369	4.8
Construction	270,000	13.2	42,121	0.7
Public utilities	89,910	4.4	[9]	[9]
Transportation and communications	194,880	9.5	77,025	1.4
Finance	7,070	0.4	...	...
Trade	100,760	4.9	112,244	2.0
Pub. admin., defense	62,410	3.1	243,449[9]	4.3[9]
Services				
Other	11,770	0.6	94,826[10]	1.7[10]
TOTAL	2,048,040	100.0	5,671,290	100.0

Tourism: n.a.
Land use (1992): forested 17.9%; meadows and pastures 56.1%; agricultural and under permanent cultivation 4.1%; other 21.9%.

Foreign trade[11]

Balance of trade (current prices)

	1988	1989	1990	1991	1992	1993
U.S.$'000,000	−612	−670	−648	−737	−716	−823
% of total	74.8%	76.1%	71.8%	69.5%	72.0%	75.7%

Imports (1990): U.S.$877,520,000 (foodstuffs 28.9%, capital equipment 22.9%, crude petroleum and derivatives 10.9%, machinery and spare parts 9.5%). *Major import sources* (1989): South Africa 23.2%; U.S.S.R. 9.8%; United States 7.1%; Portugal 6.8%; Italy 6.0%.
Exports (1992): U.S.$139,304,000 (shrimp 46.3%, cashew nuts 12.6%, cotton 7.8%, sugar 4.8%, lobster 3.5%). *Major export destinations* (1990): Spain 17.9%; United States 11.6%; Japan 10.4%; Portugal 5.6%.

Transport and communications

Transport. Railroads (1992): route length (1993) 1,946 mi, 3,131 km; passenger-mi 16,200,000, passenger-km 26,000,000; short ton-mi cargo 421,900,000, metric ton-km cargo 616,000,000. Roads (1991): total length 16,955 mi, 27,287 km (paved 17%). Vehicles (1992): passenger cars 35,000; trucks and buses 35,000. Merchant marine (1992): vessels (100 gross tons and over) 107; total deadweight tonnage 31,645. Air transport (1992): passenger-mi 252,900,000, passenger-km 407,000,000; short ton-mi cargo 7,057,000, metric ton-km cargo 10,303,000; airports (1994) with scheduled flights 8.
Communications. Daily newspapers (1993): total number 2; total circulation 81,000; circulation per 1,000 population 5.0. Radio (1993): total number of receivers 600,000 (1 per 27 persons). Television (1993): total number of receivers 35,000 (1 per 467 persons). Telephones (1991): 69,477 (1 per 211 persons).

Education and health

Education (1992)

	schools	teachers	students	student/ teacher ratio
Primary (age 5–9)[12]	3,384	22,132	1,199,847	54.2
Secondary (age 10–16)[13]	207[14]	3,614	144,671	40.0
Voc., teacher tr.	32[14]	1,126	13,749	12.2
Higher[14]	2	457	2,562	5.6

Educational attainment (1980). Percentage of population age 25 and over having: no formal schooling 80.7%; primary education 18.2%; secondary 0.9%; higher 0.2%. *Literacy* (1990): percentage of total population age 15 and over literate 32.9%; males literate 45.1%; females literate 21.3%.
Health: physicians (1989) 388 (1 per 36,428 persons); hospital beds (1988) 12,129 (1 per 1,227 persons); infant mortality rate per 1,000 live births (1990–95) 147.0.
Food (1988–90): daily per capita caloric intake 1,805 (vegetable products 97%, animal products 3%); 77% of FAO recommended minimum requirement.

Military

Total active duty personnel (1994): n.a.[15]. *Military expenditure as percentage of GNP* (1991): 13.0% (world 4.2%); per capita expenditure U.S.$10.

[1]Mozambique adopted a new multiparty constitution, which became effective on Nov. 30, 1990; the first multiparty elections took place on Oct. 27–29, 1994. [2]Detail does not add to total given because of rounding. [3]Excludes refugees in neighbouring countries estimated at about 1,200,000 in 1991; most of these refugees were repatriated between June 1993 and the fall of 1994. [4]Density is based on land area. [5]Includes refugees in nearby countries. [6]1990. [7]Metal content only. [8]Internal disorder and a lack of foreign exchange have brought importation of crude petroleum and the production of refined petroleum products practically to a halt. [9]Services includes Public utilities. [10]Unemployed. [11]Import figures are c.i.f. [12]Includes initiation classes in which pupils learn Portuguese. [13]Includes the two stages of secondary education and the upper-level primary stage. [14]1988. [15]Under the terms of the 1992 peace agreement, government and Renamo forces are to merge, forming a new army some 30,000 strong.

Myanmar (Burma)

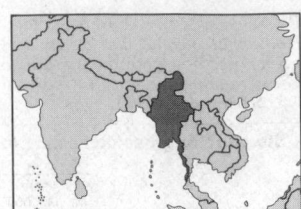

Official name: Pyidaungzu Myanma Nainngandaw (Union of Myanmar).
Form of government: military regime[1].
Head of state and government:
Chairman of the State Law and Order Restoration Council.
Capital: Yangôn (Rangoon).
Official language: Burmese.
Official religion: none.
Monetary unit: 1 Myanmar kyat (K) = 100 pyas; valuation (Oct. 7, 1994) 1 U.S.$ = K 5.82; 1 £ = K 9.26.

Area and population		area		population
				1983
Divisions	Capitals	sq mi	sq km	census
Irrawaddy (Ayeyarwady)	Bassein (Pathein)	13,567	35,138	4,994,061
Magwe (Magway)	Magwe (Magway)	17,305	44,820	3,243,166
Mandalay	Mandalay	14,295	37,024	4,577,762
Pegu (Bago)	Pegu (Bago)	15,214	39,404	3,799,791
Sagaing	Sagaing	36,535	94,625	3,862,172
Tenasserim (Tanintharyi)	Tavoy (Dawei)	16,735	43,343	917,247
Yangôn	Yangôn (Rangoon)	3,927	10,171	3,965,916
States				
Chin	Hakha	13,907	36,019	368,949
Kachin	Myitkyinā	34,379	89,041	904,794
Karen	Pa-an (Hpa-an)	11,731	30,383	1,055,359
Kayah	Loi-kaw	4,530	11,733	168,429
Mon	Moulmein (Mawlamyine)	4,748	12,297	1,680,157
Rakhine (Arakan)	Sittwe (Akyab)	14,200	36,778	2,045,559
Shan	Taunggyi	60,155	155,801	3,716,841
TOTAL		261,228	676,577	35,307,913[2]

Demography

Population (1994): 45,573,000.
Density (1994): persons per sq mi 174.5, persons per sq km 67.4.
Urban-rural (1993): urban 25.0%; rural 75.0%.
Sex distribution (1990): male 49.56%; female 50.44%.
Age breakdown (1990): under 15, 36.0%; 15–29, 29.7%; 30–44, 17.8%; 45–59, 10.1%; 60–74, 5.3%; 75 and over, 1.1%.
Population projection: (2000) 51,567,000; (2010) 61,631,000.
Doubling time: 32 years.
Ethnic composition (1983): Burman 69.0%; Shan 8.5%; Karen 6.2%; Rakhine 4.5%; Mon 2.4%; Chin 2.2%; Kachin 1.4%; other 5.8%.
Religious affiliation (1990): Buddhist 89.1%; Christian 4.9%; Muslim 3.8%; other 2.2%.
Major cities (1983): Yangôn (Rangoon) 2,513,023; Mandalay 532,949; Moulmein (Mawlamyine) 219,961; Pegu (Bago) 150,528; Bassein (Pathein) 144,096.

Vital statistics

Birth rate per 1,000 population (1994): 33.0 (world avg. 26.0).
Death rate per 1,000 population (1994): 11.0 (world avg. 9.2).
Natural increase rate per 1,000 population (1994): 22.0 (world avg. 16.8).
Total fertility rate (avg. births per childbearing woman; 1994): 4.2.
Marriage rate per 1,000 population: n.a.
Divorce rate per 1,000 population: n.a.
Life expectancy at birth (1994): male 57.0 years; female 60.0 years.
Major causes of death per 100,000 population (1978): pneumonia 16.1; heart diseases 10.5; enteritis and other diarrheal diseases 10.0; tuberculosis 9.4; malignant neoplasms (cancers) 6.5; cerebrovascular disease 4.1; malaria 3.5.

National economy

Budget (1991–92). Revenue: K 18,039,000,000 (revenue from taxes 58.1%, nontax revenue 38.0%, capital revenue 3.9%). Expenditures: K 27,621,-000,000 (defense 22.0%, education 17.4%, general public service 17.1%, transportation 10.7%, agriculture 7.3%, housing 7.3%, health 6.8%).
Public debt (external, outstanding; 1992): U.S.$4,974,000,000.
Tourism (1991): receipts from visitors U.S.$13,000,000; expenditures by nationals abroad U.S.$1,000,000.
Production (metric tons except as noted). Agriculture, forestry, fishing (1993): rice 17,434,000, sugarcane 3,410,000, pulses 842,000, peanuts (groundnuts) 433,000, plantains 275,000, sesame seeds 237,000, corn (maize) 220,000, onions 179,000, potatoes 143,000, millet 140,000, seed cotton 68,000, tobacco leaves 50,000, jute 39,000; livestock (number of live animals) 9,584,000 cattle, 2,529,000 pigs, 2,110,000 buffalo, 1,397,000 sheep and goats, 4,000,000 ducks, 25,000,000 chickens; roundwood (1992) 22,733,000 cu m; fish catch (1991) 769,236. Mining and quarrying (1991–92): gypsum 32,898; copper concentrates 18,318; refined lead 2,526; tin concentrates 170; jade 157; refined silver 1,905 troy oz. Manufacturing (value of production in '000,000 kyats; 1987–88): food and beverages 23,549.8; clothing and wearing apparel 1,606.6; industrial raw materials 1,468.9; construction materials 1,120.9; transport vehicles 719.0; personal goods 327.8. Construction (units; 1987–88)[3]: residential 1,193; nonresidential 1,483. Energy production (consumption): electricity (kW-hr; 1992) 2,674,000,000 (2,674,000,000); coal (metric tons; 1992) 69,000 (73,000); crude petroleum (barrels; 1992) 5,313,000 (5,504,000); petroleum products (metric tons; 1992) 542,000 (543,000); natural gas (cu m; 1992) 973,000,000 (973,000,000).
Household income and expenditure. Average household size (1983) 5.2; average annual income per household: n.a.; sources of income: n.a.; expenditure (1978)[4]: food and beverages 64.4%, clothing and footwear 8.0%, fuel and lighting 7.8%, household rent and repairs 3.8%, tobacco 3.7%, other 12.3%.

Gross national product (at current market prices; 1992–93): U.S.$30,707,000,-000 (U.S.$700 per capita).

Structure of gross domestic product and labour force				
	1992–93		1990–91	
	in value K '000,000	% of total value	labour force	% of labour force
Agriculture	110,859	58.8	10,867,000	69.0
Mining	1,264	0.7	79,000	0.5
Manufacturing	13,928	7.4	1,132,000	7.2
Construction	2,887	1.5	188,000	1.2
Public utilities	392	0.2	17,000	0.1
Transp. and commun.	4,642	2.5	388,000	2.5
Trade	42,355	22.5	1,396,000	8.9
Finance	326	0.2	1,205,000	7.7
Public admin., services	11,693	6.2		
Other	—	—	465,000	2.9
TOTAL	188,346	100.0	15,737,000	100.0

Population economically active (1990–91): total 15,737,000; activity rate of total population 37.2% (participation rates: ages 15–64 [1983] 64.2%; female [1987–88] 35.3%; unemployed [1987–88] 4.3%).

Price and earnings indexes (1985 = 100)						
	1987	1988	1989	1990	1991	1992	1993
Consumer price index	136.4	158.3	201.3	236.8	313.2	381.9	503.4
Monthly earnings index[5]	113.5	199.2	277.6	...	...	...	...

Land use (1992): forested 49.3%; meadows and pastures 0.5%; agricultural and under permanent cultivation 15.3%; other 34.9%.

Foreign trade[6]

Balance of trade (current prices)					
	1988	1989	1990	1991	1992	1993
K '000,000	−346.8	+274.9	+485.0	−1,055.4	−338.1	−948.4
% of total	14.2%	10.6%	13.5%	16.7%	4.9%	11.6%

Imports (1991–92): K 3,870,000,000 (1989–90; machinery and equipment 51.4%, industrial raw materials 31.4%, consumer goods 17.1%). Major import sources (1990–91): Singapore 19.7%; Japan 18.3%; China 17.0%; Malaysia 5.2%; Australia 4.0%; United States 3.2%; Thailand 2.6%.
Exports (1991–92): K 2,584,000,000 (1989–90; agricultural products 31.5%, forest products 23.8%, minerals and gems 8.7%, animal and marine products 4.5%). Major export destinations (1990–91): Singapore 13.2%; Thailand 11.1%; Japan 8.1%; China 7.4%; Hong Kong 6.5%; South Korea 4.0%; Sri Lanka 3.6%.

Transport and communications

Transport. Railroads (1990–91): route length 1,949 mi, 3,137 km; passenger-mi 2,781,000,000, passenger-km 4,476,000,000; short ton-mi cargo 395,000,000, metric ton-km cargo 576,000,000. Roads (1992–93): total length 15,118 mi, 24,330 km (paved 16%). Vehicles (1992): passenger cars 35,000; trucks and buses 35,000. Merchant marine (1992): vessels (100 gross tons and over) 144; total deadweight tonnage 1,354,005. Air transport (1990–91): passenger-mi 137,700,000, passenger-km 221,600,000; short ton-mi cargo 5,649,000, metric ton-km cargo 8,248,000; airports (1994) with scheduled flights 20.
Communications. Daily newspapers (1993): total number 2; total circulation 414,000; circulation per 1,000 population 9. Radio (1993): total receivers 3,200,000 (1 per 14 persons). Television (1993): total receivers 1,000,000 (1 per 45 persons). Telephones (1992–93): 89,318 (1 per 494 persons).

Education and health

Education (1992–93)	schools	teachers	students	student/teacher ratio
Primary (age 5–9)	36,499	198,909	6,518,800	32.8
Secondary (age 10–15)	2,920	67,503	1,633,700	24.2
Voc., teacher tr.	112	2,194	28,200	12.9
Higher	40	6,696	260,300	38.9

Educational attainment (1983). Percentage of population age 25 and over having: no formal schooling 55.8%; primary education 39.4%; secondary 4.6%; religious 0.1%; postsecondary 0.1%. Literacy (1983): total population age 15 and over literate 16,472,494 (78.5%); males literate 8,816,031 (85.8%); females literate 7,656,463 (71.6%).
Health (1992–93): physicians 13,353 (1 per 3,306 persons); hospital beds 27,830 (1 per 1,586 persons); infant mortality rate per 1,000 live births (1994) 84.
Food (1988–90): daily per capita caloric intake 2,454 (vegetable products 96%, animal products 4%); 114% of FAO recommended minimum requirement.

Military

Total active duty personnel (1994): 286,000 (army 92.7%, navy 4.2%, air force 3.1%). Military expenditure as percentage of GNP (1991): 5.8% (world 4.2%); per capita expenditure U.S.$30.

---

[1]The military government has refused to hand over power to the National League for Democracy, which won in the 1990 multiparty elections. [2]Includes 7,710 persons not distributed by area. [3]Construction Corporation activity only. [4]Based on 24 rural townships. [5]Wages in manufacturing. [6]Import figures are f.o.b. in balance of trade and c.i.f. in commodities and trading partners.

Namibia[1]

Official name: Republic of Namibia.
Political status: unitary multiparty republic with two legislative houses (National Assembly [72[2]]; National Council [26]).
Head of state and government: President.
Capital: Windhoek.
Official language: English.
Official religion: none.
Monetary unit[3]: 1 Namibian dollar (Nam$) = 100 cents; valuation (Oct. 7, 1994) 1 U.S.$ = Nam$3.57; 1 £ = Nam$5.68.

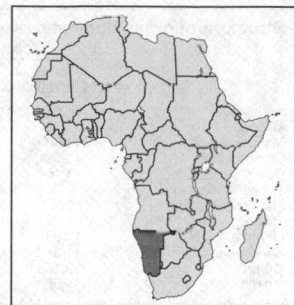

Area and population[4]

Regions	Chief towns	area sq mi	area sq km	population 1992 estimate
Erongo[4]	Omaruru	24,602	63,719	98,500
Hardap	Mariental	42,428	109,888	80,000
Karas	Keetmanshoop	62,288	161,324	73,000
Khomas	Windhoek	14,210	36,804	161,000
Kunene	Opuwo	55,697	144,254	58,500
Liambezi	Katima Mulilo	7,541	19,532	92,000
Ohangwena	Oshikango	4,086	10,582	178,000
Okavango	Rundu	16,763	43,417	136,000
Omaheke	Gobabis	32,715	84,731	55,600
Omusati	Ongandjera	5,265	13,637	158,000
Oshana	Oshakati	2,042	5,290	159,000
Oshikoto	Tsumeb	10,273	26,607	176,000
Otjozondjupa	Grootfontein	40,667	105,327	85,000
Other		2	6	1,000
TOTAL		318,580[5]	825,118	1,511,600

Demography

Population (1994): 1,596,000.
Density (1994): persons per sq mi 5.0, persons per sq km 1.9.
Urban-rural (1991): urban 32.8%; rural 67.2%.
Sex distribution (1991): male 49.78%; female 50.22%.
Age breakdown (1990): under 15, 45.7%; 15–29, 25.5%; 30–44, 15.0%; 45–59, 8.6%; 60–74, 4.3%; 75 and over, 0.9%.
Population projection: (2000) 1,957,000; (2010) 2,705,000.
Doubling time: 23 years.
Ethnic composition (1991): Ovambo 47.4%; Kavango 8.8%; Herero 7.1%; Damara 7.1%; white 6.1%; Nama 4.6%; other 18.9%.
Religious affiliation (1981): Lutheran 51.2%; Roman Catholic 19.8%; Dutch Reformed 6.1%; Anglican 5.0%; other 17.9%.
Major cities (1990): Windhoek 125,000; Swakopmund 15,500; Rundu 15,000; Rehoboth 15,000; Keetmanshoop 14,000.

Vital statistics

Birth rate per 1,000 population (1990–95): 41.6 (world avg. 26.0).
Death rate per 1,000 population (1990–95): 10.6 (world avg. 9.2).
Natural increase rate per 1,000 population (1990–95): 31.0 (world avg. 16.8).
Total fertility rate (avg. births per childbearing woman; 1990–95): 5.7.
Life expectancy at birth (1990–95): male 57.5 years; female 60.0 years.
Major causes of death per 100,000 population: n.a.; however, major diseases include malaria, tuberculosis, and trypanosomiasis (sleeping sickness).

National economy

Budget (1993–94). Revenue: R 3,009,000,000 (1991–92; customs and excise taxes 42.8%, of which general sales tax 13.9%; individual income taxes 10.7%; mining taxes 4.4%; nontax revenues 3.7%). Expenditures: R 3,366,-000,000 (education 23.5%; transportation 18.4%; health and welfare 13.1%; national defense 5.3%; agriculture 5.0%).
Tourism (1992): receipts from visitors U.S.$91,000,000; expenditures by nationals abroad U.S.$81,000,000.
Public debt (external, outstanding; 1993): U.S.$3,180,000.
Production (metric tons except as noted). Agriculture, forestry, fishing (1993): roots and tubers 250,000, cereals 81,000 (of which millet 36,000, corn [maize] 32,000, sorghum 7,000), fruits 10,000, vegetables and melons 8,000, pulses 7,000, wool 3,400[6], karakul pelts 770,627 units[7]; livestock (number of live animals) 2,900,000 sheep, 2,300,000 cattle, 1,800,000 goats; fish catch (1991) 204,517. Mining and quarrying (1993): diamonds 1,141,000 carats, mostly gem quality; zinc 54,000; copper 34,400; lead 31,200; uranium 1,967; silver 2,314,800 troy oz; gold 62,821 troy oz. Manufacturing (1991): n.a.; products include cut gems (primarily diamonds), fur products (karakul), processed foods (fish, meats, and dairy products), textiles, carved wood products, refined metals (copper and lead). Construction (value of buildings completed in R '000,000; 1990): residential 44.6; nonresidential 92.4. Energy production (consumption): electricity (kW-hr; 1992) 1,714,000,000 (1,714,000,000); coal, none (n.a.); crude petroleum, none (n.a.).
Population economically active: total (1992) 552,000; activity rate of total population, 36.5% (participation rates: ages 15–64 [1984], c. 56%, female 23.9%; unemployed [1988] c. 20%).

Price and earnings indexes (1990 = 100)

	1987	1988	1989	1990	1991	1992	1993
Consumer price index	68.7	77.5	89.3	100.0	111.9	131.7	143.0
Earnings index	...	...	...	...	...	...	...

Household income and expenditure. Average household size (1981) 4.8; average annual income per household (1980) R 3,223 (U.S.$4,143); sources of income (1989): wages and salaries 70.0%, income from property 24.4%, transfer payments 5.2%; expenditure: n.a.
Gross national product (1993): U.S.$2,598,000,000 (U.S.$1,660 per capita).

Structure of gross domestic product and labour force

	1991 in value R '000,000	1991 % of total value	1988 labour force[8,9]	1988 % of labour force[8,9]
Agriculture	700	10.8	36,071	19.5
Mining	2,052	31.7	10,062	5.5
Manufacturing	265	4.1	9,442	5.1
Construction	118	1.8	12,657	6.8
Public utilities	65	1.0	1,273	0.7
Transportation and communications	447	6.9	7,880	4.3
Trade	744	11.5	29,394	15.9
Finance	460	7.1	4,327	2.3
Services	304	4.7	25,167	13.6
Public administration and defense	1,323	20.4	48,520	26.3
TOTAL	6,478	100.0	184,793	100.0

Land use (1992): forested 21.9%; meadows and pastures 46.2%; agricultural and under permanent cultivation 0.8%; other 31.1%.

Foreign trade

Balance of trade (current prices)

	1988	1989	1990	1991	1992	1993
R '000,000	+463	+496	−57	+277	+207	+569
% of total	10.7%	9.2%	1.0%	4.3%	2.8%	7.2%

Imports (1992): R 3,358,000,000 (1988; chemical and petroleum products 21.5%; food and agricultural products 17.1%; machinery and transport equipment 6.6%; other 46.2%). *Major import source* (1991): South Africa 75–100%.
Exports (1992): R 3,673,000,000 (1991; minerals 75.9%, of which diamonds 30.5%; agricultural products 11.0%, of which cattle 5.8%, karakul pelts 0.9%). *Major export destinations* (1986): United States 25%; South Africa 19%; Japan 15%.

Transport and communications

Transport. Railroads: length (1992) 1,480 mi, 2,382 km; passenger-km 2,008,-000,000; metric ton-km 1,225,700,000. Roads (1992): total length 26,024 mi, 41,882 km (paved 11%). Number of registered motor vehicles (1991): 122,331. Merchant marine (1992): vessels (100 gross tons and over) 30; total deadweight tonnage 5,874. Air transport (1991)[10]: passenger-km 423,000,000; metric ton-km cargo 2,000,000; airports (1994) with scheduled flights 12.
Communications. Daily newspapers (1993): total number 5; total circulation 49,500; circulation per 1,000 population 32. Radio (1993): 240,000 receivers (1 per 6.4 persons). Television (1993): 39,500 receivers (1 per 39 persons). Telephones (1992): 92,970 (1 per 16 persons).

Education and health

Education (1990)

	schools	teachers	students	student/ teacher ratio
Primary (age 6–12)	1,134[11]	...	313,528	...
Secondary (age 13–19)	...	2,534	74,331	29.3
Voc., teacher tr.	9[12]	140[11]	1,666[11]	11.9[11]
Higher[13]	...	213	2,507	11.8

Educational attainment (1977). Percentage of labour force having: no formal schooling 59.8%; primary education 33.2%; secondary 5.0%; higher 2.0%.
Literacy (1985): total population age 15 and over literate 474,000 (72.5%); males literate 239,000 (74.2%); females literate 235,000 (70.8%).
Health: physicians (1992) 324 (1 per 4,594 persons); hospital beds (1989) 6,997 (1 per 216 persons); infant mortality rate per 1,000 live births (1993) 63.8.
Food (1979–81): daily per capita caloric intake 2,197 (vegetable products 77%, animal products 23%); 96% of FAO recommended minimum requirement.

Military

Total active duty personnel (1994): 8,100 (army 98.8%, navy 1.2%). *Military expenditure as percentage of GNP* (1984): 7.7% (world 5.9%); per capita expenditure U.S.$113.

[1]On March 21, 1990, Namibia achieved independence, its constitution (approved Feb. 9, 1990) became effective, the 72 member Constituent Assembly (elected Nov. 7 11, 1989) became the National Assembly, and a president (elected Feb. 6, 1990, by the Constituent Assembly) was sworn in. [2]72 elected and up to 6 appointed members. [3]As of June 1992, the Namibian dollar circulates at par and concurrently with the South African rand (R). [4]Includes the 434 sq mi (1,124 sq km) district of Walvis Bay (1992 pop. estimate, 23,000) that was jointly administered with South Africa from November 1992 to March 1994. [5]Detail does not add to total given because of rounding. [6]1992. [7]1987. [8]Employed persons only. [9]Formal sector only. [10]Namib Air only. [11]1989. [12]1988. [13]1991.

Nepal

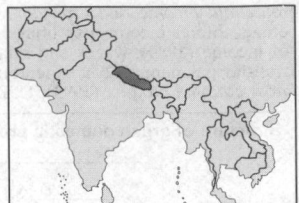

Official name: Nepāl Adhirājya
(Kingdom of Nepal).
Form of government: constitutional
monarchy with two legislative houses
(National Council [60[1]]; House of
Representatives [205]).
Chief of state: King.
Head of government: Prime Minister.
Capital: Kāthmāndu.
Official language: Nepālī.
Official religion: Hinduism.
Monetary unit: 1 Nepalese rupee
(NRs) = 100 paisa (pice); valuation
(Oct. 7, 1994) 1 U.S.$ = NRs 49.40;
1 £ = NRs 78.57.

Area and population

Development regions Zones	Capitals	area sq mi	area sq km	population 1991 census
Eastern	Dhankūtā	10,987	28,456	4,446,749
Koshī		3,733	9,669	1,728,247
Mechī		3,165	8,196	1,118,210
Sāgarmāthā		4,089	10,591	1,600,292
Central	Kāthmāndu	10,583	27,410	6,183,955
Bāgmatī		3,640	9,428	2,250,805
Janakpur		3,733	9,669	2,061,816
Nārāyanī		3,210	8,313	1,871,334
Western	Pokharā	11,351	29,398	3,770,678
Dhawalāgiri		3,146	8,148	490,877
Gandakī		4,740	12,275	1,266,128
Lumbinī		3,465	8,975	2,013,673
Mid-western	Surkhet	16,362	42,378	2,410,414
Bherī		4,071	10,545	1,103,043
Karnālī		8,244	21,351	260,529
Rāptī		4,047	10,482	1,046,842
Far-western	Dipāyal	7,544	19,539	1,679,301
Mahākālī		2,698	6,989	664,952
Setī		4,846	12,550	1,014,349
TOTAL		56,827	147,181	18,491,097

Demography

Population (1994): 19,525,000.
Density (1994): persons per sq mi 343.6, persons per sq km 132.7.
Urban-rural (1991): urban 9.6%; rural 90.4%.
Sex distribution (1991): male 51.63%; female 48.37%.
Age breakdown (1991): under 15, 42.3%; 15–29, 25.7%; 30–44, 16.7%; 45–59, 9.7%; 60–74, 4.7%; 75 and over, 0.9%.
Population projection: (2000) 21,094,000; (2010) 23,335,000.
Doubling time: 28 years.
Ethnic composition (1991): Nepalese 53.2%; Bihārī (including Maithilī and Bhojpurī) 18.4%; Tharu 4.8%; Tamang 4.7%; Newār 3.4%; Magar 2.2%; Abadhi 1.7%; other 11.6%.
Religious affiliation (1991): Hindu 86.2%; Buddhist 7.8%; Muslim 3.8%; Christian 0.2%; Jain 0.1%; other 1.9%.
Major cities (municipalities; 1991): Kāthmāndu 419,073; Birātnagar 130,129; Lalitpur 117,203; Pokharā 95,311; Birganj 68,764.

Vital statistics

Birth rate per 1,000 population (1993): 38.0 (world avg. 26.0).
Death rate per 1,000 population (1993): 13.0 (world avg. 9.2).
Natural increase rate per 1,000 population (1993): 25.0 (world avg. 16.8).
Total fertility rate (avg. births per childbearing woman; 1993): 5.4.
Marriage rate per 1,000 population: n.a.
Divorce rate per 1,000 population: n.a.
Life expectancy at birth (1993): male 54.0 years; female 53.0 years.
Major causes of death per 100,000 population: n.a.; however, the leading causes of mortality are infectious and parasitic diseases, diseases of the respiratory system, diseases of the nervous system, diseases of the circulatory system, and injuries and poisoning.

National economy

Budget (1992–93). Revenue: NRs 21,595,300,000 (internal revenue 78.7%, foreign grants 21.3%). Expenditures: NRs 33,595,200,000 (development 64.3%, regular 35.7%).
Public debt (external, outstanding; 1992): U.S.$1,747,000,000.
Tourism (1992): receipts from visitors U.S.$110,000,000; expenditures by nationals abroad U.S.$52,000,000.
Production (metric tons except as noted). Agriculture, forestry, fishing (1992): rice 2,509,000, sugarcane 1,291,000, corn (maize) 1,164,000, wheat 779,000, potatoes 733,000, millet 230,000, pulses 169,000, barley 28,000, jute 10,000, tobacco 6,000; livestock (number of live animals) 6,246,000 cattle, 5,406,000 goats, 3,058,000 buffalo, 912,000 sheep, 599,000 pigs; roundwood (1991) 18,704,000 cu m; fish catch (1991) 15,595. Mining and quarrying (1991): limestone 221,920; magnesite 25,000; talc 3,500; garnet 22,000 kg. Manufacturing (value added in NRs '000; 1990–91): cigarettes 1,129,465; carpets and rugs 880,026; wearing apparel 694,640; woven textiles 587,484; structural clay products 498,940. Construction: n.a. Energy production (consumption): electricity (kW-hr; 1991) 890,000,000 (854,000,000); coal (metric tons; 1991) none (67,000); petroleum products (metric tons; 1991) none (226,000); natural gas, none (none).
Gross national product (at current market prices; 1992): U.S.$3,285,000,000 (U.S.$170 per capita).

Structure of gross domestic product and labour force

	1992–93 in value NRs '000,000[2]	1992–93 % of total value	1991 labour force	1991 % of labour force
Agriculture	66,520	45.9	...	80.5
Mining	232	0.2	...	...
Manufacturing	11,300	7.8	...	1.7
Construction	11,824	8.2	...	0.8
Public utilities	1,457	1.0	...	0.1
Transportation and communications	9,921	6.8	...	0.6
Trade	8,721	6.0	...	3.3
Finance	13,571	9.4	...	0.3
Services	11,277	7.8	...	10.7
Other	10,136[3]	6.9[3]	...	2.0
TOTAL	144,959	100.0	...	100.0

Land use (1991): forested 18.1%; meadows and pastures 14.6%; agricultural and under permanent cultivation 19.4%; other 47.9%.
Population economically active (1990): total 8,585,370; activity rate of total population 45.4% (participation rates: ages 15–64 [1986] 82.5%; female 34.7%; unemployed [1980] 5.5%).

Price and earnings indexes (1985 = 100)

	1986	1987	1988	1989	1990	1991	1992
Consumer price index	119.0	131.8	143.6	156.3	169.2	195.5	229.1
Earnings index	...	...	...	...	...	...	...

Household income and expenditure (1984–85). Average household size (1991) 5.6; income per household NRs 14,796 (U.S.$853); sources of income: self-employment 63.4%, wages and salaries 25.1%, rent 7.5%, other 4.0%; expenditure: food and beverages 61.2%, housing 17.3%, clothing 11.7%, health care 3.7%, education and recreation 2.9%, transportation and communications 1.2%, other 2.0%.

Foreign trade[4]

Balance of trade (current prices)

	1987	1988	1989	1990	1991	1992
NRs '000,000	−7,659.6	−10,780	−10,796	−13,037	−17,059	−16,255
% of total	52.8%	54.6%	56.2%	51.4%	46.5%	33.7%

Imports (1992–93): NRs 36,978,500,000 (basic manufactured goods 31.6%[5]; machinery and transport equipment 19.5%; chemicals 12.3%; mineral fuels and lubricants 10.5%; food and live animals, chiefly for food 9.3%; crude materials except fuels 8.5%[5]). *Major import sources* (1990–91): India 32.1%; Singapore 14.0%; Japan 12.9%; New Zealand 5.0%; China 4.6%; France 3.0%.
Exports (1992–93): NRs 17,307,400,000 (basic manufactures 59.3%; food and live animals, chiefly for food 11.4%; crude materials except fuels 2.8%; animal and vegetable oils 0.9%). *Major export destinations* (1990–91): West Germany 35.9%; India 22.4%; United States 18.4%; Switzerland 6.5%; Belgium 2.3%; United Kingdom 2.2%.

Transport and communications

Transport. Railroads (1991–92): route length 33 mi, 53 km; passengers carried 884,000; freight handled 14,329 metric tons. Roads (1991): total length 5,175 mi, 8,328 km (paved 37%). Vehicles (1990–91): passenger cars 4,949; trucks and buses 3,363. Merchant marine: none. Air transport (1991): passenger-mi 439,000,000, passenger-km 706,000,000; short ton-mi cargo 7,500,000, metric ton-km cargo 11,000,000; airports (1994) with scheduled flights 17.
Communications. Daily newspapers (1990): total number 28; total circulation 150,000; circulation per 1,000 population 7.9. Radio (1993): 600,000 receivers (1 per 33 persons). Television (1993): 250,000 receivers (1 per 77 persons). Telephones (1989): 44,514 (1 per 415 persons).

Education and health

Education (1991)

	schools	teachers	students	student/ teacher ratio
Primary (age 6–10)	18,694	74,495	2,884,275	38.7
Secondary (age 11–15) } Vocational	6,124	24,632	773,808	31.4
Higher	3	4,694[6]	154,528	21.8[6]

Educational attainment (1981). Percentage of population age 25 and over having: no formal schooling 41.2%; primary education 29.4%; secondary 22.7%; higher 6.8%. *Literacy* (1991): total population age 15 and over literate 4,255,000 (37.7%); males literate 2,975,000 (51.7%); females literate 1,280,000 (23.3%).
Health (1991–92): physicians 1,497 (1 per 12,623 persons); hospital beds 4,848 (1 per 3,898 persons); infant mortality rate per 1,000 live births (1993) 96.
Food (1988–90): daily per capita caloric intake 2,205 (vegetable products 94%, animal products 6%); 100% of FAO recommended minimum requirement.

Military

Total active duty personnel (1993): 35,000 (army 99.4%, air force 0.6%). *Military expenditure as percentage of GNP* (1991): 1.1% (world 4.2%); per capita expenditure U.S.$2.

---

[1]Includes 10 members nominated by the king. [2]Preliminary. [3]Includes indirect taxes. [4]Import figures are f.o.b. in balance of trade and c.i.f. for commodities and trading partners. [5]1991–92. [6]1989.

Netherlands, The

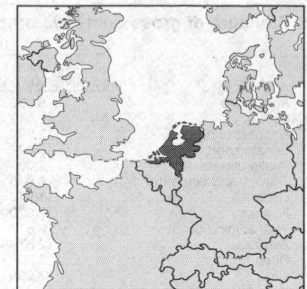

Official name: Koninkrijk der Nederlanden (Kingdom of The Netherlands).
Form of government: constitutional monarchy with a parliament (States General) comprising two legislative houses (First Chamber [75]; Second Chamber [150]).
Chief of state: Monarch.
Head of government: Prime Minister.
Seat of government: The Hague.
Capital: Amsterdam.
Official language: Dutch.
Official religion: none.
Monetary unit: 1 Netherlands guilder (f.) = 100 cents; valuation (Oct. 7, 1994) 1 U.S.$ = f. 1.73; 1 £ = f. 2.74.

Area and population		area		population
				1994[1]
Provinces	Capitals	sq mi	sq km	estimate
Drenthe	Assen	1,025	2,655	451,409
Flevoland	Lelystad	545	1,412	253,699
Friesland	Leeuwarden	1,297	3,360	607,016
Gelderland	Arnhem	1,936	5,015	1,851,402
Groningen	Groningen	906	2,347	556,607
Limburg	Maastricht	838	2,170	1,125,187
Noord-Brabant	's-Hertogenbosch	1,910	4,947	2,259,779
Noord-Holland	Haarlem	1,030	2,667	2,457,329
Overijssel	Zwolle	1,290	3,340	1,044,648
Utrecht	Utrecht	525	1,359	1,056,033
Zeeland	Middelburg	693	1,796	363,867
Zuid-Holland	The Hague	1,108	2,871	3,313,193
TOTAL LAND AREA		13,104[2]	33,939	
INLAND WATER		2,929	7,587	
TOTAL		16,033	41,526	15,341,553[3]

Demography

Population (1994): 15,401,000.
Density (1994)[4]: persons per sq mi 1,175.3, persons per sq km 453.8.
Urban-rural (1993[1]): urban 89.0%; rural 11.0%.
Sex distribution (1993[1]): male 49.44%; female 50.56%.
Age breakdown (1993[1]): under 15, 18.3%; 15–29, 23.0%; 30–44, 23.7%; 45–59, 17.4%; 60–74, 12.1%; 75 and over, 5.5%.
Population projection: (2000) 16,042,000; (2010) 16,769,000.
Doubling time: not applicable; vital rates and net migration in near balance.
Ethnic composition (by nationality; 1992[1]): Netherlander 95.2%; Turkish 1.4%; Moroccan 1.1%; German 0.3%; other 2.0%.
Religious affiliation (1992): Roman Catholic 33.0%; Dutch Reformed Church 15.0%; Calvinist 8.0%; Muslim 3.2%; other 1.8%; no religion 39.0%.
Major cities (1993[1]): Amsterdam 719,856; Rotterdam 596,023; The Hague 444,661; Utrecht 234,170; Eindhoven 195,267.

Vital statistics

Birth rate per 1,000 population (1993): 12.8 (world avg. 26.0); (1992) legitimate 87.5%; illegitimate 12.5%.
Death rate per 1,000 population (1993): 9.0 (world avg. 9.2).
Natural increase rate per 1,000 population (1993): 3.8 (world avg. 16.8).
Total fertility rate (avg. births per childbearing woman; 1992): 1.6.
Marriage rate per 1,000 population (1992): 6.2.
Divorce rate per 1,000 population (1992): 2.0.
Life expectancy at birth (1992): male 74.3 years; female 80.3 years.
Major causes of death per 100,000 population (1992): malignant neoplasms (cancers) 236.8, of which lung cancer 56.1; ischemic heart diseases 138.9; cerebrovascular diseases 85.2; accidents, poisoning, and violence 35.7.

National economy

Budget (1992). Revenue: f. 172,962,000,000 (income and corporate taxes 47.3%, value-added taxes 23.2%, excise and import taxes 8.4%, property taxes 3.5%). Expenditures: f. 194,887,000,000 (social security and public health 26.2%, education and culture 17.7%, debt service 14.0%, defense 7.6%, transportation 5.6%).
Public debt (1993[5]): U.S.$195,935,000,000.
Tourism (1992): receipts from visitors U.S.$5,004,000,000; expenditures by nationals abroad U.S.$9,330,000,000.
Production (metric tons except as noted). Agriculture, forestry, fishing (1993): sugar beets 8,251,200[6], potatoes 7,595,300[6], wheat 1,034,900, onions 605,900, barley 252,200; livestock (number of live animals) 14,964,000 pigs, 4,797,000 cattle, 1,916,000 sheep; roundwood (1991) 1,351,000 cu m; fish catch (1991) 443,097. Manufacturing (value added in f. '000,000; 1991): foodstuffs 13,314; chemicals and chemical products 12,114; electrical machinery 9,041; machinery and transport equipment 6,798; publishing and printing 6,244. Construction (buildings completed by value in f. '000; 1992): residential 10,700,000; nonresidential 10,900,000. Energy production (consumption): electricity (kW hr; 1992) 77,202,000,000 (85,880,000,000); coal (metric tons; 1992) none (12,140,000); crude petroleum (barrels; 1992) 19,497,000 (393,262,000); petroleum products (metric tons; 1992) 57,813,000 (27,823,000), natural gas (cu m; 1992) 91,013,000,000 (48,934,000,000).
Household income and expenditure (1992). Average household size 2.4; income per household f. 58,090 (U.S.$33,040); sources of income: wages 58.5%, transfer payments 28.9%, self-employment 12.6%; expenditure (1990): rent 18.5%, food, beverages, and tobacco 15.4%, medical care 12.7%, transporta-

tion and communications 12.7%, education and recreation 10.5%, household furnishings and appliances 7.2%, clothing and footwear 6.9%, other 16.1%.
Gross national product (at current market price; 1993): U.S.$316,390,000,000 (U.S.$20,710 per capita).

Structure of gross domestic product and labour force

	1992		1991	
	in value f. '000,000	% of total value	labour force	% of labour force
Agriculture	20,466	4.0	293,000	4.2
Mining	16,523	3.2	14,000	0.2
Manufacturing	102,853	20.1	1,169,000	16.7
Construction	30,126	5.9	418,000	6.0
Public utilities	8,961	1.8	44,000	0.6
Transp. and commun.	36,013	7.0	403,000	5.7
Trade	83,093	16.2	1,138,000	16.2
Finance	7	7	682,000	9.7
Pub. admin., defense	7	7	} 2,313,000	33.0
Services	234,681[7]	45.8[7]		
Other	−20,494[8]	−4.0[8]	537,000[9]	7.7[9]
TOTAL	512,230[10]	100.0	7,011,000	100.0

Population economically active (1991): total 7,011,000; activity rate of total population 46.5% (participation rates: ages 15–64, 69.6%; female 39.7%; unemployed 7.7%).

Price and earnings indexes (1990 = 100)

	1987	1988	1989	1990	1991	1992	1993
Consumer price index	95.8	96.6	97.6	100.0	103.9	107.7	109.9
Hourly earnings index	94.7	95.9	97.2	100.0	103.7	108.2	...

Land use (1992): forested 10.3%; meadows and pastures 31.4%; agricultural and under permanent cultivation 27.2%; other 31.1%.

Foreign trade

Balance of trade (current prices)

	1987	1988	1989	1990	1991	1992
f. '000,000	13,201	17,647	19,277	22,345	26,131	22,225
% of total	3.6%	4.5%	4.4%	4.9%	5.6%	4.7%

Imports (1992): f. 236,159,000,000 (machinery and transport equipment 31.6%, of which road vehicles 7.3%; foodstuffs, beverages, and tobacco 12.3%; chemicals and chemical products 10.7%; mineral fuels 8.6%; textiles 7.0%; metals and metal products 6.7%; raw materials, oils, and fats 4.7%). *Major import sources:* Germany 25.2%; Belgium-Luxembourg 14.2%; U.K. 8.6%; France 7.9%; U.S. 7.6%.
Exports (1992): f. 245,861,000,000 (machinery and transport equipment 23.8%, of which road vehicles 3.7%; foodstuffs, beverages, and tobacco 20.5%; chemicals and chemical products 15.9%; mineral fuels 8.6%; metals and metal products 6.2%; textiles 4.8%). *Major export destinations:* Germany 28.8%; Belgium-Luxembourg 14.3%; France 10.6%; U.K. 9.2%; Italy 6.4%.

Transport and communications

Transport. Railroads (1992): length 2,753 km; passenger-km 15,350,000,000; metric ton-km cargo 2,764,000,000. Roads (1993): total length 105,800 km (paved 88%). Vehicles (1993): passenger cars 5,740,000; trucks and buses 685,000. Merchant marine (1992): vessels (100 gross tons and over) 1,076; total deadweight tonnage 4,190,997. Air transport (1992): passenger-km 31,944,000,000; metric ton-km cargo 2,488,100,000; airports (1994) 5.
Communications. Daily newspapers (1990): total number 45; total circulation 4,944,000; circulation per 1,000 population 332. Radio (1991): total number of receivers 12,146,299 (1 per 1.2 persons). Television (1992): total number of receivers 5,618,000 (1 per 2.7 persons). Telephones (1991): 10,500,000 (1 per 1.4 persons).

Education and health

Education (1992–93)

	schools	teachers[11]	students	student/ teacher ratio[11]
Primary (age 6–12)	9,333	99,031	1,526,000	15.7
Secondary (age 12–18)	1,117	89,370	668,000	7.7
Voc., teacher tr.	747	18,613	498,000	28.0
Higher	206	30,952[12]	389,000	10.2

Educational attainment (1992). Percentage of population ages 15–64 having: primary education 17.1%; secondary 65.7%; higher 17.0%; other 0.2%. *Literacy* (1992): virtually 100% literate.
Health: physicians (1991) 37,481 (1 per 400 persons); hospital beds (1992) 87,860 (1 per 172 persons); infant mortality rate per 1,000 live births (1993) 6.3.
Food (1988–90): daily per capita caloric intake 3,078 (vegetable products 68%, animal products 32%); 114% of FAO recommended minimum requirement.

Military

Total active duty personnel (1994): 70,900 (army 60.9%, navy 20.2%, air force 12.7%, other[13] 6.2%). *Military expenditure as percentage of GNP* (1992): 2.6% (world 5.0%); per capita expenditure U.S.$524.

---

[1]January 1. [2]Detail does not add to total given because of rounding. [3]Includes 1,384 persons having no fixed municipality of residence. [4]Based on land area only. [5]June. [6]1992. [7]Services includes Finance and Pub. admin., defense. [8]Imputed bank service charge. [9]Unemployed. [10]Detail does not add to total given because of statistical discrepencies. [11]1990–91. [12]1985–86. [13]Includes 3,600 military police.

New Zealand

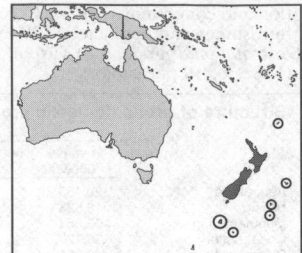

Official name: New Zealand (English); Aotearoa (Maori).
Form of government: constitutional monarchy with one legislative house (House of Representatives [99]).
Chief of state: British Monarch, represented by Governor-General.
Head of government: Prime Minister.
Capital: Wellington.
Official languages: English; Maori.
Official religion: none.
Monetary unit: 1 New Zealand dollar ($NZ) = 100 cents; valuation (Oct. 7, 1994) 1 U.S.$ = $NZ 1.65; 1 £ = $NZ 2.63.

Area and population	area		population
Islands			1993
Regional Councils	sq mi	sq km	estimate[1]
North Island	44,702	115,777	2,604,100
Auckland	...	...	982,000
Bay of Plenty	...	...	213,800
Gisborne[2]	...	...	44,400
Hawkes Bay	...	...	140,100
Manawatu-Wanganui	...	...	230,700
Northland	...	...	134,000
Taranaki	...	...	107,500
Waikato	...	...	344,600
Wellington	...	...	407,000
South Island	58,384	151,215	889,300
Canterbury	...	...	451,700
Nelson-Marlborough[2, 3]	...	...	114,400
Otago	...	...	186,900
Southland	...	...	102,600
West Coast	...	...	33,700
Remainder[4, 5]	...	...	800
Offshore islands[6]	322	854	...
Stewart Island[7]	674	1,746	...
Chatham Islands[8]	372	963	...
TOTAL	104,454	270,534	3,494,200

Demography

Population (1994): 3,525,000,000.
Density (1994): persons per sq mi 33.8, persons per sq km 13.0.
Urban-rural (1993): urban 68.5%; rural 31.5%.
Sex distribution (1993): male 49.28%; female 50.72%.
Age breakdown (1993): under 15, 23.1%; 15–29, 24.2%; 30–44, 22.5%; 45–59, 14.6%; 60–74, 11.0%; 75 and over, 4.6%.
Population projection: (2000) 3,786,000; (2010) 4,097,000.
Doubling time: 75 years.
Ethnic composition (1991): New Zealand European 73.8%; New Zealand Maori 9.6%; Pacific Island Polynesian 3.6%; multiethnic 4.5%; other 8.5%.
Religious affiliation (1991): Anglican 21.4%; Presbyterian 16.0%; Roman Catholic 14.8%; Methodist 4.1%; nonreligious 19.7%; other 24.0%.
Major cities (1992): Auckland 316,900; Christchurch 293,700; Manukau 229,-800; North Shore 153,300; Wellington 150,100.

Vital statistics

Birth rate per 1,000 population (1993): 17.2 (world avg. 26.0); (1992) legitimate 63.3%; illegitimate 36.7%.
Death rate per 1,000 population (1993): 7.9 (world avg. 9.2).
Natural increase rate per 1,000 population (1993): 9.3 (world avg. 16.8).
Total fertility rate (avg. births per childbearing woman; 1993): 2.1.
Marriage rate per 1,000 population (1993): 6.4.
Divorce rate per 1,000 population (1993): 2.7.
Life expectancy at birth (1991): male 72.0 years; female 77.9 years.
Major causes of death per 100,000 population (1991): diseases of the circulatory system 341.6, of which ischemic heart disease 199.7; malignant neoplasms (cancers) 201.1; diseases of the respiratory system 73.5; accidents 48.2; diabetes mellitus 11.9.

National economy

Budget (1992–93): $NZ 29,874,000,000 (income tax 42.6%, goods and services tax 19.9%, interest and profits 7.8%, excise duties 6.2%). Expenditures: $NZ 31,468,000,000 (social services 34.0%, education 14.4%, administration 14.0%, health 12.9%).
Public debt (year ending June 30, 1992): $NZ 26,378,000,000.
Tourism (1992): receipts U.S.$1,032,000,000; expenditures U.S.$977,000,000.
Production (metric tons except as noted). Agriculture, forestry, fishing (1993): barley 347,000, corn (maize) 171,000, wheat 171,000, peas 80,000, oats 73,-000; livestock (number of live animals) 51,000,000 sheep, 8,675,000 cattle, 470,000 goats, 430,000 pigs; roundwood (1993) 15,560,000 cu m; fish catch (1993) 580,874. Mining and quarrying (1992): limestone 3,720,686; iron ore and sand concentrate 2,934,143; serpentine 23,781; silver 22,000 kg; gold 10,-000 kg. Manufacturing (1991–92): wood pulp 1,343,300; chemical fertilizers 994,000[9]; cement 599,000; beer 362,656,000 litres[9]; carbonated soft drinks 179,378,000 litres; footwear 4,022,000 pairs[9]. Construction ($NZ '000; 1992–93): residential 2,284,800; nonresidential 1,088,500. Energy production (consumption): electricity (kW-hr; 1992) 31,271,000,000 (31,271,000,000); coal (metric tons; 1992) 2,830,000 (2,430,000); crude petroleum (barrels; 1992) 13,959,000 (32,743,000); petroleum products (metric tons; 1992) 4,635,000 (4,158,000); natural gas (cu m; 1992) 6,877,100,000 (4,605,900,000).
Gross national product (1993): U.S.$44,660,000,000 (U.S.$12,900 per capita).

Structure of gross domestic product and labour force

	1990–91		1993	
	in value $NZ '000,000	% of total value	labour force[1]	% of labour force
Agriculture	5,380	7.4	160,500	9.8
Mining	1,042	1.4	3,500	0.2
Manufacturing	12,790	17.5	242,000	14.7
Construction	3,097	4.2	79,600	4.8
Public utilities	2,081	2.8	11,000	0.7
Transp. and commun.	5,926	8.0	89,500	5.4
Trade	11,943	16.4	312,500	19.0
Finance	17,020	23.2	155,900	9.5
Pub. admin., defense	8,613	11.7 }	417,600	25.4
Services	2,379	3.2 }		
Other	3,068[10]	4.2[10]	173,600[11]	10.5[11]
TOTAL	73,339	100.0	1,645,700	100.0

Population economically active (1993[1]): total 1,645,700; activity rate 47.1% (participation rates: over age 15, 63.1%; female 43.5%; unemployed 9.7%).

Price and earnings indexes (1990 = 100)							
	1987	1988	1989	1990	1991	1992	1993
Consumer price index	83.8	89.2	94.3	100.0	102.6	103.6	105.0
Weekly earnings index	85.7	92.2	95.8	100.0	102.6	103.5	...

Household income and expenditure. Average household size (1992–93) 2.8; annual income per household (1991) $NZ 39,600 (U.S.$21,430); sources of income (1987–88): wages and salaries 68.7%, transfer payments 14.1%, self-employment 8.1%; expenditure (1992–93): housing 18.5%, food 17.4%, transportation 16.8%, household durable goods 13.8%, clothing 4.8%.
Land use (1992): forested 27.5%; meadows and pastures 50.9%; agricultural and under permanent cultivation 1.5%; other 20.1%.

Foreign trade

Balance of trade (current prices)						
	1988	1989	1990	1991	1992	1993
$NZ '000,000	+3,215.0	+1,380.6	+1,349.1	+3,359.6	+2,451.0	+1,673.4
% of total	13.6%	4.8%	4.4%	11.2%	7.2%	4.6%

Imports (1993): $NZ 17,332,700,000 (machinery 24.1%; minerals, chemicals, and plastics 20.7%; transport equipment 14.0%; basic manufactures 9.4%; metals and metal products 4.3%; textiles, clothing, and footwear 2.0%). *Major import sources:* Australia 21.6%; U.S. 18.5%; Japan 15.3%; U.K. 6.1%; Germany 4.2%.
Exports (1993): $NZ 19,006,000,000 (food and live animals 42.5%; basic manufactures 21.9%; minerals, chemicals, and plastics 6.9%; metals and metal products 6.9%). *Major export destinations:* Australia 20.0%; Japan 14.7%; U.S. 11.9%; U.K. 6.4%; South Korea 4.5%; Germany 2.6%.

Transport and communications

Transport. Railroads (1993): length 2,469 mi, 3,973 km; passenger-km (1984) 458,160,000; short ton-mi cargo (1992–93) 1,712,000,000, metric ton-km cargo 2,500,000,000. Roads (1992): total length 58,605 mi, 94,315 km (paved 73%). Vehicles (1993): passenger cars 1,562,134; trucks and buses 328,510. Merchant marine (1992): vessels (100 gross tons and over) 139; total deadweight tonnage 279,805. Air transport (1990): passenger-mi 6,591,000,000, passenger-km 10,608,000,000; short ton-mi cargo 227,000,000, metric ton-km cargo 332,000,000; airports (1994) 36.
Communications. Daily newspapers (1990): total number 35; total circulation 1,100,000; circulation per 1,000 population 322. Radio (1991): 3,100,000 receivers (1 per 1.1 persons). Television (1991): 1,100,000 receivers (1 per 3.1 persons). Telephones (1988): 2,403,000 (1 per 1.4 persons).

Education and health

Education (1993)	schools	teachers	students	student/ teacher ratio
Primary (age 5–12)[12]	2,412	21,247	434,308	20.4
Secondary (age 13–17)	339	14,946	230,132	15.4
Voc., teacher tr.	30	5,734	99,299	17.3
Higher[13]	7	4,088	97,835	23.9

Educational attainment (1991). Percentage of population age 25 and over having: primary and some secondary education 54.9%; secondary 31.1%; higher 6.9%; not specified 6.1%. *Literacy:* virtually 100.0%.
Health: physicians 10,787 (1 per 359 persons); hospital beds (1989) 29,352 (1 per 114 persons); infant mortality rate per 1,000 live births 7.3.
Food (1988–90): daily per capita caloric intake 3,461 (vegetable products 59%, animal products 41%); 131% of FAO recommended minimum requirement.

Military

Total active duty personnel (1994): 10,000 (army 45.0%, air force 33.0%, navy 22.0%). *Military expenditure as percentage of GNP* (1993): 1.5% (world, n.a.); per capita expenditure U.S.$194.

---

[1]Provisional; March 5. [2]Reorganized as a unitary authority that is administered by a district council with regional powers. [3]Reorganized as three separate unitary authorities: Nelson city, Tasman district, and Marlborough district. [4]Includes the population of Kermadec Islands and persons on oil rigs. [5]Includes the population of Chatham Islands county and Campbell Island. [6]Excludes islands in Regional Councils. [7]Part of Southland Regional Council. [8]Chatham Islands county remains outside any Regional Council. [9]1990–91. [10]Includes import duties less imputed bank service charges. [11]Includes 162,300 unemployed. [12]Includes 83 composite schools that provide both primary and secondary education. [13]Universities only.

Nicaragua

Official name: República de Nicaragua (Republic of Nicaragua).
Form of government: unitary multiparty republic with one legislative house (National Assembly [92[1]]).
Head of state and government: President.
Capital: Managua.
Official language: Spanish.
Official religion: none.
Monetary unit: 1 córdoba oro (C$)[2] = 100 centavos; valuation (Oct. 7, 1994) 1 U.S.$ = C$6.74; 1 £ = C$10.71.

Area and population

Departments	Capitals	area[3] sq mi	area[3] sq km	population 1991 estimate
Boaco	Boaco	1,639	4,244	121,561
Carazo	Jinotepe	405	1,050	154,989
Chinandega	Chinandega	1,902	4,926	335,596
Chontales	Juigalpa	2,463	6,378	141,676
Estelí	Estelí	902	2,335	171,215
Granada	Granada	359	929	154,912
Jinotega	Jinotega	3,766	9,755	178,195
León	León	1,972	5,107	350,275
Madriz	Somoto	619	1,602	98,737
Managua	Managua	1,418	3,672	1,108,720
Masaya	Masaya	228	590	211,123
Matagalpa	Matagalpa	3,291	8,523	350,627
Nueva Segovia	Ocotal	1,206	3,123	124,659
Río San Juan	San Carlos	2,885	7,473	44,576
Rivas	Rivas	832	2,155	138,676
Autonomous regions				
North Atlantic	...	12,417	32,159	} 313,694
South Atlantic	Bluefields	10,582	27,407	
TOTAL LAND AREA		46,884[4]	121,428	
INLAND WATER		3,954	10,242	
TOTAL		50,838	131,670	3,999,231

Demography

Population (1994): 4,210,000.
Density (1994)[5]: persons per sq mi 89.8, persons per sq km 34.7.
Urban-rural (1992): urban 61.6%, rural 38.4%.
Sex distribution (1992): male 50.16%; female 49.84%.
Age breakdown (1992): under 15, 45.4%; 15–29, 27.6%; 30–44, 15.3%; 45–59, 7.3%; 60–74, 3.6%; 75 and over, 0.8%.
Population projection: (2000) 4,457,000; (2010) 4,900,000.
Doubling time: 21 years.
Ethnic composition (1991): mestizo (Spanish/Indian) 69.0%; white 17.0%; black 9.0%; Amerindian 5.0%.
Religious affiliation (1992): Roman Catholic 89.3%; other (mostly Baptist, Moravian, and Pentecostal) 10.7%.
Major cities (1992)[6]: Managua 973,759; León 172,042; Masaya 101,878; Chinandega 101,605; Matagalpa 95,268; Granada 91,929.

Vital statistics

Birth rate per 1,000 population (1993): 35.6 (world avg. 26.0).
Death rate per 1,000 population (1993): 6.9 (world avg. 9.2).
Natural increase rate per 1,000 population (1993): 28.7 (world avg. 16.8).
Total fertility rate (avg. births per childbearing woman; 1993): 4.5.
Marriage rate per 1,000 population (1991): 3.3.
Divorce rate per 1,000 population (1991): 0.4.
Life expectancy at birth (1993): male 60.7 years; female 66.4 years.
Major causes of death per 100,000 population (1991)[7]: diseases of the circulatory system 141.9; infectious and parasitic diseases 100.1; accidents and violence 94.0; diseases of the respiratory system 73.0; malignant neoplasms (cancers) 56.6.

National economy

Budget (1994). Revenue: C$2,538,000,000 (indirect taxes 82.9%, direct taxes 11.0%, unspecified 6.1%). Expenditures: C$2,791,000,000 (current expenditure 79.3%, development expenditure 20.7%).
Production (metric tons except as noted). Agriculture, forestry, fishing (1993): sugarcane 2,400,000, corn (maize) 283,000, rice 178,000, bananas 136,000, sorghum 105,000, dry beans 73,000, oranges 70,000, plantains 55,000, cassava 52,000, coffee 50,000, pineapples 45,000, sesame seed 11,000; livestock (number of live animals) 1,680,000 cattle, 709,000 pigs; roundwood (1992) 3,565,000 cu m; fish catch (1991) 5,709, of which crustaceans 3,192. Mining and quarrying (1992): gold 42,568 troy oz. Manufacturing (value of production in C$'000,000; 1991[8]): food 1,579; beverages 945; tobacco products 447; cement, bricks, and tile 236; rubber products 215; textiles 188. Construction (completed; 1991): 569 cu m. Energy production (consumption): electricity (kW-hr; 1992) 1,601,000,000 (1,636,000,000); coal, none (none); crude petroleum (barrels; 1992) none (5,212,000); petroleum products (metric tons; 1992) 635,000 (720,000); natural gas, none (none).
Household income and expenditure. Average household size (1980) 6.9; income per household: n.a.; sources of income: n.a.; expenditure: n.a.
Tourism (1992): receipts from visitors U.S.$21,000,000; expenditures by nationals abroad U.S.$30,000,000.
Population economically active (1991): total 1,386,300; activity rate of total population 34.7% (participation rates: over age 15, 62.0%; female 33.2%; unemployed [1994] more than 60.0%).

---

[1]Includes two unsuccessful 1990 presidential candidates meeting special conditions.
[2]The córdoba oro (gold córdoba), introduced in August 1990, circulated simultaneously with the new córdoba until April 30, 1991, when the new córdoba ceased to be legal tender; on April 30, 1 córdoba oro equaled 5,000,000 new córdobas. The new córdoba had been introduced in February 1988 at the rate of 1 new córdoba to 1,000 (old) córdobas. [3]Lakes and lagoons are excluded from the areas of departments and autonomous regions. [4]Detail does not add to total given because of rounding. [5]Based on land area. [6]*Municipio* population. [7]Projected rates based on about 50% of total deaths. [8]At prices of 1980. [9]Estimated figures. [10]Unemployed persons previously employed. [11]Estimated percentages. [12]Railroad service halted in January 1994 because of insufficient revenue. [13]Aeronica only. [14]Number of lines.

Price and earnings indexes (1990 = 100)

	1988	1989	1990	1991	1992	1993
Consumer price index	0.03	1.32	100.0	2,842	3,418	4,303
Earnings index	...	...	...	...	...	...

Gross national product (at current market prices; 1993): U.S.$1,434,000,000 (U.S.$360 per capita).

Structure of gross domestic product and labour force

	1992 in value C$'000,000[8, 9]	1992 % of total value	1991 labour force	1991 % of labour force
Agriculture	4,349	24.1	415,400	30.0
Mining	115	0.6	9,000	0.6
Manufacturing	4,060	22.5	188,200	13.6
Construction	556	3.1	30,200	2.2
Public utilities	507	2.8	10,300	0.7
Transportation and communications	942	5.2	42,600	3.1
Trade	3,337	18.5	195,500	14.1
Finance, real estate	589	3.3	24,700	1.8
Pub. admin., defense	2,028	11.2	98,100	7.1
Services	1,570	8.7	183,900	13.3
Other	—	—	188,400[10]	13.6[10]
TOTAL	18,054[4]	100.0	1,386,300	100.0[4]

Public debt (external, outstanding; 1992): U.S.$8,994,000,000.
Land use (1992): forested 27.0%; meadows and pastures 46.3%; agricultural and under permanent cultivation 10.7%; other 16.0%.

Foreign trade

Balance of trade (current prices)

	1988	1989	1990	1991	1992	1993
U.S.$'000,000	−483.9	−236.6	−236.8	−419.1	−576.2	−393.0
% of total	51.0%	27.6%	26.4%	43.3%	57.0%	42.4%

Imports (1992): U.S.$793,700,000 (consumer goods 35.0%, petroleum products 14.6%, capital goods for industry 12.9%). *Major import sources*[11]: United States 24.0%; former U.S.S.R. 10.0%; Cuba 8.0%; Guatemala 7.0%; Costa Rica 6.0%; Japan 6.0%.
Exports (1992): U.S.$217,500,000 (coffee 20.3%, fresh and frozen meat 17.6%, cotton 11.8%, sugar 8.6%, bananas 4.5%, sesame 2.6%). *Major export destinations*[11]: United States 19.0%; Germany 15.0%; Canada 8.0%; Greece 6.0%; Japan 6.0%; Mexico 5.0%.

Transport and communications

Transport. Railroads:[12]. Roads (1993): total length 9,499 mi, 15,287 km (paved 10%). Vehicles (1992): passenger cars 35,000; trucks and buses 35,000. Merchant marine (1992): vessels (100 gross tons and over) 25; total deadweight tonnage 1,295. Air transport (1990)[13]: passenger-mi 69,000,000, passenger-km 111,000,000; short ton-mi cargo 2,470,000, metric ton-km cargo 3,600,000; airports (1994) with scheduled flights 4.
Communications. Daily newspapers (1991): total number 3; total circulation 113,000; circulation per 1,000 population 28. Radio (1993): 880,000 receivers (1 per 4.8 persons). Television (1993): 210,000 receivers (1 per 20 persons). Telephones (1991): 54,280[14] (1 per 76 persons).

Education and health

Education (1991)

	schools	teachers	students	student/ teacher ratio
Primary (age 7–12)	4,402	18,646	674,045	36.1
Secondary (age 13–18) }	407	4,191	180,112	43.0
Voc., teacher tr.				
Higher	10	3,469	34,846	10.0

Educational attainment: n.a. *Literacy* (1986): total population age 15 and over literate 74.0%.
Health (1991): physicians 2,125 (1 per 1,882 persons); hospital beds 4,974 (1 per 804 persons); infant mortality rate per 1,000 live births (1993) 71.0.
Food (1984–86): daily per capita caloric intake 2,472 (vegetable products, n.a., animal products, n.a.); 110% of FAO recommended minimum requirement.

Military

Total active duty personnel (1993): 15,200 (army 88.8%, navy 3.3%, air force 7.9%). *Military expenditure as percentage of GNP* (1991): 4.0% (world 4.2%); per capita expenditure U.S.$18.

Niger

Official name: République du Niger
(Republic of Niger).
Form of government: unitary multiparty
republic with one legislative body
(High Council of the Republic [83]).
Chief of state: President.
Head of government: Prime Minister.
Capital: Niamey.
Official language: French.
Official religion: none.
Monetary unit: 1 CFA franc
(CFAF) = 100 centimes;
valuation (Oct. 7, 1994)
1 U.S.$ = CFAF 526.67;
1 £ = CFAF 837.67.

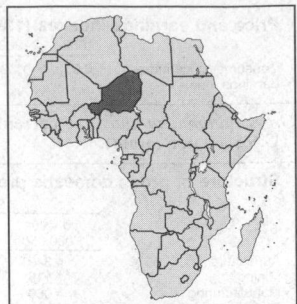

Area and population

Departments	Capitals	area[1] sq mi	area[1] sq km	population 1988 census[2]
Agadez[3]	Agadez	244,869	634,209	205,232
Diffa	Diffa	54,138	140,216	187,230
Dosso	Dosso	11,970	31,002	1,018,058
Maradi	Maradi	14,896	38,581	1,386,549
Tahoua	Tahoua	41,188	106,677	1,306,948
Tillabéry	Tillabéry	34,863	90,293	1,715,118
Zinder	Zinder	56,151	145,430	1,409,417
TOTAL		458,075	1,186,408	7,228,552

Demography

Population (1994): 8,813,000.
Density (1994)[1]: persons per sq mi 17.7, persons per sq km 6.8.
Urban-rural (1991): urban 20.2%; rural 79.8%.
Sex distribution (1990): male 49.32%; female 50.68%.
Age breakdown (1990): under 15, 47.7%; 15–29, 25.9%; 30–44, 14.6%; 45–59,
7.8%; 60 and over, 4.0%.
Population projection: (2000) 10,640,000; (2010) 14,326,000.
Doubling time: 22 years.
Ethnic composition (1988): Hausa 52.8%; Zerma-Songhai 21.0%; Tuareg
10.6%; Fulani 9.8%; Kanuri-Nanga 4.5%; Teda 0.5%; Arab 0.3%; Gurma
0.3%; other 0.2%.
Religious affiliation (1988): Muslim, primarily Sunnī, 98.6%; other, mostly
traditional beliefs, 1.4%.
Major cities (1988): Niamey 392,169; Zinder 119,838; Maradi 109,386; Tahoua
49,941; Agadez 49,361.

Vital statistics

Birth rate per 1,000 population (1990–95): 51.3 (world avg. 26.0).
Death rate per 1,000 population (1990–95): 18.7 (world avg. 9.2).
Natural increase rate per 1,000 population (1990–95): 32.6 (world avg. 16.8).
Total fertility rate (avg. births per childbearing woman; 1990): 7.1.
Marriage rate per 1,000 population: n.a.
Divorce rate per 1,000 population: n.a.
Life expectancy at birth (1990–95): male 44.9 years; female 48.1 years.
Major causes of death (1989): n.a.; however, among selected major causes
registered at medical facilities are measles, diarrhea, meningitis, malaria,
pneumonia, tetanus, viral hepatitis, and poliomyelitis.

National economy

Budget (1992). Revenue: CFAF 188,400,000,000 (current revenues 44.3%,
foreign loans 31.2%, external aid and gifts 24.5%). Expenditures: CFAF
188,400,000,000 (current expenditures 45.0%, capital expenditures 38.0%,
amortization of public debt 17.0%).
Public debt (external, outstanding; 1992): U.S.$1,362,000,000.
Tourism (1992): receipts from visitors U.S.$17,000,000; expenditures by na-
tionals abroad U.S.$9,000,000.
Gross national product (at current market prices; 1993): U.S.$2,279,000,000
(U.S.$270 per capita).

Structure of gross domestic product and labour force

	1991 in value CFAF '000,000	% of total value	labour force	% of labour force
Agriculture	245,995	37.5	3,222,000	86.9
Mining	34,516	5.3		
Manufacturing	43,921	6.7	96,000	2.6
Construction	15,085	2.3		
Public utilities	15,341	2.3		
Transportation and communications	26,727	4.1		
Trade and finance	117,083	17.8	389,000	10.5
Pub. admin., defense	143,557	21.9		
Services				
Other	14,500	2.1	...	...
TOTAL	656,725	100.0	3,707,000	100.0

Production (metric tons except as noted). Agriculture, forestry, fishing (1993):
millet 1,430,000, pulses 508,000, sorghum 305,000, vegetables and melons
257,000 (of which onions 175,000), roots and tubers 255,000, sugarcane
140,000, rice 72,000, peanuts (groundnuts) 60,000, wheat 4,000, seed cotton
3,000, corn (maize) 1,000, tobacco leaf 1,000; livestock (number of live animals) 5,407,000 goats, 3,505,000 sheep, 1,800,000 cattle, 462,000 asses, 370,000

camels, 82,000 horses; roundwood (1992) 5,289,000 cu m; fish catch (1991)
3,150. Mining and quarrying (1993): uranium 2,914. Manufacturing (1990):
processed meat 115,000; cement 27,000; butter 3,000; peanut (groundnut) oil
1,000; beer 92,000 hectolitres; cotton fabrics 36,000,000 sq m. Construction
(value added in CFAF; 1991): 15,085,000,000. Energy production (consumption): electricity (kW-hr; 1992) 171,000,000 (361,000,000); coal (metric tons;
1992) 170,000 (170,000); crude petroleum, none (n.a.); petroleum products
(metric tons; 1992) none (201,000); natural gas, none (n.a.).
Population economically active (1992): total 4,130,000; activity rate of total
population 50.0% (participation rates [1988]: over age 10, 53.5%; female
20.7%; unemployed, n.a.).

Price and earnings indexes (1985 = 100)

	1987	1988	1989	1990	1991	1992	1993
Consumer price index	90.3	89.0	86.5	85.8	79.1	75.6	74.6
Hourly earnings index[4]	100.0	100.0	100.0	100.0	100.0	100.0	...

Household income and expenditure. Average household size (1988) 6.4; income per household: n.a.; sources of income (1977): self-employment 59.5%,
family 30.1%, salary or wages 4.8%, employer 0.7%; expenditure (1983):
food and beverages 50.5%, household expenses 19.1%, clothing 7.3%.
Land use (1992): forested 1.5%; meadows and pastures 6.9%; agricultural
and under permanent cultivation 2.8%; other (largely desert) 88.8%.

Foreign trade[5]

Balance of trade (current prices)

	1986	1987	1988	1989	1990	1991
CFAF '000,000	−11,400	−12,000	−20,900	−20,900	−5,000	−12,300
% of total	4.7%	5.2%	8.6%	8.4%	2.8%	6.5%

Imports (1990): CFAF 107,200,000,000 (food and live animals 25.6%, machinery and transport equipment 22.3%, basic manufactures 16.7%, mineral
fuels 12.9%, chemicals 10.2%). *Major import sources* (1991): France 23.5%;
Côte d'Ivoire 10.0%; West Germany 5.7%; United Kingdom 5.4%; Japan
3.6%; The Netherlands 3.6%; Italy 3.4%.
Exports (1990): CFAF 106,000,000,000 (uranium 79.6%, live animals 11.1%,
beverages and tobacco 4.7%). *Major export destinations* (1991): France
81.0%; Nigeria 6.6%; United States 2.0%; Canada 1.9%; Mali 1.0%.

Transport and communications

Transport. Railroads (1992): none[6]. Roads (1991): total length 12,244 mi,
19,705 km (paved 22%). Vehicles (1990): passenger cars 31,427; trucks and
buses 8,768. Air transport (1992)[7]: passenger-mi 126,000,000, passenger-km
203,000,000; short ton-mi cargo 11,000,000, metric ton-km cargo 16,000,000;
airports (1994) with scheduled flights 1.
Communications. Daily newspapers (1991): total number 1; total circulation
5,000; circulation per 1,000 population 0.6. Radio (1993): total number of
receivers 400,000 (1 per 21 persons). Television (1993): total number of
receivers 25,000 (1 per 341 persons). Telephones (1992): 14,040 (1 per 588
persons).

Education and health

Education (1990)

	schools	teachers	students	student/ teacher ratio
Primary (age 7–12)	2,807	8,759	368,732	42.1
Secondary (age 13–19)	105[8]	2,534	74,337	29.3
Voc., teacher tr.	7[8]	190	2,421	12.7
Higher	3[8]	341[9, 10]	4,506[8]	11.1[9, 10]

Educational attainment (1988). Percentage of population age 25 and over
having: no formal schooling 85.0%; Koranic education 11.2%; primary education 2.5%; secondary 1.1%; higher 0.2%. *Literacy* (1988): percentage
of total population age 15 and over literate 10.8%; males literate 16.7%;
females literate 5.4%.
Health: physicians (1989) 140 (1 per 52,900 persons); hospital beds (1979)
3,261 (1 per 1,633 persons); infant mortality rate per 1,000 live births
(1990–95) 124.0.
Food (1988–90): daily per capita caloric intake 2,239 (vegetable products 95%,
animal products 5%); 95% of FAO recommended minimum requirement.

Military

Total active duty personnel (1994): 5,300 (army 98.1%, air force 1.9%). *Military
expenditure as percentage of GNP* (1992): 1.0% (world [1991] 4.2%); per
capita expenditure U.S.$4.

[1]The departmental areas and total shown are obsolete. The total area, according to
recent official estimates, is 497,000 sq mi (1,287,000 sq km); but subtotals distributing
this total among the departments remain unpublished. [2]De jure. [3]The peace accord
signed in October 1994 provided for an eventual limited autonomy for the Tuaregs.
[4]Guaranteed minimum wage for professionals. [5]Import figures are c.i.f. in balance
of trade, commodities, and trading partners. [6]Niger is a cofounder of the Common
Benin-Niger Organization (OCBN) for Railroads and Transport, currently maintaining
rail operations only in Benin but having the purpose of extending rail services from
the sea at Cotonou, Benin, to Dosso and, ultimately, Niamey, Niger; in the interim,
freight transported between the two countries is carried by truck. [7]Air Afrique. [8]1989.
[9]1988. [10]Université de Niamey and École Nationale d'Administration du Niger only.

Nigeria

Official name: Federal Republic of Nigeria.
Form of government: military regime[1].
Head of state and government: military leader.
Capital: Abuja (Federal Capital Territory)[2].
Official language: English.
Official religion: none.
Monetary unit: 1 Nigerian naira (₦) = 100 kobo; valuation (Oct. 7, 1994) 1 U.S.$ = ₦22.00; 1 £ = ₦34.99.

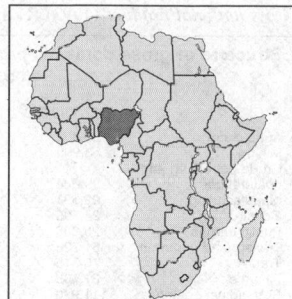

Area and population

States	Capitals	area sq mi	area sq km	population 1991 census[3]
Abia	Umuahia	[4]	[4]	2,297,978
Adamawa	Yola	35,286[5]	91,390[5]	2,124,049
Akwa Ibom	Uyo	2,734	7,081	2,359,736
Anambra	Awka	6,824[6]	17,675[6]	2,767,903
Bauchi	Bauchi	24,944	64,605	4,294,413
Benue	Makurdi	17,442[7]	45,174[7]	2,780,398
Borno	Maiduguri	44,942[8]	116,400[8]	2,596,589
Cross River	Calabar	7,782	20,156	1,865,604
Delta	Asaba	9	9	2,570,181
Edo	Benin City	13,707[9]	35,500[9]	2,159,848
Enugu	Enugu	6	6	3,161,295
Imo	Owerri	4,575[4]	11,850[4]	2,485,499
Jigawa	Dutse	10	10	2,829,929
Kaduna	Kaduna	17,781	46,053	3,969,252
Kano	Kano	16,712[10]	43,285[10]	5,632,040
Katsina	Katsina	9,341	24,192	3,878,344
Kebbi	Birnin Kebbi	11	11	2,062,226
Kogi	Lokoja	7, 12	7, 12	2,099,046
Kwara	Ilorin	25,818[12]	66,869[12]	1,566,469
Lagos	Ikeja	1,292	3,345	5,685,781
Niger	Minna	25,111	65,037	2,482,367
Ogun	Abeokuta	6,472	16,762	2,338,570
Ondo	Akure	8,092	20,959	3,884,485
Osun	Oshogbo	13	13	2,203,016
Oyo	Ibadan	14,558[13]	37,705[13]	3,488,789
Plateau	Jos	22,405	58,030	3,283,704
Rivers	Port Harcourt	8,436	21,850	3,983,857
Sokoto	Sokoto	39,589[11]	102,535[11]	4,392,391
Taraba	Jalingo	5	5	1,480,590
Yobe	Damaturu	8	8	1,411,481
Federal Capital Territory				
Abuja	Abuja	2,824	7,315	378,671
TOTAL		356,669[14]	923,768	88,514,501

Demography

Population (1994): 93,472,000.
Density (1994): persons per sq mi 262.1, persons per sq km 101.2.
Urban-rural (1992): urban 36.8%; rural 63.2%.
Sex distribution (1991): male 50.32%; female 49.68%.
Age breakdown (1990): under 15, 47.4%; 15–29, 26.0%; 30–44, 14.4%; 45–59, 8.0%; 60–74, 3.5%; 75 and over, 0.7%.
Population projection: (2000) 105,885,000; (2010) 130,344,000.
Doubling time: 22 years.
Ethnic composition (1983): Hausa 21.3%; Yoruba 21.3%; Igbo (Ibo) 18.0%; Fulani 11.2%; Ibibio 5.6%; Kanuri 4.2%; Edo 3.4%; Tiv 2.2%; Ijaw 1.8%; Bura 1.7%; Nupe 1.2%; other 8.1%.
Religious affiliation (1980): Christian 49.0%, of which Protestant 26.3%, Roman Catholic 12.1%, African indigenous 10.6%; Muslim 45.0%; other 6.0%.
Major cities (1992): Lagos 1,347,000; Ibadan 1,295,000; Kano 699,900; Ogbomosho 660,600; Oshogbo 441,600; Ilorin 430,600.

Vital statistics

Birth rate per 1,000 population (1990–95): 46.5 (world avg. 26.0).
Death rate per 1,000 population (1990–95): 14.0 (world avg. 9.2).
Natural increase rate per 1,000 population (1990–95): 32.5 (world avg. 16.8).
Total fertility rate (avg. births per childbearing woman; 1990–95): 6.6.
Life expectancy at birth (1993): male 53.5 years; female 55.9 years.

National economy

Budget (1994). Revenue: ₦110,200,000,000 (1992; petroleum royalties and rents 62.0%; petroleum profit tax 12.8%; import duties 11.6%; company income tax 3.9%). Expenditures: ₦110,200,000,000 (1992; recurrent expenditure 64.3%, of which debt service 53.7%, defense 2.9%, education 2.8%, police 2.5%, health 1.4%; capital expenditure 35.7%).
Public debt (external, outstanding; 1992): U.S.$28,458,000,000.
Production (metric tons except as noted). Agriculture, forestry, fishing (1993): cassava 21,000,000, yams 20,000,000, sorghum 4,800,000, millet 3,800,000, rice 3,400,000, plantains and bananas 2,450,000, corn (maize) 2,300,000, sugarcane 1,250,000, peanuts (groundnuts) 1,250,000; livestock (number of live animals) 24,500,000 goats, 16,316,000 cattle, 14,000,000 sheep; roundwood (1992) 114,289,000 cu m; fish catch (1991) 266,562. Mining and quarrying (1991): limestone 1,435,405; marble 52,379; tin 9,855[15]. Manufacturing (value added in U.S.$'000,000; 1990): food and beverages 703; textiles 373; chemical products 165; metal products 160; machinery and transport equipment 159; paper products 62; rubber and plastic products 61. Construction (dwellings completed; 1982): 31,038. Energy production (consumption): electricity (kW-hr; 1992) 11,800,000,000 (11,700,000,000); coal (metric tons; 1992) 95,000 (60,000); crude petroleum (barrels; 1992) 669,908,000 (87,780,-000); petroleum products (metric tons; 1992) 11,355,000 (11,509,000); natural gas (cu m; 1992) 4,900,000,000 (4,900,000,000).
Tourism (1992): receipts U.S.$29,000,000; expenditures U.S.$348,000,000.
Gross national product (1993): U.S.$32,517,000,000 (U.S.$310 per capita).

Structure of gross domestic product and labour force

	1991 in value ₦'000,000	1991 % of total value	1986 labour force	1986 % of labour force
Agriculture	98,617	30.7	13,259,000	43.1
Mining	120,850	37.6	6,800	0.1
Manufacturing	18,559	5.8	1,263,700	4.1
Construction	4,900	1.5	545,600	1.8
Public utilities	1,345	0.4	130,400	0.4
Transp. and commun.	6,388	2.0	1,111,900	3.6
Trade	42,386	13.2	7,417,400	24.1
Finance	18,199	5.7	120,100	0.4
Pub. admin., defense	8,800	2.7 }	4,902,100	15.9
Services	1,072	0.3 }		
Other	...	...	2,008,500[16]	6.5[16]
TOTAL	321,116	100.0[14]	30,765,500	100.0

Population economically active (1986): total 30,765,500; activity rate 31.1% (participation rates: ages 15–64, 58.8%; female 33.3%; unemployed [1992] 4.0%).

Price and earnings indexes (1990 = 100)

	1987	1988	1989	1990	1991	1992	1993
Consumer price index	40.1	61.9	93.1	100.0	113.0	163.4	256.8
Earnings index	...	...	...	...	...	...	...

Household income and expenditure. Avg. household size (1983) 5.0; annual income per household (1981) ₦2,300 (U.S.$3,745)[17]; sources of income (1979): self-employment 49.4%, wages 36.2%, interest 5.4%, rent 4.7%, transfer payments 4.3%; expenditures (1979): food 53.0%, fuel and light 11.4%, clothing 6.0%, transportation 4.7%, household goods 3.8%, other 21.1%.
Land use (1992): forested 12.4%; pastures 43.9%; agricultural 35.6%; other 8.1%.

Foreign trade

Balance of trade (current prices)

	1987	1988	1989	1990	1991	1992
₦'000,000	+15,401	+8,283	+29,730	+68,587	+40,696	+76,298
% of total	35.2%	14.2%	34.5%	45.4%	20.2%	22.8%

Imports (1992): ₦143,151,200,000 (machinery and transport equipment 43.2%; manufactured goods [mostly iron and steel products, textiles, and paper products] 27.8%; chemicals 16.0%; food 8.8%). *Major import sources* (1991): Germany 13.8%; U.K. 13.6%; U.S. 11.8%; France 8.9%.
Exports (1992): ₦205,613,100,000 (crude petroleum 97.9%; cocoa beans 0.6%; rubber 0.4%; fertilizer 0.2%; other exports include cocoa products, textiles, and cashew nuts). *Major export destinations* (1991): U.S. 40.7%; Spain 12.6%; Germany 8.6%; The Netherlands 5.0%; France 5.0%; Italy 4.0%.

Transport and communications

Transport. Railroads (1987): length 3,557 km[18]; passenger-km 3,808,277,000; metric ton-km cargo 1,743,000,000. Roads (1991): total length 112,140 km (paved 28%). Vehicles (1990): passenger cars 785,000; trucks and buses 625,000. Merchant marine (1992): vessels (100 gross tons and over) 271; total deadweight tonnage 733,329. Air transport (1992): passenger-km 996,-000,000; metric ton-km cargo 11,484,000; airports (1994) 12.
Communications. Daily newspapers (1990): total number 24; total circulation 1,553,000[19]; circulation per 1,000 population 18[19]. Radio (1993): 10,000,000 receivers (1 per 9.2 persons). Television (1991): 4,100,000 receivers (1 per 30 persons). Telephones (1992): 457,600 (1 per 196 persons).

Education and health

Education (1991–92)

	schools	teachers	students	student/ teacher ratio
Primary (age 6–12)[20]	35,446	353,600	13,776,854	38.9
Secondary (age 12–17)	5,594[21]	141,491	3,123,277	22.1
Voc., teacher tr.	376[21]	15,738[22]	391,593[22]	24.9[22]
Higher[23]	...	19,601	335,824	17.1

Literacy (1990): total population age 15 and over literate 29,537,300 (50.7%); males literate 17,792,300 (62.3%); females literate 11,745,000 (39.5%).
Health (1987): physicians 16,145 (1 per 5,006 persons); hospital beds 95,694 (1 per 844 persons); infant mortality rate (1993) 77.3.
Food (1988–90): daily per capita caloric intake 2,200 (vegetable products 97%, animal products 3%); 93% of FAO recommended minimum requirement.

Military

Total active duty personnel (1994): 76,500 (army 81.1%, navy 6.5%, air force 12.4%). *Military expenditure as percentage of GNP* (1991): 0.8% (world 4.2%); per capita expenditure U.S.$2.

[1]Civilian government (in place from Aug. 26, 1993) was overthrown by a military coup on Nov. 17, 1993. [2]Statutory transfer of capital from Lagos to Abuja took place in December 1991, although full transfer remains incomplete (executive offices, *e.g.,* were transferred on Jan 7, 1994). [3]Preliminary. [4]Imo includes Abia. [5]Adamawa includes Taraba. [6]Anambra includes Enugu. [7]Benue includes part of Kogi. [8]Borno includes Yobe. [9]Edo includes Delta. [10]Kano includes Jigawa. [11]Sokoto includes Kebbi. [12]Kwara includes part of Kogi. [13]Oyo includes Osun. [14]Detail does not add to total given because of rounding. [15]1990. [16]Includes 1,263,000 unemployed. [17]Urban households only. [18]1992. [19]For 15 newspapers only. [20]1990–91. [21]1987–88. [22]1988–89. [23]1989–90.

Norway

Official name: Kongeriket Norge (Kingdom of Norway).
Form of government: constitutional monarchy with one legislative house (Parliament [165]).
Chief of state: King.
Head of government: Prime Minister.
Capital: Oslo.
Official language: Norwegian.
Official religion: Evangelical Lutheran.
Monetary unit: 1 Norwegian krone (NKr) = 100 øre; valuation (Oct. 7, 1994) 1 U.S.$ = NKr 6.70; 1 £ = NKr 10.65.

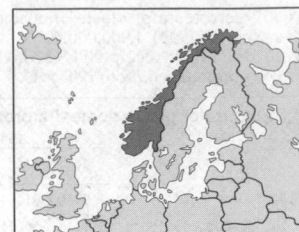

Area and population		area[1]		population
				1994[2]
Counties	Capitals	sq mi	sq km	estimate
Akershus	—	1,898	4,917	429,709
Aust-Agder	Arendal	3,557	9,212	99,145
Buskerud	Drammen	5,763	14,927	227,130
Finnmark	Vadsø	18,779	48,637	76,442
Hedmark	Hamar	10,575	27,388	187,411
Hordaland	Bergen	6,036	15,634	419,798
Møre og Romsdal	Molde	5,832	15,104	239,786
Nordland	Bodø	14,798	38,327	240,811
Nord-Trøndelag	Steinkjer	8,673	22,463	127,709
Oppland	Lillehammer	9,753	25,260	183,320
Oslo	Oslo	175	454	477,515
Østfold	Moss	1,615	4,183	238,760
Rogaland	Stavanger	3,529	9,141	350,729
Sogn og Fjordane	Leikanger	7,195	18,634	107,576
Sør-Trøndelag	Trondheim	7,271	18,831	255,381
Telemark	Skien	5,913	15,315	163,152
Troms	Tromsø	10,021	25,954	149,725
Vest-Agder	Kristiansand	2,811	7,281	148,570
Vestfold	Tønsberg	856	2,216	201,908
TOTAL		125,050	323,878	4,324,577[3]

Demography

Population (1994): 4,325,000.
Density (1994): persons per sq mi 34.6, persons per sq km 13.4.
Urban-rural (1990): urban 75.0%; rural 25.0%.
Sex distribution (1993): male 49.46%; female 50.54%.
Age breakdown (1993): under 15, 19.2%; 15–29, 22.3%; 30–44, 21.8%; 45–59, 16.1%; 60–74, 13.4%; 75 and over, 7.2%.
Population projection: (2000) 4,426,000; (2010) 4,550,000.
Doubling time: not applicable; doubling time exceeds 100 years.
Ethnic composition (by country of citizenship; 1993): Norway 96.4%; Denmark 0.4%; Sweden 0.3%; United Kingdom 0.3%; Pakistan 0.3%; United States 0.2%; Iran 0.2%; other 1.9%.
Religious affiliation (1980): Lutheran 87.9%; nonreligious 3.2%; other 8.9%.
Major cities (1994)[4]: Oslo 477,515; Bergen 219,810; Trondheim 142,015; Stavanger 102,539; Baerum 94,160.

Vital statistics

Birth rate per 1,000 population (1992): 14.0 (world avg. 26.0); legitimate 57.1%; illegitimate 42.9%.
Death rate per 1,000 population (1992): 10.5 (world avg. 9.2).
Natural increase rate per 1,000 population (1992): 3.5 (world avg. 16.8).
Total fertility rate (avg. births per childbearing woman; 1992): 1.9.
Marriage rate per 1,000 population (1992): 4.5.
Divorce rate per 1,000 population (1992): 2.4.
Life expectancy at birth (1992): male 74.2 years; female 80.3 years.
Major causes of death per 100,000 population (1992): ischemic heart disease 242.6; malignant neoplasms (cancers) 224.5; cerebrovascular disease 126.1.

National economy

Budget (1994). Revenue: NKr 318,050,000,000 (social-security taxes 24.7%, value-added taxes 23.5%, taxes on interest and dividends 10.9%, taxes on petroleum income and activity 3.4%, ordinary income tax 2.9%). Expenditures: NKr 339,977,000,000 (social security and welfare 24.6%, health 8.2%, debt service 6.3%).
Land use (1991): forested 27.1%; meadows and pastures 0.4%; agricultural and under permanent cultivation 2.8%; built-up and other 69.7%.
Tourism (1992): receipts from visitors U.S.$1,975,000,000; expenditures by nationals abroad U.S.$3,870,000,000.
Production (metric tons except as noted). Agriculture, forestry, fishing (1992): barley 663,000, oats 568,000, potatoes 415,000, wheat 246,000; livestock (number of live animals; 1993) 937,500 sheep[5], 975,800 cattle, 745,100 pigs; roundwood (1991) 10,987,000 cu m; fish catch (1993) 2,374,840, of which capelin 530,400, herring 348,700, cod 271,000, mackerel 227,000. Mining and quarrying (1993)[6]: iron ore 2,162,000, copper 36,000, zinc 29,000, lead 3,200. Manufacturing (value added in NKr '000,000; 1992): machinery and equipment 27,821, of which transport equipment 6,477, electrical equipment 4,719; food products 19,496; paper and paper products 12,176; chemical products 9,967; wood and wood products 4,115. Construction (1993): residential 2,099,000 sq m; nonresidential 2,272,000 sq m. Energy production (consumption): electricity (kW-hr; 1991) 110,950,000,000 (108,138,000,000); coal (metric tons; 1991) 339,000 (690,000); crude petroleum (barrels; 1991) 712,436,000 (94,430,000); petroleum products (metric tons; 1991) 12,415,000 (8,109,000); natural gas (cu m; 1991) 27,425,000,000 (2,049,000,000).

Gross national product (1993): U.S.$113,525,000,000 (U.S.$26,340 per capita).

Structure of gross domestic product and labour force				
	1991		1992	
	in value NKr '000,000	% of total value	labour force	% of labour force
Agriculture	20,052	2.9	114,000	5.3
Mining	3,908	0.6	25,000	1.2
Crude petroleum and natural gas	99,664	14.5	...	...
Manufacturing	92,591	13.5	308,000	14.5
Construction	24,705	3.6	133,000	6.2
Public utilities	26,386	3.8	20,000	0.9
Transp. and commun.	61,738	9.0	161,000	7.6
Trade	75,315[7]	11.0[7]	366,000	17.2
Finance	61,709	9.0	157,000	7.4
Pub. admin., defense	111,910	16.3	779,000	36.6
Services	67,231	9.8		
Other	41,479	6.0	66,000[8]	3.1[8]
TOTAL	686,686[9]	100.0	2,130,000[9]	100.0

Public debt (1990): U.S.$23,430,000,000.
Population economically active (1993): total 2,131,000; activity rate of total population 49.4% (participation rates: ages 16–64, 79.9%[10]; female 49.2%[10]; unemployed 6.0%).

Price and earnings indexes (1985 = 100)							
	1987	1988	1989	1990	1991	1992	1993
Consumer price index	116.5	124.3	130.0	135.4	140.0	143.3	146.5
Hourly earnings index	128.0	135.0	141.0	149.6	157.2	162.3	167.5[11]

Household income and expenditure. Average household size (1990) 2.4; consumption expenditure per household (1991) NKr 180,126 (U.S.$27,785); sources of income (1991): wages and salaries 58.8%, social security 24.2%, self-employment and property income 16.9%; expenditure (1991): housing 19.4%, food 18.4%, transportation 12.4%, clothing and footwear 6.8%, household furniture and equipment 6.7%, beverages and tobacco 7.0%.

Foreign trade

Balance of trade (current prices)					
	1988	1989	1990	1991	1992	1993
NKr '000,000	−2,976	+27,248	+48,231	+59,565	+61,730	+55,635
% of total	1.0%	7.9%	12.9%	15.9%	16.4%	14.0%

Imports (1993): NKr 170,991,300,000 (machinery and transport equipment 38.9%, of which ships 6.2%, road vehicles 5.9%; metals and metal products 9.2%, of which iron and steel 4.6%; food products 4.4%, of which fruits and vegetables 1.5%; petroleum products 2.8%). *Major import sources:* Sweden 14.1%; Germany 13.5%; U.K. 9.1%; Denmark 7.4%.
Exports (1993): NKr 226,626,100,000 (fuels and fuel products 45.9%, of which crude petroleum 39.5%, natural gas 6.5%; machinery and transport equipment 11.8%; metals and metal products 10.6%, of which aluminum 4.4%; food products 7.9%, of which fish 6.9%). *Major export destinations:* U.K. 24.6%; Germany 13.0%; Sweden 8.7%; The Netherlands 8.5%.

Transport and communications

Transport. Railroads (1992): route length 4,026 km; passenger-km 2,312,000,000; metric ton-km cargo 2,300,000,000. Roads (1994): total length 90,502 km (1991; paved 70%). Vehicles (1993): passenger cars 1,633,088; trucks and buses 396,090. Merchant marine (1992): vessels (100 gross tons and over) 2,499; total deadweight tonnage 38,298,755. Air transport (1992): passenger-km 8,954,504,000; metric ton-km cargo 617,462,000; airports (1994) 48.
Communications. Daily newspapers (1993): total number 62; total circulation 2,190,000; circulation per 1,000 population 507. Radio (1993): 3,300,000 receivers (1 per 1.3 persons). Television (1993): 1,500,000 receivers (1 per 2.9 persons). Telephones (1992)[12]: 2,268,486 (1 per 1.9 persons).

Education and health

Education (1992–93)	schools	teachers[13]	students	student/ teacher ratio[13]
Primary (age 7–12)	3,352	35,416	463,948	13.2
Secondary (age 13–18) and vocational	778	20,982	243,797	11.6
Higher	199	8,085	162,168	18.4

Educational attainment (1992). Percentage of population age 16 and over having: lower secondary education 40.1%; higher secondary 42.8%; higher 17.1%. *Literacy* (1992): virtually 100% literate.
Health: physicians (1994) 14,497 (1 per 299 persons); hospital beds 23,390 (1 per 183 persons); infant mortality rate per 1,000 live births 5.9.
Food (1988–90): daily per capita caloric intake 3,221 (vegetable products 65%, animal products 35%); 120% of FAO recommended minimum requirement.

Military

Total active duty personnel (1993): 29,400 (army 43.8%, navy 28.2%, air force 27.9%). *Military expenditure as percentage of GNP* (1991): 3.2% (world avg. 4.2%); per capita expenditure U.S.$769.

[1]Excludes Svalbard and Jan Mayen (24,360 sq mi [63,080 sq km]). [2]January 1. [3]Includes the Norwegian population of Svalbard and Jan Mayen, registered as residents in municipalities on the mainland. [4]Population of municipalities. [5]One year and over. [6]Metal content of ore. [7]Includes hotels. [8]Includes 53,000 unemployed not previously employed. [9]Detail does not add to total given because of rounding. [10]1992. [11]Second quarter. [12]Main lines only. [13]1991–92.

Oman

Official name: Salṭanat 'Umān
(Sultanate of Oman).
Form of government: monarchy[1].
Head of state and government: Sultan.
Capital: Muscat.
Official language: Arabic.
Official religion: Islam.
Monetary unit: 1 rial Omani
(RO) = 1,000 baizas; valuation (Oct. 7,
1994) 1 RO = U.S.$2.56 = £1.64.

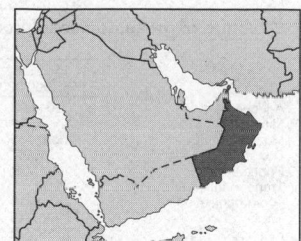

Area and population

Regions[3]	Centres[4]	area[2] sq mi	area[2] sq km	population 1993 census
al-Bāṭinah	ar-Rustāq; Ṣuḥār	5,320	13,770	538,763
ad-Dākhilīyah	Nizwā; Samā'il	29,770	77,110	220,403
al-Janūbīyah	Salālah	45,370	117,510	174,888
Masqaṭ	Muscat (Masqaṭ)	1,420	3,670	622,506
Musandam	Khaṣab	590	1,530	27,669
ash-Sharqīyah	Ibrā; Sūr	16,190	41,920	247,551
aẓ-Ẓāhirah	al-Buraymī; 'Ibri	19,490	50,490	169,710
TOTAL		118,150	306,000	2,017,591[5]

Demography

Population (1994): 2,048,000.
Density (1994): persons per sq mi 17.3, persons per sq km 6.7.
Urban-rural (1990): urban 11.0%; rural 89.0%.
Sex distribution (1992): male 54.68%; female 45.32%.
Age breakdown (1992): under 15, 36.0%; 15–29, 27.5%; 30–44, 24.1%; 45–59, 8.0%; 60–74, 3.6%; 75 and over, 0.8%.
Population projection: (2000) 2,393,000; (2010) 3,119,000.
Doubling time: 21 years.
Ethnic composition (1990): Omani Arab 73.5%; Pakistani (mostly Baluchi) 21.0%; other 5.5%.
Religious affiliation (1984): Muslim 86%; Hindu 13%; other 1%.
Major cities (1990): Muscat 85,000[6]; Nizwā 62,880; Samā'il 44,721; Salālah 10,000[6].

Vital statistics

Birth rate per 1,000 population (1992): 53.0 (world avg. 26.0).
Death rate per 1,000 population (1992): 3.9 (world avg. 9.2).
Natural increase rate per 1,000 population (1992): 49.1 (world avg. 16.8).
Total fertility rate (avg. births per childbearing woman; 1992): 6.9.
Marriage rate per 1,000 population: n.a.
Divorce rate per 1,000 population: n.a.
Life expectancy at birth (1992): male 69.8 years; female 72.6 years.
Morbidity (reported cases of illness per 100,000 population; 1989): influenza 6,823; malaria 1,235; chicken pox 1,156; mumps 1,048; amebic dysentery 376; measles 294; bacillary dysentery 206; infectious hepatitis 96; tuberculosis 33; brucellosis 15.

National economy

Budget (1994). Revenue: RO 1,732,000,000 (oil revenue 76.0%; other 24.0%). Expenditures: RO 2,033,000,000 (1993; recurrent budget 67.2%, of which defense 29.5%, education 9.1%, general public services 5.3%, fuel and energy 5.3%, health 4.6%; capital development projects 32.8%).
Public debt (external, outstanding; 1992): U.S.$2,340,000,000.
Gross national product (at current market prices; 1993): U.S.$9,500,000,000 (U.S.$5,600 per capita).

Structure of gross domestic product and labour force

	1992 in value RO '000,000[7]	1992 % of total value	1990 labour force	1990 % of labour force
Agriculture	143.7	3.3	146,400	27.7
Mining	1,887.6	42.7	2,800	0.5
Manufacturing	190.2	4.3	32,800	6.2
Construction	178.6	4.0	104,800	19.8
Public utilities	67.5	1.5	4,100	0.8
Transportation and communications	160.9	3.6	14,500	2.7
Trade	615.9	13.9	87,500	16.5
Finance	160.9	3.6	9,400	1.8
Pub. admin., defense	772.5	17.5	81,000	15.3
Services	287.1[8]	6.5[8]	45,800	8.7
Other	−47.5[9]	−1.1[9]	—	—
TOTAL	4,417.4	100.0[10]	529,100	100.0

Tourism (1992): receipts from visitors U.S.$85,000,000; expenditures by nationals abroad U.S.$47,000,000.
Household income and expenditure. Average household size (1986) 3.7; income per household: n.a.; sources of income: n.a.; food expenditure (1988): meat and fish 23.9%, fruits and vegetables 22.0%, bread and cereals 17.4%, dairy products and eggs 10.7%, other foods 26.0%.
Production (metric tons except as noted). Agriculture, forestry, fishing (1993): vegetables and melons 163,000 (of which watermelons 30,000), dates 133,000, bananas 26,000, mangoes 11,000, onions 9,000, potatoes 6,000, papayas 3,000, tobacco leaf 2,000, wheat 1,000; livestock (number of live animals) 735,000 goats, 148,000 sheep, 142,000 cattle, 94,000 camels, 3,000,000 chickens; fish catch (1992) 112,313. Mining and quarrying (1992): copper 13,600; silver 2,700 kg; gold 20 kg. Manufacturing (value added in RO '000; 1990): textiles and apparel 13,957; metal products 2,303; machinery and equipment 1,797;

chemical products 840; food products and beverages 715; wood products 439; paper products 282; other major products include refined petroleum products. Construction (1989): number of residential permits 3,408; nonresidential permits 353. Energy production (consumption): electricity (kW-hr; 1992) 6,237,000,000 (6,237,000,000); coal, none (none); crude petroleum (barrels; 1992) 269,869,000 (21,505,000); petroleum products (metric tons; 1992) 3,043,000 (1,530,000); natural gas (cu m; 1992) 1,839,200,000 (1,839,200,000).
Population economically active (1990)[11]: total 680,850; activity rate of total population 39.9% (participation rates: ages 15–64 [1986] 60.9%; female [1986] 7.5%; unemployed, n.a.).

Price and earnings indexes (1990 = 100)

	1986	1987	1988	1989	1990	1991	1992
Consumer price index	96.0	93.6	94.7	99.4	100.0	104.6	105.6
Earnings index	...	...	...	...	...	...	...

Land use (1992): meadows and pastures 4.7%; agricultural and under permanent cultivation 0.3%; other (mostly desert and developed area) 95.0%.

Foreign trade

Balance of trade (current prices)

	1986	1987	1988	1989	1990	1991
RO '000,000	+112.3	+694.2	+601.1	+780.1	+1,107.5	+776.6
% of total	8.0%	35.7%	24.9%	33.1%	39.4%	26.2%

Imports (1991): U.S.$3,193,972,000 (machinery and transport equipment 41.9%, of which road motor vehicles 11.8%, civil-engineering and construction machinery 6.4%; basic manufactured goods 17.5%, of which iron and steel 5.6%; food and live animals 13.8%; miscellaneous manufactured articles 7.8%; chemicals 5.9%; beverages and tobacco 4.0%). *Major import sources:* United Arab Emirates 25.3%; Japan 20.5%; United Kingdom 10.0%; United States 7.6%; West Germany 5.2%.
Exports (1991): U.S.$1,759,564,000 (petroleum 86.1%; road motor vehicles 4.5%; nonferrous metals [copper and aluminum] 0.9%). *Major export destinations* (1989): Japan 37.2%; South Korea 26.7%; Taiwan 8.6%; Singapore 3.9%; United Kingdom 3.4%; China 3.2%; United States 3.1%.

Transport and communications

Transport. Railroads: none. Roads (1994): total length 16,372 mi, 26,349 km (paved 20%). Vehicles (1993): automobiles 166,323, trucks and buses 83,888. Merchant marine (1992): vessels (100 gross tons and over) 26; total deadweight tonnage 11,727. Air transport (1992)[12]: passenger-mi 1,194,400,000, passenger-km 1,922,100,000; short ton-mi cargo 47,780,000, metric ton-km cargo 69,756,000; airports (1994) with scheduled flights 6.
Communications. Daily newspapers (1991): total number 4; total circulation 61,500; circulation per 1,000 population 39. Radio (1993): total number of receivers 900,000 (1 per 2.2 persons). Television (1993): total number of receivers 1,500,000 (1 per 1.3 persons). Telephones (1992)[13]: 130,110 (1 per 15 persons).

Education and health

Education (1992–93)

	schools	teachers	students	student/ teacher ratio
Primary (age 6–14)	416	10,839	289,911	26.7
Secondary (age 15–17)	128[14]	8,112	137,947	17.0
Voc., teacher tr.	25[14]	425	2,814	6.6
Higher	5[14]	433[15]	3,615[16]	...

Educational attainment: n.a. *Literacy* (1990): total population age 6 and over literate 41%; males literate 58%; females literate 24%.
Health (1990): physicians 1,393 (1 per 1,078 persons); hospital beds 3,952 (1 per 380 persons); infant mortality rate per 1,000 live births (1992) 22.6.
Food: daily per capita caloric intake, n.a.

Military

Total active duty personnel (1994): 39,200 (army 80.4%[17], navy 10.7%, air force 8.9%); foreign troops 3,700. *Military expenditure as percentage of GNP* (1993): 15% (world, n.a.); per capita expenditure U.S.$1,060.

[1]The sultan is assisted by an appointed 60-member advisory council consisting of 59 governorate (*wilāyah*) representatives and the sultan's representative, who leads the body. [2]Approximate; no comprehensive survey of surface area has ever been carried out in Oman. [3]Regions are divided into 59 governorates. [4]Centres of the regions are not administrative capitals. [5]Includes the population (16,101) of al-Wosta, which is not shown separately. [6]1982. [7]In purchasers' value at current prices. [8]Services include real estate and business services. [9]Other includes import duties less imputed bank service charges. [10]Detail does not add to total given because of rounding. [11]Non-Omani workers constitute approximately 55–60% of the labour force. [12]One-fourth apportionment of international flights of Gulf Air. [13]Includes main lines. [14]1989–90. [15]1990; universities and equivalent institutes. [16]1991–92. [17]Including personnel of Royal Household units not formally part of army table of organization.

Pakistan

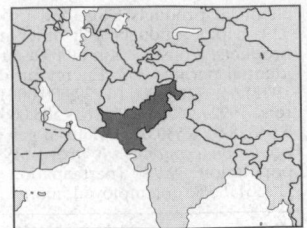

Official name: Islām-ī Jamhūrīya-e Pākistān (Islamic Republic of Pakistan).
Form of government: multiparty, federal Islamic republic with two legislative houses (Senate [87]; National Assembly [217]).
Chief of state: President.
Chief of government: Prime Minister.
Capital: Islāmābād.
Official language: Urdū.
Official religion: Islam.
Monetary unit: 1 Pakistan Rupee (PRs) = 100 paisa; valuation (Oct. 7, 1994) 1 U.S.$ = PRs 30.62; 1 £ = PRs 48.70.

Area and population

Provinces	Capitals	area[1] sq mi	sq km	population 1983 estimate[2]
Balochistān	Quetta	134,051	347,190	4,611,000
North-West Frontier	Peshāwar	28,773	74,521	11,658,000
Punjab	Lahore	79,284	205,344	50,460,000
Sindh	Karāchi	54,407	140,914	20,312,000
Federally Administered Tribal Areas	...	10,509	27,220	2,329,000
Federal Capital Area Islāmābād	...	350	906	359,000
TOTAL		307,374	796,095	89,729,000

Demography

Population (1994)[2]: 131,434,000.
Density (1994): persons per sq mi 386.9, persons per sq km 149.4.
Urban-rural (1993): urban 32.0%; rural 68.0%.
Sex distribution (1993): male 52.50%; female 47.50%.
Age breakdown (1988): under 15, 46.3%; 15–29, 24.6%; 30–44, 14.0%; 45–59, 9.0%; 60–74, 4.8%; 75 and over, 1.3%.
Population projection: (2000) 154,794,000; (2010) 197,672,000.
Doubling time: 24 years.
Linguistic composition (1981): Punjābī 48.2%; Pashto 13.1%; Sindhī 11.8%; Saraiki 9.8%; Urdū 7.6%; other 9.5%.
Religious affiliation (1981): Muslim 96.7%; Christian 1.6%; Hindu 1.5%; other 0.2%.
Major cities (1981): Karāchi 5,208,132; Lahore 2,952,689; Faisalābād 1,104,209; Rāwalpindi 794,843; Islāmābād 204,364.

Vital statistics

Birth rate per 1,000 population (1993): 40.0 (world avg. 26.0).
Death rate per 1,000 population (1993): 11.0 (world avg. 9.2).
Natural increase rate per 1,000 population (1993): 29.0 (world avg. 16.8).
Total fertility rate (avg. births per childbearing woman; 1993): 6.1.
Marriage rate per 1,000 population (1975–80): 10.7.
Divorce rate per 1,000 population (1975–80): 0.3.
Life expectancy at birth (1993): male 59.3 years; female 60.7 years.
Major causes of death (percentage of total deaths; 1987): malaria 18.2%; childhood diseases 12.1%; diseases of digestive system 9.8%; diseases of respiratory system 9.2%; infection of intestinal tract 7.7%.

National economy

Budget (1993–94). Revenue: PRs 288,693,000,000 (nontax receipts 27.1%, customs duties 25.7%, excise taxes 14.5%, income taxes 14.0%). Expenditures: PRs 272,455,000,000 (public-debt service 48.1%, defense 32.7%, subsidies 1.8%, law and order 1.7%).
Production (metric tons except as noted). Agriculture, forestry, fishing (1992–93): sugarcane 38,059,000, wheat 16,159,000, rice 3,116,000, corn (maize) 1,178,000, gram 329,000, jowar 238,000, cotton 9,054,000 bales; livestock (number of live animals) 40,200,000 goats, 27,700,000 sheep, 18,700,000 buffalo, 17,800,000 cattle, 1,100,000 camels, 182,600,000 poultry; roundwood (1992) 26,567,000 cu m; fish catch (1992) 553,118. Mining and quarrying (1992–93): limestone 9,015,000; rock salt 895,000; gypsum 533,000; silica sand 158,000; chromite 23,000. Manufacturing (1992–93): cement 8,600,000; chemical fertilizers 3,203,000, of which urea 2,306,000; refined sugar 2,397,-000; cotton yarn 1,219,000; chemicals 373,000; vegetable products 319,000; jute textiles 97,500; paper and paperboard 66,500; cotton textiles 325,-000,000 sq m; cigarettes 33,300,000,000 units; motor-vehicle tires 1,263,000 units; bicycles 573,000 units. Construction (value in PRs; 1984): residential 8,490,000,000; nonresidential 14,579,000,000. Energy production (consumption): electricity (kW-hr; 1992) 51,972,000,000 (51,972,000,000); coal (metric tons; 1992) 3,188,000 (4,222,000); crude petroleum (barrels; 1992) 27,915,000 (53,873,000); petroleum products (metric tons; 1992) 6,285,000 (10,653,000); natural gas (cu m; 1992) 13,426,000,000 (13,426,000,000).
Household income and expenditure (1988). Average household size 6.3; income per household PRs 25,572 (U.S.$1,420); sources of income: self-employment 56.0%, wages and salaries 22.0%, other 22.0%; expenditure: food 47.0%, housing 12.0%, clothing and footwear 8.0%, other 33.0%.
Land use (1992): forested 5.3%; meadows and pastures 6.5%; agricultural and under permanent cultivation 27.4%; built-on, wasteland, and other 60.8%.
Gross national product (at current market prices; 1993): U.S.$54,045,000,000 (U.S.$440 per capita).

Structure of gross domestic product and labour force

	1992–93 in value PRs '000,000	% of total value	labour force	% of labour force
Agriculture	304,603	22.4	15,030,000	44.5
Mining	8,019	0.6 }	3,920,000	11.6
Manufacturing	210,135	15.5 }		
Construction	51,297	3.8	2,100,000	6.2
Public utilities	44,774	3.3	260,000	0.8
Transportation and communications	125,219	9.2	1,660,000	4.9
Trade	196,315	14.5	4,200,000	12.4
Finance	88,722	6.5 }		
Pub. admin., defense	95,372	7.0 }	4,510,000	13.3
Services	93,000	6.8 }		
Other	141,882	10.4	2,120,000[3]	6.3[3]
TOTAL	1,359,338	100.0	33,800,000	100.0

Population economically active (1992–93): total 33,800,000; activity rate of total population 28.0% (participation rates: ages 15–64 [1991–92] 50.8%; female [1991–92] 14.2%; unemployed 6.3%).

Price index (1985 = 100)

	1987	1988	1989	1990	1991	1992	1993
Consumer price index	108.4	117.9	127.2	138.7	155.0	169.8	177.0

Tourism (1992): receipts from visitors U.S.$120,000,000; expenditures by nationals abroad U.S.$679,000,000.
Public debt (external, outstanding; 1992): U.S.$18,476,000,000.

Foreign trade[4]

Balance of trade (current prices)

	1988	1989	1990	1991	1992	1993
PRs '000,000	−27,036	−37,093	−24,896	−28,537	−31,283	−54,352
% of total	14.2%	16.1%	9.3%	8.4%	7.9%	12.6%

Imports (1992–93): PRs 258,642,900,000 (petroleum products 15.5%, specialized machinery 12.9%, road vehicles 10.1%, vegetable oil and fats 5.9%, wheat 4.7%, organic chemicals 3.6%, iron and steel manufactures 3.2%, telecommunications equipment 3.0%). *Major import sources:* Japan 15.9%; U.S. 9.4%; Germany 7.5%; Saudi Arabia 5.4%; Malaysia 5.1%; U.K. 4.8%; South Korea 4.5%; France 4.2%; China 4.2%.
Exports (1992–93): PRs 177,027,900,000 (textile fabrics 51.4%, ready-made garments 21.5%, cotton 4.7%, rice 4.7%, leather and leather goods 3.5%, fresh fish 2.7%, professional instruments 1.5%). *Major export destinations:* U.S. 13.9%; Germany 7.8%; U.K. 7.1%; Japan 6.8%; Hong Kong 6.6%; Dubai 5.9%; Saudi Arabia 4.7%; France 4.3%.

Transport and communications

Transport. Railroads (1991–92): route length (1992–93) 5,453 mi, 8,775 km; passenger-mi 11,285,000,000, passenger-km 18,161,000,000; short ton-mi cargo 4,085,000,000, metric ton-km cargo 5,964,000,000. Roads (1991–92): total length 111,693 mi, 179,752 km (paved 51%). Vehicles (1992): passenger cars 731,500; trucks and buses 213,000. Merchant marine (1992): vessels (100 gross tons and over) 73; total deadweight tonnage 513,823. Air transport (1992): passenger-km 10,104,000,000; metric ton-km cargo 408,048,000; airports (1994) with scheduled flights 34.
Communications. Daily newspapers (1992): total number 274; total circulation 809,000; circulation per 1,000 population 6. Radio (1993): total number of receivers 10,000,000 (1 per 13 persons). Television (1993): total number of receivers 2,080,000 (1 per 62 persons). Telephones (1991): 1,294,690 (1 per 95 persons).

Education and health

Education (1992–93)

	schools	teachers	students	student/teacher ratio
Primary (age 5–9)	124,171	360,100	14,120,000	39.2
Secondary (age 10–14)	19,117	276,400	4,770,000	17.3
Voc., teacher tr.	710	6,772	91,000	13.4
Higher	797	29,076	721,600	24.8

Educational attainment (1981). Percentage of population age 25 and over having: no formal schooling 78.9%; some primary education 8.7%; some secondary 10.5%; postsecondary 1.9%. *Literacy* (1993): total population age 15 and over literate 35.0%; males literate 47.3%; females literate 22.3%).
Health (1992): physicians 55,572 (1 per 2,242 persons); hospital beds 76,938 (1 per 1,619 persons); infant mortality rate per 1,000 live births (1993) 104.7.
Food (1988–90): daily per capita caloric intake 2,280 (vegetable products 87%, animal products 13%); 99% of FAO recommended minimum requirement.

Military

Total active duty personnel (1994): 587,000 (army 88.6%, navy 3.7%, air force 7.7%). *Military expenditure as percentage of GNP* (1991): 6.1% (world 4.2%); per capita expenditure U.S.$22.

---

[1]Excludes 32,323 sq mi (83,716 sq km) of Azad Jammu and Kashmir, administered, but not claimed, by Pakistan. [2]1983 provincial estimates exclude and 1994 estimate includes Afghan refugees and residents of Pakistani-occupied Jammu and Kashmir. [3]Includes unemployed. [4]Import figures are f.o.b. in balance of trade and c.i.f. for commodities and trading partners.

Palau

Official name: Belu'u era Belau (Palauan); Republic of Palau (English).
Form of government: unitary republic with two legislative houses (Senate [14]; House of Delegates [16]).
Head of state and government: President.
Capital: Koror.
Official languages: Palauan; English.
Official religion: none.
Monetary unit: 1 U.S. dollar (U.S.$) = 100 cents; valuation (Oct. 7, 1994) 1 £ = U.S.$1.59.

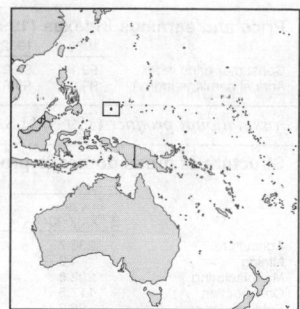

Area and population

States	area sq mi	area sq km	population 1990 census
Aimeliik	20	52	439
Airai	17	44	1,234
Angaur	3	8	206
Hatohobei	1	3	22
Kayangel	1	3	137
Koror	7	18	10,501
Melekeok	11	28	244
Ngaraard	14	36	310
Ngardmau	18	47	149
Ngaremlengui	25	65	281
Ngatpang	18	47	62
Ngchesar	16	41	287
Ngercholong	4	10	354
Ngiwal	10	26	234
Peleliu	5	13	601
Sonsorol	1	3	61
Other			
Rock Islands	18	47	—
TOTAL	188[1]	487[1]	15,122

Demography

Population (1994): 17,200.
Density (1994): persons per sq mi 91.5, persons per sq km 35.3.
Urban-rural (1990): urban 59.6%; rural 40.4%.
Sex distribution (1990): male 53.82%; female 46.18%.
Age breakdown (1990): under 15, 30.3%; 15–29, 27.8%; 30–44, 22.8%; 45–59, 10.5%; 60–74, 6.4%; 75 and over, 2.2%.
Population projection: (2000) 20,300; (2010) 25,500.
Doubling time: 28 years.
Ethnic composition (1990): Palauan 83.2%; Filipino 9.8%; other Micronesian 2.0%; Chinese 1.2%; white 0.8%; other 3.0%.
Religious affiliation (1990): Roman Catholic 40.8%; Protestant 24.8%; traditional beliefs 24.8%; other 9.6%.
Major cities (1990): Koror 9,018.

Vital statistics

Birth rate per 1,000 population (1994): 21.8 (world avg. 26.0); legitimate, n.a.; illegitimate, n.a.
Death rate per 1,000 population (1994): 7.9 (world avg. 9.2).
Natural increase rate per 1,000 population (1994): 13.9 (world avg. 16.8).
Total fertility rate (avg. births per childbearing woman; 1994): 2.9.
Marriage rate per 1,000 population: n.a.
Divorce rate per 1,000 population: n.a.
Life expectancy at birth (1994): male 69 years; female 73 years.
Major causes of death per 100,000 population (1985–86): diseases of the circulatory system 176.5; diseases of the respiratory system 99.8; accidents, poisoning, and violence 95.9; malignant and benign neoplasms (cancers) 92.1; diseases of the digestive system 34.5; endocrine, metabolic, and nutritional disorders 19.2; infectious and parasitic diseases 15.3.

National economy

Budget (1991). Revenue: U.S.$46,660,000 (cash grants from the U.S. 35.4%, tax revenue 26.4%). Expenditures: U.S.$28,871,000.
Tourism (1991): total number of visitors 32,700.
Gross national product (at current market prices; 1986): U.S.$31,600,000[2] (U.S.$2,260 per capita).

Structure of gross domestic product and labour force

	1985 in value U.S.$'000	1985 % of total value	1990 labour force	1990 % of labour force
Agriculture, fisheries	...	16.0	445	7.3
Mining	...	...	14	0.2
Manufacturing	...	...	100	1.7
Public utilities	...	1.0	78	1.3
Construction	...	11.0	919	15.1
Transportation and communications	...	3.0	416	6.8
Trade	...	19.0	1,207	19.9
Finance	...	4.0	120	2.0
Public administration, defense	...	36.0	870	14.3
Services	...	2.0	1,672	27.6
Other	...	8.0[3]	232	3.8
TOTAL	31,580	100.0	6,072	100.0

Production (metric tons except as noted). Agriculture, forestry, fishing: n.a.; livestock (number of live animals) n.a.; roundwood, n.a.; fish catch (1992) 4,068. Mining and quarrying: n.a. Manufacturing: n.a. Construction: n.a. Energy production (consumption): electricity (kW-hr; 1990) 22,000,000 (23,288,000); coal, none (n.a.); crude petroleum, none (n.a.); petroleum products, none (n.a.); natural gas, none (n.a.).
Public debt (external, outstanding; 1993): U.S.$100,000,000.
Population economically active (1990): total 6,072; activity rate of total population 40.2% (participation rates: ages 16–64, 64.1%; female 36.9%; unemployed 7.8%).
Land use: n.a.
Household income and expenditure. Average household size (1990) 5.0; income per household (1989) U.S.$8,882; sources of income (1989): wages 63.7%, social security 12.0%, self-employment 7.4%, retirement 5.5%, interest, dividend, or net rental 4.3%, remittance 4.1%, public assistance 1.0%, other 2.0%; expenditure: n.a.

Foreign trade

Imports (1993): U.S.$40,000,000 (1984; food and agricultural raw materials 28.9%; machinery and transport equipment 24.5%; chemicals and related products 4.0%). *Major import sources* (1984): United States 41.8%; Japan 38.2%.
Exports (1986): U.S.$500,000 (1984; food and agricultural raw materials 69.1%; manufactured goods 30.9%). *Major export destinations* (1984). Japan 58.8%; United States 8.0%.

Transport and communications

Transport. Railroads: none. Roads (1993): total length 38 mi, 61 km (paved 59%). Vehicles (1986): passenger cars and trucks 1,687. Merchant marine (1991): vessels (100 gross tons and over) 4; total deadweight tonnage, n.a. Air transport: n.a.; airports (1994) with scheduled flights 1.
Communications. Daily newspapers: none. Radio (1993): total number of receivers 9,000 (1 per 67 persons). Television (1993): total number of receivers 1,600 (1 per 9.4 persons). Telephones (1988): 1,500 (1 per 9.3 persons).

Education and health

Education (1990)

	schools[4]	teachers[4]	students	student/ teacher ratio
Primary (age 6–13)	26	289	2,365	...
Secondary (age 14–18)	6	5	1,275	...
Vocational	1[6]	36[6]	815[7]	...
Higher	...	...	382	...

Educational attainment (1990). Percentage of population age 25 and over having: no formal schooling 1.8%; some primary education 21.8%; completed primary 5.5%; some secondary 13.3%; completed secondary 26.6%; some postsecondary 11.1%; higher 19.9%. *Literacy* (1990): total population age 15 and over literate 10,288 (97.6%); males literate 5,677 (98.3%); females literate 4,611 (96.6%).
Health (1986): physicians 10[8] (1 per 1,396 persons); hospital beds 70 (1 per 200 persons); infant mortality rate per 1,000 live births (1994) 25.
Food: daily per capita caloric intake, n.a.

Military

Total active duty personnel: n.a.

[1]Detail does not add to total given because of rounding. [2]Gross national product comprises U.S. government spending only. [3]Includes mining and manufacturing. [4]1987. [5]Included with primary. [6]1984. [7]Figure reflects completed requirements for a program. [8]Government-employed health personnel only.

Panama

Official name: República de Panamá
  (Republic of Panama).
Form of government: multiparty
  republic with one legislative house
  (Legislative Assembly [72]).
Head of state and government:
  President assisted by Vice Presidents.
Capital: Panama City.
Official language: Spanish.
Official religion: none.
Monetary unit: 1 balboa (B) = 100 cents;
  valuation (Oct. 7, 1994)
  1 U.S.$ = B 1.00; 1 £ = B 1.59.

Area and population

Provinces	Capitals	area sq mi	area sq km	population 1992 estimate
Bocas del Toro	Bocas del Toro	3,376	8,745	88,385
Chiriquí	David	3,341	8,653	396,842
Coclé	Penonomé	1,902	4,927	177,070
Colón	Colón	1,888	4,890	222,577[1]
Darién	La Palma	6,437	16,671	45,020
Herrera	Chitré	904	2,341	108,714
Los Santos	Las Tablas	1,470	3,806	82,810
Panamá	Panama City	4,590	11,887	1,168,492
Veraguas	Santiago	4,339	11,239	224,676
Special territory				
Comarca de San Blas	El Porvenir	910	2,357	[1]
TOTAL		29,157	75,517[2]	2,514,586

Demography

Population (1994): 2,583,000.
Density (1994): persons per sq mi 88.6, persons per sq km 34.2.
Urban-rural (1990): urban 53.7%; rural 46.3%.
Sex distribution (1990): male 50.61%; female 49.39%.
Age breakdown (1990): under 15, 34.8%; 15–29, 29.2%; 30–44, 18.2%; 45–59,
  10.3%; 60–74, 5.5%; 75 and over, 2.0%.
Population projection: (2000) 2,856,000; (2010) 3,266,000.
Doubling time: 41 years.
Ethnic composition (1992): mestizo 64.0%; black and mulatto 14.0%; white
  10.0%; Amerindian 8.0%; Asian (mostly Chinese) 4.0%.
Religious affiliation (1992): Roman Catholic 80.0%; Protestant (mostly evan-
  gelical) 10.0%; Muslim 5.0%; Bahā'ī 1.0%; Hindu 0.3%; Jewish 0.3%; other
  3.4%.
Major cities (1990): Panama City 413,505[3]; San Miguelito 243,025[4]; David
  65,763[5]; Colón 54,654; Barú 46,093[5].

Vital statistics

Birth rate per 1,000 population (1993): 22.8 (world avg. 26.0); (1985) legiti-
  mate 28.1%; illegitimate 71.9%.
Death rate per 1,000 population (1993): 4.9 (world avg. 9.2).
Natural increase rate per 1,000 population (1993): 17.9 (world avg. 16.8).
Total fertility rate (avg. births per childbearing woman; 1992): 2.9.
Marriage rate per 1,000 population (1992): 4.1.
Divorce rate per 1,000 population (1992): 0.6.
Life expectancy at birth (1991): male 70.6 years; female 74.7 years.
Major causes of death per 100,000 population (1991)[6]: diseases of the circu-
  latory system 141.5, of which ischemic heart diseases 56.8, cerebrovascular
  disease 52.7; malignant neoplasms (cancers) 73.9; accidents 43.6; infectious
  and parasitic diseases 31.6; diseases of the respiratory system 27.5.

National economy

Budget (1994). Revenue: B 1,928,600,000 (current revenue 73.4%, of which
  nontax revenue 25.0%; development revenue 26.6%, of which foreign loans
  16.8%). Expenditures: B 1,928,600,000 (current expenditure 80.2%, of which
  public debt payments 25.6%, current transfers 14.0%, education 11.1%,
  administration 7.8%, health 7.2%; development expenditure 19.8%).
Public debt (external, outstanding; 1992): U.S.$3,770,000,000.
Production (metric tons except as noted). Agriculture, forestry, fishing (1992):
  sugarcane 1,400,000, bananas 1,110,000, rice 165,000, corn (maize) 95,000,
  plantains 70,000, tomatoes 30,000, oranges 26,000, coffee 12,000, tobacco
  2,000; livestock (number of live animals) 1,400,000 cattle, 257,000 pigs; roundwood 1,028,000 cu m; fish catch (value of production in B '000): shrimps
  30,400, fish 9,400, lobster 5,600. Mining and quarrying (1992): limestone
  716,000; gold 8,000 troy oz. Manufacturing (value added in B '000; 1991):
  food products 133,300; beverages 59,800; paints, soaps, and pharmaceuticals
  37,700; wearing apparel 29,800; tobacco products 25,700; cement, bricks, and
  tiles 24,600. Construction (value of construction in B '000; 1992): residential
  129,000; nonresidential 75,100. Energy production (consumption): electricity
  (kW-hr; 1993) 3,156,000,000 ([1992] 2,311,000,000); coal (metric tons; 1992)
  none (67,000); crude petroleum (barrels; 1992) none (12,937,000); petroleum
  products (metric tons; 1992) 1,731,000 (1,214,000); natural gas (cu m; 1992)
  none (59,455,000).
Household income and expenditure. Average household size (1990) 4.4; average annual income per household (1990) B 5,450 (U.S.$5,450); sources
  of income, n.a.; expenditure (1983–84)[7]: food and beverages 34.9%, transportation and communications 15.1%, housing and energy 12.6%, education
  and recreation 11.7%.
Population economically active (1991): total 858,509[8]; activity rate of total
  population 37.4% (participation rates: ages 15–69, 60.0%; female 33.8%;
  unemployed [1993] 12.5%).

Price and earnings indexes (1990 = 100)

	1988	1989	1990	1991	1992	1993	1994[9]
Consumer price index	99.1	99.2	100.0	101.3	103.1	103.6	104.6
Annual earnings index[10]	99.9	98.6	100.0	104.4	...	...	...

Gross national product (1993): U.S.$6,612,000,000 (U.S.$2,580 per capita).

Structure of gross domestic product and labour force

	1992 in value B '000,000[11]	% of total value	labour force[8]	% of labour force[8]
Agriculture	236.7	10.8	214,682	23.3
Mining	4.3	0.2	2,357	0.3
Manufacturing	202.8	9.2	86,571	9.4
Construction	117.5	5.3	49,681	5.4
Public utilities	86.2	3.9	10,774	1.2
Transp. and commun.	549.2[12]	25.0[12]	49,969	5.4
Trade	259.1	11.8	180,166	19.6
Finance, real estate	322.2	14.7	39,174	4.2
Pub. admin.	285.8	13.0	60,274	6.5
Services	189.0	8.6	177,326	19.3
Other	−54.1[13]	−2.5[13]	49,567[14]	5.4[14]
TOTAL	2,198.7	100.0	920,541	100.0

Tourism (1992): receipts from visitors U.S.$207,000,000; expenditures by na-
  tionals abroad U.S.$125,000,000.
Land use (1991): forested 42.9%; meadows and pastures 20.7%; agricultural
  and under permanent cultivation 8.6%; other 27.8%.

Foreign trade[15, 16]

Balance of trade (current prices)

	1988	1989	1990	1991	1992	1993
B '000,000	−275	−453	−894	−1,071	−1,329	−1,426
% of total	25.7%	35.3%	50.1%	54.2%	57.0%	56.3%

Imports (1992): B 2,019,000,000 (mineral fuels 15.3%, machinery and apparatus 14.9%, transport equipment 12.6%, chemicals and chemical products
  10.8%). *Major import sources:* U.S. 36.2%; Colón Free Zone 15.9%; Japan
  8.2%; Ecuador 6.0%; Aruba 3.4%.
Exports (1992): B 474,000,000 (bananas 43.4%, shrimps 11.4%, clothing 4.7%,
  raw sugar 4.2%, fish products 2.7%). *Major export destinations:* U.S. 29.8%;
  Germany 26.7%; Italy 8.1%; Costa Rica 6.6%; Sweden 4.3%.

Transport and communications

Transport. Railroads (1992): route length 220 mi, 354 km; (1989) passenger-mi
  375,000, passenger-km 600,000; (1992)[17] short ton-mi cargo 461,000, metric
  ton-km cargo 673,000. Roads (1992): total length 6,278 mi, 10,103 km (paved
  32%). Vehicles: passenger cars (1990) 150,903; trucks and buses 72,744.
  Merchant marine (1992): vessels (100 gross tons and over) 5,217; total deadweight tonnage 79,255,644. Panama Canal traffic (1993): oceangoing transits
  12,257; cargo 157,980,000 metric tons. Air transport (1992): passenger-mi
  209,000,000, passenger-km 336,000,000; short ton-mi cargo 3,608,000, metric
  ton-km cargo 5,268,000; airports (1994) with scheduled flights 8.
Communications. Daily newspapers (1990): total number 8; total circulation
  170,000; circulation per 1,000 population 70. Radio (1993): 450,000 receivers
  (1 per 5.6 persons). Television (1993): 204,539 receivers (1 per 12 persons).
  Telephones (1992): 283,168 (1 per 8.8 persons).

Education and health

Education (1992)

	schools	teachers	students	student/ teacher ratio
Primary (age 6–11)	2,712	13,751	352,994	25.7
Secondary (age 12–17) Voc., teacher tr. }	363	10,350	201,047	19.4
Higher	9	3,684	63,894	17.3

Educational attainment (1990). Percentage of population age 25 and over
  having: no formal schooling 12.3%; incomplete primary education 21.2%;
  complete primary education 22.9%; secondary 30.4%; higher 13.2%. *Literacy*
  (1990): total population age 15 and over literate 1,385,000 (88.1%); males
  literate 705,000 (88.1%); females literate 680,000 (88.2%).
Health (1992): physicians 2,947 (1 per 844 persons); hospital beds 7,435 (1
  per 335 persons); infant mortality rate per 1,000 live births (1994) 17.0.
Food (1988–90): daily per capita caloric intake 2,269 (vegetable products 80%,
  animal products 20%); 98% of FAO recommended minimum requirement.

Military

Total active duty personnel (1993): 11,800 (national police force 93.2%, national maritime service 3.4%, national air service 3.4%). U.S. forces in
  former Canal Zone 10,500. *Military expenditure as percentage of GNP* (1991):
  1.4% (world 4.2%); per capita expenditure U.S.$31.

[1]Colón includes Comarca de San Blas. [2]Detail does not add to total given because of
rounding. [3]1990 estimated pop. of Panama City urban agglomeration including San
Miguelito is 821,000. [4]Population of urban district. [5]Population of the cabecera, the
seat, or "head" of the municipality. [6]Projected rates based on about 75% of total
deaths. [7]Panama City only. [8]Excludes nonresidents in former Canal Zone and indigenous areas and institutional households. [9]April. [10]Public sector only. [11]At prices of
1970. [12]Includes trans-Panamanian oil pipeline, commission of Panama Canal, and all
activities of Colón Free Zone. [13]Net of imputed bank service charges and import fees.
[14]Includes 1,455 not adequately defined and 48,112 unemployed without previous employment. [15]Import figures are f.o.b. in balance of trade and c.i.f. in commodities and
trading partners. [16]Excludes Colón Free Zone (1992 imports f.o.b. B 4,365,000,000;
1992 reexports f.o.b. B 4,833,000,000, of which textiles and clothing 25.8%, nonelectrical and electrical machinery and apparatus 21.8%). [17]Panama Railroad only.

Papua New Guinea

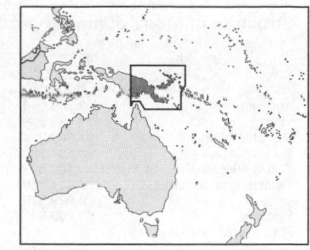

Official name: Independent State of Papua New Guinea.
Form of government: constitutional monarchy with one legislative house (National Parliament [109]).
Chief of state: British Monarch represented by Governor-General.
Head of government: Prime Minister.
Capital: Port Moresby.
Official language: English[1].
Official religion: none.
Monetary unit: 1 Papua New Guinea kina (K) = 100 toea; valuation (Oct. 7, 1994) 1 U.S.$ = K 1.09; 1 £ = K 1.73.

Area and population		area		population
Provinces	Administrative centres	sq mi	sq km	1990 census[2]
Central	Port Moresby (Central)	11,400	29,500	140,584
Eastern Highlands	Goroka	4,300	11,200	299,619
East New Britain	Rabaul	6,000	15,500	184,408
East Sepik	Wewak	16,550	42,800	248,308
Enga	Wabag	4,950	12,800	238,357
Gulf	Kerema	13,300	34,500	68,060
Madang	Madang	11,200	29,000	270,299
Manus	Lorengau	800	2,100	32,830
Milne Bay	Alotau (Samarai)	5,400	14,000	157,288
Morobe	Lae	13,300	34,500	363,535
National Capital District	Port Moresby	100	240	193,242
New Ireland	Kavieng	3,700	9,600	87,194
North Solomons (Bougainville)	Arawa (Buka)	3,600	9,300	[3]
Oro (Northern)	Popondetta	8,800	22,800	96,762
Sandaun (West Sepik)	Vanimo	14,000	36,300	135,185
Simbu (Chimbu)	Kundiawa	2,350	6,100	183,801
Southern Highlands	Mendi	9,200	23,800	302,724
Western	Daru	38,350	99,300	108,705
Western Highlands	Mount Hagen	3,300	8,500	291,090
West New Britain	Kimbe	8,100	21,000	127,547
TOTAL		178,704[4]	462,840	3,529,538[5]

Demography

Population (1994): 4,246,000.
Density (1994): persons per sq mi 23.8, persons per sq km 9.2.
Urban-rural (1990)[2]: urban 15.2%; rural 84.8%.
Sex distribution (1990)[2]: male 52.09%; female 47.91%.
Age breakdown (1990): under 15, 40.4%; 15–29, 28.8%; 30–44, 16.9%; 45–59, 9.3%; 60–74, 4.3%; 75 and over, 0.3%.
Population projection. (2000) 4,867,000, (2010) 6,023,000.
Doubling time: 30 years.
Ethnic composition (1983): New Guinea Papuan 84.0%; New Guinea Melanesian 15.0%; other 1.0%.
Religious affiliation (1980): Protestant 58.4%; Roman Catholic 32.8%; Anglican 5.4%; traditional beliefs 2.5%; Baha'i 0.6%; other 0.3%.
Major cities (1990)[2]: Port Moresby 193,242; Lae 80,655; Madang 27,057; Wewak 23,224; Goroka 17,855.

Vital statistics

Birth rate per 1,000 population (1994): 33.0 (world avg. 26.0); legitimate, n.a.; illegitimate, n.a.
Death rate per 1,000 population (1994): 10.0 (world avg. 9.2).
Natural increase rate per 1,000 population (1994): 23.0 (world avg. 16.8).
Total fertility rate (avg. births per childbearing woman; 1994): 4.7.
Marriage rate per 1,000 population: n.a.
Life expectancy at birth (1994): male 56.0 years; female 57.0 years.
Major causes of death per 100,000 population (1991): pneumonia 28.7; conditions originating from perinatal period 17.5; malaria 12.7; meningitis 8.5; tuberculosis 7.0; intestinal infections 6.8.

National economy

Budget (1993). Revenue: K 1,333,000,000 (company tax 27.7%, foreign grants 15.2%, import duties 14.9%, personal income tax 14.2%, nontax revenue 11.4%, excise duties 7.0%). Expenditures: K 1,564,500,000 (administrative 38.5%, transfers to provincial governments 21.8%, interest payments 10.1%, capital works 8.4%).
Production (metric tons except as noted). Agriculture, forestry, fishing (1992): bananas 1,250,000, coconuts 780,000, sweet potatoes 475,000, sugarcane 450,000, yams 220,000, taro 217,000, palm oil 206,000, cassava 113,000, copra 110,000, palm kernels 57,000, coffee 47,000, cacao 34,000, pineapples 13,000, tea 9,000; livestock (number of live animals) 1,010,000 pigs, 105,000 cattle, 3,000,000 chickens; roundwood 8,188,000 cu m; fish catch (1991) 25,330. Mining and quarrying (1991): copper 204,500; silver 124,900 kg; gold 60,800 kg. Manufacturing (value added, in K; 1985): food, beverages, and tobacco 162,558,000; metals, metal products, machinery, and equipment 47,493,000; wood products 29,807,000. Construction (value in K; 1986)[6]: residential K 19,369,000; nonresidential K 55,675,000. Energy production (consumption): electricity (kW-hr; 1992) 1,790,000,000 (1,790,000,000); coal (metric tons; 1992) none (1,000); crude petroleum (barrels) none (n.a.); petroleum products (metric tons; 1992) none (735,000); natural gas, none (n.a.).
Tourism: receipts from visitors (1992) U.S.$49,000,000; expenditures by nationals abroad (1990) U.S.$42,000,000.
Gross national product (1993): U.S.$4,646,000,000 (U.S.$1,120 per capita).

Structure of gross domestic product and labour force				
	1992		1980	
	in value K '000,000	% of total value	labour force[7]	% of labour force[7]
Agriculture	1,087.6	25.8	564,500	77.0
Mining	862.4	20.5	4,300	0.6
Manufacturing	364.4	8.7	14,000	1.9
Construction	222.5	5.3	21,600	2.9
Public utilities	63.7	1.5	2,800	0.4
Transp. and commun.	275.0	6.6	17,400	2.4
Trade	406.1	9.6	25,100	3.4
Finance	42.8	1.0	4,500	0.6
Pub. admin., defense } Services	883.1	21.0	77,100	10.5
Other	−0.6[8]		1,500	0.2
TOTAL	4,207.9	100.0	732,800	100.0[4]

Public debt (external, outstanding; 1992): U.S.$1,539,000,000.
Land use (1991): forested 84.4%; agricultural and under permanent cultivation 0.9%; meadows and pastures 0.2%; other 14.5%.
Population economically active (1980)[7]: total 732,800; activity rate 24.6% (participation rates: over age 10, 35.2%; female 39.8%; unemployed 12.8%[9]).

Price and earnings indexes (1985 = 100)							
	1987	1988	1989	1990	1991	1992	1993
Consumer price index	109.0	114.9	120.9	120.4	137.3	143.3	150.4
Weekly earnings index[10]	109.5	112.8	118.6	122.4	129.9	135.8	...

Household income and expenditure. Average household size (1980) 4.6; income per household (1975–76) K 2,771 (U.S.$3,483); sources of income (1970): wages and salaries 57.3%, transfer payments 1.1%, self-employment and other 41.6%; expenditure (1987)[11]: food and beverages 40.9%, transportation and communications 13.0%, housing 12.5%, clothing and footwear 6.2%, heating and lighting 4.9%, services and other 22.5%.

Foreign trade[12]

Balance of trade (current prices)						
	1988	1989	1990	1991	1992	1993
K '000,000	+214.7	−47.2	+38.5	−52.7	+475.2	+1,318.9
% of total	9.4%	2.1%	1.8%	2.0%	15.7%	37.3%

Imports (1993): K 1,110,000,000 (1990: machinery and transport equipment 38.7%; basic manufactures 20.4%; food and live animals 17.9%; chemicals 7.5%; mineral fuels, lubricants, and related materials 2.7%). *Major import sources* (1990): Australia 50.6%; Japan 14.4%; U.S. 10.4%; Singapore 9.2%; New Zealand 3.6%; U.K. 2.5%; China 2.3%.
Exports (1993): K 2,430,000,000 (gold 28.0%; timber 16.5%; copper ore and concentrates 10.5%; palm oil and copra 4.4%; coffee 3.7%; cocoa beans 1.3%). *Major export destinations* (1992): Japan 21.3%; Australia 40.9%; Germany 9.7%; South Korea 7.9%; U.K. 4.3%; Singapore 3.7%.

Transport and communications

Transport. Railroads: none. Roads (1986): total length 12,263 mi, 19,736 km (paved 6%). Vehicles (1989): passenger cars 13,150; trucks and buses 24,332. Merchant marine (1992): vessels (100 gross tons and over) 87; total deadweight tonnage 40,855. Air transport (1992): passenger-mi 439,831,000, passenger-km 707,841,000; short ton-mi cargo 56,587,000, metric ton-km cargo 82,616,000; airports (1992) with scheduled flights 121.
Communications. Daily newspapers (1990): total number 2; total circulation 49,000; circulation per 1,000 population 13. Radio (1993): 235,000 receivers (1 per 17 persons). Television (1993): 10,000 receivers (1 per 392 persons). Telephones (1990): 63,200 (1 per 59 persons).

Education and health

Education (1990)				
	schools	teachers	students	student/ teacher ratio
Primary (age 7–12)	2,606	13,105	415,195	31.7
Secondary (age 13–16)	135	2,306[13]	55,797	25.0[13]
Voc., teacher tr.	117	751[13]	9,846	12.4[13]
Higher	2	902[14]	5,007	7.1[14]

Educational attainment (1990). Percentage of population age 25 and over having: no formal schooling 82.6%; some primary education 8.2%; completed primary 5.0%; some secondary 4.2%. *Literacy* (1990): total population age 15 and over literate 52.0%; males literate 64.9%; females literate 37.8%.
Health: physicians (1990) 301 (1 per 12,874 persons); hospital beds (1989) 15,335 (1 per 234 persons); infant mortality rate (1993) 53.0.
Food: daily per capita caloric intake (1988) 2,247 (1980–82: vegetable products 90%, animal products 10%); (1984) 82% of FAO minimum.

Military

Total active duty personnel (1994): 3,800 (army 84.2%, navy 13.2%, air force 2.6%). *Military expenditure as percentage of GNP* (1991): 3.0% (world 4.2%); per capita expenditure U.S.$26.

[1]The national languages are English, Tok Pisin (English Creole), and Motu. [2]Preliminary results. [3]Data unavailable because of civil insurrection. [4]Detail does not add to total given because of rounding. [5]Excludes an estimated population of 160,000 in the North Solomons, 4,500 people in remote areas, and an estimated foreign population of about 20,000–30,000. [6]Completed new buildings. [7]Citizens of Papua New Guinea over age 10 involved in "money-raising activities" only. [8]Statistical discrepancy. [9]1977; in six urban centres. [10]Minimum wage of urban labourers. [11]Weights of retail price index components. [12]Import figures are f.o.b. in balance of trade and c.i.f. for commodities and trading partners. [13]1989. [14]1986.

Paraguay

Official name: República del Paraguay
 (Spanish); Tetä Paraguáype
 (Guaraní) (Republic of Paraguay).
Form of government: multiparty
 republic with two legislative
 houses (Senate [45]; Chamber of
 Deputies [80]).
Head of state and government:
 President.
Capital: Asunción.
Official languages: Spanish; Guaraní.
Official religion: none[1].
Monetary unit: 1 Paraguayan Guaraní
 (G) = 100 céntimos; valuation
 (Oct. 7, 1994) 1 U.S.$ = G1,919;
 1 £ = G3,053.

Area and population

Regions	Capitals	area		population
		sq mi	sq km	1992 census
Departments				
Occidental		95,338	246,925	97,208
Alto Paraguay	Fuerte Olimpo	31,795	82,349	11,816
Boquerón	Filadelfia	35,393	91,669	26,292
Presidente Hayes	Pozo Colorado	28,150	72,907	59,100
Oriental		61,710	159,827	4,026,342
Alto Paraná	Ciudad del Este	5,751	14,895	403,858
Amambay	Pedro Juan Caballero	4,994	12,933	97,158
Asunción[2]	—	45	117	502,426
Caaguazú	Coronel Oviedo	4,430	11,474	383,319
Caazapá	Caazapá	3,666	9,496	128,550
Canindiyú	Salto del Guairá	5,663	14,667	96,826
Central	Asunción	952	2,465	864,540
Concepción	Concepción	6,970	18,051	166,946
Cordillera	Caacupé	1,910	4,948	206,097
Guairá	Villarrica	1,485	3,846	162,244
Itapúa	Encarnación	6,380	16,525	375,748
Misiones	San Juan Bautista	3,690	9,556	88,624
Ñeembucú	Pilar	4,690	12,147	69,884
Paraguarí	Paraguarí	3,361	8,705	203,012
San Pedro	San Pedro	7,723	20,002	277,110
TOTAL		157,048	406,752	4,123,550[3]

Demography

Population (1994): 4,732,000[3].
Density (1994): persons per sq mi 30.1, persons per sq km 11.6.
Urban-rural (1992): urban 50.5%; rural 49.5%.
Sex distribution (1992): male 50.19%; female 49.81%.
Age breakdown (1992): under 15, 40.1%; 15–29, 27.6%; 30–44, 18.7%; 45–59, 8.3%; 60–74, 4.2%; 75 and over, 1.1%.
Population projection: (2000) 5,464,000; (2010) 6,889,000.
Doubling time: 26 years.
Ethnic composition (1980): mestizo (Spanish-Guaraní) 90.8%; Amerindian 3.0%; German 1.7%; other 4.5%.
Religious affiliation (1991): Roman Catholic 93.1%; other 6.9%.
Major cities (1992): Asunción 502,426; Ciudad del Este 133,893; San Lorenzo 133,311; Lambaré 99,681; Fernando de la Mora 95,287.

Vital statistics

Birth rate per 1,000 population (1991): 33.6 (world avg. 26.0); (1985) legitimate 68.7%[4]; illegitimate 31.3%[4].
Death rate per 1,000 population (1991): 6.4 (world avg. 9.2).
Natural increase rate per 1,000 population (1991): 27.2 (world avg. 16.8).
Total fertility rate (avg. births per childbearing woman; 1991): 4.4.
Marriage rate per 1,000 population (1990): 1.8[4].
Life expectancy at birth (1991): male 65.0 years; female 69.4 years.
Major causes of death per 100,000 population (1988)[5]: diseases of the circulatory system 200.9; malignant neoplasms (cancers) 60.8; infectious and parasitic diseases 56.4; diseases of the respiratory system 52.5.

National economy

Budget (1993). Revenue: G4,254,817,000,000 (taxes on goods and services 30.7%, income on fixed assets 23.3%, customs duties 11.6%, pension funds 6.2%, documentary tax 3.6%, real estate taxes 2.5%). Expenditures: G1,726,216,200,000 (education 19.3%, public works 14.4%, defense 10.5%, public health 7.5%, interior 7.0%, agriculture 5.8%, housing 5.4%).
Public debt (external, outstanding; 1992): U.S.$1,483,000,000.
Production (metric tons except as noted). Agriculture, forestry, fishing (1992): cassava 3,300,000, sugarcane 2,788,000, soybeans 1,315,000, seed cotton 670,000, corn (maize) 466,000, oranges 355,000, lint cotton 215,000, bananas 140,000, sweet potatoes 86,000; livestock (number of live animals) 7,800,000 cattle, 2,600,000 pigs, 18,000,000 chickens; roundwood (1991) 8,466,000 cu m; fish catch (1991) 13,000. Mining and quarrying (1992): limestone 600,000; kaolin 74,000; gypsum 4,500. Manufacturing (value of production in G'000,000; 1990): woven cotton fabric 207,600; processed meat 162,593; naphtha 76,813; gasoline 74,624; beer 70,054; soft drinks 68,197; cement 43,494; sugar 41,787; wheat flour 25,162. Construction (1985): residential 60,800 sq m; nonresidential 163,200 sq m. Energy production (consumption): electricity (kW-hr; 1992) 27,136,000,000 (2,523,000,000); coal, none (none); crude petroleum (barrels; 1992) none (2,308,000); petroleum products (metric tons; 1992) 313,000 (825,000); natural gas, none (none).
Tourism (1992): receipts from visitors U.S.$153,000,000; expenditures by nationals abroad U.S.$120,000,000.
Gross national product (1993): U.S.$6,977,000,000 (U.S.$1,500 per capita).

Structure of gross domestic product and labour force

	1992		1982	
	in value G'000,000	% of total value	labour force	% of labour force
Agriculture	2,369,044	24.5	445,518	42.9
Mining	36,368	0.4	1,406	0.1
Manufacturing	1,643,211	17.0	124,658	12.0
Construction	558,926	5.8	69,900	6.7
Public utilities	301,697	3.1	2,605	0.3
Transp. and commun.	384,728	4.0	30,524	2.9
Trade	2,929,879	30.3	85,961	8.3
Finance	203,645	2.1	18,019	1.7
Pub. admin., defense	} 1,243,340	} 12.8	174,228	16.8
Services			86,444	8.3
Other				
TOTAL	9,670,838	100.0	1,039,258[6]	100.0

Population economically active (1982): total 1,039,258; activity rate 51.5% (participation rates: ages 15–64, 57.5%; female 19.7%; unemployed [1989] 9.2%).

Price and earnings indexes (1990 = 100)

	1987	1988	1989	1990	1991	1992	1993
Consumer price index	46.7	57.2	72.4	100.0	124.3	143.1	169.2
Earnings index	...	...	...	...	...	...	...

Household income and expenditure. Average household size (1992) 4.7; sources of income (1989): wages and salaries 33.9%, transfer payments 2.5%, other 63.6%; expenditure (1980): food 48.7%, housing 16.4%, clothing 9.7%, household durable goods 6.2%, transportation and communications 4.5%.
Land use (1991): forested 33.3%; meadows and pastures 53.9%; agricultural and under permanent cultivation 5.6%; other 7.2%.

Foreign trade

Balance of trade (current prices)

	1988	1989	1990	1991	1992	1993
U.S.$'000,000	+ 15.1	+ 363.8	− 234.7	− 538.3	− 580.6	− 752.3
% of total	1.5%	21.8%	10.9%	26.7%	30.7%	34.2%

Imports (1993): U.S.$1,477,540,000 (machinery and transport equipment 37.0%, of which transport equipment 14.0%; fuels and lubricants 10.0%; tobacco and beverages 7.6%; chemicals and pharmaceuticals 6.8%; iron products 3.6%). *Major import sources:* Brazil 23.0%; United States 14.3%; Argentina 11.7%; Japan 11.6%; Taiwan 6.2%; South Korea 3.9%; United Kingdom 3.6%; Germany 2.9%.
Exports (1993): U.S.$725,218,000 (soybean flour 30.8%; cotton fibres 22.7%; timber 8.8%; hides and skins 7.4%; processed meat 6.5%; vegetable oil 5.6%, of which tung oil 0.6%; oilseed cakes 4.1%; perfume oils 1.1%; tobacco 1.0%). *Major export destinations:* Brazil 29.7%; The Netherlands 26.1%; Argentina 8.9%; United States 7.3%; Italy 2.4%; United Kingdom 1.9%; France 1.6%.

Transport and communications

Transport. Railroads (1990): route length 273 mi, 439 km; passenger-mi 7,900,000, passenger-km 12,700,000; short ton-mi cargo 7,877,000, metric ton-km cargo 11,500,000. Roads (1988): total length 15,957 mi, 25,681 km (paved 9%). Vehicles (1990): passenger cars 117,067; buses 3,375. Merchant marine (1992): vessels (100 gross tons and over) 38; total deadweight tonnage 38,513. Air transport (1992): passenger-mi 700,000,000, passenger-km 1,127,000,000; short ton-mi cargo 3,500,000[7], metric ton-km cargo 5,100,000[7]; airports (1994) with scheduled flights 1.
Communications. Daily newspapers (1993): total number 5; total circulation 148,000[8]; circulation per 1,000 population 32[8]. Radio (1993): 775,000 receivers (1 per 6.0 persons). Television (1993): 350,000 receivers (1 per 13 persons). Telephones (1992): 151,880 (1 per 30 persons).

Education and health

Education (1991–92)

	schools	teachers	students	student/ teacher ratio
Primary (age 7–12)	4,649	29,172	720,983	24.7
Secondary (age 13–18)[9]	812	12,218	169,167	13.8
Higher	2[10]	2,694[11]	32,884	

Educational attainment (1982). Percentage of population age 25 and over having: no formal schooling 13.6%; primary education 64.7%; secondary 15.5%; higher 3.4%; not stated 2.8%. *Literacy* (1990): percentage of total population age 15 and over literate 90.1%; males literate 92.1%; females literate 88.1%.
Health (1992): physicians 3,161 (1 per 1,423 persons); hospital beds 5,389 (1 per 835 persons); infant mortality rate per 1,000 live births (1990–95) 47.0.
Food (1988–90): daily per capita caloric intake 2,684 (vegetable products 82%, animal products 18%); 116% of FAO recommended minimum requirement.

Military

Total active duty personnel (1993): 16,500 (army 75.7%, navy 18.2%, air force 6.1%). *Military expenditure as percentage of GNP* (1991): 1.1% (world 4.2%); per capita expenditure U.S.$23.

[1]Roman Catholicism, although not official, enjoys special recognition in the 1992 constitution. [2]Asunción is the capital city, not a department. [3]Preliminary 1992 census figure is not adjusted for undercount. The 1994 population figure is adjusted for estimated undercount. [4]Civil Registry records only. [5]Reporting areas only (constituting about 50 percent of the total population). [6]Detail does not add to total given because of rounding. [7]1991. [8]For four newspapers only. [9]Includes vocational education and teacher training. [10]1990–91. [11]1985.

Peru

Official name: República del Perú (Spanish) (Republic of Peru).
Form of government[1]: unitary multiparty republic with one legislative house (Congress [80][2]).
Head of state and government: President.
Capital: Lima.
Official languages: Spanish; Quechua; Aymara.
Official religion: Roman Catholicism.
Monetary unit[3]: 1 nuevo sol (S/.) = 100 céntimos; valuation (Oct. 7, 1994) 1 U.S.$ = S/. 2.25; 1 £ = S/. 3.58.

Area and population

Regions	Capitals	area sq mi	area sq km	population 1993 census[4]
Andres Avelino Cáceres	...	40,707	105,430	1,909,799
Arequipa	...	24,458	63,345	924,745
Chavin	...	15,686	40,627	940,481
Grau	...	15,661	40,562	1,594,922
Inca	...	66,696	172,741	1,456,122
José Carlos Mariátegui	...	40,081	103,809	1,399,508
La Libertad	...	9,873	25,570	1,279,472
Loreto	...	142,414	368,852	673,329
Los Libertadores-Wari	...	34,340	88,939	1,434,554
Nor Oriental del Marañón	...	33,486	86,728	2,540,432
Ucayali	...	39,541	102,411	307,813
Departments				
Lima	...	13,437	34,802	6,483,901
San Martín	...	19,789	51,253	545,154
Constitutional Province				
Callao	Callao	57	147	638,234
TOTAL		496,225[5]	1,285,216	22,128,466

Demography

Population (1994): 23,383,000.
Density (1994): persons per sq mi 47.1, persons per sq km 18.2.
Urban-rural (1993): urban 71.8%; rural 28.2%.
Sex distribution (1993): male 50.32%; female 49.68%.
Age breakdown (1993): under 15, 36.4%; 15–29, 29.0%; 30–44, 18.2%; 45–59, 10.2%; 60–74, 5.0%; 75 and over, 1.2%.
Population projection: (2000) 26,276,000; (2010) 31,047,000.
Doubling time: 28 years.
Ethnic composition (1981): Quechua 47.1%; mestizo 32.0%; white 12.0%; Aymara 5.4%; other Amerindian 1.7%; other 1.8%.
Religious affiliation (1989): Roman Catholic 92.5%; Protestant 5.5%.
Major cities (1993): metropolitan Lima 5,759,676; Callao 637,755; Arequipa 620,471; Trujillo 508,716; Chiclayo 410,468.

Vital statistics

Birth rate per 1,000 population (1990–95): 29.0 (world avg. 26.0); (1977) legitimate 57.8%; illegitimate 42.2%.
Death rate per 1,000 population (1990–95): 7.6 (world avg. 9.2).
Natural increase rate per 1,000 population (1990–95): 21.4 (world avg. 16.8).
Total fertility rate (avg. births per childbearing woman; 1990–95): 3.6.
Marriage rate per 1,000 population (1982): 6.0[6].
Life expectancy at birth (1990–95): male 62.7 years; female 66.6 years.
Major causes of death per 100,000 population (1989): diseases of the circulatory system 115.3; respiratory diseases 100.2; infectious diseases 84.5; malignant neoplasms 72.9; accidents, poisoning, and violence 53.6.

National economy

Budget (1992). Revenue: S/. 5,651,680,000 (taxes on goods and services 58.8%; income taxes 13.3%; import duties 10.1%; nontax revenue 7.6%). Expenditures: S/. 7,526,990,000 (current expenditure 72.7%, of which transfer payments 32.4%, wages and salaries 13.9%; capital expenditure 14.9%; public debt amortization 12.4%).
Tourism (1992): receipts U.S.$237,000,000; expenditures U.S.$480,000,000.
Production (metric tons except as noted). Agriculture, forestry, fishing (1993): sugarcane 5,000,000, potatoes 1,475,000, rice 950,000, corn (maize) 785,000, plantains 710,000, cassava 290,000, seed cotton 94,000, coffee 86,000; livestock (number of live animals) 11,915,000 sheep, 3,950,000 cattle, 2,400,000 pigs, 60,000,000 chickens; roundwood (1992) 7,826,000 cu m; fish catch (1992) 6,842,700. Mining and quarrying (1992): iron ore 1,849,000; zinc 603,000; copper 369,000; lead 194,000; silver 1,572. Manufacturing (value in S/. '000,000[7]; 1992): processed foods 163.6; base metal products 157.0; beverages and tobacco 63.6; textiles 58.2; industrial chemicals 46.9; apparel 33.2; wood products 32.6. Construction (value in S/. '000,000[7]; 1992): residential 22.4; nonresidential 14.6. Energy production (consumption): electricity (kW-hr; 1992) 13,132,000,000 (13,132,000,000); coal (metric tons; 1992) 90,000 (280,000); crude petroleum (barrels; 1992) 42,000,000 (58,000,000); petroleum products (metric tons; 1992) 7,562,000 (5,988,000); natural gas (cu m; 1992) 1,314,000,000 (525,000,000).
Household income and expenditure. Average household size (1986) 5.2; income per household (1988) I/. 1,086,620[3] (U.S.$2,173); sources of income (1988): business income 65.1%, wages 31.2%, transfers 3.7%; expenditure (1990): food 29.4%, recreation and education 13.2%, household durables 10.1%, clothing and footwear 8.5%, transportation 7.5%, health 7.0%, other 24.3%.
Gross national product (1993): U.S.$33,973,000,000 (U.S.$1,490 per capita).

Structure of gross domestic product and labour force

	1992 in value S/. '000,000[7]	% of total value	labour force	% of labour force
Agriculture	437.7	13.2	2,658,000	33.0
Mining	354.6	10.7	198,000	2.4
Manufacturing	713.4	21.5	840,000	10.4
Construction	218.4	6.6	300,000	3.7
Public utilities	...	...	25,000	0.3
Transp. and commun.	...	...	355,000	4.4
Trade	411.5	12.4	1,297,000	16.1
Finance	...	...	192,000	2.4
Services	1,180.2[8]	35.6[8]	2,199,000[9]	27.3[9]
TOTAL	3,315.8	100.0	8,064,000	100.0

Population economically active (1992): total 8,064,000; activity rate of total population 35.9% (participation rates: over age 15 [1990] 56.4%; female [1985–86] 38.3%; unemployed 8.3%).

Price and earnings indexes (1985 = 100)

	1987	1988	1989	1990[10]	1991[10]	1992[10]	1993[10]
Consumer price index	331	2,536	88,733	6,727	34,274	59,476	88,369
Monthly earnings index[11]	379	1,406	39,141	2,130	15,041	24,774	...

Land use (1992): forest 53.1%; pasture 21.2%; agricultural 2.9%; other 22.8%.
Public debt (external, outstanding; 1992): U.S.$15,417,000,000.

Foreign trade

Balance of trade (current prices)

	1988	1989	1990	1991	1992	1993
U.S.$'000,000	+127.9	+1,523.9	+585.3	−165.0	−566.7	−623.9
% of total	2.4%	27.6%	9.8%	2.4%	7.5%	8.2%

Imports (1992): U.S.$4,051,000,000 (raw and intermediate materials 44.0%, machinery and transport equipment 27.6%, consumer goods 20.8%). Major import sources: U.S. 27.2%; Colombia 8.1%; Japan 7.7%; Argentina 6.2%; Brazil 5.2%; Germany 4.6%; Venezuela 3.4%.
Exports (1992): U.S.$3,484,000,000 (copper 23.1%, fish flour 12.6%, zinc 9.6%, gold 6.2%, petroleum and derivatives 5.6%, lead 4.6%, silver 2.2%). Major export destinations: U.S. 21.4%; Japan 9.8%; China 7.0%; U.K. 6.3%; Italy 6.0%; Brazil 4.7%; Germany 4.1%; Venezuela 3.1%.

Transport and communications

Transport. Railroads (1991): route length 2,157 mi, 3,472 km; passenger-km 319,772,000; metric ton-km cargo 826,848,000. Roads (1992): total length 43,460 mi, 69,942 km (paved 11%). Vehicles (1992): passenger cars 402,351; trucks and buses 257,884. Merchant marine (1992): vessels (100 gross tons and over) 623; total deadweight tonnage 615,582. Air transport (1992): passenger-km 1,292,000,000; metric ton-km cargo 148,000,000; airports (1994) 25.
Communications. Daily newspapers (1992): total number 59; total circulation 1,590,000; circulation per 1,000 population 71. Radio (1993): 4,400,000 receivers (1 per 5.2 persons). Television (1993): 2,000,000 receivers (1 per 11 persons). Telephones (1991): 799,000 (1 per 28 persons).

Education and health

Education (1991)

	schools	teachers	students	student/teacher ratio
Primary (age 6–11)	28,265	138,455	4,053,801	29.3
Secondary (age 12–16)	6,607	96,969	1,996,181	20.6
Voc., teacher tr.	1,704	11,289	312,669	27.7
Higher	553	44,361	751,234	16.9

Educational attainment (1981). Percentage of population age 25 and over having: no formal schooling 20.1%; less than primary education 33.2%; primary 21.1%; secondary 20.8%; higher 4.8%. Literacy (1991): total population age 15 and over literate 89.3%; males 95.9%; females 82.6%.
Health (1990): physicians (1989) 21,856 (1 per 997 persons); hospital beds 35,715 (1 per 625 persons); infant mortality rate per 1,000 live births (1990–95) 75.8.
Food (1988–90): daily per capita caloric intake 2,037 (vegetable products 86%, animal products 14%); 87% of FAO recommended minimum requirement.

Military

Total active duty personnel (1994): 115,000 (army 65.2%, navy 21.7%, air force 13.1%). Military expenditure as percentage of GNP (1991): 1.1% (world 4.2%); per capita expenditure U.S.$23.

[1]A new constitution promulgated in December 1993 replaced the 1980 constitution, which was suspended in April 1992. [2]Interim legislative body elected November 1992. The new constitution provides for a 120-seat legislature. [3]A new currency, the nuevo sol, was introduced in January 1991, replacing the inti (abbrev.: I/.) at the rate of one million intis for one nuevo sol. It was in effect from July 1, 1991, when new bills and coins became available. [4]Preliminary. [5]Detail does not add to total given because of rounding. [6]Excludes Indian jungle population; based on incomplete information. [7]At 1979 prices. [8]Includes finance, public administration, and other. [9]Includes public administration and other. [10]1985 = 0.1. [11]Estimate for Lima metropolitan area only.

Philippines

Official name: Republika ng Pilipinas
(Pilipino); Republic of the
Philippines (English).
Form of government: unitary republic
with two legislative houses (Senate
[24]; House of Representatives
[200[1]]).
Chief of state and head of government:
President.
Capital: Manila.
Official languages: Pilipino; English.
Official religion: none.
Monetary unit: 1 Philippine peso
(₱) = 100 centavos; valuation (Oct. 7,
1994) 1 U.S.$ = ₱ 25.60;
1 £ = ₱ 40.72.

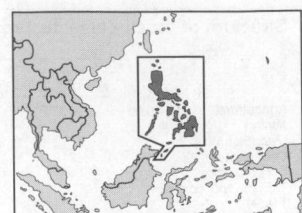

Area and population

Area and population	area		population
Regions	sq mi	sq km	1995 estimate[2]
Bicol	6,808	17,633	4,382,000
Cagayan Valley	10,362	26,838	2,656,000
Central Luzon	7,039	18,231	7,178,000
Central Mindanao	5,549	14,373	2,378,000
Central Visayas	5,773	14,951	5,225,000
Eastern Visayas	8,275	21,432	3,401,000
Ilocos	4,958	12,840	3,963,000
National Capital	246	636	9,201,000
Northern Mindanao	10,937	28,328	4,096,000
Southern Mindanao	12,237	31,693	5,242,000
Southern Tagalog	18,117	46,924	9,989,000
Western Mindanao	6,194	16,042	2,848,000
Western Visayas	7,808	20,223	6,047,000
Autonomous Regions			
Cordillera	7,063	18,294	1,304,000
Muslim Mindanao	4,493	11,638	2,103,000
TOTAL	115,860[3]	300,076	70,011,000[3]

Demography

Population (1994): 68,278,000.
Density (1994): persons per sq mi 589.3, persons per sq km 227.5.
Urban-rural (1994): urban 44.0%; rural 56.0%.
Sex distribution (1994): male 50.23%; female 49.77%.
Age breakdown (1990): under 15, 38.6%; 15–29, 28.6%; 30–44, 18.1%; 45–59, 9.3%; 60–74, 4.4%; 75 and over, 1.0%.
Population projection: (2000) 78,414,000; (2010) 94,503,000.
Doubling time: 30 years.
Ethnic composition (by mother tongue of households; 1980): Tagalog 29.7%; Cebuano 24.2%; Ilocano 10.3%; Hiligaynon Ilongo 9.2%; Bicol 5.6%; Samar-Leyte 4.0%; Pampango 2.8%; Pangasinan 1.8%; other 12.5%[3].
Religious affiliation (1980): Roman Catholic 84.1%; Aglipayan (Philippine Independent Church) 6.2%; Muslim 4.3%; Protestant 3.9%; other 1.5%.
Major cities (1990): Quezon City 1,667,000; Manila 1,599,000; Davao 850,000; Caloocan 761,000; Cebu 610,000; Zamboanga 442,000.

Vital statistics

Birth rate per 1,000 population (1994): 30.0 (world avg. 26.0); (1982) legitimate 93.9%; illegitimate 6.1%.
Death rate per 1,000 population (1994): 7.0 (world avg. 9.2).
Natural increase rate per 1,000 population (1994): 23.0 (world avg. 16.8).
Total fertility rate (avg. births per childbearing woman; 1994): 3.8.
Marriage rate per 1,000 population (1991): 6.7.
Life expectancy at birth (1994): male 64.0 years; female 68.0 years.
Major causes of death per 100,000 population (1990): heart diseases 74.4; pneumonia 66.3; vascular diseases 54.2; tuberculosis 39.1; malignant neoplasms (cancers) 35.7; diarrhea 12.0; septicemia 9.4; accidents 6.4.

National economy

Budget (1992). Revenue: ₱ 240,570,000,000 (taxes on goods and services 29.1%, international duties 28.5%, income taxes 26.0%, nontax revenues 12.5%). Expenditures: ₱ 258,680,000,000 (debt service 30.7%, education 15.4%, transportation and communications 11.0%, defense 10.2%, general public services 10.0%, agriculture 8.4%, health 4.2%).
Tourism (1992): receipts U.S.$1,674,000,000; expenditures U.S.$102,000,000.
Production. Agriculture, forestry, fishing (value in ₱ '000,000; 1992): rice 43,271, coconuts 22,012, corn (maize) 21,152, sugarcane 13,552, bananas 10,677, pineapples 5,063, mango 4,539, cassava 3,409, tobacco 3,203, coffee 2,655; livestock (number of live animals) 8,022,000 pigs, 2,577,000 buffalo, 2,240,000 goats, 1,658,000 cattle, 63,127,000 chickens; roundwood 38,652,000 cu m; fish catch 25,987. Mining and quarrying (value in ₱ '000,000; 1992): gold 6,602; silver 6,505; copper concentrate 5,909; sand and gravel 2,400; salt 2,194; coal 1,738; nickel ore 566. Manufacturing (gross value added in ₱ '000,000; 1992)[4]: food products 133,274; petroleum and coal products 35,510; industrial chemicals 27,176; footwear and wearing apparel 22,071; beverages 15,849; electrical machinery 13,211; nonmetallic mineral products 10,182. Construction (authorized; 1992): residential 3,862,000 sq m; nonresidential 4,288,000 sq m. Energy production (consumption): electricity (kW-hr; 1992) 25,682,000,000 (25,682,000,000); coal (metric tons; 1992) 1,664,000 (2,321,-000); crude petroleum (barrels; 1992) 3,045,000 (92,126,000); petroleum products (metric tons; 1992) 10,294,000 (11,684,000).
Public debt (external, outstanding; 1992): U.S.$26,004,000,000.
Gross national product (1993): U.S.$54,593,000,000 (U.S.$830 per capita).

Structure of gross domestic product and labour force

	1992			
	in value ₱ '000,000	% of total value	labour force	% of labour force
Agriculture	290,338	21.7	10,867,000	41.6
Mining	16,263	1.2	146,000	0.6
Manufacturing	327,501	24.5	2,535,000	9.7
Construction	68,695	5.1	1,055,000	4.0
Public utilities	33,875	2.5	84,000	0.3
Transp. and commun.	76,543	5.7	1,217,000	4.7
Trade	183,306	13.7	3,325,000	12.7
Finance	53,166	4.0	445,000	1.7
Services	288,734	21.6	4,202,000	16.1
Other			2,247,000[5]	8.6[5]
TOTAL	1,338,421	100.0	26,122,000[3]	100.0

Population economically active (1992): total 26,122,000; activity rate 40.7% (participation rates: ages 15–64, 65.0%; female 37.2%; unemployed 8.5%).

Price and earnings index (1985 = 100)

	1987	1988	1989	1990	1991	1992	1993
Consumer price index	104.6	113.7	127.6	145.7	172.9	188.3	202.6
Monthly earnings index[6]	129.4	150.2	176.9	...	...	...	...

Household income and expenditure (1991). Average household size 5.3; income per family ₱ 90,950 (U.S.$3,310); sources of income: wages 44.9%, business profits 44.0%, self-employment 7.4%, transfers 3.7%; expenditure: food, beverages, and tobacco 58.1%, household furnishings and operations 13.2%, transportation 5.3%, fuel and power 4.2%, clothing 3.7%.
Land use (1992): forested 33.5%; meadows and pastures 4.3%; agricultural and under permanent cultivation 30.8%; other 31.4%.

Foreign trade[7]

Balance of trade (current prices)

	1988	1989	1990	1991	1992	1993
₱ '000,000	−24,023	−57,713	−86,604	−89,465	−121,250	−176,298
% of total	7.5%	14.6%	17.0%	15.6%	19.6%	22.5%

Imports (1992): U.S.$15,465,000,000 (machinery and transport equipment 28.6%, basic manufactures 15.2%, mineral fuels and lubricants 14.0%, chemicals 10.3%, food and live animals 7.2%, inedible crude materials 4.4%). *Major import sources:* Japan 21.2%; U.S. 18.2%; Saudi Arabia 6.0%; South Korea 4.8%; Hong Kong 4.8%; Germany 4.5%; Singapore 3.7%; Australia 3.0%; Malaysia 2.7%; U.K. 2.0%.
Exports (1992): U.S.$9,790,000,000 (machinery and transport equipment 17.1%, food and live animals 11.6%, clothing and accessories 8.7%, basic manufactures 7.1%, animal and vegetable oils and fats 5.1%, inedible crude materials 5.0%). *Major export destinations:* U.S. 39.3%; Japan 17.8%; Germany 5.3%; Hong Kong 4.7%; U.K. 4.5%; The Netherlands 4.1%; Singapore 2.6%; France 1.8%; South Korea 1.8%.

Transport and communications

Transport. Railroads (1992): route length 658 mi, 1,059 km; passenger-mi 75,200,000, passenger-km 121,100,000; short ton-mi cargo 3,500,000, metric ton-km cargo 5,100,000. Roads (1991): total length 99,813 mi, 160,633 km (paved 14%). Vehicles (1992): passenger cars 480,542; trucks and buses 916,559. Merchant marine (1992): vessels (100 gross tons and over) 1,499; total deadweight tonnage 13,807,113. Air transport (1992)[8]: passenger-mi 8,010,000,000, passenger-km 12,891,000,000; short ton-mi cargo 213,667,000, metric ton-km cargo 311,948,000; airports (1994) with scheduled flights 20.
Communications. Daily newspapers (1992): total number 43; circulation 3,200,000; circulation per 1,000 population 49. Radio (1993): 4,000,000 receivers (1 per 16 persons). Television (1993): 7,000,000 receivers (1 per 9.4 persons). Telephones (1992): 1,177,870 (1 per 55 persons).

Education and health

Education (1991–92)

	schools	teachers	students	student/teacher ratio
Primary (age 7–12)	34,081	316,182	10,558,105	33.4
Secondary (age 13–16)	5,550	129,700	4,208,151	32.4
Voc., teacher tr.	1,261			
Higher	809	56,880[9]	1,656,815	23.7[9]

Educational attainment (1980). Percentage of population age 25 and over having: no grade completed 11.7%; elementary education 53.8%; secondary 18.8%; college 15.2%; not stated 0.5%. *Literacy* (1980): total population age 15 and over literate 25,139,700 (88.7%); males literate 12,772,200 (89.9%); females literate 12,367,500 (87.5%).
Health: physicians (1989) 57,270 (1 per 1,062 persons); hospital beds (1992) 83,330 (1 per 780 persons); infant mortality rate (1994) 39.
Food (1988–90): daily per capita caloric intake 2,341 (vegetable products 89%, animal products 11%); 104% of FAO recommended minimum requirement.

Military

Total active duty personnel (1994): 106,500 (army 63.8%, navy 21.6%, air force 14.6%). *Military expenditure as percentage of GNP* (1991): 2.1% (world 4.2%); per capita expenditure U.S.$15.

---

[1]Excludes 20 seats appointed by the president to represent cause-oriented groups. [2]Projection. [3]Detail does not add to total given because of rounding. [4]Manufacturing firms with 10 or more workers. [5]Mostly unemployed. [6]Wages in nonagricultural activities. [7]Import figures are f.o.b. in balance of trade and c.i.f. for commodities and trading partners. [8]Philippines Airlines only. [9]1990–91.

Poland

Official name: Rzeczpospolita Polska (Republic of Poland).
Form of government: unitary multiparty republic with two legislative houses (Senate [100]; Diet [460]).
Chief of state: President.
Head of government: Prime Minister.
Capital: Warsaw.
Official language: Polish.
Official religion: none.
Monetary unit: 1 złoty (Zł) = 100 groszy; valuation (Oct. 7, 1994) 1 U.S.$ = Zł 23,114; 1 £ = Zł 36,763.

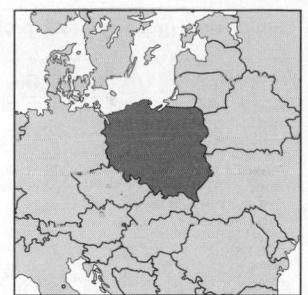

Area and population

Provinces	Capitals	area sq mi	area sq km	population 1993[1] estimate
Biała Podlaska	Biała Podlaska	2,065	5,348	308,500
Białystok	Białystok	3,882	10,055	697,900
Bielsko-Biała	Bielsko-Biała	1,430	3,704	907,300
Bydgoszcz	Bydgoszcz	3,880	10,049	1,123,000
Chełm	Chełm	1,493	3,866	249,400
Ciechanów	Ciechanów	2,456	6,362	434,400
Częstochowa	Częstochowa	2,387	6,182	781,900
Elbląg	Elbląg	2,356	6,103	486,100
Gdańsk	Gdańsk	2,855	7,394	1,437,700
Gorzów	Gorzów Wielkopolski	3,276	8,484	506,100
Jelenia Góra	Jelenia Góra	1,691	4,379	522,000
Kalisz	Kalisz	2,514	6,512	718,000
Katowice	Katowice	2,568	6,650	3,953,000
Kielce	Kielce	3,556	9,211	1,135,600
Konin	Konin	1,984	5,139	475,600
Koszalin	Koszalin	3,270	8,470	514,400
Kraków	Kraków	1,256	3,254	1,232,400
Krosno	Krosno	2,202	5,702	501,700
Legnica	Legnica	1,559	4,037	519,800
Leszno	Leszno	1,604	4,154	392,700
Łódź	Łódź	588	1,523	1,021,400
Łomża	Łomża	2,581	6,684	352,200
Lublin	Lublin	2,622	6,792	1,130,700
Nowy Sącz	Nowy Sącz	2,153	5,576	716,200
Olsztyn	Olsztyn	4,759	12,327	762,500
Opole	Opole	3,295	8,535	1,026,000
Ostrołęka	Ostrołęka	2,509	6,498	404,100
Piła	Piła	3,168	8,205	487,300
Piotrków	Piotrków Trybunalski	2,419	6,266	644,100
Płock	Płock	1,976	5,117	520,400
Poznań	Poznań	3,147	8,151	1,341,400
Przemyśl	Przemyśl	1,713	4,437	411,500
Radom	Radom	2,816	7,294	759,600
Rzeszów	Rzeszów	1,698	4,397	735,300
Siedlce	Siedlce	3,281	8,499	658,400
Sieradz	Sieradz	1,880	4,869	411,500
Skierniewice	Skierniewice	1,529	3,960	423,100
Słupsk	Słupsk	2,878	7,453	421,100
Suwałki	Suwałki	4,050	10,490	480,100
Szczecin	Szczecin	3,854	9,982	981,400
Tarnobrzeg	Tarnobrzeg	2,426	6,283	606,400
Tarnów	Tarnów	1,603	4,151	683,400
Toruń	Toruń	2,065	5,348	665,100
Wałbrzych	Wałbrzych	1,609	4,168	742,400
Warszawa	Warszawa	1,463	3,788	2,409,100
Włocławek	Włocławek	1,700	4,402	433,400
Wrocław	Wrocław	2,427	6,287	1,131,600
Zamość	Zamość	2,695	6,980	493,700
Zielona Góra	Zielona Góra	3,424	8,868	667,200
TOTAL		120,728	312,685	38,418,100

Demography

Population (1994): 38,653,000.
Density (1994): persons per sq mi 320.2, persons per sq km 123.6.
Urban-rural (1994): urban 61.8%; rural 38.2%.
Sex distribution (1993): male 48.70%; female 51.30%.
Age breakdown (1993): under 15, 24.1%; 15–29, 21.3%; 30–44, 24.2%; 45–59, 15.0%; 60–74, 11.6%; 75 and over, 3.8%.
Population projection: (2000) 39,547,000; (2010) 41,089,000.
Ethnic composition (1990): Polish 98.7%; Ukrainian 0.6%; other 0.7%.
Religious affiliation (1992): Roman Catholic 91.1%; Orthodox 1.5%.
Major cities (1993): Warsaw 1,644,500; Łódź 838,400; Kraków 744,000.

Vital statistics

Birth rate per 1,000 population (1993): 12.8 (world avg. 26.0); (1985) legitimate 95.0%; illegitimate 5.0%.
Death rate per 1,000 population (1993): 10.2 (world avg. 9.2).
Natural increase rate per 1,000 population (1993): 2.6 (world avg. 16.8).
Total fertility rate (avg. births per childbearing woman; 1992): 2.1.
Marriage rate per 1,000 population (1993): 5.4.
Divorce rate per 1,000 population (1993): 0.7.
Life expectancy at birth (1992): male 66.7 years; female 75.7 years.
Major causes of death per 100,000 population (1992): diseases of the circulatory system 556.7; malignant neoplasms 195.1; accidents, poisoning, and violence 78.3; diabetes mellitus 15.8; infectious and parasitic diseases 7.7.

National economy

Budget (1992). Revenue: Zł 312,800,000,000,000 (1991; turnover tax 29.0%, income tax 25.5%). Expenditures: Zł 381,900,000,000,000 (1991; social benefits 20.5%, interest on debts 18.9%).
Public debt (external, outstanding; 1993): U.S.$46,800,000,000.
Gross national product (1993): U.S.$87,272,400,000 (U.S.$2,270 per capita).

Structure of gross domestic product and labour force

	1992 in value Zł '000,000,000	% of total value	labour force	% of labour force
Agriculture	84,898.2	7.4	4,037,100	23.3
Mining and manufacturing	434,040.9	38.0 }	3,882,100	22.4
Public utilities	25,775.0	2.3 }		
Construction	98,481.4	8.6	1,066,200	6.1
Transp. and commun.	65,029.8	5.7	773,100	4.5
Trade	164,742.1	14.4	1,605,300	9.2
Finance			198,600	1.1
Public administration	245,956.3 }	21.5	296,600	1.7
Services			3,115,200	17.9
Other	23,505.8[2]	2.1[2]	2,394,000[3]	13.8[3]
TOTAL	1,142,429.5	100.0	17,368,200	100.0

Production (metric tons except as noted). Agriculture (value added in Zł '000,-000; 1992): potatoes 23,400,000, sugar beets 11,100,000, wheat 7,400,000, rye 4,000,000; livestock (number of live animals; 1993) 22,100,000 pigs, 8,200,000 cattle; roundwood (1992) 20,037,000 cu m; fish catch (1991) 457,389. Mining and quarrying (1992): electrolytic copper 387,000; zinc 134,600; lead 54,800; aluminum 43,600. Manufacturing (value of production in Zł '000,000,000; 1992): machinery and transport equipment 230,222.1; chemicals 93,144.7; food 964.2. Construction (1992): 79,289 units, of which residential 40,689. Energy production (consumption): electricity ('000,000 kW-hr; 1992) 132,750 (128,718); coal ('000 metric tons; 1992) 199,000 (177,000); crude petroleum (barrels; 1992) 1,476,000 (1,009,000); petroleum products ('000 metric tons; 1992) 10,959 (11,777); natural gas ('000,000 cu m; 1992) 2,730 (8,369).
Population economically active (1992): total 17,368,200; activity rate of total population 45.2% (participation rates: ages 18–64 [male], 18–59 [female] 61.0%; female [18–59] 53.5%; unemployed [1992] 13.8%).

Price and earnings indexes (1985 = 100)

	1986	1987	1988	1989	1990	1991	1992
Consumer price index	2.1	2.6	4.2	14.6	100.0	170.3	243.0
Monthly earnings index	2.5	3.1	5.6	21.5	100.0	165.4	208.9

Household income and expenditure. Avg. household size (1991) 3.6; avg. annual income (1991) Zł 40,521,000 (U.S.$3,830); sources of income (1992): wages 30.3%, transfer payments 20.5%, self-employment 5.1%, other 44.1%; expenditure (1991): food 47.9%, clothing 9.5%, housing 9.9%.
Tourism (1992): receipts U.S.$4,100,000,000; expenditures U.S.$132,000,000.
Land use (1992): forest 28.8%; meadow 13.3%; agric. 48.3%; other 9.6%.

Foreign trade

Balance of trade (current prices)

	1988	1989	1990	1991	1992	1993
Zł '000,000,000	+740	+4,612	+51,935	−6,543	+69,791	−57,609
% of total	6.6%	13.4%	25.1%	2.0%	18.6%	13.5%

Imports (1993): Zł 240,781,000,000 (machinery and transport equipment 34.6%, chemicals 17.2%, fuel and power 13.0%, consumer goods 9.4%, food 7.5%). *Major import sources* (1992): Germany 23.9%; Russia 8.5%; Italy 6.9%; U.K. 6.7%; The Netherlands 4.7%; Austria 4.5%.
Exports (1993): Zł 183,172,000,000 (1993; machinery and transport equipment 25.8%, light-industrial products 15.4%, steel products 14.7%, fuel and power 10.2%, chemicals 9.6%, food 7.5%). *Major export destinations* (1992): Germany 31.4%; Netherlands 6.0%; Italy 5.6%; Russia 5.5%; U.K. 4.3%.

Transport and communications

Transport. Railroads (1992): length 25,254 km; passenger-km 32,571,000,000; metric ton-km cargo 57,762,000,000. Roads (1991): total length 363,116 km (paved 62%). Vehicles (1992): passenger cars 6,504,716; trucks and buses 1,298,316. Merchant marine (1992): vessels (100 gross tons and over) 644; total deadweight tonnage 4,314,308. Air transport (1992): passenger-km 3,577,300,000; metric ton-km cargo 51,900,000; airports (1994) 12.
Communications. Daily newspapers (1992): 72; circulation 6,085,000; circulation per 1,000 population 158. Radio (1993): 10,895,500 (1 per 3.5 persons). Television (1993): 10,087,000 (1 per 3.8 persons). Telephones (1993): 5,854,-000 (1 per 6.6 persons).

Education and health

Education (1992–93)

	schools	teachers	students	student/ teacher ratio
Primary (age 7–14)	19,212	351,700	5,176,200	14.7
Secondary (age 15–18)	1,762	28,300	607,100	21.5
Voc., teacher tr.	8,499	84,100	1,651,800	19.6
Higher	124	63,100	495,700	7.8

Educational attainment (1988). Percentage of population age 15 and over having: no formal schooling or less than full primary education 6.4%; primary 38.8%; secondary 48.3%; higher 6.5%. *Literacy* (1988): 98.7%.
Health (1993): physicians 83,900 (1 per 459 persons); hospital beds 217,140 (1 per 177 persons); infant mortality rate per 1,000 live births 13.3.
Food (1988–90): daily per capita caloric intake 3,426 (vegetable products 66%, animal products 34%); 131% of FAO recommended minimum.

Military

Total active duty personnel (1993): 283,600 (army 65.5%, navy 6.7%, air force 27.8%). *Military expenditure as percentage of GNP:* 2.5% (world, n.a.); per capita expenditure U.S.$57.

[1]January 1. [2]Other material activities. [3]Unemployed.

Portugal

Official name: República Portuguesa
(Portuguese Republic).
Form of government: parliamentary
state with one legislative house
(Assembly of the Republic [230]).
Chief of state: President.
Head of government: Prime Minister.
Capital: Lisbon.
Official language: Portuguese.
Official religion: none.
Monetary unit: 1 escudo (Esc) = 100
centavos; valuation (Oct. 7, 1994)
1 U.S.$ = Esc 157.32; 1 £ = Esc 250.21.

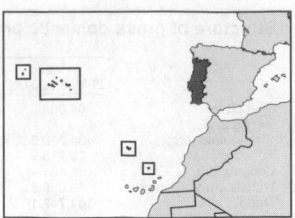

Area and population

Continental Portugal Districts	Capitals	area sq mi	area sq km	population 1992[1] estimate
Aveiro	Aveiro	1,081	2,800	657,600
Beja	Beja	3,947	10,223	166,300
Braga	Braga	1,041	2,695	748,300
Bragança	Bragança	2,547	6,597	156,500
Castelo Branco	Castelo Branco	2,555	6,616	213,300
Coimbra	Coimbra	1,533	3,971	426,400
Évora	Évora	2,856	7,396	172,900
Faro	Faro	1,925	4,986	340,600
Guarda	Guarda	2,139	5,540	186,400
Leiria	Leiria	1,354	3,508	427,700
Lisboa	Lisbon (Lisboa)	1,065	2,758	2,062,300
Portalegre	Portalegre	2,341	6,064	133,400
Porto	Porto	904	2,341	1,626,200
Santarém	Santarém	2,590	6,707	441,100
Setúbal	Setúbal	1,955	5,064	715,300
Viana do Castelo	Viana do Castelo	853	2,210	247,800
Vila Real	Vila Real	1,662	4,305	235,300
Viseu	Viseu	1,934	5,009	399,100
Azores (Açores) Autonomous Region	Ponta Delgada	868	2,247	236,500
Madeira Autonomous Region	Funchal	306	794	253,000
TOTAL		35,456[2]	91,831[2]	9,846,000

Demography

Population (1994): 9,814,000.
Density (1994): persons per sq mi 275.1, persons per sq km 106.2.
Urban-rural (1992): urban 34.7%; rural 65.3%.
Sex distribution (1992[1]): male 48.26%; female 51.74%.
Age breakdown (1987): under 15, 22.7%; 15–29, 24.6%; 30–44, 18.8%; 45–59, 16.5%; 60–74, 12.6%; 75 and over, 4.8%.
Population projection: (2000) 9,737,000; (2010) 9,611,000.
Nationality (1990): Portuguese 99.5%; Cape Verdean 0.2%; Brazilian 0.1%; Spanish, British, and American 0.1%; other 0.1%.
Religious affiliation (1981): Christian 96.0%, of which Roman Catholic 94.5%, Protestant 0.6%, other Christian (mostly Apostolic Catholic and Jehovah's Witness) 0.9%; nonreligious 3.8%; Jewish 0.1%; Muslim 0.1%.
Major cities (1988[1]): Lisbon 830,500; Porto 350,000; Amadora 95,518.

Vital statistics

Birth rate per 1,000 population (1992): 11.7 (world avg. 26.0); (1990) legitimate 85.5%; illegitimate 14.5%.
Death rate per 1,000 population (1992): 10.3 (world avg. 9.2).
Natural increase rate per 1,000 population (1992): 1.4 (world avg. 16.8).
Total fertility rate (avg. births per childbearing woman; 1990–95): 1.5.
Marriage rate per 1,000 population (1991): 7.3.
Divorce rate per 1,000 population (1990): 0.9.
Life expectancy at birth (1990–95): male 71.1 years; female 78.1 years.
Major causes of death per 100,000 population (1992): circulatory diseases 448.6, of which cerebrovascular diseases 242.2, ischemic heart disease 95.1; malignant neoplasms (cancers) 190.2; respiratory diseases 68.4.

National economy

Budget (1992). Revenue: Esc 3,132,600,000,000 (indirect taxes 55.1%, direct taxes 37.2%). Expenditures: Esc 3,362,900,000,000 (1988; education 12.4%, health 9.8%, defense 6.6%, administration 5.3%, public works 2.8%).
Public debt (1992): U.S.$39,922,000,000.
Tourism (1992): receipts from visitors U.S.$3,210,000,000; expenditures by nationals abroad U.S.$1,165,000,000.
Production (metric tons except as noted). Agriculture, forestry, fishing (1993): potatoes 1,352,000, grapes 1,300,000, tomatoes 718,000, corn (maize) 586,000, wheat 367,000, cork 180,000[3], olives 146,000, rice 85,000, carrots 83,000, oats 61,000, onions 57,000; livestock (number of live animals) 5,601,000 sheep, 2,547,000 pigs, 1,345,000 cattle; roundwood (1992) 10,907,000 cu m; fish catch (1991) 325,349. Mining and quarrying (1993): copper pyrites 615,434; kaolin 95,900[4]; zinc 5,675; tungsten 1,280. Manufacturing (value of production in Esc '000,000; 1989): cotton and synthetic fibres 222,717; refined petroleum 148,274; clothing 138,659; motor vehicles 113,924; knitted fabrics 105,339; dairy products 90,282; iron and steel 70,919; cement 57,720; alcoholic beverages 47,489. Construction (1990): residential 4,197,912 sq m; nonresidential 2,045,167 sq m. Energy production (consumption): electricity (kW-hr; 1992) 30,087,000,000 (31,624,000,000); coal (metric tons; 1992) 221,000 (4,706,000); crude petroleum (barrels; 1992) none (82,587,000); petroleum products (metric tons; 1992) 10,588,000 (10,968,000); natural gas, none (n.a.).
Gross national product (1993): U.S.$77,700,000,000 (U.S.$7,890 per capita).

Structure of gross domestic product and labour force

	1990 in value Esc '000,000	1990 % of total value	1992 labour force	1992 % of labour force
Agriculture	490,787	6.3	530,600	10.8
Mining	} 2,275,815	} 29.2	22,900	0.5
Manufacturing			1,126,100	23.0
Construction	585,382	7.5	386,000	7.9
Public utilities	250,629	3.2	34,900	0.7
Trade	1,352,031	17.4	935,600	19.1
Pub. admin., defense	} 1,653,845	} 21.2	1,290,900	26.4
Services				
Transp. and commun.	462,412	5.9	224,800	4.6
Finance	720,037	9.2	143,100	2.9
Other	...	...	194,100[5]	4.0[5]
TOTAL	7,790,937[6]	100.0[6]	4,888,900[6]	100.0[6]

Population economically active (1992): total 4,888,900; activity rate of total population 49.7% (participation rates: ages 15–64, 68.2%; female 44.3%; unemployed 4.0%).

Price and earnings indexes (1990 = 100)

	1987	1988	1989	1990	1991	1992	1993
Consumer price index	71.5	78.3	88.2	100.0	111.4	121.3	129.2
Daily earnings index	72.4	76.0	86.2	100.0	113.5	...	...

Household income and expenditure. Average household size (1991) 3.1; income per household: n.a.; sources of income (1992): wages and salaries 41.1%, property and entrepreneurial income 37.0%, transfer payments 21.9%; expenditure (1986): food 34.7%, transportation and communications 15.4%, clothing and footwear 10.3%, cafes and hotels 9.7%, housing 5.0%, health 4.5%, recreation 4.3%, other 16.1%.
Land use (1992): forested 35.9%; meadows and pastures 9.1%; agricultural and under permanent cultivation 34.5%; other 20.5%.

Foreign trade

Balance of trade (current prices)

	1987	1988	1989	1990	1991	1992
Esc '000,000	−457,800	−580,000	−705,000	−918,600	−1,067,800	−1,144.6
% of total	15.2%	16.0%	15.2%	16.4%	18.5%	18.8%

Imports (1992): Esc 4,048,797,000,000 (machinery and transport equipment 35.6%, of which road vehicles and parts 23.3%; chemicals and chemical products 8.9%; textiles 6.4%; office machines 2.1%). *Major import sources:* Spain 16.6%; Germany 15.0%; France 12.8%; Italy 10.2%; U.K. 7.2%; The Netherlands 6.9%.
Exports (1992): Esc 2,453,041,000,000 (textiles and wearing apparel 29.4%; machinery and transport equipment 19.9%, of which electrical equipment 5.6%; footwear 8.8%; cork and wood products 4.4%; chemicals and chemical products 4.2%). *Major export destinations:* Germany 19.2%; Spain 14.7%; France 14.2%; U.K. 10.1%.

Transport and communications

Transport. Railroads (1992): route length 2,066 mi[3], 3,325 km[3]; passenger-km 5,694,000,000; metric ton-km cargo 1,867,000,000. Roads (1989): total length 43,605 mi, 70,176 km (paved 86%). Vehicles (1992[1]): passenger cars 3,671,166; trucks and buses 205,568. Merchant marine (1992): vessels (100 gross tons and over) 332; total deadweight tonnage 1,129,382. Air transport (1993): passenger-km 7,896,000,000; metric ton-km cargo 183,990,000; airports (1994) 14.
Communications. Daily newspapers (1991): total number 30; total circulation 525,000[7]; circulation per 1,000 population 50[7]. Radio (1992): 2,475,000 receivers (1 per 4.0 persons). Television (1992): 1,789,703 receivers (1 per 5.5 persons). Telephones (1991): 3,565,300 (1 per 2.8 persons).

Education and health

Education (1992–93)

	schools	teachers	students	student/ teacher ratio
Primary (age 5–11)	11,771	71,788	925,936	12.9
Secondary (age 12–19)	1,368	64,479[8]	815,491	14.0[8]
Vocational	220	[8]	84,932	[8]
Higher[9]	250	30,998	214,403	6.9

Educational attainment (1981). Percentage of population age 25 and over having: no formal schooling 4.4%; primary education 76.2%; secondary 19.0%; postsecondary 0.1%; higher 0.3%. *Literacy* (1990): total population age 15 and over literate 6,769,270 (86.8%); males literate 3,208,634 (86.7%); females literate 3,560,636 (86.9%).
Health (1992): physicians 28,604 (1 per 344 persons); hospital beds 41,814 (1 per 235 persons); infant mortality rate per 1,000 live births 9.3.
Food (1988–90): daily per capita caloric intake 3,342 (vegetable products 76%, animal products 24%); 136% of FAO recommended minimum requirement.

Military

Total active duty personnel (1994): 50,700 (army 53.7%, navy 24.6%, air force 21.7%). *Military expenditure as percentage of GNP* (1991): 3.3% (world 4.2%); per capita expenditure U.S.$203.

[1]January 1. [2]Includes 117 sq mi (304 sq km) of water areas comprising the Tagus and Sado estuaries and the Aveiro Lagoon. [3]1991. [4]1992. [5]Unemployed. [6]Detail does not add to total given because of rounding. [7]For 24 newspapers only. [8]Secondary includes Vocational. [9]Includes teacher colleges.

Puerto Rico

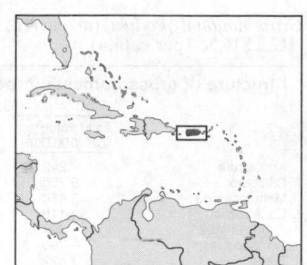

Official name: Estado Libre Asociado de Puerto Rico; Commonwealth of Puerto Rico.
Political status: self-governing commonwealth in association with the United States, having two legislative houses (Senate [29[1]]; House of Representatives [53][1]).
Chief of state: President of the United States.
Head of government: Governor.
Capital: San Juan.
Official languages: Spanish; English.
Official religion: none.
Monetary unit: 1 U.S. dollar (U.S.$) = 100 cents; valuation (Oct. 7, 1994) 1 £ = U.S.$1.59.

Population (1990 census)

Municipio	population	Municipio	population	Municipio	population
Adjuntas	19,451	Fajardo	36,882	Naguabo	22,620
Aguada	35,911	Florida	8,689	Naranjito	27,914
Aguadilla	59,335	Guánica	19,984	Orocovis	21,158
Aguas Buenas	25,424	Guayama	41,588	Patillas	19,633
Aibonito	24,971	Guayanilla	21,581	Peñuelas	22,515
Añasco	25,234	Guaynabo	92,886	Ponce	187,749
Arecibo	93,385	Gurabo	28,737	Quebradillas	21,425
Arroyo	18,910	Hatillo	32,703	Rincón	12,213
Barceloneta	20,947	Hormigueros	15,212	Río Grande	45,648
Barranquitas	25,605	Humacao	55,203	Sabana Grande	22,843
Bayamón	220,262	Isabela	39,147	Salinas	28,335
Cabo Rojo	38,521	Jayuya	15,527	San Germán	34,962
Caguas	133,447	Juana Díaz	45,198	San Juan	437,745
Camuy	28,917	Juncos	30,612	San Lorenzo	35,163
Canóvanas	36,816	Lajas	23,271	San Sebastián	38,799
Carolina	177,806	Lares	29,015	Santa Isabel	19,318
Cataño	34,587	Las Marías	9,306	Toa Alta	44,101
Cayey	46,553	Las Piedras	27,896	Toa Baja	89,454
Ceiba	17,145	Loíza	29,307	Trujillo Alto	61,120
Ciales	18,084	Luquillo	18,100	Utuado	34,980
Cidra	35,601	Manatí	38,692	Vega Alta	34,559
Coamo	33,837	Maricao	6,206	Vega Baja	55,997
Comerío	20,265	Maunabo	12,347	Vieques	8,602
Corozal	33,095	Mayagüez	100,371	Villalba	23,559
Culebra	1,542	Moca	32,926	Yabucoa	36,483
Dorado	30,759	Morovis	25,288	Yauco	42,058
				TOTAL	3,522,037

Demography

Area: 3,515 sq mi, 9,104 sq km.
Population (1994): 3,653,000.
Density (1994): persons per sq mi 1,039.2, persons per sq km 401.3.
Urban-rural (1990): urban 71.2%; rural 28.8%.
Sex distribution (1990): male 48.43%; female 51.57%.
Age breakdown (1990): under 15, 27.2%; 15–29, 25.1%; 30–44, 20.4%; 45–59, 14.1%; 60–74, 9.2%; 75 and over, 4.0%.
Population projection: (2000) 3,849,000; (2010) 4,199,000.
Doubling time: 69 years.
Ethnic composition (1980): white 80.0%; black 20.0%.
Religious affiliation (1984): Roman Catholic 85.3%; Protestant 4.7%; other 10.0%.
Major cities (1990): San Juan 426,832; Ponce 159,151; Caguas 92,429; Mayagüez 83,010; Arecibo 49,545.

Vital statistics

Birth rate per 1,000 population (1993): 18.0 (world avg. 26.0); (1990) legitimate 63.2%; illegitimate 36.8%.
Death rate per 1,000 population (1993): 7.4 (world avg. 9.2).
Natural increase rate per 1,000 population (1993): 10.2 (world avg. 16.8).
Total fertility rate (avg. births per childbearing woman; 1991): 2.2.
Marriage rate per 1,000 population (1990): 9.4.
Divorce rate per 1,000 population (1990): 3.9.
Life expectancy at birth (1988–90): male 70.2 years; female 78.5 years.
Major causes of death per 100,000 population (1990): heart disease 169.7; cancers 116.4; diabetes 47.5; cerebrovascular disease 34.0; pneumonia 33.7.

National economy

Budget (1992). Revenue: U.S.$5,857,000,000 (income taxes 36.2%, excise taxes 15.4%, service charges 5.5%, property taxes 1.1%, other receipts 41.8%). Expenditures: U.S.$5,607,000,000 (education 30.3%, public safety and protection 11.4%, welfare 10.8%, health 10.7%, debt service 6.2%).
Public debt (outstanding; 1993): U.S.$14,242,200,000.
Tourism: receipts from visitors (1993) U.S.$1,629,100,000; expenditures by nationals abroad (1991) U.S.$798,000,000.
Production (in U.S.$'000,000 except as noted). Agriculture, forestry, fishing (gross farm income; 1993): milk 191.1, poultry 90.3, vegetables 72.6, coffee 60.8, beef 43.6, fruit 34.1, pork 33.2, eggs 25.1, sugar 14.7; livestock (number of live animals; 1992) 600,000 cattle, 202,000 pigs; roundwood, n.a.; fish catch (1991) 2,291 metric tons. Mining (value of production in U.S.$'000; 1993): stone 50. Manufacturing (value added in U.S.$'000,000; 1993): chemicals, pharmaceuticals, and allied products 6,896; machinery and metal products 2,757; food products 1,761; clothing 520; printing and publishing 167; stone, clay, and glass products 163. Construction (authorized; 1985): residential 1,798,000 sq m; nonresidential 41,000 sq m. Energy production (consump-

tion): electricity (kW-hr; 1992) 16,434,000,000 (16,434,000,000); coal (metric tons; 1992) none (154,000); crude petroleum (barrels; 1991) none (39,216,-000); petroleum products (metric tons; 1992) 4,945,000 (5,461,000); natural gas, none (none).
Gross national product (1993): U.S.$24,991,200,000 (U.S.$6,902 per capita).

Structure of gross domestic product and labour force

	1993			
	in value U.S.$'000,000	% of total value	labour force	% of labour force
Agriculture	409.6	1.1	34,000	2.8
Manufacturing	14,132.5	39.4	168,000	14.0
Mining	823.2	2.3	...	...
Construction			58,000	4.8
Public utilities	2,948.2	8.2	16,000	1.4
Transp. and commun.			38,000	3.2
Trade	5,381.8	15.0	201,000	16.7
Finance, real estate	4,763.0	13.3	32,000	2.7
Pub. admin., defense	3,899.8	10.9	451,000	37.6
Services	3,848.7	10.8		
Other	−373.2	−1.0	202,000[3]	16.8[3]
TOTAL	35,833.6	100.0	1,201,000[4]	100.0

Population economically active (1993): total 1,201,000; activity rate 33.2% (participation rates: ages 16–64, 46.9%; female [1990] 37.1%; unemployed 16.8%).

Price and earnings indexes (1985 = 100)

	1987	1988	1989	1990	1991	1992	1993
Consumer price index	100.7	104.0	107.7	112.0	117.8	120.3	123.6
Hourly earnings index[5]	104.6	107.1	111.1	116.4	121.2	...	...

Household income and expenditure (1993). Average family size 3.6; income per family U.S.$24,094; sources of income: wages and salaries 54.1%, transfers 29.8%, self-employment 6.8%, rent 5.2%, other 4.1%; expenditure (1993): food and beverages 20.6%, housing and energy 11.8%, transportation 11.8%, health care 11.6%, household furnishings 11.2%, recreation 7.9%, clothing 7.4%, education 3.1%, other 14.6%.
Land use (1991): forested 20.0%; meadows and pastures 37.7%; agricultural and under permanent cultivation 14.2%; other 28.1%.

Foreign trade

Balance of trade (current prices)

	1988	1989	1990	1991	1992	1993
U.S.$'000,000	+1,327	+2,312	+3,584	+5,419	+5,857	+3,405
% of total	5.3%	7.6%	10.2%	14.6%	16.2%	9.4%

Imports (1993): U.S.$16,385,900,000 (chemicals [all forms] 22.5%, food 12.3%, electrical machinery 11.3%, transport equipment 7.5%, petroleum and petroleum products 6.3%, nonelectrical machinery 6.2%, professional and scientific instruments 4.6%). Major import sources (1990): U.S. 68.7%; Venezuela 4.4%; Japan 3.2%; Dominican Republic 2.0%; The Bahamas 1.8%; U.K. 1.0%.
Exports (1993). U.S.$19,790,700,000 (chemicals and chemical products 43.1%, food 15.2%, electrical machinery 10.0%, computers 8.0%). Major export destinations (1990): U.S. 86.9%; Dominican Republic 2.0%; U.S. Virgin Islands 1.4%; U.K. 0.8%; The Netherlands 0.7%.

Transport and communications

Transport. Railroads (1988)[6]: length 59 mi, 96 km. Roads (1992): total length 14,036 mi, 22,588 km (paved 87%). Vehicles (1992): passenger cars 1,380,213; trucks 215,115. Merchant marine: n.a. Air transport (1990–91): passenger arrivals 4,245,137, passenger departures 4,262,164; cargo loaded and unloaded 222,172 metric tons[7]; airports (1994) with scheduled flights 7.
Communications. Daily newspapers (1993): total number 3; total circulation 506,900; circulation per 1,000 population 140. Radio (1993): 2,000,000 receivers (1 per 1.8 persons). Television (1993): 830,000 receivers (1 per 4.4 persons). Telephones (1992): 1,365,520 (1 per 2.6 persons).

Education and health

Education (1985–86)

	schools	teachers	students	student/ teacher ratio
Primary (age 5–12)	1,542	18,359	427,582	23.3
Secondary (age 13–18)	395	13,612	334,661	24.6
Voc., teacher tr.	52	...	149,191	...
Higher	45	9,045	156,818	17.3

Educational attainment (1990). Percentage of population age 25 and over having: primary education 26.8%; some secondary 23.5%; complete secondary 21.0%; higher 28.7%. *Literacy* (1990): total population age 18 and over literate 2,122,860 (89.7%); males literate 1,001,878 (89.6%); females literate 1,120,982 (89.7%).
Health (1988): physicians 9,422 (1 per 349 persons); hospital beds 13,609 (1 per 254 persons); infant mortality rate per 1,000 live births (1991) 13.0.

Military

Total active duty personnel (1992): 3,518 U.S. personnel.

---

[1]Includes (1992; each house) 2 special at-large seats above usual legally mandated membership of body that were created under a constitutional provision to limit majority party's control of either house to two-thirds. [2]Statistical discrepancy. [3]Unemployed. [4]Detail does not add to total given because of rounding. [5]Manufacturing sector only. [6]Privately owned railway for sugarcane transport only. [7]Handled by the Luis Muñoz Marín International Airport only.

Qatar

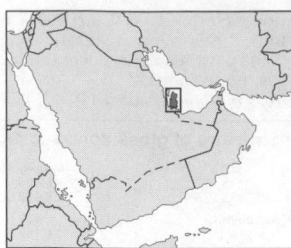

Official name: Dawlat Qaṭar (State of Qatar).
Form of government: monarchy (emirate)[1]; Islamic law is the basis of legislation in the state.
Head of state and government: Emir.
Capital: Doha.
Official language: Arabic.
Official religion: Islam.
Monetary unit: 1 riyal (QR) = 100 dirhams; valuation (Oct. 7, 1994) 1 U.S.$ = QR 3.64; 1 £ = QR 5.79.

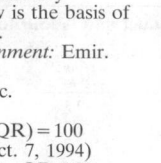

Area and population		area		population
				1992
Municipalities	Capitals	sq mi	sq km	estimate
ad-Dawḥah (Doha)	—	51	132	313,639
al-Ghuwayrīyah	al-Ghuwayrīyah	241	622	2,349
Jarayān al-Bāṭinah	Jarayān al-Bāṭinah	1,434	3,715	3,932
al-Jumaylīyah	al-Jumaylīyah	990[2]	2,565[2]	10,414
al-Khawr	al-Khawr	385	996	12,982
ar-Rayyān	ar-Rayyān	343	889	132,785
ash-Shamāl	Madinat ash-Shamāl	348	901	6,323
Umm Ṣalāl	Umm Ṣalāl Muḥammad	190	493	16,110
al-Wakrah	al-Wakrah	430	1,114	34,185
TOTAL		4,412	11,427	532,719

Demography

Population (1994): 552,000.
Density (1994): persons per sq mi 125.1, persons per sq km 48.3.
Urban-rural (1990): urban 89.5%; rural 10.5%.
Sex distribution (1992): male 70.65%; female 29.34%.
Age breakdown (1992): under 15, 23.3%; 15–29, 18.8%; 30–44, 43.8%; 45–59, 12.0%; 60–74, 1.8%; 75 and over, 0.3%.
Population projection: (2000) 614,000; (2010) 732,000.
Doubling time: 39 years.
Ethnic composition (1983): South Asian 34%; Qatari 20%; other Arab 25%; Iranian 16%; other 5%.
Religious affiliation (1980): Muslim (mostly Sunnī) 92.4%; Christian 5.9%; Hindu 1.1%; Bahā'ī 0.2%; other 0.4%.
Major cities (1987): Doha 236,131; ar-Rayyān 99,939; al-Wakrah 25,747; Umm Sa'īd 12,111.

Vital statistics

Birth rate per 1,000 population (1992): 19.6 (world avg. 26.0); legitimate, n.a.; illegitimate, n.a.
Death rate per 1,000 population (1992): 1.8 (world avg. 9.2).
Natural increase rate per 1,000 population (1992): 17.8 (world avg. 16.8).
Total fertility rate (avg. births per childbearing woman; 1992): 3.0.
Marriage rate per 1,000 population (1992): 3.0.
Divorce rate per 1,000 population (1992): 0.8.
Life expectancy at birth (1992): male 69.7 years; female 74.2 years.
Major causes of death per 100,000 population (1992): diseases of the circulatory system 56.9; injuries and poisoning 36.0; neoplasms (including benign neoplasms) 21.4; certain conditions originating in the perinatal period 11.1; diseases of the respiratory system 7.5; endocrine, metabolic, and nutritional diseases and immunity disorders 7.3; diseases of the digestive system 3.4; signs, symptoms, and ill-defined conditions 10.9.

National economy

Budget (1993–94). Revenue: QR 10,373,000,000 (1992–93; crude oil 67.3%). Expenditures: QR 13,076,000,000 (1992–93; wages and salaries 32.8%; state capital development projects 23.2%, of which electricity and water 8.5%, education 8.3%, social and health services 6.4%).
Public debt (external, outstanding; 1989): U.S.$1,100,000,000.
Production (metric tons except as noted). Agriculture, forestry, fishing (value of production in QR '000; 1992): forage 112,395, milk and dairy products 111,769, vegetables and other crops (except cereals) 94,116, beef 41,501, fruits and dates 31,849, poultry meat 28,408, eggs 16,620, cereals 2,986; livestock (number of live animals; 1992) 132,000 sheep, 103,000 goats, 29,000 camels, 11,000 cattle; roundwood, n.a.; fish catch (1992) 5,417. Mining and quarrying (1992): limestone 900,000; sulfur 52,000; gypsum, sand and gravel, and clay are also produced. Manufacturing (value added in QR '000; 1991): manufactured products 2,931,999; chemicals and petroleum products 2,428,-436; fabricated metal products and machinery 65,767; food, beverages, and tobacco 45,335; paper and paper products 40,218; furniture and wood products 19,598; clothing and textiles 13,924. Construction (1992): residential 12,420 units; nonresidential 1,416 units. Energy production (consumption): electricity (kW-hr; 1992) 4,740,000,000 (4,740,000,000); coal, none (n.a.); crude petroleum (barrels; 1992) 153,465,000 (21,075); petroleum products (metric tons; 1992) 4,980,000 (1,744,000); natural gas (cu m; 1992) 11,489,-000,000 (11,489,000,000).
Population economically active (1988): total 292,568; activity rate of total population 53.7% (participation rates: ages 15–64, 80.8%; female 11.2%; unemployed [1986] 0.5%).

Price and earnings indexes (1990 = 100)							
	1985	1986	1987	1988	1989	1990	1991
Consumer price index	86.1	87.5	89.8	94.0	97.1	100.0	104.4
Earnings index	...	...	...	...	...	...	...

Gross national product (at current market prices; 1992): U.S.$8,511,000,000 (U.S.$16,367 per capita).

Structure of gross domestic product and labour force				
	1992		1988	
	in value QR '000,000	% of total value	labour force	% of labour force
Agriculture	242	0.9	4,544	1.6
Oil sector	9,750	35.8	7,657	2.6
Manufacturing	3,450	12.7	10,627	3.6
Construction	1,110	4.1	64,213	21.9
Public utilities	309	1.1	3,672	1.3
Transportation	798	3.0	11,877	4.1
Trade	1,822	6.7	34,246	11.7
Finance	2,943	10.8	6,172	2.1
Pub. admin., defense				
Services	6,778	24.9	149,560	51.1
Other				
TOTAL	27,202	100.0	292,568	100.0

Household income and expenditure. Average household size (1986) 6.4; income per household: n.a.; sources of income (1988): wages and salaries 80.8%, rents and royalties 10.6%, self-employment 5.6%, other 3.0%; expenditure (1988): housing 26.6%, food 24.5%, transportation 13.0%, recreation and personal effects 11.1%, clothing 9.1%, education 4.3%, energy and water 1.9%, health 1.0%.
Land use (1991): meadows and pastures 4.7%; agricultural and under permanent cultivation 0.6%; built-up, desert, and other 94.7%.
Tourism (1991): receipts and expenditures, n.a.; total number of tourists staying in hotels 142,652.

Foreign trade

Balance of trade (current prices)						
	1987	1988	1989	1990	1991	1992
QR '000,000	+3,224	+2,253	+4,827	+7,992	+5,423	+6,644
% of total	28.7%	19.8%	33.9%	39.3%	30.2%	31.2%

Imports (1992): QR 7,336,000,000 (machinery and transport equipment 44.1%; manufactured goods 31.4%; food and live animals 12.7%; chemicals and chemical products 6.3%; raw materials 3.1%). *Major import sources:* Japan 15.6%; United States 11.4%; United Kingdom 11.2%; Germany 7.3%; Italy 6.6%; France 5.5%; United Arab Emirates 5.0%; Saudi Arabia 3.6%.
Exports (1992): QR 13,600,000,000 (crude petroleum, petroleum products, and liquefied gas 85.7%; non-oil exports 14.3%). *Major export destinations* (1989): Japan 54.4%; Thailand 5.0%; Singapore 4.0%; South Korea 3.6%; United Arab Emirates 3.4%; Italy 2.7%; India 2.7%; Saudi Arabia 2.5%.

Transport and communications

Transport. Railroads: none. Roads (1988): total length 671 mi, 1,080 km (paved 63%). Vehicles (1992): passenger cars 122,000; trucks and buses 55,079. Merchant marine (1992): vessels (100 gross tons and over) 65; total deadweight tonnage 635,580. Air transport (1991)[3]: passenger-mi 1,042,000,-000, passenger-km 1,676,000,000; short ton-mi cargo 35,100,000, metric ton-km cargo 51,245,000; airports (1994) with scheduled flights 1.
Communications. Daily newspapers (1992): total number 4; total circulation 80,000[4]; circulation per 1,000 population 217[4]. Radio (1991): total number of receivers 250,000 (1 per 1.8 persons). Television (1990): total number of receivers 160,000 (1 per 2.8 persons). Telephones (1992): 160,717 (1 per 3.2 persons).

Education and health

Education (1991–92)[5]				student/
	schools	teachers	students	teacher ratio
Primary (age 6–11)	155	4,250	49,770	11.7
Secondary (age 12–17)	36	1,050	9,869	9.4
Vocational	3	101	843	8.4
Higher[6]	1	569	6,666	11.7

Educational attainment (1986). Percentage of population age 25 and over having: no formal education 53.3%, of which illiterates 24.3%; primary 9.8%; preparatory (lower secondary) 10.1%; secondary 13.3%; postsecondary 13.3%; other 0.2%. *Literacy* (1986): total population age 15 and over literate 201,733 (75.7%); males literate 149,980 (76.8%); females literate 51,753 (72.5%).
Health (1992): physicians 758 (1 per 671 persons); hospital beds 1,081 (1 per 481 persons); infant mortality rate per 1,000 live births 15.8.
Food: daily per capita caloric intake, n.a.

Military

Total active duty personnel (1994): 10,100 (army 84.2%, navy 7.9%, air force 7.9%). *Military expenditure as percentage of GNP* (1992): 4.1% (world, n.a.); per capita expenditure U.S.$1,634.

---

[1]Provisional constitution of 1970 provided limited constitutional forms but has not been fully implemented. [2]Includes area of unpopulated Hawar Islands (also claimed by Bahrain). [3]One-fourth apportionment of international flights of Gulf Air. [4]1990. [5]Public schools only; available detail for private schools (1991–92) included 17,728 primary students, 1,695 secondary students, and 1,465 teachers. [6]1992–93.

Réunion

Official name: Département de la
Réunion (Department of Réunion).
Political status: overseas department
(France) with two legislative houses
(General Council [47]; Regional
Council [45]).
Chief of state: President of France.
Heads of government: Commissioner of
the Republic (for France); President
of General Council (for Réunion);
President of Regional Council (for
Réunion).
Capital: Saint-Denis.
Official language: French.
Official religion: none.
Monetary unit: 1 French franc (F) = 100
centimes; valuation (Oct. 7, 1994)
1 U.S.$ = F 5.27; 1 £ = F 8.38.

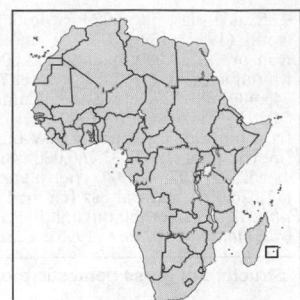

Area and population

Arrondissements	Capitals	area		population
		sq mi	sq km	1990 census
Saint-Benoît	Saint-Benoît	284	736	85,132
Saint-Denis	Saint-Denis	164	423	207,158
Saint-Paul	Saint-Paul	180	467	113,071
Saint-Pierre	Saint-Pierre	339	878	192,462
TOTAL		970[1,2]	2,512[1,2]	597,823

Demography

Population (1994): 647,000.
Density (1994): persons per sq mi 667.0, persons per sq km 257.6.
Urban-rural (1990): urban 73.4%; rural 26.6%.
Sex distribution (1992): male 49.25%; female 50.75%.
Age breakdown (1990): under 15, 31.3%; 15–29, 29.5%; 30–44, 19.6%; 45–59,
11.5%; 60–74, 6.2%; 75 and over, 1.9%.
Population projection: (2000) 718,000; (2010) 854,000.
Doubling time: 40 years.
Ethnic composition (1983): mixed race 63.5%; East Indian 28.2%; Chinese
2.2%; white 1.9%; East African 1.1%; other 3.1%.
Religious affiliation (1990): Roman Catholic 89.6%; Muslim 2.0%; other 8.4%.
Major cities (1990): Saint-Denis 100,926; Le Port 29,190; Le Tampon 27,300;
Saint-André 25,237; Saint-Pierre 23,899.

Vital statistics

Birth rate per 1,000 population (1992): 22.8 (world avg. 26.0); legitimate
46.1%; illegitimate 53.9%.
Death rate per 1,000 population (1992): 5.3 (world avg. 9.2).
Natural increase rate per 1,000 population (1992): 17.5 (world avg. 16.8).
Total fertility rate (avg. births per childbearing woman; 1992): 2.6.
Marriage rate per 1,000 population (1990): 6.4.
Divorce rate per 1,000 population (1990): 1.3.
Life expectancy at birth (1991): male 69.0 years; female 78.3 years.
Major causes of death per 100,000 population (1989): diseases of the cir-
culatory system 185.0; malignant neoplasms (cancers) 90.3; accidents and
violence 66.3; diseases of the digestive system 46.1; diseases of the respira-
tory system 43.0.

National economy

Budget (1993). Revenue: F 4,190,000,000 (receipts from the French central
government and local administrative bodies 47.6%, subsidies and related
receipts 14.2%, new loans 11.9%). Expenditures: F 4,190,000,000 (current
expenditures 66.4%, development expenditures 33.6%).
Public debt (external, outstanding; 1990)[3]: U.S.$61,000,000.
Tourism (1992): receipts U.S.$157,000,000; expenditures, n.a.
Gross national product (at current market prices; 1990): U.S.$1,848,000,000
(U.S.$3,080 per capita).

Structure of gross domestic product and labour force

	1990			
	in value F '000,000	% of total value	labour force	% of labour force
Agriculture	1,200[4]	4.1[4]	11,256	4.8
Manufacturing	2,600[4]	9.2[4]	10,087	4.3
Construction	1,800	6.2	16,519	7.1
Public utilities	1,400	4.9	1,316	0.6
Transportation and communications	1,700[5]	5.9[5]	7,309	3.1
Trade	5,500[5]	19.2[5]	17,689	7.6
Finance, real estate, business services	6,200	21.9	27,630	11.8
Pub. admin., defense, other services	8,100	28.6	54,382	23.3
Other			87,378[6]	37.4[6]
TOTAL	28,500	100.0	233,566	100.0

Production (metric tons except as noted). Agriculture, forestry, fishing (1992):
sugarcane 1,703,000[7], pe-tsai (Chinese cabbage) and black nightshade 8,291,
bananas 7,000, mangoes 6,517, pineapples 6,300, onions 5,781, eggplant
3,270, pimento 405, ginger 95, vanilla 59[7], tobacco 14[7], geranium essence 5[7];
livestock (number of live animals) 89,000 pigs, 31,000 goats, 19,000 cattle;
roundwood (1991) 36,000 cu m; fish (value of catch in F '000,000; 1993)

lobster 39, other 52. Mining and quarrying: gravel and sand for local use.
Manufacturing (value added in F '000,000; 1991): construction materials
(mostly cement) 275; alcoholic and nonalcoholic beverages (mostly rum)
206; fabricated metals 186; sugar, molasses, and related products 178; printing and publishing 176. Construction (value of public construction; 1988):
residential F 258,200,000; nonresidential F 1,587,000,000. Energy production
(consumption): electricity (kW-hr; 1993) 1,129,000,000 (993,000,000); coal,
none (none); crude petroleum, none (none); petroleum products (metric
tons; 1993) none (434,000); natural gas, none (none).
Population economically active (1990): total 233,566; activity rate of total
population 39.1% (participation rates: ages 15–64, 60.3%; female 41.1%;
unemployed [March 1993] 35–40%).

Price and earnings indexes (December 1992 = 100)[8]

	1988	1989	1990	1991	1992	1993	1994[9]
Consumer price index	86.6	90.9	94.4	97.3	100.0	102.4	106.1
Hourly earnings index	75.6	78.7	86.1	91.6	100.0	105.3	105.3

Household income and expenditure. Average household size (1990) 3.8; income per household (1987) F 89,304 (U.S.$14,858); sources of income
(1987): wages and salaries and self-employment 67.5%, transfer payments
29.7%, other 2.8%; expenditure (1986–87): transportation and communications 24.9%, food and beverages 22.4%, housing 11.8%, recreation and
education 10.1%, clothing and footwear 7.9%, household furnishings 6.0%,
other 16.9%.
Land use (1991): forested 35.2%; meadows and pastures 4.8%; agricultural
and under permanent cultivation 20.8%; other 39.2%.

Foreign trade

Balance of trade (current prices)

	1988	1989	1990	1991	1992	1993
F '000,000	−8,781	−10,067	−10,747	−11,975	−11,542	−10,765
% of total	80.6%	83.1%	84.1%	87.6%	83.9%	84.4%

Imports (1993): F 11,757,000,000 (food and agricultural products 21.1%,
electrical and nonelectrical machinery 15.3%, transport equipment 14.2%,
chemical products 10.0%, mineral fuels 6.2%). *Major import sources:* France
69.4%; other EEC countries 9.9%; Indian Ocean countries (including South
Africa) 4.6%; Bahrain 4.2%.
Exports (1993): F 992,000,000 (food products [mostly sugar; also includes
lobster, rum, and geranium essence] 75.6%, electrical and nonelectrical machinery 7.2%, transport equipment 5.4%). *Major export destinations:* France
69.5%; other EEC countries 12.3%; Indian Ocean countries (including
South Africa) 11.4%; Japan 3.8%.

Transport and communications

Transport. Railroads:[10]. Roads (1991): total length 1,750 mi, 2,800 km (paved
79%). Vehicles (1992): passenger cars 150,000; trucks and buses 50,000. Merchant marine (1992): vessels (100 gross tons and over) 7; total deadweight
tonnage 33,476. Air transport (1993): passenger arrivals 484,200, passenger
departures 480,083; cargo unloaded 11,770 metric tons, cargo loaded 3,500
metric tons; airports (1994) with scheduled flights 1.
Communications. Daily newspapers (1991): total number 3; total circulation
55,000; circulation per 1,000 population 90. Radio (1993): total number of
receivers 150,000 (1 per 4.2 persons). Television (1993): total number of
receivers 90,500 (1 per 7.0 persons). Telephones (1993): 191,647 (1 per 3.3
persons).

Education and health

Education (1993–94)

	schools	teachers	students	student/ teacher ratio
Primary (age 6–10)	349	...	72,513	...
Secondary (age 11–17) } Voc., teacher tr.	97	...	91,015	...
Higher[11,12]	1	218	7,600	34.9

Educational attainment (1986–87). Percentage of population age 25 and
over having: no formal schooling 18.8%; primary education 44.3%; lower
secondary 21.6%; upper secondary 11.0%; higher 4.3%. *Literacy* (1986–87):
total population age 15 and over literate 298,965 (78.2%); males literate
141,006 (75.9%); females literate 157,959 (80.3%).
Health (1993): physicians 1,062 (1 per 594 persons); hospital beds 2,939 (1
per 215 persons); infant mortality rate per 1,000 live births (1994) 8.0.
Food (1988–90): daily per capita caloric intake 3,082 (vegetable products 81%,
animal products 19%), 136% of FAO recommended minimum requirement.

Military

Total active duty personnel (1993): 3,400 French troops[13].

---

[1]Includes 3 sq mi (8 sq km) not distributed by arrondissement. [2]Indian Ocean islets
administered by France from Réunion are excluded from total. Areas of these islets,
which have no permanent population, are: Îles Glorieuses 1.7 sq mi (4.3 sq km), Île
Juan de Nova 1.9 sq mi (4.8 sq km), Île Tromelin 0.3 sq mi (0.8 sq km), Bassas da
India 0.1 sq mi (0.2 sq km), Île Europa 7.8 sq mi (20.2 sq km). [3]Includes long-term
private debt not guaranteed by the government. [4]Manufacturing includes sugarcane
production. [5]Transportation and communications includes hotels and restaurants.
[6]Includes 86,118 unemployed. [7]1993. [8]Indexes refer to December. [9]March. [10]No
public railways; railways in use are for sugar industry. [11]1992–93. [12]University only.
[13]Includes troops stationed on Mayotte.

Romania

Official name: România (Romania).
Form of government: unitary republic
with two legislative houses (Senate
[143]; Assembly of Deputies [341[1]]).
Chief of state: President.
Head of government: Prime Minister.
Capital: Bucharest.
Official language: Romanian.
Official religion: none.
Monetary unit: 1 Romanian leu (plural
lei) = 100 bani; valuation (Oct. 7,
1994) 1 U.S.$ = 1,746 lei;
1 £ = 2,777 lei.

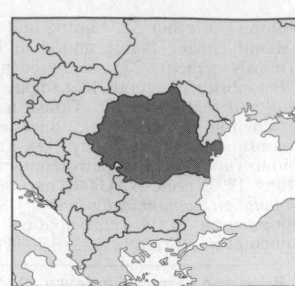

Area and population

Counties	Capitals	area sq mi	area sq km	population 1992[2] census
Alba	Alba Iulia	2,406	6,231	414,200
Arad	Arad	2,954	7,652	487,400
Argeş	Piteşti	2,626	6,801	680,600
Bacău	Bacău	2,551	6,606	736,100
Bihor	Oradea	2,909	7,535	634,100
Bistriţa-Năsăud	Bistriţa	2,048	5,305	327,200
Botoşani	Botoşani	1,917	4,965	458,900
Brăila	Brăila	1,824	4,724	392,100
Braşov	Braşov	2,066	5,351	642,500
Buzău	Buzău	2,344	6,072	516,300
Călăraşi	Călăraşi	1,959	5,074	338,800
Caraş-Severin	Reşiţa	3,283	8,503	375,800
Cluj	Cluj-Napoca	2,568	6,650	735,100
Constanţa	Constanţa	2,724	7,055	748,000
Covasna	Sfântu Gheorghe	1,431	3,705	232,600
Dâmboviţa	Târgovişte	1,559	4,036	559,900
Dolj	Craiova	2,862	7,413	761,100
Galaţi	Galaţi	1,708	4,425	639,900
Giurgiu	Giurgiu	1,356	3,511	313,100
Gorj	Târgu Jiu	2,178	5,641	400,100
Harghita	Miercurea-Ciuc	2,552	6,610	347,700
Hunedoara	Deva	2,709	7,016	548,000
Ialomiţa	Slobozia	1,718	4,449	304,000
Iaşi	Iaşi	2,112	5,469	806,800
Maramureş	Baia Mare	2,400	6,215	538,500
Mehedinţi	Drobeta-Turnu Severin	1,892	4,900	332,100
Mureş	Târgu Mureş	2,585	6,696	607,300
Neamţ	Piatra Neamţ	2,274	5,890	577,600
Olt	Slatina	2,126	5,507	521,000
Prahova	Ploieşti	1,812	4,694	873,200
Sălaj	Zalău	1,486	3,850	266,300
Satu Mare	Satu Mare	1,701	4,405	400,100
Sibiu	Sibiu	2,093	5,422	452,800
Suceava	Suceava	3,303	8,555	700,800
Teleorman	Alexandria	2,224	5,760	482,300
Timiş	Timişoara	3,356	8,692	700,300
Tulcea	Tulcea	3,255	8,430	270,200
Vâlcea	Râmnicu Vâlcea	2,203	5,705	436,300
Vaslui	Vaslui	2,045	5,297	457,800
Vrancea	Focşani	1,878	4,863	392,600
Municipality				
Bucharest	Bucharest	703	1,820	2,351,000
TOTAL		91,699[3]	237,500	22,760,500

Demography

Population (1994): 22,740,000.
Density (1994): persons per sq mi 248.0, persons per sq km 95.7.
Urban-rural (1992): urban 54.4%; rural 45.6%.
Sex distribution (1992): male 49.13%; female 50.87%.
Age breakdown (1992): under 15, 22.4%; 15–29, 22.9%; 30–44, 20.8%; 45–59, 17.1%; 60 and over, 16.8%.
Population projection: (2000) 22,645,000; (2010) 22,487,000.
Ethnic composition (1992): Romanian 89.4%; Hungarian 7.1%; Gypsy 1.8%; German 0.5%; Ukrainian 0.3%; other 0.9%.
Religious affiliation (1992): Romanian Orthodox 86.8%; Roman Catholic 5.0%; Greek Orthodox 3.5%; Pentecostal 1.0%; Muslim 0.2%; other 3.5%.
Major cities (1992): Bucharest 2,064,474; Constanţa 350,476; Iaşi 342,994; Timişoara 334,278; Cluj-Napoca 328,008.

Vital statistics

Birth rate per 1,000 population (1993): 10.9 (world avg. 26.0).
Death rate per 1,000 population (1993): 11.6 (world avg. 9.2).
Natural increase rate per 1,000 population (1993): −0.7 (world avg. 16.8).
Total fertility rate (avg. births per childbearing woman; 1992): 1.5.
Marriage rate per 1,000 population (1991): 7.9.
Divorce rate per 1,000 population (1990): 1.4.
Life expectancy at birth (1987–89): male 66.5 years; female 72.4 years.
Major causes of death per 100,000 population (1992): circulatory disease 707.7, cancer 163.4, respiratory disease 94.0, diseases of the digestive system 57.9.

National economy

Budget (1991). Revenue: 787,940,000,000 lei (income tax 35.2%, of which corporate 13.3%; social security 28.9%; value-added taxes 23.2%; customs duties 3.1%). Expenditures: 779,980,000,000 lei (social security and welfare 26.5%; defense 10.3%; education 10.0%; health 9.2%).
Tourism (1992): receipts U.S.$262,000,000; expenditures U.S.$260,000,000.
Production (metric tons except as noted). Agriculture (1993): corn (maize) 7,988,000, wheat 5,314,000, potatoes 3,709,000, sugar beets 1,776,000, grapes 1,339,000, cabbages 854,000, tomatoes 799,000, oats 554,000, dry onions 344,000, soybeans 95,000; livestock (number of live animals) 12,079,000 sheep,

9,852,000 pigs, 3,683,000 cattle, 3,186,000 goats, 88,000,000 chickens; roundwood (1992) 13,657,000 cu m; fish catch (1991) 124,933. Mining (1992): iron ore 1,229,000; bauxite 175,000; zinc 25,813; copper 24,720; lead 16,697. Manufacturing (1991): raw steel 7,115,500; fertilizers 1,091,626; sulfuric acid 745,400; 389,227 televisions; aluminum and alloys 167,451; synthetic rubber 54,583. Construction (1989): residential 5,409,000 sq m. Energy production (consumption): electricity (kW-hr; 1992) 54,195,000,000 (58,398,000,000); coal (metric tons; 1992) 37,760,000 (40,969,000); crude petroleum (barrels; 1992) 49,652,000 (97,368,000); petroleum products (metric tons; 1992) 11,974,000 (11,236,000); natural gas (cu m; 1992) 18,509,000,000 (22,143,000,000).
Public debt (external, outstanding; 1992): U.S.$1,322,000,000.
Gross national product (1993): U.S.$24,810,000,000 (U.S.$1,090 per capita).

Structure of gross domestic product and labour force

	1991 in value '000,000 lei	1991 % of total value	1992 labour force	1992 % of labour force
Agriculture	391,200	18.5	2,187,300	20.3
Mining, manufacturing, and public utilities	919,500	43.6	4,152,500	38.6
Construction	104,600	5.0	578,500	5.4
Transp. and commun.	95,600	4.5	616,800	5.7
Trade	178,500	8.5	694,200	6.5
Finance	49,300	2.3	57,100	0.5
Pub. admin.	202,800	9.6 }	1,528,000	14.2
Services	71,000	3.4 }		
Other	97,200	4.6	956,900[4]	8.8[4]
TOTAL	2,109,700	100.0	10,771,300	100.0

Population economically active (1992): total 10,771,300; activity rate 47.4% (participation rates: ages 15–64, 67.2%; female 44.2%; unemployed 8.6%).

Price and earnings indexes (1990 = 100)

	1987	1988	1989	1990	1991	1992	1993
Consumer price index	92.7	95.3	96.0	100.0	274.4	765.0	2,720.3
Annual earnings index	84.9	87.0	90.5	100.0	221.3	597.4	1,804.8

Household income and expenditure. Average household size (1992) 3.1; income per household (1989) 73,500 lei (U.S.$4,940); sources of income (1982): wages 62.6%; expenditure (1989): food 51.1%, housing 16.4%, clothing 15.7%.
Land use (1992): forest 29.0%; pasture 21.0%; agricultural 43.2%; other 6.8%.

Foreign trade

Balance of trade (current prices)

	1988	1989	1990	1991	1992	1993
U.S.$'000,000	+3,750	+2,050	−3,244	−1,182	−1,420.5	−1,127.8
% of total	19.7%	10.8%	21.7%	12.5%	14.0%	10.3%

Imports (1991): 400,103,000,000 lei (1990; raw materials 47.6%, machinery 23.7%, chemicals 6.4%). *Major import sources:* U.S.S.R. 23.6%; Germany 11.4%; Saudi Arabia 8.3%; Iran 5.9%; U.S. 4.6%; Poland 4.3%.
Exports (1991): 323,693,000,000 lei (1990; raw materials and mineral fuels 33.7%, machinery and transport equipment 30.8%, manufactured goods 21.2%, chemicals 6.5%). *Major export destinations:* U.S.S.R. 25.2%; Germany 10.2%; Italy 8.8%; U.S. 5.8%; France 3.4%; Czechoslovakia 3.2%.

Transport and communications

Transport. Railroads (1993): length 7,051 mi, 11,348 km; passenger-km 19,404,000,000; metric ton-km cargo 25,176,000,000. Roads (1992): length 95,099 mi, 153,014 km (paved 51%). Vehicles (1992): cars 1,397,118; trucks and buses 332,273. Merchant marine (1992): vessels (100 gross tons and over) 439; total deadweight tonnage 4,845,539. Air transport (1993): passenger-km 1,884,000,000; metric ton-km cargo 16,704,000; airports (1994) 16.
Communications. Daily newspapers (1990): total number 65; total circulation 1,245,000; circulation per 1,000 population 54. Radios (1993): 3,000,000 (1 per 7.6 persons). Televisions (1993): 4,000,000 (1 per 5.7 persons). Telephones (1992): 3,192,180 subscribers (1 per 7.1 persons).

Education and health

Education (1991–92)

	schools	teachers	students	student/ teacher ratio
Primary (age 6–13)	13,730	153,187	2,608,914	17.0
Secondary (age 14–17)	2,301[5]	16,791	248,748	14.8
Voc., teacher tr.	[5]	41,622	959,882	23.1
Higher	56	17,605	215,226	12.2

Educational attainment (1992). Percentage of population age 25 and over having: no schooling 5.4%; primary education 59.8%; secondary 27.4%; postsecondary 7.3%. *Literacy* (1992): total population age 15 and over literate 96.9%; males literate 98.6%; females literate 95.2%.
Health (1992): physicians 48,502 (1 per 469 persons); hospital beds 215,629 (1 per 105 persons); infant mortality rate per 1,000 live births (1993) 23.4.
Food (1988–90): daily per capita caloric intake 3,081 (vegetable products 78%, animal products 22%); 116% of FAO recommended minimum requirement.

Military

Total active duty personnel (1994): 230,500 (army 69.6%, navy 8.2%, air force 11.9%, paramilitary border guards 10.3%). *Military expenditure as percentage of GNP* (1991): 4.0% (world 4.2%); per capita expenditure U.S.$162.

[1]Includes 13 nonelective seats. [2]Preliminary results of Jan. 7, 1992, census. [3]Detail does not add to total given because of rounding. [4]Includes 929,000 unemployed. [5]Secondary includes Voc., teacher tr.

Russia

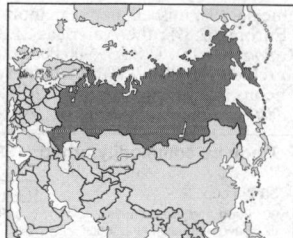

Official name: Rossiyskaya Federatsiya (Russian Federation).
Form of government: federal multiparty republic with a bicameral legislative body (Federal Assembly comprising a Federation Council [178] and a State Duma [450])[1].
Head of state: President.
Head of government: Prime Minister.
Capital: Moscow.
Official language: Russian.
Official religion: none.
Monetary unit: 1 ruble = 100 kopecks; valuation (Oct. 7, 1994) free rate, 1 U.S.$ = 2,927 Rub; 1 £ = 4,656 Rub.

Area and population

Federal Republics Other entities	Capitals	area sq mi	area sq km	population 1993 estimate
Adygea	Maykop	2,900	7,600	446,800
Bashkortostan	Ufa	55,400	143,600	4,041,500
Buryatia	Ulan-Ude	135,600	351,300	1,056,600
Chechenia[2, 3]	...	4	4	4
Chuvashia	Cheboksary	7,100	18,300	1,359,300
Dagestan	Makhachkala	19,400	50,300	1,925,200
Gorno-Altay	Gorno-Altaisk	35,700	92,600	197,600
Ingushetia[2, 3]	Grozny	7,400[4]	19,300[4]	1,306,400[4]
Kabardino-Balkaria[5]	Nalchik	4,800	12,500	785,900
Kalmykia (Khalmg Tangch)	Elista	29,400	76,100	321,700
Karachay-Cherkessia	Cherkessk	5,400	14,100	434,200
Karelia	Petrozavodsk	66,600	172,400	799,600
Khakassia	Abakan	23,900	61,900	583,500
Komi	Syktyvkar	160,600	415,900	1,245,700
Mari El	Ioshkar-Ola	9,000	23,200	764,200
Mordvinia	Saransk	10,100	26,200	964,400
North Ossetia	Vladikavkaz	3,100	8,000	651,500
Russia	Moscow	4,709,800[6]	12,198,300	124,919,300
Regions (Oblasts)				
Amur[5]	Blagoveshchensk	140,400	363,700	1,062,500
Arkhangelsk	Arkhangelsk	226,800	587,400	1,561,600
Astrakhan	Astrakhan	17,000	44,100	1,012,900
Belgorod	Belgorod	10,500	27,100	1,422,800
Bryansk	Bryansk	13,500	34,900	1,468,500
Chelyabinsk	Chelyabinsk	33,900	87,900	3,634,400
Chita	Chita	166,600	431,500	1,375,900
Irkutsk	Irkutsk	296,500	767,900	2,871,700
Ivanovo	Ivanovo	9,200	23,900	1,308,000
Kaliningrad[5]	Kaliningrad	5,800	15,100	906,100
Kaluga	Kaluga	11,500	29,900	1,085,800
Kamchatka	Petropavlovsk-Kamchatsky	182,400	472,300	456,500
Kemerovo	Kemerovo	36,900	95,500	3,176,800
Kirov	Kirov	46,600	120,800	1,700,700
Kostroma	Kostroma	23,200	60,100	811,900
Kurgan	Kurgan	27,400	71,000	1,118,100
Kursk	Kursk	11,500	29,800	1,340,700
Leningrad	St. Petersburg	33,200[7]	85,900[7]	1,674,200
Lipetsk	Lipetsk	9,300	24,100	1,241,000
Magadan	Magadan	178,100	461,400	326,500
Moskva (Moscow)	Moscow	18,100[8]	47,000[8]	6,682,300
Murmansk	Murmansk	55,900	144,900	1,117,300
Nizhny Novgorod	Nizhny Novgorod	28,900	74,800	3,696,800
Novgorod	Novgorod	21,400	55,300	751,500
Novosibirsk	Novosibirsk	68,800	178,200	2,803,000
Omsk	Omsk	53,900	139,700	2,175,500
Orenburg	Orenburg	47,900	124,000	2,219,400
Oryol (Orel)	Oryol	9,500	24,700	908,400
Penza	Penza	16,700	43,200	1,521,800
Perm	Perm	62,000	160,600	3,106,400
Pskov	Pskov	21,400	55,300	839,900
Rostov	Rostov-na-Donu	38,900	100,800	4,382,900
Ryazan	Ryazan	15,300	39,600	1,341,900
Sakhalin	Yuzhno-Sakhalinsk	33,600	87,100	713,900
Samara	Samara	20,700	53,600	3,312,100
Saratov	Saratov	38,700	100,200	2,721,900
Smolensk	Smolensk	19,200	49,800	1,165,200
Sverdlovsk[5]	Yekaterinburg	75,200	194,800	4,697,900
Tambov	Tambov	13,200	34,300	1,314,400
Tomsk	Tomsk	122,400	316,900	1,000,300
Tula	Tula	9,900	25,700	1,839,800
Tver	Tver	32,500	84,100	1,663,200
Tyumen	Tyumen	554,100	1,435,200	3,120,200
Ulyanovsk (Simbirsk)	Simbirsk	14,400	37,300	1,462,200
Vladimir	Vladimir	11,200	29,000	1,654,100
Volgograd	Volgograd	44,000	113,900	2,660,500
Vologda[5]	Vologda	56,300	145,700	1,362,400
Voronezh	Voronezh	20,200	52,400	2,487,600
Yaroslavl	Yaroslavl	14,100	36,400	1,466,800
Autonomous Region				
Yevreyskaya (Jewish)	Birobidzhan	13,900	36,000	219,400
Territories (Krays)				
Altay	Barnaul	65,300	169,100	2,682,000
Khabarovsk	Khabarovsk	304,500	788,600	1,621,000
Krasnodar	Krasnodar	29,300	76,000	4,879,100
Krasnoyarsk	Krasnoyarsk	903,400	2,339,700	3,048,200
Primorye (Maritime)[5]	Vladivostok	64,100	165,900	2,301,700
Stavropol	Stavropol	25,700	66,500	2,580,200
Autonomous cities				
Moscow	—	8	8	8,881,200
St. Petersburg[5]	—	7	7	4,952,300
Autonomous districts (Okrugs)[9]				
Aga-Buryat	Aginskoye	7,300	19,000	78,700
Chukchi (Chukotka)	Anadyr	284,800	737,700	124,300
Evonk	Tyra	296,400	767,600	23,600
Khanty-Mansi	Khanty-Mansiysk	202,000	523,100	1,301,000
Komi-Permyak	Kudymkar	12,700	32,900	161,100

Area and population (continued)			
Koryak	Palana	116,400	301,500	37,700
Nenets	Naryan-Mar	68,100	176,400	52,300
Taymyr	Dudinka	332,900	862,100	50,700
Ust-Orda Buryat	Ust-Ordynsky	8,600	22,400	142,200
Yamalo-Nenets	Salekhard	289,700	750,300	464,800
Sakha (Yakutia)	Yakutsk	1,198,200	3,103,200	1,073,800
Tatarstan	Kazan	26,300	68,000	3,723,000
Tuva (Tyva)	Kyzyl-Orda	65,800	170,500	306,000
Udmurtia	Izhevsk	16,300	42,100	1,642,800
TOTAL		6,592,800	17,075,400	148,549,000

Demography

Population (1994): 148,179,000.
Density (1994): persons per sq mi 22.5, persons per sq km 8.7.
Urban-rural (1993): urban 73.3%; rural 26.7%.
Sex distribution (1993): male 47.00%; female 53.00%.
Age breakdown (1993): under 15, 22.3%; 15–29, 20.5%; 30–44, 24.5%; 45–59, 16.0%; 60–69, 10.3%; 70 and over, 6.4%.
Population projection: (2000) 146,239,000; (2010) 143,477,000.
Doubling time: not applicable; doubling time exceeds 100 years.
Ethnic composition (1989): Russian 81.5%; Tatar 3.8%; Ukrainian 3.0%; Chuvash 1.2%; Bashkir 0.9%; Belorussian 0.8%; Mordovian 0.7%; Chechen 0.6%; German 0.6%; other 6.9%.
Religious affiliation: believers are predominantly Russian Orthodox; there are Catholic, Protestant, Muslim, Old Believer, and Jewish minorities.
Major cities (1993): Moscow 8,789,200; St. Petersburg 4,387,400; Nizhny Novgorod 1,432,900; Novosibirsk 1,430,700; Yekaterinburg 1,357,800; Samara 1,231,800; Omsk 1,166,500; Chelyabinsk 1,134,800; Kazan 1,097,700; Ufa 1,096,000; Perm 1,093,000; Rostov-na-Donu 1,025,100.

Other principal cities (1993)

	population		population		population
Astrakhan	511,400	Krasnoyarsk	919,300	Tolyattigrad	677,700
Barnaul	600,600	Naberezhnye Chelny	519,900	Tula	538,900
Irkutsk	635,000	Novokuznetsk	597,500	Ulyanovsk (Simbirsk)	661,100
Izhevsk	652,900	Orenburg	555,400	Vladivostok	643,400
Kemerovo	517,100	Penza	552,500	Volgograd	1,002,000
Khabarovsk	612,000	Ryazan	527,900	Voronezh	903,300
Krasnodar	636,100	Saratov	904,400	Yaroslavl	634,500

Mobility (1989). Population living in the same residence as in 1988: 78.8%; different residence, same oblast 11.5%; different republic 9.7%.
Emigration (1992): 618,285.
Households (1989). Total family households 40,246,000; average household size 3.2; 2 persons 34.2%; 3 persons 28.0%; 4 persons 25.2%; 5 persons or more 12.6%. Population in family households: 128,787,000 (87.0%), non-family population 19,254,000 (13.0%).

Vital statistics

Birth rate per 1,000 population (1992): 10.7 (world avg. 26.0); (1990) legitimate 85.4%; illegitimate 14.6%.
Death rate per 1,000 population (1992): 12.2 (world avg. 9.2).
Natural increase rate per 1,000 population (1992): −1.5 (world avg. 16.8).
Total fertility rate (avg. births per childbearing woman; 1993): 1.8.
Marriage rate per 1,000 population (1992): 7.2.
Divorce rate per 1,000 population (1992): 5.0.
Life expectancy at birth (1993): male 59.0 years; female 73.2 years.
Major causes of death per 100,000 population (1991): circulatory diseases 625.8; malignant neoplasms (cancers) 197.3; accidents, poisoning, and violence 143.5, of which suicide 21.0, murder 11.8; respiratory diseases 56.1; digestive diseases 29.3; infectious and parasitic diseases 12.1.

Social indicators

Educational attainment (1989). Percentage of population age 15 and over having: primary or no formal education 19.4%; some secondary 21.0%; secondary and some postsecondary 48.3%; higher and postgraduate 11.3%.
Quality of working life (1990). Average workweek: 40 hours. Annual rate per 100,000 workers of: injury or accident 569; industrial illness 5.3; death 11.2. Proportion of labour force insured for damages or income loss resulting from: injury 100%; permanent disability 100%; death 100%. Average days lost to labour stoppages per 1,000 workdays (1992): 1.1.
Access to services (1990). Proportion of dwellings having access to: electricity, virtually 100%; safe public water supply 94%; public sewage collection 92%; central heating 92%; bathroom 87%; gas 72%; hot water 79%.
Social participation. Eligible voters participating in last national election: 96%. Population participating in voluntary work: n.a. Trade union membership in total workforce (1989): 100%. Practicing religious population in total affiliated population (1991): 32%.
Social deviance. Offense rate per 100,000 population (1992) for: murder 10.9; rape 9.5; serious bodily injury 40.9; burglary and housebreaking 76.7; larceny-theft 566.9. Incidence per 100,000 in general population (1992) of: alcoholism 1,727.5; substance abuse 25.1; suicide 26.5.
Material well-being (1993). Goods possessed per 100 households: automobile 20; radio receiver 101; television receiver 112; refrigerator 95; camera 37; motorcycle 22; bicycle 54; tape recorder 59.

National economy

Budget (1994). Revenue: 124,477,000,000,000 Rub (value-added tax 31.8%; foreign activity 24.0%; enterprise profits tax 17.7%; excise taxes 8.1%). Expenditures: 194,495,000,000,000 (current expenditure 74.3%, of which economy 23.3%, defense 20.9%, education 5.8%, health 3.0%, interest on foreign debt 2.4%; development expenditure 25.7%).
Gross national product (1992): U.S.$397,786,000 (U.S.$2,680 per capita).

Structure of gross domestic product and labour force

	1991		1992	
	in value '000,000 Rub	% of total value	labour force	% of labour force
Agriculture	100,200	16.0	9,700,000	13.3
Mining				
Manufacturing }	228,100	36.4	21,800,000	29.9
Public utilities				
Construction	57,300	9.1	8,300,000	11.4
Transp. and commun.	43,100	6.9	5,600,000	7.7
Trade			5,700,000	7.8
Finance				
Services }	162,900	26.0	14,400,000	19.8
Pub. admin., defense			2,900,000	4.0
Other	34,700	5.6	4,478,000	6.1
TOTAL	626,300	100.0	72,878,000	100.0

Public debt (external, outstanding; 1993)[10]: U.S.$72,500,000,000.

Production (metric tons except as noted). Agriculture, forestry, fishing (1992): wheat 46,200,000, potatoes 38,200,000, barley 27,000,000, sugar beets 25,500,000, hay 24,700,000, rye 13,900,000, oats 11,200,000, vegetables (other than potatoes) 10,000,000, fodder crops 8,700,000, sunflower seeds 3,100,000, peas 2,600,000, corn (maize) 2,100,000, millet 1,500,000, buckwheat 1,038,000, rice 800,000; livestock (number of live animals; 1993): 52,200,000 cattle, 48,200,000 sheep, 31,500,000 pigs, 3,200,000 goats, 2,600,000 horses; roundwood 238,000,000 cu m; fish catch 5,300,000. Mining and quarrying (1992): nickel 215,000,000; chrome ore 121,400,000; iron ore 86,700,000; antimony 10,000,000; tin 6,000,000; molybdenum 5,000,000. Manufacturing (1992): crude steel 67,000,000; cement 61,700,000; rolled steel 46,800,000; pig iron 46,100,000; mineral fertilizers 12,300,000; sulfuric acid 9,700,000; cellulose 5,676,000; paper 3,608,000; cardboard 2,160,000; caustic soda 1,836,000; synthetic resins and plastics 1,295,000; detergents 532,000; synthetic fibres 474,000; soap 344,000; cotton fabrics 3,292,000,000 sq m; leather 743,000,000 sq m; silk fabrics 731,000,000 sq m; linen fabrics 415,000,000 sq m; wool fabrics 276,000,000 sq m; carpets 34,500,000 sq m; tableware 552,000,000 pieces; hats 4,200,000 pieces; cigarettes 148,000,000,000 units; watches 57,100,000 units; vacuum cleaners 4,320,000 units; washing machines 4,284,000 units; television receivers 3,641,000 units; refrigerators 3,187,000 units; tape recorders 2,758,000 units; bicycles 2,405,000 units; sewing machines 1,624,000 units; cameras 1,607,000 units; passenger cars 963,000 units; motorcycles 604,000 units; video recorders 448,000 units; forge press machines 15,500 units; machine tools 9,700 units; leather footwear 221,000,000 pairs; beer 27,500,000 hectolitres; vodka and liquors 15,100,000 hectolitres; champagne 7,600,000 hectolitres; grape wine 7,500,000 hectolitres; brandy 195,000 hectolitres. Construction (1992): residential 31,500,000 sq m.

Manufacturing, mining, and construction enterprises (1991)

	no. of enter-prises	no. of employees	monthly wages as a % of avg. of all wages[11]	value added ('000,000 Rub)
Manufacturing				
Machinery and metal products	5,429	9,970,000	98.2	3,105
Fuel and energy	1,486	1,378,000	133.3	1,652
Metallurgy	428	1,274,000	124.3	6,321
Chemicals, petrochemicals, pulp, and paper	4,796	2,840,000	94.1	4,977
Light industry	4,725	2,145,000	80.0	...
Food	6,056	1,533,000	100.1	1,041
Other industries[11]	2,729	3,018,000	...	...
Building materials	2,217	7,018,000	108.2	962

Energy production (consumption): electricity (kW-hr; 1992) 1,008,500,000 (992,208,000); coal (metric tons; 1992) 317,006,000 (316,058,000); crude petroleum (barrels; 1992) 399,337,000 (268,326,000); petroleum products (metric tons; 1992) 219,240,000 (193,581,000); natural gas (cu m; 1992) 557,677,000,000 (394,714,000,000); peat (metric tons; 1992) 4,436,000 (4,402,000); oil shale (metric tons; 1992) 3,800,000 (n.a.).

Energy production by source (1992): thermal 71.0%, hydroelectric 17.1%, nuclear and other 11.9%.

Population economically active (1992): total 72,878,000; activity rate of total population 49.0% (participation rates: ages 16–59 [male], 16–54 [female] 87.4%; female [1991] 52.4%; unemployed [1993] 10.4%).

Price and earnings indexes (1990 = 100)

	1990	1991	1992
Consumer price index	100.0	160.3	2,509.0
Monthly earnings index	100.0	185.9	2,064.2

Land use (1992): forested c. 58.3%; meadows and pastures 5.1%; agricultural and under permanent cultivation 7.7%; other 28.9%.

Household income and expenditure. Average household size (1989) 3.2; income per household: n.a.; sources of income (1992): wages 76.0%, pensions and stipends 8.7%, other 15.3%; expenditure (1992): food 39.8%, clothing 19.4%, taxes and other financial payments 7.5%, furniture and household appliances 7.5%, culture 4.6%, alcoholic beverages 2.8%, housing 0.8%.

Foreign trade

Balance of trade (current prices; non-CIS)

	1990	1991	1992
U.S.$'000,000	−10,603	+6,438	+4,986
% of total	6.9%	6.8%	6.7%

Imports (1992): U.S.$34,900,000,000 (machinery and transport equipment 39.2%, food 26.6%, textiles 11.2%, chemicals 9.8%, raw materials excluding

fuels 6.4%, miscellaneous manufactured articles 4.2%). *Major import sources:* Europe 62.8%; the Americas 21.2%; Asia 13.9%; Africa 2.0%.

Exports (1992): U.S.$39,900,000,000 (fuels and lubricants 54.3%, raw materials excluding fuels 19.9%, machinery and transport equipment 9.2%, miscellaneous manufactured articles 6.5%, chemicals 6.4%, food 2.7%). *Major export destinations:* Europe 74.8%; Asia 20.4%; the Americas 3.5%; Africa 1.2%.

Trade by commodity group (1992)

	imports		exports	
SITC group	U.S.$'000,000	%	U.S.$'000,000	%
00 Food and live animals	9,300	26.6	1,100	2.2
02 Raw materials, excl. fuels	2,300	6.4	8,100	5.8
03 Mineral fuels, lubricants	1,000	2.6	21,700	62.7
05 Chemicals	3,400	9.8	2,500	6.5
65 Textile yarn, fabrics	3,900	11.2	300	8.8
07 Machinery and transport eqpt.	13,700	39.2	3,700	10.2
08 Misc. manufactured articles	1,300	4.2	2,500	3.8
09 Goods, n.e.s.	...	...	...	...
TOTAL	39,900	100.0	39,900	100.0

Direction of trade (1990)

	imports		exports	
	U.S.$'000,000	%	U.S.$'000,000	%
Africa	1,701	1.7	1,730	2.0
Asia	17,309	17.6	15,770	18.3
Japan	3,583	3.6	2,460	2.9
South America	7,423	7.5	6,202	7.2
North and Central America	4,819	4.9	1,376	1.6
United States	3,674	3.7	953	1.1
Europe	66,632	67.7	60,987	70.8
EC	9,085	9.2	16,513	19.2
EFTA	8,416	8.5	5,714	6.6
other Europe	49,131	46.1	38,760	45.0
Oceania	615	0.6	51	0.1
TOTAL	98,499	100.0	86,116	100.0

Transport and communications

Transport. Railroads (1993): length 158,100 km; passenger-km 253,200,000,000; metric ton-km cargo 1,967,000,000. Roads (1993): total length 918,000 km (paved 76%). Vehicles (1993): passenger cars 10,499,000; trucks and buses 407,000. Merchant marine (1993): vessels (100 gross tons and over) 24; total deadweight tonnage 91,000,000. Air transport (1993): passenger-km 117,700,000,000; metric ton-km cargo 1,800,000; airports (1994) 58.

Distribution of traffic (1992)

	cargo carried ('000,000 tons)	% of national total	passengers carried ('000,000)	% of national total
Intercity transport			27,279	28.7
Road	1,923	39.2	24,792	26.1
Rail	1,640	33.4	2,372	2.4
Sea and river	398	8.1	53	0.1
Air	1	...	62	0.1
Pipeline	945	19.3	—	—
Urban transport			20,257	21.3
Road	—	—	266	0.3
Rail	—	—	19,991	21.0
TOTAL	4,907	100.0	95,072	100.0

Communications. Daily newspapers (1990): total 4,808; total circulation 166,000,000; circulation per 1,000 population 112. Radio (1992): 48,800,000 receivers (1 per 3 persons). Television (1992): 54,200,000 receivers (1 per 2.7 persons). Telephones (1992): 24,796,000 (1 per 6.0 persons).

Education and health

Education (1992–93)

	schools	teachers	students	student/teacher ratio
Primary (age 6–13) }	70,200	1,611,000	20,990,000	13.8
Secondary (age 14–17)				
Voc., teacher tr.	2,609	...	2,090,000	...
Higher	535	...	2,638,000	...

Health (1993): physicians 657,000 (1 per 225 persons); hospital beds 1,998,000 (1 per 74 persons); infant mortality rate per 1,000 live births (1992) 18.1.

Food (1992): daily per capita caloric intake 2,100 (vegetable products, n.a., animal products, n.a.); 82% of FAO recommended minimum.

Military

Total active duty personnel (1993): 2,030,000 (army 70.1%, navy 20.0%, air force 9.9%). *Military expenditure as percentage of GNP* (1992): 9.9%; per capita expenditure U.S.$265.

[1]The president of the Russian Federation dissolved the former Congress of People's Deputies on Sept. 22, 1993; a new constitution, approved by referendum Dec. 11–12, 1993, created a Federal Assembly, elections to which were held at the same time. [2]The former Chechen-Ingush republic was split into two separate republics June 4, 1992; although both are formally recognized by the Russian Federation, details on final status within the federation remain undetermined. [3]Republic is not signatory to the March 31, 1992, treaty establishing the Russian Federation. [4]Ingushetia's area and population include Chechenia. [5]Entity has formally proclaimed itself a republic; final status remains undetermined. [6]Detail does not add to total given because of rounding. [7]Leningrad region includes area of autonomous city of St. Petersburg. [8]Moskva region includes area of autonomous city of Moscow. [9]With the exception of the Chukchi autonomous district (identified in Roman type), which has formally separated from Magadan region, all autonomous districts are administratively part of another national administrative subdivision, within which their area and population are included. [10]Total as of March 31, 1993; Russia has also assumed responsibility for the governmental and commercial debts of the former U.S.S.R., estimated to constitute a further U.S.$88,000,000,000. [11]1990.

Rwanda

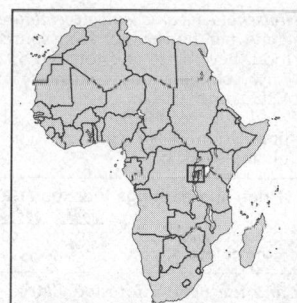

Official name: Republika y'u Rwanda (Rwanda); République Rwandaise (French) (Republic of Rwanda).
Form of government: transitional regime of Rwandan Patriotic Front[1].
Head of state and government: President assisted by Prime Minister and Vice President (Minister of Defense).
Capital: Kigali.
Official languages: Rwanda; French.
Official religion: none.
Monetary unit: 1 Rwanda franc (RF); valuation (Oct. 7, 1994) 1 U.S.$ = RF 216.20; 1 £ = RF 135.93.

Area and population		area		population
		sq mi	sq km	1991 census
Prefectures	Capitals			
Butare	Butare	709	1,837	766,839
Byumba	Byumba	1,838	4,761	783,350
Cyangugu	Cyangugu	712	1,845	515,129
Gikongoro	Gikongoro	794	2,057	464,585
Gisenyi	Gisenyi	791	2,050	734,697
Gitarama	Gitarama	845	2,189	851,516
Kibungo	Kibungo	1,562	4,046	655,368
Kibuye	Kibuye	658	1,705	470,747
Kigali	Kigali	1,159	3,002	918,869
Kigali (city)	—	45	116	237,782
Ruhengeri	Ruhengeri	642	1,663	766,112
TOTAL		9,757[2]	25,271	7,164,994[3]

Demography

Population (1994): 7,817,000.
Density (1994): persons per sq mi 801.2, persons per sq km 309.3.
Urban-rural (1991): urban 5.4%; rural 94.6%.
Sex distribution (1991): male 48.67%; female 51.33%.
Age breakdown (1990): under 15, 49.0%; 15–29, 26.1%; 30–44, 13.5%; 45–59, 7.5%; 60–74, 3.3%; 75 and over, 0.6%.
Population projection: (2000) 9,377,000; (2010) 12,698,000.
Doubling time: 21 years.
Ethnic composition (1983): Hutu 90%; Tutsi 9%; Twa 1%.
Religious affiliation (1988): Roman Catholic 65%; traditional beliefs 17%; Protestant 9%; Muslim 9%.
Major cities (1991): Kigali 237,782[3]; Ruhengeri 29,578[4]; Butare 28,645[4]; Gisenyi 21,918[4].

Vital statistics

Birth rate per 1,000 population (1990–95): 52.1 (world avg. 26.0); (1978) legitimate 94.9%; illegitimate 5.1%.
Death rate per 1,000 population (1990–95): 18.2 (world avg. 9.2).
Natural increase rate per 1,000 population (1990–95): 33.9 (world avg. 16.8).
Total fertility rate (avg. births per childbearing woman; 1990–95): 8.5.
Marriage rate per 1,000 population (1984)[5]: 2.5.
Divorce rate per 1,000 population: n.a.
Life expectancy at birth (1990–95): male 44.8 years; female 47.7 years.
Major causes of death per 100,000 population (1984)[6]: complications of pregnancy, childbirth, and birth injury 192.4; infectious and parasitic diseases (including malaria, typhoid, trypanosomiasis [sleeping sickness], pneumonia, tuberculosis, bacillary dysentery and amebiasis, diphtheria, meningococcal infection, and poliomyelitis) 11.8; diseases of the digestive system 10.3; diseases of the nervous system 10.1; accidents, poisoning, and violence 5.2.

National economy

Budget (1992). Revenue: RF 28,723,000,000 (taxes on goods and services 34.7%; import and export duties 31.1%; income tax 15.6%; property taxes 0.3%). Expenditures: RF 54,868,000,000 (current expenditure 74.1%, of which wages and salaries 26.5%, debt payment 8.7%, capital expenditure 25.9%).
Public debt (external, outstanding; 1992): U.S.$804,000,000.
Production (metric tons except as noted). Agriculture, forestry, fishing (1993): plantains 2,700,000, roots and tubers 1,377,000 (of which sweet potatoes 700,000, cassava 350,000, potatoes 260,000), cereals 199,000 (of which sorghum 109,000, corn [maize] 70,000), coffee 31,000, tea 14,000, tobacco 4,000; live-stock (number of live animals) 1,119,000 goats, 610,000 cattle, 402,000 sheep, 130,000 pigs; roundwood (1992) 5,660,000 cu m; fish catch (1991) 3,551. Mining and quarrying (1990): cassiterite (tin ore) 730; wolframite (tungsten ore) 175; gold (1992) 15,552 troy oz. Manufacturing (1991): cement 57,000; lye soap 9,000; sugar 2,969[7]; beer 915,000 hectolitres; soft drinks 101,000 hec-tolitres; footwear 24,000 pairs; blankets 406,876 units[7]; matches 70,942,000 boxes[7]. Construction (1981): residential 59,600 sq m; nonresidential 34,400 sq m. Energy production (consumption): electricity (kW-hr; 1992) 185,000,-000 (197,000,000); coal, none (n.a.); petroleum products (metric tons; 1992) none (137,000); natural gas (cu m; 1992) 153,762 (153,762).
Tourism (1992): receipts from visitors U.S.$4,000,000; expenditures by nationals abroad U.S.$17,000,000.
Land use (1992): forested 22.3%; meadows and pastures 18.3%; agricultural and under permanent cultivation 47.4%; other 12.0%.
Population economically active (1991): total 3,649,000; activity rate of total population 50.2% (participation rates: ages 14–74 [1989], 46.3%; female 53.5%; unemployed, n.a.).

Price and earnings indexes (1990 = 100)							
	1987	1988	1989	1990	1991	1992	1993
Consumer price index	92.3	95.0	96.0	100.0	119.6	131.1	147.3
Earnings index	...	...	...	...	...	...	...

Gross national product (at current market prices; 1993): U.S.$1,498,000,000 (U.S.$200 per capita).

Structure of gross domestic product and labour force	1991		1989	
	in value RF '000,000[8]	% of total value	labour force	% of labour force
Agriculture	57,151	42.0	2,832,557	90.1
Mining	281	0.2	4,691	0.2
Manufacturing	16,708	12.3	45,089	1.4
Construction	9,660	7.1	38,237	1.2
Public utilities	303	0.2	2,562	0.1
Transportation and communications	9,438	6.9	7,333	0.2
Trade	23,255	17.1	80,026	2.6
Finance	1,947	1.4	3,128	0.1
Pub. admin., defense	11,711	8.6	120,019	3.8
Services	5,684	4.2		
Other	...	...	9,414	0.3
TOTAL	136,138	100.0	3,143,056	100.0

Household income and expenditure. Average household size (1991) 4.7; average annual income per household (1983) RF 122,870 (U.S.$1,300); sources of income (1977): self-employment (profits, interest, etc.) 71.0%, salaries and wages 16.5%, transfers 9.5%; expenditure (1982)[9]: food 44.2%, housing 13.2%, clothing and footwear 11.4%, transportation 10.3%, household equipment 8.4%.

Foreign trade[10]

Balance of trade (current prices)						
	1987	1988	1989	1990	1991	1992
RF '000,000	−10,562	−11,403	−10,918	−6,834	−15,181	−17,729
% of total	37.1%	40.7%	41.7%	27.0%	39.6%	49.9%

Imports (1991): RF 38,474,500,000 (machinery and transport equipment 14.5%, of which machinery 11.1%, transport equipment 3.4%; mineral fuels and lubricants 12.8%; food, beverages, and tobacco 11.4%; construction materials 3.9%). *Major import sources:* Belgium-Luxembourg 17.1%; Kenya 13.4%; France 6.8%; Germany 6.0%; Italy 2.8%; The Netherlands 2.7%; United Kingdom 2.1%; United States 1.0%; Zaire 0.7%.
Exports (1991): RF 11,971,200,000 (coffee 60.2%; tea 23.4%). *Major export destinations:* Germany 21.3%; The Netherlands 18.8%; Belgium-Luxembourg 11.8%; United Kingdom 6.4%; United States 5.8%; Italy 1.7%.

Transport and communications

Transport. Railroads: none. Roads (1991): total length 8,283 mi, 13,330 km (paved 6%). Vehicles (1992): passenger cars 7,868; trucks and buses 2,048. Merchant marine: none. Air transport (1991): passenger arrivals 29,000, passenger departures 30,000; metric ton cargo loaded 2,674, metric ton cargo unloaded 4,794; airports (1994) with scheduled flights 3.
Communications. Daily newspapers (1994): total number, none; total circulation per 1,000 population, n.a. Radio (1992): total number of receivers 650,000 (1 per 12 persons). Television: none. Telephones (1992): 21,220 (1 per 347 persons).

Education and health

Education (1990–91)	schools	teachers	students	student/ teacher ratio
Primary (age 7–15)	1,671	19,183	1,100,437	57.4
Secondary (age 16–19)[11]	...	2,802	70,400	25.1
Higher[12]	3[13]	646	3,389	5.2

Educational attainment (1978). Percentage of population age 25 and over having: no formal schooling 76.9%; some primary education 16.8%; complete primary education 4.0%; some secondary and complete secondary education 2.0%; some postsecondary vocational and higher education 0.3%. *Literacy* (1990): percentage of total population age 15 and over literate 50.2%; males literate 63.9%; females literate 37.1%.
Health: physicians (1989) 272 (1 per 24,697 persons); hospital beds (1984) 9,046 (1 per 649 persons); infant mortality rate per 1,000 live births (1990–95) 110.0.
Food (1988–90): daily per capita caloric intake 1,913 (vegetable products 97%, animal products 3%); 82% of FAO recommended minimum requirement.

Military

Total active duty personnel (1994): 5,200 (army 96.2%, navy, none, air force 3.8%). *Military expenditure as percentage of GNP* (1991): 7.5% (world 4.2%); per capita expenditure U.S.$15.

---

[1]Civil war victory against former government declared by RPF July 18, 1994; new government established on July 19, 1994. [2]Detail does not add to total given because of rounding. [3]The population of Kigali decreased to about 100,000–120,000 because of the 1994 civil war. [4]Resident population only. [5]Excludes marriages not registered in court. [6]In hospitals only. [7]1990. [8]At factor cost. [9]Weights of consumer price index components. [10]Imports f.o.b. in balance of trade and c.i.f. in commodities and trading partners. [11]Includes vocational and teacher training. [12]1989–90. [13]1985.

Saint Kitts and Nevis

Official name: Federation of Saint Kitts and Nevis[1].
Form of government: constitutional monarchy with one legislative house (National Assembly [15[2]]).
Chief of state: British Monarch represented by Governor-General.
Head of government: Prime Minister.
Capital: Basseterre.
Official language: English.
Official religion: none.
Monetary unit: 1 Eastern Caribbean dollar (EC$) = 100 cents; valuation (Oct. 7, 1994) 1 U.S.$ = EC$2.70; 1 £ = EC$4.30.

Area and population		area		population
				1991
Islands[3]	Capitals	sq mi	sq km	census[4]
Nevis[5]	Charlestown	36.0	93.2	9,130
St. Kitts	Basseterre	68.0	176.2	32,696
TOTAL		104.0	269.4	41,826

Demography

Population (1994): 41,800.
Density (1994): persons per sq mi 401.9, persons per sq km 155.2.
Urban-rural (1990): urban 48.9%; rural 51.1%.
Sex distribution (1990): male 51.56%; female 48.44%.
Age breakdown (1990): under 15, 32.5%; 15–29, 25.6%; 30–44, 18.9%; 45–59, 10.1%; 60–74, 8.9%; 75 and over, 4.0%.
Population projection: (2000) 42,000; (2010) 42,000.
Doubling time: 56 years.
Ethnic composition (1991): black 94.9%; mixed/white/Indo-Pakistani 5.1%.
Religious affiliation (1985): Protestant 76.4%, of which Anglican 36.2%, Methodist 32.3%; Roman Catholic 10.7%; other 12.9%.
Major towns (1990): Basseterre 15,000; Charlestown 1,200.

Vital statistics

Birth rate per 1,000 population (1991): 21.9 (world avg. 26.0); (1983) legitimate 19.2%; illegitimate 80.8%.
Death rate per 1,000 population (1991): 9.5 (world avg. 9.2).
Natural increase rate per 1,000 population (1991): 12.4 (world avg. 16.8).
Total fertility rate (avg. births per childbearing woman; 1992): 2.5.
Marriage rate per 1,000 population: n.a.
Divorce rate per 1,000 population: n.a.
Life expectancy at birth (1994): male 63.0 years; female 69.0 years.
Major causes of death per 100,000 population (1985): diseases of the circulatory system 443.2, of which cerebrovascular disease 220.5, diseases of pulmonary circulation and other heart disease 122.7; malignant neoplasms (cancers) 95.5; diseases of the respiratory system 81.8; infectious and parasitic diseases 50.0; ill-defined conditions 102.3.

National economy

Budget (1992). Revenue: EC$110,800,000 (tax revenue 68.8%, of which income taxes 18.1%, import duties 17.8%, consumption taxes 15.5%; nontax revenue 29.5%). Expenditures: EC$117,000,000 (current expenditure 89.7%; development expenditure 10.3%).
Tourism (1992): receipts from visitors U.S.$67,000,000; expenditures by nationals abroad U.S.$5,000,000.
Production (metric tons except as noted). Agriculture, forestry, fishing (1993): sugarcane 200,000, coconuts 2,000, potatoes 308[6], mangoes 272[6]; livestock (number of live animals) 14,000 sheep, 10,000 goats, 5,000 cattle; roundwood, n.a.; fish catch (1991) 1,750. Mining and quarrying: excavation of sand for local use. Manufacturing (1991): raw sugar 22,500[7]; molasses 5,600[6]; aerated beverages 47,000 hectolitres; beer 17,200 hectolitres; other manufactures include garments, electronic components, plastics, and ethanol. Construction: n.a. Energy production (consumption): electricity (kW-hr; 1992) 40,000,000 (40,000,000); coal, none (none); crude petroleum, none (none); petroleum products (metric tons; 1992) none (24,000); natural gas, none (none).
Public debt (external, outstanding; 1992): U.S.$39,300,000.
Gross national product (at current market prices; 1993): U.S.$183,300,000 (U.S.$4,470 per capita).

Structure of gross domestic product and labour force				
	1991		1984	
	in value EC$'000,000[8]	% of total value	labour force[9]	% of labour force[9]
Agriculture	28.1	7.1	4,380	29.6
Mining	2.7	0.7	—	—
Manufacturing	50.7	12.8	2,170	14.7
Construction	53.3	13.5	400	2.7
Public utilities	5.0	1.3	1,030	7.0
Transportation and communications	61.9	15.6	450	3.0
Trade, restaurants	88.8	22.4	940	6.3
Finance, real estate	43.7	11.0	280	1.9
Pub. admin., defense	70.8	17.9 }	4,700	31.7
Services	13.1	3.3 }		
Other	−22.0[10]	−5.6[10]	460	3.1
TOTAL	396.1	100.0	14,810	100.0

Household income and expenditure. Average household size (1980) 3.7; income per household: n.a.; sources of income: n.a.; expenditure (1978)[11]: food, beverages, and tobacco 55.6%, household furnishings 9.4%, housing 7.6%, clothing and footwear 7.5%, fuel and light 6.6%, transportation 4.3%, other 9.0%.
Population economically active (1980): total 17,125; activity rate of total population 39.5% (participation rates: ages 15–64, 69.5%; female 41.0%; unemployed[12]).

Price and earnings indexes (1990 = 100)							
	1987	1988	1989	1990	1991	1992	1993[13]
Consumer price index	91.1	91.3	95.9	100.0	104.2	107.2	110.3
Earnings index	...	...	...	...	...	...	...

Land use (1991): forested 17.0%; meadows and pastures 3.0%; agricultural and under permanent cultivation 39.0%; other 41.0%.

Foreign trade[14]

Balance of trade (current prices)						
	1987	1988	1989	1990	1991	1992
EC$'000,000	−138.8	−173.9	−199.3	−188.4	−183.1	−202.4
% of total	47.9%	51.6%	56.3%	55.8%	53.7%	53.5%

Imports (1992): EC$290,400,000 ([15]manufactured products 73.0%, agricultural products 16.0%, fuels 6.0%). *Major import sources* (1989): United States 41.3%; Caricom countries 15.6%, of which Trinidad and Tobago 7.4%; United Kingdom 14.0%.
Exports (1992): EC$88,000,000 ([15]raw sugar 37.0%, garments 26.0%, other goods [including beer, nonalcoholic beverages, coconut oil, electronic goods, and transport equipment] 37.0%). *Major export destinations* (1989): United States 54.6%; United Kingdom 26.1%; Caricom countries 8.9%, of which Trinidad and Tobago 4.1%.

Transport and communications

Transport. Railroads (1992)[16]: length 22 mi, 36 km. Roads (1993): total length 186 mi, 300 km (paved 42%). Vehicles (1990): passenger cars 4,000; trucks and buses, n.a. Merchant marine (1992): vessels (100 gross tons and over) 1; total deadweight tonnage 550. Air transport: passenger arrivals (1992) 123,-195[17]; passenger departures, n.a.; cargo handled, n.a.; airports (1994) with scheduled flights 2.
Communications (1992). Daily newspapers[18]: none. Radio (1993): total number of receivers 25,000 (1 per 1.7 persons). Television (1993): total number of receivers 9,500 (1 per 4.4 persons). Telephones (1990): 9,600[19] (1 per 4.4 persons).

Education and health

Education (1991–92)				
	schools	teachers	students	student/ teacher ratio
Primary (age 5–12)	31	342	6,978	20.4
Secondary (age 13–17)	7	298	4,645	15.6
Voc., teacher tr.	2	35	189	5.4
Higher	1	3	36	12.0

Educational attainment (1980). Percentage of population age 25 and over having: no formal schooling 1.1%; primary education 29.6%; secondary 67.2%; higher 2.1%. *Literacy* (1990): total population age 15 and over literate 25,500 (90.0%); males literate 13,100 (90.0%); females literate 12,400 (90.0%).
Health (1990): physicians 43 (1 per 972 persons); hospital beds 268 (1 per 156 persons); infant mortality rate per 1,000 live births (1994) 20.0.
Food (1988–90): daily per capita caloric intake 2,435 (vegetable products 76%, animal products 24%); 101% of FAO recommended minimum requirement.

Military

Total active duty personnel (1993): the police force includes a 50-member paramilitary unit.

[1]Both Saint Christopher and Nevis and the Federation of Saint Christopher and Nevis are officially acceptable, variant, short- and long-form names of the country. [2]Includes 4 nonelective seats. [3]Parish subdivisions of both islands are for statistical purposes only. [4]Preliminary. [5]Nevis has full internal self-government. The Nevis legislature is subordinate to the National Assembly only with regard to external affairs and defense. [6]1990. [7]1994. [8]At factor cost. [9]Employed persons only. [10]Less imputed bank service charges. [11]Weights of consumer price index components. [12]Official data not available. Unemployment rates were thought to be low in 1992 because of labour shortages in the sugar industry and increased job creation in the manufacturing and tourism industries. [13]September. [14]Imports c.i.f.; exports f.o.b. [15]Estimated figures. [16]Light railway serving the sugar industry on Saint Kitts. [17]Saint Kitts airport only. [18]Total circulation of one weekly newspaper and one twice-weekly newspaper is 9,000. [19]Number of subscribers.

Saint Lucia

Official name: Saint Lucia.
Form of government: constitutional monarchy with two legislative houses (Senate [11]; House of Assembly [17]).
Chief of state: British Monarch represented by Governor-General.
Head of government: Prime Minister.
Capital: Castries.
Official language: English.
Official religion: none.
Monetary unit: 1 Eastern Caribbean Dollar (EC$) = 100 cents; valuation (Oct. 7, 1994) 1 U.S.$ = EC$2.70; 1 £ = EC$4.30.

Area and population

Districts	Capitals	area sq mi	area sq km	population 1992 estimate
Anse-la-Raye	Anse-la-Raye	} 18	47	5,218
Canaries	Canaries			1,864
Castries	Castries	31	79	53,883
Choiseul	Choiseul	12	31	6,638
Dennery	Dennery	27	70	11,574
Gros Islet	Gros Islet	39	101	13,996
Laborie	Laborie	15	38	7,763
Micoud	Micoud	30	78	15,636
Soufrière	Soufrière	19	51	7,962
Vieux Fort	Vieux Fort	17	44	13,617
TOTAL		238[1]	617[1]	138,151

Demography

Population (1994): 142,000.
Density (1994): persons per sq mi 596.6, persons per sq km 230.1.
Urban-rural (1990): urban 44.1%; rural 55.9%.
Sex distribution (1992): male 48.49%; female 51.51%.
Age breakdown (1992): under 15, 36.7%; 15–29, 29.4%; 30–44, 16.3%; 45–59, 8.8%; 60–74, 6.3%; 75 and over, 2.5%.
Population projection: (2000) 151,000; (2010) 169,000.
Doubling time: 35 years.
Ethnic composition (1985): black 87.0%; mixed 9.1%; East Indian 2.6%; white 1.3%.
Religious affiliation (1991): Roman Catholic 79.0%; Protestant 15.5%, of which Seventh-day Adventist 6.5%, Pentecostal 3.0%; other 5.5%.
Major city (1992): Castries city proper 2,063 (urban area 13,615).

Vital statistics

Birth rate per 1,000 population (1992): 26.2 (world avg. 26.0); legitimate 14.2%; illegitimate 85.8%.
Death rate per 1,000 population (1992): 6.3 (world avg. 9.2).
Natural increase rate per 1,000 population (1992): 19.9 (world avg. 16.8).
Total fertility rate (avg. births per childbearing woman; 1992): 3.0.
Marriage rate per 1,000 population (1992): 3.2.
Divorce rate per 1,000 population (1992): 0.3.
Life expectancy at birth (1992): male 68.7 years; female 74.6 years.
Major causes of death per 100,000 population (1992): diseases of the circulatory system 205.6, of which ischemic heart diseases 133.2, cerebrovascular disease 34.7; malignant neoplasms (cancers) 64.4; diseases of the respiratory system 48.5; infectious and parasitic diseases 31.1; ill-defined conditions 130.3.

National economy

Budget (1992–93). Revenue: EC$331,100,000 (consumption duties on imported goods 27.0%, income taxes 26.8%, import duties 18.7%, taxes on domestic goods and services 10.7%). Expenditures: EC$344,200,000 (current expenditures 69.7%, development expenditures and net lending 30.3%).
Public debt (external, outstanding; 1992): U.S.$88,300,000.
Tourism: receipts from visitors (1992) U.S.$209,300,000; expenditures by nationals abroad (1991) U.S.$17,000,000.
Production. Agriculture, forestry, fishing (export value in EC$'000 except as noted; 1992): bananas 184,000[2], copra 2,603[2], breadfruit 713, mangoes 670, cacao beans 404[2], pepper 241, plantains 216, pineapple 189; livestock (number of live animals) 16,000 sheep, 12,000 cattle, 12,000 pigs, 12,000 goats; roundwood, n.a.; fish catch 958 metric tons. Mining and quarrying: excavation of sand for local construction and pumice. Manufacturing (value of production in EC$'000; 1992): food, beverages, and tobacco 72,379; paper products and cardboard boxes 41,029; garments 10,385; electrical and electronic components 9,501; refined coconut oil 6,981; textiles 4,359. Construction (buildings approved; 1992): residential 91,900 sq m; nonresidential 43,300 sq m. Energy production (consumption): electricity (kW-hr; 1992) 152,100,000 (125,500,000); coal, none (none); crude petroleum, none (none); petroleum products (metric tons; 1992) none (325,000); natural gas, none (none).
Household income and expenditure. Average household size (1991) 4.0; income per household: n.a.; sources of income: n.a.; expenditure (1982)[3]: food 46.8%, housing 13.5%, clothing and footwear 6.5%, transportation and communications 6.3%, household furnishings 5.8%, fuel and light 4.5%, recreation and education 3.2%, beverages and tobacco 2.8%, health care 2.3%, other 8.3%.

Population economically active (1992): total 57,797; activity rate of total population 41.8% (participation rates: ages 15–64, 72.7%; female 46.5%; unemployed [1993] 20.0%).

Price and earnings indexes (1988 = 100)

	1987	1988	1989	1990	1991	1992	1993
Consumer price index	99.2	100.0	104.1	109.0	115.2	121.0	122.0
Earnings index[4]	...	100.0	103.0	106.1	109.3	...	...

Gross national product (at current market prices; 1992): U.S.$453,000,000 (U.S.$2,900 per capita).

Structure of gross domestic product and labour force

	1993 in value EC$'000,000[5]	1993 % of total value	1992 labour force[6]	1992 % of labour force[6]
Agriculture	126.0	12.3	2,824	8.9
Mining	6.9	0.7	...	...
Manufacturing	75.7	7.4	4,360	13.8
Construction	92.2	9.0	2,197	6.9
Public utilities	35.1	3.4	832	2.6
Transportation and communications	185.0	18.1	2,551	8.0
Trade, restaurants	251.3	24.6	8,714	27.5
Finance, real estate	143.1	14.0	3,488	11.0
Pub. admin., defense	134.6	13.2	6,758	21.3
Services	32.7	3.2	...	...
Other	−61.8[7]	−6.1[7]	...	...
TOTAL	1,020.7[8]	100.0[8]	31,724	100.0

Land use (1991): forested 13.0%; meadows and pastures 5.0%; agricultural and under permanent cultivation 30.0%; other 52.0%.

Foreign trade[9]

Balance of trade (current prices)

	1987	1988	1989	1990	1991	1992
EC$'000,000	−225.1	−228.9	−377.2	−321.4	−426.7	−436.7
% of total	34.3%	26.8%	39.0%	31.9%	41.8%	39.7%

Imports (1992): EC$845,500,000 (consumer goods 58.3%, of which food and live animals 19.6%; machinery and transport equipment 21.3%; chemicals and chemical products 10.0%; crude petroleum and petroleum products 6.8%). *Major import sources:* United States 33.8%; Caricom countries 17.6%, of which Trinidad and Tobago 9.2%; United Kingdom 13.7%; Japan 6.2%; Canada 3.2%.
Exports (1992): EC$331,500,000 (bananas 60.1%; clothing 15.0%[10]; paper and paperboard 5.0%[10]; beer 4.3%; coconut oil 2.0%). *Major export destinations:* United Kingdom 51.4%; United States 21.4%; Caricom countries 17.0%, of which Dominica 4.1%; Barbados 3.4%; Italy 6.3%.

Transport and communications

Transport. Railroads: none. Roads (1990): total length 500 mi, 805 km (paved 56%). Vehicles (1992): passenger cars 9,863; trucks and buses 9,075. Merchant marine (1992): vessels (100 gross tons and over) 7; total deadweight tonnage 2,070. Air transport (1992): passenger arrivals 223,467[11], passenger departures 226,630[11]; cargo unloaded 1,393 metric tons, cargo loaded 3,465 metric tons; airports (1994) with scheduled flights 2.
Communications. Daily newspapers: none[12]. Radio (1993): total number of receivers 90,000 (1 per 1.6 persons). Television (1993): total number of receivers 25,000 (1 per 5.6 persons). Telephones (1992): 35,990 (1 per 3.8 persons).

Education and health

Education (1992–93)

	schools	teachers	students	student/ teacher ratio
Primary (age 5–11)	84	1,181[13]	32,204	27.4[13]
Secondary (age 12–16)	14	466[13]	7,612	17.5[13]
Voc., teacher tr. } Higher	1	113[13]	1,125	6.3[13]

Educational attainment (1980). Percentage of population age 25 and over having: no formal schooling 17.5%; primary education 74.4%; secondary 6.8%; higher 1.3%. *Literacy* (1990): about 80%.
Health (1992): physicians 64 (1 per 2,235 persons); hospital beds 435 (1 per 318 persons); infant mortality rate per 1,000 live births 18.3.
Food (1988–90): daily per capita caloric intake 2,424 (vegetable products 75%, animal products 25%); 100% of FAO recommended minimum requirement.

Military

Total active duty personnel (1992):[14].

---

[1]Total includes the uninhabited 30 sq mi (78 sq km) Central Forest Reserve. [2]Value of production. [3]Castries administrative area only. [4]Public sector only. [5]At constant prices of 1990. [6]Data exclude workers (all self-employed and many agricultural workers) not making contributions to the national insurance plan and all unemployed. [7]Less imputed bank service charges. [8]Detail does not add to total given because of rounding. [9]Imports f.o.b. in balance of trade and c.i.f. in commodities and trading partners. [10]Estimated figure. [11]1990. [12]Two newspapers published once and thrice a week have a total circulation (1992) of 9,000. [13]1991–92. [14]The 497-member police force includes a specially trained paramilitary unit and a coast guard unit.

Saint Vincent and the Grenadines

Official name: Saint Vincent and the Grenadines.
Form of government: constitutional monarchy with one legislative house (House of Assembly [21[1]]).
Chief of state: British Monarch represented by Governor-General.
Head of government: Prime Minister.
Capital: Kingstown.
Official language: English.
Official religion: none.
Monetary unit: 1 Eastern Caribbean Dollar (EC$) = 100 cents; valuation (Oct. 7, 1994) 1 U.S.$ = EC$2.70; 1 £ = EC$4.30.

Area and population

	area		population
			1993
Constituencies[2]	sq mi	sq km	estimate[3]
Island of Saint Vincent[4]			
Barrouallie	14.2	36.8	5,319
Bridgetown	7.2	18.6	7,706
Calliaqua	11.8	30.6	20,760
Chateaubelair	30.9	80.0	6,185
Colonarie	13.4	34.7	8,073
Georgetown	22.2	57.5	7,472
Kingstown (city)	1.9	4.9	15,824
Kingstown (suburbs)	6.4	16.6	11,006
Layou	11.1	28.7	6,132
Marriaqua	9.4	24.3	9,069
Sandy Bay	5.3	13.7	2,858
Saint Vincent Grenadines			
Northern Grenadines[5]	9.0	23.3	5,642
Southern Grenadines[5]	7.5	19.4	2,919
TOTAL	**150.3**	**389.3[6]**	**108,965**

Demography

Population (1994): 110,000.
Density (1994): persons per sq mi 731.9, persons per sq km 282.6.
Urban-rural (1991)[7]: urban 24.6%; rural 75.4%.
Sex distribution (1993): male 49.92%; female 50.08%.
Age breakdown (1985): under 15, 37.4%; 15–29, 32.7%; 30–44, 14.9%; 45–59, 7.5%; 60–74, 5.6%; 75 and over, 1.9%.
Population projection: (2000) 116,000; (2010) 127,000.
Doubling time: 39 years.
Ethnic composition (1986): black 65.5%; mulatto 19.0%; East Indian 5.5%; white (mostly Portuguese) 3.5%; Amerindian/black 2.0%; other 4.5%.
Religious affiliation (1980): Protestant 80.5%, of which Anglican 41.6%, Methodist 20.9%, Baptist 5.9%, Seventh-day Adventist 4.4%; Roman Catholic 11.6%; other 7.9%.
Major city (1993): Kingstown 15,824.

Vital statistics

Birth rate per 1,000 population (1992): 24.7 (world avg. 26.0); legitimate, n.a.; illegitimate, n.a.
Death rate per 1,000 population (1992): 6.6 (world avg. 9.2).
Natural increase rate per 1,000 population (1992): 18.1 (world avg. 16.8).
Total fertility rate (avg. births per childbearing woman; 1992): 2.5.
Marriage rate per 1,000 population (1992): 3.7.
Divorce rate per 1,000 population (1992): 0.8.
Life expectancy at birth (1994): male 71.0 years; female 74.0 years.
Major causes of death per 100,000 population (1992): diseases of the circulatory system 221.2, of which hypertensive disease 110.1, diseases of pulmonary circulation and other forms of heart disease 44.1; malignant neoplasms (cancers) 99.1; endocrine and metabolic disorders 55.1; homicide, suicide, and other violence 39.5.

National economy

Budget (1994). Revenue: EC$265,000,000 (current revenue 70.2%; development revenue 29.8%, of which domestic sources 15.8%, foreign loans and grants 14.0%). Expenditures: EC$263,600,000 (current expenditure 70.0%; development expenditure 30.0%).
Land use (1992): forested 36.0%; meadows and pastures 5.0%; agricultural and under permanent cultivation 28.0%; other 31.0%.
Tourism: receipts from visitors (1992) U.S.$52,700,000; expenditures by nationals abroad (1991) U.S.$7,000,000.
Production (metric tons except as noted). Agriculture, forestry, fishing (1992): bananas 61,700[8], coconuts 23,000, eddoes and dasheens[9] 5,240, yams 2,147, mangoes 2,000, sweet potatoes 1,706; plantains 1,339, lemons and limes 1,000, oranges 1,000, ginger 834, arrowroot starch 635[10], soursops, guavas, and papaws are other important fruits; livestock (number of live animals) 12,000 sheep, 9,000 pigs, 6,000 cattle; roundwood, n.a.; fish catch (1991) 7,665, of which squid and octopus 4,298. Mining and quarrying: sand and gravel for local use. Manufacturing (value added in EC$'000; 1988): beverages and tobacco products 9,686; food products 9,499; textiles, clothing, and footwear 3,872; metal products and electrical machinery 2,510. Construction (gross floor area planned; 1992): 80,800 sq m. Energy production (consumption): electricity (kW-hr; 1992) 57,200,000 (52,900,000); coal, none (none); crude petroleum, none (none); petroleum products (metric tons; 1992) none (27,000); natural gas, none (none).

Gross national product (1993): U.S.$234,000,000 (U.S.$2,130 per capita).

Structure of gross domestic product and labour force

	1992[11]		1980	
	in value EC$'000,000	% of total value	labour force	% of labour force
Agriculture	89.8	17.8	8,928	25.7
Mining	1.5	0.3	108	0.3
Manufacturing	45.9	9.1	1,781	5.1
Construction	52.6	10.4	3,549	10.2
Public utilities	24.0	4.8	402	1.2
Transportation and communications	108.1	21.4	1,882	5.4
Trade	66.4	13.2	2,566	7.4
Finance, real estate	54.4	10.8	351	1.0
Pub. admin., defense	81.2	16.1 }	7,579	21.8
Services	9.3	1.8 }		
Other	−28.9[12]	−5.7[12]	7,593[13]	21.9[13]
TOTAL	**504.3**	**100.0**	**34,739**	**100.0**

Public debt (external, outstanding; 1992): U.S.$61,000,000.
Population economically active (1991): total 42,030; activity rate of total population 39.5% (participation rates: over age 15 [1980] 60.9%; female [1980] 36.1%; unemployed [1993] 30–40%).

Price and earnings indexes (1990 = 100)

	1988	1989	1990	1991	1992	1993	1994
Consumer price index	90.4	92.9	100.0	105.6	109.1	113.8	112.8[14]
Annual earnings index	...	...	...	...	...	...	...

Household income and expenditure. Average household size (1991) 3.9; income per household (1988) EC$4,579 (U.S.$1,696); sources of income: n.a.; expenditure (1975–76): food and beverages 59.8%, clothing 7.7%, household furnishings 6.6%, housing 6.3%, energy 6.2%, other 13.4%.

Foreign trade[15]

Balance of trade (current prices)

	1987	1988	1989	1990	1991	1992
EC$'000,000	−100.9	−69.9	−111.5	−100.0	−141.7	−95.3
% of total	26.3%	13.2%	21.7%	18.3%	28.1%	17.5%

Imports (1992): EC$360,600,000 (food products 23.2%; basic manufactures 21.6%; machinery and transport equipment 17.8%). *Major import sources:* United States 35.5%; Trinidad and Tobago 17.6%; United Kingdom 16.9%; Barbados 3.4%; Canada 3.0%.
Exports (1992): EC$213,000,000 (domestic exports 96.3%, of which bananas 52.7%, flour 11.2%, varieties of taro roots 3.5%, sweet potatoes 2.3%; re-exports 3.7%). *Major export destinations:* United Kingdom 41.2%; Trinidad and Tobago 12.0%; Saint Lucia 10.0% United States 4.4%; Antigua and Barbuda 4.4%.

Transport and communications

Transport. Railroads: none. Roads (1991): total length 586 mi, 943 km (paved 16%). Vehicles (1992): passenger cars 5,000; trucks and buses 2,000. Merchant marine (1992): vessels (100 gross tons and over) 881; total deadweight tonnage 7,044,189. Air transport (1992): passenger arrivals 112,574, passenger departures 113,699; airports (1994) with scheduled flights 4.
Communications. Daily newspapers: none[16]. Radio (1993): total number of receivers 55,000 (1 per 2.0 persons). Television (1993): total number of receivers 17,700 (1 per 6.1 persons). Telephones (1992): 17,500 (1 per 6.1 persons).

Education and health

Education (1991–92)

	schools	teachers	students	student/ teacher ratio
Primary (age 5–11)	60	1,215	24,134	19.9
Secondary (age 12–18)	21	408	7,124	17.5
Voc., teacher tr.	2	...	337	...

Educational attainment (1980). Percentage of population age 25 and over having: no formal schooling 2.4%; primary education 88.0%; secondary 8.2%; higher 1.4%. *Literacy* (1983): total population age 15 and over literate 54,000 (85.0%).
Health: physicians (1992) 40 (1 per 2,690 persons); hospital beds (1989) 500 (1 per 209 persons); infant mortality rate per 1,000 live births (1990–92 avg.) 19.0.
Food (1988–90): daily per capita caloric intake 2,460 (vegetable products 85%, animal products 15%); 102% of FAO recommended minimum requirement.

Military

Total active duty personnel (1992): 634-member police force includes a coast guard and paramilitary unit. *Military expenditure as percentage of central government expenditure* (1989–90): 5.6%[17].

[1]Includes 6 nonelective seats; excludes speaker who may be elected from within or from outside of the House of Assembly membership. [2]For statistical purposes and the election of legislative representatives. [3]January 1. [4]For local administration, the island of Saint Vincent is divided into five parishes; population by parish is not available. [5]Both a constituency and a parish. [6]Detail does not add to total given because of rounding. [7]Urban defined as Kingstown and suburbs. [8]1993. [9]Varieties of taro roots. [10]1992–93. [11]At factor cost. [12]Less imputed bank service charges. [13]Not adequately defined. [14]March. [15]Imports f.o.b. in balance of trade and c.i.f. in commodities and trading partners. [16]Weekly newspapers: 2. [17]May not agree with military expenditure as percentage of GNP because of different bases used.

San Marino

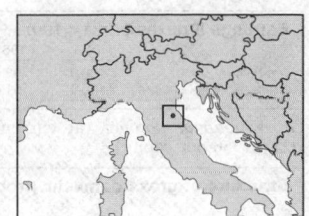

Official name: Serenissima Repubblica
di San Marino (Most Serene
Republic of San Marino).
Form of government: unitary multiparty
republic with one legislative house
(Great and General Council [60]).
Head of state and government:
Captains-Regent (2).
Capital: San Marino.
Official language: Italian.
Official religion: none.
Monetary unit: 1 Italian lira (Lit; plural
lire) = 100 centesimi; valuation (Oct.
7, 1994) 1 U.S.$ = Lit 1,569;
1 £ = Lit 2,495.

Area and population

Castles	Capitals	area sq mi	area sq km	population 1994[1] estimate
Acquaviva	Acquaviva	1.88	4.86	1,240
Borgo Maggiore	Borgo	3.48	9.01	5,127
Chiesanuova	Chiesanuova	2.11	5.46	812
Città	San Marino	2.74	7.09	4,385
Domagnano	Domagnano	2.56	6.62	2,146
Faetano	Faetano	2.99	7.75	795
Fiorentino	Fiorentino	2.53	6.56	1,716
Montegiardino	Montegiardino	1.28	3.31	672
Serravalle/Dogano	Serravalle	4.07	10.53	7,706
TOTAL		23.63[2]	61.19	24,599

Demography

Population (1994): 24,500.
Density (1994): persons per sq mi 1,036.8, persons per sq km 400.4.
Urban-rural (1994[1]): urban 89.8%; rural 10.2%.
Sex distribution (1994[1]): male 49.71%; female 50.29%.
Age breakdown (1994[1]): under 15, 14.9%; 15–29, 23.6%; 30–44, 24.0%; 45–59, 17.9%; 60–74, 13.9%; 75 and over, 5.7%.
Population projection: (2000) 26,600; (2010) 30,400.
Doubling time: not applicable; natural population growth is negligible, averaging only 0.3% during 1989–93.
Ethnic composition (1994[1]): Sammarinesi 77.7%; Italian 21.1%; other 1.2%.
Religious affiliation (1980): Roman Catholic 95.2%; no religion 3.0%; other 1.8%.
Major cities (1994[1]): Serravalle/Dogano 4,749; San Marino 2,399; Borgo Maggiore 2,355; Murata 1,491; Domagnano 1,027.

Vital statistics

Birth rate per 1,000 population (1989–93): 10.5 (world avg. 26.0); (1985) legitimate 95.2%; illegitimate 4.8%.
Death rate per 1,000 population (1989–93): 7.0 (world avg. 9.2).
Natural increase rate per 1,000 population (1989–93): 3.5 (world avg. 16.8).
Total fertility rate (avg. births per childbearing woman; 1984): 1.3.
Marriage rate per 1,000 population (1989–93): 7.9.
Divorce rate per 1,000 population (1989–93): 0.8.
Life expectancy at birth (1980–85): male 70.7 years; female 76.2 years.
Major causes of death per 100,000 population (1989–93): diseases of the circulatory system 324.5; malignant neoplasms (cancers) 216.4; accidents, violence, and suicide 42.9; diseases of the respiratory system 16.3.

National economy

Budget (1991). Revenue: Lit 379,337,000,000 (mainly receipts from postage stamp sales, tourism, and customs duties [collected by Italy and paid as a subsidy]). Expenditures: Lit 379,337,000,000 ([3]finance and economic planning 31.0%, internal affairs 11.3%, health and social security 9.0%, education and culture 7.1%, public works 6.3%).
Public debt: n.a.
Tourism: number of tourist arrivals (1993) 3,072,030; receipts from visitors (1983) U.S.$56,454,000; expenditures by nationals abroad, n.a.
Population economically active (1994[1]): total 14,874; activity rate of total population 60.5% (participation rates: ages 15–64 [1992] 72.9%; female 40.8%; unemployed 4.1%).

Price and earnings indexes (1990 = 100)

	1987	1988	1989	1990	1991	1992	1993
Consumer price index	84.1	88.4	94.0	100.0	108.0	115.7	121.9
Earnings index	...	...	...	...	...	...	...

Household income and expenditure. Total number of households (1994[1]) 9,052; average household size 2.7; income per household: n.a.; sources of income: n.a.; expenditure (1991)[4]: food, beverages, and tobacco 22.1%, housing, fuel, and electrical energy 20.9%, transportation and communications 17.6%, clothing and footwear 8.0%, education 7.1%, furniture, appliances, and goods and services for the home 7.2%, health and sanitary services 2.6%, other goods and services 14.5%.
Production (metric tons except as noted). Agriculture, forestry, fishing[3]: wheat *c.* 4,400, grapes *c.* 700, barley *c.* 500; livestock (number of live animals; 1993) 910 cattle, 725 pigs, 65 sheep. Manufacturing (1993): processed meats 342,578 kg, of which beef 238,725 kg, pork 89,000 kg, veal 13,840 kg; cheese 80,201 kg; butter 14,793 kg; milk 959,069 litres; yogurt 6,645 litres; other major products include textiles, cement, paper, leather, bricks, pot-

tery, tiles, postage stamps, gold and silver jewelry, paints, synthetic rubber, and furniture. Construction (new units completed; 1993): residential 161; nonresidential 102. Energy production (consumption): all electrical power is imported via electrical grid from Italy (consumption, n.a.); coal, none (n.a.); crude petroleum, none (n.a.); petroleum products, none (n.a.); natural gas, none (n.a.).
Gross national product (at current market prices; 1987): U.S.$188,000,000 (U.S.$8,590 per capita).

Structure of labour force (1994[1])

	labour force	% of labour force
Agriculture	294	2.0
Manufacturing	4,739	31.9
Construction and public utilities	1,195	8.0
Transportation and communications	278	1.9
Trade	2,499	16.8
Finance and insurance	390	2.6
Services	1,239	8.3
Public administration and defense	3,624	24.4
Other	616[5]	4.1[5]
TOTAL	14,874	100.0

Land use (1985): agricultural and under permanent cultivation 74%; meadows and pastures 22%; forested, built-on, wasteland, and other 4%.

Foreign trade

Balance of trade: n.a. San Marino and Italy form a single customs area; separate figures for San Marino are not available.
Imports (1993): manufactured goods of all kinds, oil, and gold. *Major import source:* Italy.
Exports (1993): wine, wheat, woolen goods, furniture, wood, ceramics, building stone, dairy products, meat, and postage stamps. *Major export destination:* Italy.

Transport and communications

Transport. Railroads: none (nearest rail terminal is at Rimini, Italy, 17 mi [27 km] northeast). Roads (1987): total length 147 mi, 237 km. Vehicles (1994[1]): passenger cars 22,159; trucks and buses 3,658. Merchant marine: vessels (100 gross tons and over) none. Air transport: airports with scheduled flights, none; there is, however, a heliport that provides passenger and cargo service between San Marino and Rimini, Italy, during the summer months.
Communications. Daily newspapers (1992): 6; circulation per 1,000 population, n.a. Radio (1993): total number of receivers 12,600 (1 per 1.9 persons). Television (1990): total number of receivers 8,000 (1 per 2.9 persons). Telephones (1988): 15,700 (1 per 1.5 persons).

Education and health

Education (1993–94)

	schools	teachers	students	student/ teacher ratio
Primary (age 6–10)	14	219	1,166	5.3
Secondary (age 11–18)	3	133	772	5.8
Voc., teacher tr.	...	...	385	
Higher	...	...	...	

Educational attainment (1994[1]). Percentage of the adult labour force having: basic literacy or primary education 22.2%; secondary 39.1%; some postsecondary 32.5%; higher degree 6.1%. *Literacy* (1986): total population age 15 and over literate 18,135 (98.0%); males literate 8,957 (98.2%); females literate 9,178 (97.7%).
Health (1987): physicians 60 (1 per 375 persons); hospital beds 149 (1 per 151 persons); infant mortality rate per 1,000 live births (1989–93) 9.7.
Food (1988–90)[6]: daily per capita caloric intake 3,498 (vegetable products 74%, animal products 26%); 139% of FAO recommended minimum requirement.

Military

Total active duty personnel (1992): none[7]. *Military expenditure as percentage of national budget* (1987): 0.9% (world 5.4%); per capita expenditure (1987) U.S.$82.

---

[1]January 1. [2]Detail does not add to total given because of rounding. [3]Early 1980s. [4]Weighting coefficients for component expenditures are those of the 1991 official Italian consumer price index for the North-Central region of Italy. [5]Unemployed. [6]Figures are for Italy. [7]Defense is provided by a public security force of about 50; all fit males ages 16–55 constitute a militia.

São Tomé and Príncipe

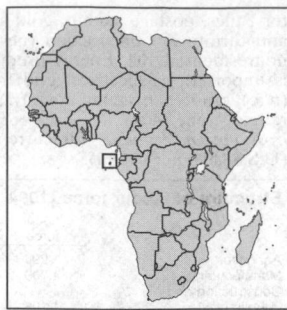

Official name: República democrática de São Tomé e Príncipe (Democratic Republic of São Tomé and Príncipe).
Form of government: Unitary multiparty[1].
Chief of state: President.
Head of government: Prime Minister.
Capital: São Tomé.
Official language: Portuguese.
Official religion: none.
Monetary unit: 1 dobra (Db) = 100 cêntimos; valuation (Oct. 7, 1994) 1 U.S.$ = Db 811.68; 1 £ = Db 1,291.

Area and population

Islands Districts	Capitals	area sq mi	area sq km	population 1991 census[2]
Príncipe		55	142	5,639
Pagué	Santo António	55	142	5,639
São Tomé		332	859	114,507
Aqua Grande	São Tomé	7	17	43,420
Cantagalo	Santana	46	119	11,421
Caué	São João Angolares	103	267	5,541
Lemba	Neves	88	229	9,448
Lobata	Guadalupe	41	105	13,101
Mé-Zóchi	Trindade	47	122	31,576
TOTAL		386	1,001	120,146

Demography

Population (1994): 128,000.
Density (1994): persons per sq mi 331.6, persons per sq km 127.9.
Urban-rural (1992): urban 44.1%; rural 55.9%.
Sex distribution (1991): male 49.42%; female 50.58%.
Age breakdown (1990): under 15, 47.6%; 15–29, 25.8%; 30–44, 12.1%; 45–59, 7.3%; 60 and over, 6.4%; not stated, 0.8%.
Population projection: (2000) 146,000; (2010) 182,000.
Doubling time: 23 years.
Ethnolinguistic composition: mestiços, angolares (descendants of Angolan slaves), forros (descendants of freed slaves), serviçais (alien contract labourers), and tongas (children of serviçais) speak Portuguese; non-Portuguese-speaking Europeans speak French and Spanish.
Religious affiliation (1991): Roman Catholic, about 80.8%; remainder mostly Protestant, predominantly Seventh-day Adventist and an indigenous Evangelical Church.
Major cities (1991): São Tomé 43,420; Trindade 11,388[3]; Santana 6,190[3]; Neves 5,919[3]; Santo Amaro 5,878[3].

Vital statistics

Birth rate per 1,000 population (1993): 35.4 (world avg. 26.0); (1977) legitimate 9.8%; illegitimate 90.2%.
Death rate per 1,000 population (1993): 9.1 (world avg. 9.2).
Natural increase rate per 1,000 population (1993): 26.3 (world avg. 16.8).
Total fertility rate (avg. births per childbearing woman; 1993): 4.6.
Marriage rate per 1,000 population: n.a.
Divorce rate per 1,000 population: n.a.
Life expectancy at birth (1993): male 63.0 years; female 61.2 years.
Major causes of death per 100,000 population (1987): malaria 160.6; direct obstetric causes 76.7; pneumonia 74.0; influenza 61.5; anemias 47.3; hypertensive disease 32.1.

National economy

Budget (1988). Revenue: Db 975,000,000 (indirect taxes 44.4%; income from property 16.0%; nondurable goods 11.3%; direct taxes 10.2%). Expenditures: Db 1,115,000,000 (current expenditure 82.4%, of which wages and salaries 45.5%; capital expenditure 17.6%).
Public debt (external, outstanding; 1992): U.S.$168,800,000.
Tourism (1990): receipts from visitors U.S.$1,000,000; expenditures by nationals abroad U.S.$2,000,000.
Production (metric tons except as noted). Agriculture, forestry, fishing (1993): coconuts 36,000, cassava 5,000, fruits (other than melons) 5,000, cacao 3,000, bananas 3,000, palmetto 3,000[4], vegetables and melons 3,000, copra 2,000, cereals 1,000, taro 742[5], palm kernels 500; livestock (number of live animals) 4,000 goats, 4,000 cattle, 3,000 pigs, 2,000 sheep; roundwood (1992) 9,000 cu m; fish catch (1991) 2,996, principally marine fish and shellfish. Mining and quarrying: some quarrying to support local construction industry. Manufacturing (1987): bread 2,459; soap 604; coconut oil 330; ice 191[6]; palm oil 177; limes 22[6]; corn (maize) flour 18[6]; sawn wood 3,272 cu m; beer 28,540 hectolitres; bottled water 13,750 hectolitres; soft drinks 10,460 hectolitres; other products include clothing, bricks, and clay products. Construction (1972): buildings authorized 44 (5,561 sq m, of which residential 3,698, mixed residential-commercial 1,361, commercial 502). Energy production (consumption): electricity (kW-hr; 1992) 15,000,000 (15,000,000); coal, none (n.a.); crude petroleum, none (n.a.); petroleum products (metric tons; 1992) none (24,000); natural gas, none (n.a.).
Household income and expenditure. Average household size (1981): 4.0; income per household: n.a.; sources of income: n.a.; expenditure: n.a.
Population economically active (1991): total 49,216; activity rate of total population 41.0% (participation rates [1981]: ages 15–64, 61.1%; female 32.4%; unemployed 30.7%[5]).

Earnings indexes (1981 = 100)

	1981	1982	1983	1984	1985	1986
Agricultural sector	100.0	93.6	98.5	103.0	97.2	96.3
Nonagricultural sectors	100.0	101.4	100.7	107.7	107.7	123.8

Gross national product (at current market prices; 1993): U.S.$43,750,000 (U.S.$350 per capita).

Structure of gross domestic product and labour force

	1992 in value Db '000,000	1992 % of total value	1991 labour force	1991 % of labour force
Agriculture	3,852	27.8	13,592	27.6
Mining	...	...		
Manufacturing	933	6.7	1,510	3.1
Public utilities			269	0.6
Construction	851	6.2	2,866	5.8
Transportation and communications	3,801	27.5	2,186	4.4
Trade			4,451	9.0
Finance	...	...	176	0.4
Pub. admin., defense	3,195	23.1	5,592	11.4
Services	1,200	8.7	2,369	4.8
Other	...	...	16,205[7]	32.9[7]
TOTAL	13,832	100.0	49,216	100.0

Land use (1992): meadows and pastures 1.0%; agricultural and under permanent cultivation 38.6%; forest, built-on, wasteland, and other 60.4%.

Foreign trade[8]

Balance of trade (current prices)

	1985	1986	1987	1988	1989	1990
Db '000,000	−571	−517	−380	−397	−1,047	−1,261
% of total	47.4%	40.5%	35.1%	19.5%	46.1%	51.2%

Imports (1992): U.S.$30,800,000 (capital goods 30.8%, food and other agricultural products 14.0%, mineral fuels and lubricants 9.1%). *Major import sources* (1987): Portugal 33.7%; East Germany 12.1%; Spain 11.3%; Angola 8.8%; West Germany 8.4%; France 6.5%; The Netherlands 5.4%; Norway 4.2%; Belgium-Luxembourg 3.5%.
Exports (1992): U.S.$5,500,000 (cocoa 60.0%). *Major export destinations* (1988): West Germany 52.3%; East Germany 20.2%; The Netherlands 12.7%.

Transport and communications

Transport. Railroads: none. Roads (1991): total length 149 mi, 240 km (paved 41.7%). Vehicles (1987): passenger cars 2,600; trucks and buses 300. Merchant marine (1992): vessels (100 gross tons and over) 4; total deadweight tonnage 2,277. Air transport (1990): passenger-mi 5,000,000, passenger-km 8,000,000; short ton-mi cargo 700,000, short ton-km cargo 1,000,000; airports (1994) with scheduled flights 2.
Communications. Daily newspapers: none; 2 government weeklies (circulation, n.a.). Radio (1993): total number of receivers 31,000 (1 per 4.0 persons). Television: none. Telephones (1991): 3,105 (1 per 39 persons).

Education and health

Education (1989)

	schools	teachers	students	student/ teacher ratio
Primary (age 6–13)	64	559	19,822	35.5
Secondary (age 14–18)	11[9]	318	7,446	23.4
Voc., teacher tr.	2[9]	18[10]	289	...
Higher	...	...	700[11]	...

Educational attainment (1981). Percentage of population age 25 and over having: no formal schooling 56.6%; incomplete primary education 18.0%; primary 19.2%; incomplete secondary 4.6%; complete secondary 1.3%; postsecondary 0.3%. *Literacy* (1981): total population age 15 and over literate 28,114 (54.2%); males literate 17,689 (70.2%); females literate 10,425 (39.1%).
Health (1989): physicians 61 (1 per 1,881 persons); hospital beds (1983) 640 (1 per 158 persons); infant mortality rate per 1,000 live births (1993) 64.9.
Food (1988–90): daily per capita caloric intake 2,153 (vegetable products 95%, animal products 5%); 92% of FAO recommended minimum requirement.

Military

Total active duty personnel: a gendarmerie of about 900 men was to be established in the early 1990s. *Military expenditure as percentage of GNP* (1980): 1.6% (world 5.4%); per capita expenditure U.S.$6.

[1]Multiparty system effective as of January 1991 elections; National People's Assembly was dissolved on July 10, 1994. Legislative elections took place on Oct. 2, 1994. [2]Preliminary. [3]1981. [4]1988. [5]1987. [6]1983. [7]Includes 15,148 unemployed. [8]Import figures are c.i.f. [9]1984–85. [10]Vocational teachers only. [11]Students abroad, 1982–83.

Saudi Arabia

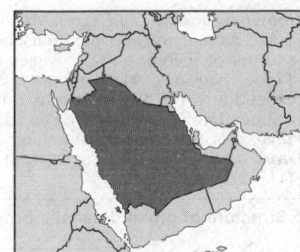

Official name: al-Mamlakah
al-'Arabīyah as-Sa'ūdīyah (Kingdom
of Saudi Arabia).
Form of government: monarchy.
Head of state and government: King.
Capital: Riyadh.
Official language: Arabic.
Official religion: Islam.
Monetary unit: 1 Saudi riyal
(SRls) = 100 halalah; valuation (Oct.
7, 1994) 1 U.S.$ = SRls 3.75;
1 £ = SRls 5.97.

Area and population

Geographic Regions		area		population
Administrative Regions [1]	Capitals	sq mi	sq km	1985 estimate
al-Gharbīyah (Western)	—	...	...	3,043,189
al-Bāḥah	al-Bāḥah	...	...	...
al-Madīnah	Medina (al-Madīnah)	...	...	...
Makkah	Mecca (Makkah)	...	...	...
al-Janūbīyah (Southern)	—	...	...	625,017
'Asīr	Abha	...	...	...
Jīzān	Jīzān	...	...	...
Najrān	Najrān	...	...	...
ash-Shamālīyah (Northern)	—	...	...	679,476
al-Hudūd ash-Shamālīyah (Northern Borders)	'Ar'ar	...	...	...
al-Jawf	Sakākah	...	...	...
Tabūk	Tabūk	...	...	...
ash-Sharqīyah (Eastern)	—	...	...	3,030,765
ash-Sharqīyah (Eastern)	ad-Dammām	...	...	...
al-Wūsṭā (Central)	—	...	...	3,632,092
Ḥā'il	Ḥā'il	...	...	...
al-Qaṣīm	Buraydah	...	...	...
ar-Riyāḍ	Riyadh (ar-Riyāḍ)	...	...	...
TOTAL		865,000	2,240,000	11,010,539[2]

Demography

Population (1994): 17,947,000.
Density (1994): persons per sq mi 20.7, persons per sq km 8.0.
Urban-rural (1990): urban 77.3%; rural 22.7%.
Sex distribution (1992): male 55.86%; female 44.14%.
Age breakdown (1992): under 15, 42.6%; 15–29, 27.0%; 30–44, 20.0%; 45–59, 6.9%; 60–74, 2.8%; 75 and over, 0.7%.
Population projection: (2000) 21,718,000; (2010) 29,074,000.
Doubling time: 24 years.
Ethnic composition (1983): Saudi 82.0%; Yemeni 9.6%; other Arab 3.4%; other 5.0%.
Religious affiliation (1980): Muslim (mostly Sunnī) 98.8%; Christian 0.8%; other 0.4%.
Major cities (1980): Riyadh (ar-Riyāḍ) 1,308,000[3]; Jiddah 1,500,000[4]; Mecca (Makkah) 550,000; aṭ-Ṭā'if 300,000.

Vital statistics

Birth rate per 1,000 population (1992): 36.1 (world avg. 26.0).
Death rate per 1,000 population (1992): 4.6 (world avg. 9.2).
Natural increase rate per 1,000 population (1992): 31.5 (world avg. 16.8).
Total fertility rate (avg. births per childbearing woman; 1992): 5.5.
Marriage rate per 1,000 population: n.a.
Divorce rate per 1,000 population: n.a.
Life expectancy at birth (1992): male 68.9 years; female 72.3 years.
Major causes of death per 100,000 population: n.a.; however, principal infectious diseases include malaria, diarrheal diseases, cholera, trachoma, cerebrospinal meningitis, yellow fever, typhoid, tuberculosis, and lung infections. Parasitic infections, motor vehicle accidents, and metabolic disorders are also significant.

National economy

Budget (1993). Revenue: SRls 169,150,000,000 (1990; oil revenues 72.8%). Expenditures: SRls 196,950,000,000 (defense and security 30.3%, education 17.3%, health and social development 7.2%, transportation and communications 4.6%, economic resource development 4.5%).
Production (metric tons except as noted). Agriculture, forestry, fishing (1993): wheat 3,600,000, barley 1,100,000, dates 560,000, tomatoes 490,000, watermelons 420,000, grapes 120,000, cucumbers and gherkins 100,000, potatoes 87,000, eggplants 75,000, pumpkins, squash, and gourds 65,000, carrots 24,000, millet 11,000; livestock (number of live animals) 7,100,000 sheep, 3,400,000 goats, 420,000 camels, 210,000 cattle, 100,000 asses, 86,000,000 chickens; fish catch (1992) 44,008. Mining and quarrying (1992): gypsum 375,000; gold 5,626 kg. Manufacturing (1992): cement 15,300,000; steel 1,900,000; fuel oils 176,000,000 barrels; diesel oil 170,500,000 barrels; gasoline and naphtha 170,000,000 barrels; jet fuel 60,000,000 barrels; asphalt and related products 35,070,000 barrels. Construction (1991): residential 16,077,677 sq m; nonresidential 2,204,894 sq m. Energy production (consumption): electricity (kW-hr; 1992) 48,620,000,000 (48,620,000,000); coal, n.a. (n.a.); crude petroleum (barrels; 1992) 3,026,000,000 (573,200,000); petroleum products (metric tons; 1992) 88,464,000 (35,022,000); natural gas (cu m; 1992) 34,407,000,000 (34,407,000,000).
Land use (1992): forested 0.9%; meadows and pastures 55.8%; agricultural and under permanent cultivation 1.7%; built-on, waste, and other 41.6%.
Tourism: receipts from visitors (1989) U.S.$2,050,000,000; expenditures by nationals abroad (1988) U.S.$2,000,000,000.
Pilgrims to Mecca from abroad (1989): 774,560.

Population economically active (1988): total 5,368,804; activity rate of total population 36.3% (participation rates: ages 15–64, 59.1%; female 3.5%).

Price and earnings indexes (1990 = 100)							
	1988	1989	1990	1991	1992	1993	1994[5]
Consumer price index	97.0	98.0	100.0	104.9	104.8	105.9	106.5
Earnings index	...	...	...	...	...	...	...

Public debt (external, outstanding; 1991): U.S.$2,893,000,000.
Gross national product (1992): U.S.$126,320,000,000 (U.S.$7,940 per capita).

Structure of gross domestic product and labour force				
	1992		1990	
	in value[6] SRls '000,000	% of total value	labour force	% of labour force
Agriculture	27,600	6.2	569,200	9.9
Mining	159,000	35.7	3,500	0.1
Oil sector			40,800	0.8
Manufacturing	31,000	7.0	374,900	6.5
Construction	37,900	8.5	944,100	16.4
Public utilities	900	0.2	126,900	2.2
Transp. and commun.	28,900	6.5	262,300	4.5
Trade	30,700	6.9	898,300	15.6
Finance	27,500[7]	6.2[7]	99,000	1.7
Pub. admin., defense	86,100	19.3	624,800	10.8
Services	8,400	1.9	1,822,000	31.6
Other	7,700[8]	1.7[8]		
TOTAL	445,700	100.0[9]	5,771,800	100.0[9]

Household income and expenditure. Average household size (1986) 6.6; income per household: n.a.; sources of income: n.a.; expenditure (1988)[10]: food 37%, housing 21%, transportation and communications 15%, clothing 8%, household furnishings 7%, education and entertainment 2%.

Foreign trade[11]

Balance of trade (current prices)						
	1986	1987	1988	1989	1990	1991
SRls '000,000,000	+8.6	+16.5	+15.1	+32.3	+82.1	+77.2
% of total	6.1%	10.5%	9.0%	17.9%	32.8%	27.5%

Imports (1991): SRls 108,881,300,000 (transport equipment 21.0%, machinery and appliances 19.4%, metals and metal articles 9.1%, textiles and clothing 8.4%, chemicals 7.4%, live animals and animal products 5.2%). *Major import sources:* U.S. 20.2%; Japan 13.7%; U.K. 11.3%; Germany 7.8%; Switzerland 4.9%; Italy 4.6%; France 4.0%; South Korea 3.0%; Taiwan 2.0%.
Exports (1991): SRls 178,974,100,000 (crude petroleum 78.1%, refined petroleum products 13.2%, other 8.7%). *Major export destinations:* U.S. 22.9%; Japan 16.0%; The Netherlands 6.0%; South Korea 5.6%; Singapore 5.1%; France 4.6%; Italy 4.3%; Bahrain 3.3%; Brazil 2.8%.

Transport and communications

Transport. Railroads (1989–90): route length (1991) 864 mi, 1,390 km; passenger-mi 93,800,000, passenger-km 151,000,000; short ton-mi cargo 487,700,000, metric ton-km cargo 712,000,000. Roads (1993): total length 94,157 mi, 151,532 km (paved 40%). Vehicles (1992): passenger cars 2,762,132; trucks and buses 2,286,541. Merchant marine (1992): vessels (100 gross tons and over) 301; total deadweight tonnage 1,381,651. Air transport (1993)[12]: passenger-mi 11,540,000,000, passenger-km 18,571,801,000; short ton-mi cargo 492,006,000, metric ton-km cargo 718,316,000; airports (1994) with scheduled flights 25.
Communications. Daily newspapers (1992): total number 10; total circulation 579,300[13]; circulation per 1,000 population 34[13]. Radio (1993): 5,000,000 receivers (1 per 3.5 persons). Television (1993): 4,500,000 receivers (1 per 3.9 persons). Telephones[14] (1992): 1,568,370 (1 per 10.7 persons).

Education and health

Education (1992–93)	schools	teachers	students	student/ teacher ratio
Primary (age 6–12)	10,228	141,930	2,025,948	14.3
Secondary (age 13–18)	4,643[15]	89,171	1,033,521	11.6
Voc., teacher tr.	190[15]	3,804	39,840	10.5
Higher	72[15]	11,682[16]	163,688[16]	14.0

Educational attainment (1986). Percentage of population age 25 and over having: no formal schooling 31.8%; primary, secondary, or higher education 68.2%. *Literacy* (1990): percentage of population age 15 and over literate 62.4%; males literate 73.1%; females literate 48.1%.
Health (1991): physicians 25,543 (1 per 523 persons); hospital beds 40,923 (1 per 359 persons); infant mortality rate per 1,000 live births 69.0.
Food (1988–90): daily per capita caloric intake 2,929 (vegetable products 84%, animal products 16%); 121% of FAO recommended minimum requirement.

Military

Total active duty personnel (1994): 104,000 (army 67.3%, navy 11.5%, air force 21.2%). *Military expenditure as percentage of GNP* (1989): 16.0% (world 4.9%); per capita expenditure U.S.$897.

[1]13 administrative regions created September 1993. [2]Preliminary 1992 census total 16,927,294; detail, n.a. [3]1981 estimate. [4]1983 estimate. [5]April. [6]In purchasers' value at current prices. [7]Finance includes real estate and business services. [8]Other includes import duties. [9]Detail does not add to total given because of rounding. [10]Urban middle-income households only. [11]Import figures are f.o.b. in balance of trade and c.i.f. in commodities and trading partners. [12]Domestic and international operation of Saudi Arabian Airlines. [13]Circulation for 9 dailies only. [14]Main telephone lines only. [15]1990–91. [16]1991–92.

Senegal

Official name: République du Sénégal
  (Republic of Senegal).
Form of government: multiparty
  republic with one legislative house
  (National Assembly [120]).
Chief of state: President.
Head of government: Prime Minister.
Capital: Dakar.
Official language: French.
Official religion: none.
Monetary unit: 1 CFA franc
  (CFAF) = 100 centimes; valuation
  (Oct. 7, 1994) 1 U.S.$ = CFAF 526.67;
  1 £ = CFAF 837.67.

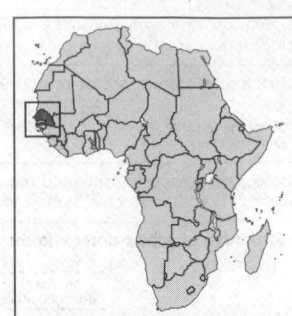

Area and population		area		population
				1992
Regions	Capitals	sq mi	sq km	estimate
Dakar	Dakar	212	550	1,735,000
Diourbel	Diourbel	1,683	4,359	705,000
Fatick	Fatick	3,064	7,935	549,000
Kaolack	Kaolack	6,181	16,010	901,000
Kolda	Kolda	8,112	21,011	656,000
Louga	Louga	11,270	29,188	515,000
Saint-Louis	Saint-Louis	17,034	44,117	719,000
Tambacounda	Tambacounda	23,012	59,602	427,000
Thiès	Thiès	2,549	6,601	1,054,000
Ziguinchor	Ziguinchor	2,834	7,339	443,000
TOTAL		75,951	196,712	7,704,000

Demography

Population (1994): 8,112,000.
Density (1994): persons per sq mi 106.8, persons per sq km 41.2.
Urban-rural (1988): urban 38.6%; rural 61.4%.
Sex distribution (1988): male 48.65%; female 51.35%.
Age breakdown (1988): under 15, 47.4%; 15–29, 26.1%; 30–44, 13.6%; 45–59,
  7.9%; 60 to 70, 3.0%; 70 and over, 2.0%.
Population projection: (2000) 9,519,000; (2010) 12,424,000.
Doubling time: 23 years.
Ethnic composition (1988): Wolof 43.7%; Peul- (Fulani-) Tukulor 23.2%;
  Serer 14.0%; Diola 5.5%; Malinke (Mandingo) 4.6%; other 9.0%.
Religious affiliation (1988): Sunnī Muslim 94.0%; Christian, predominantly
  Roman Catholic, 4.9%; traditional beliefs and other 1.1%.
Major cities (1992): Dakar 1,729,823; Thiès 201,350; Kaolack 179,894; Ziguin-
  chor 148,831; Saint-Louis 125,717.

Vital statistics

Birth rate per 1,000 population (1990–95): 44.0 (world avg. 26.0).
Death rate per 1,000 population (1990–95): 13.0 (world avg. 9.2).
Natural increase rate per 1,000 population (1991): 31.0 (world avg. 16.8).
Total fertility rate (avg. births per childbearing woman; 1991): 6.2.
Marriage rate per 1,000 population: n.a.
Divorce rate per 1,000 population: n.a.
Life expectancy at birth (1991): male 54.0 years; female 56.0 years.
Major causes of death (percentage of officially confirmed deaths from infec-
  tious diseases only; 1988): malaria 44.8%; tetanus 17.8%; meningitis 15.3%;
  tuberculosis of respiratory system 10.4%.

National economy

Budget (1993). Revenue: CFAF 479,600,000,000 (1990; current revenue 86.0%,
  of which import duties 28.0%, personal and corporate income taxes 17.0%,
  value-added taxes 16.9%, personal property taxes 3.1%; aid, grants, and
  subsidies 13.9%). Expenditures: CFAF 539,100,000,000 (1990; debt service
  22.4%; public services 16.0%; agriculture 13.9%; education 11.0%; defense
  6.1%; transportation and communications 4.9%; public order and security
  4.5%; industry 3.2%; health 2.3%).
Production (metric tons except as noted). Agriculture, forestry, fishing (1993):
  sugarcane 850,000, millet 657,000, peanuts (groundnuts) 628,000, paddy rice
  189,000, corn (maize) 125,000, sorghum 98,000, seed cotton 50,000; livestock (number of live animals) 4,400,000 sheep, 3,118,000 goats, 2,750,000
  cattle, 320,000 pigs; roundwood (1991) 5,098,000 cu m; fish catch (1991)
  338,335. Mining and quarrying (1992): calcium phosphate 2,283,500; cement 603,100; aluminum phosphate mining ceased in 1989. Manufacturing
  (1992): paint and varnish 2,774,000; refined petroleum products 600,200;
  peanut oil 164,200; fertilizers 158,900; wheat flour 136,800; fresh meat 44,-
  250; sugar 42,000; soap 42,000; canned fish 23,996; carbonated beverages
  238,000 hectolitres; beer 170,000 hectolitres; plastic footwear 644,000 pairs.
  Construction (authorized; 1992)[1]: residential 338,000 sq m; nonresidential
  18,000 sq m. Energy production (consumption): electricity (kW-hr; 1992)
  762,000,000 (762,000,000); coal, none (n.a.); crude petroleum (barrels; 1992)
  none (5,935,000); petroleum products (metric tons; 1992) 755,000 (799,000);
  natural gas, none (n.a.).
Population economically active (1992): total 2,620,000; activity rate of total
  population 34% (participation rates [1988]: over age 10, 46.2%; female
  26.0%; unemployed 12.0%).

Price and earnings indexes (1985 = 100)							
	1986	1987	1988	1989	1990	1991	1992
Consumer price index	106.4	101.8	99.9	100.4	100.7	98.9	98.8
Hourly earnings index[2]	100.0	100.0	100.0	104.7	109.5	109.5	109.5

Household income and expenditure[3]. Average household size (1988) 8.8; average annual income per household (1975) CFAF 1,105,800 (U.S.$5,160);
  sources of income (1975): wages and salaries 51.6%, remittances and gifts
  17.5%, pensions, social security, and related benefits 12.5%, other 18.4%;
  expenditure (1979): food and tobacco 57.5%, housing, maintenance, and
  utilities 18.4%, clothing 11.9%, transport 5.4%, other 6.8%.
Public debt (external, outstanding; 1992): U.S.$2,932,000,000.
Gross national product (at current market prices; 1993): U.S.$5,879,000,000
  (U.S.$730 per capita).

Structure of gross domestic product and labour force				
	1992			
	in value CFAF '000,000,000	% of total value	labour force	% of labour force
Agriculture	334.2	22.0	2,120,000	81.0
Mining	11.2	0.7		
Manufacturing	226.0	14.9		
Public utilities	31.6	2.1	160,000	6.0
Construction	48.4	3.2		
Transp. and commun.	169.5	11.2		
Trade	415.8	27.4	340,000	13.0
Finance				
Services	282.2	18.6		
Pub. admin., defense				
TOTAL	1,519.1[4]	100.0[4]	2,620,000	100.0

Tourism (1991): receipts from visitors U.S.$171,000,000; expenditures by na-
  tionals abroad U.S.$103,000,000.
Land use (1992): forested 54.3%; meadows and pastures 16.1%; agricultural
  and under permanent cultivation 12.2%; other 17.4%.

Foreign trade

Balance of trade (current prices)						
	1987	1988	1989	1990	1991	1992
CFAF '000,000,000	− 125.4	− 145.5	− 168.4	− 150.3	− 134.4	− 152.8
% of total	25.6%	29.2%	27.6%	26.6%	25.4%	30.0%

Imports (1992): CFAF 330,900,000,000 (machinery and transportation equipment 20.2%, petroleum products 12.7%, rice 7.4%, dairy products 4.8%,
  pharmaceutical products 3.6%, paper and paper products 3.5%). *Major import sources* (1979): France 32.9%; Nigeria 7.5%; United States
  5.3%; Côte d'Ivoire 4.5%; Spain 4.2%; West Germany 3.6%; Japan 3.6%;
  The Netherlands 3.1%; Thailand 2.9%; Gabon 2.7%; Pakistan 2.3%.
Exports (1992): CFAF 178,100,000,000 (petroleum products 12.3%, canned
  fish 12.2%, phosphates 8.2%, fresh fish 7.5%, peanut oil 7.4%, shellfish
  7.3%, cotton 4.1%). *Major export destinations* (1990): France 34.9%; India
  10.6%; Mali 7.1%; Italy 7.0%; The Netherlands 5.3%; Spain 2.9%; Côte
  d'Ivoire 2.8%; Cameroon 2.5%; Japan 2.0%; Philippines 1.8%.

Transport and communications

Transport. Railroads: (1993) route length 562 mi, 904 km; (1991) passenger-
  mi 108,000,000, passenger-km 174,000,000; short ton-mi cargo 418,000,000,
  metric ton-km cargo 610,000,000. Roads (1991): total length 9,625 mi, 15,490
  km (paved 27%). Vehicles (1991): passenger cars 97,000; trucks and buses
  40,000. Merchant marine (1992): vessels (100 gross tons and over) 183; total
  deadweight tonnage 27,473. Air transport (1990)[5]: passenger-mi 144,276,000,
  passenger-km 232,329,000; short ton-mi cargo 26,971,000, metric ton-km
  cargo 39,374,000; airports (1994) with scheduled flights 5.
Communications. Daily newspapers (1990): total number 1; total circulation
  45,000; circulation per 1,000 population 6.2. Radio (1993): total number of
  receivers 850,000 (1 per 10.8 persons). Television (1993): total number of
  receivers 61,000 (1 per 129 persons). Telephones (1992): 58,100 main lines
  (1 per 136 persons).

Education and health

Education (1990–91)				student/
	schools	teachers	students	teacher ratio
Primary (age 6–12)	2,458	13,394	708,299	52.9
Secondary (age 13–18)	321	4,791[6]	173,490	34.8[6]
Vocational	13	259[6]	6,435	24.6[6]
Higher	18	770[7]	18,862	19.3[7]

Educational attainment (1988). Percentage of population age 6–34 having: no
  formal schooling 62.6%; primary education 25.7%; secondary 8.4%; higher
  0.8%; other 2.5%. *Literacy* (1988): percentage of total population age 15
  and over literate 28.6%; males literate 38.8%; females literate 19.4%.
Health (1992): physicians 520 (1 per 15,350 persons); hospital beds 7,408 (1
  per 1,041 persons); infant mortality rate per 1,000 live births (1991) 86.0.
Food (1988–90): daily per capita caloric intake 2,322 (vegetable products 91%,
  animal products 9%); 98% of FAO recommended minimum requirement.

Military

Total active duty personnel (1994): 13,350 (army 89.9%, navy 5.2%, air force
  4.9%). *Military expenditure as percentage of GNP* (1992): 2.1% (world [1991]
  4.2%); per capita expenditure U.S.$16.

---

[1]Capital region only. [2]January 1; index refers to the *S.M.I.G.* (*salaire minimum interprofessionnel garanti*), a form of minimum professional wage. [3]Traditional African
households in Dakar. [4]Detail does not add to total given because of rounding. [5]Air
Afrique only. [6]1989. [7]1988.

Seychelles

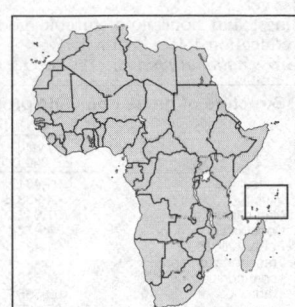

Official name: Repiblik Sesel (Creole);
Republic of Seychelles (English);
République des Seychelles (French).
Form of government: multiparty
republic with one legislative house
(National Assembly [33][1]).
Head of state and government:
President.
Capital: Victoria.
Official languages: none[2].
Official religion: none.
Monetary unit: 1 Seychelles rupee
(SR) = 100 cents; valuation (Oct. 7,
1994) 1 U.S.$ = SR 4.93;
1 £ = SR 7.85.

Area and population

Island Groups	Capital	area sq mi	area sq km	population 1987 census
Central (Granitic) group				
La Digue and satellites		6	15	1,026
Mahé and satellites	Victoria	61	158	61,183
Praslin and satellites	—	16	42	5,002
Silhouette	—	8	20	191
Other islands	—	2	4	0
Outer (Coralline) islands		83	214	296
TOTAL		176	455[3]	68,598

Demography

Population (1994): 71,800.
Density (1994): persons per sq mi 408.0, persons per sq km 157.8.
Urban-rural (1990): urban 59.3%; rural 40.7%.
Sex distribution (1989): male 49.96%; female 50.04%.
Age breakdown (1989): under 15, 35.1%; 15–29, 31.5%; 30–44, 15.3%; 45–59, 9.2%; 60–74, 6.5%; 75 and over, 2.4%.
Population projection: (2000) 75,000; (2010) 80,500.
Doubling time: 46 years.
Ethnic composition (1983): Seychellois Creole (mixture of Asian, African, and European) 89.1%; Indian 4.7%; Malagasy 3.1%; Chinese 1.6%; English 1.5%.
Religious affiliation (1987): Roman Catholic 88.6%; other Christian (mostly Anglican) 8.5%; Hindu 0.4%; other 2.5%.
Major city (1987): Victoria 24,325.

Vital statistics

Birth rate per 1,000 population (1993): 23.4 (world avg. 26.0); (1989) legitimate 27.2%; illegitimate 72.8%.
Death rate per 1,000 population (1993): 8.3 (world avg. 9.2).
Natural increase rate per 1,000 population (1993): 15.1 (world avg. 16.8).
Total fertility rate (avg. births per childbearing woman; 1993): 2.3.
Marriage rate per 1,000 population (1987): 9.4.
Divorce rate per 1,000 population (1985): 0.7.
Life expectancy at birth (1994): male 66.0 years; female 73.0 years.
Major causes of death per 100,000 population (1985–89): diseases of the circulatory system 263.5, of which cerebrovascular disease 57.4; malignant neoplasms (cancers) 116.9; diseases of the respiratory system 77.1, of which pneumonia 49.0; accidents and adverse effects 44.4; infectious and parasitic diseases 42.9; diseases of the digestive system 40.5.

National economy

Budget (1994). Revenue: SR 1,389,200,000 (customs taxes and duties 46.9%, transfers from Social Security Fund 14.4%, business taxes 9.3%, administrative fees 6.9%, fees and fines 5.2%, dividends and interest 5.2%, grants 2.6%). Expenditures: SR 1,326,700,000 (debt service 14.0%, capital projects 13.2%, education 13.0%, social security 8.3%, health 7.3%, tourism and transport 6.4%, defense 4.7%).
Tourism (1993): receipts from visitors SR 607,400,000; expenditures by nationals abroad U.S.$16,000,000[4].
Land use (1991): forested 18.5%; agricultural and under permanent cultivation 22.2%; built-on, wasteland, and other 59.3%.
Gross national product (at current market prices; 1992): U.S.$376,000,000 (U.S.$5,450 per capita).

Structure of gross domestic product and labour force

	1992 in value SR '000,000	1992 % of total value	1993 labour force[5]	1993 % of labour force
Agriculture	84.4	3.8	2,153	8.5
Mining, manufacturing, and construction	382.0	17.2	4,605	18.2
Tourism	386.5	17.4	4,570	18.1
Transportation and communications	513.1	23.1	4,092	16.2
Finance	168.0	7.6	} 9,818	} 39.0
Public admin., defense	295.4	13.3		
Other	390.9	17.6		
TOTAL	2,221.1	100.0	25,238	100.0

Production (metric tons except as noted). Agriculture, forestry, fishing (1992): coconuts 7,000, bananas 2,000, copra 1,000, cinnamon 777[6], tea 246[6]; livestock (number of live animals) 19,000 pigs, 5,000 goats, 2,000 cattle, 185,200[7] chickens; fish catch (1993) 5,447, of which (1989) jack 36.9%, snapper 20.8%,

mackerel 6.7%, kawakawa 5.3%. Mining and quarrying (1985): guano 4,500. Manufacturing (1993): canned tuna 4,531; soft drinks 70,450 hectolitres; beer and stout 65,230 hectolitres; cigarettes 65,000,000 units. Energy production (consumption): electricity (kW-hr; 1992) 109,000,000 (109,000,000); coal, none (n.a.); crude petroleum, none (n.a.); petroleum products (metric tons; 1992) none (49,000); natural gas, none (n.a.).
Population economically active (1993): total 25,238; activity rate of total population 35.4% (participation rates [1989]: ages 15–64, 74.3%; female 42.5%; unemployed [1987] 6.3%).

Price and earnings indexes (1990 = 100)

	1987	1988	1989	1990	1991	1992	1993
Consumer price index	93.0	94.8	96.3	100.0	102.0	105.3	106.7
Monthly earnings index	...	...	...	100.0	103.8	123.5	126.0

Public debt (external, outstanding; 1992): U.S.$147,200,000.
Household income and expenditure. Average household size (1987) 4.5; average annual income per household (1978) SR 18,480 (U.S.$2,658); sources of income: wages and salaries 77.2%, self employment 3.8%, transfer payments 3.2%; expenditure (1983–84): food and beverages 53.9%, housing 13.6%, energy and water 9.1%, household and personal goods 6.6%, transportation 6.4%, clothing and footwear 4.2%, recreation 1.4%.

Foreign trade

Balance of trade (current prices)

	1988	1989	1990	1991	1992	1993
SR '000,000	−546.4	−627.8	−692.3	−660.0	−760.8	−588.4
% of total	61.7%	63.9%	53.4%	56.7%	63.0%	52.7%

Imports (1993): SR 1,235,883,000 (manufactured goods 32.8%, of which metal manufactures 9.0%, paper products 2.0%; machinery and transport equipment 25.1%, of which vehicles 6.8%, communications equipment 4.0%; electrical machinery and parts 3.7%; food and live animals 15.7%, of which cereals 3.3%, vegetables and fruits 3.0%, dairy products 2.0%; mineral fuels, lubricants, and related materials 14.2%, of which petroleum products 14.0%; chemicals 6.6%; beverages and tobacco 3.5%). *Major import sources:* United Kingdom 13.3%; Yemen 13.1%; Singapore 13.1%; South Africa 12.8%; United States 7.7%; France 6.2%; Japan 5.8%; Germany 3.2%; Italy 2.6%; Thailand 2.1%; India 2.1%.
Exports (1993): SR 263,430,000[8] (petroleum products 55.5%[9]; canned tuna 22.1%; other fish 5.7%; cinnamon bark 0.7%; food, beverages, tobacco, and chemicals 0.7%[9]; copra 0.3%). *Major export destinations*[10]: United Kingdom 15.9%; France 4.2%; Réunion 2.6%.

Transport and communications

Transport. Railroads: none. Roads (1993): total length 199 mi, 321 km (paved 68%). Vehicles (1991): passenger cars 4,700; trucks and buses 1,600. Merchant marine (1992): vessels (100 gross tons and over) 9; total deadweight tonnage 3,337. Air transport (1993): passenger arrivals 119,000, passenger departures 120,000; metric ton cargo unloaded 2,982, metric ton cargo loaded 635; airports (1994) with scheduled flights 2.
Communications. Daily newspapers (1990): total number 1; total circulation 3,200; circulation per 1,000 population 47. Radio (1992): total number of receivers 30,000 (1 per 2.4 persons). Television (1992): total number of receivers 8,200 (1 per 8.7 persons). Telephones (1993): 10,909[11] (1 per 6.5 persons).

Education and health

Education (1994)

	schools	teachers	students	student/ teacher ratio
Primary (age 6–15)	25[12]	575	9,767	17.0
Secondary (age 16–18)	4[7]	425	6,315	14.9
Voc., teacher tr.	1[7]	201	1,702	8.5

Educational attainment (1987). Percentage of population age 12 and over having: no formal schooling 7.8%; primary education 51.5%; some secondary 12.2%; complete secondary 13.4%; vocational 9.9%; postsecondary 3.1%; unspecified 2.1%. *Literacy* (1987): total population age 15 and over literate 37,984 (84.2%); males literate 18,427 (82.9%); females literate 19,557 (85.7%).
Health (1993): physicians 70 (1 per 1,019 persons); hospital beds 424 (1 per 168 persons); infant mortality rate per 1,000 live births 13.0.
Food (1988–90): daily per capita caloric intake 2,356 (vegetable products 85%, animal products 15%); 101% of FAO recommended minimum requirement.

Military

Total active duty personnel (1993): 1,100[13]. *Military expenditure as percentage of GNP* (1989): 4.2% (world 4.9%); per capita expenditure U.S.$206[14].

[1]Includes 11 nonelective seats (one-half the elected number), which are appointive, allocated according to each party's share of the popular vote. [2]Creole, English, and French are all national languages per 1993 constitution. [3]Detail docs not add to total given because of rounding. [4]1992. [5]Excludes self-employed and domestic workers. [6]1993. [7]1986. [8]Includes SR 184,978,000 of reexports. [9]Items reexported. [10]Domestic export only. [11]Number of lines. [12]1988. [13]All services form part of the army. [14]At prices of 1987.

Sierra Leone

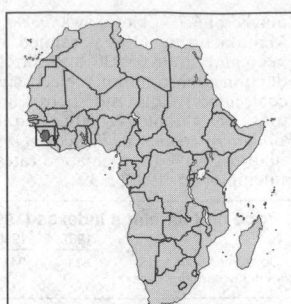

Official name: Republic of
Sierra Leone.
Form of government: military regime.
Head of state and government:
Chairman, Supreme Council of
State.
Capital: Freetown.
Official language: English.
Official religion: none.
Monetary unit: 1 leone (Le) = 100
cents; valuation (Oct. 7, 1994)
1 U.S.$ = Le 585.55; 1 £ = Le 931.32.

Area and population		area		population
Provinces				1985
Districts	Capitals	sq mi	sq km	census[1]
Eastern Province	Kenema	6,005	15,553	960,551
Kailahun	Kailahun	1,490	3,859	233,839
Kenema	Kenema	2,337	6,053	337,055
Kono	Sefadu	2,178	5,641	389,657
Northern Province	Makeni	13,875	35,936	1,262,226
Bombali	Makeni	3,083	7,985	315,914
Kambia	Kambia	1,200	3,108	186,231
Koinadugu	Kabala	4,680	12,121	183,286
Port Loko	Port Loko	2,208	5,719	329,344
Tonkolili	Magburaka	2,704	7,003	247,451
Southern Province	Bo	7,604	19,694	740,510
Bo	Bo	2,015	5,219	268,671
Bonthe (incl. Sherbro)	Bonthe	1,339	3,468	105,007
Moyamba	Moyamba	2,665	6,902	250,514
Pujehun	Pujehun	1,585	4,105	116,318
Western Area[2]	Freetown	215	557	554,243
TOTAL		27,699	71,740	3,517,530

Demography

Population (1994): 4,616,000.
Density (1994): persons per sq mi 166.6, persons per sq km 64.3.
Urban-rural (1992): urban 33.8%; rural 66.2%.
Sex distribution (1990): male 49.12%; female 50.88%.
Age breakdown (1985): under 15, 41.4%; 15–29, 26.1%; 30–44, 17.1%; 45–59, 10.3%; 60–74, 4.5%; 75 and over, 0.6%.
Population projection: (2000) 5,395,000; (2010) 6,944,000.
Doubling time: 26 years.
Ethnic composition (1983): Mende 34.6%; Temne 31.7%; Limba 8.4%; Kono 5.2%; Bullom-Sherbro 3.7%; Fulani 3.7%; Kuranko 3.5%; Yalunka 3.5%; Kissi 2.3%; other 3.4%.
Religious affiliation (1993): Sunnī Muslim 60.0%; traditional beliefs 30.0%; Christian 10.0%[3].
Major cities (1985): Freetown 469,776; Koidu–New Sembehun 80,000; Bo 26,000; Kenema 13,000; Makeni 12,000.

Vital statistics

Birth rate per 1,000 population (1990–95): 48.1 (world avg. 26.0); legitimate, n.a.; illegitimate, n.a.
Death rate per 1,000 population (1990–95): 21.6 (world avg. 9.2).
Natural increase rate per 1,000 population (1990–95): 26.5 (world avg. 16.8).
Total fertility rate (avg. births per childbearing woman; 1990–95): 6.5.
Marriage rate per 1,000 population: n.a.
Divorce rate per 1,000 population: n.a.
Life expectancy at birth (1990–95): male 41.4 years; female 44.6 years.
Major causes of death per 100,000 population: n.a.; however, the major diseases are malaria, tuberculosis, leprosy, whooping cough, measles, tetanus, and diarrhea.

National economy

Budget (1992–93). Revenue: Le 54,294,000,000 (customs and excise taxes 61.8%, direct taxes 24.3%, nontax revenue 13.9%). Expenditures: Le 82,126,-000,000 (recurrent expenditure 77.9%, development expenditure 22.1%).
Public debt (external, outstanding; 1992): U.S.$680,000,000.
Tourism (1992): receipts from visitors U.S.$17,000,000; expenditures by nationals abroad U.S.$3,000,000.
Production (metric tons except as noted). Agriculture, forestry, fishing (1993): rice 486,000, cassava 97,000, sugarcane 70,000, pulses 40,000, coffee 36,000, palm kernels 35,000, plantains 31,000, millet 26,000, sorghum 24,000, cacao beans 24,000, tomatoes 23,000, peanuts (groundnuts) 21,000, sweet potatoes 12,000, corn (maize) 12,000; livestock (number of live animals) 333,000 cattle, 278,000 sheep, 153,000 goats, 50,000 pigs, 6,000,000 chickens; roundwood (1992) 3,225,000 cu m; fish catch (1991) 50,000. Mining and quarrying (1993): bauxite 1,164,000; rutile (a titanium ore) 150,302; diamonds 200,300 carats; gold 5,314 oz. Manufacturing (1991): salt 209; nails 80; beer and stout 47,640 hectolitres; soft drinks 28,800 hectolitres; paint 9,000 litres; cigarettes 706,000,000 units. Construction (value added in Le; 1992–93): 4,972,100,000. Energy production (consumption): electricity (kW-hr; 1992) 230,000,000 (230,000,000); coal, none (n.a.); crude petroleum (barrels; 1992) none (1,554,000); petroleum products (metric tons; 1992) 162,000 (122,000); natural gas, none (n.a.).
Household income and expenditure. Average household size (1983) 4.7; average annual income per household (1984): U.S.$320; sources of income (1984): self-employment 61.6%, wages and salaries 27.9%, other 10.5%; expenditure (1986): food, beverages, and tobacco 67.7%, housing 14.1%, transportation and communications 8.2%, clothing and footwear 2.8%, furniture, furnish-

ings, and household durable goods 2.2%, recreation, entertainment, and education 1.4%, health 1.1%.
Gross national product (1993): U.S.$625,500,000 (U.S.$140 per capita).

Structure of gross domestic product and labour force				
	1992–93		1988	
	in value Le '000,000	% of total value	labour force[4]	% of labour force[4]
Agriculture	94,401.9	27.5	7,262	10.4
Mining	44,938.6	13.1	5,845	8.3
Manufacturing	37,642.0	11.0	8,616	12.3
Construction	4,972.1	1.4	7,259	10.3
Public utilities	1,436.6	0.4	2,713	3.9
Transportation and communications	34,878.9	10.2	7,718	11.0
Trade	68,695.7	20.0 }	5,058	7.2
Finance	37,462.5	10.9 }		
Pub. admin., defense	18,453.1	5.4 }	25,714	36.6
Services	621.7	0.2 }		
Other	...	...	...	...
TOTAL	343,503.1	100.0[5]	70,185	100.0

Population economically active (1985): total 1,352,000; activity rate of total population 36.9% (participation rates: ages 15–64, 62.9%; female 33.7%; unemployed [registered; 1986] 9.0%).

Price index (1990 = 100)							
	1987	1988	1989	1990	1991	1992	1993
Consumer price index	22.2	29.1	47.4	100.0	202.7	335.4	409.9

Land use (1992): forested 28.5%; meadows and pastures 30.8%; agricultural and under permanent cultivation 7.5%; other 33.2%.

Foreign trade

Balance of trade (current prices)						
	1988	1989	1990	1991	1992	1993
Le '000,000	– 1,260.3	– 1,327.9	+ 1,475.9	+ 3,903.8	+ 14,449.7	– 7,692.0
% of total	15.9%	7.4%	3.6%	4.6%	10.9%	5.4%

Imports (1993): Le 84,121,100,000 (food and live animals 38.2%; machinery and transport equipment 15.2%; minerals, fuels, and lubricants 14.8%; basic manufactured goods 10.1%; chemicals 8.5%). *Major import sources* (1990): Nigeria 29.0%; United Kingdom 14.4%; Germany 10.1%; United States 8.2%; The Netherlands 5.6%.
Exports (1993): Le 65,265,300,000 (rutile 47.0%; bauxite 21.1%; diamonds 17.0%; cocoa 3.2%; coffee 2.0%). *Major export destinations:* United States 32.2%; United Kingdom 20.2%; Germany 11.0%; The Netherlands 3.4%.

Transport and communications

Transport. Railroads (1990): length 52 mi, 84 km. Roads (1991): total length 5,505 mi, 8,860 km (paved 18%). Vehicles (1992): passenger cars 32,258; trucks and buses 11,961. Merchant marine (1992): vessels (100 gross tons and over) 62; total deadweight tonnage 18,384. Air transport (1985)[6]: passenger-mi 68,290,000, passenger-km 109,903,000; short ton-mi cargo 1,400,000, metric ton-km cargo 2,044,000; airports (1994) with scheduled flights 1.
Communications. Daily newspapers (1991): total number 1; total circulation 10,000; circulation per 1,000 population 2.3. Radio (1994): 1,000,000 receivers (1 per 4.6 persons). Television (1993): 25,000 receivers (1 per 180 persons). Telephones (1992): 56,200 (1 per 77.9 persons).

Education and health

Education (1991–92)				
	schools	teachers	students	student/ teacher ratio
Primary (age 5–11)	1,792	10,051	315,146	31.4
Secondary (age 12–18)	217	3,924	72,516	18.5
Voc., teacher tr.	30	750	6,929	9.2
Higher[7]	2	600	4,752	7.9

Educational attainment (1985). Percentage of population age 5 and over having: no formal schooling 64.1%; primary education 18.7%; secondary 9.7%; higher 1.5%. *Literacy* (1990): total population age 15 and over literate 477,600 (20.7%); males literate 343,800 (30.7%); females literate 133,800 (11.3%).
Health: physicians (1992) 404 (1 per 10,832 persons); hospital beds (1988) 4,025 (1 per 980 persons); infant mortality rate per 1,000 live births (1985–90) 154.
Food (1988–90): daily per capita caloric intake 1,899 (vegetable products 96%, animal products 4%); 83% of FAO recommended minimum requirement.

Military

Total active duty personnel (1994): 6,150 (army 97.6%, navy 2.4%, air force, none). *Military expenditure as percentage of GNP* (1991): 2.3% (world 4.2%); per capita expenditure U.S.$3.

---

[1]Preliminary figures exclude adjustment for underenumeration; adjusted total is 3,700,000. [2]Not officially a province; the administration of the Western Area is split among Greater Freetown (the city and its suburbs) and other administrative bodies. [3]Christian (1980) 9.1%, of which Protestant 4.7%, Roman Catholic 2.2%, Anglican 1.2%. [4]Registered employment only. [5]Detail does not add to total given because of rounding. [6]International flights only. [7]1989–90.

Singapore

Official name: Hsin-chia-p'o
Kung-ho-kuo (Mandarin Chinese);
Republik Singapura (Malay);
Singapore Kudiyarasu (Tamil);
Republic of Singapore (English).
Form of government: unitary multiparty
republic with one legislative house
(Parliament [87[1]]).
Chief of state: President.
Head of government: Prime Minister.
Capital: Singapore.
Official languages: Chinese; Malay;
Tamil; English.
Official religion: none.
Monetary unit: 1 Singapore dollar
(S$) = 100 cents; valuation (Oct. 7,
1994) 1 U.S.$ = S$1.48; 1 £ = S$2.36.

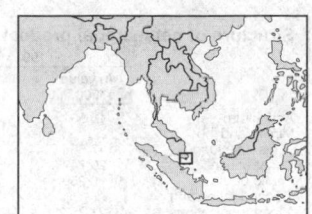

Population (1990 census)

Census division[2]	population	Census division[2]	population	Census division[2]	population
Alexandra	27,245	Henderson	18,445	Nee Soon East	58,651
Aljunied	51,669	Hong Kah Central	48,379	Nee Soon South	49,771
Ang Mo Kio	35,814	Hong Kah North	33,265	Pasir Panjang	35,824
Ayer Rajah	44,977	Hong Kah South	37,900	Paya Lebar	41,903
Bedok	22,032	Hougang	36,774	Potong Pasir	32,992
Boon Lay	39,249	Jalan Besar	28,298	Punggol	68,270
Boon Teck	22,652	Jalan Kayu	34,907	Queenstown	19,676
Braddell Heights	47,738	Joo Chiat	35,777	Radin Mas	35,730
Brickworks	10,593	Jurong	74,696	Sembawang	28,039
Bukit Batok	44,918	Kaki Bukit	32,782	Serangoon Gardens	44,702
Bukit Gombak	46,149	Kallang	34,170	Siglap	36,022
Bukit Merah	18,666	Kampong Chai Chee	33,928	Tampines East	41,474
Bukit Panjang	95,827	Kampong Glam	29,481	Tampines North	73,634
Bukit Timah	47,056	Kampong Kembangan	33,510	Tampines West	38,833
Buona Vista	23,873	Kampong Ubi	40,682	Tanah Merah	32,314
Cairnhill	48,445	Kebun Baru	36,878	Tanglin	43,544
Changi	50,003	Kim Keat	28,538	Tanjong Pagar	29,217
Changkat	41,995	Kim Seng	23,683	Teck Ghee	26,622
Cheng San	27,821	Kolam Ayer	22,420	Telok Blangah	29,157
Chong Boon	32,174	Kreta Ayer	29,631	Thomson	71,345
Chong Pang	38,613	Kuo Chuan	26,968	Tiong Bahru	27,468
Chua Chu Kang	43,465	Leng Kee	28,886	Toa Payoh	22,811
Clementi	37,635	Macpherson	23,764	Ulu Pandan	42,923
Eunos	52,976	Marine Parade	31,003	West Coast	46,052
Fengshan	27,285	Moulmein	33,872	Whampoa	18,285
Geylang Serai	36,800	Mountbatten	23,891	Yio Chu Kang	28,589
Geylang West	34,560	Noo Soon Central	47,032	Yuhua	32,733
				TOTAL	3,016,379

Demography

Area: 247.5 sq mi, 641.0 sq km.
Population (1994)[3]: 2,933,000.
Density (1994): persons per sq mi 11,851, persons per sq km 4,576.
Urban-rural: urban 100.0%.
Sex distribution (1993): male 50.45%; female 49.55%.
Age breakdown (1993): under 15, 23.1%; 15–29, 24.8%; 30–44, 28.7%; 45–59, 13.9%; 60 and over, 9.5%.
Population projection: (2000) 3,317,000; (2010) 4,072,000.
Doubling time: 56 years.
Ethnic composition (1993): Chinese 77.5%; Malay 14.2%; Indian[4] 7.1%; other 1.2%.
Religious affiliation (1991): Buddhist, Taoist, and other traditional beliefs 53.9%; Muslim 15.4%; Christian 12.6%; Hindu 3.6%; nonreligious 14.5%.
Major cities: Singapore has no separately defined cities within its borders.

Vital statistics

Birth rate per 1,000 population (1993): 17.0 (world avg. 26.0).
Death rate per 1,000 population (1993): 4.6 (world avg. 9.2).
Natural increase rate per 1,000 population (1993): 12.4 (world avg. 16.8).
Total fertility rate (avg. births per childbearing woman; 1993): 1.8.
Marriage rate per 1,000 population (1992): 9.1.
Divorce rate per 1,000 population (1992): 1.4.
Life expectancy at birth (1992): male 73.7 years; female 78.3 years.
Major causes of death per 100,000 population (1992): malignant neoplasms 123.5; cardiovascular diseases 120.1; diseases of the respiratory system 86.6; cerebrovascular diseases 59.8; accidents, poisoning, and violence 19.2.

National economy

Budget (1992–93). Revenue: S$18,577,800,000 (tax revenue 68.8%, development fund account 17.9%, nontax revenue 7.3%, sinking fund account 6.0%). Expenditures: S$16,641,600,000 (administration 28.0%, government development 16.0%, debt servicing 14.6%, manpower 14.2%, grants 10.6%).
Public debt (external, outstanding; 1990): U.S.$3,481,000,000.
Production (metric tons except as noted). Agriculture, forestry, fishing (1992): vegetables 5,198, fruits 280; livestock (number of live animals) 3,000,000 chickens, 400,000 ducks; fish catch 9,198. Mining and quarrying (value added in S$; 1992): granite 72,000,000. Manufacturing (value added in S$; 1992): electronic products 8,669,800,000; transport equipment 1,936,900,000; petroleum products 1,791,600,000; metal products 1,641,900,000; chemical products 1,487,000,000; nonelectrical machinery 1,446,300,000; printing and publishing 1,140,300,000. Construction (1992): residential 4,222,000 sq m; nonresidential 2,729,700 sq m. Energy production (consumption): electricity (kW-hr; 1991) 16,597,000,000 (16,597,000,000); crude petroleum (barrels;

1991) none (326,368,000); petroleum products (metric tons; 1991) 36,900,000 (11,104,000).
Household income and expenditure. Average household size (1984) 3.9; income per household (1987–88) S$26,560 (U.S.$12,900); sources of income (1987–88): wages 81.2%, self-employment 16.8%, transfer payments and other 2.0%; expenditure (1990): food 18.7%, recreation and education 15.3%, transportation and communications 13.7%, rent and utilities 9.2%, furniture and household equipment 8.9%, clothing and footwear 7.4%, health 4.4%.
Gross national product (1992): U.S.$44,323,000,000 (U.S.$15,790 per capita).

Structure of gross domestic product and labour force

	1993			
	in value S$'000,000[5]	% of total value	labour force[6]	% of labour force[6]
Agriculture	158.5	0.2	3,900	0.2
Quarrying	54.6	0.1	300	—
Manufacturing	19,640.1	27.6	429,500	27.0
Construction	4,761.6	6.7	102,100	6.4
Public utilities	1,450.6	2.0	7,500	0.5
Transp. and commun.	10,427.2	14.6	166,800	10.5
Trade	12,752.5	17.9	363,600	22.8
Finance	19,145.1	26.9	173,400	10.9
Services	6,971.7	9.8	345,000	21.7
Other	−4,159.0[7]	−5.8[7]	...	...
TOTAL	71,211.9	100.0	1,592,100	100.0

Population economically active (1991): total 1,554,316; activity rate of total population 56.3% (participation rates: ages 15 and over, 73.2%; female 39.8%; unemployed 1.7%).

Price and earnings indexes (1985 = 100)

	1987	1988	1989	1990	1991	1992	1993
Consumer price index	99.1	100.6	103.0	106.6	110.2	112.7	115.4
Monthly earnings index	104.0	112.6	123.6	135.1	147.6	158.6	169.6

Land use (1991): forested 4.9%; agricultural 1.6%; other 93.5%.
Tourism (1992): receipts from visitors U.S.$5,204,000,000; expenditures by nationals abroad U.S.$2,340,000,000.

Foreign trade[8]

Balance of trade (current prices)

	1988	1989	1990	1991	1992	1993
S$'000,000	−4,159	−4,143	−8,559	−5,770	−7,490	−10,338
% of total	2.6%	2.3%	4.3%	2.7%	3.5%	4.1%

Imports (1993): S$137,602,800,000 (office machines 8.8%, crude petroleum 7.5%, telecommunications apparatus 7.0%, generators 5.3%, petroleum products 3.3%, scientific instruments 3.0%, motor vehicles 2.4%). *Major import sources:* Japan 21.9%; Malaysia 16.5%; United States 16.2%; Thailand 4.1%; Taiwan 4.0%; Saudi Arabia 3.9%; Hong Kong 3.2%.
Exports (1993): S$119,473,400,000 (office machines 22.3%, petroleum products 9.9%, telecommunications apparatus 9.7%, generators 3.3%, optical instruments 2.3%, clothing 2.1%). *Major export destinations:* United States 20.3%; Malaysia 14.2%; Hong Kong 8.7%; Japan 7.5%; Thailand 5.7%; Germany 4.0%; Taiwan 3.9%; United Kingdom 3.0%.

Transport and communications

Transport. Railroads (1992): length 26 km. Roads (1993): total length 2,989 km (paved 97%). Vehicles (1993): passenger cars 321,922; trucks and buses 132,455. Merchant marine (1992): vessels (100 gross tons and over) 946; total deadweight tonnage 14,929,172. Air transport (1992): passenger-km 37,105,000,000; metric ton-km cargo 2,306,204,000; airports (1994) 1.
Communications. Daily newspapers (1992): total number 8; total circulation 916,102; circulation per 1,000 population 325. Radio (1993): 870,000 receivers (1 per 3.3 persons). Television (1993): 650,000 receivers (1 per 4.4 persons). Telephones (1992): 1,153,000[9] (1 per 2.5 persons).

Education and health

Education (1992)

	schools	teachers	students	student/ teacher ratio
Primary (age 6–11)	194	10,188	262,599	25.8
Secondary (age 12–18)	160	9,278	182,149	19.6
Voc., teacher tr.	21	1,594	27,984	17.6
Higher	7	3,721	65,775	17.7

Educational attainment (1980). Percentage of population age 25 and over having: no schooling or incomplete primary 43.7%; primary education 38.3%; secondary 14.6%; postsecondary 3.4%. *Literacy* (1990): total population age 10 and over literate 90.7%; males literate 95.7%; females literate 85.6%.
Health (1992): physicians 3,962 (1 per 725 persons); hospital beds 9,726 (1 per 295 persons); infant mortality rate per 1,000 live births 5.0.
Food (1988–90): daily per capita caloric intake 3,121 (vegetable products 76%, animal products 24%); 136% of FAO recommended minimum requirement.

Military

Total active duty personnel (1993): 55,500 (army 81.1%, navy 8.1%, air force 10.8%). *Military expenditure as percentage of GNP* (1989): 5.1% (world 4.9%); per capita expenditure U.S.$557.

[1]Includes 6 nonelected members. [2]The census divisions have no administrative function. [3]De jure population. [4]Includes Sri Lankan. [5]At prices of 1985. [6]Employed only. [7]Imputed bank service charges. [8]Import figures are f.o.b. in balance of trade and c.i.f. for commodities and trading partners. [9]Lines installed.

Slovakia

Official name: Slovenská Republika (Slovak Republic).
Form of government: unitary multiparty republic with one legislative house (National Council [150]).
Chief of state: President.
Head of government: Prime Minister.
Capital: Bratislava.
Official language: Slovak.
Official religion: none.
Monetary unit: 1 Slovak koruna[1] (Sk) = 100 halura; valuation (Oct. 7, 1994) 1 U.S.$ = Sk 31.19; 1 £ = Sk 49.61.

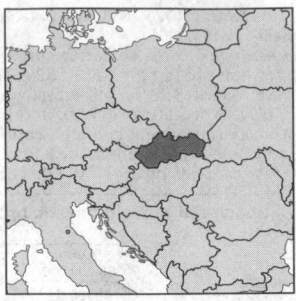

Area and population

Electoral Regions[3]	Capitals	area sq mi	area sq km	population 1993[2] estimate
Stredné Slovensko	Banská Bystrica	6,943	17,982	1,623,659
Východné Slovensko	Košice	6,253	16,193	1,523,965
Zapadné Slovensko	Bratislava	5,595	14,492	1,719,876
Capital city				
Bratislava	—	142	368	446,655
TOTAL		18,933	49,036	5,314,155

Demography

Population (1994): 5,352,000.
Density (1994): persons per sq mi 282.7, persons per sq km 109.1.
Urban-rural (1991): urban 56.8%; rural 43.2%.
Sex distribution (1993): male 48.81%; female 51.19%.
Age breakdown (1993): under 15, 24.1%; 15–29, 23.1%; 30–44, 23.0%; 45–59, 14.8%; 60–74, 11.4%; 75 and over, 3.6%.
Population projection: (2000) 5,510,000; (2010) 5,774,000.
Doubling time: not applicable; population growth is negligible.
Ethnic composition (1992): Slovak 85.7%; Hungarian 10.7%; Gypsy 1.5%; Czech 1.1%; Ruthenian 0.3%; Ukrainian 0.3%; German 0.1%; other 0.3%.
Religious affiliation (1991): Roman Catholic 60.3%; nonreligious and atheist 9.7%; Protestant 7.9%, of which Slovak Evangelical 6.2%, Reformed Christian 1.6%; Greek Catholic 3.4%; Eastern Orthodox 0.7%; other 18.0%.
Major cities (1993): Bratislava 446,655; Košice 237,336; Nitra 90,866; Prešov 90,069; Banská Bystrica 85,631; Žilina 85,005.

Vital statistics

Birth rate per 1,000 population (1993): 14.1 (world avg. 26.0); legitimate 90.2%; illegitimate 9.8%.
Death rate per 1,000 population (1993): 10.1 (world avg. 9.2).
Natural increase rate per 1,000 population (1993): 4.0 (world avg. 16.8).
Total fertility rate (avg. births per childbearing woman; 1992): 1.9.
Marriage rate per 1,000 population (1993): 6.4.
Divorce rate per 1,000 population (1993): 1.5.
Life expectancy at birth (1992): male 66.6 years; female 75.4 years.
Major causes of death per 100,000 population (1992): diseases of the circulatory system 521.0; malignant neoplasms (cancers) 200.0; diseases of the respiratory system 77.0; accidents, poisoning, and violence 76.0; diseases of the digestive system 52.0; endocrine and metabolic disorders 19.0.

National economy

Budget (1992). Revenue: Kčs 115,876,000,000 (receipts from enterprises 80.6%; taxes 17.2%). Expenditures: Kčs 124,809,000,000 (education, health, social welfare, and culture 71.9%; defense 3.5%).
Public debt (external, outstanding): n.a.
Production (metric tons except as noted). Agriculture, forestry, fishing (1992): cereals 3,528,000 (of which wheat 1,697,000, barley 1,038,000, corn [maize] 676,000, rye 76,000), sugar beets 1,326,000, potatoes 658,000; livestock (number of live animals) 2,269,000 pigs, 1,182,000 cattle (of which 429,000 dairy cows), 572,000 sheep, 12,000 horses, 13,267,000 poultry; roundwood 3,956,000 cu m; fish catch, n.a. Mining and quarrying (1993): iron ore 930,000; lead-zinc ore 320,000; copper ore 290,000. Manufacturing (1992): crude steel 3,798,000; cement 3,374,000; pig iron 2,952,000; plastic and resins 426,000; flour 409,000; phosphate fertilizers 200,269; cotton fabrics 68,767,000 m; beer 3,686,000 hectolitres; other alcoholic beverages 580,000 hectolitres; refrigerators and freezers 551,695 units; metalworking machines 2,595 units. Construction (1991): residential 1,147,000 sq m. Energy production (consumption): electricity (kW-hr; 1992) 22,255,000,000 (27,069,000,000[4]); coal (metric tons; 1993) 3,190,000 (n.a.); crude petroleum (barrels; 1991) 529,000 (n.a.); petroleum products, n.a. (n.a.); natural gas (cu m; 1992) 277,000,000 (n.a.).
Population economically active (1993): total 2,548,733; activity rate of total population 47.9% (participation rates [1992]: ages 15–64, 74.5%; female 42.8%; unemployed 14.4%).

Price and earnings indexes (1990 = 100)

	1986	1987	1988	1989	1990	1991	1992
Consumer price index[5]	88.8	89.0	89.2	90.5	100.0	156.1	171.7
Annual earnings index	88.7	90.4	93.4	95.8	100.0	115.0	136.5

Gross national product (at current market prices; 1992): U.S.$10,229,000,000 (U.S.$1,930 per capita).

Structure of net material product and labour force

	1991 in value Kčs '000,000[1]	1991 % of total value	1992 labour force	1992 % of labour force
Agriculture	15,931	5.9	247,371	10.1
Mining and manufacturing	147,566	54.6	585,093	23.9
Construction	20,747	7.7	168,431	6.9
Public utilities	3,259	1.2	45,136	1.8
Transportation and communications	21,357	7.9	163,206	6.7
Trade	23,445	8.7	216,321	8.8
Finance	5,102	1.9	145,644	5.9
Pub. admin., defense	7,305	2.7	83,591	3.4
Services	25,377	9.4	385,229	15.7
Other	—	—	412,842	16.8
TOTAL	270,089	100.0	2,452,864	100.0

Land use (1992): forested 42.7%; meadows and pastures 20.6%; agricultural and under permanent cultivation 31.9%; other 4.8%.
Household income and expenditure. Average household size (1991) 3.0; income per household (1991) Kčs 105,227[1, 6] (U.S.$3,595[6]); sources of income (1992): wages and salaries 71.8%, transfer payments 16.3%, other 11.9%; expenditure (1992): food and beverages 26.8%, taxes 14.0%, clothing and footwear 8.9%, housing 7.6%, household durable goods 3.9%, other 42.7%.
Tourism (1992): receipts U.S.$213,000,000; expenditures U.S.$155,000,000.

Foreign trade

Balance of trade (current prices)

	1991	1992
Kčs '000,000[1]	−14,064	−5,158
% of total	6.7%	2.4%

Imports (1992): Kčs 109,983,000,000[1] (machinery and transport equipment 32.7%; petroleum and petroleum products 27.8%; chemical products 9.7%; semimanufactured products 8.0%; raw materials 7.0%). *Major import sources:* former U.S.S.R. 34.7%; Germany 20.8%; Austria 10.1%; Italy 5.6%; Poland 3.2%.
Exports (1992): Kčs 104,825,000,000[1] (semimanufactured products 41.9%; machinery and transport equipment 17.3%; manufactured goods 15.2%; chemical products 11.2%; food, beverages, and tobacco 8.0%). *Major export destinations:* Germany 24.4%; former U.S.S.R. 16.8%; Poland 8.0%; Austria 7.4%; Hungary 6.9%; Italy 5.5%.

Transport and communications

Transport. Railroads (1992): length 2,275 mi, 3,661 km; passenger-mi 3,388,000,000, passenger-km 5,543,000,000; short ton-mi cargo 11,437,000,000, metric ton-km cargo 16,697,000,000. Roads (1992): total length 11,110 mi, 17,880 km (paved, n.a.). Vehicles (1992): passenger cars 953,239; trucks and buses 81,350. Merchant marine: n.a. Air transport: n.a.; airports (1994) with scheduled flights 4.
Communications. Daily newspapers (1992): total number 21; total circulation 378,000; circulation per 1,000 population 71. Radio (1992): total number of receivers 1,068,185 (1 per 5.0 persons). Television (1992): total number of receivers 1,279,101 (1 per 4.1 persons). Telephones (1992): 1,362,178 (1 per 3.9 persons).

Education and health

Education (1992–93)

	schools	teachers	students	student/ teacher ratio
Primary (age 6–14)	2,472	39,867	704,119	17.7
Secondary (age 15–18)	165	4,659	63,522	13.6
Voc., teacher tr.	234	7,812	103,793	13.3
Higher	14	8,103	64,311	7.9

Educational attainment (1991). Percentage of adult population having: incomplete primary education 0.5%; primary and incomplete secondary 30.6%; complete secondary 58.6%; higher 9.4%; unknown 0.9%. *Literacy* (1990): total population age 15 and over literate 3,980,202 (100%); males literate 1,916,410 (100%); females literate 2,063,792 (100%).
Health (1992): physicians 15,767 (1 per 336 persons); hospital beds 52,613 (1 per 100 persons); infant mortality rate per 1,000 live births 12.6.
Food (1990): daily per capita caloric intake 3,335 (vegetable products 63%, animal products 37%); 135% of FAO recommended minimum requirement.

Military

Total active duty personnel (1994): 47,000 (army 70.2%, air force 29.8%). *Military expenditure as percentage of GNP:* n.a.; per capita expenditure U.S.$53.

[1]The Slovak koruna was introduced Feb. 8, 1993, at par with the former Czechoslovak koruna (Kčs), which it replaced. For settlement of obligations existing prior to February 8 between the Czech and Slovak republics, an interim currency, the clearing koruna (XCS) was introduced. [2]January. [3]Until 1990 Slovakia comprised four regions, subdivided into 38 administrative districts. After 1990 only the districts were retained. In 1994 a new system of administration was under discussion. [4]1991. [5]Cost-of-living index; wage earners only. [6]Worker's household.

Slovenia

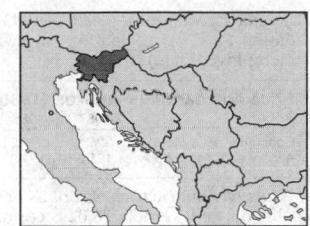

Official name: Republika Slovenija
(Republic of Slovenia).
Form of government: multiparty
republic with two legislative
houses (State Council [40]; State
Assembly [90]).
Head of state: President.
Head of government: Prime Minister.
Capital: Ljubljana.
Official language: Slovene.
Official religion: none.
Monetary unit: 1 Slovene tolar
(SIT) = 100 stotin; valuation (Oct. 7,
1994) 1 Yugoslav dinar (Din) = 1.11
tolarji; 1 U.S.$ = 121.82 tolarji;
1 £ = 193.75 tolarji.

Area and population (1991 census)

Districts	area sq km[1]	population	Districts	area sq km[1]	population
Ajdovscina	352	22,632	Metlika	108	8,184
Brežice	268	24,724	Mozirje	508	16,533
Celje	230	64,736	Murska Sobota	692	63,744
Čerknica	483	15,020	Nova Gorica	605	59,126
Crnomelj	486	18,374	Novo Mesto	759	58,970
Domžale	240	44,185	Ormož	212	17,570
Dravograd	105	8,507	Pesnica	169	18,083
Gornja Radgona	210	21,315	Piran	45	16,768
Grosuplje	421	28,151	Postojna	492	20,283
Hrastnik	58	11,059	Ptuj	645	68,753
Idrija	425	17,207	Radlje ob Dravi	346	16,929
Ilirska Bistrica	480	14,624	Radovljica	641	34,286
Izola	28	13,770	Ravne na Koroškem	304	27,377
Jesenice	375	31,939	Ribnica	256	12,736
Kamnik	289	28,766	Ruše	209	15,440
Kočevje	766	18,523	Šentjur pri Celju	240	19,101
Kopor	273	45,301	Sevnica	200	18,950
Kranj	453	72,185	Sežana	698	23,925
Krško	345	28,576	Škofja Loka	512	38,303
Lasko	250	19,014	Slovenj Gradec	286	20,976
Lenart	204	17,217	Slovenska Bistrica	369	32,516
Lendava	256	26,143	Slovenske Konjice	222	21,992
Litija	328	18,709	Šmarje pri Jelšah	400	31,888
Ljubljana-Bežigrad	46	58,150	Tolmin	939	20,975
Ljubljana-Center	5	28,351	Trbovlje	58	19,337
Ljubljana-Moste Polje	152	72,081	Trebnje	308	17,722
Ljubljana-Šiška	156	82,845	Tržič	155	14,975
Ljubljana-Vič Rudnik	543	80,180	Velenje	182	42,674
Ljutomer	179	18,744	Vrhnika	169	19,459
Logatec	173	9,764	Zagorje ob Savi	147	16,960
Maribor	359	151,221	Žalec	349	39,340
			TOTAL	20,256	1,965,986

Demography

Population (1994): 2,001,000.
Density (1994): persons per sq mi 255.9, persons per sq km 98.8.
Urban-rural (1991): urban 48.9%; rural 51.1%.
Sex distribution (1993): male 48.50%; female 51.50%.
Age breakdown (1993): under 15, 19.6%; 15–29, 22.3%; 30–44, 23.7%; 45–59, 17.6%; 60–74, 12.5%; 75 and over, 4.3%.
Population projection: (2000) 2,000,000; (2010) 1,975,000.
Doubling time: not applicable; doubling time exceeds 100 years.
Ethnic composition (1991): Slovene 87.8%; Croat 2.8%; Serb 2.4%; Bosnian 1.4%; Magyar 0.4%; other 5.2%.
Religious affiliation (1991): Roman Catholic 83.6%; other 16.4%, predominantly Christian adherents of the Slovene Old Catholic Church, a few Protestant denominations, and the Eastern Orthodox Church; there are also small Muslim and Jewish communities.
Major cities (1991): Ljubljana 276,133; Maribor 108,122; Celje 41,279; Kranj 37,318; Velenje 27,665.

Vital statistics

Birth rate per 1,000 population (1992): 10.0 (world avg. 26.0); legitimate 72.3%; illegitimate 27.7%.
Death rate per 1,000 population (1992): 9.7 (world avg. 9.2).
Natural increase rate per 1,000 population (1992): 0.3 (world avg. 16.8).
Total fertility rate (avg. births per childbearing woman; 1992): 1.3.
Marriage rate per 1,000 population (1992): 4.6.
Divorce rate per 1,000 population (1992): 1.1.
Life expectancy at birth (1990–91): male 69.5 years; female 77.4 years.
Major causes of death per 100,000 population (1992): circulatory diseases 425.6; cancers 248.7; accidents 91.4; respiratory diseases 39.1; digestive diseases 36.6; endocrine and metabolic disorders 33.6.

National economy

Budget (1992). Revenue: SIT 231,215,000,000. Expenditures: SIT 231,199,000,000.
Tourism (1990): receipts U.S.$852,000,000; expenditures, n.a.
Production (metric tons except as noted). Agriculture, forestry, fishing (1992): potatoes 368,000, grapes 213,000, corn (maize) 207,000, wheat 178,000, sugar beets 97,000, plums 9,000; livestock (number of live animals) 602,000 pigs, 504,000 cattle, 21,000 sheep, 11,400,000 poultry; roundwood (1991) 2,098,000 cu m; fish catch 4,706, of which freshwater 938. Mining and quarrying (1991): lead-zinc ore 162,000; bauxite 48,000; mercury 9. Manufacturing (1992): cement 801,000; crude steel 297,000; aluminum ingots 84,809; soap and detergents 36,355; cotton yarn 13,379; leather footwear 9,492,000 pairs; refrigerators 661,000 units; bicycles 190,000 units; telephones 123,000 units. Construction (1991): residential 147,806 sq m; nonresidential 17,547 sq m. Energy production (consumption): electricity (kW-hr; 1992) 12,033,000,000 (11,645,000,000); coal (metric tons; 1992) 5,556,000 (5,363,000); crude petroleum (barrels; 1991) 17,584 (3,680,000); petroleum products (metric tons; 1991) 126,000 (1,586,000); natural gas (cu m; 1991) 19,271,000 (837,000,000).
Gross national product (1992): U.S.$12,744,000,000 (U.S.$6,330 per capita).

Structure of gross material product and labour force

	1991		1992	
	in value SIT '000,000	% of total value	labour force	% of labour force
Agriculture	17,223	6.2	80,319	9.0
Mining	} 114,592	40.9	327,524	36.7
Manufacturing				
Construction	13,015	4.6	45,514	5.1
Public utilities	14,926	5.3	11,603	1.3
Transp. and commun.	22,284	8.0	52,654	5.9
Trade	39,480	14.1	108,878	12.2
Finance	47,385	16.9	44,622	5.0
Pub. admin., defense	}		31,235	3.5
Services	11,520	4.0	190,088	21.3
Other		...	...	...
TOTAL	280,425	100.0	892,437	100.0

Population economically active (1992): total 892,437; activity rate of total population 45.5% (participation rates: ages 18–64, 68.3%; female 47.7%; unemployed 11.5%).

Price and earnings indexes (1990 = 100)

	1986	1987	1988	1989	1990	1991	1992
Consumer price index	0.2	0.4	1.1	15	100	218	656
Earnings index[2]	135	129	115	136	100	86	83

Land use (1992): forest 50.2%; pasture 27.7%; agricultural 14.9%; other 7.2%.
Household income and expenditure. Average household size (1991) 3.1; income per household (1990) Din 161,589 (U.S.$14,277); sources of income (1990): wages 59.4%, transfers 17.5%, self-employment 14.5%, other 8.6%; expenditure (1991): food 30.8%, housing 18.3%, transportation 12.7%, clothing 8.5%, energy 7.3%, education and entertainment 6.1%, drink and tobacco 5.2%, health care 5.0%, household durable goods 3.3%.

Foreign trade

Balance of trade (current prices)

	1987	1988	1989	1990	1991	1992
U.S.$'000,000	+35	+364	+192	−609	−257	+540
% of total	0.7%	5.9%	2.9%	6.9%	3.2%	4.2%

Imports (1992): SIT 502,442,000,000 (machinery and transport equipment 26.4%; basic manufactures 19.6%; consumer goods 18.1%, of which food 7.6%; chemicals 12.4%; mineral fuels 10.8%). *Major import sources:* Germany 22.7%; Croatia 13.9%; Italy 13.7%; Austria 8.1%; France 8.0%.
Exports (1992): SIT 540,803,000,000 (machinery and transport equipment 29.4%; consumer goods 28.3%, of which food 5.1%; basic manufactures 27.1%; chemicals 9.1%; raw materials except fuels 2.0%). *Major export destinations:* Germany 27.0%; Croatia 14.2%; Italy 13.4%; France 9.2%; Austria 5.1%.

Transport and communications

Transport. Railroads (1992): length 746 mi, 1,201 km; passenger-mi 340,000,000, passenger-km 547,000,000; short ton-mi cargo 1,762,000,000, metric ton-km cargo 2,573,000,000. Roads (1992): total length 9,192 mi, 14,794 km (paved 75%). Vehicles (1992): passenger cars 606,820; trucks and buses 33,957. Merchant marine (1992): vessels (100 gross tons and over) 22; total deadweight tonnage 596,944. Air transport (1992): passenger-mi 259,000,000, passenger-km 417,000,000; short ton-mi cargo 1,192,000, metric ton-km cargo 1,918,000; airports (1994) 1.
Communications. Daily newspapers (1991): total number 4; total circulation 303,000; circulation per 1,000 population 154. Radio (1989): 687,000 receivers (1 per 2.9 persons). Television (1989): 528,500 receivers (1 per 3.7 persons). Telephones (1992): 593,000 (1 per 3.4 persons).

Education[3] and health

Education (1991–92)

	schools	teachers	students	student/ teacher ratio
Primary (age 7–14)	845	14,936	222,339	14.8
Secondary (age 15–18)	226	8,688	101,880	11.7
Voc., teacher tr.	70	986	4,605	4.7
Higher	28	2,575	36,504	14.2

Educational attainment (1991). Percentage of population age 15 and over having: less than full primary education 13.7%; primary 27.9%; secondary 45.6%; postsecondary and higher 12.8%. *Literacy* (1991): virtually 100%.
Health: physicians (1990) 4,086 (1 per 489 persons); hospital beds (1991) 11,816 (1 per 167 persons); infant mortality rate per 1,000 live births (1992) 8.9.

Military

Total active duty personnel (1993): 15,000 (army 100%). *Military expenditure as percentage of GNP:* n.a.; per capita expenditure (1992) U.S.$171.

[1]One sq km is equal to approximately 0.3861 sq mi. [2]Based on worker real net personal income. [3]Includes adult education.

Solomon Islands

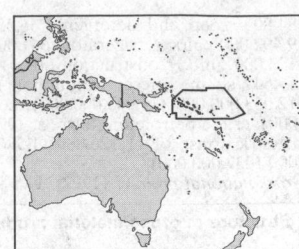

Official name: Solomon Islands.
Form of government: constitutional monarchy with one legislative house (National Parliament [47]).
Chief of state: British Monarch represented by Governor-General.
Head of government: Prime Minister.
Capital: Honiara.
Official language: English.
Official religion: none.
Monetary unit: 1 Solomon Islands dollar (SI$) = 100 cents; valuation (Oct. 7, 1994) 1 U.S.$ = SI$3.27; 1 £ = SI$5.20.

Area and population

		area		population
Provinces	**Capitals**	sq mi	sq km	1994 estimate
Central Islands	Tulagi	497	1,286	26,865
Guadalcanal	Honiara	2,060	5,336	55,104
Isabel	Buala	1,597	4,136	20,197
Makira	Kira Kira	1,231	3,188	26,037
Malaita	Auki	1,631	4,225	97,011
Temotu	Santa Cruz	334	865	19,175
Western	Gizo	3,595	9,312	83,978
Capital Territory				
Honiara	—	8	22	39,722
TOTAL		10,954[1]	28,370	368,089

Demography

Population (1994): 368,000.
Density (1994): persons per sq mi 33.6, persons per sq km 13.0.
Urban-rural (1986): urban 15.7%; rural 84.3%.
Sex distribution (1991): male 51.73%; female 48.27%.
Age breakdown (1991): under 15, 46.4%; 15–29, 27.2%; 30–44, 14.5%; 45–59, 7.8%; 60–74, 3.5%; 75 and over, 0.6%.
Population projection: (2000) 433,000; (2010) 569,000.
Doubling time: 21 years.
Ethnic composition (1986): Melanesian 94.2%; Polynesian 3.7%; other Pacific Islander 1.4%; European 0.4%; Asian 0.2%; other 0.1%.
Religious affiliation (1986): Christian 96.7%, of which Protestant 77.5%, Roman Catholic 19.2%; Baha'i 0.4%; traditional beliefs 0.2%; other and no religion 2.7%.
Major cities (1986)[2]: Honiara 35,288[3]; Gizo 3,727; Auki 3,262; Kira Kira 2,585; Buala 1,913.

Vital statistics

Birth rate per 1,000 population (1993): 37.0 (world avg. 26.0).
Death rate per 1,000 population (1993): 4.0 (world avg. 9.2).
Natural increase rate per 1,000 population (1993): 33.0 (world avg. 16.8).
Total fertility rate (avg. births per childbearing woman; 1993): 5.4.
Marriage rate per 1,000 population: n.a.
Divorce rate per 1,000 population: n.a.
Life expectancy at birth (1993): male 69.0 years; female 73.0 years.
Major causes of death per 100,000 population: n.a.; however, major diseases include malaria, influenza, diarrhea, conjunctivitis and yaws[4].

National economy

Budget (1992). Revenue: SI$228,400,000 (1991; taxes on foreign trade 46.8%, income taxes 29.2%, nontax revenue 14.3%, foreign grants 9.7%). Expenditures: SI$255,900,000 (1991; administrative 33.2%, interest payments 12.6%, capital expenditure 10.7%).
Tourism: receipts from visitors (1992) U.S.$6,000,000; expenditures by nationals abroad (1991) U.S.$13,000,000.
Land use (1991): forested 91.5%; meadows and pastures 1.4%; agricultural and under permanent cultivation 2.0%; other 5.1%.
Gross national product (at current market prices; 1993): U.S.$260,000,000 (U.S.$750 per capita).

Structure of gross domestic product and labour force

	1991		1993	
	in value SI$'000[5]	% of total value	labour force[6]	% of labour force
Agriculture	117,600	48.4	8,106	27.4
Mining	–700	–0.3	} 2,844	9.6
Manufacturing	9,000	3.7		
Construction	10,500	4.3	977	3.3
Public utilities	2,200	0.9	245	0.8
Transportation and communications	17,500	7.2	1,723	5.8
Trade	23,300	9.6	3,390	11.5
Finance	8,000	3.3	1,144	3.9
Pub. admin., defense	} 55,800	23.0	4,303	14.6
Services			6,845	23.1
Other	44,300	18.2	...	...
TOTAL	243,100[1]	100.0[1]	29,577	100.0

Household income and expenditure. Average household size (1986) 6.4; average annual income per household (1983) SI$1,010[7] (U.S.$1,160); sources of income (1983): wages and salaries 74.1%, self-employment, remittances, gifts, and other assistance 25.9%; expenditure (1990)[8]: food 51.1%, drinks and tobacco 13.7%, housing 8.8%, transportation 8.4%, clothing 3.9%.

Population economically active (1993): total 29,577[6]; activity rate of total population 8.3% (participation rates: ages 15–60 [1986] 98.6%; female 22.6%; unemployed, n.a.).

Price and earnings indexes (1985 = 100)

	1987	1988	1989	1990	1991	1992	1993
Consumer price index	126.1	147.2	169.1	183.9	211.6	234.3	255.1
Annual earnings index[6]	121.3	194.2	248.8	216.9	262.8	304.8	309.7

Production (metric tons except as noted). Agriculture, forestry, fishing (1993): palm oil and kernels 38,029, copra 29,057, coconut oil 4,286, cacao beans 3,297; livestock (number of live animals; 1992) 54,000 pigs, 13,000 cattle; roundwood 547,000 cu m; fish catch 32,486. Mining and quarrying (1992): gold 1,061 troy oz. Manufacturing (1992): processed fish 36,788; sawn timber 18,400 cu m; other major industries include beer brewing, soap and tobacco manufacturing, garment manufacturing, weaving, wood carving, fibreglass products, boatbuilding, and leatherworking. Construction (gross value in SI$ in Honiara; 1993): residential 7,764,000; nonresidential 7,661,000. Energy production (consumption): electricity (kW-hr; 1993) 48,928,000 (43,473,000); coal, none (n.a.); petroleum products (metric tons; 1992) none (52,000); natural gas, none (n.a.).
Public debt (external, outstanding; 1992): U.S.$89,300,000.

Foreign trade

Balance of trade (current prices)

	1987	1988	1989	1990	1991	1992
SI$'000	–6,646	–32,710	–45,920	–18,340	–73,100	–9,300
% of total	2.5%	8.7%	11.7%	5.0%	13.9%	1.5%

Imports (1991): SI$305,712,000 (machinery and transport equipment 32.5%, manufactured goods 22.8%, mineral fuels and lubricants 20.6%, food 14.9%). *Major import sources:* Australia 36.0%; Japan 19.8%; Singapore 11.4%; New Zealand 8.2%; United States 5.5%; United Kingdom 2.8%.
Exports (1991): SI$228,713,000 (fish products 46.5%, timber products 24.1%, palm oil products 7.7%, cacao beans 5.9%, copra 4.5%). *Major export destinations:* Japan 28.2%; United Kingdom 15.3%; Thailand 13.8%; The Netherlands 7.6%; South Korea 6.9%; Fiji 5.1%.

Transport and communications

Transport. Railroads: none. Roads (1987)[9]: total length 1,300 mi, 2,100 km (paved 8%). Vehicles (1993): passenger cars 2,052; trucks and buses 2,574. Merchant marine (1992): vessels (100 gross tons and over) 33; total deadweight tonnage 4,985. Air transport (1992): passenger-mi 117,100,000, passenger-km 188,400,000; short ton-mi cargo 25,000[10], metric ton-km cargo 37,000[10]; airports (1994) with scheduled flights 22.
Communications. Daily newspapers[11]: none. Radio (1994): total number of receivers 38,000 (1 per 9.5 persons). Television: none. Telephones (1989): 7,000 (1 per 44 persons).

Education and health

Education (1993)

	schools	teachers	students	student/ teacher ratio
Primary (age 7–12)	520	2,357	70,103	29.7
Secondary (age 13–18)	} 23	364	7,351	20.2
Voc., teacher tr.				
Higher	—	—	—	—

Educational attainment (1986)[12]. Percentage of population age 25 and over having: no schooling 44.4%; primary education 46.2%; secondary 6.8%; higher 2.6%. *Literacy* (1976): total population age 15 and over literate 55,500 (54.1%); males 33,600 (62.4%); females 21,900 (44.9%).
Health: physicians (1988) 31 (1 per 9,852 persons); hospital beds (1986) 1,479 (1 per 193 persons); infant mortality rate per 1,000 live births (1992) 26.0.
Food (1988–90): daily per capita caloric intake 2,278 (vegetable products 90%, animal products 10%); 100% of FAO recommended minimum requirement.

Military

Total active duty personnel: no military forces are maintained, but a police force of 475 provides internal security.

---

[1]Detail does not add to total given because of rounding. [2]Ward populations. [3]1990. [4]Reported cases of these diseases in 1987 were: malaria 168,196, influenza 63,681, diarrhea 18,536, and conjunctivitis 10,965. [5]At 1984 factor cost. [6]Persons employed in the monetary sector only. [7]Public-service earnings. [8]Retail price index components. [9]Includes 500 mi (800 km) of privately maintained roads mainly for plantation use. [10]1984. [11]In 1988 there were three weekly newspapers with a combined circulation of 10,000. [12]Indigenous population only.

Somalia[1]

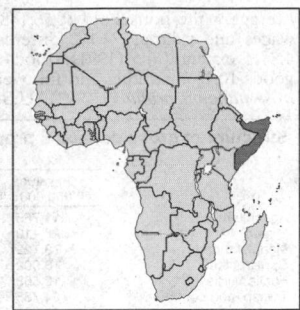

Official name: Soomaaliya (Somali)(Somalia).
Form of government: interim UN-imposed regime[2].
Head of state and government: Special Envoy assisted by military command of UN-administered operation in Somalia (for United Nations); no effective local government (for Somalia).
Capital: Mogadishu.
Official languages: Somali; Arabic.
Official religion: Islam.
Monetary unit: 1 Somali shilling (So.Sh.) = 100 cents; valuation (Oct. 7, 1994) 1 U.S.$ = So.Sh. 2,622; 1 £ = So.Sh. 4,171.

Area and population

Regions	Capitals	area sq mi	area sq km	population 1980 estimate
Bakool	Xuddur	10,000	27,000	148,700
Banaadir	Mogadishu (Muqdisho)	400	1,000	520,100
Bari	Boosaaso	27,000	70,000	222,300
Bay	Baydhabo	15,000	39,000	451,000
Galguduud	Dhuusamarreeb	17,000	43,000	255,900
Gedo	Garbahaarrey	12,000	32,000	235,000
Hiiraan	Beledweyne	13,000	34,000	219,300
Jubbada Dhexe	Bu'aale	9,000	23,000	147,800
Jubbada Hoose	Kismaayo	24,000	61,000	272,400
Mudug	Gaalkacyo	27,000	70,000	311,200
Nugaal	Garoowe	19,000	50,000	112,200
Sanaag	Ceerigaabo	21,000	54,000	216,500
Shabeellaha Dhexe	Jawhar	8,000	22,000	352,000
Shabeellaha Hoose	Marka	10,000	25,000	570,700
Togdheer	Burao	16,000	41,000	383,900
Woqooyi Galbeed	Hargeysa	17,000	45,000	655,000
TOTAL		246,000[3]	637,000	5,074,000

Demography

Population (1994): 6,667,000[4].
Density (1994): persons per sq mi 27.1, persons per sq km 10.5.
Urban-rural (1991): urban 37.2%; rural 62.8%.
Sex distribution (1990): male 49.46%; female 50.54%.
Age breakdown (1990): under 15, 47.0%; 15–29, 23.4%; 30–44, 16.6%; 45–59, 8.6%; 60–74, 3.7%; 75 and over, 0.7%.
Population projection: (2000) 9,176,000; (2010) 12,588,000.
Doubling time: 22 years.
Ethnic composition (1983): Somali 98.3%[5], Arab 1.2%; Bantu 0.4%; other 0.1%.
Religious affiliation (1980): Sunnī Muslim 99.8%; Christian 0.1%; other 0.1%.
Major cities (1984): Mogadishu 570,000; Hargeysa 90,000; Kismaayo 86,000; Berbera 83,000; Marka (1981) 60,000.

Vital statistics

Birth rate per 1,000 population (1990–95): 50.2 (world avg. 26.0); legitimate, n.a.; illegitimate, n.a.
Death rate per 1,000 population (1990–95): 18.5 (world avg. 9.2).
Natural increase rate per 1,000 population (1990–95): 31.7 (world avg. 16.8).
Total fertility rate (avg. births per childbearing woman; 1990–95): 7.0.
Marriage rate per 1,000 population: n.a.
Divorce rate per 1,000 population: n.a.
Life expectancy at birth (1990–95): male 45.4 years; female 48.6 years.
Major causes of death per 100,000 population: n.a.; however, major diseases include leprosy, malaria, tetanus, and tuberculosis.

National economy

Budget (1991). Revenue: So.Sh. 151,453,000,000 (domestic revenue sources, principally indirect taxes and import duties 60.4%; external grants and transfers 39.6%). Expenditures: So.Sh. 141,141,000,000 (general services 46.9%; economic and social services 31.2%; debt service 7.0%).
Tourism: receipts from visitors (1986) U.S.$8,000,000; expenditures by nationals abroad (1983) U.S.$13,000,000.
Production (metric tons except as noted). Agriculture, forestry, fishing (1993): fruits (excluding melons) 246,000, sugarcane 200,000, sorghum 150,000, corn (maize) 120,000, bananas 90,000, sesame seed 30,000, rice 15,000, beans 13,000, dates 9,000, seed cotton 6,000, other forest products include khat, frankincense, and myrrh; livestock (number of live animals) 12,500,000 goats, 6,500,000 sheep, 6,100,000 camels, 1,500,000 cattle; roundwood (1992) 8,755,000 cu m; fish catch (1991) 16,100. Mining and quarrying (1992): sepiolite 2,000 kilograms. Manufacturing (value added in So.Sh. '000,000; 1988): food 794; cigarettes and matches 562; hides and skins 420; paper and printing 328; plastics 320; chemicals 202; beverages 144. Construction (value added in So.Sh.; 1991): 51,100,000,000. Energy production (consumption): electricity (kW-hr; 1992) 258,000,000 (258,000,000); coal, none (n.a.); crude petroleum (barrels; 1991) n.a. (806,000); petroleum products (metric tons; 1991) none (59,000); natural gas, none (n.a.).
Household income and expenditure. Average household size (1980) 4.9; income per household: n.a.; sources of income: n.a.; expenditure (1983)[6]: food and tobacco 62.3%, housing 15.3%, clothing 5.6%, energy 4.3%, other 12.5%.
Gross national product (at current market prices; 1990): U.S.$946,000,000 (U.S.$150 per capita).

Structure of gross domestic product and labour force

	1991 in value So.Sh. '000,000	% of total value	labour force	% of labour force
Agriculture	867,500	64.5	2,275,000	70.8
Mining	2,700	0.2		
Manufacturing	59,200	4.4	336,000	10.4
Construction	51,100	3.8		
Public utilities	9,400	0.7		
Transportation and communications	80,700	6.0		
Trade	125,000	9.3		
Finance	45,700	3.4	604,000	18.8
Pub. admin., defense	80,700	6.0		
Services	30,900	2.3		
Other	–8,100	–0.6		
TOTAL	1,344,900[3]	100.0	3,215,000	100.0

Public debt (external, outstanding; 1992): U.S.$1,898,000,000.
Population economically active (1991): total 3,215,000; activity rate of total population 40.9% (participation rates [1987]: over age 10, 63.1%; female 48.7%; unemployed, n.a.).

Price and earnings indexes (1985 = 100)

	1983	1984	1985	1986	1987	1988	1989[7]
Consumer price index	38.0	72.6	100.0	135.8	174.0	316.6	707.1
Earnings index	...	...	...	...	...	...	...

Land use (1992): forested 14.4%; meadows and pastures 68.5%; agricultural and under permanent cultivation 1.7%; other 15.4%.

Foreign trade[8]

Balance of trade (current prices)

	1987	1988	1989	1990	1991	1992
U.S.$'000,000	–382	–373	–299	–274	–274	–305
% of total	64.3%	68.7%	62.4%	61.4%	61.4%	67.0%

Imports (1991): U.S.$360,000,000 (agricultural products 22.1%, of which rice 8.6%; unspecified 77.9%). *Major import sources* (1990): Italy 30.8%; The Netherlands 8.8%; Bahrain 6.0%; United Kingdom 5.9%; Djibouti 5.9%; China 4.9%; Germany 4.7%; Thailand 4.6%.
Exports (1991): U.S.$86,000,000 (agricultural products 46.1%, of which live sheep and goats 23.3%, live camels 7.0%, live cattle 6.4%, bananas 5.8%; fishery products 10.7%; other 43.2%). *Major export destinations* (1990): Italy 28.7%; Saudi Arabia 23.4%; Yemen 19.1%; United Arab Emirates 10.7%.

Transport and communications

Transport. Railroads: none. Roads (1991): total length 13,500 mi, 21,700 km (paved 28%). Vehicles (1992): passenger cars 10,500; trucks and buses 11,500. Merchant marine (1992): vessels (100 gross tons and over) 28; total deadweight tonnage 18,496. Air transport (1991): passenger-mi 81,000,000, passenger-km 131,000,000; short ton-mi cargo 3,000,000, metric ton-km cargo 5,000,000; airports (1994) with scheduled flights, n.a.
Communications. Daily newspapers (1993): total number 1; total circulation, n.a. Radio (1993): total number of receivers 400,000 (1 per 16 persons). Television (1987): total number of receivers 3,000 (1 per 2,270 persons). Telephones (1991): 9,000 (1 per 741 persons).

Education and health

Education (1986–87)

	schools	teachers	students	student/ teacher ratio
Primary (age 6–14)	1,125	8,208	171,830	20.9
Secondary (age 15–18)	82	2,109	42,764	20.3
Voc., teacher tr.	21	498	4,809	9.7
Higher	1	262[9]	1,692	...

Educational attainment: n.a. *Literacy* (1990): percentage of total population age 15 and over literate 24.1%; males literate 42.7%; females literate 14.0%.
Health: physicians (1987) 323 (1 per 19,071 persons); hospital beds (1985) 5,536 (1 per 1,053 persons); infant mortality rate per 1,000 live births (1990–95) 122.
Food (1988–90): daily per capita caloric intake 1,874 (vegetable products 69%, animal products 31%); 81% of FAO recommended minimum requirement.

Military

Total active duty personnel (1994)[2, 10]: clan militias and armed gangs have fought for control of the country since the 1991 revolution. *Military expenditure as percentage of GNP* (1986): 3.2% (world 5.5%); per capita expenditure U.S.$6.

[1]Proclamation of the "Republic of Somaliland" by the Somali National Movement in May 1991 on territory corresponding to the former British Somaliland (which unified with the former Italian Trust Territory of Somalia to form Somalia in 1960) has received no international recognition. This entity would represent about a quarter of Somalia's territory and a quarter to a third of its population; a new president was elected in May 1993; a new currency, the Somaliland shilling, was to be introduced in late 1994. [2]UN operation in Somalia (begun May 1992) is to end March 31, 1995, per official announcement of November 1994. [3]Detail does not add to total given because of rounding. [4]Excluding Somali refugees in neighbouring countries, estimated to number about 600,000. [5]The Somali are divided into six major clans, of which four are predominantly pastoral (representing c. 70% of the population) and two are predominantly agricultural (representing c. 20% of the population); the remainder are urban dwellers with less clan identification. [6]Capital city only. [7]Third quarter. [8]Imports are c.i.f. [9]1980–81. [10]As of September 1994 there were an estimated 18,900 UN-sponsored military personnel in Somalia.

South Africa

Official name: Republic of South
　Africa (English).
Form of government[1]: multiparty
　republic with two legislative houses
　(Senate [90]; National Assembly
　[400]).
Head of state and government:
　President assisted by Executive
　Deputy Presidents.
Capitals: Pretoria (executive);
　Bloemfontein (judicial); Cape Town
　(legislative).
Official languages: [2].
Official religion: none.
Monetary unit: 1 rand (R) = 100 cents;
　valuation (Oct. 7, 1994)
　1 U.S.$ = R 3.57; 1 £ = R 5.68.

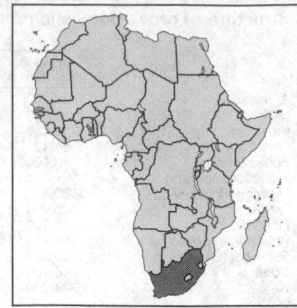

Area and population

Provinces	Capitals	area sq mi	area sq km	population 1993 estimate
Eastern Cape	Bisho	65,875	170,616	6,665,400
Eastern Transvaal	Nelspruit	31,590	81,816	2,838,500
Gauteng	Johannesburg	7,243	18,760	6,847,000
Natal	Ulundi and			
(KwaZulu/Natal)	Pietermaritzburg	35,321	91,481	8,549,000
Northern Cape	Kimberley	140,306	363,389	763,900
Northern Transvaal	Pietersburg	46,180	119,606	5,120,600
North-West	Mafikeng	45,834	118,710	3,506,800
Orange Free State	Bloemfontein	49,976	129,437	2,804,600
Western Cape	Cape Town	49,956	129,386	3,620,200
TOTAL		472,281	1,223,201	40,716,000

Demography

Population (1994): 41,749,000.
Density (1994): persons per sq mi 88.4, persons per sq km 34.1.
Urban-rural (1992): urban 60.3%; rural 39.7%.
Sex distribution (1990): male 49.73%; female 50.27%.
Age breakdown (1990): under 15, 38.8%; 15–29, 27.2%; 30–44, 17.9%; 45–59,
　10.1%; 60–74, 4.7%; 75 and over, 1.3%.
Population projection: (2000) 47,912,000; (2010) 58,446,000.
Doubling time: 27 years.
Ethnic composition (1991): black 75.8%, of which Zulu *c.* 22.0%, Xhosa *c.*
　18.0%, Pedi *c.* 9.0%, Sotho *c.* 7.0%, Tswana *c.* 7.0%, Tsonga *c.* 3.5%, Swazi
　c. 3.0%, Ndebele *c.* 2.0%, Venda *c.* 2.0%; white 13.0%; Coloured 8.7%, of
　which Cape Malay 1.0%; Asian 2.5%.
Religious affiliation (1990): Christian 78.0%, of which black independent
　churches 18.5%, Afrikaans Reformed 11.3%, Roman Catholic 7.8%,
　Methodist 7.2%, Anglican 5.3%, Lutheran 2.9%; traditional religions 10.5%;
　Hindu 1.7%; Muslim 1.1%; Jewish 0.4%; other 8.3%.
Major cities (1991)[3]: Cape Town 2,350,157; Johannesburg 1,916,063[4]; Durban
　1,137,378; Pretoria 1,080,187; Port Elizabeth 853,204.

Vital statistics

Birth rate per 1,000 population (1994): 34.0 (world avg. 26.0).
Death rate per 1,000 population (1994): 8.0 (world avg. 9.2).
Natural increase rate per 1,000 population (1994): 26.0 (world avg. 16.8).
Total fertility rate (avg. births per childbearing woman; 1992): 4.1.
Life expectancy at birth (1994): male 62.0 years; female 68.0 years.
Major causes of death per 100,000 population (1988)[5]: diseases of the cir-
　culatory system 133.9; accidents and violence 110.6; malignant neoplasms
　(cancers) 70.2; diseases of the respiratory system 69.6; infectious and para-
　sitic diseases 68.3; ill-defined conditions 97.5.

National economy

Budget (1993–94). Revenue: R 88,210,000,000 (income taxes 56.3%, sales
　and value-added taxes 28.2%, customs duties 5.8%, excise duties 5.5%).
　Expenditures: R 114,154,000,000 (education 23.9%, interest on debt 19.4%,
　economic services 14.8%, health 11.3%, defense 9.3%).
Public debt (external, December 1993): U.S.$1,480,000,000.
Production (in R '000,000 except as noted). Agriculture, forestry, fishing (in
　value of production; 1991–92): poultry and eggs 4,236, beef 2,856, corn
　(maize) 1,537, temperate fruits 1,373, wheat 1,308, hay 1,237, sugarcane
　1,141, milk 1,098, sheep and goat meat 884, grapes 750, citrus fruits 679,
　tobacco 507; roundwood (1992) 19,679,000 cu m; fish catch (1991) 498,884
　metric tons. Mining and quarrying (in value of sales; 1992): gold 19,525;
　rough diamonds 14,249[6]; coal 9,286; platinum-group metals 2,164; iron ore
　1,128; copper 1,077; manganese 600; lime and limestone 503; chrome 364.
　Manufacturing (in value added; 1991): food and beverages 10,306; soaps,
　paints, pharmaceuticals, and refined petroleum 7,742; iron and steel 5,862;
　transport equipment 5,043; metal products 4,231; nonelectrical machinery
　4,042; paper and paper products 3,349. Construction (buildings completed
　in value of construction; 1992)[7]: residential 4,027; nonresidential 4,636.
　Energy production (consumption): electricity (kW-hr; 1992) 148,620,000,000
　(163,294,000,000[8]); coal (metric tons; 1992) 174,000,000 (132,260,000[8]); crude
　petroleum (barrels; 1992) none (118,746,000[8]); petroleum products (metric
　tons; 1992) 14,799,000[8] (14,802,000[8]); natural gas, none (none).
Household income and expenditure[7]. Average household size (1983) 4.5; aver-
　age annual income per household (1990–91) R 16,814 (U.S.$6,500), of which
　average black household R 9,348 (U.S.$3,614), average Coloured household
　R 19,284 (U.S.$7,455), average Asian household R 29,712 (U.S.$11,487),

average white household R 56,148 (U.S.$21,707); sources of income (1991):
　wages and salaries 74.1%, interest, dividends, rent, etc., 21.1%, transfers
　4.8%; expenditure (1991): food 35.1%, transportation 15.0%, household
　goods 10.2%, clothing and footwear 7.5%.
Gross national product (1993): U.S.$117,960,000,000 (U.S.$2,900 per capita).

Structure of gross domestic product and labour force

	1992 in value R '000,000[7, 9]	1992 % of total value	1991 labour force[7]	1991 % of labour force
Agriculture	11,765	4.0	1,224,434	10.5
Mining	28,410	9.6	840,749	7.2
Manufacturing	73,722	24.9	1,417,128	12.2
Construction	8,902	3.0	526,373	4.5
Public utilities	12,668	4.3	102,928	0.9
Transp. and commun.	24,756	8.4	497,122	4.3
Trade	40,395	13.7	1,358,291	11.7
Finance, real estate	36,056	12.2	503,971	4.4
Pub. admin., defense	46,553	15.7 }	2,640,520	22.7
Services	5,357	1.8 }		
Other	7,257	2.4	2,512,851[10]	21.6[10]
TOTAL	295,841	100.0	11,624,367	100.0

Population economically active (1991)[7]: total 11,624,367; activity rate of total
　population 37.5% (participation rates: ages 20–64 [1985] 68.3%; female
　39.4%; unemployed (1993) 40.0%.

Price and earnings indexes (1990 = 100)

	1988	1989	1990	1991	1992	1993	1994[11]
Consumer price index	76.3	87.5	100.0	115.3	131.3	144.1	152.9
Monthly earnings index[12]	74.8	87.5	100.0	112.6	...	...	...

Tourism (1992): receipts U.S.$1,226,000,000; expenditures U.S.$1,544,000,000.
Land use (1992): forest 3.7%; pasture 66.6%; agriculture 10.8%; other 18.9%.

Foreign trade

Balance of trade (current prices)

	1988	1989	1990	1991	1992	1993
R '000,000	+10,240	+13,458	+16,717	+16,146	+13,917	+20,500
% of total	10.5%	13.1%	15.9%	14.3%	11.6%	14.8%

Imports (1992): R 52,857,000,000 (machinery and apparatus 26.8%, chemicals
　and chemical products 11.1%, motor vehicles 8.2%, food 5.9%). *Major im-
　port sources:* Germany 15.1%; U.S. 13.1%; U.K. 9.5%; Japan 9.3%; France
　3.8%; not specified 19.7%.
Exports (1992): R 66,774,000,000 (gold 27.1%, base metals and metal products
　12.7%, diamonds 9.5%, food 7.0%, coal 6.0%). *Major export destinations*[13]:
　Italy 8.0%; Germany 6.0%; Japan 6.0%; U.S. 5.0%; U.K. 4.0%.

Transport and communications

Transport. Railroads[14]: route length (1992) 21,617 km; passenger-km (1990–
　91) 1,205,400,000[15]; metric ton-km cargo (1990–91) 93,019,000,000. Roads
　(1991): length 182,329 km (paved 30%). Vehicles (1992): passenger cars
　3,488,570; trucks and buses 1,899,721. Merchant marine (1992): vessels 219;
　total deadweight tonnage 282,533. Air transport (1993)[16]: passenger-km
　10,521,000,000; metric ton-km cargo 319,957,000; airports (1994) 31.
Communications. Daily newspapers (1992): total number 19; total circulation
　1,311,926; circulation per 1,000 population 32. Radio (1993): 10,000,000 re-
　ceivers (1 per 4.1 persons). Television (1993): 3,445,000 receivers (1 per 12
　persons). Telephones (1992): 5,222,090 (1 per 7.6 persons).

Education and health

Education (1992)

	schools	teachers	students	student/ teacher ratio
Primary/Secondary	20,648	322,493	8,374,564	26.0
Voc., teacher tr.	197	14,876	147,009	9.9
Tertiary vocational	12	6,865	113,870	16.6
University	17	31,863	318,944	10.0

Educational attainment (1990). Percentage of all-age population group (black,
　white, Coloured, Asian) having: no formal schooling (34.4%, 7.8%, 15.5%,
　11.4%); primary education (45.2%, 10.3%, 32.6%, 21.8%); secondary (19.8%,
　56.4%, 48.9%, 60.3%); technical/teacher training (0.5%, 10.1%, 2.3%, 2.5%);
　undergraduate (0.06%, 6.7%, 0.3%, 1.7%); graduate (0.05%, 8.7%, 0.4%,
　2.3%). *Literacy:* total population age 15 and over literate (1990), n.a.[17]
Health: physicians[7] (1992) 25,375 (1 per 1,264 persons); hospital beds (1991)
　141,977 (1 per 222 persons); infant mortality rate (1994) 47.0.
Food (1988–90): daily per capita caloric intake 3,133 (vegetable products
　87%, animal products 13%); 128% of FAO recommended minimum.

Military

Total active duty personnel (1994): 78,500 (army 73.9%, navy 5.7%, air force
　12.7%, intraservice medical service 7.7%). *Military expenditure as percentage
　of GNP* (1991): 3.7% (world 4.2%); per capita expenditure U.S.$99.

---

[1]Interim constitution in effect from April 27, 1994. [2]Afrikaans; English; Ndebele; Pedi
(North Sotho); Sotho (South Sotho); Swazi; Tsonga; Tswana (West Sotho); Venda;
Xhosa; Zulu. [3]Population of urban areas. [4]1991 population of the Witwatersrand
(including East Rand [1,378,792] and West Rand [870,066] urban areas) is 4,164,-
921. [5]Excludes population and causes of death for formerly nominally independent
Transkei, Venda, Bophuthatswana, and Ciskei (TVBC). [6]1993. [7]Excludes TVBC.
[8]Includes Botswana, Lesotho, Namibia, and Swaziland. [9]At factor cost. [10]All not adequately defined. [11]April. [12]Manufacturing only. [13]Estimated figures. [14]South African
Railways. [15]Excludes suburban traffic. [16]SAA only. [17]Unofficial estimates range from
a high of about 65% to a low of less than 50%.

Spain

Official name: Reino de España
(Kingdom of Spain).
Form of government: constitutional
monarchy with two legislative
houses (Senate [255[1]]; Congress of
Deputies [350]).
Chief of state: King.
Head of government: Prime Minister.
Capital: Madrid.
Official language: Castilian Spanish.
Official religion: none.
Monetary unit: 1 peseta (Pta) = 100
céntimos; valuation (Oct. 7, 1994)
1 U.S.$ = Ptas 127.62;
1 £ = Ptas 202.98.

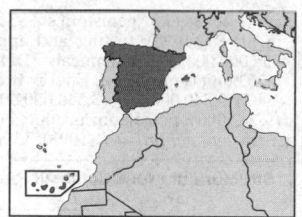

Area and population

Autonomous communities	Capitals	area sq mi	area sq km	population 1992 estimate
Andalucía	Seville	33,694	87,268	6,983,734
Aragón	Zaragoza	18,398	47,650	1,207,338
Asturias	Oviedo	4,079	10,565	1,118,610
Baleares (Balearic Islands)	Palma de Mallorca	1,936	5,014	685,686
Canarias (Canary Islands)	Santa Cruz de Tenerife	2,796	7,242	1,501,651
Cantabria	Santander	2,042	5,289	526,400
Castilla–La Mancha	Toledo	30,591	79,230	1,716,665
Castilla y León	Valladolid	36,368	94,193	2,618,228
Cataluña	Barcelona	12,328	31,930	6,018,154
Extremadura	Mérida	16,063	41,602	1,131,195
Galicia	Santiago de Compostela	11,365	29,434	2,792,802
La Rioja	Logroño	1,944	5,034	260,282
Madrid	Madrid	3,087	7,995	4,910,199
Murcia	Murcia	4,370	11,317	1,038,126
Navarra	Pamplona	4,023	10,421	521,670
País Vasco (Basque Country)	Vitoria (Gasteiz)	2,800	7,201	2,129,523
Valencia	Valencia	8,998	23,305	3,797,671
TOTAL SPAIN		194,885	504,750	38,957,934
Enclaves in Northern Morocco				
Ceuta	—	7.1	18.5	70,746
Melilla	—	5.4	14.0	56,403
Other enclaves (plazas de soberanía)	—	0.26	0.66	...
TOTAL		194,897.79[2]	504,783.10	39,085,083

Demography

Population (1994): 39,193,000[3].
Density (1994): persons per sq mi 201.1, persons per sq km 77.6.
Urban-rural (1990): urban 78.4%; rural 21.6%.
Sex distribution (1994): male 49.10%; female 50.90%.
Age breakdown (1994): under 15, 17.4%; 15–29, 24.8%; 30–44, 21.3%; 45–59, 16.5%; 60–69, 10.3%; 70 and over, 9.7%.
Population projection: (2000) 39,268,000; (2010) 40,317,000.
Doubling time: not applicable; doubling time exceeds 100 years.
Ethnolinguistic composition (1989): Spanish 72.3%; Catalan 16.3%; Galician 8.1%; Basque 2.3%; other 1.0%.
Religious affiliation (1993): Roman Catholic 94.9%; Muslim 1.2%; Protestant 0.5%; other 3.4%.
Major cities (1991)[4]: Madrid 2,909,792; Barcelona 1,623,542; Valencia 752,909; Seville 659,126; Zaragoza 586,219.

Vital statistics

Birth rate per 1,000 population (1992): 10.0 (world avg. 26.0); (1988) legitimate 92.0%; illegitimate 8.0%.
Death rate per 1,000 population (1992): 8.4 (world avg. 9.2).
Natural increase rate per 1,000 population (1992): 1.6 (world avg. 16.8).
Total fertility rate (avg. births per childbearing woman; 1990–95): 1.4.
Marriage rate per 1,000 population (1992): 5.4.
Life expectancy at birth (1990–95): male 74.6 years; female 80.5 years.
Major causes of death per 100,000 population (1991): circulatory diseases 352.7; malignant neoplasms (cancers) 208.4; respiratory diseases 80.6.

National economy

Budget (1994[5]). Revenue: Ptas 13,217,000,000,000 (direct taxes 45.8%; indirect taxes 37.5%, of which value-added tax on products 9.0%; other taxes on production 16.7%). Expenditures: Ptas 16,514,000,000,000 (current transfers between public administrations 53.2%; interest payments 17.3%; wages 16.0%).
Tourism (1992): receipts from visitors U.S.$22,181,000,000; expenditures by nationals abroad U.S.$5,542,000,000.
Production (metric tons except as noted). Agriculture, forestry, fishing (1993): barley 9,520,000, sugar beets 8,650,000, wheat 5,002,000, grapes 4,453,000, potatoes 3,977,000, tomatoes 2,699,000, oranges 2,426,000, corn (maize) 1,699,000, onions 897,000; livestock (number of live animals) 24,830,000 sheep, 18,000,000 pigs, 4,800,000 cattle, 2,800,000 goats; roundwood (1992) 17,102,000 cu m; fish catch (1992) 894,552. Mining and quarrying (metal content in metric tons; 1993): iron ore 2,475,000; zinc 170,000; lead 25,000. Manufacturing (value added, in Ptas '000,000; 1990): machinery and transport equipment 2,175,761; food products 1,564,469; chemical products 921,075; paper products 662,993; wood and cork products 379,452; clothing and footwear 338,083; textiles 306,572. Construction (1993): dwellings 237,637. Energy production (consumption): electricity (kW-hr; 1992) 158,505,000,000 (159,146,000,000); coal (metric tons; 1992) 33,399,000 (47,496,000,000); crude

petroleum (barrels; 1992) 8,054,000 (412,530,000); petroleum products (metric tons; 1992) 50,446,000 (41,588,000); natural gas (cu m; 1992) 1,189,186,000 (6,668,871,000).
Gross national product (1993): U.S.$534,056,000,000 (U.S.$13,650 per capita).

Structure of gross domestic product and labour force

	1993 in value Ptas '000,000	% of total value	labour force	% of labour force
Agriculture	2,103,800	3.4	1,410,400	9.2
Mining	} 13,800,800	} 22.7	67,900	0.4
Manufacturing			2,906,800	19.0
Public utilities			85,400	0.6
Construction	4,987,200	8.2	1,530,000	10.0
Transp. and commun.	...	...	786,800	5.1
Trade			3,184,600	20.9
Finance	} 36,515,700	} 60.0	1,080,800	7.0
Services			} 3,066,100	20.0
Pub. admin., defense				
Other	3,473,700[6]	5.7[6]	1,199,800[7]	7.8
TOTAL	60,881,000[2]	100.0	15,318,800[2]	100.0

Public debt (1993[8]): Ptas 28,709,000,000,000 (U.S.$210,000,000,000).
Population economically active (1993): total 15,318,800; activity rate of total population 39.1% (participation rates: ages [1992] 16–64, 60.0%; female 43.1%; unemployed 14.9%).

Price and earnings indexes (1990 = 100)

	1987	1988	1989	1990	1991	1992	1993
Consumer price index	83.7	87.7	93.7	100.0	105.9	112.2	117.3
Monthly earnings index	80.5	85.7	92.0	100.0	108.2	116.5	124.4

Household income and expenditure. Average household size (1991) 3.4; income per household (1992) Ptas 2,591,000 (U.S.$25,800); sources of income (1991): wages and salaries 48.5%, profits and self-employment 27.5%, social security 19.5%; expenditure (1992): food 24.2%, housing 22.9%, transportation 13.1%, clothing and footwear 9.3%, household goods and services 6.5%.
Land use (1992): forested 31.9%; meadows and pastures 20.5%; agricultural and under permanent cultivation 39.9%; other 7.7%.

Foreign trade

Balance of trade (current prices)

	1988	1989	1990	1991	1992	1993
Ptas '000,000	−1,954.7	−2,722.0	−2,765.4	−2,724.3	−3,022.5	−1,831.3
% of total	17.2%	20.6%	19.7%	19.6%	18.6%	10.2%

Imports (1993): Ptas 9,998,840,000,000 (agricultural products 11.6%; machinery 11.0%; energy products 11.0%, of which crude petroleum 10.6%; transportation equipment 8.7%). Major import sources: France 17.0%; Germany 15.5%; Italy 9.1%; U.K. 7.7%; Japan 3.9%.
Exports (1993): Ptas 7,576,522,000,000 (transport equipment 21.1%; agricultural products 15.1%; machinery 7.9%). Major export destinations: France 20.4%; Germany 16.0%; Italy 9.9%; U.K. 8.9%.

Transport and communications

Transport. Railroads (1992): route length 13,050 km; passenger-km 16,352,000,000; metric ton-km cargo 9,252,000,000. Roads (1991): length 331,961 km (paved 99%). Vehicles (1992): cars 13,102,285; trucks and buses 2,696,776. Merchant marine (1992): vessels 2,190; deadweight tonnage 5,077,275. Air transport (1993): passenger-km 26,738,000,000; metric ton-km cargo 599,016,000; airports (1994) with scheduled flights 23.
Communications. Daily newspapers (1993): total number 119; total circulation 2,516,299[9]; circulation per 1,000 population 64[9]. Radio (1993): 12,000,000 receivers (1 per 3.3 persons). Television (1993): 17,000,000 receivers (1 per 2.3 persons). Telephones (1990): 12,603,000 (1 per 3.1 persons).

Education and health

Education (1992–93)

	schools	teachers	students	student/ teacher ratio
Primary (age 6–11)	38,512[10]	267,725[10]	4,474,775	...
Secondary (age 12–18)	23,107	170,144	2,558,717	15.0
Vocational[11]	2,668	63,236	1,234,045	19.5
Higher	1,415	67,166[11]	1,261,012	18.8

Educational attainment (1986). Percentage of population age 25 and over having: no formal schooling 5.2%; less than primary education 40.3%; primary 29.9%; incomplete secondary 8.9%; completed secondary 8.7%; higher 7.0%.
Literacy (1991): total population age 10 and over literate 33,338,300 (85.4%); males literate 16,458,400 (85.1%); females literate 16,879,900 (84.3%).
Health (1991): physicians 153,306 (1 per 257 persons); hospital beds 168,514 (1 per 234 persons); infant mortality rate (1992) 7.4.
Food (1988–90): daily per capita caloric intake 3,472 (vegetable products 68%, animal products 32%); 141% of FAO recommended minimum requirement.

Military

Total active duty personnel (1994): 206,500 (army 70.2%, navy 16.0%, air force 13.8%). Military expenditure as percentage of GNP (1991): 1.7% (world 4.2%); per capita expenditure U.S.$233.

[1]At the June 1993 elections, 208 seats were directly elected and 47 indirectly elected by the parliaments of the autonomous communities. [2]Detail does not add to total given because of rounding. [3]Estimate based on 1991 census. [4]For municipios, which may include rural population. [5]Preliminary. [6]Import taxes and value-added tax on products. [7]Includes 694,100 unemployed persons not previously employed. [8]December. [9]For 51 newspapers only. [10]Includes preschool. [11]1988–89.

Sri Lanka

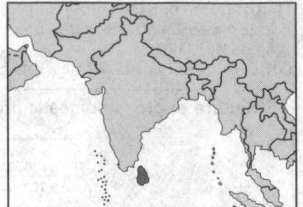

Official name: Sri Lankā Praja-
thanthrika Samajavadi Janarajaya
(Sinhala); Ilangai Jananayaka
Socialisa Kudiarasu (Tamil)
(Democratic Socialist Republic of Sri
Lanka).
Form of government: unitary multiparty
republic with one legislative house
(Parliament [225]).
Head of state and government:
President.
Capitals: Colombo (administrative)
and Sri Jayewardenepura Kotte
(legislative).
Official languages: Sinhala; Tamil.
Official religion: none.
Monetary unit: 1 Sri Lanka rupee
(SL Rs) = 100 cents; valuation
(Oct. 7, 1994) 1 U.S.$ =
SL Rs 49.24; 1 £ = SL Rs 78.32.

Area and population		area		population
		sq mi	sq km	1991 estimate
Districts	**Capitals**			
Amparai	Amparai	1,705	4,415	482,000
Anuradhapura	Anuradhapura	2,772	7,179	716,000
Badulla	Badulla	1,104	2,861	718,000
Batticaloa	Batticaloa	1,102	2,854	417,000
Colombo	Colombo	270	699	1,965,000
Galle	Galle	638	1,652	946,000
Gampaha	Gampaha	536	1,387	1,532,000
Hambantota	Hambantota	1,007	2,609	517,000
Jaffna	Jaffna	396	1,025	871,000
Kalutara	Kalutara	617	1,598	945,000
Kandy	Kandy	749	1,940	1,258,000
Kegalle	Kegalle	654	1,693	751,000
Kilinochchi	Kilinochchi	494	1,279	101,000
Kurunegala	Kurunegala	1,859	4,816	1,428,000
Mannar	Mannar	771	1,996	132,000
Matale	Matale	770	1,993	421,000
Matara	Matara	495	1,283	776,000
Monaragala	Monaragala	2,177	5,639	351,000
Mullaitivu	Mullaitivu	1,010	2,617	92,000
Nuwara Eliya	Nuwara Eliya	672	1,741	541,000
Polonnaruwa	Polonnaruwa	1,271	3,293	319,000
Puttalam	Puttalam	1,186	3,072	598,000
Ratnapura	Ratnapura	1,264	3,275	941,000
Trincomalee	Trincomalee	1,053	2,727	315,000
Vavuniya	Vavuniya	759	1,967	114,000
TOTAL		25,332	65,610	17,247,000

Demography

Population (1994): 17,830,000.
Density (1994): persons per sq mi 703.9, persons per sq km 271.8.
Urban-rural (1993): urban 22.0%; rural 78.0%.
Sex distribution (1991): male 50.98%; female 49.02%.
Age breakdown (1991): under 15, 35.2%; 15–24, 21.1%; 25–44, 26.5%; 45–59, 10.6%; 60–69, 4.0%; 70 and over, 2.6%.
Population projection: (2000) 19,117,000; (2010) 21,222,000.
Doubling time: 50 years.
Ethnic composition (1991): Sinhalese 82.7%; Tamil 8.9%; Sri Lankan Moor 7.7%; other 0.7%.
Religious affiliation (1981): Buddhist 69.3%; Hindu 15.5%; Muslim 7.6%; Christian 7.5%; other 0.1%.
Major cities (1990): Colombo 615,000; Dehiwala–Mount Lavinia 196,000; Moratuwa 170,000; Jaffna 129,000; Sri Jayewardenepura Kotte 109,000.

Vital statistics

Birth rate per 1,000 population (1994): 20.0 (world avg. 26.0); (1982) legitimate 94.6%; illegitimate 5.4%.
Death rate per 1,000 population (1994): 6.0 (world avg. 9.2).
Natural increase rate per 1,000 population (1994): 14.0 (world avg. 16.8).
Total fertility rate (avg. births per childbearing woman; 1994): 2.4.
Marriage rate per 1,000 population (1990): 8.9.
Divorce rate per 1,000 population (1988): 0.2.
Life expectancy at birth (1994): male 70.0 years; female 74.0 years.
Major causes of death per 100,000 population (1986): diseases of the circulatory system 101.9; violence and poisoning 77.8; diseases of the nervous system 45.3; respiratory diseases 36.1; infectious and parasitic diseases 32.2.

National economy

Budget (1992). Revenue: SL Rs 85,000,000,000 (sales and turnover tax 30.8%, import duties 25.6%, excise taxes 14.1%, income taxes 11.2%, nontax revenue 9.8%). Expenditures: SL Rs 118,802,000,000 (public-debt service 22.0%, transfer payments 19.4%, administration 16.4%, education 10.1%, transport 9.0%, defense 8.5%, general public services 8.2%).
Public debt (external, outstanding; 1992): U.S.$5,607,000,000.
Tourism (1992): receipts U.S.$199,000,000; expenditures U.S.$111,000,000.
Production (metric tons except as noted). Agriculture, forestry, fishing (1993): rice 2,450,000, coconuts 1,597,000, sugarcane 780,000, cassava 310,000, tea 232,000, rubber 110,000, sweet potatoes 65,000, copra 60,000; livestock (number of live animals) 1,600,000 cattle, 870,000 buffalo, 500,000 goats; roundwood (1992) 9,229,000 cu m; fish catch (1991) 198,063. Mining and quarrying (1992): quartz stone 1,130,000; limestone 600,000; titanium con-

centrate 36,000; gemstones U.S.$58,000,000. Manufacturing (value added, in SL Rs; 1990): textiles and apparel 27,930,000,000; food and tobacco 21,-955,000,000; petrochemicals 21,215,000,000. Construction (1990): residential, 6,262 units completed. Energy production (consumption): electricity (kW-hr; 1992) 3,540,000,000 (3,540,000,000); crude petroleum (barrels; 1992) none (9,742,000); petroleum products (metric tons; 1992) 1,227,000 (1,575,000).
Gross national product (1993): U.S.$10,573,000,000 (U.S.$600 per capita).

Structure of gross domestic product and labour force				
	1991		1992	
	in value SL Rs '000,000	% of total value	labour force	% of labour force
Agriculture	82,359	22.3	2,379,889	40.0
Mining	4,190	1.1	52,452	0.9
Manufacturing	62,734	17.0	635,457	10.7
Construction	26,164	7.1	248,596	4.2
Public utilities	6,500	1.8	22,621	0.4
Transp. and commun.	35,293	9.5	231,536	3.9
Trade	75,579	20.4	530,209	8.9
Finance	19,315	5.2	36,091	0.6
Pub. admin., defense	26,634	7.2 }	821,449	13.8
Services	11,261	3.0 }		
Other	19,865	5.4	989,921[1]	16.6[1]
TOTAL	369,894	100.0	5,948,221	100.0

Population economically active: total (1992) 5,948,221; activity rate 40.9% (participation rates: ages 15 and over, 56.6%; female 32.6%; unemployed 13.3%).

Price and earnings indexes (1990 = 100)							
	1987	1988	1989	1990	1991	1992	1993
Consumer price index	64.7	73.8	82.3	100.0	112.2	125.0	139.6
Average wage index[2]	58.5	73.2	84.3	100.0	111.7	128.4	155.4

Household income and expenditure (1991). Average household size (1981) 5.2; income per household SL Rs 103,400 (U.S.$2,500); sources of income: wages 48.5%, property income and self-employment 43.3%, transfers 8.2%; expenditure: food and beverages 59.5%, transportation 14.8%, clothing 6.2%, household furnishings 5.0%, housing and energy 4.6%.
Land use (1992): forested 32.5%; meadows and pastures 6.8%; agricultural and under permanent cultivation 29.5%; other 31.2%.

Foreign trade

Balance of trade (current prices)						
	1988	1989	1990	1991	1992	1993
SL Rs '000,000	−17,058	−15,135	−17,485	−29,612	−27,128	−36,037
% of total	15.4%	11.9%	9.9%	14.9%	11.0%	11.5%

Imports (1992): SL Rs 150,076,000,000 (textiles and textile articles 19.9%, machinery and appliances 13.0%, chemicals and related products 7.2%, vegetable products 6.7%, base metals and base-metal products 5.5%). *Major import sources* (1991): Japan 11.6%; India 7.1%; U.S. 5.7%; U.K. 5.4%; Iran 4.7%; China 3.3%; Pakistan 2.4%; Australia 1.2%.
Exports (1992): SL Rs 107,369,000,000 (tea 14.0%, natural rubber 2.7%, desiccated coconut 2.2%, coconut oil 1.0%). *Major export destinations* (1991): U.S. 28.4%; Germany 7.6%; U.K. 6.4%; Japan 5.2%; Canada 1.6%; Pakistan 1.6%; Australia 1.1%; India 0.6%.

Transport and communications

Transport. Railroads (1992): route length 1,427 km; passenger-km 2,818,000,-000; metric ton-km cargo 168,900,000. Roads (1991): total length 25,952 km (paved 81%). Vehicles (1992): passenger cars 189,477; trucks and buses 153,745. Merchant marine (1992): vessels (100 gross tons and over) 66; total deadweight tonnage 472,625. Air transport (1993): passenger-km 3,677,000,-000; metric ton-km cargo 104,437,000; airports (1994) 1.
Communications. Daily newspapers (1990): total number 18; total circulation 550,000; circulation per 1,000 population 32. Radio (1993): 2,200,000 receivers (1 per 8.0 persons). Television (1993): 700,000 receivers (1 per 25 persons). Telephones (1992): 190,000 (1 per 92 persons).

Education and health

Education (1991)				
	schools	teachers	students	student/ teacher ratio
Primary (age 5–10)	9,590	173,811	2,112,723	12.2
Secondary (age 11–17)	9,041	106,792	2,105,959	19.7
Voc., teacher tr.	23	437	8,908	20.4
Higher	8	1,937	31,447	16.2

Educational attainment (1981). Percentage of population age 25 and over having: no schooling 15.5%; less than complete primary education 12.1%; complete primary 52.3%; postprimary 14.7%; secondary 3.0%; higher 1.1%; unspecified 1.3%. *Literacy* (1991): percentage of population age 10 and over literate 86.9%; males literate 90.1%; females literate 83.8%.
Health (1992): physicians 3,345 (1 per 5,203 persons); hospital beds 48,061 (1 per 362 persons); infant mortality rate per 1,000 live births (1994) 23.
Food (1988–90): daily per capita caloric intake 2,246 (vegetable products 95%, animal products 5%); 101% of FAO recommended minimum.

Military

Total active duty personnel (1994): 126,000 (army 83.3%, navy 8.2%, air force 8.5%). *Military expenditure as percentage of GNP* (1991): 4.8% (world 4.2%); per capita expenditure U.S.$25.

[1]Includes unemployed. [2]Agricultural minimum rates. [3]Public schools only.

Sudan, The

Official name: Jumhūrīyat as-Sūdān (Republic of the Sudan).
Form of government: Islamic military regime with one transitional legislative house (Transitional National Assembly [302][1]).
Head of state and government: President.
Capitals: Khartoum (executive); Omdurman (legislative).
Official language: Arabic.
Official religion: [2].
Monetary unit: 1 Sudanese dinar (Sd)[3]; valuation (Oct. 7, 1994) 1 U.S.$ = Sd 31.13; 1 £ = Sd 49.51.

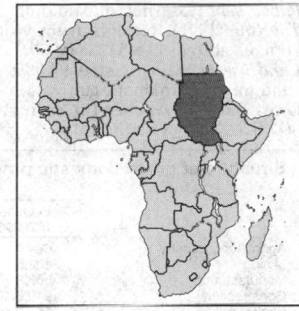

Area and population

States[4]	Capitals	area sq mi	area sq km	population 1983 census
A'ālī an-Nīl (Upper Nile)	Malakāl	92,198	238,792	1,599,605
Baḥr al-Ghazāl (Bahr el-Ghazal)	Wāw	77,566	200,894	2,265,510
Dārfūr (Darfur)	al-Fāshir	196,404	508,684	3,093,699
al-Istiwā'īyah (Equatoria)	Juba	76,436	197,969	1,406,181
al-Kharṭūm (Khartoum)	Khartoum	10,875	28,165	1,802,299
Kurdufān (Kordofan)	al-Ubayyiḍ	146,817	380,255	3,093,294
ash-Shamālīyah (Northern)	ad-Dāmir	183,800	476,040	1,083,024
ash Sharqīyah (Eastern)	Kassalā	128,987	334,074	2,208,209
al-Wusṭā (Central)	Wad Madanī	53,675	139,017	4,012,543
TOTAL		966,757[5, 6]	2,503,890[6]	20,564,364[7]

Demography

Population (1994): 25,699,000.
Density (1994): persons per sq mi 26.6, persons per sq km 10.3.
Urban-rural (1990): urban 22.5%; rural 77.5%.
Sex distribution (1990): male 50.23%; female 49.77%.
Age breakdown (1990): under 15, 45.2%; 15–29, 26.1%; 30–44, 15.4%; 45–59, 8.7%; 60–74, 3.9%; 75 and over, 0.7%.
Population projection: (2000) 30,253,000; (2010) 43,045,000.
Doubling time: 23 years.
Ethnic composition (1983): Sudanese Arab 49.1%; Dinka 11.5%; Nuba 8.1%; Beja 6.4%; Nuer 4.9%; Azande 2.7%; Bari 2.5%; Fur 2.1%; Shilluk 1.7%; Lotuko 1.5%; other 9.5%.
Religious affiliation (1992): Sunnī Muslim 74.7%; traditional beliefs 17.1%; Christian 8.2%.
Major cities (1983): Omdurman 526,287[8]; Khartoum 476,218[8]; Khartoum North 341,146[8]; Port Sudan (1990) *c.* 215,000[9]; Wad Madanī (1987) *c.* 145,000.

Vital statistics

Birth rate per 1,000 population (1993): 42.7 (world avg. 26.0).
Death rate per 1,000 population (1993): 12.5 (world avg. 9.2).
Natural increase rate per 1,000 population (1993): 30.2 (world avg. 16.8).
Total fertility rate (avg. births per childbearing woman; 1993): 6.2.
Marriage rate per 1,000 population: n.a.
Divorce rate per 1,000 population: n.a
Life expectancy at birth (1993): male 53.0 years; female 54.7 years.
Major causes of death per 100,000 population: n.a.

National economy

Budget (1993–94). Revenue: Sd 1,553,100,000 (direct taxes 38.6%; indirect taxes 35.4%; loans and grants 26.0%). Expenditures: Sd 2,337,000,000 (current expenditures 69.6%, of which social and welfare expenditure 7.5%; development expenditures 30.4%).
Tourism (1992): receipts from visitors U.S.$5,000,000; expenditures by nationals abroad U.S.$21,400,000.
Public debt (external, outstanding; 1992): U.S.$8,984,000,000.
Population economically active (1983)[10]: total 6,342,981; activity rate of total population 35.1% (participation rates: ages 15–64, 57.4%; female 29.1%; unemployed [1992] *c.* 30.0%).

Price and earnings indexes (1990 = 100)

	1988	1989	1990	1991	1992	1993	1994
Consumer price index	36.3	60.5	100.0	223.6	486.6	979.9	1,497.9[11]
Earnings index	...	...	...	...	...	...	...

Production (metric tons except as noted). Agriculture, forestry, fishing (1992): sugarcane 4,600,000, sorghum 3,700,000, wheat 895,000, peanuts (groundnuts) 454,000, millet 424,000, sesame seeds 330,000, seed cotton 261,000, cottonseed 170,000, yams 129,000, cotton lint 87,000, gum arabic 25,000[12]; livestock (number of live animals) 22,600,000 sheep, 21,600,000 cattle, 18,700,000 goats, 2,800,000 camels; roundwood 24,104,000 cu m; fish catch (1991) 33,303. Mining and quarrying: salt (1992) 75,000; gold (1993) 31,500 troy oz. Manufacturing (1991): wheat flour 733,900[13]; refined sugar 356,200[13]; cement 168,000; cattlehides and horsehides 35,000; calfskins, goatskins, and sheepskins 18,000; cigarettes 750,000,000 units. Construction: n.a. Energy production (consumption): electricity (kW-hr; 1992) 1,325,000,000 (1,325,000,000); coal, none (none); crude petroleum (barrels; 1992) none (7,477,000); petroleum products (metric tons; 1992) 853,000 (1,045,000); natural gas, none (none).
Land use (1991): forested 18.8%; meadows and pastures 46.3%; agricultural and under permanent cultivation 5.4%; desert and other 29.5%.

Gross national product (1992): U.S.$8,176,000,000 (U.S.$300 per capita).

Structure of gross domestic product and labour force

	1991 92[14] in value LSd '000,000	1991 92[14] % of total value	1983 labour force[10]	1983 % of labour force[10]
Agriculture	2,475	33.8	4,028,705	63.5
Mining	6	0.1	6,534	0.1
Manufacturing	670	9.1	266,693	4.2
Construction	395	5.4	139,282	2.2
Public utilities	155	2.1	43,728	0.7
Transportation and communications	} 2,850	} 38.9	215,474	3.4
Trade and finance			314,878	5.0
Services			550,409	8.7
Pub. admin., defense	780	10.6 }		
Other	...	...	777,480[15]	12.2[15]
TOTAL	7,331	100.0	6,342,981	100.0

Household income and expenditure. Average household size (1980) 5.3; income per household: n.a.[16]; sources of income: n.a.; expenditure (1983): food and beverages 63.6%, housing 11.5%, household goods 5.5%, clothing and footwear 5.3%, health care 4.1%, energy 3.8%.

Foreign trade

Balance of trade (current prices)

	1987	1988	1989	1990	1991	1992
U.S.$'000,000	−397	−551	−507	−667	−585	−502
% of total	27.2%	35.1%	38.3%	39.2%	49.0%	44.0%

Imports (1992): U.S.$821,000,000 (petroleum products 28.0%, trucks 9.0%, nonelectrical machinery 5.8%, metal manufactures 5.6%, tractors 4.1% animal and vegetable oils 4.0%). *Major import sources:* Saudi Arabia 21.3%; United States 7.9%; United Kingdom 7.8%; United Arab Emirates 6.4%; Yemen 5.2%; Egypt 5.2%.
Exports (1992): U.S.$319,000,000 (cotton 20.4%, sesame seeds 14.5%, sheep and lambs 11.3%, gum arabic 5.9%, hides and skins 5.3%, roselle[17] 5.3%). *Major export destinations:* Saudi Arabia 19.3%; Libya 11.7%; Italy 9.0%; Egypt 7.4%; France 6.5%; Thailand 6.0%.

Transport and communications

Transport. Railroads (1991): route length 2,960 mi, 4,764 km; passenger-mi 330,000,000, passenger-km 531,000,000; short ton-mi cargo 271,000,000, metric ton-km cargo 396,000,000. Roads (1990): total length *c.* 14,000 mi, *c.* 22,500 km (paved 9%). Vehicles (1992): passenger cars 116,000; trucks and buses 57,000. Merchant marine (1992): vessels (100 gross tons and over) 16; total deadweight tonnage 62,244. Air transport (1993)[18]: passenger-mi 360,508,000, passenger-km 580,182,000; short ton-mi cargo 25,265,000, metric ton-km cargo 36,886,000; airports (1994) with scheduled flights 12.
Communications. Daily newspapers (1990): total number 3[19]; total circulation, n.a. Radio (1993): 7,500,000 receivers (1 per 3.3 persons). Television (1993): 250,000 receivers (1 per 100 persons). Telephones (1992): 91,930 (1 per 269 persons).

Education and health

Education (1991–92)

	schools	teachers	students	student/ teacher ratio
Primary (age 7–12)	8,501	64,227	2,079,649	32.4
Secondary (age 13–18)	2,578	20,024	446,898	22.3
Voc., teacher tr.	67	1,648	26,953	16.4
Higher	24	1,943	54,345	28.0

Educational attainment: n.a. *Literacy* (1990): total population age 15 and over literate 3,750,000 (27.1%); males 2,940,000 (42.7%); females 810,000 (11.7%).
Health (1986): physicians 2,405[20] (1 per 9,439 persons); hospital beds 18,571 (1 per 1,222 persons); infant mortality rate (1993) 102.0.
Food (1988–90): daily per capita caloric intake 2,043 (vegetable products 83%, animal products 17%); 87% of FAO recommended minimum.

Military

Total active duty personnel (1993): 72,800[21] (army 93.4%, navy 2.5%, air force 4.1%). *Military expenditure as percentage of GNP* (1991): 8.6% (world 4.2%); per capita expenditure U.S.$88.

---

[1]Appointed interim legislature. Total number of seats includes seats assigned to southern Sudan (area at war with central government). [2]Islam was being imposed in 1994. [3]A new currency, the Sudanese dinar (introduced May 1992 at a value equal to 10 Sudanese pounds [Lsd]), is gradually replacing the Sudanese pound. [4]Local administrative reorganization into 26 states was officially announced in February 1994. Complete list of these new states was not available in October 1994. [5]Detail does not add to total given because of rounding. [6]Including *c.* 50,000 sq mi (130,000 sq km) of inland water area. [7]Preliminary 1993 census figure was 24,900,000, including an estimated 3,850,000 in the southern Sudan. [8]Khartoum urban agglomeration: 1993 est. (including Omdurman, Khartoum North, squatters, and displaced persons from southern Sudan) *c.* 3,500,000. [9]Excluding about 300,000 refugees from Eritrea. [10]Excludes nomads, the homeless, and institutionalized persons. [11]February. [12]1993. [13]1989. [14]At constant prices of 1981–82. [15]Includes 592,759 unemployed not previously employed. [16]Average annual income of paid worker (1992) U.S.$216. [17]Variety of hibiscus cultivated for its edible parts. [18]Sudan Airways only. [19]Government-controlled dailies. Press censorship imposed since military coup of 1989. [20]Government-employed only. [21]Excludes 30,000–50,000 members of the Islamic paramilitary group.

Suriname

Official name: Republiek Suriname (Republic of Suriname).
Form of government: multiparty republic with one legislative house (National Assembly [51]).
Head of state and government: President.
Capital: Paramaribo.
Official language: Dutch.
Official religion: none.
Monetary unit: 1 Suriname guilder (Sf) = 100 cents; valuation (Oct. 7, 1994) 1 U.S.$ = Sf 183.49[1]; 1 £ = Sf 291.85.

Area and population		area		population
				1980
Districts[2]	Capitals	sq mi	sq km	census
Brokopondo	Brokopondo	2,843	7,364	6,621
Commewijne	Nieuw Amsterdam	908	2,353	20,063
Coronie	Totness	1,507	3,902	2,777
Marowijne	Albina	1,786	4,627	16,125
Nickerie	Nieuw Nickerie	2,067	5,353	32,690
Para	Onverwacht	2,082	5,393	12,827
Saramacca	Groningen	1,404	3,636	10,808
Sipaliwini	...	50,412	130,566	23,226
Wanica	Lelydorp	171	443	60,725
Town district				
Paramaribo	Paramaribo	71	183	167,798
TOTAL		63,251[3]	163,820[3]	355,240[4]

Demography

Population (1994): 423,000.
Density (1994): persons per sq mi 6.7, persons per sq km 2.6.
Urban-rural (1992): urban 48.7%; rural 51.3%.
Sex distribution (1993): male 49.22%; female 50.78%.
Age breakdown (1993): under 15, 33.8%; 15–29, 30.2%; 30–44, 19.0%; 45–59, 10.1%; 60–74, 5.6%; 75 and over, 1.3%.
Population projection: (2000) 465,000; (2010) 534,000.
Doubling time: 43 years.
Ethnic composition (1991): Suriname Creole 35.0%; Indo-Pakistani 33.0%; Javanese 16.0%; Bush Negro 10.0%; Amerindian 3.0%; other 3.0%.
Religious affiliation (1983): Hindu 26.0%; Roman Catholic 21.6%; Muslim 18.6%; Protestant (mostly Moravian) 18.0%; other 15.8%.
Major cities (1980): Paramaribo 200,970[5]; Nieuw Nickerie 6,078; Meerzorg 5,355; Marienburg 3,633.

Vital statistics

Birth rate per 1,000 population (1991): 22.5 (world avg. 26.0); legitimate, n.a.; illegitimate, n.a.
Death rate per 1,000 population (1991): 6.4 (world avg. 9.2).
Natural increase rate per 1,000 population (1991): 16.1 (world avg. 16.8).
Total fertility rate (avg. births per childbearing woman; 1993): 2.8.
Marriage rate per 1,000 population (1991): 4.6.
Divorce rate per 1,000 population (1991): 2.4.
Life expectancy at birth (1993): male 66.6 years; female 71.8 years.
Major causes of death per 100,000 population (1987)[6]: diseases of the circulatory system 178.6, of which ischemic heart disease 60.7, diseases of pulmonary circulation and other forms of heart disease 47.2; homicide, suicide, and other violence 68.5; malignant neoplasms (cancers) 57.2; diseases of the respiratory system 33.7; ill-defined conditions 67.6.

National economy

Budget (1992). Revenue: Sf 1,430,700,000[7] (direct taxes 32.6%; indirect taxes 26.8%; bauxite levy 16.8%; aid 4.4%). Expenditures: Sf 1,815,500,000[7] (current expenditures 96.1%, of which general public services 48.9%, transfers 14.0%, debt service 10.4%; capital expenditures 3.9%).
Production (metric tons except as noted). Agriculture, forestry, fishing (1993): rice 260,000, bananas 50,000, sugarcane 45,000, oranges 15,000, plantains 13,000, coconuts 10,000, watermelons 9,000, cucumbers 5,000, cassava 4,000, tomatoes 4,000, palm oil 1,500; livestock (number of live animals) 97,000 cattle, 36,000 pigs; roundwood (1992) 154,000 cu m; fish catch (1991) 4,100. Mining and quarrying (1992): bauxite 3,160,000; gold 965 troy oz. Manufacturing (1992): alumina 1,573,000; aluminum 32,400; cement 14,339; sugar 2,000; palm oil 1,988; plywood 8,000 sq m; shoes 111,624 pairs; soft drinks 101,680 hectolitres; beer 66,690 hectolitres; cigarettes 419,000,000 units. Construction (value of buildings authorized; 1985): residential Sf 46,500,000[7]; nonresidential Sf 8,100,000[7]. Energy production (consumption): electricity (kW-hr; 1992) 1,420,000,000 (1,420,000,000); hard coal (metric tons) none (n.a.); crude petroleum (barrels; 1992) 1,730,000 (1,240,000); petroleum products (metric tons; 1992) none (446,000); natural gas, none (none).
Population economically active (1990)[8]: total 99,010; activity rate of total population 24.6% (participation rates: ages 15–64, 59.2%; female 41.3%; unemployed 15.5%).

Price and earnings indexes (1990 = 100)							
	1987	1988	1989	1990	1991	1992	1993
Consumer price index	76.0	81.5	82.1	100.0	126.0	181.0	440.7
Earnings index	...	...	...	...	...	...	...

Public debt (external, outstanding; 1990): U.S.$138,000,000.
Tourism (1992): receipts from visitors U.S.$11,000,000; expenditures by nationals abroad U.S.$12,000,000.
Land use (1992): forested 94.9%; meadows and pastures 0.1%; agricultural and under permanent cultivation 0.4%; other 4.6%.
Gross national product (at current market prices; 1992): U.S.$1,727,000,000 (U.S.$3,690 per capita).

Structure of gross domestic product and labour force				
	1992		1990[8]	
	in value Sf '000,000[7,9]	% of total value	labour force	% of labour force
Agriculture, forestry	684.0	14.7	2,890	2.9
Mining	103.5	2.2	2,380	2.4
Manufacturing	508.8	11.0	8,840	8.9
Construction	349.0	7.5	3,910	3.9
Public utilities	151.0	3.2	...	...
Transportation and communications	262.9	5.7	5,270	5.3
Trade	1,089.4	23.5	13,770	13.9
Finance, real estate	932.4	20.0	2,550	2.6
Pub. admin., defense	843.3	18.2 }	36,720	37.1
Services	36.2	0.8 }		
Other	−316.9[10]	−6.8[10]	22,680[11]	22.9[11]
TOTAL	4,643.5[12]	100.0	99,010	100.0[12]

Household income and expenditure. Average household size (1980) 3.9; income per household: n.a.; sources of income (1975): wages and salaries 74.6%, transfer payments 3.2%, other 22.2%; expenditure (1968–69)[9]: food and beverages 40.0%, household furnishings 12.3%, clothing and footwear 11.0%, transportation and communications 9.5%, recreation and education 8.4%, energy 6.9%, housing 4.4%, other 7.5%.

Foreign trade

Balance of trade (current prices)						
	1985	1986	1987	1988	1989	1990
Sf '000,000	+54.1	−5.0	+17.3	+103.6	+268.3	+93.1
% of total	4.8%	0.6%	1.6%	14.3%	16.1%	5.8%

Imports (1991): Sf 909,400,000[7] (semimanufactured goods 35.1%, machinery and transport equipment 24.5%, fuels and lubricants 15.5%). *Major import sources:* United States 38.3%; The Netherlands 22.1%; Trinidad and Tobago 11.2%; Netherlands Antilles 3.5%; Brazil 3.0%.
Exports (1991): Sf 641,300,000[7] (alumina 69.8%, shrimps 8.9%, aluminum 8.8%, rice 6.0%, bananas 2.5%, wood and wood products 0.2%). *Major export destinations:* Norway 34.2%; The Netherlands 26.3%; United States 12.9%; Brazil 8.2%; Japan 7.8%; France 2.3%.

Transport and communications

Transport. Railroads (1991): length 187 mi, 301 km; passengers, not applicable; cargo, n.a. Roads (1990): total length 5,688 mi, 9,153 km (paved 29%). Vehicles (1993): passenger cars 42,561; trucks and buses 15,774. Merchant marine (1992): vessels (100 gross tons and over) 24; total deadweight tonnage 15,721. Air transport (1990)[13]: passenger-mi 251,000,000, passenger-km 404,000,000; short ton-mi cargo 10,300,000, metric ton-km cargo 15,000,000; airports (1994) with scheduled flights 2.
Communications. Daily newspapers (1992): total number 3; total circulation 25,000; circulation per 1,000 population 61. Radio (1993): total number of receivers 290,256 (1 per 1.4 persons). Television (1993): total number of receivers 59,598 (1 per 7.0 persons). Telephones (1992): 63,000 (1 per 6.5 persons).

Education and health

Education (1991–92)				student/
	schools	teachers	students	teacher ratio
Primary (age 6–11)	301	2,918	63,083	21.6
Secondary (age 12–18)	89	1,684	26,708	15.8
Voc., teacher tr.[14]	64	1,283	15,996	12.5
Higher[15]	1	...	2,164	...

Educational attainment: n.a. *Literacy* (1990): total population age 15 and over literate 262,700 (94.9%); males literate 128,700 (95.1%); females literate 134,000 (94.7%).
Health: physicians (1990) 299 (1 per 1,348 persons); hospital beds (1989) 1,901 (1 per 212 persons); infant mortality rate per 1,000 live births (1986) 26.5.
Food (1988–90): daily per capita caloric intake 2,436 (vegetable products 86%, animal products 14%); 108% of FAO recommended minimum requirement.

Military

Total active duty personnel (1994): 1,800[16] (army 77.8%, navy 13.3%, air force 8.9%). *Military expenditure as percentage of GNP* (1991): 3.8% (world 4.2%); per capita expenditure U.S.$186.

---

[1]Floating rate introduced July 11, 1994. [2]Districts reorganized in 1985. [3]Area excludes 6,809 sq mi (17,635 sq km) of territory disputed with Guyana. [4]Detail does not add to total given because of computational discrepancies. [5]1993. [6]Based on 71.6% of total deaths. [7]Par value prior to July 11, 1994, was Sf 1.79 = U.S.$1.00; Sf 3.03 = 1 £. [8]Districts of Wanica and Paramaribo only. [9]At factor costs. [10]Imputed bank service charges. [11]Includes 15,360 unemployed. [12]Detail does not add to total given because of rounding. [13]SLM (Suriname Airways) only. [14]1984–85. [15]1989–90. [16]All services are part of the army.

Swaziland

Official name: Umbuso weSwatini (Swazi); Kingdom of Swaziland (English).
Form of government[1]: monarchy with two legislative houses (Senate [30[2]]; House of Assembly [65[3]]).
Head of state and government: King, assisted by Prime Minister.
Capitals: Mbabane (administrative); Lobamba (royal and legislative).
Official languages: Swazi; English.
Official religion: none.
Monetary unit: 1 lilangeni[4] (plural emalangeni [E]) = 100 cents; valuation (Oct. 7, 1994) 1 U.S.$ = E 3.57; 1 £ = E 5.68.

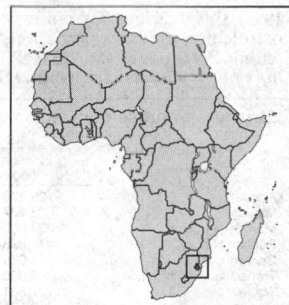

Area and population

Districts	Capitals	area sq mi	area sq km	population 1986 census[5]
Hhohho	Mbabane	1,378	3,569	178,936
Lubombo	Siteki	2,296	5,947	153,958
Manzini	Manzini	1,571	4,068	192,596
Shiselweni	Nhlangano	1,459	3,780	155,569
TOTAL		6,704	17,364	681,059

Demography

Population (1994): 883,000.
Density (1994): persons per sq mi 131.7, persons per sq km 50.8.
Urban-rural (1991): urban 34.3%; rural 65.7%.
Sex distribution (1990): male 49.37%; female 50.63%.
Age breakdown (1990): under 15, 47.4%; 15–29, 25.8%; 30–44, 14.3%; 45–59, 8.0%; 60 and over, 4.5%.
Population projection: (2000) 984,000; (2010) 1,270,000.
Doubling time: 26 years.
Ethnic composition (1983): Swazi 84.3%; Zulu 9.9%; Tsonga 2.5%; Indian 0.8%; Pakistani 0.8%; Portuguese 0.2%; other 1.5%.
Religious affiliation (1980): Christian 77.0%, of which Protestant 37.3%; African indigenous 28.9%, Roman Catholic 10.8%; traditional beliefs 20.9%; other 2.1%.
Major cities (1986): Manzini 52,000; Mbabane 38,290; Nhlangano 4,107; Piggs Peak 3,223; Siteki 2,271.

Vital statistics

Birth rate per 1,000 population (1990–95): 37.2 (world avg. 26.0); legitimate, n.a.; illegitimate, n.a.
Death rate per 1,000 population (1990–95): 10.4 (world avg. 9.2).
Natural increase rate per 1,000 population (1990–95): 26.8 (world avg. 16.8).
Total fertility rate (avg. births per childbearing woman; 1990–95): 4.9.
Marriage rate per 1,000 population: n.a.
Divorce rate per 1,000 population: n.a.
Life expectancy at birth (1990–95): male 56.2 years; female 59.8 years.
Major causes of death (1992)[6]: accidents and injuries 15.8%; infectious intestinal diseases 13.3%; tuberculosis 10.3%; malnutrition 6.2%; respiratory diseases 5.3%; circulatory diseases 5.0%; digestive diseases 4.6%.

National economy

Budget (1993–94). Revenue: E 1,240,100,000 (receipts from Customs Union of Southern Africa 45.6%; tax on income and profits 28.6%; sales tax 12.3%; foreign-aid grants 3.2%; property income 2.4%; fees, services, and fines 1.2%). Expenditures: E 1,521,900,000 (recurrent expenditure 61.6%, of which education 18.3%, general administration 13.7%, economic services 9.9%, health 5.9%, justice and police 5.6%, defense 5.3%, public-debt payments 1.8%).
Land use (1992): forested 6.9%; meadows and pastures 62.2%; agricultural and under permanent cultivation 11.1%; other 19.8%.
Tourism (1992): receipts from visitors U.S.$32,000,000; expenditures by nationals abroad U.S.$16,000,000.
Gross national product (at current market prices; 1993): U.S.$932,400,000 (U.S.$1,050 per capita).

Structure of gross domestic product and labour force

	1991 in value E '000	1991 % of total value	1986 labour force	1986 % of labour force
Agriculture	299,300	13.4	30,197	18.8
Mining	24,400	1.1	5,245	3.3
Manufacturing	603,700	27.1	14,742	9.2
Construction	53,200	2.4	7,661	4.8
Public utilities	36,800	1.7	1,315	0.8
Transp. and commun.	105,800	4.7	7,526	4.7
Trade	193,100	8.7	12,348	7.7
Finance	225,100	10.1	1,931	1.2
Pub. admin., defense	301,900	13.5 }	32,309	20.1
Services	42,500	1.9 }		
Other	342,200[7]	15.4[7]	47,081[8]	29.4[8]
TOTAL	2,228,000	100.0	160,355	100.0

Population economically active (1986): total 160,355; activity rate of total population 23.5% (participation rates: ages 15 and over, 44.1%; female 34.2%; unemployed 27.0%).

Price and earnings indexes (1990 = 100)

	1987	1988	1989	1990	1991	1992	1993
Consumer price index	74.0	83.2	90.1	100.0	110.8	119.9	140.3
Earnings index	...	...	...	...	...	...	...

Public debt (external, outstanding; 1992): U.S.$233,400,000.
Production (metric tons except as noted). Agriculture, forestry, fishing (1993): sugarcane 3,500,000, corn (maize) 84,000, grapefruit 52,000, seed cotton 50,000, lint cotton 16,000, roots and tubers 10,000 (of which potatoes 6,000, sweet potatoes 4,000), pulses 4,000; livestock (number of live animals) 753,000 cattle, 406,000 goats, 31,000 pigs, 23,000 sheep, 1,000,000 chickens; roundwood (1992) 2,297,000 cu m; fish catch (1991) 105. Mining and quarrying (1993): asbestos 33,862; diamonds 61,686 carats. Manufacturing (value added in E; 1988): food and beverages 290,900,000, of which beverage processing 168,402,000, sugarcane milling 94,934,000; paper and paper products 107,490,000; textiles and garments 17,965,000; wood and wood products 11,453,000; machinery and equipment 10,833,000; nonmetallic mineral products 9,464,000. Construction (value in E; 1993)[9]: residential 38,600,000; nonresidential 3,600,000. Energy production (consumption): electricity (kW-hr; 1991) 387,000,000 (815,000,000); coal (metric tons; 1992) 100,220 (1989; 28,454); crude petroleum, n.a. (n.a.); petroleum products, n.a. (n.a.); natural gas, n.a. (n.a.).
Household income and expenditure. Average household size (1986) 5.7; annual income per household (1985) E 332 (U.S.$151); sources of income (1985): wages and salaries 44.4%, self-employment 22.2%, transfers 12.2%, other 21.2%; expenditure (1985): food and beverages 33.5%, rent and fuel 13.4%, household durable goods 12.8%, transportation and communications 8.8%, clothing and footwear 6.0%, recreation 3.3%.

Foreign trade

Balance of trade (current prices)

	1988	1989	1990	1991	1992	1993
E '000,000	−57.3	−56.7	−77.5	−98.6	−362.7	−406.9
% of total	2.8%	2.1%	2.6%	2.9%	9.1%	8.7%

Imports (1991–92): E 2,057,690,000 (machinery and transport equipment 26.9%; minerals, fuels, and lubricants 14.5%; manufactured items 13.2%; foodstuffs 12.8%). *Major import sources:* South Africa 95.8%; United Kingdom 1.2%; Singapore 0.3%; Hong Kong 0.3%; Denmark 0.3%; The Netherlands 0.2%.
Exports (1991): E 1,711,539,000 (sugar 24.8%; wood and wood products 11.1%; canned fruits 3.9%; diamonds 0.8%; asbestos 0.8%). *Major export destinations* (1991): South Africa 47.0%; United States 3.6%; United Kingdom 3.3%; Mozambique 2.4%; South Korea 2.2%; Zimbabwe 2.2%.

Transport and communications

Transport. Railroads (1993): length 199 mi, 320 km; passengers, n.a.; short ton-mi cargo 73,300,000[10], metric ton-km cargo 107,000,000[10]. Roads (1990): total length 1,740 mi, 2,801 km (paved 26%). Vehicles (1992): passenger cars 25,283; trucks and buses 7,297. Merchant marine: none; landlocked state. Air transport (1992)[11]: passenger-mi 25,608,000, passenger-km 41,212,000; short ton-mi cargo 101,000, metric ton-km cargo 147,000; airports (1994) with scheduled flights 1.
Communications. Daily newspapers (1993): total number 3; total circulation 20,500[12]; circulation per 1,000 population 25[12]. Radio (1993): total number of receivers 65,000 (1 per 13 persons). Television (1993): total number of receivers 12,500 (1 per 65 persons). Telephones (1991): 19,546 (1 per 40 persons).

Education and health

Education (1991)

	schools	teachers	students	student/teacher ratio
Primary (age 6–13)	523	5,015	183,738	36.6
Secondary (age 14–18)	153	2,149	50,676	23.6
Voc., teacher tr.	8	280	772	2.8
Higher	1	146	1,705	11.7

Educational attainment (1986). Percentage of population age 25 and over having: no formal schooling 42.1%; some primary education 23.9%; complete primary 10.5%; some secondary 19.2%; complete secondary and higher 4.3%. *Literacy* (1986): total population age 15 and over literate 240,171 (67.0%); males literate 112,578 (69.0%); females literate 127,593 (65.0%).
Health: physicians (1990) 83 (1 per 9,265 persons); hospital beds (1984) 1,608 (1 per 396 persons); infant mortality rate per 1,000 live births (1990–95) 73.0.
Food (1988–90): daily per capita caloric intake 2,634 (vegetable products 91%, animal products 9%); 114% of FAO recommended minimum requirement.

Military

Total active duty personnel (1983): 2,657. *Military expenditure as percentage of GNP* (1989): 1.7% (world 4.9%); per capita expenditure U.S.$13.

[1]The government announced on Oct. 9, 1992, that a new constitution would be forthcoming; nonparty legislative elections took place on Sept. 25, 1993, and Oct. 11, 1993. [2]Includes 20 nonelective seats. [3]Includes 10 nonelective seats. [4]The lilangeni is at par with the South African rand. [5]Preliminary. [6]Percentage of deaths of known cause at government, mission, and private hospitals. [7]Includes indirect taxes less imputed bank service charges and subsidies. [8]Includes 43,925 unemployed. [9]Urban areas under the jurisdiction of the Manzini and Mbabane town councils only. [10]1984. [11]Royal Swazi National Airways only; international flights only. [12]Circulation for 2 newspapers only.

Sweden

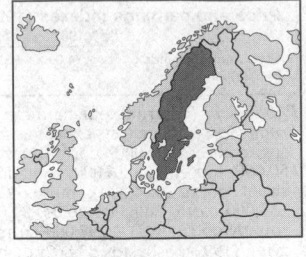

Official name: Konungariket Sverige
(Kingdom of Sweden).
Form of government: constitutional
monarchy and parliamentary
state with one legislative house
(Parliament [349]).
Chief of state: King.
Head of government: Prime Minister.
Capital: Stockholm.
Official language: Swedish.
Official religion: Church of Sweden
(Lutheran).
Monetary unit: 1 Swedish krona
(SKr) = 100 ore; valuation (Oct. 7,
1994) 1 U.S.$ = SKr 7.32;
1 £ = SKr 11.64.

Area and population

Counties	Capitals	area sq mi	area sq km	population 1994[1] estimate
Älvsborg	Vänersborg	4,400	11,395	447,437
Blekinge	Karlskrona	1,136	2,941	151,853
Gävleborg	Gävle	7,024	18,191	289,612
Göteborg och Bohus	Göteborg	1,985	5,141	754,438
Gotland	Visby	1,212	3,140	57,751
Halland	Halmstad	2,106	5,454	264,607
Jämtland	Östersund	19,090	49,443	136,073
Jönköping	Jönköping	3,839	9,944	310,872
Kalmar	Kalmar	4,313	11,170	242,528
Kopparberg	Falun	10,886	28,194	290,515
Kristianstad	Kristianstad	2,350	6,087	293,245
Kronoberg	Växjö	3,266	8,458	179,649
Malmöhus	Malmö	1,907	4,938	800,122
Norrbotten	Luleå	38,191	98,913	267,092
Örebro	Örebro	3,289	8,519	275,532
Östergötland	Linköping	4,078	10,562	411,212
Skaraborg	Mariestad	3,065	7,937	279,246
Södermanland	Nyköping	2,340	6,060	259,199
Stockholm	Stockholm	2,505	6,488	1,686,230
Uppsala	Uppsala	2,698	6,989	283,006
Värmland	Karlstad	6,789	17,584	285,220
Västerbotten	Umeå	21,390	55,401	258,171
Västernorrland	Härnösand	8,370	21,678	260,567
Västmanland	Västerås	2,433	6,302	260,932
TOTAL LAND AREA		158,661[2]	410,929	
INLAND WATER		15,071	39,035	
TOTAL		173,732	449,964	8,745,109

Demography

Population (1994): 8,773,000.
Density (1994)[3]: persons per sq mi 55.3, persons per sq km 21.3.
Urban-rural (1992): urban 84.3%; rural 15.7%.
Sex distribution (1994[1]): male 49.41%; female 50.59%.
Age breakdown (1994[1]): under 15, 18.7%; 15–29, 20.0%; 30–44, 20.3%; 45–59, 18.7%; 60–74, 14.1%; 75 and over, 8.2%.
Population projection: (2000) 8,973,000; (2010) 9,192,000.
Ethnic composition (1994[1]): Swedish 90.1%; Finnish 2.4%; other 7.5%.
Religious affiliation (1992[1]): Church of Sweden 88.2% (nominally; about 30% nonpracticing); Roman Catholic 1.7%; Pentecostal 1.1%; other 9.0%.
Major cities (1994[1]): Stockholm 692,954; Göteborg 437,313; Malmö 237,438; Uppsala 178,011; Linköping 128,610.

Vital statistics

Birth rate per 1,000 population (1993): 13.5 (world avg. 26.0); legitimate 50.5%; illegitimate 49.5%.
Death rate per 1,000 population (1993): 11.1 (world avg. 9.2).
Natural increase rate per 1,000 population (1993): 2.4 (world avg. 16.8).
Total fertility rate (avg. births per childbearing woman; 1992): 2.1.
Marriage rate per 1,000 population (1993): 3.9.
Divorce rate per 1,000 population (1993): 2.5.
Life expectancy at birth (1988–92): male 74.8 years; female 80.5 years.
Major causes of death per 100,000 population (1990): heart disease 447.2; malignant neoplasms (cancers) 237.5; cerebrovascular disease 120.2.

National economy

Budget (1993–94). Revenue: SKr 343,990,000,000 (value-added and excise taxes 55.4%, social-security contributions 15.8%, income and capital gains taxes 11.2%, nontax revenue 10.5%, property taxes 7.1%). Expenditures: SKr 549,662,000,000 (health and social affairs 23.0%, interest on national debt 17.5%, education and culture 9.9%, defense 7.1%).
Public debt (1993): U.S.$100,950,000,000.
Tourism (1992): receipts from visitors U.S.$3,086,000,000; expenditures by nationals abroad U.S.$6,794,000,000.
Production (metric tons except as noted). Agriculture, forestry, fishing (1993): sugar beets 2,136,000, wheat 1,750,000, barley 1,670,000, oats 1,295,000, potatoes 1,260,000[4]; livestock (number of live animals) 2,276,000 pigs, 1,807,000 cattle, 471,000 sheep; roundwood 46,900,000 cu m; fish catch 334,000, of which Baltic herring 64,000. Mining and quarrying (1993): iron ore 11,580,000[5]; copper 334,000; zinc 301,000; lead 150,000. Manufacturing (value added, in SKr '000,000; 1991): machinery and transport equipment 101,889; paper and paper products 34,325; food and beverages 23,037; wood and wood products 14,379; textiles and wearing apparel 4,054. Construction (1992): 57,319 dwellings completed. Energy production (consumption): electricity (kW-hr; 1992) 146,245,000,000 (144,095,000,000); coal (metric tons;

1992) 37,000 (3,368,000); crude petroleum (barrels; 1992) 7,000 (121,713,000); petroleum products (metric tons; 1992) 17,027,000 (16,296,000); natural gas (cu m; 1992) none (486,913,000).
Gross national product (1992): U.S.$233,190,000,000 (U.S.$26,800 per capita).

Structure of gross domestic product and labour force

	1992 in value SKr '000,000	1992 % of total value	1993 labour force	1993 % of labour force
Agriculture	29,520	2.3	137,000	3.2
Mining	3,407	0.3	11,000	0.3
Manufacturing	253,000	20.1	726,000	16.8
Public utilities	42,828	3.4	35,000	0.8
Construction	84,086	6.7	236,000	5.5
Transp. and commun.	89,623	7.1	277,000	6.4
Trade	137,561	10.9	567,000	13.1
Finance	315,031	25.0	368,000	8.5
Pub. admin., defense } Services	375,404	29.7	1,602,000	37.1
Other	−69,159[6]	−5.5[6]	356,000[7]	8.2[7]
TOTAL	1,261,301	100.0	4,320,000[2]	100.0[2]

Population economically active (1993): total 4,320,000; activity rate of total population 49.5% (participation rates: ages 16–64 [1992] 82.0%; female 48.0%; unemployed 8.2%).

Price and earnings indexes (1990 = 100)

	1987	1988	1989	1990	1991	1992	1993
Consumer price index	80.0	85.0	90.6	100.0	109.4	118.5	117.1
Hourly earnings index	77.0	83.0	91.0	100.0	105.0	110.0	113.0

Household income and expenditure. Average household size (1990) 2.1; median income per household SKr 119,000 (U.S.$18,400); sources of income (1991): wages and salaries 60.3%, transfer payments 24.0%, self-employment 12.6%; expenditure (1991): housing and energy 29.2%, food 21.0%, transportation 17.3%, education and recreation 9.2%.
Land use (1992): forested 59.8%; meadows and pastures 1.5%; agricultural and under permanent cultivation 7.9%; other 30.8%.

Foreign trade

Balance of trade (current prices)

	1987	1988	1989	1990	1991	1992
SKr '000,000	29,827	31,208	23,098	23,272	38,343	42,894
% of total	5.6%	5.4%	3.6%	3.5%	6.1%	7.0%

Imports (1993): SKr 331,930,000,000 (machinery and transport equipment 36.0%, of which transport equipment 8.6%, electrical machinery 10.9%; chemicals 11.5%; food 7.4%; clothing 5.4%). *Major import sources:* Germany 19.9%; U.K. 9.4%; U.S. 9.1%; Denmark 7.3%; Norway 6.4%; Finland 6.2%.
Exports (1993): SKr 388,260,000,000 (machinery and transport equipment 43.2%, of which transport equipment 15.2%, electrical machinery 10.4%; paper products 10.2%; chemicals 9.9%; wood and wood pulp 6.1%; iron and steel products 5.8%). *Major export destinations:* Germany 14.4%; U.K. 10.2%; U.S. 8.4%; Norway 8.1%; Denmark 6.6%; Finland 4.6%.

Transport and communications

Transport. Railroads (1992): length 6,863 mi, 11,045 km; passenger-mi 3,517,000,000, passenger-km 5,660,000,000; short ton-mi cargo 13,318,000,000, metric ton-km cargo 19,444,000,000. Roads (1992): total length 84,419 mi, 135,859 km (paved 72%). Vehicles (1993): passenger cars 3,566,040; trucks and buses 315,994. Merchant marine (1992): vessels (100 gross tons and over) 664; total deadweight tonnage 3,327,699. Air transport (1992): passenger-mi 5,019,234,000, passenger-km 8,077,690,000; short ton-mi cargo 115,470,000, metric ton-km cargo 168,580,000; airports (1994) 45.
Communications. Daily newspapers (1992): total number 174; total circulation 4,833,000; circulation per 1,000 population 558. Radio (1992): 7,271,556 receivers (1 per 1.2 persons). Television (1992): 3,750,000 receivers (1 per 2.3 persons). Telephones (1983): 7,410,000 (1 per 1.1 persons).

Education and health

Education (1993–94)

	schools	teachers	students	student/ teacher ratio
Primary (age 7–12)	4,826	90,234	893,932	9.9
Secondary (age 13–18)	600	29,539	313,728	10.6
Higher[8]	...	27,523[9]	272,718	9.9

Educational attainment (1990). Percentage of population age 16–64 having: primary education 37.1%; lower secondary education 29.4%; higher secondary 12.2%; some postsecondary 21.3%. *Literacy* (1993): virtually 100%.
Health: physicians (1992) 22,000 (1 per 394 persons); hospital beds (1991) 48,588 (1 per 177 persons); infant mortality rate per 1,000 live births (1993) 4.8.
Food (1988–90): daily per capita caloric intake 2,978 (vegetable products 63%, animal products 37%); 111% of FAO requirement.

Military

Total active duty personnel (1993): 64,800 (army 67.1%, navy 15.1%, air force 17.8%). *Military expenditure as percentage of GNP* (1989): 2.6% (world 4.9%); per capita expenditure U.S.$574.

[1]January 1. [2]Detail does not add to total given because of rounding. [3]Density based on land area only. [4]1992. [5]Metal content of ore. [6]Includes statistical discrepancies less imputed bank service charges. [7]Unemployed. [8]1989–90. [9]Includes graduate assistants.

Switzerland

Official name: Confédération
Suisse (French); Schweizerische
Eidgenossenschaft (German);
Confederazione Svizzera (Italian)
(Swiss Confederation).
Form of government: federal state with
two legislative houses (Council of
States [46]; National Council [200]).
Head of state and government:
President.
Capitals: Bern (administrative);
Lausanne (judicial).
Official languages: French, German,
Italian.
Official religion: none.
Monetary unit: 1 Swiss Franc
(Sw F) = 100 centimes; valuation (Oct.
7, 1994) 1 U.S.$ = Sw F 1.28;
1 £ = Sw F 2.03.

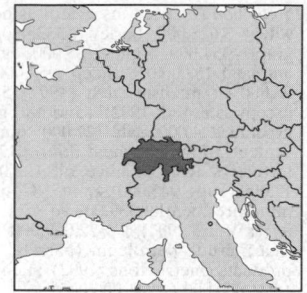

Area and population		area		population
				1993[1]
Cantons	Capitals	sq mi	sq km	estimate
Aargau	Aarau	542	1,404	512,000
Appenzell Ausser-Rhoden[2]	Herisau	94	243	53,400
Appenzell Inner-Rhoden[2]	Appenzell	67	173	14,500
Basel-Landschaft[2]	Liestal	165	428	233,200
Basel-Stadt[2]	Basel	14	37	196,600
Bern	Bern	2,336	6,051	953,500
Fribourg	Fribourg	645	1,671	214,600
Genève	Geneva	109	282	383,900
Glarus	Glarus	265	685	39,000
Graubünden	Chur	2,743	7,105	179,300
Jura	Delémont	323	836	68,300
Luzern	Luzern	576	1,493	331,800
Neuchâtel	Neuchâtel	310	803	162,600
Nidwalden[2]	Stans	107	276	34,900
Obwalden[2]	Sarnen	189	491	30,200
Sankt Gallen	Sankt Gallen	782	2,026	432,800
Schaffhausen	Schaffhausen	115	298	73,000
Schwyz	Schwyz	351	908	116,100
Solothurn	Solothurn	305	791	234,900
Thurgau	Frauenfeld	383	991	213,200
Ticino	Bellinzona	1,000	2,012	294,100
Uri	Altdorf	416	1,077	35,500
Valais	Sion	2,017	5,224	262,400
Vaud	Lausanne	1,240	3,211	593,000
Zug	Zug	92	239	87,100
Zürich	Zürich	668	1,729	1,158,100
TOTAL		15,940	41,284	6,908,000[3]

Demography

Population (1994): 6,991,000.
Density (1994): persons per sq mi 438.6, persons per sq km 169.3.
Urban-rural (1992): urban 68.1%; rural 31.9%.
Sex distribution (1992): male 48.84%; female 51.16%.
Age breakdown (1992): under 15, 17.4%; 15–29, 21.3%; 30–44, 23.3%; 45–59, 18.6%; 60–74, 12.7%; 75 and over, 6.7%.
Population projection: (2000) 7,298,000; (2010) 7,452,000.
Linguistic composition (1990): German 63.6%; French 19.2%; Italian 7.6%; Spanish 1.7%; Portuguese 1.4%; Romansch 0.6%; other 5.9%.
Religious affiliation (1990): Roman Catholic 46.2%; Protestant 40.0%; Muslim 2.2%; Orthodox Christian 1.0%; Jewish 0.3%; other 10.3%.
Major cities (1993[1]): Zürich 345,200 (841,052[4]); Basel 175,500 (360,350[4]); Geneva 170,200 (394,783[4]); Bern 130,100 (299,466[4]); Lausanne 117,600.

Vital statistics

Birth rate per 1,000 population (1992): 12.6 (world avg. 26.0); legitimate 93.8%; illegitimate 6.2%.
Death rate per 1,000 population (1992): 9.1 (world avg. 9.2).
Natural increase rate per 1,000 population (1992): 3.5 (world avg. 16.8).
Total fertility rate (avg. births per childbearing woman; 1992): 1.6.
Marriage rate per 1,000 population (1992): 6.5.
Life expectancy at birth (1991–92): male 74.3 years; female 81.2 years.
Major causes of death per 100,000 population (1991): heart disease 271.6, of which ischemic 150.9, other 120.7; malignant neoplasms (cancers) 244.0.

National economy

Budget (1993)[5]. Revenue: Sw F 36,651,000,000 (turnover taxes 29.9%, direct federal taxes 21.3%, motor fuel fees 11.9%). Expenditures: Sw F 39,737,-000,000 (welfare 23.9%, transportation 15.9%, defense 14.6%).
National debt (end of year; 1992): Sw F 55,296,000,000.
Tourism (1993): receipts from visitors U.S.$9,283,000,000; expenditures by nationals abroad U.S.$6,895,000,000.
Production (metric tons except as noted). Agriculture, forestry, fishing (1992): milk 3,845,000, sugar beets 907,000, potatoes 737,000, wheat 533,000, apples 396,000, barley 365,000, grapes 164,000; livestock (number of live animals) 1,783,000 cattle, 1,706,000 pigs; roundwood (1991) 4,070,000 cu m; fish catch (1991) 4,791. Mining (1991): salt 250,000. Manufacturing (value added in U.S.$'000,000; 1990): nonelectrical machinery 7,544; food products 5,832; electrical goods and electronics 5,713; industrial chemicals 4,800; printing and publishing 4,222; metal products 3,944. Energy production (consumption): electricity (kW-hr; 1992) 55,908,000,000 ([1991] 55,006,000,000);

coal (metric tons; 1991) none (396,000); crude petroleum (barrels; 1991) none (33,967,000); petroleum products (metric tons; 1991) 4,522,000 (11,-089,000); natural gas (cu m; 1991) 3,150,000 (2,184,000,000).
Gross national product (1992): U.S.$248,688,000,000 (U.S.$36,230 per capita).

Structure of gross domestic product and labour force				
	1990		1992	
	in value Sw F '000,000	% of total value	labour force	% of labour force
Agriculture	9,664	3.1	194,800	5.4
Manufacturing	76,722	24.4	858,000	24.0
Mining	}		25,300	0.7
Public utilities	6,011	1.9 }		
Construction	26,224	8.4	329,300	9.2
Transp. and commun.	18,556	5.9	218,400	6.1
Trade	56,531	18.0	735,600	20.6
Finance, insurance[6]	67,158	21.4	452,100	12.7
Pub. admin., defense	63,037	20.1	136,800	3.8
Services	}		620,000	17.4
Other	−9,913[7]	−3.2[7]	2,500	0.1
TOTAL	313,990	100.0	3,572,800[8]	100.0[8]

Population economically active (1992): total 3,572,800; activity rate of total population 51.5% (participation rates: age 15 and over [1988] 62.9%; female 38.3%; unemployed [February 1993–January 1994] 4.7%).

Price and earnings indexes (1985 = 100)							
	1987	1988	1989	1990	1991	1992	1993
Consumer price index	102.2	104.1	107.4	113.2	119.8	124.7	128.8
Hourly earnings index	106.5	110.4	114.8	121.7	130.9	138.0	...

Household income and expenditure. Average household size (1992) 2.4; average income per household (1990) Sw F 71,574 (U.S.$51,522); sources of income (1991): wages 64.5%, transfer payments 15.1%, other 20.4%; expenditure (1992): food 19.3%, housing 15.9%, health and personal effects 13.3%, transportation and communications 11.7%.
Land use (1991): forested 26.4%; meadows and pastures 40.5%; agricultural and under permanent cultivation 10.4%; other 22.7%.

Foreign trade[9]

Balance of trade (current prices)						
	1988	1989	1990	1991	1992	1993
Sw F '000,000	−7,519	−9,998	−7,397	−6,144	+268	+3,721
% of total	4.8%	5.6%	4.0%	3.4%	0.2%	3.2%

Imports (1993): Sw F 89,829,000,000 (machinery and electronics 20.0%; chemical products 13.2%; precision instruments, watches, and jewelry 12.6%).
Major import sources: Germany 32.6%; France 10.9%; Italy 9.8%; U.K. 7.2%; U.S. 6.2%.
Exports (1993): Sw F 93,289,000,000 (machinery and electronics 26.6%; chemical products 24.0%; precision instruments, watches, and jewelry 22.0%).
Major export destinations: Germany 22.9%; France 9.1%; U.S. 8.8%; Italy 7.8%; U.K. 6.9%.

Transport and communications

Transport. Railroads: length (1991) 3,125 mi, 5,030 km; passenger-km (1992) 11,748,000,000[10]; metric ton-km cargo (1992) 7,668,000,000[10]. Roads (1992): total length 44,191 mi, 71,118 km. Vehicles (1991): passenger cars 3,085,372; trucks and buses 291,457. Merchant marine (1992): vessels (100 gross tons and over) 24; total deadweight tonnage 602,084. Air transport (1992)[11]: passenger-km 16,154,000,000; metric ton-km cargo 1,063,000,000; airports (1994) with scheduled flights 6.
Communications. Daily newspapers (1991): total number 103; total circulation 2,851,832; circulation per 1,000 population 415. Radio (1993): 2,685,000 receivers (1 per 2.6 persons). Television (1993): 2,300,000 receivers (1 per 3.0 persons). Telephones (1991): 6,227,254 (1 per 1.1 persons).

Education and health

Education (1992–93)				
	schools	teachers	students	student/ teacher ratio
Primary (age 7–12)	...	...	420,089	...
Secondary (age 13–19)	...	...	404,249	...
Voc., teacher tr.	...	...	197,572	...
Higher	...	...	146,288	...

Educational attainment (1988). Percentage of resident Swiss (resident alien) population age 30 and over having completed: lower secondary education or less 33.9% (45.2%); upper secondary 47.5% (31.2%); higher 18.6% (23.6%).
Literacy: virtually 100.0%.
Health (1991): physicians c. 22,500 (1 per 311 persons); hospital beds 54,112 (1 per 127 persons); infant mortality rate (1992) 6.8.
Food (1988–90): daily per capita caloric intake 3,508 (vegetable products 61%, animal products 39%); 130% of FAO recommended minimum.

Military

Total active duty personnel (1993): 1,800[12]. *Military expenditure as percentage of GNP* (1991): 1.9% (world 4.2%); per capita expenditure U.S.$667.

[1]January 1. [2]Demicanton; functions as a full canton. [3]Includes 1,243,600 resident aliens. [4]1991 population of urban agglomeration. [5]Confederation-level only. [6]Includes consulting services. [7]Imputed bank charges less import duties. [8]Labour force includes 948,700 foreign workers. [9]Import figures are f.o.b. in balance of trade and c.i.f. in commodities and trading partners. [10]Swiss Federal Railways. [11]Swissair only. [12]Excludes 565,000 army reservists and 60,000 air corps reservists.

Syria

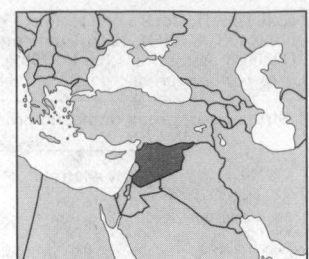

Official name: al-Jumhūrīyah al-'Arabīyah as-Sūrīyah (Syrian Arab Republic).
Form of government: unitary multiparty[1] republic with one legislative house (People's Council [250]).
Head of state and government: President.
Capital: Damascus.
Official language: Arabic.
Official religion: none[2].
Monetary unit: 1 Syrian pound (LS) = 100 piastres; valuation (nonessential [imports] rate; Oct. 7, 1994) 1 U.S.$ = LS 11.22; 1 £ = LS 17.85.

Area and population		area		population
		sq mi	sq km	1993 estimate
Governorates	**Capitals**			
Darā	Darā	1,440	3,730	593,000
Dayr az-Zawr	Dayr az-Zawr	12,765	33,060	581,000
Dimashq	Damascus	6,962	18,032	1,416,000
Ḥalab	Aleppo	7,143	18,500	2,768,000
Ḥamāh	Ḥamāh	3,430	8,883	1,079,000
al-Ḥasakah	al-Ḥasakah	9,009	23,334	1,002,000
Ḥimṣ	Homs	16,302	42,223	1,253,000
Idlib	Idlib	2,354	6,097	903,000
al-Lādhiqīyah	Latakia	887	2,297	808,000
al-Qunayṭirah	al-Qunayṭirah	719[3]	1,861[3]	42,000
ar-Raqqah	ar-Raqqah	7,574	19,616	495,000
as-Suwaydā'	as-Suwaydā'	2,143	5,550	290,000
Ṭarṭūs	Ṭarṭūs	730	1,892	666,000
Municipality				
Damascus	—	41	105	1,497,000
TOTAL		71,498[3]	185,180[3]	13,393,000

Demography

Population (1994): 13,853,000.
Density (1994): persons per sq mi 193.7, persons per sq km 74.8.
Urban-rural (1993): urban 50.0%; rural 50.0%.
Sex distribution (1992): male 50.60%; female 49.40%.
Age breakdown (1992): under 15, 48.3%; 15–29, 26.9%; 30–44, 13.2%; 45–59, 7.0%; 60–74, 3.8%; 75 and over, 0.8%.
Population projection: (2000) 16,925,000; (2010) 23,634,000.
Doubling time: 22 years.
Ethnic composition (1981): Arab 88.8%; Kurdish 6.3%; other 4.9%.
Religious affiliation (1980): Muslim (mostly Sunnī) 89.6%; Christian 8.9%; other 1.5%.
Major cities (1993): Damascus 1,497,000; Aleppo 1,494,000; Homs 537,000; Latakia 293,000; Ḥamāh 229,000.

Vital statistics

Birth rate per 1,000 population (1992): 43.8 (world avg. 26.0).
Death rate per 1,000 population (1992): 6.0 (world avg. 9.2).
Natural increase rate per 1,000 population (1992): 37.8 (world avg. 16.8).
Total fertility rate (avg. births per childbearing woman; 1992): 6.9.
Marriage rate per 1,000 population (1992)[4]: 8.4.
Divorce rate per 1,000 population (1992)[4]: 0.7.
Life expectancy at birth (1992): male 64.9 years; female 67.3 years.
Major causes of death per 100,000 population (1981): diseases of the circulatory system 60.7; accidents and adverse effects 18.3; infectious and parasitic diseases 15.1.

National economy

Budget (1992). Revenue: LS 93,043,000,000 (taxes and duties 38.0%, foreign revenues 21.0%). Expenditures: LS 93,043,000,000 (defense 26.3%, administration 17.5%, education 12.2%, agriculture 10.1%, health 3.1%).
Tourism (1992): receipts from visitors U.S.$600,000,000; expenditures by nationals abroad U.S.$260,000,000.
Land use (1992): steppe and pasture 43.8%; cultivable 32.1%; forested 3.6%; other 20.5%.
Gross national product (1991): U.S.$16,204,000,000 (U.S.$1,170 per capita).

Structure of gross domestic product and labour force				
	1992		1991	
	in value[5] LS '000,000	% of total value	labour force	% of labour force
Agriculture	103,476	29.7	916,952	26.3
Mining	46,778	13.4	6,651	0.2
Manufacturing	19,143	5.5	456,162	13.1
Construction	13,505	3.9	340,779	9.8
Public utilities	174	0.1	8,422	0.2
Transportation and communications	32,508	9.3	166,965	4.8
Trade	79,217	22.8	378,250	10.9
Finance	12,705	3.6	24,651	0.7
Pub. admin.	33,170	9.5	} 951,104	27.3
Services	6,683	1.9		
Other productive activities	130	0.1	...	...
Other	564[6]	0.2[6]	235,432[7]	6.8[7]
TOTAL	348,053	100.0	3,485,368	100.0[8]

Production (metric tons except as noted). Agriculture, forestry, fishing (1993): wheat 3,625,000, barley 1,553,000, seed cotton 639,000, tomatoes 395,000, grapes 354,000, apples 235,000, eggplants 148,000; livestock (number of live animals) 16,000,000 sheep, 950,000 goats, 770,000 cattle; roundwood (1992) 95,000 cu m; fish catch (1992) 5,400. Mining and quarrying (metric tons except as noted; 1992): sand and gravel 8,000,000; phosphate rock 1,266,000; gypsum 234,000; salt 127,000; marble 18,000 cu m. Manufacturing (1992): cement 3,700,000; wheat flour 1,171,000[9]; refined sugar 178,000; nitrogenous fertilizers 105,000; olive oil 103,000; silk and cotton textiles 26,000; soap 17,000; rugs 945,000 sq m[9]. Construction (1988): residential 2,390,000 sq m; nonresidential 339,000 sq m. Energy production (consumption): electricity (kW-hr; 1992) 13,422,000,000 (13,422,000,000); coal (metric tons) none (n.a.); crude petroleum (barrels; 1992) 176,027,000 (83,269,000); petroleum products (metric tons; 1992) 11,148,000 (9,420,000); natural gas (cu m; 1992) 1,941,000,000 (1,941,000,000).
Population economically active (1991): total 3,845,368; activity rate of total population 27.8% (participation rates: ages 15–64 [1986] 46.7%; female 10.2%; unemployed 6.1%).

Price and earnings indexes (1990 = 100)							
	1988	1989	1990	1991	1992	1993	1994[10]
Consumer price index	75.2	83.8	100.0	107.7	117.9	131.8	141.1
Earnings index	...	...	...	...	...	...	...

Public debt (external, outstanding; 1992): U.S.$14,341,000,000.
Average household size (1986): 5.7; income per household: n.a.; sources of income: n.a.; expenditure (1987)[11]: food 58.8%, rent, fuel, and light 16.0%, clothing and footwear 7.5%, household durable goods 5.8%, transportation and communications 2.4%, education and recreation 2.1%.

Foreign trade[12]

Balance of trade (current prices)						
	1988	1989	1990	1991	1992	1993
LS '000,000	−7,879	+12,140	+19,579	+2,835	−1,223	−7,312
% of total	20.7%	21.9%	27.3%	4.2%	1.7%	9.4%

Imports (1992): LS 39,178,300,000 (machinery and equipment 17.8%, food and beverages 17.5%, basic metals industries 14.7%, transportation equipment 13.1%, resins and artificial rubber 7.6%, textiles 7.5%). *Major import sources:* Germany 10.2%; Japan 9.9%; Italy 8.2%; France 6.3%; Turkey 6.2%; United States 6.1%; Romania 4.3%.
Exports (1992): LS 34,719,800,000 (crude petroleum and petroleum products 59.8%, fresh vegetables and fruits 7.6%, textiles 7.5%, raw cotton 5.9%, live animals and meat 3.7%). *Major export destinations:* Italy 35.0%; France 18.6%; Lebanon 13.0%; Saudi Arabia 4.3%; Spain 3.5%; Germany 2.5%.

Transport and communications

Transport. Railroads (1992): route length 2,261 km; passenger-km 1,248,000,000; metric ton-km cargo 1,704,000,000. Roads (1993): total length 36,255 km (paved 77%). Vehicles (1991): passenger cars 119,040; trucks and buses 135,416. Merchant marine (1992): vessels (100 gross tons and over) 94; total deadweight tonnage 210,369. Air transport (1991): passenger-km 1,157,000,000; metric ton-km cargo 14,414,000; airports (1994) with scheduled flights 5.
Communications. Daily newspapers (1990): total number 9; total circulation 236,400; circulation per 1,000 population 19.5. Radio (1993): 3,000,000 receivers (1 per 4.5 persons). Television (1993): 700,000 receivers (1 per 19.1 persons). Telephones (1992): 718,760 (1 per 18.0 persons).

Education and health

Education (1992–93)				
	schools	teachers	students	student/ teacher ratio
Primary (age 6–11)	10,079	106,164	2,573,181	24.2
Secondary (age 12–18)	2,077[13]	47,889	845,631	17.7
Voc., teacher tr.	238[13]	10,770	71,319	6.6
Higher[14]	44[13]	5,997	178,526	29.8

Educational attainment (1984). Percentage of population age 10 and over having: no schooling 31.9%; knowledge of reading and writing 28.3%; primary education 31.2%; secondary 4.8%; certificate 2.0%; higher 1.8%.
Literacy (1990): percentage of population age 15 and over literate 64.5%; males literate 78.3%; females literate 50.8%.
Health (1990): physicians 11,682 (1 per 1,037 persons); hospital beds 13,603 (1 per 891 persons); infant mortality rate per 1,000 live births (1992) 44.2.
Food (1988–90): daily per capita caloric intake 3,122 (vegetable products 88%, animal products 12%); 126% of FAO recommended minimum requirement.

Military

Total active duty personnel (1994): 408,000 (army 73.5%, navy 2.0%, air force 24.5%). *Military expenditure as percentage of GNP* (1992): 9.3% (world, n.a.); per capita expenditure U.S.$170.

[1]Parties ideologically compatible with the Ba'th Party. [2]Islam is required to be the religion of the head of state and is the basis of the legal system. [3]Includes territory in the Golan Heights recognized internationally as part of Syria (located between the 1949 Israel-Syria Armistice line [west] and the 1974 UN Disengagement of Forces zone [east]) that has been occupied by Israel since 1967. Israel's unilateral annexation of this territory in December 1981 has received no international recognition. [4]Syrian Arabs only. [5]In purchasers' value at current prices. [6]Includes import duties and imputed bank service charges. [7]Unemployed, previously employed, and never previously employed. [8]Detail does not add to total given because of rounding. [9]1991. [10]March. [11]Weights of consumer price index components for Damascus only. [12]Import figures are f.o.b. in balance of trade and c.i.f. in commodities and trading partners. [13]1989–90. [14]University-level institutions only.

Taiwan

Official name: Chung-hua Min-kuo
(Republic of China).
Form of government: multiparty
republic with a National Assembly
(402) and Legislative Yuan (161)[1].
Chief of state: President.
Head of government: Premier.
Capital: Taipei.
Official language: Mandarin Chinese.
Official religion: none.
Monetary unit: 1 New Taiwan dollar
(NT$) = 100 cents; valuation (Oct. 7,
1994) 1 U.S.$ = NT$26.16;
1 £ = NT$41.61.

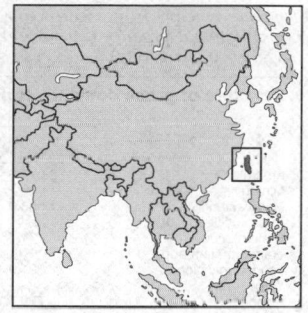

Area and population

Taiwan area Counties	Capitals	area sq mi	area sq km	population 1993 estimate
Chang-hua	Chang-hua	415	1,074	1,267,805
Chia i	Chia-i	734	1,902	558,670
Hsin-chu	Hsin-chu	551	1,428	388,551
Hua-lien	Hua-lien	1,787	4,629	356,233
I-lan	I-lan	825	2,137	459,152
Kao-hsiung	Feng-shan	1,078	2,793	1,153,738
Miao-li	Miao-li	703	1,820	553,526
Nan-t'ou	Nan-t'ou	1,585	4,106	542,095
P'ong hu	Ma-kung	49	127	94,879
P'ing-tung	P'ing-tung	1,072	2,776	902,788
T'ai-chung	Feng-yuan	792	2,051	1,334,969
T'ai-nan	Hsin-ying	778	2,016	1,051,540
T'ai-pei	Pan-ch'iao	792	2,052	3,185,535
T'ai-tung	T'ai-tung	1,357	3,515	254,752
T'ao-yüan	T'ao-yüan	471	1,221	1,429,836
Yün-lin	Tou-liu	498	1,291	753,752
Municipalities				
Chia-i	—	23	60	258,229
Chi-lung	—	51	133	360,624
Hsin-chu	—	40	104	333,540
Kao-hsiung	—	59	154	1,405,041
T'ai-chung	—	63	163	804,778
T'ai-nan	—	68	176	697,593
Taipei	—	105	272	2,675,029
non-Taiwan area Counties[2]				
Kinmen (Quemoy) Lienchiang (Matsu)	} —	69	179	50,168
TOTAL		13,969[3]	36,179	20,872,823

Demography

Population (1994)[4]: 21,151,000.
Density (1994)[4]: persons per sq mi 1,521.7, persons per sq km 587.5.
Urban-rural (1991)[5]: urban 74.7%; rural 25.3%.
Sex distribution (1993)[5]: male 51.58%; female 48.42%.
Age breakdown (1993)[5]: under 15, 25.1%; 15–29, 27.0%; 30–44, 25.0%; 45–59, 12.3%; 60–69, 6.5%; 70 and over, 4.1%.
Population projection: (2000) 22,548,000; (2010) 25,085,000.
Doubling time: 67 years.
Ethnic composition (1986): Taiwanese 84.0%; mainland Chinese 14.0%; aborigine 2.0%.
Religious affiliation (1980): Chinese folk-religionist 48.5%; Buddhist 43.0%; Christian 7.4%; Muslim 0.5%; other 0.6%.
Major cities (1993)[5]: Taipei 2,675,029; Kao-hsiung 1,405,041; T'ai-chung 804,778; T'ai-nan 697,593; Chi-lung 360,624.

Vital statistics

Birth rate per 1,000 population (1993): 15.6 (world avg. 26.0); (1992)[5] legitimate 97.7%; illegitimate 2.3%.
Death rate per 1,000 population (1993): 5.3 (world avg. 9.2).
Natural increase rate per 1,000 population (1993): 10.3 (world avg. 16.8).
Total fertility rate (avg. births per childbearing woman; 1992)[5]: 1.7.
Life expectancy at birth (1993): male 72.0 years; female 77.4 years.
Major causes of death per 100,000 population (1992)[5]: malignant neoplasms 101.5; cerebrovascular diseases 69.4; accidents and suicide 63.7; heart disease 62.9; diabetes 23.7; liver diseases 18.2; pneumonia 14.1.

National economy

Budget (1992)[6]. Revenue: NT$1,716,303,000,000 (land tax 12.7%, income taxes 12.6%, business tax 8.6%, surplus of public enterprises 8.2%, commodity tax 6.6%, customs duties 5.2%). Expenditures: NT$1,674,617,000,000 (economic development 26.7%, administration and defense 25.7%, education 20.1%).
Production (metric tons except as noted). Agriculture, forestry, fishing (1993): sugarcane 4,577,000, rice 1,820,000, citrus fruits 506,731, corn (maize) 321,-322[7], pineapples 277,263, bananas 212,748, sweet potatoes 188,000; livestock (number of live animals) 9,844,920 pigs, 293,629 goats, 165,601 cattle; timber 46,924 cu m; fish catch 1,170,707. Mining and quarrying (1990): silver 3,926 kg. Manufacturing (1993): cement 23,964,134; steel ingots 12,779,-031; paperboard 2,836,623; fertilizers 1,886,902; synthetic fibre 1,170,752; polyvinyl chloride plastics 1,078,460; electronic calculators 12,833,221 units; sound recorder 6,193,258 units; sewing machines 3,373,401 units; desktop-computer systems 3,226,046 units. Construction (1993): total residential and nonresidential 47,533,000 sq m. Energy production (consumption): electricity (kW-hr; 1993) 109,911,000,000 (92,085,000,000); coal (metric tons; 1993) 328,000 ([1992] 16,500,000); crude petroleum (barrels; 1993) 400,000 ([1992] 215,400); natural gas (cu m; 1992) 767,000,000 (n.a.).

Gross national product (1993): U.S.$220,129,000,000 (U.S.$10,566 per capita).

Structure of gross domestic product and labour force[5]

	1993 in value NT$'000,000	% of total value	labour force[8]	% of labour force[8]
Agriculture	197,794	3.5	1,005,000	11.3
Mining	34,855	0.6	19,000	0.2
Manufacturing	1,806,793	31.6	2,483,000	28.0
Construction	316,765	5.5	879,000	9.9
Public utilities	162,461	2.8	36,000	0.4
Transp. and commun.	364,864	6.4	463,000	5.2
Trade	940,905	16.5	1,806,000	20.4
Finance	1,134,789	19.9	482,000	5.4
Pub. admin., defense	638,733	11.2	1,572,000	17.7
Services	391,059	6.8		
Other	−276,499[9]	−4.8[9]	128,000[10]	1.4[10]
TOTAL	5,712,519	100.0	8,874,000[3]	100.0[3]

Public debt (1992): NT$370,887,000,000.
Tourism (1992): receipts from visitors U.S.$2,449,000,000.
Population economically active (1990): total 10,236,324; activity rate 50.5% (participation rates: age 15–64, 72.5%; female 38.5%; unemployed 1.7%).

Price and earnings indexes (1985 − 100)[5]

	1987	1988	1989	1990	1991	1992	1993
Consumer price index	101.2	102.5	107.0	111.5	115.5	120.6	124.2
Monthly earnings index[11]	121.0	134.2	153.8	176.1	195.7	213.6	228.2

Household income and expenditure (1992). Average household size 3.9; income per household NT$776,700 (U.S.$30,900[12]); sources of income: wages 68.3%, self-employment and other 28.1%, transfer payments 3.6%; expenditure: food 27.2%, rent, fuel, and power 19.3%, education 17.2%, transportation 13.2%, health care 5.3%, furniture 5.1%, clothing 4.6%, other 8.1%.
Land use (1980): forested 55.0%; agricultural 25.2%; other 19.8%.

Foreign trade

Balance of trade (current prices)

	1988	1989	1990	1991	1992	1993
NT$'000,000	306,852	359,832	330,980	350,013	231,668	199,604
% of total	9.7%	11.5%	10.1%	9.4%	6.0%	4.7%

Imports (1993): NT$2,034,746,000,000 (electronic machinery 18.7%, nonelectrical machinery 12.6%, chemicals 9.8%, iron and steel 8.5%, road motor vehicles 8.2%, crude petroleum 3.8%). *Major import sources:* Japan 30.1%; U.S. 21.7%; Germany 5.5%; Korea 3.3%; Australia 2.7%; Malaysia 2.5%.
Exports (1993): NT$2,234,350,000,000 (nonelectrical machinery 20.1%, electronic machinery 19.1%, plastic articles 5.9%, transportation equipment 5.5%, synthetic fibres 4.8%). *Major export destinations:* U.S. 27.7%; Hong Kong 21.7%; Japan 10.6%; Germany 4.1%; Singapore 3.4%.

Transport and communications

Transport. Railroads (1993): track length 3,887 km; passenger-km 9,542,118,-000; metric ton-km cargo 1,964,388,000. Roads (1993): total length 19,531 km (paved 87%). Vehicles (1993): passenger cars 3,416,848; trucks and buses 790,712. Merchant marine (1992): vessels (100 gross tons and over) 649; total deadweight tonnage 9,241,283. Air transport (1993): passenger-km 28,218,367,000; metric ton-km cargo 4,523,666,000; airports (1994) 12.
Communications. Daily newspapers (1988): total number 93; total circulation 4,000,000; circulation per 1,000 population 202. Radio (1993): 8,620,000 receivers (1 per 2.4 persons). Television (1993): 7,000,000 receivers (1 per 3.0 persons). Telephones (1992): 10,115,000 (1 per 2.1 persons).

Education and health

Education (1993–94)

	schools	teachers[13]	students	student/ teacher ratio[13]
Primary (age 6–12)	2,525	84,052	2,111,037	26.2
Secondary (age 13–18)	906	70,739	1,426,030	19.9
Vocational	209	18,332	515,211	27.4
Higher	125	31,430	689,185	20.8

Educational attainment (1992). Percentage of population age 25 and over having: no formal schooling 10.7%; less than complete primary education 6.2%; primary 26.2%; incomplete secondary 20.1%; secondary 23.1%; some college 7.7%; higher 6.0%. *Literacy* (1992): population age 15 and over literate 14,384,643 (93.2%); males 7,716,325 (96.9%); females 6,668,318 (89.2%).
Health (1992): physicians 24,982 (1 per 829 persons); hospital beds 96,084 (1 per 215 persons); infant mortality rate per 1,000 live births 5.2.
Food: daily per capita caloric intake (1990) 3,020 (1988; vegetable products 77%, animal products 23%); 118% of FAO recommended minimum.

Military

Total active duty personnel (1993): 442,000 (army 70.6%, navy 13.6%, air force 15.8%). *Military expenditure as percentage of GNP* (1989): 5.4% (world 4.9%); per capita expenditure U.S.$397.

---

[1]National Assembly functions as an electoral college or constituent body; the legislative branch is the formal lawmaking body. [2]The Nov. 7, 1992, constitutional reforms replaced the military administrations (established in 1949) on Quemoy and Matsu with civilian administrations. [3]Detail does not add to total given because of rounding. [4]Includes Quemoy and Matsu groups. [5]For Taiwan area only, excluding Quemoy and Matsu groups. [6]General government. [7]1991. [8]Civilian employed persons only. [9]Import duties less imputed bank service charge. [10]Unemployed. [11]In manufacturing. [12]Based on the average exchange rate. [13]1992–93.

Tajikistan

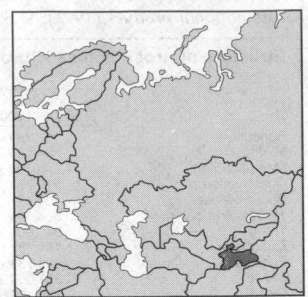

Official name: Jumhurii Tojikistan (Republic of Tajikistan).
Form of government: parliamentary republic with one legislative house (Supreme Soviet [230]).
Chief of state: Speaker of the Supreme Soviet (de facto President).
Head of government: Chairman of the Council of Ministers (Prime Minister).
Capital: Dushanbe.
Official language: Tajik (Tojik).
Official religion: none.
Monetary unit: 1 Russian ruble = 100 kopecks; valuation[1] (Oct. 7, 1994) 1 U.S.$ = 0.65 rubles; 1 £ = 1.03 rubles.

Area and population

Area and population		area		population
		sq mi	sq km	1991 estimate
Autonomous republic	**Capitals**			
Badakhshan	Khorog	24,600	63,700	167,100
Provinces				
Khudzhand	Khudzhand	10,100	26,100	1,635,900
Kulyab	Kulyab	4,600	12,000	668,100
Kurgan-Tyube	Kurgan-Tyube	4,900	12,600	1,113,500
Regions under republican juris-diction	—	11,000	28,400	1,181,800
City				
Dushanbe	—	100	300	591,900
TOTAL		55,300	143,100	5,358,300

Demography

Population (1994): 5,813,000.
Density (1994): persons per sq mi 105.1, persons per sq km 40.6.
Urban-rural (1992): urban 30.9%; rural 69.1%.
Sex distribution (1992): male 49.60%; female 50.40%.
Age breakdown (1989): under 15, 42.9%; 15–29, 28.1%; 30–44, 13.8%; 45–59, 9.0%; 60–74, 4.6%; 75 and over, 1.6%.
Population projection: (2000) 6,701,000; (2010) 8,493,000.
Doubling time: 25 years.
Ethnic composition (1991): Tajik 63.8%; Uzbek 24.0%; Russian 6.5%; Tatar 1.4%; Kyrgyz 1.3%; Ukrainian 0.7%; German 0.3%; other 2.0%.
Religious affiliation (1990): believers are predominantly Sunnī Muslim (Ḥanafīyah).
Major cities (1989): Dushanbe 582,400; Khudzhand (formerly Leninabad) 164,500; Kulyab 79,300; Kurgan-Tyube 58,400; Ura-Tyube 47,700.

Vital statistics

Birth rate per 1,000 population (1992): 34.9 (world avg. 26.0); (1989) legitimate 93.0%; illegitimate 7.0%.
Death rate per 1,000 population (1992): 6.8 (world avg. 9.2).
Natural increase rate per 1,000 population (1992): 28.1 (world avg. 16.8).
Total fertility rate (avg. births per childbearing woman; 1993): 4.7.
Marriage rate per 1,000 population (1991): 10.3.
Divorce rate per 1,000 population (1991): 1.4.
Life expectancy at birth (1993): male 65.7 years; female 71.5 years.
Major causes of death per 100,000 population (1989): diseases of the circulatory system 197.5; diseases of the respiratory system 138.8; infectious and parasitic diseases 81.2; malignant neoplasms (cancers) 51.9; violence, poisoning, and accidents 48.4; diseases of the digestive system 23.0; diseases of the nervous system 8.9; endocrine and metabolic disorders 6.9.

National economy

Production (metric tons except as noted). Agriculture, forestry, fishing (1993): seed cotton 580,000, vegetables (except potatoes) 552,000, potatoes 100,000, fruit (except grapes) 220,000, wheat 200,000, grapes 85,000, barley 40,000, corn (maize) 30,000, rice 20,000; livestock (number of live animals) 3,310,000 sheep and goats, 1,159,000 cattle, 143,000 pigs, 18,000,000 poultry; roundwood, n.a.; fish catch (1992) 39,000. Mining and quarrying: detail not available; however, antimony, mercury, and molybdenum are mined. Manufacturing (1992): cement 400,000; mineral fertilizers 50,000; vegetable oil 46,500; refrigerators 61,300 units; metal-cutting machines 400 units; leather footwear 5,500,000 pairs. Construction (1992): residential 400,000 sq m. Energy production (consumption): electricity (kW-hr; 1992) 16,800,000,000 (16,800,000,000); coal (metric tons; 1992) 200,000 (136,000); crude petroleum (barrels; 1992) 733,000 (279,000); petroleum products, n.a. (n.a.); natural gas (cu m; 1992) 99,900,000 (1,771,000,000).
Public debt (external, outstanding): n.a.
Land use (1992): forest 2.9%; pasture 24.7%; agriculture 7.0%; other 65.4%.
Population economically active (1992): total 2,575,000; activity rate of total population 46.2% (participation rates: ages 16–59 [male], 16–54 [female] 80.5%; female [1990] 39.0%; unemployed [1990] 2.0%).

Price and earnings indexes (1990 = 100)

Price and earnings indexes (1990 = 100)	1986	1987	1988	1989	1990	1991	1992
Consumer price index	...	...	...	...	100.0	184.8	1,013.0
Monthly earnings index	78.3	80.2	85.6	90.9	100.0	...	...

Tourism: receipts from visitors, n.a.; expenditures by nationals abroad, n.a.
Gross national product (at current market prices; 1992): U.S.$3,410,400,000 (U.S.$600 per capita).

Structure of gross domestic product and labour force

	1990			
	in value '000,000 rubles	% of total value	labour force[2]	% of labour force[2]
Agriculture	2,014.6	38.3	831,000	42.9
Mining } Manufacturing } Public utilities	1,503.0	28.5	260,700	13.5
Construction	771.7	14.7	160,800	8.3
Transportation and communications	221.0	4.2	64,700	3.3
Trade	—	—	145,400	7.5
Finance	750.7	14.3	—	—
Public administration, defense	—	—	38,800	2.0
Services	—	—	436,900	22.5
Other	—	—		
TOTAL	5,261.0	100.0	1,938,300	100.0

Budget (1992). Revenue: 16,875,000,000 rubles (value-added tax 30.5%, excise tax 30.0%, enterprise profits tax 10.8%, individual income tax 3.1%). Expenditures: 17,978,000,000 rubles (social welfare and culture 54.2%, law enforcement 23.2%, national economy 7.4%).
Household income and expenditure. Average household size (1989) 6.1; income per household: n.a.; sources of income: n.a.; expenditure: n.a.

Foreign trade

Balance of trade (current prices)

Balance of trade (current prices)	1991
'000,000 rubles	512.0
% of total	6.3%

Imports (1991): 3,815,600,000 rubles (machinery and transport equipment 28.1%, basic manufactures 23.2%, chemical products 22.9%, textiles 8.6%, consumer products 5.4%). *Major import sources:* former Soviet republics 90.8%; other 9.2%.
Exports (1991): 4,327,600,000 rubles (basic metal manufactures 47.6%, basic manufactures 32.7%, textiles 11.3%, chemical products 4.3%, food products 2.5%). *Major export destinations:* former Soviet republics 91.2%; other 8.8%.

Transport and communications

Transport. Railroads (1990): length 553.6 mi, 891.0 km; passenger-mi 6,094,400,000, passenger-km 9,808,000,000; short ton-mi cargo 7,617,000,000, metric ton-km cargo 11,121,000,000. Roads (1990): total length 8,324,000 mi, 13,396,000 km (paved 93%). Vehicles (1988): passenger cars 209,100; trucks and buses, n.a. Merchant marine: vessels (100 gross tons and over) n.a.; total deadweight tonnage, n.a. Air transport (1989): passenger-mi 3,214,600,000, passenger-km 5,173,400,000; short ton-mi cargo 22,124,000, metric ton-km cargo 32,300,000; airports (1994) with scheduled flights 1.
Communications. Daily newspapers (1990): total number 74; total circulation 1,598,000; circulation per 1,000 population 298.2. Radio (1992): total number of receivers 854,000 (1 per 6.7 persons). Television (1992): total number of receivers 860,000 (1 per 6.6 persons). Telephones (1992): 285,000 (1 per 19 persons).

Education and health

Education (1991–92)

Education (1991–92)	schools	teachers	students	student/ teacher ratio
Primary (age 6–13) } Secondary (age 14–17) }	3,179	99,000	1,310,000	13.2
Voc., teacher tr.	...	...	...	...
Higher	13	...	69,300	...

Educational attainment (1989). Percentage of population age 25 and over having: primary education or no formal schooling 16.3%; some secondary 21.1%; completed secondary and some postsecondary 55.1%; higher 7.5%.
Literacy: percentage of total population age 15 and over literate 97.7%; males literate 98.8%; females literate 96.6%.
Health (1992): physicians 13,500 (1 per 412 persons); hospital beds (1990) 56,500 (1 per 93 persons); infant mortality rate per 1,000 live births 40.6.
Food: daily per capita caloric intake, n.a.

Military

Total active duty personnel (1994): 6,000 (army 100%); about 24,000 Russian troops remained in Tajikistan in late 1994. *Military expenditure as percentage of GNP* (1992): 3.1% (world, n.a.); per capita expenditure U.S.$19.

---

[1]Official rate; black-market rate was about 2,900 Russian rubles to the dollar and 4,700 Russian rubles to the pound. [2]State sector.

Tanzania

Official name: Jamhuri ya Muungano wa Tanzania (Swahili); United Republic of Tanzania (English).
Form of government: unitary[1] multiparty[2] republic with one legislative house (National Assembly [255[3]]).
Head of state and government: President.
Seat of government: Dar es Salaam[4] (Capital designate, Dodoma).
Official languages: Swahili; English.
Official religion: none.
Monetary unit: 1 Tanzanian shilling (T Sh) = 100 cents; valuation (Oct. 7, 1994) 1 U.S.$ = T Sh 535.00; 1 £ = T Sh 850.92.

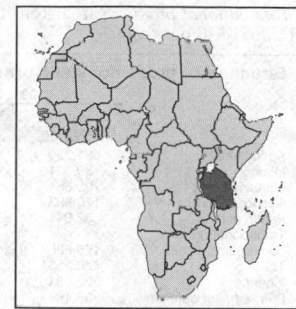

Area and population

Regions	Capitals	area sq mi	area sq km	population 1988 census
Arusha	Arusha	31,778	82,306	1,351,675
Coast	Dar es Salaam	12,512	32,407	638,015
Dar es Salaam	—	538	1,393	1,360,850
Dodoma	Dodoma	15,950	41,311	1,237,819
Iringa	Iringa	21,955	56,864	1,208,914
Kagera	Bukoba	10,961	28,388	1,326,183
Kigoma	Kigoma	14,300	37,037	854,817
Kilimanjaro	Moshi	5,139	13,309	1,108,699
Lindi	Lindi	25,501	66,046	646,550
Mara	Musoma	7,555	19,566	970,942
Mbeya	Mbeya	23,301	60,350	1,476,199
Morogoro	Morogoro	27,336	70,799	1,222,737
Mtwara	Mtwara	6,451	16,707	889,494
Mwanza	Mwanza	7,564	19,592	1,878,271
Pemba North	Wete	222	574	137,399
Pemba South	Chake Chake	128	332	127,640
Rukwa	Sumbawanga	26,500	68,635	694,974
Ruvuma	Songea	24,517	63,498	783,327
Shinyanga	Shinyanga	19,607	50,781	1,772,549
Singida	Singida	19,051	49,341	791,814
Tabora	Tabora	29,402	76,151	1,036,293
Tanga	Tanga	10,351	26,808	1,283,636
Zanzibar North	Mkokotoni	182	470	97,028
Zanzibar South and Central	Koani	330	854	70,184
Zanzibar West	Zanzibar	89	230	208,327
TOTAL LAND AREA		341,217[5]	883,749	
INLAND WATER		22,800	59,050	
TOTAL		364,017	942,799	23,174,336

Demography

Population (1994): 27,296,000[6].
Density (1994)[7]: persons per sq mi 80.0, persons per sq km 30.9.
Urban-rural (1991): urban 34.2%; rural 65.8%.
Sex distribution (1990): male 49.44%; female 50.56%.
Age breakdown (1990): under 15, 49.1%; 15–29, 25.6%; 30–44, 13.9%; 45–59, 7.6%; 60–74, 3.2%; 75 and over, 0.6%.
Population projection: (2000) 31,885,000; (2010) 41,335,000.
Doubling time: 27 years.
Ethnolinguistic composition (1987): Nyamwezi and Sukuma 26.3%; Swahili 8.8%; Haya 5.3%; Hehet and Bena 5.0%; Chagga 4.4%; Gogo 4.4%; Makonde 3.7%; other 42.1%.
Religious affiliation (1984): Muslim 35%; animist 35%; Christian 30%.
Major cities (1988): Dar es Salaam 1,360,850; Mwanza 223,013; Dodoma 203,833; Tanga 187,634; Zanzibar 157,634.

Vital statistics

Birth rate per 1,000 population (1994): 45.5 (world avg. 26.0).
Death rate per 1,000 population (1994): 19.4 (world avg. 9.2).
Natural increase rate per 1,000 population (1994): 26.1 (world avg. 16.8).
Total fertility rate (avg. births per childbearing woman; 1994): 6.0.
Life expectancy at birth (1994): male 41.5 years; female 45.0 years.
Major causes of death per 100,000 population: n.a.; however, the major diseases include malaria, bilharziasis, tuberculosis, and sleeping sickness.

National economy

Budget (1991–92). Revenue: T Sh 215,162,000,000[8] (1988–89; sales tax 46.3%, income tax 23.2%, customs and excise tax 11.8%). Expenditures: T Sh 227,973,000,000 (1988–89; public administration 17.4%, economic services 15.2%, defense 15.1%, education 5.7%, health 4.9%).
Public debt (external, outstanding; 1992): U.S.$6,280,000,000.
Tourism (1992): receipts from visitors U.S.$120,000,000; expenditures by nationals abroad (1990) U.S.$19,000,000.
Production (metric tons except as noted). Agriculture (1993): cassava 6,833,000, corn (maize) 2,284,000, sugarcane 1,470,000, bananas 800,000, plantains 800,000, sorghum 707,000, rice 631,000, coconuts 360,000, sweet potatoes 260,000, millet 221,000, potatoes 220,000; livestock (number of live animals) 13,296,000 cattle, 9,373,000 goats, 3,828,000 sheep, 335,000 pigs, 27,000,000 chickens; roundwood (1992) 34,903,000 cu m; fish catch (1992) 331,585. Mining and quarrying (1992): salt 64,000; gold 6; diamonds 68,000 carats. Manufacturing (1993): cement 540,000[9]; fresh meat and poultry 291,000; sugar 121,000; hides and skins 48,325; wheat flour 3,000[10]; soap 23,900[10]; cotton textiles 38,000,000 sq m[10]. Construction: n.a. Energy production (consumption): electricity (kW-hr; 1992) 901,000,000 (901,000,000); coal

(metric tons; 1992) 33,200 (75,000[10]); crude petroleum (barrels; 1992) none (4,075,000); petroleum products (metric tons; 1992) 565,000 (608,000).
Gross national product (1992): U.S.$2,848,000,000 (U.S.$110 per capita).

Structure of gross domestic product and labour force

	1991 In value T Sh '000,000	1991 % of total value	labour force	% of labour force
Agriculture	259,182	57.7	10,540,000	80.3
Mining	4,820	1.1		
Manufacturing	22,953	5.1		
Construction	13,468	3.0	614,000	4.7
Public utilities	7,334	1.6		
Transp. and commun.	39,393	8.8		
Trade	65,596	14.6		
Finance	27,206	6.1	1,969,000	15.0
Pub. admin., defense	18,292	4.1		
Services	17,228	3.8		
Other	−26,463[11]	−5.9[11]	...	...
TOTAL	449,009	100.0	13,123,000	100.0

Population economically active (1991): total 13,123,000; activity rate of total population 46.0% (participation rates: over age 10, 74.3%[12]; female 47.6%).

Price index (1990 = 100)

	1987	1988	1989	1990	1991	1992	1993
Consumer price index	50.6	66.4	83.5	100.0	122.3	149.3	184.3

Household income and expenditure. Avg. household size (1988) 5.2; income per household: n.a.; sources of income: n.a.; expenditure (1981): food 54.3%, clothing 10.8%, housing 8.6%, energy 6.6%, transportation 6.4%.
Land use (1992): forested 46.1%; meadows and pastures 40.7%; agricultural and under permanent cultivation 3.9%; other 9.3%.

Foreign trade[13]

Balance of trade (current prices)

	1988	1989	1990	1991	1992	1993
T Sh '000,000	−53,787	−116,840	186,418	−261,226	−325,514	−306,625
% of total	49.9%	49.5%	54.0%	63.6%	56.8%	52.2%

Imports (1993): T Sh 446,713,000,000 (1988; machinery and transport equipment 45.6%, basic manufactures 16.3%, fuel 10.2%, chemicals 8.8%, metals 5.5%, food 5.4%). *Major import sources* (1988): U.K. 16.2%; West Germany 10.5%; Japan 10.5%; Italy 8.5%; Sweden 3.8%; The Netherlands 3.5%.
Exports (1993): T Sh 140,088,000,000 (1988; coffee 25.9%, cotton 23.6%, sisal 1.4%). *Major export destinations* (1988): West Germany 22.6%; U.K. 16.6%; The Netherlands 6.9%; Singapore 5.9%; Italy 5.2%; Japan 4.8%.

Transport and communications

Transport. Railroads (1991): length 2,600 km; passenger-km 3,740,000,000; metric ton-km cargo 1,490,000,000. Roads (1994): length 88,000 km (paved 4.2%). Vehicles (1992): passenger cars 50,000; trucks and buses 40,000. Merchant marine (1992): vessels (100 gross tons and over) 43; deadweight tonnage 48,465. Air transport (1993)[14]: passenger-km 150,931,000; metric ton-km 1,893,000; airports (1994) with scheduled flights 12.
Communications. Daily newspapers: total number (1992) 3; total circulation 220,000; circulation per 1,000 population 8.5. Radio (1993): 4,000,000 receivers (1 per 6.6 persons). Television (1993): 80,000 receivers (1 per 332 persons). Telephones (1992): 150,680 (1 per 171 persons).

Education and health

Education (1992)[15]

	schools	teachers	students	student/ teacher ratio
Primary (age 7–13)	10,451[16]	101,306	3,603,488	35.6
Secondary (age 14–19)	288[17]	8,649[16]	175,776	...
Teacher training	63[17]	1,255[16]	14,051	...
Higher	4[18]	1,206[18]	6,100[19]	...

Educational attainment (1978). Percentage of population age 10 and over having: no schooling 48.6%; some primary education 40.7%; completed primary 8.7%; secondary and higher 1.9%. *Literacy* (1978): percentage of total population age 15 and over literate 46.3%; males literate 62.2%; females literate 31.4%; estimated total literacy in 1987: 94.0%.
Health: physicians (1984) 1,065 (1 per 19,775 persons); hospital beds (1986) 22,800 (1 per 924 persons); infant mortality rate (1994) 109.7.
Food (1988–90): daily per capita caloric intake 2,195 (vegetable products 94%, animal products 6%); 95% of FAO recommended minimum requirement.

Military

Total active duty personnel (1994): 49,600 (army 90.7%, navy 2.0%, air force 7.3%). *Military expenditure as percentage of GNP* (1990): 5.3% (world 4.5%); per capita expenditure U.S.$5.

[1]Federal governmental structures exist in the Zanzibar constitution and House of Representatives and in 1993 legislation authorizing a similar house in Tanganyika. [2]Multiparty system became official May 1992; multiparty elections began locally in 1993 and were scheduled to continue at various levels until completed in 1995. [3]Includes 179 directly elected, 35 indirectly elected, 15 presidential nominees, 25 ex officio members, and the president of Zanzibar. [4]Government in process of being transferred from Dar es Salaam to Dodoma; legislative branch meets in Dodoma. [5]Detail does not add to total given because of rounding. [6]Data exclude about 500,000 Burundian and 300,000 Rwandan refugees in Tanzania. [7]Based on land area. [8]Includes foreign grants and loans. [9]1992. [10]1991. [11]Less imputed bank service charges. [12]1988. [13]Import figures are c.i.f. [14]Air Tanzania only. [15]Excludes Zanzibar and Pemba. [16]1991. [17]1986–87. [18]1989. [19]1990.

Thailand

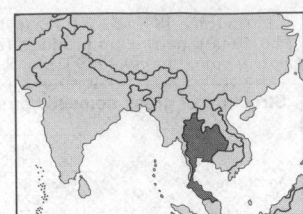

Official name: Muang Thai, or Prathet Thai (Kingdom of Thailand).
Form of government: constitutional monarchy with two legislative houses (Senate [270]; House of Representatives [360]).
Chief of state: King.
Head of government: Prime Minister[1].
Capital: Bangkok.
Official language: Thai.
Official religion: Buddhism.
Monetary unit: 1 Thai baht (B) = 100 stangs; valuation (Oct. 7, 1994) 1 U.S.$ = B 25.03; 1 £ = B 39.81.

Area and population	area		population
Regions[2]	sq mi	sq km	1992 estimate[3]
Bangkok Metropolis	2,995	7,758	8,661,228
Central	6,407	16,594	2,822,518
Eastern	14,094	36,503	3,738,670
Northeastern	65,195	168,854	20,059,015
Northern	65,500	169,644	11,682,315
Southern	27,303	70,715	7,401,746
Western	16,621	43,047	3,423,473
TOTAL	198,115	513,115	57,788,965

Demography

Population (1994): 57,586,000[4].
Density (1994): persons per sq mi 290.7, persons per sq km 112.2.
Urban-rural (1992): urban 17.7%; rural 82.3%.
Sex distribution (1992): male 50.21%; female 49.79%.
Age breakdown (1990): under 20, 44.3%; 20–39, 34.2%; 40–59, 15.4%; 60–69, 3.9%; 70 and over, 2.2%.
Population projection: (2000) 61,202,000; (2010) 66,738,000.
Doubling time: 50 years.
Ethnic composition (1983): Thai 79.5%, of which Siamese 52.6%, Lao 26.9%; Chinese 12.1%; Malay 3.7%; Khmer 2.7%; other 2.0%.
Religious affiliation (1991): Buddhist 94.8%; Muslim 4.0%; Christian 0.5%; other 0.7%.
Major cities (1991)[3]: Bangkok 5,620,591; Nonthaburi 264,201; Nakhon Ratchasima 202,503; Chiang Mai 161,541; Khon Kaen 131,478.

Vital statistics

Birth rate per 1,000 population (1993): 20.0 (world avg. 26.0).
Death rate per 1,000 population (1993): 6.0 (world avg. 9.2).
Natural increase rate per 1,000 population (1993): 14.0 (world avg. 16.8).
Total fertility rate (avg. births per childbearing woman; 1993): 2.2.
Marriage rate per 1,000 population (1992): 8.3.
Divorce rate per 1,000 population (1992): 0.8.
Life expectancy at birth (1993): male 66.0 years; female 71.0 years.
Major causes of death per 100,000 population (1990)[5]: diseases of the heart 206; malignant neoplasms (cancers) 162; accidents, homicide, and other injury 104; diseases of the digestive system 73; diseases of the respiratory system 55; cardiovascular diseases 44.

National economy

Budget (1992–93). Revenue: B 508,236,000,000 (taxes 88.6%, state enterprises 6.8%, sale of property and services 5.6%). Expenditures: B 425,512,000,000 (economic services 26.2%, education 21.1%, defense 17.2%, health 8.1%, general public services 5.7%, internal security 5.5%, external debt service 4.2%, social security 4.0%).
Production (metric tons except as noted). Agriculture, forestry, fishing (1993): sugarcane 38,500,000, tapioca 19,487,000, rice 19,440,000, corn (maize) 3,300,000, bananas 1,630,000[6], rubber 1,580,000, coconuts 1,353,000[6], soybeans 510,000, dry beans 322,000[6], cabbages 194,000[6], sorghum 140,000[6]; livestock (number of live animals; 1992) 6,820,000 cattle, 5,100,000 pigs, 4,793,000 buffalo, 136,000,000 chickens; roundwood (1991) 37,940,000 cu m; fish catch (1991) 3,065,170. Mining and quarrying (1992): limestone 25,272,000; gypsum 7,111,000; zinc ore 407,000; marble 86,995; fluorite 51,597; lead ore 27,946; tin concentrates 11,484. Manufacturing (1991): cement 19,210,000; refined sugar 3,994,828; chemical fertilizer 458,103; synthetic fibre 225,017[7]; jute products 152,263[7]; motorcycles 600,119 units. Construction (1990): residential 16,343,000 sq m; nonresidential 13,449,000 sq m. Energy production (consumption): electricity (kW-hr; 1991) 52,486,000,000 (53,041,000,000); coal (metric tons; 1991) 14,689,000 (14,868,000); crude petroleum (barrels; 1991) 8,839,000 (87,496,000); petroleum products (metric tons; 1991) 13,532,000 (20,725,000); natural gas (cu m; 1991) 5,606,000,000 (5,606,000,000).
Land use (1991): forested 27.4%; meadows and pastures 1.6%; agricultural and under permanent cultivation 45.3%; other 25.7%.
Tourism (1992): receipts from visitors U.S.$4,829,000,000; expenditures by nationals abroad U.S.$1,590,000,000.
Population economically active (1992): total 31,371,200; activity rate of total population 55.9% (participation rates: over age 13, 74.7%; female 44.4%; unemployed 4.9%).

Price and earnings indexes (1990 = 100)							
	1987	1988	1989	1990	1991	1992	1993
Consumer price index	86.3	89.6	94.4	100.0	105.7	110.0	114.0
Monthly earnings index	75.6	84.0	87.8	100.0	115.3	...	...

Gross national product (at current market prices; 1992): U.S.$106,559,000,000 (U.S.$1,840 per capita).

Structure of gross domestic product and labour force				
	1991		1992	
	in value B '000,000	% of total value	labour force[8]	% of labour force[8]
Agriculture	321,356	12.8	14,981,400	47.7
Mining	39,331	1.6	50,000	0.2
Manufacturing	706,561	28.2	4,299,000	13.7
Construction	170,893	6.8	2,055,400	6.6
Public utilities	52,941	2.1	140,400	0.4
Transportation and communications	175,686	7.0	936,500	3.0
Trade	426,233	17.0	3,820,600	12.2
Finance	205,931	8.2 }		
Pub. admin., defense	86,483	3.4 }	3,524,900	11.2
Services	324,012	12.9 }		
Other	...	...	1,563,000[9]	5.0[9]
TOTAL	2,509,427	100.0	31,371,200	100.0

Public debt (external, outstanding; 1992): U.S.$13,238,000,000.
Household income and expenditure (1990). Average household size 4.1; average annual income per household B 67,452 (U.S.$2,636); sources of income: wages and salaries 35.8%, self-employment 34.2%, transfer payments 5.8%, other 24.2%; expenditure: food, tobacco, and beverages 38.4%, housing 23.8%, transportation and communications 13.3%, clothing 6.1%, medical and personal care 5.5%, education and recreation 3.6%, other 9.3%.

Foreign trade[10]

Balance of trade (current prices)						
	1988	1989	1990	1991	1992	1993
B '000,000	−59,529	−71,417	−172,323	−139,742	−107,887	−111,602
% of total	6.9%	6.5%	12.7%	8.8%	6.1%	5.6%

Imports (1992): B 1,033,245,000,000 (nuclear reactors 17.9%, electrical machinery 14.8%, mineral fuels and lubricants 8.2%, iron and steel 8.1%, vehicles 6.5%, plastics 3.5%, organic chemicals 3.0%). *Major import sources:* Japan 29.3%; United States 11.7%; Singapore 7.3%; Taiwan 5.5%; Germany 5.3%; South Korea 4.4%; Malaysia 3.9%; China 3.0%; United Kingdom 2.3%.
Exports (1992): B 824,643,000,000 (electrical machinery 14.4%, textiles and apparel 11.7%, nuclear reactors 10.7%, fish and fish preparations 9.6%, precious stones 4.8%, rubber and rubber articles 4.6%, cereals 4.5%, vegetables 3.3%). *Major export destinations:* United States 22.2%; Japan 17.3%; Singapore 8.6%; Hong Kong 4.6%; Germany 4.3%; The Netherlands 4.3%; United Kingdom 3.6%; Malaysia 2.6%; France 2.2%.

Transport and communications

Transport. Railroads (1992)[11]: route length 2,405 mi, 3,870 km; passenger-mi 8,784,000,000, passenger-km 14,136,000,000; short ton-mi cargo 2,112,000,000, metric ton-km cargo 3,084,000,000. Roads (1990): total length 44,844 mi, 72,170 km (paved 55%). Vehicles (1992): passenger cars 890,821; trucks and buses 2,231,518. Merchant marine (1992): vessels (100 gross tons and over) 351; total deadweight tonnage 1,194,470. Air transport (1992): passenger-mi 12,737,000,000, passenger-km 20,498,000,000; short ton-mi cargo 634,495,000, metric ton-km cargo 926,347,000; airports (1994) with scheduled flights 26.
Communications. Daily newspapers (1990): total number 34; total circulation 4,000,000; circulation per 1,000 population 72. Radio (1993): 10,000,000 receivers (1 per 5.7 persons). Television (1993): 3,300,000 receivers (1 per 17 persons). Telephones (1991): 1,553,160 receivers (1 per 36 persons).

Education and health

Education (1991)	schools	teachers	students	student/ teacher ratio
Primary (age 7–12)	34,039	395,327	7,957,971	20.1
Secondary (age 13–18)	1,859	109,346	1,953,044	17.9
Voc., teacher tr.	634	36,934	653,055	17.7
Higher[12]	43	52,317	952,012	18.2

Educational attainment (1991). Percentage of population age 13 and over having: no formal schooling 7.4%; primary education 73.9%; secondary 10.4%; postsecondary 8.3%. *Literacy* (1985): total population age 15 and over literate 28,451,390 (88.8%); males literate 14,877,240 (93.2%); females literate 13,574,150 (84.5%).
Health (1991): physicians 12,803 (1 per 4,327 persons); hospital beds (1990) 90,740 (1 per 604 persons); infant mortality rate per 1,000 live births 25.0.
Food (1988–90): daily per capita caloric intake 2,280 (vegetable products 91%, animal products 9%); 103% of FAO recommended minimum requirement.

Military

Total active duty personnel (1993): 295,000 (army 64.4%, navy 21.0%, air force 14.6%). *Military expenditure as percentage of GNP* (1991): 2.7% (world 4.2%); per capita expenditure U.S.$44.

---

[1]The new constitution requires that future prime ministers be elected members of Parliament. [2]Actual local administration is based on 73 provinces. [3]Based on registration records. [4]Based on 1990 census results, which are lower than the 1990 registration records estimate. [5]Imputed rates calculated from registered deaths. [6]1992. [7]1990. [8]May; economically active persons 13 years and over. [9]Mostly unemployed. [10]Import figures are f.o.b. in balance of trade and c.i.f. for commodities and trading partners. [11]Traffic data refer to fiscal year ending September 30. [12]1989.

Togo

Official name: République Togolaise (Republic of Togo).
Form of government: multiparty republic[1] with one legislative body (National Assembly [81[2]]).
Chief of state: President[1].
Head of government: Prime Minister.
Capital: Lomé.
Official language: French.
Official religion: none.
Monetary unit: 1 CFA franc (CFAF) = 100 centimes; valuation (Oct. 7, 1994) 1 U.S.$ = CFAF 526.67; 1 £ = CFAF 837.67.

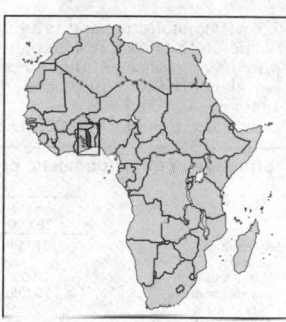

Area and population

Regions Prefectures	Capitals	area sq mi	area sq km	population 1901 census
Centrale	Sokodé			273,138
Sotouboua	Sotouboua	2,892	7,491	131,007
Tchamba	Tchamba	1,214	3,143	44,810
Tchaoudjo	Sokodé	984	2,549	96,691
De la Kara	Kara			426,651
Assoli	Bafilo	362	938	32,425
Bassar	Bassar	2,444	6,330	118,934
Binah	Pagouda	180	465	50,081
Doufelgou	Niamtougou	432	1,120	59,331
Kéran	Kandé	419	1,085	44,844
Kozah	Kara	653	1,692	121,036
Des Plateaux	Atakpamé			650,393
Amou	Amlamé	773	2,003	78,125
Haho	Notsé	1,406	3,641	110,768
Kloto	Kpalimé	1,072	2,777	186,778
Ogou	Atakpamé	2,349	6,083	165,143
Wawa	Badou	954	2,471	109,579
Des Savanes	Dapaong			329,144
Oti	Sansanné-Mango	1,453	3,762	77,803
Tône	Dapaong	1,869	4,840	251,341
Maritime	Lomé			1,040,241
Golfe	Lomé	133	345	447,806
Lacs	Aného	275	713	137,855
Vo	Vogan	290	750	150,575
Yoto	Tabligbo	483	1,250	100,682
Zio	Tsévié	1,288	3,337	203,323
TOTAL		21,925	56,785	2,719,567

Demography

Population (1994): 3,922,000.
Density (1994): persons per sq mi 178.9, persons per sq km 69.1.
Urban-rural (1991): urban 26.4%; rural 73.6%.
Sex distribution (1990): male 49.45%; female 50.55%.
Age breakdown (1990): under 15, 45.3%; 15–29, 26.0%; 30–44, 15.0%; 45–59, 8.7%; 60 and over, 5.0%.
Population projection: (2000) 4,668,000; (2010) 6,238,000.
Doubling time: 22 years.
Ethnic composition (1981): Ewe-Adja 43.1%; Tem-Kabre 26.7%; Gurma 16.1%; Kebu-Akposo 3.8%; Ana-Ife (Yoruba) 3.2%; non-African 0.3%; other 6.8%.
Religious affiliation (1981): traditional beliefs 58.9%; Roman Catholic 21.5%; Muslim 12.1%; Protestant 6.8%; other 0.7%.
Major cities (1983): Lomé 366,476; Sokodé 48,098[3]; Kpalimé 27,669[3].

Vital statistics

Birth rate per 1,000 population (1990–95): 44.5 (world avg. 26.0).
Death rate per 1,000 population (1990–95): 12.8 (world avg. 9.2).
Natural increase rate per 1,000 population (1990–95): 31.7 (world avg. 16.8).
Total fertility rate (avg. births per childbearing woman; 1991): 7.1.
Marriage rate per 1,000 population (1979): 2.3.
Life expectancy at birth (1990–95): male 53.2 years; female 56.8 years.
Morbidity (reported cases of illness per 100,000 population; 1978): infectious and parasitic diseases 26,926; diseases of the respiratory system 9,296; diseases of the digestive system 8,007; accidents, poisoning, and trauma 7,172.

National economy

Budget (1992). Revenue: CFAF 95,800,000,000 (tax revenue 82.6%, nontax revenue 17.4%). Expenditures: CFAF 95,800,000,000 (1990: general public services 25.4%, education 23.1%, defense 14.9%, debt service 14.1%, economic services 7.4%, health 5.2%).
Public debt (external, outstanding; 1992): U.S.$1,138,000,000.
Production (metric tons except as noted). Agriculture, forestry, fishing (1993): yams 529,000, cassava 389,000, corn (maize) 340,000, sorghum 126,000, millet 75,000, cottonseed 44,000, pulses 43,000, peanuts (groundnuts) 35,000, rice 33,000, coffee 28,000, bananas 16,000, coconuts 14,000, palm oil 14,000, oranges 12,000, tomatoes 9,000, palm kernels 8,000, cacao beans 7,000; livestock (number of live animals) 1,900,000 goats, 1,200,000 sheep, 850,000 pigs, 246,000 cattle, 7,000,000 chickens; roundwood (1991) 1,234,000 cu m; fish catch (1991) 12,524. Mining and quarrying (1992): phosphate rock 2,100,000; marble production ceased in the early 1990s. Manufacturing (1987): cement 399,000[4]; wheat flour 58,000; beer 452,000 hectolitres; soft drinks 142,000 hectolitres[5]; footwear 100,000 pairs[6]. Construction (value added in CFAF; 1991): 15,400,000,000. Energy production (consumption): electricity (kW-hr; 1992) 60,000,000 (355,000,000); coal, none (n.a.); crude petroleum, none (n.a.); petroleum products (metric tons; 1992) none (175,000).
Gross national product (1993): U.S.$1,329,000,000 (U.S.$330 per capita).

Structure of gross domestic product and labour force

	1991 In value CFAF '000,000	1991 % of total value	1991 labour force	1991 % of labour force
Agriculture	150,580	35.0	991,000	69.2
Mining	41,420	9.6		
Manufacturing	29,480	6.8	161,000	11.2
Construction	15,400	3.6		
Public utilities	16,000	3.8		
Transp. and commun.	29,280	6.8		
Trade	75,000	17.4		
Finance	17,800	4.1	280,000	19.6
Pub. admin., defense	40,500	9.4		
Services	14,940	3.5		
TOTAL	430,400	100.0	1,432,000	100.0

Population economically active: total (1992) 1,501,000; activity rate of total population 39.9% (participation rates [1985]: ages 15–64, 69.5%; female 37.5%; unemployed [1980] 2.3%).

Price and earnings indexes (1990 = 100)

	1987	1988	1989	1990	1991	1992	1993
Consumer price index	100.0	99.8	99.0	100.0	100.4	101.8	100.8
Hourly earnings index[7]	105.5	105.5	105.5	105.5	105.5	...	...

Household income and expenditure. Average household size (1980) 5.6; average annual income per household CFAF 102,000 (U.S.$452); sources of income: n.a.; expenditure (1970): food and beverages 60.9%, housing 9.9%, transportation 8.2%, clothing 7.7%, household durable goods 3.9%.
Tourism (1992): receipts from visitors U.S.$39,000,000; expenditures by nationals abroad U.S.$48,000,000.
Land use (1992): forested 26.6%; meadows and pastures 32.9%; agricultural and under permanent cultivation 12.3%; other 28.2%.

Foreign trade[8]

Balance of trade (current prices)

	1986	1987	1988	1989	1990	1991
CFAF '000,000,000	−29.7	−36.2	−52.5	−51.1	−63.1	−36.2
% of total	13.2%	19.8%	26.7%	24.6%	30.2%	20.2%

Imports (1991): CFAF 125,222,000,000 (1990; machinery and transport equipment 22.6%, food products 14.8%, chemicals 12.4%, cotton yarn and fabrics 11.5%, lime and cement 4.2%). *Major import sources* (1990): France 30.5%; W.Ger. 6.0%; U.S. 5.3%; Japan 4.3%; U.K. 3.8%; China 1.5%.
Exports (1991): CFAF 71,433,000,000 (1990; calcium phosphates 44.5%, cotton [ginned] 20.7%, machinery and transport equipment 7.3%, coffee 6.6%, cocoa beans 5.7%). *Major export destinations* (1990): Africa 16.2%; France 9.8%; U.S.S.R. 4.7%; W.Ger. 3.7%; U.K. 1.5%; eastern Europe 1.2%.

Transport and communications

Transport. Railroads (1993): route length 326 mi, 525 km; (1991) passenger-km 24,000,000; metric ton-km cargo 6,000,000. Roads (1991): total length 7,545 km (paved 24%). Vehicles (1991): passenger cars 26,000; trucks and buses 16,000. Merchant marine (1992): vessels (100 gross tons and over) 8; total deadweight tonnage 20,633. Air transport (1990)[9]: passenger-km 232,329,000; metric ton-km cargo 39,374,000; airports (1994) with scheduled flights 1.
Communications. Daily newspapers (1990): total number 2; total circulation 10,000[10]; circulation per 1,000 population 2.9[10]. Radio (1993): 700,000 receivers (1 per 5.4 persons). Television (1993): 150,000 receivers (1 per 25.4 persons). Telephones (1992): 30,670 (1 per 124 persons).

Education and health

Education (1990)

	schools	teachers	students	student/ teacher ratio
Primary (age 6–11)	2,494	11,105	651,962	58.7
Secondary (age 12–18)	314	4,231	117,153	27.7
Vocational	18[11]	261	8,392	32.2
Higher[12]	1[11]	276[5]	7,732[13]	26.6[5]

Educational attainment (1981). Percentage of population age 15 and over having: no formal schooling 76.5%; primary education 13.5%; secondary 8.7%; higher 1.3%. *Literacy* (1990): total population age 15 and over literate 821,600 (43.0%); males 56.0%; females 31.0%.
Health: physicians (1988) 268 (1 per 12,299 persons); hospital beds (1988) 5,275 (1 per 625 persons); infant mortality rate (1991) 110.0.
Food (1988–90): daily per capita caloric intake 2,269 (vegetable products 95%, animal products 5%); 99% of FAO recommended minimum requirement.

Military

Total active duty personnel (1994): 6,950 (army 93.5%, navy 2.9%, air force 3.6%). *Military expenditure as percentage of GNP* (1991): 3.0% (world 4.2%); per capita expenditure U.S.$12.

[1]Personal military-supported rule from 1967 continues under constitution approved by referendum in September 1992. [2]78 seats occupied in mid-1994. [3]1981. [4]1991. [5]1988. [6]1990. [7]January 1. [8]Import figures are f.o.b. in balance of trade and c.i.f. for commodities and trading partners. [9]Air Afrique only. [10]For one daily only. [11]1987. [12]Universities only. [13]1989.

Tonga

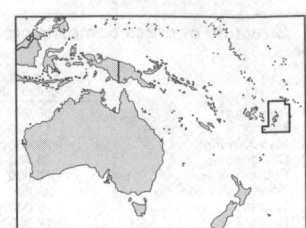

Official name: Pule'anga Fakatu'i 'o Tonga (Tongan); Kingdom of Tonga (English).
Form of government: constitutional monarchy with one legislative house (Legislative Assembly [30][1]).
Head of state and government: King assisted by Privy Council.
Capital: Nuku'alofa.
Official languages: Tongan; English.
Official religion: none.
Monetary unit: 1 pa'anga[2] (T$) = 100 seniti; valuation (Oct. 7, 1994)
1 U.S.$ = T$1.35; 1 £ = T$2.15.

Area and population

Divisions		area		population
Districts	Capitals	sq mi	sq km	1986 census
'Eua	'Ohonua	33.7	87.4	4,393
'Eua Fo'ou		...	...	1,993
'Eua Motu'a		...	...	2,400
Ha'apai	Pangai	42.5	110.0	8,919
Foa		...	...	1,410
Ha'ano		...	...	891
Lulunga		...	...	1,584
Mu'omu'a		...	...	885
Pangai		...	...	2,850
'Uiha		...	...	1,299
Niuas	Hihifo	27.7	71.7	2,368
Niua Fo'ou		...	...	763
Niua Toputapu		...	...	1,605
Tongatapu	Nuku'alofa	100.6	260.5	63,794
Kolofo'ou		...	...	15,903
Kolomotu'a		...	...	13,115
Kolovai		...	...	4,031
Lapaha		...	...	7,005
Nukunuku		...	...	5,863
Tatakamotonga		...	...	6,773
Vaini		...	...	11,104
Vava'u	Neiafu	46.0	119.2	15,175
Hahake		...	...	2,299
Hihifo		...	...	2,093
Leimatu'a		...	...	2,884
Motu		...	...	1,384
Neiafu		...	...	5,268
Pangaimotu		...	...	1,247
TOTAL LAND AREA		278.1[3]	720.3[3]	
INLAND WATER		11.4	29.6	
TOTAL		289.5	749.9	94,649

Demography

Population (1994): 99,700.
Density (1994)[4]: persons per sq mi 358.5, persons per sq km 138.4.
Urban-rural (1986): urban 30.7%; rural 69.3%.
Sex distribution (1992): male 50.28%; female 49.72%.
Age breakdown (1986): under 15, 40.6%; 15–29, 29.0%; 30–44, 13.8%; 45–59, 10.2%; 60–74, 5.0%; 75 and over, 1.4%.
Population projection: (2000) 103,000; (2010) 105,000.
Doubling time: 29 years.
Ethnic composition (1986): Tongan 95.5%; part Tongan 2.8%; other 1.7%.
Religious affiliation (1986): Free Wesleyan 43.0%; Roman Catholic 16.0%; Mormon 12.1%; Free Church of Tonga 11.0%; Church of Tonga 7.3%; other 10.6%.
Major cities (1986): Nuku'alofa 21,383; Neiafu 3,879; Haveluloto 3,070; Vaini 2,697; Tofoa-Koloua 2,298.

Vital statistics

Birth rate per 1,000 population (1993): 25.2 (world avg. 26.0).
Death rate per 1,000 population (1993): 6.8 (world avg. 9.2).
Natural increase rate per 1,000 population (1993) 18.4 (world avg. 16.8).
Total fertility rate (avg. births per childbearing woman; 1993): 3.7.
Marriage rate per 1,000 population (1992): 8.2.
Divorce rate per 1,000 population (1992): 1.1.
Life expectancy at birth (1993): male 65.5 years; female 70.2 years.
Major causes of death per 100,000 population (1992)[5]: diseases of the circulatory system 158.5; malignant neoplasms 54.9; diseases of the respiratory system 31.5; diseases of the digestive system 18.3; infectious diseases 16.3; nutritional and metabolic disorders 15.2.

National economy

Budget (1994–95). Revenue: T$52,940,000 (foreign-trade taxes 53.8%, government services revenue 15.2%, indirect taxes 12.6%, direct taxes 11.3%, interest and rent 6.3%). Expenditures: T$52,900,000 (general administration 18.1%, education 17.0%, health 12.3%, law and order 11.5%, public works and communications 11.3%, public debt 7.1%, agriculture 5.5%).
Tourism (1992): receipts from visitors U.S.$9,000,000; expenditures by nationals abroad U.S.$1,000,000.
Production (metric tons except as noted). Agriculture, forestry, fishing (1992): yams 33,000, taro 27,000, coconuts 25,000, cassava 15,000, vegetables (including melons) 15,000, sweet potatoes 14,000, fruits (excluding melons) 13,000, copra 2,000; livestock (number of live animals) 97,000 pigs, 16,000 goats, 10,000 cattle, 4,000 horses; roundwood (1991) 5,000 cu m; fish catch (1991) 1,889. Mining and quarrying (1982): coral 150,000; sand 25,000. Manufacturing (output in T$; 1992): food products and beverages 6,945,000; chemical products 3,568,000; textile and wearing apparel 3,075,000; metal products

1,576,000; publishing and printing 1,393,000; furniture 632,000. Construction (value in T$; 1984): residential 9,552,300; nonresidential 11,377,100. Energy production (consumption): electricity (kW-hr; 1991) 22,000,000 (22,000,000); petroleum (barrels; 1989) none (154,000); petroleum products (metric tons; 1991) n.a. (24,000).
Gross national product (1992): U.S.$136,000,000 (U.S.$1,350 per capita).

Structure of gross domestic product and labour force

	1993–94		1990	
	in value T$'000	% of total value	labour force	% of labour force
Agriculture	77,800	36.2	11,682	36.5
Mining	...	...	4,665	14.6
Manufacturing	9,000	4.2		
Construction	9,200	4.3	1,257	3.9
Public utilities	...	...	408	1.3
Transp. and commun.	27,000	12.6	1,821	5.7
Trade	27,000	12.6	2,597	8.1
Finance	...	...	1,188	3.7
Pub. admin., defense	23,200	10.8	7,052	22.0
Services				
Other	41,600	19.4	1,343	4.2
TOTAL	214,800	100.0[6]	32,013	100.0

Public debt (external, outstanding; 1992): U.S.$42,300,000.
Population economically active (1990): total 32,013; activity rate 33.6% (participation rates: ages 10 and over, 46.7%; female 33.0%; unemployed 4.2%).

Price and earnings indexes (1985 = 100)

	1987	1988	1989	1990	1991	1992	1993
Consumer price index	127.4	140.0	145.8	159.9	176.8	190.9	192.7
Quarterly earnings index[7]	101.7	130.9	176.2	175.0	200.0	218.0	

Household income and expenditure. Average household size (1986) 6.3; income per household: n.a.; sources of income: n.a.; expenditure (1984)[8]: food 49.3%, household operations 13.3%, housing 10.5%, tobacco and beverages 7.0%, transportation 5.8%, clothing and footwear 5.6%.
Land use (1991): forested 11.1%; meadows and pastures 5.6%; agricultural and under permanent cultivation 66.7%; other 16.6%.

Foreign trade

Balance of trade (current prices)

	1987	1988	1989	1990	1991	1992
T$'000,000	−58.0	−50.3	−54.0	−49.8	−42.1	−53.9
% of total	74.4%	70.9%	73.5%	62.1%	47.4%	63.9%

Imports (1992): T$84,280,000 (food and live animals 25.4%, basic manufactures 20.4%, machinery and transport equipment 19.3%, mineral fuels 13.0%, chemicals 6.2%). *Major import sources:* New Zealand 29.7%; Australia 23.9%; Japan 12.5%; Fiji 11.9%; U.S. 8.5%.
Exports (1992): T$17,250,000 (squash 50.3%, vanilla beans 12.1%, fish 8.9%, root crops 3.9%, coconut products 3.2%). *Major export destinations:* Japan 51.6%; U.S. 21.6%; Australia 11.1%; New Zealand 10.0%; Fiji 2.0%.

Transport and communications

Transport. Railroads: none. Roads (1993): total length 386 km (paved 76%). Vehicles (1992): passenger cars 3,297, commercial vehicles 3,757. Merchant marine (1992): vessels (100 gross tons and over) 15; total deadweight tonnage 13,740. Air transport (1992): passenger-km 68,309,000; metric ton-km cargo 1,126; airports (1994) with scheduled flights 4.
Communications. Daily newspapers (1990): 1; total circulation 7,000; circulation per 1,000 population 74. Radio (1993): 66,000 receivers (1 per 1.5 persons). Television: n.a.[9] Telephones (1992): 5,326 (1 per 18 persons).

Education and health

Education (1992)

	schools	teachers	students	student/ teacher ratio
Primary (age 6–11)	115	784	16,658	21.2
Secondary (age 12–18)	40	862	15,253	17.7
Voc., teacher tr.	8	65[10]	358	13.4[10]
Higher	1	19	226	11.9

Educational attainment (1986). Percentage of population age 25 and over having: complete primary 38.3%; lower secondary 30.3%; secondary 23.4%; postsecondary 4.9%; higher 1.0%; not stated 2.1%. *Literacy* (1976): total population age 15 and over literate 46,456 (92.8%); males 23,372 (92.9%); females 23,084 (92.8%).
Health (1992): physicians 46 (1 per 2,139 persons); hospital beds 307 (1 per 320 persons); infant mortality rate per 1,000 live births (1993) 21.4.
Food (1988–90): daily per capita caloric intake 2,967 (vegetable products 81%, animal products 19%); 130% of FAO recommended minimum requirement.

Military

Total active duty personnel (1991): Tonga has a national police (defense) force of about 300. *Military expenditure as percentage of GNP* (1989): 4.9% (world 4.9%); per capita expenditure U.S.$21.

[1]Includes 12 nonelective seats and 9 nobles elected by the 33 hereditary nobles of Tonga. [2]The pa'anga was pegged at par to the Australian dollar through Feb. 8, 1991, but beginning Feb. 11, 1991, it has been linked to a weighted basket of foreign currencies. [3]Total includes 27.6 sq mi (71.5 sq km) of uninhabited islands. [4]Density is based on land area. [5]Reported inpatient deaths at all hospitals. [6]Detail does not add to total given because of rounding. [7]In manufacturing. [8]Current weight of consumer price index components. [9]Tonga has no authorized television service, but a "pirate" station began transmitting in mid-1984. [10]1990.

Trinidad and Tobago

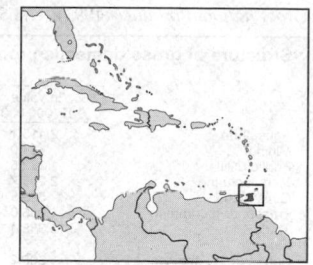

Official name: Republic of Trinidad and Tobago.
Form of government: multiparty republic with two legislative houses (Senate [31]; House of Representatives [36[1]]).
Chief of state: President.
Head of government: Prime Minister.
Capital: Port of Spain.
Official language: English.
Official religion: none.
Monetary unit: 1 Trinidad and Tobago dollar (TT$) = 100 cents; valuation (Oct. 7, 1994) 1 U.S.$ = TT$5.58; 1 £ = TT$8.88.

Area and population

Counties	Capitals	area sq mi	area sq km	population 1990 census[2]
Caroni	Chaguanas	191.0	494.7	120,508
Nariva/Mayaro	Rio Claro	349.0	903.9	36,781
St. Andrew/St. David	Sangre Grande	360.0	932.4	62,944
St. George	...	354.0	916.9	445,620
St. Patrick	Siparia	252.0	652.7	120,129
Victoria	Princes Town	315.0	815.9	210,833
Unitary State				
Tobago	Scarborough	116.0	300.4	50,282
Cities				
Port of Spain	—	4.0	10.4	50,878
San Fernando	—	3.0	7.8	30,092
Boroughs				
Arima	—	4.0	10.4	29,695
Chaguanas	—	23.0	59.6	56,601
Point Fortin	—	9.0	23.3	20,025
TOTAL		1,980.1[3]	5,128.4	1,234,388

Demography

Population (1994): 1,273,000.
Density (1994): persons per sq mi 642.9, persons per sq km 248.2.
Urban-rural (1990): urban 64.8%; rural 35.2%.
Sex distribution (1991): male 53.33%; female 46.67%.
Age breakdown (1991): under 15, 30.5%; 15–29, 26.4%; 30–44, 22.1%; 45–59, 12.6%; 60 and over, 8.4%.
Population projection: (2000) 1,337,000; (2010) 1,451,000.
Doubling time: 60 years.
Ethnic composition (1990): East Indian 40.3%; black 39.6%; mixed 18.4%; white 0.6%; Chinese 0.4%; other 0.7%.
Religious affiliation (1990): Roman Catholic 29.4%; Hindu 23.8%; Anglican 10.9%; Muslim 5.8%; other 30.1%.
Major cities (1990): Chaguanas 56,601; Port of Spain 50,878; San Fernando 30,092; Arima 29,695; Point Fortin 20,025; Scarborough 3,000.

Vital statistics

Birth rate per 1,000 population (1992): 18.4 (world avg. 26.0).
Death rate per 1,000 population (1992): 6.8 (world avg. 9.2).
Natural increase rate per 1,000 population (1992): 11.6 (world avg. 16.8).
Total fertility rate (avg. births per childbearing woman; 1992): 2.7.
Marriage rate per 1,000 population (1991): 5.7.
Divorce rate per 1,000 population (1991): 1.1.
Life expectancy at birth (1993): male 68.0 years; female 73.2 years.
Major causes of death per 100,000 population (1991): diseases of the circulatory system 260.0, of which ischemic heart diseases 113.5, cerebrovascular disease 75.9; malignant neoplasms (cancers) 83.4; diabetes mellitus 83.3.

National economy

Budget (1993). Revenue: TT$6,852,000,000 (individual income taxes 19.7%, value-added taxes 17.2%, petroleum-sector corporate taxes 10.4%, import duties 9.1%, nontax revenues 8.9%). Expenditures: TT$6,842,000,000 (current expenditures 94.3%, development expenditures 5.7%).
Tourism (1992): receipts from visitors U.S.$111,000,000; expenditures by nationals abroad U.S.$112,000,000.
Production (metric tons except as noted). Agriculture, forestry, fishing (1992): sugarcane 1,210,000[4], coconuts 40,000, rice 22,000, oranges 8,000, bananas 6,000, grapefruit 4,000, corn (maize) 3,000, cocoa 1,140, coffee 706; livestock (number of live animals) 60,000 cattle, 52,000 goats, 50,000 pigs; roundwood 87,000 cu m; fish catch (1991) 10,283. Mining and quarrying (1993): natural asphalt 19,200. Manufacturing (1993): anhydrous ammonia and urea (nitrogenous fertilizers) 2,291,900; cement 527,200; methanol 492,800; steel billets 492,100; steel wire rods 413,000; raw sugar 116,900[5]; beer and stout 424,000 hectolitres; rum 128,400 hectolitres. Construction (authorized; 1991): residential 207,400 sq m; nonresidential 32,700 sq m. Energy production (consumption): electricity (kW-hr; 1992) 3,945,000,000 (3,945,000,000); coal, none (none); crude petroleum (barrels; 1993) 45,203,000 (40,903,000[6]); petroleum products (metric tons; 1993) 5,261,000 (1,924,000[6]); natural gas (cu m; 1993) 7,038,000,000 (4,878,000,000).
Land use (1991): forested 42.7%; meadows and pastures 2.1%; agricultural and under permanent cultivation 23.4%; other 31.8%.
Public debt (external, outstanding; 1992): U.S.$1,782,000,000.
Gross national product (at current market prices; 1992): U.S.$4,995,000,000 (U.S.$3,940 per capita).

Structure of gross domestic product and labour force

	1993 in value TT$'000,000	1993 % of total value	1991 labour force	1991 % of labour force
Agriculture[7]	584	2.4	51,100	10.4
Petroleum[8], natural gas, quarrying	5,586	23.0	23,000	4.7
Manufacturing[9]	2,100	8.7	53,300	10.8
Construction	1,857	7.7	74,500	15.1
Public utilities	464	1.9	9,200	1.9
Transp. and commun.	3,181	13.1	29,600	6.0
Trade	3,764	15.5	82,800	16.8
Finance, real estate	2,123	8.7	32,400	6.6
Pub. admin., defense	2,751	11.3 }	134,900	27.4
Services	1,674	6.9 }		
Other	198[10]	0.8[10]	1,200	0.2
TOTAL	24,282	100.0	492,200[3]	100.0[3]

Population economically active (1991): total 492,200; activity rate of total population 39.3% (participation rates: ages 15–64, 60.8%; female 36.0%; unemployed [1992] 19.7%).

Price and earnings indexes (1990 = 100)

	1987	1988	1989	1990	1991	1992	1993
Consumer price index	75.0	80.8	90.1	100.0	103.9	110.6	122.5
Weekly earnings index[11]	92.2	93.8	94.5	100.0	100.1	103.0	104.1[12]

Household income and expenditure. Average household size (1990) 4.1; income per household (1988) TT$17,083 (U.S.$4,444); sources of income: n.a.; expenditure (1993): food and beverages 25.5%, housing 21.6%, transportation 15.2%, household furnishings 14.3%, clothing and footwear 10.4%, other 13.0%.

Foreign trade[13]

Balance of trade (current prices)

TT$'000,000	1988	1989	1990	1991	1992	1993
	+1,114	+1,517	+3,480	+1,352	+1,842	+1,113
% of total	11.4%	12.7%	24.5%	8.7%	13.1%	7.0%

Imports (1992): TT$6,101,000,000 (capital goods 23.6%; nondurable consumer goods 22.0%, of which food 13.8%; chemical products [mostly medicines and plastics] 12.6%; mineral fuels and lubricants 9.0%). *Major import sources* (1992): United States 41.4%; EEC 15.7%, of which United Kingdom 7.8%; Venezuela 9.7%; Japan 6.7%; Caricom 5.3%.
Exports (1992): TT$7,943,000,000 (mineral-fuel lubricants 64.2%; chemicals and chemical products 15.3%; food 4.7%, of which raw sugar 1.8%). *Major export destinations* (1992): United States 47.1%; Caricom 13.8%, of which Barbados 3.4%, Guyana 2.3%; Netherlands Antilles 7.1%; EEC 5.3%.

Transport and communications

Transport. Railroads: none. Roads (1990): total length 4,970 mi, 8,000 km (paved 50%). Vehicles (1991): passenger cars 150,196; trucks and buses 60,006. Merchant marine (1992): vessels (100 gross tons and over) 53; total deadweight tonnage 17,533. Air transport: (1992) passenger-mi 2,030,-000,000, passenger-km 3,267,000,000; (1991) short ton-mi cargo 10,100,000, metric ton-km cargo 14,800,000; airports (1994) with scheduled flights 2.
Communications. Daily newspapers (1993): total number 3; total circulation 96,000; circulation per 1,000 population 76. Radio (1993): 700,000 receivers (1 per 1.8 persons). Television (1993): 250,000 receivers (1 per 5.0 persons). Telephones (1992): 246,730 (1 per 5.1 persons).

Education and health

Education (1991–92)

	schools	teachers	students	student/ teacher ratio
Primary (age 5–11)	471	7,511	196,333	26.1
Secondary (age 12–16)	101	4,844	94,201	19.4
Higher[14]	1	471	4,541	9.6

Educational attainment (1980). Percentage of population age 25 and over having: no formal schooling 7.1%; primary education 66.5%; secondary 21.7%; higher 2.7%; other 2.0%. *Literacy* (1985): total population age 15 and over literate 751,600 (96.1%).
Health (1992): physicians 982 (1 per 1,275 persons); hospital beds[15] 4,399 (1 per 285 persons); infant mortality rate per 1,000 live births (1994) 17.0.
Food (1988–90): daily per capita caloric intake 2,770 (vegetable products 85%, animal products 15%); 114% of FAO recommended minimum requirement.

Military

Total active duty personnel (1993): 2,550 (army 78.4%, coast guard 21.6%).
Military expenditure as percentage of GNP (1991): 0.6% (world 4.2%); per capita expenditure U.S.$23.

[1]Excludes speaker, who may be elected from outside the House of Representatives. [2]Preliminary data. [3]Detail does not add to total given because of rounding. [4]1993. [5]1994. [6]1992. [7]Includes sugar industry. [8]Includes refined petroleum. [9]Excludes refined petroleum and sugar industries. [10]Net of value-added taxes less imputed bank service charges. [11]Manufacturing sector only. [12]Average of first three quarters only. [13]Exports f.o.b.; imports c.i.f. [14]University of the West Indies, St. Augustine campus. [15]Includes nursing homes.

Tunisia

Official name: al-Jumhūrīyah
at-Tūnisīyah (Republic of Tunisia).
Form of government: multiparty
republic with one legislative house
(Chamber of Deputies [163]).
Chief of state: President.
Head of government: Prime Minister.
Capital: Tunis.
Official language: Arabic.
Official religion: Islam.
Monetary unit: 1 dinar (D) = 1,000
millimes; valuation (Oct. 7, 1994)
D 1.00 = U.S.$1.02 = £0.64.

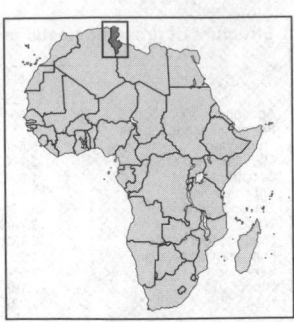

Area and population		area		population
				1994
Governorates	Capitals	sq mi	sq km	census[1]
al-Ariānah	al-Ariānah	602	1,558	566,247
Bājah	Bājah	1,374	3,558	301,898
Banzart	Bizerte (Banzart)	1,423	3,685	475,053
Bin 'Arūs	Bin 'Arūs	294	761	369,552
Jundūbah	Jundūbah	1,198	3,102	402,487
al-Kāf	al-Kāf	1,917	4,965	270,996
Madanīn	Madanīn	3,316	8,588	382,699
al-Mahdīyah	al-Mahdīyah	1,145	2,966	334,208
al-Munastīr	al-Munastīr	393	1,019	363,126
Nābul	Nābul	1,076	2,788	577,813
Qābis	Qābis	2,770	7,175	310,643
Qafṣah	Qafṣah	3,471	8,990	304,665
al-Qaṣrayn	al-Qaṣrayn	3,114	8,066	385,450
al-Qayrawān	al-Qayrawān	2,591	6,712	528,899
Qibilī	Qibilī	8,527	22,084	131,661
Ṣafāqis	Ṣafāqis	2,913	7,545	732,471
Sīdī Bū Zayd	Sīdī Bū Zayd	2,700	6,994	374,835
Siliānah	Siliānah	1,788	4,631	243,536
Sūsah	Sūsah	1,012	2,621	432,312
Tatāuīn	Tatāuīn	15,015	38,889	133,676
Tawzar	Tawzar	1,822	4,719	89,088
Tūnis	Tunis (Tūnis)	134	346	881,560
Zaghwān	Zaghwān	1,069	2,768	143,010
TOTAL		63,378[2]	164,150[2]	8,735,885

Demography

Population (1994): 8,757,000.
Density (1994): persons per sq mi 138.2, persons per sq km 53.3.
Urban-rural (1985): urban 53.0%; rural 47.0%.
Sex distribution (1992): male 50.70%; female 49.30%.
Age breakdown (1992): under 15, 36.6%; 15–29, 28.9%; 30–44, 16.9%; 45–59, 10.1%; 60–74, 5.9%; 75 and over, 1.6%.
Population projection: (2000) 9,781,000; (2010) 11,296,000.
Doubling time: 37 years.
Ethnic composition (1983): Arab 98.2%; Berber 1.2%; French 0.2%; Italian 0.1%; other 0.3%.
Religious affiliation (1980): Sunnī Muslim 99.4%; Christian 0.3%; Jewish 0.1%; other 0.2%.
Major cities (commune; 1989): Tunis 620,149; Ṣafāqis 221,770; Aryānah 131,-403; Ettadhamen 111,793; Sūsah 101,071.

Vital statistics

Birth rate per 1,000 population (1992): 25.3 (world avg. 26.0); (1974) legitimate 99.8%; illegitimate 0.2%.
Death rate per 1,000 population (1992): 6.2 (world avg. 9.2).
Natural increase rate per 1,000 population (1992): 19.1 (world avg. 16.8).
Total fertility rate (avg. births per childbearing woman; 1990–95): 3.4.
Marriage rate per 1,000 population (1992): 7.7.
Divorce rate per 1,000 population (1992): 1.5.
Life expectancy at birth (1990–95): male 66.9 years; female 68.7 years.
Major causes of death per 100,000 population: n.a.; however, of approximately 12,000 deaths[3] for which a cause was reported in 1992, complications of pregnancy and childbirth 31.6%; circulatory diseases 22.4%; accidents and poisoning 14.9%; respiratory diseases 7.2%; endocrine and metabolic disorders 5.2%; infectious and parasitic diseases 4.8%.

National economy

Budget (1992). Revenue: D 4,925,400,000 (indirect taxes 42.2%, direct taxes 11.4%, investment 9.4%). Expenditures: D 5,662,800,000 (finance 17.9%, education 12.4%, interior affairs 5.8%, national economy 4.9%, health 4.9%).
Public debt (external, outstanding; 1992): U.S.$7,644,000,000.
Land use (1991): forested 4.3%; meadows and pastures 27.9%; agricultural and under permanent cultivation 31.4%; other 36.4%.
Production (metric tons except as noted). Agriculture, forestry, fishing (1992): wheat 1,584,000, olives 630,000, barley 611,000, tomatoes 550,000, watermelons 380,000, sugar beets 290,000, potatoes 218,000, grapes 110,000, oranges 98,000, dates 75,000, alfalfa 46,000; livestock (number of live animals) 6,400,-000 sheep, 1,300,000 goats, 636,000 cattle; roundwood (1991) 3,320,000 cu m; fish catch (1991) 90,710. Mining and quarrying (1993): phosphate rock 6,707,-000[4]; iron ore 295,000; zinc 2,000. Manufacturing (1993): cement 4,499,000; phosphoric acid 858,400; flour 626,400; crude steel 192,000[5]. Construction (1982): residential building authorized 2,679,000 sq m. Energy production (consumption): electricity (kW-hr; 1992) 5,750,000,000 (5,746,000,000); coal (metric tons; 1992) none (15,000); crude petroleum (barrels; 1991) 38,599,000 (12,648,000); petroleum products (metric tons; 1992) 1,664,000 (3,284,000); natural gas (cu m; 1992) 314,600,000 (787,500,000).

Gross national product (1993): U.S.$15,152,000,000 (U.S.$1,780 per capita).

Structure of gross domestic product and labour force				
	1992		1989	
	in value D '000,000	% of total value	labour force	% of labour force
Agriculture	2,415.1	17.6	543,100	23.0
Mining	787.0	5.7 }	36,600	1.6
Public utilities	252.5	1.8 }		
Manufacturing	2,295.7	16.7	422,300	17.9
Construction	529.5	3.9	295,200	12.5
Transp. and commun.	1,006.0	7.3		
Trade	3,388.4	24.7 }	349,000	14.8
Finance				
Pub. admin., defense }	1,809.2	13.2 }	465,400	19.7
Services				
Other	1,248.1	9.1	249,000[6]	10.5[6]
TOTAL	13,731.5	100.0	2,360,600	100.0

Population economically active (1989): total 2,360,000, activity rate of total population 28.8% (participation rates: ages 15–64, 42.2%; female 20.9%; unemployed 13.4%).

Price and earnings indexes (1990 = 100)							
	1987	1988	1989	1990	1991	1992	1993
Consumer price index	81.3	87.2	93.9	100.0	107.8	113.8	118.7
Hourly earnings index[7]	86.0	89.9	92.2	100.0	101.6	105.5	113.3

Household income and expenditure. Average household size (1994) 5.1; income per household: n.a.; sources of income: n.a.; expenditure (1985): food and beverages 39.0%, household durable goods 11.2%, housing 10.7%, transportation 9.0%, recreation 7.1%, clothing and footwear 6.0%, energy 5.1%, health care 3.0%, education 1.8%, other 7.1%.
Tourism (1992): receipts from visitors U.S.$1,074,000,000; expenditures by nationals abroad U.S.$167,000,000.

Foreign trade

Balance of trade (current prices)						
	1988	1989	1990	1991	1992	1993
D '000,000	−898.9	−1,089.8	−1,439.7	−1,037.5	−1,726.1	−1,999.2
% of total	17.9%	16.3%	18.9%	13.1%	17.4%	20.7%

Imports (1993): D 6,237,000,000 (textiles 13.4%, chemical products 4.5%, tubes and pipes 2.9%, clothing and accessories 2.8%, iron and steel products 2.3%, pharmaceutical products 1.9%, plastics and plastic products 1.7%). *Major import sources:* France 26.9%; Italy 18.2%; Germany 13.0%; U.S. 5.8%; Belgium 4.3%; Spain 3.2%; Japan 2.3%.
Exports (1993): D 3,818,000,000 (clothing and accessories 32.0%, petroleum and petroleum products 9.7%, olive oil 4.6%, phosphoric acid 3.2%, chemical products 2.9%, phosphates 2.8%). *Major export destinations:* France 30.0%; Italy 17.2%; Germany 17.1%; Belgium 7.3%; Libya 5.0%.

Transport and communications

Transport. Railroads (1992): route length 1,404 mi, 2,260 km; passenger-mi 670,000,000, passenger-km 1,078,000,000; short ton-mi cargo 1,380,000,000, metric ton-km cargo 2,015,000,000. Roads (1989): total length 18,133 mi, 29,183 km (paved 60%). Vehicles (1989): passenger cars 321,101; trucks and buses 208,596. Merchant marine (1992): vessels (100 gross tons and over) 77; total deadweight tonnage 443,290. Air transport (1992): passenger-mi 1,000,000,000, passenger-km 1,668,000,000; short ton-mi cargo 11,700,000, metric ton-km cargo 17,100,000; airports (1994) 5.
Communications. Daily newspapers (1993): total number 6; total circulation 132,000[8]; circulation per 1,000 population 15[8]. Radio (1993): 1,700,000 receivers (1 per 5.0 persons). Television (1993): 650,000 receivers (1 per 13 persons). Telephones (1992): 337,063 (1 per 24 persons).

Education and health

Education (1992–93)				
	schools	teachers	students	student/ teacher ratio
Primary (age 6–11)	4,044	54,560	1,440,960	26.4
Secondary (age 12–18)	625	26,097	639,403	24.5
Teacher tr.[9, 10]	...	237	3,839	16.2
Higher	...	5,360	87,780	16.4

Educational attainment (1989). Percentage of population age 25 and over having: no formal schooling 54.9%; primary 26.9%; secondary 14.3%; higher 3.4%; unspecified 0.5%. *Literacy* (1990): total population age 15 and over literate 65.3%; males literate 74.2%; females literate 56.3%.
Health (1992): physicians 4,670 (1 per 1,799 persons); hospital beds 16,116 (1 per 521 persons); infant mortality rate (1990–95) 43.0.
Food (1988–90): daily per capita caloric intake 3,122 (vegetable products 91%, animal products 9%); 131% of FAO recommended minimum requirement.

Military

Total active duty personnel (1993): 35,500 (army 76.0%, navy 14.1%, air force 9.9%). *Military expenditure as percentage of GNP* (1991): 3.4% (world 4.2%); per capita expenditure U.S.$52.

[1]Preliminary. [2]Total includes 3,714 sq mi (9,620 sq km) of territory in the southwest part of Tunisia that is not distributed by governorate. [3]Recorded deaths from urban areas only, including complete figures for Tunis. [4]1990. [5]1989. [6]Includes 218,300 unemployed. [7]Year-end; index refers to the *S.M.I.G.* (*salaire minimum interprofessionel garanti*), a form of minimum professional wage. [8]Circulation for two dailies only. [9]1987–88. [10]Teacher training only.

Turkey

Official name: Türkiye Cumhuriyeti
(Republic of Turkey).
Form of government: multiparty
republic with one legislative
house (Turkish Grand National
Assembly [450]).
Chief of state: President.
Head of government: Prime Minister.
Capital: Ankara.
Official language: Turkish.
Official religion: none.
Monetary unit: 1 Turkish lira (LT) = 100
kurush; valuation (Oct. 7, 1994)
1 U.S.$ = LT 34,441;
1 £ = LT 54,779.

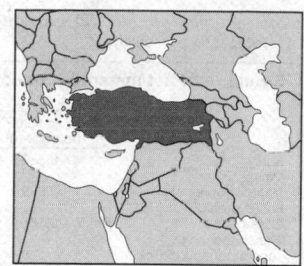

Area and population

Geographic regions[1]	area		population
	sq mi	sq km	1990 census
Akdeniz kıyısı (Mediterranean Coast)	22,933	59,395	5,443,867
Batı Anadolu (West Anatolia)	29,742	77,031	3,864,661
Doğu Anadolu (East Anatolia)	68,074	180,180	6,867,415
Güneydoğu Anadolu (Southeast Anatolia)	15,347	35,880	2,699,776
İç Anadolu (Central Anatolia)	91,254	236,347	13,096,179
Karadeniz kıyısı (Black Sea Coast)	31,388	81,295	6,827,304
Marmara ve Ege kıyıları (Marmara and Aegean coasts)	33,035	85,560	11,698,384
Trakya (Thrace)	9,175	23,764	5,975,449
TOTAL	300,948	779,452	56,473,035

Demography

Population (1994): 61,183,000.
Density (1994): persons per sq mi 203.3, persons per sq km 78.5.
Urban-rural (1990): urban 59.0%; rural 41.0%.
Sex distribution (1990): male 50.66%; female 49.34%.
Age breakdown (1990): under 15, 35.0%; 15–29, 28.6%; 30–44, 18.4%; 45–59, 10.9%; 60 and over, 7.1%.
Population projection: (2000) 69,694,000; (2010) 80,724,000.
Doubling time: 35 years.
Ethnolinguistic composition (1992)[2]: Turkish 92.0%; Kurdish 6.2%; Arabic 1.4%; other 0.4%.
Religious affiliation (1992): Sunnī Muslim *c.* 80.0%; Alevi (nonorthodox Shīʿi sect) *c.* 19.8%; Christian *c.* 0.2%.
Major cities (1990): Istanbul 6,620,241; Ankara 2,559,471; İzmir 1,757,414; Adana 916,150; Bursa 834,576; Gaziantep 603,434; Konya 513,346.

Vital statistics

Birth rate per 1,000 population (1994): 26.0 (world avg. 26.0).
Death rate per 1,000 population (1994): 6.0 (world avg. 9.2).
Natural increase rate per 1,000 population (1994): 20.0 (world avg. 16.8).
Total fertility rate (avg. births per childbearing woman; 1994): 3.2.
Marriage rate per 1,000 population (1991): 8.0.
Divorce rate per 1,000 population (1991): 0.5.
Life expectancy at birth (1994): male 69.0 years; female 73.0 years.
Major causes of death per 100,000 population (1990)[3]: diseases of the circulatory system represented 344; malignant neoplasms (cancers) 75; infectious and parasitic diseases 27; ill-defined conditions 87.

National economy

Budget (1993). Revenue: LT 359,850,000,000,000 (indirect taxes 37.8%; direct taxes 35.7%; nontax revenue 24.1%). Expenditures: LT 489,255,000,000,000 (current expenditures 88.3%, of which interest payments 23.8%; development expenditures 11.7%).
Public debt (external, outstanding; December 1993): U.S.$48,823,000,000.
Tourism (1993): receipts from visitors U.S.$3,959,000,000; expenditures by nationals abroad U.S.$934,000,000.
Production (in '000 metric tons except as noted). Agriculture, forestry, fishing (1993): wheat 21,000, sugar beets 15,563, barley 7,500, potatoes 4,650, grapes 3,700, corn (maize) 2,500, apples 2,080, oranges 840, cottonseed 834, sunflower seeds 815, lentils 735, cotton (lint) 556, olives 550, tobacco 324, hazelnuts 305, sultana raisins 180, attar of roses 800 kg; livestock (number of live animals; 1992) 40,433,000 sheep, 11,973,000 cattle; roundwood (1992) 15,252,000 cu m; fish catch (1991) 364,640. Mining (1992): boron (concentrate) 1,059; pumice 736; chromite 531; celestite (concentrate) 38. Manufacturing (1990)[4]: refined petroleum 11,805; spinning and weaving of textiles 6,723; food products 6,629; motor vehicles 4,034; industrial chemicals 3,957; nonelectrical machinery 3,711. Construction (completed; 1993): residential 65,966,000 sq m; nonresidential 17,133,000 sq m. Energy production (consumption): electricity (kW-hr; 1993) 73,727,000,000 ([1991] 60,591,000,000); coal (metric tons; 1993) 48,681,000 ([1991] 57,511,000); crude petroleum (barrels; 1993) 27,828,000 ([1991] 165,475,000); petroleum products (metric tons; 1991) 20,124,000 (18,726,000); natural gas (cu m; 1991) 219,000,000 (3,540,000,000).
Household income and expenditure. Average household size (1990) 5.0; income per household (1987) LT 3,680,500 (U.S.$4,294); sources of income (1987): self-employment 51.4%, wages and salaries 24.1%, rent and interest 13.7%, transfers 10.8%; expenditure (1987): food and beverages 33.1%, housing 14.7%, clothing 12.3%, household furnishings 11.5%.
Gross national product (at current market prices; 1992): U.S.$114,234,000,000 (U.S.$1,950 per capita).

Structure of gross domestic product and labour force

	1993		1992	
	in value LT '000,000'000[5]	% of total value	labour force	% of labour force
Agriculture	248,356	14.6	8,914,033	42.1
Mining	19,264	1.1	213,210	1.0
Manufacturing	326,642	19.2	3,416,822	16.1
Construction	122,261	7.2	1,180,541	5.0
Public utilities	49,575	2.9	67,427	0.3
Transportation and communications	225,267	13.3	865,459	4.1
Trade	311,310	18.3	2,612,669	12.3
Finance, real estate	124,818	7.3	476,820	2.3
Pub. admin., defense	203,922	12.0 }	2,640,239	12.5
Services	68,994	4.1 }		
Other	—	—	788,093[6]	3.7[6]
TOTAL	1,700,409	100.0	21,184,313	100.0

Population economically active (1992): total 21,184,313; activity rate of total population 36.2% (participation rates [1991]: ages 15–64, 58.4%; female 30.9%; unemployed 7.8%).

Price and earnings indexes (1990 = 100)

	1988	1989	1990	1991	1992	1993	1994[7]
Consumer price index	38.2	62.4	100.0	166.0	282.3	468.8	695.9
Daily earnings index[8]	24.1	53.6	100.0	243.8	423.9	750.3	...

Land use (1991): forested 26.3%; meadows and pastures 11.0%; agricultural and under permanent cultivation 36.0%; other 26.7%.

Foreign trade[9]

Balance of trade (current prices)

	1987	1988	1989	1990	1991	1992
U.S.$'000,000	−3,204	−1,900	−3,316	−8,140	−6,318	−6,922
% of total	13.6%	7.5%	12.5%	23.9%	18.9%	19.0%

Imports (1993): U.S.$29,428,000,000 (nonelectrical machinery 17.7%; mineral fuels 13.5%; iron and steel 9.0%; road vehicles 7.3%; electrical and electronic equipment 7.1%). *Major import sources:* Germany 15.4%; United States 11.4%; Italy 8.7%; former U.S.S.R. 7.8%; France 6.6%; Japan 5.5%.
Exports (1993): U.S.$15,349,000,000 (textiles and clothing 35.5%; iron and steel 11.2%; edible fruits 6.0%; electrical machinery 4.1%). *Major export destinations:* Germany 23.8%; former U.S.S.R. 6.8%; United States 6.4%; United Kingdom 5.4%; France 5.0%; Italy 4.9%.

Transport and communications

Transport. Railroads (1992): route length 5,238 mi, 8,430 km; passenger-mi 3,889,000,000, passenger-km 6,259,000,000; short ton-mi cargo 5,742,000,000, metric ton-km cargo 8,383,000,000. Roads (1992): total length 240,286 mi, 386,704 km (paved 15%). Vehicles (1992): passenger cars 2,181,388; trucks and buses 816,244. Merchant marine (1992): vessels (100 gross tons and over) 880; total deadweight tonnage 7,114,289. Air transport (1993)[10]: passenger-mi 4,484,000,000, passenger-km 7,217,000,000; short ton-mi cargo 110,518,000, metric ton-km cargo 161,354,000; airports (1994) with scheduled flights 22.
Communications. Daily newspapers (1991)[11]: total number 31; total circulation 4,054,000; circulation per 1,000 population 71. Radio (1993): total number of receivers 7,100,000 (1 per 8.4 persons). Television (1993): total number of receivers 10,530,000 (1 per 5.7 persons). Telephones (1991): 8,199,568 (1 per 7.1 persons).

Education and health

Education (1991–92)

	schools	teachers	students	student/ teacher ratio
Primary (age 6–10)	50,701	234,961	6,878,923	29.3
Secondary (age 11–16)	8,064	117,702	3,010,672	25.6
Voc., teacher tr.	2,971	57,425	977,010	17.0
Higher	424	35,132	759,047	21.6

Educational attainment (1985). Percentage of population age 25 and over having: no formal schooling 40.1%; primary education 44.4%; secondary 11.6%; higher 3.9%. *Literacy* (1990): total population age 15 and over literate 29,106,000 (79.2%); males literate 16,581,000 (89.9%); females literate 12,525,000 (68.5%).
Health (1992): physicians 29,679[12] (1 per 1,974[12] persons); hospital beds 126,611 (1 per 463 persons); infant mortality rate per 1,000 live births (1994) 49.0.
Food (1988–90): daily per capita caloric intake 3,196 (vegetable products 92%, animal products 8%); 127% of FAO recommended minimum requirement.

Military

Total active duty personnel (1993): 480,000 (army 77.1%, navy 10.4%, air force 12.5%). *Military expenditure as percentage of GNP* (1991): 5.4% (world 4.2%); per capita expenditure U.S.$99.

---

[1]Administratively divided into 76 provinces in 1993. [2]Official data based on mother tongue. Unofficially, Kurds as an ethnic group are estimated to constitute about 20% of the population. [3]Projected rates based on about 35% of total deaths. [4]Value added in LT '000,000,000. [5]At factor cost. [6]Unemployed persons not previously employed. [7]March. [8]Private sector only. [9]Imports are f.o.b. in balance of trade and c.i.f. in commodities and trading partners. [10]Turkish Airlines only. [11]Principal daily newspapers in Istanbul, Ankara, and five other large cities. [12]Ministry of Health doctors only (excludes Ministry of Defense).

Turkmenistan

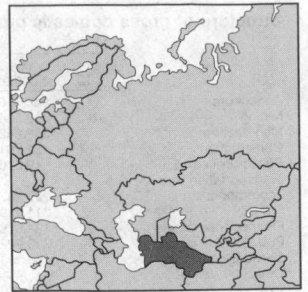

Official name: Türkmenistan
Jumhuriyäti (Republic of
Turkmenistan).
Form of government: republic with one
legislative body (Majlis [175][1]).
Head of state and government:
President.
Capital: Ashgabat.
Official language: Turkmen.
Official religion: none.
Monetary unit: manat[2]; valuation (Oct.
7, 1994) 1 U.S.$ = 10 manat;
1 £ = 15.91 manat.

Area and population

| | | area | | population |
| | | | | 1991 |
Provinces	Capitals	sq mi	sq km	estimate
Balkan	Nebitdag	90,300	233,900	925,500
Chärjew	Chärjew	36,200	93,800	774,700
Mary	Mary	33,500	86,800	859,500
Dashhowuz	Dashhowuz	28,400	73,600	738,000
City				
Ashgabat	—	...	...	416,400
TOTAL		188,500[3]	488,100	3,714,100

Demography

Population (1994): 4,044,000.
Density (1994): persons per sq mi 21.5, persons per sq km 8.3.
Urban-rural (1992): urban 45.1%; rural 54.9%.
Sex distribution (1989): male 49.30%; female 50.70%.
Age breakdown (1989): under 15, 40.5%; 15–29, 28.8%; 30–44, 15.5%; 45–59, 9.1%; 60–74, 4.7%; 75 and over, 1.4%.
Population projection: (2000) 4,691,000; (2010) 6,007,000.
Doubling time: 27 years.
Ethnic composition (1992): Turkmen 73.3%; Russian 9.8%; Uzbek 9.0%; Kazakh 2.0%; Tatar 0.9%; other 5.0%.
Religious affiliation: believers are predominantly Sunnī Muslim (Ṣūfī).
Major cities (1991): Ashgabat 416,400; Chärjew 166,400; Dashhowuz 117,000; Mary 94,900; Nebitdag 89,100.

Vital statistics

Birth rate per 1,000 population (1992): 33.4 (world avg. 26.0); (1989) legitimate 96.5%; illegitimate 3.5%.
Death rate per 1,000 population (1992): 7.2 (world avg. 9.2).
Natural increase rate per 1,000 population (1992): 26.2 (world avg. 16.8).
Total fertility rate (avg. births per childbearing woman; 1993): 3.8.
Marriage rate per 1,000 population (1992): 11.1.
Divorce rate per 1,000 population (1992): 1.5.
Life expectancy at birth (1993): male 61.4 years; female 68.6 years.
Major causes of death per 100,000 population (1989): diseases of the circulatory system 275.3; diseases of the respiratory system 160.6; infectious and parasitic diseases 79.3; malignant neoplasms (cancers) 65.1; accidents, poisoning, and violence 62.4; diseases of the digestive system 32.2; diseases of the nervous system 9.1; endocrine and metabolic disorders 8.0.

National economy

Budget (1992). Revenue: 62,719,000,000 rubles (tax revenue 52.5%, of which turnover tax 26.3%, company profit tax 19.6%, individual income tax 4.8%, excise tax 1.9%, nontax revenue 47.5%). Expenditures: 94,882,000,000 rubles (1991; social and cultural affairs 56.9%, of which social security 26.7%, education and science 19.7%, health 9.4%; national economy 39.0%; government administration 2.7%).
Public debt (external, outstanding; 1992): U.S.$650,000,000.
Production (metric tons except as noted). Agriculture, forestry, fishing (1992): seed cotton 1,290,000, vegetables 360,000, grain 320,000, fruit 228,000; livestock (number of live animals) 5,600,000 sheep and goats, 1,400,000 cattle, 300,000 pigs, 8,000,000 poultry; roundwood (1990) 4,000,000 cu m; fish catch 20,949. Mining and quarrying (1989): sulfur 5,547,000; sodium sulphate 261,-000. Manufacturing (1992): cement 1,051,000; cotton fibre 437,000; mineral fertilizers 103,000; centrifugal pumps 1,069,000 units; rugs 1,071,000 sq m. Construction (1992): 20,754,000 sq m. Energy production (consumption): electricity (kW-hr; 1992) 13,100,000,000 (13,100,000,000); coal (metric tons; 1992) none (269,000); crude petroleum (barrels; 1992) 35,184,000 (43,386,-000); petroleum products (metric tons; 1991) 500,000 (500,000); natural gas (cu m; 1992) 60,107,000,000 (11,197,000,000).
Population economically active (1992): total: 1,572,900; activity rate of total population 40.8% (participation rates: ages 16–59 [male], 16–54 [female] 81.0%; female 50.5%; unemployed [1991] 20–25%).

Price and earnings indexes (1990 = 100)

	1986	1987	1988	1989	1990	1991	1992
Consumer price index	80.8	81.6	85.6	89.9	100	185.7	1,921.8
Monthly earnings index	79.2	81.4	85.5	90.8	100	170.1	1,573.7

Household income and expenditure. Average household size (1989) 5.6; income per household: n.a.; sources of income (1992): wages and salaries 73.5%, pensions and grants 17.3%, income from agriculture sales 6.6%, nonwage income of workers 2.6%; expenditure (1992): food and clothing 65.4%, services 9.7%, taxes and other payments 8.6%.

Gross national product (at current market prices; 1993): U.S.$4,898,390,000 (U.S.$1,270 per capita)[4].

Structure of net material product and labour force

| | 1991 | | 1992 | |
	in value '000,000 rubles	% of total value	labour force	% of labour force
Agriculture	6,389.7	46.4	695,200	44.2
Mining	}			
Manufacturing	2,699.1	19.6	154,300	9.8
Public utilities	}			
Construction	3,126.1	22.7	163,500	10.4
Transportation and and communications	578.4	4.2	56,400	3.6
Trade	—	—	88,500	5.6
Finance	—	—	...	...
Public administration, defense	—	—	49,800	3.2
Services	—	—	338,700	21.5
Other	977.7	7.1	26,500	1.7
TOTAL	13,771.0	100.0	1,572,900	100.0

Tourism: n.a.
Land use (1986): forested 35.4%; meadows and pastures 62.3%; agricultural and under permanent cultivation 2.3%.

Foreign trade

Balance of trade (current prices)

	1987	1988	1989	1990	1991	1992
'000,000 rubles	−477	−284	−676	−971	+898	+2,409
% of total	8.9%	5.1%	11.3%	15.5%	6.1%	17.9%

Imports (1992): 5,497,000,000 rubles (machinery and transport equipment 30.3%, manufactured items 21.8%, food 17.1%, chemicals 6.5%). *Major import sources:* former Soviet republics 83.8%; foreign countries 16.2%.
Exports (1992): 7,906,000,000 (fuels and lubricants 42.3%, manufactured items 38.1%, chemicals 5.5%, food 4.0%). *Major export destinations:* former Soviet republics 85.8%; foreign countries 14.2%.

Transport and communications

Transport. Railroads (1991): length 1,317 mi, 2,120 km; passengers transported 5,900,000; short ton cargo 20,700,000, metric ton cargo 22,800,000. Roads (1990): total length 8,300 mi, 13,400 km (paved 86%). Vehicles (1988): passenger cars 170,600; trucks and buses, n.a. Merchant marine: vessels (100 gross tons and over) n.a.; total deadweight tonnage, n.a. Air transport (1989): passenger-mi 2,021,000,000, passenger-km 3,253,000,000; short ton-mi cargo 222,000,000, metric ton-km cargo 324,200,000; airports (1994) with scheduled flights 1.
Communications. Daily newspapers (1989): total number 66; total circulation 1,141,000; circulation per 1,000 population 319. Radio (1991): 823,000 receivers (1 per 5.2 persons). Televisions (1991): 705,000 receivers (1 per 6.1 persons). Telephones (1992): 266,000 (1 per 15 persons).

Education and health

Education (1991–92)

	schools	teachers	students	student/ teacher ratio
Primary (age 6–13) } Secondary (age 14–17) }	1,791	60,000	842,000	14.1
Voc., teacher tr.	41	...	33,700	...
Higher	9	...	41,700	...

Educational attainment (1989). Percentage of population age 25 and over having: primary education or no formal schooling 13.6%; some secondary 21.3%; completed secondary and some postsecondary 56.8%; higher 8.3%.
Literacy: n.a.
Health (1992): physicians 13,500 (1 per 412 persons); hospital beds 41,800 (1 per 92 persons); infant mortality rate per 1,000 live births 43.6.
Food: daily per capita caloric intake, n.a.

Military

Total active duty personnel (1994): CIS joint-control forces 28,000 (100% army). *Military expenditure as a percentage of GNP* (1992): 8.8% (world 5.0%); per capita expenditure U.S.$112.

[1]The legislative body per the 1992 constitution was to be a 50-member Majlis, but the 175-seat Supreme Soviet elected in January 1990 acts as the Majlis until expiration of its 5-year term or new elections are held. The People's Council (created per the 1992 constitution as a supreme representative body including the Majlis) is a supervisory, not legislative, body. [2]Sole legal tender as of November 1993. [3]Detail does not add to total given because of rounding. [4]Ruble-area GNP and exchange-rate data are very speculative.

Tuvalu

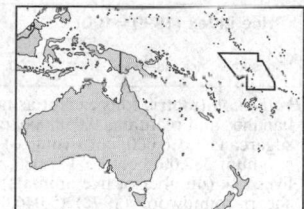

Official name: Tuvalu.
Form of government: constitutional monarchy with one legislative house (Parliament [12]).
Chief of state: British Monarch, represented by Governor-General.
Head of government: Prime Minister.
Capital: Fongafale, on Funafuti atoll.
Official language: none.
Official religion: none.
Monetary unit[1]: 1 Tuvalu Dollar = 1 Australian Dollar ($T = $A) = 100 Tuvalu and Australian cents; valuation (Oct. 7, 1994) 1 U.S.$ = $A 1.35; 1 £ = $A 2.15.

Area and population

Islands[2]	area		population
	sq mi	sq km	1987 estimate
Funafuti	0.91	2.36	2,718
Nanumaga	1.00	2.59	717
Nanumea	1.38	3.57	965
Niulakita	0.16	0.41	75
Niutao	0.82	2.12	867
Nui	1.27	3.29	622
Nukufetau	1.18	3.06	722
Nukulaelae	0.64	1.66	335
Vaitupu	1.89	4.90	1,437
TOTAL	9.253[3]	23.963[3]	8,458[4,5]

Demography

Population (1994): 9,300.
Density (1994): persons per sq mi 989.4, persons per sq km 381.1.
Urban-rural (1991): urban 43.0%; rural 57.0%.
Sex distribution (1991): male 48.39%; female 51.61%.
Age breakdown (1991): under 15, 34.7%; 15–64, 59.4%; 65 and over, 5.9%.
Population projection: (2000) 11,000; (2010) 12,500.
Doubling time: 39 years.
Ethnic composition (1979): Tuvaluan (Polynesian) 91.2%; mixed (Polynesian/Micronesian/other) 7.2%; European 1.0%; other 0.6%.
Religious affiliation (1979): Church of Tuvalu (Congregational) 96.9%; Seventh-day Adventist 1.4%; Bahā'ī 1.0%; Roman Catholic 0.2%; other 0.5%.
Major locality (1990): Fongafale, on Funafuti atoll, 3,432.

Vital statistics

Birth rate per 1,000 population (1992): 29.0 (world avg. 26.0); (1989) legitimate 82.2%; illegitimate 17.8%.
Death rate per 1,000 population (1992): 11.0 (world avg. 9.2).
Natural increase rate per 1,000 population (1992): 18.0 (world avg. 16.8).
Total fertility rate (avg. births per childbearing woman; 1992): 3.3.
Marriage rate per 1,000 population: n.a.
Divorce rate per 1,000 population: n.a.
Life expectancy at birth (1990): male 60.0 years; female 63.0 years.
Major causes of death per 100,000 population (1985): diseases of the digestive system 170.0; diseases of the circulatory system 150.0; diseases of the respiratory system 120.0; diseases of the nervous system 120.0; malignant neoplasms (cancers) 70.0; infectious and parasitic diseases 40.0; endocrine and metabolic disorders 20.0; ill-defined conditions 430.0; in 1992 the leading causes of death included liver diseases, meningitis, tuberculosis, and still and perinatal deaths; other health problems included acute respiratory infections, diarrhea, filariasis, conjunctivitis, fish poisoning, diabetes, rheumatism, and hypertension.

National economy

Budget (1990). Recurrent revenue: $A 5,301,000 (local sources [including fisheries licenses, import duties, sales tax, and income and company taxes] 77.4%; Tuvalu Trust Fund[6] 22.6%). Expenditures: $A 10,826,000[7] (1987; capital [development] expenditures 68.9%, of which marine transport 20.7%, education 13.0%, fisheries 5.6%, health 3.1%; current expenditures 31.1%).
Gross domestic product (at current market prices; 1990): U.S.$8,750,000 (U.S.$967 per capita).

Structure of gross domestic product and labour force

	1990		1991	
	in value $A	% of total value	labour force	% of labour force
Agriculture, fishing, forestry	2,699,000	24.1	4,020	68.0
Mining	302,000	2.7	—	—
Manufacturing[8]	358,000	3.2	60	1.0
Construction	1,635,000	14.6	240	4.0
Public utilities	235,000	2.1	—	—
Transportation and communications	403,000	3.6	60	1.0
Trade, hotels, and restaurants	1,669,000	14.9	240	4.0
Finance	997,000	8.9	—	—
Pub. admin., defense } Services	2,901,000	25.9	1,290	22.0
TOTAL	11,199,000	100.0	5,910	100.0

Production (metric tons except as noted). Agriculture[9], forestry, fishing (1993): coconuts 2,000, fruits 1,000, hens' eggs 12, other agricultural products include breadfruit, pulaka (taro), bananas, pandanus fruit, sweet potatoes, and pawpaws; livestock (number of live animals) 13,000 pigs[10]; forestry, n.a.; fish catch (1991) 1,460, of which tuna 71.2%. Mining and quarrying: n.a.[11]. Manufacturing (1988): copra 90 metric tons; handicrafts and baked goods are also important. Construction: n.a.; however, the main areas of construction activity are roadworks, coastal protection, government facilities, and water-related infrastructure projects. Energy production (consumption): electricity (kW-hr; 1992) 1,300,000 (1,300,000); coal, none (none); crude petroleum, none (n.a.); petroleum products, none (n.a.); natural gas, none (none).
Public debt: n.a.
Tourism (1991): number of visitors 976; receipts from visitors $A 169,700[12]; hotel occupancy 95%[12].
Population economically active (1991): total 5,910; activity rate of total population 65.3% (participation rates: ages 15–64, 85.5%; female [1979] 51.3%; unemployed [1979] 4.0%).

Price and earnings indexes (1986 = 100)

	1987	1988	1989	1990	1991	1992	1993
Consumer price index	111.0	113.3	116.3	123.2	130.0	132.9	134.9
Earnings index[13]	102.5	105.0	110.0	112.5	...	...	...

Household income and expenditure. Average household size (1979) 6.4; average annual income per household $A 2,575; sources of income (1987): agriculture and other 45.0%, cash economy only 38.0%, overseas remittances 17.3%; expenditure (1992)[14]: food 45.5%, housing and household operations 11.5%, transportation 10.5%, alcohol and tobacco 10.5%, clothing 7.5%, other 14.5%.
Land use (1987): agricultural and under permanent cultivation 73.6%[15]; scrub 16.1%; other 10.3%.

Foreign trade

Balance of trade (current prices)

	1984	1985	1986	1987	1988	1989
$A '000	−3,637	−3,969	−4,076	−4,946	−6,780	−5,158
% of total	85.4%	92.7%	99.9%	99.9%	99.7%	99.5%

Imports (1989): $A 5,170,000 (food 29.3%, manufactured goods 28.2%, petroleum and petroleum products 12.8%, machinery and transport equipment 12.2%, chemicals 7.1%, beverages and tobacco 3.9%). *Major import sources* (1986): Australia 40.6%; New Zealand 10.9%; United Kingdom 5.1%; Japan 3.0%; United States 1.0%.
Exports (1990): $A 30,400 (1989; clothing and footwear 29.5%, copra 21.5%, fruits and vegetables 8.0%). *Major export destinations:* n.a.

Transport and communications

Transport. Railroads: none. Roads (1985): total length 5 mi, 8 km (paved, none). Vehicles[16]: passenger cars, n.a.; trucks and buses, n.a. Merchant marine (1992): vessels (100 gross tons and over) 6; total deadweight tonnage 16,005. Air transport (1977): passenger arrivals (Funafuti) 1,443; cargo, n.a.; airports (1994) with scheduled flights 1.
Communications. Daily newspapers: none. Radio (1993): total number of receivers 4,000 (1 per 2.4 persons). Television: none. Telephones (1992): 190 (1 per 48 persons).

Education and health

Education (1990)

	schools	teachers	students	student/teacher ratio
Primary (age 5–11)	9	72	1,485	20.6
Secondary (age 12–18)	1	21	314	15.0
Vocational[17]	8	16	354	22.1
Higher	—	—	—	—

Educational attainment (1979). Percentage of population age 25 and over having: no formal schooling 0.4%; primary education 93.0%; secondary 6.1%; higher 0.5%. *Literacy* (1990): total population literate in Tuvaluan 8,593 (95.0%); literacy in English estimated at 45.0%.
Health (1990): physicians 4 (1 per 2,261 persons); hospital beds 30 (1 per 302 persons); infant mortality rate per 1,000 live births 78.6.
Food: daily per capita caloric intake, n.a.

Military

Total active duty personnel (1987): there is a police force numbering 32.

[1]The value of the Tuvalu Dollar is pegged to the value of the Australian Dollar, which is also legal currency in Tuvalu. [2]Local government councils have been established on all islands except Niulakita. [3]A recent survey puts the area at 9.4 sq mi (24.4 sq km). [4]De facto population. [5]1991 census total is 9,043. [6]The Tuvalu Trust Fund was capitalized in 1987 with $A 27,700,000 to replace recurrent grant aid from the United Kingdom; the fund was valued at $A 36,000,000 in late 1991. [7]Figure includes $A 5,200,000 of capital expenditures, paid for, primarily, by foreign-aid contributions that are not part of recurrent revenue. [8]Including cottage industry. [9]Because of poor soil quality, only limited subsistence agriculture is possible on the islands. [10]Other livestock include goats. [11]Research into the mineral potential of Tuvalu's maritime exclusive economic zone (289,500 sq mi [750,000 sq km] of the Pacific Ocean) is currently being conducted by the South Pacific Geo-Science Commission. [12]1990. [13]Average minimum wage. [14]Weights of consumer price index components. [15]Capable of supporting coconut palms, pandanus, and breadfruit. [16]There are several cars, tractors, trailers, and light trucks on Funafuti; a few motorcycles are in use on most islands. [17]1982–83.

Uganda

Official name: Republic of Uganda.
Form of government: transitional military regime with a constituent assembly (Constituent Assembly [214[1]][2]).
Head of state and government: President assisted by Prime Minister.
Capital: Kampala.
Official languages: English; Swahili.
Official religion: none.
Monetary unit: 1 Uganda shilling (U Sh) = 100 cents; valuation (Oct. 7, 1994) 1 U.S.$ = U Sh 920.87; 1 £ = U Sh 1,465.

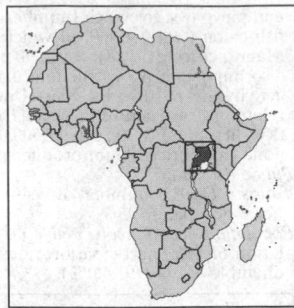

Area and population

Regions Districts	Capitals	area sq mi	area sq km	population 1991 census[3]
Central				
Kalangala	...	...	...	16,400
Kampala	Kampala	70	180	773,500
Kiboga	...	...	...	140,800
Luwero	Luwero	3,550	9,200	449,200
Masaka	Kasawa Bukoto	6,310	16,330	831,300
Mpigi	Mpigi	2,400	6,220	915,400
Mubende	Bageza	3,980	10,310	497,500
Mukono	Kawuga Mukono	5,500	14,240	816,200
Rakai	Byakabanda	1,920	4,970	382,000
Eastern				
Iganga	Bulamogi	5,060	13,110	944,000
Jinja	Jinja	280	730	284,900
Kamuli	Namwendwa	1,680	4,350	480,700
Kapchorwa	Kaptanya	670	1,740	116,300
Kumi	Kumi	1,100	2,860	237,000
Mbale	Bunkoko	980	2,550	706,600
Pallisa	...	...	...	355,000
Soroti	Soroti	3,880	10,060	430,900
Tororo	Sukulu	1,780	4,550	554,000
Northern				
Apac	Apac	2,510	6,490	460,700
Arua	Olaki	3,020	7,830	624,600
Gulu	Bungatira	4,530	11,740	338,700
Kitgum	Labongo	8,230	16,140	350,300
Kotido	Kotido	5,100	13,210	190,700
Lira	Lira	2,800	7,250	498,300
Moroto	Katikekile	5,450	14,110	171,500
Moyo	Moyo	1,930	5,010	178,500
Nebbi	Nebbi	1,120	2,890	315,900
Western				
Bundibugyo	Busaru	900	2,340	116,000
Bushenyi	Bumbaire	2,080	5,400	734,800
Hoima	Hoima	3,820	9,900	197,800
Kabale	Rubale	960	2,490	412,800
Kabarole	Karambe	3,230	8,360	741,400
Kasese	Rukoki	1,240	3,200	343,000
Kibaale	...	...	...	219,300
Kisoro	...	...	...	184,900
Masindi	Nyangeya	3,720	9,640	253,500
Mbarara	Kakika	4,190	10,840	929,600
Rukungiri	Kagunga	1,060	2,750	388,000
TOTAL LAND AREA		76,080	197,040	
INLAND WATER[4]		16,990	44,000	
TOTAL		93,070[5]	241,040[5]	16,582,700[5]

Demography

Population (1994): 18,194,000.
Density (1994)[6]: persons per sq mi 239.1, persons per sq km 92.3.
Urban-rural (1992): urban 11.7%; rural 88.3%.
Sex distribution (1991): male 49.00%; female 51.00%.
Age breakdown (1990): under 15, 49.6%; 15–29, 25.4%; 30–44, 13.9%; 45–59, 7.1%; 60 and over, 4.0%.
Population projection: (2000) 21,168,000; (2010) 27,244,000.
Doubling time: 19 years.
Ethnic composition (1983): Ganda 17.8%; Teso 8.9%; Nkole 8.2%; Soga 8.2%; Gisu 7.2%; Chiga 6.8%; Lango 6.0%; Rwanda 5.8%; other 31.1%.
Religious affiliation (1980): Roman Catholic 49.6%; Protestant 28.7%; Muslim 6.6%; other 15.1%.
Major cities (1991): Kampala 773,000; Jinja 61,000; Mbale 54,000.

Vital statistics

Birth rate per 1,000 population (1990–95): 51.5 (world avg. 26.0).
Death rate per 1,000 population (1990–95): 14.1 (world avg. 9.2).
Natural increase rate per 1,000 population (1990–95): 37.4 (world avg. 16.8).
Total fertility rate (avg. births per childbearing woman; 1990–95): 7.3.
Life expectancy at birth (1990–95): male 51.4 years; female 54.7 years.

National economy

Budget (1991–92). Revenue: U Sh 434,335,000,000 (external assistance grants 52.9%; tax revenue 45.6%). Expenditures: U Sh 528,647,000,000 (1990–91; current expenditures 79.2%, of which security 51.7%, education 16.5%, public services 16.2%, health 5.5%; capital expenditures 20.8%).
Tourism (1991): receipts from visitors U.S.$15,000,000; expenditures by nationals abroad U.S.$18,000,000.
Land use (1992): forested 27.6%; meadows and pastures 9.0%; agricultural and under permanent cultivation 33.9%; other 29.5%.
Population economically active (1991): total 8,365,000; activity rate of total population 49.6% (participation rates: ages 15–64, 78.9%[7]; female 35.2%).

Price index (1990 = 100)

	1987	1988	1989	1990	1991	1992	1993
Consumer price index	16.0	47.0	75.0	100.0	128.0	195.0	207.0

Production (metric tons except as noted). Agriculture, forestry, fishing (1993): bananas and plantains 9,058,000, cassava 3,982,000, sweet potatoes 1,894,000, sugarcane 1,010,000, corn (maize) 681,000, millet 652,000, dry beans 441,000, sorghum 382,000, coffee 177,000, peanuts (groundnuts) 150,000, tea 12,000; livestock (number of live animals) 5,200,000 cattle, 3,400,000 goats, 1,760,000 sheep; roundwood (1992) 15,046,000 cu m; fish catch (1991) 254,900. Mining and quarrying (1992): tungsten (wolfram) 66.0; tin ore 30.0; gold 57,900 troy oz. Manufacturing (1990): soap 30,600; sugar 28,900; animal feed 15,000; cement 14,960; metal products 1,300; footwear 319,000 pairs; fabrics 8,200,000 sq m; 1,289,700,000 cigarettes; beer 194,000 hectolitres. Construction: n.a. Energy production (consumption): electricity (kW-hr; 1992) 786,000,000 (674,000,000); petroleum products (metric tons; 1992) none (303,000).
Gross national product (1993): U.S.$3,425,000,000 (U.S.$190 per capita).

Structure of gross domestic product and labour force

	1991 in value U Sh '000,000	1991 % of total value	1991 labour force	1991 % of labour force
Agriculture	1,082,040	51.4	6,724,000	80.4
Mining	8,490	0.4		
Manufacturing	89,540	4.3	478,000	5.7
Construction	134,470	6.4		
Public utilities	15,000	0.7		
Transp. and commun.	163,010	7.8		
Trade	258,820	12.3		
Finance	145,890	6.9	1,163,000	13.9
Pub. admin., defense	67,260	3.2		
Services	139,370	6.6		
TOTAL	2,103,890	100.0	8,365,000	100.0

Household size. Average household size (1983) 4.8; income per household: n.a.; expenditure (1989–90)[8]: food 57.1%, rent, education, and health 15.7%, fuel and lighting 7.3%, transportation 5.9%, clothing 5.5%.
Public debt (external, outstanding; 1992): U.S.$2,495,000,000.

Foreign trade

Balance of trade (current prices)

	1987	1988	1989	1990	1991	1992
U Sh '000,000	−19,051	−55,716	−23,471	−48,013	+23,012	−363,753
% of total	41.0%	48.9%	17.4%	27.1%	8.5%	53.3%

Imports (1991): U Sh 137,250,000,000 (producer goods 18.8%, of which construction materials 5.0%, machinery 4.8%; consumer goods 10.5%, of which automobiles 2.5%, drugs and pharmaceuticals 2.0%, sugar 1.7%; other goods 70.7%). *Major import sources:* Kenya 23.3%; U.K. 15.0%; Japan 9.3%; Germany 6.9%.
Exports (1991): U Sh 146,661,000,000 (unroasted coffee 66.9%; cotton 6.1%; gold 4.7%; tea 3.2%). *Major export destinations:* The Netherlands 21.5%; France 16.2%; U.S. 11.9%; Spain 11.1%; Germany 10.9%; Italy 7.9%.

Transport and communications

Transport. Railroads (1991): route length 1,240 km[9]; passenger-km 330,000,000; metric ton-km cargo 87,000,000. Roads (1991): total length 28,660 km (paved 16%). Vehicles (1990): passenger cars 35,492; trucks and buses 14,902. Merchant marine (1992): vessels (100 gross tons and over) 2; total deadweight tonnage 8,600[10]. Air transport (1990)[11]: passenger-km 67,000,000; metric ton-km cargo 3,000,000; airports (1994) 1.
Communications. Daily newspapers (1992): total number 4; total circulation 55,000; circulation per 1,000 population 3.2. Radio (1993): 3,500,000 receivers (1 per 5.1 persons). Television (1993): 115,000 receivers (1 per 154 persons). Telephones (1992): 55,270 (1 per 313 persons).

Education and health

Education (1989)

	schools	teachers	students	student/ teacher ratio
Primary (age 5–11)	7,905	75,561	2,633,764	34.8
Secondary (age 12–15)	774	13,356	240,334	18.0
Voc., teacher tr.	136	2,081	23,179	11.1
Higher	9	934[12]	5,778	8.8[12]

Educational attainment (1969). Percentage of population age 25 and over having: no formal schooling or less than one full year 58.2%; primary education 33.9%; lower secondary 5.0%; upper secondary 2.5%; higher 0.4%.
Literacy (1990): population age 15 and over literate 4,586,000 (48.3%); males literate 2,900,000 (62.2%); females literate 1,686,000 (34.9%).
Health (1989): physicians 774 (1 per 20,720 persons); hospital beds 20,136 (1 per 817 persons); infant mortality rate (1990–95) 94.0.
Food (1988–90): daily per capita caloric intake 2,178 (vegetable products 94%, animal products 6%); 93% of FAO recommended minimum requirement.

Military

Total active duty personnel (1994): 50,000 (army 97.6%, navy 0.8%, air force 1.6%). *Military expenditure as percentage of GNP* (1991): 2.6% (world 4.2%); per capita U.S.$4.

[1]Elective seats only. [2]Body elected and appointed in 1994 to debate and enact a draft constitution. [3]Preliminary. [4]Includes swamps; excludes 30,960 sq km of Uganda's Lake Victoria territorial waters. [5]Detail does not add to total given because of rounding. [6]Based on land area. [7]1985. [8]Kampala and Entebbe only. [9]1990. [10]1988. [11]Uganda Airlines only. [12]1984.

Ukraine

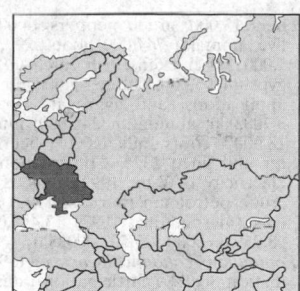

Official name. Ukrayina (Ukraine).
Form of government: unitary multiparty republic with a single legislative body (Supreme Council [450]).
Head of state: President.
Head of government: Prime Minister.
Capital: Kiev (Kyyiv).
Official language: Ukrainian.
Official religion: none.
Monetary unit: karbovanets[1] (no decimal unit); valuation (Oct. 7, 1994) free rate, 1 U.S.$ = 30,028 karbovantsy; 1 £ = 47,760 karbovantsy.

Area and population

Autonomous republic	Capitals	area sq mi	area sq km	population 1991 estimate
Crimea (Krym)	Simferopol	10,400	27,000	2,596,000
Provinces				
Cherkasy	Cherkasy	8,100	20,900	1,531,800
Chernihiv	Chernihiv	12,300	31,900	1,398,000
Chernivtsi	Chernivtsi	3,100	8,100	940,500
Dnipropetrovsk	Dnipropetrovsk	12,300	31,900	3,918,600
Donetsk	Donetsk	10,200	26,500	5,352,600
Ivano-Frankivsk	Ivano-Frankivsk	5,400	13,900	1,451,500
Kharkiv	Kharkiv	12,100	31,400	3,186,600
Kherson	Kherson	11,000	28,500	1,270,000
Khmelnytsky	Khmelnytsky	8,000	20,600	1,521,500
Kirovohrad	Kirovohrad	9,500	24,600	1,247,500
Kyyiv (Kiev)	Kiev	11,200	28,900	4,588,900
Luhansk	Luhansk	10,300	26,700	2,877,400
Lviv	Lviv	8,400	21,800	2,771,300
Mykolayiv	Mykolayiv	9,500	24,600	1,350,800
Odessa	Odessa	12,900	33,300	2,634,500
Poltava	Poltava	11,100	28,800	1,762,800
Rivne	Rivne	7,800	20,100	1,181,600
Sumy	Sumy	9,200	23,800	1,430,700
Ternopil	Ternopil	5,300	13,800	1,177,100
Vinnytsya	Vinnytsya	10,200	26,500	1,908,400
Volyn	Volodymyr-Volynsky	7,800	20,200	1,072,700
Zakarpatska	Uzhhorod	4,900	12,800	1,271,600
Zaporizhzhya	Zaporizhzhya	10,500	27,200	2,108,500
Zhytomyr	Zhytomyr	11,600	29,900	1,503,700
TOTAL		233,100	603,700	52,056,600

Demography

Population (1994): 52,304,000.
Density (1994): persons per sq mi 224.4, persons per sq km 86.6.
Urban-rural (1993): urban 67.8%; rural 32.2%.
Sex distribution (1993): male 46.36%; female 53.63%.
Age breakdown (1991): under 15, 21.5%; 15–29, 21.0%; 30–44, 20.6%; 45–59, 18.5%; 60–69, 10.7%; 70 and over, 7.7%.
Population projection: (2000) 52,970,000; (2010) 54,098,000.
Ethnic composition (1991): Ukrainian 72.6%; Russian 22.2%; Jewish 0.7%; Belarusian 0.9%; Moldovan 0.6%; Tatar 0.4%; other 2.6%.
Religious affiliation: believers are predominantly Ukrainian Orthodox; there is a Ukrainian Catholic minority.
Major cities (1993): Kiev 2,646,000; Kharkiv 1,615,000; Dnipropetrovsk 1,186,000; Donetsk 1,121,000; Odessa 1,087,000.

Vital statistics

Birth rate per 1,000 population (1992): 11.5 (world avg. 26.0); legitimate 88.1%; illegitimate 11.9%.
Death rate per 1,000 population (1992): 13.4 (world avg. 9.2).
Natural increase rate per 1,000 population (1992): −1.9 (world avg. 16.8).
Total fertility rate (avg. births per childbearing woman; 1993): 1.8.
Marriage rate per 1,000 population (1992): 7.6.
Divorce rate per 1,000 population (1992): 4.3.
Life expectancy at birth (1993): male 65.3 years; female 74.7 years.
Major causes of death per 100,000 population (1992): circulatory diseases 690.0; cancers 203.0; accidents 128.0; respiratory diseases 74.0; diseases of the digestive system (1989) 30.1; infectious diseases (1989) 11.6.

National economy

Budget (1993). Revenue: 8,121,300,000,000 karbovantsy (tax revenue 87.6%, of which value-added tax 24.5%, corporate tax 16.6%, foreign trade tax 12.4%; nontax revenue 12.4%). Expenditures: 9,094,600,000,000 karbovantsy (current expenditure 92.4%, of which social safety net 20.3%, national economy 14.6%, education 13.6%, health care 11.4%; capital expenditure 7.6%).
Production (metric tons except as noted). Agriculture, forestry, fishing (1993): sugar beets 33,717,000, wheat 21,831,000, potatoes 21,009,000, corn (maize) 3,786,000, sunflower seeds 2,075,000, grapes 666,000; livestock (number of live animals) 22,457,000 cattle, 16,175,000 pigs, 7,237,000 sheep and goats; roundwood (1992) 8,900,000 cu m; fish catch (1992) 1,300,000. Mining and quarrying (1992): iron ore 75,700,000; manganese 5,800,000. Manufacturing (1993): iron rails 75,700,000, crude steel 41,800,000; pig iron 35,300,000; rolled metals 32,500,000; cement 20,100,000; paper products 653,500; caustic soda 401,800; detergents 211,800; synthetic fibre 119,000; cellulose 75,800; pesticides 21,700; fertilizer 3,300; sulfuric acid 3,000; bricks 9,300,000,000 units; automobiles 176,500 units; metal-cutting machines 33,900 units; forge press machines 7,900 units; earth-moving equipment 6,900 units; reinforced concrete 20,500,000 cu m. Construction (1991): residential 14,454,000 sq m. Energy production (consumption): electricity (kW-hr; 1992) 252,400,000,-

000 (246,800,000,000); coal (metric tons; 1992) 133,600,000 (138,900,000,-000); crude petroleum (barrels; 1992) 32,800,000 (298,500,000); petroleum products 32,500,000 (28,800,000); natural gas (cu m; 1992) 18,200,000,000 (96,900,000,000).
Gross national product (1993): U.S.$99,589,000,000 (U.S.$1,910 per capita)[2].

Structure of net material product and labour force

	1991 in value '000,000 rubles	1991 % of total value	1992 labour value	1992 % of labour force
Agriculture	60,400	28.7	4,989,000	20.8
Mining	}	}	7,401,000	30.9
Manufacturing	90,800	43.1		
Public utilities			898,000	3.7
Construction	29,100	13.8	1,910,000	8.0
Transp. and commun.	9,400	4.5	1,623,000	6.8
Trade	12,000	5.7	1,751,000	7.3
Finance	—	—	144,000	0.6
Pub. admin., defense	—	—	562,000	2.3
Services	—	—	3,920,000	16.3
Other	8,900	4.2	787,000	3.3
TOTAL	210,600	100.0	23,985	100.0

Population economically active (1992): total 23,985,000; activity rate of total population 46.1% (participation rates: ages 16–59 [male], 16–54 [female] 79.9%; [1991] female 54.5%; unemployed [1991] 3.1%).

Price and earnings indexes (1990 = 100)

	1986	1987	1988	1989	1990	1991	1992
Consumer price index	68.4	70.3	76.3	85.5	100.0	191.2	3,132
Monthly earnings index	69.4	71.3	78.0	86.3	100.0	190.8	2,677

Land use (1992): forested 17.0%; meadows and pastures 12.4%; agricultural and under permanent cultivation 57.1%; other 13.5%.
Household income and expenditure (1992). Average household size 3.0; income per household 12,825 karbovantsy[1]; sources of income (1991): wages 51.8%, pensions 20.4%, financial receipts 11.7%, sales of agricultural products 7.2%, other 8.9%; expenditure (1991): food and nonalcoholic beverages 39.2%, consumer goods 32.2% (of which furniture and household appliances 6.8%), entertainment and culture 6.3%, alcoholic beverages 2.1%, housing 1.7%.

Foreign trade

Balance of trade (current prices)

	1987	1988	1989	1990	1991	1992
'000,000,000 rubles	−6.2	−2.9	−6.5	−8.1	−12.1	−188.0
% of total	6.6%	3.0%	6.3%	8.1%	10.6%	4.3%

Imports (1992): 2,255,000,000,000 rubles (machinery 38.3%, transport equipment 10.7%, chemicals 9.8%, textiles 8.4%, food products 3.9%). *Major import sources:* Western countries 69.0%, of which Spain 12.3%, Britain 10.9%, Germany 10.6%, Italy 4.1%; former Soviet republics 31.0%.
Exports (1992): 2,067,000,000,000 rubles (oil and gas 27.2%, ferrous metals 14.0%, transport equipment 10.5%, machinery 7.8%, food 4.2%). *Major export destinations:* Western countries 51.0%; former Soviet republics 49.0%.

Transport and communications

Transport. Railroads (1992): length 22,799 km; passenger-km 75,600,000,000; metric ton-km cargo 338,000,000,000. Roads (1992): total length 170,000 km (paved 95%). Vehicles (1988): passenger cars 2,920,000. Air transport (1992): passenger-km 8,400,000,000; metric ton-km cargo 100,000,000; airports (1994) with scheduled flights 20.
Communications (1991). Daily newspapers: total number 1,891; total circulation 26,804,000; circulation per 1,000 population 52. Radio: 14,520,000 receivers (1 per 4.1 persons). Television: 17,024,000 receivers (1 per 3.0 persons). Telephones (1992): 8,434,000 (1 per 6.2 persons).

Education and health

Education (1992–93)

	schools	teachers	students	student/teacher ratio
Primary (age 6–13) Secondary (age 14–17)	22,000	579,000	7,087,000	12.2
Voc., teacher tr.	754	...	1,368,000	...
Higher	156	...	856,000	...

Educational attainment (1989). Percentage of population age 15 and over having: some primary education 6.8%; completed primary 13.8%; some secondary 18.4%; completed secondary 31.1%; some postsecondary 19.5%; higher 10.4%. *Literacy* (1989): percentage of total population age 15 and over literate 98.4%; males literate 99.5%; females literate 97.4%.
Health (1992): physicians 228,900 (1 per 228 persons); hospital beds 700,300 (1 per 75 persons); infant mortality rate per 1,000 live births 13.8.

Military

Total active duty personnel (1994): 517,000 (army 59.6%, air force and air defense 40.4%). *Military expenditure as percentage of GNP* (1993) 3.9%. The Black Sea Fleet of the former U.S.S.R. remained to be divided with Russia and Georgia at year-end. Commonwealth of Independent States- (CIS-) controlled Strategic Nuclear Forces constituted a third military establishment during a two-year transition period.

---

[1]On Nov. 12, 1992, Ukraine replaced the Russian ruble with the karbovanets, or Ukrainian coupon, a temporary national currency; a prospective permanent national currency, the hryvnya, had not been issued as of December 1994. [2]Ruble-area GNP and exchange-rate data are very speculative.

United Arab Emirates

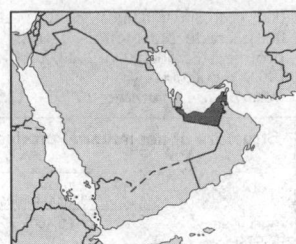

Official name: al-Imārāt al-ʿArabīyah al-Muttaḥidah (United Arab Emirates).
Form of government: federation of seven emirates with one appointive advisory body (Federal National Council [40[1]]).
Chief of state: President.
Head of government: Prime Minister.
Capital: Abu Dhabi.
Official language: Arabic.
Official religion: Islam.
Monetary unit: 1 U.A.E. dirham (Dh) = 100 fils; valuation (Oct. 7, 1994) 1 U.S.$ = Dh 3.67; 1 £ = Dh 5.84.

Area and population

Emirates	Capitals	area sq mi	area sq km	population 1991 estimate
Abu Dhabi (Abū Ẓaby)	Abu Dhabi	28,210[2]	73,060[2]	798,000
ʿAjmān (Ajman)	ʿAjmān	100	260	76,000
Dubayy (Dubai)	Dubayy	1,510	3,900	501,000
Al-Fujayrah (Fujairah)	Al-Fujayrah	500	1,300	63,000
Raʾs al-Khaymah (Ras al-Khaimah)	Raʾs al-Khaymah	660	1,700	130,000
Ash-Shāriqah (Sharjah)	Ash-Shāriqah	1,000	2,600	314,000
Umm al-Qaywayn (Umm al-Qaiwain)	Umm al-Qaywayn	300	780	27,000
TOTAL		32,280	83,600	1,909,000

Demography

Population (1994): 2,125,000.
Density (1994): persons per sq mi 65.8, persons per sq km 25.4.
Urban-rural (1990): urban 77.8%; rural 22.2%.
Sex distribution (1992): male 63.35%; female 36.65%.
Age breakdown (1992)[3]: under 15, 32.1%; 15–29, 17.9%; 30–44, 34.4%; 45–59, 12.9%; 60–74, 2.2%; 75 and over, 0.4%.
Population projection: (2000) 2,393,000; (2010) 2,917,000.
Doubling time: 35 years.
Ethnic composition (1983): Arab 87.1%, of which Arab from United Arab Emirates 30.7%; Pakistani and Indian 9.1%; Persian 1.7%; Baluchi 0.8%; African 0.8%; British 0.2%; American 0.1%; other 0.2%.
Religious affiliation (1980): Muslim 94.9% (Sunnī 80%, Shīʿī 20%); Christian 3.8%; other 1.3%.
Major cities (1989): Dubayy 585,189; Abu Dhabi 363,432; al-ʿAyn 176,411; ash-Shāriqah 125,000[4]; Raʾs al-Khaymah 42,000[4].

Vital statistics

Birth rate per 1,000 population (1992): 23.3 (world avg. 26.0); legitimate, n.a.; illegitimate, n.a.
Death rate per 1,000 population (1992): 4.3 (world avg. 9.2).
Natural increase rate per 1,000 population (1992): 19.0 (world avg. 16.8).
Total fertility rate (avg. births per childbearing woman; 1992): 4.1.
Marriage rate per 1,000 population (1990): 2.6.
Divorce rate per 1,000 population (1990): 0.9.
Life expectancy at birth (1992): male 69.6 years; female 73.8 years.
Major causes of death per 100,000 population (1989)[5]: accidents and poisoning 43.7; diseases of the circulatory system 34.3; malignant neoplasms (cancers) 13.7; respiratory diseases 8.1.

National economy

Budget (1994). Revenue: Dh 16,200,000,000 (1992; domestic revenues 74.8%; other sources 25.2%). Expenditures: Dh 17,600,000,000 (1992; current expenditures 95.4%, of which [1989] defense 43.9%, education 15.0%, public safety 13.5%, health 6.9%, economic services 4.3%; development expenditures 4.5%).
Gross national product (at current market prices; 1993): U.S.$47,749,000,000 (U.S.$22,470 per capita).

Structure of gross domestic product and labour force

	1993 In value Dh '000,000[6]	1993 % of total value	1990 labour force	1990 % of labour force
Agriculture	2,838	2.2	43,100	6.3
Mining	51,719	39.3	10,000	1.5
Manufacturing	10,891	8.3	63,400	9.2
Construction	11,582	8.8	119,200	17.3
Public utilities	2,961	2.2	20,600	3.0
Transportation and communications	7,390	5.6	71,700	10.4
Trade	13,382	10.2	101,400	14.7
Finance, real estate	15,139	11.5	18,800	2.7
Pub. admin., defense	14,881	11.3	} 241,300	} 35.0
Services	3,745[7]	2.8[7]		
Other	−2,868[8]	−2.2[8]	—	—
TOTAL	131,660	100.0	689,500	100.0[3]

Public debt (external, outstanding; 1991): U.S.$1,067,000,000.
Tourism (1992): total number of tourist arrivals 50,000.
Production (metric tons except as noted). Agriculture, forestry, fishing (1993): dates 176,000, tomatoes 90,000, eggplants 61,000, cabbages 58,000, lemons and limes 25,000, pumpkins and squash 18,000, cauliflowers 15,000, cucum-

bers 15,000, green peppers 14,000, mangoes 10,000; livestock (number of live animals) 747,000 goats, 277,000 sheep, 130,000 camels, 58,000 cattle, 7,000,000 chickens; fish catch (1991) 92,300. Mining and quarrying (1992): gypsum 95,000; sulfur 75,000; lime 45,000; also marble, shale for ceramic applications, and aggregate for cement. Manufacturing (1992): cement 3,700,000; aluminum 240,000; mutton and lamb meat 23,000[9]; goat's milk 18,000[9]; cow's milk 6,000[9]; beef and veal 6,000[9]; goat meat 5,000[9]; butter and ghee 232[9]. Construction: n.a. Energy production (consumption): electricity (kW-hr; 1992) 17,460,000,000 (17,460,000,000); coal, none (n.a.); crude petroleum (barrels; 1992) 778,000,000 (65,831,000); petroleum products (metric tons; 1992) 13,485,000 (6,574,000); natural gas (cu m; 1992) 28,959,000,000 (25,503,000,000).
Population economically active (1992): total 733,500; activity rate of total population 36.9% (participation rates [1986]: ages 15–64, 76.7%; female 6.6%; unemployed, n.a.).

Price and earnings indexes (1990 = 100)

	1986	1987	1988	1989	1990	1991	1992
Consumer price index[10]	91.2	93.9	95.0	98.8	100.0	105.5	102.1
Earnings index	...	...	...	...	...	...	...

Household income and expenditure. Average household size (1986) 6.8; income per household: n.a.; sources of income: n.a.; expenditure (1991): rent, fuel, and light 23.9%, food 22.7%, transportation and communications 14.1%, durable household goods 11.6%, education, recreation, and entertainment 8.6%.
Land use (1992): forested, virtually none; meadows and pastures 2.4%; agricultural and under permanent cultivation 0.5%; built-on, wasteland, and other 97.1%.

Foreign trade

Balance of trade (current prices)

	1987	1988	1989	1990	1991	1992
Dh '000,000	+25,928	+19,090	+27,420	...	+30,200	+21,800
% of total	33.9%	28.9%	28.1%	...	22.8%	14.6%

Imports (1989): Dh 35,080,000,000 (1987; machinery and transport equipment 30.5%, basic manufactures 16.8%, food and live animals 15.8%, chemicals 6.9%, mineral fuels 4.0%, crude minerals 1.8%). *Major import sources:* Japan 15.0%; United Kingdom 9.4%; United States 8.4%; West Germany 7.6%; Italy 4.7%; France 3.7%; Thailand 3.4%; Saudi Arabia 3.1%; China 2.9%; The Netherlands 2.5%; Australia 2.5%; Singapore 2.3%; Belgium-Luxembourg 1.2%; Switzerland 1.2%; Turkey 1.2%.
Exports (1989): Dh 62,500,000,000 (crude petroleum 65.6%, nonpetroleum exports and reexports 34.4%). *Major export destinations:* Japan 32.1%; Singapore 4.8%; India 4.4%; South Korea 4.3%; United States 3.9%; Oman 3.0%; Australia 2.4%; France 1.8%; Italy 1.7%; United Kingdom 1.4%; West Germany 1.2%; Brazil 1.1%; Bangladesh 0.8%; The Netherlands 0.6%; Belgium-Luxembourg 0.6%; Iran 0.4%; Iraq 0.3%.

Transport and communications

Transport. Railroads: none. Roads (1984): total length 2,709 mi, 4,360 km (paved [1981] 61%). Vehicles (1990): passenger cars 302,000; trucks and buses 157,000. Merchant marine (1992): vessels (100 gross tons and over) 276; total deadweight tonnage 1,491,728. Air transport (1993)[11]: passenger-mi 3,469,700,000, passenger-km 5,583,990,000; short ton-mi cargo 189,900,000, metric ton-km cargo 277,313,000; airports (1994) with scheduled flights 4.
Communications. Daily newspapers (1991): total number 9; total circulation 246,600[12]; circulation per 1,000 population 127[12]. Radio (1993): total number of receivers 420,000 (1 per 5.0 persons). Television (1993): total number of receivers 170,000 (1 per 12.2 persons). Telephones (1991): 777,179 (1 per 2.5 persons).

Education and health

Education (1991–92)

	schools	teachers	students	student/teacher ratio
Primary (age 6–11)	} 354[13]	13,139	231,674	17.6
Secondary (age 12–18)		9,430	} 117,118	12.4
Vocational	9[14]		893	
Higher	1	728	8,668	11.9

Educational attainment (1975). Percentage of population age 25 and over having: no formal schooling 72.2%; primary education 5.2%; secondary 16.6%; higher 6.0%. *Literacy* (1986): total population age 15 and over literate 858,149 (73.0%); males literate 657,579 (74.5%); females literate 200,570 (68.4%).
Health (1991): physicians 3,090 (1 per 618 persons); hospital beds 6,540 (1 per 292 persons); infant mortality rate per 1,000 live births (1992) 23.4.
Food (1987–89): daily per capita caloric intake 3,295 (vegetable products 77%, animal products 23%); 136% of FAO recommended minimum requirement.

Military

Total active duty personnel (1994): 61,500 (army 92.7%, navy 3.2%, air force 4.1%). *Military expenditure as percentage of GNP* (1992): 6.0% (world, n.a.); per capita expenditure U.S.$1,044.

[1]All appointed seats. [2]Approximate, based on reported total and on reported partial areas for smaller emirates. [3]Detail does not add to total given because of rounding. [4]1980. [5]Registered; Abu Dhabi Emirate only. [6]At factor cost. [7]Services include domestic help. [8]Less imputed bank service charges. [9]1993. [10]City of Abu Dhabi only. [11]Emirates Airlines only. [12]Based on seven dailies only. [13]1987–88. [14]1985–86.

United Kingdom

Official name: United Kingdom of Great Britain and Northern Ireland.
Form of government: constitutional monarchy with two legislative houses (House of Lords [1,183]; House of Commons [651]).
Chief of state: Sovereign.
Head of government: Prime Minister.
Capital: London.
Official language: English.
Official religion: Churches of England and Scotland "established" (protected by the state, but not "official") in their respective countries, no established church in Northern Ireland or Wales.
Monetary unit: 1 pound sterling (£) = 100 new pence; valuation (Oct. 7, 1994) 1 £ = U.S.$1.59; 1 U.S.$ = £0.63.

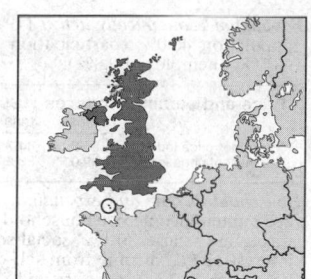

Area and population

		area		population
				1992
Countries	Capitals	sq mi	sq km	estimate
England	London	50,363	130,439	48,378,400[1]
Counties				
Avon	Bristol	520	1,346	968,400
Bedfordshire	Bedford	477	1,235	536,500
Berkshire	Reading	486	1,259	758,100
Buckinghamshire	Aylesbury	727	1,883	645,700
Cambridgeshire	Cambridge	1,316	3,409	677,700
Cheshire	Chester	899	2,329	966,900
Cleveland	Middlesbrough	225	583	560,000
Cornwall[2]	Truro	1,376	3,564	475,400
Cumbria	Carlisle	2,629	6,810	490,200
Derbyshire	Matlock	1,016	2,631	947,400
Devon	Exeter	2,591	6,711	1,045,100
Dorset	Dorchester	1,025	2,654	664,300
Durham	Durham	941	2,436	607,000
East Sussex	Lewes	693	1,795	720,600
Essex	Chelmsford	1,418	3,672	1,555,800
Gloucestershire	Gloucester	1,020	2,643	541,400
Greater London[3]	London	610	1,579	6,904,600
Greater Manchester[3]	Manchester	497	1,287	2,573,500
Hampshire	Winchester	1,458	3,777	1,587,500
Hereford & Worcester	Worcester	1,516	3,927	690,400
Hertfordshire	Hertford	631	1,634	994,200
Humberside	Hull	1,356	3,512	881,400
Isle of Wight	Newport	147	381	125,600
Kent	Maidstone	1,441	3,731	1,538,300
Lancashire	Preston	1,183	3,064	1,413,600
Leicestershire	Leicester	986	2,553	902,300
Lincolnshire	Lincoln	2,284	5,915	596,800
Merseyside[3]	Liverpool	252	652	1,445,600
Norfolk	Norwich	2,073	5,368	763,000
North Yorkshire	Northallerton	3,208	8,309	723,000
Northamptonshire	Northampton	914	2,367	590,100
Northumberland	Newcastle upon Tyne	1,943	5,032	307,200
Nottinghamshire	Nottingham	836	2,164	1,025,200
Oxfordshire	Oxford	1,007	2,608	587,100
Shropshire	Shrewsbury	1,347	3,490	412,800
Somerset	Taunton	1,332	3,451	472,400
South Yorkshire[3]	Barnsley	602	1,560	1,304,400
Staffordshire	Stafford	1,049	2,716	1,051,900
Suffolk	Ipswich	1,466	3,797	648,000
Surrey	Kingston upon Thames	648	1,679	1,036,700
Tyne and Wear[3]	Newcastle upon Tyne	208	540	1,134,400
Warwickshire	Warwick	765	1,981	492,000
West Midlands[3]	Birmingham	347	899	2,630,600
West Sussex	Chichester	768	1,989	712,600
West Yorkshire[3]	Wakefield	787	2,039	2,093,500
Wiltshire	Trowbridge	1,344	3,480	579,300
Northern Ireland[4]	Belfast	5,452	14,120	1,610,000
Scotland	Edinburgh	30,418	78,783	5,111,200
Regions				
Borders	Newton Saint Boswells	1,814	4,698	104,800
Central	Stirling	1,042	2,700	272,700
Dumfries and Galloway	Dumfries	2,481	6,425	147,900
Fife	Glenrothes	509	1,319	349,900
Grampian	Aberdeen	3,379	8,752	522,400
Highland	Inverness	10,092	26,137	205,900
Lothian	Edinburgh	683	1,770	750,600
Strathclyde	Glasgow	5,318	13,773	2,290,700
Tayside	Dundee	2,951	7,643	394,600
Island areas[5] (TOTAL)	—	2,149	5,566	71,700
Wales	Cardiff	8,019	20,768	2,898,600[1]
Counties				
Clwyd	Mold	937	2,427	414,600
Dyfed	Carmarthen	2,227	5,768	351,100
Gwent	Newport	531	1,376	449,300
Gwynedd	Caernarvon	1,494	3,869	239,800
Mid Glamorgan	Cardiff	393	1,018	542,800
Powys	Llandrindod Wells	1,960	5,077	119,400
South Glamorgan	Cardiff	161	416	410,500
West Glamorgan	Swansea	316	817	371,200
TOTAL		94,251	244,110	57,998,200

Demography

Population (1994): 58,422,000.
Density (1994): persons per sq mi 619.8, persons per sq km 239.3.
Urban-rural (1985): urban 91.5%; rural 8.5%.
Sex distribution (1992): male 48.89%; female 51.11%.
Age breakdown (1992): under 15, 19.3%; 15–29, 22.0%; 30–44, 21.1%; 45–59, 16.9%; 60–74, 13.8%; 75 and over, 6.9%.

Population projection: (2000) 59,648,000; (2010) 61,100,000.
Doubling time: not applicable; doubling time exceeds 100 years.
Ethnic composition (1991)[6]: white 94.2%; Asian Indian 1.4%; Pakistani 0.9%; West Indian 0.8%; African 0.3%; Chinese 0.3%; Bangladeshi 0.2%; Arab 0.1%; other and not stated 1.8%.
Religious affiliation (religious participation of about 8,400,000 active members only; 1990): Christian *c.* 80%, of which Roman Catholic *c.* 21%, Anglican *c.* 20%, Presbyterian *c.* 14%, Methodist *c.* 5%, Baptist *c.* 3%; Muslim *c.* 11%; Sikh *c.* 4%; Hindu *c.* 2%; Jewish *c.* 1%; other *c.* 2%.
Major cities (1992): Greater London 6,904,600; Birmingham 1,009,100; Leeds 721,800; Glasgow 684,300; Sheffield 531,000; Liverpool 479,000; Bradford 477,500; Edinburgh 439,900; Manchester 434,600; Bristol 396,600.
Place of birth (1991): native-born 93.2% (52,721,000); foreign-born 6.8%, of which India 1.5%, Ireland 1.1%, Caribbean 0.9%, Pakistan 0.9%, other 2.2%.
Mobility (1981). Population living in the same residence as 1980: 90.9%; different residence, same country (of the U.K.) 8.2%; different residence, different country within the U.K. 0.4%; from outside the U.K. 0.5%.
Households (1990–91)[6, 7]. Average household size 2.5 (3.1); 1 person 26% (20%), 2 persons 34% (26%), 3 persons 17% (16%), 4 persons 16% (17%), 5 persons 6% (10%), 6 or more persons 2% (11%). Family households (1987): 17,836,500 (77.4%), nonfamily 5,208,500 (22.6%, of which 1-person 9.9%).
Immigration (annual average; 1988–92): permanent residents 242,600, from Australia 10.6%, United States 10.4%, New Zealand 5.2%, Bangladesh, India, and Sri Lanka 5.0%, Pakistan 3.9%, South Africa 3.3%.

Vital statistics

Birth rate per 1,000 population (1992): 13.5 (world avg. 26.0); legitimate 69.1%; illegitimate 30.9%.
Death rate per 1,000 population (1992): 10.9 (world avg. 9.2).
Natural increase rate per 1,000 population (1992): 2.6 (world avg. 16.8).
Total fertility rate (avg. births per childbearing woman; 1992): 1.8.
Marriage rate per 1,000 population (1991): 6.5.
Divorce rate per 1,000 population (1991)[6]: 3.0.
Life expectancy at birth (1991): male 73.2 years; female 78.6 years.
Major causes of death per 100,000 population (1992): diseases of the circulatory system 501.0, of which ischemic heart disease 287.5, cerebrovascular disease 130.8; malignant neoplasms (cancers) 280.8; diseases of the respiratory system 120.4, of which pneumonia 54.4; diseases of the digestive system 36.7; accidents and violence 34.2; diseases of the endocrine system 19.5, of which diabetes mellitus 14.8; diseases of the genitourinary system 11.1.

Social indicators

Educational attainment (1981). Percentage of population age 25 and over having: primary or secondary education only 89.7%; some postsecondary 4.8%; bachelor's or equivalent degree 4.9%; higher university degree 0.6%.

Distribution of disposable income (1991)

percentage of household income by quintile

1	2	3	4	5 (highest)
7.7	12.1	16.4	22.5	41.3

Quality of working life (1991). Average workweek (hours): male 42.2, female 37.4 (overtime [1986]; male 8.6%, female 2.1%). Annual rate per 100,000 workers for: injury or accident 752.6; industrial diseases 0.5[8]; death 1.5. Proportion of labour force (employed persons) insured for damages or income loss resulting from: injury 100%; permanent disability 100%; death 100%. Average days lost to labour stoppages per 1,000 employee workdays 1992: 0.1. Principal means of transport to work (1991; London only): public transportation 81%, private automobile 15%, motor or pedal cycle 2%, other 2%.
Access to services (1990)[6]. Proportion of households having access to: bath or shower 98%; toilet 99%; central heating 80%.
Social participation. Eligible voters participating in last national election: 76.9%. Population age 16 and over participating in voluntary work (1987)[6]: 22%. Trade union membership in total workforce (1990) 34.9%.
Social deviance (1992)[9]. Offense rate per 100,000 population for: theft and handling stolen goods 5,561.2; burglary 2,643.1; violence against the person 393.5; fraud and forgery 328.8; robbery 103.2; sexual offense 57.5. Incidence per 100,000 population of: registered drug addicts 36.5[9]; suicide 7.9.
Leisure (1991). Favourite leisure activities (hours weekly): watching television 26.0; listening to radio 10.1; reading 2.6[10]; cultural activities 1.5[10].
Material well-being (1992). Households possessing: automobile 68%, telephone 88%, television receiver 98% (colour 95%), refrigerator 99%, central heating 82%, washing machine 88%, videocassette recorder 69%.

National economy

Gross national product (1992): U.S.$1,024,025,000,000 (U.S.$17,770 per capita).

Structure of gross domestic product and labour force

	1992			
	in value £'000,000	% of total value	labour force	% of labour force
Agriculture	9,309	1.8	577,000	2.1
Mining	9,842	1.9	11	11
Manufacturing	114,098	22.2	4,985,000[11]	18.0[11]
Construction	32,002	6.2	1,515,000	5.5
Public utilities	13,717	2.7	414,000	1.5
Transp. and commun.	41,613	8.1	1,497,000	5.4
Trade	72,549	14.1	5,351,000	19.3
Finance	121,704	23.6	3,086,000	11.1
Pub. admin., defense	89,114	17.3		
Services	32,892	6.4 }	10,914,000[12]	37.1[12]
Other	22,846[13]	–4.4 }		
TOTAL	514,594	100.0[1]	27,739,000	100.0

Budget (1993–94). Revenue: £208,979,000,000 (income tax 35.1%, taxes on expenditures 18.7%, social-security contributions 17.7%). Expenditures: £256,865,000,000 (social-security benefits 30.5%, national health service 13.5%, education and science 12.5%, defense 9.0%, debt interest 7.0%).
Total national debt (March 1992): £204,174,000,000.

Financial aggregates

	1988	1989	1990	1991	1992	1993	1994[14]
Exchange rate:							
U.S. dollar per £	1.78	1.64	1.78	1.77	1.76	1.50	1.54
SDRs per £	1.34	1.22	1.36	1.31	1.10	1.08	1.06
International reserves (U.S.$)							
Total (excl. gold; '000,000,000)	44.10	34.77	35.85	41.89	36.64	36.78	39.24[15]
SDRs ('000,000,000)	1.32	1.14	1.25	1.31	0.54	0.29	0.41
Reserve pos. in IMF ('000,000,000)	1.67	1.64	1.68	1.85	2.01	1.86	1.91
Foreign exchange ('000,000,000)	41.12	31.99	32.93	38.73	34.09	34.63	37.04[15]
Gold ('000,000 fine troy oz)	19.00	18.99	18.97	18.89	18.61	18.45	18.44[15]
% world reserves	2.0	2.0	2.0	2.0	2.0	2.0	2.0[15]
Interest and prices							
Central bank discount (%)	...	...	...	...	...	...	...
Govt. bond yield (%) long term	9.36	9.58	11.08	9.92	9.15	7.87	8.41
Industrial share prices (1990=100)	85.0	101.9	100.0	109.8	114.7	131.7	135.0[16]
Balance of payments (U.S.$'000,000)							
Balance of visible trade,	−36,994	−39,157	−32,400	−17,990	−24,618	−20,570	...
Imports, f.o.b.	180,527	190,898	214,693	201,081	212,058	201,802	...
Exports, f.o.b.	143,534	151,741	182,293	183,091	187,440	181,232	...
Balance of invisibles	8,205	3,570	3,010	6,768	3,904	4,179	...
Balance of payments, current account	−28,789	−35,587	−29,390	−11,222	−20,714	−16,391	...

Tourism (1992): receipts from visitors U.S.$13,683,000,000; expenditures by nationals abroad U.S.$19,831,000,000.

Manufacturing, mining, and construction enterprises (1991)

	no. of enter-prises[17]	no. of employees	annual wages as a % of avg. of all wages[10]	annual value added (£'000,000)
Manufacturing				
Food, beverages, and tobacco	8,916	577,000	103.0	14,875
Mechanical engineering	23,322	588,000[18]	108.4	13,300[18]
Paper and paper products; printing and publishing	21,495	442,000	133.8	12,102
Electrical and data-processing equipment	9,644	534,000	96.8	12,008
Transport equipment	4,233	503,000	...	11,574
Chemical engineering	3,137	283,000	118.1	11,100
Rubber and plastics	4,785	224,000	118.1	4,976
Clothing and footwear	11,207	270,000	85.6	3,219
Timber and wood products	13,794	189,000	98.1	3,165
Metal manufacturing	1,186	124,000	102.8	3,063
Textiles	4,466	182,000	79.2	2,842
Mineral-oil processing	123	13,000	118.1	1,484
Mining				
Extraction of coal, mineral oil, and natural gas	...	99,000	118.1	9,391
Extraction of minerals other than fuels	793	8,000	103.1	368
Construction	185,854	1,035,000	...	18,306

Production (metric tons except as noted). Agriculture, forestry, fishing (1993): wheat 12,890,000, sugar beets 8,500,000[19], potatoes 7,065,000, barley 6,013,000, turnips and rutabagas 3,451,000[20, 21], corn (maize) 1,657,000[20, 21], rapeseed 1,166,000[19], cabbage 642,000, oats 477,000; livestock (number of live animals) 29,333,000 sheep, 11,709,000 cattle, 7,869,000 pigs; roundwood (1992) 6,353,000 cu m; fish catch (1991) 823,225. Mining (1992): limestone 89,398,000; iron 13,200[22]; tin 2,000; lead 1,440[22]. Manufacturing (total sales in £'000,000; 1992): motor vehicles and parts 19,909; aerospace equipment 9,351; electronic data-processing and telecommunications equipment 6,486; basic electrical equipment 3,999; mechanical lifting and handling equipment 2,471; constructional steelwork 2,445; boilers 2,265. Construction (value in £; 1992)[6]: residential 6,076,000,000; nonresidential 13,000,000,000, of which commercial 6,592,000,000, industrial 2,232,000,000.

Retail trade enterprises (1991)

	no. of enter-prises	no. of employees	weekly wage as a % of all wages	annual turnover (£'000,000)[23]
Food and grocery,	62,009	813,000	...	48,718
of which				
large grocery	74	522,000	...	37,827
other grocery	19,130	95,000	...	4,073
meats	12,773	66,000	...	2,555
Household goods,	49,248	322,000	...	21,035
of which				
electrical and musical goods	12,043	97,000	...	7,365
furniture	12,341	61,000	...	4,543
Drink, confectionery, and tobacco,	49,109	274,000	...	13,497
of which				
tobacco and confectionery	43,357	234,000	...	10,533
Clothing and footwear,	27,321	289,000	...	12,446
of which				
women's, girls', and infants' wear	14,709	122,000	...	4,723
footwear	3,610	74,000	...	2,673
men's and boys' wear	4,036	37,000	...	2,145
Pharmaceuticals	8,098	85,000	...	4,849
Mail order	36	32,000	...	3,942

Energy production (consumption): electricity (kW-hr; 1990) 318,979,000,000 (330,922,000,000); coal (metric tons; 1990) 89,303,000 (100,249,000); crude petroleum (barrels; 1990) 656,722,000 (568,604,000); petroleum products (metric tons; 1990) 81,919,000 (79,470,000); natural gas (cu m; 1990) 53,895,000,000 (61,895,000,000).

Population economically active (1992): total 27,739,000; activity rate of total population 48.0% (participation rates: ages 15–64 [1988], 61.1%; female 48.3%; unemployed 9.8%).

Price and earnings indexes (1990=100)

	1987	1988	1989	1990	1991	1992	1993
Consumer price index	80.8	84.7	91.3	100.0	105.9	109.8	111.5
Monthly earnings index	92.0	83.5	91.1	100.0	108.0	114.6	118.5

Household income and expenditure (1992). Average household size 2.4; average annual income per household £14,440 (U.S.$25,490); sources of income: wages and salaries 61.9%, social-security benefits 15.1%, rent, dividends, and interest 12.5%, income from self-employment 10.5%; expenditure: food and beverages 18.2%, transport and vehicles 16.8%, housing 15.1%, household goods 6.3%, clothing 5.6%, energy 3.8%.
Land use (1991): forested 10.0%; meadows and pastures 46.3%; agricultural and under permanent cultivation 27.3%; other 16.4%.

Foreign trade

Balance of trade (current prices)

	1988	1989	1990	1991	1992	1993
£'000,000	−37,446	−39,157	−31,131	−17,990	−24,618	−20,570
% of total	11.5%	11.4%	7.8%	4.7%	6.2%	5.4%

Imports (1993): £135,477,000,000 (machinery and transport equipment 39.2%, of which electrical equipment 17.6%, road vehicles 10.6%; chemicals and chemical products 9.5%, of which organic chemicals 2.2%; food and live animals 8.5%, of which vegetables and fruits 2.3%, meat and meat preparations 1.4%; petroleum and petroleum products 4.2%; textile yarn and fabrics 2.9%; nonferrous metals 2.9%; paper and paperboard 2.8%; iron and steel products 1.9%). *Major import sources:* Germany 14.8%; U.S. 12.1%; France 10.0%; The Netherlands 6.7%; Japan 6.3%; Italy 5.0%; Belgium-Luxembourg 5.0%; Ireland 4.1%; Switzerland 3.5%; Norway 3.1%.
Exports (1992): £118,488,000,000 (machinery and transport equipment 40.7%, of which electrical equipment 17.5%, road vehicles 7.0%, chemicals and chemical products 14.5%, of which organic chemicals 3.7%; petroleum and petroleum products 6.6%; professional, scientific, and controlling instruments 4.0%; iron and steel products 2.6%; clothing and footwear 2.3%). *Major export destinations:* Germany 13.4%; United States 12.4%; France 10.1%; The Netherlands 6.8%; Belgium-Luxembourg 5.9%; Ireland 5.3%; Italy 5.1%; Spain 3.6%; Sweden 2.4%; Japan 2.2%; Switzerland 1.9%.

Transport and communications

Transport. Railroads (1993)[24]: length 23,518 mi[18], 37,849 km[18]; passenger-mi 19,693,000,000, passenger-km 31,693,000,000; short ton-mi cargo 10,623,000,000, metric ton-km cargo 15,509,000,000. Roads (1992): total length 240,241 mi, 386,631 km (paved 100%). Vehicles (1993)[6]: passenger cars 20,344,000; trucks and buses 2,753,000. Merchant marine (1992): vessels (100 gross tons and over) 1,631; total deadweight tonnage 4,355,063. Air transport (1992): passenger-mi 53,892,300,000, passenger-km 86,731,400,000; short ton-mi cargo 1,811,100,000, metric ton-km cargo 2,644,100,000; airports (1994) with scheduled flights 54.
Communications. Daily newspapers (1990): total number 99; total circulation 22,253,500; circulation per 1,000 population 388. Radio (1993): 70,000,000 receivers (1 per 0.8 person). Television (1991): 19,546,000 licenses (1 per 3.0 persons). Telephones (1984): 29,517,991 receivers (1 per 1.9 persons).

Education and health

Education (1991–92)[25]

	schools	teachers	students	student/ teacher ratio
Primary (age 5–10)	23,958	222,600	4,849,500	21.8
Secondary (age 11–19)	4,731	232,700	3,534,500	15.2
Voc., teacher tr.[26, 27]	724	93,000[28]	539,718	...
Higher[29]	48	32,638	401,657	12.3

Literacy (1990): total population literate, virtually 100%[30].
Health (1981): physicians 92,172 (1 per 611 persons); hospital beds (1987) 388,700 (1 per 146 persons); infant mortality rate (1992) 6.6.
Food (1988–90): daily per capita caloric intake 3,270 (vegetable products 66%, animal products 34%); 130% of FAO recommended minimum requirement.

Military

Total active duty personnel (1993): 274,800 (army 49.0%, navy 21.6%, air force 29.4%). *Military expenditure as percentage of GNP* (1989): 4.2% (world 4.9%); per capita expenditure U.S.$605.

[1]Detail does not add to total given because of rounding. [2]Includes separately administered Isles of Scilly (area 6 sq mi [16 sq km]; pop. 2,000). [3]Geographic entity only; since April 1, 1986, the administrative functions of the former metropolitan county councils have been dispersed among other local authorities. [4]Comprises 26 local government districts not shown separately. [5]Includes three separately administered island groups (Orkney 377 sq mi [976 sq km], pop. 19,710; Shetland 553 sq mi [1,432 sq km], pop. 22,640; Western Isles 1,119 sq mi [2,898 sq km], pop. 29,350). [6]Great Britain only. [7]Figures in parentheses are for Northern Ireland (1984). [8]1982. [9]England and Wales only. [10]1984. [11]Manufacturing includes Mining. [12]Includes 2,732,000 unemployed not distributed by sector. [13]Plus rent; less imputed bank service charges. [14]July. [15]May. [16]June. [17]1988. [18]1990. [19]1992. [20]Primarily for fodder. [21]1987. [22]1991. [23]Includes value-added taxes. [24]British Rail only. [25]Public sector only. [26]Third level. [27]1987–88. [28]1984–85. [29]Universities only. [30]A survey in 1986–87, however, put the number of functional illiterates at 9–12% of the adult population.

United States

Official name: United States of America.
Form of government: federal republic with two legislative houses (Senate [100]; House of Representatives [435[1]]).
Head of state and government: President.
Capital: Washington, D.C.
Official language: none.
Official religion: none.
Monetary unit: 1 dollar (U.S.$) = 100 cents; valuation (Oct. 7, 1994) 1 U.S.$ = £0.63; 1 £ = U.S.$1.59.

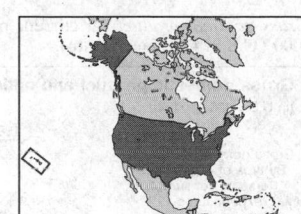

Major cities (1990): New York 7,322,564; Los Angeles 3,485,398; Chicago 2,783,726; Houston 1,630,553; Philadelphia 1,585,577; San Diego 1,110,549; Detroit 1,027,974; Dallas 1,006,877; Phoenix 983,403; San Antonio 935,933.

Other principal cities (1990)

	population		population		population
Akron	223,019	Fort Worth	447,619	Oklahoma City	441,719
Albuquerque	384,736	Fresno	354,202	Omaha	335,795
Anaheim	266,406	Honolulu	365,272	Pittsburgh	369,879
Anchorage	226,338	Indianapolis	741,952	Portland (Ore.)	437,319
Arlington (Tex.)	261,721	Jacksonville	672,971	Riverside	226,505
Atlanta	394,017	Jersey City	228,537	Rochester (N.Y.)	231,636
Aurora (Colo.)	222,103	Kansas City (Mo.)	435,146	Sacramento	369,365
Austin	465,622	Las Vegas	258,295	St. Louis	396,685
Baltimore	736,014	Lexington (Ky.)	225,366	St. Paul	272,235
Baton Rouge	219,531	Long Beach	429,433	St. Petersburg	238,629
Birmingham	265,968	Louisville	269,063	San Francisco	723,959
Boston	574,283	Memphis	610,337	San Jose	782,248
Buffalo	328,123	Mesa	288,091	Santa Ana	293,742
Charlotte	395,934	Miami	358,548	Seattle	516,259
Cincinnati	364,040	Milwaukee	628,088	Tampa	280,015
Cleveland	505,616	Minneapolis	368,383	Toledo	332,943
Colorado Springs	281,140	Nashville	510,784	Tucson	405,390
Columbus	632,910	New Orleans	496,938	Tulsa	362,307
Corpus Christi	257,453	Newark	275,221	Virginia Beach	393,069
Denver	467,610	Norfolk	261,229	Washington, D.C.	606,900
El Paso	515,342	Oakland	372,242	Wichita	304,011

Place of birth (1990): native-born 227,078,000 (91.3%); foreign-born 21,632,-000 (8.7%), of which Mexico 4,447,000, Germany (East and West) 1,163,000, Philippines 998,000, Canada 871,000, United Kingdom 765,000, Cuba 751,-000, South Korea 663,000, Italy 640,000, Vietnam 556,000, China 543,000, India 463,000, Japan 422,000, Poland 397,000, U.S.S.R. 337,000, Portugal 219,000, Greece 189,000, other 8,208,000.

Vital statistics

Birth rate per 1,000 population (1993): 15.7 (world avg. 26.0); (1991) legitimate 70.5%; illegitimate 29.5%.
Death rate per 1,000 population (1993): 8.8 (world avg. 9.2).
Natural increase rate per 1,000 population (1993): 6.9 (world avg. 16.8).
Total fertility rate (avg. births per childbearing woman; 1993): 2.1.
Marriage rate per 1,000 population (1993): 9.0; median age at first marriage (1991): men 26.3 years, women 24.1 years.
Divorce rate per 1,000 population (1993): 4.6.
Life expectancy at birth (1992): white male 73.2 years, black and other male 67.8 years; white female 79.7 years, black and other female 75.6 years.
Major causes of death per 100,000 population (12 months ending May 1993): cardiovascular diseases 350.0, of which ischemic heart disease 180.0, other forms of heart disease 76.2, cerebrovascular diseases 57.4, atherosclerosis 5.3, other cardiovascular diseases 10.5; malignant neoplasms (cancers) 195.3; diseases of the respiratory system 71.9, of which pneumonia 30.2; accidents and adverse effects 31.6, of which motor-vehicle accidents 14.1; diabetes mellitus 21.3; AIDS 13.7; suicide 12.2; chronic liver disease and cirrhosis 9.1; homicide 8.5.
Morbidity rates of infectious diseases per 100,000 population (1992): gonorrhea 196.1; chicken pox 62.0; syphilis 44.2; AIDS 17.8; salmonellosis 16.0; tuberculosis 10.4; shigellosis 9.4; hepatitis A (infectious) 9.0; hepatitis B (serum) 6.3; aseptic meningitis 4.8; mumps 1.6.
Incidence of chronic health conditions per 1,000 population (1992): chronic sinusitis 143.5; arthritis 130.4; deformities or orthopedic impairments 123.7; hypertension 108.9; hay fever 100.6; hearing impairment 93.1; heart conditions 84.5; chronic bronchitis 52.8; asthma 48.4; hemorrhoids 37.4.

Social indicators

Educational attainment (1991). Percentage of population age 25 and over having: incomplete primary education 6.2%; primary 4.4%; incomplete secondary 11.0%; secondary 38.6%; some postsecondary 18.4%; 4-year higher degree or more 21.4%. Number of earned degrees (1991–92): bachelor's degree 1,105,000; master's degree 344,000; doctor's degree 39,800; first-professional degrees (in fields such as medicine, theology, and law) 74,900.

Distribution of income (1992)

percentage of disposable household income by quintile

1	2	3	4	5 (highest)
3.8	9.4	15.8	24.2	46.9

Quality of working life (1993). Average workweek: 39.3 hours. Annual rate per 100,000 workers for (1992): injury or accident 2,700; death 6.0. Proportion of labour force insured for damages or income loss resulting from: injury, permanent disability, and death (1988) 56.6%. Average days per 1,000 workdays lost to labour stoppages (1993): 0.1. Average duration of journey to work (1979): 22.5 minutes (private automobile 85.7%, public transportation 5.9%, bicycle or motorcycle 1.3%, foot 3.9%, work at home 2.3%, other 0.9%). Rate per 1,000 employed workers of discouraged workers (unemployed no longer seeking work; 1992): 6.9.
Access to services (1991). Proportion of occupied dwellings having access to: electricity, virtually 100.0%; safe public water supply 97.9% (13.2% from wells); public sewage collection 75.4%; septic tanks 24.1%; public fire protection, n.a.
Social participation. Eligible voters participating in last presidential election (1992): 54.0%. Population age 18 and over participating in voluntary work (1991): 51.1%. Trade-union membership in total workforce (1993): 15.8%. Practicing religious population in total affiliated population (church attendance; 1987): once a week 47%; once in six months 67%; once a year 74%.
Social deviance (1992). Offense rate per 100,000 population for: murder 9.3; rape 42.8; robbery 263.6; aggravated assault 441.8; motor-vehicle theft 631.5; burglary and housebreaking 1,168.2; larceny-theft 3,103.0; drug-abuse

Area and population

States	Capitals	area[2] sq mi	area[2] sq km	population 1994 estimate
Alabama	Montgomery	51,705	133,915	4,229,000
Alaska	Juneau	591,004	1,530,693	619,000
Arizona	Phoenix	114,000	295,259	3,994,000
Arkansas	Little Rock	53,187	137,754	2,445,000
California	Sacramento	158,706	411,407	31,902,000
Colorado	Denver	104,091	269,594	3,631,000
Connecticut	Hartford	5,018	12,997	3,276,000
Delaware	Dover	2,045	5,294	709,000
Florida	Tallahassee	58,664	151,939	13,973,000
Georgia	Atlanta	58,910	152,576	6,987,000
Hawaii	Honolulu	6,471	16,760	1,200,000
Idaho	Boise	83,564	216,430	1,126,000
Illinois	Springfield	57,871	149,885	11,782,000
Indiana	Indianapolis	36,413	94,309	5,769,000
Iowa	Des Moines	56,275	145,752	2,845,000
Kansas	Topeka	82,277	213,096	2,575,000
Kentucky	Frankfort	40,410	104,659	3,820,000
Louisiana	Baton Rouge	47,752	123,677	4,336,000
Maine	Augusta	33,265	86,156	1,236,000
Maryland	Annapolis	10,460	27,091	5,023,000
Massachusetts	Boston	8,284	21,455	5,983,000
Michigan	Lansing	97,102	251,493	9,531,000
Minnesota	St. Paul	86,614	224,329	4,573,000
Mississippi	Jackson	47,689	123,514	2,649,000
Missouri	Jefferson City	69,697	180,514	5,255,000
Montana	Helena	147,046	380,847	849,000
Nebraska	Lincoln	77,355	200,349	1,632,000
Nevada	Carson City	110,561	286,352	1,429,000
New Hampshire	Concord	9,279	24,032	1,125,000
New Jersey	Trenton	7,787	20,168	7,885,000
New Mexico	Santa Fe	121,593	314,924	1,645,000
New York	Albany	52,735	136,583	18,159,000
North Carolina	Raleigh	52,669	136,412	7,049,000
North Dakota	Bismarck	70,702	183,117	637,000
Ohio	Columbus	44,787	115,998	11,143,000
Oklahoma	Oklahoma City	69,956	181,185	3,251,000
Oregon	Salem	97,073	251,418	3,086,000
Pennsylvania	Harrisburg	46,043	119,251	12,093,000
Rhode Island	Providence	1,212	3,139	1,002,000
South Carolina	Columbia	31,113	80,582	3,690,000
South Dakota	Pierre	77,116	199,730	727,000
Tennessee	Nashville	42,144	109,152	5,161,000
Texas	Austin	266,807	691,027	18,291,000
Utah	Salt Lake City	84,899	219,887	1,901,000
Vermont	Montpelier	9,614	24,900	576,000
Virginia	Richmond	40,767	105,586	6,558,000
Washington	Olympia	68,139	176,479	5,376,000
West Virginia	Charleston	24,232	62,758	1,820,000
Wisconsin	Madison	66,215	171,496	5,109,000
Wyoming	Cheyenne	97,809	253,324	480,000
District				
Dist. of Columbia	—	69	179	567,000
TOTAL		3,679,192[3]	9,529,063	260,711,000[3]

Demography

Population (1994)[4]: 260,967,000.
Density (1994)[4]: persons per sq mi 70.9, persons per sq km 27.3.
Urban-rural (1992): urban 75.6%; rural 24.4%.
Sex distribution (1992): male 48.80%; female 51.20%.
Age breakdown (1992): under 15, 21.9%; 15–29, 22.1%; 30–44, 24.4%; 45–59, 14.9%; 60–74, 11.3%; 75 and over, 5.4%.
Population projection: (2000) 275,512,000; (2010) 298,865,000.
Doubling time: 101 years.
Population by race and Hispanic[5] origin (1992): non-Hispanic white 74.8%; non-Hispanic black 11.9%; Hispanic 9.5%; Asian and Pacific Islander 3.1%; American Indian and Eskimo 0.7%.
Religious affiliation (1990): Christian 86.5%, of which Protestant 52.7%, Roman Catholic 26.2%, other Christian 7.6%; Muslim 1.9%; Jewish 1.8%; nonreligious 7.5%; other 2.3%.
Mobility (1992). Population living in the same residence as in 1991: 83.0%; different residence, same county 11.0%; different county, same state 3.0%; different state 3.0%; moved from abroad 1.0%.
Households (1993). Total households 96,391,000 (married-couple families 53,-171,000 [55.2%]). Average household size 2.6; 1 person 24.5%, 2 persons 32.4%, 3 persons 17.5%, 4 persons 15.5%, 5 or more persons 10.1%. Family households: 68,144,000 (70.7%); nonfamily 28,247,000 (29.3%), of which 1-person 83.7%.
Immigration (1992[6]): permanent immigrants admitted 974,000, from Mexico 21.9%, Vietnam 8.0%, Philippines 6.3%, former U.S.S.R. 4.5%, Dominican Republic 4.3%, China 3.8%, India 3.8%, El Salvador 2.7%, Poland 2.6%, South Korea 2.0%, Jamaica 1.9%, Taiwan 1.7%, Canada 1.6%, Ukraine 1.5%, Colombia 1.4%, Iran 1.4%. Refugee arrivals (1992[6]): 117,037.

violation 309.2[7]; drunkenness 260.1[7]. Drug and substance users (population age 26 and over; 1992): alcohol 47.8%; tobacco (cigarettes) 26.2%; marijuana 4.4%; cocaine 0.6%; tranquilizers 0.5%[7]; analgesics 0.5%[7]; stimulants 0.2%[7]; hallucinogens 0.1%[7]; heroin, n.a. Rate per 100,000 population of suicide (1993): 12.2.

Crime rates per 100,000 population in metropolitan areas (1992)

	violent crime			
	total	murder	rape	robbery	assault
Atlanta	940.2	12.7	59.6	370.1	497.8
Baltimore	1,359.4	16.7	53.9	637.1	651.7
Boston	686.5	3.5	33.6	183.3	466.1
Chicago	...	14.6	...	577.4	653.7
Dallas	1,124.5	17.5	64.1	422.7	620.2
Detroit	980.8	16.5	66.6	366.1	531.6
Houston	1,012.0	17.6	57.6	399.2	537.3
Los Angeles	1,778.6	20.9	42.0	750.1	965.6
Miami	2,037.0	17.0	54.2	902.5	1,063.2
Minneapolis	478.0	4.3	53.5	180.4	239.8
New York	2,163.7	27.1	38.2	1,237.1	861.4
Philadelphia	673.1	11.0	33.6	329.6	298.9
Pittsburgh	409.7	4.3	29.3	179.1	197.0
St. Louis	1,003.4	15.7	173.2	276.5	537.9
San Francisco	1,085.9	11.0	38.2	578.1	458.5
Washington, D.C.	774.9	15.7	30.7	328.1	400.4

	property crime			
	total	burglary	larceny	auto theft
Atlanta	6,991.7	1,631.7	4,488.9	871.1
Baltimore	6,022.9	1,358.0	3,824.3	840.6
Boston	4,040.5	982.7	2,321.6	736.2
Chicago	5,357.0	1,129.1	3,384.3	843.6
Dallas	7,327.2	1,686.0	4,584.1	1,057.1
Detroit	5,506.3	1,065.5	3,397.0	1,043.7
Houston	5,935.7	1,480.2	3,124.8	1,330.7
Los Angeles	5,629.0	1,400.3	2,779.3	1,449.5
Miami	10,299.5	2,348.6	6,172.4	1,778.4
Minneapolis	5,108.3	1,051.5	3,576.0	480.8
New York	6,326.8	1,403.0	3,202.2	1,721.4
Philadelphia	3,769.0	784.3	2,225.2	759.5
Pittsburgh	2,872.1	612.7	1,623.0	636.5
St. Louis	4,904.6	1,194.3	3,105.6	604.7
San Francisco	5,960.1	1,107.0	3,821.4	1,031.6
Washington, D.C.	4,796.6	837.2	3,286.3	673.1

Leisure (1992). Favourite leisure activities (percentage of total population that undertook activity at least once in the previous year): movie 59.0%, amusement park 50.0%, sports event 37.0%, live play 31.0%, art museum 27.0%; exercising 60.0%, reading literature 54.0%, playing sports 39.0%.
Material well-being (1992). Occupied dwellings with householder possessing: automobile 84.9%[8]; telephone 93.9%; radio receiver 99.0%; television receiver 98.3%; air conditioner 69.9%[9]; washing machine 76.3%[9]; videocassette recorder 72.5%; cable television 60.2%.
Recreational expenditures (1991): U.S.$258,700,000,000[10] (television and radio receivers 21.7%; nondurable toys and sports equipment 11.0%; sports supplies 10.2%; magazines and newspapers 7.8%; golfing, bowling, and other participatory activities 7.3%; books and maps 6.0%; spectator amusements 4.0%, of which spectator sports 1.5%, theatre and opera 1.4%, movies 1.1%; flowers, seeds, and potted plants 3.6%).

National economy
Budget (1994). Revenue: U.S.$1,259,900,000,000 (individual income tax 43.6%, social-insurance taxes and contributions 36.5%, corporation income tax 11.1%, other 8.8%). Expenditures: U.S.$1,480,000,000,000 (social security and medicare 31.5%, defense 18.9%, income security 14.4%, interest on debt 13.8%, health 7.3%, other 14.1%).
Total national debt (Oct. 17, 1994): U.S.$4,613,524,000,000.

Manufacturing, mining, and construction enterprises (1993)

	no. of enterprises[11]	no. of employees	hourly wage as a % of all wages	value added (U.S.$'000,000)[7]
Manufacturing				
Chemical and related products	12,109	1,078,200	137.4	154,793
Transportation equipment	10,500	1,698,500	146.1	151,979
Food and related products	20,624	1,733,100	96.6	145,336
Machinery, except electrical	52,135	1,882,100	118.1	124,235
Electric and electronic machinery	15,962	1,503,100	104.4	106,669
Instruments and related products	10,326	875,600	113.6	82,536
Fabricated metal products	36,105	1,306,900	108.3	76,670
Paper and related products	6,342	683,100	124.4	58,281
Rubber and plastic products	14,515	889,700	97.9	50,295
Primary metals	6,771	673,500	129.8	46,605
Apparel and related products	22,872	975,700	65.6	33,432
Stone, clay, and glass products	16,166	523,300	110.2	31,839
Lumber and wood	33,982	698,800	89.8	26,995
Textile-mill products	6,412	666,900	82.7	26,925
Tobacco products	138	46,200	161.4	24,484
Petroleum and coal products	2,254	158,100	170.2	24,024
Furniture and fixtures	11,613	481,000	86.6	20,669
Leather and leather products	2,193	116,400	70.7	4,293
Miscellaneous manufacturing industries	16,544	362,400	86.4	19,999
Mining				
Oil and gas extraction	22,910	352,600	130.5	80,049[11]
Coal mining	3,905	95,900	158.7	17,068[11]
Nonmetallic, except fuels	5,775	104,300	118.7	9,233[11]
Metal mining	1,027	48,000	140.4	4,610[11]
Construction				
Special trade contractors	342,000	3,019,900	136.7	117,480[11]
Heavy construction contractors	36,600	779,800	132.5	44,940[11]
General contractors and operative builders	157,600	1,117,400	126.1	33,802[11]

Gross national product (at current market prices; 1993): U.S.$6,378,100,000,000 (U.S.$24,700 per capita).

Gross domestic product and national income
(in U.S.$'000,000,000)

	1989	1990	1991	1992	1993
Gross domestic product	5,200.8	5,465.1	5,677.5	6,038.6	6,377.9
By type of expenditure					
Personal consumption expenditures	3,450.1	3,657.3	3,887.7	4,139.9	4,391.8
Durable goods	474.6	480.3	446.1	497.3	537.9
Nondurable goods	1,130.1	1,193.7	1,251.5	1,300.9	1,350.0
Services	1,845.5	1,983.3	2,190.1	2,341.6	2,503.9
Gross private domestic investment	771.2	741.0	721.1	796.5	891.7
Fixed investment	742.9	746.1	731.3	789.1	876.1
Changes in business inventories	28.3	−5.0	−10.2	7.3	15.6
Net exports of goods and services	−46.1	−31.2	−21.8	−29.6	−63.6
Exports	626.2	672.8	598.2	640.5	661.7
Imports	672.3	704.0	620.0	670.1	725.3
Government purchases of goods and services	1,025.6	1,098.1	1,090.5	1,131.8	1,158.1
Federal	400.1	424.0	447.3	448.8	443.4
State and local	625.6	674.1	643.2	313.8	714.6
By major type of product					
Goods output	2,072.7	2,143.3	2,182.5	2,312.8	2,421.9
Durable goods	906.6	928.0	888.4	977.9	1,047.9
Nondurable goods	1,166.0	1,215.2	1,294.1	1,334.9	1,374.0
Services	2,671.2	2,864.2	3,030.3	3,221.1	3,410.5
Structures	456.9	457.4	464.7	504.6	545.5
National income (incl. capital consumption adjustment)	4,223.3	4,418.4	4,544.2	4,836.6	5,140.3
By type of income					
Compensation of employees	3,079.0	3,244.2	3,390.8	3,582.0	3,772.2
Proprietors' income	379.3	402.5	368.0	414.3	321.0
Rental income of persons	8.2	6.9	−10.4	−8.9	12.6
Corporate profits	275.2	298.3	346.3	407.2	466.6
Net interest	324.0	466.7	449.5	442.0	445.6
By industry division (excl. capital consumption adjustment)					
Agriculture, forestry, fishing	101.0	103.4	90.9	100.9	105.3
Mining and construction	261.5	267.3	246.8	251.3	268.1
Manufacturing	803.8	806.5	841.0	895.3	929.0
Durable	465.6	461.5	464.2	501.7	523.0
Nondurable	338.2	345.0	376.8	393.6	406.1
Transportation	136.6	144.0	140.8	151.0	161.8
Communications	87.4	92.8	95.3	103.7	107.4
Public utilities	90.2	92.0	99.0	101.5	106.9
Wholesale and retail trade	607.5	638.8	669.3	700.3	742.8
Finance, insurance, real estate	613.8	647.5	685.0	748.9	815.6
Services	883.0	963.4	1,002.5	1,085.8	1,171.0
Government and government enterprise	41.7	648.4	699.5	734.5	765.3
Other	37.6	41.7	17.4	7.3	0.2

Structure of gross domestic product and labour force

	1991		1993	
	in value U.S.$'000,000,000	% of total value	labour force[12]	% of labour force[12]
Agriculture	109	1.9	3,074,000	2.4
Mining	92	1.6	669,000	0.5
Manufacturing	1,026	17.9	19,557,000	15.3
Construction	223	3.9	7,220,000	5.6
Public utilities	170	3.0 }	8,481,000	6.6
Transp. and commun.	336	5.9 }		
Trade	907	15.8	24,769,000	19.3
Finance	1,040	18.2	7,962,000	6.2
Public administration, defense	721	12.6 }	47,573,000	37.2
Services	1,090	19.0 }		
Other	10[13]	0.2[13]	8,734,000[14]	6.8[14]
TOTAL	5,723[3]	100.0	128,040,000[3]	100.0[3]

Business activity (1990): number of businesses 20,054,000 (sole proprietorships 73.7%, active corporations 18.5%, active partnerships 7.8%), of which services 8,631,000, wholesaling and retailing 3,849,000; business receipts $12,186,000,000,000 (active corporations 89.6%, sole proprietorships 6.0%, active partnerships 4.4%), of which wholesaling and retailing $3,563,000,000,000, services $1,140,000,000,000; net profit $529,000,000,000 (active corporations 70.1%, sole proprietorships 26.7%, partnerships 3.2%), of which services $122,000,000,000, wholesaling and retailing $47,000,000,000. New business concerns and business failures (1993): total number of new incorporations 667,341[15]; total failures 85,982, of which commercial service 24,311, retail trade 15,600; failure rate per 10,000 concerns 95.9; current liabilities of failed concerns $48,281,000,000, of which retail trade $9,644,000,000, manufacturing and mining $4,931,300,000; average liability $561,500. Business expenditures for new plant and equipment (1993): total $584,600,000,000, of which trade, services, and communications $297,700,000,000, manufacturing businesses $179,500,000,000 (nondurable goods 54.6%, durable goods 45.4%), public utilities $75,000,000,000, transportation $22,400,000,000, mining $10,100,000,000.
Production. Agriculture, forestry, fishing (value of production/catch in U.S.$'000,000 except as noted; 1992): corn (maize) 19,378, soybeans 11,843, hay 10,506, wheat 7,979, cotton lint 4,248, tobacco 3,059, potatoes 2,160, grapes 1,825, sorghum 1,693, oranges 1,599, apples 1,422, tomatoes 1,310, peanuts (groundnuts) 1,285, sugar beets 1,157, rice 1,099, barley 951, sugarcane 844, lettuce 822, strawberries 685, almonds 670, onions 613, cottonseed 607, dry edible beans 467, grapefruit 426, oats 391, peaches 373, carrots 338, cantaloupe 291, broccoli 280, pears 274, walnuts 268, lemons 256, sunflower seeds 246, pecans 240, cranberries 213, celery 206; livestock (number of live animals) 99,559,000 cattle, 57,684,000 pigs, 10,750,000 sheep, 5,450,000 horses, 1,437,000,000 chickens; roundwood 495,800,000 cu m; fish and shellfish catch

3,678, of which fish 2,013 (including salmon 582, Alaska pollack 324), shellfish 1,665 (including shrimp 480, crabs 471). Mining (metal content in metric tons, except as noted; 1993): iron 34,617,000; copper 1,787,000; zinc 488,000; lead 354,000; molybdenum 45,400; vanadium 1,700; mercury 70; silver 1,700,000 kg; gold 330,000 kg; helium 93,000,000 cu m. Quarrying (metric tons; 1993): sand and gravel 812,000,000; crushed stone 780,000,000; cement 72,600,000; clay 42,200,000; common salt 38,000,000; phosphate rock 31,800,000; lime 16,600,000; gypsum 15,500,000. Manufacturing (metric tons except as noted; 1993): crude steel 87,343,000; paper and paperboard 76,688,000; wood pulp 57,189,000; pig iron 48,275,000; sulfuric acid 40,153,000; coke 21,237,000[15]; phosphoric acid 10,474,000; cheese 5,877,000; newsprint 5,833,000; aerospace vehicles (sales) U.S.$121,852,000,000[15]; machine tools (new orders for metal-cutting-type tools) U.S.$2,322,400,000; cotton fabric 4,402,000,000 sq m; carpets and rugs 1,134,300,000 sq m[15]; footwear 167,803,000 pairs[15]; motor-vehicle tires 237,448,000 units; major household appliances 51,277,000 units, of which 8,109,000 refrigerators, 7,703,000 microwave ovens, 6,793,000 washing machines, 5,074,000 clothes driers; television receivers 21,304,000 units[15]; radio receivers 18,405,000 units; new passenger cars (factory sales) 5,955,000 units; new trucks and buses (factory sales) 4,786,000 units. Construction (completed; 1993): private U.S.$299,563,000,000, of which residential U.S.$208,092,000,000, nonresidential U.S.$91,471,000,000; public U.S.$55,103,000,000, of which residential U.S.$5,139,000,000, nonresidential U.S.$49,964,000,000.

Retail and wholesale trade and services (1993)

	no. of establish-ments	no. of employees	hourly wage as a % of all wages	annual sales or receipts (U.S.$'000,000)
Retail trade[16]	1,547,300	19,954,000	67.1	2,081,600
Automotive dealers	84,200	1,432,300	101.8	454,400
Food stores	187,800	3,227,800	71.8	392,400
General merchandise group stores	36,900	2,416,500	67.6	267,000
Eating and drinking places	415,200	7,044,300	49.4[17]	211,000
Gasoline service stations	101,900	626,400	61.7	133,500
Building materials, hardware, garden supply, and mobile home dealers	71,700	805,500	80.0	115,900
Furniture, home furnishings, equipment stores	110,700	824,100	87.9	113,700
Apparel and accessory stores	147,600	1,152,000	64.2	106,100
Drugstores and proprietary stores	49,100	588,000	75.1	80,900
Liquor stores	30,600	114,200	...	21,200
Wholesale trade[18]	466,700	5,984,000	108.7	1,922,600
Durable goods	292,800	3,119,000	112.0	979,400
Machinery, equipment, and supplies	114,400	721,900	110.9	180,900
Motor vehicles, automotive equipment	43,000	456,100	98.5	176,700
Professional and commercial equipment	...	744,900	135.3	150,700
Electrical goods	35,300	445,000	116.8	143,200
Lumber and other construction materials	19,100	222,200	103.6	80,800
Metals and minerals, except petroleum	11,100	132,600	112.0	70,000
Hardware, plumbing, heating equipment and supplies	23,100	268,700	105.8	47,100
Furniture and home furnishings	14,500	138,200	98.8	34,900
Miscellaneous durable goods	...	289,300	87.8	95,000
Nondurable goods	173,900	2,565,000	104.3	943,200
Groceries and related products	42,100	856,000	106.6	209,500
Petroleum and petroleum products	16,700	165,700	98.6	121,600
Farm-products raw materials	12,600	113,200	77.7	96,900
Apparel and accessories	16,900	206,900	100.2	75,600
Drugs, drug proprietaries, and druggists' sundries	4,900	198,900	124.7	72,800
Paper and paper products	16,800	246,800	110.4	58,800
Beer, wine, and distilled alcoholic beverages	5,800	151,400	119.8	54,500
Chemicals and allied products	12,700	140,300	122.2	38,000
Miscellaneous nondurable goods	45,300	486,100	88.2	135,000
Services[16, 19]	2,141,700	30,658,000	99.1	1,299,400
Health	447,900	8,823,500	108.9	285,000
Business, except computer services	265,900	4,997,400	97.9	201,900
Computer and data-processing services	43,800	911,600	153.2	100,700
Legal services	145,900	938,400	142.3	96,200
Automotive repair, services, garages	162,800	960,900	85.9	79,500
Management and public relations	43,800	699,000	130.3	70,000
Hotels and motels	40,900	1,626,100	68.2	62,100
Engineering services	34,000	580,800	150.0	61,500
Personal services	193,900	1,095,800	72.8	59,100
Amusement and recreation	79,800	1,449,000	71.7	51,100
Motion pictures	30,000	420,800	113.8	43,800

Energy production (consumption): electricity (kW-hr; 1992) 2,797,000,000,000 (2,757,000,000,000); coal (metric tons; 1992) 907,400,000 (809,700,000); crude petroleum (barrels; 1992) 2,617,000,000 (4,895,000,000); petroleum products (metric tons; 1991) 758,400,000 (828,600,000); natural gas (cu m; 1992) 503,332,000,000 (558,946,000,000). Domestic production of energy by source (1993): natural gas 32.5%, coal 31.1%, crude petroleum 22.0%, other[20] 14.4%.

Energy consumption by source (1993): petroleum and petroleum products 40.2%, natural gas 24.8%, coal 23.4%, other[20] 11.6%; by end use (1992): industrial 37.2%, residential and commercial 35.5%, transportation 27.3%.

Household income and expenditure. Average household size (1992) 2.6; average (mean) annual income per household U.S.$39,020, of which average white household U.S.$40,780, average Hispanic[5] household U.S.$29,602, average black household U.S.$25,409; sources of income: wages and salaries 57.8%, transfer payments 16.7%, self-employment 8.1%, other 17.4%; expenditure: transportation 21.4%, housing 15.5%, food 10.8%, fuel and utilities 8.0%, wearing apparel 7.0%, recreation 6.8%, health 6.7%, expenditures in restaurants and hotels 5.5%, household furnishings 4.8%, education 1.7%, other 13.5%.

Selected household characteristics (1993). Total number of households 96,391,000, of which (by race) white 85.2%, black 11.6%, other 3.2%; in central cities 31.4%, in suburbs 46.3%, outside metropolitan areas 22.3%; (by tenure) owned 62,220,000 (64.5%), rented 32,499,000 (33.7%); family households 68,144,000, of which married couple 78.0%, female head with own children[21] under age 18, 7.5%, female head without own children[21] under 18, 4.9%; nonfamily households 28,247,000, of which female living alone 50.3%, male living alone 33.2%, other 16.5%.

Financial aggregates

	1988	1989	1990	1991	1992	1993	1994[22]
Exchange rate, U.S.$ per:							
£[23]	1.78	1.64	1.78	1.77	1.76	1.50	1.54
SDR[23]	1.34	1.28	1.36	1.37	1.41	1.40	1.46
International reserves (U.S.$)[24]							
Total (excl. gold; '000,000,000)	36.74	63.55	72.26	66.66	60.27	62.35	64.39
SDRs ('000,000,000)	9.64	9.95	10.99	11.24	8.50	9.02	9.70
Reserve pos. in IMF ('000,000,000)	9.75	9.05	9.00	9.49	11.70	11.80	12.18
Foreign exchange ('000,000,000)	17.36	44.55	52.19	45.93	40.01	41.53	42.51
Gold ('000,000 fine troy oz)	261.87	261.93	261.91	261.91	261.84	261.79	261.76
% world reserves	27.62	27.78	27.84	27.86	28.13	28.67	28.70
Interest and prices							
Central bank discount (%)[24]	6.5	7.0	6.5	3.5	3.0	3.0	3.50
Govt. bond yield (%)[23]	8.24	8.56	8.25	6.01	5.31	4.44	6.48
Industrial share prices[23] (1990 = 100)	78.5	94.7	100.0	114.1	125.5	132.3	134.5
Balance of payments ($'000,000,000)							
Balance of visible trade	−126.97	−115.71	−108.84	−73.44	−96.14	−112.74	...
Imports, f.o.b.	−447.31	−477.38	−497.55	−489.40	−536.28	580.51	...
Exports, f.o.b.	320.34	361.67	388.71	415.96	440.14	467.77	...
Balance of invisibles	0.60	14.51	18.38	69.75	29.84	3.49	...
Balance of payments, current account	−126.37	−101.20	−90.46	−3.69	−66.30	−109.25	...

Population economically active (1993): total 128,040,000[12]; activity rate of total population 49.6% (participation rates: ages 15–64, 76.2%; female 45.6%; unemployed 6.8%).

Price and earnings indexes (1990 = 100)

	1988	1989	1990	1991	1992	1993	1994[22]
Consumer price index	90.5	94.9	100.0	104.2	107.4	110.6	113.6
Hourly earnings index[25]	96.5	99.0	100.0	98.1	99.6	101.7	...

Average employee earnings

	average hourly earnings in U.S.$		average weekly earnings in U.S.$	
	July 1993	July 1994	July 1993	July 1994
Manufacturing				
Durable goods	12.29	12.63	511.26	531.7
Lumber and wood products	9.64	9.87	391.38	404.67
Furniture and fixtures	9.28	9.57	368.42	383.76
Stone, clay, and glass products	11.90	12.16	511.70	533.82
Primary metal industries	14.07	14.39	613.45	637.48
Fabricated metal products	11.65	11.88	482.31	500.15
Machinery, except electrical	12.76	12.95	543.58	558.15
Electrical and electronic equipment	11.25	11.58	462.38	479.41
Transportation equipment	15.57	16.42	650.83	696.21
Instruments and related products	12.26	12.46	497.76	515.84
Miscellaneous manufacturing	9.37	9.58	364.49	378.41
Nondurable goods	11.02	11.29	444.11	460.63
Food and kindred products	10.47	10.70	425.08	445.12
Tobacco manufactures	18.62	20.38	670.32	772.40
Textile mill products	8.88	9.12	363.19	375.74
Apparel and other textile products	7.02	7.30	259.74	272.29
Paper and allied products	11.34	11.83	492.20	516.97
Printing and publishing	11.91	12.13	453.77	465.79
Chemicals and allied products	14.82	15.21	637.26	655.55
Petroleum and coal products	18.43	18.94	812.76	829.57
Rubber and miscellaneous plastics products	10.61	10.74	436.07	446.78
Leather and leather products	7.55	7.96	288.41	300.89
Nonmanufacturing				
Metal mining	15.10	16.03	649.30	708.53
Coal mining	17.18	17.54	731.87	747.20
Oil and gas extraction	14.08	13.92	613.89	623.62
Nonmetallic minerals, except fuels	12.78	13.14	604.49	632.03
Construction	14.35	14.72	566.83	585.86
Transportation and public utilities	13.65	13.82	546.00	556.95
Wholesale trade	11.71	11.99	448.49	460.42
Retail trade	7.24	7.44	214.30	220.97
Finance, insurance, and real estate	11.24	11.71	400.14	418.05
Hotels, motels, and tourist courts	7.38	7.58	233.95	239.53
Health services	11.76	12.12	386.90	398.75
Legal services	15.22	15.61	528.13	540.11
Miscellaneous services	15.62	14.55	573.25	568.91

Tourism (1993): receipts from visitors U.S.$74,560,000,000; expenditures by nationals abroad U.S.$52,585,000,000; number of foreign visitors (1992) 16,450,000 (6,979,000 from Europe, 4,699,000 from Asia, 1,423,000 from South America, 1,201,000 from Central America and the Caribbean); number of nationals traveling abroad[26] (1992) 15,965,000 (7,136,000 to Europe, 5,285,000 to Latin America[27]).

Land use (1991): forested 31.3%; meadows and pastures 26.1%; agricultural and under permanent cultivation 20.5%; other 22.1%.

Foreign trade

Balance of trade (current prices)

	1987	1988	1989	1990	1991	1992	1993
U.S.$'000,000,000	−152.1	−118.5	−109.4	−101.7	−99.2	−84.5	−115.7
% of total	23.0%	15.5%	13.1%	11.4%	9.8%	8.6%	11.1%

Imports (1993): U.S.$580,644,000,000 (machinery and transport equipment 44.8%, of which motor vehicles and parts 13.7%; basic and miscellaneous manufactures 29.4%; mineral fuels and lubricants 9.6%; chemicals and related products 5.0%; food and live animals 4.0%). *Major import sources:* Canada 19.1%; Japan 18.5%; Mexico 6.9%; Taiwan 5.4%; Germany 4.9%; U.K. 3.7%; South Korea 2.9%; France 2.6%; Italy 2.3%; Singapore 2.2%; Hong Kong 1.6%; Saudi Arabia 1.3%.

Exports (1993): U.S.$464,767,000,000 (machinery and transport 45.0%, of which motor vehicles and parts 17.2%; basic and miscellaneous manufactures 18.8%; chemicals and related products 9.7%; food and live animals 7.1%; inedible crude materials 5.2%). *Major export destinations:* Canada 21.6%; Japan 10.3%; Mexico 9.0%; U.K. 5.6%; Germany 4.1%; Taiwan 3.5%; South Korea 3.2%; France 2.9%; The Netherlands 2.8%; Belgium-Luxembourg 2.0%.

Trade by commodity group (1993)

	imports		exports	
SITC Group	U.S.$'000,000	%	U.S.$'000,000	%
00 Food and live animals	22,984	4.0	32,895	7.1
01 Beverages and tobacco	5,512	0.9	6,503	1.4
02 Crude materials, excluding fuels	15,374	2.6	24,341	5.2
03 Mineral fuels, lubricants, and related materials	55,582	9.6	9,736	2.1
04 Animal and vegetable oils, fat, and waxes	1,000	0.2	1,461	0.3
05 Chemicals and related products, n.e.s.	29,166	5.0	45,066	9.7
06 Basic manufactures	66,168	11.4	36,609	7.9
07 Machinery and transport equipment	259,975	44.8	208,986	45.0
08 Miscellaneous manufactured articles	104,485	18.0	50,630	10.9
09 Goods not classified by kind	20,398	3.5	48,540	10.4
TOTAL	580,644	100.0	464,767	100.0

Direction of trade (1993)

	imports		exports	
	U.S.$'000,000	%	U.S.$'000,000	%
Africa	14,547	2.5	9,169	2.0[3]
South Africa	1,847	0.3	2,967	0.6
Other Africa	12,700	2.2	6,202	1.3
Americas	185,260	31.9[3]	178,469	38.4[3]
Canada	110,922	19.1	100,177	21.6
Caribbean countries and Central America	10,289	1.8	12,684	2.7
Mexico	39,930	6.9	41,636	9.0
South America	24,119	4.2	23,972	5.2
Asia	257,742	44.4	150,730	32.4
Japan	107,268	18.5	47,950	10.3
Other Asia	150,474	25.9	102,780	22.1
Europe	117,451	20.2[3]	115,766	24.9
EU	97,824	16.9	96,957	20.9
EFTA	15,802	2.7	12,701	2.7
Russia	1,744	0.3	2,967	0.6
Other Europe	2,081	0.4	3,141	0.7
Oceania	4,730	0.8	9,823	2.1
Australia	3,294	0.6	8,272	1.8
Other Oceania	1,436	0.2	1,551	0.3
Other	914	0.2	810	0.2
TOTAL	580,664	100.0	464,767	100.0

Transport and communications

Transport. Railroads (1993): length 136,000 mi[15], 219,000 km[15]; passenger-mi 6,062,000,000, passenger-km 9,756,000,000; short ton-mi cargo 1,088,990,000,000, metric ton-km cargo 1,590,048,000,000. Roads (1992): total length 3,902,000 mi, 6,280,000 km (paved 88.9%). Vehicles (1992): passenger cars 144,213,000; trucks and buses 46,149,000. Merchant marine (1993): vessels (1,000 gross tons and over) 603; total deadweight tonnage 20,419,000. Air transport (1993): passenger-mi 480,463,000,000, passenger-km 773,232,000,000; short ton-mi cargo 13,320,000,000, metric ton-km cargo 19,447,000,000; localities (1993) with scheduled flights 834[28]. Certified route passenger/cargo air carriers (1992) 77; operating revenue (U.S.$'000,000; 1991) 74,942, of which domestic 56,119, international 18,823; operating expenses 76,669, of which domestic 56,596, international 20,073.

Intercity passenger and freight traffic by mode of transportation (1992)

	cargo traffic ('000,000,000 ton-mi)	% of nat'l total	passenger traffic ('000,000,000 passenger-mi)	% of nat'l total
Rail	1,107	37.4	14	0.7
Road	815	27.6	1,687	81.6
Inland water	454	15.3	—	—
Air	11	0.4	367	17.8
Petroleum pipeline	571	19.3	—	—
TOTAL	2,958	100.0	2,066[3]	100.0[3]

Communications. Daily newspapers (1992): total number 1,570; total circulation 62,160,000; circulation per 1,000 population 243. Radio (1993[29]): total number of receivers 538,000,000 (1 per 0.5 persons). Television (1994[29]): total number of receivers 211,000,000 (1 per 1.2 persons). Telephones (1992; access lines): 140,000,000 (1 per 1.8 persons).

Other communications media (1993)

Print	titles		titles
Books (new)	42,217	Home economics	90
of which		Industrial arts	106
Agriculture	443	Journalism and	
Art	1,124	communications	90
Biography	1,801	Labour and industrial	
Business	1,186	relations	70
Education	1,065	Law	273
Fiction	4,841	Library and information	
General works	1,482	sciences	118
History	1,960	Literature and language	158
Home economics	731	Mathematics and science	238
Juvenile	5,062	Medicine	182
Language	548	Philosophy and religion	130
Law	904	Physical education and	
Literature	1,867	recreation	151
Medicine	2,651	Political science	136
Music	315	Psychology	138
Philosophy, psychology	1,589	Sociology and anthropology	149
Poetry, drama	839	Zoology	94
Religion	2,274		
Science	2,153	**Cinema**[15]	
Sociology, economics	6,408	Feature films	431
Sports, recreation	914		
Technology	1,720		traffic
Travel	340	**Cellular telephones**	
Periodicals[8]	3,731	Number of	
of which		subscribers	16,009,000
Agriculture	153		
Business and economics	262		(pieces of mail)
Chemistry and physics	170	**Post**[7]	
Children's periodicals	78	Mail	165,851,000,000
Education	203	Domestic	165,058,000,000
Engineering	265	International	793,000,000
Fine and applied arts	145		
General interest	181		
History	151		

Education and health

Education (1992–93)

	schools	teachers	students	student/ teacher ratio
Primary (age 5–13)[30]		1,478,000	35,031,000	23.7
Secondary and vocational (age 14–17)	84,578	1,076,000	12,841,000	11.9
Higher, including teacher-training colleges	5,758	880,000	14,558,000	18.2

Literacy: studies in the late 1980s indicated that adult "functional" literacy may not exceed 85%.

Health (1992): doctors of medicine 653,100[31] (1 per 391 persons), of which office-based practice 387,900 (including specialties in internal medicine 16.8%, general and family practice 15.1%, pediatrics 7.5%, obstetrics and gynecology 7.0%, general surgery 6.4%, psychiatry 5.6%, anesthesiology 5.2%, orthopedics 4.1%, ophthalmology 3.8%); doctors of osteopathy 33,500; nurses 1,853,024 (1 per 138 persons); dentists 155,058 (1 per 1,647 persons); hospital beds 1,174,000 (1 per 218 persons), of which nonfederal 92.4% (community hospitals 80.9%, psychiatric 11.8%, long-term general and special 1.8%), federal 7.6%; infant mortality rate per 1,000 live births (1993) 8.3.

Food (1988–90): daily per capita caloric intake 3,642 (vegetable products 70%, animal products 30%); 138% of FAO recommended minimum requirement. Per capita consumption of major food groups (pounds annually; 1992): milk 230.8; grains 187.0; sweeteners 143.3; potatoes 133.5; red meat 114.1; fresh vegetables 109.3; fresh fruits 98.7; fats and oils 65.6; poultry products 60.1; fish and shellfish 14.7.

Military

Total active duty personnel (1993): 1,729,700 (army 33.9%, navy 29.5%, air force 26.0%, marines 10.6%). *Military expenditure as percentage of GNP* (1991): 4.9% (world 4.2%); per capita expenditure U.S.$1,110. *Military aid* (1993): total $4,143,000,000 (Middle East 76.2%, of which Israel 43.4%, Egypt 31.4%; Europe 20.8%, of which Turkey 10.9%; Latin America 1.8%).

[1]Excludes 4 delegates having only committee voting privileges. [2]Total area excluding U.S. share of Great Lakes is 3,618,770 sq mi (9,372,571 sq km). [3]Detail does not add to total given because of rounding. [4]Includes military personnel residing overseas. [5]Persons of Hispanic origin may be of any race. [6]Fiscal year ending September 30. [7]1991. [8]1988. [9]1990. [10]Constant 1987 dollars. [11]1987. [12]Excludes military personnel overseas. [13]Statistical discrepancy. [14]Unemployed. [15]1992. [16]Number of establishments for 1991. [17]Excludes tips. [18]Number of establishments for 1987. [19]Annual receipts for 1992. [20]Includes hydroelectric, nuclear, and geothermal power. [21]"Own children" includes adopted children and stepchildren. [22]July. [23]Period average. [24]End-of-year. [25]Manufacturing sector only. [26]Excludes Canada and Mexico. [27]Includes Central and South America. [28]Includes 292 localities in Alaska. [29]January 1. [30]Primary includes kindergarten. [31]578,100 professionally active.

Uruguay

Official name: República Oriental del Uruguay (Oriental Republic of Uruguay).
Form of government: republic with two legislative houses (Senate [31][1]; Chamber of Representatives [99]).
Head of state and government: President.
Capital: Montevideo.
Official language: Spanish.
Official religion: none.
Monetary unit: 1 peso uruguayo (Uruguayan peso)[2]; valuation (Oct. 7, 1994) 1 U.S.$ = Ur$5.61; 1 £ = Ur$8.92.

Area and population		area		population
		sq mi	sq km	1985 census
Departments	**Capitals**			
Artigas	Artigas	4,605	11,928	69,145
Canelones	Canelones	1,751	4,536	364,248
Cerro Largo	Melo	5,270	13,648	78,416
Colonia	Colonia del Sacramento	2,358	6,106	112,717
Durazno	Durazno	4,495	11,643	55,077
Flores	Trinidad	1,986	5,144	24,739
Florida	Florida	4,022	10,417	66,474
Lavalleja	Minas	3,867	10,016	61,466
Maldonado	Maldonado	1,851	4,793	94,314
Montevideo	Montevideo	205	530	1,311,976
Paysandú	Paysandú	5,375	13,922	103,763
Río Negro	Fray Bentos	3,584	9,282	48,644
Rivera	Rivera	3,618	9,370	89,475
Rocha	Rocha	4,074	10,551	66,601
Salto	Salto	5,468	14,163	108,487
San José	San José de Mayo	1,927	4,992	89,893
Soriano	Mercedes	3,478	9,008	79,439
Tacuarembó	Tacuarembó	5,961	15,438	83,498
Treinta y Tres	Treinta y Tres	3,679	9,529	46,869
TOTAL LAND AREA		67,574	175,016	
INLAND WATER		463	1,199	
TOTAL		68,037	176,215	2,955,241

Demography

Population (1994): 3,168,000.
Density (1994): persons per sq mi 46.6, persons per sq km 18.0.
Urban-rural (1992): urban 89.3%; rural 10.7%.
Sex distribution (1992): male 48.74%; female 51.26%.
Age breakdown (1990): under 15, 25.8%; 15–29, 23.0%; 30–44, 18.9%; 45–59, 15.8%; 60–74, 11.9%; 75 and over, 4.6%.
Population projection: (2000) 3,274,000; (2010) 3,453,000.
Doubling time: 87 years.
Ethnic composition (1990): white (mostly Spanish, Italian, or mixed Spanish-Italian) 86.0%; mestizo 8.0%; mulatto or black 6.0%.
Religious affiliation (1988): Roman Catholic 66.0%; Protestant 2.0%; Jewish 0.8%; nonreligious and atheist 31.2%.
Major cities (1985): Montevideo 1,311,976; Salto 80,823; Paysandú 76,191; Las Piedras 58,288; Rivera 57,316.

Vital statistics

Birth rate per 1,000 population (1991): 17.6 (world avg. 26.0); (1983) legitimate 73.8%; illegitimate 26.2%.
Death rate per 1,000 population (1991): 9.6 (world avg. 9.2).
Natural increase rate per 1,000 population (1991): 8.0 (world avg. 16.8).
Total fertility rate (avg. births per childbearing woman; 1990): 2.3.
Marriage rate per 1,000 population (1991): 6.6.
Divorce rate per 1,000 population (1991): 3.1.
Life expectancy at birth (1990–95): male 69.3 years; female 75.7 years.
Major causes of death per 100,000 population (1990): diseases of the circulatory system 378.4; malignant neoplasms (cancers) 222.8; respiratory diseases 76.3; accidents 47.0; diseases of the digestive system 39.1.

National economy

Budget (1993). Revenue: Ur$10,109,681,000 (direct taxes 80.3%, receipts from foreign trade 7.0%). Expenditures: Ur$10,704,929,000 (social security and welfare 58.8%, general public services 15.3%, capital investments 7.8%, interest on public debt 7.2%, subsidies 3.7%).
Public debt (external, outstanding; 1992): U.S.$3,092,000,000.
Tourism (1992): receipts U.S.$381,000,000; expenditures U.S.$104,000,000.
Production (metric tons except as noted). Agriculture, forestry, fishing (1992): rice 622,000, sugarcane 430,000, barley 214,000, sugar beets 160,000, corn (maize) 82,000, wheat 73,000; livestock (number of live animals) 25,702,000 sheep, 9,508,000 cattle, 475,000 horses; roundwood (1991) 3,829,000 cu m; fish catch 125,758. Mining and quarrying (1991): hydraulic cement 500,000; gypsum 145,000. Manufacturing (value added in NUr$'000,000; 1988): food products (excluding beverages) 128,600; petroleum products 69,873; chemicals and chemical products 68,178; textiles 63,459; beverages 51,012; transport equipment 46,570; tobacco products 31,004; leather products 28,155; paper and paper products 25,002. Construction (approvals; 1992): residential 295,350 sq m; nonresidential 155,616 sq m. Energy production (consumption): electricity (kW-hr; 1991) 7,017,000,000 (5,226,000,000); coal, none (none); crude petroleum (barrels; 1991) none (9,742,000); petroleum products (metric tons; 1991) 1,139,000 (1,276,000); natural gas, none (n.a.).
Gross national product (1992): U.S.$10,444,000,000 (U.S.$3,340 per capita).

Structure of gross domestic product and labour force

	1992		1985	
	in value NUr$'000,000	% of total value	labour force	% of labour force
Agriculture	3,720,173	10.8	170,183	14.5
Mining	65,434	0.2	1,771	0.1
Manufacturing	7,493,693	21.7	214,945	18.3
Construction	1,570,105	4.5	64,385	5.4
Public utilities	785,152	2.3	17,377	1.5
Transp. and commun.	2,063,285	6.0	59,289	5.0
Trade	4,501,501	13.0	139,242	11.9
Finance	3,583,271	10.4	42,688	3.6
Pub. admin., defense	3,379,347	9.8 }	369,260	31.4
Services	8,817,939	25.5 }		
Other	−1,456,698[3]	−4.2[3]	97,668[4]	8.3[4]
TOTAL	34,523,202	100.0	1,176,808	100.0

Population economically active (1991): total 1,239,400; activity rate 44.7% (participation rates: ages 14 and over, 57.5%; female 40.7%; unemployed 2.5%).

Price and earnings indexes (1985 = 100)

	1987	1988	1989	1990	1991	1992	1993
Consumer price index	288.5	467.9	844.4	1,794	3,624	6,105	9,408
Monthly earnings index[5]	319.8	524.8	946.1	1,844	3,909	6,706	10,844

Household income and expenditure. Avg. household size (1985) 3.3; avg. annual income per household (1985) NUr$266,261 (U.S.$2,625); sources of income[6]: wages 53.5%, self-employment 17.0%, transfer payments and other 29.5%; expenditure (1982–83)[7]: food 39.9%, housing 17.6%, transportation and communications 10.4%, health care 9.3%, clothing 7.0%, durable goods 6.3%, recreation 3.1%, education 1.3%, personal effects and other 5.1%.
Land use (1991): forested 3.8%; meadows and pastures 77.3%; agricultural and under permanent cultivation 7.5%; other 11.4%.

Foreign trade[8]

Balance of trade (current prices)						
	1988	1989	1990	1991	1992	1993
U.S.$'000,000	+300.3	+478.8	+435.4	+44.9	−248.9	−536.7
% of total	12.0%	17.6%	14.8%	1.4%	6.8%	14.0%

Imports (1993): U.S.$2,324,372,000 (machinery and appliances 23.4%; transport equipment 17.5%; chemical products 11.5%; mineral products 9.7%; synthetic plastics, resins, and rubber 6.1%; base metals and products 5.7%; textile products 5.4%). *Major import sources:* Brazil 27.3%; Argentina 20.8%; United States 9.6%; Italy 4.2%; Germany 3.9%; France 3.0%.
Exports (1993): U.S.$1,645,312,000 (textiles and textile products 23.6%; live animals and live-animal products 21.6%; vegetable products 15.2%; hides and skins 10.7%; synthetic plastics, resins, and rubber 3.6%; mineral products 3.5%). *Major export destinations:* Brazil 22.3%; Argentina 19.2%; United States 9.0%; Germany 6.3%; United Kingdom 3.9%; Italy 3.0%.

Transport and communications

Transport. Railroads[9]: route length (1992) 3,004 km; passenger-km (1987) 140,600,000; metric ton-km cargo (1990) 204,000,000. Roads (1985): length 52,000 km (paved 23%). Vehicles (1992): passenger cars 310,833; trucks and buses 148,644. Merchant marine (1992): vessels (100 gross tons and over) 93; deadweight tonnage 172,520. Air transport (1991): passenger-km 471,000,000; metric ton-km cargo 2,600,000; airports (1994) 7.
Communications. Daily newspapers (1990): total number 30; total circulation 720,000; circulation per 1,000 population 233. Radio (1993): total receivers 1,800,000 (1 per 1.7 persons). Television (1993): total receivers 700,000 (1 per 4.5 persons). Telephones (1992): 668,407 (1 per 4.7 persons).

Education and health

Education (1992)	schools	teachers	students	student/ teacher ratio
Primary (age 6–11)	2,419	16,376	338,020	20.6
Secondary (age 12–17)	351	15,522	208,015	13.4
Vocational	103	...	55,042	...
Higher	2	6,666	62,842	9.4

Educational attainment (1985). Percentage of population age 25 and over having: no formal schooling 7.5%; less than primary education 26.6%; primary 31.2%; secondary 19.9%; higher 14.8%. *Literacy* (1985): population age 15 and over literate 95.0%; males 975,200 (94.5%); females 1,074,300 (95.4%).
Health (1992): physicians 10,608 (1 per 295 persons); hospital beds (1987) 14,133 (1 per 215 persons); infant mortality rate per 1,000 live births 18.7.
Food (1988–90): daily per capita caloric intake 2,668 (vegetable products 65%, animal products 35%); 100% of FAO recommended minimum requirement.

Military

Total active duty personnel (1993): 24,700 (army 69.6%, navy 18.2%, air force 12.2%). *Military expenditure as percentage of GNP* (1991): 2.1% (world 4.2%); per capita expenditure U.S.$64.

---

[1]Includes the vice president, who serves as ex officio presiding officer. [2]The peso uruguayo (Uruguayan peso [Ur$]) replaced the new Uruguayan peso (Nur$) on March 1, 1993, at the rate of 1 Uruguayan peso = 1,000 new Uruguayan pesos. [3]Includes indirect taxes less subsidies. [4]Includes unemployed not previously employed. [5]From urban areas only. [6]Salaried employees only. [7]Weights of consumer price index components in Montevideo. [8]Import figures are f.o.b. in balance of trade and c.i.f. for commodities and trading partners. [9]Passenger service ceased in 1988.

Uzbekistan

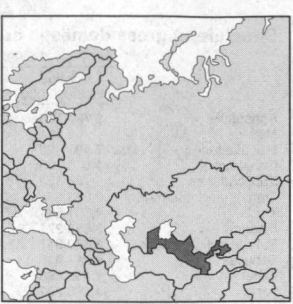

Official name: Ozbekistan Jumhuriyäti (Republic of Uzbekistan).
Form of government: multiparty republic with a single legislative body (Supreme Soviet [500][1]).
Head of state: President.
Head of government: Prime Minister.
Capital: Tashkent (Toshkent).
Official language: Uzbek.
Official religion: none.
Monetary unit: sum[2] (plural sumy); valuation (Oct. 3, 1994) 1 U.S.$ = 16 sumy; 1 £ = 25.45 sumy.

Area and population

Autonomous Republic	Administrative centres	area sq mi	area sq km	population 1992 estimate
Karakalpakstan	Nukus	63,700	164,900	1,311,000
Provinces				
Andizhan (Andijan)	Andizhan	1,600	4,200	1,839,000
Bukhara	Bukhara	54,900	142,100	1,232,000
Dzhizak (Djizak)	Dzhizak	7,900	20,500	806,000
Fergana	Fergana	2,700	7,100	2,282,000
Kashka Darya	Karshi	11,000	28,400	1,756,000
Khorezm	Urgench	2,400	6,300	1,100,000
Namangan	Namangan	3,100	7,900	1,604,000
Samarkand	Samarkand	9,500	24,500	2,265,000
Surkhan Darya	Termez	8,000	20,800	1,385,000
Syr Darya	Gulistan	2,000	5,100	587,000
Tashkent (Toshkent)	Tashkent	6,000	15,600	4,331,000
TOTAL		172,700[3]	447,400	20,498,000

Demography

Population (1994): 22,382,000.
Density (1994): persons per sq mi 129.6, persons per sq km 50.0.
Urban-rural (1992): urban 40.0%; rural 60.0%.
Sex distribution (1992): male 49.40%; female 50.60%.
Age breakdown (1989): under 15, 40.8%; 15–29, 28.4%; 30–44, 15.0%; 45–59, 9.3%; 60–74, 4.7%; 75 and over, 1.8%.
Population projection: (2000) 25,466,000; (2010) 31,577,000.
Doubling time: 26 years.
Ethnic composition (1991): Uzbek 73.0%; Russian 7.7%; Tajik 4.8%; Tatar 2.3%; Kyrgyz 0.9%; Ukrainian 0.7%; Turkmen 0.6%; other 10.0%.
Religious affiliation (1993): believers are predominantly Sunnī Muslim (Ḥanafīyah).
Major cities (1992): Tashkent 2,119,900; Samarkand 372,000; Namangan 333,000; Andizhan 302,000; Bukhara 235,000.

Vital statistics

Birth rate per 1,000 population (1992): 33.1 (world avg. 26.0); (1989) legitimate 95.8%; illegitimate 4.2%.
Death rate per 1,000 population (1992): 6.5 (world avg. 9.2).
Natural increase rate per 1,000 population (1992): 26.6 (world avg. 16.8).
Total fertility rate (avg. births per childbearing woman; 1993): 3.8.
Marriage rate per 1,000 population (1992): 11.0.
Divorce rate per 1,000 population (1992): 1.5.
Life expectancy at birth (1990): male 65.1 years; female 71.8 years.
Major causes of death per 100,000 population (1989): diseases of the circulatory system 251.3; diseases of the respiratory system 119.3; accidents, poisoning, and violence 60.1; malignant neoplasms (cancers) 55.9; infectious and parasitic diseases 44.5; diseases of the digestive system 27.1; diseases of the nervous system 9.1; endocrine and metabolic disorders 6.5.

National economy

Budget (1992). Revenue: 74,700,000,000 rubles (price differential tax 36.1%, turnover tax 26.2%, excise tax 12.7%, corporate income tax 12.7%, individual income tax 5.5%). Expenditures: 86,200,000,000 rubles (social and cultural affairs 27.3%, subsidies 24.7%, national economy 18.9%).
Household income and expenditure (1992). Average household size (1989) 5.5; income per household 2,343 rubles; sources of income: wages and salaries 61.8%, subsidies, grants, and nonwage income 22.8%, other 15.4%; expenditure: food and consumer goods 72.4%, other 27.6%.
Public debt (external, outstanding; 1992): U.S.$123,000,000.
Production (metric tons except as noted). Agriculture, forestry, fishing (1993): seed cotton 4,300,000, vegetables 3,500,000, fruit (except grapes) and berries 1,000,000, rice 500,000, grapes 480,000, potatoes 425,000, corn (maize) 341,000, barley 300,000, rye 10,000; livestock (number of live animals; 1994) 9,400,000 sheep, 5,300,000 cattle, 530,000 pigs, 33,000,000 chickens; roundwood (1990) 15,000 cu m; fish catch (1991) 27,400. Mining and quarrying (1992): copper 80,000; lead 22,000; gold 80. Manufacturing (1992): cement 5,934,500; cotton fibre 1,399,400; mineral fertilizers 1,361,000; rolled metals 604,000; plastic 94,000; synthetic fibre 32,600; textiles 690,000,000 sq m; refrigerators 84,200,000 units; compressors 8,123,000 units; tractors 16,900 units; television receivers 5,000 units; cotton harvesters 2,350 units; footwear 39,200,000 pairs. Construction (1992): residential 7,000,000,000 sq m. Energy production (consumption): electricity (kW-hr; 1992) 50,900,000,000 (50,769,000,000); coal (metric tons; 1992) 9,231,000 (10,681,000); crude petroleum (barrels; 1992) 8,063,000 (39,238,000); petroleum products (metric tons; 1992) 4,901,000 (4,901,000); natural gas (cu m; 1992) 42,800,000,000 (41,300,000,000).

Gross national product (1993): U.S.$21,030,000,000 (U.S.$960 per capita).

Structure of net material product and labour force

	1992 in value '000,000 rubles	% of total value	labour force	% of labour force
Agriculture	20,729	48.8	3,577,000	43.4
Mining			1,135,000	13.8
Manufacturing	12,925	30.4		
Public utilities			182,000	2.2
Construction	3,518	8.3	622,000	7.5
Transp. and commun.	1,845	4.3	360,000	4.4
Trade	2,766	6.5	462,000	5.6
Finance	—	—	25,000	0.3
Pub. admin., defense	—	—	96,000	1.2
Services	—	1.7	1,664,000	20.2
Other	711	—	119,800	1.4
TOTAL	42,494	100.0	8,242,800	100.0

Population economically active (1992): total 8,242,800; activity rate of total population 39.0% (participation rates: ages 16–59 [male], 16–54 [female] 79.7%; female 43.8%; unemployed 1.1%).

Price and earnings indexes (1990 = 100)

	1990	1991	1992
Consumer price index	100.0	161.1	1,428
Earnings index	...	...	...

Land use (1992): forested 3.0%; meadows and pastures 51.1%; agricultural and under permanent cultivation 10.8%; other 35.1%.

Foreign trade

Balance of trade (current prices)

	1987	1988	1989	1990	1991
'000,000,000 rubles	−3.9	−1.2	−3.5	−3.7	−0.6
% of total	20.8%	8.5%	17.0%	18.4%	1.5%

Imports (1992): U.S.$929,300,000 (1991; textiles 20.6%, food products 10.0%, machinery 20.4%, basic manufactures 19.7%, chemicals 7.4%). *Major import sources:* Switzerland 21.3%; China 7.3%; Belgium 4.3%; Turkey 3.8%; Afghanistan 3.5%.
Exports (1992): U.S.$869,300,000 (1991; textiles 20.6%, food products 10.0%, metal manufactures 5.4%, transport equipment 3.6%, machinery 2.2%). *Major export destinations:* U.K. 13.5%; Belgium 12.9%; Germany 10.8%; Turkey 8.9%; Poland 5.5%.

Transport and communications

Transport. Railroads (1991): length 4,225 mi, 6,800 km; passenger-mi 3,231,000,000, passenger-km 5,200,000,000; short ton-mi cargo 48,357,000,000, metric ton-km cargo 70,600,000,000. Roads (1990): total length 55,431 mi, 89,207 km (paved 83%). Vehicles (1988): passenger cars 790,800; trucks and buses, n.a. Merchant marine: vessels (100 gross tons and over) n.a.; total deadweight tonnage, n.a. Air transport (1991): passenger-mi 6,524,000,000, passenger-km 10,500,000,000; short ton-mi cargo 60,754,000,000; metric ton-km cargo 88,700,000,000; airports (1994) with scheduled flights 1.
Communications. Daily newspapers (1990): total number 279; total circulation 5,158,400; circulation per 1,000 population 249.1. Radio (1991): total number of receivers 3,677,000 (1 per 5.6 persons). Television (1991): total number of receivers 3,308,000 (1 per 6.3 persons). Telephones (1991): 1,458,000 (1 per 14.3 persons).

Education and health

Education (1991–92)

	schools	teachers	students	student/ teacher ratio
Primary (age 6–13)	8,557	384,000	4,721,400	12.3
Secondary (age 14–17)				
Voc., teacher tr.	243	...	254,400	...
Higher	52	...	337,400	...

Educational attainment (1989). Percentage of population age 25 and over having: primary education or no formal schooling 13.3%; some secondary 19.8%; completed secondary and some postsecondary 57.7%; higher 9.2%.
Literacy (1989): percentage of total population age 15 and over literate 97.2%; males literate 98.5%; females literate 96.0%.
Health (1992): physicians 75,900 (1 per 282 persons); hospital beds 236,200 (1 per 83 persons); infant mortality rate per 1,000 live births 37.1.

Military

Total active duty personnel (1994): 45,000[4] (army 99.0%, air force 1.0%).
Military expenditure as percentage of GNP (1992): 0.2%; per capita expenditure U.S.$17.

[1]Elections to new 150-seat legislature (Supreme Assembly) were held Dec. 25, 1994. The Supreme Soviet was to continue to exercise legislative powers until the seating of the new legislature. [2]The sum was introduced on July 1, 1994, to replace the sum-coupon (an interim currency introduced in November 1993 to replace the Russian ruble) at a rate of 1 sum to 1,000 sum-coupons. The Russian ruble was banned from circulation in Uzbekistan from mid-April 1994. [3]Detail does not add to total given because of rounding. [4]Includes CIS centrally controlled units. About 5,000 Russian troops remained in Uzbekistan in late 1994.

Vanuatu

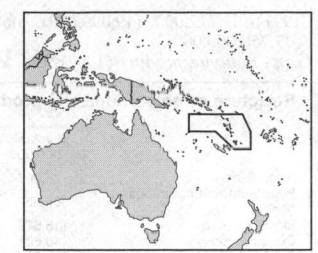

Official name: Ripablik blong Vanuatu
 (Bislama); République de Vanuatu
 (French); Republic of Vanuatu
 (English).
Form of government: republic with a
 single legislative house (Parliament
 [46]).
Chief of state: President.
Head of government: Prime Minister.
Capital: Vila.
Official languages: Bislama; French;
 English.
Official religion: none.
Monetary unit: vatu (VT); valuation
 (Oct. 7, 1994) 1 U.S.$ = VT 113.50;
 1 £ = VT 180.52.

Area and population

		area		population
Local Government Regions	Capitals	sq mi	sq km	1989 census
Ambae/Maéwo	Longana	270	699	10,958
Ambrym	Eas	257	666	7,191
Banks/Torres	Sola	341	882	5,985
Éfaté	Vila	356	923	30,868
Épi	Ringdove	172	446	3,628
Malekula	Lakatoro	793	2,053	19,298
Paama	Liro	23	60	1,696
Pentecost	Loltong	193	499	11,341
Santo/Malo	Luganville	1,640	4,248	25,581
Shepherd	Morua	33	86	3,975
Taféa	Isangel	629	1,628	22,423
TOTAL		4,707	12,190	142,944

Demography

Population (1994): 164,000.
Density (1994): persons per sq mi 34.8, persons per sq km 13.5.
Urban-rural (1989): urban 18.4%[1]; rural 81.6%.
Sex distribution (1989): male 51.60%; female 48.40%.
Age breakdown (1989)[2]: under 15, 45.5%; 15–29, 26.6%; 30–44, 15.2%; 45–59,
 8.4%; 60–74, 3.7%; 75 and over, 0.6%.
Population projection: (2000) 189,000; (2010) 231,000.
Doubling time: 25 years.
Ethnic composition (1989): Ni-Vanuatu 97.9%; European 1.0%; other Pacific
 Islanders 0.4%; other 0.7%.
Religious affiliation (1989): Christian 77.2%, of which Presbyterian 35.8%,
 Roman Catholic 14.5%, Anglican 14.0%, Seventh-day Adventist 8.2%; Cus-
 tom 4.6%; nonreligious 1.7%; unknown 4.0%; other 12.5%.
Major towns (1989): Vila (Port-Vila) 19,400; Luganville (Santo) 6,900; Port
 Olry 884[3]; Isangel 752[3].

Vital statistics

Birth rate per 1,000 population (1994): 35.0 (world avg. 26.0).
Death rate per 1,000 population (1994): 7.0 (world avg. 9.2).
Natural increase rate per 1,000 population (1994): 28.0 (world avg. 16.8).
Total fertility rate (avg. births per childbearing woman; 1994): 4.6.
Marriage rate per 1,000 population (1985): *c.* 7.4.
Divorce rate per 1,000 population (1985): less than 0.7.
Life expectancy at birth (1994): male 64.0 years; female 68.0 years.
Major causes of death per 100,000 population (1985)[4]: infectious and para-
 sitic diseases 69.3; diseases of the respiratory system 60.5; diseases of the
 circulatory system 37.6; accidents and violence 23.6; malignant neoplasms
 (cancers) 22.9; ill-defined conditions 117.3.

National economy

Budget (1989). Revenue: VT 4,154,700,000 (taxes on international trade
 58.6%; taxes on goods and services 22.7%; nontax revenue 16.8%). Expenditures: VT 7,287,200,000 (manufacturing, mining, and construction 21.4%;
 public services 13.7%; education 12.6%; transportation and communications
 10.5%; agriculture 6.7%; health 6.6%).
Public debt (external, outstanding; 1992): U.S.$39,600,000.
Tourism: receipts from visitors (1992) U.S.$27,000,000; expenditures by na-
 tionals abroad (1991) U.S.$1,000,000.
Production (metric tons except as noted). Agriculture, forestry, fishing (1993):
 coconuts 259,000, roots and tubers 50,000, copra 35,000, bananas 13,000,
 vegetables and melons 8,000, cacao beans 3,000, peanuts (groundnuts) 2,000,
 corn (maize) 1,000; livestock (number of live animals) 128,000 cattle, 59,000
 pigs; roundwood (1991) 63,000 cu m; fish catch (1991) 3,200. Mining and
 quarrying (1985): small quantities of coral-reef limestone, crushed stone,
 sand, and gravel. Manufacturing (value added in '000 VT; 1984): food,
 beverages, and tobacco 358,000; wood products 96,000; fabricated metal
 products 60,000; paper products, including printing and publishing, 48,800;
 nonmetallic mineral products 24,600; handicrafts 14,600; textiles, clothing,
 and leather 12,900. Construction (approvals in Vila and Luganville; 1992):
 residential 20,386 sq m; nonresidential 19,876 sq m. Energy production
 (consumption): electricity (kW-hr; 1992) 28,681,000 (28,681,000); coal, none
 (none); crude petroleum, none (none); petroleum products (metric tons;
 1991) none (26,000); natural gas, none (none).
Population economically active (1989): total 66,957; activity rate of total
 population 47.0% (participation rates: ages 15–64, 85.0%; female 46.3%;
 unemployed 0.5%).

Price and earnings indexes (1985 = 100)

	1987	1988	1989	1990	1991	1992	1993
Consumer price index	118.3	132.2	142.7	151.1	160.6	168.1	173.3
Earnings index	...	...	...	...	...	...	...

Gross national product (at current market prices; 1992): U.S.$189,000,000
 (U.S.$1,220 per capita).

Structure of gross domestic product and labour force

	1990		1989	
	in value VT '000,000	% of total value	labour force	% of labour force
Agriculture	3,582	20.0	49,811	74.4
Mining	...	...	1	—
Manufacturing	1,050	5.9	891	1.3
Construction	1,033	5.8	1,302	1.9
Public utilities	339	1.9	109	0.2
Transportation and communications	1,517	8.5	1,031	1.5
Trade	5,772	32.2	2,713	4.1
Finance	1,743	9.7	646	1.0
Pub. admin., defense	1,985	11.1 }	7,892	11.8
Services	1,278	7.1 }		
Other	−400[5]	−2.2[5]	2,561	3.8
TOTAL	17,899	100.0	66,957	100.0

Household income and expenditure (1985)[1]. Average household size (1989)
 5.1; income per household U.S.$11,299; sources of income: wages and
 salaries 59.0%, self-employment 33.7%; expenditure (1990)[1, 6]: food and
 nonalcoholic beverages 30.5%, housing 20.7%, transportation 13.2%, health
 and recreation 12.3%, tobacco and alcohol 10.4%.
Land use (1992): forested 75.0%; meadows and pastures 2.0%; agricultural
 11.8%; other 11.2%.

Foreign trade[7]

Balance of trade (current prices)

	1987	1988	1989	1990	1991	1992
VT '000,000	−5,508	−5,000	−5,319	−8,566	−7,364	−6,689
% of total	58.6%	54.8%	50.9%	66.0%	67.0%	56.8%

Imports (1992): VT 9,228,000,000 (machinery and transport equipment 27.5%;
 food and live animals 17.4%; basic manufactures 14.9%; mineral fuels
 9.0%; chemical products 6.6%; beverages and tobacco 4.1%). *Major import
 sources:* Australia 38.7%; New Zealand 10.0%; Japan 9.1%; France 7.9%;
 New Caledonia 6.3%; Fiji 5.2%; Hong Kong 3.5%; Singapore 2.8%.
Exports (1992): VT 2,539,000,000 (domestic exports 74.5%, of which copra
 32.8%, beef and veal 13.3%, seashells 8.0%, cacao beans and preparations
 6.5%, timber 3.5%; reexports 25.5%). *Major export destinations*[8]: Japan
 19.9%; Australia 10.9%; New Caledonia 5.9%; South Korea 5.6%.

Transport and communications

Transport. Railroads: none. Roads (1993): total length 702 mi, 1,130 km
 (paved 21%). Vehicles (1992): passenger cars 4,500; trucks and buses 3,000.
 Merchant marine (1992): vessels (100 gross tons and over) 280; total
 deadweight tonnage 3,259,594. Air transport (1992): international passenger arrivals 52,188, international passenger departures 52,837; international
 cargo unloaded 571 metric tons, international cargo loaded 188 metric tons;
 airports (1994) with scheduled flights 29.
Communications. Daily newspapers: none. Radio (1993): total number of
 receivers 55,000 (1 per 2.9 persons). Television (1987): total number of
 receivers 1,000 (1 per 136 persons). Telephones (1986): 3,240 (1 per 40
 persons).

Education and health

Education (1992)

	schools	teachers	students	student/ teacher ratio
Primary (age 6–11)[9]	272	852	26,267	30.8
Secondary (age 11–18)	21[10]	220	4,269	19.4
Voc., teacher tr.	...	...	444	...
Higher	1	...	124[11]	...

Educational attainment (1989). Percentage of population age 6 and over
 having: no formal schooling or less than one year 22.3%; some primary
 education 52.6%; lower-level secondary 18.3%; upper-level secondary and
 higher 4.8%; not stated 2.0%. *Literacy* (1979): total population age 15 and
 over literate 32,120 (52.9%); males 18,550 (57.3%); females 13,570 (47.8%).
Health (1990): physicians 20 (1 per 7,345 persons); hospital beds 364 (1 per
 404 persons); infant mortality rate per 1,000 live births (1994) 44.0.
Food (1988–90): daily per capita caloric intake 2,736 (vegetable products 81%,
 animal products 19%); 120% of FAO recommended minimum requirement.

Military

Total active duty personnel: Vanuatu has a paramilitary force of about 300.

[1]Vila and Luganville only. [2]For indigenous population only. [3]1979. [4]Deaths reported
to the Ministry of Health only. [5]Imputed bank service charges. [6]Weights of consumer
price index components. [7]Imports c.i.f.; exports f.o.b. [8]Destination of domestic exports
only. [9]Excludes independent private schools. [10]1986. [11]1991.

Venezuela

Official name: República de Venezuela
(Republic of Venezuela).
Form of government: federal multiparty
republic with two legislative
houses (Senate [49[1]]; Chamber of
Deputies [199]).
Head of state and government:
President.
Capital: Caracas.
Official language: Spanish.
Official religion: none.
Monetary unit: 1 bolívar (B, plural
Bs) = 100 céntimos; valuation[2] (Oct. 7,
1994) 1 U.S.$ = Bs 170;
1 £ = Bs 270.38.

Area and population

States	Capitals	area sq mi	area sq km	population 1994 estimate
Amazonas	Puerto Ayacucho	67,900	175,750	65,252
Anzoátegui	Barcelona	16,700	43,300	1,006,124
Apure	San Fernando de Apure	29,500	76,500	360,616
Aragua	Maracay	2,700	7,014	1,306,974
Barinas	Barinas	13,600	35,200	503,811
Bolívar	Ciudad Bolívar	91,900	238,000	1,090,624
Carabobo	Valencia	1,795	4,650	1,755,339
Cojedes	San Carlos	5,700	14,800	219,938
Delta Amacuro	Tucupita	15,500	40,200	106,318
Falcón	Coro	9,600	24,800	673,701
Guárico	San Juan de Los Morros	25,091	64,986	572,388
Lara	Barquisimeto	7,600	19,800	1,392,727
Mérida	Mérida	4,400	11,300	670,875
Miranda	Los Teques	3,070	7,950	2,262,017
Monagas	Maturín	11,200	28,900	541,569
Nueva Esparta	La Asunción	440	1,150	316,776
Portuguesa	Guanare	5,900	15,200	700,964
Sucre	Cumaná	4,600	11,800	761,959
Táchira	San Cristóbal	4,300	11,100	926,976
Trujillo	Trujillo	2,900	7,400	544,201
Yaracuy	San Felipe	2,700	7,100	453,154
Zulia	Maracaibo	24,400	63,100	2,676,856
Other federal entities				
Dependencias Federales	—	50	120	...
Distrito Federal	Caracas	745	1,930	2,267,990
TOTAL		352,144[3]	912,050	21,177,149

Demography

Population (1994): 21,177,000.
Density (1994): persons per sq mi 60.1, persons per sq km 23.2.
Urban-rural (1992): urban 84.6%; rural 15.4%.
Sex distribution (1994): male 50.40%; female 49.60%.
Age breakdown (1992): under 15, 37.4%; 15–29, 28.0%; 30–44, 19.0%; 45–59, 9.7%; 60 and over, 5.9%.
Population projection: (2000) 23,799,000; (2010) 27,816,000.
Doubling time: 30 years.
Ethnic composition (1993): mestizo 67%; white 21%; black 10%; Indian 2%.
Religious affiliation (1991): Roman Catholic 92.1%; other 7.1%.
Major cities (1990): Caracas 1,290,087; Maracaibo 1,206,726; Valencia 955,005; Barquisimeto 723,587; Maracay 538,616.

Vital statistics

Birth rate per 1,000 population (1992): 27.7 (world avg. 26.0); (1974) legitimate 47.0%; illegitimate 53.0%.
Death rate per 1,000 population (1992): 4.5 (world avg. 9.2).
Natural increase rate per 1,000 population (1992): 23.2 (world avg. 16.8).
Total fertility rate (avg. births per childbearing woman; 1992): 3.3.
Marriage rate per 1,000 population (1992): 5.4.
Divorce rate per 1,000 population (1992): 0.9.
Life expectancy at birth (1993): male 69.8 years; female 75.8 years.
Major causes of death per 100,000 population (1992): heart diseases 79.9; malignant neoplasms (cancers) 53.7; accidents 43.6; perinatal problems 33.0; cerebrovascular diseases 29.7; pneumonia 17.3.

National economy

Budget (1993). Revenue: Bs 961,495,000,000 (tax revenues 41.4%, oil revenues 38.3%, nontax revenues 20.3%). Expenditures: Bs 1,192,848,000,000 (subsidies 29.8%, goods and services 28.9%, capital transfers 17.6%, interest payments 16.6%).
Public debt (external, outstanding; 1992): U.S.$25,252,000,000.
Tourism (1992): receipts U.S.$432,000,000; expenditures U.S.$1,428,000,000.
Production (metric tons except as noted). Agriculture, forestry, fishing (1992): sugarcane 6,700,000, bananas 1,215,000, corn (maize) 904,000, rice 595,000, sorghum 528,000, plantains 510,000, cassava 382,000, coffee 72,000, cacao 14,000; livestock (number of live animals) 14,192,000 cattle; roundwood (1991) 1,290,000 cu m; fish catch (1991) 352,835. Mining and quarrying (1992): iron ore 18,054,000; bauxite 1,530,000; aluminum ore 620,000; gold 7,500 kg. Manufacturing (value added in Bs '000; 1990): base metals 60,320,000; food products 56,737,000; chemicals 51,838,000; beverages 27,350,000; metal products 15,770,000; textiles 13,658,000; paper and paper products 12,982,000; electrical machinery 11,506,000. Construction (in Bs; 1992): residential 77,648,000,000; nonresidential 356,982,000,000. Energy production (consumption): electricity (kW-hr; 1991) 57,150,000,000 (57,150,000,000); coal (metric tons; 1991) 2,696,000 (400,000); crude petroleum (barrels; 1991) 857,826,000 (357,155,000); petroleum products (metric tons;

1991) 53,212,000 (19,090,000); natural gas (cu m; 1991) 23,750,000,000 (23,750,000,000).
Gross national product (1992): U.S.$58,901,000,000 (U.S.$2,900 per capita).

Structure of gross domestic product and labour force

	1992 in value Bs '000,000[4]	% of total value	labour force	% of labour force
Agriculture	26,793	4.8	805,843	10.7
Petroleum and natural gas } Mining	95,687	17.1	81,977	1.1
Manufacturing	116,573	20.8	1,214,979	16.1
Construction	40,681	7.3	725,410	9.6
Public utilities	9,154	1.6	68,306	0.9
Transp. and commun.	28,763	5.1	462,802	6.1
Trade	80,392	14.3	1,610,180	21.4
Finance	77,065	13.7	446,184	5.9
Pub. admin., defense	47,823	8.5 }	2,045,748	27.1
Services	34,926	6.2 }		
Other	2,773	0.5	76,388	1.0
TOTAL	560,630	100.0[3]	7,537,817	100.0[3]

Population economically active (1992): total 7,537,817; activity rate 37.2% (participation rates: over age 15, 59.5%; female 31.9%; unemployed 7.1%).

Price and earnings indexes (1985 = 100)

	1987	1988	1989	1990	1991	1992	1993
Consumer price index	142.9	185.0	340.9	480.1	644.3	846.8	1,169.7
Monthly earnings index[5]	115.6	139.3	207.8	309.5	...	...	...

Household income and expenditure. Average household size (1990) 5.1; average annual income per household (1981) Bs 42,492 (U.S.$9,899); sources of income: n.a.; expenditure (1990): food 37.1%, rent and utilities 9.4%, clothing 8.3%, transportation and communications 5.1%, education and recreation 4.9%, household furnishings and maintenance 2.8%.
Land use (1991): forested 33.9%; meadows and pastures 20.1%; agricultural and under permanent cultivation 4.4%; other 41.6%.

Foreign trade

Balance of trade (current prices)

	1988	1989	1990	1991	1992	1993
Bs '000,000	−65,434	+232,261	+529,115	+286,500	+154,700	+274,600
% of total	18.2%	33.5%	46.7%	20.1%	9.3%	12.1%

Imports (1992): Bs 866,560,087,000 (machinery 33.0%, transport equipment 18.5%, chemicals 10.5%, basic metal manufactures 8.0%; textile products 4.3%, animal products 4.1%, processed food products 3.4%). *Major import sources:* U.S. 46.2%; Japan 7.5%; Ger. 6.5%; Italy 4.6%; Brazil 3.9%; Colombia 3.9%; U.K. 2.3%; Spain 2.3%.
Exports (1992): Bs 984,595,359,000 (crude petroleum and petroleum products 79.2%, iron ore 1.8%). *Major export destinations:* U.S. 50.3%; The Netherlands 4.0%; Puerto Rico 3.8%; Colombia 3.5%; Japan 2.6%; Germany 2.4%; Brazil 1.8%; Trinidad and Tobago 1.8%.

Transport and communications

Transport. Railroads (1992): route length 226 mi, 363 km; passenger-km 46,670,000; metric ton-km cargo 36,240,000. Roads (1992): total length 58,081 mi, 93,472 km (paved 32%). Vehicles (1992): passenger cars 1,565,872; trucks and buses 456,425. Merchant marine (1992): vessels (100 gross tons and over) 271; total deadweight tonnage 1,355,419. Air transport (1992): passenger-km 6,791,000,000; metric ton-km cargo 782,000,000; airports (1994) with scheduled flights 25.
Communications. Daily newspapers (1990): total number 54; total circulation 2,800,000; circulation per 1,000 population 142. Radio (1993): 8,100,000 receivers (1 per 2.6 persons). Television (1993): 3,700,000 receivers (1 per 5.6 persons). Telephones (1992): 1,804,220 (1 per 11.0 persons).

Education and health

Education (1991–92)

	schools	teachers	students	student/ teacher ratio
Primary (age 7–12)	15,800	183,298	4,190,047	22.9
Secondary (age 13–17)[6]	1,621	32,572	289,430	8.9
Higher	99[7]	43,833	550,783	12.6

Educational attainment (1990). Percentage of population age 10 and over having: no formal schooling 9.5%; primary education 45.7%; secondary 35.9%; higher 8.9%. *Literacy* (1990): total population age 15 and over literate 13,371,743 (92.2%); males 6,742,992 (93.5%); females 6,628,751 (91.1%).
Health (1992): physicians (1989) 32,616 (1 per 576 persons); hospital beds 52,786 (1 per 382 persons); infant mortality rate per 1,000 live births 25.2.
Food (1988–90): daily per capita caloric intake 2,443 (vegetable products 84%, animal products 16%); 99% of FAO recommended minimum.

Military

Total active duty personnel (1993): 75,000 (army 76.0%, navy 14.7%, air force 9.3%). *Military expenditure as percentage of GNP* (1991): 3.6% (world 4.2%); per capita expenditure U.S.$96.

[1]In addition, four former presidents hold lifetime membership. [2]Fixed exchange rate to U.S.$ introduced July 1994. [3]Detail does not add to total given because of rounding. [4]At 1984 prices. [5]Blue-collar workers. [6]Includes vocational and teacher training. [7]1990–91.

Vietnam

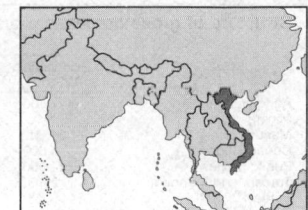

Official name: Cong Hoa Xa Hoi Chu Nghia Viet Nam (Socialist Republic of Vietnam).
Form of government: socialist republic with one legislative house (National Assembly [395]).
Chief of state: President.
Head of government: Prime Minister.
Capital: Hanoi.
Official language: Vietnamese.
Official religion: none.
Monetary unit: 1 dong (D) = 10 hao = 100 xu; valuation (Oct. 7, 1994) 1 U.S.$ = D 11,053; 1 £ = D 17,581.

Area and population

Regions Provinces	Capitals	area sq mi	area sq km	population 1992 estimate
Dong bang song Cuu Long		15,280	39,575[1]	15,214,300
An Giang	Long Xuyen	1,322	3,424	1,896,800
Ben Tre	Ben Tre	868	2,247	1,286,100
Can Tho	Can Tho	1,179	3,054	1,741,700
Dong Thap	Cao Lanh	1,265	3,276	1,433,800
Kien Giang	Rach Gia	2,410	6,243	1,296,500
Long An	Tan An	1,675	4,338	1,198,400
Minh Hai	Bac Lieu	2,969	7,689	1,682,100
Soc Trang		1,200	3,107	1,146,300
Tien Giang	My Tho	903	2,339	1,590,200
Tra Vinh	...	915	2,369	919,200
Vinh Long	...	574	1,487	1,023,200
Dong bang song Hong		4,810[1]	12,457[1]	13,547,000
Ha Tay		831	2,153	2,177,500
Hai Hung	Hai Duong	985	2,552	2,613,600
Haiphong (MUNICIPALITY)	—	580	1,503	1,556,600
Hanoi (CAPITAL)	—	355	920	2,099,600
Nam Ha	...	934	2,419	2,537,600
Ninh Binh	...	536	1,387	821,500
Thai Binh	Thai Binh	588	1,524	1,740,600
Dong Nam Bo		9,066[1]	23,481	8,445,500
Ba Ria–Vung Tau	...	756	1,957	636,400
Dong Nai	Bien Hoa	2,264	5,864	1,721,600
Ho Chi Minh City (MUNICIPALITY)	—	807	2,090	4,181,600
Song Be	Thu Dau Mot	3,686	9,546	1,057,400
Tay Ninh	Ho Chi Minh City	1,554	4,024	848,500
Duyen hai mien trung		17,692[1]	45,823	7,199,800[1]
Binh Dinh	Quy Nhon	2,346	6,076	1,339,600
Binh Thuan		3,086	7,992	436,800
Khanh Hoa	Nha Trang	2,030	5,258	901,200
Ninh Thuan		1,324	3,430	834,500
Phu Yen	Tuy Hoa	2,017	5,223	691,700
Quang Nam–Da Nang	Da Nang	4,629	11,988	1,873,500
Quang Ngai	Quang Ngai	2,261	5,856	1,122,500
Khu Bon cu		19,703	51,187	9,300,300
Ha Tinh	...	2,337	6,054	1,265,800
Nghe An	...	6,325	16,381	2,620,900
Quang Binh	Dong Hoi	3,082	7,983	718,000
Quang Tri	Dong Ha	1,773	4,592	507,400
Thanh Hoa	Thanh Hoa	4,312	11,168	3,243,800
Thua Thien–Hue	Hue	1,934	5,009	950,400
Mien nui va trung du		39,749[1]	102,949	11,843,600
Bac Thai	Thai Nguyen	2,511	6,503	1,117,800
Cao Bang	Cao Bang	3,261	8,445	614,500
Ha Bac	Bac Giang	1,781	4,614	2,218,400
Ha Giang	...	3,024	7,831	507,200
Hoa Binh	...	1,781	4,612	697,500
Lai Chau	Lai Chau	6,618	17,140	485,700
Lang Son	Lang Son	3,150	8,167	658,800
Lao Cai	...	3,108	8,049	517,700
Quang Ninh	Hai Duong	2,293	5,939	878,800
Son La	Son La	5,487	14,210	753,400
Tuyen Quang	...	2,240	5,801	614,400
Vinh Phu	Viet Tri	1,867	4,836	2,160,000
Yen Bai	...	2,626	6,802	621,400
Tay Nguyen		21,455[1]	55,569	2,803,900
Dac Lac	Buon Me Thoat	7,645	19,800	1,126,900
Gia Lai	...	6,047	15,662	713,600
Kon Tum	...	3,835	9,934	241,100
Lam Dong	Da Lat	3,929	10,173	722,300
TOTAL		127,816[1]	331,041	69,405,200[2]

Demography

Population (1994): 72,342,000.
Density (1994): persons per sq mi 566.0, persons per sq km 218.5.
Urban-rural (1993): urban 20.4%; rural 79.6%.
Sex distribution (1993): male 48.64%; female 51.36%.
Age breakdown (1989): under 15, 39.0%; 15–29, 28.7%; 30–44, 16.0%; 45–59, 9.1%; 60–74, 5.6%; 75 and over, 1.6%.
Population projection: (2000) 81,516,000; (2010) 97,097,000.
Ethnic composition (1989): Vietnamese 87.1%; Tho (Tay) 1.8%; Chinese (Hoa) 1.5%; Tai 1.5%; Khmer 1.4%; Muong 1.4%; Nung 1.1%; other 4.2%.
Religious affiliation (1992): Buddhist *c.* 67.0%; Roman Catholic *c.* 8.0%.
Major cities (1992): Ho Chi Minh City 4,181,600; Hanoi 2,099,600.

Vital statistics

Birth rate per 1,000 population (1994): 27.1 (world avg. 26.0).
Death rate per 1,000 population (1994): 7.8 (world avg. 9.2).
Natural increase rate per 1,000 population (1994): 19.3 (world avg. 16.8).
Total fertility rate (avg. births per childbearing woman; 1994): 3.3.
Life expectancy at birth (1994): male 63.4 years; female 67.6 years.
Morbidity (cases of reportable infectious disease per 100,000 population; 1990): malaria 2,564; trachoma 241; diarrhea 183.

National economy

Budget (1994). Revenue: D 38,660,000,000,000 (transfers from state enterprises 52.5%; taxes 31.8%; oil revenues 15.3%). Expenditures: D 46,853,-000,000,000 (current expenditures 74.4%, of which social services 28.8%).
Public debt (external, outstanding; 1993): U.S.$17,700,000,000.
Gross national product (1993): U.S.$12,053,000,000[3] (U.S.$170 per capita[3]).

Structure of net material product and labour force

	1993 in value D '000,000,000	1993 % of total value	1993 labour force	1993 % of labour force
Agriculture, forestry, fishing	37,328	29.8	23,815,000	72.8
Mining, manufacturing	26,960	21.6	3,500,000	10.7
Construction	8,495	6.8	830,000	2.5
Transp. and commun.	5,116	4.1	539,000	1.6
Trade, tourism, and restaurants	28,557	22.8	}	
Finance, insurance	2,318	1.8	} 3,026,000	9.2
Pub. admin. Services }	15,100	12.1	}	
Other	1,202	1.0	1,008,000	3.1
TOTAL	125,076	100.0	32,718,000	100.0[1]

Tourism (1992): receipts from visitors U.S.$50,000,000.
Production (metric tons except as noted). Agriculture, forestry, fishing (1993). rice 22,300,000, sugarcane 6,656,000, cassava 2,631,000, coconuts 1,207,000, corn (maize) 800,000; livestock (number of live animals) 14,861,000 pigs, 3,320,000 cattle, 2,956,000 buffalo; roundwood (1992) 29,620,000 cu m; fish catch (1992) 1,080,300. Mining and quarrying (1992): phosphate rock 280,-000; gold 10,000 kg. Manufacturing (1993): cement 4,600,000; sugar 478,000; steel 175,200[4]; fish sauce 131,700,000 litres[4]. Energy production (consumption): electricity (kW-hr; 1992) 9,800,000,000 (9,800,000,000); coal (metric tons; 1992) 4,792,000 (3,424,000); crude petroleum (barrels; 1992) 38,880,000 (283,300); petroleum products (metric tons; 1992) 38,000 (2,878,000).
Population economically active (1989): total 30,521,019; activity rate 47.4% (participation rates: ages 15–64, 79.9%; female 51.7%; unemployed 5.8%).
Household income and expenditure. Average household size (1989) 4.8; income per household (1990)[5] D 577,008 (U.S.$93); expenditure (1990): food 62.4%, clothing 5.0%, household goods 4.6%, education 2.9%, housing 2.5%.
Land use (1992): forest 29.6%; pasture 1.0%; agricultural 20.6%; other 48.8%.

Foreign trade[6]

Balance of trade (current prices)

	1988	1989	1990	1991	1992	1993
U.S.$'000,000	−679	−350	−41	−63	−60	−655
% of total	31.7%	11.7%	1.2%	1.5%	1.2%	10.3%

Imports (1993): U.S.$3,505,000,000 (crude petroleum 19.5%, machinery and spare parts 15.7%, steel 5.4%, fertilizers 4.5%). *Major import sources:* Singapore 28.1%; Japan 14.1%; North and South Korea 12.5%; France 7.8%.
Exports (1993): U.S.$2,850,000,000 (crude petroleum 29.6%, agricultural and forestry products 21.1%, fish and fish products 13.0%, rice 12.3%). *Major export destinations:* Japan 33.7%; Singapore 17.5%; Hong Kong 6.3%.

Transport and communications

Transport. Railroads (1991): length 3,220 km; passenger-km 1,767,000,000; metric ton-km cargo 1,103,300,000. Roads (1991): total length 88,000 km (paved 11%). Vehicles (1976): passenger cars 100,000; trucks and buses 200,000. Merchant marine (1992): vessels (100 gross tons and over) 230; total deadweight tonnage 872,752. Air transport (1990): passenger-km 87,000,000; metric ton-km cargo 1,000,000; airports (1994) with scheduled flights 12.
Communications. Daily newspapers (1993): 5. Radio (1993): 8,000,000 receivers. Television (1993): 2,500,000 receivers. Telephones (1992)[7]: 260,000.

Education and health

Education (1993–94)

	schools	teachers	students	student/ teacher ratio
Primary (age 7–12)	13,092[8]	275,640	9,725,095	35.3
Secondary (age 13–18)[9]	6,298[10]	166,968	3,815,852	22.9
Vocational	451	12,197	137,405	11.3
Higher	104	20,648	118,589	5.7

Educational attainment (1989). Percentage of population 25 and over having: no formal education (illiterate) 16.6%; some primary 46.6%; complete primary 23.5%; secondary 6.5%; postsecondary and higher 6.8%. *Literacy* (1991): persons 15 and over literate 88.0%; males 93.0%; females 84.0%.
Health (1991): physicians 25,900 (1 per 2,617 persons); hospital beds 206,000 (1 per 329 persons); infant mortality rate (1994) 45.5.
Food (1991): daily per capita caloric intake 1,943.

Military

Total active duty personnel (1994): 572,000 (army 87.4%, navy 7.3%, air force 5.3%). *Military expenditure as percentage of GNP* (1992): 7.2%.

[1]Detail does not add to total given because of rounding. [2]Total includes 1,044,800 persons in special enumeration groups not distributed in province and region estimates. [3]Other international sources have accounted domestic growth performance and estimate the gross national product to be U.S.$72,000,000,000 (U.S.$1,000 per capita). [4]1992. [5]Wage workers and government officials only. [6]Data reflects trade with the convertible currency area; import figures are f.o.b. [7]Main telephone lines. [8]Includes 2,955 institutions that provide primary and first cycle of secondary education. [9]Includes first and second cycle of secondary education. [10]Includes 534 institutions that provide both the first and second cycle of secondary education.

Western Samoa

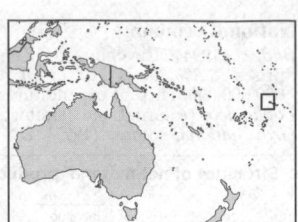

Official name: Malo Sa'oloto Tuto'atasi o Samoa i Sisifo (Samoan); Independent State of Western Samoa (English).
Form of government: constitutional monarchy[1] with one legislative house (Legislative Assembly [48][2]).
Chief of state: Head of State.
Head of government: Prime Minister.
Capital: Apia.
Official languages: Samoan; English.
Official religion: none.
Monetary unit: 1 tala (WS$, plural tala) = 100 sene; valuation (Oct. 7, 1994) 1 U.S.$ = WS$2.54; 1 £ = WS$4.04.

Area and population

Islands	area		population
Political Districts	sq mi	sq km	1986 census
Savaii	659	1,707	44,930
Fa'aseleleaga			...
Gaga'emauga			...
Gaga'ifomauga			...
Palauli			...
Satupa'iteā			...
Vaisigano			...
Upolu	432	1,119	112,228
A'ana			...
Aiga-i-le-Tai			...
Atua			...
Tuamasaga			...
Vaa-o-Fonoti			...
TOTAL	1,093[3]	2,831[3]	157,158[4]

Demography

Population (1994): 164,000.
Density (1994): persons per sq mi 150.0, persons per sq km 57.9.
Urban-rural (1993): urban 23.0%; rural 77.0%.
Sex distribution (1991): male 52.45%; female 47.55%.
Age breakdown (1986): under 15, 41.2%; 15–29, 30.8%; 30–44, 13.3%; 45–59, 9.1%; 60–74, 4.4%; 75 and over, 1.2%.
Population projection: (2000) 174,000; (2010) 192,000.
Doubling time: 28 years.
Ethnic composition (1982): Samoan (Polynesian) *c.* 88%; Euronesian *c.* 10%; European *c.* 2%.
Religious affiliation (1986): Congregational 47.2%; Roman Catholic 22.3%; Methodist 15.1%; Mormon 8.6%; other 6.8%.
Major city (1981): Apia 33,170.

Vital statistics

Birth rate per 1,000 population (1992): 31.7 (world avg. 26.0); (1978) legitimate 43.5%; illegitimate 56.5%.
Death rate per 1,000 population (1992): 6.8 (world avg. 9.2).
Natural increase rate per 1,000 population (1992): 24.9 (world avg. 16.8).
Total fertility rate (avg. births per childbearing woman; 1991): 4.5.
Marriage rate per 1,000 population (1989)[5]: 5.3.
Divorce rate per 1,000 population (1989)[5]: 0.2.
Life expectancy at birth (1992): male 63.8 years; female 70.0 years.
Major causes of death per 100,000 population (1985)[5]: diseases of the circulatory system 42.0; malignant neoplasms (cancers) 18.2; diseases of the respiratory system 13.2; infectious and parasitic diseases 8.8; diabetes mellitus 5.6.

National economy

Budget (1990). Revenue: WS$121,100,000 (tax revenue 74.5%, of which taxes on international trade 43.2%, income tax 17.4%, taxes on goods and services 13.5%; nontax revenue 25.5%, of which rents, royalties, and interest 6.9%). Expenditures: WS$158,700,000 (development expenditure 59.2%; current expenditure 40.8%).
Public debt (external, outstanding; 1992): U.S.$117,400,000.
Production (metric tons except as noted). Agriculture, forestry, fishing (1993): coconuts 130,000, taro 37,000, copra 11,000, bananas 10,000, papayas 10,000, pineapples 6,000, mangoes 5,000, avocados 2,000, cow's milk 1,000; livestock (number of live animals) 1,000,000 goats, 178,000 pigs, 25,000 cattle; roundwood (1992) 131,000 cu m; fish catch (1991) 565. Mining and quarrying: n.a. Manufacturing (in WS$'000; 1990): beer 8,708, cigarettes 6,551, coconut cream 5,576, sawn wood 3,662, coconut oil 3,442, coconut meat 2,905, soap 1,487, paints 1,457. Construction (permits issued in WS$; 1990): residential 4,421,000; commercial, industrial, and other 12,874,000. Energy production (consumption): electricity (kW-hr; 1992) 48,000,000 (48,000,000); coal, none (n.a.); crude petroleum, none (n.a.); petroleum products (metric tons; 1992) none (42,000).
Household income and expenditure. Average household size (1981) 5.1; income per household (1972) WS$1,518 (U.S.$2,200); sources of income (1972): wages 49.4%, self-employment 22.8%, remittances, gifts, and other assistance 18.0%, land rent 8.7%, other 1.1%; expenditure (1987)[6]: food 58.8%, transportation 9.0%, housing and furnishings 5.1%, fuel and light 5.0%, clothing 4.2%, other goods and services 1.9%, other 16.0%.
Gross national product (at current market prices; 1993): U.S.$160,000,000 (U.S.$980 per capita).

Structure of gross domestic product and labour force

	1989		1986	
	in value WS$'000	% of total value	labour force	% of labour force
Agriculture	117,100	47.1	29,023	63.6
Mining	...	...	...	...
Manufacturing	31,600	12.7 }	1,587	3.5
Construction	4,600	1.9	62	0.1
Public utilities	11,000	4.4	855	1.9
Transp. and commun.	5,200	2.1	1,491	3.3
Trade	25,600	10.3	1,710	3.7
Finance	...	...	842	1.8
Pub. admin., defense, government services	31,000	12.5 }	9,436	20.7
Other services }	22,300	9.0		
Other }			629	1.4
TOTAL	248,400	100.0	45,635	100.0

Population economically active (1994): total 47,207; activity rate of total population 28.7% (participation rates: ages 15–64 [1981] 48.6%; female [1986] 18.8%).

Price and earnings indexes (1985 = 100)

	1987	1988	1989	1990	1991	1992	1993
Consumer price index	110.6	120.0	127.7	147.2	145.2	157.6	160.3
Earnings index	...	...	...	...	...	...	...

Tourism (1992): receipts from visitors U.S.$19,000,000; expenditures by nationals abroad U.S.$2,000,000.
Land use (1992): forested 47.3%; meadows and pastures 0.4%; agricultural and under permanent cultivation 43.1%; other 9.2%.

Foreign trade[7]

Balance of trade (current prices)

	1988	1989	1990	1991	1992	1993
WS$'000	−111,729	−109,249	−137,300	−196,994	−238,965	−228,318
% of total	64.0%	65.4%	77.0%	83.9%	89.3%	87.4%

Imports (1993): WS$269,079,000 (1983; food 21.3%, machinery 21.0%, petroleum products 18.4%, miscellaneous manufactured articles 7.4%, chemicals 5.9%, animal oils and fats 0.5%). *Major import sources* (1991): New Zealand 38.3%; Australia 22.0%; United States 10.3%; Japan 9.5%; Fiji 6.5%; Germany 1.9%; American Samoa 1.9%.
Exports (1993): WS$16,522,000 (1991; taro 37.5%, coconut cream 28.8%, automotive wiring harnesses 15.3%, beer 4.6%, cigarettes 3.8%). *Major export destinations* (1991): New Zealand 49.1%; Australia 23.0%; American Samoa 13.8%; United States 7.1%.

Transport and communications

Transport. Railroads: none. Roads (1987): total length[8] 1,296 mi, 2,085 km (paved 19%). Vehicles (1990): passenger cars 2,295; trucks and buses 3,252. Merchant marine (1992): vessels (100 gross tons and over) 7; total deadweight tonnage 6,501. Air transport: passengers, n.a.; cargo, n.a.; airports (1994) with scheduled flights 2.
Communications. Daily newspapers: none. Radio (1993): 75,000 receivers (1 per 2.2 persons). Television (1990): 9,000 receivers (1 per 18 persons). Telephones (1992): 9,000 (1 per 18 persons).

Education and health

Education (1986–87)

	schools	teachers	students	student/ teacher ratio
Primary (age 5–11)	164[9]	1,511[10]	40,755	27.0
Secondary (age 12–18)	38[11]	492	11,395	23.2
Voc., teacher tr.	4[9]	37	228	6.2
Higher[9]	6	25	271	10.8

Educational attainment (1981). Percentage of population age 25 and over having: some primary education 16.5%; complete primary 24.5%; some secondary 52.1%; complete secondary 3.1%; higher 2.0%; unknown 1.8%.
Literacy (1981): virtually 100%.
Health: physicians (1990) 50 (1 per 3,183 persons); hospital beds (1989) 644 (1 per 255 persons); infant mortality rate per 1,000 live births (1991) 47.0.
Food (1988–90): daily per capita caloric intake 2,695 (vegetable products 81%, animal products 19%); 118% of FAO recommended minimum requirement.

Military

No military forces are maintained; New Zealand is responsible for defense.

[1]According to the constitution, the current Head of State, paramount chief HH Malietoa Tanumafili II, will hold office for life. Upon his death, the monarchy will functionally cease, and future Heads of State will be elected by the Legislative Assembly. [2]Includes the Head of State as an ex officio member. [3]Total includes 2 sq mi (5 sq km) of uninhabited islands. [4]The provisional total for the 1991 census is 159,862. [5]Registered only. [6]Consumer price index components. [7]Import figures are f.o.b. in balance of trade and c.i.f. in commodities and trading partners. [8]Total length includes 733 mi (1,180 km) of plantation roads. [9]1983. [10]Includes some secondary teachers. [11]1982.

Yemen

Official name: al-Jumhūrīyah
al-Yamanīyah (Republic of Yemen).
Form of government: multiparty republic
with one legislative house (Council of
Representatives [301]).
Head of state: President[1].
Head of government: Prime Minister.
Capital: Ṣanʿāʾ.
Official language: Arabic.
Official religion: Islam.
Monetary unit: 1 Yemen rial
(YRls) = 100 fils; valuation (Oct. 7,
1994): official rate (pegged to U.S.$)
1 U.S.$ = YRls 12.01, 1 £ = YRls 19.10;
parallel market rate 1 U.S.$ =
YRls 84.00, 1 £ = 133.60 YRls.

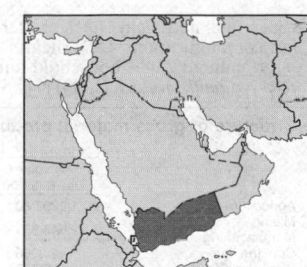

Area and population

Governorates	Capitals	area sq mi	area sq km	population 1986 estimate[2]
North Yemen				
al-Bayḍāʾ	al-Bayḍāʾ	4,310	11,170	295,439
Dhamār	Dhamār	3,430	8,870	698,823
Ḥajjah	Ḥajjah	3,700	9,590	720,000
al-Ḥudaydah	al-Ḥudaydah	5,240	13,580	1,052,086
Ibb	Ibb	2,480	6,430	1,254,128
al-Jawf	al-Jawf	...	...	42,762
al-Maḥwīt	al-Maḥwīt	830	2,160	260,836
Maʾrib	Maʾrib	15,400	39,890	95,326
Ṣaʿdah	Ṣaʿdah	4,950	12,810	323,124
Ṣanʿāʾ	Ṣanʿāʾ	7,840	20,310	1,664,518
Taʿizz	Taʿizz	4,020	10,420	1,419,708
South Yemen				
Abyān	Zinjibār	8,297	21,489	279,241
ʿAdan	Aden	2,695	6,980	326,919
Ḥaḍramawt	al-Mukallā	59,991	155,076	507,005
Laḥij	Laḥij	4,928	12,766	458,385
al-Mahrah	al-Ghaydah	25,618	66,350	44,225
Shabwah	ʿAtāq	28,536	73,908	192,324
TOTAL		182,278[3, 4]	472,099[3]	9,664,939

Demography

Population (1994): 12,961,000.
Density (1994)[5]: persons per sq mi 63.1, persons per sq km 24.4.
Urban-rural (1990): urban 29.3%; rural 70.7%.
Sex distribution (1992): male 49.68%; female 50.32%.
Age breakdown (1992): under 15, 50.6%; 15–29, 22.9%; 30–44, 13.6%; 45–59,
7.7%; 60–74, 4.0%; 75 and over, 1.2%.
Population projection: (2000) 15,859,000; (2010) 21,797,000.
Doubling time: 21 years.
Ethnic composition (1986): predominantly Arab.
Religious affiliation (1980): Muslim 99.9%, of which Sunnī 53.0%, Shīʿī
46.9%; other 0.1%.
Major cities (1986): Ṣanʿāʾ 427,150; Aden 318,000[6]; Taʿizz 178,043; al-Ḥuday-
dah 155,110; al-Mukallā 59,100[6].

Vital statistics

Birth rate per 1,000 population (1992): 48.1 (world avg. 26.0).
Death rate per 1,000 population (1992): 14.2 (world avg. 9.2).
Natural increase rate per 1,000 population (1992): 33.9 (world avg. 16.8).
Total fertility rate (avg. births per childbearing woman; 1992): 8.4.
Marriage rate per 1,000 population: n.a.
Life expectancy at birth (1992): male 53.3 years; female 55.5 years.
Major causes of death per 100,000 population: n.a.; however, major diseases
include malaria, tuberculosis, leprosy, and intestinal infections.

National economy

Budget (1992). Revenue: YRls 32,008,000,000 (excise tax 30.2%, taxes on
income and profits 29.3%, import duties 29.1%). Expenditures: YRls 53,-
637,000,000 (defense 21.9%, education 14.3%, general public services 6.3%,
health 3.5%).
Production (metric tons except as noted). Agriculture, forestry, fishing (1993):
sorghum 465,000, potatoes 213,000, tomatoes 204,000, wheat 160,000, grapes
144,000, watermelons 120,000, bananas 62,000, onions 61,000, millet 60,000,
papayas 56,000, livestock (number of live animals) 3,715,000 sheep, 3,297,000
goats, 1,163,000 cattle, 500,000 asses, 173,000 camels, 3,000 horses, 24,000,-
000 chickens; roundwood (1992) 324,000 cu m; fish catch (1991) 85,261.
Mining and quarrying (1992): salt 250,000; gypsum 100,000. Manufacturing
(1988)[7]: flour 23,700; wheat bran 10,500; canned tomatoes 1,265; cotton lint
800; foam rubber 715; soft drinks 49,000,000 bottles; beer 5,200,000 litres;
textiles 2,600,000 metres; cigarettes 1,166,000,000 units. Construction: n.a.
Energy production (consumption): electricity (kW-hr; 1992) 1,810,000,000
(1,810,000,000); coal, none (n.a.); crude petroleum (barrels; 1992) 62,139,000
(45,710,000); petroleum products (metric tons; 1992) 5,650,000 (2,808,000).
Population economically active (1986): total 2,043,237; activity rate of total
population 19.6% (participation rates: 15–64, 41.2%; female [1992] 14.0%;
unemployed [1993] c. 40%).

Price index (1990 = 100)[8]

	1985	1986	1987	1988	1989	1990
Consumer price index	41.7	50.5	58.5	64.7	74.5	100.0

Gross national product (at current market prices; 1991): U.S.$6,746,000,000
(U.S.$540 per capita).

Structure of gross domestic product and labour force

	1992 in value[9] YRls '000,000	1992 % of total value	1986 labour force	1986 % of labour force
Agriculture	24,144	19.9	1,151,348	56.3
Mining	6,623	5.5	11,771	0.6
Manufacturing	11,738	9.7	94,913	4.6
Public utilities	1,694	1.4	160,952	7.9
Construction	6,098	5.0	32,852	1.6
Transp. and commun.	9,240	7.0	107,011	5.3
Trade	15,794	13.0	248,979	12.2
Finance	7,085	5.8	8,757	0.4
Pub. admin., defense	30,452	25.1	226,054	11.1
Services	1,023	0.8	...	...
Other	7,460[10]	6.1[10]	...	...
TOTAL	121,341	100.0[4]	2,043,237	100.0

Household income and expenditure. Average household size (1986) 5.6; income per household: n.a.; sources of income: n.a.; expenditure: n.a.
Tourism: receipts from visitors (1992) U.S.$47,000,000; expenditures by na-
tionals abroad (1989) U.S.$81,000,000.
Public debt (external, outstanding; 1991): U.S.$5,207,000.
Land use (1992): forested 3.8%; meadows and pastures 30.4%; agricultural
and under permanent cultivation 2.8%; other 63.0%.

Foreign trade[11]

Balance of trade[8]

	1986	1987	1988	1989	1990	1991
YRls '000,000	−10,540	−15,182	−13,344	−10,839	−13,797	−8,582
% of total	93.7%	87.4%	56.9%	44.5%	49.4%	37.7%

Imports (1991): YRls 15,667,000,000 (1987[12]; food and live animals 31.6%,
basic manufactured goods 28.6%, machinery and transport equipment
21.9%, chemical products 9.3%, raw materials 5.8%, beverages and tobacco
2.4%). *Major import sources* (1987)[12]: Japan 12.0%; United States 10.8%;
The Netherlands 10.0%; West Germany 7.1%; France 6.3%; Italy 5.3%;
Saudi Arabia 5.3%.
Exports (1991): YRls 7,084,700,000 (1987[12]; coffee 16.6%, cigarettes 15.6%,
biscuits 13.6%, leather 12.5%, grapes 8.6%, sesame seeds 4.2%). *Major
export destinations* (1987)[12]: Saudi Arabia 53.6%; South Yemen 24.0%; Italy
8.2%; Japan 4.0%.

Transport and communications

Transport. Railroads: none. Roads (1988): total length 39,200 km (paved
5.7%). Vehicles (1993): passenger cars 186,172; trucks and buses 254,355.
Merchant marine (1992): vessels (100 gross tons and over) 40; deadweight
tonnage 13,653. Air transport (1990): passenger-km 1,032,248,000; metric
ton-km cargo 11,661,000; airports (1994) with scheduled flights 11.
Communications. Daily newspapers (1990)[12]: total number 2; total circulation
120,000; circulation per 1,000 population 10. Radio (1993): 325,000 receivers
(1 per 39 persons). Television (1991): 335,000 receivers (1 per 34 persons).
Telephones (1992): 146,000 (1 per 83 persons).

Education and health

Education (1990–91)[12]

	schools	teachers	students	student/ teacher ratio
Primary (age 7–12)	7,313[13]	35,350	1,291,372	36.5
Secondary (age 13–18)	942[14]	12,106	394,578	32.6
Voc., teacher tr.	73[14]	1,247	26,119	20.9
Higher[13]	1	470	23,457	49.9

Educational attainment (1986)[12]. Percentage of population age 10 and over
having: no formal schooling 74.2%; reading and writing ability 19.8%; primary education 4.0%; secondary education 0.6%; higher 0.6%; not specified
0.8%. *Literacy* (1990): percentage of total population age 15 and over literate
38.5%; males literate 53.3%; females literate 26.3%.
Health (1986): physicians 1,886 (1 per 5,531 persons); hospital beds 10,485 (1
per 995 persons); infant mortality rate per 1,000 live births (1992) 114.8.
Food (1986–88): daily per capita caloric intake 2,284 (vegetable products 90%,
animal products 10%); 94% of FAO recommended minimum requirement.

Military

Total active duty personnel (1994): 66,000 (army 92.4%, navy 2.3%, air force
5.3%). *Military expenditure as percentage of GNP* (1991): 15.7% (world 5.0%);
per capita expenditure U.S.$89.

[1]Presidential Council assisting the President was abolished per constitutional amendment of September 1994. [2]Based on North Yemen's 1986 census results and South
Yemen's 1986 estimates. [3]Former North Yemeni territorial claims with regard to
alignment of the long-undemarcated eastern boundary with Saudi Arabia (which
increased Yemen's claimed total area to 205,356 sq mi [531,869 sq km]) are under
negotiation with Saudi Arabia in 1994. [4]Detail does not add to total given because
of rounding. [5]Based on the higher total area estimate of 205,356 sq mi (531,869 sq
km). [6]1984. [7]Democratic Republic of Yemen only. [8]Urban areas only. [9]In purchasers'
value at current prices. [10]Includes import duties of 7.9 million Yemeni rials less
imputed bank service charges. [11]Imports are f.o.b. [12]Yemen Arab Republic only.
[13]1988–89. [14]1985–86.

Yugoslavia

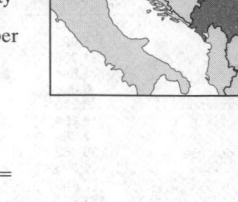

Official name: Savezna Republika
 Jugoslavija (Federal Republic of
 Yugoslavia).
Form of government: federal multiparty
 republic with two legislative houses
 (Chamber of Republics [40]; Chamber
 of Citizens [138]).
Chief of state: Federal President.
Head of government: Prime Minister.
Capital: Belgrade.
Official language: Serbo-Croatian.
Official religion: none.
Monetary unit[1]: 1 new dinar (second) =
 100 paras; valuation (Sept. 26, 1994)
 1 U.S.$ = 1.56 new dinars (second);
 1 £ = 2.47 new dinars (second).

Area and population		area		population
		sq mi	sq km	1993 estimate
Republics	**Capitals**			
Montenegro	Podgorica	5,333	13,812	626,000
Serbia	Belgrade	21,609	55,968	5,809,000
Autonomous provinces[2]				
Kosovo and Metohia	Priština	4,203	10,887	2,043,000
Vojvodina	Novi Sad	8,304	21,506	2,002,000
TOTAL		39,449	102,173	10,480,000

Demography

Population (1994): 10,515,000.
Density (1994): persons per sq mi 266.5, persons per sq km 102.9.
Urban-rural (1991): urban 52.0%; rural 48.0%.
Sex distribution (1991): male 49.6%; female 50.4%.
Age breakdown (1991): under 15, 22.8%; 15–29, 21.6%; 30–44, 21.7%; 45–59,
 17.1%; 60–74, 12.2%; 75 and over, 3.5%; unknown, 1.1%.
Population projection: (2000) 10,724,000; (2010) 11,084,000.
Doubling time: not applicable; doubling time exceeds 100 years.
Ethnic composition (1991): Serb 62.3%; Albanian 16.6%; Montenegrin 5.0%;
 Yugoslav 3.3%; Hungarian 3.3%; Muslim 3.1%; Croat 1.1%; other 5.3%.
Religious affiliation (1991): most believers are affiliated with the Serbian
 Orthodox Church; there are also Muslim, Roman Catholic, and Protes-
 tant minorities.
Major cities (1993): Belgrade 1,168,454; Novi Sad 179,626; Niš 175,391; Kragu-
 jevac 147,305; Subotica 100,386.

Vital statistics

Birth rate per 1,000 population (1992): 13.5 (world avg. 26.0).
Death rate per 1,000 population (1992): 10.1 (world avg. 9.2).
Natural increase rate per 1,000 population (1992): 3.4 (world avg. 16.8).
Total fertility rate (avg. births per childbearing woman; 1991): 2.1.
Marriage rate per 1,000 population (1992): 6.1.
Divorce rate per 1,000 population (1992): 0.6.
Life expectancy at birth (1991): male 69.0 years; female 74.6 years.
Major causes of death per 100,000 population (1992): diseases of the circula-
 tory system 528.3; malignant neoplasms (cancers) 154.7; accidents, violence,
 and poisoning 56.6; diseases of the respiratory system 47.2; diseases of the
 digestive system 26.4.

National economy

Budget (1993). Revenue: Din 30,353,000,000[3] (social security tax 50.9%,
 turnover tax 20.9%, income tax 9.7%). Expenditure[4] Din 30,353,000,000[3]
 (social security 50.9%, current transfers 46.6%).
Land use (1990): forested 29.5%; meadows and pastures 20.7%; agricultural
 and under permanent cultivation 35.7%; other 14.1%.
Production (metric tons except as noted). Agriculture, forestry, fishing (1993):
 corn (maize) 4,004,000, wheat 3,049,000, potatoes 591,000, plums 509,000,
 grapes 397,000; livestock (number of live animals) 4,092,000 pigs, 2,752,000
 sheep, 1,991,000 cattle, 23,293,000 poultry; roundwood (1993) 1,755,000 cu
 m; fish catch (1991) 36,511. Mining and quarrying (1993): copper ore 18,189,-
 000; lead-zinc ore 337,000; lime 318,000; bauxite 102,000; magnesite 55,000;
 salt 39,000; aluminum and ingots 25,778; asbestos ore 9,000; refined silver
 25,144 kg. Manufacturing (1993): wheat flour 986,000; crude steel 183,000;
 nitric acid 116,000; sulfuric acid 75,000; canned fruit 65,000; electrolytic
 copper 51,300; welded pipes 31,000; rolled aluminum 11,000; canned meat
 10,000; cotton yarn 10,000; rolled copper 10,000; medicines 9,500; refined
 lead 6,000; linoleum flooring 5,000; knitted clothing 4,103; woolen fabrics
 16,380,000 sq m; parquet flooring 826,000 cu m; liquor 27,628,000 hectolitres;
 hosiery 19,000,000 pairs; leather footwear 10,435,000 pairs; furniture 961,000
 units; kitchen ranges 119,000 units; refrigerators 39,000 units; television receivers 24,000 units; gasoline engines 15,000 units; telephones 14,000 units;
 bicycles 11,000 units; automobiles 8,000 units; tractors 5,000 units; radios
 642 units; trucks 278 units; railway-goods cars 50 units. Construction (residential units constructed; 1993): 20,013. Energy production (consumption):
 electricity (kW-hr; 1992) 36,488,000,000 (38,088,000,000); coal (metric tons;
 1992) 40,105,000 (41,102,000); crude petroleum (barrels; 1992) 8,539,000,000
 (23,199,000); petroleum products (metric tons; 1992) 1,983,000 (2,288,000);
 natural gas (cu m; 1992) 772,000,000 (1,984,000,000).
Household income and expenditure. Average household size (1992) 3.6; income per household (1992) Din 1,155,094[3] (U.S.$1,540); sources of income
 (1992): wages and salaries 53.1%, transfer payments 15.3%, self-employment
 9.3%, other 22.3%; expenditure (1992): food 48.0%, clothing and footwear

8.6%, fuel and light 7.3%, beverages and tobacco 7.3%, transportation
 and communications 4.9%, health care 3.9%, housing 3.8%, education and
 entertainment 2.9%, household durable goods 2.2%.
Gross national product (1990)[5]: U.S.$31,867,000,000 (U.S.$3,093 per capita).

Structure of gross material product and labour force				
	1992		1993	
	in value Din '000,000[3]	% of total value	labour force	% of labour force
Agriculture	1,220,080	19.5	126,000	3.9
Mining	2,548,855	40.7	916,000	28.5
Manufacturing }				
Construction	443,988	7.1	159,000	5.0
Public utilities	65,739	1.0	50,000	1.6
Transp. and commun.	339,443	5.4	152,000	4.7
Trade	1,414,012	22.5	326,000	10.1
Finance			85,000	2.6
Pub. admin., defense	235,714	3.8	91,000	2.8
Services }			350,000	10.9
Other			960,000[6]	29.9[6]
TOTAL	6,267,831	100.0	3,215,000	100.0

Population economically active (1993): total 3,215,000; activity rate 30.6% (participation rates: ages 15–64, n.a.; female [1992] 45.3%; unemployed 23.0%).

Price and earnings indexes (1990 = 100)							
	1986	1987	1988	1989	1990[3]	1991[3]	1992[3]
Consumer price index	0.0	0.2	0.9	13	100	324	...
Monthly earnings index[7]	0.2	0.4	1	19	100	195	295

Tourism (1992): receipts from visitors U.S.$88,000,000; expenditures, n.a.

Foreign trade

Balance of trade (current prices)						
	1987	1988	1989	1990	1991	1992
Din '000,000[3]	−1,465	−1,315	−1,887	−3,750	−1,825	−4,036
% of total	8.3%	6.9%	9.5%	13.9%	8.6%	28.4%

Imports (1991): Din 104,591,000,000[3] (machinery and transport equipment
 22.7%, of which road vehicles 6.8%; mineral fuels and lubricants 19.0%;
 chemicals 13.7%; manufactured goods 10.4%, of which textiles 3.2%; food
 and live animals 8.4%, of which beverages 0.8%). *Major import sources:* Germany 20.2%; former U.S.S.R. 12.6%; Italy 10.6%; U.S. 4.1%; Austria 3.9%.
Exports (1991): Din 89,707,000,000[3] (manufactured goods 49.9%, of which
 clothing 14.2%, iron and steel 5.4%, textile products 4.3%; machinery and
 transport equipment 19.6%; food and live animals 11.8%, of which fruits
 and vegetables 3.7%; chemicals 9.1%). *Major export destinations:* Germany
 23.1%; former U.S.S.R. 17.8%; Italy 14.0%; U.S. 4.4%; Romania 4.3%.

Transport and communications

Transport. Railroads (1993): length 2,460 mi, 3,960 km; passenger-mi 1,802,-
 000,000; passenger-km 2,901,000,000; short ton-mi cargo 1,055,000,000, metric ton-km cargo 1,698,000,000. Roads (1992): total length 29,771 mi, 47,912
 km (paved 59%). Vehicles (1991): passenger cars 1,406,000; trucks and buses
 132,100. Merchant marine (1992): fishing vessels 12. Air transport: (1993):
 passenger-mi 65,000,000, passenger-km 104,000,000, short ton-mi cargo 74,-
 000,000, metric ton-km cargo 119,000,000; airports (1994) 5.
Communications. Daily newspapers (1990)[5]: total number 12; total circulation 1,006,000; circulation per 1,000 population 98. Radio (1993): 2,692,000
 receivers (1 per 3.9 persons). Television (1989): 1,642,522 receivers (1 per
 4.8 persons). Telephones (1992): 2,159,000 (1 per 4.8 persons).

Education and health

Education (1992–93)				
	schools	teachers	students	student/ teacher ratio
Primary (age 7–14)	4,433	51,489	945,237	18.4
Secondary (age 15–18)	539	25,580	359,568	14.1
Higher	141	11,586[8]	142,372[8]	12.2

Educational attainment (1981)[5]. Percentage of population age 15 and over
 having: less than full primary education 44.6%; primary 24.4%; secondary
 24.7%; postsecondary and higher 5.7%. *Literacy* (1981)[5]: total population
 age 10 and over literate 7,411,500 (89.2%); males literate 4,236,900 (95.4%;
 females literate 3,174,600 (83.2%).
Health (1992): physicians (1991) 25,873 (1 per 402 persons); hospital beds
 58,339 (1 per 179 persons); infant mortality rate per 1,000 live births 21.7.
Food (1990)[5]: daily per capita caloric intake 3,545 (1988–90; vegetable products 93%, animal products 7%); 140% of FAO recommended minimum.

Military

Total active duty personnel (1994): 126,500 (army 71.2%, air force 22.9%, navy
 5.9%). *Military expenditure as percentage of government expenditure:* 76.6%.

---

[1]Yugoslavia experienced extreme hyperinflation between early 1993 and January 1994.
The new dinar (second), or "super dinar," introduced on Jan. 24, 1994, was pegged to
the German Mark at a rate of one-to-one and equaled 13,000,000,000,000,000,000,000
new dinars. The new dinar had been introduced Jan. 1, 1990, at the rate of 1 new
dinar = 10,000 (old) dinars. Inflation was close to zero between January 1994 and
September 1994. [2]The autonomous provinces are administratively part of the Republic
of Serbia. [3]In new dinars before extreme hyperinflation. [4]External analysts estimate
defense expenditure at 76.7% of government expenditure. [5]Data refer to Yugoslavia
as constituted prior to 1991. [6]Includes 220,000 workers in the private sector. [7]Based
on worker nominal net personal income. [8]Number of teachers and students is reduced
because of a boycott of Serbian schools by Albanians.

Zaire

Official name: République du Zaïre
(Republic of Zaire).
Form of government: Transitional
regime[1].
Chief of state: President[1].
Head of government: Prime Minister[1].
Capital: Kinshasa.
Official language: French.
Official religion: none.
Monetary unit: new zaïre (NZ)[2];
valuation (Oct. 7, 1994)
1 U.S.$ = NZ 2,022;
1 £ = NZ 3,216.

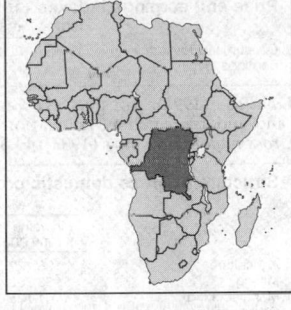

Area and population

Regions	Capitals	area sq mi	area sq km	population 1991 estimate
Bandundu	Bandundu	114,154	295,658	4,458,000
Bas-Zaïre	Matadi	20,819	53,920	2,357,000
Equateur	Mbandaka	155,712	403,292	4,022,000
Haute-Zaïre	Kisangani	194,302	503,239	5,017,000
Kasai-Occidental	Kananga	59,746	154,742	2,502,000
Kasai-Oriental	Mbuji-Mayi	65,754	170,302	2,851,000
Kinshasa	—	3,848	9,965	3,919,000
Maniema	Kindu	51,062	132,250	926,000
Nord-Kivu	Goma	22,967	59,483	3,089,000
Shaba	Lubumbashi	191,845	496,877	4,771,000
Sud-Kivu	Bukavu	25,147	65,130	2,758,000
TOTAL		905,354[3]	2,344,858	36,672,000[3]

Demography

Population (1994): 43,775,000.
Density (1994): persons per sq mi 48.4, persons per sq km 18.7.
Urban-rural (1985): urban 44.2%; rural 55.8%.
Sex distribution (1990): male 49.28%; female 50.72%.
Age breakdown (1985): under 15, 45.2%; 15–29, 26.0%; 30–44, 15.5%; 45–59, 8.7%; 60–74, 3.9%; 75 and over, 0.7%.
Population projection: (2000) 52,644,000; (2010) 70,841,000.
Doubling time: 22 years.
Ethnic composition (1983): Luba 18.0%; Kongo 16.1%; Mongo 13.5%; Rwanda 10.3%; Azande 6.1%; Bangi and Ngale 5.8%; Rundi 3.8%; Teke 2.7%; Boa 2.3%; Chokwe 1.8%; Lugbara 1.6%; Banda 1.4%; other 16.6%.
Religious affiliation (1980): Roman Catholic 48.4%; Protestant 29.0%; indigenous Christian 17.1%; traditional beliefs 3.4%; Muslim 1.4%; other 0.7%.
Major cities (1991): Kinshasa 3,804,000; Lubumbashi 739,082; Mbuji-Mayi 613,027; Kisangani 373,397; Kananga 371,862.

Vital statistics

Birth rate per 1,000 population (1990–95): 45.3 (world avg. 26.0).
Death rate per 1,000 population (1990–95): 13.0 (world avg. 9.2).
Natural increase rate per 1,000 population (1990–95): 32.3 (world avg. 16.8).
Total fertility rate (avg. births per childbearing woman; 1990–95): 6.1.
Marriage rate per 1,000 population: n.a.
Divorce rate per 1,000 population: n.a.
Life expectancy at birth (1990–95): male 52.3 years; female 55.7 years.
Major causes of death per 100,000 population (1977)[4]: measles 9.6; meningitis 1.1; influenza 0.4; whooping cough 0.3.

National economy

Budget (1992–93). Revenue: Z 3,513,084,000,000,000,000[5] (1991; revenue from mining 30.4%, external trade taxes 26.8%, income tax 18.6%, petroleum tax 15.8%, other revenue 8.4%). Expenditures: Z 4,525,450,000,000,000,000[5] (1991; service of external and internal debt 28.4%, capital expenditure 20.5%, administration 20.0%).
Tourism (1990): receipts from visitors U.S.$7,000,000; expenditures by nationals abroad U.S.$16,000,000.
Production (metric tons except as noted). Agriculture, forestry, fishing (1993): cassava 20,835,000, plantains 2,291,000, sugarcane 1,400,000, corn (maize) 1,201,000, peanuts (groundnuts) 604,000, rice 458,000, bananas 406,000, sweet potatoes 385,000, yams 315,000, mangoes 212,000, papayas 210,000, palm oil 181,000, oranges 156,000, pineapples 145,000, dry beans 123,000, coffee 78,000, seed cotton 77,000, palm kernels 72,000, dry peas 64,000, avocados 47,000, tomatoes 41,000, onions 32,000, cabbage 30,000, natural rubber 5,000; livestock (number of live animals) 4,120,000 goats, 1,650,000 cattle, 1,130,000 pigs, 985,000 sheep, 35,000,000 chickens; roundwood (1992) 43,243,000 cu m; fish catch (1992) 150,000. Mining and quarrying (1993): copper 46,372; zinc 4,158; cobalt 2,174; cassiterite 1,002; gold 389 kg; diamonds 15,327,000 carats. Manufacturing (1990): cement 457,000; sulfuric acid 164,000; sugar 70,000; soap 47,109; animal feedstuff 20,000; explosives 19,500; plastics 7,586[6]; iron and steel products 5,875; paint 2,458; medicine 45[6]; printed fabrics 44,370,000 sq m; cigarettes 5,236,000,000 units; tires 102,000 units; bicycles 5,830 units; automobiles 2,038 units; beer 4,590,000 hectolitres; carbonated beverages 1,923,000 hectolitres; leather shoes 2,954,-000 pairs. Construction (1985): residential 20,000 sq m; nonresidential 39,000 sq m. Energy production (consumption): electricity (kW-hr; 1992) 6,180,000 (5,984,000); coal (metric tons; 1992) 128,000 (170,000); crude petroleum (barrels; 1992) 10,080,000 (2,750,000); petroleum products (metric tons; 1992) 346,000 (1,012,000); natural gas, none (n.a.).
Household income and expenditure. Average household size (1982) 6.0; average annual income per household Z 1,200 (U.S.$209); sources of income: n.a.; expenditure (1985): food 61.7%, housing and energy 11.5%, clothing and footwear 9.7%, transportation 5.9%, furniture and utensils 4.9%, medical care 2.6%, recreation and education 2.0%.
Gross national product (1991): U.S.$8,123,000,000 (U.S.$220 per capita).

Structure of gross domestic product and labour force

	1991 in value Z '000,000	1991 % of total value	labour force	% of labour force
Agriculture	197,903	31.4	9,021,000	65.1
Mining	152,327	24.2		
Manufacturing	8,636	1.4		
Construction	34,874	5.5	2,200,000	15.9
Public utilities	394	0.1		
Transp. and commun.	5,047	0.0		
Trade	110,356	17.5		
Finance	18,316	2.9		
Pub. admin., defense	60,830	9.7	2,627,000	19.0
Services	42,010	0.7		
Other	−1,328	−0.2		
TOTAL	629,374	100.0	13,848,000	100.0

Public debt (external, outstanding; 1992): U.S.$8,895,000,000.
Population economically active (1991): total 13,848,000; activity rate 35.9% (participation rates [1987]: over age 10, 57.4%; female 40.8%; unemployed, n.a.).

Price and earnings indexes (1990 = 1)

	1987	1988	1989	1990	1991	1992	1993
Consumer price index	0.14	0.27	0.55	1	23	953	19,897
Earnings index	...	...	...	...	...	...	...

Land use (1992): forested 76.7%; meadows and pastures 6.6%; agricultural and under permanent cultivation 3.5%; other 13.2%.

Foreign trade

Balance of trade (current prices)

	1987	1988	1989	1990	1991	1992
NZ⁰	+12.1	+28.9	+66.3	+56.0	+1,128.2	+13,882.4
% of total	19.9%	26.1%	26.3%	13.3%	15.1%	8.2%

Imports (1990): NZ 368,800 (machinery and transport equipment 31.7%, basic manufactures 21.1%, food and live animals 19.6%, chemicals 10.2%, mineral fuels 7.5%). *Major import sources* (1991): Belgium-Luxembourg 21.2%; France 12.4%; Germany 11.6%; China 7.0%; U.S. 6.8%; The Netherlands 4.9%; Italy 4.5%.
Exports (1990): NZ 512,400 (copper 47.6%, diamonds 11.4%, crude petroleum 10.8%, coffee 5.7%). *Major export destinations* (1991): Belgium-Luxembourg 44.7%; U.S. 18.3%; Germany 8.4%; Italy 5.8%; Japan 5.5%; France 2.6%; Canada 2.2%.

Transport and communications

Transport. Railroads (1991)[7]: length 3,162 mi, 5,088 km; passenger-mi 360,-000,000, passenger-km 580,000,000; short ton-mi cargo 1,258,000,000, metric ton-km cargo 1,836,000,000. Roads (1991): total length 91,200 mi, 146,800 km (paved 2%). Vehicles (1992): passenger cars 105,000; trucks and buses 95,000. Merchant marine (1992): vessels (100 gross tons and over) 27; total deadweight tonnage 30,692. Air transport (1991)[8]: passenger-mi 89,627,000, passenger-km 144,242,000; short ton-mi cargo 14,415,000, metric ton-km cargo 21,046,000; airports (1994) with scheduled flights 11.
Communications. Daily newspapers (1988): total number 7; total circulation 45,000; circulation per 1,000 population 1.4. Radio (1993): 3,400,000 receivers (1 per 12 persons). Television (1993): 22,000 receivers (1 per 1,929 persons). Telephones (1988): 32,116 (1 per 1,144 persons).

Education and health

Education (1987–88)

	schools	teachers	students	student/teacher ratio
Primary (age 6–11)	10,817	113,468[9]	4,356,516	36.6[9]
Secondary (age 12–17)	4,276[10]	49,153[10]	507,944	21.7[10]
Voc., teacher tr.	[10]	[10]	558,407	[10]
Higher	...	3,506	52,800	15.1

Educational attainment: n.a. *Literacy* (1984): percentage of total population age 15 and over literate 38.2%; males literate 57.4%; females literate 20.4%.
Health: physicians (1990) 2,469 (1 per 15,584 persons); hospital beds (1986) 68,508 (1 per 487 persons); infant mortality rate per 1,000 live births (1985–90) 83.
Food (1988–90): daily per capita caloric intake 2,130 (vegetable products 97%, animal products 3%); 96% of FAO recommended minimum requirement.

Military

Total active duty personnel (1994): 28,100 (army 89.0%, navy 4.6%, air force 6.4%). *Military expenditure as percentage of GNP* (1988): 2.6% (world 5.0%); per capita expenditure U.S.$8.

---

[1]Transitional government from April 9, 1994, per promulgation of Transitional Constitutional Act. [2]The new zaïre (NZ) replaced the (old) zaïre (Z) at a rate of 3,000,000 (old) zaïres to 1 NZ on Oct. 22, 1993. [3]Detail does not add to total given because of rounding. [4]Infectious diseases only. [5]Zaire is experiencing hyperinflation. [6]1987. [7]Traffic statistics are for services operated by the Zaire National Railways (SNCZ), which controls more than 90% of the country's total rail facility. [8]Air Zaire only. [9]1986–87. [10]Secondary includes Voc., teacher tr.

Zambia

Official name: Republic of Zambia.
Form of government: multiparty
  republic with one legislative house
  (National Assembly [151[1]]).
Head of state and government:
  President.
Capital: Lusaka.
Official language: English.
Official religion: none.
Monetary unit: 1 Zambian kwacha
  (K) = 100 ngwee; valuation (Oct.
  7, 1994) 1 U.S.$ = K 671;
  1 £ = K 1,067.

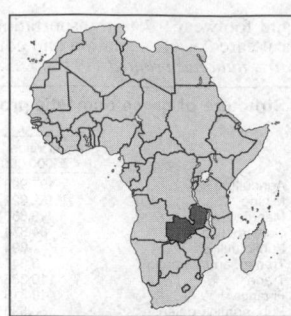

Area and population		area		population
		sq mi	sq km	1990 census
Provinces	Capitals			
Central	Kabwe	36,446	94,395	725,611
Copperbelt	Ndola	12,096	31,328	1,579,542
Eastern	Chipata	26,682	69,106	973,818
Luapula	Mansa	19,524	50,567	526,705
Lusaka	Lusaka	8,454	21,896	1,207,980
Northern	Kasama	57,076	147,826	867,795
North-Western	Solwezi	48,582	125,827	383,146
Southern	Livingstone	32,928	85,283	946,353
Western	Mongu	48,798	126,386	607,497
TOTAL		290,586	752,614	7,818,447

Demography

Population (1994): 9,132,000.
Density (1994): persons per sq mi 31.4, persons per sq km 12.1.
Urban-rural (1992): urban 42.4%; rural 57.6%.
Sex distribution (1990): male 49.16%; female 50.84%.
Age breakdown (1990): under 15, 48.4%; 15–29, 27.2%; 30–44, 13.7%; 45–59, 7.0%; 60–74, 3.1%; 75 and over, 0.6%.
Population projection: (2000) 10,672,000; (2010) 13,885,000.
Doubling time: 19 years.
Ethnolinguistic composition (1980): Bemba peoples 36.2%; Maravi (Nyanja) peoples 17.6%; Tonga peoples 15.1%; North-Western peoples 10.1%; Barotze peoples 8.2%; Mambwe peoples 4.6%; Tumbuka peoples 4.6%; other 3.6%.
Religious affiliation (1980): Christian 72.0%, of which Protestant 34.2%, Roman Catholic 26.2%, African Christian 8.3%; traditional beliefs 27.0%; Muslim 0.3%; other 0.7%.
Major cities (1990): Lusaka 982,362; Ndola 376,311; Kitwe 348,571; Mufulira 175,025.

Vital statistics

Birth rate per 1,000 population (1990–95): 50.3 (world avg. 26.0); legitimate, n.a.; however, marriage is both early and universal, suggesting that legitimate births are a relatively high proportion of all births.
Death rate per 1,000 population (1990–95): 12.4 (world avg. 9.2).
Natural increase rate per 1,000 population (1990–95): 37.9 (world avg. 16.8).
Total fertility rate (avg. births per childbearing woman; 1990–95): 7.2.
Marriage rate per 1,000 population: n.a.
Divorce rate per 1,000 population: n.a.
Life expectancy at birth (1993): male 45.0 years; female 46.2 years.
Major causes of death per 100,000 population: n.a.; almost two-thirds of the reported illnesses are related to nutritional deficiencies and infectious and parasitic diseases.

National economy

Budget (1994). Revenue: K 686,600,000,000 (1992; customs duties and excise taxes 62.6%, income tax 24.8%, mineral revenue 5.4%). Expenditures: K 686,600,000,000 (current expenditures 67.3%, capital expenditures 32.7%).
Production (metric tons except as noted). Agriculture, forestry, fishing (1993): corn (maize) 1,598,000, sugarcane 1,300,000, cassava 570,000, fruits and vegetables 363,000 (of which onions 26,000, tomatoes 26,000, oranges 4,000), wheat 71,000, seed cotton 58,000, sweet potatoes 56,000, peanuts (groundnuts) 42,000, millet 37,000, sorghum 35,000, soybeans 28,000, sunflower seeds 21,000, tobacco 7,000; livestock (number of live animals) 3,204,000 cattle, 600,000 goats, 293,000 pigs, 67,000 sheep, 21,000,000 chickens; roundwood (1992) 13,790,000 cu m; fish catch (1991) 65,945. Mining and quarrying (1993): copper 432,206; zinc 7,287; cobalt 4,797; lead 3,003; silver 20,972 kg; gold 8,713 troy oz. Manufacturing (1992): smelter copper 483,700; refined copper 441,600; cement 372,000[2]; sulfuric acid 276,000[3]; raw sugar 147,000[4]; refined zinc 7,320; refined lead 3,600; cigarettes 1,500,000,000 units[4]. Construction (value in K; 1985): buildings 151,100,000; other construction 43,200,000. Energy production (consumption): electricity (kW-hr; 1992) 7,780,000,000 (6,300,000,000); coal (metric tons; 1992) 395,000 (674,000); crude petroleum (barrels; 1992) none (3,995,000); petroleum products (metric tons; 1992) 502,000 (440,000); natural gas, none (n.a.).
Household income and expenditure. Average household size (1981) 5.8; average annual income per household (1981) K 1,041 (U.S.$908); sources of income (1981): wages and salaries 94.0%, other 6.0%; expenditure (1977): food 37.7%, housing 11.0%, clothing 8.3%, transportation 4.3%, education 2.1%, health 1.0%.
Population economically active (1990): total 2,716,000; activity rate of total population 34.9% (participation rates: ages 15–64, 60.1%[5]; female 28.2%[5]; unemployed 17.4%[6]).

Price and earnings indexes (1990 = 100)

Price and earnings indexes (1990 = 100)	1987	1988	1989	1990	1991	1992	1993
Consumer price index	13.0	20.2	46.0	100.0	192.6	572.8	1,655.4
Earnings index	...	...	...	...	...	...	...

Land use (1992): forested 38.6%; meadows and pastures 40.4%; agricultural and under permanent cultivation 7.1%; other 13.9%.
Gross national product (1993): U.S.$3,155,000,000 (U.S.$370 per capita).

Structure of gross domestic product and labour force				
	1991		1990	
	in value K '000,000	% of total value	labour force	% of labour force
Agriculture	28,132	12.8	1,872,000	68.9
Mining	33,755	15.3	56,800	2.1
Manufacturing	61,725	28.0	50,900	1.9
Construction	10,911	5.0	29,100	1.1
Public utilities	1,909	0.9	8,900	0.3
Transportation and communications	15,812	7.2	25,600	0.9
Trade	24,021	10.9	30,700	1.1
Finance	24,832	11.3	24,200	0.9
Public admin., defense } Services	19,254	8.7	111,600	4.1
Other	...	...	506,100	18.6
TOTAL	220,351	100.0[7]	2,716,000[7]	100.0[7]

Public debt (external, outstanding; 1992): U.S.$4,809,000,000.
Tourism (1992): receipts from visitors U.S.$51,000,000; expenditures by nationals abroad U.S.$56,000,000.

Foreign trade

Balance of trade (current prices)						
	1987	1988	1989	1990	1991	1992
K '000,000	+1,431.1	+2,888.1	+5,833.5	+2,589.6	+17,884.6	−14,633
% of total	9.7%	17.3%	18.8%	3.4%	14.7%	5.3%

Imports (1990): K 27,307,900,000 (1988; machinery and transport equipment 38.3%; basic manufactures 19.8%; chemicals 16.9%; mineral fuels, lubricants, and electricity 12.3%; food 3.8%). *Major import sources:* South Africa 16.9%; United Kingdom 12.2%; Germany 11.6%; United States 10.2%; Japan 6.7%.
Exports (1990): K 33,802,600,000 (1988; copper 85.2%; cobalt 6.1%; zinc 1.6%; tobacco 0.3%; lead 0.2%). *Major export destinations:* Japan 31.0%; France 13.6%; Thailand 6.8%; India 6.1%; Belgium-Luxembourg 5.8%.

Transport and communications

Transport. Railroads (1993): length 791 mi, 1,273 km; passenger-mi 166,690,000[4], passenger-km 268,262,000[4]; short ton-mi cargo 735,600,000, metric ton-km cargo 1,074,000. Roads (1992): total length 23,214 mi, 37,359 km (paved 18%). Vehicles (1992): passenger cars 100,000; trucks and buses 75,000. Merchant marine: vessels (100 gross tons and over) none. Air transport (1992): passenger-mi 313,000,000, passenger-km 504,000,000; short ton-mi cargo 11,425,000, metric ton-km cargo 16,680,000; airports (1994) with scheduled flights 8.
Communications. Daily newspapers (1990): total number 2; total circulation 105,000; circulation per 1,000 population 13. Radio (1993): total number of receivers 1,660,380 (1 per 5.4 persons). Television (1993): total number of receivers 200,000 (1 per 44 persons). Telephones (1992): 112,630 (1 per 77 persons).

Education and health

Education (1989)	schools	teachers	students	student/ teacher ratio
Primary (age 7–13)	3,489	32,348[3]	1,446,847	44.1[3]
Secondary (age 14–18)	480	5,786[3]	161,349[3]	27.9[3]
Voc., teacher tr.	26	846	8,218	9.7
Higher	2	320	6,247	19.5

Educational attainment (1980). Percentage of population age 25 and over having: no formal schooling 54.7%; some primary education 34.4%; some secondary 10.5%; higher 0.4%. *Literacy* (1990): population age 15 and over literate 3,131,000 (72.8%); males literate 1,676,000 (80.8%); females literate 1,455,000 (65.3%).
Health: physicians (1984) 798 (1 per 8,437 persons); hospital beds (1989) 22,461 (1 per 349 persons); infant mortality rate per 1,000 live births (1990–95) 72.0.
Food (1988–90): daily per capita caloric intake 2,016 (vegetable products 95%, animal products 5%); 87% of FAO recommended minimum requirement.

Military

Total active duty personnel (1994): 23,820 (army 87.4%; navy, none; air force 6.7%; paramilitary 5.9%). *Military expenditure as percentage of GNP* (1990): 2.4% (world 4.5%); per capita expenditure U.S.$10.

---

[1]President may appoint a maximum of 8 additional members. [2]1991. [3]1988. [4]1990. [5]1985. [6]1987. [7]Detail does not add to total given because of rounding.

Zimbabwe

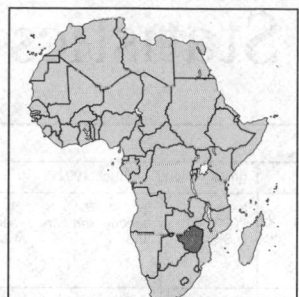

Official name: Republic of Zimbabwe.
Form of government: multiparty republic with one legislative house (House of Assembly [150[1]]).
Head of state and government: President.
Capital: Harare.
Official language: English.
Official religion: none.
Monetary unit: 1 Zimbabwe dollar (Z$) = 100 cents; valuation (Oct. 7, 1994) 1 U.S.$ = Z$8.36; 1 £ = Z$13.30.

Area and population		area		population
		sq mi	sq km	1992 census[2]
Provinces	**Capitals**			
Bulawayo	—	185	479	620,936
Harare	—	337	872	1,478,810
Manicaland	Mutare	14,077	36,459	1,537,676
Mashonaland Central	Bindura	10,945	28,347	857,318
Mashonaland East	Marondera	12,444	32,230	1,033,336
Mashonaland West	Chinhoyi	22,178	57,441	1,116,928
Masvingo	Masvingo	21,840	56,566	1,221,845
Matabeleland North	...	28,967	75,025	640,957
Matabeleland South	Gwanda	20,916	54,172	591,747
Midlands	Gweru	18,983	49,166	1,302,214
TOTAL		150,872	390,757	10,401,767

Demography

Population (1994): 10,971,000.
Density (1994): persons per sq mi 72.7, persons per sq km 28.1.
Urban-rural (1988): urban 26.4%; rural 73.6%.
Sex distribution (1992): male 48.80%; female 51.20%.
Age breakdown (1990): under 15, 45.5%; 15–29, 28.3%; 30–44, 15.1%; 45–59, 7.2%; 60–74, 3.1%; 75 and over, 0.8%.
Population projection: (2000) 13,194,000; (2010) 16,808,000.
Doubling time: 23 years.
Ethnolinguistic composition (1982): African 97.6%, of which Shona-speaking Bantu 70.8%, Ndebele-speaking Bantu 15.8%; European 2.0%; Asian 0.1%; other 0.3%.
Religious affiliation (1980): Christian 44.8%, of which Protestant (including Anglican) 17.5%, African indigenous 13.6%, Roman Catholic 11.7%; animist 40.4%; other 14.8%.
Major cities (1992): Harare 1,184,169; Bulawayo 620,936; Chitungwiza 274,035; Mutare 131,808; Gweru 124,735.

Vital statistics

Birth rate per 1,000 population (1990–95): 40.6 (world avg. 26.0).
Death rate per 1,000 population (1990–95): 11.0 (world avg. 9.2).
Natural increase rate per 1,000 population (1990–95): 29.6 (world avg. 16.8).
Total fertility rate (avg. births per childbearing woman; 1992): 4.6.
Marriage rate per 1,000 population: n.a.
Divorce rate per 1,000 population: n.a.
Life expectancy at birth (1990–95): male 54.4 years; female 57.3 years.
Major causes of death per 100,000 population: n.a.; major causes of death include malnutrition, measles, pneumonia, malaria, and diarrheal diseases.

National economy

Budget (1993–94). Revenue: Z$13,300,000,000 (income tax 45.6%; customs duties 16.2%; sales tax 15.3%; revenue from investments and property 6.5%; international grants 5.3%; excise tax 3.8%). Expenditures: Z$14,684,870,000 (recurrent expenditures 78.7%, of which goods and services 48.7%, transfer payments 29.9%).
Population economically active (1986–87): total 3,260,000; activity rate of total population 38.3% (participation rates: over age 15, 76.5%; female 36.6%; unemployed 7.2%[3]).

Price and earnings indexes (1985 = 100)							
	1987	1988	1989	1990	1991	1992	1993
Consumer price index	128.6	138.1	155.9	183.0	227.5	332.7	409.1
Monthly earnings index	139.5	134.3	173.9	...	...	...	...

Production (metric tons except as noted). Agriculture, forestry, fishing (1993): corn (maize) 2,562,000, sugarcane 700,000, wheat 300,000, tobacco leaves 205,000, vegetables (including melons) 140,000, cottonseed 119,000, sorghum 90,000, soybeans 65,000, peanuts (groundnuts) 64,000; livestock (number of live animals) 4,000,000 cattle, 2,500,000 goats, 530,000 sheep, 270,000 pigs, 12,000,000 chickens; roundwood (1992) 8,033,000 cu m; fish catch (1991) 22,155 metric tons. Mining and quarrying (value of production in Z$; 1993): gold 1,393,240,000; asbestos 475,681,000; coal 404,771,000; nickel 369,141,000; copper 87,761,000; chrome 54,878,000. Manufacturing (value in Z$; 1990): metals and metal products 2,355,800,000; foodstuffs 2,145,200,000; chemicals and petroleum products 1,721,300,000; textiles 1,293,400,000; beverages and tobacco 1,197,100,000; clothing and footwear 836,500,000; paper, printing, and publishing 734,500,000; transport equipment 549,700,000; wood and furniture 357,100,000; nonmetallic mineral products 306,400,000; other manufactured goods 127,600,000. Construction (Z$; 1992): residential 364,428,000; commercial 332,968,000; industrial 148,830,000. Energy production (consumption): electricity (kW-hr; 1992) 9,000,000,000 (10,520,000,000); coal (metric tons; 1992) 6,000,000 (5,880,000); crude petroleum, none (none);

petroleum products (metric tons; 1991) none (836,000); natural gas, none (none).
Public debt (external, outstanding; 1992): U.S.$2,783,000,000.
Household income and expenditure. Average household size (1992) 4.8; income per household Z$1,689 (U.S.$2,628); sources of income: n.a.; expenditure (1987): food, beverages, and tobacco 30.1%, household durable goods 11.1%, clothing, footwear, and textiles 10.3%, energy 7.3%, housing 6.5%, transportation 6.1%, education 6.0%, health service 3.8%, recreation 0.6%.
Gross national product (1992): U.S.$5,896,000,000 (U.S.$670 per capita).

Structure of gross domestic product and labour force				
	1992			
	in value Z$'000,000	% of total value	labour force[4]	% of labour force[4]
Agriculture	5,692	22.1	292,100	23.9
Mining	1,226	4.8	49,300	4.0
Manufacturing	7,760	30.2	199,200	16.3
Construction	499	1.9	92,700	7.6
Public utilities	687	2.7	8,900	0.7
Transp. and commun.	1,865	7.3	51,500	4.2
Trade	2,145	8.3	98,700	8.1
Finance	1,271	5.0	16,600	1.4
Pub. admin., defense	1,311	5.1 }	412,500	33.8
Services	2,569	10.0 }		
Other	681[5]	2.6[5]	...	...
TOTAL	25,706	100.0	1,221,500	100.0

Land use (1992): forested 49.1%; meadows and pastures 12.5%; agricultural and under permanent cultivation 7.4%; other 31.0%.
Tourism (1992): receipts from visitors U.S.$105,000,000.

Foreign trade

Balance of trade (current prices)						
	1986	1987	1988	1989	1990	1991
Z$'000,000	529.9	629.7	896.5	...	−296.8	−1,867.4
% of total	13.9%	15.3%	17.8%	...	3.4%	14.4%

Imports (1992): Z$11,232,300,000 (machinery and transport equipment 35.9%, of which transport equipment 8.9%; manufactured goods 14.4%, of which paper and paperboard 1.6%, bars, rods, and sections 1.0%; fuels 12.1%, of which petroleum products 11.9%; chemicals 11.8%). *Major import sources:* South Africa 24.4%; United Kingdom 11.3%; United States 9.0%; Germany 6.4%; Japan 5.3%; Italy 2.1%; Switzerland 1.8%; France 1.7%; The Netherlands 1.5%.
Exports (1992): Z$7,333,600,000 (domestic exports 87.4%, of which tobacco 28.5%; gold sales 11.4%; ferroalloys 7.9%; nickel metal 5.0%; asbestos 3.9%; corn [maize] 1.9%; cotton 1.9%; sugar 1.5%; copper 1.4%). *Major export destinations[6]:* South Africa 11.9%; United Kingdom 9.9%; Germany 6.1%; United States 5.6%; Japan 5.4%; Botswana 4.5%; Switzerland 4.4%; Zambia 3.4%; Italy 3.3%; China 3.0%.

Transport and communications

Transport. Railroads (1991): route length 1,714 mi, 2,759 km; passenger-mi 355,057,000, passenger-km 571,410,000; short ton-mi cargo 3,695,000, metric ton-km cargo 5,394,000. Roads (1992): total length 56,593 mi, 91,078 km (paved 16%). Vehicles (1992): passenger cars 310,412; trucks and buses 30,182. Merchant marine: none. Air transport (1991): passenger-mi 508,000,000, passenger-km 817,000,000; short ton-mi cargo 44,000,000, metric ton-km cargo 64,000,000; airports (1994) with scheduled flights 5.
Communications. Daily newspapers (1992): total number 2; total circulation 208,032; circulation per 1,000 population 21. Radio (1993): 522,000 receivers (1 per 20 persons). Television (1993): 137,090 receivers (1 per 80 persons). Telephones (1991): 312,380 (1 per 31 persons).

Education and health

Education (1992)				
	schools	teachers	students	student/teacher ratio
Primary (age 7–13)	4,567	60,834	2,306,809	37.9
Secondary (age 14–19)	1,518	23,233	657,344	28.3
Voc., teacher tr.	25	1,479	27,431	18.5
Higher[7]	28	2,414	39,406	16.3

Educational attainment (1986–87). Percentage of employed population age 15 and over having: no formal schooling 24.5%; primary 42.9%; secondary and tertiary 31.7%. *Literacy* (1985): total population age 15 and over literate 3,413,000 (76.0%); males literate 1,846,000 (81.5%); females literate 1,567,000 (66.8%).
Health: physicians (1990) 1,320 (1 per 7,371 persons); hospital beds (1985) 19,913 (1 per 411 persons); infant mortality rate per 1,000 live births (1989) 67.
Food (1988–90): daily per capita caloric intake 2,256 (vegetable products 93%, animal products 7%); 94% of FAO recommended minimum requirement.

Military

Total active duty personnel (1994): 46,900 (army 91.5%, air force 8.5%). *Military expenditure as percentage of GNP* (1991): 5.5% (world 4.2%); per capita expenditure U.S.$29.

[1]Includes 30 nonelective seats. [2]Preliminary results. [3]Does not take into consideration seasonal unemployment of communal workers. [4]Wage-earning workers only. [5]Less imputed bank service charges. [6]Excludes gold sales and reexports. [7]Includes postsecondary vocational and teacher training at the higher level.

Comparative National Statistics

World and regional summaries

region/bloc	area and population, 1994						gross national product, 1992						labour force, 1990		
	area		population			population projection, 2010	total ('000,000 U.S.$)	% agriculture	% industry	% services	growth rate, 1985–92	GNP per capita (U.S.$)	total ('000)	% male	% female
	square miles	square kilometres	total	per sq mi	per sq km										
World	52,499,780	135,973,730	5,589,422,000	106.5	41.1	6,942,172,000	23,020,153	5	34	61	2.8	4,250	2,363,545	63.9	36.1
Africa	11,724,320	30,365,720	683,021,000	58.3	22.5	1,030,581,000	434,270	19	35	46	2.2	650	242,784	65.6	34.4
Central Africa	2,553,070	6,612,400	81,986,000	32.1	12.4	129,328,000	34,900	22	36	42	0.2	470	26,428	64.7	35.3
East Africa	2,471,320	6,400,640	214,314,000	86.7	33.5	336,949,000	49,390	32	22	46	3.1	240	85,082	58.8	41.2
North Africa	3,287,810	8,515,370	152,714,000	46.4	17.9	221,568,000	160,940	15	38	47	2.3	1,100	40,016	84.6	15.4
Southern Africa	1,033,890	2,667,770	47,605,000	46.0	17.8	67,526,000	114,340	4	42	54	1.5	2,520	14,532	64.3	35.7
West Africa	2,378,230	6,159,540	186,402,000	78.4	30.3	275,210,000	74,700	37	28	35	3.7	390	76,726	63.8	36.2
Americas	16,297,750	42,211,010	762,800,000	46.8	18.1	929,173,000	7,697,600	3	30	67	2.0	10,440	293,723	66.5	33.5
Anglo-America[3]	8,368,970	21,675,560	290,276,000	34.7	13.4	334,054,000	6,472,950	2	29	69	2.0	22,840	135,438	58.7	41.3
Canada	3,849,670	9,970,610	29,107,000	7.6	2.9	35,050,000	565,790	2	32	66	1.7	20,320	13,360	60.2	39.8
United States	3,679,190	9,529,060	261,045,000	71.0	27.4	298,865,000	5,904,820	2	29	69	2.0	23,120	122,005	58.6	41.4
Latin America	7,928,780	20,535,450	472,524,000	59.6	23.0	595,119,000	1,224,650	9	34	57	2.1	2,700	158,285	73.1	26.9
Caribbean	90,650	234,750	35,029,000	386.4	149.2	41,458,000	72,900	8	38	54	1.3	2,120	13,813	66.9	33.1
Central America	202,040	523,280	31,577,000	156.3	60.3	44,457,000	33,170	18	22	60	2.7	1,120	9,520	78.5	21.5
Mexico	756,070	1,958,200	91,840,000	121.5	46.9	118,455,000	294,830	8	29	63	2.9	3,470	30,487	72.9	27.1
South America	6,880,020	17,819,220	314,078,000	45.7	17.6	390,749,000	823,750	10	35	55	1.8	2,700	104,465	73.6	26.4
Andean Group	2,110,520	5,466,280	111,994,000	53.1	20.5	144,726,000	178,690	10	38	52	3.6	1,630	34,715	75.6	24.4
Brazil	3,286,500	8,512,000	159,000,000	48.4	18.7	194,002,000	425,410	11	37	52	1.1	2,770	55,026	72.6	27.4
Other South America	1,483,000	3,840,940	43,084,000	29.1	11.2	52,021,000	219,650	7	31	62	1.9	5,210	14,724	72.4	27.6
Asia	12,325,690	31,923,320	3,385,495,000	274.7	106.1	4,192,400,000	6,086,070	9	39	52	5.0	1,860	1,436,522[4]	64.7[4]	35.3[4]
Eastern Asia	4,546,920	11,776,450	1,414,498,000	311.1	120.1	1,567,636,000	4,575,690	5	41	54	5.1	3,310	775,590	57.4	42.6
China	3,696,120	9,572,900	1,192,300,000	322.6	124.5	1,323,800,000	442,350	27	35	38	7.5	380	669,693	56.7	43.3
Japan	145,850	377,750	124,960,000	856.8	330.8	130,344,000	3,507,840	2	42	56	4.4	28,220	62,202	62.1	37.9
South Korea	38,330	99,270	44,436,000	1,159.3	447.6	49,683,000	296,350	8	45	47	9.5	6,790	18,664	66.2	33.8
Other Eastern Asia	666,620	1,726,530	52,802,000	79.2	30.6	63,809,000	329,150	4	37	59	6.9	6,400	25,031	58.8	41.2
South Asia	1,971,490	5,106,110	1,217,884,000	617.7	238.5	1,627,758,000	361,910	32	26	42	5.0	310	411,136	77.4	22.6
India	1,222,240	3,165,600	913,744,000	747.6	288.6	1,189,396,000	271,640	32	27	41	5.4	310	322,944	74.8	25.2
Pakistan	339,700	879,810	131,434,000	386.9	149.4	197,672,000	49,480	27	27	46	4.8	410	33,698	87.5	12.5
Other South Asia	409,550	1,060,700	172,706,000	421.7	162.8	240,690,000	40,790	35	20	45	2.9	250	54,494	86.2	13.8
Southeast Asia	1,735,800	4,495,710	475,515,000	273.9	105.8	606,070,000	481,690	22	35	43	6.1	1,060	189,297	63.0	37.0
ASEAN	1,185,080	3,069,370	343,332,000	289.7	111.9	426,866,000	378,590	15	39	46	7.4	1,160	132,060	65.6	34.4
Non-ASEAN	550,720	1,426,340	132,183,000	240.0	92.7	179,204,000	103,100	46	19	35	2.4	820	57,237	57.1	42.9
Southwest Asia	4,071,480	10,545,050	277,598,000	68.2	26.3	390,936,000	666,780	14	38	48	3.1	2,520	60,499[4]	76.2[4]	23.8[4]
Central Asia	1,542,250	3,994,400	53,681,000	34.8	13.4	68,946,000	58,250	31	41	28	−0.9	1,110	4	4	4
Gulf Cooperation Council	1,026,860	2,659,550	24,693,000	24.0	9.3	38,851,000	202,220	5	53	42	4.0	9,300	6,511	91.7	8.3
Iran	632,460	1,638,060	59,614,000	94.3	36.4	85,775,000	130,910	23	29	48	2.3	2,190	15,253	82.0	18.0
Other Southwest Asia	869,910	2,253,040	139,610,000	160.5	62.0	197,364,000	275,400	14	30	56	4.0	2,100	38,735[4]	71.3[4]	28.7[4]
Europe	8,868,200	22,968,600	729,943,000	82.3	31.8	754,991,000	8,448,430	4	35	61	2.3	11,680	378,335[4]	57.7[4]	42.3[4]
Eastern Europe	7,437,180	19,262,210	346,027,000	46.5	18.0	348,014,000	802,760	14	48	38	0.0	2,340	208,749[4]	53.0[4]	47.0[4]
Russia	6,592,850	17,075,400	148,174,000	22.5	8.7	143,477,000	397,790	13	48	39	2.3	2,680	146,634[4]	52.0[4]	48.0[4]
Other Eastern Europe	844,330	2,186,810	197,853,000	234.3	90.5	204,537,000	404,970	15	48	37	−2.0	2,090	62,115[4]	55.4[4]	44.6[4]
Western Europe	1,431,020	3,706,390	383,916,000	268.3	103.6	406,977,000	7,645,670	3	33	64	2.6	20,090	169,586	63.6	36.4
EFTA	517,360	1,339,950	33,473,000	64.7	25.0	35,009,000	889,630	3	34	63	1.6	26,890	15,917	58.1	41.9
European Union	912,450	2,363,250	349,633,000	383.2	147.9	371,072,000	6,774,840	3	33	64	2.7	19,450	153,330	64.1	35.9
France	210,030	543,970	57,982,000	276.1	106.6	63,263,000	1,278,650	3	29	68	2.8	22,300	25,404	60.1	39.9
Germany	137,820	356,960	81,966,000	594.7	229.6	93,324,000	1,846,060	2	39	59	2.8	23,030	38,981	60.7	39.3
Italy	116,330	301,300	57,257,000	492.2	190.0	56,270,000	1,186,570	3	32	65	2.5	20,510	23,339	68.1	31.9
Spain	194,900	504,780	39,193,000	201.1	77.6	40,317,000	547,950	4	32	64	4.0	14,020	14,456	75.5	24.5
United Kingdom	94,250	244,110	58,422,000	619.9	239.3	61,100,000	1,024,770	2	34	64	1.8	17,760	27,766	61.4	38.6
Other EU	159,120	412,130	54,813,000	344.5	133.0	56,798,000	860,840	5	29	66	2.8	15,770	23,384	66.5	33.5
Other Western Europe	1,210	3,190	810,000	667.8	253.8	896,000	11,200	5	20	75	5.3	14,340	339	68.1	31.9
Oceania	3,283,810	8,505,080	28,163,000	8.6	3.3	35,027,000	353,783	4	29	67	2.1	12,910	12,181	63.0	37.0
Australia	2,966,150	7,682,300	17,875,000	6.0	2.3	21,598,000	299,320	3	30	67	2.3	17,070	7,963	61.9	38.1
Pacific Ocean Islands	317,660	822,780	10,288,000	32.4	12.5	13,429,000	54,463	10	26	64	0.9	5,520	4,218	65.0	35.0

[1]Refers only to the long-term external public and publicly guaranteed debt of the 129 countries that report under the World Bank's Debtor Reporting System (DRS). [2]Continental and regional totals may

Africa

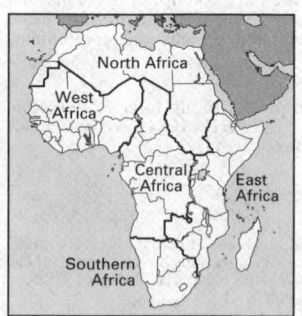

Americas

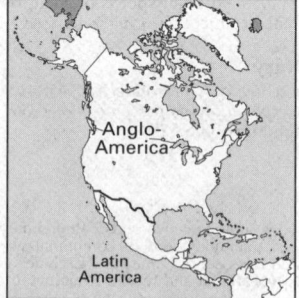

Asia

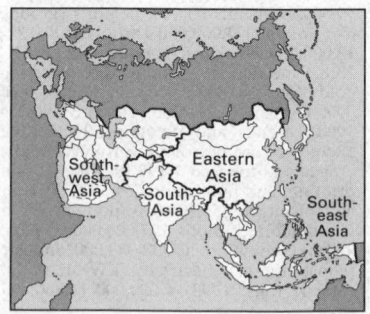

pop. per 1,000 ha of arable land, 1992	electricity consumption (kW-hr per capita), 1992	imports (c.i.f.)	exports[2] (f.o.b.)	balance[2]	total	% of GNP	male	female	pop. per doctor	infant mortality per 1,000 births	pop. having safe water (%)	food (% FAO recommended minimum), 1988–90	male	female	region/bloc
		trade ('000,000 U.S.$), 1993			debt ('000,000 U.S.$), 1992[1]		life expectancy (years)		health				literacy (%)		
4,020	2,188	3,800,890	3,682,110	−118,780	1,097,735	26.4	64.1	68.2	730	64.3	77	114	81.8	69.1	World
3,960	476	110,900	96,560	−14,340	228,083	78.2	53.9	57.1	4,180	94.8	50	100	61.8	42.2	Africa
3,520	163	6,110	5,340	−770	30,704	88.0	51.0	54.4	12,870	100.1	42	91	71.8	47.4	Central Africa
4,870	136	15,530	12,410	−3,120	39,313	92.0	49.1	52.2	13,070	107.5	40	85	60.3	45.6	East Africa
4,010	663	43,670	39,150	−4,520	97,220	72.1	62.1	65.7	1,900	69.0	74	122	61.7	35.0	North Africa
3,090	3,605	21,670	14,660	−7,010	1,213	20.8	61.4	67.3	1,430	50.9	56	124	77.1	74.9	Southern Africa
3,610	112	23,920	20,980	−2,940	59,632	81.3	51.8	54.6	6,830	100.8	46	95	54.6	32.8	West Africa
2,050	5,765	934,680	910,030	−24,650	322,516	27.0	66.2	74.0	500	38.1	88	123	90.4	88.7	Americas
1,230	12,734	742,900	719,090	−23,810	—	—	72.5	79.2	400	8.2	100	136	95.8	95.4	Anglo-America[3]
630	18,117	138,290	135,530	−2,750	—	—	74.0	80.6	460	6.8	100	122	96.6	96.6	Canada
1,380	12,160	603,310	582,350	−20,950	—	—	72.3	79.0	390	8.3	100	138	95.7	95.3	United States
3,510	1,462	191,680	186,830	−4,850	322,516	27.6	65.6	71.4	760	48.6	78	114	86.4	83.5	Latin America
7,450	1,365	18,770	18,320	−440	10,538	49.6	65.5	69.9	520	52.4	77	114	87.0	84.2	Caribbean
5,440	537	13,630	21,270	+7,650	23,437	70.7	64.1	69.1	1,490	47.9	66	103	75.0	68.1	Central America
3,810	1,369	63,880	59,860	−4,020	72,219	24.5	66.5	73.1	890	41.0	76	131	88.7	83.5	Mexico
3,140	1,593	95,410	87,370	−8,040	216,322	26.3	65.5	71.2	730	51.1	79	110	86.7	84.8	South America
5,900	1,390	44,040	38,200	−5,840	77,017	43.1	66.2	71.7	900	44.5	75	98	90.0	84.8	Andean Group
3,110	1,722	25,680	25,020	−660	86,251	20.3	63.5	69.1	850	60.0	87	114	82.1	81.2	Brazil
1,450	1,639	25,690	24,150	−1,550	53,054	24.4	71.5	77.7	360	34.0	62	126	95.1	94.4	Other South America
6,950	924	1,086,840	1,001,700	−85,140	369,458	20.3	64.2	67.0	1,000	64.7	75	109	78.8	61.1	Asia
13,550	1,424	647,910	591,520	−56,390	82,690	11.2	69.3	73.0	640	24.3	76	114	89.0	73.0	Eastern Asia
12,640	650	103,550	110,440	+6,890	58,475	13.2	68.6	71.8	650	26.0	72	112	87.0	68.0	China
30,590	7,192	240,710	215,800	−24,910	—	—	76.1	82.1	580	4.5	97	125	100.0	100.0	Japan
22,980	3,348	84,340	72,390	−11,950	23,919	8.1	69.0	76.0	900	15.0	97	120	99.1	93.5	South Korea
12,740	3,375	219,310	192,890	−26,420	296	14.1	70.2	75.7	520	18.2	99	121	97.4	92.4	Other Eastern Asia
5,000	335	41,070	41,080	+10	105,952	29.5	59.6	60.3	2,410	93.8	80	99	60.7	36.4	South Asia
5,300	374	22,490	24,020	+1,530	67,721	24.9	60.4	61.2	2,190	88.0	85	101	63.9	39.4	India
6,040	417	9,490	9,590	+100	18,476	37.3	59.3	60.7	2,240	104.7	56	99	47.3	22.3	Pakistan
8,270	84	9,090	7,470	−1,620	19,755	52.3	55.3	55.2	5,890	109.6	71	89	51.8	29.2	Other South Asia
7,810	415	233,780	215,830	−17,950	108,742	29.4	60.6	64.7	2,650	66.3	55	112	88.3	76.6	Southeast Asia
8,200	534	225,910	208,700	−17,210	101,877	30.8	61.4	65.4	2,490	67.6	65	114	88.7	77.3	ASEAN
6,960	102	7,870	7,130	−740	6,865	17.7	58.5	63.0	3,210	63.2	28	106	87.0	74.8	Non-ASEAN
2,560	1,845	164,080	149,320	−14,760	72,074	20.4	64.8	69.3	600	49.9	86	126	82.3	67.5	Southwest Asia
1,210	3,274	2,360	2,080	−280	41	0.1	64.6	72.0	280	36.2	100	132	98.8	96.2	Central Asia
6,250	4,137	74,920	70,020	−4,900	2,340	21.9	69.4	72.8	560	23.1	95	123	72.7	50.0	Gulf Cooperation Council
3,420	864	15,620	14,260	−1,360	3,065	21.3	64.4	66.2	2,000	62.1	89	125	64.5	43.3	Iran
3,320	1,353	71,180	62,060	−9,120	66,628	42.2	64.0	69.1	720	53.8	78	124	85.0	67.9	Other Southwest Asia
2,430	5,729	1,608,100	1,566,860	−41,240	175,626	20.2	68.7	77.1	290	11.6	98	134	98.8	96.9	Europe
1,570	5,025	116,840	106,510	−10,330	154,219	19.5	63.3	74.1	270	16.8	97	132	98.7	95.8	Eastern Europe
1,140	6,659	34,710	30,060	−4,650	64,703	16.3	59.0	73.2	230	18.1	100	132	98.6	95.2	Russia
2,190	3,802	82,130	74,610	−7,530	89,516	22.7	66.5	74.8	320	15.9	95	132	98.8	96.2	Other Eastern Europe
4,830	6,371	1,491,260	1,460,350	−30,910	21,406	28.2	73.4	79.8	310	6.8	100	135	98.9	97.9	Western Europe
4,130	13,097	192,960	191,870	−1,090	—	—	73.6	80.2	340	6.3	99	122	100.0	100.0	EFTA
4,910	5,738	1,294,980	1,265,010	−29,960	21,277	29.0	73.3	79.8	300	6.9	100	136	98.8	97.7	European Union
3,180	7,140	200,400	199,320	−1,080	—	—	72.9	81.1	370	6.4	100	143	98.9	98.7	France
7,030	6,627	329,510	326,670	−2,850	—	—	73.2	79.6	310	6.1	100	132	100.0	100.0	Germany
6,330	4,525	147,540	134,250	−13,280	—	—	73.6	80.2	190	7.4	100	139	97.8	96.4	Italy
2,570	4,071	82,390	73,730	−8,670	—	—	74.6	80.5	260	7.4	100	141	97.5	94.2	Spain
8,860	5,933	205,390	196,930	−8,450	—	—	73.2	78.6	450	6.6	100	130	100.0	100.0	United Kingdom
5,270	5,228	329,750	334,120	+4,370	21,277	29.0	73.0	79.1	340	8.1	98	136	97.6	94.7	Other EU
24,860	3,234	3,330	3,470	+140	129	5.0	73.2	78.6	520	7.9	100	131	98.3	98.1	Other Western Europe
530	7,098	60,470	54,490	−5,980	2,053	33.8	70.7	76.0	520	21.7	88	123	93.9	90.9	Oceania
340	9,043	45,630	41,460	−4,160	—	—	75.0	80.9	440	6.1	99	124	99.5	99.5	Australia
12,510	3,663	14,850	13,030	−1,820	2,053	33.8	63.4	67.3	780	36.5	67	122	82.7	72.7	Pacific Ocean Islands

contain undistributable detail.   [3]Anglo-America includes Canada, the United States, Greenland, Bermuda, and St. Pierre and Miquelon.   [1]Data for Russia refer to all 15 republics of the former U.S.S.R.

Europe

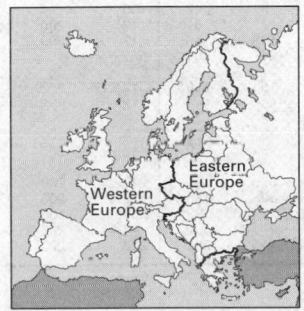

Eastern Europe

Oceania

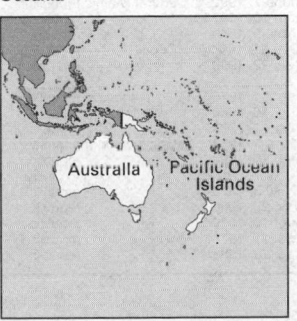

Government and international organizations

This table summarizes principal facts about the governments of the countries of the world, their branches and organs, the topmost layers of local government constituting each country's chief administrative subdivisions, and the participation of their central governments in the principal intergovernmental organizations of the world.

In this table "date of independence" may refer to a variety of circumstances. In the case of the newest countries, those that attained full independence after World War II, the date given is usually just what is implied by the heading—the date when the country, within its present borders, attained full sovereignty over both its internal and external affairs. In the case of longer established countries, the choice of a single date may be somewhat more complicated, and grounds for the use of several different dates often exist. The reader should refer to *Macropædia* and *Micropædia* articles on national histories and relevant historical acts. In cases of territorial annexation or dissolution, the date given here refers either to the final act of union of a state composed of smaller entities or to the final act of separation from a larger whole (*e.g.*, the separation of Bangladesh from Pakistan in 1971).

The date of the current, or last, constitution is in some ways a less complicated question, but governments sometimes do not, upon taking power, either adhere to existing constitutional forms or trouble to terminate the previous document and legitimize themselves by the installation of new constitutional forms. Often, however, the desire to legitimize extraconstitutional political activity by associating it with existing forms of long precedent leads to partial or incomplete modification, suspension, or abrogation of a constitution, so that the actual day-to-day conduct of government may be largely unrelated to the provisions of a constitution still theoretically in force. When a date in this column is given in italics, it refers to a document that has been suspended, abolished by extraconstitutional action, or modified extensively.

The characterizations adopted under "type of government" represent a compromise between the forms provided for by the national constitution and the more pragmatic language that a political scientist might adopt to describe these same systems. For an explanation of the application of these terms in the Britannica World Data, *see* the Glossary at page 541.

The positions denoted by the terms "chief of state" and "head of government" are usually those identified with those functions by the constitution. The duties of the chief of state may range from largely ceremonial responsibilities, with little or no authority over the day-to-day conduct of government, to complete executive authority as the effective head of government. In certain countries, an official of a political party or a revolutionary figure outside the constitutional structure may exercise the powers of both positions.

Membership in the legislative house(s) of each country as given here includes all elected or appointed members, as well as ex officio members (those who by virtue of some other office or title are members of the body), whether voting or nonvoting. The legislature of a country with a unicameral system is shown as the upper house in this table.

The number of administrative subdivisions for each country is listed down to the second level. A single country may, depending on its size, complexity, and historical antecedents, have as many as five levels of administrative subordination or it may have none at all. Each level of subordination may have several kinds of subdivisions.

Government and international organizations

country	date of independence[a]	date of current or last constitution[b]	type of government	executive branch[c] chief of state	head of government	legislative branch[d] upper house (members)	lower house (members)	admin. subdivisions first-order (number)	second-order (number)	seaward claims territorial (nautical miles)	fishing/ economic (nautical miles)
Afghanistan	Aug. 19, 1919	Sept. 27, 1993[1]	republic	president	prime minister[2]	...	—	...	...	—	—
Albania	Nov. 28, 1912	April 29, 1991[1]	republic	president	prime minister	140	—	27	c. 200	12	3
Algeria	July 5, 1962	Feb. 23, 1989	republic[5]	president HCS	prime minister	200[6,7]	—	48	1,541	12	12
American Samoa		July 1, 1967	territory (U.S.)	U.S. president	governor	18	21	3	15	12	200
Andorra	Dec. 6, 1288	May 4, 1993	parl. coprincipality	[8]	head of the govt.	28	—	7	...	—	—
Angola	Nov. 11, 1975	Aug. 27, 1992	republic	president		220	—	18	163	20	200
Antigua and Barbuda	Nov. 1, 1981	Nov. 1, 1981	constitutional monarchy	British monarch	prime minister	17	17	30	—	12[9]	200[9]
Argentina	July 9, 1816	Aug. 24, 1994[11]	federal republic	president		48	259	24	...	12	200
Armenia	Sept. 23, 1991	April 1978	republic	president	prime minister	185	—	37	...	—	—
Aruba		Jan. 1, 1986	overseas territory (Neth.)	Dutch monarch	[12]	21	—	...	...	12	200
Australia	Jan. 1, 1901	July 9, 1900	federal parl. state[14]	British monarch	prime minister	76	147	8	c. 900	12	200
Austria	Oct. 30, 1918	Oct. 1, 1920	federal republic	president	chancellor	63	183	9	99	—	—
Azerbaijan	Aug. 30, 1991	April 1978	republic	president	prime minister	50	—	2	64	—	—
Bahamas, The	July 10, 1973	July 10, 1973	constitutional monarchy	British monarch	prime minister	16	49	—	...	3	200
Bahrain	Aug. 15, 1971	June 1973	monarchy (emirate)	emir	prime minister	30[6]	—	1	—	12	15
Bangladesh	March 26, 1971	Dec. 16, 1972	republic	president	prime minister	330	—	4	64	12	200
Barbados	Nov. 30, 1966	Nov. 30, 1966	constitutional monarchy	British monarch	prime minister	21	28	—	...	12	200
Belarus	Aug. 25, 1991	March 30, 1994	republic	president		360	—	6	118[16]	—	—
Belgium	Oct. 4, 1830	May 5, 1993	fed. const. monarchy	monarch	prime minister	185	212	10	589	12	15
Belize	Sept. 21, 1981	Sept. 21, 1981	constitutional monarchy	British monarch	prime minister	9	29	6	...	12[17]	200
Benin	Aug. 1, 1960	Dec. 2, 1990	republic	president		64	—	6	84	200	200
Bermuda		June 8, 1968	colony (U.K.)	British monarch	[18]	11	40	11	—	12	200
Bhutan	March 24, 1910	—	[19]	king		154	—	4	18	—	—
Bolivia	Aug. 6, 1825	Feb. 2, 1967	republic	president		27	130	9	111	—	—
Bosnia and Herzegovina	March 3, 1992	1990	republic[20,21]	president CP	prime minister	240[7]	—	100	...	...	—
Botswana	Sept. 30, 1966	Sept. 30, 1966	republic	president		15[6]	44	21	...	—	—
Brazil	Sept. 7, 1822	Oct. 5, 1988	federal republic	president		81	513	27	4,491	12	200
Brunei	Jan. 1, 1984	*Sept. 29, 1959*	monarchy (sultanate)	sultan		21[6]	—	4	—	12	200
Bulgaria	Oct. 5, 1908	July 12, 1991	republic	president	prime minister	240	—	9	328	12	200
Burkina Faso	Aug. 5, 1960	June 11, 1991[1]	republic	president	prime minister	107	—	30	109	—	—
Burundi	July 1, 1962	March 13, 1992[1]	republic	president[22]		81	—	15	122	—	—
Cambodia	Nov. 9, 1953	Sept. 24, 1993	constitutional monarchy	king	[23]	120	—	22	...	12	200
Cameroon	Jan. 1, 1960	June 2, 1972	republic	president	prime minister	180	—	10	49	50	3
Canada	July 1, 1867	April 17, 1982	federal parl. state[14]	Canadian GG[24]	prime minister	110[25]	295	12	...	12	200
Cape Verde	July 5, 1975	Sept. 25, 1992	republic	president	prime minister	79	—	14	31	12[9]	200[9]
Central African Republic	Aug. 13, 1960	Nov. 21, 1986	republic	president	prime minister	85	—	17	52	—	—
Chad	Aug. 11, 1960	April 6, 1993[1]	republic	president	prime minister	57	—	14	54	—	—
Chile	Sept. 18, 1810	March 11, 1981	republic	president		47	120	13	51	12	200
China	1523 BC	Dec. 4, 1982	people's republic	president	premier SC	2,978	—	30	338	12	3
Colombia	July 20, 1810	July 5, 1991	republic	president		102	163	33	1,011	12	200
Comoros	July 6, 1975	June 7, 1992[26]	federal Islamic republic	president	prime minister	42	—	3	7	12[9]	200[9]
Congo	Aug. 15, 1960	March 15, 1992[26]	republic	president	prime minister	60	125	15	47	200	3
Costa Rica	Sept. 15, 1821	Nov. 9, 1949	republic	president		57	—	7	81	12	200
Côte d'Ivoire	Aug. 7, 1960	Oct. 31, 1960	republic	president	prime minister	175	—	10	49	12	200
Croatia	June 25, 1991	Dec. 22, 1990	republic	president	prime minister	68	138	21	101	...	...
Cuba	May 20, 1902	Feb. 24, 1976	socialist republic	president		589	—	15	168	12	200
Cyprus[28]	Aug. 16, 1960	Aug. 16, 1960	republic	president		80[7]	—	...	...	12	3
Czech Republic	Jan. 1, 1993	Jan. 1, 1993	republic	president	prime minister	81[29]	200	8	75	—	—
Denmark	c. 800	June 5, 1953	constitutional monarchy	monarch	prime minister	179	—	16	275	3	200
Djibouti	June 27, 1977	Sept. 15, 1992	republic	president		65	—	5	9	12	200
Dominica	Nov. 3, 1978	Nov. 3, 1978	republic	president		31	—	37	...	12	200
Dominican Republic	Feb. 27, 1844	Nov. 28, 1966	republic	president		30	120	30	136	6	200
Ecuador	May 24, 1822	Aug. 10, 1979	republic	president		77	—	21	193	200	200
Egypt	Feb. 28, 1922	Sept. 11, 1971	republic	president	prime minister	454	—	27	...	12[30]	200[30]
El Salvador	Jan. 30, 1841	Dec. 20, 1983	republic	president		84	—	14	262	200	200

Finally, in the second half of the table are listed the memberships each country maintains in the principal international intergovernmental organizations of the world. This part of the table may also be utilized to provide a complete membership list for each of these organizations as of Dec. 1, 1994.

Notes for the column headings

a. The date may also be either that of the organization of the present form of government or the inception of the present administrative structure (federation, confederation, union, etc.).
b. Constitutions whose dates are in italic type had been wholly or substantially suspended or abolished as of late 1994.
c. For abbreviations used in this column see the list on the facing page.
d. When a legislative body has been adjourned or otherwise suspended, figures in parentheses indicate the number of members in the legislative body as provided for in constitution or law.
e. Vatican City also a member.
f. States contributing funds to or receiving aid from UNICEF in 1994.
g. Palestine (Liberation Organization) also a member.

International organizations, conventions

ACP	African, Caribbean, and Pacific (Lomé IV) convention
ADB	Asian Development Bank
APEC	Asia-Pacific Economic Cooperation Council
CARICOM	Caribbean Community and Common Market
EU	The European Union
ECOWAS	Economic Community of West African States
EEC	European Economic Community
FAO	Food and Agriculture Org.
GATT (WTO)	General Agreement on Tariffs and Trade (World Trade Org. as of January 1995)
GCC	Gulf Cooperation Council
I-ADB	Inter-American Development Bank
IAEA	International Atomic Energy Agency
IBRD	International Bank for Reconstruction and Development
ICAO	International Civil Aviation Org.
ICJ	International Court of Justice
IDA	International Development Assn.
IDB	Islamic Development Bank
IFC	International Finance Corporation
ILO	International Labour Org.
IMF	International Monetary Fund
IMO	International Maritime Org.
ITU	International Telecommunication Union
LAS	League of Arab States
OAS	Organization of American States
OAU	Organization of African Unity
OPEC	Organization of Petroleum Exporting Countries
SPC	South Pacific Commission
UNCTAD	United Nations Conference on Trade and Development
UNESCO	United Nations Educational Scientific and Cultural Org.
UNICEF	United Nations Children's Fund
UNIDO	United Nations Industrial Development Org.
UPU	Universal Postal Union
WHO	World Health Org.
WIPO	World Intellectual Property Org.
WMO	World Meteorological Org.

Abbreviations used in the executive-branch column

AFPRC	Armed Forces Provisional Ruling Council
CP	Collective Presidency
CS	Council of State
FC	Federal Council
GG	Governor-General
GPC	General People's Committee
HCS	High Committee of State
PNA	Palestine National Authority
PRC	Provisional Ruling Council
SC	State Council
SLORC	State Law and Order Restoration Council
SCS	Supreme Council of State

membership in international organizations																							Commonwealth of Nations	regional multipurpose						economic									country
United Nations (date of admission)	UN organs★ and affiliated intergovernmental organizations																								EU	GCC	LAS	OAS	OAU	SPC	ACP	ADB	APEC	CARICOM	ECOWAS	EEC	I-ADB	IDB	OPEC	
	UNCTAD★	UNICEF★	ICJ★	FAO	GATT (WTO)	IAEA	IBRD	ICAO	IDA	IFC	ILO	IMF	IMO	ITU	UNESCO	UNIDO	UPU	WHO	WIPO	WMO																				
1946	●	●	●	●		●	●	●	●	●	●	●	●	●	●	●	●	●	●	●														●				●		Afghanistan
1955	●	●	●	●		●	●	●	●	●	●	●	●	●	●	●	●	●	●	●																				Albania
1962	●	●	●	●	●[4]	●	●	●	●	●	●	●	●	●	●	●	●	●	●	●			●		●											●		●	Algeria
—	●													●			●			●							●												American Samoa
1993	●													●	●			●																					Andorra
1976	●	●	●	●		●	●	●	●	●	●	●	●	●	●	●	●	●	●	●						●			●										Angola
1981	●	●	●	●		●	●	●	●	●	●	●	●	●	●	●[10]	●	●	●	●	●			●			●				●							Antigua and Barbuda
1945	●	●	●	●		●	●	●	●	●	●	●	●	●	●	●	●	●	●	●				●			●							●			Argentina
1992	●	●	●	●	●[4]	●	●	●	●[10]	●	●	●	●	●	●	●	●	●	●	●															●			Armenia
—													●[13]																										Aruba
1945	●	●	●	●		●	●	●	●	●	●	●	●	●	●	●	●	●	●	●	●					●		●	●								Australia
1955	●	●	●	●		●	●	●	●	●	●	●	●	●	●	●[10]	●	●	●	●													●[10]	●			Austria
1992	●	●	●	●	●[4]	●	●	●	●	●	●	●	●	●	●	●	●	●	●	●														●			Azerbaijan
1973	●	●	●	●	●[10]	●	●	●	●	●	●	●	●	●	●	●	●	●	●	●	●			●			●			●			●				Bahamas, The
1971	●	●	●	●	●[4]	●	●	●	●	●	●	●	●	●	●	●	●	●	●	●		●	●												●		Bahrain
1974	●	●	●	●		●	●	●	●	●	●	●	●	●	●	●	●	●	●	●	●					●		●							●		Bangladesh
1966	●	●	●	●		●	●	●	●	●	●	●	●	●	●	●	●	●	●	●	●			●			●			●			●				Barbados
1945	●	●	●	●	●[4]	●	●	●	●	●	●	●	●	●	●	●	●	●	●	●																	Belarus
1945	●	●	●	●		●	●	●	●	●	●	●	●	●	●	●	●	●	●	●								●					●	●			Belgium
1981	●	●	●	●		●	●	●	●	●	●	●	●	●	●	●	●	●	●	●	●			●			●			●			●				Belize
1960	●	●	●	●		●	●	●	●	●	●	●	●	●	●	●	●	●	●	●					●			●				●			●		Benin
—																																					Bermuda
1971	●	●	●	●			●	●	●	●	●	●	●	●	●	●	●	●	●	●								●						●			Bhutan
1945	●	●	●	●		●	●	●	●	●	●	●	●	●	●	●	●	●	●	●				●			●							●			Bolivia
1992	●	●	●	●	●[10]	●	●	●	●	●	●	●	●	●	●	●	●	●	●	●																	Bosnia and Herzegovina
1966	●	●	●	●			●	●	●	●	●	●	●	●	●	●	●	●	●	●	●					●		●							●		Botswana
1945	●	●	●	●		●	●	●	●	●	●	●	●	●	●	●	●	●	●	●				●			●							●			Brazil
1984	●	●	●	●			●	●		●	●	●	●	●	●	●	●	●	●	●	●							●			●						Brunei
1955	●	●	●	●	●[4]	●	●	●	●	●	●	●	●	●	●	●	●	●	●	●																	Bulgaria
1960	●	●	●	●			●	●	●	●	●	●	●	●	●	●	●	●	●	●					●			●				●			●		Burkina Faso
1962	●	●	●	●			●	●	●	●	●	●	●	●	●	●	●	●	●	●					●			●							●		Burundi
1955	●	●	●	●	●[10]		●	●	●	●	●	●	●	●	●	●	●	●	●	●								●	●						●		Cambodia
1960	●	●	●	●			●	●	●	●	●	●	●	●	●	●	●	●	●	●					●			●							●		Cameroon
1945	●	●	●	●		●	●	●	●	●	●	●	●	●	●	●	●	●	●	●	●					●		●	●				●	●			Canada
1975	●	●	●	●	●[10]		●	●	●	●	●	●	●	●	●	●	●	●	●	●					●			●				●			●		Cape Verde
1960	●	●	●	●			●	●	●	●	●	●	●	●	●	●	●	●	●	●					●			●							●		Central African Republic
1960	●	●	●	●			●	●	●	●	●	●	●	●	●	●	●	●	●	●					●			●							●		Chad
1945	●	●	●	●		●	●	●	●	●	●	●	●	●	●	●	●	●	●	●				●			●							●			Chile
1945	●	●	●	●		●	●	●	●	●	●	●	●	●	●	●	●	●	●	●								●							●		China
1945	●	●	●	●		●	●	●	●	●	●	●	●	●	●	●	●	●	●	●				●			●							●			Colombia
1975	●	●	●	●	●[10]		●	●	●	●	●	●	●	●	●	●	●	●	●	●					●			●							●		Comoros
1960	●	●	●	●			●	●	●	●	●	●	●	●	●	●	●	●	●	●					●			●				●			●		Congo
1945	●	●	●	●			●	●	●	●	●	●	●	●	●	●	●	●	●	●				●			●							●			Costa Rica
1960	●	●	●	●			●	●	●	●	●	●	●	●	●	●	●	●	●	●					●			●			●	●			●		Côte d'Ivoire
1992	●	●	●	●	●[4]	●	●	●	●	●	●	●	●	●	●	●	●	●	●	●														●			Croatia
1945	●	●	●	●		●		●			●		●	●	●	●	●	●	●	●				●[27]			●										Cuba
1960	●	●	●	●		●	●	●	●	●	●	●	●	●	●	●	●	●	●	●	●							●							●[13]		Cyprus[28]
1993	●	●	●	●		●	●	●	●	●	●	●	●	●	●	●	●	●	●	●														●			Czech Republic
1945	●	●	●	●		●	●	●	●	●	●	●	●	●	●	●	●	●	●	●								●					●	●			Denmark
1977	●	●	●	●	●[10]		●	●	●	●	●	●	●	●	●	●	●	●	●	●			●		●			●							●		Djibouti
1978	●	●	●	●			●	●	●	●	●	●	●	●	●	●	●	●	●	●	●			●			●			●			●				Dominica
1945	●	●	●	●			●	●	●	●	●	●	●	●	●	●	●	●	●	●				●			●					●[4]		●			Dominican Republic
1945	●	●	●	●	●[4]	●	●	●	●	●	●	●	●	●	●	●	●	●	●	●				●			●							●		●	Ecuador
1945	●	●	●	●		●	●	●	●	●	●	●	●	●	●	●	●	●	●	●			●											●	●		Egypt
1945	●	●	●	●			●	●	●	●	●	●	●	●	●	●	●	●	●	●				●			●							●			El Salvador

Government and international organizations (continued)

country	date of independence[a]	date of current or last constitution[b]	type of government	chief of state	head of government	upper house (members)	lower house (members)	first-order (number)	second-order (number)	territorial (nautical miles)	fishing/economic (nautical miles)
Equatorial Guinea	Oct. 12, 1968	Nov. 16, 1991[26]	republic[5]	president	prime minister	80	—	7	18	12	200
Eritrea	May 24, 1993	1993[31]	republic[5]	—president—		60[32]	—	10	...	...	...
Estonia	Aug. 20, 1991	July 3, 1992	republic	president	prime minister	101	—	15	...	12	...
Ethiopia	c. 1000 BC	July 1991[1]	republic	—president[22]—		548[33]	—	9[34]	...	...	...
Faeroe Islands	—	April 1, 1948	part of Danish realm	Danish monarch	[35]	32	—	7	50	3	200
Fiji	Oct. 10, 1970	July 25, 1990	republic	president	prime minister	34	70	...	...	12[9]	200[9]
Finland	Dec. 6, 1917	July 17, 1919	republic	president	prime minister	200	—	12	455	4	12
France	August 843	Oct. 4, 1958	republic	president	prime minister	321	577	22	96	12	200
French Guiana	—	Feb. 28, 1983	overseas dept. (Fr.)	French president	[36]	19	31	2	21	12	200
French Polynesia	—	Sept. 6, 1984	overseas territory (Fr.)	French president	[37]	41	—	5	48	12	200
Gabon	Aug. 17, 1960	March 26, 1991	republic	president	prime minister	120	—	9	37	12	200
Gambia, The	Feb. 18, 1965	*April 24, 1970*	republic	—chairman AFPRC—		—	—	7	35	12	200
Gaza Strip	—	May 4, 1994[38]	interim authority	—chairman PNA—		—	—	...	—	...	...
Georgia	April 9, 1991	1921[39]	republic	chairman (parl.)	prime minister	235[7]	—	3	65	...	...
Germany	May 5, 1955	May 23, 1949	federal republic	president	chancellor	68	672	16	29	40	200
Ghana	March 6, 1957	Jan. 7, 1993	republic	—president—		200	—	110	...	12	200
Gibraltar	—	May 23, 1969	colony (U.K.)	British monarch	governor	18	—	...	...	...	...
Greece	Feb. 3, 1830	June 11, 1975	republic	president	prime minister	300	—	13	52	6/10	3
Greenland	—	May 1, 1979	part of Danish realm	Danish monarch	[35]	27	—	3	18	3	200
Grenada	Feb. 7, 1974	Feb. 7, 1974	constitutional monarchy	British monarch	prime minister	13	15	9	...	12	200
Guadeloupe	—	Feb. 28, 1983	overseas dept. (Fr.)	French president	[36]	42	41	3	34	12	200
Guam	—	Aug. 1, 1950	territory (U.S.)	U.S. president	governor	21	—	19	...	12	200
Guatemala	Sept. 15, 1821	Jan. 14, 1986	republic	—president—		80	—	22	330	12	200
Guernsey	—	Jan. 1, 1949[41]	crown dependency (U.K.)	British monarch[42]	bailiff	60	—	1	2	...	...
Guinea	Oct. 2, 1958	Dec. 23, 1990[1]	republic	—president—		15[43]	—	31	175	12	200
Guinea-Bissau	Sept. 10, 1974	May 16, 1984	republic	president	prime minister	100	—	9	37	12	200
Guyana	May 26, 1966	Oct. 6, 1980	cooperative republic	—president—		65	—	10	71	12	200
Haiti	Jan. 1, 1804	March 29, 1987	republic	president	prime minister	27	83	9	...	12	200
Honduras	Nov. 5, 1838	Jan. 20, 1982	republic	—president—		128	—	18	289	12	200
Hong Kong	—	41	crown colony (U.K.)	British monarch	governor	60	—	...	19	12	3
Hungary	Nov. 16, 1918	Oct. 18, 1989[1]	republic	president	prime minister	394	—	20	184	—	—
Iceland	June 17, 1944	June 17, 1944	republic	president	prime minister	63	—	8	199	12	200
India	Aug. 15, 1947	Jan. 26, 1950	federal republic	president	prime minister	245	545	32	477	12	200
Indonesia	Aug. 17, 1945	Aug. 17, 1945	republic	—president—		1,000	500	27	298	12[9]	200[9]
Iran	Oct. 7, 1906	Dec. 2–3, 1979	Islamic republic	—president[44]—		270	—	25	229	12	50[45]
Iraq	Oct. 3, 1932	Sept. 22, 1968[39]	republic	—president—		250	—	16[46]	96	12	3
Ireland	Dec. 6, 1921	Dec. 29, 1937	republic	president	prime minister	60	166	32	81	12	200
Isle of Man	—	1961[41]	crown dependency (U.K.)	British monarch[42]	chief minister	10	24	24	...	12[47]	...
Israel	May 14, 1948	June 1950[41]	republic	president	prime minister	120	—	6	15	12	3
Italy	March 17, 1861	Jan. 1, 1948	republic	president	prime minister	326	630	20	94	12	12
Jamaica	Aug. 6, 1962	Aug. 6, 1962	constitutional monarchy	British monarch	prime minister	21	60	13	—	12	200
Japan	c. 660 BC	May 3, 1947	constitutional monarchy	emperor	prime minister	252	511	47	3,260	12[48]	200
Jersey	—	Jan. 1, 1949[41]	crown dependency (U.K.)	British monarch[42]	bailiff	58	—	—	—	3	...
Jordan	May 25, 1946	Jan. 8, 1952	constitutional monarchy	—king[22]—		40	80	8	44	3	3
Kazakhstan	Dec. 16, 1991	Jan. 28, 1993	republic	president	prime minister	177	—	19	218	—	—
Kenya	Dec. 12, 1963	Dec. 12, 1963	republic	—president—		202	—	8	40	12	200
Kiribati	July 12, 1979	July 12, 1979	republic	—president—		41	—	24	...	12[9]	200[9]
Korea, North	Sept. 9, 1948	Dec. 27, 1972	socialist republic	president	premier	687	—	13	172	12	200
Korea, South	Aug. 15, 1948	Feb. 25, 1988	republic	president	prime minister	299	—	15	204	12[49]	12
Kuwait	June 19, 1961	Nov. 16, 1962	const. mon. (emirate)	—emir[22]—		50	—	—	—	12	3
Kyrgyzstan	Aug. 31, 1991	May 5, 1993	republic	president	prime minister	35[50]	70[50]	7	89	—	—
Laos	Oct. 23, 1953	Aug. 15, 1991	republic	president	prime minister	85	—	17	114	—	—
Latvia	Aug. 21, 1991	Nov. 7, 1922	republic	president	prime minister	100	—	33	49	12	...
Lebanon	Nov. 26, 1941	Sept. 21, 1990	republic	president	prime minister	128	—	...	...	12	3
Lesotho	Oct. 4, 1966	April 2, 1993	constitutional monarchy	king	prime minister	33[6]	65	11	...	—	—
Liberia	July 26, 1847	July 25, 1993[51]	republic[5]	—chairman CS[52]—		35[43]	—	...	...	200	3
Libya	Dec. 24, 1951	March 2, 1977	socialist state[53]	rev. leader	sec. GPC	750	—	13	c. 1,500	12[54]	3
Liechtenstein	July 12, 1806	Oct. 5, 1921	constitutional monarchy	prince	head of govt.	25	—	11	—	—	—
Lithuania	Sept. 6, 1991	Nov. 6, 1992	republic	president	prime minister	141	—	55	81	12	...
Luxembourg	May 10, 1867	Oct. 17, 1868	constitutional monarchy	grand duke	prime minister	21[6]	60	3	12	—	—
Macau	—	May 10, 1990	special terr. (Port.)	—governor—		23	—	2	7	6	12
Macedonia	April 1992	Nov. 17, 1991	republic	president	prime minister	120	—	34	...	—	—
Madagascar	June 26, 1960	Sept. 21, 1992	republic	president	prime minister	138	—	6	113	12	200
Malawi	July 6, 1964	July 6, 1966	republic	—president—		177	—	3	24	—	—
Malaysia	Aug. 31, 1957	Aug. 31, 1957	fed. const. monarchy	paramount ruler	prime minister	69	180	15	144	12	200
Maldives	July 26, 1965	Nov. 11, 1968	republic	—president—		48	—	21	202	12[9]	30
Mali	Sept. 22, 1960	Jan. 5, 1992	republic	president	prime minister	116	—	9	46	—	—
Malta	Sept. 21, 1964	Dec. 13, 1974	republic	president	prime minister	65	—	...	...	12	25
Marshall Islands	Dec. 22, 1990	May 1, 1979	republic	—president—		12[6]	33	26	—	12[9]	200
Martinique	—	Feb. 28, 1983	overseas dept. (Fr.)	French president	[36]	45	41	3	34	12	200
Mauritania	Nov. 28, 1960	July 21, 1991	republic	—president—		56	79	13	53	12	200
Mauritius	March 12, 1968	March 12, 1992	republic	president	prime minister	70	—	11	105	12	200
Mayotte	—	Dec. 24, 1976	terr. collectivity (Fr.)	French president	[55]	17	—	17	...	12	200
Mexico	Sept. 16, 1810	Feb. 5, 1917	federal republic	—president—		128	500	32	2,378	12	200
Micronesia	Dec. 22, 1990	May 10, 1979	federal republic	—president—		14	—	4	...	12	200
Moldova	Aug. 27, 1991	Aug. 27, 1994	republic	president	prime minister	104	—	...	...	—	—
Monaco	Feb. 2, 1861	Dec. 17, 1962	constitutional monarchy	prince	min. of state	18	—	...	...	12	3
Mongolia	March 13, 1921	Feb. 12, 1992	republic	president	prime minister	76	—	22	258	—	—
Morocco	March 2, 1956	Oct. 9, 1992	constitutional monarchy	—king[22]—		333	—	46[56]	...	12	200
Mozambique	June 25, 1975	Nov. 30, 1990	republic	—president—		250	—	11	c. 150	12	200
Myanmar (Burma)	Jan. 4, 1948	*Jan. 4, 1974*	republic	—chairman SLORC—		(492)	—	14	314	12	200
Namibia	March 21, 1990	March 21, 1990	republic	—president—		26	72	14	—	12	200
Nauru	Jan. 31, 1968	Jan. 31, 1968	republic	—president—		18	—	...	...	12	200
Nepal	Nov. 13, 1769	Nov. 9, 1990	constitutional monarchy	king	prime minister	60	205	14	75	—	—
Netherlands, The	March 30, 1814	Feb. 17, 1983	constitutional monarchy	monarch	prime minister	75	150	12	646	12	200

membership in international organizations																																				country
United Nations (date of admission)	UN organs★ and affiliated intergovernmental organizations																				Commonwealth of Nations	regional multipurpose						economic									
	UNCTAD★[e]	UNICEF★[f]	ICJ★	FAO	GATT (WTO)	IAEA[g]	IBRD	ICAO	IDA	IFC	ILO	IMF	IMO	ITU[e]	UNESCO	UNIDO	UPU[e]	WHO	WIPO[e]	WMO		EU	GCC	LAS[g]	OAS	OAU	SPC	ACP	ADB	APEC	CARICOM	ECOWAS	EEC	I-ADB	IDB[g]	OPEC	
1968	●	●	●	●	●[10]		●	●	●[10]	●	●	●	●	●	●	●	●	●		●						●		●									Equatorial Guinea
1993	●	●		●			●[10]	●		●[10]	●	●		●	●	●	●	●		●				●[10]		●											Eritrea
1991	●	●	●	●	●[4]	●	●	●		●	●	●	●	●	●	●	●	●	●	●																	Estonia
1945	●	●	●	●	●	●	●	●	●	●	●	●	●	●	●	●	●	●	●	●						●		●									Ethiopia
—																		●		●																	Faeroe Islands
1970	●	●	●	●	●	●	●	●	●	●	●	●	●	●	●	●	●	●	●	●	●						●	●	●	●							Fiji
1955	●	●	●	●	●	●	●	●	●	●	●	●	●	●	●	●	●	●	●	●		●[10]							●				●[10]	●			Finland
1945	●	●	●	●	●	●	●	●	●	●	●	●	●	●	●	●	●	●	●	●		●					●						●				France
—																	●			●							●										French Guiana
—																	●										●										French Polynesia
1960	●	●	●	●	●	●	●	●	●	●	●	●	●	●	●	●	●	●	●	●						●		●							●	●	Gabon
1965	●	●	●	●	●	●	●	●	●	●	●	●	●	●	●	●	●	●	●	●	●					●		●				●					Gambia, The
—																																					Gaza Strip
1992	●	●		●			●[10]	●			●	●		●	●		●	●	●	●																	Georgia
1973	●	●	●	●	●	●	●	●	●	●	●	●	●	●	●	●	●	●	●	●		●							●				●	●	●		Germany
1957	●	●	●	●	●	●	●	●	●	●	●	●	●	●	●	●	●	●	●	●	●					●		●				●					Ghana
—																																					Gibraltar
1945	●	●	●	●	●	●	●	●	●	●	●	●	●	●	●	●	●	●	●	●		●							●				●				Greece
—																		●		●																	Greenland
1974	●	●	●	●	●		●	●	●	●	●	●	●	●	●		●	●			●				●			●			●						Grenada
—																																					Guadeloupe
—																											●										Guam
1945	●	●	●	●	●	●	●	●	●	●	●	●	●	●	●	●	●	●	●	●					●									●			Guatemala
—																																					Guernsey
1958	●	●	●	●	●[10]	●	●	●	●	●	●	●	●	●	●	●	●	●	●	●						●		●				●			●		Guinea
1974	●	●	●	●	●		●	●	●	●	●	●	●	●	●	●	●	●	●	●						●		●				●					Guinea-Bissau
1966	●	●	●	●	●		●	●	●	●	●	●	●	●	●	●	●	●	●	●	●				●			●			●			●			Guyana
1945	●	●	●	●	●	●	●	●	●	●	●	●	●	●	●	●	●	●	●	●					●			●			●[4]			●			Haiti
1945	●	●	●	●	●	●	●	●	●	●	●	●	●	●	●	●	●	●	●	●					●									●			Honduras
—		●		●	●[13]						●						●												●	●							Hong Kong
1955	●	●	●	●	●	●	●	●	●	●	●	●	●	●	●	●	●	●	●	●																	Hungary
1946	●	●	●	●	●	●	●	●	●	●	●	●	●	●	●	●	●	●	●	●																	Iceland
1945	●	●	●	●	●	●	●	●	●	●	●	●	●	●	●	●	●	●	●	●	●							●	●					●	●		India
1950	●	●	●	●	●	●	●	●	●	●	●	●	●	●	●	●	●	●	●	●								●	●					●	●	●	Indonesia
1945	●	●	●	●	●[4]	●	●	●	●	●	●	●	●	●	●	●	●	●	●	●				●										●	●	●	Iran
1945	●	●	●	●		●	●	●	●	●	●	●	●	●	●	●	●	●	●	●				●										●	●	●	Iraq
1955	●	●	●	●	●	●	●	●	●	●	●	●	●	●	●	●	●	●	●	●		●						●					●				Ireland
—																																					Isle of Man
1949	●	●	●	●	●	●	●	●	●	●	●	●	●	●	●	●	●	●	●	●									●				●	●			Israel
1955	●	●	●	●	●	●	●	●	●	●	●	●	●	●	●	●	●	●	●	●		●						●					●				Italy
1962	●	●	●	●	●		●	●	●	●	●	●	●	●	●	●	●	●	●	●	●				●			●			●			●			Jamaica
1956	●	●	●	●	●	●	●	●	●	●	●	●	●	●	●	●	●	●	●	●									●	●	●			●			Japan
—																																					Jersey
1955	●	●	●	●	●[4]	●	●	●	●	●	●	●	●	●	●	●	●	●	●	●				●										●			Jordan
1992	●	●		●	●[4]	●	●	●	●	●	●	●	●	●	●	●	●	●	●	●																	Kazakhstan
1963	●	●	●	●	●		●	●	●	●	●	●	●	●	●	●	●	●	●	●	●					●		●									Kenya
—		●		●	●[10]												●										●	●									Kiribati
1991	●	●		●				●			●		●	●	●	●	●	●	●	●																	Korea, North
1991	●	●	●	●	●	●	●	●	●	●	●	●	●	●	●	●	●	●	●	●								●	●					●			Korea, South
1963	●	●	●	●	●	●	●	●	●	●	●	●	●	●	●	●	●	●	●	●			●	●										●	●	●	Kuwait
1992	●	●		●	●[4]		●			●	●	●		●	●		●	●		●																	Kyrgyzstan
1955	●	●	●	●			●	●	●	●	●	●	●	●	●	●	●	●	●	●									●								Laos
1991	●	●	●	●	●[4]	●	●	●	●	●	●	●	●	●	●	●	●	●	●	●																	Latvia
1945	●	●	●	●		●	●	●	●	●	●	●	●	●	●	●	●	●	●	●				●										●			Lebanon
1966	●	●	●	●			●	●	●	●	●	●		●	●	●	●	●		●	●					●		●									Lesotho
1945	●	●	●	●	●		●	●	●	●	●	●	●	●	●	●	●	●	●	●						●		●				●					Liberia
1955	●	●	●	●		●	●	●	●	●	●	●	●	●	●	●	●	●	●	●				●		●		●						●	●	●	Libya
1990	●	●	●								●		●	●	●		●[4]	●	●	●																	Liechtenstein
1991	●	●	●	●	●[4]	●	●	●	●	●	●	●	●	●	●	●	●	●	●	●																	Lithuania
1945	●	●	●	●	●	●	●	●	●	●	●	●	●	●	●	●	●	●	●	●		●						●					●				Luxembourg
—													●[13]																●								Macau
1993	●	●		●	●[4]	●	●[10]	●	●	●	●	●	●	●	●	●	●	●	●	●																	Macedonia
1960	●	●	●	●	●		●	●	●	●	●	●	●	●	●	●	●	●	●	●						●		●							●		Madagascar
1964	●	●	●	●	●		●	●	●	●	●	●	●	●	●	●	●	●	●	●	●					●		●									Malawi
1957	●	●	●	●	●	●	●	●	●	●	●	●	●	●	●	●	●	●	●	●	●							●	●					●			Malaysia
1965	●	●	●	●	●		●	●	●	●	●	●	●	●	●	●	●	●	●	●	●							●	●					●			Maldives
1960	●	●	●	●	●		●	●	●	●	●	●	●	●	●	●	●	●	●	●						●		●				●			●		Mali
1964	●	●	●	●	●	●	●	●	●	●	●	●	●	●	●	●	●	●	●	●	●												●[13]				Malta
1991	●	●		●									●[10]	●			●										●		●								Marshall Islands
—																	●																				Martinique
1961	●	●	●	●	●		●	●	●	●	●	●	●	●	●	●	●	●	●	●				●		●		●							●		Mauritania
1968	●	●	●	●	●		●	●	●	●	●	●	●	●	●	●	●	●	●	●	●					●		●									Mauritius
—																																					Mayotte
1945	●	●	●	●	●	●	●	●	●	●	●	●	●	●	●	●	●	●	●	●					●					●	●[4]			●			Mexico
1991	●	●		●									●[10]	●			●												●								Micronesia
1992	●			●	●[4]		●		●[10]	●	●	●		●	●		●	●		●																	Moldova
1993	●	●		●							●			●	●		●	●		●																	Monaco
1961	●	●	●	●	●[4]	●	●	●	●	●	●	●		●	●	●	●	●	●	●									●								Mongolia
1956	●	●	●	●	●	●	●	●	●	●	●	●	●	●	●	●	●	●	●	●				●		●		●						●			Morocco
1975	●	●	●	●			●	●	●	●	●	●	●	●	●	●	●	●	●	●						●		●									Mozambique
1948	●	●	●	●	●		●	●	●	●	●	●	●	●	●	●	●	●	●	●								●	●								Myanmar (Burma)
1990	●	●	●	●	●[10]		●	●	●	●	●	●		●	●	●	●	●		●	●[57]					●		●									Namibia
—		●												●			●										●							●			Nauru
1955	●	●	●	●	●[4]		●	●	●	●	●	●	●	●	●	●	●	●	●	●									●								Nepal
1945	●	●	●	●	●	●	●	●	●	●	●	●	●	●	●	●	●	●	●	●		●						●					●				Netherlands, The

Government and international organizations (continued)

country	date of independence[a]	date of current or last constitution[b]	type of government	executive branch[c]		legislative branch[d]		admin. subdivisions		seaward claims	
				chief of state	head of government	upper house (members)	lower house (members)	first-order (number)	second-order (number)	territorial (nautical miles)	fishing/economic (nautical miles)
Netherlands Antilles	—	Dec. 29, 1954	overseas territory (Neth.)	Dutch monarch	[12]	22	—	5	—	12	200
New Caledonia	—	Nov. 9, 1988	overseas territory (Fr.)	French president	[58]	54	—	3	32	12	200
New Zealand	Sept. 26, 1907	June 30, 1852[41]	constitutional monarchy	British monarch	prime minister	99	—	12	74	12	200
Nicaragua	April 30, 1838	Jan. 9, 1987	republic	president		92	—	17	143	200	200
Niger	Aug. 3, 1960	Dec. 26, 1992[26]	republic	president	prime minister	83	—	7	36	—	—
Nigeria	Oct. 1, 1960	*Oct. 1, 1979*	federal republic	chairman PRC		(91)	(593)	31	589	30	200
Northern Mariana Is.	—	Jan. 9, 1978	commonwealth (U.S.)	U.S. president	governor	9	18	4	—	12	200
Norway	June 7, 1905	May 17, 1814	constitutional monarchy	king	prime minister	165	—	19	439	4	200
Oman	Dec. 20, 1951	—	monarchy (sultanate)	sultan		60[6]	—	59	—	12	200
Pakistan	Aug. 14, 1947	Aug. 14, 1973	federal Islamic republic	president	prime minister	87	217	16[59]	...	12	200
Panama	Nov. 3, 1903	Oct. 11, 1972[34]	republic	president[60]		72	—	10	67	200	[3]
Papua New Guinea	Sept. 16, 1975	Sept. 16, 1975	constitutional monarchy	British monarch	prime minister	109	—	20	...	12[9]	200[9]
Paraguay	May 14, 1811	June 22, 1992	republic	president		45	80	18	217	—	—
Peru	July 28, 1821	Dec. 29, 1993	republic	president		80[43]	—	14	190	200	200
Philippines	July 4, 1946	Feb. 11, 1987	republic	president		24	200[61]	15	90	[30]	200[9]
Poland	Nov. 10, 1918	Dec. 8, 1992[62]	republic	president	prime minister	100	460	49	2,465	12	[63]
Portugal	*c.* 1140	April 25, 1976	parliamentary state	president	prime minister	230	—	20	305	12	200
Puerto Rico	—	July 25, 1952	commonwealth (U.S.)	U.S. president	governor	29	53	78	...	12	200
Qatar	Sept. 3, 1971	July 1970[39]	monarchy	emir		35[6]	—	9	—	12	[64]
Réunion	—	Feb. 28, 1983	overseas dept. (Fr.)	French president	[36]	47	45	4	24	12	200
Romania	May 21, 1877	Dec. 13, 1991	republic	president	prime minister	143	341	41	260	12[30]	200[30]
Russia	Dec. 8, 1991	Dec. 24, 1993	federal republic	president	prime minister	178	450	89	1,863	12	...
Rwanda	July 1, 1962	June 10, 1991	republic[5]	president	prime minister	70	—	11	145	—	—
St. Kitts and Nevis	Sept. 19, 1983	Sept. 19, 1983	constitutional monarchy	British monarch	prime minister	15	—	1	—	12	200
St. Lucia	Feb. 22, 1979	Feb. 22, 1979	constitutional monarchy	British monarch	prime minister	11	17	10	—	12	200
St. Vincent	Oct. 27, 1979	Oct. 27, 1979	constitutional monarchy	British monarch	prime minister	21	—	7	—	12	200
San Marino	855	Oct. 8, 1600	republic	captains-regent (2)		60	—	9	—	—	—
São Tomé and Príncipe	July 12, 1975	Sept. 10, 1990	republic	president	prime minister	55	—	2	7	12[9]	200[9]
Saudi Arabia	Sept. 23, 1932	—	monarchy	king		62[6]	—	13	...	12	[3]
Senegal	Aug. 20, 1960	March 7, 1963	republic	president	prime minister	120	—	10	31	12[30]	200[30]
Seychelles	June 29, 1976	June 18, 1993	republic	president		33	—	...	...	12	200
Sierra Leone	April 27, 1961	*Oct. 1, 1991*	republic	chairman SCS		(127)	—	4	148	200	[3]
Singapore	Aug. 9, 1965	June 3, 1959[41]	republic	president	prime minister	87	—	—	—	3	12
Slovakia	Jan. 1, 1993	Jan. 1, 1993	republic	president	prime minister	150	—	4	38	—	—
Slovenia	June 25, 1991	Dec. 23, 1991	republic	president	prime minister	40	90	62	...	...	...
Solomon Islands	July 7, 1978	July 7, 1978	constitutional monarchy	British monarch	prime minister	47	—	8	...	12[9]	200[9]
Somalia	July 1, 1960	July 1, 1960	UN-imposed regime[65]	[66]		...	—	...	...	200	200
South Africa	May 31, 1910	April 27, 1994	republic	president[67]		90	400	9	349	12	200
Spain	1492	Dec. 29, 1978	constitutional monarchy	king	prime minister	255	350	17	50	12	200
Sri Lanka	Feb. 4, 1948	Sept. 7, 1978	republic	president		225	—	...	...	12	200
Sudan, The	Jan. 1, 1956	*Oct. 10, 1985*	Islamic military regime	president		302	—	26[69]	...	12	[3]
Suriname	Nov. 25, 1975	Nov. 25, 1987	republic	president		51	—	10	—	12	200
Swaziland	Sept. 6, 1968	*Sept. 6, 1968*	monarchy	king[22]		30	65	4	40	—	—
Sweden	before 836	Jan. 1, 1975	constitutional monarchy	king	prime minister	349	—	24	286	12	[15]
Switzerland	Sept. 22, 1499	May 29, 1874	federal state	president FC		46	200	26	3,003	—	—
Syria	April 17, 1946	March 14, 1973	republic	president		250	—	14	59	35	[3]
Taiwan	Oct. 25, 1945	Dec. 25, 1947[41]	republic	president	premier	402[70]	161	5	25	24	200
Tajikistan	Sept. 9, 1991	April 1978	republic	de facto president	prime minister	230	—	5	...	—	—
Tanzania	Dec. 9, 1961	April 25, 1977	republic	president		255	—	25	99	12	200
Thailand	1350	Dec. 9, 1991	constitutional monarchy	king	prime minister	270	360	73	711	12	200
Togo	April 27, 1960	Sept. 27, 1992[26]	republic	president	prime minister	81	—	5	21	30	200
Tonga	June 4, 1970	Nov. 4, 1875	constitutional monarchy	monarch[71]		30	—	5	23	12	200
Trinidad and Tobago	Aug. 31, 1962	July 27, 1976	republic	president	prime minister	31	36	12	...	12[9]	200[9]
Tunisia	March 20, 1956	June 1, 1959	republic	president	prime minister	163	—	23	246	12	[3]
Turkey	Oct. 29, 1923	Nov. 7, 1982	republic	president	prime minister	450	—	76	829	12[72]	[15]
Turkmenistan	Oct. 27, 1991	May 18, 1992	republic	president		175	—	5	...	—	—
Tuvalu	Oct. 1, 1978	Sept. 15, 1986	constitutional monarchy	British monarch	prime minister	12	—	8	—	12[9]	200[9]
Uganda	Oct. 9, 1962	*Sept. 8, 1967*	republic[5]	president[22]		214[33, 61]	—	38	...	—	—
Ukraine	Aug. 24, 1991	April 1978	republic	president	prime minister	450	—	25	485	12	200
United Arab Emirates	Dec. 2, 1971	Dec. 2, 1971[39]	federation of emirates	president	prime minister	40[6]	—	7	—	12	200
United Kingdom	Oct. 14, 1066	[73]	constitutional monarchy	monarch	prime minister	1,183	651	3[74]	86[75]	12[47]	200
United States	July 4, 1776	March 4, 1789	federal republic	president		100	435	51	3,043[76]	12	200
Uruguay	Aug. 25, 1828	Feb. 15, 1967	republic	president		31	99	19	...	200	200
Uzbekistan	Aug. 31, 1991	Dec. 8, 1992	republic	president	prime minister	150[50]	—	13	...	...	...
Vanuatu	July 30, 1980	July 30, 1980	republic	president	prime minister	46	—	11	...	12[9]	200[9]
Venezuela	July 5, 1811	Jan. 23, 1961	federal republic	president		53	199	24	202	12	200
Vietnam	Sept. 2, 1945	April 15, 1992	socialist republic	president	prime minister	395	—	53	467	12	200
Virgin Islands (U.S.)	—	July 22, 1954	territory (U.S.)	U.S. president	governor	15	—	2	—	12	200
West Bank	—	—	Israeli military[77]	—	area commander	—	—	...	—	—	—
Western Sahara	—	—	annexture of Morocco	—	—	—	—	5	...	12	200
Western Samoa	Jan. 1, 1962	Oct. 28, 1960	[79]	head of state	prime minister	48	—	...	—	12	200
Yemen	December 1918	May 16, 1991	republic	president	prime minister	301	—	17	...	12	200
Yugoslavia	Dec. 1, 1918	April 27, 1992	federal republic	federal president	prime minister	40	138	2	...	12	...
Zaire	June 30, 1960	April 9, 1994[81]	republic[5]	president	prime minister	738	—	11	41	12	200
Zambia	Oct. 24, 1964	Aug. 30, 1991	republic	president		159	—	9	57	—	—
Zimbabwe	April 18, 1980	April 18, 1980	republic	president		150	—	10	80	—	—

[1]Transitional constitution. [2]Office vacant from June 1994. [3]Territorial sea claim assumed to claim fishing/economic rights within the same zone. [4]Observer status. [5]Transitional government. [6]Body with limited or no legislative authority. [7]Includes unoccupied seats. [8]President of France and Bishop of Seu d'Urgell, Spain. [9]Measured from claimed archipelagic baselines. [10]Full membership pending. [11]Promulgation date of significant amendments to July 9, 1853, constitution. [12]Executive responsibilities divided between (for The Netherlands) the governor and (locally) the prime minister. [13]Associate member. [14]Formally a constitutional monarchy. [15]Defined by equidistant line. [16]1990. [17]3 nautical miles from mouth of Sarstoon River (southern boundary with Guatemala) to Ranguana Caye. [18]Executive responsibilities divided between (for the U.K.) the governor and (locally) the premier of the Cabinet. [19]Resembles a constitutional monarchy without a formal constitution. [20]Central government has ineffective control because of civil war. [21]Government assumed interim status as of June 1994; expect implementation of joint Bosnian-Muslim–Bosnian-Croatian government from December 1994. [22]Assisted by the prime minister. [23]First prime minister assisted by second prime minister. [24]Governor-general can exercise all the powers of the reigning monarch of the Commonwealth. Royal assent to the monarch is a matter of choice. [25]Temporarily increased from 104. [26]Date of referendum approving new constitution. [27]Suspended membership. [28]Republic of Cyprus only. [29]Seats not occupied as of mid-1994. [30]Zone defined by geographic coordinates. [31]Official proclamations organizing government. [32]Excludes the central committee for the People's Front for Democracy and Justice. [33]Constituent assembly; body writing new constitution. [34]Pending approval of new constitution. [35]Executive responsibilities divided between (for Denmark) the high commissioner and (locally) the prime minister. [36]Executive responsibilities divided among (for France) the commissioner and (locally) the president of the General Council and the president of the Regional Council. [37]Executive responsibilities divided between (for France) the high commissioner and (locally) the president of the Council of Ministers. [38]Date of agreement providing for Palestinian self-rule in the Gaza Strip and Jericho area of the West Bank. [39]Provisional constitution. [40]3 nautical miles in Baltic Sea, 16 nautical miles in North Sea. [41]Evolving body of constitutional law.

membership in international organizations

United Nations (date of admission)	UN organs★ and affiliated intergovernmental organizations																				Commonwealth of Nations	regional multipurpose						economic									country
	UNCTAD★[e]	UNICEF★[f]	ICJ★	FAO	GATT (WTO)	IAEA[e]	IBRD	ICAO	IDA	IFC	ILO	IMF	IMO	ITU[e]	UNESCO	UNIDO	UPU[e]	WHO	WIPO[e]	WMO		EU	GCC	LAS[g]	OAS	OAU	SPC	ACP	ADB	APEC	CARICOM	ECOWAS	EEC	I-ADB	IDB[g]	OPEC	
—															●[13]		●			●											●[4]						Netherlands Antilles
—																	●			●							●										New Caledonia
1945	●	●	●	●	●	●	●	●	●	●	●	●	●	●	●	●	●	●	●	●	●						●			●							New Zealand
1945	●	●	●	●	●	●	●	●	●	●	●	●	●	●	●	●	●	●	●	●					●				●					●			Nicaragua
1960	●	●	●	●	●	●	●	●	●	●	●	●		●	●	●	●	●	●	●						●		●				●			●		Niger
1960	●	●	●	●	●	●	●	●	●	●	●	●	●	●	●	●	●	●		●	●					●		●				●				●	Nigeria
—																	●										●										Northern Mariana Is.
1945	●	●	●	●	●	●	●	●	●	●	●	●	●	●	●	●	●	●	●	●									●					●			Norway
1971	●	●	●	●			●	●	●	●		●	●	●	●	●	●	●		●			●	●											●		Oman
1947	●	●	●	●	●	●	●	●	●	●	●	●	●	●	●	●	●	●	●	●	●								●						●		Pakistan
1945	●	●	●	●	●[4]	●	●	●	●	●	●	●	●	●	●	●	●	●	●	●					●									●			Panama
1975	●	●	●	●	●[10]		●	●	●	●	●	●	●	●	●	●	●	●		●	●						●	●	●	●							Papua New Guinea
1945	●	●	●	●	●	●	●	●	●	●	●	●	●	●	●	●	●	●	●	●					●									●			Paraguay
1945	●	●	●	●	●	●	●	●	●	●	●	●	●	●	●	●	●	●	●	●					●									●			Peru
1945	●	●	●	●	●	●	●	●	●	●	●	●	●	●	●	●	●	●	●	●									●	●							Philippines
1945	●	●	●	●	●	●	●	●	●	●	●	●	●	●	●	●	●	●	●	●																	Poland
1955	●	●	●	●	●	●	●	●		●	●	●	●	●	●	●	●	●	●	●		●											●	●			Portugal
—																	●	●[13]													●[4]						Puerto Rico
1971	●	●	●	●	●	●	●	●			●	●	●	●	●	●	●	●	●	●			●	●											●	●	Qatar
—																	●																				Réunion
1955	●	●	●	●	●	●	●	●	●	●	●	●	●	●	●	●	●	●	●	●																	Romania
1991	●	●			●[4]	●	●	●	●		●	●	●	●	●	●	●	●	●	●																	Russia
1962	●	●	●	●	●		●	●	●	●	●	●		●	●	●	●	●	●	●						●		●									Rwanda
1983	●	●	●	●	●		●		●			●			●	●	●	●			●				●			●			●						St. Kitts and Nevis
1979	●	●	●	●	●		●	●	●	●	●	●	●		●	●	●	●	●	●	●				●			●			●						St. Lucia
1980	●	●	●	●	●		●	●	●			●	●	●	●	●	●	●			●				●			●			●						St. Vincent
1992	●		●					●			●	●		●	●		●	●	●	●																	San Marino
1975	●	●	●	●	●[10]		●	●	●		●	●	●	●	●	●	●	●		●						●		●									São Tomé and Príncipe
1945	●	●	●	●	●[4]	●	●	●	●	●	●	●	●	●	●	●	●	●	●	●			●	●											●	●	Saudi Arabia
1960	●	●	●	●	●	●	●	●	●	●	●	●	●	●	●	●	●	●	●	●						●		●				●			●		Senegal
1976	●	●	●	●	●[10]		●	●		●	●	●	●		●	●	●	●		●	●					●		●									Seychelles
1961	●	●	●	●	●	●	●	●	●	●	●	●	●	●	●	●	●	●	●	●	●					●		●				●			●		Sierra Leone
1965	●	●	●		●	●	●	●		●	●	●	●	●			●	●	●	●	●								●	●							Singapore
1993	●	●		●	●	●	●	●	●	●	●	●	●	●	●	●	●	●	●	●																	Slovakia
1992	●	●		●	●		●	●	●		●	●	●	●	●	●	●	●	●	●																	Slovenia
1978	●	●	●	●	●[10]		●	●	●	●	●	●	●	●			●	●		●	●						●	●	●								Solomon Islands
1960	●	●	●	●			●	●	●	●	●	●	●	●	●	●	●	●	●	●				●		●		●							●		Somalia
1945	●	●	●	●	●	●	●	●	●	●		●		●			●	●	●	68	●					●											South Africa
1955	●	●	●	●	●	●	●	●	●	●	●	●	●	●	●	●	●	●	●	●		●							●				●	●			Spain
1955	●	●	●	●	●	●	●	●	●	●	●	●	●	●	●	●	●	●	●	●	●								●								Sri Lanka
1956	●	●	●	●		●	●	●	●	●	●	●	●	●	●	●	●	●	●	●				●		●		●							●		Sudan, The
1975	●	●	●	●	●		●	●			●	●	●	●	●	●	●	●	●	●					●			●			●[4]			●			Suriname
1968	●	●	●	●	●		●	●	●	●	●	●		●	●	●	●	●	●	●	●					●		●									Swaziland
1946	●	●	●	●	●	●	●	●	●	●	●	●	●	●	●	●	●	●	●	●		●[10]						●	●				●[10]	●			Sweden
—	●	●	●	●	●	●	●	●	●	●	●	●	●	●	●	●	●	●	●	●									●					●			Switzerland
1945	●	●	●	●		●	●	●	●	●	●	●	●	●	●	●	●	●		●				●											●		Syria
—					●[4]																								●	●							Taiwan
1992	●	●					●		●			●			●	●	●[10]	●		●																	Tajikistan
1961	●	●	●	●	●	●	●	●	●	●	●	●	●	●	●	●	●	●	●	●	●					●		●									Tanzania
1946	●	●	●	●	●	●	●	●	●	●	●	●	●	●	●	●	●	●	●	●									●	●							Thailand
1960	●	●	●	●	●		●	●	●	●	●	●	●	●	●	●	●	●	●	●						●		●				●					Togo
—	●	●		●	●[10]		●	●	●	●		●		●	●	●	●	●			●						●	●	●								Tonga
1962	●	●	●	●	●		●	●	●	●	●	●	●	●	●	●	●	●	●	●	●				●			●			●			●			Trinidad and Tobago
1956	●	●	●	●	●	●	●	●	●	●	●	●	●	●	●	●	●	●	●	●				●		●									●		Tunisia
1945	●	●	●	●	●	●	●	●	●	●	●	●	●	●	●	●	●	●	●	●									●				●[13]		●		Turkey
1992	●	●			●[4]		●	●	●[10]		●	●	●	●	●		●	●		●															●		Turkmenistan
—		●			●[10]										●		●				●[57]						●	●	●								Tuvalu
1962	●	●	●	●	●	●	●	●	●	●	●	●		●	●	●	●	●	●	●	●					●		●							●		Uganda
1945	●				●[4]	●	●	●	●[10]		●	●	●	●	●	●	●	●	●	●																	Ukraine
1971	●	●	●	●	●	●	●	●	●	●	●	●	●	●	●	●	●	●	●	●			●	●											●	●	United Arab Emirates
1945	●	●	●	●	●	●	●	●	●	●	●	●	●	●	●[4]	●	●	●	●	●	●	●					●		●				●	●			United Kingdom
1945	●	●	●	●	●	●	●	●	●	●	●	●	●	●	●[4]	●	●	●	●	●					●		●		●	●				●			United States
1945	●	●	●	●	●	●	●	●		●	●	●	●	●	●	●	●	●	●	●					●									●			Uruguay
1992	●	●			●[4]		●	●	●		●	●		●	●		●[10]	●	●	●																	Uzbekistan
1981	●	●	●	●			●	●	●	●		●	●	●		●	●	●		●	●						●	●	●								Vanuatu
1945	●	●	●	●	●	●	●	●		●	●	●	●	●	●	●	●	●	●	●					●						●[4]			●		●	Venezuela
1977	●	●	●	●	●[4]	●	●	●	●	●	●	●	●	●	●	●	●	●	●	●									●								Vietnam
—																	●														●						Virgin Islands (U.S.)
—																																					West Bank
—																										●[78]											Western Sahara
1976	●	●	●	●			●		●	●		●		●	●		●	●			●						●	●	●								Western Samoa
1947	●	●	●	●	●[10]		●	●	●	●	●	●	●	●	●	●	●	●	●	●				●											●		Yemen
[80]	●	●	●	●	●	●	●	●[10]	●[10]	●	●	●	●	●	●	●	●	●	●	●														●			Yugoslavia
1960	●	●	●	●	●	●	●	●	●	●	●	68	●	●	●	●	●	●	●	●						●		●									Zaire
1964	●	●	●	●	●	●	●	●	●	●	●	●		●	●	●	●	●	●	●	●					●		●									Zambia
1980	●	●	●	●	●	●	●	●	●	●	●	●		●	●	●	●	●	●	●	●					●		●									Zimbabwe

[42]Represented by the lieutenant governor. [43]Interim legislature. [44]Shares coexecutive authority with spiritual leader. [45]Sea of Oman only; median line boundaries in the Persian Gulf. [46]De facto administration. [47]Median line between the Isle of Man and the United Kingdom. [48]3 nautical miles in 5 straits. [49]3 nautical miles in Korean Strait. [50]As of December 1994 elections. [51]UN-brokered peace agreement. [52]National Transitional Government inaugurated in March 1994 had no effective power outside Monrovia in November 1994. [53]Formally a *jamahiriya,* translated as "the masses of people." [54]Based on Gulf of Sidra closing line (32° 30′ N), in part. [55]Executive responsibilities divided between (for France) the high commissioner and (locally) the president of the General Council. [56]Excludes Western Sahara. [57]Special member. [58]Executive responsibilities divided between (for France) the high commissioner and (locally) the president of the Territorial Congress. [59]Includes 11 federally administered tribal areas; excludes Jammu and Kashmir. [60]Assisted by vice president. [61]Elective seats only. [62]"Little constitution." [63]Defined by international treaties. [64]Limits of continental shelf or median line boundaries. [65]Somaliland (the former colonially administered area of British Somaliland in northern Somalia) declared its unilateral independence from Somalia in May 1991. [66]Special Envoy assisted by the military command of the UN-administered operation in Somalia. [67]Assisted by executive deputy presidents. [68]Suspended membership. [69]Per official announcement of February 1994. [70]Occupied seats mid-1994. [71]Assisted by Privy Council. [72]Black Sea and Mediterranean Sea; 6 nautical miles in Aegean Sea. [73]Based on evolving body of statutes and common law. [74]England and Wales form a single administrative entity. [75]Excludes former metropolitan county councils whose administrative functions have been dispersed among other local authorities. [76]County governments. [77]Jericho area administered by the interim Palestine National Authority. [78]Membership held by the Sahrawi Arab Democratic Republic. [79]Mixed political system approximating a constitutional monarchy. [80]Seat in the UN General Assembly was not recognized as of Sept. 15, 1992. [81]Date of Transitional Constitutional Act.

Area and population

This table provides the area and population for each of the countries of the world and for all but the smallest political dependencies having a permanent civilian population. The data represent the latest published and unpublished data for both the surveyed area of the countries and their populations, the latter both as of a single year (1993) to provide the best comparability and as of the most recent census to provide the fullest comparison of certain demographic measures that are not always available between successive national censuses. The 1994 midyear estimates represent a combination of national, United Nations (UN) or other international organizations, and *Encyclopædia Britannica* estimates so as to give the best fit to available published series, to take account of unpublished information received in correspondence, and to incorporate the results of very recent censuses for which published analyses are not yet available.

One principal point to bear in mind when studying these statistics is that all of them, whatever degree of precision may be implied by the exactness of the numbers, are estimates—all of varying, and some of suspect, accuracy—even when they *contain* a very full enumeration. The United States—which has a long tradition both of census taking and of the use of the most sophisticated analytical tools in processing the data—is unable to determine within 2.1% (the estimated 1990 undercount) its total population nationally. And that is an *average* underenumeration. In states and larger cities, where enumeration of particular populations, both legal and illegal, is most difficult, the accuracy of the enumerated count may be off as much as 4% at a state level and as much as 10% for a single city. The high accuracy attained by census operations in China may approach 0.25% of rigorously maintained civil population registers. Other national census operations not so based, however, are inherently less accurate. For example, Ethiopia's first-ever census in 1984 resulted in figures that were 30% or more above prevailing estimates; Nigeria's 1991 census corrected decades of miscounts and was well below prevailing estimates. An undercount of 2–8% is more typical, but even census operations offering results of 30% or more above or below prevailing estimates can still represent well-founded benchmarks from which future planning may proceed. The editors have tried to take account of the range of variation and accuracy in published data, but it is difficult to establish a value for many sources of inaccuracy unless some country or agency has made a conscientious effort to establish both the relative accuracy (precision) of its estimate and the absolute magnitude of the quantity it is trying to measure—for example, the number of people in Cambodia who died at the hands of the Khmer Rouge. If a figure of 1,000,000 is adopted, what is its accuracy: ± 1%, 10%, 50%? Are the original data documentary or evidentiary, complete or incomplete, analytically biased or unbiased, in good agreement with other published data?

Many similar problems exist and in endless variations: What is the extent of southern European immigration to western Europe in search of jobs? How many refugees from Afghanistan, Liberia, Rwanda, or Burundi are there in surrounding countries? How many undocumented aliens are there in the United States? How many Palestinians are there in the Middle East (they are politically inconvenient to enumerate everywhere)? How many Amerindians exist (remain, preserving their original language and a mode of life unassimilated by the larger national culture) in the countries of South America? How many people have died or emigrated as a result of the civil violence in Central America?

Still, much information is accurate, well founded, and updated regularly.

Area and population

country	area			population (latest estimate)					population (latest census)				
	square miles	square kilo- metres	rank	total midyear 1994	rank	density		% annual growth rate 1989–94	census year	total	male (%)	female (%)	urban (%)
						per sq mi	per sq km						
Afghanistan	251,825	652,225	41	16,903,000	53	67.1	25.9	2.0	1979	13,051,358[1]	51.4	48.6	15.1
Albania	11,100	28,748	142	3,374,000	125	304.0	117.4	1.1	1989	3,182,417	51.5	48.5	35.7
Algeria	919,595	2,381,741	11	27,815,000	33	30.2	11.7	2.7	1987	23,038,942	49.9	50.1	49.7
American Samoa	77	199	204	54,900	206	713.0	275.9	3.8	1990	46,773	51.4	48.6	33.4
Andorra	181	468	192	62,400	203	344.8	133.3	4.2	1992[2]	61,599	53.1	46.9	66.2[3]
Angola	481,354	1,246,700	24	11,233,000	62	23.3	9.0	2.9	1970	5,673,046	52.1	47.9	14.2
Antigua and Barbuda	171	442	194	66,000	201	386.0	149.3	0.0	1991	65,962	48.0[4]	52.0[4]	32.0[4]
Argentina	1,073,518	2,780,400	8	33,880,000	31	31.6	12.2	1.3	1991	32,615,528	48.9	51.1	86.2[5]
Armenia	11,500	29,800	141	3,553,000	122	309.0	119.2	1.6	1989	3,287,677	49.3	50.7	67.8
Aruba	75	193	205	72,100	197	961.3	373.6	3.5	1991	66,687	49.2	50.8	...
Australia	2,966,200	7,682,300	6	17,875,000	49	6.0	2.3	1.2	1991	17,284,036	49.6	50.4	85.4[6]
Austria	32,378	83,859	115	8,027,000	84	247.9	95.7	1.0	1991	7,795,786	48.2	51.8	64.5
Azerbaijan	33,400	86,600	113	7,424,000	88	222.3	85.7	0.9	1989	7,037,867	48.7	51.3	53.8
Bahamas, The	5,382	13,939	158	272,000	174	50.5	19.5	1.6	1990	255,095	49.0	51.0	64.3
Bahrain	268	695	186	552,000	162	2,059.7	794.2	3.4	1991	508,037	57.9	42.1	88.4
Bangladesh	57,295	148,383	93	117,404,000	9	2,049.1	791.2	2.0	1991	109,876,977	51.4	48.6	16.4[5]
Barbados	166	430	195	264,000	176	1,590.4	614.0	0.3	1990[7]	257,083	47.7	52.3	37.9[5]
Belarus	80,153	207,595	85	10,404,000	67	129.8	50.1	0.3	1989	10,199,709	46.9	53.1	65.5
Belgium	11,787	30,528	139	10,118,000	72	858.4	331.4	0.4	1991	9,978,681	48.9	51.1	96.6[3]
Belize	8,867	22,965	150	210,000	179	23.7	9.1	2.7	1991	189,392	50.9	49.1	47.5
Benin	43,500	112,680	101	5,235,000	102	120.3	46.5	3.2	1992	4,855,349	48.7	51.3	37.7[5]
Bermuda	21	54	211	61,700	204	2,938.1	1,142.6	1.0	1991[7]	58,460	48.5	51.5	100.0
Bhutan	18,150	47,000	131	800,000	154	44.1	17.0	2.1	...	...	50.6[5]	49.4[5]	5.3[5]
Bolivia	424,164	1,098,581	28	7,888,000	85	18.6	7.2	2.4	1992	6,420,792	49.4	50.6	57.5
Bosnia and Herzegovina	19,741	51,129	127	4,447,000	111	225.3	87.0	0.6	1991	4,365,639	49.7[8]	50.3[8]	36.2[8]
Botswana	224,607	581,730	47	1,448,000	146	6.4	2.5	3.3	1991	1,326,796	47.8	52.2	23.9
Brazil	3,286,500	8,511,996	5	159,000,000	5	48.4	18.7	1.7	1991	146,917,459	49.4	50.6	75.5
Brunei	2,226	5,765	167	283,000	173	127.1	49.1	2.8	1991	260,482	52.8	47.2	59.4[8]
Bulgaria	42,855	110,994	103	8,452,000	82	197.2	76.1	−1.2	1992	8,472,724	49.1	50.9	67.1
Burkina Faso	105,946	274,400	73	10,044,000	73	94.8	36.6	2.7	1985[7]	7,964,705	48.1	51.9	11.7
Burundi	10,740	27,816	145	5,799,000	96	539.9	208.5	2.2	1990[3]	5,292,793	48.6	51.4	6.3
Cambodia	70,238	181,916	89	9,525,000	76	135.6	52.4	2.6	1981	6,682,000	46.3[9]	53.7[9]	10.3[9]
Cameroon	183,569	475,442	53	12,905,000	61	70.3	27.1	2.9	1987	10,516,232	49.0	51.0	38.3
Canada	3,849,674	9,970,610	2	29,107,000	32	7.6	2.9	1.2	1991	27,296,859	49.3	50.7	76.6
Cape Verde	1,557	4,033	169	355,000	172	228.0	88.0	1.3	1990	336,798	48.0	52.0	44.8
Central African Republic	240,324	622,436	43	3,069,000	128	12.8	4.9	2.4	1988	2,688,426	49.1	50.9	36.5
Chad	495,755	1,284,000	22	6,495,000	92	13.1	5.1	2.6	1993	6,158,992	49.3[5]	50.7[5]	30.0[5]
Chile	292,135	756,626	38	13,805,000	58	47.3	18.2	1.6	1992	13,231,677	49.1	50.9	85.1[10]
China	3,696,100	9,572,900	3	1,192,300,000	1	322.6	124.5	1.3	1990	1,133,682,501	51.6	48.4	26.4
Colombia	440,831	1,141,748	26	34,520,000	30	78.3	30.2	1.7	1985	30,062,193	49.5	50.5	67.2[4]
Comoros	719	1,862	175	527,000	163	733.0	283.0	3.3	1980	335,150	49.9	50.1	23.2
Congo	132,047	342,000	63	2,856,000	131	21.6	8.4	5.4	1984[7]	1,909,248	48.7	51.3	52.0
Costa Rica	19,730	51,100	128	3,308,000	126	167.7	64.7	2.5	1984	2,416,809	50.0	50.0	43.9
Côte d'Ivoire	123,847	320,763	68	13,895,000	56	112.2	43.3	3.8	1988	10,815,694	51.1	48.9	39.0
Croatia	21,829	56,538	126	4,788,000	106	219.3	84.7	0.4	1991	4,784,265	48.5	51.5	54.3
Cuba	42,804	110,861	104	10,994,000	64	256.8	99.2	0.9	1981	9,723,605	50.6	49.4	69.0
Cyprus[11]	3,572	9,251	164	769,000	156	215.3	83.1	0.5	1992[7, 12]	602,025	49.8	50.2	76.7
Czech Republic	30,450	78,864	116	10,345,000	69	339.7	131.2	0.1	1991	10,302,215	48.5	51.5	...
Denmark	16,639	43,094	133	5,205,000	104	312.8	120.8	0.3	1993[2]	5,180,614	49.3	50.7	84.9[10]
Djibouti	8,950	23,200	149	569,000	160	63.6	24.5	3.0	1960–61	81,200	...	...	80.7[5]
Dominica	290	750	184	72,000	198	248.3	96.0	0.1	1991	71,794	50.0	50.0	...
Dominican Republic	18,704	48,443	130	7,803,000	87	417.2	161.1	2.2	1993	7,089,000	50.1[8]	49.9[8]	52.0[8]
Ecuador	105,037	272,045	74	11,221,000	66	106.8	41.2	2.4	1990	9,648,189	49.7	50.3	55.4
Egypt	385,229	997,739	30	58,466,000	17	151.8	58.6	2.5	1986	48,205,049	51.1	48.9	43.9
El Salvador	8,124	21,041	151	5,642,000	97	694.5	268.1	2.2	1992	5,047,925	48.0	52.0	44.3[4]

The sources of these data are censuses; national population registers (cumulated periodically); registration of migration, births, deaths, and so on; sample surveys to establish demographic conditions; and the like.

The statistics provided for area and population by country are ranked, and the population densities based on those values are also provided. The population densities, for purposes of comparison within this table, are calculated on the bases of the 1994 midyear population estimate as shown and of total area of the country. Elsewhere in individual country presentations the reader may find densities calculated on more specific population figures and more specialized area bases: land area for Finland (because of its many lakes) or ice-free area for Greenland (most of which is ice cap). The data in this section conclude with the estimated average annual growth rate for the country (including both natural growth and net migration) during the five-year period, 1989–94.

In the section containing census data, information supplied includes the census total (usually de facto, the population actually present, rather than de jure, the population legally resident, who might be anywhere); the male-female breakdown; the proportion that is urban (according to the country's own definition of the term "urban," which differs very much from country to country); and finally an analysis of the age structure of the population by 15-year age groups. This last analysis may be particularly useful in distinguishing the type of population being recorded—young, fast-growing nations show a high proportion of people under 30 (most countries in sub-Saharan Africa and the Middle East have nearly one-half of their population under 15 years), while other nations (for example Sweden, which suffered no age-group losses in World War II) exhibit quite uniform proportions.

Finally, a section is provided giving the population of each country at 10-year intervals from 1940 to 2010. The data for years past represent the best available analysis of the published data by the country itself, by the demographers of the United Nations, or by the editors of Britannica. The projections for 2000 and 2010 similarly represent the best fit of available data through the early 1990s with projected population structure and growth rates during the next two decades. The evidence of the last 25 years with respect to similar estimates published about 1970, however, shows how cloudy is the glass through which these numbers are read. In 1970 no respectable Western analyst would have imagined proposing that mainland China could achieve the degree of birth control that it apparently has since then (as evidenced by the results of 1982 and 1990 censuses); on the other hand, even the Chinese admit that their methods have been somewhat Draconian and that they have already seen some backlash in terms of higher birth rates among those who have so far postponed larger families. How much is "some" by 2000? Compound that problem with all the social, economic, political, and biological factors that can affect 216 countries' populations, and the difficulty facing the prospective compiler of such projections may be appreciated.

Specific data about the vital rates affecting the data in this table may be found in great detail in both the country statistical boxes in "The Nations of the World" section and in the *Vital statistics, marriage, family* table, beginning at page 786.

Percentages in this table for male and female population will always total 100.0, but percentages by age group may not, for reasons such as nonresponse on census forms, "don't know" responses (which are common in countries with poor birth registration systems), and the like.

age distribution (%)						population (by decade, '000s)								country
0–14	15–29	30–44	45–59	60–74	75 and over	1940	1950	1960	1970	1980	1990	2000 projection	2010 projection	
44.5	26.9	15.8	8.6	3.6	0.6	...	8,150	9,829	12,431	14,985	15,332	25,725	32,889	Afghanistan
33.0	28.9	18.5	11.7	5.9	1.9	1,088	1,215	1,607	2,136	2,671	3,256	3,610	4,016	Albania
43.9	28.0	13.9	8.4	4.2	1.6	7,688	8,956	10,800	14,330	18,666	25,012	32,693	41,311	Algeria
38.1	29.0	18.1	9.4	4.3	1.1	13	19	20	27	33	47	67	86	American Samoa
16.3	27.7	27.2	15.1	9.0	3.8	5	6	8	19	33	53	63	71	Andorra
41.7	23.2	17.0	7.4	3.8	1.0	3,738	4,131	4,816	5,588	7,722	10,020	13,400	18,082	Angola
37.2[4]	30.8[4]	12.8[4]	11.5[4]	6.4[4]	1.3[4]	34	45	55	66	66	66	66	66	Antigua and Barbuda
30.6	23.3	19.3	13.9	9.6	3.3	14,169	17,150	20,611	23,788	27,820	32,201	36,239	40,170	Argentina
30.3	25.7	20.8	13.6	6.4	3.2	1,320	1,354	1,867	2,520	3,067	3,335	3,870	4,163	Armenia
24.4	22.0	27.0	16.1	7.2	3.0	31	51	57	61	60	63	76	83	Aruba
22.1	24.2	23.4	15.0	11.1	4.4	7,079	8,219	10,315	12,552	14,741	17,065	19,236	21,598	Australia
17.4	23.7	21.6	17.2	13.4	6.7	6,684	6,935	7,048	7,447	7,549	7,718	8,181	8,294	Austria
32.8	29.7	16.8	12.8	5.7	2.2	3,274	2,896	3,895	5,172	6,165	7,134	7,834	8,568	Azerbaijan
32.2	30.8	19.7	10.6	5.0	1.8	70	79	113	169	210	255	295	327	Bahamas, The
31.7	28.4	28.2	8.0	3.1	0.6	90	127	162	215	342	484	653	831	Bahrain
41.4[5]	29.5[5]	15.5[5]	8.8[5]	3.9[5]	0.9[5]	41,259	45,482	54,699	68,171	88,687	108,362	132,402	161,775	Bangladesh
24.1[5]	27.0[5]	22.1[5]	11.4[5]	—15.4[5]—		179	209	232	235	249	261	270	279	Barbados
23.0	22.4	20.6	18.0	11.5	4.5	9,046	7,745	8,190	9,040	9,650	10,260	10,634	11,028	Belarus
18.2	21.8	22.5	16.9	14.1	6.6	8,301	8,639	9,153	9,690	9,859	9,967	10,338	10,717	Belgium
43.9	27.9	14.9	7.2	4.4	1.6	56	68	90	120	146	189	235	268	Belize
46.6[5]	25.7[5]	14.7[5]	8.4[5]	3.8[5]	0.8[5]	...	2,046	2,273	2,693	3,459	4,622	6,269	8,357	Benin
19.5	24.0	26.8	16.4	—13.3—		31	37	43	53	55	59	65	72	Bermuda
40.6[5]	26.5[5]	17.1[5]	10.4[5]	4.6[5]	0.8[5]	...	...	...	...	600	737	900	1,100	Bhutan
41.2	26.2	16.8	8.9	—6.5—		2,508	2,765	3,405	4,265	5,581	7,171	9,038	11,087	Bolivia
27.5[8]	29.0[8]	19.2[8]	15.8[8]	6.3[8]	2.0[8]	...	2,662	3,240	3,703	4,107	4,347	4,601	4,871	Bosnia and Herzegovina
46.1[5]	27.5[5]	14.1[5]	7.2[5]	4.0[5]	1.3[5]	278	407	490	581	905	1,276	1,713	2,210	Botswana
34.7[5]	28.3[5]	19.4[5]	10.5[5]	5.6[5]	1.5[5]	41,525	52,901	71,539	93,139	121,286	149,042	172,777	194,002	Brazil
34.5	29.3	24.2	7.9	—4.1—		36	48	84	129	185	253	334	432	Brunei
20.2[3]	20.8[3]	21.4[3]	18.3[3]	14.4[3]	4.8[3]	6,344	7,251	7,867	8,490	8,862	8,991	8,361	8,212	Bulgaria
48.3	23.4	13.4	8.7	4.7	1.4	3,036	3,584	4,350	5,412	6,599	9,012	11,884	15,549	Burkina Faso
46.4	25.3	15.4	7.0	4.0	1.7	1,887	2,435	2,908	3,350	4,120	5,280	6,674	8,437	Burundi
44.2[9]	28.2[9]	14.7[9]	8.4[9]	4.0[9]	0.5[9]	3,400	4,346	5,433	6,938	6,400	8,592	10,031	13,357	Cambodia
46.4	24.5	14.6	8.7	4.1	1.6	...	4,466	5,296	6,612	8,655	11,524	15,293	20,225	Cameroon
20.9	22.7	25.1	15.3	11.3	4.7	11,693	13,737	17,909	21,324	24,593	27,791	31,325	35,050	Canada
44.8	30.8	10.2	7.5	—6.7—		181	148	199	272	296	337	383	436	Cape Verde
43.2	27.5	15.0	9.2	4.1	0.8	991	1,311	1,500	1,793	2,257	2,793	3,528	4,449	Central African Republic
43.3[5]	25.8[5]	15.6[5]	9.6[5]	4.8[5]	0.9[5]	2,351	2,658	3,064	3,652	4,715	5,836	7,647	9,722	Chad
30.6[10]	27.0[10]	21.2[10]	12.2[10]	6.8[10]	2.2[10]	5,063	6,091	7,585	9,368	11,104	12,958	15,037	16,918	Chile
27.7	31.0	20.7	12.1	6.9	1.7	530,000	556,613	667,070	818,316	981,242	1,133,683	1,276,200	1,323,800	China
36.1	31.2	17.2	9.5	4.6	1.4	9,097	11,268	15,321	20,884	26,906	32,300	37,822	42,959	Colombia
47.2	23.2	14.8	7.6	5.1	1.8	119	148	177	245	333	464	640	883	Comoros
44.7	27.2	13.3	9.1	4.6	0.7	...	815	960	1,182	1,631	2,264	3,374	4,390	Congo
37.9	31.5	15.8	9.2	4.4	1.2	619	862	1,236	1,731	2,246	2,994	3,798	4,534	Costa Rica
46.8	27.3	14.9	7.5	—3.4—		2,350	2,775	3,799	5,515	8,194	11,980	17,065	23,657	Côte d'Ivoire
19.4	20.7	22.7	18.3	12.9	4.5	...	3,851	4,140	4,411	4,588	4,770	4,786	4,782	Croatia
30.3	27.6	19.1	12.1	8.2	2.7	4,566	5,752	7,019	8,565	9,724	10,631	11,502	12,181	Cuba
26.1[10]	22.5[10]	22.5[10]	15.0[10]	9.8[10]	4.1[10]	413	494	573	615	658	758	813	893	Cyprus[11]
21.0	21.8	22.6	16.8	12.7	5.1	...	8,925	9,539	9,830	10,292	10,298	10,449	10,536	Czech Republic
17.0	22.1	21.7	19.0	13.2	7.0	3,832	4,271	4,581	4,929	5,123	5,141	5,303	5,310	Denmark
45.2[5]	24.9[5]	16.1[5]	9.0[5]	—4.8[5]—		44	60	78	158	355	505	680	916	Djibouti
35.1[13]	28.1[13]	14.5[13]	9.5[13]	—11.7[13]—		45	51	60	70	75	72	73	74	Dominica
40.6[8]	30.1[8]	15.1[8]	8.7[8]	—5.5[8]—		1,759	2,313	3,160	4,343	5,648	7,168	8,621	9,903	Dominican Republic
38.8	28.5	17.3	9.0	4.7	1.7	2,546	3,307	4,421	5,958	8,123	10,264	12,646	14,899	Ecuador
39.5	26.4	16.9	10.6	5.2	1.0	16,942	20,461	26,085	33,329	40,540	53,153	65,998	78,905	Egypt
44.4[5]	27.6[5]	13.4[5]	8.9[5]	4.6[5]	1.1[5]	1,550	1,931	2,527	3,534	4,525	5,172	6,425	7,772	El Salvador

Area and population (continued)

country	area square miles	area square kilometres	area rank	population (latest estimate) total midyear 1994	rank	density per sq mi	density per sq km	% annual growth rate 1989–94	population (latest census) census year	total	male (%)	female (%)	urban (%)
Equatorial Guinea	10,831	28,051	144	386,000	168	35.6	13.8	2.5	1983	300,000	48.3	51.7	28.2
Eritrea	45,300	117,400	100	3,779,000	119	83.4	32.2	3.0	1984	2,703,998	49.9	50.1	15.1
Estonia	17,462	45,226	132	1,499,000	144	85.8	33.1	–0.9	1989	1,572,916	46.9	53.1	71.6
Ethiopia	437,794	1,133,882	27	53,384,000	22	121.9	47.1	3.0	1984	39,480,954	50.0	50.0	9.9
Faeroe Islands	540	1,399	177	45,000	209	83.3	32.2	–1.2	1993[2]	46,801	51.9	48.1	...
Fiji	7,056	18,274	155	771,000	155	109.3	42.2	1.3	1986	715,375	50.7	49.3	38.7
Finland	130,559	338,145	64	5,083,000	105	38.9	15.0	0.5	1990	4,998,478	48.5	51.5	79.7
France	210,026	543,965	48	57,982,000	19	276.1	106.6	0.5	1990	56,625,026	48.7	51.3	74.3[5]
French Guiana	33,399	86,504	114	146,000	185	4.4	1.7	5.7	1990	114,808	52.1	47.9	73.4[14]
French Polynesia	1,544	4,000	170	215,000	178	139.2	53.8	2.3	1988	188,814	52.1	47.9	55.0
Gabon	103,347	267,667	76	1,139,000	149	11.0	4.3	1.7	1993	1,011,710	49.2[5]	50.8[5]	45.7[5]
Gambia, The	4,127	10,689	162	1,060,000	151	256.8	99.2	3.8	1993	1,025,867	50.2	49.8	21.2[15]
Gaza Strip	140	363	198	756,000	157	5,400.0	2,082.6	4.6	1992[2]	716,800	50.3	49.7	...
Georgia	26,900	69,700	121	5,503,000	98	204.6	79.0	0.2	1989	5,443,359	47.2	52.8	55.7
Germany	137,823	356,959	62	81,966,000	12	594.7	229.6	0.8	1987[16]	61,077,042	48.0	52.0	85.3[5]
Ghana	92,098	238,533	81	16,050,000	54	174.3	67.3	2.6	1984	12,296,081	49.3	50.7	32.0
Gibraltar	2.2	5.8	215	28,800	213	13,090.9	4,965.5	–1.0	1991[17]	26,703	51.0	49.0	...
Greece	50,949	131,957	96	10,365,000	68	203.4	78.5	0.6	1991	10,264,156	49.0	51.0	62.5[5]
Greenland	840,000	2,175,600	14	55,500	205	0.1	0.0	0.1	1994[2]	55,419	53.5	46.5	80.6
Grenada	133	344	200	91,800	194	690.2	266.9	0.2	1991	91,158	49.4	50.6	32.2
Guadeloupe	687	1,780	176	426,000	164	620.1	239.3	2.2	1990	387,034	48.9	51.1	48.4
Guam	209	541	190	145,000	186	693.8	268.0	2.4	1990	133,152	53.3	46.7	38.2
Guatemala	42,042	108,889	105	10,322,000	70	245.5	94.8	2.9	1981[7]	6,043,559	49.8	50.2	34.3
Guernsey	30	78	209	64,300	202	2,143.3	824.4	1.2	1991[19]	58,867	48.1	51.9	...
Guinea	94,926	245,857	78	6,501,000	91	68.5	26.4	3.1	1983	5,781,014	48.6	51.4	26.0
Guinea-Bissau	13,948	36,125	137	1,050,000	152	75.3	29.1	2.2	1979	767,739	48.2	51.8	14.0
Guyana	83,044	215,083	84	733,000	158	8.8	3.4	–0.4	1980	758,619	49.5	50.5	30.5[9]
Haiti	10,695	27,700	146	6,491,000	93	606.9	243.3	1.6	1982	5,053,792	48.5	51.5	20.6
Honduras	43,277	112,088	102	5,302,000	101	122.5	47.3	3.2	1988	4,376,839	49.6	50.4	43.7[5]
Hong Kong	415	1,075	179	5,979,000	94	14,408.1	5,563.0	1.0	1991[7]	5,674,114	51.1	48.9	93.1[6]
Hungary	35,920	93,033	110	10,257,000	71	285.6	110.3	–0.3	1990	10,375,323	48.1	51.9	61.8
Iceland	39,699	102,819	106	267,000	175	6.7	2.6	1.1	1993[2]	264,922	50.2	49.8	91.4
India	1,222,243	3,165,596	7	913,744,000	2	747.4	288.6	1.9	1991	846,302,688	51.9	48.1	25.7
Indonesia	741,052	1,919,317	16	194,746,000	4	262.8	101.5	2.1	1990	179,378,946	49.9	50.1	30.9
Iran	632,457	1,638,057	18	59,614,000	16	94.3	36.4	2.5	1991[7]	55,473,187	51.5	48.5	57.3
Iraq	167,975	435,052	58	19,869,000	44	118.3	45.7	2.9	1987	16,335,199	51.4	48.6	70.2
Ireland	27,137	70,285	120	3,512,000	124	129.4	50.0	–0.1	1991	3,525,719	49.7	50.3	57.0
Isle of Man	221	572	189	70,000	200	316.7	122.4	0.7	1991[7]	69,788	48.3	51.7	51.1
Israel[20, 21]	7,992	20,700	152	5,331,000	100	667.0	257.5	3.7	1983[7, 22]	4,037,620	49.8	50.2	86.9
Italy	116,334	301,303	71	57,257,000	21	492.2	190.0	0.1	1991	57,103,833	48.6	51.4	67.1
Jamaica	4,244	10,991	161	2,497,000	134	588.4	227.2	1.0	1991	2,391,700	48.9	51.1	50.2
Japan	145,850	377,750	61	124,960,000	8	856.8	330.8	0.3	1990	123,611,167	49.1	50.9	77.4
Jersey	45	116	208	86,800	195	1,928.9	748.3	1.0	1991	84,082	48.6	51.4	...
Jordan[23]	34,342	88,946	112	4,224,000	115	123.0	47.5	6.7	1979	2,132,997	52.3	47.7	59.5
Kazakhstan	1,049,200	2,717,300	9	16,954,000	52	16.2	6.2	0.4	1989	16,536,511	48.5	51.5	57.2
Kenya	224,961	582,646	46	27,450,000	34	122.0	47.1	3.4	1989	21,443,636	50.0[5]	50.0[5]	23.6[5]
Kiribati	313	811	181	78,600	196	251.1	96.9	2.3	1990	72,298	49.6	50.4	34.8
Korea, North	47,399	122,762	98	23,067,000	39	486.7	187.9	1.9	[24]	[24]	49.0[5]	51.0[5]	59.8[5]
Korea, South	38,330	99,274	108	44,436,000	25	1,159.3	447.6	1.0	1990[7]	43,410,899	50.2	49.8	74.4
Kuwait	6,880	17,818	156	1,469,000	145	213.5	82.4	–6.0	1985	1,697,301	56.9	43.1	100.0
Kyrgyzstan	76,600	198,500	86	4,488,000	110	58.6	22.6	0.7	1989	4,290,442	48.9	51.1	38.2
Laos	91,429	236,800	83	4,743,000	107	51.9	20.0	3.1	1990	4,201,660	49.1	50.9	18.6[5]
Latvia	24,946	64,610	124	2,551,000	133	102.3	39.5	–1.0	1989	2,680,029	46.6	53.4	71.1
Lebanon	3,950	10,230	163	2,965,000	129	750.6	289.8	1.8	1970	2,126,325	50.8	49.2	60.1
Lesotho	11,720	30,355	140	1,929,000	142	164.6	63.5	2.5	1986[7]	1,577,536	48.2	51.8	16.0
Liberia	38,250	99,067	109	2,377,000	135	62.1	24.0	0.3	1984	2,101,628	50.6	49.4	38.8
Libya	678,400	1,757,000	17	5,225,000	103	7.7	3.0	3.6	1984	3,637,488	53.6	46.4	64.5[4]
Liechtenstein	62	160	207	30,500	211	491.9	190.6	1.5	1980	25,215	49.6	50.4	...
Lithuania	25,213	65,301	123	3,724,000	120	147.7	57.0	0.1	1989	3,689,779	47.4	52.6	68.0
Luxembourg	999	2,586	172	398,000	167	398.4	153.9	1.0	1991	384,634	49.0	51.0	85.9[3]
Macau	7.5	19.3	214	416,000	166	60,289.9	23,111.1	5.4	1991	339,464	48.5	51.5	97.0
Macedonia	9,928	25,713	148	2,089,000	138	210.4	81.2	0.8	1991	2,033,964	50.5	49.5	58.1
Madagascar	226,658	587,041	45	13,702,000	59	60.5	23.3	3.3	1993[7]	12,092,157	49.5	50.5	21.9[5]
Malawi	45,747	118,484	99	9,732,000	75	212.7	82.1	1.9	1987	7,988,507	48.4	51.6	10.7
Malaysia	127,584	330,442	65	19,506,000	46	152.9	59.0	2.4	1991	17,566,982	50.4	49.6	50.6
Maldives	115	298	202	244,000	177	2,121.7	818.8	3.3	1990	213,215	51.3	48.7	25.9
Mali	482,077	1,248,574	23	8,825,000	78	18.3	7.1	2.0	1987	7,696,348	48.9	51.1	22.0
Malta	122	316	201	368,000	170	3,016.4	1,164.6	0.9	1985	345,418	49.2	50.8	85.3
Marshall Islands	70	181	206	54,100	207	772.9	298.9	4.0	1988	43,380	51.1	48.9	64.5
Martinique	436	1,128	178	381,000	169	873.9	337.8	1.4	1990	359,579	48.4	51.6	80.5
Mauritania	398,000	1,030,700	29	2,069,000	139	5.2	2.0	1.9	1988	1,864,236	49.5	50.5	39.1
Mauritius	788	2,040	174	1,120,000	150	1,421.3	549.0	1.2	1990	1,056,827	49.9	50.1	39.3
Mayotte	144	374	197	110,000	189	763.9	294.1	5.5	1991	94,385	52.0	48.0	59.7[25]
Mexico	756,066	1,958,201	15	91,840,000	11	121.5	46.9	2.1	1990	81,249,645	49.1	50.9	71.3
Micronesia	271	701	185	104,000	191	383.8	148.4	1.1	1980	73,160	51.1	48.9	19.4
Moldova	13,000	33,700	138	4,358,000	112	335.2	129.3	0.0	1989	4,337,592	47.5	52.5	46.9
Monaco	0.75	1.95	216	30,300	212	40,400.0	15,538.5	0.5	1990	29,972	47.5	52.5	100.0
Mongolia	604,800	1,566,500	19	2,266,000	136	3.7	1.4	1.8	1989	2,043,100	50.1	49.9	57.1
Morocco	177,117	458,730	55	26,544,000	36	149.9	57.9	2.2	1982	20,419,555[26]	50.1	49.9	42.7
Mozambique	313,661	812,379	36	17,346,000	51	55.3	21.4	4.2	1980	12,130,000	48.7	51.3	13.2
Myanmar (Burma)	261,228	676,577	40	45,573,000	24	174.5	67.4	2.2	1983	35,313,905	49.6	50.4	24.0
Namibia	318,580	825,118	35	1,596,000	143	5.0	1.9	4.1	1991	1,401,711	48.6	51.4	32.8
Nauru	8.2	21.2	213	10,200	215	1,243.9	481.1	2.1	1983	8,042	...	...	...
Nepal	56,827	147,181	94	19,525,000	45	343.6	132.7	1.9	1991	18,491,097	49.9	50.1	9.6
Netherlands, The	16,033	41,526	134	15,401,000	55	960.6	370.9	0.7	1993[2]	15,239,182	49.4	50.6	89.0[26]

0–14	15–29	30–44	45–59	60–74	75 and over	1940	1950	1960	1970	1980	1990	2000 projection	2010 projection	country
		age distribution (%)						population (by decade, '000s)						
41.7	25.1	15.7	11.2	5.0	1.0	...	211	244	291	255	350	448	573	Equatorial Guinea
46.1	23.0	15.9	8.9	4.4	1.6	...	1,255	1,551	1,963	2,484	3,351	4,523	6,140	Eritrea
22.2	21.4	21.0	18.5	11.7	5.1	1,054	1,101	1,216	1,365	1,473	1,571	1,450	1,450	Estonia
46.6	22.7	15.6	8.9	4.5	1.7	...	10,318	22,640	28,660	36,265	47,423	63,726	85,605	Ethiopia
24.4	—59.0—			—16.6—		27	31	35	39	43	48	45	45	Faeroe Islands
38.2	29.5	17.8	9.6	3.8	0.8	218	289	394	520	634	732	826	917	Fiji
19.3	20.5	24.6	17.1	12.9	5.7	3,698	4,009	4,430	4,606	4,780	4,986	5,159	5,226	Finland
19.1	22.6	22.8	15.6	12.8	7.1	41,300	41,736	45,684	50,770	53,880	56,735	60,008	60,200	France
33.4	27.3	23.2	10.2	4.4	1.5	30	27	33	49	69	117	163	206	French Guiana
36.0	29.7	18.9	10.4	4.1	0.9	50	62	84	109	151	197	246	296	French Polynesia
33.0[5]	29.3[5]	15.8[5]	12.9[5]	7.3[5]	1.7[5]	442	469	486	504	808	1,078	1,244	1,445	Gabon
43.8[15]	26.5[15]	15.7[15]	7.3[15]	—5.7[15]—		193	232	357	458	632	917	1,227	1,546	Gambia, The
51.0	—38.8—			—10.2—		...	...	...	370	456	630	911	1,243	Gaza Strip
24.8	24.1	19.2	17.5	10.8	3.6	3,612	3,527	4,160	4,708	5,075	5,460	5,569	5,680	Georgia
14.6	24.0	20.1	20.6	13.6	7.2	57,400	68,373	72,673	77,772	78,289	79,433	85,053	93,324	Germany
45.0	26.4	14.6	8.1	4.1	1.8	3,636	5,297	6,050	8,789	11,222	14,470	18,749	24,293	Ghana
19.0	21.3	22.6	18.2	12.9	5.3	14	23	24	26	30	31	29	29	Gibraltar
18.4[3]	22.0[3]	20.5[3]	18.6[3]	14.0[3]	6.3[3]	7,319	7,566	8,327	8,793	9,643	10,089	10,493	10,518	Greece
27.4	24.7	26.1	14.6	—7.2—		19	23	33	41	50	56	57	60	Greenland
35.9[18]	28.5[18]	14.2[18]	8.5[18]	—11.3[18]—		71	76	90	95	89	91	93	95	Grenada
24.9	29.5	21.4	12.5	8.3	3.4	180	206	265	320	327	390	473	541	Guadeloupe
30.0	30.0	22.6	10.8	5.5	1.1	22	59	67	85	107	133	167	198	Guam
44.9	26.8	14.8	8.5	3.9	1.1	2,201	2,969	3,964	5,246	6,917	9,197	12,222	15,827	Guatemala
17.0	23.3	22.2	16.8	13.5	7.2	44	44	45	51	55	61	69	78	Guernsey
46.3[4]	26.1[4]	14.9[4]	8.4[4]	3.7[4]	0.6[4]	...	2,550	3,136	3,900	4,461	5,755	7,759	10,301	Guinea
44.3	25.5	15.1	8.2	4.7	2.2	341	505	542	525	795	964	1,192	1,473	Guinea-Bissau
40.8	30.5	14.0	8.8	4.4	1.2	344	423	560	702	759	754	755	755	Guyana
39.2	26.9	15.6	10.0	5.4	2.9	2,827	3,097	3,723	4,605	5,473	6,052	7,102	8,121	Haiti
44.6[5]	28.3[5]	14.4[5]	7.8[5]	3.9[5]	1.1[5]	1,146	1,390	1,873	2,553	3,316	4,681	6,251	7,890	Honduras
23.0	25.0	26.2	—25.8—			1,786	1,974	3,074	3,942	5,063	5,706	6,350	7,020	Hong Kong
21.3	19.4	22.5	17.9	13.4	5.6	9,280	9,338	9,984	10,337	10,693	10,365	10,170	9,951	Hungary
24.8	23.7	22.7	13.9	10.2	4.7	121	143	176	204	228	255	278	294	Iceland
36.0[5]	27.7[5]	18.0[5]	11.2[5]	5.9[5]	1.2[5]	317,000	357,561	442,344	554,911	688,856	846,191	1,018,673	1,189,396	India
36.6	28.3	18.1	10.6	5.2	1.1	70,500	75,449	92,701	119,467	146,449	178,302	210,625	236,841	Indonesia
44.3	26.6	15.1	8.2	4.8	0.8	14,000	16,913	21,554	28,359	38,783	54,051	68,329	85,775	Iran
45.2	27.2	14.2	7.0	3.7	1.4	3,745	5,180	6,847	9,356	13,043	17,751	23,521	30,761	Iraq
26.7	24.1	20.2	13.8	10.6	4.6	2,958	2,969	2,834	2,954	3,421	3,526	3,492	3,459	Ireland
17.3	20.7	20.4	17.0	15.3	9.2	52	55	49	52	64	69	73	78	Isle of Man
32.6	26.4	18.0	12.3	9.4	3.1	...	...	2,114	2,958	3,862	4,613	5,990	6,647	Israel[20, 21]
17.3[5]	24.2[5]	20.5[5]	18.5[5]	13.7[5]	6.1[5]	43,840	46,769	50,223	53,565	56,235	57,003	57,274	56,270	Italy
32.5[10]	30.9[10]	17.3[10]	9.3[10]	—10.0[10]—		1,212	1,403	1,629	1,891	2,133	2,403	2,651	2,929	Jamaica
18.2	21.7	22.2	20.1	12.6	4.8	73,075	83,200	93,419	103,720	116,807	123,478	127,287	130,344	Japan
15.5	24.9	23.9	17.0	11.9	6.8	51	57	63	71	76	84	92	101	Jersey
51.6	23.4	13.4	7.4	3.1	1.1	...	1,095	1,384	1,795	2,175	3,202	5,171	6,961	Jordan[23]
31.9	26.3	19.4	13.2	6.9	2.3	6,148	6,703	9,996	13,110	14,940	16,742	17,312	17,925	Kazakhstan
49.1[5]	26.5[5]	13.4[5]	6.5[5]	3.5[5]	1.0[5]	4,470	6,018	8,115	11,225	16,667	24,000	33,310	44,850	Kenya
40.3	27.5	17.3	9.2	4.8	0.9	29	33	41	49	57	72	88	106	Kiribati
28.6[5]	34.6[5]	19.8[5]	10.5[5]	5.2[5]	1.3[5]	...	9,740	10,568	14,388	17,999	21,412	25,491	28,491	Korea, North
25.7	30.4	22.9	13.4	6.1	1.5	...	21,147	25,142	32,976	38,124	42,869	46,789	49,683	Korea, South
36.8	28.3	24.1	8.6	1.8	0.4	...	145	292	748	1,358	2,125	1,702	2,177	Kuwait
37.5	27.0	16.3	10.9	6.2	2.1	1,528	1,740	2,173	2,965	3,631	4,395	4,653	4,944	Kyrgyzstan
44.2[25]	25.2[25]	14.4[25]	9.9[25]	4.9[25]	1.4[25]	1,075	1,755	2,177	2,713	3,205	4,202	5,592	7,119	Laos
21.4	21.7	20.3	19.2	12.0	5.3	1,886	1,949	2,129	2,374	2,544	2,684	2,602	2,681	Latvia
42.6	23.8	16.7	9.1	—7.7—		965	1,443	1,857	2,469	2,669	2,740	3,312	3,777	Lebanon
40.7	25.1	16.6	10.7	5.6	1.3	566	734	870	1,064	1,330	1,747	2,233	2,821	Lesotho
43.2	28.2	14.7	7.7	4.4	1.8	...	758	1,004	1,393	1,879	2,365	2,785	3,755	Liberia
46.4[4]	25.0[4]	16.2[4]	8.6[4]	3.3[4]	0.6[4]	900	1,029	1,349	1,986	3,043	4,545	6,386	8,720	Libya
23.0	26.5	24.1	14.1	9.2	3.1	11	14	16	21	26	29	34	39	Liechtenstein
22.6	23.8	20.0	17.9	10.9	4.8	2,925	2,567	2,779	3,148	3,439	3,737	3,725	3,727	Lithuania
17.3	21.5	23.8	17.5	12.8	7.1	296	296	314	339	364	382	407	415	Luxembourg
24.1	27.2	29.4	9.6	7.3	2.3	375	188	169	221	243	332	492	580	Macau
29.1[8]	27.1[8]	19.6[8]	14.8[8]	7.1[8]	2.2[8]	...	1,229	1,392	1,629	1,900	2,024	2,185	2,356	Macedonia
45.6[5]	26.7[5]	15.0[5]	7.7[5]	—5.0[5]—		4,034	4,230	5,309	6,742	8,790	12,010	16,579	22,431	Madagascar
46.1	25.4	14.5	8.0	—6.0—		1,696	3,033	3,481	4,511	6,128	9,289	11,405	13,233	Malawi
38.1[5]	28.1[5]	18.4[5]	9.6[5]	4.5[5]	1.2[5]	...	6,187	7,908	10,466	13,764	17,756	21,592	24,280	Malaysia
46.9	26.7	12.3	9.0	4.0	0.8	81	82	106	128	155	216	286	360	Maldives
46.1	23.9	15.0	8.9	4.9	1.2	3,000	3,426	4,224	5,690	6,816	8,130	9,980	12,252	Mali
24.1	23.2	23.0	15.4	10.5	3.8	270	300	329	326	324	354	378	394	Malta
51.0	24.5	14.6	5.5	3.6	0.8	...	11	15	22	32	46	68	100	Marshall Islands
23.1	28.9	20.5	13.5	9.7	4.3	200	222	252	287	326	361	415	458	Martinique
44.1	26.6	15.0	8.1	4.7	1.4	666	781	970	1,245	1,483	1,906	2,467	3,307	Mauritania
29.7	28.9	22.3	10.9	6.6	1.6	428	479	662	824	957	1,075	1,207	1,365	Mauritius
47.0	27.4	15.0	6.5	3.0	1.2	16	17	25	35	52	89	150	250	Mayotte
38.3	29.4	16.6	8.9	4.5	1.7	19,815	25,828	34,993	48,934	67,046	84,486	102,555	118,455	Mexico
46.4	26.8	12.6	8.5	4.5	1.1	...	30	40	57	73	101	110	120	Micronesia
27.9	22.9	21.0	15.6	9.7	2.9	2,468	2,341	3,004	3,595	4,002	4,364	4,301	4,420	Moldova
12.3	16.7	21.2	20.4	17.9	10.8	20	22	23	24	27	30	31	31	Monaco
41.9	29.2	14.6	8.5	—5.8—		750	747	931	1,248	1,663	2,122	2,525	3,025	Mongolia
42.2	28.0	14.1	9.2	4.8	1.5	7,750	8,953	11,640	15,126	19,177	24,294	30,351	37,949	Morocco
44.4	26.7	15.9	8.7	3.6	0.7	...	6,458	7,584	9,390	12,103	14,438	20,868	27,381	Mozambique
40.7	27.7	15.0	10.5	—6.1—		...	17,832	21,746	27,102	33,821	41,825	51,567	61,631	Myanmar (Burma)
44.4[5]	25.8[5]	15.2[5]	8.6[5]	5.0[5]	1.0[5]	336	405	522	761	1,002	1,387	1,957	2,705	Namibia
...	...	...	...	...		3	4	5	7	8	9	11	13	Nauru
42.3	25.7	16.7	9.7	4.7	0.9	7,000	8,000	9,180	11,232	14,634	18,111	21,094	23,335	Nepal
18.3	23.0	23.7	17.4	12.1	5.5	8,834	10,027	11,417	12,958	14,150	14,952	16,042	16,769	Netherlands, The

Area and population (continued)

country	area			population (latest estimate)					population (latest census)				
	square miles	square kilo- metres	rank	total midyear 1994	rank	density		% annual growth rate 1989-94	census year	total	male (%)	female (%)	urban (%)
						per sq mi	per sq km						
Netherlands Antilles	308	800	182	193,000	181	626.6	241.3	0.1	1992	189,474	47.9	52.1	...
New Caledonia	7,172	18,576	154	183,000	182	25.5	9.9	2.1	1989	164,173	51.1	48.9	59.4
New Zealand	104,454	270,534	75	3,525,000	123	33.7	13.0	1.1	1991	3,434,950	49.3	50.7	75.9
Nicaragua	50,838	131,670	97	4,210,000	116	82.8	32.0	2.4	1971	1,877,952	48.3	51.7	48.0
Niger	496,900	1,287,000	20	8,813,000	79	17.7	6.8	3.3	1988[7]	7,228,552	49.5	50.5	15.3
Nigeria	356,669	923,768	32	93,471,000	10	262.1	101.2	2.1	1991	88,514,501	50.3	49.7	35.2[5]
Northern Mariana Islands	184	477	191	46,300	208	251.6	97.1	2.7	1990	46,300	52.6	47.4	28.0
Norway	125,050	323,878	67	4,332,000	113	34.6	13.4	0.5	1990	4,247,546	49.4	50.6	75.0[5]
Oman	118,150	306,000	70	2,048,000	140	17.3	6.7	2.6	1993	2,017,591	51.0[27]	49.0[27]	10.6[5]
Pakistan	339,697	879,811	34	131,434,000	7	386.9	149.4	2.8	1981[28]	84,253,644	52.5	47.5	28.3
Panama	29,157	75,517	118	2,583,000	132	88.6	34.2	1.9	1990	2,329,329	50.6	49.4	53.7
Papua New Guinea	178,704	462,840	54	4,246,000	114	23.8	9.2	2.3	1990	3,529,538[29]	52.1[29]	47.9[29]	15.2[29]
Paraguay	157,048	406,752	59	4,732,000	108	30.1	11.6	2.6	1992	4,123,550	50.2	49.8	50.5
Peru	496,225	1,285,216	21	23,383,000	38	47.1	18.2	2.1	1993	22,639,443	49.7[8]	50.3[8]	64.9[8]
Philippines	115,860	300,076	72	68,278,000	14	589.3	227.5	2.4	1990	60,684,887	50.3	49.7	48.6
Poland	120,728	312,685	69	38,653,000	29	320.2	123.6	0.4	1988	37,878,641	48.7	51.3	61.2
Portugal	35,574	92,135	111	9,814,000	74	275.1	106.2	-0.1	1991	9,830,779	48.2	51.8	29.7[8]
Puerto Rico	3,515	9,104	165	3,653,000	121	1,039.3	401.3	0.9	1990	3,522,037	48.4	51.6	71.2
Qatar	4,412	11,427	160	552,000	161	125.1	48.3	3.9	1986	369,079	67.2	32.8	88.0[4]
Réunion	970	2,512	173	647,000	159	667.0	257.6	1.9	1990	597,828	49.2	50.8	73.4
Romania	91,699	237,500	82	22,740,000	40	248.0	95.7	-0.4	1992	22,760,449	49.1	50.9	54.4
Russia	6,592,800	17,075,400	1	148,174,000	6	22.5	8.7	0.1	1989	147,400,537	46.9	53.1	73.6
Rwanda	10,169	26,338	147	7,817,000	86	768.7	296.8	3.1	1991	7,164,994	48.7	51.3	5.4
St. Kitts and Nevis	104	269	203	41,800	210	401.9	155.4	-0.1	1991	41,862	51.6[5]	48.4[5]	48.9[5]
St. Lucia	238	617	188	142,000	187	596.6	230.1	1.5	1991	133,308	48.5	51.5	46.4[5]
St. Vincent and the Grenadines	150	389	196	110,000	190	733.3	282.8	1.0	1991	106,499	49.9	50.1	24.6
San Marino	24	61	210	24,500	214	1,036.8	400.4	1.4	1976	19,149	50.4	49.6	90.1[3]
São Tomé and Príncipe	386	1,001	180	128,000	188	331.6	127.9	2.2	1991	120,146	49.4	50.6	40.5[18]
Saudi Arabia	865,000	2,240,000	13	17,947,000	48	20.7	8.0	3.4	1992	16,929,294	55.9	44.1	77.3[5]
Senegal	75,951	196,712	87	8,112,000	83	106.8	41.2	2.7	1988	6,928,405	48.7	51.3	38.6
Seychelles	176	455	193	71,800	199	408.0	157.8	0.7	1987	68,598	49.7	50.3	35.5
Sierra Leone	27,699	71,740	119	4,616,000	109	166.6	64.3	2.7	1985	3,517,530	49.6	50.4	31.8
Singapore	247	641	187	2,933,000	130	11,850.9	4,575.7	2.1	1990[7]	2,705,115	50.6	49.4	100.0
Slovakia	18,933	49,035	129	5,352,000	99	282.7	109.1	0.3	1991	5,268,935	48.9	51.1	56.8
Slovenia	7,821	20,256	153	2,001,000	141	255.8	98.8	0.0	1991	1,974,839	48.5	51.5	48.9
Solomon Islands	10,954	28,370	143	360,000	171	32.9	12.7	3.2	1986	285,176	51.9	48.1	15.7
Somalia	246,000	637,000	42	6,667,000	90	27.1	10.5	0.0	1975	4,089,203	50.1	49.9	25.4
South Africa[30]	472,281	1,223,201	25	41,749,000	27	88.4	34.1	2.4	1991[31]	26,504,191	48.8	51.2	60.3
Spain	194,898	504,783	51	39,193,000	28	201.1	77.6	0.2	1991	38,999,181	49.1	50.9	75.3
Sri Lanka	25,332	65,610	122	17,830,000	50	703.9	271.8	1.2	1981	14,848,364	50.8	49.2	21.5
Sudan, The	966,757	2,503,890	10	25,699,000	37	26.6	10.3	1.6	1993	24,940,683	50.2[5]	49.8[5]	22.5[5]
Suriname	63,251	163,820	92	423,000	165	6.7	2.6	1.0	1980	354,860	49.5	50.5	44.8[9]
Swaziland	6,704	17,364	157	883,000	153	131.7	50.9	3.5	1986	681,059	47.2	52.8	22.8
Sweden	173,732	449,964	56	8,773,000	80	50.5	19.5	0.7	1993[2]	8,745,109	49.4	50.6	84.3[10]
Switzerland	15,940	41,284	135	6,991,000	89	438.6	169.3	1.0	1990[32]	6,873,687	49.3	50.7	59.7[3]
Syria	71,498	185,180	88	13,853,000	57	193.8	74.8	3.4	1981	9,052,628	51.1	48.9	47.1
Taiwan	13,969	36,179	136	21,074,000	43	1,508.6	582.5	1.0	1990[7]	20,393,628	52.1	47.9	74.5
Tajikistan	55,300	143,100	95	5,813,000	95	105.1	40.6	2.4	1989	5,108,576	49.7	50.3	32.6
Tanzania	364,017	942,799	31	27,296,000	35	75.0	29.0	2.8	1988	23,174,336	48.9	51.1	32.8[5]
Thailand	198,115	513,115	50	57,586,000	20	290.7	112.2	1.3	1990	54,532,300	49.6	50.4	18.7
Togo	21,925	56,785	125	3,922,000	118	178.9	69.1	2.9	1981	2,719,567	48.7	51.3	15.2
Tonga	290	750	183	100,000	193	344.8	133.3	0.7	1986[7]	94,649	50.3	49.7	30.7
Trinidad and Tobago	1,980	5,128	168	1,273,000	147	642.9	248.2	1.0	1990	1,234,388	50.1	49.9	69.1[5]
Tunisia	63,378	164,150	91	8,757,000	81	138.2	53.3	2.1	1994	8,735,885	50.8[33]	49.2[33]	52.8[33]
Turkey	300,948	779,452	37	61,183,000	15	203.3	78.5	2.2	1990	56,473,035	50.7	49.3	59.0
Turkmenistan	188,500	488,100	52	4,044,000	117	21.5	8.3	2.5	1989	3,533,925	49.3	50.7	45.4
Tuvalu	9.4	24.4	212	9,700	216	1,031.9	397.5	2.0	1985	8,229	47.4	52.6	...
Uganda	93,070	241,040	80	18,194,000	47	195.5	75.5	2.6	1991	16,671,705	49.1	50.9	11.3
Ukraine	233,100	603,700	44	52,304,000	23	224.4	86.6	0.2	1989	51,706,746	46.3	53.7	66.9
United Arab Emirates	30,000	77,700	117	2,125,000	137	70.8	27.3	4.1	1985	1,622,464	64.9	35.1	76.9[4]
United Kingdom	94,251	244,110	79	58,422,000	18	619.9	239.3	0.4	1991[7]	56,467,000	48.4	51.6	89.1[5]
United States	3,679,192	9,529,063	4	260,967,000	3	70.9	27.4	1.1	1990[35]	248,709,873	48.7	51.3	75.2
Uruguay	68,037	176,215	90	3,168,000	127	46.6	18.0	0.6	1985	2,955,241	48.7	51.3	86.2
Uzbekistan	172,700	447,400	57	22,382,000	41	129.6	50.0	2.2	1989	19,905,158	49.3	50.7	40.7
Vanuatu	4,707	12,190	159	164,000	183	34.8	13.5	2.7	1989	142,630	51.6	48.4	17.7
Venezuela	352,144	912,050	33	21,177,000	42	60.1	23.2	2.3	1990	19,405,429	49.7	50.3	84.0
Vietnam	127,246	329,566	66	72,342,000	13	568.5	219.5	2.2	1989	64,411,713	48.7	51.3	20.1
Virgin Islands (U.S.)	136	352	199	104,000	192	764.7	295.5	0.5	1990	101,809	48.3	51.7	37.2
West Bank[36]	2,270	5,900	166	1,219,000	148	537.0	206.6	4.6	1992[2]	1,051,500	50.3	49.7	...
Western Sahara	97,344	252,120	77	208,000	180	2.1	0.8	1.8	1970	76,425	...	...	...
Western Samoa	1,093	2,831	171	164,000	184	150.0	57.9	0.7	1991	159,682	53.0[6]	47.0[6]	20.5[6]
Yemen	205,356	531,869	49	12,961,000	60	63.1	24.4	3.6	1986[37]	9,274,173[38]	47.3[8]	52.7[8]	10.2[8]
Yugoslavia	39,449	102,173	107	10,515,000	66	266.5	102.9	0.1	1991	10,394,026	49.6	50.4	46.8[8]
Zaire	905,446	2,345,095	12	43,775,000	26	48.3	18.7	3.3	1984	29,671,407	49.2	50.8	36.6[4]
Zambia	290,586	752,614	39	9,132,000	77	31.4	12.1	3.0	1990	7,818,447	49.2	50.8	42.0
Zimbabwe	150,872	390,757	60	10,971,000	65	72.7	28.1	3.1	1992	10,401,767	48.8	51.2	23.0[14]

[1]Settled population only.   [2]Civil register; not a census.   [3]1991 estimate.   [4]1985 estimate.   [5]1990 estimate.   [6]1986 census.   [7]Data are for de jure population.   [8]1981 census.   [9]1980 estimate.   [10]1992 estimate.   [11]Except census, data are for the island of Cyprus.   [12]Republic of Cyprus only.   [13]1989 estimate.   [14]1982 census.   [15]1983 census.   [16]Former West Germany only.   [17]Excludes visitors, transients, and family members of British servicemen.   [18]1988 estimate.   [19]Data exclude Alderney (population 2,297) and Sark (population 604).   [20]Area figures exclude the West Bank, East Jerusalem, Gaza Strip, and Golan Heights.   [21]Population figures include the Golan Heights and East Jerusalem, and exclude Israelis in the West Bank and Gaza Strip.   [22]Includes East Jerusalem and Israelis in the West Bank, Gaza Strip, and Golan Heights.   [23]Excludes the West Bank.   [24]No census ever taken.   [25]1985 census.   [26]Including 163,868 in Western Sahara.   [27]Omani nationals only.

age distribution (%)						population (by decade, '000s)								country
0–14	15–29	30–44	45–59	60–74	75 and over	1940	1950	1960	1970	1980	1990	2000 projection	2010 projection	
26.0	23.9	25.5	14.3	7.3	3.0	77	112	136	163	174	192	193	194	Netherlands Antilles
32.6	28.6	19.8	12.1	5.4	1.6	53	59	79	110	140	168	204	238	New Caledonia
23.2	24.6	22.4	14.4	10.9	4.5	1,637	1,909	2,377	2,820	3,144	3,363	3,786	4,097	New Zealand
48.1	25.6	14.1	7.4	3.8	1.1	825	1,109	1,472	1,972	2,771	3,871	4,457	4,900	Nicaragua
48.7	24.8	14.6	6.8	3.6	1.5	1,700	2,291	2,913	4,016	5,565	7,735	10,640	14,326	Niger
47.4[5]	26.0[5]	14.4[5]	8.0[5]	3.5[5]	0.6[5]	...	33,320	42,366	56,346	69,875	86,015	105,885	130,344	Nigeria
23.8	33.5	30.7	9.1	2.3	0.5	48	6	9	10	17	44	50	58	Northern Mariana Islands
18.8	22.9	22.1	15.1	13.9	7.2	2,973	3,265	3,581	3,877	4,086	4,241	4,426	4,550	Norway
46.7[5]	23.6[5]	17.2[5]	8.3[5]	3.5[5]	0.7[5]	...	413	505	654	988	1,851	2,393	3,120	Oman
44.5	23.9	15.4	9.3	5.3	1.6	28,300	39,513	49,955	65,706	85,299	118,122	154,794	197,672	Pakistan
34.8	29.2	18.2	10.2	5.5	2.0	620	893	1,148	1,531	1,950	2,398	2,856	3,266	Panama
40.4[5]	28.6[5]	17.0[5]	9.3[5]	4.3[5]	0.3[5]	1,308	1,613	1,920	2,422	3,086	3,875	4,867	6,023	Papua New Guinea
40.1	27.6	18.7	8.3	4.2	1.1	1,111	1,351	1,778	2,290	3,147	4,277	5,464	6,889	Paraguay
41.2[8]	27.9[8]	15.6[8]	9.3[8]	4.4[8]	1.6[8]	6,784	7,632	9,931	13,193	17,295	21,550	26,276	31,047	Peru
39.6	28.7	17.3	9.2	4.2	1.1	16,459	20,988	27,561	36,850	48,286	62,049	78,414	94,503	Philippines
25.4	21.2	23.3	16.6	10.4	4.2	31,500	24,824	29,561	32,526	35,578	38,111	39,547	41,089	Poland
25.5[8]	23.5[8]	18.0[8]	17.2[8]	11.9[8]	3.9[8]	7,696	8,405	8,826	9,040	9,766	9,868	9,737	9,611	Portugal
27.2	25.1	20.4	14.1	9.2	4.0	1,878	2,218	2,360	2,721	3,204	3,528	3,849	4,199	Puerto Rico
27.8	29.3	32.3	8.6	1.6	0.4	...	47	59	151	229	484	613	732	Qatar
29.5	29.8	20.3	11.7	6.5	2.1	221	244	338	447	507	601	718	854	Réunion
23.9[13]	22.4[13]	20.8[13]	17.6[13]	11.3[13]	4.0[13]	15,907	16,311	18,403	20,253	22,201	23,201	22,645	22,487	Romania
23.1	22.0	21.9	17.6	11.2	4.2	110,098	105,018	119,906	130,392	138,914	148,292	146,239	143,477	Russia
45.6	28.6	12.4	8.4	3.9	0.9	1,910	2,120	2,742	3,728	5,113	6,925	9,377	12,698	Rwanda
32.5[5]	25.6[5]	18.9[5]	10.1[5]	8.9[5]	4.0[5]	43	49	51	46	43	42	42	42	St. Kitts and Nevis
36.8	29.4	16.3	8.7	6.3	2.5	70	79	86	101	122	134	151	169	St. Lucia
37.4[4]	32.7[4]	14.9[4]	7.5[4]	5.6[4]	1.9[4]	61	67	80	86	99	105	116	127	St. Vincent and the Grenadines
24.4	23.0	19.9	17.4	11.4	3.9	10	13	15	19	21	23	27	30	San Marino
46.3[8]	25.0[8]	11.6[8]	10.8[8]	5.3[8]	1.8[8]	60	60	64	74	94	117	146	182	São Tomé and Príncipe
42.9[5]	24.6[5]	19.9[5]	8.4[5]	3.4[5]	0.7[5]	...	3,201	4,075	5,745	10,006	15,713	21,718	29,074	Saudi Arabia
47.5	26.1	13.6	7.8	——5.0——		1,857	2,600	3,076	4,207	5,651	7,292	9,519	12,424	Senegal
33.6	30.3	15.3	10.7	7.1	2.9	32	34	42	54	64	70	75	81	Seychelles
43.9[4]	25.6[4]	15.7[4]	9.6[4]	4.5[4]	0.7[4]	1,700	1,944	2,241	2,656	3,263	4,151	5,395	6,944	Sierra Leone
23.2	27.3	27.7	12.7	6.9	2.2	751	1,022	1,639	2,075	2,282	2,705	3,317	4,072	Singapore
25.0	22.7	22.8	14.6	10.7	4.2	3,553	3,463	3,994	4,528	4,984	5,298	5,510	5,774	Slovakia
20.0	22.4	23.7	17.4	11.9	4.6	1,450	1,467	1,580	1,727	1,901	1,998	2,000	1,975	Slovenia
47.3	25.7	13.9	8.1	——4.9——		94	104	125	163	230	319	433	569	Solomon Islands
45.6	24.9	15.5	7.4	——5.4——		...	2,438	2,956	3,667	5,799	6,763	9,170	12,588	Somalia
32.1	20.4	20.7	10.5	5.7	1.6	10,353	13,683	17,396	22,458	29,529	37,959	47,912	58,446	South Africa[30]
18.4[10]	25.1[10]	20.6[10]	——35.9[10]——			25,757	27,868	30,303	33,779	37,581	38,959	39,879	40,317	Spain
35.3	29.6	17.9	10.6	5.2	1.4	5,972	7,678	9,889	12,514	14,747	16,993	19,117	21,222	Sri Lanka
45.2[5]	26.1[5]	15.5[5]	8.7[5]	3.9[5]	0.7[5]	8,500	9,322	11,256	14,090	19,449	24,023	30,253	43,045	Sudan, The
39.3	29.5	13.8	10.0	4.5	2.8	193	215	247	292	355	403	465	534	Suriname
47.3	26.6	13.4	7.4	3.4	1.3	154	200	320	409	550	769	1,004	1,344	Swaziland
18.7	20.0	20.3	18.7	14.1	8.2	6,371	7,041	7,490	8,081	8,310	8,559	8,973	9,193	Sweden
16.8	22.8	23.2	18.0	12.5	6.7	4,234	4,715	5,429	6,270	6,362	6,712	7,297	7,452	Switzerland
48.5	25.8	12.5	8.3	3.7	1.2	2,597	3,495	4,561	6,305	8,704	12,116	16,925	23,634	Syria
27.1	27.8	23.1	12.3	7.9	1.8	5,987	7,619	10,668	14,583	17,705	20,279	22,364	24,693	Taiwan
42.9	28.1	13.8	9.0	4.6	1.6	1,525	1,532	2,083	2,942	3,968	5,303	6,701	8,493	Tajikistan
47.2[5]	26.7[5]	14.2[5]	7.8[5]	3.3[5]	0.7[5]	...	7,892	10,073	13,273	18,441	24,403	31,885	41,336	Tanzania
28.8	30.4	21.2	12.3	5.7	1.6	15,296	20,010	26,392	35,745	46,718	54,677	61,202	66,738	Thailand
49.8	24.8	13.1	6.8	3.3	2.0	834	1,201	1,465	1,954	2,614	3,493	4,668	6,238	Togo
40.6	29.0	13.8	10.1	5.0	1.4	37	50	65	80	92	97	103	105	Tonga
31.3[5]	26.9[5]	21.5[5]	12.2[5]	——8.1[5]——		503	668	828	941	1,082	1,227	1,337	1,451	Trinidad and Tobago
39.7[33]	28.8[33]	14.2[33]	10.7[33]	5.4[33]	1.2[33]	2,887	3,530	4,221	5,137	6,392	8,074	9,781	11,296	Tunisia
35.0	28.6	18.4	10.9	——7.1——		17,723	20,800	27,509	35,321	44,438	56,098	69,694	80,724	Turkey
40.5	28.8	15.5	9.1	4.7	1.4	1,302	1,211	1,594	2,189	2,860	3,668	4,691	6,007	Turkmenistan
31.8[34]	31.7[34]	15.2[34]	13.2[34]	6.3[34]	1.7[34]	4	5	5	6	8	9	11	13	Tuvalu
48.3[5]	26.6[5]	13.9[5]	7.2[5]	3.4[5]	0.7[5]	4,233	5,969	7,551	9,806	12,779	16,447	21,168	27,244	Uganda
21.5	21.0	20.6	18.5	10.7	7.7	41,340	36,906	42,783	47,317	50,034	51,892	52,970	54,098	Ukraine
31.9[4]	24.9[4]	32.1[4]	8.7[4]	1.9[4]	0.5[4]	...	70	90	223	1,015	1,844	2,393	2,917	United Arab Emirates
19.1	21.9	21.2	16.7	14.1	7.0	48,226	50,290	52,372	55,632	56,330	57,561	59,648	61,100	United Kingdom
21.5	23.4	23.9	14.4	11.5	5.3	132,594	152,271	180,671	204,879	227,726	249,908	275,512	298,865	United States
26.6	22.8	18.3	16.5	11.4	4.3	1,974	2,194	2,531	2,824	2,914	3,094	3,274	3,453	Uruguay
40.8	28.4	15.0	9.3	4.7	1.8	6,551	6,314	8,559	11,973	15,977	20,515	25,466	31,577	Uzbekistan
45.5	26.6	15.2	8.4	3.7	0.6	43	52	65	86	115	148	189	231	Vanuatu
38.3	28.1	18.6	9.3	4.5	1.2	3,740	5,009	7,502	10,604	15,024	19,325	23,799	27,816	Venezuela
39.0	28.7	16.0	9.1	5.6	1.6	20,209	22,725	30,172	41,063	53,722	66,233	81,516	97,097	Vietnam
28.9	23.7	22.0	16.0	7.3	2.2	25	27	32	75	97	102	107	113	Virgin Islands (U.S.)
48.4	——40.2——		——11.4——			...	...	...	608	733	1,011	1,525	2,216	West Bank[36]
42.9	27.2	16.3	7.4	4.4	1.8	...	14	32	76	155	193	233	282	Western Sahara
41.1[6]	30.9[6]	13.3[6]	9.1[6]	4.4[6]	1.2[6]	61	82	111	143	155	160	174	192	Western Samoa
46.7[8]	23.0[8]	15.1[8]	10.5[8]	4.7[8]	0.8[8]	...	4,529	5,538	6,276	7,936	11,282	15,859	21,797	Yemen
22.8	21.6	21.7	17.1	12.2	3.5	...	7,131	8,050	8,910	9,842	10,529	10,724	11,084	Yugoslavia
45.2[4]	25.9[4]	15.5[4]	8.7[4]	3.9[4]	0.7[4]	10,370	13,055	16,151	21,368	27,009	38,476	52,433	70,260	Zaire
48.4[5]	27.2[5]	13.7[5]	7.0[5]	3.1[5]	0.7[5]	1,484	2,440	3,141	4,189	5,738	8,138	10,672	13,885	Zambia
51.0[14]	26.3[14]	13.4[14]	6.5[14]	1.2[14]	1.6[14]	1,940	2,730	3,840	5,308	7,100	9,730	13,194	16,808	Zimbabwe

[28]Excludes Afghan refugees and residents of Pakistani-occupied Jammu and Kashmir. [29]Excludes North Solomons province and five remote census districts. [30]Includes the former black independent states of Bophuthatswana, Ciskei, Transkei, and Venda. [31]Excludes the former black independent states of Bophuthatswana, Ciskei, Transkei, and Venda. [32]Includes resident aliens; excludes seasonal workers. [33]1984 census. [34]1979 census. [35]Excludes 515,000 armed forces overseas. [36]Excludes East Jerusalem. [37]Former Yemen Arab Republic only. [38]Includes 1,168,199 nationals abroad.

Major cities and national capitals

The following table lists the principal cities or municipalities (those exceeding 100,000 in population [50,000 for Anglo-America]) of the countries of the world, together with figures for each national capital (indicated by a ★), regardless of size.

Most of the populations given refer to a so-called city proper, that is, a legally defined, incorporated, or chartered area defined by administrative boundaries and by national or state law. Some data, however, refer to the municipality, or commune, similar to the medieval city-state in that the city is governed together with its immediately adjoining, economically dependent areas, whether urban or rural in nature. Some countries define no other demographic or legal entities within such communes or municipalities, but many identify a centre, seat, head (*cabecera*), or locality that corresponds to the most densely populated, compact, contiguous core of the municipality. Because the amount of work involved in carefully defining these "centres" may be considerable, the necessary resources usually exist only at the time of a national census (generally 5 or 10 years apart). Between censuses, therefore, it may be possible only to track the growth of the municipality as a whole. Thus, in order to provide the most up-to-date data for cities in this table, figures referring to municipalities or communes may be given (identified by the abbreviation "MU"), even though the country itself may define a smaller, more closely knit city proper. Specific identification of municipalities is provided in this table *only* when

the country also publishes data for a more narrowly defined city proper; it is *not* provided when the sole published figure is the municipality, whether or not this is the proper local administrative term for the entity.

Problems also exist in the identification of cities in terms of named legal entities. There is, for example, a single municipality (*commune*) named Brussel (Brussels) at the centre of the Brussels agglomeration in Belgium; the *commune* numbers only about 136,000 population, while the agglomeration, which is understood by most people to constitute the city, numbers nearly a million. Both are shown so as to apprise the reader of the existence of a problem.

For certain countries, more than one form of the name of the city is given, usually to permit recognition of recent place name changes or of *forms* of the place name likely to be encountered in press stories if the title of the city's entry in the *Encyclopædia Britannica* is spelled according to a different romanization or spelling policy. Chinese names, for example, are given first in their Wade-Giles spelling (the scholarly system used by Britannica) and then, parenthetically, in their Pinyin spelling, the official Chinese system now encountered in press reports, official documents, and maps.

Sources for this data were usually the national census and statistical abstracts of the countries concerned, supplemented by correspondence with most national statistical offices to solicit unpublished data.

Major cities and national capitals

country / city	population	country / city	population	country / city	population	country / city	population	country / city	population
Afghanistan (1988 est.)		Rosario	875,664[3]	Naogaon	109,156	Tuzla	131,861	Maracanaú	133,206
Herāt	177,300	Salta	373,857	Nārāyanganj	288,008	Zenica	145,577	Marília	144,906
★ Kābul	700,000[1]	San Fernando	144,761	Narsinghdi	100,120			Maringá	225,516
Kandahār		San Isidro	299,022	Nawābganj	131,260	**Botswana** (1991)		Mauá	294,631
(Qandahār)	225,500	San Juan	119,399	Pābna	113,146	★ Gaborone	133,468	Mogi das Cruzes	125,992
Mazār-e Sharīf	130,600	San Justo	946,715[3]	Rājshāhi	324,532			Montes Claros	223,046
		San Luis	121,146	Rangpur	220,849	**Brazil** (1991)		Mossoró	117,020
Albania (1990)		San Miguel de		Saidpur	110,494	Alvorada	132,582	Natal	459,827
★ Tiranë	243,000	Tucumán	473,014	Sirājganj	100,003	Americana	153,592	Nilópolis	104,671
		San Salvador de		Sylhet	114,284	Anápolis	222,400	Niterói	400,586
Algeria (1987)		Jujuy	124,950[3]	Tangail	111,783	Aracaju	401,676	Nova Friburgo	111,020
★ Algiers	1,507,241	Santa Fe	442,214	Tongi	165,099	Araçatuba	145,751	Nova Iguaçu	562,062
Annaba	222,518	Santiago del Estero	201,709			Arapiraca	124,790	Novo Hamburgo	199,479
Batna	181,601	Tigre	256,005	**Barbados** (1990)		Araraquara	101,302	Olinda	341,059
Béchar	107,311	Tres de Febrero	349,221	★ Bridgetown	6,070	Barra Mansa	145,112	Osasco	566,949
Bejaïa	114,534	Vicente López	289,142			Bauru	254,211	Parnaíba	105,131
Biskra	128,280	Villa Nueva		**Belarus** (1991 est.)		Belém	765,476	Passo Fundo	135,158
Blida (el-Boulaida)	127,284	(Guaymallén)	157,334[2]	Baranovichi	166,700	Belo Horizonte	1,529,566	Pelotas	260,510
Constantine				Bobruysk	223,000	Betim	152,846	Petrolina	123,857
(Qacentina)	440,842	**Armenia** (1991 est.)		Borisov	150,200	Blumenau	185,200	Petrópolis	164,849
Mostaganem	114,037	Gyumri (Kumayri;		Brest	277,000	Boa Vista	118,928	Piracicaba	223,170
Oran (Wahran)	609,823	Leninakan)	120,000[4]	Gomel	503,300	★ Brasília	1,492,542	Poços de Caldas	104,800
Sétif	170,182	★ Yerevan	1,283,000	Grodno	284,800	Cachoeiro de Itapemirim	112,099	Ponta Grossa	219,648
Sidi bel Abbès	152,778			★ Minsk	1,633,600	Campina Grande	298,331	Porto Alegre	1,237,223
Skikda	128,747	**Aruba** (1991)		Mogilyov	363,000	Campinas	748,076	Porto Velho	226,198
Tébessa	107,559	★ Oranjestad	20,046	Mozyr	103,000	Campo Grande	516,403	Presidente Prudente	157,618
Tlemcen (Tilimsen)	107,632			Orsha	125,300	Campos	275,508	Recife	1,296,995
		Australia (1993 est.)		Pinsk	123,800	Canoas	269,234	Ribeirão Prêto	416,186
American Samoa		Adelaide	1,070,200[5]	Vitebsk	361,500	Carapicuíba	207,264	Rio Branco	167,457
(1990)		Brisbane	777,280			Caruaru	180,654	Rio Claro	130,364
★ Pago Pago	3,519	★ Canberra	278,904	**Belgium** (1993 est.)		Cascavel	175,294	Rio de Janeiro	5,473,909
		Fairfield	185,250	Antwerp	465,102	Caxias do Sul	262,983	Rio Grande	157,608
Andorra (1993 est.)		Geelong	151,806[6]	Brugge (Bruges)	116,871	Colombo	105,464	Salvador	2,070,296
★ Andorra la Vella	22,387	Gold Coast-Tweed	300,200[6]	★ Brussels	136,424[7]	Contagem	195,705	Santa Bárbara d'Oeste	140,208
		Hobart	193,300[5]	Agglomeration	950,339	Cuiabá	252,784	Santa Maria	193,294
Angola (1990 est.)		Liverpool	104,650	Charleroi	207,045	Curitiba	841,882	Santarém	168,153
★ Luanda	1,544,400	Melbourne	3,187,500[5]	Ghent	229,828	Diadema	305,068	Santo André	518,272
Lubango	105,000[2]	Newcastle	455,700[6]	Liège (Luik)	196,632	Divinópolis	141,984	Santos	415,554
		Perth	1,221,300[5]	Namur	104,372	Dourados	116,754	São Bernardo	
Antigua and Barbuda		Randwick	117,850			Duque de Caxias	325,903	do Campo	550,030
(1986 est.)		Stirling	178,734	**Belize** (1992 est.)		Embu	155,851	São Caetano do Sul	149,203
★ Saint John's	36,000	Sydney	3,719,000[5]	★ Belmopan	3,687	Feira de Santana	340,034	São Carlos	100,502
		Wanneroo	190,965			Florianópolis	191,664	São Gonçalo	296,021
Argentina (1991; MU)		Wollongong	182,210	**Benin** (1992 est.)		Fortaleza	743,335	São João de Meriti	220,742
Almirante Brown	449,105			Abomey-Calavi	125,565	Foz do Iguaçu	186,362	São José	
Avellaneda	346,620	**Austria** (1991)		★ Cotonou (official)	533,212	Franca	227,613	do Rio Prêto	263,454
Bahía Blanca	271,467	Graz	237,810	Djougou	132,192	Goiânia	912,136	São José dos	
Berazategui	243,690	Innsbruck	118,112	Parakou	106,708	Governador		Campos	385,879
★ Buenos Aires	2,960,976	Linz	203,044	★ Porto-Novo		Valadares	210,396	São Leopoldo	160,228
Caseros	340,343[3]	Salzburg	143,978	(de facto)	177,660	Gravataí	166,954	São Luís	164,334
Catamarca	110,489	★ Vienna	1,539,848			Guarapuava	107,046	São Paulo	9,393,753
Concordia	138,905			**Bermuda** (1991)		Guarulhos	544,698	São Vicente	268,467
Córdoba	1,179,067	**Azerbaijan** (1991 est.)		★ Hamilton	1,100	Ilhéus	135,117	Sapucaia do Sul	104,626
Corrientes	267,742	★ Baku (Baky)	1,080,500			Imperatriz	209,970	Sete Lagoas	137,537
Esteban Echeverría	276,017	Ganja (Gyandzha)	282,200	**Bhutan** (1993 est.)		Ipatinga	120,025	Sorocaba	348,952
Florencio Varela	253,554	Sumqayıt (Sumgait)	236,200	★ Paro (administrative)	3,000[8]	Itabuna	170,434	Susano (Suzano)	110,414
Formosa	165,700			★ Thimphu (official)	30,340	Itajaí	114,558	Taboão da Serra	159,894
General San Martín	407,506	**Bahamas, The** (1990)				Itapevi	107,983	Taubaté	185,790
General Sarmiento	646,891	★ Nassau	172,196	**Bolivia** (1992)		Itaquaquecetuba	164,665	Teresina	556,073
Godoy Cruz	141,553[3]			Cochabamba	404,102	Jaboatão	217,905	Uberaba	198,565
La Matanza	1,121,164	**Bahrain** (1991)		El Alto	404,367	Jacareí	143,468	Uberlândia	354,710
La Plata	542,567	★ al-Manāmah	120,937	★ La Paz		Jequié	114,542	Uruguaiana	103,160
La Rioja	106,281			(administrative)	711,036	João Pessoa	497,306	Vila Velha	263,897
Lanús	466,755	**Bangladesh** (1991)		Oruro	183,194	Joinville	326,208	Vitória	258,243
Lomas de Zamora	572,769	Barisāl	180,014	Potosí	112,291	Juàzeiro do Norte	163,527	Vitória da	
Mar del Plata	414,696[3]	Brāhmanbāria	114,297	Santa Cruz	694,616	Juiz de Fora	377,538	Conquista	179,868
Mendoza	121,696	Chittagong	1,566,070	★ Sucre (judicial)	130,952	Jundiaí	253,177	Volta Redonda	219,988
Merlo	390,031	Comilla	164,509			Lages	137,169		
Moreno	287,188	★ Dhākā (Dacca)	3,637,892	**Bosnia and Herzegovina**		Limeira	177,016	**Brunei** (1991)	
Morón	641,541	Dinājpur	136,657	(1991; MU)		Londrina	355,062	★ Bandar Seri	
Paraná	277,338	Gāzipur	100,690	Banja Luka	195,139	Luziânia	194,128	Begawan	21,484
Posadas	219,824	Jamālpur	108,416	Doboj	102,546	Macapá	146,523		
Quilmes	509,445	Jessore	176,398	Mostar	126,067	Maceió	554,727	**Bulgaria** (1992 est.)	
Resistencia	218,438[3]	Khulna	601,051	Prijedor	112,470	Manaus	1,005,634	Burgas	211,597
Río Cuarto	217,717	Mymensingh	198,662	★ Sarajevo	525,980	Marabá	102,364	Dobrich	116,066

country / city	population
Pleven	137,466
Plovdiv	379,112
Ruse	190,229
Shumen	112,091
Sliven	114,596
★ Sofia	1,140,795
Stara Zagora	162,368
Varna	316,231
Burkina Faso (1985)	
Bobo Dioulasso	228,668
★ Ouagadougou	441,514
Burundi (1990)	
★ Bujumbura	235,440
Gitega	101,827
Cambodia (1991 est.)	
★ Phnom Penh	900,000
Cameroon (1987)	
Bafoussam	112,920
Bamenda	110,690
Douala	810,490
Garoua	142,170
Maroua	123,450
★ Yaoundé	650,540
Canada (1991)	
Barrie	62,728
Beauport	69,158
Brampton	234,445
Brantford	81,997
Brossard	64,793
Burlington	129,575
Burnaby	158,858
Calgary	710,677
Cambridge	92,772
Charlesbourg	70,788
Chicoutimi	62,670
Dartmouth	67,798
Delta	88,978
East York	102,696
Edmonton	616,741
Etobicoke	309,993
Guelph	87,976
Halifax	114,455
Hamilton	318,499
Hull	60,707
Jonquière	57,933
Kamloops	67,057
Kelowna	75,950
Kingston	56,597
Kitchener	168,282
Laval	314,398
Lethbridge	60,974
London	303,165
Longueuil	129,874
Markham	153,811
Mississauga	463,388
Moncton	57,010
Montreal	1,017,666
Montreal-Nord	85,516
Nanaimo	60,129
Niagara Falls	75,399
North Bay	55,405
North York	562,564
Oakville	114,670
Oshawa	129,344
★ Ottawa	313,987
Peterborough	68,371
Prince George	69,653
Quebec	167,517
Red Deer	58,134
Regina	179,178
Richmond	126,624
Saint Catharines	129,300
Saint-Hubert	74,027
Saint John	74,969
Saint John's	95,770
Saint-Laurent	72,402
Sainte-Foy	71,133
Sarnia-Clearwater	74,167
Saskatoon	186,058
Sault Sainte Marie	81,476
Scarborough	524,598
Sherbrooke	76,429
Sudbury	92,884
Surrey	245,173
Thunder Bay	110,740
Toronto	635,395
Vancouver	471,844
Verdun	61,307
Victoria	71,228
Waterloo	71,181
Windsor	191,435
Winnipeg	616,790
York	140,525
Cape Verde (1990)	
★ Praia	61,797
Central African Republic (1990 est.)	
★ Bangui	706,000[9]
Chad (1993)	
Abéché	187,757
Bongor	194,992
Doba	185,477
Moundou	281,477
★ N'Djamena	529,555
Sarh	198,113
Chile (1990 est.; MU)	
Antofagasta	227,985
Arica	206,600
Calama	120,602
Chillán	166,669
Concepción	318,140
Copiapó	100,946[10]
Coquimbo	122,872[10]
Curicó	103,919[10]
Iquique	161,914
La Serena	123,552
Los Angeles	142,136[10]
Osorno	140,370
Puente Alto	220,039
Puerto Montt	128,537
Punta Arenas	132,396
Quilpué	115,782
Rancagua	210,473
San Bernardo	217,154
★ Santiago (administrative)	4,628,320
Talca	190,255
Talcahuano	257,767
Temuco	262,624
Valdivia	125,067
★ Valparaíso (legislative)	301,677
Viña del Mar	319,440
China (1990)[11]	
A-ch'eng (Acheng)	197,595
A-k'o-su (Aksu)	164,092
An-ch'ing (Anqing)	250,718
An-k'ang (Ankang)	142,170
An-shan (Anshan)	1,203,986
An-shun (Anshun)	174,142
An-ta (Anda)	136,446
An-yang (Anyang)	420,332
Canton (Guangzhou)	2,914,281
Chan-chiang (Zhanjiang)	400,997
Ch'ang-chi (Changji)	132,260
Chang-chia-k'ou (Zhangjiakou)	529,136
Ch'ang-chih (Changzhi)	317,144
Ch'ang-chou (Changzhou)	531,470
Chang-chou (Zhangzhou)	181,424
Ch'ang-ch'un (Changchun)	1,679,270
Ch'ang-sha (Changsha)	1,113,212
Ch'ang-shu (Changshu)	181,805
Ch'ang-te (Changde)	301,276
Chao-ch'ing (Zhaoqing)	194,784
Ch'ao-chou (Chaozhou)	313,469
Ch'ao-hsien (Chaoxian)	123,676
Chao tung (Zhaodong)	170,076
Ch'ao-yang (Chaoyang)	222,394
Chen-chiang (Zhenjiang)	368,316
Cheng-chou (Zhengzhou)	1,159,679
Ch'eng-te (Chengde)	246,799
Ch'eng-tu (Chengdu)	1,713,255
Chi-an (Ji'an)	148,583
Chi-hsi (Jixi)	683,885
Chi-lin (Jilin)	1,036,858
Chi-nan (Jinan)	1,480,915
Chi-ning (Jining) (*Inner Mongolia*)	163,552
Chi-ning (Jining) (*Shantung*)	265,248
Ch'i-t'ai-ho (Qitaihe)	214,957
Ch'i-tung (Qidong)	126,872
Chia-hsing (Jiaxing)	211,526
Chia-mu-ssu (Jiamusi)	493,409
Chiang-men (Jiangmen)	230,587
Chiang-yin (Jiangyin)	213,659
Chiang-yu (Jiangyou)	175,753
Chiao-hsien (Jiaoxian)	153,364
Chiao-nan (Jiaonan)	121,397
Chiao-tso (Jiaozuo)	409,100
Ch'ien-chiang (Qianjiang)	205,504
Ch'ih-feng (Chifeng)	350,077
Chin-ch'ang (Jinchang)	105,287
Chin-ch'eng (Jincheng)	136,396
Chin-chou (Jinzhou)	569,518
Ch'in-chou (Qinzhou)	114,586
Chin-hsi (Jinxi)	357,052
Chin-hua (Jinhua)	144,280
Ch'in-huang-tao (Qinhuangdao)	364,972
Ch'ing-chou (Qingzhou)	128,258
Ch'ing-tao (Qingdao)	1,459,195
Ching-te-chen (Jingdezhen)	281,183
Ch'ing-yüan (Qingyuan)	164,641
Chiu-chiang (Jiujiang)	291,187
Chiu-t'ai (Jiutai)	180,130
Chou-k'ou (Zhoukou)	146,288
Chou-shan (Zhoushan)	156,317
Chu-ch'eng (Zhucheng)	102,134
Ch'ü-ching (Qujing)	178,669
Ch'u-chou (Quzhou)	112,373
Chu-chou (Zhuzhou)	409,924
Chu-hai (Zhuhai)	164,747
Ch'u-hsien (Chuxian)	125,341
Chu-ma-tien (Zhumadian)	123,232
Ch'üan-chou (Quanzhou)	185,154
Chung-shan (Zhongshan)	278,829
Chungking (Chongqing)	2,266,772
Feng-ch'eng (Fengcheng)	193,784
Fo-shan (Foshan)	303,160
Fu-chin (Fujin)	103,104
Fu-chou (Fuzhou) (*Fukien*)	874,809
Fu-chou (Fuzhou) (*Kiangsi*)	121,949
Fu-hsin (Fuxin)	635,473
Fu-ling (Fuling)	173,878
Fu-shun (Fushun)	1,202,388
Fu-yang (Fuyang)	179,572
Fu-yü (Fuyu)	192,981
Ha-mi (Hami)	161,315
Hai-ch'eng (Haicheng)	205,560
Hai-k'ou (Haikou)	280,153
Hai-la-erh (Hailar)	180,650
Hai-lun (Hailun)	133,565
Hai-ning (Haining)	100,478
Han-chung (Hanzhong)	169,930
Han-tan (Handan)	837,552
Hang-chou (Hangzhou)	1,099,660
Harbin	2,443,398
Heng-shui (Hengshui)	104,269
Heng-yang (Hengyang)	487,148
Ho-fei (Hefei)	700,270
Ho-kang (Hegang)	522,747
Ho-pi (Hebi)	212,976
Ho-tse (Heze)	189,293
Ho-yuan (Heyuan)	120,101
Hsi-ch'ang (Xichang)	134,419
Hsi-ning (Xining)	551,776
Hsia-men (Xiamen)	368,786
Hsiang-fan (Xiangfan)	410,407
Hsiang-t'an (Xiangtan)	441,968
Hsiao-kan (Xiaogan)	166,280
Hsiao-shan (Xiaoshan)	162,930
Hsien-ning (Xianning)	136,811
Hsien-t'ao (Xiantao)	222,884
Hsien-yang (Xianyang)	352,125
Hsin-hsiang (Xinxiang)	473,762
Hsin-t'ai (Xintai)	281,248
Hsin-yang (Xinyang)	192,509
Hsin-yu (Xinyu)	173,524
Hsing-ch'eng (Xingcheng)	102,384
Hsing-hua (Xinghua)	161,910
Hsing-t'ai (Xingtai)	302,789
Hsü-ch'ang (Xuchang)	208,815
Hsü-chou (Xuzhou)	805,695
Hsuan-ch'eng (Xuancheng)	112,673
Hu-chou (Huzhou)	218,071
Hu-ho-hao-t'e (Hohhot)	652,534
Hua-tien (Huadian)	175,873
Huai-an (Huai'an)	131,149
Huai-hua (Huaihua)	120,785
Huai-nan (Huainan)	703,934
Huai-pei (Huaibei)	366,549
Huai-yin (Huaiyin)	239,675
Huang-shan (Huangshan)	102,628
Huang-shih (Huangshi)	457,601
Hui-chou (Huizhou)	161,023
Hun-chiang (Hunjiang)	482,043
Hung-hu (Honghu)	190,772
I-ch'ang (Yichang)	371,601
I-cheng (Yizheng)	109,268
I-ch'un (Yichun)	795,789
I-ch'un (Yichun) (*Kiangsi*)	151,585
I-hsing (Yixing)	200,824
I-ning (Yining)	177,193
I-pin (Yibin)	241,019
I-yang (Yiyang)	185,818
Jen-ch'iu (Renqiu)	114,256
Jih-chao (Rizhao)	185,048
Jui-an (Rui'an)	156,468
K'ai-feng (Kaifeng)	507,763
K'ai-li (Kaili)	113,958
K'ai-yuan (Kaiyuan)	124,219
Kan-chou (Ganzhou)	220,129
Kashgar (Kashi)	174,570
Ko-chiu (Gejiu)	214,294
K'o-la-ma-i (Karamay)	197,602
K'u-erh-le (Korla)	159,344
Kuang-shui (Guangshui)	102,770
Kuang-yüan (Guangyuan)	182,241
Kuei-hsien (Guixian)	114,025
Kuei-lin (Guilin)	364,130
K'uei-t'un (Kuitun)	118,553
Kuei-yang (Guiyang)	1,018,619
K'un-ming (Kunming)	1,127,411
K'un-shan (Kunshan)	102,052
Kung-chu-ling (Gongzhuling)	226,569
Lai-chou (Laizhou)	198,664
Lai-wu (Laiwu)	246,833
Lai-yang (Laiyang)	137,080
Lan-chou (Lanzhou)	1,194,640
Lang-fang (Langfang)	148,105
Lao-ho-k'ou (Laohekou)	123,366
Le-shan (Leshan)	341,128
Lei-yang (Leiyang)	130,115
Leng-shui-chiang (Lengshuijiang)	137,994
Lhasa	106,885
Li-ling (Liling)	108,504
Li-yang (Liyang)	109,520
Liang-ch'eng (Liangcheng)	156,307
Liao-ch'eng (Liaocheng)	207,844
Liao-yang (Liaoyang)	492,559
Liao-yüan (Liaoyuan)	354,141
Lien-yüan (Lianyuan)	118,858
Lien-yün-kang (Lianyungang)	354,139
Lin-ch'ing (Linqing)	123,958
Lin-fen (Linfen)	187,309
Lin-ho (Linhe)	133,183
Lin-i (Linyi)	324,720
Liu-chou (Liuzhou)	609,320
Liu-p'an-shui (Liupanshui)	363,954
Lo-ho (Luohe)	126,438
Lo-yang (Luoyang)	759,752
Long-yen (Longyan)	134,481
Lou-ti (Loudi)	120,410
Lu-an (Lu'an)	144,248
Lu-chou (Luzhou)	262,892
Lung-ching (Longjing)	139,417
Lung-k'ou (Longkou)	140,002
Ma-an-shan (Ma'anshan)	305,421
Man-chou-li (Manzhouli)	120,023
Mao-ming (Maoming)	178,683
Mei-ho-k'ou (Meihekou)	209,038
Mei-hsien (Meixian)	132,156
Mi-shan (Mishan)	132,744
Mien-yang (Mianyang)	262,947
Mu-tan-chiang (Mudanjiang)	571,705
Nan-ch'ang (Nanchang)	1,086,124
Nan-ch'ung (Nanchong)	180,273
Nan-ning (Nanning)	721,877
Nan-p'ing (Nanping)	195,064
Nan-t'ung (Nantong)	343,341
Nan-yang (Nanyang)	243,303
Nanking (Nanjing)	2,090,204
Nei-chiang (Neijiang)	256,012
Ning-po (Ningbo)	552,540
O-ch'eng (Echeng)	190,123
Pai-ch'eng (Baicheng)	217,987
Pai-yin (Baiyin)	204,970
P'an-chih-hua (Panzhihua) (Tu-k'ou [Dukou])	415,466
P'an-shan (Panshan)	362,773
Pang-pu (Bengbu)	449,245
Pao-chi (Baoji)	337,765
Pao-ting (Baoding)	483,155
Pao-t'ou (Baotou)	983,508
Pei-an (Bei'an)	204,899
Pei-hai (Beihai)	112,673
Pei-p'iao (Beipiao)	194,301
★ Peking (Beijing)	5,769,607
Pen-hsi (Benxi)	768,778
Pin-chou (Binzhou)	133,555
P'ing-hsiang (Pingxiang)	425,579
P'ing-ting-shan (Pingdingshan)	410,775
P'ing-tu (Pingdu)	150,123
Po-chou (Bozhou)	106,346
P'u-ch'i (Puqi)	117,264
P'u-yang (Puyang)	175,988
San-men-hsia (Sanmenxia)	120,523
San-ming (Sanming)	160,691
San-ya (Sanya)	102,820
Sha-shih (Shashi)	281,352
Shan-t'ou (Shantou)	578,630
Shan-wei (Shanwei)	107,847
Shao-hsing (Shaoxing)	179,818
Shao-kuan (Shaoguan)	350,043
Shao-yang (Shaoyang)	247,227
Shang-chih (Shangzhi)	215,373
Shang-ch'iu (Shangqiu)	164,880
Shang-jao (Shangrao)	132,455
Shanghai	7,496,509
Shen-chen (Shenzhen)	350,727
Shen-yang (Shenyang)	3,603,712
Shih-chia-chuang (Shijiazhuang)	1,068,439
Shih-ho-tzu (Shihezi)	299,676
Shih-shou (Shishou)	104,571
Shih-tsui-shan (Shizuishan)	257,862
Shih-yen (Shiyan)	273,786
Shuang-ch'eng (Shuangcheng)	142,659
Shuang-ya-shan (Shuangyashan)	386,081
Sian (Xi'an)	1,959,044
Ssu-p'ing (Siping)	317,223
Su-ch'ien (Suqian)	105,021
Su-chou (Suzhou) (*Anhwei*)	151,862
Su-chou (Suzhou) (*Kiangsu*)	706,459
Sui-hua (Suihua)	227,881
Sui-ning (Suining)	146,086
Ta-an (Da'an)	138,963
Ta-ch'ing (Daqing)	657,297
Ta-hsien (Daxian)	188,101
Ta-li (Dali)	136,554
Ta-lien (Dalian)	1,723,302
Ta-t'ung (Datong)	798,319
T'ai-an (Tai'an)	350,696
T'ai-chou (Taizhou)	152,442
T'ai-yüan (Taiyuan)	1,533,884
Tan-chiang (Danjiang)	103,211
Tan-tung (Dandong)	523,699
Tan-yang (Danyang)	169,603
T'ang-shan (Tangshan)	1,044,194
T'ao-nan (Taonan)	150,168
Te-chou (Dezhou)	195,485
Te-yang (Deyang)	182,488
T'eng-hsien (Tengxian)	315,083
T'ieh-fa (Tiefa)	131,807
T'ieh-li (Tieli)	265,683
T'ieh-ling (Tieling)	254,842
T'ien-men (Tianmen)	100,002
T'ien-shui (Tianshui)	244,974
Tientsin (Tianjin)	4,574,689
Tsa-lan-t'un (Zalantun)	130,031
Ts'ang-chou (Cangzhou)	242,708
Tsao-chuang (Zaozhuang)	380,846
Tsao-yang (Zaoyang)	102,198
Tsitsihar (Qiqihar)	1,070,051
Tsun-i (Zunyi)	261,862
Tu-chiang-yen (Dujiangyan)	123,357
Tu-yun (Duyun)	132,971
Tun-hua (Dunhua)	235,100
T'ung-ch'uan (Tongchuan)	280,657
T'ung-hua (Tonghua)	324,600
Tung-kuan (Dongguan)	308,669
T'ung-liao (Tongliao)	255,129
T'ung-ling (Tongling)	228,017
Tung-t'ai (Dongtai)	192,247
Tung-ying (Dongying)	281,728
Tz'u-hsi (Cixi)	107,329
Tzu-hsing (Zixing)	110,048
Tzu-kung (Zigong)	393,184
Tzu-po (Zibo)	1,138,074
Wa-fang-tien (Wafangdian)	251,733
Wan-hsien (Wanxian)	156,823
Wei-fang (Weifang)	428,522
Wei-hai (Weihai)	128,888
Wei-nan (Weinan)	140,169
Wen-chou (Wenzhou)	401,871
Wen-teng (Wendeng)	133,910
Wu-chou (Wuzhou)	210,452
Wu-hai (Wuhai)	264,081
Wu-han (Wuhan)	3,284,229
Wu-hsi (Wuxi)	826,833
Wu-hu (Wuhu)	425,740
Wu-lan-hao-t'e (Ulanhot)	159,538
Wu-lu-mu-ch'i (Ürümqi)	1,046,898
Wu-wei (Wuwei)	133,101
Ya-k'o-she (Yakeshi)	377,869

Major cities and national capitals (continued)

country city	population	country city	population	country city	population	country city	population	country city	population
Yang-chiang		**Czech Republic** (1991)		Besançon	119,194	Magdeburg	272,516	**Iceland** (1993 est.)	
(Yangjiang)	215,196	Brno	387,986	Bordeaux	213,274	Mainz	184,646	★ Reykjavík	101,855
Yang-chou		Liberec	101,934	Boulogne-Billancourt	101,971	Mannheim	318,446		
(Yangzhou)	312,892	Olomouc	105,690	Brest	153,099	Moers	106,384	**India** (1991)	
Yang-ch'üan		Ostrava	327,553	Caen	115,624	Mönchengladbach	265,069	Abohar	107,016
(Yangquan)	362,268	Plzen	173,129	Clermont-Ferrand	140,167	Mülheim an der		Ādoni	135,718
Yen-an (Yan'an)	113,277	★ Prague	1,212,010	Dijon	151,636	Ruhr	176,962	Agartala	157,636
Yen-ch'eng (Yancheng)	296,831			Grenoble	153,973	Munich (München)	1,256,638	Āgra	899,195
Yen-chi (Yanji)	230,892	**Denmark** (1993 est.; MU)		Le Havre	197,219	Münster	267,072	Ahmadābād	2,872,865
Yen-t'ai (Yantai)	452,127	Ålborg	152,270	Le Mans	148,465	Neuss	149,017	Ahmadnagar	181,015
Yin-ch'uan		Århus	271,272	Lille	178,301	Nürnberg	500,198	Āizawl	154,343
(Yinchuan)	356,652	★ Copenhagen	1,339,395[9, 15]	Limoges	136,407	Oberhausen	226,025	Ajmer	401,930
Ying-k'ou (Yingkou)	421,589	Odense	180,799	Lyon	422,444	Offenbach am Main	117,000	Akola	327,946
Yü-lin (Yulin)	144,467			Marseille	807,726	Oldenburg	146,816	Alandur	125,009
Yü-men (Yumen)	109,234	**Djibouti** (1991 est.)		Metz	123,920	Osnabrück	166,837	Alīgarh	479,978
Yü-shu (Yushu)	131,861	★ Djibouti	317,000	Montpellier	210,866	Paderborn	128,453	Allahābād	806,447
Yü-tz'u (Yuci)	191,356			Mulhouse	109,905	Pforzheim	116,733	Alleppey	174,606
Yu-yao (Yuyao)	114,065	**Dominica** (1991)		Nancy	102,410	Potsdam	138,618	Alwar	206,107
Yüan-chiang		★ Roseau	15,853	Nantes	252,029	Recklinghausen	126,647	Ambāla	119,535
(Yuanjiang)	107,004			Nice	345,674	Regensburg	124,398	Ambattur	223,332
Yüeh-yang		**Dominican Republic**		Nîmes	133,607	Remscheid	124,106	Amrāvati	433,746
(Yueyang)	302,800	(1993)		Orléans	107,965	Reutlingen	106,638	Amritsar	709,456
Yun-ch'eng (Yuncheng)	108,359	La Romana	136,000[16]	★ Paris	2,175,200	Rostock	241,106	Amroha	136,893
Yung-an (Yong'an)	111,762	La Vega	189,000[16]	Perpignan	108,049	Saarbrücken	192,332	Anand	110,144
		San Pedro		Reims	185,164	Salzgitter	116,750	Anantapur	174,792
Colombia (1994 est.)		de Macorís	137,000[16]	Rennes	203,533	Schwerin	124,084	Āra (Arrah)	156,871
Armenia	217,670	Santiago de los		Rouen	105,470	Siegen	111,130	Āsānsol	261,836
Barrancabermeja	177,718	Caballeros	690,000	Saint-Étienne	201,569	Solingen	167,112	Aurangābād	572,634
Barranquilla	1,049,170	★ Santo Domingo	2,100,000	Strasbourg	255,937	Stuttgart	599,415	Āvadi	180,291
Bello	295,279			Toulon	170,167	Ulm	114,066	Baharampur	115,036
Bucaramanga	351,061	**Ecuador** (1990)		Toulouse	365,933	Wiesbaden	268,069	Bahraich	135,352
Buenaventura	260,301	Ambato	124,166	Tours	133,403	Witten	105,834	Bally	181,978
Cali	1,687,280	Cuenca	194,981	Villeurbanne	119,848	Wolfsburg	128,996	Bālurghāt	119,829
Cartagena	726,256	Guayaquil	1,508,444			Wuppertal	388,102	Bangalore	2,650,659
Cartago	115,517	Machala	144,197	**French Guiana** (1990)		Würzburg	128,796	Bānkura	114,927
Ciénaga	143,452	Manta	125,505	★ Cayenne	41,659	Zwickau	110,583	Barāhanagar	223,770
Cúcuta	469,579	Portoviejo	132,937					Bārāsat	107,365
Dosquebradas	157,024	★ Quito	1,100,847	**French Polynesia** (1988)		**Ghana** (1988 est.)		Barddhamān	
Envigado	107,650	Santo Domingo	114,422	★ Papeete	23,555	★ Accra	949,113	(Burdwān)	244,789
Florencia	114,730					Kumasi	385,192	Bareilly	583,473
Floridablanca	235,086	**Egypt** (1991 est.)		**Gabon** (1988 est.)		Sekondi-Takoradi	103,653	Barrackpore	133,429
Ibagué	342,504	Alexandria	3,382,000[17]	★ Libreville	352,000	Tamale	151,069	Basīrhāt	101,652
Itagüí	166,353	Aswān	215,000	Port-Gentil	164,000	Tema	109,975	Bathinda (Bhatinda)	159,144
Magangué	103,386	Asyūṭ	313,000					Beāwar	105,357
Malambo	104,752	Banhā	133,000	**Gambia, The** (1986 est.)		**Gibraltar** (1994 est.)		Belgaum	325,639
Manizales	332,529	Banī Suwayf	174,000	★ Banjul	44,188[20]	★ Gibraltar	28,800[21]	Bellary	245,758
Medellín	1,608,379	Būr Sa'īd (Port Said)	460,000[17]	Serekunda	102,600			Bhāgalpur	254,993
Montería	272,669	★ Cairo	6,849,000[17]			**Greece** (1991)		Bharatpur	148,506
Neiva	242,945	Damanhūr	216,000	**Gaza Strip** (1988 est.)		★ Athens	748,110	Bharūch (Broach)	132,312
Palmira	253,664	al-Fayyūm	244,000	Gaza (Ghazzah)	57,000	Iráklion	117,167	Bhātpāra	304,298
Pasto	318,084	Hulwan (Helwan)	352,300[18]			Kallithéa	110,738	Bhāvnagar	400,636
Pereira	347,024	al-Ismā'īlīyah	247,000	**Georgia** (1991 est.)		Larissa	113,426	Bhilainagar	389,601
Popayán	216,550	al-Jīzah (Giza)	2,096,000	Batumi	137,500	Pátrai (Patras)	155,180	Bhīlwāra	183,791
Quibdó	126,867	Kafr ad-Dawwar	221,000	Kutaisi	238,200	Peristérion	145,854	Bhīmavaram	125,495
Ríohacha	136,889	Kafr ash-Shaykh	102,910[19]	Rustavi	161,900	Piraiévs (Piraeus)	169,622	Bhind	109,731
Santa Marta	301,633	al-Maḥallah al-Kubrā	400,000	Sukhumi	120,000	Thessaloníki	377,951	Bhiwandi	378,546
★ Santafé de Bogotá,		al-Manṣūrah	362,000	★ Tbilisi	1,279,000			Bhiwāni	121,449
D.C.	5,131,582	al-Minyā	203,000			**Greenland** (1994 est.)		Bhopāl	1,063,662
Sincelejo	175,864	Qinā	137,000	**Germany** (1993 est.)		★ Nuuk (Godthåb)	12,935	Bhubaneshwar	411,542
Soacha	243,668	Sawhāj	152,000	Aachen	245,627			Bhusāwal	144,804
Soledad	253,832	Shibīn al-Kawm	153,000	Augsburg	264,852	**Grenada** (1991)		Bīd (Bhīr)	112,351
Tuluá	137,184	Shubrā al-Khaymah	812,000	Bergisch Gladbach	104,887	★ Saint George's	4,439	Bīdar	107,542
Tumaco	113,527	as-Suways (Suez)	376,000	Berlin	3,465,748			Bihār Sharīf	200,976
Tunja	117,570	Ṭanṭā	372,000	Bielefeld	324,287	**Guadeloupe** (1990)		Bijāpur	186,846
Turbo	121,278	al-Uqṣur (Luxor)	155,000[17]	Bochum	400,356	★ Basse-Terre	14,107	Bīkaner	415,355
Valledupar	260,859	az-Zaqāzīq	279,000	★ Bonn	298,227			Bilāspur	190,911
Villavicencio	246,043			Bottrop	119,377	**Guam** (1990)		Bokāro	350,540
		El Salvador (1992; MU)		Braunschweig	258,347	★ Agana	1,139	Bombay (Greater)	9,909,547
Comoros (1990 est.)		Mejicanos	145,000	Bremen	554,377			Brahmapur	210,585
★ Moroni	23,432	Nueva San Salvador	116,575	Bremerhaven	131,468	**Guatemala**		Budaun	116,706
		San Miguel	182,817	Chemnitz	283,590	(1994 est.; MU)		Bulandshahr	126,737
Congo (1992 est.)		★ San Salvador	422,570	Cologne (Köln)	960,631	★ Guatemala City	1,150,452	Burhānpur	172,809
★ Brazzaville	937,579	Santa Ana	202,337	Cottbus	122,883	Mixco	413,002	Burnpur	174,704
Pointe-Noire	576,206	Soyapango	104,470[16]	Darmstadt	141,431	Villa Nueva	154,508	Calcutta	4,388,262
				Dortmund	600,669			Calicut (Kozhikode)	419,531
Costa Rica (1993 est.)		**Equatorial Guinea**		Dresden	481,676	**Guernsey** (1991)		Chandannagar	122,351
★ San José	280,613[12]	(1983)		Duisburg	539,094	★ St. Peter Port	16,648	Chandīgarh	502,992
		★ Malabo	30,418	Düsseldorf	578,135			Chandrapur	225,841
Côte d'Ivoire				Erfurt	203,134	**Guinea** (1990 est.)		Chhapra	136,824
(1988)		**Eritrea** (1991 est.)		Erlangen	102,794	★ Conakry	1,127,000	Chittoor	133,233
★ Abidjan	1,929,079	★ Asmera	367,300	Essen	627,269			Cochin	564,038
Bouaké	329,850			Frankfurt am Main	663,952	**Guinea-Bissau** (1988 est.)		Coimbatore	853,402
Daloa	121,842	**Estonia** (1994 est.)		Freiburg im		★ Bissau	125,000	Cuddalore	143,774
Korhogo	109,445	★ Tallinn	442,679	Breisgau	195,789			Cuddapah	121,422
Yamoussoukro	106,786	Tartu	105,844	Fürth	107,239	**Guyana** (1990 est.)		Cuttack	402,390
				Gelsenkirchen	295,368	★ Georgetown	234,000	Darbhanga	218,274
Croatia (1991)		**Ethiopia** (1989 est.)		Gera	124,925			Dāvangere	265,971
Osijek	129,792	★ Addis Ababa	1,732,080	Göttingen	128,299	**Haiti** (1992 est.)		Dehra Dūn	270,028
Rijeka	167,964	Dire Dawa	121,887	Hagen	214,912	Carrefour	241,223	Delhi	7,174,755
Split	200,459			Halle	299,884	Delmas	200,251	Dewās	163,699
★ Zagreb	867,865	**Faeroe Islands**		Hamburg	1,688,785	★ Port-au-Prince	752,600	Dhānbād	151,334
		(1994 est.)		Hamm	182,640			Dhūle (Dhūlia)	277,957
Cuba (1991 est.)		★ Tórshavn	16,200	Hannover	523,627	**Honduras** (1992 est.; MU)		Dibrugarh	118,374
Bayamo	128,167			Heidelberg	140,282	San Pedro Sula	339,600	Dindigul	182,293
Camagüey	286,404	**Fiji** (1990 est.)		Heilbronn	121,052	★ Tegucigalpa	703,500[22]	Durg	150,513
Cienfuegos	125,000	★ Suva	200,000[9]	Herne	180,082			Durgāpur	415,986
Guantánamo	203,371			Hildesheim	106,450	**Hong Kong** (1994 est.)		Elūru	212,918
★ Havana	2,119,059	**Finland** (1994 est.)		Ingolstadt	108,448	Hong Kong	5,979,000[21]	Erode	158,774
Holguín	232,770	Espoo	182,647	Jena	100,390			Etāwah	124,032
Las Tunas	120,897	★ Helsinki	508,588	Kaiserslautern	101,803	**Hungary** (1994 est.)		Faizābād	125,012
Manzanillo	107,650[13]	Oulu	104,346	Karlsruhe	279,329	★ Budapest	1,996,000	Farīdābād	613,828
Matanzas	115,466	Tampere	176,149	Kassel	199,935	Debrecen	218,000	Farrukhābād-cum-	
Pinar del Río	124,100	Turku	160,390	Kiel	249,199	Győr	131,000	Fatehgarh	193,624
Santa Clara	197,189	Vantaa	161,103	Koblenz	109,654	Kecskemét	106,000	Fatehpur	117,203
Santiago de Cuba	418,721			Krefeld	248,413	Miskolc	190,000	Fīrozābād	215,089
		France (1990)		Leipzig	496,647	Nyíregyháza	115,000	Gadag-Betigeri	133,918
Cyprus (1993 est.)[9]		Aix-en-Provence	126,854	Leverkusen	162,011	Pécs	173,000	Gāndhīdhām	104,392
Limassol	137,000	Amiens	136,234	Lübeck	217,500	Szeged	180,000	Gāndhīnagar	121,746
★ Nicosia	177,000[14]	Angers	146,163	Ludwigshafen	167,541	Székesfehérvár	110,000	Gangānagar	161,377

country city	population
Gaya	291,220
Ghāziābād	460,949
Gonda	106,078
Gondia	109,271
Gorakhpur	489,850
Gudivāda	101,635
Gulbarga	303,139
Guna	100,389
Guntakal	107,560
Guntūr	471,020
Gurgaon	120,790
Guwāhāti (Gauhāti)	577,591
Gwalior	692,982
Hābra	100,142
Haldīa	100,109
Haldwāni-cum-Kāthgodam	102,744
Hālisahar	113,670
Hāpur	146,591
Haridwār (Hardwār)	148,882
Hāthras	113,653
Hindupur	104,635
Hisār (Hissār)	172,070
Hoshiārpur	122,528
Howrah (Hāora)	946,732
Hubli-Dhārwād	647,640
Hugli-Chunchura	142,388
Hyderābād	2,991,884
Ichalkaranji	214,835
Imphāl	196,268
Indore	1,086,673
Ingrāj Bāzār	139,018
Jabalpur	739,961
Jaipur	1,454,678
Jalandhar (Jullundur)	519,530
Jalgaon	241,603
Jālna	174,958
Jammu	206,135[11]
Jāmnagar	325,475
Jamshedpur	461,212
Jaunpur	136,287
Jhānsi	301,304
Jodhpur	648,621
Jūnāgadh	130,132
Kākināda	279,875
Kalyān	1,014,062
Kāmārhāti	266,625
Kānchipuram	145,028
Kānchrāpāra	100,059
Kānpur	1,958,282
Karīmnagar	148,349
Karnāl	173,742
Katihār	135,348
Khammam	127,812
Khandwa	145,111
Kharagpur	189,010
Kolhāpur	405,118
Kota	536,444
Krishnanagar	120,918
Kukatpalle	185,378
Kulti-Barākar	108,930
Kumbakonam	139,449
Kurnool	236,313
Lātūr	197,164
Lucknow	1,592,010
Ludhiana	1,012,062
Machilīpatnam (Masulipatam)	159,007
Madras	3,795,028
Madurai	951,696
Mahbūbnagar	116,775
Mālegaon	342,431
Mālkājgiri	126,066
Mandya	119,970
Mangalore	272,819
Māngo	110,024
Mathura	226,850
Maunāth Bhanjan	136,447
Medinīpur (Midnāpore)	125,098
Meerut	752,078
Miraj	121,564
Mirzāpur-cum-Vindhyāchal	169,368
Modinagar	102,307
Moga	108,213
Morādābād	416,836
Morena	147,095
Munger (Monghyr)	150,042
Murwāra (Katni)	163,699
Muzaffarnagar	240,057
Muzaffarpur	240,450
Mysore	480,006
Nadiād	166,852
Nāgercoil	189,482
Nāgpur	1,622,225
Naihāti	132,032
Nānded	274,626
Nandyāl	120,171
Nāshik (Nāsik)	646,896
Navadwīp	125,247
Navsāri	125,980
Nellore	316,445
★ New Delhi	294,149
Neyveli	117,471
Nizāmābād	240,924
Noida	167,440
North Barrackpore	100,513
North Dum Dum	151,298
Ongole	100,544
Pālghāt	122,964
Pāli	136,797
Pallavaram	111,194
Pānihāti	275,359
Pānīpat	191,010
Parbhani	190,235
Pathānkot	142,862
Patiala	253,341
Patna	916,980
Pīlībhīt	106,329
Pimpri-Chinchwad	515,962
Pondicherry	202,648
Porbandar	116,546
Proddatūr	133,860
Pune	1,559,558
Puri	124,835
Pūsa	122,086
Quilon	139,717
Qutubullapur	105,380
Rāe Bareli	130,101
Rāichūr	157,477
Rāiganj	151,454
Raipur	437,887
Rāj Nāndgaon	125,394
Rājahmundry	326,071
Rājapālaiyam	114,042
Rājkot	556,137
Rāmagundam	213,962
Rāmpur	242,752
Rānchi	598,498
Ratlām	183,370
Raurkela Steel Township	215,489
Rewa	128,918
Rishra	102,649
Rohtak	215,844
Sāgar	195,106
Sahāranpur	373,904
Salem	363,934
Sambalpur	130,766
Sambhal	150,012
Sāngli	193,181
Satna	156,321
Shāhjahānpur	237,663
Shāntipur	109,911
Shiliguri (Silīguri)	226,677
Shillong	130,691
Shimoga	178,882
Shivpuri	108,271
Sholāpur (Solapur)	603,870
Shrīrāmpur	137,087
Sīkar	148,235
Silchar	115,045
Sirsa	112,542
Sitāpur	120,595
Sonīpat	142,992
South Dum Dum	230,507
Srīnagar	586,038[11]
Sūrat	1,496,943
Surendranagar	105,973
Tambaram	106,590
Tellicherry	103,577
Tenāli	143,836
Thāne (Thāna)	796,620
Thanjāvūr	200,216
Tiruchchirāppalli	386,628
Tirunelveli	135,762
Tirupati	174,393
Tirupper (Tiruppūr)	235,076
Tiruvannāmalai	108,291
Tiruvottiyūr	167,851
Titāgarh	113,831
Tonk	100,020
Trivandrum	523,733
Tumkūr	138,598
Tuticorin	205,105
Udaipur	307,682
Ujjain	366,787
Ulhāsnagar	368,822
Uluberia	155,188
Unnāo	107,246
Uttarpāra-Kotrung	100,867
Vadodara (Baroda)	1,021,084
Vārānasi (Benares)	925,962
Vellore	172,467
Vijayawāda	701,351
Vishākhapatnam	750,024
Vizianagaram	159,461
Warangal	446,760
Wardha	102,974
Yamunanagar	144,250
Yavatmāl (Yeotmāl)	108,591
Indonesia (1990)	
Ambon	206,260
Balikpapan	309,492
Banda Aceh	143,409
Bandar Lampung	458,215
Bandung	2,026,893
Banjarmasin	443,738
Bengkulu	146,439
Binjai	127,222
Blitar	113,064
Bogor	271,711
Cilacap	113,893[23]
Cimahi	105,940[23]
Cirebon	245,307
Denpasar	261,263[23]
★ Jakarta	8,259,266
Jambi	301,359
Jayapura	149,618[23]
Jember	140,105[23]
Kediri	235,602
Madiun	165,999
Magelang	123,213
Malang	650,295
Manado	275,374
Mataram	141,387[23]
Medan	1,685,972
Padang	477,344
Palembang	1,084,483
Pangkal Pinang	108,411
Pasuruan	134,019
Pekalongan	227,535
Pekanbaru	341,328
Pematangsiantar	203,834
Pontianak	387,112
Probolinggo	131,291
Purwokerto	105,395[23]
Samarinda	335,016
Semarang	1,005,316
Sukabumi	119,981
Sumba	355,073[23]
Surabaya	2,421,016
Surakarta	504,176
Tanjung Balai	102,095
Tanjung Karang-Telukbetung	284,275[23]
Tasikmalaya	165,297[23]
Tebing Tinggi	116,767
Tegal	225,770
Ujung Pandang	913,196
Yogyakarta	412,392
Iran (1991)	
Ahvāz	724,653
Āmol	139,923
Arāk	331,354
Ardabīl	311,022
Bābol	137,348
Bākhtarān	624,084
Bandar 'Abbās	249,504
Bandar-e Būshehr	132,824
Bīrjand	101,177
Bojnūrd	112,426
Borūjerd	201,016
Dezfūl	181,309
Eṣfahān (Isfahan)	1,127,030
Gorgān	162,468
Hamadān	349,653
Īlām	116,428
Islāmshahr (Eslāmshahr)	230,183
Karaj	442,387
Kāshān	155,188
Kermān	311,643
Khomeynīshahr	118,348
Khorramābād	249,258
Khvoy	137,885
Malāyer	130,458
Marāgheh	117,388
Mashhad (Meshed)	1,559,155
Masjed-e Soleymān	107,539
Najafābād	160,004
Neyshābūr	135,681
Orūmīyeh	357,399
Qā'emshahr	123,684
Qazvīn	278,826
Qom	681,253
Rājaishahr	160,362
Rasht	340,637
Sabzevār	148,065
Sanandaj	244,039
Sārī	167,602
Shīrāz	965,117
Sīrjān	107,887
Tabrīz	1,088,985
★ Tehrān	6,475,527
Yazd	275,298
Zāhedān	361,623
Zanjān	254,100
Iraq (1985 est.)	
al-'Amārah	131,758
★ Baghdad	4,044,000[13]
Ba'qūbah	114,516
Basra	616,700
al-Hillah	215,249
Irbīl	333,903
Karbalā'	184,574
Kirkūk	570,000[24]
Mosul	570,926
an-Najaf	242,603
an-Nāṣirīyah	138,842
ar-Ramādī	137,388
as-Sulaymānīyah	279,424
Ireland (1991)	
Cork	127,253[25]
★ Dublin	478,389[25]
Isle of Man (1991)	
★ Douglas	22,214
Israel (1993 est.)	
Bat Yam	145,300
Beersheba (Be'er Sheva')	134,700
Bene Beraq	124,400
Haifa (Hefa)	249,800
Holon	162,800
★ Jerusalem (Yerushalayim, Al-Quds)	556,500
Netanya	141,800
Petaḥ Tiqwa	150,900
Ramat Gan	124,100
Rishon le-Ẕiyyon	150,400
Tel Aviv–Yafo	356,900
Italy (1993 est.; MU)	
Ancona	100,701
Bari	342,129
Bergamo	115,053
Bologna	401,308
Brescia	192,883
Cagliari	180,309
Catania	329,898
Ferrara	137,099
Florence (Firenze)	397,434
Foggia	155,674
Forlì	109,080
Genoa (Genova)	667,563
La Spezia	100,458
Latina	107,611
Lecce	100,508
Livorno	166,394
Messina	232,911
Milan (Milano)	1,358,627
Modena	176,972
Monza	120,054
Naples (Napoli)	1,071,744
Novara	102,029
Padua (Padova)	213,656
Palermo	696,735
Parma	170,555
Perugia	146,160
Pescara	121,424
Piacenza	102,161
Prato	166,108
Ravenna	136,099
Reggio di Calabria	178,312
Reggio nell'Emilia	133,191
Rimini	129,876
★ Rome (Roma)	2,723,327
Salerno	147,564
Sassari	121,961
Siracusa (Syracuse)	126,800
Taranto	230,207
Terni	108,140
Torre del Greco	100,686
Trento	101,538
Trieste	228,398
Turin (Torino)	952,736
Venice (Venezia)	305,617
Verona	255,492
Vicenza	107,481
Jamaica (1991)	
★ Kingston	103,771
Japan (1993 est.)	
Abiko	123,320
Ageo	203,451
Aizuwakamatsu	119,920
Akashi	280,795
Akishima	107,097
Akita	307,862
Amagasaki	496,313
Anjō	147,937
Aomori	288,291
Asahikawa	362,176
Asaka	107,961
Ashikaga	167,424
Atsugi	206,186
Beppu	129,441
Chiba	850,631
Chigasaki	209,575
Chōfu	199,209
Daitō	126,967
Ebetsu	106,798
Ebina	110,638
Fuchu	215,048
Fuji	228,069
Fujieda	123,501
Fujinomiya	119,397
Fujisawa	362,088
Fukui	254,667
Fukuoka	1,268,626
Fukushima	282,654
Fukuyama	370,873
Funabashi	539,740
Gifu	409,558
Habikino	116,817
Hachinohe	241,229
Hachiōji	488,187
Hadano	161,692
Hakodate	304,286
Hamamatsu	560,660
Handa	104,540
Higashi-Hiroshima	104,053
Higashi-Kurume	112,760
Higashi-Murayama	136,369
Higashi-Ōsaka	515,375
Hikone	102,046
Himeji	463,197
Hino	167,339
Hirakata	396,867
Hiratsuka	251,991
Hirosaki	175,444
Hiroshima	1,102,047
Hitachi	201,831
Hōfu	119,086
Ibaraki	255,500
Ichihara	270,332
Ichikawa	447,165
Ichinomiya	266,648
Iida	106,876
Ikeda	104,018
Ikoma	103,621
Imabari	120,942
Iruma	142,195
Ise	102,980
Isesaki	119,356
Ishinomaki	121,528
Itami	188,125
Iwaki	359,098
Iwakuni	108,986
Iwatsuki	109,221
Izumi	149,809
Joetsu	131,197
Kadoma	142,233
Kagoshima	539,911
Kakamigahara	132,387
Kakogawa	249,390
Kamakura	172,638
Kanazawa	446,325
Kariya	125,246
Kashihara	119,207
Kashiwa	316,725
Kasugai	273,116
Kasukabe	196,576
Katsuta	113,557
Kawachi-Nagano	113,994
Kawagoe	316,313
Kawaguchi	451,345
Kawanishi	142,541
Kawasaki	1,199,707
Kiryū	123,296
Kisarazu	125,792
Kishiwada	189,991
Kita-Kyūshū	1,019,996
Kitami	108,706
Kobe	1,509,395
Kochi	319,243
Kodaira	169,855
Kofu	199,841
Koganei	107,458
Kokubunji	104,339
Komaki	133,820
Komatsu	106,692
Koriyama	322,255
Koshigaya	294,966
Kumagaya	155,000
Kumamoto	639,699
Kurashiki	418,450
Kure	211,616
Kurume	232,846
Kushiro	202,297
Kuwana	100,779
Kyōto	1,452,240
Machida	358,891
Maebashi	287,912
Matsubara	134,514
Matsudo	463,517
Matsue	144,712
Matsumoto	203,707
Matsuyama	454,374
Matsuzaka	120,002
Minō	125,031
Misato	133,276
Mishima	107,049
Mitaka	166,473
Mito	246,851
Miyakonojō	130,845
Miyazaki	293,590
Moriguchi	156,272
Morioka	283,398
Muroran	114,297
Musashino	137,341
Nagano	352,378
Nagaoka	188,745
Nagareyama	146,178
Nagasaki	441,308
Nagoya	2,158,713
Naha	301,679
Nara	355,869
Narashino	154,700
Neyagawa	257,137
Niigata	400,237
Niihama	128,716
Niiza	142,231
Nishinomiya	424,719
Nobeoka	128,271
Noda	118,172
Numazu	213,062
Obihiro	170,328
Odawara	197,460
Ōgaki	149,812
Ōita	420,361
Okayama	604,513
Okazaki	318,983
Okinawa	109,954
Ōme	134,393
Ōmiya	422,023
Ōmuta	146,917

Major cities and national capitals (continued)

country city	population	country city	population	country city	population	country city	population	country city	population
Ōsaka	2,588,989	Haeju	195,000	**Macedonia** (1991; MU)		Orizaba	114,216	Enschede	147,349
Ōta	143,411	Hamhŭng-Hungnam	701,000	Bitola	124,003	Pachuca	174,013	Groningen	170,038
Otaru	161,033	Hŭich'ŏn	163,000	Giostivar	116,065	Poza Rica	151,739	Haarlem	149,315
Ōtsu	268,583	Kaesŏng	120,000	Kumanovo	135,482	Puebla	1,007,170	Haarlemmermeer	102,781
Oyama	147,713	Kanggye	211,000	★ Skopje (Skopije)	563,102	Querétaro	385,503	Leiden	113,838
Saga	170,257	Kimch'aek (Songjin)	179,000	Tetovo	180,605	Reynosa	265,663	Maastricht	118,285
Sagamihara	560,366	Kusŏng	177,000			Salamanca	123,190	Nijmegen	146,993
Sakai	806,263	Namp'o	370,000	**Madagascar** (1993)		Saltillo	420,947	Rotterdam	596,023
Sakata	100,707	★ P'yŏngyang	2,355,000	★ Antananarivo	1,052,835	San Luis Potosí	488,238	★ The Hague (seat of	
Sakura	156,507	Sinp'o	158,000	Antsirabe	120,239	San Nicolás de los		government)	444,661
Sapporo	1,731,670	Sinŭiju	289,000	Mahajanga	100,807	Garza	436,603	Tilburg	162,398
Sasebo	245,108	Sunch'ŏn	356,000	Toamasina	127,441	San Pedro Garza		Utrecht	234,170
Sayama	162,046	Tanch'ŏn	284,000			García	113,017	Zaanstad	131,785
Sendai	950,893	Tōkch'ŏn	217,000	**Malaŵi** (1993 est.)		Soledad de Graciano		Zoetermeer	102,937
Seto	128,788	Wŏnsan	274,000	Blantyre	399,263	Sanchez	123,943		
Shimizu	241,152			★ Lilongwe	267,659	Tampico	272,690	**Netherlands Antilles**	
Shimonoseki	259,898	**Korea, South** (1990)				Tapachula	138,858	(1985 est.)	
Shizuoka	474,219	Andong	116,958	**Malaysia** (1991)		Tehuacán	139,450	★ Willemstad	125,000[4]
Sōka	214,254	Ansan	252,418	Alor Setar	125,026	Tepic	206,967		
Suita	339,970	Anyang	481,291	George Town (Pinang)	219,376	Tijuana	698,752	**New Caledonia** (1989)	
Suzuka	178,890	Ch'angwŏn	323,223	Ipoh	382,633	Tlaquepaque	328,031	★ Nouméa	65,110
Tachikawa	154,900	Cheju	232,643	Johor Baharu	328,646	Toluca	327,865		
Takamatsu	331,031	Chinhae	120,212	Kelang	243,698	Tonala	151,190	**New Zealand** (1993 est.)	
Takaoka	175,261	Chinju	255,695	Kota Baharu	219,713	Torreón	439,436	Auckland	321,100
Takarazuka	205,207	Ch'ŏnan	211,363	Kota Kinabalu	208,484	Tuxtla	289,626	Christchurch	297,600
Takasaki	238,055	Ch'ŏngju	477,783	★ Kuala Lumpur	1,145,075	Uruapan	187,623	Dunedin	118,400
Takatsuki	361,283	Chŏnju	517,059	Kuala Terengganu	228,659	Veracruz	438,821	Hamilton	103,600
Tama	149,132	Ch'unch'ŏn	174,224	Kuantan	198,356	Villahermosa	261,231	Manukau	233,600
Tokorozawa	315,517	Ch'ungju	128,425	Kuching	147,729	Xalapa (Jalapa)		North Shore	155,500
Tokushima	265,243	Hanam	101,325	Melaka	295,999	Enríquez	279,451	Waitakere	141,900
Tokuyama	110,097	Inch'ŏn	1,817,919	Petaling Jaya	254,849	Zacatecas	100,051	★ Wellington	150,800
★ Tokyo	8,080,296	Iri	203,382	Port Kelang	192,080	Zamora de Hidalgo	109,751		
Tomakomai	166,625	Kangnŭng	152,678	Sandakan	223,432	Zapopan	668,323	**Nicaragua** (1992 est.; MU)	
Tondabayashi	117,733	Kimhae	106,206	Seloyang Baru	124,606			Chinandega	101,605
Tottori	144,854	Kumi	206,121	Seremban	182,584	**Micronesia**		León	172,042
Toyama	324,073	Kunp'o	100,059	Shah Alam	101,733	★ Palikir	—	★ Managua	973,759
Toyohashi	349,590	Kunsan	218,205	Sibu	126,384			Masaya	101,878
Toyokawa	114,058	Kuri	109,374	Taiping	183,165	**Moldova** (1991 est.)			
Toyonaka	403,224	Kwangju	1,139,003	Tawai	244,765	Bălţi (Beltsy)	164,900	**Niger** (1988)	
Toyota	341,453	Kwangmyŏng	328,593			★ Chişinău (Kishinyov)	676,700	Maradi	112,965
Tsu	162,488	Kyŏngju	141,896	**Maldives** (1990)		Tighina (Bendery)	141,500	★ Niamey	398,265
Tsuchiura	131,100	Masan	493,731	★ Male'	55,130	Tiraspol	186,000	Zinder	120,892
Tsukuba	152,233	Mokp'o	243,064						
Ube	175,146	P'ohang	317,768	**Mali** (1992 est.)		**Monaco** (1990)		**Nigeria** (1994 est.)[27]	
Ueda	121,121	Puch'ŏn	667,993	★ Bamako	745,787	★ Monaco	29,972[21]	Aba	284,400
Uji	182,287	Pusan	3,798,113					Abeokuta	406,500
Urawa	442,023	★ Seoul (Sŏul)	10,612,577	**Malta** (1994 est.)		**Mongolia** (1993 est.)		★ Abuja (capital	
Urayasu	122,091	Shihŭng	107,176	★ Valletta	9,144	★ Ulaanbaatar (Ulan		designate)	298,300[28]
Utsunomiya	434,029	Sŏngnam	540,754			Bator)	619,000	Ado-Ekiti	341,900
Wakayama	395,496	Sunch'ŏn	167,214	**Marshall Is.** (1990 est.)				Akure	154,400
Yachiyo	153,838	Suwŏn	644,805	★ Majuro	20,000	**Morocco** (1982)		Awka	105,800
Yaizu	114,756	Taegu	2,229,040			Agadir	110,479	Benin City	218,300
Yamagata	251,354	Taejŏn	1,049,578	**Martinique** (1990)		Casablanca		Bida	119,400
Yamaguchi	132,602	Ŭijŏngbu	212,352	★ Fort-de-France	101,540	(Dar el-Beida)	2,139,204	Calabar	165,900
Yamato	202,200	Ulsan	682,411			Fès (Fez)	448,823	Deba Habe	131,800
Yao	276,324	Wŏnju	162,415	**Mauritania** (1992)		Kenitra	188,194	Ede	292,100
Yatsushiro	107,579	Yŏsu	173,169	★ Nouakchott	480,408	Khouribga	127,181	Effon-Alaiye	145,600
Yokkaichi	282,197					Marrakech	439,728	Ejigbo	100,700
Yokohama	3,288,464	**Kuwait** (1985)		**Mauritius** (1992 est.)		Meknès	319,783	Enugu	300,700
Yokosuka	435,383	Ḥawallī	145,215	★ Port Louis	142,850	Mohammedia	105,120	Gombe	102,600
Yonago	132,708	★ Kuwait (al-Kuwayt)	44,224			Oujda	260,082	Gusau	150,300
Zama	117,025	as-Sālimīyah	153,220	**Mayotte** (1985)		★ Rabat	518,616	Ibadan	1,362,000
				★ Mamoudzou	7,325	Safi	197,309	Ife	282,400
Jersey (1991)		**Kyrgyzstan** (1991 est.)				Salé	289,391	Igboho	101,500
★ St. Helier	28,123	★ Bishkek (Frunze)	641,400	**Mexico** (1990)		Tanger	266,346	Ijebu-Ode	148,800
		Osh	238,200	Acapulco	515,374	Tétouan	199,615	Ikare	134,000
Jordan (1993 est.)				Aguascalientes	440,425			Ikerre	232,700
★ Amman	1,272,000	**Laos** (1990 est.; MU)		Atizapán de Zaragoza		**Mozambique** (1991 est.)		Ikire	117,300
Irbid	385,000	★ Vientiane	442,000	(Ciudad López		Beira	298,847	Ikirun	172,600
al-Mafraq	105,000			Mateos)	315,059	Chimoio	108,818	Ikorodu	175,900
as-Salṭ	171,000	**Latvia** (1992 est.)		Campeche	150,518	★ Maputo (Lourenço		Ila	251,100
az-Zarqā'	605,000	Daugavpils	127,279	Cancún	167,730	Marques)	931,591	Ilawe-Ekiti	175,500
		Liēpāja	113,815	Celaya	214,856	Matala	337,239	Ilesha	359,900
Kazakhstan (1991 est.)		★ Rīga	897,078	Chihuahua	516,153	Nacala	125,208	Ilobu	189,300
Aktyubinsk	266,600			Ciudad Apodaca	103,364	Nampula	250,473	Ilorin	452,700
★ Almaty (Alma-Ata)	1,156,200	**Lebanon** (1985 est.)		Ciudad Madero	160,331	Quelimane	146,206	Inisa	114,000
Aqmola (Tselinograd)	286,000	★ Beirut (Bayrūt)	1,910,000[9,13]	Ciudad Obregón	219,980	Tete	112,221	Iseyin	206,600
Aqtau (Shevchenko)	169,000	an-Nabaṭīyah	100,000	Ciudad Santa Catarina	162,707			Iwo	344,300
Atyrau (Guryev)	156,700	Sidon (Ṣaydā)	100,000	Ciudad Victoria	194,996	**Myanmar (Burma)** (1983)		Jos	196,300
Auliye-Ata (Dzhambul)	312,300	Tripoli (Ṭarābulus)	500,000	Coatzacoalcos	198,817	Bassein (Pathein)	144,096	Kaduna	325,500
Chimkent	438,800	Zaḥlah	200,000	Colima	106,967	Mandalay	532,949	Kano	641,200
Dzhezkazgan	111,100			Córdoba	130,695	Monywa	106,843	Katsina	196,500
Ekibastuz	138,900	**Lesotho** (1990 est.)		Cuautla	110,242	Moulmein		Kumo	140,800
Karaganda	608,600	★ Maseru	170,000[9]	Cuernavaca	279,187	(Mawlamyine)	219,961	Lafia	116,500
Kokchetav	143,300			Culiacán	415,046	Pegu (Bago)	150,528	★ Lagos	1,444,000
Oral (Uralsk)	214,000	**Liberia** (1990 est.)		Durango	348,036	Sittwe (Akyab)	107,621	Maiduguri	304,500
Oskemen		★ Monrovia	668,000[9]	Ensenada	169,426	Taunggye	108,231	Makurdi	117,100
(Ust-Kamenogorsk)	332,900			Gómez Palacio	164,092	★ Yangŏn (Rangoon)	2,513,023	Minna	130,200
Pavlodar	342,500	**Libya** (1988 est.)		Guadalajara	1,650,042			Mushin	317,000
Petropavlovsk	248,300	Banghāzi	446,250	Guadalupe	535,332	**Namibia** (1992 est.)		Offa	187,600
Qostanay (Kustanay)	233,900	Misrātah	121,669	Hermosillo	406,417	★ Windhoek	161,000	Ogbomosho	694,400
Qyzylorda (Kzyl-Orda)	158,200	★ Tripoli (Ṭarābulus)	591,062	Heroica Nogales	105,873			Oka	136,200
Rudny	128,800			Irapuato	265,042	**Nauru** (1983)		Ondo	161,400
Semey (Semipalatinsk)	344,700	**Liechtenstein** (1993 est.)		Juárez	789,522	★ Yaren	559	Onitsha	353,800
Taldy-Kurgan	136,100	★ Vaduz	5,072	La Paz	137,641			Oshogbo	453,600
Temirtau	213,100			León	758,279	**Nepal** (1991; MU)		Owo	174,600
		Lithuania (1993 est.)		Los Mochis	162,659	Birātnagar	129,388	Oyo	244,000
Kenya (1984 est.)		Kaunas	429,000	Matamoros	266,055	★ Kāthmāndu	421,258	Port Harcourt	389,900
Kisumu	167,100	Klaipēda	206,400	Mazatlán	262,705	Lalitpur	115,865	Sapele	132,400
Mombasa	425,600	Panevēžys	132,000	Mérida	523,422			Shagamu	111,500
★ Nairobi	1,504,900[13]	Šiauliai	147,800	Mexicali	438,377	**Netherlands, The**		Shaki	165,600
Nakuru	101,700	★ Vilnius	590,100	★ Mexico City	9,815,795[26]	(1993 est.)		Shomolu	140,500
				Minatitlán	142,060	Amersfoort	106,923	Sokoto	195,000
Kiribati (1990)		**Luxembourg** (1991)		Monclova	177,792	★ Amsterdam (capital)	719,856	Warri	119,900
★ Bairiki	2,226	★ Luxembourg	75,622	Monterrey	1,068,996	Apeldoorn	149,504	Zaria	360,800
				Morelia	428,486	Arnhem	133,272		
Korea, North (1987 est.)		**Macau** (1991)		Nezahualcóyotl	1,255,456	Breda	128,185	**Northern Mariana Is.**	
Anju	186,000	★ Macau (Santo Nome		Nuevo Laredo	218,413	Dordrecht	112,687	(1990)	
Ch'ŏngjin	520,000	de Deus)	326,460	Oaxaca	212,818	Eindhoven	195,267	★ Saipan	38,896

country city	population	country city	population	country city	population	country city	population	country city	population
Norway (1994 est.; MU)		Muntilupa	278,000	Suceava	114,355	Oryol	347,000	St.-Louis	125,717
Bergen	219,810	Naga	115,000	Timişoara	334,278	Penza	552,000	Thiès	201,350
★ Oslo	477,515	Navotas	187,000	Tîrgu Mureş	163,625	Perm	1,093,000	Ziguinchor	148,831
Stavanger	102,539	Olongapo	193,000			Pervouralsk	144,000		
Trondheim	142,015	Ormoc	129,000	**Russia** (1993 est.)		Petropavlovsk-		**Seychelles** (1987)	
		Pagadian	106,000	Abakan	158,000	Kamchatsky	265,000	★ Victoria	24,325
Oman (1982 est.)		Parañaque	308,000	Achinsk	122,000	Petrozavodsk	270,000		
★ Muscat	85,000	Pasay	367,000	Almetyevsk	135,000	Podolsk	206,000	**Sierra Leone** (1990 est.)	
		Pasig	395,000	Angarsk	269,000	Prokopyevsk	269,000	★ Freetown	669,000[9]
Pakistan (1981)		Quezon City	1,667,000	Anzhero-Sudzhensk	106,000	Pskov	208,000		
Bahāwalpur	180,263	Roxas	103,000	Arkhangelsk	411,000	Pyatigorsk	132,000	**Singapore** (1994 est.)[21]	
Chiniot	105,559	San Carlos (Negros		Armavir	163,000	Rostov-na-Donu	1,025,000	★ Singapore	2,933,000
Dera Ghāzi Khān	102,007	Occidental)	106,000	Arzamas	112,000	Rubtsovsk	172,000		
Faisalābād (Lyallpur)	1,104,209	San Carlos		Astrakhan	511,000	Ryazan	528,000	**Slovakia** (1993 est.)	
Gujrānwāla	658,753	(Pangasinan)	124,000	Balakovo	205,000	Rybinsk (Andropov)	251,000	★ Bratislava	446,655
Gujrāt	155,058	San Juan del Monte	127,000	Balashikha	137,000	Saint Petersburg		Košice	237,336
Hyderābād	751,529	San Pablo	161,000	Barnaul	601,000	(Leningrad)	4,952,000		
★ Islamābād	204,364	Surigao	100,000	Belgorod	315,000	Salavat	154,000	**Slovenia** (1994 est.)	
Jhang	195,558	Tacloban	138,000	Berezniki	197,000	Samara		★ Ljubljana	270,759
Jhelum	106,462	Tagig	267,000	Biysk	234,000	(Kuybyshev)	1,232,000	Maribor	103,512
Karāchi	5,208,132	Toledo	120,000	Blagoveshchensk	213,000	Saransk	321,000		
Kasūr	155,523	Valenzuela	340,000	Bratsk	259,000	Sarapul	111,000	**Solomon Islands**	
Lahore	2,952,089	Zamboanga	442,000	Bryansk	461,000	Saratov	904,000	(1990 est.)	
Lahore				Cheboksary	444,000	Sergiev Posad		★ Honiara	35,288
Cantonment	237,000	**Poland** (1993 est.)		Chelyabinsk	1,135,000	(Zagorsk)	115,000		
Lārkāna	123,890	Białystok	274,100	Cherepovets	319,000	Serov	103,000	**Somalia** (1985 est.)	
Mardān	147,977	Bielsko-Biała	179,700	Cherkessk	119,000	Serpukhov	140,000	★ Mogadishu	700,000
Mīrpur Khās	124,371	Bydgoszcz	383,600	Chita	369,000	Severodvinsk	245,000		
Multān	730,070	Bytom	229,200	Dimitrovgrad	131,000	Shakhty	228,000	**South Africa** (1985)	
Nawābshāh	102,139	Chorzów	128,800	Dzerzhinsk	287,000	Shchyolkovo	109,000	★ Bloemfontein	
Okāra	153,483	Czestochowa	259,500	Elektrostal	152,000	Simbirsk		(judicial)	300,150[7, 30]
Peshāwar	566,248	Dąbrowa Górnicza	131,600	Engels	184,000	(Ulyanovsk)	661,000	Boksburg	110,832
Quetta	285,719	Elbląg	127,300	Glazov	107,000	Smolensk	352,000	★ Cape Town	
Rahīm Yār Khān	119,036	Gdańsk	461,700	Grozny	364,000	Sochi	352,000	(legislative)	776,617
Rāwalpindi	794,843	Gdynia	250,200	Irkutsk	635,000	Solikamsk	109,000	Metro Cape Town	1,869,144[7]
Sāhīwāl	150,954	Gliwice	214,400	Ivanovo	478,000	Stary Oskol	188,000	Durban	634,301
Sargodha	291,362	Gorzów		Izhevsk	653,000	Stavropol	333,000	Metro Durban	1,137,378[7]
Sheikhūpura	141,168	Wielkopolski	124,600	Kaliningrad	413,000	Sterlitamak	254,000	Germiston	116,718
Siālkot	302,009	Grudziądz	103,400	Kaliningrad		Surgut	259,000	Johannesburg	632,369
Sukkur	190,551	Jastrzębie-Zdrój	104,200	(Moscow oblast)	136,000	Syktyvkar	226,000	Metro	
Wāh Cantonment	122,335	Kalisz	106,600	Kaluga	346,000	Syzran	176,000	Johannesburg	1,916,063[7]
		Katowice	359,900	Kamensk-Uralsky	208,000	Taganrog	292,000	Mdantsane	242,823
Panama (1992 est.)		Kielce	213,600	Kamyshin	127,000	Tambov	312,000	Pietermaritzburg	228,549[7, 30]
Colón	137,825	Koszalin	110,800	Kansk	110,000	Tolyatti (Toliatti)	678,000	Port Elizabeth	272,844
★ Panama City	625,150	Kraków	744,000	Kazan	1,098,000	Tomsk	500,000	★ Pretoria (executive)	443,059
San Miguelito	242,529[29]	Legnica	106,600	Kemerovo	517,000	Tula	539,000	Metro Pretoria	1,080,187[7]
		Łódź	838,400	Khabarovsk	612,000	Tver (Kalinin)	455,000	Roodepoort	141,764
Papua New Guinea		Lublin	350,400	Khimki	135,000	Tyumen	493,000	Soweto	596,632[7, 9]
(1990)		Olsztyn	164,900	Kineshma	104,000	Ufa	1,096,000		
★ Port Moresby (National		Opole	129,600	Kirov	491,000	Ukhta	111,000	**Spain** (1992 est.; MU)	
Capital District)	193,242	Płock	125,000	Kiselyovsk	126,000	Ulan-Ude	365,000	Albacete	131,425
		Poznań	582,900	Kislovodsk	119,000	Usolye-Sibirskoye	107,000	Alcalá de Henares	159,355[7]
Paraguay (1992)		Radom	230,400	Kolomna	163,000	Ussuriysk	162,000	Alcorcón	139,641[7]
★ Asunción	502,426	Ruda Śląska	167,700	Kolpino	144,000	Ust-Ilimsk	113,000	Algeciras	101,063[7]
Ciudad del Este	133,893	Rybnik	140,100	Komsomolsk-na-		Velikiye Luki	117,000	Alicante	266,542
San Lorenzo	133,311	Rzeszów	156,700	Amure	315,000	Vladikavkaz		Almería	156,476
		Słupsk	102,000	Kostroma	282,000	(Ordzhonikidze)	307,000	Badajoz	123,592
Peru (1993)		Sosnowiec	251,300	Kovrov	162,000	Vladimir	339,000	Badalona	206,585[7]
Arequipa	620,471	Szczecin	416,400	Krasnodar	636,000	Vladivostok	643,000	Baracaldo	104,883[7]
Ayacucho	114,809	Tarnów	121,900	Krasnoyarsk	919,000	Volgodonsk	183,000	Barcelona	1,615,921
Callao	637,755	Toruń	201,800	Kurgan	363,000	Volgograd	1,002,000	Bilbao	367,255
Chiclayo	410,468	Tychy	136,600	Kursk	437,000	Vologda	289,000	Burgos	161,105
Chimbote	296,600[13]	Wałbrzych	140,600	Kuznetsk	101,000	Volzhsky	283,000	Cádiz	153,064
Cuzco	257,751	★ Warsaw		Leninsk-Kuznetsky	132,000	Vorkuta	114,000	Cartagena	166,736[7]
Huancayo	256,666	(Warszawa)	1,644,500	Lipetsk	466,000	Voronezh	903,000	Castellón de la	
Huánuco	117,335	Włocławek	122,300	Lyubertsy	164,000	Votkinsk	105,000	Plana	135,683
Ica	163,080	Wrocław	640,700	Magadan	142,000	Yakutsk	196,000	Córdoba	304,305
Iquitos	266,175	Zabrze	203,500	Magnitogorsk	440,000	Yaroslavl	635,000	Coruña, La	247,651
Juliaca	134,700[13]	Zielona Góra	115,100	Makhachkala	328,000	Yekaterinburg		Donostia (San	
★ Lima	421,570[13]			Maykop	163,000	(Sverdlovsk)	1,358,000	Sebastián)	171,571
Metro Lima-Callao	5,759,676	**Portugal** (1991)		Mezhdurechensk	108,000	Yelets	120,000	Elche	181,658[7]
Piura	286,475	★ Lisbon	677,790	Miass	171,000	Yoshkar-Ola	248,000	Fuenlabrada	144,723[7]
Pucallpa	153,000[13]	Porto	310,600	Michurinsk	109,000	Yuzhno-Sakhalinsk	165,000	Getafe	138,704[7]
Sullana	154,800[13]			★ Moscow	8,881,000	Zelenograd	174,000	Gijón	259,054[7]
Tacna	172,393	**Puerto Rico** (1990)		Murmansk	455,000	Zhukovsky	101,000	Granada	256,167
Trujillo	508,716	Bayamón	202,103	Murom	127,000	Zlatoust	207,000	Hospitalet de	
Ucayali	171,007	Carolina	162,404	Mytishchi	153,000			Llobregat	269,241[7]
		Ponce	159,151	Naberezhnye Chelny		**Rwanda** (1991)		Huelva	143,351
Philippines (1990)		★ San Juan	426,832	(Brozhnev)	520,000	★ Kigali	232,733	Jaén	104,235
Angeles	237,000			Nakhodka	165,000			Jerez de la Frontera	182,939[7]
Bacolod	364,000	**Qatar** (1990 est.)		Nalchik	241,000	**St. Kitts and Nevis**		La Laguna	109,485[7]
Bago	124,000	★ Doha	293,000[9]	Nevinnomyssk	127,000	(1990 est.)		Leganés	171,400[7]
Baguio	183,000			Nikolo-Beryozovka		★ Basseterre	15,000	León	143,579
Batangas	185,000	**Réunion** (1990)		(Neftekamsk)	115,000			Lleida (Lérida)	112,255
Butuan	228,000	★ Saint-Denis	100,926	Nizhnekamsk	203,000	**St. Lucia** (1992 est.)		Logroño	121,066[7]
Cabanatuan	173,000			Nizhnevartovsk	242,000	★ Castries	13,615[30]	★ Madrid	2,909,792[7]
Cadiz	120,000	**Romania** (1992)		Nizhny Novgorod				Málaga	522,781
Cagayan de Oro	340,000	Arad	190,088	(Gorky)	1,433,000	**St. Vincent and The**		Mataró	101,501[7]
Calbayog	115,000	Bacău	204,495	Nizhny Tagil	434,000	**Grenadines** (1991)		Móstoles	192,018[7]
Caloocan	761,000	Baia Mare	148,815	Noginsk	121,000	★ Kingstown	15,466	Murcia	318,838[7]
Cebu	610,000	Botoşani	126,204	Norilsk	167,000			Ourense (Orense)	102,893
Cotabato	127,000	Brăila	234,706	Novgorod	234,000	**San Marino** (1994 est.)		Oviedo	195,673
Dagupan	122,000	Braşov	323,835	Novocheboksarsk	121,000	★ San Marino	2,399	Palma (de Mallorca)	296,754[7]
Davao	850,000	★ Bucharest	2,064,474	Novocherkassk	188,000			Palmas de Gran	
General Santos	250,000	Buzău	148,247	Novokuybyshevsk	113,000	**São Tomé and Príncipe**		Canaria, Las	
Iligan	227,000	Cluj-Napoca	328,008	Novokuznetsk	598,000	(1990 est.)		(Is. Canarias)	357,745
Iloilo	310,000	Constanţa	350,476	Novomoskovsk		★ São Tomé	43,420	Pamplona	179,251[7]
Lapu-Lapu	146,000	Craiova	303,520	(Tula oblast)	145,000			Sabadell	184,460[7]
Las Piñas	286,000	Drobeta-Turnu Severin	115,526	Novorossiysk	192,000	**Saudi Arabia** (1980 est.)		Salamanca	163,136
Legaspi	121,000	Focşani	101,296	Novoshakhtinsk	107,000	ad-Dammām	200,000	Santa Coloma de	
Lipa	160,000	Galaţi	325,788	Novosibirsk	1,431,000	Jiddah	1,500,000[11]	Gramanet	132,173[7]
Lucena	151,000	Iaşi	342,994	Novotroitsk	108,000	Mecca (Makkah)	550,000	Santa Cruz de	
Makati	453,000	Oradea	220,848	Obninsk	106,000	Medina (al-Madinah)	290,000	Tenerife	201,241
Malabon	277,000	Piatra Neamţ	123,175	Odintsovo	130,000	★ Riyadh (ar-Riyad)	1,308,000[24]	Santander	191,058
Mandaluyong	247,000	Piteşti	179,479	Oktyabrsky	107,000	aṭ-Ṭā'if	300,000	Sevilla (Seville)	677,962
Mandaue	180,000	Ploieşti	252,073	Omsk	1,167,000			Tarragona	110,514
★ Manila	1,599,000	Râmnicu Vâlcea	113,356	Orekhovo-Zuyevo	135,000	**Senegal** (1992 est.)		Terrassa	154,300[7]
Metro Manila	7,832,000	Satu Mare	131,859	Orenburg	555,000	★ Dakar	1,729,823	Valencia	750,726
Marikina	000,000	Sibiu	169,696	Orsk	274,000	Kaolack	179,894	Valladolid	331,367

Major cities and national capitals (continued)

country city	population
Vigo	274,629[7]
Vitoria (Gasteiz)	207,609
Zaragoza (Saragossa)	596,454
Sri Lanka (1990 est.)	
★ Colombo (administrative)	615,000
Dehiwala-Mount Lavinia	196,000
Jaffna	129,000
Kandy	104,000
Moratuwa	170,000
★ Sri Jayawardenepura Kotte (legislative and judicial)	109,000[32]
Sudan, The (1983)	
Juba	116,000[33]
★ Khartoum (executive)	476,218
Khartoum North	341,146
Nyala	111,693
★ Omdurman (legislative)	526,287
Port Sudan	206,727
al-Qaḍārif	116,876
al-Ubayyiḍ	140,024
Wad Madanī	141,065
Waw	116,000[33]
Suriname (1986 est.)	
★ Paramaribo	77,558
Swaziland (1990 est.)	
★ Mbabane	47,000
Sweden (1994 est.; MU)	
Borås	103,367
Göteborg	437,313
Helsingborg	111,853
Jönköping	113,557
Linköping	128,610
Malmö	237,438
Norrköping	121,028
Örebro	124,164
★ Stockholm	692,954
Uppsala	178,011
Västerås	121,593
Switzerland (1993 est.)	
Basel (Bâle)	175,500
★ Bern (Berne)	130,100
Geneva (Genève)	170,200
Lausanne	117,600
Zürich	345,200
Syria (1993 est.)	
Aleppo (Ḥalab)	1,494,000
★ Damascus (Dimashq)	1,497,000
Dayr az-Zawr	125,000[15]
Ḥamāh	229,000[15]
al-Ḥasakah	106,000[15]
Homs (Ḥims)	537,000
Latakia (al-Ladhiqiyah)	293,000
al-Qāmishlī	151,000[15]
ar-Raqqah	130,000[15]
Taiwan (1993 est.)	
Chang-hua	219,536
Chi-lung (Keelung)	363,134[17]
Chia-i	258,451[17]
Chung-ho	383,516
Chung-li	282,643
Feng-shan (Kao-hsiung-hsien)	294,471
Fêng-yüan	155,959
Hsin-chu	335,924[17]
Hsin-chuang	314,980
Hsin-tien	240,558
Hua-lien	107,090
Kao-hsiung	1,407,444
Pan-ch'iao (T'ai-pei-hsien)	543,982
P'ing-tung	213,309
San-chu'ung	382,003
T'ai-chung	820,383[17]
T'ai-nan	700,576[17]
T'ai-tung	108,353[17]
★ Taipei (T'ai-pei)	2,650,511[17]
T'ao-yuan	251,520
Yung-ho	246,355
Tajikistan (1991 est.)	
★ Dushanbe	582,400
Khodzhent (Leninabad)	164,500
Tanzania (1988)	
★ Dar es Salaam	1,360,850
Dodoma (capital designate)	203,833
Mbeya	194,000[28]
Mwanza	223,013
Tabora	214,000[28]
Tanga	187,634
Zanzibar	157,634
Thailand (1992 est.)	
★ Bangkok	5,562,141
Chiang Mai	170,269
Hat Yai	124,295
Khon Kaen	120,090
Nakhon Ratchasima	190,730
Nonthanburi	259,028
Togo (1990 est.)	
★ Lomé	513,000[9]
Tonga (1990 est.)	
★ Nuku'alofa	34,000
Trinidad and Tobago (1991 est.)	
★ Port-of-Spain	51,076
Tunisia (1989)	
Aryānah	131,403
Ettadhamen	111,793
Ṣafāqis (Sfax)	221,770
Sūsah	101,071
★ Tunis	620,149
Turkey (1990)	
Adana	916,150
Adapazari	171,225
Adıyaman	100,045
★ Ankara	2,559,471
Antakya	123,871
Antalya	378,208
Aydın	107,011
Balıkesir	170,589
Batman	147,347
Bursa	834,576
Çorum	116,810
Denizli	204,118
Diyarbakır	381,144
Edirne	102,345
Elazığ	204,603
Erzurum	242,391
Eskişehir	413,082
Gaziantep	603,434
Gebze	159,116
İçel	422,357
İskenderun	154,807
Isparta	112,117
İstanbul	6,620,241
İzmir	1,757,414
İzmit	256,882
Kahramanmaraş	228,129
Karabük	105,373
Kayseri	421,362
Kırıkkale	185,431
Konya	513,346
Kütahya	130,944
Malatya	281,776
Manisa	158,928
Ordu	102,107
Osmaniye	122,307
Samsun	303,979
Sivas	221,512
Tarsus	187,508
Trabzon	143,941
Urfa (Şanlıurfa)	276,528
Uşak	105,270
Van	153,111
Zonguldak	116,725
Turkmenistan (1991 est.)	
★ Ashkhabad (Ashgabat)	517,200[1]
Chardzhev (Chardzhou)	166,400
Tashauz	117,000
Tuvalu (1985 est.)	
★ Funafuti	2,810
Uganda (1991)	
★ Kampala	773,463
Ukraine (1993 est.)	
Alchevsk	129,000
Berdyansk	137,000
Bila Tserkva (Belaya Tserkov)	213,000
Cherkasy (Cherkassy)	312,000
Chernihiv (Chernigov)	313,000
Chernivtsi (Chernovtsy)	263,000
Dniprodzerzhynsk (Dneprodzerzhinsk)	287,000
Dnipropetrovsk (Dnepropetrovsk)	1,186,000
Donetsk	1,121,000
Horlivka (Gorlovka)	336,000
Ivano-Frankivsk (Ivano-Frankovsk)	234,000
Kamyanets-Podilsky (Kamenets-Podolsky)	108,000
Kerch	183,000
Kharkiv (Kharkov)	1,615,000
Kherson	371,000
Khmelnytsky (Khmelnitsky)	253,000
★ Kiev (Kyyiv)	2,646,000
Kirovohrad	281,000
Konotop	100,000
Kostyantynivka (Konstantinovka)	106,000
Kramatorsk	204,000
Krasny Luch	115,000
Kremenchuk (Kremenchug)	248,000
Kryvy Rih (Krivoy Rog)	737,000
Luhansk (Voroshilovgrad)	504,000
Lutsk	217,000
Lviv (Lvov)	810,000
Lysychansk (Lisichansk)	127,000
Makiyivka (Makeyevka)	424,000
Mariupol (Zhdanov)	524,000
Melitopol	178,000
Mykolayiv (Nikolayev)	519,000
Nikopol	161,000
Odesa (Odessa)	1,087,000
Oleksandriya (Aleksandriya)	106,000
Pavlohrad	137,000
Poltava	326,000
Rivne (Rovno)	245,000
Sevastopol	375,000
Severodonetsk	135,000
Simferopol	358,000
Slovyansk (Slavyansk)	138,000
Stakhanov	114,000
Sumy	307,000
Ternopil (Ternopol)	229,000
Uzhhorod	126,000
Vinnytsya (Vinnitsa)	387,000
Yenakiyeve (Yenakiyevo)	120,000
Yevpatoriya	115,000
Zaporizhzhya (Zaporozhye)	900,000
Zhytomyr (Zhitomir)	302,000
United Arab Emirates (1989 est.)	
★ Abu Dhabi (Abū Ẓaby)	363,432
Al-'Ayn	176,441
Dubai (Dubayy)	585,189
Sharjah (ash-Shāriqah)	125,123[23]
United Kingdom (1992 est.)[34]	
Aberdeen	218,220[1]
Barnsley	224,800
Belfast	288,700
Birmingham	1,009,100
Blackburn	136,612[7]
Blackpool	146,069[7]
Bolton	263,800
Bournemouth	151,302[7]
Bradford	477,500
Brighton	143,582[7]
Bristol	396,600
Cardiff	295,600
Coventry	304,600
Derby	227,100
Doncaster	293,500
Dudley	311,000
Dundee	170,120[1]
Edinburgh	439,880
Gateshead	203,100
Glasgow	681,470[1]
Gloucester	101,608[7]
Huddersfield	148,544[35]
Ipswich	116,956[7]
Kingston upon Hull	268,500
Kirklees	383,200
Leeds	721,800
Leicester	285,400
Liverpool	479,000
★ London	6,679,699[7]
Luton	171,671[7]
Manchester	434,600
Middlesbrough	140,849
Newcastle upon Tyne	281,700
Newport	133,311[7]
Northampton	180,567[7]
Norwich	120,895[7]
Nottingham	282,500
Ogwr	132,442[7]
Oldbury/Smethwick	153,461[35]
Oldham	220,200
Oxford	110,103[7]
Peterborough	153,166[7]
Plymouth	257,500
Poole	133,050[7]
Portsmouth	174,697[7]
Preston	126,082[7]
Reading	128,877[7]
Renfrew	201,150[1]
Rochdale	205,700
Rotherham	255,100[7]
St. Helens	178,764[7]
Salford	230,300
Sandwell	294,100
Sefton	294,900
Sheffield	531,000
Slough	101,066[7]
Solihull	200,900
Southampton	208,100
Southend-on-Sea	158,517
Stockport	288,800
Stoke-on-Trent	252,900
Sunderland	297,100
Sutton Coldfield	103,097[35]
Swansea	181,906[7]
Swindon	128,493
Tameside	221,000
Trafford	215,900
Wakefield	317,100
Walsall	263,400
West Bromwich	154,531
Wigan	312,400
Wirral	335,300
Wolverhampton	247,500
United States (1992 est.)	
Abilene (*Texas*)	108,095
Akron (*Ohio*)	223,621
Alameda (*Calif.*)	78,940
Albany (*Ga.*)	79,635
Albany (*N.Y.*)	99,708
Albuquerque (*N.M.*)	398,492
Alexandria (*Va.*)	113,134
Alhambra (*Calif.*)	83,214
Allentown (*Pa.*)	106,429
Altoona (*Pa.*)	52,477
Amarillo (*Texas*)	161,065
Anaheim (*Calif.*)	274,162
Anchorage (*Alaska*)	245,866
Anderson (*Ind.*)	60,360
Ann Arbor (*Mich.*)	109,766
Antioch (*Calif.*)	69,106
Appleton (*Wis.*)	68,462
Arlington (*Texas*)	275,907
Arlington (*Va.*)	171,582[36]
Arlington Heights (*Ill.*)	76,518
Arvada (*Colo.*)	93,330
Asheville (*N.C.*)	62,791
Atlanta (*Ga.*)	394,848
Aurora (*Colo.*)	239,626
Aurora (*Ill.*)	105,929
Austin (*Texas*)	492,329
Bakersfield (*Calif.*)	187,985
Baldwin Park (*Calif.*)	71,047
Baltimore (*Md.*)	726,096
Baton Rouge (*La.*)	224,704
Battle Creek (*Mich.*)	54,435
Bayonne (*N.J.*)	61,804
Baytown (*Texas*)	66,447
Beaumont (*Texas*)	115,494
Beaverton (*Ore.*)	57,232
Bellevue (*Wash.*)	85,627
Bellflower (*Calif.*)	64,503
Bellingham (*Wash.*)	55,295
Berkeley (*Calif.*)	101,122
Bethlehem (*Pa.*)	72,373
Billings (*Mont.*)	84,011
Binghamton (*N.Y.*)	52,054
Birmingham (*Ala.*)	264,984
Bismarck (*N.D.*)	51,319
Bloomington (*Ill.*)	54,142
Bloomington (*Ind.*)	61,503
Bloomington (*Minn.*)	85,181
Boca Raton (*Fla.*)	64,338
Boise City (*Idaho*)	135,506
Bossier City (*La.*)	52,874
Boston (*Mass.*)	551,675
Boulder (*Colo.*)	85,616
Bridgeport (*Conn.*)	137,020
Bristol (*Conn.*)	61,146
Brockton (*Mass.*)	89,191
Broken Arrow (*Okla.*)	62,604
Brooklyn Park (*Minn.*)	57,399
Brownsville (*Texas*)	105,757
Bryan (*Texas*)	56,545
Buena Park (*Calif.*)	70,936
Buffalo (*N.Y.*)	323,284
Burbank (*Calif.*)	96,325
Burnsville (*Minn.*)	53,742
Camarillo (*Calif.*)	54,812
Cambridge (*Mass.*)	93,554
Camden (*N.J.*)	86,926
Canton (*Ohio*)	84,788
Cape Coral (*Fla.*)	81,523
Carlsbad (*Calif.*)	64,360
Carrollton (*Texas*)	88,908
Carson (*Calif.*)	87,113
Cary (*N.C.*)	51,881
Cedar Rapids (*Iowa*)	111,659
Cerritos (*Calif.*)	53,527
Champaign (*Ill.*)	64,350
Chandler (*Ariz.*)	100,173
Charleston (*S.C.*)	81,301
Charleston (*W.V.*)	57,083
Charlotte (*N.C.*)	416,294
Chattanooga (*Tenn.*)	152,888
Chesapeake (*Va.*)	166,005
Cheyenne (*Wyo.*)	51,873
Chicago (*Ill.*)	2,768,483
Chicopee (*Mass.*)	56,115
Chino (*Calif.*)	63,217
Chula Vista (*Calif.*)	144,752
Cicero (*Ill.*)	71,604
Cincinnati (*Ohio*)	364,278
Clarksville (*Tenn.*)	84,394
Clearwater (*Fla.*)	98,121
Cleveland (*Ohio*)	502,539
Cleveland Heights (*Ohio*)	53,306
Clifton (*N.J.*)	72,519
Clovis (*Calif.*)	55,031
College Station (*Texas*)	55,682
Colorado Springs (*Colo.*)	295,815
Columbia (*Mo.*)	73,078
Columbia (*S.C.*)	98,832
Columbus (*Ga.*)	185,744
Columbus (*Ohio*)	642,987
Compton (*Calif.*)	95,608
Concord (*Calif.*)	112,688
Coon Rapids (*Minn.*)	59,945
Coral Springs (*Fla.*)	86,306
Corona (*Calif.*)	86,340
Corpus Christi (*Texas*)	266,412
Costa Mesa (*Calif.*)	96,240
Council Bluffs (*Iowa*)	54,884
Cranston (*R.I.*)	76,703
Dallas (*Texas*)	1,022,497
Daly City (*Calif.*)	93,358
Danbury (*Conn.*)	65,297
Danville (*Va.*)	53,571
Davenport (*Iowa*)	97,508
Dayton (*Ohio*)	183,189
Daytona Beach (*Fla.*)	64,634
Dearborn (*Mich.*)	88,296
Dearborn Heights (*Mich.*)	59,521
Decatur (*Ala.*)	50,444
Decatur (*Ill.*)	84,273
Denton (*Texas*)	67,833
Denver (*Colo.*)	483,852
Des Moines (*Iowa*)	194,540
Des Plaines (*Ill.*)	54,037
Detroit (*Mich.*)	1,012,110
Diamond Bar (*Calif.*)	55,915
Dothan (*Ala.*)	54,787
Downey (*Calif.*)	95,250
Dubuque (*Iowa*)	58,575
Duluth (*Minn.*)	85,431
Durham (*N.C.*)	140,926
Eagan (*Minn.*)	52,886
East Orange (*N.J.*)	72,250
East Providence (*R.I.*)	50,394
Eau Claire (*Wis.*)	57,970
Edmond (*Okla.*)	57,128
El Cajon (*Calif.*)	92,483
El Monte (*Calif.*)	106,935
El Paso (*Texas*)	543,813
Elgin (*Ill.*)	81,108
Elizabeth (*N.J.*)	107,915
Elyria (*Ohio*)	57,268
Encinitas (*Calif.*)	56,635
Erie (*Pa.*)	109,267
Escondido (*Calif.*)	113,161
Euclid (*Ohio*)	54,265
Eugene (*Ore.*)	115,965
Evanston (*Ill.*)	74,188
Evansville (*Ind.*)	127,566
Everett (*Wash.*)	75,124
Fairfield (*Calif.*)	82,192
Fall River (*Mass.*)	91,066
Fargo (*N.D.*)	77,052
Farmington Hills (*Mich.*)	76,892
Fayetteville (*N.C.*)	76,651
Flint (*Mich.*)	139,311
Florissant (*Mo.*)	51,456
Fontana (*Calif.*)	98,633
Fort Collins (*Colo.*)	93,335
Fort Lauderdale (*Fla.*)	148,524
Fort Smith (*Ark.*)	74,291
Fort Wayne (*Ind.*)	173,717
Fort Worth (*Texas*)	454,430
Fountain Valley (*Calif.*)	54,043
Fremont (*Calif.*)	179,300
Fresno (*Calif.*)	376,130
Fullerton (*Calif.*)	115,476
Gainesville (*Fla.*)	86,763
Galveston (*Texas*)	59,582
Garden Grove (*Calif.*)	145,874
Gardena (*Calif.*)	51,244
Garland (*Texas*)	191,186
Gary (*Ind.*)	116,702
Gastonia (*N.C.*)	57,076
Glendale (*Ariz.*)	156,165
Glendale (*Calif.*)	177,671
Grand Prairie (*Texas*)	104,482
Grand Rapids (*Mich.*)	191,230
Great Falls (*Mont.*)	56,628
Greeley (*Colo.*)	61,774

[1]1993 estimate. [2]1984 estimate. [3]City proper; 1980 census. [4]1989 census. [5]Population of the statistical division containing the city. [6]Statistical district. [7]1991 census. [8]1982 estimate. [9]Population refers to widest officially defined agglomeration or metropolitan area. [10]1992 census. [11]Excludes the agricultural population of the named civil division. [12]Central canton. [13]1990 estimate. [14]Excludes population of Lefkoşa (Turkish-occupied Nicosia), estimated at 37,400 in 1985. [15]1992 estimate. [16]1989 estimate. [17]1994 estimate. [18]1986 estimate. [19]1986 census. [20]1983 census.

country / city	population
Green Bay (Wis.)	100,459
Greensboro (N.C.)	189,924
Greenville (S.C.)	59,042
Gresham (Ore.)	74,434
Hamilton (Ohio)	63,827
Hammond (Ind.)	84,256
Hampton (Va.)	137,048
Harlingen (Texas)	51,962
Harrisburg (Pa.)	53,430
Hartford (Conn.)	131,995
Haverhill (Mass.)	52,167
Hawthorne (Calif.)	71,349
Hayward (Calif.)	115,189
Henderson (Nev.)	84,358
Hesperia (Calif.)	57,077
Hialeah (Fla.)	191,702
High Point (N.C.)	70,752
Hollywood (Fla.)	121,732
Honolulu (Ha.)	371,320
Houston (Texas)	1,690,180
Huntington (W.V.)	54,094
Huntington Beach (Calif.)	105,055
Huntington Park (Calif.)	55,450
Huntsville (Ala.)	163,319
Independence (Mo.)	112,713
Indianapolis (Ind.)	746,538
Inglewood (Calif.)	111,496
Iowa City (Iowa)	59,313
Irvine (Calif.)	119,389
Irving (Texas)	161,261
Jackson (Miss.)	196,231
Jackson (Tenn.)	50,844
Jacksonville (Fla.)	661,177
Janesville (Wis.)	54,295
Jersey City (N.J.)	228,575
Johnson City (Tenn.)	50,389
Joliet (Ill.)	78,917
Kalamazoo (Mich.)	81,253
Kansas City (Kan.)	146,507
Kansas City (Mo.)	431,553
Kenner (La.)	73,737
Kenosha (Wis.)	83,506
Kettering (Ohio)	60,152
Killeen (Texas)	66,574
Knoxville (Tenn.)	167,287
La Crosse (Wis.)	51,347
La Habra (Calif.)	52,100
La Mesa (Calif.)	53,568
Lafayette (La.)	97,002
Lake Charles (La.)	71,135
Lakeland (Fla.)	72,628
Lakewood (Calif.)	76,144
Lakewood (Colo.)	125,957
Lakewood (Ohio)	58,805
Lancaster (Calif.)	106,139
Lancaster (Pa.)	57,171
Lansing (Mich.)	126,722
Laredo (Texas)	136,508
Largo (Fla.)	67,401
Las Cruces (N.M.)	66,466
Las Vegas (Nev.)	295,516
Lawrence (Kan.)	67,824
Lawrence (Mass.)	65,493
Lawton (Okla.)	87,168
Lee's Summit (Mo.)	51,327
Lexington-Fayette (Ky.)	232,562
Lincoln (Neb.)	197,488
Little Rock (Ark.)	176,870
Livermore (Calif.)	60,045
Livonia (Mich.)	101,375
Lodi (Calif.)	53,174
Long Beach (Calif.)	438,771
Longmont (Colo.)	54,627
Longview (Texas)	72,695
Lorain (Ohio)	71,483
Los Angeles (Calif.)	3,489,779
Louisville (Ky.)	271,038
Lowell (Mass.)	99,873
Lubbock (Texas)	187,941
Lynchburg (Va.)	66,097
Lynn (Mass.)	78,652
Lynwood (Calif.)	63,216
McAllen (Texas)	90,252
Macon (Ga.)	107,257
Madison (Wis.)	195,161
Malden (Mass.)	53,709
Manchester (N.H.)	97,307
Mansfield (Ohio)	53,226
Medford (Mass.)	56,702
Melbourne (Fla.)	64,276
Memphis (Tenn.)	610,275
Merced (Calif.)	59,661
Meriden (Conn.)	58,585
Mesa (Ariz.)	296,645
Mesquite (Texas)	108,324
Miami (Fla.)	367,016
Miami Beach (Fla.)	90,896
Midland (Texas)	95,167
Midwest City (Okla.)	52,845
Milpitas (Calif.)	53,764
Milwaukee (Wis.)	617,043
Minneapolis (Minn.)	362,696
Minnetonka (Minn.)	50,096
Mission Viejo (Calif.)	76,045
Mobile (Ala.)	201,896
Modesto (Calif.)	172,292
Monroe (La.)	56,174
Montebello (Calif.)	60,368
Monterey Park (Calif.)	59,357
Montgomery (Ala.)	192,125
Moreno Valley (Calif.)	132,105
Mount Prospect (Ill.)	53,315
Mount Vernon (N.Y.)	67,050
Mountain View (Calif.)	66,941
Muncie (Ind.)	72,419
Murfreesboro (Tenn.)	50,397
Napa (Calif.)	63,282
Naperville (Ill.)	91,928
Nashua (N.H.)	79,720
Nashville-Davidson (Tenn.)	495,012
National City (Calif.)	57,408
New Bedford (Mass.)	96,892
New Britain (Conn.)	72,919
New Haven (Conn.)	123,966
New Orleans (La.)	489,595
New Rochelle (N.Y.)	67,578
New York City (N.Y.)	7,311,966
Newark (N.J.)	267,849
Newport Beach (Calif.)	67,900
Newport News (Va.)	177,286
Newton (Mass.)	82,120
Niagara Falls (N.Y.)	61,703
Norfolk (Va.)	253,768
Norman (Okla.)	83,678
North Charleston (S.C.)	74,379
North Las Vegas (Nev.)	55,571
North Little Rock (Ark.)	62,328
North Miami (Fla.)	51,254
North Richland Hills (Texas)	50,358
Norwalk (Calif.)	97,767
Norwalk (Conn.)	78,528
Oak Lawn (Ill.)	56,345
Oak Park (Ill.)	54,217
Oakland (Calif.)	373,219
Oceanside (Calif.)	139,718
Odessa (Texas)	93,760
Ogden (Utah)	66,236
Oklahoma City (Okla.)	450,995
Olathe (Kan.)	67,610
Omaha (Neb.)	339,671
Ontario (Calif.)	138,981
Orange (Calif.)	113,501
Orem (Utah)	69,437
Orlando (Fla.)	174,215
Oshkosh (Wis.)	56,292
Overland Park (Kan.)	119,260
Owensboro (Ky.)	53,366
Oxnard (Calif.)	144,805
Palm Bay (Fla.)	70,119
Palmdale (Calif.)	84,430
Palo Alto (Calif.)	56,189
Parma (Ohio)	86,631
Pasadena (Calif.)	132,605
Pasadena (Texas)	125,418
Passaic (N.J.)	56,960
Paterson (N.J.)	139,358
Pawtucket (R.I.)	71,058
Pembroke Pines (Fla.)	70,800
Penn Hills (Pa.)	52,029
Pensacola (Fla.)	59,773
Peoria (Ariz.)	52,920
Peoria (Ill.)	113,983
Philadelphia (Pa.)	1,552,572
Phoenix (Ariz.)	1,012,230
Pico Rivera (Calif.)	60,743
Pine Bluff (Ark.)	57,675
Pittsburg (Calif.)	50,205
Pittsburgh (Pa.)	366,852
Plano (Texas)	142,106
Plantation (Fla.)	71,608
Pleasanton (Calif.)	54,217
Plymouth (Minn.)	54,834
Pomona (Calif.)	140,364
Pompano Beach (Fla.)	72,870
Pontiac (Mich.)	69,350
Port Arthur (Texas)	59,677
Port St. Lucie (Fla.)	63,461
Portland (Maine)	62,756
Portland (Ore.)	445,458
Portsmouth (Va.)	104,361
Providence (R.I.)	155,418
Provo (Utah)	91,194
Pueblo (Colo.)	98,552
Quincy (Mass.)	84,457
Racine (Wis.)	86,121
Raleigh (N.C.)	220,524
Rancho Cucamonga (Calif.)	111,161
Rapid City (S.D.)	57,053
Reading (Pa.)	79,028
Redding (Calif.)	71,523
Redlands (Calif.)	60,994
Redondo Beach (Calif.)	62,790
Redwood City (Calif.)	67,213
Reno (Nev.)	139,884
Rialto (Calif.)	75,079
Richardson (Texas)	76,364
Richmond (Calif.)	90,157
Richmond (Va.)	202,263
Riverside (Calif.)	238,601
Roanoke (Va.)	96,754
Rochester (Minn.)	73,913
Rochester (N.Y.)	234,163
Rochester Hills (Mich.)	64,161
Rockford (Ill.)	141,679
Rocky Mount (N.C.)	50,399
Rosemead (Calif.)	52,451
Roseville (Mich.)	51,124
Roswell (Ga.)	50,667
Royal Oak (Mich.)	67,298
Sacramento (Calif.)	382,816
Saginaw (Mich.)	70,719
St. Charles (Mo.)	57,274
St. Clair Shores (Mich.)	67,363
St. Joseph (Mo.)	71,929
St. Louis (Mo.)	383,733
St. Paul (Minn.)	268,266
St. Petersburg (Fla.)	235,306
Salem (Ore.)	112,050
Salinas (Calif.)	114,762
Salt Lake City (Utah)	165,835
San Angelo (Texas)	86,099
San Antonio (Texas)	966,437
San Bernardino (Calif.)	172,451
San Diego (Calif.)	1,148,851
San Francisco (Calif.)	728,921
San Jose (Calif.)	801,331
San Leandro (Calif.)	68,932
San Mateo (Calif.)	86,538
Sandy (Utah)	81,003
Santa Ana (Calif.)	288,024
Santa Barbara (Calif.)	85,119
Santa Clara (Calif.)	93,989
Santa Clarita (Calif.)	118,676
Santa Fe (N.M.)	59,004
Santa Maria (Calif.)	64,112
Santa Monica (Calif.)	87,064
Santa Rosa (Calif.)	116,554
Santee (Calif.)	54,923
Sarasota (Fla.)	50,920
Savannah (Ga.)	138,908
Schaumburg (Ill.)	71,146
Schenectady (N.Y.)	65,395
Scottsdale (Ariz.)	137,022
Scranton (Pa.)	79,746
Seattle (Wash.)	519,598
Sheboygan (Wis.)	50,199
Shreveport (La.)	196,645
Simi Valley (Calif.)	103,813
Sioux City (Iowa)	81,907
Sioux Falls (S.D.)	105,634
Skokie (Ill.)	58,989
Somerville (Mass.)	72,303
South Bend (Ind.)	105,942
South Gate (Calif.)	88,622
South San Francisco (Calif.)	55,610
Southfield (Mich.)	81,088
Sparks (Nev.)	56,188
Spokane (Wash.)	187,429
Springfield (Ill.)	106,429
Springfield (Mass.)	153,466
Springfield (Mo.)	145,438
Springfield (Ohio)	70,421
Stamford (Conn.)	107,590
Sterling Heights (Mich.)	118,314
Stockton (Calif.)	219,621
Suffolk (Va.)	53,276
Sunnyvale (Calif.)	118,438
Sunrise (Fla.)	67,145
Syracuse (N.Y.)	162,835
Tacoma (Wash.)	183,890
Tallahassee (Fla.)	130,357
Tampa (Fla.)	284,737
Taunton (Mass.)	50,697
Taylor (Mich.)	70,250
Tempe (Ariz.)	142,139
Terre Haute (Ind.)	59,196
Thornton (Colo.)	58,881
Thousand Oaks (Calif.)	107,522
Toledo (Ohio)	329,325
Topeka (Kan.)	120,257
Torrance (Calif.)	135,642
Trenton (N.J.)	87,807
Troy (Mich.)	78,719
Troy (N.Y.)	54,153
Tucson (Ariz.)	415,079
Tulsa (Okla.)	375,307
Tuscaloosa (Ala.)	78,732
Tustin (Calif.)	53,307
Tyler (Texas)	76,072
Union City (Calif.)	54,798
Union City (N.J.)	57,256
Upland (Calif.)	64,668
Utica (N.Y.)	66,849
Vacaville (Calif.)	77,902
Vallejo (Calif.)	113,703
Victoria (Texas)	57,388
Vineland (N.J.)	54,664
Virginia Beach (Va.)	417,061
Visalia (Calif.)	81,323
Vista (Calif.)	76,036
Waco (Texas)	103,997
Walnut Creek (Calif.)	61,017
Waltham (Mass.)	56,698
Warren (Mich.)	142,404
Warren (Ohio)	51,147
Warwick (R.I.)	85,823
★ Washington, D.C.	585,221
Waterbury (Conn.)	106,904
Waterloo (Iowa)	67,124
Waukegan (Ill.)	69,686
Waukesha (Wis.)	59,172
West Allis (Wis.)	62,149
West Covina (Calif.)	98,777
West Haven (Conn.)	54,169
West Palm Beach (Fla.)	67,723
West Valley City (Utah)	91,733
Westland (Mich.)	85,524
Westminster (Calif.)	78,185
Westminster (Colo.)	80,721
Wheaton (Ill.)	53,757
Whittier (Calif.)	00,533
Wichita (Kan.)	311,746
Wichita Falls (Texas)	95,018
Wilmington (Del.)	72,411
Wilmington (N.C.)	59,487
Winston-Salem (N.C.)	144,791
Worcester (Mass.)	163,414
Wyoming (Mich.)	64,123
Yakima (Wash.)	58,448
Yonkers (N.Y.)	186,063
Yorba Linda (Calif.)	56,806
Youngstown (Ohio)	94,387
Yuma (Ariz.)	61,047
Uruguay (1992 est.)	
★ Montevideo	1,383,660
Uzbekistan (1992 est.)	
Andijon (Andizhan)	302,000
Angren	133,000
Bukhara	235,000
Chirchik	158,000
Dzhizak	115,000
Fergana	193,000
Marghilon (Margilan)	128,000
Namangan	333,000
Nawoiy (Navoi)	113,000
Nukus	182,000
Olmaliq (Almalyk)	116,000
Qarshi (Karshi)	175,000
Quqon (Kokand)	177,000
Samarqand (Samarkand)	372,000
★ Tashkent (Toshkent)	2,126,000
Urgench	132,000
Vanuatu (1989)	
★ Vila	19,311
Venezuela (1990)	
Acarigua	116,551
Barcelona	221,792
Barinas	153,630
Barquisimeto	625,450
Baruta	182,941[9]
Cabimas	165,755[9]
★ Caracas	1,822,465
Catla la Mar	100,104
Ciudad Bolívar	225,340
Ciudad Guayana (San Felix de Guayana)	453,047
Cumaná	212,432
Guacara	100,766
Guarenas	134,158
Los Teques	140,617
Maracaibo	1,249,670
Maracay	354,196
Maturín	206,654
Mérida	170,902
Petare	338,417
Puerto Cabello	128,825
Puerto La Cruz	155,731
San Cristóbal	220,675
Santa Ana de Coro	124,506
Turmero	174,280
Valencia	903,621
Vietnam (1989)	
Bien Hoa	273,879
Cam Pha	105,336
Cam Rahn	114,041
Can Tho	208,078
Da Lat	102,583
Da Nang	369,734
Haiphong	449,747
★ Hanoi	2,099,600[15]
Ho Chi Minh City (Saigon)	4,181,600[15]
Hong Gai	123,102
Hue	211,718
Long Xuyen	128,017
My Tho	104,724
Nam Dinh	165,629
Nha Trang	213,460
Phan Thiet	114,236
Qui Nhon	159,852
Rach Gia	137,784
Thai Nguyen	124,871
Vinh	110,793
Vung Tau	123,528
Virgin Islands (U.S.) (1990)	
★ Charlotte Amalie	12,331
West Bank (1987 est.)	
Nābulus	106,944
★ —	—
Western Sahara (1982)	
★ El Aaiún (Laayoune)	93,075
Western Samoa (1991)	
★ Apia	32,859
Yemen (1986)	
★ Aden (economic)	318,000[2]
Al-Ḥudaydah	155,110
★ San'ā' (political)	427,185
Ta'izz	178,430
Yugoslavia (1991)	
★ Belgrade (Beograd)	1,136,786
Kragujevac	146,607
Niš	175,555
Novi Sad	178,896
Podgorica (Titograd)	118,059
Priština	148,656[35]
Subotica	100,219
Zaire (1991 est.)	
Boma	246,207
Bukavu	209,566
Kananga	371,862
Kikwit	182,850
★ Kinshasa	3,804,000
Kisangani	373,397
Kolwezi	544,497
Likasi	279,839
Lubumbashi	739,082
Matadi	172,926
Mbandaka	165,623
Mbuji-Mayi	613,027
Zambia (1990)	
Chingola	167,954
Kabwe	166,519
Kitwe	338,207
Luanshya	146,275
★ Lusaka	982,362
Mufulira	152,944
Ndola	376,311
Zimbabwe (1992)	
Bulawayo	620,936
Chitungwiza	274,035
Gweru	124,735
★ Harare	1,184,169
Mount Darwin	164,362
Mutare	131,808

[21]No separate areas within the state are distinguished administratively as cities. [22]Population includes Comayagüela. [23]1980 census. [24]1981 estimate. [25]County borough. [26]Distrito Federal. [27]Projections based on a repudiated census taken in 1963. [28]Federal Capital Territory; 1992 estimate. [29]1990 census. [30]Urban area. [31]1983 estimate. [32]Population refers to Kotte only. [33]1980 estimate. [34]Population of local authority areas. [35]1981 census. [36]Census-designated place (CDP).

Language

This table presents estimated data on the principal language communities of the countries of the world. The countries, and the principal languages (occasionally, language families) represented in each, are listed alphabetically. A bullet (●) indicates those languages that are official in each country. The sum of the estimates equals the 1994 population of the country given in the "Area and population" table.

The estimates represent, so far as national data collection systems permit, the distribution of mother tongues (a mother tongue being the language spoken first and, usually, most fluently by an individual). Many countries do not collect any official data whatever on language use, and published estimates not based on census or survey data usually span a substantial range of uncertainty. The editors have adopted the best-founded distribution in the published literature (indicating uncertainty by the degree of rounding shown) but have also adjusted or interpolated using data not part of the base estimate(s). Such adjustments have not been made to account for large-scale refugee movements, as these are of a temporary nature.

A variety of approaches have been used to approximate mother-tongue distribution when census data were unavailable. Some countries collect data on ethnic or "national" groups only; for such countries ethnic distribution often had to be assumed to conform roughly to the distribution of language communities. This approach, however, should be viewed with caution, because a minority population is not always free to educate its children in its own language and because better economic opportunities often draw minority group members into the majority-language community. For some countries, a given individual may be visible in national statistics only as a passport-holder of a foreign country, however long he may remain resident. Such persons, often guest workers, have sometimes had to be assumed to be speakers of the principal language of their home country. For other countries, the language mosaic may be so complex, the language communities so minute in size, scholarly study so inadequate, or the census base so obsolete that it was possible only to assign percentages to entire groups, or families, of related languages, despite their mutual unintelligibility (Papuan and Melanesian languages in Papua New Guinea, for instance). For some countries in the Americas, so few speakers of any single indigenous language remain that it was necessary to combine these groups as *Amerindian* so as to give a fair impression of their aggregate size within their respective countries.

No systematic attempt has been made to account for populations that may legitimately be described as bilingual, unless the country itself collects data on that basis, as does Bolivia or the Comoros, for example. Where a nonindigenous official or excolonial language constitutes a lingua franca of the country, however, speakers of the language as a second tongue are shown in italics, even though very few may speak it as a mother tongue. No comprehensive effort has been made to distinguish between dialect communities *usually* classified as belonging to the same language, though such distinctions were possible for some countries—*e.g.*, between French and Occitan (the dialect of southern France) or among the various dialects of Chinese.

In giving the names of Bantu languages, grammatical particles specific to a language's autonym (name for itself) have been omitted (the form *Rwanda* is used here, for example, rather than *kinyaRwanda*, and *Tswana* instead of *seTswana*). Parenthetical alternatives are given for a number of languages that differ markedly from the name of the people speaking them (such as Kurukh, spoken by the Oraon tribes of India) or that may be combined with other groups sometimes distinguishable in national data but appearing here under the name of the largest member—*e.g.*, "Tamil (and other South Asian languages)" combining data on South Asian Indian populations in Singapore. The term *creole* as used here refers to distinguishable dialectal communities related to a national, official, or former colonial language (such as the French creole that survives in Mauritius from the end of French rule in 1810).

Language

Major languages by country	Number of speakers
Afghanistan[1]	
Indo-Aryan languages	
Pashai	100,000
Iranian languages	
Balochi	160,000
● Dari (Persian)	
Chahar Aimak	470,000
Ḥazāra	1,490,000
Tajik	3,450,000
Nūristānī group	130,000
Pamir group	100,000
● Pashto	8,850,000
Turkic languages	
Turkmen	330,000
Uzbek	1,490,000
Other	320,000
Albania[1]	
● Albanian	3,410,000
Greek	64,000
Macedonian	5,000
Other	1,000
Algeria	
● Arabic	23,090,000
Berber	4,690,000
French	13,000,000
Other	40,000
American Samoa	
● English	2,000
English (lingua franca)	*54,000*
● Samoan	50,000
Tongan	2,000
Other	2,000
Andorra[2]	
● Catalan (Andorran)	18,000
English	1,000
French	5,000
Portuguese	7,000
Spanish	29,000
Other	3,000
Angola[1]	
Ambo (Ovambo)	270,000
Chokwe	470,000
Herero	80,000
Kongo	1,480,000
Luchazi	270,000
Luimbe-Nganguela	610,000
Lunda	130,000
Luvale (Luena)	400,000
Mbunda	130,000
Mbundu	2,420,000
Nyaneka-Humbe	610,000
Ovimbundu	4,180,000
● Portuguese	*3,900,000*
Other	170,000
Antigua and Barbuda	
● English	...
English/English Creole	63,000
Other	3,000
Argentina	
Amerindian languages	100,000
Italian	590,000
● Spanish	32,810,000
Other	380,000
Armenia	
● Armenian	3,320,000
Azerbaijani	90,000
Other	140,000
Aruba	
● Dutch	4,000
English	6,000
Papiamento	55,000
Spanish	5,000
Other	1,000
Australia	
Aboriginal languages	50,000
Arabic	179,000
Cantonese	179,000
Dutch	52,000
● English	15,188,000
English (lingua franca)	*17,300,000*
Filipino languages	64,000
French	50,000
German	123,000
Greek	313,000
Hindī	25,000
Hungarian	32,000
Indonesian (Malay)	32,000
Italian	458,000
Japanese	23,000
Korean	21,000
Macedonian	70,000
Mandarin	59,000
Maltese	57,000
Polish	73,000
Portuguese	29,000
Russian	27,000
Serbo-Croatian	97,000
Spanish	98,000
Turkish	46,000
Vietnamese	120,000
Other	409,000
Austria	
Czech	19,000
● German	7,385,000
Hungarian	34,000
Polish	18,000
Romanian	17,000
Serbo-Croatian	174,000
Slovene	30,000
Turkish	122,000
Other	228,000
Azerbaijan	
Armenian	350,000
● Azerbaijani	6,110,000
Lezgian	160,000
Russian	560,000
Other	240,000
Bahamas, The	
● English	...
English/English Creole	220,000
French (Haitian) Creole	50,000
Bahrain[2]	
● Arabic	400,000
Other	150,000
Bangladesh[1]	
● Bengali	114,740,000
Chakma	430,000
● English	*3,100,000*
Gāro	110,000
Khāsī	90,000
Marma (Magh)	220,000
Mro	40,000
Santhālī	80,000
Tripuri	80,000
Other	1,610,000
Barbados	
Bajan (English Creole)	237,000
● English	27,000
Belarus	
● Belarusian	6,830,000
Polish	60,000
Russian	3,320,000
Ukrainian	140,000
Other	60,000
Belgium[2,3]	
Arabic	160,000
● Dutch	6,000,000
● French	3,310,000
● German	90,000
Italian	240,000
Spanish	50,000
Turkish	90,000
Other	180,000
Belize	
Black Carib (Garífuna)	14,000
● English	106,000
English Creole (lingua franca)	*160,000*
German	3,000
Mayan languages	20,000
Spanish	66,000
Spanish (lingua franca)	*120,000*
Benin[1]	
Adja	580,000
Bariba	440,000
Dendi	110,000
Djougou	160,000
Fon	2,050,000
● French	*810,000*
Fulani (Peul)	290,000
Houéda (Péda)	450,000
Somba (Otamary)	340,000
Yoruba (Nago)	620,000
Other	190,000
Bermuda	
● English	62,000
Bhutan[1]	
Assamese	120,000
● Dzongkha (Bhutiā)	400,000
Nepālī (Hindī)	280,000
Bolivia	
● Aymara	174,000
Guaraní	2,000
● Quechua	413,000
● Spanish	3,476,000
Spanish-Aymara	1,487,000
Spanish-Guaraní	25,000
Spanish-Quechua	1,948,000
Spanish-others	140,000
Other	222,000
Bosnia and Herzegovina	
● Serbo-Croatian	4,410,000
Other	40,000
Botswana[1]	
● English (lingua franca)	*580,000*
Khoikhoin (Hottentot)	36,000
Ndebele	19,000
San (Bushmen)	50,000
Shona	180,000
Tswana	1,093,000
Tswana (lingua franca)	*1,160,000*
Other	71,000
Brazil[1]	
Amerindian languages	270,000
German	870,000
Italian	670,000
Japanese	760,000
● Portuguese	154,950,000
Other	1,480,000
Brunei	
Chinese	26,000
English	10,000
● Malay	129,000
Malay-Chinese	2,000
Malay-Chinese	82,000
English-Chinese	6,000
Malay-Chinese-English	11,000
Other	15,000
Bulgaria[1]	
● Bulgarian	7,030,000
French	*240,000*
Macedonian	210,000
Romany	310,000
Turkish	800,000
Other	100,000
Burkina Faso[1,4]	
● French	*600,000*
Fulani	840,000
Hausa	20,000
Mande languages	
Busansi (Bisa)	200,000
Dyula	80,000
Marka (Soninke)	240,000
Samo	290,000
Songhai	150,000
Tamashek (Tuareg)	330,000
Voltaic (Gur) languages	
Bobo	680,000
Gurunsi (Grusi)	520,000
Gurma	490,000
Lobi	700,000
Mossi	4,820,000
Senufo	530,000
Other	70,000
Burundi[1]	
● French	*540,000*
● Rundi	5,650,000
Hutu	4,750,000
Tutsi	780,000
Twa	60,000
Other[5]	150,000
Cambodia[1]	
Cham	220,000
Chinese	300,000
● Khmer	8,440,000
Vietnamese	520,000
Other[6]	50,000
Cameroon[1]	
Chadic languages	
Buwal	250,000
Hausa	150,000
Kotoko	140,000
Mandara (Wandala)	730,000
Masana (Masa)	510,000
● English	...
● French	*1,940,000*
Niger-Congo languages	
Adamawa-Eastern languages	
Chamba	310,000
Gbaya	150,000
Mbum	170,000
Benue-Congo languages	
Bamileke (Medumba)-Widikum (Mogha-mo)-Bamum (Mum)	2,390,000
Basa (Bassa)	140,000
Duala	1,410,000
Fang (Pangwe)-Beti-Bulu	2,530,000
Ibibio (Efik)	20,000
Jukun	80,000

Major languages by country	Number of speakers
Lundu	350,000
Maka	630,000
Tikar	960,000
Tiv	340,000
Wute	40,000
Kwa languages	
Igbo	70,000
West Atlantic languages	
Fulani	1,240,000
Saharan languages	
Kanuri	40,000
Semitic languages	
Arabic	130,000
Other	100,000
Canada	
● English	17,700,000
● French	6,986,000
English-French	233,000
English-other	431,000
French-other	49,000
English-French-other	32,000
Aboriginal (Amerindian and Eskimo [Inuktitut]) languages	210,000
Arabic	47,000
Chinese	306,000
Czech	26,000
Danish	23,000
Dutch	143,000
Filipino (Pilipino)	49,000
Finnish	29,000
German	504,000
Greek	128,000
Hungarian	79,000
Italian	524,000
Polish	143,000
Portuguese	178,000
Punjābī	73,000
Russian	29,000
Serbo-Croatian	47,000
Spanish	96,000
Ukrainian	239,000
Vietnamese	47,000
Yiddish	26,000
Other	733,000
Cape Verde	
Crioulo (Portuguese Creole)	355,000
● Portuguese	...
Central African Republic[1]	
Banda	880,000
Baya (Gbaya)	750,000
● French	350,000
Kare	80,000
Mbaka	130,000
Mbum	130,000
Ngbandi	330,000
Sango (lingua franca)	770,000
Sara	210,000
Zande (Azande)	300,000
Other	270,000
Chad[1]	
● Arabic	1,700,000
Dagu	150,000
● French	840,000
Hausa	150,000
Kanuri	150,000
Kotoko	140,000
Masa	150,000
Masalit, Maba, and Mimi	410,000
Mbum	420,000
Mubi	270,000
Sara, Bagirmi, and Kreish	1,980,000
Tama	410,000
Teda (Tubu)	470,000
Other	110,000
Chile[1]	
Araucanian (Mapuche)	500,000
Aymara	140,000
Rapa Nui	3,000
● Spanish	12,650,000
Other	510,000
China[1]	
Achang	30,000
Bulang (Blang)	90,000
Ch'iang (Qiang)	210,000
Chinese (Han)	1,096,380,000
Cantonese (Yüeh [Yue])	55,000,000
Hakka	41,000,000
Hsiang (Xiang)	53,000,000
Kan (Gan)	26,000,000
● Mandarin	784,000,000
Min	45,000,000
Wu	93,000,000
Chingpo (Jingpo)	130,000
Chuang (Zhuang)	16,290,000
Daghur (Daur)	130,000
Evenk (Ewenki)	30,000

Major languages by country	Number of speakers
Gelo	460,000
Hani (Woni)	1,320,000
Hui	9,050,000
Kazakh	1,170,000
Korean	2,020,000
Kyrgyz	150,000
Lahu	430,000
Li	1,170,000
Lisu	600,000
Manchu	10,330,000
Maonan	80,000
Miao	7,780,000
Mongol	5,060,000
Mulam	170,000
Nakhi (Naxi)	290,000
Nu	30,000
Pai (Bai)	1,680,000
Pumi	30,000
Puyi (Chung-chia)	2,680,000
Salar	90,000
She	660,000
Shui	360,000
Sibo (Xibo)	180,000
Tai (Dai)	1,080,000
Tajik	40,000
Tibetan	4,830,000
Tu	200,000
T'u-chia (Tujia)	6,000,000
Tung (Dong)	2,640,000
Tung hsiang (Dongxiang)	390,000
Uighur	7,590,000
Wa (Va)	370,000
Yao	2,240,000
Yi	6,910,000
Other	940,000
Colombia[1]	
Amerindian languages	290,000
Arawakan	30,000
Cariban	20,000
Chibchan	140,000
Other	90,000
English Creole	40,000
● Spanish	34,180,000
Comoros	
● Arabic	...
Comorian	396,000
Comorian-French	68,000
Comorian Malagasy	29,000
Comorian-Arabic	9,000
Comorian-Swahili	2,000
Comorian-French-other	21,000
● French	30,000
Other	2,000
Congo[1]	
Bubangi	30,000
● French	830,000
Kongo	1,470,000
Kota	30,000
Lingala (lingua franca)	...
Maka	50,000
Mbete	140,000
Mboshi	330,000
Monokutuba (lingua franca)	1,700,000
Punu	90,000
Sango	80,000
Teke	490,000
Other	150,000
Costa Rica	
Chibchan languages	10,000
Bribrí	6,000
Cabécar	4,000
Chinese	6,000
English Creole	66,000
● Spanish	3,226,000
Côte d'Ivoire[1]	
Akan (including Baule and Anyi)	4,180,000
● French	4,900,000
Kru (including Bete)	1,460,000
Malinke (including Dyula and Bambara)	1,590,000
Southern Mande (including Dan and Guro)	1,070,000
Voltaic ([Gur] including Senufo and Lobi)	1,630,000
Other (non-Ivoirian population)	3,970,000
Croatia	
● Serbo-Croatian	4,600,000
Other	190,000
Cuba	
● Spanish	10,994,000
Cyprus[1]	
● Greek	590,000
● Turkish	150,000
Other	30,000

Major languages by country	Number of speakers
Czech Republic[1]	
Bulgarian	3,000
● Czech	8,398,000
German	40,000
Greek	3,000
Hungarian	20,000
Moravian	1,331,000
Polish	60,000
Romanian	1,000
Romany	33,000
Russian	5,000
Ruthenian	2,000
Silesian	44,000
Slovak	317,000
Ukrainian	8,000
Other	70,000
Denmark[2]	
● Danish	5,013,000
English	18,000
German	9,000
Iranian languages	8,000
Norwegian	10,000
South Slavic languages	11,000
Swedish	8,000
Turkish	34,000
Other	82,000
Djibouti[1]	
Afar	110,000
● Arabic	30,000
● French	50,000
Somali	350,000
Gadaboursi	90,000
Issa	190,000
Issaq	80,000
Other	70,000
Dominica	
● English	3,000
French Creole	50,000
French Creole-English	19,000
Dominican Republic	
French (Haitian) Creole	160,000
● Spanish	7,650,000
Ecuador	
Quechua (and other Indian languages)	790,000
● Spanish	10,440,000
Egypt[1]	
● Arabic	57,760,000
French	260,000
Other	700,000
El Salvador	
● Spanish	5,642,000
Equatorial Guinea[1]	
Bubi	40,000
Fang	320,000
French	...
● Spanish	...
Other[7]	30,000
Eritrea	
Cushitic languages	
Afar	160,000
Agew (Awngi)	120,000
Beja	150,000
Saho	110,000
Nilotic languages	
Kunama	100,000
Nara	80,000
Semitic languages	
Amharic	60,000
● Arabic	...
Tigré	1,170,000
● Tigrinya	1,810,000
Other	10,000
Estonia	
● Estonian	930,000
Russian	520,000
Other	50,000
Ethiopia[1]	
● Amharic	16,040,000
Gurage	2,500,000
Oromo (Galla)	16,550,000
Sidamo	1,710,000
Somali	2,160,000
Tigrinya	3,840,000
Walaita (Welayta)	1,480,000
Other	9,100,000
Faeroe Islands	
● Danish	...
● Faeroese	45,000
Fiji[1]	
● English	160,000
Fijian	377,000
Hindī	356,000
Other	38,000

Major languages by country	Number of speakers
Finland	
● Finnish	4,739,000
● Swedish	298,000
Other	46,000
France	
Arabic[8]	1,470,000
English[8]	80,000
● French[8, 9, 10]	54,300,000
Basque	80,000
Breton	580,000
Catalan (Roussillonais)	210,000
Corsican	170,000
Dutch (Flemish)	100,000
German (Alsatian)	1,320,000
Occitan	1,570,000
Italian[8]	260,000
Polish[8]	50,000
Portuguese[8]	670,000
Spanish[8]	220,000
Turkish[8]	200,000
Other[8]	740,000
French Guiana	
Amerindian languages	4,000
English Creole	2,000
● French	...
French Creoles	132,000
Other	7,000
French Polynesia[11]	
Chinese	12,000
● French	173,000
Polynesian languages	196,000
Other	42,000
Gabon[1]	
Fang	470,000
● French	440,000
Kota	50,000
Mbete	190,000
Mpongwe (Onyènè)	200,000
Punu, Sira, Nzebi	220,000
Teke	20,000
Other	180,000
Gambia, The	
Dyola	110,000
● English	...
Fulani	200,000
Malinke	430,000
Soninke	90,000
Wolof	150,000
Other	80,000
Gaza Strip	
Arabic	751,000
Hebrew	5,000
Georgia	
Abkhaz	90,000
Armenian	380,000
Azerbaijani	310,000
● Georgian	3,930,000
Ossetian	130,000
Russian	490,000
Other	170,000
Germany[2]	
● German	77,440,000
Greek	340,000
Italian	570,000
Polish	280,000
Portuguese	100,000
South Slavic languages	800,000
Spanish	140,000
Turkish	1,820,000
Kurdish	400,000
Other	480,000
Ghana[1]	
Akan	8,420,000
● English	...
Ewe	1,910,000
Ga-Adangme	1,250,000
Gurma	530,000
Hausa (lingua franca)	9,600,000
Mole-Dagbani (Mossi)	2,540,000
Yoruba	220,000
Other	1,190,000
Gibraltar[2]	
Arabic	2,000
● English	26,000
Spanish	...
Other	1,000
Greece[1]	
Albanian	60,000
● Greek	9,900,000
Macedonian	160,000
Turkish	90,000
Other	150,000
Greenland[2]	
● Danish	7,000
● Greenlandic	48,000

Major languages by country	Number of speakers
Grenada	
● English	...
English/English Creole	92,000
Guadeloupe	
French Creole/French	405,000
● French	...
Other	21,000
Guam	
● Chamorro	42,000
Chinese	2,000
Chuukese (Trukese)	2,000
● English	54,000
English (lingua franca)	144,000
Japanese	3,000
Korean	5,000
Palauan	2,000
Philippine languages	29,000
Other	6,000
Guatemala	
Black Carib (Garifuna)	20,000
Mayan languages	3,620,000
Cakchiquel	920,000
Kekchí	500,000
Mam	280,000
Quiché	1,050,000
● Spanish	6,680,000
Guernsey	
English	64,000
French	...
Guinea[1]	
● French	550,000
Mande languages	
Kpelle	300,000
Loma	150,000
Malinke	1,510,000
Susu	720,000
Yalunka	190,000
Other	450,000
West Atlantic languages	
Basari-Koniagi	80,000
Fulani (Peul)	2,510,000
Kissi	390,000
Other	200,000
Other	10,000
Guinea-Bissau	
Balante	153,000
Crioulo (Portuguese Creole)	45,000
Crioulo-Portuguese	23,000
Crioulo-other (except Portuguese)	314,000
Fulani	174,000
Malinke	72,000
Mandyako	52,000
Pepel	29,000
● Portuguese	—
Portuguese-other (except Crioulo)	85,000
Other	103,000
Guyana	
Amerindian languages	24,000
Arawakan	14,000
Cariban	10,000
● English	...
English Creoles	572,000
Other (includes Caribbean Hindī and English)	137,000
Haiti	
● French	60,000
French-Haitian (French) Creole	780,000
● Haitian (French) Creole	5,650,000
Honduras	
Black Carib (Garifuna)	72,000
English Creole	11,000
Miskito	10,000
● Spanish	5,207,000
Other	2,000
Hong Kong	
Chinese	
● Cantonese	5,302,000
Cantonese (lingua franca)	5,730,000
Chiu Chau	84,000
Fukien (Min)	114,000
Hakka	96,000
Putonghua (Mandarin)	66,000
Putonghua (lingua franca)	1,080,000
Sze Yap	24,000
● English	132,000
English (lingua franca)	1,890,000

Language (continued)

Major languages by country	Number of speakers
Filipino (Pilipino)	6,000
Japanese	12,000
Other	144,000
Hungary	
German	40,000
• Hungarian	10,110,000
Romanian	10,000
Romany	50,000
Serbo-Croatian	20,000
Slovak	10,000
Other	20,000
Iceland[2]	
• Icelandic	251,000
Other	16,000
India	
Austro-Asiatic languages	
Ho	1,080,000
Kharia	260,000
Khāsī	850,000
Korkū	490,000
Muṇḍā	470,000
Mundari	1,010,000
Santālī	5,640,000
Savara (Sora)	320,000
Dravidian languages	
Goṇḍī	2,620,000
Kannaḍa	36,060,000
Khond	270,000
Koyā	330,000
Kui	680,170
Kurukh (Oraon)	1,700,000
Malayālam	34,800,000
Tamil	59,980,000
Telugu	72,720,000
Tulu	1,850,000
English	310,000
• English (lingua franca)	30,000,000
Indo-Iranian (Indo-Aryan) languages	
Assamese	14,960,000
Bengali	69,060,000
Bhīlī (Bhilodī)	5,970,000
Barel	400,000
Bhilalī	400,000
Dogrī	2,040,000
Gujarātī	44,510,000
Halabī	700,000
• Hindī	354,270,000
Anga (Angika)	700,000
Baghelkhaṇḍī	400,000
Bāgrī	1,800,000
Banjārī	800,000
Bhojpurī	23,900,000
Bundelkhaṇḍī	600,000
Chhattīsgaṛhī	11,200,000
Garhwālī	2,100,000
Gojrī	600,000
Hāṛautī	600,000
Khorthā (Khoṭṭā)	800,000
Kumaunī	2,100,000
Lamānī (Banjārī)	2,000,000
Magahī (Magadhī)	11,100,000
Maithilī	10,200,000
Mālvī	1,100,000
Maṇḍeālī	400,000
Mārwāṛī	7,900,000
Mewāṛī	1,400,000
Nagpurī	600,000
Nīmāḍī	1,300,000
Pahāṛī	2,100,000
Rājasthānī	3,500,000
Sadānī (Sadrī)	1,300,000
Surgujiā	900,000
Hindī (lingua franca)	411,000,000
Kashmīrī	4,260,000
Khandeshī	1,590,000
Kiṣan	210,000
Konkanī	2,120,000
Marāṭhī	66,550,000
Nepali (Gorkhali)	1,680,000
Oriyā	30,680,000
Punjābī	24,930,000
Sindhī	2,610,000
Kachchī	800,000
Urdū	47,370,000
Sino-Tibetan languages	
Adi	160,000
Āo	140,000
Gāro	550,000
Lushai (Mizo)	520,000
Meithei (Manipurī)	1,210,000
Nissī	190,000
Tripuri	660,000
Other	15,390,000
Indonesia	
Balinese	3,230,000
Banjarese	3,410,000
Batak	4,320,000
Buginese	4,280,000
• Indonesian (Malay)	23,580,000
Javanese	76,790,000
Maderese	8,430,000
Minang	4,600,000
Sundanese	30,710,000
Other	35,390,000
Iran[1]	
Armenian	290,000
Iranian languages	
Bakhtyārī (Lurī)	1,000,000
Balochi	1,360,000
• Farsī (Persian)	27,200,000
Farsī (lingua franca)	49,300,000
Gīlakī	3,150,000
Kurdish	5,440,000
Lurī	2,580,000
Māzandarānī	2,150,000
Other	1,290,000
Semitic languages	
Arabic	1,290,000
Other	140,000
Turkic languages	
Afshari	670,000
Azerbaijani	10,020,000
Qashqa'i	760,000
Shahsavani	360,000
Turkish (mostly Pishagchi, Bayat, and Qajar)	430,000
Turkmen	930,000
Other	120,000
Other	440,000
Iraq[1]	
• Arabic	15,320,000
Assyrian	160,000
Azerbaijani	340,000
Kurdish	3,770,000
Persian	160,000
Other	120,000
Ireland	
• English	3,340,000
• Irish	180,000
Isle of Man	
• English	70,000
Israel[12]	
• Arabic	980,000
English	64,000
French	44,000
German	35,000
• Hebrew	3,667,000
Hungarian	30,000
Romanian	83,000
Russian	92,000
Spanish	45,000
Yiddish	114,000
Other	178,000
Italy[1]	
Albanian	120,000
Catalan	30,000
French	300,000
German	300,000
Greek	40,000
• Italian	53,860,000
Rhaetian	730,000
Friulian	710,000
Ladin	20,000
Sardinian	1,520,000
Slovene	120,000
Other	230,000
Jamaica	
• English	...
English/English Creoles	2,350,000
Hindī and other Indian languages	50,000
Other	100,000
Japan[2]	
Ainu	25,000
Chinese	200,000
English	70,000
• Japanese	123,830,000
Korean	690,000
Philippine languages	60,000
Other	90,000
Jersey	
English	87,000
• French	...
Jersey Norman French	6,000
Jordan[1]	
• Arabic	4,190,000
Other	40,000
Kazakhstan	
German	540,000
• Kazakh	6,660,000
Russian	8,030,000
Tatar	230,000
Uighur	180,000
Ukrainian	340,000
Uzbek	330,000
Other	650,000
Kenya[1]	
Bantu languages	
Bajun (Rajun)	70,000
Basuba	110,000
Embu	320,000
Gusii (Kisii)	1,690,000
Kamba	3,090,000
Kikuyu	5,740,000
Kuria	160,000
Luhya	3,800,000
Mbere	110,000
Meru	1,500,000
Nyika (Mijikenda)	1,310,000
Pokomo	70,000
Swahili	10,000
• Swahili (lingua franca)	18,000,000
Taita	270,000
Cushitic languages	
Oromo languages	
Boran	120,000
Gabbra	50,000
Gurreh	150,000
Orma	60,000
Somali languages	
Degodia	170,000
Ogaden	50,000
Somali	280,000
English (lingua franca)	2,100,000
Nilotic languages	
Kalenjin	2,960,000
Luo	3,500,000
Masai	430,000
Sambur	130,000
Teso	240,000
Turkana	370,000
Semitic languages	
Arabic	70,000
Other	610,000
Kiribati[1]	
• English	...
Kiribati (Gilbertese)	77,700
Tuvaluan (Ellice)	400
Other	500
Korea, North[1]	
Chinese	40,000
• Korean	23,030,000
Korea, South[1]	
Chinese	40,000
• Korean	44,390,000
Kuwait[2]	
• Arabic	1,420,000
Other	50,000
Kyrgyzstan	
• Kyrgyz	2,360,000
Russian	1,150,000
Uzbek	570,000
Other	410,000
Laos[1]	
• Lao-Lum (Lao)	3,180,000
Lao-Soung (Miao [Hmong] and Man [Yao])	250,000
Lao-Tai (Tai)	370,000
Lao-Theung (Mon-Khmer)	780,000
Other[13]	160,000
Latvia	
• Latvian	1,330,000
Russian	1,070,000
Other	150,000
Lebanon[1]	
• Arabic	2,760,000
Armenian	180,000
French	710,000
Other	30,000
Lesotho[1]	
• English	...
• Sotho	1,640,000
Zulu	290,000
Liberia[1]	
• English	480,000
Krio (English Creole)	2,100,000
Kwa (Kru) languages	
Bassa	329,000
Belle (Bellleh)	12,000
De (Dey)	9,000
Grebo	213,000
Krahn	90,000
Kru	174,000
Mande (Northern) languages	
Gbandi	67,000
Kpelle	462,000
Loma	134,000
Malinke (Mandingo)	121,000
Mende	19,000
Vai	85,000
Mande (Southern) languages	
Gio (Dan)	186,000
Mano	169,000
West Atlantic (Mel) languages	
Gola	94,000
Kissi	96,000
Other	117,000
Libya[1]	
• Arabic	5,020,000
Berber	160,000
Other[14]	50,000
Liechtenstein[2]	
• German	27,000
Italian	900
Other	2,500
Lithuania	
• Lithuanian	2,990,000
Polish	220,000
Russian	430,000
Other	80,000
Luxembourg[2]	
Belgian	11,000
Danish	2,000
Dutch	3,000
English	4,000
French	14,000
German	9,000
Greek	1,000
Italian	20,000
Luxemburgian	280,000
Portuguese	40,000
Spanish	3,000
Other	13,000
Macau	
Chinese	
• Cantonese	360,000
Mandarin	5,000
Other Chinese languages	40,000
English	2,000
• Portuguese	10,000
Other	4,000
Macedonia[1]	
Albanian	520,000
• Macedonian	1,550,000
Romany	60,000
Turkish	90,000
Other	160,000
Madagascar[1]	
• French	1,400,000
• Malagasy	13,560,000
Other	140,000
Malaŵi[1]	
Chewa (Maravi)	5,680,000
• English	490,000
Lomwe	1,790,000
Ngoni	650,000
Yao	1,290,000
Other	330,000
Malaysia	
Bajau	120,000
Chinese	1,130,000
Chinese-others	640,000
Dusan	200,000
• English	100,000
English-others	220,000
English (lingua franca)	6,000,000
Iban	460,000
Iban-others	80,000
• Malay	8,410,000
Malay-others	2,990,000
Tamil	760,000
Tamil-others	10,000
Other	4,390,000
Maldives	
• Divehi (Maldivian)	244,000
Mali[1]	
Afro-Asiatic languages	
Berber languages	
Tamashek (Tuareg)	650,000
Semitic languages	
Arabic (Maure)	140,000
• French	700,000
Niger-Congo languages	
Mande languages	
Bambara	2,810,000
Bobo Fing	10,000
Dyula	260,000
Malinke, Khasonke, and Wasulunka	590,000
Samo (Duun)	60,000
Soninke	770,000
Voltaic (Gur) languages	
Bwa (Bobo)	210,000
Dogon	350,000
Mossi	40,000
Senufo and Minianka	1,060,000
West Atlantic languages	
Fulani and Tukulor	1,230,000
Nilo-Saharan languages	
Songhai	630,000
Other	20,000
Malta[1]	
• English	8,000
• Maltese	352,000
Other	8,000
Marshall Islands[2]	
• English	...
• Marshallese	52,400
Other	1,700
Martinique	
French Creole/French	368,000
• French	...
Other	13,000
Mauritania[1]	
• Arabic	...
French	120,000
Fulani	20,000
Ḥassānīyah Arabic	1,690,000
Soninke	60,000
Tukulor	110,000
Wolof	140,000
Zenaga	20,000
Other	30,000
Mauritius	
Bhojpurī	214,000
Bhojpurī-other	23,000
• English	2,000
French	38,000
French Creole	691,000
French Creole-other	100,000
Hindī	14,000
Marāṭhī	8,000
Tamil	9,000
Telugu	7,000
Urdū	7,000
Other	3,000
Mayotte[15]	
Mahorais (local dialect of Comorian Swahili)	96,000
Other Comorian Swahili dialects	42,000
Malagasy	37,000
• French	46,000
Other	7,000
Mexico	
Amerindian languages	7,250,000
Amuzgo	40,000
Aztec (Nahuatl)	1,650,000
Chatino	40,000
Chinantec	150,000
Chocho	20,000
Chol	180,000
Chontal	50,000
Cora	20,000
Cuicatec	20,000
Huastec	170,000
Huave	20,000
Huichol	30,000
Kanjobal	20,000
Mame	20,000
Mayo	50,000
Mazahua	180,000
Mazatec	230,000
Mixe	130,000
Mixtec	530,000
Otomí	390,000
Popoluca	40,000
Purepecha	130,000
Tarahumara	70,000
Tepehua	10,000
Tepehuan	30,000
Tlapanec	90,000
Tojolabal	50,000
Totonac	290,000
Triqui	20,000
Tzeltal	360,000
Tzotzil	320,000
Yaqui	10,000
Yucatec (Mayan)	970,000
Zapotec	540,000
Zoque	60,000
Other	320,000
• Spanish	84,590,000
Spanish-Amerindian languages	5,890,000
Micronesia	
Chuukese (Trukese)	43,300
• English	500
Kosraean	7,600
Mortlockese	7,900
Palauan	400

Major languages by country	Number of speakers
Pohnpeian	24,700
Woleaian	3,800
Yapese	6,000
Other	9,800
Moldova	
Gagauz	140,000
• Romanian (Moldovan)	2,700,000
Russian	1,010,000
Ukrainian	370,000
Other	130,000
Monaco[2]	
English	2,000
• French	12,000
Italian	5,000
Monegasque	5,000
Other	6,000
Mongolia[1]	
Bayad	45,000
Buryat	40,000
Darhat	17,000
Dariganga	33,000
Dörbed	64,000
Dzakhchin	26,000
Kazakh	139,000
• Khalkha (Mongolian)	1,858,000
Ould	9,000
Torgut	12,000
Uryankhai	24,000
Other	92,000
Morocco[1]	
• Arabic	17,610,000
Berber	8,940,000
Other[6]	540,000
Mozambique	
Chopi	500,000
Chuabo	990,000
Koti	60,000
Kunda	10,000
Lomwe	1,350,000
Makonde	330,000
Makua	4,820,000
Marendje	600,000
Mwani	80,000
Nqulu	20,000
Nsenga	40,000
Nyanja	580,000
Nyungwe	390,000
Phimbi	20,000
• Portuguese	210,000
Ronga	630,000
Sena	1,620,000
Shona	1,130,000
Swahili	10,000
Swazi	20,000
Tonga	330,000
Tsonga	2,150,000
Tswa	1,040,000
Yao	290,000
Zulu	10,000
Other	120,000
Myanmar (Burma)[1]	
• Burmese	31,430,000
Chin	990,000
Kachin (Chingpo)	620,000
Karen (Karan)	2,830,000
Kayah	190,000
Mon	1,100,000
Rakhine (Arakanese)	2,050,000
Shan	3,860,000
Other	2,500,000
Namibia[1]	
Bergdama (Damara)	120,000
East Caprivian (mostly Lozi)	60,000
• English	130,000
Herero	120,000
Kavango (Okavango)	150,000
Nama	70,000
Ovambo (Ambo [Kwanyama])	790,000
San (Bushmen)	50,000
Other	230,000
Nauru	
Chinese	900
English	800
English (lingua franca)	10,100
Kiribati (Gilbertese)	1,800
• Nauruan	5,900
Tuvaluan (Ellice)	900
Nepal	
Austro-Asiatic (Munda) languages	
Santali	30,000
Indo-Aryan languages	
Bengali	20,000
Bhojpuri	1,290,000
Dhanwar	20,000
Hindi	170,000

Major languages by country	Number of speakers
Hindi (Awadhi dialect)	330,000
Maithili	2,310,000
• Nepali (Eastern Pahari)	10,380,000
Rajbansi	90,000
Tharu	950,000
Urdu	200,000
Tibeto-Burman languages	
Bhutia (Sherpa)	120,000
Chepang	20,000
Gurung	220,000
Limbu	260,000
Magar	440,000
Newari	670,000
Rai and Kiranti	380,000
Tamang	910,000
Thakali	10,000
Thami	10,000
Other	690,000
Netherlands, The[2]	
Arabic	166,000
• Dutch	14,656,000
Dutch and Frisian	580,000
Turkish	219,000
Other	360,000
Netherlands Antilles	
• Dutch	...
English	15,000
Papiamento	166,000
Other	12,000
New Caledonia[1]	
• French	61,000
Melanesian languages	84,000
Polynesian languages (mostly Wallisian)	21,000
Other	17,000
New Zealand	
• English	3,205,000
English-Maori	150,000
• Maori	50,000
Other	120,000
Nicaragua	
English Creole	42,000
Misumalpan languages	
Miskito	166,000
Sumo	10,000
• Spanish	3,989,000
Other	4,000
Niger[1]	
Berber languages	
Tamashek (Tuareg)	910,000
Chadic languages	
Hausa	4,670,000
Hausa (lingua franca)	6,170,000
• French	1,320,000
Saharan languages	
Kanuri	390,000
Teda (Tubu)	40,000
Semitic languages	
Arabic	30,000
Songhai and Zerma	1,870,000
Voltaic (Gur) languages	
Gurma	20,000
West Atlantic languages	
Fulani (Fulfulde)	860,000
Other	10,000
Nigeria[1]	
Arabic	300,000
Bura	1,500,000
Edo	3,100,000
• English (lingua franca)	14,000,000
English Creole (lingua franca)[16]	33,000,000
Fulani	10,500,000
Hausa	19,900,000
Hausa (lingua franca)	47,000,000
Ibibio	5,300,000
Igbo (Ibo)	10,000,000
Ijo (Ijaw)	1,700,000
Kanuri	3,900,000
Nupe	1,200,000
Tiv	2,100,000
Yoruba	19,900,000
Other	7,300,000
Northern Mariana Islands	
Carolinian	2,200
Chamorro	13,800
Chinese	3,300
Chuukese (Trukese)	1,100
• English	2,200
English (lingua franca)	41,900
Japanese	900
Korean	3,000
Palauan	1,600
Philippine languages	15,800
Other	2,300

Major languages by country	Number of speakers
Norway[2]	
Danish	18,000
English	23,000
• Norwegian	4,182,000
Swedish	12,000
Other	97,000
Oman	
• Arabic (Omani)	1,500,000
Balochi	380,000
Farsi (Persian)	60,000
Swahili	30,000
Urdu	50,000
Other	20,000
Pakistan	
Balochi	3,960,000
Brahui	1,580,000
English (lingua franca)	15,000,000
Pashto	17,270,000
Punjabi	
Punjabi	63,310,000
Hindko	3,190,000
Sindhi	
Sindhi	15,470,000
Siraiki	12,920,000
• Urdu	9,990,000
Other	3,750,000
Panama	
Amerindian languages	215,000
Bokotá	4,000
Chibchan	192,000
Cuna	52,000
Guaymí	137,000
Teribe	2,000
Chocó	19,000
Embera	16,000
Waunama	3,000
Chinese	8,000
English Creoles	362,000
• Spanish	1,998,000
Papua New Guinea[1]	
• English	60,000
Melanesian languages	850,000
Motu (Hiri)	130,000
Papuan languages	3,310,000
Tok Pisin (English Creole)	2,810,000
Other	80,000
Paraguay	
German	41,000
• Guaraní	1,900,000
Guaraní-Spanish	2,301,000
Portuguese	150,000
• Spanish	307,000
Other	35,000
Peru	
Aymara	210,000
• Quechua	1,780,000
• Spanish	17,070,000
Spanish-Aymara	370,000
Spanish-Quechua	3,320,000
Spanish-others	330,000
Other	300,000
Philippines	
Aklanon	670,000
Bicol	4,750,000
Bolinao (Zambal)	290,000
Cebuano	16,660,000
Chavacano	350,000
Chinese	170,000
Davaweno	200,000
• English (lingua franca)	36,000,000
• Filipino (Pilipino; Tagalog)	16,260,000
Hamtikanon	560,000
Hiligaynon/Ilonggo	6,820,000
Ibanag	400,000
Ifugao	210,000
Ilocano	7,600,000
Kankanai	250,000
Maguindanao	820,000
Manobo	210,000
Maranao	980,000
Masbate	500,000
Pampango	2,340,000
Pangasinan	1,540,000
Romblon	280,000
Samal	400,000
Samar-Leyte (Waray-Waray)	3,160,000
Subanon	230,000
Sulu-Moro (Tau Sug)	540,000
Other	2,080,000
Poland	
Belarusian	190,000
German	500,000
• Polish	37,730,000
Ukrainian	230,000
Portugal[2]	
• Portuguese	9,720,000
Other	100,000

Major languages by country	Number of speakers
Puerto Rico	
English	19,000
• Spanish	1,875,000
Spanish-English	1,713,000
Other	47,000
Qatar[2]	
• Arabic	220,000
Other[17]	330,000
Réunion	
• French	190,000
French Creole	600,000
Other[18]	60,000
Romania	
Bulgarian	9,000
German	118,000
Hebrew	9,000
Hungarian	1,619,000
• Romanian	20,334,000
Romany	409,000
Russian	39,000
Serbo-Croatian	34,000
Slovak	20,000
Tatar	25,000
Turkish	30,000
Ukrainian	66,000
Other	27,000
Russia	
Adyghian	120,000
Armenian	360,000
Avar	540,000
Azerbaijani	280,000
Bashkir	990,000
Belarusian	440,000
Buryat	360,000
Chechen	900,000
Chuvash	1,390,000
Dargin	350,000
Georgian	90,000
German	350,000
Ingush	210,000
Kabardinian	380,000
Kalmyk	160,000
Karachay	150,000
Kazakh	560,000
Komi	240,000
Komi-Permyak	110,000
Kumyk	270,000
Lak	100,000
Lezgian	240,000
Mari	530,000
Mordovinian	750,000
Ossetian	380,000
Romanian	120,000
Romany	130,000
• Russian	128,300,000
Tabasaran	90,000
Tatar	4,760,000
Tuvinian	200,000
Udmurt	510,000
Ukrainian	1,880,000
Uzbek	100,000
Yakut	360,000
Other	1,460,000
Rwanda	
• French	530,000
• Rwanda	7,820,000
St. Kitts and Nevis	
• English	...
English/English Creole	42,000
St. Lucia	
• English	28,000
English/French Creole	114,000
St. Vincent and the Grenadines	
• English	...
English/English Creole	109,000
Other	1,000
San Marino[1]	
• Italian	25,000
São Tomé and Príncipe	
Crioulo (Portuguese Creole)	110,000
• Portuguese	...
Other	17,000
Saudi Arabia[1]	
• Arabic	17,050,000
Other	900,000
Senegal[1]	
Diola (Dyola)	450,000
• French	410,000
Fulani (Peul)-Tukulor	1,880,000
Malinke (Mandingo)	370,000
Serer	1,200,000
Wolof	3,550,000
Wolof (lingua franca)	5,650,000
Other	660,000

Major languages by country	Number of speakers
Seychelles	
English	2,000
French	1,000
• Seselwa (French Creole)	66,000
Other	3,000
Sierra Leone[1]	
• English	700,000
Krio (English Creole [lingua franca])	4,400,000
Mande languages	
Kono-Vai	240,000
Koranko	160,000
Mende	1,600,000
Susu	70,000
Yalunka	160,000
West Atlantic languages	
Bullom-Sherbro	170,000
Fulani	170,000
Kissi	110,000
Limba	390,000
Temne	1,460,000
Other	80,000
Singapore[1]	
Chinese	2,275,000
• English	1,097,000
• Malay	416,000
• Mandarin Chinese	...
• Tamil (and other Indian languages)	208,000
Other	34,000
Slovakia[1]	
Czech, Moravian, and Silesian	59,000
German	5,000
Hungarian	572,000
Polish	3,000
Romany	81,000
Russian	2,000
Ruthenian and Ukrainian	31,000
• Slovak	4,585,000
Other	13,000
Slovenia	
Serbo-Croatian	140,000
• Slovene	1,830,000
Other	40,000
Solomon Islands[1]	
• English	...
Melanesian languages	308,000
Papuan languages	31,000
Polynesian languages	13,000
Other[19]	8,000
Somalia[1]	
• Arabic	...
English	...
• Somali	6,550,000
Other	110,000
South Africa[20]	
• Afrikaans	6,540,000
• English	3,620,000
Nguni	18,120,000
• Ndebele	850,000
• Swazi	980,000
• Xhosa	7,280,000
• Zulu	9,020,000
Sotho	10,240,000
• North Sotho (Pedi)	3,630,000
• South Sotho	2,800,000
• Tswana (Western Sotho)	3,800,000
Tsonga	1,420,000
Venda	810,000
Other	1,000,000
Spain[2]	
Basque (Euskera)	590,000
• Castilian Spanish	31,530,000
Catalan (Català)	5,120,000
English	100,000
Galician (Gallego)	1,570,000
Other	270,000
Sri Lanka	
English	10,000
English-Sinhala	980,000
English-Sinhala-Tamil	640,000
English-Tamil	200,000
• Sinhala	10,760,000
Sinhala-Tamil	1,670,000
• Tamil	3,500,000
Other	60,000
Sudan, The[1]	
• Arabic	12,690,000
Azande (Zande)	690,000
Bari	630,000
Beja	1,640,000
Dinka	2,970,000
Fur	530,000
Lotuko	380,000
Nubian	2,080,000

Language (continued)

Major languages by country	Number of speakers		Major languages by country	Number of speakers		Major languages by country	Number of speakers		Major languages by country	Number of speakers		Major languages by country	Number of speakers
Nuer	1,260,000		Tatoga	200,000		**Turkmenistan**			Mon-Khmer (mostly			**Western Sahara**	
Shilluk	440,000		Yao	670,000		Russian	480,000		Cambodian)	140,000		Arabic	218,000
Other	2,390,000		Other	4,200,000		● Turkmenian	2,910,000		Navajo	170,000			
						Uzbek	350,000		Norwegian	90,000		**Western Samoa**	
Suriname			**Thailand**[1]			Other	310,000		Pennsylvania Dutch	90,000		● English	1,000
● Dutch	...		Chinese	6,990,000					Persian	230,000		● Samoan	78,000
English	...		Karen	210,000		**Tuvalu**			Polish	820,000		Samoan-English	85,000
Sranantonga	170,000		Malay	2,100,000		● English	...		Portuguese	490,000			
Sranantonga-other	170,000		Mon-Khmer			Kiribati (Gilbertese)	700		Punjābī	60,000		**Yemen**[1]	
Other (mostly Hindī,			languages			Tuvaluan (Ellice)	9,000		Romanian	70,000		● Arabic	12,710,000
Javanese, and			Khmer	730,000					Russian	270,000		Other	260,000
Saramacca)	80,000		Kuy	620,000		**Uganda**[1]			Samoan	40,000			
			Other	200,000		Bantu languages			Serbo-Croatian	130,000		**Yugoslavia**	
Swaziland[1]			Thai languages			Ganda (Luganda)	3,230,000		Slovak	90,000		Albanian	1,440,000
● English	...		Lao	15,480,000		Gisu	1,310,000		Spanish	19,640,000		Hungarian	400,000
● Swazi	790,000		● Thai (Siamese)	30,270,000		Gwere	520,000		Swedish	90,000		Romanian	60,000
Zulu	20,000		Other	400,000		Kiga (Chiga)	1,240,000		Syriac	40,000		Romany	100,000
Other	70,000		Other	590,000		Konjo	250,000		Tagalog	950,000		● Serbo-Croatian	8,120,000
						Nkole	1,490,000		Thai (including Laotian)	230,000		Slovak	70,000
Sweden[2]			**Togo**[1]			Nyoro	600,000		Turkish	50,000		Vlach	140,000
Arabic	60,000		● French	670,000		Rundi	560,000		Ukrainian	110,000		Other	200,000
Danish	41,000		Chadic languages			Rwanda	1,060,000		Vietnamese	570,000			
English	32,000		Hausa	11,000		Soga	1,490,000		Yiddish	240,000		**Zaire**[1]	
Finnish	211,000		Kwa languages			Swahili (lingua			Other	770,000		Azande (Zande)	2,670,000
German	45,000		Adja-Ewe group			franca)	6,400,000					Boa	1,020,000
Iranian languages	48,000		Adja	122,000		Toro	580,000		**Uruguay**			Chokwe	800,000
Norwegian	47,000		Ane (Mina)	222,000		Central Sudanic			● Spanish	3,060,000		● French	3,400,000
Polish	39,000		Anlo	3,000		languages			Other	110,000		Kongo	7,030,000
South Slavic			Ewe	910,000		Lugbara	700,000					Kongo (lingua	
languages	75,000		Fon	39,000		Madi	250,000		**Uzbekistan**			franca)	13,000,000
Spanish	55,000		Hwe	5,000		English	180,000		Crimean Tatar	200,000		Lingala (lingua	
● Swedish	7,901,000		Kpessi	3,000		Nilotic languages			Karakalpak	440,000		franca)	30,000,000
Turkish	29,000		Peda-Hula (Pla)	16,000		Acholi	850,000		Kazakh	850,000		Luba	7,870,000
Other	190,000		Watyi (Ouatchi)	404,000		Alur	310,000		Korean	120,000		Lugbara	700,000
			Ana-Ife group			Karamojong	370,000		Kyrgyz	160,000		Mongo	5,900,000
Switzerland			Ahlo	7,000		Kuman	190,000		Russian	2,430,000		Ngala and Bangi	2,530,000
● French	1,340,000		Ana (Ana-Ife)	98,000		Lango	1,100,000		Tajik	990,000		Rundi	1,690,000
● German	4,450,000		Anyana	8,000		Padhola	300,000		Tatar	410,000		Rwanda	4,500,000
● Italian	530,000		Nago	10,000		Teso	1,620,000		Turkish	110,000		Swahili (lingua	
Romansch	40,000		Yoruba	7,000		Other	180,000		Turkmenian	120,000		franca)	21,000,000
Other	620,000		Kebu-Akposo group						Ukrainian	90,000		Teke	1,200,000
			Adele	8,000		**Ukraine**			● Uzbek	15,960,000		Other	7,870,000
Syria[1]			Akposo	105,000		Belarusian	160,000		Other	500,000			
● Arabic	12,300,000		Kebu	45,000		Bulgarian	170,000					**Zambia**[24]	
Armenian	390,000		Voltaic (Gur)			Hungarian	160,000		**Vanuatu**			Bemba group	3,310,000
Kurdish	870,000		languages			Polish	30,000		● Bislama (English			Aushi (Ushi)	160,000
Other	290,000		Kabre-Tem group			Romanian	340,000		Creole)	130,000		Bemba	2,280,000
			Kabre	541,000		Russian	17,180,000		● English	...		Bisa	130,000
Taiwan			Kotokoli (Tem)	226,000		● Ukrainian	33,820,000		● French	50,000		Lala	260,000
Austronesian			Namba (Lamba)	119,000		Other	450,000		Melanesian			Lamba	210,000
languages	340,000		Naudemba						languages	161,000		Other	270,000
Ami	126,000		(Losso)	161,000		**United Arab Emirates**[2]			Other	3,000		● English	800,000
Atayal	80,000		para-Gurma group			● Arabic	890,000					Lozi (Barotse) group	750,000
Bunun	39,000		Basari	69,000		Other[17]	1,230,000		**Venezuela**			Lozi (Barotse)	550,000
Paiwan	61,000		Chekossi (Akan)	46,000					● Amerindian languages	210,000		Luyi (Luyana)	140,000
Puyuma	8,000		Chamba	38,000		**United Kingdom**			Goajiro	80,000		Nkoya	50,000
Rukai	8,000		Dye (Gangam)	37,000		● English	56,830,000		Warrau (Warao)	30,000		Other	10,000
Saisiyat	4,000		Gurma	133,000		Scots-Gaelic	80,000		Other	100,000		Mambwe group	420,000
Tsou	6,000		Konkomba	55,000		Welsh	560,000		● Spanish	20,510,000		Lungu	90,000
Yami	4,000		Moba	211,000		Other	950,000		Other	460,000		Mambwe	150,000
Chinese			Mossi	10,000								Mwanga	
Hakka	2,140,000		Tamberma	22,000		**United States**			**Vietnam**[1]			(Winamwanga)	170,000
● Mandarin	2,780,000		Yanga	11,000		Amharic	40,000		Bahnar	150,000		Other	20,000
Min (South			West Atlantic (Mel)			Arabic	400,000		Cham	110,000		North-Western group	920,000
Fuklen)	15,810,000		languages			Armenian	170,000		Chinese (Hoa)	1,010,000		Chokwe	60,000
Other	20,000		Fulani (Peul)	53,000		Bengali	40,000		Hre	110,000		Kaonde	250,000
			Other	166,000		Cajun	40,000		Jarai	270,000		Luchazi	60,000
Tajikistan						Chinese (including			Khmer	1,010,000		Lunda	240,000
Russian	570,000		**Tonga**			Formosan)	1,470,000		Ko'ho	100,000		Luvale (Luena)	180,000
● Tajik	3,610,000		● English	...		Czech	100,000		Man (Mien, or Yao)	540,000		Mbunda	140,000
Uzbek	1,350,000		● Tongan	98,000		Danish	40,000		Miao (Meo, or Hmong)	630,000		Nyanja (Maravi) group	1,610,000
Other	290,000		Other	2,000		Dutch	160,000		Mnong	70,000		Chewa	480,000
						● English	224,900,000		Muong	1,030,000		Ngoni	180,000
Tanzania[1]			**Trinidad and Tobago**			English (lingua			Nung	800,000		Nsenga	420,000
Chaga (Chagga),			● English	...		franca)	253,410,000		Rhadé	220,000		Nyanja (Maravi)	470,000
Pare	1,340,000		English Creole[21]	36,000		Finnish	60,000		Roglai	80,000		Other	50,000
● English	800,000		Caribbean Hindī	44,000		French	1,930,000		San Chay (Cao Lan)	130,000		Tonga (Ila-Tonga)	
Gogo	1,070,000		Trinidad English	1,190,000		French Creole			San Diu	110,000		group	1,380,000
Ha	940,000		Other	3,000		(mostly Haitian)	210,000		Sedang	110,000		Ila	70,000
Haya	1,610,000					German	1,750,000		Stieng	60,000		Lenje	160,000
Hehet	1,880,000		**Tunisia**			Greek	440,000		Tai	1,170,000		Soli	70,000
Iramba	780,000		● Arabic	6,120,000		Gujarātī	120,000		Tho (Tay)	1,340,000		Tonga	1,000,000
Luguru	1,340,000		Arabic-French	2,300,000		Hebrew	160,000		● Vietnamese	62,810,000		Other	70,000
Luo	230,000		Arabic-French-			Hindī (including			Other	490,000		Tumbuka group	420,000
Makonde	1,610,000		English	280,000		Urdū)	380,000					Senga	70,000
Masai	270,000		Arabic-other	10,000		Hungarian	170,000		**Virgin Islands (U.S.)**			Tumbuka	340,000
Ngoni	360,000		Other-no Arabic	20,000		Ilocano	50,000		● English	85,000		Other	330,000
Nyakyusa	1,470,000		Other	30,000		Italian	1,480,000		French	3,000			
Nyamwezi						Japanese	480,000		Spanish	14,000		**Zimbabwe**	
(Sukuma)	5,760,000		**Turkey**[1]			Korean	710,000		Other	3,000		● English	240,000
Shambala	1,170,000		Arabic	840,000		Kru (Gullah)	70,000					Ndebele (Nguni)	1,780,000
● Swahili	2,410,000		Kurdish[22]	6,490,000		Lithuanian	60,000		**West Bank**[23]			Nyanja	250,000
Swahili (lingua			● Turkish	53,580,000		Malayālam	40,000		Arabic	1,110,000		Shona	7,920,000
franca)	25,000,000		Other	280,000		Miao (Hmong)	90,000		Hebrew	110,000		Other	790,000

---

[1]Figures given represent ethnolinguistic groups. [2]Data refer to nationality (usually resident aliens holding foreign passports). [3]Data are partly based on place of residence. [4]Majority of population speak Moré (language of the Mossi); Dyula is language of commerce. [5]Swahili also spoken. [6]French also spoken. [7]Pidgin English and Portuguese Creole also spoken. [8]Based on "nationality" at 1982 census. [9]Includes naturalized citizens. [10]French is the universal language throughout France; traditional dialects and minority languages are retained regionally in the approximate numbers shown, however. [11]Data reflect multilingualism; 1994 population estimate is 215,000. [12]Includes the population of the Golan Heights and East Jerusalem; excludes the Israeli population in the West Bank and Gaza Strip. [13]English and French also spoken. [14]English and Italian also spoken. [15]Data reflect ability to speak the language, not mother tongue; 1994 population estimate is 110,000. [16]Includes speakers of standard English. [17]Mostly Pakistanis, Indians, and Iranians. [18]Gujarātī and Chinese also spoken. [19]Solomon Islands Pidgin (English) is the lingua franca. [20]Includes the former Black independent states of Bophuthatswana, Ciskei, Transkei, and Venda. [21]Spoken on Tobago only. [22]Other estimates of the Kurdish population range from 6 percent to 20–25 percent. [23]Excludes East Jerusalem. [24]Groups are officially defined geographic divisions; elements comprising them are named by language.

Religion

The following table presents statistics on religious affiliation for each of the countries of the world. An assessment was made for each country of the available data on distribution of religious communities within the total population; the best available figures, whether originating as census data, membership figures of the churches concerned, or estimates by external analysts in the absence of reliable local data, were applied as percentages to the estimated 1994 midyear population of the country to obtain the data shown below.

Several concepts govern the nature of the available data, each useful separately but none the basis of any standard of international practice in the collection of such data. The word "affiliation" was used above to describe the nature of the relationship joining the religious bodies named and the populations shown. This term implies some sort of formal, usually documentary, connection between the religion and the individual (a baptismal certificate, a child being assigned the religion of its parents on a census form, maintenance of one's name on the tax rolls of a state religion, etc.) but says nothing about the nature of the individual's personal religious practice, in that the individual may have lapsed, never been confirmed as an adult, joined another religion, or may have joined an organization that is formally atheist.

The user of these statistics should be careful to note that not only does the nature of the affiliation (with an organized religion) differ greatly from country to country, but the social context of religious practice does also. A country in which a single religion has long been predominant will often show more than 90% of its population to be *affiliated,* while in actual fact, no more than 10% may actually *practice* that religion on a regular basis. Such a situation often leads to undercounting of minority religions (where someone [head of household, communicant, child] is counted at all), blurring of distinctions seen to be significant elsewhere (a Hindu country may not distinguish Protestant [or even Christian] denominations; a Christian country may not distinguish among its Muslim or Buddhist citizens), or double-counting in countries where an individual may conscientiously practice more than one "religion" at a time.

Until 1989 communist countries had for long consciously attempted to ignore, suppress, or render invisible religious practice within their borders. Countries with large numbers of adherents of traditional, often animist, religions and belief systems usually have little or no formal methodology for defining the nature of local religious practice. On the other hand, countries with strong missionary traditions, or good census organizations, or few religious sensitivities may have very good, detailed, and meaningful data.

The most comprehensive work available is DAVID B. BARRETT (ed.), *World Christian Encyclopedia* (1982); it examines both the theoretical and practical problems of collecting and analyzing religious statistics, assembles a mine of national detail, and establishes a basis for further study.

Religion

Religious affiliation	1994 population
Afghanistan	
Sunnī Muslim	14,200,000
Shī'ī Muslim	2,540,000
other	170,000
Albania	
Muslim	2,190,000
Albanian Orthodox	670,000
Roman Catholic	440,000
other	70,000
Algeria	
Sunnī Muslim	27,680,000
Ibāḍīyah Muslim	110,000
other	30,000
American Samoa	
Congregational	31,000
Roman Catholic	11,000
other	13,000
Andorra	
Roman Catholic	57,000
other	5,000
Angola	
Roman Catholic	7,720,000
Protestant	2,220,000
traditional beliefs	1,070,000
other	230,000
Antigua and Barbuda	
Anglican	29,000
Protestant	27,000
Roman Catholic	7,000
other	2,000
Argentina	
Roman Catholic	31,030,000
other	2,850,000
Armenia	
Armenian Apostolic (Orthodox)	3,340,000
other (mostly Roman Catholic and Muslim)	210,000
Aruba	
Roman Catholic	64,000
other	8,000
Australia	
Roman Catholic	4,660,000
Anglican	4,260,000
Uniting Church and Methodist	1,350,000
Presbyterian	640,000
other Protestant	1,110,000
Orthodox	490,000
nonreligious	2,270,000
other	3,100,000
Austria	
Roman Catholic	6,260,000
Evangelical Lutheran	390,000
atheist and nonreligious	690,000
other	690,000
Azerbaijan	
Muslim (mostly Shī'ī)	6,460,000
Russian Orthodox	420,000
Armenian Apostolic (Orthodox)	420,000
other	130,000
Bahamas, The	
Protestant	150,000
Anglican	55,000
Roman Catholic	51,000
other	16,000
Bahrain	
Shī'ī Muslim	330,000
Sunnī Muslim	140,000
other	80,000
Bangladesh	
Muslim	101,730,000
Hindu	14,240,000
other	1,430,000
Barbados	
Anglican	105,000
Protestant	67,000
other	92,000
Belarus	
Believers are predominantly Belarusian Orthodox; Roman Catholic and Jewish minorities.	
Belgium	
Roman Catholic	9,110,000
other	1,010,000
Belize	
Roman Catholic	121,000
Protestant	57,000
Anglican	15,000
other	17,000
Benin	
traditional beliefs	3,250,000
Roman Catholic	1,100,000
Muslim	630,000
other	260,000
Bermuda	
Anglican	23,000
Methodist	10,000
Roman Catholic	9,000
other	20,000
Bhutan	
Buddhist	560,000
Hindu	140,000
other	50,000
Bolivia	
Roman Catholic	7,300,000
other	590,000
Bosnia and Herzegovina	
Sunnī Muslim	1,780,000
Serbian Orthodox	1,380,000
Roman Catholic	670,000
Protestant	180,000
other	440,000
Botswana	
traditional beliefs	710,000
Protestant	390,000
African Christian	170,000
Roman Catholic	140,000
other	40,000
Brazil	
Roman Catholic (including syncretic Afro-Catholic cults having Spiritist beliefs and rituals)	120,800,000
Evangelical Protestant	17,500,000
other	20,700,000
Brunei	
Muslim	188,000
other	95,000
Bulgaria	
Bulgarian Orthodox	7,400,000
Muslim	890,000
other	170,000
Burkina Faso	
traditional beliefs	5,910,000
Muslim	3,080,000
Christian	1,060,000
Burundi	
Roman Catholic	3,770,000
nonreligious	1,080,000
other (mostly Protestant)	940,000
Cambodia	
Buddhist	9,050,000
Muslim	200,000
other	270,000
Cameroon	
Roman Catholic	4,480,000
traditional beliefs	3,350,000
Muslim	2,810,000
Protestant	2,260,000
Canada	
Roman Catholic	13,160,000
Protestant	8,270,000
Anglican	2,360,000
Eastern Orthodox	440,000
Jewish	350,000
Muslim	120,000
Sikh	80,000
Hindu	80,000
nonreligious	3,610,000
other	640,000
Cape Verde	
Roman Catholic	330,000
Protestant	25,000
Central African Republic	
Protestant	770,000
Roman Catholic	770,000
traditional beliefs	740,000
Muslim	460,000
other	340,000
Chad	
Muslim	2,860,000
traditional beliefs	1,480,000
Roman Catholic	1,360,000
Protestant	750,000
other	40,000
Chile	
Roman Catholic	11,100,000
Evangelical Protestant	1,840,000
other	870,000
China	
nonreligious	681,000,000
Chinese folk-religionist	240,000,000
atheist	143,000,000
Buddhist	101,000,000
Muslim	17,000,000
Christian	9,000,000
traditional beliefs	1,000,000
Colombia	
Roman Catholic	32,140,000
other	2,380,000
Comoros	
Sunnī Muslim	523,000
Christian	4,000
Congo	
traditional beliefs	1,430,000
Roman Catholic	1,020,000
Protestant	350,000
Muslim	60,000
Costa Rica	
Roman Catholic	2,690,000
other	620,000
Côte d'Ivoire	
Muslim	5,400,000
Roman Catholic	2,900,000
traditional beliefs	2,400,000
nonreligious	1,900,000
Protestant	900,000
other	400,000
Croatia	
Roman Catholic	3,660,000
Serbian Orthodox	530,000
Protestant	70,000
Sunnī Muslim	60,000
other	470,000
Cuba	
Roman Catholic	4,350,000
nonreligious	5,350,000
atheist	700,000
other	580,000
Cyprus	
Greek Orthodox	590,000
Muslim (mostly Sunnī)	150,000
other (mostly Christian)	30,000
Czech Republic	
Roman Catholic	4,040,000
Evangelical Church of Czech Brethren	200,000
Czechoslovak Hussite	180,000
Silesian Evangelical	30,000
Eastern Orthodox	20,000
atheist and nonreligious	4,130,000
other	1,760,000
Denmark	
Evangelical Lutheran	4,592,000
other	613,000
Djibouti	
Sunnī Muslim	535,000
Christian[1]	34,000
Dominica	
Roman Catholic	55,000
other	17,000
Dominican Republic	
Roman Catholic	7,120,000
other	680,000
Ecuador	
Roman Catholic	10,440,000
other	790,000
Egypt	
Sunnī Muslim	52,600,000
Christian (mostly Coptic[2])	5,800,000
El Salvador	
Roman Catholic	4,230,000
other (mostly Protestant)	1,410,000
Equatorial Guinea	
Roman Catholic	380,000
other	10,000
Eritrea	
Christian (mostly Ethiopian Orthodox)	1,900,000
Muslim	1,900,000
Estonia	
Believers are predominantly affiliated with the Evangelical Lutheran Church of Estonia; Russian Orthodox and Protestant minorities.	
Ethiopia	
Ethiopian Orthodox	28,120,000
Muslim (mostly Sunnī)	16,060,000
traditional beliefs	6,510,000
other	2,680,000

Religion (continued)

Religious affiliation	1994 population
Faeroe Islands	
Evangelical Lutheran	33,000
other	12,000
Fiji	
Christian (mostly Methodist and Roman Catholic)	408,000
Hindu	294,000
Muslim	60,000
other	9,000
Finland	
Evangelical Lutheran	4,408,000
other	675,000
France	
Roman Catholic	42,850,000
nonreligious	7,070,000
Muslim	3,190,000
atheist	1,970,000
Jewish	640,000
other	2,260,000
French Guiana	
Roman Catholic	107,000
other	39,000
French Polynesia	
Protestant	100,000
Roman Catholic	85,000
other	30,000
Gabon	
Roman Catholic	600,000
traditional beliefs	400,000
African Christian	110,000
other	30,000
Gambia, The	
Muslim (mostly Sunnī)	1,010,000
other	50,000
Gaza Strip	
Muslim (mostly Sunnī)	747,000
other	9,000
Georgia	
Georgian Orthodox	3,580,000
Sunnī Muslim	610,000
Russian Orthodox	550,000
Armenian Apostolic (Orthodox)	440,000
other (mostly nonreligious)	330,000
Germany	
Evangelical Lutheran	32,960,000
Roman Catholic	28,970,000
Muslim	1,750,000
other (mostly nonreligious or unaffiliated)	18,290,000
Ghana	
traditional beliefs	6,100,000
Muslim	4,820,000
Roman Catholic	1,940,000
Protestant	790,000
African Christian	780,000
Anglican	340,000
other	1,280,000
Gibraltar	
Roman Catholic	22,000
other	7,000
Greece	
Greek Orthodox	10,120,000
Muslim	160,000
other	90,000
Greenland	
Evangelical Lutheran	55,000
other	1,000
Grenada	
Roman Catholic	49,000
Anglican	13,000
other	30,000
Guadeloupe	
Roman Catholic	390,000
other	40,000
Guam	
Roman Catholic	115,000
Protestant	23,000
other	7,000
Guatemala	
Roman Catholic	7,280,000
Protestant	2,430,000
Guernsey	
Anglican	42,000
other	22,000
Guinea	
Muslim	5,530,000
Christian	520,000
traditional beliefs	460,000
Guinea-Bissau	
traditional beliefs	680,000
Muslim	320,000
Christian	50,000
Guyana	
Hindu	249,000
Roman Catholic	133,000
Protestant	127,000
Anglican	121,000
Muslim	66,000
other	37,000
Haiti	
Roman Catholic	5,210,000
Baptist	630,000
Pentecostal	230,000
other	420,000
Honduras	
Roman Catholic	4,510,000
Protestant	530,000
other	270,000
Hong Kong	
Buddhist and Taoist	4,410,000
Roman Catholic	270,000
Protestant	220,000
other	1,060,000
Hungary	
Roman Catholic	6,950,000
Protestant	2,570,000
nonreligious and atheist	490,000
Jewish	55,000
other	180,000
Iceland	
Evangelical Lutheran	246,000
other	21,000
India	
Hindu	734,000,000
Sunnī Muslim	75,000,000
Shī'ī Muslim	25,000,000
Sikh	18,000,000
Roman Catholic	13,000,000
Protestant	9,000,000
Buddhist	6,000,000
Jain	5,000,000
Zoroastrian (Parsi)	130,000
other	29,000,000
Indonesia	
Muslim	169,840,000
Protestant	11,760,000
Roman Catholic	6,970,000
Hindu	3,560,000
Buddhist	2,010,000
other	600,000
Iran	
Shī'ī Muslim	55,770,000
Sunnī Muslim	3,370,000
other	470,000
Iraq	
Shī'ī Muslim	12,300,000
Sunnī Muslim	6,820,000
other (mostly Christian)	750,000
Ireland	
Roman Catholic	3,268,000
other	243,000
Isle of Man	
Anglican	43,000
other	27,000
Israel	
Jewish[3]	4,330,000
Muslim (mostly Sunnī)	760,000
other	240,000
Italy	
Roman Catholic	47,580,000
nonreligious	7,790,000
atheist	1,490,000
other	410,000
Jamaica	
Protestant	1,230,000
Anglican	180,000
Roman Catholic	120,000
other	970,000
Japan	
Shintoist[4]	110,200,000
Buddhist[4]	97,320,000
Christian	1,470,000
other	10,620,000
Jersey	
Anglican	53,000
Roman Catholic	20,000
other	13,000
Jordan	
Sunnī Muslim	3,930,000
other	300,000
Kazakhstan	
Muslim (mostly Sunnī)	7,970,000
Russian Orthodox	2,540,000
Protestant	340,000
other (mostly nonreligious)	6,100,000
Kenya	
Roman Catholic	7,250,000
Protestant	5,300,000
traditional beliefs	5,190,000
African Christian	4,830,000
Anglican	1,980,000
Muslim	1,650,000
other	1,250,000
Kiribati	
Roman Catholic	42,000
Congregational	31,000
other	6,000
Korea, North	
atheist and nonreligious	15,660,000
traditional beliefs	3,600,000
Ch'ŏndogyo	3,210,000
other	600,000
Korea, South	
Buddhist	16,130,000
Confucian	10,860,000
Protestant	10,370,000
Roman Catholic	2,290,000
Wonbulgyo	1,160,000
Ch'ŏndogyo	1,030,000
Taejong	500,000
other	2,090,000
Kuwait	
Sunnī Muslim	930,000
Shī'ī Muslim	400,000
other	150,000
Kyrgyzstan	
Muslim (mostly Sunnī)	3,140,000
other (mostly non-religious and Russian Orthodox)	1,350,000
Laos	
Buddhist	2,740,000
traditional beliefs	1,590,000
other	410,000
Latvia	
Believers are predominantly affiliated with the Latvian Evangelical Lutheran Church; Russian Orthodox, Roman Catholic, and Protestant minorities.	
Lebanon	
Shī'ī Muslim	1,070,000
Sunnī Muslim	700,000
Maronite Christian	590,000
Druze	200,000
Greek Orthodox	160,000
Greek Catholic	100,000
Armenian Christian	100,000
other	30,000
Lesotho	
Roman Catholic	840,000
Protestant	570,000
other	520,000
Liberia	
Christian	1,610,000
traditional beliefs	440,000
Muslim	330,000
Libya	
Sunnī Muslim	5,070,000
other	160,000
Liechtenstein	
Roman Catholic	25,000
other	6,000
Lithuania	
Roman Catholic	2,980,000
other (mostly Russian Orthodox, Old Believer, Evangelical Lutheran, and nonreligious)	740,000
Luxembourg	
Roman Catholic	375,000
other	23,000
Macau	
nonreligious	191,000
Buddhist	188,000
other	37,000
Macedonia	
Macedonian Orthodox	1,230,000
Sunnī Muslim	540,000
other	310,000
Madagascar	
traditional beliefs	7,540,000
Protestant	2,740,000
Roman Catholic	2,740,000
Muslim	690,000
Malaŵi	
Protestant (mostly Presbyterian)	4,870,000
Roman Catholic	1,950,000
Muslim	1,950,000
traditional beliefs	970,000
Malaysia	
Muslim	10,320,000
Buddhist	3,370,000
Chinese folk-religionist	2,260,000
Hindu	1,370,000
Christian	1,250,000
other	940,000
Maldives	
Sunnī Muslim	244,000
Mali	
Muslim	7,940,000
traditional beliefs	790,000
Christian	90,000
Malta	
Roman Catholic	363,000
other	5,000
Marshall Islands	
Believers are predominantly Protestant (mainly Congregational); Roman Catholic minority.	
Martinique	
Roman Catholic	340,000
other	40,000
Mauritania	
Sunnī Muslim	2,060,000
other	10,000
Mauritius	
Hindu	570,000
Roman Catholic	300,000
Muslim	180,000
other	70,000
Mayotte	
Sunnī Muslim	107,000
Christian	3,000
Mexico	
Roman Catholic	82,370,000
Protestant and Evangelical Catholic	4,490,000
Jewish	70,000
nonreligious	2,980,000
other	1,930,000
Micronesia	
Believers are about equally Roman Catholic and Protestant (mainly Congregational).	
Moldova	
Russian (Moldovan) Orthodox	4,340,000
other	20,000
Monaco	
Roman Catholic	27,000
other	3,000
Mongolia	
Tantric Buddhist (Lamaist)	2,130,000
Muslim	140,000
Morocco	
Muslim (mostly Sunnī)	26,240,000
other	300,000
Mozambique	
traditional beliefs	8,290,000
Roman Catholic	5,450,000
Muslim	2,250,000
other	1,360,000
Myanmar (Burma)	
Buddhist	40,760,000
Christian	2,240,000
Muslim	1,750,000
traditional beliefs	520,000
Hindu	230,000
other	70,000
Namibia	
Lutheran	817,000
Roman Catholic	316,000
Dutch Reformed	97,000
Anglican	80,000
other	286,000
Nauru	
Congregational	5,600
other	4,600
Nepal	
Hindu	16,820,000
Buddhist	1,520,000
Muslim	740,000
other	440,000
Netherlands, The	
Roman Catholic	5,080,000
Dutch Reformed Church (NHK)	2,310,000
Reformed Churches	1,230,000
Muslim	490,000
nonreligious	6,010,000
other	280,000
Netherlands Antilles	
Roman Catholic	162,000
other	31,000
New Caledonia	
Roman Catholic	111,000
other	72,000
New Zealand	
Anglican	750,000
Presbyterian	560,000
Roman Catholic	520,000
Methodist	140,000
Baptist	70,000
Ratana	50,000
Mormon	50,000
nonreligious	690,000
other	680,000
Nicaragua	
Roman Catholic	3,760,000
other (mostly Protestant)	450,000
Niger	
Sunnī Muslim	8,690,000
other	130,000
Nigeria	
Muslim	42,060,000
Protestant	24,580,000
Roman Catholic	11,310,000

Religious affiliation	1994 population
African Christian	9,910,000
traditional beliefs	5,230,000
other	370,000
Northern Mariana Islands	
Roman Catholic	41,000
other	5,000
Norway	
Evangelical Lutheran (Church of Norway)	3,807,000
other	525,000
Oman	
Muslim	1,760,000
other	290,000
Pakistan	
Muslim (mostly Sunnī)	127,230,000
Christian	2,050,000
Hindu	1,980,000
other	170,000
Panama	
Roman Catholic	2,070,000
Protestant	260,000
other	250,000
Papua New Guinea	
Protestant	2,480,000
Roman Catholic	1,390,000
Anglican	230,000
other	150,000
Paraguay	
Roman Catholic	4,410,000
other (mostly Protestant)	320,000
Peru	
Roman Catholic	21,090,000
other (mostly Protestant)	1,870,000
Philippines	
Roman Catholic	56,670,000
Protestant	3,210,000
Muslim	2,910,000
Aglipayan	2,120,000
Church of Christ (Iglesia ni Cristo)	1,570,000
other	1,780,000
Poland	
Roman Catholic	35,560,000
nonreligious	2,160,000
Polish Orthodox	580,000
other	353,000
Portugal	
Roman Catholic	9,270,000
other	540,000
Puerto Rico	
Roman Catholic	3,120,000
other	540,000
Qatar	
Muslim (mostly Sunnī)	510,000
other	40,000
Réunion	
Roman Catholic	570,000
other	80,000
Romania	
Romanian Orthodox	19,740,000
Roman Catholic	1,140,000
other	1,860,000
Russia	

Russia — Believers are predominantly affiliated with the Russian Orthodox Church; Roman Catholic, Protestant, Muslim, Jewish, and Buddhist minorities.

Religious affiliation	1994 population
Rwanda	
Roman Catholic	5,080,000
traditional beliefs	1,950,000
Protestant	700,000
Muslim	80,000
St. Kitts and Nevis	
Anglican	14,000
Methodist	12,000
other	16,000
St. Lucia	
Roman Catholic	112,000
other	30,000
St. Vincent and the Grenadines	
Anglican	46,000
Methodist	23,000
Roman Catholic	13,000
other	28,000
San Marino	
Roman Catholic	23,000
other	1,000
São Tomé and Príncipe	
Roman Catholic	110,000
Protestant	20,000
Saudi Arabia	
Sunnī Muslim	17,130,000
Shīʿī Muslim	600,000
other	210,000
Senegal	
Sunnī Muslim	7,630,000
Christian	400,000
other	90,000
Seychelles	
Roman Catholic	64,000
other	8,000
Sierra Leone	
Sunnī Muslim	2,770,000
traditional beliefs	1,380,000
Christian	460,000
Singapore	
Buddhist and Taoist	1,581,000
Muslim	451,000
Protestant	229,000
Roman Catholic	142,000
Hindu	104,000
nonreligious	411,000
other	16,000
Slovakia	
Roman Catholic	3,230,000
Slovak Evangelical	330,000
atheist	520,000
other	1,270,000
Slovenia	
Roman Catholic	1,880,000
other	120,000
Solomon Islands	
Protestant	150,000
Anglican	122,000
Roman Catholic	69,000
other	19,000
Somalia	
Sunnī Muslim	6,650,000
other	20,000
South Africa[5]	
Christian	22,990,000
Protestant	11,460,000
Dutch (Afrikaans) Reformed Churches	4,130,000
Nederduitse Gereformeerde	3,650,000
Gereformeerde Nederduitsch	180,000
Hervormde	300,000
other Protestant	7,320,000
Methodist	2,110,000
Presbyterian	460,000

Religious affiliation	1994 population
United	
Congregational	430,000
Lutheran	850,000
Apostolic Faith Mission of South Africa	450,000
New Apostolic Church	160,000
other Apostolic	470,000
Baptist	290,000
Pentecostal Protestant	80,000
African Protestant Church	40,000
Full Gospel	230,000
Pentecostal	20,000
Salvation Army	30,000
Seventh-day Adventist	100,000
Swiss	50,000
Assemblies of God	170,000
other	1,380,000
Roman Catholic	2,630,000
Anglican	1,350,000
Greek Orthodox	30,000
black independent churches	7,500,000
Zion Christian Church	1,580,000
other	5,930,000
Mormon	10,000
Hindu	440,000
Muslim	380,000
Jewish	120,000
other beliefs	30,000
nonreligious	410,000
not stated	9,530,000
Spain	
Roman Catholic	37,190,000
Muslim	450,000
other	1,550,000
Sri Lanka	
Buddhist	12,360,000
Hindu	2,760,000
Muslim	1,350,000
Roman Catholic	1,230,000
other	140,000
Sudan, The	
Sunnī Muslim	18,760,000
traditional beliefs	4,290,000
Christian[1]	2,340,000
other	310,000
Suriname	
Hindu	116,000
Roman Catholic	96,000
Muslim	83,000
Protestant	79,000
other	48,000
Swaziland	
Christian[1]	680,000
traditional beliefs	180,000
other	20,000
Sweden	
Church of Sweden (Lutheran)	7,741,000
other	1,032,000
Switzerland	
Roman Catholic	3,230,000
Protestant	2,800,000
other	970,000
Syria	
Sunnī Muslim	10,250,000
Shīʿī Muslim	2,080,000
Christian	1,250,000
other	280,000
Taiwan	
Chinese folk-religionist	10,220,000
Buddhist	9,060,000
Christian[1]	1,250,000
other	240,000
Tajikistan	
Sunnī Muslim	4,650,000
Shīʿī Muslim	290,000

Religious affiliation	1994 population
other (mostly nonreligious)	870,000
Tanzania	
Muslim	9,550,000
Christian	9,550,000
traditional beliefs	8,190,000
Thailand	
Buddhist	54,340,000
Muslim	2,270,000
Christian	310,000
other	660,000
Togo	
traditional beliefs	2,310,000
Roman Catholic	840,000
Sunnī Muslim	470,000
Protestant	270,000
other	30,000
Tonga	
Free Wesleyan	43,000
Roman Catholic	16,000
other	41,000
Trinidad and Tobago	
Protestant	383,000
Roman Catholic	374,000
Hindu	303,000
Anglican	139,000
Muslim	74,000
Tunisia	
Sunnī Muslim	8,710,000
other	50,000
Turkey	
Muslim (mostly Sunnī)	60,690,000
other	490,000
Turkmenistan	
Muslim (mostly Sunnī)	3,520,000
Russian Orthodox	440,000
other	80,000
Tuvalu	
Congregational	9,400
other	300
Uganda	
Roman Catholic	9,020,000
Anglican	4,770,000
traditional beliefs	2,290,000
Muslim (mostly Sunnī)	1,200,000
other	910,000
Ukraine	

Ukraine — Believers are predominantly affiliated with the Ukrainian Orthodox Church; Ukrainian Autocephalous Orthodox and Ukrainian Catholic (Uniate) minorities.

Religious affiliation	1994 population
United Arab Emirates	
Sunnī Muslim	1,700,000
Shīʿī Muslim	340,000
other	90,000
United Kingdom	
Christian[1]	50,910,000
Church of England	33,330,000
Protestant	8,760,000
Roman Catholic	7,650,000
Eastern Orthodox	350,000
other Christian	820,000
Muslim	820,000
Hindu	410,000
Jewish	320,000
Sikh	230,000
nonreligious and atheist	5,550,000
other	180,000
United States	
Christian (professing)	222,580,000
Christian (affiliated)	179,000,000
Protestant	105,070,000
Roman Catholic	54,800,000

Religious affiliation	1994 population
Eastern Orthodox	5,580,000
Anglican	2,330,000
other Christian	11,220,000
Christian (unaffiliated)	43,580,000
nonreligious	23,120,000
Jewish	5,560,000
Muslim	5,060,000
New-Religionist	940,000
Hindu	900,000
atheist	860,000
Baha'i	300,000
Buddhist	230,000
Sikh	190,000
other	1,230,000
Uruguay	
Roman Catholic	2,090,000
other	1,080,000
Uzbekistan	
Muslim (mostly Sunnī)	19,700,000
Russian Orthodox	2,010,000
other (mostly nonreligious)	670,000
Vanuatu	
Presbyterian	59,000
Roman Catholic	24,000
Anglican	23,000
other	58,000
Venezuela	
Roman Catholic	19,500,000
other	1,670,000
Vietnam	
Buddhist	48,220,000
Roman Catholic	6,110,000
New-Religionist	
Cao Dai	2,550,000
Hoa Hao	1,530,000
other	13,940,000
Virgin Islands (U.S.)	
Protestant	48,000
Roman Catholic	35,000
other	21,000
West Bank	
Muslim (mostly Sunnī)	1,010,000
Jewish[6]	110,000
Christian and other	100,000
Western Sahara	
Sunnī Muslim	208,000
Western Samoa	
Congregational	78,000
Roman Catholic	36,000
other	50,000
Yemen	
Muslim	12,940,000
other	20,000
Yugoslavia	
Serbian Orthodox	6,830,000
Sunnī Muslim	2,000,000
Roman Catholic	420,000
Protestant	110,000
other	1,160,000
Zaire	
Roman Catholic	21,190,000
Protestant	12,690,000
African Christian	7,490,000
traditional beliefs	1,490,000
Muslim	610,000
other	310,000
Zambia	
Christian[1]	6,630,000
traditional beliefs	2,490,000
other	90,000
Zimbabwe	
Christian[1]	6,360,000
traditional beliefs	4,440,000
other	170,000

[1]Includes affiliated and nominal Christians. [2]Official 1986 census figure is 5.9 percent. [3]Includes the Golan Heights and East Jerusalem; excludes the West Bank and Gaza Strip. [4]Many Japanese practice both Shintoism and Buddhism. [5]Excludes the former black independent states of Bophuthatswana, Ciskei, Transkei, and Venda, in which there are about 5,800,000 Christians and 2,100,000 practicers of traditional beliefs. [6]Excludes East Jerusalem.

Vital statistics, marriage, family

This table provides some of the basic measures of the factors that influence the size, direction, and rates of population change within a country. The accuracy of these data depends on the effectiveness of each respective national system for registering vital and civil events (birth, death, marriage, etc.) and on the sophistication of the analysis that can be brought to bear upon the data so compiled.

Data on birth rates, for example, depend not only on the completeness of registration of births in a particular country but also on the conditions under which those data are collected: Do all births take place in a hospital? Are the births reported comparably in all parts of the country? Are the records of the births tabulated at a central location in a timely way with an effort to eliminate inconsistent reporting of birth events, perinatal mortality, etc.? Similar difficulties attach to death rates but with the added need to identify "cause of death." Even in a developed country such identifications are often left to nonmedical personnel, and in a developing country with, say, only one physician for every 10,000 population, there will be too few physicians to perform autopsies to assess accurately the cause of death after the fact and also too few to provide ongoing care at a level where records would permit inference about cause of death based on prior condition or diagnosis.

Calculating natural increase, which at its most basic is simply the difference between the birth and death rates, may be affected by the differing degrees of completeness of birth and death registration for a given country. The total fertility rate may be understood as the average number of children that would be borne per woman if all childbearing women lived to the end of their childbearing years and bore children at each age at the average rate for that age. Calculating a meaningful fertility rate requires analysis of changing age structure of the female population over time, changing mortality rates among mothers and their infants, and changing medical practice at births, each improvement of natural survivorship or medical support leading to greater numbers of live-born children and greater numbers of children who survive their first year (the basis for measurement of infant mortality, another basic indicator of demographic conditions and trends within a population).

As indicated above, data for causes of death are not only particularly difficult to obtain, since many countries are not well equipped to collect the data, but also difficult to assess, as their accuracy may be suspect and their meaning may be subject to varying interpretation. Take the case of a citizen of a less developed country who dies of what is clearly a lung infection: Was the death complicated by chronic malnutrition, itself complicated by a parasitic infestation, these last two together so weakening the subject that he died of an infection that he might have survived had his general health been better? Similarly, in a developed country: Someone may die from what is identified in an autopsy as a cerebrovascular accident, but if that accident occurred in a vascular system that was weakened by diabetes, what was the actual cause of death? Statistics on causes of death seek to identify the "underlying" cause (that which sets the final train of events leading to death in motion) but often must settle for the most proximate cause or symptom. Even this kind of analysis may be misleading for those charged with interpreting the data with a view to ordering health-care priorities for a particular country. The eight groups of causes of death utilized here include most, but not all, of the detailed

Vital statistics, marriage, family

country	vital rates						causes of death (rate per 100,000 population)								
	year	birth rate per 1,000 population	death rate per 1,000 population	infant mortality rate per 1,000 live births	rate of natural increase per 1,000 population	total fertility rate	year	infectious and parasitic diseases	malignant neoplasms (cancers)	endocrine and metabolic disorders	diseases of the nervous system	diseases of the circulatory system	diseases of the respiratory system	diseases of the digestive system	accidents, poisoning, and violence
Afghanistan	1993	51.0	22.0	161.0	29.0	6.7		...	...	...	...	...	...	...	...
Albania	1990	25.2	5.6	28.2[2]	19.6	2.9[2]		...	...	...	...	...	...	...	...
Algeria	1992	30.4	5.3	54.0[3]	25.1	4.0[3]		...	...	...	...	...	...	...	...
American Samoa	1990	39.3	5.1	13.5	34.2	5.2	1990	16.4[5]	46.8	16.4[6]	...	131.1[7]	65.6[8]	...	58.5
Andorra	1992	12.1	3.6	6.4[9]	8.7	1.7[3]									
Angola	1990–95	51.3	19.2	127.0	32.1	7.2		...	...	...	...	...	...	...	...
Antigua and Barbuda	1993	17.5	5.5	19.2	12.0	1.7	1988	14.0	44.5	25.4	7.6	237.5	44.5	15.2	5.1
Argentina	1992	20.0	9.0	34.0	11.0	2.8	1990	26.4	142.5	25.7	9.3	358.1	50.8	34.6	51.5
Armenia	1992	21.6	6.5	17.9	15.1	2.6[12]	1990	13.8	103.9	16.9	4.1	323.5	53.2	22.3	58.8
Aruba	1992	18.1	5.8	9.6[12]	12.3	1.8[13]	1991	9.8	124.9	47.7	4.2	189.5	30.9	23.9	11.2
Australia	1993	14.7	6.9	6.1	7.8	1.9	1992	5.0	179.9	13.5	14.9	307.8	56.8	22.0	40.3
Austria	1993	11.8	10.3	7.4[14]	1.5	1.6[14]	1992	3.3	246.1	24.2	15.1	555.3	49.8	53.4	64.6
Azerbaijan	1994	26.0	6.0	25.0	20.0	2.7	1989	42.1	72.1	8.6	9.7	292.4	88.9	25.6	42.1
Bahamas, The	1992	25.6	5.0	23.8[2]	20.6	2.1	1990	18.0	80.4	72.2	11.0	126.3	52.2	29.0	40.8
Bahrain	1992	29.8	4.8	25.1	25.0	3.9	1991	2.8	32.3	16.8	3.8	86.6	27.7	10.2	19.0
Bangladesh	1993	35.4	11.9	109.2	23.5	4.6		...	...	...	...	...	...	...	...
Barbados	1992	16.2	9.1	9.1	7.1	1.8	1988	19.8	160.7	79.8	15.2	338.9	47.9	36.6	44.0
Belarus	1994	12.0	11.0	12.0	1.0	1.7	1990	7.1	171.8	7.1[16]	9.7	545.8	73.6	22.2	100.5
Belgium	1992	11.5	10.6	8.9	0.9	1.6[17]	1989	10.6	274.6	23.0	39.2	412.8	93.1	40.9	64.7
Belize	1993	35.7	6.1	36.5	29.6	4.5	1990	...	52.4	37.0[6]	...	164.0	57.1	32.8	92.6[18]
Benin	1992	44.0	15.0	119.0[2]	29.0	7.0[2]		...	...	...	...	...	...	...	...
Bermuda	1990	15.0	7.5	7.8	7.5	1.8[12]	1990	...	181.5	...	...	344.4	25.2	...	38.6
Bhutan	1993	39.6	16.3	123.3	23.3	5.5		...	...	...	...	...	...	...	...
Bolivia	1993	32.8	8.6	75.1[17]	24.2	4.3	1989	9.9	122.6[19]	12.6	11.9	344.1	29.0	29.2	47.1
Bosnia and Herzegovina	1994	14.0	7.0	15.2	7.0	1.6									
Botswana	1990–95	38.4	9.3	60.0	29.1	5.1		...	...	...	...	...	...	...	...
Brazil	1991	25.3	6.6	60.0[21]	18.7	2.8[14]	1989[22]	41	72	22	9	210	61	30	94
Brunei	1992	27.2	3.3	9.6	23.9	3.5	1986	5.3	27.0	...	...	80.0	23.4	...	39.8
Bulgaria	1993	10.0	12.9	16.9	−2.9	1.6[14]	1992	7.0	181.4	22.3	5.7	768.1	70.7	37.6	68.5
Burkina Faso	1990–95	46.7	17.6	118.0	29.1	6.5		...	...	...	...	...	...	...	...
Burundi	1991	47.0	15.0	111.0	32.0	6.9		...	...	...	...	...	...	...	...
Cambodia	1993	40.0	15.0	112.0	25.0	4.6		...	...	...	...	...	...	...	...
Cameroon	1990–95	40.7	12.2	63.0	28.5	5.7		...	...	...	...	...	...	...	...
Canada	1991	15.2	7.2	6.8	8.0	1.7[4]	1991	5.3	197.7	24.3	18.5	278.6	61.6	26.8	48.5
Cape Verde	1992	48.0	10.0	61.0	38.0	5.3[17]	1980	153.7	43.8	20.6	16.5	135.8	72.3	27.7	30.1
Central African Republic	1988	41.6	16.7	219.0[2]	24.9	6.1		...	...	...	...	...	...	...	...
Chad	1990–95	43.7	18.0	122.0	25.7	5.9		...	...	...	...	...	...	...	...
Chile	1991	21.3	5.6	14.6	15.7	2.6[15]	1989	21.1	105.7	11.1	8.7	157.8	64.5	45.8	74.7
China	1992	18.2	6.6	26.0[3]	11.6	2.3[2]	1990[23]	18.4	121.5	8.1[16]	4.4	203.6	121.2	27.3	52.5
Colombia	1990–95	25.8	5.9	37.0	19.9	2.9	1990[22]	26	83	17	10	193	53	23	159
Comoros	1993	46.7	11.3	81.8	35.4	6.9		...	...	...	...	...	...	...	...
Congo	1990–95	44.7	14.7	82.0	30.0	6.3		...	...	...	...	...	...	...	...
Costa Rica	1993	26.1	3.6	11.6	22.5	3.1	1991	10.5	74.6	13.6	8.2	111.3	38.5	19.9	39.7
Côte d'Ivoire	1990–95	50.0	13.2	87.0	36.8	7.4[2]		...	...	...	...	...	...	...	...
Croatia	1992	9.8	10.8	11.6	−1.0	1.7[2]	1991	10.8	226.1[19]	14.9[16]	6.9	571.8	29.5	53.2	91.8
Cuba	1990–95	17.4	6.7	9.4[21]	10.7	1.9	1990	9.4	128.7	23.3	10.6	294.7	58.0	26.3	79.9
Cyprus	1992	20.0	8.9	11.0	11.1	2.4[4]									
Czech Republic	1993	11.7	11.5	8.5	0.2	1.9[15]	1992	3.6	270.0	14.9	8.5	649.8	49.4	43.0	84.2
Denmark	1993	13.0	12.1	6.5[14]	0.9	1.8	1992	9.2	292.2	21.1	13.0	505.2	89.2	42.8	71.9
Djibouti	1990–95	46.5	16.5	112.0	30.0	6.6		...							
Dominica	1993	20.8	5.1	18.4[15]	15.7	2.5[14]	1990	37.5	116.6	51.4	9.7	273.5	43.0	20.8	18.0
Dominican Republic	1993	25.7	6.4	53.6	19.3	2.9	1985	51.4	27.4	12.3	8.6	100.3	35.4	22.3	33.7
Ecuador	1993	26.5	5.8	36.9	20.7	3.2	1992	52.0	50.0	11.8[6]	1.9[26]	93.1	40.6	13.2	66.7
Egypt	1992	30.4	6.3	59.0	24.1	4.2	1987	98.9	22.0	9.1	13.6	314.4	140.7	45.8	39.1
El Salvador	1994	33.0	6.0	41.0	27.0	3.8	1990[22]	52	43	17	12	120	49	38	137

causes classified by the World Health Organization and would not, thus, aggregate to the country's crude death rate for the same year. Among the lesser causes excluded by the present classification are: benign neoplasms; nutritional disorders; anemias; mental disorders; kidney and genitourinary diseases not classifiable under the main groups; maternal deaths (for which data *are* provided, however, in the "Health services" table); diseases of the skin and musculoskeletal systems; congenital and perinatal conditions; and general senility and other ill-defined (ill-diagnosed) conditions, a kind of "other" category.

Expectation of life is probably the most accurate single measure of the quality of life in a given society. It summarizes in a single number all of the natural and social stresses that operate upon individuals in that society. The number may range from as few as 40 years of life in the least developed countries to as much as 80 years for women in the most developed nations. The lost potential in the years separating those two numbers is prodigious, regardless of how the loss arises—wars and civil violence, poor public health services, or poor individual health practice in matters of nutrition, exercise, stress management, and so on.

Data on marriages and marriage rates probably are less meaningful in terms of international comparisons than some of the measures mentioned above because the number, timing, and kinds of social relationships that substitute for marriage depend on many kinds of social variables—income, degree of social control, heterogeneity of the society (race, class, language communities), or level of development of civil administration (if one must travel for a day or more to obtain a legal civil ceremony, one may forgo it). Nevertheless, the data for a single country say specific things about local practice in terms of the age at which a man or woman typically marries, and the overall rate will at least define the number of legal civil marriages, though it cannot say anything about other, less formal arrangements (here the figure for the legitimacy rate for children in the next section may identify some of the societies in which economics or social constraints may operate to limit the number of marriages that are actually confirmed on civil registers). The available data usually include both first marriages and remarriages after annulment, divorce, widowhood, or the like.

The data for families provide information about the average size of a family unit (individuals related by blood or civil register) and the average number of children under a specified age (set here at 15 to provide a consistent measure of social minority internationally, though legal minority depends on the laws of each country). When well-defined family data are not collected as part of a country's national census or vital statistics surveys, data for households are substituted on the assumption that most households worldwide represent families in some conventional sense. In the older countries of Europe and North America, increasing numbers of households are composed of unrelated individuals (unmarried heterosexual couples, aged [or younger] groups sharing limited [often fixed] incomes for reasons of economy, or homosexual couples); such arrangements are not yet so common in the rest of the world that they represent great numbers overall. Very few census programs, even in developed countries, make adequate provision for distinguishing these households.

expectation of life at birth (latest year)		nuptiality, family, and family planning														country
		marriages			age at marriage (latest)						families (F), households (H) (latest)					
		year	total number	rate per 1,000 population	groom (percent)			bride (percent)			families (households)		children		induced abortions	
male	female				19 and under	20–29	30 and over	19 and under	20–29	30 and over	total ('000)	size	number under age 15	percent legiti-mate	number	ratio per 100 live births	
44.0	43.0	...	...	...	...	...	...	...	...	...	H 2,110	H 6.2	H 2.8[1]	...	...	...	Afghanistan
69.3	75.4	1990	28,992	8.9	1.3	78.8	19.9	21.0	74.0	5.0	F 675	F 4.7	F 1.6	...	...	...	Albania
66.3	68.4	1988	139,930	5.9	0.7[4]	67.1[4]	32.2[4]	29.8[4]	61.4[4]	8.8[4]	H 3,322	H 0.9	H 3.0	...	...	...	Algeria
69.0	74.0	1990	370	7.8	...	...	...	...	...	...	H 7	H 7.0	H 2.7	72.0	...	...	American Samoa
75.3	81.3	1992	135	2.2	...	...	...	...	...	...	...	...	...	...	...	...	Andorra
44.9	48.1	...	...	...	...	...	...	...	...	...	...	H 4.8	...	...	...	...	Angola
70.8	74.9	1988	382	4.9	1.0[10]	37.4[11]	61.6	3.7[10]	52.4[11]	43.9	H 20	H 3.5	H 1.2	23.4	...	...	Antigua and Barbuda
67.0	74.0	1983	177,010	6.0	5.6	71.5	22.9	26.0	58.6	15.4	H 10,097	H 3.2	H 1.0	67.5	...	...	Argentina
67.4	73.3	1989	27,267	7.8	2.7	77.0	20.3	34.0	54.2	11.8	H 559	H 4.7	H 1.8	92.1	26,141	34.7	Armenia
71.1	77.1	1992	566	7.9	...	...	...	...	...	...	H 19	H 3.6	...	63.2	...	...	Aruba
75.0	80.9	1991	113,869	6.6	1.1	58.0	40.9	5.4	65.1	29.5	H 5,853	H 3.0	H 0.6	77.0	...	...	Australia
72.9	79.4	1991	44,106	5.6	1.7	60.9	37.4	6.8	68.1	25.1	H 3,021	H 2.6	H 0.5	75.2	...	...	Austria
67.0	75.0	1989	71,874	10.4	1.2	80.4	18.4	24.8	63.9	11.3	H 1,381	H 4.8	H 1.7	97.5	42,134	23.2	Azerbaijan
68.0	75.3	1992	2,407	9.1	1.3[15]	53.8[15]	44.9[15]	5.3[15]	61.1[15]	33.6[15]	H 68	H 3.8	...	41.2	...	...	Bahamas, The
68.7	72.9	1990	2,942	5.8	1.8	69.8	28.4	26.2	59.9	13.9	H 67	H 6.5	H 2.2	...	...	...	Bahrain
55.0	54.4	1990	1,130,000	10.8	...	...	...	...	...	...	H 19,700	H 5.3	...	...	...	...	Bangladesh
72.9	77.9	1989	2,047	8.0	0.2	43.2	56.6	1.7	58.7	39.6	H 67	H 3.7	H 1.5	26.9	...	...	Barbados
66.0	76.0	1989	97,929	9.6	4.1	74.7	21.2	26.2	55.6	18.2	H 2,796	H 3.2	H 0.8	91.0	140,900	86.3	Belarus
72.4	79.1	1992	58,156	5.8	1.4[13]	74.5[13]	24.1[13]	9.3[13]	73.6[13]	17.7[13]	F 3,613	F 2.7	F 0.5	90.8	...	...	Belgium
67.0	72.0	1991	1,047	5.4	7.8	58.1	34.1	27.4	50.6	22.0	H 38	H 4.9	H 2.2	42.5	822	12.1	Belize
49.0	52.0	1980–85	...	12.8	...	...	...	...	...	...	...	H 5.4	...	...	...	...	Benin
73.0	79.0	1990	907	15.2	0.2	37.4	62.4	1.5	49.4	49.1	H 22	H 2.6	H 0.5	63.9	92	11.0	Bermuda
50.7	49.6	...	...	...	...	...	...	...	...	...	...	H 5.4	...	...	...	...	Bhutan
60.3	65.3	1980	26,990	4.8	8.3	75.1	16.6	26.1	55.4	18.5	H 1,655	H 3.8	H 1.6	80.9	...	...	Bolivia
66.0	76.0	1990	31,449	7.0	2.3[12]	76.0[12]	21.7[12]	28.5[12]	59.3[12]	12.2[12]	H 1,203	H 3.6	H 1.1[20]	...	...	...	Bosnia and Herzegovina
58.0	64.0	1986	1,638	1.5	...	33.0	67.0	5.0	69.2	25.8	H 125	H 5.7	H 2.0	28.8	17	0.1	Botswana
63.5	69.1	1990	777,460	5.2	7.5	72.6	19.9	33.3	55.2	11.5	F 31,888	F 4.2	...	...	...	...	Brazil
69.3	72.7	1992	1,795	6.7	5.6[4]	72.5[4]	21.9[4]	12.5[4]	58.9[4]	28.6[4]	H 45	H 5.8	H 2.0	99.6	...	...	Brunei
68.0	74.7	1991	48,820	5.3	5.9[15]	76.6[15]	17.5[15]	30.0[16]	51.8[15]	10.2[15]	F 2,627	F 3.3	F 0.7	88.0	144,644	137.5	Bulgaria
46.6	49.9	...	...	...	...	...	...	...	...	...	...	H 6.2	...	...	...	...	Burkina Faso
50.0	54.0	...	...	...	...	...	...	...	...	...	...	H 4.6	...	...	...	...	Burundi
49.0	52.0	...	...	...	...	...	...	...	...	...	...	H 5.6	...	...	...	...	Cambodia
54.5	57.5	...	...	...	...	...	...	...	...	...	...	H 5.2	...	...	...	...	Cameroon
74.0	80.6	1990	187,737	7.1	1.2	57.5	41.3	5.0	64.1	30.9	H 10,018	H 2.7	H 0.6	83.8	71,092	17.3	Canada
60.0	64.0	1988	1,040	3.2	2.3	62.4	35.3	17.0	61.1	21.9	F 59	F 5.1	...	55.2	...	...	Cape Verde
48.0	53.0	...	...	...	...	...	...	...	...	...	...	H 4.7	...	...	...	...	Central African Republic
45.9	49.1	...	...	...	...	...	...	...	...	...	...	H 3.0	...	...	...	...	Chad
68.5	75.6	1990	98,702	7.5	4.9	72.9	22.2	20.3	64.6	15.1	H 3,261	H 4.1	H 1.2	65.7	29	—	Chile
68.6	71.8	1992	9,545,047	8.2	...	...	...	...	...	...	H 278.6[24]	H 4.1	H 1.1	...	10,500,000	47.7	China
66.4	72.3	1980	102,448	3.8	6.4	69.6	24.0	31.5	56.5	12.0	F 4,772	F 5.4	F 2.5	75.2	...	...	Colombia
55.2	59.5	...	...	...	...	...	...	...	...	...	...	H 5.6	...	...	...	...	Comoros
49.1	54.0	...	...	...	...	...	...	...	...	...	H 326	H 4.7	H 2.0	...	...	...	Congo
75.6	79.5	1990	22,703	7.6	7.5	65.6	26.9	27.8	54.6	17.6	H 681.6	H 4.5	H 1.6	62.8	...	...	Costa Rica
52.8	56.2	...	...	...	...	...	...	...	...	...	...	H 5.4	...	...	...	...	Côte d'Ivoire
66.8	74.8	1992	22,169	4.6	1.2[12]	72.4[12]	26.4[12]	19.5[12]	64.8[12]	15.7[12]	H 1,544	H 3.1	H 0.6	...	...	...	Croatia
73.9	77.6	1991	161,160	15	8.3[12]	57.0[12]	34.7[12]	24.3[12]	49.9[12]	25.8[12]	F 2,860	F 3.7	H 1.0	...	147,530	79.0	Cuba
74.1	78.6	1991	7,178	9.5	0.8[12]	70.5[12]	28.7[12]	17.8[12]	66.0[12]	16.2[12]	H 180	H 3.5	H 1.1	99.8	...	...	Cyprus
68.5	76.1	1991	71,973	6.2	9.1	67.0	23.8	33.2	50.4	16.3	H 3,981	H 2.7	H 0.5	90.3	126,055	96.2	Czech Republic
72.4	77.8	1992	32,188	6.2	0.4	43.1	56.5	2.1	55.6	42.3	F 2,833	F 1.8	F 0.3	53.5	19,729	30.7	Denmark
47.4	50.6	...	...	...	...	...	...	...	...	...	...	H 5.6	...	96.8	...	...	Djibouti
73.9	79.7	1990	228	3.3	—	41.2	58.8	3.1	58.3	38.6	H 18	H 4.3	H 2.2	...	...	...	Dominica
65.9	70.2	1987	15,642	2.3	8.0[25]	63.0[25]	29.0[25]	29.7[25]	51.0[25]	19.3[25]	H 753	H 5.1	H 2.5	32.8	562	0.5	Dominican Republic
67.1	72.3	1992	68,337	6.4	12.2[12]	64.5[12]	23.3[12]	33.7[12]	52.2[12]	14.1[12]	...	H 4.1	...	67.9	...	...	Ecuador
65.0	60.3	1990	458,000	8.3	5.9[4]	61.8[4]	32.3[4]	40.4[4]	49.2[4]	10.4[4]	H 9,733	H 4.9	H 2.1	100.0	...	...	Egypt
63.0	68.0	1989	23,167	4.4	6.2	57.0	36.8	22.1	52.9	25.0	H 1,046	H 4.9	H 2.4	32.0	...	...	El Salvador

Vital statistics, marriage, family (continued)

country	vital rates						causes of death (rate per 100,000 population)								
	year	birth rate per 1,000 population	death rate per 1,000 population	infant mortality rate per 1,000 live births	rate of natural increase per 1,000 population	total fertility rate	year	infectious and parasitic diseases	malignant neoplasms (cancers)	endocrine and metabolic disorders	diseases of the nervous system	diseases of the circulatory system	diseases of the respiratory system	diseases of the digestive system	accidents, poisoning, and violence
Equatorial Guinea	1993	41.1	15.1	117.0[17]	26.0	5.3	...	...	...	...	...	...	...	...	...
Eritrea[27]	...														
Estonia	1993	10.2	14.0	15.8[14]	–3.8	1.8[14]	1990	8.1	194.2	5.0[6]	1.3[26]	746.7	24.6	11.0	129.8
Ethiopia[27]	1990–95	49.1	18.5	122.0	30.6	7.0	...	...	...	...	...	...	...	...	...
Faeroe Islands	1992	16.8	8.4	8.5[2]	8.4	2.7[15]	1992	4.3	191.3	14.9[6]	—	352.8	59.5	14.9	57.4
Fiji	1993	24.8	5.0	27.0[13]	19.8	3.1[15]	1987	18.2	35.5	27.3[6]	2.4[26]	153.4	31.7	15.5	32.2
Finland	1992	13.2	9.8	5.9[2]	3.4	1.9	1992	6.7	198.0	12.4	17.4	482.3	72.2	38.7	90.0
France	1992	12.9	9.1	6.7	3.8	1.8[2]	1991	12.1	244.2	25.9	19.5	307.9	63.1	46.7	82.7
French Guiana	1990	31.5	5.2	15.8	26.3	3.7[2]	1989	61.7	58.1	16.3	10.9	114.3	20.9	13.6	98.0
French Polynesia	1990	27.4	4.6	10.4	22.8	3.9	1985–89	25.0	78.0	12.0	10.0	121.0	29.0	11.0	89.0
Gabon	1990–95	42.6	15.9	94.0	26.7	5.3	...	...	...	...	...	...	...	...	...
Gambia, The	1990–95	44.1	19.4	132.0	24.7	6.1	...	...	...	...	...	...	...	...	...
Gaza Strip	1994	56.0	6.0	43.0	50.0	7.7									
Georgia	1994	17.0	9.0	16.0	8.0	2.2	1989	13.5	98.6	12.0	4.1	553.2	51.4	32.1	58.2
Germany	1991	10.4	11.4	6.8[14]	–0.1	1.3[21]	1991	6.9	263.2	29.2	16.4	569.8	67.3	53.8	58.4
Ghana	1990–95	41.7	11.7	81.0	30.0	6.0	...	...	...	...	...	...	...	...	...
Gibraltar	1991	20.2	9.1	5.7	11.1	2.8	1987	17.0	203.9	—	—	601.4	34.0	23.8	3.4
Greece	1993	10.0	9.4	8.5	0.6	1.5[17]	1991	5.5	195.5	13.1	8.3	484.8	52.1	24.4	41.0
Greenland	1993	30.8	6.5	12.7	24.4	2.9[14]	1992	14.5	152.0	3.6[6]	1.8[26]	197.3	45.2	10.9	255.2
Grenada	1989	33.0	8.3	29.0[2]	24.7	3.0[2]	1984	13.5	90.5	62.9	11.4	290.3	54.1	39.5	47.9
Guadeloupe	1992	17.8	5.6	10.4	12.2	2.2[17]	1990	20.8[13]	121.2	23.0[13]	12.3[13]	186.8	30.5	29.7	72.9
Guam	1994	30.0	4.0	9.8	26.0	3.3	1992	4.9	65.2	29.5[6]	9.8	123.4	14.7[31]	11.2	68.7
Guatemala	1993	36.2	7.7	55.6	28.5	4.9	1984	211.5	29.8	29.6	9.0	57.2	145.7	21.7	52.0
Guernsey	1993	10.7	9.5	1.3[15]	1.2	1.6[12]	1990	8.4	314.3	11.8	15.1	430.3	112.6	30.3	20.2
Guinea	1994	46.0	21.0	147.0	25.0	6.0	...	...	...	...	...	...	...	...	...
Guinea-Bissau	1994	43.0	21.0	140.0	22.0	5.8	...	...	...	...	...	...	...	...	...
Guyana	1994	20.0	7.0	49.0	13.0	2.6[14]	1984	19.3	37.1	33.3	11.6	202.5	39.8	74.0	56.5
Haiti	1994	40.0	19.0	109.0	21.0	4.7[14]									
Honduras	1993	35.8	6.4	47.2	29.4	4.9	1983	46.6	12.4	5.3	7.8	48.4	26.3	16.7	42.2
Hong Kong	1993	12.0	5.1	4.7	6.9	1.2[15]	1992	15.9	157.2	9.5	4.5	141.5	93.9	22.6	29.2
Hungary	1993	11.3	14.4	14.0	–3.1	1.8[14]	1992	9.1	313.0	19.5	11.8	738.6	67.3	105.1	126.8
Iceland	1992	17.6	6.6	4.8	11.0	2.2	1992	5.4	164.4	4.2	18.8	290.4	91.2	17.2	40.6
India	1991	29.3	9.8	88.0[17]	19.5	3.9[14]	...	...	...	...	...	...	...	...	...
Indonesia	1991	32.2	11.7	90.0	20.5	3.7	...	...	...	...	...	...	...	...	...
Iran	1993	43.0	8.1	62.1	34.9	6.1[14]	...	...	...	...	...	...	...	...	...
Iraq	1992	36.5	6.5	56.3	30.0	5.8	...	...	...	...	...	...	...	...	...
Ireland	1992	14.6	8.7	9.1[2]	5.9	2.1[17]	1991	5.2	206.0	17.1	17.1	403.2	124.1	24.1	38.8
Isle of Man	1993	12.3	14.5	5.7	–2.2	1.8[12]	1993	8.6	337.8	4.3[6]	—	701.6	258.8	18.7	50.3
Israel	1993	21.3	6.3	7.8	15.0	2.9[15]	1990	12.8	125.6	21.1	7.9	249.7	44.4	17.9	38.2
Italy	1992	9.9	9.6	8.3	0.3	1.4[17]	1990	3.5	251.5	39.1	16.5	407.1	61.8	50.2	50.6
Jamaica	1992	23.9	5.4	27.0[12]	18.5	2.6	1985	30.0	91.4	29.1	13.6	229.6	36.8	21.4	17.4
Japan	1993	9.6	7.0	4.5[14]	2.6	1.5[14]	1992	10.8	187.8	9.9	5.5	251.4	74.4	44.4	47.7
Jersey	1991	12.5	9.9	6.0[12]	2.6	1.3[12]	...	...	...	...	...	...	...	...	...
Jordan	1992	37.8	5.2	33.8	32.6	5.9									
Kazakhstan	1994	20.0	8.0	27.0	12.0	2.5	1990	23.0	135.7	6.4	6.1	344.3	73.6	24.8	103.9
Kenya	1990–95	43.7	10.3	66.0	33.4	6.3	...	...	...	...	...	...	...	...	...
Kiribati	1993	32.0	12.3	98.4	19.7	3.8	...	...	...	...	...	...	...	...	...
Korea, North	1993	23.0	5.0	24.0	18.0	2.4	1986	19.4	69.0	3.0[16]	6.5	224.9	46.7	51.6	38.2
Korea, South	1993	15.0	6.0	15.0	11.0	1.6	1991[22]	15	111	14[16]	7	166	23	45	90
Kuwait	1992	39.9	2.4	16.4	37.5	5.6	1989	6.0	28.7	7.4	7.2	81.4	13.7	5.2	29.4
Kyrgyzstan	1994	29.0	7.0	52.0	22.0	3.6	1990	27.9	76.4	4.0	6.7	267.9	123.9	27.7	92.8
Laos	1994	44.0	16.0	107	28.0	6.3	...	...	...	...	...	...	...	...	...
Latvia	1992	12.0	13.5	17.4	–1.5	2.0[12]	1990	11.3	205.8	10.1	6.9	759.9	44.2	34.7	139.6
Lebanon	1992	25.2	4.5	28.0	20.7	2.9	...	...	...	...	...	...	...	...	...
Lesotho	1990–95	34.4	9.7	79.0	24.7	4.7	...								
Liberia	1990–95	47.3	14.2	126.0	33.1	6.8	...	...	...	...	...	...	...	...	...
Libya	1990–95	41.9	8.0	68	33.8	6.4	...	...	...	...	...	...	...	...	...
Liechtenstein	1992	12.6	6.0	—	6.6	...	1992	6.7	144.0	...	...	160.7	33.5	13.4	20.1
Lithuania	1992	14.3	11.0	16.5	3.3	2.0[12]	1990	9.1	187.5	7.0	7.5	620.1	49.0	23.3	120.2
Luxembourg	1993	13.4	9.9	6.0	3.5	1.7	1992	7.4	255.4	24.2	15.5	429.0	65.9	48.3	66.2
Macau	1992	17.9	3.9	7.3	14.0	1.6[2]	1992	10.0	75.9	7.4	2.9	136.0	53.0	20.2	23.6
Macedonia	1994	16.0	7.0	24.5	9.0	1.9	1989	20.3	102.4[19]	13.3	5.1	346.2	49.8	18.2	34.5
Madagascar	1990–95	45.5	12.7	110.0	32.8	6.6	...	...	...	...	...	...	...	...	...
Malawi	1990–95	54.5	21.5	142.0	33.0	7.6	1986[33]	711	27	25	60	50	265	34	78
Malaysia	1991	27.0	5.0	13.0	22.0	3.6[3]	1989[34]	62	60	11	7[16]	117	14	11	67
Maldives	1993	38.0	8.0	53.0	30.0	6.1	1988	31.3	—	—	—	170.1	66.2	—	9.9
Mali	1993	51.7	20.8	108.0	30.9	7.3	...	...	...	...	...	...	...	...	...
Malta	1993	14.0	7.3	10.3[14]	6.7	2.1[14]	1992	5.5	176.8	41.7	12.4	363.0	68.5	22.9	36.2
Marshall Islands	1991	47.0	8.0	30.3	39.0	7.1	1991	102.0	29.1	—	—	74.9	52.0	41.6	35.4
Martinique	1993	15.8	6.0	6.2[14]	9.8	1.9	1990	22.0	135.5	30.7	10.7[25]	208.0	34.2	31.3	54.8
Mauritania	1994	46.0	18.0	117.0	28.0	6.5	...	...	...	...	...	...	...	...	...
Mauritius	1991	20.7	6.6	23.0	14.1	2.2	1992	15.3	62.5	36.1	5.0	279.5	67.0	33.1	45.5
Mayotte	1991	43.7	6.0	38.0	37.7	6.8[12]	...	...	...	...	...	...	...	...	...
Mexico	1992	31.7	4.6	27.1	27.1	3.7[15]	1991	34.9	48.6	40.7	6.8	99.3	47.1	39.7	68.6
Micronesia	1985–89	37.9	8.0	52.2	29.9	5.6	1984	20.4	27.1	6.8	4.5	53.2	47.5	5.7	23.8
Moldova	1994	16.0	10.0	19.0	6.0	2.1	1989	12.4	131.6	8.3	8.2	452.2	64.2	85.4	105.3
Monaco	1988	22.9	18.5	9.0[12]	4.4	1.2[12]	...	...	...	...	...	...	...	...	...
Mongolia	1994	34.0	7.7	48	26.3	4.5	...	...	...	...	...	...	...	...	...
Morocco	1990–95	32.3	8.3	68.0	24.0	4.4	...	...	...	...	...	...	...	...	...
Mozambique	1990–95	45.1	18.2	147.0	26.9	6.5	...								
Myanmar (Burma)	1994	33.0	11.0	84.0	22.0	4.2	...	...	...	...	...	...	...	...	...
Namibia	1990–95	42.5	10.7	70.0	31.8	6.0	...	...	...	...	...	...	...	...	...
Nauru	1989	21.0	5.0	41.0	16.0	2.5	1976–81[35]	33.0	38.0	24.0	13.0	89.0	16.0	53.0	116.0
Nepal	1993	38.0	13.0	96.0	25.0	5.4	...	...	...	...	...	...	...	...	...
Netherlands, The	1993	12.8	9.0	6.3	3.8	1.6[14]	1991	6.0	236.5	29.6	18.3	344.3	70.9	31.4	34.5

male	female	year	total number	rate per 1,000 population	groom 19 and under	groom 20–29	groom 30 and over	bride 19 and under	bride 20–29	bride 30 and over	families total ('000)	size	children number under age 15	percent legitimate	abortions number	ratio per 100 live births	country
49.6	53.8	...	...	...	...	...	...	...	...	...		H 4.5	...	...	...	...	Equatorial Guinea
...	...																Eritrea[27]
65.0	75.0	1990	11,774	8.0	7.1	61.1	31.8	23.2	50.1	26.7	H 427	H 3.1	H 0.8	66.1	21,404	95.9	Estonia
45.4	48.7	...	...									H 4.5					Ethiopia[27]
72.8	79.6	1990	203	4.3	1.0[28]	68.8[28]	30.2[28]	8.8[28]	70.7[28]	20.5[28]	F 14	F 3.0	F 0.9	57.5	26	3.3	Faeroe Islands
61.0	65.0	1987	6,039	8.4	6.6	68.7	24.7	31.0	55.8	13.2	F 97	F 6.0	F 2.5	82.7	...	...	Fiji
71.3	79.3	1992	20,093	4.6	1.3[12]	61.1[12]	37.6[12]	5.0[12]	68.0[12]	27.0[12]	H 2,200	H 2.3	H 0.4	72.6	12,232	18.7	Finland
72.9	81.1	1992	269,940	4.7	0.4[10]	61.7[10]	37.9[10]	3.3[10]	69.5[10]	27.2[10]	H 20,899	H 2.7	H 1.0	68.1	161,646	21.2	France
63.4	69.7	1990	465	4.1	...	...	...	...	...	...	H 33	H 3.4	H 1.2	20.3	388	16.8	French Guiana
66.1	71.3	1990	987	4.9	11.3[28,29]	75.8[28,29]	12.9[28,29]	41.5[28,29]	52.5[28,29]	6.0[28,29]	H 40	H 4.7	H 1.7	41.5	...	...	French Polynesia
51.9	55.2	...	...								H 136	H 4.0			...	...	Gabon
43.4	46.6	...										H 8.3			...	...	Gambia, The
65.0	67.0	...															Gaza Strip
69.0	76.0	1989	38,288	7.0	5.7	66.2	28.1	27.8	55.7	16.5	H 1,244	H 4.1	H 1.1	82.3	68,883	75.6	Georgia
72.2[30]	78.7[30]	1991	454,291	6.2	0.8	55.0	40.0	4.0	65.8	29.9	H 34,827	H 2.3	H 0.3	84.9	149,196	16.9	Germany
54.2	57.8	...									H 2,355	H 4.9	H 2.2				Ghana
73.4	80.4	1991	229	8.2	...	...	...	...	...	...	H 8	H 3.2	H 0.7	97.1	...	...	Gibraltar
74.6	79.8	1991	65,568	6.2	0.9	58.3	40.8	14.6	66.6	18.8	H 2,990	H 3.3	H 0.7	96.1	180	0.2	Greece
60.7	68.4	1991	451	8.1	1.1	44.6	54.3	2.7	59.6	37.7	F 31	F 1.8	F 0.5	28.0	962	80.7	Greenland
67.8	72.5	...									H 24	H 3.7	H 2.2				Grenada
70.0	77.0	1992	1,880	4.7	0.6[4]	56.8[4]	42.6[4]	8.8[4]	67.5[4]	23.7[4]	H 112	H 3.4	H 0.9	39.3	561	8.7	Guadeloupe
69.5	75.6	1992	1,477	10.6	3.0	55.5	41.5	9.2	59.3	31.5	H 31	H 4.0	H 1.3	67.8	...	...	Guam
61.5	66.7	1988	46,155	5.4	15.9	55.7	28.4	41.5	38.0	20.5	H 1,611	H 5.4	H 5.4	34.8	...	...	Guatemala
...	...	1990	403	6.8	...	...	...	...	...	...	H 21	H 2.6	H 0.5	80.2			Guernsey
41.0	45.0	...									H 1,064	H 4.7					Guinea
42.0	45.0	...									H 124	H 4.1	H 2.8	11.3	...	...	Guinea-Bissau
62.0	68.0	...									H 150	H 5.1	H 2.1				Guyana
43.0	47.0	...									H 1,147	H 4.4	H 1.8				Haiti
64.8	60.2	1993	19,875	4.9	7.7	65.1	27.2	27.9	58.5	13.6	H 463	H 5.7	H 2.8	...	...	...	Honduras
75.1	80.7	1992	45,702	7.9	0.6[12]	50.6[12]	48.8[12]	3.3[12]	66.2[12]	30.5[12]	H 1,582	H 3.4	H 0.7	94.5	17,600	25.2	Hong Kong
64.6	73.7	1991	66,000	6.4	5.2	72.4	22.4	27.3	57.5	15.2	F 3,058	F 2.9	F 0.8	81.5	89,931	70.7	Hungary
75.7	80.9	1992	1,241	4.7	0.2	53.5	46.3	2.3	64.4	33.3	H 85	H 2.9	H 1.3	43.6	658	14.5	Iceland
57.7	58.7	...									H 97,093	H 5.5	H 2.4	...	596,345	2.4	India
55.6	58.9	1989–90[32]	1,210,570	7.9	...	...	...	...	...	...	H 39,695	H 4.5	H 1.8		...	...	Indonesia
64.4	66.2	1989	458,708	8.5	...	...	...	...	...	...	H 9,759	H 5.1	H 2.2				Iran
46.0	57.0	1990	143,518	8.1	...	...	...	...	...	...	H 1,873	H 8.9	H 4.1				Iraq
71.0	76.7	1992	16,109	4.6	1.1[12]	72.2[12]	26.7[12]	3.7[12]	80.6[12]	15.7[12]	H 726	H 3.9	H 1.3	82.0	...	...	Ireland
...	...	1993	417	6.0	0.7	55.9	43.4	4.6	61.6	33.8				73.5	...	...	Isle of Man
75.1	78.5	1990	30,683	6.5	3.4	74.0	22.6	22.5	66.8	10.7	H 1,355	H 3.7	H 1.1	98.5	15,800	14.9	Israel
73.6	80.2	1990	312,585	5.4	1.0[13]	69.9[13]	29.1[13]	10.0[13]	75.7[13]	14.3[13]	F 19,766	F 2.8	F 0.5	93.7	165,456	29.8	Italy
71.4	75.8	1991	13,254	5.3	...	...	...	...	...	...	H 554	H 4.2	H 1.4	14.9			Jamaica
70.1	82.2	1990	722,138	5.8	1.2[29]	61.8[29]	37.0[29]	3.4[29]	79.6[29]	17.0[29]	F 22,240	F 5.4	F 1.2	99.0	436,299	35.7	Japan
											H 29	H 2.6	H 0.4	88.1	313	29.2	Jersey
64.4	69.9	1990	32,706	8.2	4.6	74.3	21.1	39.5	54.6	5.9	H 375	H 6.9	H 3.4	...	...	...	Jordan
64.0	73.0	1989	165,380	10.0	3.8	76.0	20.2	26.0	58.2	15.8	H 3,824	H 4.0	H 1.4	88.0	358,124	93.7	Kazakhstan
57.1	60.8	...									H 1,938	H 6.2	H 2.7				Kenya
52.6	55.8	1988	352	5.2	...	...	...	...	...	...	H 11	H 6.6	H 2.5	...			Kiribati
68.0	74.0	1987	188,007	9.3	...	...	...	...	...	...	H 4,054	H 4.8	H 1.7				Korea, North
69.0	76.0	1989	309,872	7.3	0.3	77.1	22.6	2.7	89.5	7.8	H 11,355	H 3.8	H 1.0	99.5	...	...	Korea, South
74.3	78.1	1989	11,051	5.4	3.2	69.5	27.3	31.2	57.3	11.5	H 246	H 7.4	H 1.6				Kuwait
65.0	73.0	1989	41,790	9.7	2.2	82.4	15.4	29.8	59.5	10.7	H 856	H 4.2	H 1.9	87.0	87,212	66.3	Kyrgyzstan
49.0	52.0	...										H 6.0					Laos
63.7	74.5	1991	22,337	8.4	6.5[12]	63.5[12]	30.0[12]	22.7[12]	51.8[12]	25.6[12]	H 732	H 3.1	H 0.8	81.6	45,149	119.1	Latvia
72.5	77.9	...									H 405	H 5.3	H 2.2				Lebanon
58.0	63.0	...									H 330	H 4.8	H 2.0				Lesotho
54.0	57.0	...									H 474	H 5.0					Liberia
61.6	65.0	...									F 383	F 5.4	F 2.9				Libya
69.5	73.6	1992	202	6.8	—	54.5	44.5	0.0	66.3	29.2	H 8	H 3.0	H 0.7	85.3	...	...	Liechtenstein
65.3	76.1	1990	36,310	9.8	7.4	70.0	22.6	24.2	56.5	19.3	H 1,000	H 3.2	H 0.8	93.3	26,598	47.3	Lithuania
72.6	79.1	1992	2,512	6.4	1.0	55.2	43.8	3.9	64.9	31.2	H 145	H 2.8	H 0.5	87.3	...	...	Luxembourg
68.1	71.8	1992	2,148	5.8	0.3	41.7	58.0	2.6	67.1	30.3	H 99	H 3.5	H 0.9	99.3	...	...	Macau
70.0	74.0	1990	15,973	7.5	4.2[12]	79.0[12]	16.8[12]	27.5[12]	64.3[12]	8.2[12]	H 435[20]	H 4.4[20]	H 1.3[20]	...	...	...	Macedonia
54.0	57.0	...									H 1,709	H 4.7	H 2.0				Madagascar
43.5	44.9	...										H 4.3					Malawi
69.0	73.0	...									H 3,580	H 4.9					Malaysia
65.0	62.0	...									H 23	H 6.1	H 2.7				Maldives
43.9	47.0	...									H 1,364	H 5.6					Mali
73.0	77.8	1993	2,476	6.8	2.5	73.1	23.8	9.9	76.9	13.2	H 76	H 3.6	H 1.2	98.2	...	...	Malta
60.0	63.0	...									H 5	H 8.7					Marshall Islands
74.9	81.0	1993	1,555	4.2	0.1[13]	46.8[13]	53.1[13]	3.3[13]	61.5[13]	35.2[13]	H 107	H 3.3	H 0.8	34.1	1,753	30.6	Martinique
45.0	48.0	...									H 246	H 5.0					Mauritania
65.0	73.0	1990	11,252	10.6	1.5	60.2	38.3	21.7	60.3	18.0	F 155	F 5.3	F 2.0	72.8	...	...	Mauritius
54.0	58.0	...									H 19	H 4.9	H 2.3	89.2			Mayotte
66.5	73.1	1992	667,590	7.6	16.9	64.7	18.4	36.4	52.4	11.2	H 17,152	H 5.1	H 2.0	72.5	...	...	Mexico
64.0	68.1	...									H 11	H 7.0					Micronesia
65.0	72.0	1989	39,928	9.4	3.9	76.3	19.8	31.6	52.5	15.9	H 1,144	H 3.4	H 1.1	89.6	90,860	110.5	Moldova
72.0	80.0	1987	...	7.5	...	...	...	...	...	...	H 14	H 2.2	H 0.3	96.8	...	...	Monaco
63.0	67.0	1989	16,100	7.8	...	...	...	...	...	...	F 428	F 4.8					Mongolia
61.6	65.0	...									H 2,819	H 5.8	H 2.5				Morocco
45.2	48.4	...	...	...							F 1,860	F 4.4	F 2.0	73.1			Mozambique
56.0	60.0	...	...	...								H 5.2	...	...	...	...	Myanmar (Burma)
57.5	60.0	...										H 4.8					Namibia
64.0	69.0	...									H 1	H 8.0	H 2.6				Nauru
54.0	53.0	...									H 3,345	H 5.5	H 2.3				Nepal
74.3	80.3	1992	93,638	6.2	0.4	53.0	46.6	2.1	65.6	32.3	H 6,185	H 2.4	H 0.4	87.5	18,384	9.3	Netherlands, The

Vital statistics, marriage, family (continued)

country	vital rates						causes of death (rate per 100,000 population)								
	year	birth rate per 1,000 population	death rate per 1,000 population	infant mortality rate per 1,000 live births	rate of natural increase per 1,000 population	total fertility rate	year	infectious and parasitic diseases	malignant neoplasms (cancers)	endocrine and metabolic disorders	diseases of the nervous system	diseases of the circulatory system	diseases of the respiratory system	diseases of the digestive system	accidents, poisoning, and violence
Netherlands Antilles	1991	18.3	5.8	6.3[12]	12.5	...	1987[36]	...	150.6	31.9	10.8	205.4	41.0	21.1	41.6
New Caledonia	1994	25.0	5.0	21.0	20.0	2.9									
New Zealand	1992	17.2	7.9	7.3	9.3	2.1	1991	4.6	201.2	17.9	13.9	345.0	78.0	24.1	53.4
Nicaragua	1993	35.6	6.9	71.0	28.7	4.5	1991[34]	100	56	18	13	142	73	34	93
Niger	1990–95	51.3	18.7	124.0	32.6	7.1									
Nigeria	1990–95	45.2	13.9	96.0	31.3	6.4									
Northern Mariana Islands	1987	45.6	5.5	4.1	40.1	...	1987	18.7	70.2[19]	23.4	14.0	135.7	70.2	9.4	145.1
Norway	1992	14.0	10.5	5.9	3.5	1.9	1991	6.3	229.6	17.6	19.1	488.5	101.9	30.0	59.7
Oman	1992	61.3	4.5	24.2	56.8	7.9									
Pakistan	1993	40.0	11.0	104.7	29.0	6.1									
Panama	1991	25.5	5.2	21.3	20.3	2.9[14]	1990	20.0	57.8	11.0[6]	1.9[26]	111.4	18.9	7.4	51.0
Papua New Guinea	1993	33.0	11.0	53.0	22.0	4.8									
Paraguay	1991	33.6	6.4	39.0[17]	27.2	4.4	1988[38]	56	61	23	11	201	53	21	49
Peru	1990–95	29.0	7.6	75.8	21.4	3.6	1989[34]	85	73	19	11	115	100	36	67
Philippines	1994	30.0	7.0	39.0	23.0	3.8	1984	179.8	30.2	13.4	...	100.6	...	...	16.8
Poland	1992	13.4	10.2	14.2	3.2	2.1[2]	1992	7.5	200.0	16.7	8.0	537.3	34.6	32.5	78.2
Portugal	1992	12.0	13.5	10.8[2]	−1.5	1.5[17]	1992	7.5	190.2	37.6	8.9	448.6	68.4	49.2	66.9
Puerto Rico	1993	18.0	7.4	13.0[2]	10.2	2.2[2]	1991	16.8	120.0	93.0	15.7	238.4	72.0	42.3	70.2
Qatar	1992	19.6	1.8	15.8	17.8	5.7[14]	1992	3.4	21.4[19]	7.3[15]	2.6	59.9	7.5	3.4	36.0
Réunion	1992	22.8	5.3	8.0[21]	17.5	2.6	1989	11.0	90.3	24.9[16]	18.1[39]	185.0	43.0	46.1	66.3
Romania	1993	10.9	11.6	23.4	−0.7	2.2[12]	1992	12.4	163.4	11.7	8.2	707.7	94.0	57.9	74.3
Russia	1992	10.7	12.2	18.0	−1.5	1.6	1991	12.1	197.3	8.0	7.6	625.8	56.1	29.3	143.5
Rwanda	1990–95	52.1	18.2	110.0	33.9	8.5									
St. Kitts and Nevis	1991	21.9	9.5	20.0[21]	12.4	2.5[14]	1985	50.0	95.5	20.5[6]	11.4	443.2	81.8	25.0	29.5
St. Lucia	1992	26.2	6.3	18.3	19.9	3.0	1990	27.8	48.3	25.8	6.6	209.5	33.7	28.4	36.4
St. Vincent and the Grenadines	1991	24.3	6.1	20.3[40]	18.2	2.5[14]	1991	20.6	107.8	49.7	12.2	189.4	30.0	15.9	42.2
San Marino	1989–93	10.5	7.0	9.7	3.5	...	1989–93[35]	1.7	216.4	2.6[6]	...	324.5	16.3	9.4	42.9
São Tomé and Príncipe	1993	35.4	9.1	58.0[9]	26.3	4.6	1987	240.7	19.6	5.3[6]	2.7[26]	143.5	86.5	15.2	14.3
Saudi Arabia	1992	42.7	4.6	23.6	38.1	7.0									
Senegal	1994	43.0	16.0	80.0	27.0	6.0									
Seychelles	1993	23.4	8.3	13.0	15.1	2.8[2]	1985–89[35]	42.9	116.9	10.6	7.9	263.5	77.1	40.5	67.0
Sierra Leone	1990–95	50.2	18.5	122.0	31.7	7.0									
Singapore	1993	17.0	4.6	5.0[14]	12.4	1.8	1992	11.6	123.5	9.5	4.3	183.9	86.6	12.0	19.2
Slovakia	1993	14.1	10.1	12.6	4.0	1.9[14]	1992	4.0	200.0[19]	19.0	8.0	521.0	77.0	52.0	76.0
Slovenia	1991	10.0	9.7	8.9[14]	0.3	1.3[14]	1992	6.2	248.7	33.6	1.0[26]	425.6	39.1	36.6	91.4
Solomon Islands	1993	37.0	4.0	26.0[14]	33.0	5.4									
Somalia	1990–95	50.2	18.5	122.0	31.7	6.5									
South Africa	1994	34.0	8.0	47.0	26.0	4.1[14]	1988	68.3	70.2	24.8[16]	10.7	133.9	69.6	17.0	110.6
Spain	1991	9.9	8.7	7.7[14]	1.2	1.7[17]	1990	10.0	197.2	31.5	11.9	348.0	83.0	48.4	48.4
Sri Lanka	1991	21.2	5.8	24.0[3]	15.4	2.5[3]	1986	32.2	27.7	9.0	45.3	101.9	36.1	15.5	77.8
Sudan, The	1993	42.7	12.5	102.0	30.2	6.2									
Suriname	1990–95	25.6	5.6	28.0	20.0	2.7	1987[41]	35	57	42	10	179	34	25	69
Swaziland	1990–95	37.2	10.4	107.0	26.8	4.9									
Sweden	1992	14.1	10.9	5.6	3.2	2.1	1990	7.3	237.5	22.2	13.0	567.4	83.5	35.0	58.4
Switzerland	1992	12.6	9.1	6.8	3.5	1.6	1992	16.7	240.8	24.6[16]	17.7	391.8	62.5	27.5	75.1
Syria	1990–95	42.4	5.8	39.0	36.6	6.2	1981[21]	22	12	7	13	86	19	8	27
Taiwan	1993	15.6	5.3	5.2[14]	10.3	1.7[14]	1992	...	101.5	23.7[6]	...	140.1[3]	24.3[41]	18.2[42]	63.7[42]
Tajikistan	1994	35.0	6.0	40.0	29.0	4.5	1989	81.2	51.9	6.9	8.9	197.5	138.8	23.0	48.4
Tanzania	1994	48.0	15.0	102.0	33.0	6.3									
Thailand	1993	20.0	6.0	25.0[2]	14.0	2.2	1991	...	162.0	...	...	250.0	55.0	73.0	104.0
Togo	1994	49.0	12.0	94.0	37.0	7.0									
Tonga	1993	25.2	6.8	21.4	18.4	3.7	1992	16.3	54.9	15.2	6.1	158.5	31.5	18.3	4.1
Trinidad and Tobago	1992	18.4	6.8	17.0[21]	11.6	2.7	1991	22.5	83.4	83.3[6]	2.4[26]	260.0	31.1	13.7	51.4
Tunisia	1992	25.3	6.2	43.0[17]	19.1	3.4[17]									
Turkey	1994	26.0	6.0	49.0	20.0	3.2	1990[42]	23	79	9[6]	3[26]	358	29	12	28
Turkmenistan	1994	33.0	7.0	45.0	26.0	4.1	1989	79.3	65.1	8.0	9.1	275.3	160.6	32.2	62.4
Tuvalu	1991	29.0	10.0	33.0	19.0	3.1	1985	40.0	70.0	20.0	120.0	150.0	120.0	170.0	...
Uganda	1990–95	51.0	21.0	104	30.0	7.3									
Ukraine	1994	12.0	13.0	14.0	−0.2	1.7	1990	11.6	196.3	6.7[16]	7.4	671.0	60.5	31.3	107.7
United Arab Emirates	1990–95	21.2	3.9	22.0	17.3	4.5									
United Kingdom	1992	13.5	10.9	6.6	2.6	1.8	1992	5.1	280.8	19.5	21.8	501.0	120.4	36.7	34.2
United States	1993	15.7	8.5	8.5[14]	7.2	2.0[2]	1993	27.5[43]	206.0	21.3[6]	0.3[26]	364.7	70.1[31]	15.2	54.9
Uruguay	1991	17.6	9.6	18.7[9]	8.0	2.3[15]	1990	16.0	222.8	25.5	16.2	378.4	76.3	39.1	61.7
Uzbekistan	1994	33.0	6.0	35.0	27.0	4.0	1989	44.5	55.9	6.5	9.1	251.3	119.3	24.7	60.1
Vanuatu	1994	35.0	7.0	44.0	28.0	4.6	1985[44]	69.3	22.9	16.2	11.8	37.6	60.5	12.5	23.6
Venezuela	1992	27.7	4.5	25.2	23.2	3.3	1989	30.0	51.1	18.6	7.4	115.0	29.0	18.8	61.4
Vietnam	1994	30.0	7.0	36.0	23.0	3.7	1979	48.0	54.0	...	...	123.8	...	...	...
Virgin Islands (U.S.)	1988	22.0	5.0	13.1	17.0	2.6[12]	1989	10.8	78.9	36.5[5]	—	232.7	14.8[31]	12.8	56.2
West Bank	1994	46.0	7.0	40.0	39.0	5.7									
Western Sahara	1994	48.0	20.0	177.0[2]	28.0	7.3[2]									
Western Samoa	1991	34.0	6.0	47.0	28.0	4.5									
Yemen	1992	48.7	14.2	114.8	34.5	8.4									
Yugoslavia	1992	13.5	10.1	21.7	3.4	2.1[2]	1991	9.3	155.8[19]	21.6	8.2	528.3	47.5	26.6	57.0
Zaire	1990–95	47.5	14.6	93.0	32.9	6.7									
Zambia	1990–95	46.4	18.0	84.0	28.4	6.3									
Zimbabwe	1990–95	40.6	11.0	55.0	29.6	4.6									

[1]Excludes nomadic tribes. [2]1991. [3]1993. [4]1986. [5]Septicemia only. [6]Diabetes mellitus only. [7]Cerebrovascular disease and heart disease only. [8]Chronic obstructive pulmonary diseases, pneumonia, and influenza only. [9]1991–92 average. [10]Under 21 years of age. [11]21–29 years of age. [12]1989. [13]1988. [14]1992. [15]1990. [16]Includes nutritional disorders. [17]1990–95. [18]Accidents only. [19]Includes benign neoplasms. [20]1981. [21]1994. [22]Rates based on about 75 percent of total deaths. [23]Results based on a sample population of about 100,000. [24]Millions of households. [25]1985. [26]Meningitis only. [27]Ethiopia includes Eritrea. [28]1987. [29]First marriages only. [30]Former West Germany only. [31]Bronchitis, pneumonia, and influenza. [32]Muslims only.

expectation of life at birth (latest year)		nuptiality, family, and family planning													country
		marriages			age at marriage (latest)						families (F), households (H) (latest)				
		year	total number	rate per 1,000 population	groom (percent)			bride (percent)			families (households)		children		induced abortions	
male	female				19 and under	20–29	30 and over	19 and under	20–29	30 and over	total ('000)	size	number under age 15	percent legitimate	number	ratio per 100 live births
71.1	75.8	1991	1,220	6.4	...	...	...	...	...	...	H 41	H 3.7	H 2.1	51.6	...	...	Netherlands Antilles
69.0	76.0	1987	729	4.5	0.5	54.5	45.0	10.2	61.9	27.9		H 4.1		48.1			New Caledonia
72.0	77.9	1989	22,733	6.8	1.2	58.7	40.1	5.5	66.0	28.5	H 1,178	H 2.9	H 0.7	63.3	10,200	17.6	New Zealand
60.7	66.4	1991	13,122	3.3	18.1[10,25]	—81.9[25,37]—		48.2[10,25]	—51.8[25,37]—			H 6.9					Nicaragua
44.9	48.1	...	...	...							H 1,130	H 6.4					Niger
50.8	54.3	...	...	...							H 14,411	H 5.0					Nigeria
59.0	64.0	1987	685	31.2	2.5	50.2	47.3	5.7	70.4	23.9	H 7	H 4.6	H 1.5	53.9			Northern Mariana Islands
74.2	80.3	1992	19,266	4.5	0.7[15]	56.2[15]	43.1[15]	3.7[15]	68.9[15]	27.4[15]	F 1,983	F 2.2	F 0.4	57.1	15,528	25.5	Norway
69.8	72.7	...	...	...							H 350	H 3.7					Oman
59.3	60.7	...	...	...								H 6.3					Pakistan
70.6	74.7	1991	10,528	4.5	3.6[12]	55.0[12]	41.4[12]	15.6[12]	55.8[12]	28.6[12]	H 524	H 4.4	H 1.5	28.1			Panama
55.0	57.0	...	...	...							H 674	H 4.6					Papua New Guinea
65.0	69.4	1987	17,741	4.5	3.8	64.4	31.8	34.0	46.5	19.5	H 868	H 4.7	1.9	68.7			Paraguay
62.7	66.6	1982	109,200	6.0	5.5	60.4	34.1	25.9	51.4	22.6	H 3,099	H 5.2		57.8			Peru
64.0	68.0	1989	395,933	6.6	6.4	69.6	24.0	21.9	63.9	14.2	F 9,566	F 5.7	F 2.4	93.9			Philippines
66.7	75.7	1991	233,206	6.1	4.4	76.6	19.0	21.8	65.0	13.2	F 9,435	F 3.6	F 0.9	95.0	30,878	5.7	Poland
71.1	78.1	1990	71,654	7.3	4.2	75.2	20.6	19.0	67.3	13.7	H 2,954	H 3.8	H 0.8	85.5			Portugal
70.2	78.5	1990	21,498	9.4	16.7	70.0	13.3	33.1	57.8	9.1	H 1,005	H 3.6	H 1.0	63.2			Puerto Rico
65.2	67.6	1992	1,578	3.0	4.8	71.7	23.5	34.0	56.9	9.1	H 61	H 6.4					Qatar
69.0	78.3	1990	3,831	6.4	1.2	65.2	33.6	12.5	66.8	20.7	H 158	H 3.8	H 1.1	46.1	4,302	31.7	Réunion
66.5	72.4	1991	183,388	7.9	3.8	77.1	19.1	30.2	57.9	11.9	H 7,115	H 3.1			866,934	314.9	Romania
59.0	73.2	1991	1,277,232	8.6	7.2	65.6	27.2	31.3	45.6	23.1	H 40,426	H 3.2	H 0.8	85.4	4,242,028	196.3	Russia
44.8	47.7	1982	14,313	2.6	...	...	...	...	...	...	H 1,509	H 4.7	2.3	94.9			Rwanda
63.0	69.0	...	...	...							H 12	H 3.7	H 1.4	19.2			St. Kitts and Nevis
68.6	74.4	1992	436	3.2	0.8[12]	34.4[12]	64.8[12]	3.5[12]	45.1[12]	51.4[12]	H 25	H 4.6	H 2.0	10.0			St. Lucia
68.0	72.0	1991	444	4.2	0.5[4]	41.6[4]	57.9[4]	6.4[4]	59.5[4]	34.1[4]	H 27	H 3.9	H 2.0				St. Vincent and the Grenadines
70.7	76.2	1989	169	7.4	0.6	75.1	24.3	5.3	85.3	9.5	H 9	H 2.7	H 0.4	95.2			San Marino
63.0	61.2	...	...	...				...						9.8			São Tomé and Príncipe
68.9	72.3	...	...	...							H 1,513	H 6.6					Saudi Arabia
48.0	50.0	...	...	...							H 1,167	H 4.8					Senegal
66.0	73.0	1987	622	9.4	1.0	54.2	44.8	6.4	65.1	28.5	H 13	H 4.8	H 1.9	27.2	9	0.5	Seychelles
41.4	44.6	...	...	...							H 749	H 4.7					Sierra Leone
73.7	78.3	1992	25,784	9.1	0.4[13]	66.5[13]	33.1[13]	5.1[13]	79.1[13]	15.8[13]	H 510	H 3.9	H 1.3		17,798	36.2	Singapore
66.6	75.4	1990	40,435	7.7	7.0	78.2	14.8	32.8	57.7	9.5	H 1,778	H 3.0	H 0.7	92.8	56,176	69.9	Slovakia
69.5	77.4	1992	9,119	4.6	10.3	73.0	16.7	0.9	69.6	29.5	H 641	H 3.1	H 0.6				Slovenia
69.0	73.0	...	...	...							F 41	F 5.6	F 2.3				Solomon Islands
45.4	48.6	...	...	...								H 4.9					Somalia
62.0	68.0	...	...	...								H 4.5		75.9			South Africa
74.6	80.5	1992	211,228	5.4	2.6[13]	76.4[13]	21.0[13]	11.6[13]	77.0[13]	11.4[13]	F 10,665	F 3.5		92.0			Spain
70.0	74.0	1989	141,533	8.4	0.5[25]	71.1[25]	28.4[25]	16.9[25]	73.0[25]	10.1[25]	H 2,721	H 5.2	H 1.9	94.6			Sri Lanka
53.0	54.7	...	...	...							H 3,471	H 5.3					Sudan, The
67.8	72.8	1991	1,974	4.6	...	...	...	...	...	...		H 3.9					Suriname
56.2	59.8	...	...	...							H 122	H 5.7			1,145		Swaziland
74.8	80.5	1991	39,805	4.3	0.4	41.2	58.4	2.6	53.6	43.8	H 3,670	H 2.2	H 0.5	50.5	34,849	28.4	Sweden
74.1	80.9	1992	45,080	6.5	0.3	52.1	47.6	2.6	66.1	31.3	H 2,859	H 2.4	0.4	93.8			Switzerland
65.2	69.2	1988	101,946	7.5	...	...	...	...	...	...	F 1,151	F 6.2	F 2.4				Syria
72.0	77.4	1990	143,886	7.1	1.5	62.3	36.2	6.0	77.7	16.3	H 5,093	H 4.0	H 1.0	97.7			Taiwan
67.0	72.0	1989	47,616	9.2	2.1	86.8	11.1	39.0	54.3	6.7	H 799	H 6.1	H 2.7	93.0	54,494	27.2	Tajikistan
49.0	52.0	...	...	...							H 3,435	H 5.1	H 2.3				Tanzania
66.0	71.0	1992	449,913	8.3	...	...	...	...	...	...	H 10,418	H 5.3	H 1.9				Thailand
54.0	58.0	...	...	...							H 479	H 5.6					Togo
65.5	70.2	1992	806	8.2	...	...	...	...	...	...	F 15	F 6.1	F 2.7	80.6			Tonga
68.0	73.2	1992	7,009	5.7	5.9	61.0	33.1	25.5	52.6	21.9	H 301	H 4.1	H 1.3		9	—	Trinidad and Tobago
66.9	68.7	1992	64,694	7.7	0.4[12]	63.6[12]	36.0[12]	21.5[12]	66.8[12]	11.7[12]	H 1,703	H 5.1	H 1.9	99.8	23,300	10.9	Tunisia
69.0	73.0	1991	459,624	8.0	8.5[13]	75.9[13]	15.6[13]	36.1[13]	56.5[13]	7.4[13]	H 11,189	H 5.0	H 1.7				Turkey
63.0	70.0	1989	34,890	9.0	3.0	87.4	9.6	16.1	77.1	6.8	H 598	H 5.6	H 2.4	96.5	39,068	31.3	Turkmenistan
61.0	63.0	...	...	...							H 1	H 6.4	H 2.2	82.2			Tuvalu
40.8	42.9	...	...	...							H 2,766	H 4.8					Uganda
64.0	74.0	1989	489,330	9.5	5.5	70.2	24.3	32.9	46.7	20.4	H 14,507	H 3.2	H 0.8	89.2	1,019,038	155.1	Ukraine
69.8	74.1	...	...	...							H 247	H 6.8					United Arab Emirates
73.2	78.6	1990	375,410	6.5	1.9	59.7	38.4	6.6	64.7	28.7	H 21,672	H 2.7	H 1.7	69.1	178,416	22.5	United Kingdom
72.0	78.9	1992	2,362,000	9.2	4.5[13]	54.1[13]	41.4[13]	11.8[13]	55.7[13]	32.5[13]	F 63,550	F 2.6	F 1.0	76.6	1,354,000	35.5	United States
69.3	75.5	1991	54,754	6.6	7.2[28]	63.3[28]	29.5[28]	24.7[28]	54.2[28]	21.1[28]	H 863	H 3.3	H 0.9	73.8			Uruguay
66.0	72.0	1989	200,681	10.0	2.3	87.4	10.3	37.9	55.2	6.9	H 3,415	H 5.5	H 2.4	95.8	226,276	33.8	Uzbekistan
64.0	68.0	...	...	...							H 28	H 5.1	H 2.2				Vanuatu
69.8	75.8	1991	107,136	5.4	10.7	61.3	28.0	30.4	51.7	17.9	H 2,707	H 5.3	H 2.2	47.0			Venezuela
63.0	67.0	...	...	...							H 12,958[45]	H 4.8[45]	H 1.9[45]				Vietnam
66.7	70.7	1987	1,906	18.0	4.5	50.9	44.6	1.0	38.4	60.6	H 32	H 3.1	H 1.0	38.4			Virgin Islands (U.S.)
68.0	71.0	...	...	...													West Bank
39.0	41.0	...	...	...													Western Sahara
64.0	69.0	1989	833	5.3	0.5	52.7	46.8	8.6	61.3	30.1	F 20	F 7.8	F 3.8	43.5			Western Samoa
53.3	55.5	...	...	...							H 1,848	H 5.6					Yemen
69.0	74.6	1992	61,521	6.1	2.4	66.7	30.9	22.4	60.6	17.0	H 2,774	H 3.6	H 0.9				Yugoslavia
50.0	53.7	...	...	...								H 6.0					Zaire
43.5	44.8	...	...	...							H 1,370	H 4.4	H 2.1				Zambia
54.4	57.3	...	...	...							H 2,166	H 4.8	1.1	95.8			Zimbabwe

[33]Projected rates based on about 10 percent of total deaths. [34]Projected rates based on about 45 percent of total deaths. [35]Average annual rates for the period. [36]Includes Aruba. [37]Over 21 years of age. [38]Reporting areas only (constituting about 50 percent of the total population). [39]Includes mental disorders. [40]1989–91 average. [41]Projected rates based on about 70 percent of total deaths. [42]Projected rates based on about 35 percent of total deaths. [43]Of which AIDS, 14.3. [44]Registered events only. [45]Private households only.

National product and accounts

The national product and accounts table furnishes, for most of the countries of the world, breakdowns of (1) gross national product (GNP) and its global and per capita growth rates (1985–92), (2) principal accounting and industrial components of gross domestic product (GDP), (3) recent growth rates of real GDP, and (4) principal elements of each country's balance of payments, including international goods trade, invisibles, and tourism payments.

Measures of national output. The two most commonly used measures of national output (except for the accounting systems of centrally planned economies) are GDP and GNP. Each of these measures represents an aggregate value of goods and services produced by a specific country. The GDP, the more basic of these, is a measure of the total value of goods and services produced entirely within a given country. The GNP, the more comprehensive value, is composed of both domestic production (GDP) *and* the net income from current (short-term) transactions with other countries. When the income received from other countries is greater than payments to them, a country's GNP is greater than its GDP. In theory, if all national accounts could be equilibrated, the global summation of GDP would equal GNP.

In the first section of the table, data are provided for the nominal GNP. ("Nominal" refers to value in current prices for the year indicated and is distinguished from a "real" valuation, which is one adjusted to eliminate the effect of recent inflation [most often] or, occasionally, of deflation between two given dates.) Both the total and per capita values of this product are denominated in U.S. dollars for ease of comparison. Beside these are

given figures for average annual growth of total and per capita real GNP. GNP per capita provides a rough measure of annual national income per person, but values should be compared cautiously, as they are subject to a number of distortions, notably of exchange rate, but also of purchasing power parity (the differing ability [by more than an exchange rate] of any two currencies to purchase comparable goods in their respective domestic markets), and in the existence of elements of national production that do not enter the monetary economy in such a way as to be visible to fiscal authorities (*e.g.,* food, clothing, or housing produced and consumed within families or communal groups or services exchanged).

In a number of countries with centrally planned economies, the conventional concept for the aggregated national income/product is net material product (NMP), which includes only material goods and "productive" services. These NMP accounts are not directly comparable to the GDP values presented in this table for market economies. The GDP value is more comprehensive and includes a number of sectors (especially personal and financial services) excluded from the NMP value. Estimated GNPs have been supplied for most countries (including the centrally planned), based either on the country's own, or on external, analysis.

The internal structure of the national product. GDP/GNP values allow comparison of the relative size of national economies, but further information is provided when these aggregates are analyzed according to their component kinds of expenditure, cost components, and industrial sectors of origin.

There are three major domestic components of GDP expenditure: private

National product and accounts

country	gross national product (GNP)					gross domestic product (GDP) by type of expenditure, 1991 (%)					cost components of gross domestic product (GDP), 1991 (%)			
	nominal, 1992 ('000,000 U.S.$)	per capita, 1992 (U.S.$)	average annual growth rates, 1985–92			consumption		gross domestic investment	foreign trade		indirect taxes net of subsidies	consumption of fixed capital	compensation of employees	net operating surplus
			real GNP (%)	population (%)	real GNP per capita (%)	private	government		exports	imports				
Afghanistan	3,000[1]	200[1]	...	2.5	...	...	...	...	...		...	...	...	...
Albania	2,500	760	...	1.7	...	73[2]	10[2]	24[2]	——— −7[2] ———		...	13[2]	62[2]	25[2]
Algeria	48,326	1,830	0.7	2.7	−2.0	49	16	29	31	−25	18[1]	8[1]	39[1]	35[1]
American Samoa	128[7]	2,600[7]	...	1.5	...	...	...	...	...		...	...	...	...
Andorra	760	14,000	...	4.7	...	...	...	...	...		...	...	...	...
Angola	5,100[7]	490[7]	...	2.9	...	41[1]	35[1]	16[1]	42[1]	−35[1]	9[1]	8	43[1]	47[1,8]
Antigua and Barbuda	395	4,870	2.1	1.0	1.1	66[9]	16[9]	22[9]	39	−79	16[10]	——— 84[10] ———		
Argentina	200,282	6,050	1.8	1.3	0.5	——— 84 ———		15	8	−6	...	...	...	...
Armenia	2,719	780	...	1.2	...	——— 95[5] ———		33[5]	——— −28[5] ———		...	...	...	...
Aruba	900[7]	14,000[7]	...	1.6	...	66[10]	21[10]	17[10]	——— −3[10] ———		...	...	...	...
Australia	299,323	17,070	2.3	1.6	0.7	61	18	20	18	−17	11	15	51	22
Austria	174,767	22,110	3.0	0.6	2.4	55	18	26	41	−40	13	12	53	21
Azerbaijan	6,290	870	...	1.0	...	——— 73[5] ———		12[5]	——— 15[5] ———		...	...	...	...
Bahamas, The	3,161	12,020	0.7	1.9	−1.2	75	14	23	46	−60	13	8	43	56[8]
Bahrain	4,300	7,800	...	3.5	...	36[2]	26[2]	31[2]	119[2]	−102[2]	3[2]	16[2]	47[2]	35[2]
Bangladesh	24,672	220	3.9	2.2	1.7	87[2]	9[2]	12[2]	9[2]	−17[2]	...	...	...	...
Barbados	1,693	6,530	0.9	0.3	0.6	67	19	17	45	−48	...	...	...	...
Belarus	30,127	2,910	...	0.5	...	52[2]	12[2]	34[2]	49[2]	−47[2]	...	...	...	...
Belgium	209,594	20,880	3.1	0.3	2.8	63	15	20	72	−68	9	10	54	27
Belize	442	2,210	8.9	2.6	6.3	66	19	30	71	−87	16	7	——— 77 ———	
Benin	2,058	410	1.7	3.2	−1.5	83	12	14	22	−31	4[1]	8	20[1]	76[1,8]
Bermuda	1,300[7]	22,000[7]	...	0.9	...	71	13	11	59	−54	...	...	...	...
Bhutan	263	180	7.4	2.2	5.2	54[2]	25[2]	33[2]	30[2]	−42[2]	3[2]	10[2]	——— 87[2] ———	
Bolivia	5,084	680	3.5	2.5	1.0	71	11	13	27	−23	...	...	...	...
Bosnia and Herzegovina	14,000[7]	3,200[7]	...	0.2	...	...	...	...	...		...	...	...	...
Botswana	3,797	2,790	11.5	3.4	8.1	46[2]	31[2]	26[2]	50[2]	−52[2]	6[18]	15[18]	28[18]	51[18]
Brazil	425,412	2,770	1.1	1.8	−0.7	64	14	19	9	−7	12[2]	——— 88[2] ———		
Brunei	3,500[2]	13,890[2]	...	3.2	...	...	...	...	...		...	...	...	...
Bulgaria	11,906	1,330	−3.6	0.0	−3.6	70	5	28	——— −4 ———		20	5	43	52[20]
Burkina Faso	2,908	290	3.7	2.8	0.9	83[9]	16[9]	21[9]	11[9]	−31[9]	4[9]	8	27[9]	69[8,9]
Burundi	1,193	210	3.9	2.9	1.0	90	11	18	10	−28	11[2]	5[2]	22[2]	62[2]
Cambodia	2,000[7]	280[7]	...	2.7	...	...	...	...	...		...	...	...	...
Cameroon	10,003	820	−3.7	3.0	−6.7	69[9]	14[9]	16[9]	15[9]	−14[9]	...	...	...	...
Canada	565,787	20,320	1.7	1.4	0.3	61	21	20	24	−25	12	12	57	18
Cape Verde	330	850	4.5	2.7	1.8	83	20	26	3	−32	9[18]	——— 91[18] ———		
Central African Republic	1,307	410	0.3	2.7	−2.4	88[2]	14[2]	11[2]	16[2]	−28[2]	...	...	...	...
Chad	1,261	220	3.8	2.5	1.3	88[9]	23[9]	10[9]	12[9]	−33[9]	8[10]	——— 92[10] ———		
Chile	37,064	2,730	7.8	1.7	6.1	64	10	22	33	−29	...	...	...	...
China	442,346	380	7.5	1.5	6.0	56[5]	9[5]	34[5]	21[5]	−18[5]	...	...	...	...
Colombia	44,555	1,290	4.2	1.8	2.4	65	10	17	21	−14	9	8	38	53[8]
Comoros	262	510	1.4	3.7	−2.3	92	23	10	9	−34	8[18]	——— 92[18] ———		
Congo	2,502	1,030	0.3	3.3	−3.0	73[9]	14[9]	15[9]	40[9]	−42[9]	14[1]	19[1]	32[1]	35[1]
Costa Rica	6,261	2,000	5.1	2.5	2.6	59	16	25	39	−39	12[2]	2[2]	51[2]	34[2]
Côte d'Ivoire	8,655	670	−1.7	4.0	−5.7	66[22]	18[22]	9[22]	34[22]	−27[22]	19[18]	——— 81[18] ———		
Croatia	26,300[7]	5,600[7]	...	0.4	...	...	...	...	...		11[2]	13[2]	62[2]	14[2]
Cuba	14,900	1,370	...	1.0	...	95[1,5]	9[1,5]	18[1,5]	——— −21[1,5] ———		...	...	...	...
Cyprus	7,070	9,820	6.1	1.0	5.1	64	15	26	47	−53	9[2]	11[2]	——— 80[2] ———	
Czech Republic	25,313	2,440	−5.2	0.1	−5.3	45	19	30	——— 7 ———		...	...	...	...
Denmark	133,941	25,930	1.3	0.1	1.2	52	25	17	37	−31	14	9	54	23
Djibouti	358[2]	690[2]	...	2.9	...	80	30	16	41	−67	21[18]	——— 79[18] ———		
Dominica	181	2,520	4.8	−0.3	5.1	71	20	41	46	−79	17	——— 83 ———		
Dominican Republic	7,611	1,040	2.2	1.9	0.3	83	4	20	23	−31	5	6	——— 89 ———	
Ecuador	11,843	1,070	3.1	2.5	0.6	69	8	22	31	−30	12	8	12	76[8]
Egypt	34,514	630	3.2	2.4	0.8	73	11	24	28	−36	7[1]	——— 93[1] ———		
El Salvador	6,283	1,170	2.7	1.8	0.9	88	11	14	15	−27	6	4	——— 90 ———	

consumption (analyzed in greater detail in the "Household budgets and consumption" table), government spending, and gross domestic investment. The fourth, nondomestic, component of GDP expenditure is net foreign trade; values are given for both exports (a positive value) and imports (a negative value, representing obligations to other countries). The sum of these five percentages, excluding statistical discrepancies and rounding, should be 100% of the GDP.

The structure of GDP as accounted by cost components here comprises four general categories: indirect taxes (excise or value-added taxes), net of subsidies; consumption of fixed capital (depreciation); and two income categories: (a) compensation of employees (salaries, wages, etc.) and (b) net operating surplus ("profits," interests, rent, etc.).

The distribution of GDP for ten industrial sectors is aggregated into three major industrial groups:

1. The primary sector, composed of agriculture (including forestry and fishing) and mineral production (including fossil fuels).
2. The secondary sector, composed of manufacturing, construction, and public utilities.
3. The tertiary sector, which includes transportation and communications, trade (wholesale and retail), financial services (including banking, real estate, insurance, and business services), other (community, social, and personal) services, and government services.

Percentages in this section of the table may not add to 100 because the value of each economic sector is calculated as a percentage of the total GDP, which may contain adjustments such as import duties and bank service charges that are not distributed by sector.

Average annual growth rate of real GDP. These columns show average annual growth rates of real product for the decade from 1975 to 1985, as well as for the seven years from 1985 to 1992. Real GDP growth rates indicate the change in total output achieved by each country during the periods indicated excluding inflation.

Balance of payments (external account transactions). The external account records the sum (net) of all economic transactions of a current nature between one country and the rest of the world. The account shows a country's net of overseas receipts and obligations, including not only the trade of goods and merchandise but also such invisible items as services, interest and dividends, short- and long-term investments, tourism, transfers to or from overseas residents, etc. Each transaction gives rise either to a foreign claim for payment, recorded as a deficit (e.g., from imports, capital outflows), or a foreign obligation to pay, recorded as a surplus (e.g., from exports, capital inflows) or a domestic claim on another country. Any international transaction automatically creates a deficit in the balance of payments of one country and a surplus in that of another. Values are given in U.S. dollars for comparability.

Tourist trade. Net income or expenditure from tourism (in U.S. dollars for comparability) is often a significant element in a country's balance of payments. Receipts from foreign nationals reflect payments for goods and services from foreign currency resources by tourists in the given country. Expenditures by nationals abroad are also payments for goods and services, but in this case made by the residents of the given country as tourists abroad.

| origin of gross domestic product (GDP) by economic sector, 1991 (%) | | | | | | | | | | avg. annual growth rate of real GDP (%) | | balance of payments, 1993 (current external transactions; '000,000 U.S.$) | | | tourist trade, 1992 ('000,000 U.S.$) | | country |
| primary | | secondary | | | tertiary | | | | | | | net transfers | | current balance of payments | receipts from foreign nationals | expenditures by nationals abroad | |
agriculture	mining	manufacturing	construction	public utilities	transp., communications	trade	financial svcs.	other svcs.	government	1975–1985	1985–1992	goods, merchandise	invisibles				
52[2]	3	26[2,3]	7[2]	3	4[2]	9[2]		2[2]	—	...	-5.3[4]	-371[1]	228[1]	-143[1]	1[2]	1[2]	Afghanistan
36[2,5]	3	42[2,3,5]	6[2]	3	3[2,5]	4[2,5]		8[2,5]	—	...	0.4	-179[2]	...	...	10[7]	...	Albania
5[2]	17[2,6]	16[2]		16[2]	6	5[2]	13[2]	—28[2]—		6.1	0.7[4]	2,560	-3,570	1,010	75	163	Algeria
...	...	...	...	...	...	...	...	...	...	...	...	-54[2]	...	...	10[7]	...	American Samoa
...	...	...	...	...	...	...	...	...	...	...	...	-1,151[2]	...				Andorra
10	58	3	2	—	2	6	1	—18—		2.4	3.0[4]	2,080[7]	...	...	13[2]	75	Angola
4[2]	2[2]	3[2]	11[2]	4[2]	18[2]	26[2]	22[2]	—18[2]—		4.5	6.0	-206[9]	197[9]	-9[9]	394	187	Antigua and Barbuda
7	2	24	5	2	5	16	15	—25—		-0.0	2.6	-2,455	-5,113	-7,568	3,090	2,211	Argentina
28[5]	3	46[3,5]	15[5]	3	3[5]	5[5]	—35—			6.7[5]	0.5[5]						Armenia
...	...	...	...	...	...	...	...	...	...		12.0[11]	074[9]	318[5]	569	443	50	Aruba
3	5	15	8	4	8	14	23	19	4	3.0	2.6	-157	-10,686	-10,843	3,992	3,994	Australia
3	12	26[12]	7	3	6	16	17	4	14	2.4	2.8	-7,825	8,700	-875	14,832	8,371	Austria
41[5]	3	37[3,5]	8[5]	3	3[5]	4[5]	—6[5]—				-7.0[5]						Azerbaijan
9[2]	3[2]	24[2]	0[2]	2[2]	5[2]	15[2]	15[2]	—20[2]—		4.5	2.6[13]	-841[9]	714[9]	-127[9]	1,244	187	Bahamas, The
1	19	17	6	2	12	11	17	5	20	4.7	2.3[4]	-313[9]	-680[9]	-993[9]	177	141	Bahrain
36	—	9	6	1	12	8	2	22	5	4.5	4.0	-1,283	1,480	197	8	111	Bangladesh
5	1	7	5	3	7	26	13	3	16	2.3	1.2[14]	-307[9]	444[9]	-137[9]	463	41	Barbados
25[5]	3	46[3,5]	10[5]	3	4[5]	7[5]	—75—			5.2[5]	0.3[5]						Belarus
2	—	21	6	3	8	21	17	12	13	1.7	3.0	215[9,15]	5,194[9,15]	5,409[9,15]	4,053	6,603	Belgium
20[9]	1[9]	15[9]	7[9]	2[9]	14[9]	18[9]	10[9]	7[9]	9[9]	2.3	8.1	-119	70	-49	108	14	Belize
37	12	8[12]	3	1	8	17	—12—		9	4.5	0.8[4]	-183[9]	154[9]	-29[9]	32	12	Benin
...	...	...	...	...	...	...	...	...	...	1.8	1.1[4]	-481[2]	447[2]	-34[2]	444	134	Bermuda
43	1	9	8	7	7	8	8	—11—		8.3	7.1[14]	-32[1]	411	9[1]	3	...	Bhutan
21	15	14	3	1	9	13	12	—12—		0.1	2.5	-432[9]	-101[9]	-533[9]	105	68	Bolivia
11[1,16]	14	58[1,12,16]	71[1,16]	11[1,16]	6[1,16]	14[1,16]	—3[1,16]—			3.6[17]	0.3[13,17]	...	...	...			Bosnia and Herzegovina
5	42	4	6	2	3	14	5	2	19	11.7	9.8[14]	147[2]	-11[2]	138[2]	79[7]	407[7]	Botswana
11	2	25	7	4	5	7[19]	24	14[19]	10	3.8	1.5	15,525[9]	-9,250[9]	6,275[9]	1,307	1,332	Brazil
3	39	8	4	1	4	13	7	—24—		3.0	0.9[14]	84[9]	...	...	32[1]	...	Brunei
15	3	43[3]	5	3	8	8	—21—			-0.6	-1.3[4]	-381[9]	...	...	49	23	Bulgaria
31[9]	19	15[9]	6[9]	19	4[9]	15[9]	2[9]	22[9]		4.1	3.6	-362[9]	263[9]	-99[9]	9	36	Burkina Faso
49	1[6]	12	4	6	3	9	—2—		11	5.3	3.4	-102[9]	48[9]	-54[9]	4	21	Burundi
...	...	...	...	...	...	...	...	...	...			-190[1]	...				Cambodia
24[1]	14[1]	13[1]	5[1]	1[1]	6[1]	25[1]	—21—		10[1]	9.0	-3.8[4]	381[7]	-704[7]	-323[7]	10	182[7]	Cameroon
2[9]	4[9]	18[9]	7[9]	4[9]	9[9]	12[0]	18[9]	23[9]	7[9]	3.4	1.9	9,859	-29,460	-19,601	5,679	11,265	Canada
22[2]	12,[6]	6[2]	11[2]	6	12[2]	25[2]	—23[2]—			4.4	5.5[4]	-169[9]	165[9]	-4[9]	...	...	Cape Verde
42	3	9	2	—	—38—					0.5	1.7[4]	-42[9]	-15[9]	-57[9]	9[2]	41[2]	Central African Republic
45[2]	—	12[2]	—	12	1[2]	7	19	—29—		-5.0	4.0[4]	-100[1]	207	-80[7]	21	30	Chad
8	7	21	6	3	7	19	—29—			3.5	7.4	740[0]	-1,331[9]	-583[9]	706	459	Chile
24[9]	3	42[3,9]	6[9]	3	6[9]	6[9]	—10[0]—			9.5[21]	8.5	5,183[9]	1,218[9]	6,401[9]	3,948	812	China
17	8	20	5	3	9	11	—28—			3.8	4.1	1,233[9]	-321[9]	912[9]	705	641	Colombia
40[9]	...	4[9]	6[9]	29	4[9]	26[9]	—18[9]—			4.2	3.2[4]	-29[7]	20[7]	0[7]	8	6	Comoros
14[1]	28[1]	6[1]	2[1]	2[1]	14[1]	9[1]	—25[1]—			8.8	-0.0[4]	650[9]	-958[9]	-308[9]	6	83	Congo
18	12	19[12]	3	4	5	20	12	6	14	2.7	4.6	-498[9]	127[9]	-371[9]	431	223	Costa Rica
34[22]	—	6[22]	2[22]	6[22]	8[22]	7[22]	—9[22]—		13[22]	3.7	-1.1[4]	994[9]	-2,418[9]	-1,424[9]	53	228	Côte d'Ivoire
16[9,17]	...	49[3,9,17]	6[17]	19,[17]	9[9,17]	11[9,17]	—89,[17]—			2.8[17]	-1.7[4,17]	...	...	...			Croatia
16[1,23]	41,[23]	39[1,23]	9[1,23]	31,[23]	8[1,23]	20[1,23]	—11,[23,24]—			5.7[5]	-1.4[5,13]	-817[9]	...	...	382	...	Cuba
9	—	12	6	2	9	20	7	6	19	8.1	6.3	-2,087[9]	1,846[9]	-241[9]	1,539	132	Cyprus
6	3	44[3]	6	3	4	10	10	5	7	0.7	-2.1	-1,834[9,25]	1,803[9,25]	-31[9,25]	1,280[9,5]	670[9,26]	Czech Republic
4	1	19	6	2	10	14	20	0	22	2.6	1.4	7,848	-2,501	5,347	3,784	3,770	Denmark
3[1]	—	5[1]	6[1]	6[1]	13[1]	34[1]	—3[1]—		30[1]	1.4	2.2[4]	-433[9]	...	...	6[2]	...	Djibouti
26	1	7	7	3	16	13	15	1	18	5.4	4.8[14]	-43[9]	18[9]	-25[9]	25	6	Dominica
15	3	16	7	2	9	15	13	10	10	3.2	2.6	-1,612[9]	1,199[9]	-393[9]	1,054	115	Dominican Republic
18	12	15	3	2	9	15	11	—15—		4.3	2.6	644[9]	-1,111[9]	-467[9]	192	178	Ecuador
20	3	17	6	2	8	20	6	8	10	8.0	5.3	-5,501[9]	8,313[9]	2,812[9]	2,730	918	Egypt
10[9]	—	19[9]	3[9]	2[9]	5[9]	35[9]	8[9]	10[9]	7[9]	0.4	2.5	-706[9]	493[9]	-213[9]	49	577	El Salvador

National product and accounts (continued)

country	gross national product (GNP)					gross domestic product (GDP) by type of expenditure, 1991 (%)					cost components of gross domestic product (GDP), 1991 (%)			
	nominal, 1992 ('000,000 U.S.$)	per capita, 1992 (U.S.$)	average annual growth rates, 1985–92			consumption		gross domestic invest-ment	foreign trade		indirect taxes net of subsidies	consump-tion of fixed capital	compen-sation of employ-ees	net operating surplus
			real GNP (%)	popu-lation (%)	real GNP per capita (%)	private	govern-ment		exports	imports				
Equatorial Guinea	146	330	2.0	2.3	−0.3	76	14	16	28	−35	...	...	...	...
Eritrea	400	110	...	3.6	...	...	...	...	...	...	...	...	...	...
Estonia	4,297	2,750	...	0.2	...	52	14	25	33	−28	12	6	41	37
Ethiopia	6,206	110	1.4	3.4	−2.0	78	22	10	8	−18	9[18]	—91[18]—		
Faeroe Islands	635[27]	13,500[27]	...	0.5	...	53[1]	25[1]	19[1]	34[1]	−31[1]	12[18]	8	62[18]	26[8,18]
Fiji	1,510	2,010	3.5	0.9	2.6	65[2]	15[2]	19[2]	64[2]	−64[2]	11[1]	7[1]	41[1]	41[1]
Finland	116,309	22,980	1.1	0.4	0.7	56	24	20	22	−23	12	17	58	14
France	1,278,652	22,300	2.8	0.6	2.2	60	19	20	23	−22	13	13	52	22
French Guiana	891[1,27]	8,020[1,27]	...	6.2	...	67[1]	36[1]	45[1]	71[1]	−120[1]	...	...	...	...
French Polynesia	3,007[2,27]	15,260[2,27]	...	2.8	...	60[3]	40[3]	21[3]	9[3]	−31[3]	...	...	...	...
Gabon	5,341	4,450	0.6	2.7	−2.1	47[9]	15[9]	27[9]	39[9]	−28[9]	18[1]	14[1]	35[1]	34[1]
Gambia, The	367	390	5.0	3.2	1.8	73	18	19	4	−14	18[2]	10[2]	—72[2]—	
Gaza Strip	840[7]	1,270[7]	...	4.3	...	133	16	27	16	−93	...	...	...	...
Georgia	4,659	850	...	0.5	...	59[2]	38[2]	8[2]	40[9]	−46[2]	...	...	...	...
Germany	1,846,064	23,030	2.8	0.6	2.2	54	18	22	38	−31	11	13	55	21
Ghana	7,066	450	4.5	3.3	1.2	84	11	13	16	−24	...	...	...	...
Gibraltar	431[7]	15,080[7]	...	−0.1	...	...	...	...	...	...	...	...	...	...
Greece	75,106	7,180	1.8	0.7	1.1	72[22]	19[22]	19[22]	23[22]	−33[22]	14	9	39	39
Greenland	987[2]	17,780[2]	...	0.5	...	...	...	...	...	...	6[30]	8	76[30]	18[8,30]
Grenada	210	2,310	4.2	−0.2	4.4	69	19	44	45	−77	...	...	...	...
Guadeloupe	2,024[1,27]	5,790[1,27]	...	1.7	...	89[1]	32[1]	30[1]	6[1]	−57[1]	13[30]	8	71[30]	15[8,30]
Guam	2,000[7]	14,000[7]	...	3.2	...	...	...	...	...	...	...	...	...	...
Guatemala	9,586	980	3.5	2.9	0.6	84	6	14	18	−22	6[2]	2[2]	—92[2]—	
Guernsey[31]	1,531	26,000	11.1	1.2	9.9	...	...	...	...	...	...	...	...	...
Guinea	3,103	510	3.6	2.8	0.8	78[9]	10[9]	18[9]	24[9]	−30[9]	12[18]	—88[18]—		
Guinea-Bissau	217	210	2.5	2.1	0.4	95[9]	7[9]	24[9]	3[9]	−29[9]	11[30]	—89[30]—		
Guyana	268	330	−5.1	0.3	−5.4	56	12	36	68	−73	13[2]	—87[2]—		
Haiti	2,479	370	−0.9	2.0	−2.9	—96—		13	15	−24	10[2]	2[2]	—88[2]—	
Honduras	3,142	580	3.6	3.1	0.5	67	11	25	35	−38	11[2]	7[2]	43[2]	39[2]
Hong Kong	89,274	15,380	6.5	0.9	5.6	60	8	28	139	−135	5[2]	8	50[2]	45[2,8]
Hungary	30,671	3,010	−2.1	−0.6	−1.5	56	26	21	36	−39	13	8	59	20
Iceland	6,177	23,670	1.7	1.2	0.5	62	20	19	33	−34	18	11	52	19
India	271,638	310	5.4	2.1	3.3	61[9]	11[9]	25[9]	—39—		11	10	—79—	
Indonesia	122,825	670	6.5	1.8	4.7	55	9	35	28	−27	7	5	—88—	
Iran	130,910	2,190	2.3	3.7	−1.4	62	10	32	14	−19	2[2]	15[2]	—83[2]—	
Iraq	35,000[1]	1,940[1]	...	3.3	...	56[2]	33[2]	8[2]	27[2]	−24[2]	1[1]	9[1]	28[1]	62[1]
Ireland	42,798	12,100	4.9	−0.1	5.0	58	16	19	61	−54	10	10	51	29
Isle of Man	490[30]	7,570[30]	...	1.4	...	...	...	...	...	...	...	...	...	...
Israel	67,658	13,230	5.0	2.7	2.3	61	30	24	30	−45	17	14	48	21
Italy	1,186,568	20,510	2.5	0.2	2.3	62	18	20	18	−18	9	12	45	34
Jamaica	3,216	1,340	3.7	0.8	2.9	68	13	27	45	−54	15[1]	8[1]	44[1]	33[1]
Japan	3,507,841	28,220	4.4	0.4	4.0	57	9	32	10	−9	7	15	56	22
Jersey	2,884[7]	34,200[7]	...	1.1	...	...	...	...	...	...	...	...	...	...
Jordan	4,406	1,120	−1.2	5.8	−7.0	91	27	24	43	−85	16[18]	8[18]	42[18]	35[18]
Kazakhstan	28,584	1,680	...	1.0	...	75	17	16	—8—		...	...	...	...
Kenya	8,453	330	4.1	3.5	0.6	65	17	21	27	−29	14	8	35	51[8]
Kiribati	52	700	1.0	2.1	−1.1	70[1]	45[1]	31[1]	22[1]	−70[1]	12[10]	12[10]	52[10]	25[10]
Korea, North	22,000	990	...	1.9	...	...	...	...	...	...	...	...	...	...
Korea, South	296,349	6,790	9.5	1.0	8.5	53	11	39	29	−32	11	10	47	32
Kuwait	15,300	10,680	...	−2.3	...	67	164	56	15	−202	—	8[18]	34[18]	58[18]
Kyrgyzstan	3,667	810	...	1.7	...	49	20	33	—2—		—	16[1]	50[1]	34[1]
Laos	1,104	250	4.7	2.9	1.8	...	...	...	...	...	...	...	...	...
Latvia	5,080	1,930	...	0.0	...	10	46	34	35	−25	7	4	43	47
Lebanon	4,800[7]	1,400[7]	...	2.3	...	110[2]	44[2]	10[2]	32[2]	−96[2]	...	...	...	...
Lesotho	1,090	590	3.5	2.7	0.8	132	17	75	14	−138	19[2]	—81[2]—		
Liberia	984[1]	390[1]	...	3.1	...	58[2]	13[2]	10[2]	42[2]	−23[2]	4[18]	—96[18]—		
Libya	26,100	5,350	...	3.6	...	32[2]	23[2]	15[2]	59[2]	−29[2]	...	...	...	...
Liechtenstein	978[7]	33,510[7]	...	1.4	...	...	...	...	...	...	...	...	...	...
Lithuania	4,922	1,310	...	0.7	...	52	17	22	—9—		...	...	...	...
Luxembourg	13,716	35,260	3.9	0.8	3.1	57	17	31	94	−100	15	11	65	10
Macau	5,056[27]	13,390[27]	...	3.0	...	30	8	29	80	−47	...	...	...	...
Macedonia	...	...	...	1.1	...	...	...	...	...	...	...	...	...	...
Madagascar	2,809	230	1.4	3.1	−1.7	92	9	8	11	−26	13[18]	—87[18]—		
Malawi	1,896	210	3.1	3.4	−0.3	78	14	20	23	−36	10[1]	—90[1]—		
Malaysia	51,917	2,790	8.2	2.5	5.7	55	14	36	82	−87	14[2]	—86[2]—		
Maldives	114	500	11.8	3.3	8.5	49[2]	22[2]	19[2]	62[2]	−53[2]	...	...	...	...
Mali	2,730	300	0.9	2.8	−1.9	83[9]	14[9]	18[9]	12[9]	−27[9]	8[18]	—92[18]—		
Malta	2,606	7,240	6.1	0.7	5.4	61	18	32	87	−98	12[2]	5[2]	43[2]	40[2]
Marshall Islands	77[7,27]	1,580[7,27]	...	3.7	...	...	...	...	...	...	4	4	70	22
Martinique	2,835[1,27]	7,970[1,27]	...	1.0	...	84[1]	30[1]	25[1]	8[1]	−47[1]	12[30]	8	68[30]	20[8,30]
Mauritania	1,109	530	2.6	2.7	−0.1	54[9]	15[9]	18[9]	35[9]	−22[9]	13[18]	—87[18]—		
Mauritius	2,965	2,700	7.4	1.1	6.3	64	12	28	65	−69	16	8	40	44[8]
Mayotte	134[7,27]	1,430[7,27]	...	3.7	...	47[2]	92[2]	3[2]	—42[2]—		...	...	...	...
Mexico	294,831	3,470	2.9	1.8	1.1	72	9	22	14	−17	10	10	26	55
Micronesia	157[1]	1,560[1]	...	2.4	...	...	...	...	...	...	...	...	...	...
Moldova	5,485	1,260	...	0.6	...	63	10	27	33	−33	...	...	...	...
Monaco	475[7]	16,000[7]	...	1.0	...	...	...	...	...	...	...	...	...	...
Mongolia	2,100[7,27]	900[7,27]	...	2.8	...	73[2]	24[2]	30[2]	23[2]	−50[2]	20	22[2]	39[2]	40[2,20]
Morocco	27,210	1,040	3.8	2.5	1.3	67	15	23	22	−27	15[18]	—85[18]—		
Mozambique	1,034	60	1.4	2.7	−1.3	89	20	43	23	−75	6[18]	—94[18]—		
Myanmar (Burma)	28,000[27]	660[27]	...	2.2	...	—86—		16	2	−3	4	5	43	48
Namibia	2,502	1,610	4.2	3.1	1.1	69	29	11	61	−70	13[1]	4[1]	44[1]	38[1]
Nauru	90[1]	10,000[1]	...	2.0	...	...	...	...	...	...	...	...	...	...
Nepal	3,285	170	4.7	2.6	2.1	81	12	21	14	−28	7[2]	—93[2]—		
Netherlands, The	312,340	20,590	2.8	0.7	2.1	60	14	21	54	−49	10	11	53	27

origin of gross domestic product (GDP) by economic sector, 1991 (%)										avg. annual growth rate of real GDP (%)		balance of payments, 1993 (current external transactions; '000,000 U.S.$)			tourist trade, 1992 ('000,000 U.S.$)		country
primary		secondary			tertiary					1975–1985	1985–1992	net transfers		current balance of payments	receipts from foreign nationals	expenditures by nationals abroad	
agriculture	mining	manufacturing	construction	public utilities	transp., communications	trade	financial svcs.	other svcs.	government			goods, merchandise	invisibles				
50	12	1[12]	3	3	2	7		13	14	6.0	2.2[24]	24[7]	-1[7]	-25[7]	...	...	Equatorial Guinea
...	...	...	...	...	...	...	...	...	...	...	...	...	...	...	...	...	Eritrea
17	2	33	6	2	6	8	2	4	6	-0.2[26]	-1.6[14]	55[9]	95[9]	150[9]	4	2	Estonia
41[2]	—	11[2]	4[2]	1[2]	7[2]	10[2]	4[2]	7[2]	13[2]	1.6	2.1[14]	-823[9]	703[9]	-120[9]	23	77	Ethiopia
15[22]	—	13[22]	4[22]	1[22]	9[22]	11[22]	7[22]	24[22]	16[22]	2.5	1.4[4]	140[7]	...	...	...	...	Faeroe Islands
21[9]	—	12[9]	6[9]	1[9]	14[9]	19[9]	13[0]	——17[0]——		1.4	3.0[14]	-126[9]	113[9]	-13[4]	223	44	Fiji
5	—	19	9	3	8	11	20	7	21	2.9	0.6	6,392	-7,372	-980	1,315	2,403	Finland
6	12	18[12]	5	2	6	15	4	23	16	2.3	2.6	8,416	3,504	11,920	25,000	13,910	France
11[1]	3	9[1,3]	14[1]	3	28	11[1]	——6[1,20]——			...	13.2[29]	-618[9]	...	...	...	...	French Guiana
5[6]	12	76,[12]	6[6]	26	76	20[6]	——53[6]——			5.2	5.6[4]	-788[9]	...	...	170	...	French Polynesia
11[7]	48[7]	57	6[7]	27	8[7]	12[7]	——7[7]——			-2.1	-6.9[4]	1,412[9]	-1,547[9]	-135[9]	5	143	Gabon
23	—	6	7	1	17	24	7	3	12	-0.8	3.5[14]	-31[9]	68[9]	379	56	13	Gambia, The
16	3	13[3]	18	3	——53——					2.8	4.8[14]	-235[18]	219[18]	-16[18]	6[18]	10[18]	Gaza Strip
47[5,9]	5[9]	34[3,5,9]	8[5]	3	35,[9]	25,[9]	——65,[9]——			6.1[5]	-1.8[5]	-661[7]	...	...	...	...	Georgia
1[9]	3[9]	28[9]	6[9]	...	5[9]	8[9]	13[9]	19[9]	10[9]	2.2	2.9	43,130	-64,520	-21,390	10,982	37,309	Germany
48[2]	2[2]	9[2]	3[2]	2[2]	4[2]	19[2]	4[2]	—	8[2]	0.3	4.7	-470[9]	92[9]	-378[9]	167	17	Ghana
...	...	...	...	...	...	...	...	...	...	...	...	-365[7]	...	...	82	...	Gibraltar
16	1	17	7	3	7	——15——		8	19	2.8	1.7	-10,557	9,810	-747	3,268	1,186	Greece
...	...	...	...	...	...	...	...	...	...	...	...	-123[9]	...	...	...	...	Greenland
16	—	5	11	3	15	20	10	3	21	4.9	4.4	-83[9]	58[9]	-25[9]	38	57	Grenada
9[1]	3	6[1,3]	7[1]	3	28	17[1]	——67[1,28]——			2.3	3.3[29]	-1,418[9]	...	...	269	...	Guadeloupe
...	...	...	...	...	...	...	...	...	...	...	...	...	...	...	1,579	589[30]	Guam
26	—	15	2	3	8	24	9	6	7	2.2	3.2	-1,044[9]	338[9]	-706[9]	243	103	Guatemala
...	...	...	...	...	...	...	...	...	...	...	...	...	...	...	146[22]	...	Guernsey[31]
28[2]	24[2]	4[2]	6[2]	1[2]	4[2]	22[2]	——11[2]——			2.9	5.3[4]	-185[9]	...	...	...	...	Guinea
45[1]	—	5[1]	6[1]	1	1[1]	28[1]	——6[1]——		8[1]	1.7	4.1[32]	-95[9]	...	...	...	...	Guinea-Bissau
25	11	12[32]	7	32	8	9	8	4	17	-3.2	0.5	-93[9]	...	...	31	...	Guyana
0[4]	—	13	0	1	2	16	6	4	14	2.3	-1.4	-138[7]	128[7]	-10[7]	46	337	Haiti
23	2	17	4	3	5	13	14	11	7	4.4	3.5	-140[9]	-124[9]	-264[9]	32	38	Honduras
—	—	15	5	2	9	24	32	——15——		8.9	7.0	-3,406	...	...	6,037	...	Hong Kong
10	12	25[12]	6	3	8	12	8	——15——		2.7	2.5	-4,021	-241	-4,262	1,251	661	Hungary
17	—	12	9	4	8	14	18	6	15	4.1	0.7	2[9]	-212[9]	-210[9]	129	288	Iceland
32	2	19	6	2	7	12	8	6	6	4.4	5.2	-6,110[2]	-716[2]	-6,826[2]	1,415	425[2]	India
19	14	21	6	1	6	17	7	3	6	6.2	6.3	6,021[9]	-9,700[9]	-3,679[9]	2,729	1,166	Indonesia
24	9	16	4	1	7	18	12	2	8	1.4	1.0	-6,560[7]	-1,349[7]	-7,909[7]	577	734[7]	Iran
20[2]	12[2]	10[2]	8[2]	1[2]	8[2]	16[2]	11[2]	——14[2]——		2.9	4.9[13]	-90[9]	...	...	55[2]	...	Iraq
8[2]	3	30[2,3]	5[2]	3	5[2]	12[2]	5[2]	13[2]	14[2]	3.5	5.1	6,804[9]	-4,175[9]	2,629[9]	1,620	1,361	Ireland
...	...	...	...	...	...	...	...	...	...	-1.7	...	...	...	...	36[10]	...	Isle of Man
2	12	22[12]	8	2	8	10	24	4	23	3.2	4.8	-5,607	4,234	-1,373	1,876	1,674	Israel
3	12	21[12]	6	5	6	18	12	14	13	3.1	2.5	3,088	-31,082	-27,994	21,577	16,617	Italy
6	11	18	13	3	9	21	13	5	7	-1.6	3.5[4]	-409[9]	521[9]	117[9]	858	64	Jamaica
2	—	32	9	4	6	14[19]	16	16[19]	6	4.4	4.0	141,570	-10,100	131,470	3,588	26,837	Japan
5[2]	—	——2[2]——			————93[2]————					...	7.2[14]	...	...	...	526[2]	...	Jersey
7[9]	4[9]	15[9]	5[9]	3[9]	15[9]	10[9]	19[9]	4[9]	20[9]	8.6	1.5	-1,780[9]	1,015[9]	-765[9]	462	350	Jordan
34[5]	3	37[3,5]	14[5]	3	8[5]	5[5]	——15——			2.7[5]	-3.0[5]	-1,670[9]	-410[9]	-2,080[9]	...	...	Kazakhstan
25	—	10	7	1	6	10	13	4	13	4.9	4.3	-591[9]	493[9]	-98[9]	442	29	Kenya
24[1]	—	2[1]	4[1]	2[1]	14[1]	14[1]	8[1]	3[1]	25[1]	-11.5	0.9[33]	-16[30]	22[30]	6[30]	2	27	Kiribati
...	...	...	...	...	...	...	...	...	...	...	...	-128[9]	...	...	...	...	Korea, North
7	—	34	9	3	8	12	14	5	6	8.0	9.2	-2,146[9]	-2,383[9]	-4,529[9]	3,272	3,794	Korea, South
—	42[9]	14[9]	2[9]	-1[9]	2[9]	8[9]	3[9]	——30[9]——		-2.4	3.0[33]	85[9]	788[9]	873[9]	273	1,705	Kuwait
28	3	38[3]	7	3	4	————23————				...	1.5[14]	-77	...	...	...	...	Kyrgyzstan
53	—	13	4	2	6	8	3	5	6	3.4[26]	-6.9	-134[9]	...	...	...	...	Laos
20	—	34	6	2	7	11	5	4	5			679[7]	...	...	...	...	Latvia
9[1]	5[1,6]	13[1]	3[1]	6	4[1]	28[1]	——38[1]——			-9.4	-22.5[13]	-3,854	...	...	...	...	Lebanon
12	—	12	19	1	3	8	5	8	16	4.7	6.6[14]	-823[9]	861[9]	38[9]	19	11	Lesotho
34[1]	10[1]	7[1]	2[1]	2[1]	7[1]	5[1]	12[1]	3[1]	12[1]	0.0	1.2[4]	63[18]	-181[18]	-118[18]	6[10]	...	Liberia
5[1]	28[1]	8[1]	13[1]	2[1]	6[1]	7[1]	9[1]	1[1]	21[1]	-3.1	1.2[4]	3,780[2]	-1,577[2]	2,203[2]	6	154	Libya
...	...	...	...	...	...	...	...	...	...	...	...	574[7]	...	...	...	...	Liechtenstein
21[7]	3	48[3,7]	5[7]	3	5[7]	9[7]	——14[7]——			4.2[26]	1.2[14]	305[9]	69	311[9]	...	...	Lithuania
1	—	24	7	2	7	16	14	15	15	2.4	7.8	15	15	15	290[2]	...	Luxembourg
...	...	...	...	...	...	...	...	...	...	...	7.9	-201[9]	...	...	2,234	57	Macau
17[1,17]	12	55[1,12,17]	51[1,17]	11,[17]	6[1,17]	13[1,17]	——3[1,17]——			3.1[17]	1.0[13,17]	...	...	...	11	...	Macedonia
39[2]	12,[6]	8[2]	2[2]	6	5[2]	7[2]	——38[2]——			0.2	1.1	138[9]	2[9]	-136[9]	39	37	Madagascar
35	...	13	4	2	6	12	11	4	14	3.1	2.1	44[30]	-97[30]	-53[30]	13[7]	3[2]	Malawi
17	9	29	4	2	7	11	10	2	10	6.8	7.3	3,409	-5,600	-2,103	1,768	1,740	Malaysia
24	2	6[34]	9	34	6	17	4	24	8	15.5	9.2	-111[9]	-78[9]	-33[9]	113	22	Maldives
46	1	7	4	1	4	16	1	——15——		1.8	4.6	-145[9]	54[9]	-91[9]	45	68	Mali
3	35	26	4[35]	36	6	14	14	9	23[36]	6.5	5.9	-599[2]	544[2]	-55[2]	568	138	Malta
...	...	...	...	...	...	...	...	...	...	...	...	...	...	...	4	...	Marshall Islands
6[1]	3	11[1,3]	5[1]	3	28	15[1]	——68[1,28]——			3.9	4.0[29]	1,508[9]	...	...	282	...	Martinique
31[1]	10[1]	6[1]	6[1]	1[1]	11[1]	19[1]	——5[1]——		14[1]	2.0	3.0[4]	377	-55[7]	-18[7]	15[2]	31[2]	Mauritania
11	—	24	7	2	11	18	12	4	11	4.2	6.9	254	158	-96	299	142	Mauritius
...	...	...	...	...	...	...	...	...	...	...	...	-83[9]	...	...	...	...	Mayotte
9	2	22	4	1	8	27	12	——16——		4.1	1.9	-20,677[9]	-2,134[9]	-22,811[9]	5,996	6,108	Mexico
...	...	...	...	...	...	...	...	...	...	...	...	...	...	...	...	...	Micronesia
42[5]	3	38[3,5]	7[5]	3	4[5]	5[5]	——5[5]——			2.5[26]	-3.6	-37[9]	2[9]	-35[9]	...	...	Moldova
...	...	...	...	...	...	...	...	...	...	...	...	...	...	...	...	...	Monaco
20[2]	3	34[2,3]	6[2]	3	13[2]	9[2]	——18[2]——			...	4.1[37]	-807	-317	-111[7]	...	...	Mongolia
18	2	17	5	6	6	21	...	11	12	3.0	3.4	2,706[9]	2,309[9]	-427[9]	1,360	242	Morocco
37[2]	12	23[2,12]	13[2]	...	10[2]	——17[2]——				-1.0	2.2	650[9]	278[9]	-901[9]	...	...	Mozambique
57	1	8	2	—	3	23	——4——			5.8	-0.2	-205[30]	29[30]	-176[30]	13[7]	1[7]	Myanmar (Burma)
15[2]	22[2]	6[2]	2[2]	2[2]	7[2]	12[2]	7[2]	22	21[2]	0.0	3.5[32]	110[9]	32[9]	142[9]	91	81	Namibia
...	...	...	...	...	...	...	...	...	...	...	...	...	...	...	...	...	Nauru
55	—	6	7	1	4	6	7	——7——		3.6	4.9	-376[9]	195[9]	-181[9]	110	52	Nepal
4	4	21	6	2	7	16	——45——			1.8	2.9	10,956[9]	-4,206[9]	6,750[9]	5,004	9,330	Netherlands, The

National product and accounts (continued)

country	gross national product (GNP)					gross domestic product (GDP) by type of expenditure, 1991 (%)					cost components of gross domestic product (GDP), 1991 (%)			
	nominal, 1992 ('000,000 U.S.$)	per capita, 1992 (U.S.$)	average annual growth rates, 1985–92			consumption		gross domestic investment	foreign trade		indirect taxes net of subsidies	consumption of fixed capital	compensation of employees	net operating surplus
			real GNP (%)	population (%)	real GNP per capita (%)	private	government		exports	imports				
Netherlands Antilles	1,600[27]	8,320[27]	...	0.9	...	67[30]	29[30]	26[30]	66[30]	-87[30]	...	...	...	...
New Caledonia	1,000[7]	6,000[7]	...	2.1	...	45[1]	31[1]	20[1]	32[1]	-29[1]	6[1]	11[1]	44[1]	40[1]
New Zealand	41,186	12,060	0.3	0.7	-0.4	63	17	17	29	-26	14	9	45	32
Nicaragua	1,325	410	-5.0	2.8	-7.8	90	20	20	21	-51	...	...	...	...
Niger	2,466	300	1.7	3.2	-1.5	78	15	8	12	-13	...	...	...	...
Nigeria	32,944	320	6.3	2.9	3.4	44	4	13	63	-24	1	5	14	80
Northern Mariana Is.	541	12,080	...	7.1	...	...	...	...	...	...	...	...	...	...
Norway	110,465	25,800	0.6	0.4	0.2	52	22	18	43	-36	11	15	52	23
Oman	10,683	6,490	4.8	3.8	1.0	38	36	17	48	-39	20	8	33	67[8,20]
Pakistan	49,477	410	4.8	3.1	1.7	69	14	19	11	-18	12	6	—82—	
Panama	6,133	2,440	0.9	2.1	-1.2	61	17	18	39	-36	9	8	46	37
Papua New Guinea	3,846	950	2.2	2.3	-0.1	60	22	27	42	-52	11	12	37	40
Paraguay	6,038	1,340	3.9	2.9	1.0	80	7	25	20	-32	6[2]	11[2]	24[2]	59[2]
Peru	21,272	950	-2.2	2.1	-4.3	80	5	17	9	-12	15	14	37	34
Philippines	49,462	770	4.2	2.3	1.9	73	9	21	28	-32	9	8	34	48
Poland	75,268	1,960	-1.5	0.4	-1.9	58	20	22	23	-23	...	...	...	...
Portugal	73,336	7,450	4.8	-0.7	5.5	66	18	28	27	-40	13	8	45	42[8]
Puerto Rico	23,603	6,610	2.7	0.8	1.9	62	14	16	72	-64	5	6	42	47
Qatar	8,511	16,240	-0.9	6.0	-6.9	32[18]	44[18]	14[18]	41[18]	-32[18]	1[10]	—99[10]—		
Réunion	6,225[27]	9,980[27]	...	1.5	...	79[9]	29[9]	27[9]	4[9]	-39[9]	10[30]	8	57[30]	33[8,30]
Romania	24,865	1,090	-5.4	0.1	-5.5	69	6	29	17	-21	11[2]	13[2]	71[2]	4[2]
Russia	397,786	2,680	...	0.5	...	57	7	39	—-3—		...	...	...	...
Rwanda	1,813	250	0.2	3.0	-2.8	81	21	12	8	-23	7[1]	8[1]	25[1]	61[1]
St. Kitts	181	3,990	4.9	-0.4	5.3	65[2]	18[2]	56[2]	51[2]	-90[2]	...	...	...	...
St. Lucia	453	2,900	7.1	1.9	5.2	68[9]	17[9]	33[9]	9[9]	-44[9]	...	...	...	...
St. Vincent	217	1,990	5.6	0.9	4.7	70[9]	25[9]	24[9]	13[9]	-32[9]	...	...	...	...
San Marino	400[7,27]	17,000[7,27]	...	0.9	...	...	...	...	...	...	...	...	...	...
São Tomé and Príncipe	44	370	0.5	2.3	-1.8	75[9]	50[9]	29[9]	—9	-54[9]	...	...	...	...
Saudi Arabia	126,355	7,940	4.8	3.5	1.3	39	38	19	46	-42	-0.2[1]	8	46[1]	54[1,8]
Senegal	6,124	780	3.3	3.0	0.3	78	13	14	16	-21	18[18]	—82[18]—		
Seychelles	378	5,480	4.9	0.8	4.1	51[9]	28[9]	22[9]	48[9]	-49[9]	23[2]	8[2]	35[2]	33[2]
Sierra Leone	726	170	2.5	2.5	0.0	78	10	12	25	-26	8[2]	6[2]	14[2]	73[2]
Singapore	44,315	15,750	7.7	1.8	5.9	43	11	37	—9—		...	...	...	...
Slovakia	10,249	1,920	-6.6	0.4	-7.0	49	24	35	—8—		...	...	...	...
Slovenia	12,744	6,330	...	0.7	...	...	...	...	...	...	...	...	...	...
Solomon Islands	237	710	5.6	2.9	2.7	69[1]	31[1]	33[1]	52[1]	-85[1]	14[18]	7[18]	48[18]	32[18]
Somalia	946[6]	150[6]	...	3.1	...	95[1]	11[1]	40[1]	8[1]	-55[1]	3[18]	—97[18]—		
South Africa	106,019	2,670	1.1	2.4	-1.3	60	21	16	25	-20	10	16	54	20
Spain	547,947	14,020	4.0	0.2	3.8	63	16	25	17	-20	8	11	46	35
Sri Lanka	9,459	540	3.5	1.3	2.2	77	10	23	29	-39	13	5	44	39
Sudan, The	10,107[2]	400[2]	...	2.8	...	81[1]	10[1]	15[1]	9[1]	-15[1]	...	...	...	...
Suriname	1,728	3,700	-0.9	2.3	-3.2	51	32	21	20	-24	9	11	48	32
Swaziland	930	1,080	10.3	3.9	6.4	79	20	19	60	-78	15[18]	7[18]	45[18]	34[18]
Sweden	233,209	26,780	1.0	0.6	0.4	53	27	18	28	-27	13	12	62	14
Switzerland	248,688	36,230	2.0	0.9	1.1	58	14	27	35	-34	5	10	64	21
Syria	17,700[27]	1,370[27]	...	3.3	...	78	14	16	25	-33	-4	4	—100—	
Taiwan	210,722	10,180	8.8	1.1	7.7	54	18	23	48	-43	10	9	53	28
Tajikistan	2,723	480	...	3.0	...	...	...	...	...	...	...	...	...	...
Tanzania	2,858	110	4.4	3.0	1.4	85	10	38	16	-50	17	2	9	72
Thailand	106,559	1,840	10.0	1.7	8.3	56	9	42	35	-42	13	9	24	53
Togo	1,575	400	2.2	3.7	-1.5	70[2]	19[2]	23[2]	41[2]	-53[2]	21[18]	—79[18]—		
Tonga	136	1,350	0.8	0.9	-0.1	...	...	...	...	...	...	...	...	...
Trinidad and Tobago	4,995	3,940	-1.7	1.3	-3.0	63	15	13	41	-33	3[2]	10[2]	50[2]	33[2]
Tunisia	14,615	1,740	4.1	2.0	2.1	65	17	23	39	-43	12[1]	11[1]	—78[1]—	
Turkey	114,234	1,950	4.9	2.2	2.7	60[2]	19[2]	24[2]	20[2]	-23[2]	9[2]	6[2]	33[2]	52[2]
Turkmenistan	4,895	1,270	...	2.5	...	...	...	...	...	...	...	...	...	...
Tuvalu	8.8[2,27]	970[2,27]	...	1.8	...	...	...	...	...	...	...	...	...	...
Uganda	2,968	170	4.9	3.1	1.8	95[1]	10[1]	24[1]	18[1]	-49[1]	65[10]	—35[10]—		
Ukraine	87,025	1,670	...	0.3	...	...	...	...	...	...	...	...	...	...
United Arab Emirates	37,068	22,220	3.1	3.1	0.0	41	17	21	67	-47	-1[2]	13[2]	23[2]	66[2]
United Kingdom	1,024,769	17,760	1.8	0.3	1.5	64	22	16	23	-25	13	11	58	18
United States	5,904,822	23,120	2.0	0.9	1.1	68	17	15	11	-11	8	13	61	18
Uruguay	10,444	3,340	3.5	0.6	2.9	70	14	13	23	-20	19	8	44	37[8]
Uzbekistan	18,377	860	...	2.4	...	61	19	26	—-5—		...	...	...	...
Vanuatu	189	1,220	2.9	2.4	0.5	63[2]	28[2]	44[2]	46[2]	-77[2]	20[1]	8	41[1]	38[1,8]
Venezuela	58,901	2,900	3.6	2.5	1.1	67	10	19	31	-26	4	7	33	56
Vietnam	15,000[7]	220[7]	...	2.3	...	78	15	11	—-5—		11[1]	7[1]	59[1]	22[1]
Virgin Islands (U.S.)	1,246[18,27]	11,740[18,27]	...	-1.4	...	...	...	...	...	...	...	...	...	...
West Bank	2,020[7]	2,060[7]	...	3.5	...	106[18]	10[18]	29[18]	19[18]	-64[18]	...	...	...	...
Western Sahara	60[7,27]	300[7,27]	...	2.4	...	...	...	...	...	...	...	...	...	...
Western Samoa	153	940	0.4	0.5	-0.1	...	...	...	...	...	...	...	...	...
Yemen	8,000	780	...	4.4	...	75[2]	27[2]	16[2]	14[2]	-33[2]	9[2]	5[2]	—86[2]—	
Yugoslavia	32,000[27]	3,000[27]	...	0.8	...	...	...	...	...	...	...	...	...	...
Zaire	9,200	240	...	3.3	...	82	14	5	23	-24	...	...	...	...
Zambia	2,580	290	1.4	3.5	-2.1	52	16	15	34	-17	7[2]	9[2]	57[2]	26[2]
Zimbabwe	5,896	570	2.4	3.0	-0.6	58[2]	24[2]	21[2]	31[2]	-33[2]	14[2]	—86[2]—		

[1]1989. [2]1990. [3]Manufacturing includes mining and public utilities. [4]1985–90. [5]Net material product (NMP). [6]Mining includes public utilities. [7]1991. [8]Net operating surplus includes consumption of fixed capital. [9]1992. [10]1986. [11]1986–91. [12]Manufacturing includes mining. [13]1985–89. [14]1985–91. [15]Data refer to the Belgium-Luxembourg Economic Union (BLEU). [16]Gross material product. [17]Social product. [18]1987. [19]Services includes restaurants and hotels. [20]Net operating surplus includes indirect taxes net of subsidies. [21]1978–85. [22]1993. [23]Global social product. [24]Activities in the material sphere not elsewhere specified. [25]Data refer to former Czechoslovakia. [26]1980–85. [27]Gross domestic product (GDP). [28]Services includes transportation,

agriculture	mining	manufacturing	construction	public utilities	transp., communications	trade	financial svcs.	other svcs.	government	1975–1985	1985–1992	goods, merchandise	invisibles	current balance of payments	receipts from foreign nationals	expenditures by nationals abroad	country
1[30]	—	6[30]	9[30]	5[30]	14[30]	26[30]	14[30]	11[30]	20[30]	1.9[38]	...	−863[9]	900[9]	37[0]	529	...	Netherlands Antilles
2[1]	26[1,6]	5[1]	5[1]	6	4[1]	21[1]	——37[1]——			−0.2	...	−518[9]	...	...	94	...	New Caledonia
7	1	17	4	3	8	16	23	3	12	1.6	0.3	1,663[9]	−2,690[9]	−1,027[9]	1,032	977	New Zealand
31	1	17	3	1	4	24	6	4	9	−1.8	−2.2	−392	−65	−457	21	30	Nicaragua
37	5	7	2	2	4	18	——22——			1.7	1.1[4]	−48[9]	3[9]	−45[9]	17	9	Niger
39	13	8	2	1	3	13	9	3	0	0.7	5.2	4,611[9]	−2,343[9]	2,268[4]	29	340	Nigeria
...	...	...	...	...	...	...	...	...	...	...	...	...	...	...	528		Northern Mariana Is.
3	15	13	4	4	9	11	9	10	16	4.0	1.8	8,016	−5,563	2,453	1,975	3,870	Norway
4	42	4	4	2	4	14	9	2	17	13.6	3.9[14]	2,047[9]	−2,413[9]	−366[9]	85	47	Oman
22	1	15	4	3	8	15	6	7	7	6.4	6.0	−2,700[9]	680[9]	−2,020[9]	120	679	Pakistan
11	—	9	3	4	25	12	14	10	12	4.6	1.5	−986	931	−55	207	125	Panama
26	17	10	6	2	7	10	4	——19——		1.2	3.9	−231	−332[1]	−355[1]	49	42[1]	Papua New Guinea
27	—	17	5	3	4	30	2	——12——		6.3	4.9	−552[7]	86[7]	−466[7]	153	120	Paraguay
7	2	25	9	1	6	19	18	12	3	0.6	−1.3	−580	−1,195	−1,775	237	480	Peru
21	1	26	5	2	6	14	4	——21——		2.8	3.2	−6,222	2,933	−3,289	1,674	102	Philippines
7	12	40[12]	10	2	6	13	——20——			−0.2	−1.6[14]	−85[9]	−3,017[9]	−3,102[9]	4,100	132	Poland
6[2]	12	29[2,12]	8[2]	3[2]	6[2]	17[2]	9[2]	8[2]	13[2]	3.1	3.6	−9,540[9]	9,356[9]	−184[9]	3,721	1,165	Portugal
1	35	39	2[35]	39	8[39]	15	13	10	11	3.3	4.3[14]	1,730[7]	−5,131[7]	−3,401[7]	1,511	760	Puerto Rico
1	34	13	4	2	3	6	11	——27——		0.0	...	1,608[9]	...	...	...	...	Qatar
6[2]	...	12[2]	8[2]	7[2]	——67[2]——					5.1	4.1[4]	−2,187[9]	...	...	157	...	Réunion
19	3	44[3]	5	3	5	8	2	8	10	−0.1	−5.5	−1,194[9]	−312[9]	−1,506[9]	262	260	Romania
16	3	36[3]	9	3	7	——26——				3.9[5]	2.3[5,14]	−4,300[9]	—	−4,300[9]	...	...	Russia
40[1]	—	13[1]	7[1]		7[1]	13[1]	8[1]	——8[1]——		5.0	1.0	−172[9]	87[9]	−85[9]	4	17	Rwanda
7	1	13	13	1	16	22	11	3	18	2.9	5.8	−60[9]	39[9]	−21[9]	67	5	St. Kitts
14[2]	1[2]	8[2]	6[2]	3[2]	17[2]	24[2]	13[2]	4[2]	15[2]	4.6	6.0	−153[9]	98[9]	−55[9]	208	177	St. Lucia
18	—	9	10	5	22	14	11	2	15	6.3	6.7	−41[9]	24[9]	−17[9]	54	77[7]	St. Vincent
...	...	...	...	...	...	...	...	...	...	...	...	...	...	...	...	...	San Marino
25[1]	...	10[1]	9[1]	2[1]	12[1]	10[1]	1[1]	——31[1]——		1.8	3.2[4]	−6[2]	−2[2]	−8[2]	1[2]	2[2]	São Tomé and Príncipe
6[2]	35[2]	9[2]	9[2]	—	6[2]	8[2]	7[2]	3[2]	16[2]	2.8	4.9	12,991[9]	−32,422[9]	−19,431[9]	1,884[2]	2,000[18]	Saudi Arabia
21[2]	3	16[2,3]	3[2]	2	9[2]	24[2]	——27[2]——			2.0	3.4[4]	−284[7]	467	−238[7]	171[7]	103[7]	Senegal
5	40	17[40]	40	40	23	18	8	15	13	2.5	5.4[14]	−143[9]	141[9]	−2[9]	117	16	Seychelles
35	10	9	1	—	9	20	12	——3——		1.4	2.5[14]	−1[2]	−68[2]	−69[2]	17	3	Sierra Leone
—	—	29	6	2	14	18	27	——10——		7.4	7.5	−4,900[9]	7,829[9]	2,929[9]	5,204	2,340	Singapore
6	3	53[3]	7	3	8	10	2	12	3	...	1.4[4]	...	...	...	213	155	Slovakia
6	1	33	4	5	6	10	21	2	12	...	−4.4[41]	...	...	...	670	234	Slovenia
31	—	——7——		39	8[39]	——13——		——23——		6.8	3.4[13]	−8[7]	−29[7]	−37[7]	6	13[7]	Solomon Islands
65	—	4	4	1	6	9	3	2	6	1.4	2.5[4]	−279[1]	122[1]	−157[1]	8[10]	...	Somalia
5	10	25	3	4	8	14	15	2	15	2.6	0.8	5,944	−4,130	1,814	1,226	1,544	South Africa
49[3]	3	23[3,9]	9[9]	3	——58[9]——					1.7	3.7	−16,064	9,807	−6,257	22,181	5,542	Spain
22	1	17	7	2	10	20	5	3	7	5.3	3.6[14]	−715[9]	264[9]	−451[9]	199	111	Sri Lanka
36[1]	12	8[1,12]	5[1]	2[1]	——38[1]——				12[1]	−0.1	1.9[4]	−597[9]	919	−506[9]	5	33	Sudan, The
12	3	9	9	6	7	17	22	1	22	0.8	1.4[14]	68[9]	−57[9]	11[9]	11	12	Suriname
13	1	27	2	2	5	9	10	2	14	3.6	5.4[4]	−90[9]	115[9]	25[9]	32	16	Swaziland
3	—	21	7	3	7	11	23	——29——		1.6	1.2	7,708	−9,544	−1,836	3,086	6,794	Sweden
3[2]	12	24[2,12]	8[2]	2[2]	6[2]	18[2]	21[2]	——20[2]——		1.6	1.9	−251[9]	13,670[9]	13,419[9]	7,650	6,068	Switzerland
28[2]	14[2]	6[2]	4[2]	−1[2]	9[2]	25[2]	4[2]	2[2]	10[2]	4.5	4.0	159[9]	−104[9]	55[9]	600	260	Syria
4	—	34	5	3	6	16	19	4	11	8.6	8.2	11,443	−5,601	5,842	2,449	5,678[7]	Taiwan
44[5]	3	31[3,5]	13[5]	3	3[5]	6[5]	——35——			3.7[5]	1.8[4,5]	...	...	...	...	...	Tajikistan
47[2]	1.0[2]	4[2]	3[2]	1[2]	7[2]	12[2]	5[2]	——6[2]——		2.0	4.1	−779[2]	353[2]	−426[2]	120	192[2]	Tanzania
13	2	28	7	2	7	23	9	6	3	6.8	10.0[14]	−4,155[9]	−2,449[9]	−6,604[9]	4,829	1,590	Thailand
35[1]	8[1]	7[1]	4[1]	4[1]	7[1]	23[1]	——3[1]——		10[1]	1.3	4.5[4]	−96[9]	−9[9]	−105[9]	39	48	Togo
34[1]	1[1]	9[1]	6[1]	1[1]	6[1]	10[1]	4[1]	——17[1]——		6.6	...	−36[9]	35[9]	−1[9]	9	1	Tonga
3	23	10	8	2	10	14	10	7	12	2.0	−1.1[14]	666[9]	−544[9]	122[9]	111	112	Trinidad and Tobago
18	6	17	4	2	7	24	——13——			5.2	4.1	−2,044[9]	1,099[9]	−945[9]	1,074	167	Tunisia
17	2	19	7	3	15	18	7	2	10	3.6	6.0[4]	−14,162	7,782	−6,380	3,639	776	Turkey
46[5]	3	20[3,5]	18[5]	3	7[5]	——9[5]——				1.9[5]	3.5[5,14]	194[9]	1[9]	195[9]	...	...	Turkmenistan
24[2]	3[2]	3[2]	15[2]	2[2]	4[2]	15[2]	9[2]	——26[2]——		...	...	41	...	...	0.3	...	Tuvalu
35[2]	12	7[2,12]	7[2]	1[2]	10[2]	21[2]	5[2]	3[2]	10[2]	−1.4	4.8	−271[9]	171[9]	−100[9]	157[7]	187	Uganda
29[5]	3	43[3,5]	14[5]	3	4[5]	6[5]	——45——			3.4[5]	1.0[5,14]	...	...	...	...	...	Ukraine
2[9]	41[9]	8[9]	9[9]	2[9]	6[9]	10[9]	11[9]	3[9]	11[9]	6.9	1.9	4,528[9]	...	...	...	...	United Arab Emirates
2	6[6]	21	7	6	7	15	18	7	17	1.8	2.0	−20,172	4,108	−16,064	13,683	19,831	United Kingdom
2[1]	2[1]	19[1]	5[1]	3[1]	6[1]	16[1]	17[1]	19[1]	12[1]	2.9	2.2	−132,470	23,220	−109,250	53,861	39,872	United States
10	—	25	4	3	6	12	13	24	9	0.7	4.1	−239[9]	32[9]	−207[9]	381	104	Uruguay
36[9]	3	29[3,9]	13[9]	3	——22[9]——					4.4[5]	0.9[5]	−61[9]	49[9]	57[9]	...	...	Uzbekistan
20[2]	—	6[2]	6[2]	2[2]	8[2]	32[2]	10[2]	7[2]	11[2]	5.1	1.7[4]	−49[9]	53[9]	4[9]	27	17	Vanuatu
5	18	22	6	2	5	13	13	6	9	1.0	4.5	1,689[9]	−5,054[9]	−3,365[9]	432	1,428	Venezuela
41	3	20[3]	3	3	4	12	11	——9——		3.7[5]	...	−1,093[9]	...	...	85[2]	...	Vietnam
...	...	...	...	...	...	...	...	...	...	−0.4	...	−500[2]	...	...	792	...	Virgin Islands (U.S.)
19[18]	12	8[12,18]	17[18]	42	——56[18,42]——					4.8	5.2[14]	−391[10]	525[18]	134[18]	10[18]	46[18]	West Bank
...	...	...	...	...	...	...	...	...	...	...	...	...	...	...	...	...	Western Sahara
47[1]	...	13[1]	2[1]	4[1]	4[1]	10[1]	...	9[1]	12[1]	1.3	...	−84[9]	33[9]	−51[9]	19	2	Western Samoa
21[2]	9[2]	9[2]	4[2]	2[2]	8[2]	12[2]	6[2]	——12[2]——		...	...	...	...	...	47	81[1]	Yemen
14[16]	12	40[12,16]	7[16]	1[16]	7[16]	20[16]	——10[16]——			...	...	...	...	...	88	...	Yugoslavia
31[1]	24[1]	1[1]	6[1]	—	1[1]	21[1]	——7[1]——		10[1]	−0.1	0.7[4]	600[2]	−1,243[2]	−643[2]	72	16[2]	Zaire
18[2]	9[2]	32[2]	4[2]	1[2]	5[2]	12[2]	7[2]	—	6[2]	0.2	1.2[4]	420[2]	−727[2]	−307[2]	51	56	Zambia
20	6	26	2	3	7	10	6	12	6	2.4	4.2[4]	487	−537[7]	−489[7]	105	70[7]	Zimbabwe

communications. [29] 1982–89. [30] 1988. [31] Excludes Alderney and Sark. [32] 1987–92. [33] 1985–88. [34] Manufacturing includes public utilities. [35] Construction includes mining. [36] Government includes public utilities. [37] 1984–90. [38] Includes Aruba. [39] Transportation includes public utilities. [40] Manufacturing includes mining, construction, and public utilities. [41] 1987–91. [42] Tertiary sector includes public utilities.

Employment and labour

This table provides international comparisons of the world's national labour forces—giving their size; composition by demographic component and employment status; and structure by industry.

The table focuses on the concept of "economically active population," which the International Labour Organisation (ILO) defines as persons of all ages who are either employed or looking for work. In general, "economically active population" does not include students, persons occupied solely in domestic duties, retired persons, persons living entirely on their own means, and persons wholly dependent on others. Persons engaged in illegal economic activities—smugglers, prostitutes, drug dealers, bootleggers, black marketeers, and others—also fall outside the purview of the ILO definition. Countries differ markedly in their treatment, as part of the labour force, of such groups as members of the armed forces, inmates of institutions, the unemployed (both persons seeking their first job and those previously employed), seasonal and international migrant workers, and persons engaged in informal, subsistence, or part-time economic activities. Some countries include all or most of these groups among the economically active, while others may treat the same groups as inactive.

Three principal structural comparisons of the economically active total are given in the first part of the table: (1) participation rate, or the proportion of the economically active who possess some particular characteristic, is given for women and for those of working age (usually ages 15 to 64), (2) activity rate, the proportion of the total population who *are* economically active, is given for both sexes and as a total, and (3) employment status, usually (and here) grouped as employers, self-employed, employees, family workers (usually unpaid), and others.

Each of these measures indicates certain characteristics in a given national labour market; none should be interpreted in isolation, however, as the meaning of each is influenced by a variety of factors—demographic structure and change, social or religious customs, educational opportunity, sexual differentiation in employment patterns, degree of technological development, and the like. Participation and activity rates, for example, may be high in a particular country because it possesses an older population with few children, hence a higher proportion of working age, or because, despite a young population with many below working age, the economy attracts eligible immigrant workers, themselves almost exclusively of working age. At the same time, low activity and participation rates might be characteristic of a country having a young population with poor employment possibilities or of a country with a good job market distorted by the presence of large numbers of "guest" or contract workers who are not part of the domestic labour force. An illiterate woman in a strongly sex-differentiated labour force is likely to begin and end as a family or

Employment and labour

| country | year | economically active population | | | | | | | | | distribution by economic sector | | | |
| | | total ('000) | participation rate (%) | | activity rate (%) | | | employment status (%) | | | | agriculture, forestry, fishing | | manufacturing; mining, quarrying; public utilities | |
			female	ages 15–64	total	male	female	employers, self-employed	employees	unpaid family workers	other	number ('000)	% of econ. active	number ('000)	% of econ. active
Afghanistan	1979	3,941	7.9	49.1	30.3	54.2	4.9	...	...	...	...	2,369	60.1	494	12.5
Albania	1989[3]	1,458	45.8	78.7[4]	45.6	48.0	43.1	...	...	...	...	799	54.8	279	19.1
Algeria	1987	5,341	9.2	44.3	23.6	42.4	4.4	16.8	61.7	2.6	18.9	725	13.6	622	11.6
American Samoa	1990	14.2	41.1	52.6[6]	30.4	34.8	25.7	2.1	92.6	0.2	5.1	0.3	2.3	4.8	33.7
Andorra	1989	25	45.6	74.3	55.1	...	...	...	...	...	...	0.3	1.2	2.7	11.0
Angola	1988	3,936	39.0	61.5[8]	41.5	51.5	31.9	...	...	...	...	2,810	71.4	400[9]	10.2[9]
Antigua and Barbuda	1985	32	40.1	56.2[11, 12]	42.6	53.3	32.9	12.3[13]	69.9[13]	0.6[13]	17.2[13]	2.1[14, 15]	9.0[14, 15]	2.1[14, 15]	9.1[14, 15]
Argentina	1990	12,305	27.9	59.6	38.1	55.4	21.0	25.1[16]	71.2[16]	3.3[16]	0.4[16]	1,201[16]	12.0[16]	2,136[16]	21.3[16]
Armenia	1990	2,044	49.4	79.9[18]	61.3	63.2	59.5	...	...	...	...	117	5.7	453	22.2
Aruba	1991	31.1	42.5	67.1	46.7	54.5	39.0	...	...	...	...	0.2	0.5	2.3	7.3
Australia	1992[21]	8,586	41.8	73.0	49.1	57.3	41.0	14.1	74.5	0.9	10.5	430	5.0	1,431	16.7
Austria	1991[21]	3,607	41.1	68.1	46.1	56.6	36.4	9.9	83.1	3.6	3.4	259	7.2	1,020	28.3
Azerbaijan	1990	3,242	42.6[22]	71.8[18]	45.4	52.1	38.8	...	...	...	...	...	...	...	...
Bahamas, The	1990	114	46.7	75.2	44.9	48.8	41.0	76.5[22]	11.1[22]	0.3[22]	12.1[22]	5.8	5.1	6.4	5.6
Bahrain	1991	226	17.5	66.8	44.6	63.5	18.5	9.5[24]	85.9[24]	0.1[24]	4.6[24]	5	2.3	33	14.6
Bangladesh	1989	50,744	41.4	79.9	46.9	53.2	40.2	29.3	9.4	45.2	16.1	32,569	64.2	7,081	14.0
Barbados	1992[21]	125	48.3	77.3	50.2	54.4	46.4	8.8[14]	76.4[14]	0.2[14]	14.6[14]	6.0	4.8	11.7	9.4
Belarus	1992	4,887	49.0[22]	86.1[18]	47.8	...	...	...	...	...	...	981	20.1	1,432	29.3
Belgium	1990	4,179	41.6	51.2[27]	41.9	50.1	34.1	12.7	73.9	3.4	10.0	100	2.4	820	19.6
Belize	1991	58.1	26.4	56.1[27]	31.5	45.8	16.8	23.4[28]	55.1[28]	7.5[28]	14.0[28]	18.3	31.4	7.0	12.0
Benin	1988	2,100	47.8	72.5[8]	47.2	50.2	44.3	...	...	...	...	1,310	62.4	173[9]	8.2[9]
Bermuda	1991	35.2	48.2[29]	76.0[12]	59.7[29]	63.5[29]	56.1[29]	7.7[16]	88.6[16]	0.5[16]	3.2[16]	0.6[30]	1.7[30]	1.4[30]	3.9[30]
Bhutan	1985	632	32.9	69.0	44.6	58.0	30.3	...	...	...	...	531[16]	92.5[16]	16[9, 16]	2.8[9, 16]
Bolivia	1992	2,530	38.2	64.0	39.4	48.7	30.4	41.2	31.5	7.1	20.2	984	38.9	281	11.1
Bosnia and Herzegovina	1990[32]	1,026	36.9	...	22.7	...	...	...	...	...	...	39	3.8	519	50.5
Botswana	1991[21]	443	38.4	59.2	33.4	43.1	24.6	6.5	62.5	17.2	13.8	100	22.7	46	10.5
Brazil	1990[21]	64,468	35.5	63.6[28]	43.8	57.5	30.5	26.3	62.3	7.7	3.7	14,181	22.0	10,217	15.9
Brunei	1991	112	32.9	67.6	43.0	54.6	30.0	3.5	91.4	0.4	4.7	2.2	1.9	11.6	10.4
Bulgaria	1985	4,686	47.7	75.7	52.4	55.1	49.6	0.3	98.2	—	1.5	772	16.5	1,778	37.9
Burkina Faso	1988	4,547	46.4	78.1[8]	53.3	57.6	49.1	...	...	...	...	3,869	85.1	223[9]	4.9[9]
Burundi	1990	2,780	52.6	91.4	52.1	51.2	53.8	62.8	5.1	30.3	1.8	2,574	92.6	37	1.3
Cambodia	1992	3,964	55.7	91.2[33]	43.1	41.2	44.7	...	...	...	...	2,454[16]	74.4[16]	220[9, 16]	6.7[9, 16]
Cameroon	1988	4,392	33.8	57.1[8]	41.2	52.5	26.1	60.2[14]	14.6[14]	18.0[14]	7.1[14]	2,901[34]	74.0[34]	180[34]	4.6[34]
Canada	1992[21]	13,797	45.0	75.2	49.7	55.5	44.2	9.0	89.8	0.5	0.8	466	3.4	2,354	17.1
Cape Verde	1990	121	37.1	64.3	35.3	46.9	24.9	24.7	53.7	2.0	19.6	29.9	24.8	6.8	5.7
Central African Republic	1988	1,187	46.8	78.3	48.2	52.2	44.3	75.3	8.0	8.1	8.6	881	74.2	31	2.6
Chad	1988	1,899	21.4	51.0	35.2	56.1	14.8	...	...	...	...	1,452	76.5	124[9]	6.5[9]
Chile	1992[21]	4,990	32.0	58.0	37.5	52.1	23.5	26.2	66.0	3.4	4.4	860	17.2	925	18.5
China	1987[21]	584,569	44.5	76.8[27]	54.7	59.6	49.7	...	...	...	...	414,740	71.0	95,977	16.4
Colombia	1985	9,558	32.8	49.4[35]	34.3	46.6	22.3	...	...	...	...	2,412[16]	28.5[16]	1,231[16]	14.5[16]
Comoros	1988	197	40.6	68.4[8]	45.3	54.2	36.5	47.6[16]	25.6[16]	—26.8[16]—		53[16]	53.3[16]	4.1[16]	4.2[16]
Congo	1984	563	45.6	54.0	29.5	33.0	26.2	64.3	31.4	1.2	3.1	294	52.2	50	8.8
Costa Rica	1992	1,087	29.9	55.6[27]	37.0	52.4	21.9	23.7	72.2	3.4	0.7	259	23.8	219	20.1
Côte d'Ivoire	1988	4,263	32.3	66.6	39.4	52.2	26.0	...	...	...	...	2,451	57.5	433[9]	10.2[9]
Croatia	1991	2,040	42.9	65.2	45.3	53.9	37.4	12.7	73.7	2.0	11.6	341	16.7	571	28.0
Cuba	1989	4,570[36]	36.1[36]	56.9[27, 36]	43.7[36]	55.4[36]	31.7[36]	4.8[24]	94.1[24]	0.2[24]	0.9[24]	721[32]	20.4[32]	768[32]	21.8[32]
Cyprus[37, 38]	1991	280	37.9	73.0	48.2	59.9	36.5	18.1	72.2	6.2	3.5	34	12.3	51	18.1
Czech Republic	1991	5,421	47.6	77.9	52.6	56.8	48.7	2.2	88.7	7.6	1.5	628	11.6	2,021	37.3
Denmark	1991	2,912	46.5	82.4	56.6	61.5	51.8	8.4	89.5	1.7	0.4	161	5.5	609	20.9
Djibouti	1988	230	40.4	67.0[8]	44.9	52.7	36.9	...	...	...	...	176	76.6	21[9]	9.0[9]
Dominica	1989	30.6	41.8	62.3	37.5	47.1	29.3	29.2	50.6	1.9	18.3	7.7	25.2	3.6	11.8
Dominican Republic	1981	1,915	28.9	53.6	33.9	48.1	19.7	36.5	51.3	3.3	8.9	420	22.0	243	12.7
Ecuador	1990	3,360	26.4	55.7	34.8	51.5	18.3	45.7	42.5	4.4	7.4	1,036	30.8	404	12.0
Egypt	1989[21]	16,034	28.8	54.0	30.7	42.8	18.0	26.7	45.7	20.7	6.9	6,335	39.5	2,102	13.1
El Salvador	1980[21]	1,593	34.8	62.4	35.4	47.5	24.0	28.2	59.2	10.9	1.7	637	40.0	262	16.4
Equatorial Guinea	1983	103	35.7	66.7	39.2	52.5	26.9	29.0	16.0	29.9	25.1	59.4	57.9	1.8	1.8
Eritrea[39]	...	...	...	...	...	...	...	...	...	...	...	...	...	...	...
Estonia	1989	856	50.0	79.7	54.7	58.5	51.3	...	...	...	...	100	11.7	270	31.5
Ethiopia[39]	1992	23,518	41.1	70.1	41.3	48.5	34.1	58.5[40]	6.5[40]	34.0[40]	1.0[40]	16,101[40]	88.3[40]	312[40]	1.7[40]
Faeroe Islands	1977	17.6	27.2	64.0	41.9	58.2	23.9	11.9	86.1	...	2.0	3.3	18.8	3.9	21.9

traditional agricultural worker. Loss of working-age men to war, civil violence, or emigration for job opportunities may also affect the structure of a particular labour market.

The distribution of the economically active population by employment status reveals that a large percentage of economically active persons in some less developed countries falls under the heading "employers, self-employed." This occurs because the countries involved have poor, largely agrarian economies in which the average worker is a farmer who tills his own small plot of land. In countries with well-developed economies, "employees" will usually constitute the largest portion of the economically active.

Caution should be exercised when using the economically active data to make intercountry comparisons, as countries often differ in their choices of classification schemes, definitions, and coverage of groups and in their methods of collection and tabulation of data. The population base containing the economically active population, for example, may range, in developing countries, from age 9 or 10 with no upper limit to, in developed countries, age 18 or 19 upward to a usual retirement age of from 55 to 65, with sometimes a different range for each sex. Data on female labour-force participation, in particular, often lack comparability. In many less developed countries, particularly those dominated by the Islamic faith, a cultural bias favouring traditional roles for women results in the under counting of economically active women. In other less developed countries, particularly those in which subsistence workers are deemed economically active, the role of women may be overstated.

The second major section of the table provides data on the distribution by economic (also conventionally called industrial) sector of the "economically active population." The data usually include such groups as unpaid family workers, members of the armed forces, and the unemployed, the last distributed by industry as far as possible.

The categorization of industrial sectors is based on the divisions listed in the *International Standard Industrial Classification of All Economic Activities*. The "other" category includes persons whose activities were not adequately defined and the unemployed who were not distributable by industrial sector.

A substantial part of the data presented in this table is summarized from various issues of the ILO's *Year Book of Labour Statistics,* which compiles its statistics both from official publications and from information submitted directly by national census and labour authorities. The editors have supplemented and updated ILO statistical data with information from Britannica's holdings of relevant official publications and from direct correspondence with national authorities.

construction		transportation, communications		trade, hotels, restaurants		finance, real estate		public administration, defense		services		other		country
number ('000)	% of econ. active	number ('000)	% of econ. active	number ('000)	% of econ. active	number ('000)	% of econ. active	number ('000)	% of econ. active	number ('000)	% of econ. active	number ('000)	% of econ. active	
51	1.3	66	1.6	138	3.5	1	1	1	1	749[1]	19.0[1]	78[2]	2.0[2]	Afghanistan
49	3.4	44	3.0	49	3.3	1	1	1	1	220[1]	15.1[1]	17	1.2	Albania
690	12.9	216	4.1	391	7.3	143	2.7	5	5	1,180[5]	22.1[5]	1,374	25.7	Algeria
1.2	8.3	0.8	5.5	1.8	13.0	0.3	2.1	1.4	10.0	2.8	19.8	0.7[7]	5.1[7]	American Samoa
2.9	11.8	...	...	6.0	24.2	1.3	5.4	2.6	10.3	4.1	16.7	0.1	0.5	Andorra
9	9	10	10	10	10	10	10	10	10	726[10]	18.5[10]	—	—	Angola
2.6[14,15]	11.1[14,15]	2.6[14,15]	11.1[14,15]	5.2[14,15]	22.4[14,15]	0.8[14,15]	3.4[14,15]	5	5	7.9[5,14,15]	33.9[5,14,15]	—	—	Antigua and Barbuda
1,003[16]	10.0[16]	460[16]	4.6[16]	1,702[16]	17.0[16]	396[16]	3.9[16]	5	5	2,399[5,16]	23.0[5,16]	700[17]	7.0[17]	Argentina
162	7.9	88	4.3	88	4.3	18	0.9	8	0.4	413	20.2	697[19]	34.1[19]	Armenia
3.2	10.4	2.3	7.5	11.0	35.4	2.4	7.8	5	5	8.6[5]	27.7[5]	1 1[20]	3.5[20]	Aruba
594	6.9	520	6.1	1,697	19.8	935	10.9	373	4.3	2,189	25.5	418[17]	4.9[17]	Australia
313	8.7	228	6.3	689	19.1	236	6.6	5	5	822[5]	22.8[5]	40	1.1	Austria
...	...	...	...	...	...	...	...	...	...	...	...	...	...	Azerbaijan
10.8	9.4	8.7	7.6	85.0	30.0	9.0	7.9	5	5	35.5[5]	31.0[5]	3.2[23]	2.8[23]	Bahamas, The
27	11.8	14	6.1	30	13.2	17	7.6	5	5	84[5]	37.1[5]	16[20]	7.3[20]	Bahrain
661	1.3	1,278	2.5	4,130	8.1	238	0.5	5	5	3,439[5]	6.8[5]	1,341[25]	2.6[25]	Bangladesh
7.4	5.9	4.1	3.3	14.2	11.4	4.1	3.3	5	5	39.1[5]	31.3[5]	38.2[20]	30.5[20]	Barbados
382	7.8	33.1	6.8	327	6.7	26	26	172	3.5	853[26]	17.5[26]	409	8.3	Belarus
236	5.6	257	6.2	634	15.2	328	7.8	5	5	1,389[5]	33.2[5]	415[20]	9.9[20]	Belgium
4.1	7.0	2.9	5.0	10.0	17.2	1.8	3.1	5.4	9.2	6.0	10.3	2.8	4.8	Belize
9	9	10	10	10	10	10	10	10	10	616[10]	29.4[10]	—	—	Benin
3.4	9.7	2.7	7.6	9.5	27.1	4.6	13.0	2.4	6.8	6.4	18.0	4.3[31]	12.1[31]	Bermuda
9	9	10	10	10	10	10	10	10	10	27[10,16]	4.7[10,16]	—	—	Bhutan
129	5.1	117	4.6	232	9.2	54	2.1	59	2.3	350	13.8	323[17]	12.7[17]	Bolivia
75	7.3	69	6.7	131	12.8	39	3.8	5	5	155[5]	15.1[5]	—	—	Bosnia and Herzegovina
57	12.9	10	2.3	34	7.7	13	3.0	5	5	103[5]	23.2[5]	79[20]	17.0[20]	Botswana
3,823	5.9	2,440	3.6	7,976	12.4	1,716	2.7	5	5	21,694[5]	33.7[5]	2,367[7]	3.77	Brazil
14.1	12.6	5.4	4.8	15.4	13.8	5.8	5.2	5	5	52.1[5]	46.6[5]	5.3[20]	4.7[20]	Brunei
407	8.7	315	6.7	397	8.5	25	0.5	5	5	993[5]	21.2[5]	1		Bulgaria
9	9	10	10	10	10	10	10	10	10	455[10]	10.0[10]	—	—	Burkina Faso
20	0.7	9	0.3	26	0.9	2.0	0.1	5	5	85[5]	3.1[5]	27[20]	1.0[20]	Burundi
9	9	10	10	10	10	10	10	10	10	625[10,16]	18.9[10,16]	—	—	Cambodia
67[34]	1.7[34]	52[34]	1.3[34]	154[34]	3.9[34]	8[34]	0.2[34]	5	5	293[5,34]	7.5[5,34]	228[5,20]	5.8[5,20]	Cameroon
879	6.4	1,002	7.3	2,412	17.5	809	5.9	5	5	5,767[5]	41.8[5]	106[7]	0.77	Canada
22.7	18.8	6.1	5.1	12.7	10.6	0.8	0.7	5	5	17.4[5]	14.4[5]	24.1	20.0	Cape Verde
6	0.5	7	0.6	92	7.8	0.7	0.1	5	5	70[5]	5.9[5]	100[20]	8.5[20]	Central African Republic
9	9	10	10	10	10	10	10	10	10	323[10]	17.0[10]	—	—	Chad
339	6.8	335	6.7	849	17.0	244	4.9	5	5	1,221[5]	24.5[5]	218[20]	4.4[20]	Chile
13,298	2.3	10,898	1.9	20,785	3.6	1,268	0.2	9,704	1.7	17,414	3.0	487	0.1	China
242[16]	2.9[16]	353[16]	4.2[16]	1,262[16]	14.9[16]	278[16]	3.3[16]	5	5	1,998[5,16]	23.6[5,16]	691[16,17]	8.2[16,17]	Colombia
3.3[16]	3.3[16]	2.1[16]	2.1[16]	1.9[16]	1.9[16]	0.2[16]	0.2[16]	2.4[16]	2.4[16]	4.6[16]	4.7[16]	28[10]	27.8[16]	Comoros
25	4.5	29	5.1	67	11.8	3	0.5	5	5	85[5]	15.1[5]	10	2.0	Congo
66	6.1	50	4.6	180	16.6	39	3.5	5	5	258[5]	23.8[5]	16[17]	1.5[17]	Costa Rica
9	9	10	10	10	10	10	10	10	10	1,377[10]	32.3[10]	—	—	Côte d'Ivoire
93	4.5	112	5.5	223	10.9	58	2.8	104	5.1	204	10.0	329[20]	16.1[20]	Croatia
344[32]	9.8[32]	236[32]	6.7[32]	395[32]	11.2[32]	22[32]	0.6[32]	152[32]	4.3[32]	836[32]	23.7[32]	53[32]	1.5[32]	Cuba
23	8.3	15	5.5	61	21.8	17	6.1	5	5	54[5]	19.3[5]	24[25]	8.6[25]	Cyprus[37,38]
412	7.6	366	6.8	551	10.2	26	26	238	4.4	1,005[26]	18.5[26]	200	3.7	Czech Republic
199	6.8	195	6.7	422	14.5	253	8.7	218	7.5	802	27.6	52[17]	1.8[17]	Denmark
9	9	10	10	10	10	10	10	10	10	33[10]	14.4[10]	—	—	Djibouti
2.6	8.5	1.6	5.2	2.9	9.5	0.7	2.3	5	5	5.7[5]	18.6[5]	5.4[25]	17.6[25]	Dominica
81	4.3	40	2.1	192	10.0	22	1.2	5	5	360[5]	18.9[5]	553[17]	20.9[17]	Dominican Republic
197	5.9	131	3.9	477	14.2	81	2.4	5	5	838[5]	24.9[5]	106[17]	5.0[17]	Ecuador
990	6.2	780	4.9	1,340	8.4	255	1.6	5	5	3,116[5]	19.4[5]	1,115[20]	7.0[20]	Egypt
80	5.0	66	4.1	256	16.1	16	1.0	5	5	250[5]	15.7[5]	27[23]	1.7[23]	El Salvador
1.9	1.9	1.8	1.7	3.1	3.0	0.4	0.4	5	5	8.4[5]	8.2[5]	25.8[20]	25.2[20]	Equatorial Guinea
...	...	...	...	...	...	...	...	...	...	...	...	...	...	Eritrea[39]
73	8.5	73	8.5	75	8.8	4	0.5	19	2.2	182	21.3	60	7.0	Estonia
46[40]	0.3[40]	77[40]	0.4[40]	696[40]	3.8[40]	15[40]	0.1[40]	5	5	933[5,40]	5.1[5,40]	56[2,40]	0.3[2,40]	Ethiopia[39]
2.0	11.1	1.9	11.1	2.1	11.9	0.3	1.9	5	5	3.5[5]	20.1[5]	0.6	3.2	Faeroe Islands

Employment and labour (continued)

country	year	economically active population						employment status (%)				distribution by economic sector			
		total ('000)	participation rate (%)		activity rate (%)							agriculture, forestry, fishing		manufacturing; mining, quarrying; public utilities	
			female	ages 15–64	total	male	female	employers, self-employed	employees	unpaid family workers	other	number ('000)	% of econ. active	number ('000)	% of econ. active
Fiji	1986	241	21.2	56.0	33.7	52.4	14.5	33.6	42.2	16.3	7.9	106	44.1	22	9.0
Finland	1992	2,526	46.9	74.2	50.1	54.8	45.8	12.8	84.5	0.7	2.0	203	8.0	520	20.6
France	1991[21]	24,609	43.3	66.9	44.5	51.1	38.3	12.6	77.1	1.0	9.3	1,257	5.1	4,841	19.7
French Guiana	1990	48.8	38.2	67.3	42.5	50.5	33.9	10.6	62.7	2.5	24.2	4.2	8.6	3.1	6.4
French Polynesia	1988	75	37.1	64.8	39.9	48.2	30.9	13.0	55.0	4.0	28.0	7.6	10.0	5.4	7.2
Gabon	1988	473	37.6	57.0[8]	43.3	54.8	32.1	...	...	...	...	326	69.0	62[9]	13.1[9]
Gambia, The	1983	326	46.3	78.2	47.3	51.1	43.6	0.5	78.0	14.3	7.1	240	73.7	9	2.9
Gaza Strip	1992	119	1.7	35.3[27]	16.5	32.1	0.8	...	...	...	...	21.3	18.0	11.1[41]	9.4[41]
Georgia	1991	2,514	45.9[22]	90.1[18,22]	46.4	...	...	...	...	...	...	386	15.3	690[9]	27.4[9]
Germany	1991	39,405	42.3	72.6	50.2	60.0	41.1	7.3	91.4	1.3	—	1,487	3.8	11,898	30.2
Ghana	1984	5,580	51.2	82.5[27]	45.4	44.9	45.8	67.7	15.7	12.2	4.4	3,311	59.3	631	11.3
Gibraltar	1991	14.8	33.4	66.9[27]	53.8	71.9	35.4	6.6[24]	89.7[24]	...	3.6[24]	—	—	1.1	7.5
Greece	1990[21]	4,000	37.1	57.7[36]	39.6[36]	50.8[36]	28.7[36]	32.4	50.6	12.0	5.0	893	22.3	808	20.2
Greenland	1976	21.4	33.4	63.5[27]	43.1	53.0	31.4	12.6	82.5	0.4	4.5	3.2	15.1	3.3	15.3
Grenada	1988	38.9	48.6	72.7[42]	39.9	42.9	37.2	...	...	...	...	5.6	14.3	3.3	8.6
Guadeloupe	1990	172	45.5	66.4	44.5	49.6	39.7	13.2	53.7	2.0	31.1	9.4[43]	7.2[43]	6.8[43]	5.3[43]
Guam	1990	66.1	37.4	75.7[6]	49.7	58.4	39.7	2.4	94.4	0.1	3.1	0.5	0.8	3.5	5.3
Guatemala	1989[21]	2,898	25.5	59.1	33.5	50.8	16.7	32.7	47.6	16.2	3.5	1,416	48.9	405	14.0
Guernsey[44]	1991	30.2	43.2	74.2	51.2	60.6	42.6	13.7	86.3	—	...	2.4	7.8	2.4	7.9
Guinea	1983	1,823	39.4	63.5	39.1	48.7	30.1	36.2	15.6	37.6	10.6	1,424	78.1	27	1.5
Guinea-Bissau	1988	446	41.3	66.9[8]	47.2	57.2	37.8	...	...	...	...	354	79.4	17[9]	3.9[9]
Guyana	1987[45]	270	29.9	60.4	35.7	50.9	21.0	14.3[16]	63.8[16]	1.9[16]	20.0[16]	50[16]	20.4[16]	41[16]	16.8[16]
Haiti	1990	2,679	40.0	64.8	41.1	50.3	32.3	59.1	16.5	10.4	14.0	1,535	57.3	178	6.6
Honduras	1992[21]	1,729	31.2	58.3[27]	34.8	49.0	21.2	36.5	48.7	10.7	4.1	640	37.0	264	15.3
Hong Kong	1992[21]	2,793	36.8	69.2	49.5	61.6	36.9	10.7	86.5	0.9	2.0	19	0.7	671	24.0
Hungary	1993	5,015	48.5	82.8[18]	48.6	52.3	45.3	...	...	...	...	431	8.6	1,304	26.0
Iceland	1993	149	45.9	81.6[46]	56.2	60.7	51.7	...	...	...	...	13.5	9.5	24.2	16.3
India	1991	314,904	29.0	60.7[24,27]	37.6	51.5	22.7	8.8[24]	16.3[24]	3.6[24]	71.3[24]	172,713[24]	66.4[24]	28,846[24]	11.1[24]
Indonesia	1989	75,508	39.9	67.7	42.6	51.2	34.0	42.4	26.2	28.6	2.8	41,284	54.7	7,909	10.5
Iran	1986	12,855	10.3	46.8	26.0	45.6	5.5	36.9	41.5	3.9	17.7	3,209	25.0	1,584	12.3
Iraq	1988	4,127	12.0	45.3	24.7	42.3	6.1	25.4[47]	59.5[47]	11.4[47]	3.7[47]	477	11.6	439	10.6
Ireland	1991	1,334	32.2	59.7	37.8	51.4	24.3	18.2	77.8	1.4	2.6	155	11.6	246	18.4
Isle of Man	1991	33.2	42.3	73.2	47.6	56.9	38.9	15.8	80.1	—	4.1	1.2	3.7	3.9	11.6
Israel	1992[21]	1,858	41.8	58.3	43.5	41.4	29.6	15.0	72.9	0.9	11.2	61	3.3	386	20.8
Italy	1991[21]	24,245	37.1	65.1[48]	42.5	54.9	30.7	21.6	63.8	3.7	10.9	1,823	7.5	4,958	20.4
Jamaica	1993	1,083	47.2	71.6[29,49]	43.8	46.2	41.4	34.1[50]	47.2[50]	2.7[50]	16.0[50]	221	20.4	110	10.2
Japan	1992	65,780	40.7	71.2	52.9	63.9	42.3	12.8	77.8	6.9	2.4	4,110	6.2	16,080	24.4
Jersey	1991	47.5	43.2	66.9[27]	56.5	66.1	47.5	12.6	84.0	...	3.4	2.2	4.7	3.8	8.0
Jordan	1988	644	11.4	43.2	22.8	39.3	5.3	22.8[51]	67.2[51]	0.8[51]	9.2[51]	33	5.1	55	8.6
Kazakhstan	1992	7,450	54.0[22]	80.1[18]	43.7	...	...	...	...	...	...	1,355	18.2	1,290	17.3
Kenya	1988	9,220	40.0	65.1[8]	39.9	47.9	32.0	...	...	...	...	7,182	77.9	696[9]	7.5[9]
Kiribati	1990	32.6	46.4	75.6[27]	45.1	48.9	41.4	71.9	25.3	...	2.8	23.1	71.0	0.9	2.8
Korea, North	1985	9,084	46.0	75.3	44.6	48.6	40.6	...	...	...	...	3,726[14]	44.1[14]	2,790[9,14]	33.0[9,14]
Korea, South	1992[21]	19,385	40.1	63.7	45.4	54.0	36.6	28.1	59.3	10.2	2.4	3,025	15.6	4,894	25.2
Kuwait	1988	730	24.3	61.5	38.9	53.5	21.0	3.9	94.1	0.1	1.9	9	1.3	69	9.4
Kyrgyzstan	1991	1,754	48.6[22]	79.2[18]	39.1	...	...	...	...	...	...	623	35.5	319	18.2
Laos	1985	2,014	45.3	84.2	48.9	53.1	44.6	...	...	...	...	1,393[16]	75.7[16]	130[9,16]	7.1[9,16]
Latvia	1991	1,462	50.0[22]	80.0[22]	55.1[22]	59.3[22]	51.5[22]	—— 95.5 ——		—— 4.5 ——		248	17.0	371	25.4
Lebanon	1988	904	16.6	44.0	26.5	43.9	8.9	...	...	...	...	132[43]	19.1[43]	131[43]	18.9[43]
Lesotho	1986	504	27.0	44.0	31.6	47.3	16.7	16.8	55.7	20.5	7.0	131	25.9	142	28.2
Liberia	1984	704	41.0	56.3	33.5	39.1	27.8	59.1	21.6	14.4	5.0	481	68.3	31	4.4
Libya	1989	994	8.7[36]	37.5[8,36]	24.9[36]	43.3[36]	4.6[36]	23.7[52]	69.6[52]	4.2[52]	2.6[52]	192	19.2	144	14.5
Liechtenstein	1993	15.1	37.7	70.5	50.0	63.9	36.7	6.3	91.6	0.1	2.0	0.3	2.2	4.9	32.2
Lithuania	1992	1,869	48.9[22]	76.9[22]	52.4[22]	56.6[22]	48.6[22]	...	...	...	...	343	18.4	594	31.8
Luxembourg	1991[53]	168	36.5	62.5	43.5	56.4	31.2	9.2	85.3	1.1	4.4	5	3.2	26	15.8
Macau	1991[21]	175	41.5	66.4[54]	50.1	60.2	40.4	9.5	86.3	1.2	3.0	0.1	0.1	57	32.5
Macedonia	1993	632	...	...	30.5	...	...	5.7	66.6	—	27.7	34	5.4	170	26.9
Madagascar	1988	4,945	40.8	65.3[8]	44.0	52.5	35.4	...	...	...	...	3,830	77.5	509[9]	10.3[9]
Malawi	1987	3,458	51.0	89.4	43.3	43.9	42.8	4.9	16.2	77.6	1.3	2,968	85.8	114	3.3
Malaysia	1990[21]	6,685	35.5	63.5	37.6	48.2	26.9	25.6[36]	61.9[36]	12.5[36]	...	1,889[36]	30.6[36]	1,059[36]	17.1[36]
Maldives	1990	56	19.9	50.2	26.5	41.3	10.8	39.7	49.3	4.5	6.5	14.1	25.0	9.4	16.6
Mali	1987	3,438	37.4	67.4	44.7	57.2	32.7	35.4	5.2	57.6	1.8	2,803	81.5	191	5.6
Malta	1990	132	25.4	47.4[54]	39.2	56.1	18.7	14.1[11]	77.4[11]	...	8.5[11]	3	2.5	38	28.8
Marshall Islands	1988	11.5	30.1	54.1[27]	26.5	37.7	14.8	21.6	58.9	7.1	12.5	2.2	18.7	1.0	9.0
Martinique	1990	165	47.5	68.1	45.9	49.8	42.2	9.5	56.9	1.5	32.1	10.4[43]	7.1[43]	7.1[43]	4.9[43]
Mauritania	1988	593	21.8	45.8[8]	31.0	49.1	13.3	...	...	...	...	390	65.7	60[9]	10.2[9]
Mauritius[56]	1991	463	35.2	68.0	44.5	57.9	31.2	12.2[29]	80.1[29]	1.9[29]	5.9[29]	81	17.5	146	31.5
Mayotte	1991	27.3	29.4	56.4	28.9	39.2	17.7	12.0	42.9	7.3	37.8	3.1	11.4	1.3	4.7
Mexico	1991	31,229	30.7	59.9	37.5	53.1	22.6	30.8	54.0	12.7	2.5	8,190	26.2	5,175	16.6
Micronesia	1990	30.5	29.8[16]	60.6	30.3	...	...	2.7[16]	74.4[16]	0.1[16]	22.7[16]	12.7	41.5	1.6	5.2
Moldova	1991	2,070	50.0[22]	86.3[29]	47.4	...	...	...	...	...	...	739	35.7	424	20.5
Monaco	1990	12.6	39.7	...	42.0	53.2	31.8	17.4	75.1	0.3	7.2	—	0.3	2.7	21.8
Mongolia	1990	694	45.5[34]	82.2[34]	46.9[34]	50.9[34]	42.8[34]	...	...	...	...	192	27.6	123	17.8
Morocco	1982	5,999	19.7	48.9	29.3	47.1	11.6	27.1	40.5	17.6	14.8	2,352	39.2	1,016	16.9
Mozambique	1980	5,671	52.4	87.3[27]	48.6	47.6	49.5	44.4[13]	40.0[13]	14.5[13]	1.1[13]	4,755	83.8	347	6.1
Myanmar (Burma)	1989–90[21]	15,701	35.3[11]	64.2[11]	40.2[11]	52.4[11]	28.2[11]	...	...	...	...	10,614[58]	67.6[58]	1,232	7.8
Namibia	1985	477	23.9	55.4	30.8	47.3	14.6	...	...	...	...	185[16]	43.4[16]	93[9,16]	21.8[9,16]
Nauru	1977	2.2	...	...	30.5	...	...	...	...	...	...	...	...	...	...
Nepal	1990	8,585	34.7	82.5[43]	45.4	57.5	32.6	86.2[24]	9.1[24]	2.5[24]	2.2[24]	6,244[24]	91.1[24]	37[24]	0.5[24]
Netherlands, The	1991	7,011	39.7	67.6	46.6	56.9	36.5	8.8	82.7	1.5	7.0	293	4.2	1,227	17.5
Netherlands Antilles	1988[21]	73	43.1	59.5[43]	38.5	45.1	32.3	...	...	...	...	0.5	0.7	5.8	8.0
New Caledonia	1989	66	37.5	70.7[48]	40.2	49.1	30.8	16.3	64.3	1.6	17.8	7.8	11.8	6.2	9.3
New Zealand	1992[21]	1,635	43.6	70.8[50]	47.1[50]	53.9[50]	40.6[50]	18.0	70.2	1.1	10.7	159	9.7	255	15.6
Nicaragua	1991	1,386	33.2	62.0[32]	34.7	47.8	22.3	...	...	...	...	415	30.0	208	15.0
Niger	1988[60]	2,316	20.4	55.2	31.9	51.1	13.0	51.4	5.0	40.3	3.3	1,764	76.2	73	3.1

construction		transportation, communications		trade, hotels, restaurants		finance, real estate		public administration, defense		services		other		country
number ('000)	% of econ. active	number ('000)	% of econ. active	number ('000)	% of econ. active	number ('000)	% of econ. active	number ('000)	% of econ. active	number ('000)	% of econ. active	number ('000)	% of econ. active	
12	4.9	13	5.5	26	10.8	6	2.5	5	5	375[5]	15.2[5]	20[20]	8.2[20]	Fiji
208	8.2	177	7.0	357	14.1	206	8.2	131	5.2	666	26.4	58[23]	2.3[23]	Finland
1,581	6.4	1,405	5.7	3,778	15.4	2,227	9.1	5	5	6,982[5]	28.4[5]	2,537[20]	10.3[20]	France
4.4	9.1	1.9	3.8	4.2	8.5	1.7	3.5	5	5	17.5[5]	35.9[5]	11.8[7]	24.2[7]	French Guiana
5.5	7.4	2.8	3.7	10.3	13.7	1.2	1.5	5	5	21.5[5]	28.6[5]	21.1[20]	28.0[20]	French Polynesia
9	9	10	10	10	10	10	10	10	10	85[10]	17.9[10]	—	—	Gabon
4	1.3	8	2.5	17	5.1	1	1	1	1	22[1]	6.8[1]	25	7.7	Gambia, The
41.4	34.9	6.3	5.3	17.7	14.9	41	41	5	5	11.1[5]	9.4[5]	9.5[25,41]	8.0[25,41]	Gaza Strip
0	9	100	4.0	184	7.3	...	...	60	2.4	534	21.2	561	22.3	Georgia
2,503	6.4	2,290	5.8	5,694	14.4	2,763	7.0	5	5	12,773[5]	32.4[5]	—	—	Germany
65	1.2	123	2.2	792	14.2	27	0.5	98	1.7	376	6.7	158[7]	2.8[7]	Ghana
2.8	19.0	0.7	4.6	3.0	20.0	1.5	10.1	2.6	17.3	3.2	21.6	—	—	Gibraltar
260	6.5	259	6.5	672	16.8	187	4.7	5	5	721[5]	18.0[5]	201[23]	5.0[23]	Greece
3.1	14.6	1.8	8.6	2.7	12.6	0.3	1.6	5	5	6.3[5]	29.5[5]	0.6	2.8	Greenland
3.5	9.1	1.7	4.4	5.4	13.9	0.8	2.0	5	5	5.9[5]	15.3[5]	12.7[20]	32.5[20]	Grenada
8.8[43]	6.8[43]	4.0[43]	3.1[43]	9.6[43]	7.4[43]	18.7[43]	14.5[43]	5	5	31.4[5,43]	24.3[5,43]	40.6[7,43]	31.4[7,43]	Guadeloupe
8.0	12.1	4.5	6.8	11.5	17.5	3.9	6.0	17.7	26.7	14.5	21.9	2.0[7]	3.1[7]	Guam
114	3.9	72	2.5	375	12.9	38	1.3	5	5	417[5]	14.4[5]	60[20]	2.1[20]	Guatemala
3.2	10.5	1.4	4.5	7.4	24.6	5.8	19.3	1.9	6.4	5.3	17.7	0.4	1.3	Guernsey[44]
9	0.5	29	1.6	37	2.0	4	0.2	5	5	138[5]	7.5[5]	156	8.5	Guinea
9	9	10	10	10	10	10	10	10	10	75[10]	16.7[10]	—	—	Guinea-Bissau
7[16]	2.8[16]	9[16]	3.8[16]	15[16]	6.2[16]	3[16]	1.2[16]	30[16]	12.1[16]	29[16]	11.9[16]	61[16,20]	24.7[16,20]	Guyana
28	1.0	21	0.8	353	13.2	5	0.2	5	5	155[5]	5.8[5]	404[20]	15.1[20]	Haiti
72	4.2	52	3.0	282	16.3	30	1.7	5	5	334[5]	19.3[5]	55[20]	3.2[20]	Honduras
231	8.3	295	10.6	740	26.8	232	8.3	5	5	542[5]	19.4[5]	55[7]	2.0[7]	Hong Kong
271	5.4	369	7.4	654	13.0	26	26	274	5.5	1,049[26]	20.9[26]	663[7]	13.2[7]	Hungary
9.0	6.1	9.8	6.6	25.7	17.3	13.0	8.7	8.2	5.5	37.0	24.9	7.7[7]	5.2[7]	Iceland
3,864[24]	1.5[24]	6,207[24]	2.4[24]	12,638[24]	4.9[24]	1,822[24]	0.7[24]	5	5	18,515[5,24]	7.1[5,24]	15,670[24]	6.0[24]	India
1,829	2.4	2,192	2.9	10,891	14.4	397	0.5	5	5	8,969[5]	11.7[5]	2,138[20]	2.8[20]	Indonesia
1,207	9.4	631	4.9	876	6.8	114	0.9	5	5	3,051[5]	23.7[5]	2,183[20]	17.0[20]	Iran
461	11.2	266	6.4	282	6.8	42	1.0	5	5	2,160[5]	52.3[5]	—	—	Iraq
80	6.0	65	4.9	201	15.0	95	7.1	5	5	286[5]	21.5[5]	209[23]	15.7[23]	Ireland
3.4	10.3	2.4	7.3	6.1	18.4	4.4	13.1	5	5	10.4[5]	31.4[5]	1.4[7]	4.1[7]	Isle of Man
121	6.5	109	5.9	245	13.3	180	9.7	5	5	625[5]	33.7[5]	128[23]	6.9[23]	Israel
1,957	8.1	1,149	4.7	4,660	19.2	1,003	4.1	5	5	6,042[5]	24.9[5]	2,652[7]	10.9[7]	Italy
62	5.7	40	3.7	191	17.6	43	4.0	5	5	229[5]	21.1[5]	187[20]	17.2[20]	Jamaica
6,190	9.4	3,850	5.9	14,360	21.8	5,460	8.3	5	5	14,010[5]	21.3[5]	1,720[20]	2.6[20]	Japan
4.4	9.3	2.4	5.0	6.8	14.4	7.4	15.6	3.1	6.5	16.7	33.1	1.6[20]	3.4[20]	Jersey
51	7.9	52	8.1	76	11.8	18	2.8	5	5	358[5]	55.6[5]	—	—	Jordan
588	7.9	520	7.0	916	12.3	44	0.6	159	2.1	1,055	14.2	1,522	20.4	Kazakhstan
9	9	10	10	10	10	10	10	10	10	1,342[10]	14.6[10]	—	—	Kenya
0.3	1.0	0.9	2.8	1.3	4.1	0.4	1.4	2.1	6.5	2.3	7.0	1.1[20]	3.4[20]	Kiribati
9	9	10	10	10	10	10	10	10	10	1,939[10,14]	22.9[10,14]	—	—	Korea, North
1,652	8.5	1,008	5.2	4,244	21.9	1,126	5.8	5	5	2,972[5]	15.3[5]	464[7]	2.4[7]	Korea, South
115	15.7	38	5.2	83	11.4	22	3.0	5	5	384[5]	52.6[5]	11[2]	1.5[2]	Kuwait
147	8.4	94	5.4	88	5.0	7	0.4	37	2.1	383	21.7	57	3.3	Kyrgyzstan
9	9	10	10	10	10	10	10	10	10	316[10,16]	17.2[10,16]	—	—	Laos
130	8.9	107	7.3	178	12.2	85	5.8	24	1.6	254	17.4	65	4.5	Latvia
43[43]	6.2[43]	48[43]	7.0[43]	115[43]	16.5[43]	24[43]	3.5[43]	5	5	200[5,43]	28.8[5,43]	—	—	Lebanon
28	5.5	8	1.6	24	4.7	2	0.5	5	5	157[5]	31.1[5]	13	2.6	Lesotho
4	0.6	14	2.0	47	6.7	1	1	1	1	63[1]	9.0[1]	64[20]	9.1[20]	Liberia
156	15.7	79	7.9	53	5.3	15	1.5	308	31.0	48	4.8	—	—	Libya
1.2	7.7	0.5	3.1	2.1	13.7	1.1	7.5	0.9	6.0	3.7	24.6	0.5[20]	3.0[20]	Liechtenstein
169	9.1	124	6.6	227	12.2	14	0.8	26	1.4	290	15.5	81	4.3	Lithuania
14	8.4	11	6.3	29	17.5	15	9.2	21	12.8	31	18.7	14[25]	8.1[25]	Luxembourg
15	8.4	8	4.6	37	20.9	6	3.4	5	5	47[5]	27.1[5]	5[20]	3.1[20]	Macau
37	5.8	10	10	10	10	10	10	10	10	180[10]	28.5[10]	211[20]	33.4[20]	Macedonia
9	9	10	10	10	10	10	10	10	10	606[10]	12.2[10]	—	—	Madagascar
46	1.4	25	0.7	94	2.7	6	0.2	5	5	147[5]	4.3[5]	57	1.7	Malawi
340[36]	5.5[36]	266[36]	4.3[36]	1,120[36]	18.1[36]	231[36]	3.7[36]	844[36]	13.7[36]	427[36]	6.9[36]	—	—	Malaysia
3.2	5.6	5.3	9.4	8.9	15.7	1.1	1.9	5	5	11.8[5]	21.0[5]	2.7[55]	4.7[55]	Maldives
13	0.4	6	0.2	159	4.6	0.3	—	75	2.2	84	2.4	107	3.1	Mali
6	4.4	9	6.9	13	9.8	5	3.7	5	5	53[5]	40.0[5]	57	3.8[7]	Malta
1.1	9.4	0.5	4.7	1.4	12.1	0.8	7.3	5	5	3.1[5]	26.4[5]	1.4[20]	12.5[20]	Marshall Islands
6.9[43]	4.7[43]	5.9[43]	4.0[43]	12.4[43]	8.5[43]	19.3[43]	13.2[43]	5	5	32.9[5,43]	22.6[5,43]	51.1[7,40]	35.0[7,43]	Martinique
9	9	10	10	10	10	10	10	10	10	143[10]	24.1[10]	—	—	Mauritania
24	5.2	32	6.9	61	13.2	11	2.4	5	5	94[5]	20.3[5]	14[20]	3.1[20]	Mauritius[56]
3.1	11.4	1.5	5.4	2.0	7.2	0.1	0.4	5	5	5.7[5]	21.0[5]	10.5[20]	38.4[20]	Mayotte
1,872	6.0	1,141	3.7	6,150	19.7	1,295	4.1	5	5	6,527[5]	20.9[5]	880[20]	2.8[20]	Mexico
1.8	6.1	57	57	57	57	57	57	6.3	20.8	3.7[57]	12.1[57]	4.1[7]	13.5[7]	Micronesia
159	7.4	67	3.2	137	6.6	1	1	1	1	519[1]	25.1[1]	31	1.5	Moldova
0.7	5.3	...	...	2.5	20.2	1.0	8.0	2.8	22.4	1.9	14.9	0.9[25]	7.1[25]	Monaco
45	6.4	55	7.9	49	7.1	1	1	1	1	184[1]	26.5[1]	47[20]	6.7[20]	Mongolia
437	7.3	141	2.3	498	8.3	26	26	533	8.9	474[26]	7.9[26]	548[2]	9.1[2]	Morocco
42	0.7	7.7	1.4	112	2.0	1	1	1	1	243[1]	4.3[1]	95[7]	1.7[7]	Mozambique
174	1.1	385	2.5	1,405	8.9	1	1	1	1	956[1]	6.1[1]	935[59]	6.0[59]	Myanmar (Burma)
9	9	10	10	10	10	10	10	10	10	148[10,16]	34.7[10,16]	—	—	Namibia
														Nauru
2[24]	—	7[24]	0.1[24]	109[24]	1.6[24]	10[24]	0.1[24]	5	5	314[5,24]	4.6[5,24]	127[24]	1.9[24]	Nepal
418	6.0	403	5.7	1,138	16.2	682	9.7	5	5	2,313[5]	33.0[5]	537[20]	7.7[20]	Netherlands, The
5.4	7.4	4.7	6.4	15.9	21.8	4.6	6.3	5	5	21.3[5]	29.3[5]	14.7	20.2[7]	Netherlands Antilles
4.5	8.8	3.1	4.7	9.5	14.3	2.5	3.8	5	5	22.0[5]	33.4[5]	13.5[7]	16.0[7]	New Caledonia
80	4.9	89	5.4	308	18.9	158	9.6	5	5	416[5]	25.4[5]	171[20]	10.5[20]	New Zealand
30	2.2	43	3.1	196	14.1	25	1.8	98	7.1	184	13.3	188[2]	13.6[2]	Nicaragua
14	0.6	15	0.6	209	9.0	2	0.1	5	5	123[5]	5.3[5]	117[25]	5.0[25]	Niger

Employment and labour (continued)

country	year	economically active population										distribution by economic sector			
		total ('000)	participation rate (%)		activity rate (%)			employment status (%)				agriculture, forestry, fishing		manufacturing; mining, quarrying; public utilities	
			female	ages 15–64	total	male	female	employers, self-employed	employees	unpaid family workers	other	number ('000)	% of econ. active	number ('000)	% of econ. active
Nigeria	1986[21]	30,766	33.3	58.8	31.1	41.1	20.9	64.6	18.8	10.7	5.9	13,259	43.1	1,401	4.6
Northern Mariana Islands	1990	26.6	43.2	83.3[6]	61.3	66.2	55.9	1.4	96.1	0.2	2.3	0.6	2.3	6.0	22.5
Norway	1992	2,130	45.2	79.9[48]	49.7	55.1	44.5	8.3	84.3	1.2	6.2	114	5.3	353	16.6
Oman	1988	644	6.3	57.2	38.2	60.7	5.9	...	...	...	...	399	62.0	33	5.1
Pakistan	1992–93[21]	33,829	14.2	50.8	28.0	46.4	8.2	41.2	32.4	20.2	6.2	15,034	44.5	4,190	12.4
Panama	1991[21]	859	33.8	60.0[61]	37.4	48.9	25.6	28.4	61.0	4.4	6.2	196	22.9	91	10.6
Papua New Guinea	1980[62]	733	39.8	35.2[8]	24.6	28.3	20.5	72.7	26.4	—	0.9	564	77.0	21	2.9
Paraguay	1982	1,039	19.7	57.5	34.3	54.8	13.6	43.1	37.7	9.2	9.9	446	42.9	129	12.4
Peru	1990	7,435	38.3[63]	54.6[27]	34.5	..	..	39.8[24]	41.8[24]	8.4[24]	10.0[24]	2,497	34.0	969	13.2
Philippines	1992[21]	26,938	37.2	66.5	41.1	51.3	30.7	36.9	40.5	13.9	8.6	10,869	41.5	2,781	10.6
Poland	1992	17,529	45.9	69.5	46.1	51.1	41.4	20.3	60.4	5.6	13.7	3,758	21.4	3,827	21.8
Portugal	1992[21]	4,737	44.3	68.2	48.2	56.2	40.9	22.8	74.5	1.7	1.0	531	11.2	1,184	25.0
Puerto Rico	1993[21]	1,211	39.1	53.7[6]	33.5	42.3	24.1	14.0	84.1	0.7	1.2	35	2.9	217	17.9
Qatar	1988	293	11.2	80.8	53.7	77.3	22.2	1.8[43]	97.7[43]	...	0.5[43]	4.5	1.6	22.0	7.5
Réunion	1990[21]	234	41.1	60.3	39.1	46.8	31.6	8.4	53.1	1.1	37.4	11	4.8	11	4.8
Romania	1992	10,290	44.3	67.2	45.2	51.2	39.3	11.7	82.5	1.5	4.3	2,187	21.3	4,153	40.4
Russia	1992	72,878	48.5[22]	77.1[22]	52.6[22]	57.9[22]	47.9[22]	...	...	...	...	9,700	13.3	21,800	29.9
Rwanda	1989	3,143	53.5	77.6[8,36]	46.3	44.6	48.0	38.8[64]	7.2[64]	53.8[64]	0.2[64]	2,833	90.1	52	1.7
St. Kitts and Nevis	1980	17.1	41.0	69.5	39.5	48.4	31.2	9.7	78.5	0.4	11.4	4.5	26.1	3.8	22.3
St. Lucia	1980	42.2	39.1	69.9	37.2	47.1	28.0	21.0	55.8	1.6	21.6	10.7	25.5	3.7	8.7
St. Vincent	1980	34.7	36.1	60.9[27]	35.5	46.6	25.0	18.0[13]	82.5[13]	1.5[13]	—	8.9	25.7	2.3	6.6
San Marino	1991	13.3	40.8	72.9	53.3	61.8	44.4	21.7	77.8	0.6	—	0.3	2.2	4.5	33.7
São Tomé and Príncipe	1981	31	32.4	61.1	31.7	43.1	20.4	15.8	79.4	0.1	4.7	16	53.9	1.9	6.2
Saudi Arabia	1988	5,369	3.6	59.1	36.3	54.9	3.6	...	...	...	...	192	3.6	595	11.1
Senegal	1990	2,433	26.0	46.2[8]	33.5	50.9	17.0	...	...	...	...	...	...	...	...
Seychelles	1991	29[22]	42.5[22]	74.3[22]	44.0[22]	50.7[22]	37.3[22]	10.7[24]	76.6[24]	0.3[24]	12.4[24]	2.2[65]	8.8[65]	4.4[9,65]	17.9[9,65]
Sierra Leone	1988	1,452	33.1	54.4[8]	36.8	50.2	23.9	...	...	...	...	929	64.0	244[9]	16.8[9]
Singapore	1992[21]	1,620	40.1	69.3	50.2	59.4	40.7	12.3	84.1	0.9	2.7	5	0.3	443	27.3
Slovakia	1991	2,618	46.9	76.0	49.6	54.0	45.5	1.4	87.9	8.2	2.5	365	13.9	867	33.1
Slovenia	1991	946	46.7	66.7	48.1	52.9	43.6	2.2	88.8	1.9	7.1	121	12.8	335	35.4
Solomon Islands	1992[67]	26.8	25.6[43]	24.9[43,54]	13.7[43]	19.7[43]	7.3[43]	29.6[43]	68.6[43]	—	1.8[43]	6.4	23.7	2.5	9.0
Somalia	1988	2,972	41.2	65.1[8]	43.3	52.8	34.8	...	...	...	...	2,118	71.3	290	9.7
South Africa[68]	1991	11,624	39.4	68.3[34,48]	37.5	45.5	29.5	7.0	74.8	...	18.2	1,224	10.5	2,361	20.3
Spain	1992[21]	15,155	36.2	60.0[6]	39.0	51.0	27.6	17.5	71.1	3.9	7.5	1,446	9.5	3,178	21.0
Sri Lanka	1992	5,948	32.7	56.6[28]	40.9	55.3	26.6	24.0	51.5	11.2	13.3	2,380	40.0	711	11.9
Sudan, The	1983[60]	6,343	29.1	57.4	35.1	50.0	20.4	59.2[52]	25.3[52]	9.9[52]	5.6[52]	4,029	63.5	317	5.0
Suriname	1990[21,69]	99	41.3	59.2	43.8	51.9	35.9	...	...	...	...	2.9	2.9	11.2	11.3
Swaziland	1988	302	39.4	62.8[8]	41.0	50.3	31.9	...	...	...	...	220	73.0	33[9]	11.0[9]
Sweden	1992[21]	4,464	48.0	82.0[6]	51.5	54.2	48.8	8.7	86.1	0.4	4.8	137	3.1	857	19.2
Switzerland	1992	3,573	38.3	62.2[27]	51.5	64.7	38.8	9.7[16]	90.3[16]	...	...	194	5.4	859	24.0
Syria	1991[21]	3,485	18.0	46.7[43]	27.8	44.6	10.2	31.0	49.3	13.0	6.7	917	26.3	471	13.5
Taiwan	1993[21]	8,874	38.1	58.8[28]	42.3	50.9	33.3	22.4	67.8	8.4	1.4	1,005	11.3	2,538	28.6
Tajikistan	1990	2,468	39.0	78.1[18]	46.1	..	..	...	...	...	...	831[32]	42.9[32]	261[32]	13.5[32]
Tanzania	1988	12,003	48.3	74.3[8]	47.4	49.6	45.2	...	...	...	...	9,836	82.0	558[9]	4.7[9]
Thailand	1992[21,70]	31,371	44.4	77.6[27]	54.4	60.4	48.4	30.4	36.0	23.1	10.5	14,981[60]	47.8[60]	4,489	14.3
Togo	1988	1,334	36.8	61.4[8]	41.1	52.6	29.9	70.3[24]	10.4[24]	11.3[24]	8.0[24]	936	70.2	145[9]	10.9[9]
Tonga	1990	32.0	33.0	57.0	33.6	45.2	22.0	33.7	45.4	16.8	4.1	11.7	36.5	5.1	15.8
Trinidad and Tobago	1991	492	36.0	60.8	39.3	47.3	30.2	17.0	79.2	2.9	0.9	51	10.4	86	17.4
Tunisia	1989	2,361	20.9	52.8	29.8	46.5	12.7	20.9	54.9	7.4	16.8	510	21.6	418	17.7
Turkey	1992[21]	21,184	30.9	58.4	36.2	48.7	22.7	29.4	39.0	27.9	3.7	8,785	41.5	3,440	16.2
Turkmenistan	1992	1,573	52.2[29]	80.3[18]	40.8	...	...	...	...	...	...	695	44.2	154	9.8
Tuvalu	1991	5.9	51.3[51]	85.5	65.3	...	...	0.35[51]	22.25[51]	—77.5[51]—		4.2	68.0	0.1	2.0
Uganda	1988	7,687	41.4	69.5[8]	44.7	52.9	36.7	...	...	...	...	6,307	82.1	404[9]	5.2[9]
Ukraine	1992	23,985	49.2[22]	83.1[18]	46.1	...	...	...	...	...	...	4,989	20.8	7,401	30.9
United Arab Emirates	1990	690	10.4[36]	69.0[36]	47.0[36]	67.6[36]	12.9[36]	6.8[16]	92.7[16]	0.1[16]	0.5[16]	43	6.3	94	13.6
United Kingdom	1991	28,295	43.0	75.4	49.2	57.7	41.0	11.1	80.8	...	8.1	557	2.0	7,076[9]	25.0[9]
United States	1992[71]	128,548	45.1	74.9	50.4	56.7	44.4	8.0	91.0	0.3	0.8	3,653	2.8	24,005	18.7
Uruguay	1991	1,239	40.7	67.7[49]	44.7	55.7	34.7	23.2	72.5	1.6	2.7	56	4.5	265	21.4
Uzbekistan	1992	8,243	43.8[50]	79.7[18]	39.0	...	...	...	...	...	...	3,577	43.4	1,317	16.0
Vanuatu	1989	67.0	46.3	85.0	47.0	49.0	44.9	...	...	...	...	49.8	74.4	1.0	1.5
Venezuela	1991[21]	7,418	32.2	62.2	37.3	50.1	24.2	28.2	61.1	2.0	8.7	837	11.3	1,346	18.1
Vietnam	1989	30,521	51.7	79.9	47.4	47.0	47.7	...	...	...	...	20,471	67.1	3,390	11.1
Virgin Islands (U.S.)	1990[21]	47.4	47.8	67.5[12]	46.6	50.3	43.1	7.6	85.5	0.2	6.7	0.6	1.2	3.7	7.8
West Bank	1992	215	12.6	41.2[27]	20.4	35.5	5.2	...	...	...	...	42.6	19.8	27.6[41]	12.8[41]
Western Sahara	...	...	...	...	...	...	...	...	...	...	...	...	...	...	...
Western Samoa	1986	45.6	18.8	48.6[24]	29.0	44.5	11.6	21.1[24]	43.5[24]	35.0[24]	0.4[24]	29.0	63.6	2.4	5.4
Yemen	1988	3,029	31.6	52.6	26.4	36.8	16.4	...	...	...	...	2,152	71.1	129	4.3
Yugoslavia	1993	3,215	41.6[73]	...	30.7	...	...	...	...	...	...	121	3.8	1,011	31.4
Zaire	1988	12,869	35.8	57.4[8]	38.1	49.6	27.0	...	...	...	...	8,483	66.9	1,910[9]	15.0[9]
Zambia	1988	2,628	29.3	52.6[8]	33.5	48.0	19.4	22.9[16]	42.5[16]	3.6[16]	31.0[16]	1,833	69.8	286[9]	10.9[9]
Zimbabwe	1986–87	3,260	47.8	76.5[27]	42.1	44.8	39.6	...	...	...	...	2,110	64.7	179	5.5

[1]Services includes finance, real estate and public administration, defense. [2]Unemployed, not previously employed only. [3]Employed persons only. [4]Ages 15–59 (male) and 15–54 (female). [5]Services includes public administration, defense. [6]Ages 16–64. [7]Unemployed only. [8]Over age 10. [9]Manufacturing; mining, quarrying; public utilities includes construction. [10]Services includes transportation, communications; trade, hotels, restaurants; finance, real estate; and public administration, defense. [11]1983. [12]Over age 16. [13]1970. [14]1982. [15]Wage earners and self-employed only. [16]1980. [17]Includes unemployed, not previously employed. [18]Ages 16–59 (male) and 16–54 (female). [19]Includes self-employed and unemployed. [20]Mostly unemployed. [21]Excludes all or some classes or elements of the military. [22]1989. [23]Mostly unemployed, not previously employed. [24]1981. [25]Includes unemployed. [26]Services includes finance, real estate. [27]Over age 15. [28]1983–84. [29]1990. [30]Agriculture includes mining, quarrying. [31]Mostly employees of international companies and unemployed. [32]State sector only. [33]Ages 16–60. [34]1985. [35]Over age 12. [36]1988. [37]Republic of Cyprus only. [38]1992 population economically active for Turkish Republic of Northern Cyprus is 74,065. [39]Ethiopia includes Eritrea. [40]1984. [41]Other includes public utilities and finance, real estate.

construction number ('000)	construction % of econ. active	transportation, communications number ('000)	transportation, communications % of econ. active	trade, hotels, restaurants number ('000)	trade, hotels, restaurants % of econ. active	finance, real estate number ('000)	finance, real estate % of econ. active	public administration, defense number ('000)	public administration, defense % of econ. active	services number ('000)	services % of econ. active	other number ('000)	other % of econ. active	country
546	1.8	1,112	3.6	7,417	24.1	120	0.4	5	5	4,902[5]	15.9[5]	2,009[20]	6.5[20]	Nigeria
5.0	21.7	1.4	5.3	5.3	19.8	1.0	3.8	1.4	5.3	4.5	16.9	0.6[7]	2.3[7]	Northern Mariana Islands
133	6.2	161	7.6	366	17.2	157	7.4	5	5	779[5]	36.6[5]	66[23]	3.1[23]	Norway
52	8.0	26	4.0	23	3.6	1	0.2	5	5	110[5]	17.1[5]	—	—	Oman
2,099	6.2	1,663	4.9	4,198	12.4	283	0.8	5	5	4,207[5]	12.4[5]	2,146[20]	6.3[20]	Pakistan
34	3.9	54	6.3	167	19.5	34	4.0	5	5	227[5]	26.4[5]	54[23]	6.3[23]	Panama
22	2.9	1.7	2.4	25	3.4	4	0.6	5	5	77[5]	10.5[5]	2	0.2	Papua New Guinea
70	6.7	31	2.9	86	8.3	18	1.7	5	5	174[5]	16.8[5]	86[17]	8.3[17]	Paraguay
272	3.7	323	4.4	1,146	15.6	176	2.4	5	5	1,961[5]	26.7[5]	—	—	Peru
1,035	4.0	1,221	4.7	3,283	12.5	452	1.7	5	5	4,254[5]	16.2[5]	2,284[20]	8.7[20]	Philippines
995	5.7	831	4.7	1,636	9.3	204	1.2	5	5	3,884[5]	22.2[5]	2,304[7]	13.7[7]	Poland
386	8.1	225	4.7	936	19.8	143	3.0	5	5	1,291[5]	27.3[5]	42[2]	0.9[2]	Portugal
92	7.6	44	3.6	258	21.3	37	3.1	5	5	513[5]	42.4[5]	15[2]	1.2[2]	Puerto Rico
64.2	22.0	11.9	4.1	34.2	11.7	6.2	2.1	5	5	149.6[5]	51.1[5]	—	—	Qatar
17	7.1	7	3.1	18	7.7	3	1.3	5	5	79[5]	33.9[5]	87[20]	37.4[20]	Reunion
579	5.6	617	6.0	694	6.7	57	0.6	5	5	1,528[5]	14.8[5]	475[23]	4.6[23]	Romania
8,300	11.4	5,600	7.7	5,700	7.8	26	26	2,900	4.0	14,400[26]	19.8[26]	4,478[25]	6.1[25]	Russia
38	1.2	7	0.2	80	2.5	3	0.1	5	5	120[5]	3.8[5]	9	0.3	Rwanda
0.4	2.5	0.3	1.6	1.3	7.3	0.8	4.7	1.0	5.7	2.9	17.0	2.2[20]	12.8[20]	St. Kitts and Nevis
2.6	6.3	1.5	3.5	2.8	6.5	0.5	1.1	2.4	5.6	7.9	18.8	10.1[20]	24.0[20]	St. Lucia
3.5	10.2	1.9	5.4	2.6	7.4	0.4	1.0	5	5	7.6[5]	21.8[5]	7.6	21.9	St. Vincent
1.1	7.9	0.2	1.7	2.2	16.7	0.3	2.2	2.1	15.7	2.1	16.0	0.57	3.77	San Marino
1.8	5.9	1.0	3.4	2.0	6.5	0.2	0.5	2.4	7.8	3.5	11.3	1.47	4.67	São Tomé and Príncipe
1,181	22.0	321	6.0	964	18.0	151	2.8	5	5	1,965[5]	36.6[5]	—	—	Saudi Arabia
...	...	...	...	...	...	...	...	...	...	...	...	...	...	Senegal
9	9	66	66	8.6[65,66]	35.3[65,66]	1	1	1	1	9.3[1,65]	38.1[1,65]	—	—	Seychelles
9	9	10	10	10	10	10	10	10	10	280[10]	19.2[10]	—	—	Sierra Leone
103	6.4	158	9.8	356	22.0	171	10.6	5	5	339[5]	20.9[5]	44[20]	2.7[20]	Singapore
243	9.3	165	6.3	246	9.4	26	26	99	3.8	498[26]	19.0[26]	135	5.2	Slovakia
42	4.4	53	5.6	103	10.9	44	4.7	5	5	177[5]	18.7[5]	71[20]	7.5[20]	Slovenia
1.1	4.1	1.4	5.3	3.2	11.9	1.2	4.5	4.3	15.9	6.9	25.6	—	—	Solomon Islands
9	9	10	10	10	10	10	10	10	10	565[10]	19.0[10]	—	—	Somalia
526	4.5	497	4.3	1,358	11.7	504	4.3	5	5	2,641[5]	22.7[5]	2,513[20]	21.6[20]	South Africa[68]
1,538	10.1	783	5.2	2,905	19.2	818	5.4	5	5	3,467[5]	22.9[5]	1,020[23]	6.7[23]	Spain
249	4.2	232	3.9	530	8.9	36	0.6	5	5	821[5]	13.8[5]	990[20]	16.6[20]	Sri Lanka
139	2.2	215	3.4	294	4.6	21	0.3	5	5	550[5]	8.7[5]	777[23]	12.3[23]	Sudan, The
3.9	3.9	5.3	5.3	13.8	13.9	2.6	2.6	5	5	37.2[5]	37.1[5]	22.7[20]	22.9[20]	Suriname
9	9	10	10	10	10	10	10	10	10	48[10]	16.0[10]	—	—	Swaziland
273	6.1	305	6.8	604	13.5	399	8.9	5	5	1,668[5]	37.4[5]	221[20]	5.0[20]	Sweden
320	9.0	215	6.0	713	20.0	374	10.5	5	5	805[5]	22.5[5]	92[7]	2.6[7]	Switzerland
341	9.8	167	4.8	378	10.9	25	0.7	5	5	951[5]	27.3[5]	2.05[7]	0.0[7]	Syria
879	9.9	463	5.2	1,806	20.4	482	5.4	313	3.5	1,259	14.2	128[7]	1.4[7]	Taiwan
161[32]	8.3[32]	65[32]	3.3[32]	145[32]	7.5[32]	...	...	39[32]	2.0[32]	437[32]	22.5[32]	—	—	Tajikistan
9	9	10	10	10	10	10	10	10	10	1,608[10]	13.4[10]	—	—	Tanzania
2,055	6.6	936	3.0	3,821	12.2	1	1	1	1	3,525[1]	11.2[1]	1,562[20]	5.0[20]	Thailand
9	9	10	10	10	10	10	10	10	10	253[10]	18.9[10]	—	—	Togo
1.3	3.9	1.8	5.7	2.6	8.1	1.2	3.7	5	5	7.1[5]	22.0[5]	1.37	4.27	Tonga
75	15.1	30	6.0	83	16.8	32	6.6	5	5	135[5]	27.4[5]	1	0.2	Trinidad and Tobago
248	10.5	96	4.1	217	9.2	15	0.7	5	5	444[5]	18.8[5]	412[20]	17.5[20]	Tunisia
1,049	5.0	798	3.8	2,471	11.7	446	2.1	5	5	2,539[5]	12.0[5]	1,656[7]	7.8[7]	Turkey
164	10.4	56	3.6	89	5.6	26	26	50	3.2	373[26]	23.7[26]	27	1.7	Turkmenistan
0.2	4.0	0.1	1.0	0.2	4.0	—	—	5	5	1.3[5]	22.0[5]	—	—	Tuvalu
9	9	10	10	10	10	10	10	10	10	976[10]	12.7[10]	—	—	Uganda
1,910	8.0	1,623	6.8	1,751	7.3	144	0.6	562	2.3	4,818	20.1	787	3.3	Ukraine
119	17.3	72	10.4	101	14.7	19	2.7	5	5	241[5]	35.0[5]	—	—	United Arab Emirates
9	9	57	57	57	57	57	57	1,931	6.8	16,193[57]	57.2[57]	2,241[7]	7.9[7]	United Kingdom
8,118	6.3	7,018	5.5	26,431[72]	20.6[72]	13,359	10.4	5	5	44,939[5,72]	35.0[5,72]	1,018[23]	0.8[23]	United States
82	6.6	66	5.3	219	17.7	60	4.8	5	5	459[5]	37.0[5]	32[23]	2.6[23]	Uruguay
622	7.5	360	4.4	462	5.6	25	0.3	96	1.2	1,664	20.2	120	1.5	Uzbekistan
1.3	1.9	1.0	1.5	2.7	4.1	0.6	1.0	5	5	7.9[5]	11.8[5]	2.6	3.8	Vanuatu
685	9.2	421	5.7	1,549	20.9	426	5.7	5	5	2,062[5]	27.8[5]	92[23]	1.2[23]	Venezuela
581	1.9	576	1.9	1,880	6.2	90	0.3	305	1.0	1,374	4.5	1,854[20]	6.1[20]	Vietnam
5.7	12.0	3.7	7.8	9.0	18.9	2.5	5.3	5.1	10.8	14.0	29.5	3.2	6.7	Virgin Islands (U.S.)
67.5	31.4	10.2	4.7	25.2	11.7	41	41	5	5	23.1[5]	10.8[5]	19.2[20,41]	8.9[20,41]	West Bank
...	...	...	...	...	...	...	...	...	...	...	...	...	...	Western Sahara
0.1	0.1	1.5	3.3	1.7	3.7	0.8	1.8	5	5	9.4[5]	20.7[5]	0.6	1.4	Western Samoa
178	5.9	90	3.0	84	2.8	4	0.1	5	5	391[5]	12.9[5]	—	—	Yemen
159	4.9	152	4.7	287	8.9	85	2.6	5	5	441[5]	13.7[5]	960[74]	29.9[74]	Yugoslavia
9	9	10	10	10	10	10	10	10	10	2,297[10]	18.1[10]	—	—	Zaire
9	9	10	10	10	10	10	10	10	10	500[10]	19.3[10]	—	—	Zambia
51	1.0	70	2.3	128	3.9	24	0.7	5	5	307[5]	12.2[5]	277[20]	8.5[20]	Zimbabwe

[42]Ages 15–65. [43]1986. [44]Excludes Alderney and Sark. [45]Data are for the economically active population ages 15–64 only. [46]Ages 16–74. [47]1977. [48]Ages 20–64. [49]Ages 14–64. [50]1991. [51]1979. [52]1973. [53]Excludes about 30,000 foreign border workers. [54]Over age 14. [55]Includes unemployed, previously employed. [56]Island of Mauritius only. [57]Services includes transportation, communications; trade, hotels, restaurants; and finance, real estate. [58]Includes unemployed seasonal agricultural workers. [59]Includes underemployed seasonal nonagricultural workers. [60]Excludes nomadic population. [61]Ages 15–69. [62]Citizens over age 10 involved in money-raising activities only. [63]1985–86. [64]1978. [65]Excludes self-employed and domestic workers. [66]Trade, hotels, restaurants, includes transportation, communications. [67]Wage earners only. [68]Excludes the former black independent states of Bophuthatswana, Ciskei, Transkei, and Venda. [69]Districts of Wanica and Paramaribo only. [70]May survey. [71]Excludes armed forces overseas. [72]Services includes hotels. [73]1992. [74]Private sector 6.8%, unemployed 23.1%.

Agriculture and land use

This table provides data on the structure of national agricultural sectors from the perspective of farms and farmland use. The data are taken mainly from national agricultural censuses and surveys, supplemented by reports of the United Nations Food and Agriculture Organization's (FAO's) *World Census of Agriculture*. Many of these national censuses, of course, are taken under guidelines established by the FAO for the *World Census of Agriculture* programs (the 1990 census is the fifth and will include national censuses taken during the decade 1986–95). It represents a cooperative effort by FAO member countries to collect agricultural data within a general framework that permits international harmonization of concepts and definitions; transfer of technical expertise; and increased effectiveness in the collection, analysis, publication, and policy-related use of such statistics. More than 100 countries were expected to participate in the 1990 census.

All agricultural statistics are subject to quality-control problems, including errors or biases arising from such factors as incomplete or inaccurate lists of holdings, ambiguous questions, respondents who inadvertently or willfully give inaccurate information, failure to record data for all parts of fragmented holdings, respondents' misunderstandings of the definitions of land use and cropping methods, or a failure to report livestock temporarily absent from the holding on public or common pasture land or in transit. Frequently, subjects studied, classification schemes, and definitions vary from the FAO guidelines (economic planners need different information

about a commercial, high-technology, multicrop agricultural sector than they do for a family-subsistence, low-technology, one-crop sector). When a complete census of agriculture is impossible, a sample survey may be taken. This is a limited census of a predetermined number of carefully screened holdings. From these results, nationwide projections may be prepared.

With respect to the first section of the table, number and size of farms, many countries impose a minimum size limit for holdings that may be covered in their census reports, and this cutoff, if not sufficiently low, can result in a substantial undercount of smaller holdings; conversely Soviet-bloc nations formerly published statistics only on state collective or cooperative farms and excluded production from privately held plots of land, even though these often represented a significant fraction of agricultural output.

The land tenure statistics classify farms (a single parcel of land, or holding, or a group of holdings operated as a single farm) according to the rights under which the farmer holds the land or operates the enterprise represented by the farm. Owner-operated includes two types of ownership: outright ownership in which the holder has title and has the right to determine use and transfer of the land; and ownerlike possession in which the holder lacks the legal title but uses it under perpetual lease, hereditary tenure, or leases of 30 years or more with nominal, or no, rent. Farms classed as owner-operated are divided into individual and family, corporate or state, and socialized or collective proprietorships. Rented includes

Agriculture and land use

country	farms (latest census of agriculture)[a]														
	year	number of farms ('000)	size of holding								tenure (% of farms)				
			average (ha)	size class (%)							owner-operated			rented (including share-croppers)	tribal/com-munal	other[b]
				under 1 ha	1–5 ha	5–10 ha	10–20 ha	20–50 ha	50–200 ha	over 200 ha	individual/family	corporate/state	socialized/collective			
Afghanistan	1981	126[1]	3.5[1]	44.8[1]	35.2[1]			20.0[1]			55.1[1]	—		25.1[1]	—	19.8[1]
Albania	1990	0.5[2]	1,182[2,3]	...	...	...	...	...	...	...	97.0[4]	3.0[4]		—	—	—
Algeria	1987	899[7]	6.2[7]	1.1[7]	12.7[7]	15.8[7]	21.7[7]	25.6[7]	18.0[7]	5.1[7]	...	...	...	...	...	...
American Samoa	1990	1.1	2.9	44.7[9]	40.0[10]	13.8[11]			1.6[12]		93.9	...	...	2.2	—	3.9
Andorra	—	—	—													
Angola	1970–71	1,067	3.9	3.3	13.5	9.3	11.3	13.7	19.2	29.7	80.5	1.1	—	—	18.2	0.2
Antigua and Barbuda	1984	2.3	2.1	61.7	33.8	2.9	0.6	0.6	0.4	—	32.1[14]	22.9[14]		40.5[14]	—	4.5[14]
Argentina	1988	421	469	15.1		8.4	14.0[15]	12.0[16]	25.1	25.5	85.1[14]	—	—	8.3[14]	—	6.6[14]
Armenia	1992	...	...	...	...	...	...	...	...	...	...	...	...	...	...	...
Aruba	...	...	...	...	...	...	...	...	...	...	...	...	...	...	...	...
Australia	1993–94	123	3,710[8]	15.7					9.2[18]	75.1[19]	...	...	...	...	...	...
Austria	1993	267	26.4[23]	3.3[23]	32.2[23]	17.8[23]	20.0[23]	21.5[23]	4.6[23]	0.7[23]	38.9[23]	1.5[23]	—	59.5[23]	—	0.1[23]
Azerbaijan	1992	...	...	...	...	...	...	...	...	...	...	...	...	...	...	...
Bahamas, The	1978	4.2	8.5	55.2[9]	30.1[10]	12.3[11]		1.1[24]	0.4[25]	1.0[26]	74.9	0.6	—	4.0	—	20.5
Bahrain	1980	0.8	4.4	19.4	52.9	17.4	8.2	2.0	0.1		37.9	0.1	—	62.0	—	—
Bangladesh	1983–84	10,045	0.9	70.3	27.0[27]	2.5[28]		0.2[29]			62.8	...	...	1.4	...	35.8
Barbados	1969	0.2	95.8	...	...	...	...	...	...	...	...	...	...	...	...	...
Belarus	1990	...	...	...	...	...	...	...	...	...	...	...	...	...	...	...
Belgium	1991	84	16.5	13.9	24.1	14.8	19.1	22.1	6.0		33.4[14]	...	...	65.7[14]	—	0.9[14]
Belize	1974	8.9	26.7	69.4			16.7	8.6	4.4	0.9	43.6	56.4	—			
Benin	1983	...	...	...	...	...	...	...	...	...	...	...	...	...	...	...
Bermuda	1990	0.08[34]	3.1[34]	...	...	...	...	...	...	...	...	...	...	...	...	...
Bhutan	1984	160	0.8	51.3[9,35]	42.9[10,35]	5.8[35,36]					...	...	...	...	...	...
Bolivia	1984	315	72.1	25.3	42.1	12.1	6.8	6.1	4.9	2.8	70.3	...	...	2.0	4.3	23.3
Bosnia and Herzegovina[37]	1981	540	...	33.4	48.9	13.7	2.3	0.6			100.0	—	—			
Botswana	1990	90.3[38]	5.0	9.1	56.1	26.9	7.9				—	0.4	—	—	99.6	—
Brazil	1985	5,835	64.5	11.1	28.6	13.2	14.0	15.6	12.4	4.9	63.2	1.0	—	17.9	—	18.4[40]
Brunei	1964	6.3	2.6	44.1[9]	40.4[10]	15.5[36]					52.3	1.0	—	22.0	—	24.7
Bulgaria	1991	2.2[6,42]	2,467[6,42]	...	...	...	...	...	...	...	—	84.6[6,42]	—	15.4[6]	—	—
Burkina Faso	1984	1,860	4.8	...	...	...	...	...	...	...	...	...	...	...	...	...
Burundi	1983	...	...	...	...	...	...	...	...	...	...	...	...	...	...	...
Cambodia	1962[43]	840	3.6	30.7	54.9	10.4	3.4	0.6			...	...	...	...	...	...
Cameroon	1973	926	1.6	42.7	53.8	3.2	0.3	—			2.4	63.5	—	5.2	59.5	32.9
Canada	1991	280	242	1.4[9]	3.5[10]	24.2[44]		70.9[45]			36.5	...	...	...	...	...
Cape Verde	1979	...	...	...	...	...	...	...	...	...	...	...	...	...	...	...
Central African Republic	1974	283	1.7	32.2	65.2	2.5	—	—	—	—	0.3[14]	—	—	0.1[14]	98.6[14]	1.2[14]
Chad	1973	366	2.6	19.7	69.5	10.0	0.8		—	—	...	...	...	...	...	...
Chile	1975–76	306	94.1	16.0	32.5	13.4	12.3	11.8	9.2	4.8	84.0		—	7.2	8.8	
China	1987	1,650[48]	...	...	...	...	...	...	...	...	—	10.0[49]	90.0[49]			
Colombia	1971	1,177	26.3	22.8	36.7	13.6	10.0	8.5	6.3	2.1	68.7	—	—	5.8	4.1	21.4
Comoros	1982	...	...	...	...	...	...	...	...	...	...	...	...	...	...	...
Congo	1986	143[7]	1.4[7]	37.3[7]	62.2[7]	0.5[7]					91.7[14]	8.3[14]	—	...	...	...
Costa Rica	1973	82	38.3	23.3	25.5	11.2	10.8	15.2	10.7	3.3	97.9	1.7	—	0.1	—	0.3
Côte d'Ivoire	1975	550	5.0	9.5	54.4	24.9	9.4	1.7	0.1	—	...	...	...	...	...	...
Croatia[37]	1981	569	...	30.7	51.1	14.7	2.3	0.3			100.0	—	—			
Cuba	1988	1.8[42]	1,047[42]	...	...	...	...	...	...	...	—	79.0	—	9.4	—	11.6[50]
Cyprus	1985	48.0	3.8	24.4	56.8	15.0	2.9	0.9			—	—	—	—	—	—
Czech Republic[51]	1980	1,391	8.1	89.9[52]	9.9[53]			0.2[54]			6.0[14]	30.8[14]	63.2[14]	—	0.6	—
Denmark	1992[56]	74.5	35.9[57]	2.8		15.4	22.5	37.2	22.1		64.4[2]			35.6[2]		
Djibouti	1988–89	1.2	0.4	c. 100	...	...	...	...	...	...	...	...	...	...	...	...
Dominica	1986–88	1.9	...	89[58]	9[59]			2			33			15		52
Dominican Republic	1981	385	6.3	16.0	65.7	8.5	5.4	2.6	1.5	0.3	53.2	18.5	4.5	1.6	—	17.4
Ecuador	1974	517	15.4	27.8	38.8	10.6	8.0	8.2	5.6	0.9	70.3	0.3	—	7.7	7.4	14.3
Egypt	1990	3,896	0.7[34]	95.8[60]	2.3[61]	1.9[62]					...	...	...	...	...	...
El Salvador	1970–71	271	5.4	48.9	37.9	5.8	3.4	2.6	1.2	0.2	41.5	—	—	28.2	6.3	24.1

sharecropping; communal/tribal includes types of customary or traditional arrangements in which title or goods do not change hands. "Other" usually includes farms operated on several parcels of land and held under multiple forms of tenure.

Statistics on types of farms by commodities produced refer to FAO categories. The terms "mainly crops" and "mainly livestock" indicate that more than half of the for-sale production was that indicated.

The section on technology provides some measures of the role modern technology plays in the farm activities of each country (although, of course, irrigation may employ technology developed in ancient times). Ratios referred to area mean area of "arable" (cultivated and cultivable) land, roughly "cropland," less area of permanent crops (see below).

The classification of farmland by economic use is also subject to differing treatment internationally. For purposes of this table, "cropland" comprises: (1) land under temporary crops (those requiring replanting after each harvest), (2) land under permanent crops (those *not* requiring replanting, including tree, bush and shrub, and vine crops), and (3) land temporarily (less than five years) fallow (unused, but capable of being returned to cultivation with no special preparation). "Meadows and pastures" includes land (both permanent and temporary use) whose principal purpose is the raising of animal fodder or forage. "Woodland and forest" includes both natural and planted tracts of timber (*e.g.*, plantings of Christmas trees),

whether harvested or not. "Other" comprises: (1) mixed and multiple use lands, (2) residue of farmland holdings not classifiable according to categories listed above (including areas of farm buildings, roads, ornamental gardens, watercourses and flooded land, wasteland, etc.), (3) land not classified by respondents in census, or (4) detail not distinguishable as one of categories above by reason of its summarization in a published source. When "cropland" is indicated to compose 100 percent of farmland, it should usually be understood to mean only that woodland, pasture, etc., were not part of the published data, rather than that those classes of land use do not exist.

Measurements of area are given in hectares (ha; 1 hectare is equal to 2.471 acres). A kilogram (kg) is equal to 2.205 pounds (1 kg/ha = 0.89 lb/ac). The following notes further define the column headings:

a. All properties used wholly or partly for agricultural production. A property need not have agricultural land to be considered a farm; piggeries, hatcheries, and poultry batteries are farms because they engage in agricultural production, *i.e.*, raise livestock and produce livestock products.

b. All forms of tenure not included in the preceding categories. Includes land operated by schools, religious bodies, squatters, seasonally by nomads, and built-on, waste, and similar types of alienation.

... Not available, or no agricultural census or survey ever taken.

— None, less than half the smallest unit shown, or not applicable.

activity (% of farms)			technology (latest)				farmland use									country
							land in farms		land use (%)							
									cropland							
mainly crops	mainly live-stock	mixed/ other	tractors (per 1,000 ha)	electri-city (% of farms having)	irriga-tion (% of land irrig.)	artificial fertilizer (kg/ha)	total ('000 ha)	% of total land area	perma-nent crops	tempo-rary crops	fallow	total crop-land	mead-ows and pastures	wood-land and forest	other	
...	...	...	0.1	...	35	7	39,810	61.0	1.8	46.3	51.9	19.9	75.4	4.8	—	Afghanistan
57.9[5]	36.2[5]	5.9[5]	21.2	...	75	158	1,111[6]	40.0[6]	17.8	82.2		19.9	35.7[6]	...	—	Albania
55.7[5]	44.3[5]	...	12.5	...	6	15	39,814[8]	16.7[8]	6.9[8]	55.2[8]	37.9[8]	20.4[8]	77.2[8]	...	2.4[8]	Algeria
...	...	—	7.5	38.5	...	...	3.2	16.4	88.7		11.3	71.4	5.3	...	23.3	American Samoa
...	...	...	...	...	...	...	...	2.0				2.8	69.4	27.8	...	Andorra
32.9	44.1	23.0	3.4	...	89[13]	7	4,180	3.4	36.8	63.2	—	1.7	82.0	...	16.2	Angola
...	...	...	30.0	...	...	...	2.5	9.0	26.0	57.1	16.9	62.6	36.0	1.4		Antigua and Barbuda
10.6[17]	78.9[17]	10.5[17]	8.2	...	7	4	177,437	64.8	4.8	71.5	23.7	15.4	56.4	21.3	6.9	Argentina
...	...	...	31.0	...	64	...	1,200	40.0	...	...	...	33.3	58.3	...	8.4	Armenia
...	...	...	...	...	...	...	...	...	...	...	...	...	...	...	...	Aruba
27.8[20]	54.7	17.5[21]	6.2	...	4	28	466,000[8]	60.7[8]	1.1	98.9		3.5	6.6	3.5	89.9[22]	Australia
59.8[23]	—	40.2[23]	245	...	0.3	201	7,530	91.0	5.3	93.5	1.2	20.0	26.0	43.0	11.0	Austria
...	...	...	24.0	...	90	...	4,200	48.3	...	...	...	38.1	52.4	—	9.5	Azerbaijan
...	...	...	10.0	...	10[13]	...	36.2	2.6	23.3	59.9	16.8	23.3	6.9	25.7	44.0	Bahamas, The
...	...	...	...	21.3	100	...	3.5	5.2	50.7	49.3	—	45.9	...	...	54.1	Bahrain
91.3[30]	8.7[30]	—	0.6	...	35	98	9,137[31]	70.2[31]	88.2		11.8[31]	89.5[31]	10.5[31]			Bangladesh
...	...	...	38.0	...	...	91	19.8	45.9	...	...	...	13.7	86.3			Barbados
78.7[32]	19.4[32]	1.9[32]	20.9	...	2	...	9,400[32]	45.2[32]	...	...	...	64.8[32]	35.2[32]			Belarus
...	2.5[33]	...	148.0	...	0.1	496	1,392	45.6	1.2	98.4	0.4	51.9	45.2	0.5	2.4	Belgium
...	...	...	25.6	...	4	88	233	10.0	13.1	81.1	5.8	36.5	15.9	36.1	11.6	Belize
...	...	...	0.1	...	0.5	2	3,300	29.3	...	...	...	100.0	—	—	—	Benin
...	...	...	12.5	...	...	...	2.4	4.4	18.6	72.9	8.5	91.1	8.9	...	—	Bermuda
...	...	...	...	...	30	1	156	3.4	11.7	88.3		100.0	—	—	—	Bhutan
...	...	...	2.5	...	8	3	22,670	20.6	55.0		45.0	6.9	47.7	39.0	6.4	Bolivia
...	...	...	429	...	0.2	...	2,525	49.4	8.9	70.9	20.2	44.2	55.4	...	0.4	Bosnia and Herzegovina[37]
13.6[34]	27.9[34]	58.5[34]	5.1	...	0.1	1	343[39]	5.9[39]	—	100.0[39]		83.5[39]	...	...	...	Botswana
80.0[41]	16.2[41]	3.8[41]	14.8	4.1[41]	6	43	376,287	44.5	18.2[39]	66.9[39]	14.9[39]	15.8[39]	47.8[39]	24.2[39]	12.2[39]	Brazil
...	...	...	24.0	...	33	57	16.4	2.8	78.0	22.0	—	54.8	0.1	16.4	28.7	Brunei
43.9[4]	56.1[4]	—	11.7	...	31	195	6,159[4]	55.7[4]	6.3[4]	93.7		75.4[4]	24.6[4]	...	...	Bulgaria
...	...	...	0.04	...	0.7	6	8,919	32.6	...	...	...	...	...	...	...	Burkina Faso
...	...	...	0.1	...	7	4	2,388	85.8	73.8		26.2	56.7	37.7	5.6	—	Burundi
...	...	...	0.6	...	4	1	2,984	16.5	94.9	3.5	1.6	96.1	...	3.9	—	Cambodia
...	...	...	0.2	...	0.6	6[2]	1,490	3.3	...	...	...	100.0	—	—	—	Cameroon
43.9	42.9	13.2	16.3	...	1.5	47	67,754	7.3	80.9		19.1	61.1	6.1	32.7		Canada
...	...	...	0.4	...	5	—	25[46]	6.2[46]	20.8[46]	79.1[46]		100.0[46]	—	—	—	Cape Verde
...	...	...	0.1	...	...	2	491	0.8	11.8	80.2	—	100.0	—	—	—	Central African Republic
...	...	...	0.05	...	0.4	2	23,877[47]	45.8[47]	50.0[47]	50.0[47]		23.7[47]	76.3[47]	—	—	Chad
...	...	...	10.1	...	32	69	8,746[32]	11.7[32]	26.5[32]	59.5[32]	14.0[32]	15.3[32]	52.4[32]	...	32.3[32]	Chile
...	...	...	8.3	...	53	261	166,902	17.4	4.1	95.9		100.0	—	—	—	China
...	...	...	9.3	...	13	101	30,993	27.0	30.6	27.6	41.8	24.7	56.4	...	18.9	Colombia
6.2[5]	93.8[5]	—	...	...	...	...	83	44.3	56.4	43.6		100.0	—	—	—	Comoros
...	...	...	4.9	...	3	0	226	0.7	14.8	85.2	—	100.0	—	—	—	Congo
...	...	...	24.6	...	42	203	3,122	60.0	42.2	57.8	—	15.7	49.9	22.9	11.4	Costa Rica
...	...	...	1.5	...	3	11	2,753	8.6	65.9	34.1	—	100.0	—	—	—	Côte d'Ivoire
...	...	...	0.4	...	0.3	...	3,220	57.0	8.8	81.8	9.4	50.4	48.5	...	1.1	Croatia[37]
...	...	...	30.0	...	35	199	8,679	78.3	...	...	...	33.0	32.1	31.9	2.1	Cuba
72.7	27.3	...	130	...	35	144	210	35.6	34.7	54.3	11.0	74.9	25.1		Cyprus
34.3	24.4	41.3	26.1[4,55]	100.0	6	314	4,283[4,55]	54.3[4,55]	2.6[4,55]	97.4[4,55]		74.8[4,55]	20.4[4,55]	4.8[4,55]		Czech Republic[51]
48.1	32.8	19.1	60.9	...	17	255	2,756	64.8	...	99.8	0.2	79.7	20.3	...	—	Denmark
...	...	...	...	...	...	...	1	0.5	...	6.8	—	100.0	—	—	—	Djibouti
...	...	...	12.9	...	...	259	20	26.3	...	...	...	...	...	...	...	Dominica
44.0	56.0	...	2.4	60.0	23	50	2,412	49.8	38.0	40.2	21.8	34.1	51.6	13.0	0.9	Dominican Republic
67.8	12.4	19.8	5.4	...	31	29	7,954[32]	30.5[32]	50.1[32]	20.7[32]	29.2[32]	34.7[32]	62.0[32]	3.2[32]		Ecuador
...	...	...	27.5	...	119	373	5,279[3,57]	5.3[3,57]	7.1[57]	92.9[57]		100.0[57]				Egypt
95.3	4.7	—	6.1	...	21	106	1,452	69.0	25.1	58.6	16.4	44.9	38.2	11.6	5.3	El Salvador

Agriculture and land use (continued)

country	farms (latest census of agriculture)[a]			size class (%)							tenure (% of farms)					
	year	number of farms ('000)	average (ha)	under 1 ha	1–5 ha	5–10 ha	10–20 ha	20–50 ha	50–200 ha	over 200 ha	owner-operated individual/ family	corporate/ state	socialized/ collective	rented (including share-croppers)	tribal/ com-munal	other[b]
Equatorial Guinea	...	...	...	...	...	...	...	...	...	...	...	...	...	...	...	...
Eritrea[63]	—															
Estonia[37]	1993	10.2	...	—— 8.0 ——		12.8	27.8	42.2	—— 9.2 ——		93.5	—— 6.5 ——				
Ethiopia[63]	1976–77	4,893	1.4	49.9	46.5	3.4	0.2	—	—		98.4	1.6	—	—	—	—
Faeroe Islands	...	...	...	...	...	...	...	...	...		...	...	...	...	...	...
Fiji	1978–79	66	4.2	64.3	20.6	8.1	3.7	2.1	—— 1.2 ——			—— 78.7 ——		3.5	95.1	1.4
Finland	1992[65]	198	12.8[23]	—	34.4	21.5	23.4	18.1	—— 2.6 ——					21.3		
France	1990	924	26.6[39]	—— 37.5 ——			31.9[66]	11.2[67]	—— 19.4 ——		65.2[49]	—	—	33.5[49]	—	1.2[49]
French Guiana	1989	4.5	4.6	16.5	73.6	6.0	1.5	—— 2.4 ——			36.5	—	—	6.3	—	57.1
French Polynesia	1987	5.6	...	37.7		—— 62.3 ——										
Gabon	1975	71	1.0	68.0	—— 32.0 ——						81.8	—	—	0.3	5.3	12.5
Gambia, The	1989–90	...	...	...	...	...	...	...	...		...	...	...	...	...	...
Gaza Strip	1968	...	...	...	...	...	...	...	...		...	...	...	...	...	...
Georgia	1990	...	...	...	...	...	...	...	...		...	...	...	...	...	...
Germany	1992[3, 65]	601	28.0	12.4[58]	17.1[69]	16.4	19.5	24.5	—— 10.1 ——							
Ghana	1970	805	3.2	36.6	48.7	9.0	3.9	1.8								
Gibraltar	—	...	...	...	...	...	...	...	...		...	...	...	...	...	...
Greece	1981	999	3.5	24.7	54.2	15.0	4.7	1.2	—— 0.2 ——							
Greenland	—	...	...	...	...	...	...	...	...							
Grenada	1981	8	1.7	88.3[58]	6.9[70]	3.3[71]	0.7	0.4[24]	—— 0.3[72] ——			—— 73.2 ——		14.1	—	12.7
Guadeloupe	1988–89	17	2.8	32.1	58.3	7.0	1.6		—— 0.9 ——		46.6[73]	—	—	19.1[73]	—	34.3[73]
Guam	1987	0.4	15.1	42.2[9]	33.9[10]	—— 19.4[11] ——			—— 4.6[12] ——		64.4	—	—	4.3	—	31.3
Guatemala	1979	600	6.8	39.7[75]	49.8[76]	—— 8.2[77] ——			—— 2.2[78] ——			—— 74.0[79] ——		6.3[79]	5.8[79]	13.9[79]
Guernsey	1993	0.089	16.2[57]	6.7[17]	24.0[17]	23.1[17]	—— 46.1[17] ——				32.4[2, 14]	—	—	67.6[2, 14]	—	—
Guinea	1984–85[3]	...	2.4	...	...	...	...	...	...		...	...	...	...	...	...
Guinea-Bissau	1961	87	3.0	13.4	73.3	10.0	3.0	0.3			...	90.0	...	...	...	...
Guyana	1964	...	...	...	...	—— 3.8 ——										10.0
Haiti	1971	617	1.4	58.7	37.5						66.6	—	—	25.0	—	8.4
Honduras	1974	195	13.5	17.3	46.6	14.5	9.8	7.8	3.3	0.8	99.7	0.1	—		0.2	
Hong Kong	1986	11	0.3	97.5	2.3	0.1	—— 0.1 ——				—— 9.0 ——			77.0	—	14.0
Hungary	1992	2.9[81]	...	90[57]	—— 9.9[57] ——			—— 0.1[57] ——			6.8[82]	13.3[82]	74.5[82]	—	—	—
Iceland	1981	7.0	...	15.7	9.3	11.7	23.7	35.8	—— 3.7 ——		92.7	...	...	1.2	—	6.1
India	1985–86	97,700	...	58.1	31.9[27]	8.1[71]	—— 1.9 ——				74.8[6]	—[7]	—[7]	3.2[7]	—[7]	22.1[7]
Indonesia	1987	19,501[84]	c.1[84]	70.7[84]	—— 29.3[84] ——											
Iran	1988	3,330	...	...	...	...	...	...	...							
Iraq	1979	470	13.3	25.9[85]	27.6[86]	23.2[87]	11.5[88]	9.4	1.9[89]	0.5[90]	52.5[13]	—	—	40.9[13]	—	6.6[13]
Ireland	1986	279[41]	25.0[17]	2.7[41]	—— 37.8[41] ——		—— 52.4[41] ——		7.1[41]		72.4	...	...	27.6	—	—
Isle of Man	1987	0.8	59.7	—— 25.8[91] ——			14.0[92]	18.2[24]	23.4[25]	18.5[26]	84.0	—	1.4			14.6
Israel	1981	52	11.3	26.5	57.6	8.3	4.0	2.0	—— 1.8 ——		81.5[41]	—	—	6.7[41]	—	11.8[41]
Italy	1990–91	3,023	7.5	33.0	43.0	11.7	6.7	3.8	—— 1.8 ——							
Jamaica	1978–79	184	2.9	32.5[93]	60.7[94]	4.8[71]	0.9	0.4[24]	0.3[25]	0.4[26]	99.5[95]	0.2[95]	—			0.3[95]
Japan	1992	2,888	1.4	57.6	40.5		—— 1.9 ——				79.4[41]	—	—		...	20.6[41]
Jersey	1990	0.6	11.1	—— 45.0[96] ——		16.4[97]	19.7[98]	—— 19.0[99] ——			31.4[35]	—	—	68.6[35]	...	6.1
Jordan	1983	57	6.3	25.3	44.6	15.6	8.6	4.5	1.3	0.1	80.5	—	—	13.1	0.3	...
Kazakhstan	1992	...	...	...	...	...	...	...	...							
Kenya	1976–79[102]	2,750	2.5	65.5	27.3	2.7[103]	—— 4.4[104] ——									
Kiribati	...	...	...	...	...	...	...	...	...		...	...	...	...	...	...
Korea, North	...	...	...	...	...	...	...	...	...		...	...	...	...	...	...
Korea, South	1990[3]	1,767	1.2	60.8[2]	—— 39.2[2] ——						82.5[40]	—	—	17.4[41]	—	0.1[41]
Kuwait	1991–92	2.3	2.4[105]	48.6[41]	25.4[41]	10.2[41]	8.7[41]	4.0[41]	3.1[41]	—	95.3	...	...			4.7
Kyrgyzstan	1992	...	...	...	...	...	...	...	...		...	...	...	...	...	...
Laos	1983	...	...	...	...	...	...	...	...		...	...	...	...	...	...
Latvia	1992	52.3[106]	...	...	...	...	...	...	...							
Lebanon	1970	143	4.3	47.7	—— 44.5 ——		—— 6.5 ——		1.2	0.1						
Lesotho	1986	207	2.0[41]	27.0[41]	67.5[41]	—— 5.5[41] ——										
Liberia	1971[107]	122	3.0	52.8	31.0	12.0	—— 3.7 ——		—— 0.5 ——		40.0[14]	—	—	—	43.3[14]	16.7[14]
Libya	1974	144	14.0	12.7	34.1	20.6	17.4	12.0	—— 3.2 ——							
Liechtenstein	1990	0.42	8.7	33.8	25.7	10.3	10.8	18.7	—— 0.7 ——		31.7	—— 57.2 ——		24.5	—— 42.8 ——	43.8
Lithuania	1993	4.3	...	...	...	...	...	...	...							
Luxembourg	1993	3.4	37	14.6[58]	11.6	8.1	8.6	22.6	—— 34.3 ——		45.4[14]	...	...			
Macau	...	...	...	...	...	...	...	...	...		...	...	...	...	...	...
Macedonia[37]	1981	176	...	44.7	43.0	6.7	1.2	—— 0.2 ——			100.0	—— 87.3[14] ——		4.9[14]	...	7.4[14]
Madagascar	1984–85	1,453	1.3	54.8	44.2	1.0	0.2	0.1	—— 0.1 ——							
Malawi	1980–81[102]	1,136	1.2	54.9	40.1[109]	—— 5.0[110] ——					53.2[41]	18.2[41]	—	19.6[41]	...	9.0[41]
Malaysia	1980[102, 111]	920	2.2	...	...	...	...	...	...							
Maldives	1985	...	...	...	...	...	...	...	...		...	...	...	...	...	...
Mali	1982–83	562	4.0	20.1	54.1	17.4	—— 8.4 ——				96.8[113]	3.2	—	70.4	—	13.6[50]
Malta	1983	12	1.1	67.8	30.0	2.0	—— 0.2 ——				16.0	—	—			
Marshall Islands	...	...	...	...	...	...	...	...	...		...	...	...	...	...	...
Martinique	1988–89	16.0	2.3	64.9	28.2	4.0	1.6	—— 1.4 ——								
Mauritania	1984–85	100	2.0	49.2	41.0[27]	7.0[71]	2.0	0.5[24]	—— 0.3[72] ——		68.4	...	...	4.4	10.4	17.0
Mauritius	1980	32.5	1.1	61.3	36.2	1.9	0.3	0.2	—— 0.1 ——		95.8	...	...	4.2	—	—
Mayotte	1987	5.9[84]	1.7[100]	...	...	...	...	...	...							
Mexico	1970[115]	2,848	49	23.5	39.4	21.1	8.8	2.7	2.9	1.5	—— 97.6 ——			1.0	—	1.5
Micronesia	...	...	...	...	...	...	...	...	...		...	...	...	...	...	...
Moldova	1991	1.3	...	...	...	...	...	...	...		—	30.8	55.2	—	—	14.0
Monaco	—	...	...	...	...	...	...	...	...		—	16.0	84.0	—	—	—
Mongolia	1985	0.3	385,000	...	...	...	...	...	...							
Morocco	1985–86	1,900[100]	3.9[100]	29.8[7]	44.0[7]	14.9[7]	7.7[7]	3.0[7]	—— 0.7[7] ——		0.2	0.1	—		99.7	—
Mozambique	1973	1,605	3.1	...	...	...	...	...	...							
Myanmar (Burma)	1987–88	4,308[116]	2.3[116]	61.2[58, 116]	24.7[70, 116]	11.5[116, 117]	2.5[92, 116]	—— 0.8[12, 116] ——			45.0	...	...	55.0		
Namibia	1989	6.3[118]	...	...	...	...	...	...	...							
Nauru	...	...	...	...	...	...	...	...	...		...	...	...	...	...	...
Nepal	1981–82	2,194	1.1	66.7	29.9	2.7	—— 0.7 ——				97.5	—	—	1.6	—	0.9
Netherlands, The	1993[56]	120[119]	15.5[33]	9.9	24.4	16.1	18.7	25.3	—— 5.6 ——		—— 31.5[14, 33] ——			12.2[14, 33]	—	56.4[14, 33]

activity (% of farms) — mainly crops	mainly live-stock	mixed/ other	technology (latest) — tractors (per 1,000 ha)	electricity (% of farms having)	irrigation (% of land irrig.)	artificial fertilizer (kg/ha)	land in farms — total ('000 ha)	% of total land area	land use (%) — cropland — permanent crops	temporary crops	fallow	total cropland	meadows and pastures	wood-land and forest	other	country
...	...	...	0.8	...	...	...	...	...	...	...	...	...	...	...	...	Equatorial Guinea
...	...	...	0.4	...	...	...	...	...	...	...	...	...	...	...	...	Eritrea[63]
...	...	...	21.1	...	...	...	252.3[64]	22.7[64]	...	...	...	44.0[64]	10.0[64]	34.0[64]	12.0[64]	Estonia[37]
...	...	...	0.3	...	1	7	6,971	5.7	7.4	76.8	15.8	86.9	9.1	...	4.0	Ethiopia[63]
...	...	...	...	...	...	...	...	...	...	...	...	...	...	...	...	Faeroe Islands
52.3	—47.6—		39.4	...	1	96	277	15.2	...	...	...	...	...	...	...	Fiji
36.6[08]	38.0	25.4	93.1	100.0	0	210	14,914	49.0	0.3[41]	97.6[41]	2.1[41]	17.3	0.8	61.7	20.2	Finland
...	...	...	81.0	...	7	319	30,340	55.3	7.3	89.5	3.2	54.3	36.6	—9.1—		France
...	...	...	30.5	...	20	64	21.7[32]	0.3[32]	16.6	80.4	3.0	57.0	43.0	...	...	French Guiana
...	...	...	31.2	...	19.4	33	36.8	10.4	90.0	7.1	2.9	62.0	8.5	1.9	27.6	French Polynesia
...	...	...	5.1	...	...	3	73.0	0.3	...	...	...	...	...	...	...	Gabon
...	...	...	0.2	...	8	11	176.4	16.5	...	100.0	...	100.0	...	...	...	Gambia, The
...	...	...	83.9	...	133	...	16.5[32]	50.0[32]	68.8[32]	31.2[32]	...	100.0	...	...	...	Gaza Strip
...	...	...	31.3	...	60	...	3,200	45.7	...	...	...	25.0	62.5	...	12.5	Georgia
...	...	...	115.3	...	4	384	19,185[57]	54.9[57]	1.8[57]	—98.2[57]—		61.3[57]	27.4[57]	8.0[57]	3.3[57]	Germany
...	...	...	3.6	...	1	3	2,574	10.8	61.4	38.6	...	100.0	—	—	—	Ghana
...	...	...	...	...	...	4	...	...	...	...	...	...	...	...	...	Gibraltar
...	...	...	79.5	...	43	175	3,546	26.9	29.2	61.1	9.7	98.1	1.9	...	...	Greece
...	c. 100	...	6.0	...	...	...	13.9	40.2	...	...	...	...	...	...	...	Greenland
...	...	...	6.0	...	...	...	...	...	...	...	...	...	...	...	...	Grenada
72.2[74]	17.2[74]	10.5[74]	36.4	...	14	307	46.7[32]	35.3[32]	14.5[32]	39.1[32]	46.5[32]	56.7[32]	43.3[32]	...	...	Guadeloupe
...	...	...	13.3	68.7	...	...	5.3	9.8	—51.2[35]—		48.8[35]	17.8[35]	34.3[35]	—47.9[35]—		Guam
...	71.9	...	3.1	...	9	66	4,147	38.1	27.6	—72.4—		42.0	27.3	27.2	3.4	Guatemala
...	...	...	...	...	...	...	2	27.6	—	100.0	—	12.3	87.7	...	...	Guernsey
...	...	...	0.5	...	4	1	1,600[23]	6.5	...	...	...	...	...	...	...	Guinea
...	...	...	0.1	...	...	3	169	4.7	...	...	...	...	...	...	...	Guinea-Bissau
...	...	...	7.6	...	27	33	10,652	26.2	...	...	...	8.4	91.6	...	...	Guyana
...	...	...	0.4	...	13	4	1,579	57.0	...	...	...	54.4	33.3	12.0	...	Haiti
56.3	37.3	6.4	2.1	...	6	18	2,630	23.5	15.4[80]	34.6[80]	50.0[80]	52.0[80]	48.0[80]	...	...	Honduras
...	...	...	1.2	...	33	100.0[34]	7.3	6.8	7.4	37.0	55.6	100.0	—	—	—	Hong Kong
43.4[5]	44.3[5]	12.3[5]	8.5	...	5	231	7,960[4]	85.6[4]	3.4[4]	96.6[4]	—	57.3[4]	14.5[4]	22.2[4]	6.0[4]	Hungary
...	...	...	1,809	87.0[46]	...	2,529	...	...	...	...	...	...	...	...	...	Iceland
86.8[7]	—7	13.2[7]	6.8	...	28	69	169,603[83]	56.4[83]	—84.4[83]—		15.6[83]	97.9[83]	...	—2.1[83]—		India
...	...	...	2.1	...	50	110	48,583	25.3	27.0	45.2	27.8	60.7	5.1	18.9	15.3	Indonesia
...	...	...	7.1	...	56	80	104,900[35]	63.8[35]	4.9[35]	62.0[35]	33.2[35]	14.2[35]	85.8[32]	...	...	Iran
87.9	11.2	0.8	6.1	...	49	40	5,702	13.1	3.0	62.4	34.6	87.2	0.7	0.2	11.9	Iraq
...	...	...	182	...	...	741	5,692	82.6	0.5	99.5	—	9.5	69.5	—21.0—		Ireland
...	...	...	...	...	...	...	48	83.3	3.5	—96.5—		12.8	87.2	...	...	Isle of Man
...	...	...	72.2	...	52	252	432[32]	21.2[32]	25.0[32]	—75.0[32]—		81.5[32]	...	—18.5[32]—		Israel
...	...	...	163	...	35	151	22,702[23]	75.3[23]	25.5[23]	—74.5[23]—		48.1[23]	18.2[23]	24.7[23]	9.0[23]	Italy
80.8[39]	...	—10.2[39]—	19.9	...	23	116	603[95]	54.8[95]	22.2[95]	72.2[95]	5.6[95]	11.3[95]	21.0[95]	13.5[83]	23.6[95]	Jamaica
85.1[100]	14.9[100]		493	...	69	414	5,165	13.9	9.1	—90.9—		95.5	...	...	4.5	Japan
58.2[74,101]	14.9[74,101]	26.9[74,101]	...	...	...	...	6.5	56.2	—98.9—		1.1	63.4		—36.6—		Jersey
...	...	...	18.6	1.5	21	61	364	4.1	13.3	63.0	23.7	87.7	1.0	0.3	11.0	Jordan
...	...	...	6.2	...	6	...	180,000	66.2	...	...	...	19.2	00.5	...	0.3	Kazakhstan
...	...	...	7.3	...	3	48	6,922	11.9	11.5	—88.5—		71.0	23.8	1.9	3.3	Kenya
...	...	...	...	...	...	...	...	...	...	...	...	...	...	...	...	Kiribati
...	...	...	43.7	...	85	407	...	...	...	...	...	...	...	...	...	Korea, North
82.3[5]	17.7[5]	—	33.8	...	70	454	2,109	21.2	6.7	—93.3—		100.0	—	—	—	Korea, South
38.9	61.1	—	20.0	100.0	40	200	7.9	0.4	20.6	79.4	—	70.0	—30.0—			Kuwait
...	...	...	20.8	...	73	...	9,900	50.0	...	...	...	14.1	84.8	...	1.1	Kyrgyzstan
...	...	...	1.1	...	16	2	1,680	7.1	2.3	—97.7—		52.4	47.6	...	...	Laos
...	...	...	33.6	...	...	...	2,500	38.5	...	...	...	68.0	—32.0—			Latvia
77.0[74]	8.1[74]	14.0[74]	13.9	...	40	92	275[39]	27.0[39]	36.7[39]	39.7[39]	23.6[39]	100.0[39]	—	—		Lebanon
37.3	—	62.7	5.4	...	...	14	372[41]	12.3[41]	—	89.6[41]	10.4[41]	98.8[41]	...	...	1.2[41]	Lesotho
...	...	...	2.6	...	2	7	370[82]	3.8[82]	66.2[82]	33.8[82]	...	98.3[82]	...	1.7[82]	...	Liberia
...	...	...	19.0	...	14	37	8,800[82]	5.1[82]	—33.3[82]—		66.7[82]	20.5[82]	79.5[82]	...	...	Libya
23.9[34]	61.6[34]	14.5[34]	112	...	...	...	3.9	24.2	1.1	—98.9—		39.9	57.5	1.1	1.5	Liechtenstein
...	...	...	20.7	...	...	...	3,524	54.0	...	...	...	76.3	13.0	—10.7—		Lithuania
25.6[108]	59.0	15.4	146	...	...	...	138	53.3	—96.8—		3.2	41.7	49.5	6.7	2.1	Luxembourg
...	...	...	...	...	...	...	...	...	...	...	...	...	...	...	...	Macau
...	...	...	72.7	...	12	...	1,320	51.3	9.3	65.4	25.3	46.4	53.4	—	1.2	Macedonia[37]
...	...	...	1.1	...	36	2	2,044	3.5	15.4	84.6	—	100.0	—	—	—	Madagascar
22.1	...	77.9	0.8	...	1	23	1,332	14.1	0.2	99.8	—	94.8	...	5.2	—	Malawi
...	...	...	12.0[112]	...	33[112]	170[112]	4,100[35]	31.2[35]	84.8[35]	15.2[35]	...	100.0[35]	...	...	...	Malaysia
...	...	...	...	...	...	...	10	63.5	...	...	...	...	...	...	...	Maldives
...	...	...	0.4	...	10	9	2,277	1.8	—	100.0	—	100.0	...	...	...	Mali
...	...	...	37.5	...	8	39	13.0	41.2	5.0	—95.0—		87.5	—12.5—			Malta
...	...	...	...	...	...	...	...	...	...	...	...	...	...	...	...	Marshall Islands
...	...	...	110	...	50	945	37.2[32]	39.0[32]	46.6[32]	50.7[32]	2.7[32]	52.1[32]	47.9[02]	...	—	Martinique
...	...	...	1.7	...	7	12	196[33]	0.2[33]	—	56.2	43.8	100.0	—	—	—	Mauritania
...	...	...	3.7	...	17	304	100[114]	53.8[114]	4.2[114]	95.8[114]	—	90.0[114]	—10.0[114]—			Mauritius
...	...	...	...	...	...	...	14.6	39.0	33.3	66.7	—	100.0	—	—	—	Mayotte
83.9	12.9	3.2	7.4	...	26	70	139,868	72.7	6.3	58.1	35.6	16.5	53.3	14.2	16.0	Mexico
61.4[5]	15.7[5]	22.9[5]	7.4	45	0	...	5.8	12.2	—9.3—		90.7	32.9	30.2	—36.9—		Micronesia
...	...	...	31.0	...	18	...	2,500[32]	73.5[32]	...	...	...	60.0[32]	12.0[32]	—	20.0[32]	Moldova
...	...	...	...	...	...	...	...	...	...	...	...	...	...	...	...	Monaco
...	...	...	8.4	...	6	12	124,587	79.6	...	66.8	33.2	0.9	99.1	...	...	Mongolia
...	...	...	4.6	...	14	35	8,944[31,56]	20.0[31,56]	7.2[31,56]	71.5[31,56]	21.3[31,56]	100.0[31,56]	...	...	...	Morocco
...	...	...	1.9	...	4	1	13,626	17.8	—44.9—		55.1	55.0	45.0	...	...	Mozambique
1.3[5]	94.4[5]	4.3[5]	1.1	...	10	8	12,560	10.0	3.0	79.5	17.5	97.0	3.0	...	—	Myanmar (Burma)
...	...	...	4.7	...	0.6	...	662	0.8	0.3	—99.7—		100.0	—	—	—	Namibia
...	...	...	...	...	...	...	...	...	...	...	...	...	...	...	...	Nauru
31.1	57.7	11.2	2.0	...	37	25	2,464	16.7	1.3	97.1	1.6	94.0	1.7	0.6	3.7	Nepal
...	...	...	227	...	63	628	1,986	58.5	—98.8—		1.2	46.5	53.5	...	...	Netherlands, The

Agriculture and land use (continued)

country	year	number of farms ('000)	average (ha)	under 1 ha	1–5 ha	5–10 ha	10–20 ha	20–50 ha	50–200 ha	over 200 ha	individual/ family	corporate/ state	socialized/ collective	rented (including share-croppers)	tribal/ communal	other[b]
Netherlands Antilles	...	...	...	...	...	...	...	...	...	...	...	...	...	...	...	...
New Caledonia	1983–84	12.7	23	71.2[58]	13.8[69]	3.7	2.3	2.5	3.8	2.8	85.7[34]	10.9[34]	...	...	...	3.4[34]
New Zealand	1992	79.7	217[57]	—12.5[34]—		10.3[34]	8.4[34]	—46.5[34]—		22.3[34]	...	...		...		
Nicaragua	1984	...	...	—26.2—				—30.6—		43.3	64.4[14,35]	—35.6[14,35]—		...		
Niger	1980[3]	699	4.9	3.8	54.1	37.8	—4.3—				...	...		...		
Nigeria	1971	...	...	92.0	7.8	0.2	—	—	—	—	...	...		...		
Northern Mariana Is.	1990	0.1	49.1	26.1[122]	35.3[123]	—24.4[11]—		—14.3—			56.3	...		23.5	...	20.2
Norway	1993[56]	88.3[124]	10.2[2]	—31.0—		24.9	28.6	14.2	—1.3—		—65.4[2]—			34.6[2]	—	—
Oman	1978–79	83	1.0	70.5	25.0	2.8	1.3[125]	0.3[126]	0.1	—	...	...		...		
Pakistan	1990	5,076	...	27.0	54.0	12.2	4.7	—2.1—			64.1[14,39]	0.3[14,39]		35.6[14,39]		
Panama	1991	209	14.2	47.4	25.0	7.6	7.0	7.5	5.0	0.7	28.6	...		1.4	—	70.0
Papua New Guinea	1985[127]	0.8	483	—26.8[59]—					28.3[84]	44.9[84]	26.9[14,84]	71.0[14,84]		2.1[14,84]		
Paraguay	1981	249	88	8.6	27.4	19.9	22.7	14.5	4.4	2.5	54.5	0.4		9.2	—	35.9[40]
Peru	1984	1,574	9.5	24.1	47.7	13.2	6.7	5.5	—2.8—		75.5	—		0.8	6.8	16.9
Philippines	1980	3,420	2.6	22.7	63.3	13.0	—3.5—				58.3	—		27.4	—	14.3
Poland	1992	2,144[106]	7.0[106]	17.8[106]	35.3[106]	14.8[106]	—32.1[106]—				78.3[4,14]	13.9[4,14]	3.3[4,14]			4.5[4,14]
Portugal	1979	784	6.6	44.5	41.9	7.7	3.3	1.5	0.7	0.4	68.1			8.7		23.2
Puerto Rico	1987	20	17.2	—48.7[128]—		19.5[129]	16.7[130]	6.7[131]	—8.3[72]—		—77.5—			7.1		15.4
Qatar	1990	0.8	7.0	20.5	41.8	18.0	12.6	5.8	—1.4—							
Réunion	1989	15	4.1	35.6	47.9	12.5	2.7	—1.3—			46.1[7]			22.5[7]		31.4[7]
Romania	1989	3.6[42]	3,900[42]	...	...	...	...	...	...	...	9.0[14]	13.9[14]	60.7[14]	—		16.4[14]
Russia	1992	28.4[42]														
Rwanda	1984	1,112	1.2	56.8	26.8[132]	—16.4[133]—					50.9			1.4		47.7[50]
St. Kitts and Nevis	1981	...	...	...	...	...	...	...	...	...	46.8[14]	48.0[14]		5.2[14]		
St. Lucia	1986	12	2.0	75.9[58]	10.3[70]	4.9[71]	0.9	0.3[24]	0.2[25]	0.4[26]	72.0			15.5		12.5
St. Vincent	1985–86	8[73]	1.8[73]	48.0[73,93]	40.7[73,134]	8.5[70,73]	2.4[11,73]	—0.5[12,73]—			62.0[73]			8.8[73]		19.2[73]
San Marino	1975	0.7	7.0	21.3	47.8	—24.7—		5.1	—1.1—		39.9[14]	15.5[14]		29.9[14]		14.7[14]
São Tomé and Príncipe	1964	11.1	8.7	88.5	9.8	0.7	0.2	0.2	0.2	0.4	77.2			20.5		2.3
Saudi Arabia	1982–83	212	10.1	36.6	35.8	11.3	8.2	5.0	2.6	0.5	85.9			2.6		11.5
Senegal	1976	362	7.0	—99.4—				—0.6—			...	...	0.6	...		99.4
Seychelles	1993	0.9[135]	...	...	...	...	...	...	...	...	98.9	—1.1—		6.4	—	
Sierra Leone	1971	286	1.8	38.8	55.0	—6.1—		—0.1—			93.6			88.8		
Singapore	1973	16	0.8	77.4	22.2	0.3	—0.1—				7.4					3.8
Slovakia	1991	...	...								...	...		...		
Slovenia[37]	1991	157	...	28.4	36.0	18.0	—17.6—				100.0					
Solomon Islands	1975[102]	92	1.0	...	...	...	...	...	...	...	—	—		—	100.0	—
Somalia	1984	198	3.6	...	...	...	...	...	...	...	99.9	0.1				
South Africa	1992	67[138]	1,193[100]	...	...	...	...	...	...	...	72.5			19.8	—7.7—	
Spain	1989	2,285	19.0	27.7	36.6	13.2	9.5	6.8	3.9	2.3	72.5			19.8	—7.7—	
Sri Lanka	1982	1,817	1.1	77.5[9]	—22.2[140]—		0.1[141]	0.1[24]	—0.1[72]—		59.0[142]	27.2[142]		8.2[142]		5.6[142]
Sudan, The	1982	...	...	...	...	...	...	...	...	...	22.3	2.2		28.0	42.0	5.5
Suriname	1981	22	7.5	21.9[95]	61.2[95]	11.1[95]	3.6[95]	1.6[95]	0.3[95]	0.3[95]	20.2[95]	0.9[95]		49.5[95]		29.4[95]
Swaziland	1990–91	1.0[143]	...	—45.7—				—54.3[19]—			84.4			—15.6—		
Sweden	1993[56]	91	29.5[23]		15.2		21.3	26.7	—16.9—		48.3			15.2		36.5[50]
Switzerland	1990	108	9.1[34]	23.1[34]	18.7[34]	14.6[34]	27.5[34]	15.2[34]	0.9[34]		36.2[39]		0.8[39]	58.5[39]		4.5[39]
Syria	1988	444	8.9	16.7	36.8[27]	22.8[71]	13.1	8.5	2.0[148]	0.2[149]	65.8[14,113]	1.8[14]	32.5[14]	...	—	...
Taiwan	1989	723	1.2	72.6	27.4	...	...	...	...	...	86.4			3.7	—	9.9
Tajikistan	1992	...	...	...	...	...	...	...	...	...	...	...		...		...
Tanzania	1986–87	3,626	0.9[3]	70.1	28.8	1.0	—0.1—				87.3[73]			3.6[73]	—	9.1[73]
Thailand	1988	4,877	3.7	14.3	72.0[150]	—13.1[151]—		—0.5[152]—			87.0			3.6	—	9.3
Togo	1982–83	263	1.5	48.8	38.6[109]	—12.7[110]—					70.7[14]			21.1[14]	8.2[14]	2.8
Tonga	1985	10.1	3.3	18.9	67.9	12.7	—	0.5	—	—	52.1	—97.2—				2.8
Trinidad and Tobago	1982	30.6	4.3	35.1	50.7	9.6	4.1	—	0.4	0.1	52.1			36.5	—	11.4
Tunisia	1988	376	13.6	—45.7—		20.6	17.9	11.4	—4.4—		89.3			10.6		0.1
Turkey	1990	4,091	...	16.0	51.1	18.0	9.7	4.4	—0.8—		...	...		...		...
Turkmenistan	1992	...	...	...	...	...	...	...	...	...	99.9			...	0.1	
Tuvalu	1976	1.5	1.7	...	...	...	...	...	...	...	97.4			...		2.6
Uganda	1964	1,171	3.9	20.7	59.8	11.2	—8.3—				...	...		...		...
Ukraine	1990	...	...	...	...	...	...	...	...	...	...	...		...		...
United Arab Emirates	1986–87	17.9	2.3	45.4	38.8[154]	—15.9[155]—					...	...		...		...
United Kingdom	1992	242	107.3[57,156]	5.6[58]	8.4[69]	11.9	15.2	24.7	28.0	6.2	—74.3[157]—			25.7[157]	—	—
United States	1987	2,040[64]	193.4[64]	—8.7[94]—		—19.8[11]—		30.9[158]	22.9[159]	17.7[160]	52.8	6.1		11.5	—	29.2
Uruguay	1990	54	280.5[114]	—	8.2	12.1	13.2	16.5	23.3	26.7	—59.1[39]—			17.3[39]	—	23.6[39]
Uzbekistan	1992	...	...	...	...	...	...	...	...	...	65.3[39]	34.7[39]		...		...
Vanuatu	1983–84	27	6.9													
Venezuela	1984–85	381	82.0	8.3	36.3	15.7	13.0	10.4	9.3	7.1	61.5[49]			6.1[49]	...	31.3[32,49]
Vietnam	1991	31[42]	28.0[3]								—100—				—	
Virgin Islands (U.S.)	1987	0.3	27.0	30.0[161]	30.3[162]	12.0	13.9	6.0	3.7[163]	4.1[164]	75.3			8.6	—	16.1
West Bank	1965	55	3.4	49.8	34.4	10.6	4.0	1.0	0.2	0.0	7.16			6.4	—	22.0
Western Sahara	1983	...	...								...	...		...		...
Western Samoa	1989	11	6.1	...	...	...	...	...	...	...	...	—		...	86.0	14.0
Yemen[165]	1977–83	591	2.3	57.5	30.9	7.4	3.3	0.8	0.1	—	90.3[14]			9.4[14]	—	0.3[14]
Yugoslavia	1981	1,198	...	24.7	48.8	19.9	4.4	—0.7—			83.0[57]	—17.0[57]—				
Zaire	1970	2,538	2.3	41.6	57.3	1.0	0.2	—	—		4.2	0.1			95.6	0.1
Zambia	1971	768	3.1	50.5	45.2	—3.8—		—0.5—			...	...		...	98.0	—
Zimbabwe	1974	765	38.7	—16.7[91]—		52.8[168]	29.8[169]	—0.7[19]—			—2.0—			...	98.0	—

[1]1967. [2]1989. [3]Cultivated area only. [4]1993. [5]Based on value of output by sector. [6]1987. [7]1973. [8]1991–92. [9]Less than 1.2 ha. [10]1.2 to 4.0 ha. [11]4.0 to 20 ha. [12]20 ha or more. [13]Percentage of farms having irrigation. [14]Based on area, not number, of holdings. [15]10 to 25 ha. [16]25 to 50 ha. [17]1974. [18]50 to 100 ha. [19]100 ha or more. [20]Includes fruits and vegetables. [21]Includes houseplants and cut flowers. [22]Includes fallow and grazing lands. [23]1990. [24]20 to 40 ha. [25]40 to 61 ha. [26]61 ha or more. [27]1.0 to 4.0 ha. [28]4.0 to 10.1 ha. [29]10.1 ha or more. [30]1977. [31]1990–91. [32]1988. [33]1985. [34]0 ha or more. [35]1982. [36]4.0 ha or more. [37]Holdings and tenure refer to private plots only; land use 1990. [38]Includes about 21,000 farms without land; distribution by size refers to traditional farms with land only. [39]1980. [40]Almost all squatters. [41]1970. [42]State farms and cooperatives only. [43]Precollectivization. [44]4.0 to 52.2 ha. [45]52.2 ha and over. [46]Irrigated land only. [47]1968. [48]1984. [49]1971. [50]Owned and rented holdings. [51]Data for Czech Republic include Slovakia unless otherwise noted. [52]Less than 0.5 ha. [53]0.5 to 50 ha. [54]50 to 1,000 ha. [55]Excludes Slovakia. [56]Arable area for Eritrea, but data for tractors is separate. [57]1991. [58]Less than 2.0 ha. [59]2.0 to 20 ha. [60]2.1 ha or less. [61]2.1 to 4.2 ha. [62]4.2 ha or more. [63]Data for Ethiopia include Eritrea; values shown for Ethiopia would remain broadly representative for Eritrea, but data for tractors is separate. [64]January 1994. [65]Excludes holdings of less than 1.0 ha. [66]10 to 35 ha. [67]35 to 50 ha. [68]Includes fruit-growing and viticulture. [69]2.0 to 5.0 ha. [70]2.0 to 4.0 ha. [71]4.0 to 10 ha. [72]40 ha or more. [73]1972. [74]Commercial farms only. [75]Less than 0.7 ha. [76]0.7 to 7.1 ha. [77]7.1 to 45 ha. [78]45 ha or more. [79]Excludes holdings of 0.04 ha (500 sq m) or less. [80]1979. [81]Agricultural cooperatives only. [82]1981. [83]1986–87. [84]1983. [85]Less than 2.5 ha. [86]2.5 to 7.5 ha. [87]7.5 to 12.5 ha. [88]12.5 to 20 ha. [89]50 to 250 ha. [90]250 ha or more. [91]Less than 8.0 ha. [92]8.0 to 20 ha. [93]Less than 0.4 ha. [94]0.4 to 4.0 ha. [95]1969. [96]Less than 4.5 ha. [97]4.5 to 9.0 ha. [98]9.0 to 18 ha. [99]18 ha or more. [100]1978. [101]1975. [102]Excludes large commercial farms.

mainly crops	mainly live-stock	mixed/ other	tractors (per 1,000 ha)	electricity (% of farms having)	irrigation (% of land irrig.)	artificial fertilizer (kg/ha)	total ('000 ha)	% of total land area	permanent crops	temporary crops	fallow	total cropland	meadows and pastures	woodland and forest	other	country
...	...	...	2.5	...	...	...	293	15.8	51.7	34.8	13.5	6.5	93.5	...	...	Netherlands Antilles
			194	...	...	00										New Caledonia
12.5	68.1	19.4	197	...	74	741	17,300	63.9	85.5		14.5	2.8	78.1	7.7[120]	11.4[121]	New Zealand
			2.4	...	8	28	5,651	47.7								Nicaragua
			0.05	...	1	1	3,806[114]	3.0[114]								Niger
...	...	...	0.4	...	3	12	34,290	37.1	20.0		80.0	31.4	27.5	41.1	...	Nigeria
64.3[5]	36.7[5]	...	22	45	...	...	5.8	12.2				32.9	30.2	36.9		Northern Mariana Is.
24.3[5]	70.6[5]	3.9[5]	177	...	11	242	1,013	3.3	95.0		5.0	43.7		56.3		Norway
...	...	...	9.4	...	92	111	83	0.3	68.6	31.4	—	49.2		50.8		Oman
...	...	...	13.7	...	83	91	21,350	27.7	76.5		23.5	98.9		1.1		Pakistan
...	...	...	10.1	0.5[49]	6	58	2,942	39.0	23.7	41.3	35.0	22.2	50.0	24.1	3.6	Panama
			28.5	...	...	40	386	0.8	100.0			33.7	26.4		39.9	Papua New Guinea
33.0	67.0		7.5	...	3	9	21,941	53.9	4.2	76.6	19.2	12.6	47.5	38.5	1.4	Paraguay
4.9	93.0	2.1	4.8	6.5	38	41	14,893	11.6	24.1	75.9	—	27.1	47.5	19.8	5.6	Peru
98.2	1.5	0.3	2.0	...	29	67	9,034	30.1	57.5	42.5	—	86.3	6.8	6.9		Philippines
53.8[5]	46.2[5]	—	81.8	...	0.7	219	18,664	59.7	1.9[4]	98.1[4]		78.3[4]	21.7[4]	...	...	Poland
			55.4	...	27	73	5,183	56.1	26.1	44.6	29.3	52.6	3.2	34.5	9.7	Portugal
61.0	33.4	5.6	61.5	...	60	...	349	39.3	70.4		29.6	28.0	46.4	19.1	6.6	Puerto Rico
50.4[5]	49.6[5]	...	19.1	...	114	230	5.7	0.5	25.2	74.8	—	100.0				Qatar
			39.5	...	14	282	59.8[32]	28.4[32]	3.2[32]	94.1[32]	2.7[32]	80.1[32]	19.9[32]	...	...	Réunion
			15.7	...	29	133	14,750[57]	61.9[57]	5.8[57]	94.2[57]		68.1[57]	31.9[57]	...	...	Romania
			10.0	...	4	...	210,600	12.3	90.1		9.9	61.7	37.2	—	1.1	Russia
			0.1	...	0.5	1	1,350	51.3	85.6		14.4	63.7	10.6	5.2	20.5	Rwanda
			27.0	...	...	...	12	45.3	31.5		68.5	58.1		41.9		St. Kitts and Nevis
25.0[17]	75.0[17]		17.4	...	20	...	23	38.0	68.5[17]	31.5[17]		57.9[17]	10.2[17]	26.4[17]	5.5[17]	St. Lucia
...	...	...	20.0	...	25	...	17.9	34.8	64.3	16.1	19.6	84.3	15.7	...	...	St. Vincent
...	...	...		...	...	...	4.7	76.5	60.9	6.5	32.6	69.2	6	8.2	16.4	San Marino
...	...	...	62.5	...	6	...	96	100.0	99.4		0.6	38.3	...	50.7	2.0	São Tomé and Príncipe
...	...	...	0.6	...	27	401	2,135	1.0	4.1	18.7	77.2	88.5	...	11.5		Saudi Arabia
...	...	...	0.2	...	8	2	11,338	59.1	0.1	99.9		22.4	77.6	...	...	Senegal
1.8[136]	32.4	65.8[137]	40.0	...	...	...	7.5	27.8	89.6	10.4		100.0	—	—	—	Seychelles
50.3	49.7		1.1	...	7	1	2,732	38.1	20.7	79.3		19.3	80.7	...	...	Sierra Leone
12.5	6.2	81.3	65.0	...	100	5,600	5.6[48]	9.0[48]	75.0	25.0	—	66.7	...	33.3	...	Singapore
			22.2[32]	...	...	98[32]	2,447[32]	49.9[32]	3.2	92.1	4.7	60.7[32]	34.0[32]	5.3[32]		Slovakia
50.7	11.9	37.4	286	...	0.8	...	864	42.7	19.0	80.0	1.0	35.2	64.7	—	0.1	Slovenia[37]
43.4	56.6			...	...	...	93	3.4	40.0	45.2	14.8	100.0	—	—	—	Solomon Islands
20.0	60.0	20.0	2.1	...	12	3										Somalia
34.2[5,57]	45.0[5,57]	20.8[5,57,139]	13.4	...	9	59	98,890	82.7	5.9[100]	94.1[100]		12.6	83.0	2.2	2.2	South Africa
...	...	...	50.0	...	22	101	24,740	57.6	79.4		20.6	48.9	34.3	16.8	—	Spain
...	...	...	35.5	...	59	111	2,009	30.6	56.4	43.6	—	86.0	1.0	2.7	8.8	Sri Lanka
...	...	...	0.8	...	15	4	31,500	13.3	0.8	88.7	10.5	20.0	70.2	...	...	Sudan, The
33.0[95]	12.5[95]	54.5[95]	23.3	...	105	26	165	1.0	15.0	53.0	32.0	40.4	23.1	19.1	17.4	Suriname
45.8[144]	25.3[144]	28.9[120,144]	24.1	...	34	46	900	52.2	88.4		11.6	21.6	31.3[145]	12.5	34.6[146]	Swaziland
14.1	42.3	43.6[147]	66.8	...	4	127	7,878	19.2	91.0		9.0	35.3	4.2	50.3	10.2	Sweden
58.0	42.0		288	...	6	430	1,071	27.1	6.2	93.8	—	31.1	68.1	...	0.8	Switzerland
...	...	...	13.9	...	18	45	6,065	32.8	77.3		22.7	91.7	...	...	8.3	Syria
41.9	30.3	27.8	...	...	38	400[100]	2,827	78.5	27.5	72.5	—	31.7	...	65.7	2.4	Taiwan
...	...	...	44.2	...	81	...	4,300	30.1	...	...	...	20.9	76.7	—	2.4	Tajikistan
44.1	4.7	51.2	2.3	...	5	9	7,545[73]	8.5[73]	19.1[73]	72.5[73]	8.4[73]	49.8[73]	10.2[73]	24.7[73]	15.3[73]	Tanzania
...	...	...	9.6	...	26	36	14,178	27.6	13.5	86.5		93.8	0.9	2.1	3.2	Thailand
...	...	...	0.6	...	1	8	406	7.1	17.3[30]	82.7[30]		71.0[30]	29.0[30]	...	...	Togo
...	...	...	6.8	...	...	2	33	44.5	62.7		37.3	81.2	6.7	10.1	1.9	Tonga
63.7[153]	36.3[153]		35.3	40.7	29	57	132	25.8	55.9	44.1		62.3	4.4	0.1	27.2	Trinidad and Tobago
...	...	...	9.4	...	8	22	10,040[32]	64.6[32]	87.1[32]		12.9[32]	74.5[32]	25.6[32]	...	...	Tunisia
...	3.6	96.4	29.5	...	15	64	35,642	46.3	11.0	70.5	18.5	77.1		22.9		Turkey
...	...	...	45.7	...	100	...	32,200	66.0	...	...	...	4.0	95.6	—	0.4	Turkmenistan
...	...	...	...	...	...	...			...	...	...		...	...	...	Tuvalu
...	...	...	0.9	...	0.2	...	2,262	11.3	29.8	70.2	—	100.0	...	...	...	Uganda
...	...	...	13.2	...	8	...	41,400	68.5	...	...	...	80.7	16.9	—	2.4	Ukraine
...	...	...	6.4	...	17	311	17.5[100]	0.2[100]	64.8[100]	18.2[100]	17.1[100]	97.6[100]	...	1.3[100]	1.1[100]	United Arab Emirates
...	...	...	76.4	...	2	376	18,493	76.8	0.7	98.3	1.0	35.7	60.0	4.3		United Kingdom
40.7	55.4	3.8	25.9	68.8	11	99	394,502[64]	43.1[64]	1.0	90.5	8.5	46.0	42.5	8.3	3.2	United States
37.1[39]	58.7[39]	4.2[39]	26.2	...	11	54	15,623	88.7	3.1[114]	96.9[114]		8.8[114]	85.3[114]	4.2[114]	1.7[114]	Uruguay
...	...	...	42.4	...	96	...	25,600	57.1	...	...	...	16.0	82.0	—	2.0	Uzbekistan
92.2	7.2	0.6	3.8	...	...	...	183	15.0	62.5	3.0	34.5	84.9	15.1	...	...	Vanuatu
27.6	9.0	63.4	15.2	...	6	130	31,278	34.3	19.0[49]	59.0[49]	22.0[49]	13.2[49]	57.0[49]	22.8[49]	7.0[49]	Venezuela
74.5[5]	25.5[5]	—	6.8	...	34	82	9,060	27.4	7.4	92.6		100.0	...	...	...	Vietnam
48.3	40.8	10.9	15.4	15.6	...	...	7.2	20.9	18.3	13.7	68.0	10.7	75.3	10.3	3.7	Virgin Islands (U.S.)
...	...	...	14.1[35]	...	5	...	185[39]	31.4[39]	62.2[39]	37.8[39]		100.0[39]	...	...	...	West Bank
							5,002	18.8	—	—	—	—	100.0			Western Sahara
35.5[14,166]	56.9[14,166]	7.6[14,166]	1.4	...	...	...	70[101]	24.8[101]	71.2[101]	28.8[101]	—	93.8[101]	6.2[101]	...	...	Western Samoa
...	...	...	4.0	...	26	12	1,351	0.1	6.7	69.7	23.6	98.8	...	...	1.2	Yemen[165]
12.7[95,167]	87.3[95,167]		110	...	2	115	6,228[57]	61.1[57]	8.6[57]	88.8[57]	2.6[57]	65.4[57]	33.9[57]	...	0.7[57]	Yugoslavia
92.3	9.7		0.3	...	0.2	1	5,897	2.6	7.7	92.3	—	70.6	20.1	2.0	7.3	Zaire
15.8	9.7	74.5	1.1	...	0.7	15	938	1.3	4.5	95.5	—	14.2	38.1	...	47.7	Zambia
1.8[14,100]	26.7[14,100]	71.5[14,100]	5.9	...	8	53	29,620	76.6	2.5	97.5	—	34.5	65.7	...	...	Zimbabwe

[103]5.0 to 8.0 ha. [104]8.0 ha or more. [105]1985–86. [106]Private farms only. [107]Excludes temporary rangeland available for agricultural use to subsistence farms. [108]Two-fifths under horticulture and viticulture. [109]1.0 to 3.0 ha. [110]3.0 ha or more. [111]West Malaysia except as noted. [112]Malaysia. [113]Includes some rented farms. [114]1986. [115]Preliminary 1991 census reported 4,310,000 farms and an average size of 50 ha. [116]Family farms only. [117]4.0 to 8.0 ha. [118]Commercial farms owned mostly by whites. [119]Includes agricultural and horticultural farms. [120]Includes timber plantations. [121]Includes conservation planting and plantations of native trees. [122]Less than 0.8 ha. [123]0.8 to 4.0 ha. [124]Excludes holdings of less than 0.5 ha. [125]0.5 to 50 ha. [126]50 ha. [127]Large holdings only. [128]1.0 to 3.9 ha. [129]0.9 to 7.9 ha. [130]7.9 to 19.7 ha. [131]19.7 to 40 ha. [132]1.0 to 2.0 ha. [133]2.0 ha or more. [134]0.4 to 2.0 ha. [135]Includes 700 part time farmers. [136]Includes root crops. [137]Includes fruits, vegetables, coconuts, and cinnamon. [138]Total indicates white commercial farmers, of which 60 percent have viable farming units. [139]Includes horticulture. [140]1.2 to 12 ha. [141]12 to 20 ha. [142]1988–89. [143]Includes individual-tenured farms; total incudes 60 percent unused holdings. [144]1983–84. [145]Includes meadows and pastures on individual-tenured farms. [146]Includes all unallocated communal grazing land and uplands in Swaziland National Land area. [147]Includes 36 percent of small farms not identified by activity. [148]50 to 300 ha. [149]300 ha or more. [150]1.0 to 6.4 ha. [151]6.4 to 22.4 ha. [152]22.4 ha or more. [153]1963. [154]1.0 to 7.5 ha. [155]7.5 ha or more. [156]Full-time operations only. [157]Excludes Northern Ireland. [158]20 to 72 ha. [159]72 to 202 ha. [160]202 ha or more. [161]Less than 3.0 ha. [162]3.0 to 10 ha. [163]100 to 260 ha. [164]260 ha or more. [165]Former Yemen Arab Republic only. [166]1976. [167]Data refer to Yugoslavia as constituted prior to 1991. [168]0.8 to 16 ha. [169]16 to 100 ha.

Crops and livestock

This table provides comparative data for selected categories of agricultural production for the countries of the world. The data are taken mainly from the United Nations Food and Agriculture Organization's (FAO) annual *Production Yearbook*.

The FAO depends largely on questionnaires supplied to each country for its statistics, but, where no official or semiofficial responses are returned, the FAO makes estimates, using incomplete, unofficial, or other similarly limited data. And, although the FAO provides standardized guidelines upon which many nations have organized their data collection systems and methods, persistent, often traditional, variations in standards of coverage, methodology, and reporting periods reduce the comparability of statistics that *can* be supplied on such forms. FAO data are based on calendar-year periods; that is, data for any particular crop refer to the calendar year in which the harvest (or the bulk of the harvest) occurred.

In spite of the often tragic food shortages in a number of countries in recent years, worldwide agricultural production is probably more often underreported than overreported. Many countries do not report complete domestic production. Some countries, for example, report only crops that are sold commercially and ignore subsistence crops produced for family or communal consumption, or barter; others may limit reporting to production for export only, to holdings above a certain size, or represent a sampling only.

Methodological problems attach to much smaller elements of the agricultural whole, however. The FAO's cereals statistics relate, ideally, to weight or volume of crops harvested for dry grain (excluding cereal crops used for grazing, harvested for hay, or harvested green for food, feed, or silage). Some countries, however, collect the basic data they report to the FAO on sown or cultivated areas instead and calculate production statistics from estimates of yield. Millet and sorghum, which in many European and North American countries are used primarily as livestock or poultry feed, may be reportable by such countries as animal fodder only, while elsewhere many nations use the same grains for human consumption and report them as cereals. Statistics for tropical fruits are frequently not compiled by producing countries, and coverage is not uniform, with some countries reporting only commercial fruits and others including those consumed for subsistence as well. Figures on wild fruits and berries are seldom included

Crops and livestock

country	grains				roots and tubers[a]				pulses[b]				fruits[c]		vegetables[d]	
	production ('000 metric tons)		yield (kg/hectare)		production ('000 metric tons)		yield (kg/hectare)		production ('000 metric tons)		yield (kg/hectare)		production ('000 metric tons)		production ('000 metric tons)	
	1979–81 average	1993	1979–81 average	1993	1979–81 average	1993	1979–81 average	1993	1979–81 average	1993	1979–81 average	1993	1979–81 average	1993	1979–81 average	1993
Afghanistan	4,060	2,540	1,337	1,155	265	228	14,881	16,889	41	35	989	946	807	612	516	487
Albania	916	610	2,500	2,345	112	56	6,967	7,000	23	15	512	604	154	134	333	287
Algeria	1,958	2,012	656	681	540	900	6,878	8,036	52	48	431	408	1,197	1,072	824	2,001
American Samoa	...	...	...	...	3	2	4,116	3,361	...	...	...	...	2	1	...	...
Andorra	...	...	...	...	...	...	...	...	...	...	...	...	...	...	...	...
Angola	379	335	533	363	1,464	2,080	4,028	4,444	42	36	385	267	432	425	231	195
Antigua and Barbuda	—	—	1,809	1,833	—	—	4,673	5,357	...	...	...	...	9	9	1	3
Argentina	24,457	24,756	2,183	2,828	2,328	2,410	14,087	15,752	239	321	918	1,518	6,184	5,517	2,279	2,758
Armenia	270	305	1,783	2,088	240	350	12,213	11,812	...	2	...	1,497	407	270	468	413
Aruba	...	...	...	...	...	...	...	...	...	...	...	...	...	...	...	...
Australia	21,150	28,549	1,321	1,941	843	1,137	23,413	28,869	192	2,247	912	1,294	2,121	2,495	1,044	1,662
Austria	4,388	4,042	4,131	5,015	1,356	715	25,387	22,344	23	113	2,876	3,485	950	885	666	455
Azerbaijan	1,105	1,105	2,253	1,588	142	200	7,359	10,000	2,167	...	9	...	1,647	1,358	852	700
Bahamas, The	1	1	1,142	1,250	2	2	8,998	9,250	1	1	1,238	1,309	12	12	28	28
Bahrain	...	...	...	...	—	—	19,048	14,857	...	...	917	900	35	23	15	11
Bangladesh	20,983	29,250	1,938	2,513	1,705	1,818	10,062	10,392	637	517	646	725	1,303	1,358	1,066	1,419
Barbados	2	2	2,538	2,500	11	7	11,653	9,269	1	1	1,209	1,254	3	3	10	6
Belarus	4,108	7,355	1,438	2,844	12,672	11,600	16,085	15,065	101	150	496	1,364	510	290	799	1,000
Belgium[1]	2,069	2,287	4,861	6,442	1,468	2,100	39,246	41,176	7	24	3,080	3,562	386	755	980	1,680
Belize	27	26	1,924	1,563	3	4	20,000	21,765	1	2	526	630	72	141	3	5
Benin	366	719	698	1,020	1,363	2,255	7,449	9,593	34	59	445	557	142	161	121	240
Bermuda	...	...	...	...	1	1	9,041	20,636	...	...	...	...	1	—	2	3
Bhutan	159	106	1,439	1,088	40	56	6,767	10,673	2	2	592	800	29	64	11	10
Bolivia	663	1,078	1,183	1,524	1,063	1,288	5,185	6,479	18	33	1,014	1,104	547	821	317	378
Bosnia and Herzegovina	...	1,256	...	3,666	...	230	...	4,600	...	17	...	945	...	123	...	80
Botswana	35	34	203	280	7	9	5,513	6,000	19	13	622	433	9	11	16	16
Brazil	30,805	43,044	1,496	2,357	27,265	24,903	11,570	12,149	2,206	2,486	464	625	18,607	31,210	4,089	5,771
Brunei	3	1	1,640	1,625	1	1	1,470	2,813	...	...	...	...	5	5	8	8
Bulgaria	8,130	5,749	3,853	2,953	376	500	10,175	11,111	68	64	984	1,187	1,975	1,093	2,021	1,454
Burkina Faso	1,166	2,495	575	879	126	86	8,927	5,931	46	62	1,004	861	56	73	155	254
Burundi	219	300	1,081	1,361	1,036	1,449	6,775	6,696	317	376	959	1,033	1,243	1,673	151	225
Cambodia	1,334	2,560	964	1,385	178	227	6,569	8,404	14	14	588	583	125	260	368	483
Cameroon	866	970	849	1,211	1,663	1,966	3,866	5,819	105	76	542	548	1,715	1,135	370	463
Canada	42,729	52,241	2,174	2,649	2,626	3,333	23,818	26,667	199	1,430	1,577	1,605	697	714	1,747	1,878
Cape Verde	6	6	465	300	10	8	3,901	5,845	4	—	353	200	12	15	1	8
Central African Republic	103	83	529	669	1,106	874	3,270	3,369	7	16	556	1,032	165	203	44	65
Chad	508	747	587	580	424	658	4,505	5,568	47	36	413	612	97	114	59	74
Chile	1,742	2,642	2,124	4,244	901	933	10,262	14,477	171	94	843	1,113	1,657	3,032	1,760	2,310
China	286,456	412,262	3,027	4,587	144,354	144,988	13,594	15,213	6,648	5,894	1,223	1,310	8,814	23,093	83,196	125,509
Colombia	3,339	3,614	2,452	2,507	4,144	4,632	11,043	12,778	128	184	604	786	3,905	5,530	1,362	1,296
Comoros	18	19	1,058	1,276	55	61	4,745	5,532	5	8	1,237	828	36	58	3	4
Congo	15	27	825	922	679	701	6,685	6,626	5	10	572	838	126	187	33	44
Costa Rica	337	204	2,498	3,099	45	142	5,764	23,894	12	33	498	565	1,362	2,397	58	174
Côte d'Ivoire	866	1,305	867	997	3,414	4,191	5,154	5,200	8	8	667	667	1,549	1,709	317	446
Croatia	...	2,733	...	4,257	...	507	...	7,835	...	22	...	950	...	571	...	239
Cuba	551	277	2,458	1,776	997	744	6,092	4,944	12	25	306	342	810	1,307	466	476
Cyprus	87	194	1,793	3,177	182	172	23,108	20,023	6	3	1,047	1,020	358	334	102	126
Czech Republic	...	6,475	...	4,025	...	2,396	...	23,302	...	220	...	2,423	...	533	...	573
Denmark	7,346	8,217	4,040	4,389	913	1,500	26,904	32,609	14	466	3,420	3,820	124	112	263	314
Djibouti	—	—	833	3,250	...	...	...	...	...	...	...	...	...	...	13	22
Dominica	—	—	1,427	1,333	26	23	10,241	9,297	—	—	467	450	46	89	7	6
Dominican Republic	447	589	3,004	4,007	214	289	5,783	6,132	73	79	958	966	1,333	1,550	209	215
Ecuador	686	1,434	1,633	1,823	552	538	9,595	6,697	39	36	547	431	3,769	5,257	243	365
Egypt	8,134	14,147	4,053	6,164	1,330	1,878	18,336	21,644	283	321	2,000	2,423	2,310	4,998	7,345	7,474
El Salvador	719	922	1,702	1,986	27	48	12,350	15,987	41	69	850	947	257	319	96	127
Equatorial Guinea	...	...	...	...	53	82	2,926	2,645	...	...	...	...	11	17	...	...
Eritrea	...	73	...	...	...	109	...	2,804	...	13	...	368	...	4	...	25
Estonia	796	675	1,862	1,791	1,031	652	14,257	13,872	1	...	1,333	1,212	46	26	117	116
Ethiopia	...	6,617	1,186	...	...	1,965	...	3,619	...	802	...	901	...	230	...	574
Faeroe Islands	...	...	...	...	1	2	...	13,872	...	...	...	...	...	...	...	...

in national reports at all. FAO vegetable statistics include vegetables and melons grown for human consumption only. Some countries do not make this distinction in their reports, and some exclude the production of kitchen gardens and small family plots, although in certain countries, such small-scale production may account for 20 to 40 percent of total output.

Livestock statistics may be distorted by the timing of country reports. Ireland, for example, takes a livestock enumeration in December that is reported the following year and that appears low against data for otherwise comparable countries because of the slaughter and export of animals at the close of the grazing season. It balances this, however, with a June enumeration, when numbers tend to be high. Milk production as defined by the FAO includes whole fresh milk, excluding milk sucked by young animals but including amounts fed by farmers or ranchers to livestock, but national practices vary. Certain countries do not distinguish between milk cows and other cattle, so that yield per dairy cow must be estimated. Some countries do not report egg production statistics (here given in metric tons), and external estimates must be based on the numbers of chickens and reported or assumed egg-laying rates. Other countries report egg pro-

duction by number, and this must be converted to weight, using conversion factors specific to the makeup by species of national poultry flocks.

Metric system units used in the table may be converted to English system units as follows:

metric tons × 1.1023 = short tons
kilograms × 2.2046 = pounds
kilograms per hectare × 0.8922 = pounds per acre.

The notes that follow, keyed by references in the table headings, provide further definitional information.
a. Includes such crops as potatoes and cassava.
b. Includes beans and peas harvested for dry grain only. Does not include green beans and green peas.
c. Excludes melons.
d. Includes melons, green beans, and green peas.
e. From milk cows only.
f. From chickens only.

livestock														country
cattle		sheep		hogs		chickens		milk[e]				eggs[f]		
stock ('000 head)		stock ('000 head)		stock ('000 head)		stock ('000 head)		production ('000 metric tons)		yield (kg/animal)		production (metric tons)		
1979–81 average	1993	1979–81 average	1993	1979–81 average	1993	1979–81 average	1993	1979–81 average	1993	1979–81 average	1993	1979–01 average	1993	
3,723	1,500	18,667	14,200	...	...	6,000	7,000	552	300	491	395	14,000	14,450	Afghanistan
606	450	1,232	1,200	174	140	3,000	5,000	296	250	1,326	1,471	9,333	11,300	Albania
1,356	1,460	13,111	18,800	4	6	24,000	78,000	514	650	975	970	24,550	140,000	Algeria
...	...	...	...	10	11	...	...	—	—	800	800	34	30	American Samoa
...	...	...	...	...	...	...	...	...	...	...	...	...	...	Andorra
3,083	3,200	225	250	600	810	5,000	6,000	153	157	497	491	3,650	3,900	Angola
14	16	12	13	4	4	...	...	6	6	959	969	138	120	Antigua and Barbuda
55,620	50,320	31,473	24,500	3,751	2,200	38,000	58,000	5,311	6,800	1,746	2,267	253,731	336,800	Argentina
766	549	2,242	850	231	243	9,000	9,000	501	200	1,677	1,000	25,367	20,000	Armenia
...	...	...	...	...	...	...	...	...	...	...	...	...	...	Aruba
26,161	24,062	134,871	138,102	2,416	2,646	40,000	90,000	5,598	7,554	2,994	4,617	197,870	162,000	Australia
2,553	2,401	193	312	3,906	3,720	15,000	13,000	3,434	3,270	3,509	3,940	96,804	102,000	Austria
1,765	1,570	5,128	5,055	179	123	17,000	26,000	800	700	1,208	1,000	40,200	48,000	Azerbaijan
4	6	35	40	14	15	1,000	2,000	1	2	1,000	1,000	356	600	Bahamas, The
6	16	7	9	...	...	...	1,000	6	19	2,703	2,639	3,238	3,000	Bahrain
25,053	23,923	750	989	...	...	59,000	109,000	833	767	221	206	80,745	73,401	Bangladesh
17	33	52	66	44	45	1,000	2,000	7	15	1,294	1,310	1,489	1,000	Barbados
6,760	6,221	525	361	4,520	4,308	35,000	47,000	6,082	5,500	2,215	2,477	166,267	185,000	Belarus
3,104	3,303	110	156	5,083	6,963	29,000	35,000	4,042	3,762	3,876	4,691	200,655	182,570	Belgium[1]
50	58	3	4	16	26	...	1,000	4	7	1,021	1,015	1,034	1,400	Belize
810	1,100	972	940	400	550	11,000	26,000	12	16	120	130	7,860	18,720	Benin
1	1	...	...	2	2	...	...	2	2	2,836	3,056	435	500	Bermuda
299	429	10	54	55	74	...	...	26	29	257	257	159	350	Bhutan
4,570	5,800	8,967	7,512	1,553	2,273	17,000	33,000	71	120	1,396	1,412	22,500	54,000	Bolivia
...	685	...	1,080	...	550	...	8,000	...	560	...	1,474	...	17,000	Bosnia and Herzegovina
2,906	2,700	147	325	5	16	1,000	2,000	90	87	350	350	786	1,800	Botswana
116,645	153,350	18,414	19,701	34,102	31,050	426,000	620,000	11,378	15,671	712	784	765,117	1,334,000	Brazil
3	1	...	...	11	14	1,000	2,000	...	...	...	...	1,787	3,200	Brunei
1,782	974	10,358	4,814	3,803	2,680	39,000	17,000	1,843	1,350	2,638	2,809	131,679	60,000	Bulgaria
2,760	4,178	3,200	5,500	198	540	11,000	18,000	81	121	175	175	7,448	16,500	Burkina Faso
614	420	301	390	44	100	3,000	4,000	42	32	350	350	2,356	3,192	Burundi
809	2,468	...	...	162	2,043	3,000	10,000	14	19	170	170	5,400	10,000	Cambodia
3,521	4,867	2,167	3,770	1,139	1,434	8,000	20,000	88	120	500	500	8,400	12,600	Cameroon
12,096	11,786	480	662	9,548	10,572	96,000	96,000	7,354	7,045	4,137	5,105	330,863	315,240	Canada
12	21	1	6	40	105	...	1,000	1	1	500	500	200	700	Cape Verde
1,662	2,781	84	137	243	474	2,000	3,000	23	49	200	225	966	1,350	Central African Republic
4,360	4,600	2,620	2,100	9	14	3,000	4,000	118	123	270	270	2,850	3,870	Chad
3,650	3,575	6,059	4,629	1,068	1,288	23,000	45,000	1,111	1,650	1,561	1,919	66,046	103,071	Chile
52,567	82,641	101,864	109,720	313,660	393,965	906,000	2,688,000	1,143	5,230	1,802	1,529	2,325,749	9,240,000	China
24,110	25,324	2,399	2,540	2,013	2,635	30,000	62,000	2,187	4,467	965	994	176,972	284,690	Colombia
70	47	8	15	...	...	1,000	2,000	3	4	500	500	564	640	Comoros
64	67	69	111	28	56	1,000	2,000	1	1	500	500	825	1,200	Congo
2,183	2,122	2	3	223	244	5,000	14,000	318	470	1,067	1,473	16,760	23,000	Costa Rica
664	1,205	1,020	1,219	315	392	17,000	26,000	12	21	110	102	10,253	16,400	Côte d'Ivoire
...	590	...	524	...	1,202	...	12,000	...	673	...	1,923	...	47,470	Croatia
5,166	4,500	356	310	1,443	1,603	24,000	25,000	1,045	700	1,579	1,458	98,936	70,000	Cuba
22	56	290	295	162	297	2,000	3,000	33	110	3,601	4,681	5,309	6,150	Cyprus
...	2,512	...	254	...	4,599	...	28,000	...	3,454	...	3,951	...	155,018	Czech Republic
2,970	2,115	55	63	9,699	10,870	15,000	18,000	5,126	4,660	4,920	6,555	77,130	87,100	Denmark
47	190	417	470	...	...	...	...	2	7	350	350	...	...	Djibouti
7	9	6	8	8	5	...	...	3	5	1,000	1,000	177	158	Dominica
1,918	2,371	65	128	298	850	19,000	33,000	427	380	1,742	1,696	19,267	43,300	Dominican Republic
2,987	4,819	1,148	1,602	3,417	2,540	33,000	57,000	924	1,550	1,446	2,084	43,056	58,600	Ecuador
1,906	3,226	1,791	3,707	21	26	28,000	38,000	648	890	674	674	78,100	128,000	Egypt
1,234	1,345	4	5	455	325	5,000	4,000	268	280	958	933	36,822	47,700	El Salvador
4	5	33	36	4	6	...	...	...	...	...	...	116	190	Equatorial Guinea
...	1,550	...	1,510	...	...	...	4,000	...	36	...	194	...	5,934	Eritrea
821	661	164	144	1,038	772	6,000	5,000	1,149	900	3,633	4,091	29,267	25,000	Estonia
...	29,450	...	21,700	...	20	...	54,000	...	738	...	209	...	73,370	Ethiopia
2	2	67	68	...	...	...	...	...	...	...	...	...	...	Faeroe Islands

Crops and livestock (continued)

country	grains				roots and tubers[a]				pulses[b]				fruits[c]		vegetables[d]	
	production ('000 metric tons)		yield (kg/hectare)		production ('000 metric tons)		yield (kg/hectare)		production ('000 metric tons)		yield (kg/hectare)		production ('000 metric tons)		production ('000 metric tons)	
	1979–81 average	1993	1979–81 average	1993	1979–81 average	1993	1979–81 average	1993	1979–81 average	1993	1979–81 average	1993	1979–81 average	1993	1979–81 average	1993
Fiji	19	22	2,004	2,338	24	66	7,928	12,360	—	1	540	1,200	11	12	6	13
Finland	2,993	3,341	2,511	3,621	629	777	15,578	21,352	13	30	2,182	2,362	107	89	130	214
France	46,078	55,817	4,700	6,531	6,735	5,801	28,465	35,269	340	3,826	3,304	4,911	14,124	9,953	6,999	7,229
French Guiana	1	25	1,159	3,571	13	18	10,842	10,056	...	...	...	...	2	5	3	10
French Polynesia	...	...			17	13	13,874	12,476					4	8	6	6
Gabon	11	25	1,718	1,764	372	381	5,209	5,509	—	—	528	667	181	265	22	31
Gambia, The	78	102	1,189	1,097	6	6	3,000	3,000	4	4	267	267	4	4	7	8
Gaza Strip	5	1	2,793	529	5	25	18,333	22,273	...	...	...	...	200	125	61	157
Georgia	573	397	1,942	1,438	412	190	12,400	9,500	10	...	711	...	1,678	1,267	960	1,100
Germany	32,044	36,222	4,166	5,800	19,465	12,074	23,587	38,322	116	202	1,902	2,514	4,448	4,293	3,206	3,927
Ghana	726	1,645	807	1,340	3,183	6,436	6,721	6,585	14	20	101	100	966	1,467	299	450
Gibraltar	...	...	...	...	...	...	...	...					...	...	...	...
Greece	4,951	4,924	3,090	3,579	1,041	1,008	16,378	20,499	94	46	1,262	1,524	3,437	4,464	3,636	4,013
Greenland	...	...														
Grenada	—	—	949	1,000	3	4	4,582	5,177	1	1	1,607	1,125	29	23	2	2
Guadeloupe					22	23	8,459	11,625	—	—	514	600	115	166	17	24
Guam			3,000	2,000	2	2	13,756	14,904					2	2	2	5
Guatemala	1,122	1,520	1,578	1,831	52	63	3,535	4,630	77	116	840	890	734	857	277	374
Guernsey			...	...									...	...	...	...
Guinea	678	956	958	881	644	997	7,116	8,139	42	60	646	857	664	984	410	420
Guinea-Bissau	102	181	711	1,350	47	65	5,986	7,283	2	2	971	600	45	66	21	20
Guyana	267	303	2,907	3,280	16	32	6,626	7,273	1	1	487	591	41	71	9	12
Haiti	419	385	1,009	944	689	768	3,778	3,828	90	88	471	680	1,007	882	281	219
Honduras	492	765	1,170	1,447	21	38	4,896	7,202	38	54	517	654	1,650	1,365	95	175
Hong Kong	—	—	1,712	2,000	—	—	25,407	23,500	...	...	...	...	3	4	189	86
Hungary	13,001	9,040	4,519	3,136	1,507	1,203	15,894	13,189	127	294	1,547	2,426	2,389	1,750	1,841	1,657
Iceland	...	...	...	...	11	11	11,858	11,000							1	2
India	138,182	201,479	1,324	1,995	16,777	22,160	12,926	15,366	10,509	13,145	461	556	20,409	31,850	42,616	60,010
Indonesia	33,605	54,398	2,837	3,910	16,153	19,373	9,054	11,893	352	504	882	1,269	4,941	7,341	2,434	4,912
Iran	8,855	17,368	1,108	1,744	1,284	2,800	14,324	18,666	247	542	799	737	3,234	7,987	4,966	7,820
Iraq	1,803	3,283	832	1,019	96	230	18,464	17,692	36	40	802	1,148	1,161	1,559	1,992	2,681
Ireland	2,009	1,607	4,733	5,856	822	650	20,799	29,545	...	7	3,444	4,667	22	24	283	228
Isle of Man	...	...	...	...	...	...										
Israel	239	229	1,840	2,171	201	225	36,551	36,877	8	5	955	1,021	1,913	1,435	762	1,268
Italy	18,025	19,549	3,548	4,658	2,962	2,027	18,274	21,144	321	211	1,335	1,668	20,661	18,630	13,401	13,035
Jamaica	7	6	1,667	1,315	230	288	11,666	14,922	8	7	882	1,051	332	372	104	149
Japan	14,318	10,738	5,252	4,428	5,342	5,463	22,838	25,588	108	108	1,258	1,509	6,330	4,552	15,230	14,137
Jersey	...	...													...	...
Jordan	91	82	516	745	9	50	16,866	23,810	8	6	588	1,316	90	253	437	820
Kazakhstan	26,790	21,500	1,063	978	1,918	2,300	10,220	10,698	...	120	...	1,000	379	230	1,185	1,002
Kenya	2,281	2,112	1,364	1,215	1,257	1,680	7,993	8,077	185	200	430	286	650	974	490	655
Kiribati	...	...	...	...	9	8	8,011	7,813					5	5	4	5
Korea, North	7,352	5,210	3,741	2,878	1,909	2,250	12,486	12,500	280	290	849	817	851	1,363	2,630	3,866
Korea, South	8,452	7,099	4,986	5,608	1,653	721	17,787	20,028	56	35	940	1,193	994	2,200	9,070	10,276
Kuwait	—	2	3,087	5,042	—	1	16,934	20,000	...	...	...	...	1	1	36	89
Kyrgyzstan	1,413	1,603	2,452	2,501	272	300	12,348	12,500	2	...	...	1,000	247	136	396	305
Laos	1,056	1,298	1,402	2,294	184	215	10,114	8,830	17	41	1,728	1,984	89	149	184	237
Latvia	859	1,199	1,278	1,759	1,371	1,272	12,979	14,501	7	5	1,167	1,622	106	85	229	226
Lebanon	41	81	1,307	1,947	130	282	16,923	20,443	10	36	940	1,895	704	1,332	354	911
Lesotho	198	158	977	890	6	8	15,526	15,000	8	3	536	508	16	18	21	26
Liberia	254	71	1,251	1,092	346	361	6,894	6,933	3	3	500	500	121	130	64	71
Libya	225	303	430	661	97	155	6,671	8,158	9	14	1,079	1,157	203	316	527	791
Liechtenstein	...	...	...	...	11	12[2]	18,742	17,974[2]								
Lithuania	1,742	2,240	1,642	1,882	1,832	1,200	13,022	10,435	110	10	...	1,143	202	120	333	280
Luxembourg[1]	...	...	...	...												
Macau	...	...			4	8	11,174	13,351	...	1	...	...	...	...	2	1
Macedonia	...	497		2,318	...	90	...	7,500	...	26	...	1,964	...	298	...	294
Madagascar	2,178	2,732	1,664	1,998	2,267	3,251	5,704	6,438	53	63	852	853	719	813	283	343
Malawi	1,341	2,137	1,161	1,489	562	586	4,458	3,427	204	264	609	580	376	498	212	251
Malaysia	2,061	2,137	2,828	3,111	468	533	8,951	9,780	...	...	...	...	931	1,184	314	383
Maldives	—	—	806	1,000	7	8	5,176	4,816	...	—	600	636	8	10	15	19
Mali	1,064	2,074	790	975	123	145	8,349	8,529	47	64	338	218	13	16	173	267
Malta	8	9	3,252	3,431	21	24	8,948	20,167	1	1	2,333	2,295	11	12	47	53
Marshall Islands	...	...	...	...	...	...	...	...					...	...	...	...
Martinique					22	23	6,997	8,523					178	263	27	25
Mauritania	48	164	384	867	7	4	2,888	1,871	29	15	407	296	15	12	7	8
Mauritius	1	2	2,536	3,795	12	21	17,368	17,452	1	2	491	800	6	12	26	48
Mayotte			...	...									...	...	...	...
Mexico	20,692	25,825	2,152	2,604	1,120	1,323	12,906	16,757	1,311	937	719	742	7,316	9,462	3,947	6,045
Micronesia	...	...											...	...	...	...
Moldova	2,565	3,255	3,221	5,232	324	300	7,969	7,500	53	111	1,463	1,592	1,994	1,430	1,609	1,430
Monaco																
Mongolia	320	510	573	917	50	74	7,878	9,250	—	3	292	833	3	...	26	15
Morocco	3,583	2,930	811	590	504	884	14,221	15,531	229	277	571	604	1,623	2,329	1,320	2,700
Mozambique	649	766	603	565	3,679	3,643	4,194	4,243	59	79	381	271	327	292	184	114
Myanmar (Burma)	12,984	17,945	2,521	2,809	167	240	8,087	8,541	365	842	588	778	838	1,013	1,872	2,225
Namibia	73	81	626	787	203	250	9,242	8,333	6	7	944	1,046	8	10	6	8
Nauru													...	...	...	...
Nepal	3,640	5,325	1,615	1,871	349	875	5,455	7,584	140	206	536	616	135	542	517	1,179
Netherlands, The	1,280	1,343	5,696	7,743	6,329	7,699	37,752	46,380	24	28	3,145	4,000	535	695	2,527	3,702
Netherlands Antilles																
New Caledonia	3	1	2,134	1,438	21	21	5,692	5,978	—	—	772	567	9	4	3	3
New Zealand	785	778	4,077	5,219	220	275	26,301	25,822	63	85	2,882	2,537	364	834	382	567
Nicaragua	392	566	1,475	1,749	28	80	9,107	12,422	39	73	576	641	313	328	47	59
Niger	1,702	1,813	440	300	212	255	7,210	7,435	292	508	269	1,224	37	46	142	257

livestock														country
cattle		sheep		hogs		chickens		milk[e]				eggs[f]		
stock ('000 head)		stock ('000 head)		stock ('000 head)		stock ('000 head)		production ('000 metric tons)		yield (kg/animal)		production (metric tons)		
1979–81 average	1993	1979–81 average	1993	1979–81 average	1993	1979–81 average	1993	1979–81 average	1993	1979–81 average	1993	1979–81 average	1993	
212	295	...	...	64	95	1,000	3,000	54	63	1,701	1,703	1,976	2,800	Fiji
1,747	1,232	107	62	1,430	1,309	9,000	5,000	3,236	2,566	4,572	5,828	77,967	69,700	Finland
23,825	20,328	12,133	10,380	11,472	12,564	177,000	210,000	27,084	24,993	3,707	5,347	849,667	928,200	France
6	12	3	4	6	10	...	...	—	—	2,080	2,154	292	254	French Guiana
8	5	2	...	24	34			2	2	2,771	2,135	923	1,700	French Polynesia
5	30	105	170	126	105	2,000	3,000	...	1	250	250	1,050	1,500	Gabon
293	400	136	121	10	11	...	1,000	5	7	175	175	402	894	Gambia, The
5	3	15	24	...	...	1,000	3,000	11	8	4,185	4,000	2,265	5,600	Gaza Strip
1,552	1,130	1,961	1,350	926	600	17,000	18,000	643	400	1,055	825	35,900	30,000	Georgia
20,672	16,200	3,148	2,298	...	26,466	...	121,000	31,725	28,200	4,178	5,369	1,123,573	882,000	Germany
804	1,200	1,942	2,200	379	450	11,000	12,000	16	23	130	130	12,203	14,310	Ghana
...	...	...	...	...	...			...	...	...	...	...	...	Gibraltar
929	631	8,040	9,659	944	1,040	30,000	27,000	666	695	1,867	1,986	122,540	121,090	Greece
...	...	20	22	...	...									Greenland
7	4	14	12	2	3			1	1	769	820	948	920	Grenada
91	56	3	4	44	30	...	...	1	1	507	508	778	1,925	Guadeloupe
1	...	...		13	4							1,071	700	Guam
1,886	2,055	615	430	737	850	14,000	16,000	263	260	749	732	40,590	71,600	Guatemala
...	4	...		...	...			9	...	4,202	...			Guernsey
1,500	1,650	436	435	39	33	7,000	14,000	41	47	185	105	7,420	14,490	Guinea
290	475	177	255	256	310	...	1,000	9	12	170	170	300	612	Guinea-Bissau
193	160	115	130	90	30	11,000	11,000	13	28	832	933	8,033	8,300	Guyana
1,000	800	88	85	1,533	200	5,000	5,000	20	22	229	250	2,943	3,250	Haiti
1,980	2,315	5	8	418	596	5,000	14,000	224	380	538	950	19,093	31,500	Honduras
7	2	...	...	520	104	6,000	4,000	4	1	3,022	2,905	2,737	1,240	Hong Kong
1,936	1,159	2,960	1,752	8,232	5,364	62,000	36,000	2,559	2,070	3,727	4,814	250,000	228,000	Hungary
60	76	838	500	11	21			121	115	3,635	3,966	3,000	2,500	Iceland
186,500	192,700	44,987	44,608	9,400	10,547	160,000	435,000	13,420	30,500	530	959	568,333	1,516,000	India
6,502	11,000	4,124	6,300	3,234	8,200	168,000	620,000	79	380	762	1,169	177,767	420,000	Indonesia
5,450	7,000	31,672	45,200	17	...	97,000	176,000	1,125	1,915	700	760	155,333	345,000	Iran
1,630	1,200	10,842	6,000	...	...	26,000	40,000	290	260	750	650	48,362	47,500	Iraq
6,043	6,265	2,374	6,125	1,122	1,423	8,000	10,000	4,729	5,314	3,178	4,228	35,000	34,000	Ireland
...	...	...	...	...	...			...	...	...	...	...	...	Isle of Man
299	357	243	330	96	100	25,000	23,000	702	1,081	6,817	9,291	91,675	113,445	Israel
8,697	7,783	9,120	10,403	8,885	8,307	138,000	136,000	10,546	10,300	3,478	3,887	659,163	710,000	Italy
279	330	4	2	208	180	5,000	8,000	48	53	1,000	1,000	16,500	20,000	Jamaica
4,261	5,024	13	27	9,851	10,783	284,000	334,000	6,526	8,625	4,526	6,074	1,998,041	2,595,181	Japan
7	6[2]	...	...	...	...									Jersey
29	40	950	1,900	...	...	28,000	75,000	18	96	1,000	3,000	19,000	51,000	Jordan
8,349	8,313	34,162	33,000	3,017	2,459	44,000	57,000	4,490	4,500	1,546	1,406	187,867	185,000	Kazakhstan
10,418	11,000	5,100	5,500	75	105	17,000	25,000	958	1,830	460	489	19,896	42,000	Kenya
...	...	...		10	9			...		105	130	...		Kiribati
945	1,300	292	390	2,100	3,300	18,000	22,000	55	88	2,244	2,316	103,833	148,000	Korea, North
1,634	2,814	6	4	2,153	5,928	41,000	78,000	449	1,860	4,864	6,643	255,786	484,000	Korea, South
17	12	250	150	...	...	9,000	10,000	24	14	2,653	3,549	8,573	4,000	Kuwait
968	1,002	9,853	9,000	320	264	9,000	13,000	676	800	1,803	1,778	23,283	30,000	Kyrgyzstan
437	1,010	...	...	1,117	1,559	5,000	9,000	6	11	200	200	22,167	36,000	Laos
1,413	1,144	207	165	1,623	867	10,000	4,000	1,668	1,219	2,898	2,287	40,467	18,500	Latvia
56	77	152	250	18	40	19,000	24,000	85	130	2,290	2,766	41,275	61,000	Lebanon
581	650	1,062	1,665	75	76	1,000	1,000	20	24	290	290	789	826	Lesotho
39	36	200	210	103	120	2,000	4,000	1	1	130	130	2,336	3,600	Liberia
164	135	5,380	5,650	...	...	6,000	26,000	63	150	1,499	1,429	16,233	38,500	Libya
6	6	2	3	3	3			9	12	3,310	4,444			Liechtenstein
2,195	1,701	61	52	2,568	1,360	13,600	8,000	2,565	2,500	2,955	3,369	54,000	55,000	Lithuania
...	...	...	...	...	...			...	...	...	...			Luxembourg[1]
				3	1							575	640	Macau
...	285	...	2,351	...	173	...	22,000	...	100	...	1,429	...	18,600	Macedonia
10,147	10,280	695	735	1,175	1,495	18,000	22,000	440	479	255	274	12,717	17,400	Madagascar
817	970	84	195	192	240	8,000	9,000	35	41	458	450	10,503	11,400	Malawi
539	735	65	308	1,869	2,983	51,000	95,000	25	33	549	559	131,100	350,000	Malaysia
...	...	...	...	...	...			...	...	...	...	...	...	Maldives
5,670	5,554	6,247	6,971	48	84	12,000	22,000	139	136	245	245	6,720	11,880	Mali
13	24	5	6	12	109	1,000	1,000	29	24	4,111	3,810	6,256	6,800	Malta
...	...	...	...	...	...			...	...	...	...	...	...	Marshall Islands
57	38	77	135	37	63	...	...	5	2	754	681	1,500	1,350	Martinique
1,262	1,000	5,166	4,800	...	...	3,000	4,000	85	87	350	350	2,720	4,420	Mauritania
27	34	10	7	7	14	2,000	3,000	25	25	2,500	2,500	2,800	4,400	Mauritius
...	...	...	...	...	...			...	...	...	...	...	...	Mayotte
27,706	30,649	6,484	5,876	16,895	16,832	177,000	285,000	6,949	7,450	1,284	1,150	636,256	1,189,585	Mexico
...	...	...	...	...	...			...	...	...	...	...	...	Micronesia
1,138	909	1,208	1,070	2,020	1,600	16,000	22,000	1,189	1,000	2,780	2,857	48,633	45,000	Moldova
...	...	...	...	...	...			...	...	...	...	...	...	Monaco
2,452	2,819	14,261	14,657	32	40	...	...	210	248	355	318	983	1,200	Mongolia
3,362	2,924	15,228	16,302	7	10	24,000	78,000	753	814	640	538	72,900	187,200	Morocco
1,400	1,250	106	118	120	170	17,000	22,000	64	57	170	170	8,733	11,400	Mozambique
8,565	9,584	235	305	2,263	2,529	23,000	25,000	283	435	245	245	31,435	37,299	Myanmar (Burma)
2,318	2,300	4,084	2,900	15	15	1,000	2,000	68	71	412	410	900	1,500	Namibia
...	...	...	...	2	3			...	...	...	...	8	16	Nauru
6,893	6,237	730	911	375	630	6,000	7,000	190	261	325	373	14,300	18,000	Nepal
5,071	4,794	856	2,000	10,058	13,709	91,000	108,000	11,832	11,010	5,025	6,439	540,409	600,000	Netherlands, The
2	1	8	7	7	3	...	...	1	—	1,262	1,250	517	510	Netherlands Antilles
113	125	4	4	16	39	...	1,000	3	4	600	600	887	1,350	New Caledonia
8,063	8,675	67,393	51,000	433	430	7,000	10,000	6,586	8,360	3,016	3,068	56,855	49,000	New Zealand
2,373	1,645	3	4	625	530	5,000	6,000	234	182	814	700	28,833	26,500	Nicaragua
3,343	1,800	3,007	3,505	31	39	10,000	21,000	97	161	200	420	6,800	9,010	Niger

Crops and livestock (continued)

country	grains production ('000 metric tons)		grains yield (kg/hectare)		roots and tubers[a] production ('000 metric tons)		roots and tubers[a] yield (kg/hectare)		pulses[b] production ('000 metric tons)		pulses[b] yield (kg/hectare)		fruits[c] production ('000 metric tons)		vegetables[d] production ('000 metric tons)	
	1979–81 average	1993	1979–81 average	1993	1979–81 average	1993	1979–81 average	1993	1979–81 average	1993	1979–81 average	1993	1979–81 average	1993	1979–81 average	1993
Nigeria	7,480	14,360	1,264	1,237	18,789	42,415	8,794	10,193	647	1,650	444	797	6,238	7,850	3,355	5,495
Northern Mariana Islands	...	...	...	...	...	...	...	...	...	...	...	...	...	...	...	...
Norway	1,129	1,403	3,634	3,967	524	455	25,884	24,851	...	...	...	...	117	117	189	164
Oman	2	5	982	2,180	1	6	13,663	22,917	...	...	...	...	111	202	105	167
Pakistan	17,200	23,766	1,608	1,954	423	939	10,495	12,260	595	555	397	377	2,569	4,285	2,084	4,099
Panama	253	327	1,524	2,044	76	77	7,796	6,243	5	9	443	379	1,208	1,289	44	76
Papua New Guinea	4	3	2,087	1,729	1,125	1,291	7,087	7,197	2	2	500	523	1,327	1,779	286	376
Paraguay	659	864	1,538	1,806	2,080	2,768	13,100	14,100	69	48	803	872	826	792	229	243
Peru	1,429	1,933	1,944	2,725	2,477	2,232	7,574	8,073	111	105	856	916	1,487	1,713	720	938
Philippines	10,942	14,281	1,611	2,108	3,100	2,683	6,632	6,894	37	37	652	786	6,816	6,541	3,477	4,430
Poland	18,466	23,417	2,345	2,753	39,508	36,271	16,808	20,600	216	639	1,232	1,916	1,584	2,706	4,573	6,137
Portugal	1,210	1,307	1,102	1,836	1,141	1,375	8,947	14,798	76	62	228	293	2,055	2,047	1,529	1,800
Puerto Rico	6	—	8,925	5,000	39	18	6,470	1,683	6	2	916	658	296	243	28	38
Qatar	1	4	2,623	3,079	—	—	13,367	10,000	...	...	...	...	6	15	18	42
Réunion	12	15	5,064	5,712	11	16	13,295	11,429	1	1	2,626	1,551	23	50	15	59
Romania	18,109	15,493	2,854	2,423	4,317	3,709	14,728	14,895	115	85	258	1,284	2,952	3,505	4,202	3,834
Russia	82,466	94,907	1,147	1,644	37,632	38,000	9,962	11,343	2,659	4,102	815	1,334	3,075	3,100	12,696	10,450
Rwanda	271	199	1,134	1,013	1,743	1,377	8,809	5,182	221	208	727	740	2,162	2,763	169	134
St. Kitts and Nevis	...	...	...	...	2	1	3,649	3,371	—	—	1,000	1,000	1	2	1	1
St. Lucia	—	—	703	714	10	11	4,250	4,116	—	—	2,187	2,000	90	193	1	1
St. Vincent and the Grenadines	1	1	3,294	3,524	24	18	8,049	4,673	—	—	913	1,000	35	91	2	3
San Marino	...	...	...	...	...	...	...	...	...	...	...	...	...	...	...	...
São Tomé and Príncipe	1	1	1,538	1,935	14	20	12,701	14,741	...	...	...	...	4	5	3	3
Saudi Arabia	303	4,897	820	4,466	4	87	9,931	17,059	6	8	1,813	1,875	499	933	682	2,470
Senegal	850	1,070	690	823	43	58	4,344	3,498	21	44	398	372	75	111	82	142
Seychelles	...	...	...	...	—	—	5,000	5,000	...	...	...	...	2	2	1	2
Sierra Leone	542	550	1,249	1,172	124	112	3,315	3,832	31	40	579	655	128	167	153	173
Singapore	...	...	...	...	2	—	11,330	10,000	...	...	...	...	9	...	39	5
Slovakia	...	3,201	...	3,747	...	530	...	11,253	...	127	...	1,512	...	322	...	522
Slovenia	...	404	...	3,463	...	340	...	11,724	...	5	...	943	...	226	...	49
Solomon Islands	13	—	3,513	—	87	99	15,048	16,865	2	2	840	1,000	11	14	5	6
Somalia	305	286	474	586	39	49	10,863	10,426	10	13	494	310	182	246	27	47
South Africa	14,036	12,004	2,117	2,120	793	1,250	12,002	14,045	110	44	1,051	484	3,140	3,938	1,662	1,921
Spain	14,709	17,319	1,986	2,707	5,670	4,019	15,986	18,712	365	172	704	714	12,603	12,649	8,547	9,945
Sri Lanka	2,132	2,487	2,464	2,996	717	455	9,685	8,700	47	39	845	750	1,717	695	535	659
Sudan, The	2,962	3,151	659	506	296	154	3,329	2,963	99	115	1,260	1,095	754	846	789	880
Suriname	258	260	3,972	3,766	3	4	5,301	12,690	—	—	849	733	52	81	6	30
Swaziland	92	88	1,345	1,706	13	10	1,993	2,000	3	4	576	613	121	146	12	12
Sweden	5,407	5,394	3,595	4,944	1,191	1,150	28,914	28,750	32	67	2,248	2,488	207	199	228	246
Switzerland	843	1,291	4,883	6,407	924	908	37,834	48,804	1	10	3,354	3,636	724	542	306	307
Syria	3,069	5,386	1,156	1,486	279	452	15,302	19,800	180	198	799	849	733	1,369	2,973	1,714
Taiwan	...	...	...	...	...	...	...	...	...	...	...	...	...	...	...	...
Tajikistan	285	303	1,295	1,062	152	100	16,926	9,091	6	10	792	1,000	431	220	495	552
Tanzania	3,010	3,908	1,063	1,318	6,158	7,323	9,491	13,037	315	312	454	491	1,953	2,154	973	899
Thailand	20,316	22,226	1,911	2,108	15,512	19,828	14,226	13,037	342	440	685	835	6,304	6,628	2,711	2,604
Togo	301	633	729	905	922	966	8,722	7,489	23	43	238	311	41	48	65	159
Tonga	...	...	...	...	91	101	5,970	6,680	...	...	...	...	14	13	7	8
Trinidad and Tobago	13	22	3,167	3,083	20	11	12,206	9,820	4	2	1,638	1,643	57	64	30	17
Tunisia	1,146	1,918	828	1,216	127	199	12,905	9,707	89	89	560	829	518	843	1,044	1,526
Turkey	25,232	31,749	1,869	2,270	2,958	4,652	16,664	24,201	817	1,972	1,140	959	7,682	9,645	13,338	18,468
Turkmenistan	281	900	2,142	2,254	16	16	7,833	8,201	...	...	...	...	90	205	279	597
Tuvalu	...	...	...	...	—	—	...	...	...	...	...	...	...	1	...	...
Uganda	1,171	1,795	1,555	1,528	3,548	6,146	5,802	6,594	236	556	638	794	6,300	9,104	290	413
Ukraine	33,181	42,725	2,208	3,290	18,429	21,009	11,017	13,696	1,551	2,934	1,238	2,329	3,973	3,464	7,773	6,369
United Arab Emirates	3	8	5,608	4,160	2	4	14,558	16,667	...	...	...	...	62	238	130	385
United Kingdom	18,840	19,317	4,791	6,373	6,601	7,069	32,891	41,460	240	737	3,168	3,247	524	545	3,762	4,160
United States	301,405	260,205	4,150	4,305	15,487	19,524	28,795	34,534	1,466	1,281	1,614	1,661	26,531	28,565	25,476	32,199
Uruguay	1,012	1,435	1,644	2,686	197	220	5,497	9,263	5	6	909	981	273	444	172	186
Uzbekistan	2,597	2,101	2,208	1,769	264	425	10,409	9,884	7	...	952	...	1,284	1,000	2,718	3,500
Vanuatu	1	1	513	515	32	50	19,630	9,940	...	...	...	...	11	19	6	8
Venezuela	1,550	1,595	1,904	2,517	599	722	8,058	8,943	37	60	509	577	2,029	2,666	402	500
Vietnam	12,222	23,105	2,049	3,314	6,284	5,531	6,592	7,639	117	212	558	692	2,584	4,158	2,504	3,905
Virgin Islands (U.S.)	...	...	...	...	...	...	...	...	...	...	...	...	...	...	...	...
West Bank	...	...	...	...	...	...	...	...	...	...	...	...	...	...	...	...
Western Sahara	...	...	...	...	...	...	...	...	...	...	...	...	...	...	...	...
Western Samoa	...	...	...	...	39	41	6,929	6,164	...	...	...	...	53	43	...	1
Yemen	903	825	1,045	1,097	133	214	11,992	14,047	80	76	1,087	1,421	173	346	335	517
Yugoslavia	...	7,663	...	2,940	...	592	...	5,920	...	53	...	921	...	1,407	...	581
Zaire	900	1,752	807	830	13,595	21,672	6,901	7,906	155	196	604	623	2,624	3,552	479	577
Zambia	990	1,758	1,676	2,294	333	636	5,458	5,304	7	24	340	611	76	101	209	262
Zimbabwe	2,273	3,072	1,359	1,805	76	162	3,823	4,537	23	48	566	683	109	153	136	140

livestock								milk[e]				eggs[f]		country
cattle		sheep		hogs		chickens		production		yield		production		
stock ('000 head)		stock ('000 head)		stock ('000 head)		stock ('000 head)		('000 metric tons)		(kg/animal)		(metric tons)		
1979–81 average	1993	1979–81 average	1993	1979–81 average	1993	1979–81 average	1993	1979–81 average	1993	1979–81 average	1993	1979–81 average	1993	
12,066	16,316	8,022	14,000	1,000	6,660	80,000	120,000	289	380	209	233	198,333	310,000	Nigeria
...	...	...	...	...	...	...	...	...	...	...	...	...	...	Northern Mariana Islands
989	976	2,033	2,316	675	745	4,000	4,000	1,926	1,879	5,125	5,583	44,665	52,712	Norway
141	142	114	148	...	...	...	3,000	18	19	420	420	710	6,160	Oman
15,268	17,779	22,580	27,668	...	...	44,000	92,000	2,189	3,928	864	1,090	96,367	231,900	Pakistan
1,425	1,427	...	...	205	207	5,000	8,000	94	125	988	1,106	14,553	12,600	Panama
130	105	2	4	870	1,022	2,000	3,000	—	220	100	...	1,810	3,450	Papua New Guinea
5,066	8,074	387	371	1,090	2,915	12,000	12,000	163	250	1,903	1,894	26,025	36,800	Paraguay
4,276	3,950	13,767	11,915	2,116	2,400	40,000	60,000	796	795	1,298	1,407	59,700	107,000	Peru
1,885	1,781	30	30	7,712	7,954	53,000	65,000	13	14	994	903	201,285	264,000	Philippines
12,494	7,643	4,105	1,260	20,343	18,860	77,000	46,000	16,250	12,680	2,778	3,087	488,642	344,700	Poland
1,332	1,345	4,440	5,601	3,367	2,547	18,000	22,000	750	1,467	2,123	3,871	62,008	83,425	Portugal
497	552	6	8	225	115	7,000	13,000	420	378	2,324	4,182	21,902	19,832	Puerto Rico
9	11	48	145	...	...	1,000	3,000	4	4	1,561	1,520	281	3,600	Qatar
20	23	2	2	61	93	6,000	8,000	5	5	526	506	3,040	4,840	Réunion
6,351	3,683	15,766	12,079	10,926	9,852	92,000	88,000	3,987	2,900	1,914	1,871	323,833	300,000	Romania
58,414	52,226	63,566	48,183	36,218	31,520	507,000	625,000	46,953	42,600	2,113	2,104	2,193,000	2,128,000	Russia
625	610	303	402	124	130	1,000	1,000	61	91	510	615	860	1,950	Rwanda
5	5	14	14	2	2	...	...	...	...	...	...	297	350	St. Kitts and Nevis
10	12	13	16	10	13	...	...	1	1	1,390	1,513	497	540	St. Lucia
8	6	13	12	6	9	...	...	1	1	1,362	1,340	530	640	St. Vincent and the Grenadines
...	...	...	...	...	...	...	...	...	...	...	...	...	...	San Marino
3	4	...	2	2	3	...	...	—	—	170	170	148	172	São Tomé and Príncipe
374	210	4,040	7,100	...	...	19,000	86,000	64	303	443	6,379	40,791	112,750	Saudi Arabia
2,424	2,750	1,966	4,400	180	320	8,000	34,000	87	103	357	360	6,353	27,000	Senegal
3	2	...	...	10	18	...	...	1	...	519	536	811	1,520	Seychelles
349	333	268	278	36	50	4,000	6,000	18	17	250	250	4,669	6,000	Sierra Leone
1	...	...	...	1,017	150	14,000	2,000	...	...	...	...	26,870	15,546	Singapore
...	1,203	...	407	...	2,281	...	10,000	...	1,277	...	3,115	...	60,000	Slovakia
...	504	...	21	...	602	...	11,000	...	280	...	1,647	...	25,400	Slovenia
23	12	...	...	45	54	3,000	3,000	1	1	600	850	284	280	Solomon Islands
4,437	1,500	10,467	6,500	9	6	3,000	3,000	477	180	414	400	2,320	2,000	Somalia
13,647	13,239	31,625	30,000	1,339	1,499	30,000	41,000	2,553	2,400	2,809	2,609	159,952	223,000	South Africa
4,608	4,800	14,721	24,800	10,392	18,000	51,000	51,000	5,984	5,800	3,255	4,143	665,560	603,200	Spain
1,662	1,600	27	19	71	90	6,000	9,000	182	190	448	306	28,857	45,400	Sri Lanka
18,376	21,600	17,628	22,500	...	...	27,000	35,000	1,352	2,500	500	481	31,745	34,000	Sudan, The
46	97	3	9	19	36	5,000	6,000	7	17	1,209	1,737	2,638	3,100	Suriname
658	753	32	23	17	31	1,000	1,000	36	42	252	271	272	335	Swaziland
1,928	1,773	392	448	2,711	2,390	13,000	12,000	3,452	3,349	5,257	6,367	113,633	113,000	Sweden
2,008	1,745	350	424	2,113	1,692	6,000	6,000	3,653	3,927	4,194	5,041	43,186	37,500	Switzerland
778	770	9,311	16,000	...	1	15,000	18,000	504	800	1,353	2,402	68,759	100,000	Syria
135	166	...	...	5,021	9,845	41,411	92,329	47	278	4,127	4,830	...	...	Taiwan
1,177	1,159	2,377	2,550	130	143	6,000	5,000	452	500	1,025	1,053	19,000	16,000	Tajikistan
12,616	13,296	3,754	3,828	160	335	18,000	27,000	374	545	160	169	35,392	60,050	Tanzania
4,228	7,190	25	136	3,344	4,800	60,000	132,000	19	145	1,950	1,142	145,500	450,000	Thailand
229	246	592	1,200	231	850	2,000	7,000	7	10	225	225	1,677	6,325	Togo
10	10	...	...	105	94	...	...	—	—	2,106	1,500	229	260	Tonga
77	55	10	14	59	48	7,000	12,000	6	11	1,169	1,565	7,433	9,500	Trinidad and Tobago
583	659	4,651	7,110	4	6	24,000	39,000	216	441	878	1,696	36,383	53,700	Tunisia
15,467	11,951	46,199	39,416	13	12	55,000	153,000	7,737	8,750	1,300	1,450	217,164	415,000	Turkey
606	711	4,277	5,405	159	209	5,000	7,000	311	400	1,372	1,600	13,550	14,500	Turkmenistan
...	...	...	...	6	13	...	...	...	...	...	...	11	12	Tuvalu
4,919	5,200	1,319	1,760	187	900	13,000	20,000	344	455	350	350	10,587	16,000	Uganda
25,433	22,457	8,912	6,597	20,197	16,175	209,000	180,000	21,044	18,199	2,272	2,274	850,167	660,440	Ukraine
26	58	132	277	...	...	2,000	7,000	4	6	446	207	2,533	10,900	United Arab Emirates
13,321	11,708	21,643	29,333	7,856	7,520	116,000	126,000	15,917	14,780	4,755	5,407	834,000	623,613	United Kingdom
112,152	100,611	12,670	10,191	64,045	59,815	1,068,000	1,486,000	58,139	68,700	5,377	7,067	4,116,200	4,235,800	United States
10,965	10,093	19,219	25,702	308	223	6,000	9,000	811	1,171	1,442	1,743	16,903	22,400	Uruguay
3,391	5,275	7,949	8,407	441	529	22,000	33,000	2,123	2,800	1,627	1,647	81,567	88,000	Uzbekistan
94	128	...	...	68	59	...	...	2	3	201	257	237	280	Vanuatu
10,527	14,660	333	525	2,241	2,100	42,000	74,000	1,356	1,655	1,163	1,306	128,745	123,900	Venezuela
1,646	3,320	...	...	9,396	14,861	55,000	83,000	26	41	800	800	55,317	115,000	Vietnam
8	8	4	3	5	3	...	...	3	2	3,477	2,703	196	160	Virgin Islands (U.S.)
...	...	...	...	...	...	...	...	...	...	...	...	...	...	West Bank
...	...	...	...	...	...	...	...	...	...	...	...	...	...	Western Sahara
26	25	...	...	71	178	...	...	1	1	1,000	1,000	152	200	Western Samoa
973	1,163	3,002	3,715	...	...	5,000	21,000	70	155	361	608	7,083	19,072	Yemen
...	1,991	...	2,752	...	4,092	...	21,000	...	1,778	...	1,754	...	68,100	Yugoslavia
1,159	1,650	726	985	685	1,130	14,000	35,000	6	8	827	851	7,247	8,400	Zaire
2,238	3,204	29	67	217	293	18,000	21,000	60	87	300	300	27,880	33,440	Zambia
5,378	4,000	481	530	155	270	8,000	12,000	455	400	431	455	10,400	15,300	Zimbabwe

¹Belgium includes Luxembourg.   ²1990.

Extractive industries

Extractive industries are generally defined as those exploiting in situ natural resources and include such activities as mining, forestry, fisheries, and agriculture; the definition is often confined, however, to nonrenewable resources only. For the purposes of this table, agriculture is excluded; it is covered in the two tables immediately preceding.

Extractive industries are divided here into three parts: mining, forestry, and fisheries. These major headings are each divided into two main subheadings, one that treats production and one that treats foreign trade. The production sections are presented in terms of volume except for mining, and the trade sections are presented in terms of U.S. dollars. Volume of production data usually imply output of primary (unprocessed) raw materials only, but, because of the way national statistical information is reported, the data may occasionally include some processed and manufactured materials as well, since these are often indistinguishably associated with the extractive process (sulfur from petroleum extraction, cured or treated lumber, or "processed" fish). This is also the case in the trade sections, where individual national trade nomenclatures may not distinguish some processed and manufactured goods from unprocessed raw materials.

Mining. In the absence of a single international source publication or standard of practice for reporting volume or value of mineral production, single-country sources predominantly have been used to compile mining production figures, supplemented by U.S. Bureau of Mines data, by the United Nations' *Industrial Statistics Yearbook* (2 vol.), and by industry sources, especially *Mining Journal*'s *Mining Annual Review*. Each country

has its own methods of classifying mining data, which do not always accord with the principal mineral production categories adopted in this table—namely, "metals," "nonmetals," and "energy." The available data have therefore been adjusted to accord better with the definition of each group. Included in the "metal" category are all ferrous and nonferrous metallic ores, concentrates, and scrap; the "nonmetal" group includes all nonmetallic minerals (stone, clay, precious gems, etc.) except the mineral fuels; the last group, "energy," is composed predominantly of the natural hydrocarbon fuels, though it may also include manufactured gas.

The contribution (value) of each national mineral sector to its country's gross domestic product is given, as is the distribution by group of that contribution (to gross domestic product and to foreign trade), although statistics regarding the value of mineral production are less readily available in country sources than those regarding trade or volume of minerals produced. Figures for value added by mineral output, though not always available, were sought first, as they provide the most consistent standard to compare the importance of minerals both within a particular national economy and among national mineral sectors worldwide. Where value added to the gross domestic product was not available, gross value of production or sales was substituted and the exception footnoted. Figures for value of production are reported here in millions of U.S. dollars to permit comparisons to be made from country to country. Comparisons can also be made as to the relative importance of each mineral group within a given country.

Extractive industries

country	mining														
	% of GDP, 1992	mineral production (value added)					trade (value)								
		year	total ('000,000 U.S.$)	by kind (%)			year	exports				imports			
				metals[a]	non-metals[b]	energy[c]		total ('000,000 U.S.$)	by kind (%)			total ('000,000 U.S.$)	by kind (%)		
									metals[a]	non-metals[b]	energy[c]		metals[a]	non-metals[b]	energy[c]
Afghanistan	...	1988[1]	16.2	—	17.7	82.3	1989–90[2]	1.1	—	100.0	—	...	...	...	...
Albania	...	1990	124.4	—32.7—		67.3						...	...	...	...
Algeria	18.6[3]	1987	9,569.7	—2.4—		97.6	1991	9,117.3	0.1	0.3	99.6	102.9	3.2	34.0	62.8
American Samoa	...	1992	...	—	100.0	—	1989	0.1	100.0	—	—	0.1	—	—	100.0
Andorra	...	...	...	...	...	...	1990	0.3	—	100.0	—	26.9	—	95.1	4.9
Angola	58.2[3]	1989	2,609.0		4.9	95.1	1991	3,340.4	—	6.4	93.6	—	—	—	—
Antigua and Barbuda	1.9[4]	1989	3.3	—	100.0	—	1984	—	—	—	—	1.1	—	—	100.0
Argentina	2.3[3]	1990	4,033.2	2.7	3.9	93.4	1992	400.5	1.1	0.7	98.2	441.5	46.0	7.8	46.2
Armenia	...	...	...	...	...	...									
Aruba	...	1992	...	—	100.0	—									
Australia	4.9	1991–92	12,876.9	37.5[5]	7.1[5]	55.4[5]	1992	10,364.2	30.5	5.9	63.6	1,736.9	7.2	12.6	80.2
Austria	0.3[3]	1990	715.0	5.3	30.8	63.9	1992	353.0	38.6	61.0	0.4	2,594.8	15.6	10.5	73.9
Azerbaijan	...	...	...	...	...	...	1990	620.8	14.9	5.9	79.2	...	...	...	...
Bahamas, The	...	1988[1]	11.3	—	100.0	—	1989	1,850.2	—	0.6	99.4	1,556.7	—	—	100.0
Bahrain	18.6[3]	1990	861.4	—	1.2[6]	98.8[6]	1992	188.4	2.2	32.1	65.7	1,598.0	1.1	4.2	94.7
Bangladesh	—	1991–92	3.2	—	0.3[7]	99.7[7]	1990	—	—	—	—	304.3	5.7	6.3	88.0
Barbados	0.5	1992	6.3	—100.0—			1991	—	—	—	—	8.5	—	29.3	70.7
Belarus	...	...	...	...	...	...	1990	1,177.4	14.2	14.7	71.1	2,180.6	47.8	5.5	46.7
Belgium	0.2[3]	1991	503.7	—	44.6[8]	55.4[8]	1992[9]	8,793.5	5.2	93.6	1.2	16,622.2	13.0	49.6	37.4
Belize	0.9	1993	4.9	—	100.0	—	1992	—	—	—	—	3.4	—	33.3	66.7
Benin	4.2[3]	1991	62.6[10]	—100.0[10]—			1990	22.5	—	—	100.0	—	—	—	—
Bermuda	...	...	...	...	...	...	1992	70.8	—	100.0	—	1.7[8]	—	42.0[8]	58.0[8, 11]
Bhutan	1.0[3]	1991	2.0	—100.0—			1987	1.5	13.8	85.9	0.3[11, 12]	0.9	—	9.7	90.3[11, 12]
Bolivia	7.7[13]	1993	562.8	—56.5[14]—		43.5[14]	1992	400.6	67.7	0.8	31.5	6.1	—	100.0	—
Bosnia and Herzegovina	...	...	...	...	...	...									
Botswana	50.6[3]	1991	1,680.0	...	...	...	[15]								
Brazil	1.6	1992	5,738.7	...	...	...	1992	2,745.5	93.4	6.6	—	5,060.8	9.1	2.5	88.4
Brunei	36.1[14]	1991	1,476.0[16]	...	...	...	1990	1,783.7	—	—	100.0	13.2	—	100.0	—
Bulgaria	0.4[14]	1991[1]	582.1	24.6	28.2	47.2	1992	...	...	...	...	1,125.6	7.5	2.0	90.5
Burkina Faso	0.9	1992	28.4	—	100.0	—	1990	...	...	...	...	3.2	—	100.0	—
Burundi	0.5[3]	1991	4.7	—	100.0	—	1992	...	...	...	...	1.1	—	100.0	—
Cambodia	...	1991	...	—	100.0	—									
Cameroon	13.1[3]	1991	1,441.0[10]	—	—	100.0	1991	1,371.9	—	—	100.0	143.0	90.7	9.3	—
Canada	3.9	1990	25,411.4	24.6	6.4	69.0	1992	15,346.1	20.7	5.8	73.5	6,189.2	26.5	8.1	65.4
Cape Verde	0.3[3]	1991	0.8	—	100.0	—	1990	...	...	...	...	1.3	—	—	100.0
Central African Republic	2.7[3]	1991	32.5[17]	—100.0[17]—		—	1989	60.7	—	100.0	—	1.0	—	100.0	—
Chad	0.5[3]	1991	5.0	—	100.0	—	1989–90[2]	2.9	100.0	—	—	...	...	...	...
Chile	8.2	1992	2,066.4	...	...	...	1991	1,236.7	96.1	3.9	—	976.0	—	3.0	97.0
China	2.7[3]	1991	9,885.2	10.7	11.8	77.5	1992	4,398.3	3.1	16.9	80.0	3,806.3	44.8	6.6	48.6
Colombia	7.6	1991	3,587.4	...	...	...	1992	1,881.1	0.3	9.6	90.1	73.1	34.3	65.7	—
Comoros	—[13]	1993	...	—	100.0	—	...	...	...	...	...	...	...	...	...
Congo	21.0[3]	1991	586.2[10]	—	—	...	1986	785.6	1.7	5.9	92.4	3.8	—	100.0	—
Costa Rica	...	1990	3.8	12.8	87.2	—	1991	0.4	100.0	—	—	62.0	—	14.6	85.4
Côte d'Ivoire	2.5[3]	1991	248.1[10]	...	...	...	1985	37.2	6.4	0.9	92.7	313.1	0.2	3.6	96.2
Croatia	...	1991	119.7	1.3	71.3	27.4	1992	70.2	20.3	—	79.7	478.9	6.7	13.6	79.7
Cuba	...	1987	...	...	...	...	1987	431.4	83.6	1.8	14.6	1,257.3	—	1.8	98.2
Cyprus	0.3	1992	17.2	1.1	98.9	—	1992	5.6	100.0	—	—	129.1	—	18.2	81.8
Czech Republic	...	1991[1]	2,225.4	—8.4—		91.6	1990[19]	627.2[12, 20]	2.5[20]	12.1[20]	85.4[12, 20]	1,282.7	24.0	8.6	67.4
Denmark	0.9	1991	1,100.7	—	11.9	88.1	1992	847.4	15.2	8.7	76.1	881.8	3.9	14.4	81.7
Djibouti	—[3]	1987	...	—	100.0	—	1989	...	...	...	...	14.6[12]	0.2	9.7	90.1[12]
Dominica	1.0[3]	1991	1.4	—	100.0	—	1990	...	...	...	...	1.5	—	41.9	58.1
Dominican Republic	2.7	1992	141.0	...	...	...	1991	261.6	99.6	0.4	—	367.2[8]	14.7[8]	—	85.3[8]
Ecuador	9.0	1991	882.6	0.6	0.2	99.2	1992	1,270.1	1.3	0.2	98.5	9.3	—	100.0	—
Egypt	10.1	1988	1,960.0	0.4	6.7	92.9	1992	1,186.9	1.1	0.9	98.0	231.1	44.0	21.7	34.3
El Salvador	0.2	1992	10.8	100.0	—	—	1991	...	...	...	...	91.8	—	2.6	97.4

Since the data for value of mineral production are obtained mostly from country sources, there is some variation (from a standard calendar year) in the time periods to which the data refer. In addition, the time period for which production data are available does not always correspond with the year for which mineral trade data are available.

The Standard International Trade Classification (SITC), Revision 3, was used to determine the commodity groupings for foreign trade statistics. The actual trade data for these groups is taken largely from the United Nations' *International Trade Statistics Yearbook* (2 vol.) and national sources.

Forestry. Data for the production and trade sections of forestry are based on the Food and Agriculture Organization (FAO) of the United Nations' *Yearbook of Forest Products*. Production of roundwood (all wood obtained in removals from forests) is the principal indicator of the volume of each country's forestry sector; this total is broken down further (as percentages of the roundwood total) into its principal components: fuelwood and charcoal, and industrial roundwood. The latter group was further divided to show its principal component, sawlogs and veneer; lesser categories of industrial roundwood could not be shown for reasons of space. These included pitprops (used in mining, a principal consumer of wood) and pulpwood (used in papermaking and plastics). Value of trade in forest products is given for both imports and exports, although exports alone tend to be the significant indicator for producing countries, while imports of wood are rarely a significant fraction of the trade of most importing countries.

Fisheries. Data for nominal (live weight) catches of fish, crustaceans, mollusks, etc., in all fishing areas (marine areas and inland waters) are taken from the FAO *Yearbook of Fishery Statistics* (*Catches and Landings*). Total catch figures are given in metric tons; the catches in inland waters and marine areas are given as percentages of the total catch, as are the main kinds of catch—fish, crustaceans, and mollusks. The total catch figures exclude marine mammals, such as whales and seals; and such aquatic animal products as corals, sponges, and pearls; but include frogs, turtles, and jellyfish. The subtotals by kind of catch, however, exclude the last group, which do not belong taxonomically to the fish, crustaceans, or mollusks.

Figures for trade in fishery products (including processed products and preparations like oils, meals, and animal feeding stuffs) are taken from the FAO's *Yearbook of Fishery Statistics* (*Fishery Commodities*). Value figures for trade in fish products are given for both imports and exports.

The following notes further define the column headings:
a. Includes ferrous and nonferrous metallic ores, concentrates, and scraps, such as iron ore, bauxite and alumina, copper, zinc, gold (except unwrought or semimanufactured), lead, or uranium.
b. Includes natural fertilizers; stone, sand, and aggregate; and pearls, precious and semiprecious stones, worked and unworked.
c. Includes hydrocarbon solids, liquids, and gases.
1 cubic metre = 35.3147 cubic feet
1 metric ton = 1.1023 short tons

forestry, 1992						fisheries, 1991								country
production of roundwood				trade (value, '000 U.S.$)		catch (nominal)						trade (value, '000 U.S.$)		
total ('000 cubic metres)	fuelwood, charcoal (%)	industrial roundwood (%)		exports	imports	total ('000 metric tons)	by source (%)		by kind of catch (%)			exports	imports	
		total	sawlogs, veneer				marine	inland	fish	crustaceans	mollusks			
7,314	77.5	22.5	11.7	...	221	1.5	—	100.0	100.0	—	—	...	...	Afghanistan
2,556	60.9	39.1	39.1	763	1,005	12.0	55.2	44.8	81.1	1.8	17.1	6,987	120	Albania
2,307	87.0	13.0	2.0	...	497,636	80.1	99.5	0.5	95.9	3.2	0.9	1,944	1,714	Algeria
...	...	...	...			0.1	100.0	—	100.0	—	—	305,947[4]	6,204[4]	American Samoa
				11	145		—	100.0	100.0	—	—			Andorra
6,378	85.9	14.1	1.0	550	6,548	75.1	90.7	9.3	90.9	0.8	0.3	5,896	49,052	Angola
...	...	...	...	...	3,161	2.3	100.0	—	91.3	8.7	—	460	1,190	Antigua and Barbuda
11,865	36.1	63.9	29.0	127,195	298,472	640.6	98.3	1.7	92.4	1.4	7.6	448,012	18,763	Argentina
...	...	...	...	13	1	4.5	...	...	...	...	...	...	...	Armenia
...	...	...	...	...	61	0.8	100.0	—	100.0	—	—	160	4,750	Aruba
19,450	14.9	85.1	41.4	477,317	1,558,005	227.3	98.1	1.9	65.2	20.1	14.7	577,592	359,809	Australia
13,875	17.6	82.4	59.6	3,343,713	1,694,901	4.5	—	100.0	100.0	—	—	3,011	161,550	Austria
				21	1	39.7	...	...	...	...	...			Azerbaijan
115	—	100.0	13.0	28	18,450	9.2	100.0	—	13.3	82.2	4.5	27,500	6,490	Bahamas, The
—	—	—	—	16	13,332	7.6	100.0	—	78.6	19.6	1.8	3,557	3,540	Bahrain
31,907	97.2	2.8	1.5	96	19,685	892.7	29.0	71.0	90.8	9.2	—	178,932	—	Bangladesh
...	...	...	...		12,627	2.7	100.0	—	100.0	—	—	208	6,796	Barbados
				20,527	780	15.5	...	...	...	...	...			Belarus
4,370[9]	11.6[9]	88.4[9]	60.7[9]	2,115,658[9]	3,219,248[9]	40.2	97.9	2.1	95.2	3.6	1.2	227,557[9]	779,104[9]	Belgium
188	67.0	33.0	33.0	3,094	3,371	1.6	99.9	0.1	25.3	60.7	14.0	5,620	500	Belize
5,371	94.5	5.5	0.9	30	5,394	41.0	22.0	78.0	81.2	18.8	—	—	5,129	Benin
					579	0.4	100.0	—	99.3	0.7	—	—	7,465	Bermuda
1,610	82.7	17.3	14.9	9,506	...	1.0	—	100.0	100.0	—	—	...	...	Bhutan
1,633	84.3	15.7	14.9	29,854	4,000	5.4	—	100.0	100.0	—	—	105	2,425	Bolivia
5,379[4]	...	...	...	23,133	3,512	3.6[4]	—	100.0[4]	...	...	...			Bosnia and Herzegovina
1,398	93.8	6.2	—	...	...	1.9	—	100.0	100.0	—	—	1,000	6,695	Botswana
268,905	71.1	28.9	15.3	1,889,803	231,551	800.0	73.2	26.8	89.2	10.0	0.8	157,398	180,800	Brazil
295	26.8	73.2	69.8	11	14,159	1.7	93.6	6.4	71.8	27.6	0.6	440	6,780	Brunei
3,668	40.0	60.0	25.9	70,908	63,691	49.9	82.9	17.1	97.0	—	3.0	15,966	602	Bulgaria
9,251	95.5	4.5	...	...	5,848	7.0	—	100.0	100.0	—	—	—	5,560	Burkina Faso
4,483	98.8	1.2	0.1	...	1,234	23.1	—	100.0	100.0	—	—	197	257	Burundi
6,840	83.4	16.6	7.4	97,236	...	111.1	32.8	67.2	91.4	5.8	2.8	...	...	Cambodia
14,600	78.7	21.3	15.7	269,527	43,015	78.0	71.8	28.2	83.8	16.2	—	2,265	22,293	Cameroon
186,049	3.7	96.3	70.6	18,167,104	1,841,318	1,529.0	96.7	3.3	83.7	8.5	7.8	2,168,121	675,242	Canada
...	...	...	...	...	1,679	8.5	100.0	—	99.2	0.7	—	2,380	225	Cape Verde
3,448	88.6	11.4	3.4	15,372	68	13.5	—	100.0	100.0	—	—	—	2,056	Central African Republic
4,158	85.8	14.2	0.1	...	534	60.0	—	100.0	100.0	—	—	—	...	Chad
25,773	31.0	69.0	27.7	1,094,122	79,056	6,002.9	99.9	0.1	97.1	0.5	2.0	1,066,922	5,000	Chile
206,557[18]	68.7[18]	31.3[18]	16.2[18]	904,832[18]	4,316,872[18]	13,135.0	57.9	42.1	77.0	0.9	12.4	1,181,989	438,090	China
20,619	82.1	17.9	13.0	14,940	188,978	108.7	77.0	23.0	88.0	11.6	0.4	117,737	52,100	Colombia
...	...	...	...	11	...	6.5	100.0	—	99.2	0.8	—	—	750	Comoros
3,624	59.8	40.2	18.6	149,608	1,251	45.0	40.3	59.7	99.2	0.8	—	2,600	22,175	Congo
4,000	72.8	27.2	21.9	15,986	102,425	17.9	89.0	11.0	80.2	19.5	0.3	61,609	12,955	Costa Rica
13,302	78.9	21.1	15.0	279,078	22,445	85.2	72.0	28.0	97.4	2.6	—	173,067	114,947	Côte d'Ivoire
3,244	...	...	...	245,209	132,153	33.8	78.4	21.6	...	...	...			Croatia
3,140	80.5	19.5	6.1	1,847	192,232	165.2	86.9	13.1	86.5	9.3	3.8	129,612	15,361	Cuba
51	33.3	66.7	47.1	587	85,408	2.7	97.4	2.6	89.6	0.1	10.3	4,422	26,295	Cyprus
15,289[19]	9.9[19]	90.1[19]	47.0[19]	569,630[19]	167,371[19]	22.5[19]	—	100.0[19]	100.0[19]	—	—	17,034[19]	61,343[19]	Czech Republic
2,315	19.7	80.3	43.6	393,759	1,937,106	1,793.2	98.0	2.0	92.3	0.7	7.0	2,302,299	1,148,265	Denmark
...	...	...	...	...	1,997	0.4	100.0	—	99.7	0.3	—	186	601	Djibouti
...	...	...	...	...	3,752	0.6	100.0	—	100.0	—	—	—	1,310	Dominica
982	99.4	0.6	0.4	...	81,788	17.2	93.7	6.3	68.5	5.8	25.7	620	25,920	Dominican Republic
7,499	56.4	43.6	37.2	24,254	170,967	383.6	99.4	0.6	67.9	31.3	0.8	587,635	5,752	Ecuador
2,352	95.4	4.6	—	...	1,070,052	298.0	27.6	72.4	96.8	2.9	0.3	11,050	73,172	Egypt
4,672	96.9	3.1	1.9	1,288	51,628	11.3	61.5	38.5	73.0	22.0	4.7	14,482	2,325	El Salvador

Extractive industries (continued)

country	mining % of GDP, 1992	mineral production (value added) year	total ('000,000 U.S.$)	by kind (%) metals[a]	non-metals[b]	energy[c]	trade (value) year	exports total ('000,000 U.S.$)	metals[a]	non-metals[b]	energy[c]	imports total ('000,000 U.S.$)	metals[a]	non-metals[b]	energy[c]
Equatorial Guinea	...	1992	...	—	—	100.0	1990	...	...	...	...	2.1	—	100.0	—
Eritrea[21]	...	...					...	...	...	...	...	...	...	...	...
Estonia	2.4	1992[1]	40.8	—16.9—		83.1	...	...	...	...	...	29.4	—	0.8	99.2
Ethiopia[21]	0.2[23]	1991	5.0	—100.0—			1991	2.5	—	100.0	—	0.1	—	100.0	—
Faeroe Islands	0.1[14]	1988	1.2	—	—	100.0	1990	...	...	...	...	...	...	...	...
Fiji	0.2	1990	11.2	95.2	4.8	—	1988	0.2	99.8	0.2	—	2.6	1.2	42.7	56.1
Finland	0.4	1991	341.2	28.3	71.7	—	1992	142.8	40.0	53.0	7.0	2,581.8	22.4	9.2	68.4
France	0.8	1991	5,459.0	2.9	22.3	74.8	1992	2,308.9	45.6	35.6	18.8	17,743.0	9.6	6.6	83.8
French Guiana		1990		—100.0—			1990					2.0	—	—	100.0
French Polynesia	...	...					1990	58.8	—	100.0	—	3.9[14]	—	25.5[14]	74.5[14]
Gabon	30.6[3]	1991	1,055.9	20.1[23]	—	79.9[23]	1992	2,086.9	11.3	—	88.7	...	...	...	...
Gambia, The	—	1992–93	—	—	100.0	—	1986	3.3	—	100.0	—	...	...	...	...
Gaza Strip	...	...					...	...	...	...	...	...	...	...	...
Georgia	...	...					1990	275.2	74.7	9.9	15.4	547.0	55.8	12.4	31.8
Germany	3.4[23,24]	1989[24]	11,803.2	0.6	20.0	79.4	1992	3,876.1	49.7	28.2	22.1	26,407.8	16.6	7.6	75.8
Ghana	1.9	1992	130.7	—100.0—			1989	97.6	23.5	76.5	—	...	...	...	...
Gibraltar	...	...					1986	1.0	—	100.0	—	0.3	—	100.0	—
Greece	1.4[3]	1990	666.2	13.6	34.6	51.8	1991	308.0	40.5	30.3	29.2	1,681.7	7.8	6.7	85.5
Greenland	...	1990	...	100.0	—	—	1992	...	100.0	—	—	1.4	—	100.0	—
Grenada	0.3[3]	1991	0.7	—	100.0	—	1986	—				1.2	—	38.7	61.3
Guadeloupe	...	1992		—	100.0	—	1992	0.7	100.0	—	—	3.5	—	—	100.0
Guam	...	1987[1]	2.3	—	100.0	—	1986[25]		100.0	—	—	...	...	...	...
Guatemala	0.2	1990	25.3[10]	...	...	...	1991	20.0	—	—	100.0	140.8	...	3.9	96.1
Guernsey	...	...					...	...	...	...	...	...	...	...	...
Guinea	22.0[3]	1991	592.8[27]	—100.0[27]—			1989–90[2]	581.5	90.7	9.3		...	...	...	...
Guinea-Bissau	—[3]	1992[1]	8.0	—	100.0	—	1986	1.0	—	100.0	—	...	...	...	...
Guyana	11.7	1992	37.9[28]	—100.0—			1989	86.3	97.8	2.2	—	1.1[6]	—	100.0[6]	—
Haiti	0.1	1992	1.2	100.0	—	—	1989–90[2]					...	...	...	...
Honduras	1.9	1992	51.8	—100.0—			1992	19.1	100.0	—	—	51.4	—	21.3	78.7
Hong Kong	—	1992	30.5	—	100.0	—	1992	1,461.9	23.4	75.0	1.6	3,251.2	9.0	76.6	14.4
Hungary	...	1989	939.5	4.8	4.3	90.9	1991	242.7	89.0	4.3	6.7	1,529.7	10.3	3.9	85.8
Iceland	...	1992		—	100.0	—	1992	8.5	—	100.0	—	56.9	75.3	17.0	7.7
India	2.3[29]	1990–91	4,999.8	9.4	10.3	80.3	1991	3,370.2	21.0	78.1	0.9	6,452.0	7.4	36.8	55.8
Indonesia	12.6	1992	15,902.2	—6.5[20]—		93.5[20]	1992	11,103.8	8.6	0.9	90.5	1,717.5	24.0	14.1	61.9
Iran	9.1[29]	1989–90	16,995.0[16]	...	...	...	1987	9,417.7	0.1	0.1	99.8	23.9	14.9	24.8	60.3
Iraq	11.8[4]	1990	9,589.6[10]	...	...	...	1986	8,784.3	—	0.4	99.6	4.6	23.5	74.9	1.6
Ireland	...	1989	512.1[30]	30.3	68.7	1.0[30]	1992	347.9	94.2	5.8	—	700.3	15.4	7.4	77.2
Isle of Man	...	1992		—	100.0	—	...	...	...	...	...	...	...	...	...
Israel	...	1990	352.6	...	...	...	1992	3,904.7	0.2	98.1	1.7	4,528.1	—	70.6	29.4
Italy	...	1989	2,554.5	3.4	25.2	71.4	1992	716.9	29.5	55.2	15.3	15,084.0	14.3	8.6	77.1
Jamaica	9.4	1991	397.5	99.2	0.8	—	1991	658.6	99.8	0.2	—	138.0	0.1	—	99.9
Japan	0.3[3]	1988	1,771.4	7.5	36.6	55.9	1992	689.8	43.4	55.6	1.0	57,718.3	13.2	7.3	79.5
Jersey	...	...					...	...	...	...	...	...	...	...	...
Jordan	4.2	1993	145.2	—	100.0	—	1992	314.5	1.9	98.1	—	358.4	1.0	3.1	95.9
Kazakhstan	...	...					...	...	...	...	...	...	...	...	...
Kenya	0.3[13]	1993	12.1	—100.0—			1990	26.2	4.2	95.8	—	208.3	4.6	1.7	93.7
Kiribati	—	1992		...	...	...	1987	0.03	98.6	1.4	—	0.04	—	67.4	32.6
Korea, North	...	...					...	...	...	...	...	...	...	...	...
Korea, South	0.4[13]	1990	1,384.7	3.9	41.3	54.8	1992	188.5	35.1	58.6	6.3	15,022.9	14.4	3.7	81.9
Kuwait	42.1	1992	9,014.0	—	—	100.0	1992	5,202.6	0.4	—	99.6	2.9	—	100.0	—
Kyrgyzstan	...	...					...	...	...	...	...	...	...	...	...
Laos	0.1[3]	1991	1.4	—100.0—			...	...	...	...	...	...	...	...	...
Latvia	0.2	1991	30.9	—100.0—			1990	111.2	58.9	38.0	3.1	607.9	47.2	6.9	45.9
Lebanon	—[4]	...					1986	45.8	28.3	71.7	—	28.9	2.2	78.3	19.5
Lesotho	0.2[3]	1991	1.1	—	100.0	—	[15]	...	...	...	...	...	...	...	...
Liberia	3.0[4]	1989	122.3[32]	—100.0[32]—			1989–90[2]	129.0	85.9	8.5	5.6	...	...	...	...
Libya	26.3[3]	1991	9,988.9[16]	—	—	100.0[16]	1991	9,906.0	—	—	100.0	14.6	—	100.0	—
Liechtenstein	...	...					...	...	...	...	...	...	...	...	...
Lithuania	...	...					1992	3.6	—	100.0	—	324.8	—	3.5	96.5
Luxembourg	0.3[3]	1991	29.2	—	100.0	—	[9]	...	...	...	...	...	...	...	...
Macau	...	1991	1.8	—	100.0	—	1992	—	—	—	—	20.3	—	58.4	41.6
Macedonia	...	...					...	...	...	...	...	...	...	...	...
Madagascar	0.3[3]	1991	8.1	—100.0—			1991	19.5	48.5	51.5	—	26.4	—	—	100.0
Malawi	...	1986	0.1	—	100.0	—	1985					6.1	—	60.5	39.5
Malaysia	8.0[13]	1990	5,542.9	2.1	2.4	95.5	1991	5,170.1	2.6	2.0	95.4	812.8	44.9	27.8	27.3
Maldives	1.9	1992	2.9	—	100.0	—	1990	0.05	100.0	—	—	24.2[12]	0.1	10.3	89.6[12]
Mali	1.5[3]	1991	40.1	—100.0—			1992	35.0	—	100.0	—	0.3	—	100.0	—
Malta	...	1988	3.1	—	100.0	—	1990	8.9	53.9	46.1	—	24.4	—	54.1	45.9
Marshall Islands	...	...					...	...	...	...	...	...	...	...	...
Martinique	...	1992		—	100.0	—	1992	2.3	17.2	—	82.8	136.8	—	—	100.0
Mauritania	10.6	1992	122.1	—100.0—			1989–90[2]	231.3	97.2	0.1	2.7	0.3[6]	—	100.0[6]	—
Mauritius	0.1	1993	3.1	—	100.0	—	1992	22.5	—	100.0	—	36.4	—	70.8	29.2
Mayotte	...	...					...	...	...	...	...	...	...	...	...
Mexico	3.5[13]	1991	5,946.9[12]	18.9	27.9	53.2[12]	1992	8,020.6	3.0	3.2	93.8	1,952.2	11.0	9.6	79.4
Micronesia	—	...					...	...	...	...	...	...	...	...	...
Moldova	...	1992		—	100.0	—	1990	75.1	54.4	45.6	—	664.5	40.0	12.6	47.4
Monaco	...	...					...	...	...	...	...	...	...	...	...
Mongolia	...	...					...	...	...	...	...	...	...	...	...
Morocco	2.2[3]	1991	567.4	—93.6[14]—		6.4[14]	1992	432.9	19.6	80.4	—	1,298.6	0.7	18.3	81.0
Mozambique	0.2[3]	1991	2.4	0.4[1,20]	79.7[1,20]	19.9[1,20]	1988	0.4	—	—	100.0	...	...	...	...
Myanmar (Burma)	0.6[34]	1991–92	172.5[16]	—100.0—			1989–90[2]	36.7	23.4	76.6	—	...	...	...	...
Namibia	31.7[3]	1991	744.5	—100.0—			[15]	...	...	...	...	...	...	...	...
Nauru	...	1990		—	100.0	—	1992	108.1	—	100.0	—	...	...	...	...
Nepal	0.2[29]	1992–93	5.2	—	100.0	—	1990					5.0	43.8	0.1	56.1
Netherlands, The	3.2	1991	10,052.9	—	6.5	93.5	1992	5,774.2	17.6	8.9	73.5	11,112.0	9.8	7.7	82.5

forestry, 1992						fisheries, 1991								country
production of roundwood				trade (value, '000 U.S.$)		catch (nominal)						trade (value, '000 U.S.$)		
total ('000 cubic metres)	fuelwood, charcoal (%)	industrial roundwood (%)		exports	imports	total ('000 metric tons)	by source (%)		by kind of catch (%)			exports	imports	
		total	sawlogs, veneer				marine	inland	fish	crusta- ceans	mollusks			
613	72.9	27.1	27.1	29,959	...	3.5	90.0	10.0	81.5	11.1	3.7	—	1,580	Equatorial Guinea
														Eritrea[21]
...	...	...	...	36,092	4,280	317.4	...	...	...	...	...	...	...	Estonia
45,603	96.2	3.8	—	...	4,229	4.5	38.9	61.1	100.0	—	—	...	113	Ethiopia[21]
...	...	...	...	...	26	246.0	100.0	—	93.5	5.2	1.3	407,731	17,099	Faeroe Islands
307	12.1	87.9	86.6	40,854	16,026	31.1	86.9	13.1	78.8	4.4	14.8	33,015	25,700	Fiji
38,667	7.6	92.4	42.3	8,159,907	673,252	82.8	91.1	8.9	100.0	—	—	10,663	128,946	Finland
44,840	23.3	76.7	48.5	4,097,031	5,909,685	812.8	94.3	5.7	63.9	2.6	33.4	925,560[22]	2,925,994[22]	France
254	26.0	74.0	70.5	2,214	2,138	7.3	98.9	1.1	49.1	50.9	—	37,274	3,685	French Guiana
...	...	...	...	14	15,366	2.6	99.4	0.6	96.1	3.6	0.3	370	6,390	French Polynesia
4,344	62.4	37.6	37.6	124,850	5,985	22.0	90.9	9.1	80.8	19.2	—	4,450	12,580	Gabon
946	97.8	2.2	1.5	15	491	23.7	89.5	10.5	90.1	4.4	5.5	5,710	5,310	Gambia, The
...	...	...	...	...	...	0.5	100.0	—	100.0	—	—	...	...	Gaza Strip
...	...	...	...	771	63	56.0[3]	...	...	...	...	...	...	...	Georgia
37,264	12.1	87.9	44.0	7,292,538	12,684,162	300.2	84.4	15.6	84.4	4.7	10.9	715,975	2,114,720	Germany
17,211	90.1	9.9	7.7	132,627	11,455	365.0	84.4	15.6	98.6	0.4	1.0	15,619	31,320	Ghana
...	...	...	...	...	65	30.0	100.0	—	100.0	—	—	...	...	Gibraltar
2,546	53.0	47.0	23.0	90,727	610,341	149.0	93.2	6.8	88.9	4.0	7.1	86,013	172,982	Greece
...	...	—	—	...	9	113.4	100.0	—	35.5	64.5	—	325,735	5,854	Greenland
...	...	...	...	...	...	2.0	100.0	—	98.0	0.5	0.8	50	1,630	Grenada
22	68.2	31.8	31.8	...	32,850	8.4	99.5	0.5	91.5	2.3	6.0	200	22,009	Guadeloupe
...	...	...	...	7	...	0.8	76.2	23.8	100.0	—	—	...	...	Guam
11,256	99.0	1.0	0.9	25,888	59,848	6.7	55.5	44.5	61.9	37.8	0.3	14,980	2,204	Guatemala
...	...	...	...	...	...	26	26	26	26	26	26	5,703	...	Guernsey
4,235	86.6	13.4	3.3	3,010	4,398	37.5	90.7	9.3	100.0	—	—	—	4,750	Guinea
572	73.8	26.2	7.0	1,925	375	5.0	96.0	4.0	79.4	20.5	0.1	1,600	420	Guinea-Bissau
177	7.9	92.1	83.6	3,056	1,613	40.0	98.0	2.0	88.5	11.5	—	17,550	—	Guyana
6,051	96.1	3.9	3.7	...	10,187	5.2	93.2	6.8	74.7	17.5	7.8	2,130	4,170	Haiti
6,229	91.0	9.0	8.7	10,162	69,204	21.0	99.1	0.9	22.0	41.9	36.1	59,781	1,161	Honduras
193	100.0	—	—	1,019,242	2,074,847	230.9	97.4	2.6	90.1	5.3	4.6	641,927	1,236,578	Hong Kong
5,218	45.5	54.5	27.7	176,999	246,402	29.4	—	100.0	100.0	—	—	5,060	17,963	Hungary
—	—	—	—	678	59,223	1,051.4	99.9	0.1	95.2	3.8	1.0	1,280,006	13,981	Iceland
282,359	91.3	8.7	6.5	17,585	255,687	4,036.9	57.9	42.1	92.6	6.6	0.8	570,317	—	India
185,629	78.8	21.2	19.5	3,975,904	482,814	3,186.0	74.7	25.3	88.6	9.1	1.9	1,192,082	47,395	Indonesia
6,840	36.7	63.3	4.7	...	450,116	277.4	70.3	29.7	96.0	2.0	0.5	63,718	12,220	Iran
155	67.7	32.3	12.0	...	117,378	12.0	25.0	75.0	100.0	—	—	...	...	Iraq
1,834	2.7	97.3	61.5	164,790	586,649	240.7	99.7	0.3	88.0	3.5	8.5	308,147	97,985	Ireland
...	...	...	...	...	...	4.6	100.0	—	23.3	2.7	74.0	...	...	Isle of Man
113	11.5	88.5	31.9	20,663	314,890	20.7	16.3	83.7	98.6	1.0	0.4	7,175	88,620	Israel
8,423	58.2	41.8	23.0	1,825,738	6,392,336	548.2	89.7	10.3	56.4	6.4	37.2	249,039[31]	2,689,639[31]	Italy
169	7.7	92.3	56.8	145	63,920	10.4	69.0	31.0	98.7	1.2	—	6,962	27,348	Jamaica
28,063	1.2	98.8	62.1	1,632,729	13,040,097	9,306.8	97.8	2.2	81.8	1.9	15.2	839,200	12,043,577	Japan
...	...	...	...	...	...	2.8[26]	100.0[26]	—[26]	14.4[26]	81.5[26]	4.1[26]	3,052	...	Jersey
11	63.6	36.4	—	3,330	99,411	—	9.1	90.9	100.0	—	—	968	15,017	Jordan
...	...	...	...	1,121	25	82.7	...	...	...	...	...	...	...	Kazakhstan
37,311	95.1	4.9	1.2	192	15,167	198.6	3.7	96.3	99.5	0.4	0.1	24,480	540	Kenya
...	...	...	...	...	...	30.0	100.0	—	85.5	0.7	13.8	235	234	Kiribati
4,783	87.5	12.5	12.5	6,125	863	1,700.1	94.1	5.9	100.0	—	—	61,400	...	Korea, North
6,485	69.3	30.7	16.4	618,634	2,697,320	2,515.3	98.8	1.2	61.7	4.4	32.9	1,490,616	568,201	Korea, South
...	...	...	...	1,769	50,919	2.0	100.0	—	60.9	39.1	—	11,200	10,100	Kuwait
...	...	...	...	43	...	1.0	...	...	...	...	...	...	...	Kyrgyzstan
4,398	94.0	6.0	3.5	33,604	950	20.0	—	100.0	100.0	—	—	...	...	Laos
...	...	...	...	36,462	2,418	369.9	...	...	...	...	...	...	...	Latvia
488	98.6	1.4	1.4	3	42,536	1.8	94.4	5.6	97.2	1.4	1.4	...	...	Lebanon
635	100.0	...	...	...	2,937	...	—	100.0	...	...	...	15	15	Lesotho
6,099	82.6	17.4	14.6	79,399	306	9.6	58.4	41.6	98.8	1.2	—	1,320	8,170	Liberia
646	83.0	17.0	9.8	4	37,959	7.8	100.0	—	99.6	—	0.4	1,120	9,350	Libya
...	...	...	...	...	...	—	—	100.0	100.0	—	—	33	33	Liechtenstein
...	...	...	...	22,135	1,684	317.0	...	...	...	...	...	...	...	Lithuania
9	9	9	9	9	9	—	—	100.0	100.0	—	—	9	9	Luxembourg
...	...	...	...	2,473	15,488	2.3	100.0	—	58.5	38.8	2.7	6,878	15,022	Macau
756	...	...	...	...	...	1.6[4]	—	100.0[4]	...	...	...	...	...	Macedonia
8,597	90.6	9.4	5.4	2,414	1,565	101.0	72.5	27.5	87.6	11.5	0.3	51,912	399	Madagascar
9,706	95.3	4.7	0.8	83	3,841	63.7	—	100.0	100.0	—	—	355	790	Malawi
54,008	17.0	83.0	80.6	3,703,512	485,285	620.0	97.7	2.3	75.2	12.7	10.0	264,938	170,478	Malaysia
...	...	...	...	...	6,353	80.7	100.0	—	99.5	—	—	36,969	—	Maldives
5,953	93.6	6.4	0.2	...	1,915	60.0	—	100.0	100.0	—	—	352	1,730	Mali
...	...	...	...	50	49,692	0.7	100.0	—	98.5	0.8	0.7	2,280	18,050	Malta
...	...	...	...	...	...	0.2	100.0	—	100.0	—	—	580	210	Marshall Islands
13	76.9	23.1	23.1	...	28,344	3.6	97.6	2.4	94.8	4.4	—	237	31,095	Martinique
13	61.5	38.5	7.7	...	94	90.0	93.3	6.7	56.2	0.3	43.5	147,156	679	Mauritania
13	15.4	84.6	53.8	181	39,307	18.9	99.7	0.3	97.6	0.5	1.9	20,695	15,406	Mauritius
...	...	...	...	...	...	0.8[6]	...	...	...	...	...	...	...	Mayotte
22,966	67.3	32.7	23.8	154,213	981,799	1,421.9	88.0	12.0	86.8	6.0	7.1	393,493	46,710	Mexico
...	...	...	...	...	...	1.4	99.6	0.4	98.3	0.7	0.5	1,060	293	Micronesia
...	...	...	...	299	218	5.2	...	...	...	...	...	...	...	Moldova
...	...	...	...	...	...	—	100.0	—	100.0	—	—	22	22	Monaco
1,960	68.9	31.1	31.1	309	1,494	0.1	—	100.0	100.0	—	—	—	2,260	Mongolia
2,356	60.5	39.5	6.6	42,341	251,665	592.9	99.8	0.2	83.3	1.0	15.7	808,919	1,241	Morocco
15,993	93.9	6.1	0.3	470	4,886	34.0	98.5	1.5	81.7	17.7	0.0	61,800	11,140	Mozambique
22,733	82.0	18.0	12.3	363,388	5,682	769.2	77.2	22.8	99.1	0.9	—	26,250	—	Myanmar (Burma)
35	35	35	35	35	35	204.5	100.0	—	99.8	0.2	—	15	15	Namibia
...	...	...	...	...	...	0.2	100.0	—	100.0	—	—	...	...	Nauru
19,591	96.8	3.2	3.2	...	340	16.0	—	100.0	100.0	—	—	...	...	Nepal
1,210	15.8	84.2	40.2	2,503,161	4,545,229	443.1	99.1	0.9	85.4	1.8	11.3	1,356,212	977,450	Netherlands, The

Extractive industries (continued)

country	mining % of GDP, 1992	mineral production (value added) year	total ('000,000 U.S.$)	by kind (%) metals[a]	non-metals[b]	energy[c]	trade (value) year	exports total ('000,000 U.S.$)	by kind (%) metals[a]	non-metals[b]	energy[c]	imports total ('000,000 U.S.$)	by kind (%) metals[a]	non-metals[b]	energy[c]
Netherlands Antilles	...	1988	7.4	—	100.0	—	1991	152.2		4.3	95.7	1,407.9	—	—	100.0
New Caledonia	23.6[23]	1989	516.8	100.0			1992	115.6[36]	100.0[36]			7.7	—	—	100.0
New Zealand	1.0[34]	1990–91	552.8	—17.3—		82.7	1992	238.0	15.0	6.3	78.7	667.4	17.0	15.8	67.2
Nicaragua	0.6	1991	16.5	82.2	17.8	—	1992	0.6	100.0	—	—	115.5	—	1.1	98.9
Niger	7.2[3]	1991	145.7	—100.0—			1992	378.0[37]	100.0[37]	—	—				
Nigeria	17.0[3]	1991	12,239.4	—	0.6	99.4	1986	5,451.9	0.2	0.2	99.6	70.3	21.9	78.1	—
Northern Mariana Islands	—	—	—									...			
Norway	15.1[3]	1991	13,949.0	0.4	1.2	98.4	1992	16,516.1	1.1	1.5	97.4	1,575.7	68.6	11.0	20.4
Oman	50.6[4]	1991	4,341.0	—	0.6	99.4	1991	4,312.0	0.2	—	99.8	13.3	—	100.0	—
Pakistan	0.6[29]	1992–93	301.5	—22.0[1,38]—		78.0[1,38]	1992	86.8	5.9	18.5	75.6	831.2	19.7	4.6	75.7
Panama	0.2	1992	15.1	—100.0—			1992	78.9	1.8	98.2	—	248.7	1.5	—	98.5
Papua New Guinea	20.5	1992	894.1	100.0			1990	583.6	100.0	—	—	3.8	—	100.0	—
Paraguay	0.4	1992	24.2	—	100.0	—	1992					76.6	5.3	4.5	90.2
Peru	10.7	1991	1,098.1	—52.9[40]—		47.1	1990	696.0	98.1	0.2	1.7	161.8	6.5	3.4	90.1
Philippines	1.2	1992	637.5	67.3	29.1	3.6	1992	442.0	72.1	1.4	26.5	2,114.3	9.3	4.1	86.6
Poland	...	1990	1,903.5	17.9	17.6	64.5	1991	1,366.4	9.4	21.9	68.7	2,624.7	9.8	2.3	87.9
Portugal	...	1986	129.2	14.4	77.7	7.9	1992	422.6	66.3	33.7	—	2,040.7	1.4	6.8	91.8
Puerto Rico	0.1[34]	1991	32.0	—	100.0	—	1986[25]	50.7	2.4	95.9	1.7	52.1	0.4	28.8	70.8
Qatar	35.8	1992	2,678.6[16]	...	...	...	1991	2,363.8	—	0.1	99.9	42.4	78.8	21.2	—
Réunion	...	1992	—	—	100.0	—	1992	0.5	100.0	—	—	12.5	—	—	100.0
Romania	...	1991	1,315.6	1.7	7.8	90.5	1991	27.9	43.9	56.1	—	2,156.2	12.3	3.6	84.1
Russia[42]	...	1989[1]	90,630.0	21.6	12.4	65.8	1991	43,926.7	6.9	5.4	87.7	2,395.1	43.6	17.0	39.4
Rwanda	0.2[3]	1991	2.2	...	...	...	1990	5.1	100.0	—	—	5.7	—	100.0	—
St. Kitts and Nevis	0.7[3]	1991	1.0	—	100.0	—	1988	—	—	—	—	0.6	—	—	100.0
St. Lucia	0.7[13]	1993	2.6	—	100.0	—	1991	—	—	—	—	5.0	—	61.5	38.5
St. Vincent	0.3	1992	0.6	—	100.0	—	1990	—	—	—	—	1.4	—	—	100.0
San Marino	...	...	...	...	...	...	...	...	...	...	...	...	...	...	...
São Tomé and Príncipe	0.1[3]	1992	—	—	100.0	—	...	...	...	...	...	...	...	...	...
Saudi Arabia	35.5[4]	1990	33,110.8	—1.4—		98.6	1989	20,083.7	0.4	0.6	99.0	190.6	65.6	34.4	—
Senegal	2.0[3]	1991	94.9	—	100.0	—	1990	72.9	3.8	96.2	—	170.6	—	17.8	82.2
Seychelles	...	1991	—	—	100.0	—	1991	—	—	—	—	37.8[12]	—	0.4	99.6[12]
Sierra Leone	13.1[29]	1992–93	84.2	—100.0—		—	1986	112.6	57.0	43.0	—	0.1	—	100.0	—
Singapore	0.1[13]	1993	24.8	—	100.0	—	1992	418.2	42.2	36.7	21.1	6,792.1	1.4	5.3	93.3
Slovakia	...	...	...	...	...	...	...	...	...	...	...	...	...	...	...
Slovenia	...	1991	207.7	0.7	15.2	84.1	...	...	...	...	...	...	...	...	...
Solomon Islands	−0.3[3]	1991	−0.5	—100.0—		—	1988	0.7[44]	100.0[44]	—	—	0.7	—	51.1	48.9
Somalia	0.2[3]	1991	1.0	—	100.0	—	1989–90[2]	...	...	...	...	...	...	...	...
South Africa	9.6	1989	9,012.6	—86.6—		13.4	1990[15]	4,351.6[45]	33.3	29.4	37.3[45]	374.9[45]	28.1	64.5	7.4[45]
Spain	...	1990	3,786.9	8.6	32.3	59.1	1992	551.0	44.6	52.1	3.3	10,478.9	12.6	4.2	83.2
Sri Lanka	1.1[3]	1991	101.3[46]	—100.0[46]—		—	1992	179.6	4.0	96.0	—	261.4	2.2	36.0	61.8
Sudan, The	—[3]	1991	17.1	—100.0—		—	1989–90[2]	...	...	...	...	...	...	...	...
Suriname	2.9[3]	1991	49.9[28]	...	...	...	1990	355.5	98.3	—	1.7	7.0	23.9	76.1	—
Swaziland	1.1[3]	1991	8.9	...	...	...	[15]	...	...	...	...	...	...	...	...
Sweden	0.3	1991	771.6	69.5	30.5	—	1992	955.7	81.4	13.4	5.2	3,206.9	14.3	7.5	78.2
Switzerland	1.1[8]	1992	...	—	100.0	—	1992	2,783.3	5.5	94.3	0.2	4,218.5	4.0	72.9	23.1
Syria	14.4[4]	1991	3,504.6[10]	—	—100.0[10]—		1990	1,510.2	—	2.7	97.3	63.2	3.3	10.3	86.4
Taiwan	0.6	1992	1,091.8	—	90.1	9.9	1991	467.2	...	...	...	6,509.6	—35.2—		64.8
Tajikistan	...	...	...	...	...	...	...	...	...	...	...	...	...	...	...
Tanzania	1.1[3]	1991	22.0	—	100.0	—	1988	8.4	—	100.0	—	113.5	—	24.1	75.9
Thailand	1.6[3]	1991	1,541.4	1.3	36.2	62.5	1992	1,230.0	2.2	84.7	13.1	2,789.4	8.7	28.1	63.2
Togo	9.6[3]	1991	146.8	—	100.0	—	1991	124.7	—	100.0	—	3.1	—	100.0	—
Tonga	0.8[3]	1988–89	0.5	—	100.0	—	1991	—	—	—	—	0.6	—	37.9	62.1
Trinidad and Tobago	13.5	1992	706.6	—	1.2[14]	98.8[14]	1992	484.5	—	0.2	99.8	161.1	21.6	5.7	72.7
Tunisia	5.7	1992	889.9	—9.1[6]—		90.9[6]	1992	569.7	1.0	8.2	90.8	338.4	2.6	40.4	57.0
Turkey	1.1[13]	1990	2,077.0	10.6	19.9	69.5	1992	296.0	22.2	73.6	4.2	4,176.0	15.5	2.1	82.4
Turkmenistan	...	...	...	...	...	...	1986	0.4	100.0	—	—	...	—	—	100.0
Tuvalu	...	1992	...	...	...	...	1989–90[2]	...	...	...	...	...	...	...	...
Uganda	0.4[3]	1991	11.6	...	...	...	1990	7,590.9	80.2	4.5	15.3	10,662.0	35.9	2.7	61.4
Ukraine	...	...	...	...	...	...	1986	9,043.3	0.3	0.1	99.6	33.3	19.7	79.5	0.8
United Arab Emirates	41.5	1992	14,596.6	—	0.6	99.4									
United Kingdom	1.9	1992	17,376.1	—	5.0[1,23]	95.0[1,23]	1992	12,786.6	6.3	28.5	65.2	14,618.4	14.0	25.5	60.5
United States	1.6[3]	1991	92,000.0	2.6[20]	6.5[20]	90.9[20]	1992	11,683.7	30.8	26.3	42.9	54,774.8	6.5	10.9	82.6
Uruguay	0.2	1992	21.6	—	100.0	—	1992	3.1	—	100.0	—	156.5	0.4	5.5	94.1
Uzbekistan	...	...	...	...	...	...	...	...	...	...	...	...	...	...	...
Vanuatu	...	1992	...	—	100.0	—	1986	—	—	—	—	0.5	—	38.0	62.0
Venezuela	14.8	1992	9,648.0	—4.6—		95.4	1992	7,359.4	0.9	0.3	98.8	199.5	37.9	36.3	25.8
Vietnam	...	1989	1,062.9	...	...	...	...	...	...	...	...	...	...	...	...
Virgin Islands (U.S.)	...	1987[1]	2.7	—	100.0	—	1986[25]	0.3	18.3	81.7	—	966.5	—	0.2	99.8
West Bank	...	...	...	...	...	...	...	...	...	...	...	...	...	...	...
Western Sahara	...	...	...	...	47		...	...	...	...	...	...	...	...	...
Western Samoa	...	1992	—	—	—100.0—		1985[48]	0.4	—	100.0	—	86.5[12]	—	...	100.0[12]
Yemen	9.1[4]	1990	585.8	—	—100.0—		1990[49]	369.7	90.5	6.5	3.0	3,313.8	8.7	5.3	86.0
Yugoslavia	3.2[3,49]	1991[49]	2,205.9	33.6	8.5	57.9	1989–90[2]	257.4	2.4	33.1	64.5	...	...	...	...
Zaire	24.2[3]	1991	708.0	...	...	...	1992	57.2	—	100.0	—	...	...	...	...
Zambia	15.3[3]	1991	546.8	96.1[20]	3.9[20]	—	1991	70.6	7.4	91.2	1.4	34.2	38.8	61.2	—
Zimbabwe	4.8	1992	240.6[50]	—100.0[50]—		—									

[1]Gross value of production (output). [2]Average for the two-year period. [3]1991. [4]1990. [5]1988–89. [6]1986. [7]1989–90. [8]1985. [9]Belgium includes Luxembourg. [10]Mostly crude petroleum. [11]Includes coke and briquettes. [12]Includes petroleum products. [13]1993. [14]1988. [15]South Africa includes Botswana, Lesotho, Namibia, and Swaziland. [16]Mostly crude petroleum and natural gas. [17]Mostly diamonds, some gold. [18]China includes Taiwan. [19]Data refer to former Czechoslovakia. [20]1987. [21]Ethiopia includes Eritrea. [22]France includes Monaco. [23]1989. [24]Former West Germany only. [25]Trade with the United States only. [26]Jersey includes Guernsey. [27]Mostly bauxite and diamonds. [28]Mostly bauxite. [29]1992–93. [30]Excludes crude petroleum and natural gas.

forestry, 1992						fisheries, 1991								country
production of roundwood				trade (value, '000 U.S.$)		catch (nominal)						trade (value, '000 U.S.$)		
total ('000 cubic metres)	fuelwood, charcoal (%)	industrial roundwood (%)		exports	imports	total ('000 metric tons)	by source (%)		by kind of catch (%)			exports	imports	
		total	sawlogs, veneer				marine	inland	fish	crusta-ceans	mollusks			
6	—	100.0	66.7	...	13,705	1.1	100.0	—	100.0	—	—	281	7,355	Netherlands Antilles
...	—	100.0	...	...	8,999	4.9	100.0	—	58.1	13.9	2.7	4,365	3,730	New Caledonia
15,042	0.3	99.7	65.6	963,813	242,754	609.0	99.8	0.2	83.6	0.6	15.7	460,766	37,084	New Zealand
3,565	91.6	8.4	7.0	697	10,291	5.7	95.5	4.5	44.1	55.9	—	18,079	1,332	Nicaragua
5,289	93.8	6.2	...	...	5,020	3.2	—	100.0	100.0	—	—	...	1,400	Niger
114,289	93.1	6.9	4.9	11,619	75,802	266.6	65.9	34.1	95.8	4.2	—	15,590	191,460	Nigeria
...	...	...	...	...	...	0.1	100.0	—	98.3	1.7	—	18	...	Northern Mariana Islands
10,884	8.6	91.4	52.4	1,401,823	725,516	2,095.9	100.0	—	97.4	2.4	0.2	2,282,247	307,051	Norway
...	...	...	...	...	41,090	117.8	100.0	—	97.5	0.9	1.6	34,515	3,947	Oman
26,567	91.8	8.2	6.7	87	146,864	515.5	77.5	22.5	92.5	6.4	1.1	110,365	—	Pakistan
1,028	88.5	11.5	5.6	3,216	87,467	147.4	99.8	0.2	89.4	9.3	1.3	74,757[39]	10,610[39]	Panama
8,188	67.6	32.4	30.3	245,726	5,701	25.3	47.5	52.5	90.1	5.9	—	12,470	35,400	Papua New Guinea
8,502	63.5	36.5	31.7	27,838	20,947	13.0	—	100.0	100.0	—	—	92	803	Paraguay
7,826	87.1	12.0	11.0	4,209	117,233	6,944.2	99.6	0.4	98.5	0.2	1.3	491,076	1,000	Peru
38,625	90.6	9.45	1.6	78,677	220,134	2,311.8	73.5	26.5	85.2	4.9	9.7	467,729	96,109	Philippines
20,478	15.7	84.3	44.6	496,683	126,178	457.4	89.5	10.5	90.6	2.1	7.3	188,743	37,450	Poland
10,907	5.5	94.5	35.8	1,133,270	584,568	325.3	99.2	0.8	91.4	0.4	8.6	287,214	757,843	Portugal
...	...	...	...	...	...	2.3	92.3	7.7	82.6	12.6	4.8	[41]	[41]	Puerto Rico
...	...	...	...	...	10,727	8.1	100.0	—	87.6	11.5	0.9	—	2,700	Qatar
36	86.1	13.9	11.1	12	54,204	2.3	99.9	0.1	84.9	13.8	—	9,115	38,095	Réunion
13,657	19.7	80.3	34.0	112,790	76,022	124.9	67.6	32.4	100.0	—	—	330	10,840	Romania
377,100	24.1	75.9	35.0	1,545,946	145,785	9,216.9	88.8	11.2	95.1	2.4	2.4	837,169	46,068	Russia[42]
5,660	95.3	4.7	1.1	...	5,508	3.6	—	100.0	100.0	—	—	...	240	Rwanda
...	...	...	...	...	4	1.8	100.0	—	87.4	12.6	—	150[43]	900[43]	St. Kitts and Nevis
...	...	...	...	...	28	0.9	100.0	—	99.6	0.4	—	...	2,630	St. Lucia
...	...	...	...	...	1,840	7.7	100.0	—	42.9	1.0	56.1	17,077	505	St. Vincent
...	...	...	...	...	...	—	—	100.0	100.0	—	—	[31]	[31]	San Marino
9	—	100.0	100.0	...	...	3.5	100.0	—	99.1	0.1	0.8	...	600	São Tomé and Principe
...	...	...	...	...	510,652	43.3	95.4	4.6	93.1	6.9	—	4,068	78,171	Saudi Arabia
4,908	86.3	13.7	0.8	...	22,992	319.7	94.5	5.5	90.3	1.8	7.9	233,400	38,635	Senegal
...	...	...	...	...	...	5.9	100.0	—	98.8	0.4	0.8	16,045	5,372	Seychelles
3,225	96.3	3.7	—	66	2,071	50.0	70.0	30.0	92.8	2.0	5.2	10,500	1,460	Sierra Leone
...	...	...	...	688,474	959,917	13.1	99.8	0.2	77.9	11.5	10.6	499,950	460,545	Singapore
...	...	...	...	...	...	...	...	...	...	...	...	...	...	Slovakia
2,098[3]	...	...	...	188,937	150,564	6.9[4]	87.2[4]	12.0[4]	...	...	...	...	...	Slovenia
468	29.5	70.5	70.5	61,722	265	69.3	100.0	—	98.5	—	0.1	40,909	179	Solomon Islands
8,755	98.8	1.2	0.3	...	877	16.1	98.1	1.9	95.0	3.1	1.9	9,240	10	Somalia
19,679[35]	36.0[35]	64.0[35]	24.3[35]	519,158[35]	282,288[35]	498.9	99.5	0.5	97.2	0.7	2.1	140,536[15]	143,417[15]	South Africa
17,102	11.6	88.4	27.7	1,160,662	2,944,870	1,350.0	97.8	2.2	75.7	2.2	22.1	772,651	2,748,305	Spain
9,229	92.8	7.2	0.5	27	41,860	198.1	88.0	12.0	96.9	3.0	0.1	21,477	53,116	Sri Lanka
24,109	90.7	9.3	...	...	16,774	33.3	4.5	95.5	100.0	—	—	100	2,300	Sudan, The
154	12.3	87.7	70.8	1,442	4,400	4.1	96.3	3.7	73.9	26.1	—	4,480	300	Suriname
2,297	24.4	75.6	13.9	74,516	...	0.1	—	100.0	100.0	—	—	15	15	Swaziland
53,574	8.3	91.7	46.1	9,006,921	1,081,544	245.0	97.7	2.3	98.0	1.3	0.7	167,623	441,095	Sweden
4,553	18.6	81.4	64.1	1,383,589	1,987,824	4.8	—	100.0	100.0	—	—	7,506[33]	392,668[33]	Switzerland
95	26.3	73.7	53.7	113	48,759	5.5	27.3	72.7	98.8	1.2	—	47	451	Syria
94	20.7	79.3	...	...	...	1,316.7	80.0	20.0	...	...	...	589,980[14]	118,195[14]	Taiwan
...	...	...	...	3	25	3.9	...	...	...	...	...	...	...	Tajikistan
34,903	94.1	5.9	0.9	3,648	13,014	400.3	13.8	86.2	99.4	0.4	0.1	...	...	Tanzania
37,591	92.7	7.3	0.3	155,703	1,395,921	3,065.2	91.2	8.8	76.7	9.9	11.7	2,901,366	1,049,962	Thailand
1,264	84.8	15.2	0.6	...	3,329	12.5	96.6	3.4	100.0	—	—	1,170	18,500	Togo
5	—	100.0	100.0	...	2,125	1.9	100.0	—	100.0	—	—	1,199	364	Tonga
87	25.3	74.7	71.3	384	50,204	10.3	100.0	—	87.5	12.5	—	2,796	5,584	Trinidad and Tobago
3,303	95.9	4.1	0.2	7,876	153,461	90.7	100.0	—	82.6	2.5	14.9	82,156	1,335	Tunisia
15,252	63.9	36.1	21.0	51,570	284,610	364.6	87.1	12.9	92.0	0.6	7.4	60,984	24,768	Turkey
...	...	...	...	85	450	43.0	...	...	...	...	...	...	...	Turkmenistan
...	...	...	...	...	...	0.5	100.0	—	100.0	—	—	...	...	Tuvalu
15,046	87.1	12.9	0.5	...	2,109	254.9	—	100.0	100.0	—	—	...	...	Uganda
...	...	...	...	7,307	4,113	900.0	...	...	...	...	...	...	...	Ukraine
...	...	...	...	...	...	92.3	100.0	—	99.9	0.1	—	17,970	16,840	United Arab Emirates
6,353	4.4	95.6	56.6	1,847,274	8,780,721	823.2	97.7	2.3	86.0	5.2	8.8	1,121,885	1,911,905	United Kingdom
495,800	18.8	81.2	48.7	14,946,676	13,616,398	5,473.3	95.0	5.0	75.4	9.3	14.7	3,279,343[41]	5,997,616[41]	United States
4,081	74.4	25.6	19.2	29,591	36,031	143.7	99.7	0.3	98.3	—	1.7	111,738	3,381	Uruguay
...	...	...	...	...	107	27.4	...	...	...	...	...	...	...	Uzbekistan
63	38.1	61.9	61.9	294	177	3.2	100.0	—	65.5	9.1	23.8	—	579	Vanuatu
1,526	50.9	49.1	47.4	2	220,827	352.8	94.0	6.0	90.3	3.6	6.1	89,530	4,574	Venezuela
29,620	84.9	15.1	8.7	48,608	9,742	877.0	69.6	30.4	88.0	8.2	3.8	112,816	...	Vietnam
...	...	...	...	...	...	0.9	100.0	—	87.7	8.4	3.9	...	...	Virgin Islands (U.S.)
...	...	...	...	...	...	...	...	...	...	...	...	...	...	West Bank
...	...	...	...	...	...	—	100.0	—	...	...	...	...	...	Western Sahara
131	53.4	46.6	44.3	11	1,694	0.6	100.0	—	99.1	0.4	0.5	110	1,000	Western Samoa
324	100.0	—	—	29	7,957	85.3	99.0	1.0	94.8	2.7	2.5	13,600	2,550	Yemen
3,452	...	...	...	251,049	102,322	8.1[4]	5.7[4]	94.3[4]	...	...	...	2,582[49]	33,567[40]	Yugoslavia
43,243	92.7	7.3	0.9	41,116	7,279	100.0	1.3	98.7	100.0	—	—	...	62,760	Zaire
13,790	93.9	6.1	2.5	...	20,174	65.9	—	100.0	100.0	—	—	630	470	Zambia
8,033	78.0	22.0	6.5	8,080	17,777	22.2	—	100.0	100.0	—	—	96	1,129	Zimbabwe

[31]Italy includes San Marino.   [32]Mostly iron ore.   [33]Switzerland includes Liechtenstein.   [34]1990–91.   [35]South Africa includes Namibia.   [36]Mostly nickel.   [37]Radioactive materials only.   [38]1985–86.   [39]Excludes the Free Zone of Colón and the Canal Zone.   [40]Includes coal mining.   [41]United States includes Puerto Rico.   [42]Data refer to the former U.S.S.R.   [43]Includes Anguilla.   [44]Gold only.   [45]Excludes crude petroleum.   [46]Mostly precious and semiprecious stones.   [47]Accounts for 5% to 6% of 1988 phosphate production of Morocco.   [48]Former Yemen Arab Republic only.   [49]Data refer to former Yugoslavia only.   [50]Mostly gold, nickel, and asbestos.

Manufacturing industries

This table provides a summary of manufacturing activity by industrial sector for the countries of the world, providing figures for total manufacturing value added, as well as the percentage contribution of 29 major branches of manufacturing activity to the gross domestic product. U.S. dollar figures for total value added by manufacturing are given but should be used with caution because of uncertainties with respect to national accounting methods, purchasing power parities, price structures and preferments, exchange rates, and so on, especially for countries having nonconvertible currencies.

Manufacturing activity is classified here according to a modification of the International Standard Industrial Classification (ISIC), revision 2, published by the United Nations. A summary of the 2-, 3-, and 4-digit ISIC codes (groups) defining these 29 sectors follows, providing definitional detail beyond that possible in the column headings.

The collection and publication of national manufacturing data is usually carried out by one of three methods: a full census of manufacturing (usually done every 5 to 10 years for a given country), a periodic survey of manufacturing (usually taken at annual or other regular intervals between censuses), and the onetime sample survey (often limited in geographic, sectoral, or size of enterprise coverage). The full census is, naturally, the

most complete, but, since up to 10 years may elapse between such censuses, it is sometimes necessary to substitute a survey of more recent date but less complete coverage. In certain instances, in order to provide the most timely data, the estimate series maintained by the United National Industrial Development Organization (UNIDO) in Vienna for its *Industry and Development Global Report* and other studies has been used.

ISIC code(s)	Products manufactured
31	Food, beverages, and tobacco
311 + 312	food including prepared animal feeds
313	alcoholic and nonalcoholic beverages
314	tobacco manufactures
32	Textiles, wearing apparel, and leather goods
321	spinning of textile fibres, weaving and finishing of textiles, knitted articles, carpets, rope, etc.
322	wearing apparel (including leather clothing; excluding knitted articles and footwear)
323 + 324	leather products (including footwear; excluding wearing apparel), leather substitutes, and fur products

Manufacturing industries

country	year	total manufacturing value added ('000,000 U.S.$)	(31) food (311+312)	bever-ages (313)	tobacco manufac-tures (314)	(32) textiles (exc. wearing apparel) (321)	wearing apparel (322)	leather and fur products (323+324)	(33) wood products (exc. furniture) (331)	wood furniture (332)	(34) paper, paper products (341)	printing and pub-lishing (342)	(35) industrial chemi-cals (351)	paints, soaps, etc. (352 exc. 3522)	drugs and medicines (3522)
Afghanistan	1988–89[1]	435	18.3	1.9	—	8.0	0.4	16.7	—0.5—		0.9	4.9	4.8	0.2	2.7
Albania	1990[2,3]	2,053	—34.1—		1.1	5.0	9.2	7.2	—4.6—		1.1	0.9	6.0[4]	[4]	[4]
Algeria	1990	5,739	14.2	3.0	3.8	7.3	6.4	3.5	3.3	1.6	3.9	0.4	0.4	—3.0—	
American Samoa	1990	297	...	...	...	...	...	...			...	...	...	...	...
Andorra	1989[7]	22	0.6	20.6	—	...	45.9	0.2	—0.4—		2.3	0.7	—	0.2	...
Angola	1989	319	20.0	—12.2—		—11.6—			—3.7—		—0.3—		9.1[8]	[8]	[8]
Antigua and Barbuda	1991	13	...	...	...	...	...	...			...	...	...	...	...
Argentina	1990	31,156	15.1	3.0	1.5	7.1	1.6	1.7	0.8	0.8	2.8	2.2	5.9	—5.7—	
Armenia	1991[10]	1,348[11]	6.4	19.9	2.3	15.6	21.5	8.6	2.7	...	0.3	0.4	−1.3	—	0.8
Aruba	...	...													
Australia	1991–92[12]	40,244	14.5	3.4	0.7	3.1	2.2	0.6	3.2	1.4	2.6	6.6	3.0	3.0	1.1
Austria	1990[10]	31,318	7.4	2.7	4.5	4.1	1.7	0.9	2.8	3.2	4.3	3.7	4.1	1.7	1.7
Azerbaijan	1990[2,3]	12,166[13]	—38.0—		...	—18.4—			...	...	1.7	—8.7—		5.9[8]	[8]	[8]
Bahamas, The	1991[3,12]	96	8.0	49.3	—	0.6	2.6	—	—	3.1	...	...	—13.3—		
Bahrain	1991	702	...	...	...	...	...	...			...	...	...	...	...
Bangladesh	1988–89[12]	1,476	17.7	0.2	4.9	30.9	8.4	3.3	0.8	0.1	2.3	1.7	10.8	1.6	5.1
Barbados	1990	90	33.7	11.2	1.1	1.1	5.6	—	—4.7—		1.1	9.0	—4.5—		
Belarus	1989[2,3]	39,976[13]	—14.3—		...	—18.1—			—4.7—		...	...	8.7[8]	[8]	[8]
Belgium	1990	42,392	14.2	1.7	0.6	4.2	2.3	0.6	1.1	3.6	2.6	3.9	10.6	—2.8—	
Belize	1991[10]	56	51.4	12.7	2.0	—4.1—			5.0	6.1	0.7	1.3	—4.0—		
Benin	1986	56	—62.5—			—8.8—			—3.4—		—4.0—				—5.5—
Bermuda	1990	173	...	...	...	...	...	...			...	...	...	...	...
Bhutan	1989[10]	21	6.0	10.1	—	—5.6—			18.1	2.7	0.4	1.0	21.5	—1.7—	
Bolivia	1989[10,15]	539	13.5	13.3	1.0	0.9	0.3	1.8	2.1	0.1	0.4	2.6	0.4	1.1	1.9
Bosnia and Herzegovina	1989	4,252	8.3	0.9	1.1	3.5	10.5	6.5	—12.0—		3.3	1.0	7.3[16]	[16]	[16]
Botswana	1990	148	38.8	19.0	—	9.5	1.4	0.7	0.7	0.7	2.7	0.7	0.7	—0.7—	
Brazil	1991[3,12]	89,977[17]	13.1	2.1	1.2	4.9	—4.2—		1.1	0.9	4.0	3.3	12.0	1.0	1.9
Brunei	1990	582	...	...	...	...	...	...			...	...	...	...	...
Bulgaria	1991[2]	9,041	15.5	3.2	5.3	4.4	1.7	1.3	1.3	1.0	2.1	0.9	6.0	1.7	3.8
Burkina Faso	1991	390	—54.2—			—24.2—			...	...	—1.3—				—5.5—
Burundi	1990	109	52.3	23.4	6.5	2.8	3.7	—	...	...	...	0.9	2.8	—0.9—	
Cambodia	1988[2,3]	25	—70.2—			—10.3—		...	...	...	...	...	...	—	—2.5—	
Cameroon	1990	826	22.4	35.6	2.8	−10.5	−3.3	1.0	7.4	3.1	1.3	0.7	2.1	—2.5—	
Canada	1990[10]	112,213	11.3	2.6	0.9	2.7	2.5	0.4	4.0	2.0	7.8	6.8	4.3	3.3	2.2
Cape Verde	1986[3]	24	—45.5—		8.3	—	...	...	—20.8—		—	...	...	...	...
Central African Republic	1990	48	27.1	12.5	20.8	2.1	...	—	18.8	2.1	—	4.2	2.1	—4.2—	
Chad	1990	161	...	...	...	...	...	...			...	...	...	...	...
Chile	1990[10,21]	8,737	17.7	4.3	3.5	3.9	1.9	1.8	3.1	0.6	6.4	2.6	2.8	4.9	2.2
China	1991	94,468	5.3	3.0	6.3	10.0	2.4	1.1	0.6	0.5	2.0	1.2	8.9	1.3	2.6
Colombia	1991	6,714	15.7	12.9	2.1	8.6	2.9	2.1	—1.2—		4.2	2.4	6.9	5.6	3.4
Comoros	1991	11	...	...	...	...	...	...			...	...	...	—3.9—	
Congo	1990	104	22.3	23.3	8.7	1.9	1.0	1.9	6.8	3.9	1.0	1.0	7.8	—3.9—	
Costa Rica	1991	973	31.3	14.7	3.5	3.0	3.5	1.2	2.1	1.8	4.5	3.4	3.5	3.8	2.0
Côte d'Ivoire	1990	1,409	24.1	4.8	4.2	11.5	0.6	1.3	2.3	0.8	0.7	0.9	1.3	—5.7—	
Croatia	1991	5,974	20.4	3.9	3.7	7.1	6.0	2.8	3.1	3.0	3.2	5.4	5.7	3.5	3.6
Cuba	1990[17]	5,990	17.2	6.0	43.9	1.8	1.5	1.2	0.9	0.7	0.2	1.4	1.1	—4.8—	
Cyprus[22]	1991	824	13.4	8.3	5.2	4.3	14.4	4.7	5.3	4.5	2.0	4.6	0.3	3.3	0.7
Czech Republic	1992[2,3]	23,958	—25.6—		...	—6.8—		2.1	—1.7—		—3.8—		—5.7—		
Denmark	1991[12,15]	23,588	18.7	3.5	1.2	2.5	1.1	0.5	2.1	2.8	2.8	6.6	4.7	2.1	4.6
Djibouti	1990	68	...	...	...	...	...	...			...	...	...	...	...
Dominica	1991	13	...	...	...	...	...	...	...	...	...	...	—3.4—		
Dominican Republic	1990	1,298	31.9	13.8	5.2	3.5	1.2	3.0	0.2	1.5	2.9	1.7	1.6	—3.4—	
Ecuador	1990[10,25]	1,196	19.1	2.8	0.1	7.9	0.9	0.8	1.3	0.8	2.9	2.2	1.5	5.6	0.7
Egypt	1988–89[12,26]	12,980	22.1	1.8	3.5	15.5	0.6	0.7	0.6	1.4	1.2	1.5	3.1	4.0	2.2
El Salvador	1992[3]	1,209	37.0	14.2	4.4	6.3	4.6	1.5	1.5	2.3[27]	1.6	1.6	—5.5—		
Equatorial Guinea	1990[2]	1.9	27.6	4.1	—	...	2.6	—	...	49.3	...	1.2	—13.8—		
Eritrea	1983–84	151	17.1	19.4	2.0	7.6	0.3	2.2	—	0.1	0.6	1.3	0.1	3.1	...
Estonia	1992[2]	886	—37.3—			13.9	—6.2—		4.4	5.3	1.3	...	8.9[28]	[28]	[28]
Ethiopia[30]	1990–91[2]	649	25.9	15.5	8.0	14.5	4.6	11.7	—	0.8	2.4	3.4	—1.7—		
Faeroe Islands	1988[3,12]	186	50.2[31]	...	...	...	...	...			...	...	...	...	...

ISIC code(s)	Products manufactured
33	Wood and wood products
331	sawlogs, wood products (excluding furniture), cane products, and cork products
332	wood furniture
34	Paper and paper products, printing and publishing
341	wood pulp, paper, and paper products
342	printing, publishing, and bookbinding
35	Chemicals and chemical, petroleum, coal, rubber, and plastic products
351	basic industrial chemicals (including fertilizers, pesticides, and synthetic fibres)
352 minus 3522	chemical products not elsewhere specified (including paints, varnishes, and soaps and other toiletries)
3522	drugs and medicines
353 + 354	refined petroleum and derivatives of petroleum and coal
355	rubber products
356	plastic products (excluding synthetic fibres)
36	Glass, ceramic, and nonmetallic mineral products
361 + 362	pottery, china, glass, and glass products
369	bricks, tiles, cement, cement products, plaster products, etc.

ISIC code(s)	Products manufactured
37	Basic metals
371	iron and steel
372	nonterrous basic metals and processed nickel and cobalt
38	Fabricated metal products, machinery and equipment
381	fabricated metal products (including cutlery, hand tools, fixtures, and structural metal products)
382 minus 3825	nonelectrical machinery and apparatus not elsewhere specified
3825	office, computing, and accounting machinery
383 minus 3832	electrical machinery and apparatus not elsewhere specified
3832	radio, television, and communications equipment (Including electronic parts)
384 minus 3843	transport equipment not elsewhere specified
3843	motor vehicles (excluding motorcycles)
385	professional and scientific equipment; photographic and optical goods; watches and clocks
39	Other manufactured goods
390	jewelry, musical instruments, sporting goods, artists' equipment, toys, etc.

refined petroleum and products (353+354)	rubber products (355)	plastic products (356)	pottery, china, and glass (361+362)	bricks, tiles, cement, etc. (369)	iron and steel (371)	non-ferrous metals (372)	fabricated metal products (381)	nonelectrical machinery (382 exc. 3825)	office equip., computers (3825)	electrical equip. (383 exc. 3832)	radio, television (3832)	transport equip. exc. motor vehicles (384 exc. 3843)	motor vehicles (3843)	professional equip. (385)	jewelry, musical instruments (390)	country
—	—	2.1	—1.1—		0.4	—	—						0.1	—	37.1	Afghanistan
5.6[5]	[4]	...	1.0	6.1	...	[6]	10.4[6]	—5.9—		—[6]—						Albania
2.9	0.4	1.0	1.2	8.9	10.0	0.6	10.0	—1.6—		—4.6—		—5.5—		1.2	1.3	Algeria
...	...	...	...	...	...	...	...	...	...	...	...	...	...	...	...	American Samoa
—	0.1	4.6	0.2	0.1	0.8	1.6	—	—3.3—		—14.6—				2.4	1.3	Andorra
20.0	[8]	[8]	—11.3—		—1.9—			—5.0—				—4.7—		[9]	0.3[9]	Angola
...	...	...	...	...	...	...	...	...	...	...	...	...	...	...	...	Antigua and Barbuda
19.9	1.2	1.4	1.3	3.0	5.3	1.0	5.2	—2.7—		—3.3—		—6.9—		0.4	0.3	Argentina
...	0.3	1.4	0.0	...	0.3	4.4	...			—15.5—		—	0.4		...	Armenia
...	...	...	...	...	...	...	...	...	...	...	...	...	...	...	...	Aruba
3.7	0.9	3.4	1.2	3.6	4.7	8.8	7.2	—3.6—		3.3	2.9	3.3	6.1	1.0	0.8	Australia
1.8	1.0	1.7	2.0	4.7	6.7	1.4	8.1	—10.5—		9.8	2.8	1.1	4.2	0.7	0.8	Austria
9.2	[8]	[8]		2.7	—3.4—		—18.7—								...	Azerbaijan
...	...	...	—6.8—		2.3	—		...						—	...	Bahamas, The
...	...	...	...	...	...	...	...	...	...	...	...	...	...	...	...	Bahrain
0.7	0.6	0.4	0.5	2.1	1.3	...	1.7	—0.5—		—2.4—		—1.7—			0.4	Bangladesh
5.6	2.3	2.3	1.1	5.6	—		9.0	—2.3—		—1.1—		—1.1—			—	Barbados
4.5	[8]	[8]	...	4.0	...	...	—38.7—								...	Belarus
0.9	0.7	5.2	2.2	2.1	5.9	2.7	6.7	—8.7—		—6.9—		—7.5—		0.6	1.8	Belgium
—0.6—				6.1	...		3.1	—0.1—				—2.1—			0.7	Belize
—10.1—								—5.0—							0.7	Benin
...	...	...	...	...	...	...	...	...	...	...	...	...	...	...	...	Bermuda
...	0.7	2.2	—29.0—		...	...	...			—1.0[14]—					[14]	Bhutan
50.2	...	1.3	0.5	4.6	—	1.9	1.0	—0.1—		0.2		—0.5—		0.1	—	Bolivia
-0.7	0.2	[16]	—2.4—		5.8	7.0	11.6	—5.8—		—6.3—		—7.1—		...	0.3	Bosnia and Herzegovina
—	0.7	—	—4.3—		...		7.5	—0.7—		—0.7—		—0.7—		—	14.3	Botswana
...	1.3	2.3	...	...	11.3[18]		[19]	—11.4—		—7.6—		7.3		...	...	Brazil
...	...	...	...	...	...	...	...	...	...	...	...	...	...	...	...	Brunei
9.0	1.4	1.3	1.2	2.5	6.1	2.6	3.8	—6.9[19]—		5.1	2.3	2.8	1.4	[19]	5.5	Bulgaria
			—3.5—													Burkina Faso
—	—	—	—	1.9	—	—	4.7	—		—		—		—	—	Burundi
...	...	...	...	...	...	...	...	...	...	...	...	...	...	...	...	Cambodia
13.8	0.1	3.0	1.7	1.9	3.6	2.8	2.1	—3.9—		—1.1—		—0.4—			0.7	Cameroon
2.3	1.2	2.6	0.6	2.5	2.9	2.9	5.8	5.8	1.0	3.0	3.7	3.8	8.8	0.8	1.5	Canada
							[20]					10.8[20]			—	Cape Verde
												—4.2—			2.1	Central African Republic
...	...	...	...	...	...	...	...	...	...	...	...	...	...	...	...	Chad
6.3	0.0	2.0	0.7	2.5	3.2	19.6	4.2	—1.7—		1.3	0.1	0.8	0.9	0.1	0.2	Chile
3.6	1.8	2.0	—6.8—		7.5	2.1	3.2	—11.3—		4.8	3.7	—4.9—		1.0	2.0	China
2.2	1.9	3.4	2.2	4.0	3.3	0.6	3.3	1.8	—	2.6	0.6	0.9	3.3	1.0	0.9	Colombia
—	—	—	—	—	—	—									—	Comoros
1.9	1.0	1.0	1.0		—		4.9	—1.9—		—1.9—		—2.9—		—		Congo
2.7	1.5	3.0	1.4	3.2	—	0.1	2.0	1.3		1.2	2.6	0.7	0.7		0.3	Costa Rica
16.5	0.3	—	0.1	1.8	0.2	0.1	4.0	—0.1—		—1.1—		—15.8—			1.6	Côte d'Ivoire
-11.9	0.5	2.1	2.3	3.9	1.8	1.4	5.8	5.8	0.7	6.2	2.1	6.4	0.4	0.5	0.5	Croatia
...	1.4	1.2	0.4	1.9	0.6	1.1	1.3	—2.9—		—0.9—		—3.8—		0.2	3.6	Cuba
1.0	0.3	3.5	0.4	8.5	—		7.3	3.2		1.3		0.4	0.7		2.3	Cyprus[22]
5.4	—2.0—		—4.6—		16.1[18]		[18]	—9.5[23]—		—4.4[24]—		—8.5—			...	Czech Republic
1.5	0.5	2.7	0.7	3.8	1.1	0.3	8.1	—13.0—		2.5	2.6	—5.2—		2.6	2.3	Denmark
...	...	...	...	...	...	...	...	...	...	...	...	...	...	...	...	Djibouti
—															0.2	Dominica
16.2	0.8	1.6	0.7	3.5	1.8	0.2	3.7	—0.5—		—0.8—		—0.1—		0.2	0.2	Dominican Republic
31.6	1.4	3.6	1.3	5.0	1.8	0.2	3.7	—0.2—		2.3	0.4	—	1.8	0.2	0.3	Ecuador
3.2	0.4	1.8	1.5	7.4	5.3	8.0	4.0	3.7		1.4	0.8	1.4	2.2	0.7	0.1	Egypt
6.0	0.7	...	—5.2—		—2.7—		0.9	—0.7—		—1.7—		—0.3—				El Salvador
...	...	...	...	0.8	...	...	0.6	...	...	...	...	...	...	...	...	Equatorial Guinea
38.4	[28]	3.0	1.0	1.6	0.8	...	1.2		0.1						...	Eritrea
	—1.4—				—2.6[18]—			—2.7—		—4.6[29]—		—4.2—		[29]	2.7	Estonia
—	1.3	0.9	0.5	4.8	...		3.9								...	Ethiopia[30]
			...	...	...	...	...					21.8[32]			...	Faeroe Islands

Manufacturing industries (continued)

country	year	total manufacturing value added ('000,000 U.S.$)	food (311+312)	beverages (313)	tobacco manufactures (314)	textiles (exc. wearing apparel) (321)	wearing apparel (322)	leather and fur products (323+324)	wood products (exc. furniture) (331)	wood furniture (332)	paper, paper products (341)	printing and publishing (342)	industrial chemicals (351)	paints, soaps, etc. (352 exc. 3522)	drugs and medicines (3522)
Fiji	1990	142	42.5	9.8		11.3		0.6	7.6	2.2	3.6	4.4	—	5.2	
Finland	1991[12,34]	21,657	11.7	3.4	0.8	1.4	1.5	0.5	4.4	1.8	12.7	8.7	4.6	1.7	1.4
France	1991[10]	249,127	10.4	2.5	0.7	2.6	2.2	1.0	1.5	1.6	2.5	5.6	3.7	3.5	1.9
French Guiana	1991[25]	45	...	...	...	35			38.2[35]		...	...	—	—	—
French Polynesia	1990[3]	213	27.4			...	...	...	...	...	—	—	—		
Gabon	1990	268	9.7	7.5	6.3	1.1	1.9	0.7	19.8	2.6	0.7	1.5	2.6	1.1	
Gambia, The	1990	13	45.5	18.2	—	...	...	...	—	9.1	...	...	...	...	...
Gaza Strip	1991	71	36.7			21.9			3.5		...	...	4.0[8]	[8]	[8]
Georgia	1988[2,3]	11,879[13]													
Germany[37]	1990[10,15]	535,545	5.3	2.2	2.4	2.2	1.1	0.4	1.2	1.5	2.5	1.9	6.6	3.2	2.0
Ghana	1990	620	12.2	14.0	11.2	8.0	0.2	0.3	9.0	1.1	0.6	1.6	0.8	4.3	
Gibraltar	...	...	...	...	...	...	...	...	...	...	...	...	...	...	...
Greece	1990[12,25]	9,293	14.5	5.1	3.0	11.9	5.9	1.8	1.9	1.0	2.9	3.1	3.1	4.4	2.4
Greenland	1991	27													
Grenada	1992[12]	10													
Guadeloupe	1991[25]	95	...	...	...	35			25.8[35]		...	...	...	...	...
Guam	1986	9.1													
Guatemala	1988[10,34]	842	24.1	5.3	2.5	6.5	3.2	2.7	1.2	0.6	1.4	4.8	4.9	9.1	6.8
Guernsey	1993[39]	61	5.1		—	1.5			...	...	—	17.6	—		7.8
Guinea	1990	115													
Guinea-Bissau	1990	10													
Guyana	1992[40]	49	...	...	...	...	...	...	...	...	...	...	...	...	...
Haiti	1992–93[41]	22	...	...	...	11.7	55.5	1.8	...	...	...	...	...	...	...
Honduras	1989	589	31.0	9.9	4.6	4.1	2.8	0.9	6.2	1.7	3.3	2.7	0.6	4.1	1.5
Hong Kong	1991	11,865	3.7	1.3	2.4	15.1	19.9	0.7	0.2	0.5	2.6	7.6	2.2		
Hungary	1989	7,109	7.4	1.8	0.5	4.6	2.6	1.6	1.0	1.6	1.7	2.0	7.3	0.3	5.3
Iceland	1990[12]	819	45.5	2.0	—	2.7	1.2	0.6	0.1	4.7	1.1	9.9	7.9	1.6	
India	1988–89[12,42]	20,395	9.7	1.0	2.0	11.0	1.0	0.7	10.0	0.4	2.2	1.3	3.9	4.0	
Indonesia	1990	12,268	10.5	0.7	9.4	11.2	2.2	0.9	2.0	0.5	1.6	2.0	3.1	6.5	
Iran	1989–90[10,25]	28,194	11.6	2.7	1.4	18.5	1.1	2.6	2.0	0.5	1.6	2.0		9.7	
Iraq	1990	3,807	7.6	2.9	3.3	5.8	1.2	1.3	0.1	0.4	2.1	1.1	4.0	9.7	
Ireland	1990[43]	14,780	20.5	5.4	1.1	2.3	1.4	0.3	1.2	0.6	1.3	3.8	2.8	1.4	12.6
Isle of Man	1985–86[3,12]	45	16.9			...	...	...	...	...	...	...	...	...	...
Israel	1990[10,34]	10,193	12.0	1.4	0.3	4.0	4.2	0.7	1.1	1.3	2.4	4.6	7.1[44]	2.2	1.9
Italy	1990	164,069	5.4	2.2	0.4	7.2	3.4	2.3	1.1	2.0	2.4	4.3	5.8	4.6	
Jamaica	1990	734	16.6	12.3	11.5	0.7	3.8	2.3	0.6	1.9	1.4	3.6	7.6	1.4	
Japan	1991[45]	1,016,524	7.5	1.1	0.3	3.0	1.4	0.4	1.5	1.0	2.4	5.4	4.1	2.4	2.7
Jersey	1991	45													
Jordan	1991[10]	609	9.4	4.9	12.8	3.5	2.4	1.1	3.2		3.6	2.3	8.0	3.7	5.1
Kazakhstan	1988[2,3]	28,438[13]	16.2			16.2			2.7		...	...	7.3[8]	[8]	[8]
Kenya	1991[12,15]	897	28.8	10.2	1.4	5.8	1.7	1.4	1.8	1.2[27]	4.4	3.0	1.9	5.5	1.6
Kiribati	1989	0.66	...	...	—	—			...	...	—	—	...		
Korea, North	...	...	...	...	...	...	...	...	...	...	...	...	...	...	...
Korea, South	1990[10,34]	100,211	6.0	1.9	2.8	6.8	3.4	1.7	0.9	1.0	2.1	2.5	4.2	2.7	2.2
Kuwait	1992	3,177	4.0			3.0			1.9		2.5		3.8[8]	[8]	[8]
Kyrgyzstan	1991[2,3]	6,219[13]	20.9			31.4			...	...	2.1	...	...	...	...
Laos	1991	137													
Latvia	1991[2]	24,420[11]	25.5	1.4	0.4	15.4	4.9	3.2	2.4	1.7	2.0	1.4	2.4	4.5	1.1
Lebanon	1990	422	...	...	...	...	...	...	...	...	...	2.3		2.8	
Lesotho	1991[3]	113	52.4			32.6			1.6		...	...	...		
Liberia	1985[2,10,15]	64	10.8	42.7	...	—		0.3		4.5	0.6	1.3	0.4	7.2	
Libya	1990	1,211	5.5	2.8	10.8	2.7	0.7	7.1	0.9	0.7	0.4	0.3	7.2	5.8	
Liechtenstein	...	...													
Lithuania	1991[2,3]	34,569[11]	32.2			22.1			6.0[47]		[47]		3.1[8]	[8]	[8]
Luxembourg	1990	2,208	2.1	2.4	0.6	2.7	0.6	...	0.1	0.1	1.4	1.7	11.7	5.9	
Macau	1991[10]	474	1.3	0.6	—	20.2	53.0	2.7	0.2	1.0	0.7	2.2		0.4	0.7
Macedonia	1989	2,095	7.3	3.2	6.4	14.3	15.4	6.8	3.7		0.9	0.7	7.6[16]	[16]	[16]
Madagascar	1990	147	15.3	11.1	0.7	41.7	2.8	2.8	—	—	3.5	0.7		6.2	
Malawi	1990	133	20.2	9.0	6.7	13.4	1.5	3.0	1.5	0.7	0.7	6.7	3.7	15.7	
Malaysia	1990[12]	9,069	9.5	2.2	1.4	3.3	3.1	0.1	6.4	0.8	1.7	2.9	8.2	2.2	0.4
Maldives	1991	6.0[40]	...	...	...	...	...	...	...	...	—	0.8	0.8	0.8	
Mali	1990	122	13.9	1.6	10.7	41.8	10.7	—	...	...	...	...	...	...	...
Malta	1990	554	10.1	9.7	1.4	2.5	16.2	2.3	0.4	4.5	1.1	5.6	0.5	2.5	
Marshall Islands	1981[1]	0.16	39.7	—	—	35				8.8	—	51.5	...		
Martinique	1991[25]	191	...	...	...	35			16.8[35]		...	...	...		
Mauritania	1989[3]	103	63.1[31]	...	...	...	...	...	...	...	...	...	...	...	...
Mauritius	1990[10]	480	16.7	5.1	1.7	5.9	42.5	1.6	1.0	0.9	0.7	2.5	2.5	2.1	
Mayotte	1990	...	...	...	...	...	...	...	...	...	...	...	...	...	...
Mexico	1988[10,48]	30,308	12.4	4.3	2.4	5.3	1.5	1.3	0.9	0.8	2.9	2.2	6.9	3.6	2.7
Micronesia	...	...	...	...	...	...	...	...	...	...	...	...	...	...	...
Moldova	1991[2]	21,908[11]	46.3	...	...	11.9	6.7	4.2	3.4[49]		[49]	...	2.8		
Monaco	...	...													16.1
Mongolia	1990[3]	621	33.1			20.6	6.7	14.5	6.3		...	2.1	...	...	...
Morocco	1991[25]	3,071	8.6	22.4		11.4	8.7	2.3	2.5		4.2	1.4	15.4	0.9	
Mozambique	1988	292	28.6	9.2	5.4	18.2	4.1	1.4	1.3	0.8	2.9	2.2	0.5	5.1	
Myanmar (Burma)	1984–85[3]	731	38.8			9.4			...	...	...	3.4	...		
Namibia	1990	117	...	...	...	...	...	...	...	...	...	...	...	...	...
Nauru	1989	—													
Nepal	1990–91[3,10,25]	238	14.0	7.2	14.7	20.1	8.8	2.1	0.9	0.7	1.2	0.6		5.0	0.7
Netherlands, The	1991	44,527	21.8			2.2	0.5	0.3	2.0		3.7	7.5	14.6		
Netherlands Antilles	1988	78	...	...	...	...	...	...	...	...	...	...	...	...	...
New Caledonia	1989[3]	371	...	...	...	...	...	...	6.1		7.5	7.3	3.4	2.9	
New Zealand	1990–91	7,352	22.8	9.2		3.2	4.1		2.1	0.6	0.5	1.8	4.1		
Nicaragua	1991[3]	426	36.9	22.1	10.4	4.4	0.5	1.1	...	...	...	...	...	...	...
Niger	1991	156	...	...	...	...	...	...	...	...	...	...	...	...	...

| | | | (36) | | (37) | | (38) | | | | | | | | (39) | country |
| refined petroleum and products | rubber products | plastic products | pottery, china, and glass | bricks, tiles, cement, etc. | iron and steel | nonferrous metals | fabricated metal products | nonelectrical machinery | office equip., computers | electrical equip. | radio, television | transport equip. exc. motor vehicles | motor vehicles | professional equip. | jewelry, musical instruments | |
(353+354)	(355)	(356)	(361+362)	(369)	(371)	(372)	(381)	(382 exc. 3825)	(3825)	(383 exc. 3832)	(3832)	(384 exc. 3843)	(3843)	(385)	(390)	
—	0.6	2.4	—	3.6[33]			3.9	0.9				0.5	0.2	—	0.8	Fiji
3.2	0.4	1.5	1.0	3.6	3.4	1.4	6.7	10.1	0.7	3.6	2.2	3.7	1.7	1.5	0.7	Finland
6.5	1.4	2.6	1.2	3.1	3.4	1.7	7.5	9.2		9.9		3.7	7.1	1.6	1.5	France
...	...	...	61.8[36]		[36]		[36]								...	French Guiana
—	...	...	...				42.5								...	French Polynesia
11.6	—	—	1.1	6.3	1.5	1.5	7.5	1.1		4.5		6.3		0.4	2.6	Gabon
—	—	—	—		—		—	...	...	...	...	...	...	...	27.3	Gambia, The
...	[8]	[8]	—	5.2	...	...	15.7								...	Gaza Strip
...	...	...	...	...	...	...	...	...	...	...	...	...	...	...	...	Georgia
3.7	1.2	3.2	1.2	2.2	3.6	1.4	7.3	13.7	1.8	6.5	7.1	1.5	11.1	1.5	0.5	Germany[37]
7.2	0.8	0.5	0.2	3.7	0.5	19.4	2.2	0.3		0.8		0.6		0.2	0.2	Ghana
...	...	...	...	...	...	...	...	...	...	...	...	...	...	...	...	Gibraltar
2.6	0.9	3.0	1.3	6.9	3.0	3.7	4.8	1.9		3.7	1.1	4.3	1.0	0.2	0.5	Greece
...	...	...	...	...	...	...	...	...	...	...	...	...	...	...	...	Greenland
...	...	...	...	...	...	...	...	...	...	...	...	...	...	...	...	Grenada
			[38]		[38]		64.1[38]	10.0							...	Guadeloupe
1.1	2.3	3.6	3.4	5.9	3.1	0.1	2.8	0.7	0.1	2.4	0.4	0.1	0.2	0.2	0.5	Guam
—		10.9	—	1.9			—	7.4			40.3	3.0			4.6	Guatemala
...	...	...	...	...	...	...	...	...	...	...	...	...	...	...	...	Guernsey
...	...	...	...	...	...	...	...	...	...	...	...	...	...	...	...	Guinea
...	...	...	...	...	...	...	...	...	...	...	...	...	...	...	...	Guinea-Bissau
—	1.4							6.5							...	Guyana
1.9	2.2	4.3	0.2	7.0	0.9	0.2	5.0	0.9	—	1.1	0.5	0.2	0.3	0.2	22.9	Haiti
0.1	0.1	5.7	1.1		0.8		6.4	6.9	4.8	2.0	5.6	2.9		4.1	1.6	Honduras
...	...	...	...	...	...	...	...	...	...	...	...	...	...	...	3.3	Hong Kong
3.8	1.4	1.9	2.0	2.8	6.4	4.3	4.0	10.7		4.0	7.5	2.6	3.8	5.1	2.0	Hungary
—	2.9	3.2	0.5	4.1	1.1	4.3	9.9					2.2			3.2	Iceland
5.0	2.9	1.1	0.8	3.6	11.7	2.2	3.3	7.1	0.1	6.8	2.2	3.4	4.5	0.8	0.4	India
13.0	4.2	1.2	0.9	1.9	6.0	—	6.0	0.9		2.4		6.3		0.1	0.5	Indonesia
1.0	2.0	2.3	1.8	10.4	6.6	2.1	5.2	7.9		2.4		4.1		0.3	0.3	Iran
32.2	0.3	1.0	0.8	15.4	0.5	—	2.0	3.4		3.9		1.1			—	Iraq
0.2	0.8	2.2	1.2	3.8	0.6	0.1	3.2	2.6	11.2	2.9	9.5	1.5	0.6	4.1	0.9	Ireland
[44]	0.8	4.6	0.7	3.0	1.1	0.6	12.1	1.7	1.0	2.8	18.7	6.2	1.1	1.2	1.2	Isle of Man
1.3	1.7	3.4	3.2	3.9	5.2	1.4	5.2	12.8		9.0		10.7		0.8	0.3	Italy
11.0	2.1	3.3	1.6	3.7	1.2	—	2.6	1.8		1.9		6.0		—	1.1	Jamaica
1.0	1.2	3.6	1.2	3.0	5.4	1.2	7.4	10.8	3.5	6.7	8.5	1.2	9.1	1.4	1.6	Japan
...	...	...	...	...	...	...	...	...	...	...	...	...	...	...	...	Jersey
8.5	0.1	3.2	1.2	14.1	3.9	1.2	3.6	2.1		1.8				0.3	0.1	Jordan
...	[8]	[8]	...	6.4	...	...	17.5								...	Kazakhstan
0.8	3.6	2.8	0.6	4.5	0.2		6.0[16]	0.6		5.2		2.8	1.4	—	1.9	Kenya
...	...	...	—	—	—	—	...	—	—	...	...	...	...	...	...	Kiribati
3.4	3.1	2.7	1.3	3.7	6.2	1.2	5.1	6.3	0.7	8.9	6.1	2.5	7.8	1.1	1.8	Korea, North
75.7	[8]	[8]	3.2		0.5		4.9								0.6	Korea, South
0.9	...	...	...	4.9	4.7		28.0								...	Kuwait
...	...	...	...	...	...	...	...	...	...	...	...	...	...	...	...	Kyrgyzstan
0.1	0.7	0.7	1.4	2.9	0.7	0.1	1.7	5.9	0.1	2.7	6.7	2.9	1.6	0.2	5.3	Laos
...	...	...	4.2		1.5		...	...	...	...	...	...	...	...	...	Latvia
...	...	...	...	...	...	...	...	...	...	...	...	...	...	...	...	Lebanon
...	...	0.6	0.2	20.7	—		9.5	0.3		0.7		—	—		—	Liberia
30.9	0.1	0.8	0.1	18.3	—		1.7	—		—		—	—		3.2	Libya
3.7	[8]	[8]	...	5.4	...	...	19.0								...	Liechtenstein
0.1	8.4	2.0	3.0	6.9	29.1	2.8	9.6	6.1		1.4		0.6		0.5	0.1	Lithuania
—	0.2	1.7[16]	0.5	0.2	—	—	1.8	0.5		0.7	0.2	1.0		—	...	Luxembourg
—	1.4	[16]	6.1		5.8	3.7	5.1	2.5		8.1		3.7		0.9	9.5	Macau
6.2	0.7	0.7	0.7	2.1	—	—	2.8	1.4		0.7		0.7		—	0.1	Macedonia
—	—	3.7	—	6.0			3.7	2.2		0.7		0.7		—	—	Madagascar
2.6	5.8	2.9	1.2	4.9	3.2	0.7	3.5	3.5	0.3	3.4	18.0	1.1	4.4	1.1	1.2	Malawi
0.8	—	—	—	0.8	—		4.1	1.6		1.6		9.8			...	Maldives
...	3.1	1.8	0.4	2.0	—		4.3	2.2		17.7		4.1		4.0	3.8	Mali
...	...	...	...	...	...	...	...	...	...	...	...	...	...	...	...	Malta
52.2	...	...	[38]		[38]		20.8[30]	2.2							...	Marshall Islands
...	...	...	...	...	...	...	...	...	...	...	...	...	...	...	...	Martinique
...	...	...	...	...	...	...	...	...	...	...	...	...	...	...	...	Mauritania
—	0.4	1.4	0.1	2.2	0.9		2.9	0.8		1.1		0.6	0.2	2.7	3.3	Mauritius
7.3	1.5	2.5	2.8	2.9	4.5	1.5	4.7	2.9	1.0	5.3	2.3	0.5	12.3	0.3	0.6	Mexico
...	...	...	...	...	...	...	...	...	...	...	...	...	...	...	...	Micronesia
...	...	...	0.7	4.1	1.0		15.9								3.1	Moldova
...	...	...	0.6	7.4	...	...	...	...	...	...	...	...	...	...	...	Monaco
	3.6		0.5		2.2	0.3	6.3			4.1		5.2			...	Mongolia
0.8	2.5	1.2	0.9	2.9	0.8	0.4	2.7	0.8		4.3		2.6			0.1	Morocco
...	...	...	...	...	...	...	...	...	...	...	...	...	...	...	...	Mozambique
...	...	...	...	10.0	...	...	...	1.4		1.1		5.3			...	Myanmar (Burma)
—	—	...	...	...	...	...	...	...	...	...	...	...	...	...	...	Namibia
—	0.8	1.2	...	12.8	3.1		3.0			1.0	0.3				...	Nauru
3.1	3.7		3.8		3.7		7.5	8.2		10.9		5.5			0.9	Nepal
...	...	...	...	...	...	...	...	...	...	...	...	...	...	0.7	0.4	Netherlands, The
...	...	...	...	...	...	80.8	...			7.1		...	...	...	...	Netherlands Antilles
2.0	0.8	3.1	3.6		3.4		6.5	4.6		3.5		4.4		0.3	1.2	New Caledonia
0.1	5.0	...	5.5				2.3	0.8				0.1			...	New Zealand
...	...	...	...	...	...	...	...	...	...	...	...	...	...	...	...	Nicaragua
...	...	...	...	...	...	...	...	...	...	...	...	...	...	...	...	Niger

Manufacturing industries (continued)

country	year	total manufacturing value added ('000,000 U.S.$)	(31) food (311+312)	beverages (313)	tobacco manufactures (314)	(32) textiles (exc. wearing apparel) (321)	wearing apparel (322)	leather and fur products (323+324)	(33) wood products (exc. furniture) (331)	wood furniture (332)	(34) paper, paper products (341)	printing and publishing (342)	(35) industrial chemicals (351)	paints, soaps, etc. (352 exc. 3522)	drugs and medicines (3522)
Nigeria	1990	3,606	14.0	12.0	2.0	12.4	0.1	3.0	0.7	0.9	3.2	3.0	0.5	—12.8—	
Northern Mariana Islands	1987[1,3]	58	—3.3—			26.0	—62.7[50]—		...	...	...	1.3	...	...	...
Norway	1992[25]	13,594	13.2	—9.9—		1.6	0.5	0.2	3.2	1.6	4.3	10.1	4.7	1.5	1.9
Oman	1990[3]	393													
Pakistan	1990	4,299	16.1	1.8	10.2	18.4	1.7	1.3	0.3	0.1	1.1	0.9	6.5	—7.2—	
Panama	1991	454	29.4	13.2	5.7	1.2	6.6	1.9	1.8	2.2	5.2	3.0	0.7	—8.3—	
Papua New Guinea	1989	451	48.4	13.1	4.9	—	0.4	—	11.6	2.0	1.1	2.4	1.1	—1.1—	
Paraguay	1990	633	35.4	8.7	1.4	6.5	0.5	5.1	14.5	1.4	0.2	5.1	0.3	—0.9—	
Peru	1991	3,130	22.4	—9.2—		8.9	5.2	1.2	—4.9—		1.0	2.6	2.8	3.7	1.6
Philippines	1992	12,076	40.7	4.8	2.7	2.9	—6.8—		1.8	1.5	0.9	1.3	8.3[16]	[16]	[16]
Poland	1990	23,017	11.3	8.0	1.6	5.3	1.9	1.7	1.4	1.3	1.5	0.7	4.6	1.6	1.3
Portugal	1990	11,680	11.6	3.5	1.9	14.9	4.2	3.3	2.5	1.2	5.9	2.8	5.2	—4.6—	
Puerto Rico	1991	12,672	5.2	8.4	1.4	0.3	4.0	1.0	—0.4—		0.7	1.4	0.4	3.1	43.5
Qatar	1991	917	1.9	0.4		—	—2.4—		1.2	0.2	—	1.4	35.7	—0.3—	
Réunion	1991[52]	323	33.0	11.3	—	—0.7—			—2.7—		4.6[53]	9.7	[54]	—3.2—	
Romania	1991	11,509	7.6	6.4	1.1	11.5	4.8	3.0	2.8	3.9	1.8	0.5	3.8	1.3	0.5
Russia[55]	1990	502,639[56]	17.1	1.7	0.5	7.4	4.8	1.6	1.3	1.1	0.8	0.8	3.9	—1.9—	
Rwanda	1990	180	32.6	19.3	8.8	...	...	...	4.4	0.6	1.1	1.1	7.7	—	
St. Kitts and Nevis	1991	19	...			...	...	...	...	...	30.2	...	0.5	...	
St. Lucia	1991[2,57]	42	—44.7—			3.4	11.6								
St. Vincent	1988[3,12]	14	24.9	—25.4—		—10.1—			—1.9—		—5.3—		...	...	
San Marino		...	...	...		...	...		...	...	...	...	...	...	
São Tomé and Príncipe	1990	1.0	...	...		...	...		...	...	...	...	...	...	
Saudi Arabia	1990	5,387	5.9	0.8	0.6	0.4	0.1	0.1	0.2	0.7	2.0	1.1	35.4	—3.1—	
Senegal	1990	639	36.4	3.0	0.9	1.6	0.6		0.8	0.9	3.0	4.1	10.3	—4.1—	
Seychelles	1989	26	—79.6—			—0.6—			—2.1—		—6.0—			—4.1—	
Sierra Leone	1985–86[25]	43	—60.6—			—0.5—			—15.8—		—0.5—		3.0	—5.3—	—4.1—
Singapore	1993[25]	17,522	2.4	1.0	0.7	0.4	1.5	0.2	0.2	0.8	1.3	4.8	22.5[8]	[8]	[8]
Slovakia	1991	10,471[2]	—15.7—			3.4	1.2	2.5	—3.4—		3.5	0.9	3.7	2.4	4.7
Slovenia	1991	5,223	10.2	2.9	1.8	13.2	0.2	2.8	3.6	2.3	5.0	4.6			
Solomon Islands	1990	7.1	...	...		...	...		...	0.1	—	—10.9—		—6.7—	
Somalia	1988	18	26.5	4.8	18.7	3.3	0.4	14.0	1.5	1.2	5.0	3.7	4.9	—11.6[61]—	
South Africa	1991[12,60]	24,151	10.6	4.8	0.4	3.4	3.1	1.6	2.5	1.8	2.4	5.0	3.9	3.7	2.7
Spain	1990[12,15]	87,325	12.3	4.2	1.0	3.8	2.6	1.6	0.9	—	1.7	1.5	1.1	3.0	1.2
Sri Lanka	1990[10,34]	1,005	17.4	4.4	15.5	8.2	16.9	2.0							
Sudan, The	1988	354	44.1	2.3	12.7	9.3	0.3	2.5	0.3	0.3	1.7	2.3	0.8	—4.0—	
Suriname	1990[2,12,57]	360	39.9	19.6	9.2	...	1.6	1.1	5.0	1.2	2.3	2.2	...	—8.3—	—0.6—
Swaziland	1988	204	26.5	36.4	—	—4.5—			—2.9—		—23.3—				
Sweden	1990[12,34]	51,431	8.3	1.4	0.5	1.2	0.4	0.2	5.9	1.1	8.8	6.1	3.9	2.0	3.0
Switzerland	1990	58,051	10.3	1.7	0.5	3.0	2.0	0.8	3.9	2.5	2.4	7.3	7.2	—7.8—	—9.4—
Syria	1990[12]	1,743	—35.0—			—28.8—			—4.3—		—1.5—		6.2	—2.5—	
Taiwan	1992	67,871	5.4	—5.7—		7.3	3.1	1.2	—1.2—		—5.4—		5.2[8]	[8]	[8]
Tajikistan	1990[2]	4,432[11]	—20.0—			—47.8—			—1.3—		3.4	2.3	13.6	—2.3—	
Tanzania	1990	87	12.5	5.7	10.2	17.0	1.1	2.3	2.3	1.1	1.7	16.5	1.2	1.4	2.2
Thailand	1988[10,25]	11,405	17.4	3.8	0.1	10.2	3.7	1.2	1.4	1.4					
Togo	1989[3]	115	—50.8—			—14.1—			—7.1—		—3.8—			—5.9—	
Tonga	1991[2,62]	13	—42.3—			3.0	5.6	5.2	1.6	[63]	[63]	6.2		—13.3—	
Trinidad and Tobago	1991[3]	758	—29.9—			—2.3—			—1.7[49]—		[49]	5.1	28.0[64]	[64]	[64]
Tunisia	1990	1,612	7.4	5.8	2.2	5.1	7.6	3.0	1.3	1.0	2.1	1.6	2.7	—8.7—	
Turkey	1990[10,65]	28,958	8.8	3.1	4.1	11.1	3.3	0.4	0.6	0.3	1.9	1.5	5.2	2.4	2.6
Turkmenistan	1990[2,3]	4,550[11]	—15.4—		...	38.4	—6.2—		...	...	1.4	...	4.2[8]	[8]	[8]
Tuvalu	1990	0.3	...	...	...	...	...		—	—	—	—	—	—2.5—	
Uganda	1982	406	33.9	11.7	9.4	27.1	2.3	1.3	2.1	0.8	[49]	...	6.7[8]	[8]	
Ukraine	1991[2]	294,656[11]	—29.6—		...	—14.0—			—3.3[49]—		[49]	...	...	...	
United Arab Emirates	1992[12,17]	2,736	...	...		...			...		...		...		
United Kingdom	1991	188,919	9.1	3.8	1.1	2.7	2.2	0.8	1.2	1.8	3.3	8.0	5.1	2.0	3.6
United States	1991	1,313,829	9.0	2.0	1.9	2.0	2.5	0.3	2.1	1.6	4.4	7.9	5.3	3.2	3.3
Uruguay	1988[10,34]	1,877	19.1	7.6	4.6	9.4	2.5	5.1	0.8	0.2	3.7	2.4	2.8	3.3	4.1
Uzbekistan	1991[2,3]	53,417[11]	—14.4—		...	38.4	5.5	2.6	—1.4—		0.3		0.28[8]	[8]	
Vanuatu	1985[3]	4.6	33.8	8.8		—8.7—			—5.4—		—17.2—				
Venezuela	1992	11,044	14.2	7.5	3.5	2.7	2.8	1.7	1.1	1.0	2.5	1.7	4.8	—6.4—	
Vietnam	1989[66,67]	5,533	—28.2—			—17.7[68]—			[69]		[69]	[68]		—9.9—	
Virgin Islands (U.S.)		...[70]	...	...		...	...		...	...	...		...	...	
West Bank	1991	100	...	...	...	...	...		...		...		...		
Western Sahara		...												8.6	
Western Samoa	1990	15	36.0	25.5	19.2	—	...		10.7	—	—	—0.5—		—9.2—	
Yemen[71]	1986	540	—51.9—			—8.7—			—3.9—		1.2	2.0	3.9	—7.6—	
Yugoslavia	1991[3]	1,998	11.5	1.5	1.8	3.5	10.6	2.8	1.0	2.8	—	1.0	8.2	—7.1—	
Zaire	1990	96	5.1	28.9	15.5	5.1	2.1	5.1	2.1	—	1.1	2.3	3.6	—7.1—	
Zambia	1990	1,028	8.5	23.0	9.4	6.0	4.5	3.4	2.7	2.0	1.9	2.9	3.2[44]	3.5	1.0
Zimbabwe	1989[12]	2,359	12.1	11.9	4.1	9.9	4.0	2.7	1.5	1.0					

[1]Gross output in value of sales. [2]Gross output of production. [3]Percentage breakdown by ISIC category is incomplete. [4]351 includes 352 and 355. [5]Includes petroleum extraction. [6]381 includes 37 and 383. [7]Value of manufactured exports (excluding duty-free reexports). [8]351 includes 352, 355, and 356. [9]390 includes 385. [10]In producer's prices. [11]Rubles of former U.S.S.R. [12]In factor values. [13]Constant rubles of 1982 of the former U.S.S.R. [14]38 includes 39. [15]Establishments employing 20 or more persons. [16]351 includes 352 and 356. [17]Excludes petroleum refining. [18]37 includes 381. [19]382 includes 385. [20]384 minus 3843 includes 381. [21]Establishments employing 50 or more persons. [22]Republic of Cyprus only. [23]Includes professional equipment. [24]Includes optical goods. [25]Establishments employing 10 or more persons. [26]Private establishments employing 10 or more persons, and all public establishments. [27]Includes metal furniture. [28]351 includes 352, 353, and 354. [29]383 includes 385. [30]Ethiopia includes Eritrea. [31]Processed fish only. [32]Ship repair only. [33]369 includes 371. [34]Establishments employing five or more persons. [35]33 includes 32. [36]36 includes 37 and 38. [37]Former West Germany only. [38]381 includes 36 and 37. [39]Value of manufactured exports. [40]Includes public utilities. [41]Value added of assembled

refined petroleum and products	rubber products	plastic products	(36) pottery, china, and glass	bricks, tiles, cement, etc.	(37) iron and steel	non-ferrous metals	(38) fabricated metal products	nonelectrical machinery	office equip., computers	electrical equip.	radio, television	transport equip. exc. motor vehicles	motor vehicles	professional equip.	(39) jewelry, musical instruments	country
(353+354)	(355)	(356)	(361+362)	(369)	(371)	(372)	(381)	(382 exc. 3825)	(3825)	(383 exc. 3832)	(3832)	(384 exc. 3843)	(3843)	(385)	(390)	
1.2	1.8	3.0	0.5	6.3	0.7	2.0	5.6	——1.2——		——2.2——		——10.7——		—	0.3	Nigeria
...	50	50	——4.9——											...		Northern Mariana Islands
1.5	0.2	2.0	0.7	2.0	2.3	4.0	5.6	12.9	0.5	3.2	2.4	6.6	1.0	0.8	0.8	Norway
9.5[51]	...	...	...	...	...	...	...	...	...	...	...	...	...	...	...	Oman
6.9	0.9	0.5	1.1	7.9	6.8	—	1.0	——1.8——		——3.2——		——3.6——		0.3	0.4	Pakistan
3.8	0.3	3.9	0.9	5.4	0.7	0.0	3.6	——0.1——		——0.5——		——0.2——		0.4	0.6	Panama
—	—	0.4	0.7	1.6			6.7	——1.3——		——0.7——		——2.4——			...	Papua New Guinea
9.8	—	1.9	0.3	4.1	—	0.3	1.9	——0.2——				——0.9——		—	0.5	Paraguay
1.0	——1.9——		——5.1——		2.1	18.4	1.5	——0.9——		——2.1——		——2.1——		9	1.5[9]	Peru
10.8	1.3	16	——3.1——		——2.5——		2.4	——1.1——		——4.0——		——1.2——		9	1.8[9]	Philippines
7.2	0.9	1.2	1.5	2.6	8.2	4.1	4.7	11.0	0.3	3.7	2.5	4.6	3.5	0.8	1.1	Poland
2.9	0.9	2.4	4.0	6.1	2.7	0.5	4.7	——2.6——		——6.9——		——4.1——		0.4	0.2	Portugal
0.6	——1.3——		——1.4——		——0.3——		0.9	——5.4——		——11.3——		——0.3——		7.7	0.9	Puerto Rico
40.5	0.1	0.5	——3.0——		9.6	...	——2.6——								0.1	Qatar
—	—	50	3.1[54]	15.1	—	—	10.2	——6.3——						—	—	Réunion
3.6	2.1	0.6	1.8	3.3	7.2	1.7	4.3	10.9	0.3	——4.7——		3.9	4.1	1.7	0.7	Romania
4.2	1.1	0.6	1.0	3.5	3.1	1.6	2.3	——26.1——		——3.0——		——3.8——		3.2	3.7	Russia[55]
...	...	...	—	13.3			9.4	——0.6——		——0.6——		——0.6——		...	...	Rwanda
...	...	2.1	...	...	...	...	...	...	...	——7.5——		...	...	...	...	St. Kitts and Nevis
																St. Lucia
...	...	0.4	...	...	...	...	6.6[58]	...	...	58	58	...	...	...	...	St. Vincent
...	...	...	...	...	...	...	...	...	...	...	...	...	...	...	...	San Marino
...	...	...	...	...	...	...	...	...	...	...	...	...	...	...	...	São Tomé and Príncipe
17.1	0.1	2.7	0.9	12.6	6.4	0.3	5.0	——1.1——		——2.0——		——0.6——		0.1	0.7	Saudi Arabia
10.3	—	—	—	8.0	—	—	6.7	——2.7——		——1.1——		——5.5——		—	—	Senegal
			——5.2——		—	—				——2.4——				...		Seychelles
			——6.8[59]——		——59——			4 1							7.7	Sierra Leone
7.0	0.3	2.3	0.3	1.5	0.8	0.3	6.4	——5.0——		3.8	40.9	——7.2——		1.8	0.7	Singapore
2.6	8	8	1.0	3.3	12.6	2.7	10.7[58]	——14.0——		58	58				...	Slovakia
0.6	1.5	1.8	——4.5——		3.9	1.3	6.2	——8.0——		——8.7——		1.5	2.7	0.4	1.4	Slovenia
—	—	10.7	—	2.1	—	0.3	1.5	...		...		...		...	...	Solomon Islands
61	1.6	2.6	1.4	3.2	8.8	3.6	6.4	——6.1——		——4.3——		1.6	6.0	0.8	1.7	South Africa
2.0	1.7	2.8	1.8	5.5	4.3	1.5	6.2	6.1	0.4	4.2	2.6	2.8	9.0	0.4	1.0	Spain
10.6	5.0	0.9	1.1	2.8	0.8	0.3	1.5	0.9	—	0.6	0.1	1.7			1.0	Sri Lanka
2.0	2.0	1.1	0.3	1.1	—	4.5	4.0	...		——2.5——		——1.7——		0.3	0.3	Sudan, The
—	—	0.2	——7.6——		—	—	—	...	...	...		1.4	—	0.2	0.3	Suriname
			——2.3——		—	—	2.4	——0.2——							0.9	Swaziland
3.0	0.8	1.5	0.8	2.2	4.1	1.2	8.6	11.1	1.0	3.4	4.4	2.9	9.7	2.3	0.3	Sweden
2.9	1.2	3.2	1.1	1.6	2.0	1.7	6.7	——13.2——		——10.0——		——1.8——		4.8	0.3	Switzerland
			——7.5——		——1.2——			——12.0——						—	0.3	Syria
7.6	1.4	6.0	——4.0——		——6.4——		5.8	——4.5——		——13.6——		——7.8——		1.3	3.5	Taiwan
0.4	8	8	...	3.5	——11.8——			——10.0——							...	Tajikistan
3.4	1.1	1.1	—	4.6	2.3	1.1	4.6	——1.1——		——1.1——		——5.7——		—	—	Tanzania
8.6	3.1	0.5	2.9	3.4	2.1	0.6	2.9	0.4	—	2.3	3.1	3.1	2.9	0.4	1.4	Thailand
			——10.9——		2.2	—	4.3	...	...	...	...	...	...	...	...	Togo
			——3.8——		—	—	7.0	——0.4——		...		3.3	—	...	8.3[63]	Tonga
16.9	64	64	——64——					——14.2——						—	...	Trinidad and Tobago
0.9	1.2	2.2	1.6	15.2	8.9	0.7	9.4	——0.2——		——5.3——		——5.3——		0.1	0.6	Tunisia
17.2	1.6	1.1	3.4	4.7	4.9	2.0	3.1	4.9	0.1	2.5	2.6	0.7	5.3	0.3	0.3	Turkey
21.7	8	8	...	6.3	...	...	——5.4——							...	...	Turkmenistan
—	—	—	—	—	—	—	—	—	—	—	—	—	—	—	...	Tuvalu
—	—	—	0.7	6.6	1.5	—	—	—	—	—	—	—	—	—	...	Uganda
...	8	8	...	4.2	11.2	1.1	——29.9——								...	Ukraine
...	...	...	...	...	...	...	...	...	...	...	...	...	...	...	...	United Arab Emirates
1.4	1.3	3.3	1.7	2.6	2.1	0.8	5.4	11.8	2.1	4.1	5.0	6.4	4.5	1.7	1.2	United Kingdom
1.8	1.2	2.7	0.9	1.6	2.1	1.4	5.8	7.4	2.1	3.3	4.8	6.0	5.6	6.3	1.5	United States
10.4	3.0	2.0	1.5	1.8	0.9	0.2	3.2	0.4	0.1	3.2	0.3	1.4	5.5	0.1	0.4	Uruguay
4.4	8	8	...	3.8	——5.0——		——10.1——								...	Uzbekistan
...	...	...	...	...	——11.1——										...	Vanuatu
20.6	1.4	1.9	1.8	3.4	5.4	1.8	5.3	——2.1——		——2.4——		——2.3——		0.3	1.3	Venezuela
5.7	...	...	——16.8[69]——		——1.6——		——15.8——								...	Vietnam
...	...	...	...	...	...	...	...	...	...	...	...	...	...	...	...	Virgin Islands (U.S.)
...	...	...	...	...	...	...	...	...	...	...	...	...	...	...	...	West Bank
...	...	...	...	...	...	...	...	...	...	...	...	...	...	...	...	Western Sahara
—	—	—	——15.3——		—	—	8.7	—	—	—	—	—	—	—	—	Western Samoa
1.9	2.2	...		4.3	3.0	1.8	9.0	——6.7——		——4.8——		——10.8——		...	1.8	Yemen[71]
1.0			—	2.1	2.1	1.0	3.1	——3.1——		——2.1——		——3.1——		...	0.3	Yugoslavia
0.9	2.2	1.2	0.5	5.3	0.7	0.1	8.0	——1.9——		——1.7——		——3.8——		—	0.1	Zaire
11	2.0	3.0	0.5	2.8	17.8	0.5	5.3	——1.0——		2.5	0.4	0.7	3.2	0.1	0.5	Zimbabwe

reexports only. [42]Establishments with electric power and 10 or more employees, or without electric power and 20 or more employees. [40]Establishments employing three or more persons. [44]351 includes 353 + 354 [45]Establishments employing four or more persons. [46]Excludes metal furniture. [47]33 includes 34. [48]Includes production of *maquiladores* (foreign-owned assembly plants). [49]33 includes 341. [50]322 and 323 + 324 includes 355 + 356. [51]Refined petroleum only [52]Establishments employing six or more persons. [53]341 includes 356. [54]361 + 362 includes 351. [55]Data refer to former U.S.S.R. [56]In constant U.S.$ of 1980. [57]Selected industries only. [58]381 includes 383. [59]36 includes 37. [60]Excludes Bophuthatswana, Ciskei, Venda, and Transkei, formerly nominally independent republics officially reincorporated into South Africa as of March April 1994. [61]352 includes 353 + 354. [62]Tongatapu Island only. [63]39 includes 332 and 341. [64]351 includes 352, 355, 356, and 36. [65]Private establishments employing 25 or more persons, and all public establishments. [66]Includes electricity. [67]Includes mining. [68]32 includes 342. [69]36 includes 33 and 341. [70]Data withheld for reasons of confidentiality. [71]Former Yemen Arab Republic only.

Energy

This table provides data about the commercial energy supplies (reserves, production, consumption, and trade) of the various countries of the world, together with data about oil pipeline networks and traffic. Many of the data and concepts used in this table are adapted from the United Nations' *Energy Statistics Yearbook*.

Electricity. Total installed electrical power capacity comprises the sum of the rated power capacities of all main and auxiliary generators in a country. "Total installed capacity" (kW) is multiplied by 8,760 hours per year to yield "Total production capacity" (kW-hr).

Production of electricity comprises the total gross production of electricity by publicly or privately owned enterprises and also that generated by industrial establishments for their own use, but usually excludes consumption by the utility itself. Measured in millions of kilowatt-hours (kW-hr), annual production of electricity ranges generally between 50% and 60% of total production capacity. The data are further analyzed by type of generation: fossil fuels, hydroelectric power, and nuclear fuel.

The great majority of the world's electrical and other energy needs are met by the burning of fossil hydrocarbon solids, liquids, and gases, either for thermal generation of electricity or in internal combustion engines. Many renewable and nontraditional sources of energy are being developed worldwide (wood, biogenic gases and liquids, tidal, wave, and wind power, geothermal and photothermal [solar] energy, and so on), but collectively these sources are still negligible in the world's total energy consumption.

For this reason only hydroelectric and nuclear generation are considered here separately with fossil fuels.

Trade in electrical energy refers to the transfer of generated electrical output via an international grid. Total electricity consumption (residential and nonresidential) is equal to total electricity requirements less transformation and distribution losses.

Coal. The term coal, as used in the table, comprises all grades of anthracite, bituminous, subbituminous, and lignite that have acquired or may in the future, by reason of new technology or changed market prices, acquire an economic value. These types of coal may be differentiated according to heat content (density) and content of impurities. Most coal reserve data are based on proven recoverable reserves only, of all grades of coal. Exceptions are footnoted, with proven in-place reserves reported only when recoverable reserves are unknown. Production figures include deposits removed from both surface and underground workings as well as quantities used by the producers themselves or issued to the miners. Wastes recovered from mines or nearby preparation plants are excluded from production figures.

Natural gas. This term refers to any combustible gas (usually chiefly methane) of natural origin from underground sources. The data for production cover, to the extent possible, gas obtained from gas fields, petroleum fields, or coal mines that is actually collected and marketed. (Much natural gas in Middle Eastern and North African oil fields is

Energy

country	electricity installed capacity, 1992 ('000 kW)	electricity production, 1992 capacity ('000,000 kW-hr)	electricity production, 1992 amount ('000,000 kW-hr)	power source, 1992 fossil fuel (%)	power source, 1992 hydro-power (%)	power source, 1992 nuclear fuel (%)	trade, 1992 exports ('000,000 kW-hr)	trade, 1992 imports ('000,000 kW-hr)	consumption amount, 1992 ('000,000 kW-hr)	consumption per capita, 1992 (kW-hr)	consumption resi-dential, 1990 (%)	consumption non-resi-dential, 1990 (%)	coal reserves, latest ('000,000 metric tons)	coal pro-duction, 1992 ('000 metric tons)	coal con-sump-tion, 1992 ('000 metric tons)
Afghanistan	494	4,327	703	32.0	68.0	—	—	131	834	44	...	...	66	8	8
Albania	770	6,745	3,357	3.9	96.1	—	560	—	2,797	844	...	...	15[1]	366	576
Algeria	5,369	47,032	18,286	98.9	—	—	1,061	133	17,358	659	...	...	43	15	1,315
American Samoa	33	289	90	100.0	—	—	—	—	90	1,800	27.5[3]	72.5[3]	...	...	...
Andorra	...	...	...	...	...	...	...	...	...	...	...	...	...	...	...
Angola	617	5,405	1,855	25.9	74.1	—	—	—	1,855	188	27.5[2]	72.5[2]	...	—	—
Antigua and Barbuda	26	228	95	100.0	—	—	—	—	95	1,439	42.4[4]	57.6[4]	...	—	—
Argentina	17,326	151,776	56,273	52.6	34.8	12.6	10	2,602	58,865	1,778	45.9	54.1	130	215	1,393
Armenia	4,200	36,792	9,000	100.0	—	—	—	—	9,000	2,580	...	...	...	...	141
Aruba	90	788	350	100.0	—	—	—	—	350	5,645	...	...	...	...	...
Australia	36,117	316,385	159,116	90.4	9.6	—	—	—	159,116	9,043	30.1[2]	69.9[2]	90,940	225,788	103,406
Austria	17,231	150,944	51,180	29.5	70.5	—	8,621	9,175	51,734	6,653	23.1[2]	83.4[2]	59	1,771	5,000
Azerbaijan	5,220	45,727	20,000	100.0	...	...	—	—	20,000	2,746	...	...	...	—	27
Bahamas, The	401	3,513	975	100.0	—	—	—	—	975	3,693	33.6[4]	66.4[4]	...	...	...
Bahrain	1,050	9,198	3,510	100.0	—	—	—	—	3,510	6,585	...	...	...	—	—
Bangladesh	2,738	23,985	9,554	91.7	8.3	—	—	—	9,554	80	43.8	56.2	1,054[1]	—	338
Barbados	140	1,226	537	100.0	—	—	—	—	537	2,073	33.7	66.3	...	...	...
Belarus	7,005	61,363	37,600	99.9	0.1	...	3,685	13,762	47,677	4,631	...	...	...	—	1,600
Belgium	14,038	122,973	72,259	38.2	1.6	60.2	5,721	5,849	72,387	7,240	26.9[8]	73.1[8]	410	1,197	14,387
Belize	23	201	110	100.0	—	—	—	—	110	556	...	...	...	...	...
Benin	15	131	5	100.0	—	—	—	198	203	41	...	...	...	...	...
Bermuda	140	1,226	517	100.0	—	—	—	—	517	8,339	39.6	60.4	...	...	...
Bhutan	361	3,162	1,627	0.4	99.6	—	1,445	3	185	115	29.2[3]	69.8[3]	...	2	18
Bolivia	726	6,360	2,412	44.0	56.0	—	3	15	2,424	322	76.1	23.9	...	—	—
Bosnia and Herzegovina	3,400	29,784	13,000	73.1	26.9	—	...	...	13,000	2,921	21.8	78.2	...	15,000	15,000
Botswana	10	10	522[10, 11]	10	10	10	10	82[10, 11]	10	10	...	...	3,500	10	10
Brazil	55,129	482,930	241,241	6.7	92.6	0.7	8	24,148	265,381	1,722	46.2	53.8	2,359	4,731	16,041
Brunei	382	3,346	1,257	100.0	—	—	—	—	1,257	4,656	55.3[4]	44.7[4]	...	—	—
Bulgaria	11,025	96,579	35,587	61.7	5.8	32.5	584	3,289	38,292	4,277	41.2[3]	58.8[3]	3,730	30,340	33,621
Burkina Faso	59	517	195	100.0	—	—	—	—	195	20	...	...	...	...	...
Burundi	43	377	107	1.9	98.1	—	—	23	130	22	...	...	...	...	...
Cambodia	35	307	150	53.3	46.7	—	—	—	150	17	...	...	...	—	—
Cameroon	627	5,493	2,720	2.8	97.2	—	—	—	2,720	223	...	...	...	1	1
Canada	108,090	946,868	520,857	23.8	60.8	15.4	31,528	6,477	495,806	18,117	28.8[4]	71.2[4]	8,623	65,362	52,386
Cape Verde	7	61	37	100.0	—	—	—	—	37	96	...	...	...	—	—
Central African Republic	43	377	96	18.7	81.3	—	—	—	96	30	...	...	4	...	...
Chad	29	254	85	100.0	—	—	—	—	85	15	...	...	...	...	...
Chile	4,809	42,127	22,362	33.7	66.3	—	—	—	22,362	1,644	32.7	67.3	1,181	1,668	2,685
China	162,000	1,419,120	753,940	82.4	17.6	—	—	4,980	758,920	650	7.7	92.3	114,500	1,116,369	1,090,809
Colombia	10,218	89,510	35,993	37.8	62.2	—	—	338	36,331	1,087	69.8	30.2	4,539	23,776	6,049
Comoros	5	44	16	87.5	12.5	—	—	—	16	27	...	...	...	...	...
Congo	118	1,034	428	0.7	99.3	—	—	108	536	226	...	...	...	—	—
Costa Rica	1,042	9,128	4,144	14.1	85.9	—	98	34	4,080	1,278	72.1	27.9	...	—	—
Côte d'Ivoire	1,173	10,275	1,850	42.4	57.6	—	—	—	1,850	143	29.6	70.4	...	—	—
Croatia	3,494	30,607	8,894	51.2	48.8	—	632	3,532	11,794	2,419	50.6	49.4	...	120	1,065
Cuba	3,988	34,935	12,492	99.3	0.7	—	—	—	12,492	1,155	56.0	44.0	—	—	151
Cyprus	546	4,783	2,404	100.0	—	—	—	—	2,404	3,358	77.3	22.7	—	—	26
Czech Republic	14,488	126,915	59,132	76.5	2.8	20.7	3,340	304	56,096	5,391	23.6[3, 12]	76.4[3, 12]	5,370[12]	88,975	76,097
Denmark	10,031	87,872	30,849	97.0	0.1	2.9[13]	4,901	8,647	34,595	6,707	32.5[8]	67.5[8]	63[5]	—	11,044
Djibouti	85	745	180	100.0	—	—	—	—	180	385	...	...	...	—	—
Dominica	8	70	31	48.4	51.6	—	—	—	31	431	53.5[4]	46.5[4]	...	...	...
Dominican Republic	1,447	12,676	5,330	84.1	15.9	—	—	—	5,330	713	...	...	...	—	58
Ecuador	2,229	19,526	7,165	30.9	69.1	—	—	—	7,165	648	68.2	31.8	24	—	—
Egypt	11,829	103,622	45,000	78.4	21.6	—	—	—	45,000	821	29.6	70.4	53	—	1,155
El Salvador	751	6,579	2,457	25.2	58.9	15.9[13]	46	98	2,509	465	68.8	31.2	...	—	—

flared [burned] because it is often not economical to capture and market it.) Manufactured gas is generally a by-product of industrial operations such as gasworks, coke ovens, and blast furnaces. It is usually burned at the point of production and rarely enters the marketplace. Production of manufactured gas is, therefore, only reported as a percentage of domestic gas consumption.

Crude petroleum. Crude petroleum is the liquid product obtained from oil wells; the term also includes shale oil, tar sand extract, and field or lease condensate. Production and consumption data in the table refer, so far as possible, to the same year so that the relationship between national production and consumption patterns can be clearly seen; both are given in barrels.

Proven reserves are that oil remaining underground in known fields whose existence has been "proved" by the evaluation of nearby producing wells or by seismic tests in sedimentary strata known to contain crude petroleum, and that is judged recoverable within the limits of present technology and economic conditions (prices). The published proven reserve figures do not necessarily reflect the true reserves of a country, because government authorities or corporations often have political or economic motives for withholding or altering such data.

The estimated exhaustion rate of petroleum reserves is an extrapolated ratio of published proven reserves to the current rate of withdrawal/production. Present world published proven reserves will last about 40 to 45 years at the present rate of withdrawal, but there are large country-to-country variations above or below the average.

Data on petroleum and refined product pipelines are provided because of the great importance to both domestic and international energy markets of this means of bringing these energy sources from their production or transportation points to refineries, intermediate consumption and distribution points, and final consumers. Their traffic may represent a very significant fraction of the total movement of goods within a country. Available data for petroleum pipelines are often incomplete and their basis varies internationally, some countries reporting only international shipments, others reporting domestic shipments of 50 kilometres or more, and so on.

For data in the hydrocarbons portions of the table (coal, natural gas, and petroleum), extensive use has been made of a variety of international sources, such as those of the United Nations, the International Energy Agency (of the Organization for Economic Cooperation and Development), the World Energy Conference (in its *Survey of Energy Resources* [triennial]); the U.S. Department of Energy (especially its *International Energy Annual*); and of various industry surveys, such as those published by the *International Petroleum Encyclopedia*, the *Oil and Gas Journal*, and *World Oil*.

natural gas						crude petroleum							country
published proven reserves, 1994 ('000,000,-000 cu m)	production		consumption			reserves, 1994		produc-tion, 1993 ('000,000 barrels)	consump-tion, 1992 ('000,000 barrels)	refining capacity, 1994 ('000 barrels per day)	pipelines (latest)		
	natural gas, 1993 ('000,000 cu m)	manufac-tured gas, 1992 (% of total gas con-sumption)	amount, 1992 ('000,000 cu m)	resi-dential, 1990 (%)	non-resi-dential, 1990 (%)	published proven ('000,000 barrels)	years to exhaust proven reserves				length (km)	traffic ('000,000 metric ton-km)	
99	294	...	189	...	...	165	...	3	8	40	...	...	Afghanistan
10	136	...	246	...	...	165	55	3	8	40	200	...	Albania
3,625	50,591	27.3	19,922	26.8[2]	70.2[2]	9,200	34	274	169	530	6,910	...	Algeria
...	...	...	...	...	...	...	...	—	—	—	—	...	American Samoa
—	—	—	—	—	—	—	—	—	—	—	—	—	Andorra
51	561	10.4	167	...	...	1,500	8	182	10	32	179	...	Angola
...	...	...	...	...	...	...	...	—	—	—	—	—	Antigua and Barbuda
750	17,282	10.2	28,256	49.2	50.8	1,570	7	210	182	709	6,990	...	Argentina
...	170[5]	...	1,860	...	...	...	...	—	...	...	...	...	Armenia
...	...	...	...	...	...	...	...	—	3	...	—	—	Aruba
555	24,052	28.8	17,859	...	...	1,615	9	187	203	705	3,000	...	Australia
19	1,450	13.7	8,888	25.7[2]	74.3[2]	95	11	9	62	210	725	5,319	Austria
170[6]	11,655[7]	...	11,523	...	...	3,300[6]	38[6]	75	92	406	1,760	1,705	Azerbaijan
...	—	—	...	...	...	...	...	—	...	...	—	—	Bahamas, The
167	5,222	5.9	5,177	...	...	70	5	13	95	250	72	...	Bahrain
714	6,046	0.2	5,570	34.2	65.8	4	10	0.4	8	31	—	—	Bangladesh
0.2	20	7.0	22	62.6	37.4	4	10	0.4	1	3	—	—	Barbados
...	210[7]	...	15,907	...	...	...	...	15	158	832	2,570	...	Belarus
—	145	19.8	13,230	43.4[8]	56.6[8]	...	...	—	212[9]	607	1,328	1,011	Belgium
...	...	...	...	...	...	...	...	—	—	—	—	—	Belize
—	...	...	...	...	...	20	20	1.0	—	—	—	—	Benin
...	...	...	...	...	...	...	...	—	—	—	—	—	Bermuda
...	...	...	...	...	...	...	...	—	—	—	—	—	Bhutan
111	3,067	26.6	674	—	100.0	108	15	7	8	45	2,380	...	Bolivia
...	—	7.4	436	...	...	...	...	—	15	...	174	—	Bosnia and Herzegovina
...	...	10	...	...	...	...	...	—	10	...	—	—	Botswana
137	3,330	59.9	3,731	—	100.0	3,600	16	230	429	1,253	5,804	...	Brazil
396	8,484	0.8	2,207	...	...	1,350	23	58	0.01	9	553	...	Brunei
7	11	10.8	4,848	...	...	15	38	0.4	18	300	718	...	Bulgaria
...	...	...	...	...	...	...	...	—	—	—	—	—	Burkina Faso
...	...	...	...	...	...	...	...	—	—	—	—	—	Burundi
...	...	...	...	...	...	...	...	—	—	—	—	—	Cambodia
110	—	100.0	...	...	...	400	9	43	5	42	—	—	Cameroon
2,685	155,016	23.4	69,413	20.6[2]	79.4[2]	5,096	8	615	469	1,880	23,564	99,908	Canada
...	...	...	...	...	...	...	...	—	—	—	—	—	Capo Verde
...	...	...	...	...	...	...	...	—	—	—	—	—	Central African Republic
...	...	...	...	...	...	...	...	—	—	—	—	—	Chad
110	1,153	30.3	2,093	23.4	76.6	300	60	5	46	165	1,540	...	Chile
1,671	16,602	50.2	15,753	12.2	87.8	24,000	23	1,067	983	2,200	10,800	...	China
283	4,066	27.7	4,307	12.8	87.2	1,935	12	164	83	249	4,935	...	Colombia
...	...	...	...	...	...	...	...	—	—	—	—	—	Comoros
76	2[7]	61.3	3	...	...	830	11	73	9	21	25	...	Congo
...	—	10.0	—	—	—	—	...	—	4	15	176	...	Costa Rica
14	—	60.0	—	—	—	50	250	0.2	15	63	—	—	Côte d'Ivoire
35	1,900	13.6	2,511	...	...	151	10	15	29	293	690	3,482	Croatia
3	31[5]	85.9	37	3.4	96.6	100	11	9	37	280	—	—	Cuba
...	...	61.8	—	—	—	...	...	—	5	22	—	—	Cyprus
13[12]	699[12]	27.3	7,606	...	...	15[12]	21	0.7[12]	45	307	...	...	Czech Republic
121	4,188	18.2	2,284	...	...	780	13	59	64	184	688	1,898	Denmark
...	...	...	...	...	...	...	...	—	—	—	—	—	Djibouti
...	...	...	...	...	...	...	...	—	—	—	—	—	Dominica
...	...	18.9	...	...	...	...	...	—	14	48	104	...	Dominican Republic
108	102	42.7	100	...	...	2,014	16	124	44	148	2,158	...	Ecuador
436	8,690	12.3	8,396	5.3	94.7	6,300	19	326	176	532	1,767	...	Egypt
—	—	47.3	—	—	—	...	...	—	6	18	—	—	El Salvador

Energy (continued)

country	electricity installed capacity, 1992 ('000 kW)	production, 1992 capacity ('000,000 kW-hr)	production, 1992 amount ('000,000 kW-hr)	power source, 1992 fossil fuel (%)	power source, 1992 hydro-power (%)	power source, 1992 nuclear fuel (%)	trade, 1992 exports ('000,000 kW-hr)	trade, 1992 imports ('000,000 kW-hr)	consumption amount, 1992 ('000,000 kW-hr)	consumption per capita, 1992 (kW-hr)	consumption resi-dential, 1990 (%)	consumption non-resi-dential, 1990 (%)	coal reserves, latest ('000,000 metric tons)	coal pro-duction, 1992 ('000 metric tons)	coal consump-tion, 1992 ('000 metric tons)
Equatorial Guinea	5	44	19	89.5	10.5	—	—	—	19	51	...	...	...	...	...
Eritrea	...	...	...	...	...	...	...	...	...	...	...	...	...	...	...
Estonia	3,405	29,828	11,831	99.9	0.1	...	3,492	...	8,339	5,271	...	...	...	18,849	20,760
Ethiopia	464	4,065	1,257	7.2	87.4	5.4[13]	—	...	1,257	24	...	...	11	—	—
Faeroe Islands	91	797	205	63.4	36.6	—	—	—	205	4,362	...	...	...	—	—
Fiji	200	1,752	477	18.2	81.8	—	—	—	477	645	10.5	89.5	...	—	20
Finland	13,356	116,999	57,431	40.1	26.4	33.5	673	9,067	65,825	13,144	18.6[2]	81.3[2]	...	—	4,980
France	105,249[14]	921,981[14]	462,263[14]	11.1[14]	15.7[14]	73.2[14]	58,533[14]	4,737[14]	408,467[14]	7,140[14]	30.3[8]	69.7[8]	210	11,056[14]	28,565[14]
French Guiana	175	1,533	450	100.0	—	—	—	—	450	4,327	...	58.7[2, 15]	...	—	—
French Polynesia	79	692	275	74.5	25.5	—	—	—	275	1,329	...	...	...	—	—
Gabon	310	2,716	919	22.5	77.5	—	—	—	919	743	55.1	44.9	...	—	...
Gambia, The	29	254	71	100.0	—	—	—	—	71	78	...	...	...	—	...
Gaza Strip	...	...	...	...	...	...	...	...	...	...	...	...	...	...	...
Georgia	4,275	37,449	9,300	100.0	...	...	—	—	9,300	1,700	...	...	...	500	736
Germany	115,015	1,007,531	537,134	66.5	3.9	29.6	33,738	28,418	531,814	6,627	26.3[8, 16]	73.7[8, 16]	80,069	313,960	327,500
Ghana	1,187	10,398	6,152	0.7	99.3	—	286	4	5,870	368	...	...	...	—	3
Gibraltar	33	289	88	100.0	—	—	—	—	88	2,839	...	...	...	—	...
Greece	8,968	78,560	37,410	93.6	6.4	—	—	362	967	38,015	3,734	30.6[8]	69.4[8]	3,000	55,051	56,424
Greenland	96	841	216	100.0	—	—	—	—	216	3,789	35.3[17]	64.7[17]	183	...	...
Grenada	9	79	62	100.0	—	—	—	—	62	681	46.8[4]	53.2[4]	...	...	...
Guadeloupe	319	2,794	690	100.0	—	—	—	—	690	1,725	...	32.9[15, 17]	...	...	...
Guam	302	2,646	800	100.0	—	—	—	—	800	5,755	39.7	60.3	...	...	...
Guatemala	696	6,097	2,340	10.3	89.7	—	—	—	2,340	240	27.0[1]	73.0[2]	...	...	...
Guernsey	...	...	227	100.0	—	—	...	...	227	4,997	...	...	...	...	...
Guinea	176	1,542	531	65.0	35.0	—	—	—	531	87	...	...	...	...	...
Guinea-Bissau	11	96	41	100.0	—	—	—	—	41	41	...	...	...	...	...
Guyana	114	999	235	97.8	2.2	—	—	—	235	291	32.5[18]	67.5[18]	13[1]	...	...
Haiti	153	1,340	475	60.0	40.0	—	—	—	475	70	...	...	21[1]	...	...
Honduras	290	2,540	2,313	8.6	91.4	—	5	200	2,508	459	51.7	48.3	...	...	10,214
Hong Kong	8,932	78,244	34,914	100.0	—	—	4,963	—	29,951	5,164	70.8	29.2	...	—	...
Hungary	6,741	59,051	31,514	55.3	0.5	44.2	1,521	4,987	35,080	3,337	30.7[3]	69.3[3]	4,461	15,812	17,531
Iceland	1,068	9,356	4,541	0.1	94.8	5.1[13]	—	—	4,541	17,465	20.9[2]	79.1[2]	...	—	50
India	81,204	711,347	327,913	76.6	21.3	2.1	73	1,500	329,340	374	45.8	54.2	62,548	254,600	256,750
Indonesia	12,005	105,164	45,760	80.4	19.1	0.5[13]	—	—	45,760	239	55.0	45.0	32,063	21,146	5,520
Iran	19,080	167,141	53,200	87.8	12.2	—	—	—	53,200	864	21.1[11]	78.9[11]	193	1,500	2,000
Iraq	7,168	62,792	25,300	97.2	2.8	—	—	—	25,300	1,312	...	...	...	—	3,091
Ireland	3,933	34,453	16,011	93.4	6.6	—	—	—	16,011	4,593	41.4[8]	58.6[8]	14	1	...
Isle of Man	...	...	188[4]	100.0	—	—	—	350	172[3]	2,530[3]	48.1[8]	51.9[8]	...	—	4,945
Israel	4,140	36,266	24,475	99.9	0.1	—	—	—	24,125	4,702	68.4	31.6	34	825[19]	18,389[19]
Italy	61,625[19]	539,835[19]	226,243[19]	78.2[19]	20.2[19]	1.6[4, 19]	647[19]	35,947[19]	261,543[19]	4,525[19]	25.0[8]	75.0[8]	...	—	66
Jamaica	732	6,412	2,735	95.2	4.8	—	—	—	2,735	1,108	25.6	74.4	...	—	66
Japan	205,144	1,797,061	895,336	64.9	10.0	25.1	—	—	895,336	7,192	20.8[2]	79.2[2]	844	7,613	116,813
Jersey	...	...	440	...	...	...	...	...	440	6,579	...	...	...	...	...
Jordan	1,048	9,180	4,422	99.7	0.3	—	—	—	4,422	1,031	60.0	40.0	...	...	...
Kazakhstan	21,250	186,150	81,293	100.0	...	...	...	...	81,293	4,768	...	...	25,000	131,033	91,742
Kenya	805	7,052	3,215	4.5	87.0	8.5[13]	—	240	3,455	137	35.1	64.9	...	—	110
Kiribati	2	18	7	100.0	—	—	—	—	7	95	...	...	...	—	...
Korea, North	9,500	83,220	38,000	36.8	63.2	—	—	—	38,000	1,680	...	...	600	94,000	96,050
Korea, South	26,945	236,038	147,843	58.5	3.3	38.2	—	—	147,843	3,348	34.0	66.0	203	11,970	39,814
Kuwait	7,070	61,933	11,200	100.0	—	—	—	—	11,200	5,685	92.1	7.9	...	—	...
Kyrgyzstan	3,504	30,695	11,892	22.6	77.4	...	7,406	5,318	9,804	2,170	...	...	...	3,262	3,577
Laos	256	2,243	910	4.7	95.3	—	638	26	298	67	...	...	...	1	1
Latvia	2,033	17,809	3,834	34.2	65.8	—	2	4,080	7,912	2,953	...	...	...	—	663
Lebanon	1,220	10,687	2,500	86.0	14.0	—	—	40	2,540	895	...	...	...	—	...
Lesotho	[10]	[10]	[10]	[10]	[10]	[10]	[10]	[10]	[10]	[10]	...	...	...	[10]	[10]
Liberia	332	2,908	460	65.2	34.8	—	—	—	460	167	...	...	...	—	5
Libya	4,600	40,296	16,950	100.0	—	—	—	—	16,950	3,477	...	...	—	—	21
Liechtenstein	[21]	[21]	[21]	[21]	[21]	[21]	[21]	[21]	[21]	[21]	...	...	...	...	...
Lithuania	6,129	53,690	18,707	20.1	1.7	78.2	10,642	5,338	13,403	3,569	...	...	...	...	657
Luxembourg	1,238	10,845	1,198	49.2	50.8	—	533	4,511	5,176	13,693	15.3[8]	84.7[8]	...	—	288
Macau	260	2,278	992	100.0	—	—	—	114	1,106	2,248	75.0[4]	25.0[4]	...	—	—
Macedonia	1,700	14,892	5,100	88.2	11.8	—	...	...	5,100	2,459	27.4	72.6	1,075[1]	...	...
Madagascar	220	1,927	569	43.8	56.2	—	—	—	569	44	...	...	12	—	—
Malawi	185	1,621	792	2.0	98.0	—	—	—	792	76	52.8	47.2	4	—	12
Malaysia	6,700	58,692	32,082	84.2	15.8	—	175	159	32,066	1,706	51.6	48.4	...	190	2,225
Maldives	14	123	30	100.0	—	—	—	—	30	132	50.9[3]	49.1[3]	...	...	...
Mali	87	762	313	40.3	59.7	—	—	—	313	32	...	...	...	...	...
Malta	250	2,190	1,120	100.0	—	—	—	—	1,120	3,120	25.1[11]	74.9[11]	...	—	300
Marshall Islands	99[7]	867[7]	...	...	...	...	...	...	...	...	...	...	...	...	...
Martinique	110	964	735	100.0	—	—	—	—	735	1,997	...	40.9[15, 17]	...	...	...
Mauritania	105	920	146	82.2	17.8	—	—	—	146	68	...	...	...	—	6
Mauritius	336	2,943	925	87.8	12.2	—	—	—	925	842	...	...	...	—	62
Mayotte	8	70	18	100.0	—	—	...	...	18	180	...	...	...	...	...
Mexico	28,783	252,139	121,762	75.1	17.3	7.6[13]	2,042	989	120,709	1,369	17.4[11]	82.6[11]	1,720	6,539	6,932
Micronesia	...	...	...	...	...	...	...	...	...	...	...	...	...	...	...
Moldova	3,086	27,033	11,248	97.7	2.3	—	4,636	4,609	11,221	2,572	...	...	...	—	2,409
Monaco	[14]	[14]	[14]	[14]	[14]	[14]	[14]	[14]	[14]	[14]	...	...	...	[14]	[14]
Mongolia	901	7,893	3,300	100.0	—	—	—	70	3,370	1,459	29.8[3]	70.2[3]	24,000[1]	7,535	7,035
Morocco	2,620	22,951	10,325	90.5	9.5	—	—	932	11,257	428	66.6	33.4	45	576	1,791
Mozambique	2,358	20,656	490	89.8	10.2	—	—	325	815	55	...	...	240	40	60
Myanmar (Burma)	1,090	9,548	2,674	52.2	47.8	—	—	—	2,674	61	...	59.1[2, 15]	2	69	73
Namibia	[10]	[10]	[10]	[10]	[10]	[10]	[10]	[10]	[10]	[10]	...	...	...	[10]	[10]
Nauru	10	88	30	100.0	—	—	—	—	30	3,000	...	...	...	...	...
Nepal	277	2,427	931	6.6	93.4	—	85	80	926	45	67.3	32.7	...	...	92
Netherlands, The	17,518	153,458	77,202	94.7	0.2	5.1	227	8,905	85,880	5,666	25.0[4]	75.0[4]	497	—	12,140

natural gas						crude petroleum					pipelines (latest)		country
published proven reserves, 1994 ('000,000,-000 cu m)	production natural gas, 1993 ('000,000 cu m)	production manufactured gas, 1992 (% of total gas consumption)	consumption amount, 1992 ('000,000 cu m)	consumption residential, 1990 (%)	consumption non-residential, 1990 (%)	reserves, 1994 published proven ('000,000 barrels)	years to exhaust proven reserves	production, 1993 ('000,000 barrels)	consumption, 1992 ('000,000 barrels)	refining capacity, 1994 ('000 barrels per day)	length (km)	traffic ('000,000 metric ton-km)	
37	...	...	...	...	...	4	3	1.5	...	—	—	—	Equatorial Guinea
						...			...	...	...	...	Eritrea
...	...	2.2	785	...	...	...	...	...	...	...	...	...	Estonia
23	—	100.0	—	...	...	...	...	—	5	18	—	—	Ethiopia
...	...	...	...	...	...	...	...	—	—	—	—	—	Faeroe Islands
—	—	...	—	—	—	...	...	—	—	—	—	—	Fiji
—	—	31.4	2,990	0.6[8]	99.4[8]	...	...	—	68	200	—	—	Finland
35	3,551	21.3[14]	33,750[14]	32.4[8]	67.6[8]	177	9	20	543[14]	1,861	7,546	22,969	France
...	...	...	...	...	...	...	...	—	—	—	—	—	French Guiana
...	...	...	...	...	...	...	...	—	—	—	—	—	French Polynesia
14	102	14.2	51	19.7	80.3	730	7	108	7	17	284	...	Gabon
—	—	—	...	...	...	...	...	—	—	—	—	—	Gambia, The
...	...	...	...	...	...	...	...	—	—	—	—	—	Gaza Strip
...	45[7]	...	4,856	...	...	...	...	0.9	6	106	670	—	Georgia
343	17,684	19.3	86,487	36.6[8,16]	63.4[8,16]	449	20	22	729	2,265	7,590	14,136	Germany
—	...	94.4	...	...	...	0.5	0.25	2	7	27	—	—	Ghana
...	...	...	...	...	...	...	...	—	—	—	—	—	Gibraltar
8	74	96.5	148	...	...	41	10	4	96	396	573	...	Greece
...	...	...	...	...	...	...	...	—	—	—	—	—	Greenland
...	...	...	...	...	...	...	...	—	—	—	—	—	Grenada
...	...	...	...	...	...	...	...	—	—	—	...	—	Guadeloupe
...	—	100.0[5]	—	...	...	...	...	—	—	—	—	—	Guam
0.3	8	6.5	9	...	...	207	104	2	6	20	275	...	Guatemala
...	...	...	...	...	...	...	...	—	—	—	—	—	Guernsey
24[6]	...	...	...	...	...	...	...	—	—	—	—	—	Guinea
...	...	...	...	...	...	...	...	—	—	—	—	—	Guinea-Bissau
...	...	...	...	...	...	...	...	—	—	—	—	—	Guyana
...	...	...	...	...	...	...	...	—	—	—	—	—	Haiti
—	—	30.7	—	—	—	...	...	—	3	14	—	—	Honduras
...	...	66.8	...	...	...	...	...	...	...	...	—	—	Hong Kong
97	5,411	11.6	8,968	14.0[8]	86.0[8]	139	12	12	57	242	1,204	3,367	Hungary
—	...	...	...	...	...	...	...	—	—	—	—	—	Iceland
718	16,347	23.2	12,102	53.7	46.3	5,921	31	191	396	1,086	5,200	...	India
1,823	53,270	16.4	20,623	—	100.0	5,779	12	483	313	860	2,961	...	Indonesia
20,671	29,082	10.1	24,786	—	100.0[4]	92,860	70	1,329	341	1,162	9,800	...	Iran
3,101	1,892	13.7	3,010	...	...	100,000	629	159	156	348	6,075	...	Iraq
17	2,500	3.6	2,220	13.9[8]	86.1[8]	...	...	—	15	53	—	—	Ireland
...	...	...	...	...	...	...	...	—	—	—	—	—	Isle of Man
0.4	23	111.5	23	—	100.0	3	30	0.1	73	208	998	...	Israel
302	19,193	13.1[19]	50,216[19]	45.6[8]	54.4[8]	621	20	31	559[19]	2,262	3,851	9,900	Italy
—	—	46.1	—	—	—	...	...	—	9	36	10	—	Jamaica
30	2,152	39.9	53,602	61.3[8]	38.7[8]	54	9	6	1,532	4,810	406	...	Japan
...	...	...	...	...	...	...	...	—	—	—	—	—	Jersey
6	207	83.7	—	—	—	1.0	10	0.1	21	100	209	...	Jordan
...	5,416	...	18,480	...	...	...	...	168	112	390	4,350	22,300	Kazakhstan
—	—	103.7	—	—	—	...	...	—	16	90	483	...	Kenya
...	...	...	...	...	...	...	...	—	—	—	—	—	Kiribati
...	...	30.5	4,915	...	...	...	...	—	18	42	37	...	Korea, North
—	—	...	...	...	...	...	...	—	511	1,147	455	...	Korea, South
1,498	4,497	52.6	2,620	25.0	75.0	96,500	141	684	117	624	917	...	Kuwait
...	68[6]	...	1,876	...	...	...	...	0.9[6]	0.2	...	...	...	Kyrgyzstan
...	...	...	...	...	...	...	...	—	—	—	136	...	Laos
...	...	...	2,729	...	...	...	...	—	...	—	1,530	...	Latvia
—	—	1.8	...	...	...	...	...	—	3	38	72	...	Lebanon
—	—	10	—	...	...	...	...	—	10	—	—	—	Lesotho
...	...	50.5[20]	...	...	...	...	...	—	—	15	—	—	Liberia
1,297	6,352	9.8	5,470	...	...	22,800	46	499	113	348	4,826	—	Libya
...	...	21	21	...	...	...	...	—	21	—	—	—	Liechtenstein
...	...	4.0	3,437	...	...	...	...	...	30	263	105	...	Lithuania
...	—	38.1	544	48.0[8]	52.0[8]	...	...	...	9	—	48	...	Luxembourg
...	...	...	...	...	...	...	...	—	—	—	—	—	Macau
...	—	8.3	256	...	...	...	...	—	8	51	—	—	Macedonia
2	—	33.6	—	...	...	...	...	—	1.4	16	—	—	Madagascar
...	—	...	...	...	...	...	...	—	—	—	—	—	Malawi
2,172	20,739	10.5	7,507	6.6	93.4	4,300	18	234	73	270	1,307	...	Malaysia
...	...	...	...	...	...	...	...	—	—	—	—	—	Maldives
...	...	...	...	...	...	...	...	—	—	—	—	—	Mali
—	...	...	...	...	...	...	...	—	—	—	—	—	Malta
...	...	...	...	...	...	...	...	—	—	—	—	—	Marshall Islands
—	—	212.6	...	...	...	...	...	—	4	16	—	—	Martinique
...	...	88.4	...	...	...	...	...	—	7	—	—	—	Mauritania
...	...	...	...	...	...	...	...	—	—	—	—	—	Mauritius
...	...	...	...	...	...	...	...	—	—	—	—	—	Mayotte
2,009	37,027	27.3	24,109	3.9[11]	96.1[11]	50,925	52	972	471	1,524	38,350	...	Mexico
...	...	...	...	...	...	...	...	—	—	—	—	—	Micronesia
...	—	...	3,652	...	...	...	...	—	52[5]	—	—	—	Moldova
...	...	14	14	...	...	...	...	—	—	—	—	—	Monaco
...	...	...	...	...	...	...	...	—	—	—	—	—	Mongolia
1	25	32.1	24	—	100.0	1.1	11	0.1	48	155	982	...	Morocco
65	—	...	—	...	...	...	...	—	...	...	595	...	Mozambique
278	833	0.5	973	—	100.0[4]	50	10	5	6	32	1,343	...	Myanmar (Burma)
147	—	10	...	...	...	...	...	—	10	—	—	—	Namibia
...	...	...	...	...	...	...	...	—	—	—	—	—	Nauru
...	...	...	...	...	...	...	...	—	—	—	—	—	Nepal
1,930	85,515	17.0	48,934	46.8[4]	53.4[4]	132	8	17	368	1,184	1,383	4,560	Netherlands, The

Energy (continued)

country	electricity													coal		
	installed capacity, 1992 ('000 kW)	production, 1992		power source, 1992			trade, 1992		consumption					reserves, latest ('000,000 metric tons)	production, 1992 ('000 metric tons)	consumption, 1992 ('000 metric tons)
		capacity ('000,000 kW-hr)	amount ('000,000 kW-hr)	fossil fuel (%)	hydropower (%)	nuclear fuel (%)	exports ('000,000 kW-hr)	imports ('000,000 kW-hr)	amount, 1992 ('000,000 kW-hr)	per capita, 1992 (kW-hr)	residential, 1990 (%)	nonresidential, 1990 (%)				
Netherlands Antilles	200	1,752	853	100.0	—	—	—	—	853	4,874	...	...		...	...	...
New Caledonia	253	2,216	1,170	70.5	29.5	—	—	—	1,170	6,763	...	...		2	...	170
New Zealand	7,520	65,875	31,271	26.8	66.0	7.2[13]	—	—	31,271	9,051	37.5[4]	62.5[4]		117	2,830	2,430
Nicaragua	457	4,003	1,601	54.2	16.6	29.2[13]	—	35	1,636	414	67.1	32.9		...	...	...
Niger	63	552	171	100.0	—	—	—	190	361	44	50.0	50.0		70	170	170
Nigeria	4,574	40,068	11,800	72.9	27.1	—	100	—	11,700	101	80.4	19.6		190	95	60
Northern Mariana Islands	114	999	...	...	...	...	...	...	...	...	...	...		...	...	...
Norway	27,281	238,982	117,682	0.4	99.6	—	10,103	1,359	108,938	25,382	27.0[2]	73.0[2]		13	391	703
Oman	1,539	13,482	6,237	100.0	—	—	—	—	6,237	3,810	...	...		...	...	...
Pakistan	10,184	89,212	51,972	59.6	39.6	0.8	—	—	51,972	417	64.5	35.5		524	3,188	4,222
Panama	957	8,383	3,016	37.3	62.7	—	63	211	3,164	1,258	26.8[11]	73.2[11]		...	...	67
Papua New Guinea	490	4,292	1,790	74.3	25.7	—	—	—	1,790	441	27.5	72.5		...	...	1
Paraguay	6,533	57,229	27,141	0.1	99.9	—	24,619	1	2,523	558	...	...		...	...	...
Peru	4,187	36,678	13,132	25.5	74.5	—	—	—	13,132	585	35.8	64.2		1,060	90	280
Philippines	6,771	59,314	21,775	54.3	19.5	26.2[13]	—	—	21,775	334	53.0	47.0		262	1,663	2,321
Poland	31,119	272,602	132,750	97.3	2.7	—	9,066	5,034	128,718	3,351	33.5[3]	66.5[3]		41,200	198,449	176,682
Portugal	8,222	72,025	30,087	83.1	16.9	—	1,197	2,538	31,428	3,185	36.4[2]	63.6[2]		36	221	4,706
Puerto Rico	4,230	37,055	16,434	98.2	1.8	—	—	—	16,434	4,573	31.0[11]	69.0[11]		...	—	154
Qatar	1,515	13,271	4,740	100.0	—	—	—	—	4,740	10,464	83.0	17.0		...	...	...
Réunion	175	1,533	1,009	31.4	68.6	—	—	—	1,009	1,617	...	...		...	...	...
Romania	22,177	194,271	54,195	78.4	21.6	—	218	4,421	58,398	2,503	23.6[3]	76.4[3]		3,118	37,760	40,969
Russia	213,099	1,866,747	1,008,450	71.0	17.1	11.9	43,952	27,710	992,208	6,659	21.6[3, 22]	78.4[3, 22]		265,657	317,006	316,058
Rwanda	60	526	185	2.2	97.8	—	—	12	197	26	...	...		...	...	...
St. Kitts and Nevis	15	131	40	100.0	—	—	—	—	40	952	...	...		...	...	...
St. Lucia	22	193	107	100.0	—	—	—	—	107	781	26.6[3]	73.4[3]		...	...	...
St. Vincent and the Grenadines	14	123	51	23.5	76.5	—	—	—	51	468	45.3[4]	54.7[4]		...	...	...
San Marino	19	19	19	19	19	19	19	19	19	19	...	...		...	19	19
São Tomé and Príncipe	6	53	15	46.7	53.3	—	—	—	15	121	...	...		...	...	...
Saudi Arabia	17,550	153,738	48,620	100.0	—	—	—	—	48,620	3,054	69.3[17]	30.7[17]		...	...	...
Senegal	231	2,024	762	100.0	—	—	—	—	762	99	...	...		...	...	...
Seychelles	28	245	109	100.0	—	—	—	—	109	1,514	...	...		...	...	...
Sierra Leone	126	1,104	230	100.0	—	—	—	—	230	53	...	...		...	—	1
Singapore	3,550	31,098	17,543	100.0	—	—	—	—	17,543	6,336	48.0	52.0		...	—	—
Slovakia	6,295	55,144	22,520	39.5	11.2	49.3	...	1,500	24,020	4,511	18.0	82.0		...	4,000	11,500
Slovenia	3,232	28,312	12,026	38.9	28.1	33.0	2,034	—	9,992	4,966	18.0	82.0		...	5,556	5,556
Solomon Islands	12	105	30	100.0	—	—	...	...	30	88	69.4	30.6		...	...	...
Somalia	70	613	258	100.0	—	—	—	—	258	28	...	...		...	...	...
South Africa	25,854[10]	226,481[10]	169,145[10]	97.0[10]	0.5[10]	2.5[10]	6,185[10]	334	163,294[10]	3,605[10]	...	...		55,333	174,910[10]	132,260[10]
Spain	43,825	383,907	158,505	51.6	13.2	35.2	3,710	4,351	159,146	4,071	16.7[2]	83.2[2]		1,450	33,399	47,496
Sri Lanka	1,409	12,343	3,540	18.1	81.9	—	—	—	3,540	200	65.1	34.9		...	—	1
Sudan, The	500	4,380	1,325	29.1	70.9	—	—	—	1,325	50	...	...		...	—	—
Suriname	415	3,635	1,420	20.8	79.2	—	—	—	1,420	3,242	...	...		...	—	—
Swaziland	10	10	10	10	10	10	10	10	10	10	18.7[18]	81.3[18]		999	10	10
Sweden	34,557	302,719	146,245	5.3	51.2	43.5	10,995	8,845	144,095	16,655	26.4[2]	73.6[2]		1	37	3,368
Switzerland	16,311[21]	142,884[21]	59,117[21]	2.7[21]	57.6[21]	39.7[21]	26,046[21]	21,757[21]	54,828[21]	8,015[21]	26.6[8]	73.4[8]		...	—	263[21]
Syria	4,157	36,415	13,422	45.0	55.0	—	—	—	13,422	1,011	21.2[8]	78.8[8]		...	...	—
Taiwan	19,247	168,604	93,885	56.5	8.9	34.6	—	—	85,290	4,110	31.9	68.1		100	335	—
Tajikistan	4,050	35,478	16,800	20.0	80.0	—	...	...	16,800	3,007	...	...		...	200	136
Tanzania	439	3,846	901	30.7	69.3	—	—	—	901	32	...	...		200	—	—
Thailand	12,806	112,181	59,698	92.9	7.1	—	41	481	60,138	1,071	51.0	49.0		999	15,357	15,567
Togo	34	298	60	91.7	8.3	—	—	295	355	94	...	...		...	...	...
Tonga	7	61	27	100.0	—	—	—	—	27	278	...	...		...	...	...
Trinidad and Tobago	1,150	10,074	3,945	100.0	—	—	—	—	3,945	3,119	41.0	59.0		...	...	...
Tunisia	1,414	12,387	5,750	98.4	1.6	—	125	121	5,746	684	42.8	57.2		—	—	15
Turkey	18,714	163,935	67,342	60.4	39.4	0.2[13]	314	189	67,217	1,152	14.2[9]	85.8[9]		7,148	51,431	58,503
Turkmenistan	3,950	34,602	13,100	100.0	...	...	...	...	13,100	3,393	...	...		...	—	269
Tuvalu	...	...	...	...	...	...	...	...	...	...	...	...		...	...	...
Uganda	162	1,419	786	0.8	99.2	—	112	—	674	36	...	...		...	...	...
Ukraine	54,360	476,194	252,524	67.6	3.2	29.2	5,762	...	246,762	4,731	...	...		...	133,597	138,915
United Arab Emirates	4,756	41,663	17,460	100.0	—	—	131	—	17,460	10,455	...	...		...	...	...
United Kingdom	65,356	572,519	326,879	73.5	2.2	24.3	32	16,725	343,572	5,933	35.4[8]	64.6[8]		3,800	84,874	100,388
United States	751,717	6,585,041	3,074,504	71.1	8.1	20.8	8,855	37,204	3,102,853	12,160	34.9[8]	65.1[8]		240,116	904,959	808,346
Uruguay	2,065	18,089	8,898	11.0	89.0	—	3,396	12	5,514	1,762	60.6	39.4		...	...	1
Uzbekistan	17,625	154,395	50,900	100.0	...	...	131	—	50,769	2,367	...	...		...	9,231	10,681
Vanuatu	11	96	29	100.0	—	—	—	—	29	185	...	...		...	...	...
Venezuela	18,741	164,171	69,460	32.2	67.8	—	360	—	69,100	3,423	42.0	58.0		417	2,427	350
Vietnam	2,200	19,272	9,800	39.8	60.2	—	—	—	9,800	141	36.4[3]	63.6[3]		150	4,792	3,424
Virgin Islands (U.S.)	316	2,768	1,020	100.0	—	—	—	—	1,020	9,533	40.2[4]	59.8[4]		...	—	205
West Bank	...	...	...	...	...	...	...	...	...	...	...	...		...	...	...
Western Sahara	56	491	85	100.0	—	—	—	—	85	340	...	...		...	...	...
Western Samoa	19	166	48	58.3	41.7	—	—	—	48	304	...	...		...	...	...
Yemen	810	7,096	1,810	100.0	—	—	—	—	1,810	144	...	...		...	...	...
Yugoslavia	9,863	86,400	36,488	68.7	31.3	—	400	2,000	38,088	3,614	26.0	74.0		16,570[23]	40,105	41,105
Zaire	2,831	24,800	6,180	2.6	97.4	—	198	2	5,984	150	...	89.1[2, 15]		600	128	170
Zambia	2,436	21,339	7,780	0.5	99.5	—	1,500	20	6,300	729	31.8	68.2		55	395	390
Zimbabwe	2,038	17,853	9,000	65.3	34.7	—	80	1,600	10,520	994	44.2	55.8		734	6,000	5,880

natural gas — published proven reserves, 1994 ('000,000,000 cu m)	production — natural gas, 1993 ('000,000 cu m)	production — manufactured gas, 1992 (% of total gas consumption)	consumption — amount, 1992 ('000,000 cu m)	consumption — residential, 1990 (%)	consumption — non-residential, 1990 (%)	crude petroleum reserves, 1994 — published proven ('000,000 barrels)	reserves, 1994 — years to exhaust proven reserves	production, 1993 ('000,000 barrels)	consumption, 1992 ('000,000 barrels)	refining capacity, 1994 ('000 barrels per day)	pipelines — length (km)	pipelines — traffic ('000,000 metric ton-km)	country
—	—	111.1	...	...	...	...	...	—	88	477	—	—	Netherlands Antilles
...	—	...	...	...	...	...	...	—	...	...	—	—	New Caledonia
89	4,763	6.4	4,897	4.8[4]	95.2[4]	156	12	13	32	93	310	...	New Zealand
...	...	97.1	—	—	—	...	...	—	5	16	56	...	Nicaragua
...	—	—	...	...	...	...	...	—	...	...	...	—	Niger
3,398	4,701	1.4	4,900	—	100.0	17,900	20	692	88	433	5,042	...	Nigeria
...	...	...	...	...	...	...	...	...	...	...	...	...	Northern Mariana Islands
1,996	24,707	49.7	2,033	...	...	9,284	11	820	106	287	53	9,618	Norway
566	3,548	11.7	1,839	...	...	4,700	17	283	22	76	1,300	...	Oman
650	14,762	1.5	13,426	41.5	58.5	203	9	23	54	133	1,135	...	Pakistan
—	—	22.8	50	—	—	...	...	—	13	100	130	...	Panama
425	82	...	—	—	—	253	6	45	—	—	—	—	Papua New Guinea
—	—	3.4	...	...	...	...	...	—	2	8	—	...	Paraguay
199	1,303	31.7	525	61.4	38.6	381	8	46	58	184	800	...	Peru
84	—	58.4	...	...	...	279	70	4	92	279	357	...	Philippines
155	5,100	32.0	10,410	...	...	37	31	1.2	95	333	2,346	17,661	Poland
—	—	59.0	...	...	...	...	...	—	83	294	69	...	Portugal
—	—	93.3	...	...	...	...	...	—	40	127	—	—	Puerto Rico
7,079	8,068	11.8	11,489	—	100.0	3,729	24	156	21	58	235	...	Qatar
...	...	...	...	...	...	...	...	...	...	...	...	...	Réunion
227	22,042	8.6	22,143	...	...	1,569	31	51	97	681	4,229	6,654	Romania
48,677	643,000[6]	8.0	334,491	...	...	156,700	54	2,595	1,924	6,463	83,100	1,240,000	Russia
57	0.2[7]	—	0.2	...	...	...	...	—	...	—	—	—	Rwanda
...	...	...	...	...	...	...	...	—	—	—	—	—	St. Kitts and Nevis
...	...	...	...	...	...	...	...	—	—	—	—	—	St. Lucia
...	...	...	...	...	...	...	...	—	—	—	—	—	St. Vincent and the Grenadines
...	...	19	19	...	...	...	...	—	19	—	—	—	San Marino
...	...	...	...	...	...	...	...	—	...	—	—	—	São Tomé and Príncipe
5,263	32,131	51.7	34,407	9.8[8]	90.2[8]	261,203	88	2,979	573	1,614	6,550	...	Saudi Arabia
—	...	14.3	...	...	...	...	...	—	6	23	—	—	Senegal
...	...	...	...	...	...	...	...	...	2	10	—	—	Seychelles
—	...	...	...	...	...	...	...	—	...	10	—	—	Sierra Leone
—	—	377.5	...	...	...	...	...	—	354	1,055	—	—	Singapore
8	313[7]	7.4	5,826	...	...	7	14	0.5[6]	31	193	...	...	Slovakia
...	24[5]	—	333	...	...	...	...	0.02[5]	3	15	290	128	Slovenia
—	—	...	—	—	—	...	...	—	...	10	15	...	Solomon Islands
6	—	...	...	...	...	...	...	—	...	10	15	...	Somalia
27	—	100.0[10]	—	...	...	41	27	1.5	119[10]	364	2,679	...	South Africa
20	702	42.6	6,669	...	...	23	3	7	413	1,283	2,059	4,664	Spain
—	—	59.4	...	...	...	...	...	—	10	50	62	...	Sri Lanka
85	—	54.5	...	...	...	300	429	0.7	7	22	815	...	Sudan, The
—	...	...	...	...	...	56	29	1.9	1	—	—	—	Suriname
...	...	10	...	...	...	...	...	...	10	—	—	—	Swaziland
—	—	42.9	487	...	...	...	...	—	122	428	—	—	Sweden
...	—	12.4[21]	2,619[21]	38.3[8]	61.7[8]	...	...	...	30[21]	132	314	1,110	Switzerland
198	3,704	11.2	1,941	...	...	1,700	8	210	83	242	1,819	...	Syria
68	725	...	...	...	...	4	10	0.4	...	543	615	...	Taiwan
...	49	...	1,771	...	...	...	...	0.7[7]	0.3	...	...	...	Tajikistan
116	—	100.0	...	...	...	...	...	—	4	17	982	...	Tanzania
163	8,889	15.1	8,078	—	100.0	179	9	19	102	314	67	...	Thailand
—	...	...	...	...	...	...	...	...	...	—	—	—	Togo
...	...	...	...	...	...	...	...	...	...	—	—	—	Tonga
240	5,111	4.5	5,931	1.8	98.2	466	11	44	41	305	1,051	...	Trinidad and Tobago
91	235	13.4	780	9.1	90.9	1,700	46	37	13	34	883	...	Tunisia
11	201	31.3	4,766	...	...	488	17	28	166	713	4,059	55,492	Turkey
326[6]	84,300[7]	...	11,198	...	...	740[6]	17	32	43	236	250	...	Turkmenistan
...	...	...	...	...	...	...	...	...	...	—	—	—	Tuvalu
...	...	...	...	...	...	...	...	...	...	—	—	—	Uganda
...	19,502	1.5	96,596	...	...	...	...	36[7]	299	1,244	3,930	200,000	Ukraine
5,794	24,336	12.9	25,503	...	...	98,100	123	799	66	193	830	...	United Arab Emirates
610	63,051	13.6	66,220	52.7[8]	47.3[8]	4,554	7	681	602	1,867	3,926	9,836	United Kingdom
4,673	543,941	17.9	563,699	33.4[11]	66.6[11]	23,745	9	2,517	4,873	15,142	275,800	871,618	United States
—	—	83.5	...	...	...	...	...	—	10	35	—	...	Uruguay
...	41,600[6]	...	41,275	...	...	...	...	29	30	173	290	200	Uzbekistan
...	...	...	...	...	...	...	...	...	...	—	—	—	Vanuatu
3,650	22,277	17.1	21,573	9.1	90.9	63,330	74	851	335	1,167	6,850	...	Venezuela
105	697	...	3	...	...	500	11	45	0.3	—	150	...	Vietnam
—	—	95.0	...	...	...	...	...	...	108	545	—	—	Virgin Islands (U.S.)
...	...	...	...	...	...	...	...	...	...	...	—	—	West Bank
...	...	...	...	...	...	...	...	...	...	...	...	—	Western Sahara
...	...	...	...	...	...	...	...	...	...	—	—	—	Western Samoa
425	...	32.5	...	...	...	4,000	53	76	46	120	676	—	Yemen
45	898	2.8	2,176	...	...	78	9	9	23	282	545	...	Yugoslavia
28	—	7.8	—	—	—	187	21	9	3	17	390	...	Zaire
—	—	100.0	—	—	—	...	...	...	4	24	1,724	...	Zambia
...	...	90.8	—	—	—	...	...	...	...	—	212	...	Zimbabwe

[1]Estimated reserves in place. [2]1981. [3]1985. [4]1984. [5]1990. [6]1992. [7]1991. [8]1983. [9]Belgium includes Luxembourg. [10]South Africa includes Botswana, Lesotho, Namibia, and Swaziland. [11]1982. [12]Data refer to former Czechoslovakia. [13]Geothermally generated electricity. [14]France includes Monaco. [15]Transportation and industry only; excludes agricultural, commercial, and public-service sectors. [16]Data refer to former West Germany only. [17]1988. [18]1980. [19]Italy includes San Marino. [20]1989. [21]Switzerland includes Liechtenstein. [22]Data refer to former U.S.S.R. [23]Data refer to Yugoslavia as constituted prior to 1991.

Transportation

This table presents data on the transportation infrastructure of the various countries and dependencies of the world and on their commercial passenger and cargo traffic. Most states have roads and airports, with services corresponding to the prevailing level of economic development. A number of states, however, lack railroads or inland waterways because of either geographic constraints or lack of development capital and technical expertise. Pipelines, one of the oldest means of bulk transport if aqueducts are considered, are today among the most narrowly developed transportation modes worldwide for shipment of bulk materials. Because the principal contemporary application of pipeline technology is to facilitate the shipment of hydrocarbon liquids and gases, coverage of pipelines will be found in the "Energy" table. It is, however, also true that pipelines now find increasing application for slurries of coal or other raw materials.

While the United Nations' *Statistical Yearbook* and *Monthly Bulletin of Statistics* provide much data on infrastructure and traffic and have established basic definitions and classifications for transportation statistics, the number of countries covered is limited. Several commercial publications maintain substantial databases and publishing programs for their particular areas of interest: highway and vehicle statistics are provided by the International Road Federation's annual *World Road Statistics;* the International Union of Railways' *International Railway Statistics* and Jane's *World Railways* provide similar data for railways; Lloyd's *Register of Shipping Statistical Tables* summarizes the world's merchant marine; the *Official Airline Guide*, the International Civil Aviation Organization's *Digest of Statistics: Commercial Air Carriers,* and the International Air Transport Association's *World Air Transport Statistics* have also been used to supplement and update data collected by the UN. Because several of these agencies are commercially or insurance-oriented, their data tend to be more complete, accurate, and timely than those of intergovernmental organizations, which depend on periodic responses to questionnaires or publication of results in official sources. All of these international sources have been extensively supplemented by national statistical sources to provide additional data. Such diversity of sources, however, imposes limitations on the comparability of the statistics from country to country because the basis and completeness of data collection and the frequency and timeliness of analysis and publication may vary greatly. Data shown in italic are from 1989 or earlier.

The categories adopted in the table also have special problems of comparability. Total road length is subject to wide international variation of interpretation, as "roads" can mean anything from mere tracks to highly developed highways. Each country also has individual classifications that differ according to climate, availability of road-building materials, traffic patterns, administrative responsibility, and so on. "Paved roads," by contrast, is a much more tightly definable category, but the proportion of paved to total roads may be distorted by the less comparable total road statistics. Automobile and truck and bus fleet statistics, which are usually

Transportation

country	roads and motor vehicles (latest)								railroads (latest)					
	roads			motor vehicles			cargo		track length		traffic			
	length		paved (percent)	automobiles	trucks and buses	persons per vehicle	short ton-mi ('000,000)	metric ton-km ('000,000)	mi	km	passengers		cargo	
	mi	km									passenger-mi ('000,000)	passenger-km ('000,000)	short ton-mi ('000,000)	metric ton-km ('000,000)
Afghanistan	*11,930*	*19,200*	*47*	38,000	35,000	242	*1,993*	*2,910*	*6*	*10*	...	...	...	...
Albania	4,629	7,450	38	16,000	32,900	68	818.5	1,195	447	720	484.2	779.2	400	584
Algeria	59,388	95,576	66	800,000	600,000	19	9,589	14,000	2,941[2]	4,733[2]	1,804	2,904	1,728	2,523
American Samoa	217	350	43	5,010	339	9.5	...	...	—	—	—	—	—	—
Andorra	167	269	74	36,418	4,436	1.4	...	...	—	—	—	—	—	—
Angola	45,128	72,626	25	120,000	40,000	64	...	...	*1,739*[2]	*2,798*[2]	*203*	*326*	*1,178*	*1,720*
Antigua and Barbuda	724	1,165	33	13,650	3,550	3.8	...	...	—	—	—	—	—	—
Argentina	131,338	211,369	27	4,417,882	1,552,893	5.5	...	...	21,198[2]	34,115[2]	6,618	10,651	5,790	8,453
Armenia	4,800	7,700	99	*230,100*	...	...	780.8	1,140	511	823	199	320	2,861	4,177
Aruba	236	380	100	32,060	814	2.1	...	...	—	—	—	—	—	—
Australia	503,474	810,264	36	7,913,200	2,041,300	1.8	604,160	882,059	23,174[2,7]	37,295[2,7]	7,152	11,510	61,000	89,000
Austria	68,400	110,000	100	3,244,920	278,643	2.2	3,755	5,482	4,136	6,657	5,988[7]	9,636[7]	8,080[7]	11,796[7]
Azerbaijan	22,800	36,700	87	*235,600*	...	...	3,549	5,181	1,299	2,090	1,012	1,629	9,439	13,781
Bahamas, The	1,450	2,334	56	66,696	14,322	3.3	...	...	—	—	—	—	—	—
Bahrain	1,660	2,671	75	107,657	24,523	3.8	...	...	—	—	—	—	—	—
Bangladesh	120,100	193,283	4	67,000	63,000	868	...	...	1,706[2]	2,746[2]	3,323	5,348	492	718
Barbados	977	1,573	95	39,406	9,318	5.3	...	...	—	—	—	—	—	—
Belarus	30,600	49,300	96	700,000	46,200	14	15,321	22,369	3,459	5,567	9,815	15,795	44,899	65,551
Belgium	85,672	137,876	97	4,109,601	389,812	2.2	18,833	27,495	2,132[2]	3,432[2]	4,224	6,798	5,540	8,089
Belize	1,684	2,710	18	12,075	2,800	13	...	...	—	—	—	—	—	—
Benin	3,770	6,070	20	25,000	13,000	129	...	...	359	578	39.4	63.4	111.3	162.5
Bermuda	120	193	100	19,712	3,316	2.6	...	...	—	—	—	—	—	—
Bhutan	1,600	2,500	72	2,590	1,367	348	...	...	—	—	—	—	—	—
Bolivia	26,612	42,828	4	265,000	60,000	23	*1,133*	*1,654*	2,264[2]	3,643[2]	244.2	393.0	414.5	605.2
Bosnia and Herzegovina	13,153	21,168	54	438,080	50,578	8.9	2,708	3,954	646	1,039	...	...	...	...
Botswana	11,933	19,204	13	23,500	47,175	19	...	...	551	887	160	257	666	972
Brazil	934,566	1,504,041	10	12,974,991	1,371,127	11	*178,359*	*260,400*	18,751[2]	30,177[2]	11,430	18,395	83,169	121,425
Brunei	1,502	2,417	51	122,104	13,658	2.0	...	...	12[13]	19[13]	—	—	...	...
Bulgaria	22,942	36,922	92	1,358,976	130,000	5.8	7,596	11,090	4,076	6,560	3,351	5,393	5,314	7,758
Burkina Faso	8,161	13,134	*12*	12,000	13,000	360	...	...	*308*[2]	*495*[2]	*422*	*680*	*322*	*470*
Burundi	*3,893*	*6,265*	*16*	*14,483*	*14,914*	*188*	...	...	—	—	—	—	—	—
Cambodia	*9,200*	*14,800*	*18*	*4,000*	*7,100*	*737*	...	...	403	649	33.6	54.0	6.9	10.0
Cameroon	*29,950*	*48,200*	*7*	95,000	80,000	70	175	255	686[2]	1,104[2]	284	457	514	751
Canada	527,794	849,404	35	13,322,457	3,688,433	1.7	29,033	42,388	53,985	86,880	852	1,371	166,057	242,439
Cape Verde	*3,489*	*5,615*	*29*	10,000	5,000	23	...	...	—	—	—	—	—	—
Central African Republic	14,750	23,738	2	8,221	8,541	171	*2.8*	*4.1*	—	—	—	—	—	—
Chad	*24,855*	*40,000*	*1*	9,000	7,000	385	...	...	—	—	—	—	—	—
Chile	49,457	79,593	14	826,794	437,520	11	...	...	2,778[2]	4,470[2]	710	1,142	1,845	2,694
China	656,606	1,056,707	88	2,261,600	4,655,800	168	230,011	335,810	42,564	68,500	217,800	350,500	817,548	1,193,600
Colombia	66,721	107,377	12	854,160	430,611	26	4,265	6,227	2,007[2]	3,230[2]	9.6	15.5	166.4	242.9
Comoros	466	750	28	*1,000*	*4,000*	84	...	...	—	—	—	—	—	—
Congo	7,919	12,745	10	28,000	17,418	59	*46*	*67*	494	795	340	547	273	399
Costa Rica	22,096	35,560	16	194,846	100,356	11	1,536	2,243	590[2]	950[2]	26.5	42.6	*102.7*	*150.0*
Côte d'Ivoire	42,250	68,000	8	170,000	92,000	47	...	...	410[2]	660[2]	634[15]	1,021[15]	396[15]	578[15]
Croatia	16,732	26,928	81	669,761	35,452	6.8	958.2	1,399	1,676	2,699	610	981	1,212	1,770
Cuba	*28,928*	*46,555*	*27*	*241,300*	*208,400*	*23*	2,482	3,623	3,033	4,881	1,880	3,025	937	1,368
Cyprus	6,492	10,448	55	197,779	84,326	2.1	...	...	—	—	—	—	—	—
Czech Republic	34,734	55,896		2,522,360	362,732	3.6	5,569[17]	8,131[17]	5,865	9,439	6,694	10,773	17,566	25,646
Denmark	44,143	71,042	100	1,604,638	315,511	2.7	7,100	10,400	1,763	2,838	2,858	4,600	1,281	1,870
Djibouti	1,789	2,879	13	13,000	3,000	33	...	...	66	106	*182*	*293*	*81.7*	*119.3*
Dominica	466	750	49	4,696	4,616	7.7	...	...	—	—	—	—	—	—
Dominican Republic	7,500	12,000	48	150,000	110,000	29	...	...	65	104	—	—	—	—
Ecuador	27,159	43,709	12	335,903	48,348	27	2,147	3,135	600[2]	965[2]	51	82	3.4	5.0
Egypt	29,445[19]	47,387[19]	73[19]	1,119,727	466,650	36	21,394	31,235	5,487	8,831	26,834	43,185	2,166	3,162
El Salvador	9,371	15,081	12	221,870	33,229	21	...	...	374[2]	602[2]	3.9	6.3	26.2	38.2

based upon registration, are relatively accurate, though some countries round off figures, and unregistered vehicles may cause substantial undercount. There is also inconsistent classification of vehicle types; in some countries a vehicle may serve variously as an automobile, a truck, or a bus, or even as all three on certain occasions. Relatively few countries collect and maintain commercial road traffic statistics.

Data on national railway systems are generally given for railway track length rather than the length of routes, which may be multitracked. Siding tracks usually are not included, but some countries fail to distinguish them. The United States data include only class 1 railways, which account for about 94 percent of total track length. Passenger traffic is usually calculated from tickets sold to fare-paying passengers. Such statistics are subject to distortion if there are large numbers of nonpaying passengers, such as military personnel, or if season tickets are sold and not all the allowed journeys are utilized. Railway cargo traffic is calculated by weight hauled multiplied by the length of the journey. Changes in freight load during the journey should be accounted for but sometimes are not, leading to discrepancies.

Merchant fleet and tonnage statistics collected by Lloyd's registry service for vessels over 100 gross tons are quite accurate. Cargo statistics, however, reflect the port and customs requirements of each country and the reporting rules of each country's merchant marine authority (although these, increasingly, reflect the recommendations of the International Mar-

itime Organization); often, however, they are only estimates based on customs declarations and the count of vessels entered and cleared. Even when these elements are reported consistently, further uncertainties may be introduced because of ballast, bunkers, ships' stores, or transshipped goods included in the data.

Airport data are based on scheduled flights reported in the commercial *Official Airline Guide* and are both reliable and current. The comparability of civil air traffic statistics suffers from differing characteristics of the air transportation systems of different countries; data for an entire country may be two to three years behind those for a single airport.

Outside of Europe, where standardization of data on inland waterways is necessitated by the volume of international traffic, comparability of national data declines markedly. Calculations as to both the length of a country's waterway system (or route length of river, lake, and coastal traffic) and the makeup of its stock of commercially significant vessels (those for which data will be collected) are largely determined by the nature and use of the country's hydrographic net—its seasonality, relief profile, depth, access to potential markets—and inevitably differ widely from country to country. Data for coastal or island states may refer to scheduled coastwise or interisland traffic.

merchant marine				air					canals and inland waterways (latest)				country
fleet, 1992 (vessels over 100 gross tons)	total dead-weight tonnage, 1992 ('000)	international cargo (latest)		airports with scheduled flights, 1994	traffic (latest)				length		cargo		
		loaded metric tons ('000)	off-loaded metric tons ('000)		passengers		cargo		mi	km	short ton-mi ('000,000)	metric ton-km ('000,000)	
					passenger-mi ('000,000)	passenger-km ('000,000)	short ton-mi ('000,000)	metric ton-km ('000,000)					
—	—	—	—	1	127[1]	205[1]	18.5[1]	27.0[1]	750	1,200	...	...	Afghanistan
24	81.0	1,065	664	1	...	...	...	...	27	43	24	35	Albania
149	1,093.4	57,607	14,284	11	2,010[3]	3,234[3]	13.8[3]	20.2[3]	...	...	...	...	Algeria
3	0.1	380	733	3	...	...	...	...	...	...	...	...	American Samoa
—	—	—	—	—	...	...	...	...	—	—	—	—	Andorra
113	123.5	21,102	1,242	17	771[4]	1,241[4]	28.8[4]	42.0[4]	805	1,295	...	...	Angola
292	997.4	28	113	2	121	195	0.1	0.2	...	...	...	...	Antigua and Barbuda
423	1,173.1	36,792	6,861	49	5,585[5]	8,989[5]	110[5]	161[5]	6,800	11,000	19,326	28,215	Argentina
...	...	...	...	2	3,453	5,557	33.6	49.0	...	...	...	...	Armenia
6	6	...	...	1	...	...	...	...	...	...	...	...	Aruba
695	3,857.3	315,912	37,020	428	23,033	37,068	1,004	1,466	5,200	8,368	66,439	97,000	Australia
26	208.5	1,453	4,637	6	4,328	6,965	68.7	100.4	277	446	5,608	8,041	Austria
...	...	...	...	1	3,025	4,869	...	...	...	...	3,775	5,512	Azerbaijan
1,061	33,081.7	6,020	5,705	24	215	346	0.2	0.3	...	...	...	...	Bahamas, The
87	192.5	13,285	3,512	1	1,194[8]	1,922[8]	47.7[8]	69.6[8]	...	...	...	...	Bahrain
301	566.8	996	6,840	7	1,506	2,424	208	303	5,000	8,046	...	...	Bangladesh
37	84.0	206	538	1	93[9]	149[9]	0.8[10]	1.1[10]	...	...	...	...	Barbados
...	18,373.0	...	...	1	3,487	5,611	23	34	...	...	678	990	Belarus
232	218.5	57,168	88,908	2	4,026	6,480	287.4	419.7	1,269	2,043	3,580	5,227	Belgium
32	45.7	178	241	8	...	...	...	...	513	825	...	...	Belize
12	0.2	124	995	1	126[11]	203[11]	11[11]	16[11]	...	...	...	...	Benin
94	5,206.5	130	470	1	...	...	...	...	...	...	...	...	Bermuda
—	—	—	—	1	2.7	4.4	...	...	...	...	...	—	Bhutan
1	15.8	...	...	21	739	1,190	99.9	145.9	6,214	10,000	90	132	Bolivia
...	...	...	...	1	...	...	...	...	...	...	...	...	Bosnia and Herzegovina
—	—	—	—	4	52[12]	84[12]	0.4[12]	0.6[12]	...	...	...	...	Botswana
635	9,348.3	168,026	52,570	110	18,491	29,758	882	1,288	31,069	50,000	56,030	81,803	Brazil
51	349.7	13,554	1,325	1	1,008	1,623	44.4	64.8	130	209	...	...	Brunei
222	1,938.2	5,290	20,080	3	1,863	2,999	29.5	43.0	292	470	573	837	Bulgaria
—	—	—	—	2	158	254	12.3	18.0	...	...	...	...	Burkina Faso
1	0.4	35	188	1	...	...	...	...	...	...	...	...	Burundi
3	3.8	11	95	6	...	...	...	...	2,300	3,700	...	...	Cambodia
47	39.8	10,081	3,396	5	349	561	25	37	1,299	2,090	...	...	Cameroon
1,185	2,896.8	153,795	69,080	106	24,084	38,760	3,569	5,210	1,860	3,000	...	...	Canada
42	30.9	128	273	9	100	161	0.7	1.0	...	...	...	...	Cape Verde
—	—	53	126	1	144[11]	232[11]	12.1[11]	17.7[11]	500	800	91.1	133	Central African Republic
—	—	...	...	1	131	211	11	16	1,240	2,000	...	...	Chad
392	854.9	21,768	13,464	18	2,249	3,620	590	862	450	725	5,629	8,218	Chile
2,390	20,058.0	105,852	101,688	94	33,000	51,500	1,100	1,600	86,100	138,600	793,979	1,159,190	China
101	403.0	21,588	10,032	68	2,847	4,582	655	956	8,000	14,300	7,038	10,276	Colombia
6	3.6	11	104	4	1.9	3.0	...	...	...	...	...	...	Comoros
22	10.8	8,987	736	14	157	253	12	17	696	1,120	...	...	Congo
24	8.4	1,605	1,892	13	885[14]	1,425[14]	25.9[14]	37.9[14]	454	730	...	...	Costa Rica
51	98.6	3,984	6,178	7	196.9[16]	316.8[16]	32.2[16]	47.0[16]	609	980	...	...	Côte d'Ivoire
203	140.9	3,816	6,384	4	0.1	0.1	0.9	1.3	488	785	36	52	Croatia
303	924.6	8,092	15,440	12	1,908	3,070	23.8	34.8	149	240	2,085	3,044	Cuba
1,416	36,198.1	2,544	5,088	2	1,579	2,541	22.8	33.3	...	...	...	...	Cyprus
22[17]	446.2[17]	...	...	4	1,573	2,531	52.5	76.6	295	475	2,040	2,978	Czech Republic
456	7,569.1	17,508	34,368	12	2,480[18]	3,991[18]	79.9[18]	116.7[18]	259	417	1,100	1,600	Denmark
10	4.1	414	958	3	...	...	...	...	...	...	...	...	Djibouti
7	3.2	40	63	2	...	...	...	...	...	...	...	...	Dominica
28	10.4	2,550	4,182	5	889	1,431	51	75	...	...	...	...	Dominican Republic
154	504.1	11,783	1,958	14	589	948	100	146	932	1,500	...	...	Ecuador
444	1,005.2	12,252	21,456	9	3,279	5,277	84.1	122.8	2,175	3,500	1,715	2,504	Egypt
15	...	221	1,023	1	801[20]	1,289[20]	4.8[20]	7.0[20]	...	...	...	...	El Salvador

Transportation (continued)

country	roads and motor vehicles (latest) roads length mi	km	paved (percent)	motor vehicles automobiles	trucks and buses	persons per vehicle	cargo short ton-mi ('000,000)	metric ton-km ('000,000)	railroads (latest) track length mi	km	traffic passengers passenger-mi ('000,000)	passenger-km ('000,000)	cargo short ton-mi ('000,000)	metric ton-km ('000,000)
Equatorial Guinea	1,667	2,682	19	5,500	3,500	40	...	...	—	—	—	—	—	—
Eritrea	559	899	63	...	...	...	...	...	...	...	...	...	...	...
Estonia	9,194	14,797	54	283,400	83,000	4.2	998	1,457	633	1,018	590	950	2,497	3,646
Ethiopia	17,381	27,972	15	37,799	20,939	856	...	...	486[21]	782[21]	172	277	86	126
Faeroe Islands	269	433	...	13,080	3,505	2.9	...	...	—	—	—	—	—	—
Fiji	2,996	4,821	13	43,979	30,899	10	...	...	370[13]	595[13]	...	...	...	...
Finland	47,693	76,755	62	1,936,345	271,230	2.3	16,300	23,800	3,637[2]	5,853[2]	1,543	2,484	5,375	7,848
France	504,055	811,200	92	24,020,000	5,040,000	2.0	101,200	147,700	21,173[2]	34,074[2]	39,140	62,990	34,501	50,370
French Guiana	706	1,137	40	25,000	9,000	3.4	...	...	—	—	—	—	—	—
French Polynesia	584	940	42	39,000	16,000	3.7	...	...	—	—	—	—	—	—
Gabon	4,286	6,898	11	23,000	17,000	28	...	...	414	668	21	34	126	184
Gambia, The	1,483	2,386	32	6,000	2,500	112	...	...	—	—	—	—	—	—
Gaza Strip	...	...	...	18,116	3,937	28	...	...	—	—	—	—	—	—
Georgia	21,000	33,900	87	427,400	...	...	4,168	6,085	976	1,570	10.6	17.0	...	...
Germany	395,367	636,282	99	39,086,000	2,923,000	1.9	138,975	202,900	56,813	91,432	35,439	57,034	56,315	82,219
Ghana	22,800	36,700	32	90,000	43,000	115	873	1,275	592[2]	953[2]	84	135	75	109
Gibraltar	27	43	100	18,149	2,576	1.4	...	...	—	—	—	—	—	—
Greece	80,800	130,000	92	1,829,100	820,462	3.9	8,457	12,347	1,570[2]	2,527[2]	1,245	2,004	386	563
Greenland	50	80	...	1,816	1,403	17	...	...	—	—	—	—	—	—
Grenada	700	1,127	51	4,784	981	16	...	...	—	—	—	—	—	—
Guadeloupe	1,480	2,384	80	95,962	28,134	2.7	...	...	—	—	—	—	—	—
Guam	419	674	100	76,736	30,254	1.3	...	...	—	—	—	—	—	—
Guatemala	7,477	12,033	26	145,000	105,000	37	...	...	570[2]	917[2]	6.3	10.1	29.2	42.7
Guernsey	...	...	...	32,691	6,466	1.6	...	...	—	—	—	—	—	—
Guinea	17,600	28,400	4	23,155	13,000	169	...	...	411[2]	662[2]	...	...	...	...
Guinea-Bissau	2,175	3,500	15	3,500	2,500	168	...	...	—	—	—	—	—	—
Guyana	4,474	7,200	10	24,000	9,000	23	...	...	116[13]	187[13]	...	...	...	...
Haiti	2,485	4,000	24	33,000	22,000	118	...	...	—	—	—	—	—	—
Honduras	8,825	14,203	17	65,430	101,986	30	...	...	488	785	4.8	7.7	20.7	30.2
Hong Kong	1,010	1,625	100	291,913	159,891	13	...	...	21	34	1,939	3,120	41.0	60.0
Hungary	18,610	29,950	99	2,058,334	229,191	4.5	2,314	3,379	8,200	13,200	5,706	9,183	6,860	10,015
Iceland	7,067	11,373	22	116,195	15,644	2.0	318	464	—	—	—	—	—	—
India	1,266,000	2,037,000	49	2,806,533	2,396,738	165	144,000	210,000	38,800[2]	62,500[2]	186,500	300,100	176,100	257,100
Indonesia	176,168	283,516	44	1,876,230	1,666,195	52	17,000	25,000	4,090	6,583	6,544	10,532	2,586	3,775
Iran	94,130	151,488	34	1,557,000	561,000	27	46,750	68,250	2,838[2]	4,567[2]	2,848	4,584	5,277	7,704
Iraq	28,305	45,554	84	672,000	368,000	18	...	...	1,493[2]	2,403[2]	572	920	79	115
Ireland	57,369	92,327	94	858,498	149,355	3.5	3,519	5,138	1,749	2,814	761.8	1,226	454.3	663.3
Isle of Man	357	574	58	43,184	4,753	0.7	...	...	37[2]	59[2]	...	...	...	...
Israel	8,364	13,461	100	923,000	186,000	4.5	...	...	356[2]	573[2]	123	198	751	1,096
Italy	188,597	303,518	100	28,200,000	2,521,000	1.9	125,171	182,746	12,176	19,595	30,050	48,361	15,091	22,033
Jamaica	10,212	16,435	29	97,500	18,000	21	...	...	129[2]	208[2]	12.1	19.5	1.7	2.5
Japan	691,488	1,112,844	71	38,963,861	22,698,045	2.0	194,370	283,776	23,690	38,125	249,947	402,252	18,263	26,664
Jersey	...	...	...	60,396	8,029	1.3	...	...	—	—	—	—	—	—
Jordan	3,958	6,370	100	172,248	44,209	18	19,133	27,934	490[2]	788[2]	3.7	6.0	542	791
Kazakhstan	102,500	164,900	69	734,800	...	...	30,316	44,260	13,200	21,200	12,100	19,400	256.3	374.2
Kenya	39,400	63,400	14	157,166	172,023	76	134	196	1,885[2]	3,034[2]	288	464	899	1,312
Kiribati	398	640	5	307	130	147	...	...	—	—	—	—	—	—
Korea, North	18,600	30,000	8	248,000	...	...	...	...	5,302	8,533	2,100	3,400	6,200	9,100
Korea, South	34,659	55,778	61	3,461,057	1,745,097	8.4	5,921	8,645	4,049	6,517	21,616	34,787	9,765	14,256
Kuwait	2,655	4,273	100	579,841	126,754	2.0	...	...	—	—	—	—	—	—
Kyrgyzstan	11,900	19,100	86	173,800	...	...	3,858	5,632	490	789	81.5	131.2	1,088	1,589
Laos	8,780	14,130	16	20,233	12,987	135	165.1	241.1	—	—	—	—	—	—
Latvia	37,421	60,224	55	340,000	87,000	6.2	3,333	4,866	1,489	2,397	2,441	3,929	11,465	16,739
Lebanon	4,579	7,370	85	473,372	49,560	5.0	...	...	259	417	5.3	8.6	29	42
Lesotho	2,607	4,195	20	6,363	15,379	73	...	...	1.6	2.6	...	...	...	...
Liberia	5,011	8,064	9	8,000	4,000	198	...	...	304[2]	490[2]	...	...	1,746[13]	2,549[13]
Libya	11,992	19,300	56	448,000	322,000	6.3	...	...	—	—	—	—	—	—
Liechtenstein	201	323	...	17,697	1,787	1.5	...	...	12	19	...	...	...	...
Lithuania	27,700	44,500	80	565,320	92,056	5.7	3,417	4,989	1,862	2,996	1,703	2,740	7,765	11,337
Luxembourg	3,163	5,091	99	208,847	22,425	1.7	164	239	168[2]	271[2]	175	282	488	713
Macau	60	97	100	29,894	5,692	11	...	...	—	—	—	—	—	—
Macedonia	6,581	10,591	48	230,993	22,594	8.0	1,819	2,655	431	693	...	...	488	712
Madagascar	22,214	35,750	15	50,000	35,000	151	220	321	655[2]	1,054[2]	121.5	195.5	144.0	210.3
Malawi	7,590	12,215	22	16,118	17,394	254	—	—	495[2]	797[2]	57.0	91.7	40.5	59.1
Malaysia	57,505	92,545	75	2,147,974	472,414	7.1	...	...	1,381	2,222	1,148[29]	1,848[29]	945[29]	1,380[29]
Maldives	...	...	...	804	1,114	120	...	...	—	—	—	—	—	—
Mali	11,185	18,000	8	23,000	10,000	256	...	...	399[2]	642[2]	304.2	489.5	187.2	273.3
Malta	988	1,588	92	120,320	27,978	2.4	...	...	—	—	—	—	—	—
Marshall Islands	...	...	...	763	80	43	...	...	—	—	—	—	—	—
Martinique	1,286	2,069	75	135,269	7,328	2.3	...	...	—	—	—	—	—	—
Mauritania	4,683	7,536	24	10,000	5,000	133	...	...	416[2]	670[2]	4.4	7.0	3,860	5,635
Mauritius	1,138	1,831	93	32,751	2,097	31	...	...	—	—	—	—	—	—
Mayotte	143	230	49	——1,528——		40	...	...	—	—	—	—	—	—
Mexico	151,309	243,509	35	7,497,128	3,607,282	7.9	74,579	108,884	12,784[2]	20,515[2]	2,408	3,875	23,973	35,001
Micronesia	140	226	17	...	...	...	...	...	—	—	—	—	—	—
Moldova	9,015	14,508	85	221,883	20,409	18	2,587	3,777	715	1,150	5,515	8,875	10,279	15,007
Monaco	31	50	100	16,500	3,500	1.5	...	...	1	2	...	...	...	...
Mongolia	30,600	49,200	2	5,660	29,794	58	1,438	2,099	1,445	2,325	326	524	3,485	5,088
Morocco	36,955	59,474	50	811,896	291,973	23	830	1,212	1,176[2]	1,893[2]	1,387	2,232	3,427	5,004
Mozambique	16,955	27,287	17	35,000	35,000	224	...	...	1,857	2,988	49.0	78.9	288.6	421.4
Myanmar (Burma)	14,579	23,463	38	35,000	35,000	611	71	103.7	1,949[2]	3,137[2]	2,781	4,476	395	576
Namibia	26,024	41,882	11	52,767	57,173	14	...	...	1,481	2,383	1,248	2,008	840	1,226
Nauru	17	27	78	——1,448——		6.3	...	...	3[13]	5[13]	...	...	4.7	6.8
Nepal	5,175	8,328	37	4,949	3,363	2,259	984	1,437	33[2]	53[2]	...	...	...	...
Netherlands, The	73,455	118,214	89	5,658,000	797,000	2.4	16,752	24,458	1,711	2,753	9,538	15,350	1,893	2,764

merchant marine				air					canals and inland waterways (latest)				country
fleet, 1992 (vessels over 100 gross tons)	total dead-weight tonnage, 1992 ('000)	international cargo (latest)		airports with scheduled flights, 1994	traffic (latest)				length		cargo		
		loaded metric tons ('000)	off-loaded metric tons ('000)		passengers		cargo		mi	km	short ton-mi ('000,000)	metric ton-km ('000,000)	
					passenger-mi ('000,000)	passenger-km ('000,000)	short ton-mi ('000,000)	metric ton-km ('000,000)					
3	6.7	110	64	1	4	7	0.7	1.0	...	...	...	...	Equatorial Guinea
...	...	...	...	2	...	...	...	...	...	...	...	...	Eritrea
234	680.4	6,072	5,664	1	118.7	191.1	4.1	6.0	311	500	0.4	0.6	Estonia
27	84.3	520	3,014	25	974	1,568	54	79	...	...	...	...	Ethiopia
191	59.8	207	472	1	...	...	...	...	...	...	...	...	Faeroe Islands
64	60.4	568	625	13	146.9	236.5	20.0	29.2	126	200	...	...	Fiji
263	989.3	31,872	32,556	25	5,333	8,582	77.5	113.2	4,148	6,675	2,260	3,300	Finland
729	4,981.0	61,200	182,400	63	26,770[22]	43,082[22]	5,343[22]	7,801[22]	9,278	14,932	5,912	8,631	France
7	0.7	62	688	8	...	...	...	...	286	460	...	...	French Guiana
41	16.5	15	666	36	...	...	...	...	...	...	...	...	French Polynesia
29	30.2	12,828	212	17	276.7	445.3	17.9	26.1	994	1,600	...	...	Gabon
11	2.0	109	212	1	...	...	...	...	250	400	...	...	Gambia, The
—	—	...	...	—	...	...	...	...	...	...	...	...	Gaza Strip
...	...	...	...	1	3,291	5,296	...	...	...	...	...	...	Georgia
1,375	6,832.3	58,176	117,648	40	71,030	114,312	3,021	4,410	4,686	7,541	37,877	55,300	Germany
155	131.0	1,810	2,842	1	206	331	13	19	803	1,293	75	110	Ghana
49	1,136.1	5	400	1	...	...	...	...	...	...	...	...	Gibraltar
1,872	45,276.6	20,400	37,788	34	4,513	7,262	73.3	107.0	50	80	585	854	Greece
82	17.2	298	288	5	16.3	26.3	0.23	0.34	...	...	...	...	Greenland
3	0.5	25	190	2	...	...	...	...	...	...	...	...	Grenada
20	4.4	388	2,486	6	...	...	...	...	...	...	...	...	Guadeloupe
5	0.1	195	1,524	1	...	...	...	...	...	...	...	...	Guam
8	0.4	1,624	2,529	2	142.9	230.0	6.3	9.2	162	260	...	...	Guatemala
—	...	...	...	1	...	...	...	...	...	...	...	...	Guernsey
23	1.7	12,210	712	1	17.9	28.8	1.7	2.5	805	1,295	...	...	Guinea
19	1.8	33	263	2	6	9	0.7	1.0	...	...	...	...	Guinea-Bissau
82	13.5	1,730	673	1	229	369	1.9	2.8	3,700	6,000	...	...	Guyana
4	0.4	170	704	1	...	...	...	...	60	100	...	...	Haiti
966	1,437.3	1,316	1,002	8	321[23]	516[23]	2.0[23]	3.0[23]	289	465	...	...	Honduras
387	11,688.6	27,216[24]	57,312[24]	1	...	...	...	...	...	...	...	...	Hong Kong
15	134.5	...	...	1	924.0	1,487	7.0	10.2	1,008	1,622	3,540	5,169	Hungary
394	114.9	834	1,677	24	1,273	2,049	24.9	36.4	...	...	58	84	Iceland
888	10,365.9	45,255	54,134	95	8,897	14,318	245.2	357.9	10,054	16,180	...	...	India
2,014	3,130.2	151,536	36,012	126	9,270	14,919	315.2	460.2	13,409	21,579	17,000	25,000	Indonesia
403	8,345.3	113,207	16,719	19	3,001	4,830	41.1	60.0	562	904	...	...	Iran
131	1,578.8	97,830	8,638	...	970	1,570	37.4	54.6	631	1,015	...	...	Iraq
189	208.6	6,367	17,637	10	2,364	3,804	296	432	...	...	...	...	Ireland
101	2,836.5	6	203	1	115.5	185.9	0.2	0.3	...	...	...	...	Isle of Man
50	723.4	7,812	20,220	7	5,332[25]	8,581[25]	589.5[25]	860.7[25]	...	...	...	...	Israel
1,636	10,940.1	46,032	225,408	32	15,234[26]	24,516[26]	1,338.00	1,953[26]	1,500	2,400	59	86	Italy
12	16.2	8,802	5,285	4	888.6	1,430	14.2	20.0	...	...	...	...	Jamaica
10,091	27,816.8	100,032	707,688	75	65,699	105,732	4,914	7,175	1,100	1,770	170,005	248,203	Japan
—	—	...	...	1	...	...	...	...	...	...	...	...	Jersey
5	113.6	8,868	6,168	2	2,488	4,004	146.3	213.6	...	...	19,202	28,035	Jordan
...	...	...	...	6	7,800	12,600	48.0	70.0	...	...	235	343	Kazakhstan
29	11.6	2,320	5,689	14	828.3[27]	1,333[27]	82.9[27]	121.1[27]	...	...	...	...	Kenya
7	2.7	15	26	18	5.3	8.6	0.5	0.8	3	5	...	...	Kiribati
100	951.2	635	5,520	1	...	...	...	...	1,400	2,253	...	...	Korea, North
2,138	11,724.9	62,856	222,516	13	12,401	19,957	1,825	2,664	1,000	1,609	11,382	16,617	Korea, South
209	3,188.5	51,400	4,522	1	2,519	4,054	174.0	254.1	...	...	...	...	Kuwait
...	...	...	...	1	1,602	2,578	158.8	231.9	...	...	...	...	Kyrgyzstan
1	1.5	—	—	11	11	18	1.4	2.0	2,850	4,587	307	448	Laos
261	1,436.9	22,548	3,984	1	1,863	2,999	15.1	22.0	180	300	277	404	Latvia
163	438.2	152	1,150	1	798	1,285	25.5	37.2	...	...	...	...	Lebanon
—	—	—	—	1	4.8	7.7	0.2	0.3	—	—	—	—	Lesotho
1,672	97,374.0	14,900	1,520	1	11	17	0.07	0.1	...	...	...	...	Liberia
150	1,223.6	55,299	7,586	12	693[28]	1,116[28]	2.6[28]	3.8[28]	—	—	...	...	Libya
—	...	...	...	—	...	...	...	...	...	...	...	...	Liechtenstein
52	373.9	...	...	3	569.8	917.0	3.6	5.3	373	600	31	45	Lithuania
54	2,603.6	—	—	1	79.5	128	606.9	886.1	23	37	232	338	Luxembourg
6	0.1	755	3,935	—	...	...	...	...	...	...	...	...	Macau
...	...	...	...	1	...	...	...	...	...	...	...	...	Macedonia
85	82.1	527	792	50	152	244	52.5	76.7	...	...	...	...	Madagascar
1	0.3	...	...	6	33.2	53.4	1.6	2.3	891	1,434	6.7	9.8	Malawi
552	2,916.3	66,025	30,083	40	9,321	15,001	400.8	585.1	4,534	7,296	...	...	Malaysia
44	79.0	27	78	1	...	...	...	...	...	...	...	...	Maldives
—	—	...	...	1	68	110	0.4	0.6	1,128	1,815	18	27	Mali
889	17,073.2	90	2,458	1	630	1,014	3.8	5.6	...	...	...	...	Malta
35	4,182.4	29	123	24	...	...	2.4	3.5	...	...	...	...	Marshall Islands
6	1.1	552	1,728	2	...	...	...	...	...	...	...	...	Martinique
126	23.9	10,037	674	10	173	278	11	16	...	...	...	...	Mauritania
35	152.2	855	1,842	1	1,659	2,670	63.9	93.3	...	...	...	...	Mauritius
1	1.1	—	—	1	...	...	...	...	...	...	...	...	Mayotte
635	1,495.3	125,448	52,092	57	11,936[30]	19,154[30]	1,241[30]	1,812[30]	1,800	2,900	...	...	Mexico
17	6.9	...	...	4	...	...	...	...	...	...	...	...	Micronesia
1	...	...	...	1	1,461	2,352	13.0	19.0	...	...	18	27	Moldova
...	...	...	...	1	...	...	...	...	...	...	...	...	Monaco
...	...	...	...	1	254	408	2.6	3.8	247	397	2.9	4.3	Mongolia
492	586.2	18,300	17,916	16	1,700	2,700	24.0	35.0	...	...	2,622	3,028	Morocco
107	31.6	2,578	3,379	7	253	407	7.1	10.3	2,330	3,750	...	...	Mozambique
144	1,354.0	1,200	876	20	137.7	221.6	5.6	8.2	7,954	12,800	236.5	345.3	Myanmar (Burma)
30	5.9	483	260	12	263	423	1.4	2.0	...	...	...	...	Namibia
2	5.8	1,650	59	1	148[31]	238[31]	1.1[31]	1.6[31]	...	...	...	...	Nauru
...	...	...	...	17	439	706	7.5	11.0	...	...	...	...	Nepal
1,076	4,191.0	89,016	289,176	5	19,849	31,944	1,704	2,488	3,939	6,340	4,088	5,969	Netherlands, The

Transportation (continued)

country	roads and motor vehicles (latest) roads length mi	km	paved (per-cent)	motor vehicles auto-mobiles	trucks and buses	persons per vehicle	cargo short ton-mi ('000,000)	metric ton-km ('000,000)	railroads (latest) track length mi	km	traffic passengers passen-ger-mi ('000,000)	passen-ger-km ('000,000)	cargo short ton-mi ('000,000)	metric ton-km ('000,000)
Netherlands Antilles	525	845	...	60,000	13,000	2.6	...	...	—	—	—	—	—	—
New Caledonia	3,580	5,762	22	55,000	20,000	2.3	...	...	—	—	—	—	—	—
New Zealand	58,605	94,315	73	1,577,951	324,852	1.8	...	...	2,627	4,227	285	458	1,800	2,628
Nicaragua	9,499	15,287	10	35,000	35,000	59	...	...	186[2]	300[2]	15.8	25.5	46.6	68.0
Niger	6,997	11,258	29	31,427	8,768	192	1,044	1,524	—	—	—	—	—	—
Nigeria	69,680	112,140	28	800,000	625,000	63	...	...	2,210	3,557	2,366	3,808	1,194	1,743
Northern Mariana Islands	186	300	18	11,633	6,190	2.5	...	...	—	—	—	—	—	—
Norway	56,235	90,502	70	1,633,088	396,090	2.1	5,143	7,508	2,502[2]	4,026[2]	1,437	2,312	1,575	2,300
Oman	16,123	25,948	19	175,000	90,787	7.3	...	...	—	—	—	—	—	—
Pakistan	111,693	179,752	51	721,150	200,160	132	...	...	5,453[2]	8,775[2]	11,285	18,161	4,085	5,964
Panama	6,278	10,103	32	150,903	72,744	11	...	...	220[2]	354[2]	0.3	0.6	0.5	0.7
Papua New Guinea	12,263	19,736	6	13,150	24,332	101	...	...	—	—	—	—	—	—
Paraguay	15,957	25,681	9	117,067	3,375	36	...	...	273[2]	439[2]	7.9	12.7	7.9	11.5
Peru	43,460	69,942	11	402,351	257,884	34	...	...	2,157[2]	3,472[2]	198.7	319.8	566.3	826.8
Philippines	99,813	160,633	14	480,542	916,559	47	...	...	658[2]	1,059[2]	75.2	121.1	3.5	5.1
Poland	227,027	365,365	63	6,112,171	1,329,650	5.1	40,309	58,850	16,061	25,848	24,926	40,115	44,621	65,146
Portugal	43,605	70,176	86	2,020,000	695,700	3.6	7,482	10,923	2,066[2]	3,325[2]	3,538	5,694	1,279	1,867
Puerto Rico	14,036	22,588	87	1,380,213	215,115	2.2	...	...	—	—	—	—	—	—
Qatar	671	1,080	63	122,000	55,079	3.0	...	...	—	—	—	—	—	—
Réunion	1,750	2,800	79	150,000	50,000	3.1	...	...	—	—	—	—	—	—
Romania	95,099	153,014	51	1,397,118	332,273	13	10,460	15,271	7,051	11,348	12,057	19,404	17,244	25,176
Russia	570,000	918,000	76	10,499,000	407,000	14	172,751	252,212	98,239	158,100	157,331	253,200	1,347	1,967
Rwanda	8,185	13,173	9	7,868	2,048	697	140	200	—	—	—	—	—	—
St. Kitts and Nevis	186	300	42	4,000	700	10	...	...	—	—	—	—	—	—
St. Lucia	500	805	56	9,863	9,075	7.3	...	...	—	—	—	—	—	—
St. Vincent and the Grenadines	586	943	16	5,000	2,000	15	...	...	—	—	—	—	—	—
San Marino	147	237	...	22,159	3,658	0.9	...	...	—	—	—	—	—	—
São Tomé and Príncipe	149	240	42	2,600	900	39	...	...	—	—	—	—	—	—
Saudi Arabia	94,157	151,532	40	2,762,773	2,340,630	3.3	...	...	864[2]	1,390[2]	94	151	523	763
Senegal	8,772	14,117	27	100,000	45,000	53	375	547	562	904	108	174	418	610
Seychelles	199	321	68	4,700	1,600	11	...	...	—	—	—	—	—	—
Sierra Leone	5,505	8,860	18	32,258	11,961	99	36	53	52	84	...	...	...	...
Singapore	1,857	2,989	97	321,922	132,455	6.3	...	...	16	26	...	...	...	...
Slovakia	11,110	17,880	...	953,239	81,350	5.1	...	...	2,275	3,661	3,444	5,543	11,436	16,697
Slovenia	9,192	14,794	75	606,820	33,957	3.1	4.4	6.4	746	1,201	340	547	1,762	2,573
Solomon Islands	1,300	2,100	8	2,052	2,574	75	...	...	—	—	—	—	—	—
Somalia	13,845	22,281	14	10,500	11,500	300	...	...	—	—	—	—	—	—
South Africa	113,294	182,329	30	3,488,570	1,899,721	7.4	1,053	1,538	13,432[2]	21,617[2]	749	1,205	63,713	93,019
Spain	206,271	331,961	99	13,102,285	2,696,776	2.5	105,824	154,500	8,109[2]	13,050[2]	10,161	16,352	6,337	9,252
Sri Lanka	16,126	25,952	81	189,477	153,745	51	3,373	4,925	887[2]	1,427[2]	1,751	2,818	115.7	168.9
Sudan, The	14,000	22,500	9	116,000	57,000	143	...	...	2,960[2]	4,764[2]	330	531	271	396
Suriname	5,687	9,153	29	42,561	15,774	7.1	...	...	187	301	...	...	73	107
Swaziland	1,740	2,801	26	25,283	7,297	25	20,100	29,400	199	320	...	...	13,318	19,444
Sweden	84,419	135,859	72	3,566,040	315,994	2.2	6,863	10,020	6,863	11,045	3,517	5,660	5,252	7,668
Switzerland	44,191	71,118	96	3,085,372	291,457	2.0	6,863	10,020	3,125	5,030	7,300	11,748	5,252	7,668
Syria	19,616	31,569	77	117,842	152,833	48	1,075	1,570	1,097[2]	1,766[2]	775	1,248	1,167	1,704
Taiwan	12,136	19,531	87	3,416,848	790,712	5.0	7,906	11,543	2,415	3,887	5,929	9,542	1,345	1,964
Tajikistan	8,324	13,396	93	209,100	...	...	3,518	5,136	554	891	6,094	9,808	7,617	11,121
Tanzania	34,500	55,600	37	50,000	40,000	287	...	...	2,218	3,569	2,324	3,740	1,021	1,490
Thailand	44,844	72,170	55	890,821	2,231,518	18	...	...	2,405[2]	3,870[2]	8,784	14,136	2,112	3,084
Togo	4,688	7,545	24	25,000	12,500	99	...	...	326	525	82	132	12	17
Tonga	240	386	76	3,297	3,757	14	...	...	—	—	—	—	—	—
Trinidad and Tobago	4,970	8,000	50	150,196	60,006	5.9	...	...	—	—	—	—	—	—
Tunisia	18,133	29,183	60	321,101	208,596	15	678	990	1,404[2]	2,260[2]	670	1,078	1,380	2,015
Turkey	240,286	386,704	15	2,181,388	816,244	20	46,373	67,704	5,238[2]	8,430[2]	3,889	6,259	5,742	8,383
Turkmenistan	8,300	13,400	86	170,600	...	...	3,283	4,793	1,317	2,120	...	...	...	...
Tuvalu	5	8	—	...	...	...	...	...	—	—	—	—	—	—
Uganda	17,808	28,660	16	17,804	25,246	402	...	...	770[2]	1,240[2]	205	330	60	87
Ukraine	106,000	170,000	95	2,920,000	...	...	44,218	64,557	14,167	22,799	47,000	75,600	232,000	338,000
United Arab Emirates	2,709	4,360	61	353,000	188,000	3.7	...	...	—	—	—	—	—	—
United Kingdom	240,241	386,631	100	20,344,000	2,753,000	2.5	84,635	123,565	23,518[43]	37,849[43]	19,693	31,693	10,623	15,509
United States	3,902,000	6,280,000	89	144,213,000	46,149,000	1.3	758,013	1,106,680	136,000	219,000	6,062	9,756	1,089,092	1,590,048
Uruguay	32,311	52,000	23	310,833	148,644	6.8	500	730	1,865[2]	3,002[2]	87.4	140.6	139.7	204.0
Uzbekistan	55,431	89,207	83	790,800	...	...	15,037	21,954	4,200	6,800	3,300	5,200	48,400	70,600
Vanuatu	702	1,130	21	4,500	3,000	21	...	...	—	—	—	—	—	—
Venezuela	58,081	93,472	32	1,565,872	456,425	10	...	...	226[2]	363[2]	29.0	46.7	24.8	36.2
Vietnam	56,000	90,000	10	...	...	...	1,845	2,693	2,001	3,220	1,189	1,913	755	1,103
Virgin Islands (U.S.)	532	856	100	49,231	12,723	1.7	...	...	—	—	—	—	—	—
West Bank	...	...	...	40,033	14,324	16	...	...	...	...	...	...	...	...
Western Sahara	3,900	6,200	23	6,284	424	20	...	...	—	—	—	—	—	—
Western Samoa	1,296	2,085	19	2,295	3,252	29	...	...	—	—	—	—	—	—
Yemen	31,933	51,392	9	186,172	254,355	27	...	...	—	—	—	—	—	—
Yugoslavia	29,771	47,912	59	1,406,000	132,100	6.8	14,929[46]	21,796[46]	2,461	3,960	1,803	2,901	1,163	1,698
Zaire	91,031	146,500	12	105,000	95,000	206	...	...	3,275	5,270	162[47]	260[47]	1,186[47]	1,732[47]
Zambia	23,214	37,359	18	100,000	75,000	49	...	...	791	1,273	166.7	268.3	735.6	1,074
Zimbabwe	56,593	91,078	16	310,412	30,182	30	...	...	1,714[2]	2,759[2]	355.1	571.4	3.7	5.4

[1]Bakhtar Afghan Airlines only. [2]Route length. [3]Air Algérie international flights only. [4]TAAG-Angola Airlines only. [5]Aerolineas Argentinas only. [6]Included with Netherlands Antilles. [7]Government railways only. [8]Including Gulf Air international traffic. [9]Caribbean Airways only. [10]Caribbean Air Cargo only. [11]Air Afrique only. [12]Air Botswana only. [13]For industrial purposes only. [14]Lasca only. [15]Traffic between Ouagadougou, Burkina Faso, and Abidjan, Côte d'Ivoire. [16]Air Ivoire only. [17]Data refer to former Czechoslovakia. [18]Including SAS international and domestic traffic. [19]National roads only. [20]TACA airlines only. [21]Includes 100 km of the Chemin de Fer Djibouti-Ethiopien (CDE) in Djibouti. [22]Air France, UTA, and Air Inter only. [23]TAN and SAHSA airlines only. [24]Includes

merchant marine				air					canals and inland waterways (latest)				country
fleet, 1992 (vessels over 100 gross tons)	total dead-weight tonnage, 1992 ('000)	international cargo (latest)		airports with scheduled flights, 1994	traffic (latest)				length		cargo		
		loaded metric tons ('000)	off-loaded metric tons ('000)		passengers		cargo		mi	km	short ton-mi ('000,000)	metric ton-km ('000,000)	
					passenger-mi ('000,000)	passenger-km ('000,000)	short ton-mi ('000,000)	metric ton-km ('000,000)					
154[32]	1,053.6[32]	18,560	18,715	5	234[33]	377[33]	1.2[33]	1.8[33]	...	...	...	...	Netherlands Antilles
17	18.1	1,040	930	10	79.7[34]	128[34]	0.3[34]	0.5[04]	...	...	...	...	New Caledonia
139	279.8	15,960	9,672	36	8,254	13,284	325	474	1,000	1,609	1,503	2,195	New Zealand
25	1.3	320	1,629	4	69	111	2.5	3.6	1,379	2,220	...	...	Nicaragua
—	—	—	—	1	144.3	232.3	27.0	39.4	186	300	...	...	Niger
271	733.3	80,607	10,812	12	619	996	7.9	11.5	5,328	8,575	...	...	Nigeria
2	0.9	...	...	3									Northern Mariana Islands
1,630	2,143.3	109,440	19,884	48	5,564[18]	8,954[18]	423.0[18]	617.5[10]	980	1,577	6,109	8,919	Norway
20	11.7	33,843	2,492	6	1,194[8]	1,922[8]	47.8[8]	69.8[8]	...	...	...	...	Oman
73	513.8	6,036	23,052	34	6,278	10,104	279.5	408.0	...	...	...	...	Pakistan
5,217	79,255.6	100,992	62,148	8	209	336	3.6	5.3	497	800	...	...	Panama
87	40.9	2,463	1,784	121	439.8	707.8	56.6	82.6	6,798	10,940	...	...	Papua New Guinea
38	38.5	...	...	1	700	1,127	3.5	5.1	1,900	3,100	...	...	Paraguay
623	615.6	10,197	5,077	25	803	1,292	101	148	5,300	8,600	...	...	Peru
1,499	13,807.1	14,100	30,396	20	8,010[35]	12,891[35]	213.7[35]	311.9[35]	2,000	3,219	...	...	Philippines
644	4,311.3	31,755	15,384	12	2,230	3,589	30.8	45.0	2,484	3,997	514	750	Poland
326	1,129.3	4,068	16,044	14	4,906	7,896	126	184	510	820	...	...	Portugal
13	—	...	...	7									Puerto Rico
65	635.6	18,145	2,588	1	1,042[8]	1,676[8]	35.1[8]	51.2[8]	...	...	...	...	Qatar
7	33.5	287	1,815	1									Réunion
439	4,845.5	11,352	16,008	16	1,171	1,884	11.4	16.7	1,071	1,724	1,295	1,891	Romania
4,543	16,592.3	27,072	7,320	58	73,135	117,700	1,233	1,800	63,380	102,000	93,010	135,792	Russia
—	—	—	—	3	...	...	...	...	...	...	...	...	Rwanda
1	0.6	24	36	2	...	...	...	...	...	...	...	...	St. Kitts and Nevis
7	2.1	150	234	2	...	...	...	...	...	...	...	...	St. Lucia
881	7,044.2	80	140	4	...	...	...	...	...	...	...	...	St. Vincent and the Grenadines
—	—	—	—	—	—	—	—	—	—	—	—	—	San Marino
4	2.3	16	25	2	5.0	8.0	0.7	1.0	...	...	...	...	São Tomé and Príncipe
301	1,381.7	214,070	46,437	24	10,913	17,563	465	679	...	...	...	...	Saudi Arabia
183	27.5	2,591	2,477	9	144.3[28]	232.3[28]	27.0[28]	39.4[28]	557	897	...	...	Senegal
9	3.3	11	348	2	...	...	...	...	...	...	...	...	Seychelles
62	18.4	1,802	533	1	68.3[36]	109.9[36]	1.4[36]	2.0[36]	500	800	447	652	Sierra Leone
946	14,929.2	114,804	158,904	1	23,056	37,105	1,579	2,306	...	...	...	...	Singapore
...	...	...	...	4	...	...	...	...	...	...	...	...	Slovakia
22	596.9	...	...	1	259	417	1,314	1,918	...	...	2.3	3.4	Slovenia
33	5.0	278	349	22	117.1[37]	188.4[37]	0.02[37]	0.04[07]	...	...	...	...	Solomon Islands
28	18.5	324	1,118	...	154	248	1.4	2.0	...	...	...	...	Somalia
219	202.5	95,904	13,560	31	6,537[38]	10,521[38]	219[38]	320[38]	...	...	...	...	South Africa
2,190	5,077.3	40,836	133,956	23	16,614	26,738	410	599	649	1,045	21,836[39]	31,880[39]	Spain
66	472.6	4,104	7,176	1	2,285	3,677	71.5	104.4	267	430	...	...	Sri Lanka
16	62.2	1,195	3,467	12	360.5[40]	580.2[40]	25.3[40]	36.9[40]	3,300	5,310	...	...	Sudan, The
24	15.7	5,776	1,286	2	251[41]	404[41]	10.3[41]	15.0[41]	746	1,200	...	...	Suriname
—	—	—	—	1	25.6	41.2	0.1	0.1	—	—	...	...	Swaziland
664	3,327.7	48,048	56,976	45	5,019[18]	8,078[18]	115.5[18]	168.6[18]	1,275	2,052	5,300	7,800	Sweden
24	602.8	...	...	6	10,038	16,154	728.1	1,063	40	65	34	50	Switzerland
94	210.4	17,868	5,676	5	719	1,157	9.9	14.4	541	870	...	...	Syria
649	9,241.3	128,125	217,154	12	17,534	28,218	3,099	4,524	...	...	...	...	Taiwan
...	...	...	...	1	3,214	5,173	22.1	32.3	...	...	...	...	Tajikistan
43	48.5	1,249	2,721	12	97	156	1.3	1.9	...	...	...	...	Tanzania
351	1,194.5	21,192	40,152	26	12,737	20,498	634.5	926.3	2,300	3,701	...	...	Thailand
8	20.6	2,362	1,050	1	126	203	11	16	31	50	...	...	Togo
15	13.7	15	104	4	42.4	68.3	0.01	0.01	...	...	...	...	Tonga
53	17.5	9,622	10,961	2	2,030	3,267	10.1	14.8	...	...	...	...	Trinidad and Tobago
77	443.3	6,648	9,612	5	1,036	1,668	11.7	17.1	...	...	...	...	Tunisia
880	7,114.3	22,956	61,720	22	4,484[42]	7,217[42]	110.5[42]	161.4[42]	750	1,200	209	305	Turkey
...	...	...	...	1	2,021	3,253	222	324	...	...	...	...	Turkmenistan
6	16.0	...	...	1									Tuvalu
2	...	...	...	1	41.6	67.0	2.1	3.0	...	...	...	...	Uganda
...	...	34,200	...	20	5,200	8,400	68	100	1,039	1,672	5,628	8,217	Ukraine
276	1,491.7	88,153	9,595	4	1,859[8]	2,992[8]	99[8]	144[8]	...	...	...	...	United Arab Emirates
1,631	4,687.3	133,740	176,316	54	53,892	86,731	1,811	2,644	1,424	2,291	35,900	52,500	United Kingdom
5,710	25,646.4	392,316[44]	483,516[44]	834	480,463	773,232	13,320	19,447	25,482	41,009	462,008	674,520	United States
93	172.5	710[45]	1,450[45]	7	293	471	1.8	2.6	1,000	1,600	...	...	Uruguay
...	...	...	...	1	6,500	10,500	60,800	88,700	...	...	...	...	Uzbekistan
280	3,259.6	80	55	29	—	—	—	—	...	...	...	...	Vanuatu
271	1,355.4	101,435	17,932	25	4,220	6,791	536	782	4,400	7,100	...	...	Venezuela
230	872.8	303	1,510	12	54	87	0.7	1.0	11,000	17,702	...	...	Vietnam
1	...	105.5	648.3	4	...	...	...	...	...	...	...	...	Virgin Islands (U.S.)
—	—	...	...	—									West Bank
—	—	40	15	1	...	...	...	...	...	...	...	...	Western Sahara
7	6.5	28	68	2	...	...	...	...	...	...	...	...	Western Samoa
40	13.7	1,936	7,829	12	641	1,032	8.0	11.7	...	...	...	...	Yemen
462[46]	5,173.1[46]	8,520[46]	10,176[46]	5	65	104	82	119	1,616[46]	2,600[46]	3,430[46]	5,007[46]	Yugoslavia
27	30.7	2,395	1,453	24	89.6[48]	144.2[48]	14.4[48]	21.0[48]	9,300	15,000	678	990	Zaire
—	—	—	—	8	313	504	11.4	16.7	1,398	2,250	...	...	Zambia
—	—	—	—	5	508	817	44	64	...	...	...	...	Zimbabwe

transshipments. [25]El Al only. [26]Alitalia only. [27]Kenya Airways only. [28]International traffic only. [29]Peninsular Malaysia and Singapore. [30]Aeronaves de Mexico and Mexicana only. [31]Air Nauru only. [32]Includes Aruba. [33]Antillean Airlines only. [34]Air Caledonie only. [35]PAL only. [36]Sierra Leone Airlines international traffic only. [37]Solair only. [38]SAA only. [39]Coastal shipping only. [40]Sudan Airways only. [41]Suriname Airways only. [42]Turkish Airlines only. [43]British Railways only; excludes Northern Ireland. [44]Includes Puerto Rico. [45]Port of Montevideo only. [46]Data refer to Yugoslavia as constituted prior to 1991. [47]Zaire National Railways only. [48]Air Zaire only.

Communications

Virtually all the states of the world have a variety of communications media and services available to their citizens: book publishing and newspapers (although only daily papers are included in this table); postal services; radio and television broadcast systems; telephones; and cinema. Unfortunately, the availability of information about the structure and volume of these national services and sectors often runs behind the capabilities of the services themselves. Certain countries publish no official information; others publish data analyzed according to a variety of fiscal, calendar, religious, or other years; still others, while they possess such data almost simultaneously with the end of the business year, may not see them published except in company or parastatal reports of limited distribution. Even when such data are published in national statistical summaries, it may be only after a delay of up to several years. Figures in italics are from 1989 or earlier.

The data also differ in their completeness and reliability. Figures for book production, for example, generally include all works published in separate bindings except advertising works, timetables, telephone directories, price lists, catalogs of businesses or exhibitions, musical scores, maps, atlases, and the like. The figures include government publications, school texts, theses, offprints, series works, and illustrated works, even those consisting principally of illustrations. Figures refer to works actually published during the year of survey, usually by a registered publisher, and deposited for copyright. A book is defined as a work of 49 or more pages, a pamphlet as a work of from 5 to 48 pages. A work published simultaneously in more than one country is counted as having been published in each. Newspaper statistics are especially difficult to collect and compare. Newspapers continually are founded, cease publication, merge, or change frequency of publication. Data on circulation, sales, and readership are often incomplete, slow to be aggregated at the national level, or regarded as proprietary. In some countries circulation data are virtually nonexistent. In others no daily newspaper exists.

Post office statistics are compiled mainly from the Universal Postal Union's annual summary *Statistique des services postaux*. Postal services, unlike the other media discussed earlier, tend most often to be operated by a single national service, to cover a country completely, and to record traffic data according to broadly similar schemes (although the details of *classes* of mail handled may differ). Some countries do not enumerate domestic traffic or may record only international traffic requiring handling charges.

Data for some kinds of communications apparatus and traffic are rel-

Communications

country	publishing (latest)								daily newspapers (latest)		
	number of titles			number of copies ('000)					number	total circulation ('000)	circulation per 1,000 population
	books		periodicals	pamphlets	books		periodicals	pamphlets			
	total	school textbooks			total	school textbooks					
Afghanistan	1,776	150	105	1,019	...	...	...	...	14	180	11
Albania	363	190	143	18	3,498	3,110	3,477	270	2	135	42
Algeria	475	1	48	19	...	...	803	...	10	1,274	51
American Samoa	...	...	...	...	...	...	...	...	—	—	—
Andorra	49	4	15	...	...	...	15	...	1	3	54
Angola	14	...	...	...	130	...	...	...	4	115	11
Antigua and Barbuda	...	...	...	...	...	...	...	...	1	6	79
Argentina	4,836	...	...	...	...	...	...	...	159	4,000	124
Armenia	817[9]	...	76	[9]	10,100[9]	...	28,800	[9]	82	1,678	496
Aruba	...	...	...	...	...	...	...	...	5	...	...
Australia	6,800	487	...	3,923	...	...	...	...	62	4,200	249
Austria	9,315	...	2,619	990	...	...	...	...	25	2,706	357
Azerbaijan	829[9]	...	91	[9]	12,500[9]	...	49,100	[9]	154	2,900	416
Bahamas, The	...	...	...	...	...	...	...	...	3	35	135
Bahrain	46	...	...	...	...	...	...	...	2	29	56
Bangladesh	1,209	...	41	...	...	...	163	...	52	700	6
Barbados	17	...	52	60	...	...	...	...	2	41	160
Belarus	2,432	71	129	779	37,887	5,031	4,596	15,024	28	2,937	286
Belgium	13,913[9]	...	13,014	[9]	...	...	...	...	33	3,000	305
Belize	12	...	...	...	156	...	...	...	—	—	—
Benin	...	...	...	...	...	...	...	...	1	12	3
Bermuda	...	...	...	...	...	...	...	...	1	18	310
Bhutan	...	...	...	...	...	...	...	...	—	—	—
Bolivia	365	...	...	82	365	...	...	46	17	400	55
Bosnia and Herzegovina	966	...	92	...	7,540	...	1,887	...	3	149	34
Botswana	97	4	20	61	...	...	153	...	1	18	14
Brazil	13,973	...	3,782	3,675	...	...	980	...	356	8,100	54
Brunei	25	6	4	...	56	22	363	...	1	10	38
Bulgaria	2,659	773	907	601	34,695	8,350	6,006	6,185	24	4,065	451
Burkina Faso	4	...	37	...	9	...	24	...	1	3	0.3
Burundi	37	9	...	17	274	229	...	174	1	20	4
Cambodia	...	...	58	...	...	...	...	...	1	25	3
Cameroon	...	...	58	...	...	...	127	...	1	66	5
Canada	12,750	...	1,503	...	...	...	39,510	...	105	5,115	187
Cape Verde	9	—	...	1	9	—	...	1	—	—	—
Central African Republic	...	...	...	...	...	...	...	...	1	2	0.7
Chad	...	...	10	...	...	...	...	...	1	2	0.3
Chile	1,527	...	241	439	...	...	1,980	...	45	6,000	445
China	73,923	11,107	6,078	...	5,387,020	2,657,140	1,840,000	...	44	...	...
Colombia	1,481	44	...	...	11,314	700	...	...	31	1,441	23
Comoros	...	...	...	...	...	...	...	...	—	—	—
Congo	...	...	3	...	...	...	34	...	5	17	7
Costa Rica	230	1	...	14	...	...	...	...	4	314	102
Côte d'Ivoire	...	...	...	...	...	...	...	...	1	90	8
Croatia	2,239	...	352	...	12,220	...	6,357	...	9	636	133
Cuba	1,575	346	160	283	37,607	6,989	2,797	7,767	19	1,824	172
Cyprus	530	67	48	325	769	353	244	585	11	78	111
Czech Republic	6,743[9]	...	2,898	[9]	...	...	...	...	76	5,002	484
Denmark	7,066	721	210	3,132	...	...	7,906	...	47	1,810	352
Djibouti	...	...	7	...	...	...	6	...	1	4	8
Dominica	...	...	...	...	...	...	...	...	—	—	—
Dominican Republic	...	...	277	...	...	...	...	...	12	230	32
Ecuador	717[9]	...	...	[9]	...	...	...	...	25	920	87
Egypt	1,311	256	265	140	20,096	14,267	2,017	2,967	14	3,000	57
El Salvador	15	6	...	—	63	21	...	—	5	457	87
Equatorial Guinea	...	17	...	...	...	17	...	...	2	2	6
Eritrea[20]	...	...	...	...	...	...	...	...	...	...	...
Estonia	1,142	98	351	512	17,506	1,846	19,000	5,794	111	2,556	1,620
Ethiopia[20]	2,147	23	3	93	426	69	14	248	3	42	0.8
Faeroe Islands	148	...	...	...	...	...	...	...	...	...	...

atively easy to collect; telephones, for example, must be installed, and service recorded so that it may be charged. But in most countries radios may be purchased by anyone and turned on whenever desired; car radios are seldom enumerated or licensed separately. As a result, data on distribution and use of radio and television apparatus may be collected in a variety of ways—on the basis of numbers of subscribers, licenses issued, periodic sample surveys, census or housing surveys, or private consumer surveys. Statistics on commercial cinema attendance (usually those of the United Nations Educational, Scientific and Cultural Organization [Unesco] or national data) may refer to a variety of screening facilities, including fixed, mobile, or drive-in facilities.

The *Statistical Yearbook* of Unesco contains extensive data on book publishing, newspapers, radio and television, and cinema that have been collected from standardized questionnaires. The quality and recency of its data, however, depend on the completion and timely return of each questionnaire by national authorities, and response rates depend on a variety of factors. In general, however, response rates for inquiries by international organizations in communications are better than in other fields because these organizations and the responsible authorities in each country must conduct day-to-day business and, hence, have a better ongoing relationship. The commercially published annual *World Radio TV Handbook* (Andrew G. Sennitt, editor) is a valuable source of information on broadcast media and has complete and timely coverage. It depends on data received from broadcasters, but, because some do not respond, local correspondents and monitors are used in many countries, and some unconfirmed or unofficial data are included as estimates. The statistics on telephones are derived mainly from the UN-affiliated International Telecommunication Union's *ITU Statistical Yearbook* and from a variety of national and regional intergovernmental sources. A number of countries report incomplete telephone data: the national total may exclude figures for some telephone companies, or some portion of the national territory; some countries supply statistics only on telephone exchange lines, some island states report only radio telephones. A number of countries omit data on public coin box telephones; their statistics thus reflect an undercount.
... Not available.
—None, nil, or not applicable.

post offices, 1992				radio, 1993		television, 1993		telephones, 1992		cinema (latest) annual attendance		country
number	persons per office	pieces of mail handled ('000)	pieces of mail handled per capita	receivers (all types; '000)	persons per receiver	receivers (all types; '000)	persons per receiver	receivers ('000)	persons per receiver	number ('000,000)	per 1,000 population	
358[1]	41,400[1]	36,981[1,2]	2.5[1,2]	1,500	14	100	203	31[3]	433[3]	...	...	Afghanistan
613[4]	5,020[4]	13,763[4]	4.5[4]	210	16	246[5]	13[5]	59	57	6.9	2,160	Albania
2,828[6]	8,840[6]	401,378[6]	16[6]	3,500	7.7	2,000	14	1,239	23	21.0	880	Algeria
...	...	...	...	20	2.6	8.0	6.6	7.3[7]	5.0[7]	...	...	American Samoa
...	...	3,483[8]	90[8]	15	4.2	6.0[1]	8.6[1]	43	1.4	...	...	Andorra
76	145,000	2,063	0.2	450	24	51	214	78[5]	132[5]	3.2	370	Angola
...	...	...	...	75	0.9	28	2.3	16[6]	4.0[6]	...	...	Antigua and Barbuda
4,998	6,620	98,688[2]	2.0[2]	21,582	1.6	7,165	4.7	4,622[6]	7.0[6]	18.0	550	Argentina
898[10]	3,840[10]	49,000[11]	14[11]	642[5]	5.6[5]	722[5]	5.0[5]	650[5]	5.3[5]	13.4	4,020	Armenia
...	...	...	...	40	1.8	19	3.8	35	1.9	...	...	Aruba
4,361[6]	3,910[6]	3,493,185[6]	200[6]	20,000	0.9	8,000	2.2	8,540	2.0	39.8	2,360	Australia
2,665[1,12]	2,860[12]	3,406,656[1]	450[1]	4,700	1.7	2,706	2.9	4,957	1.6	10.5	1,340	Austria
1,821[10]	3,970[10]	538,885	75	3,682[13]	1.9[13]	1,522[5]	4.7[5]	1,174[5]	6.15[5]	31.0	4,290	Azerbaijan
128[1]	1,960[1]	60,526[1]	240[1]	200	1.3	60	4.5	142[5]	1.8[5]	...	...	Bahamas, The
12	42,300	45,050[14]	89[14]	320	1.7	270	2.0	183	2.8	0.6	1,230	Bahrain
7,985[1]	13,100[1]	197,363	1.8	4,500	26	350	328	276	408	302.3	3,000	Bangladesh
17	14,900	18,749[15]	74[15]	200	1.2	69	3.8	111	2.4	...	...	Barbados
3,997	2,602	240,412[14]	23[14]	6,140[5]	3.3[5]	3,538[5]	2.9[5]	1,862	5.5	94.0	9,120	Belarus
1,816	5,520	3,436,030	343	5,000	2.0	4,200	2.4	5,898	1.7	16.1	1,630	Belgium
112[7]	1,520[7]	3,096[7]	187	100	2.0	27	7.6	20	9.9	...	...	Belize
189	25,700	5,535	1.1	350	15	20	254	18	273	1.3	330	Benin
17	3,530	21,700	360	100	0.6	30	2.0	54[5]	1.1[5]	0.2	3,630	Bermuda
83	18,800	1,817	1.2	30	26	0.28	6,180[8]	5.0	160	...	...	Bhutan
201	31,900	15,213	2.4	4,000	1.9	610[5]	125	198[5]	38[5]	4.6	650	Bolivia
656[5]	6,630[5]	128,886[5]	30[5]	733[6]	5.9[6]	629[6]	6.9[6]	727[6]	6.0[6]	4.3	1,000	Bosnia and Herzegovina
167	8,070	32,178[16]	24[16]	1,100	1.3	14	100	66	21	...	...	Botswana
12,606	11,900	3,294,509[17]	22[17]	60,000	2.6	30,000	5.2	15,000	10	91.3	680	Brazil
13	20,000	11,070	43	100	2.8	67	4.1	67	4.0	2.3	11,000	Brunei
3,119	2,880	254,813[14]	28[14]	3,000	2.8	3,127	2.7	2,839[18]	3.0[18]	25.7	2,860	Bulgaria
66	121,200	13,689	1.7	200	49	46	212	18[13]	485[13]	6.0	720	Burkina Faso
33[5]	182,000[5]	4,400[5]	0.7[5]	500	11	4.5	1,259	14	395	0.1	24	Burundi
...	...	...	...	1,000	9.2	70	133	6.0	1,510	...	...	Cambodia
1,595	7,520	22,590[14]	1.9[14]	2,000	6.3	15	837	61[13]	185[13]	...	...	Cameroon
16,734[1]	1,570[1]	9,004,547[1,17]	340[1,17]	22,600	1.2	17,400	1.6	20,126[4]	1.3[4]	76.3	2,750	Canada
60	6,170	1,963	5.3	100	3.5	5.0[4]	65[4]	12	29	...	...	Cape Verde
53[5]	54,600[5]	...	...	550	5.5	7.5	400	7.3[5]	399[5]	...	...	Central African Republic
88	69,400	4,270	0.7	1,260	5.0	5.0[4]	1,050[4]	9.1	677	...	...	Chad
1,133	12,000	270,441	20	4,250	3.2	2,000	6.8	1,404	9.0	9.7	740	Chile
51,411	22,800	5,718,409[15,17]	4.9[15,17]	209,205[6]	5.4[6]	35,000[6]	32[6]	18,888	62	16,878	15,300	China
1,678[6]	19,700[6]	220,456[6]	6.7[6]	34,487	1.0	5,500	6.2	4,100	8.1	41.0	1,290	Colombia
56	8,930	1,016[16]	2.0[16]	50	10	0.2[6]	2,310[6]	5.7	87	...	...	Comoros
124[6]	18,300[6]	2,582[6,16]	1.1[6,16]	250	11	8.5	326	26[1]	86[1]	...	...	Congo
279[5]	8,660[5]	19,493	8.1	255	13	340	9.4	486	6.4	0.2	76	Costa Rica
868[5]	13,800[5]	40,642[5]	3.4[5]	1,500	8.9	810	17	207	62	...	...	Côte d'Ivoire
1,087[6]	4,390[6]	232,707[5]	49[5]	761[5]	6.3[5]	1,027[6]	4.6[6]	1,107	4.3	3.1	640	Croatia
903[13]	11,500[13]	116,244[13]	11[13]	2,140	5.1	2,500	4.4	614	17	29.9	2,790	Cuba
774	935	52,685[15,16]	73[13,16]	275	2.8	234	3.3	349[5]	1.6[5]	...	...	Cyprus
3,522	2,927	2,334,248	226	2,883[19]	3.6[19]	3,185[19]	3.2[19]	3,238	3.2	36.4	3,530	Czech Republic
1,321	3,920	1,904,100	368	2,235	2.3	2,500	2.1	5,000[6]	1.0[6]	9.2	1,790	Denmark
5[8]	76,600[8]	1,623[8]	4.2[8]	30	18	17	32	14	37	...	...	Djibouti
63[8]	1,210[8]	2,051[8]	278	45	1.6	5.2	14	17	4.2	...	...	Dominica
240	31,167	4,609[4]	0.74	1,150	6.7	728	11	631	12	...	...	Dominican Republic
508[5]	21,200[5]	19,329[5]	1.8[5]	3,000	3.7	900	12	544	20	6.8	650	Ecuador
7,048[5]	8,090[5]	269,097[5]	4.7[5]	14,000	4.1	5,000	11	2,600	22	26.9	520	Egypt
307	18,400	18,572	3.3	1,935	2.9	501	11	297	18	...	...	El Salvador
20[1]	17,100[1]	...	...	100	3.8	2.5	151	2.0[4]	163[4]	...	...	Equatorial Guinea
...	...	...	...	...	...	...	...	...	...	...	...	Eritrea[20]
602	2,540	22,939[18]	15[10]	926[1]	1.7[1]	600	2.5	386	4.0	7.3	4,640	Estonia
554	99,500	26,192[16]	0.5[16]	3,300	16	100	555	155	358	...	...	Ethiopia[20]
45	1,029	10,260[14]	221[14]	21	2.4	14	3.3	32	1.4	...	500	Faeroe Islands

Communications (continued)

country	number of titles — books total	number of titles — books school textbooks	number of titles — periodicals	number of titles — pamphlets	number of copies ('000) — books total	number of copies ('000) — books school textbooks	number of copies ('000) — periodicals	number of copies ('000) — pamphlets	daily newspapers number	daily newspapers total circulation ('000)	daily newspapers circulation per 1,000 population
Fiji	10	6	...	3	20	12	...	6	1	27	35
Finland	8,261	541	5,711	2,947	...	...	...	...	66	2,780	559
France	43,682[9]	3,084	2,588	9	...	...	118,354	...	79	11,792	210
French Guiana	...	...	...	...	...	...	...	...	1	1	10
French Polynesia	...	...	...	...	...	...	...	...	2	21	102
Gabon	...	...	...	...	...	...	...	...	1	20	17
Gambia, The	15	2	10	6	6	22	885	1	2	2	2
Gaza Strip	...	...	...	...	...	...	...	...	—	—	—
Georgia	1,659[9]	...	75	9	20,100[9]	...	29,700	9	147	3,677	671
Germany	67,890	3,084	9,040	...	...	...	332,913	...	354	30,083	424
Ghana	338	27	121	12	...	...	774	...	2	200	13
Gibraltar	...	...	15	...	...	...	4	...	2	4	133
Greece	4,066[9]	...	309	9	...	...	...	...	117	1,400	140
Greenland	...	...	...	...	...	...	...	...	—	—	—
Grenada	...	...	...	...	...	...	...	...	—	—	—
Guadeloupe	...	...	...	...	...	...	...	...	1	20	57
Guam	...	...	...	...	...	...	...	...	1	22	183
Guatemala	...	...	...	...	...	...	...	...	5	190	21
Guernsey	...	...	...	...	...	...	...	...	1	16	277
Guinea	...	...	3	...	...	...	5	...	—	—	—
Guinea-Bissau	...	...	...	...	...	...	...	...	1	6	6
Guyana	9	—	...	37	...	—	...	...	2	80	101
Haiti	188	17	...	83	...	...	...	...	4	45	7
Honduras	...	...	...	...	...	...	...	...	5	199	39
Hong Kong	3,642	538	617	2,039	27,483	7,771	...	16,829	38	3,700	632
Hungary	7,210	1,088	1,201	923	91,406	20,883	15,146	8,558	34	2,460	233
Iceland	1,036	141	598	566	...	...	...	...	6	148	572
India	11,607	210	...	2,330	...	...	...	...	2,281	17,000	21
Indonesia	1,742	189	117	32	...	...	4,281	...	64	5,144	28
Iran	5,018	...	318	...	24,310	...	6,166	...	21	1,500	27
Iraq	82	...	...	...	452	...	...	...	6	650	34
Ireland	628	...	257	2,051	...	...	2,975	...	7	591	159
Isle of Man	...	...	...	...	...	...	...	...	...	...	...
Israel	2,038	291	807	176	8,872	3,961	...	...	30	1,200	261
Italy	25,157	1,823	9,121	2,594	200,251	50,125	79,103	15,395	76	6,093	107
Jamaica	23	3	...	48	...	...	...	...	3	155	63
Japan	42,345[9]	1,657	3,918	9	466,100[9]	2,117	...	9	121	71,690	580
Jersey	...	...	...	...	...	...	...	...	1	24	300
Jordan	...	...	31	...	...	...	43	...	4	225	56
Kazakhstan	2,055[9]	...	88	9	28,800[9]	...	33,300	9	456	8,622	512
Kenya	343	...	...	5	686	...	...	9	5	350	15
Kiribati	...	...	...	...	...	...	...	...	—	—	—
Korea, North	...	...	...	...	...	...	...	...	11	5,000	230
Korea, South	26,780	3,840	...	2,652	137,692	87,990	...	22,859	39	12,000	280
Kuwait	749	...	73	44	...	...	257	...	9	450	221
Kyrgyzstan	936[9]	...	50	9	9,700[9]	...	34,400	9	128	1,622	367
Laos	79	9	...	30	423	180	...	143	3	14	3
Latvia	1,509[9]	...	187	9	...	...	...	9	172	5,231	1,637
Lebanon	...	...	...	...	...	...	...	...	14	320	118
Lesotho	...	...	...	...	...	...	...	...	4	20	11
Liberia	...	...	...	...	...	...	...	...	8	35	14
Libya	121	20	...	...	553	180	...	...	3	70	15
Liechtenstein	...	...	79	...	...	...	220	...	2	9	307
Lithuania	2,686[9]	...	135	9	23,700[9]	...	40,400	9	140	2,595	712
Luxembourg	362	13	508	158	...	...	...	...	5	145	389
Macau	...	...	11	...	...	...	...	...	8	240	501
Macedonia	559	131	74	...	1,683	...	347	...	2	52	26
Madagascar	36	2	121	10	82	8	261	29	5	50	4
Malawi	66	5	14	75	...	...	124	...	1	25	3
Malaysia	3,682	772	1,631	66	13,449	6,028	1,689	171	45	2,500	140
Maldives	...	...	64	...	...	...	70	...	2	2	7
Mali	160	76	...	...	92	56	...	...	2	10	1
Malta	337	11	332	123	...	...	...	...	3	54	153
Marshall Islands	...	...	...	...	...	...	...	...	—	...	...
Martinique	...	...	...	...	...	...	...	...	1	32	92
Mauritania	...	...	...	...	...	...	...	...	1	1	0.5
Mauritius	36	2	48	22	65	7	...	92	7	80	74
Mayotte	...	...	...	...	...	...	...	...	1	12	160
Mexico	2,587	107	178	21	...	...	28,388	...	285	11,237	127
Micronesia	...	...	...	...	...	...	...	...	...	...	...
Moldova	1,277[9]	...	68	9	19,800[9]	...	38,400	9	189	2,400	561
Monaco	41[9]	...	6	9	722[9]	...	8	9	1	8	286
Mongolia	193	...	45	524	6,397[9]	...	6,361	9	1	162	74
Morocco	...	...	...	...	...	...	...	...	13	320	13
Mozambique	29	...	5	37	3,130	...	2,263	360	2	81	5
Myanmar (Burma)	673	...	...	...	...	...	...	...	2	200	5
Namibia	131	10	...	62	...	...	...	...	6	220	124
Nauru	...	...	...	...	...	...	...	...	—	—	—
Nepal	...	122	...	...	...	7,243	...	...	28	150	8
Netherlands, The	13,691	2,119	367	...	...	...	19,283	...	86	4,592	311
Netherlands Antilles	...	...	...	...	...	...	...	...	6	55	293
New Caledonia	11	...	...	3	...	...	...	...	1	19	114
New Zealand	1,601	14	5,788	1,851	...	...	...	...	35	1,100	324
Nicaragua	27	—	...	14	271	—	...	192	6	250	65
Niger	...	...	...	...	...	...	...	...	1	5	0.6

post offices, 1992				radio, 1993		television, 1993		telephones, 1992		cinema (latest) annual attendance		country
number	persons per office	pieces of mail handled ('000)	pieces of mail handled per capita	receivers (all types; '000)	persons per receiver	receivers (all types; '000)	persons per receiver	receivers ('000)	persons per receiver	number ('000,000)	per 1,000 population	
265	2,790	24,287	33	450	1.7	10[6]	73[6]	83	9.1	...	...	Fiji
2,073	2,410	2,006,100	401	4,950	1.0	1,900	2.7	3,800	1.3	6.0	1,450	Finland
16,855[21]	3,390[21]	22,311,000[21]	400[21]	49,000	1.2	29,300	2.0	34,346[22]	1.6[22]	117.5	2,060	France
...	...	...	...	447	2.1[7]	6.5	22	31[6]	3.8[6]	...	...	French Guiana
95	2,210	20,439	97	84	2.5	27	7.8	44[4]	4.3[4]	0.4	2,190	French Polynesia
52[6]	22,500[6]	6,478[2,6,16]	5.5[2,6,16]	250	5.1	40	32	26[6]	57[6]	0.1	95	Gabon
...	...	...	...	180	5.7	...	...	9.3[1]	92[1]	...	...	Gambia, The
...	...	...	...	...	...	...	...	...	...	...	...	Gaza Strip
...	...	138,000[6,11]	25[6,11]	...	...	...	...	1,002	5.5	47.0	8,680	Georgia
36,291	2,200	8,839,012	110	30,000	2.7	30,500	2.7	45,711[13]	1.7[13]	119.9	1,500	Germany
1,011	15,200	145,576	9.5	4,000	3.9	250	63	81	188	3.9	340	Ghana
4	7,750	12,280	400	17	1.7	7.5	3.8	19	1.5	0.17	5,830	Gibraltar
1,245	8,270	455,549	44	4,085	2.5	2,300	4.5	5,290	1.9	...	...	Greece
...	...	...	...	25	2.2	21	2.6	17[1]	3.4[1]	...	...	Greenland
191[5,12]	450[5,12]	...	...	80	1.2	30	3.1	24	3.8	...	...	Grenada
...	...	...	...	100	4.0	150	2.8	121[6]	3.2[6]	...	...	Guadeloupe
...	...	...	...	105	1.4	75	1.9	41[13]	3.1[13]	...	...	Guam
540	17,600	117,418	12	400	25	475	21	300	33	7.7	910	Guatemala
15	4,000	15,272[17]	250[17]	...	...	...	...	60[13]	1.0[13]	...	...	Guernsey
755	80,000[5]	14,383[5]	2.4[5]	130	49	65	97	19[5]	382[5]	3.9	780	Guinea
24	41,700	410[2,16,23]	0.4[2,16,23]	40	26	...	...	15[5]	67[5]	...	...	Guinea-Bissau
63[12]	12,700[12]	4,577[2,14]	5.7[2,14]	310	2.4	40[5]	19[5]	33[7]	23[7]	13.0	17,200	Guyana
132	50,200	586,035	89	3,000	2.1	25	255	50[13]	126[13]	2.1	380	Haiti
...	...	...	...	1,800	2.9	160	32	107	47	...	...	Honduras
167	35,300	960,337[15]	160[15]	3,000	2.0	1,749	3.4	3,649	1.6	58.5	10,290	Hong Kong
3,210	3,210	1,599,810	155	6,000	1.7	4,262	2.4	2,048	5.0	21.6	2,070	Hungary
120	2,190	67,940	260	155	1.7	76	3.5	140	1.9	1.3	5,160	Iceland
150,346	5,620	13,314,660	16	55,000	16	20,000	45	6,706	131	4,297.3	5,010	India
26,291	7,000	545,972	3.0	22,000	8.6	11,000	17	1,622	114	133.2	770	Indonesia
4,426[5]	10,100[5]	239,151[16]	4.1[16]	12,000	4.9	2,250	26	3,627	16	66.6	1,200	Iran
343	57,100	488,070[16]	2.5[16]	3,500	5.5	1,000	19	712[6]	25[6]	...	...	Iraq
2,002	1,760	540,000[14]	150[14]	2,000	1.8	1,000	3.5	1,096	3.2	11.6	3,290	Ireland
32	2,180	33,085[23]	470[23]	...	...	...	...	...	...	...	...	Isle of Man
1,698	3,060	489,000[15]	94[15]	2,250	2.3	1,500	3.5	2,545[5]	2.0[5]	...	...	Israel
14,411	4,020	7,711,808	130	15,000	3.8	17,000	3.4	32,037[6]	1.8[6]	88.6	1,550	Italy
825[5]	2,930[5]	80,147[15,23]	33[15,23]	1,500	1.6	484	5.1	102[5]	13[5]	143.6	1,170	Jamaica
24,181[5]	5,110[5]	22,723,628[5]	180[5]	97,000	1.3	100,000	1.3	57,640	2.2	...	...	Japan
23	3,650	48,275	570	...	...	...	...	120	0.9	...	...	Jersey
842[6]	3,760[6]	58.981	15	700	5.8	250	16	320	12	0.9	290	Jordan
5,450[5,10]	3,100[5,10]	1,602,917[5]	95[5]	4,188[5]	4.0[5]	4,795[5]	3.5[5]	3,504[5]	4.8[5]	150.0	8,890	Kazakhstan
1,086	20,400	352,884	16	4,200	6.3	260	102	420	61	...	...	Kenya
24	3,010	707	9.7	10.0	7.7	...	...	1.6	47	...	...	Kiribati
...	...	...	...	4,700	4.8	338	66	1,089	30	187.4	9,560	Korea, North
3,421	12,800	2,884,392[15,17]	66[15,17]	42,000	1.0	9,101	4.8	17,697[5]	2.5[5]	55.3	1,300	Korea, South
54[13]	36,300[13]	115,215[1,14]	56[1,14]	1,000	1.4	800	1.8	362[13]	5.5[13]	0.9	480	Kuwait
1,020[10]	4,350[10]	355,300[5]	80[5]	825[5]	5.4[5]	875[5]	5.1[5]	352	13	32.0	7,190	Kyrgyzstan
126	34,900	4,100	0.9	425	11	80	57	8.2	545	1.0	229	Laos
1,062	2,640	311,155	110	2,000	1.2	1,200	2.2	704	3.7	19.7	7,340	Latvia
...	...	...	...	2,150	1.4	1,100	2.6	310[5]	9.1[5]	...	...	Lebanon
140[6]	12,600[6]	77,615[6]	44[6]	425	4.4	50	38	22	84	...	...	Lesotho
44[13]	55,400[13]	26,803[1]	11[1]	600	4.0	45	53	28[4]	86[4]	...	...	Liberia
317[12]	14,300[12]	1,707,397[2,14]	380[2,14]	1,000	5.0	500	9.9	480	9.8	...	...	Libya
12	2,490	17,192[17]	580[17]	11	2.7	10	3.0	18	1.6	...	...	Liechtenstein
1,037[12]	3,620[12]	44,083	12	1,420	2.6	1,400	2.7	1,634[5]	2.3[5]	13.9	3,690	Lithuania
106	3,640	121,900[17]	320[17]	240	1.6	101	3.9	192[5]	2.0[5]	0.5	1,330	Luxembourg
20	24,000	12,681	26	250[5]	1.4[5]	70	5.6	146	2.6	2.7	6,400	Macau
257[5]	7,880[5]	38,401[5]	19[5]	365[6]	5.5[6]	331[6]	6.1[6]	357[6]	5.7[6]	2.1	1,060	Macedonia
8,433	1,410	28,464	2.4	1,500	8.8	130	102	68	189	0.4	32	Madagascar
263[22]	28,000[22]	113,975[22]	15[22]	1,100	9.7	...	...	57	182	...	...	Malawi
5,049	3,690	870,765	47	3,500	5.5	2,000	9.5	2,023[6]	8.9[6]	41.6	2,400	Malaysia
40	5,780	1,979	8.6	25	9.5	4.8	4.9	2.5[24]	75[24]	...	...	Maldives
88[6]	92,600[6]	5,660[6]	0.7[6]	150	58	10	865	15[6]	564[6]	...	...	Mali
50	7,140	47,240	130	90	4.1	133	2.7	202	1.8	0.3	860	Malta
...	...	...	...	...	...	...	...	1.0	57	...	...	Marshall Islands
...	...	...	...	60	6.3	65	5.8	159[6]	2.3[6]	1.1	3,150	Martinique
60	33,700	...	...	300	7.2	1.1	1,974	7.8[5]	208[5]	...	...	Mauritania
113	9,920	36,961	33	250	4.4	157	7.1	100	11	0.6	550	Mauritius
...	...	...	...	30	3.5	3.5	30	3.2[6]	29[6]	...	...	Mayotte
7,300	12,190	862,477	10	16,325	5.5	12,350[5]	6.7[5]	11,537	7.6	351.0	4,500	Mexico
...	...	...	...	70	1.5	7.0	16	5.7	18	...	...	Micronesia
1,398[10]	3,120[10]	536,331[5]	123[5]	1,421[5]	3.1[5]	1,264[5]	3.5[5]	553	7.9	30.0	6,880	Moldova
...	...	...	...	15	2.0	20	1.5	56	0.5	0.1	3,390	Monaco
424[13]	4,790[13]	12,820[13,15,23]	6.3[13,15,23]	200	11	120	19	69[5]	31[5]	20.1	9,720	Mongolia
1,313	19,500	206,511	8.1	4,500	5.9	1,210	22	714	36	30.2	1,240	Morocco
312	53,900	8,744	0.5	600	25	35	435	75	198	4.1	300	Mozambique
1,152	36,200	70,499	1.7	3,200	14	1,000	45	81[13]	501[13]	...	...	Myanmar (Burma)
104	13,480	89,743	64	240[6]	5.6[6]	39	40	93	16	...	...	Namibia
1[22]	8,500[22]	168[22]	20[22]	4.0	2.5	...	...	1.5[13]	5.9[13]	...	...	Nauru
3,921	4,710	41,529	2.2	600	32	250	77	67[1]	275[1]	...	...	Nepal
2,624[4]	5,580[4]	6,105,000[1]	410[1]	12,146	1.3	5,618	2.7	10,500[5]	1.4[5]	14.7	975	Netherlands, The
16[1]	11,800[1]	17,427[1]	92[1]	125	1.5	35	5.5	60[1]	0.0[1]	...	...	Netherlands Antilles
274	616	22,257[16]	132[10]	50	3.6	36	5.0	315	5.6[5]	0.2	1,260	New Caledonia
1,242[7]	2,670[7]	838,656[7,16]	250[7,16]	3,100	1.1	1,100	3.2	2,403[4]	1.4[4]	5.0	1,750	New Zealand
...	...	...	...	880	4.7	210	20	50[5]	81[5]	...	...	Nicaragua
65[12]	122,830[12]	4,930	0.6	400	21	25	341	14	589	...	...	Niger

Communications (continued)

country	number of titles — books total	number of titles — books school textbooks	number of titles — periodicals	number of titles — pamphlets	number of copies ('000) — books total	number of copies ('000) — books school textbooks	number of copies ('000) — periodicals	number of copies ('000) — pamphlets	daily newspapers — number	daily newspapers — total circulation ('000)	daily newspapers — circulation per 1,000 population
Nigeria	900	800	92	566	...	...	495	...	31	1,700	16
Northern Mariana Islands	...	...	...	...	...	...	...	...	—	...	...
Norway	2,998	...	6,498	714	...	...	...	...	85	2,588	614
Oman	...	...	11	...	...	...	90	...	4	62	41
Pakistan	...	...	282	...	...	...	7,674	...	237	1,817	15
Panama	...	...	8	...	...	...	18	...	8	170	70
Papua New Guinea	...	...	...	...	...	...	...	...	2	49	13
Paraguay	...	...	...	...	...	...	...	...	5	165	39
Peru	359	3	45	122	...	...	90	...	66	1,700	79
Philippines	763	323	1,570	62	...	...	9,468	...	47	3,400	54
Poland	8,912	313	3,007	2,376	107,191	22,288	41,194	18,318	67	4,889	127
Portugal	6,430[9]	1,545	937	[9]	24,928[9]	11,458	6,359	[9]	24	390	38
Puerto Rico	...	...	...	...	...	...	...	...	3	456	131
Qatar	448	334	190	73	...	...	120	...	5	80	217
Réunion	41	—	...	32	...	—	...	...	3	65	109
Romania	1,828	...	435	350	49,562	...	22,675	2,915	65	...	...
Russia	41,234[9]	...	3,681	[9]	1,553,100[9]	...	5,010,200	[9]	4,808	166,000	1,119
Rwanda	131	42	15	76	746	552	101	2,109	1	0.5	0.1
St. Kitts and Nevis	—	—	10	3	—	—	43	3	—	—	—
St. Lucia	44	25	...	19	89	84	...	7	—	—	—
St. Vincent	...	...	...	...	...	...	...	...	—	—	—
San Marino	...	...	15	...	...	...	...	...	6	2	87
São Tomé and Príncipe	...	...	...	...	...	...	...	...	...	...	...
Saudi Arabia	...	...	58	...	...	...	...	...	12	600	42
Senegal	42	8	123	...	169	70	381	...	1	50	7
Seychelles	...	...	2	...	...	...	2	...	1	3.2	47
Sierra Leone	...	16	...	...	...	...	...	...	1	10	2
Singapore	1,524	389	1,786	403	8,947	4,081	...	2,179	8	763	280
Slovakia	6,743[9]	...	...	[9]	...	...	...	...	12	1,291	246
Slovenia	1,853	...	274	...	6,267	...	7,194	...	4	303	154
Solomon Islands	...	...	...	...	...	...	...	...	1	9	1
Somalia	...	...	...	...	...	...	...	...	1	9	1
South Africa	3,254	274	...	1,582	28,467	11,797	...	6,473	22	1,340	38
Spain	33,752	2,725	1,998	5,330	174,577	28,703	...	23,516	102	3,200	82
Sri Lanka	1,160	128	170	1,375	15,093	12,365	1,770	5,158	18	550	32
Sudan, The	...	...	10	...	...	...	136	...	5	610	24
Suriname	...	...	22	...	...	...	44	...	2	40	95
Swaziland	...	...	...	...	...	...	...	...	3	10	13
Sweden	9,498	420	46	2,368	...	...	4,947	...	107	4,499	533
Switzerland	14,886[9]	308	3,079	[9]	...	...	...	...	94	3,213	463
Syria	119	1	...	...	553	...	...	...	10	280	22
Taiwan	16,156	...	4,134	...	...	...	...	...	93	4,000	202
Tajikistan	787[9]	...	36	[9]	12,000[9]	...	27,200	[9]	74	1,598	309
Tanzania	127	23	...	45	275	46	...	89	3	200	7
Thailand	7,589	604	1,293	87	...	...	...	...	34	4,000	72
Togo	...	...	...	...	...	...	...	...	1	10	3
Tonga	...	...	...	...	...	...	...	...	1	7	74
Trinidad and Tobago	...	...	...	...	...	...	...	...	2	95	77
Tunisia	293	...	...	...	879	...	...	...	6	300	37
Turkey	5,935	173	1,325	430	...	...	1,325	...	399	4,000	72
Turkmenistan	759[9]	...	33	[9]	7,600[9]	...	12,800	[9]	66	1,141	319
Tuvalu	...	...	...	...	...	...	...	...	—	—	—
Uganda	...	...	26	...	...	...	158	...	2	30	2
Ukraine	4,351	173	185	1,506	99,783	25,183	9,957	36,634	127	13,026	251
United Arab Emirates	...	281	80	...	...	4,423	922	...	8	250	157
United Kingdom	80,787	2,773	6,408	5,786	...	...	...	...	104	22,494	395
United States	48,146	...	11,593	...	...	...	...	...	1,611	62,328	250
Uruguay	790	48	465	353	1,391	110	...	579	30	720	233
Uzbekistan	2,080[9]	...	95	[9]	51,000[9]	...	171,800	[9]	279	6,600	322
Vanuatu	...	...	...	...	...	...	...	...	—	—	—
Venezuela	3,000	...	...	461	...	...	...	...	54	2,800	142
Vietnam	...	...	...	...	...	...	...	...	5	600	9
Virgin Islands (U.S)	...	...	...	...	...	...	...	...	2	19	166
West Bank	...	...	...	...	...	...	...	...	—	—	—
Western Sahara	...	...	...	...	...	...	...	...	—	—	—
Western Samoa	...	...	...	...	...	...	...	...	—	—	—
Yemen	...	...	...	...	...	...	...	...	5	135	12
Yugoslavia	2,618[9]	...	397	[9]	11,350[9]	...	4,651	[9]	12	1,006	98
Zaire	...	...	68	...	...	...	...	...	7	45	1
Zambia	454	215	...	...	...	...	...	...	2	99	12
Zimbabwe	145	17	28	204	...	...	680	...	2	206	21

post offices, 1992				radio, 1993		television, 1993		telephones, 1992		cinema (latest)		country
number	persons per office	pieces of mail handled ('000)	pieces of mail handled per capita	receivers (all types; '000)	persons per receiver	receivers (all types; '000)	persons per receiver	receivers ('000)	persons per receiver	annual attendance number ('000,000)	per 1,000 population	
3,547[5]	25,000[5]	590,596[5]	6.7[5]	10,000	9.0	4,100[5]	21[5]	722[13]	118[13]	4.6	51	Nigeria
...	...	...	...	10.5	4.3	4.1	11	4.9[4]	4.4[4]	...	...	Northern Mariana Islands
2,543[5]	1,680[5]	2,092,646	490	3,300	1.3	1,500	2.9	2,268	1.9	10.7	2,510	Norway
76[5]	19,700[5]	27,089[2]	18[2]	900	2.2	1,500	1.3	263[5]	6.1[5]	...	...	Oman
13,380	9,030	725,845[17]	6.0[17]	10,000	13	2,080	62	1,461	85	25.3	230	Pakistan
268[6]	9,020[6]	13,249	5.7	450	5.6	205	12	283	8.8	...	...	Panama
114[6]	34,200[6]	36,478[2,6]	9.4[2,6]	235	18	10	415	636	59[6]	...	...	Papua New Guinea
293	14,600	6,935	1.6	775	6.0	350	13	152	30	...	...	Paraguay
1,017[5]	17,400[5]	15,295[24]	0.7[24]	4,400	5.2	2,000	12	816	28	33.0	1,910	Peru
2,832	22,700	1,140,055	18	4,000	17	7,000	9.5	1,178	55	...	...	Philippines
8,041[6]	4,740[6]	1,060,187,100[15]	28[15]	10,400	3.7	10,000	3.9	5,854	6.6	20.9	550	Poland
7,532	1,310	752,596	76	2,475	4.0	1,770	5.6	3,375	2.9	9.6	974	Portugal
...	...	...	...	2,000	1.8	830	4.4	1,366	2.6	...	...	Puerto Rico
29	13,800	25,993[2]	65[2]	250	1.8	250	1.8	154	2.9	0.3	710	Qatar
...	...	...	...	150	4.2	91	7.0	168[6]	3.6[6]	...	...	Réunion
5,226	4,360	256,788	110	3,000	7.6	4,000	5.7	3,192	7.1	203.4	8,790	Romania
52,989	2,800	15,075,068	100	90,000	1.7	54,200[5]	2.7[5]	24,796	6.0	750	5,040	Russia
43	184,000	9,972	1.3	650	12	...	...	22	335	0.3	56	Rwanda
8	5,580	2,473	55	25	1.7	9.5	4.4	9.4[6]	4.6[6]	...	...	St. Kitts and Nevis
58	2,600	5,095	34	90	1.6	25	5.6	36	3.8	...	...	St. Lucia
56	1,960	...	...	55	2.0	18	6.0	20	5.4	...	...	St. Vincent
10	2,700	...	...	13	1.9	8.0[6]	2.9[6]	41	0.6	0.03	1,300	San Marino
11	10,700	101,525	860	31	4.0	...	...	3.5	35	...	...	São Tomé and Príncipe
609[6,12]	23,200[6,12]	551,909[23]	32[23]	5,000	3.5	4,500	3.9	1,466[5]	11[5]	...	...	Saudi Arabia
133[5]	52,600[5]	14,210[5]	2.0[5]	850	9.3	61	130	50	154	...	...	Senegal
5	14,000	4,254	60	40	1.8	13	5.5	18	3.9	...	...	Seychelles
78	51,300	2,036	0.5	1,000	4.5	25	180	35[5]	125[5]	...	...	Sierra Leone
794	3,590	524,965	180	870	3.0	650	4.4	1,153	2.5	30.7	20,600	Singapore
...	...	...	...	1,068,000	5.0	1,279,000	4.1	1,362	3.9	13.8	2,630	Slovakia
505	3,880	207,207	110	601[6]	3.3[6]	445[6]	4.4[6]	593	3.4	2.8	1,440	Slovenia
117[5]	2,900[5]	2,164[6,15]	6.8[6,15]	38	9.2	...	...	7.0[1]	46[1]	...	...	Solomon Islands
...	...	...	...	400	16	3.0[4]	2,270[4]	8.0[13]	882[13]	...	...	Somalia
...	...	...	...	10,000	4.1	3,445	12	5,222	7.6	26.0	680	South Africa
41,833[6]	950[6]	5,608,624[6]	140[6]	12,600[19]	3.1	17,240[19]	2.3	15,477[4]	2.5[4]	79.1	2,080	Spain
4,025	4,320	432,160	25	2,200	8.0	700	25	190	92	37.2	2,270	Sri Lanka
808[6]	35,000[6]	8,966	0.3	7,500	3.3	250	100	92	269	13.0	600	Sudan, The
...	...	...	...	250	1.7	43	9.7	63	6.5	...	...	Suriname
70	12,200	15,024	18	65	13	13	66	26	32	...	...	Swaziland
1,978	4,390	2,849,623[15,16,24]	328[15,16,24]	7,272	1.2	3,750	2.3	7,410[8]	1.1[8]	15.6	1,810	Sweden
3,716	1,850	3,002,418[15,16]	432[15,16]	2,685	2.6	2,300	3.0	6,227[5]	1.1[5]	15.4	2,270	Switzerland
617	21,000	15,042	1.1	3,000	4.5	700	19	719	19	6.9	590	Syria
13,233[5]	1,550[5]	1,754,119[5]	86[5]	13,600[5]	1.5[5]	6,660[5]	3.1[5]	8,040[6]	2.4[6]	64.2	3,200	Taiwan
785[5,10]	6,920[5,10]	020,049[6]	59[6]	854[5]	6.4[5]	860[5]	6.3[5]	285[5]	19[5]	30.0	5,520	Tajikistan
846	27,400	153,548	6.6	4,000	6.6	80	332	151	171	1.8	72	Tanzania
4,266	13,500	867,682	15	10,000	5.7	3,300	17	1,553[5]	36[5]	...	...	Thailand
420[5]	8,560[5]	...	...	700	5.4	23	165	31	119	...	...	Togo
...	...	...	...	66	1.5	...	...	7.1	14	...	...	Tonga
232	5,300	23,288	19	700	1.8	250	5.0	247	5.1	...	...	Trinidad and Tobago
826	10,100	144,522	17	1,700	5.1	650	13	465	18.1	...	...	Tunisia
41,590[12]	14,000[12]	1,631,531	28	7,100	8.4	10,530	5.7	11,830	5.0	16.5	287	Turkey
580[5,10]	6,490[5,10]	244,027[5]	65[5]	823[5]	4.6[5]	705[5]	5.3[5]	266	14	46.0	12,200	Turkmenistan
9[13]	970[13]	88[2,13]	102[2,13]	4.0	2.4	...	...	0.19	49	...	...	Tuvalu
319	51,700	16,311	1	3,500	5.1	115	154	55	314	...	...	Uganda
16,515	3,200	1,397,027	27	15,000[6]	3.5[6]	17,200[6]	3.0[6]	8,434	0.2	415.8	8,000	Ukraine
186	10,800	121,370	60	420	5.0	170	12	1,046	1.9	...	...	United Arab Emirates
19,958	2,750	16,364,000[17]	300[17]	70,000	0.8	20,000	2.9	29,518[3]	1.9[3]	102	1,770	United Kingdom
40,037	6,397	165,228,428[17]	645[17]	520,000	0.5	215,000	1.2	181,091[3]	1.33	981.9	3,890	United States
361[6]	8,570[6]	16,343	6	1,800	1.8	600	5.2	668	5.4	6.2	2,110	Uruguay
3,800[5,10]	5,520[5,10]	1,537,874[5]	73[5]	3,677[5]	5.7[5]	3,308[5]	6.3[5]	1,488	14	126.0	6,010	Uzbekistan
...	...	...	...	55	2.9	1.0[6]	148[6]	4.1[5]	37[5]	...	...	Vanuatu
556	35,500	94,854	4.8	8,100	2.5	3,700	5.5	2,165	9.4	18	1,590	Venezuela
...	...	...	...	8,000	8.8	2,500	28	123[1]	563[1]	239.9	3,760	Vietnam
...	...	...	...	90	1.2	32	3.2	59[6]	1.7[6]	...	...	Virgin Islands (U.S.)
...	...	...	...	...	...	...	...	...	...	...	...	West Bank
...	...	...	...	...	...	...	...	...	...	...	...	Western Sahara
45[5]	3,560[5]	3,514[2]	22[2]	75	2.2	6.0[6]	27[6]	9.0	18	...	...	Western Samoa
406[1]	27,700[1]	9,999	0.9	325	39	335[6]	34[6]	146	83	...	...	Yemen
1,569	6,590	234	—	2,692	3.9	1,643	6.4	2,159	4.8	2.9	280	Yugoslavia
307	122,800	45,394[6,16]	1.3[6,16]	3,400	13	22	1,929	32[13]	1,026[13]	...	...	Zaire
463[5]	16,900[5]	76,475[15,16]	9.8[15,16]	1,660	5.0	200	44	113	76	...	...	Zambia
294[6]	31,900[6]	175,141[6]	19[6]	522	20	137	78	313[5]	31[5]	5.6	690	Zimbabwe

[1]1989. [2]Foreign-received and foreign-sent only. [3]1984. [4]1987. [5]1991. [6]1990. [7]1986. [8]1983. [9]Books includes pamphlets. [10]Includes telephone and telegraph offices. [11]Letters sent only. [12]Permanent post offices only. [13]1988. [14]Letters only. [15]Excludes small packets. [16]Excludes postcards. [17]Domestic and foreign-sent only. [18]1993. [19]1992. [20]Ethiopia includes Eritrea. [21]Includes overseas departments and Monaco. [22]1985. [23]Excludes printed matter. [24]Domestic only.

Trade: external

The following table presents comparative data on the international, or foreign, trade of the countries of the world. The table analyzes data for both imports and exports in two ways: (1) into several major commodity groups defined in accordance with the United Nations system called the Standard International Trade Classification (SITC) and (2) by direction of trade for each country with major world trading blocs and partners. These commodity groupings are defined by the SITC code numbers beneath the column headings. The single-digit numbers represent broad SITC categories (in the SITC, called "sections"); the double-digit numbers represent subcategories ("divisions") of the single-digit categories (27 is a subcategory of 2); the three-digit number is a subcategory ("group") of the double-digit (667 is a subcategory of 66). Where a plus or minus sign is used before one of these SITC numbers, the SITC category or subcategory is being added to or subtracted from the aggregate implied by the total of the preceding sections. The SITC commodity aggregations used here are listed in the table at the end of this headnote. The full SITC commodity breakdown—some 3,118 basic headings—is presented in the 1986 United Nations publication *Standard International Trade Classification, Revision 3*.

The SITC was developed by the United Nations through its Statistical Commission as an outgrowth of the need for a standard system of aggregating commodities of external trade to provide international comparability of foreign trade statistics. The United Nations Statistical Commission has defined external merchandise trade as "all goods whose movement into or out of the customs area of a country compiling the statistics adds to or subtracts from the material resources of the country." Goods passing through a country for transport only are excluded, but goods entering for reexport, or deposited (as in a bonded warehouse, or free trade area) for reimport, are included. Statistics in this table refer only to goods and exclude purely financial transactions that are covered in the "Finance" and "National product and accounts" tables. Gold for fabrication (*e.g.*, as jewelry) is included; monetary and reserve gold are excluded.

For purposes of comparability of data, total value of imports and exports is given in this table in U.S. dollars. Conversions from currencies other than U.S. dollars are determined according to the average market rates for the year for which data are supplied; these are mainly as calculated by the International Monetary Fund (IMF) or other official sources. The commodity categories are given in terms of percentages of the total value of the country's import or export trade (with the exclusions noted above). Value is based on transaction value: for imports, the value at which the goods were purchased by the importer plus the cost of transportation and insurance to the frontier of the importing country (c.i.f. [cost, insurance, and freight] valuation); for exports, the value at which the goods were sold by the exporter, including the cost of transportation and insurance to bring

Trade: external

country	year	imports total value ('000,000 U.S.$)	food and agricultural raw materials (0+1+2 −27−28 +4)	mineral ores and concentrates (27+28 +667)	fuels and other energy (3)	total[a] (5+6 −667 +7+8 +9)	of which chemicals and related products (5)	of which machinery and transport equipment (7)	of which other[a] (6−667 +8+9)	from European Union (EU)[b]	from United States	from Eastern Europe[c]	from Japan	from all other[d]
Afghanistan	1991[1]	936.4	15.0	—[2]	2.1	84.6[3]	2.1	48.2	34.3[3]	4.5[4]	0.2[4]	59.9[4,5]	7.9[4]	27.6[4]
Albania	1990	446.5	25.7	——24.5——		49.8	9.3	31.0	9.5	37.7[6]	...	27.9[5]	0.1	34.4
Algeria	1992	8,647.8	31.4	0.8	1.4	66.4	10.9	30.7	24.9	63.3	11.0	1.2	4.5	20.0
American Samoa	1989[7]	377.9	65.1	—[2]	7.1	27.8[3]	1.2	6.7	20.0[3]	...	28.0	—	3.9	68.1
Andorra	1987	700.4	——28.3[2]——		3.7	68.0[3]	7.3	19.9	40.8[3]	84.9	2.8	0.2[5]	6.3	5.9
Angola	1991	1,970.0	——32.4[2,8]——		0.7[8]	66.9[3,8]	10.6[8]	25.0[8]	31.3[3,8]	67.4[4]	10.8[4]	...	8.0[4]	13.7[4]
Antigua and Barbuda	1987	247.0	——17.8[2]——		9.9	72.3[3]	6.2	26.8	39.4[3]	41.3	29.5	—	—	29.2
Argentina	1992	14,863.9	7.9	1.6	2.9	87.7	14.0	47.6	26.1	24.4	21.7	0.6	4.7	48.5
Armenia	1991	208.2[9]	——26.1[2]——		12.9	61.1[3]	8.2	17.7	35.2[3]	1.1[4]	7.1[4]	77.0[4]	0.7[4]	14.1[4]
Aruba	1988	330.9	22.3	0.1	7.6	70.0	8.0	19.7	42.3	22.8	40.7	0.1[5]	3.7	32.8
Australia	1992	42,949.1	6.5	0.8	5.5	87.2	9.3	39.6	38.2	20.8	22.7	0.5	17.3	38.7
Austria	1993	50,361.5	8.2	1.1	5.0	85.7	10.4	37.7	37.5	66.6	4.4	5.6	4.4	19.0
Azerbaijan	1992	939.9[9]	——31.9[2]——		5.1	63.0[3]	12.1	22.7	28.2[3]	10.3	2.5	58.4	—	28.8
Bahamas, The	1988	2,263.5	10.2	0.1	56.7	33.0	6.4	9.6	17.1	7.7	39.6	1.0[5]	0.6	51.1
Bahrain	1992	4,263.1	9.0	0.2	39.8	51.0	7.1	25.2	18.7	23.0[4]	13.0[4]	...	5.7[4]	58.4[4]
Bangladesh	1992[11]	2,251.5	37.7	5.0	13.9	43.3	9.7	13.5	20.1	10.1	4.3	2.4[5]	7.2	76.1
Barbados	1992	553.0	23.8	0.3	11.3	64.6	12.6	20.5	31.5	15.6	38.2	0.1	3.9	42.1
Belarus	1992	3,368.6[9]	——37.3[2]——		11.1	51.6[3]	10.0	31.7	10.0[3]	3.1	1.4	83.6	0.1	11.7
Belgium[12]	1992	125,122.1	12.9	8.3	7.6	71.2	11.9	25.6	33.7	73.5	4.4	1.6	2.2	18.2
Belize	1992	274.2	22.0	0.4	11.9	65.7	9.2	24.7	31.8	15.5	57.0	—	1.7	25.8
Benin	1987	348.2	——35.0[2]——		7.3	57.7[3]	5.6	13.5	38.5[3]	41.1	3.9	1.3[5]	5.6	48.0
Bermuda	1992	511.1[13]	22.5	0.1[2]	6.2	71.2[3]	13.3	21.8	36.2[3]	12.7	65.8	—	5.2	16.2
Bhutan	1990	78.1	24.0	0.5	13.1	62.4	5.5	26.0	30.9	3.4	1.3	—	5.4	89.9[14]
Bolivia	1993	1,249.6	10.6	1.6	4.7	83.2	11.2	47.7	24.3	18.6	22.6	1.3	10.9	46.5
Bosnia and Herzegovina	1990	1,866.9	...	...	31.6	...	...	...	...	...	...	...	...	...
Botswana	1991	1,946.5	15.5	2.5	6.3	75.7	7.1	33.0	35.6	6.1	1.2	—	0.3	92.3[17]
Brazil	1992	23,123.7	11.8	2.6	23.8	61.8	15.3	33.2	13.4	24.7	23.2	1.6	5.4	45.1
Brunei	1989	856.4	19.4	0.6	0.9	79.1	6.2	35.9	37.1	19.2	12.7	—	14.8	53.3
Bulgaria	1992	4,344.9	10.4	2.4	36.0	51.2	9.6	22.6	19.0	31.4	2.9	32.2	1.9	31.6
Burkina Faso	1990	539.6	23.1	0.6	11.2	65.1	13.7	24.7	26.7	47.9[4]	3.0[4]	0.2[4]	4.0[4]	44.9[4]
Burundi	1992	229.5	11.2	0.5	12.2	76.2	14.1	27.5	34.5	44.1	4.3	0.5	8.1	43.1
Cambodia	1989	215.0[4]	...	...	30.2[22]	...	1.2[22]	36.9[22]	...	1.9[4]	—[4]	96.1[4,23]	1.7[4]	0.3[4]
Cameroon	1991	2,306.2	16.8	6.2	3.4	73.6	14.7	27.1	31.7	58.5	6.6	0.4[5]	2.9	31.6
Canada	1993	131,478.9	7.7	1.7	4.0	86.6	7.7	50.7	28.3	8.7	67.0	0.4	6.3	17.6
Cape Verde	1990	136.3	30.7	—	7.5	61.8	6.1	30.7	24.9	64.7	2.4	3.0[5]	3.8	26.1
Central African Republic	1989	159.1	20.1	0.7	6.7	72.6	14.0	33.2	25.3	56.7	1.3	0.3	7.6	34.2
Chad	1991	296.6	15.9[26]	0.6[26]	14.2[26]	69.3[26]	16.4[26]	28.8[26]	24.1[26]	38.6[4]	5.1[4]	—	1.7[4]	54.7[4]
Chile	1993	10,425.3	7.9	0.5	9.0	82.6	11.6	44.0	27.0	21.8	28.3	0.2	6.9	42.8
China	1993	103,959.0	6.0	2.3	5.6	86.1	9.4	42.9	33.9	13.9	10.3	6.4	22.4	47.1
Colombia	1992	6,683.9	12.8	1.1	5.5	80.6	20.9	33.4	26.4	18.1	35.8	0.5	8.7	36.9
Comoros	1990	52.0	——46.7[2]——		15.0	38.3[3]	3.3	11.7	23.3	73.0[4]	—[4]	...	5.0[4]	22.1[4]
Congo	1989	517.6	18.9[27]	0.7[27]	1.7[27]	78.7[27]	9.1[27]	35.3[27]	34.3[27]	77.0	5.8	1.7[5]	4.2	11.2
Costa Rica	1991	2,234.6	9.3	0.4	9.4	80.9	17.8	19.4	43.7	9.2	51.3	0.2	5.3	33.9
Côte d'Ivoire	1989	2,185.3	——23.7——		21.3	55.0	14.8	16.4	23.8	53.5	4.3	1.0[5]	2.7	38.6
Croatia	1993	4,666.4	11.0	1.6	9.9	77.5	12.4	24.2	41.0	48.2	2.7	10.6	0.9	37.6
Cuba	1989	8,122.1	14.9	0.5[2]	32.4	52.2[3]	6.2	27.5	18.5[3]	10.3	...	76.5[5]	0.6	12.6
Cyprus	1992	3,290.1	17.4	0.7	8.6	73.3	7.3	32.5	33.6	52.8	8.4	7.2	10.5	21.1
Czech Republic	1993	12,566.8	——12.7[2]——		11.4	75.9[3]	12.0	35.8	28.0[3]	42.3	3.0	32.7	1.7	20.3
Denmark	1992	33,613.1	16.4	0.5	6.3	76.8	11.8	29.9	35.2	52.9	5.1	2.8	4.1	35.0
Djibouti	1991	214.4	38.3	0.2	9.1	52.3	6.0	15.5	30.8	45.6	3.7	0.7[5]	7.2	42.7
Dominica	1991	109.6	27.6	0.3	7.9	64.2	12.0	21.6	30.5	21.0	31.4	0.3	5.6	41.8
Dominican Republic	1991	1,988.1	13.7[22]	0.3[22]	35.2[22]	50.7[22]	11.7[22]	23.2[22]	15.9[22]	14.3[4]	45.7[4]	—[4]	5.2[4]	34.8[4]
Ecuador	1992	2,501.3	6.8	0.7	4.0	88.6	17.7	44.6	26.3	21.4	32.5	1.0[5]	13.1	32.0
Egypt	1992	8,293.0	35.7	1.8	1.4	61.1	13.0	26.2	21.9	36.3	17.5	3.7	4.3	38.1
El Salvador	1992	1,537.5	17.3	0.5	14.0	68.2	18.0	25.8	24.4	9.8	40.0	0.6	5.2	44.4

the goods onto the transporting vehicle at the frontier of the exporting country (f.o.b. [free-on-board] valuation).

The largest part of the information presented here comes from the United Nations' *Commodity Trade Statistics* (including microfiche format) and *International Trade Statistics Yearbook*. These publications, however, cannot always provide the most recent data for all countries listed in this table and must be supplemented by national and regional sources. In some cases where the original data were only available for an alternative trade classification, an approximation has been made of the SITC commodity groupings.

a. Also includes any unallocated commodities.

b. EU of 12 countries (Belgium, Denmark, France, Germany, Greece, Ireland, Italy, Luxembourg, The Netherlands, Portugal, Spain, and the United Kingdom). From Jan. 1, 1993, the method of compilation of external trade statistics for countries within the European Union was changed for countries within the group, because of the abolition of customs control; intra-EU trade is no longer based on customs documents for its estimation but on a system of direct reporting. The method of compiling trade statistics with countries outside the EU is unchanged.

c. Includes Albania, Bulgaria, Czech Republic, Hungary, Poland, Romania, Slovakia, and European republics of the former U.S.S.R. (Belarus, Estonia, Latvia, Lithuania, Moldova, Russia, and Ukraine).

d. May include value of trade shown as not available (...) in any of the four preceding columns. May include any unspecified areas or countries.

... Not available.

— None, less than 0.05%, or not applicable.

Detail may not add to 100.0 or indicated subtotals because of rounding.

SITC category codes	
0	food and live animals
1	beverages and tobacco
2	crude materials, inedible, except fuels
27	crude fertilizers and crude minerals (excluding coal, petroleum, and precious stones)
28	metalliferous ores and metal scrap
3	mineral fuels, lubricants, and related materials (including coal, petroleum, natural gas, and electric current)
4	animal and vegetable oils, fats, and waxes
5	chemicals and related products not elsewhere specified
6	manufactured goods classified chiefly by material
667	pearls, precious and semiprecious stones, unworked or worked
7	machinery and transport equipment
8	miscellaneous manufactured articles
9	commodities and transactions not classified elsewhere

exports								direction of trade (%)					country
total value ('000,000 U.S.$)	food and agricultural raw materials (0+1+2 −27−28 +4)	mineral ores and concentrates (27+28 +667)	fuels and other energy (3)	total[a] (5+6 −667 +7+8 +9)	of which chemicals and related products (5)	of which machinery and transport equipment (7)	of which other[a] (6−667 +8+9)	to European Union (EU)[b]	to United States	to Eastern Europe[c]	to Japan	to all other[d]	
235.1	63.0[2]			37.0[3]				7.1[4]	0.5[4]	70.2[4,5]	0.3[4]	22.0[4]	Afghanistan
267.4	37.9	46.8		15.3	1.5	0.8	13.0	23.1[6]	...	38.2[5]	2.1	36.6	Albania
11,136.8	0.7	0.3	96.6	2.4	0.6	0.8	0.9	72.8	13.9	1.8	0.7	10.7	Algeria
307.5	100.0		—	—					100.0	—	—	—	American Samoa
24.6	29.6[2]		—	70.4[3]	7.2	10.9	52.4[3]	99.9		—	—	0.1	Andorra
3,409.7	0.3	4.9	94.8	—	—	—	—	26.9	61.4	0.4[5]	0.0	11.3	Angola
19.4	7.4[2]		17.8	74.7[3]	0.5	24.0	41.3[3]	15.0	15.4	—	—	69.5	Antigua and Barbuda
12,234.9	63.8	0.1	8.8	27.2	5.8	7.5	13.9	30.6	11.0	1.8	3.1	53.5	Argentina
141.1[9]	26.8[2]			73.2[3]	6.5	26.5	40.1[3]	1.1[4]	0.3[4]	85.8[4]	—[4]	12.8[4]	Armenia
30.5	54.0	1.2	0.2	44.5	7.1	7.9	29.5	5.6	22.3	—	—	72.1	Aruba
45,110.0	21.9	8.0	17.0	53.1	2.8	9.2	41.1	13.0	10.1	0.4	24.2	52.3	Australia
40,233.1	6.3	0.8	1.2	91.7	9.3	37.2	45.2	60.3	3.1	10.2	1.4	25.0	Austria
1,484.0[9]	16.2[2]		8.7	75.1[3]	45.2[10]	16.9	13.0[3]	12.6	2.6	38.1	0.1	46.7	Azerbaijan
2,163.8	2.8	0.8	77.7	18.7	16.8	0.8	1.2	2.2	79.6	—	2.2	16.0	Bahamas, The
3,464.4	1.5	0.2	79.0	19.3	2.2	0.9	16.1	5.1[4]	1.9[4]	...	8.1[4]	84.9[4]	Bahrain
1,902.8	18.3	—	0.4	81.3	0.8	0.3	80.2	38.0	31.8	1.9[5]	2.7	25.5	Bangladesh
132.7	44.5	0.5		55.0	15.4	18.3	21.2	29.9	21.1	—	1.0	47.9	Barbados
3,200.6[9]	14.1[2]		2.1	83.7[3]	19.0	45.9	18.8	2.7	0.6	77.5	0.1	19.0	Belarus
123,459.9	12.3	7.0	3.5	77.2	14.7	27.0	35.5	75.0	3.9	1.4	1.0	18.7	Belgium[12]
135.9	75.2		3.0	21.8	1.1	3.0	17.7	27.6	47.2	—	0.8	24.3	Belize
114.0	68.1[2]		27.5	4.4[3]	1.2	1.2	2.0[3]	50.4	16.8	0.1[5]	0.9	31.8	Benin
84.3	...	...	...	...	90.3	...	...	27.0	62.3	—	—	10.6	Bermuda
68.1	35.0	3.9	32.6[15]	28.4	16.6	0.1	11.8	0.2	—	—	—	99.8[16]	Bhutan
808.9	23.1	24.0	12.7	40.2	0.7	2.0	37.5	33.6	26.1	—	0.3	40.0	Bolivia
2,056.1	...	...		...	9.4	20.8	...	...				...	Bosnia and Herzegovina
1,853.5	0.7	86.6	—	6.7	1.0	2.4	3.3	2.9	0.3	—	—	96.8[18]	Botswana
36,206.8	28.7	7.6	1.6	62.1	6.1	20.8	35.3	29.6	19.7	1.0	6.4	43.2	Brazil
1,883.1	0.5[2]		96.9	2.6[3]	...	1.3	1.2[3]	0.1	4.9	—	58.1	36.8	Brunei
4,070.6	24.1[19]	10.5[19,20]		65.4[19,21]	11.9[19]	30.6[19]	22.9[19,21]	15.6[19]	3.4[19]	55.0[5,19]	0.7[19]	25.4[19]	Bulgaria
151.1	74.3			25.7	0.1	0.8	24.8	23.1	0.8[4]	—	1.3	74.8[4]	Burkina Faso
74.7	82.3	—		17.7	—		17.7	77.8[4]	7.8[4]	—[4]	1.7[4]	12.7[4]	Burundi
25.0[4]	82.9[22,24]	...		...	...	...	...	4.0[4]	1.4[4]	78.8[4,23]	9.2[4]	6.5[4]	Cambodia
2,892.5	35.3	—	47.5	17.2	0.7	7.5	9.0	61.3	0.4	0.3[5]	0.3	37.7	Cameroon
144,730.5	16.6	2.3	10.5	70.6	5.2	39.5	26.0	5.7	80.7	0.4	4.5	8.6	Canada
28.6	18.4		65.1	16.5	0.9	11.1	4.5	11.4	—	—	—	88.5[25]	Cape Verde
140.3	54.3	43.2		2.5	0.2	0.2	2.0	89.2	0.6	—	—	10.2	Central African Republic
193.9	85.6[2]		11.0	3.4[3]	0.7	0.7	2.1[3]	28.6[4]	0.1[4]	...	4.8[4]	66.5[4]	Chad
9,308.3	38.8	12.7	0.2	48.3	3.9	2.7	41.8	26.1	16.4	0.3	16.6	40.6	Chile
91,744.0	12.9	0.9	4.5	81.7	5.0	16.6	60.0	12.8	18.5	3.8	17.2	47.7	China
6,916.1	42.2		28.5	29.3	5.4	2.3	21.6	25.7	39.4	0.5	2.9	31.6	Colombia
18.0	59.8	—	1.8	38.4	35.3		3.1	75.1[4]	19.2[4]	...	2.6[4]	3.1[4]	Comoros
1,154.8	8.4[27]	1.4[27]	89.1[27]	1.2[27]	0.1[27]	0.5[27]	0.6[27]	48.7	46.2	1.2[5]	0.1	3.8	Congo
1,827.6	65.8	0.1	0.5	33.6	5.1	3.1	25.4	26.8	47.6	0.2	1.3	24.2	Costa Rica
2,931.2	75.4		9.6	14.9	3.4	2.9	8.7	62.2	6.6	5.0[5]	1.3	24.8	Côte d'Ivoire
3,903.8	17.7	0.6	9.7	72.1	14.5	14.2	43.5	53.5	2.1	7.7	—	36.6	Croatia
5,392.0	91.7[2]		...	8.3[3]	1.2	0.8	6.3[3]	13.4	—	70.1[5]	1.9	14.6	Cuba
1,002.8	37.9	1.5	5.2	55.4	5.8	12.3	37.4	40.8	1.5	6.7	0.3	50.7	Cyprus
12,770.6	14.0[2]		6.2	79.9[3]	9.3	27.4	43.1[3]	43.6	1.8	30.9	0.5	23.1	Czech Republic
39,577.3	30.0	0.5	4.0	65.5	10.0	26.9	28.6	51.2	4.2	2.7	3.4	38.5	Denmark
17.3	32.5	—		67.5	0.4	8.3	58.7	62.6	0.8	—	0.9	35.7	Djibouti
54.2	67.2	0.4	—	32.4	23.7	4.2	4.4	61.2	5.2	—	—	33.6	Dominica
658.3	49.1	39.7[2]		11.2[3]	3.5	...	7.6[3]	21.6	63.7	—	3.6	11.1	Dominican Republic
3,042.3	51.2	0.6	43.9	4.3	0.6	0.7	3.0	15.9	46.7	1.7[5]	2.1	33.7	Ecuador
3,050.0	14.0	0.4	43.8	41.8	5.3	1.2	35.2	39.3	9.4	6.4	2.4	42.4	Egypt
555.1	49.4	0.3	0.3	50.0	12.7	2.9	34.4	10.3	33.6	—	0.7	55.5	El Salvador

Trade: external (continued)

country	year	total value ('000,000 U.S.$)	food and agricultural raw materials (0+1+2 -27-28 +4)	mineral ores and concentrates (27+28 +667)	fuels and other energy (3)	manufactured goods total[a] (5+6 -667 +7+8 +9)	of which chemicals and related products (5)	of which machinery and transport equipment (7)	of which other[a] (6-667 +8+9)	from European Union (EU)[b]	from United States	from Eastern Europe[c]	from Japan	from all other[d]
Equatorial Guinea	1990	61.6	13.5	3.4	7.7	75.4	3.9	58.2	13.3	30.6	39.9	—	0.3[4]	29.1
Eritrea	...	...	...	...	...	...	...	...	...	...	...	...	...	...
Estonia	1993	895.5	21.8	0.7	15.3	62.1	8.9	31.9	21.3	23.3	2.7	28.6[5]	4.2	41.1
Ethiopia	1991	471.8	6.5	0.2	10.6	82.6	15.4	44.6	22.6	37.4	13.1	1.9[5]	9.6	38.0
Faeroe Islands	1993	249.8	30.4	0.6	15.5	53.5	9.5	15.3	28.7	60.3	3.0	3.2	1.6	31.8
Fiji	1992	630.7	16.8	0.4	14.1	68.7	8.3	24.6	35.8	7.1	8.7	0.3	10.3	73.6
Finland	1993	18,033.4	9.5	4.0	12.8	73.7	13.3	33.9	26.5	45.6	7.3	10.6	5.8	30.7
France[29]	1993	210,095.8	13.3	1.2	8.9	76.7	11.4	34.5	30.8	58.4	8.7	2.4	4.1	26.4
French Guiana	1993	571.4	19.6	0.1	2.8	77.5	7.1	44.5	25.8	85.4[4]	2.6	0.1	2.3	9.6[4]
French Polynesia	1988	808.3	20.4	0.2	5.4	74.1	6.4	35.9	31.8	65.2	11.3	0.1	4.4	18.9
Gabon	1990	918.2	—12.1[2,4]—		1.9[4]	86.0[3,4]	8.3[4]	42.0[4]	35.7[3,4]	69.6	6.4[4]	0.1[4]	4.9	19.0[4]
Gambia, The	1992	234.2	—39.6[2]—		8.0	52.4[3]	5.8	19.9	26.7[3]	40.8[4]	2.9[4]	2.6[4,5]	3.0[4]	50.7[4]
Gaza Strip	1992	366.2	...	...	...	...	...	...	...	...	...	...	...	100.0[30]
Georgia	1991	179.1[9]	—23.1—		17.8	59.1	9.7	14.7	34.7	2.8[6]	1.0	75.6	—	20.7
Germany	1993	329,537.8	12.4	1.5	8.3	77.8	8.3	34.5	34.9	46.3	7.4	6.5	6.3	33.6
Ghana	1990	1,412.3	—7.9[2,32]—		14.0[32]	78.1[3,32]	12.0[32]	28.1[23]	38.0[3,32]	49.7	10.8	0.8[5]	5.5	33.2
Gibraltar	1988	257.9	—24.4[2]—		20.7	54.9[3]	4.3	21.4	29.2[3]	73.4[33]	5.4[33]	...	10.4[33]	10.8[33]
Greece	1992	23,438.1	16.9	0.4	9.8	72.9	10.6	34.0	28.3	63.1	3.6	4.0	6.4	22.9
Greenland	1993	346.6	17.6	0.3	11.2	70.8	4.4	22.5	44.0	82.0	4.0	0.7	3.6	9.7
Grenada	1991	117.2	28.4	0.2	7.4	64.1	8.5	24.2	31.3	19.8	32.2	0.1	7.1	40.8
Guadeloupe	1993	1,476.7	24.7	0.2	2.0	73.1	10.1	30.0	33.0	79.7[4]	3.3	0.2	2.5	14.3[4]
Guam	1983	610.7	16.9	0.1	46.9	36.2	2.3	19.1	14.8	...	23.4	...	19.9	56.6
Guatemala	1992	2,462.8	12.4	0.3	13.8	73.4	17.8	31.8	23.8	11.8	45.4	0.4[5]	6.0	36.5
Guernsey[35]	...	...	...	...	...	...	...	...	...	...	...	...	...	...
Guinea	1990	693.0	—12.8[2,36]—		13.7[36]	73.5[3,36]	...	17.0[36]	56.5[3,36]	61.3[4]	9.0	...	3.5[4]	26.2[4]
Guinea-Bissau	1990	85.7	20.1[37]	2.2[37]	6.2[37]	71.5[37]	5.6[37]	36.4[37]	29.5[37]	57.8[4]	1.0[4]	3.1[4]	10.6[4]	27.5[4]
Guyana	1990	311.1	5.6[38]	0.5[38]	43.2[38]	50.7[38]	9.4[38]	23.2[38]	18.1[38]	26.4[4]	34.5[4]	0.8[4]	5.8[4]	32.5[4]
Haiti	1992[27]	278.0	—47.9—		22.0	30.1	8.0	6.6	15.6	16.9[4]	56.3[4]	0.1[4]	0.6[4]	26.1[4]
Honduras	1992	667.8	13.1	1.2	14.2	71.5	21.3	23.7	26.5	7.1	54.2	0.3	4.8	33.6
Hong Kong	1993	141,307.6	7.2	2.2	1.8	88.8	6.1	34.5	48.2	9.8	7.5	0.2	16.3	66.2
Hungary	1993	12,530.3	8.3	0.6[2]	13.3	77.8[3]	11.9	36.6	29.3[3]	40.1	3.9	28.2	2.7	25.0
Iceland	1993	1,344.7	13.4	3.1	9.2	74.3	9.2	29.1	36.1	48.4	9.3	3.6	5.5	33.1
India	1993[1]	23,995.5	7.5	16.1	29.5	46.9	14.2	14.1	18.6	28.7	9.5	2.2	6.5	53.1
Indonesia	1993	28,327.8	11.7	2.4	7.6	78.3	14.3	42.9	21.1	20.0	11.5	0.7[5]	22.1	45.8
Iran	1990[1]	12,807.0	—28.2[2]—		2.5	69.3[3]	16.0	30.0	23.4[3]	39.9	—	4.7[5]	7.6	47.8
Iraq	1989	11,730.0[4]	17.6[39]	0.2[39]	0.3[39]	81.9[39]	7.5[39]	39.8[39]	34.6[39]	31.6[4]	11.0[4]	11.9[4,5]	4.6[4]	40.9[4]
Ireland	1992	22,478.2	13.1	0.7	5.2	81.0	13.0	35.6	32.4	66.5	14.2	0.8	5.0	13.5
Isle of Man[35]	...	...	...	...	...	...	...	...	...	...	...	...	...	...
Israel	1993	22,619.0	8.4	17.9	7.4	66.3	9.3	32.7	24.3	48.9	17.8	1.2	5.1	27.0
Italy[40]	1993	156,958.7	18.0	2.1	9.3	70.6	12.4	28.4	29.7	55.4	5.3	5.1	2.6	31.6
Jamaica	1992	1,692.8	16.7	0.1	17.4	65.8	12.7	21.7	31.4	9.6	52.3	0.2	5.0	32.9
Japan	1993	240,670.2	24.7	4.7	20.5	50.1	7.3	17.0	25.8	12.6	23.2	1.4	—	62.9
Jersey	1980	537.1	23.9	0.4	9.3	66.5	6.5	24.8	35.2	84.9[41]	...	...	...	15.1
Jordan	1993	3,560.7	21.5	0.7	12.8	65.0	10.1	26.9	28.0	30.7	12.7	5.8	5.0	45.8
Kazakhstan	1992	3,318.8[9]	—19.2[2,8]—		9.9[8]	71.0[3,8]	9.7[8]	30.9[8]	30.4[3,8]	4.6	0.6	52.7	0.4	41.7
Kenya	1991	2,101.1	10.5	0.5	32.9	56.0	15.0	25.6	15.5	32.7	3.8	0.9	10.8	51.8
Kiribati	1992	36.7	27.5	—	7.8	64.7	3.5	47.3	13.9	10.5	2.9	—	22.7	64.0
Korea, North	1991	2,280.0	...	...	...	...	...	...	...	2.9[6]	—	37.6[6]	9.8	49.7
Korea, South	1992	81,775.3	12.5	3.3	17.9	66.2	9.4	35.4	21.4	11.7	22.4	1.0	23.8	41.1
Kuwait	1989	6,302.2	20.2	0.4	1.0	78.4	7.5	29.5	41.4	29.9	13.2	1.6	12.9	42.4
Kyrgyzstan	1992	504.1[9]	—15.0[2]—		30.9	54.1[3]	11.0	24.1	19.0[3]	0.8	1.5	57.7	—	40.1
Laos	1992	265.0	32.1[43]	0.2[43]	11.2[43]	56.4[43]	6.1[43]	25.7[43]	24.7[43]	3.5[4]	0.4[4]	...	11.6[4]	84.5[4]
Latvia	1993	996.1	—16.9[2,8]—		9.4[8]	73.7[3,8]	11.6[8]	31.3[8]	30.9[3,8]	17.1	1.2	50.8	0.4	30.5
Lebanon	1992	4,202.9[4]	—17.3[2,38]—		3.6[38]	79.1[3,38]	7.8[38]	29.3[38]	42.0[3,38]	43.9[4]	8.1[4]	6.3[4,6]	3.6[4]	38.2[4]
Lesotho	1990	696.5	23.2[27]	0.4[27]	8.7[27]	67.8[27]	7.4[27]	16.7[27]	43.7[27]	2.5	0.2[4]	—[4]	0.1[4]	97.2[4,44]
Liberia	1988	272.3	—19.8[2]—		20.3	59.9[3]	5.6	30.2	24.1[3]	37.7	21.2	...	4.4	36.7
Libya	1991	5,357.5	25.7	0.3	0.4	73.7	7.6	33.8	32.2	58.2	1.3	0.9[5]	3.3	36.3
Liechtenstein	1992	764.2	3.3	0.3[2]	0.9	95.5[3]	5.2	28.9	61.4[3]	...	...	...	...	...
Lithuania	1993	1,303.4	—75.5[2,20]—			24.5[3,21]	4.4	8.9	11.2[3,21]	6.8	1.9	82.6	0.6	8.1
Luxembourg	1991	8,115.0	11.4	—11.9[2]—		76.7[3]	12.6	32.9	31.2[3]	90.6	2.0	...	1.7	5.7
Macau	1993	1,897.1	15.3	4.2	4.6	75.9	4.6	20.0	51.3	11.2	5.8	0.3	15.8	66.9
Macedonia	1990	1,113.4	...	...	19.1	...	...	7.2	...	36.8	...	...	...	63.2
Madagascar	1991	402.5	12.5	0.1	12.2	75.2	11.1	41.1	22.9	56.2	6.3	1.2[5]	7.1	29.2
Malawi	1989	507.7	9.1[22]	1.3[22]	13.3[22]	76.3[22]	20.2[22]	29.4[22]	26.8[22]	32.1	3.4	...	6.3	58.2
Malaysia	1992	39,924.9	7.6	1.5	4.2	86.8	8.1	54.9	23.7	12.5	15.8	0.4[5]	26.0	45.4
Maldives	1992	189.4	—25.9—		12.1	62.0	5.9	23.4	32.8	7.3	1.0	0.2	3.8	87.7
Mali	1987	374.1	—22.3[2]—		14.8	62.9[3]	15.0	22.1	25.8[3]	48.8	5.0	0.9	3.3	42.0
Malta	1992	2,338.5	11.2	0.5	4.7	83.6	6.8	48.4	28.4	76.7	3.2	1.8	4.1	14.2
Marshall Islands	1991	56.4	—40.9[2]—		11.1	48.0[3]	2.7	16.3	29.0[3]	...	58.5	—	9.6	31.9
Martinique	1993	1,631.2	22.3	0.2	7.5	70.0	10.0	30.1	29.9	78.0	2.9	0.2	2.5	16.4
Mauritania	1990	388.1	30.6[36]	...	7.0[36]	62.4[36]	...	51.0[36]	11.4[36]	76.0[6]	7.4	...	2.8	13.8
Mauritius	1992	1,782.9	15.6	1.5	8.7	74.3	7.2	25.2	41.9	31.5	3.0	0.3	9.5	55.7
Mayotte	1992	87.5	—20.1—		3.6	76.3	9.4	41.1	25.8	74.0[45]	...	...	3.3	22.7
Mexico	1992	47,877.9	14.3	0.8	3.5	81.4	9.5	48.2	23.8	14.9	62.9	0.3[5]	6.3	15.5
Micronesia	1991	88.6	—36.6[2]—		13.2	50.2[3]	4.1	14.1	31.9[3]	...	36.2[36]	...	22.0[36]	41.8[36]
Moldova	1991	422.2[9]	—18.1[2]—		16.2	65.8[3]	13.7	15.3	36.7[3]	1.8	2.8	76.6	0.4	18.4
Monaco[29]	...	...	...	...	...	...	...	...	...	...	...	...	...	...
Mongolia	1990	828.6	8.8	—27.2[20]—		64.0[21]	5.3	31.1	27.6[21]	5.0[6]	—	87.4[5]	1.1	6.6
Morocco	1993	6,857.4	22.4	2.1	14.3	61.2	11.0	28.7	21.5	54.5	10.1	3.1	1.7	30.7
Mozambique	1988	715.0	—37.3[2]—		8.5	54.2[3]	6.5	33.4	14.3[3]	43.2[4]	7.9	13.7[23]	4.0[4]	31.2[4]
Myanmar (Burma)	1992[1]	845.2	—11.2[2]—		3.5	85.3[3,47]	7.2	32.2	45.8[3,47]	10.8	2.7[4]	1.1[5]	21.1	64.2[4]
Namibia	1991	1,167.1	—24.1[2]—		9.3	66.6[3]	7.9	28.5	30.2[3]	...	...	...	...	100.0[48]
Nauru	1989[49]	13.9	—33.7[2]—		0.4	65.9[3]	2.7	22.3	40.9[3]	...	...	...	...	...
Nepal	1990[11]	404.5	17.1	0.5	12.2	70.1	15.6	23.7	30.8	15.3	1.6	2.8	13.7	66.6
Netherlands, The	1993	129,754.5	16.8	1.6	9.6	72.0	11.5	31.2	29.3	56.8	8.5	2.4	4.1	28.2

total value ('000,000 U.S.$)	food and agricultural raw materials (0+1+2 -27-28 +4)	mineral ores and concen- trates (27+28 +667)	fuels and other energy (3)	manufactured goods total[a] (5+6 -667 +7+8 +9)	of which chemicals and related products (5)	of which machinery and transport equipment (7)	of which other[a] (6-667 +8+9)	to European Union (EU)[b]	to United States	to Eastern Europe[c]	to Japan	to all other[d]	country
61.7	48.6	—	—	51.4	0.1	39.8[28]	11.5	47.2	—	—	—	52.8	Equatorial Guinea
...	...	...	...	...	...	...	...	...	...	...	...	...	Eritrea
804.4	34.9	1.8	7.0	56.3	5.9	18.4	32.0	17.8	1.9	45.1[15]	...	35.2	Estonia
188.6	84.4	—	1.0	14.7	1.2	—	13.4	58.2	4.3	0.5[5]	20.3	16.6	Ethiopia
377.8	95.8	—	—	4.2	0.1	3.9	0.2	85.2	2.5	0.3	2.6	0.5	Faeroe Islands
428.0	53.1	0.1	8.9	37.0	1.0	5.4	31.6	31.9	14.0	—	5.3	48.9	Fiji
23,502.6	11.3	0.6	2.7	85.4	6.5	31.4	47.4	45.4	7.7	9.1	1.6	36.2	Finland
216,247.6	17.4	0.8	2.7	79.1	14.3	38.4	26.5	59.7	7.2	2.1	2.0	29.0	France[29]
107.6	39.8	—	—	60.2	0.4	21.9	37.9	78.6[4]	1.9	—	—	19.5[4]	French Guiana
74.7	5.9	31.3	—	62.8	1.6	38.6	22.6	40.0	18.9	—	22.5	18.6	French Polynesia
2,463.8	11.7	10.6[2,20]	74.2	3.6[3,21]	1.7	0.2	1.7[3,21]	46.1	29.7	0.4[5]	4.1	19.7	Gabon
63.7	73.4[8]	0.2[2,8,20]	—[8]	26.4[3,8,21]	—[8]	0.7[8]	25.6[3,8,21]	76.3[4]	0.4[4]	0.2[4]	14.4[4]	8.7[4]	Gambia, The
79.3	...	...	...	...	...	...	...	...	...	...	...	100.0[31]	Gaza Strip
177.9[9]	—32.6—		0.9	66.5	6.4	27.9	32.2	0.1[6]	—	82.3	—	17.5	Georgia
365,254.6	6.5	0.7	1.2	91.5	13.1	49.5	28.9	47.9	7.7	6.9	2.6	34.9	Germany
1,072.3	52.1	21.2[2,20]	3.4	23.3[3,21]	0.1	0.3	22.9[3,21]	63.3[4]	13.1[4]	4.4[4,5]	5.0[4]	14.3[4]	Ghana
82.1	—8.2[22]—		51.5	40.3[3]	2.8	18.1	19.4[3]	22.2	—	—	—	77.8[34]	Gibraltar
9,842.0	35.6	2.2	5.3	57.0	3.8	4.8	48.4	78.4	3.9	6.2	0.9	10.7	Greece
312.3	92.7	—	1.2	6.1	—	1.6	4.5	80.9	1.9	—	13.1	4.1	Greenland
20.1	77.0	—	—	23.0	4.5	2.1	16.4	44.1	14.2	—	2.6	39.2	Grenada
133.3	74.7	0.4	—	24.8	1.1	17.8	6.0	79.5[4]	1.6	—	0.3	18.6[4]	Guadeloupe
39.2	23.5	2.7	3.5	70.3	5.6	11.5	53.2	...	24.9	—	4.8	70.4	Guam
1,295.3	67.8	0.3	2.0	30.0	11.1	1.5	17.4	10.7	35.4	0.5[5]	1.7	51.7	Guatemala
...	...	...	...	...	...	...	...	...	...	...	...	...	Guernsey[35]
788.0	6.3	86.5	—	7.2	...	...	7.2	56.1[4]	23.0	—	1.1[4]	19.8[4]	Guinea
19.3	87.1[37]	0.3[37]	—[37]	12.6[37]	0.3[37]	—[37]	12.3[37]	27.9[4]	0.4[4]	—[4]	0.6[4]	71.1[4]	Guinea-Bissau
250.6	40.6	29.2[2,20]	—	30.3[3,21]	3.5	6.7	20.1[3,21]	44.2[4]	19.0[4]	1.9[4]	5.8[4]	29.1[4]	Guyana
77.7	—23.5—			76.5	...	...	...	20.3[4]	74.7[4]	0.1[4]	0.7[4]	4.2[4]	Haiti
515.7	84.3	2.8	0.5	12.4	2.1	0.3	10.0	30.0	52.5	0.6[5]	2.5	14.4	Honduras
135,384.6	4.2	1.1	0.9	93.8	5.1	30.6	58.1	15.0	23.0	0.5	5.1	56.4	Hong Kong
8,906.9	24.0	1.8[2]	4.1	70.2[3]	12.1	24.1	34.0[3]	46.5	4.2	22.8	1.0	25.5	Hungary
1,396.1	82.6	0.8	0.1	16.6	0.1	2.2	14.2	59.9	15.9	0.4	9.3	14.5	Iceland
20,328.0	17.8	18.6	2.8	60.8	6.7	7.0	47.1	28.4	19.0	4.3	7.7	40.5	India
36,822.8	15.0	2.8	28.2	54.0	2.3	6.0	45.8	14.4	14.2	0.6[5]	30.3	40.4	Indonesia
14,409.4	3.4	0.3[20]	92.5	3.8[21]	—	0.1	3.7[21]	49.6[4]	0.1[4]	10.5[4]	14.3[4]	25.6[4]	Iran
14,520.0[4]	0.5		99.5		—	—		23.2[4]	16.0[4]	16.6[4,5]	7.5[4]	36.6[4]	Iraq
28,332.5	26.0	1.5	0.6	71.9	19.1	27.0	25.9	74.3	8.2	0.9	2.9	13.6	Ireland
...	...	...	...	...	...	...	...	...	...	...	...	...	Isle of Man[35]
14,825.5	7.5	28.5	0.6	63.3	14.9	31.0	17.4	29.7	31.2	3.2	5.2	30.7	Israel
178,937.3	7.5	0.3	2.2	90.0	7.4	36.7	45.9	53.3	7.7	3.9	1.0	33.1	Italy[40]
1,052.8	23.8	53.3	1.0	22.0	2.5	1.9	17.6	23.6	36.5	0.4	1.4	38.0	Jamaica
360,911.1	1.0	0.2	0.5	90.2	5.6	72.0	20.6	15.8	29.5	0.6	—	54.2	Japan
200.2	27.6	4.3[42]	—	68.0	1.2	31.1	35.7	67.3[41]	...	...	...	32.7	Jersey
1,255.7	18.8	21.9	—	59.2	24.9	12.5	21.9	8.7	3.1	3.8	1.1	83.3	Jordan
3,259.3[9]	—27.8[2,8]—		14.3[8]	58.0[3,8]	11.6[8]	8.4[8]	38.0[3,8]	8.7	3.1	51.6	1.6	35.1	Kazakhstan
1,118.0	61.2	3.4	10.9	24.4	4.2	0.9	19.4	41.1	3.7	0.1	1.0	54.1	Kenya
4.7	82.5	—	—	17.5	—	—	17.5	6.0	12.3	—	—	81.7	Kiribati
1,240.0	...	...	...	...	...	...	...	7.3[6]	—	45.4[6]	22.9	24.4	Korea, North
76,631.5	4.1	0.2	2.3	93.4	5.8	42.5	45.1	12.1	23.7	1.1	15.1	48.0	Korea, South
11,476.0	0.7	0.2	91.0	8.2	2.4	2.5	3.3	22.7[4]	8.2[4]	1.3[4]	18.5[4]	49.3[4]	Kuwait
376.9[9]	—9.7[2]—		8.1	82.1[3]	1.8	40.8	39.6[3]	4.0	—	54.5	0.4	41.0	Kyrgyzstan
132.0	46.5[22]	3.4[22]	50.1[22]	—22	—22	—22	—22	21.4[4]	4.4[4]	...	8.2[4]	66.0[4]	Laos
1,079.4	—26.2[2,8]—		1.8[8]	72.0[3,8]	12.4[8]	27.9[8]	31.7[3,8]	23.7	0.6	50.0	0.6	25.0	Latvia
550.5[4]	—14.4[2,38]—		—38	85.6[3,30]	1.1[38]	18.2[38]	66.2[3,38]	18.0[4]	4.6[4]	4.5[4,6]	0.4[4]	72.5[4]	Lebanon
59.0	—28.4[2]—		—	71.6[3]	1.4	0.4	69.8[3]	16.1	12.4	—	—	71.4	Lesotho
396.3	39.4	57.7	0.5	2.4	—	0.5	1.9	66.6	18.8	...	1.2	13.3	Liberia
11,211.7	0.7	—	95.4	3.9	3.4	—	0.5	86.2	—	1.6	—	12.2	Libya
1,437.7	3.8	—2	0.1	96.0[3]	8.7	45.1	42.2[3]	44.9	...	...	...	55.1	Liechtenstein
1,242.2	—58.6[2,20]—			41.4[3,21]	4.7	10.6	26.1[3,21]	13.5	0.4	75.7	0.1	10.4	Lithuania
6,277.2	6.6	—1.1[2]—		92.3[3]	17.6	20.2	54.5[3]	82.4	3.3	...	0.7	13.5	Luxembourg
1,718.8	5.9			94.0	1.4	4.4	88.2	32.7	32.8	0.1	1.4	33.0	Macau
579.2	...		...	...	5.4	14.2	...	42.3	...	...	...	57.7	Macedonia
291.7	72.4	8.0	0.5	19.1	2.8	2.3	14.1	49.9	14.6	6.1[5]	8.9	20.6	Madagascar
266.5	95.0[22]	—22	—22	5.0[22]	0.5[22]	—22	4.5[22]	48.6	12.6	...	12.6	26.3	Malawi
40,624.6	20.8	0.6	12.8	65.8	2.1	43.9	19.8	14.9	18.6	0.2	13.3	53.0	Malaysia
39.4	79.7	0.1	—	20.2	—	—	20.2	44.0	13.6		3.3	39.0	Maldives
170.0	—69.0[2]—		—	31.0[3]	...	...	...	9.4	—	12.4	1.0	77.2	Mali
1,537.3	3.1	0.2	2.0	94.7	2.5	59.2	33.0	75.3	5.8	2.3	0.1	16.5	Malta
2.9	99.9	—	—	0.1	—	—	0.1	—38	70.4[38]	—38	—30	20.6[38]	Marshall Islands
202.0	59.1	0.5	19.9	20.6	3.0	12.5	5.1	65.8	0.6	—	—	33.6	Martinique
409.1	47.7	48.6[2,20]	1.9	1.6[3,21]	—	0.3	1.3[3,21]	51.6[6]	3.1	11.9[23]	21.2	12.2	Mauritania
1,335.5	31.6	1.7	1.9	64.7	1.0	1.5	62.2	75.0	12.0	0.1	0.2	12.6	Mauritius
4.8	39.9[46]	—46	—46	60.1[46]	60.1[46]	—46	0.1[46]	70.0[45]	...	...	...	30.0	Mayotte
27,207.1	13.2	1.8	29.8	55.1	7.7	31.6	15.8	11.9	68.6	0.1[5]	3.2	16.1	Mexico
11.0	87.2[36]	—36	—36	12.8[36]	...	...	...	...	0.3[36]	...	58.2[30]	41.5[36]	Micronesia
407.0[9]	—48.0[2]—		0.6	51.4[3]	2.3	19.1	30.0[3]	1.2	0.1	88.5	0.1	10.1	Moldova
...	...	...	...	...	...	...	...	...	...	...	...	...	Monaco[29]
592.6	27.3	—48.1[20]—		24.6[21]	...	...	...	4.0[6]	0.1	90.7[5]	1.2	4.0	Mongolia
3,800.2	29.1	10.2	2.7	58.0	19.5	5.5	33.0	62.4	3.4	1.1	1.9	27.2	Morocco
103.0	82.4	7.7[2,20]	1.3	8.7[3,21]	0.3	0.8	7.6[3,21]	28.7[6]	16.5	...	16.6	39.2	Mozambique
464.3	—73.5[2]—		0.2	26.3[3,47]	0.1	—	26.2[3,47]	2.2	0.4[4]	—	6.5	90.9[4]	Myanmar (Burma)
1,244.4	35.9	59.2	0.1	4.8	—	—	4.8	...	25.0[27]	—	15.0[27]	60.0[27]	Namibia
80.3	—	99.8	—	0.2	—	—	0.2	...	...	...	...	...	Nauru
149.2	6.1	—	—	93.9	0.1	—	93.8	45.5	32.9	2.7[5]	0.5	18.3	Nepal
146,999.0	25.5	1.3	8.9	64.3	14.2	24.9	25.1	67.0	3.7	2.3	0.8	26.1	Netherlands, The

Trade: external (continued)

country	year	imports total value ('000,000 U.S.$)	food and agricultural raw materials (0+1+2-27-28+4)	mineral ores and concentrates (27+28+667)	fuels and other energy (3)	manufactured goods total[a] (5+6-667+7+8+9)	of which chemicals and related products (5)	of which machinery and transport equipment (7)	of which other[a] (6-667+8+9)	from European Union (EU)[b]	from United States	from Eastern Europe[c]	from Japan	from all other[d]
Netherlands Antilles	1991	2,188.9	5.9	0.1	70.7	23.3	3.6	9.2	10.6	8.2	14.5	0.1	1.7	75.4
New Caledonia	1991	864.4	—18.5[2]—		9.7	71.8[3]	6.8	35.8	29.3[3]	60.8	7.0	0.2	5.8	26.2
New Zealand	1993	9,654.8	9.0	2.5	6.4	82.1	13.9	38.5	29.7	17.5	18.0	0.2	16.2	48.1
Nicaragua	1992	906.8	24.0	0.1	14.9	60.9	12.8	26.2	21.9	8.1	25.6	1.9[5]	6.0	58.5
Niger	1990	388.8	—32.1[2]—		12.9	55.0[3]	10.2	22.3	22.5[3]	48.4[4]	3.3[4]	—[4]	3.5[4]	44.8[4]
Nigeria	1987	3,918.7	12.8	2.7	0.4	84.1	16.9	38.2	29.0	56.4	8.3	5.0[5]	9.0	21.3
Northern Mariana Islands	1989	313.7	16.6	—	19.2	64.1	2.8	28.8	32.6	—	24.6	—	15.5	60.0
Norway	1993	24,355.5	8.4	4.9	3.3	83.4	9.5	38.9	34.9	48.7	8.1	2.5	8.0	32.7
Oman	1992	3,769.2	19.7	0.6	1.8	77.8	5.8	43.7	28.3	23.5	6.8	0.1	23.3	46.3
Pakistan	1992	9,573.0	18.8	2.1	16.3	62.8	15.7	34.8	12.3	25.5	10.5	1.2	14.2	48.7
Panama	1992	2,018.8	11.0	0.4	15.0	73.6	12.9	27.9	32.8	6.5	36.9	0.1	8.2	48.2
Papua New Guinea	1990	1,233.1	18.8	0.3	6.8	74.1	7.0	38.3	28.8	6.5	9.7	1.1[5]	13.0	69.7
Paraguay	1992	1,420.4	13.3	0.5	13.6	72.6	10.3	41.1	21.2	13.9	14.0	0.5[5]	12.3	59.4
Peru	1990	3,469.8	25.3	0.6	12.5	61.6	14.6	32.7	14.3	17.1	28.2	0.7[5]	3.4	50.5
Philippines	1993	18,772.7	10.1	1.7	11.5	76.7	9.7	32.7	34.3	10.0	20.0	1.2	22.8	45.9
Poland	1991	15,521.7	15.7	2.0	18.9	63.4	9.5	34.1	19.8	49.9	2.3	19.0[5]	1.6	27.2
Portugal	1992	30,610.5	15.2	0.6	8.0	76.2	9.0	38.0	29.1	73.8	3.0	0.6	3.1	19.5
Puerto Rico	1988[11]	11,859.1	19.7	0.6	10.7	69.0	15.6	23.7	29.7	6.5	66.8	0.1	4.9	21.7
Qatar	1992	2,015.4	15.3	2.3	0.7	81.8	6.3	44.1	31.4	35.8	11.4	0.5	15.6	36.7
Réunion	1993	2,171.7	22.3	0.2	5.1	72.4	10.6	29.0	32.8	79.3[4]	0.3	0.5	2.0	17.9[4]
Romania	1991	5,722.8	16.4	6.0	40.0	37.5	7.4	16.2	13.9	25.2	3.2	24.7[5]	1.3	45.6
Russia	1992	55,300.0[9]	—14.4[2,8]—		7.0[8]	78.7[3,8]	8.0[8]	47.5[8]	23.1[3,8]	22.4[4]	4.9[4]	32.0[4]	2.8[4]	37.8[4]
Rwanda	1990	291.1	18.2	1.9	15.3	64.6	10.2	16.1	38.3	43.3	1.2	1.4[5]	7.7	46.4
St. Kitts and Nevis	1988	93.3	21.0	—	5.5	73.5	7.5	32.0	34.0	21.2	47.4	—	3.8	27.5
St. Lucia	1991	295.2	25.8	1.1	7.0	66.1	10.1	21.0	34.9	22.6	37.2	0.1	6.1	34.0
St. Vincent and the Grenadines	1990	136.1	27.4	0.2[2]	6.1	66.4[3]	11.0	21.7	33.7[3]	25.8	36.0	0.1	3.3	34.8
San Marino[40]	...	...	...	...	...	...	...	...	...	...	...	...	...	...
São Tomé and Príncipe	1988	21.7	—35.2—		6.5	58.3	...	30.5	27.8	63.1[4]	31.3[4]	...	1.1[4]	4.5[4]
Saudi Arabia	1991	29,073.8	13.9	0.7	0.3	85.2	8.6	40.4	36.1	34.4	20.2	0.9[5]	13.7	30.8
Senegal	1990	1,620.4	30.5	1.9	16.0	51.7	9.7	21.3	20.7	56.1	5.3	1.2[5]	3.6	33.7
Seychelles	1991	172.5	21.7	0.1	21.9	56.4	6.0	23.1	27.2	31.4	2.5	0.1[5]	5.2	60.7
Sierra Leone	1992	130.5	—40.4[2]—		10.4	49.2[3]	10.9	18.9	19.4[3]	38.5[4]	11.1[4]	0.8[4]	2.3[4]	47.4[4]
Singapore	1993	85,160.8	6.8	0.6	10.8	81.7	7.0	52.3	22.5	11.5	16.2	0.4[5]	21.9	50.0
Slovakia[53]	1992	3,563.2	—12.1[2]—		29.5	58.3[3]	9.8	31.9	16.7[3]	34.2	1.8	44.2[5]	...	19.8
Slovenia	1993	6,501.0	—13.7[2]—		10.8	75.5[3]	11.5	30.3	33.7[3]	55.7	2.9	9.0[5]	1.9	30.4
Solomon Islands	1989	113.1	—18.2[2]—		9.7	72.1[3]	4.3	36.4	31.4[3]	4.6	2.8	0.1[5]	23.2	69.3
Somalia	1990	397.8[4]	30.3[27]	0.2[27]	4.6[27]	64.9[27]	5.1[27]	37.1[27]	22.7[27]	49.9[4]	3.1[4]	—[4]	2.3[4]	44.6[4]
South Africa[54]	1993	20,042.6	9.5[19]	1.1[19]	0.5[19,55]	88.8[19,56]	14.3[19]	43.0[19]	31.5[19,56]	40.3	13.1	0.5[5]	12.6	33.4
Spain	1993	88,423.2	15.9	2.0	10.6	71.5	10.9	35.6	25.0	61.1	6.8	1.8	3.9	26.3
Sri Lanka	1992	3,472.7	18.2	2.7	8.9	70.2	9.0	21.3	39.8	14.9	4.7	1.9[5]	12.2	66.5
Sudan, The	1992	820.9	15.2	0.7	28.0	56.2	6.6	30.6	19.1	22.8	7.9	2.6	3.5	63.2
Suriname	1990	472.0	11.8	1.5	18.0	68.7	21.4	24.7	22.6	29.4	41.0	—	2.8	26.8
Swaziland	1990	666.0	18.3	1.0	15.8	64.9	10.0	23.8	31.2	5.0	0.3	—	0.8	94.0[59]
Sweden	1993	46,369.8	9.5	1.4	9.2	79.9	11.5	36.0	32.4	55.0	9.1	3.0	5.0	28.0
Switzerland[60]	1993	62,028.6	8.7	5.2	3.9	82.2	13.5	29.6	39.1	72.6	6.4	1.1	3.9	16.0
Syria	1990	2,399.7	33.0	0.3	3.0	63.7	13.5	19.8	30.4	40.7	10.7	8.3[5]	3.3	36.9
Taiwan	1992	72,132.4	10.8	1.3	7.8	80.1	12.5	39.4	28.2	13.1	21.9	1.3	30.2	33.4
Tajikistan	1992	302.5[9]	—58.0[2,20]—		15.1	26.9[3,21]	11.3	7.0	8.6[3,21]	13.9[4]	2.9[4]	33.5[4]	0.3[4]	49.5[4]
Tanzania	1990	1,021.5	5.4	1.5	10.3	82.8	9.8	45.6	27.4	53.7	1.6	0.8[5]	7.7	36.2
Thailand	1991	37,588.3	10.4	5.7	9.2	74.7	9.6	39.7	25.4	14.0	10.6	1.6[5]	29.4	44.5
Togo	1991	443.9	24.4	0.7	9.8	65.1	11.9	28.3	25.0	55.6	6.4	0.1	6.7	31.1
Tonga	1991	59.3	30.1	0.4	15.8	53.7	8.1	19.0	26.5	2.1	9.9	—	9.0	78.9
Trinidad and Tobago	1993	1,462.9	16.3	1.5	15.9	66.3	11.0	32.9	22.4	19.6	39.6	0.1	3.8	36.9
Tunisia	1992	6,432.0	12.0	2.3	7.5	78.2	8.4	30.4	39.4	71.1	5.0	3.5[5]	2.3	18.2
Turkey	1993	29,429.3	10.5	3.4	13.5	72.6	12.1	38.2	22.4	44.0	11.4	10.3	5.5	28.8
Turkmenistan	1991	3,140.0[9]	—28.1[2]—		2.8	69.1[3]	6.5	30.3	32.4[3]	4.8[4]	0.5[4]	56.4[4]	0.5[4]	37.8[4]
Tuvalu	1989	4.1	—38.2[2]—		12.8	49.0[3]	7.1	12.2	29.6[3]	5.4[27]	1.0[27]	—[27]	3.1[27]	90.6[27]
Uganda	1990	466.4[4]	—8.4[2]—		15.7	75.9[3]	10.9	35.8	29.2[3]	45.9[4]	6.1[4]	—[4]	5.8[4]	42.2[4]
Ukraine	1992	7,950.0[9]	—9.0[2,8]—		22.3[8]	68.7[3,8]	8.9[8]	37.6[8]	22.2[3,8]	7.0[4]	1.1[4]	73.6[4]	0.5[4]	17.8[4]
United Arab Emirates	1988	8,523.1	—17.2[2]—		2.9	79.9[3]	7.0	32.2	40.8[3]	27.0	9.5	...	16.4	47.1
United Kingdom[35]	1993	206,380.4	12.7	3.0	5.3	78.9	9.3	38.7	30.9	49.1	11.9	1.5	6.2	31.2
United States[62]	1993	603,153.6	7.3	1.7	9.8	81.2	5.1	44.0	32.1	16.8	—	0.6	18.3	64.3
Uruguay	1993	2,332.9	10.5	0.4	8.6	80.5	14.0	41.0	25.5	21.9	9.0	1.1	5.4	62.5
Uzbekistan	1992	2,700.0[9]	—43.8[2,20]—		25.5	30.7[3,21]	11.0	10.5	9.1[3,21]	1.5	0.4	64.5	0.1	33.5
Vanuatu	1992	81.8	—24.4[2]—		9.7	65.9[3]	6.6	29.3	30.1[3]	8.0[45]	1.9[4]	—	9.4	80.7[4]
Venezuela	1991	10,037.6	13.6	1.8	2.4	82.2	15.0	43.5	23.8	22.7	47.8	0.6[5]	5.0	24.0
Vietnam	1991	2,194.0	—9.4[2]—		22.9	67.8[3]	16.3	26.1	25.4[3]	10.3	—	17.8[5]	6.2	65.7
Virgin Islands (U.S.)	1992	3,550.8	...	...	71.4	...	...	...	...	...	49.8	...	...	...
West Bank	1992	89.3[64]	...	...	...	...	...	...	...	...	...	...	...	...
Western Sahara	...	...	...	...	...	...	...	...	...	...	...	...	...	...
Western Samoa	1989	76.9	24.3[38]	0.3[38]	17.5[38]	57.9[38]	7.4[38]	22.9[38]	27.6[38]	8.7[4]	5.6	—[4]	12.8	72.9[4]
Yemen	1992	2,589.6	35.2	0.6[2]	6.1	58.2[3]	6.6	21.8	29.7[3]	28.1	9.2	1.9[5]	7.0	53.8
Yugoslavia	1991	5,548.6	12.4	1.3	19.0	67.4	13.7	22.7	31.0	43.1	4.2	24.5[5]	2.3	26.0
Zaire	1990	886.1	—20.0[32]—		13.8[32]	66.2[32]	4.4[32]	45.5[32]	16.3[32]	59.1[4]	9.8[4]	0.1[4]	2.7[4]	28.3[4]
Zambia	1990	1,237.7	3.7	1.1[2]	15.2	79.9[3]	12.6	47.0	20.3[3]	35.2	10.1	0.2[5]	6.7	47.8
Zimbabwe	1991	2,007.1	5.0	1.7	12.5	80.8	16.3	41.0	23.5	34.3	5.5	0.3	6.0	53.9

[1]Year ending March. [2]Excluding precious stones, etc. (667). [3]Including precious stones, etc. (667). [4]Estimate. [5]Including also Asian republics of the former U.S.S.R. [6]Main countries only. [7]Year ending September 30. [8]1990. [9]External trade figures originally quoted in rubles have been converted to U.S. dollars using a market exchange rate. This total in U.S. dollars can vary markedly according to the exchange rate used. [10]Includes petrochemicals. [11]Year ending June 30. [12]Figures for Belgium-Luxembourg Economic Union (Luxembourg is also shown separately). [13]Free-on-board valuation (f.o.b.). [14]Includes 83.6% from India. [15]Mainly electricity. [16]Includes 84.8% to India. [17]Includes 83.8% from South Africa and Namibia. [18]Includes 78.3% to Switzerland. [19]1991. [20]Including metals. [21]Excluding metals. [22]1985. [23]Former U.S.S.R. only. [24]Rubber only. [25]Includes ships' bunkers and stores. [26]1975. [27]1986. [28]Includes 38.7% for ships and boats. [29]Figures for France include Monaco. [30]Includes 89.7% from Israel. [31]Includes 80.5% to Israel and 15.0% to Jordan. [32]1987. [33]Excluding petroleum products. [34]Includes 51.5% for ships' bunkers. [35]Figures for United Kingdom include Guernsey, Isle of Man, and Jersey (the latter is also shown separately). [36]1988. [37]1980. [38]1983. [39]1986; commercial imports only (excluding oil companies' imports). [40]Figures for Italy include San Marino. [41]United Kingdom only. [42]Including coins. [43]1974. [44]Includes 94.1% from rest of Customs Union of Southern Africa. [45]France only.

total value ('000,000 U.S.$)	food and agricultural raw materials (0+1+2 −27−28 +4)	mineral ores and concentrates (27+28 +667)	fuels and other energy (3)	manufactured goods total (5+6 −667 +7+8 +9)	of which chemicals and related products (5)	of which machinery and transport equipment (7)	of which other[a] (6−667 +8+9)	to European Union (EU)[b]	to United States	to Eastern Europe[c]	to Japan	to all other[d]	country
1,599.2	0.6	0.5	96.0	3.0	1.4	0.8	0.7	4.6	28.4	—	2.9	64.1	Netherlands Antilles
444.5	—	32.9	—	67.1	—	—	67.1	47.0	4.8	—	29.5	18.6	New Caledonia
10,558.2	63.1	0.5	2.5	33.9	5.9	7.4	20.6	15.1	11.6	1.0	14.6	57.7	New Zealand
236.5	86.8	0.5	0.9	11.9	2.8	0.2	8.8	25.5	26.0	0.2[5]	9.1	39.3	Nicaragua
282.6	—92.0[2]—		1.1	7.0[3]	0.1	1.0	5.9[3]	73.3[4]	15.3[4]	—[4]	-[4]	11.5[4]	Niger
7,383.4	3.7		95.4	0.9	0.2	—	0.7	41.4	47.0		0.1	11.5	Nigeria
130.5[50]	...	...	...	...	...	...	100.0	—	—	—	—	100.0	Northern Mariana Islands
32,329.0	9.7	1.2	51.3	37.8	5.9	13.0	18.5	66.6	6.2	1.6	1.8	23.7	Norway
5,427.8	3.4	0.2	83.7	12.8	0.4	9.2	3.2	3.1[4]	3.4[4]	—[4]	32.9[4]	60.5[4]	Oman
7,370.7	19.5	0.3	1.2	79.0	0.5	0.9	77.7	28.1	12.8	0.4	7.7	51.1	Pakistan
474.2	78.2	0.3	0.7	20.9	4.9	1.0	15.0	39.1	31.9	—	0.2	28.9	Panama
1,261.7	25.5	46.3	0.1	28.2	0.1	5.7	22.4	21.3	2.4	—	27.9	48.4	Papua New Guinea
656.6	84.2	0.1	0.5	15.2	3.2	0.2	11.0	34.3	5.3	0.1[5]	0.4	60.0	Paraguay
3,230.9	24.5	20.8	10.0	44.7	2.1	1.0	41.6	32.2	23.1	3.3[5]	12.7	28.8	Peru
11,374.8	16.8	1.9	2.0	79.2	2.3	18.6	58.3	17.4	38.5	0.2	16.1	27.8	Philippines
14,903.4	20.0	2.9	10.7	66.5	9.2	18.5	38.8	55.5	2.5	16.8[5]	0.6	24.6	Poland
18,540.6	12.1	2.3	2.9	82.7	4.2	21.6	56.8	75.2	3.5	0.4	0.8	20.1	Portugal
13,952.8	16.9	1.0	2.2	79.9	39.8	19.7	20.4	3.3	88.0	—	0.1	8.5	Puerto Rico
3,840.7	0.3	0.2	83.3	16.2	8.2	2.1	5.9	2.5[4]	2.0[4]	—[4]	56.9[4]	38.6[4]	Qatar
186.8	75.8	0.4	0.2	23.7	3.1	12.3	8.3	81.6[4]	0.1	—	3.8	14.5[4]	Réunion
4,163.6	8.2	0.4	12.8	78.6	7.7	26.7	44.2	34.3	3.0	28.2[5]	2.4	32.1	Romania
63,600.0[9]	—6.5[2,8]—		35.2[8]	58.3[3,8]	7.0[8]	32.7[8]	18.6[3,8]	25.8[4]	1.0[4]	35.8[4]	2.3[4]	35.2[4]	Russia
131.9	72.8	3.9	—	23.3[51]	—	—	23.3[51]	64.1[4]	6.1[4]	—[4]	1.9[4]	27.9[4]	Rwanda
27.4	42.0	—	0.9	57.0	0.1	34.2	22.8	22.3	62.3	—	—	15.4	St. Kitts and Nevis
109.9	65.1	—	0.1	34.8	0.7	8.8	25.3	57.7	21.7	—	—	20.6	St. Lucia
82.7	76.1	—[2]	—	23.8[3]	1.6	4.7	17.6[3]	54.6	10.4	—	—	35.0	St. Vincent and the Grenadines
...	...	...	....	...	...	...	...	...	...	...	...	...	San Marino[40]
11.6	100.0	...	....	—	...	...	—	85.2[5]	10.4[4]	—	—[4]	4.4[4]	Sao Tomé and Príncipe
47,790.2	1.0	0.2	91.4	7.4	5.0	0.9	1.5	20.7	23.4	0.7[5]	15.8	39.4	Saudi Arabia
782.6	55.8	9.3	12.4	22.5	14.9	2.4	5.2	53.3	0.1	—	2.0	44.6	Senegal
48.7	34.1	0.1	60.6	5.2	—	4.0	1.2	28.9	1.2	—	0.1	69.9[52]	Seychelles
149.9	3.2	90.4	—	6.4	—	...	...	46.8	30.6	—	—	22.6	Sierra Leone
73,940.7	6.3	0.5	12.2	80.9	6.4	58.3	16.2	14.0	20.3	0.9[5]	7.5	57.2	Singapore
3,488.8	—13.4[2]—		0.8	85.8[3]	11.4	17.3	57.0[3]	41.6	...	34.2[5]		24.2	Slovakia[50]
6,083.0	—6.6[2]—		5.1	88.3[3]	9.1	27.4	51.8[3]	57.4	3.6	10.3[5]	0.4	28.4	Slovenia
74.8	93.9	0.6	—	5.5	—	—	5.5	28.0	0.1	—	33.2	38.6	Solomon Islands
81.0	97.2	1.1[2,20]	0.2	1.5[3,21]	—	0.6	0.9[3,21]	58.9	0.3[4]	—	0.5	40.3[4]	Somalia
24,353.7	11.2[19]	14.5[19]	6.3[19]	68.1[19,57]	4.3[19]	5.0[19]	58.9[19,57]	20.7	6.9	1.0[5]	5.5	65.9[58]	South Africa[54]
67,550.2	17.4	0.7	2.9	79.0	8.2	41.3	29.5	68.5	4.6	1.5	0.8	24.5	Spain
2,490.0	26.7	7.2	0.5	65.6	1.0	1.8	62.8	32.4	34.1	1.1[6]	5.2	27.1	Sri Lanka
319.3	87.4	5.3	—	7.2	—	—	7.2	28.5	1.2	—	5.0	65.2	Sudan, The
472.6	15.7	74.0	1.2	9.0	—	0.3	8.7	36.9	11.4	—	6.8	45.0	Suriname
566.2	80.9[46]	3.2[46]	0.9[46]	14.9[46]	0.2[46]	2.1[46]	12.6[46]	24.3[46]	6.9[46]	0.7[46]	—	68.0[46]	Swaziland
54,120.6	8.4	1.6	3.4	86.6	9.9	43.3	33.5	53.0	8.4	2.8	2.5	33.2	Sweden
64,541.2	3.6	4.9	0.1	91.4	24.5	29.1	37.9	56.7	8.9	2.1	3.5	28.8	Switzerland[60]
4,213.7	18.2	1.0	45.2	35.7	12.8	0.2	22.7	41.7	0.9	33.8[5]	0.1	23.6	Syria
81,332.9	11.2	0.1	0.7	88.0	5.2	41.6	38.4	15.2	28.9	0.1	10.9	44.9	Taiwan
228.2[9]	—67.4[2,20]—		1.3	31.3[3,21]	2.5	14.6	14.2[3,21]	5.1[4]	0.8[4]	39.6[4]	4.8[4]	49.6[4]	Tajikistan
416.1	82.0	1.0	2.0	15.1	1.0	2.2	11.8	39.2	6.8	0.7[5]	3.9	49.5	Tanzania
28,420.9	31.5	3.8	1.0	63.7	2.6	24.0	37.2	20.7	21.3	1.9[5]	18.1	38.0	Thailand
253.2	42.0	49.2	2.3	6.5	1.1	1.0	4.4	29.4	0.1	5.5[6]	—	65.0	Togo
16.5	84.5	—		15.5	0.6	0.9	14.0	1.6	16.0	—	58.0	24.4	Tonga
1,662.1	7.9	0.1	57.6	34.4	16.9	2.8	14.7	4.8	47.7	—	1.1	46.4	Trinidad and Tobago
4,039.9	10.7	1.3	15.1	72.9	12.8	8.7	51.3	78.0	0.8	1.4[5]	0.3	19.5	Tunisia
15,348.9	24.4	1.6	1.1	72.8	4.0	8.4	60.4	47.5	6.4	7.7	1.0	37.4	Turkey
4,520.0[9]	—10.2[2]—		40.0	49.8[3]	5.5	1.2	43.1[3]	3.3[4]	0.1[4]	57.3[4]	0.3[4]	39.0[4]	Turkmenistan
0.1	92.2	—	—	7.8	—	—	7.8	—	—	—	—	100.0[61]	Tuvalu
152.1	98.9	0.1	—	1.1	0.1	0.6	0.3	75.9	8.1[4]	0.4[5]	3.3	12.3[4]	Uganda
7,740.0[9]	—10.6[2,8]—		6.9[8]	82.4[3,8]	7.5[8]	46.4[8]	28.5[3,8]	4.9[4]	0.3[4]	62.3[4]	1.0[4]	31.5[4]	Ukraine
9,029.0	—5.4[2]—		72.2	22.4[3]	1.1	6.3	15.0[3]	5.2[4]	4.0[4]	—[4]	34.8[4]	56.0[4]	United Arab Emirates
181,645.1	8.3	3.1	6.8	81.8	14.2	39.9	27.7	52.4	12.7	1.7	2.2	31.0	United Kingdom[35]
464,757.3	13.3	1.4	2.1	83.2	9.9	48.4	24.9	20.9	—	1.2	10.3	67.6	United States[62]
1,606.5	56.8	0.4	—	42.8	5.5	8.1	29.3	20.9	9.1	0.8	0.9	68.3	Uruguay
2,510.0[9]	—17.1[2,20]—		11.6	71.4[3,21]	7.6	15.0	48.8[3,21]	8.4	0.8	64.3	0.1	26.4	Uzbekistan
23.6	82.3[46]	—[46]	17.7[46]	17.7[46]	...	...	...	49.8[46]	...	—[46]	18.7[46]	31.4[46]	Vanuatu
15,129.9	2.3	3.0	80.9	13.9	2.2	1.1	10.5	11.8	52.0	0.2[5]	2.7	33.2	Venezuela
1,970.0	—48.9[2]—		35.6	15.5[3]	0.7	0.1	14.7[3]	3.0	—	10.4[5]	35.1	51.5	Vietnam
2,303.5	...	...	84.2[63]	...	...	...	...	—	94.1	—	...	...	Virgin Islands (U.S.)
27.1[65]	...	...	...	...	...	...	...	...	...	...	...	...	West Bank
...	...	...	...	...	...	...	...	...	...	...	...	...	Western Sahara
12.9	88.4	—	—	11.6	—	—	11.6	27.6	8.1	—	0.4	63.9	Western Samoa
474.4	20.5[46]	2.7[46]	74.4[46]	2.4[46]	1.5[46]	0.1[46]	0.8[46]	17.5[46]	35.3[46]	—[46]	16.9[46]	30.3[46]	Yemen
4,704.1	15.9	0.6	4.4	79.1	9.1	19.6	50.3	48.6	4.5	29.1[5]	0.2	17.6	Yugoslavia
999.2	13.2	55.2[2,20]	12.7	18.9[3,21]	0.1	0.8	18.0[3,21]	74.6[4]	12.5[4]	—[4]	1.7[4]	11.2[4]	Zaire
1,350.2	5.3[66]	83.4[2,20,66]	0.1[66]	11.3[3,21,66]	0.1[66]	0.3[66]	10.9[3,21,66]	30.5	1.6	—	31.0	36.8	Zambia
1,251.0	54.6	5.6	0.5	39.4	2.0	2.1	35.3	41.3	5.8	0.6	7.2	45.0	Zimbabwe

[46]Domestic exports only. [47]Includes border trade. [48]Includes 89.7% from South Africa. [49]Based on trade with Australia and New Zealand only. [50]All reexports. [51]Includes 19.8% for nonmonetary gold. [52]Includes 61.1% for bunkers. [53]Excluding trade with the Czech Republic. [54]Figures for South Africa refer to Customs Union of Southern Africa (includes South Africa, Botswana, Lesotho, and Swaziland, also shown separately). [55]Excluding crude oil. [56]Including crude oil (included in "unclassified goods" accounting in total for 12.3%). [57]Includes gold (included in "unclassified goods" accounting in total for 38.7%). [58]Including unspecified destinations of 29.0%. [59]Includes 90.1% from South Africa; this includes imports passing through South Africa in transit, which may have had their origin from other countries. [60]Figures for Switzerland include Liechtenstein. [61]All to the South Pacific region in 1985. [62]Figures for United States include American Samoa, Guam, Puerto Rico, and Virgin Islands (U.S.), also shown separately. [63]Exports of refined petroleum to United States only. [64]Excluding imports from Israel ($580.7 million in 1987). [65]Excluding exports to Israel ($160.5 million in 1987). [66]1989.

Trade: domestic

The following table presents data relating to domestic wholesale and retail trade for the countries of the world. The section on wholesale trade is based for the most part on establishments (service points from which a business enterprise operates [see note a]) engaged primarily in selling goods to retailers and distributors for resale or to purchasers who buy for business and farm uses. The retail trade section is based on businesses engaged in selling merchandise for personal or household consumption; restaurants are, when possible, included, hotels excluded.

The data presented here are based on information from a variety of country and international sources. The country sources include statistical abstracts, correspondence, annual reports, and censuses of business and trade.

Because there is no single published source or common international methodology for the compilation of data on wholesale and retail trade, nor a single current year on which, by common agreement, the various national reports would be based, allowance must be made for variations in the meaning and recency of the information provided for any single country and for its comparability internationally. Variations occur in part because of the ways in which countries define wholesale and retail trade; the conventional free-enterprise distinction between wholesale and retail activity (of a single enterprise or an entire national trade sector) may not exist in the business practice of some countries. Variations also exist in the kind and level of detail reported. For example, countries may design surveys differently according to the size (number of employees, sales, surface area) of establishments surveyed, their profitability, or other less direct criteria,

such as ownership or location. The depth of analysis to which the data are subjected may also vary. The structure of a national trade sector is also affected by the degree of government involvement, which may range from total control of wholesale distribution in some socialist countries to partial involvement in some strategic sectors, or to relative noninvolvement in fully private trade sectors of capitalist countries. In some smaller countries data may refer to a single trading enterprise.

At the table's extreme left, preceding the year to which the trade data refer, the combined value of the country's wholesale and retail trade as a percentage of gross domestic product or net material product is given. Unless otherwise noted, GDP data include restaurants and exclude hotels.

Both the wholesale and retail sections of the table provide similar detail: establishments or outlets, employees, sales, and certain derived values for relationships among these measures; the retail section provides an additional breakdown of sales by an end-use classification of retail sales outlets.

Although all sales figures are given in U.S. dollars, the comparability of these dollar figures may differ considerably; for instance, the purchasing power of various national currencies in domestic transactions may bear only a distant relationship to the exchange rate of the same currency in international transactions, especially for countries having nonconvertible currencies. The price of goods may also vary, depending on the degree to which they are subject to direct subsidies and artificial cost controls such as tax, investment, or free-trade preferences by a central government seeking to influence social or economic conditions.

Trade: domestic

country	domestic trade as percentage of GDP, 1991	year	wholesale trade					retail trade		
			establishments[a]	employees[b]	sales[c] (U.S.$'000,000)	employees per establishment	sales per establishment (U.S.$'000)	outlets[a]	employees[b]	sales[c] (U.S.$'000,000)
Afghanistan	7.9[1,2]	1981–82	...	3	...	...	...	...	126,100[3]	...
Albania	4.6[4]	1990	...	3	...	...	...	11,741[5]	62,000[3]	1,570[5]
Algeria	17.8[6]	1986	...	3	...	...	...	3,600[7,8]	390,990[1,3,9]	16,200
American Samoa	...	1990	177	255	...	1.4	...	583	1,495	...
Andorra	24.2[10]	1988	...	...	...	...	...	592[11]	7,227	...
Angola	6.1	1973	3	...	...	...	...	29,138[3]	...	...
Antigua and Barbuda	25.6[1,4]	1980	25	350	...	14.0	...	199	1,000	23[12]
Argentina	13.0[4]	1974	45,700	275,000[13]	10,922[14]	6.0[13]	...	445,798[15]	930,000[13,15]	15,540[12]
Armenia	5.6	1990	...	3	...	...	...	...	88,100[3]	...
Aruba	37.2[1,16]	1990	...	723	...	...	...	...	5,700	17
Australia	14.2[18]	1991–92	15,514	153,092	44,553	9.9	2,872	209,909	1,290,173	107,230
Austria	16.5[1]	1992	17,149[6]	191,000	83,160	10.2[6]	3,526[6]	33,601[6]	253,000	42,650
Azerbaijan	2.2	...	...	...	...	...	...	...	...	...
Bahamas, The[19]	26.2[1,20]	1980	23	1,066	143	46.3	6,235	132	4,059	460[20]
Bahrain	10.6[1]	1983	3	3	...	...	3	255[3]	12,551[3]	1,601
Bangladesh	8.2[1,21]	1985	...	3	...	...	...	271,000	3,610,000[3]	5,500[20]
Barbados	26.3[1]	1990	...	3	...	...	...	1,911[22]	20,800[3]	264[12]
Belarus	5.5[23]	1991	3	3	3	...	...	22,300[3]	299,900[3]	19,900[3]
Belgium	20.9[1]	1984	60,589	160,600	65,110	2.6	1,075	135,534	193,500	20,957
Belize	17.7[1,23]	1983	...	3	...	...	...	...	4,558[3]	33[20]
Benin	19.5[1,6]	1979	...	...	...	...	...	170[7]	1,910[13,20]	150[12]
Bermuda	32.8[24]	1985	60[24]	820	...	...	...	310[7,24]	4,342[13]	116[15,25]
Bhutan	7.6[1]	1982	...	3	...	...	...	...	9,000[3,5,13]	...
Bolivia	13.0	1989	...	3	...	...	...	...	244,907[3,5]	1,570[20]
Bosnia and Herzegovina	13.9[6]	1990	...	3	18,469[6]	...	...	...	130,914[3]	18,065[6]
Botswana	14.2[21]	1983–84	205	3,500	494[12]	...	...	1,660	10,700	165[12]
Brazil	7.1	1985	44,994	498,280	51,475	11.1	1,144	674,695	3,086,751	65,264
Brunei	10.5[1,4]	1986	3	3	...	3	...	833[3,26]	4,261[3,26]	...
Bulgaria	10.5[1,4,27]	1987	...	7,700[28]	...	...	...	41,339[15]	79,820[15]	34,700[15]
Burkina Faso	15.2[6]	1975	...	3	...	...	...	...	19,354[3,13]	...
Burundi	9.1	1986	...	...	...	...	...	...	...	210
Cambodia	...	...	...	...	...	...	...	...	...	...
Cameroon	25.1[1,6]	1980	...	3	...	...	...	1,312[7]	13,776[13,20]	1,430[20]
Canada	11.5[23]	1993	...	3	232,900[6]	...	...	...	2,428,000[3,4]	150,200
Cape Verde	28.4[6]	1980	...	3	...	...	...	...	3,930[3]	...
Central African Republic	26.4[6]	1989	113	302	...	2.7	...	14,543	23,078	230
Chad	29.5[6]	1983	...	3	...	...	...	...	1,661[3,7,29]	497[3]
Chile	18.5	1983	561[7]	15,300[7]	2,312[7]	27.2[7]	4,121[7]	1,125[15,20]	21,700[15,20]	1,403[15,20]
China	4.5	1992	435,000	1,550,000[13]	...	15.6[13]	...	10,063,000[13,15]	24,345,000[15]	175,980[15]
Colombia	11.0	1985	...	...	...	...	...	1,110[32]	49,000[32]	8,600[20]
Comoros	26.3[1,23]	1980	...	3	...	...	...	...	1,873[3,7]	...
Congo	14.4[6]	1984	...	3	...	...	...	...	13,240[3]	...
Costa Rica	20.0	1975	332[33]	4,073[33]	35[33]	12.3[33]	104[33]	9,713	26,486	475[34]
Côte d'Ivoire	12.9[6]	1981	...	...	...	...	...	2,023[7]	16,720[7]	1,800[20]
Croatia	26.4	1992	...	27,376	38,117[6]	...	...	17,969	78,287	39,231[6]
Cuba	20.1[6,27]	1989	...	...	15,174	...	...	56,916[28]	230,000[9,13]	8,124
Cyprus	21.3[1]	1991	1,559[25]	13,645	86	5.3[25]	720[25]	8,474[25]	36,551	196
Czech Republic[35]	12.1[11]	1990	63,110[28]	251,000[28]	40,083[28]	4.0[28]	635[28]	62,667[6]	258,127	21,235
Denmark	13.6	1991	22,230	177,106	72,601	8.0	3,266	36,750	211,085	29,872
Djibouti	10.8[20]	1985	28	371[16]	...	...	...	431	1,877[16]	...
Dominica	13.2[1]	1989	...	3	...	...	...	...	3,700[3]	790[20]
Dominican Republic	14.3[23]	1983	670	...	3,136	...	4,681	11,220[16]	...	1,259[16]
Ecuador	15.1	1990	426	18,014	139	42.3	326	554	20,168	102
Egypt	19.9[18]	1983–84	2,552	45,500[13]	4,492	18.0[13]	1,760	2,545	55,800[13]	29,700[20]
El Salvador	8.2[23]	1983	396	6,400	1,038	16.2	2,621	1,416	10,700	485

The data on distribution of retail sales by kind of consumer goods may have their origin in several different types of data or analysis. One country may aggregate sales data by kind of establishment only (this may be perfectly satisfactory in a country of small, independent outlets); another may aggregate data directly by kind of goods (most easily done in a country with well-developed statistical, tax-reporting, and commercial systems). Other countries may find it impolitic to publish data that reflect the poverty of their distribution network or their supply of consumer goods and may aggregate or publish data for only a few sectors: food or nonfood goods, for example. For countries with only a few trading enterprises in a particular sector, detail must often be withheld to preserve the confidentiality of individual businesses.

The notes that follow further define the column headings.

a. The number of establishments or outlets refers to economic units that operate at a single physical location in one principal kind of activity, whether singly owned or part of a multiunit firm. Such units are not necessarily identical with a company or enterprise.

b. Number of employees refers to full-time and part-time paid workers, including salaried managers and officers; it usually excludes owner-operators, partners, vendors, and unpaid relatives.

c. Total sales (also called turnover) includes the value of merchandise sold for cash or credit; amounts received from customers for layaway purchases; receipts from rental or leasing of vehicles, equipment, tools, instruments, etc.; receipts for delivery, installation, maintenance, repair, alteration, storage, and other services.

d. Outlets engaged primarily in the sale of food and nonalcoholic beverages, such as grocery stores, meat and fish markets, and bakeries.

e. Outlets engaged primarily in the sale of clothing and shoes; also includes outlets that sell accessory items, such as millinery, furs, and leather goods.

f. Outlets engaged primarily in the sale of home furnishings, including furniture, draperies, floor coverings, household appliances, and home entertainment equipment.

g. Outlets that primarily serve food and drink, including restaurants, lunchrooms, cafeterias, social caterers, refreshment places, contract feeders, ice cream parlors, and bars and taverns.

h. Outlets engaged primarily in the sale of pharmaceuticals, cosmetics, and perfumes.

i. Outlets engaged primarily in the sale of building materials, hardware, garden supplies, paint, electrical supplies, and farm equipment.

j. Outlets engaged primarily in the sale of motor vehicles, motorcycles, bicycles, and tires, batteries, and other automotive supplies and parts; includes service stations.

k. Outlets engaged in the sale of multiple lines of merchandise, such as department stores, variety stores, and rural general stores.

l. Miscellaneous specialized outlets such as those engaged primarily in the sale of liquors, sporting goods, books, jewelry, photographic and optical goods, gifts, flowers, tobacco products, home fuels, and newspapers.

retail trade (continued)

food[d]	clothing, shoes[e]	home furnishings[f]	eating, drinking[g]	drugs, pharmaceuticals[h]	building materials[i]	automobile parts[j]	general merchandise[k]	other[l]	employees per outlet	sales per outlet (U.S.$'000)	population per outlet	country
...	...	...	...	...	...	...	...	...	...	...	...	Afghanistan
62.4				37.6					...	134[5]	277[5]	Albania
...	...	...	...	...	...	...	...	...	5.0[7,8]	...	5,146[7,8]	Algeria
...	...	...	...	...	...	...	...	...	...	...	81	American Samoa
...	...	...	...	...	...	...	...	...	3.8[11]	...	39[11]	Andorra
...	...	...	...	...	...	...	...	...	...	...	...	Angola
...	...	...	...	...	...	...	...	...	5.0	100	378	Antigua and Barbuda
...	...	...	...	...	...	...	...	...	2.1[13,15]	...	58[15]	Argentina
...	...	...	...	...	...	...	...	...	...	...	...	Armenia
...	...	...	...	...	...	...	...	...	...	...	...	Aruba
28.9	3.6	8.9	3.7	2.9	2.4	31.9	7.9	10.7	6.1	511	82.8	Australia
33.2	13.4	7.0	...	30.4	2.0	19.7	4.7	16.5	7.1[6]	857[6]	227[6]	Austria
...	...	...	...	...	...	...	...	...	...	...	...	Azerbaijan
24.4[16]	7.7[16]	7.1[16]	—	3.7[16]	8.4[16]	30.1[16]	7.6[16]	11.0[16]	30.8	1,881	1,026	Bahamas, The[19]
...	...	...	...	...	...	...	...	...	49.2[3]	...	1,507[3]	Bahrain
...	...	...	...	...	...	...	...	...	...	...	...	Bangladesh
...	...	...	...	...	...	...	...	...	...	...	130[22]	Barbados
...	...	...	...	...	...	...	...	...	13.4[3]	892[3]	460[3]	Belarus
35.1				64.9					1.4	155	73	Belgium
...	...	...	...	...	...	...	...	...	...	...	...	Belize
...	...	...	...	...	...	...	...	...	11.3[13,20]	...	19,871[20]	Benin
...	...	...	...	...	...	...	...	...	11.0[12,15]	...	178[7,24]	Bermuda
...	...	...	...	...	...	...	...	...	...	...	...	Bhutan
...	...	...	...	...	...	...	...	...	...	...	...	Bolivia
...	...	...	...	...	...	...	...	...	...	...	...	Bosnia and Herzegovina
...	...	...	...	...	...	...	...	...	6.4	99.4	604	Botswana
14.8	10.7	6.3	...	4.8	12.8	29.5	17.7	3.6	4.6	98	201	Brazil
...	...	...	...	...	...	...	...	...	5.1[3,26]	...	279[3,26]	Brunei
50.9	10.9	3.4	...	5.9	...	...	0.2	28.7	1.9[15]	839[15]	217[15]	Bulgaria
...	...	...	...	...	...	...	...	...	...	...	...	Burkina Faso
...	...	...	...	...	...	...	...	...	...	...	...	Burundi
...	...	...	...	...	...	...	...	...	...	...	...	Cambodia
...	...	...	...	...	...	...	...	...	10.5[7,13]	...	6,481[7]	Cameroon
26.1	5.8	5.5	...	6.1	...	34.3	10.8	11.4	...	...	...	Canada
...	...	...	...	...	...	...	...	...	...	...	...	Cape Verde
...	...	...	...	...	...	...	...	...	1.6	16	187	Central African Republic
...	...	...	...	...	...	...	...	...	...	...	...	Chad
28.3[16]	30	5.0[16]	1.6[16]	5.4[16]	4.7[16]	18.0[16]	17.1[16,30]	19.9[16]	19.3[15,20]	1,247[15,20]	10,210[15,20]	Chile
55.4	16.3	...	...	4.4	31	2.8	13.7[31]	7.4	2.4[13,15]	171[5]	140,250[15]	China
...	...	...	...	...	...	...	...	...	44.1[32]	1,522[32]	...	Colombia
...	...	...	...	...	...	...	...	...	...	...	...	Comoros
...	...	...	...	...	...	...	...	...	...	...	...	Congo
37.7	13.5	6.9	...	8.2	7.0	15.1	5.9	5.7	2.7	59	202	Costa Rica
...	...	...	...	...	...	...	...	...	8.3[7]	...	4,257[7]	Côte d'Ivoire
23.8	6.1	3.2	...	...	5.8	19.8	32.0	9.3	4.4	1,973[6]	266	Croatia
35.8	17.2	9.9	...	5.3	0.8	5.1	...	25.9	4.0[9,13]	184[28]	177[20]	Cuba
9.8[6]	7.8[6]	2.2[6]	46.2[6]	1.6[6]	3.5[6]	11.2[6]	6.4[6]	11.5[6]	1.0[25]	124[25]	77[25]	Cyprus
42.9	15.1	12.8	...	3.6	2.9	10.0	...	12.7	4.2[6]	362[6]	249[6]	Czech Republic[35]
9.7	9.5	...	40.9	2.2	3.2	12.3	...	22.2	5.7[6]	813[6]	140[6]	Denmark
...	...	...	...	...	...	...	...	...	...	...	998	Djibouti
...	...	...	...	...	...	...	...	...	...	...	...	Dominica
26.3	2.0	11.5	3.9	1.6	7.2	38.2	6.2	3.1	...	112[16]	519[16]	Dominican Republic
...	...	...	...	...	...	...	...	...	36.4	184	18,520	Ecuador
...	...	...	...	...	...	...	...	...	21.9[13]	1,278	17,756	Egypt
11.9[8,36]	7.6[8,36]	16.2[8,36]	...	7.9[8,36]	6.3[8,36]	12.4[8,36]	28.2[8,36]	9.5[8,36]	7.6	342	3,336	El Salvador

Trade: domestic (continued)

country	domestic trade as percentage of GDP, 1991	year	wholesale trade					retail trade		
			establishments[a]	employees[b]	sales[c] (U.S.$'000,000)	employees per establishment	sales per establishment (U.S.$'000)	outlets[a]	employees[b]	sales[c] (U.S.$'000,000)
Equatorial Guinea	8.4[6]	1983	...	36	...	...	...	...	2,701	...
Eritrea[37]	...									
Estonia	4.6	1993	...	...	370	...	...	...	70,000[4]	546
Ethiopia[37]	9.6[1,2]	1984	375[7,38]	3,200[7,38]	...	8.5[7,38]	...	7,416[7,38]	17,100[7,38]	273
Faeroe Islands	13.1[23]	1987	78	3	19	...	241	430	1,484[1,3,34]	38
Fiji	19.0[1,23]	1990	209	2,887	363	13.8	1,737	1,095	6,522	419
Finland	10.8[1]	1992	9,367[10]	80,394[10]	46,334[10]	8.6[10]	4,946[10]	38,433[39]	150,151[39]	41,885[39]
France	15.2	1990	85,817	942,778	381,241	11.0	4,442	379,240	1,643,246	256,764
French Guiana	12.2[6]	1991	175	905	1,798	5.2	10,274	820	2,522	1,984
French Polynesia	22.7[4]	1986	3	3	...	...	...	947[3]	5,038[3]	...
Gabon	12.1[1,4]	1982	...	3	...	...	...	...	12,683[3,13,24]	...
Gambia, The	23.6[18]	1983	...	3	...	...	...	...	16,551[3]	...
Gaza Strip	...	1986	...	3	...	...	...	...	13,400[3]	...
Georgia	5.6[4]	1988	...	3	...	...	...	...	172,400[3]	...
Germany	8.3[23]	1991	...	1,336,200	624,396	...	...	152,629	2,240,700	365,023
Ghana	19.0[4]	1983	460[41]	1,100[41]	115[41]	2.4[41]	250[41]	1,500	16,000	252[20]
Gibraltar	...	1991	...	737	...	...	...	1,835	...	
Greece	12.8[1,6]	1988	31,032	115,979	...	3.7	...	184,821	388,132	12,263[42]
Greenland	8.0[22]	1992	...	3	139	...	...	...	2,214[3,9]	211
Grenada	10.0[1]	1988	...	3	3	...	...	...	5,421[3]	63[3,12]
Guadeloupe	17.0[1,16]	1991	736	4,053	1,066	5.5	145	4,005	11,754	1,306
Guam	51.5[16]	1992	169	2,045	3	12.1	3	768	12,060	1,400[3]
Guatemala	24.0[23]	1989	...	3	...	...	...	88,200[16]	374,690[3]	1,200[20]
Guernsey	...	1991	...	642	...	...	...	...	2,573	...
Guinea	21.9[4]	1979	...	3	...	...	...	...	12,808[3,41]	...
Guinea-Bissau	27.5[1,6]	1979	3	3	...	...	...	685[3,41]	5,085[3]	44[3,26]
Guyana	8.6	1980	...	3	...	...	...	147[7]	14,690[3]	93[12]
Haiti	16.4	1983	...	3	...	...	...	653[7,43]	303,353[3]	500[20]
Honduras	13.0	1991	...	3	...	...	...	...	156,500[3]	401[12]
Hong Kong	23.9	1991	21,298	85,498	5,443	4.0	2,556	62,238	411,626	9,106
Hungary	12.4	1992	206[16]	122,600[16]	13,121[24]	595[24]	...	176,697	652,300[39]	19,870
Iceland	13.9	1990	1,509[12,45]	5,132[24]	...	598[34,45]	...	1,719	8,013[46]	1,251
India	12.4[2]	1980	3	3	...	...	...	3,132,000[3,15]	3,615,000[3,15]	108,300[12]
Indonesia	16.6	1980	3	3	3	3	3	54,632[3]	85,400[3]	3,451[3]
Iran	18.5	1986–87	118,698	3	2,429[48]	...	133[48]	634,084	521,708[3,49]	37,350
Iraq	16.1[1]	1987–88[26]	1,942	3,902	130	2.0	67	108,460	165,594	7,077
Ireland	11.2[1,9]	1988	3,972	39,101	11,420	9.8	2,875	31,699	89,680	10,952
Isle of Man	12.0[12]	1981	...	775	...	...	...	...	3,146	...
Israel	11.6[1,6]	1988	17,967	67,300	16,875	3.8	939	43,844	103,100	10,763
Italy	18.5[1]	1983	...	3	...	...	...	1,033,725	1,369,200[3]	122,978
Jamaica	24.9[1,23]	1991	...	3	...	...	...	10,150[34]	173,500[3]	1,457[12]
Japan	13.8	1991	475,967	4,773,000[13]	4,253,448	10.0[13]	8,963	1,591,186[15]	6,936,000[13,15]	1,043,976[15]
Jersey	...	1986	...	855	...	...	...	...	7,046	...
Jordan	9.7[23]	1991	488	2,862	147	5.9	301	34,086	69,393	1,002
Kazakhstan	5.1	1991	...	...	...	...	...	42,168	484,800	...
Kenya	9.5[4]	1985	3,079[9]	27,481	...	13.6	...	5,033[8]	34,628	1,085[12]
Kiribati	13.5[6]	1987	...	3	...	...	...	30	1,127[3,28]	3.8
Korea, North	...									
Korea, South	12.4	1990	90,621	502,476	70,389	5.5	777	1,040,490[1]	2,356,800[1]	76,057[1]
Kuwait	7.6[23]	1989	2,982	25,897	65	8.7	22	14,521	54,588	145
Kyrgyzstan	...	1992	...	3	...	...	...	...	92,900[3,10]	138
Laos	7.8	1990	...	...	...	...	...	15,000	...	576
Latvia	13.6[4]	1991	...	...	...	...	...	7,214	95,300	20,425
Lebanon	31.7[4]	1986	...	3	...	...	...	...	114,706[3]	1,662[13]
Lesotho	7.7									
Liberia	19.1[1,6]	1984	...	3	...	...	...	...	46,850[3]	115[20]
Libya	6.8[6]	1973	1,126	4,148[13]	...	3.7[13]	...	26,825	44,605[13]	9,205[12]
Liechtenstein	...	1975	67	216	...	3.2	...	228	740	...
Lithuania	9.5	1991	...	3	...	...	...	...	188,600[3]	25,864
Luxembourg	16.4	1991	1,860	11,099	6,539	6.0	3,419	3,591	18,588	4,394
Macau	...	1991	...	3	...	...	...	...	47,706[3]	...
Macedonia	14.4[6]	1990	...	3	9,522[6]	...	...	...	65,593[6]	9,238[6]
Madagascar	13.0[6]	1976	1,104	...	...	...	...	1,570	...	696[24]
Malawi	10.9	1984	439	23,000	522	52	1,189	500	8,600	127
Malaysia	11.3	1980	19,663	116,200	15,461	5.9	786	95,993	73,000	8,200[20]
Maldives	17.5[1]	1990	...	3	...	...	...	...	8,884[3]	5[20]
Mali	15.5[1]	1979	...	3	...	...	...	...	5,200[3]	...
Malta	14.3[1]	1983	3	3	1.0	...	333	4[20]	11,936[3,7]	2.3
Marshall Islands	83.7[1,24]	1988	...	3	...	...	...	...	1,394[3]	...
Martinique	19.4[1,25]	1991	740	3	...	...	...	5,489	12,399[3,20]	234[12]
Mauritania	19.1[1,6]	1971[7]	23	100	102	4.3	4,445	59	700	103
Mauritius	17.9[1]	1986	3	3	...	3	...	207[1,3,7]	10,107[1,3,7]	164[1,3,7]
Mayotte	...	1983	3	3	3	...	3	41[3]	597[3,9]	27[3]
Mexico	26.7	1988	36,512	3	23,506	...	644	713,315	3,875,100[3,4]	39,810
Micronesia	11.9[12]	1980	...	348[13]	...	...	...	...	489[1,13]	...
Moldova	9.4	1990	...	3	...	...	...	...	148,000[3]	...
Monaco	...	1975	...	273	...	...	...	...	1,439	...
Mongolia	21.7[6]	1983[3,51]	...	...	...	...	...	4,828	21,100	1,235[28]
Morocco	20.9	1972	...	...	...	...	...	4,000[7]	20,000[7]	5,750[20]
Mozambique	...	1980	...	...	...	...	...	...	63,058[3]	...
Myanmar (Burma)	22.9[18]	1983	...	3	...	...	...	...	1,405,000[2,3]	2,116
Namibia	12.4[4]	1977	222	5,035	377	22.7	1,698	1,248	7,569	254
Nauru	...									
Nepal	5.8[1,4]	1983	...	3	...	...	...	...	119,000[3,13,24]	736
Netherlands, The	16.0	1991	48,900	262,000	170,990	5.4	3,497	81,700	180,000	59,514

retail trade (continued)									employees per outlet	sales per outlet (U.S.$'000)	population per outlet	country
percentage breakdown of sales												
food[d]	clothing, shoes[e]	home furnishings[f]	eating, drinking[g]	drugs, pharmaceuticals[h]	building materials[i]	automobile parts[j]	general merchandise[k]	other[l]				
...	...	...	...	...	...	...	...	...	...	...	...	Equatorial Guinea
...	...	...	...	...	...	...	...	...	...	...	...	Eritrea[37]
...	...	...	...	...	...	...	...	...	...	...	...	Estonia
15.9	45.2	...	...	...	7.9	9.8	10.5	10.7	2.3[7,38]	277[38]	55,200[7,38]	Ethiopia[37]
...	...	...	...	...	...	...	...	...	...	89	109	Faeroe Islands
5.7	5.5	7.7	7.8	3.6	14.7	11.5	41.9	1.6	6.0	382	668	Fiji
30.0	6.1	2.3	3.8	9.4	24.2	11.7	12.5		3.9[39]	1,000[30]	130[39]	Finland
53.8	10.5	12.5	8.2	...	2.4	4.2	8.4		4.3	677	150	France
...	...	...	...	...	...	...	...	...	3.1	2,419	155	French Guiana
...	...	...	...	...	...	...	...	...	5.3[3]		188[3]	French Polynesia
50.5	9.6	...	...	...	33.8	6.1	...	...	...	...	...	Gabon
...	...	...	...	...	...	...	...	...	...	...	...	Gambia, The
...	...	...	...	...	...	...	...	...	...	...	...	Gaza Strip
...	...	...	...	...	...	...	...	...	...	...	...	Georgia
27.9	12.6	5.1	...	6.7	2.0	18.4	[40]	27.3[40]	14.6	2,392	520	Germany
...	...	...	...	...	...	...	...	...	1.1	108[41]	7,993	Ghana
...	...	...	...	...	...	...	...	...	...	...	...	Gibraltar
60.0[42]	18.1[42]	9.5[42]	...	...	...	...	...	12.4[42]	2.1	...	54	Greece
...	...	...	...	...	...	...	...	...	...	...	...	Greenland
...	...	...	...	...	...	...	...	...	...	...	...	Grenada
44.8	13.4	19.6	...	7.1	...	...	...	15.1	2.9	326	91	Guadeloupe
11.6[9]	10.9[9]	4.9[9]	8.0[9]	0.3[9]	5.2[9]	26.9[9]	3.3[9]	28.9[9]	15.7	1,494[3]	181	Guam
...	...	...	...	...	...	...	...	...	...	...	83[16]	Guatemala
...	...	...	...	...	...	...	...	...	...	...	...	Guernsey
...	...	...	...	...	...	...	...	...	...	...	...	Guinea
...	...	...	...	...	...	...	...	...	0.8[3,41]	...	1,080[3,41]	Guinea-Bissau
9.7	18.9	13.8	4.5	2.8	17.7	18.6	...	14.0	...	743	5,884	Guyana
...	...	...	...	...	...	...	...	...	...	...	7,034[7,43]	Haiti
...	...	...	...	...	...	...	...	...	...	...	...	Honduras
16.1	9.5	...	20.2	...	...	8.9	...	45.3[44]	6.3	140	88	Hong Kong
29.3	8.1	...	11.6	3.1	19.2	14.7	3.1	10.9	4.2[39]	112	58	Hungary
63.2[47]	8.7	...	...	...	...	...	[47]	28.1	4.7[46]	728	152	Iceland
...	...	...	...	...	...	...	...	...	1.2[3,15]	...	219[3,15]	India
...	...	...	...	...	...	...	...	...	1.6[3]	63[3]	2,681[3]	Indonesia
...	...	...	...	...	...	...	...	...	...	59	78	Iran
...	...	...	...	...	...	...	...	...	1.5	20	158	Iraq
40.6	9.1	1.4	10.4	2.9	5.1	21.6	2.8	6.1	2.8	345	112	Ireland
...	...	...	...	...	...	...	...	...	...	...	...	Isle of Man
35.4	12.2	20.0	...	...	...	...	6.2	26.2	2.4	245	103	Israel
50.8	15.1	...	...	3.4	...	...	...	30.7	...	119	55	Italy
...	...	...	...	...	...	...	...	...	...	...	214[34]	Jamaica
29.5	10.6	8.5	—	2.8	...	13.5	14.1	21.0	4.4[13,15]	656[15]	77.9[15]	Japan
...	...	...	...	...	...	...	...	...	...	...	...	Jersey
28.9	12.1	6.6	...	1.6	7.4	22.6	9.5	11.3	2.0	29	108	Jordan
...	...	...	...	...	...	...	...	...	11.5	...	400	Kazakhstan
...	...	...	...	...	...	...	...	...	7.0	...	4,057[9]	Kenya
...	...	...	...	...	...	...	...	...	...	127	2,226	Kiribati
...	...	...	...	...	...	...	...	...	...	...	...	Korea, North
29.4[22]	13.1[22]	8.9[22]	18.9[22]	5.0[22]	2.4[22]	5.4[22]	1.2[22]	15.6[22]	2.3[1]	73[1]	41[1]	Korea, South
18.4[47]	14.5	17.3	...	2.6	6.5	16.4	[47]	24.3	3.8	10	138	Kuwait
...	...	...	...	...	...	...	...	...	...	...	...	Kyrgyzstan
...	...	...	...	...	...	...	...	...	...	38	278	Laos
...	...	...	...	...	...	...	...	...	13.2	2,831	373	Latvia
...	...	...	...	...	...	...	...	...	...	...	...	Lebanon
...	...	...	...	...	...	...	...	...	...	...	...	Lesotho
...	...	...	...	...	...	...	...	...	...	...	...	Liberia
...	...	...	...	...	...	...	...	...	1.7[13]	...	84	Libya
...	...	...	...	...	...	...	...	...	3.2	...	105	Liechtenstein
...	...	...	...	...	...	...	...	...	...	...	...	Lithuania
24.7	10.1	11.3	...	3.3	...	42.9	...	7.7	5.2	1,224	108	Luxembourg
...	...	...	...	...	...	...	...	...	...	...	...	Macau
...	...	...	...	...	...	...	...	...	...	...	...	Macedonia
...	...	...	...	...	...	...	...	...	...	...	4,977	Madagascar
...	...	...	...	...	...	...	...	...	17.2	254	14,196	Malawi
32.9[50]	7.3[50]	10.8[50]	...	2.5[50]	1.1[50]	33.3[50]	4.4[50]	7.7[50]	0.8	64	143	Malaysia
...	...	...	...	...	...	...	...	...	...	...	...	Maldives
...	...	...	...	...	...	...	...	...	...	...	...	Mali
...	...	...	...	...	...	...	...	...	...	578[7]	83,378[7]	Malta
...	...	...	...	...	...	...	...	...	...	...	...	Marshall Islands
...	...	...	...	...	...	...	...	...	...	...	68	Martinique
...	...	...	...	...	...	...	...	...	11.9	1,742	20,300	Mauritania
...	...	...	...	...	...	...	...	...	48.8[1,3,7]	792[1,3,7]	4,976[1,3,7]	Mauritius
...	...	...	...	...	...	...	...	...	...	652[3]	1,477[3]	Mayotte
33.8	...	...	...	...	37.0	23.7	...	5.8	...	59	113	Mexico
...	...	...	...	...	...	...	...	...	...	...	...	Micronesia
...	...	...	...	...	...	...	...	...	...	...	...	Moldova
...	...	...	...	...	...	...	...	...	...	...	...	Monaco
...	...	...	...	...	...	...	...	...	4.3	225	372	Mongolia
...	...	...	...	...	...	...	...	...	5.0[7]	...	c. 4,000[7]	Morocco
...	...	...	...	...	...	...	...	...	...	...	...	Mozambique
...	...	...	...	...	...	...	...	...	...	...	...	Myanmar (Burma)
31.4	11.9	5.3	...	2.8	1.7	...	41.9	5.0	5.9	196	713	Namibia
...	...	...	...	...	...	...	...	...	...	...	...	Nauru
...	...	...	...	...	...	...	...	...	...	...	...	Nepal
40.1	12.1	11.4	...	2.2	4.5	6.0	11.9	11.8	2.2	728	184	Netherlands, The

Trade: domestic (continued)

country	domestic trade as percentage of GDP, 1991	year	wholesale trade					retail trade		
			establishments[a]	employees[b]	sales[c] (U.S.$'000,000)	employees per establishment	sales per establishment (U.S.$'000)	outlets[a]	employees[b]	sales[c] (U.S.$'000,000)
Netherlands Antilles	13.6[10]	1988	...	3	...	...	...	...	15,890[3]	149[13,17]
New Caledonia	20.8[10]	1991	...	3	...	...	...	1,023	4,995[3]	...
New Zealand	16.4[1,2]	1992	8,263[52]	76,664[52]	16,295[52]	9.3[52]	1,972[52]	29,961[15,52]	116,301[15,52]	16,550
Nicaragua	23.8	1987	...	3	...	...	...	20,610[16]	94,600[3]	790[20]
Niger	13.2[1,6]	...	...	...	...	...	...	...	...	...
Nigeria	13.1	1983[7]	154	16,000	2,220	104	14,415	421	20,000	2,202
Northern Mariana Islands	...	1987	28	187	49	6.7	1,777	383	2,304	155
Norway	11.0[1]	1992	18,390	101,385[46]	56,056	5.5[46]	3,048	40,154	121,677[46]	31,264
Oman	11.4[4]	1990	3	3	...	...	...	25,840[1,3,6]	87,500[3]	2,449[12]
Pakistan	14.8[1,18]	1983	...	...	...	...	...	276,701[43]	501,773[14,43]	12,848
Panama	12.1	1982[54]	560	13,115	1,491	23.4	2,662	7,561	15,765[7]	1,334
Papua New Guinea	9.9	1985	...	3	...	...	...	...	25,100[3,34]	669[1]
Paraguay	30.0[1]	1982	...	3	...	...	...	...	85,961[3]	2,645[20]
Peru	12.4[23]	1973	4,210	34,100	2,163	8.1	514	103,010	72,200	8,500[20]
Philippines	13.9	1981	20,642	122,717	4,538	5.9	220	279,968	241,872	4,836
Poland	13.1	1991	...	119,600[28,46]	33,482[28]	...	...	630,000	606,700[28,46]	43,164
Portugal	17.4[4]	1983	4,522	135,400[13]	9,260	29.9[13]	2,048	4,889	74,400[13]	3,057
Puerto Rico	14.7[23]	1991	1,876	34,571	7,365[28]	18.4	3,165[28]	9,164	106,239	7,206[28]
Qatar	6.3	1990	134	3,801	85	28.4	636	4,956	18,238	1,048[10]
Réunion	20.3[6]	1992	...	...	...	...	...	3,506	12,927	2,114
Romania	7.0[1,4]	1989	...	...	...	...	...	82,035	465,200	19,926
Russia	15.1[4]	1992	...	...	...	...	...	319,500	3,135,000	18,771
Rwanda	18.5[1,6]	1978	...	3	...	...	...	...	8,014[1,3]	350[20]
St. Kitts and Nevis	22.4[1]	1984	...	3	...	...	...	...	940[3]	...
St. Lucia	24.1[4]	1980	...	3	...	...	...	...	4,770[1,3,13]	...
St. Vincent	11.4[1,5]	...	...	...	...	...	...	...	...	...
San Marino	...	1993	224	3	...	...	...	1,120	2,499[3]	...
São Tomé and Príncipe	10.0[6]	1981	...	3	...	...	...	...	1,994[3]	...
Saudi Arabia	8.1[4]	1991[15]	4,460	31,481[13]	1,354	7.1[13]	304	80,266	174,187[13]	2,292
Senegal	24.5[4]	1987	97[7]	1,843[7]	...	19[7]	...	289[7]	4,964[7]	664[12]
Seychelles	11.3[4]	1985	3	3	...	3	...	131[3]	1,298[3]	...
Sierra Leone	20.3[2]	1983–84	...	3	...	...	...	...	7,211[3]	177[12]
Singapore	17.1[1,23]	1992	24,820	158,993	132,480	6.4	5,338	17,798[15]	78,152[15]	12,058[15]
Slovakia	8.9[27]	1992	...	...	...	...	...	5,590	24,638	1,313
Slovenia	15.3	1990	...	3	29,509	...	...	...	97,981[3]	22,738
Solomon Islands	9.0[4]	1991	...	3	...	...	...	405[20]	2,849[3]	139[20]
Somalia	9.3	...	...	...	...	...	...	...	...	...
South Africa	13.5	1991	...	...	46,541	...	...	58,100[34]	373,200[34]	35,592
Spain	20.5[1,28]	1984	40,000[22]	...	...	...	...	710,865[22]	1,400,000[22]	54,777
Sri Lanka	20.4[1]	1983[7]	190	15,000	3	78.9	...	1,348	44,300	1,116[3,25]
Sudan, The	12.8[6]	1981	...	3	...	...	...	...	...	3,278
Suriname	17.3	1985	...	3	...	...	...	13,000[14]	12,840[3]	110[20]
Swaziland	8.7[1]	1984	67	1,000	...	14.9	...	656	3,700	23[20]
Sweden	10.9	1990	31,960[25]	167,800[25]	37,518[25]	5.2[25]	1,174[25]	61,095	253,522	38,349
Switzerland	18.0[4]	1985	15,019	143,470	...	9.6	...	53,465	259,674	23,620[25]
Syria	24.8[4]	1983	2,827[43]	...	...	...	...	75,865[43]	110,000[13,43]	7,330[20]
Taiwan	16.1[1,23]	1987	55,654[12]	169,100	7,572[28]	2.9[12]	101[12]	355,760[12]	181,200	14,291[28]
Tajikistan	17.0[6]	...	...	3	...	...	...	...	145,400[3]	...
Tanzania	11.6[1,4]	1983	...	...	...	...	...	1,620[7]	16,524[7]	3,975[20]
Thailand	15.2[4]	1988	16,740	139,252	14,535	8.3	868	260,030	280,886	13,683
Togo	22.6[6]	1980	...	...	...	...	...	181[7]	1,815[7]	112 .
Tonga	9.8[56]	1976	...	14[13]	...	...	...	...	654[13]	...
Trinidad and Tobago	15.3[1,23]	1977	124	6,786	509	54.7	4,102	370	15,986	1,670[20]
Tunisia	23.7[1]	1984	...	3	...	...	...	...	153,860[3,28]	2,814
Turkey	17.5	1990	54,567	225,427	68,961	4.1	1,264	445,365	560,796	73,834
Turkmenistan	...	1990	...	3	...	...	...	...	90,000[3]	4,150
Tuvalu	14.9[1]	1979	...	3	...	...	...	...	113[3,13]	...
Uganda	20.5[4]	1977	226	4,100	...	18.1	...	251	3,200	5,285[24]
Ukraine	5.7	1991	...	3	...	...	...	...	1,753,000[3,4]	70,800
United Arab Emirates	10.0[23]	1983	...	...	...	3	...	13,906[1,3,41]	121,278[3,41]	5,910[20]
United Kingdom	14.1[1,23]	1991[57]	120,580[4]	939,000[4]	401,652[4]	7.8[4]	3,331[4]	342,321	2,367,000	234,520
United States	14.2	1993	478,000[39]	6,113,000	1,922,600	12.7[39]	3,686[39]	1,547,000[39]	19,743,000	2,081,600
Uruguay	12.5	1985	...	3	...	...	...	...	139,242[3]	5,397[15,25]
Uzbekistan	8.7	1991	...	3	...	...	...	...	462,000[3]	...
Vanuatu	32.2[4]	1983[49]	18	187[13]	...	10.4[13]	...	256	1,439[13]	...
Venezuela	13.4	1979	...	...	...	...	...	...	161,596	12,345[20]
Vietnam	18.0	1990	...	...	...	...	...	25,723	419,400	4,414
Virgin Islands (U.S.)	...	1987	84	1,322	211	15.7	2,509	1,311	8,529	703
West Bank	...	1986	...	3	...	...	...	...	23,000[3]	...
Western Sahara	...	...	...	...	...	...	...	...	...	...
Western Samoa	10.3[6]	1986	...	3	...	...	...	...	842[3]	...
Yemen[58]	12.4[4]	1986	...	3	...	...	...	...	201,606[3]	2,195[12]
Yugoslavia	20.3	1992	5,723	17,693	8,671	3.1	1,515	51,159	125,348	8,958
Zaire	20.7[6]	1981	...	...	...	...	...	3,036[7]	33,398[7]	3,300[12]
Zambia	12.1[4]	1974	494[7]	15,500[7]	977[7]	31.4[7]	1,978[7]	1,636[7]	13,700[7]	768[12]
Zimbabwe	10.0	1990	...	...	...	...	...	...	95,400[3]	693[28]

[1]Includes hotels. [2]1989–90. [3]Retail-trade data include wholesale trade. [4]1990. [5]Excludes retail-trade network of the agricultural cooperatives. [6]1989. [7]Data refer to larger establishments only. [8]1971. [9]1987. [10]1988. [11]1972. [12]1983. [13]All persons engaged, including proprietors. [14]1973. [15]Excludes restaurants (eating and drinking establishments). [16]1982. [17]Netherlands Antilles. [18]1991–92. [19]Data refer to New Providence Island only. [20]1986. [21]1990–91. [22]1979. [23]1992. [24]1981. [25]1984. [26]Privately owned establishments only. [27]Percentage of net material product. [28]1985. [29]1976. [30]General merchandise includes clothing and shoes. [31]General merchandise includes building materials. [32]For major cities only. [33]Wholesale selling directly to the public only. [34]1980. [35]Data refer to former Czechoslovakia. [36]Selected outlets in urban areas only. [37]Ethiopia includes Eritrea. [38]Excludes Addis Ababa and Asmera. [39]1991. [40]Other includes general

retail trade   (continued)

food[d]	clothing, shoes[e]	home furnishings[f]	eating, drinking[g]	drugs, pharmaceuticals[h]	building materials[i]	automobile parts[j]	general merchandise[k]	other[l]	employees per outlet	sales per outlet (U.S.$'000)	population per outlet	country
…	…	…	…	…	…	…	…	…	…	…	…	Netherlands Antilles
…	…	…	…	…	…	…	…	…	…	…	169	New Caledonia
23.7	5.5	6.6	15.1	3.2	2.3	30.8	4.5	8.3	3.9[15,52]	346[15,52]	106[15,52]	New Zealand
…	…	…	…	…	…	…	…	…	…	…	143[16]	Nicaragua
…	…	…	…	…	…	…	…	…	…	…	…	Niger
									47.5	5,230	226,615	Nigeria
27.0	[53]	2.3	8.8	…	7.2	[53]	4.7	50.0[53]	6.0	406	50	Northern Mariana Islands
34.9	9.9	7.3	…	…	4.8	27.0	4.0	12.1	0.0[40]	779	107	Norway
…	…	…	…	…	…	…	…	…	…	…	56[1,3,6]	Oman
64.0	12.0	4.0	…	…	…	…	…	20.0	1.8[14,43]	…	273[43]	Pakistan
									13.9[7]	176	270	Panama
…	…	…	7.1[1]	…	…	26.0	…	66.9	…	…	…	Papua New Guinea
…	…	…	…	…	…	…	…	…	…	…	…	Paraguay
…	…	…	…	…	…	…	…	…	0.7	20	145	Peru
25.4	12.3	6.7	…	…	11.3	29.5	…	14.8	0.9	17	177	Philippines
31.1[41]	9.9[41]	11.1[41]	…	2.0[41]	4.9[41]	6.7[41]	…	34.3[41]	2.4[28,46]	68	61	Poland
21.5[42]	14.1[42]	11.2[42]	…	3.3[42]	5.6[42]	35.2[42]	9.1[42]	…	15.3[13]	625	2,047	Portugal
30.5[16]	9.9[16]	4.5[16]	7.5[16]	4.3[16]	5.9[16]	23.2[16]	8.9[16]	5.3[16]	11.6	201[28]	387	Puerto Rico
9.0[10]	9.6[10]	13.2[10]	…	2.7[10]	7.2[10]	29.7[10]	9.1[10]	19.5[10]	3.7	177[10]	98	Qatar
54.4	11.5	17.8	…	6.9	…	…	…	9.4	3.7	603	178	Réunion
30.0[34]	10.0[34]	5.9[34]	25.0[34]	1.6[34]	0.8[34]	…	…	26.7[34]	5.7	243	282	Romania
…	…	…	…	…	…	…	…	…	9.8	59	563	Russia
…	…	…	…	…	…	…	…	…	…	…	…	Rwanda
…	…	…	…	…	…	…	…	…	…	…	…	St. Kitts and Nevis
…	…	…	…	…	…	…	…	…	…	…	…	St. Lucia
…	…	…	…	…	…	…	…	…	…	…	…	St. Vincent
…	…	…	…	…	…	…	…	…	1.9[3]	…	18.3[3]	San Marino
…	…	…	…	…	…	…	…	…	…	…	…	São Tomé and Príncipe
…	…	…	…	…	…	…	…	…	2.2[13]	29	201	Saudi Arabia
…	…	…	…	…	…	…	…	…	17.2[7]	…	23,430[7]	Senegal
…	…	…	…	…	…	…	…	…	9.9[3]	…	498[3]	Seychelles
…	…	…	…	…	…	…	…	…	…	…	…	Sierra Leone
17.7[47]	20.4	11.6	…	…	…	24.2	[47]	26.1	4.4	677	158	Singapore
42.1	7.7	9.3	…	1.9	0.8	3.7	1.7	32.8	1.4	235	948	Slovakia
…	…	…	…	…	…	…	…	…	…	…	…	Slovenia
…	…	…	…	…	…	…	…	…	…	…	…	Solomon Islands
…	…	…	…	…	…	…	…	…	…	…	…	Somalia
35.0	13.9	8.1	…	3.3	…	18.7	4.5	16.5	6.4[34]	383[34]	c. 540[34]	South Africa
39.2	10.5	16.7	…	…	…	4.2	…	29.4	2.0[22]	119[22]	52[22]	Spain
…	…	…	…	…	…	…	…	…	32.9	…	11,436	Sri Lanka
…	…	…	…	…	…	…	…	…	…	…	…	Sudan, The
…	…	…	…	…	…	…	…	…	…	…	…	Suriname
52.5[20]	25.1[20]	22.4[20]	…	…	…	…	…	…	5.6	…	969	Swaziland
42.3[6]	13.7[6]	16.7[6]	…	2.1[6]	…	…	12.5[6]	12.7[6]	4.1	628	140	Sweden
46.4[25]	13.5[25]	…	…	4.0[25]	…	…	…	36.1[25]	4.9	…	122[25]	Switzerland
16.0	2.5	…	…	3.5	12.3	39.5[55]	3.5	22.7	1.4[13,43]	…	97[43]	Syria
21.5[24]	3.2[24]	8.8[24]	…	4.1[24]	3.1[24]	8.7[24]	3.1[24]	47.5[24]	0.3[12]	33[12]	52[12]	Taiwan
…	…	…	…	…	…	…	…	…	…	…	…	Tajikistan
…	…	…	…	…	…	…	…	…	10.0[7]	…	12,600[7]	Tanzania
10.5	3.4	4.6	…	1.0	7.2	43.2	12.4	17.7	1.1	53	209	Thailand
…	…	…	…	…	…	…	…	…	10.0[7]	…	15,600[7]	Togo
…	…	…	…	…	…	…	…	…	…	…	…	Tonga
18.6	…	8.5	2.7	…	10.7	28.2	15.3	15.9	43.2	1,467	2,798	Trinidad and Tobago
…	…	…	…	…	…	…	…	…	…	…	…	Tunisia
15.0	10.6	15.5	3.8	2.8	2.9	27.3	10.6	11.5	1.3	166	126	Turkey
…	…	…	…	…	…	…	…	…	…	…	…	Turkmenistan
…	…	…	…	…	…	…	…	…	…	…	…	Tuvalu
…	…	…	…	…	…	…	…	…	12.7	…	47,200	Uganda
…	…	…	…	…	…	…	…	…	…	…	…	Ukraine
…	…	…	…	…	…	…	…	…	…	…	49[2,3,41]	United Arab Emirates
36.8	9.4	5.3	10.2	3.6	10.6	…	17.5	6.6	6.9	685	158	United Kingdom
18.8	5.1	5.5	10.1	3.9	5.6	28.2	12.8	10.0	12.5[39]	1,177[39]	163[39]	United States
…	…	…	…	…	…	…	…	…	…	…	…	Uruguay
…	…	…	…	…	…	…	…	…	…	…	…	Uzbekistan
…	…	…	…	…	…	…	…	…	5.6[13]	…	484	Vanuatu
50.2	10.1	7.6	…	…	…	5.0	…	27.1	…	…	…	Venezuela
…	…	…	…	…	…	…	…	…	16.6	171	2,575	Vietnam
17.6	7.9	6.4	12.0	2.3	4.8	11.4	1.9	35.7	6.5	536	81	Virgin Islands (U.S.)
…	…	…	…	…	…	…	…	…	…	…	…	West Bank
…	…	…	…	…	…	…	…	…	…	…	…	Western Sahara
…	…	…	…	…	…	…	…	…	…	…	…	Western Samoa
…	…	…	…	…	…	…	…	…	…	…	…	Yemen[58]
…	…	…	…	…	…	…	…	…	2.5	175	205	Yugoslavia
…	…	…	…	…	…	…	…	…	11.0[7]	…	9,676[7]	Zaire
…	…	…	…	…	…	…	…	…	8.4[7]	359[7]	2,873[7]	Zambia
…	…	…	…	…	…	…	…	…	…	…	…	Zimbabwe

merchandise.   [41]1977.   [42]1978.   [43]1975.   [44]Includes home furnishings, building materials, and general merchandise.   [45]Excludes fuels, automobiles, alcohol and tobacco, building materials.   [46]Full-time equivalents.   [47]Food includes general merchandise.   [48]1972–73.   [49]Urban establishments only.   [50]Peninsular Malaysia only.   [51]State- and cooperative-owned establishments, including public catering.   [52]1982–83.   [53]Other includes clothing, shoes, and automobile parts.   [54]Excludes Colón Free Trade Zone.   [55]Includes machinery, transport equipment, and petroleum products.   [56]1988–89.   [57]Great Britain only.   [58]Data refer to former Yemen Arab Republic only.

Finance

This table presents major statistical aggregates comprising national financial structure or constituting a basis for certain international financial comparisons. It includes such data as international reserves, money supply, central banking activity and discount rates, commercial (or "deposit money") banking activity, and external indebtedness of the central government. The country models are broadly similar and permit comparison of internal structure and external position at a high level of generalization.

One of the principal financial criteria of the relative economic position of a country is the size of its international reserves. International reserves as represented in this table comprise the sum of a country's (1) reserve position in the International Monetary Fund (IMF), a quota subscribed in the country's own currency, constituting a level up to which transactions may be effected within the IMF system, (2) holdings of foreign exchange, (3) holdings of gold, and (4) holdings of Special Drawing Rights (SDRs; an unconditional credit allocation, within a quota system set by the IMF, of currency needed by a country to maintain stability of foreign exchange transactions or markets). At appropriate accounting intervals these four elements are valued in a single unit of account (the SDR) and summed. The portion of this reserve total comprised by foreign exchange is very significant as an indication of the country's international liquidity (ability to pay its debts immediately in hard, or convertible, currencies). The ratio of external debt to total reserves, however, is less susceptible of interpretation in isolation: a low ratio, for example, may characterize the situation of a country with little need to borrow or of one with substantial debt but also

the means to repay it. Much higher ratios, on the other hand, may be manageable, despite small reserves, if a country's export earnings are also high.

The section on money supply for the country, both as a total and as a per capita amount, refers to one particular measure of money in circulation: M1, the sum of money in private sector demand deposit accounts and outside banks in circulation; it is distinguished from a broader measure of supply, M2, which is roughly M1 plus "quasi-money" (the time, savings, and foreign-currency deposits of residents).

The section of the table outlining banking activity and the principal monetary aggregates encompasses both central bank authorities and commercial (deposit) banks. For both, the principal component aggregates are grouped under assets and liabilities. For certain countries, the four principal aggregates under assets and liabilities do not comprise the entire total, and the percentages shown, therefore, may add to less than 100% (occasionally more, when the net of other liabilities [capital, reserves, undistributed profits, checks, and other transit items] is negative, reducing the total against which these percentages are calculated). The items excluded by the choice of categories are the least significant worldwide but may be important locally; they include such items as quasi-money, money seasonally adjusted, unused bank overdrafts, and so on. In the case of the central bank authority, data are also provided for the central bank discount rate, generally the controlling interest rate for banking and commercial activity in the country.

The largest share of assets in the case of both central and commercial

Finance

country	international reserves, 1994[a]			money supply, 1993[b]		central bank authority, 1993[b]									
	total ('000,000 SDRs)	% foreign exchange	ratio of external debt to total reserves, 1992[b]	stock ('000,000,000 national currency)	M1 per capita	assets (%)				liabilities (%)				central bank discount rate, 1994[a]
						claims on government	claims on private sector	claims on banks	claims on foreign assets	reserve money	government deposits	foreign liabilities	capital accounts	
Afghanistan	199[1]	78.4[1]	18.6[2,3]	...	...	96.0[3,4]	—[3]	0.3[3]	3.6[3]	76.7[3]	4.6[3]	7.9[3]	2.0[3]	...
Albania	...	...	...	...	...	...	...	...	...	...	...	...	...	...
Algeria	1,680	88.3	14.3	447.6	16,300	80.1	—	8.6	11.3	73.3	0.9	6.6	—	...
American Samoa	...	...	...	...	...	...	...	...	...	...	...	...	...	...
Andorra	...	...	...	...	...	...	...	...	...	...	...	...	...	...
Angola	...	...	...	...	...	...	...	...	...	...	...	...	...	...
Antigua and Barbuda	31	100.0	3.9[3,5]	0.185	2,800	27.6	—	1.0	71.3	100.0	—	—	—	7.0[7,8]
Argentina	10,183	95.6	4.6	15.245	450	22.6	—	46.3	31.2	30.2	2.7	7.4	14.3	7[9]
Armenia	...	...	...	...	...	...	...	...	...	...	...	...	...	...
Aruba	151	98.0	1.3[2,5]	0.378	5,260	—	—	—	100.0	67.4	15.8	—	15.8	9.5
Australia	8,852	91.8	...	71.027	4,000	40.1	—	—	59.9	61.4	7.4	0.3	—	5.8
Austria	12,882	90.5	...	308.7	38,900	3.2	—	22.5	74.3	72.0	0.1	—	31.7	4.8
Azerbaijan	...	...	...	18.535[3]	2,590[3]	...	...	...	...	...	...	...	...	...
Bahamas, The	171	95.9	4.1[2,3]	0.372	1,380	40.9	—	1.1	58.0	71.1	3.2	—	31.2	6.5
Bahrain	851	93.3	1.2[2,3]	0.365	670	—	—	—	100.0	32.5	32.1	—	44.2	5.1[10]
Bangladesh	1,897	98.9	6.7	93.281	800	4.1[4]	—	25.1	70.8	62.1	6.7	22.2	4.4	5.5
Barbados	145	100.0	2.9	0.477	1,810	37.6	—	5.2	57.2	55.3	17.9	36.4	5.8	8.0
Belarus	...	...	...	35.985[3]	3,490[3]	...	...	...	...	...	...	...	...	20.0[1]
Belgium	10,534	85.2	...	...	...	6.6[1]	...	—	93.4[1]	54.9[1]	...	—	...	4.5
Belize	30	90.0	2.9	0.136	660	44.3	—	—	55.7	75.4	10.9	9.8	12.4	12.0
Benin	89	97.8	5.4	111.3	21,600	15.9	—	34.6	49.4	73.9	12.0	9.1	—	12.0
Bermuda	...	...	...	...	...	...	...	...	...	...	...	...	...	...
Bhutan	64[1]	98.4[1]	1.1	0.841[1]	550[1]	—	—	2.1[1]	97.9[1]	60.7[1]	1.0[1]	—	—	8.0[7,9]
Bolivia	212	68.4	16.5	2.499	320	55.7[4]	—	14.9	29.4	25.7	25.4	16.4	10.8	20.1[9]
Bosnia and Herzegovina	...	...	...	...	...	...	...	...	...	...	...	...	...	...
Botswana	3,088	98.6	0.1	0.607[1]	440[1]	—	—	—	100.0[1]	9.0[1]	59.6[1]	—	15.9[1]	14.3[7]
Brazil	26,078	99.5	3.8	...	...	62.8[4]	—	2.2	35.0	8.3	17.0	48.2	7.7	10,944
Brunei	...	...	—	...	...	...	...	...	...	...	...	...	...	...
Bulgaria	...	...	...	...	...	...	...	...	...	...	...	...	...	...
Burkina Faso	158	91.8	2.9	121.6	12,300	17.7	—	6.7	75.7	81.5	5.7	8.9	—	12.0
Burundi	119	94.1	5.4	...	...	20.6[4]	0.6	3.7	75.1	29.1	12.1	22.5	20.2	...
Cambodia	...	...	...	...	...	...	...	...	...	...	...	...	...	...
Cameroon	127[7]	8.3[7]	159.0	267.5	21,000	85.0	—	13.9	1.1	34.6	4.0	57.8	1.0	12.0[1]
Canada	8,219	80.4	...	114.4	4,030	43.3	—	—	56.7	95.4	—	—	—	7.0
Cape Verde	...	...	...	9.907[1]	28,500[1]	42.7[1,4]	25.6[1]	1.6[1]	30.0[1]	53.7[1]	4.4[1]	1.1[1]	16.4[1]	4.0[9]
Central African Republic	82[7]	98.8[7]	8.0	59.4	19,600	42.8	—	5.5	51.7	79.1	2.5	13.2	1.9	12.0[1]
Chad	29[7]	96.6[7]	8.1	45.5	7,090	64.5	—	11.2	24.3	73.0	1.1	15.5	2.4	12.0[1]
Chile	7,498	99.1	1.0	937.5[1]	69,800[1]	33.8[1,4]	1.4[1]	24.1[1]	40.6[1]	51.6[1]	11.8[1]	11.3[1]	8.3[1]	21.0[9]
China	21,559	94.0	2.8	1,424.4	1,200	12.3[1]	7.3[1]	67.2[1]	13.2[1]	91.5[1]	2.3[1]	—	6.8[1]	...
Colombia	5,567	96.2	1.8	5,138.0	150,000	9.9[4]	—	5.1	85.0	58.4	5.3	6.2	14.2	32.3
Comoros	24[7]	95.8[7]	6.0	10.857[1]	21,600[1]	25.0[1]	—	—	75.0[1]	58.6[1]	6.6[1]	5.0[1]	29.7[1]	...
Congo	1[7]	—[7]	235.0	95.8	34.000	95.8	—	2.0	2.2	83.8	6.5	11.0	2.8	12.0[1]
Costa Rica	642	98.3	3.1	117.2	36,300	29.1[4]	—	12.4	58.5	75.1	5.1	83.7	9.0	33.0
Côte d'Ivoire	6	66.7	1,110.1	494.0	36,200	34.5	—	65.4	0.1	37.4	1.7	59.7	—	12.0
Croatia	...	...	...	...	...	...	...	...	...	...	...	...	...	...
Cuba	...	...	...	...	...	...	...	...	...	...	...	...	...	...
Cyprus[11]	843	95.0	...	0.549	920	36.4	—	12.0	51.6	69.3	13.8	2.5	—	6.5
Czech Republic	3,377	97.7	1.7[12]	296.056	28,600	15.1[4]	—	24.9	60.0	53.3	10.8	38.6	3.0	8.0
Denmark	6,623	93.5	...	283.0	54,500	5.2	0.1	57.6	37.0	32.8	46.8	0.4	—	5.0
Djibouti	55	98.2	2.1	36.404	65,000	—	—	0.3	99.7	84.0	4.3	—	10.6	...
Dominica	12	100.0	4.2	0.076	1,050	30.8	—	0.5	68.8	89.3	—	10.7	—	6.4[7,8]
Dominican Republic	281	97.5	7.5	13.549	1,750	14.8[4]	—	12.1	73.0	131.7	—	157.4	-8.2	...
Ecuador	877[7]	95.9[7]	11.1	1,860.2[1]	171,000[1]	71.3[4]	0.3	1.4	27.0	20.6	12.0	76.5	5.5	36.0
Egypt	9,087	97.8	3.3	34.571	600	43.5[4]	—	11.2	45.3	34.5	31.2	32.9	—	21.3[3]
El Salvador	455	96.3	4.5	7.353	1,320	45.3[4]	—	13.2	41.5	58.3	10.0	15.9	14.4	14.0[9]

banks is usually either claims on government and government agencies or foreign assets and holdings, though some of the latter, such as the large outstanding loans to socialist and less developed countries, have become the chief liabilities. The chief liability of a central bank is usually reserve money (the currency and notes issued by the bank). When government deposits represent a substantial share, budgetary surpluses have usually been deposited by the central government. Large foreign liabilities imply extensive foreign investment. Among the deposit money banks, loans to the private sector normally represent the largest share of assets; occasionally, a trade- or banking-oriented country such as Belgium or Luxembourg will show major foreign assets. The chief liabilities of these banks will usually be savings deposits. If the country commands a high degree of confidence internationally, foreign liabilities may comprise a substantial share of liabilities.

Because the majority of the world's countries are in the less developed bloc, and because their principal financial concern is often external debt and its service, data are given for outstanding external public and publicly guaranteed long-term debt rather than for total public debt, which is the major concern in the developed countries. For comparability, the data are given in U.S. dollars. The volume of debt by itself does not create external payment problems. If the country's external debt service (interest payments plus principal repayment) needs can be met by a strong, dependable export market, by export of services, or, occasionally, by direct remittances from abroad (by residents working abroad and sending wages home in foreign

currencies, for example), no debt problem need exist. Countries whose debt service ratio (total debt service as a percent of exports of goods and services) is relatively high, however, must often base their external borrowing policy on maintenance of domestic conditions of strict efficiency and, sometimes, austerity. The failure to adhere to such policies may lead to eventual crises of financial liquidity, deflation, and slower growth.

Ideally, the data presented here should be obtained by utilizing a single international methodology to provide a universally comparable set of international statistics. No international agency, however, can collect such data for all countries because of differences, both overall and in detail, in national definitions of financial aggregates, in accounting methodology, and in the completeness with which it is possible to survey a country's financial activity. The greater part of the data presented in the table comes from the IMF's *International Financial Statistics* and the World Bank's *World Debt Tables*. These sources are supplemented by other recent data from national, regional, or other international sources. In a few cases the desired data are negligible or unavailable, as noted.

Detailed percentages may not add to 100.0 because of rounding, statistical discrepancy, or nonaccounting of negligible quantities.
—None, less than half the last significant figure, or not applicable.
... Not available.
a. Latest month.
b. Year-end.

deposit money banks, 1993[b]										external public debt outstanding (long-term, disbursed only), 1992						country
assets (%)				liabilities						total ('000,000 U.S.$)	creditors (%)		debt service				
loans to govern-ment	loans to private sector	re-serves	foreign assets	deposits ('000,000,000 national currency)	composition (%)						offi-cial	private	total ('000,000 U.S.$)	repayment (%)		debt service ratio (%)	
					demand depos.	savings depos.	govt. depos.	foreign liabilities						princi-pal	inter-est		
1.4[4,5]	51.2[5]	31.1[5]	16.3[5]	51.160[5]	35.6[5]	49.4[5,6]	0.5[5]	0.6[5]		5,269[2,3]	...	...	68[2,3]	16.2[2,3]	83.8[2,3]	7.3[2,3]	Afghanistan
										112.2	51.7	48.3	1.9	—	100.0	2.3	Albania
71.5[4]	19.4	6.2	2.9	579.9	32.2	31.0	17.9	22.2		24,762	25.1	74.9	8,841	78.6	21.4	68.5	Algeria
...	...	...	...		...	...	...	...		...	...	...	...	...	...	...	American Samoa
...	...	...	...		...	...	...	...		...	...	...	...	...	...	...	Andorra
										7,628	43.7	56.3	196	74.0	26.0	5.7	Angola
13.2[4]	62.0	9.0	15.8	0.974	12.6	61.5[6]	4.1	14.6		107[2,5]	...	...	50[2,5]	...	...	14.1[2,5]	Antigua and Barbuda
19.8[4]	63.0	8.1	9.1	67.5	7.0	45.3[6]	7.4	14.6		46,835	26.9	73.1	3,521	35.4	64.6	23.6	Argentina
...	...	...	...		...	...	...	...		2.8	100.0	—	...	...	...	...	Armenia
3.1	57.2	12.1	27.6	1.386	21.1	40.0	1.5	21.0		198[2,5]	...	...	7[2,5]	...	...	1.3[2,5]	Aruba
10.2[4]	82.7	1.3	5.8	350.522	15.3	51.6	1.0	17.5		...	...	...	...	...	...	...	Australia
28.9[4]	45.9	2.1	23.1	3,603.6	5.0	45.6	1.4	25.0		...	...	...	...	...	...	...	Austria
...	...	...	...		...	...	...	...		...	...	...	...	...	...	...	Azerbaijan
24.4[4]	82.4	6.1	−13.0	1.711	16.8	72.3[6]	1.7	—		743[2,3]	...	...	66[2,3]	36.4[2,3]	63.6[2,3]	7.6[2,3]	Bahamas, The
6.6	32.0	3.7	56.9	2.004	13.0	43.2	18.6	22.9		1,810[2,3]	...	...	144[2,3]	45.1[2,3]	54.9[2,3]	4.1[2,3]	Bahrain
27.2[4]	55.3	13.1	4.4	367.807	13.1	64.2	8.8	2.5		12,226	98.6	1.4	468	64.7	35.3	13.7	Bangladesh
28.0	57.0	6.1	9.0	2.128	13.2	65.3	4.8	14.3		400.6	52.2	47.8	91.1	64.7	35.3	15.7[3]	Barbados
...	...	...	...		...	...	...	...		181.2	12.6	87.4	0.6	—	100.0	...	Belarus
22.0[4,5]	21.9[5]	0.2[5]	55.9[5]	10,652.2[5]	5.5[5]	17.8[5,6]	—	69.7[5]		...	...	...	...	...	...	...	Belgium
9.2[4]	72.5	9.4	8.9	0.532	15.3	54.2[6]	9.3	13.0		153.1	83.9	16.1	16.0	66.3	33.7	6.3[3]	Belize
3.6	34.5	47.4	14.4	196.4	43.1	30.2	13.0	7.6		1,322	99.6	0.4	24	58.3	41.7	4.1	Benin
...	...	...	...	8.835[5]	...	...	...	...		796[2,3]	...	...	69[2,3]	52.2[2,3]	47.8[2,3]	...	Bermuda
34.5[1,4]	19.0[1]	37.0[1]	9.5[1]	2.240[1]	22.1[1]	33.3[1,6]	8.9[1]	15.9[1]		82.7	83.6	16.4	5.9	69.5	30.5	7.9[3]	Bhutan
—	85.2	12.2	2.6	12.602	11.6	56.9[6]	—	11.3		3,694	92.6	7.4	223	56.5	43.5	28.2	Bolivia
...	...	...	...		...	...	...	...		...	...	...	...	...	...	...	Bosnia and Herzegovina
4.2[4]	64.5	24.4	6.9	2.272	22.7	61.0	—	6.1		537.5	96.3	3.7	84.4	60.5	39.5	3.4[3]	Botswana
...	...	...	...		...	...	...	...		86,251	30.7	69.3	6,271	61.1	38.9	16.1	Brazil
...	...	...	...		...	...	...	...		—		12,5	...	...	...	...	Brunei
...	...	...	...		...	...	...	...		9,951	22.7	77.3	264	30.9	69.1	4.4	Bulgaria
8.5	55.6	25.9	9.9	158.2	26.5	36.3	30.2	7.9		994	99.5	0.5	28	50.0	50.0	7.9[6]	Burkina Faso
21.4[3,4]	67.4[3]	7.5[3]	3.7[3]	33.879[3]	36.8[3]	32.9[3]	...	4.8[3]		947	99.6	0.4	35	60.0	40.0	35.4	Burundi
...	...	...	...		...	...	...	...		1,564[2,3]	...	...	15[2,3]	—	100.0[2,3]	...	Cambodia
33.5[4]	60.3	2.0	4.2	617.0	42.0	54.1	32.0	10.9		5,465	84.1	15.9	159	47.8	52.2	7.4	Cameroon
14.3[4]	75.2	1.1	9.4	552.6	16.6	54.5[6]	0.4	14.9		...	...	...	...	...	...	...	Canada
...	...	...	...		...	...	...	...		151.4	98.7	1.3	7.0	60.0	40.0	9.9[3]	Cape Verde
34.8[4]	56.9	1.1	7.2	28.0	25.9	18.4	7.1	12.7		807.2	97.4	2.6	13.7	55.1	44.9	8.0	Central African Republic
34.0[4]	54.3	5.2	6.6	38.4	20.9	5.7	17.0	20.3		658.8	98.9	1.1	10.0	41.5	58.5	4.4	Chad
2.6[1,4]	88.0[1]	6.7[1]	2.7[1]	7,832.6[1]	5.8[1]	58.7[1,6]	4.6[1]	19.0[1]		9,578	54.2	45.8	1,438	43.9	56.1	11.1	Chile
—	77.5	18.3	4.1	3,622.4	21.2	42.0	—	3.5		58,475	32.7	67.3	8,027	64.8	35.2	8.8	China
4.8[4]	71.0	21.0	3.1	11,708.9	24.6	36.0[6]	7.0	11.4		13,245	59.1	40.9	3,445	68.7	31.3	32.4	Colombia
—	78.1[1]	12.5[1]	9.4[1]	12.795[1]	30.2[1]	44.7[1]	—	10.2[1]		185.1	100.0	—	3.5	41.4	58.6	6.6	Comoros
22.5[4]	51.3	7.5	18.8	129.7	32.3	22.0	2.0	13.4		3,878	81.0	19.0	120	78.8	21.2	8.8	Congo
2.4[4]	50.5	41.1	6.0	302.8	16.3	78.8[6]	1.5	3.6		3,207	80.1	19.9	480	60.2	39.8	18.1	Costa Rica
19.0	74.0	1.7	4.4	1,182.0	18.5	28.0	7.8	12.1		10,685	74.9	25.1	517	50.3	49.7	14.6	Côte d'Ivoire
...	...	...	...		...	...	...	...		...	...	...	...	...	...	...	Croatia
...	...	...	...		...	...	...	...		26,755[2,3]	...	...	260[2,3]	45.0[2,3]	55.0[2,3]	24.2[2,3]	Cuba
12.1	56.6	12.5	18.8	4.303	7.4	56.7	0.9	26.4		...	...	...	...	...	...	...	Cyprus[11]
31.2[4]	52.7	7.4	8.7	965.839	20.9	44.3[6]	1.9	4.5		5,550[12]	26.0[12]	74.0[12]	1,645[12]	77.5[12]	22.5[12]	9.2[3,12]	Czech Republic
7.4	47.9	3.7	40.9	947.6	27.0	33.6	—	19.4		...	...	...	...	...	...	...	Denmark
0.7[4]	44.3	1.3	53.8	72.432	30.7	30.5	1.3	20.8		173.8	99.9	0.1	10.1	76.2	23.8	3.6	Djibouti
16.7[4]	60.8	8.9	13.6	0.479	10.0	51.1[6]	9.0	17.5		85.9	100.0	—	4.6	58.7	41.3	12.8[3]	Dominica
5.7[4]	64.2	23.7	6.3	31.514	20.9	54.7	8.1	1.6		9,761	74.8	25.2	280	61.8	38.2	11.1	Dominican Republic
0.6[1]	73.6[1]	19.3[1]	6.5[1]	3,339.7[1]	28.5[1]	39.6[1]	—	4.3[1]		9,831	44.8	55.2	812	54.3	45.7	22.4	Ecuador
41.9[4]	22.8	13.7	21.6	168.329	8.9	58.6[6]	4.1	3.6		35,724	89.4	10.6	1,995	58.5	41.5	12.2	Egypt
4.5	63.8	28.1	3.6	22.570	16.3	69.3[6]	2.5	1.9		2,017	91.6	8.4	203	61.6	38.4	12.4	El Salvador

Finance (continued)

country	international reserves, 1994[a]			money supply, 1993[b]		central bank authority, 1993[b]									central bank discount rate, 1994[a]
	total ('000,000 SDRs)	% foreign exchange	ratio of external debt to total reserves, 1992[b]	stock ('000,000,000 national currency)	M1 per capita	assets (%)				liabilities (%)				
						claims on government	claims on private sector	claims on banks	claims on foreign assets	reserve money	government deposits	foreign liabilities	capital accounts	
Equatorial Guinea	—	—	14.9	2.6	6,690	98.9	—	—	1.1	20.0	1.4	65.7	1.6	12.0[1]
Eritrea	...	...	...	...	...	...	...	...	...	...	...	...	...	...
Estonia	...	...	...	...	...	...	...	...	...	...	...	...	...	...
Ethiopia	352	96.9	17.5	7.450	140	57.6	—	18.5	23.9	56.2	17.8	9.2	4.1	12.0
Faeroe Islands	...	...	...	...	...	...	...	...	...	...	...	...	...	...
Fiji	155	89.0	0.7	0.364	470	2.1[4]	—	—	97.9	51.9	1.1	—	14.8	6.0
Finland	6,643	94.7	...	141.759	27,900	3.8	9.3	16.0	70.9	80.5	1.7	0.4	14.6	5.3
France	20,153	76.3	...	1,645.0[1]	28,600[1]	9.4	0.5	46.9	43.3	35.5	24.7	15.1	28.1	9.5
French Guiana	...	...	...	5.565	39,000	...	...	...	...	...	...	...	...	...
French Polynesia	...	...	...	52.910	249,000	...	...	...	...	...	...	...	...	...
Gabon	43[7]	97.7[7]	41.9	134.4	103,000	74.4	—	23.6	2.0	69.5	3.7	17.4	2.3	12.0[7]
Gambia, The	72[7]	97.2[7]	3.6	0.435[1]	470[1]	23.1[1,4]	—	—	76.9[1]	25.7[1]	34.2[1]	39.7[1]	6.4[1]	13.5
Gaza Strip	...	...	...	...	...	...	...	...	...	...	...	...	...	...
Georgia	...	...	...	...	...	...	...	...	...	...	...	...	...	...
Germany	61,253	88.8	...	697.6	8,560	6.5	—	61.4	32.1	74.6	3.2	5.5	—	4.5
Ghana	261	89.3	9.3	461.4	29,100	69.8[4]	—	0.5	29.6	20.1	3.7	62.4	6.8	30.0
Gibraltar	...	...	...	...	...	...	...	...	...	...	...	...	...	...
Greece	5,423	95.7	4.6[2,3]	2,651.2	256,000	62.4	—	6.1	31.5	26.4	2.5	40.3	—	22.5
Greenland	...	...	...	...	...	...	...	...	...	...	...	...	...	...
Grenada	18	100.0	3.7	0.124	1,350	27.9	—	0.5	71.6	99.3	0.7	—	—	6.5[8]
Guadeloupe	...	...	...	6.282	14,900	...	...	...	...	...	...	...	...	...
Guam	...	...	...	...	...	...	...	...	...	...	...	...	...	...
Guatemala	610	96.9	2.7	5.048	500	8.1[4]	—	28.5	63.4	348.6	94.3	34.6	8.8	13.8[9]
Guernsey	...	...	...	...	...	...	...	...	...	...	...	...	...	...
Guinea	...	...	...	...	...	...	...	...	...	...	...	...	...	...
Guinea-Bissau	...	...	32.5	201.9	194,000	31.9[4]	—	43.2	24.9	40.0	5.6	93.8	11.1	30.0
Guyana	173	99.4	8.8	11.677	15,900	76.9	—	—	23.1	8.5	11.1	79.1	1.8	17.5
Haiti	13	92.3	33.7[3]	...	...	...	...	...	...	...	...	...	...	...
Honduras	40	97.5	16.1	2.876	550	49.1[4]	—	28.5	22.4	44.8	26.9	113.5	26.4	26.1[1]
Hong Kong	...	...	...	187.608	31,500	...	...	...	...	...	...	...	...	...
Hungary	4,934[7]	98.7[7]	4.0	549.2[3]	53,100[3]	51.9[3]	0.2[3]	25.6[3]	22.3[3]	49.1[3]	7.3[3]	90.2[3]	—	22.2
Iceland	273	95.6	...	31.625	119,000	28.3	0.7	5.5	65.5	33.3	24.6	30.2	—	5.2
India	11,960	94.5	10.7	1,312.4	1,450	68.6	—	6.9	24.5	75.2	—	9.2	9.1	12.0
Indonesia	8,308[7]	96.3[7]	4.9	28,801.0[1]	154,000[1]	13.6[1,4]	1.6[1]	25.1[1]	59.7[1]	26.6[1]	30.5[1]	6.1[1]	10.3[1]	11.5[1,10]
Iran	...	...	...	18,305.4	311,000	61.8[4]	—	12.3	25.9	54.1	16.3	9.6	2.6	...
Iraq	...	...	...	...	...	...	...	...	...	...	...	...	...	...
Ireland	4,588	94.2	...	3.996	1,140	6.9	—	—	93.1	54.0	31.0	—	29.7	6.3
Isle of Man	...	...	...	...	...	...	...	...	...	...	...	...	...	...
Israel	4,459	100.0	2.9[2,3]	10.536[1]	1,980[1]	29.2[1]	—	31.0[1]	39.8[1]	61.4[1]	32.8[1]	4.1[1]	—	11.5
Italy	24,911	84.3	...	545,020.0[1]	9,529,000[1]	70.6[1]	—	2.9[1]	26.4[1]	76.3[1]	—	2.7[1]	—	7.0
Jamaica	109[1]	100.0[1]	34.0[3]	16.903	6,810	35.9	—	—	64.1	94.5	87.7	66.1	9.2	52.0[8]
Japan	79,943	90.0	...	145,610.0	1,166,000	52.5	—	34.8	12.7	118.0	5.1	—	—	1.8
Jersey	...	...	...	...	...	...	...	...	...	...	...	...	...	...
Jordan	264	84.5	8.6	1.837	440	44.7	—	—	55.3	108.0	5.6	—	—	8.5
Kazakhstan	...	...	...	...	...	...	...	...	...	...	...	...	...	...
Kenya	470	96.4	82.2	59.322	2,200	58.3[1]	—	—	41.7[1]	206.0[1]	—	47.1[1]	15.0[1]	32.5
Kiribati	...	...	...	...	...	...	...	...	...	...	...	...	...	...
Korea, North	...	...	...	...	...	...	...	...	...	...	...	...	...	...
Korea, South	15,089	97.3	1.4	29,041.0	656,000	6.5[4]	—	59.5	33.9	47.1	10.3	0.1	—	5.0
Kuwait	2,727	89.2	0.2[2,3]	1.097	760	8.3	—	—	91.7	40.1	39.6	—	16.8	5.8
Kyrgyzstan	...	...	...	...	...	...	...	...	...	...	...	...	...	...
Laos	...	...	...	...	...	...	...	...	...	...	...	...	...	...
Latvia	...	...	...	...	...	...	...	...	...	...	...	...	...	...
Lebanon	2,776	87.3	0.2	1.143.2	390,000	4.0	0.4	1.8	93.8	20.2	11.6	0.1	0.9	19.3
Lesotho	150[7]	97.3[7]	2.8	0.351[1]	190[1]	21.9[1]	—	1.0[1]	77.1[1]	30.6[1]	55.7[1]	0.9[1]	8.7[1]	13.5[7]
Liberia	...	...	...	0.428	150	41.4[4]	57.8	0.8	0.1	16.3	0.7	18.5	2.2	7.7[1,9]
Libya	4,622[1]	84.4[1]	0.5[2,3]	4.987[1]	1,110[1]	71.0[1]	0.1	—	28.9[1]	61.5[1]	12.4[1]	—	—	...
Liechtenstein	...	...	...	...	...	...	...	...	...	...	...	...	...	...
Lithuania	...	...	...	...	...	...	...	...	...	...	...	...	...	11.0[3]
Luxembourg	...	...	...	81.8[1]	209,000[1]	...	...	...	...	...	...	...	...	6.0[7,9]
Macau	...	...	...	20.988[1]	55,100[1]	...	...	...	...	...	...	...	...	...
Macedonia	...	...	...	...	...	...	...	...	...	...	...	...	...	...
Madagascar	62[3]	100.0[3]	42.9[3]	915.3[1]	70,200[1]	85.9[1,4]	—	3.2[1]	10.9[1]	38.1[1]	22.4[1]	30.9[1]	2.9[1]	...
Malawi	19	84.2	37.7	1.021	90	82.1[4]	—	—	17.9	66.9	26.7	23.7	—	25.0
Malaysia	24,553	98.4	0.8	35.544[1]	1,890[1]	1.5[1]	1.1[1]	−29.1[1]	126.5[1]	67.8[1]	15.2[1]	0.1[1]	—	7.8[1]
Maldives	20	95.0	3.2	0.695	2,890	75.3[4]	—	0.6	24.0	71.2	5.8	14.0	6.1	5.0[10]
Mali	171	94.2	8.0	117.8	13,500	25.2	—	14.7	60.2	88.3	3.4	11.3	—	12.0
Malta	1,162	94.4	0.1	0.425	1,160	3.1	—	—	96.9	77.5	3.6	—	—	5.5
Marshall Islands	...	...	...	...	...	...	...	...	...	...	...	...	...	...
Martinique	...	...	...	6.294[1]	16,800[1]	...	...	...	...	...	...	...	...	...
Mauritania	33	100.0	30.0	20.938	9,500	67.6[4]	1.8	8.5	22.1	81.0	26.9	94.0	17.6	7.0[1]
Mauritius	505	94.1	0.9	7.423	6,700	6.5	—	3.3	90.2	60.4	0.1	0.1	2.9	8.3
Mayotte	...	...	...	0.783[1]	7,690[1]	...	...	...	...	...	...	...	...	...
Mexico	20,967	99.4	3.8	143.485	1,580	−11.8	0.6	4.9	106.2	67.9	—	20.4	1.8	19.5[10]
Micronesia	...	...	...	...	...	...	...	...	...	...	...	...	...	...
Moldova	...	...	...	...	...	...	...	...	...	...	...	...	...	...
Monaco	...	...	...	...	...	...	...	...	...	...	...	...	...	...
Mongolia	75[1]	49.4[1]	...	7.947[3]	3,680[3]	...	...	...	...	...	...	...	...	...
Morocco	2,756	97.5	5.6	92.080[3]	3,550[3]	23.7[3]	14.7[3]	15.3[3]	46.4[3]	87.2[3]	1.0[3]	10.7[3]	—	...
Mozambique	...	...	...	...	...	21.9[3,4]	36.8[3]	—	41.3[3]	43.9[3]	17.9[3]	154.2[3]	—	...
Myanmar (Burma)	276	97.1	17.0	30.587[5]	730[5]	80.7[5]	—	16.5[5]	2.8[5]	80.0[5]	—	3.2[5]	—	9.0[7,9]
Namibia	...	...	...	1.467	1,910	57.1	—	—	42.9	21.5	20.4	56.3	—	14.5
Nauru	...	...	...	...	...	...	...	...	...	...	...	...	...	...
Nepal	422	97.4	3.7	20.428[1]	1,070[1]	44.3[1]	1.2[1]	1.8[1]	52.7[1]	49.0[1]	19.4[1]	9.3[1]	20.4[1]	11.0[7]
Netherlands, The	24,745	90.0	...	149.6	9,750	4.9	—	5.3	89.8	66.4	9.4	—	—	5.0[7]

deposit money banks, 1993[b] — assets (%) loans to government	loans to private sector	reserves	foreign assets	liabilities — deposits ('000,000,000 national currency)	composition (%) demand depos.	savings depos.	govt. depos.	foreign liabilities	external public debt outstanding (long-term, disbursed only), 1992 — total ('000,000 U.S.$)	creditors (%) official	private	debt service total ('000,000 U.S.$)	repayment (%) principal	interest	debt service ratio (%)	country
9.9[4]	40.4	25.4	24.3	4.9	27.2	14.0	10.8	13.0	205.5	92.2	7.8	3.0	66.7	33.3	4.8	Equatorial Guinea
...	...	...	...		...	...	...	...	26.5	41.9	58.1	7.3	100.0	—	...	Eritrea
49.0[4]	17.6	19.4	14.0	8.439	31.7	38.5	4.9	5.4								Estonia
...	...	...	...		...	...	...	...	4,168	87.1	12.9	105	60.5	30.5	13.5	Ethiopia
...	...	...	...		...	...	...	...								Faeroe Islands
15.7[4]	67.8	10.4	6.2	1.408	17.1	69.1	1.5	6.8	225	98.2	1.8	59	71.2	28.8	6.3	Fiji
2.0	70.9	4.9	22.2	562.680	23.3	27.3	1.8	32.7								Finland
6.6[1]	65.8[1]	0.3[1]	27.3[1]	10,357.0[1]	13.4[1]	25.1[1]	0.9[1]	27.9[1]								France
...	...	...	...		...	...	...	...	36[2,5]			8[2,5]			5.3[2,5]	French Guiana
...	...	...	(iii)						38[2,3]			46[2,3]	82.6[2,3]	17.4[2,3]	...	French Polynesia
37.0[4]	55.0	2.7	5.3	294.8	38.6	36.0	10.2	12.5	2,998	79.5	20.5	334	29.6	70.4	13.2	Gabon
28.8[1,4]	37.7[1]	14.1[1]	19.4[1]	0.591[1]	38.6[1]	51.3[1]	—	2.1[1]	339.9	97.3	2.7	25.6	74.0	26.0	11.5	Gambia, The
...	...	...	...		...	...	...	...								Gaza Strip
...	...	...	...		...	...	...	...								Georgia
17.5[4]	63.5	2.3	16.6	4,792.5	10.1	28.2	5.1	10.3								Germany
5.5[4]	23.6	38.4	32.5	792.5	29.7	25.7	8.0	16.7	3,096	93.5	6.5	188	61.2	38.8	16.7	Ghana
39.6[3]		...	0.1[3]	4,418.2[3]	39.7[3]				866[2,3]			97[2,3]	52.6[2,3]	47.4[2,3]	...	Gibraltar
42.1[1,4]	30.8[1]	18.0[1]	9.2[1]	11,007.7[1]	6.6[1]	54.0[1]	—	26.5[1]	24,565[2,3]			3,166[2,3]	52.8[2,3]	47.2[2,3]	36.5[2,3]	Greece
...	...	...	...		...	...	...	...								Greenland
19.3[4]	59.5	7.6	13.7	0.704	11.0	51.8[6]	2.9	14.3	97.7	88.2	11.8	5.5	70.9	29.1	3.3[3]	Grenada
...	...	...	...		...	...	...	...	58[2,5]			5[2,5]			5.9[2,5]	Guadeloupe
...	...	...	...		...	...	...	...								Guam
14.8	61.5	23.3	0.4	12.094	15.9	73.5	0.6	5.4	2,104	82.4	17.6	449	66.6	33.4	24.4	Guatemala
...	...	...	...		...	...	...	...								Guernsey
...	...	...	...		...	...	...	...	2,466	95.9	4.1	80	58.8	41.2	11.6	Guinea
7.4[4]	38.8	27.9	26.0	478.800	14.3	32.0[6]	1.8	1.6	580.1	95.0	5.0	5.7	56.1	43.9	87.7	Guinea-Bissau
51.2[4]	26.0	13.9	8.1	39.546	13.1	70.5	8.0	7.1	1,665	96.5	3.5	92	53.3	46.7	31.6[3]	Guyana
...	...	...	...		...	...	...	...	625.9	92.7	7.3	0.4	—	100.0	3.1[3]	Haiti
13.9[4]	72.1	6.1	7.9	6.957	18.9	49.3[6]	5.0	3.0	3,192	93.0	7.0	347	55.0	45.0	32.4	Honduras
...	...	...	...	6,061.6	...	...	...	...	7,178[2,3]			1,108[2,3]	58.2[2,3]	41.8[2,3]	1.1[2,3]	Hong Kong
9.5[3,4]	54.7[3]	29.7[3]	6.1[3]	1,705.3[3]	15.6[3]	35.1[3,6]	1.0[3]	7.8[3]	17,836	21.6	78.4	4,351	63.6	36.4	31.2	Hungary
12.8	80.1	4.7	2.4	242.825	11.4	54.4	—	17.4								Iceland
26.9	58.8	14.4	—	3,344.5	15.3	75.2	—		67,721	64.9	35.1	5,411	49.7	50.3	20.9	India
7.5[1,4]	75.2[1]	9.5[1]	7.8[1]	166,401.0[1]	10.2[1]	54.2[1,6]	3.9[1]	9.7[1]	49,289	81.3	18.7	7,442	63.3	36.7	20.3	Indonesia
3.4	60.6	29.0	7.0	36,517.6	33.3	63.5	—	16.4	3,065	6.2	93.8	263	74.1	25.9	1.3	Iran
...	...	...	...		...	...	...	...	12,954[2,3]			403[2,3]	—	100.0[2,3]	133.4[2,3]	Iraq
11.3	59.9	3.0	25.9	21.957	9.9	58.7	0.5	19.1								Ireland
...	...	...	...		...	...	...	...								Isle of Man
27.1	50.3	9.6	13.0	240.897	3.5	44.0	8.2	15.4	18,504[2,3]			2,412[2,3]	50.1[2,3]	49.9[2,3]	20.6[2,3]	Israel
13.9[1]	63.3[1]	11.8[1]	11.0[1]	1,144,340.0[1]	39.0[1]	31.3[1]	—	22.2[1]								Italy
15.1[4]	42.8	24.8	17.2	55.099	21.2	53.9	4.2	14.0	3,596	88.1	11.9	560	70.5	29.5	20.1	Jamaica
10.1[4]	78.8	1.0	10.1	708,920.0	14.8	52.6	—	11.0								Japan
...	...	...	...		...	...	...	...								Jersey
6.1	41.9	25.8	26.2	5.729	13.6	47.8	2.0	24.7	6,914	62.6	37.4	657	57.5	42.5	18.4	Jordan
...	...	...	...		...	...	...	...								Kazakhstan
18.6[1]	48.4	15.4	17.6	135.391	24.9	47.5[6]	3.5	2.5	4,635	82.1	17.9	325	61.8	38.2	13.7	Kenya
...	...	...	...		...	...	...	...	16[2,5]			9[2,8]			3.6[2,5]	Kiribati
...	...	...	...		...	...	...	...	3,770[2,3]			149[2,3]	18.1[2,3]	81.9[2,3]	...	Korea, North
2.7	79.6	10.7	7.1	184,844.0	9.4	45.0[6]	5.2	6.5	23,919	37.9	62.1	4,589	66.2	33.8	5.0	Korea, South
58.4	15.9	0.8	24.9	5.877	12.4	77.2	1.0	8.7	792[2,3]			74[2,3]	51.4[2,3]	48.6[2,3]	8.5[2,3]	Kuwait
...	...	...	...		...	...	...	...								Kyrgyzstan
...	...	...	...		...	...	...	...	1,891	100.0	—	11	63.6	36.4	9.7[3]	Laos
...	...	...	...		...	...	...	...	26.0	65.8	34.2	0.2	—	100.0	...	Latvia
21.8	32.1	7.8	38.3	18,386.7	2.3	76.1[6]	0.8	11.2	304	67.8	32.2	64	60.9	39.1	3.3	Lebanon
15.6[1,4]	35.9[1]	15.4[1]	33.0[1]	0.881[1]	35.4[1]	42.2[1]	4.5[1]	2.8[1]	441.8	93.5	6.5	33.9	58.7	41.3	5.5	Lesotho
19.0[4]	26.5	44.4	10.2	0.482	31.1	57.0	6.3	3.7	1,101	82.3	17.7					Liberia
...	59.6[1]	37.5[1]	2.9[1]	4.764[1]	56.5[1]	26.4[1]	3.8[1]	4.4[1]	3,030[2,3]			674[2,3]	69.7[2,3]	30.3[2,3]	6.3[2,3]	Libya
...	...	...	...		...	...	...	...								Liechtenstein
...	...	...	...		...	...	...	...	9.5	100.0						Lithuania
—	4.4[1]	...	95.6[1]	13,070.8[1]	0.8[1]	10.6[1]	—	81.4[1]								Luxembourg
43.3[1]		...	53.5[1]	77.361[1]	7.4[1]	57.1[1]	...	25.5[1]	92[2,3]			13[2,3]	15.4[2,3]	84.6[2,3]	0.8[2,3]	Macau
...	...	...	...		...	...	...	...								Macedonia
1.4[1]	66.9[1]	17.4[1]	14.3[1]	1,373.0[1]	43.6[1]	20.2[1]	10.1[1]	3.2[1]	3,805	93.2	6.8	73	54.8	45.2	15.8	Madagascar
28.3[4]	45.3	21.9	4.5	1.733	32.3	53.3	—	6.3	1,557	97.6	2.4	78	61.5	38.5	18.0	Malawi
7.9[1]	82.5[1]	6.0[1]	3.6[1]	143.845[1]	13.2[1]	55.7[1]	1.0[1]	13.0[1]	13,346	33.1	66.9	2,518	67.8	32.2	5.4	Malaysia
15.8[4]	34.7	39.5	10.0	1.148	24.5	29.6	5.3	17.8	92.6	93.8	6.2	6.9	78.3	21.7	3.5	Maldives
1.9	50.9	43.1	4.2	184.4	28.6	28.5	17.9	6.8	2,472	99.8	0.2	32	59.4	40.6	2.4[3]	Mali
11.0	53.9	6.4	28.7	1.295	4.6	72.7	—	8.0	129.4	100.0	—	20.1	76.1	23.9	0.4[5]	Malta
...	...	...	...		...	...	...	...	53[2,5]			12[2,5]				Marshall Islands
...	...	...	...		...	...	...	...							1.9[2,5]	Martinique
2.2[4]	73.0	19.1	5.7	56.440	20.4	11.8	2.3	23.4	1,855	95.3	4.7	69	72.5	27.5	14.5[3]	Mauritania
20.6	59.0	13.0	7.4	40.521	7.9	81.9	—	1.3	742	84.6	15.4	137	64.2	35.8	7.1	Mauritius
...	...	...	...		...	...	...	...								Mayotte
3.5[4]	91.2	1.4	4.0	462.869	21.2	43.9[6]	5.4	15.2	72,219	35.0	65.0	15,253	66.4	33.6	32.7	Mexico
...	...	...	...		...	...	...	...								Micronesia
...	...	...	...		...	...	...	...	37.5	100.0	—	5.0	100.0	—	...	Moldova
...	...	...	...		...	...	...	...								Monaco
...	...	...	...		...	...	...	...	296.2	64.9	35.1	65.0	86.0	14.0	16.6	Mongolia
...	...	...	...		...	...	...	...	20,332	78.3	21.7	1,857	49.9	50.1	22.7[3]	Morocco
17.3[3]	42.1[3]	32.3[3]	8.3[3]	313.900[3]	71.4[3]	6.6[3]	19.6[3]	9.1[3]	4,136	90.8	9.2	24	54.2	45.8	6.6	Mozambique
-46.3[4,5]	35.0[5]	111.3[5]	—	20.619[5]	6.7[5]	57.2[5,6]			4,974	94.9	5.1	52	50.0	50.0	11.0[3]	Myanmar (Burma)
8.5	82.5	3.0	5.9	3.279	40.7	46.8[6]	3.5	4.9	24[2,5]			179[2,5]			...	Namibia
...	...	...	...		...	...	...	...	113[2,5]			142[2,5]				Nauru
28.2[3,4]	47.5[3]	8.0[3]	15.5[3]	33.870[3]	12.7[3]	68.6[3]	—	4.5[3]	1,747	95.3	4.7	65	58.5	41.5	11.3	Nepal
12.2[4]	50.0	0.3	37.0	1,026.5	10.9	34.6[6]	—	32.0								Netherlands, The

Finance (continued)

country	international reserves, 1994[a]			money supply, 1993[b]		central bank authority, 1993[b]									central bank discount rate, 1994[a]
	total ('000,000 SDRs)	% foreign exchange	ratio of external debt to total reserves, 1992[b]	stock ('000,000,000 national currency)	M1 per capita	assets (%)				liabilities (%)				
						claims on government	claims on private sector	claims on banks	claims on foreign assets	reserve money	government deposits	foreign liabilities	capital accounts	
Netherlands Antilles	191	90.1	5.3[2,3]	0.785	4,070	11.7	—	...	88.3	72.1	12.8	—	11.9	5.0
New Caledonia	...	...	...	58.597	323,000									
New Zealand	3,143	96.7	...	24.547	7,000	25.1	...	8.8	66.1	18.7	59.1	1.9	—	6.2
Nicaragua	...	...	...	...	...									
Niger	94	89.4	6.0	79.5	9,170	28.3	—	23.1	48.6	68.3	2.8	19.9	—	12.0
Nigeria	983	97.6	28.5	48.708[3]	550[3]	64.1[3]	1.1[3]	0.7[3]	34.1[3]	26.9[3]	43.0[3]	—	3.2[3]	13.0
Northern Mariana Islands	...	...	...											
Norway	12,971	94.2	...	342.3	79,200	14.8	...	8.6	76.6	21.6	54.0	—	...	6.8
Oman	687	92.3	1.2	0.452	260	6.4	—	—	93.6	37.0	8.1	0.1	28.6	4.2[7,9]
Pakistan	1,580	95.4	19.5	378.111	2,910	60.9	—	22.6	16.5	70.8	10.8	14.6	—	10.0[7]
Panama	438	97.0	7.5	0.708	280	53.3[4]	16.4	—	30.3	12.6	78.7	22.7	9.9	...
Papua New Guinea	101	98.0	6.4	0.530	130	75.2	—	—	24.8	35.5	65.6	8.4	31.2	6.3[7]
Paraguay	655	87.3	2.6	1,054.0	226,000	45.6[4]	0.2	4.6	49.6	54.7	5.2	4.5	11.7	18.0
Peru	3,896	98.8	5.2	2.884[1]	130[1]	1.5[1,4]	—	6.2[1]	92.2[1]	61.3[1]	0.9[1]	44.2[1]	3.8[1]	15.4
Philippines	4,607	95.8	5.7	117.5[1]	1,830[1]	39.9[4]	—	9.3	56.8	65.3	71.6	83.9	2.8	7.5
Poland	3,475	97.3	10.4	196,460.0	5,092,000	48.8[4]	0.1	19.7	31.4	49.6	7.0	11.9	0.7	35.0
Portugal	10,944	92.3	1.1	3,774.5	384,000	7.2[4]	—	6.3	86.5	69.0	12.4	0.1	11.4	12.0
Puerto Rico	...	...	...	...	...									
Qatar	501	83.6	0.2[2,3]	4.156	7,600	—	—	5.0	95.0	72.4	7.2	—	7.3	...
Réunion	...	...	...	10.187[1]	16,200[1]	...	...	...	...	...	...	...	...	
Romania	1,036	85.3	1.4	2,196.3	96,600	10.7	—	50.0	39.3	79.8	15.5	57.6	11.3	20.0[1]
Russia	...	...	...	...	...									11.0[7]
Rwanda	35[7]	65.7[7]	10.3	25.041	3,250	69.8[4]	0.3	2.3	27.6	33.8	18.0	14.4	20.7	6.5[7,8]
St. Kitts and Nevis	24	100.0	1.5	0.076	1,820	9.5	—	—	90.5	100.0	—	—	—	7.0[7,8]
St. Lucia	42	95.2	1.6	0.226	1,600	6.8	—	—	93.2	96.6	3.4	—	—	
St. Vincent and the Grenadines	21	100.0	1.8	0.091	830	10.5	—	—	89.5	100.0	—	—	—	6.5[7,8]
San Marino	...	...	...	...	...									
São Tomé and Príncipe	...	...	...	...	...	—	—	—	100.0[3]	26.1[3]	11.7[3]	...	...	
Saudi Arabia	4,693	74.5	0.2[2,3]	120.0[3]	7,260[3]									
Senegal	9	77.8	213.2	197.8	24,700	47.7	—	52.0	0.3	38.1	1.7	42.3	—	12.0
Seychelles	26	96.2	4.7	0.336	4,690	59.9	—	4.3	35.8	76.2	11.7	—	2.8	9.5
Sierra Leone	35	74.3	33.0	35.053	7,700	19.7	—	—	80.3	105.9	28.0	962.9	—	16.0[8]
Singapore	36,285	99.4	0.1[2,3]	22,882	7,880	—	—	—	100.0	18.8	38.6	—	—	3.6[10]
Slovakia	...	...	...	...	...									
Slovenia	...	...	...	...	...									
Solomon Islands	17	100.0	3.8	0.124	350	42.6[4]	—	—	57.4	41.4	5.3	5.0	46.1	11.3[8]
Somalia	...	...	...	...	...									
South Africa	469	66.3	...	49.858[5]	1,320[5]	26.7[5]	—	12.5[5]	60.7[5]	115.9[5]	62.3[5]	6.5[5]	—	12.0
Spain	29,311	95.0	...	17,409.0	444,000	-1.8	—	52.4	49.4	62.6	1.5	—	17.7	7.5
Sri Lanka	1,341	98.1	6.0	59.355	3,350	29.9	—	4.1	66.0	48.5	1.5	34.8	14.5	17.0
Sudan, The	277[7]	100.0[7]	363.0	44,305[3]	1,500[3]	97.3[3,4]	—	0.9[3]	1.8[3]	87.2[3]	—	83.3[3]	1.0[3]	...
Suriname	2	—	23.4[2,3]	3.221[1]	7,960[1]	98.1[1]	—	—	1.9[1]	92.7[1]	0.4[1]	2.3[1]	1.5[1]	11.0
Swaziland	181	95.0	0.8	0.291	350	—	—	0.8	99.2	29.0	57.6	0.6	4.1	4.5
Sweden	15,311	95.4	...	...	...	35.9	—	0.5	63.7	59.4	7.9	—	—	3.5
Switzerland	25,657	85.8	...	91.2	12,900	7.5	—	2.0	90.5	58.1	0.7	—	—	
Syria	...	...	...	181.979[1]	13,800[1]	58.8[1,4]	—	22.4[1]	18.9[1]	64.9[1]	24.9[1]	18.8[1]	0.2[1]	5.5
Taiwan	61,970	99.5	0.0[2,3]	2,806.4	134,000	0.1	—	9.6	90.2	54.0	3.9	—	—	
Tajikistan	...	...	...	...	...									
Tanzania	207	95.2	18.5	237.9	8,840	72.5	—	0.6	26.9	42.1	—	124.2	—	30.0
Thailand	18,987	98.0	0.6	249.7[1]	4,360[1]	6.8	—	6.2	87.0	38.6	28.6	—	35.3	9.0[7]
Togo	88	98.9	4.2	46.0	11,900	42.8	—	8.4	48.8	65.4	6.5	16.4	—	12.0
Tonga	24	91.7	1.3	0.028	280	18.2	—	—	81.8	38.9	3.7	—	4.5	4.3[7,9]
Trinidad and Tobago	33	93.9	10.2	3.137	2,470	35.4	—	5.1	59.5	36.6	7.4	24.4	41.4	13.0
Tunisia	697	98.7	8.6	3.093	360	5.5	—	52.8	41.7	63.7	5.7	14.5	4.8	8.8[10]
Turkey	2,717	93.7	6.2	125,858.0	2,079,000	51.8[4]	—	6.3	41.9	43.3	5.5	36.4	2.9	262.8[10]
Turkmenistan	...	...	...	13.060[3]	4,210[3]	...	...	...	...	...	...	...	...	
Tuvalu														
Uganda	146	100.0	26.3	214.463[1]	12,200[1]	75.1[1,4]	0.9[1]	1.9[1]	22.1[1]	27.8[1]	55.7[1]	79.6[1]	15.2[1]	24.0
Ukraine				173.4[3]	3,330[3]									5.4[3]
United Arab Emirates	4,715	95.0	0.2[2,3]	18.174	8,640	—	—	0.2	99.8	56.1	29.0	1.3	7.2	...
United Kingdom	27,818	91.8	...	252.2	4,320	29.6	—	0.7	69.6	56.7	—	55.9	—	5.0[10]
United States	53,818	54.9	...	1,230.3	4,740	82.7	—	—	17.3	94.3	8.5	0.1	—	4.0
Uruguay	662	87.8	5.1	4.053	1,280	48.5[4]	0.8	18.9	31.8	18.7	31.4	27.7	—	186.4
Uzbekistan	...	...	...	...	...									
Vanuatu	33	90.9	1.0	5.679	35,000	—	—	0.1	99.9	54.4	41.9	0.4	13.5	6.0[10]
Venezuela	5,733	84.4	2.5	416.9	19,900	20.6[4]	—	2.0	77.4	24.8	8.6	36.8	6.7	67.0
Vietnam	...	...	...	...	...									
Virgin Islands (U.S.)	...	...	...	...	...									
West Bank	...	...	...	...	...									
Western Sahara	...	...	...	...	...									
Western Samoa	36	94.4	1.9	0.042	260	1.5	—	0.5	98.0	50.9	56.4	—	...	5.5[9]
Yemen	140[7]	98.6[7]	16.5	...	...									
Yugoslavia[13]	...	...	...	...	...									
Zaire	132[7]	79.5[7]	56.3	6,495	150	37.8[4]	0.7	1.2	60.3	63.2	0.3	229.3	40.9	60.0[1]
Zambia	130[3]	99.2[3]	41.8	22.360[3]	2,780[3]	8.1[3]	2.4[3]	—	89.5[3]	144.5[3]	-186.7[3]	793.2[3]	—	95.0
Zimbabwe	389	94.6	11.2	5.788	540	24.2[4]	—	—	75.8	62.8	—	84.9	—	72.2

deposit money banks, 1993[b]									external public debt outstanding (long-term, disbursed only), 1992							country
assets (%)				liabilities					total ('000,000 U.S.$)	creditors (%)		debt service				
loans to government	loans to private sector	reserves	foreign assets	deposits ('000,000,000 national currency)	composition (%)					official	private	total ('000,000 U.S.$)	repayment (%)		debt service ratio (%)	
					demand depos.	savings depos.	govt. depos.	foreign liabilities					principal	interest		
3.5[4]	50.1	5.0	41.4	3.568	14.1	42.7[6]	1.1	39.1	1,077[2,3]	...	...	88[2,3]	47.7[2,3]	52.3[2,3]	5.6[2,3]	Netherlands Antilles
									273[2,3]	...	...	43[2,3]	86.0[2,3]	14.0[2,3]	9.6[2,3]	New Caledonia
10.1	80.9	3.7	5.3	76.092	30.6	48.8[6]	—	21.0	...	...	...	...	...	...	...	New Zealand
									8,994	78.9	21.1	80	56.3	43.8	24.9	Nicaragua
2.0	62.0	28.6	6.7	104.7	27.5	39.5	20.5	16.6	1,362	99.9	0.1	8	50.0	50.0	2.3	Niger
5.9[1]	46.8[1]	27.3[1]	20.0[1]	99.264[1]	31.3[1]	41.7[1]	3.6[1]	1.3[1]	28,458	65.0	35.0	3,722	55.6	44.4	30.2	Nigeria
									...	...	...	...	...	...	...	Northern Mariana Islands
6.8[4]	83.9	0.5	8.8	562.2	43.9	24.8[6]	1.1	12.0	...	...	...	...	...	...	...	Norway
9.7	68.4	3.1	18.8	1.591	13.7	54.3	9.6	4.0	2,340	21.4	78.6	493	69.0	31.0	12.1[5]	Oman
31.8	51.4	10.4	6.4	665.290	29.2	35.2	2.9	13.5	18,476	97.3	2.7	1,723	65.8	34.2	17.4	Pakistan
1.0	24.9	—	74.2	17.172	3.8	19.2	—	66.0	3,770	34.8	65.2	632	63.4	36.6	21.7	Panama
27.5	61.9	2.0	8.6	1.830	16.0	54.3	2.4	0.4	1,539	76.6	23.4	196	60.7	39.3	9.0	Papua New Guinea
0.1[4]	64.1	20.7	15.1	3,630.9	10.1	59.8	5.8	7.4	1,462	79.1	20.9	609	62.1	37.9	39.7	Paraguay
18.6[1,4]	42.9[1]	21.4[1]	17.0[1]	9.5[1]	13.6[1]	54.1[1,6]	10.9[1]	6.8[1]	15,417	72.6	27.4	760	58.4	41.6	17.0	Peru
10.7[4]	53.4	15.6	20.3	749.5	6.6	63.7	5.6	10.8	26,004	71.6	28.4	4,394	71.0	29.0	24.9	Philippines
46.2[4]	26.2	10.3	17.4	726,505.0	13.3	49.9[6]	3.7	4.3	43,034	76.6	23.4	1,306	38.9	61.1	8.1	Poland
23.8[4]	47.0	12.9	15.7	16,756.2	17.4	41.4	2.6	24.9	21,277	21.6	78.4	4,832	69.2	30.8	19.6[3]	Portugal
...	...	...	...	...	...	...	...	...	...	...	...	...	...	...	...	Puerto Rico
—	67.4	3.0	29.6	27.778	10.1	42.3	15.5	0.6	368[2,3]	...	...	44[2,3]	50.0[2,3]	50.0[2,3]	1.4[2,3]	Qatar
...	...	...	...	...	...	...	...	...	61[2,5]	...	...	9[2,5]	77.8[2,5]	22.2[2,5]	0.5[2,5]	Réunion
5.2	64.3	13.0	17.4	7,603.4	17.7	10.3	11.3	9.4	1,322	87.7	12.3	129	65.1	34.9	3.2	Romania
									64,703	19.2	80.8	1,600	68.4	31.6	...	Russia
15.5[4]	63.4	17.3	13.9	33.464	38.5	39.9	8.5	2.7	804[3]	90.8	0.2	18.3	63.4	36.6	13.7[6]	Rwanda
13.8[4]	53.3	9.0	23.8	0.707	6.8	47.0[6]	15.9	22.5	39.3	98.7	1.3	2.4	58.3	41.7	3.3[3]	St. Kitts and Nevis
9.8[4]	71.6	9.7	9.0	1.055	15.0	51.9[6]	16.5	10.2	88.3	99.3	0.7	11.4	64.0	36.0	3.5[3]	St. Lucia
14.7[4]	48.9	13.3	23.1	0.549	11.1	45.5[6]	17.5	14.2	61.0	100.0	—	4.5	62.2	37.8	3.7[3]	St. Vincent and the Grenadines
...	...	...	...	...	...	...	...	...	...	...	...	...	...	...	...	San Marino
...	42.7[1]	5.2[1]	52.1[1]	204.2[1]	41.1[1]	45.4[1,6]	0.7[1]	15.9[1]	168.8	99.3	0.7	3.3	66.7	33.3	31.7	São Tomé and Príncipe
—									2,893[2,3]	...	...	522[2,3]	79.7[2,3]	20.3[2,3]	1.1[2,3]	Saudi Arabia
5.6	83.7	6.7	4.0	508.8	19.9	27.3	23.2	9.0	2,932	96.2	3.8	121	65.3	34.7	7.6	Senegal
78.1[4]	13.1	18.8	3.0	1.322	15.2	58.1	8.1	2.9	147.2	83.0	17.0	17.6	68.2	31.8	6.7	Seychelles
21.9[4]	37.8	7.3	33.0	39.303	32.4	40.6	—	3.9	680	92.2	7.8	22	50.0	50.0	4.9[5]	Sierra Leone
8.6	53.5	3.9	34.0	148.212	9.4	40.0	4.3	34.8	3,914[2,3]	...	...	494[2,3]	52.6[2,3]	47.4[2,3]	0.8[2,3]	Singapore
...	...	...	...	...	...	...	...	...	...	...	...	...	...	...	...	Slovakia
...	...	...	...	...	...	...	...	...	...	...	...	...	...	...	...	Slovenia
58.2[4]	36.7	2.1	3.0	0.230	35.6	54.8	2.3	2.5	89.3	91.6	8.4	9.6	77.1	22.9	9.5[3]	Solomon Islands
									1,800	98.2	1.8	—	—	—	...	Somalia
7.1[5]	88.5[5]	3.5[5]	0.9[5]	134.074[5]	30.6[5]	53.0[5]	...	5.0[5]	...	...	...	...	—	—	...	South Africa
10.4[1]	55.3	5.2	20.1	82,825.0	13.1	38.7	2.0	15.0	...	...	...	...	...	...	...	Spain
15.1[4]	60.4	10.9	13.6	188.133	14.4	53.8	3.4	17.8	5,607	90.0	10.0	372	65.3	34.7	9.7	Sri Lanka
—	42.4[3]	30.4[3]	27.2[3]	33.122[3]	56.5[3]	28.5[3]	5.2[3]	4.8[3]	8,984	83.6	16.4	25	56.0	44.0	5.1	Sudan, The
4.81	53.1[1]	41.3[1]	0.8[1]	4.640[1]	39.2[1]	50.5[1]	0.5[1]	3.6[1]	68[2,3]	...	...	13[2,0]	53.8[2,3]	46.2[2,3]	3.3[2,3]	Suriname
2.7	65.1	16.5	15.8	1.128	19.1	64.8	0.5	5.9	233.4	98.5	1.5	25.0	67.4	32.6	3.4[3]	Swaziland
11.4	61.9	1.6	25.1	1,313.9	—48.5[6]—		—	40.5	...	...	...	...	...	...	...	Sweden
4.0	68.0	0.9	27.0	844.0	5.4	39.1	—	22.7	...	...	...	...	...	...	...	Switzerland
56.2[1,4]	18.2[1]	12.2[1]	13.4[1]	195.153[1]	27.3[1]	28.1[1]	3.1[1]	3.4[1]	14,341	94.3	5.7	810	79.3	20.7	25.2[5]	Syria
12.4[4]	74.3	9.9	3.4	10,816.8	21.6	59.5	5.9	4.1	3,244[2,3]	...	...	960[2,3]	78.1[2,3]	21.9[2,3]	1.6[2,3]	Taiwan
...	...	...	...	...	...	...	...	...	9.7	100.0	—	—	—	—	...	Tajikistan
54.3[4]	30.0	10.0	5.6	349.400	33.0	33.3	1.5	16.4	6,048	96.0	4.0	169	64.5	35.5	30.5	Tanzania
5.4[1,4]	89.0[1]	2.5[1]	3.1[1]	2,419.9[1]	2.7[1]	77.2[1]	3.2[1]	6.9[1]	13,238	60.3	39.7	2,144	67.4	32.6	4.9[3]	Thailand
1.1	58.3	30.8	9.8	175.8	20.0	38.0	24.5	10.9	1,138	95.3	4.7	20	50.0	50.0	3.6	Togo
8.0[4]	36.3	55.8	—	0.086	22.6	37.4	14.3	—	42.3	100.0	—	1.5	66.7	33.3	2.8	Tonga
12.7[4]	66.9	10.2	10.1	11.951	19.0	62.7	1.2	3.2	1,782	44.2	55.8	393	67.7	32.3	19.1	Trinidad and Tobago
5.8	86.0	2.0	6.2	9.195	18.2	41.1	—	15.6	7,418	81.4	18.6	1,252	68.2	31.8	18.5	Tunisia
17.5[4]	48.2	12.5	21.8	711,525.0	10.3	25.8	28.0	26.2	39,640	43.1	56.9	7,432	61.3	38.7	26.2	Turkey
...	...	...	...	...	...	...	...	...	...	...	...	...	...	...	...	Turkmenistan
...	...	...	...	...	...	...	...	...	...	...	...	...	...	...	...	Tuvalu
12.9[1,4]	40.2[1]	13.3[1]	36.6[1]	261.359[1]	41.2[1]	22.1[1]	3.1[1]	10.1[1]	2,495	92.1	7.9	43	57.0	43.0	21.8	Uganda
...	...	...	...	...	...	...	...	...	415.3	14.3	85.7	5.0	—	100.0	...	Ukraine
10.1	40.6	5.0	44.2	149.352	8.4	33.6	10.1	17.8	1,067[2,3]	...	...	380[2,3]	74.2[2,3]	25.8[2,3]	1.6[2,3]	United Arab Emirates
2.2[4]	49.6	0.5	47.8	1,428.1	16.4	25.3[6]	—	49.5	...	...	...	...	...	...	...	United Kingdom
10.3[4]	84.7	2.6	2.4	4,554.1	19.8	48.6	0.9	4.9	...	...	...	...	...	...	...	United States
5.6[4]	35.9	16.3	42.3	40,716.2	4.3	42.6[6]	2.7	36.8	3,092	36.6	63.4	438	53.7	46.3	16.4	Uruguay
...	...	...	...	...	...	...	...	...	15.5	100.0	—	—	—	—	...	Uzbekistan
3.2[4]	26.9	6.1	63.8	29.873	14.9	62.9[6]	2.4	11.9	39.6	97.5	2.5	1.4	60.7	39.3	0.9[1]	Vanuatu
14.2[4]	55.8	19.8	10.2	1,543.2	16.6	70.9[6]	1.8	4.3	25,252	14.3	85.7	1,807	16.8	83.2	10.7	Venezuela
...	...	...	...	...	...	...	...	...	16,694[2,3]	...	...	228[2,3]	17.0[2,3]	83.0[2,3]	14.3[2,3]	Vietnam
...	...	...	...	...	...	...	...	...	...	...	...	...	...	...	...	Virgin Islands (U.S.)
...	...	...	...	...	...	...	...	...	...	...	...	...	...	...	...	West Bank
...	...	...	...	...	...	...	...	...	...	...	...	...	...	...	...	Western Sahara
3.0[4]	56.8	32.4	7.8	0.137	20.2	55.6	2.2	2.8	117.4	99.3	0.7	4.6	71.7	28.3	8.8	Western Samoa
...	...	...	...	...	...	...	...	...	5,341	97.5	2.5	110	77.3	22.7	6.8[3]	Yemen
...	...	...	...	...	...	...	...	...	11,015	56.2	43.8	968	42.2	57.8	12.5[3]	Yugoslavia[13]
0.7[4]	5.4	46.3	47.6	4.582	35.3	23.5[6]	2.2	20.9	8,895	90.4	9.6	58	52.6	47.4	5.9[5]	Zaire
22.5[3]	35.7[3]	22.7[3]	19.1[3]	63.005[3]	20.9[3]	41.2[3]	5.0[3]	4.8[3]	4,809	91.5	8.5	251	62.5	37.5	20.6	Zambia
22.5[4]	61.3	11.3	5.0	10.519	38.8	31.7	9.5	7.7	2,783	67.7	32.3	468	71.8	28.4	25.3	Zimbabwe

[1]1992. [2]Includes long-term private debt not guaranteed by the government. [3]1991. [4]Includes claims on nonfinancial government (public) enterprises and/or local governments. [5]1990. [6]Includes foreign-currency deposits. [7]1993. [8]Treasury bill rate. [9]Short-term deposit rate. [10]Money market rate. [11]Republic of Cyprus only. [12]Data refer to former Czechoslovakia. [13]Data refer to the former Socialist Federal Republic of Yugoslavia.

Housing and construction

The present table summarizes data about the housing stock and the construction industries of the countries of the world. The principal focus is on the elements that are most comparable internationally: the age of the housing (by decade, so far as possible), the legal tenure of the householder, construction of exterior walls, principal physical amenities, sanitary arrangements, and the amount of space both absolutely (total area of the average dwelling in square metres [1 square metre equals 1.20 square yards, or 10.76 square feet]) and relatively (persons per room). The data on construction characterize the industry in terms of: (1) the portion of national gross domestic product (GDP) represented by each country's construction industry, (2) the number of new dwelling units constructed annually, their area, and the rate (in years) required to replace the total national stock of dwellings shown on the extreme left of the table, and (3), for nonresidential construction, the number of buildings or portions of buildings built for nonresidential purposes and their area in square metres.

Because housing patterns differ greatly from country to country, the portion of each country's housing stock for which data are compared was defined as specifically as possible. In general, the numbers refer to permanent, private dwelling units that are usually occupied year-round, whether or not actually occupied on the date of the housing census or survey. That definition implies the exclusion of certain housing that is often part of national housing censuses: vacation homes, second homes occupied less than half the year, collective or communal dwellings, and so on. The housing unit to which the data on tenure refer may be either the individual dwelling or the household, according to the reporting practice of the country concerned.

The data are collected mostly from national housing censuses and surveys. The majority of countries combine the housing census with the population census at five- to ten-year intervals. Some countries, however, can conduct a meaningful housing census only in the capital city or in the few largest cities; others may be able to collect and process data for only a few of the most important housing characteristics even when national coverage is complete. These choices may be dictated by the lack of funding to collect data for the entire country or by the perception, particularly in a tropical, rural country where adequate dwellings can be built by hand, that no urgent housing problem exists. These choices may be complex, however, as

Housing and construction

country	housing stock			decade built (percent)					tenure[c] (percent)			construction of exterior walls (percent)			
	year	dwelling units[a]	median age[b] (years)	1949 or earlier	1950–59	1960–69	1970–79	1980 or later	owned	rented	collective, vacant, other	traditional materials	sawn/ framed wood	masonry or cement	other
Afghanistan	1979	3,940,000[1]	...	...	...	...	...	...	55.2	23.5	21.3	...	...	...	...
Albania	1989	385,769[4]	22.6	14.0[5]	20.3[6]	19.0[7]	24.3[8]	22.4[9]	91.2	8.8	—	...	...	...	...
Algeria	1987	3,050,812	...	—51.4[13]—		6.4[14]	18.6	23.6	63.0[15]	24.6[15]	12.4[15]	...	...	...	...
American Samoa	1990	6,959	13.9	4.4	7.5	21.9	22.7	43.5	78.1	21.9	—	4.1[18]	56.3[18]	34.9[18]	4.7[18]
Andorra	1990	...	18.1	18.0	5.7	20.8	—55.5—		...	...	...	...	...	...	...
Angola	...	...	...	...	...	...	...	...	...	...	...	...	...	...	...
Antigua and Barbuda	1970	15,405[20]	11.1	23.3	31.4	46.1	—	—	55.9	40.4	3.7	...	...	...	...
Argentina	1980	10,096,888[12]	21.6	24.0	17.3	22.0	18.3	18.4	67.7	14.8	17.5	6.1	6.7	84.2	3.0
Armenia	1989	559,000[22]	...	...	...	...	...	...	...	...	...	...	...	...	...
Aruba	1991	19,224	27.7	17.0[24]	25.8[25]	12.1	16.8	28.3	70.6	26.7	2.7	—	7.7	90.6	1.7
Australia	1986	6,450,152[12]	26.1[26]	37.9[26]	10.4[26]	18.6[26]	—33.1[26]—		69.1[22]	26.7[22]	5.1[22]	...	...	...	...
Austria	1991	3,393,271	33.8	33.05	14.7[6]	18.17	18.5[8]	15.7[9]	50.0	38.7	11.3	—	5.1[4]	81.9[4]	13.0[4]
Azerbaijan	1989	1,381,000[22]	...	...	...	...	...	...	...	...	...	...	...	...	...
Bahamas, The	1980	54,308	30.7	—54.7—		25.6	—19.7—		51.4	37.4	11.2	4.0[33]	32.3	54.7	9.0
Bahrain	1981	52,810	15.2	58.3	14.5	—27.2—			48.2	33.6	18.2	—	—	93.6	6.4
Bangladesh	1981	14,785,048	...	...	...	...	...	...	89.7	5.0	5.3	20.0	11.6	5.0	63.4
Barbados	1990	75,211	19.1	—48.6—			22.9	28.5	76.1	20.4	3.5	0.2	61.2[36]	35.4	3.2
Belarus	1989	2,796,000[22]	...	...	...	...	...	...	...	...	...	...	...	...	...
Belgium	1991	3,748,165	...	37.0[5]	21.5[38]	13.1[39]	18.5[8]	9.9[9]	64.5	34.2	1.3	...	...	...	...
Belize	1991	37,658	...	—26.3—			17.8	55.9	65.9	22.8	11.3	5.1	65.6	24.8	4.5
Benin	1979	612,041	...	...	...	...	...	...	76.8	10.1	13.1	...	...	...	...
Bermuda	1991	22,061	...	—56.0—		15.8	12.0	16.2	43.4	52.4	4.2	—	1.7[18, 36]	95.1[18]	3.2[18]
Bhutan	...	...	...	...	...	...	...	...	...	...	...	...	...	...	...
Bolivia	1988	1,318,800	...	...	...	...	...	...	69.1	13.4	17.5	72.3	2.3	21.1	4.2
Bosnia and Herzegovina	1989	...	...	...	...	...	...	...	...	...	...	...	...	...	...
Botswana	1991	276,209	...	...	...	...	...	...	59.2	22.9	17.9	48.7	—	49.3	2.0
Brazil	1990	35,578,857	...	...	...	...	...	...	67.0	17.7	15.3	...	...	...	...
Brunei	1981	28,676	...	...	...	...	...	...	83.8	11.8	4.4	0.2	54.8	36.5	8.5
Bulgaria	1975	3,326,000[35]	17.9	—81.9—		11.1	—7.0—		77.3	22.7	—	...	...	...	...
Burkina Faso	1985	1,274,546[22]	...	...	...	...	...	...	...	...	...	...	...	...	...
Burundi	1979	938,000[45]	...	...	...	...	...	...	98.7	1.1	0.2	...	...	...	...
Cambodia	...	...	...	...	...	...	...	...	...	...	...	...	...	...	...
Cameroon	1976	1,390,896[20]	...	...	...	...	...	...	83.4	11.2	5.4	75.5	13.9	9.5	1.1
Canada	1986	10,079,442[12]	10.5	20.3[5]	20.0[6]	19.4[7]	—40.3[47]—		62.1	37.5	0.5	36.1	—	60.1	3.8
Cape Verde	1990	67,619	...	—73.6—				26.4	...	15.4[18]	...	82.2	7.1	2.5	8.2
Central African Republic	1975	519,314[35]	...	...	...	...	...	...	...	...	...	...	...	...	...
Chad	...	...	...	...	...	...	...	...	...	...	...	13.0	44.4	41.6	1.0
Chile	1982	2,510,275	20.4	—46.2—		21.1	—32.7—		63.1	18.7	18.2	...	...	...	...
China	1990	276,947,962	...	...	...	...	...	...	18.5[2, 27]	81.5[2, 27]	...	...	...	...	...
Colombia	1985	5,824,857	20.6[49]	54.6[49]	26.2[49]	19.2[49]	—		67.6	23.6	8.8	16.7	7.0	75.6	0.7
Comoros	1980	81,791	...	5.3	7.7	21.3	—63.7—		87.4	3.1	9.5	73.5	1.8	16.9	7.8
Congo	1984	363,140[22]	...	...	...	...	...	...	61.4	24.1	14.5	10.5	15.9	54.9	18.7
Costa Rica	1984	500,788	...	...	...	...	...	...	65.8	20.7	13.5	1.1	60.1	35.6	3.2
Côte d'Ivoire	1985	1,146,370[50]	...	...	...	...	...	...	64.0	35.4	0.6	...	...	...	...
Croatia	1991	1,575,644	...	...	...	...	...	...	...	...	...	3.8	33.2	61.5	1.4
Cuba	1981	2,363,364	24.6	23.2[51]	21.3[52]	21.6	—25.6—		60.0	16.5	23.5	11.9	—	87.6	0.5
Cyprus	1982	168,588	22.8	—39.9—		15.4	—44.7—		...	...	...	...	32.0[53]	67.1	0.9
Czech Republic	1991	3,705,691	42.4	41.7[5]	10.2[6]	14.5[7]	19.6[8]	14.0[9]	44.7[18]	41.7[18]	13.6[18]	...	...	...	...
Denmark	1991	2,374,970	36.6	44.3	10.0	16.4	18.1	11.2	53.8	44.5	1.7	...	73.0[54]	22.5	4.5
Djibouti	1982	25,000[48]	27.6	...	...	...	...	...	...	...	...	...	...	...	...
Dominica	1981	17,310[22]	...	58.4[40]	16.9[40]	21.1[40]	—3.6[40]—		66.4	21.9	11.7	—	75.1	20.8	4.1
Dominican Republic	1981	1,125,785[20]	...	...	...	...	...	...	72.0	17.0	11.0	31.1	31.3	31.4	6.2
Ecuador	1990	2,111,121	...	...	...	...	...	...	68.1	22.6	9.3	32.2	9.3	57.7	0.8
Egypt	1986	9,732,728	...	—37.1[2]—		—62.9[2]—			64.0	27.2	8.8	...	...	...	...
El Salvador	1971	680,456	...	...	...	...	...	...	56.7[55]	22.3[55]	21.0[55]	37.9	9.6	46.9	5.6
Equatorial Guinea	...	...	...	...	...	...	...	...	...	...	...	...	...	...	...
Eritrea	...	...	...	...	...	...	...	...	...	...	...	—	18.2	77.4	4.4
Estonia	1989	663,708	19.1	18.5[56]	11.8[57]	22.5[7]	27.0[8]	20.2[9]	18.3	81.5	0.2	...	...	...	...
Ethiopia	1984	9,300,000	...	...	...	...	...	...	48.8[2]	47.2[2]	4.0[2]	89.5	...	5.9	4.6
Faeroe Islands	1977	11,172[15]	32.5	—60.1—		21.8	—15.0—		84.5	9.9	5.6	—	43.9	53.5	2.6
Fiji	1986	124,098	...	...	...	...	...	...	75.5	11.1	13.4	9.0	26.4	29.8	34.8
Finland	1990	2,152,938	17.1	—29.6—		16.5	26.4	27.5	71.5	20.5	8.0	14.0[4, 15]	81.8[4, 15]	—4.2[4, 15]—	
France	1990	21,535,677	19.1[41]	—43.5[41, 60]—		11.6[41, 61]	27.3[41, 62]	17.7[41, 63]	54.4	39.6	6.0	...	...	...	...
French Guiana	1990	33,285	...	...	...	23.2[40]	...	...	41.3	—58.7—		29.4	—70.6—		2.2
French Polynesia	1988	39,513	10.8	—11.3—		16.0	27.6	45.1	68.5	21.2	10.3	36.9	15.8	45.2	2.2

planners are always aware that much housing is physically inadequate to protect dwellers from the elements, is disadvantageously placed in relation to tainted or disease-infested water supply or to the outfall of unprocessed sewage, or is built of materials (mud, skins, thatch, etc.) that may harbour pests or disease. In the developed countries, median age and the distribution of physical amenities provide strong indicators of the quality and availability of housing.

The data for the construction industry refer to the most recent year in which a broad range of countries could be surveyed.

The broadest indication of total activity in a national construction industry is its contribution to the national gross domestic product, since that figure, in addition to construction of buildings, also includes civil engineering projects, such as dams, roads and other transportation infrastructure, recreational facilities, irrigation and land reclamation works, and the like. The scope of the data relating to construction of buildings may be limited in several respects. It may be confined to activity capable of being surveyed in the modern or urban sectors only, may be limited to private new construction only or to government and government-financed activity only, or may refer to construction mortgaged or financed through certain organizations only. Depending on national data-collection systems, it usually excludes remodeling of old premises but may include extensions or enlargements of existing buildings. The data for new construction are usually of two principal types: authorized new construction or certification after construction that newly built structures meet building and fire codes and the like. Data for construction completed are naturally more meaningful but are not available for every country, necessitating the substitution of authorized construction data, which are usually available only for areas regulated by certain types of governmental authorities.

The following notes further define the column headings:
a. Data refer to permanent, private dwelling units that are usually occupied year-round, whether or not occupied on the census date.
b. Data are estimates unless specifically provided by a country source.
c. Data may be either for dwellings or for households, depending on country reporting practice.
d. Data may be either for construction completed or for construction authorized, depending on country reporting practice.

| physical amenities (percent) | | | sewage disposal (percent) | | | space[b] | | | construction industry (1991) | | | | | | country |
piped water	electricity	inside toilet or WC	closed public sewer or septic tank	open public sewer	other	average area (sq m)	rooms per dwelling unit	persons per room	percent of GDP	new residential[d] total no. of dwellings	floor area ('000 sq m)	years to replace nat'l stock	new nonresidential[d] number of units	floor area ('000 sq m)	
25.3[2]	66.5[2]	5.5[2]	5.5	77.9	16.6	...	5.5	2.1	5.8[3]	...	...	...	...	...	Afghanistan
33.0	...	21.3	...	...	...	35.7	1.8	2.6	6.4[10,11]	12,428[12]	...	37.4[12]	...	...	Albania
72.7	73.3[15]	...	51.0[15]	22.8[15]	26.2[15]	...	2.9	2.6	19.5[16]	71,433[17]	...	42.6[17]	...	...	Algeria
96.2	94.4	93.4	68.5	—31.5—		...	4.5	1.6	...	218[19]	...	21.5[19]	...	...	American Samoa
—	—	—	—	—	—	...	...	...	19.9[11]	...	91[18]	...	14[18]	47.5[18]	Andorra
									1.9						Angola
85.4	...	...	17.0	—83.0—		...	3.1	...	11.0[11]	764[19]	...	20.2[19]	210[18]	164.5[18]	Antigua and Barbuda
72.9	86.8	95.1	77.1	—22.9—		...	3.9	1.3	1.9[11]	67,528[21]	...	105.2[16]	...	...	Argentina
...	...	...	...	...	...	...	...	...	13.8	...	1,910[23]	...	...	...	Armenia
97.9	98.7[26]	89.2[26]	...	...	...	...	5.2	0.7	8.2[27]	158[12]	...	94.5[12]	113[12]	...	Aruba
97.1[28]	98.4[29]	92.2[26]	99.0[26]	—1.0[26]—		...	5.1[26]	0.6[26]	8.0[30]	132,700	11,170[31]	48.6	23,340[15]	13,727[31]	Australia
95.0[26]	...	88.7	94.3[26]	—	5.7[26]	85.0	4.3[19]	0.6[19]	7.3	36,553[11]	3,981	92.8[11]	500[15]	100[15]	Austria
...	...	...	...	...	...	...	...	...	10.6[10]	...	2,600[32]	...	...	[32]	Azerbaijan
83.0[34]	77.9	...	63.2	2.2	34.6	...	4.0	1.2	3.1[19]	1,027[17]	...	52.9[17]	62[17]	...	Bahamas, The
97.5	98.2	...	44.7	...	55.3	...	3.0[35]	2.3[29]	5.7	1,919[19]	...	27.5[19]	1,444[19]	...	Bahrain
56.0	6.6	2.6	1.5	—90.7—		...	2.0	2.9	5.7[31]	300,900[21]	...	49.1	...	...	Bangladesh
94.0	92.6	66.2	66.8	0.4	32.8	...	4.3	0.8	4.8	1,960[19]	...	...	...	...	Barbados
...	...	...	...	...	...	...	...	...	11.8[10,37]	...	5,395[32]	...	...	[32]	Belarus
99.6	100.0	91.9	62.5[40]	—37.5[40]—		86.3	4.3	0.6	6.0	30,100	23,636	72.3[16]	9,101[16]	36,684	Belgium
54.9	67.2	34.7	34.7	—65.3—		...	...	...	7.4[37]	...	6,185[41]	...	...	...	Belize
...	...	...	...	...	...	...	...	...	5.8[16]	...	...	...	...	...	Benin
97.4[18]	...	96.7[18]	96.7[18]	—3.3[18]—		...	3.2[18]	0.7[18]	4.9[42]	666[16]	...	36.6[16]	...	...	Bermuda
...	...	...	...	...	...	...	...	...	8.4	...	...	...	...	...	Bhutan
60.2	59.0	23.2	22.5	—77.5—		...	...	...	2.7	24,980[16]	...	52.8[16]	...	...	Bolivia
66.2	94.2	53.2	...	...	...	56.0	...	...	7.1[10,16]	26,568[12]	...	...	...	...	Bosnia and Herzegovina
77.0	5.4[26]	25.4[26]	8.6[26]	20.4[26]	71.0[26]	...	2.6	1.8	5.7[31]	...	96[17]	...	472[15]	132[17]	Botswana
73.4	87.8	...	60.1[19]	—39.9[19]—		...	5.1[18]	0.9[18]	7.1	...	20,090[17]	...	5,01?[15]	8,180[17]	Brazil
90.3	64.2	94.2	57.4	—42.6—		...	4.2	1.0	2.8[11]	1,954[41]	...	147.0	5	...	Brunei
74.6	99.8	33.2	33.2	—67.8—		45.3[43]	2.5[44]	1.1[44]	9.4[10,35]	62,800[16]	1,386[12]	53.0[16]	...	...	Bulgaria
...	...	...	...	...	...	...	...	...	0.6[17]	...	...	...	...	...	Burkina Faso
11.0	0.6	...	1.6	—98.4—		87.2[27]	2.4[27]	0.6[27]	4.1	...	...	...	...	...	Burundi
...	...	...	...	...	...	...	...	...	5.3[46]	...	...	...	...	...	Cambodia
22.0	5.9	2.2	2.2	70.4	27.6	...	4.1	1.2	5.5[16]	...	230[1]	...	53[1]	51.1[1]	Cameroon
99.8[35]	100.0	99.4[35]	98.9[26]	—1.1—		...	5.7	0.5	6.6[37]	218,304[16]	...	44.0[16]	14,846[15]	...	Canada
16.2	24.9	25.1	—3.4[18]—		96.6[18]	...	1.8[18]	2.8[18]	15.6[19]	...	31[27]	...	3[27]	0.5[27]	Cape Verde
...	...	...	...	...	...	...	...	...	1.7	...	15[11,48]	...	1[11,48]	...	Central African Republic
...	...	...	...	...	...	...	...	...	1.2[16]	...	...	...	...	...	Chad
81.4	84.7	...	63.2	36.4	0.4	59.9[35,43]	3.6	1.3	5.8	87,500	5,145	32.1[16]	...	2,003	Chile
89.4[2,17]	...	25.2[2,17]	47.0[2,17]	—53.0[2,17]—		37.0[17]	2.2[17]	1.8[17]	5.3	...	940,020	...	...	251,050	China
70.5	78.5	77.9	69.6	—30.4—		...	3.3	1.6	4.6	74,996[17]	5,648[16]	70.2[17]	...	1,994[16]	Colombia
12.9	5.7	...	2.1	—97.9—		33.7	2.5	2.1	5.9[37]	...	...	...	...	...	Comoros
30.5	8.8	16.6	—86.2[22]—		13.8[2]	...	3.7[2]	1.7[2]	1.8[16]	...	...	...	...	...	Congo
86.9	97.3	...	66.5	—33.5—		...	4.0	1.4	2.7	...	760[15]	...	2,868[15]	178[15]	Costa Rica
23.0	39.6	23.9	—68.5—		31.5	...	2.8	...	2.2[41]	...	...	...	...	...	Côte d'Ivoire
86.2	98.6	80.3	80.8	—19.2—		70.4	2.8	1.1	8.4	12,623	996	...	477	147	Croatia
74.1	82.9	45.2	60.9	9.3	30.1	71.0[43]	4.1	1.0	9.3[10,16]	25,344[35]	1,800[35]	93.2[35]	469[15]	1,803[15]	Cuba
100.0	98.1	74.5	95.6	—4.4—		...	4.6	0.8	10.2[37]	6,639[17]	979[17]	25.4[17]	1,103[13]	411[15]	Cyprus
96.9	100.0	88.5	...	—1.9—		70.5	2.7	1.0	11.3[11]	69,300	2,212	53.4	...	...	Czech Republic
100.0	100.0	99.2[16]	98.6[26]	—1.4[26]—		107.8	3.8	0.6	5.6[37]	15,888	1,449	149.5	6,141[17]	4,195	Denmark
45.0	58.0	82.0	26.0	23.0	51.0	...	1.9	6.9	5.8[16]	...	24.3[17]	...	26[17]	13.7[17]	Djibouti
91.1[1]	...	12.3[40]	12.3[40]	—87.7[40]—		...	2.8[40]	1.7[40]	7.3	...	...	...	...	...	Dominica
64.4	36.7[40]	14.1	52.1[40]	22.6[40]	25.3[40]	...	2.8[40]	1.5[40]	8.2[37]	...	648[17]	...	856[17]	508[17]	Dominican Republic
62.7[20]	77.7[20]	49.6[20]	39.5[20]	25.1[20]	35.4[20]	...	2.8	1.7	2.8	...	3,825[15]	...	596[15]	412.7[15]	Ecuador
73.1	87.0	...	...	...	...	...	3.3	1.5	6.1[30]	183,505[16]	...	53.0[16]	...	...	Egypt
48.0	34.1	6.3[29]	20.0[29]	—80.0[29]—		...	1.5[55]	3.3[55]	2.9[37]	694	341[15]	...	271	0.7[15]	El Salvador
...	...	...	...	...	...	...	...	...	5.6[16]	...	...	...	...	...	Equatorial Guinea
...	...	...	...	...	...	...	...	...	...	...	...	...	...	[32]	Eritrea
92.7	99.9	...	...	...	...	34.5	2.5	0.9	5.0	...	329[32]	...	...	[32]	Estonia
67.9[2]	...	55.2[2]	...	...	...	...	1.9	2.1	3.0[6]	...	260[58]	...	92[1]	63.3[58]	Ethiopia
99.7	99.5	95.0	80.7	8.1	2.2	...	5.5	1.1	10.6	223[37]	...	37.5[17]	...	...	Faeroe Islands
73.7	48.5	56.0	35.4[59]	—64.6[59]—		...	3.3	1.8	6.4[37]	2,767[17]	49	45.1[17]	105[17]	37	Fiji
95.1	95.9[4,15]	92.7	96.4	—3.6—		74.2	3.5	0.6	8.6	51,803	4,127	41.6	32,886[28]	34,050[23]	Finland
99.7[35]	...	93.5	73.8[50]	—26.2[50]—		77.0[55]	3.9	0.7	5.3	248,400[37]	...	83.2	...	42,950	France
77.0	86.7	62.0	34.3[27]	—65.7[27]—		...	2.8	1.2	9.3[16]	1,209	195	35.7[11]	...	28.5[15]	French Guiana
92.5	91.0	78.9	2.0[1]	67.0[1]	31.0[1]	...	3.8	1.3	6.1[11]	700[17]	85[32]	59.3[17]	156[17]	[32]	French Polynesia

Housing and construction (continued)

country	year	dwelling units[a]	median age[b] (years)	decade built (percent): 1949 or earlier	1950–59	1960–69	1970–79	1980 or later	tenure[c] (percent): owned	rented	collective, vacant, other	construction of exterior walls (percent): traditional materials	sawn/framed wood	masonry or cement	other
Gabon	1967	15,886[48]	...	...	...	...	...	...	—87.0—		13.0	...		...	...
Gambia, The	1983	202,199	...	...	...	...	...	...	63.9	21.9	14.2	82.9	—	12.9	4.2
Gaza Strip	1992	66,819[64]	23.0	4.7	31.2	14.3	25.8	23.9	89.1[15,65]	7.6[15,65]	3.3[15,65]	—		96.0	4.0
Georgia	1989	1,244,000[22]	...												
Germany[66]	1987	34,173,581[12]	...	30.6[60]	15.2[67]	23.6[68]	19.8[69]	10.8[70]	39.0	60.3	0.7	...		...	...
Ghana	1984	1,216,677	...						47.7[50]	25.3[50]	27.0[50]				
Gibraltar	1991	7,604[20]	25.0	37.3[72]	16.7[73]	15.6[74]	23.0[75]	7.4[76]	15.2	84.8	—				
Greece	1981	3,999,332	29.2	30.2[5]	27.4[6]	20.7[7]	—21.5—		73.1[77]	26.9[77]					
Greenland	1989	18,401	10.2	11.9[28]	18.8[28]	46.5[28]	—22.8[28]—		39.3[15]	—60.7[15]—					
Grenada	1981	21,017	18.3[40]	48.0[40]	29.0[40]	22.2[40]		—0.8[40]—	74.5	14.4	11.1	—	80.3	13.2	6.5
Guadeloupe	1990	112,478	...				8.1[77]		62.6	—37.4—		29.5		—70.5—	
Guam	1990	35,223	15.8	2.3	7.1	19.2	41.5	29.9	45.6	54.4	—	0.0	5.1	85.8	9.1
Guatemala	1981	1,259,598	12.5		—62.0—	10.0		—28.0—	64.7	11.3	24.0	55.6	21.1	19.3	4.0
Guernsey	1991	21,215[20]	...						68.4	31.6	—				
Guinea	1983	674,152[22]	...												
Guinea-Bissau	1979	123,936	...						...	...	...	95.7	0.1	2.3	1.9
Guyana	1980	149,734[22]	17.6		—43.5—	19.4		—37.1—	57.2	27.3	15.5	1.8	85.6	6.6	6.0
Haiti	1987	1,164,136	...			—75.9—		—24.1—	73.2	4.5	22.3	37.0	57.4	5.4	0.2
Honduras	1988	809,263	12.1[77]		—38.9[77]—	37.8[69,77]		—23.3[77]—	71.8[77]	16.5[77]	12.7[77]	61.0[77]	26.4[77]	11.7[77]	0.9[77]
Hong Kong	1991	1,580,072	...		—48.1—	13.6[26]		—38.3[26]—	42.6	53.0	4.4	...		...	...
Hungary	1990	3,817,000	16.4	32.9[5]	11.8[52]	14.9	23.2	17.2	75.9	23.7	0.4	21.8	14.6	63.6	—
Iceland	1984	70,777	25.6	—46.0—			—54.1—		70.3[78]	—29.7[78]—				71.9[78]	
India	1981	142,954,921	...						84.6[29]	15.4[29]	—				
Indonesia	1989	38,881,106[22]	...						87.0[29]	5.0[29]	8.0[29]				
Iran	1986	8,211,375	...		—82.5[28]—		—17.5[28]—		77.0	12.2	9.8	28.8	0.7	69.2	1.3
Iraq	1956	741,000	...						83.0	12.8	4.2				
Ireland	1981	1,038,000[12]	47.2		—60.0—	12.8		—26.2—	67.9	20.9	11.2				
Isle of Man	1991	27,316	...						66.5	32.5	1.0				
Israel	1983	1,104,270	...	9.5[79]		—90.5[80]—			74.3	23.1	2.6				
Italy	1991	19,509,362[22]	19.4[26]	30.8[5]	19.7[38]	27.5[81]	—22.0[47]—		58.9[26]	35.5[26]	5.6[26]				
Jamaica	1982	517,297[22]	17.0		—33.6—	28.8		—39.6—	46.7	32.6	20.7	7.1	28.4	54.4	10.1
Japan	1988	37,393,000	11.0	7.3[83]		—67.8[84]—		—24.9[45]—	62.1	33.8	4.2		73.1	25.5	1.4
Jersey	1991	32,463	...						49.6	48.0	2.4				
Jordan	1979	378,815	...						62.6	30.8	6.6				
Kazakhstan	1989	3,824,000[22]	...												
Kenya	1979	2,956,369[22]	...												
Kiribati	1990	11,301[22]	...						68.2[55]	17.9[55]	13.9[55]	64.4[55]		—35.6[55]—	
Korea, North	1987	4,054,027[22]	...												
Korea, South	1990	11,301,006	13.1	13.2	6.6	12.7	23.7	43.8	79.0	17.7	3.3	7.8	18.9	73.0	0.3
Kuwait	1985	228,781	14.5[18]		—12.2[18]—	38.8[18]		—34.5[18]—	38.2	53.6	8.2	46.5[4]		36.5[4]	17.0[4]
Kyrgyzstan	1989	856,000[22]	...												
Laos		...	...												
Latvia	1989	732,000[22]	...												
Lebanon	1970	483,908[20]	...	30.1[87]	40.2[88]	—29.4—									
Lesotho	1986	317,161[20]	...												
Liberia	1974[48]	263,333	...						62.5[49]	28.0[49]	9.5[49]				
Libya	1984	569,679	...												
Liechtenstein	1980	9,336	29.4	27.1[87]	15.0[88]	27.1	—30.8—		53.6	41.7	4.7				
Lithuania	1991	1,165,700[22]	...												
Luxembourg	1991	144,683	33.1	34.5[5]	17.6[6]	12.5[7]	17.8[8]	17.6[9]	66.1	28.3	5.6				
Macau	1991	89,193	...						65.9	32.0	2.1	—	0.5[40]	99.3[40]	0.2[40]
Macedonia	1989	...	...												
Madagascar	1975	1,671,473[22]	...												
Malawi	1987	1,859,572	...						39.6	—60.4—		51.6	3.1	44.4	0.9
Malaysia	1991	3,447,597	...						63.4[18]	25.0[18]	11.6[18]				
Maldives	1990	37,114	11.6	15.1	7.9	13.7	21.7	41.6	96.4	3.6	—	53.8	2.7	41.1	2.4
Mali	1987	1,364,079	...						84.2	8.5	7.3	75.9	8.5	10.3	5.3
Malta	1985	101,509	...		—81.8[90]—		—18.2[91]—		53.9	43.0	3.1	93.0[64]	...	92.9[64]	0.21[64]
Marshall Islands	1980	4,163	...	6.4	13.3	24.7	—55.5—		60.0	33.0	7.0	10.7	63.5	15.9	9.9
Martinique	1990	123,317	19.0		—54.5[92]—		17.9[63]	—27.6[76]—	60.9	32.5	6.6	20.4[27]		—79.6[27]—	
Mauritania	1977	246,462[22]	...		—19.7[1]—		24.3[1,93]	—56.0[1,94]—	75.9	15.2	8.9	—	4.2[1]	66.8[1]	28.9[1]
Mauritius	1990	223,821	...						77.8	14.8	7.3	50.4		—48.2—	1.4
Mayotte	1991	19,227	...						77.9	14.6	7.5	19.0	8.1	69.5	3.4
Mexico	1990	16,197,802	...		—51.4[18]—		15.4[18]	—33.2[18]—							
Micronesia	1980	11,562	...	3.8	5.2	21.3	—69.7—		51.8	39.2	9.0	6.0	41.8	14.6	37.6
Moldova	1989	1,144,000[22]	...												
Monaco	1990	16,122	30.0		—39.5[60]—	13.0[61]	19.7[62]	27.8[95]	23.3	60.5	16.2				
Mongolia	1969	242,000	...						100.0	—	—				
Morocco	1982	3,419,282[22]	...						41.2[2]	43.3[2]	15.5[2]	24.5	—	73.5	1.8
Mozambique	1980	2,712,439[22]	...									86.5	2.3	8.3	2.9
Myanmar (Burma)	1983	6,750,884	...						...	...		80.3	14.8	3.2	1.7
Namibia		...	...												
Nauru	1977	508[96]	...		—88.6[96]—		—11.4[96]—		11.0[86]	80.6[86]	8.4[86]				
Nepal	1981	2,585,154[22]	...						75.3[86]	10.7[86]	14.0[86]				
Netherlands, The	1990	5,802,400	25.4	28.2	11.8	18.0	21.7	20.3	43.2[15]	56.8[15]					
Netherlands Antilles	1981	56,070	21.0		—49.8—	19.7		—30.5—	64.8	35.2	—		18.3	78.8	2.9
New Caledonia	1989	44,047	...		—19.3—		—80.7—		56.4	29.7	13.9	6.4	11.7	61.7	20.2
New Zealand	1991	1,185,396	...		—64.1[26]—	19.2[26]		—16.2[26]—	72.4	22.7	4.9	30.8	45.6	21.8	1.8
Nicaragua	1971	330,422	...						64.4	20.3	15.3	66.5			
Niger	1988	1,163,424[22]	...												
Nigeria	1982[97]	...	...						37.0	46.0	17.0	29.0	—	71.0	—
Northern Mariana Islands	1990	8,210	...	1.0	2.5	6.4	13.3	76.8	39.5	56.6	3.9	0.0	13.5	66.5	20.0
Norway	1990	1,769,000	25.3	44.1[5]	20.6[6]	17.8[7]	20.7[8]	16.0[9]	80.3	—19.7—					
Oman	1989	2,469[27]	...						70.2	19.8	20.8				
Pakistan[98]	1980	12,597,000	17.2	17.1[87]	36.7[99]	24.9[100]		—21.3[101]—	78.4	7.7	13.9	49.2	2.4	41.4	7.1

physical amenities (percent)			sewage disposal (percent)			space[b]			construction industry (1991)						country
									percent of GDP	new residential[d]			new nonresidential[d]		
piped water	electricity	inside toilet or WC	closed public sewer or septic tank	open public sewer	other	average area (sq m)	rooms per dwelling unit	persons per room		total no. of dwellings	floor area ('000 sq m)	years to replace nat'l stock	number of units	floor area ('000 sq m)	
...	50.5	...	...	...	...	...	3.0	1.3	6.2[11]	...	216[50]	...	75[50]	119.4[50]	Gabon
21.9	...	...	...	...	...	...	2.0	2.0	6.5[30]	...	...	...	14[50]	...	Gambia, The
97.2[15]	97.6	98.4	...	...	...	144.3[43]	2.6[15]	2.5[15]	18.2	1,247[17]	180[17]	53.6[17]	...	31.1[17]	Gaza Strip
...	...	...	...	...	...	...	...	...	7.8[37]	...	1,005[16]	...	...	...	Georgia
100.0	99.7	98.3	97.1[18]	—2.9[18]—		82.1[12]	4.3[12]	0.6[12]	5.7[37]	275,951	32,272	123.8	48,662	39,420	Germany[66]
34.0[71]	...	...	...	...	...	...	...	...	3.1[11]	...	...	...	...	...	Ghana
96.7[26]	100.0[26]	99.2	100.0[26]	—	—	...	3.3	1.1	...	...	...	...	...	...	Gibraltar
81.3[29]	89.0[29]	93.0[29]	...	...	...	138.4[19]	3.3[19]	0.9[00]	6.6	107,034[35]	46,434[11,23]	37.4[35]	11,471[28]	12,536[11,23]	Greece
82.7[28]	84.2[28]	30.1[28]	39.1[28]	—60.9[28]—		72.0[43]	2.8	1.1	16.7	255[16]	18[16]	71.1[16]	...	12.3[15]	Greenland
86.5[40]	...	23.0[40]	23.0[40]	—77.0[40]—		...	2.9	1.6	10.8	...	...	...	...	...	Grenada
83.2	89.4	78.2	24.6[27]	—75.4[27]—		...	3.3	1.0	4.7[27]	676[16]	...	126.7[16]	...	166[19]	Guadeloupe
99.2	98.4	97.0	97.0	—3.0—		...	5.0	0.8	7.9[27]	417[17]	...	67.4[17]	500[17]	...	Guam
52.0	37.0	14.3	20.1	3.4	76.5	...	2.4	2.2	2.0	...	495[16,32]	...	...	32	Guatemala
96.5[28]	...	98.8	65.9	—34.1—		...	5.8[19]	0.5[19]	...	165[16]	...	128.6[16]	...	...	Guernsey
...	...	...	...	...	...	...	...	...	5.6[11]	...	...	...	...	...	Guinea
3.7	3.9	...	4.2	—95.8—		...	1.4	4.5	6.4[16]	...	...	...	...	...	Guinea-Bissau
38.1	69.0	29.0	10.4	—89.6—		...	2.9	1.8	5.2[11]	...	...	...	56[21]	...	Guyana
5.8	21.9	45.8	2.0[27]	—98.0[27]—		...	2.3	2.1	6.2	...	...	...	...	...	Haiti
55.0[18]	25.0[18]	13.0[18]	14.4[18]	—85.6[18]—		...	2.4[18]	2.3[18]	4.4	1,442[41]	214[19]	...	148[19]	98[19]	Honduras
85.7[26]	...	69.2[49]	65.4[49]	—34.6[49]—		53.2[29]	3.1[49]	2.8[49]	5.0	67,579[17]	714[37]	25.5[17]	303[17]	1,578[37]	Hong Kong
90.1	98.8[41]	75.9	85.5	—14.5—		52.3	2.6	1.0	5.8	50,600[35]	4,353[16]	78.3[35]	3,433[15]	21,886[15,23]	Hungary
99.1[78]	94.6[78]	93.6[78]	86.5[70]	—13.5[78]—		...	4.8[78]	0.9[78]	8.6	1,594	660[23]	...	552	729[23]	Iceland
67.0[49]	53.5[2,49]	20.0[49]	...	...	...	...	2.0[29]	2.6[29]	5.7[31]	...	...	...	13,908[41]	...	India
12.9	44.0	26.6[18]	22.8[29]	—77.2[29]—		59.0	3.3	1.7[29]	5.7	...	...	...	...	...	Indonesia
74.6	84.1	43.6	...	...	...	60.0[28]	2.8	1.8	3.8[30]	124,891[15]	13,081[35]	65.0[15]	5,235[16]	853[35]	Iran
20.8	17.1	...	...	...	...	...	2.4	...	8.0[11]	...	11,521[17]	...	11,799[15]	1,176[17]	Iraq
94.8	94.7[29]	93.0	72.3[29]	—27.7[29]—		...	3.7[15]	1.0[15]	5.0[17]	23,568[37]	2,741[11]	44.0[37]	...	3,146[11]	Ireland
...	...	99.5	...	...	...	...	...	0.4[26]	9.8[17]	168[17]	...	161.0[17]	...	...	Isle of Man
96.5[29]	96.5[29]	98.8	99.0[77]	—1.0[77]—		149.8[43]	3.0	1.2	5.3[16]	69,600[37]	7,452[37]	25.9[12]	...	1,464[37]	Israel
98.7[26]	99.0[29]	94.0[26]	95.7[29]	—4.3[29]—		85.3[26]	4.0[15]	0.8[26]	5.9	197,978	93,214[23]	98.5	29,235[16]	103,628[23]	Italy
76.9	48.6	35.2	...	...	...	...	2.4[40]	4.3	12.9[37]	...	...	136.4	...	6,989[82]	Jamaica
94.0[1]	...	65.8	61.2[1]	—38.8[1]—		89.9	4.9	0.7	8.7	1,370,000	117,219	28.7	...	127,560[11]	Japan
94.0[85]	...	93.0[26]	96.0[85]	...	...	...	5.0	0.5	...	354[17]	...	82.5[17]	...	...	Jersey
77.2	77.3	55.4[86]	15.7	—84.3—		...	...	...	5.5[37]	6,292[19]	1,709[19]	60.2[19]	820[19]	557[19]	Jordan
50.0	...	...	...	—41.0—		...	...	...	9.0	...	6,125	...	...	...	Kazakhstan
...	...	...	...	...	...	...	...	...	6.9[11]	...	828	...	85[19]	184[19]	Kenya
33.1	23.7[55]	53.3	...	...	...	...	...	...	3.0[16]	...	...	...	...	...	Kiribati
...	...	...	...	...	...	...	...	...	...	...	...	...	...	...	Korea, North
74.1	49.9[40]	51.3	...	...	...	80.6	2.3	1.5	9.1	750,000[16]	60,407	9.8[10]	36,801[17]	67,410	Korea, South
53.9[18]	99.5[18]	...	95.9[10]	—64.1[18]—		...	4.0[18]	1.8[18]	2.0[11]	9,735[19,45]	2,563[16]	23.5[17,45]	370[17]	416[16]	Kuwait
...	...	...	...	...	...	...	...	...	7.7	...	1,232	...	...	...	Kyrgyzstan
...	...	...	...	...	...	...	...	...	3.7	...	...	...	...	...	Laos
...	...	...	...	...	...	...	...	...	7.2[10,37]	...	432	...	...	...	Latvia
...	93.4	82.9	...	...	...	...	...	...	3.7[37]	...	4,938[17,32]	...	...	32	Lebanon
...	...	...	...	...	...	...	...	...	18.9	...	...	...	52[19]	...	Lesotho
...	...	...	...	...	...	...	2.3[15]	1.7	2.2[16]	...	...	...	...	...	Liberia
70.1[49]	72.1[49]	40.6[49]	40.6[49]	—59.4[49]—		...	3.3[49]	1.8[49]	12.7[16]	...	...	...	...	...	Libya
96.5	96.6	86.7	90.2	—9.8—		102.0	3.0	1.4	...	...	257[32]	...	...	271[32]	Liechtenstein
96.0	...	...	...	...	...	57.9	...	...	4.9	15,300[11,20]	872[37]	...	...	...	Lithuania
99.4	...	99.4	93.0[40]	—7.0[40]—		114.2	5.4[18]	0.5[18]	7.5	2,982[37]	560[37]	53.6	91[37]	273[37]	Luxembourg
98.0	99.8	97.9	...	...	...	...	3.1	1.3	...	10,796	886	20.2	1,003[11]	406[11]	Macau
72.0	96.4	56.3	...	...	...	68.6	...	...	5.7[16]	10,189[11]	...	...	...	...	Macedonia
...	...	...	...	...	...	...	...	...	3.8[17]	...	24[17]	...	...	8.9[17]	Madagascar
23.6	22.8[18]	33.4[18]	33.0[64]	—67.0[64]—		...	1.9	1.7	4.4[37]	...	...	...	...	...	Malawi
65.0[18]	64.4[18]	...	56.4[18]	4.4[18]	30.2[18]	...	2.3[40,89]	2.6[40,89]	3.8	...	8,809[19]	...	...	960[10]	Malaysia
...	53.4[15]	...	43.2	—56.8—		...	4.4	1.5	8.7	680[17]	...	54.6[17]	...	...	Maldives
3.8	3.6	1.3	...	...	...	...	2.6	2.2	4.0	10,025[21]	...	...	...	...	Mali
98.0	98.0	98.8	98.0	15.4[64]	6.1[64]	...	3.2[64]	1.3[64]	...	4,605[34]	...	22.5[34]	2,319[17]	...	Malta
49.8[35]	56.0[35]	43.7[35]	28.6	—71.4—		...	...	...	7.5[26]	...	...	...	...	...	Marshall Islands
94.1	90.2	89.0	41.8[27]	—58.2[27]—		...	3.2	0.9	3.6[27]	1,528	...	55.8	...	56.2[26]	Martinique
...	...	...	...	...	...	...	...	...	7.9[41]	...	42[32,41]	...	...	32	Mauritania
94.7	96.2	63.3	63.3	—36.7—		...	3.6[1]	1.4[1]	7.3[37]	4,592[21]	887	48.7	552[17]	227	Mauritius
42.5	32.2	6.7	54.4	—45.6—		...	2.2	2.2	...	616[19]	...	21.3[19]	...	...	Mayotte
79.4	87.5	45.0[18]	60.9	2.7	36.4	...	3.4	1.5	3.9	...	...	...	61,386[26]	...	Mexico
40.0	28.3	...	8.0	—92.0—		...	...	...	...	...	...	...	...	...	Micronesia
...	...	...	...	...	...	...	...	...	6.9	...	1,594[11]	...	...	...	Moldova
100.0	100.0	96.2	98.4[50]	—1.6[50]—		...	2.8	0.8	...	...	...	...	...	...	Monaco
0.3	47.5	...	...	...	...	...	...	...	5.8[16]	...	112	...	...	176[19]	Mongolia
30.5[2]	37.2[2]	50.2[2]	...	...	...	...	2.7	2.2	5.3	51,911[19]	2,156[15]	65.9[19]	1,014[15]	457[15]	Morocco
12.7	4.2	...	...	...	...	...	...	...	13.2[11]	...	247[77]	...	...	127[77]	Mozambique
...	...	...	...	...	...	...	...	...	1.6[90]	1,193[50]	...	...	1,483[58]	...	Myanmar (Burma)
...	...	...	...	...	...	...	...	...	2.3[11]	...	...	...	...	...	Namibia
...	49.2	...	...	...	...	...	3.6[86]	1.6[86]	...	...	...	...	...	...	Nauru
47.7	30.2	6.1	...	...	...	...	3.7	2.0	7.2[30]	...	...	...	...	...	Nepal
100.0	98.0	100.0	90.0[17]	—10.0[17]—		...	4.1[15]	0.7[16]	5.8	82,888	35,616[18,23]	70.0	15,091[16]	49,968[16,23]	Netherlands, The
79.6	96.9	82.0	...	...	...	...	4.2	1.0	9.5[35]	547	...	150.2	173	...	Netherlands Antilles
90.1	85.3	70.9	76.7	—23.3—		...	3.3	1.2	4.9[35]	772	46[19]	57.1	1[41]	...	New Caledonia
92.7[29]	...	97.1[29]	...	...	...	126.3[17,43]	5.6	0.5	4.2[31]	19,092[16]	2,543[17]	61.2[16]	...	3,218[17]	New Zealand
27.9	40.9	19.3	19.2	—80.8—		...	2.2	2.1	3.5	...	569[32]	...	...	32	Nicaragua
...	...	...	...	...	...	...	...	...	2.3	...	...	...	...	...	Niger
...	81.3	7.0	...	...	...	...	1.4	3.0	1.8	91,008[87]	...	...	1,592[18]	...	Nigeria
91.0	94.1[18]	79.5	81.7	—18.3—		...	3.6	1.1	...	...	...	...	...	...	Northern Mariana Islands
97.5[40]	...	94.6	86.8[18]	—13.2[18]—		103.5	4.1	0.6	3.6	21,689	2,696	82.2	4,954[15]	2,228	Norway
...	...	...	...	...	...	...	...	...	3.1[11]	1,043[19]	...	...	266[19]	...	Oman
20.3	30.6	25.1	...	...	...	...	1.9	3.3	3.8[30]	...	...	...	...	...	Pakistan[98]

Housing and construction (continued)

country	housing stock			decade built (percent)					tenure[c] (percent)			construction of exterior walls (percent)			
	year	dwelling units[a]	median age[b] (years)	1949 or earlier	1950–59	1960–69	1970–79	1980 or later	owned	rented	collective, vacant, other	traditional materials	sawn/ framed wood	masonry or cement	other
Panama	1990[102]	524,284[20]	18.0[18]	47.4[18]	12.8[18]	18.1[18]	——21.7[18]——		75.5	15.7	8.8	16.9	...	81.2	1.9
Papua New Guinea	1980	556,519[22]	...						40.0[50]	——60.0[50]——		...	...	...	...
Paraguay	1982	868,284[37]	21.1	——56.0——		17.0	——27.0——		80.4	10.5	9.1	21.5	29.7	47.6	1.2
Peru	1981	4,049,000[12]	...	——30.9——			——69.1——		72.6	14.8	12.6	54.3	7.0	37.8	0.9
Philippines	1980	11,380,000[11, 22]	...	——78.5[40]——			——21.5[40]——		80.2	12.4	7.4	36.3	33.6	23.8	6.3
Poland	1988	11,967,021	...	35.0[83]	——33.7[84]——		——31.3[47]——		35.2	64.3	0.9	——14.1[55]——		——85.9[55]——	
Portugal	1981	4,188,655[12]	33.7	——53.3——		17.5	——29.2——		56.7	38.8	4.6	—	0.7	61.0	38.3
Puerto Rico	1990	1,188,985	18.0	9.0	12.8	22.9	29.5	25.8	72.1	27.9	...	—	15.1	83.6	1.3
Qatar	1986	64,543	...	...	...	...	...	...	21.9	72.0	6.1	...	...	...	...
Réunion	1990	157,853	14.3	——47.6[92]——		19.9[63]	——32.5[76]——		54.6[27]	34.5[27]	10.9[27]	...	...	...	...
Romania	1992	7,632,000	...	...	...	...	...	...	78.6	20.8	0.6	...	...	...	...
Russia	1989	40,246,000[22]	...	...	...	...	...	...	...	...	...	...	...	...	...
Rwanda	1978	1,055,950[22]	...	...	...	...	...	...	95.3	1.7	3.0	88.6	7.9	1.3	2.2
St. Kitts and Nevis	1980	11,615[22]	24.2	——63.5——		17.9	——14.7——		54.7	29.5	15.8	—	76.2	21.3	2.5
St. Lucia	1991	33,079	13.5	——17.0——		12.4	26.0	44.6	72.4	26.8	0.8	—	53.4	46.1	0.5
St. Vincent and the Grenadines	1980	27,110	...	—					72.1	16.0	11.9	—	53.8	42.9	3.3
San Marino	1979	8,384[11]	...	...	...	...	...	...	73.5	21.9	4.6	...	...	...	...
São Tomé and Príncipe	1981	30,056	...	...	...	...	...	...	...	...	...	2.2	29.8	67.2	0.8
Saudi Arabia	1955[48, 104]	...	...	...	...	...	...	...	...	...	...	...	...	...	...
Senegal		13,000							——84.6——		15.4	...	...	...	...
Seychelles	1987	15,050	...	...	...	...	...	...	63.7	25.1	11.2	1.0	40.0	52.0	7.0
Sierra Leone		...	...	...	...	...	...	...	...	...	...	...	...	...	...
Singapore	1980	513,224	...	——63.2——			——36.8——		55.0	39.6	5.4	4.7	——95.3——		
Slovakia	1991	1,617,829	26.9	17.1[5]	17.3[6]	20.3[7]	25.4[8]	19.9[9]	...	...	...	—	38.0[53]	61.4	0.6
Slovenia	1989														
Solomon Islands	1986	43,842[22]	...	...	...	...	...	...	27.4[28]	43.0[28]	29.6[28]	...	...	...	...
Somalia		...	...	...	...	...	...	...	...	...	...	...	...	...	...
South Africa	1991	3,599,518[105]	18.6[40]	40.6[40]	24.2[40]	35.2[40]			54.5	34.0	11.5	...	...	...	...
Spain	1991	11,824,851[20]	39.4[18]	39.2[18, 106]	23.4[18, 107]	18.5[7, 18]	——18.9[18, 47]——		67.5	14.9	17.6	...	...	...	...
Sri Lanka	1981	2,811,406	...	...	...	...	...	...	69.4	10.1	20.5	...	...	...	...
Sudan, The	1983	...	...	...	...	...	...	...	86.2	8.1	5.7	76.5	4.4	16.7	2.4
Suriname	1980	77,658	...	——52.4——			——47.6——		...	...	...	38.9[109]	——61.1[109]——		
Swaziland	1986	122,369	...	...	...	...	...	...	...	...	...	65.9	——34.1——		
Sweden	1990	3,830,037	20.0	33.2	14.2	22.4	22.2	10.6	55.9	40.0	4.1	...	...	...	...
Switzerland	1990	2,800,953	28.5	33.2[87]	15.9[88]	19.4[7]	17.2[8]	14.3[9]	31.3	66.5	2.2	...	...	...	...
Syria	1987	1,836,195	...	——91.3[40]——			——8.7[40]——		81.6[40]	15.5[40]	2.8[40]	...	...	...	...
Taiwan	1990	4,237,174[20]	17.2	6.1[5]	6.7[6]	15.8[7]	42.6[8]	28.8[9]	78.5	12.8	8.7	...	...	...	...
Tajikistan	1989	799,000[22]	...	...	...	...	...	...	...	...	...	...	...	...	...
Tanzania	1978	3,554,793	...	——17.0——			——83.0——		75.4	19.4	5.2	83.0		16.3	0.7
Thailand	1980	12,224,400[11, 22]	...	22.0[40]	25.0[40]	53.0[40]	—		84.3[19]	9.3[19]	6.4[19]	15.1	70.0	6.3	8.6
Togo	1958–60[2]	22,274	...	...	...	...	...	...	...	...	...	...	...	...	...
Tonga	1986	15,091	22.5	——59.4[110]——		20.3[111]	——20.3[112]——		82.0	3.5	14.5	35.1[28]	45.4[28]	15.3[28]	4.2[28]
Trinidad and Tobago	1980	314,739[11]	...	——56.3——		14.5	——29.2——		64.6	34.0	1.4	3.3	32.6	53.8	10.3[36]
Tunisia	1984	1,703,279[113]	...	...	...	...	...	...	78.9	12.6	8.5	...	...	...	...
Turkey	1986	10,855,495	8.4	16.2[110]	6.2[114]	19.6[100]	——58.0[101]——		77.2	12.0	10.8	——28.8——		——71.2——	
Turkmenistan	1989	598,000[22]	...	...	...	...	...	...	...	...	...	...	...	...	...
Tuvalu	1979	1,079	...	...	...	...	...	...	81.6	12.1	6.6	64.9	4.2	31.0	—
Uganda		...	...	...	...	...	...	...	...	...	...	...	...	...	...
Ukraine	1989	14,057,000[22]	...	...	...	...	...	...	...	...	...	...	...	...	...
United Arab Emirates	1980	153,009	15.0	0.8	1.3	11.4	——86.5——		36.2	45.2	18.6	2.9	7.3	87.3	2.5
United Kingdom[116]	1991	21,897,322	32.6[26]	54.0[26]	13.0[26]	16.6[26]	——16.4[26]——		66.4	33.6	—	...	...	...	...
United States	1990	102,263,678	25.0	32.9[15]	14.0[15]	16.6[15]	——36.5[15]——		64.2	35.8	—	...	...	...	...
Uruguay	1985	852,400	...	...	...	...	...	...	57.6	23.2	19.2	...	...	...	...
Uzbekistan	1989	3,415,000[22]	...	...	...	...	...	...	...	...	...	...	...	...	...
Vanuatu	1979	28,252[16, 22]	...	...	...	...	...	...	40.9[48]	25.7[48]	33.4[48]	61.4	7.7	13.6	17.2
Venezuela	1990	3,534,507	...	...	...	...	...	...	75.8	13.9	10.3	14.6	0.5	84.9	—
Vietnam	1989	12,958,041[22]	...	...	...	...	...	...	...	...	...	...	...	...	...
Virgin Islands (U.S.)	1990	39,290	14.7	10.0[18]	8.9[18]	42.7[18]	——38.4[18]——		44.6	55.4	—	...	...	...	...
West Bank	1992	119,165[64]	12.2	8.0	12.7	24.6	26.2	28.6	86.2[65]	11.5[65]	2.3[65]	23.0	—	75.3	1.7
Western Sahara	1982	19,559	...	...	...	...	...	...	32.2[51]	62.3[51]	5.5[51]	...	...	...	...
Western Samoa	1981	33,402	...	...	...	...	...	...	80.1	2.0	17.9	62.3	24.4	8.6	4.7
Yemen[117]	1988[118]	1,701,203	...	...	...	...	...	...	83.9	5.2	10.9	...	...	...	...
Yugoslavia	1981[119]	3,074,000[37]	...	31.1	12.7	26.8	——29.4——		67.1	25.0	7.9	...	——82.6——		17.4
Zaire	1984	5,669,600[22]	...	...	...	...	...	...	47.4[48, 64]	38.3[48, 64]	14.3[48, 64]	52.4[48]	——45.5[48]——		2.1[48]
Zambia	1980	1,128,356	...	...	...	...	...	...	78.8[120]	21.1[120]	...	...	...	...	...
Zimbabwe	1969	925,581	...	...	...	...	...	...	65.1[105]	32.6[105]	2.3[105]	55.9[121]	——44.1[121]——		

[1]1983. [2]Urban only. [3]1989–90. [4]Data refer to buildings. [5]1945 or earlier. [6]1946–60. [7]1961–70. [8]1971–80. [9]1981 or later. [10]Percentage of net material product. [11]1990. [12]1991. [13]1962 or earlier. [14]1963–69. [15]1985. [16]1989. [17]1987. [18]1980. [19]1986. [20]Occupied dwellings only; may include seasonal and/or temporary housing. [21]Average annual gain in housing stock during intercensal interval. [22]Data refer to households. [23]Volume in cubic metres. [24]1940 or earlier. [25]1940–59. [26]1981. [27]1982. [28]1976. [29]1971. [30]1991–92. [31]1990–91. [32]Residential includes nonresidential. [33]Stucco. [34]1993. [35]1988. [36]Includes wood and brick, and wood and concrete. [37]1992. [38]1946–61. [39]1962–70. [40]1970. [41]1984. [42]1983–85 average. [43]Average size of dwelling unit in year to which new dwellings and floor area data refer. [44]1986–87. [45]Data refer to compound dwellings, which usually contain two or three dwelling units each. [46]1966. [47]1971 or later. [48]Capital city only. [49]1973. [50]1975. [51]1934–45. [52]1946–59. [53]Includes prefabricated units. [54]Includes corrugated steel. [55]1978. [56]1950 or earlier. [57]1951–60. [58]1987–88. [59]1977. [60]1948 or earlier. [61]1949–61. [62]1962–74. [63]1975–81. [64]1967. [65]Excludes refugee camps. [66]Former West Germany. [67]1949–57. [68]1958–68. [69]1969–78. [70]1979 or later. [71]1979. [72]1952

physical amenities (percent)			sewage disposal (percent)			space			percent of GDP	construction industry (1991) new residential			new nonresidential		country
piped water	electricity	inside toilet or WC	closed public sewer or septic tank	open public sewer	other	average area (sq m)	rooms per dwelling unit	persons per room		total no. of dwellings	floor area ('000 sq m)	years to replace nat'l stock	number of units	floor area ('000 sq m)	
80.7	65.7[18]	74.3[18]	44.2	—55.8—		...	2.8	1.6	5.3[37]	15,149[17]	...	34.6[17]	90[15]	142.5[15]	Panama
50.0	56.0	40.0	...	...		...	...	...	6.2	587[19]	...	...	...	...	Papua New Guinea
...	...	26.4	...	...		...	2.2[103]	2.4[103]	5.5	...	61[28]	...	2,715[17]	365[17]	Paraguay
73.4	89.5	78.0	58.1	—41.9—		42.4	2.6	2.0	6.6[37]	...	952[19]	...	...	...	Peru
41.4	46.0	35.0	44.1	—55.9—		...	2.4[103]	2.3[103]	4.1	...	3,486[35]	...	2,807[15]	3,222[35]	Philippines
84.3	96.2[55]	68.9	67.0[55]	—33.0[55]—		55.6[41]	3.2	1.0	10.2	129,492	13,856[17]	56.9[16]	41,914[4]	...	Poland
99.1[12]	99.4[12]	78.1[12]	75.5	—24.5—		75.4[16,43]	5.0[35]	0.8	7.5[11]	62,081	4,240	62.5	6,880[17]	2,045	Portugal
95.6	97.4[85]	94.7	95.7	—4.3—		...	4.8[18]	0.8[18]	2.1[35]	11,710[17]	1,740[17]	82.8[17]	900[15]	41.0[15]	Puerto Rico
...	93.2	...	—50.5—	49.5		...	4.1	1.3	3.9	1,095[17]	391[19]	58.9[17]	258[19]	168[19]	Qatar
70.0[27]	81.6[27]	50.7[27]	52.4[27]	—47.6[27]—		...	3.6[27]	1.2[27]	9.9[16]	8,499[16]	...	16.6[16]	...	...	Réunion
...	48.6[46]	...	12.2[46]	—87.8[46]—		89.6[43]	2.6	1.4	5.7[11]	60,400[16]	5,409[16]	98.6[16]	...	...	Romania
...	...	...	...	...		...	...	...	9.1	...	49,400	...	...	...	Russia
...	...	...	...	...		...	...	...	6.8[16]	435[41]	60[26]	...	...	...	Rwanda
46.3	57.5	33.5	31.8[23]	—68.2[23]—		...	3.0	1.1	13.5	171[21]	...	68.0[21]	63[41]	34[26]	St. Kitts and Nevis
64.7	72.9	35.7	35.7	—64.3—		...	3.4	1.2	6.0[11]	471[4,17]	70	57.2[4,17]	121[19]	18.3	St. Lucia
95.0[1]	...	...	22.0[1]	—78.0[1]—		...	2.8	1.8	9.5	465[17,32]	88[17,32]	...	32	32	St. Vincent and the Grenadines
99.8	100.0	98.3	98.3	—1.7—		...	4.5	0.8	...	131	...	64.0	60	...	San Marino
...	22.0	9.2	9.8	...		...	...	...	8.8[16]	...	...	...	...	...	São Tomé and Príncipe
...	...	...	...	...		...	...	...	9.1[11]	...	16,078	...	2,205	...	Saudi Arabia
87.7	95.9	...	...	...		...	2.3	1.5	2.9[11]	...	257[17]	...	34[17]	33[17]	Senegal
77.0	75.8	95.0	33.1[59]	—66.9[59]—		...	4.1	1.1	4.2[11]	4,802[32,59]	...	...	46[19]	32	Seychelles
...	...	...	...	...		...	...	...	1.3[31]	...	...	...	...	...	Sierra Leone
90.6[40]	98.3	63.6[40]	63.6[40]	—36.4[40]—		...	1.8[40]	2.5[40]	6.7[37]	14,170[11]	2,957	36.2[11]	1,991	2,226[11]	Singapore
91.8	...	80.1	87.6	—12.4—		71.7	2.9	1.1	12.0[11]	...	1,147	...	...	...	Slovakia
93.0	98.9	75.3	...	...		66.1	...	...	8.7	7,759[16]	148	...	18	...	Slovenia
92.7[28]	79.6[28]	89.2	89.2[28]	—10.8[28]—		10.8[28]	2.3[28]	2.0[28]	4.3[11]	...	...	...	...	...	Solomon Islands
...	...	...	...	...		...	...	...	3.8	...	...	...	...	...	Somalia
...	...	...	...	...		117.6[43]	3.4[40]	...	3.1	39,266[16]	4,619[16]	34.5[16]	...	1,316[16]	South Africa
98.7	99.2	97.1	87.9[18]	—12.1[18]—		86.6	4.4[40]	...	8.6	281,059	...	43.9	...	...	Spain
18.2	14.9	4.7	4.7	—95.3—		18.6[40]	2.5	2.1	7.1	59,637[19]	...	47.2[19]	...	...	Sri Lanka
29.4	9.9	70.2[2,46]	2.6[2,46]	—97.4[2,46]—		...	2.2[46]	2.5[46]	4.5[100]	...	...	...	...	...	Sudan, The
62.9	82.0	40.4	19.6[109]	—80.4[109]—		...	2.1	1.9	8.6	...	355[15,23]	...	161[15]	...	Suriname
42.5	11.6	21.4	...	...		...	...	...	2.4	...	...	...	28[41]	...	Swaziland
99.0[15]	96.2[18]	98.0	96.3[18]	—3.7[18]—		...	3.4	0.6	7.5	66,886	...	57.3	...	3,818[41]	Sweden
100.0[18]	...	93.3[18]	92.2[18]	—	7.8[18]	93.0	3.7	0.6	8.4[11]	37,597	...	84.6	8,109[19]	...	Switzerland
40.2[1]	41.7[1]	...	36.0[1]	—64.0[1]—		93.0	3.0	2.0	3.6[11]	55,572[17]	2,390[35]	33.0[17]	...	300[36]	Syria
79.4[18]	99.7[18]	94.2[18]	69.3[18]	...		30.5	4.1	1.2	5.2[37]	...	36,914[32,37]	...	...	32	Taiwan
37.2	6.0	...	...	...		...	...	...	14.7[11]	...	1,224	...	...	...	Tajikistan
...	...	...	...	...		...	2.5	1.9	2.6[11]	...	...	...	...	...	Tanzania
29.7[11]	89.3[11]	40.9[85]	40.9[28]	9.8[28]	49.3[28]	...	1.9[28]	...	7.2[11]	...	16,343	...	...	13,499	Thailand
4.1	10.3	...	—	—100.0—		...	1.8	3.4	3.6[16]	...	...	...	...	...	Togo
61.3[28]	20.9[28]	42.3[28]	11.2[28]	—88.8[28]—		...	...	...	5.6[108]	...	...	...	...	...	Tonga
64.3	83.3	41.1	41.0	—59.0—		...	3.3	1.4	8.4[37]	...	211	...	69[19]	27.2	Trinidad and Tobago
26.4	64.3	43.3	69.2[16]	—30.8[16]—		...	1.9	2.4	7.0	34,566[17]	...	43.8[17]	...	...	Tunisia
68.0	56.8	70.6	42.0	52.0	6.0	110.5[43]	2.4[15]	2.2[40]	6.6	250,480[16]	46,377	43.3[16]	3,933[19]	16,165	Turkey
...	...	...	...	...		...	...	...	22.7	...	20,754[32,37]	...	...	32	Turkmenistan
65.4	7.4	37.3	...	...		...	...	...	14.6[11]	...	...	...	...	...	Tuvalu
...	...	...	...	...		...	...	...	7.2[11]	...	...	...	65[103]	26.8[103]	Uganda
...	...	...	...	...		...	...	...	13.8	...	14,454	...	...	...	Ukraine
30.9[115]	24.2[115]	84.5	...	...		...	2.8	1.8	8.6[37]	...	...	...	133[41]	...	United Arab Emirates
...	...	99.8	...	...		...	5.0	0.5	6.8	188,503	...	122.2	...	32	United Kingdom[116]
98.5	96.9	98.9	99.2	—0.8—		147.1	5.2	0.5	4.4[11]	1,308,000	214,900[19]	78.2	...	140,100[19]	United States
89.3	84.7	73.3	...	92.0		...	3.4	1.7	3.8	...	160[15]	...	105[15]	21.4[15]	Uruguay
...	...	...	...	...		...	...	...	10.7	...	9,363	...	...	...	Uzbekistan
39.2[16]	14.2	27.5[16]	...	...		...	...	...	5.8[11]	...	5.7[19]	...	...	15.3[19]	Vanuatu
86.2	89.8	84.4[26]	80.2	—19.8—		53.5[43]	4.2	1.3	5.8	91,666[19]	4,904[19]	29.5[19]	678[19]	1,067[19]	Venezuela
...	...	...	...	...		...	...	...	4.4[10]	...	...	...	53[41]	59.3[41]	Vietnam
96.3[18]	98.1[18]	86.0[18]	93.6[18]	—6.4[18]—		...	4.3	0.6	...	...	...	...	262[18]	...	Virgin Islands (U.S.)
75.2[15]	75.3	98.4	...	...		127.2[43]	2.4[15]	2.7[15]	14.1[17]	5,740	730	20.8	...	175.8	West Bank
78.5	95.3	...	...	...		...	4.5	1.2	4.4[16]	...	...	...	...	...	Western Sahara
80.7	37.7	71.0	16.6	—83.4—		...	3.9[28,104]	1.5[28,104]	1.9[16]	132[15]	...	...	118[15]	...	Western Samoa
5.7[50]	4.6[50]	...	...	...		...	2.0[50]	2.8[50]	4.4[11]	...	1,988[15]	...	...	...	Yemen[117]
67.8	95.7	53.3	...	...		67.2[37]	2.9[37]	1.2[37]	7.3	59,909	...	51.3	2,805	2,073[23]	Yugoslavia
...	...	...	...	...		...	...	...	2.0[35]	...	20[15]	...	73[15]	39[15]	Zaire
12.4[120]	27.5[78]	15.1[120]	...	82.3[120]		...	1.9[120]	2.6[120]	3.9[11]	...	...	...	...	...	Zambia
...	...	9.3[121]	...	...		...	2.8	1.2	1.9	...	...	...	...	...	Zimbabwe

or earlier. [73]1953–62. [74]1963–72. [75]1973–81. [76]1982 or later. [77]1974. [78]1960. [79]1947 or earlier. [80]1948–83. [81]1961–71. [82]Factory space only. [83]1944 or earlier. [84]1945–70. [85]Minimum. [86]1961. [87]1946 or earlier. [88]1947–60. [89]Peninsular Malaysia only. [90]1957 or earlier. [91]1958–67. [92]1974 or earlier. [93]1960–68. [94]1969 or later. [95]1975–82. [96]Dwellings of indigenous population only. [97]Lagos only. [98]Excludes Islāmābād, North-West Frontier, and federally administered tribal lands. [99]1947–65. [100]1966–75. [101]1970 or later. [102]Excludes areas under U.S. military control in the provinces of Panama and Colón. [103]1972. [104]European-style dwellings only. [105]White, Coloured, and Asian dwellings only; excludes Bantu. [106]1940 or earlier. [107]1941–60. [108]1988–89. [109]1964. [110]1955 or earlier. [111]1956–66. [112]1907 or later. [113]1994. [114]1956–65. [115]1968. [116]Excludes Northern Ireland. [117]Former Yemen Arab Republic only. [118]Combined from 1986 and 1988 census data. [119]Data refer to Yugoslavia as constituted prior to 1991. [120]1969. [121]Bantu dwellings only.

Household budgets and consumption

This table provides international data on household income, on the consumption expenditure of households for goods and services, and on the principal object of such expenditure (in most countries), food consumption (by kind). For purposes of this compilation, income comprises pretax monetary payments and payment in kind. The first part of the table provides data on distribution of income by households and by sources of income; the second part analyzes the largest portion of income use—consumption expenditure. Such expenditure is defined as the purchase of goods and services to satisfy current wants and needs. This definition excludes income expended on taxes, debts, savings and investments, and insurance policies. The third and last part of the table focuses on food, which usually, and often by a wide margin, represents the largest share of consumer spending worldwide. The data provided include daily available calories per capita and consumption of major food groups.

For both sources of income and consumption expenditure, the primary basis of analysis for most countries is the household, an economic unit that can be as small as a single person or as large as an extended family. For some of the countries that do not compile information by household, the table provides data on personal income and personal expenditure—*i.e.*, the income and expenditure of all the individuals constituting a society's households. When no expenditure data at all is available, the table reports the weights of each major class of goods and services making up a given country's consumer (or retail) price index (CPI). The weighting of the components of the CPI usually reflects household spending patterns within the country or its principal urban or rural areas.

The data on distribution of income show, collectively for an entire country, the proportion of total income earned (occasionally, expended) by households constituting the lowest quintile and highest decile (poorest 20% and wealthiest 10%) within the country. These figures show the degree to which either group represents a disproportionate share of poverty or wealth.

The data on sources of income illuminate patterns of economic structure in the gaining of an income. They indicate, for example, that in poor, agrarian countries income often derives largely from self-employment (usually farming) or that in industrial countries, with well-developed systems of salaried employment and social welfare, income derives mainly from wages and salaries and secondarily from transfer payments (*see* note a). Because household sizes and numbers of income earners vary so greatly internationally, and because the frequency and methodology of household and CPI surveys do not permit single-year comparisons for more than a few countries at once, no summary of total *household* income or expenditure was possible. Instead, U.S. dollar figures are supplied for *per capita* private final consumption expenditure (for a single, recent year) that are more comparable internationally and refer to the same date. The figures on distribution of consumption expenditure by end use reveal patterns of personal and family use of disposable income and indicate, inter alia, that in developing countries food may absorb 50% or more of disposable income, while in the larger household budgets of the developed countries, by contrast, food purchases may account for only 20–30% of spending. In either type of country, the cost of transportation often rivals that of housing, once the more basic need. Each category of expenditure betrays similar complexities of local habit, necessity, and aspiration.

The reader should exercise caution when using these data to make intercountry comparisons. Most of the information comes from single-country surveys, which often differ markedly in their coverage of economically or

Household budgets and consumption

country	income (latest)						consumption expenditure						
	percent received by		by source (percent)				per capita private final, U.S.$ 1992	by kind or end use (percent of household or personal budget; latest)					
	lowest 20% of households	highest 10% of households	wages, salaries	self-employment	transfer payments[a]	other[b]		food[c]	housing[d]	clothing[e]	health care	energy, water	education
Afghanistan	...	...	20.7	28.0	8.2	43.1		33.9	3.0	...	1.1	0.7	...
Albania	...	...	...	...	...	...	680[1]	...	...	...	...	...	...
Algeria	6.9	31.7	...	...	...	...	700	55.7	5.4[2]	9.1	3.1	[2]	[3]
American Samoa	...	...	...	...	...	...	1,877[4]	44.3	23.4[5]	5.8	...	...	...
Andorra	...	...	...	...	...	...		...	...	...	...	...	...
Angola	...	...	...	...	...	...	420[6]	...	...	...	...	...	...
Antigua and Barbuda	...	...	...	...	...	...	2,170[7]	42.9	23.3	7.5	...	5.5	...
Argentina	4.4	35.2	...	...	...	...	5,870	38.2	9.3	8.0	7.9	9.0	2.6
Armenia	...	...	68.1	—— 31.9 ——			560	47.3	...	17.4	...	...	...
Aruba	...	...	...	...	...	...		26.9	12.6	8.4	2.9	5.6	1.9
Australia	4.8	28.1	58.2	15.2	15.8	10.8	10,450	18.9	18.1	5.6	7.4	2.2	1.6
Austria	4.0	28.7	55.6	[8]	24.5	19.9[8]	12,920	17.8	13.6	9.2	5.3	4.2	0.4
Azerbaijan	...	...	81.0	—— 19.0 ——				...	...	...	...	...	...
Bahamas, The	3.6	32.1	...	...	...	...	3,950[6]	19.8	19.2	7.2	3.4	4.3	7.8
Bahrain	...	...	...	...	...	...	2,800[1]	32.4	21.2	5.9	2.3	2.2	2.3
Bangladesh	9.5[9]	24.6[9]	26.1	50.8	0.5	22.6	170	63.3	8.8	5.9	1.1	8.4	1.2
Barbados	6.8	...	...	...	...	...	4,540[10]	43.2	13.1	5.1	...	6.2	...
Belarus	...	...	76.4	—— 23.6 ——			3,650[1]	29.0	2.7	...	...	...	...
Belgium	7.9[11]	21.5[11]	49.6	10.9	20.7	18.8	13,720	16.9	12.2	7.9	11.2	4.4	[3]
Belize	...	...	84.1	—— 15.9 ——			1,350[10]	51.5[12]	2.3	11.1	3.4	6.0	1.5
Benin	8.0	39.0	26.3	—— 73.7 ——			390	37.0	10.0	14.0	5.0	2.0	4.0
Bermuda	7.2	24.7	72.2	6.7	2.4	18.7	12,690[13]	20.7[12]	21.8	6.0	6.8	4.5	[3]
Bhutan	...	...	...	...	...	...	220	72.3	...	21.2	...	3.7	...
Bolivia	5.6[9]	31.7[9]	...	...	...	...	560	39.4	7.8	5.1	2.1	4.6	0.3
Bosnia and Herzegovina	...	...	53.2	12.0	18.2	16.6	1,890[1]	44.7	1.6	8.3	3.4	7.8	[3]
Botswana	3.7	42.9	73.3	15.4	10.8	0.4	1,290[6]	39.5[12]	13.3[2]	5.6	2.3	[2]	[3]
Brazil	2.1[14]	51.3[14]	...	...	...	...	1,520	35.0	9.0	10.0	6.0	2.0	5.0
Brunei	...	...	...	...	...	...		45.1	5.0[2]	6.1	...	[2]	[3]
Bulgaria	10.4[14]	21.9[14]	58.3	3.8	27.3	10.6	890	43.4	1.1	4.7	6.7	4.4	[15]
Burkina Faso	...	...	...	...	...	...	230	38.7[16]	5.1[16]	4.4[16]	5.2[16]	13.7[16]	[3]
Burundi	...	...	...	...	...	...	164	59.6[16]	4.4[16]	11.1[16]	...	5.8[16]	...
Cambodia	...	...	...	...	...	...		...	...	...	...	...	...
Cameroon	...	...	34.7	51.3	10.4	3.6	660	24.0	13.0	7.0	12.0	3.0	9.0
Canada	5.7	24.1	63.8	6.6	16.6	12.9	10,420	13.7	24.1[2]	5.4	4.3	[2]	3.1
Cape Verde	...	...	...	...	...	...	880[1]	60.0	8.5	2.5	0.5	4.9	[15]
Central African Republic	...	...	...	...	...	...	370	70.5[16]	0.6[16]	9.5[16]	1.0[16]	6.5[16]	...
Chad	8.0	30.0	...	...	...	...	210	45.3[16]	3.5[16]	11.9[16]	...	5.8[16]	...
Chile	3.7[14]	48.9[14]	40.8	...	8.0	51.2	2,000	27.9	15.2	22.5	...	...	...
China	6.4[14]	24.6[14]	79.8[18]	—— 20.2[18] ——			170[10]	53.8[12,18]	2.3[18]	13.7[18]	2.2[18]	3.7[18]	2.3[18]
Colombia	3.6[14]	39.5[14]	44.4	36.9	11.3	7.4	980	32.5	8.2	4.7	6.6	2.4	1.6
Comoros	...	...	25.6	64.5	8.7	1.2	430[1]	56.0	...	10.0	5.0	14.4	...
Congo	7.0	43.5	...	...	...	...	480	37.0	6.0	6.0	6.0	3.0	8.0
Costa Rica	4.0[14]	34.1[14]	...	...	...	...	1,270	33.0	8.0	8.0	7.0	1.0	8.0
Côte d'Ivoire	7.3[9]	26.9[9]	44.9	49.9	—— 5.2 ——		460	39.0	4.0	9.0	9.0	1.0	6.0
Croatia	...	...	40.2	40.8	12.1	6.9	5,050[1]	37.8	2.9	8.6	4.3	7.6	[3]
Cuba	...	...	57.3	...	...	42.7	1,510[6]	26.7	...	...	...	2.5	...
Cyprus	7.9[18]	...	...	...	...	...	6,500[10]	23.9	5.9	9.4	3.1	1.2	1.4
Czech Republic	10.0[19]	21.8[19]	49.8	...	27.4	22.8[8]	1,800	26.1	5.5[2]	7.3	[20]	[2]	...
Denmark	3.5	25.6	48.2	33.6	18.2	...	12,420	18.1	21.8	5.4	2.2	5.4	1.8
Djibouti	...	...	51.6	36.0	10.5	1.9	1,030[1]	50.3	6.4	1.7	2.4	13.1	...
Dominica	...	...	...	...	...	...	1,800[6]	43.1	16.1	6.5	...	5.4	...
Dominican Republic	4.2[14]	39.6[14]	41.7	31.8	1.5	25.0	770	46.0	10.0	3.0	8.0	5.0	3.0
Ecuador	2.9	51.5	14.5	78.9	4.4	2.2	800	36.2	4.1	10.4	4.2	1.2	[15]
Egypt	5.8	33.2	...	...	...	...	480	49.0	6.0	11.0	3.0	3.0	6.0
El Salvador	5.5[11]	29.5[11]	...	...	...	...	1,050	33.0	5.0	9.0	8.0	2.0	5.0

demographically stratified groups, in sample design, or in the methods employed for collection, classification, and tabulation of data. Further, the reference period of the data varies greatly; while a significant portion of the data is from 1980 or later, information for some countries dates from the 1970s. This older information is typeset in italic. Finally, intercountry comparisons of annual personal consumption expenditure may be misleading because of the distortions of price and purchasing power present when converting a national currency unit into U.S. dollars.

The table's food consumption data include total daily available calories per capita (food supply), which amounts to domestic production and imports minus exports, animal feed, and nonfood uses, and a percentage breakdown of the major food groups that make up food supply.

The data for daily available calories per capita provide a measure of the nutritional adequacy of each nation's food supply. The following list, based on estimates from the United Nations Food and Agriculture Organization (FAO), indicates the regional variation in recommended daily minimum nutritional requirements, which are defined by factors such as climatic ambience, physical activity, and average body weight: Africa (2,320 calories), formerly Centrally Planned Asia (2,300 calories), Far East (2,240 calories), Latin America (2,360 calories), Near East (2,440 calories).

The breakdown of diet by food groups describes the character of a nation's food supply. A typical breakdown for a low-income country might show a diet with heavy intake of vegetable foods, such as cereals, potatoes, or cassava. In the high-income countries, a relatively larger portion of total calories derives from animal products (meat, eggs, and milk). The reader should note that these data refer to total national *supply* and often do not reflect the differences that may exist within a single country.

In compiling this table, Britannica editors rely on both numerous national reports and principal secondary sources such as the World Bank's *World Development Report* (annual), the International Labour Organisation's *Statistical Sources and Methods, vol. 1 Consumer Price Indices* (2nd ed.), the UN's *Yearbook of National Accounts Statistics* (annual) and *National Accounts Statistics: Compendium of Income Distribution Statistics,* and the FAO's *Food Balance Sheets 1988–90.*

The following terms further define the column headings:
a. Includes pensions, family allowances, unemployment payments, remittances from abroad, and social security and related benefits.
b. Includes interest and dividends, rents and royalties, and all other income not reported under the three preceding categories.
c. Includes alcoholic and nonalcoholic beverages and meals away from home when identifiable. Excludes tobacco except as noted.
d. Rent, maintenance of dwellings, and taxes only; excludes energy and water (heat, light, power, and water) and household durables (furniture, appliances, utensils, and household operations), shown separately.
e. Includes footwear.
f. Furniture, appliances, and utensils; usually includes expenditure on household operation.
g. Includes expenditure on cultural activities other than education.
h. May include data not shown separately in preceding categories, including meals away from home (*see* note c).
i. Represents pure fats and oils only.
j. Consists mainly of peas, beans, and lentils; spices; stimulants; alcoholic beverages (when combined with "other"); sugars and honey; and nuts and oilseeds.

transportation, communications	household durable goods[f]	recreation[g]	personal effects, other[h]	daily available calories per capita (1988–90)	cereals	potatoes, cassava	meat, poultry	fish	eggs, milk	fruits, vegetables	fats, oils[i]	other[j]	country
...	...	...	61.3	1,764	75.5	1.2	4.8	—	3.3	2.8	7.9	4.5	Afghanistan
...	...	...	...	2,585	63.4	1.6	5.3	0.2	7.4	3.5	7.7	10.9	Albania
6.7	6.4	3.4[43]	10.2	2,945	55.0	2.5	1.7	0.4	6.5	4.3	14.7	14.9	Algeria
14.9	5	...	11.6	...	...	...	...	...	...	...	...	...	American Samoa
...	...	...	...	*3,667*	*23.8*	*5.5*	*18.0*	*1.5*	*9.4*	*6.7*	*15.9*	*19.1*	Andorra
...	...	...	...	1,880	32.5	32.4	4.4	3.0	2.8	3.6	9.9	11.2	Angola
10.0	...	...	*10.8*	2,307	26.9	1.0	16.7	3.0	11.0	7.2	13.0	21.2	Antigua and Barbuda
11.6	...	7.5	5.9	3,068	30.9	5.5	18.1	0.3	9.0	4.1	12.8	19.4	Argentina
...	6.6	...	28.7	...	...	...	...	...	...	...	...	...	Armenia
17.4	9.1	3.1	12.1	...	...	...	...	...	...	...	...	...	Aruba
15.2	6.4	7.7	16.9	3,302	24.3	3.0	19.9	0.8	11.1	4.9	13.6	22.4	Australia
16.9	7.6	7.0	18.0	3,486	19.8	3.3	13.7	0.6	10.5	6.6	22.2	23.2	Austria
...	...	...	...	...	...	...	...	...	...	...	...	...	Azerbaijan
18.9	10.2	5.3	3.9	2,776	25.2	1.9	17.4	1.3	7.6	9.6	9.3	27.6	Bahamas, The
8.5	9.8	6.4	9.0	...	...	...	...	...	...	...	...	...	Bahrain
0.9	...	...	10.4	2,038	82.9	1.3	0.5	0.6	1.2	1.1	5.4	6.9	Bangladesh
4.6	*9.6*	...	*16.2*	3,217	28.1	3.9	13.7	2.5	7.4	3.3	13.4	27.7	Barbados
...	...	...	68.3	...	...	...	...	...	...	...	...	...	Belarus
13.2	10.8	6.5[3]	16.9	3,925	19.0	4.7	18.6	1.0	9.1	5.6	21.3	20.7	Belgium
6.5	10.1	2.2	5.4	2,575	32.9	1.9	8.7	0.4	10.9	6.2	11.7	27.3	Belize
14.0	5.0	...	9.0	2,383	35.0	30.0	2.3	0.8	0.9	2.9	7.8	11.3	Benin
17.1	14.7	8.4[3]	6.0	2,960	20.5	2.3	19.7	2.7	8.9	9.5	13.4	23.0	Bermuda
...	0.7	...	2.1	...	85.2	2.4	0.4	0.1	0.6	1.4	5.3	4.6	Bhutan
17.7	9.7	2.7	10.6	2,012	41.2	11.2	9.7	0.1	2.5	8.4	9.2	17.6	Bolivia
6.0	4.1	3.5[3]	2.3	...	...	...	...	...	...	...	...	...	Bosnia and Herzegovina
13.1	14.0	8.3[3]	3.9	2,260	62.7	0.8	4.0	0.3	7.1	1.4	5.5	18.2	Botswana
8.0	8.0	...	17.0	2,730	34.4	6.4	6.8	0.4	6.4	5.0	15.0	25.5	Brazil
17.2	8.3	8.9[3]	9.4	2,859	47.6	1.0	11.9	1.6	5.7	4.0	7.0	21.1	Brunei
8.3	3.2	15	28.2[15]	3,695	39.6	1.5	10.3	0.4	8.8	5.1	15.2	19.2	Bulgaria
18.6[16]	3.0[16]	2.3[3, 16]	9.0[16]	2,218	71.8	1.4	2.3	0.2	1.4	0.8	4.1	17.6	Burkina Faso
...	6.0[16]	...	13.1[16, 17]	1,947	21.1	29.0	1.0	0.2	0.8	9.6	2.6	35.8	Burundi
...	...	...	...	2,122	83.4	3.1	3.2	0.8	0.4	3.2	1.2	4.8	Cambodia
12.0	3.0	...	17.0	2,208	38.9	15.9	3.5	1.1	1.6	11.8	8.6	18.6	Cameroon
14.7	8.8	8.0	17.9	3,242	22.6	3.4	15.1	1.4	9.9	6.4	18.5	22.7	Canada
8.8	6.9	15	7.9[15]	2,780	51.5	5.0	3.7	0.9	3.0	2.4	13.9	19.6	Cape Verde
4.1[16]	0.8[16]	1.3[16]	5.7[16]	1,847	25.6	33.4	7.3	0.5	1.2	5.7	7.3	19.2	Central African Republic
...	...	...	33.5[16]	1,703	50.2	16.3	3.5	1.8	2.8	2.8	5.0	17.3	Chad
6.4	...	...	28.0	2,484	45.7	4.3	8.3	1.4	6.5	5.5	8.6	19.7	Chile
1.4[18]	...	6.0[18]	14.6[10]	2,642	69.7	5.0	8.0	0.6	1.4	2.6	4.7	7.1	China
17.9	5.7	4	10.2	2,453	31.4	8.1	7.4	0.2	6.6	9.1	9.9	27.2	Colombia
6.6	...	3.0	5.0	1,760	44.9	17.8	1.7	1.5	1.6	8.9	7.3	16.3	Comoros
15.0	4.0	...	15.0	2,295	18.6	43.9	2.7	3.2	1.0	7.4	11.6	11.6	Congo
8.0	9.0	...	18.0	2,711	35.7	0.8	5.1	0.3	8.8	4.9	13.0	31.3	Costa Rica
10.0	3.0	...	19.0	2,565	36.7	27.2	2.5	1.2	1.4	9.4	9.9	11.6	Côte d'Ivoire
9.3	4.5	4.1[3]	1.5	...	...	...	...	...	...	...	...	...	Croatia
5.4	...	...	65.4	3,129	32.9	4.8	6.5	1.1	7.9	3.8	14.1	29.0	Cuba
15.8	10.1	6.5	22.8	...	40.0	2.5	13.7	0.4	7.9	7.0	10.1	18.4	Cyprus
3.1	4.5	0.8[20]	52.7	3,574[21]	29.9[21]	4.2[21]	13.0[21]	0.5[21]	9.5[21]	4.2[21]	17.5[21]	21.2[21]	Czech Republic
15.7	6.2	10.1	13.3	3,630	20.4	3.6	23.7	2.0	8.7	3.9	17.7	20.1	Denmark
...	1.5	...	24.6	2,363	53.5	0.6	4.1	0.3	6.0	2.8	11.9	20.9	Djibouti
11.6	6.0	...	11.3	2,911	27.9	8.5	8.9	1.0	9.2	9.6	9.3	25.6	Dominica
4.0	8.0	...	13.0	2,310	32.7	3.5	5.2	0.3	5.2	15.2	14.1	23.7	Dominican Republic
12.5	7.7	15	23.7[15]	2,399	33.4	3.2	4.8	1.0	6.9	11.1	20.7	19.0	Ecuador
4.0	3.0	...	15.0	3,310	63.2	1.8	2.8	0.4	1.0	6.3	11.1	12.6	Egypt
10.0	7.0	...	21.0	2,331	53.8	0.8	2.3	0.1	6.2	4.5	8.3	24.0	El Salvador

Household budgets and consumption (continued)

country	income (latest) percent received by		by source (percent)				consumption expenditure per capita private final, U.S.$ 1992	by kind or end use (percent of household or personal budget; latest)					
	lowest 20% of households	highest 10% of households	wages, salaries	self-employment	transfer payments[a]	other[b]		food[c]	housing[d]	clothing[e]	health care	energy, water	education
Equatorial Guinea	...	...	...	...	...	...	380[1]	...	...	...	...	...	...
Eritrea[22]	...	...	...	...	...	...	...	...	...	...	...	...	...
Estonia	6.5	28.8	66.0	—————34.0—————			180	47.3[12]	13.8	9.2	...	...	1.7
Ethiopia[22]	8.6[9]	27.5[9]	0.2	79.5	—	20.3	80	49.0	7.0	6.0	3.0	7.0	4.0
Faeroe Islands	...	...	...	...	...	...	...	40.9	11.0	8.0	...	18.9	...
Fiji	3.7	37.8	81.5	9.1	—	9.4	1,280[1]	34.7	15.6[2]	9.3	2.4	[2]	[3]
Finland	3.7	26.9	59.7	11.1	24.1	5.1	10,430	20.8	16.1	5.2	4.6	3.8	[3]
France	5.6	26.1	51.7	14.2	27.0	7.1	13,800	17.9	16.0	6.3	9.7	4.0	0.6
French Guiana	...	...	74.6	—————25.4—————			...	30.0[12]	16.1[2]	6.7	4.4	[2]	[3]
French Polynesia	...	...	63.7	[8]	14.8	21.5[8]	4,310[23]	32.1	...	6.3	1.0	8.1	[3]
Gabon	3.3	54.4	...	...	...	...	2,100	54.7[12, 16, 24]	13.0[16, 24]	17.5[16, 24]	1.9[16, 24]	...	...
Gambia, The	...	...	...	...	...	...	220[1]	58.0[25]	5.1[25]	17.5[25]	...	5.4[25]	...
Gaza Strip	...	...	...	...	...	...	910[7]	...	...	...	...	...	...
Georgia	...	...	74.9	—————25.1—————			2,500[1]	38.3	...	14.8	...	0.3	...
Germany	7.0[26]	24.4[26]	57.8	[8]	20.9	21.3	11,990	19.5	16.3	8.2	3.5	4.0	[3]
Ghana	7.0[9]	29.0[9]	41.6[27]	47.1[27]	—	11.3[27]	380	57.4	11.5[2]	14.3	1.3	[2]	[3]
Gibraltar	...	...	...	...	...	...	...	39.1[12]	12.6	11.0	...	...	...
Greece	...	...	37.2	[8]	16.8	46.0[8]	4,790	33.3	9.8	8.7	3.5	2.7	0.7
Greenland	...	...	...	...	...	...	...	29.5	8.9	7.6	...	7.1	...
Grenada	...	...	...	...	...	...	1,610[10]	40.7[12]	11.9	5.2	[28]	3.9	[3]
Guadeloupe	...	...	78.9	13.7	7.4	—	4,080[7]	31.6[12]	11.3[2]	9.3	4.6	[2]	[3]
Guam	...	...	...	...	...	...	...	24.1	28.6	10.6	4.8	...	...
Guatemala	2.1[14]	46.6[14]	...	...	...	...	910	64.4	16.0[2]	3.1	0.6	[2]	0.3
Guernsey	...	...	...	...	...	...	...	23.7	12.1	7.5	...	8.2	...
Guinea	...	...	...	...	...	...	430	61.5	7.3[2]	7.9	11.1	[2]	...
Guinea-Bissau	2.1[9]	42.4[9]	...	...	...	...	260	...	...	...	...	...	...
Guyana	...	...	73.0	...	6.3	20.7	240[10]	42.5[12]	21.4	8.6	...	5.2	[3]
Haiti	...	...	...	...	...	...	370[10]	77.9	8.3	3.2	...	...	...
Honduras	2.7[14]	47.9[14]	58.3	[8]	1.8	39.9[8]	410	44.4	22.4[2]	9.1	7.0	[2]	[3]
Hong Kong	5.4[19]	31.3[19]	...	...	...	...	8,170	16.9	15.8[2]	21.2	5.9	[2]	1.2
Hungary	10.9[14]	20.8[14]	46.1	11.9	22.4	19.6	2,390	38.1	5.7	7.4	1.5	6.1	0.7
Iceland	4.7	27.3	74.4	3.0	16.6	6.0	15,550[10]	23.7	12.9	8.2	1.8	2.6	1.3
India	8.8[9]	27.1[9]	42.2	39.7	...	18.1	160	52.2	6.1[29]	10.0	2.4	4.7[29]	1.8
Indonesia	8.7[9]	27.9[9]	42.1	41.5	2.5	13.9	360	47.5[18]	20.1[2, 18]	5.5[18]	...	[2]	[3]
Iran	3.8	41.7	37.4[18]	30.5[18]	—————32.1[18]—————		1,120	42.6[12]	24.9[2]	11.8	3.9	[2]	[3]
Iraq	2.1	...	23.9	33.9	23.0	18.6	1,710[13]	50.2	19.9[2]	10.6	1.6	[2]	[3]
Ireland	4.6	26.5	58.6	13.3	19.9	8.2	6,890	35.0	7.8	6.9	[28]	4.5	[3]
Isle of Man	6.4	26.6	64.1	6.6	16.9	12.4	...	31.0	7.9	7.0	...	11.0	...
Israel	8.4	23.1	86.9[18, 24]	2.4[18, 24]	—————10.6[18, 24]—————		7,910	26.1[12]	22.6	4.8	6.3	2.1	3.1
Italy	6.8	25.3	41.7	25.9	20.3	12.1	13,480	18.8	11.4	9.9	6.7	3.8	[3]
Jamaica	6.0[9]	32.6[9]	63.6	13.9	14.0	8.5	880[10]	35.7	5.7	4.6	2.8	4.9	0.2
Japan	10.9	31.6[30]	58.5	11.0	18.9	11.6	16,830	23.9	5.3	6.8	2.7	5.4	4.5
Jersey	...	...	...	...	...	...	...	28.3	14.9	8.3	...	6.5	...
Jordan	6.5[9]	32.6[9]	...	...	...	...	970	40.6	15.8	6.7	2.2	5.0	3.5
Kazakhstan	...	...	73.3	—————26.7—————			1,040	29.6	2.6	...	...	...	...
Kenya	3.4	47.9	...	...	...	...	180	46.5	10.0	7.7	2.2	2.6	1.0
Kiribati	...	...	69.7	21.4	6.0	2.9	370[4]	50.0[12]	7.5[2, 5]	8.0	...	[2]	...
Korea, North	...	...	...	...	...	...	...	46.5[31]	0.6[31]	29.9[31]	...	3.3[31]	...
Korea, South	7.4	27.6[29]	53.8	25.1	13.1	8.0	3,450[10]	35.1[12]	11.2[2]	4.4	7.5	[2]	[3]
Kuwait	...	...	53.8	20.8	—————25.4—————		3,460	28.1[12]	15.5	8.1	0.7	9.6	[3]
Kyrgyzstan	...	...	72.8	—————27.2—————			2,370[1]	33.5	2.2	...	...	...	...
Laos	...	...	...	...	...	...	140[6]	...	...	...	...	...	...
Latvia	...	...	63.2	5.3	16.6	14.9	3,950[1]	45.2	...	...	...	...	...
Lebanon	5.0	45.0	27.9	...	3.0	69.1	780[4]	42.8[16]	16.8[16]	8.6[16]	7.2[16]	4.5[16]	3.9[16]
Lesotho	2.9[9]	43.6[9]	22.4	27.8	44.7	5.1	330	48.0[12]	10.1	16.4	...	...	...
Liberia	5.3	...	...	...	...	...	330[6]	34.4[16]	14.9[16]	13.8[16]	...	5.0[16]	...
Libya	10.1	...	...	...	...	...	2,330[6]	37.2[12]	32.2[2]	6.9	3.3	[2]	[3]
Liechtenstein	...	...	92.9[32]	7.1[32]	...	...	...	21.3[12]	18.0	6.6	7.7	4.4	[3]
Lithuania	...	...	66.4	9.7	18.7	5.2	680	50.3	...	...	...	...	...
Luxembourg	...	...	88.6	9.1	2.3	—	13,880[10]	12.8	13.7	5.9	7.3	6.1	[3]
Macau	...	...	...	...	...	...	4,160[10]	44.2[12]	22.8	7.3	...	4.8	...
Macedonia	...	...	57.7	17.2	16.2	9.0	1,800[1]	40.6	1.9	7.8	3.0	7.8	[3]
Madagascar	5.2	...	58.8[16, 33]	14.1[16, 33]	—	27.1[16, 33]	190	59.0	6.0	6.0	2.0	6.0	4.0
Malawi	10.4	40.1	83.3	6.0	...	11.7	130	30.0	4.0	9.0	4.0	5.0	10.0
Malaysia	4.6[14]	37.9[14]	...	...	...	...	1,610	28.7	10.2[2]	4.3	2.5	[2]	0.6
Maldives	...	...	...	...	...	...	270[6]	57.4	1.6	8.0	2.5	...	[3]
Mali	...	...	...	...	...	...	280	57.0	2.0	6.0	2.0	6.0	4.0
Malta	...	...	62.4	20.1	—	17.5	4,100[1]	31.2	3.5	7.6	3.5	2.0	0.4
Marshall Islands	...	...	...	...	...	...	...	57.7	15.6[2, 5]	12.0	...	[2]	...
Martinique	...	...	80.0	...	...	20.0	4,840[7]	32.1[12]	10.6[2]	8.0	5.2	[2]	[3]
Mauritania	3.5[9]	30.2[9]	...	...	...	...	450	51.2	2.3	7.7	1.4	7.9	0.3
Mauritius	4.0	46.7	51.7	29.0	11.2	8.1	1,510	41.9	8.8	8.4	3.0	6.4	2.9
Mayotte	...	...	...	...	...	...	...	79.6	—	7.1	...	...	...
Mexico	4.0	38.2	52.4	23.6	5.6	18.4	2,760	34.8[12]	12.3	7.2	4.1	[2]	[3]
Micronesia	...	...	67.2	18.0	...	14.8	...	73.5	...	...	...	...	...
Moldova	...	...	69.1	6.7	12.6	11.6	790	...	...	...	...	...	...
Monaco	...	...	...	...	...	...	...	...	...	...	...	...	...
Mongolia	...	...	81.9	—————18.1—————			780[1]	39.1	5.9[2]	23.4	0.5	[2]	2.9
Morocco	6.6[9]	30.5[9]	...	...	...	...	730	38.0	7.0	11.0	5.0	2.0	8.0
Mozambique	...	...	...	...	...	...	70	...	...	...	...	...	...
Myanmar (Burma)	8.0	...	...	...	...	...	750	49.1[16]	10.4[16]	15.3[16]	2.4[16]	4.0[16]	5.9[16]
Namibia	...	...	73.3	0.4	3.4	22.9	930	...	...	...	...	...	...
Nauru	...	...	...	...	...	...	...	...	...	...	...	...	...
Nepal	9.1[9]	25.0[9]	25.1	63.4	—————11.5—————		110	61.2	17.3	11.7	3.7	...	[3]
Netherlands, The	8.2	21.9	48.4	10.8	28.7	12.1	12,660	14.0	14.8	7.0	12.7	3.6	0.7

transportation, communications	household durable goods[f]	recreation[g]	personal effects, other[h]	daily available calories per capita (1988–90)	cereals	potatoes, cassava	meat, poultry	fish	eggs, milk	fruits, vegetables	fats, oils[i]	other[j]	country
...	...	...	...	...	...	...	...	...	...	...	...	...	Equatorial Guinea
...	...	...	...	...	...	...	...	...	...	...	...	...	Eritrea[22]
7.8	4.4	3.6	12.2	...	...	...	...	...	...	...	...	...	Estonia
8.0	2.0	...	14.0	1,690	71.5	4.1	3.1	—	2.4	0.8	3.6	14.5	Ethiopia[22]
...	6.6	...	14.6	...	29.3	5.5	15.8	3.9	7.0	3.3	18.0	17.2	Faeroe Islands
13.8	9.3	4.3[3]	10.6	2,768	38.7	6.1	3.9	3.1	4.6	1.5	14.1	27.9	Fiji
16.7	6.4	10.9[3]	15.5	3,066	23.4	4.9	16.7	1.9	15.4	4.9	12.8	20.0	Finland
15.9	7.6	6.9	15.2	3,593	23.9	3.7	16.0	1.2	12.5	4.9	18.9	18.9	France
17.5	7.9	0.2[3]	11.2	2,805	29.1	4.3	17.0	3.0	7.7	8.7	8.0	22.1	French Guiana
12.2	12.3	6.9[3]	21.1	2,765	36.5	5.2	12.4	2.4	5.1	4.3	11.5	22.7	French Polynesia
6.3[16,24]	...	...	6.6[16,24]	2,442	24.4	25.5	6.3	2.1	1.4	14.7	7.9	17.7	Gabon
...	...	...	14.0[25]	2,290	67.2	1.0	2.4	1.3	1.7	1.1	9.7	15.5	Gambia, The
...	...	...	...	...	50.4	1.6	4.2	0.2	4.9	9.0	13.8	15.9	Gaza Strip
...	5.9	...	40.7	...	...	...	...	...	...	...	...	...	Georgia
18.0	9.4	10.1[3]	11.1	3,522	22.3	4.8	13.9	0.8	10.1	6.0	18.8	23.3	Germany
3.3	3.8	3.9[3]	4.5	2,141	20.0	39.3	1.9	2.5	0.3	8.5	8.6	9.9	Ghana
13.3	10.0	...	14.0	...	...	...	...	...	...	...	...	...	Gibraltar
14.9	8.0	5.0	13.4	3,775	27.7	3.9	12.2	0.8	10.1	9.5	18.4	17.3	Greece
7.7	9.3	12.4	17.5	...	...	...	...	...	...	...	...	...	Greenland
9.1	13.7	4.6[3]	10.9[28]	2,400	26.5	2.4	7.6	2.4	12.3	8.3	10.0	30.6	Grenada
20.5	9.3	4.7[3]	8.7	2,777	34.4	3.3	11.2	3.2	7.5	8.0	11.2	21.3	Guadeloupe
18.0	...	5.1	8.8	...	...	...	...	...	...	...	...	...	Guam
7.0	5.0	0.9	2.7	2,254	60.5	0.4	1.4	—	2.9	2.1	7.2	25.4	Guatemala
15.7	8.3	...	24.7	...	...	...	...	...	...	...	...	...	Guernsey
5.1	2.9	4.1	0.1	2,243	48.2	13.2	1.5	0.7	1.2	14.4	12.0	8.7	Guinea
...	...	...	...	2,235	63.6	6.1	4.6	0.3	1.5	4.2	13.0	6.7	Guinea-Bissau
4.8	2.9	6.4[3]	8.2	2,495	48.4	2.1	4.5	3.0	5.6	5.0	6.9	24.6	Guyana
...	4.0	...	6.6	2,005	37.4	12.4	3.5	0.3	1.7	9.8	6.1	28.7	Haiti
3.0	8.3	2.4[3]	3.1	2,211	50.9	0.5	2.3	0.3	5.1	6.8	13.3	20.9	Honduras
9.6	12.5	7.3	9.6	2,860	35.4	1.0	16.2	3.0	4.8	4.5	16.2	18.8	Hong Kong
15.2	8.8	5.9	10.6	3,608	29.1	2.8	12.6	0.3	8.8	4.5	20.8	21.1	Hungary
16.1	8.7	10.5	14.2	3,473	27.5	2.7	12.5	5.0	15.8	3.3	10.3	22.9	Iceland
10.6	3.1	1.8	5.7	2,229	63.1	1.8	0.7	0.3	4.8	3.2	7.2	18.9	India
...	2.9[18]	...	24.0	2,605	66.5	6.2	1.3	1.2	0.6	2.3	7.7	14.3	Indonesia
5.0	6.4	1.7[3]	3.7	3,022	62.8	2.1	3.3	0.3	3.2	7.1	10.8	10.3	Iran
6.5	6.7	0.8[3]	3.7	3,092	61.5	0.5	3.5	0.1	3.0	6.4	12.7	12.4	Iraq
12.8	7.0	12.1[3]	13.9[28]	3,951	24.3	6.0	14.8	0.8	14.5	3.6	17.4	18.7	Ireland
14.9	5.7	...	22.5	...	...	...	...	...	...	...	...	...	Isle of Man
11.3	10.5	3.9	9.3	3,220	31.3	1.9	8.1	1.1	9.6	9.0	19.1	19.9	Israel
12.1	9.1	9.5[3]	10.6	3,498	32.1	2.1	11.0	1.1	8.6	7.4	21.7	15.9	Italy
12.4	5.5	2.1	26.1	2,558	32.6	7.3	6.5	1.4	6.1	7.0	11.5	27.7	Jamaica
9.0	1.4	9.5	31.5	2,921	39.7	2.6	5.6	6.9	6.2	4.4	11.2	23.3	Japan
13.9	7.1	...	21.0	...	...	...	...	...	...	...	...	...	Jersey
11.2	6.1	4.0	4.0	2,710	51.8	1.0	6.2	0.2	4.6	4.6	11.0	20.9	Jordan
...	...	...	67.8	...	...	...	...	...	...	...	...	...	Kazakhstan
8.4	9.4	3.1	9.1	2,064	52.0	7.4	4.1	0.5	8.4	3.2	6.4	17.9	Kenya
8.0	5	...	26.5	2,516	39.0	10.9	3.7	5.7	1.2	5.8	8.2	25.5	Kiribati
...	3.8[31]	...	15.9	2,843	62.1	5.7	3.4	2.6	1.1	5.8	3.3	16.0	Korea, North
11.0	6.1	11.3[3]	13.4	2,826	52.5	0.7	5.2	3.5	2.2	6.9	9.1	19.8	Korea, South
13.7	11.2	5.2[3]	7.9	3,057	36.0	1.2	10.7	0.7	9.5	8.1	15.8	17.9	Kuwait
...	...	...	64.3	...	...	...	...	...	...	...	...	...	Kyrgyzstan
...	...	...	...	2,465	74.7	4.6	7.0	0.4	1.7	2.5	1.9	7.2	Laos
...	...	...	54.8	2,490	...	...	...	...	...	...	...	...	Latvia
5.4[16]	2.6[16]	1.9[16]	6.3[16]	3,142	37.6	3.1	6.0	...	5.9	11.4	15.7	20.3	Lebanon
4.7	11.9	...	8.8	2,121	75.3	0.6	4.2	0.2	1.5	1.7	3.9	12.5	Lesotho
...	6.1[16]	...	25.8[16]	2,264	46.7	22.6	2.0	1.1	0.5	4.9	14.4	7.7	Liberia
9.4	1.6	8.5[3]	2.5	3,293	45.4	1.7	5.6	0.2	6.7	7.5	16.5	16.3	Libya
13.3	5.8	16.3[3]	6.6	...	...	...	...	...	...	...	...	...	Liechtenstein
...	...	...	49.7	2,110	...	...	...	...	...	...	...	...	Lithuania
19.1	10.8	4.2[3]	20.1	3,925	19.0	4.7	18.6	1.0	9.1	5.6	21.3	20.7	Luxembourg
4.9	2.9	...	13.1	2,295	42.7	2.0	16.0	1.4	4.6	5.3	12.8	15.3	Macau
6.5	4.2	3.3[3]	1.8	...	...	...	...	...	...	...	...	...	Macedonia
4.0	1.0	...	12.0	2,156	55.8	19.2	6.2	0.7	3.3	4.2	3.5	7.1	Madagascar
10.0	3.0	...	25.0	2,048	68.8	4.0	1.5	0.9	0.7	4.6	1.7	17.9	Malawi
20.9	7.7	11.0	14.1	2,671	40.3	3.4	7.3	1.7	4.9	3.4	19.2	19.7	Malaysia
2.6	17.0	5.9[3]	5.0	2,400	52.6	3.9	0.6	12.6	—	4.2	4.8	21.4	Maldives
10.0	1.0	...	12.0	2,260	72.7	1.9	3.3	0.6	4.2	0.8	7.8	8.6	Mali
16.4	9.9	7.1	18.4	3,169	30.1	1.5	10.7	1.0	11.3	6.6	15.9	22.9	Malta
...	5	...	14.7	...	...	...	...	...	...	...	...	...	Marshall Islands
20.7	9.4	5.4[3]	8.6	2,768	31.2	3.7	11.3	2.7	7.7	10.9	11.2	21.2	Martinique
2.0	1.9	0.5	24.8	2,447	54.8	0.4	4.0	0.6	12.5	1.6	8.3	17.9	Mauritania
10.0	0.4	—	12.2	2,897	50.0	1.2	3.7	1.4	6.4	1.5	12.2	23.5	Mauritius
5.4	...	...	7.9	...	...	...	...	...	...	...	...	...	Mayotte
11.5	10.9	4.9[3]	14.3	3,061	46.7	0.7	8.5	0.6	5.8	3.3	12.5	21.0	Mexico
...	...	...	26.5	...	...	...	...	...	...	...	...	...	Micronesia
...	...	...	...	...	...	...	...	...	...	...	...	...	Moldova
...	...	...	...	3,593	23.9	3.7	16.0	1.2	12.5	4.9	18.9	18.9	Monaco
3.5	8.0	0.4	16.2	2,361	46.5	2.0	24.1	0.1	6.4	0.8	6.2	13.8	Mongolia
8.0	5.0	...	16.0	3,031	54.5	1.7	2.1	0.6	1.8	4.4	10.9	24.0	Morocco
...	...	...	...	1,804	32.0	43.3	1.5	0.3	0.7	1.8	12.7	7.7	Mozambique
3.8[16]	0.5[16]	1.1[16]	7.5[16]	2,453	79.5	0.4	1.8	1.0	1.0	2.5	6.3	7.5	Myanmar (Burma)
...	...	...	...	1,960	55.0	15.5	8.1	0.7	0.0	1.7	7.1	8.9	Namibia
...	...	...	...	...	...	...	...	...	...	...	...	...	Nauru
1.2	...	2.9[3]	2.0	2,206	80.9	3.0	1.2	—	4.1	0.9	4.4	5.4	Nepal
12.7	7.2	9.8	17.5	3,078	17.8	5.3	12.2	0.6	13.1	6.1	20.2	24.6	Netherlands, The

Household budgets and consumption (continued)

country	income (latest)						consumption expenditure						
	percent received by		by source (percent)				per capita private final, U.S.$ 1992	by kind or end use (percent of household or personal budget; latest)					
	lowest 20% of households	highest 10% of households	wages, salaries	self-employment	transfer payments[a]	other[b]		food[c]	housing[d]	clothing[e]	health care	energy, water	education
Netherlands Antilles	...	...	52.1	23.3	23.5	...	4,110[13]	21.2[12,34]	16.8[2,34]	8.4[34]	2.3[34]	2	3
New Caledonia							5,410[35]	25.7	21.5[2,5]	4.7	[21]	2	...
New Zealand	5.1[19]	28.7[19]	52.1	5.6	21.0	21.3	7,680	16.1	20.0	5.2	6.4	2.4	3
Nicaragua	3.1[36]	...	...	...	...	...	320						
Niger			...	...	...	...	230	50.5	19.1[5]	7.3	...	...	...
Nigeria	...	...	36.2	49.4	4.3	10.1	230	48.0	3.0	5.0	3.0	1.0	4.0
Northern Mariana Islands								49.2[12]	19.5[2,5]	9.1	[20]	2	0.6
Norway	2.6	26.6	58.8	9.9	24.2	7.1	13,700	23.5	13.7	7.0	5.4	6.2	0.6
Oman							2,510[10]	40.6	24.6	5.1	2.4	3.2	3
Pakistan	8.4[9]	25.2[9]	22.0	56.0	...	22.0	240	37.0	11.0	6.0	1.0	5.0	1.0
Panama	2.0[14]	42.1[14]	85.3	[8]	9.2	5.5[8]	1,420	34.9	12.6[2]	5.1	3.5	2	3
Papua New Guinea	...	...	57.3	[8]	1.1	41.6[8]	610	40.9	12.5[5]	6.2	...	4.9	...
Paraguay	...	...	33.9	[8]	2.5	63.6[8]	1,120	48.7	16.4	9.7	3.4	—	1.5
Peru	4.9[9]	35.4[9]	31.2	65.1	3.7	...	800	31.5[12]	0.8[2]	10.7	4.5	2	3
Philippines	6.5[9]	32.1[9]	44.9	44.0	3.7	7.4	580	55.1	4.2[2]	3.7	...	...	...
Poland	9.2[14]	21.6[14]	34.0	4.3	20.7	41.0	1,010	41.2	2.8	10.9	8.1	1.0	3
Portugal	5.2	33.4	42.6	25.0	21.3	11.1	4,520[10]	34.8	2.0	10.3	4.5	3.0	1.4
Puerto Rico	3.2	34.7	54.1	6.8	29.8	9.3	5,880	20.6	11.8[2]	7.4	11.6	2	3.1
Qatar	...	...	80.8	5.6	...	13.6	3,600[4]	24.5	35.1[5]	9.1	1.0	1.9	4.3
Réunion	3.1[19]	51.4[19]	67.5		29.7	2.8	4,820[35]	29.2[12]	13.0[2]	8.8	4.3	2	3
Romania	...	...	62.6	37.4			680	51.1	16.4[2,5]	15.7	1.2	2	3
Russia	...	...	76.0	5.7	8.7	9.6	1,042	34.8	2.7	22.3	...	...	...
Rwanda	9.7[9]	24.6[9]	16.5	[8]	9.5	74.0[8]	160	29.0	9.0	11.0	3.0	6.0	6.0
St. Kitts and Nevis	...	...	...	...	...	...	2,580[1]	55.6[12]	7.6	7.5	...	6.6	...
St. Lucia	...	...	...	...	...	...		49.6[12]	13.5	6.5	2.3	4.5	3
St. Vincent and the Grenadines	...	...	...	...	...	...	1,240[1]	59.8	6.3	7.7	...	6.2	...
San Marino	...	...	...	...	...	...		22.1[11]	20.9[2]	8.0	2.6	2	3
São Tomé and Príncipe	...	...	...	...	...	...	400[1]						
Saudi Arabia	...	...	...	...	...	...	2,790[10]	52.2[18,38]	17.2[18,38]	6.6[18,38]	2.1[18,38]	1.8[18,38]	1.1[18,38]
Senegal	3.5	42.2	51.6[16]		48.4[16]		650	49.0	7.0	11.0	2.0	4.0	6.0
Seychelles	4.1	35.6	77.2	3.8	3.2	15.8	3,110[1]	53.9	13.6	4.2	0.4	9.1	...
Sierra Leone	5.6	37.8	27.9	61.6	...	10.5	115	63.8	5.8[2]	10.0	3.5	2	3
Singapore	5.1	33.5	81.2	16.8	2.0		7,020	17.1	9.5[2]	7.3	4.5	2	1.2
Slovakia	...	...	71.8	[8]	16.3	11.9[8]	1,600	26.8	7.6[2]	8.9	...	2	...
Slovenia	...	...	59.4	14.5	17.5	8.6	2,770	30.8	18.3	8.5	5.0	7.3	3
Solomon Islands	...	...	74.1	25.9			820[4]	46.8	21.9[2,5]	5.7	[20]	2	4.3[17]
Somalia	...	...	...	...	...	...	17[1]	62.3[12,16]	15.3[16]	5.6[16]	...	2	...
South Africa	1.9	39.4	74.1	[8]	4.8	21.1[8]	1,560	35.1	9.4[2]	7.5	4.9	2	0.3
Spain	8.3[11]	21.8[11]	48.1	24.1	19.7	8.1	9,270	20.9[12]	12.6[2]	8.7	4.1	2	3
Sri Lanka	8.9[9]	25.2[9]	48.5	[8]	8.2	43.3[8]	380	53.7	1.8	6.2	1.5	2.9	1.2
Sudan, The	4.0	34.6	...	...	...	...	760[1]	63.6	11.5	5.3	4.1	3.8	3
Suriname	9.3	...	74.6	...	3.2	22.2	2,260[1]	39.9[16]	4.4[16]	11.0[16]	3.6[16]	6.9[16]	2.6[16]
Swaziland	2.8	54.5	44.4	22.2	12.2	21.2	650[1]	33.5[12]	13.4[2]	6.0	1.8	2	3
Sweden	5.3	18.6	62.2	7.1	24.8	5.9	13,760	19.2	24.0	6.7	2.7	5.2	0.2
Switzerland	6.0[39]	27.0[39]	64.5	[8]	15.1	20.4[8]	20,720	27.1[12]	15.2	4.3	10.5	4.8	3
Syria	6.0	...	...	...	...	...	1,630	48.8[12]	17.7	9.1	...	4.6	3
Taiwan	7.5	38.6[30]	68.3	[8]	3.6	28.1[8]	4,670	27.4	18.8[29]	4.7	5.4	2.9[29]	3
Tajikistan	...	...	64.3	4.4	23.5	7.8	440						
Tanzania	2.4[9]	46.5[9]	33.8	59.8	...	6.4	77	53.8[11]	8.6	10.8	4.5	6.6	0.8
Thailand	6.1[9]	35.3[9]	36.4	45.0	0.9	17.7	1,080	29.0	6.3	11.6	8.0	1.7	0.5
Togo	8.0	30.5	...	...	...	...	280	60.9	9.9[2]	7.7	1.6	2	0.6
Tonga	...	...	...	...	...	...		49.3	10.5	5.6	0.3	2.7	...
Trinidad and Tobago	2.6	33.6	...	...	...	...	2,690[10]	25.5[12]	21.6	10.4	[15]	...	1.5
Tunisia	5.9[9]	30.7[9]	...	...	...	...	2,620	39.0	10.7	...	3.0	5.1	1.8
Turkey	3.5[11]	41.5[11]	24.1	51.4	10.8	13.7	1,070	40.0	6.0	15.0	4.0	7.0	1.0
Turkmenistan	...	...	73.5	6.6	17.3	2.6	2,410[1]	49.0	12.5[5]	4.0	...	2	...
Tuvalu	...	...	17.9	76.1	...	6.0		57.1[12,16]	...	5.5[16]	...	7.3[16]	...
Uganda	8.5[9]	27.2[9]	...	...	...	...	165	41.3	1.7	...	...	2	3
Ukraine	...	...	71.9	5.5	22.6		930	24.1	23.7	9.1	1.1	1.2	3.9
United Arab Emirates	...	...	...	...	...	...	9,920						
United Kingdom	4.6[11]	27.8[11]	60.4	13.7	13.5	12.4	9,970	19.1	14.6	5.9	1.6	4.0	1.1
United States	3.8	46.9[30,40]	63.8	8.2	11.9	16.2	15,530	15.0	14.3	5.4	15.5	2.9	[15]
Uruguay	6.0[11,18]	29.3[11,18]	53.5	20.8	30.1		2,660	39.9	17.6[2]	7.0	9.3	2	1.3
Uzbekistan	...	...	61.8	—	22.8	15.4	320[1]	30.5[12]	29.0[2,5]	4.7	[20]	2	...
Vanuatu	...	...	56.7	[8]	7.7	35.6[8]	660[1]						
Venezuela	4.8[14]	33.2[14]	...	...	...	...	2,140	39.3	7.6	8.1	2.2	1.7	0.6
Vietnam	...	...	17.2	64.6	17.6	0.5	...	62.4	2.5	5.0	...	...	2.9
Virgin Islands (U.S.)	...	...	65.7	2.6	13.0	12.7	1,380[7]	25.3[41]	24.9[41]	5.4[41]	...	6.5[41]	...
West Bank	...	...	...	...	...	...							
Western Sahara	...	...	...	...	...	...							
Western Samoa	...	...	49.4	22.8	...	27.8	710[1]	58.8	5.1[5]	4.2	...	5.0	...
Yemen	...	...	...	...	...	...	590	61.0[42]	13.2[42]	...	1.1[42]	6.1[42]	...
Yugoslavia	5.3[14,43]	27.4[14,43]	53.1	9.3	15.3	22.3	2,480[10]	48.0	2.8	8.5	4.5	9.1	3
Zaire	...	...	...	...	...	...	190	61.7	11.5[2]	9.7	2.6	2	3
Zambia	5.6[9]	34.2[9]	79.9	17.8	1.3	1.0	350	36.0	7.0	10.0	8.0	4.0	14.0
Zimbabwe	4.0	46.9	...	...	...	...	350	30.1[11]	6.5	10.3	7.1	8.9	6.0

[1]1990. [2]Housing includes energy, water. [3]Recreation includes education. [4]1988. [5]Housing includes household durable goods. [6]1989. [7]1986. [8]Other includes self-employment. [9]Data refer to expenditure shares by fractiles of persons. [10]1991. [11]Based on posttax income. [12]Includes tobacco. [13]1985. [14]Data refer to income shares by fractiles of persons. [15]Personal effects, other includes education and recreation. [16]Capital city only. [17]Includes wage taxes. [18]Urban areas only. [19]Based on posttax per capita income. [20]Recreation includes health care. [21]Data refer to former Czechoslovakia. [22]Ethiopia includes Eritrea. [23]1984. [24]Wage earners only. [25]Low-income population in Banjul and Kombo St. Mary only. [26]Former West Germany only. [27]Urban areas of

transportation, communications	household durable goods[f]	recreation[g]	personal effects, other[h]	food consumption daily available calories per capita (1988–90)	percent of total calories (latest) derived from: cereals	potatoes, cassava	meat, poultry	fish	eggs, milk	fruits, vegetables	fats, oils[i]	other[i]	country
23.6[34]	10.2[34]	6.6[3,34]	10.9[34]	2,681	33.5	3.3	16.0	1.9	9.3	6.6	11.4	18.1	Netherlands Antilles
24.0	5	11.6	12.5	2,909	40.2	6.4	10.0	1.2	5.7	4.5	13.1	18.9	New Caledonia
15.7	6.9	7.8[3]	19.4	3,460	22.3	2.8	16.8	1.6	10.8	6.3	16.4	23.0	New Zealand
...	...	...	...	2,234	51.1	1.6	2.1	—	4.7	2.9	8.3	29.3	Nicaragua
...	5	...	23.1	2,240	73.9	3.6	2.1	—	2.1	1.1	3.0	14.2	Niger
3.0	6.0	...	27.0	2,199	36.8	34.2	1.3	0.4	0.5	3.3	11.8	11.6	Nigeria
8.3	5	13.9[20]	...	...	...	...	...	...	...	...	...	...	Northern Mariana Islands
12.8	0.9	8.8	15.1	3,221	27.0	5.3	10.6	4.2	13.2	4.9	10.9	18.0	Norway
8.9	7.1	4.1[3]	4.0	...	...	...	...	...	...	...	...	...	Oman
13.0	5.0	...	21.0	2,283	58.9	0.4	2.2	0.1	7.3	2.6	13.8	14.6	Pakistan
15.1	8.4	11.7[3]	8.7	2,269	37.7	3.1	7.5	1.3	7.0	6.6	13.8	23.0	Panama
13.0	5	...	22.5	2,589	23.0	26.5	5.9	1.9	0.8	24.8	4.8	12.1	Papua New Guinea
4.5	6.2	2.3	7.3	2,684	29.2	17.0	11.7	0.2	4.2	8.0	10.7	19.0	Paraguay
6.8	11.3	11.2[3]	23.2	2,035	42.9	9.3	5.2	1.7	5.2	4.9	7.2	23.7	Peru
5.3	13.2	...	18.5	2,343	56.3	4.5	5.3	3.2	1.9	7.3	5.8	16.7	Philippines
8.9	8.3	15.0[3]	3.8	3,426	33.3	5.8	12.1	0.9	10.8	3.3	15.4	18.4	Poland
15.4	8.6	4.4	15.6	3,342	30.8	5.5	11.9	2.6	6.6	5.8	17.1	19.6	Portugal
11.8	11.2	7.9	14.7	...	...	...	...	...	...	...	...	...	Puerto Rico
13.0	5	—11.1—		...	...	...	...	...	...	...	...	...	Qatar
21.2	8.4	6.3[3]	8.7	3,083	47.8	2.3	10.5	1.5	5.3	5.1	10.3	17.2	Réunion
6.6	5	4.5[3]	4.5	3,001	44.1	4.0	8.3	0.7	7.9	5.3	13.6	16.0	Romania
...	9.4	...	30.8	3,380[37]	36.8[37]	5.3[37]	10.6[37]	2.1[37]	8.8[37]	3.4[37]	13.2[37]	19.8[37]	Russia
9.0	9.0	...	18.0	1,915	18.0	31.0	1.0	—	1.4	16.0	2.5	30.1	Rwanda
4.3	9.4	...	9.0	2,435	18.7	3.8	11.3	3.4	7.9	4.2	18.6	32.1	St. Kitts and Nevis
6.3	5.8	3.2[3]	8.3	2,424	26.7	5.7	14.0	1.3	7.7	9.8	11.0	23.8	St. Lucia
3.7	6.6	...	9.7	2,460	34.6	10.6	8.8	0.4	5.2	4.1	7.4	28.9	St. Vincent and the Grenadines
17.6	7.2	7.1[3]	14.5	3,498	32.1	2.1	11.0	1.1	8.6	7.4	21.7	15.9	San Marino
...	...	...	...	2,153	31.3	13.9	1.3	2.5	1.2	2.9	16.4	30.5	São Tomé and Príncipe
4.5[18,38]	5.9[18,38]	...	8.6[18,38]	2,932	49.5	0.8	6.0	0.5	6.7	10.5	11.4	13.6	Saudi Arabia
5.0	2.0	...	12.0	2,323	63.3	1.3	3.7	1.9	2.6	1.2	12.4	13.6	Senegal
6.4	6.6	1.4	4.4	2,356	48.9	1.1	5.3	2.4	5.9	3.5	11.6	21.3	Seychelles
4.4	3.9	3.8[3]	4.8	1,899	52.7	5.8	1.1	1.4	0.8	3.6	21.7	13.0	Sierra Leone
13.8	8.9	14.8	22.9	3,121	41.4	2.3	15.0	1.8	4.8	7.2	5.7	21.9	Singapore
...	3.9	...	26.2	...	...	...	...	...	...	...	...	...	Slovakia
12.7	3.3	6.1[3]	8.0	...	...	...	...	...	...	...	...	...	Slovenia
9.9	5	...	15.7	2,277	25.3	36.6	3.6	5.4	0.7	2.0	0.7	16.8	Solomon Islands
...	...	...	12.1[10]	1,873	52.8	0.9	6.6	0.3	21.2	2.2	8.6	7.4	Somalia
15.0	10.2	6.1	11.5	3,134	53.0	1.7	7.6	0.7	4.0	2.4	9.5	20.3	South Africa
15.2	6.5	6.6[3]	25.4	3,472	21.3	5.2	20.0	1.6	8.6	7.3	17.5	18.5	Spain
14.8	5.0	2.8	10.1	2,246	57.5	3.1	0.4	1.4	2.8	4.7	3.8	26.1	Sri Lanka
1.5	5.5	0.7[3]	9.7	2,042	56.0	0.8	4.2	0.1	11.3	3.0	10.6	14.0	Sudan, The
9.5[16]	12.3[16]	5.8[16]	4.0[16]	2,436	52.1	2.0	0.5	0.5	6.2	4.1	9.9	18.8	Suriname
8.8	12.8	3.3[3]	20.4	2,634	53.9	1.1	4.7	—	3.7	3.6	7.5	25.5	Swaziland
17.3	6.1	9.0	9.6	2,976	21.1	4.4	10.1	2.3	15.3	5.5	20.1	21.3	Sweden
11.7	4.9	10.3[3]	11.2	3,508	20.3	2.4	17.6	0.7	12.9	5.8	18.3	22.0	Switzerland
3.8	5.1	3.1[3]	7.8	3,121	53.1	1.4	3.0	—	6.3	7.2	13.1	15.8	Syria
13.4	3.0	17.3[3]	7.1	2,872	36.8	2.5	14.3	1.9	3.1	8.3	14.4	18.7	Taiwan
...	...	...	...	...	...	...	...	...	...	...	...	...	Tajikistan
6.4	6.3	1.6	0.6	2,195	48.5	22.6	2.3	1.2	1.7	6.0	5.0	12.6	Tanzania
12.9	10.9	4.2	14.9	2,280	58.7	1.1	5.0	1.6	1.4	5.6	5.3	21.4	Thailand
8.2	3.9	0.4	6.8	2,269	47.7	29.0	2.3	1.2	0.6	1.8	9.3	8.0	Togo
5.8	10.6	0.5	14.7	2,967	15.7	35.1	12.2	2.0	2.1	4.5	8.0	20.5	Tonga
15.2	14.3	15	6.2[15]	2,769	42.1	2.5	5.0	0.5	6.5	3.4	13.1	26.9	Trinidad and Tobago
9.0	11.2	7.1	7.1	3,123	53.0	1.3	2.7	0.6	4.7	5.5	17.6	14.5	Tunisia
5.0	...	...	22.0	3,197	48.4	3.7	2.5	0.4	2.9	8.5	15.8	18.0	Turkey
...	...	...	...	...	...	...	...	...	...	...	...	...	Turkmenistan
12.0	5	...	22.5	...	...	...	...	...	...	...	...	...	Tuvalu
5.9[16]	...	...	24.2[16]	2,179	23.5	30.8	2.4	1.1	1.7	17.3	1.8	21.3	Uganda
...	6.8	6.3[3]	43.9	...	...	...	...	...	...	...	...	...	Ukraine
14.1	11.6	4.7	6.5	3,286	34.6	1.3	11.5	1.4	9.3	14.6	10.8	16.4	United Arab Emirates
17.2	6.5	8.7	21.3	3,270	22.1	6.1	14.7	0.9	11.8	4.5	17.8	22.1	United Kingdom
11.4	7.9	15	27.6[15]	3,642	21.7	2.7	14.7	0.8	11.4	5.6	18.1	25.0	United States
10.4	6.3	3.1	5.1	2,668	36.8	3.9	18.3	0.2	13.0	3.7	9.6	14.4	Uruguay
...	...	...	...	...	...	...	...	...	...	...	...	...	Uzbekistan
13.2	5	12.3[20]	10.3	2,736	21.7	24.5	12.2	2.2	1.8	3.3	10.4	23.9	Vanuatu
6.5	4.1	1.9	28.0	2,440	36.4	2.0	5.9	1.2	7.4	7.3	16.1	23.6	Venezuela
...	4.6	...	22.6	2,216	72.7	7.5	0.0	0.9	0.5	4.3	1.8	6.2	Vietnam
11.7[41]	4.3[41]	...	21.9[41]	...	...	...	...	...	...	...	...	...	Virgin Islands (U.S.)
...	...	...	...	...	44.4	1.9	6.1	0.1	6.2	11.0	12.5	17.8	West Bank
...	...	...	...	...	...	...	...	...	...	...	...	...	Western Sahara
9.0	5	...	17.9	2,469	20.1	19.1	12.0	3.6	1.2	13.2	8.4	22.4	Western Samoa
1.9[42]	3.0[42]	...	13.7[42]	2,231	66.9	1.0	3.5	0.4	3.7	3.5	6.5	14.4	Yemen
8.7	3.3	4.6[3]	10.8	3,545[42]	43.2[42]	2.3[42]	8.2[42]	0.2[42]	7.9[42]	3.7[42]	16.9[42]	17.7[42]	Yugoslavia
5.9	4.8	3.8[3]	—	2,129	16.4	55.8	1.8	0.7	0.1	7.7	7.0	10.4	Zaire
5.0	1.0	...	15.0	2,016	75.0	4.8	2.4	0.7	1.3	1.6	3.2	11.0	Zambia
1.1	12.9	0.6	16.5	2,256	59.4	1.4	2.5	0.2	1.5	1.1	9.6	24.3	Zimbabwe

Eastern Region only.   [28]Personal effects, other includes health care.   [29]Housing includes water.   [30]Highest 20%.   [31]Workers and clerical workers only.   [32]Earned income only.   [33]Malagasy households only.   [34]Curaçao and Bonaire only.   [35]1987.   [36]Rural areas only.   [37]Data refer to former U.S.S.R.   [38]Middle-income population only.   [39]Excludes transfer payments and property income.   [40]Income of highest 5% of households is 18.6%.   [41]St. Thomas only.   [42]Data refer to former Yemen Arab Republic.   [43]Data refer to former Socialist Republic of Yugoslavia.

Health services

The provision of health services in most countries is both a principal determinant of the quality of life and a large and growing sector of the national economy. This table summarizes the basic indicators of health personnel; hospitals, by kind and utilization; mortality rates that are most indicative of general health services; external controls on health (adequacy of food supply and availability of safe drinking water); and sources and amounts of expenditure on health care. Each datum refers more or less directly to the availability or use of a particular health service in a country, and, while each may be an accurate measure at a national level, each may also conceal considerable differences in availability of the particular service to different segments of a population or regions of a country. In the United States, for example, the availability of physicians ranges from about one per 775 persons in the least well-served states to one per 283 in the best-served, with a rate of one per 148 in the national capital. Such disparities are even more pronounced in most other countries, unless the government has made some special effort to achieve a more even distribution of personnel and facilities. In addition, even when trained personnel exist and facilities have been created, the country may lose health professionals via the "brain drain" to foreign countries; or low levels of financial support at the national level may leave facilities underserved; or lack of good transportation may prevent those most in need from reaching a clinic or hospital that could help them.

Definitions and limits of data have been made as specific as possible in the compilation of this table. For example, despite wide variation worldwide in the nature of the qualifying or certifying process that permits an individual to represent himself as a physician, organizations such as the World Health Organization (WHO) try to maintain more consistent international standards for training and qualification. International statistics presented here for "physicians" refer to persons qualified according to WHO standards and exclude traditional health practitioners, whatever the local custom with regard to the designation "doctor." Statistics for health personnel in this table uniformly include all those actually working in the health service field, whether in the actual provision of services or in teaching, administration, research, or other tasks. One group of practitioners for whom this type of guideline works less well is that of midwives, whose training and qualifications vary enormously from country to country but who must be included, as they represent, after nurses, perhaps the largest and most important category of health auxiliary worldwide. The statistics here refer to those midwives working in some kind of institutional setting (a hospital, clinic, community health-care centre, or the like) and exclude rural noninstitutional midwives and traditional birth attendants.

Hospitals also differ considerably worldwide in terms of staffing and services. In this tabulation, the term hospital refers generally to a permanent facility offering inpatient services and/or nursing care and staffed by at least one physician. Establishments offering only outpatient or custodial care are excluded. These statistics are broken down into data for general hospitals (those providing care in more than one specialty), specialized facilities (with care in only one specialty), local medical centres, and rural health-care centres; the last two generally refer to institutions that provide a more limited range of medical or nursing care, often less than full-time. Hospital data are further analyzed into three categories of administrative classification: public, private nonprofit, and private for profit. Statistics on

Health services

country	health personnel year	physicians	dentists	nurses	pharmacists	midwives	population per physician	hospitals year	number	general	specialized	medical centres	rural	government	private nonprofit	private for profit	hospital beds per 10,000 pop.
Afghanistan	1989–91	2,233	267	1,451	510	338	7,414	1982	68	66.2	16.2	—	17.6	86.8	13.2	—	5
Albania	1990	4,467	1,099	...	772[4]	9,936[4]	729	1989	895	—17.9—		—82.1—		100.0	—	—	57
Algeria	1990	23,550	7,199	24,700[7]	2,134	3,800[7]	1,062	1990	284[8]	...	...	...	...	...	...	...	24
American Samoa	1989	34	7	140	2	1	1,384	1990	1	100.0	—	—	—	100.0	—	—	27
Andorra	1990	105	...	...	2[9]	...	502	1990	1	100.0	—	—	—	100.0	—	—	23
Angola	1990	662	...	9,145	...	1,237[11]	15,136	1990	58	...	...	...	...	...	...	...	12
Antigua and Barbuda	1991	59	13	179	13	...	1,119	1991	2	50.0	50.0	—	—	100.0	—	—	63
Argentina	1988	96,000	21,900[15]	18,000[10]	681[9]	...	328	1980	3,189	84.2	15.8	—	—	41.9	3.6	54.5	48[4]
Armenia	1992	13,600[16]	16	34,000[17]	...	17	254[16]	1991	183	...	...	...	...	100.0	—	—	83[18]
Aruba	1992	74	19	515[15]	13	3	936	1992	2	50.0	—	50.0	—	100.0	—	—	44
Australia	1986	36,610	6,310	182,236[17]	10,637	[17]	438	1990	1,071[14]	...	...	...	...	65.5[14]	—34.5[14]—		50
Austria	1992	24,049	3,354	31,920	2,004[20]	825	327	1992	323	39.3	60.7	—	—	...	...	...	95
Azerbaijan	1992	29,100[16]	16	72,200[17]	...	17	251[16]	1991	749	...	...	...	...	100.0	—	—	100[18]
Bahamas, The	1992	357	31[9]	682[21]	52[21]	...	714	1990	5	60.0	20.0	20.0	—	60.0	—40.0—		45
Bahrain	1991	535	38	1,607	121	...	937	1991	12	58.3	42.7	—	—	75.0	16.7	8.3	23
Bangladesh	1991	21,004	523	9,655	...	7,713	5,264	1991	890	68.9[11]	5.1[11]	23.1[11]	2.9[11]	68.5	—31.5—		3
Barbados	1990	294	33	836	...	436[9]	886	1982	11	27.3	18.2	—	54.5	81.8	—	18.2	80[21]
Belarus	1992	42,700[16]	16	115,700[17]	...	17	242[16]	1991	868	...	...	...	...	36.3	—63.7—		127[18]
Belgium	1993	36,178	6,850	...	12,896	...	278	1982	531	53.3	46.7	—	—	100.0	—	—	80[15]
Belize	1991	96	12	282	15	114	2,021	1991	7	...	...	...	...	100.0	—	—	30
Benin	1989	323	16	1,384	86	453	13,879	1980	131	4.6	9.9	80.9	4.6	87.8	12.2	—	13[29]
Bermuda	1992	59	27	548	36	...	1,022	1989	2	50.0	50.0	—	—	...	...	...	68
Bhutan	1990	141	9	233	5	70	5,226	1993	27	...	...	...	...	...	...	...	12
Bolivia	1991	2,868	1,298[4,31]	2,319[4,31]	...	...	2,561	1987[32]	553	—14.8—		27.3	57.9	...	...	...	8[21]
Bosnia and Herzegovina	1989	6,929	1,368	...	781	...	624	1989	...	...	...	...	...	...	...	...	46
Botswana	1988	240	21	2,488	40	...	4,964	1990	30	...	...	...	...	80.0	10.0	10.0	25
Brazil	1988	169,488	97,675	...	42,347	...	848	1990	35,701	—18.3—		—81.7—		66.8	—33.2—		37[24]
Brunei	1992	197	27	1,228	10	254	1,359	1992	10	90.0	—	—	10.0	90.0	—10.0—		36
Bulgaria	1993	28,457	5,727	52,038	2,376	6,903	298	1993	286	74.7[15]	25.3[15]	—	—	...	...	...	107
Burkina Faso	1991[31]	341	19	2,627	113	339	27,158	1993	78	—14.1—		85.9		100.0	—	—	5[15]
Burundi	1990	317	9	670[31]	55	97[31]	16,657	1988	264	—12.5—		—87.5—		87.5	—12.5—		19[21]
Cambodia	1988	425	36[18]	7,271	262[18]	2,232	18,518	1988	188[32]	...	...	...	...	100.0	—	—	16
Cameroon	1989	945	55	6,053	206	...	11,849	1988	629	—27.0—		—73.0—		72.3	—27.7—		26[4]
Canada	1991	60,559	14,621	262,288	22,121	...	464	1989	1,079	81.8	16.6	1.6	—	95.8	—	4.2	70
Cape Verde	1988	112	...	205	9	10[9]	2,931	1980	21	9.5	4.8	61.9	23.8	100.0	—	—	15[4]
Central African Republic	1990	170	8	1,353	22	166	16,447	1988	133	—21.1—		—78.9—		79.7	—20.3—		15
Chad	1989	147	5	86	19	40	38,910	1978	4	100.0	—	—	—	82.9	—17.1—		8
Chile	1992	15,062	1,125[15,28]	204[15,28]	...	...	889	1992	217	...	...	...	...	100.0	—	—	32
China	1992	1,808,000[35]	...	1,040,000	408,000[15]	59,000[15]	648[35]	1991	63,101	15.6	6.0	—78.4—		100.0	—	—	26[18]
Colombia	1989	29,498	14,050	45,735	...	...	1,078	1989	947	...	...	...	...	...	...	...	14
Comoros	1990	57	6	155	6	86	8,135	1980	17	17.7	—	23.5	58.8	100.0	—	—	23[29]
Congo	1990	613	35	1,624	175	498	4,028	1978	473	0.6	0.2	97.3	1.9	94.9	5.1	—	22[10]
Costa Rica	1991	3,123	1,167	4,755	1,260	...	981	1980	39	48.7	28.2	—23.1—		92.3	—	7.7	23[15]
Côte d'Ivoire	1990	2,020	219	3,691	135	1,533	5,931	1988	...	...	...	...	...	...	...	...	9
Croatia	1992	9,261	1,984	...	1,696	...	517	1992	98	32.7	61.3	—	—	...	...	...	61
Cuba	1990	38,800	6,482[10]	58,589[10]	650[11]	...	274	1990	274	38.0	—37.9—		24.1	100.0	—	—	56
Cyprus[38]	1991	1,264	461	2,476[17]	96[21]	17	457	1991	...	...	...	...	...	...	...	...	59
Czech Republic	1992	31,935	5,918	...	...	...	323	1992	285	63.2	36.8	—	—	100.0	—	—	98
Denmark	1994	14,497	5,088	63,841	1,498[24]	915[7]	358	1992	163	42.9	57.1	—	—	42.9	57.1	—	35
Djibouti	1989	97	10	359[9]	14	175[9]	5,258	1989[32]	13	—69.2—		30.8		100.0	—	—	27
Dominica	1991	38	4[21]	273[17,24]	12[21]	17	1,889	1990	10	—30.0—		—70.0—		100.0	—	—	41
Dominican Republic	1990	7,332	689	5,398	129[11]	...	934	1987	103	—44.7—		—55.3—		...	...	...	20
Ecuador	1992	12,853	1,826	4,215	...	667	836	1992	429	16.1	6.1	—77.8—		...	...	...	16
Egypt	1990	31,312	5,910	44,022	9,774	...	1,698	1982	1,521	32.3	13.2	15.9	38.6	83.1	3.8	13.1	20[15]
El Salvador	1991	4,080	800[24]	4,898[24]	597[9]	1,940	1,322	1989	42	45.2	14.3	40.5	—	69.0	—	31.0	10

number of beds refer to beds that are maintained and staffed on a full-time basis for a succession of inpatients to whom care is provided.

Data on hospital utilization refer to institutions defined as above. Admission and discharge, the two principal points at which statistics are normally collected, are the basis for the data on the amount and distribution of care by kind of facility. The data on numbers of patients exclude babies born during a maternal confinement but include persons who die before being discharged. The bed-occupancy and average length-of-stay statistics depend on the concept of a "patient-day," which is the annual total of daily censuses of inpatients. The bed-occupancy rate is the ratio of total patient-days to potential days based on the number of beds; the average length-of-stay rate is the ratio of total patient-days to total admissions. Bed-occupancy rates may exceed 100% because stays of partial days are counted as full days.

Two measures that give health planners and policy makers an excellent indication of the level of ordinary health care are those for mortality of children under age five and for maternal mortality. The former reflects the probability of a newborn infant dying before age five. The latter refers to deaths attributable to delivery or complications of pregnancy, childbirth, the puerperium (the period immediately following birth), or abortion.

Levels of nutrition and access to safe drinking water are two of the most basic limitations imposed by the physical environment in which health-care activities take place. The nutritional data are based on recommendations of the United Nations' Food and Agriculture Organization for the necessary daily intake (in calories) for a moderately active person of average size in a climate of a particular kind (fewer calories are needed in a hot climate) to remain in average *good* health. Excess intake in the many developed countries ranges to more than 40% above the minimum required to maintain health (the excess usually being construed to diminish, rather than raise, health). The range of deficiency is less dramatic numerically but far more critical to the countries in which deficiencies are chronic, because the deficiencies lead to overall poor health (raising health service needs and costs), to decreased productivity in nearly every area of national economic life, and to the loss of social and economic potential through early mortality. By "safe" water is meant only water that has no substantial quantities of chemical or biological pollutants—*i.e.*, quantities sufficient to cause "immediate" health problems.

Two principal kinds of public health-care finance data are given, health insurance and central government expenditure. The data on insurance refer to public programs only and identify the mandated basis or extent of responsibility for costs or funding required under the relevant law of the principal participants (individuals, employers, and government). Data on public health-care expenditure refer to a consolidated statement of expenditure, budgetary and otherwise, by all elements of the central government but exclude expenditure by other levels of government (state, city, etc.) and parastatal expenditures. In a number of countries significant government expenditures for health-care services are made at these other levels, amounting to 2, 10, and sometimes 20 times the level of central government expenditure. These expenditures may include costs for national health insurance, family-planning programs, and workers' compensation. Expenditures at the national level for social security are excluded.

admissions or discharges					mortality				popu-lation with access to safe water (latest) (%)	food supply (% of FAO require-ment) 1988–90	financing of public health care, latest year					country
	by kinds of hospital (%)				bed occu-pancy rate (%)	aver-age length of stay (days)	under age 5 per 1,000 live newborn 1992	maternal mortality per 100,000 live births 1990–91			health-care insurance			public health expendi-tures (% of natl. budget)	public health expendi-tures per capita (U.S.$)	
rate per 10,000 pop.	general	special-ized	medical centres	rural							indiv. (% of earn-ings)	em-ployer (% of payroll)	govt (% of covered earnings)			
76[1]	52.8[1]	46.7[1]	—	0.5[1]	58.0[1]	8[1]	257	640[2]	23	72	3.0[3]		3.0[3]	...	...	Afghanistan
	...	...	...	...	...	...	34		97	107	10.0[3]	26.0[3]	5	...	23[6]	Albania
568[9]	...	...	...	...	...	...	72	140[2]	68	123	1.5	12.5	—	...	36[6]	Algeria
965	100.0	—	—	—	38.4	4	11[10]		...	...	...	...	...	25.5	320	American Samoa
...	...	...	...	...	...	...	...		100	...	...	...	...	...	...	Andorra
238	...	...	...	...	44.5[12]	16[12]	292	000[13]	41	80	...	...	...	7.5	6[6]	Angola
63[14]	...	...	...	...	49.9[14]	7[14]	25		100	95	2.5	2.5	—	...	...	Antigua and Barbuda
...	...	...	...	...	...	...	24	48.6[4]	65	116	3.0	5.4	—	3.0	7	Argentina
...	...	...	...	...	...	...	34	40.1	...	...	...	...	...	10.3	150[6]	Armenia
...	...	...	...	...	92.2		...		...	...	...	...	...	...	...	Aruba
...	...	...	...	...	...	...	9	3.5[18]	99	124	1.3[19]	—	5	12.7	580	Australia
2,559	...	...	...	...	78.2	11	9	3.1[18]	100	133	4.0[19]	4.0[19]	—	13.0	1,070	Austria
...	...	...	...	...	...	...	53	28.6[10]	...	...	...	...	...	8.2	98[6]	Azerbaijan
865[8]	...	...	...	...	86.8[8]	14[8]	29	69.3[4]	100	115	1.7[3, 22]	7.1[3, 23]	—	14.5	290	Bahamas, The
1,274[24]	...	...	...	...	80.0[24]	7[24]	16	7.9[4]	100	...	—	—	—	9.0	260	Bahrain
853[4]	...	...	...	...	...	...	127	600[2]	84	88	—	25, 26	27	4.8	2	Bangladesh
842	93.9	4.6	—	1.5	89.8[8]	34[8]	12	26.7[24]	100	133	0.7	0.7	—	11.9	260	Barbados
...	...	...	...	...	...	...	23	24.8[10]	...	...	1.0[3]	4.7[3, 22]	5	2.5	3	Belarus
1,552	91.0	9.0	—	—	85.3	19	11	6.6[10]	100	149	4.7	6.1	—	1.7	130	Belgium
...	...	...	...	...	...	...	52	43.2[28]	75	114	19	19	19	10.2	88	Belize
...	...	...	...	...	...	...	147	160[2]	51	104	—	0.2[30]	—	5.6	3	Benin
1,327	96.6	3.4	—	—	83.0	16	9[21]		...	112	19	19	—	14.5	680	Bermuda
...	...	...	...	...	...	...	201	1,310[2]	34	128	...	...	...	4.8	3	Bhutan
...	...	...	...	...	...	...	118	600[2]	52	84	5.0	10.0	—	8.2	12	Bolivia
529[14]	...	...	...	...	82.4[14]	11[14]	...	56.0[10]	...	...	...	...	...	...	...	Bosnia and Herzegovina
...	...	...	...	...	93.1[10]		58	250[2]	90	97	—	19	—	4.7	46	Botswana
1,277	...	...	...	...	...	...	65	65.3[11]	87	114	19	20.3	19	6.9	46	Brazil
1,069[29]	98.5[29]	—	—	1.5[29]	38.0[29]	4[29]	10		100	128	—	...	—	3.4	190	Brunei
2,118[29]	...	...	...	...	84.4[29]	16[29]	20	15.7[18]	99	148	—	35.0[3]	5	4.8	61	Bulgaria
...	...	...	...	...	...	...	150	810[2]	68	94	—	11.5[33]	—	7.2	4	Burkina Faso
109[7]	...	...	...	...	...	...	179	800[13]	57	84	—	...	—	...	6[6]	Burundi
...	...	...	...	...	...	...	184	500[2]	36	96	...	...	...	...	...	Cambodia
...	...	...	...	...	...	...	117	430[2]	48	95	—	7.0[33]	—	3.4	7	Cameroon
1,677[34]	93.9[34]	6.0[34]	0.1[34]	—	75.7[29]	13[29]	8	3.0	100	122	19	10	19	5.2	250	Canada
...	...	...	...	...	...	...	60		71	118	3.0	2.0	—	...	...	Cape Verde
326[9]	...	...	...	...	41.9[9]	7[9]	179	600[2]	24	82	—	12.0[30, 33]	—	...	5[6]	Central African Republic
...	...	...	...	...	...	...	209	960[2]	57	73	—	6.0[30, 33]	—	...	1[6]	Chad
797[4]	...	...	...	...	73.8[4]	8[4]	18	48.3[5]	86	102	19	—	19	11.1	73	Chile
460	—60.8—		—39.2—		80.9	16	43	115[5]	72	112	—	36	...	...	5[6]	China
614	41.4	16.7	—41.9—		57.2	6	20	77.0[11]	86	106	2.3	4.7	—	5.3	11	Colombia
...	...	...	...	...	...	...	130	500[13]	63	75	—	...	—	7.3	12	Comoros
...	...	...	...	...	...	...	110	900[2]	38	103	—	0.2[30]	—	...	21[6]	Congo
1,192	77.8	16.7	—5.5—		75.7	8	16	30.8	93	121	5.5	9.3	0.3	32.0	150	Costa Rica
...	...	...	...	...	...	...	124	680[13]	76	111	—	0.5[37]	—	...	106	Côte d'Ivoire
1,172	80.1	19.9	—	—	78.9	15	13[15]	3.6[10]	...	...	...	...	...	...	...	Croatia
1,619[11]	32.3[11]	—64.2[11]—		3.5[11]	74.4[29]	11[29]	11	38.8[24]	98	135	—	10.0[3]	5	...	49[6]	Cuba
789[8]	96.1[8]	0.8[8]	—	3.1[8]	76.2[8]	12[8]	11	10[13]	100	...	6.3[3]	6.3[3]	4.0[3]	6.5	200	Cyprus[38]
1,909	96.5	3.5	—	—	72.6	14	12	9.9[18]	100	145[39]	5.7	4.5	5	5.6[39]	63[39]	Czech Republic
1,253	92.9	7.1	—	—	80.4	8	8	7.4[18]	100	135	—	—	5	1.1	110	Denmark
...	...	...	...	...	...	...	168	740[13]	45	...	...	...	...	7.2	22	Djibouti
1,016[40]	...	...	...	...	84.3[40]	8[40]	22	48.2[28]	77	120	3.0[3]	6.8[3]	—	12.9	90	Dominica
488	...	...	...	...	55.3	4	50	93.6[7]	67	102	2.5[3]	7.0[3]	2.5[3]	14.0	16	Dominican Republic
518	...	...	...	...	57.5	7	59	122.9[24]	55	105	19	19	19	11.0	17	Ecuador
...	...	...	...	...	...	...	55	65.2[4]	90	132	1.0	4.0	—	2.8	14	Egypt
384	59.7	20.4	19.9	—	64.6	6	63	58.8[7]	47	102	2.5	6.3	19	7.3	9	El Salvador

Health services (continued)

country	health personnel							hospitals		kinds (%)				ownership (%)			hospital beds per 10,000 pop.
	year	physicians	dentists	nurses	pharma- cists	midwives	popu- lation per physi- cian	year	number	gen- eral	spe- cial- ized	medical centres	rural	govern- ment	private non- profit	private for profit	
Equatorial Guinea	1990	99	...	154	...	55	3,532	1982	...	...	...	...	...	...	...	...	112
Eritrea	1986–87	78	...	...	...	...	36,000	1986–87	...	...	...	...	...	...	...	...	9
Estonia	1992	5,360	739	7,671	930[15]	802	288	1992	118	...	...	...	...	100.0	...	...	96
Ethiopia	1988	1,466	...	3,496	364	...	30,195	1986–87	86	...	...	...	...	...	...	...	3
Faeroe Islands	1991	83	42	359	10[24]	17	571	1991	3	33.3	—	—	66.7	100.0	—	—	67
Fiji	1990	300	47	1,651	...	...	2,438	1986	25	...	...	...	...	...	...	...	24[21]
Finland	1992	12,929	4,614	119,213	574[20]	736	390	1991	427	88.5	11.5						123
France	1991	152,096	38,146	308,141	50,940	10,872	374	1991	3,819	—91.6—			8.4	27.9	—72.1—		122
French Guiana	1992	200	32	489	33	31	644	1991	6[4]	50.0[4]	—	—	50.0[4]	50.0[4]	—50.0[4]—		66
French Polynesia	1989	317	88	477	38	89	607	1981	34	8.8	5.9	52.9	32.4	94.1	—	5.9	70[10]
Gabon	1989	448	32	759	71	240	2,504	1985	105	—26.7—		—73.3—		100.0	—	—	45
Gambia, The	1991	61	...	430[10]	...	...	14,536	1989	7	...	...	...	...	57.1	—42.9—		7[15]
Gaza Strip	1984	250	...	...	...	...	2,000	1992	6	...	...	...	...	83.3	—16.7—		14
Georgia	1990	32,100[16]	16	64,100[17]	...	17	170[16]	1990	422	...	...	...	...	100.0	...	...	110
Germany	1992	251,877	56,342	708,000[17]	42,369	17	313	1991	2,411	...	...	...	...	51.5	34.8	13.7	83
Ghana	1989[31]	628	39	11,808	67	1,736	22,452	1991	121	90.9	9.1	—	—	60.3	—39.7—		13
Gibraltar	1992	29	2[24]	302[15]	3[24]	8[24]	981	1991	2	50.0	50.0	—	—	100.0	...	...	78
Greece	1990	34,336	10,038	32,722	7,463[20]	1,860	294	1990	396	46.0	54.0	—	—	37.6	—62.4—		50
Greenland	1991	89	43	356	10	17	621	1990	16	6.3	—	—	93.7	100.0	—	—	75
Grenada	1990	56	7	296	28	36	1,617	1982	39	7.7	7.7	69.2	15.4	100.0	...	...	45[21]
Guadeloupe	1991	590	119	1,476	192	107	680	1991	29[7]	...	...	...	...	37.9[7]	—62.1[7]—		80
Guam	1986	147	...	594[17]	...	17	823	1982	4	25.0	25.0	50.0	—	50.0	—50.0—		21[46]
Guatemala	1987	3,579	810[9]	9,093[9]	411[9]	...	2,356	1985	...	...	...	...	...	...	...	...	17[4]
Guernsey	1993	79	...	...	...	...	804	1993	1	100.0	...	...	...	100.0	...	...	91[29]
Guinea	1990	773	22[24]	243[24]	261[24]	343[24]	7,445	1988	38	—100.0—		...	...	100.0	...	...	6
Guinea-Bissau	1986	274	13	674[7]	12	111[7]	3,245	1981	17	11.8	—	—	88.2	...	...	...	27[11]
Guyana	1990	286	15[10]	854[10]	29[10]	172[10]	2,552	1979	55	20.0	12.7	27.3	40.0	87.3	3.6	9.1	29[4]
Haiti	1989	944	98	2,262[24]	...	...	6,083	1989	87	—77.8[41]—		22.2[41]—		61.1[41]	—38.9[41]—		8
Honduras	1990	2,900	459[24]	1,001[24]	792[24]	...	1,586	1992	59	...	...	...	...	45.8	—54.2—		11
Hong Kong	1993[48]	7,625	1,575	23,239	874	981[18]	776	1982	71	43.7	15.5	39.4	1.4	50.7	26.8	22.5	46[49]
Hungary	1992	36,201	4,668	51,518[21]	4,652[15]	2,695[21]	252	1992	148	75.5[50]	15.3[50]	—9.2[50]—		...	...	...	99
Iceland	1990	726	219	1,793	132	202	353	1990	25	92.0	8.0	—	—	...	...	...	112
India	1992[48]	405,253	11,300	340,208[15]	...	181,323[4]	2,170	1981	25,452	26.7	0.3	65.8	7.2	71.6	—28.4—		9[15]
Indonesia	1990	25,752	3,821[24]	98,842[17]	1,777[24]	17	6,861	1992	985	...	...	...	...	...	...	...	6
Iran	1993	29,000	4,770[18]	43,291[4]	...	...	2,000	1982	581	71.1	15.5	9.8	3.6	66.4	13.9	19.7	15[49]
Iraq	1991	9,366	1,577	13,206	1,552	...	1,922	1990	177	72.9	27.1	—	—	...	...	...	18
Ireland	1988	5,590	1,205	23,127	...	...	632	1991[8, 52]	104	81.7	18.3	—	—	100.0	...	...	39
Isle of Man	1988	86	...	...	...	...	745	1986	3	33.3	33.3	—	33.3	100.0	...	...	109[41]
Israel	1987	11,895	2,900[45]	14,785[45]	2,540[45]	12,110[45]	345	1992	209	22.0	78.0	—	—	21.5	40.7	37.8	59
Italy	1992	296,385	10,814[10]	170,409[10]	53,948[10]	...	193	1991	1,886	71.6	28.4	—	—	60.9	—39.1—		68
Jamaica	1992	1,589	270	1,687	65[31]	340[31]	1,541	1992	30	80.0	20.0	—	—	80.0	—20.0—		22[8]
Japan	1990	211,797	74,028	721,403	150,627	22,918	583	1991	10,066	89.2	10.8	—	—	70.2	—29.8—		136
Jersey	1992	88	...	...	...	...	967	1990	6	16.7	83.3	—	—	100.0	...	...	88
Jordan	1991	6,395	1,477	6,466	2,220	513[21]	574	1992	53[21]	...	...	...	...	52.8[21]	—47.2[21]—		11
Kazakhstan	1992	69,100[16]	16	229,600[17]	...	17	246[16]	1991	1,805	...	...	...	...	100.0	...	...	135[18]
Kenya	1989	3,266	561	25,489	413	...	7,313	1989	558	—47.3—		—52.7—		...	...	...	14
Kiribati	1990	16	17	116	3[7]	...	4,483	1982	34	2.9	97.1	—		100.0	...	...	40[21]
Korea, North	1989	57,690	...	...	...	...	370	1982	7,924	19.3	12.4	—68.3—		...	...	...	135[10]
Korea, South	1990	42,554	9,619	89,032	37,118	7,643	1,007	1990	924	—60.2—		39.8	—	...	...	...	23
Kuwait	1992	2,506	326[31]	9,041[31]	873[31]	137[24]	558	1992[8]	16	...	...	...	...	100.0	...	...	29
Kyrgyzstan	1992	15,758[16]	16	47,669[17]	...	17	283[16]	1992	392	...	...	...	...	100.0	...	...	117
Laos	1990	1,173	...	6,753[7, 17]	...	17	3,555	1990	1,074	0.7	—99.3—			100.0	...	...	25
Latvia	1991	10,696	1,507	16,754	...	...	246	1991	187	...	...	...	...	100.0	...	...	135
Lebanon	1989–91	6,638	1,015	1,248	1,390	153	407	1982	...	...	...	...	...	...	...	...	38
Lesotho	1990	74	...	874	60	...	15,728	1987	22	90.9	9.1	—	—	54.5	45.5		15
Liberia	1985	89	5	908	...	443	24,600	1981	85[47]	...	...	...	...	60.0[47]	—40.0[47]—		15
Libya	1989–91	4,749	686	13,849	618[45]	...	690	1982	64	68.8	31.2	—	—	100.0	...	...	48
Liechtenstein	1992	31	12	...	2	...	956	1985	1	...	...	...	...	...	...	...	37
Lithuania	1992	13,764	2,088	78,300	...	4,900	274	1992	199	...	...	...	...	100.0	...	...	118
Luxembourg	1992	780	198[15]	...	316[15]	134[15]	500	1991	32	56.3	43.7			...	...	...	115
Macau	1992	473	35	848	41	...	798	1992	39	5.1	—	94.9	—	35.9	—64.1—		30
Macedonia	1991	4,487	1,094[10]	...	404[10]	...	454	1991	...	...	...	...	...	...	...	...	54
Madagascar	1990	1,392	89	3,124	19	1,703	8,628	1978	749	0.8	1.1	75.7	22.4	100.0	...	...	23[29]
Malawi	1989	186	...	284	5	...	49,118	1987	395	12.2	0.8	—87.0—		59.2	—40.8—		16
Malaysia	1990	7,012	1,288	36,076[10]	1,084	...	2,475	1989	264	...	...	...	...	38.6	—61.4—		22
Maldives	1992	35	1[21]	152	13[7]	141[7]	6,560	1992	5	20.0	—	80.0	—	100.0	...	...	8
Mali	1988	435	13	1,509	57	321	18,046	1983	162	...	...	...	...	100.0	...	...	6
Malta	1993	860	110	4,011	520	281	424	1991	6	...	...	...	...	...	...	...	93
Marshall Islands	1991	20	2[7]	130	...	4	2,402	1985	2	100.0	...	...	...	100.0	...	...	14
Martinique	1991	625	121	1,567	199	130	584	1991	...	...	...	...	...	...	...	...	103
Mauritania	1991	135	20	819	6	141	14,259	1990	16	...	...	...	...	100.0	...	...	8[24]
Mauritius	1991	990	145	2,682[17]	147	17	1,098	1991	46	23.9	8.7	—67.4—		95.7	—4.3—		28
Mayotte	1985	9	1	51	1	2	7,427	1985	2	100.0	...	...	...	100.0	...	...	12
Mexico	1991	93,371	4,600	141,404	...	...	924	1991	772	...	...	...	...	100.0	...	...	8
Micronesia	1993	50	7	230	7	...	2,069	1993	4	100.0	...	...	...	100.0	...	...	31
Moldova	1992	17,200[16]	16	48,600[17]	...	17	253[16]	1991	335	...	...	...	...	100.0	...	...	128[18]
Monaco	1992	85	31[10]	293[10]	64[10]	8[10]	354	1982	1	100.0	...	...	...	100.0	...	...	199[18]
Mongolia	1991[31]	6,318	200[11]	10,340[21]	30[21]	...	337	1981	1,659	2.1	5.4	71.9	20.6	100.0	...	...	121[15]
Morocco	1990	5,665	701	22,925	1,697	87	4,415	1990[32]	203	31.0	—	69.0	—	100.0	...	...	11
Mozambique	1989	388	118[24]	3,086[24]	332[24]	1,080[24]	35,763	1988	238	4.2	0.8	84.5	13.5	100.0	...	...	9
Myanmar (Burma)	1993	13,353	970	9,177	...	14,281[15]	3,341	1982	614	49.7	2.4	—	47.9	...	...	...	6[15]
Namibia	1992	324	51	4,471	91[15]	...	4,594	1992	47	...	...	...	...	91.5	—8.5—		60[24]
Nauru	1980	11	...	...	...	...	700	1980	...	...	...	...	...	...	...	...	250
Nepal	1992	1,497	...	2,781	427[11]	2,379[11]	12,623	1992	114	...	...	...	...	...	...	...	3
Netherlands, The	1992	37,461[15]	7,900[15]	121,000[10]	2,287	1,167	400[15]	1992	238	66.0	34.0			...	...	...	58

admissions or discharges					bed occu-pancy rate (%)	aver-age length of stay (days)	mortality		popu-lation with access to safe water (latest) (%)	food supply (% of FAO require-ment) 1988–90	financing of public health care, latest year			public health expendi-tures (% of natl. budget)	public health expendi-tures per capita (U.S.$)	country
rate per 10,000 pop.	by kinds of hospital (%)						under age 5 per 1,000 live newborn 1992	maternal mortality per 100,000 live births 1990–91			health-care insurance					
	general	special-ized	medical centres	rural							indiv. (% of earn-ings)	em-ployer (% of payroll)	govt. (% of covered earnings)			
...	...	...	...	...	...	...	182	800[13]	...	...	4.5[3]	21.5[3]	19	...	...	Equatorial Guinea
							208	...	...	...	...	...	...	...	...	Eritrea
...	...	...	...	...	...	...	24	31.4	...	...	—	13.0	5	3.9	170	Estonia
							208	560[2]	25	73	—	—	—	3.0	1	Ethiopia
1,812[11]	76.6[11]	—	—	24.3[11]	60.6	11[11]	...	...	...	...	...	...	...	13.3	1,310	Faeroe Islands
886	...	...	...	...	72.6	7	29	41.1[7]	80	104	—	—	—	7.9	50	Fiji
2,265	96.8	3.2	—	—	100.3	20	7	4.5[10]	95	113	1.0	1.5	5	3.2	290	Finland
2,318[21]	...	...	...	...	83.0[24]	16[24]	9	11.9	100	143	6.8	12.8	...	16.0	1,440	France
1,903	...	...	...	...	75.1	10	...	129.7[9]	...	124	...	...	...	...	...	French Guiana
1,472	70.9	...	3.2	25.9	51.7	8	...	...	...	104	...	...	...	...	...	French Polynesia
258[41]	...	...	...	...	23.6[41]	13[41]	158	190[2]	68	104	—	4.6	—	...	57[6]	Gabon
...	...	...	...	...	...	...	220	1,000[13]	75	100	...	...	...	6.5	5	Gambia, The
1,441	...	...	...	...	80.8	4	...	...	...	...	...	...	...	...	...	Gaza Strip
							29	54.9[10]	...	...	...	...	...	...	...	Georgia
1,823	...	...	...	...	83.8	15	8	8.7	100	132	6.4[19,42]	6.4[19,42]	19	10.1[43]	1,010[43]	Germany
...	...	...	...	...	...	...	170	1,000[2]	52	93	—	19	—	9.0	5	Ghana
1,474	...	...	...	...	41.4	...	...	...	...	...	...	...	...	13.2	640	Gibraltar
1,269	78.3	21.7	—	...	67.6	10	9	2.9	98	151	3.0	5.9	3.8	8.2	360	Greece
2,450	29.2	—	—	70.8	69.4	8	21	...	...	...	...	...	...	10.5	1,510	Greenland
749[44]	...	...	...	...	...	...	35	65.4[4]	85	99	4.0[3]	4.0[3]	...	15.6	22	Grenada
2,136	...	...	...	...	82.3	11	...	89.3[45]	...	114	...	...	...	...	...	Guadeloupe
738[46]	97.6[46]	2.4[46]	—	—	78.8[46]	8[46]	15[10]	...	100	...	...	...	...	8.2	320	Guam
284	...	...	...	...	57.7	9	76	92.3[24]	62	103	2.0	4.0	2.0	9.9	11	Guatemala
1,100	100.0	...	...	...	83.9[29]	28[29]	...	—	...	...	1.6	2.4	...	23.6	900	Guernsey
...	...	...	...	...	...	...	230	800[2]	53	97	1.6	2.4	...	...	5[6]	Guinea
326	59.8	—	—	40.2	57.5	11	239	700[2]	41	97	...	...	...	1.4	4	Guinea-Bissau
...	...	...	...	...	...	...	65	200[13]	61	110	4.4[3]	6.6[3]	—	...	18[6]	Guyana
123[41]	...	...	...	...	...	...	133	340[2]	39	89	...	...	...	...	4[6]	Haiti
429[47]	75.6[47]	16.7[47]	—	7.7[47]	70.2[47]	8[47]	58	220[2]	77	98	2.5	5.0	2.5	...	30[6]	Honduras
1,494	93.6	3.2	3.2	—	82.4	0	7	5.9	100	114	—	—	—	10.8	320	Hong Kong
2,228	...	...	...	...	76.4	12	16	9.9[18]	98	137	4.0	19.5	...	6.2	130	Hungary
2,623	94.7	5.3	—	—	90.2	13	7	0.0[18]	100	131	—	—	51	23.1	2,010	Iceland
...	...	...	...	...	...	...	124	460[2]	85	101	1.5	4.0	—	1.6	1	India
...	...	...	...	...	...	...	111	450[2]	51	121	—	6.0	—	2.8	3	Indonesia
...	...	...	...	...	...	...	58	120[2]	89	125	7.0[3]	20.0[3]	3.0[3]	7.3	24	Iran
645	...	...	...	...	42.4	4	80	120[2]	77	128	5.0[3]	12.0[3]	...	...	15[6]	Iraq
1,478	81.9	18.1	—	—	70.9	7	6	7.6	100	157	1.3	1.3	5	13.0	670	Ireland
1,274[41]	83.9[41]	7.0[41]	—	9.1[41]	81.2[41]	25[41]	4	...	...	...	...	...	...	26.0	520	Isle of Man
1,813	...	...	...	...	92.6	11	11	14.5	100	125	5.6	5.0	0.2	4.4	260	Israel
1,491	90.7	9.3	—	—	70.0	12	10	8.6	100	139	1.0	10.8	...	11.3	770	Italy
550[8]	81.7[8]	18.3[8]	—	—	63.8[8,14]	6[8,14]	14	102[18]	100	114	2.5[3]	2.5[3]	...	...	47[6]	Jamaica
643[29]	97.9[29]	2.1[29]	—	—	83.3[29]	56[29]	6	9.2[18]	97	125	4.1	4.1	...	...	1,247[6]	Japan
1,718	84.0	16.0	—	—	86.8[45]	24[45]	...	...	...	...	...	...	...	19.9	1,240	Jersey
408[8]	...	...	...	...	68.7[8]	30	30	48[2]	99	110	—	—	—	5.2	22	Jordan
...	...	...	...	...	...	...	50	54.8	...	...	...	...	...	8.3	150[6]	Kazakhstan
...	...	...	...	...	...	...	74	170[2]	49	89	19	—	—	5.4	5	Kenya
633	47.6	—	52.4	...	58.0	15	81	...	44	95	—	—	—	13.0	32	Kiribati
...	...	...	...	...	...	...	33	26[2]	100	121	...	...	...	...	13[6]	Korea, North
519[53]	97.8	2.2	—	...	80.6[53]	13[53]	9	9.9[10]	97	120	1.5[22]	1.5[22]	...	1.2	14	Korea, South
927	...	...	...	...	71.7[29]	8[29]	17	1.9[4]	100	126	—	—	51	6.0	570	Kuwait
...	...	...	...	...	...	...	60	62.9	...	...	—	5.2	5	13.2	120[6]	Kyrgyzstan
...	...	...	...	...	...	...	145	300[2]	36	111	...	...	...	...	...	Laos
...	...	...	...	...	...	...	26	23.7	...	...	1.0[3]	37.0[3]	5	6.1	...	Latvia
...	...	...	...	...	...	...	44	200[13]	92	127	3.0	12.0	...	...	...	Lebanon
221[14]	...	...	...	...	...	...	156	350[13]	47	93	...	...	...	11.5	22	Lesotho
...	...	...	...	...	...	...	217	600[13]	50	98	...	...	—	5.1	6	Liberia
719	...	...	...	...	52.7	13	104	70[2]	97	139	1.5	1.4	2.2	2.7	62	Libya
...	...	...	...	...	...	...	5[21]	...	...	...	...	...	...	...	...	Liechtenstein
1,877	...	...	...	...	...	...	20	22.9	...	...	1.0[3]	30.0[3]	5	...	160[6]	Lithuania
1,970	91.7	8.3	—	—	82.2	17	11	0.0[18]	100	149	4.5	4.5	...	4.6	420	Luxembourg
635	...	...	...	...	58.9	10	10[20]	13.2[10]	...	100	...	...	...	...	...	Macau
646[10,14]	...	...	...	...	58.2[10,14]	9[10,14]	...	16.7[10]	...	...	...	...	...	...	...	Macedonia
699[14]	...	...	...	...	57.9[14]	2[14]	168	570[2]	23	95	—	8.3[30,33]	—	6.6	2	Madagascar
436[7]	...	...	...	...	90.6[7]	8[7]	226	400[2]	56	88	—	—	...	7.4	4	Malawi
717[8]	...	...	...	...	...	...	19	59[2]	78	120	...	...	...	5.8	51	Malaysia
291[7]	...	...	...	...	57.5[7,54]	5[7,54]	78	315.6[24]	95	...	...	...	...	9.7	33	Maldives
...	...	...	...	...	...	...	220	2,000[2]	41	96	—	2.0[30]	—	2.1	2	Mali
1,569[29]	...	...	...	...	83.7[29]	19[29]	11	0.0[18]	100	128	8.3[3]	10.0[3]	—	7.4	230	Malta
...	...	...	...	...	...	...	92	...	...	...	—	—	—	18.9	140	Marshall Islands
2,139	...	...	...	...	61.0	11	...	94.8[4]	...	114	...	...	...	...	...	Martinique
...	...	...	...	...	...	...	206	000[10]	66	106	—	2.0[30]	—	...	9[6]	Mauritania
1,301[8,21]	...	...	...	...	84.5[8,47]	8[8,47]	24	99.2[4]	96	128	—	—	51	8.8	56	Mauritius
770	100.0	—	—	—	74.8	6	...	...	...	...	...	...	...	...	...	Mayotte
403	...	...	...	...	64.7	5	33	51.3	76	131	3.1	8.8	0.6	1.9	10	Mexico
2,171[7]	100.0[7]	—	—	—	...	...	29	...	...	...	...	...	...	11.8	190	Micronesia
...	...	...	...	...	...	...	36	34.1[10]	...	...	...	...	...	12.2	140[6]	Moldova
2,630	100.0	...	...	...	77.6	14	...	...	100	...	...	...	...	...	26[6]	Monaco
2,508	25.9	33.0	1.1	40.0	89.1	14	80	140[2]	80	97	...	...	...	7.4	...	Mongolia
238	93.6[50]	—	6.4[50]	—	52.9	9	61	300[2]	56	125	0.2	0.4	...	3.0	9	Morocco
92[14,47]	...	...	...	...	70.2[14,47]	9[14,47]	287	300[2]	22	77	...	...	...	...	2[6]	Mozambique
289	75.7	10.1	—	14.2	78.1	9	113	400[2]	32	114	1.5	1.5	...	6.8	7	Myanmar (Burma)
...	...	...	...	...	...	...	79	070[9]	52	...	...	...	...	9.7	72	Namibia
...	...	...	...	...	...	...	...	...	...	...	...	...	...	14.2	180	Nauru
54[24]	...	...	...	...	...	...	128	830[2]	42	100	...	...	...	4.7	1	Nepal
1,057	97.5	2.5	—	—	78.6	16	7	6.0	100	114	10.0	11.2	5	13.9	1,550	Netherlands, The

Health services (continued)

country	year	physicians	dentists	nurses	pharmacists	midwives	population per physician	year	number	general	specialized	medical centres	rural	government	private non-profit	private for profit	hospital beds per 10,000 pop.
Netherlands Antilles	1992	273	62	998	31	12	701	1992	11	36.4	36.4	27.2	—	...	...	...	75
New Caledonia	1990	216	64	...	46	38	776	1990	8	12.5	12.5	75.0	—	62.5	—37.5—		62
New Zealand	1993	10,787	1,865	43,948	3,478	...	323	1992	337[15]	12.5	12.5	...	...	43.3[15]	—56.7[15]—		77[15]
Nicaragua	1991	2,125	310	2,360	...	...	1,882	1985	52	55.1	8.2	36.7	...	...	...		12[15]
Niger	1990	142	5	2,036	29	457	54,472	1979	...	...	...	...	...	...	...		6
Nigeria	1989	17,954	1,088	64,503	5,318	52,378	4,692	1985	11,588	6.6	0.5	—92.9—		81.4	—18.6—		12[4]
Northern Mariana Islands	1986	23	4	103	2	2	1,324	1988	1	100.0	—	—	—	100.0	—		19
Norway	1994	14,497	5,088	61,367	3,041[45]	...	305	1992	333	21.0	79.0	—	—	...	...		55
Oman	1990	1,579	97	3,944	239	33[45]	969	1989	180	—28.3—		—71.7—		100.0	...		26[21]
Pakistan	1992	60,223	2,279	27,442	3,772	17,678	2,072	1992	10,905	—7.1—		—92.9—		...	...		6
Panama	1992	2,947	571	2,483	...	...	844	1992	57	...	...	...	...	87.0[50]	—13.0[50]—		30
Papua New Guinea	1990	301	...	2,447	...	...	12,874	1980	390	5.1	—	53.6	41.2	46.2	53.8	—	42[10]
Paraguay	1991	2,992	1,017[24]	3,584[9]	...	...	1,470	1991	...	...	...	...	...	...	...		12
Peru	1991	23,098	5,500	16,719	5,940	3,520	952	1992	427	...	...	...	...	56.7	—43.3—		17
Philippines	1993	78,445	1,614[31]	14,853[31]	730[24,31]	12,339[31]	849	1992	1,696	...	...	...	...	34.4	—65.6—		13
Poland	1993	83,724	16,615	203,635	16,338	23,635	459	1992	775	88.3	11.7	—	—	...	...		66
Portugal	1992	28,604	1,267[21]	29,525[7]	5,656[21]	824[7]	344	1989	621	24.8	13.7	61.5	—	86.3	—13.7—		46
Puerto Rico	1988	9,422	...	...	...	...	349	1988	67	...	...	...	...	100.0	—		39
Qatar	1992	758	114	1,829[31]	175[31]	...	671	1992	3	33.3	66.7	—	—	100.0	—		20
Réunion	1993	1,062	281	2,371	239[20]	123	594	1992	...	...	...	...	...	71.1[50]	—28.9[50]—		49
Romania	1992[31]	42,808	6,414	...	6,432[10]	...	531	1992	...	...	...	...	...	...	...		95
Russia	1992	657,000[16]	[16]	1,691,000[17]	...	17	226[16]	1992	12,700	...	...	...	...	100.0	...		135
Rwanda	1989	272	7	835	25	...	24,697	1985[8]	220	—13.6—		—86.4—		100.0	...		9
St. Kitts and Nevis	1990	43	11	190	7[7]	...	975	1990	4	...	...	...	...	...	...		64
St. Lucia	1992	64	6	256	13[9]	...	2,235	1992	4	25.0	25.0	—	50.0	...	...		31
St. Vincent	1992	40	6	224	27[15]	...	2,690	1990	9[4]	11.1[4]	22.2[4]	11.1[4]	55.6[4]	88.9[4]	—11.1[4]—		49[10]
San Marino	1987	60	...	...	...	...	375	1987	...	...	...	...	...	...	...		66
São Tomé and Príncipe	1989	61	5	223	1	54	1,881	1978	16	12.5	—	87.5	—	...	...		63[45]
Saudi Arabia	1991	25,543	1,967	48,066	1,811	...	523	1990	229	...	...	...	...	71.2	—28.8—		21
Senegal	1988	407	58	934	200	474	17,072	1984	87	18.4	29.9	51.7	—	100.0	—		9[24]
Seychelles	1993	70	10	367	5	...	1,018	1993	7	14.3	14.3	71.4	—	100.0	—		59
Sierra Leone	1988	300	18[9]	1,318[9,17]	14[9]	17	13,150	1988	219	—25.6—		—74.4—		...	...		10
Singapore	1993	4,146	743	11,127	720	522	693	1993	21	...	...	...	...	52.4	—47.6—		36
Slovakia	1992	15,767	2,444	...	499	...	336	1991	111	72.1	27.9	—	—	100.0	—		91
Slovenia	1990	4,086	1,148	...	1,019	...	489	1991[14]	27	...	...	...	...	...	...		59
Solomon Islands	1990	52	15[7]	447	...	...	6,129	1986	8	100.0	—	—	—	75.0	25.0		53
Somalia	1986	450	2	1,834	180	556	13,315	1985	...	...	...	...	...	...	...		9
South Africa[58]	1992[48]	25,375	3,998	155,079	9,277	...	1,264	1987	737	51.4	—48.6—			...	...		49
Spain	1991	153,306	11,249	161,285	37,648	6,250	257	1989	830	54.9	45.1	—	—	42.8	—57.2—		43
Sri Lanka	1991[31]	2,962	333[10]	9,955	520[10]	5,030[10]	5,823	1991[8]	420	...	...	...	...	100.0	—		28[21]
Sudan, The	1986[31]	2,405	...	...	...	...	9,439	1981	160	21.9	5.6	—	72.5	...	...	...	9
Suriname	1989	299	22[9]	922[24]	...	...	1,346	1980	17	29.4	17.6	47.1	5.9	58.8	29.4	11.8	47[10]
Swaziland	1990	83	7	1,264	13	...	9,265	1984	23	30.4	8.7	—60.9—		56.5	—43.5—		25
Sweden	1992	22,000	4,900	82,700[17]	5,416	17	394	1991	...	...	...	...	...	...	...		56
Switzerland	1991	22,500	5,000	...	...	...	302	1983	372	52.7	47.3	—	—	...	...		79[15]
Syria	1989–91	10,114	3,362	11,957	3,634	3,201[24]	1,198	1988	213	80.3	19.7	—	—	23.0	—77.0—		12
Taiwan	1993	26,192	6,664	50,296	19,374	1,012	797	1990	827	...	...	...	...	11.5	—88.5—		48[49]
Tajikistan	1992	13,500[16]	[16]	40,800[17]	...	17	412[16]	1991	374	...	...	...	...	100.0	—		108[18]
Tanzania	1984	1,065	...	...	...	...	19,775	1982	3,032	4.9	—	87.2	7.9	...	...		11[9]
Thailand	1991	12,803	2,408	78,240	4,333	10,582	4,327	1991	1,064	92.4	7.6	—	—	75.8	—24.2—		17
Togo	1991	319	22	1,187	65	222	11,270	1979	65	10.8	4.6	61.5	23.1	96.9	3.1	—	16[24]
Tonga	1991	49	11[10]	266[10]	2[10]	37[10]	1,994	1989	4	...	...	...	...	...	...		32
Trinidad and Tobago	1992	982	131	2,347[17]	567	17	1,275	1992	31[7]	...	...	...	...	...	...		35
Tunisia	1992	4,670	836	12,143	1,596	...	1,799	1991[8]	138	5.8	3.6	—90.6—		100.0	—		20
Turkey	1990	50,639	10,514	44,904	15,792	30,415	1,108	1990	857	74.9	8.5	—16.6—		85.4	—14.6—		22
Turkmenistan	1992	13,600[16]	[16]	40,600[17]	...	17	282[16]	1991	368	...	...	...	...	100.0	—		113[18]
Tuvalu	1990	4	2[4]	31[4]	1[7]	...	2,261	1985	8	11.1	—	—	88.9	100.0	—		36
Uganda	1989	704	...	2,332	...	...	22,781	1981	485	15.5	1.2	83.3	—	84.5	15.5	—	12[10]
Ukraine	1992	230,000[16]	[16]	618,000[17]	...	17	227[16]	1992	3,900	...	...	...	...	100.0	—		135
United Arab Emirates	1991	3,090	388[21]	7,130[21]	190[7]	...	618	1993	35	...	...	...	...	82.9	—17.1—		21
United Kingdom	1981	92,172[59]	17,472	182,897	17,589	...	611[59]	1988	2,423[7]	...	...	...	...	100.0	—		64[10]
United States	1992	653,100	179,000	1,853,000	198,000	3,000	389	1992	6,639	82.1	17.9	—	—	31.0	51.1	17.9	46
Uruguay	1992	10,608	3,660	1,841	885	576	295	1992[8]	...	...	...	...	...	...	...		25
Uzbekistan	1992	75,900[16]	[16]	247,000[17]	...	17	282[16]	1991	1,388	...	...	...	...	100.0	—		109[18]
Vanuatu	1990	20	...	321	...	...	7,345	1990	21	—23.8—		—76.2—		...	...		25
Venezuela	1989	32,616	7,945	52,260	5,615	...	590	1992	610	...	...	...	...	37.0	—63.0—		26
Vietnam	1990	23,300[16]	[16]	58,912[15]	12,100[4]	14,813[15]	2,843[16]	1984	10,768	14.6	6.5	78.9	...	100.0	—		25[21]
Virgin Islands (U.S.)	1985	167	...	...	...	...	622	1985	...	...	...	...	...	...	...		49
West Bank	1984	510	...	...	...	...	1,535	1992	16	...	...	...	...	56.3	—43.7—		14
Western Sahara[61]	1982	11	—	...	2	...	13,000	1982[32]	2	50.0	—	50.0	—	100.0	—		9
Western Samoa	1990	50	10[10]	285[10]	...	...	3,183	1984	30	3.3	—	—	96.7	100.0	—		39[10]
Yemen	1990	2,708	144	6,430	188	199	4,166	1990	74	...	...	...	...	...	...		9
Yugoslavia	1991	21,230	4,643	...	2,651	...	497	1991	...	...	...	...	...	...	...		57
Zaire	1990	2,469	41	27,601	59	...	15,584	1979	942	37.3	38.9	23.8	—	40.9	44.6	14.5	21[7]
Zambia	1990	713	26	1,503	24	311	11,414	1987	965	8.2	0.3	19.0	72.5	80.9	19.1	—	29[10]
Zimbabwe	1990	1,320	131	6,116	347	2,651	7,371	1985	1,202	3.7	1.3	—95.0—		72.5	—27.5—		24

[1]Excludes four specialized hospitals. [2]1980–91 UN estimate. [3]Includes funds for old-age retirement, incapacitating disability, work injury, and life insurance. [4]1987. [5]Government provides remainder of the cost of benefits. [6]May include parastatal expenditures and expenditures at the intermediate and local levels of government and/or the costs of additional services such as national health insurance and family-planning programs. [7]1985. [8]Government hospitals only. [9]1984. [10]1989. [11]1986. [12]Excludes specialized hospitals and medical centres. [13]1988 UN estimate. [14]General hospitals only. [15]1991. [16]Physicians includes dentists. [17]Nurses includes midwives. [18]1992. [19]Amounts vary internally. [20]Number of pharmacies. [21]1990. [22]Minimum on a graduated scale. [23]Maximum on a graduated scale. [24]1988. [25]Employer provides the cost of benefits. [26]Factory and shop workers only. [27]Government provides hospital facilities. [28]1982–87 average. [29]1982. [30]Employed women only. [31]Government-employed health personnel only. [32]Public sector only. [33]Includes family allowances. [34]1978. [35]Includes physicians practicing dentistry and doctors of traditional Chinese medicine (330,000 in 1991). [36]Employer provides the cost of benefits; government provides subsidies as needed. [37]Employed women and workers' wives only; special system for

| | admissions or discharges | | | | | bed occupancy rate (%) | average length of stay (days) | mortality | | population with access to safe water (latest) (%) | food supply (% of FAO requirement) 1988–90 | financing of public health care, latest year | | | public health expenditures (% of natl. budget) | public health expenditures per capita (U.S.$) | country |
| rate per 10,000 pop. | by kinds of hospital (%) | | | | | | | under age 5 per 1,000 live newborn 1992 | maternal mortality per 100,000 live births 1990–91 | | | health-care insurance | | | | | |
	general	specialized	medical centres	rural								indiv. (% of earnings)	employer (% of payroll)	govt. (% of covered earnings)			
1,165[14]	...	...	...	...	84.8[14]	8[14]	...	...	...	111	...	...	...	6.7	120	Netherlands Antilles
										109						New Caledonia
1,293[8,52]	...				80.3[8,52]	8[8,52]	10	14.0	100	131	...	...	[51]	12.2	540	New Zealand
634	—91.7—		8.3		...	...	76	58[2]	54	99	2.0	6.0	2.3	5.2	27[6]	Nicaragua
							320	700[2]	53	95		11.0[30,33]	—	5.2	6	Niger
							191	800[2]	36	93	6.0[3]	6.0[3]		1.4	1	Nigeria
1,550	100.0	...	—	—	54.7	4									510	Northern Mariana Islands
1,548	90.8	9.2	—	—	82.2	11	8	8.2	100	120	7.8[3]	16.7[3]	[5]	10.3	1,160	Norway
1,226	...	...	...	...	83.0[14]	5[14]	31	220[13]	84		—	7.0		5.7	170	Oman
...					...	...	137	500[2]	56	99		7.0		0.7	1	Pakistan
1,453	...	...	...	...	60.1	8	20	38.2[4]	83	98	7.3[3]	10.8[3]		21.8	140	Panama
253[14,24]					...	...	77	900[2]	33	114				8.7	32	Papua New Guinea
...					...	...	34	379.5[11]	35	116	9.5[3]	13.0[3]	1.5[3]	4.3	5	Paraguay
416[29]	...	...	...	...	88.2[29]	14[29]	65	300[2]	56	87	8.0	1.0		5.1	19	Peru
...					...	...	60	100[2]	88	104	1.3	1.7	[5]	4.1	7	Philippines
1,288	96.0	4.0	—	—	72.5	14	16	9.9[18]	89	131	—	45.0[3]	[5]	10.8	65	Poland
1,006	—94.7—		5.3		66.6	11	13	9.6[18]	92	136	11.0[3]	24.5[3]	...	8.0	200	Portugal
1,156	...	...	...	...	66.2	7	16[10]	20.2	...					10.7	230	Puerto Rico
...					71.7[55]	7[55]	33	...	100					0.8	70	Qatar
3,118					80.1	4	...	...	...	136						Réunion
...					70.0[57]	6[57]	28	60.3[18]	95	116	—	25.0[3]	[5]	9.2	41	Romania
...					...	...	32	52.4	100[56]	132[56]	—	9.0		...	160[6]	Russia
85[53]	...	...	...	...	42.8[53]	7[53]	222	210[2]	66	82				3.3	1	Rwanda
1,028[14,47]	...	...	...	...	58.9[14,47]	10[14,47]	42	...	100	101	5.0[3]	5.0[3]		12.4	84	St. Kitts and Nevis
955[24]					...	...	21	12.4[28]	67	100	5.0[3]	5.0[0]		6.3	83	St. Lucia
717[14]	...	...	...	...	64.1[14]	6[14]	25	...	75	102	2.5[3]	3.0[3]		15.1	81	St. Vincent
1,435[47]					69.5[47]	11[47]								...	...	San Marino
1,733	76.1	—	23.9	—	68.7	12	85	76.7[4]	52	92	4.0[3]	6.0[3]		...	...	São Tomé and Príncipe
749[47]	...	...	...	...	...	...	40	41[2]	95	121	—	...			246[6]	Saudi Arabia
...					...	...	145	600[2]	48	98	3.0[23]	3.0[23]		2.3	5	Senegal
1,558[37]	...	...	...	...	70.0[57]	6[57]	20	50[2]	100	104	5.0[3]	10.0[3,22]	—	7.1	230	Seychelles
13[14,47]	...	...	...	...	77.1[14,47]	18[14,47]	249	450[2]	37	83				9.6	1	Sierra Leone
1,192	...	...	...	...	73.0[41]	10[41]	7	4.1	100	136	19	19	19	6.2	210	Singapore
1,679	94.9	5.1	—	—	73.2	14	14	...	100		1.4	4.1	...	...	...	Slovakia
1,497	...	...	...	...	77.9	11	11	4.3[10]			6.4	7.0		...	...	Slovenia
...	...	...	...	...	...	...	...	10[13]	82	86	—	—	—	6.2	14	Solomon Islands
...					...	...	211	1,100[2]	37	81				...	1[6]	Somalia
1,597	...	...	...	...	71.7	8	70	84[2]	...	128	—	—	—	10.7	84	South Africa[58]
946	...	...	.	...	76.9	12	9	5.5	100	141	4.9[0]	24.4[3]		7.0	300	Spain
1,464[21]	...	...	...	...	88.3[29]	6[29]	19	46.5[11]	60	101				4.8	7	Sri Lanka
81[14]	...	...	...	...	...	...	166	550[2]	48	87	—	—	—	1.3	1	Sudan, The
820	83.6	2.4	8.0	6.0	41.6	15	35	31.1[4]	68	108	—	—	—	3.7	49	Suriname
506	...	...	...	...	...	...	107	400[13]	30	114	—	—	—	5.9	25	Swaziland
1,998	...	...	...	...	77.1	8	7	3.2	100	111	1.0	8.4	[5]	0.8	98	Sweden
1,278	85.9	14.1	—	—	80.8	24	9	4.6[18]	100	130	19	...	[5]	...	1,430[6]	Switzerland
474	...	...	...	...	57.9	5	40	140[2]	74	126	—	—	—	1.9	11	Syria
...					...	...	8	7.8	...	...	1.4[3]	5.6[3]	2.8[3]	...	135[6]	Taiwan
...					...	...	85	38.9[10]	...	...				...	100[6]	Tajikistan
706	66.5	—	13.1	20.4	...	...	176	340[2]	49	94				3.7	1	Tanzania
...					...	...	33	50[2]	77	103	1.5	1.5	1.5	8.2	24	Thailand
718[29]	...	...	...	...	56.6[20]	10[29]	137	420[2]	60	99	—	2.0[30]	—	5.2	5	Togo
...					...	...	25	...	75	112				6.6	51	Tonga
652[9]	...	...	...	...	65.5[9]	8[9]	22	49.2	97	114	2.8[3]	5.6[3]		...	104[6]	Trinidad and Tobago
568	78.3[41]	19.1[41]	—	2.6[41]	44.1[41]	9[41]	38	70[2]	99	131	5.0	16.0	—	6.6	31	Tunisia
...					...	...	87	150[8]	78	127	5.0	7.0	—	3.5	20	Turkey
...	...	...	...	...	...	...	91	55.2[10]	60	99	—	...		9.4	130[3]	Turkmenistan
1,308	40.9	...	—	59.1	51.5[14]	12.2[14]	56	...	...	...				3.1	34	Tuvalu
...					...	...	185	300[2]	33	93	—	—	—	5.5	1	Uganda
...					...	...	25	3.5	...	...				11.4	130[6]	Ukraine
1,032[29]	...	...	...	...	69.6[29]	7[29]	22	130[13]	95	136	—	—	—	6.9	140	United Arab Emirates
1,434	...	...	...	...	80.6[11]	15[11]	9	5.6[18]	100	130	2.0[3,22]	4.6[3,22]	[5]	13.9	950	United Kingdom
1,220[60]	...	...	...	...	65.6[60]	7[60]	10	8.2	100	138	1.5	1.5		16.0	900	United States
399	...	...	...	...	69.3	16	22	25.3[10]	75	101	3.0	4.0		5.0	44	Uruguay
...					...	...	68	42.8[10]	...	...				...	120[3]	Uzbekistan
912[47]	...	...	...	...	55.0	8[47]	85	...	100	103	—	—	—	6.6	29	Vanuatu
...	...	...	...	...	...	...	24	55.0[4]	80	99	4.0	4.3[22]	1.5[3,22]	10.0	73	Venezuela
1,587	12.4	8.1	56.6	22.9	80.7	7	49	120[2]	24	103				...	...	Vietnam
...					...	...	16[24]	...	...	...				15.7	330	Virgin Islands (U.S.)
857	...	...	...	...	80.1	5	...	...	...	...				...	...	West Bank
226	98.2	...	1.8	...	36.9	5										Western Sahara[61]
823	62.0	—	...	38.0	25.4	7	58	...	83	101				7.1	21	Western Samoa
95[9,62]	89.0[9,62]	0.4[9,62]	—	10.6[9,62]	73.4[9,62]	18	177	800[13]	36	...				4.7	13	Yemen
1,188	50.7	13.8	—35.5—		75.6	13	22[63]	16.8[10]	83[63]	140[63]	15.2[23]	15.2[23]		...	122[6,63]	Yugoslavia
474[14]	...	...	...	...	71.6[14]	12[14]	188	800[2]	39	96				...	2[6]	Zaire
1,249	—75.7—		—24.3—		68.5	7	202	150[2]	53	87				7.4	10	Zambia
767	40.8	25.7	—33.5—		64.1	7	86	330[10]	84	94				7.0	20	Zimbabwe

public employees. [38]Republic of Cyprus only. [39]Data refer to former Czechoslovakia. [40]Princess Margaret Hospital only. [41]1981. [42]Average contributions. [43]Former West Germany only. [44]Excludes medical centres. [45]1983. [46]1979. [47]1980. [48]Registered personnel; all may not be present and working in the country. [49]1993. [50]Based on bed ownership. [51]Government provides entire cost of benefits. [52]Excludes psychiatric hospitals. [53]General and specialized hospitals only. [54]Central Hospital only. [55]Hamad General Hospital only. [56]Data refer to former U.S.S.R. [57]Victoria Hospital only. [58]Data exclude the former black independent states of Bophuthatswana, Ciskei, Transkei, and Venda. [59]OECD estimate for 1990 is 80,400 physicians (1 per 714 persons). [60]5,292 community hospitals only. [61]Settlements of Smara, Boujdour, and El Aaiún only. [62]Former Yemen Arab Republic only. [63]Data refer to former Socialist Federal Republic of Yugoslavia.

Social protection

This table summarizes three principal areas of social protective activity for the countries of the world: social security, crime and law enforcement, and military affairs. Because the administrative structure, financing, manning, and scope of institutions and programmed tasks in these fields vary so greatly from country to country, no well-accepted or well-documented body of statistical comparisons exists in international convention to permit objective assessment of any of these subjects, either from the perspective of a single country or internationally. The data provided within any single subject area do, however, represent the most consistent approach to problems of international comparison found in the published literature for that field.

The provision of social security programs to answer specific social needs, for example, is summarized simply in terms of the existence or nonexistence of a specific type of benefit program because of the great complexity of national programs in terms of eligibility, coverage, term, age limits, financing, payments, and so on. Activities connected with a particular type of benefit often take place at more than one governmental level, through more than one agency at the same level, or through a mixture of public and private institutions. The data shown here are summarized from the U.S. Social Security Administration's *Social Security Programs Throughout the World* (biennial). A bullet symbol (●) indicates that a country has at least one program within the defined area; in some cases it may have several. A blank space indicates that no program existed providing the benefit shown; ellipses [...] indicate that no information was available as to whether a program existed.

Data given for social security expenditure as a percentage of total central governmental expenditure are taken from the International Monetary Fund's *Government Finance Statistics Yearbook*, which provides the most comparable analytic series on the consolidated accounts of central governments, governmentally administered social security funds, and independent national agencies, all usually separate accounting entities, through which these services may be provided in a given country.

Data on the finances of social security programs are taken in large part from the International Labour Office's *The Cost of Social Security* (triennial), supplemented by national data sources.

Figures for criminal offenses known to police, usually excluding civil offenses and minor traffic violations, are taken in part from Interpol's *International Crime Statistics* (biennial) and a variety of national sources. Statistics are usually based on the number of offenses reported to police, not the number of offenders apprehended or tried in courts. Attempted offenses are counted as the offense that was attempted. A person identified as having committed multiple offenses is counted only under the most serious offense. Murder refers to all acts involving the voluntary taking of life, including infanticide, but excluding abortion, or involuntary acts such as those normally classified as manslaughter. Assault includes "serious," or aggravated, assault—that involving injury, endangering life, or perpetrated with the use of a dangerous instrument. Burglary involves theft from the premises of another; although Interpol statistics are reported as "breaking and entering," national data may not always distinguish cases of forcible

Social protection

country	social security — programs available, 1993					expenditures, 1991 (% of total central govt.)	finances — year	receipts total ('000,000 natl. cur.)	insured persons (%)	employers (%)	government (%)	other (%)	expenditures total ('000,000 natl. cur.)	benefits (%)	administration (%)	other (%)
	old-age, invalidity, death[a]	sickness and maternity[b]	work injury[c]	unemployment[d]	family allowances[e]											
Afghanistan	●	●	●		●	...	...	...	...	...	...	...	...	...	...	...
Albania	●	●	●	●	●	...	1990	967.0	—	—	88.8	11.2	1,440.0	99.5	—0.5—	...
Algeria	●	●	●		●	...	1990	27,700.0	...	...	...	...	28,748.0	61.8	30.6	7.6
American Samoa	●	...	...	...	...	...	1990						13.0	100.0	...	...
Andorra	...	...	...	...	...	...	1993	11,832.2	...	...	...	...	7,937.2	90.2	4.6	5.2
Angola	...	...	...	...	...	...	...	...	...	...	...	...	...	...	...	...
Antigua and Barbuda	●	●	●			...	1983	13.0	29.2	48.7	—	22.1	4.2	66.1	33.9	—
Argentina	●	●	●	●	●	35.3[4]	1986	4,994.5	31.3	45.6	19.5	3.6	4,500.2	97.4	2.3	0.3
Armenia	●	●	●	●	●	...	...	...	...	...	...	...	...	...	...	...
Aruba	●	...	●	...	...	12	1992	66.3	...	...	...	...	60.4	...	...	...
Australia	●	●	●	●	●	27.5	1986	24,310.5	1.8	12.5	84.8	0.9	23,896.9	98.8	1.2	—
Austria	●	●	●	●	●	44.8[13]	1986	368,562.0	29.5	46.8	21.2	2.5	361,191.0	96.2	2.4	1.4
Azerbaijan	●	●	●	●	●	...	...	...	...	...	...	...	...	...	...	...
Bahamas, The	●	●	●			9.3[9]	1986	73.6	26.8	40.7	1.3	31.2	31.8	75.6	23.2	1.2
Bahrain	●		●			2.1[13]	1986	35.8	21.1	42.2	—	36.7	7.6	73.2	19.7	7.1
Bangladesh		●	●		●	9.8[13, 14]	1986	154.3	37.4	41.8	1.4	19.4	57.9	95.8	4.2	—
Barbados	●	●	●	●		19.8[4]	1986	148.0	37.7	39.4	5.6	17.3	129.5	92.9	5.2	1.9
Belarus	●	●	●	●	●	...	1986	3,199.0	—	—	93.2	6.8	3,199.0	100.0	—	—
Belgium	●	●	●	●	●	41.3[4]	1986	1,347,070.0	24.4	39.7	31.6	4.3	1,322,636.0	94.5	4.3	1.2
Belize	●	●	●			3.0	1986	11.2	9.4	56.4	—	34.2	2.4	52.1	46.2	1.7
Benin	●		●		●	8.7[13, 15]	1986	4,539.2	15.9	78.4	—	5.7	3,906.3	65.5	3.0	1.0
Bermuda	●		●			...	...	...	...	...	...	...	...	...	...	...
Bhutan	...	...	...	...	...	0.5	1990						26.0[13]	...	...	...
Bolivia	●	●	●		●	17.9	1986	70,737,008.0	25.6	39.4	23.4	11.5	52,958.650.0	82.0	17.6	0.4
Bosnia and Herzegovina	●	●	●	●	●	...	...	...	...	...	...	...	...	...	...	...
Botswana			●			0.6[13]	1988						33.0[13]	...	...	...
Brazil	●	●	●	●	●	32.1	1986	201,807,600.0	38.5	53.5	3.8	4.2	184,814,900.0	91.7	6.4	1.9
Brunei	●	...	●	...	...	...	1984						39.5	...	...	...
Bulgaria	●	●	●		●	16.7[6]	1986	3,707.4	—	17.8	0.4	—	3,593.0	99.8	0.2	—
Burkina Faso	●		●		●	8.4[9, 13]	1986	8,057.5	15.6	64.3	—	20.1	2,060.4	99.2	—	0.8
Burundi	●		●			0.7[16]	1986	1,368.9	30.9	51.1	—	18.0	933.1	82.2	14.8	3.0
Cambodia	...	...	...	...	...	...	...	...	...	...	...	...	...	...	...	...
Cameroon	●		●		●	6.5[4, 13]	1986	56,770.0	14.0	68.2	—	17.8	19,869.0	100.0	—	—
Canada	●	●	●	●	●	28.6[4]	1986	87,538.9	11.7	16.6	61.2	10.5	77,122.0	96.2	2.7	1.1
Cape Verde	●	●	●		●	...	1986	499.9	27.5	62.5	1.5	8.5	210.3	62.3	14.7	23.0
Central African Republic	●		●		●	6.2[3, 13]	1986	4,549.0	9.8	88.5	—	1.7	5,550.0	45.7	13.6	40.7
Chad	●		●		●	1.9[18]	1986	1,221.9	26.3	65.9[13]	—	7.8	841.4	41.4	55.3	3.3
Chile	●	●	●	●	●	31.8	1986	588,205.0	30.1	2.0	48.9	19.0	425,099.0	92.0	7.4	0.6
China	●	●	●			...	...	...	...	...	...	...	...	...	...	...
Colombia	●	●	●		●	19.6[3]	1986	169,872.0	21.5	56.5	1.7	20.2	133,837.0	51.6	42.3	6.1
Comoros	...	...	●	...	...	...	1983	40.7	100.0	—	—	—	54.3	17.4	62.3	20.3
Congo	●		●		●	0.4[21]	1983	15,272.8	12.1	80.2	—	7.7	7,256.7	66.6	21.3	12.1
Costa Rica	●	●	●		●	12.5[13]	1986	23,387.4	25.5	49.2	2.7	22.6	18,080.1	81.8	3.8	14.4
Côte d'Ivoire	●		●		●	3.6[3]	1986	40,277.4	13.6	53.1	—	33.3	22,866.5	79.6	14.1	6.3
Croatia	●	●	●	●	●	...	...	...	...	...	...	...	...	...	...	...
Cuba	●	●	●			...	1986	1,887.7	—	41.8	58.2	—	1,887.7	96.4	—	3.6
Cyprus[23]	●	●	●	●		19.6	1986	141.6	29.4	39.9	17.2	13.5	81.7	98.5	1.4	0.1
Czech Republic[24]	●	●	●	●	●	23.0	1986	120,692.0	—	3.7	94.5	1.8	120,692.0	99.7	0.3	—
Denmark	●	●	●	●	●	37.6[6]	1986	178,991.9	3.5	8.0	85.7	2.8	174,349.8	97.1	2.9	—
Djibouti	●		●	...	...	6.2[13, 17]	1979	1,352.2	...	...	...	...	1,115.7	...	...	...
Dominica	●	●	●			1.4[15]	1986	12.3	22.6	50.9	—	26.5	4.4	68.0	32.0	—
Dominican Republic	●	●	●			4.7[6]	1986	77.9	20.1	72.9	—	6.8	74.3	75.9	24.1	—
Ecuador	●	●	●		●	1.9[6]	1986	101,137.5	16.4	24.3	11.0	48.3	41,625.0	88.1	11.9	—
Egypt	●	●	●	●		12.0[4]	1988	2,633.0	38.6	61.4	—	—	2,596.0	...	...	...
El Salvador	●	●	●			2.2	1986	287.4	23.2	54.0	—	22.8	210.9	75.0	25.0	—

entry. Automobile theft excludes brief use of a car without the owner's permission, "joyriding," and implies intent to deprive the owner of the vehicle permanently. Criminal offense data for certain countries refer to cases disposed of in court, rather than to complaints. Police manpower figures refer, for the most part, to full-time, paid professional staff, excluding clerical support and volunteer staff. Personnel in military service who perform police functions are presumed to be employed in their principal activity, military service.

The figures for military manpower refer to full-time, active-duty military service and exclude reserve, militia, paramilitary, and similar organizations. Because of the difficulties attached to the analysis of data on military manpower and budgets (including problems such as data withheld on national security grounds, or the publication of budgetary data specifically intended to hide actual expenditure, or the complexity of long-term financing of purchases of military matériel [how much was actually spent as opposed to what was committed, offset by nonmilitary transfers, etc.]), extensive use is made of the principal international analytic tools: publications such as those of the International Institute for Strategic Studies (*The Military Balance* and *Strategic Survey*) and the U.S. Arms Control and Disarmament Agency (*World Military Expenditures and Arms Transfers*), both annuals.

The data on military expenditures are from the sources identified above, as well as from the IMF's *Government Finance Statistics Yearbook* and country statistical publications.

The following notes further define the column headings:

a. Programs providing cash payments for *each* of the three types of long-term benefit indicated to persons (1) exceeding a specified working age (usually 50–65, often 5 years earlier for women) who are qualified by a term of covered employment, (2) partially or fully incapacitated for their usual employment by injury or illness, and (3) qualified by their status as spouse, cohabitant, or dependent minor of a qualified person who dies.

b. Programs providing cash payments (jointly, or alternatively, medical services as well) to occupationally qualified persons for *both* of the short-term benefits indicated: (1) illness and (2) maternity.

c. Programs providing cash or medical services to employment-qualified persons who become temporarily or permanently incapacitated (fully or partially) by work-related injury or illness.

d. Programs providing term-limited cash compensation (usually 40–75% of average earnings) to persons qualified by previous employment (of six months minimum, typically) for periods of involuntary unemployment.

e. Programs providing cash payments to families or mothers to mitigate the cost of raising children and to encourage the formation of larger families.

f. A police officer is a full-time, paid professional, performing domestic security functions. Data include administrative staff but exclude clerical employees, volunteers, and members of paramilitary groups.

g. Includes all active-duty personnel, regular and conscript, performing national security functions. Excludes reserves, paramilitary forces, border patrols, and gendarmeries.

crime and law enforcement (latest)					military protection									country
offenses reported to the police per 100,000 population					population per police officer[f]	manpower, 1994[g]		expenditure, 1991				arms trade, 1991 ('000,000 U.S.$)		
total	personal		property			total ('000)	per 1,000 population	total '000,000	per capita	% of central government expenditure	% of GDP or GNP	imports	exports	
	murder	assault	burglary	automobile theft										
...	...	...	...	...	540[1]	2	2	287[3]	213[3]	64.4[3]	7.7[3]	1,900	0	Afghanistan
...	...	...	...	...	550	73.0	21.0	157[4]	49[4]	11.4[5]	4.1[4]	0	0	Albania
2,080	...	109.0	...	...	840	121.7	4.4	730	28	7.7[6]	1.8	100	0	Algeria
5,183	13.1	995.0	696.0	52.4	460	—	7	—	—	—	—	...	...	American Samoa
5,430	...	46.0	1,510.0	254.0	220	—	—	—	—	—	—	...	...	Andorra
237	10.9	0.8	...	0.1	140[0]	82.0	7.3	1,127[9]	161[9]	28.8[10]	23.0[9]	30	0	Angola
2,668	...	297.3	844.0	...	120	11	11	...	...	...	...	...	...	Antigua and Barbuda
637	8.5	0.6	—	110.4	1,270	69.8	2.1	2,449	75	26.0	1.9	10	5	Argentina
363	6.1	7.0	...	...	...	32.7	9.2	...	...	...	...	...	...	Armenia
4,544	24.9	280.1	...	...	...	—	7	—	—	—	—	...	...	Aruba
6,773	4.5	369.6	1,962.8	770.6	450	61.6	0.4	7,400	427	9.5	2.6	210	30	Australia
6,007	2.3	1.9	1,151.8	26.7	470	51.3	6.4	1,667	213	2.5	1.0	10	10	Austria
305	...	...	...	...	...	56.0	7.5	...	...	...	...	...	...	Azerbaijan
6,752	17.6	115.7	1,336.5	...	125	2.6	9.4	9[3]	40[3]	2.5[3]	0.5[3]	...	...	Bahamas, The
3,723	...	...	...	...	180	8.1	14.7	278	520	26.0	7.7	50	0	Bahrain
16.8	2.0	2.1	4.4	0.3	2,560	115.5	1.0	312	3	8.4	1.4	40	0	Bangladesh
4,519	11.7	109.0	323.0	13.6	280	11	11	10[4]	38[4]	1.8[4]	0.6[4]	0	0	Barbados
650	2.9	7.0	...	...	...	92.5	8.9	...	...	...	...	...	...	Belarus
3,338	2.2	120.7	690.9	281.0	640	63.0	6.2	4,625	463	4.7	2.4	210	30	Belgium
1,968	23.2	349.0	643.8	...	290	0.9	4.3	4[3]	25[0]	4.0[3]	2.0[3]	...	...	Belize
1,234	...	...	...	...	3,250	4.5	0.9	35[6]	8[6]	19.4[4]	2.0[6]	0	0	Benin
7,413	10.8	154.6	2,092.3	...	370	—	7	—	—	—	—	...	...	Bermuda
...	...	...	...	...	...	4.0[14]	3.1[11]	...	...	...	...	...	...	Bhutan
...	...	...	...	...	...	33.5	4.2	117	16	12.8	2.4	10	0	Bolivia
558	...	...	...	...	...	110.0	24.7	...	...	...	...	...	...	Bosnia and Herzegovina
6,693	19.5	442.6	411.8	...	750	7.5	5.2	159	126	6.0[4]	4.9	5	0	Botswana
116	...	...	...	...	...	336.8	2.1	5,295	34	2.1[6]	1.3	20	70	Brazil
358	0.4	3.7	113.9	10.8	100	4.4	15.5	305[3]	1,398[3]	24.5[3]	8.1[3]	...	...	Brunei
70	2.1	4.0	14.8	...	...	101.9	12.1	1,464	164	29.7[4]	4.0	0	70	Bulgaria
41	0.2	4.1	—	—	...	10.0	1.0	100	11	17.5[5]	3.6	0	0	Burkina Faso
87	3.3	7.4	...	...	...	14.6	2.5	28	5	13.4	2.4	5	0	Burundi
...	...	...	...	...	1,980	88.5	9.3	...	...	...	...	40	0	Cambodia
...	0.2	0.1	0.2	0.3	1,170	14.6	1.1	168	14	6.6[4]	1.6	0	0	Cameroon
11,442.6	5.7	134.3	1,331.7	382.7	8,640	78.1	2.7	11,510	427	7.9	2.0	200	420	Canada
...	...	...	...	...	110	1.1	3.1	12[17]	47[17]	13.5[17]	11.8[17]	0	0	Cape Verde
135	1.6	22.8	2.7	...	2,740[1]	5.0	1.6	21[6]	8[6]	6.6[4]	1.7[6]	0	0	Central African Republic
...	...	...	...	...	990	30.4	4.7	67	13	16.5	5.2	10	0	Chad
1,347	5.8	107.0	...	11.2	470	93.0	6.7	1,010	76	12.2	3.4	70	0	Chile
201	1.9	4.1	17.5	...	1,360[19]	2,930.0	2.5	51,040	44	17.4	3.3	240	925	China
840	40.5	266.9	...	...	420	146.4	4.2	1,037	31	20.5	2.6	60	0	Colombia
...	...	...	...	...	960	—	20	...	...	...	...	...	...	Comoros
32	1.5	4.7	0.2	0.2	870	10.0	3.5	99[22]	49[22]	12.5[22]	5.1[22]	0	0	Congo
868	5.3	11.1	232.4	23.1	480	7.5	2.3	20	6	1.4	0.4	0	0	Costa Rica
262	2.6	47.9	12.2	19.9	4,640	8.4	0.6	131	10	4.3	2.1	0	0	Côte d'Ivoire
1,087	...	...	...	...	...	105.0	21.9	...	...	...	...	...	...	Croatia
...	...	...	...	...	650	106.0	9.6	1,400[6]	137[6]	...	4.2[6]	525	0	Cuba
671	3.2	12.3	208.7	2.8	180	10.0	16.3	415	585	22.5	7.1	0	0	Cyprus[23]
1,911	2.0	89.4	621.5	95.7	640	92.9	9.0	2,804	179	17.3	2.6	50	270	Czech Republic[24]
10,270	4.6	163.4	2,382.9	575.9	600	27.0	5.2	2,672	510	5.3	2.1	50	10	Denmark
487	4.8	67.0	14.4	9.8	...	8.4	14.8	27[3]	67[9]	22.4[0]	8.1[3]	...	...	Djibouti
22,432	9.3	47.0	1,025.0	11.0	600	11	11	...	...	...	...	...	...	Dominica
946	11.9	30.8	154.0	24.8	580	24.5	3.1	53	7	7.4	0.8	0	0	Dominican Republic
333	5.1	4.0	...	4.3	260	57.5	5.1	232	22	14.8	2.1	10	0	Ecuador
3,314	1.6	0.7	...	3.4	580	440.0	7.5	1,022	19	10.7[4]	3.4	525	0	Egypt
...	...	...	...	...	1,000	30.7	5.4	171	31	23.8	2.9	50	0	El Salvador

Social protection (continued)

country	programs available, 1993 old-age, invalid-ity, death[a]	sickness and mater-nity[b]	work injury[c]	unem-ploy-ment[d]	family allow-ances[e]	expendi-tures, 1991 (% of total central govt.)	year	receipts total ('000,000 natl. cur.)	insured persons (%)	em-ployers (%)	govern-ment (%)	other (%)	expenditures total ('000,000 natl. cur.)	benefits (%)	admin-istration (%)	other (%)
Equatorial Guinea	●	●	●		●	...	1983	43.0	4.7	95.3	—	—	20.0	30.0	70.0	—
Eritrea[26]	...	...	...	...	...	...	...									
Estonia	●	●	●	●	●	41.9[13]	...	90.1	...	...	...	...				
Ethiopia[26]	●	...	●	...	...	3.9[4]	1986	162.1	32.5	63.2	—	4.2	116.3	98.2	1.8	—
Faeroe Islands	●	...	...	...	...											
Fiji	●	...	●	...	...	4.0	1986	111.6	26.5	26.5	—	47.0	34.4	94.8	5.2	—
Finland	●	●	●	●	●	44.8[13]	1986	90,413.3	8.3	39.7	44.7	7.3	82,164.8	96.8	3.2	—
France	●	●	●	●	●	43.2[6]	1986	1,431,025.0	23.4	50.6	23.0	3.0	1,439,788.7	95.1	4.0	0.9
French Guiana	●	...	...	...	●	...	1990	659.4	...				705.3			
French Polynesia						...	1990	19,268.0					17,832.0			
Gabon	●	●	●	...	●	...	1986	37,788.0	8.3	84.8	—	6.9	42,326.0	80.7	15.1	4.2
Gambia, The	●	...	●	...	...	3.5[29]	1982	—					5.6			
Gaza Strip	...	...	...	...	...											
Georgia	●	●	●	●	●											
Germany	●	●	●	●	●	48.5[4,13]	1986[30]	459,340.0	36.6	35.0	25.8	2.6	451,885.0	97.2	2.8	—
Ghana	●	...	●	...	...	6.4[5]	...									
Gibraltar	●	●	●	●	●											
Greece	●	●	●	●	●	28.8[17]	1986	872,503.0	29.4	42.5	21.4	6.7	898,814.0	93.7	6.3	—
Greenland	●	●	...	...	●											
Grenada	●	●	...	...	...	5.0[13,16]	1986	15.2	27.7	57.9	—	14.4	6.0	91.0	9.0	—
Guadeloupe	●	...	...	...	●		1990	2,641.2					4,071.9			
Guam	●	...	...	...	●		1989						7.3			
Guatemala	●	●	●	...	...	5.2[4,13]	1986	209.0	26.9	55.9	—	17.2	134.4	86.0	10.9	3.1
Guernsey	●	●	...	●	●	...	1993	66,369	—44.3—		45.5	10.2	62,458	94.2	5.8	—
Guinea	●	●	●	...	●	...	1986	269.2	3.0	90.9	—	6.1	268.7	85.2	1.8	13.0
Guinea-Bissau	...	...	...	...	...	8.8[13]	1986	138.0	22.8	63.4	10.3	3.8	61.9	59.6	40.4	—
Guyana	●	●	●	...	...	3.7[10]	1986	200.2	17.3	21.4	0.7	60.6	62.1	80.2	18.2	1.6
Haiti	●	●	●	...	...	5.1[13]	1977	60.5	—26.6—		69.9	3.5	52.4	92.7	7.3	—
Honduras	●	●	●	...	...	4.5[15]	1986	166.2	23.9	40.8	3.3	32.0	76.8	84.6	15.4	—
Hong Kong	●	●	●	●	●		1992–93						7,076.5	74.2	25.8	—
Hungary	●	●	●	●	●	27.7[6]	1986	149,400.0	21.1	78.9	—		142,939.0	99.3	0.7	—
Iceland	●	●	●	●	●[31]	18.5	1991	14,406.0	—	54.3	45.7	—	69,255.0	98.1	1.9	—
India	●	●	●	...	...	...	1986	87,807.7	9.8	66.9	9.6	13.7	40,362.2	98.4	1.6	—
Indonesia	●	●	●	...	...	—	1986	97.9	17.3	58.1	—	24.6	92.2	12.5	19.4	68.1
Iran	●	●	●	●	...	13.7[6]	1986	346,460.0	83.2	0.1	8.2	8.5	167,879.0	43.4	6.3	50.0
Iraq	●	●	●	...	●	...	1977	107.8	9.9	55.6	21.9	12.6	71.0	94.0	2.4	3.6
Ireland	●	●	●	●	●	26.2[6]	1986	4,299.6	13.0	24.4	61.7	0.9	4,302.2	95.2	4.7	0.1
Isle of Man	●	●	●	●	●	37.0[32]	1985						14.4			
Israel	●	●	●	●	●	21.0	1986	6,723.0	23.9	37.3	30.7	8.1	6,146.8	89.9	5.4	4.7
Italy	●	●	●	●	●	28.5[5]	1986	90,646.0	19.5	51.7	17.6	11.2	100,251.0	89.3	2.0	8.7
Jamaica	●	●	●	...	...	3.2[16]	1986	330.4	11.8	14.3	36.1	37.8	171.5	93.4	6.0	0.6
Japan	●	●	●	●	●		1986	50,525,725.0	27.2	30.6	26.8	15.4	40,145,652.0	94.6	1.7	3.7
Jersey	●	●	●	...	●	9.5	1991	60.9	—63.8—		23.4	12.8	52.8			
Jordan	●	...	●	...	...	6.9	1986	53.6	28.7	55.3	—	16.0	9.5	77.4	14.0	8.6
Kazakhstan	●	●	●	●	...											
Kenya	●	...	●	...	...	0.1	1986	1,660.0	27.7	27.7	1.2	43.4	268.0	85.1	14.9	—
Kiribati	●	...	●	...	...											
Korea, North	...	...	...	...	...											
Korea, South	●	...	●	...	...	7.8	1990	1,286,000.0	31.6	68.4	—		2,037,000.0			
Kuwait	●	...	...	...	...	1.8	1986	385.8	6.3	12.4	54.6	26.7	169.5	96.3	3.7	—
Kyrgyzstan	●	●	●	●	●											
Laos	...	...	...	...	...											
Latvia	●	●	●	●	●											
Lebanon	●	●	●	...	●											
Lesotho	...	...	...	...	...	1.5[13]	1988	—					5.3			
Liberia	●	...	●	...	...	1.0[5]	1983	2.9	—	69.0	13.8	17.2	2.6	54.4	45.6	—
Libya	●	●	●	...	...	...	1977	192.9	9.1	28.7	58.7	3.5	128.2	96.2	3.2	0.5
Liechtenstein	●	●	●	●	●											
Lithuania	●	●	●	●	●								24,981.7			
Luxembourg	●	●	●	●	●	44.6[6]	1986	59,427.9	24.7	34.2	34.5	6.6	51,643.0	96.8	2.7	0.5
Macau	...						1992	117.9					111.9			
Macedonia	●	●	●	●	●											
Madagascar	●	...	●	...	●	1.5[13]	1986	10,288.2	22.2	77.8	—		10,075.3	87.0	13.0	—
Malawi	●	...	●	...	...	1.0[9]	1986	—					5.4			
Malaysia	●	...	●	...	...	5.3[13]	1986	6,304.0	21.6	40.5	2.5	35.4	1,589.3	93.9	6.1	—
Maldives	...	...	...	...	...	1.0	1989						6.4			
Mali	●	●	●	...	●	3.0[5]	1986	8,128.8	16.6	74.3	—	9.1	7,924.6	63.7	34.7	1.6
Malta	●	●	●	●	●	29.8	1986	71.6	26.8	33.5	39.7	—	94.0	94.4	5.6	—
Marshall Islands	●	...	...	...	...	...										
Martinique	●	...	...	...	●		1991	2,958.8					4,873.3			
Mauritania	●	...	●	...	●	3.7[15]	1986	584.6	6.3	87.7	—	6.0	583.3	81.8	18.2	—
Mauritius	●	●	●	...	●	14.7[13]	1986	993.8	9.6	35.0	37.7	17.7	654.1	95.1	4.1	0.8
Mayotte	...	...	...	...	...											
Mexico	●	●	●	...	...	12.3[6]	1986	2,463,649.0	19.6	63.1	5.0	12.3	2,115,574.0	73.6	17.3	9.1
Micronesia	...					...										
Moldova	●	●	●	●	●											
Monaco	●	●	●	●	●											
Mongolia	●	●	●	...	●											
Morocco	●	●	●	...	●	5.4[6,13]	1986	3,660.7	27.6	41.2	—	31.2	2,506.5	94.5	3.5	1.9
Mozambique	●	...	●	...	...		1986	228.2	—	86.2	13.7	0.1	145.0	100.0	—	—
Myanmar (Burma)	●	●	●	...	...	0.3	1986	44.3	19.9	59.6	18.5	2.0	35.9	51.5	15.6	32.9
Namibia	●	...	...	...	...	6.8										
Nauru	...	...	...	...	...											
Nepal	●	...	●	...	...	0.7[14]	1985						59.3			
Netherlands, The	●	●	●	●	●	34.4	1986	140,734.0	38.0	33.4	15.6	13.0	122,791.0	97.0	3.0	—

	crime and law enforcement (latest)					military protection						arms trade, 1991 ('000,000 U.S.$)		country
	offenses reported to the police per 100,000 population				population per police officer[f]	manpower, 1994[g]		expenditure, 1991						
total	personal		property			total ('000)	per 1,000 population	total '000,000	per capita	% of central government expenditure	% of GDP or GNP	imports	exports	
	murder	assault	burglary	automobile theft										
...	...	...	...	...	190	1.3	3.4	2[25]	9[25]	21.0[25]	...	0	0	Equatorial Guinea
						[27]	[27]					...	...	Eritrea[26]
2,672	15.5	24.4	516.8	...		2.5	1.7					...	...	Estonia
94	6.7	24.8	1.9	...	1,100	[28]	28	1,384[6]	28[6]	52.1[6]	21.9[6]	80	0	Ethiopia[26]
						—	7							Faeroe Islands
1,915	4.3	31.6	411.1	...	440	3.9	5.1	32	44	0.5	2.2	0	0	Fiji
9,631	0.6	47.2	1,432.0	364.8	640	31.2	6.1	2,454	492	5.9	2.0	5	0	Finland
6,169	4.4	88.5	712.0	519.6	630	409.6	7.1	42,430	744	8.1	3.6	130	1,100	France
8,936	27.2	178.7	1,367.3	150.6		—	7	—	—	—	—			French Guiana
1,799	0.9	98.9	232.7			—	7							French Polynesia
323	2.2	25.3	62.2	20.9	1,290	4.7	3.6	148[6]	143[6]	13.7[6]	3.6[6]	0	0	Gabon
					3,310	0.8	0.8	1[4]	2[4]	2.0[4]	0.7[4]	0	0	Gambia, The
1,355						—	—					...	...	Gaza Strip
						—	—							Georgia
7,108[30]	3.9[30]	107.0[30]	1,749.1[30]	115.1[30]	...	367.3	4.6	39,520[30]	494[30]	7.5[30]	2.5[30]	520	1,310	Germany
864	2.0	95.9	4.7	...	620	6.9	0.4	37	2	3.1[5]	0.6	0	0	Ghana
10,039	—	860.2			170	—	7						...	Gibraltar
3,306	2.0	97.6	265.0	68.4	380	159.3	15.4	3,807	379	9.1	5.5	130	0	Greece
9,360	18.1	845.0	1,883.5	...	340	—	7							Greenland
2,679	10.0	880.0	153.0	...	230	11	11							Grenada
4,533	10.2	154.8	554.5	146.9	...	—	7						...	Guadeloupe
10,080	7.9	169.3	634.2	333.6		—	7						...	Guam
510	27.4	77.1	27.9	58.1	670	44.2	4.3	89	10	11.0	1.0	0	0	Guatemala
						—	7							Guernsey
32.4	1.0	0.8	1.3	0.5	1,140	6.9	1.1	37	5	5.1[6]	1.3	5	0	Guinea
						9.3	8.8	3[22]	4[22]	4.1[22]	2.4[22]	5	0	Guinea-Bissau
1,980	15.6	28.1	434.7	...	190	1.7	2.3	3	4	2.1	1.0	0	0	Guyana
701	...	...	...		400	7.3	1.1	52	8	13.4[40]	2.0	0	0	Haiti
	9.4	7.7	...	3.3	1,040	16.8	3.2	47	9	9.1	1.7	20	0	Honduras
1,395	1.5	99.5	229.7	79.4	221	—	7	—				...	...	Hong Kong
3,287	3.1	66.0	742.9	77.6	710	74.5	7.3	1,261	122	4.1[6]	2.1	0	40	Hungary
1,550	0.9	64.3	704.8	112.8	940	—	7	—				0	0	Iceland
187	3.5	...	19.3	...	820	1,265.0	1.4	7,189	8	16.4	2.7	800	0	India
134	0.9	6.2	28.4	6.0	1,340	276.0	1.4	1,732	9	7.4	1.6	70	0	Indonesia
76.6	0.5	47.7			...	513.0	8.6	5,647	96	24.9	5.7	1,600	30	Iran
91	1.7	21.7	40.8	1.4	140	382.0	19.2	9,459	528	50.8[29]	74.9	0	0	Iraq
2,476	0.8	2.1	821.5	31.6	310	13.0	3.7	511	145	3.3	1.3	0	10	Ireland
					...	—	7							Isle of Man
5,234	2.2	202.5	2,483.0	315.8	210	172.0	32.3	4,992	1,100	20.5	8.1	460	380	Israel
4,358	6.4	33.8	...	546.0	680	322.3	5.6	24,340	421	4.3	2.1	180	100	Italy
1,927	20.9	476.0	305.6	14.8	430	3.3	1.3	25	10	3.4	0.7	5	0	Jamaica
1,397	1.0	15.7	184.3	27.6	480	237.7	1.9	32,560	263	6.1	1.0	775	10	Japan
					...	—	7						...	Jersey
762.6	2.1	19.4	11.9	12.3	630	98.6	23.3	426	125	26.6	11.2	60	0	Jordan
815						[33]	[33]					...	...	Kazakhstan
364	4.2	57.3	63.5	6.6	1,500	24.2	0.9	218	9	9.1	2.8	10	0	Kenya
285	12.4	5.5	73.3	...	330									Kiribati
					460	1,128.0	48.9	4,660	214	40.7[5]	20.0	90	160	Korea, North
2,637	1.5	42.5	12.3	...	420	633.0	14.2	10,580	242	19.2	3.8	775	30	Korea, South
709	10.2[34]	92.2	66.8	17.1	80	16.6	11.3	16,740	19,940	19.9[4]	102.2	50	0	Kuwait
987	10.4[34]	12.6	482.4	...		12.0	2.7							Kyrgyzstan
					280	37.0	7.8	55[9]	15[9]	21.3[3]	10.5[3]	10	0	Laos
1,571	8.0	...	18.3	...		6.9	2.7							Latvia
366	13.2	14.1	65.7	67.3	530	44.3	14.9	168	50	12.9	3.5	5	0	Lebanon
1,896	51.1	204.3	201.3	...	1,130	2.0	1.0	56[6]	33[6]	17.1[6]	5.4[6]	0	0	Lesotho
					1,570	[35]	[35]	58[4]	23[4]	13.3[4]	4.8[4]	0	0	Liberia
1,007	2.9	5.7	...	...		70.0	13.4	2,670	613	28.0[4]	8.7	370	30	Libya
					660	—	[36]					...	...	Liechtenstein
1,507	8.1[34]	9.2	702	...		8.9	2.4							Lithuania
6,628	2.2	84.1	1,047.3	131.5	730	0.8	2.0	108	277	2.4	0.8	20	0	Luxembourg
1,226	1.8	133.8	152.2	47.4	...	—	7	...	...		...	...	...	Macau
686	...	...	...	...	...	10.4	5.0					...	...	Macedonia
					2,900	21.0	1.5	30	2	7.5	1.2	0	0	Madagascar
1,001	2.6	96.5	15.6	...	1,670	10.4	1.1	24	3	4.3	1.1	0	0	Malawi
451	1.9	14.3	97.7	18.4	760	114.5	5.9	1,651	92	12.0	3.7	30	0	Malaysia
2,353	1.9	3.3	36.1	...	35,710	—	7						...	Maldives
33	—	3.9	...	...	160	7.4	0.8	41[4]	5[4]	8.0[4]	2.0[4]	0	0	Mali
2,802	10.4	50.6	1,907.1	367.1	230	1.9	5.0	22	61	2.4[6]	0.8	0	0	Malta
2,273	...	...	...	...	400	—	[37]	—	—	—	—		...	Marshall Islands
3,924	7.9	156.4	689.0	102.6		—	7						...	Martinique
					710	15.7	7.6	43[4]	25[4]	15.9[4]	4.3[4]	0	0	Mauritania
2,770	2.5	15.1	50.0	...	240	—	—	10	9	1.5	0.4	0	0	Mauritius
					...	—	[7]					...	...	Mayotte
108	7.3	30.2	...	...	...	175.0	1.9	1,185	13	3.0	0.4	40	20	Mexico
...	...	...				—	[37]					...	...	Micronesia
						11.1	2.5	...	...	...	...			Moldova
4,614	...	170.2	373.7	140.1								...	...	Monaco
					120	21.3	9.4	113	50	...	4.9	0	0	Mongolia
769	1.5	170.5	...	...	840	195.5	7.2	1,147	44	18.1[6]	4.3	30	0	Morocco
...						[38]	[38]	144	10	40.7[5]	13.0	10	0	Mozambique
262	4.9	35.5	0.1	50.2	650	286.0	6.3	1,280	31	13.4	2.4	370	0	Myanmar (Burma)
						8.1	5.1					...	...	Namibia
	25.0	400.0	100.0	...	110									Nauru
29.1	2.2	0.5	0.2	...	1,000	35.0	1.8	30	2	5.9	1.1	0	0	Nepal
7,613	14.8	148.3	2,621.8	181.8	510	70.9	4.6	7,246	482	4.7	2.5	360	120	Netherlands, The

Social protection (continued)

country	social security					expenditures, 1991 (% of total central govt.)	finances									
	programs available, 1993						year	receipts					expenditures			
	old-age invalidity, death[a]	sickness and maternity[b]	work injury[c]	unemployment[d]	family allowances[e]			total ('000,000 natl. cur.)	insured persons (%)	employers (%)	government (%)	other (%)	total ('000,000 natl. cur.)	benefits (%)	administration (%)	other (%)
Netherlands Antilles	●	...	●	...	...	33.0[12]	1992	139.2	100.0	—	—	—	142.0	...	...	...
New Caledonia	...	...	...	...	...		1987	15,834.0	...	...	...	...	14,598.0	...	...	...
New Zealand	●	●	●	●	●	34.0	1986	9,645.5	1.6	3.1	92.5	2.9	9,534.5	97.4	2.4	0.2
Nicaragua	●	●	●	...	●	3.3[25]	1983	832.9	20.4	53.5	10.4	15.7	427.5	65.5	28.5	6.0
Niger	●	...	●	...	●	1.7[13, 25]	1986	12,890.6	12.3	39.2	37.8	10.7	10,032.1	49.0	32.4	18.6
Nigeria	●	...	●	...	...	2.5[41]	1986	108.4	17.9	24.4	—	57.7	17.5	44.7	55.3	—
Northern Mariana Islands	...	...	...	...	...											
Norway	●	●	●	●	●	38.0[6, 13]	1986	157,853.7	17.5	24.6	55.7	2.2	153,249.6	99.0	1.0	...
Oman	●	...	...	...	...	3.4[13]	1990						38.0[13]	...	...	...
Pakistan	●	●	●	...	...	0.2[9]	1986	5,134.8	1.0	10.1	83.6	5.3	4,629.5	98.4	1.2	0.4
Panama	●	●	●	...	...	20.9	1986	500.5	30.0	44.9	3.4	21.7	425.9	94.3	5.5	0.2
Papua New Guinea	●	...	●	...	...	0.8	1983	45.0	40.5	32.1	8.0	19.4	9.4	82.3	9.7	8.0
Paraguay	●	●	●	...	...	11.7[6]	1988	49,272.0	...	...	...	...	40,588.0	...	...	...
Peru	●	●	●	...	...	0.2[10]	1986	7,041,677.0	31.1	68.9	—	—	6,136,672.0	39.5	51.6	8.9
Philippines	●	●	●	...	...	1.6	1986	10,705.0	18.6	26.5	—	54.9	4,244.8	86.9	13.1	...
Poland	●	●	●	●	●		1986	2,242,443.0	2.6	60.7	35.3	1.4	1,830,162.0	99.2	0.8	—
Portugal	●	●	●	●	●	27.3[6, 13]	1986	494,527.0	24.6	66.0	7.0	2.4	459,353.8	95.4	4.6	—
Puerto Rico	●	●	●	●	...		1980						1,041.3	100.0	—	—
Qatar	...	...	...	...	...		1986	80.0	—	—	100.0	—	80.0	100.0	—	—
Réunion	...	...	...	...	...								8,470.4	...	...	...
Romania	●	●	●	...	●	25.1	1983	72,064.9	—	54.0	46.0	—	63,927.5	100.0	—	—
Russia	●	●	●	●	●											
Rwanda	●	...	●	...	...	2.9[29]	1986	2,123.8	24.5	41.0	—	34.5	585.9	65.0	35.0	...
St. Kitts and Nevis	●	●	●	...	...	9.4[13, 22]	1989	14.3	...	...	...	...	7.9	...	...	...
St. Lucia	●	●	...	...	...		1986	14.6	28.6	28.6	—	42.8	3.4	61.4	38.6	...
St. Vincent and the Grenadines	●	●	●	...	...	2.3[13]	1989									
San Marino	●	●	...	●	...		1983	51,673.0	12.0	48.7	36.1	3.2	46,179.0	95.7	3.7	0.6
São Tomé and Príncipe	●	●	●	...	...		1986	46.4	37.7	56.3	—	6.0	23.7	100.0	—	—
Saudi Arabia	●	...	●	...	...											
Senegal	●	●	●	...	●	2.6[3, 13]	1986	22,094.0	21.2	69.9	—	8.7	18,827.0	84.8	15.3	...
Seychelles	●	●	●	...	...	5.3[16]	1983	69.1	30.1	60.2	—	9.7	42.7	69.6	4.9	25.5
Sierra Leone	●	...	●	...	...	1.9[6]	1977	10.5	—26.7—		73.3	—	10.0	100.0	—	—
Singapore	●	...	●	...	...	1.9	1986	6,691.0	51.0	23.2	0.1	25.7	5,601.2	71.9	0.4	27.7
Slovakia	●	●	●	●	●		1992	28,013	13.9	85.3	—	0.8	13,823	...	...	...
Slovenia	●	●	●	●	●											
Solomon Islands	●	...	●	...	...	0.6[5]	1986	13.7	27.9	41.8	—	30.3	6.8	40.8	11.5	47.7
Somalia	●	...	●	...	●	1.7[13, 41]										
South Africa	●	●	●	●	...		1987	976.0	—	100.0	—	—	668.0	...	...	...
Spain	●	●	●	●	●	36.4[6]	1986	5,893,481.0	16.4	54.0	27.1	2.5	5,801,152.0	95.0	2.7	2.3
Sri Lanka	●	...	●	...	...	17.6[13]	1986	10,432.8	20.9	24.2	32.2	22.7	4,022.6	98.8	1.1	0.1
Sudan, The	●	...	●	...	...	2.2[29]	1986	42.1	14.3	28.7	—	57.0	8.5	49.4	50.6	...
Suriname	●	...	...	...	●	6.0[9]	1983	125.8	35.8	26.5	36.6	1.1	106.3	98.1	1.9	—
Swaziland	●	...	●	...	...	0.4[13]	1986	10.7	31.4	31.4	—	37.2	3.9	45.8	54.2	—
Sweden	●	●	●	●	●	50.7	1986	318,641.9	1.8	38.5	49.2	10.5	291,962.1	95.9	4.1	...
Switzerland	●	●	●	●	●	49.9[3]	1986	37,602.7	45.1	23.2	26.3	5.4	35,691.2	91.5	2.8	5.7
Syria	●	...	●	...	...	1.6	1989						1,150.0	...	...	...
Taiwan	●	●	●	...	...	13.8[6]										
Tajikistan	●	●	●	●	●											
Tanzania	●	...	●	...	...	0.5[14]	1986	1,286.6	26.9	33.7	2.0	37.4	487.7	41.4	55.3	3.3
Thailand	...	●	...	...	...	3.4	1986	284.8	—	100.0	—	—	246.0	88.8	11.2	...
Togo	●	...	●	...	●	6.5[22]	1986	9,588.0	9.3	70.9	—	19.8	4,671.0	70.7	29.3	...
Tonga	...	...	...	...	...	0.8										
Trinidad and Tobago	●	...	●	...	...	5.3[17]	1986	505.4	15.7	31.5	34.9	17.9	383.2	77.1	11.8	11.1
Tunisia	●	●	●	...	●	12.2	1989	325.3	36.9	63.1	—	—	358.3	90.0[16]	6.1[16]	3.9[16]
Turkey	●	●	●	...	...	0.8	1986	1,753,294.0	28.2	32.5	15.9	23.4	1,417,940.0	97.1	2.6	0.3
Turkmenistan	●	●	●	●	●											
Tuvalu	●	...	...	...	...		1981						0.1	67.6	32.4	...
Uganda	●	...	●	...	...	2.1[9]	1986	75.1	44.6	44.6	—	10.8	0.5	100.0	—	...
Ukraine	●	●	●	●	●		1986	16,835.0	—	—	94.7	5.3	16,835.0	100.0	—	—
United Arab Emirates	...	...	...	...	...	3.2[4, 13]	1989	42.0	...	...	...	...	420.0[13]	...	...	...
United Kingdom	●	●	●	●	●	33.1[13]	1986	78,737.0	18.3	23.4	55.1	3.2	76,059.0	95.4	2.9	1.7
United States	●	●	●	●	...	20.6	1986	644,464.0	24.5	33.7	30.2	11.6	525,855.0	95.9	3.2	0.9
Uruguay	●	●	●	●	●	53.9[13]	1986	92,849.0	33.3	37.2	24.0	5.4	93,379.0	92.7	6.0	1.3
Uzbekistan	●	●	●	●	●											
Vanuatu	●	...	●	...	...	0.9[9]										
Venezuela	●	●	●	●	...	6.9[9]	1986	7,457.6	21.3	40.7	12.7	25.3	6,355.7	86.1	14.9	—
Vietnam	●	●	●	...	...											
Virgin Islands (U.S.)	●	●	●	●	...											
West Bank	...	...	...	...	...											
Western Sahara	...	...	...	...	...											
Western Samoa	●	...	...	...	...	—							—			
Yemen	●	...	...	...	...	—							—			
Yugoslavia	●	●	●	●	●	6.0[48]	1986[48]	2,777,651.0	63.3	32.2	3.4	1.1	2,732,679.0	90.3	1.9	7.8
Zaire	●	...	●	...	●	0.4[17]	1986	1,238.3	28.6	60.2	—	11.2	1,044.2	27.9	72.1	—
Zambia	●	...	●	...	...	1.5[5]	1986	179.2	28.4	28.4	—	43.2	67.7	40.6	59.4	—
Zimbabwe	...	...	●	...	...	2.5[22]	1983	167.0	25.9	7.6	64.2	2.3	112.2	93.7	6.2	0.1

[1]Rural areas only. [2]The bulk of the national armed forces disintegrated after the fall of the central government in April 1992, with only the northern corps retaining its integrity. [3]1984. [4]1989. [5]1988. [6]1990. [7]Political dependency; defense is the responsibility of the administering country. [8]Includes civilian militia. [9]1986. [10]1983. [11]Paramilitary unit of a country participating in the U.S.-sponsored Regional Security System, a defense pact among eastern Caribbean states. [12]Netherlands Antilles includes Aruba. [13]Includes welfare. [14]1985. [15]1979. [16]1977. [17]1981. [18]1976. [19]Local officers only. [20]Military defense is the responsibility of France. [21]1971. [22]1987. [23]Republic of Cyprus only. [24]Data refer to former Czechoslovakia, except military manpower, 1994. [25]1980. [26]Ethiopia includes Eritrea. [27]Demobilization of some Eritrean forces began in late 1993. Estimated strength of these forces is currently about 70,000. [28]Following the declaration of independence by Eritrea in April 1993, estimated strength of Ethiopian armed forces was some 120,000. [29]1982. [30]Former West Germany. [31]Coverage is through tax system. [32]1988–89. [33]Russian-controlled forces on

crime and law enforcement (latest)					population per police officer	military protection								country
offenses reported to the police per 100,000 population						manpower, 1994		expenditure, 1991				arms trade, 1991 ('000,000 U.S.$)		
total	personal		property			total ('000)	per 1,000 population	total '000,000	per capita	% of central government expenditure	% of GDP or GNP	imports	exports	
	murder	assault	burglary	automobile theft										
6,496[39]	...	479	...	...	330	—	7	—	—	—	—	...	...	Netherlands Antilles
...					...		7					...	...	New Caledonia
13,247	4.1	136.9	2,477.6	1,026.4	630	10.0	2.8	559	168	3.5	1.4	40	0	New Zealand
772	18.3	140.0	110.7	...	90[8]	15.2	3.6	5,225[22]	1,597[14]	26.2[22]	17.2[22]	0	0	Nicaragua
32	0.2	2.5	1.0	0.1	2,350[40]	5.3	0.6	30	4	4.2[4]	1.3	0	0	Niger
312	...	...	...	...	1,140	76.5	0.8	244	2	2.0[6]	0.8	5	0	Nigeria
290	4.5	109.4	67.1	24.6	...	—	7	—	—	—	—	...	...	Northern Mariana Islands
5,656	0.9	37.6	83.1	493.6	660	33.5	7.7	3,288	769	6.2	3.2	200	10	Norway
162	...	...	...	...	430	42.9	20.9	1,450	945	35.5	15.8	40	0	Oman
221	5.6	0.1	9.1	4.1	720	587.0	4.5	2,672	23	24.7	6.1	120	10	Pakistan
703	6.1	18.9	...	125.1	180	11.7	4.5	73[6]	31[6]	5.6[6]	1.6[6]	5	0	Panama
750.6	7.9	43.7	96.4	14.4	720	3.8	0.9	97	25	4.4	3.0	0	0	Papua New Guinea
461	10.0	111.6	...	109.1	310	16.5	3.5	107	22	8.9	1.7	0	0	Paraguay
474	12.0	8.9	243.7	...	730	115.0	4.9	506	23	12.4	1.1	10	0	Peru
230	30.1	41.8	...	1.2	1,100	106.5	1.6	947	14	10.5	2.1	80	0	Philippines
2,311	2.8	50.5	1,027.7	...	370	283.6	7.3	7,362	192	32.9	4.6	0	90	Poland
805	2.8	6.9	34.5	48.2	660	50.7	5.2	2,115	203	6.2	3.3	550	0	Portugal
3,601	24.1	188.5	989.5	526.9	380	—	7	—	—	—	—	...	...	Puerto Rico
358	3.0	54.7	1.5	7.8	...	10.1	18.3	608[25]	2,638[25]	20.1[22]	9.3[22]	20	0	Qatar
2,097	7.8	123.1	181.3	137.9	220	—	7	...	...	...	...	...	...	Réunion
276	3.4	3.0	45.7	6.7	...	230.5	10.1	3,747	162	11.4	4.0	170	0	Romania
1,857	15.5[34]	50.4	860.1	...	...	1,714.0	11.7	...	...	...	...	...	...	Russia
327	6.1	58.9	4.0	...	4,650	5.0	0.6	117	15	10.6[4]	7.5	0	0	Rwanda
15,468	...	...	...	...	300	11	11	...	...	...	...	...	...	St. Kitts and Nevis
4,386	17.0	1,193.0	778.0	...	430	11	11	...	...	...	...	...	...	St. Lucia
3,977	10.3	986.9	...	...	250	11	11	...	...	...	...	...	...	St. Vincent and the Grenadines
...					...	—	—					...	...	San Marino
558	4.0	...	...	...	400	—	7	1[25]	7[25]	2.5[25]	1.6[25]	0	0	São Tomé and Príncipe
120	0.6	10.2	...	16.9	280	104.0	5.8	35,510	2,151	60.5[6]	16.5	6,900	0	Saudi Arabia
149	1.0	13.5	5.1	0.3	730	13.4	1.6	108	14	6.3[4]	1.9	0	0	Senegal
4,583	7.4	648.6	1,028.5	...	120	0.8	11.1	8[3]	124[3]	7.4[3]	5.6[3]	...	...	Seychelles
...					600	13.4	2.9	12	3	9.8[6]	2.3	0	0	Sierra Leone
1,507	1.5	4.7	126.2	15.9	230	54.0	18.4	2,107	764	25.3	5.2	120	30	Singapore
1,982	2.2	84.2	...	...	...	47.0	8.8	...	...	...	...	...	...	Slovakia
1,930	...	...	...	...	...	8.1	4.0	...	...	...	...	...	...	Slovenia
...					620	—	—					...	...	Solomon Islands
144	1.5	8.0	31.2	...	540	42	42	43[9]	6[9]	30.0[9]	3.2[9]	0	0	Somalia
...	...	...	...	...	870	78.5	1.9	3,839	95	11.7	3.7	90	20	South Africa
2,635	2.4	26.2	1,212.0	342.8	580	206.5	5.3	9,115	233	7.0	1.7	150	60	Spain
309	11.6	40.3	57.8	...	860	126.0	7.1	432	25	15.0	4.8	50	0	Sri Lanka
509	30.5	60.3	107.7	6.9	740	118.5	4.6	2,157	79	102.7	7.7	90	0	Sudan, The
17,819	7.6	1,024.4	...	...	330	1.8	4.3	75	186	5.3[6]	3.8	0	0	Suriname
4,310	87.8	542.0	922.9	...	610	—	—	12	14	4.1	1.4	0	0	Swaziland
14,188	7.0	36.2	1,801.8	879.0	330	64.0	7.3	6,432	751	6.4	2.8	40	20	Sweden
5,275	3.2	50.0	1,076.0	1,504.6[43]	640	1.8	0.3	4,528	667	19.4	1.9	110	50	Switzerland
73	1.6	5.5	27.3	2.2	1,970	408.0	29.5	4,526	342	60.3	17.9	650	0	Syria
673	7.4	...	...	111.7	720	425.0	30.7	9,748	472	32.4	5.2	450	5	Taiwan
317	2.5	4.6	...	...	...	...	...	...	...	...	...	...	...	Tajikistan
1,250	6.4	0.5	97.3	0.9	1,330	49.6	1.8	124	5	15.6	5.3	10	0	Tanzania
1,449	9.5	21.8	25.0	4.2	530	256.0	4.4	2,438	43	17.0	2.7	430	0	Thailand
11	...	...	...	...	1,970	7.0	1.8	47	12	13.8[6]	3.0	0	0	Togo
2,100	...	...	...	...	330	—	44	—	—	—	—	...	...	Tonga
5,335	8.4	164.5	611.3	...	280	2.6	2.0	29	23	1.7	0.6	0	0	Trinidad and Tobago
1,240	2.1	104.0	143.6	11.1	340	35.5	4.1	433	52	9.9	3.4	20	0	Tunisia
134.3	1.7	55.8	...	9.5	1,570	503.8	8.2	5,671	97	17.9	5.4	800	20	Turkey
...					...	45	45					...	...	Turkmenistan
...	...	...	...	—	290	...	...	...	...	...	...	...	...	Tuvalu
...	...	...	...	...	1,090	50.0	2.7	78	4	21.8	2.6	10	0	Uganda
923	7.1[34]	15.5	407.1	...	...	517.0	9.9	...	...	...	...	...	...	Ukraine
1,496	1.8	5.4	...	...	140	61.5	28.9	4,900	2,053	127.7	15.6	150	0	United Arab Emirates
8,986[46]	2.2[46]	353.5[46]	1,991.2[46]	977.4[46]	420	254.3	4.4	43,200	750	11.4	4.3	525	3,700	United Kingdom
5,652	9.3	441.8	1,168.2	631.5	345	1,650.5	6.3	280,300	1,110	19.6	4.9	1,900	9,600	United States
6,806	4.1	160.6	56.9	...	170	25.6	8.1	198	63	11.2	2.1	5	0	Uruguay
420	5.1	15.6	...	...	...	45.0	2.0	...	...	...	...	...	...	Uzbekistan
...	...	...	...	...	450	—	—	...	...	...	...	...	...	Vanuatu
1,194	16.3	171.3	...	161.6	320	79.0	3.7	1,900	94	18.2	3.6	140	0	Venezuela
...					...	572.0	7.9	720	11	40.0	4.8	200	0	Vietnam
10,441	22.3	1,943.2	3,183.7	954	240	—	7	—	—	—	—	...	...	Virgin Islands (U.S.)
2,226	...	...	...	...	...	...	...	...	...	...	...	...	...	West Bank
...	...	...	...	...	...	—	7	...	...	...	...	...	...	Western Sahara
...					...	—	44	—	—	—	—	...	...	Western Samoa
170[47]	...	...	...	...	1,940	66.0	5.1	1,061[47]	105[47]	28.3[47]	14.4[47]	200	0	Yemen
1,135[48]	5.4[48]	35.5[48]	...	...	140[48]	126.5	12.0	4,210[6,40]	184[6,48]	55.0[6,48]	4.0[6,48]	0	30	Yugoslavia
...	...	...	...	...	910	49.1	1.1	49[5]	1[5]	1.6[5]	0.8[5]	0	0	Zaire
2,088	8.3	17.5	406.8	18.6	540	24.0	2.6	80[6]	10[6]	14.4[4]	2.4[4]	10	0	Zambia
3,033	17.1	526.5	462.4	20.3	750	46.9	4.3	316	29	14.0	5.5	5	0	Zimbabwe

Kazakhstan territory, estimated at about 40,000. [34]Includes attempted murders. [35]As a result of civil war, the armed forces of Liberia, a combat strength of about 3,000–5,000, are now confined to the capital, Monrovia. [36]Military defense is the responsibility of Switzerland. [37]Military defense is the responsibility of the United States. [38]Under the terms of 1992 peace accord, government and Renamo forces are to merge to form a new National Army some 30,000 strong. [39]Curaçao only. [40]Includes paramilitary forces. [41]1978. [42]Following the 1991 revolution, no national armed forces have yet been formed. [43]Includes bicycles and motorcycles. [44]Military defense is the responsibility of New Zealand. [45]Forces under joint Turkmenistan/Russian control. [46]England and Wales. [47]Former Yemen Arab Republic only. [48]Data refer to Yugoslavia as constituted prior to 1991.

Education

This table presents international data on education analyzed to provide maximum comparability among the different educational systems in use among the nations of the world. The principal data are, naturally, numbers of schools, teachers, and students, arranged by four principal levels of education—the first (primary); general second level (secondary); vocational second level; and third level (higher). Whenever possible, data referring to preprimary education programs have been excluded from this compilation. The ratio of students to teachers is calculated for each level. These data are supplemented at each level by a figure for enrollment ratio, an indicator of each country's achieved capability to educate the total number of children potentially educable in the age group usually represented by that level. At the first and second levels this is given as a net enrollment ratio and at the third level as a gross enrollment ratio. Two additional comparative measures are given at the third level: students per 100,000 population and proportion (percentage) of adults age 25 and over who have achieved some level of higher or postsecondary education. Data in this last group are confined as far as possible to those who have completed their educations and are no longer in school. No enrollment ratio is provided for vocational training at the second level because of the great variation worldwide in the academic level at which vocational training takes place, in the need of countries to encourage or direct students into vocational programs (to support national development), and, most particularly, in the age range of students who normally constitute a national vocational system (some will be as young as 14, having just completed a primary cycle; others will be much older).

At each level of education, differences in national statistical practice, in national educational structure, public-private institutional mix, training and deployment of teachers, and timing of cycles of enrollment or completion of particular grades or standards all contribute to the problems of comparability among national educational systems.

Reporting the number of schools in a country is not simply a matter of counting permanent red-brick buildings with classrooms in them. Often the resources of a less developed country are such that temporary or outdoor facilities are all that can be afforded, while in a developed but sparsely settled country students might have to travel 80 km (50 mi) a day to find a classroom with 20 students of the same age, leading to the institution of measures such as traveling teachers, radio or televisual instruction at home under the supervision of parents, or similar systems. According to UNESCO definitions, therefore, a "school" is defined only as "a body of students . . . organized to receive instruction."

Such difficulties also limit the comparability of statistics on numbers of teachers, with the further complications that many at any level must work part-time, or that the institutions in which they work may perform a mixture of functions that do not break down into the tidy categories required by a table of this sort. In certain countries teacher training is confined to higher education, in others as a vocational form of secondary training, and so on. For purposes of this table, teacher training at the secondary level has been treated as vocational education. At the higher level, teacher training is classified as one more specialization in higher education itself.

The number of students may conceal great variation in what each country defines as a particular educational "level." Many countries do, indeed, have a primary system composed of grades 1 through 6 (or 1 through 8)

Education

country	year	first level (primary)					general second level (secondary)					vocational second level[a]	
		schools	teachers[c]	students[d]	student/ teacher ratio	net enroll- ment ratio[b]	schools	teachers[c]	students[d]	student/ teacher ratio	net enroll- ment ratio[b]	schools	teachers[c]
Afghanistan	1989	553	16,756	586,014	35.0	19	819	5,715	271,000	47.4	...	33	556
Albania	1990	1,726	28,796	557,000	19.3	...	47	2,318	68,000	29.3	...	466	7,390
Algeria	1993	13,970	162,066	4,436,363	27.4	90	3,424	135,730	2,305,196	17.0	53	147[1]	6,343[1]
American Samoa	1989	122	461	10,209	22.1	...	7	207	3,097	15.0	...	1	15
Andorra	1991	...	...	...	...	...	12	...	2,303	...	...	6	...
Angola	1991	6,308[5]	31,062	990,155	31.9	91	5,276[5]	5,138[6]	166,812	30.2[6]	10	...	566[6]
Antigua and Barbuda	1992	43	549	10,770	19.6	...	12	353	4,373	12.5	...	1[7]	45[7]
Argentina	1989	21,207	259,579	4,998,963	19.3	...	7,224[8]	262,000[8]	1,862,000[8]	7.1[8]	...	8	8
Armenia	1992	1,374[10]	54,000[10]	592,000[10]	11.0[10]	...	10	10	10	10	...	69	...
Aruba	1990	29	317	6,640	20.9	...	10	166	2,988	18.0	...	16	221
Australia	1993	11	98,526	1,816,066	18.4	98	9,865[11]	103,385	1,282,309	12.4	79	234[5, 12]	52,587[5, 12]
Austria	1993	3,702	35,603	401,974	11.3	91	1,607	52,545	431,027	8.2	90	1,318	24,706
Azerbaijan	1992	4,332[10]	139,000[10]	1,375,000[10]	9.9[10]	...	10	10	10	10	...	77	...
Bahamas, The	1991	100[14]	1,409[9]	27,264[14]	20.9[9]	100	37[14]	1,555[9]	23,616[14]	19.1[9]	87	...	...
Bahrain	1992	114	3,085	66,694	21.6	85	35[13]	2,118	42,435	20.0	86	9[13]	809
Bangladesh	1991	48,146	202,847	13,035,000	64.3	69	9,731	110,313	3,662,000	33.2	17	153	1,440
Barbados	1990	104	1,602	29,539	18.4	90	33	1,406	21,259	15.1	80	8[13]	79[13]
Belarus	1992	5,187[10]	123,300[10]	1,488,500[10]	12.1[10]	...	10	10	10	10	...	148	...
Belgium	1991	4,584	71,064[13, 17]	744,882	...	95	2,055	114,628[13]	793,599	...	87	397	14,548[13]
Belize	1993	237	1,804	47,210	26.2	...	31	782	8,901	11.4	...	8[18]	...
Benin	1991	2,952	13,180[6]	505,970	34.7[6]	45	151[13]	2,178	76,672	35.2	13	13[13]	687[13]
Bermuda	1990	24	310	5,472	17.7	...	12	331	3,555	10.7	...	20	20
Bhutan	1990	156	1,757	52,029	29.6	...	31	662	15,984	24.1	...	8	149
Bolivia	1990	9,758[9]	51,763	1,278,775	24.7	81	724[9]	12,434[8]	219,232[8]	17.6[8]	27	479[9]	8
Bosnia and Herzegovina	1991	2,205	23,369	539,875	23.1	...	238	9,030	172,063	19.1	...	...	...
Botswana	1992	654	9,708	308,840	31.8	96	169	3,743	68,137	18.2	44	40	759
Brazil	1991	206,526	1,253,029	28,742,471	22.7	86	10,160[6]	248,705	3,558,946	14.3	16	...	...
Brunei	1992	161	3,047	50,434	16.6	93	23	1,939	25,309	13.1	62	6	340
Bulgaria	1994	3,360[10]	70,131[10]	987,999[10]	14.1[10]	80	10	10	10	10	60	494	18,991
Burkina Faso	1992	2,587	8,565	530,002	61.9	29	173	2,419	60,629	25.1	7	22	537
Burundi	1992	1,342[18]	9,582	631,039	65.9	51	113[18]	2,026[18]	46,508	21.8[18]	5	...	...
Cambodia	1993	4,539	42,405	1,465,958	35.6	...	440	19,540	239,363	12.2	...	65	2,618
Cameroon	1991	6,709	38,430	1,964,146	51.1	76	388[9]	11,400[6]	409,729	32.2[6]	15	220[9]	6,267[6]
Canada	1994	16,231[10]	300,797[10]	5,360,900[10]	17.8[10]	100	10	10	10	10	93	...	...
Cape Verde	1990	367	2,028	67,761	33.4	95	16[9]	238	7,114	29.9	11	3[9]	56[21]
Central African Republic	1991	930	4,004	308,409	77.0	56	46[8]	845[8]	46,989[8]	55.6[8]	...	8	8
Chad	1991	2,544	9,238	591,417	67.2	38	66[3]	2,062	72,641	35.2	...	25[9]	285[3]
Chile	1991	8,626	81,742	2,033,862	36.0	83	1,694[13]	...	436,892	...	53	1,262[13]	...
China	1992	885,479	6,342,000	146,295,000	23.1	96	84,021	3,141,000	47,708,000	15.2	...	13,763	483,000
Colombia	1991	41,044	143,193	4,310,970	30.1	83	6,134[8, 13]	119,742[8]	2,377,947[8]	19.9[8]	38	8	8
Comoros	1990	257[13]	1,777[13]	64,737[13]	36.4[13]	56	32[24]	557	14,472	26.0	...	4[24]	41[9]
Congo	1990	1,604	7,704	492,595	63.9	...	238[13]	4,774	165,840	34.7	...	60[13]	1,965[13]
Costa Rica	1991	3,317	14,078	453,297	32.2	91	179[6]	4,968	108,344	21.8	39	77[6]	2,281
Côte d'Ivoire	1992	6,844	39,237	1,447,785	36.9	52	147[25]	9,263[25]	289,510[25]	31.3[25]	...	15	1,947[24]
Croatia	1991	2,074	23,988	434,901	18.1	...	220	12,201	188,305	15.4	...	3	122
Cuba	1992	9,346	74,354	917,889	12.3	97	2,175[6]	61,804	597,997	9.7	67	618[6]	33,892
Cyprus[28]	1992	390	3,257	63,454	19.5	98	113[8]	3,848[8]	47,908[8]	12.5[8]	90	8	8
Czech Republic	1993	4,142	65,186	1,115,027	17.1	...	285	8,574	117,765	13.7	...	708	14,537
Denmark	1992	2,127[29]	59,800[29]	613,329[29]	10.3[29]	95	154[30]	7,500[30]	74,000[30]	9.6[3, 30]	89	204	...
Djibouti	1991	69	737	31,926	43.3	34	26[8]	362[8, 31]	9,363[8]	28.6	11	8	8
Dominica	1992	65	605	12,120	20.0	...	13[18]	199[18]	5,983[18]	22.0[18]	...	...	108[9, 32]
Dominican Republic	1990	4,854[31]	21,850[31]	1,032,055[31]	47.23[1]	73	...	...	426,926	...	...	9	16,838[13, 19]
Ecuador	1990	16,146[9]	60,608	1,843,819	30.4	...	2,027[8, 9]	36,730[13, 19]	504,481[13, 19]	13.7[13, 19]	...	8	...
Egypt	1992	16,481[33]	279,315[33]	6,964,306[33]	24.9[33]	...	6,558[6, 33]	155,941[13, 33]	4,165,362[33]	20.0[13, 33]	...	519[34]	79,167
El Salvador	1989	4,160	25,318	1,016,181	40.1	70	468[8]	...	28,370	28.2[8, 13]	15	8	...

that passes students on to some kind of postprimary education. But the age of intake, the ability of parents to send their children or to permit them to finish that level, or the need to withdraw the children seasonally for agricultural work all make even a simple enrollment figure difficult to assess in isolation. All of these difficulties are compounded when a country has instruction in more than one language or when its educational establishment is so small that higher, sometimes even secondary, education cannot take place within the country. Enrollment figures in this table may, therefore, include students enrolled outside the country.

Student-teacher ratio, however, usually provides a good measure of the ratio of trained educators to the enrolled educable. In general, at each level of education both students and teachers have been counted on the basis of full-time enrollment or employment, or full-time equivalent when country statistics permit. At the primary and secondary levels, net enrollment ratio is the ratio of the number of children within the usual age group for a particular level who are actually enrolled to the total number of children in that age group (× 100). This ratio is usually less than (occasionally, equal to) 100 and is the most accurate measure of the completeness of enrollment at that particular level. It is not always, however, the best indication of utilization of teaching staff and facilities. Utilization, provided here for higher education only, is best seen in a gross enrollment ratio, which compares total enrollment (of all ages) to the population within the normal age limits for that level. For a country with substantial adult literacy or general educational programs, the difference may be striking: typically, for a less developed country, even one with a good net enrollment ratio of 90 to 95, the gross enrollment ratio may be 20%, 25%, even 30% higher,

indicating the heavy use made by the country of facilities and teachers at that level.

Literacy data provided here have been compiled as far as possible from data for the population age 15 and over for the best comparability internationally. Standards as to what constitutes literacy may also differ markedly; sometimes completion of a certain number of years of school is taken to constitute literacy; elsewhere it may mean only the ability to read or write at a minimal level testable by a census taker; in other countries studies have been undertaken to distinguish among degrees of functional literacy. When a country reports an official 100% (or near) literacy rate, it should usually be viewed with caution, as separate studies of "functional" literacy for such a country may indicate 10%, 20%, or even higher rates of inability to read, or write, effectively.

Finally, the data provided for public expenditure on education are complete in that they include all levels of public expenditure (national, state, local) but are incomplete for certain countries in that they do not include data for private expenditure; in some countries this fraction of the educational establishment may be of significant size. Occasionally data for external aid to education may be included in addition to domestic expenditure.

The following notes further define the column headings:

a. Usually includes teacher training at the second level.
b. Latest.
c. Full-time.
d. Full-time; may include students registered in foreign schools.

third level (higher)									literacy[b]				public expenditure on education (percent of GNP)[b]	country
students[d]	student/ teacher ratio	institutions	teachers[c]	students[d]	student/ teacher ratio	gross enrollment ratio[b]	students per 100,000 population[b]	percent of population age 25 and over with postsecondary education[b]	over age	total (%)	male (%)	female (%)		
8,537	15.4	5	198	1,419	7.5	1.6	147	3.2	15	29.4	44.1	13.9	2.0	Afghanistan
138,000	18.7	8	1,806	27,000	15.0	7.2	689	...	15	100.0	100.0	100.0	...	Albania
127,963[1]	20.2[1]	15[2]	14,379	243,397	16.9	11.8	1,163	0.0	15	57.4	69.8	45.5	5.7	Algeria
139	9.3	2	...	909	...	...	...	12.6	15	95.9	95.6	96.3	8.3	American Samoa
1,455	...	...	...	802[3,4]	...	...	...	24.9	15	100.0	100.0	100.0	...	Andorra
19,687	...	1[5]	439	6,534	14.9	0.9	71	...	15	41.7	55.6	28.5	7.3	Angola
5907	13.1[7]	7	7	7	7	7	...	...	15	90.0	...	...	2.7	Antigua and Barbuda
8	8	1,540[9]	70,000	959,000	13.7	43.4	3,293	6.9	15	95.3	95.5	95.1	3.1	Argentina
40,600	...	14	...	66,100	...	...	2,030	...	15	98.8	99.4	98.1	...	Armenia
2,678	11.7	1	20	180	9.0	...	...	...	15	95.0	...	...	...	Aruba
985,942[1]	...	95[13]	25,916[13]	420,640[3]	16.2[3]	38.6	3,178	21.5	15	99.5	...	...	5.5	Australia
315,376	12.8	94	14,809	216,765	14.6	34.5	2,847	6.1	15	100.0	100.0	100.0	5.8	Austria
60,100	...	18	...	108,000	...	...	1,470	...	15	97.3	98.9	95.9	...	Azerbaijan
...	...	1[15]	300[15]	2,200[15]	7.3[15]	19.6	1,945	...	15	95.0	...	...	4.4	Bahamas, The
6,165	7.6	2	561	7,090	12.6	17.5	1,456	3.8	15	69.7	76.5	58.6	5.0	Bahrain
27,891	19.4	997	23,332	767,385	32.9	3.8	382	1.3	15	34.8	45.2	23.7	2.3	Bangladesh
996[13]	12.6[13]	3	153[3]	4,242	8.6[3]	17.3	1,657	3.3	15	98.0[16]	...	...	7.9	Barbados
139,000	...	33	...	184,600	...	...	1,700	...	15	97.9	99.4	96.6	5.2	Belarus
137,175	...	21	10,517[13]	111,845	...	38.2	2,772	...	...	100.0	100.0	100.0	5.2	Belgium
1,726[19]	...	7	7	7	7	...	...	6.6	15	93.0	...	...	5.8	Belize
6,870[13]	10.0[13]	13[13]	956[6]	10,873[6]	11.4	2.8	235	0.3	15	23.4	31.7	15.6	5.1	Benin
20	...	1[20]	56[20]	498[20]	8.9[20]	...	...	7.4	15	96.9	96.7	97.0	3.2	Bermuda
1,822	12.2	2	57	519	9.1	0.9	18	...	15	18.0	31.0	9.0	3.4	Bhutan
8	8	10[9]	4,261[1]	109,503[1]	...	22.6	2,028	9.8	15	77.5	84.7	70.7	2.7	Bolivia
...	...	44	2,801	37,541	13.4	...	...	...	10	85.5	96.5	76.7	...	Bosnia and Herzegovina
7,057	9.3	1	370	3,352	9.1	3.3	487	0.5	15	73.6	83.7	65.1	7.5	Botswana
...	...	918[6]	133,135	1,565,056	11.8	11.6	1,075	5.0	15	81.7	82.1	81.2	4.6	Brazil
1,756	5.2	4	289	1,372	4.7	4.5	259	9.4	15	85.1	90.9	78.7	4.6	Brunei
214,558	11.8	87	21,248	203,601	9.6	30.4	2,078	...	15	95.5	...	...	6.4	Bulgaria
8,022	14.9	9	437	7,387	16.9	0.7	60	3.8	15	18.2	27.9	8.9	2.3	Burkina Faso
...	...	8[18]	492	3,830	7.8	0.8	73	...	7	74.3	73.7	74.9	3.7	Burundi
15,537	5.9	9	268	22,182	82.5	...	...	...	15	74.3	85.0	65.0	...	Cambodia
90,543	14.8[6]	5[9]	1,086	33,177	30.5	3.4	288	...	15	54.1	66.3	42.6	3.1	Cameroon
...	...	272	64,100	921,300	14.4	98.8	7,197	44.4	14	95.6	95.6	95.7	7.4	Canada
752	...	...	...	...	...	—	...	0.5	15	47.4	61.4	38.6	4.1	Cape Verde
8	8	1[6,22]	134[6,22]	2,534[6,22]	18.9[6,22]	1.8	146	...	15	37.7	51.8	24.9	2.8	Central African Republic
3,819	15.1[3]	4[3]	59	2,969	50.3	0.8	70	...	15	29.8	42.2	17.9	2.3	Chad
262,563	...	201[13]	15,101[00]	286,962	...	23.3	2,144	7.1	15	93.4	93.5	93.2	2.9	Chile
5,836,000	12.1	1,053	388,000	2,184,000	5.6	4.2	191	1.1	15	77.7	87.0	68.0	1.7	China
8	8	235[9]	51,725[3]	474,787[3]	9.2[3]	13.7	1,554	6.8	15	86.7	87.5	85.9	3.1	Colombia
349	14.6[9]	—	32	248	7.8	—	...	0.2	15	46.3	54.2	39.0	6.5	Comoros
20,722[13]	10.5	12[13]	641[13]	10,310[13]	16.1[13]	6.0	524	3.0	15	56.6	70.0	43.9	5.6	Congo
30,959	13.6	5[1,22]	7,534[1,22]	60,145[1,22]	8.0[1,22]	27.6	2,584	14.2	15	92.8	92.6	93.1	4.5	Costa Rica
3,094	...	1[26]	1,204[2]	19,660[23]	...	2.5	204	...	15	53.8	66.9	40.2	7.2	Côte d'Ivoire
1,839	15.1	54	6,303	66,881	10.6	...	...	9.4[27]	10	98.0	98.9	97.0	...	Croatia
314,168	9.3	35[6]	24,668	242,434	9.8	20.9	2,285	4.2	15	96.0	...	...	6.7	Cuba
8	8	29	485	5,952	12.3	15.0	1,029	...	15	94.0	98.0	90.0	4.0	Cyprus[28]
201,209	13.8	23	12,007	114,185	8.9	...	...	7.2	15	100.0	100.0	100.0	5.0	Czech Republic
149,000	...	94[18]	...	126,221[18]	...	35.6	2,917	...	...	100.0	100.0	100.0	7.4	Denmark
8	8	1	13	106	8.2	—	...	...	20	33.7	...	...	3.5	Djibouti
...	...	2[18]	40	658	16.5	...	...	1.7	15	94.4	...	...	5.8	Dominica
3,602[9,32]	...	7[22]	5,319[18,22]	86,504[18,22]	16.3[18,22]	18.6	1,929	2.3	15	83.3	84.8	81.8	1.5	Dominican Republic
260,850[13,19]	15.5[13,19]	21	12,856	206,541	16.1	20.1	1,958	12.7	15	88.3	90.5	86.2	2.7	Ecuador
1,110,184	14.0	12[18,22]	34,553[18,22,33]	600,600[10,02,03]	...	19.2	1,697	4.1[27]	15	48.4	62.9	33.8	5.0	Egypt
88,708	8	8[6,22]	2,637[6,22]	51,277[6,22]	19.4[6,22]	16.1	1,512	2.3	15	73.0	76.2	70.0	1.7	El Salvador

Education (continued)

country	year	first level (primary)					general second level (secondary)					vocational second level[a]	
		schools	teachers[c]	students[d]	student/ teacher ratio	not enroll- ment ratio[b]	schools	teachers[c]	students[d]	student/ teacher ratio	net enroll- ment ratio[b]	schools	teachers[c]
Equatorial Guinea	1988	703	1,065	61,009	57.3	...	9	319	9,226	28.9	...	...	...
Eritrea	1993	447	4,954	184,492	37.2	...	86	1,759	59,962	34.1	...	4	53
Estonia	1993	715[10]	15,783[10]	216,427[10]	13.7[10]	81	10	10	10	10	73	92	...
Ethiopia[35]	1991	8,434	68,399	2,063,636	30.2	28	1,209[5]	23,110	775,211	33.5	...	...	763[13]
Faeroe Islands	1991	67[10]	611[3, 10]	5,440[3]	14.0[3, 10]	...	10	10	2,979[3]	10	...	9[13]	...
Fiji	1991	681[6]	4,664	144,924	31.1	99	140[5]	2,684[6]	55,622	19.6[6]	...	44[5]	369[6]
Finland	1992	4,819[36]	42,178[36]	591,252[36]	14.0[36]	...	465[37]	6,262[37]	105,511[37]	17.0[37]	93	541	...
France	1992	44,131[18]	277,826	4,068,000	14.6	100	11,325[8]	365,417[8]	2,511,300	11.7[8]	87	8	8
French Guiana	1990	84[13]	...	14,256	...	...	11[13]	...	10,722[8]	...	...	8[13]	...
French Polynesia	1990	278	2,503	44,734	17.9	...	32[8]	1,341[8]	20,159[8]	15.0[8]	...	8	8
Gabon	1987	992	4,229	195,049	46.1	...	51[38]	1,512	32,922	21.8	...	29[38]	759
Gambia, The	1991	233	2,757	86,101	31.2	56	14	279	6,434	26.1	19	18	477
Gaza Strip	1989	331[10]	4,429[10]	185,410[10]	41.9[10]	...	10	10	10	10	...	10	10
Georgia	1990	3,788[10]	...	924,700[10]	10	...	10	...	10	...	...	10	10
Germany	1993	43,941[10]	656,809[10]	9,345,162[10]	14.2[10]	89[37]	10	...	10	...	85[39]	8,951	105,546
Ghana	1990	11,056[1]	66,068[1]	1,796,490[1]	27.2[1]	...	5,513	45,429	793,388	17.5	...	58	2,317
Gibraltar	1991	21[10]	92[3]	5,308[10]	31.9[3]	...	10	124[3]	10	...	...	1	29[3]
Greece	1993	7,634[31]	37,549[31]	745,666[31]	19.9[31]	93	2,988	45,794	700,488	15.3	87	695	14,349
Greenland	1990	90[3, 10]	994[10]	7,674	9.1[10]	...	10	10	1,387	10	...	...	...
Grenada	1994	57	781	21,311	27.3	...	19	352	6,939	19.7	...	...	...
Guadeloupe	1993	340	3,135	39,075	12.5	...	78[8]	3,813[8]	49,295[8]	12.9[8]	...	8	8
Guam	1990	36	850	16,819	19.8	...	24	736	15,733	21.4	...	40	176[40]
Guatemala	1991	9,362	36,757	1,249,413	34.0	58	1,274	13,588	207,935	15.3	13	626	7,129
Guernsey	1992	22	231	4,469	19.3	...	8	286	3,521	12.3	...	1	228[41]
Guinea	1990	2,476	8,699	346,807	39.9	26	225[13]	4,846	75,674	15.6	7	35[13]	1,130
Guinea-Bissau	1988	632[9]	3,065[9]	79,035	24.6[9]	45	12[5]	824[5]	5,505	7.5[5]	3	4[9]	107
Guyana	1990	423	4,010[3]	118,015[3]	29.4[3]	...	93	...	72,096[3]	...	...	8	176
Haiti	1993	7,306[18]	27,607	787,553	28.5	26	...	10,174[8]	193,624[8]	19.0[8]	...	8	8
Honduras	1992	8,074	26,420	959,466	36.3	93	590	9,708	144,456	14.9	19	5[3]	581[3]
Hong Kong	1994	633	19,346[1]	485,061	26.7[1]	95	489	20,360[1]	472,200	22.5[1]	61	9	2,488[13]
Hungary	1993	3,959	96,223	1,092,563	11.8	86	876	26,335	335,153	12.7	77	343	6,624
Iceland	1992	...	25,809	...	...	...	...	29,985	...	...	...	...	...
India	1993	572,541	1,681,970	105,370,216	62.6	...	235,793	2,435,293	59,255,258	24.3	...	...	...
Indonesia	1991[45]	147,064	1,331,993	26,308,423	19.8	97	28,834	707,987	8,236,018	11.6	38	3,823	108,536
Iran	1992	59,280[18]	312,273	9,787,593	31.3	98	18,445[6]	199,451	5,311,988	26.6	47	1,006[6]	19,480
Iraq	1992	8,875	127,578	3,316,036	26.0	78	2,746	43,937	1,084,715	24.7	37	296	9,957
Ireland	1992	3,425	20,430[46]	542,898	...	90	474	12,034	216,740	18.0	81	317	9,004
Isle of Man	1989	32	240[34]	5,458	...	...	7	276[34]	4,908	...	...	1	...
Israel	1993	1,735	51,321	661,063	12.9	...	816	50,392	449,409	8.9	...	386	...
Italy	1993	22,710	182,390	2,959,564	16.2	...	9,857	105,964	2,059,044	19.4	...	7,930	133,685
Jamaica	1993[31]	788[36]	10,147	386,688	38.1	100	126	7,927	152,367	19.2	61	18	976
Japan	1992	24,730	441,000	8,947,000	20.3	100	16,801	567,000	10,256,000	18.1	97	6,679[18]	53,000[18]
Jersey	1990	32	294[9]	5,794	19.2[9]	...	14	372[9]	4,405	12.3[9]	...	1	...
Jordan	1992	2,421	44,649[10]	1,065,945[10]	23.9[10]	99	622	10	10	10	36	49	2,105
Kazakhstan	1992	8,841[10]	262,600[10]	3,226,400[10]	12.3[10]	...	10	10	10	10	...	3,115	...
Kenya	1993	15,804	173,002	5,428,600	31.4	91	2,639	31,657	517,577	16.3	...	24[32]	1,332[3, 32]
Kiribati	1992	95	545	16,020	29.4	...	9[6]	194	3,069	15.8	...	6[6]	43
Korea, North	1987	6,122	138,945	1,543,000	11.1	...	10	111,000	2,468,000	22.2	...	473[5]	...
Korea, South	1993	6,057	139,159	4,336,252	31.2	100	4,358[8]	194,565[8]	4,497,242[8]	23.1[8]	88	8	8
Kuwait	1994	239	8,217	130,877	15.9	45	390	17,340	188,399	10.9	...	36	650
Kyrgyzstan	1993	1,862	76,300[10]	954,700[10]	12.5[10]	...	1,472	10	10	10	...	37	...
Laos	1992	7,140	21,036	580,792	27.6	59	750[6]	8,936	117,504	13.1	15	139[3]	1,262
Latvia	1992	943[10]	33,712[10]	330,468[10]	9.8[10]	82	10	10	10	10	...	57[18]	10
Lebanon	1989	2,130[2]	22,810[2]	346,534	...	...	1,405[2]	21,344[24]	241,964	...	...	181[2]	4,792
Lesotho	1992	1,198	6,685	361,144	54.0	70	179	2,407	46,572	19.3	17	10	227
Liberia	1986	1,651[26]	9,099[26]	80,048	25.0[26]	35	419[26]	1,129[26]	43,273[23]	45.8[26]	17	6[26]	63[26]
Libya	1992	2,744[34]	99,623	1,238,986	12.4	...	1,555[34]	11,429	138,860	12.1	...	195[34]	7,072
Liechtenstein	1993	14	118	1,912	16.2	...	8	74	1,161	15.7	...	1[3]	74[3]
Lithuania	1993	2,219[10]	43,900[10]	512,411[10]	11.7[10]	...	10	10	10	10	...	104	4,638
Luxembourg	1992	...	2,032[31]	26,197[31]	12.9[31]	85	...	1,953[8, 31]	8,465	...	60	...	8
Macau	1991	69	1,088	34,972	32.1	...	21	913	17,601	19.3	...	2	30
Macedonia	1991	1,067	12,976	266,813	20.6	...	90	4,227	70,696	16.7	...	...	...
Madagascar	1991	13,791	38,933	1,570,721	40.3	64	1,142[3]	14,856	322,772	21.7	...	61[13]	1,484
Malawi	1990	2,624	20,580	1,325,453	64.4	48	94	1,096	29,326	26.8	2	13	250
Malaysia	1992	6,891	125,916	2,641,000	21.0	...	1,336	77,149	1,400,000	18.1	...	75	3,489
Maldives	1986	243	1,138	41,812	36.7	...	9	291	3,581	12.3	...	10	52
Mali	1992	1,514	7,963	375,131	47.1	19	307[49]	5,883	88,529	19.8[18]	5	...	...
Malta	1992	168	1,455[18]	35,626	25.4[18]	99	46	1,594[18]	24,462	16.2[18]	80	31	738
Marshall Islands	1992	102	515	12,248	23.8	...	8[9]	137	2,215	16.2	...	...	8
Martinique	1993	282	2,711	33,170	12.2	...	79[8]	3,830[8]	47,295[8]	12.3[8]	...	...	8
Mauritania	1992	1,309	3,967	187,202	47.2	...	56	1,905	36,882	19.4	...	5	169
Mauritius	1992	283	6,389	129,738	20.2	89	122	3,949	83,784	20.5	...	19	69[2]
Mayotte	1990	88	427	19,078	44.7	...	4	66	2,280	34.5	...	2	17
Mexico	1993	86,636	481,466	14,500,000	30.1	100	25,131	352,865	5,980,000	16.9	46	6,571	77,347
Micronesia	1988	177	1,051[23]	25,139	22.2[23]	...	16	314[23]	5,385	13.2[23]	...	...	...
Moldova	1992	1,654[10]	53,000[10]	725,000[10]	13.6[10]	...	10	10	10	10	...	53	...
Monaco	1990	6[9]	735[10]	5,523[10]	7.5[10]	...	3[9]	10	10	10	...	...	...
Mongolia	1991	11	11	11	11	94	634[11]	20,600[11]	440,900[11]	21.4[11]	...	75	2,500
Morocco	1991	4,052	87,839	2,483,691	28.3	59	1,080[31]	69,915[31]	1,121,193[31]	16.0[31]	29	562[21]	5,359[21]
Mozambique	1992	3,384[50]	22,132[50]	1,199,847[50]	54.2[50]	42	207[51]	3,614[51]	144,671[51]	40.0[51]	...	32[13]	1,126
Myanmar (Burma)	1993	36,499	198,909	6,518,800	32.8	...	2,920	67,503	1,633,700	24.2	...	112	2,194
Namibia	1990	1,134[3]	...	313,528	...	81	...	2,534	74,331	29.3	...	9[13]	140[3]
Nauru	1989	3	61	1,367	22.4	...	2	34	629	18.5	...	1	3
Nepal	1991	18,694	74,495	2,884,275	38.7	61	6,124[8]	24,632[8]	773,808[8]	31.4[8]	23	8	8
Netherlands, The	1993	9,333	99,031[18]	1,526,000	15.7[18]	95	1,117	89,370[18]	668,000	7.7[18]	81	747	18,613[18]

students[d]	student/ teacher ratio	third level (higher) institutions	teachers[c]	students[d]	student/ teacher ratio	gross enroll-ment ratio[b]	students per 100,000 popula-tion[b]	percent of population age 25 and over with post-secondary education[b]	literacy[b] over age	total (%)	male (%)	female (%)	public expenditure on education (percent of GNP)[b]	country
...	...	5	133	1,542	11.6	...	...	1.1[27]	15	62.8	77.8	48.6	1.7	Equatorial Guinea
774	14.6	1	144	2,032	14.1	...	55	...	...	20.0	...	...	...	Eritrea
30,687	...	14	3,168[18]	24,464	8.2[18]	...	1,593	...	15	99.7	99.9	99.6	...	Estonia
8,243[13]	10.8[13]	11[23]	1,697	22,358	13.3	0.8	66	...	15	24.3	32.7	16.4	4.9	Ethiopia[35]
1,387[13]	...	1	20	100	5.0	...	...	...	15	100.0	100.0	100.0	...	Faeroe Islands
5,000	0.9[6]	5[34]	277	7,008	28.5	12.8	1,080	3.3	15	87.0	90.0	84.0	5.6	Fiji
180,019	...	20	7,002	115,358	14.8	50.7	3,757	11.2	15	100.0	100.0	100.0	7.4	Finland
1,777,200	8	1,062[3]	57,409	1,700,800	29.6	43.2	3,414	...	15	98.8	98.9	98.7	5.7	France
8	8	...	...	...	...	...	...	6.4	16	82.0	82.5	81.3	17.6	French Guiana
8	8	4[3]	70[3]	701[3]	10.0[3]	...	...	...	15	95.0	94.9	95.0	9.8	French Polynesia
15,352	20.2	1[13,22]	363[13,22]	2,896[13,22]	8.0[13,22]	3.3	368	...	15	60.7	73.5	48.5	2.9	Gabon
13,966	29.3	9[38]	177[38]	1,489[38]	8.4[38]	—	...	...	15	27.2	39.0	16.0	2.7	Gambia, The
10	10	1[34]	30[2]	2,387[34]	...	—	...	9.5						Gaza Strip
19	...	19	...	93,100	...	...	1,900	...	15	99.0	99.5	98.5	...	Georgia
2,470,837	23.4	314	171,025[1]	1,858,455	10.7[18]	36.1[39]	3,051	26.5	15	100.0	100.0	100.0	4.0	Germany
30,221	13.0	3	700	9,274	13.2	1.5	126	3.5	15	60.4	70.0	50.9	3.1	Ghana
772	14.1[5]	—	—	—	—	—	...	...	15	99.0	99.0	99.0	6.0	Gibraltar
290,443	20.2	82[13]	12,760[13]	189,173[13]	14.8[13]	25.0	1,928	7.4	15	93.2	97.6	89.1	3.1	Greece
2,297[3]	...	4	35[9]	200[13]	5.7[9]	...	...	...	15	100.0	100.0	100.0	...	Greenland
...	...	1	66	651	9.9	...	709	1.5	15	85.0	...	...	4.6	Grenada
8	8	1	310	4,296	13.9	...	1,028	5.2	15	90.1	89.7	90.5	14.3	Guadeloupe
1,095[40]	6.2[40]	1	206	2,208	10.7	...	...	34.4	15	96.4	96.4	96.5	8.5	Guam
94,485	13.3	5[3]	4,346[3]	69,532[3]	16.0[3]	8.6	741	3.0	15	60.3	69.7	51.7	1.2	Guatemala
4,952[42]	21.7	—	—	—	—	—	...	...	15	100.0	100.0	100.0	...	Guernsey
10,268	9.1	10[13]	805[22]	6,245[22]	7.8[22]	1.4	122	...	15	24.0	34.9	13.4	2.2	Guinea
825	7.7	—	—	—	—	—	...	...	15	36.5	50.2	24.0	2.8	Guinea-Bissau
5,388	30.6	1[1,22]	370[1,22]	2,391[1,22]	6.5[1,22]	5.1	588	1.8	15	96.4	97.6	95.4	4.7	Guyana
0	8	2[43]	554[43]	6,678[43]	12.1[43]	1.2	107	0.7	15	53.0	59.1	47.4	1.8	Haiti
76,388	13.7[3]	5	2,512	36,870	14.7	9.1	854	3.3	15	73.1	75.5	70.6	4.0	Honduras
53,604	18.5[13]	12	1,422[13]	70,426	32.4[13]	17.6	1,534	7.1	15	88.1	94.7	80.9	3.0	Hong Kong
212,932	32.2	91	17,743	119,828	6.8	15.3	1,117	7.0	15	98.9	99.2	98.6	7.2	Hungary
...	...	5[18]	369[18,44]	5,450[18]	14.0[18,44]	29.2	2,397	3.7	15	100.0	100.0	100.0	5.8	Iceland
...	...	7,513	...	4,610,000	...	6.7	556	2.5	15	48.2	61.8	33.7	3.9	India
1,352,009	12.5	900[6]	141,094[6]	1,485,894[6]	10.5[6]	8.7	1,032	1.2	15	77.6	85.6	70.0	2.2	Indonesia
307,069	15.8	44[22]	25,208	636,255	25.2	12.2	1,061	7.8	15	54.0	64.5	43.3	4.6	Iran
152,903	15.4	20	10,520	197,786	18.8	13.8	1,240	...	15	59.7	69.8	49.3	5.1	Iraq
132,117	14.7	48	3,934[3]	76,809	16.0[3]	33.8	2,895	24.4	15	100.0	100.0	100.0	6.1	Ireland
425[18]	...	...	...	...	...	...	...	...	15	...	...	...	...	Isle of Man
122,223	...	7	6,150[1]	84,990	...	34.4	2,790	31.2	15	94.8	97.1	92.7	5.8	Israel
2,833,150	21.2	50[22]	56,723[22]	1,538,606[22]	27.1[22]	31.7	2,795	4.1	15	97.1	97.8	96.4	5.4	Italy
15,617	16.0	15[3]	1,047[13]	19,173[6]	17.9[13]	6.0	662	2.0	15	98.4	98.2	98.6	4.1	Jamaica
1,242,000[18]	23.4[18]	1,114	150,000	2,817,000	18.8	31.3	2,338	31.7	15	100.0	100.0	100.0	4.7	Japan
283[9]	...	...	...	...	...	...	...	...	15	100.0	100.0	100.0	4.1	Jersey
26,175	12.4	55[3]	3,734	83,777	22.4	21.5	2,497	...	15	80.1	89.3	70.3	4.0	Jordan
1,091,600	...	61	...	288,000	...	...	1,710	...	15	97.5	99.1	96.1	...	Kazakhstan
14,456[32]	13.4[3,32]	14	4,392	88,180	...	2.2	187	1.3	15	69.0	79.8	58.5	7.0	Kenya
288	6.7	—	—	54[6]	—	—	...	0.6	15	90.0	...	...	6.5	Kiribati
220,000	...	281	27,000	390,000	14.4	...	...	...	15	99.0	...	...	3.7	Korea, North
8	8	605	48,535	1,652,665	34.0	39.9	4,208	14.2	15	96.3	99.1	93.5	4.1	Korea, South
2,524	3.9	1[47]	927[6]	11,284	15.2[3]	13.8	1,135	11.1	15	79.7	83.3	74.9	6.0	Kuwait
40,922	...	12	...	53,670	...	...	1,330	30.0	15	97.0	98.6	95.5	7.0	Kyrgyzstan
8,198	6.5	9[6]	698[6]	4,730[6]	6.8[6]	1.3	116	...	15	83.9	92.0	75.8	1.2	Laos
38,100[18]	...	14	...	46,279	...	...	1,536	...	15	99.5	99.8	99.2	...	Latvia
32,708	6.8	18[2]	5,400[1]	85,495[1]	15.8[1]	27.8	3,071	3.1	15	80.1	87.8	73.1	2.0	Lebanon
2,167	9.5	1	204	1,421	7.0	2.7	114	0.6	15	73.6	62.4	84.5	6.4	Lesotho
2,322[26]	36.9[26]	3[26]	470[9]	5,095[9]	...	2.5	220	1.5	15	39.5	49.8	28.8	5.7	Liberia
76,648	10.8	10[3]	...	47,300	...	18.0	1,548	...	15	63.8	75.4	50.4	9.6	Libya
147[3]	...	1	163[48]	214	1.3[48]	—	...	11.2	15	100.0	100.0	100.0	...	Liechtenstein
42,000	9.1	17	9,003[13]	55,000	7.3[13]	...	1,758	...	...	...	...	...	...	Lithuania
11,877	6.1	...	...	4,957[18]	...	2.4	207	...	15	100.0	100.0	100.0	4.3	Luxembourg
388	12.9	9	478	7,037	14.7	...	...	15.9	10	61.3	76.4	46.2	...	Macau
...	...	27	2,101	26,413	12.6	...	...	5.1	10	89.1	94.2	83.8	...	Macedonia
17,419	11.7	5[3]	939	35,824	38.2	3.4	333	...	15	80.2	87.7	72.9	1.5	Madagascar
3,679	14.7	4	235	2,685	11.4	0.7	63	0.2	15	41.6	...	...	3.4	Malawi
33,000	9.5	54	11,471[10]	136,000[18]	11.9[18]	7.2	679	1.9	15	78.4	86.5	70.4	5.5	Malaysia
462	8.9	—	—	—	—	0.8	...	0.4	15	90.4	90.6	90.1	6.9	Maldives
...	...	7[18]	701	6,703	9.6	...	73	...	6	18.8	26.7	11.4	3.2	Mali
...	...	1	320	3,150	9.8	13.1	882	3.9	15	96.0	96.2	95.9	4.0	Malta
7,093	9.6	...	...	...	...	...	...	11.4	15	91.2	92.4	90.0	...	Marshall Islands
8	8	1	71	3,670	51.7	...	...	6.3	15	92.5	91.8	93.2	15.3	Martinique
1,782	10.5	4	176	5,850	33.2	3.3	281	...	15	34.0	47.1	21.4	4.9	Mauritania
2,052	...	2	382[3]	2,159	5.7[3]	2.1	208	1.9	15	79.9	85.2	74.7	3.7	Mauritius
392	23.1	—	—	—	—	—	...	...	15	31.8	...	...	...	Mayotte
1,076,700	13.9	1,832	128,212	1,256,100	9.8	15.2	1,478	8.3	15	87.3	89.5	85.1	4.5	Mexico
...	...	...	...	920[9]	...	...	...	8.0	15	76.7	67.0	87.2	...	Micronesia
47,200	...	11	...	52,200	...	...	1,250	...	15	96.4	98.6	94.4	26.4	Moldova
1,218[2]	...	...	...	...	...	...	...	6.8						Monaco
47,600	19.0	9	1,465	13,829	9.4	13.6	1,254	8.1	10	97.9	...	...	8.5	Mongolia
68,802[21]	12.8[21]	35	7,713	225,001	29.2	10.2	958	0.6	15	49.5	61.3	38.0	5.8	Morocco
13,740	12.2	2[13]	457[13]	2,582[10]	5.6[13]	0.1	11	0.2	15	32.9	45.1	21.3	6.2	Mozambique
28,200	12.9	40	6,696	260,300	38.9	5.4	459	0.1	15	78.5	85.8	71.6	2.4	Myanmar (Burma)
1,666[3]	11.9[3]	...	213[18]	2,507[18]	11.8[18]	3.3	280	2.0	15	72.5	74.2	70.8	1.6	Namibia
30	10.0	1[52]	...	c. 200[52]	...	...	...	...	15	99.0	...	...	...	Nauru
8	8	3	4,694[3]	154,528	21.8[3]	6.6	549	6.8	15	37.7	51.7	23.3	2.0	Nepal
498,000	28.0[18]	206	30,952[5]	389,000	...	37.6	3,280	17.2	15	100.0	100.0	100.0	6.2	Netherlands, The

Education (continued)

country	year	first level (primary) schools	teachers[c]	students[d]	student/teacher ratio	net enrollment ratio[b]	general second level (secondary) schools	teachers[c]	students[d]	student/teacher ratio	net enrollment ratio[b]	vocational second level[a] schools	teachers[c]
Netherlands Antilles	1989	85[9]	1,231[9]	21,778	17.9[9]	...	23[9]	664[9]	8,698	14.2[9]	...	36[9]	50[5]
New Caledonia	1990	279	1,696	34,242	20.2	...	44	1,685[8]	14,237	12.5[8]	...	29	[8]
New Zealand	1993	2,412[53]	21,247[53]	434,306[53]	20.4[53]	100	339	14,946	230,132	15.4	85	30	5,734
Nicaragua	1991	4,402	18,646	674,045	36.1	80	407[8]	4,191[8]	180,112[8]	43.0[8]	25	[8]	[8]
Niger	1990	2,807	8,759	368,732	42.1	25	105[3]	2,534	74,337	29.3	6	7[3]	190
Nigeria	1992	35,446	353,600	13,776,854	38.9	...	5,594[13]	141,491	3,123,277	22.1	...	376[13]	15,738[3]
Northern Mariana Islands	1989	18	240	4,882	20.3	...	9[8]	163[8]	2,075[8]	12.7[8]	...	[8]	[8]
Norway	1993	3,352	35,416[1]	463,948	13.2[1]	99	778[8]	20,982[1,8]	243,797[8]	11.6[1,8]	89	[8]	[8]
Oman	1992	436	10,184	277,370	27.2	85	128[6]	6,841	116,817	17.1	50	25[6]	423
Pakistan	1993	124,171	360,100	14,200,000	39.2	...	19,117	276,400	4,770,000	17.3	...	710	6,772
Panama	1992	2,712	13,751	352,994	25.7	92	363[8]	10,350[8]	201,047[8]	19.4[8]	50	[8]	[8]
Papua New Guinea	1990	2,606	13,105	415,194	31.7	72	135	2,306[3]	55,797	25.0[3]	...	117	751[3]
Paraguay	1992	4,649	29,172	720,983	24.7	98	812[8,19]	12,218[8,19]	169,167[8,19]	13.8[8,19]	28	[8,19]	[8,19]
Peru	1991	28,265	138,455	4,053,801	29.3	95	6,607	96,969	1,996,181	20.6	42	1,704	11,289
Philippines	1992	34,081	316,182	10,558,105	33.4	96	5,550	122,688[18]	4,033,597[18]	32.9[18]	58	1,262[18]	13,265[18]
Poland	1993	19,212	351,700	5,178,200	14.7	96	1,762	28,300	607,100	21.5	78	8,499	84,100
Portugal	1993	11,771	71,788	925,936	12.9	100	1,368	64,479	815,491	12.6	...	220	...
Puerto Rico	1989[31]	1,145	33,357[10]	661,693[10]	19.8[10]	...	315	[10]	[10]	[10]	...	525[5]	...
Qatar	1992[31]	155	4,250	49,770	11.7	88	36	1,050	9,869	9.4	69	3	101
Réunion	1994	349	...	72,513	...	...	95[8]	...	91,015[8]	...	...	[8]	...
Romania	1992	13,730	153,187	2,608,914	17.0	78	1,209	16,791	248,748	14.8	72	1,101	41,622
Russia	1993	70,200[10]	1,611,000[10]	20,990,000[10]	13.8[10]	...	[10]	[10]	[10]	[10]	...	2,609	...
Rwanda	1992	1,724	18,937	1,104,903	58.3	72	192[8]	4,054[8]	62,701[8]	15.5[8]	8	[8]	[8]
St. Kitts and Nevis	1992	31	342	6,978	20.4	...	7	298	4,645	15.6	...	2	35
St. Lucia	1993	84	1,181[1]	32,204	27.4[1]	...	14	466[1]	7,612	17.5[1]	...	1[7]	113[1]
St. Vincent and the Grenadines	1992	60	1,215	24,134	19.9	...	21	408	7,124	17.5	...	2	...
San Marino	1994	14	219	1,166	5.3	...	3	133	772	5.8	...	...	...
São Tomé and Príncipe	1989	64	559	19,822	35.5	...	11[55]	318	7,446	23.4	...	2[55]	18[56]
Saudi Arabia	1989	8,631	105,937	1,694,394	16.0	64	4,153	52,818	739,088	14.0	36	321[13]	3,295[13]
Senegal	1991	2,458	13,394	708,299	52.9	48	321	4,791[3]	173,490	34.8[3]	13	13	259[3]
Seychelles	1993	25[13]	685	12,851	18.8	...	4[5]	553	7,337	13.3	...	1[5]	190
Sierra Leone	1992	1,792	10,051	315,146	31.4	...	217	3,924	72,516	18.5	...	30	750
Singapore	1992	194	10,188	266,599	25.8	100	180	9,278	182,149	19.6	...	21	1,594
Slovakia	1993	2,472	39,867	704,119	17.7	...	165	4,659	63,522	13.6	...	234	7,812
Slovenia	1992	845	14,936	222,339	14.8	...	226	8,688	101,880	11.7	...	79	985
Solomon Islands	1993	520	2,357	70,103	29.7	...	23[8]	364[8]	7,351[8]	20.2[8]	...	[8]	[8]
Somalia	1987	1,125	8,208	171,830	20.9	8	82	2,109	42,764	20.3	3	21	498
South Africa	1992	20,648	322,493	8,374,564	26.0	...	197	14,876	147,009	9.9	...	12	6,865
Spain	1990	19,821	135,747	2,961,955	21.8	100	22,633[3]	200,633[3]	3,611,860[3]	18.3[3]	90	2,668[3]	63,236[3]
Sri Lanka	1991	9,590	173,811	2,112,723	12.2	100	9,041	106,792	2,105,959	19.7	...	23	437
Sudan, The	1992	8,501	64,227	2,079,649	32.4	...	5,578[8]	20,024[8]	446,898[8]	22.3[8]	...	[8]	[8]
Suriname	1992	301	2,918	63,083	21.6	100	89	1,684	26,708	15.8	45	64[55]	1,283[55]
Swaziland	1991	523	5,015	183,738	36.6	91	153	2,149	50,676	23.6	...	8	280
Sweden	1994	4,826	90,234	893,932	9.9	100	600[8]	29,539[8]	313,728[8]	10.6[8]	90	[8]	[8]
Switzerland	1993	...	...	420,089	...	96	...	...	404,249	...	80	...	...
Syria	1992	9,934	102,617	2,539,081	24.7	97	2,077[9]	46,218	849,530	18.4	44	238[9]	8,811
Taiwan	1994	2,525	84,052	2,111,037	26.2	...	906	70,739	1,426,030	19.9	...	209	18,332
Tajikistan	1992	3,179[10]	99,000[10]	1,310,000[10]	13.2[10]	...	[10]	[10]	[10]	[10]	...	...	...
Tanzania	1991[58]	10,437	98,174	3,512,347	35.8	50	288[9]	8,649	166,812	19.3	...	63[9]	1,255
Thailand	1991	34,039	395,327	7,957,971	20.1	...	1,859	109,346	1,953,044	17.9	...	634	36,934
Togo	1990	2,494	11,105	651,962	58.7	76	358[23]	4,231	117,153	27.7	...	18[9]	261
Tonga	1992	115	784	16,658	21.2	...	40	862	15,253	17.7	...	8	65[6]
Trinidad and Tobago	1992	471	7,511	196,333	26.1	90	101	4,844	96,201	19.4	73	...	237[13,32]
Tunisia	1993	4,044	54,560	1,440,960	26.4	100	625	26,097	639,403	24.5	44	...	...
Turkey	1992	50,701	234,961	6,878,923	29.3	100	8,064	117,702	3,010,672	25.6	44	2,971	57,425
Turkmenistan	1992	1,791[10]	60,000[10]	842,000[10]	14.0[10]	...	[10]	[10]	[10]	[10]	...	41	...
Tuvalu	1990	9	72	1,485	20.6	100	1	21	314	15.0	...	8[34]	16[34]
Uganda	1989	7,905	75,561	2,632,764	34.8	55	774	13,356	240,334	18.0	...	136	2,081
Ukraine	1993	22,000[10]	579,000[10]	7,087,000[10]	12.2[10]	...	[10]	[10]	[10]	[10]	...	754	...
United Arab Emirates	1992	354[10,13]	13,139	231,674	17.6	100	[10]	9,430[8]	117,118	12.4	64	9[5]	[8]
United Kingdom	1992[31]	23,958	222,600	4,849,500	21.8	97	4,730	232,700	3,534,500	15.2	80	724[13,59]	93,000[55,59]
United States	1991	61,340[31,53]	1,680,000	33,978,000	20.2	98	20,406[8,31]	1,072[8]	12,472,000[8]	11.6[8]	80	[8]	[8]
Uruguay	1992	2,419	16,376	338,020	20.6	91	351	15,522	208,015	13.4	...	103	...
Uzbekistan	1992	...	384,000[10]	4,721,400[10]	13.0[10]	...	[10]	[10]	[10]	[10]	...	243	...
Vanuatu	1992	272	852	26,267	30.8	...	21[21]	220	4,269	19.4	...	...	...
Venezuela	1992	15,800	183,298	4,190,047	22.9	91	1,621[9]	32,572[8]	289,430[8]	8.9[8]	19	[8]	[8]
Vietnam	1994	13,092	275,640	9,725,095	35.3	...	6,298	166,968	3,815,852	22.9	...	451	12,197
Virgin Islands (U.S.)	1989[60]	41[9]	965	12,263	12.7	...	10[9]	799	9,741	12.2	...	3[5]	275[5]
West Bank[61]	1990	410	5,458[3]	198,740	34.2[3]	...	...	5,892[9]	108,610	20.1[9]	...	...	170
Western Sahara	1989[31]	27	596	14,794	24.8	...	18	577	9,218	16.0	...	...	...
Western Samoa	1987	164[34]	1,511[62]	40,755	27.0	...	38[2]	492	11,395	23.2	...	4[34]	37
Yemen[63]	1991	7,313[3]	35,350	1,291,372	36.5	...	942[5]	12,106	394,578	32.6	...	73[5]	1,247
Yugoslavia	1993	4,433	51,489	945,237	18.4	79[64]	539	25,580	359,600	14.1	76[64]	...	...
Zaire	1988	10,817	113,468[9]	4,356,416	36.6[9]	58	4,276[8]	49,153[8]	507,944	21.7[8]	17	27	27
Zambia	1989	3,489	32,348[13]	1,446,847	44.1[13]	81	480	5,786[13]	161,349[13]	27.9[13]	16	26	846
Zimbabwe	1992	4,567	60,834	2,306,809	37.9	100	1,518	23,233	657,344	28.3	...	25	1,479

[1]1992. [2]1982. [3]1989. [4]Students registered abroad. [5]1986. [6]1990. [7]Vocational second level includes third level. [8]General second level includes vocational second level. [9]1987. [10]First level includes second level. [11]General second level includes first level. [12]Includes special education. [13]1988. [14]Data exclude 86 combined primary-secondary schools with 12,286 students. [15]College of the Bahamas only. [16]National literacy standard based solely on school attendance. [17]Includes preschool. [18]1991. [19]General second level includes teacher training at second level. [20]Third level includes vocational second level. [21]Excludes teacher training. [22]Universities only. [23]1984. [24]1981. [25]Data exclude 208 private schools with 107,096 students. [26]1980. [27]Age 15 and over. [28]Republic of Cyprus only. [29]Includes preschool, primary, and lower secondary (to age 15). [30]Upper second level only. [31]Public schools only. [32]Teacher training only. [33]Data exclude 1,399 primary and 1,290 secondary schools, as well as the university, in the al-Azhar education system. [34]1983. [35]Data includes Eritrea. [36]Includes lower-secondary students at all-age schools.

students[d]	student/teacher ratio	third level (higher)							literacy[b]				public expenditure on education (percent of GNP)[b]	country
		institutions	teachers[c]	students[d]	student/teacher ratio	gross enrollment ratio[b]	students per 100,000 population[b]	percent of population age 25 and over with post-secondary education[b]	over age	total (%)	male (%)	female (%)		
6,526	13.0[5]	2[5]	80[5]	578	8.8[5]	...	...	6.4	15	95.0	...	...	2.8	Netherlands Antilles
6,765	[8]	6	141[3]	1,207	9.9[3]	...	...	...	15	57.9	57.4	58.3	13.4	New Caledonia
99,299	17.3	7[22]	4,008[22]	97,835[22]	23.9[22]	44.8	4,232	6.9	15	100.0	100.0	100.0	7.2	New Zealand
[8]	[8]	10	3,469	34,846	10.0	10.1	814	...	15	74.0	...	...	4.1	Nicaragua
2,421	12.7	3[13]	341[54]	4,506[13]	11.1[54]	0.7	60	0.2	15	10.8	16.7	5.4	3.1	Niger
391,583	24.9[3]	...	19,601[3]	335,824[3]	17.1[3]	3.7	320	...	15	42.4	60.0	31.5	1.7	Nigeria
[8]	[8]	1	102	1,097	10.8	...	...	21.9	15	96.3	96.9	95.6	...	Northern Mariana Islands
[8]	[8]	100	8,085	162,168	18.4	45.3	3,083	18.8	15	100.0	100.0	100.0	8.7	Norway
2,680	6.3	5	433	3,615	...	6.2	463	...	6	41.0	58.0	24.0	3.8	Oman
91,000	13.4	797	29,076	721,600	24.8	2.8	266	1.9	15	25.6	36.0	15.2	2.7	Pakistan
[8]	[8]	9	3,684	63,894	17.3	23.6	2,377	13.2	15	88.1	88.1	88.2	5.5	Panama
9,846	12.4[3]	2	902[5]	5,007	7.1[5]	1.7	146	...	15	52.0	64.9	37.8	4.7	Papua New Guinea
[8,19]	[8,19]	2[18]	2,694[55]	32,884	...	8.2	769	3.4	15	90.1	92.1	88.1	1.9	Paraguay
312,669	27.7	553	44,361	751,234	16.9	35.6	3,465	4.8	15	...	95.9	82.6	1.5	Peru
361,736[18]	27.3[18]	809	70,012[13]	1,656,815	22.6[13]	27.8	2,596	15.2	15	88.7	89.9	87.5	2.9	Philippines
1,651,000	19.6	124	63,100	495,700	7.8	21.5	1,521	6.5[27]	15	98.7	99.2	98.3	5.6	Poland
84,932	...	250	30,998	214,403	6.9	22.7	1,935	0.4	15	86.8	86.7	86.9	4.8	Portugal
149,191[5]	...	45	9,045	156,818	17.3	48.1	4,091	18.4	15	89.1	89.7	88.5	8.2	Puerto Rico
843	8.4	1[47]	569[47]	6,666[1]	11.7[1]	25.9	1,608	13.3	15	75.7	76.8	72.5	3.0	Qatar
[8]	...	1[22]	218[22]	7,600[22]	34.9[22]	...	...	4.3	15	78.2	75.9	80.3	15.6	Réunion
959,882	23.1	56	17,605	215,226	12.2	8.7	1,010	7.3	15	96.9	98.6	95.2	3.6	Romania
2,090,000	...	535	...	2,638,000	...	...	1,900	...	15	98.0	99.5	96.8	8.2	Russia
[8]	[8]	3[55]	646[6]	3,454	5.2[6]	0.6	50	0.3	15	50.4	49.8	50.9	3.8	Rwanda
189	5.4	1	3	36	12.0	...	...	2.1	15	98.0	...	...	2.8	St. Kitts and Nevis
1,125[7]	6.3[1]	7	...	7	...	...	...	1.3	15	80.0	...	...	5.5	St. Lucia
337	...	...	...	...	...	...	...	1.4	15	85.0	...	...	6.7	St. Vincent and the Grenadines
385	...	...	...	332[4,9]	...	...	...	...	15	98.0	98.2	97.7	...	San Marino
289	...	...	...	700[4,34]	...	...	...	0.3	15	54.2	70.2	39.1	4.3	São Tomé and Príncipe
31,354[13]	9.5[13]	82	9,631	115,006	11.0	13.3	1,064	...	15	62.4	73.1	48.1	6.8	Saudi Arabia
6,435	24.6[3]	18	770[22]	18,862	19.3[22]	2.9	266	0.8	15	28.6	38.8	19.4	3.7	Senegal
1,682	8.9	...	...	...	...	...	...	3.1	15	84.2	82.9	85.7	8.5	Seychelles
6,929	9.2	2[6]	600[6]	4,752[6]	7.9[6]	1.3	114	...	15	20.7	30.7	11.3	1.4	Sierra Leone
27,984	17.6	7	3,721	65,775	17.7	7.9	963	3.4	10	90.7	95.7	85.6	3.4	Singapore
103,793	13.3	14	8,103	64,311	7.9	...	...	9.4	15	100.0	100.0	100.0	7.0	Slovakia
4,695	4.7	28	2,575	36,504	14.2	...	...	5.9[23]	10	99.2	99.3	99.1	5.7	Slovenia
[8]	[8]	—	—	—	—	...	...	2.6	15	54.1	62.4	44.9	4.2	Solomon Islands
4,809	9.7	1	202[24]	1,692	...	2.3	195	...	10	54.8	60.9	47.9	0.4	Somalia
113,870	16.6	17	31,863	318,944	10.0	...	1,231	2.3	15	76.4	77.8	75.1	3.8	South Africa
1,234,045[3]	19.5[3]	789[3]	59,135	1,169,141	19.8	35.5	3,335	7.0	15	94.7	97.0	92.5	4.6	Spain
8,900	20.4	8	1,937	31,447	16.2	5.2	505	1.1	10	86.9	90.1	83.8	3.3	Sri Lanka
[8]	[8]	24	1,943	54,345	28.0	2.9	258	...	15	27.1	42.7	11.7	4.8	Sudan, The
15,996[55]	12.5[55]	1[6]	...	2,164[6]	...	9.2	1,023	...	15	94.9	95.1	94.7	8.3	Suriname
772	2.0	1	146	1,705	11.7	4.7	382	4.3	15	67.0	69.0	65.0	6.4	Swaziland
[8]	[8]	...	27,523[6,57]	272,718[6]	9.9[6]	33.8	2,407	15.4	15	100.0	100.0	100.0	8.8	Sweden
197,572	...	...	...	146,288	...	29.1	2,417	...	15	100.0	100.0	100.0	5.2	Switzerland
53,289	6.0	44[9]	4,605[9]	183,079	...	18.8	1,695	3.9	15	64.5	78.3	50.8	4.2	Syria
515,211	27.4	125	31,430	689,185	20.8	...	2,225	6.0	15	93.2	96.9	89.2	3.6	Taiwan
...	...	13	...	69,300	...	...	1,280	...	15	97.7	98.8	96.6	...	Tajikistan
16,297	13.0	4[3]	1,206[3]	6,100[6]	4.4[3]	0.2	21	...	...	94.0	...	...	5.8	Tanzania
653,055	17.7	43[3]	52,317[3]	952,012[3]	18.2[3]	16.3	2,060	2.9	15	88.8	93.2	84.5	3.6	Thailand
8,392	32.2	1[22]	276[22]	7,732[3,22]	26.6[22]	2.6	226	1.3	15	43.0	56.0	31.0	5.7	Togo
358	13.4[6]	1	19	226	11.9	—	...	1.0	15	92.8	92.9	92.8	4.2	Tonga
731[18]	...	1	471	4,541	9.6	6.5	591	2.7	15	96.1	...	...	4.1	Trinidad and Tobago
3,839[13,32]	16.2	...	5,360	87,780	16.4	9.4	1,045	3.4	15	65.3	74.2	56.3	6.2	Tunisia
977,010	17.0	424	35,132	759,047	21.6	14.8	1,569	3.9	15	79.2	89.9	68.5	4.0	Turkey
33,700	...	9	...	41,700	...	...	1,130	65.1[12]	15	97.7	98.8	96.6	...	Turkmenistan
354	22.1	—	...	...	...	...	...	0.5	15	95.5	95.5	95.5	...	Tuvalu
23,179	11.1	9	934[23]	5,778	8.8[23]	1.1	115	0.4	15	48.3	62.2	34.9	1.7	Uganda
1,368,000	...	156	...	856,000	...	...	1,700	29.9	15	98.4	99.5	97.4	...	Ukraine
893	[8]	1	728	8,668	11.9	10.6	637	6.0	15	73.0	74.5	68.4	1.9	United Arab Emirates
539,718[13,59]	...	48[22]	32,638[22]	401,657[22]	12.3[22]	27.8	2,406	11.0	15	100.0	100.0	100.0	5.2	United Kingdom
[8]	[8]	3,559	824,000	13,710,000	16.6	76.2	5,653	39.8	15	95.5	95.7	95.3	5.3	United States
55,042	...	2	6,666	62,842	9.4	32.0	2,180	14.8	15	95.0	94.5	95.4	2.8	Uruguay
254,400	...	52	...	337,400	...	...	1,650	...	15	97.2	98.5	96.0	...	Uzbekistan
444	...	1	...	124[18]	...	—	...	...	15	52.9	57.3	47.0	4.5	Vanuatu
[8]	[8]	99[18]	40,033	550,783	12.6	29.5	2,847	7.0	15	92.2	93.5	91.1	5.2	Venezuela
137,405	11.3	104	20,648	118,589	6.1	2.3	153	...	15	87.6	93.0	82.8	3.0	Vietnam
775[5]	28.7[5]	1[9]	979	757[9]	8.3[9]	...	...	17.6	15	90.0	...	...	7.5	Virgin Islands (U.S.)
1,595	9.4	4[34]	988[3]	14,434[3]	14.6	...	...	8.1	...	...	...	...	...	West Bank[61]
...	...	...	...	...	...	...	...	...	...	...	...	...	...	Western Sahara
228	6.2	6[34]	373[31]	562[34]	15.2[34]	...	...	2.0	15	100.0	100.0	100.0	4.2	Western Samoa
26,119	20.9	1[3]	470[3]	23,457[3]	49.9[3]	2.9	276	...	15	38.5	53.3	26.3	4.6	Yemen[63]
...	...	141	11,568	142,372	12.2	18.2[64]	1,374[64]	5.7[27]	10	89.2	95.4	83.2	6.1	Yugoslavia[64]
558,407	[8]	...	3,506	52,800	15.1	2.1	176	...	10	71.8	83.6	60.7	1.0	Zaire
8,218	9.7	2	320	6,247	19.5	2.1	189	0.4	15	72.8	80.8	65.3	2.3	Zambia
27,431	18.5	3	935	11,975	12.8	0.1	528	...	15	76.0	81.5	66.8	7.4	Zimbabwe

[37]Excludes lower-secondary students. [38]Vocational second level includes third level. [39]Former West Germany only. [40]Postsecondary associate-degree program only. [41]Includes part-time teachers. [42]Includes part-time students. [43]Port-au-Prince universities only. [44]Based on data for four schools only. [45]Schools under Department of Education and Culture only. [46]National schools only. [47]1993. [48]Part-time teachers only. [49]Excludes vocational. [50]Includes Portuguese-language initiation classes. [51]Includes upper first level. [52]University of South Pacific extension centre. [53]Includes 83 composite schools that provide both primary and secondary education. [54]University of Niger and National School of Administration only. [55]1985. [56]Vocational teachers only. [57]Includes graduate assistants. [58]Excludes Zanzibar and Pemba. [59]Third-level vocational and teacher training. [60]Excludes 42 private schools with 0,556 students. [61]Excludes East Jerusalem. [62]Includes some secondary teachers. [63]Data refer to former Yemen Arab Republic only. [64]Data refer to Yugoslavia as constituted up to 1991.

The following list indicates the principal sources used in the compilation of *Britannica World Data*. It is by no means a complete list, either for international or for national sources, but is indicative only of the range of materials to which reference has been made in preparing this compilation. For example, in addition to the kinds of works cited below, reference has also been made to the constitution of each country, to the publications of its central or commercial banks, to unpublished information received in correspondence from the countries, and to other more specialized sources.

International Statistical Sources

Asian Development Bank. *Asian Development Outlook* (annual); *Key Indicators of Developing Member Countries of ADB* (annual, with supplements).

Billboard Ltd. *World Radio TV Handbook* (annual).

Caribbean Development Bank. *Annual Report.*

Comité Monétaire de la Zone Franc. *La Zone Franc: Rapport* (annual).

Commonwealth of Independent States. *Strany-Chleny SNG: Statistichesky Yezhegodnik (Member States of the CIS: Statistical Yearbook).*

Eastern Caribbean Central Bank. *Report and Statement of Accounts* (annual).

Europa Publications Ltd. *Africa South of the Sahara* (annual); *Eastern Europe and the Commonwealth of Independent States; The Europa Year Book* (2 vol.); *The Far East and Australasia* (annual); *The Middle East and North Africa* (annual).

Food and Agriculture Organization. *Food Balance Sheets; Production Yearbook; Trade Yearbook; World Census of Agriculture* (decennial); *Yearbook of Fishery Statistics* (2 vol.); *Yearbook of Forest Products.*

FT Caribbean. *The Caribbean Handbook* (annual).

Her Majesty's Stationery Office. *The Commonwealth Yearbook.*

Instituts d'Émission d'Outre-Mer et des Départements d'Outre-Mer (France). *Rapport annuel, Bulletin trimestriel* (quarterly).

Inter-American Development Bank. *Economic and Social Progress in Latin America* (annual).

Inter-Parliamentary Union. *Chronicle of Parliamentary Elections and Developments* (annual); *World Directory of Parliaments* (annual).

International Air Transport Association. *World Air Transport Statistics* (annual).

International Bank for Reconstruction and Development/The World Bank. *World Bank Atlas* (annual); *World Debt Tables* (annual); *World Development Report* (annual).

International Civil Aviation Organization. *Civil Aviation Statistics of the World* (annual); *Digest of Statistics.*

International Institute for Strategic Studies. *The Military Balance* (annual).

International Labour Organisation. *Year Book of Labour Statistics; The Cost of Social Security: Basic Tables* (triennial).

International Monetary Fund. *Annual Report on Exchange Arrangements and Exchange Restrictions; Direction of Trade Statistics Yearbook; Government Finance Statistics Yearbook; IMF Economic Reviews* (irreg.); *International Financial Statistics* (monthly, with supplements and yearbook).

International Road Federation. *World Road Statistics* (annual).

International Telecommunication Union. *ITU Statistical Yearbook.*

Jane's Publishing Co., Ltd. *Jane's World Railways* (annual).

Lloyd's Register of Shipping. *Lloyd's Register of Shipping: Statistical Tables* (annual).

Longman Group U.K. Ltd. *Keesing's Record of World Events* (monthly).

Macmillan Press Ltd. *The Statesman's Year-Book.*

Middle East Economic Digest Ltd. *Africa Economic Digest* (semimonthly); *Middle East Economic Digest* (semimonthly).

Mining Journal. *Mining Annual Review* (2 vol.).

Nordic Council. *Yearbook of Nordic Statistics.*

Official Airline Guides, Inc. *Official Airline Guide* (monthly).

Organization of Eastern Caribbean States. *Statistical Pocket Digest.*

Organization for Economic Cooperation and Development. *Economic Surveys* (annual); *Financing and External Debt of Developing Countries* (annual); *National Accounts of Developing Countries* (irreg.).

Oxford University Press. *World Christian Encyclopedia* (David B. Barrett, ed. [1982]).

PennWell Publishing Co. *International Petroleum Encyclopedia* (annual).

René Moreux et Cie. *Marchés tropicaux & Méditerranéens* (weekly).

South Pacific Commission. *Key Economic Indicators* (irreg.); *South Pacific Economies: Statistical Summary* (biennial).

United Nations (UN). *Demographic Yearbook; International Trade Statistics Yearbook* (2 vol.); *Energy Statistics Yearbook; Industrial Statistics Yearbook* (2 vol.); *Monthly Bulletin of Statistics; Population Studies* (irreg.); *National Accounts Statistics* (3 vol.; annual); *Population and Vital Statistics Report* (quarterly); *Statistical Yearbook; World Population Prospects 19*** (biennial).

UN: Conference on Trade and Development. *Handbook of International Trade and Development Statistics* (annual); *The Least Developed Countries* (annual).

UN: Economic Commission for Africa. *African Socio-Economic Indicators* (annual); *African Statistical Yearbook* (2 vol. in 4 parts); *Demographic and Related Socio-Economic Data Sheets for ECA Member States* (irreg.); *Survey of Economic and Social Conditions in Africa* (annual).

UN: Economic Commission for Europe. *Annual Bulletin of Housing and Building Statistics for Europe; Annual Bulletin of Transport Statistics for Europe.*

UN: Economic Commission for Latin America. *Economic Survey of Latin America and the Caribbean* (annual); *Statistical Yearbook for Latin America and the Caribbean.*

UN: Economic and Social Commission for Asia and the Pacific. *Foreign Trade Statistics of Asia and the Pacific* (annual); *Statistical Indicators for Asia and the Pacific* (quarterly); *Statistical Yearbook for Asia and the Pacific.*

UN: Economic and Social Commission for Western Asia. *Demographic and Related Socio-Economic Data Sheets* (irreg.); *National Accounts Studies of the ESCWA Region* (irreg.); *Population Bulletin* (irreg.); *The Population Situation in the ESCWA Region* (irreg.); *Prices and Financial Statistics in the ESCWA Region* (irreg.); *Statistical Abstract of the Region of the Economic and Social Commission for Western Asia* (annual).

UN: Educational, Scientific, and Cultural Organization. *Statistical Yearbook.*

United Nations Development Programme. *Human Development Report* (annual).

United Nations Industrial Development Organization. *Industrial Development Review Series* (irreg.); *Industry and Development: Global Report* (annual).

United States: Central Intelligence Agency, *The World Factbook* (annual); Dept. of Commerce, *World Population Profile* (irreg.); Dept. of Energy, *International Energy Annual;* Dept. of Health and Human Services, *Social Security Programs Throughout the World* (biennial); Dept. of Interior, *Minerals Yearbook* (3 vol. in 8); Dept. of State, *Background Notes* (irreg.).

Vatican (Central Statistics Office of the Church). *Statistical Yearbook of the Church.*

World Energy Conference. *Survey of Energy Resources* (triennial).

World Health Organization. *World Health Statistics Annual; World Health Statistics Quarterly.*

World Tourism Organization. *World Tourism Statistics* (2 vol.; annual).

National Statistical Sources

Afghanistan. *First Seven-Year Economic and Social Development Plan, 1355–1361 (March 1976–March 1983); Preliminary Results of the First Afghan Population Census, 1979).*

Albania. *IMF Economic Reviews: Albania* (1994); *Population and Housing Census 1989; Statistical Yearbook of Albania.*

Algeria. *Annuaire statistique; Recensement général de la population et de l'habitat, 1987.*

American Samoa. *American Samoa Statistical Digest* (annual); *Population of American Samoa* (ESCAP; Country Monograph Series No. 7.1 [1979]); *1990 Census of Population and Housing* (U.S.).

Andorra. *Estadístiques* (annual); *Recull Estadístic General de la Població Andorra 90.*

Angola. *Angola: an Introductory Economic Review* (A World Bank Country Study [1991]); *Informação Estatística* (annual); *Perfil estatístico de Angola* (annual).

Antigua. *Statistical Yearbook.*

Argentina. *Anuario estadístico de la República Argentina; Boletín estadístico trimestral* (quarterly); *Censo nacional de población y vivienda, 1991; Encuesta permanente de hogares* (irreg.).

Armenia. *Economic Reviews: Armenia* (IMF [1993]); *Statisticheskii Yezhegodnik Armenii* (Statistical Yearbook of Armenia).

Aruba. *Statistical Yearbook; Third Population and Housing Census October 6, 1991.*

Australia. *Census of Manufacturing Establishments: Summary of Operations by Industry Subdivision, Australia* (annual); *Foreign Trade Australia: Comparative and Summary Tables* (annual); *Monthly Summary of Statistics, Australia; National Income and Expenditure* (annual); *Social Indicators* (irreg.); *Year Book Australia; 1991 Census of Population and Housing.*

Austria. *Grosszählung 1991* (General Census 1991). *Österreichisches Jahrbuch* (annual); *Sozialstatistische Daten* (irreg.); *Statistisches Jahrbuch für die Republik Österreich.*

Azerbaijan. *A World Bank Country Study: Azerbaijan, from Crisis to Sustained Growth* (1993); *Economic Reviews: Azerbaijan* (IMF [1993]); *Narodnoye Khozyaystvo Azerbaydzhanskoy SSR* (National Economy of the Azerbaijan S.S.R. [annual]).

Bahamas, The. *Census of Population and Housing 1990; Quarterly Statistical Summary; Statistical Abstract* (annual); *Vital Statistics Report* (annual).

Bahrain. *Statistical Abstract* (annual); *1981 Census of Bahrain.*

Bangladesh. *Bangladesh Population Census, 1991; Population of Bangladesh* (ESCAP; Country Monograph Series No. 8 [1981]); *Statistical Yearbook of Bangladesh.*

Barbados. *Barbados Economic Report* (annual); *Monthly Digest of Statistics.*

Belarus. *Economic Reviews: Belarus* (IMF [1993]); *Narodnoye Kozyaystvo Belorusskoy S.S.R.* (National Economy of the Belorussian S.S.R. [annual]).

Belgium. *Annuaire statistique de la Belgique; Recensement de la population et des logements au 1er mars 1991.*

Belize. *Abstract of Statistics* (annual); *Belize Economic Survey* (annual); *Belize Today: Development Plan 1990–94; Labour Force Survey (1983–84); 1991 Population Census: Major Findings.*

Benin. *Annuaire statistique; Recensement des Entreprises 1980* (2 parts); *Recensement général de la population et de l'habitation (1979).*

Bermuda. *Bermuda Digest of Statistics* (annual); *Report of the Manpower Survey* (annual); *The 1991 Census of Population and Housing.*

Bhutan. *Bhutan: Development Planning in a Unique Environment* (A World Bank Country Study [1988]); *Statistical Yearbook of Bhutan* (annual).

Bolivia. *Bolivia en Cifras* (annual); *Censo Nacional de población y vivienda 1992; Compendio Estadístico* (annual); *Estadísticas Socio-económicas* (annual); *Estrategia de Desarrollo Económico y Social 1989–2000; Resumen estadístico* (annual).

Botswana. *National Development Plan 7, 1991–1997; 1991 Population and Housing Census.*

Brazil. *Anuário Econômico-Fiscal; Anuário Estatístico do Brasil; Censo Demografico 1991; Comercio Exterior do Brasil* (2 vol.; annual).

Brunei. *Brunei Statistical Yearbook; Population Survey 1986: Demographic Report; Report on the Census of Population, 1981.*

Bulgaria. *Prebroyavaneto na naselenieto kŭm 4.12.1985 godina* (Census of Population of Dec. 4, 1985); *Statisticheska godishnikna Republika Bŭlgariya* (Statistical Yearbook of the Republic of Bulgaria).

Burkina Faso. *Annuaire Statistique; Recensement général de la population du 10 au 20 decembre 1985; Statistiques Sociales* (irreg.).

Burundi. *Annuaire statistique; Recensement général de la population, 1990.*

Cambodia. *Cambodia: A Country Study* (1990); *Intersectoral Basic Needs Assessment Mission to Cambodia* (Unesco; 1991); *Report of the Kampuchea Needs Assessment Study* (UNDP; 1989).

Cameroon. *Note annuelle de statistique; Recensement général de la population et de l'habitat 1987.*

Canada. *Canada Year Book* (biennial); *Census Canada 1991: Population.*

Cape Verde. *Boletím Anual de Estatística; I.º Recenseamento Geral da População e Habitação—1990.*

Central African Republic. *Annuaire statistique; Economic and Social Development Plan 1986–90; Recensement général de la population 1988.*

Chad. *Annuaire statistique; Chad: a Country Study* (1990).

Chile. *Chile XVI censo nacional de población y V de vivienda, 22 de abril 1992; Compendio estadístico* (annual); *Plan nacional indicativo de desarrollo* (quinquennial).

China, People's Republic of. *China: A Statistics Survey in 19*** (annual); *People's Republic of China Year-Book; Statistical Yearbook of China; 10 Percent Sampling Tabulation on the 1990 Population Census of the People's Republic of China.*

Colombia. *Colombia estadística* (2 vol.; annual); *XV Censo nacional de población y IV de vivienda* (1985).

Comoros. *Plan interimaire de développement économique et sociale (1983–1986); Recensement général de la population et de l'habitat 15 septembre 1980.*

Congo. *Annuaire statistique; Recensement Général de la Population et de l'Habitat de 1984.*

Costa Rica. *Anuario estadístico; Censo de Población 1984; Plan Nacional de Desarrollo, 1986–90* (2 vol.).

Côte d'Ivoire. *Annuaire statistique; La Côte d'Ivoire en chiffres* (irreg.); *L'Économie Ivoirienne* (irreg.); *Enquête permanente aupres des menages: resultats provisoires 1985; Recensement général de la population et de l'habitat 1988.*

Croatia. *Census of Population, Households, Dwellings and Farms 31st March 1991; Statistical Yearbook.*

Cuba. *Anuario estadístico; Censo de población y viviendas, 1981; Compendio estadístico de Cuba* (annual); *Cuba Half-Yearly Economic Report.*

Cyprus. *Census of Industrial Production* (annual); *Economic Report* (annual); *Statistical Abstract* (annual).

Czech Republic. *Statistická ročenka České Republiky* (Statistical Yearbook of the Czech Republic).

Denmark. *Folke- og boligtaellingen, 1981* (Population and Housing Census); *Statistisk årbog* (Statistical Yearbook).

Djibouti. *Annuaire statistique de Djibouti.*

Dominica. *Statistical Digest* (irreg.).

Dominican Republic. *República Dominicana en cifras* (annual); *VI Censo nacional de población y vivienda, 1981*

Ecuador. *Encuesta anual de manufactura y minería; Serie estadística* (quinquennial); *Censo de población (V) y de vivienda (IV) 1990.*

Egypt. *Population, Housing, and Establishment Census, 1986; Statistical Yearbook.*

El Salvador. *Anuario estadístico* (8 vol.); *El Salvador en cifras* (annual); *Indicadores Económicos y Sociales* (annual).

Equatorial Guinea. *Censos Nacionales, I de Población y I de Vivienda—4 al 17 de Julio de 1983; Guinea en cifras* (irreg.).

Eritrea. *Ethiopia and Eritrea: A Documentary Study* (1993).

Estonia. *Eesti Statistika Aastaraamat* (Estonia Statistical Yearbook); *Estonia: The Transition to a Market Economy* (1993).

Ethiopia. *Ethiopia 1984 Population and Housing Census; Ethiopia Statistical Abstract* (annual).

Faeroe Islands. *Arbog for Færøerne* (Yearbook for the Faeroe Islands); *Rigsombudsmanden på Færøerne: Beretning* (annual).

Fiji. *Annual Employment Survey; Census of Industries* (annual); *Current Economic Statistics* (quarterly); *1986 Census of the Population.*

Finland. *Annual Statistics of Agriculture; Economic Survey* (annual); *Population Census 1990; Statistical Yearbook of Finland.*

France. *Annuaire statistique de la France; Données sociales* (triennial); *Recensement général de la population de 1990; Métropole; Tableaux de l'Economie Française* (annual).

French Guiana. *Recensement général de la population de 1990: logements-population-emplois, 973: Guyane; Tableaux economiques regionaux: Guyane* (biennial).

French Polynesia. *Résultats du Recensement Général de la Population de la Polynésie Française, du 6 Septembre 1988; Tableaux de l'economie polynesienne* (irreg.); *Te avei'a: Bulletin d'information statistique* (monthly).

Gabon. *Situation économique, financière et sociale de la République Gabonaise* (annual).

Gambia, The. *Statistical Abstract* (annual?).

Gaza Strip. *Judaea, Samaria, and Gaza Area Statistics Quarterly; Palestinian Statistical Abstract* (annual).

Georgia. *Economic Reviews: Georgia* (IMF [1993]); *Narodnoye Khozyaystvo Gruzinskoy SSR* (National Economy of the Georgian S.S.R. [annual]).

Germany. *Statistisches Jahrbuch für die Bundesrepublik Deutschland; Volkszählung vom 25. Mai 1987* (Census of Population).

Ghana. *Population Census of Ghana, 1984; Quarterly Digest of Statistics.*

Gibraltar. *Abstract of Statistics* (annual); *Census of Gibraltar, 1991.*

Greece. *Recensement des industries manufacturières: Artisanat, du commerce et autres services* (1978); *Recensement de la population et des habitations, 1991; Statistical Yearbook of Greece.*

Greenland. *Grønland* (annual); *Grønlands befolkning* (Greenland Population [annual]).

Grenada. *Abstract of Statistics* (annual); *1991 Population and Housing Census.*

Guadeloupe. *Recensement général de la population de 1990: logements-population-emplois, 971: Guadeloupe; Tableaux economiques regionaux: Guadeloupe* (biennial).

Guam. *Guam Annual Economic Review; Census '90: Guam.*

Guatemala. *Anuario Estadística; Censos nacionales, 1981: IX de población—IV de habitación.*

Guernsey. *Guernsey Census 1991; Statistical Digest* (annual).

Guinea. *Situation Économique et Conjoncturelle au 31 decembre 1985 et éléments sur la mise en oeuvre de la réform économique au cours du première trimestre 1986.*

Guinea-Bissau. *Boletim Trimestral de Estatística; Recenseamento Geral da População e da Habitação, 16 de Abril de 1979.*

Guyana. *Annual Statistical Abstract; Guyana: From Economic Recovery to Sustained Growth* (1993); *Guyana and Belize: Country Studies (1993).*

Haiti. *Bulletin trimestriel de statistique; Dominican Republic and Haiti: Country Studies* (1991); *Résultats préliminaires du recensement général* (*Septembre 1982*).

Honduras. *Anuario estadístico; Censo nacional de Población y Vivienda 1988; Honduras en cifras* (annual); *Plan nacional de desarrollo, 1987–90.*

Hong Kong. *Annual Digest of Statistics; Hong Kong* (annual); *Hong Kong 1991 Population Census; Hong Kong in Figures* (annual); *Hong Kong Social and Economic Trends* (biennial).

Hungary. *Statisztikai évkönyv* (Statistical Yearbook); *1990, Évi népszámlálás* (Census of Population).

Iceland. *Hagtidhindi* (monthly); *Landshagir* (Statistical Abstract of Iceland [annual]); *Verslunarskýrslur* (External Trade [annual]).

India. *Census of India, 1991; Economic Survey* (annual); *India: A Reference Annual; Statistical Abstract* (annual).

Indonesia. *Indonesia: An Official Handbook* (1989); *Hasil Sensus penduduk Indonesia, 1990* (Census of Population); *Statistical Yearbook of Indonesia.*

Iran. *National Census of Population and Housing, October 1986; A Statistical Reflection of the Islamic Republic of Iran* (annual); *Iran Statistical Yearbook.*

Iraq. *Iraq: A Country Study* (1990); *Annual Abstract of Statistics.*

Ireland. *Census of Population of Ireland, 1991; National Income and Expenditure* (annual); *Statistical Abstract* (annual).

Isle of Man. *Census Report 1991; Isle of Man Digest of Economic and Social Statistics* (annual).

Israel. *1983 Census of Population and Housing; Statistical Abstract* (annual).

Italy. *Annuario di statistica agraria: Annuario di statistiche demografiche; Annuario di statistiche industriali; Annuario statistico dell'istruzione; Annuario statistico Italiano; Statistiche forestale* (annual); *Statistiche sociali* (1981); *13° Censimento generale della popolazione e delle Abitazioni 20 Ottobre 1991.*

Jamaica. *Economic and Social Survey* (annual); *Statistical Abstract* (annual); *Statistical Yearbook of Jamaica.*

Japan. *Japan Statistical Yearbook; Statistical Indicators on Social Life* (annual); *1990 Population Census of Japan.*

Jersey. *Report of the Census for 1991; Statistical Digest* (annual).

Jordan. *Census 1979; Family Expenditure Survey* (1980); *National Accounts* (irreg.); *Statistical Yearbook.*

Kazakhstan. *Economic Reviews: Kazakhstan* (IMF [1993]); *Statistichesky Yezhegodnik* (Statistical Yearbook).

Kenya. *Economic Survey* (annual); *Statistical Abstract* (annual).

Kiribati. *Annual Abstract of Statistics; Kiribati Population Census 1990; Sixth National Development Plan, 1987–1991.*

Korea, North. *North Korea: A Country Study* (1981); *The Population of North Korea* (1990).

Korea, South. *Korea Statistical Yearbook; Social Indicators in Korea* (irreg.); *The 5th Five-Year Economic and Development Plan, 1982–1986; 1990 Population and Housing Census.*

Kuwait. *Annual Statistical Abstract; Economic Report* (annual); *General Census of Population and Housing and Buildings 1985.*

Kyrgyzstan. *Economic Reviews: Kyrgyz Republic* (IMF [1993]); *Statistichesky Yezhegodnik Kyrgyzstana* (Statistical Yearbook of Kyrgyzstan).

Laos. *Lao People's Democratic Republic: Industrial Transition* (UNIDO; 1994).

Latvia. *Latvia: The Transition to a Market Economy* (1993); *Statistical Yearbook of Latvia.*

Lebanon. *Lebanon: A Country Study* (1989).

Lesotho. *Statistical Yearbook; 1986 Population Census.*

Liberia. *Economic Survey* (annual); *1974 Census of Population and Housing.*

Libya. *The Five-Year Development Plan 1981–85; Libya Population Census, 1973; Statistical Abstract for Libya* (annual).

Liechtenstein. *Statistisches Jahrbuch; Volkszählung, 2 Dezember 1980* (Census of Population).

Lithuania. *Lithuania: The Transition to a Market Economy* (1993); *Lithuania's Statistics Yearbook.*

Luxembourg. *Annuaire statistique; Bulletin du STATEC* (monthly); *Recensement général de la population du 31 mars 1991.*

Macau. *Anuário Estatístico; Inquerito Industrial* (annual); *XIII Recenseamento Geral da População, 1991.*

Macedonia. *Basic Statistical Data* (annual).

Madagascar. *Recensement général de la population et de l'habitat, aout 1993; Situation économique* (annual).

Malaŵi. *Malawi Population and Housing Census, 1987; Malawi Statistical Yearbook; Malawi Yearbook.*

Malaysia. *Fifth Malaysia Plan, 1986–1990; Malaysia Official Year Book; Malaysian Annual Statistical Bulletin; Population and Housing Census of Malaysia 1991.*

Maldives. *National Development Plan 1991–1993; Population and Housing Census of Maldives 1990; Statistical Year Book of Maldives.*

Mali. *Annuaire statistique du Mali; Comptes Economiques du Mali* (annual); *Recensement général de la population et de l'habitat (du 1er au 14 avril 1987).*

Malta. *Annual Abstract of Statistics; Census of Industrial Production Report for 19*** (annual); *Malta Year Book* (annual).

Marshall Islands. *Marshall Islands Statistical Abstract* (annual).

Martinique. *Bulletin de statistique* (quarterly); *Recensement de la population de 1990: logements-population-emplois, 972: Martinique; Tableaux economiques regionaux: Martinique* (biennial).

Mauritania. *Annuaire Statistique; Mauritania: A Country Study* (1990).

Mauritius. *Annual Digest of Statistics; 1990 Housing and Population Census of Mauritius.*
Mayotte. *Recensement général de la population de la Collectivité territoriale de Mayotte: août 1991.*
Mexico. *Anuario estadístico; XI Censo general de población y vivienda, 1990; La Economia Mexicana en Cifras* (1990); *Informe de Gobierno: Estadístico* (annual).
Micronesia. *Second National Development Plan 1992–1996.*
Moldova. *Economic Reviews: Moldova* (IMF [1993]); *Republica Moldova in Cifre* (annual).
Monaco. *Annuaire Officiel.*
Mongolia. *National Economy of the MPR, 1921–86* (1986; quinquennial?); *The Mongolian People's Republic: Towards a Market Economy* (1991).
Morocco. *Annuaire statistique du Maroc; Economic and Social Development Report, 1981; Recensement général de la population et de l'habitat de 1982.*
Mozambique. *Informação Estatística* (annual); *1° Recenseamento Geral da População, 1980.*
Myanmar (Burma). *Report to the Pyithu Hluttaw on the Financial, Social, and Economic Conditions for 19*** (annual); *1983 Population Census.*
Namibia. *Budget 19**–19*** (annual); *Population Census 1981; Statistical/Economic Review* (annual).
Nepal. *Census of Manufacturing Establishments of Nepal, 1986–87; Economic Survey* (annual); *Population Monograph of Nepal* (1987); *The Seventh Plan (1985–90); Statistical Pocket Book* (irreg.); *Statistical Yearbook of Nepal.*
Netherlands, The. *Statistical Yearbook of the Netherlands; 14e Algemene volkstelling, 28 februari 1971* (14th General Population Census).
Netherlands Antilles. *Tweede Algemene Volks- en Woningtelling Nederlandse Antillen: toestand per 1 Februari 1981; Statistical Yearbook of the Netherlands Antilles.*
New Caledonia. *Annuaire statistique; Enquête socio-économique, 1980–1981; Recensement de la population de la Nouvelle-Calédonie au 4 avril 1989; Tableaux de l'economie Caledonienne* (annual).
New Zealand. *1991 New Zealand Census of Population and Dwellings; New Zealand Official Yearbook.*
Nicaragua. *Anuario estadístico de Nicaragua; Nicaragua: A Country Study* (1982); *Plan Económico, 1987* (irreg.).
Niger. *Annuaire statistique; Les comptes economiques de la nation* (triennial); *Plan de developpement economique et social du Niger 1987–91; 2ème Recensement général de la population 1988.*
Nigeria. *Annual Abstract of Statistics; Fourth National Development Plan* (1981); *Nigeria: A Country Study* (1992).
Norway. *Folke- og boligtelling 1990* (Population and Housing Census); *Industristatistikk* (annual); *Statistisk årbok* (Statistical Yearbook).
Oman. *Statistical Year Book; Fourth Five-Year Development Plan (1991–1995).*
Pakistan. *Economic Survey* (annual); *Pakistan Statistical Yearbook; Population Census of Pakistan, 1981; Some Socio-Economic Trends* (annual); *10 Years of Pakistan in Statistics, 1972–1982* (1983).
Palau. *Abstract of Statistics* (annual); *Census '90.*
Panama. *Indicadores económicos y sociales* (annual); *Censos nacionales de 1990: IX de población y V de vivienda, 13 de mayo de 1990; Panama en cifras* (annual); *Situacion económica: Cuentas nacionales* (annual); *Situacion económica: Industria* (annual).
Papua New Guinea. *Abstract of Statistics* (quarterly); *National Accounts Statistics—Statistical Bulletin* (quarterly); *Population of Papua New Guinea (ES-CAP;* Country Monograph Series No. 7.2 [1982]); *Social Indicators of Papua New Guinea, 1980–85; Summary of Statistics* (annual); *1990 National Population Census.*
Paraguay. *Anuario estadístico del Paraguay; Censo nacional de población y viviendas, 1992.*
Peru. *Censos nacionales; VIII de población: III de vivienda, 12 de julio de 1981; Compendio estadístico* (3 vol.; annual); *Informe estadístico* (annual).
Philippines. *Philippine Statistical Yearbook; Philippine Yearbook; 1990 Census of Population and Housing.*
Poland. *Narodowy spis powszechny 1988* (Census of Population); *Rocznik statystyczny* (Statistical Yearbook).
Portugal. *Anuário Estatístico; Estatísticas Agricolas* (annual); *Estatísticas do Comercio Externo* (annual); *Estatísticas Demograficas* (annual); *Estatísticas Industriais* (2 vol.; annual); *Estatísticas Monetarias e Financeiras* (annual); *Recenseamento Agricola, 1979; XIII Recenseamento Geral da População: III Recenseamento Geral da Habitação, 1991.*
Puerto Rico. *Anuario estadístico; Estadisticas socio-economicas* (annual); *Informe económico al gobernador* (Economic Report to the Governor [annual]); *1990 Census of Population and Housing* (U.S.).
Qatar. *Annual Statistical Abstract; Economic Survey of Qatar* (annual); *Qatar Year Book.*
Réunion. *Recensement général de la population de 1990: logements-population-emploi, 974; Réunion; Tableau Economique de la Réunion* (biennial).
Romania. *Anuarul statistic al României; Population and Housing Census January 7, 1992; Romania Yearbook.*
Russia. *Economic Reviews: Russian Federation* (IMF [1993]); *Rossiyskaya Federatsiya v 1992 godu: statisticheskiy yezhegodnik.*
Rwanda. *Bulletin de Statistique: Supplement Annuel; IIIème Plan de Developpement Economique, Social et Culturel 1982–86; Recensement General de la Population et de l'Habitat 1991.*
St. Kitts and Nevis. *Annual Digest of Statistics; St. Christopher and Nevis: Economic Report* (World Bank Country Study) (1985).
St. Lucia. *Annual Statistical Digest.*
St. Vincent and the Grenadines. *Digest of Statistics* (annual); *Population and Housing Census 1991.*
San Marino. *Annuario statistico, 1981–84* (4 vol.?; irreg.); *3 Censimento generale dell agricoltura* (1977); *5 Censimento generale della popolazione* (1979).
São Tomé and Príncipe. *1° Recenseamento Geral da População e da Habitação 1981.*
Saudi Arabia. *The Statistical Indicator* (annual); *Statistical Summary* (Saudi Arabian Monetary Agency [annual]); Statistical Year Book.
Senegal. *Le Sénégal en chiffres* (irreg.); *Recensement de la Population et de l'Habitat 1988; Situation économique du Senegal* (annual).
Seychelles. *National Development Plan, 1990–94;* (2 vol.); *Statistical Abstract* (annual); *1987 Census Report.*
Sierra Leone. *Sierra Leone: 12 Years of Economic Achievement and Political Consolidation under the APC and Dr. Siaka Stevens, 1968–80.*
Singapore. *Census of Population, 1990; Report on the Census of Industrial Production* (annual); *Singapore Yearbook; Yearbook of Statistics Singapore.*
Slovakia. *Sčítanie L'udu, Domov a Bytov 1991* (Census of Population, Housing, and Families 1991); *Statistical Yearbook of the Slovak Republic.*
Slovenia. *Statistični Letopis Republike Slovenija* (Statistical Yearbook of the Republic of Slovenia).
Solomon Islands. *Solomon Islands 1986 Population Census; Statistical Bulletin* (irreg.).
Somalia. *Statistical Abstract* (annual).
South Africa. *1991 Population Census; South Africa: Official Yearbook of the Republic of South Africa; South African Statistics* (biennial).
Spain. *Anuario estadístico; Censo de población de 1991.*
Sri Lanka. *Census of Population and Housing, 1981; Report on the Survey on Manufacturing Industries, 1979; Sri Lanka Year Book; Statistical Pocketbook of the Democratic Socialist Republic of Sri Lanka* (annual).
Sudan, The. *Third Population Census, 1983.*
Suriname. *General Population Census 1980; Statistisch Jaarboek van Suriname.*
Swaziland. *Annual Statistical Bulletin; Fourth Five-Year Development Plan (1986/87–90/91 Fiscal Years); Report on the 1986 Swaziland Population Census.*
Sweden. *Folk- och bostadsräkningen, 1990* (Population and Housing Census); *Statistisk årsbok för Sverige* (Statistical Abstract of Sweden [annual]).
Switzerland. *Recensement fédéral de la population, 1990; Statistisches Jahrbuch* (Statistical Yearbook).
Syria. *General Census of Housing and Inhabitants, 1981; Statistical Abstract* (annual).
Taiwan. *Industry of Free China* (monthly); *Social Indicators of the Republic of China* (annual); *Statistical Abstract* (annual); *Statistical Yearbook of the Republic of China; Taiwan Statistical Data Book* (annual); *Yearbook of Labor Statistics; 1990 Census of Population and Housing.*
Tajikistan. *Narodnoye Khozyaystvo Tadzhikskoy SSR* (National Economy of the Tadzhik S.S.R. [annual]).
Tanzania. *Tanzania Statistical Abstract* (irreg.); *1978 Population Census.*
Thailand. *Report of the Survey of Business Trade and Services* (biennial); *Foreign Trade Statistics* (monthly); *Report of the Industrial Survey, Whole Kingdom* (biennial); *Report of the Labor Force Survey: Whole Kingdom* (quarterly); *Statistical Handbook of Thailand* (annual); *Statistical Yearbook; 1990 Population and Housing Census.*
Togo. *Annuaire statistique du Togo; Eurostat Country Profile: Togo* (1991); *Plan de développement économique & social, 1981–1985; Recensement Général de la Population et de l'Habitat 1981.*
Tonga. *Population Census, 1986; Sixth Development Plan 1991–95; Statistical Abstract* (irreg.).
Trinidad and Tobago. *Annual Statistical Digest; 1990 Population and Housing Census.*
Tunisia. *Annuaire statistique de la Tunisie; Recensement général de la population et des logements, 30 mars 1984.*
Turkey. *Diş Ticaret İstatistikleri* (Annual Foreign Trade Statistics); *Genel Sanayi ve İşyerleri Sayımı* (Census of Industry and Business Establishments [1980]); *1990 Genel Nüfus Sayımı* (1990 Census of Population); *Genel Tarım Sayımı, 1980* (Census of Agriculture); *İnşaat İstatistikleri* (Construction Statistics [annual]); *Türkiye İstatistik Yilliği* (Statistical Yearbook of Turkey).
Turkmenistan. *Economic Reviews: Turkmenistan* (IMF [1994]); *Narodnoye Khozyaystvo Turkmenskoy SSR* (National Economy of the Turkmen S.S.R. [annual]).
Tuvalu. *1992–94 Medium-Term Economic Framework Programme.*
Uganda. *Uganda: A Country Study.*
Ukraine. *Economic Reviews: Ukraine* (IMF [1993]); *Narodne Hospodarstvo Ukrayini u 19** rotsi* (National Economy of Ukraine in the Year 19** [annual]).
United Arab Emirates. *Statistical Yearbook* (Abu Dhabi).
United Kingdom. *Annual Abstract of Statistics; Britain: An Official Handbook* (annual); *Census 1991; Report on the Census of Production: Summary Tables* (annual); *United Kingdom National Accounts.*
United States. *Agricultural Statistics* (annual); *Annual Energy Review; Current Population Reports* (Series P-20, P-23, P-25, P-26, P-27, P-28, P-60); *Digest of Education Statistics* (annual); *Minerals Yearbook* (3 vol.; annual); *National Transportation Statistics* (annual); *Statistical Abstract* (annual); *U.S. Exports: SIC-Based Products* (annual); *U.S. Imports: SIC-Based Products* (annual); *Vital and Health Statistics* (series 1–20); *1987 Census of Agriculture; 1987 Census of Construction Industries; 1987 Census of Manufacturing; 1987 Census of Retail Trade; 1987 Census of Service Industries; 1987 Census of Wholesale Trade; 1990 Census of Population and Housing.*
Uruguay. *Anuario Estadístico; Censo General: VI de población: IV de viviendas, Octubre 1985. Encuesta Nacional de Hogares* (annual).
Uzbekistan. *Economic Reviews: Uzbekistan* (IMF [1994]); *Narodnoye Khozyaystvo Respubliki Uzbekistan v 19** g.* (National Economy of Uzbekistan in the Year 19** [annual]).
Vanuatu. *National Population Census 1989; Second National Development Plan 1987–1991* (2 vol.); *Vanuatu Statistical Yearbook.*
Venezuela. *Anuario estadístico; Censo General de la Población y Vivienda 1990; Encuesta de hogares por muestreo* (annual); *Encuesta industrial* (annual).
Vietnam. *IMF Economic Reviews: Vietnam* (1994); *Nien Giam Thong Ke* (Statistical Yearbook); *Tong Dieu Tra Dan So Viet Nam—1989* (*Vietnam Population Census—1989*); *Vietnam: A Country Study* (1989).
Virgin Islands of the United States. *Annual Report; Economic Review, 1986; 1990 Census of Population and Housing* (U.S.).
West Bank. *Judaea, Samaria, and Gaza Area Statistics Quarterly; Palestinian Statistical Abstract* (annual).
Western Sahara. *Recensement General de la Population et de l'Habitat* (1982 [Morocco]).
Western Samoa. *Annual Statistical Abstract; Census of Population and Housing,* 1981; *Seventh Development Plan 1992–1994.*
Yemen. *Country Presentation: Republic of Yemen* (1990); *The Yemens: Country Studies* (1986).
Yugoslavia. *Popis stanovištva, domaćinstava, stanova i poljoprivrednih gazdinstava 1991 godine* (Census of Population, Households, Housing, and Agricultural Holdings 1991); *Statistički godišnjak Jugoslavije* (Statistical Yearbook of Yugoslavia).
Zaire. *Annuaire statistique* (irreg.); Conjoncture Economique (semiannual); *Recensement Scientifique de la Population du 1er juillet 1984.*
Zambia. *Country Profile: Zambia 1985; Monthly Digest of Statistics; National Development Plan, 1989–93; 1990 Census of Population, Housing, Agriculture.*
Zimbabwe. *Population Census 1991; Statistical Yearbook* (irreg.).

Aamodt / Ambulocetus 897

Index

This index covers both *Britannica Book of the Year* (cumulative for ten years) and *Britannica World Data*.

Entries in dark type are titles of articles in the *Book of the Year;* an accompanying year in dark type gives the year the reference appears, and the accompanying page number in light type shows where the article appears. References for previous years are preceded by the year in dark type. For example, "Archaeology 95:101; 94:95; 93:96; 92:95; 91:125; 90:143; 89:125; 88:125; 87:141; 86:164" indicates that the article "Archaeology" appeared every year from 1986 through 1995. Other references that appear with a page number but without a year refer to references from the current yearbook.

Indented entries in light type that follow dark type article titles refer by page number to other places in the text where the subject of the article is discussed. Light type entries that are not indented refer by page number to subjects that are not themselves article titles. Names of people covered in biographies and obituaries are followed by the abbreviation "(biog.)" or "(obit.)" with the year in dark type and a page number in light type, *e.g.,* Ailey, Alvin (obit.) **90:**103, or Reagan, Ronald Wilson (biogs.) **89:**82; **88:**80; **87:**93; **86:**108. In cases where a person has both a biography and an obituary, the words appear as subentries under the main entry and are alphabetized accordingly, *e.g.:*

Berlin, Irving
  biography **89:**66
  obituary **90:**105

References to illustrations are by page number and are preceded by the abbreviation *il.*

The index uses word-by-word alphabetization (treating a word as one or more characters separated by a space from the next word). Names beginning with "Mc" and "Mac" are alphabetized as "Mac"; "St." is treated as "Saint."

A

Aamodt, Kjetil Andre 313
AAPO (pol. party, Eth.): *see* All Amhara People's Organization
ABA: *see* American Booksellers Association
Abacha, Sani 451
Abad Faciolince, Héctor 226
"Abadanis, The" (motion picture) 246
ABB: *see* Asea Brown Boveri
Abbado, Claudio 250
Abbott, Berenice (obit.) **92:**54
Abbott, Tony 371
ABC: *see* American Broadcasting Company
'Abd al-Wahab, Muhammad (obit.) **92:**54
'Abd ar-Rahman Ahmad Ali Tur 471
Abdul, Paula (biog.) **91:**64
Abdul Rahman (obit.) **91:**86
Abe Kobo, *or* Abe Kimifusa (obit.) **94:**54
Abedi, Agha Hassan
  crime 148
  United Arab Emirates 489
Abel, Iorwith Wilbur (obit.) **88:**87
Abernathy, Ralph David (obit.) **91:**86
Abiola, Moshood ("MKO") 452
Abkhazia
  Georgia 409
  refugees 258
Aborigine (people, Austr.)
  Australia 373
aborigine (people, N. and S.Am.): *see* Native American peoples
abortion
  court decisions 206
  Roman Catholic Church 272
  violence 266
Abraham, William 220
Abravanel, Maurice (obit.) **94:**54
Abruzzo, Ben (obit.) **86:**120
Abs, Hermann Josef (obit.) **95:**60
"Absolute Turkey, An" (play) 344
abstinence
  sexuality 267
ABT: *see* American Ballet Theatre
Abu Dhabi
  Islam 274
  United Arab Emirates 489
Abu Jihad: *see* Wazir, Khalil Ibrahim al-
Abu Rishah, 'Umar (obit.) **91:**86
Abubakr III (obit.) **89:**88
AC Milan (soccer) 300
Academy Award, *or* Oscar (U.S.)
  film awards *table* 242
"Accumulator 1" (motion picture) 246
acetic acid
  natural gas 142
Achelous River (riv., Gr.)
  environment 187
"Achille Lauro" (ship) 348
achondroplasia
  genetic studies 195
acquired immune deficiency syndrome: *see* AIDS
ACS: *see* Caribbean States, Association of
acting (arts)
  film awards *table* 242
  theatre 343
Acton, Sir Harold Mario Mitchell (obit.) **95:**60
Acuff, Roy Claxton (obit.) **93:**54
Adams, Bryan (biog.) **93:**33
Adams, Diana (obit.) **94:**54
Adams, Gerry (biog.) **95:**39
Adams, John 250
Adams, John Michael Geoffrey Manningham (obit.) **86:**120
Adamson, George (obit.) **90:**103
Addams, Charles Samuel (obit.) **89:**88
Ademola, Sir Adetokunbo Adegboyega (obit.) **94:**54
Aden: *see* Yemen, People's Democratic Republic of
Adidas AG (Ger. co.) 123
Adler, Lawrence James (obit.) **89:**88
Adler, Stella (obit.) **93:**54
Adobe Systems Inc. (Am. co.)
  information processing 202
Adonis 228
adoption
  court decisions 206
ADPKD: *see* autosomal dominant polycystic kidney disease
ADRs: *see* American Depository Receipts
adultery
  literature 218
advanced composites 132
Advanced Micro Devices, *or* AMD
  microelectronics 133
Advanced Photo System 134
Advanced Warfighting Experiment (U.S.)
  military affairs 239
"Adventures of Priscilla, Queen of the Desert, The" (motion picture) 244
advertising 121, *table*
  collectibles 118
  magazines 262
  newspapers 259
  radio 342
aerial sports **94:**278; **93:**279; **92:**305; **91:**305; **90:**321; **89:**306; **88:**308; **87:**346; **86:**380
aerospace 121
  advanced composites 132
  light metals 131
Afanasyev, Viktor Grigoryevich (obit.) **95:**60
AFC: *see* American Football Conference
AFDC (U.S.): *see* Aid to Families with Dependent Children
Afewerke, Issayas (biog.) **92:**33
affiliate station (television) 339
Afghanistan 95:367; **94:**402; **93:**402; **92:**401; **91:**428; **90:**447; **89:**429; **88:**429; **87:**471; **86:**502
  food emergencies 91
  military affairs 237
  museums 248
  new flag *illus.* **94:**345; **93:**345
  refugees 258
  special reports **94:**377; **93:**233
  Uzbekistan 501
  see also WORLD DATA
'Aflaq, Michel (obit.) **90:**103
Aford (pol. org., Malawi): *see* Alliance for Democracy
African affairs 94:352; **93:**354; **92:**348; **91:**378; **90:**399; **89:**382; **88:**382; **87:**421; **86:**453
  "Africa's Second Liberation" (spotlight) 453
  agriculture 90
  anthropology 100
  archaeology 101
  arts and entertainment
    literature 222
    motion pictures 247
  consumer affairs 144
  demographic statistics 255
  disasters 32
  economic affairs 158
    currency 407
    equity markets (special report) **95:**173
  international drug traffic *map* 147
  meteorology 156
  military affairs 238
  refugees 258
  Rwandan history 265
  special report **92:**349
  see also Middle Eastern and North African affairs; *and* individual countries by name
African-American, *or* Afro-American: *see* black American
African National Congress, *or* ANC (pol. party, S.Af.) 352, 471
  military affairs 239
African Party for the Independence of Guinea-Bissau and Cape Verde, *or* PAIGC (pol. party, Guinea-Bissau) 415
African Unity, Organization of, *or* OAU
  Egypt 403
  South Africa 474
Afrikaner Weerstandsbeweging, *or* AWB (pol. party, S.Af.) 472
"After Easter" (play) 344
Ağaoğlu, Adalet 228
Agassi, Andre 316, *il.* 336
Agawa, Hiroyuki 229
"Age of Extremes: The Short Twentieth Century, 1914–1991" (Hobsbawm) 218
"Age of Rubens, The" (art exhibition) 110
age of the universe 113
Agee, Arthur *il.* 244
Agfa (Ger. co.)
  photography 134
Agracetus (Am. co.)
  soybeans 92
Agrarian Democratic Party (pol. party, Moldova) 445
Agrarian Union (pol. party, Russ.) 461
Agriculture, United States Department of, *or* USDA 92
Agriculture and Food Supplies 95:90; **94:**83; **93:**83; **92:**83; **91:**113; **90:**129; **89:**113; **88:**113; **87:**127; **86:**150
  archaeology 102
  Canada 389
  economic affairs 164
    stock exchanges 174
  Russia 463
  special reports **92:**167; **90:**140
  world production *tables* 90–96
  see also WORLD DATA; *and* individual countries by name
Ahtissari, Martti 405
Ai Bei 229
AIA: *see* American Institute of Architects
aid: *see* relief
Aid to Families with Dependent Children, *or* AFDC (U.S.) 276
  welfare reform 494, 499
AIDS, *or* acquired immune deficiency syndrome
  agriculture 91
  court decisions 207
  dance 151
  French literature 222
  special reports **94:**263; **88:**206
  street children (special report) **95:**278
  theatre 343
  veterinary medicine 200
Aidt, Naja Marie 224
Ailey, Alvin (obit.) **90:**103
air-conditioning
  buildings 182
Air Force, The United States: *see* United States Air Force, The
Air France (Fr. co.) 122
  France 407
  labour-management relations 203
air pollution
  lawn and garden tools 194
  United Kingdom 185
  urban mass transit 349
Air Products Co. (Br. co.) 99
Airbus Industrie (Eur. co.)
  aerospace 122
airlift
  United Nations 355
airline: *see* aviation
airport
  Japan 182
Aitken, Sir John William Maxwell (obit.) **86:**120
Aizu, University of (Japan) 176
Akalaitis, JoAnne (biog.) **92:**33
Akashi, Yasushi (biog.) **93:**33
  United Nations 354
Akashi-Kaikyo Bridge (Japan) 182
Akayev, Askar 435
Akebono (biog.) **94:**33
  sumo wrestling 320
Akhromeyev, Sergey Fedorovich (obit.) **92:**54
Akihito, *or* Heisei (biog.) **89:**65
  Japan 430
"Akron Beacon Journal" (Am. news.) 260
Aksyonov, Vasily 227
Akzo Nobel (paint co.) 133
Alabama (state, U.S.)
  equal protection 206
Alabama, University of
  college football 302
Alaska (state, U.S.)
  Arctic Regions 361
  energy 178
  special report **92:**168
  state government 498
  tourism *il.* 140
Albania 95:367; **94:**421; **93:**424; **92:**418; **91:**468; **90:**485; **89:**468; **88:**468; **87:**513; **86:**541
  Greece 413
  new flag *illus.* **93:**345
  Orthodox Church 272
  special report **93:**144
  see also WORLD DATA
Albanian (people)
  Macedonia 440
Albee, Edward 221, 343, 345
Albert, Stephen 250
Albert II (biog.) **94:**33
Alberts, Bruce (biog.) **95:**39
Albery, Sir Donald Arthur Rolleston (obit.) **89:**88
"Albuquerque Tribune" (Am. news.) 260
alcoholic beverages: *see* beer; spirits; wine
Aldus Corp. (Am. corp.)
  information processing 202
Alessandri Rodríguez, Jorge (obit.) **87:**100
Alexander, Bill 344
Alexander, Kelly Miller, Sr. (obit.) **86:**120
Alexander, Lincoln (biog.) **86:**89
Alfred Dunhill Cup (golf) 304
Algeria 95:368; **94:**379; **93:**380; **92:**378; **91:**404; **90:**424; **89:**407; **88:**407; **87:**448; **86:**479
  disasters 34
  education 177
  France 408
  Morocco 447
  motion pictures 246
  refugees 258
  special reports **94:**378; **92:**350
  terrorism 145
  see also WORLD DATA
Ali, Salim (obit.) **88:**87
Ali Mahdi Muhammad 471
  United Nations 353
Alia, Ramiz (biog.) **86:**89
Aliev, Geidar **94:**424
Aliyev, Heydar 376
All Amhara People's Organization, *or* AAPO (pol. party, Eth.) 404
All Anglophone Conference
  Cameroon 386
All-4-One (Am. mus. group) 252
"All in the Timing" (play) 346
All Ordinaries Index 172
Allais, Maurice (biog.) **89:**65
Allégret, Yves Edouard (obit.) **88:**87
Allen, Clabon Walter (obit.) **88:**87
Allen, George Herbert (obit.) **91:**86
Allen, Sir George Oswald Browning (obit.) **90:**103
Allen, Guy 311
Allen of Fallowfield, Alfred Walter Henry Allen (obit.) **86:**120
Alley Theatre (Houston, Tex., U.S.) 347
Alliance (pol. party, N.Z.) 450
Alliance for Democracy, *or* Aford (pol. org., Malawi) 440
Alliance for Democracy in Mali (pol. party, Mali) 442
Alliance for Freedom (pol. party, It.) 426
Alliance of Macedonia, *or* SM (pol. party, Maced.) 440
Allied Domecq (spirits) 125
Allison, Davey (obit.) **94:**54
Allison, Fran (obit.) **90:**103
"Alma-Ata Declaration: Health for All by the Year 2000, The" (Warren) **90:**21
Almendros, Nestor (obit.) **93:**54
Almirante, Giorgio (obit.) **89:**88
Almodóvar, Pedro (biog.) **91:**64
Alnæs, Karsten 224
ALP (pol. party, Austr.): *see* Australian Labor Party
Alpha AXP 21164
  microelectronics 133
alpine skiing 313
  1994 Olympic champions *table* 309
Alsgaard, Thomas 314
Alsinidendron trinerve (plant) 118
Alsop, Joseph Wright (obit.) **90:**103
Alston, Richard 151
Altman, Roger 495
Altman, Sidney (biog.) **90:**81
Alumax Inc. (Am. co.) 132
aluminum
  light metals 131, *il.* 132
  metalworking 132
  mining 240
Aluminum Co. of America (Am. co.)
  mining 241, *il.* 132
aluminum vehicle
  automobiles 125
Alvarez, Luis Walter (obit.) **89:**88
Alvin Ailey American Dance Theater 150
Alzado, Lyle (obit.) **93:**54
Alzheimer's disease 200
Amado, Jorge 226
amateur radio 342
amateur sports
  Cuba 286
  golf 305
Amato, Giuliano (biog.) **93:**33
Ambulocetus natans (fossil species) 210
